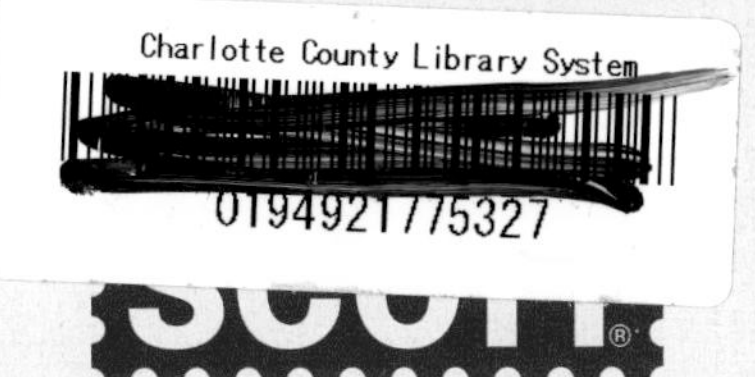

2023 STANDARD POSTAGE STAMP CATALOGUE

ONE HUNDRED AND EIGHTIETH EDITION IN SIX VOLUMES

Volume 6B

Thai-Z

EDITOR-IN-CHIEF Jay Bigalke
EDITOR-AT-LARGE Donna Houseman
CONTRIBUTING EDITOR Charles Snee
EDITOR EMERITUS James E. Kloetzel
SENIOR EDITOR /NEW ISSUES AND VALUING Martin J. Frankevicz
CATALOGUE COORDINATOR Eric Wiessinger
SENIOR GRAPHIC DESIGNER Cinda McAlexander
SALES DIRECTOR David Pistello
SALES DIRECTOR Eric Roth
SALES DIRECTOR Brenda Wyen
SALES REPRESENTATIVE Julie Dahlstrom

Released September 2023
Includes New Stamp Listings through the July 2023 *Scott Stamp Monthly* Catalogue Update

AMOS MEDIA

1660 Campbell Road, Suite A, Sidney, OH 45365
Publishers of *Linn's Stamp News, Scott Stamp Monthly, Coin World* and *Coin World Monthly.*

Table of contents

Information on philatelic societies 3A
Letter from the editor .... Vol. 6A, 3A
Acknowledgments .... Vol. 6A, 3A
Expertizing services .... Vol. 6A, 4A
Information on catalogue values, grade and condition .... Vol. 6A, 5A
Pronunciation symbols 6A
Grading illustrations .... Vol. 6A, 6A
Currency conversion 7A
2024 Volume 6A-6B catalogue number additions, deletions and changes 8A
Gum chart .... Vol. 6A, 8A
Catalogue listing policy .... Vol. 6A, 9A
Understanding the listings .... Vol. 6A, 10A
Special notices .... Vol. 6A, 12A
Abbreviations .... Vol. 6A, 12A
Basic stamp information .... Vol. 6A, 14A
Terminology .... Vol. 6A, 26A
The British Commonwealth of Nations .... Vol. 6A, 44A
Colonies, former colonies, offices, territories controlled by parent states .... Vol. 6A, 46A
Dies of British Colonial stamps referred to in the catalogue .... Vol. 6A, 47A
British Colonial and Crown Agents watermarks .... Vol. 6A, 48A

Countries of the World Thai-Z 1

Index and Identifier 874
Index to advertisers 885
Dealer directory yellow pages 886

See the following volumes for other country listings:
Volume 1A: United States, United Nations, Abu Dhabi-Australia; Volume 1B: Austria-B
Volume 2A: C-Cur; Volume 2B: Cyp-F
Volume 3A: G; Volume 3B: H-I
Volume 4A: J-L; Volume 4B: M
Volume 5A: N-Phil; Volume 5B: Pit-Sam
Volume 6A: San-Tete

Scott Catalogue Mission Statement

The Scott Catalogue Team exists to serve the recreational, educational and commercial hobby needs of stamp collectors and dealers.

We strive to set the industry standard for philatelic information and products by developing and providing goods that help collectors identify, value, organize and present their collections.

Quality customer service is, and will continue to be, our highest priority. We aspire toward achieving total customer satisfaction.

Copyright Notice

Trademark Notice

ISBN 978-0-89487-708-7

Library of Congress Card No. 2-3301

Addresses, telephone numbers, web sites, email addresses of general and specialized philatelic societies

Collectors can contact the following groups for information about the philately of the areas within the scope of these societies, or inquire about membership in these groups. Aside from the general societies, we limit this list to groups that specialize in particular fields of philately, particular areas covered by the Scott *Standard Postage Stamp Catalogue*, and topical groups. Many more specialized philatelic society exist than those listed below. These addresses are updated yearly, and they are, to the best of our knowledge, correct and current. Groups should inform the editors of address changes whenever they occur. The editors also want to hear from other such specialized groups not listed.

Unless otherwise noted all website addresses begin with http://

General Societies

American Philatelic Society, 100 Match Factory Place, Bellefonte, PA 16823-1367; (814) 933-3803; https://stamps.org; apsinfo@stamps.org

International Society of Worldwide Stamp Collectors, Joanne Murphy, M.D., P.O. Box 19006, Sacramento, CA 95819; www.iswsc.org; executivedirector@iswsc.org

Royal Philatelic Society of Canada, P.O. Box 69080, St. Clair Post Office, Toronto, ON M4T 3A1 Canada; (888) 285-4143; www.rpsc.org; info@rpsc.org

Royal Philatelic Society London, 15 Abchurch Lane, London EX4N 7BW, United Kingdom; +44 (0) 20 7486 1044; www.rpsl.org.uk; secretary@rpsl.org.uk

Libraries, Museums, and Research Groups

American Philatelic Research Library, 100 Match Factory Place, Bellefonte, PA 16823; (814) 933-3803; www.stamplibrary.org; library@stamps.org.

V. G. Greene Philatelic Research Foundation, P.O. Box 69100, St. Clair Post Office, Toronto, ON M4T 3A1, Canada; (416) 921-2073; info@greenefoundation.ca

Aero/Astro Philately

American Air Mail Society, Stephen Reinhard, P.O. Box 110, Mineola, NY 11501; www.americanairmailsociety.org; sreinhard1@optonline.net

Postal History

Auxiliary Markings Club, Jerry Johnson, 6621 W. Victoria Ave., Kennewick, WA 99336; www.postal-markings.org; membership-2010@postal-markings.org

Postage Due Mail Study Group, Bob Medland, Camway Cottage, Nanny Hurn's Lane, Cameley, Bristol BS39 5AJ, United Kingdom; 01761 45959; www.postageduemail.org.uk; secretary.pdmsg@gmail.com

Postal History Society, Yamil Kouri, 405 Waltham St. #347, Lexington, MA 02421; www.postalhistorysociety.org; yhkouri@massmed.org

Post Mark Collectors Club, Bob Milligan, 7014 Woodland Oaks Drive, Magnolia, TX 77354; (281) 259-2735; www.postmarks.org; bob.milligan0@gmail.com

U.S. Cancellation Club, Roger Curran, 18 Tressler Blvd., Lewisburg, PA 17837; rdcnrc@ptd.net

Revenues and Cinderellas

American Revenue Association, Lyman Hensley, 473 E. Elm St., Sycamore, IL 60178-1934; www.revenuer.org; ilrno2@netzero.net

Christmas Seal and Charity Stamp Society, John Denune Jr., 234 E. Broadway, Granville, OH 43023; (740) 814-6031; www.seal-society.org

National Duck Stamp Collectors Society, Anthony J. Monico, P.O. Box 43, Harleysville, PA 19438-0043; www.ndscs.org; ndscs@ndscs.org

State Revenue Society, Kent Gray, P.O. Box 67842, Albuquerque, NM 87193; www.staterevenue.org; srssecretary@comcast.net

Thematic Philately

Americana Unit, Dennis Dengel, 17 Peckham Road, Poughkeepsie, NY 12603-2018; www.americanaunit.org; ddengel@americanaunit.org

American Topical Association, Jennifer Miller, P.O. Box 2143, Greer, SC 29652-2143; (618) 985-5100; americantopical.org; ata@americantopical.org

Astronomy Study Unit, Leonard Zehr, 1411 Chateau Ave., Windsor, ON N8P 1M2, Canada; (416) 833-9317; www.astronomystudyunit.net; lenzehr@gmail.com

Bicycle Stamps Club, Corey Hjalseth, 1102 Broadway, Suite 200, Tacoma, WA 98402; (253) 318-6222; www.bicyclestampsclub.org; coreyh@evergreenhomeloans.com

Biology Unit, Chris Dahle, 1401 Linmar Drive NE, Cedar Rapids, IA 52402-3724; www.biophilately.org; chris-dahle@biophilately.org

Bird Stamp Society, Mr. S. A. H. (Tony) Statham, Ashlyns Lodge, Chesham Road, Berkhamsted, Herts HP4 2ST United Kingdom; www.bird-stamps.org/bss; tony.statham@sky.com

Captain Cook Society, Jerry Yucht, 8427 Leale Ave., Stockton, CA 95212, www.captaincooksociety.com; us@captaincooksociety.com

The CartoPhilatelic Society, Marybeth Sulkowski, 2885 Sanford Ave., SW, #32361, Grandville, MI 49418-1342; www.mapsonstamps.org; secretary@mapsonstamps.org

Casey Jones Railroad Unit, Jeff Lough, 2612 Redbud Land, Apt. C, Lawrence, KS 66046; www.uqp.de/cjr; jeffydplaugh@gmail.com

Cats on Stamps Study Unit, Robert D. Jarvis, 2731 Teton Lane, Fairfield, CA 94533; www.catstamps.info; catmews1@yahoo.com

Chemistry and Physics on Stamps Study Unit, Dr. Roland Hirsch, 13830 Metcalf Ave., Apt. 15218, Overland Park, KS 66223-8017; (301) 792-6296; www.cpossu.org; rfhirsch@cpossu.org

Chess on Stamps Study Unit, Barry Keith, 511 First St. N., Apt. 106; Charlottesville, VA 22902; www.chessonstamps.org; keithfam@embarqmail.com

Cricket Philatelic Society, A. Melville-Brown, 11 Weppons, Ravens Road, Shorham-by-Sea, West Sussex BN43 5AW, United Kingdom; www.cricketstamp.net; mel.cricket.100@googlemail.com

Earth's Physical Features Study Group, Fred Klein, 515 Magdalena Ave., Los Altos, CA 94024; http://epfsu.jeffhayward.com; epfsu@jeffhayward.com

Ebony Society of Philatelic Events and Reflections (ESPER), Don Neal, P.O. Box 5245, Somerset, NJ 08875-5245; www.esperstamps.org; esperdon@verizon.net

Europa Study Unit, Tonny E. Van Loij, 3002 S. Xanthia St.; Denver, CO 80231-4237; (303) 752-0189; www.europastudyunit.org; tvanloij@gmail.com

Fire Service in Philately, John Zaranek, 81 Hillpine Road, Cheektowaga, NY 14227-2259; (716) 668-3352; jczaranek@roadrunner.com

Gastronomy on Stamps Study Unit, David Wolfersburger, 5062 NW 35th Lane Road, Ocala, FL 34482; (314) 494-3795; www.gastronomystamps.org

Gay and Lesbian History on Stamps Club, Joe Petronie, P.O. Box 190842, Dallas, TX 75219-0842; www.glhsonline.org; glhsc@aol.com

Gems, Minerals and Jewelry Study Unit, Fred Haynes, 10 Country Club Drive, Rochester, NY 14618-3720; fredmhaynes55@gmail.com

Graphics Philately Association, Larry Rosenblum. 1030 E. El Camino Real, PMB 107, Sunnyvale, CA 94087-3759; www.graphics-stamps.org; larry@graphics-stamps.org

Journalists, Authors and Poets on Stamps, Christopher D. Cook, 7222 Hollywood Road, Berrien Springs, MI 49103; cdcook2@gmail.com

Lighthouse Stamp Society, www.lighthousestampsociety.org

Lions International Stamp Club, David McKirdy, s-Gravenwetering 248, 3062 SJ Rotterdam, Netherlands; 31(0) 10 212 0313; www.lisc.nl; davidmckirdy@aol.com

Masonic Study Unit, Gene Fricks, 25 Murray Way, Blackwood, NJ 08012-4400; genefricks@comcast.net

Medical Subjects Unit, Dr. Frederick C. Skvara, P.O. Box 6228, Bridgewater, NJ 08807; fcskvara@optonline.net

Napoleonic Age Philatelists, Ken Berry, 4117 NW 146th St., Oklahoma City, OK 73134-1746; (405) 748-8646; www.nap-stamps.org; krb4117@att.net

Old World Archaeological Study Unit, Caroline Scannell, 14 Dawn Drive, Smithtown, NY 11787-176; www.owasu.org; editor@owasu.org

Petroleum Philatelic Society International, Feitze Papa, 922 Meander Drive, Walnut Creek, CA 94598-4239; www.ppsi.org.uk; oildad@astound.net

Rotary on Stamps Fellowship, Gerald L. Fitzsimmons, 105 Calle Ricardo, Victoria, TX 77904; www.rotaryonstamps.org; glfitz@suddenlink.net

Scouts on Stamps Society International, Woodrow (Woody) Brooks, 498 Baldwin Road, Akron, OH 44312; (330) 612-1294; www.sossi.org; secretary@sossi.org

Ships on Stamps Unit, Erik Th. Matzinger, Voorste Havervelden 30, 4822 AL Breda, Netherlands; www.shipsonstamps.org; erikships@gmail.com

Space Topic Study Unit, David Blog, P.O. Box 174, Bergenfield, NJ 07621; www.space-unit.com; davidblognj@gmail.com

Stamps on Stamps Collectors Club, Michael Merritt, 73 Mountainside Road, Mendham, NJ 07945; www.stampsonstamps.org; michael@mischu.me

Windmill Study Unit, Walter J. Hallien, 607 N. Porter St., Watkins Glenn, NY 14891-1345; (607) 229-3541; www.windmillworld.com

Wine On Stamps Study Unit, David Wolfersburger, 5062 NW 35th Lane Road, Ocala, FL 34482; (314) 494-3795; www.wine-on-stamps.org;

United States

American Air Mail Society, Stephen Reinhard, P.O. Box 110, Mineola, NY

11501; www.americanairmailsociety.org; sreinhard1@optonline.net

American First Day Cover Society, P.O. Box 246, Colonial Beach VA 22443-0246; (520) 321-0880; www.afdcs.org; afdcs@afdcs.org

Auxiliary Markings Club, Jerry Johnson, 6621 W. Victoria Ave., Kennewick, WA 99336; www.postal-markings.org; membership-2010@postal-markings.org

American Plate Number Single Society, Rick Burdsall, APNSS Secretary, P.O. BOX 1023, Palatine, IL 60078-1023; www.apnss.org; apnss.sec@gmail.com

American Revenue Association, Lyman Hensley, 473 E. Elm St., Sycamore, IL 60178-1934; www.revenuer.org; ilrno2@netzero.net

American Society for Philatelic Pages and Panels, Ron Walenciak, P.O. Box 1042, Washington Township, NJ 07676; www.asppp.org; ron.walenciak@asppp.org

Canal Zone Study Group, Mike Drabik, P.O. Box 281, Bolton, MA 01740, www.canalzonestudygroup.com; czsgsecretary@gmail.com

Carriers and Locals Society, John Bowman, 14409 Pentridge Drive, Corpus Christi, TX 78410; (361) 933-0757; www.pennypost.org; jbowman@stx.rr.com

Christmas Seal & Charity Stamp Society, John Denune Jr., 234 E. Broadway, Granville, OH 43023; (740) 814-6031; www.seal-society.org; john@christmasseals.net

Civil War Philatelic Society, Patricia A. Kaufmann, 10194 N. Old State Road, Lincoln, DE 19960-3644; (302) 422-2656; www.civilwarphilatelicsociety.org; trishkauf@comcast.net

Error, Freaks, and Oddities Collectors Club, Scott Shaulis, P.O. Box 549, Murrysville, PA 15668-0549; (724) 733-4134; www.efocc.org; scott@shaulisstamps.com

National Duck Stamp Collectors Society, Anthony J. Monico, P.O. Box 43, Harleysville, PA 19438-0043; www.ndscs.org; ndscs@ndscs.org

Plate Number Coil Collectors Club (PNC3), Gene Trinks, 16415 W. Desert Wren Court, Surprise, AZ 85374; (623) 322-4619; www.pnc3.org; gctrinks@cox.net

Post Mark Collectors Club, Bob Milligan, 7014 Woodland Oaks Drive, Magnolia, TX 77354; (281) 259-2735; www.postmarks.org; bob.milligan0@gmail.com

Souvenir Card Collectors Society, William V. Kriebel, www.souvenircards.org; kriebewv@drexel.edu

United Postal Stationery Society, Dave Kandziolka, 404 Sundown Drive, Knoxville, TN 37934; www.upss.org; membership@upss.org

U.S. Cancellation Club, Roger Curran, 18 Tressler Blvd., Lewisburg, PA 17837; rdcnrc@ptd.net

U.S. Philatelic Classics Society, Rob Lund, 2913 Fulton St., Everett, WA 98201-3733; www.uspcs.org; membershipchairman@uspcs.org

US Possessions Philatelic Society, Daniel F. Ring, P.O. Box 113, Woodstock, IL 60098; http://uspps.tripod.com; danielfring@hotmail.com

United States Stamp Society, Rod Juell, P.O. Box 3508, Joliet, IL 60434-3508; www.usstamps.org; execsecretary@usstamps.org

Africa

Bechuanalands and Botswana Society, Otto Peetoom, Roos, East Yorkshire HU12 0LD, United Kingdom; 44(0)1964 670239; www.bechuanalandphilately.com; info@bechuanalandphilately.com

Egypt Study Circle, Mike Murphy, 11 Waterbank Road, Bellingham, London SE6 3DJ United Kingdom; (44) 0203 6737051; www.egyptstudycircle.org.uk; secretary@egyptstudycircle.org.uk

Ethiopian Philatelic Society, Ulf Lindahl, 21 Westview Place, Riverside, CT 06878; (203) 722-0769; https://ethiopianphilatelicsociety.weebly.com; ulindahl@optonline.net

Liberian Philatelic Society, P.O. Box 1570, Parker, CO 80134; www.liberiastamps.org; liberiastamps@comcast.net

Orange Free State Study Circle, J. R. Stroud, RDPSA, 24 Hooper Close, Burnham-on-sea, Somerset TA8 1JQ United Kingdom; 44 1278 782235; www.orangefreestatephilately.org.uk; richard@richardstroud.plus.com

Philatelic Society for Greater Southern Africa, David McNamee, 15 Woodland Drive, Alamo, CA 94507; www.psgsa.org; alan.hanks@sympatico.ca

Rhodesian Study Circle, William R. Wallace, P.O. Box 16381, San Francisco, CA 94116; (415) 564-6069; www.rhodesianstudycircle.org.uk; bwall8rscr@earthlink.net

Society for Moroccan and Tunisian Philately, S.P.L.M., 206, Bld Pereire, 75017 Paris, France; http://splm-philatelie.org; splm206@aol.com

South Sudan Philatelic Society, William Barclay, 1370 Spring Hill Road, South Londonderry, VT 05155; barclayphilatelics@gmail.com

Sudan Study Group, Andy Neal, Bank House, Coedway, Shrewsbury SY5 9AR United Kingdom; www.sudanstamps.org; andywneal@gmail.com

Transvaal Study Circle, c/o 9 Meadow Road, Gravesend, Kent DA11 7LR United Kingdom; www.transvaalstamps.org.uk; transvaalstudycircle@aol.co.uk

West Africa Study Circle, Martin Bratzel, 1233 Virginia Ave., Windsor, ON N8S 2Z1 Canada; www.wasc.org.uk; marty_bratzel@yahoo.ca

Asia

Aden & Somaliland Study Group, Malcom Lacey, 108 Dalestorth Road, Sutton-in-Ashfield, Nottinghamshire NG17 3AA, United Kingdom; www.stampdomain.com/aden; neil53williams@yahoo.co.uk

Burma (Myanmar) Philatelic Study Circle, Michael Whittaker, 1, Ecton Leys, Hillside, Rugby, Warwickshire CV22 5SL United Kingdom; https://burmamyanmarphilately.wordpress.com/burma-myanmar-philatelic-study-circle; manningham8@mypostoffice.co.uk

Ceylon Study Circle, Rodney W. P. Frost, 42 Lonsdale Road, Cannington, Bridgwater, Somerset TA5 2JS United Kingdom; 01278 652592; www.ceylonsc.org; rodney.frost@tiscali.co.uk

China Stamp Society, H. James Maxwell, 1050 W. Blue Ridge Blvd., Kansas City, MO 64145-1216; www.chinastampsociety.org; president@chinastampsociety.org

Hong Kong Philatelic Society, John Tang, G.P.O. Box 446, Hong Kong; www.hkpsociety.com; hkpsociety@outlook.com

Hong Kong Study Circle, Robert Newton, www.hongkongstudycircle.com/index.html; newtons100@gmail.com

India Study Circle, John Warren, P.O. Box 7326, Washington, DC 20044; (202) 488-7443; https://indiastudycircle.org; jw-kbw@earthlink.net

International Philippine Philatelic Society, James R. Larot, Jr., 4990 Bayleaf Court, Martinez, CA 94553; (925) 260-5425; www.theipps.info; jlarot@ccwater.com

International Society for Japanese Philately, P.O. Box 1283, Haddonfield NJ 08033; www.isjp.org; secretary@isjp.org

Iran Philatelic Study Circle, Nigel Gooch, Marchwood, 56, Wickham Ave., Bexhill-on-Sea, East Sussex TN39 3ER United Kingdom; www.iranphilately.org; nigelmgooch@gmail.com

Korea Stamp Society, Yong Sok Yi, 180 Stevens Bridges Lane, Tracy, CA 95377; yiyongsok_96204@yahoo.com; www.koreastampsociety.org

Nepal & Tibet Philatelic Study Circle, Colin Hepper, 12 Charnwood Close, Peterborough, Cambs PE2 9BZ United Kingdom; http://fuchs-online.com/ntpsc; ntpsc@fuchs-online.com

Pakistan Philatelic Study Circle, Jeff Siddiqui, P.O. Box 7002, Lynnwood, WA 98046; jeffsiddiqui@msn.com

Society of Indo-China Philatelists, Ron Bentley, 2600 N. 24th St., Arlington, VA 22207; (703) 524-1652; www.sicp-online.org; ron.bentley@verizon.net

Society of Israel Philatelists, Inc., Sarah Berezenko, 100 Match Factory Place, Bellefonte, PA 16823-1367; (814) 933-3803 ext. 212; www.israelstamps.com; israelstamps@gmail.com

Australasia and Oceania

Australian States Study Circle of the Royal Sydney Philatelic Club, Ben Palmer, G.P.O. 1751, Sydney, NSW 2001 Australia; http://club.philas.org.au/states

Fellowship of Samoa Specialists, Trevor Shimell, 18 Aspen Drive, Newton Abbot, Devon TQ12 4TN United Kingdom; www.samoaexpress.org; trevor.shimell@gmail.com

Malaya Study Group, Michael Waugh, 151 Roker Lane, Pudsey, Leeds LS28 9ND United Kingdom; http://malayastudygroup.com; mawpud43@gmail.com

New Zealand Society of Great Britain, Michael Wilkinson, 121 London Road, Sevenoaks, Kent TN13 1BH United Kingdom; 01732 456997; www.nzsgb.org.uk; mwilkin799@aol.com

Pacific Islands Study Circle, John Ray, 24 Woodvale Ave., London SE25 4AE United Kingdom; www.pisc.org.uk; secretary@pisc.org.uk

Papuan Philatelic Society, Steven Zirinsky, P.O. Box 49, Ansonia Station, New York, NY 10023; (718) 706-0616; www.papuanphilatelicsociety.com; szirinsky@cs.com

Pitcairn Islands Study Group, Dr. Everett L. Parker, 207 Corinth Road, Hudson, ME 04449-3057; (207) 573-1686; www.pisg.net; eparker@hughes.net

Ryukyu Philatelic Specialist Society, Laura Edmonds, P.O. Box 240177, Charlotte, NC 28224-0177; (336) 509-3739; www.ryukyustamps.org; secretary@ryukyustamps.org

Society of Australasian Specialists / Oceania, Steve Zirinsky, P.O. Box 230049, New York, NY 10023-0049; www.sasoceania.org; president@sosoceania.org

Sarawak Specialists' Society, Stephen Schumann, 2417 Cabrallo Drive, Hayward, CA 94545; (510) 785-4794; www.britborneostamps.org.uk; vpnam@s-s-s.org.uk

Western Australia Study Group, Brian Pope, P.O. Box 423, Claremont, WA 6910 Australia; (61) 419 843 943; www.wastudygroup.com; wastudygroup@hotmail.com

Europe

American Helvetia Philatelic Society, Richard T. Hall, P.O. Box 15053, Asheville, NC 28813-0053; www.swiss-stamps.org; secretary2@swiss-stamps.org

American Society for Netherlands Philately, Hans Kremer, 50 Rockport Court, Danville, CA 94526; (925) 820-5841; www.asnp1975.com; hkremer@usa.net

Andorran Philatelic Study Circle, David Hope, 17 Hawthorn Drive,

Stalybridge, Cheshire SK15 1UE United Kingdom; www.andorranpsc.org.uk; andorranpsc@btinternet.com

Austria Philatelic Society, Ralph Schneider, P.O. Box 978, Iowa Park, TX 76376; (940) 213-5004; www.austriaphilatelicsociety.com; rschneiderstamps@gmail.com

Channel Islands Specialists Society, Richard Flemming, Burbage, 64 Falconers Green, Hinckley, Leicestershire, LE102SX, United Kingdom; www.ciss.uk; secretary@ciss.uk

Cyprus Study Circle, Rob Wheeler, 47 Drayton Ave., London W13 0LE United Kingdom; www.cyprusstudycircle.org; robwheeler47@aol.com

Danish West Indies Study Unit of Scandinavian Collectors Club, Arnold Sorensen, 7666 Edgedale Drive, Newburgh, IN 47630; (812) 480-6532; www.scc-online.org; valbydwi@hotmail.com

Eire Philatelic Association, John B. Sharkey, 1559 Grouse Lane, Mountainside, NJ 07092-1340; www.eirephilatelicassoc.org; jsharkeyepa@me.com

Faroe Islands Study Circle, Norman Hudson, 40 Queen's Road, Vicar's Cross, Chester CH3 5HB United Kingdom; www.faroeislandssc.org; jntropics@hotmail.com

France & Colonies Philatelic Society, Edward Grabowski, 111 Prospect St., 4C, Westfield, NJ 07090; (908) 233-9318; www.franceandcolsps.org; edjjg@alum.mit.edu

Germany Philatelic Society, P.O. Box 6547, Chesterfield, MO 63006-6547; www.germanyphilatelicusa.org; info@germanyphilatelicsocietyusa.org

Gibraltar Study Circle, Susan Dare, 22, Byways Park, Strode Road, Clevedon, North Somerset BS21 6UR United Kingdom; www.gibraltarstudycircle.wordpress.com; smldare@yahoo.co.uk

International Society for Portuguese Philately, Clyde Homen, 1491 Bonnie View Road, Hollister, CA 95023-5117; www.portugalstamps.com; ispp1962@sbcglobal.net

Italy and Colonies Study Circle, Richard Harlow, 7 Duncombe House, 8 Manor Road, Teddington, Middlesex TW118BE United Kingdom; 44 208 977 8737; www.icsc-uk.com; richardharlow@outlook.com

Liechtenstudy USA, Paul Tremaine, 410 SW Ninth St., Dundee, OR 97115-9731; (503) 538-4500; www.liechtenstudy.org; tremaine@liechtenstudy.org

Lithuania Philatelic Society, Audrius Brazdeikis, 9915 Murray Landing, Missouri City, TX 77459; (281) 450-6224; www.lithuanianphilately.com/lps; audrius@lithuanianphilately.com

Luxembourg Collectors Club, Gary B. Little, 7319 Beau Road, Sechelt, BC V0N 3A8 Canada; (604) 885-7241; http://lcc.luxcentral.com; gary@luxcentral.com

Plebiscite-Memel-Saar Study Group of the German Philatelic Society, Clayton Wallace, 100 Lark Court, Alamo, CA 94507; claytonwallace@comcast.net

Polonus Polish Philatelic Society, Daniel Lubelski, P.O. Box 2212, Benicia, CA 94510; (419) 410-9115; www.polonus.org; info@polonus.org

Rossica Society of Russian Philately, Alexander Kolchinsky, 1506 Country Lake Drive, Champaign, IL 61821-6428; www.rossica.org; alexander.kolchinsky@rossica.org

Scandinavian Collectors Club, Alan Warren, Scandinavian Collectors Club, P.O. Box 39, Exton PA 19341-0039; (612) 810-8640; www.scc-online.org; alanwar@att.net

Society for Czechoslovak Philately, Tom Cossaboom, P.O. Box 4124, Prescott, AZ 86302; (928) 771-9097; www.csphilately.org; klfck1@aol.com

Society for Hungarian Philately, Alan Bauer, P.O. Box 4028, Vineyard Haven, MA 02568; (617) 645-4045; www.hungarianphilately.org; alan@hungarianstamps.com

Spanish Study Circle, Edith Knight, www.spaincircle.wixsite.com/spainstudycircle; spaincircle@gmail.com

Ukrainian Philatelic & Numismatic Society, Martin B. Tatuch, 5117 8th Road N., Arlington, VA 22205-1201; www.upns.org; treasurer@upns.org

Vatican Philatelic Society, Dennis Brady, 4897 Ledyard Drive, Manlius NY 13104-1514; www.vaticanphilately.org; dbrady7534@gmail.com

Yugoslavia Study Group, Michael Chant, 1514 N. Third Ave., Wausau, WI 54401; 208-748-9919; www.yugosg.org; membership@yugosg.org

Interregional Societies

American Society of Polar Philatelists, Alan Warren, P.O. Box 39, Exton, PA 19341-0039; (610) 321-0740; www.polarphilatelists.org; alanwar@att.net

First Issues Collector's Club, Kurt Streepy, 3128 E. Mattatha Drive, Bloomington, IN 47401; www.firstissues.org; secretary@firstissues.org

Former French Colonies Specialist Society, Col.fra, BP 628, 75367 Paris, France; www.colfra.org; postmaster@colfra.org

France & Colonies Philatelic Society, Edward Grabowski, 111 Prospect St., 4C, Westfield, NJ 07090; (908) 233-9318, www.franceandcolsps.org; edjjg@alum.mit.edu

Joint Stamp Issues Society, Richard Zimmermann, 29A, Rue Des Eviats, 67220 Lalaye, France; www.philarz.net; richard.zimmermann@club-internet.fr

The King George VI Collectors Society, Brian Livingstone, 21 York Mansions, Prince of Wales Drive, London SW11 4DL United Kingdom; www.kg6.info; livingstone484@btinternet.com

International Society of Reply Coupon Collectors, Peter Robin, P.O. Box 353, Bala Cynwyd, PA 19004; peterrobin@verizon.net

Italy and Colonies Study Circle, Richard Harlow, 7 Duncombe House, 8 Manor Road, Teddington, Middlesex TW118BE United Kingdom; 44 208 977 8737; www.icsc-uk.com; richardharlow@outlook.com

St. Helena, Ascension & Tristan Da Cunha Philatelic Society, Dr. Everett L. Parker, 207 Corinth Road, Hudson, ME 04449-3057; (207) 573-1686; www.shatps.org; eparker@hughes.net

United Nations Philatelists, Blanton Clement, Jr., P.O. Box 146, Morrisville, PA 19067-0146; www.unpi.com; bclemjunior@gmail.com

Latin America

Asociación Filatélica de Panamá, Edward D. Vianna B. ASOFILPA, 0819-03400, El Dorado, Panama; http://asociacionfilatelicadepanama.blogspot.com; asofilpa@gmail.com

Asociacion Mexicana de Filatelia (AMEXFIL), Alejandro Grossmann, Jose Maria Rico, 129, Col. Del Valle, 3100 Mexico City, DF Mexico; www.amexfil.mx; amexfil@gmail.com

Associated Collectors of El Salvador, Pierre Cahen, Vipsal 1342, P.O. Box 02-5364, Miami FL 33102; www.elsalvadorphilately.org; sfes-aces@elsalvadorphilately.org

Association Filatelic de Costa Rica, Giana Wayman (McCarty), #SJO 4935, P.O. Box 025723, Miami, FL 33102-5723; 011-506-2-228-1947; scotland@racsa.co.cr

Brazil Philatelic Association, William V. Kriebel, www.brazilphilatelic.org, info@brazilphilatelic.org

Canal Zone Study Group, Mike Drabik, P.O. Box 281, Bolton, MA 01740; www.canalzonestudygroup.com; czsgsecretary@gmail.com

Colombia-Panama Philatelic Study Group, Allan Harris, 26997 Hemmingway Ct, Hayward CA 94542-2349; www.copaphil.org; copaphilusa@aol.com

Falkland Islands Philatelic Study Groups, Morva White, 42 Colton Road, Shrivenham, Swindon SN6 8AZ United Kingdom; 44(0) 1793 783245; www.fipsg.org.uk; morawhite@supanet.com

Federacion Filatelica de la Republica de Honduras, Mauricio Mejia, Apartado Postal 1465, Tegucigalpa, D.C. Honduras; 504 3399-7227; www.facebook.com/filateliadehonduras; ffrh@hotmail.com

International Cuban Philatelic Society (ICPS), Ernesto Cuesta, P.O. Box 34434, Bethesda, MD 20827; (301) 564-3099; www.cubafil.org; ecuesta@philat.com

International Society of Guatemala Collectors, Jaime Marckwordt, 449 St. Francis Blvd., Daly City, CA 94015-2136; (415) 997-0295; www.guatemalastamps.com; president@guatamalastamps.com

Mexico-Elmhurst Philatelic Society International, Eric Stovner, P.O. Box 10097, Santa Ana, CA 92711-0097; www.mepsi.org; treasurer@mepsi.org

Nicaragua Study Group, Erick Rodriguez, 11817 S. W. 11th St., Miami, FL 33184-2501; nsgsec@yahoo.com

North America (excluding United States)

British Caribbean Philatelic Study Group, Bob Stewart, 7 West Dune Lane, Long Beach Township, NJ 08008; (941) 379-4108; www.bcpsg.com; bcpsg@comcast.net

British North America Philatelic Society, Andy Ellwood, 10 Doris Ave., Gloucester, ON K1T 3W8 Canada; www.bnaps.org; secretary@bnaps.org

British West Indies Study Circle, Steve Jarvis, 5 Redbridge Drive, Andover, Hants SP10 2LF United Kingdom; 01264 358065; www.bwisc.org; info@bwisc.org

Bermuda Collectors Society, John Pare, 405 Perimeter St., Mount Horeb, WI 53572; (608) 852-7358; www.bermudacollectorssociety.com; pare16@mhtc.net

Haiti Philatelic Society, Ubaldo Del Toro, 5709 Marble Archway, Alexandria, VA 22315; www.haitiphilately.org; u007ubi@aol.com

Hawaiian Philatelic Society, Gannon Sugimura, P.O. Box 10115, Honolulu, HI 96816-0115, www.hpshawaii.com; hiphilsoc@gmail.com

Stamp Dealer Associations

American Stamp Dealers Association, Inc., P.O. Box 513, Centre Hall PA 16828; (800) 369-8207; www.americanstampdealer.com; asda@americanstampdealer.com

National Stamp Dealers Association, Sheldon Ruckens, President, 3643 Private Road 18, Pinckneyville, IL 62274-3426; (618) 357-5497; www.nsdainc.org; nsda@nsdainc.org

Youth Philately

Young Stamp Collectors of America, 100 Match Factory Place, Bellefonte, PA 16823; (814) 933-3803; https://stamps.org/learn/youth-in-philately; ysca@stamps.org

Pronunciation Symbols

ə .... banana, collide, abut

ˈə, ˌə .... humdrum, abut

ᵊ .... immediately preceding \l\, \n\, \m\, \ŋ\, as in battle, mitten, eaten, and sometimes open \ˈō-pᵊm\, lock and key \-ᵊŋ-\; immediately following \l\, \m\, \r\, as often in French table, prisme, titre

ər .... further, merger, bird

ˈər-, ˈə-r .... as in two different pronunciations of hurry \ˈhər-ē, ˈhə-rē\

a .... mat, map, mad, gag, snap, patch

ā .... day, fade, date, aorta, drape, cape

ä .... bother, cot, and, with most American speakers, father, cart

ȧ .... father as pronounced by speakers who do not rhyme it with *bother;* French patte

au̇ .... now, loud, out

b .... baby, rib

ch .... chin, nature \ˈnā-chər\

d .... did, adder

e .... bet, bed, peck

ˈē, ˌē .... beat, nosebleed, evenly, easy

ē .... easy, mealy

f .... fifty, cuff

g .... go, big, gift

h .... hat, ahead

hw .... whale as pronounced by those who do not have the same pronunciation for both *whale* and *wail*

i .... tip, banish, active

ī .... site, side, buy, tripe

j .... job, gem, edge, join, judge

k .... kin, cook, ache

k̲ .... German ich, Buch; one pronunciation of loch

l .... lily, pool

m .... murmur, dim, nymph

n .... no, own

ⁿ .... indicates that a preceding vowel or diphthong is pronounced with the nasal passages open, as in French *un bon vin blanc* \œⁿ-bōⁿ-vaⁿ-bläⁿ\

ŋ .... sing \ˈsiŋ\, singer \ˈsiŋ-ər\, finger \ˈfiŋ-gər\, ink \ˈiŋk\

ō .... bone, know, beau

ȯ .... saw, all, gnaw, caught

œ .... French boeuf, German Hölle

œ̄ .... French feu, German Höhle

ȯi .... coin, destroy

p .... pepper, lip

r .... red, car, rarity

s .... source, less

sh .... as in shy, mission, machine, special (actually, this is a single sound, not two); with a hyphen between, two sounds as in *grasshopper* \ˈgras-ˌhä-pər\

t .... tie, attack, late, later, latter

th .... as in thin, ether (actually, this is a single sound, not two); with a hyphen between, two sounds as in *knighthood* \ˈnīt-ˌhu̇d\

t̲h̲ .... then, either, this (actually, this is a single sound, not two)

ü .... rule, youth, union \ˈyün-yən\, few \ˈfyü\

u̇ .... pull, wood, book, curable \ˈkyu̇r-ə-bəl\, fury \ˈfyu̇r-ē\

ue .... German füllen, hübsch

ue̅ .... French rue, German fühlen

v .... vivid, give

w .... we, away

y .... yard, young, cue \ˈkyü\, mute \ˈmyüt\, union \ˈyün-yən\

ʸ .... indicates that during the articulation of the sound represented by the preceding character the front of the tongue has substantially the position it has for the articulation of the first sound of *yard,* as in French *digne* \dēnʸ\

z .... zone, raise

zh .... as in vision, azure \ˈa-zhər\ (actually, this is a single sound, not two); with a hyphen between, two sounds as in *hogshead* \ˈhȯgz-ˌhed, ˈhägz-\

\ .... slant line used in pairs to mark the beginning and end of a transcription: \ˈpen\

ˈ .... mark preceding a syllable with primary (strongest) stress: \ˈpen-mən-ˌship\

ˌ .... mark preceding a syllable with secondary (medium) stress: \ˈpen-mən-ˌship\

\- .... mark of syllable division

( ) .... indicate that what is symbolized between is present in some utterances but not in others: *factory* \ˈfak-t(ə-)rē\

÷ .... indicates that many regard as unacceptable the pronunciation variant immediately following: *cupola* \ˈkyü-pə-lə, ÷-ˌlō\

Currency conversion

Country	Dollar	Pound	S Franc	Yen	HK $	Euro	Cdn $	Aus $
Australia	1.5072	1.8875	1.6878	0.0110	0.1920	1.6597	1.1097	–
Canada	1.3582	1.7009	1.5209	0.0099	0.1730	1.4957	–	0.9011
European Union	0.9081	1.1372	1.0169	0.0066	0.1157	–	0.6686	0.6025
Hong Kong	7.8499	9.8300	8.7905	0.0574	–	8.6443	5.7796	5.2083
Japan	136.85	171.38	153.25	–	17.433	150.70	100.76	90.798
Switzerland	0.8930	1.1183	–	0.0065	0.1138	0.9834	0.6575	0.5925
United Kingdom	0.7985	–	0.8942	0.0058	0.1017	0.8793	0.5879	0.5298
United States	–	1.2523	1.1198	0.0073	0.1274	1.1012	0.7363	0.6635

Country	Currency	U.S. $ Equiv.
Thailand	baht	.0293
Timor	U.S. dollar	1.0000
Togo	Community of French Africa (CFA) franc	.0017
Tokelau	New Zealand dollar	.6174
Tonga	pa'anga	.4233
Niuafoíou	pa'anga	.4233
Trinidad & Tobago	dollar	.1475
Tristan da Cunha	British pound	1.2523
Tunisia	dinar	.3293
Turkey	lira	.0514
Turk. Rep. of Northern Cyprus	lira	.0514
Turkmenistan	manat	.2862
Turks & Caicos Islands	U.S. dollar	1.0000
Tuvalu	Australian dollar	.6635
Uganda	shilling	.0003
Ukraine	hryvnia	.0271
United Arab Emirates	dirham	.2723
Uruguay	peso	.0259
Uzbekistan	sum	.0001
Vanuatu	vatu	.0084
Vatican City	euro	1.1012
Venezuela	bolivar	.0000
Viet Nam	dong	.00004
Virgin Islands	U.S. dollar	1.0000
Wallis & Futuna Islands	Community of French Pacific (CFP) franc	.0092
Yemen	rial	.0040
Zambia	kwacha	.0557
Zaire (Congo Dem. Rep.)	franc	.0005
Zimbabwe	U.S. dollar	1.0000

Source: xe.com May 1, 2023. Figures reflect values as of May 1, 2023.

Vols. 6A-6B number additions, deletions and changes

Number in 2023 Catalogue	Number in 2024 Catalogue
Sarawak	
new	136a
new	N2a
new	N3a
new	N4a
new	N5a
new	N6a
new	N8a
new	N9a
new	N10a
new	N11a
new	N12Ab
new	N14a
new	N15a
new	N16a
new	N17a
new	N17b
new	N18a
new	N19b
new	N19Ac

THAILAND

'tī-ˌland

(Siam)

LOCATION — Western part of the Malay peninsula in southeastern Asia
GOVT. — Constitutional Monarchy
AREA — 198,250 sq. mi.
POP. — 60,609,046 (1999 est.)
CAPITAL — Bangkok

32 Solot = 16 Atts = 8 Sio =
4 Sik = 2 Fuang = 1 Salung
4 Salungs = 1 Tical
100 Satangs (1909) = 1 Tical
= 1 Baht (1912)

Catalogue values for unused stamps in this country are for Never Hinged items, beginning with Scott 264 in the regular postage section, Scott B34 in the semi-postal section, Scott C20 in the airpost section, and Scott O1 in the official section.

Watermarks

Wmk. 176 — Chakra

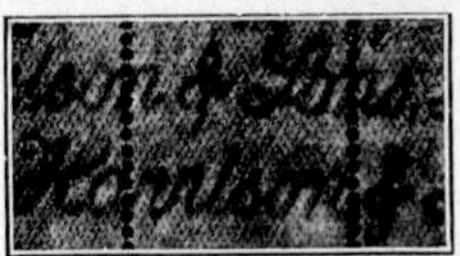

Wmk. 233 — Harrison & Sons, London in Script Letters

Wmk. 299 — Thai Characters and Wavy Lines

Wmk. 329 — Zigzag Lines

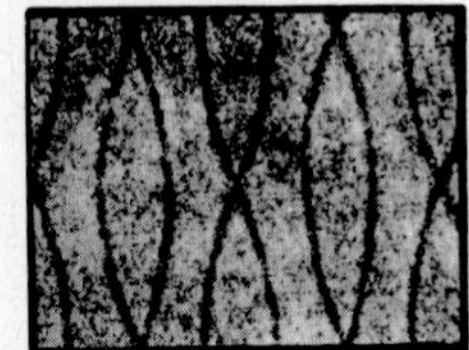

Wmk. 334 — Rectangles

Wmk. 340 — Alternating Interlaced Wavy Lines

Wmk. 356 — POSTAGE

Wmk. 368 — JEZ Multiple

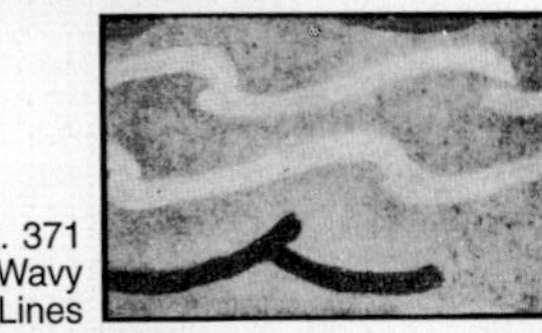

Wmk. 371 — Wavy Lines

Wmk. 374 — Circles and Crosses

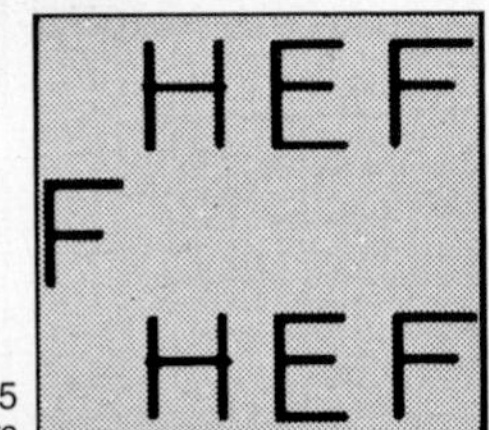

Wmk. 375 — Letters

Wmk. 377 — Interlocking Circles

Wmk. 385 — CARTOR

Wmk. 387 — Squares and Rectangles

King Chulalongkorn
A1 A2

A4

1883, Aug. 4 Unwmk. Engr.
Perf. 14½, 15

No.				Unused	Used
1	A1	1sol	dark blue	15.00	13.00
b.			Imperf., pair		*4,000.*
2	A1	1att	carmine	16.50	15.00
3	A1	1sio	vermilion	32.50	30.00
4	A2	1sik	yellow	16.50	15.00
5	A4	1sa	orange	45.00	45.00
a.			1sa ocher	52.50	52.50
			Nos. 1-5 (5)	125.50	118.00

There are three types of No. 1, differing mainly in the background of the small oval at the top.

A 1 fuang red, of similar design to the foregoing, was prepared but not placed in use. Value, $2,000.

For surcharges see Nos. 6-8, 19.

No. 1 Handstamp Surcharged in Red

a

b

c

d

e

1885, July 1

No.			Unused	Used
6	A1 (a)	1t on 1sol blue	*4,800.*	*3,600.*
7	A1 (b)	1t on 1sol blue	*450.*	*350.*
c.		"1" inverted	*4,000.*	*4,000.*
8	A1 (c)	1t on 1sol blue	*3,000.*	*2,750.*

Surcharges of Nos. 6-8 have been counterfeited.

Types "d" and "e" are typeset *official reprints.*

As is usual with handstamps, double impressions, etc., exist.

King Chulalongkorn — A7

1887-91 Typo. Wmk. 176 *Perf. 14*

No.				Unused	Used
11	A7	1a	green ('91)	6.50	2.00
12	A7	2a	green & car	6.50	2.00
13	A7	3a	grn & blue	12.00	4.00
14	A7	4a	grn & org brn	12.00	4.75
15	A7	8a	green & yel	12.00	7.00
16	A7	12a	lilac & car	17.50	3.50
17	A7	24a	lilac & blue	24.00	4.00
18	A7	64a	lil & org brn	87.50	29.00
			Nos. 11-18 (8)	178.00	56.25

Nos. 11-18 were printed with fugitive ink. Immersion in water will discolor the stamps.

The design of No. 11 has been redrawn and differs in many minor details from Nos. 12-18.

Issue dates: Nos. 12-18, Apr. 1; No. 11, Feb.

For surcharges see Nos. 20-69, 109, 111, 126.

No. 3 Handstamp Surcharged

Type I - the lower right corner character is squared.

Type II - the lower right corner character is rounded.

1889, Aug. Unwmk. *Perf. 15*

No.			Unused	Used
19	A1	1a on 1sio	21.00	21.00
a.		Type II	*150.00*	*150.00*
b.		Pair as "a," one without ovpt.	*1,500.*	
c.		Double surcharge	*300.00*	*300.00*
d.		Inverted surcharge	*900.00*	

Type I exists in three different subtypes. Type Ia - the top character is 0.6mm to 0.7mm above the top of the left character, and the box portion of the lower right character is closed. Type Ib - the top character is 0.7mm to 0.8mm above the top of the left character and has a partial bar on top of the box portion of the lower right character. Type Ic - the top character is 0.8mm to 1mm above the top of the left character and the box portion of the lower right character has no top. Type IIa - the rounded box portion of the lower right character is closed. Type IIb - the rounded box portion of the lower right character is open. Type I used a device supplied by Bradley's Printing, Publishing and Binding House. Type II used a device supplied by the Bangkolem Printing Office and Publishing House.

Nos. 12 and 13 Handstamp Surcharged

1889-90 Wmk. 176 *Perf. 14*

No.			Unused	Used
20	A7	1a on 2a	10.00	6.00
a.		"1" omitted	*450.00*	*450.00*
c.		1st Siamese character invtd.	950.00	950.00
d.		First Siamese character omitted	*950.00*	*950.00*
e.		Double surcharge	*240.00*	*240.00*
f.		Inverted surcharge	*1,900.*	*1,900.*
g.		Double surcharge, one inverted	*3,500.*	
21	A7	1a on 3a ('90)	9.00	9.00
a.		Inverted "1"	*150.00*	*150.00*

The first setting of No. 20 was done in three operations resulting in an irregular placement of both the Siamese and English numerals in relation to the script. The process was streamlined in the second setting to one operation. Eight different handstamps varying in length from 14.1mm to 15.2mm were used in the second setting.

No. 21 was applied using four different handstamps varying in length between 14.5mm and 15.5mm.

English numeral is 6mm high, with prominent serif and foot.

For surcharge see No. 29.

22	A7	1a on 2a grn & car	*475.00*	*475.00*

English numeral is 5mm high, with a narrow vertical and serif.

24	A7	1a on 2a grn & car	*350.00*	*350.00*

English numeral is short and thick, with a short, thick serif.

25	A7	1a on 2a grn & car	*2,000.*	*1,000.*

The surcharge on No. 25 was applied in three stages resulting in an irregular placement of both the Siamese and English numerals in relation to the script.

English numeral is 6.2mm high, without a foot. The serif is a thin perpendicular line.

26 A7 1a on 3a grn & bl

English numeral is 6mm high. The length of the surcharge is 14.8mm to 15mm wide. The Siamese numeral is angled rather than flat on top. The left script character has a slight point in the bottom line. The bottom right character is smoothly curved on the bottom rather than squared.

Only 36 examples of No. 26 are known: 17 mint and 19 used.

Some experts believe No. 26 to be a forgery, however this issue is currently unresolved.

No. 13 Handstamp Surcharged

1891

27	A7 2a on 3a grn & bl	95.00	65.00

The English numeral is thick, 6.3mm high and has a straight foot that is 3mm long with a slight upstroke at the end. The surcharge is 17.9mm long.

28	A7 2a on 3a grn & bl	55.00	55.00
a.	Double surcharge	*250.00*	*250.00*
b.	"2" omitted	*250.00*	

The English numeral is thin, 6mm high and has a straight foot that is 2.5mm long without an upstroke at the end. The surcharge measures 16.3mm long.

No. 21 with Additional 2 Att Surcharge

29	A7 2a on 1a on 3a grn & bl	*2,000.*	*1,800.*

On No. 29 the 2a surcharge consists of Siamese numeral like No. 27 and English numeral like No. 28.

Most examples of No. 29 show attempts to remove the "1" of the first surcharge.

Typeset Surcharge

30	A7 2a on 3a grn & bl	60.00	45.00

Seven types of this surcharge exist from one setting. The variations arise from differences in the top Siamese character and the English numeral. Type I - the top Siamese character is angled upward. Type II - the top Siamese character is mostly horizontal. Type a - the right curve of the "2" is rounded, and the "2" has a long tail. Type b - the right curve of the "2" is straight, the bottom bar is thick, and the tail is long. Type c - the right curve of the "2" is rounded, and the "2" has a vestigial tail. Type d - the "2" is 4.5mm tall, as opposed to 4mm on the other types. The right curve of the "2" is straight, the bottom bar is thick and uneven on top, and the tail is long. It is estimated that only 100 sheets were surcharged. On each sheet Type 1a appears 42 times; Type 1b, 17 times; Type 1c, 15 times; Type 1d, 1 time; Type 2a, 38 times, Type 2b, 2 times, Type 2c, 5 times.

Issued: #27-28, Jan.; #29, Feb.; #30, Mar.

No. 17 Handstamp Surcharged

f

g

1892, Oct.

33	A7 (f) 4a on 24a lil & bl	60.00	50.00
34	A7 (g) 4a on 24a lil & bl	55.00	35.00

Surcharges exist double on Nos. 33-34 and inverted on No. 33.

Nos. 33-34 Handstamp Surcharged in English

1892, Nov.

35	A7 4a on 24a lil & bl	12.00	9.00
c.	Inverted "s"	*75.00*	*60.00*

36	A7 4a on 24a lil & bl	20.00	10.00
a.	Inverted "s"	*90.00*	*90.00*

37	A7 4a on 24a lil & bl	15.00	12.50

38	A7 4a on 24a lil & bl	20.00	15.00

Numerous inverts., doubles, etc., exist.

Nos. 35 and 37 are surcharged examples of No. 33. Nos. 36 and 38 are surcharged examples of No. 34. The "4 atts" surcharge is in small Roman type on Nos. 35 and 36 and in large Roman type on Nos. 37 and 38. During the typesetting, Antique characters were mixed with the Roman characters and are often found on the same stamp. These are worth more.

Type I

Type II

Two fonts of Siamese characters exist:

Type I — the left character is narrower, the upper right of the right character is at approximately a 45-degree angle, and the bottom part of the lower right character is kinked. Type I occurs on Nos. 39-46, 50d, 51-66, and 68-69.

Type II — the left character is wider, the upper right of the right character is vertical, and the bottom part of the lower right character is rounded. Type II occurs on Nos. 47-50, and 67.

Large Roman Type

Nos. 18 and 17 Typeset Srchd. in English and Siamese

1894

39	A7 1a on 64a lil & org brn	3.50	3.50
a.	Inverted "s"	*70.00*	*60.00*
b.	Inverted surcharge	*900.00*	*900.00*
d.	Italic "s"	*200.00*	*200.00*
e.	Italic "1"	*350.00*	*300.00*

Two spacings exist on each sheet between the English and the Siamese portions of the surcharge: 10mm (72 positions) and 8.5mm (48 positions).

No. 40

No. 40e

40	A7 1a on 64a lil & org brn	2.00	1.50
a.	Inverted capital "S" added to the surcharge	*75.00*	*60.00*
b.	Capital "S" added to the surcharge	*60.00*	*60.00*
c.	Small "S" added to the surcharge	*60.00*	*60.00*
d.	Inverted small "S" added to the surcharge	*75.00*	*75.00*
e.	Narrow font	*20.00*	*18.00*

The dimensions are the same for the letters in No. 40e as No. 40, however No. 40e lacks the bold thick lines in the letters that No. 40 exhibits.

Two spacings exist on each sheet between the English and the Siamese portions of the surcharge: 10mm (72 positions) and 8.5mm (48 positions).

h

i

j

k

l m

41	A7 (h) 2a on 64a	20.00	15.00
a.	Inverted "s"	*90.00*	*60.00*
b.	Double surcharge	*100.00*	*100.00*
42	A7 (i) 2a on 64a	*2,000.*	*2,000.*
43	A7 (j) 2a on 64a	80.00	70.00
44	A7 (k) 2a on 64a	40.00	30.00
45	A7 (l) 2a on 64a	65.00	45.00
46	A7 (m) 2a on 64a	6.00	3.00
a.	"Att.s"	*60.00*	*60.00*

Nos. 41-46 were in one plate of 120 subjects. The differences in the numeral "2" are as follows. No. 41 is 2.75mm tall with a straight foot. No. 42 is 3.5mm tall with a curved foot. No. 43 is 3.5mm tall with a straight foot. No. 44 is 2.75mm tall with a curved foot. No. 45 is 2.6mm tall in script style. No. 46 is 2mm tall with a straight foot.

Two spacings exist on each sheet between the English and the Siamese portions of the surcharge: 10mm and 8.5mm.

The quantities on each sheet of each type and spacing are: h (8.5mm), 9; h (10mm), 29; i (8.5mm), 1; j (10mm), 8; k (8.5mm), 13; k (10mm), 5; l (8.5mm), 5; 1 (10mm), 6; m (8.5mm), 20; m (10mm), 24.

A second setting was also printed made entirely of No. 46.

Small Roman Type

1894, Oct. 12

47	A7 1a on 64a	5.00	3.00
a.	Surcharged on face and back	*150.00*	
b.	As "a," surcharge on back inverted	*200.00*	
c.	Double surcharge	*475.00*	
d.	Inverted surcharge	*600.00*	
e.	Siamese surcharge omitted	*300.00*	

The first setting, issued Oct. 12, 1894, has an English surcharge that is 10mm in length.

See No. 67.

48	A7 2a on 64a	4.00	3.00
a.	"Att"	*75.00*	*45.00*
b.	Inverted surcharge	*750.00*	*650.00*
c.	Surch. on face and back	*200.00*	*200.00*
d.	Surcharge on back inverted	*210.00*	*210.00*
e.	Double surcharge	*150.00*	*150.00*
f.	Double surch., one inverted	*900.00*	*800.00*
g.	Inverted "s"	*35.00*	*30.00*

The first setting, issued Oct. 12, 1894, has an English surcharge that is 12mm in length. The second setting has an English surcharge that is 10mm in length.

1895, July 23

49	A7 10a on 24a lil & bl	9.00	2.00
a.	Inverted "s"	*60.00*	*30.00*
b.	Surch. on face and back	*240.00*	*200.00*
c.	Surcharge on back inverted	*240.00*	*240.00*

Large Roman Type

No. 16 Surcharged in English and Siamese

1896

50	A7 4a on 12a lil & car	25.00	8.00
a.	Inverted "s"	90.00	60.00
b.	Surcharged on face and back	225.00	200.00
c.	Double surcharge on back	175.00	175.00
d.	Small Roman type	30.00	15.00

No. 50 is in large Roman type, and the distance between the English and the Siamese portion of the surcharges is 11mm. No. 50d is in small Roman type, and the distance between the English and Siamese portions of the surcharge is 8.5mm.

Nos. 16-18 Surcharged in English and Siamese Antique Surcharges

a

b

c

d

e

f

Antique Letters **Atts.**

Roman Letters **Atts.**

1898-99

51	A7 (a) 1a on 12a	450.00	400.00
52	A7 (b) 1a on 12a	20.00	7.00
53	A7 (c) 2a on 64a ('99)	35.00	9.00
54	A7 (d) 3a on 12a	12.00	4.00
a.	Double surcharge	*500.00*	*450.00*
55	A7 (e) 4a on 12a	15.00	5.00
a.	Double surcharge	*400.00*	*375.00*
56	A7 (e) 4a on 24a ('99)	45.00	14.00
57	A7 (f) 10a on 24a ('99)	825.00	825.00
	Nos. 51-57 (7)	1,402.	1,264.

Roman Surcharges

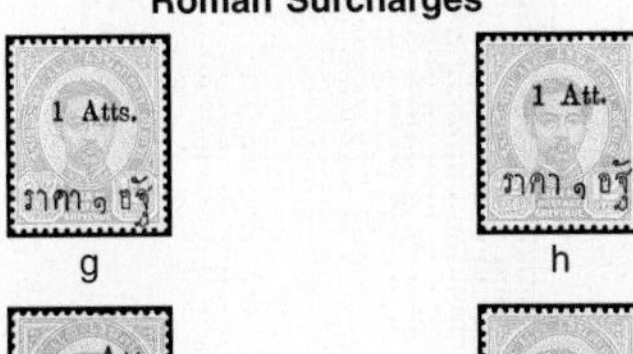

g h

i j

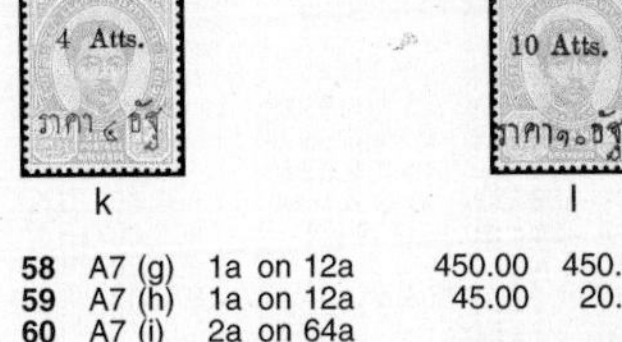

k l

No.	Type	Description	Unused	Used
58	A7 (g)	1a on 12a	450.00	450.00
59	A7 (h)	1a on 12a	45.00	20.00
60	A7 (i)	2a on 64a ('99)	35.00	10.00
61	A7 (j)	3a on 12a	85.00	19.00
62	A7 (k)	4a on 12a	40.00	14.00
a.		Double surcharge	*175.00*	*175.00*
b.		No period after "Atts."	*35.00*	*35.00*
63	A7 (k)	4a on 24a ('99)	60.00	29.00
64	A7 (l)	10a on 24a ('99)	750.00	750.00
		Nos. 58-64 (7)	1,465.	1,292.

There are two settings of "Atts." referred to as general settings. When new values were needed the numbers were replaced in the type setting but the letters remained in place. This applies to all values of Nos. 51-57. Nos. 58-64 with complete Roman characters come only from general setting 2.

General Setting 1 contains the following varieties of Roman characters: "A," 1st "t," 2nd "t," and "s."

General Setting 2 contains the following varieties of Roman characters: "A," "Atts," "ts," 2nd "t," "Att," and "s."

The 1a on 12a surcharges were printed in 3 settings. No. 52 - the English surcharge in the first setting (General Setting 1) reading "Att." is 12mm long and the distance between the English and Siamese portions is 8mm. Nos. 51 and 58 - In the second setting (General Setting 2), the English surcharge reads "Atts." is 11.5mm long, and the distance between the English and Siamese portions is 8.5mm to 9mm. Nos. 52 and 59 - In the third setting (General Setting 2), the English surcharge reads "Att." is 10mm long, and the distance between the English and Siamese portions is 8.5mm to 9mm.

Nos. 53 and 60 -There are two setting both using General Setting 2: the first setting the distance between the fourth Siamese character and the Siamese numeral is 2mm; in the second setting the distance is 1mm.

Nos. 54 and 61 - the English surcharge in the first setting (General Setting 1) is 13.5mm long. In the second setting (General Setting 1), the English surcharge is 12mm long and the distance between the English and Siamese portions is 8mm. In the third setting (General Setting 2), the English surcharge is 12mm long and the distance between the English and Siamese portions is 8.5mm to 9mm.

Nos. 55 and 62 - In the first setting (General Setting 1), the English surcharge is 12mm long and the distance between the English and Siamese portions is 8mm. In the second setting (General Setting 2), the English surcharge is 11.5mm to 12mm long and the distance between the English and Siamese portions is 8.5mm to 9mm.

Nos. 56 and 63 - Only one setting was used from General Setting 2.

Nos. 57 and 64 - Only one setting was used from General Setting 2.

Nos. 16 and 18 Surcharged in English and Siamese Surcharged

m

n

o

p

r

1894-99

No.	Type	Description	Unused	Used
65	A7 (m)	1a on 12a	20.00	6.00
66	A7 (n)	1a on 12a	20.00	6.00
a.		Inverted "1"	*300.00*	*200.00*
b.		Inverted 1st "t"	*200.00*	*175.00*
67	A7 (o)	1a on 64a	5.00	5.00
68	A7 (p)	2a on 64a	35.00	8.00
a.		"1 Atts."	*500.00*	*500.00*
69	A7 (r)	2a on 64a	24.00	8.00
		Nos. 65-69 (5)	104.00	33.00

Both the 1a on 12a and the 2a on 64a surcharges were printed such that Nos. 65 and 68 were printed on the left half of the sheet and Nos. 66 and 69 were printed on the right side of the sheet.

No. 65 is in large Roman font, measuring 13mm to 14mm wide. No. 66 is in small widely spaced Roman font, measuring 14mm to 15mm wide. No. 68 is in large Roman font, and No. 69 is in small widely spaced Roman font.

No. 67 is the second setting of No. 47. It has an English surcharge that is 8.75mm in length.

Issued: No. 67, 12/29/95; others, 2/14/99.

See No. 47.

A13

1899, Oct. Typo. Unwmk.

No.	Type	Description	Unused	Used
70	A13	1a dull green	450.	85.
71	A13	2a dl grn & rose	550.	150.
72	A13	3a car & blue	800.	200.
73	A13	4a black & grn	3,000.	600.
74	A13	10a car & grn	3,000.	600.
		Nos. 70-74 (5)	7,800.	1,635.

The King rejected Nos. 70-74 in 1897, but some were released by mistake to three post offices in Oct. 1899. Used values are for stamps canceled to order at Korat in Dec. 1899. Values for postally used stamps are listed in the Scott Classic Specialized catalog.

A14

1899-1904

No.	Type	Description	Unused	Used
75	A14	1a gray green	5.00	.75
76	A14	2a yellow green	3.50	.75
77	A14	2a scarlet & bl	6.00	1.25
78	A14	3a red & blue	8.50	2.00
79	A14	3a green	20.00	12.00
80	A14	4a dark rose	5.50	1.25
81	A14	4a vio brn & rose	12.00	1.75
82	A14	6a dk rose	35.00	14.00
83	A14	8a dk grn & org	10.00	2.00
84	A14	10a ultra	10.50	2.50
85	A14	12a brn vio & rose	40.00	2.00
86	A14	14a ultra	23.00	18.00
87	A14	24a brn vio & bl	300.00	25.00
88	A14	28a vio brn & bl	25.00	25.00
89	A14	64a brn vio & org brn	70.00	11.00
		Nos. 75-89 (15)	574.00	119.25

Two types of 1a differ in size and shape of Thai "1" are in drawing of spandrel ornaments.

Issue dates: 6a, 14a, 28a, Nos. 77, 79, 81, Jan. 1, 1904; others, Sept. 1899.

For surcharges see Nos. 90-91, 112, 125, 127.

Nos. 78 and 85 With Typewritten Srch. of 6 or 7 Siamese Characters (1 line) in Violet

1902

No.	Type	Description	Unused	Used
78a	A14	2a on 3a	*5,000.*	*5,250.*
85a	A14	10a on 12a	*5,000.*	*5,250.*

Nos. 78a and 85a were authorized provisionals, surcharged and issued by the Battambang postmaster.

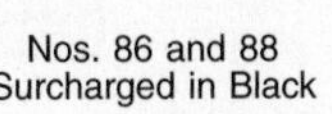

Nos. 86 and 88 Surcharged in Black

1905, Feb.

No.	Type	Description	Unused	Used
90	A14	1a on 14a	10.00	10.00
a.		No period after "Att"	60.00	60.00
b.		Double surcharge	*175.00*	*175.00*
91	A14	2a on 28a	12.00	10.00
a.		Double surcharge	*150.00*	*150.00*
b.		No period after "Att"	60.00	60.00

King Chulalongkorn — A15

1905-08 Engr.

No.	Type	Description	Unused	Used
92	A15	1a orange & green	3.50	1.25
93	A15	2a violet & slate	3.50	1.25
94	A15	2a green ('08)	12.50	5.50
95	A15	3a green	7.50	2.00
96	A15	3a vio & sl ('08)	15.00	9.00
97	A15	4a gray & red	10.00	1.25
98	A15	4a car & rose ('08)	12.00	2.50
99	A15	5a carmine & rose	12.00	3.00
100	A15	8a blk & ol bis	13.00	1.50
101	A15	9a blue ('08)	30.00	9.00
102	A15	12a blue	18.00	4.00
103	A15	18a red brn ('08)	80.00	27.50
104	A15	24a red brown	35.00	8.00
105	A15	1t dp bl & brn org	47.50	8.00
		Nos. 92-105 (14)	299.50	83.75

Issue dates: Dec. 1905, Apr. 1, 1908.

For surcharges and overprints see Nos. 110, 113-117, 128-138, 161-162, B15, B21.

King Chulalongkorn — A16

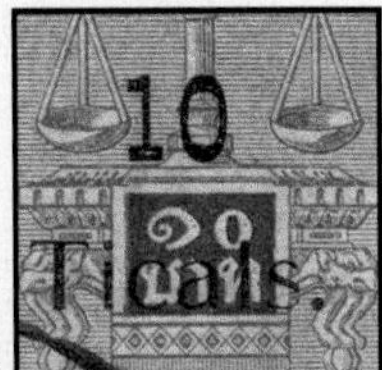

No. 106

No. 107

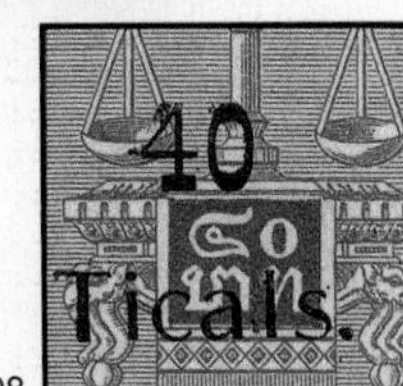

No. 108

1907, Apr. 24 Black Surcharge

No.	Type	Description	Unused	Used
106	A16	10t gray green	*750.00*	*100.00*
107	A16	20t gray green	*6,750.*	*350.00*
108	A16	40t gray green	*5,100.*	*600.00*
		Nos. 106-108 (3)	*12,600.*	*1,050.*

Counterfeits of Nos. 106-108 exist. In the genuine, the surcharged figures correspond to the Siamese value inscriptions on the basic revenue stamps.

No. 17 Surcharged

1907, Dec. 16

No.	Type	Description	Unused	Used
109	A7	1a on 24a lil & bl	5.50	1.50
a.		Double surcharge	450.00	

No. 99 Surcharged

1908, Sept.

No.	Type	Description	Unused	Used
110	A15	4a on 5a car & rose	12.00	4.00

The No. 110 surcharge is found in two spacings of the numerals: normally 15mm apart, and a narrow, scarcer spacing of 13½mm.

Nos. 17 and 84 Surcharged in Black

No.	Type	Description	Unused	Used
111	A7	2a on 24a lil & bl	4.50	1.20
a.		Inverted surcharge	*350.00*	*350.00*
112	A14	9a on 10a ultra	16.00	5.00
a.		Inverted surcharge	*450.00*	*450.00*

Jubilee Issue

Nos. 92, 95, 110, 100 and 103 Overprinted in Black or Red

1908, Nov. 11

No.	Type	Description	Unused	Used
113	A15	1a	4.50	1.25
a.		Siamese date "137" instead of "127"	*1,050.*	*1,050.*
b.		Pair, one without ovpt.	1,500.	1,500.
114	A15	3a	7.50	3.25
115	A15	4a on 5a	9.00	4.50
a.		Pair, imperf on 3 sides	*2,400.*	
116	A15	8a (R)	24.00	24.00
117	A15	18a	32.50	21.00
		Nos. 113-117 (5)	77.50	54.00

40th year of the reign of King Chulalongkorn.

Nos. 113 to 117 exist with a small "i" in "Jubilee."

Statue of King Chulalongkorn — A19

1908, Nov. 11 Engr. *Perf. 13½*

No.	Type	Description	Unused	Used
118	A19	1t green & vio	60.00	9.00
119	A19	2t red vio & org	120.00	20.00
120	A19	3t pale ol & bl	175.00	21.00
121	A19	5t dl vio & dk grn	240.00	42.50
122	A19	10t bister & car	*1,050.*	125.00
123	A19	20t gray & red brn	700.00	125.00
124	A19	40t sl bl & blk brn	950.00	400.00
		Nos. 118-124 (7)	*3,295.*	742.50

The inscription at the foot of the stamps reads: "Coronation Commemoration-Forty-first year of the reign-1908."

Stamps of 1887-1904 Surcharged

1909 *Perf. 14*

No.	Type	Description	Unused	Used
125	A14	6s on 6a dk rose	3.00	1.50
126	A7	14s on 12a lil & car	135.00	120.00
127	A14	14s on 14a ultra	27.50	22.50
		Nos. 125-127 (3)	165.50	144.00

Nos. 92-102 Surcharged with Bar and

1909, Aug. 15

No.	Type	Description	Unused	Used
128	A15	2s on 1a #92	3.00	1.20
129	A15	2s on 2a #93	60.00	60.00
130	A15	2s on 2a #94	3.00	1.20
a.		"2" omitted	*600.00*	600.00
131	A15	3s on 3a #95	15.00	12.00
132	A15	3s on 3a #96	6.00	1.25
133	A15	6s on 4a #97	45.00	35.00
134	A15	6s on 4a #98	9.00	2.00

135 A15 6s on 5a #99 13.00 8.75
136 A15 12s on 8a #100 9.00 1.50
137 A15 14s on 9a #101 11.00 1.75
138 A15 14s on 12a #102 27.00 21.00
Nos. 128-138 (11) 201.00 145.65

King Chulalongkorn — A20

1910 Engr. *Perf. 14x14½*
139 A20 2s org & green 3.00 1.50
140 A20 3s green 4.50 1.50
141 A20 6s carmine 7.50 2.50
142 A20 12s blk & ol brn 16.00 2.50
143 A20 14s blue 25.00 3.50
144 A20 28s red brown 47.50 10.00
Nos. 139-144 (6) 103.50 21.50

Issue dates: 12s, June 5. Others, May 5.
For surcharges see Nos. 163, 223-224.

A21

King Vajiravudh — A22

Printed at the Imperial Printing Works, Vienna

1912 *Perf. 14½*
145 A21 2s brn org 1.75 .60
a. Vert. pair, imperf. btwn. *600.00 600.00*
b. Horiz. pair, imperf. btwn. *600.00 600.00*
146 A21 3s yellow green 1.75 .60
a. Horiz. pair, imperf. btwn. *600.00 600.00*
b. Vert. pair, imperf. btwn. *600.00 600.00*
147 A21 6s car rose 3.00 1.00
148 A21 12s gray blk & brn 3.50 1.00
149 A21 14s ultramarine 5.50 1.50
150 A21 28s chocolate 20.00 10.00
151 A22 1b blue & blk 30.00 2.40
a. Vert. pair, imperf. btwn. *1,800. 1,800.*
b. Horiz. pair, imperf. btwn. *1,800. 1,800.*
152 A22 2b car rose & ol brn 35.00 3.00
153 A22 3b yel grn & bl blk 42.50 4.50
154 A22 5b vio & blk 65.00 7.50
155 A22 10b ol grn & vio brn 325.00 60.00
156 A22 20b sl bl & red brn 500.00 65.00
Nos. 145-156 (12) 1,033. 157.10

See Nos. 164-175.
For surcharges and overprints see Nos. 157-160, 176-186, 206, B1-B14, B16-B20, B22, B31-B33.

Nos. 147-150 Surcharged in Red or Blue

1914-15
157 A21 2s on 14s (R) ('15) 3.00 .70
a. Vert. pair, imperf. btwn. *600.00 600.00*
b. Double surcharge 450.00 450.00
158 A21 5s on 6s (Bl) 5.50 .50
a. Horiz. pair, imperf. btwn. *600.00 600.00*
b. Double surcharge 300.00 300.00
159 A21 10s on 12s (R) 5.50 .75
a. Double surcharge 300.00 300.00
160 A21 15s on 28s (Bl) 10.00 1.25
Nos. 157-160 (4) 24.00 3.20

The several settings of the surcharges on Nos. 157-160 show variations in the figures and letters.

Nos. 92-93 Surcharged

1915, Apr. 3
161 A15 2s on 1a org & grn 8.00 4.00
a. Pair, one without surcharge *600.00 600.00*
162 A15 2s on 2a vio & slate 8.25 4.00

No. 143 Surcharged in Red

1916, Oct.
163 A20 2s on 14s blue 6.00 2.00

Types of 1912 Re-engraved

Printed by Waterlow & Sons, London

1917, Jan. 1 *Perf. 14*
164 A21 2s orange brown 1.50 .30
165 A21 3s emerald 2.50 .60
166 A21 5s rose red 4.00 .30
167 A21 10s black & olive 3.50 .30
168 A21 15s blue 6.00 1.00
170 A22 1b bl & gray blk 28.00 4.00
171 A22 2b car rose & brn 100.00 42.50
172 A22 3b yellow grn & blk 450.00 275.00
173 A22 5b dp violet & blk 350.00 190.00
174 A22 10b ol gray & vio brn 525.00 25.00
a. Perf. 12½ 600.00 37.50
175 A22 20b sea grn & brn 700.00 70.00
a. Perf. 12½ 750.00 75.00
Nos. 164-175 (11) 2,171. 609.00

The re-engraved design of the satang stamps varies in numerous minute details from the 1912 issue. Four lines of the background appear between the vertical strokes of the "M" of "SIAM" in the 1912 issue and only three lines in the 1917 stamps.

The 1912 stamps with value in bahts are 37½mm high; those of 1917 are 39mm. In the latter the king's features, especially the eyes and mouth, are more distinct and the uniform and decorations are more sharply defined.

The 1912 stamps have seven pearls between the earpieces of the crown. The "A" and "M" of "SIAM" are connected. On the 1917 stamps there are nine pearls in the same place. The "A" and "M" of "SIAM" are not connected. Nos. 174 and 175 exist imperforate.

Nos. 164-173 Overprinted in Red

1918, Dec. 2
176 A21 2s orange brown 2.00 .50
a. Double overprint 175.00 175.00
177 A21 3s emerald 2.50 1.00
a. Double overprint 175.00 175.00
178 A21 5s rose red 2.50 1.50
a. Double overprint 240.00 240.00
179 A21 10s black & olive 4.50 3.00
180 A21 15s blue 8.00 6.00
181 A22 1b bl & gray blk 35.00 24.00
182 A22 2b car rose & brn 65.00 47.50
183 A22 3b yel grn & blk 175.00 125.00
184 A22 5b dp vio & blk 475.00 325.00
Nos. 176-184 (9) 769.50 533.50

Counterfeits of this overprint exist.

Nos. 147-148 Surcharged in Green or Red

1919-20
185 A21 5s on 6s (G) 2.75 .50
186 A21 10s on 12s (R) ('20) 4.50 .60

Issue dates: 5s, Nov. 11. 10s, Jan. 1.

King Vajiravudh — A23

Perf. 14-15, 12½ (#192)

1920-26 Engr.
187 A23 2s brn, *yel* ('21) 2.00 .50
188 A23 3s grn, *grn* ('21) 3.50 .60
189 A23 3s chocolate ('24) 1.75 .50
190 A23 5s rose, *pale rose* 3.00 .50
191 A23 5s green ('22) 30.00 4.00
192 A23 5s dk vio, *lil* ('26) 8.00 .50
193 A23 10s black & org ('21) 6.00 .50
194 A23 15s bl, *bluish* ('21) 9.50 .60
a. Perf. 12½ ('25) 500.00 *4.25*
195 A23 15s carmine ('22) 42.50 6.00
196 A23 25s chocolate ('21) 24.00 3.00
197 A23 25s dk blue ('22) 35.00 1.40
198 A23 50s ocher & blk ('21) 45.00 2.00
a. Perf. 12½ ('25) 170.00 *2.90*
Nos. 187-198 (12) 210.25 20.10

For overprints see Nos. 205, B23-B30.

Throne Room — A24

1926, Mar. 5 *Perf. 12½*
199 A24 1t gray vio & grn 16.00 3.50
200 A24 2t car & org red 35.00 6.00
201 A24 3t ol grn & bl 67.50 25.00
202 A24 5t dl vio & ol grn 110.00 25.00
203 A24 10t red & ol bis 400.00 32.50
204 A24 20t gray bl & brn 450.00 100.00
Nos. 199-204 (6) 1,079. 192.00

This issue was intended to commemorate the fifteenth year of the reign of King Vajiravudh. Because of the King's death the stamps were issued as ordinary postage stamps.

Nos. 195 and 150 with Surcharge similar to 1914-15 Issue in Black or Red

1928, Jan.
205 A23 5s on 15s car 5.50 2.75
206 A21 10s on 28s choc (R) 12.00 1.00

King Prajadhipok
A25 A26

1928 Engr. *Perf. 12½*
207 A25 2s dp red brn 1.00 .30
208 A25 3s deep green 1.50 .50
209 A25 5s dark violet 1.00 .30
210 A25 10s deep rose 1.20 .30
211 A25 15s dark blue 2.40 .45
212 A25 25s black & org 4.50 .60
213 A25 50s brn org & blk 7.50 .90
214 A25 80s blue & black 7.50 .90
216 A26 1b dk blue & blk 14.00 1.25
217 A26 2b car rose & blk brn 21.00 2.50
218 A26 3b yellow grn & blk 22.50 4.00
219 A26 5b dp vio & gray blk 30.00 6.00
220 A26 10b ol grn & red vio 65.00 10.00
221 A26 20b Prus grn & brn 120.00 20.00
222 A26 40b dk grn & ol brn 210.00 90.00
Nos. 207-222 (15) 509.10 138.00
Set, never hinged 650.00

On the single colored stamps, type A25, the lines in the background are uniform; those of the bicolored values are shaded and do not extend to the frame.

Issue dates: 5s, 10s, 2b-40b, Apr. 15; 2s, 3s, 15s, 25s, 50s, May 1; 1b, June 1; 80s, Nov. 15.

For overprints & surcharge see Nos. 300-301, B34.

Nos. 142, 144 Surcharged in Red or Blue

1930 *Perf. 14*
223 A20 10s on 12s blk & ol brn 8.75 1.50
224 A20 25s on 28s red brn (Bl) 30.00 2.25
Set, never hinged 50.00

King Prajadhipok and Chao P'ya Chakri
A27 A28

Statue of Chao P'ya Chakri — A29

1932, Apr. 1 Engr. *Perf. 12½*
225 A27 2s dark brown 2.00 .40
226 A27 3s deep green 3.50 1.00
227 A27 5s dull violet 2.00 .40
228 A28 10s red brn & blk 2.00 .25
229 A28 15s dull blue & blk 11.00 1.50
230 A28 25s violet & black 18.00 2.00
231 A28 50s claret & black 62.50 3.00
232 A29 1b blue black 100.00 16.00
Nos. 225-232 (8) 201.00 24.55
Set, never hinged 275.00

150th anniv. of the Chakri dynasty, the founding of Bangkok in 1782, and the opening of the memorial bridge across the Chao Phraya River.

Assembly Hall, Bangkok — A30

1939, June 24 Litho. *Perf. 11, 12*
233 A30 2s dull red brown 4.50 1.50
234 A30 3s green 12.00 3.50
235 A30 5s dark violet 6.50 .60
236 A30 10s carmine 16.00 .60
237 A30 15s dark blue 35.00 1.50
Nos. 233-237 (5) 74.00 7.70
Set, never hinged 95.00

7th anniv. of the Siamese Constitution.

Chakri Palace, Bangkok — A31

1940 Typo. *Perf. 12½*
238 A31 2s dull brown 6.50 1.00
239 A31 3s dp yellow grn 11.00 3.50
a. Cliché of 5s in plate of 3s 900.00 *725.00*
240 A31 5s dark violet 8.00 .50
241 A31 10s carmine 20.00 .50
242 A31 15s dark blue 40.00 1.50
Nos. 238-242 (5) 85.50 7.00
Set, never hinged 135.00

Issued: 2s, 3s, 5/13; 5s, 5/24; 15s, 5/28; 10s, 5/30.

King Ananda Mahidol A32

Plowing Rice Field A33

Royal Pavilion at Bang-pa-in — A34

1941, Apr. 17 Engr.
243 A32 2s brown 2.50 .55
244 A32 3s deep green 3.25 1.00
245 A32 5s violet 2.00 .55
246 A32 10s dark red 2.00 .55
247 A33 15s dp bl & gray blk 4.00 1.00
248 A33 25s slate & org 5.50 1.25
249 A33 50s red org & slate 5.00 1.50
250 A34 1b brt ultra & gray 22.50 5.00
251 A34 2b dk car rose & gray 14.00 2.50
252 A34 3b dp grn & gray 55.00 7.00

253 A34 5b blk & rose red 90.00 27.50
a. Horiz. pair, imperf. btwn.
254 A34 10b ol blk & yel 140.00 80.00
Nos. 243-254 (12) 345.75 128.40
Set, never hinged 450.00

King Ananda Mahidol — A35

1943, May 1 Unwmk. *Perf. 11*
255 A35 1b dark blue 30.00 3.00
a. Horiz. pair, imperf. btwn. 140.00 140.00
b. Vert. pair, imperf. btwn. 140.00 140.00
c. Imperf. pair 140.00 140.00

See No. 274.

Indo-China War Monument — A36

1943 Engr. *Perf. 11, 12½*
256 A36 3s dark green 25.00 21.00

Litho.
Perf. 12½x11
257 A36 3s dull green 6.50 3.00

Issue dates: No. 256, June 1. No. 257, Nov. 2.

Bangkhaen Monument — A37

Two types of 10s:
I — Size 19½x24mm.
II — Size 20¾x25¼mm.

1943, Nov. 25 *Perf. 12½, 12½x11*
258 A37 2s brown orange 2.50 3.25
259 A37 10s car rose (I) 10.00 6.00
a. Type II 5.50 1.75

10th anniv. of the quelling of a counter-revolution led by a member of the royal family on Oct. 11, 1933.
Stamps of similar design, but with values in "cents," are listed under Malaya, Occupation Stamps. See Nos. 2N1-2N6.

King Bhumibol Adulyadej — A38

1947, Dec. 5 *Pin-perf. 12½x11*
260 A38 5s orange 6.50 4.50
261 A38 10s olive ('48) 7.50 4.50
a. 10s light brown 90.00 85.00
262 A38 20s blue 12.00 4.50
263 A38 50s blue green 18.00 7.50
Nos. 260-263 (4) 44.00 21.00

Coming of age of King Bhumibol Adulyadej. Issued with and without gum.

Catalogue values for unused stamps in this section, from this point to the end of the section, are for Never Hinged items.

King Bhumibol Adulyadej — A39

1947-49 Unwmk. Engr. *Perf. 12½*
Size: 20x25mm
264 A39 5s violet 3.00 .45
265 A39 10s red 3.25 .45
266 A39 20s chocolate 3.50 .45
267 A39 50s olive 6.50 .60

Size: 22x27mm
268 A39 1b vio & dp bl 22.50 .70
269 A39 2b ultra & green 80.00 2.25
270 A39 3b brn red & blk 100.00 4.50
271 A39 5b bl grn & brn red 120.00 8.50
272 A39 10b dk brn & pur 325.00 3.00
273 A39 20b blk & rose brn 450.00 10.00
Nos. 264-273 (10) 1,114. 30.90

Issued: 5s, 20s, 11/15/47; 10s, 50s, 1/3/49; 1b-20b, 11/1/48.
For surcharges see Nos. 302-303.

Type of 1943
Perf. 11½, 12½x11½
1948, Jan. Litho.
274 A35 1b chalky blue 80.00 12.00
a. Horiz. pair, imperf. btwn. 175.00 175.00
b. Vert. pair, imperf. btwn. 175.00 175.00
c. Imperf. pair 175.00 175.00

King Bhumibol Adulyadej and Palace — A40

Perf. 12½
1950, May 5 Unwmk. Engr.
275 A40 5s red violet 4.00 .40
276 A40 10s red 4.00 .40
277 A40 15s purple 16.00 7.50
278 A40 20s chocolate 4.00 .30
279 A40 80s green 45.00 7.50
280 A40 1b deep blue 10.00 .60
281 A40 2b orange yellow 45.00 2.50
282 A40 3b gray 120.00 12.00
Nos. 275-282 (8) 248.00 31.20

Coronation of Bhumibol Adulyadej as Rama IX, May 5, 1950.

King Bhumibol Adulyadej — A41

1951-60 *Perf. 12½*
283 A41 5s rose lilac 3.50 .25
a. Perf. 13x12½ 8.50 1.10
284 A41 10s deep green 3.50 .25
a. Perf. 13x12½ 8.50 .85
285 A41 15s red brown 4.50 .30
b. Perf. 13x12½ 22.00 4.25
285A A41 20s chocolate 6.00 .30
c. Perf. 13x12½ 27.50 1.60
286 A41 25s carmine 2.40 .25
a. Perf. 13x12½ 8.50 .50
287 A41 50s gray olive 6.00 .30
a. Perf. 13x12½ 14.00 1.60
288 A41 1b deep blue 12.00 .40
a. Perf. 13x12½ 22.00 2.75
289 A41 1.15b deep blue 2.40 .30
290 A41 1.25b orange brn 13.00 .75
291 A41 2b dull blue grn 27.50 .75
a. Perf. 13x12½ 50.00 3.75
292 A41 3b gray 35.00 .90
a. Perf. 13x12½ 60.00 5.00
293 A41 5b aqua & red 90.00 1.50
a. Perf. 13x12½ 150.00 6.00
294 A41 10b black brn & vio 325.00 6.00
295 A41 20b gray & olive 350.00 21.00
Nos. 283-295 (14) 880.80 33.25

Issued: 25s, 2/15; 5s, 10s, 1b, 6/4; 2b, 3b, 12/1; 15s, 2/15/52; 1.15b, 9/1/53; 1.25b, 10/1/54; 5b, 10b, 20b, 2/1/55; 50s, 10/15/56; 20s, 1960.

United Nations Day — A42

1951, Oct. 24
296 A42 25s ultramarine 5.00 4.75

Overprinted in Carmine

1952, Oct.
297 A42 25s ultramarine 4.50 2.75

Overprinted in Carmine

1953, Oct.
298 A42 25s ultramarine 2.75 2.00

Overprinted in Carmine

1954, Oct. 24
299 A42 25s ultramarine 6.00 4.00
Nos. 296-299 (4) 18.25 13.50

For more overprints see Nos. 315, 320.

Nos. 209 and 210 Overprinted in Black

1955, Jan. 4 *Perf. 12½*
300 A25 5s dark violet 12.00 *12.00*
301 A25 10s deep rose 12.00 *12.00*

No. 266 Surcharged with New Value in Black or Carmine
302 A39 5s on 20s choc 3.50 1.00
303 A39 10s on 20s choc (C) 5.50 1.00
Nos. 300-303 (4) 33.00 26.00

King Naresuan (1555-1605), on War Elephant — A43

Perf. 13½
1955, Feb. 15 Unwmk. Engr.
304 A43 25s brt carmine 2.75 .45
305 A43 80s rose violet 25.00 5.00
306 A43 1.25b dark olive grn 70.00 3.00
307 A43 2b deep blue 15.00 2.00
308 A43 3b henna brown 60.00 3.00
Nos. 304-308 (5) 172.75 13.45

Tao Suranari — A44

1955, Apr. 15 *Perf. 12x13½*
309 A44 10s purple 4.50 .60
310 A44 25s emerald 4.50 .60
311 A44 1b brown 40.00 3.00
Nos. 309-311 (3) 49.00 4.20

Lady Mo, called Tao Suranari (Brave Woman) for her role in stopping an 1826 rebellion.

King Taksin Statue at Thonburi — A45

1955, May 1 *Perf. 12½x12*
312 A45 5s violet blue 4.50 .60
313 A45 25s Prus green 11.00 .30
314 A45 1.25b red 45.00 3.00
Nos. 312-314 (3) 60.50 3.90

King Somdech P'ya Chao Taksin (1734-1782).

No. 296 Overprinted in Red

1955, Oct. 24 *Perf. 12½*
315 A42 25s ultramarine 5.50 4.00

United Nations Day, Oct. 24, 1955.

Don Jedi Monument — A46

1956, Feb. 1 *Perf. 13½x13*
316 A46 10s emerald 4.75 3.00
317 A46 50s reddish brown 27.50 2.00
318 A46 75s violet 8.00 1.50
319 A46 1.50b brown orange 25.00 1.50
Nos. 316-319 (4) 65.25 8.00

No. 296 Overprinted in Red Violet

1956, Oct. 24
320 A42 25s ultramarine 6.00 4.50

United Nations Day, Oct. 24, 1956.

Dharmachakra and Deer — A47

20s, 25s, 50s, Hand of peace and Dharmachakra. 1b, 1.25b, 2b, Pagoda of Nakon Phatom.

Wmk. 329
1957, May 13 Photo. *Perf. 13½*
321 A47 5s dark brown 1.50 .65
322 A47 10s rose lake 1.50 .65
323 A47 15s brt green 3.25 1.75
324 A47 20s orange 3.25 2.00
325 A47 25s reddish brown 1.10 .65
326 A47 50s magenta 2.50 .70
327 A47 1b olive brown 2.90 .85
328 A47 1.25b slate blue 35.00 6.00
329 A47 2b deep claret 8.00 1.25
Nos. 321-329 (9) 59.00 14.50

2500th anniversary of birth of Buddha.

UN Day — A48

1957, Oct. 24 *Perf. 13½*
330 A48 25s olive 1.60 .80
331 A48 25s bright ocher ('58) 1.60 .80
332 A48 25s indigo ('59) 2.40 .80
Nos. 330-332 (3) 5.60 2.40

Issued: Oct. 24.

Thai Archway — A49

Designs (inscribed "SEAP Games 1959"): 25s, Royal tiered umbrellas. 1.25b, Thai archer, ancient costume. 2b, Wat Arun pagoda and prow of royal barge.

1959, Oct. 15 Photo. *Perf. 13½*

333 A49 10s orange 1.10 .25
334 A49 25s dk carmine rose 1.40 .25
335 A49 1.25b bright green 5.50 1.50
336 A49 2b light blue 4.75 .85
Nos. 333-336 (4) 12.75 2.85

Issued to publicize the South-East Asia Peninsula Games, Bangkok, Dec. 12-17.

Wat Arun, WRY Emblem — A50

1960, Apr. 7

337 A50 50s chocolate 1.00 .40
338 A50 2b yellow green 2.10 1.20

WRY, July 1, 1959-June 30, 1960.

Wat Arun, Bangkok — A51

1960, Aug. Wmk. 329 *Perf. 13½*

339 A51 50s carmine rose 1.20 .25
340 A51 2b ultramarine 4.75 1.00

Anti-leprosy campaign.

Elephants in Teak Forest — A52

1960, Aug. 29 Photo. *Perf. 13½*

341 A52 25s emerald 1.25 .25

5th World Forestry Cong., Seattle, WA, Aug. 29-Sept. 10.

Globe and SEATO Emblem — A53

1960, Sept. 8

342 A53 50s chocolate 1.25 .25

SEATO Day, Sept. 8.

Siamese Child — A54

1960, Oct. 3 Wmk. 329

343 A54 50s magenta 1.75 .25
344 A54 1b orange 6.00 .95

Children's Day, 1960.

Hand with Pen and Globe — A55

1960, Oct. 3

345 A55 50s carmine rose 1.50 .25
346 A55 2b blue 6.00 1.25

Intl. Letter Writing Week, Oct. 3-9.

UN Emblem and Globe — A56

1960, Oct. 24 *Perf. 13½*

347 A56 50s purple 1.60 .40

15th anniversary of the United Nations. See Nos. 369, 390.

King Bhumibol Adulyadej — A57

Perf. 13½x13

1961-68 Engr. Wmk. 334

348 A57 5s rose cl ('62) .80 .25
349 A57 10s green ('62) .80 .25
350 A57 15s red brn ('62) .80 .25
351 A57 20s brown ('62) .80 .25
352 A57 25s carmine ('63) .80 .25
353 A57 50s olive ('62) .80 .25
354 A57 80s orange ('62) 5.00 2.00
355 A57 1b vio bl & brn 5.00 .30
355A A57 1.25b red & citron ('65) 8.50 2.00
356 A57 1.50b dk vio & yel green 2.50 .45
357 A57 2b red & violet 2.50 .25
358 A57 3b brn & bl 13.00 .45
358A A57 4b olive bis & blk ('68) 15.00 2.50
359 A57 5b blue & green 32.50 .60
360 A57 10b red org & blk 90.00 1.00
361 A57 20b emer & ultra 100.00 3.50
362 A57 25b green & blue 45.00 2.00
362A A57 40b yellow & blk ('65) 110.00 4.50
Nos. 348-362A (18) 433.80 21.05

For overprint see No. 588.

Children in Garden — A58

Wmk. 329

1961, Oct. 2 Photo. *Perf. 13½*

363 A58 20s indigo 1.50 .30
364 A58 2b purple 6.25 1.10

Issued for Children's Day.

Pen and Envelope with Map — A59

1b, 2b, Pen and letters circling globe.

1961, Oct. 9

365 A59 25s gray green 1.20 .25
366 A59 50s rose lilac 1.00 .25
367 A59 1b bright rose 2.75 .60
368 A59 2b ultramarine 3.25 .75
Nos. 365-368 (4) 8.20 1.85

Intl. Letter Writing Week, Oct. 2-8.

UN Type of 1960

1961, Oct. 24 Wmk. 329 *Perf. 13½*

369 A56 50s maroon 1.25 .45

Issued for United Nations Day, Oct. 24.

Scout Emblem A60

Scouts Saluting and Tents A61

Design: 2b, King Vajiravudh and Scouts.

1961, Nov. 1 Photo.

370 A60 50s carmine rose .90 .25
371 A61 1b bright green 2.25 .65
372 A61 2b bright blue 2.75 .90
Nos. 370-372 (3) 5.90 1.80

Thai Boy Scouts, 50th anniversary.

Malaria Eradication Emblem and Siamese Designs
A62 A63

1962, Apr. 7 Wmk. 329 *Perf. 13*

373 A62 5s orange brown .30 .25
374 A62 10s sepia .30 .25
375 A62 20s blue 1.10 .25
376 A62 50s carmine rose .30 .25
377 A63 1b green 1.50 .25
378 A63 1.50b dk car rose 3.50 .65
379 A63 2d dark blue 2.00 .35
380 A63 3b violet 5.50 2.50
Nos. 373-380 (8) 14.50 4.75

WHO drive to eradicate malaria.

View of Bangkok and Seattle Fair Emblem — A64

1962, Apr. 21 Wmk. 329 *Perf. 13*

381 A64 50s red lilac 1.50 .25
382 A64 2b deep blue 7.50 .95

"Century 21" Intl. Expo., Seattle, WA, Apr. 21-Oct. 12.

Mother and Child — A65

Wmk. 329

1962, Oct. 1 Photo. *Perf. 13*

383 A65 25s lt blue green 1.25 .50
384 A65 50s bister brown 1.50 .25
385 A65 2b bright pink 6.75 1.00
Nos. 383-385 (3) 9.50 1.75

Issued for Children's Day.

Globe, Letters, Carrier Pigeons — A66

Design: 1b, 2b, Quill pen and scroll.

1962, Oct. 8

386 A66 25s violet .70 .30
387 A66 50s red .50 .25
388 A66 1b lemon 3.50 .60
389 A66 2b lt bluish green 7.00 .70
Nos. 386-389 (4) 11.70 1.85

Intl. Letter Writing Week, Oct. 7-13.

UN Type of 1960

1962, Oct. 24 *Perf. 13½*

390 A56 50s carmine rose 1.25 .45

United Nations Day, Oct. 24.

Exhibition Emblem — A67

1962, Nov. 1 Unwmk.

391 A67 50s olive bister 1.40 .25

Students' Exhibition, Bangkok.

Woman Harvesting Rice — A68

Wmk. 334

1963, Mar. 21 Engr. *Perf. 14*

392 A68 20s green 2.00 .65
393 A68 50s ocher 1.50 .25

FAO "Freedom from Hunger" campaign.

Temple Lion — A69

1963, Apr. 1 Wmk. 329 *Perf. 13½*

394 A69 50s green & bister 1.25 .25

1st anniv. of the formation of the Asian-Oceanic Postal Union, AOPU.

New and Old Post and Telegraph Buildings A70

Wmk. 334

1963, Aug. 4 Engr. *Perf. 14*

395 A70 50s org, bluish blk & grn 1.75 .30
396 A70 3b grn, dk red & brn 7.50 1.75

80th anniv. of the Post and Telegraph Dept.

King Bhumibol Adulyadej — A71

Perf. 13x13½

1963-71 Wmk. 329 Photo.

397 A71 5s dk car rose .25 .25
398 A71 10s dark green .25 .25
399 A71 15s red brown .25 .25
400 A71 20s black brown .25 .25
401 A71 25s carmine .25 .25
402 A71 50s olive gray .25 .25
402A A71 75s brt vio ('71) 1.25 .25
403 A71 80s dull orange 6.50 1.00
404 A71 1b dk bl & dk brn 6.00 .60
404A A71 1.25b org brn & ol ('65) 16.00 1.75
405 A71 1.50b vio bl & grn 5.00 .90
406 A71 2b dk red & vio 3.00 .25
407 A71 3b brn & dk bl 6.50 .45
407A A71 4b dp bis & blk ('68) 10.00 .60
408 A71 5b blue & green 17.50 .45
409 A71 10b orange & blk 30.00 .75
410 A71 20b brt grn & ind 125.00 4.50
411 A71 25b dk grn & bl 30.00 2.75
411A A71 40b yel & blk ('65) 150.00 6.50
Nos. 397-411A (19) 408.25 22.25

Nos. 397-403 were issued in 1963; Nos. 404, 405-407, 408-411 in 1964.

For overprint see No. 589.

Child with Dolls — A72

1963, Oct. 7 Litho. *Perf. 13½*

412 A72 50s rose red 1.75 .25
413 A72 2b dull blue 7.75 .95

Issued for Children's Day.

Garuda Carrying Letter — A73

Design: 2b, 3b, Thai women writing letters.

1963, Oct. 7 Wmk. 329

414 A73 50s lt blue & claret 2.75 .30
415 A73 1b lt grn & vio brn 4.75 1.50
416 A73 2b yel brn & turq bl 34.00 1.75
417 A73 3b org brn & yel grn 18.00 3.00
Nos. 414-417 (4) 59.50 6.55

Intl. Letter Writing Week, Oct. 6-12.

UN Emblem — A74

1963, Oct. 24 Wmk. 329 *Perf. 13½*
418 A74 50s bright blue 1.25 .25

United Nations Day, Oct. 24.

King Bhumibol Adulyadej A75

1963, Dec. 5 Photo. *Perf. 13½*
419 A75 1.50b blue, org & ind 9.00 1.10
420 A75 5b brt lil rose, org & blk 24.00 4.00

King Bhumibol's 36th birthday.

UNICEF Emblem — A76

1964, Jan. 13 Litho.
421 A76 50s blue 1.50 .25
422 A76 2b olive green 5.50 1.00

17th anniv. of UNICEF.

Hand (flags), Pigeon and Globe — A77

Designs: 1b, Girls and world map. 2b, Pen, pencil and unfolded world map. 3b, Globe and hand holding quill.

1964, Oct. 5 Wmk. 329 *Perf. 13½*
423 A77 50s lilac & lt grn 2.40 .40
424 A77 1b red brown & grn 6.00 1.50
425 A77 2b yellow & vio bl 14.50 1.50
426 A77 3b blue & dk brown 9.50 3.25
Nos. 423-426 (4) 32.40 6.65

Intl. Letter Writing Week, Oct. 5-11.

UN Emblem and Globe — A78

1964, Oct. 24 Photo. *Perf. 13½*
427 A78 50s gray 1.25 .25

United Nations Day, Oct. 24.

King and Queen — A79

1965, Apr. 28 Wmk. 329 *Perf. 13½*
428 A79 2b brown & multi 17.50 .60
429 A79 5b violet & multi 30.00 3.00

15th wedding anniversary of King Bhumibol Adulyadej and Queen Sirikit.

ITU Emblem, Old and New Communications Equipment — A80

1965, May 17 Photo.
430 A80 1b bright green 7.00 .45

Cent. of the ITU.

World Map, Letters and Goddess A81

2b, 3b, World map, letters and handshake.

1965, Oct. 3 Wmk. 329 *Perf. 13½*
431 A81 50s dp plum, gray & sal 1.75 .30
432 A81 1b dk vio bl, lt vio & yel 5.00 .45
433 A81 2b dk gray, bis & dp org 14.00 .90
434 A81 3b multicolored 17.50 2.50
Nos. 431-434 (4) 38.25 4.15

Intl. Letter Writing Week, Oct. 3-9.

A82

Gates of Royal Chapel of Emerald Buddha.

Engr. & Litho.
Perf. 13½x14
1965, Oct. 24 Wmk. 356
435 A82 50s slate grn, bl & ocher 1.50 .25

International Cooperation Year, 1965.

A83

Map of Thailand and UPU monument, Bern.

Wmk. 329
1965, Nov. 1 Litho. *Perf. 13½*
436 A83 20s dk blue & lilac 1.00 .30
437 A83 50s gray & blue 2.25 .45
438 A83 1b orange brn & vio bl 7.00 .90
439 A83 3b green & bister 14.00 2.50
Nos. 436-439 (4) 24.25 4.15

80th anniv. of Thailand's admission to the UPU.

Lotus Blossom and Child — A84

Design: 1b, Boy with book walking up steps.

1966, Jan. 8 Wmk. 334 *Perf. 13½*
440 A84 50s henna brn & blk 1.50 .25
441 A84 1b green & black 4.50 1.00

Issued for Children's Day, 1966.

Bicycling A85

1966, Aug. 4 Photo. Wmk. 329
442 A85 20s shown 1.00 .30
443 A85 25s Tennis 1.40 .60
444 A85 50s Running 1.00 .25
445 A85 1b Weight lifting 4.50 1.50
446 A85 1.25b Boxing 6.50 3.50
447 A85 2b Swimming 9.50 1.40
448 A85 3b Netball 19.00 4.50
449 A85 5b Soccer 52.50 14.00
Nos. 442-449 (8) 95.40 26.05

5th Asian Games, Bangkok.

Trade Fair Emblem and Temple of Dawn — A86

1966, Sept. 1 Litho. *Perf. 13½*
450 A86 50s lilac 1.75 .60
451 A86 1b brown red 4.50 1.25

1st Intl. Asian Trade Fair, Bangkok.

Letter Writer — A87

Design: 50s, 1b, Letters, maps and pen.

1966, Oct. 3 Photo. Wmk. 329
452 A87 50s scarlet 1.50 .30
453 A87 1b orange brown 4.50 .90
454 A87 2b brt violet 12.00 1.20
455 A87 3b brt blue grn 12.00 2.40
Nos. 452-455 (4) 30.00 4.80

Intl. Letter Writing Week, Oct. 6-12.

UN Emblem — A88

Wmk. 334
1966, Oct. 24 Litho. *Perf. 13½*
456 A88 50s ultramarine 1.25 .25

United Nations Day, Oct. 24.

Rice Field — A89

1966, Nov. 1 Engr. Wmk. 329
457 A89 50s dp bl & grnsh bl 4.50 .90
458 A89 3b plum & pink 16.00 5.50

Intl. Rice Year under sponsorship of the FAO.

Pra Buddha Bata Monastery, UNESCO Emblem — A90

1966, Nov. 4 Photo. Wmk. 329
459 A90 50s black & yel grn 1.10 .25

20th anniv. of UNESCO.

Thai Boxing — A91

Designs: 1b, Takraw (three men playing ball). 2b, Kite fighting. 3b, Cudgel play.

1966, Dec. 9 Wmk. 329 *Perf. 13½*
460 A91 50s black, brn & red 1.95 .30
461 A91 1b black, brn & red 10.00 1.50
462 A91 2b black, brn & red 24.75 4.25
463 A91 3b black, brn & red 23.00 9.00
Nos. 460-463 (4) 59.70 15.05

5th Asian Games.

Snakehead A92 — Pigmy Mackerel A93

Fish: 3b, Barb. 5b, Siamese fighting fish.

1967, Jan. 1 Photo.
464 A92 1b brt blue & multi 7.00 1.50
465 A93 2b multicolored 27.50 3.00
466 A93 3b yel grn & multi 15.00 7.00
467 A92 5b pale grn & multi 20.00 8.00
Nos. 464-467 (4) 69.50 19.50

Dharmachakra, Globe and Temples — A94

Wmk. 329
1967, Jan. 15 Litho. *Perf. 13½*
468 A94 2b black & yellow 6.50 .75

Establishment of the headquarters of the World Fellowship of Buddhists in Thailand.

Great Hornbill — A95

Birds: 25s, Hill myna. 50s, White-rumped shama. 1b, Diard's fireback pheasant. 1.50b, Spotted dove. 2b, Sarus crane. 3b, White-breasted kingfisher. 5b, Asiatic open-bill (stork).

1967, Feb. 1 Photo.
469 A95 20s tan & multi 1.60 .75
470 A95 25s lt gray & multi 3.25 1.50
471 A95 50s yel grn & multi 2.60 .65
472 A95 1b olive & multi 7.25 1.50
473 A95 1.50b dull yel & multi 7.75 2.00
474 A95 2b pale sal & multi 24.00 3.25
475 A95 3b gray & multi 15.00 7.75
476 A95 5b multicolored 24.00 8.00
Nos. 469-476 (8) 85.45 25.40

Ascocentrum Curvifolium — A96

Orchids: 20s, Vandopsis parishii. 80s, Rhynchostylis retusa. 1b, Rhynchostylus gigantea. 1.50b, Dendrobium falconerii. 2b, Paphiopedilum callosum. 3b, Dendrobium formosum. 5b, Dendrobium primulinum.

1967, Apr. 1 Wmk. 329 *Perf. 13½*
477 A96 20s black & multi 1.40 .60
478 A96 50s brt blue & multi 2.40 .30
479 A96 80s black & multi 3.50 1.50
480 A96 1b blue & multi 6.50 1.25
481 A96 1.50b black & multi 6.50 1.25
482 A96 2b ver & multi 19.00 3.25
483 A96 3b brown & multi 14.00 7.75
484 A96 5b multicolored 19.00 6.50
Nos. 477-484 (8) 72.30 22.40

Thai Architecture A97

1967, Apr. 6 Engr.
485 A97 50s Mansion 1.75 .60
486 A97 1.50b Pagodas 7.25 3.00
487 A97 2b Bell tower 20.00 3.00
488 A97 3b Temple 17.00 8.50
Nos. 485-488 (4) 46.00 15.10

Grand Palace and Royal Barge on Chao Phraya River — A98

1967, Sept. 15 Wmk. 329 *Perf. 13½*
489 A98 2b ultra & sepia 10.00 1.25

International Tourist Year, 1967.

Globe, Dove, People and Letters — A99

2b, 3b, Clasped hands, globe and doves.

1967, Oct. 8 **Photo.**
490 A99 50s dk blue & multi 1.50 .25
491 A99 1b multicolored 3.00 .65
492 A99 2b brt yel grn & blk 9.00 .90
493 A99 3b brown & blk 12.00 3.00
Nos. 490-493 (4) 25.50 4.80

Intl. Letter Writing Week, Oct. 6-12.

UN Emblem — A100

1967, Oct. 24 **Wmk. 329** ***Perf. 13½***
494 A100 50s multicolored 1.50 .25

Issued for United Nations Day, Oct. 24.

Flag and Map of Thailand A101

1967, Dec. 5 **Photo.** ***Perf. 13½***
495 A101 50s greenish blue, red & vio bl 2.40 .25
496 A101 2b ol gray, red & vio bl 9.00 1.25

50th anniversary of the flag.

Elephant Carrying Teakwood A102

1968, Mar. 1 **Engr.** **Wmk. 329**
497 A102 2b rose claret & gray ol 6.50 .60

See Nos. 537, 566.

Syncom Satellite over Thai Tracking Station — A103

1968, Apr. 1 **Photo.** ***Perf. 13***
498 A103 50s multicolored .70 .25
499 A103 3b multicolored 4.00 1.60

Earth Goddess A104

1968, May 1 **Wmk. 329** ***Perf. 13***
500 A104 50s blk, gold, red & bl grn 2.40 .40

Hydrological Decade (UNESCO), 1965-74.

Snake-skinned Gourami — A105

Fish: 20s, Red-tailed black "shark." 25s, Tor tambroides. 50s, Pangasius sanitwongsei. 80s, Bagrid catfish. 1.25b, Vaimosa rambaiae. 1.50b, Catlocarpio siamensis. 4b, Featherback.

1968, June 1 **Photo.** ***Perf. 13***
501 A105 10s multicolored .75 .25
502 A105 20s multicolored 1.10 .30
503 A105 25s multicolored 1.55 .30
504 A105 50s multicolored 1.95 .30
505 A105 80s multicolored 6.00 2.75
506 A105 1.25b multicolored 11.00 5.00
507 A105 1.50b multicolored 26.50 4.50
508 A105 4b multicolored 49.50 17.50
Nos. 501-508 (8) 98.35 30.90

Arcturus Butterfly A106

Various butterflies.

1968, July 1 **Wmk. 329** ***Perf. 13***
509 A106 50s lt blue & multi 3.00 .45
510 A106 1b multicolored 9.00 2.00
511 A106 3b multicolored 21.00 8.00
512 A106 4b buff & multi 27.00 9.00
Nos. 509-512 (4) 60.00 19.45

Queen Sirikit — A107

Designs: Various portraits of Queen Sirikit.

Photogravure and Engraved
Perf. 13½x14

1968, Aug. 12 **Wmk. 334**
513 A107 50s gold & multi 1.20 .30
514 A107 2b gold & multi 4.75 1.75
515 A107 3b gold & multi 7.50 3.00
516 A107 5b gold & multi 13.50 4.00
Nos. 513-516 (4) 26.95 9.05

Queen Sirikit's 36th birthday, or third 12-year "cycle."

WHO Emblem and Medical Apparatus A108

1968, Sept. 1 **Photo.** ***Perf. 12½***
517 A108 50s olive, blk & gray 1.10 .25

20th anniv. of the WHO.

Globe, Pen and Envelope A109

1b, 3b, Pen nib, envelope and globe.

1968, Oct. 6 **Wmk. 329** ***Perf. 13½***
518 A109 50s brown & multi .90 .25
519 A109 1b pale brown & multi 2.10 .40
520 A109 2b multicolored 3.50 .60
521 A109 3b violet & multi 6.00 2.00
Nos. 518-521 (4) 12.50 3.25

Intl. Letter Writing Week, Oct. 7-13.

UN Emblem and Flags — A110

1968, Oct. 24
522 A110 50s multicolored 1.20 .25

Issued for United Nations Day.

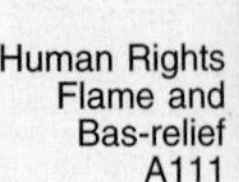

Human Rights Flame and Bas-relief A111

1968, Dec. 10 **Photo.** ***Perf. 13½***
523 A111 50s sl grn, red & vio 1.25 .25

International Human Rights Year.

King Rama II — A112

1968, Dec. 30 **Engr.** **Wmk. 329**
524 A112 50s sepia & bister 1.40 .25

Rama II (1768-1824), who reigned 1809-24.

National Assembly Building A113

Photogravure and Engraved

1969, Feb. 10 **Wmk. 329** ***Perf. 13½***
525 A113 50s multicolored 1.20 .25
526 A113 2b multicolored 5.50 1.10

First constitutional election day.

ILO Emblem and Cogwheels A114

1969, May 1 **Photo.** ***Perf. 13½***
527 A114 50s rose vio & dk bl .85 .25

50th anniv. of the ILO.

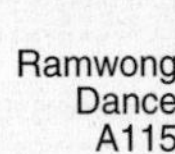

Ramwong Dance A115

Designs: 1b, Candle dance. 2b, Krathop Mai dance. 3b, Nohra dance.

1969, July 15 **Wmk. 329** ***Perf. 13***
528 A115 50s multicolored .60 .25
529 A115 1b multicolored 1.75 .65
530 A115 2b multicolored 3.50 .65
531 A115 3b multicolored 5.75 2.00
Nos. 528-531 (4) 11.60 3.55

Posting and Receiving Letters A116

Design: 2b, 3b, Writing and posting letters.

1969, Oct. 5 **Photo.** **Wmk. 334**
532 A116 50s multicolored .90 .25
533 A116 1b multicolored 1.75 .50
534 A116 2b multicolored 2.40 .75
535 A116 3b multicolored 3.50 1.10
Nos. 532-535 (4) 8.55 2.60

International Letter Writing Week.

Hand Holding Globe — A117

1969, Oct. 24 **Wmk. 329** ***Perf. 13***
536 A117 50s multicolored 1.10 .25

Issued for United Nations Day.

Teakwood Type of 1968

1969, Nov. 18 **Engr.** ***Perf. 13½***
537 A102 2b Tin mine 4.25 .30

Issued to publicize tin export, and the 2nd Technical Conf. of the Intl. Tin Council, Bangkok.

Loy Krathong Festival A118

Designs: 1b, Marriage ceremony. 2b, Khwan ceremony. 5b, Songkran festival.

1969, Nov. 23 **Photo.** **Wmk. 329**
538 A118 50s gray & multi .60 .25
539 A118 1b multicolored 2.00 .65
540 A118 2b multicolored 2.50 .55
541 A118 5b multicolored 4.75 1.50
Nos. 538-541 (4) 9.85 2.95

Biplane, Mailmen and Map of First Thai Airmail Flight, 1919 — A119

1969, Dec. 10 **Engr.** ***Perf. 13½***
542 A119 1b multicolored 1.75 .30

50th anniversary of Thai airmail service.

Shadow Play — A120

Photogravure and Engraved

1969, Dec. 18 **Wmk. 329**
543 A120 50s Phra Rama .60 .25
544 A120 2b Ramasura 3.75 .35
545 A120 3b Mekhala 3.25 1.10
546 A120 5b Ongkhot 3.75 1.40
Nos. 543-546 (4) 11.35 3.10

Symbols of Agriculture, Industry and Shipping A121

1970, Jan. 1 **Photo.**
547 A121 50s multicolored .90 .25

Productivity Year 1970.

World Map, Thai Temples and Emblem A122

1970, Jan. 31 **Litho.**
548 A122 50s brt blue & blk 1.25 .30

19th triennial meeting of the Intl. Council of Women, Bangkok.

Earth Station Radar and Satellite — A123

Perf. 14½x15

1970, Apr. 1 **Litho.** **Wmk. 356**
549 A123 50s multicolored .90 .25

Communication by satellite.

Household and Population Statistics A124

Perf. 13x13½

1970, Apr. 1 **Photo.** **Wmk. 329**
550 A124 1b multicolored 1.10 .25

Issued to publicize the 1970 census.

Inauguration of New UPU Headquarters, Bern — A125

Lithographed and Engraved

1970, June 15 Wmk. 334 ***Perf. 13½***

551 A125 50s lt bl, lt grn & grn .95 .25

Khun Ram Kamhang Teaching (Mural) A126

1970, July 1 **Litho.**

552 A126 50s black & multi 1.00 .25

Issued for International Education Year.

Swimming Stadium A127

1.50b, Velodrome. 3b, Subhajalasaya Stadium. 5b, Kittikachorn Indoor Stadium.

Lithographed and Engraved

1970, Sept. 1 Wmk. 329 ***Perf. 13½***

553 A127 50s yellow, red & pur .90 .25
554 A127 1.50b ultra, grn & dk red 1.75 .65
555 A127 3b gold, black & dk red 2.10 .90
556 A127 5b brt grn, ultra & dk red 3.50 1.10
Nos. 553-556 (4) 8.25 2.90

6th Asian Games, Bangkok.

Children Writing Letters A128

Designs: 1b, Woman writing letter. 2b, Two women reading letters. 3b, Man reading letter.

1970, Oct. 4 Photo. ***Perf. 13½***

557 A128 50s black & multi .90 .25
558 A128 1b black & multi 1.75 .55
559 A128 2b black & multi 2.75 .60
560 A128 3b black & multi 3.00 1.25
Nos. 557-560 (4) 8.40 2.65

Intl. Letter Writing Week, Oct. 6-12.

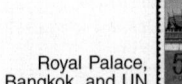

Royal Palace, Bangkok, and UN Emblem — A129

1970, Oct. 24 Photo. ***Perf. 13½***

561 A129 50s multicolored 1.25 .25

25th anniversary of the United Nations.

Heroes of Bangrachan A130

1b, Monument to Thao Thepkrasattri & Thao Sri Sunthon. 2b, Queen Suriyothai riding elephant. 3b, Phraya Phichaidaphak and battle scene.

1970, Oct. 25 Engr. ***Perf. 13½***

562 A130 50s pink & violet .90 .30
563 A130 1b violet & maroon 1.50 .90
564 A130 2b rose & brown 3.50 .90
565 A130 3b blue & green 3.00 .90
Nos. 562-565 (4) 8.90 3.00

Heroes from Thai history.

Teakwood Type of 1968

1970, Nov. 1 **Engr.**

566 A102 2b Rubber plantation 3.25 .70

Issued to publicize rubber export.

King Bhumibol Lighting Flame — A131

1970, Dec. 9 Photo. Wmk. 329

567 A131 1b multicolored 1.75 .25

Opening of 6th Asian Games, Bangkok.

Woman Playing So Sam Sai — A132

Women Playing Classical Thai Musical Instruments: 2b, Khlui Phiang-O. 3b, Krachappi. 5b, Thon Rammana.

1970, Dec. 20

568 A132 50s multicolored .90 .25
569 A132 2b multicolored 2.00 .65
570 A132 3b multicolored 3.25 .95
571 A132 5b multicolored 5.25 1.25
Nos. 568-571 (4) 11.40 3.10

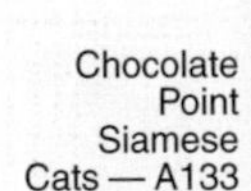

Chocolate Point Siamese Cats — A133

Siamese Cats: 1b, Blue point. 2b, Seal point. 3b, Pure white cat and kittens.

Perf. 13½x14

1971, Mar. 15 Litho. Wmk. 356

572 A133 50s multicolored .65 .45
573 A133 1b multicolored 4.50 1.00
574 A133 2b multicolored 6.00 1.10
575 A133 3b multicolored 8.50 2.75
Nos. 572-575 (4) 19.65 5.30

Muang Nakhon Temple — A134

Temples: 1b, Phanom. 3b, Pathom Chedi. 4b, Doi Suthep.

Lithographed and Engraved

1971, Mar. 30 Wmk. 329 ***Perf. 13½***

576 A134 50s rose, black & brn .90 .25
577 A134 1b emerald, bis & pur 1.75 .40
578 A134 3b org, brn & dk brn 2.75 .65
579 A134 4b ultra, ocher & brn 4.50 2.50
Nos. 576-579 (4) 9.90 3.80

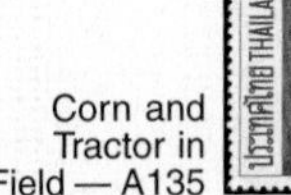

Corn and Tractor in Field — A135

1971, Apr. 20 Engr. Wmk. 329

580 A135 2b multicolored 2.40 .30

Export promotion.

Buddha's Birthplace, Lumbini, Nepal — A136

Buddha's: 1b, Place of Enlightenment, Bihar. 2b, Place of first sermon, Benares. 3b, Place of death, Kusinara.

1971, May 9 Engr. ***Perf. 13½***

581 A136 50s violet blue & blk .75 .25
582 A136 1b green & black 1.60 .55
583 A136 2b dull yellow & blk 2.75 .75
584 A136 3b red & black 3.25 1.25
Nos. 581-584 (4) 8.35 2.80

20th anniv. of World Fellowship of Buddhists.

King Bhumibol and Subjects — A137

Perf. 13½

1971, June 9 Unwmk. Litho.

585 A137 50s silver & multi 1.50 .25

King Bhumibol's Silver Jubilee.

Floating Market — A138

1971, June 20 Photo. Wmk. 329

586 A138 4b gold & multi 2.50 .45

Visit Asia Year.

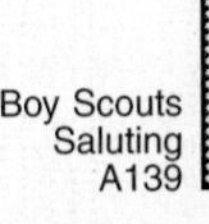
Boy Scouts Saluting A139

1971, July 1 **Litho.**

587 A139 50s orange & multi 1.25 .25

60th anniversary of Thai Boy Scouts.

Blocks of four of Nos. 354 and 403 Overprinted in Dark Blue

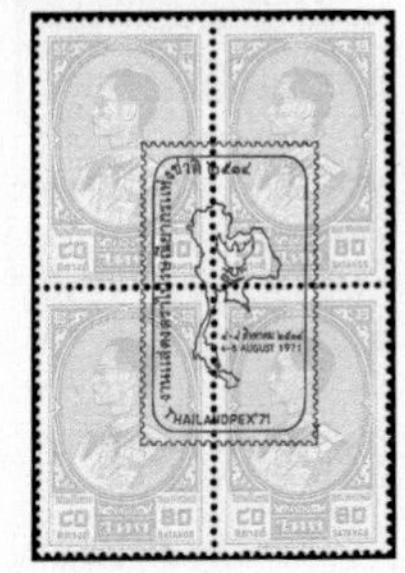
a

b

Perf. 13½x13

1971, Aug. Wmk. 334 Engr.

588 A57 (a) Block of 4 8.00 8.00
a. 80s orange, single stamp 2.00 2.00

Perf. 13x13½

Photo. Wmk. 329

589 A71 (b) Block of 4 8.00 8.00
a. 80s dull orange, single stamp 2.00 2.00

THAILANDPEX '71, Philatelic Exhib., Aug. 4-8.

Woman Writing Letter — A140

Designs: 1b, Women reading mail. 2b, Woman sitting on porch. 3b, Man handing letter to woman.

Wmk. 334

1971, Oct. 3 Litho. ***Perf. 13½***

590 A140 50s gray & multi .60 .25
591 A140 1b red brown & multi 1.40 .35
592 A140 2b ultra & multi 2.25 .50
593 A140 3b lt gray & multi 4.00 1.10
Nos. 590-593 (4) 8.25 2.20

Intl. Letter Writing Week, Oct. 6-12.

Wat Benchamabopit (Marble Temple), Bangkok — A141

Perf. 13½x14

1971, Oct. 24 Litho. Unwmk.

594 A141 50s multicolored 1.25 .25

United Nations Day, Oct. 24.

Duck Raising A142

Rural occupations: 1b, Raising tobacco. 2b, Fishermen. 3b, Rice winnowing.

Wmk. 329

1971, Nov. 15 Photo. ***Perf. 12½***

595 A142 50s lt blue & multi .65 .25
596 A142 1b multicolored 1.50 .65
597 A142 2b blue & multi 2.40 .60
598 A142 3b buff & multi 3.50 .90
Nos. 595-598 (4) 8.05 2.40

UNICEF Emblem, Mother and Child — A143

1971, Dec. 11 Wmk. 334 ***Perf. 13½***

599 A143 50s blue & multi .95 .25

25th anniv. of UNICEF.

Thai Costumes, 17th Century A144

Thai Costumes: 1b, 13th-14th cent. 1.50b, 14th-17th cent. 2b, 18th-19th cent.

Perf. 13½x14

1972, Jan. 12 Litho. Unwmk.
600 A144 50s multicolored .80 .30
601 A144 1b multicolored 1.75 .50
602 A144 1.50b multicolored 3.00 .95
603 A144 2b blue & multi 4.50 .95
Nos. 600-603 (4) 10.05 2.70

Globe — A145

Perf. 13x13½

1972, Apr. 1 Photo. Wmk. 334
604 A145 75s violet blue .90 .25

Asian-Oceanic Postal Union, 10th anniv.

King Bhumibol Adulyadej — A146

Perf. 13½x13

1972-77 Litho. Wmk. 329
Size: 21x26mm
605 A146 10s yellow green .30 .25
606 A146 20s blue .45 .25
607 A146 25s rose red .45 .25
608 A146 75s lilac .60 .25

Engr.
609 A146 1.25b yel grn & pink 1.25 .30
610 A146 2.75b red brn & blue grn 1.50 .65
611 A146 3b brn & dk blue ('74) 7.00 .65
612 A146 4b blue & org red ('73) 2.10 .30
613 A146 5b dk vio & red brown 2.10 .25
614 A146 6b green & vio 6.50 .60
615 A146 10b ver & black 3.25 .25
616 A146 20b org & yel grn 9.25 .60
617 A146 40b dp bis & lilac ('74) 36.00 7.50
618 A146 50b pur & brt grn ('77) 45.00 1.75
619 A146 100b dp org & dk bl ('77) 77.50 3.00
Nos. 605-619 (15) 193.25 16.85

See Nos. 835-838, 907-908.
For surcharges, see Nos. 2248, 2281-2282.

Iko Women A147

Hill Tribes: 2b, Musoe musician. 4b, Yao weaver. 5b, Maeo farm woman.

Wmk. 334

1972, May 11 Photo. ***Perf. 13½***
620 A147 50s multicolored .65 .25
621 A147 2b dark gray & multi 2.60 .60
622 A147 4b multicolored 7.00 4.00
623 A147 5b multicolored 8.00 1.10
Nos. 620-623 (4) 18.25 5.95

Ruby — A148

Precious Stones: 2b, Yellow sapphire. 4b, Zircon. 6b, Star sapphire.

1972, June 7 Litho.
624 A148 75s gray & multi 1.20 .40
625 A148 2b multicolored 8.00 1.50
626 A148 4b multicolored 13.00 4.50
627 A148 6b crimson & multi 12.00 4.50
Nos. 624-627 (4) 34.20 10.90

Prince Vajiralongkorn — A149

Perf. 13½x13

1972, July 28 Photo. Wmk. 329
628 A149 75s tan & multi 1.25 .25

20th birthday of Prince Vajiralongkorn, heir apparent.

Thai Costume — A150

Designs: Costumes of Thai women.

Perf. 14x13½

1972, Aug. 12 Litho. Wmk. 356
629 A150 75s tan & multi .60 .25
630 A150 2b multicolored 2.00 .70
631 A150 4b yellow & multi 4.00 3.00
632 A150 5b gray & multi 4.75 .90
a. Souvenir sheet of 4, #629-632 *40.00* 27.00
Nos. 629-632 (4) 11.35 4.85

Rambutan A151

Fruits: 1b, Mangosteen. 3b, Durian. 5b, Mango.

1972, Sept. 7 Wmk. 334 ***Perf. 13½***
633 A151 75s multicolored .90 .25
634 A151 1b multicolored 2.40 .95
635 A151 3b pink & multi 4.75 1.40
636 A151 5b lt ultra & multi 12.00 2.25
Nos. 633-636 (4) 20.05 4.85

Lod Cave, Phangnga A152

1.25b, Kang Krachan Reservoir. 2.75b, Erawan Waterfalls, Kanchanaburi. 3b, Nok-Kaw Cliff, Loei.

1972, Nov. 15 Litho. Wmk. 334
637 A152 75s multicolored .80 .25
638 A152 1.25b multicolored 1.60 1.00
639 A152 2.75b multicolored 5.50 .45
640 A152 3b multicolored 4.50 1.10
Nos. 637-640 (4) 12.40 2.80

Intl. Letter Writing Week, Oct. 9-15.

Princess Mother Visiting Old People A153

1972, Oct. 21 Photo. Wmk. 329
641 A153 75s dk green & ocher 4.50 .50

Princess Mother Sisangwan, 72nd birthday.

UN Emblem and Globe — A154

Wmk. 334

1972, Nov. 15 Litho. ***Perf. 14***
642 A154 75s blue & multi .75 .25

25th anniversary of the Economic Commission for Asia and the Far East (ECAFE).

Educational Center and Book Year Emblem A155

1972, Dec. 8 ***Perf. 13½***
643 A155 75s multicolored .75 .25

International Book Year 1972.

Crown Prince Vajiralongkorn — A156

1972, Dec. 28 Photo. Wmk. 329
644 A156 2b brt blue & multi 1.75 .30

Investiture of Prince Vajiralongkorn Salayacheevin as Crown Prince.

Flag, Soldiers and Civilians A157

1973, Feb. 3 Wmk. 334 ***Perf. 13½***
645 A157 75s multicolored .90 .25

25th anniversary of Veterans Day.

Savings Bank, Emblem and Coin — A158

1973, Apr. 1 Wmk. 329
646 A158 75s emerald & multi .90 .25

60th anniv. of Government Savings Bank.

WHO Emblem and Deity — A159

1973, Apr. 1 Wmk. 329
647 A159 75s brt green & multi .90 .25

25th World Health Organization Day.

Water Lily — A160

Designs: Various water lilies (Thai lotus).

Perf. 11x13

1973, May 15 Litho. Wmk. 356
648 A160 75s violet & multi 1.00 .25
649 A160 1.50b brown & multi 2.00 .35
650 A160 2b dull grn & multi 3.50 .75
651 A160 4b black & multi 9.00 3.50
Nos. 648-651 (4) 15.50 4.85

King Bhumibol Adulyadej — A161

Perf. 14x13½

1973-81 Photo. Wmk. 334
652 A161 5s purple 5.50 .30
653 A161 20s blue 2.40 .25
a. Perf. 14½, wmk. 233 1.00 .25
654 A161 25s rose carmine 2.75 .25

Wmk. 233 ***Perf. 14½***
655 A161 25s brown red ('81) .90 .25
656 A161 50s dk olive grn ('79) 2.75 .25
657 A161 75s violet 3.60 .25
a. Perf. 14x13½, wmk. 334 1.40 .25

Wmk. 334

Engr. ***Perf. 13***
658 A161 5b vio & brn 18.00 1.40
659 A161 6b grn & vio 12.00 1.40
660 A161 10b red & black 29.00 1.40
661 A161 20b org & yel grn ('75) 140.00 8.00
Nos. 652-661 (10) 216.90 13.75

For surcharges see Nos. 1168A, 1548, 2249.

Silversmiths A162

1973, June 15 Litho. ***Perf. 13½***
662 A162 75s shown .65 .25
663 A162 2.75b Lacquerware 2.25 .55
664 A162 4b Pottery 5.50 3.00
665 A162 5b Paper umbrellas 5.75 1.00
Nos. 662-665 (4) 14.15 4.80

Thai handicrafts.

Fresco from Temple of the Emerald Buddha A163

Designs: Frescoes illustrating Ramayana in Temple of the Emerald Buddha.

1973, July 17 Photo. Wmk. 329
666 A163 25s multicolored .90 .25
667 A163 75s multicolored .60 .25
668 A163 1.50b multicolored 2.75 1.60
669 A163 2b multicolored 4.00 1.60
670 A163 2.75b multicolored 3.00 .90
671 A163 3b multicolored 9.00 3.00
672 A163 5b multicolored 14.50 7.00
673 A163 6b multicolored 4.50 2.10
Nos. 666-673 (8) 39.25 16.70

Development of Postal Service A164

2b, Telecommunications development.

1973, Aug. 4 ***Perf. 13½***
674 A164 75s multicolored .75 .30
675 A164 2b multicolored 2.25 .75

90th anniv. of Post and Telegraph Dept.

No. 1 and Other Stamps A165

Various Stamps and: 1.25b, No. 147. 1.50b, No. 209. 2b, No. 244.

1973, Aug. 4 Photo. & Engr.
676 A165 75s dp rose & dk bl .65 .25
677 A165 1.25b blue & dp rose 1.75 .50
678 A165 1.50b olive & vio blk 5.50 1.60
679 A165 2b org & sl grn 4.00 .65
a. Souvenir sheet of 4 20.00 12.00
Nos. 676-679 (4) 11.90 3.00

2nd Natl. Phil. Exhib., THAIPEX '73, Aug. 4-8. No. 679a contains 4 stamps with simulated perforations similar to Nos. 676-679.

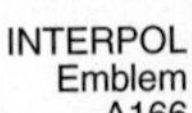

INTERPOL Emblem A166

1973, Sept. 3 **Photo.**
680 A166 75s gray & multi 1.00 .25

Intl. Criminal Police Organization, 50th anniv.

"Lilid Pralaw" A167

Designs: Scenes from Thai literature.

Perf. 11x13
1973, Oct. 7 **Litho.** **Wmk. 368**
681 A167 75s green & multi 1.00 .30
682 A167 1.50b blue & multi 2.30 1.10
683 A167 2b multicolored 3.75 1.40
684 A167 5b blue & multi 7.25 1.75
a. Souvenir sheet of 4, #681-684, perf. 13x14 37.50 25.00
Nos. 681-684 (4) 14.30 4.55

Intl. Letter Writing Week, Oct. 7-13.

Wat Suan Dok, Chiangmai; UN Emblem — A168

1973, Oct. 24 ***Perf. 13x11***
685 A168 75s blue & multi 1.20 .25

United Nations Day.

Schomburgk's Deer — A169

25s, Kouprey. 75s, Gorals. 1.25b, Water buffalos. 1.50b, Javan rhinoceros. 2b, Eld's deer. 2.75b, Asiatic 2-horned rhinoceros. 4b, Serows.

Wmk. 329
1973, Nov. 14 **Photo.** ***Perf. 13½***
686 A169 20s shown .90 .30
687 A169 25s multicolored .90 .30
688 A169 75s multicolored 1.20 .30
689 A169 1.25b multicolored 3.00 1.50
690 A169 1.50b multicolored 5.50 3.00
691 A169 2b multicolored 11.00 3.00
692 A169 2.75b multicolored 6.00 1.25
693 A169 4b multicolored 7.25 7.00
Nos. 686-693 (8) 35.75 16.65

Protected animals.

Human Rights Flame A170

Wmk. 371
1973, Dec. 10 **Litho.** ***Perf. 12½***
694 A170 75s multicolored 1.25 .25

25th anniversary of the Universal Declaration of Human Rights.

Children and Flowers — A171

1974, Jan. 12 **Litho.** ***Perf. 13***
695 A171 75s multicolored 1.50 .25

Children's Day.

Siriraj Hospital and Statue of Prince Nakarin A172

Perf. 13x13½
1974, Mar. 17 **Photo.** **Wmk. 368**
696 A172 75s multicolored 1.10 .25

84th anniversary of Siriraj Hospital, oldest medical school in Thailand.

Phala Piang Lai — A173

Classical Thai Dances: 2.75b, Phra Lux Phlaeng Rit. 4b, Chin Sao Sai. 5b, Charot Phra Sumen.

Wmk. 334
1974, June 25 **Litho.** ***Perf. 14***
697 A173 75s pink & multi .90 .30
698 A173 2.75b gray bl & multi 2.50 .75
699 A173 4b gray & multi 5.00 2.75
700 A173 5b yellow & multi 5.00 1.75
Nos. 697-700 (4) 13.40 5.55

Large Teak Tree in Uttaradit Province A174

1974, July 5 **Wmk. 329** ***Perf. 12½***
701 A174 75s multicolored 1.10 .25

15th Arbor Day.

People and WPY Emblem A175

Perf. 10½x13
1974, Aug. 19 **Litho.** **Wmk. 368**
702 A175 75s multicolored .95 .25

World Population Year, 1974.

Ban Chiang Painted Vase — A176

75s, Royal chariot. 2.75b, Avalokitesavara Bodhisattva. 3b, King Mongkut, Rama IV.

1974, Sept. 19 **Wmk. 262** ***Perf. 12½***
703 A176 75s blue & multi .75 .30
704 A176 2b black, brn & bis 2.25 .85
705 A176 2.75b black, brn & tan 3.00 .60
706 A176 3b black & multi 3.00 .90
Nos. 703-706 (4) 9.00 2.65

Centenary of National Museum. Inscribed "BATH" in error.

Purging Cassia A177

1974, Oct. 6 **Wmk. 368** ***Perf. 11x13***
707 A177 75s shown .60 .25
708 A177 2.75b Butea 2.10 .30
709 A177 3b Jasmine 4.25 .90
710 A177 4b Lagerstroemia 2.75 1.40
a. Souvenir sheet of 4, #707-710, perf. 13½x14 35.00 25.00
Nos. 707-710 (4) 9.70 2.85

Intl. Letter Writing Week, Oct. 6-12.

"UPU" and UPU Emblem A178

1974, Oct. 9 **Wmk. 371** ***Perf. 12½***
711 A178 75s dk green & multi .95 .25

Centenary of Universal Postal Union.

Wat Suthat Thepvararam A179

Wmk. 329
1974, Oct. 24 **Photo.** ***Perf. 13***
712 A179 75s multicolored 1.25 .25

United Nations Day.

Elephant Roundup A180

Wmk. 371
1974, Nov. 16 **Engr.** ***Perf. 12½***
713 A180 4b multicolored 1.00 2.00

Tourist publicity.

Vanda Coerulea A181

Orchids: 2.75b, Dendrobium aggregatum. 3b, Dendrobium scabrilingue. 4b, Aerides falcata.

Perf. 11x13
1974, Dec. 5 **Photo.** **Wmk. 368**
714 A181 75s red & multi .95 .30
715 A181 2.75b multicolored 2.25 .60
716 A181 3b olive & multi 4.00 .90
717 A181 4b green & multi 3.00 1.25
a. Souvenir sheet of 4, #714-717, perf. 13½x14 45.00 45.00
Nos. 714-717 (4) 10.20 3.05

See Nos. 745-748.

Boy — A182

Perf. 14x13½
1975, Jan. 11 **Litho.** **Wmk. 374**
718 A182 75s vermilion & multi 1.50 .25

Children's Day.

Democracy Monument A183

Designs: 2b, Mother with children and animals, bas-relief from Democracy Monument. 2.75b, Workers, bas-relief from Democracy Monument. 5b, Top of Democracy Monument and quotation from speech of King Rama VII.

Perf. 14x14½
1975, Jan. 26 **Wmk. 233**
719 A183 75s dull grn & multi .95 .30
720 A183 2b multicolored 2.10 .60
721 A183 2.75b blue & multi 3.00 .45
722 A183 5b multicolored 4.00 1.10
Nos. 719-722 (4) 10.05 2.45

Movement of Oct. 14, 1973, to re-establish democratic institutions.

Marbled Tiger Cat — A184

1975, Mar. 5 **Wmk. 334** ***Perf. 13½***
723 A184 20s shown 1.50 .30
724 A184 75s Gaurs 3.50 .60
725 A184 2.75b Asiatic elephant 5.00 .45
726 A184 3b Clouded leopard 6.50 1.10
Nos. 723-726 (4) 16.50 2.45

Protected animals.

White-eyed River Martin — A185

Birds: 2b, Paradise flycatchers. 2.75b, Long-tailed broadbills. 5b, Sultan tit.

Wmk. 371
1975, Apr. 2 **Litho.** ***Perf. 12½***
727 A185 75s ocher & multi 1.60 .30
728 A185 2b lt blue & multi 3.75 1.10
729 A185 2.75b lt violet & multi 4.00 .60
730 A185 5b rose & multi 8.00 1.75
Nos. 727-730 (4) 17.35 3.75

King Bhumibol Adulyadej and Queen Sirikit — A186

3b, King, Queen, different background design.

Perf. 10½x13
1975, Apr. 28 **Photo.** **Wmk. 368**
731 A186 75s violet bl & multi 1.60 .35
732 A186 3b multicolored 4.00 .60

25th wedding anniversary of King Bhumibol Adulyadej and Queen Sirikit.

Round-house Kick — A187

Thai Boxing: 2.75b, Reverse elbow. 3b, Flying knee. 5b, Ritual homage.

Wmk. 371
1975, May 20 **Litho.** ***Perf. 12½***
733 A187 75s green & multi 1.20 .35
734 A187 2.75b blue & multi 5.00 1.00
735 A187 3b orange & multi 4.50 1.75
736 A187 5b orange & multi 10.50 2.50
Nos. 733-736 (4) 21.20 5.60

Tosakanth Mask — A188

Masks: 2b, Kumbhakarn. 3b, Rama. 4b, Hanuman.

1975, June 10 **Litho.** **Wmk. 371**
737 A188 75s dark gray & multi 1.75 .30
738 A188 2b dull vio & multi 4.75 1.20
739 A188 3b purple & multi 5.50 1.75
740 A188 4b multicolored 13.00 3.50
Nos. 737-740 (4) 25.00 6.75

Thai art and literature.

THAIPEX 75 Emblem A189

THAIPEX 75 Emblem and: 2.75b, Stamp designer. 4b, Stamp printing plant. 5b, Stamp collector.

1975, Aug. 4 Wmk. 371 ***Perf. 12½***

741 A189 75s yellow & multi .65 .25
742 A189 2.75b orange & multi 1.75 .35
743 A189 4b lt blue & multi 2.75 1.40
744 A189 5b carmine & multi 3.25 .75
Nos. 741-744 (4) 8.40 2.75

THAIPEX 75, Third National Philatelic Exhibition, Aug. 4-10.

Orchid Type of 1974

Orchids: 75s, Dendrobium cruentum. 2b, Dendrobium parishii. 2.75b, Vanda teres. 5b, Vanda denisoniana.

Perf. 11x13

1975, Aug. 12 Photo. Wmk. 368

745 A181 75s olive & multi .90 .30
746 A181 2b multicolored 1.75 .60
747 A181 2.75b scarlet & multi 2.75 .60
748 A181 5b ultra & multi 4.50 1.25
a. Souv. sheet, #745-748, perf 13½ 50.00 35.00
Nos. 745-748 (4) 9.90 2.75

Mytilus Smaragdinus A190

Sea Shells: 1b, Turbo marmoratus. 2.75b, Oliva mustelina. 5b, Cypraea moneta.

Perf. 14x14½

1975, Sept. 5 Litho. Wmk. 375

749 A190 75s yellow & multi 2.00 1.25
750 A190 1b ver & multi 1.75 .30
751 A190 2.75b blue & multi 5.50 1.10
752 A190 5b green & multi 11.00 2.90
Nos. 749-752 (4) 20.25 5.55

Yachting and Games Emblem A191

Designs: 1.25b, Badminton. 1.50b, Volleyball. 2b, Target shooting.

Perf. 11x13

1975, Sept. 20 Litho. Wmk. 368

753 A191 75s ultra & black 1.00 .25
754 A191 1.25b brt rose & blk 1.40 .85
755 A191 1.50b red & black 2.50 1.75
756 A191 2b apple grn & blk 3.50 1.50
a. Souv. sheet, #753-756, perf 13½ 30.00 20.00
Nos. 753-756 (4) 8.40 4.35

8th SEAP Games, Bangkok, Sept. 1975.

Pataya Beach A192

Views: 2b, Samila Beach. 3b, Prachuap Bay. 5b, Laem Singha Bay.

1975, Oct. 5 Wmk. 371 ***Perf. 12½***

757 A192 75s orange & multi .90 .25
758 A192 2b orange & multi 2.40 1.50
759 A192 3b orange & multi 4.00 .85
760 A192 5b orange & multi 4.50 2.00
Nos. 757-760 (4) 11.80 4.60

Intl. Letter Writing Week, Oct. 6-12.

"u n," UN Emblem, Food and Education for Children A193

1975, Oct. 24 Litho. Wmk. 371

761 A193 75s ultra & multi 1.40 .25

United Nations Day.

Morse Telegraph A194

Design: 2.75b, Teleprinter and radar.

Perf. 14x14½

1975, Nov. 4 Litho. Wmk. 334

762 A194 75s multicolored 1.00 .40
763 A194 2.75b blue & multi 1.50 .45

Centenary of telegraph system.

Sukhrip Khrong Mueang Barge — A195

Thai ceremonial barges: 1b, Royal escort barge Anekchat Phuchong. 2b, Royal barge Anantanakarat. 2.75b, Krabi Ran Ron Rap barge. 3b, Asura Wayuphak barge. 4b, Asura paksi barge. 5b, Royal barge Sri Suphanahong, 6b, Phali Rang Thawip barge.

Wmk. 371

1975, Nov. 18 Litho. ***Perf. 12½***

764 A195 75s multicolored 1.50 .30
765 A195 1b multicolored 3.00 .90
766 A195 2b lilac & multi 4.50 1.25
767 A195 2.75b multicolored 5.00 1.00
768 A195 3b yellow & multi 7.00 1.75
769 A195 4b multicolored 6.00 3.50
770 A195 5b gray & multi 11.00 5.75
771 A195 6b blue & multi 7.50 3.50
Nos. 764-771 (8) 45.50 17.95

Thai Flag, Arms of Chakri Royal Family A196

King Bhumibol Adulyadej A197

Perf. 15x14

1975, Dec. 5 Litho. Wmk. 375

772 A196 75s multicolored 1.75 .45
773 A197 5b multicolored 5.00 1.10

King Bhumibol's 48th birthday.

Shot Put and SEAP Emblem A198

2b, Table tennis. 3b, Bicycling. 4b, Relay race.

1975, Dec. 9 Wmk. 368 ***Perf. 11x13***

774 A198 1b orange & black .70 .25
775 A198 2b brt green & blk 2.00 1.10
776 A198 3b ocher & blk 3.00 1.25
777 A198 4b violet & blk 3.50 2.00
a. Souvenir sheet of 4, #774-777, perf. 13½ 30.00 20.00
Nos. 774-777 (4) 9.20 4.60

8th SEAP Games, Bangkok, Dec. 9-20.

IWY Emblem and Globe — A199

Perf. 14x14½

1975, Dec. 20 Wmk. 375

778 A199 75s blk, org & vio bl 1.20 .30

International Women's Year.

Children Writing on Slate — A200

Perf. 13x14

1976, Jan. 10 Litho. Wmk. 368

779 A200 75s lt green & multi 1.75 .40

Children's Day.

Macrobrachium Rosenbergii — A201

Designs: 2b, Penaeus merguiensis. 2.75b, Panulirus ornatus. 5b, Penaeus monodon.

1976, Feb. 18 ***Perf. 11x13***

780 A201 75s multicolored 2.50 .30
781 A201 2b multicolored 4.00 1.75
782 A201 2.75b multicolored 4.00 1.25
783 A201 5b multicolored 9.50 3.25
Nos. 780-783 (4) 20.00 6.55

Shrimp and lobster exports.

Golden-backed Three-toed Woodpecker — A202

Birds: 1.50b, Greater green-billed malcoha. 3b, Pomatorhinus hypoleucos. 4b, Green magpie.

Wmk. 371

1976, Apr. 2 Litho. ***Perf. 12½***

784 A202 1b multicolored .60 .25
785 A202 1.50b multicolored 1.25 .65
786 A202 3b yellow & multi 4.00 1.20
787 A202 4b rose & multi 3.25 .95
Nos. 784-787 (4) 9.10 3.05

Ban Chiang Vase — A203

Designs: Ban Chiang painted pottery, various vessels, Bronze Age.

Perf. 14½x14

1976, May 5 Litho. Wmk. 375

788 A203 1b olive & multi .90 .25
789 A203 2b dp blue & multi 5.25 .90
790 A203 3b green & multi 3.75 .65
791 A203 4b org red & multi 4.00 2.50
Nos. 788-791 (4) 13.90 4.30

Mailman, 1883 — A204

Designs: 3b, Mailman, 1935. 4b, Mailman, 1950. 5b, Mailman, 1974.

Wmk. 377

1976, Aug. 4 Litho. ***Perf. 12½***

792 A204 1b multicolored .95 .30
793 A204 3b multicolored 2.75 .75
794 A204 4b multicolored 4.25 2.40
795 A204 5b multicolored 6.00 1.10
Nos. 792-795 (4) 13.95 4.55

Development of mailmen's uniforms.

Kinnari A205

Thai Mythology: 2b, Suphan-mat-cha. 4b, Garuda. 5b, Naga.

1976, Oct. 3 Wmk. 368 ***Perf. 11x13***

796 A205 1b green & multi 6.00 1.40
797 A205 2b ultra & multi 1.60 .30
798 A205 4b gray & multi 2.40 .30
799 A205 5b slate & multi 3.50 .45
Nos. 796-799 (4) 13.50 2.45

International Letter Writing Week.

UN Emblem, Drug Addicts, Alcohol, Cigarettes, Drugs — A206

Wmk. 329

1976, Oct. 24 Photo. ***Perf. 13½***

800 A206 1b ultra & multi 1.15 .25

United Nations Day.

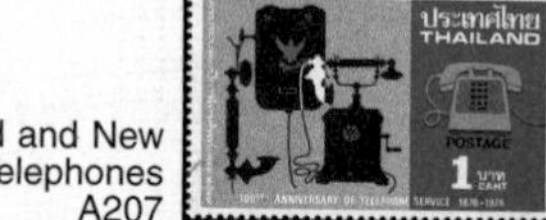

Old and New Telephones A207

Perf. 14x14½

1976, Nov. 10 Litho. Wmk. 375

801 A207 1b multicolored 1.00 .25

Centenary of first telephone call by Alexander Graham Bell, Mar. 10, 1876.

Sivalaya-Mahaprasad Hall — A208

Royal Houses: 2b, Cakri-Mahaprasad. 4b, Mahisra-Prasad. 5b, Dusit-Mahaprasad.

Perf. 14x15

1976, Dec. 5 Wmk. 375 Litho.

802 A208 1b multicolored .95 .25
803 A208 2b multicolored 7.00 1.00
804 A208 4b multicolored 4.00 2.10
805 A208 5b multicolored 1.25 1.25
Nos. 802-805 (4) 16.20 4.60

Banteng A209

Protected animals: 2b, Tapir and young. 4b, Sambar deer and fawn. 5b, Hog deer family.

Wmk. 334

1976, Dec. 26 Litho. *Perf. 11*

No.	Type	Description	Unused	Used
806	A209	1b multicolored	4.75	1.25
807	A209	2b multicolored	5.50	1.50

Wmk. 368

No.	Type	Description	Unused	Used
808	A209	4b multicolored	2.25	.45
809	A209	5b multicolored	3.00	.45
		Nos. 806-809 (4)	15.50	3.65

Child Casting Shadow of Man — A210

Wmk. 329

1977, Jan. 8 Photo. *Perf. 13½*

No.	Type	Description	Unused	Used
810	A210	1b multicolored	1.40	.25

National Children's Day.

Alsthom Diesel-electric Engine A211

Locomotives: 2b, Davenport Diesel-electric engine. 4b, Pacific steam engine. 5b, George Egestoff's steam engine.

Perf. 11x13

1977, Mar. 26 Litho. Wmk. 368

No.	Type	Description	Unused	Used
811	A211	1b multicolored	2.00	.35
812	A211	2b multicolored	5.50	.65
813	A211	4b multicolored	12.50	4.50
814	A211	5b multicolored	20.00	3.50
		Nos. 811-814 (4)	40.00	9.00

80th anniv. of State Railroad of Thailand.

Chulalongkorn University Auditorium A212

1977, Mar. 26 Photo.

No.	Type	Description	Unused	Used
815	A212	1b multicolored	1.40	.25

Chulalongkorn University, 60th anniversary.

Flags of AOPU Members A213

Wmk. 371

1977, Apr. 1 Litho. *Perf. 12½*

No.	Type	Description	Unused	Used
816	A213	1b multicolored	1.40	.25

Asian-Oceanic Postal Union (AOPU), 15th anniv.

Invalid in Wheelchair and Soldiers A214

Wmk. 329

1977, Apr. 2 Photo. *Perf. 13½*

No.	Type	Description	Unused	Used
817	A214	5b multicolored	1.75	.30

Sai-Jai-Thai Day, to publicize Sai-Jai-Thai Foundation which helps wounded soldiers.

Phra Aphai Mani and Phisua Samut A215

Puppets: 3b, Rusi and Sutsakhon. 4b, Nang Vali and Usren. 5b, Phra Aphai Mani and Nang Laweng's portrait.

Perf. 11x13

1977, June 16 Wmk. 368

No.	Type	Description	Unused	Used
818	A215	2b multicolored	.90	.25
819	A215	3b multicolored	1.75	.30
820	A215	4b multicolored	1.50	.30
821	A215	5b multicolored	1.75	.45
		Nos. 818-821 (4)	5.90	1.30

Thai plays and literature.

Drum Dance — A216

Designs: 3b, Dance of dip nets. 4b, Harvest dance. 5b, Kan dance.

1977, July 14 Photo. *Perf. 13x11*

No.	Type	Description	Unused	Used
822	A216	2b rose & multi	.75	.25
823	A216	3b lt green & multi	2.10	.40
824	A216	4b yellow & multi	1.10	.30
825	A216	5b lt violet & multi	1.60	.30
		Nos. 822-825 (4)	5.55	1.25

Thailand No. 609, Various Stamps and Thaipex Emblem A217

Wmk. 377

1977, Aug. 4 Litho. *Perf. 12½*

No.	Type	Description	Unused	Used
826	A217	75s multicolored	1.60	.25

THAIPEX 77, 4th National Philatelic Exhibition, Aug. 4-12.

Scenes from Thai Literature A218

Perf. 11x13

1977, Oct. 5 Photo. Wmk. 368

No.	Type	Description	Unused	Used
827	A218	75s multicolored	1.25	.25
828	A218	2b multi, diff.	2.50	1.00
829	A218	5b multi, diff.	3.00	.30
830	A218	6b multi, diff.	3.50	.65
		Nos. 827-830 (4)	10.25	2.20

Intl. Letter Writing Week, Oct. 6-12.

Old and New Buildings, UN Emblem A219

1977, Oct. 5 Litho. *Perf. 11x13*

No.	Type	Description	Unused	Used
831	A219	75s multicolored	1.40	.25

United Nations Day.

King Bhumibol as Scout Leader, Camp and Emblem A220

1977, Nov. 21 Photo. Wmk. 368

No.	Type	Description	Unused	Used
832	A220	75s multicolored	2.25	.25

9th National Jamboree, Nov. 21-27.

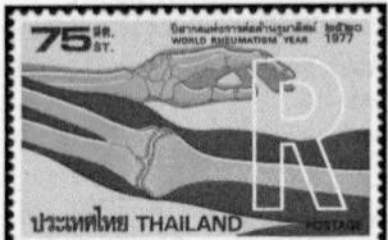

Diseased Hand and Elbow A221

1977, Dec. 20 *Perf. 11x13*

No.	Type	Description	Unused	Used
833	A221	75s multicolored	1.10	.25

World Rheumatism Year.

Map of South East Asia and ASEAN Emblem A222

Wmk. 377

1977, Dec. 1 Litho. *Perf. 12½*

No.	Type	Description	Unused	Used
834	A222	5b multicolored	2.00	.30

ASEAN, 10th anniv.

King Type of 1972-74 Redrawn

1976 *Perf. 12½x13*

Size: 21x27mm

No.	Type	Description	Unused	Used
835	A146	20s blue	4.50	.30
836	A146	75s lilac	4.50	.30

Engr.

No.	Type	Description	Unused	Used
837	A146	10b vermilion & blk	45.00	2.00
838	A146	40b bister & lilac	12.00	1.60
		Nos. 835-838 (4)	66.00	4.20

Numerals are taller and thinner and leaves in background have been redrawn.

Children Carrying Flag of Thailand A223

Wmk. 329

1978, Jan. 9 Photo. *Perf. 13½*

No.	Type	Description	Unused	Used
839	A223	75s multicolored	1.75	.25

Children's Day.

Dendrobium Heterocarpum A224

Orchids: 1b, Dendrobium pulchellum. 1.50b, Doritis pulcherrima. 2b, Dendrobium hercoglossum. 2.75b, Aerides odorata. 3b, Trichoglottis fasciata. 5b, Dendrobium wardianum. 6b, Dendrobium senile.

Perf. 11x14

1978, Jan. 18 Wmk. 368

No.	Type	Description	Unused	Used
840	A224	75s multicolored	1.35	.75
841	A224	1b multicolored	2.25	1.00
842	A224	1.50b multicolored	4.40	2.00
843	A224	2b multicolored	1.05	.25
844	A224	2.75b multicolored	5.50	.45
845	A224	3b multicolored	1.05	.60
846	A224	5b multicolored	1.35	.60
847	A224	6b multicolored	1.35	.60
		Nos. 840-847 (8)	18.30	6.25

9th World Orchid Conference.

Census Chart, Symbols of Agriculture A225

Wmk. 377

1978, Mar. 1 Litho. *Perf. 12½*

No.	Type	Description	Unused	Used
848	A225	75s multicolored	1.00	.25

Agricultural census, Apr. 1978.

Anabas Testudineus A226

Fish: 2b, Datnioides microlepis. 3b, Kryptopterus apogon. 4b, Probarbus Jullieni.

Perf. 11x13

1978, Apr. 13 Photo. Wmk. 368

No.	Type	Description	Unused	Used
849	A226	1b multicolored	2.40	.90
850	A226	2b multicolored	.90	.30
851	A226	3b multicolored	.90	.30
852	A226	4b multicolored	1.75	.60
		Nos. 849-852 (4)	5.95	2.10

Birth of Prince Siddhartha A227

Murals: 3b, Prince Siddhartha cuts his hair. 5b, Buddha descending from Tavatimsa Heaven. 6b, Buddha entering Nirvana.

Wmk. 329

1978, June 15 Photo. *Perf. 13½*

No.	Type	Description	Unused	Used
853	A227	2b multicolored	1.40	.70
854	A227	3b multicolored	2.40	1.00
855	A227	5b multicolored	9.00	2.40
856	A227	6b multicolored	4.50	2.40
		Nos. 853-856 (4)	17.30	6.50

Story of Gautama Buddha, murals in Puthi Savan Hall, National Museum, Bangkok.

Bhumibol Dam — A228

Dams and Reservoirs: 2b, Sirikit dam. 2.75b, Vajiralongkorn dam. 6b, Ubol Ratana dam.

Perf. 14x14½

1978, July 28 Litho. Wmk. 233

No.	Type	Description	Unused	Used
857	A228	75s multicolored	1.50	.45
858	A228	2b multicolored	1.50	.60
859	A228	2.75b multicolored	2.75	.60
860	A228	6b multicolored	3.75	2.00
		Nos. 857-860 (4)	9.50	3.65

Idea Lynceus A229

Butterflies: 3b, Sephisa chandra. 5b, Charaxes durnfordi. 6b, Cethosia penthesilea methypsia.

Perf. 11x13

1978, Aug. 25 Litho. Wmk. 368

No.	Type	Description	Unused	Used
861	A229	2b lilac, blk & red	2.00	.75
862	A229	3b multicolored	2.25	.75
863	A229	5b multicolored	6.00	1.40
864	A229	6b multicolored	4.00	2.25
		Nos. 861-864 (4)	14.25	5.15

Chedi Chai Mongkhon Temple — A230

Temples: 2b, That Hariphunchai. 2.75b, Borom That Chaiya. 5b, That Choeng Chum.

1978, Oct. 8 *Perf. 13x11*

No.	Type	Description	Unused	Used
865	A230	75s multicolored	1.10	.30
866	A230	2b multicolored	1.40	.45
867	A230	2.75b multicolored	4.50	.45
868	A230	5b multicolored	2.75	1.10
		Nos. 865-868 (4)	9.75	2.30

Intl. Letter Writing Week, Oct. 6-12.

Mother and Children, UN Emblem — A231

Perf. 14½x14

1978, Oct. 24 Litho. Wmk. 375

No.	Type	Description	Unused	Used
869	A231	75s multicolored	.95	.25

United Nations Day.

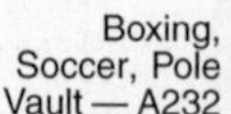

Boxing, Soccer, Pole Vault — A232

Designs: 2b, Javelin, weight lifting, running. 3b, Ball games and sailing. 5b, Basketball, hockey stick and boxing gloves.

Perf. 14x14½

1978, Oct. Wmk. 233 Litho.

870	A232	75s multicolored	.60	.25
871	A232	2b multicolored	.90	.25
872	A232	3b multicolored	1.75	.45
873	A232	5b multicolored	3.25	.90
		Nos. 870-873 (4)	6.50	1.85

8th Asian Games, Bangkok.

Five Races and World Map — A233

1978, Nov.

874	A233	75s multicolored	.85	.25

Anti-Apartheid Year.

Children Painting Thai Flag — A234

Children and Children's SOS Village, Tambol Bangpu — A235

1979, Jan. 17 ***Perf. 14x14½***

875	A234	75s multicolored	.65	.25
876	A235	75s multicolored	1.40	.35

International Year of the Child.

Matuta Lunaris A236

Crabs: 2.75b, Matuta planipes fabricius. 3b, Portunus pelagicus. 5b, Scylla serrata.

Wmk. 377

1979, Mar. 22 Litho. ***Perf. 12½***

877	A236	2b multicolored	1.90	.60
878	A236	2.75b multicolored	4.50	.60
879	A236	3b multicolored	2.50	.90
880	A236	5b multicolored	5.75	1.50
		Nos. 877-880 (4)	14.65	3.60

A237

1979, June 25

881	A237	1b Sweetsop	1.40	.45
882	A237	2b Pineapple	1.40	.45
883	A237	5b Bananas	3.30	1.40
884	A237	6b Longans (litchi)	3.10	1.60
		Nos. 881-884 (4)	9.20	3.90

See Nos. 1145-1148.

Arbor Day, 20th Anniv. — A238

Young man and woman planting tree.

Perf. 13x11

1979, July 10 Litho. Wmk. 368

885	A238	75s multicolored	.80	.25

Pencil, Pen, Thaipex '79 Emblem A239

Thaipex '79 Emblem and: 2b, Envelopes. 2.75b, Stamp album. 5b, Magnifying glass and tongs.

1979, Aug. 4 ***Perf. 11x13***

886	A239	75s multicolored	.65	.25
887	A239	2b multicolored	1.00	.30
888	A239	2.75b multicolored	1.65	.40
889	A239	5b multicolored	3.25	.90
		Nos. 886-889 (4)	6.55	1.85

Thaipex '79, 5th National Philatelic Exhibition, Bangkok, Aug. 4-12.

Floral Arrangement — A240

Designs: Decorative arrangements.

Perf. 14½x14

1979, Oct. 7 Litho. Wmk. 233

890	A240	75s multicolored	.60	.25
891	A240	2b multicolored	.90	.30
892	A240	2.75b multicolored	2.25	.40
893	A240	5b multicolored	2.25	.90
		Nos. 890-893 (4)	6.00	1.85

Intl. Letter Writing Week, Oct. 8-14.

UN Day — A241

1979, Oct. 24 Litho. ***Perf. 14½x14***

894	A241	75s multicolored	.95	.25

Frigate Makut Rajakumarn A242

Thai Naval Ships: 3b, Frigate Tapi. 5b, Fast strike craft, Prabparapak. 6b, Patrol boat T-91.

Wmk. 329

1979, Nov. 20 Photo. ***Perf. 13½***

895	A242	2b multicolored	1.60	.90
896	A242	3b multicolored	2.60	.90
897	A242	5b multicolored	5.50	1.75
898	A242	6b multicolored	6.00	2.50
		Nos. 895-898 (4)	15.70	6.05

Thai Royal Orders (Medallions and Ribbons) — A243

Designs: #900a, Rajamitrabhorn Order. #902a, House of Chakri. #904a, The nine gems. #906a, Chula Chom Klao. Pairs have continuous design.

Perf. 13x11

1979, Dec. 5 Litho. Wmk. 368

899	1b multicolored	1.40	.40
900	1b multicolored	1.40	.40
a.	A243 Pair, #899-900	3.00	3.00
901	2b multicolored	1.40	.40
902	2b multicolored	1.40	.40
a.	A243 Pair, #901-902	3.00	3.00
903	5b multicolored	2.50	.70
904	5b multicolored	2.50	.70
a.	A243 Pair, #903-904	5.50	5.50
905	6b multicolored	3.00	1.10
906	6b multicolored	3.00	1.10
a.	A243 Pair, #905-906	7.00	7.00
	Nos. 899-906 (8)	16.60	5.20

See Nos. 1278-1285.

King Type of 1972-77

Perf. 13½x13

1979, Dec. 23 Litho. Wmk. 329

Size: 21x26mm

907	A146	50s olive green	.60	.25

Engr.

908	A146	2b org red & lilac	1.25	.25

Rice Planting — A245

Children's Day: No. 910, Family in rice field.

Perf. 13x11

1980, Jan. 12 Litho. Wmk. 368

909	A245	75s multicolored	.85	.25
910	A245	75s multicolored	.85	.25

Family, House, Map of Thailand — A246

Perf. 15x14

1980, Feb. 1 Litho. Wmk. 233

911	A246	75s multicolored	.85	.30

Natl. Population & Housing Census, Apr.

Gold-fronted Leafbird — A247

2b, Yellow-cheeked tit. 3b, Chestnut-tailed siva. 5b, Scarlet minivet.

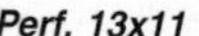

Perf. 13x11

1980, Feb. 26 Wmk. 368

912	A247	75s shown	.90	.25
913	A247	2b multicolored	1.30	.45
914	A247	3b multicolored	2.45	.60
915	A247	5b multicolored	3.25	1.25
		Nos. 912-915 (4)	7.90	2.55

Intl. Commission for Bird Preservation, 9th Conf. of Asian Section, Chieng-mai, 2/26-29.

Smokers and Lungs, WHO Emblem A248

1980, Apr. 7 Wmk. 329 ***Perf. 13½***

916	A248	75s multicolored	.70	.25

World Health Day; fight against cigarette smoking.

Garuda and Rotary Emblem — A249

1980, May 6 Wmk. 368 ***Perf. 13x11***

917	A249	5b multicolored	1.75	.45

Rotary International, 75th anniversary.

Sai Yok Falls, Kanchanaburi A250

2b, Punyaban Falls, Ranong. 5b, Heo Suwat Falls, Nakhon Ratchasima. 6b, Siriphum Falls, Chiang Mai.

Perf. 14x15

1980, July 1 Litho. Wmk. 233

918	A250	1b shown	.65	.25
919	A250	2b multicolored	.80	.25
920	A250	5b multicolored	2.40	.75
921	A250	6b multicolored	2.10	.90
		Nos. 918-921 (4)	5.95	2.15

Queen Sirikit — A251

Family with Cattle, Ceres Medal (Reverse) A252

No. 924, Ceres medal (obverse), potters.

Perf. 13½, 11x13 (5b)

Wmk. 329, 368 (5b)

1980, Aug. 12 Litho.

922	A251	75s multicolored	.90	.25
		Complete booklet, 10 #922	17.50	
923	A252	5b multicolored	1.75	.80
924	A252	5b multicolored	1.75	.80
		Nos. 922-924 (3)	4.40	1.85

Queen Sirikit's 48th birthday.

Khao Phanomrung Temple, Buri Ram — A253

Intl. Letter Writing Week, Oct. 6-12 (Temples): 2b, Prang Ku, Chailyaphum. 2.75b, Phimai, Nakhon Ratchasima. 5b, Sikhoraphum, Surin.

Perf. 11x13

1980, Oct. 5 Litho. Wmk. 368

925 A253 75s multicolored .80 .25
Complete booklet, 10 #925 14.00
926 A253 2b multicolored .80 .25
927 A253 2.75b multicolored 1.20 .30
928 A253 5b multicolored 2.00 1.00
Nos. 925-928 (4) 4.80 1.80

Princess Mother — A254

Perf. 15x14

1980, Oct. 21 Litho. Wmk. 233

929 A254 75s multicolored 3.00 .45
Complete booklet, 10 #929 40.00

Princess Mother, 80th birthday.

Golden Mount, Bangkok — A255

1980, Oct. 24

930 A255 75s multicolored .95 .30
Complete booklet, 10 #930 14.00

United Nations Day.

King Bhumibol Adulyadej — A256

Type I

Type II Redrawn

Two types of Nos. 936-938: Type I, asymmetrical shape to mouth and small eye pupils. Type II, symmetrical mouth and large eye pupils.

Perf. 11x13

1980-86(?) Litho. Wmk. 368

932 A256 25s salmon 1.10 .25
933 A256 50s olive green 5.50 .25
b. Wmk. 233, perf. 14x15 4.00 .25
c. Wmk. 387, perf. 11x13 1.00 .25
934 A256 75s lilac .50 .25
Complete booklet, 10 #934 11.00
935 A256 1.25b yellow green .50 .25
a. Wmk. 387, perf. 11x13 1.25 .25
b. Wmk. 233, perf. 14x15 4.00 .25

Perf. 13½x13

Engr. Wmk. 329

936 A256 3b brn & dk bl (II) .90 .25
a. Type I 15.00 .50
937 A256 5b pur & brn (II) 1.25 .30
a. Type I 17.00 .65
938 A256 6b dk grn & pur (II) 1.40 .25
a. Type I 15.00 .65
939 A256 8.50b grn & brn org 1.50 .30
940 A256 9.50b olive & dk grn 1.50 .55
Nos. 932-940 (9) 14.15 2.65

Issued: 25s, 75s, 12/5/80; Nos. 933, 935, 9/7/81; #933b, 12/5/81; Nos. 933b, 935b, 6/8/83; Nos. 936a, 937a, 938a, 8.50b, 9.50b, 12/5/83. Nos. 933c, 935a, 1984. Nos. 936-938, 1985-86.

See Nos. 1080-1093. For surcharges see Nos. 1226-1226A, 2250.

King Rama VII Monument Inauguration — A257

Perf. 15x14

1980, Dec. 10 Wmk. 233

946 A257 75s multicolored .75 .25

Bencharongware Bowl — A258

Perf. 11x13

1980, Dec. 15 Wmk. 368

947 A258 2b shown 1.05 .30
948 A258 2.75b Covered bowls 1.05 .30
949 A258 3b Covered jar 1.65 .45
950 A258 5b Stem plates 1.65 .75
Nos. 947-950 (4) 5.40 1.80

King Vajiravudh Birth Centenary — A259

1981, Jan. 1 Wmk. 233 *Perf. 15x14*

951 A259 75s multicolored 1.50 .25
Complete booklet, 10 #951 27.50

Children's Day — A260

Perf. 13x11

1981, Jan. 16 Wmk. 368

952 A260 75s multicolored .60 .25
Complete booklet, 10 #952 14.00

Hegira, 1500th Anniv. A261

Wmk. 377

1981, Jan. 18 Litho. *Perf. 12½*

953 A261 5b multicolored 2.75 .60

Dolls in Native Costumes A262

Wmk. 368

1981, Feb. 6 Litho. *Perf. 13½*

954 A262 75s Palm-leaf fish mobile .45 .25
Complete booklet, 10 #954 12.50
955 A262 75s Teak elephants .45 .25
Complete booklet, 10 #955 12.50
956 A262 2.75b shown 1.25 .60
957 A262 2.75b Baskets 1.25 .60
Nos. 954-957 (4) 3.40 1.70

CONEX '81 International Crafts Exhibition.

Scout Leader and Boy on Crutches — A263

1981, Feb. 28 *Perf. 13x11*

958 A263 75s shown .30 .25
Complete booklet, 10 #958 14.00
959 A263 5b Diamond cutter in wheelchair 1.60 .50

International Year of the Disabled.

Dindaeng-Tarua Expressway Opening — A264

1981, Oct. 29 *Perf. 13½*

960 A264 1b Klongtoey .65 .25
961 A264 5b Vipavadee Rangsit Highway 2.25 .65

Ongkhot, Khon Mask — A265

Designs: Various Khon masks.

1981, July 1 Litho. *Perf. 13x11*

962 A265 75s shown .45 .25
963 A265 2b Maiyarab 1.00 .25
964 A265 3b Sukrip 1.60 .50
965 A265 5b Indrajit 2.00 1.25
Nos. 962-965 (4) 5.05 2.25

Exhibition Emblem, No. 83 — A266

Wmk. 370

1981, Aug. 4 Litho. *Perf. 12*

966 A266 75s shown .50 .25
967 A266 75s No. 144 .50 .25
968 A266 2.75b No. 198 1.35 .60
969 A266 2.75b No. 226 1.35 .60
Nos. 966-969 (4) 3.70 1.70

A267

Perf. 15x14

1981, Aug. 26 Wmk. 233

970 A267 1.25b multicolored .85 .25
Complete booklet, 10 #970 14.00

Luang Praditphairo, court Musician, birth centenary. THAIPEX '81 Intl. Stamp Exhibition.

A268

Designs: Dwarfed trees.

1981, Oct. 4 Wmk. 329

971 A268 75s Mai hok-hian .50 .25
972 A268 2b Mai kam-ma-lo .85 .30
973 A268 2.75b Mai khen 1.40 .25
974 A268 5b Mai khabuan 2.40 .90
Nos. 971-974 (4) 5.15 1.70

25th Intl. Letter Writing Week, Oct. 6-12.

World Food Day — A269

Wmk. 370

1981, Oct. 16 Litho. *Perf. 12*

975 A269 75s multicolored 1.00 .25

United Nations Day — A270

1981, Oct. 24 Wmk. 368 *Perf. 13½*

976 A270 1.25b Samran Mukha-mat Pavilion .65 .25
Complete booklet, 10 #976 14.00

King Cobra A271

1981, Dec. 1 Wmk. 329 *Perf. 13½*

977 A271 75s shown .65 .25
978 A271 2b Banded krait 1.40 .65
979 A271 2.75b Thai cobra 1.60 .45
980 A271 5b Malayan pit viper 2.00 1.00
Nos. 977-980 (4) 5.65 2.35

Children's Day — A272

1982, Jan. 9 Wmk. 370 *Perf. 12*

981 A272 1.25b multicolored .75 .25
Complete booklet, strip of 4 #981 12.50

Scouting Year — A273

1982, Feb. 22

982 A273 1.25b multicolored .70 .25
Complete booklet, strip of 4 #982 5.00

Bicentenary of Bangkok (Thai Capital) — A274

Chakri Dynasty kings. (Rama I-Rama IX) — 1b, Buddha Yod-Fa (1736-1809). 2b, Buddha Lert La Naphalai (1767-1824). 3b, Nang Klao (1787-1851). 4b, Mongkut (1804-1868). 5b, Chulalongkorn (1853-1910). 6b, Vajiravudh (1880-1925). 7b, Prachathipok (1893-1941).

8b, Ananda Mahidol (1925-1946). 9b, Bhumibol Adulyadej (b. 1927).

1982, Apr. 4 Litho. *Perf. 12*

983 A274 1b multicolored .60 .30
984 A274 1.25b shown .60 .30
Complete booklet, strip of 4 #984 6.50
985 A274 2b multicolored .90 .30
986 A274 3b multicolored 2.00 .45
987 A274 4b multicolored 1.50 .60
988 A274 5b multicolored 2.75 .85
989 A274 6b multicolored 2.75 .85
990 A274 7b multicolored 3.00 1.60
991 A274 8b multicolored 2.00 .90
992 A274 9b multicolored 2.40 1.25
a. Souv. sheet of 10, 205x142mm 45.00 30.00
b. Souv. sheet of 10, 195x180mm 45.00 30.00
Nos. 983-992 (10) 18.50 7.40

Nos. 992a-992b each contain Nos. 983-992. No. 992a sold for 60b, No. 992b for 70b. Values for #992a-992b include folder.

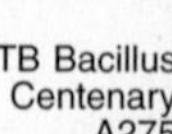

TB Bacillus Centenary A275

Wmk. 368

1982, Apr. 7 Litho. *Perf. 13½*

993 A275 1.25b multicolored .95 .25
Complete booklet, strip of 4 #993 6.00

Local Flowers A276

1.25b, Quisqualis indica. 1.50b, Murraya aniculata. 6.50b, Mesua ferrea. 7b, Desmos chinensis.

Perf. 14x14½

1982, June 30 Wmk. 233

994 A276 1.25b multicolored .35 .25
Complete booklet, strip of 4 #994 2.00
995 A276 1.50b multicolored .60 .25
996 A276 6.50b multicolored 2.10 .60
997 A276 7b multicolored 1.65 .60
Nos. 994-997 (4) 4.70 1.70

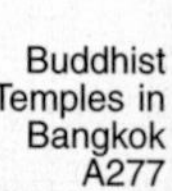

Buddhist Temples in Bangkok A277

4.25b, Wat Pho. 6.50b, Mahathat Yuwarat Rangsarit. 7b, Phra Sri Rattana Satsadaram.

1982, Aug. 4 Wmk. 368 *Perf. 13½*

998 A277 1.25b shown .45 .25
Complete booklet, strip of 4 #998 3.00
999 A277 4.25b multicolored .75 .30
1000 A277 6.50b multicolored 1.40 .60
1001 A277 7b multicolored 1.60 .45
a. Souv. sheet of 4, #998-1001, perf. 12½ 87.50 45.00
Nos. 998-1001 (4) 4.20 1.60

BANGKOK '83 Intl. Stamp Exhibition, Aug. 4-13, 1983. No. 1001a sold for 30b.
See Nos. 1025-1026.

A278

Design: LANDSAT Satellite.

1982, Aug. 9 Wmk. 370 *Perf. 12*

1002 A278 1.25b multicolored .60 .25
Complete booklet, strip of 4 #1002 6.00

2nd UN Conference on Peaceful Uses of Outer Space, Vienna, Aug. 9-21.

A279

Prince Purachatra of Kambaengbejra (1882-1936).

1982, Sept. 14 Wmk. 233 *Perf. 14*

1003 A279 1.25b multicolored 1.25 .25
Complete booklet, strip of 4 #1003 8.00

26th Intl. Letter Writing Week, Oct. 6-12 — A280

Sangalok Pottery — 1.25b, Covered glazed jar. 3b, Painted jar. 4.25b, Glazed plate. 7b, Painted plate.

1982, Oct. 3 Wmk. 329 *Perf. 13½*

1004 A280 1.25b multicolored .45 .25
Complete booklet, strip of 4 #1004 2.00
1005 A280 3b multicolored 1.25 .30
1006 A280 4.25b multicolored .90 .45
1007 A280 7b multicolored 1.60 .60
Nos. 1004-1007 (4) 4.20 1.60

UN Day — A281

Design: Loha Prasat Tower.

1982, Oct. 24

1008 A281 1.25b multicolored .60 .25
Complete booklet, strip of 4 #1008 6.00

Musical Instruments A282

50s, Chap, ching. 1b, Pi nai, pi nok. 1.25b, Klong that, taphon. 1.50b, Khong mong, krap. 6b, Khong wong yai. 7b, Khong wong lek. 8b, Ranat ek. 9b, Ranat thum.

1982, Nov. 30 Wmk. 370 *Perf. 12*

1009 A282 50s multicolored .40 .25
1010 A282 1b multicolored .95 .25
1011 A282 1.25b multicolored .55 .25
Complete booklet, strip of 4 #1011 2.00
1012 A282 1.50b multicolored .95 .30
1013 A282 6b multicolored 3.90 1.10
1014 A282 7b multicolored 1.95 .50
1015 A282 8b multicolored 1.80 .50
1016 A282 9b multicolored 1.95 .50
Nos. 1009-1016 (8) 12.45 3.65

Pileated Gibbon — A283

3b, Pig-tailed macaque. 5b, Slow loris. 7b, Silvered leaf monkey.

1982, Dec. 26

1017 A283 1.25b shown .45 .25
Complete booklet, strip of 4 #1017 5.25
1018 A283 3b multicolored 1.75 .30
1019 A283 5b multicolored 1.50 .55
1020 A283 7b multicolored 1.60 .75
Nos. 1017-1020 (4) 5.30 1.85

ASEAN Members' Flags — A284

1982, Dec. 26 Wmk. 233

1021 A284 6.50b multicolored 1.60 .30

15th Anniv. of Assoc. of Southeast Asian Nations.

Children's Day — A285

Perf. 14½x14

1983, Jan. 8 Litho. Wmk. 233

1022 A285 1.25b multicolored .75 .25
Complete booklet, strip of 4 #1022 5.00

First Anniv. of Postal Code — A286

1983, Feb. 25 Wmk. 329 *Perf. 13½*

1023 A286 1.25b Codes .75 .25
Complete booklet, strip of 4 #1023 6.00
1024 A286 1.25b Code on envelope .75 .25
Complete booklet, strip of 4 #1024 6.00

BANGKOK '83 Type of 1982

Design: Old General Post Office.

1983, Feb. 25 Wmk. 368 Photo.

1025 A277 7b multicolored 1.50 .25
1026 A277 10b multicolored 2.10 .35
a. Souv. sheet of 2, #1025-1026, perf. 12½ 27.50 14.00

25th Anniv. of Intl. Maritime Org. — A287

Perf. 14x14½

1983, Mar. 17 Litho. Wmk. 233

1029 A287 1.25b Chinese junks .60 .25
Complete booklet, strip of 4 #1029 5.00

Civil Servants' Day — A288

1983, Apr. 1 Wmk. 370 *Perf. 12*

1030 A288 1.25b multicolored .75 .25
Complete booklet, strip of 4 #1030 5.00

Prince Sithiporn Kridakara (1883-1971) — A289

Perf. 14½x14

1983, Apr. 11 Wmk. 233

1031 A289 1.25b multicolored .75 .25
Complete booklet, strip of 4 #1031 5.00

Domestic Satellite Communications System Inauguration — A290

Design: Map, dish antenna, satellite.

Wmk. 368

1983, Aug. 4 Litho. *Perf. 13½*

1032 A290 2b multicolored .95 .25

BANGKOK '83 Intl. Stamp Show, Aug. 4-13 — A291

1.25b, Mail collection. 7.50b, Posting letters. 8.50b, Mail transport. 9.50b, Mail delivery.

1983, Aug. 4 Wmk. 370 *Perf. 12*

1033 A291 1.25b multicolored .30 .25
Complete booklet, strip of 4 #1033 1.50
1034 A291 7.50b multicolored 1.25 .35
1035 A291 8.50b multicolored 1.00 .45
1036 A291 9.50b multicolored 1.00 .45
a. Souv. sheet of 4, #1033-1036 25.00 15.00
Nos. 1033-1036 (4) 3.55 1.50

No. 1036a exist imperf, sold for 50b. Values: unused $150; used $110.

A292

Prince Bhanurangsi memorial statue.

Perf. 15x14

1983, Aug. 4 Litho. Wmk. 233

1037 A292 1.25b multicolored 1.10 .25
Complete booklet, strip of 4 #1037 6.00

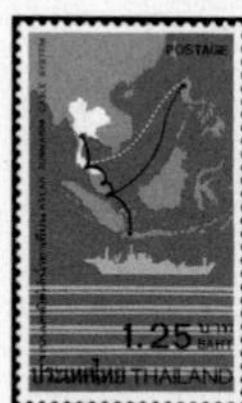

A293

Wmk. 370

1983, Sept. 27 Litho. *Perf. 12*

1038 A293 1.25b multicolored .30 .25
Complete booklet, strip of 4 #1038 1.75
1039 A293 7b multicolored 1.10 .45

Malaysia/ Thailand/ Singapore submarine cable inauguration.

Intl. Letter Writing Week — A294

1983, Oct. 6 Wmk. 329 *Perf. 13½*

1040 A294 2b Acropora asper .70 .25
1041 A294 3b Platygyra lamellina 1.60 .25
1042 A294 4b Fungia 1.00 .45
1043 A294 7b Pectinia lactuca 2.00 .75
Nos. 1040-1043 (4) 5.30 1.70

Prince Mahidol of Songkhla — A295

Wmk. 370

1983, Oct. 10 Litho. *Perf. 12*
1044 A295 9.50b multicolored 1.90 .60

Siriraj Hospital Faculty of Medicine and Rockefeller Foundation, 60th Anniv. of cooperation.

World Communications Year — A296

3b, Telecommunications equipment, diff.

Perf. 14x14½

1983, Oct. 24 Litho. Wmk. 233
1045 A296 2b multicolored .60 .25
1046 A296 3b multicolored .60 .25

United Nations Day — A297

1983, Oct. 24
1047 A297 1.25b multicolored .50 .25
Complete booklet, strip of 4 #1047 4.50

Thai Alphabet, 700th Anniv. A298

Designs: 3b, Painted pottery, Sukothai period. 7b, Thai characters, reign of King Ramkamhaeng. 8b, Buddha, Sukothai period. 9b, Mahathat Temple, Sukothai province.

1983, Nov. 17 Wmk. 370 *Perf. 12*
1048 A298 3b multicolored .90 .25
1049 A298 7b multicolored 1.50 .30
1050 A298 8b multi, vert. 1.10 .35
1051 A298 9b multi, vert. 1.10 .35
Nos. 1048-1051 (4) 4.60 1.25

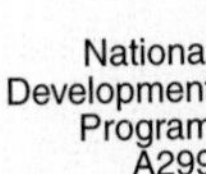

National Development Program A299

#1052, King and Queen initiating Royal Projects. #1053, Technical aid. #1054, Terrace farming, Irrigation dam. #1055, Gathering grain. #1056, Receiving the peoples' gratitude.

1984, May 5
1052 A299 1.25b multicolored .65 .25
1053 A299 1.25b multicolored .65 .25
1054 A299 1.25b multicolored .65 .25
1055 A299 1.25b multicolored .65 .25
1056 A299 1.25b multicolored .65 .25
a. Strip of 5, #1052-1056 3.25 3.25

Children's Day — A300

1984, Jan. 14 Wmk. 329 *Perf. 13½*
1057 A300 1.25b multicolored .85 .25
Complete booklet, strip of 4 #1057 5.00

17th Natl. Games, Jan. 22-28 — A301

1984, Jan. 22
1058 A301 1.25b Running .75 .25
Complete booklet, strip of 4 #1058 3.50
1059 A301 3b Soccer .75 .25

5th Rheumatology Congress, Jan. 22-27 — A302

Design: Rheumatic joints.

Perf. 14x15

1984, Jan. 22 Wmk. 233
1060 A302 1.25b multicolored .60 .25
Complete booklet, strip of 4 #1060 5.00

Armed Forces Day — A303

Design: King Naresuan, tanks, jet, ship.

1984, Jan. 25 *Perf. 15x14*
1061 A303 1.25b multicolored .60 .25
Complete booklet, strip of 4 #1061 7.00

50th Anniv. of Royal Institute — A304

1984, Mar. 31
1062 A304 1.25b multicolored .75 .25
Complete booklet, strip of 4 #1062 5.00

Thammasat University, 50th Anniv. A305

1984, June 27 *Perf. 14x15*
1063 A305 1.25b Dome Building .60 .25
Complete booklet, strip of 4 #1063 5.00

Asia-Pacific Broadcasting Union, 20th Anniv. A306

1984, July 1 Wmk. 387 *Perf. 12*
1064 A306 4b Map, emblem 1.10 .25

Seated Buddha, Chiang Saen Style — A307

Seated Buddhas in various styles.

Perf. 14½x14

1984, July 12 Wmk. 233
1065 A307 1.25b shown 1.10 .25
1066 A307 7b Sukhothai 1.40 .60
1067 A307 8.50b U-Thong 1.10 .60
1068 A307 9.50b Ayutthaya .75 .60
Nos. 1065-1068 (4) 4.35 2.05

Intl. Letter Writing Week — A308

Medicinal Succulents: 1.50b, Alocasia indica. 2b, Aloe barbadensis. 4b, Gynura pseudochina DC. 10b, Rhoeo spathacea.

Wmk. 385

1984, Oct. 7 Litho. *Perf. 13½*
1069 A308 1.50b multicolored .50 .25
1070 A308 2b multicolored .85 .35
1071 A308 4b multicolored 1.10 .45
1072 A308 10b multicolored 2.60 1.25
Nos. 1069-1072 (4) 5.05 2.30

Princess Mother (b. 1900) — A309

Perf. 15x14

1984, Oct. 21 Wmk. 233
1073 A309 1.50b Portrait 1.00 .25

UN Day — A310

Design: Woman threshing rice.

1984, Oct. 24 Wmk. 233
1074 A310 1.50b multicolored .35 .25

Local Butterflies A311

2b, Bhutanitis lidderdalei. 3b, Stichophthalma louisa. 5b, Parthenos sylvia. 7b, Stichophthalma godfreyi.

Wmk. 329

1984, Nov. 27 Photo. *Perf. 13½*
1075 A311 2b multicolored .75 .25
1076 A311 3b multicolored 1.10 .25
1077 A311 5b multicolored 1.55 .60
1078 A311 7b multicolored 2.50 .60
Nos. 1075-1078 (4) 5.90 1.70

King Type of 1980

Perf. 13½x13, 14x15 (1.50b, 2b)

Wmk. 329, 233 (1.50b, 2b)

1984-87 Litho.
1080 A256 1b Prus blue .45 .25
1081 A256 1.50b brt yel org ('85) 2.50 1.50
1082 A256 2b dk car ('85) 1.75 .25
a. Wmk. 387, perf. 11x13½ ('86?) 2.50 .25
b. Wmk. 387, perf. 14½x14 ('87) 1.10 .25

Engr.
1083 A256 2b hn brn & gray vio 12.00 .30
1084 A256 4b turq bl & hn brn 1.00 .25
1085 A256 6.50b dk yel grn & ol brn 1.25 .50
1086 A256 7b dl red brn & sep 1.25 .30
1087 A256 7.50b dk org & saph ('85) 1.20 .50
1088 A256 8b brn vio & ol grn ('85) 1.40 .35
1089 A256 9b int bl & dk ol bis ('85) 1.25 .40
1090 A256 10b hn brn & sl grn 2.25 .35
1091 A256 20b dk org & grn 2.75 .40
1092 A256 50b dp vit & grn 12.00 1.20
1093 A256 100b dp org & dk bl 20.00 1.75
Nos. 1080-1093 (14) 61.05 8.30

For surcharges see Nos. 1212, 2251.

Issued: 1b, 1/25/84; No. 1083, 4b, 6.50b, 7b, 10b, 50b, 100b, 12/5/84; 7.50b, 8b, 9b, 1/25/85; 1.50b, 4/6/85; No. 1082, 8/4/85; No. 1082a, 3/3/86; No. 1082b, 6/19/87.

Children's Day — A313

Children's drawings — No. 1101, Pedestrians, overpass. No. 1102, Climbing overpass, vert.

Wmk. 385

1985, Jan. 12 Litho. *Perf. 13½*
1101 A313 1.50b multicolored .35 .25
1102 A313 1.50b multicolored .35 .25

Bangkok Mail Center Opening A314

1985, Feb. 25
1103 A314 1.50b multicolored .35 .25

Phuket Province Heroes Bicent. — A315

Perf. 15x14

1985, Mar. 13 Litho. Wmk. 233
1104 A315 2b multicolored .60 .25

Tao-Thep-Krasattri, Tao-Sri-Sundhorn Monument.

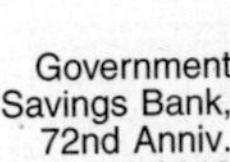

Government Savings Bank, 72nd Anniv. A316

Design: King Rama VI, headquarters.

1985, Apr. 1 *Perf. 14x15*
1105 A316 1.50b multicolored .40 .25

Intl. Telecommunications Satellite Org., 20th Anniv. — A317

1985, Apr. 6 Wmk. 387 *Perf. 12*
1106 A317 2b multicolored .60 .25

Thai Airways Intl., 25th Anniv. A318

Wmk. 385

1985, May 1 Litho. *Perf. 13*
1107 A318 2b DC-6 .40 .25
1108 A318 7.50b DC-10 1.60 .45
1109 A318 8.50b Airbus A-300 2.00 .60
1110 A318 9.50b Boeing 747 2.40 .60
Nos. 1107-1110 (4) 6.40 1.90

Natl. Flag and UPU Emblem — A319

10b, Flag and ITU emblem.

1985, July 1 Wmk. 387 *Perf. 12*
1111 A319 2b shown .35 .25

Perf. 13½
Wmk. 385

1112 A319 10b multicolored 1.60 .60

Thai membership to UPU and Intl. Telecommunications Union, cent.

Natl. Communications Day, Aug. 5 — A320

1985, Aug. 4 Wmk. 329 *Perf. 13½*
1113 A320 2b multicolored .60 .25

THAIPEX '85, Aug. 4-13 — A321

2b, Aisvarya Pavilion, vert. 3b, Varopas Piman Pavilion. 7b, Vehas Camrun Pavilion. 10b, Vitoon Tassana Tower, vert.

1985, Aug. 4 Wmk. 385
1114 A321 2b multicolored .65 .25
1115 A321 3b multicolored .90 .25
1116 A321 7b multicolored 1.60 .65
1117 A321 10b multicolored 1.75 .95
a. Souv. sheet of 4, #1114-1117 52.50 35.00
Nos. 1114-1117 (4) 4.90 2.10

No. 1117a exists imperf, sold for 40b. Value, $600.

Natl. Science Day, Aug. 18 — A322

Design: King Rama IV, solar eclipse.

1985, Aug. 18 Wmk. 387 *Perf. 12*
1118 A322 2b multicolored .90 .25

1885 Seal, Modern Map and Crest — A323

Perf. 14½x15

1985, Sept. 3 Wmk. 233
1119 A323 2b multicolored .90 .25

Royal Thai Survey Department, Cent.

13th SEA Games, Bangkok, Dec. 8-17 — A324

Designs: a, Boxing. b, Shot put. c, Badminton. d, Javelin. e, Weight lifting.

1985, Oct. 1 Wmk. 387 *Perf. 12*
1120 Strip of 5 .475 2.50
a.-e. A324 2b, any single .65 .25
f. Souv. sheet of 5, #a.-e. + label 27.50 27.50

No. 1120f sold for 20b.

Climbing Plants — A325

2b, Allemanda cathartica. 3b, Jasminum auriculatum. 7b, Passiflora laurifolia. 10b, Antigonon leptopus.

1985, Oct. 6 Wmk. 385 *Perf. 13½*
1121 A325 2b multicolored .65 .25
1122 A325 3b multicolored .90 .25
1123 A325 7b multicolored 1.60 .60
1124 A325 10b multicolored 2.00 .85
Nos. 1121-1124 (4) 5.15 1.95

International Letter Writing Week.

UN Child Survival Campaign — A326

1985, Oct. 24
1125 A326 2b multicolored .60 .25

UN Day.

Prince Kromamun Bidyalabh Bridhyakorn (1885-1974), Govt. Minister — A327

1985, Nov. 7
1126 A327 2b multi 5.25 .25
1126A A327 2b multi, diff. .70 .25
b. Pair, #1126-1126A 30.00 22.50

No. 1126A has flower design framing portrait reversed.

Rangsit (1885-1951), Prince of Jainad — A328

Perf. 15x14½

1985, Nov. 12 Wmk. 233
1127 A328 1.50b multicolored .75 .25

Asian-Pacific Postal Union, 5th Congress, Nov. 25-Dec. 4 — A329

1985, Nov. 25 Wmk. 385 *Perf. 13½*
1128 A329 2b multicolored .40 .25
1129 A329 10b multicolored 2.00 .50

Intl. Youth Year — A330

Perf. 14x15

1985, Nov. 26 Wmk. 233
1130 A330 2b multicolored .70 .25

12th Asian-Pacific Dental Congress, Bangkok, Dec. 5-10 — A331

1985, Dec. 5
1131 A331 2b multicolored .70 .25

13th SEA Games — A332

1985, Dec. 8 Wmk. 387 *Perf. 12*
1132 A332 1b Volleyball .30 .25
1133 A332 2b Sepak-takraw .60 .25
1134 A332 3b Women's gymnastics .95 .25
1135 A332 4b Bowling 1.15 .30
a. Souv. sheet, #1132-1135 + label 25.00 20.00
Nos. 1132-1135 (4) 3.00 1.05

No. 1135a sold for 20b.

French Envoys — A333

1985, Dec. 12 Wmk. 385 *Perf. 13½*
1136 A333 2b shown .45 .25
1137 A333 8.50b Thai envoys 1.40 .70

Diplomatic relations with France, 300th anniv.

Domestic Express Mail Service Inauguration A334

1986, Jan. 1
1138 A334 2b multicolored .60 .25
Complete booklet, strip of 5 #1138 7.00

Intl. Express Mail Service, EMS, 3rd anniv.

Wildlife Conservation A335

Marine turtles — 1.50b, Chelonia mydas. 3b, Eretmochelys imbricata. 5b, Dermochelys coriacea. 10b, Lepidochelys olivacea.

1986, Jan. 8 Wmk. 329
1139 A335 1.50b multicolored *.55* .25
1140 A335 3b multicolored *1.00* .25
1141 A335 5b multicolored *2.60* .45
1142 A335 10b multicolored *2.60* .65
Nos. 1139-1142 (4) *6.75* 1.60

Natl. Children's Day — A336

Design: Children picking lotus, by Areeya Makarabhundhu, age 12.

1986, Jan. 11 Wmk. 385
1143 A336 2b multicolored .60 .25
Complete booklet, strip of 5 #1143 6.00

Statue of Sunthon Phu, Poet — A337

1986, June 26
1144 A337 2b multicolored .60 .25
Complete booklet, strip of 5 #1144 6.00

Fruit Type of 1979

1986, June 26 Wmk. 385
1145 A237 2b Watermelon *1.25* .25
Complete booklet, strip of 5 #1145 12.50
1146 A237 2b Malay apple *1.25* .25
Complete booklet, strip of 5 #1146 12.50
1147 A237 6b Pomelo *1.50* .65
1148 A237 6b Papaya *1.50* .65
Nos. 1145-1148 (4) *5.50* 1.80

Nos. 1145-1148 horiz.

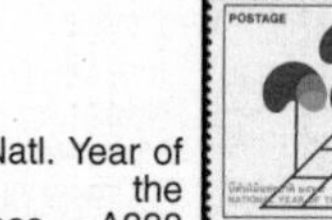
Natl. Year of the Trees — A338

1986, July 21
1149 A338 2b multicolored .75 .25
Complete booklet, strip of 5 #1149 6.00

Communications Day — A339

1986, Aug. 4
1150 A339 2b multicolored .75 .25
Complete booklet, strip of 5 #1150 6.00

Bamboo Baskets — A340

1986, Oct. 5
1151 A340 2b Chalom .50 .25
Complete booklet, strip of 5 #1151 4.50
1152 A340 2b Krabung .50 .25
Complete booklet, strip of 5 #1152 4.50
1153 A340 6b Kratib 1.00 .30
1154 A340 6b Kaleb 1.00 .30
Nos. 1151-1154 (4) 3.00 1.10

Intl. Letter Writing Week.

Intl. Peace Year — A341

1986, Oct. 24
1155 A341 2b multicolored .60 .25
Complete booklet, strip of 5 #1155 6.50

Productivity Year — A342

1986, Oct. 24 **Wmk. 329**
1156 A342 2b multicolored .75 .25
Complete booklet, strip of 5 #1156 6.00

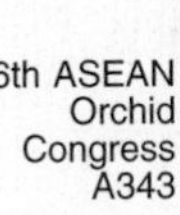

6th ASEAN Orchid Congress A343

2b, Vanda varavuth, vert. 3b, Ascocenda emma, vert. 4b, Dendrobium sri-siam. 5b, Dendrobium ekapol panda.

1986, Nov. 7 **Wmk. 385**
1157 A343 2b multicolored .70 .25
Complete booklet, strip of 5 #1157 6.00
1158 A343 3b multicolored .90 .25
1159 A343 4b multicolored 1.50 .75
1160 A343 5b multicolored 1.65 .75
a. Souv. sheet of 4, #1157-1160 90.00 80.00
Nos. 1157-1160 (4) 4.75 2.00

No. 1160a sold for 25b.

Fungi — A344

No. 1161, Volvariella volvacea. No. 1162, Pleurotus ostreatus. No. 1163, Auricularia polytricha. No. 1164, Pleurotus cystidiosus.

Perf. 13x13½
1986, Nov. 26 **Wmk. 329** **Photo.**
1161 A344 2b multicolored .70 .25
Complete booklet, strip of 5 #1161 6.50
1162 A344 2b multicolored .70 .25
Complete booklet, strip of 5 #1162 6.50
1163 A344 6b multicolored 1.75 .40
1164 A344 6b multicolored 1.75 .40
Nos. 1161-1164 (4) 4.90 1.30

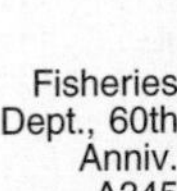

Fisheries Dept., 60th Anniv. A345

No. 1165, Morulius chrysophekadion. No. 1166, Notopterus blanci. No. 1167, Scleropages formosus. No. 1168, Pangasianodon gigas.

Wmk. 385
1986, Dec. 16 **Litho.** ***Perf. 13½***
1165 A345 2b multicolored .60 .25
Complete booklet, strip of 5 #1165 5.00
1166 A345 2b multicolored .60 .25
Complete booklet, strip of 5 #1166 5.00
1167 A345 7b multicolored 1.25 .65
1168 A345 7b multicolored 1.25 .65
Nos. 1165-1168 (4) 3.70 1.80

No. 653 Surcharged in Dark Olive Green

Perf. 14x13½
1986, Dec. **Photo.** **Wmk. 233**
1168A A161 1b on 20s blue .50 .25

Children's Day A346

Child's drawing.

Perf. 14½x15
1987, Jan. 10 **Litho.** **Wmk. 387**
1169 2b School, playground .60 .25
1170 2b Pool .60 .25
a. A346 Pair, #1169-1170 1.60 1.25

No. 1170a has continuous design.

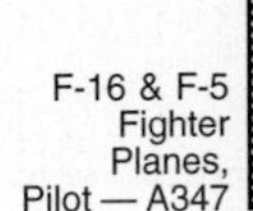

F-16 & F-5 Fighter Planes, Pilot — A347

1987, Mar. 27 **Wmk. 385** ***Perf. 13½***
1171 A347 2b multicolored .70 .25
Complete booklet, strip of 5 #1171 10.00

Royal Thai Air Force, 72nd anniv.

King Rama III (Nang Klao, 1787-1851) A348

Perf. 15x14½
1987, Mar. 31 **Wmk. 387**
1172 A348 2b multicolored .75 .25
Complete booklet, strip of 5 #1172 9.00

Ministry of Communications, 75th Anniv. — A349

1987, Apr. 1
1173 A349 2b multicolored .50 .25
Complete booklet, strip of 5 #1173 6.00

Forestry Year — A350

1987, July 11 **Wmk. 385** ***Perf. 13½***
1174 A350 2b multicolored .50 .25
Complete booklet, strip of 5 #1174 6.00

THAIPEX '87 — A351

Gold artifacts — No. 1175, Peacock, vert. No. 1176, Hand mirrors, vert. No. 1177, Water urn, finger bowls. No. 1178, Dragon vase.

1987, Aug. 4 **Wmk. 385**
1175 A351 2b multicolored .45 .25
Complete booklet, strip of 5 #1175 3.75
1176 A351 2b multicolored .45 .25
Complete booklet, strip of 5 #1176 3.75
1177 A351 6b multicolored 1.20 .35
1178 A351 6b multicolored 1.20 .35
a. Souv. sheet of 4, #1175-1178 45.00 30.00
Nos. 1175-1178 (4) 3.30 1.20

No. 1178a exists imperf. Value, $325.

ASEAN, 20th Anniv. A352

1987, Aug. 20
1179 A352 2b multicolored .30 .25
Complete booklet, strip of 5 #1179 3.75
1180 A352 3b multicolored .50 .25
1181 A352 4b multicolored .60 .35
1182 A352 5b multicolored .90 .45
Nos. 1179-1182 (4) 2.30 1.30

Natl. Communications Day — A353

1987, Aug. 4
1183 A353 2b multicolored .60 .25
Complete booklet, strip of 5 #1183 7.00

Chulachamklao Royal Military Academy, Cent. — A354

Design: School crest, King Rama V, and King Rama IX conferring sword on graduating officer.

1987, Aug. 5
1184 A354 2b multicolored 1.75 .30
Complete booklet, strip of 5 #1184 15.00

Intl. Literacy Day — A355

1987, Sept. 8
1185 A355 2b multicolored .90 .25
Complete booklet, strip of 5 #1185 6.00

Tourism Year — A356

2b, Flower-offering ceremony, Saraburi province. 3b, Duan Sib Festival, Nakhon Si Thammarat province. 5b, Bang Fai Festival, Yasothon province. 7b, Loi Krathong Festival, Sukhothai province.

1987, Sept. 18
1186 A356 2b multicolored .30 .25
Complete booklet, strip of 5 #1186 3.00
1187 A356 3b multicolored .60 .25
1188 A356 5b multicolored .90 .30
1189 A356 7b multicolored 1.25 .40
Nos. 1186-1189 (4) 3.05 1.20

Auditor General's Office, 72nd Anniv. A357

1987, Sept. 18
1190 A357 2b multicolored .60 .25
Complete booklet, strip of 5 #1190 6.00

Diplomatic Relations Between Thailand and Japan, Cent. — A358

1987, Sept. 26 **Wmk. 329**
1191 A358 2b multicolored .70 .25
Complete booklet, strip of 5 #1191 7.50

Intl. Letter Writing Week — A359

Floral garlands.

1987, Oct. 4 **Wmk. 385**
1192 A359 2b Floral tassel .30 .25
Complete booklet, strip of 5 #1192 2.25
1193 A359 3b Tasselled garland .55 .25
1194 A359 5b Wrist garland .80 .25
1195 A359 7b Double-ended garland 1.10 .50
Nos. 1192-1195 (4) 2.75 1.25

Thai Pavilion A360

1987, Oct. 9 **Wmk. 387** ***Perf. 15***
1196 A360 2b multicolored .75 .25
Complete booklet, strip of 5 #1196 8.00

Social Education and Cultural Center inauguration.

A361

A362

King Bhumibol Adulyadej, 60th Birthday A363

Royal ciphers and: #1197, Adulyadej as a child. #1198, King and Queen, wedding portrait, 1950. #1199, King taking the Oath of Accession, 1950. #1200, King dressed as a monk, collecting alms. #1201, Greeting 100 year-old woman. #1202, In military uniform holding pen and with hill tribes. #1203, Royal couple visiting wounded servicemen. #1204, Visiting farm. #1205, Royal family. #1206, King, Queen Sirikit. #1207, Princess Mother Somdej Phra Sri Nakarindra Boromrajjonnani, emblem of Medical Volunteer Assoc. #1208, Crown Prince Maha Vajiralongkorn, crown prince's royal standard. #1209, Princess Maha Chakri Sirindhorn, emblem of Sai Jai Thai

Foundation. #1210, Princess Chulabhorn, Albert Einstein gold medal awarded by UNESCO.

Wmk. 329

1987, Dec. 5 Photo. *Perf. 13½*

1197 A361 2b shown .50 .25
Complete booklet, strip of 5 #1197 6.00
1198 A361 2b multicolored .50 .25
1199 A361 2b multicolored .50 .25
1200 A361 2b multicolored .50 .25
1201 A361 2b multicolored .50 .25
1202 A361 2b multicolored .50 .25
1203 A361 2b multicolored .50 .25
1204 A361 2b multicolored .50 .25
a. Souv. sheet, #1197-1204 37.50 37.50

Litho.

Wmk. 385

1205 A362 2b multicolored 1.00 .25
1206 A362 2b multicolored 1.00 .25
1207 A362 2b multicolored 1.00 .25
1208 A362 2b multicolored 1.00 .25
1209 A362 2b multicolored 1.00 .25
1210 A362 2b multicolored 1.00 .25

Litho. & Embossed

1211 A363 100b vio blue & gold 60.00 45.00
Nos. 1197-1211 (15) 70.00 48.50

Size of Nos. 1206-1210: 45x27mm. No. 1211 printed in sheets of 10. Value, $750. No. 1204a sold for 40b.

No. 1081 Surcharged

1987 Litho. Wmk. 233 *Perf. 14x15*

1212 A256 2b on 1.50b brt yel org .60 .25

Children's Day — A364

Perf. 14x14½

1988, Jan. 9 Litho. Wmk. 387

1213 A364 2b multicolored .90 .25
Complete booklet, strip of 5 #1213 6.00

Thai Agricultural Cooperatives, 72nd Anniv. — A365

Design: Prince Bridhyalongkorn, founder.

1988, Feb. 26 Wmk. 387

1214 A365 2b multicolored .90 .25
Complete booklet, strip of 5 #1214 5.25

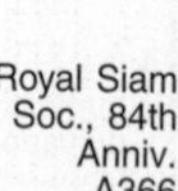

Royal Siam Soc., 84th Anniv. A366

1988, Mar. 10 *Perf. 14½x14*

1215 A366 2b multicolored .75 .25
Complete booklet, strip of 5 #1215 5.25

Cultural Heritage Preservation A367

Ruins in Sukhothai Historic Park — 2b, Wat Phra Phai Luang. 3b, Wat Traphang Thonglang. 4b, Wat Maha That. 6b, Thewalai Maha Kaset.

1988, Apr. 2 *Perf. 14½x14*

1216 A367 2b multicolored .30 .25
Complete booklet, strip of 5 #1216 4.00
1217 A367 3b multicolored .60 .25
1218 A367 4b multicolored .90 .35
1219 A367 6b multicolored 1.25 .40
Nos. 1216-1219 (4) 3.05 1.25

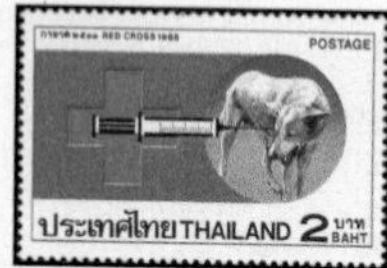

Red Cross Fair — A368

Design: Prevention of rabies.

1988, Apr. Wmk. 387 *Perf. 14*

1220 A368 2b multicolored .90 .25
Complete booklet, strip of 5 #1220 6.00

King Rama V, Founder — A369

Perf. 14x14½

1988, Apr. 26 Wmk. 387

1221 A369 5b multicolored 2.40 .60

Siriraj Hospital, cent.

Pheasants A370

Wmk. 329

1988, June 15 Photo. *Perf. 13½*

1222 A370 2b Crested fireback .30 .25
Complete booklet, strip of 5 #1222 2.75
1223 A370 3b Kalij .60 .25
1224 A370 6b Silver pheasant 1.25 .30
1225 A370 7b Hume's pheasant 1.50 .40
Nos. 1222-1225 (4) 3.65 1.20

Nos. 935a, 935 Surcharged

a

b

Perf. 11x13

1988-92 Litho. Wmk. 387

1226 A256(a) 1b on 1.25b .60 .25
1226A A256(b) 1b on 1.25b .60 .25
b. Wmk. 368 1.40 .25

Issued: #1226, 1988; #1226A, Dec. 5, 1992.

Intl. Council of Women, Cent. — A371

1988, June 26 Wmk. 385 *Perf. 13½*

1227 A371 2b multicolored .60 .25
Complete booklet, strip of 5 #1227 5.25

King Bhumibol Adulyadej
A372 A372a

Perf. 13½x13

1988-95 Litho. Wmk. 387

1228 A372 25s brown .40 .25

Perf. 14x14½

1229 A372 50s olive .55 .25
a. Wmk. 329, perf. 13½x13 .65 .25
1230 A372 1b brt blue .55 .25
Complete booklet, 5 #1230 4.25
a. Photo, wmk. 233 .80 .25
b. Photo., wmk. 340, perf. 13½x13¾ .55 .25
1233 A372 2b scarlet .70 .25
Complete booklet, 5 #1233 5.00
a. Wmk. 329 .55 .25
b. Photo., wmk. 340, perf. 13½x13¾ .70 .25
Complete booklet, 5 #1233b 6.00

Photo.

Wmk. 233

Perf. 14½

1236 A372 1b bright blue .80 .25
Nos. 1228-1236 (5) 3.00 1.25

No. 1236 has blue background without halo effect around head. See #1230.

Issued: 25s, 8/12/92; 1b-2b, 7/2/88; 50s, 7/28/93; #1230a, 1236, 1990; #1233a, 1992; #1230b, 1233b, 12/5/94; #1229a, 1995.

Perf. 13½x13

1988-90 Engr. Wmk. 329

1241 A372a 3b brn & bluish gray .80 .25
1242 A372a 4b brt bl & red brn .95 .30
1243 A372a 5b violet & brn 1.10 .30
1244 A372a 6b green & vio 1.10 .35
1245 A372a 7b red brn & dk brn .80 .25
1246 A372a 8b red brn & gray ol 1.10 .40
1247 A372a 9b dk blue & brn 1.75 .40
1248 A372a 10b hen brn & blk 1.60 .25
1249 A372a 20b brn org & sage grn 2.40 1.75
1250 A372a 25b ol grn & dk bl 4.50 .90
1251 A372a 50b violet & grn 8.00 1.00
1252 A372a 100b brn org & bluish blk 13.00 2.25
Nos. 1241-1252 (12) 37.10 8.40

Issued:3b, 10b, 50b, 100b, 12/5; 5b, 6b, 8b, 9b, 7/1/89; 4b, 7b, 20b, 12/5/89; 25b, 1/9/90.

A373

A374

King Bhumibol's Reign (since 1950) — A375

Designs: No. 1253, King Bhumibol.

Regalia: No. 1254, Great Crown of Victory. No. 1255, Sword of Victory and matching scabbard. No. 1256, Scepter. No. 1257, Fan and feather fly swatter. No. 1258, Royal slippers.

Canopied thrones in the Grand Palace: No. 1259, Queen's round ottoman on 1-tier dais in front of decorative screen. No. 1260, King's throne on 1-tier dais in front of decorative screen. No. 1261, 3-Tier throne with 3 gilded trees. No. 1262, 3-Canopy throne on high gold dais. No. 1263, 3-Tier throne with 4 gilded trees, altar in background. No. 1264, 3-Canopy throne on 5-stair dais, in front of arch flanked by columns.

Wmk. 385

1988, July 2 Litho. *Perf. 13½*

1253 A373 2b shown 2.75 .40
Complete booklet, strip of 5 #1253 27.50

Photo.

Wmk. 329

1254 A374 2b multi, vert. .75 .25
1255 A374 2b multicolored .75 .25
1256 A374 2b multicolored .75 .25
1257 A374 2b multicolored .75 .25
1258 A374 2b multicolored .75 .25

Litho.

Perf. 14x14½

Wmk. 387

1259 A375 2b multicolored .80 .30
1260 A375 2b multicolored .80 .30
1261 A375 2b multicolored .80 .30
1262 A375 2b multicolored .80 .30
1263 A375 2b multicolored .80 .30
1264 A375 2b multicolored .80 .30
a. Souv. sheet of 6, #1259-1264 60.00 60.00
Nos. 1253-1264 (12) 11.30 3.45

No. 1264a sold for 25b.

Arbor Year — A376

Perf. 14½x14

1988, July 29 Litho. Wmk. 387

1265 A376 2b multicolored .65 .25
Complete booklet, strip of 5 #1265 5.25

Natl. Communications Day — A377

Wmk. Alternating Interlaced Wavy Lines (340)

1988, Aug. 4 *Perf. 13½*

1266 A377 2b multicolored .95 .25
Complete booklet, strip of 5 #1266 7.50

Intl. Letter Writing Week — A378

Designs: Coconut leaf sculptures.

Perf. 14½x14

1988, Oct. 9 Wmk. 387

1267 A378 2b Grasshopper .35 .25
Complete booklet, strip of 5 #1267 3.00
1268 A378 2b Fish .35 .25
Complete booklet, strip of 5 #1268 3.00
1269 A378 6b Bird .95 .50
1270 A378 6b Takro (box) .95 .50
Nos. 1267-1270 (4) 2.60 1.50

Housing Development A379

Wmk. 233

1988, Oct. 24 Litho. *Perf. 14*

1271 A379 2b multicolored .65 .25
Complete booklet, strip of 5 #1271 5.25

Traffic Safety — A380

1988, Nov. 11 Wmk. 329 ***Perf. 13½***
1272 A380 2b multicolored 1.10 .25
Complete booklet, strip of 5 #1272 5.50

King's Bodyguard, 120th Anniv. — A381

1988, Nov. 11 Wmk. 385
1273 A381 2b Chulalongkorn 3.50 .45
Complete booklet, strip of 5 #1273 32.50

New Year — A382

Flowers — No. 1274, Crotalaria sessiliflora. No. 1275, Uvaria grandiflora. No. 1276, Reinwardtia trigyna. No. 1277, Impatiens griffithii.

1988, Dec. 1 Wmk. 387
1274 A382 1b multicolored .60 .25
1275 A382 1b multicolored .60 .25
1276 A382 1b multicolored .60 .25
1277 A382 1b multicolored .60 .25
Nos. 1274-1277 (4) 2.40 1.00

Thai Royal Orders Type of 1979

Floral background: Nos. 1278-1279, Knight Grand Commander, Order of Rama, 1918. Nos. 1280-1281, Knight Grand Cordon, Order of the White Elephant, 1861. Nos. 1282-1283, Knight Grand Cordon, Order of the Crown of Thailand, 1869. Nos. 1284-1285, Ratana Varabhorn Order of Merit, 1911. Pairs have continuous designs.

1988, Dec. 5 Wmk. 385
1278 A243 2b multicolored .30 .25
1279 A244 2b multicolored .30 .25
a. Pair, #1278-1279 .80 .40
1280 A243 3b multicolored .65 .25
1281 A244 3b multicolored .65 .25
a. Pair, #1280-1281 1.75 .90
1282 A243 5b multicolored 1.00 .40
1283 A244 5b multicolored 1.00 .40
a. Pair, #1282-1283 2.75 1.40
1284 A243 7b multicolored 1.20 .55
1285 A244 7b multicolored 1.20 .55
a. Pair, #1284-1285 4.00 2.00
Nos. 1278-1285 (8) 6.30 2.90

A383

Buddha Monthon Celebrations, Tambol Salaya — A384

2b, Birthplace. 3b, Enlightenment place. 4b, Location of 1st sermon. 5b, Place Buddha achieved nirvana. 6b, Statue.

Perf. 14x15, 15x14

1988, Dec. 5 Wmk. 233
1286 A383 2b multicolored .35 .25
Complete booklet, strip of 5 #1286 2.75
1287 A383 3b multicolored .45 .25
1288 A383 4b multicolored .65 .45

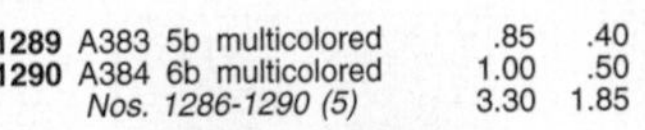

1289 A383 5b multicolored .85 .40
1290 A384 6b multicolored 1.00 .50
Nos. 1286-1290 (5) 3.30 1.85

Souvenir Sheet

Perf. 14½x14

1291 A384 6b like No. 1290 27.50 27.50

No. 1291 sold for 15b.

Children's Day — A385

"Touch" paintings by blind youth: No. 1292, *Floating Market,* by Thongbai Siyam. No. 1293, *Flying Bird,* by Kwanchai Kerd-Daeng. No. 1294, *Little Mermaid,* by Chalermpol Jiengmai. No. 1295, *Golden Fish,* by Natetip Korsantirak.

Wmk. 387

1989, Jan. 14 Litho. ***Perf. 13½***
1292 A385 2b multicolored .45 .25
Complete booklet, strip of 5 #1292 3.50
1293 A385 2b multicolored .45 .25
Complete booklet, strip of 5 #1293 3.50
1294 A385 2b multicolored .45 .25
Complete booklet, strip of 5 #1294 3.50
1295 A385 2b multicolored .45 .25
Complete booklet, strip of 5 #1295 3.50
Nos. 1292-1295 (4) 1.80 1.00

Communications Authority of Thailand, 12th Anniv. — A386

1989, Feb. 25 ***Perf. 14½x14***
1296 A386 2b multicolored .75 .25
Complete booklet, strip of 5 #1296 5.25

Chulalongkorn University, 72nd Anniv. A387

Design: 2b, Statue of Chulalongkorn and King Vajiravudh in front of university auditorium.

1989, Mar. 26
1297 A387 2b multicolored .90 .25
Complete booklet, strip of 5 #1297 7.00

A388

Perf. 15x14

1989, Mar. 31 Litho. Wmk. 233
1298 A388 2b shown .75 .30
Complete booklet, strip of 5 #1298 5.25

Wmk. 387

Perf. 13½

1299 A388 10b Emblem 1.25 .35

Thai Red Cross Society, 96th anniv. (2b); Intl. Red Cross and Red Crescent organizations, 125th annivs. (10b).

A389

Phra Nakhon Khiri Historical Park: 2b, Wat Phra Kaeo. 3b, Chatchawan Wiangchai Observatory. 5b, Phra That Chom Phet Stupa. 6b, Wetchayan Wichian Phrasat Throne Hall.

Perf. 14x14½

1989, Apr. 2 Wmk. 387
1300 A389 2b multicolored .55 .25
Complete booklet, strip of 5 #1300 4.50
1301 A389 3b multicolored .90 .45
1302 A389 5b multicolored 1.40 .95
1303 A389 6b multicolored 1.60 1.10
Nos. 1300-1303 (4) 4.45 2.75

Natl. Lottery Office, 50th Anniv. A390

1989, Apr. 5 ***Perf. 13½***
1304 A390 2b multicolored .75 .25
Complete booklet, strip of 5 #1304 5.25

Seashells A391

2b, Conus thailandis. 3b, Spondylus princeps. 6b, Cyprea guttata. 10b, Nautilus pompilius.

1989, June 28 Wmk. 329 ***Perf. 13½***
1305 A391 2b multicolored .30 .25
Complete booklet, strip of 5 #1305 2.75
1306 A391 3b multicolored .55 .25
1307 A391 6b multicolored .85 .65
1308 A391 10b multicolored 3.00 1.60
Nos. 1305-1308 (4) 4.70 2.75

Arts and Crafts Year — A392

No. 1309, Gold niello figurines, vert. No. 1310, Ceramic ginger jar, chicken, vert. No. 1311, Textiles. No. 1312, Gemstone flower ornament.

Wmk. 387

1989, June 28 Litho. ***Perf. 13½***
1309 A392 2b multicolored .30 .25
Complete booklet, strip of 5 #1309 2.75
1310 A392 2b multicolored .30 .25
Complete booklet, strip of 5 #1310 2.75
1311 A392 6b multicolored .95 .50
1312 A392 6b multicolored .95 .50
Nos. 1309-1312 (4) 2.50 1.50

Asia-Pacific Telecommunications Organization, 10th Anniv. — A393

APT emblem, map of submarine cable network and satellites of member nations.

1989, July 1 Wmk. 329 ***Perf. 13½***
1313 A393 9b multicolored 1.25 .25

Phya Anuman Rajadhon (1888-1969), Ethnologist — A394

1989, July 1 Wmk. 387 ***Perf. 13½***
1314 A394 2b multicolored .75 .25
Complete booklet, strip of 5 #1314 5.25

9th Natl. Phil. Exhib., Aug. 4-13 — A395

Various mailboxes.

1989, Aug. 4 Wmk. 233 ***Perf. 15x14***
1315 A395 2b multicolored .30 .25
Complete booklet, strip of 5 #1315 2.75
1316 A395 3b multi, diff. .45 .25
1317 A395 4b multi, diff. .45 .30
1318 A395 5b multi, diff. .70 .30
1319 A395 6b multi, diff. .90 .40
a. Souv. sheet, #1315-1319, perf 14 35.00 35.00
Nos. 1315-1319 (5) 2.80 1.50

No. 1319a sold for 30b. No. 1319a exists imperf. Value, $110.

A396

Wmk. 387

1989, June 26 Litho. ***Perf. 13½***
1320 A396 2b multicolored .50 .25
Complete booklet, strip of 5 #1320 5.25

Intl. Anti-drug Day.

A397

1989, Aug. 4 Wmk. 233 ***Perf. 14x15***
1321 A397 2b multicolored .90 .25
Complete booklet, strip of 5 #1321 5.25

Post and Telecommunications School, cent.

A398

1989, Aug. 4 Wmk. 387 ***Perf. 13½***
1322 A398 2b multicolored .55 .25
Complete booklet, strip of 5 #1322 5.25

Natl. Communications Day.

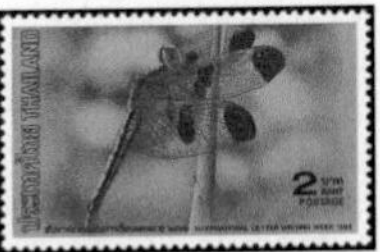

Dragonflies A399

Wmk. 329

1989, Oct. 8 Photo. *Perf. 13½*

1323 A399 2b shown .35 .25
Complete booklet, strip of 5 #1323 5.25
1324 A399 5b multi, diff. .75 .30
1325 A399 6b multi, diff. 1.10 .35
1326 A399 10b Damselfly 1.40 1.00
a. Souv. sheet of 4, #1323-1326 30.00 30.00
Nos. 1323-1326 (4) 3.60 1.90

Intl. Letter Writing Week. #1326a sold for 40b.

Transport and Communications Decade for Asia and the Pacific — A400

Perf. 14½x14

1989, Oct. 24 Litho. Wmk. 387

1327 A400 2b multicolored .75 .25
Complete booklet, strip of 5 #1327 5.25

Mental Health Care, Cent. — A401

1989, Nov. 1 Wmk. 233 *Perf. 15x14*

1328 A401 2b multicolored .55 .25
Complete booklet, strip of 5 #1328 5.25

New Year 1990 — A402

Flowering plants.

Perf. 14x14½

1989, Nov. 15 Wmk. 387

1329 A402 1b Hypericum uralum .35 .30
1330 A402 1b Uraria rufescens .35 .30
1331 A402 1b Manglietia garrettii .35 .30
1332 A402 1b Aeschynanthus macranthus .35 .30
a. Souv. sheet of 4, #1329-1332 8.00 8.00
Nos. 1329-1332 (4) 1.40 1.20

No. 1332a sold for 14b.

Insects A403

2b, Catacanthus incarnatus. 3b, Aristobia approximator. 6b, Chrysochroa chinensis. 10b, Enoplotrupes sharpi.

Wmk. 329

1989, Nov. 15 Photo. *Perf. 13½*

1333 A403 2b multicolored .30 .25
Complete booklet, strip of 5 #1333 2.75
1334 A403 3b multicolored .60 .30
1335 A403 6b multicolored .80 .40
1336 A403 10b multicolored 1.40 .85
Nos. 1333-1336 (4) 3.10 1.80

Population and Housing Census of 1990 — A404

Wmk. 387

1990, Jan. 1 Litho. *Perf. 13½*

1337 A404 2b multicolored .90 .25
Complete booklet, strip of 5 #1337 5.75

Children's Day — A405

Perf. 15x14

1990, Jan. 13 Wmk. 233

1338 A405 2b Jumping rope, horiz. .55 .25
Complete booklet, strip of 5 #1338 4.00
1339 A405 2b Sports .55 .25
Complete booklet, strip of 5 #1339 4.00

Emblems — A406

1990, Mar. 29 Wmk. 387 *Perf. 13½*

1340 A406 2b multicolored .55 .25
Complete booklet, strip of 5 #1340 5.00

WHO Fight AIDS Worldwide campaign and the Natl. Red Cross Soc.

Thai Heritage Conservation Day — A407

Prize-winning inlaid mother-of-pearl containers: No. 1341, Tiap (footed bowl with lid), vert. No. 1342, Phan waenfa (two-tiered vessel), vert. No. 1343, Lung (lidded bowl). No. 1344, Chiat klom (spade-shaped lidded container signifying noble rank).

1990, Apr. 2 Photo. Wmk. 329

1341 A407 2b multicolored .30 .25
1342 A407 2b multicolored .30 .25
1343 A407 8b multicolored 1.05 .45
1344 A407 8b multicolored 1.05 .45
Nos. 1341-1344 (4) 2.70 1.40

A408

Minerals.

Perf. 14x14½

1990, June 29 Litho. Wmk. 387

1345 A408 2b Tin .45 .25
1346 A408 3b Zinc .70 .40
1347 A408 5b Lead .85 .60
1348 A408 6b Fluorite 1.00 .80
a. Souv. sheet of 4, #1345-1348 4.50 4.50
Nos. 1345-1348 (4) 3.00 2.05

No. 1348a sold for 30b. Exists imperf, value same as perf.

A409

1990, May 16

1349 A409 2b multicolored .50 .25
Complete booklet, strip of 5 #1349 5.25

Faculty of Dentistry, Chulalongkorn Univ., 50th anniv.

Communications Day — A410

1990, Aug. 4 *Perf. 14½x14*

1350 A410 2b multicolored .65 .25
Complete booklet, strip of 5 #1350 5.75

Asian-Pacific Postal Training Center, 20th Anniv. A411

1990, Sept. 10

1351 A411 2b multicolored .35 .25
Complete booklet, strip of 5 #1351 2.25
1352 A411 8b multicolored 1.00 .60

Rotary Intl. in Thailand, 60th Anniv. A412

1990, Sept. 16 *Perf. 13½*

1353 A412 2b Health care .35 .25
Complete booklet, strip of 5 #1353 4.00
1354 A412 3b Immunizations .55 .30
1355 A412 6b Literacy project .70 .35
1356 A412 8b Thai museum project .85 .45
Nos. 1353-1356 (4) 2.45 1.35

Intl. Letter Writing Week, 1990 A413

1990, Oct. 7 *Perf. 14*

1357 A413 2b multicolored .35 .25
1358 A413 3b multi, diff. .50 .25
1359 A413 5b multi, diff. .75 .25
1360 A413 6b multi, diff. .90 .25
a. Souv. sheet of 4, #1357-1360 4.50 4.50
Nos. 1357-1360 (4) 2.50 1.00

No. 1360a sold for 30b. Exists imperf, value same as perf.

Dept. of Comptroller-General, Cent. — A414

1990, Oct. 7 *Perf. 14½x14*

1361 A414 2b multicolored .90 .25
Complete booklet, strip of 5 #1361 5.00

A415

1990, Oct. 21 *Perf. 14x14½*

1362 A415 2b multicolored 2.75 .50
Complete booklet, strip of 5 #1362 30.00

Princess Mother, 90th birthday.

A416

Flowers: No. 1363, Cyrtandromoea grandiflora. No. 1364, Rhododendron arboreum. No. 1365, Merremia vitifolia. No. 1366, Afgekia mahidolae.

1990, Nov. 15 Wmk. 233 *Perf. 14½*

1363 A416 1b multicolored .35 .25
1364 A416 1b multicolored .35 .25
1365 A416 1b multicolored .35 .25
1366 A416 1b multicolored .35 .25
a. Sheet of 4, #1363-1366 3.00 3.00
Nos. 1363-1366 (4) 1.40 1.00

New Year 1991. No. 1366a sold for 10b. Exists imperf, value same as perf.
See Nos. 1417-1420.

Wiman Mek Royal Hall — A417

Royal Throne Rooms in the Dusit Palace: 3b, Ratcharit Rungrot Royal House. 4b, Aphisek Dusit Royal Hall. 5b, Amphon Sathan Palace. 6b, Udon Phak Royal Hall. 8b, Anantasamakhom Throne Hall.

Wmk. 329

1990, Dec. 5 Photo. *Perf. 13½*

1367 A417 2b multicolored .30 .25
Complete booklet, strip of 5 #1367 3.25
1368 A417 3b multicolored .40 .25
1369 A417 4b multicolored .50 .25
1370 A417 5b multicolored .50 .25
1371 A417 6b multicolored .70 .45
1372 A417 8b multicolored 1.00 .65
Nos. 1367-1372 (6) 3.40 2.10

Somdet Phra Maha Samanachao Kromphra Paramanuchitchinorot (1790-1853), Supreme Patriarch — A418

1990, Dec. 11 Wmk. 387 *Perf. 13½*

1373 A418 2b multicolored .70 .25
Complete booklet, strip of 5 #1373 6.25

Petroleum Authority, 12th Anniv. A419

Perf. 14½x14

1990, Dec. 29 Litho. Wmk. 387

1374 A419 2b multicolored .80 .25
Complete booklet, strip of 5 #1374 5.25

Locomotives A420

Designs: 2b, No. 6, Krauss & Co., Germany, 1908. 3b, No. 32, Kyosan Kogyo, Japan, 1949. 5b, No. 715, C56, Japan, 1946. 6b, No. 953, Mikado, Japan, 1949-1951.

Perf. 14½x14

1990, Dec. 29 Litho. Wmk. 387

1375 A420 2b multicolored 1.00 .25
1376 A420 3b multicolored 1.35 .25
1377 A420 5b multicolored 1.70 1.40
1378 A420 6b multicolored 1.95 1.40
a. Souv. sheet of 4, #1375-1378 7.00 7.00
Nos. 1375-1378 (4) 6.00 3.30

No. 1378a sold for 25b. Exists imperf, value same as perf.

Children's Day — A421

Children's games: 2b, Tops. 3b, Blindfolded child breaking pot with stick. 5b, Race. 6b, Blind-man's buff.

1991, Jan. 12

1379 A421 2b multicolored .30 .25
Complete booklet, strip of 5 #1379 3.50
1380 A421 3b multicolored .45 .25
1381 A421 5b multicolored .55 .30
1382 A421 6b multicolored .80 .35
Nos. 1379-1382 (4) 2.10 1.15

A422

1991, Feb. 17 ***Perf. 14x14½***

1383 A422 2b multicolored .75 .25
Complete booklet, strip of 5 #1383 5.50

Land titling project.

A423

Perf. 14x14½

1991, Mar. 30 Litho. Wmk. 387

1384 A423 2b Princess Maha 1.25 .25
Complete booklet, strip of 5 #1384 16.00
a. Souvenir sheet of 1 4.50 4.50

Red Cross. No. 1384a sold for 8b. Exists imperf, value same as perf.

Cultural Heritage — A424

Floral decorations: 2b, Indra's heavenly abode. 3b, Celestial couch. 4b, Crystal ladder. 5b, Crocodile.

Wmk. 329

1991, Apr. 2 Photo. ***Perf. 13½***

1385 A424 2b multicolored .30 .25
1386 A424 3b multicolored .45 .25
1387 A424 4b multicolored .55 .25
1388 A424 5b multicolored .70 .30
a. Souv. sheet of 4, #1385-1388 4.00 3.00
Nos. 1385-1388 (4) 2.00 1.05

No. 1388a sold for 30b. Exists imperf, value same as perf.

Songkran Day — A425

Perf. 14x14½

1991, Apr. 13 Wmk. 387 Litho.

1389 A425 2b Demon on sheep 3.25 .75
Complete booklet, strip of 5 #1389 22.50
a. Souvenir sheet of 1 15.00 15.00

No. 1389a sold for 8b. Exists imperf, value same as perf.

See #1467, 1530, 1566, 1606, 1662, 1724, 1801, 1869, 1940, 1970, 2017.

Prince Narisranuvattivongs (1863-1947) — A426

1991, Apr. 28 ***Perf. 14½x14***

1390 A426 2b brown & yellow .50 .25
Complete booklet, strip of 5 #1390 5.00

Mosaics A427

Various lotus flowers.

1991, May 28 ***Perf. 13½***

1391 A427 2b multi, vert. .30 .25
Complete booklet, strip of 5 #1391 4.00
1392 A427 3b multi, vert. .40 .25
1393 A427 5b multi .60 .30
1394 A427 6b multi .75 .35
Nos. 1391-1394 (4) 2.05 1.15

Natl. Communications Day — A428

Wmk. 387

1991, Aug. 4 Litho. ***Perf. 13½***

1395 A428 2b multicolored .75 .25
Complete booklet, strip of 5 #1395 7.25

Thaipex '91, Natl. Philatelic Exhibition — A429

Various fabric designs.

1991, Aug. 4 ***Perf. 14x14½***

1396 A429 2b multicolored .30 .25
1397 A429 4b multicolored .40 .25
1398 A429 6b multicolored .65 .30
1399 A429 8b multicolored .80 .45
a. Souv. sheet of 4, #1396-1399 6.00 6.00
Nos. 1396-1399 (4) 2.15 1.25

No. 1399a sold for 30b. Exists imperf, value $25. No. 1399a overprinted with Philanippon emblem in lower left corner of margin sold for 200b. Value, $190.

Intl. Productivity Congress A430

Perf. 14½x14

1991, Sept. 3 Litho. Wmk. 387

1400 A430 2b multicolored .75 .25
Complete booklet, strip of 5 #1400 4.25

26th Intl. Council of Women Triennial — A431

Wmk. 387

1991, Sept. 23 Litho. ***Perf. 13½***

1401 A431 2b multicolored .80 .25
Complete booklet, strip of 5 #1401 4.25

Bantam Chickens A432

Wmk. 329

1991, Oct. 6 Photo. ***Perf. 13½***

1402 A432 2b Black bantams .35 .25
1403 A432 3b Black-tailed buff bantams .65 .25
1404 A432 6b Fancy bantams .90 .25
1405 A432 8b White bantams 1.35 .65
a. Souv. sheet of 4, #1402-1405 5.50 5.50
Nos. 1402-1405 (4) 3.25 1.40

No. 1405a sold for 35b. Exists imperf, value same as perf.
Intl. Letter Writing Week.

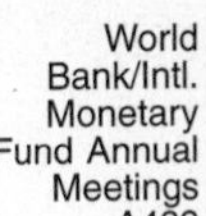

World Bank/Intl. Monetary Fund Annual Meetings A433

Temples, meeting emblem and: 2b, Silver coin of King Rama IV. 4b, Pod Duang money. 8b, Chieng and Hoi money. 10b, Funan, Dvaravati and Srivijaya money.

Perf. 14½x14

1991, Oct. 15 Litho. Wmk. 387

1406 A433 2b multicolored .25 .25
Complete booklet, strip of 5 #1406 3.25
1407 A433 4b multicolored .45 .30
1408 A433 8b multicolored .90 .60
1409 A433 10b multicolored 1.10 .75
a. Souv. sheet of 4, #1406-1409 4.00 4.00
Nos. 1406-1409 (4) 2.70 1.90

No. 1409a sold for 35b. Exists imperf, value same as perf.

1993 World Philatelic Exhibition, Bangkok — A434

1991, Oct. 23 ***Perf. 14x14½***

1410 A434 2b No. 118 .30 .25
Complete booklet, strip of 5 #1410 4.25
1411 A434 3b No. 119 .30 .25
1412 A434 4b No. 120 .35 .25
1413 A434 5b No. 121 .50 .30
1414 A434 6b No. 122 .65 .30
1415 A434 7b No. 123 .70 .35
1416 A434 8b No. 124 .90 .45
a. Souvenir sheet of 1 4.00 4.00
Nos. 1410-1416 (7) 3.70 2.15

No. 1416a sold for 15b. Exists imperf, value same as perf.

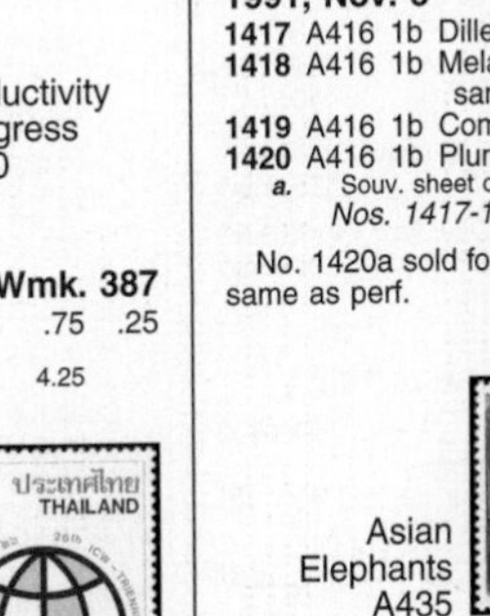

Flower Type of 1990

1991, Nov. 5 ***Perf. 13½***

1417 A416 1b Dillenia obovata .30 .25
1418 A416 1b Melastoma sanguineum .30 .25
1419 A416 1b Commelina diffusa .30 .25
1420 A416 1b Plumbago indica .30 .25
a. Souv. sheet of 4, #1417-1420 2.00 2.00
Nos. 1417-1420 (4) 1.20 1.00

No. 1420a sold for 10b. Exists imperf, value same as perf.

Asian Elephants A435

Wmk. 329

1991, Nov. 5 Photo. ***Perf. 13½***

1421 A435 2b shown .40 .25
Complete booklet, strip of 5 #1421 4.25
1422 A435 4b Pulling logs .75 .25
1423 A435 6b Lying down .90 .40
1424 A435 8b In river 1.60 .75
a. Souvenir sheet of 1, litho. 5.50 5.50
Nos. 1421-1424 (4) 3.65 1.65

No. 1424a sold for 22b and stamp does not have border. No. 1424a exists imperf, value same as perf.

Wild Animals A436

Perf. 14½x14

1991, Dec. 26 Wmk. 387 Litho.

1425 A436 2b Viverra zibetha .45 .25
Complete booklet, strip of 5 #1425 2.75
1426 A436 3b Prionodon linsang .60 .25
1427 A436 6b Felis temmincki .85 .30
1428 A436 8b Ratufa bicolor 1.25 .45
a. Sheet of 4, #1425-1428 4.50 4.50
Nos. 1425-1428 (4) 3.15 1.25

No. 1428a sold for 30b. Exists imperf, value same as perf.

Prince Mahidol of Songkla (1891-1929), Medical Pioneer — A437

1992, Jan. 1 ***Perf. 14x14½***

1429 A437 2b multicolored .95 .25
Complete booklet, strip of 5 #1429 7.25

Department of Mineral Resources, Cent. — A438

No. 1430, Locating fossils. No. 1431, Mining excavation. No. 1432, Drilling for natural gas and petroleum. No. 1433, Digging artesian wells.

Perf. 14½x14

1992, Jan. 1 Litho. Wmk. 387

1430 A438 2b multicolored .90 .25
Complete booklet, strip of 5 #1430 4.50
1431 A438 2b multicolored .90 .25
Complete booklet, strip of 5 #1431 4.50
1432 A438 2b multicolored .90 .25
Complete booklet, strip of 5 #1432 4.50
1433 A438 2b multicolored .90 .25
Complete booklet, strip of 5 #1433 4.50
Nos. 1430-1433 (4) 3.60 1.00

Children's Day — A439

Children's drawings on "World Under the Sea": 2b, Divers, fish. 3b, Fish, sea grass. 5b, Mermaid.

1992, Jan. 11 Wmk. 329 ***Perf. 13½***

1434 A439 2b multicolored .35 .25
Complete booklet, strip of 5 #1434 3.00
1435 A439 3b multicolored .35 .25
1436 A439 5b multicolored, vert. .75 .30
Nos. 1434-1436 (3) 1.45 .80

Duel on Elephants, 400th Anniv. A440

Perf. 14½x14

1992, Jan. 18 Litho. Wmk. 387

1437 A440 2b multicolored .75 .25
Complete booklet, strip of 5 #1437 6.00

Orchids (Paphiopedilum) — A441

1992, Jan. 20

1438 A441 2b Bellatulum .30 .25
1439 A441 2b Exul .30 .25
1440 A441 3b Concolor .30 .25
1441 A441 3b Godefroyae .30 .25
1442 A441 6b Niveum .60 .30
1443 A441 6b Villosum .60 .30
1444 A441 10b Parishii 1.00 .60
a. Souv. sheet of 4, #1438, 1440, 1442, 1444 7.00 7.00
1445 A441 10b Sukhakulii 1.00 .60
a. Souv. sheet of 4, #1439, 1441, 1443, 1445 7.00 7.00
Nos. 1438-1445 (8) 4.40 2.80

Fourth Asia Pacific Orchid Conference.
Nos. 1444a-1445a each sold for 30b. Each exists imperf, value same as perf.

21st Intl. Society of Sugar Cane Technologists Conf. — A442

1992, Mar. 5 *Perf. 14x14½*

1446 A442 2b multicolored .75 .25
Complete booklet, strip of 5 #1446 6.00

Intl. Red Cross — A443

Perf. 14½x14

1992, Mar. Litho. Wmk. 387

1447 A443 2b multicolored .75 .25
Complete booklet, strip of 5 #1447 4.00

Ministry of Justice, Cent. — A444

Designs: 3b, Prince Rabi Badhanasakdi of Ratchaburi, founder of Thailand's School of Law. 5b, King Rama V, reformer of court system.

1992, Mar. 25 *Perf. 13½*

1448 A444 3b multicolored .65 .25
1449 A444 5b multicolored 1.25 .30

Ministry of Agriculture and Cooperatives, Cent. — A445

1992, Apr. 1 *Perf. 14½x14*

1450 A445 2b gray & multi .35 .25
Complete booklet, strip of 5 #1450 3.25
1451 A445 3b lil & multi .45 .25
1452 A445 4b pink & multi .60 .30
1453 A445 5b gray bl & multi .75 .35
Nos. 1450-1453 (4) 2.15 1.15

A446

Ministry of Interior, Cent.: No. 1454, Prince Damrong Rajanubharb, first Minister of the Interior. No. 1455, People voting. No. 1456, Police and fire protection. No. 1457, Water and electricity provided to remote areas.

1992, Apr. 1 *Perf. 14x14½*

1454 A446 2b multicolored .60 .25
Complete booklet, strip of 5 #1454 4.00
1455 A446 2b multicolored .60 .25
Complete booklet, strip of 5 #1455 4.00
1456 A446 2b multicolored .60 .25
Complete booklet, strip of 5 #1456 4.00
1457 A446 2b multicolored .60 .25
Complete booklet, strip of 5 #1457 4.00
Nos. 1454-1457 (4) 2.40 1.00

A447

1992, Apr. 1

1458 A447 2b Ships, truck .30 .25
Complete booklet, strip of 5 #1458 3.25
1459 A447 3b Truck, bus, train .35 .25
1460 A447 5b Airplanes .55 .30
1461 A447 6b Truck, satellites .65 .40
Nos. 1458-1461 (4) 1.85 1.20

Ministry of Transport and Communications, 80th anniv.

Ministry of Education, Cent. — A448

Perf. 14x14½

1992, Apr. 1 Litho. Wmk. 387

1462 A448 2b multicolored .75 .25
Complete booklet, strip of 5 #1462 4.00

Carts — A449

1992, Apr. 2 *Perf. 14½x14*

1463 A449 2b West .30 .25
Complete booklet, strip of 5 #1463 3.50
1464 A449 3b North .35 .25
1465 A449 5b Northeast .50 .35
1466 A449 10b East 1.00 .65
a. Souv. sheet of 4, #1463-1466 4.00
Nos. 1463-1466 (4) 2.15 1.50

Heritage Conservation Day. No. 1466a sold for 30b. Exists imperf without sheet price in margin, value same as perf.

Songkran Day Type of 1991

1992, Apr. 13 *Perf. 14x14½*

1467 A425 2b Demon on monkey, zodiac 1.10 .25
Complete booklet, strip of 5 #1467 5.50
a. Souvenir sheet of 1 4.00 4.00

No. 1467a sold for 8b. Exists imperf with sale price in different colors, value same as perf.

Department of Livestock Development, 50th Anniv. A451

Perf. 14½x14

1992, May 5 Litho. Wmk. 387

1468 A451 2b multicolored .90 .25
Complete booklet, strip of 5 #1468 4.00

Wisakhabucha Day — A452

Scenes from Buddha's life: 2b, Birth. 3b, Enlightenment. 5b, Death.

Wmk. 387

1992, May 16 Litho. *Perf. 14½*

1469 A452 2b multicolored .35 .25
1470 A452 3b multicolored .70 .30
1471 A452 5b multicolored 1.00 .65
Nos. 1469-1471 (3) 2.05 1.20

Meteorological Department, 50th Anniv. — A453

1992, June 23 *Perf. 14x14½*

1472 A453 2b multicolored .90 .25
Complete booklet, strip of 5 #1472 4.00

1993 World Philatelic Exhibition, Bangkok — A454

Perf. 14x14½

1992, July 1 Litho. Wmk. 387

1473 A454 2b No. 18 .30 .25
Complete booklet, strip of 5 #1473 3.25
1474 A454 3b No. 156 .35 .25
1475 A454 5b No. 222 .50 .30
1476 A454 7b No. 255 .60 .40
1477 A454 8b No. 273 .80 .50
a. Souv. sheet of 5, #1473-1477 + label 5.25 5.25
Nos. 1473-1477 (5) 2.55 1.70

No. 1477a sold for 35b. Exists imperf. with sheet price in blue, value same as #1477a.

Visit ASEAN Year — A455

Designs: 2b, Bua Tong field, Mae Hong Son Province. 3b, Klong Larn Waterfall, Kamphaeng Phet Province. 4b, Coral, Chumphon Province. 5b, Khao Ta-Poo, Phangnga Province.

1992, July 1

1478 A455 2b multicolored .30 .25
Complete booklet, strip of 5 #1478 3.75
1479 A455 3b multicolored .40 .25
1480 A455 4b multicolored .50 .35
1481 A455 5b multicolored .60 .40
Nos. 1478-1481 (4) 1.80 1.25

Prince Chudadhuj Dharadilok of Bejraburna (1892-1923) — A456

Wmk. 368

1992, July 5 Litho. *Perf. 13½*

1482 A456 2b multicolored .75 .25
Complete booklet, strip of 5 #1482 4.25

Natl. Communications Day — A457

Perf. 14½x14

1992, Aug. 4 Litho. Wmk. 387

1483 A457 2b multicolored .75 .25
Complete booklet, strip of 5 #1483 4.00

ASEAN, 25th Anniv. — A458

Flags and: 2b, Cultures and sports. 3b, Tourist attractions. 5b, Transportation, communications. 7b, Agriculture.

1992, Aug. 8 Wmk. 368 *Perf. 13½*

1484 A458 2b multicolored .30 .25
Complete booklet, strip of 5 #1484 3.25
1485 A458 3b multicolored .35 .25
1486 A458 5b multicolored .55 .40
1487 A458 7b multicolored .85 .55
Nos. 1484-1487 (4) 2.05 1.45

Queen Sirikit, 60th Birthday A459

#1488, Wedding, with King, Queen being anointed. #1489, Coronation, King and Queen on throne. #1490, Being crowned, Queen with crown, being anointed. #1491, Formal portrait, Queen seated. #1492, Visiting wounded. #1493, Visiting public.

Wmk. 329

1992, Aug. 12 Photo. *Perf. 13½*

1488 A459 2b multicolored .60 .25
Complete booklet, strip of 5 #1488 5.00
1489 A459 2b multicolored .60 .25
Complete booklet, strip of 5 #1489 5.00
1490 A459 2b multicolored .60 .25
Complete booklet, strip of 5 #1490 5.00
1491 A459 2b multicolored .60 .25
Complete booklet, strip of 5 #1491 5.00
1492 A459 2b multicolored .60 .25
Complete booklet, strip of 5 #1492 5.00
1493 A459 2b multicolored .60 .25
Complete booklet, strip of 5 #1493 5.00
a. Souv. sheet of 6, #1488-1493 6.00 6.00
Nos. 1488-1493 (6) 3.60 1.50

No. 1493a sold for 30b. Exists imperf with sale price in different colors, value same as perf.

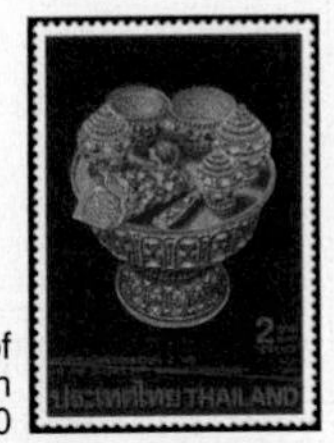

Royal Regalia of Queen Sirikit — A460

No. 1494, Tray. No. 1495, Kettle. No. 1496, Bowl. No. 1497, Box. No. 1498, Covered dish.

1992, Aug. 12 Background Colors

1494 A460 2b dark blue	.45	.25
1495 A460 2b violet	.45	.25
1496 A460 2b yellow green	.45	.25
1497 A460 2b Prussian blue	.45	.25
1498 A460 2b dark green	.45	.25
Nos. 1494-1498 (5)	2.25	1.25

Opening of Sirikit Medical Center A461

Perf. 14½x14

1992, Aug. 12 Litho. Wmk. 387

1499 A461 2b multicolored .45 .25
Complete booklet, strip of 5 #1499 4.00

Queen Sirikit, 60th Birthday A462

Litho. & Embossed

1992, Aug. 12 ***Perf. 13½***

1500 A462 100b blue & gold 15.00 15.00

No. 1500 was printed in sheets of 10. Value, $160.

A463

Wmk. 387

1992, Aug. 25 Litho. ***Perf. 13½***

1501 A463 2b multicolored .60 .25
Complete booklet, strip of 5 #1501 4.25

Prince Wan Waithayakon Krommun Naradhip Bongsprabandh (1891-1976).

A464

1992, Sept. 15 ***Perf. 14x14½***

1502 A464 2b multicolored .75 .25
Complete booklet, strip of 5 #1502 4.25

Professor Silpa Bhirasri, Sculptor, cent. of birth.

Coral — A465

2b, Catalaphyllia jardinei. 3b, Porites lutea. 6b, Tubastraea coccinea. 8b, Favia pallida.

Perf. 14½x14

1992, Oct. 4 Litho. Wmk. 387

1503 A465 2b multicolored .45 .25
Complete booklet, strip of 5 #1503 2.75
1504 A465 3b multicolored .75 .25
1505 A465 6b multicolored .85 .30
1506 A465 8b multicolored 1.25 .45
a. Souv. sheet of 4, #1503-1506 4.25
Nos. 1503-1506 (4) 3.30 1.25

Intl. Letter Writing Week. No. 1506a sold for 30b.

New Year 1993 — A466

Flowers: No. 1507, Rhododendron simsii. No. 1508, Cynoglossum lanceolatum. No. 1509, Tithonia diversifolia. No. 1510, Agapetes parishii.

Perf. 14x13½

1992, Nov. 15 Wmk. 368 Litho.

1507 A466 1b multicolored .30 .25
1508 A466 1b multicolored .30 .25
1509 A466 1b multicolored .30 .25
1510 A466 1b multicolored .30 .25
a. Souv. sheet of 4, #1507-1510 3.00 2.00
Nos. 1507-1510 (4) 1.20 1.00

Nos. 1510a sold for 10b. Exists imperf with sheet price in green, value same as perf.

1st Asian Congress of Allergies and Immunology — A467

1992, Nov. 22 ***Perf. 13½***

1511 A467 2b black, red & yellow .50 .25
Complete booklet, strip of 5 #1511 5.00

Natl. Assembly, 60th Anniv. A468

Wmk. 387

1992, Dec. 10 Litho. ***Perf. 13½***

1512 A468 2b multicolored .75 .25
Complete booklet, strip of 5 #1512 4.25

Bank of Thailand, 50th Anniv. A469

1992, Dec. 10 ***Perf. 14½x14***

1513 A469 2b multicolored .60 .25
Complete booklet, strip of 5 #1513 4.25

Children's Day — A470

Children's drawings: No. 1514, River scene. No. 1515, Wild animals, forest. No. 1516, Trains, planes, monorail.

1993, Jan. 9 Wmk. 368 ***Perf. 13½***

1514 A470 2b multicolored .35 .25
Complete booklet, strip of 5 #1514 3.50
1515 A470 2b multicolored .35 .25
Complete booklet, strip of 5 #1515 3.50
1516 A470 2b multicolored .35 .25
Complete booklet, strip of 5 #1516 3.50
Nos. 1514-1516 (3) 1.05 .75

Pottery A471

Designs: 3b, Jug with bird's neck spout, two bottles. 6b, Pear-shaped vase, two jars. 7b, Three bowls. 8b, Three jars.

1993, Jan. 9 Photo. Wmk. 329

1517 A471 3b multicolored .35 .25
1518 A471 6b multicolored .70 .50
1519 A471 7b multicolored .80 .55
1520 A471 8b multicolored .95 .70
a. Souv. sheet of 4, #1517-1520 4.00 3.50
Nos. 1517-1520 (4) 2.80 2.00

1993 World Philatelic Exhibition, Bangkok. No. 1520a sold for 35b.

Thai Teachers' Training Institute, Cent. — A472

Perf. 13½x14

1993, Jan. 16 Litho. Wmk. 368

1521 A472 2b multicolored .75 .25
Complete booklet, strip of 5 #1521 5.00

Kasetsart University, 50th Anniv. A473

1993, Feb. 2 Wmk. 329 ***Perf. 13½***

1522 A473 2b multicolored .90 .25
Complete booklet, strip of 5 #1522 5.00

Maghapuja Day — A474

Wmk. 387

1993, Mar. 7 Litho. ***Perf. 14½***

1523 A474 2b multicolored .90 .25

Queen Sri Bajarindra — A475

1993, Mar. 27 ***Perf. 14x14½***

1524 A475 2b multicolored .70 .25
Complete booklet, strip of 5 #1524 6.00

Thai Red Cross, cent.

Office of Attorney General, Cent. — A476

1993, Apr. 1 Wmk. 368 ***Perf. 12½***

1525 A476 2b multicolored .75 .25
Complete booklet, strip of 5 #1525 5.00

Heritage Conservation Day — A477

Historical landmarks, Si Satchanalai Park: 3b, Wat Chedi Chet Thaeo. 4b, Wat Chang Lom. 6b, Wat Phra Si Rattanamahathat (Chaliang). 7b, Wat Suan Kaeo Utthayan Noi.

Wmk. 368

1993, Apr. 2 Litho. ***Perf. 13½***

1526 A477 3b multicolored .35 .25
1527 A477 4b multicolored .45 .30
1528 A477 6b multicolored .70 .50
1529 A477 7b multicolored .80 .55
a. Souv. sheet of 4, #1526-1529 3.50 2.75
Nos. 1526-1529 (4) 2.30 1.60

No. 1529a sold for 25b.

See Nos. 1561-1564, 1650-1653, 1797-1800.

Songkran Day Type of 1991

Design: Demon on rooster's back, zodiac.

Perf. 14x14½

1993 Litho. Wmk. 387

1530 A425 2b multicolored .75 .25
Complete booklet, strip of 5 #1530 2.50
a. Souvenir sheet of 1 1.75 1.00
b. As "a," ovptd. in gold 15.00 15.00

No. 1530b overprinted on sheet margin in both Thai and Chinese for Chinpex '93.

Nos. 1530a-1530b sold for 8b and exist imperf. with sale price in different colors. Values same as for perf.

Issued: Nos. 1530, 1530a, 4/13.

Mushrooms A478

Wmk. 368

1993, July 1 Litho. ***Perf. 13½***

1531 A478 2b Marasmius .30 .25
Complete booklet, strip of 5 #1531 3.50
1532 A478 4b Coprinus .50 .30
1533 A478 6b Mycena .70 .45
1534 A478 8b Cyathus 1.00 .60
a. Souv. sheet of 4, #1531-1534 3.75 3.75
Nos. 1531-1534 (4) 2.50 1.60

No. 1534a sold for 30b.

Natl. Communications Day — A479

1993, Aug. 4 Wmk. 387 ***Perf. 13½***

1535 A479 2b multicolored .45 .25
Complete booklet, strip of 5 #1535 4.00

Post and Telegraph Department, 110th Anniv. A480

Wmk. 387

1993, Aug. 4 Litho. ***Perf. 13½***

1536 A480 2b multicolored 1.10 .25
Complete booklet, strip of 5 #1536 9.00

Queen Suriyothai's Monument A481

1993, Aug. 12

1537 A481 2b multicolored .60 .25
Complete booklet, strip of 5 #1537 5.00

Fruit — A482

Wmk. 368

1993, Oct. 1 Photo. *Perf. 13½*

1538 A482 2b Citrus reticulata .30 .25
Complete booklet, strip of 5 #1538 3.50
1539 A482 3b Musa sp. .40 .25
1540 A482 6b Phyllanthus distichus .75 .45
1541 A482 8b Bouea burmanica 1.00 .60
Nos. 1538-1541 (4) 2.45 1.55

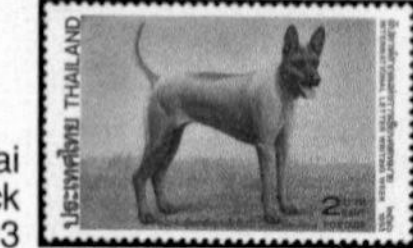

Thai Ridgeback Dogs — A483

Various dogs.

1993, Oct. 1

1542 A483 2b multicolored .45 .25
Complete booklet, strip of 5 #1542 2.75
1543 A483 3b multicolored .45 .25
1544 A483 5b multicolored .65 .30
1545 A483 10b multicolored 1.75 .65
a. Souv. sheet of 4, #1542-1545 3.75 3.50
Nos. 1542-1545 (4) 3.30 1.45

Intl. Letter Writing Week. No. 1545a sold for 30b.

5th Conference & Exhibition of ASEAN Council on Petroleum (ASCOPE) A484

Wmk. 387

1993, Nov. 2 Litho. *Perf. 13½*

1546 A484 2b multicolored .75 .25
Complete booklet, strip of 5 #1546 5.00

King Rama VII (1893-1941) — A485

1993, Nov. 8 *Perf. 14x14½*

1547 A485 2b multicolored 1.00 .25
Complete booklet, strip of 5 #1547 7.50

No. 655 Surcharged

1993 Photo. Wmk. 233 *Perf. 14½*

1548 A161 1b on 25s brown red .70 .25

Bencharong and Lai Nam Thong Wares — A486

Designs: 3b, Bencharong cosmetic jar, divinity design. 5b, Bencharong cosmetic jar, gold knob. 6b, Lai Nam Thong cosmetic jar, floral design. 7b, Lai Nam Thong cosmetic jar, floral design, diff.

Wmk. 368

1993, Oct. 1 Photo. *Perf. 13½*

1549 A486 3b multicolored .40 .25
1550 A486 5b multicolored .60 .30
1551 A486 6b multicolored .70 .45
1552 A486 7b multicolored .90 .50
a. Souv. sheet of 4, #1549-1552 3.00 3.00
Nos. 1549-1552 (4) 2.60 1.50

Bangkok '93. No. 1552a sold for 30b. No. 1552a exists imperf. Value, $14.

New Year 1994 — A487

Perf. 14½x14

1993, Nov. 15 Litho. Wmk. 387

1553 A487 1b Ipomoea cairica .30 .25
1554 A487 1b Decaschistia parviflora .30 .25
1555 A487 1b Hibiscus tiliaceus .30 .25
1556 A487 1b Passiflora foetida .30 .25
a. Souv. sheet of 4, #1553-1556 2.50 1.75
Nos. 1553-1556 (4) 1.20 1.00

No. 1556a sold for 10b.

THAICOM, Natl. Satellite Project — A488

1993, Dec. 1 *Perf. 14x14½*

1557 A488 2b multicolored .75 .25
Complete booklet, strip of 5 #1557 4.50

Children's Day — A489

1994, Jan. 8 *Perf. 14½x14*

1558 A489 2b Play land .75 .25
Complete booklet, strip of 5 #1558 4.00

Administrative Building, Chulalongkorn Hospital, 80th Anniv. A490

Perf. 14½x14

1994, Mar. 30 Litho. Wmk. 387

1559 A490 2b multicolored .75 .25
Complete booklet, strip of 5 #1559 4.00

Thai Red Cross.

Royal Institute, 60th Anniv. — A491

1994, Mar. 31 *Perf. 14x14½*

1560 A491 2b multicolored .75 .25
Complete booklet, strip of 5 #1560 3.50

Heritage Conservation Day Type of 1993

Historical landmarks, Phra Nakhon Si Ayutthaya Park: 2b, Wat Ratchaburana. 3b, Wat Maha That. 6b, Wat Maheyong. 9b, Wat Phra Si Samphet.

1994, Apr. 2 *Perf. 14½x14*

1561 A477 2b multicolored .30 .25
Complete booklet, strip of 5 #1561 2.50
1562 A477 3b multicolored .35 .25
1563 A477 6b multicolored .75 .45
1564 A477 9b multicolored 1.00 .70
a. Souv. sheet of 4, #1561-1564 3.00 3.00
Nos. 1561-1564 (4) 2.40 1.65

No. 1564a sold for 25b.

Opening of Friendship Bridge, Thailand-Laos A492

1994, Apr. 8

1565 A492 9b multicolored 1.60 .35

Songkran Day Type of 1991

Design: Demon on dog's back, zodiac.

1994, Apr. 13 Litho.

1566 A425 2b multicolored .35 .25
Complete booklet, strip of 5 #1566 3.00
a. Souvenir sheet of 1 1.50 1.75
b. As "a," inscribed in margin 4.50 4.50

No. 1566a sold for 8b and exists imperf with frame around stamp and sale price in different color. Value same as perf.

Sheet margin of No. 1566b has no value inscription and is overprinted in violet with Thai and Chinese inscriptions for Beijing Stamp Exhibition. Issued: May 1994. No. 1566b also exists imperf. Value same as perf.

Intl. Olympic Committee, Cent. — A493

Wmk. 387

1994, June 23 Litho. *Perf. 14*

1567 A493 2b Soccer .30 .25
Complete booklet, strip of 5 #1567 1.75
1568 A493 3b Running .35 .25
1569 A493 5b Swimming .60 .45
1570 A493 6b Weight lifting .80 .55
1571 A493 9b Boxing 1.10 .80
Nos. 1567-1571 (5) 3.15 2.30

Thammasat University, 60th Anniv. A494

Wmk. 387

1994, June 27 Litho. *Perf. 14*

1572 A494 2b multicolored .75 .35
Complete booklet, strip of 5 #1572 4.00

Asalhapuja Day — A495

1994, July 22 Wmk. 329 *Perf. 13½*

1573 A495 2b multicolored .45 .25

Natl. Communications Day — A496

1994, Aug. 4 Wmk. 368

1574 A496 2b multicolored .45 .25
Complete booklet, strip of 5 #1574 4.00

Crabs — A497

3b, Phricotelphusa limula. 5b, Thaipotamon chulabhorn. 6b, Phricotelphusa sirindhorn. 10b, Thaiphusa sirikit.

Wmk. 340 (340)

1994, Aug. 12 Photo. *Perf. 13½x13*

1575 A497 3b multicolored .50 .25
1576 A497 5b multicolored .75 .35
1577 A497 6b multicolored .75 .45
1578 A497 10b multicolored 1.50 .75
a. Souv. sheet of 4, #1575-1578 4.00 4.00
b. As "a," inscribed in margin 6.00 5.00
Nos. 1575-1578 (4) 3.50 1.80

No. 1578b has PHILAKOREA '94 Exhibition emblem added to sheet margin.

Intl. Letter Writing Week — A498

Winning paintings in design contest: 2b, Gold niello bowls, octagonal footed tray. 6b, Pumpkin shaped bowls. 8b, Silver niello betel-nut set. 9b, Covered square bowl with gold finial, small lotus-shaped footed tray.

Wmk. 368

1994, Oct. 9 Photo. *Perf. 13½*

1579 A498 2b multicolored .30 .25
Complete booklet, 5 #1579 3.50
1580 A498 6b multicolored .95 .55
1581 A498 8b multicolored 1.20 .70
1582 A498 9b multicolored 1.30 .80
a. Souv. sheet of 4, #1579-1582 3.50 3.50
Nos. 1579-1582 (4) 3.75 2.30

No. 1582a sold for 30b.

ILO, 75th Anniv. A499

Perf. 15x14

1994, Oct. 29 Litho. Wmk. 387

1583 A499 2b multicolored .75 .25
Complete booklet, 5 #1583 3.50

New Year 1995 — A500

Herbs: No. 1584, Utricularia delphinioides. No. 1585, Utricularia minutissima. No. 1586, Eriocaulon odoratum. No. 1587, Utricularia bifida.

1994, Nov. 15 *Perf. 14x14½*

1584 A500 1b multicolored .30 .25
1585 A500 1b multicolored .30 .25
1586 A500 1b multicolored .30 .25
1587 A500 1b multicolored .30 .25
a. Souv. sheet of 4, #1584-1587 2.25 1.50
Nos. 1584-1587 (4) 1.20 1.00

No. 1587a sold for 10b.

Suan Dusit Teachers College, 60th Anniv. A501

Perf. 14½x14

1994, Dec. 4 Litho. Wmk. 387

1588 A501 2b multicolored .90 .25
Complete booklet, 5 #1588 5.00

Council of State, 120th Anniv. A502

1994, Dec. 5 Wmk. 368 *Perf. 13½*

1589 A502 2b multicolored 1.10 .25
Complete booklet, 5 #1589 4.75

ICAO, 50th Anniv. A503

Perf. 14½x14

1994, Dec. 7 **Wmk. 387**

1590 A503 2b multicolored .75 .25
Complete booklet, 5 #1590 4.25

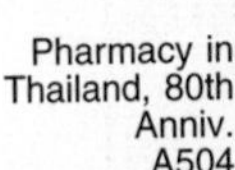

Pharmacy in Thailand, 80th Anniv. A504

Grinding stones: 2b, Dvaravati, 7th-11th cent. 6b, Lopburi Period, 11th-13th cent. 9b, Bangkok Period, 18th-20th cent.

1994, Dec. 13

1591 A504 2b multicolored .30 .25
Complete booklet, 5 #1591 3.00
1592 A504 6b multicolored .80 .50
1593 A504 9b multicolored 1.10 .80
Nos. 1591-1593 (3) 2.20 1.55

Bar Assoc., 80th Anniv. A505

Design: 2b, First Bar Assoc. headquarters, King Vajiravudh, King Bhumibol.

1995, Jan. 1 **Wmk. 368** ***Perf. 13½***

1594 A505 2b multicolored .90 .25
Complete booklet, 5 #1594 5.00

A506

Children's drawings: No. 1595, Kites Decorate the Summer Sky. No. 1596, Trees and Streams, horiz. No. 1597, Youths and Religion, horiz.

1995, Jan. 14 **Wmk. 387** ***Perf. 14***

1595 A506 2b multicolored .55 .25
Complete booklet, 5 #1595 3.50
1596 A506 2b multicolored .55 .25
Complete booklet, 5 #1596 3.50
1597 A506 2b multicolored .55 .25
Complete booklet, 5 #1597 3.50
Nos. 1595-1597 (3) 1.65 .75

Children's Day.

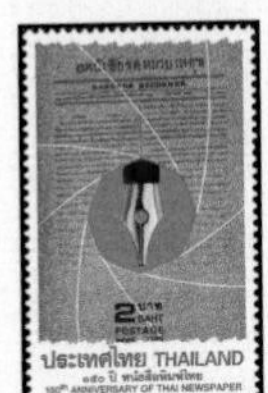

A507

1995, Mar. 4

1598 A507 2b multicolored .75 .25
Complete booklet, 5 #1598 4.25

First Thai newspaper, Bangkok Recorder, 150th anniv.

Royal Thai Air Force, 80th Anniv. A508

1995, Mar. 27 **Wmk. 368** ***Perf. 13½***

1599 A508 2b multicolored .75 .25
Complete booklet, 5 #1599 5.00

Red Cross Floating Clinic, Wetchapha A509

1995, Mar. 30

1600 A509 2b multicolored .35 .25
Complete booklet, 5 #1600 5.00

Phimai Historical Park — A510

Paintings: 3b, Naga Bridge. 5b, Brahmin Hall. 6b, Gateway of the Inner Wall. 9b, Main Pagoda.

Perf. 14½x14

1995, Apr. 2 **Wmk. 387**

1601 A510 3b multicolored .35 .25
1602 A510 5b multicolored .60 .35
1603 A510 6b multicolored .80 .50
1604 A510 9b multicolored 1.10 .80
a. Souv. sheet of 4, #1601-1604 4.00 4.00
Nos. 1601-1604 (4) 2.85 1.90

Heritage Conservation Day.
No. 1604a sold for 30b.

Ministry of Defense, 108th Anniv. A511

Design: 2b, Admin. building, King Rama V.

1995, Apr. 8 **Wmk. 387** ***Perf. 14***

1605 A511 2b multicolored .60 .25
Complete booklet, 5 #1605 5.00

Songkran Day Type of 1991

Design: Demon on boar's back, zodiac.

1995, Apr. 13 ***Perf. 11x13***

1606 A425 2b multicolored .75 .25
a. Souvenir sheet of 1 1.75 1.00
Complete booklet, 5 #1606 4.50

No. 1606a sold for 8b and exists imperf with sale price in different color. Value same as perf. No. 1606a and the similar imperf sheet exist with a red marginal inscription in Thai and Chinese (without sale price). Value, each $5.50.

Ministry of Foreign Affairs, 120th Anniv. A512

2b, Saranrom Palace, King Rama V.

1995, Apr. 14 ***Perf. 14***

1607 A512 2b multicolored .90 .25
Complete booklet, 5 #1607 5.00

Visakhapuja Day — A513

Sculptures of Buddha: 2b, Emerald Buddha, temple of Wat Phra Si Rattana Satsadaram, Bangkok. 6b, Phra Phuttha Chinnarat, Wat Phra Si Rattana Maha That, Phitsanulok Province. 8b, Phra Phuttha Sihing, Wat Phra Sing, Chiang Mai Province. 9b, Phra Sukhothai Traimit, Wat Traimit Witthayaram, Bangkok.

Wmk. 340

1995, May 13 **Photo.** ***Perf. 13½***

1608 A513 2b multicolored .30 .25
1609 A513 6b multicolored .90 .40
1610 A513 8b multicolored 1.20 .60
1611 A513 9b multicolored 1.25 .70
a. Souv. sheet of 4, #1608-1611 4.50 4.50
Nos. 1608-1611 (4) 3.65 1.95

No. 1611a sold for 35b.

ASEAN Environment Year — A514

1995, June 5 **Litho.** **Wmk. 368**

1612 A514 2b multicolored .75 .25
Complete booklet, 5 #1612 3.50

Information Technology Year — A515

1995, June 9 **Wmk. 340**

1613 A515 2b multicolored .75 .25
Complete booklet, 5 #1613 3.50

Thailand-People's Republic of China Diplomatic Relations, 20th Anniv. — A516

#1614, Elephants walking right into water. #1615, Elephants walking left into water.

Wmk. 340

1995, July 1 **Photo.** ***Perf. 13½***

1614 A516 2b multicolored .50 .25
1615 A516 2b multicolored .50 .25
a. Pair, Nos. 1614-1615 1.75 1.75
b. Souv. sheet, #1614-1615 3.00
c. As "b," diff. inscriptions in sheet margin *21.00*

No. 1615c contains Jakarta '95 exhibition emblem and does not have sheet value in margin.

#1615b sold for 8b. #1615c sold for 28b.

No. 1615b exists with serial number in sheet margin, The same number is on China (PRC) No. 2462a. These two souvenir sheets were sold as a set. Value, set $26.50.

See People's Republic of China Nos. 2579-2580.

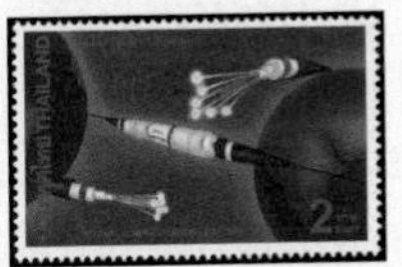

Natl. Communications Day — A517

1995, Aug. 4 **Litho.** ***Perf. 14½x14***

1616 A517 2b multicolored .75 .25
Complete booklet, 5 #1616 3.50

A518

Domestic cats: 3b, Khoa Manee. 6b, Korat or Si-Sawat. 7b, Seal point Siamese. 9b, Burmese.

1995, Aug. 4 **Photo.** ***Perf. 13½***

1617 A518 3b multicolored .50 .25
1618 A518 6b multicolored .75 .45
1619 A518 7b multicolored .95 .50
1620 A518 9b multicolored 1.50 .70
a. Souv. sheet, Nos. 1617-1620 5.50 5.50
b. As "a," diff. inscriptions in margin 17.50 17.50
Nos. 1617-1620 (4) 3.70 1.90

Thaipex '95.

No. 1620b contains Singapore '95 exhibition emblem added to sheet margin and does not have value inscription.

No. 1620a sold for 35b. No. 1620b sold for 46b.

No. 1620a exists imperf. Value $21.00.

Revenue Department, 80th Anniv. — A519

1995, Sept. 2 **Litho.** ***Perf. 14x14½***

1621 A519 2b multicolored .75 .25
Complete booklet, 5 #1621 3.50

Natl. Auditing & Office of Auditor General, 120th Anniv. A520

1995, Sept. 18 ***Perf. 14½x14***

1622 A520 2b multicolored .75 .25
Complete booklet, 5 #1622 3.50

Intl. Letter Writing Week — A521

Wicker: No. 1623, Vase with handles, legs. No. 1624, Oval-shaped container. No. 1625, Lamp shade. No. 1626, Vase.

Wmk. 340

1995, Oct. 8 **Photo.** ***Perf. 13½***

1623 A521 2b multicolored .30 .25
Complete booklet, 5 #1623 2.25
1624 A521 2b multicolored .30 .25
Complete booklet, 5 #1624 2.25
1625 A521 9b multicolored 1.20 .80
1626 A521 9b multicolored 1.20 .80
a. Souv. sheet, #1623-1626 4.50 4.50
Nos. 1623-1626 (4) 3.00 2.10

FAO, 50th Anniv. A522

1995, Oct. 16 **Litho.** ***Perf. 14½x14***

1627 A522 2b multicolored .75 .25
Complete booklet, 5 #1627 3.00

Total Solar Eclipse in Thailand A523

1995, Oct. 24 ***Perf. 13½***

1628 A523 2b multicolored .45 .25
Complete booklet, 5 #1628 2.50

UN, 50th Anniv. A524

Perf. 13½x14

1995, Oct. 24 **Wmk. 387**

1629 A524 2b multicolored .75 .25
Complete booklet, 5 #1629 2.50

World Agricultural and Industrial Exhibition, Nkhon Ratchasima Province A525

2b, Worldtech '95 Thailand Symbol Tower, vert. 5b, Farming equipment, food products, vert. 6b, Computers, equipment. 9b, Factory, beach.

Perf. 14x14½, 14½x14

1995, Nov. 4 **Wmk. 340**

1630 A525 2b multicolored .30 .25
Complete booklet, 5 #1630 2.50
1631 A525 5b multicolored .60 .40
1632 A525 6b multicolored .80 .50
1633 A525 9b multicolored 1.10 .80
Nos. 1630-1633 (4) 2.80 1.95

New Year 1996 — A526

No. 1634, Adenium obesum. No. 1635, Bauhinia acuminata. No. 1636, Cananga odorata. No. 1637, Thumbergia erecta.

1995, Dec. 9 ***Perf. 13½***

1634 A526 2b multicolored .30 .25
1635 A526 2b multicolored .30 .25
a. Souvenir sheet, #1634-1635 4.50
1636 A526 2b multicolored .30 .25
1637 A526 2b multicolored .30 .25
a. Souvenir sheet, #1634-1637 2.75 2.25
b. As "a," inscribed in margin 12.00 8.00
c. Souvenir sheet, #1636-1637 8.00 7.00
Nos. 1634-1637 (4) 1.20 1.00

No. 1637a sold for 15b.

Nos. 1635a, 1637c have "CHINA '96" emblem inscribed in sheet margin and sold for 22b each. No. 1637b is inscribed in sheet margin with "Indonesia '96" emblem and has the gold 15b value removed. No. 1637b sold for 14b.

Issued: #1635a, 1637b-1637c, 5/18/96.

Veterinary Science in Thailand, 60th Anniv. A527

1995, Dec. 9 ***Perf. 14½x14***

1638 A527 2b multicolored .75 .25
Complete booklet, 5 #1638 4.00

A528

Perf. 14x14½

1996, Jan. 12 **Litho.** **Wmk. 340**

1639 A528 2b multicolored .75 .25
Complete booklet, 5 #1639 4.00

Siriraj School of Nursing and Midwifery, cent.

A529

Paintings of Buddha instructing people with: No. 1640, Bright light, deer. No. 1641, Children, animal, person reclined, horiz. No. 1642, Followers, large tree, river.

1996, Jan. 13 **Wmk. 387** ***Perf. 13½***

1640 A529 2b multicolored .40 .25
Complete booklet, 5 #1640 2.50
1641 A529 2b multicolored .40 .25
Complete booklet, 5 #1641 2.50
1642 A529 2b multicolored .40 .25
Complete booklet, 5 #1642 2.50
Nos. 1640-1642 (3) 1.20 .75

Natl. Children's Day.

Natl. Aviation Day — A530

Perf. 14½x14

1996, Jan. 13 **Wmk. 340**

1643 A530 2b multicolored .40 .25
Complete booklet, 5 #1643 3.50

Asia-Europe Economic Meeting — A531

Perf. 14x14½

1996, Mar. 1 **Litho.** **Wmk. 340**

1644 A531 2b multicolored .75 .25
Complete booklet, 5 #1644 4.00

Maghapuja Day — A532

Scenes from the Ten Jataka stories: 2b, Man on knee, another holding chariot. 6b, Two people flying over sea. 8b, Archer approaching man with arrow in side. 9b, Charioteer pointing.

Wmk. 340

1996, Mar. 3 **Photo.** ***Perf. 13½***

1645 A532 2b multicolored .30 .25
1646 A532 6b multicolored .75 .45
1647 A532 8b multicolored 1.00 .60
1648 A532 9b multicolored 1.10 .75
a. Souvenir Sheet, #1645-1548 4.25 3.50
Nos. 1645-1648 (4) 3.15 2.05

No. 1648a sold for 36b.

Cremation of Princess Mother Somdej Phra Sri Nakharindra Barommarajjonnani — A533

Litho. & Embossed

Perf. 14½x14

1996, Mar. 10 **Wmk. 340**

1649 A533 2b gold & multi .80 .25
Complete booklet, 5 #1649 5.00

Heritage Conservation Day Type of 1993

Historical landmarks, Kamphaeng Phet Park: 2b, Wat Phra Kaeo. 3b, Wat Phra Non. 6b, Wat Chang Rop. 9b, Wat Phra Si Iriyabot.

Wmk. 387

1996, Apr. 2 **Litho.** ***Perf. 13½***

1650 A477 2b multicolored .30 .25
Complete booklet, 5 #1650 2.75
1651 A477 3b multicolored .45 .25
1652 A477 6b multicolored .80 .50
1653 A477 9b multicolored 1.10 .80
a. Souvenir sheet, #1650-1653 3.50 3.50
Nos. 1650-1653 (4) 2.65 1.80

No. 1653a sold for 28b.

Chiang Mai, 700th Anniv. A534

Anniv. logo of Chiang Mai and: 2b, Buddhist Pagoda of Wat Chiang Man. 6b, Sculpted angel on wall, Wat Chet Yot's Pagoda. 8b, Insignia of Wat Phan Tao's Vihara. 9b, Sattaphanta.

Wmk. 340

1996, Apr. 12 **Photo.** ***Perf. 13½***

1654 A534 2b multicolored .30 .25
Complete booklet, 5 #1654 3.50
1655 A534 6b multicolored .70 .45
1656 A534 8b multicolored .90 .60
1657 A534 9b multicolored 1.00 .70
a. Souvenir sheet, #1654-1657 4.00 4.00
Nos. 1654-1657 (4) 2.90 2.00

No. 1657a sold for 37b.

Second Intl. Asian Hornbill Workshop — A535

No. 1658, White-crowned. No. 1659, Rufous-necked. No. 1660, Plain-pouched. No. 1661, Rhinoceros.

1996, Apr. 12

1658 A535 3b multicolored .35 .25
1659 A535 3b multicolored .35 .25
1660 A535 9b multicolored 1.10 .80
1661 A535 9b multicolored 1.10 .80
a. Souvenir sheet, #1658-1661 4.50 4.50
b. As "a," inscribed in margin 8.00 6.50
Nos. 1658-1661 (4) 2.90 2.10

No. 1661a sold for 35b. No. 1661b was issued 6/8/96, contains CAPEX '96 exhibition emblem in sheet margin, no value inscription, and sold for 47b.

Songkran Day Type of 1991

Design: Demon on rat's back, zodiac.

Perf. 13½x14

1996, Apr. 13 **Litho.** **Wmk. 387**

1662 A425 2b multicolored .75 .25
Complete booklet, 5 #1662 3.00
a. Souvenir sheet of 1 3.50 3.50
b. Souv. sheet, #1389, 1467, 1530, 1566, 1606, 1662 3.50 3.50
c. As "a," inscribed in margin 5.00 5.00
d. As "b," inscribed in margin 12.00 12.00

No. 1662c contains CHINA '96 exhibition emblem and "CHINA '96-9th Asian International Philatelic Exhibition" in Chinese and English and no value inscription in sheet margin. No. 1662d contains CHINA '96 and Hong Kong '96 exhibition emblems in margin and no value inscription.

#1662a sold for 8b. #1662b sold for 20b. #1662c, issued 5/15/96, sold for 14b. #1662d, issued 5/10/96, sold for 25b. #1662a-1662d exist imperf.

A536

King Bhumibol Adulyadej, 50th Anniv. of Accession to the Throne — A537

Designs: No. 1663, Royal Ablutions Ceremony. No. 1664, Pouring of the Libation. No. 1665, Grand Audience. No. 1666, Royal Progress by Land. No. 1667, Audience from Balcony.

1996, June 9 **Photo.** ***Perf. 11½***

Granite Paper

1663 A536 3b multicolored .40 .25
a. Souvenir sheet 2.00
1664 A536 3b multicolored .40 .25
a. Souvenir sheet 2.00
1665 A536 3b multicolored .40 .25
a. Souvenir sheet 2.00
1666 A536 3b multicolored .40 .25
a. Souvenir sheet 2.00
1667 A536 3b multicolored .40 .25
a. Souvenir sheet 2.00

Litho. & Typo.

Wmk. 387

Perf. 13½

1668 A537 100b gold & multi 10.50 8.00
Nos. 1663-1668 (6) 12.50 9.25

Nos. 1663a 1664a, 1665a, 1666a, 1667a have a continuous design and each sold for 8b.

No. 1668 was issued in panes of 10. Value, $150.

Development Programs of King Bhumibol Adulyadej — A538

No. 1669, Using Vetiver grass to prevent soil erosion. No. 1670, Chai pattana aerator to improve water quality. No. 1671, Rain making project to counter droughts. No. 1672, Dam, natural water resource development. No. 1673, Reforestation.

Wmk. 340

1996, June 9 **Litho.** ***Perf. 13½***

1669 A538 3b multicolored .50 .25
1670 A538 3b multicolored .50 .25
1671 A538 3b multicolored .50 .25
1672 A538 3b multicolored .50 .25
1673 A538 3b multicolored .50 .25
a. Souv. sheet, #1669-1673+label 5.00 3.50
Nos. 1669-1673 (5) 2.50 1.25

No. 1671 has a holographic image. Soaking in water may affect the hologram. No. 1673a sold for 25b.

Royal Utensils A539

#1674, Gold-enameled cuspidor, golden spittoon. #1675, Royal betel, areca-nut set, vert. #1676, Royal water urn, vert.

Wmk. 329

1996, June 9 **Photo.** ***Perf. 13½***

1674 A539 3b green & multi .40 .25
1675 A539 3b blue & multi .40 .25
1676 A539 3b purple & multi .40 .25
a. Souvenir sheet, #1674-1676 2.50 2.00
Nos. 1674-1676 (3) 1.20 .75

No. 1676a sold for 17b.

Modern Olympic Games, Cent. — A540

2b, Pierre de Coubertin, grave site. 3b, 1st lighting of Olympic torch, Olympia, Greece. 5b, Olympic Stadium, Athens, Olympic flag. 9b, Discus thrower, medal from 1896 games.

Perf. 14x14½

1996, June 23 **Litho.** **Wmk. 340**

1677 A540 2b multicolored .30 .25
Complete booklet, 5 #1677 3.50
1678 A540 3b multicolored .35 .25
1679 A540 5b multicolored .60 .45
1680 A540 9b multicolored 1.10 .80
Nos. 1677-1680 (4) 2.35 1.75

Nat. Communications Day — A541

1996, Aug. 4 Wmk. 340

1681 A541 2b King using radio .55 .25
Complete booklet, 5 #1681 3.50

Royal Forest Department, Cent. — A542

Perf. 14½x14

1996, Sept. 18 Litho. Wmk. 340

Type of Forest

1682 A542 3b Tropical rain .30 .25
1683 A542 6b Hill evergreen .80 .50
1684 A542 7b Swamp .90 .60
1685 A542 9b Mangrove 1.10 .80
a. Souvenir sheet, #1682-1685 4.50 4.50
Nos. 1682-1685 (4) 3.10 2.15

No. 1685a sold for 35b.

Intl. Letter Writing Week — A543

Classical Thai novels, characters: No. 1686, "Ramayana," King Rama following deer. No. 1687, "Inao," Inao kidnapping Budsaba, taking her to cave. No. 1688, "Ngao Pa," Lumhap touring forest. No. 1689, "Mathanapatha," Nang Mathana being cursed.

Wmk. 340

1996, Oct. 6 Photo. *Perf. 13½*

1686 A543 3b multicolored .35 .25
1687 A543 3b multicolored .35 .25
1688 A543 9b multicolored 1.10 .80
1689 A543 9b multicolored 1.10 .80
a. Souvenir sheet, #1686-1689 4.50 4.50
Nos. 1686-1689 (4) 2.90 2.10

No. 1689a sold for 36b. For surcharges, see Nos. 2530-2531.

Rotary Intl. 1996 Asia Regional Conference — A544

Perf. 14x14½

1996, Oct. 25 Litho. Wmk. 340

1690 A544 2b multicolored .75 .25
Complete booklet, 5 #1609 3.00

UNESCO, 50th Anniv. A545

1996, Nov. 4 *Perf. 14½x14*

1691 A545 2b multicolored .75 .25
Complete booklet, 5 #1691 2.50

Royal Barge A546

1996, Nov. 7 Unwmk. *Perf. 11½*

Granite Paper

1692 A546 9b multicolored 1.40 1.10
a. Souvenir sheet of 1 2.75 2.25

No. 1692a sold for 16b.

New Year 1997 — A547

Designs: No. 1693, Limnocharis flava. No. 1694, Crinum thaianum, vert. No. 1695, Monochoria hastata, vert. No. 1696, Nymphoides indicum.

Perf. 14x14½, 14½x14

1996, Nov. 15 Litho. Wmk. 387

1693 A547 2b multicolored .30 .25
1694 A547 2b multicolored .30 .25
1695 A547 2b multicolored .30 .25
1696 A547 2b multicolored .30 .25
a. Souvenir sheet, #1693-1696 2.25 2.25
b. As "a," inscribed in margin 6.00 6.00
Nos. 1693-1696 (4) 1.20 1.00

No. 1696a sold for 15b. No. 1696b inscribed in sheet margin with Hong Kong '97 emblem and vertical Chinese inscription.
No. 1696b issued 2/12/97.

Ducks A548

No. 1697, Sarkidiornis melanotos. No. 1698, Dendrocygna javanica, vert. No. 1699, Cairina scutulata, vert. No. 1700, Nettapus coromandelianus.

Wmk. 340

1996, Dec. 1 Photo. *Perf. 13½*

1697 A548 3b multicolored .35 .25
1698 A548 3b multicolored .35 .25
1699 A548 7b multicolored .90 .60
1700 A548 7b multicolored .90 .60
a. Souvenir sheet, #1697-1700 4.50 4.50
Nos. 1697-1700 (4) 2.50 1.70

No. 1700a sold for 33b.

UNICEF, 50th Anniv. — A549

Perf. 14½x14

1996, Dec. 11 Litho. Wmk. 340

1701 A549 2b multicolored .75 .25
Complete booklet, 5 #1701 2.50

King Bhumibol Adulyadej — A550

Perf. 14x14½

1996, Dec. 5 Litho. Wmk. 340

1702 A550 2b carmine .35 .25
Complete booklet, 5 #1702 4.50
a. Unwmkd., granite paper .50 .25

No. 1702a issued 9/1/98.
See Nos. 1725-1729, 1743-1745, 1756-1757, 1794-1795, 1819-1820, 1876-1879, 2067, 2212-2213, 2435, 2465A.

Thailand's 1st Olympic Gold Medal, 1996 — A552

Litho. & Embossed

Perf. 14½x14

1996, Dec. 16 Wmk. 340

1704 A552 6b multicolored 1.00 .50

Mahavajiravudh School, Songkhla, Cent. — A553

Perf. 14x14½

1997, Jan. 1 Wmk. 387

1705 A553 2b multicolored .75 .25
Complete booklet, 5 #1705 2.50

Children's Day — A554

Children' paintings: No. 1706, Children processing fish. No. 1707, Monument, children in praise.

1997, Jan. 11 Wmk. 340

1706 A554 2b multicolored .45 .25
Complete booklet, 5 #1706 1.75
1707 A554 2b multicolored .45 .25
Complete booklet, 5 #1707 1.75

Communications Authority of Thailand, 20th Anniv. — A555

Perf. 14½x14

1997, Feb. 25 Litho. Wmk. 340

1708 A555 2b multicolored .75 .25
Complete booklet, 5 #1708 2.50

Statue of Prince Bhanurangsi — A556

1997, Feb. 25 *Perf. 14x14½*

1709 A556 2b multicolored .75 .25
Complete booklet, 5 #1709 2.50

Laksi Mail Center A557

No. 1710, Outside view of building. No. 1711, Computerized mail sorting machine.

1997, Feb. 25 *Perf. 14½x14*

1710 A557 2b multicolored .45 .25
1711 A557 2b multicolored .45 .25
a. Pair, #1710-1711 1.00 .50

State Railway, Cent. — A558

3b, 0-6-0 Type. 4b, Garratt. 6b, Sulzer diesel. 7b, Hitachi diesel leaving tunnel.

Wmk. 387

1997, Mar. 26 Litho. *Perf. 13*

1712 A558 3b multicolored .35 .25
a. Souvenir sheet of 1 2.00 2.00
1713 A558 4b multicolored .50 .35
1714 A558 6b multicolored .80 .50
1715 A558 7b multicolored 1.00 .60
a. Souv. sheet of 4, #1712-1715 4.00 4.00
Nos. 1712-1715 (4) 2.65 1.70

No. 1712a sold for 20b, No. 1715a sold for 30b.

Chulalongkorn University, 80th Anniv. A559

Designs: No. 1716, Palace of Prince Maha Vajirunhis. No. 1717, Faculty of Arts building.

Perf. 14½x14

1997, Mar. 26 Wmk. 340

1716 A559 2b yellow & multi .45 .25
Complete booklet, 5 #1716 2.00
1717 A559 2b rose & multi .45 .25
Complete booklet, 5 #1717 2.00

Thai Red Cross — A560

1997, Mar. 28

1718 A560 3b Rajakarun building .75 .25

Govt. Savings Bank, 84th Anniv. A561

1997, Apr. 1

1719 A561 2b multicolored .75 .25
Complete booklet, 5 #1719 2.25

Heritage Conservation Day — A562

Phanomrung historical Park: No. 1720, Outer stairway. No. 1721, Pavilion. No. 1722, Passage, stairway to sanctuary. No. 1723, Naga balustrade, Central Gate of Eastern Gallery.

1997, Apr. 2

1720 A562 3b multicolored .40 .25
1721 A562 3b multicolored .40 .25
1722 A562 7b multicolored 1.00 .60
1723 A562 7b multicolored 1.00 .60
a. Souvenir sheet, #1720-1723 4.00 4.00
Nos. 1720-1723 (4) 2.80 1.70

No. 1723a sold for 30b.

Songkran Day Type of 1991

Design: Demon on ox's back, zodiac.

1997-2002 Wmk. 340 *Perf. 14x14½*

1724 A425 2b multicolored .75 .25
Complete booklet, 5 #1724 3.50
a. Souvenir sheet of 1 1.90 1.40
b. Unwmkd., granite paper .25 .25

Issued: Nos. 1724, 1724a, 4/13/97; No. 1724b, 4/13/02. No. 1724b issued only in No. 2017b.
No. 1724a sold for 8b and exists imperf. Values same.

King Bhumibol Adulyadej Type of 1996

Litho, Litho & Engraved (#1728-1729)

Perf. 14x14½

1997, May 5 Wmk. 340

1725 A550 4b blue & red brown 1.25 .25
a. Perf. 13¼, unwmkd. 1.00 .25
b. Unwmkd., granite paper 1.00 .25
1726 A550 5b pur & org brn 1.25 .30
a. Perf. 13½, unwmk., granite paper 1.75 .30
b. Unwmkd., granite paper 1.25 .25
1727 A550 7b pink & green 1.40 1.40

Wmk. 329

Perf. 13½x13

1728 A550 10b org & dk brn 2.25 .90
1729 A550 20b violet & maroon 3.75 1.75
Nos. 1725-1729 (5) 9.90 4.60

Issued: No. 1726a, 12/28/98; No. 1725a, 10/8/99. 1725b, 1726b, 12/1/00.

Waterfowl A563

Designs: No. 1730, Pheasant-tailed jacana. No. 1731, Bronze-winged jacana. No. 1732, Painted stork. No. 1733, Black-winged stilt.

Perf. 11½x12

1997, May 15 Photo. Unwmk.

Granite Paper

No.	Type	Description	Unused	Used
1730	A563	3b multicolored	.55	.55
1731	A563	3b multicolored	.55	.55
1732	A563	7b multicolored	1.25	1.25
1733	A563	7b multicolored	1.25	1.25
a.		Souvenir sheet, #1730-1733	5.50	5.50
b.		As "a," with added inscription	9.00	9.00
		Nos. 1730-1733 (4)	3.60	3.60

No. 1733a sold for 30b. No. 1733b has PACIFIC 97 emblem in sheet margin, while sales price has been removed from sheet margin. No. 1728b sold for 42b.

King Bhumibol Adulyadej, National Telecommunications — A564

2b, King using hand-held radio, "Suthee" aerial. 3b, King using hand-held radio for communication in local areas. 6b, King using computer. 9b, King, classroom using satellite information.

Perf. 14½x14

1997, June 9 Litho. Wmk. 340

No.	Type	Description	Unused	Used
1734	A564	2b multicolored	.35	.35
		Complete booklet, 5 #1734	2.50	
1735	A564	3b multicolored	.50	.50
1736	A564	6b multicolored	1.00	1.00
1737	A564	9b multicolored	1.50	1.50
a.		Souvenir sheet, #1734-1737	6.00	6.00
		Nos. 1734-1737 (4)	3.35	3.35

No. 1737a sold for 30b. For surcharges, see Nos. 2407-2408, 2532, 2586.

Motion Pictures in Thailand, Cent. — A565

Designs: No. 1738, King Rama VII filming movie, film showing King Chulalongkorn's state visit to Europe. No. 1739, Early motion picture equipment, advertisement, Prince Sanbassatra, founder of Thai motion picures. No. 1740, Poster from "Double Luck," band playing in front of movie theater. No. 1741, Open air theater, poster from "Going Astray."

1997, June 10

No.	Type	Description	Unused	Used
1738	A565	3b multicolored	.55	.55
1739	A565	3b multicolored	.55	.55
1740	A565	7b multicolored	1.25	1.25
1741	A565	7b multicolored	1.25	1.25
		Nos. 1738-1741 (4)	3.60	3.60

Faculty of Medicine, Chulalongkorn University, 50th Anniv. A566

King Rama VIII, building, operating room.

1997, June 11

No.	Type	Description	Unused	Used
1742	A566	2b multicolored	.75	.25
		Complete booklet, 5 #1742	2.50	

King Bhumibol Adulyadej Type of 1996

Perf. 14x14½

1997, July 19 Litho. Wmk. 340

No.	Type	Description	Unused	Used
1743	A550	6b grn & gray vio	1.50	.30
1744	A550	9b dk bl & brn org	1.25	.40

Litho. & Engr.

Wmk. 329

Perf. 13½x13

No.	Type	Description	Unused	Used
1745	A550	100b lem & dk bl grn	15.00	4.75
		Nos. 1743-1745 (3)	17.75	5.45

Thai-Russian Diplomatic Relations, Cent. — A567

Design: Peterhof Palace, King Chulalongkorn (King Rama V).

1997, July 3 Litho. ***Perf. 14½x14***

No.	Type	Description	Unused	Used
1746	A567	2b multicolored	.75	.25
		Complete booklet, 5 #1746	3.00	

Asalhapuja Day — A568

3b, Mahosathajataka (scene with man on elephant). 4b, Bhuridattajataka (scene with two men, large snake). 6b, Candakumarajataka (scene with pot of fire, three men on knees, man in sky, Buddha). 7b, Naradajataka (scene with people praising human figure with four arms hovering above roof).

Perf. 11½ Syncopated

1997, July 19 Photo. Unwmk.

Granite Paper

No.	Type	Description	Unused	Used
1747	A568	3b multicolored	.65	.65
a.		Souvenir sheet of 1	1.75	.90
b.		As "a," inscribed in margin	3.25	3.25
1748	A568	4b multicolored	.80	.80
a.		Souvenir sheet of 1	1.75	.90
b.		As "a," inscribed in margin	3.25	3.25
1749	A568	6b multicolored	1.30	1.30
a.		Souvenir sheet of 1	1.75	.90
b.		As "a," inscribed in margin	3.25	3.25
1750	A568	7b multicolored	1.45	1.45
a.		Souvenir sheet of 1	2.75	1.75
b.		Souvenir sheet, #1747-1750	6.00	4.50
c.		As "a," inscribed in margin	27.50	27.50
		Nos. 1747-1750 (4)	4.20	4.20

No. 1747a sold for 6b; No. 1748a for 8b; No. 1749a for 10b; No. 1750a for 12b; No. 1750b for 30b.

Sheet margins of lack value inscriptions, but contain Shanghai '97 exhibition emblem (#1747b, 1748b), Chinese insription; Bangkok '97 exhibition emblem (#1749b, 1750c).

No. 1750b exists imperf. It was issued for sale only at overseas stamp exhibitions.

For surcharges see Nos. 2380, 2382.

1997 Thailand Philatelic Exhibition A569

Houses from: 2b, Northern region. 5b, Central region. 6b, Northeastern region. 9b, Southern region.

Wmk. 329

1997, Aug. 2 Litho. ***Perf. 13½***

No.	Type	Description	Unused	Used
1751	A569	2b multicolored	.30	.25
		Complete booklet, 5 #1751	1.75	
1752	A569	5b multicolored	.80	.70
1753	A569	6b multicolored	.90	.80
1754	A569	9b multicolored	1.40	1.25
a.		Souvenir sheet, #1751-1754	4.50	4.50
		Nos. 1751-1754 (4)	3.40	3.00

No. 1754a sold for 32b.

No. 1754a exists imperf, sold with an exhibition book. Value, $15.

Natl. Communications Day — A570

Perf. 14x14½

1997, Aug. 4 Wmk. 340

No.	Type	Description	Unused	Used
1755	A570	2b multicolored	.75	.25
		Complete booklet, 5 #1755	2.00	

Greeting Stamps — A570a

Lotus flowers: No. 1755A, Nymphaea capensis. No. 1755B, Nymphaea stellata.

Perf. 14x14½

1997, Aug. 4 Litho. Wmk. 387

Booklet Stamps

No.	Type	Description	Unused	Used
1755A	A570a	(2b) multi	*1.50*	*1.50*
1755B	A570a	(2b) multi	*1.50*	*1.50*
c.		Bklt. pane, 5 ea #1755A-1755B + 4 labels	*30.00*	
		Complete bklt., #1755Bc	*35.00*	

Nos. 1755A-1755B were sold only at 7-11 stores, not at post offices or philatelic agencies.

King Bhumibol Adulyadej Type of 1996

Litho. & Engr.

Perf. 13½x13

1997, Aug. 8 Wmk. 329

No.	Type	Description	Unused	Used
1756	A550	25b bl grn & ol blk	8.00	3.25
1757	A550	200b lil rose & vio blk	17.50	9.00

ASEAN, 30th Anniv. A571

Designs: No. 1758, Thi Lo Su Falls, Tak. No. 1759, Luang Chiang Dao Mountain, Chiang Mai. No. 1760, Phromthep Cape, Phuket. No. 1761, Thalu Island, Chumphon.

Perf. 14½x14

1997, Aug. 8 Wmk. 340

No.	Type	Description	Unused	Used
1758	A571	2b multicolored	.25	.25
		Complete booklet, 5 #1758	1.75	
1759	A571	2b multicolored	.25	.25
		Complete booklet, 5 #1759	1.75	
1760	A571	9b multicolored	1.25	1.25
1761	A571	9b multicolored	1.25	1.25
		Nos. 1758-1761 (4)	3.00	3.00

Dinosaurs A572

Designs: 2b, Phuwiangosaurus sirindhornae. 3b, Siamotyrannus isanensis. 6b, Siamosaurus suteethorni. 9b, Psittacosaurus sattayaraki.

Perf. 13½x13 Syncopated

1997, Aug. 28 Photo. Unwmk.

No.	Type	Description	Unused	Used
1762	A572	2b multicolored	.30	.25
		Complete booklet, 5 #1762	1.75	
1763	A572	3b multicolored	.35	.25
1764	A572	6b multicolored	.50	.35
1765	A572	9b multicolored	1.00	.60
a.		Souvenir sheet, #1762-1765	3.25	2.00
		Nos. 1762-1765 (4)	2.15	1.45

No. 1765a sold for 30b.

For surcharge see No. 2355.

King Chulalongkorn's Visit to Switzerland, Cent. — A573

Perf. 14x14½

1997, Sept. 12 Litho. Wmk. 340

No.	Type	Description	Unused	Used
1766	A573	2b multicolored	.75	.25
		Complete booklet, 5 #1766	5.25	

Intl. Letter Writing Week — A574

Winning drawings: No. 1767, Tricycle, combining rickshaw and tricycle. No. 1768, Tricycle with side seat. No. 1769, Motor tricycle. No. 1770. Motor tricycle with light on roof.

Perf. 11½x12

1997, Oct. 5 Photo. Unwmk.

Granite Paper

No.	Type	Description	Unused	Used
1767	A574	3b multicolored	.30	.25
1768	A574	3b multicolored	.30	.25
1769	A574	9b multicolored	.90	.50
1770	A574	9b multicolored	.90	.50
a.		Souvenir sheet, #1767-1770	2.50	2.00
		Nos. 1767-1770 (4)	2.40	1.50

No. 1770a sold for 30b.

Shells of Thailand and Singapore — A575

Designs: No. 1771, Drupa morum. No. 1772, Nerita chamaelon. No. 1773, Littoraria melanostoma. No. 1774, Cryptospira elgans.

1997, Oct. 9 Litho. ***Perf. 11½***

Granite Paper

No.	Type	Description	Unused	Used
1771	A575	2b multicolored	.30	.25
		Complete booklet, 5 #1771	1.75	
1772	A575	2b multicolored	.30	.25
		Complete booklet, 5 #1772	1.75	
1773	A575	9b multicolored	.90	.45
1774	A575	9b multicolored	.90	.45
a.		Souvenir sheet, #1771-7774	2.75	2.75
		Nos. 1771-1774 (4)	2.40	1.40

No. 1774a sold for 30b. See Singapore Nos. 825-828A.

Chalerm Prakiat Energy Conserving Building A576

Perf. 14½x14

1997, Nov. 10 Litho. Wmk. 340

No.	Type	Description	Unused	Used
1775	A576	2b multicolored	.75	.25
		Complete booklet, 5 #1775	2.50	

Christening of Suphannahong Royal Barge, 86th Anniv. — A577

Perf. 11½

1997, Nov. 13 Photo. Unwmk.

Granite Paper

No.	Type	Description	Unused	Used
1776	A577	9b multicolored	.80	.50
a.		Souvenir sheet of 1	2.10	1.50
b.		As "a," ovptd. in margin	4.50	3.00
c.		As "a," ovptd. in margin	7.25	7.25

#1776a, 1776b, 1776c sold for 20b.

The sheet margin of #1776b is ovptd in gold with Thai and Chinese inscriptions for Bangkok/China 98. Issued 10/16/98.

No. 1776c overprinted in margin with World Stamp Expo 2000 emblem in gold. Issued 7/7/00.

For surcharge, see No. 2512.

New Year 1998 — A578

Flowers: No. 1777, Cassia alata. No. 1778, Strophanthus caudatus. No. 1779, Clinacanthus nutans. No. 1780, Acanthus ilicifolius.

1997, Nov. 15 Litho. ***Perf. 13½x13***

Granite Paper

No.	Type	Description	Unused	Used
1777	A578	2b multicolored	.30	.25
1778	A578	2b multicolored	.30	.25
1779	A578	2b multicolored	.30	.25
1780	A578	2b multicolored	.30	.25
a.		Souvenir sheet, #1777-1780	1.40	.90
b.		As "a," with added inscription	3.00	2.75
		Nos. 1777-1780 (4)	1.20	1.00

No. 1780a sold for 15b. No. 1780b contains Indepex '97 exhibition emblem, but no value inscription in sheet margin.

King Bhumibol Adulyadej's 70th Birthday A579

#1781, Playing saxophone. #1782, Painting picture. #1783, Building sailboat. #1784, Wearing gold medal, sailboats. 6b, Taking photograph. 7b, Writing book. 9b, Working at computer.

1997, Dec. 5 Photo. *Perf. 11½*
Granite Paper

1781 A579 2b multicolored .30 .25
1782 A579 2b multicolored .30 .25
1783 A579 2b multicolored .30 .25
1784 A579 2b multicolored .30 .25
1785 A579 6b multicolored .45 .30
1786 A579 7b multicolored .55 .40
1787 A579 9b multicolored .75 .40
Nos. 1781-1787 (7) 2.95 2.10

For surcharge see No. 2381.

A580

Winners in Yuvabadhana Foundation, "Sports Develop Mind and Body" drawing competition: No. 1788, Children in wheelchair race. No. 1789, Flying kites. No. 1790, Gymnastics. No. 1791, Windsurfing.

Perf. 14x14½
1998, Jan. 10 Litho. Wmk. 340

1788 A580 2b multicolored .30 .25
Complete booklet, 5 #1788 3.00
1789 A580 2b multicolored .30 .25
Complete booklet, 5 #1789 3.00
1790 A580 2b multicolored .30 .25
Complete booklet, 5 #1790 3.00
1791 A580 2b multicolored .30 .25
a. Complete booklet, 5 #1791 3.00
Nos. 1788-1791 (4) 1.20 1.00

Natl. Childrens' Day.

A581

1998, Jan. 17 Unwmk.
Granite Paper

1792 A581 2b multicolored .40 .25
Complete booklet, 5 #1792 3.50

20th Asia Pacific Dental Congress.

A582

1998, Feb. 3 Wmk. 340

1793 A582 2b multicolored .30 .25
Complete booklet, 5 #1793 3.25

Veteran's Day, 50th anniv.

King Bhumibol Adulyadej Type of 1996

1998, Feb. 25 Photo. *Perf. 11½x12*
Granite Paper

1794 A550 50s dk ol & lt ol .35 .25

Litho. & Engr.
Perf. 13½x13
Wmk. 329

1795 A550 50b dp vio & dk grn 6.00 2.25

A583

Perf. 14x14½
1998, Mar. 27 Litho. Wmk. 340

1796 A583 2b Queen Sirikit .75 .25
Complete booklet, 5 #1796 4.25

1998 Thai Red Cross Fair.

Heritage Conservation Day Type of 1993

Paintings of Phanomrung Historical Park: 3b, Main Tower. 4b, Minor Tower. 6b, Scripture Repository. 7b, Lintel depicting Vishnu sleeping in ocean, doorway of Main Tower.

Perf. 14½x14
1998, Apr. 2 Litho. Wmk. 340

1797 A477 3b multicolored .30 .25
1798 A477 4b multicolored .35 .25
1799 A477 6b multicolored .45 .45
1800 A477 7b multicolored .55 .50
a. Souvenir sheet, #1797-1800 2.75 2.75

No. 1800a sold for 27b.

Songkran Day Type of 1991

Design: Demon on tiger's back, zodiac.

1998-2002 *Perf. 14x14½*

1801 A425 2b multicolored .75 .25
Complete booklet, 5 #1801 3.25
a. Souvenir sheet of 1 1.75 1.00
b. As "a," inscribed in margin 3.50 2.25
c. Unwmkd., granite paper .25 .25

Issued: Nos. 1801-1801b, 4/13/98. No. 1801c, 4/13/02. No. 1801c issued only in No. 2017b.

No. 1801a sold for 8b and exists imperf. Values same.

Sheet margin of No. 1801b contains flags of Thailand and China (PRC), Thai and Chinese inscriptions, no value inscription, and exists imperf.

No. 1801b sold for 8b and was issued 10/16/98.

Wild Cats — A584

Paintings: 2b, Felis viverrina. 4b, Panthera tigris. 6b, Panthera pardus. 8b, Felis chaus.

1998, Apr. 13 *Perf. 14½x14*

1802 A584 2b multicolored .40 .25
Complete booklet, 5 #1802 3.50
1803 A584 4b multicolored .60 .25
1804 A584 6b multicolored .60 .45
1805 A584 8b multicolored .85 .50
a. Souvenir sheet, #1802-1805 2.75 2.25
Nos. 1802-1805 (4) 2.45 1.45

No. 1805a sold for 30b.

AEROTHAI (Aeronautical Radio of Thailand, Ltd.), 50th Anniv. A585

1998, Apr. 15

1806 A585 2b multicolored .40 .25
Complete booklet, 5 #1806 3.00

Visakhapuja Day — A586

Paintings of the "Ten Jataka Stories:" 3b, Riding horse above buildings, Vidhurajataka. 4b, In chariot, Vessantarajataka. 6b, Two figures seated before larger figure, Vessantarajataka. 7b, Figures in front of building, Vessantarajataka.

1998, May 10 *Perf. 13½*

1807 A586 3b multicolored .30 .25
1808 A586 4b multicolored .35 .25
1809 A586 6b multicolored .55 .35
1810 A586 7b multicolored .65 .45
a. Souvenir sheet, #1807-1810 2.50 1.75
Nos. 1807-1810 (4) 1.85 1.30

No. 1810a sold for 30b.

Adm. Abhakara Kiartiwongse (1880-1923), Father of Royal Thai Navy — A587

1998, May 19 *Perf. 14½x14*

1811 A587 2b multicolored .35 .25
Complete booklet, 5 #1811 5.00

Educational Development A588

Perf. 14½x14
1998, June 15 Litho. Wmk. 340

1812 A588 2b multicolored .30 .25
Complete booklet, 5 #1812 4.00

King Chulalongkorn's 1st State Visit to Europe, Cent. — A589

Unwmk.
1998, July 1 Litho. *Perf. 13*
Granite Paper

1813 A589 6b multicolored .70 .45

Litho. & Embossed

1814 A589 20b multicolored 1.60 1.10

Intl. Year of the Ocean A590

2b, Orchaella brevirostris. 3b, Tursiops truncatus. 6b, Physeter catodon. 9b, Dugong dugon.

1998, July 19 Litho. *Perf. 14½x14*
Granite Paper

1815 A590 2b multicolored .35 .25
Complete booklet, 5 #1815 2.75
1816 A590 3b multicolored .35 .25
1817 A590 6b multicolored .50 .40
1818 A590 9b multicolored .80 .50
a. Souvenir sheet, #1815-1818 2.75 2.75
Nos. 1815-1818 (4) 2.00 1.40

No. 1818a sold for 30b.
For surcharges see Nos. 2356-2357.

King Bhumibol Adulyadej Type of 1996

1998 Photo. Unwmk. *Perf. 11½x12*
Granite Paper

1819 A550 2b carmine .50 .25
1820 A550 9b violet & brn org 1.25 .45

For surcharges, see Nos. 2335, 2585.

Irrigation Engineering in Thailand, 60th Anniv. A591

Perf. 14½x14
1998, Aug. 1 Litho. Unwmk.
Granite Paper

1821 A591 2b multicolored .75 .25
Complete booklet, 5 #1821 3.00

Natl. Communications Day — A592

1998, Aug. 4 Granite Paper

1822 A592 2b multicolored .75 .25
Complete booklet, 5 #1822 3.00

School of Political Science, Chulalongkorn University, 50th Anniv. A593

1998, Aug. 19 Granite Paper

1823 A593 2b multicolored .75 .25
Complete booklet, 5 #1823 3.00

Sukhothai Thammathirat Open University, Award for Excellence A594

1998, Sept. 5 Litho. *Perf. 14½x14*
Granite Paper

1824 A594 2b multicolored .75 .25
Complete booklet, 5 #1824 3.00

Amazing Thailand, 1998-99, Thai Arts and Culture — A595

1998, Sept. 15 *Perf. 13½*
Granite Paper

1825 A595 3b With bow & arrow .30 .25
1826 A595 3b Combat .30 .25
1827 A595 7b Seizing opponent .70 .50
1828 A595 7b Sky hovering .70 .50
Nos. 1825-1828 (4) 2.00 1.50

Chinese Stone Statues — A596

Warriors holding: No. 1829, Staff with loop. No. 1830, Spear with slightly curved blade. No. 1831, Mace. No. 1832, Spear with jagged blade.

1998, Sept. 15 *Perf. 14x14½*
Granite Paper

1829 A596 2b multicolored .30 .25
Complete booklet, 5 #1829 2.50
1830 A596 2b multicolored .30 .25
Complete booklet, 5 #1830 3.25
1831 A596 10b multicolored .75 .50
1832 A596 10b multicolored .75 .50
a. Souvenir sheet, #1829-1832, perf 13¼ 2.75 2.00
b. As "a," with added marginal inscription 10.00 8.00
Nos. 1829-1832 (4) 2.10 1.50

China 1999 World Philatelic Exhibition (#1832b). #1832a-1832b sold for 35b. #1832 is perf 13¼ and was issued 8/21/99.

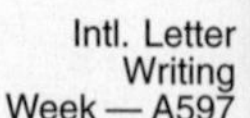

Intl. Letter Writing Week — A597

Himavanta mythical animals created by ancient Thai artists: No. 1836, Kraisara Rajasiha, 3 king lions, white body, golden collars. No. 1837, Gajasiha, 2 tusked lions. No. 1838, Kesara Singha, 2 hoofed lions. No. 1839, Singha, 3 gray lions.

Perf. 11½

1998, Oct. 3 Photo. Unwmk.

Granite Paper

1836 A597 2b multicolored .30 .25
Complete booklet, 5 #1836 3.00
1837 A597 2b multicolored .30 .25
Complete booklet, 5 #1837 3.25
1838 A597 12b multicolored .80 .60
1839 A597 12b multicolored .80 .60
a. Souvenir sheet, #1836-1839 3.00 2.50
Nos. 1836-1839 (4) 2.20 1.70

No. 1839a sold for 40b.

Thai Presidency of the Intl. Assoc. of Lions Clubs — A598

1998, Oct. 8 Litho. *Perf. 14½x14*

Granite Paper

1840 A598 2b multicolored .40 .25
Complete booklet, 5 #1840 4.00

New Year 1999 — A599

Flowers: No. 1841, Barleria lupulina. No. 1842, Gloriosa superba. No. 1843, Asclepias curassavica. No. 1844, Sesamum indicum.

Perf. 14½x14

1998, Nov. 15 Photo. Unwmk.

Granite Paper

1841 A599 2b multicolored .30 .25
1842 A599 2b multicolored .30 .25
1843 A599 2b multicolored .30 .25
1844 A599 2b multicolored .30 .25
a. Souvenir sheet, #1841-1844 1.90 1.25
Nos. 1841-1844 (4) 1.20 1.00

No. 1844a sold for 15b.

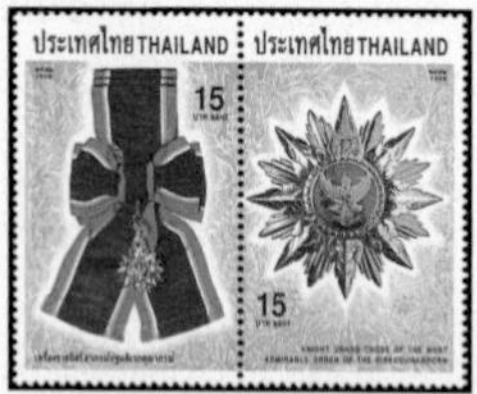

Knight Grand Cross, Most Admirable Order of the Direkgunabhorn — A600

Perf. 14x14½

1998, Dec. 5 Litho. Unwmk.

Granite Paper

1845 15b shown .90 .45
1846 15b Decoration .90 .45
a. A600 Pair, #1845-1846 2.00 .90

Children's Day — A601

Paintings from competition, "Sports develop body and mind:" No. 1847, Sepak Takraw (game of kicking ball over net). No. 1848, Swimming. No. 1849, Volleyball. No. 1850, Equestrian sports.

Perf. 14½x14

1999, Jan. 9 Litho. Unwmk.

Granite Paper

1847 A601 2b multicolored .30 .25
Complete booklet, 5 #1847 3.00
1848 A601 2b multicolored .30 .25
Complete booklet, 5 #1848 3.00
1849 A601 2b multicolored .30 .25
Complete booklet, 5 #1849 3.00
1850 A601 2b multicolored .30 .25
Complete booklet, 5 #1850 3.00
Nos. 1847-1850 (4) 1.20 1.00

Asian and Pacific Decade of Disabled Persons A602

1999, Jan. 10 Granite Paper

1851 A602 2b multicolored .45 .25
a. Complete booklet, 5 #1851 3.25

Thai Rice Production A603

#1852, Planting rice. #1853, Harvesting rice by hand. #1854, Harvesting rice with machinery. #1855, Rice in field, bowl of rice.

1999, Feb. 25 Litho. *Perf. 14½x14*

Granite Paper

1852 A603 6b multicolored .55 .40
1853 A603 6b multicolored .55 .40
1854 A603 12b multicolored .95 .75
1855 A603 12b multicolored .95 .75
a. Souvenir sheet, #1852-1855 3.25 3.25
Nos. 1852-1855 (4) 3.00 2.30

No. 1855a sold for 45b.

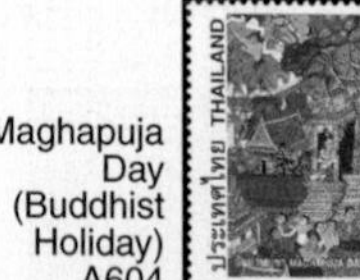

Maghapuja Day (Buddhist Holiday) A604

Designs: 3b, Birth of Mahajanaka. 6b, Mani Mekkhala carrying Mahajanaka to Mithila City. 9b, Two mango trees. 15b, Mahajanaka founding an educational institution.

1999, Mar. 1 Litho. *Perf. 13½*

Granite Paper

1856 A604 3b multicolored .30 .25
1857 A604 6b multicolored .60 .45
1858 A604 9b multicolored .80 .60
1859 A604 15b multicolored 1.25 1.00
a. Souvenir sheet, #1856-1859 3.75 3.00
Nos. 1856-1859 (4) 2.95 2.30

No. 1859a sold for 45b.

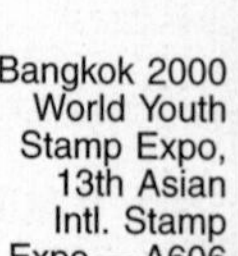

Somdetch Phra Sri Savarindira Baromma Raja Devi Phra Phan Vassa Ayika Chao, Queen Grandmother — A605

Perf. 14x14½

1999, Mar. 30 Litho. Wmk. 340

1860 A605 2b multicolored .75 .25
Complete booklet, 5 #1860 4.25

1999 Red Cross Fair.

Bangkok 2000 World Youth Stamp Expo, 13th Asian Intl. Stamp Expo — A606

Thai children's games: No. 1861, Kite flying. No. 1862, Wheel rolling. No. 1863, Catching last one in line (children going under arms). No. 1864, Snatching baby from mother snake.

Perf. 14½x14

1999, Mar. 30 Unwmk.

Granite Paper

1861 A606 2b multicolored .35 .25
1862 A606 2b multicolored .35 .25
1863 A606 15b multicolored 1.10 1.00
1864 A606 15b multicolored 1.10 1.00
a. Souvenir sheet, #1861-1864, perf. 13½ 3.50 3.00
Nos. 1861-1864 (4) 2.90 2.50

No. 1864a sold for 45b.

Heritage Conservation Day — A607

Various Thai silk designs for "Mudmee" textiles.

1999, Apr. 2 *Perf. 14x14½*

Granite Paper

1865 A607 2b bl grn & multi .30 .25
Complete booklet, 5 #1865 3.00
1866 A607 4b red & multi .45 .25
1867 A607 12b vermilion & multi 1.00 .90
1868 A607 15b black & multi 1.40 1.10
a. Souvenir sheet, #1865-1868 3.50 3.00
Nos. 1865-1868 (4) 3.15 2.50

No. 1868a sold for 45b. No. 1868a exists imperforate.

Songkran Day Type of 1991

Design: Woman on rabbit's back, zodiac.

1999, Apr. 13 Granite Paper

1869 A425 2b multicolored .75 .25
Complete booklet, 5 #1869 3.00
a. Souvenir sheet of 1 1.40 1.40
b. As "a," with added marginal inscription 5.00 5.00

China 1999 World Philatelic Exhibition (#1869b). #1869a-1869b sold for 8b and exist imperf. Values same.

Issued: #1869b, 8/21.

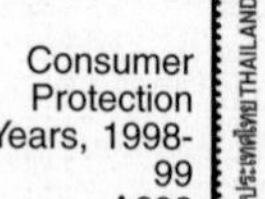

Consumer Protection Years, 1998-99 A608

1999, Apr. 30 *Perf. 14½x14*

Granite Paper

1870 A608 2b multicolored .75 .25
Complete booklet, 5 #1870 3.50

King Bhumibol Adulyadej's 72nd Birthday — A609

Royal palaces: No. 1871, Chitralada Villa, Dusit Palace, Bangkok, tree branch at UL. No. 1872, Phu Phing Ratchaniwet Palace, circular drive, white fence. No. 1873, Phu Phan Ratchaniwet Palace, adjoining buildings, light posts. No. 1874, Thaksin Ratchaniwet Palace, four trees reaching to second story windows.

1999, May 5 Photo. *Perf. 11½*

Granite Paper

1871 A609 6b multicolored .65 .45
1872 A609 6b multicolored .65 .45
1873 A609 6b multicolored .65 .45
1874 A609 6b multicolored .65 .45
a. Souvenir sheet, #1871-1874 3.75 3.00
Nos. 1871-1874 (4) 2.60 1.80

No. 1874a sold for 40b.

Political Science Dept., Thammasat University, 50th Anniv. — A610

1999, June 14 Litho. *Perf. 14x14½*

1875 A610 3b multicolored .75 .25

King Bhumibol Adulyadej Type of 1996

Litho. & Engr.

1999 Wmk. 329 *Perf. 13*

1876 A550 12b bl grn & bl 1.25 .80
1877 A550 15b yel brn & grn 2.00 .45
1878 A550 30b pink & brown 2.90 2.00

Size: 25x30mm

Perf. 12¾x13¼

1879 A550 500b org & claret 35.00 19.00
Nos. 1876-1879 (4) 41.15 22.25

Issued: 12b, 15b, 30b, 7/1; 500b, 9/10.

UPU, 125th Anniv. A611

Designs: 2b, Floating Vessel of Light Festival. 15b, Buddhist Candle Festival, Ubon Ratchathani.

1999, July 1 Litho. *Perf. 14½x14*

Granite Paper

1880 A611 2b multicolored .35 .25
Complete booklet, 5 #1880 2.90
1881 A611 15b multicolored 1.10 1.00

Customs Dept., 125th Anniv. A612

1999, July 3

1882 A612 6b multicolored .75 .45

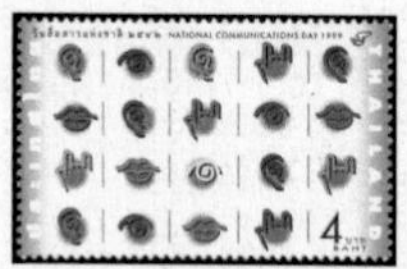

Natl. Communications Day — A613

1999, Aug. 4 Litho. *Perf. 14½x14*

Granite Paper

1883 A613 4b multicolored .75 .25

Thaipex '99 — A614

1999, Aug. 4 Granite Paper

Color of Rabbits

1884 A614 6b black & white .55 .40
1885 A614 6b gldn brn, brn .55 .40
1886 A614 12b white .95 .70
1887 A614 12b gray .95 .70
a. Souvenir sheet, #1884-1887, perf. 13½ 4.25 4.25
Nos. 1884-1887 (4) 3.00 2.20

No. 1887a sold for 50b and exists imperf. Value, $15.

Bangkok 2000 Stamp Exhibition A615

Scenes from Thai folk tales and literature: No. 1888, Boy on dragon-like horse. No. 1889, Rishi transforming tiger cub and calf into humans. No. 1890, Boy exiting conch shell. No. 1891, Children playing with kitchenware.

1999, Aug. 4 *Perf. 14½x14*

Granite Paper

1888 A615 2b multicolored .35 .25
1889 A615 2b multicolored .35 .25
1890 A615 15b multicolored 1.10 1.00
1891 A615 15b multicolored 1.10 1.00
a. Souvenir sheet, #1888-1891, perf. 13½ 3.75 3.00
Nos. 1888-1891 (4) 2.90 2.50

No. 1891a sold for 45b.

King Bhumibol Adulyadej's 72nd Birthday — A616

King: No. 1892, On father's knee. No. 1893, With mother, sister and brother. No. 1894, With brother, in suits. No. 1895, With brother, in military uniforms. No. 1896, With wife on wedding day. No. 1897, At coronation ceremony. No. 1898, As Buddhist monk. No. 1899, With Queen, Prince and Princesses. No. 1900, Wearing royal robe.

1999, Sept. 10 Photo. *Perf. 11¾*
Granite Paper

1892 A616 3b multicolored .35 .25
1893 A616 3b multicolored .35 .25
1894 A616 3b multicolored .35 .25
1895 A616 6b multicolored .60 .35
1896 A616 6b multicolored .60 .35
1897 A616 6b multicolored .60 .35
1898 A616 12b multicolored 1.25 .80
1899 A616 12b multicolored 1.25 .80
1900 A616 12b multicolored 1.25 .80
a. Souvenir sheet, #1892-1900 10.50 9.00
Nos. 1892-1900 (9) 6.60 4.20

No. 1900a sold for 90b.

Intl. Year of Older Persons A617

1999, Oct. 1 Litho. *Perf. 14½x14*
Granite Paper

1901 A617 2b multi .75 .25
Complete booklet, 5 #1901 3.50

Bauhinia Variegata — A618

Intl. Letter Writing Week: No. 1903, Bombax ceiba. No. 1904, Radermachera ignea (orange flowers). No. 1905, Bretschneidera sinensis (pink flowers).

1999, Oct. 2 *Perf. 14x14½*
Granite Paper

1902 A618 2b shown .35 .25
Complete booklet, 5 #1902 2.40
1903 A618 2b multi .35 .25
Complete booklet, 5 #1903 3.25
1904 A618 12b multi 1.10 .80
1905 A618 12b multi 1.10 .80
a. Souvenir sheet, #1902-1905, perf. 13¼ 3.00 2.75
Nos. 1902-1905 (4) 2.90 2.10

No. 1905a sold for 35b.

King Bhumibol Adulyadej's 72nd Birthday A619

King: #1906, And vehicle. #1907, And Buddhist monks. #1908, And Queen. #1909, And soldiers. #1910, And crowd. #1911, And disabled boy. #1912, Wearing green army uniform. #1913, In white suit with camera. #1914, With crowd waving flags.

1999, Oct. 21 Photo. *Perf. 14½*
Granite Paper

1906 A619 3b multi .30 .25
1907 A619 3b multi .30 .25
1908 A619 3b multi .30 .25
1909 A619 6b multi .50 .35
1910 A619 6b multi .50 .35
1911 A619 6b multi .50 .35
1912 A619 12b multi 1.10 .80
1913 A619 12b multi 1.10 .80
1914 A619 12b multi 1.10 .80
a. Souvenir sheet, #1906-1914 7.25 6.25
Nos. 1906-1914 (9) 5.70 4.20

No. 1914a sold for 90b. Numbers have been reserved for additional stamps in this set.

Design A39 — A620

Litho. & Embossed with Foil Application

1999, Dec. 5 Wmk. 387 *Perf. 13¼*

1915 A620 100b blue & bronze 7.50 7.50
1916 A620 100b blue & silver 7.50 7.50
1917 A620 100b blue & gold 7.50 7.50
a. Souvenir sheet, #1915-1917 27.50 20.00
Nos. 1915-1917 (3) 22.50 22.50

King Bhumibol Adulyadej's 72nd birthday.
No. 1917a sold for 350b.

New Year 2000 — A621

Medicinal plants: No. 1918, Thunbergia laurifolia. No. 1919, Gmelina arborea. No. 1920, Prunus cerasoides. No. 1921, Fagraea fragrans.

Perf. 14½x14¼
1999, Nov. 15 Litho.
Granite Paper

1918 A621 2b multi .30 .25
1919 A621 2b multi .30 .25
1920 A621 2b multi .30 .25
a. Souv. sheet, 5 ea #1918-1920 + 10 labels 30.00
1921 A621 2b multi .35 .25
a. Souvenir sheet, #1918-1921 2.00 1.75
Nos. 1918-1921 (4) 1.25 1.00

No. 1921a sold for 15b.
No. 1920a was issued 3/25/00 and sold for 60b. For an additional fee the blank labels could be personalized with photos taken at a booth not operated by the Thailand postal authorities at the Bangkok 2000 Stamp Exhibition.

Investiture of Crown Prince Vajiralongkorn, 27th Anniv. — A622

1999, Dec. 28 *Perf. 14x14½*
Granite Paper

1922 A622 3b multi .60 .25

Lake of Lilies, Thale Noi A623

Kulap Khao Flowers, Doi Chang Dao A624

Krachieo Flowers, Pa Hin Ngam A625

Bua Tong Flowers, Doi Mae Ukor A626

Perf. 14½x14¼
2000 Litho. Unwmk.
Granite Paper

1923 A623 Sheet of 12, #a-l 5.00 3.50
a.-l. 3b Any single .35 .35
1924 A624 Sheet of 12, #a-l 5.00 3.50
a.-l. 3b Any single .35 .35
1925 A625 Sheet of 12, #a-l 5.00 3.50
a.-l. 3b Any single .35 .35
1926 A626 Sheet of 12, #a-l 5.00 3.50
a.-l. 3b Any single .35 .35
Nos. 1923-1926 (4) 20.00 14.00

Issued: #1923, 1/1; #1924, 2/25; #1925, 7/16. #1926, 11/15.

Bees — A627

#1927, Apis andreniformis. #1928, Apis florea. #1929, Apis cerana. #1930, Apis dorsata.

2000, Mar. 19 Photo. *Perf. 11¾*
Granite Paper

1927-1930 A627 3b Set of 4 1.75 1.40

Souvenir Sheets of 1

1927a-1930a Set of 4 4.50 3.00

Nos. 1927a-1930a do not have white margin on stamps and sold for 8b each.

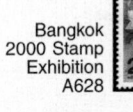

Bangkok 2000 Stamp Exhibition A628

Ceremonies: #1931, 2b, 1st month blessing (family & baby). #1932, 2b, Tonsure. #1933, 15b, Teacher respect (teacher, 3 children). #1934, 15b, Novice ordination.

2000, Mar. 25 Litho. *Perf. 14½x14*
Granite Paper

1931-1934 A628 Set of 4 3.25 3.25
a. Souvenir sheet, #1931-1934, perf. 13½x14 4.00 3.50

No. 1934a sold for 45b. No 1934a exists imperf. Value, $15.

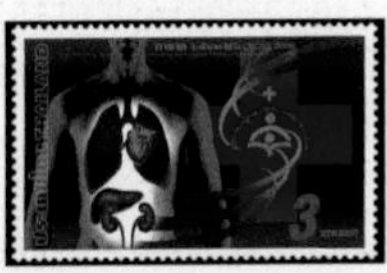
Thai Red Cross Fair — A629

2000, Mar. 30 *Perf. 14½x14*
Granite Paper

1935 A629 3b multi .75 .35

Thai Heritage Conservation A630

Chok cloths from: 3b, Hat Seio. 6b, Mae Chaem. 8b, Ban Rai. 12b, Khu Bua.

2000, Apr. 2 Wmk. 387 *Perf. 13¼*

1936-1939 A630 Set of 4 3.50 3.25
a. Souvenir sheet, #1936-1939 4.00 3.50

No. 1939a sold for 40b.

Songkran Day Type of 1991
Perf. 14x14½
2000, Apr. 13 Litho. Unwmk.
Granite Paper

1940 A425 2b Angel on serpent .75 .25
Booklet, 5 #1940 3.75
a. Souvenir sheet of 1 1.40 .75

No. 1940a sold for 8b and exists imperf.

50th Wedding Anniv. of King and Queen A631

No. 1941 — King Bhumibol Adulyadej and Queen Sirikit: a, Sitting on grass. b, Standing. c, Sitting on thrones. d, With family. e, Standing, wearing regalia.

2000, Apr. 28 Photo. *Perf. 11¾*
Granite Paper

1941 Vert. strip of 5 5.00 5.00
a.-e. A631 10b Any single 1.00 1.00

Asalhapuja Day — A632

2000, July 16 Litho. *Perf. 14x14½*
Granite Paper

1942 A632 3b multi .75 .35

Crown Prince Maha Vajiralongkorn, 48th Birthday — A633

2000, July 28 *Perf. 14½x14*
Granite Paper

1943 A633 2b multi .75 .25
Booklet, 5 #1943 5.00
a. Souvenir sheet of 1, perf. 13¼ 1.40 .80

No. 1943a sold for 8b.

Natl. Communications Day — A634

2000, Aug. 4 Granite Paper

1944 A634 3b multi .75 .25

A635

Intl. Letter Writing Week — A636

Various tea sets.

Perf. 14½x14

2000, Oct. 7 Litho. Unwmk.

Granite Paper

1945 A635 6b shown .55 .55
1946 A635 6b multi, diff. .55 .55
1947 A636 12b shown 1.05 1.10
1948 A636 12b multi, diff. 1.05 1.10
a. Souvenir sheet, #1945-1948, perf. 13¼ 4.00 3.50
Nos. 1945-1948 (4) 3.20 3.30

No. 1948a sold for 45b.

Princess Srinagarindra, Birth Cent. — A637

2000, Oct. 21 Granite Paper

1949 A637 2b multi .75 .25
Booklet, 5 #1949 3.75
a. Souvenir sheet of 1, perf. 13¼ 1.60 .80

No. 1949a sold for 8b.

Royal Barge Anantanakkharat — A638

Perf. 13¼x14

2000, Nov. 15 Photo. Wmk. 340

1950 A638 9b multi 1.00 .75
a. Souvenir sheet of 1 2.00 1.60

No. 1950a sold for 15b. No. 1950a exists with margin emblems for the Anaheim 2000 Exhibition.

New Year 2001 — A639

Flowers: No. 1951, 2b, Clerodendrum philippinum. No. 1952, 2b, Capparis micracantha. No. 1953, 2b, Belamcanda chinensis. No. 1954, 2b, Memecylon caeruleum.

Perf. 14½x14¼

2000, Nov. 15 Litho. Unwmk.

Granite Paper

1951-1954 A639 Set of 4 1.25 .85
a. Souvenir sheet, #1951-1954 2.00 1.60

No. 1954a sold for 15b.

Parrots — A640

Designs: 2b, Psittacula alexandri. 5b, Psittacula eupatria. 8b, Psittinus cyanurus. 10b, Psittacula roseata.

2001, Jan. 13 ***Perf. 14x14½***

Granite Paper

1955-1958 A640 Set of 4 3.00 2.25
Booklet, 5 #1955 3.75
a. Souvenir sheet, #1955-1958, perf. 13¼ 4.50 3.25
b. As "a," without price and with show emblem in margin 20.00 15.00

No. 1955a sold for 35b. No. 1955b, Hong Kong 2001 Stamp Exhibition, sold for 50b.

King Chulalongkorn and Land Deed — A641

2001, Feb. 17 Granite Paper

1959 A641 5b multi .75 .45

Dept. of Lands, cent.

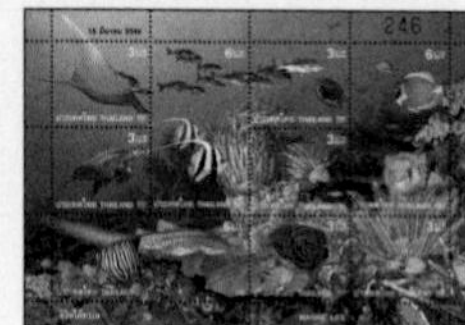

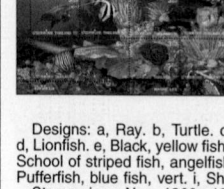

Marine Life A642

Designs: a, Ray. b, Turtle. c, Jellyfish, fish. d, Lionfish. e, Black, yellow fish, coral. f, Eel. g, School of striped fish, angelfish, coral, vert. h, Pufferfish, blue fish, vert. i, Shark, fish.

Stamp sizes: Nos. 1960a-1960f, 29x24mm, Nos. 1960g-1960h, 29x48mm. No. 1960i, 58x42mm.

Perf. 13¾x14¼

2001, Mar. 15 Photo.

Granite Paper

1960 A642 Sheet of 9 5.50 5.50
a.-f. 3b Any single .45 .35
g.-i. 6b Any single .65 .55

For surcharge, see No. 2511.

Gems — A643

Designs: 3b, Diamond. 4b, Green sapphire. 6b, Pearl. 12b, Blue sapphire.

2001 Litho. ***Perf. 14½x14***

Granite Paper

1961-1964 A643 Set of 4 2.25 2.25
a. Souvenir sheet, #1961-1964, perf. 13½x14 4.50 3.25
b. As "a," ovptd. in margin in gold 13.00 11.00

Issued, Nos. 1961-1964a, 3/30; No. 1964b, 6/9.

No. 1964a sold for 35b.

No. 1964b has Belgica 2001 emblem overprint.

Red Cross — A644

Perf. 14½x14

2001, Apr. 1 Litho. Unwmk.

Granite Paper

1965 A644 4b multi .75 .25

Ancient Brocades From Nakhon Si Thammarat National Museum — A645

Colors of brocade: 2b, Orange red, lilac, and gold. 3b, Green and gold. No. 1968, 10b, Orange and gold. No. 1969, 10b, Bright pink and gold.

2001, Apr. 2 ***Perf. 14x14½***

Granite Paper

1966-1969 A645 Set of 4 2.75 2.25
Booklet, 5 #1966 3.00
a. Souvenir sheet, #1966-1969, perf. 13¼ 3.25 3.25

Heritage Conservation Day.

No. 1969a sold for 35b.

Songkran Day Type of 1991

2b, Man on snake, zodiac.

Perf. 13½x13¾

2001-2002 Wmk. 387

1970 A425 2b multicolored .75 .25
Booklet, 5 #1970 3.00
a. Souvenir sheet of 1 1.40 1.10
b. Unwmkd., granite paper, perf. 14x14½ *3.00 3.00*

Issued: Nos. 1970-1970a, 4/13/01. No. 1970b, 4/13/02. No. 1970b issued only in No. 2017b.

No. 1970a sold for 8b and exists imperf.

Visakhapuja Day — A646

2001, May 7 Unwmk. ***Perf. 14x14½***

Granite Paper

1971 A646 3b multi .75 .35

Demon Statues — A647

Designs: 2b, Maiyarap. 5b, Wirunchambang. 10b, Thotsakan. 12b, Sahatsadecha.

Perf. 14x14½

2001, June 13 Litho. Unwmk.

Granite Paper

1972-1975 A647 Set of 4 3.50 2.60
Booklet, 5 #1972 4.00
a. Souvenir sheet, #1972-1975, perf. 13½ 4.50 3.25

No. 1975a sold for 33b.

Prince Purachartra Jayakara and Rotary Intl. Emblem — A648

2001, July 1 Granite Paper

1976 A648 3b multi .50 .25

Rotary Intl. in Thailand, 66th anniv.

Mushrooms A649

Designs: 2b, Schizophyllum commune. 3b, Lentinus giganteus. 5b, Pleurotus citrinopileatus. 10b, Pleurotus flabellatus.

2001, July 4 Photo. ***Perf. 13¾x14***

Granite Paper

1977-1980 A649 Set of 4 2.75 2.00
Booklet, 5 # 1977 3.75
a. Souvenir sheet, #1977-1980, perf. 13½ 4.50 3.25

No. 1980 sold for 26b.

Insects A650

Designs: 2b, Cheirotonus parryi. 5b, Mouhotia batesi. 6b, Cladognathus giraffa. 12b, Mormolyce phyllodes.

2001, July 4 Wmk. 329 ***Perf. 13½***

1981-1984 A650 Set of 4 2.90 2.25
Booklet, 5 #1981 3.75
a. Souvenir sheet, #1981-1984 4.00 4.00
b. As "a," with Phila Nippon '01 emblem in margin 13.00 12.00

No. 1984a sold for 34b.

No. 1984b sold for 34b, and was issued 8/1.

Natl. Communications Day — A651

Perf. 14½x14

2001, Aug. 4 Litho. Unwmk.

Granite Paper

1985 A651 4b multi .75 .45

Thaipex '01 — A652

Various domesticated fowl: 3b, 4b, 6b, 12b.

2001, Aug. 4 Photo. ***Perf. 13¼***

Granite Paper

1986-1989 A652 Set of 4 3.00 2.25
a. Souvenir sheet, #1986-1989 4.50 3.25

No. 1989a sold for 33b. No. 1989a also exists imperf. Value, $13.

Queen Suriyothai, Heroine of Thailand — A653

2001, Aug. 12 Litho. ***Perf. 14x14¾***

Granite Paper

1990 A653 3b multi .75 .45
a. Souvenir sheet of 1, perf. 13¼ 2.75 1.25

No. 1990a sold for 10b.

Queen Sirikit's Visit to the People's Republic of China — A654

2001, Aug. 12 ***Perf. 14¾x14***

Granite Paper

1991 A654 5b multi .75 .45

Butterflies A655

Designs: 2b, Pachliopta aristolochiae goniopeltis. 4b, Rhinopalpa polynice. 10b, Poritia erycinoides. 12b, Spindasis lohita.

Perf. 13½ Syncopated

2001, Sept. 10 Photo.

1992-1995 A655 Set of 4 3.25 2.75
Booklet, 5 #1992 3.00
a. Souvenir sheet, #1992-1995 4.00 4.00
b. As "a," with Hafnia '01 emblem in margin 16.00 16.00

No. 1995a sold for 40b.

No. 1995b issued 11/16. No. 1995b sold for 43b.

Intl. Letter Writing Week — A656

Medicinal herbs: 2b, Piper nigrum. 3b, Solanum trilobatum. 5b, Boesenbergia rotunda. 10b, Ocimum tenuiflorum.

Perf. 14x14½

2001, Oct. 6 Litho. Unwmk.

Granite Paper

1996-1999 A656 Set of 4 2.75 1.90
Booklet, 5 #1996 3.75
a. Souvenir sheet, #1996-1999, perf. 13½x13¼ 3.75 3.25

No. 1999a sold for 25b.

Police Cadet Academy, Cent. — A657

2001, Oct. 13 Litho. *Perf. 14½x14*

Granite Paper

2000 A657 5b multi .75 .55

Royal Barge Anekkachat Puchong — A658

2001, Nov. 15 Photo. *Perf. 14¼*

Granite Paper

2001 A658 9b multi 1.00 .90
a. Souvenir sheet of 1 2.25 2.25

No. 2001a sold for 17b.

New Year 2002 — A659

Flowers: No. 2002, 2b, Pedicularis siamensis. No. 2003, 2b, Schoutenia glomerata. No. 2004, 2b, Gentiana crassa. No. 2005, 2b, Colquhounia coccinea.

2001, Nov. 15 Litho. *Perf. 14x14½*

Granite Paper

2002-2005 A659 Set of 4 1.10 1.00
a. Souvenir sheet, #2002-2005 2.25 1.75

No. 2005a sold for 11b.

Laying of Foundation Stone for Suvarnabhumi Airport Passenger Terminal A660

2002, Jan. 19 Litho. *Perf. 14½x14*

Granite Paper

2006 A660 3b multi .50 .35

Rose — A661

2002, Feb. 1 *Perf. 13¾*

Granite Paper

2007 A661 4b multi 3.75 1.50

12th World Congress of Gastroenterology A662

2002, Feb. 24 *Perf. 14x14½*

Granite Paper

2008 A662 3b multi .50 .30

Communications Authority of Thailand, 25th Anniv. — A663

No. 2009: a, Satellite dish, CAT Telecom Co. emblem. b, Envelope, mailbox, Thailand Post emblem.

2002, Feb. 25 *Perf. 14½x14*

Granite Paper

2009 A663 3b Horiz. pair, #a-b 1.10 .75
c. Souvenir sheet, #2009, perf. 13¼x13½ 1.60 1.10

No. 2009c sold for 10b.

Maghapuja Day — A664

2002, Feb. 26 *Perf. 14½x14*

Granite Paper

2010 A664 3b multi 1.60 1.10

2002 Red Cross Fair — A665

2002, Mar. 30 Granite Paper

2011 A665 4b multi .50 .40

Ministry of Transport and Communications, 90th Anniv. — A666

2002, Apr. 1 Litho. *Perf. 14½x14*

Granite Paper

2012 A666 3b multi .75 .30

Heritage Conservation Day — A667

String puppets: No. 2013, 3b, Man. No. 2014, 3b, Woman. 4d, Demon. 15b, Monkey.

2002, Apr. 2 *Perf. 14x14½*

Granite Paper

2013-2016 A667 Set of 4 2.50 2.50
a. Souvenir sheet, #2013-2016, perf. 13¼ 4.50 3.50

No. 2016a sold for 30b.

Songkran Day Type of 1991

Design: Angel on horse, zodiac.

2002, Apr. 13 *Perf. 14x14½*

Granite Paper

2017 A425 2b multicolored .75 .25
a. Souvenir sheet of 1 *2.00 2.00*
b. Souvenir sheet, #1724b, 1801c, 1869, 1940, 1970b, 2017 *3.00 3.00*
c. As "b," with Beijing 2002 emblem in margin and selling price removed *17.50 17.50*

Nos. 2017a and 2017b sold for 8b and 14b respectively. Both exist imperf.

Issued: No. 2017c, 9/29. No. 2017c sold for 30b.

Fighting Fish — A668

Designs: No. 2018, 3b, Betta imbellis. No. 2019, 3b, Betta splendens. 4b, Betta splendens, diff. 15b, Betta splendens, diff.

2002, May 15 Litho. *Perf. 14½x14*

Granite Paper

2018-2021 A668 Set of 4 3.50 3.25
a. Souvenir sheet, #2018-2021, perf. 13½ 3.50 3.25
b. As "a," with Amphilex 2002 emblem and selling price removed 12.50 12.50

Issued: No. 2021b, 8/30. No. 2021a sold for 30b; No. 2021b sold for 31b.

Temples A669

Designs: No. 2022, 3b, Wat Phra Si Rattanasatsadaram. No. 2023, 3b, Wat Phra Chetuphon Wimon Mangkhalaram. 4b, Wat Arun Ratchawararam. 12b, Wat Benchamabophit Dusit Wanaram.

2002, June 17 *Perf. 14½x14*

Granite Paper

2022-2025 A669 Set of 4 3.00 2.25
a. Souvenir sheet, #2022-2025, perf. 13½ 3.25 2.75
b. As "a," with Philakorea 2002 emblem and selling price removed 15.00 15.00

Issued: No. 2025b, 8/2. Nos. 2025a and 2025b each sold for 27b.

Crown Prince Maha Vajiralongkorn, 50th Birthday — A670

2002, July 28 *Perf. 14x14½*

Granite Paper

2026 A670 3b multi .55 .30

Natl. Communications Day — A671

2002, Aug. 4 Granite Paper

2027 A671 4b multi .75 .40

Thailand — Australia Diplomatic Relations, 50th Anniv. — A672

Designs: No. 2028, 3b, Nelumbo nucifera (pink flower). No. 2029, 3b, Nymphaea immutabilis (purple flower).

2002, Aug. 6 *Perf. 14½x14*

Granite Paper

2028-2029 A672 Set of 2 1.10 .75
a. Souvenir sheet, #2028-2029, perf. 13½ 1.50 1.50

See Australia Nos. 2072-2073. No. 2029a sold for 9b.

Queen Sirikit, 70th Birthday A673

Designs: No. 2030, 3b, Queen and roses. No. 2031, 3b, Queen Sirikit rose. 4b, Queen Sirikit orchid. 15b, Queen Sirikit dona shrub.

2002, Aug. 12 *Perf. 14½x14*

Granite Paper

2030-2033 A673 Set of 4 2.25 2.25
a. Souvenir sheet, #2030-2033, perf. 13½ 3.75 3.50

No. 2033a sold for 31b.

National Archives, 50th Anniv. — A674

2002, Aug. 18 *Perf. 14½x14*

2034 A674 3b multi .50 .30

Thai Bank Notes, Cent. — A675

2002, Sept. 7 Engr. *Perf. 13½*

Granite Paper

2035 A675 5b org & brown .75 .50
a. Souvenir sheet of 1 1.75 1.75

No. 2035a sold for 11b.

Vimanmek Mansion Art Objects A676

Designs: No. 2036, 3b, Round, lidded betel nut box. No. 2037, 3b, Bowl. 4b, Bowl, diff. 12b, Rectangular betel nut box.

2002, Sept. 7 Litho. *Perf. 14½x14*

Granite Paper

2036-2039 A676 Set of 4 2.00 2.00
a. Souvenir sheet, #2036-2039, perf. 13½ 3.00 3.00

No. 2039a sold for 26b.

Royal Palaces — A677

Designs: No. 2040, 4b, Thailand. No. 2041, 4b, Sweden.

Perf. 12½x13½ Syncopated

2002, Oct. 5 Litho. & Engr.

2040-2041 A677 Set of 2 1.10 .75

See Sweden No. 2445.

Intl. Letter Writing Day — A678

Designs: No. 2042, 3b, Animal-shaped coconut grater. No. 2043, 3b, Strainer. 4b, Coconut shell ladle. 15b, Earthenware stove and pot.

2002, Oct. 5 Litho. *Perf. 14½x14*

Granite Paper

2042-2045 A678 Set of 4 2.25 2.00
a. Souvenir sheet, #2042-2045, perf. 13½ 4.00 3.25

No. 2045a sold for 31b.

Bangkok 2003 World Philatelic Exhibition A679

Foods from: No. 2046, 3b, Central Thailand (red tablecloth). No. 2047, 3b, Southern Thailand (brown and yellow tablecloth). 4b, Northeastern Thailand. 15b, Northern Thailand.

2002, Oct. 5 ***Perf. 14½x14***

2046-2049 A679 Set of 4 2.90 2.25
a. Souvenir sheet, #2046-2049, perf. 13½ 4.00 3.50

No. 2049a sold for 30b.

New Year 2003 — A680

Flowers: No. 2050, 3b, Guaiacum officinale. No. 2051, 3b, Nyctanthes arbor-tristis. No. 2052, 3b, Barleria cristata. No. 2053, 3b, Thevetia peruviana.

Perf. 14½x14¼

2002, Nov. 15 **Litho.**

Granite Paper

2050-2053 A680 Set of 4 1.50 1.10
a. Souvenir sheet, #2050-2053 2.25 2.25

No. 2053a sold for 16b.

20th World Scout Jamboree A681

Designs: 3b, Scouts. 12b, Jamboree site.

2002, Dec. 28 ***Perf. 14½x14***

Granite Paper

2054-2055 A681 Set of 2 1.90 1.25

New Year 2003 (Year of the Goat) — A682

2003, Jan. 1 ***Perf. 13***

Granite Paper

2056 A682 3b multi .75 .25

See Nos. 2108, 2161, 2341a.

National Children's Day — A683

Pangpond and his: a, Dog, Big (blue background). b, Friend, Hanuman (orange background). c, Girlfriend, Namo (green background). d, Teacher (red background).

2003, Jan. 11 ***Perf. 14½x14***

Granite Paper

2057 A683 3b Block of 4, #a-d 1.25 1.00

Rose — A684

2003, Feb. 1 ***Perf. 13***

Granite Paper

2058 A684 4b multi .75 .30

No. 2058 is impregnated with rose scent. Compare with Type A716.

Blue Green, by Fua Haribhitak A685

Portrait of Chira Chongkon, by Chamras Kietkong A686

Moonlight, by Prasong Padmanuja — A687

Lotus Flowers, by Thawee Nandakwang A688

2003, Feb. 24 ***Perf. 13¼***

Granite Paper

2059	A685	3b multi	.35	.25
2060	A686	3b multi	.35	.25
2061	A687	3b multi	.35	.25
2062	A688	15b multi	1.40	1.25
		Nos. 2059-2062 (4)	2.45	2.00

Bangkok 2003 World Philatelic Exhibition A689

Tourist attractions: No. 2063, 3b, Doi Inthanon Temple, Chiang Mai. No. 2064, 3b, River Kwai Bridge, Kanchanaburi. No. 2065, 3b, Phu Kradung (cliff), Loei. 15b, Maya Bay, Krabi.

2003, Mar. 3 ***Perf. 14½x14***

Granite Paper

2063-2066 A689 Set of 4 2.60 2.10
a. Souvenir sheet, #2063-2066, perf. 13¼ 4.50 3.25

No. 2066a sold for 29b.

King Bhumibol Adulyadej Type of 1996

Perf. 14x14½

2003, Mar. 14 **Litho.** **Unwmk.**

Granite Paper

2067 A550 1b blue .45 .25

2003 Red Cross Fair — A690

2003, Mar. 28 ***Perf. 14x14½***

Granite Paper

2068 A690 3b multi .75 .30

Kick Boxing A691

Designs: No. 2069, 3b, Boxers punching. No. 2070, 3b, Boxer in black trunks with knee raised. No. 2071, 3b, Boxer in red trunks kicking. 15b, Boxer in red trunks kicking, diff.

2003, Apr. 2 **Litho.** ***Perf. 13¼***

Granite Paper

2069-2072 A691 Set of 4 3.00 2.10
a. Souvenir sheet, #2069-2072 2.75 2.50
b. As "a," with China 2003 Philatelic Exhibition emblem in margin 13.00 11.00

No. 2072a sold for 29b.

Issued: No. 2072b, 11/20. No. 2072b sold for 29b.

Princess Maha Chakri Sirindhorn, 48th Birthday — A692

2003, Apr. 2 ***Perf. 14x14½***

Granite Paper

2073 A692 3b multi .75 .25

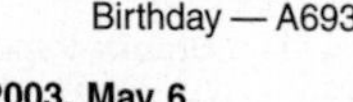

Princess Galyani Vadhana, 80th Birthday — A693

2003, May 6 **Granite Paper**

2074 A693 3b multi .75 .50

Kings Chulalongkorn and Vajiravudh — A694

2003, May 6 **Granite Paper**

2075 A694 3b multi .75 .30

Inspector General Dept., cent.

King Prajadhipok Day — A695

2003, May 30 ***Perf. 14½x14***

Granite Paper

2076 A695 3b multi .75 .30

Bantam Chickens — A696

Designs: No. 2077, 3b, White ears jungle fowl. No. 2078, 3b, Sugarcane husk colored. No. 2079, 3b, Black-tailed white. 15b, Dark gray.

2003 **Litho.** ***Perf. 13***

Granite Paper

2077-2080 A696 Set of 4 2.00 1.75
a. Souvenir sheet, #2077-2080 2.50 1.75
b. As "a," with Lanka Philex 2003 emblem in margin 20.00 16.00

Issued: Nos. 2077-2080, 2080a, 6/10; No. 2080b, 7/31. Nos. 2080a and 2080b each sold for 29b.

Asalhapuja Day — A697

2003, July 13 ***Perf. 14x14½***

Granite Paper

2081 A697 3b multi 1.40 .40

National Communications Day — A698

2003, Aug. 4 ***Perf. 14½x14***

Granite Paper

2082 A698 3b multi .75 .25

Communications Organization Emblems — A699

No. 2083: a, Thailand Post Company Limited. b, Communications Authority of Thailand (23x27mm). c, CAT Telecom Public Company Limited.

Perf. 14¼x14½

2003, Aug. 14 **Litho.** **Wmk. 340**

2083 A699 3b Horiz. strip of 3, #a-c 1.25 .90

King Chulalongkorn (1853-1910) A700

Litho. & Embossed

2003, Sept. 20 **Unwmk.** ***Perf. 13¼***

2084 A700 100b gold & multi 7.50 6.50
a. Souvenir sheet of 4 27.50 27.50

No. 2084a issued 9/30.

No. 2084a exists imperf. with Bangkok 2003 emblem at lower left. Value, $37.50.

Government Housing Bank, 50th Anniv. — A701

2003, Sept. 24 **Litho.** ***Perf. 14½x14***

Granite Paper

2085 A701 3b multi .75 .25

Bangkok 2003 World Philatelic Exhibition A702

Handicrafts: No. 2086, 3b, Basketry. No. 2087, 3b, Pottery. No. 2088, 3b, Leatherwork. 15b, Wood carving.

2003, Oct. 4 **Granite Paper**

2086-2089 A702 Set of 4 2.60 2.10
a. Souvenir sheet, #2086-2089, perf. 13¼ 3.75 3.25

A varnish with a rough surface was applied to portions of the designs.

No. 2089a sold for 29b. No 2089a exists imperf. Value, $16.

Trees of Thailand and Canada A703

No. 2090: a, Cassia fistula (Thailand). b, Maple leaves (Canada).

2003, Oct. 4 ***Perf. 14x14½***

Granite Paper

2090 A703 3b Horiz. pair, #a-b 1.25 1.10
c. Souvenir sheet, #2090, perf. 13¼ 2.50 2.50

No. 2090c sold for 9b.

Lychees A704 Rose Apples A705

Fruit: No. 2093, Coconuts. 15b, Jackfruit.

2003, Oct. 4 **Granite Paper**

2091 A704 3b shown .45 .25
2092 A705 3b shown .45 .25
2093 A704 3b multi .45 .25
2094 A704 15b multi 1.60 1.25
a. Souvenir sheet, #2091-2094, perf. 13¼ 4.50 3.25
Nos. 2091-2094 (4) 2.95 2.00

International Letter Writing Week. No. 2094a sold for 29b.

Oct. 14, 1973 Student Uprisings, 30th Anniv. — A706

2003, Oct. 14 ***Perf. 14½x14***

Granite Paper

2095 A706 3b multi .50 .25

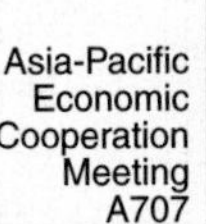

Asia-Pacific Economic Cooperation Meeting A707

2003, Oct. 20 **Granite Paper**

2096 A707 3b multi .75 .25

New Year 2004 — A708

Flowers: No. 2097, 3b, Bougainvillea spectabilis. No. 2098, 3b, Eucrosia bicolor. No. 2099, 3b, Canna x generalis. No. 2100, 3b, Zinnia violacea.

2003, Nov. 15 ***Perf. 14½x14¼***

Granite Paper

2097-2100 A708 Set of 4 1.25 1.10
a. Souvenir sheet, #2097-2100 1.50 1.25
b. As "a," with 2004 Hong Kong Stamp Expo emblem in margin 7.00 6.50

No. 2100a sold for 16b.

Issued: No. 2100b, 1/30/04. No. 2100b sold for 16b.

Thailand Flag A709

Thai Pavilion A710

Elephants A711

Cassia Fistula A712

2003, Dec. 1 ***Perf. 14¼x14½***

Granite Paper

2101 A709 3b multi .75 .25
2102 A710 3b multi .75 .25
2103 A711 3b multi .75 .25
2104 A712 3b multi .75 .25
Nos. 2101-2104 (4) 3.00 1.00

Compare with types A865a-A865d.

Elephants — A713

No. 2105: a, Asian elephant. b, African elephants.

2003, Dec. 9 ***Perf. 14½x14***

Granite Paper

2105 A713 3b Horiz. pair, #a-b 1.00 .75
c. Souvenir sheet, #2105a, perf. 13¼ 2.75 2.25

No. 2105c sold for 9b.

Thailand-South Africa diplomatic relations, 10th anniv. See South Africa No. 1330.

King Bhumibol Adulyadej Type of 1996

2003, Dec. 3 **Litho.** ***Perf. 14x14½***

Granite Paper

2106 A550 50s olive brown .75 .25
2107 A550 1b blue .75 .25

Issued: 50s, 12/3, 1b, 1/22/04

Zodiac Animal Type of 2003

2004, Jan. 1 **Litho.** ***Perf. 13***

Granite Paper

2108 A682 3b Monkey .50 .25

See No. 2341b.

Children's Day — A714

2004, Jan. 10 ***Perf. 14½x14***

Granite Paper

2109 A714 3b multi .75 .25

Paintings of Hem Vejakorn — A715

Designs: No. 2110, 3b, A Scene in Thai History (dancers). No. 2111, 3b, Maha Bharatayudh (charioteer). No. 2112, 3b, Khun Chang — Khun Phaen (women with horse). No. 2113, 3b, Phra Lor (woman and rooster).

2004, Jan. 17 ***Perf. 13¼***

Granite Paper

2110-2113 A715 Set of 4 1.40 1.10
a. Souvenir sheet, #2110-2113 3.25 2.25

No. 2113a sold for 16b.

Rose — A716

2004, Feb. 1 ***Perf. 13***

Granite Paper

2114 A716 4b multi .65 .30

Compare with type A684. No. 2114 is impregnated with rose scent.

Turtles A717

Designs: No. 2115, 3b, Cuora amboinensis. No. 2116, 3b, Platysternon megacephalum. No. 2117, 3b, Indotestudo elongata. No. 2118, 3b, Heosemys spinosa.

2004, Mar. 1 ***Perf. 14½x14***

Granite Paper

2115-2118 A717 Set of 4 1.75 1.25
a. Souvenir sheet, #2115-2118, perf. 13¼ 3.25 3.00
b. Similar to "a," with 2004 Singapore World Stamp Championship emblem in margin 8.75 7.50

Issued: No. 2118b, 8/28.

Nos. 2118a and 2118b sold for 16b.

Siam Society, Cent. — A718

2004, Mar. 10 ***Perf. 14½x14***

2119 A718 3b multi .75 .25

2004 Red Cross Fair — A719

2004, Mar. 29 ***Perf. 14x14½***

Granite Paper

2120 A719 3b multi .75 .25

Heritage Conservation Day — A720

Fringe colors of hand woven clothes: No. 2121, 3b, Rose red. No. 2122, 3b, Blue. No. 2123, 3b, Green. No. 2124, 3b, Orange red. Denomination is at LL on Nos. 2122, 2124.

2004, Apr. 2 **Litho.** ***Perf. 14x14½***

Granite Paper

2121-2124 A720 Set of 4 1.60 1.25
a. Souvenir sheet, #2121-2124, perf. 13¼ 2.75 2.50
b. As "a," with España 2004 emblem in margin, perf. 13¼ 7.50 6.75

Issued: No. 2124b, 5/22. No. 2124a sold for 16b; No. 2124b for 18b.

Architecture in Thailand and Italy — A721

No. 2125: a, Golden Mountain Temple, Bangkok. b, Colosseum, Rome.

2004, Apr. 21 ***Perf. 14½x14***

Granite Paper

2125 A721 3b Horiz. pair, #a-b 2.75 2.50
c. Souvenir sheet, #2125, perf. 13¼ 24.00 20.00

No. 2125c sold for 10b.

See Italy No. 2602.

Sculpture — A722

Designs: No. 2126, 3b, One-sided Drum, by Chit Rienpracha (yellow green background). No. 2127, 3b, Dance Drama, by Sitthidet Saenghiran (rose red background). No. 2128, 3b, Heavenly Flute, by Khien Yimsiri (Prussian blue background). No. 2129, 3b, The Calf, by Paitun Muangsomboom, horiz.

2004, May 3 ***Perf. 13¼***

2126-2129 A722 Set of 4 1.40 .95

Unseen Tourist Attractions — A723

No. 2130: a, Non Ngai Buddha, Suphan Buri. b, Khao Laem Dam, Kanchanaburi. c, Mural, Temple fo the Emerald Buddha, Bangkok. d, Ko Li-Pe, Satun. e, Buddha, Wat Phra Thong, Phuket. f, Khao Luang National Park, Nakhon Si Thammarat. g, Miracle Beach, Ko Damikhwan, Krabi. h, Hornbill, Hala-Bala Forest, Narathiwat. i, Long Ru Waterfall, Ubon Ratchathani. j, Prasat Hin Phanom Rung, Buri Ram. k, Red maple leaves, Phu Kradueng National Park, Loei. l, Phukhao Ya, Ranong. m, Ko Kradat, Trat. n, Op Luang National Park, Chiang Mai. o, Dusky leaf monkey, Phetchaburi. p, Lalu, Sra Kaeo. q, Pu Kai, Mu Ko Similan, Phang-Nga. r, Tha Le Noi Waterfowl Park. Phatthalung. s, Phu Pha Thoep, Mukdahan National Park. t, Phi Maen Cave, Mae Hong Son.

2004, May 31 ***Perf. 13***

Granite Paper

2130 A723 3b Sheet of 20, #a-t 10.00 8.00

See Nos. 2137, 2147, 2158.

Buddha Sculptures — A724

No. 2131: a, Phra Nangpaya. b, Phra Kampaeng Soumkhor. c, Phra Somdej Wat Rakangkhositaram. d, Phar Rod. e, Phra Phongsuphan.

Litho. & Embossed

2004, June 1 ***Perf. 13¼***

Granite Paper

2131 Horiz. strip of 5 7.50 6.00
a.-e. A724 9b Any single 1.50 1.10
f. Souvenir sheet, #2131a-2131e 20.00 20.00

No. 2131f sold for 53b.

Visakhapuja Day — A725

2004, June 2 **Litho.** ***Perf. 14x14½***

Granite Paper

2132 A725 3b multi .75 .25

Bridges A726

Designs: No. 2133, 5b, Phra Buddha Yodfa Bridge. No. 2134, 5b, Rama VI Bridge. No. 2135, 5b, Rama VIII Bridge. No. 2136, 5b, Rama IX Bridge.

2004, July 1 Litho. *Perf. 14¼x14½*
Granite Paper

2133-2136 A726 Set of 4 2.25 1.25

On Nos. 2135 and 2136 portions of the design were produced by a thermographic process which produces a shiny, raised effect.

Unseen Tourist Attractions Type of 2004

No. 2137: a, Wat Pho Prathap Chang, Phichit. b, Phra Prathan Chaturathit, Wat Phumin, Nan. c, Thalenai, Angthong Archipelago, Surat Thani. d, Wat Na Phra Men, Phra Nakhon Si Ayutthaya. e, Sanam Chan Palace, Nakhon Pathom. f, Piyamitr Tunnel, Yala. g, Ban Khamchanot, Udon Thani. h, Rail line along Pasak Cholasit Dam, Lop Buri. i, Khlong Lan Waterfall, Khlong Lan National Park, Kamphaeng Phet. j, Mo-I-Daeng Cliff, Khao Phra Wihan National Park, Si Sa Ket. k, Changkra Wild Orchid Park, Khon Kaen. l, Canoeists at Ti Lo Re, Tak. m, Khao Ta Mong Lai, Prachuap Khiri Khan. n, Suriya Patithin solar calendar, Prasat Phu Phek, Sakon Nakhon. o, Traditional boat racing, Chumphon. p, Mokochu Range Mae Wong National Park, Nakhon Sawan. q, Ordination by elephant in the sixth month, Surin. r, Rock climbing, Tan Rattana Waterfall, Khao Yai National Park, Prachin Buri. s, Monks collecting alms on horseback, Chiang Rai. t, Cycling in Thung Salaeng Luang, Phitsanulok.

2004, July 28 *Perf. 13*
Granite Paper

2137 A723 3b Sheet of 20, #a-t 10.00 8.00

Jasmine Flower — A727

Litho. & Embossed
2004, Aug. 2 *Perf. 13*
Granite Paper

2138 A727 5b multi .75 .30

No. 2138 is impregnated with a jasmine scent.

Princess Maha Chakri Sirindhorn Information Technology Program — A728

2004, Aug. 4 Litho. *Perf. 14x14½*
Granite Paper

2139 A728 3b multi .75 .25

National Communications Day — A729

2004, Aug. 4 *Perf. 14½x14*
Granite Paper

2140 A729 3b multi .75 .25

Opening of First Subway Line — A730

2004, Aug. 12 Litho. *Perf. 14½x14*
Granite Paper

2141 A730 3b multi .75 .25

Queen Sirikit, 72nd Birthday — A731

Litho. & Embossed
2004, Aug. 12 *Perf. 13¼*

2142 A731 100b multi 6.25 4.50
a. Souvenir sheet of 4 25.00 18.00

Boats A732

Designs: No. 2143, 3b, Thai junk. No. 2144, 3b, Sampan boat. No. 2145, 3b, Krachaeng boat. 15b, Packet boat.

2004-05 Litho. *Perf. 14½x14*
Granite Paper

2143-2146 A732 Set of 4 2.00 1.40
a. Souvenir sheet, #2143-2146, perf. 13¼ 2.75 2.60
b. As "a," with Pacific Explorer 2005 emblem in margin 9.00 8.00

No. 2146a sold for 29b. No. 2146b sold for 30b.

Issued: Nos. 2143-2146a, 9/1/04; No. 2146b, 4/21/05.

Unseen Tourist Attractions Type of 2004

No. 2147: a, Phra Nang Din, Phayad. b, Phra That Kong Khao Noi, Yasothon. c, Phra Atchana, Wat Sri Chum, Sukothai. d, Wat Bang Kung, Samut Songkhram. e, Ku Kut, Wat Phrathat Chamthewi, Lamphun. f, Dolphin watching, Chachoengsao. g, Tak Bat Dok Mai tradition, Saraburi. h, Hat Chao Lao, Chanthaburi. i, Phu Kum Khao dinosaur fossils, Kalasin. j, Reversed stupa, Wat Phra That Lampang Luang, Lampang. k, Khu Khut Waterfowl Park, Songkhla. l, Plant Market Khlong 15, Nakhon Nayok. m, Huppatad, Uthai Thani. n, Thai Muang Beach, Nakhon Phanom. o, Wild gaur, Khao Yai National Park, Nakhon Ratchasima. p, Canoeing, Le Khao Kop Cave, Trang. q, Sea of flowers, Pru Soi Dao, Uttaradit. r, Kolae boat, Ban Paseyawo, Pattani. s, Sea of Mist, Thap Boek, Phu Hin Rongkla National Park, Phetchabun. t, Bats, Khao Chung Phran, Ratchaburi.

2004, Sept. 28 *Perf. 13*
Granite Paper

2147 A723 3b Sheet of 20, #a-t 10.00 8.00

Intl. Letter Writing Week — A733

Kites: No. 2148, 3b, Snake. No. 2149, 3b, Star-shaped. No. 2150, 3b, Diamond-shaped with tail. 15b, Buffalo.

2004, Oct. 9 Litho. *Perf. 14x14½*
Granite Paper

2148-2151 A733 Set of 4 2.00 1.40
a. Souvenir sheet, #2148-2151, perf. 13¼ 3.25 3.00
b. Similar to "a," with Beijing 2004 emblem in margin 6.00 5.50

Issued: No. 2151b, 10/28. No. 2151a sold for 29b; No. 2151b for 30b.

King Mongkut (1804-68) — A734

2004, Oct. 18 *Perf. 14x14½*
Granite Paper

2152 A734 4b multi .75 .25

E-customs System A735

2004, Nov. 15 *Perf. 14½x14*
Granite Paper

2153 A735 3b multi .75 .25

New Year 2005 — A736

Flowers: No. 2154, 3b, Wrightia sirikitiae. No. 2155, 3b, Eria amica. No. 2156, 3b, Burmannia coelestris. No. 2157, 3b, Utricularia bifida.

2004, Nov. 15 *Perf. 14¼x14½*
Granite Paper

2154-2157 A736 Set of 4 2.00 1.40
a. Souvenir sheet, #2154-2157, perf. 14¼x14½ 4.75 4.75

No. 2157a sold for 16b.

Unseen Tourist Attractions Type of 2004

No. 2158: a, Phra That Cho Hae, Phrae. b, Wat Karuna, Chai Nat. c, Wat Nang Sao, Samut Sakhon. d, Phra Mutao Pagoda, Nonthaburi. e, Phu Kao Phu Phan Kham National Park, Nong Bua Lam Phu. f, Airvata (three-headed elephant), Erawan Museum, Samut Prakan. g, Wat Chedi Hoi, Pathum Thani. h, White krajiaw field, Chaiyaphum. i, Chet Si Waterfall, Nong Khai. j, Summer Palace, Ko Si Chang, Choi Buri. k, Traditional Drum-making village (Ban Bang Phae), Ang Thong. l, Ko Thalu, Rayong. m, Kosamphi Forest Park, Maha Sarakham. n, Cannonball tree, Wat Phra Non Chaksi, Sing Buri. o, Tung Kula Rong Hai, Roi Et. p, Phu Sra Dok Bua, Amnat Charoen.

2004, Nov. 26 *Perf. 13*
Granite Paper

2158 A723 3b Sheet of 16, #a-p, + 4 labels 9.00 8.00

Bangkok Fashion City Initiative A737

No. 2159: a, 3b, Man and woman. b, 3b, Woman in pink dress. c, 3b, Woman with green shirt. d, 15b, Woman with brown eyeshade.

2004, Dec. 5 *Perf. 14x14½*
Granite Paper

2159 A737 Horiz. strip of 4, #a-d 2.25 2.25
e. Souvenir sheet, #2159a-2159d, perf. 13½ 3.25 2.75

No. 2159e sold for 30b.

Queen Rambhai Bharni (1904-84) — A738

2004, Dec. 20 *Perf. 14x14½*
Granite Paper

2160 A738 3b multi .75 .25

Zodiac Animal Type of 2003
2005, Jan. 1 *Perf. 13*
Granite Paper

2161 A682 3b Cock .75 .30

See No. 2341c.

Children's Day — A739

2005, Jan. 8 *Perf. 14½x14*
Granite Paper

2162 A739 3b multi .75 .25

Thailand - Argentina Diplomatic Relations, 50th Anniv. — A740

No. 2163: a, Tango dancers, Argentina. b, Tom-tom dancers, Thailand.

2005, Feb. 2 *Perf. 13¼*
Granite Paper

2163 A740 3b Horiz. pair, #a-b 1.10 1.00

See Argentina Nos. 2312-2313.

Rose — A741

2005, Feb. 10 *Perf. 12½*
Flocked Paper

2164 A741 10b multi 1.10 .80

No. 2164 is impregnated with rose scent.

Maghapuja Day — A742

2005, Feb. 23 *Perf. 14x14½*
Granite Paper

2165 A742 3b multi .75 .25

Rotary International, Cent. — A743

2005, Feb. 23 *Perf. 14½x14*
Granite Paper

2166 A743 3b multi .75 .25

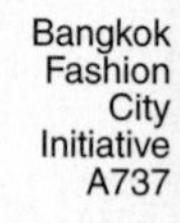

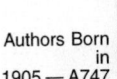

Red Cross A744

2005, Mar. 30 Litho.

Granite Paper

2167 A744 3b multi .75 .25

Princess Maha Chakri Sirindhorn, 50th Birthday — A774a

2005, Apr. 2 Litho. *Perf. 13¼*

Granite Paper

2167A A774a 3b multi .75 .25

A745

Hanging Art — A746

2005, Apr. 2 Litho. *Perf. 13¼*

Granite Paper

2168 A745 3b shown .35 .25
2169 A746 3b shown .35 .25
2170 A746 3b multi, diff. .35 .25
2171 A745 15b multi, diff. 1.40 .55
a. Souvenir sheet, #2168-2171 3.25 2.75
Nos. 2168-2171 (4) 2.45 1.30

Heritage Conservation Day. No. 2171 sold for 30b.

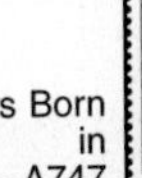

Authors Born in 1905 — A747

Designs: No. 2172, 3b, Dokmaisod (olive green background). No. 2173, 3b, Sri Burapha (Prussian blue background). No. 2174, 3b, Maimuangderm (dark blue background). No. 2175, 3b, Arkatdumkeung Rabibhadana (rose pink background).

2005, May 5 *Perf. 14½x14*

Granite Paper

2172-2175 A747 Set of 4 2.25 2.10
a. Souvenir sheet, #2172-2175, perf. 13¼ 4.00 3.75

No. 2175a sold for 17b.

Insects — A748

No. 2176: a, Coccinella transversalis. b, Chrysochroa buqueti rugicollis (47x28mm). c, Sagra femorata. d, Chrysochroa maruyamai (47x28mm).

Litho. & Embossed

2005, May 31 *Perf. 14¼x14½*

Granite Paper

2176 Horiz. strip or block of 4 2.25 1.60
a.-d. A748 5b Any single .55 .40
e. Sheet, 2 each #2176a-2176d 3.00 3.00

Embossed portions of stamps are covered with a glossy varnish.

No. 2176e issued May 2006, Washington 2006 World Philatelic Exhibition. No. 2176e sold for 54b.

Heart Balloons and Mail Truck — A749

Balloons — A749a

2005 Litho. *Perf. 13*

Granite Paper

2177 A749 3b multi .75 .50
2177A A749a 3b multi .75 .50

Issued: No. 2177, June; No. 2177A, 7/15. Nos. 2177 and 2177A were issued in sheets of 12 + 12 personalizable labels the same size as the stamp.

Buddha Amulets — A750

No. 2178: a, Phra Ruang Lang Rang Puen. b, Phra Hu Yan. c, Phra Chinnarat Bai Sema. d, Phra Mahesuan. e, Phra Tha Kradan.

Litho. & Embossed

2005, June 19 *Perf. 13¼*

Granite Paper

2178 Horiz. strip of 5 4.50 4.50
a.-e. A750 9b Any single .90 .90
f. Souvenir sheet, #2178a-2178e 7.50 7.50
g. As "f," with Taipei 2005 emblem in margin 13.25 13.25

No. 2178f sold for 55b.

No. 2178g issued 8/19/05. No. 2178g sold for 85b.

Thailand - People's Republic of China Diplomatic Relations, 30th Anniv. — A751

Panda: a, Showing tongue. b, Feeding on bamboo.

2005, July 1 Litho. *Perf.*

Granite Paper

2179 A751 Horiz. pair 1.10 .90
a.-b. 3b Either single .45 .30
c. Souvenir sheet, #2179a-2179b 4.50 3.75

No. 2179 has perf. 13¼ line of perforations between the two stamps, and the surrounding selvage is rouletted 11¾. No. 2179c, which sold for 15b, lacks the perforations between the stamps and has no rouletting.

Thaipex 2005 — A752

Dancers in play "Chuck Nark": No. 2180, 3b, Pra Rama and Princess Srida. No. 2181, 3b, Hanuman (white mask). No. 2182, 3b, Thotsakan (green mask). 15b, Pra Rama and Thotsakan.

Litho. with Foil Application

2005, Aug. 3 *Perf. 13¼*

Granite Paper

2180-2183 A752 Set of 4 2.60 2.00
a. Souvenir sheet, #2180-2183 4.50 3.25

No. 2183a sold for 30b. No. 2183a exists imperf. Value $15.

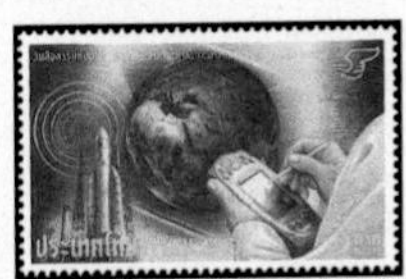

Natl. Communications Day — A753

2005, Aug. 4 Litho. *Perf. 14½x14*

Granite Paper

2184 A753 3b multi .75 .25

Building Gables A754

No. 2185: a, Prasat Phanom Rung. b, Phra Prang at Wat Phra Phai Luang. c, Uposatha Hall at Wat Khao Bandai It. d, Scripture Library at Wat Phra Sing Woramahawihan.

Perf. 13¼x13½

2005, Aug. 4 Photo. Wmk. 340

2185 Horiz. strip of 4 + central label 2.75 2.25
a.-d. A754 5b Any single .55 .40

Orchids — A755

Designs: No. 2189, 3b, Rhynchostylis gigantea Alba (white flowers). No. 2190, 3b, Rhynchostylis gigantea (pink and red flowers). No. 2191, 3b, Dendrobium gratiosissimum. 15b, Dendrobium thyrsiflorum.

Perf. 14½

2005, Sept. 1 Litho. Unwmk.

Granite Paper

2189-2192 A755 Set of 4 2.50 2.50
a. Souvenir sheet, #2189-2192, perf. 13¼ 3.50 3.50

No. 2192a sold for 30b.

Intl. Day of Peace — A756

2005, Sept. 21 *Perf. 13*

Granite Paper

2193 A756 3b multi .75 .25

Intl. Letter Writing Week — A757

Water buffalo: No. 2194, 3b, Head. No. 2195, 3b, Standing in field. No. 2196, 3b, In mud. 15b, Attached to plow.

Perf. 14½x14

2005, Oct. 8 Litho. Unwmk.

Granite Paper

2194-2197 A757 Set of 4 2.50 2.50
a. Souvenir sheet, #2194-2197, perf. 13¼ 4.50 3.25

National Library, Cent. — A758

2005, Oct. 12 *Perf. 14½x14*

Granite Paper

2198 A758 3b multi .75 .25

Abolition of Slavery, Cent. — A759

2005, Oct. 23 Litho.

Granite Paper

2199 A759 3b multi .75 .30

New Year 2006 — A760

Flowers: No. 2200, 3b, Beaumontia murtonii. No. 2201, 3b, Hibiscus mutabilis. No. 2202, 3b, Hibiscus rosa-sinensis. No. 2203, 3b, Cochlospermum religiosum.

2005, Nov. 15 *Perf. 14x14½*

Granite Paper

2200-2203 A760 Set of 4 1.25 1.25
a. Souvenir sheet, #2200-2203 2.25 2.00

No. 2203a sold for 17b.

Princess Bejaratana, 80th Birthday — A761

2005, Nov. 24 *Perf. 14x14½*

Granite Paper

2204 A761 3b multi .75 .30

Siamese Roosters — A762

Designs: No. 2205, 3b, Golden Rooster, by Pichai Nirand (olive green panel). No. 2206, 3b, Rooster at Dawn, by Prayat Pongdam (black panel). No. 2207, 3b, Legendary Rooster, by Chakrabhand Posayakrit (dancing woman, brown panel). No. 2208, 3b, Divine Rooster, by Chalermchai Kositpipat (blue panel), horiz.

Perf. 14x14½, 14½x14

2005, Nov. 24

2205-2208 A762 Set of 4 1.25 1.25

King Bhumibol Adulyadej's "New Theory" Agriculture A763

No. 2209: a, King, easel, farmers, animals. b, King and farmers.

2005, Dec. 5 *Perf. 14¼x14½*

Granite Paper

2209 Horiz. pair, #a-b, + central label .85 .85
a.-b. A763 3b Either single .35 .30

Buddhist Monks — A764

No. 2210: a, Somdet Phra Phutthachan (1788-1872). b, Phra Ratchamuni Samiram Khunupamachan (1582-1682). c, Phra Achan Man Bhuridatto (1870-1949). d, Khruba Si wichai (1877-1938).

Litho. & Engr.
2005, Dec. 5 *Perf. 13½*
Granite Paper
2210 Horiz. strip of 4 2.25 2.25
a.-d. A764 5b Any single .55 .50
e. Souvenir sheet, #2210a-2210d 3.00 3.00

No. 2210e sold for 30b.

Dec. 26, 2004 Tsunami, 1st Anniv. A765

No. 2211: a, Wave. b, Undivided Kindness of Thai People, by Chanipa Temprom.

2005, Dec. 26 **Litho.** *Perf. 14½x14*
Granite Paper
2211 A765 3b Horiz. pair, #a-b 1.50 1.00

King Bhumibol Adulyadej Type of 1996

2006 **Litho.** *Perf. 14x14½*
Granite Paper
2212 A550 10b orange & brown 2.00 1.00
2213 A550 15b yel brn & green 3.00 1.50

New Year 2006 (Year of the Dog) — A766

2006, Jan. 1 **Litho.** *Perf. 13*
Granite Paper
2214 A766 3b multi .75 .30

Prince Chaturantarasmi Krom Phra Chakrabardibongse (1856-1900), Finance Minister — A767

2006, Jan. 13 *Perf. 14x14½*
Granite Paper
2215 A767 3b multi .75 .30

Natl. Children's Day — A768

Winning designs in children's stamp design competition with panel colors of: No. 2216, 3b, Orange brown. No. 2217, 3b, Blue. No. 2218, 3b, Red violet. No. 2219, 3b, Green.

2006, Jan. 14 *Perf. 14½x14*
Granite Paper
2216-2219 A768 Set of 4 1.25 1.25

Rose — A769

Litho. & Embossed
2006, Feb. 7 *Perf. 13*
Granite Paper
2220 A769 5b multi .75 .50

Diplomatic Relations Between Thailand and Iran, 50th Anniv. A770

2006, Feb. 11 **Litho.** *Perf. 14½x14*
Granite Paper
2221 A770 3b multi .75 .30

Queen Sirikit Center for Breast Cancer A771

2006, Mar. 29 *Perf. 14½x14*
Granite Paper
2222 A771 3b multi .75 .25

Heritage Conservation Day — A772

Sites in Phu Phrabat Historical Park: No. 2223, 3b, Buddha's Footprint (monument). No. 2224, 3b, Upright rocks and trees, horiz. No. 2225, 3b, Thao Barot horse stable (rock overhang), horiz. 15b, Nang Usa rock pillar.

2006, Apr. 2 *Perf. 14x14½, 14½x14*
Granite Paper
2223-2226 A772 Set of 4 2.50 2.50
a. Souvenir sheet, #2223-2226, perf. 13¼ 4.50 3.25

No. 2226a sold for 36b.

Thon Buri Palace A773

No. 2227: a, Throne Hall. b, King Taksin's Shrine. c, Two Chinese-style residences. d, King Pinklao's residence.

2006, Apr. 2 *Perf. 14½x14*
Granite Paper
2227 A773 3b Block of 4, #a-d 1.40 1.40
e. Souvenir sheet, #2227, perf. 13¼ 2.75 2.25

No. 2227e sold for 17b.

A774

King Bhumibol Adulyadej, 60th Anniv. of Accession A775

King Bhumibol Adulyadej: No. 2228, 3b, Wearing tie, red brown background (shown). No. 2229, 3b, Wearing tie, blue background. No. 2230, 3b, Wearing tie, olive brown background. No. 2231, 3b, Without tie, blue violet background. No. 2232, Without tie, green background. No. 2233, 3b, Without tie, brown background.

2006 **Photo.** *Perf. 13¼*
Granite Paper
2228-2233 A774 Set of 6 8.00 7.00
a. Miniature sheet, #2228-2233 5.00 4.50

Litho. & Embossed With Foil Application
2234 A775 100b gold & multi 11.00 11.00

Issued: Nos. 2228-2233, 2233a, 5/5; No. 2234, 6/9. No. 2233a sold for 30b.

Visakhapuja Day — A776

2006, May 12 **Litho.** *Perf. 14x14½*
Granite Paper
2235 A776 3b multi .75 .30

Buddhadasa Bhikkhu (1906-93), Buddhist Philosopher — A777

No. 2236: a, Buddhadasa seated between trees. b, Profile of Buddhadasa. c, Gathering of monks. d, Stone fence.

2006, May 27 *Perf. 13*
Granite Paper
2236 Horiz. strip of 4 1.60 1.60
a.-d. A777 3b Any single .30 .30
e. Miniature sheet, #2236a-2236d 2.00 2.00

No. 2236e sold for 17b.

Anemonefish A778

Designs: No. 2237, 3b, Amphiprion clarkii. No. 2238, 3b, Amphiprion perideraion. No. 2239, 3b, Amphiprion ocellaris. No. 2240, 3b, Amphiprion polymnus.

2006, June 24 *Perf. 14½x14*
Granite Paper
2237-2240 A778 Set of 4 1.40 1.40
a. Miniature sheet, #2237-2240, perf. 13½ 2.75 2.25
b. As "a," with Belgica '06 emblem in margin 9.00 9.00

Issued: Nos. 2237-2240, 2240a, 6/24; No. 2240b, Dec. No. 2240a sold for 20b; No. 2240b, for 30b.

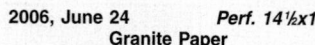

Natl. Communications Day — A779

2006, Aug. 4 **Litho.**
Granite Paper
2241 A779 3b multi .75 .30

Mitrephora Sirikitiae — A780

Litho. & Embossed
2006, Aug. 12 *Perf. 13*
Granite Paper
2242 A780 5b multi .75 .40

Royal Dog Tongdaeng A781

Dog: No. 2243, 3b, Sitting. No. 2244, 3b, Standing. No. 2245, 3b, Laying down. No. 2246, 3b, With puppies.

2006 **Litho.** *Perf. 13½*
Granite Paper
2243-2246 A781 Set of 4 1.40 1.10
a. Miniature sheet, #2243-2246 2.25 2.25
b. As "a," with MonacoPhil 2006 emblem in margin 9.00 9.00

Issued: Nos. 2243-2246, 2246a, 9/1; No. 2246b, Dec. No. 2246a sold for 17b; No. 2246b, for 26b.

Suvarnabhumi Airport — A782

2006, Sept. 28 *Perf. 14½x14*
Granite Paper
2247 A782 3b multi .75 .30

Nos, 606, 653a, 934 and 1081 Surcharged

Methods, Perfs and Watermarks As Before

2006, Sept. 15
2248 A146 2b on 20s #606 16.00 16.00
2249 A161 2b on 20s #653a 1.10 .35
a. 2b on 20s #653 75.00 75.00
2250 A256 2b on 75s #934 2.75 2.75
2251 A256 2b on 1.50b #1081 2.75 2.75
Nos. 2248-2251 (4) 22.60 21.85

Location and size of surcharges differs.

Fireworks A783

2006, Apr. 20 Litho. *Perf. 13*
Granite Paper

2252 A783 3b multi + label 2.75 2.75

Printed in sheets of 10 stamps + 10 labels that could be personalized. Sheets sold for 100b. Value, $32.50.

Intl. Letter Writing Week — A784

Carnivorous plants: No. 2253, 3b, Nepenthes mirabilis. No. 2254, 3b, Rafflesia kerrii. No. 2255, 3b, Sapria poilanei. 15b, Drosera burmannii.

2006 Litho. Unwmk. *Perf. 14½x14*
Granite Paper

2253-2256 A784 Set of 4 2.50 1.60
a. Miniature sheet, #2253-2256, perf. 13½ 3.25 2.75
b. As "a," with Beijing 2006 emblem in margin 9.00 9.00

Issued: Nos. 2253-2256, 2256a, 10/9; No. 2256b, Dec. No. 2256a sold for 29b; No. 2256b, for 44b.

New Year 2007 — A785

Flowers: No. 2257, 3b, Hypoxis aurea. No. 2258, 3b, Murdannia gigantea. No. 2259, 3b, Impatiens phuluangensis. No. 2260, 3b, Caulokaempferia alba.

2006, Nov. 15 *Perf. 14½x14*
Granite Paper

2257-2260 A785 Set of 4 1.25 .90
a. Miniature sheet, #2257-2260 2.50 2.25

No. 2260a sold for 16b.

Royal Thai Naval Academy, Cent. — A786

2006, Nov. 20 Granite Paper

2261 A786 3b multi .75 .30

King Bhumibol Adulyadej, 60th Anniv. of Accession — A787

King Bhumibol Adulyadej: No. 2262, 5b, Standing in forest. No. 2263, 5b, Seated on walkway, taking notes. No. 2264, 5b, Standing on wooden plank over water. No. 2265, 5b, Pointing to ground. No. 2266, 5b, Riding cow. No. 2267, 5b, Walking up hill.

2006, Dec. 5 Photo. *Perf. 13½*
Granite Paper

2262-2267 A787 Set of 6 3.25 2.50
a. Miniature sheet, #2262-2267 4.00 4.00

No. 2267a sold for 44b. No. 2267a exists imperf. Value, $275.

Opening of Second Thai-Lao Friendship Bridge — A788

No. 2268 — Bridge and flag of: a, Thailand (denomination at LL). b, Laos (denomination at LR).

2006, Dec. 20 Litho. *Perf. 14½x14*
Granite Paper

2268 A788 3b Horiz. pair, #a-b 1.10 1.10

New Year 2007 (Year of the Pig) — A789

2007, Jan. 1 *Perf. 13*
Granite Paper

2269 A789 3b multi .75 .30

See No. 2341d.

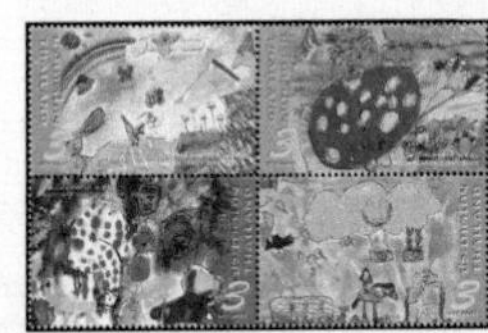

Natl. Children's Day — A790

No. 2270 — Children's drawings: a, Rainbow, birds and butterflies. b, Cat with green face and butterflies. c, Spotted animals. d, Birds, cloud, sun and girl riding horse.

2007, Jan. 13 *Perf. 14½x14*
Granite Paper

2270 A790 3b Block of 4, #a-d 1.50 1.25

Siam Commercial Bank Public Company, Cent. — A791

2007, Jan. 30 *Perf. 14x14½*
Granite Paper

2271 A791 3b multi .75 .30

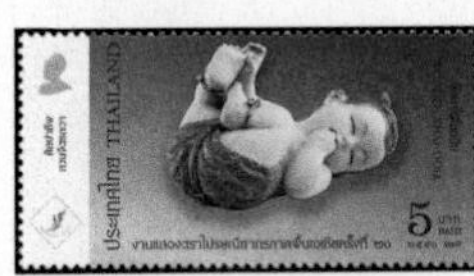

Bangkok 2007 Intl. Stamp Exhibition — A792

Various carved wooden dolls depicting Thai children with background colors of: No. 2272, 5b, Blue. No. 2273, 5b, Olive green. No. 2274, 5b, Brown olive. No. 2275, 5b, Rose.

Litho. With Foil Application
2007, Feb. 1 *Perf. 13*
Granite Paper

2272-2275 A792 Set of 4 2.25 1.75
a. Miniature sheet, #2272-2275 3.25 3.25

No. 2275a sold for 33b.

Yellow Rose — A793

2007, Feb. 7 Litho. *Perf. 13*
Granite Paper

2276 A793 5b multi .75 .40

No. 2276 is impregnated with a rose scent.

A794

A795

A796

Carved Fruits and Vegetables A797

2007, Mar. 1 Litho. *Perf. 14½x14*
Granite Paper

2277 A794 5b multi .50 .40
2278 A795 5b multi .50 .40
2279 A796 5b multi .50 .40
2280 A797 5b multi .50 .40
a. Souvenir sheet, #2277-2280, perf. 13¼ 3.50 3.25
Nos. 2277-2280 (4) 2.00 1.60

No. 2280a sold for 26b.

No. 617 Surcharged in Bronze and Black

Methods, Perfs and Watermarks As Before
2007, Mar. 29

2281 A146 50b on 40b #617 5.25 5.25
2282 A146 100b on 40b #617 7.75 7.75

Postman on Scooter — A798

Unwmk.
2007, Mar. 29 Litho. *Perf. 13*
Granite Paper

2283 A798 3b multi .75 .30

Booklet Stamp
Self-Adhesive
Serpentine Die Cut 11

2284 A798 3b multi — —
a. Booklet pane of 10 + 4 stickers —

No. 2283 was printed in sheets of 10 and in sheets of 10 + 10 labels that could be personalized.

Thailand Red Cross Tuberculosis Laboratory A799

2007, Mar. 29 Litho. *Perf. 14½x14*

2285 A799 3b multi .75 .30

A800

A801

A802

Buddhist Ecclesiastical Ceremonial Fans of King Chulalongkorn Era — A803

Litho. With Foil Application
2007, Apr. 2 *Perf. 13¼*
Granite Paper

2286 A800 5b multi .55 .40
2287 A801 5b multi .55 .40
2288 A802 5b multi .55 .40
2289 A803 5b multi .55 .40
a. Souvenir sheet, #2286-2289 3.75 3.25
Nos. 2286-2289 (4) 2.20 1.60

No. 2289a sold for 27b.

Flowers — A804

No. 2290: a, Lotus flower at UR, sunflowers in center and LR. b, Sunflower at UR, two lotus flowers. c, Rose, sunflower and lotus flowers. d, Three roses.

2007, Apr. 23 Litho. *Perf. 13*
Granite Paper

2290 Vert. strip of 4 4.50 4.50
a.-d. A804 3b Any single 1.00 1.00

King Bhumibol Adulyadej, 80th Birthday A805

Litho. & Embossed With Foil Application
2007, May 5 *Perf. 13¼*
Granite Paper

2291 A805 9b multi 1.40 1.40

Princess Galyani Vadhana, 84th Birthday — A806

2007, May 6 Litho. *Perf. 14x14½*

2292 A806 3b multi .75 .50

Visakhapuja Day — A807

2007, May 31 *Perf. 14¼x14½*
Granite Paper

2293 A807 3b multi .75 .40

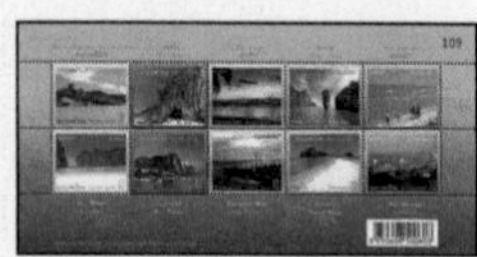

Seaside Tourist Areas — A808

No. 2294: a, Mu Ko Similan National Park. b, Ko Khai. c, Ko Chang. d, Khao Tapu. e, Hat Cha-am. f, Ao Maya. g, Ko Panyi. h, Hat Chao Mai. i, Thale Waek. j, Hat Pattaya.

2007, June 1 ***Perf. 14½x14***

Granite Paper

2294 A808 Sheet of 10 11.00 11.00
a.-j. 15b Any single 1.10 1.10

The original printing of No. 2294 has the bar code in the bottom margin. A later printing with a smaller margin has the bar code at the right side.

Waterfalls A809

Waterfall at: No. 2295, 3b, Doi Inthanon National Park. No. 2296, 3b, Thung Salaeng Luang National Park. No. 2297, 3b, Khuean Srinagarindra National Park. No. 2298, 3b, Phu Hin Rong Kla National Park.

2007, June 1 ***Perf. 14½x14***

Granite Paper

2295-2298 A809 Set of 4 1.40 1.40
a. Souvenir sheet, #2295-2298, perf. 13½ 2.90 2.25

No. 2298a sold for 16b.

Phi Takhon Masks A810

No. 2299 — Masks with rice steamer hat in: a, White, black background. b, Black, white background. c, Red, black background. d, White, white background.
10b, Two people wearing masks.

2007, June 23 ***Perf. 13¼***

Granite Paper

2299 A810 3b Horiz. strip of 4, #a-d 1.60 1.60

Souvenir Sheet

Perf. 14x14½

2300 A810 10b multi 2.00 2.00

No. 2300 contains one 60x48mm stamp.

A811

A812

A813

Rock Formations in Pa Hin Ngam National Park — A814

2007, July 2 **Litho.** ***Perf. 13¼x12¾***

2301 A811 5b multi .55 .40
2302 A812 5b multi .55 .40
2303 A813 5b multi .55 .40
2304 A814 5b multi .55 .40
a. Souvenir sheet, #2301-2304 4.75 3.75
Nos. 2301-2304 (4) 2.20 1.60

No. 2304a sold for 39b. Portions of the designs of Nos. 2301-2304 and 2304a were printed with a thermographic process producing a shiny, raised effect. A gritty substance was added to these areas to produce a rough texture.

Temples A815

Designs: No. 2305, 5b, Wat Rajaorasaram. No. 2306, 5b, Wat Rajapradit Sathitmahasimaram. No. 2307, 5b, Wat Rajabopit Sathitmahasimaram. No. 2308, 5b, Wat Suthatthepwararam.

2007, July 2 **Litho.** ***Perf. 14½x14***

Granite Paper

2305-2308 A815 Set of 4 2.25 1.75
a. Souvenir sheet, #2305-2308, perf. 13¼ 3.50 3.25

No. 2308a sold for 27b.

Bird Figurines — A816

Bird figurines covered with beetle wing: No. 2309, 5b, Duck with wings spread. No. 2310, 5b, Bird on rock. No. 2311, 5b, Bird with long tail feathers. No. 2312, 5b, Rooster.

Litho. With Foil Application

2007, Aug. 3 ***Perf. 14x14½***

Granite Paper

2309-2312 A816 Set of 4 1.75 1.75
a. Souvenir sheet, #2309-2312 3.00 2.75

No. 2312a sold for 33b. Bangkok 2007 Intl. Stamp Exhibition.

Natl. Communications Day — A817

2007, Aug. 4 **Litho.** ***Perf. 14½x14***

Granite Paper

2313 A817 3b multi .75 .30

24th Summer Universiade, Bangkok — A818

2007, Aug. 8 ***Perf. 13¼***

Granite Paper

2314 A818 3b multi .75 .30

Miniature Sheet

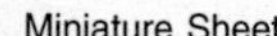

Association of South East Asian Nations (ASEAN), 40th Anniv. — A819

No. 2315: a, Secretariat Building, Bandar Seri Begawan, Brunei. b, National Museum of Cambodia. c, Fatahillah Museum, Jakarta, Indonesia. d, Typical house, Laos. e, Malayan Railway Headquarters Building, Kuala Lumpur, Malaysia. f, Yangon Post Office, Myanmar (Burma). g, Malacañang Palace, Philippines. h, National Museum of Singapore. i, Vimanmek Mansion, Bangkok. j, Presidential Palace, Hanoi, Viet Nam.

2007, Aug. 8 ***Perf. 13¼***

Granite Paper

2315 A819 3b Sheet of 10, #a-j 4.50 3.75

See Brunei No. 607, Burma No. 370, Cambodia No. 2339, Indonesia Nos. 2120-2121, Laos Nos. 1717-1718, Malaysia No. 1170, Philippines Nos. 3103-3105, Singapore No. 1265, and Viet Nam Nos. 3302-3311.

Miniature Sheet

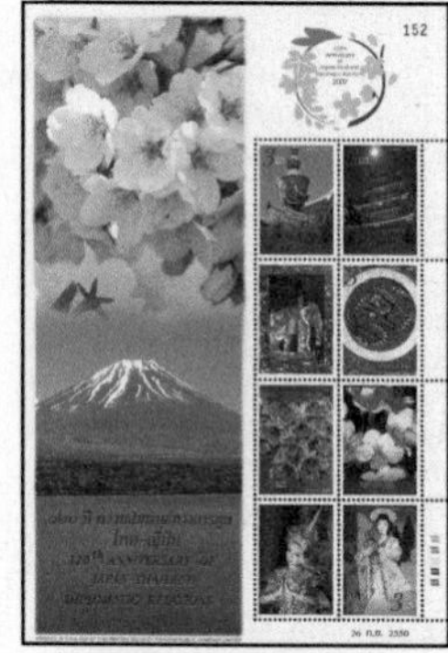

Diplomatic Relations Between Thailand and Japan, 120th Anniv. — A820

No. 2316: a, Buddhist statue. b, Pagoda. c, Elephant. d, Dragon. e, Pink and white orchids. f, White flowers. g, Thai dancer. h, Japanese dancer.

2007, Sept. 26 **Litho.** ***Perf. 13¼***

Granite Paper

2316 A820 3b Sheet of 8, #a-h 4.50 3.25

See Japan No. 2998.

Intl. Letter Writing Week — A821

Utensils: No. 2317, 3b, Betel nut scissors. No. 2318, 3b, Betel nut masher. No. 2319, 3b, Cylinder-and-piston igniter. No. 2320, 3b, Earthenware oil lamp or incense dish.

2007, Oct. 8 **Litho.** ***Perf. 14½x14***

Granite Paper

2317-2320 A821 Set of 4 1.75 1.10
a. Miniature sheet, #2317-2320, perf. 13¼ 3.00 2.75

No. 2320a sold for 18b.

Miniature Sheets

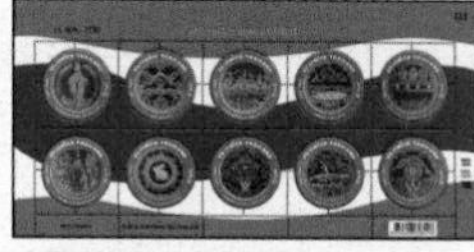

Provincial Seals — A822

No. 2321, 3b — Seals of: a, Bangkok. b, Krabi. c, Kanchanaburi. d, Kalasin. e, Kamphaeng Phet. f, Khon Kaen. g, Chanthaburi. h, Chachoengsao. i, Chon Buri. j, Chai Nat.

No. 2322, 3b — Seals of: a, Chaiyaphum. b, Chumphon. c, Chiang Rai. d, Chiang Mai. e, Trang. f, Trat. g, Tak. h, Nakhon Nayok. i, Nakhon Pathom. j, Nakhon Phanom.

Litho. & Embossed With Foil Application

2007, Oct. 11 ***Perf. 13½***

Granite Paper

Sheets of 10, #a-j

2321-2322 A822 Set of 2 5.50 5.50

Miniature Sheet

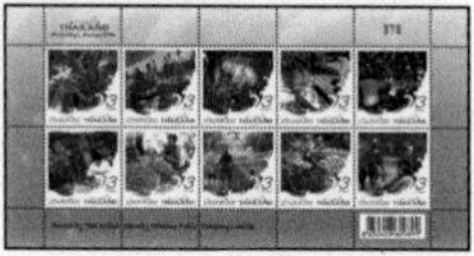

People at Work A823

No. 2323: a, People in palm tree. b, Cook feeding people on wooden walkway. c, People near elephant carving. d, Buddhist monk in canoe. e, People under lanterns. f, Artisan with hammer. g, Woman with flowers. h, Man weaving fishing basket. i, People in boats filled with fruits and vegetables. j, People logging with elephants.

2007, Oct. 26 **Litho.** ***Perf. 13***

Granite Paper

2323 A823 3b Sheet of 10, #a-j 5.50 5.50
k. Sheet of 5, #2323b, 2323c, 2323e, 2323f, 2323j 1.25 1.25
l. Sheet of 5, #2323c, 2323f, 2323g, 2323i, 2323j 1.25 1.25

Nos. 2323k and 2323l each sold for 20b at Thailand 7-11 stores. No. 2323k exists with three different sheet margins.

Ministry of Defense, 120th Anniv. — A824

2007, Nov. 11 ***Perf. 14x14½***

Granite Paper

2324 A824 3b multi .75 .30

New Year 2008 — A825

Designs: No. 2325, 3b, Pink Plumeria rubra, denomination in red. No. 2326, 3b, Plumeria obtusa. No. 2327, 3b, White and yellow Plumeria rubra, denomination in pink. No. 2328, 3b, Red Plumeria rubra, denomination in red.

2007, Nov. 15 ***Perf. 14x14½***

Granite Paper

2325-2328 A825 Set of 4 2.00 2.00
a. Souvenir sheet, #2325-2328 .75 2.90

No. 2328a sold for 18b.

Patrol Boat — A826

Perf. 14½x14¼

2007, Nov. 20 Litho.

Granite Paper

2329 A826 3b multi .55 .30

White Elephant of King Bhumibol Adulyadej A827

Designs: No. 2330, 5b, King touching elephant's trunk. No. 2331, 5b, Elephant on lawn. No. 2332, 5b, Elephant on lawn with handlers, vert. No. 2333, 5b, King touching elephant's head, vert.

Perf. 14¾x14, 14x14¾

2007, Dec. 5 Litho.

Granite Paper

2330-2333 A827 Set of 4 1.75 1.75
a. Souvenir sheet, #2333, perf. 13½ 2.75 2.25

No. 2333a sold for 10b.

Miniature Sheet

King Bhumibol Adulyadej, 80th Birthday — A828

No. 2334 — King: a, 5b, As small boy. b, 5b, As boy, sitting in wagon. c, 5b, As student, reading book. d, 5b, Wearing suit, sepia photograph. e, 5b, Wearing cap. f, 5b, Wearing red uniform. g, 5b, Wearing suit and red tie. h, 5b, Wearing gold robe. i, 80b, Wearing Buddhist robe.

Litho., Litho. & Embossed With Hologram Affixed (80b)

2007, Dec. 5 ***Perf. 13¼x13½***

2334 A828 Sheet of 9, #a-i 10.00 7.50

No. 1820 Surcharged in Gold

Methods and Perfs As Before

2007, Dec. 18 Granite Paper

2335 A550 15b on 9b #1820 2.00 .75

Busabok Mala — A829

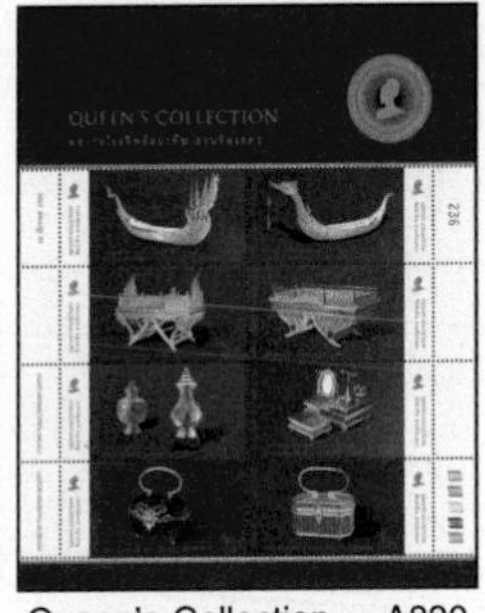

Queen's Collection — A830

No. 2337: a, Miniature model of royal barge Anantanakharai. b, Miniature model of royal barge Suphannahongse. c, Sappagab Phragajatarn. d, Sappagab Khram. e, Water jars. f, Miniature vanity set. g, Yan Lipao basketry. h, Evening bag.

Litho. & Embossed With Foil Application

2007, Dec. 18 ***Perf. 13¼x13½***

2336 A829 20b multi 2.00 2.00
a. Souvenir sheet of 1 6.00 6.00

Granite Paper

Perf. 13

2337 A830 5b Sheet of 8, #a-h 4.50 3.75

No. 2336a sold for 40b.

Nos. B78-B79 Surcharged in Black

Methods, Perfs and Watermarks As Before

2007, Jan. 16

2338 Horiz. strip of 4 (#B78) — —
a.-d. SP13 5b on 2b+1b #B78a-B78d, Any single — —

2339 Horiz. strip of 4 (#B79) — —
a.-d. SP13 5b on 2b+1b #B79a-B79d, Any single — —

New Year Types of 2003-2007 and

New Year 2008 (Year of the Rat) — A831

Unwmk.

2008, Jan. 1 Litho. ***Perf. 13***

Granite Paper

2340 A831 3b multi .75 .30

2341 Sheet of 6, #2214, 2340, 2341a-2341d 4.00 3.25
a. A682 3b As #2056, with gold rings with colored centers .30 .30
b. A682 3b As #2108, with gold rings with colored centers — —
c. A682 3b As #2161, with gold rings with colored centers .30 .30
d. A789 3b As #2269, with gold rings and dots .30 .30
e. As #2341, with Taipei 2008 emblem in margin 10.00 10.00

No. 2341 sold for 30b. On Nos. 2056, 2108 and 2161, gold rings have white centers. No. 2269 has gold dots only.

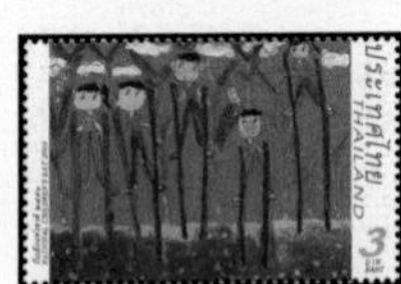

A832

A833

A834

A835

Children's Art — A836

No. 2342: a, Stilt walkers, by Kemtis Kumsrijan. b, Flying kites, by Natapol Saelim. c, Puppet show, by Sirada Chokeyangkul. d, Thien Phansa, by Salinthip Narongpun. e, People thanking rice plants, by Amornthep Jitnak.

2008, Jan. 12 Litho. ***Perf. 14½x14***

Granite Paper

2342 Horiz. strip of 5 2.00 2.00
a. A832 3b multi .35 .30
b. A833 3b multi .35 .30
c. A834 3b multi .35 .30
d. A835 3b multi .35 .30
e. A836 3b multi .35 .30

Children's Day.

Chinese New Year A837

No. 2343: a, Mask, black denomination at UR (29x48mm). b, Mask, black denomination at LL (29x48mm). c, Masks, green denomination at UL (29x24mm). d, People celebrating, green denomination at LL (29x24mm).

2008, Feb. 1 Litho. ***Perf. 14½x14¼***

Granite Paper

2343 A837 5b Block of 4, #a-d 1.75 1.75
e. Souvenir sheet, #2343a-2343b 2.50 2.50

No. 2343e sold for 20b. For surcharges, see No. 2358.

Pink Rose — A838

2008, Feb. 7 Litho. ***Perf. 13***

Granite Paper

2344 A838 5b multi .75 .40

No. 2344 is impregnated with a rose scent.

Postman in Boat — A839

2008, Mar. 3 ***Perf. 14¼***

Granite Paper

2345 A839 3b multi .75 .25

Stylized People Holding Heart — A840

2008, Mar. 17 Granite Paper

2346 A840 3b multi .75 .30

Printed in sheets of 10 and in sheets of 10 + 10 labels that could be personalized.

Nos. B78-B79 Surcharged in Gold and Black

Methods, Perfs and Watermarks As Before

2008, Mar. 26

2347 Horiz. strip of 4 (#B78) 4.00 3.00
a.-d. SP13 15b on 2b+1b #B78a-B78d, Any single 1.00 .75

2348 Horiz. strip of 4 (#B79) 4.00 3.00
a.-d. SP13 15b on 2b+1b #B79a-B79d, Any single 1.00 .75

Miniature Sheet

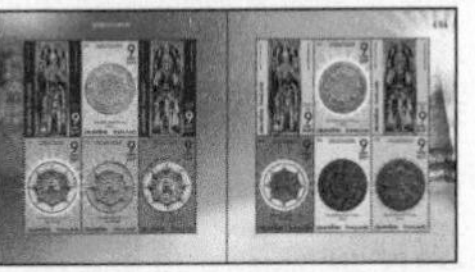

Chatukham Rammathep — A841

No. 2349: a, Statue, maroon panels, "Chatukham" above denomination. b, Gold amulet, light gray background. c, Statue, maroon panels, "Rammathep" above denomination. d, Statue, yellow panels, "Chatukham" above denomination. e, Gold amulet with inner ring, dark gray background. f, Statue, yellow panels, "Rammathep" above denomination. g, Silver and brown amulet, bister background. h, Silver amulet, blue background. i, Silver and red amulet, orange brown background. j, Silver and red amulet, olive green background. k, Black amulet, pale blue green background. l, Red brown amulet, pink background.

Litho. & Embossed

Perf. 13½x13¼

2008, Mar. 29 Unwmk.

2349 A841 9b Sheet of 12, #a-l 8.00 8.00

No. 2349 was printed in sheets of 12 with and without a row of perforations through the center of the sheet. For surcharges, see No. 2588.

A842

A843

A844

Angels and Demons — A845

2008, Apr. 2 Litho. *Perf. 14x14½*

Granite Paper

2350 A842 3b multi		.35	.30
2351 A843 3b multi		.35	.30
2352 A844 3b multi		.35	.30
2353 A845 3b multi		.35	.30
a.	Miniature sheet, #2350-2353, perf. 13¼	3.00	3.00
	Nos. 2350-2353 (4)	1.40	1.20

No. 2353a sold for 20b.

Miniature Sheet

Provincial Seals — A846

No. 2354 — Seals of: a, Nakhon Ratchasima. b, Nakhon Si Thammarat. c, Nakhon Sawan. d, Nonthaburi. e, Narathiwat. f, Nan. g, Buri Ram. h, Pathum Thani. i, Prachuap Khiri Khan. j, Prachin Buri.

Litho. & Embossed With Foil Application

2008, Apr. 2 *Perf. 13*

Granite Paper

2354 A846 3b Sheet of 10, #a-j	3.25	3.25

Nos. 1764, 1817-1818 Surcharged in Gold and Black

c

Methods and Perfs As Before

2008

2355 A572(c) 15b on 6b #1764	.95	.95

Granite Paper

2356 A590(c) 15b on 6b #1817	.95	.95
2357 A590(c) 15b on 9b #1818	.95	.95
Nos. 2355-2357 (3)	2.85	2.85

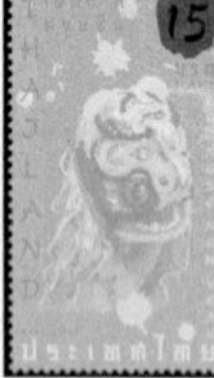

Nos. 2343a, 2343c, 2343d, and Items Similar to Nos. 2343b and 2343e Surcharged in Gold and Black — d

Methods and Perfs As Before

2008, Apr. 25 Granite Paper

2358	Block of 4 (#2343)	4.50	4.50
a.	A837(d) 15b on 5b #2343a	1.10	1.10
b.	A837(d) 15b on 5b stamp similar to #2343a	1.10	1.10
c.-d.	A837(c) 15b on 5b Either single, #2343c-2343d	1.10	1.10
e.	A837(d) 15b on 5b sheet similar to #2343e	4.50	3.75

No. 2358b is a surcharge on an unissued stamp similar to No. 2343b that was printed with the incorrectly-spelled inscription "Chinese Neww Year." The extra "w" is obliterated by a gold circle in the surcharge on No. 2358b found in in the block of four or in the souvenir sheet, No. 2358e.

Diplomatic Relations Between Thailand and Turkey, 50th Anniv. — A847

No. 2359: a, Flag of Thailand, Wat Rajannada, Bangkok. b, Flag of Turkey, Blue Mosque, Istanbul.

2008, May 12 Litho. *Perf. 13¼*

Granite Paper

2359 A847 3b Horiz. pair, #a-b	.75	.55

See Turkey Nos. 3108-3109.

Sunflowers — A848

2008, May 16 *Perf. 13*

Granite Paper

2360 A848 3b multi	.75	.25

Visakhapuja Day — A849

2008, May 19 *Perf. 14¼x14½*

Granite Paper

2361 A849 3b multi	.35	.30

A850

A851

A852

World Environment Day — A853

2008, June 5 *Perf. 13½*

Granite Paper

2362 A850 3b multi	.30	.25
2363 A851 3b multi	.30	.25
2364 A852 3b multi	.30	.25
2365 A853 3b multi	.30	.25
Nos. 2362-2365 (4)	1.20	1.00

Miniature Sheet

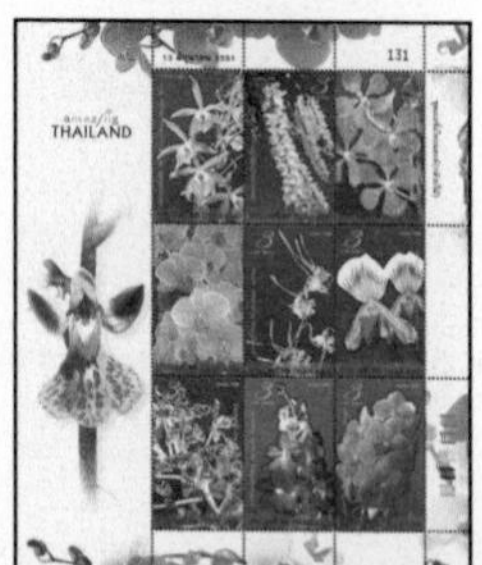

Orchids A854

No. 2366: a, Brassocattleya Ploenpit Star. b, Aerides falcata. c, Arachnis Hookeriana x Vanda Doctor Anek. d, Phalaenopsis Little Mary. e, Dendrobium sutiknoi. f, Paphiopedilum callosum. g, Grammatophyllum speciosum. h, Vascostylis Prapawan. i, Vanda Robert's Delight.

2008, June 13 Litho. *Perf. 14x14½*

Granite Paper

2366 A854 3b Sheet of 9, #a-i	3.25	3.25

A855

A856

A857

A858

A859

A860

A861

A862

A863

Bangkok Attractions A864

2008, July 11 *Perf. 13¼x13½*

Granite Paper

2367	Sheet of 10	4.00	4.00
a.	A855 3b multi	.35	.25
b.	A856 3b multi	.35	.25
c.	A857 3b multi	.35	.25
d.	A858 3b multi	.35	.25
e.	A859 3b multi	.35	.25
f.	A860 3b multi	.35	.25
g.	A861 3b multi	.35	.25
h.	A862 3b multi	.35	.25
i.	A863 3b multi	.35	.25
j.	A864 3b multi	.35	.25

Miniature Sheet

Mountain Region Attractions — A865

No. 2368: a, Phu Chi Fa. b, Phu Pha Thoep. c, Heo Narok Waterfall. d, Phang-Ung. e, Sun Crack. f, Phu Khao Hin Pakarang. g, Phae Mueang Phi Earth Pillar. h, Phu Kradueng. i, Phu Soi Dao. j, Khun Mae Ya.

2008, July 11 Litho.

Granite Paper

2368	A865 15b Sheet of 10, #a-j	11.00	11.00
o.	Sheet of 3, #2368a, 2368b, 2368g	3.75	3.75

No. 2368o sold for 60b at Thailand 7-11 stores. No. 2368o exists with two different sheet margins.

Thailand Flag — A865a

Thai Pavilion — A865b

Elephants — A865c

Cassia Fistula — A865d

2008, July 25 Litho. *Perf. 14¼x14½*

2368K A865a 3b multi	.45	.25
2368L A865b 3b multi	.45	.25
2368M A865c 3b multi	.45	.25
2368N A865d 3b multi	.45	.25
Nos. 2368K-2368N (4)	1.80	1.00

Nos. 2368K-2368N were printed by a different printer than Nos. 2101-2104.

No. 2368K has a taller, rounder "3" than No. 2101.

No. 2368L has a black line under the building railing at bottom. On No. 2102, the railing touches the white frame of the stamp.

On No. 2368M, the country name, having small dots of color in the lettering, appears pale gray, and the entire vignette has a fuzzy appearance. On No. 2103, the country name is all white and the vignette is sharper.

On No. 2368N, the area without flowers has a blue appearance, and the flowers have a greener appearance. On No. 2104, the area without flowers has a purple appearance, and the flowers appear browner. The screens used on these stamps differ, with No. 2368N having coarser dots than No. 2104. Under magnification the bottom edge of the vignette has more of a saw-tooth appearance on No. 2368N than on No. 2104.

Postman, Tree and Dove — A866

2008, Aug. 1 *Perf. 14¼*

Granite Paper

2369	A866 3b multi	.75	.30
a.	Perf. 13	4.50	4.50

A867

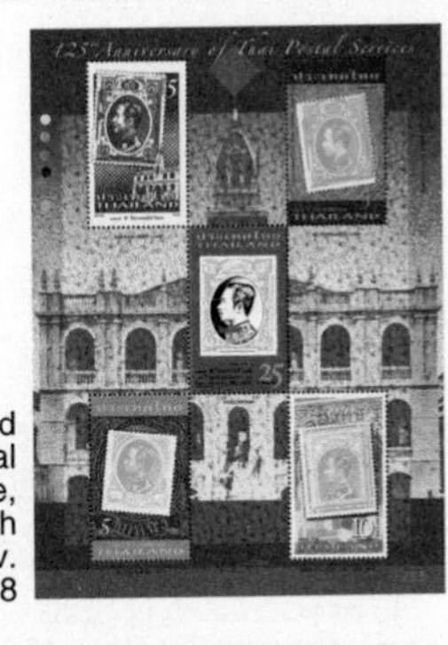

Thailand Postal Service, 125th Anniv. A868

Designs: No. 2370, 3b, Unissued 1-fuang stamp of 1883 and various modern Thailand stamps. No. 2371, 3b, Old and modern post offices. No. 2372, 3b, Old and modern post office counters. No. 2373, 3b, Old and modern postal delivery men. No. 2374, 3b, Old and modern postal trucks.

No. 2375: a, 5b, Thailand #2 in black and Post Office. b, 5b, Thailand #3. c, 5b, Thailand #4. d, 10b, Thailand #5a. e, 25b, Hologram of Thailand #1 with added Thai words.

Litho., Litho. With Hologram Affixed (#2375e)

2008, Aug. 4 ***Perf. 14½x14***

Granite Paper

2370-2374 A867 Set of 5 1.60 1.10

Perf. 13¼x13½

2375 A868 Sheet of 5 #a-e 4.50 4.50

Communications Day — A869

2008, Aug. 4 Litho. ***Perf. 14x14½***

Granite Paper

2376 A869 3b multi .75 .30

End of telegraph message service in Thailand.

Painting of Flowers by Princess Maha Chakri Sirindhorn — A870

2008, Aug. 4 ***Perf. 13½x13¼***

Granite Paper

2377 A870 5b multi .75 .40

Peacocks — A871

Designs: No. 2378, 10b, Peacock on branch. No. 2379, 10b, Peacock with tail feathers raised.

Litho. & Embossed With Hologram Affixed

2008, Aug. 9 ***Perf. 13¼***

Granite Paper

2378-2379 A871 Set of 2 2.00 1.60
a. Souvenir sheet, #2378-2379 3.75 3.25

No. 2379a sold for 30b.

Nos. 1749-1750, 1785 Surcharged in Black

Methods and Perfs As Before

2008, Oct. 1 **Granite Paper**

2380 A568 10b on 6b #1749 3.25 3.25
2381 A579 10b on 6b #1785 3.25 3.25
2382 A568 50b on 7b #1750 7.50 7.50
Nos. 2380-2382 (3) 14.00 14.00

Diplomatic Relations Between Thailand and Republic of Korea, 50th Anniv. — A872

No. 2383: a, Chakri Maha Prasat Throne Hall, Thailand (denomination at L). b, Juhamnu Mansion, Changdeok Palace, Korea (denomination at R).

2008, Oct. 1 Litho. ***Perf. 14½x14***

Granite Paper

2383 A872 3b Horiz. pair, #a-b .75 .55

See South Korea No. 2295.

Intl. Letter Writing Week — A873

Shadow puppets: No. 2384, 3b, Rishi. No. 2385, 3b, Shiva. No. 2386, 3b, Shadow play preluder. No. 2387, 3b, Theng the Jester.

2008, Oct. 4 ***Perf. 14x14½***

Granite Paper

2384-2387 A873 Set of 4 1.10 1.10
a. Souvenir sheet, #2384-2387, perf. 13½ 1.50 1.50

No. 2387a sold for 18b.

Miniature Sheet

Provincial Seals — A874

No. 2388 — Seal of: a, Pattani. b, Phra Nakhon Si Ayutthaya. c, Phang-Nga. d, Phatthalung. e, Phayao. f, Phichit. g, Phitsanulok. h, Phetchaburi. i, Phetchabun. j, Phrae.

Litho. & Embossed With Foil Application

2008, Oct. 10 ***Perf. 13¾***

Granite Paper

2388 A874 3b Sheet of 10, #a-j 4.50 4.50

Thailand No. 119 — A875

2008, Oct. 23 Litho. ***Perf. 13½x13¼***

Granite Paper

2389 A875 5b multi .75 .40

Equestrian statue of King Chulalongkorn, cent.

New Year 2009 — A876

Water lilies: No. 2390, 3b, Nymphaea "Suwanna." No. 2391, 3b, Nymphaea "Tankhwan." No. 2392, 3b, Nymphaea "Tanpong." No. 2393, 3b, Nymphaea "Mangala-Ubol."

2008, Nov. 15 Litho. ***Perf. 14x14½***

Granite Paper

2390-2393 A876 Set of 4 1.40 .55
a. Souvenir sheet of 4, #2390-2393 1.40 .75

No. 2393a sold for 17b. A sheet similar to No. 2393a, with the China 2009 World Stamp Exhibition emblem in the sheet margin, sold for 30b.

Miniature Sheet

Cremation of Princess Galyani Vadhana (1933-2008) — A877

No. 2394 — Princess: a, As child. b, Wearing sash. c, Wearing cap. d, Wearing red dress.

2008, Nov. 11 ***Perf. 14x14¾***

Granite Paper

2394 A877 5b Sheet of 4, #a-d 2.00 1.75

No. 2394 exists imperf. Value, $160.

King Bhumibol Adulyadej, 81st Birthday — A878

2008, Dec. 3 ***Perf. 13¼***

Granite Paper

2395 A878 3b multi .75 .25

Somdet Chao Phraya Borom Maha Sisuriyawong (1808-83), Regent of King Chulalongkorn A879

2008, Dec. 23 ***Perf. 14x14¾***

Granite Paper

2396 A879 3b multi .75 .30

New Year 2009 (Year of the Ox) — A880

2009, Jan. 2 Litho. ***Perf. 14¼***

Granite Paper

2397 A880 3b multi .75 .30
a. Perf. 13 (#2796a) .30 .25

Issued: No. 2397a, 1/1/14.

Miniature Sheet

Children's Day — A881

No. 2398 — Characters from "Phra Abhai Manee," poem by Phra Sunthorn Voharn: a, Sri Suvan with pole. b, Phra Abhai Manee with flute. c, Mermaid and fish. d, Giant woman in water. e, Sud Sakhon falling. f, Old man with tiger skin clothes. g, Naked man with stick. h, King's daughter.

2009 ***Perf. 14¾x14***

Granite Paper

2398 A881 3b Sheet of 8, #a-h 5.50 5.50
i. Souvenir sheet, #2398a-2398d, perf. 13¼ 9.00 9.00

Issued: No. 2398, 1/10, No. 2398i, May. Honk Kong 2009 Intl. Philatelic Exhibition (No. 2398i).

A882

A883

A884

Prince Bhanurangsi (1860-1928), Founder of Thai Postal Service — A885

2009, Jan. 11 ***Perf. 14x14¾***

Granite Paper

2399 A882 3b multi .35 .30
2400 A883 3b multi .35 .30
2401 A884 3b multi .35 .30
2402 A885 3b multi .35 .30
a. Souvenir sheet of 4, #2399-2402, perf. 13½ 2.25 2.25
Nos. 2399-2402 (4) 1.40 1.20

No. 2402a sold for 20b. No. 2402a exists imperf. Value, $27.50.

White Rose — A886

Litho. & Embossed

2009, Feb. 6 ***Perf. 13***

Granite Paper

2403 A886 5b multi .75 .40

School of Postal Services A887

2009, Feb. 22 Litho. *Perf. 14¾x14*

Granite Paper

2404 A887 3b multi .75 .30

Red Cross — A888

2009, Mar. 30 Granite Paper

2405 A888 3b multi .75 .30

Prince Krom Luang Wongsa Dhiraj Snid (1808-71), Physician — A889

2009, Mar. 30 *Perf. 14x14¾*

Granite Paper

2406 A889 3b multi .65 .30

Nos. 1736-1737 Surcharged in Gold

Methods, Perfs and Watermarks As Before

2009, Apr. 1

2407 A564 30b on 6b #1736 *15.00 11.00*
2408 A564 46b on 9b #1737 *25.00 16.00*

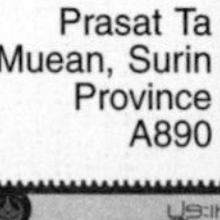

Prasat Ta Muean, Surin Province A890

Prasat Ta Muean Thom, Surin Province A891

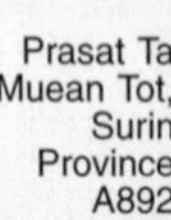

Prasat Ta Muean Tot, Surin Province A892

Prasat Sadok Kok Thom, Sa Kaeo Province A893

Perf. 14¾x14

2009, Apr. 2 Litho. Unwmk.

Granite Paper

2409 A890 3b multi .35 .30
2410 A891 3b multi .35 .30
2411 A892 3b multi .35 .30
2412 A893 3b multi .35 .30
a. Souvenir sheet of 4, #2409-2412, perf. 13½ 2.00 2.00
Nos. 2409-2412 (4) 1.40 1.20

Royal Headgear — A894

Designs: No. 2413, 5b, Gold brocade hat. No. 2414, 5b, Felt hat. No. 2415, 5b, Battle helmet. No. 2416, 5b, Grand diamond hat.

2009, Apr. 6 *Perf. 13*

Granite Paper

2413-2416 A894 Set of 4 1.75 1.75
a. Souvenir sheet of 4, #2413-2416 2.40 2.40

No. 2416a sold for 25b.

Visakhapuja Day — A895

2009, May 8 *Perf. 14¼x14½*

Granite Paper

2417 A895 3b multi .75 .30

Statues of Hindu Gods — A896

Designs: No. 2418, 5b, Ganesa. No. 2419, 5b, Brahma. No. 2420, 5b, Narayana. No. 2421, 5b, Siva.

Litho. & Embossed

2009, June 2 *Perf. 13¼*

Granite Paper

2418-2421 A896 Set of 4 1.75 1.75
a. Souvenir sheet of 4, #2418-2421 1.90 1.90

No. 2421a sold for 25b. No. 2421a exists imperf. Value, $125.

Orchids A897

Designs: No. 2422, 3b, Cattleya Queen Sirikhit. No. 2423, 3b, Paphiopedilum Princess Sangwan. No. 2424, 3b, Sirindhornia pulchella. No. 2425, 3b, Phalaenopsis Princess Chulabhorn. No. 2426, 3b, Dendrobium "Pink Nagarindra." No. 2427, 3b, Ascocenda Sukontharat. No. 2428, 3b, Dendrobium "Soamsawali."

2009, June 5 Litho. *Perf. 14½x14*

Granite Paper

2422-2428 A897 Set of 7 1.75 .95
a. Sheet of 7, #2422-2428, perf. 13¼ 6.00 4.75

No. 2428a sold for 30b.

Diplomatic Relations Between Thailand and the Philippines, 60th Anniv. — A898

No. 2429 — Stick dancers with denomination in: a, Pale yellow. b, Light blue.

2009, June 14 Granite Paper

2429 A898 3b Horiz. pair, #a-b .75 .30

Thammasat University, 75th Anniv. — A899

2009, June 27 *Perf. 14x14½*

2430 A899 3b multi .75 .30

A900

A901

A902

Candle Procession Festival — A903

2009, July 6 *Perf. 14x14½*

2431 A900 3b multi .55 .50
2432 A901 3b multi .55 .50
2433 A902 3b multi .55 .50
2434 A903 3b multi .55 .50
a. Souvenir sheet of 4, #2431-2434, perf. 13¼ 3.00 3.00
Nos. 2431-2434 (4) 2.20 2.00

No. 2434a sold for 20b.

King Bhumibol Adulyadej Type of 1996

Die Cut Perf. 13¼x13¾

2009, Aug. 4 Litho.

Self-Adhesive

2435 A550 3b bister brn & bl .75 .30

Natl. Communications Day — A904

2009, Aug. 4 *Perf. 14½x14*

Granite Paper

2436 A904 3b multi .75 .30

Hun Lakorn Lek Puppetry A905

Puppets and puppeteers with: No. 2437, 25b, Orange panel at right. No. 2438, 25b, Orange panel at left.
No. 2439, 25b, No orange panel.

Litho. With Three-Dimensional Plastic Affixed

2009, Aug. 4 *Perf. 17*

Self-Adhesive

2437-2438 A905 Set of 2 5.50 5.50

Souvenir Sheet

Perf. 12¼x12

2439 A905 25b multi 5.50 5.50

Miniature Sheet

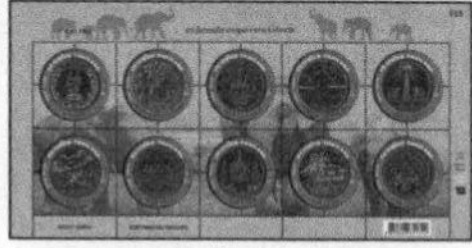

Provincial Seals — A906

No. 2440 — Seals of: a, Phuket. b, Maha Sarakham. c, Mukdahan. d, Mae Hong Son. e, Yasothon. f, Yala. g, Roi Et. h, Ranong. i, Rayong. j, Ratchaburi.

Litho. & Embossed With Foil Application

2009, Sept. 7 *Perf. 13*

Granite Paper

2440 A906 3b Sheet of 10, #a-j 2.40 2.40

Guan Yin Bodhisat — A907

2009, Sept. 9 Litho. *Perf. 14½x14¼*

Granite Paper

2441 A907 9b multi 1.00 1.00
a. Souvenir sheet of 1 1.60 1.60

No. 2441a sold for 15b. No. 2441a exists imperf. without gum. Value, $160.

Natl. Telecommunications Commission — A908

2009, Oct. 1 *Perf. 14x14½*

Granite Paper

2442 A908 3b multi .75 .30

Royal Carriages A909

Designs: No. 2443, 3b, Four-wheeled dog cart. No. 2444, 3b, Postillion landau. No. 2445, 3b, C-spring phaeton. No. 2446, 3b, Glass state coach.

2009, Oct. 7 *Perf. 13¼x13½*

Granite Paper

2443-2446 A909 Set of 4 1.25 1.25
a. Souvenir sheet of 4, #2443-2446 2.25 2.25

No. 2446a sold for 20b.

A910

A911

A912

Intl. Letter Writing Week — A913

2009, Oct. 9 *Perf. 14x14½*

Granite Paper

2447 A910 3b multi .30 .30
2448 A911 3b multi .30 .30
2449 A912 3b multi .30 .30
2450 A913 3b multi .30 .30
a. Souvenir sheet of 4, #2447-2450, perf. 13½ 1.60 1.60
Nos. 2447-2450 (4) 1.20 1.20

No. 2450a sold for 20b.

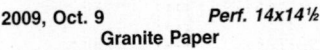

New Year 2010 — A914

Flowers: No. 2451, 3b, Drosera peltata. No. 2452, 3b, Sonerila griffithii. No. 2453, 3b, Cyanotis arachnoidea. No. 2454, 3b, Caulokaempferia saxicola.

2009, Nov. 15 *Perf. 14½x14*

Granite Paper

2451-2454 A914 Set of 4 1.25 1.25
a. Souvenir sheet of 4, #2451-2454 1.60 1.60

No. 2454a sold for 15b.

Princess Bejaratana Ratsuda, 84th Birthday — A915

2009, Nov. 24 *Perf. 13¼*

Granite Paper

2455 A915 3b multi .75 .40

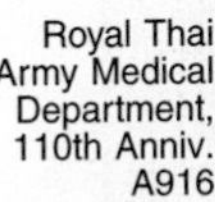

Royal Thai Army Medical Department, 110th Anniv. A916

Designs: No. 2456, 3b, Building, medic treating soldier. No. 2457, 3b, Soldier with rifle, knapsack and medical bag, soldiers carrying litter to medical helicopter. No. 2458, 3b, Medic treating soldier, doctors in surgery. No. 2459, 3b, Hospital, soldier saluting.

2009, Nov. 25 *Perf. 14½x14*

Granite Paper

2456-2459 A916 Set of 4 1.25 1.25
a. Souvenir sheet of 4, #2456-2459 16.00 —

King Bhumibol Adulyadej, 82nd Birthday A917

2009, Dec. 5 *Perf. 14½x14*

Granite Paper

2460 A917 9b multi 1.00 1.00

Thailand Earth Observation Satellite A918

2009, Dec. 5 **Litho.**

Granite Paper

2461 A918 3b multi .75 .30

A gritty substance has been applied to portions of the design.

Education for the Blind — A919

2009, Dec. 12 **Litho. & Embossed**

Granite Paper

2462 A919 3b multi .75 .30

New Year 2010 (Year of the Tiger) — A920

2010, Jan. 1 **Litho.** *Perf. 13*

Granite Paper

2463 A920 3b multi .75 .25

2010 Population and Housing Census A921

2010, Jan. 5 **Litho.** *Perf. 13½*

Granite Paper

2465 A921 3b multi .75 .25

King Bhumibol Adulyadej Type of 1996

2010, Jan. 8 *Perf. 14x14½*

Granite Paper

2465A A550 3b bister brn & bl .75 .25

Young Phra Sang — A922

Chao Ngo and Nang Rotchana A923

Phra Sang — A924

Phra Sang Playing Polo — A925

2010, Jan. 9 *Perf. 14½x14*

Granite Paper

2466 A922 3b multi .35 .25
2467 A923 3b multi .35 .25
2468 A924 3b multi .35 .25
2469 A925 3b multi .35 .25
Nos. 2466-2469 (4) 1.40 1.00

Characters from Sang Thong. National Children's Day.

Euah Suntornsanan (1910-81), Composer and Musician — A926

2010, Jan. 21 *Perf. 14x14½*

Granite Paper

2470 A926 3b multi .75 .25

Child Praying A927

Birthday Cake A928

Flowers A929

Heart A930

Moon and Stars A931

Balloons A932

2010, Jan. 28 **Litho.** *Perf. 14x14½*

Granite Paper (#2471-2476)

2471 A927 3b multi .35 .25
2472 A928 3b multi .35 .25
2473 A929 3b multi .35 .25
2474 A930 3b multi .35 .25
2475 A931 3b multi .35 .25
2476 A932 3b multi .35 .25
Nos. 2471-2476 (6) 2.10 1.50

Litho. With Holographic Film

Self-Adhesive

Die Cut Perf. 13½x13¾

2477 A927 3b multi .35 .25
2478 A928 3b multi .35 .25
2479 A929 3b multi .35 .25
2480 A930 3b multi .35 .25
2481 A931 3b multi .35 .25
2482 A932 3b multi .35 .25
a. Sheet of 6, #2477-2482 2.10
Nos. 2477-2482 (6) 2.10 1.50

No. 2482a sold for 25b.

Red Rose — A933

Litho. & Embossed

2010, Feb. 5 *Perf. 13*

Granite Paper

2483 A933 5b multi .75 .25

A rose-scented scratch-and-sniff panel was applied over a rose leaf. A souvenir sheet containing one No. 2483 sold for 14b.

A934

A935

Chinese Deities — A936

2010, Feb. 8 **Litho.** *Perf. 14x14½*

Granite Paper

2484 A934 5b multi .30 .25
2485 A935 5b multi .30 .25
2486 A936 5b multi .30 .25
a. Souvenir sheet of 3, #2484-2486, perf. 13½x13¼ 1.50 1.10
Nos. 2484-2486 (3) .90 .75

No. 2486a sold for 24b.

A937

A938

A939

Fantasy World Painting Competition A940

2010, Feb. 25 **Litho.** *Perf. 13½*

Granite Paper

2487 A937 5b multi .45 .25
2488 A938 5b multi .45 .25
2489 A939 5b multi .45 .25
2490 A940 5b multi .45 .25
a. Souvenir sheet of 4, #2487-2490 2.50 1.40
Nos. 2487-2490 (4) 1.80 1.00

Bangkok 2010 Intl. Stamp Exhibition. No. 2490a sold for 28b.

Red Cross — A941

2010, Mar. 30 *Perf. 13½*

Granite Paper

2491 A941 3b multi .75 .25

Postman Carrying Parcel — A942

2010, Mar. 30 ***Perf. 13***
Granite Paper
2492 A942 3b multi .75 .25

Heritage Conservation Day — A943

Designs: No. 2493, 3b, Jalimangalasana Residence, Sanam Chandra Palace. No. 2494, 3b, Phiman Chakri Hall, Phyathai Palace. No. 2495, 3b, Phra Ram Ratchaniwet Palace. No. 2496, 3b, Main Building, Srapathum Palace.

2010, Apr. 2 ***Perf. 14½x14***
Granite Paper
2493-2496 A943 Set of 4 .75 .55
a. Souvenir sheet of 4, #2493-2496, perf. 13½ 1.25 .95

No. 2496a sold for 19b.

King Chao Phraya Chakkri (Rama I) (1736-1809) A944

2010, Apr. 6 ***Perf. 13¼***
Granite Paper
2497 A944 3b multi .75 .25

Wedding of King Bhumibol Adulyadej and Queen Sirikit, 60th Anniv. — A945

King and Queen: No. 2498, 15b, As young couple. No. 2499, 15b, As older couple.

Litho. & Embossed With Foil Application
2010, Apr. 28 ***Perf. 13¼***
2498-2499 A945 Set of 2 1.90 1.40
a. Souvenir sheet of 2, #2498-2499 3.75 3.00

Values for Nos. 2498-2499 are for stamps with surrounding selvage. No. 2499a sold for 60b.

Thai Airways International, 50th Anniv. — A946

Airplanes: No. 2500, 3b, DC-6. No. 2501, 3b, DC-10. No. 2502, 3b, Boeing 747-400. No. 2503, 3b, Airbus A340-600.

Litho. & Embossed
2010, May 1 ***Perf. 14¼x14½***
Granite Paper
2500-2503 A946 Set of 4 .75 .55
a. Souvenir sheet of 4, #2500-2503 1.40 1.10

No. 2503a sold for 22b.

Coronation of King Bhumibol Adulyadej, 60th Anniv. — A947

2010, May 5 **Litho.** ***Perf. 13¼***
Granite Paper
2504 A947 9b multi .55 .40

Visakhapuja Day — A948

2010, May 28 ***Perf. 14¼x14½***
Granite Paper
2505 A948 3b multi .75 .25
a. Souvenir sheet of 4, #2293, 2361, 2417, 2505 1.25 .95

No. 2505a sold for 20b.

Tourism Authority of Thailand, 50th Anniv. A949

Designs: No. 2506, 3b, Wat Arun, Bangkok. No. 2507, 3b, Royal barge. No. 2508, 3b, Canoeists near shore. No. 2509, 3b, Tourists on elephants fording river.

2010, June 1 **Litho.**
Granite Paper
2506-2509 A949 Set of 4 .75 .55

Election Commission, 12th Anniv. — A950

2010, June 9 ***Perf. 13½***
Granite Paper
2510 A950 3b multi .75 .25

No. 1960 Surcharged in Silver
Miniature Sheet

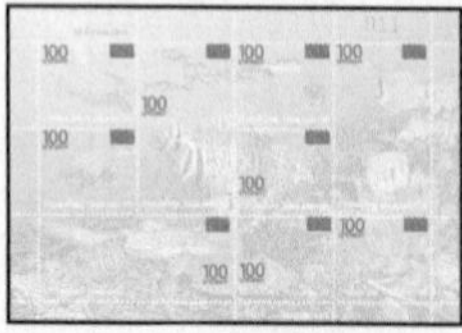

Designs as before.

Method and Perf. As Before
2010, June 16 **Granite Paper**
2511 A642 Sheet of 9 70.00 42.50
a.-f. 100b on 3b Any single 6.00 4.50
g.-i. 100b on 6b Any single 6.00 4.50

No. 1776 Surcharged in Gold

Method and Perf. As Before
2010, June 16 **Granite Paper**
2512 A577 200b on 9b #1776 17.50 13.25

Bangkok General Post Office Building, 70th Anniv. — A951

Designs: No. 2513, 3b, Sculptures of Type A15 stamp, Garuda. No. 2514, 3b, Sculptures of Type A29 stamp, man at table. 5b, General Post Office Building, horiz. (57x23mm).

Perf. 14x14½, 14½x14
2010, June 24 **Litho.**
Granite Paper
2513-2515 A951 Set of 3 .70 .55

King Nang Khlao Chao Youhua (Rama III) (1787-1851) A952

2010, July 21 ***Perf. 13¼***
Granite Paper
2516 A952 3b multi .75 .25

Miniature Sheet

Provincial Seals — A953

No. 2517 — Seals of: a, Lop Buri. b, Lampang. c, Lamphun. d, Loei. e, Si Sa Ket. f, Sakon Nakhon. g, Songkhla. h, Satun. i, Samut Prakan. j, Samut Songkhram.

Litho. With Foil Application
2010, July 23 ***Perf. 13***
Granite Paper
2517 A953 3b Sheet of 10, #a-j 2.10 1.40

National Communications Day — A954

2010, Aug. 4 **Litho.** ***Perf. 14½x14***
Granite Paper
2518 A954 3b multi .75 .25

Peacock — A955

Inscriptions: No. 2519, 15b, Thai Silk. No. 2520, 15b, Thai Silk Blend. No. 2521, 25b, Classic Thai Silk. No. 2522, 25b, Royal Thai Silk.

Litho. With Foil Application on Affixed Silk Oval
2010, Aug. 4 ***Perf. 13¼***
2519-2522 A955 Set of 4 5.00 3.75

Bangkok 2010 Intl. Stamp Exhibition. A souvenir sheet containing one No. 2522 sold for 60b.

Orchids — A956

Rhynchostylis gigantea varieties: No. 2523, 3b, Speckle. No. 2524, 3b, Kultana strain. No. 2525, 3b, Alba. No. 2526, 3b, Rubrum.

2010, Aug. 5 **Litho.** ***Perf. 14x14½***
Granite Paper
2523-2526 A956 Set of 4 .75 .55
a. Souvenir sheet of 4, #2523-2526, perf. 13½ 1.25 .95

No. 2526a sold for 20b. A sheet similar to No. 2526a with the emblem of the 4th Siam Paragon Bangkok Royal Orchid Paradise sold for 80b.

Thai Literature Heritage A957

2010, Aug. 7 ***Perf. 14½x14***
Granite Paper
2527 A957 3b multi .75 .25

Flag of Thailand A958

Cassia Flowers A959

2010, Aug. 12 ***Perf. 14¼x14½***
Granite Paper
2528 A958 3b multi .30 .25
2529 A959 3b multi .30 .25

Nos. 1687 and 1689 Surcharged

Methods, Perfs. and Watermarks As Before
2010, Aug. 27
2530 A543 10b on 9b #1688 .65 .50
2531 A543 10b on 9b #1689 .65 .50

No. 1736 Surcharged in Gold

Method, Perf. and Watermark As Before
2010, Sept. 1
2532 A564 10b on 6b #1736 .65 .50

Miniature Sheet

Queen Savang Vadhana (1862-1955) — A960

No. 2533: a, Queen Savang Vadhana. b, Prince Mahidol and his wife, Princess Srinagarindra. c, King Bhumibol Adulyadej and women (denomination in yellow), horiz. d, King Bhumibol Adulyadej and Queen Sirikit (denomination in dark blue), horiz.

Perf. 13¼ (#2533a), 13¼x13¼x14½x13¼ (#2533b), 14½x14

2010, Sept. 10 Litho. Unwmk.

Granite Paper

2533	A960	3b Sheet of 4, #a-d	.80	.60

Royal Thai Mint, 150th Anniv. — A961

No. 2534: a, Coin, old Mint building, denomination at LR. b, Coin, new Mint building, denomination at LL.

Litho. & Embossed

2010, Sept. 17 ***Perf. 13¼***

Granite Paper

2534	A961	Horiz. pair	.70	.55
a.-b.		5b Either single	.35	.25
c.		Souvenir sheet of 2, #2534a-2534b	1.40	1.10

No. 2534c sold for 20b.

National Youth Day — A962

2010, Sept. 20 Litho. ***Perf. 14½x14***

Granite Paper

2535	A962	3b multi	.75	.25

Tin Toys — A963

Designs: No. 2536, 3b, Wind-up rabbit and chicken. No. 2537, 3b, Chinese rattle drums. No. 2538, 3b, Pop gun. No. 2539, 3b, Boats. No. 2540, 3b, Boy on tricycle. No. 2541, 3b, Tops.

2010, Oct. 5 ***Perf. 13***

Granite Paper

2536-2541	A963	Set of 6	1.25	.95

A souvenir sheet containing Nos. 2536-2538 and a souvenir sheet containing Nos. 2539-2541 exist. Each sold for 20b.

Curves — A964

2010, Oct. 5 ***Perf. 13¼***

Granite Paper

2542	A964	3b green	.30	.25
2543	A964	3b lemon	.30	.25
2544	A964	3b blue	.30	.25
		Nos. 2542-2544 (3)	.90	.75

Department of Comptroller General, 120th Anniv. A965

2010, Oct. 7 ***Perf. 14½x14***

Granite Paper

2545	A965	3b multi	.75	.25

Goddess Guan Yin — A966

2010, Oct. 10 ***Perf. 14½x14¼***

Granite Paper

2546	A966	9b multi	.60	.45
a.		Souvenir sheet of 1	1.10	.85

No. 2546a sold for 15b.

King Bhumibol Adulyadej — A967

2010 Litho. ***Perf. 13½x13¼***

Granite Paper

2547	A967	1b blue	.30	.25
2548	A967	2b lake	.30	.25
2549	A967	3b green	.30	.25
2550	A967	5b fawn	.35	.30
2551	A967	6b violet	.40	.30
2552	A967	7b lilac rose	.55	.35
2553	A967	9b yel bister	.65	.45
2554	A967	10b brown & blk	.75	.55
2555	A967	12b bl grn & gray bl	.85	.60
2556	A967	15b bis & dk grn	1.05	.75
a.		Souvenir sheet of 10, #2547-2556	7.50	4.25

Litho. & Engr.

2557	A967	50b pur & bl grn	3.75	2.60
2558	A967	100b apple grn & grn	7.25	5.25
2559	A967	200b rose & brn	14.50	10.00

Size:24x29mm

2560	A967	500b org brn & brn	36.50	26.00
a.		Souvenir sheet of 4, #2557-2560	85.00	45.00
		Nos. 2547-2560 (14)	67.50	47.90

Issued: Nos. 2547-2556, 2556a, 10/10; Nos. 2557-2560, 2560a, 11/11.

King Chulalongkorn (Rama V) (1853-1910) A968

2010, Oct. 15 Litho. ***Perf. 13¼***

Granite Paper

2561	A968	9b multi	.60	.45

Vajiravudh College, Cent. — A969

2010, Nov. 11 ***Perf. 13½***

Granite Paper

2562	A969	3b multi	.75	.25

A970

A971

A972

Fireworks A973

2010, Nov. 15 ***Perf. 13½***

Granite Paper

2563	A970	3b multi	.30	.25
2564	A971	3b multi	.30	.25
2565	A972	3b multi	.30	.25
2566	A973	3b multi	.30	.25
a.		Souvenir sheet of 4, #2563-2566	1.20	1.10
		Nos. 2563-2566 (4)	1.20	1.00

No. 2566a sold for 20b.

King Bhumibol Adulyadej, 83rd Birthday — A974

Litho. With Rice Grain Affixed

2010, Dec. 5 ***Perf. 13¼***

Granite Paper

2567	A974	9b multi	.60	.45

New Year 2011 (Year of the Rabbit) — A975

2011, Jan. 1 Litho. ***Perf. 13***

Granite Paper

2568	A975	3b multi	.75	.25

Khun Chang A976

Khun Phaen A977

Kumanthong A978

Pimpiralai A979

2011, Jan. 8 ***Perf. 13¼***

Granite Paper

2569	A976	3b multi	.30	.25
2570	A977	3b multi	.30	.25
2571	A978	3b multi	.30	.25
2572	A979	3b multi	.30	.25
		Nos. 2569-2572 (4)	1.20	1.00

Khun Chang Khun Phaen, epic poem.

Fruits and Vegetables — A980

Designs: No. 2573, 3b, Bottle gourd. No. 2574, 3b, Lime. No. 2575, 3b, Tomato. No. 2576, 3b, Pumpkin.

2011, Jan. 15 ***Perf. 13½***

Granite Paper

2573-2576	A980	Set of 4	.80	.60

Li Tie Guai — A981

Han Zhong Li — A982

Lu Dong Bin — A983

Zhang Guo Lao — A984

Lan Cai He — A985

He Xian Gu — A986

Han Xiang Zi — A987

Cao Guo Jiu — A988

2011, Feb. 1 Litho. & Embossed

Granite Paper

2577	A981	3b multi	.40	.25
2578	A982	3b multi	.40	.25
2579	A983	3b multi	.40	.25
2580	A984	3b multi	.40	.25
2581	A985	3b multi	.40	.25
2582	A986	3b multi	.40	.25
2583	A987	3b multi	.40	.25
2584	A988	3b multi	.40	.25
a.		Souvenir sheet of 8, #2577-2584	3.00	2.00
		Nos. 2577-2584 (8)	3.20	2.00

Eight Chinese Immortals.

No. 1820 Surcharged in Gold

No. 1737 Surcharged in Gold

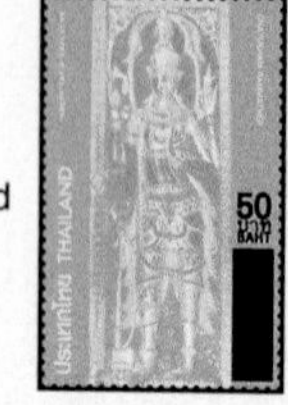
No. 2349 Surcharged

Methods, Perfs and Papers As Before

2011

2585 A550 12b on 9b #1820 .80 .60
2586 A564 50b on 9b #1737 3.25 2.50
2588 A841 Sheet of 12 39.00 39.00
a.-l. 50b on 9b Any single, #2349a-2349l 3.25 2.50

Issued: Nos. 2585, 2586, 2588, 2/2.

Charoen Krung Road, 150th Anniv. — A989

2011, Feb. 5 Litho. ***Perf. 14½x14¼***
Granite Paper

2589 A989 3b multi .75 .25

Love A990

No. 2590 — Heart of: a, Roses. b, Concentric lines.

2011, Feb. 7 ***Perf. 13***
Granite Paper

2590 A990 5b Horiz. pair, #a-b .65 .50

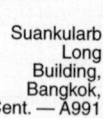

Suankularb Long Building, Bangkok, Cent. — A991

2011, Mar. 8 ***Perf. 14½x14***
Granite Paper

2591 A991 3b multi .75 .25

Fine Arts Department, Cent. — A992

2011, Mar. 27 ***Perf. 14x14½***
Granite Paper

2592 A992 3b multi .75 .25

Princess Maha Chakri Sirindhorn Wearing Red Cross Uniform — A993

2011, Mar. 30 ***Perf. 13¼***
Granite Paper

2593 A993 3b multi .75 .25

A994

A995

A996

Muang Tam Religious Sanctuary, Prakhon Chai — A997

2011, Apr. 2 ***Perf. 14½x14***
Granite Paper

2594 A994 3b multi .30 .25
2595 A995 3b multi .30 .25
2596 A996 3b multi .30 .25
2597 A997 3b multi .30 .25
a. Souvenir sheet of 4, #2594-2597 1.40 1.10
Nos. 2594-2597 (4) 1.20 1.00

Thai Heritage Conservation Day. No. 2597a sold for 20b.

Momrajawongse Kukrit Pramoj (1911-95), Prime Minister — A998

Kukrit Pramoj: No. 2598, 3b, Wearing uniform with sash, yellow orange panel at right. No. 2599, 3b, Wearing traditional costume, olive green panel at right. No. 2600, 3b, With dogs, brown panel at right, horiz. No. 2601, 3b, With Mao Zedong, gray panel at right, horiz.

2011, Apr. 20 ***Perf. 13¼***
Granite Paper

2598-2601 A998 Set of 4 1.60 .60

Diplomatic Relations Between Thailand and Laos, 60th Anniv. — A999

No. 2602: a, Woman, denomination at LR. b, Woman, denomination at LL. c, Cassia fistula flowers, denomination at LR. d, Plumeria flowers, denomination at LL.

2011, Apr. 22 ***Perf. 14x14½***
Granite Paper

2602 A999 3b Block of 4, #a-d .80 .60

See Laos Nos. 1836-1839.

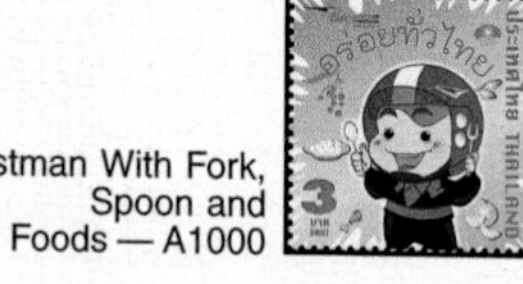
Postman With Fork, Spoon and Foods — A1000

2011, May 10 Litho. ***Perf. 13***
Granite Paper

2603 A1000 3b multi .75 .25

Self-Adhesive
Serpentine Die Cut 12

2604 A1000 3b multi .75 .25

Pridi Banomyong (1900-83), Prime Minister — A1001

No. 2605 — Banomyong: a, In suit and tie. b, Wearing uniform and sash.

2011, May 11 ***Perf. 13¼***
Granite Paper

2605 A1001 3b Horiz. pair, #a-b .75 .30

Panyananda Bhikkhu (1911-2007), Buddhist Monk — A1002

Bhikkhu and: No. 2606, 3b, Thai text. No. 2607, 3b, Buddhist temple. No. 2608, 3b, Sculpture. No. 2609, 3b, Shell-shaped award.

2011, May 11 ***Perf. 13¼***
Granite Paper

2606-2609 A1002 Set of 4 1.15 .60

No. 2606 and 2608 exist in a souvenir sheet. No. 2607 exists in a souvenir sheet of 1.

Visakhapuja Day — A1003

2011, May 17 ***Perf. 14½x14¼***
Granite Paper

2610 A1003 3b multi .70 .25

A souvenir sheet containing one example of No. 2610 sold for 10b.

Orchid Varieties — A1004

Designs: No. 2611, 3b, Dendrobium "Cherluk Red." No. 2612, 3b, Dendrobium "Lai Sirin." No. 2613, 3b, Dendrobium "Suree Peach." No. 2614, 3b, Dendrobium "Cheetah."

2011, June 2 ***Perf. 14x14½***
Granite Paper

2611-2614 A1004 Set of 4 2.50 .60
a. Souvenir sheet of 4, #2611-2614, perf. 13½ 1.40 1.10

No. 2614a sold for 20b. A sheet similar to No. 2614a, but with the emblem of the 5th Siam Paragon Bangkok Royal Orchid Paradise and the date of the show, sold for 100b.

Department of Science Service, 120th Anniv. A1005

2011, June 23 ***Perf. 14½x14***
Granite Paper

2615 A1005 3b multi .70 .25

No. 2615 was printed in sheets of 20 with stamps from the right column having purple engine turning lines in the background.

Scouting in Thailand, Cent. A1006

2011, July 1 ***Perf. 13¼***
Granite Paper

2616 A1006 3b multi .75 .25

A1007

Diplomatic Relations Between Thailand and Portugal, 500th Anniv. — A1008

No. 2617: a, Portuguese caravel, rowboats, Thai buildings and temples. b, Elephant and riders at dockside.

No. 2618: a, Portuguese caravel, Thai buildings. b, Thai boats and buildings.

2011, July 20 ***Perf. 13½***
Granite Paper

2617 A1007 3b Horiz. pair, #a-b .40 .30
2618 A1008 3b Horiz. pair, #a-b .40 .30

See Portugal Nos. 3334-3335.

Miniature Sheet

Provincial Seals — A1009

No. 2619 — Seals of: a, Samut Sakhon. b, Sa Kaeo. c, Saraburi. d, Sing Buri. e, Sukhothai. f, Suphan Buri. g, Surat Thani. h, Surin. i, Nong Khai. j, Nong Bua Lam Phu.

Litho. & Embossed With Foil Application

2011, July 20 *Perf. 13½*

Granite Paper

2619 A1009 3b Sheet of 10, #a-j 2.00 1.50

Sheets of ten identical stamps were available, but these appear to have been sold locally and not through the philatelic bureau.

Thai Alphabet — A1010

No. 2620 — Various characters of Thai alphabet that are the first consonants of the word for: a, Chicken. b, Eggs. c, Bottles. d, Water buffalo. e, Person wearing red shirt. f, Bell. g, Snake. h, Plates. i, Cymbals on string. j, Elephant. k, Chain on stump. l, Trees. m, Woman weaing pink blouse. n, Headdress. o, Javelin. p, Pedestal. q, Mandodari (girl wearing headdress). r, Old man. s, Child wearing Buddhist monk's robe. t, Child in overalls. u, Turtle. v, Bags. w, Soldier. x, Flag.

No. 2621 — Various characters of Thai alphabet that are the first consonants of the word for: a, Mouse. b, Leaves. c, Fish. d, Bee on flowers. e, Lids of pots. f, Bowl. g, Teeth. h, Sailboat. i, Horse. j, Yaksha (Buddhist giant). k, Boat. l, Monkey. m, Ring. n, Pavilion. o, Hermit in cave. p, Tiger. q, Chest. r, Kite. s, Basin with flower. t, Owl.

2011, July 29 **Litho.** *Perf. 14¼*

Granite Paper

2620	Sheet of 24	6.00	6.00
a.-x.	A1010 1b Any single	.30	.25
2621	Sheet of 20 + 4 labels	5.00	5.00
a.-t.	A1010 1b Any single	.30	.25

Communications Day — A1011

2011, Aug. 4 *Perf. 14x14½*

Granite Paper

2622 A1011 3b multi .75 .25

A1012

A1013

A1014

Likay Performers — A1015

Litho. With Glitter Affixed

2011, Aug. 4 *Perf. 14x14½*

Granite Paper

2623	A1012 5b multi	.35	.30
2624	A1013 5b multi	.35	.30
2625	A1014 5b multi	.35	.30
2626	A1015 5b multi	.35	.30
a.	Souvenir sheet of 4, #2623-2626, perf. 13½	2.00	1.50
	Nos. 2623-2626 (4)	1.40	1.20

Thaipex 2011 Intl. Philatelic Exhibition, Bangkok. No. 2626a sold for 30b.

Philatelists Association of Thailand A1016

2011, Aug. 9 **Litho.** *Perf. 13¼*

Granite Paper

2627 A1016 3b multi .75 .25

Miniature Sheet

Queen Savang Vadhana (1862-1955) — A1017

No. 2628 — Queen Savang Vadhana: a, As child, with King Chulalongkorn (pink background). b, With Crown Prince Maha Vajirunhis (olive green background. c, With Prince Mahitala Dhibesra Adulyadej Vikrom and Princess Valaya Alongkorn (blue violet background), horiz. d, With King Ananda Mahidol, King Bhumibol Adulyadej, Princess Galyani Vadhana, and Prince Rangsit Prayurasakdi (blue green background), horiz.

2011, Sept. 10 *Perf. 13¼*

Granite Paper

2628 A1017 3b Sheet of 4, #a-d .80 .60

Worldwide Fund for Nature (WWF) — A1018

Cats: No. 2629, 3b, Marbled cat. No. 2630, 3b, Asiatic golden cat. No. 2631, 3b, Leopard cat. No. 2632, 3b, Flat-headed cat.

2011, Sept. 26 *Perf. 13*

Granite Paper

2629-2632	A1018 Set of 4	.80	.60
a.	Souvenir sheet of 4, #2629-2632, + label	1.40	1.10

No. 2632a sold for 20b.

International Letter Writing Week — A1019

Designs: No. 2633, 3b, Girl and boy writing letters. No. 2634, 3b, Girl bringing letter to mail box. No. 2635, 3b, Postman delivering letter to girl. No. 2636, 3b, Boy and girl reading letters.

2011, Oct. 4 **Granite Paper**

2633-2636	A1019 Set of 4	.80	.60
a.	Souvenir sheet of 4, #2633-2636	1.40	1.10

No. 2636a sold for 20b.

King Bhumibol Adulyadej in Carpentry Shop A1020

2011, Oct. 21 *Perf. 13¼*

Granite Paper

2637 A1020 3b multi .75 .25

Cabinet declaration of King Bhumibol Adulyadej as "Father of the Thai Workmanship Standard."

Princess Mother Srinigarindra (1900-95) — A1021

2011, Oct. 21 **Litho.**

Granite Paper

2638 A1021 3b multi .75 .25

Children's Projects of Princess Maha Chakri Sirindhorn, 30th Anniv. — A1022

2011, Oct. 21 *Perf. 13¼*

Granite Paper

2639 A1022 3b multi .75 .25

Lotus Flower — A1023

2011, Nov. 7 *Perf. 13*

Granite Paper

2640 A1023 3b multi .75 .25

Festivals A1024

Designs: No. 2641, 3b, Loy Krathong and Candle Festival, Sukhothai. No. 2642, 3b, Festival of Illuminated Boat Procession, Nakhon Phanom. No. 2643, 3b, Yi-Peng Festival, Chiang Mai. No. 2644, 3b, Loi Krathong Sai Festival, Tak.

2011, Nov. 10 *Perf. 13¼*

Granite Paper

2641-2644	A1024 Set of 4	1.10	.60
a.	Souvenir sheet of 4, #2641-2644	1.50	1.10

No. 2644a sold for 22b.

Medallions of Monks — A1025

Designs: No. 2645, 9b, Luang Pho Klan, Wat Phrayathkaram. No. 2646, 9b, Luang Pu Iam, Wat Nang Ratchaworawihan. No. 2647, 9b, Luang Pu Suk, Wat Pak Khlong Makham Thao. No. 2648, 9b, Luang Pho Khong, Wat Bang Kaphom. No. 2649, 9b, Luang Pho Chui, Wat Khongkharam.

Litho. & Embossed

2011, Nov. 11 *Perf. 13¼*

Granite Paper

2645-2649	A1025 Set of 5	3.00	2.25
a.	Souvenir sheet of 5, #2645-2649	7.00	5.00

No. 2649a sold for 60b.

A1026

A1027

A1028

Fireworks A1029

Stamps With White Frames

Litho. With Glitter Affixed

2011, Nov. 15 **Granite Paper**

2650	A1026 3b multi	.45	.25
2651	A1027 3b multi	.45	.25
2652	A1028 3b multi	.45	.25
2653	A1029 3b multi	.45	.25
	Nos. 2650-2653 (4)	1.00	1.00

Souvenir Sheet

Stamps Without White Frames

2654	Sheet of 4	1.50	1.10
a.	A1026 3b multi	.35	.25
b.	A1027 3b multi	.35	.25
c.	A1028 3b multi	.35	.25
d.	A1029 3b multi	.35	.25

No. 2654 sold for 22b.

A1030

A1031

A1032

A1033

A1034

A1035

A1036

Coins Depicting King Bhumibol Adulyadej A1037

Awards of King Bhumibol Adulyadej — A1038

No. 2663: a, Agricola Medal inscribed: "Golden Jubilee of His Majesty's Reign". b, World Health Organization Award (plate on stand). c, Human Development Lifetime Achievement Award (silver bowl on stand). d, International Rice Award (medallion dated 1996). e, Award inscribed "Glory to the Greatest Inventor." f, WIPO Global Leader Award. g, Brussels Eureka medal.

Litho. & Embossed With Foil Application

2011, Dec. 5 ***Perf. 12¼***

Granite Paper

2655 A1030 5b multi .35 .25
2656 A1031 5b multi, inscribed "7 Cycle" .35 .25
a. Inscribed "7th Cycle" .65 .50
2657 A1032 5b multi .35 .25
2658 A1033 5b multi .35 .25
2659 A1034 5b multi .35 .25
2660 A1035 5b multi .35 .25
2661 A1036 5b multi .35 .25
a. Sheet of 7, #2655, 2656a, 2657-2661 4.75 3.50
2662 A1037 100b multi 6.50 5.00
Nos. 2655-2662 (8) 8.95 6.75

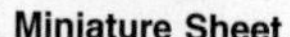
Miniature Sheet

2663 A1038 5b Sheet of 7, #a-g 8.00 6.50

King Bhumibol Adulyadej, 84th birthday. No. 2661a sold for 70b.

Diplomatic Relations Between Thailand and Pakistan, 60th Anniv. — A1039

2011, Dec. 13 Litho. ***Perf. 13¼***

Granite Paper

2664 A1039 3b multi .75 .25

New Year 2012 (Year of the Dragon) — A1040

2012, Jan. 1 ***Perf. 13***

Granite Paper

2665 A1040 3b multi .75 .25

Prince Mahidol Adulyadej (1892-1929), Father of King Bhumibol Adulyadej — A1041

2012, Jan. 1 ***Perf. 13¼***

Granite Paper

2666 A1041 3b multi .75 .25

A1042

A1043

A1044

Children's Day — A1045

2012, Jan. 14 ***Perf. 14½x14***

Granite Paper

2667 A1042 3b multi .30 .25
2668 A1043 3b multi .30 .25
2669 A1044 3b multi .30 .25
2670 A1045 3b multi .30 .25
Nos. 2667-2670 (4) 1.00 1.00

King Bhumibol Adulyadej and Map — A1046

2012, Jan. 16 ***Perf. 13¼***

Granite Paper

2671 A1046 3b multi .75 .25

Caishenye, God of Wealth — A1047

Various depictions with background color of: No. 2672, 3b, Red. No. 2673, 3b, Olive green.

2012, Jan. 23 Litho.

Granite Paper

2672-2673 A1047 Set of 2 .75 .30

A souvenir sheet containing Nos. 2672-2673 sold for 15b.

Chiang Rai, 750th Anniv. — A1048

2012, Jan. 26 ***Perf. 14x14½***

Granite Paper

2674 A1048 3b multi .75 .25

Love A1049

No. 2675, 5b: a, Heart as padlock. b, Heart on key.
No. 2676, 5b: a, Teddy bear with padlock heart. b, Teddy bear with key.

2012, Feb. 7 ***Perf. 13***

Granite Paper
Horiz. Pairs, #a-b

2675-2676 A1049 Set of 2 1.40 1.10

Excise Department, 80th Anniv. A1050

2012, Feb. 17 ***Perf. 13¼***

Granite Paper

2677 A1050 3b multi .75 .25

Red Cross — A1051

2012, Mar. 30 ***Perf. 14x14½***

Granite Paper

2678 A1051 3b multi .75 .25

Asian-Pacific Postal Union, 50th Anniv. A1052

2012, Apr. 1 ***Perf. 14½x14***

Granite Paper

2679 A1052 3b multi .75 .25

King Vajiravudh (1881-1925) and Bank Building A1053

King Prajadhipok (1893-1941) and Bank Building A1054

King Ananda Mahidol (1925-46) and Bank Building A1055

King Bhumibol Adulyadej and Bank Building A1056

2012, Apr. 1 ***Perf. 14x14½***

Granite Paper

2680 A1053 3b multi .30 .25
2681 A1054 3b multi .30 .25
2682 A1055 3b multi .30 .25
2683 A1056 3b multi .30 .25
Nos. 2680-2683 (4) 1.00 1.00

Government Savings Bank, 99th anniv.

Ministry of Transport, Cent. — A1057

Designs: No. 2684, 3b, Aerial view of highway. No. 2685, 3b, Bridge and train. No. 2686, 3b, Ship. No. 2687, 3b, Airplane and airport.

2012, Apr. 1 Litho.

Granite Paper

2684-2687 A1057 Set of 4 .80 .60
a. Sheet of 4, #2684-2687 5.50 5.50

Cultural Preservation — A1058

No. 2688, 3b: a, Monument No. 1, Muang Sing Historical Park. b, Radiating Bodhisattva Avalokitesavara, Muang Sing Historical Park.
No. 2689, 3b: a, Prang Si Thep, Si Thep Historical Park. b, Stone Dharmachakra, Si Thep Historical Park.

2012, Apr. 2 ***Perf. 13¼***

Granite Paper
Horiz. Pairs, #a-b

2688-2689 A1058 Set of 2 1.10 .60
c. Souvenir sheet of 4, #2688a-2688b, 2689a-2689b 1.40 1.10

No. 2689c sold for 20b.

Miniature Sheets

Royal Thai Air Force, Cent. A1059

No. 2690, 3b: a, Nieuport IIN. b, Breguet III. c, Biplane (Thai inscriptions). d, Ki-30. e, F8F-1. f, F-84G. g, F-86F. h, F-5A.

No. 2691, 3b: a, F-5B. b, F-5E. c, F-16 ADF. d, Gripen C. e, Avro. f, Boeing 737-800. g, Bell 412EP helicopter. h, S-92A helicopter.

2012 Sheets of 8, #a-h Litho.

Granite Paper

2690-2691 A1059 Set of 2 3.00 2.25

Issued: No. 2690, 4/9; No. 2691, 7/2.

Four sheets, containing Nos. 2690a-2690d, 2690e-2690h, 2691a-2691d and 2691e-2691h, respectively, sold for 35b each.

Buddha Statues — A1060

Designs: No. 2692, 5b, Phra Phutthasothon, Wat Sothonwararam Worawihan (olive brown inscriptions). No. 2693, 5b, Luang Pho To, Wat Bang Phli Yai Nai (dark blue inscriptions). No. 2694, 5b, Luang Pho Wat Rai Khing, Wat Rai Khing (red brown inscriptions). No. 2695, 5b, Luang Pho Wat Ban Laem, Wat Phetchasamut Worawihan (green inscriptions). No. 2696, 5b, Luang Pho Wat Khao Ta-Khrao, Wat Khao Ta-Khrao (purple inscriptions).

2012, May 5 ***Perf. 13¼***

Granite Paper

2692-2696 A1060 Set of 5 2.90 1.25
a. Souvenir sheet of 5, #2692-2696 4.50 2.00

No. 2696a sold for 40b.

2012 Rotary International Convention, Bangkok — A1061

2012, May 6 ***Perf. 14x14½***

Granite Paper

2697 A1061 3b multi .75 .25

Vesak Day — A1062

2012, June 2 ***Perf. 13¼***

Granite Paper

2698 A1062 3b multi .75 .25

Miniature Sheet

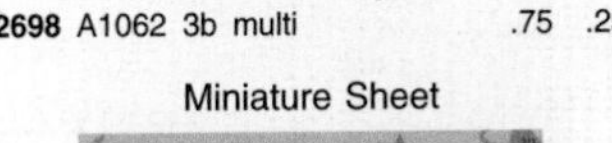

Provincial Seals — A1063

No. 2699 — Seals of: a, Ang Thong. b, Udon Thani. c, Uttaradit. d, Uthai Thani. e, Ubon Ratchathani. f, Amnat Charoen. g, Chang Thai. h, Ratchaphruek. i, Sala Thai. j, Bueng Kan.

Litho. & Embossed With Foil Application

2012, June 28 Granite Paper

2699 A1063 3b Sheet of 10, #a-j 3.50 1.40

Sheets of ten identical stamps were available, but these appear to have been sold locally and not through the philatelic bureau.

Office of the Prime Minister, 80th Anniv. A1064

2012, June 28 Litho. ***Perf. 14½x14***

Granite Paper

2700 A1064 3b multi .75 .25

Miniature Sheet

Coastlines — A1065

No. 2701: a, Phromthep Cape, Phuket, denomination at LR. b, Phromthep Cape, denomination at UR. c, Muko Ang Thong National Park, Surat Thani, denomination at LR. d, Muko Ang Thong National Park, denomination at UR. e, Rai Le Bay, Krabi, denomination at LR. f, Rai Le Bay, denomination at UR. g, Hong Island, Krabi, denomination at LR. h, Hong Island, denomination at UR. i, Panyi Island, Phang-nga, denomination at LR. j, Panyi Island, denomination at UR.

2012, July 5 ***Perf. 14¼x14½***

Granite Paper

2701 A1065 15b Sheet of 10, #a-j 15.00 7.25

Ranong, 150th Anniv. A1066

2012, July 21 ***Perf. 14½x14***

Granite Paper

2702 A1066 3b multi .75 .25

Prince Maha Vajiralongkorn, 60th Birthday — A1067

Litho. With Foil Application

2012, July 28 ***Perf. 13¼***

Granite Paper

2703 A1067 9b multi .60 .45

National Communications Day — A1068

2012, Aug. 4 Litho. ***Perf. 14½x14***

Granite Paper

2704 A1068 3b multi .75 .25

Miniature Sheet

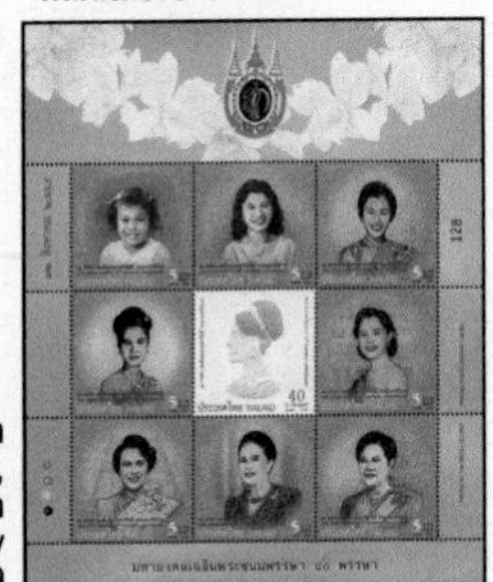

Queen Sirikit, 80th Birthday A1069

No. 2705 — Queen Sirikit: a, 5b, As child, with ribbon in hair. b, 5b, As young girl, wearing white dress and necklace. c, 5b, As young woman, with necklace. d, 5b, As young woman, with hair decoration. e, 5b, With bare shoulder showing, color photograph. f, 5b, With bird decoration on shoulder. g, 5b, Wearing red dress. h, 5b, Wearing blue earring. i, 40b, Profile.

Litho., Litho. & Embossed With Foil Application (#2705i)

2012, Aug. 12 ***Perf. 13***

Granite Paper

2705 A1069 Sheet of 9, #a-i 8.50 4.00
j. Souvenir sheet of 4, #2705a-2705d 4.00 1.60
k. Souvenir sheet of 4, #2705e-2705h 4.00 1.60

Nos. 2705j and 2705k each sold for 33b.

Miniature Sheet

Queen Savang Vadhana (1862-1955) — A1070

No. 2706 — Queen Savang Vadhana: a, As child (brown background). b, As young woman (green background). c, As woman (gray background). d, As older woman (blue background).

2012, Sept. 10 Litho. ***Perf. 13¼***

Granite Paper

2706 A1070 3b Sheet of 4, #a-d .80 .60

Thailand 2013 World Stamp Exhibition — A1071

No. 2707: a, Lanna-style lantern. b, Paper umbrellas. c, Bung Fai rocket. d, Reed mouth organ, circular panpipes. e, Courtier dolls. f, Pottery. g, Kolek boat. h, Wooden bird cage.

2012, Oct. 3 Granite Paper

2707 A1071 Block of 8 3.75 2.00
a.-h. 5b Any single .35 .25
i. Souvenir sheet of 2, #2702a-2702b 1.75 .75
j. Souvenir sheet of 2, #2702c-2702d 1.75 .75
k. Souvenir sheet of 2, #2702e-2702f 1.75 .75
l. Souvenir sheet of 2, #2702g-2702h 1.75 .75

Nos. 2707i-2707l each sold for 15b.

Somdet Phra Nyanasamvara, Supreme Buddhist Patriarch of Thailand, 99th Birthday — A1072

2012, Oct. 3 ***Perf. 13¼***

Granite Paper

2708 A1072 5b multi .75 .25

A souvenir sheet containing one of No. 2708 sold for 15b.

International Letter Writing Week A1073

Designs: No. 2709, 3b, Girl bowing to grandparents, girl writing letter (denomination in red at LL). No. 2710, 3b, Girl and mother on parke bench, girl writing letter (denomination in dark blue at LR). No. 2711, 3b, Girl and boy, girl writing letter (denomination in red at LR). No. 2712, 3b, Classmates, girl writing letter (denomination in blue at LL).

2012, Oct. 8 Litho.

Granite Paper

2709-2712 A1073 Set of 4 2.10 .60
a. Souvenir sheet of 4, #2709-2712 2.75 1.10

No. 2712a sold for 20b.

Prince Nares Vararidhi (1855-1925) A1074

2012, Oct. 14 ***Perf. 13¼***

Granite Paper

2713 A1074 3b multi .75 .25

Souvenir Sheet

Visit of King Chulalongkorn to Austria, 115th Anniv. — A1075

No. 2714: a, 5b, King Chulalongkorn. b, 15b, Emperor Franz Josef of Austria.

2012, Nov. 10 Litho.

Granite Paper

2714 A1075 Sheet of 2, #a-b 1.40 1.10

See Austria No. 2409.

Fireworks — A1076

Various fireworks with background color of: No. 2715, 3b, Violet blue. No. 2716, 3b, Green. No. 2717, 3b, Red. No. 2718, 3b, Light blue.

Litho. With Glitter Affixed

2012, Nov. 15 Granite Paper

2715-2718 A1076 Set of 4 1.75 .60
a. Souvenir sheet of 4, #2715-2718 3.50 1.25

No. 2718a sold for 24r.

Princess Chulabhorn A1077

Litho. With Foil Application

2012, Dec. 1 **Granite Paper**

2719 A1077 5b multi .75 .25

Prince Damrong Rajanubhab (1862-1943) and Military Parade A1078

Prince Damrong Rajanubhab and Luk Khun Hall — A1079

Prince Damrong Rajanubhab and Books Written by Him — A1080

Prince Damrong Rajanubhab and Woradis Palace A1081

2012, Dec. 1 **Litho.**

Granite Paper

2720 A1078 3b multi .55 .25
2721 A1079 3b multi .55 .25
2722 A1080 3b multi .55 .25
2723 A1081 3b multi .55 .25
a. Souvenir sheet of 4, #2720-2723 3.50 1.10
Nos. 2720-2723 (4) 2.20 1.00

King Bhumibol Adulyadej, 85th Birthday — A1082

Litho. with Foil Application

2012, Dec. 5 **Granite Paper**

2724 A1082 9b multi .90 .45

Princess Bajrakitiyabha, Chairperson of the United Nations Commission on Crime Prevention and Criminal Justice — A1083

2012, Dec. 7 ***Perf. 13¼***

Granite Paper

2725 A1083 5b multi .75 .25

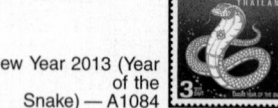

New Year 2013 (Year of the Snake) — A1084

2013, Jan. 1 **Litho.** ***Perf. 13***

Granite Paper

2726 A1084 3b multi .75 .25

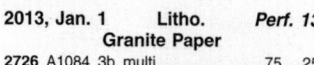

Children's Day — A1085

2013, Jan. 12 ***Perf. 13***

Granite Paper

2727 A1085 5b multi .75 .25

Tai Sui God — A1086

Tai Sui God with background color of: No. 2728, 5b, Red. No. 2729, 5b, Blue. No. 2730, 5b, Green.

Litho. With Foil Application

2013, Feb. 7 **Granite Paper**

2728-2730 A1086 Set of 3 1.80 .75
a. Souvenir sheet of 3, #2728-2730 2.25 1.50

No. 2730a sold for 30b.

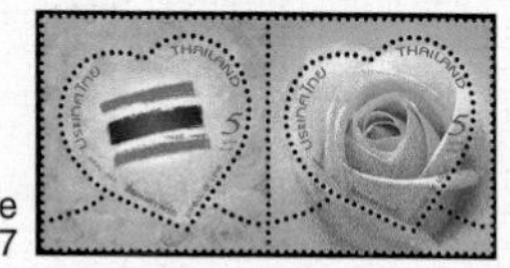

Love A1087

No. 2731: a, Flag of Thailand. b, Pink rose.

2013, Feb. 7 **Litho.**

2731 A1087 5b Horiz. pair, #a-b .70 .55

Miniature Sheet

Thailand 2013 World Stamp Exhibition, Bangkok — A1088

No. 2732: a, Gilded black lacquer cabinet (lai rot nam technique). b, Plaster dragon. c, Khon mask. d, Vessel with mother-of-pearl inlay. e, Figurine of elephant (metal beating). f, Molded sculpture of mythical being. g, Carved wood Buddha. h, Figurine with mirrored-glass inlay.

2013, Mar. 22 **Litho.** ***Perf. 13***

Granite Paper

2732 A1088 5b Sheet of 8, #a-h 2.75 2.10
i. Souvenir sheet of 2, #2732a-2732b 1.25 .95
j. Souvenir sheet of 2, #2732c-2732d 1.25 .95
k. Souvenir sheet of 2, #2732e-2732f 1.25 .95
l. Souvenir sheet of 2, #2732g-2732h 1.25 .95

Nos. 2732i-2732l each sold for 18b.

First Government Savings Bank, 1913 A1090

Government Savings Bank, 1934 A1091

Government Savings Bank, 1950 A1092

Government Savings Bank, 1966 A1093

King Chulalongkorn and Queen Srisavarindira A1089

2013, Mar. 29 **Litho.** ***Perf. 13¼***

Granite Paper

2733 A1089 3b multi .75 .25

Thai Red Cross, 120th anniv.

2013, Apr. 1 ***Perf. 14¾x14***

Granite Paper

2734 A1090 3b multi .35 .25
2735 A1091 3b multi .35 .25
2736 A1092 3b multi .35 .25
2737 A1093 3b multi .35 .25
Nos. 2734-2737 (4) 1.40 1.00

Government Savings Bank, cent.

A numbered souvenir sheet containing Nos. 2734-2737 exists.

Heritage Conservation Day — A1094

No. 2738 — Theatrical masks: a, Phra Shiva. b, Phra Vishnu. c, Phra Brahma. d, Phra Parakontap. e, Phra Panjasikorn. f, Phra kanes. g, Phra Vishnukam. h, Phra Indra.

2013, Apr. 2 ***Perf. 13¼***

Granite Paper

2738 A1094 3b Block of 8, #a-h 1.75 1.40

A souvenir sheet containing Nos. 2738a-2738c sold for 20b. This souvenir sheet also exists imperforate.

Bangkok, 2013 World Book Capital A1095

2013, Apr. 23 ***Perf. 14x13¼***

2739 A1095 5b multi .75 .25

A souvenir sheet containing No. 2739 sold for 20b. This sheet also exists imperforate.

Vesak Day A1096

2013, May 24 **Litho.** ***Perf. 14¼x14½***

Granite Paper

2740 A1096 3b multi .75 .25

Thai Engineering, Cent. A1097

Designs: No. 2741, 5b, Electrical engineering (workers and generators, gear at left). No. 2742, 5b, Civil engineering (workers and bridge, gear at left). No. 2743, 5b, Mechanical engineering (workers and machine, gear at right).

Litho. & Embossed

2013, June 1 ***Perf. 13½x13¾***

2741-2743 A1097 Set of 3 1.75 .75

Royal Irrigation Department, 111th Anniv. A1098

2013, June 13 **Litho.** ***Perf. 13¼***

Granite Paper

2744 A1098 3b multi .75 .25

Owls — A1099

Designs: No. 2745, 5b, Bubo sumatranus. No. 2746, 5b, Tyto alba. No. 2747, 5b, Otus lettia. No. 2748, 5b, Glaucidium brodiei.

2013, July 29 **Litho.** ***Perf. 14x14½***

Granite Paper

2745-2748 A1099 Set of 4 2.00 .95
a. Souvenir sheet of 4, #2745-2748, perf. 13¼ 4.50 1.75

No. 2748a sold for 35b.

Phra Si Sakkaya Thotsaphonlayan Phrathan Phutthamonthon Suthat Statue, by Silpa Bhirasri — A1100

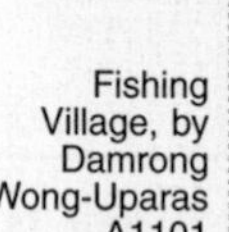

Fishing Village, by Damrong Wong-Uparas A1101

Lord Buddha's Footprint, by Pichai Nirand — A1102

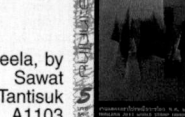

Leela, by Sawat Tantisuk A1103

Phra Mahathat Chalermaj Sattha, by Wanida Phuensuntom A1104

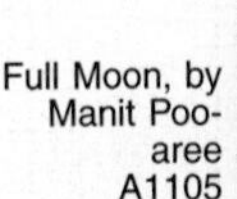

Full Moon, by Manit Poo-aree A1105

White Ubosot of Wat Rong Khun, by Chalermchai Kositpipat — A1106

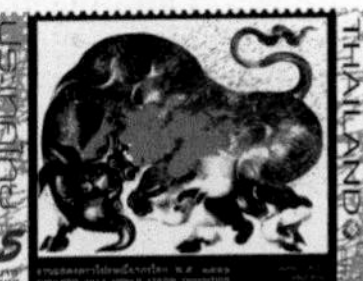

Bull, by Thawan Duchanee A1107

2013, Aug. 2 Litho. *Perf. 13¼*
Granite Paper

2749	Sheet of 8 + 4 labels	2.80	2.00
a.	A1100 5b multi	.35	.25
b.	A1101 5b multi	.35	.25
c.	A1102 5b multi	.35	.25
d.	A1103 5b multi	.35	.25
e.	A1104 5b multi	.35	.25
f.	A1105 5b multi	.35	.25
g.	A1106 5b multi	.35	.25
h.	A1107 5b multi	.35	.25
i.	Souvenir sheet of 2, #2749a-2749b	2.00	1.40
j.	Souvenir sheet of 2, #2749c-2749d	2.00	1.40
k.	Souvenir sheet of 2, #2749e-2749f	2.00	1.40
l.	Souvenir sheet of 2, #2749g-2749h	2.00	1.40

Thailand 2013 World Stamp Exhibition, Bangkok. Nos. 2749i-2749l each sold for 20b.
No. 2749a exists imperforate.

National Communications Day — A1108

Die Cut Perf. 11x10
2013, Aug. 4 Litho.
Self-Adhesive

2750	A1108 9b multi	.60	.45

A lottery code number appears under the scratch-off panel on the stamp. Values for unused stamps are for stamps with unscratched panel.

Thailand No. 1 Under Magnifying Glass — A1109

2013, Aug. 4 Litho. *Perf. 13¼*
Granite Paper

2751	A1109 5b multi	.75	.25

Thai postal services, 130th anniv.

Bangkok General Post Office Building A1110

Designs: No. 2753, Plaster renditions of Thailand Nos. 1 and 75. No. 2754, Garuda emblem from Post Office door.

2013, Aug. 4 Litho. *Perf. 14½x14*
Granite Paper

2752	A1110 5b shown	.55	.25

Litho. & Embossed

2753	A1110 5b multi	.55	.25

Litho. & Embossed With Foil Application

2754	A1110 5b multi	.55	.25
	Nos. 2752-2754 (3)	1.65	.75

A souvenir sheet with one perf. 13¼ example of No. 2754 sold for 16b.

A1111

A1112

A1113

A1114

A1115

Queen Sirikit — A1116

2013, Aug. 12 Litho. *Perf. 14x14½*
Granite Paper

2755	Miniature sheet of 6	1.50	1.10
a.	A1111 3b multi	.30	.25
b.	A1112 3b multi	.30	.25
c.	A1113 3b multi	.30	.25
d.	A1114 3b multi	.30	.25
e.	A1115 3b multi	.30	.25
f.	A1116 3b multi	.30	.25

Designation of Queen Sirikit as "Pre-eminent Protector of Arts and Crafts."

Paknam Incident, 120th Anniv. — A1117

2013, Aug. 13 Litho. *Perf. 13x13¼*
Granite Paper

2756	A1117 5b multi	.75	.25

A souvenir sheet of one sold for 16b.

Thailand Post as Public Company, 10th Anniv. — A1118

2013, Aug. 14 Litho. *Perf. 14¼*
Granite Paper

2757	A1118 10b multi	.65	.50

A1119 A1120

A1121 A1122

A1123 A1124

A1125 A1126

A1127

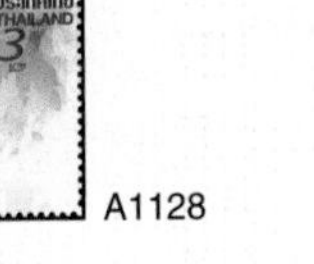

A1128

A1129

A1130

A1131

A1132

A1133

A1134

2013, Sept. 4 Litho. *Perf. 13¼x14¼*
Granite Paper

2758	A1119 3b multi	.30	.25
2759	A1120 3b multi	.30	.25
2760	A1121 3b multi	.30	.25
2761	A1122 3b multi	.30	.25
2762	A1123 3b multi	.30	.25
2763	A1124 3b multi	.30	.25
2764	A1125 3b multi	.30	.25
2765	A1126 3b multi	.30	.25

Perf. 14¼x13¼

2766	A1127 3b multi	.30	.25
2767	A1128 3b multi	.30	.25
2768	A1129 3b multi	.30	.25
2769	A1130 3b multi	.30	.25
2770	A1131 3b multi	.30	.25
2771	A1132 3b multi	.30	.25
2772	A1133 3b multi	.30	.25
2773	A1134 3b multi	.30	.25
	Nos. 2758-2773 (16)	4.80	4.00

Flag of Thailand — A1135

2013, Sept. 12 Litho. *Perf. 13¼*

2774	A1135 3b multi	.75	.25

Granite Paper
Perf. 14¼x13¼

2775	A1135 15b multi	.95	.70

Government Housing Bank, 60th Anniv. — A1136

2013, Sept. 24 Litho. *Perf. 14x14½*
Granite Paper

2776	A1136 3b multi	.75	.25

Somdet Phra Nyanasamvara (1913-2013), Supreme Patriarch of Thailand — A1137

Somdet Phra Nyanasamvara: No. 2777, 5b, As young monk. No. 2778, 5b, As older monk. No. 2779, 5b, Holding bowl for food offerings. No. 2780, 5b, Seated, giving donations to students.

2013, Oct. 3 Litho. *Perf. 13¼*
Granite Paper

2777-2780	A1137 Set of 4	2.75	1.10
a.	Souvenir sheet of 4, #2777-2780	1.90	1.90

No. 2780a sold for 30b.

A1138

A1139

A1140

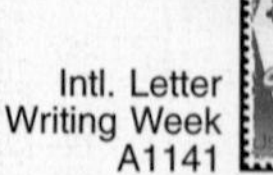

Intl. Letter Writing Week A1141

2013, Oct. 7 Litho. *Perf. 13¼*
Granite Paper

2781	A1138	3b multi	.50	.25
2782	A1139	3b multi	.50	.25
2783	A1140	3b multi	.50	.25
2784	A1141	3b multi	.50	
a.		Souvenir sheet of 4, #2781-2784	1.50	1.50
		Nos. 2781-2784 (4)	2.00	.75

No. 2784a sold for 23b.

Silpakorn University, 70th Anniv. — A1142

Depictions of Ganesh with denomination in: No. 2785, 3b, Silver. No. 2786, 3b, Black.

2013, Oct. 12 Litho. *Perf. 13¼*
Granite Paper

2785-2786 A1142 Set of 2 .75 .30

Use of Family Names in Thailand, Cent. — A1143

2013, Oct. 14 Litho. *Perf. 13*
Granite Paper

2787 A1143 3b multi .75 .25

Democracy Day A1144

2013, Oct. 14 Litho. *Perf. 13¼*
Granite Paper

2788 A1144 5b multi .75 .25

King Prajadhipok (1893-1941) A1145

2013, Nov. 8 Litho. *Perf. 13¼*
Granite Paper

2789 A1145 3b multi .75 .25

Prince Narisaranuvattiwongse (1863-1947) and Wat Rajathiwas Rajaworavihara — A1146

2013, Nov. 11 Litho. *Perf. 14½x14*
Granite Paper

2790 A1146 3b multi .75 .25

Miniature Sheet

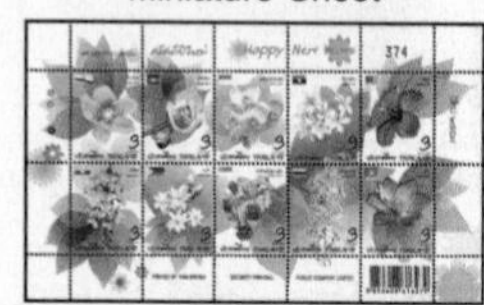
Flags and National Flowers of ASEAN Countries — A1147

Designs: a, Dillenia suffruticosa, flag of Brunei. b, Mitrella mesnyi, flag of Cambodia. c, Phalaenopsis amabilis, flag of Indonesia. d, Plumeria alba, flag of Laos. e, Hibiscus rosa-sinensis, flag of Malaysia. f, Pterocarpus macrocarpus, flag of Myanmar. g, Jasminum sambac, flag of Philippines. h, Vanda "Miss Joaquim" orchid, flag of Singapore. i, Cassia fistula, flag of Thailand. j, Nelumbo nucifera, flag of Viet Nam.

Perf. 14¼x14½
2013, Nov. 15 Litho.
Granite Paper

2791 A1147 3b Sheet of 10, #a-j 3.50 1.90

King Bhumibol Adulyadej and Humanitarian Soil Scientist Medal — A1148

Litho. With Foil Application
2013, Dec. 5 *Perf. 13¼x13*
Granite Paper

2792 A1148 9b multi .80 .45

86th birthday of King Bhumibol Adulyadej.

Jasminum Bhumibolianum A1149

2013, Dec. 5 Litho. *Perf. 13*
Granite Paper

2793 A1149 3b multi .75 .25

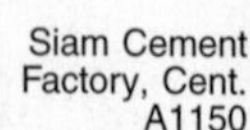
Siam Cement Factory, Cent. A1150

2013, Dec. 8 Litho. *Perf. 14½x14*
Granite Paper

2794 A1150 3b multi .75 .25

Map of Thailand and Digital Television Mascot A1151

2013, Dec. 11 Litho. *Perf. 13¼*
Granite Paper

2795 A1151 3b multi .75 .25

New Year 2014 (Year of the Horse) — A1152

2014, Jan. 1 Litho. *Perf. 13*
Granite Paper

2796	A1152	3b multi	.75	.25
a.		Souvenir sheet of 6, #2397a, 2463, 2568, 2665, 2726, 2796	1.90	1.90

No. 2796a sold for 30b. A sheet containing twelve 3b stamps similar to the 2003-14 New Year stamps but with reflective gold animals sold for 99b.

Chiang Mai University, 50th Anniv. A1153

2014, Jan. 1 Litho. *Perf. 14½x14*
Granite Paper

2797 A1153 3b multi .75 .25

National Children's Day — A1154

Children in national costume, greetings, and flags from: a, Thailand and Viet Nam. b, Philippines and Singapore. c, Malaysia and Myanmar. d, Indonesia and Laos. e, Brunei and Cambodia

2014, Jan. 11 Litho. *Perf. 14½x14*
Granite Paper

2798	Vert. strip of 5	.95	.70
a.-e.	A1154 3b Any single	.30	.25

No. 2798 was printed in sheets containing two vertical strips.

Thammasat University, 80th Anniv. A1155

2014, Jan. 15 Litho. *Perf. 14½x14*
Granite Paper

2799 A1155 3b multi .75 .25

Laughing Buddha A1156

Litho. With Foil Application
2014, Jan. 24 *Perf. 13¼*
Granite Paper

2800 A1156 5b multi .75 .25

Chinese New Year.

Khon Kaen University, 50th Anniv. A1157

2014, Jan. 25 Litho. *Perf. 13¼*
Granite Paper

2801 A1157 3b multi .75 .25

Love A1158

Cut-out in center of stamp: a, Hand signing "I love you." b, Heart.

2014, Feb. 7 Litho. *Perf. 13¾*
Granite Paper

2802 A1158 5b Horiz. pair, #a-b .65 .50

No. 2802 is impregnated with a rose scent.

Zoological Park Organization, 60th Anniv. — A1159

2014, Feb. 15 Litho. *Perf. 14x14½*
Granite Paper

2803 A1159 3b multi .75 .25

Postal School, 125th Anniv. A1160

2014, Feb. 22 Litho. *Perf. 14½x14*
Granite Paper

2804 A1160 3b multi .75 .25

Queen Saovabha Phongsri (1861-1919) — A1161

2014, Apr. 1 Litho. *Perf. 13¼*
Granite Paper

2805 A1161 3b multi .75 .25

Thai Heritage Conservation Day — A1162

Masks: a, Tosakanth. b, Kumbhakarn. c, Pipek. d, Thut. e, Khorn. f, Trisian. g, Samanakkha. h, Indrajit.

2014, Apr. 2 Litho. *Perf. 13¼*
Granite Paper

2806 A1162 3b Block of 8, #a-h 1.50 1.10

A souvenir sheet of 1 containing No. 2806a sold for 13b.

First Thailand-Laos Friendship Bridge, 20th Anniv. — A1163

Bridge and: a, Sai Buddha Image Procession Festival, Nong Khai, Thailand. b, Pho Chai Temple, Nong Khai, and On Thu Temple, Vientiane, Laos.

2014, Apr. 5 Litho. *Perf. 14½x14*
Granite Paper

2807 A1163 3b Horiz. pair, #a-b .75 .30

See Laos No. 1881.

Thailand Tobacco Monopoly, 75th Anniv. A1164

2014, Apr. 19 Litho. *Perf. 13¼*
Granite Paper

2808 A1164 3b multi .75 .25

Vesak Day A1165

2014, May 13 Litho. *Perf. 13*
Granite Paper

2809 A1165 3b multi .75 .25

Kings Chulalongkorn and Vajiravudh, King Chulalongkorn Memorial Hospital — A1166

2014, May 30 Litho. *Perf. 14x14½*
Granite Paper

2810 A1166 3b multi .75 .25

King Chulalongkorn Memorial Hospital, cent.

Pomegranates, Mangosteens, Flags of Israel and Thailand A1167

2014, June 5 Litho. *Perf. 13¼*
Granite Paper

2811 A1167 3b multi .75 .25

Diplomatic relations between Thailand and Israel, 60th anniv. See Israel No. 2020.

Don Mueang International Airport, Bangkok, Cent. A1168

Centenary emblem and: No. 2812, 3b, Breguet 14 B mail plane. No. 2813, 3b, Terminal, 1973. No. 2814, 3b, Terminal and movable boarding platform, 2014. No. 2815, 3b, Prince Chakrabongse Bhuvanath (1883-1920), commander of Royal Aeronautical Service, vert.

Perf. 14½x14, 14x14½
2014, July 1 Granite Paper Litho.

2812-2815 A1168 Set of 4 .75 .55
a. Perf. 13¼x14x13¼x13¼ .30 .25
b. Sheet of 4, #2812-2814, 2815a .75 .75

Amphibians A1169

Designs: No. 2816, 5b, Ingerophrynus macrotis. No. 2817, 5b, Rhacophorus kio. No. 2818, 5b, Megophrys nasuta. No. 2819, 5b, Hylarana erythraea.

2014, July 10 Litho. *Perf. 14½x14*
Granite Paper

2816-2819 A1169 Set of 4 1.25 .95
a. Souvenir sheet of 4, #2816-2819, perf. 13¼ 2.25 2.25

No. 2819a sold for 35b.

Communications Day — A1170

2014, Aug. 4 Litho. *Perf. 14½x14*
Granite Paper

2820 A1170 3b multi .75 .25

Thailand Waterworks, Cent. A1171

2014, Aug. 15 Litho. *Perf. 13¼*
Granite Paper

2821 A1171 3b multi .75 .25

Synod of Ayutthaya, 350th Anniv. — A1172

2014, Aug. 15 Litho. *Perf. 13¼*
Granite Paper

2822 A1172 5b multi .75 .25

See Vatican City No. 1573.

World Post Day — A1173

2014, Oct. 9 Litho. *Perf. 14¼*
Granite Paper

2823 A1173 3b multi .75 .25

Sports Authority of Thailand, 50th Anniv. A1174

2014, Oct. 17 Litho. *Perf. 14½x14*
Granite Paper

2824 A1174 3b multi .75 .25

General Post Offices A1175

No. 2825 — General Post Office in: a, Bangkok, Thailand. b, Macao.

2014, Nov. 1 Litho. *Perf. 13x13¼*
Granite Paper

2825 A1175 3b Pair, #a-b .75 .30

See Macao No. 1426.

A1176

A1177

A1178

A1179

A1180

A1181

A1182

New Year 2015 — A1183

2014, Nov. 14 Litho. *Perf. 13¼*
Granite Paper

2826	A1176 3b multi	.30	.25
2827	A1177 3b multi	.30	.25
2828	A1178 3b multi	.30	.25
2829	A1179 3b multi	.30	.25
2830	A1180 3b multi	.30	.25
2831	A1181 15b multi	.90	.70
2832	A1182 15b multi	.90	.70
2833	A1183 15b multi	.90	.70
	Nos. 2826-2833 (8)	4.20	3.35

Naval Vessels A1184

Designs: No. 2834, 5b, HTMS Pinklao. No. 2835, 5b, HTMS Phutthayodfachulalok. No. 2836, 5b, HTMS Phutthaloetlanaphalai. No. 2837, 5b, HTMS Chakri Naruebet (81x30mm).

Perf. 14½x14, 13¼ (#2837)
2014, Nov. 20 Litho.
Granite Paper

2834-2837 A1184 Set of 4 1.25 .95

A souvenir sheet containing one No. 2837 sold for 15b.

Chiang Mai Rajabhat University, 90th Anniv. — A1185

2014, Dec. 1 Litho. *Perf. 14x14½*
Granite Paper

2838 A1185 3b multi .75 .25

King Bhumibol Adulyadej, 87th Birthday — A1186

2014, Dec. 5 Litho. *Perf. 13¼*
Granite Paper

2839 A1186 5b multi .75 .25

Luang Pu Thuat High-Relief Amulet — A1187

Litho. & Embossed
2014, Dec. 15 *Perf. 14x14½*
Granite Paper

2840 A1187 9b multi .85 .40
a. Souvenir sheet of 1, perf. 13¼ 3.50 .95

No. 2840a sold for 15b.

New Year 2015 (Year of the Goat) — A1188

2015, Jan. 1 Litho. *Perf. 13¼*
Granite Paper

2841 A1188 3b multi .75 .25

National Children's Day — A1189

No. 2842 — Children, various forms of transportation and flags of: a, Thailand and Viet Nam. b, Philippines and Singapore. c, Malaysia and Myanmar. d, Indonesia and Laos. e, Brunei and Cambodia.

2015, Jan. 10 Litho. *Perf. 14½x14*
Granite Paper

2842 Vert. strip of 5 1.25 1.25
a.-e. A1189 3b Any single .30 .25

Kasetsart University, 72nd Anniv. A1190

2015, Feb. 2 Litho. *Perf. 13¼*
Granite Paper

2843 A1190 3b multi .75 .25

Princess Maha Chakri Sirindhorn Rose — A1191

2015, Feb. 9 Litho. *Perf. 13*
Granite Paper

2844 A1191 5b multi — —

No. 2844 has a rose-scented scratch-and-sniff coating.

Chinese New Year — A1192

No. 2845: a, Oranges. b, Red envelope and banknotes.

Litho. With Foil Application
2015, Feb. 9 *Perf. 13¼*
Granite Paper

2845 A1192 5b Pair, #a-b .65 .50

60th Birthday of Princess Maha Chakri Sirindhorn, Director of Thai Red Cross Society — A1193

2015, Mar. 30 Litho. *Perf. 13¼*
Granite Paper

2846 A1193 3b multi .75 .25

Princess Maha Chakri Sirindhorn, 60th Birthday — A1194

Litho. With Foil Application
Perf. 14½x14¼

2015, Apr. 2 Granite Paper

2847 A1194 5b multi .75 .25

A souvenir sheet containing one example of No. 2847 sold for 15b.
No. 2847 exists imperforate.

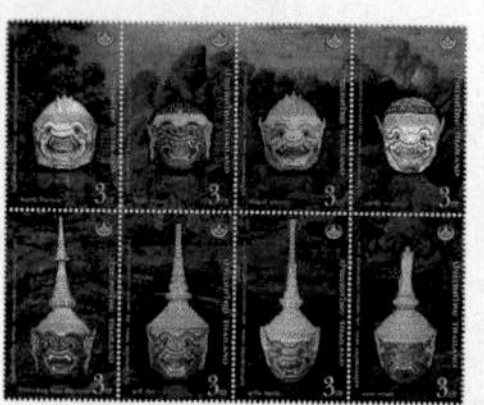
Thai Heritage Conservation Day — A1195

No. 2848 — Masks: a, Hanuman. b, Nilapat. c, Nilanon. d, Asuraphat. e, Praya Mahachompu. f, Pali. g, Sukrip. h, Ongot.

2015, Apr. 2 Litho. *Perf. 14x14½*
Granite Paper

2848 A1195 3b Block of 8, #a-h 1.50 1.10

A souvenir sheet containing one perf. 13¼ example of No. 2848a sold for 13b.

Pathum Thani, 200th Anniv. A1196

2015, Apr. 3 Litho. *Perf. 13¼*
Granite Paper

2849 A1196 3b multi .75 .25

Songkran Festival A1197

Inscriptions: No. 2850, 3b, Purifying the Buddha statue. No. 2851, 3b, Pouring scented water on the elders. No. 2852, 3b, Building the sand pagoda. No. 2853, 3b, Splashing water.

2015, Apr. 7 Litho. *Perf. 14½x14*
Granite Paper

2850-2853 A1197 Set of 4 .75 .60
2853a Souvenir sheet of 4, #2850-2853, perf. 13¼ 1.40 1.40
2853b As No. 2853a with Taipei 2015 emblem in sheet margin 10.00 10.00

No. 2853a sold for 23b.

Diplomatic Relations Between Thailand and Korea, People's Democratic Republic, 40th Anniv. — A1198

No. 2845: a, Siamese fireback (denomination at LL). b, Northern goshawk (denomination at LR).

2015, May 8 Litho. *Perf. 13¼*
Granite Paper

2854 A1198 3b Pair, #a-b .75 .25

See North Korea No.

International Telecommunication Union, 150th Anniv. — A1199

2015, May 17 Litho. *Perf. 14½x14*
Granite Paper

2855 A1199 3b multi .75 .25

Princess Prem Purachatra, 100th Birthday — A1200

2015, June 7 Litho. *Perf. 13¼*
Granite Paper

2856 A1200 3b multi .75 .25

Marine Life — A1201

Designs: No. 2857, 3b, Hymenocera picta. No. 2858, 3b, Trapezia areolata. No. 2859, 3b, Hypselodoris bullockii. No. 2860, 3b, Phyllorhiza punctata.

2015, June 8 Litho. *Perf. 13¼*
Granite Paper

2857-2860 A1201 Set of 4 .75 .60
2860a Souvenir sheet of 4, #2857-2860 1.40 1.40

See Malaysia Nos. 1550-1553.

Vesak Day — A1202

Emerald Buddha in: No. 2861, 5b, Summer season attire. No. 2862, 5b, Rainy season attire. No. 2863, 5b, Winter season attire.

Litho. With Foil Application

2015, June 15 *Perf. 13¼*
Granite Paper

2861-2863 A1202 Set of 3 .90 .70
2863a Souvenir sheet of 3, #2861-2863 1.60 1.60
2863b As No. 2863a, with Singapore 2015 emblem in sheet margin .90 .90

No. 2863a sold for 26b.

Ratsadkom Pipat Hall Revenue Department Building A1203

Krom Phra Kampaengpet Palace Revenue Department Building A1204

Jakrapong Revenue Department Building A1205

Soi Arisamphan Revenue Department Building A1206

2015, July 2 Litho. *Perf. 14½x14*
Granite Paper

2864 A1203 3b multi .30 .25
2865 A1204 3b multi .30 .25

Perf. 14x14½

2866 A1205 3b multi .30 .25
2867 A1206 3b multi .30 .25
Nos. 2864-2867 (4) 1.20 1.00

Revenue Department, Cent.

Miniature Sheet

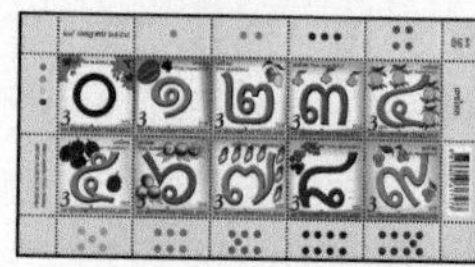
Thai Numerals — A1207

No. 2868 — Thai numeral and corresponding number of fruit: a, 0. b, 1. c, 2. d, 3. e, 4. f, 5. g, 6. h, 7. i, 8. j, 9.

2015, July 29 Litho. *Perf. 13*
Granite Paper

2868 A1207 3b Sheet of 10, #a-j 1.75 1.75

Musical Instruments A1208

Designs: No. 2869, 3b, Ranat ayk. No. 2870, 3b, Saw sam sai, vert. No. 2871, 3b, Saw duang, vert. No. 2872, 3b, Jakhay.

Perf. 14½x14, 14x14½

2015, Aug. 3 Litho.
Granite Paper

2869-2872 A1208 Set of 4 .70 .55
a. Souvenir sheet of 4, #2869-2872 + label, different perforations 1.40 1.40

Thaipex 2015 Philatelic Exhibition, Bangkok. No. 2872a sold for 23b and each stamp has at least one side that is perf. 13¼.

National Communications Day — A1209

2015, Aug. 4 Litho. *Perf. 13¼*
Granite Paper

2873 A1209 3b multi .75 .25

Army Training Command, 120th Anniv. A1210

2015, Aug. 6 Litho. *Perf. 13¼*
Granite Paper

2874 A1210 3b multi .75 .25

Flags and Emblem of Association of Southeast Asian Nations — A1211

2015, Aug. 8 Litho. *Perf. 14¼*
Granite Paper

2875 A1211 15b multi 1.40 .65
a. Souvenir sheet of 1 3.50 1.50

No. 2875a sold for 26b.

See Brunei No. 656, Burma Nos. 417-418, Cambodia No. 2428, Indonesia No. 2428, Laos No. 1906, Malaysia No. 1562, Philippines No. 3619, Singapore No. , Viet Nam No. 3529.

Diplomatic Relations Between Thailand and Singapore, 50th Anniv. — A1212

No. 2876: a, Khao Niew Manuang (sticky rice with mango). b, Ice cream sandwiches.

2015, Sept. 18 Litho. *Perf. 13¼*
Granite Paper

2876 A1212 3b Horiz. pair, #a-b .75 .25

See Singapore Nos. 1746-1747.

World Dental Congress, Bangkok A1213

2015, Sept. 22 Litho. *Perf. 14½x14*
Granite Paper

2877 A1213 3b multi .75 .25

World Post Day — A1214

2015, Oct. 9 Litho. *Perf. 13*
Granite Paper

2878 A1214 3b multi .75 .25

Former Bangkok Remand Prison A1215

Department of Corrections Administration Building A1216

Prison Security Control Room A1217

Corrections Officers Training and in Riot Gear A1218

2015, Oct. 13 Litho. *Perf. 14½x14*
Granite Paper

2879 A1215 3b multi .30 .25
2880 A1216 3b multi .30 .25
2881 A1217 3b multi .30 .25
2882 A1218 3b multi .30 .25
a. Souvenir sheet of 4, #2879-2882, perf. 13¼ 1.00 1.00
Nos. 2879-2882 (4) 1.20 1.00

100th Anniv. of the Department of Corrections.

Diplomatic Relations Between Thailand and Sri Lanka, 60th Anniv. — A1219

No. 2883: a, Phrapathomchedi Pagoda, flag of Thailand. b, Jethavana Stupa, flag of Sri Lanka.

2015, Nov. 2 Litho. *Perf. 13¼*
Granite Paper

2883 A1219 3b Horiz. pair, #a-b .75 .25

A souvenir sheet containing Nos. 2883a and 2883b sold for 16b. See Sri Lanka Nos. 1988-1989.

Exacum Affine A1220

No. 2884: a, Flowers in vase. b, Painting of flowers by Princess Maha Chakri Sirindhorn.

2015, Nov. 16 Litho. *Perf. 14¼*
Granite Paper

2884 A1220 15b Horiz. pair, #a-b 2.75 1.40

Miniature Sheet

New Year 2016 A1221

No. 2885: a, Boesenbergia alba. b, Etlingera araneosa. c, Alpinia malaccensis. d, Zingiber sirindhorniae. e, Curcuma supraneeana. f, Hedychium flavescens. g, Monolophus appendiculatus. h, Alpinia conchigera. i, Etlingera hemisphaerica. j, Curcuma alismatifolia. k, Zingiber spectabile. l, Rhynchanthus longiflorus.

2015, Nov. 23 Litho. *Perf. 14x14½*
Granite Paper

2885 A1221 3b Sheet of 12, #a-l 2.00 2.00

Luang Phor Ngern Amulet — A1222

Litho. & Embossed
2015, Dec. 1 *Perf. 14x14½*
Granite Paper

2886 A1222 9b multi .50 .40

A souvenir sheet containing a perf. 13¼ example of No. 2886 sold for 20b.

King Bhumibol Adulyadej, 88th Birthday A1223

King Bhumibol Adulyadej and: No. 2887, 5b, Farm, cattle, flame. No. 2888, 5b, Village, high tension wires, light bulb. No. 2889, 5b, Classroom, graduate, satellite dish, wind generators. No. 2890, 5b, Man at computer, solar panels, city skyline.

2015, Dec. 5 Litho. *Perf. 13¼*
Granite Paper

2887-2890 A1223 Set of 4 1.10 .85
a. Souvenir sheet of 4, #2887-2890 1.75 1.75

No. 2890a sold for 32b.

New Year 2016 (Year of the Monkey) — A1224

2016, Jan. 1 Litho. *Perf. 13¼*
Granite Paper

2891 A1224 3b multi .75 .25

Miniature Sheet

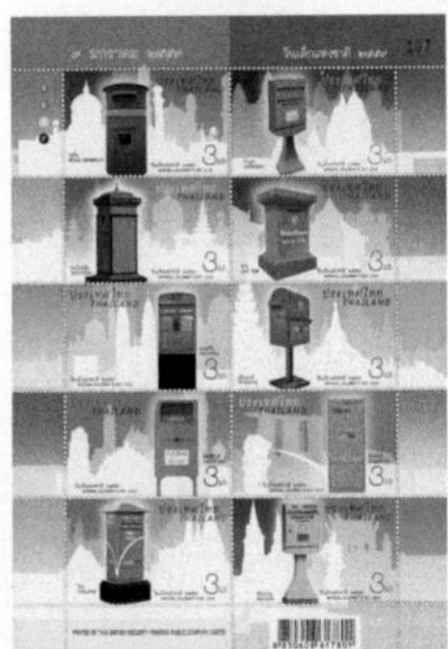
Mailboxes of Members of Association of South East Asian Nations — A1225

No. 2892 — Mailbox from: a, Brunei. b, Cambodia. c, Indonesia. d, Laos. e, Malaysia. f, Myanmar. g, Philippines. h, Singapore. i, Thailand. j, Viet Nam.

2016, Jan. 9 Litho. *Perf. 14½x14*
Granite Paper

2892 A1225 3b Sheet of 10, #a-j 1.75 1.75

National Children's Day.

National Institute of Development Administration, 50th Anniv. — A1226

2016, Feb. 1 Litho. *Perf. 13¼*
2893 A1226 3b multi .75 .25

No. 2893 has 50th anniversary emblem printed on back of stamp.

Chinese New Year — A1227

2016, Feb. 4 Litho. *Perf. 13*
Granite Paper

2894 A1227 5b multi .75 .25

Queen Sirikit Rose — A1228

2016, Feb. 8 Litho. *Perf. 13*
Granite Paper

2895 A1228 5b multi .75 .25

No. 2895 has a rose-scented scratch-and-sniff coating.

Office of the Auditor General, Cent. A1229

2016, Feb. 18 Litho. *Perf. 13¼*
Granite Paper

2896 A1229 3b multi .75 .25

Prince Bidyalongkorn (1876-1945) A1230

2016, Feb. 26 Litho. *Perf. 13¼*
Granite Paper

2897 A1230 3b multi .75 .25

Thai Cooperatives, cent.

Burapha University, 60th Anniv. (in 2015) A1231

2016, Mar. 1 Litho. *Perf. 14½x14*
Granite Paper

2898 A1231 3b multi .75 .25

Princess Valaya Alongkorn (1884-1938) — A1232

2016, Mar. 8 Litho. *Perf. 13¼*
Granite Paper

2899 A1232 3b multi .75 .25

Petchburiwittayalongkorn Teacher's Training School, 84th anniv.

A1233

A1234

A1235

Puey Ungphakorn (1916-99), Economist — A1236

2016, Mar. 9 Litho. *Perf. 13¼*
Granite Paper

2900 A1233 3b multi .30 .25
2901 A1234 3b multi .30 .25
2902 A1235 3b multi .30 .25
2903 A1236 3b multi .30 .25
Nos. 2900-2903 (4) 1.20 1.00

Ananta Samagom Throne Hall, Cent. A1237

2016, Mar. 14 Litho. *Perf. 13¼*
Granite Paper

2904 A1237 5b multi .75 .25

Chulalongkorn University, Cent. — A1238

2016, Mar. 26 Litho. *Perf. 13¼*
Granite Paper

2905 A1238 3b multi .75 .25

Queen Sirikit, 84th Birthday — A1239

2016, Mar. 30 Litho. *Perf. 13¼*
2906 A1239 3b multi .75 .25

Red Cross. No. 2906 has QR code and building printed in blue on back.

A1240

A1241

A1242

Women's Clothing — A1243

2016, Apr. 2 Litho. *Perf. 14x14½*
Granite Paper

2907	A1240	3b multi	.30	.25
2908	A1241	3b multi	.30	.25
2909	A1242	3b multi	.30	.25
2910	A1243	3b multi	.30	.25
		Nos. 2907-2910 (4)	1.20	1.00

Thai Heritage Conservation. A souvenir sheet of four stamps containing perf. 13¼ examples of Nos. 2907-2910 sold for 25b.

Chiang Mai, 720th Anniv. — A1244

2016, Apr. 7 Litho. *Perf. 13¼*
Granite Paper

2911 A1244 3b multi .75 .25

Miniature Sheet

Songkran Festival — A1245

No. 2912: a, Tao Kabilaprom and his seven daughters. b, Tung-sa Dhevi and Garuda. c, Ko-ra-ka Dhevi and tiger. d, Rak-sad Dhevi and pig. e, Mon-ta Dhevi and donkey. f, Kirinee Dhevi and elephant. g, Kimi-ta Dhevi and water buffalo. h, Maho-torn Dhevi and peacock.

2016, Apr. 7 Litho. *Perf. 14½x14*
Granite Paper

2912 A1245 5b Sheet of 8, #a-h 2.40 2.40

Princess Maha Chakri Sirindhorn and World Intellectual Property Organization Award for Creative Excellence
A1246

2016, May 3 Litho. *Perf. 13¼*
Granite Paper

2913 A1246 5b multi .75 .25

Diplomatic Relations Between Thailand and Indonesia — A1247

No. 2914 — Scenes from the epic poem *Ramayana*: a, Characters kneeling. b, Four characters and tree.

2016, May 5 Litho. *Perf. 13¼*
Granite Paper

2914 A1247 3b Horiz. pair, #a-b .75 .30

See Indonesia Nos. 2446-2447.

Vesak Day — A1248

Inscription: No. 2915, 3b, Conquer anger by love. No. 2916, 3b, Conquer evil by good. No. 2917, 3b, Conquer the miser by liberality. No. 2918, 3b, Conquer the liar by truth.

2016, May 20 Litho. *Perf. 13¼*
Granite Paper

2915-2918 A1248 Set of 4 .70 .55

A souvenir sheet containing Nos. 2915-2918 sold for 25b.

UEFA European Soccer Champions — A1249

No. 2919 — Inscriptions: a, Soviet Union, 1960. b, Spain, 1964. c, Italy, 1968. d, West Germany, 1972. e, Czechoslovakia, 1976. f, West Germany, 1980. g, France, 1984. h, Netherlands, 1988. i, Denmark, 1992. j, Germany, 1996. k, France, 2000. l, Greece, 2004. m, Spain, 2008. n, Spain, 2012. o, 2016 @France.

Die Cut Perf. 6¾x7
2016, June 10 Litho.
Self-Adhesive

2919	A1249	Booklet pane of 15	2.60	
a.-o.		3b Any single	.30	.25

Bangkok Railway Station, Cent. A1250

Various images of Bangkok Railway Station with denomination at: No. 2920, 3b, LL. No. 2921, 3b, LR. No. 2922, 3b, UL. No. 2923, 3b, UR.

2016, June 25 Litho. *Perf. 14½x14*
Granite Paper

2920-2923 A1250 Set of 4 .70 .55

A souvenir sheet containing perf. 13¼ examples of Nos. 2920-2923 sold for 25b.

A1251

Crown Prince Maha Vajiralongkorn, 64th Birthday — A1252

No. 2924: a, Monument and statue, drawing of finish line of "Bike for Dad" bicycle race. b, Drawing of family on tandem bicycle and cart.

No. 2925: a, Crown Prince riding bicyle with both hands on handlebars. b, Crown Prince riding bicycle and waving.

2016, July 28 Litho. *Perf. 14½x14*
Granite Paper

2924 A1251 5b Horiz. pair, #a-b .60 .45

Perf. 14x14½

2925	A1252	5b Vert. pair, #a-b	.60	.45
c.		Souvenir sheet of 4, #2924a, 2924b, 2925a, 2925b, perf. 13¼	2.00	2.00

No. 2925c sold for 35b.

National Communications Day — A1253

2016, Aug. 4 Litho. *Perf. 13¼*
Granite Paper

2926 A1253 3b multi .75 .25

Diplomatic Relations Between Thailand and Viet Nam, 40th Anniv. — A1254

No. 2927: a, Three Thai figurines in boat. b, Four Vietnamese figurines in boat.

2016, Aug. 5 Litho. *Perf. 13¼*
Granite Paper

2927 A1254 3b Horiz. pair, #a-b .75 .25

See Viet Nam Nos. 3551-3552.

Nymphaea "Queen Sirikit" A1255

2016, Aug. 10 Litho. *Perf. 13¼*
Granite Paper

2928 A1255 5b multi .75 .25

Thailand 2016 International Stamp Exhibition, Bangkok.

Queen Sirikit, 84th Birthday A1256

Litho. & Embossed With Foil Application
2016, Aug. 12 *Perf. 12*
Granite Paper

2929 A1256 100b gold & multi 9.00 4.50

Values are for stamps with surrounding selvage.

King Bhumibol Adulyadej and Queen Sirikit — A1257

2016, Aug. 16 Litho. *Perf. 13¼*
Granite Paper

2930 A1257 3b multi .75 .25

Thai rice research, cent.

World Post Day A1258

No. 2931 — Various people and postal workers with denomination in: a, Red at LR. b, Dark blue at LL.

2016, Oct. 3 Litho. *Perf. 13*
Granite Paper

2931 A1258 3b Horiz. pair, #a-b .75 .25

A1259 A1260

A1261 A1262

Canna Lilies
A1263 A1264

2016, Nov. 15 Litho. *Perf. 13¼x13*
Granite Paper

2932	A1259	3b multi	.30	.25
2933	A1260	3b multi	.30	.25
2934	A1261	3b multi	.30	.25
2935	A1262	3b multi	.30	.25
2936	A1263	15b multi	.85	.65
2937	A1264	15b multi	.85	.65
		Nos. 2932-2937 (6)	2.90	2.30

Phra Kring Chinabanchorn Amulet, by Luang Pu Tim Wat Lahanrai — A1265

Litho. & Embossed
2016, Dec. 1 *Perf. 14x14½*
Granite Paper

2938 A1265 9b multi 1.00 .40

A souvenir sheet containing one perf. 13¼ example of No. 2938 sold for 20b. No. 2938 exists imperforate.

New Year 2017 (Year of the Rooster) — A1266

2017, Jan. 1 Litho. *Perf. 13¼*
Granite Paper

2939 A1266 3b multi .75 .25

National Children's Day — A1267

2017, Jan. 14 Litho. *Perf. 14½x14*
Granite Paper

2940 A1267 3b multi .75 .25

Stylized Rose — A1268

Litho. & Silk-Screened

2017, Feb. 7 ***Perf. 13¼x13***

Granite Paper

2941 A1268 5b multi .75 .25

State Railway of Thailand, 120th Anniv. A1269

Various locomotives with identification number of: No. 2942, 3b, #4004. No. 2943, 3b, #3118. No. 2944, 3b, #4552. No. 2945, 3b, #5102.

2017, Mar. 26 **Litho.** ***Perf. 13***

Granite Paper

2942-2945 A1269 Set of 4 .70 .55

Values are for stamps with surrounding selvage. A souvenir sheet containing perf. 13½x13 examples of Nos, 2942-2945 sold for 28b.

Accession to the Throne of King Bhumibol Adulyadej (1927-2016), 70th Anniv. (in 2016) — A1270

2017, Apr. 1 **Litho.** ***Perf. 13½***

Granite Paper

2946 A1270 9b multi .55 .40

No. 2946 is shown sideways.

A1271

A1272 A1273

Lanna-Style Murals — A1274

2017, Apr. 2 **Litho.** ***Perf. 14½x14***

Granite Paper

2947 A1271 3b multi .30 .25
2948 A1272 3b multi .30 .25

Perf. 14x14½

2949 A1273 3b multi .30 .25
2950 A1274 3b multi .30 .25
Nos. 2947-2950 (4) 1.20 1.00

Thai Heritage Conservation Day. A souvenir sheet containing a perf. 13¼ example of No. 2950 sold for 15b.

A1275

A1276

A1277

Long Boat Racing A1278

2017, Apr. 7 **Litho.** ***Perf. 14½x14***

Granite Paper

2951 A1275 3b multi .30 .25
2952 A1276 3b multi .30 .25
2953 A1277 3b multi .30 .25
2954 A1278 3b multi .30 .25
Nos. 2951-2954 (4) 1.20 1.00

Vesak Day — A1279

Statues of Buddha and text from the Dhammapada: No. 2955, 3b "Happy is virtue until old age." No. 2956, 3b, "Happy is faith that firmly stands." No. 2957, 3b, "Happy is it to gain insight." No. 2958, 3b, "Happy is it to commit no sin."

2017, May 3 **Litho.** ***Perf. 13¼***

Granite Paper

2955-2958 A1279 Set of 4 .70 .55

A souvenir sheet containing Nos. 2955-2958 sold for 25b.

Suan Sunandha University, 80th Anniv., Bangkok, 80th Anniv. A1280

2017, May 17 **Litho.** ***Perf. 14½x14***

Granite Paper

2959 A1280 3b multi .75 .25

A1281

A1282

A1283

Chao Phraya River A1284

2017, June 5 **Litho.** ***Perf. 14x14¼***

Granite Paper

2960 A1281 3b multi .30 .25
2961 A1282 3b multi .30 .25
2962 A1283 3b multi .30 .25
2963 A1284 3b multi .30 .25
Nos. 2960-2963 (4) 1.20 1.00

1897 Meeting of King Chulalongkorn of Thailand and Tsar Nicholas II of Russia — A1285

2017, July 3 **Litho.** ***Perf. 13¼***

Granite Paper

2964 A1285 3b multi .75 .25

Diplomatic relations between Thailand and Russia, 120th anniv. See Russia No. 7834.

Princess Chulabhorn, 60th Birthday — A1286

2017, July 4 **Litho.** ***Perf. 13¼***

Granite Paper

2965 A1286 5b multi .75 .25

King Maha Vajiralongkorn, 65th Birthday — A1287

Litho. With Foil Application

2017, July 28 ***Perf. 13¼***

Granite Paper

2966 A1287 10b gold & multi .60 .45

Cassia Fistula — A1288

2017, Aug. 8 **Litho.** ***Perf. 13¼***

Granite Paper

2967 A1288 3b multi .75 .25

Association of Southeast Asian Nations, 50th anniv.

Thai Pavilion — A1289

2017, Aug. 14 **Litho.** ***Perf. 14x14½***

Granite Paper

2968 A1289 1b deep blue .45 .25
2969 A1289 2b red .45 .25
2970 A1289 3b green, roof length 21mm .45 .25
a. Perf. 14½x14, 22mm roof width — —
2971 A1289 6b dp mauve .60 .30
2972 A1289 7b magenta .65 .35
2973 A1289 9b yel & ocher .80 .40
2974 A1289 10b peach & black .90 .45
2975 A1289 50b lilac & blue 4.50 2.25
2976 A1289 100b ol yel & dk grn 9.00 4.50
Nos. 2968-2976 (9) 17.80 9.00

Issued: 2970a, 2019? Paper size on No. 2970a is slightly taller than No. 2970.

See Nos. 3092-3094.

Flag of Thailand, Cent. A1290

2017, Sept. 28 **Litho.** ***Perf. 14½x14***

Granite Paper

2977 A1290 3b multi .75 .25

World Post Day — A1291

2017, Oct. 5 **Litho.** ***Perf. 14x14½***

Granite Paper

2978 A1291 3b multi .75 .25

King Bhumibol Adulyadej (1927-2016) — A1292

Items Used at Cremation of King Bhumibol Adulyadej — A1293

Royal Crematorium — A1294

No. 2979 — King Bhumibol Adulyadej: a, Wearing gray suit and tie. b, Gesturing with hands. c, Wearing blue suit and tie, d, With camera strap around neck. e, Wearing military uniform and cap. f, Wearing blue jacket and striped shirt. g, Wearing tan shirt. h, Wearing blue plaid suit. i, Wearing brown striped shirt.

No. 2980: a, Honor guard around urn. b, Palanquin, horiz. c, Chariot.

2017, Oct. 25 Litho. *Perf. 13¼*

Granite Paper (#2979, 2981)

2979 A1292 9b Sheet of 9, #a-i 14.00 10.00

Souvenir Sheets

Litho., Sheet Margin Litho. With Foil Application

2980 A1293 3b Sheet of 3, #a-c .55 .45

Litho. With Foil Application

Perf. 14x14½

2981 A1294 9b gold & multi .55 .45

King Taksin the Great Monument, Talat — A1295

2017, Nov. 6 Litho. *Perf. 13¼*

Granite Paper

2982 A1295 3b multi .65 .25

King Taksin the Great (1734-82).

A1296 A1297

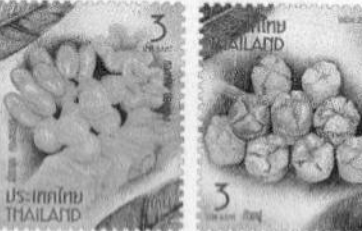

A1298 A1299

New Year 2018

A1300 A1301

2017, Nov. 15 Litho. *Perf. 14x14½*

Granite Paper

2983 A1296 3b multi .30 .25
2984 A1297 3b multi .30 .25
2985 A1298 3b multi .30 .25
2986 A1299 3b multi .30 .25
2987 A1300 15b multi .95 .75
2988 A1301 15b multi .95 .75
Nos. 2983-2988 (6) 3.10 2.50

Khruba Siwichai Amulet — A1302

Litho. & Embossed

2017, Dec. 1 *Perf. 14x14½*

Granite Paper

2989 A1302 9b multi .55 .45

A souvenir sheet containing one example of No. 2989 sold for 20b.

National Day — A1303

Litho. With Foil Application

2017, Dec. 5 *Perf. 13¼*

Granite Paper

2990 A1303 5b gold & multi .75 .25

New Year 2018 (Year of the Dog) — A1304

2018, Jan. 1 Litho. *Perf. 13¼*

Granite Paper

2991 A1304 3b multi .75 .25

A1305 A1306

A1307 Children's Day — A1308

2018, Jan. 13 Litho. *Perf. 13¼*

2992 A1305 3b multi .30 .25
2993 A1306 3b multi .30 .25
2994 A1307 3b multi .30 .25
2995 A1308 3b multi .30 .25
Nos. 2992-2995 (4) 1.20 1.00

Knitted Heart — A1309

Litho. & Embossed

2018, Feb. 7 *Perf. 13*

Granite Paper

2996 A1309 5b multi .75 .25

A1310

A1311 A1312

Murals — A1313

2018, Apr. 2 Litho. *Perf. 14½x14*

Granite Paper

2997 A1310 3b multi .30 .25
2998 A1311 3b multi .30 .25

Perf. 14x14½

2999 A1312 3b multi .30 .25
3000 A1313 3b multi .30 .25
Nos. 2997-3000 (4) 1.20 1.00

Thai heritage conservation. A souvenir sheet containing a perf. 13½ example of No. 3000 sold for 15b.

A1314

A1315

A1316

Skyrocket Festival A1317

2018, Apr. 4 Litho. *Perf. 13¼*

3001 A1314 3b multi .30 .25
3002 A1315 3b multi .30 .25
3003 A1316 3b multi .30 .25
3004 A1317 3b multi .30 .25
Nos. 3001-3004 (4) 1.20 1.00

Diplomatic Relations Between Thailand and Turkey, 60th Anniv. — A1318

No. 3005: a, Thai kick boxers. b, Turkish wrestlers.

2018, May 12 Litho. *Perf. 13¼*

Granite Paper

3005 A1318 3b Horiz. pair, #a-b .75 .30

See Turkey No. 3610.

Vesak Day — A1319

Designs: No. 3006, 3b, Phra That Gate Kaew Chulamanee, Chiang Mai. No. 3007, 3b, Phra That Doi Tung, Chiang Rai. No. 3008, 3b, Phra That Sri Jomthong, Chiang Mai. No. 3009, 3b, Phra That Lampang Luang, Lampang.

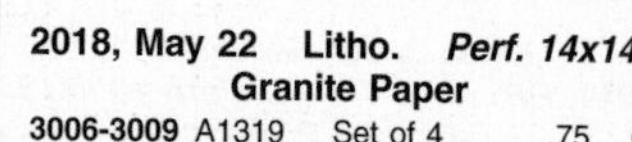

2018, May 22 Litho. *Perf. 14x14½*

Granite Paper

3006-3009 A1319 Set of 4 .75 .60

A souvenir sheet containing perf. 13½ examples of Nos. 3006-3009 sold for 25b.

Diplomatic Relations Between Thailand and Romania, 45th Anniv. — A1320

No. 3010: a, Flag, man and woman from Thailand. b, Flag, man and woman from Romania.

2018, May 31 Litho. *Perf. 13¼*

Granite Paper

3010 A1320 3b Horiz. pair, #a-b .75 .30

See Romania No. 6110.

A1321

2018 World Cup Soccer Championships, Russia — A1322

No. 3011 — Soccer ball, map of Russia and player: a, Ready to kick ball. b, Heading ball. c, Catching ball. d, Making scissor kick. e, Dribbling ball.

No. 3012 — Soccer ball, map of Russia, two players in action and: a, Cathedral. b, Nesting doll. c, Clock tower.

Die Cut Perf. 10x9¾

2018, June 14 Litho.

Self-Adhesive

3011 Booklet pane of 5 1.25

Die Cut Perf. 9¾x10

a.-e. A1321 3b Any single .30 .25
3012 Booklet pane of 3 2.75
a.-c. A1322 15b Any single .90 .70

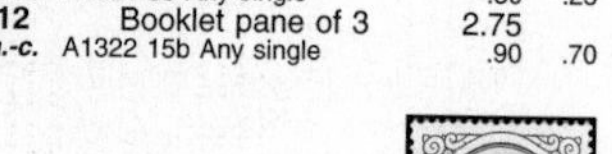

King Maha Vajiralongkorn — A1323

2018, July 28 Litho. *Perf. 14x14½*

Granite Paper

Frame Color

3013 A1323 1b bluish vio .30 .25
3014 A1323 2b red .30 .25
3015 A1323 3b green .30 .25
3016 A1323 5b brown .30 .25
3017 A1323 6b brn pur .40 .30
3018 A1323 7b magenta .45 .35
3019 A1323 9b yellow brown .55 .40
3020 A1323 10b reddish org .60 .45
3021 A1323 12b Prussian blue .75 .60
3022 A1323 15b orange brown .90 .65

Litho. With Foil Application

3023 A1323 50b metallic pink 3.00 2.25
3024 A1323 100b gold 6.00 4.50
a. Souvenir sheet of 12, #3013-3024 15.00 15.00
Nos. 3013-3024 (12) 13.85 10.50

No. 3024a sold for 250b.

King Maha Vajiralongkorn, 66th Birthday — A1324

Litho. With Foil Application

2018, July 28 ***Perf. 13¼***

Granite Paper

3025 A1324 10b gold & multi 1.50 .45

Metropolitan Electricity Authority, 60th Anniv. A1325

2018, Aug. 1 **Litho.** ***Perf. 13¼***

Granite Paper

3026 A1325 3b multi .75 .25

A1326

A1327

A1328

Thai Postal Services, 135th Anniv. A1329

2018, Aug. 4 **Litho.** ***Perf. 13¼***

Granite Paper

3027 A1326 3b multi .30 .25
3028 A1327 3b multi .30 .25
3029 A1328 3b multi .30 .25
3030 A1329 3b multi .30 .25
Nos. 3027-3030 (4) 1.20 1.00

Queen Sirikit, 86th Birthday — A1330

Litho. With Foil Application

2018, Aug. 31 ***Perf. 13¼***

Granite Paper

3031 A1330 9b gold & multi .55 .40

World Post Day — A1331

2018, Oct. 9 **Litho.** ***Perf. 13¼***

Granite Paper

3032 A1331 3b multi .75 .25

Miniature Sheet

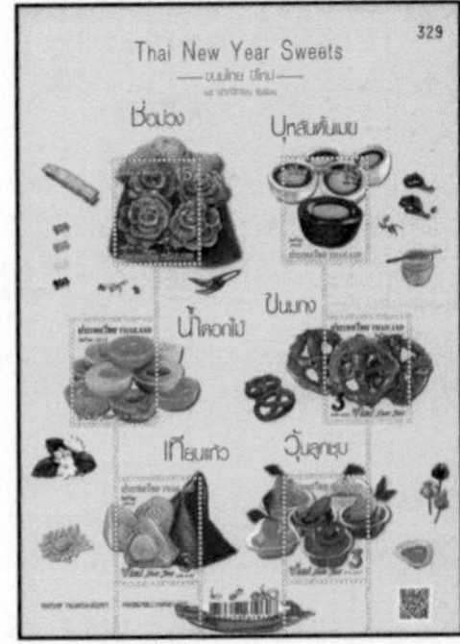

New Year Sweets A1332

No. 3033 — Various sweets with denomination color of: a, 3b, Red. b, 3b, Purple. c, 3b, Light blue. d, 3b, Orange. e, 15b, Yellow. f, 15b, Magenta.

2018, Nov. 15 **Litho.** ***Perf. 14x14½***

Granite Paper

3033 A1332 Sheet of 6, #a-f 4.00 2.00

Phitsanulok Tourism A1333

Inscriptions: No. 3034, 3b, Kaeng Sopha Waterfall. No. 3035, 3b, Tree ordination ceremony. No. 3036, 3b, Pak Thong Chai tradition. No. 3037, 3b, Phra Buddha Chinnarat.

2018, Nov. 28 **Litho.** ***Perf. 13¼***

Granite Paper

3034-3037 A1333 Set of 4 1.20 .60

Thailand 2018 World Stamp Exhibition, Bangkok A1334

Exhibition emblem and: No. 3038, 3b, Khao Tha Chomphu Bridge, Lamphun. No. 3039, 3b, Lotus Memorial Park, Sakon Nakhon. No. 3040, 3b, Black Sand Beach, Trat. No. 3041, 3b, Drum Making Village, Ang Thong. 15b, Khai Island, Satun.

2018, Nov. 28 **Litho.** ***Perf. 14½x14***

Granite Paper

3038-3042 A1334 Set of 5 1.75 1.40

Phra Achan Fan Acharo Amulet — A1335

Litho., Silk-Screened & Embossed

2018, Dec. 3 ***Perf. 13¼***

Granite Paper

3043 A1335 9b multi .55 .45

A souvenir sheet of 1 of No. 3043 sold for 20b.

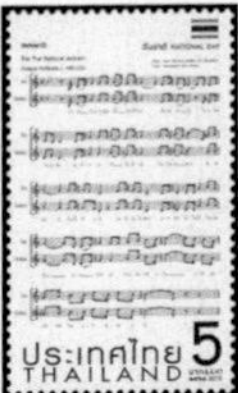

Flag and National Anthem of Thailand — A1336

2018, Dec. 5 **Litho.** ***Perf. 13¼***

Granite Paper

3044 A1336 5b multi .75 .25

New Year 2019 (Year of the Pig) — A1337

2019, Jan. 1 **Litho.** ***Perf. 13¼***

Granite Paper

3045 A1337 3b multi .75 .25

A1338

A1339

A1340

Children's Day — A1341

2019, Jan. 12 **Litho.** ***Perf. 13***

Granite Paper

3046 A1338 3b multi .30 .25
3047 A1339 3b multi .30 .25
3048 A1340 3b multi .30 .25
3049 A1341 3b multi .30 .25
Nos. 3046-3049 (4) 1.20 1.00

Roses — A1342

Litho. & Embossed

2019, Feb. 7 ***Perf. 14x14½***

Granite Paper

3050 A1342 5b multi .75 .25

No. 3050 is impregnated with a rose scent.

A1343

A1344

A1345

Thai Heritage Conservation Day — A1346

2019, Apr. 2 **Litho.** ***Perf. 14½x14***

Granite Paper

3051 A1343 3b multi .30 .25
3052 A1344 3b multi .30 .25
3053 A1345 3b multi .30 .25
3054 A1346 3b multi .30 .25
Nos. 3051-3054 (4) 1.20 1.00

A souvenir sheet containing a perf. 13½ example of No. 3054 sold for 15b.

Coronation of King Maha Vajiralongkorn — A1347

Litho. & Embossed on Foil

2019, May 4 ***Perf. 13¼***

3055 A1347 10b multi .65 .50

Vesak Day — A1348

Designs: No. 3056, 3b, Phra That Cho Hae, Phrae. No. 3057, 3b, Phra That Chae Haeng, Nan. No. 3058, 3b, Phra That Chedi Wat Phra Singh, Chiang Mai. No. 3059, 3b, Phra That Chedi Jed Yod, Chiang Mai.

2019, May 10 **Litho.** ***Perf. 14x14½***

Granite Paper

3056-3059 A1348 Set of 4 .80 .80

A souvenir sheet containing perf. 13½ examples of Nos. 3056-3059 sold for 25b.

Thailand Foundation for the Blind, 80th Anniv. A1349

Litho. & Embossed

2019, May 10 ***Perf. 14½x14***

Granite Paper

3060 A1349 3b multi .75 .25

Flowers and Association of Southeast Asian Nations Summit Emblem — A1350

2019, June 1 **Litho.** ***Perf. 14x14½***

Granite Paper

3061 A1350 3b multi .75 .25

Diplomatic Relations Between Thailand and Philippines, 70th Anniv. — A1351

No. 3062 — Flags of Thailand and Philippines and: a, Elephant. b, Carabao.

Perf. 13¼x13½

2019, June 14 **Litho.**

Granite Paper

3062 A1351 3b Horiz. pair, #a-b .75 .30

See Philippines No. 3820.

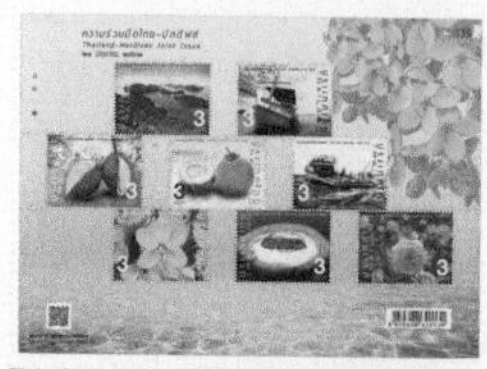

Diplomatic Relations Between Thailand and Maldive Islands, 40th Anniv. — A1352

No. 3063: a, Ang Thong National Marine Park (archipelago), Thailand. b, Boat with flag of Thailand. c, Split durians. d, Whole and halved coconuts. e, Fishermen on Maldivian boat. f, Golden shower flowers. g, Maldivian island. h, Roses.

2019, June 21 Litho. *Perf. 13½*
Granite Paper

3063 A1352 3b Sheet of 8, #a-h, + 2 labels 1.60 1.25

King Maha Vajiralongkorn, 67th Birthday — A1353

Litho. & Embossed With Foil Application
2019, July 28 *Perf. 13¼*
Granite Paper

3064 A1353 10b gold & multi .65 .50

Traditional Costumes of Thai Men and Women and ASEAN Post Emblem — A1354

2019, Aug. 8 Litho. *Perf. 14x14½*
Granite Paper

3065 A1354 3b multi .75 .25

Kamphol Vacharaphol (1919-96), Newspaper Publisher A1355

Litho. With Foil Application
2019, Aug. 19 *Perf. 13¼*

3066 A1355 5b multi .35 .25

Queen Mother Sirikit, 87th Birthday — A1356

Litho. & Embossed With Foil Application
2019, Aug. 30 *Perf. 13¼*
Granite Paper

3067 A1356 9b gold & multi .60 .45

Lighthouses — A1357

Designs: No. 3068, 3b, Bang Pa-in Lighthouse. No. 3069, 3b, Koh Sichang Lighthouse. No. 3070, 5b, His Majesty the King's 80th Birthday Anniversary Lighthouse. No. 3071, 5b, Kanchanaphisek Lighthouse.

2019, Sept. 30 Litho. *Perf. 13½*

3068-3071 A1357 Set of 4 1.10 .85
3071a Souvenir sheet of 4, #3068-3071, perf. 14x14½ 1.50 1.50

No. 3071a sold for 23b.

A1358

A1359

A1360

Lotus Receiving A1361

2019, Oct. 7 Litho. *Perf. 13½*

3072 A1358 3b multi .30 .25
3073 A1359 3b multi .30 .25
3074 A1360 3b multi .30 .25
3075 A1361 3b multi .30 .25
Nos. 3072-3075 (4) 1.20 1.00

Universal Postal Union, 145th Anniv. — A1362

2019, Oct. 9 Litho. *Perf. 13½*

3076 A1362 3b multi .75 .25

Worldwide Fund for Nature (WWF) A1363

Designs: No. 3077, 3b, Bryde's whale. No. 3078, 3b, Omura's whale. No. 3079, 3b, Whale shark. No. 3080, 3b, Leatherback turtle.

2019, Sept. 11 Litho. *Perf. 13¼*
Granite Paper

3077-3080 A1363 Set of 4 .80 .60

Souvenir sheets of 1 of Nos. 3077 and 3080 each sold for 10b. A souvenir sheet with Nos. 3077-3080 exists.

Prince Mahidol of Songkla (1892-1929) — A1364

2019, Sept. 24 Litho. *Perf. 13¼*
Granite Paper

3081 A1364 3b multi .75 .25

Ministry of Public Health, cent.

Chaipattana Water Aerator Invented by King Bhumibol Adulyadej A1365

2019, Oct. 28 Litho. *Perf. 13¼*
Granite Paper

3082 A1365 3b multi .75 .25

National Research Center of Thailand, 60th anniv.

Kha-nom Krok A1366

Kha-nom Krachao Sida A1367

Kha-nom A-Lua A1368

Kha-nom Tan A1369

Perf. 14¼x14½
2019, Nov. 15 Litho.
Granite Paper

3083 Block of 4 .80 .60
a. A1366 3b multi .30 .25
b. A1367 3b multi .30 .25
c. A1368 3b multi .30 .25
d. A1369 3b multi .30 .25

New Year 2020.

Thailand No. 496 — A1370

Litho. With Foil Application
2019, Dec. 5 *Perf. 13¼*

3084 A1370 5b gold & multi .75 .25

National Day.

Princess Chulabhorn and Chulabhorn Oncology Medical Center A1371

2019, Dec. 29 Litho. *Perf. 13¼*
Granite Paper

3085 A1371 3b multi .75 .25

Chulabhorn Oncology Medical Center, 10th anniv.

New Year 2020 (Year of the Rat) — A1372

2020, Jan. 2 Litho. *Perf. 13¼*
Granite Paper

3086 A1372 3b multi .75 .25
a. Souvenir sheet of 6, #2841, 2891, 2939, 2991, 3045, 3086 2.00 2.00

No. 3086a sold for 30b.

Children's Day — A1373

Children and: No. 3087, 3b, Cat. No. 3088, 3b, Dog. No. 3089, 3b, Bird. No. 3090, 3b, Fish.

2020, Jan. 11 Litho. *Perf. 13*
Granite Paper

3087-3090 A1373 Set of 4 1.30 .60

Teddy Bear and Hearts — A1374

Litho. With Glitter Affixed
2020, Feb. 7 *Perf. 13*
Granite Paper

3091 A1374 5b multi .75 .25

Thai Pavilion Type of 2017
2020, Mar. 6 Litho. *Perf. 14x14½*
Granite Paper

3092 A1289 5b lt brn & dk brn .30 .25
3093 A1289 12b lt bl & dk bl .75 .55
3094 A1289 15b lt org & dk grn .90 .70
Nos. 3092-3094 (3) 1.95 1.50

Fresco, Pradu Song Tham Temple, Phra Nakhon Si Ayutthaya A1375

Fresco, Pathumwanaram Temple, Ratchaworawihan A1376

Fresco, Bang Khae Yai Temple, Samut Songkhram A1377

Fresco, Born Niwat Temple, Bangkok — A1378

2020, Apr. 2 Litho. *Perf. 13¼x13½*
Granite Paper

3095 A1375 3b multi .30 .25
3096 A1376 3b multi .30 .25

Perf. 13½x13¼

3097 A1377 3b multi .30 .25
3098 A1378 3b multi .30 .25
Nos. 3095-3098 (4) 1.20 1.00

Thai heritage conservation. A souvenir sheet of 1 of No. 3098 sold for 15b.

Temples — A1379

Designs: No. 3099, 3b, Phra Borommathat, Tak. No. 3100, 3b, Phra That Doi Suthep, Chiang Mai. No. 3101, 3b, Phra That Phanom,

Nakhon Phanom. No. 3102, 3b, Phra That Hari Phun chai, Lamphun.

2020, May 2 Litho. *Perf. 13½x13¼*
Granite Paper

3099-3102 A1379 Set of 4 .75 .55

Vesak Day. A souvenir sheet containing Nos. 3099-3102 sold for 25b.

General Post Office Building, Bangkok, 80th Anniv. A1380

Perf. 13¼x13½
2020, June 24 Litho.
Granite Paper

3103 A1380 5b multi .75 .25

A1381

A1382

A1383

Buddhist Lent Festival of Floral Offerings, Wat Phra Phuttabat — A1384

2020, July 12 Litho. *Perf. 13¼x13½*
Granite Paper

3104 A1381 3b multi .30 .25
3105 A1382 3b multi .30 .25

Perf. 13½x13¼

3106 A1383 3b multi .30 .25
3107 A1384 3b multi .30 .25
Nos. 3104-3107 (4) 1.20 1.00

King Maha Vajiralongkorn, 68th Birthday — A1385

Litho. With Foil Application
2020, July 28 *Perf. 13¼*
Granite Paper

3108 A1385 10b multi — —

Princess Maha Chakri Sirindhorn, 65th Birthday — A1386

Litho. With Foil Application
2020, Aug. 4 *Perf. 13¼*
Granite Paper

3109 A1386 5b multi .75 .25

Campaign Against COVID-19 Pandemic — A1387

No. 3110 — Various people and health care workers with denomination at: a, UL. b, LR.

2020, Aug. 14 Litho. *Perf. 13¼*
Granite Paper

3110 A1387 3b Horiz. pair, #a-b — —

Ministry of Commerce, Cent. A1388

Perf. 13¼x13½
2020, Aug. 20 Litho.
Granite Paper

3111 A1388 3b multi .75 .25

A1389

A1390

A1391

Betta Splendens A1392

2020, Sept. 21 Litho. *Perf. 13¼*
Granite Paper

3112 A1389 5b multi — —
3113 A1390 5b multi — —
a. Souvenir sheet of 2, #3112-3113 — —
3114 A1391 5b multi — —
3115 A1392 5b multi — —
a. Souvenir sheet of 2, #3114-3115 — —

Nos. 3113a and 3115a each sold for 20b.

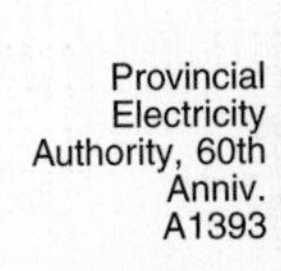

Provincial Electricity Authority, 60th Anniv. A1393

2020, Sept. 28 Litho. *Perf. 13¼*
Granite Paper

3116 A1393 3b multi .75 .25

Thong Muan A1394

Coconut Balls A1395

Lamduan Petals A1396

Sampanni A1397

Piakpun A1398

Crispy Jellies A1399

Pudding With Coconut Topping A1400

Sweet Noodles A1401

2020, Nov. 16 Litho. *Perf. 14x14½*
Granite Paper

3117 Block of 8 — —
a. A1394 3b multi — —
b. A1395 3b multi — —
c. A1396 3b multi — —
d. A1397 3b multi — —
e. A1398 3b multi — —
f. A1399 3b multi — —
g. A1400 3b multi — —
h. A1401 3b multi — —

Traditional New Year desserts.

National Day — A1402

2020, Dec. 5 Litho. *Perf. 13¼*
Granite Paper

3118 A1402 5b multi .75 .25

Queen Mother Sirikit, 88th Birthday — A1403

Litho. With Foil Application
2020, Dec. 5 *Perf. 13¼*
Granite Paper

3119 A1403 9b multi .90 .25

Princess Srinagarinda (1900-95) — A1404

2020, Dec. 21 Litho. *Perf. 13¼*
Granite Paper

3120 A1404 3b multi — —

Royal Regalia A1405

Designs: No. 3121, 5b, Royal upturned slippers. No. 3122, 5b, Sword of victory. No. 3123, 5b, Royal fan and whisk. No. 3124, 5b, Royal scepter. No. 3125, 5b, Great crown of victory, vert.

2020, Dec. 21 Litho. *Perf. 13¼*
Silver-faced Paper

3121-3125 A1405 Set of 5 — —

King Maha Vajiralongkorn at Coronation Ceremony — A1406

Litho. & Embossed With Foil Application
2020, Dec. 21 *Perf. 13¼*
Granite Paper

3126 A1406 100b multi — —

New Year 2021 (Year of the Ox) — A1407

2021, Jan. 4 Litho. *Perf. 13¼*
Granite Paper

3127 A1407 3b multi .75 .25

A1408

A1409

A1410

Children's Day — A1411

2021, Jan. 9 Litho. *Perf. 13¼*
Granite Paper

3128 A1408 3b multi .45 .25
3129 A1409 3b multi .45 .25
3130 A1410 5b multi .45 .25
3131 A1411 5b multi .45 .25
Nos. 3128-3131 (4) 1.80 1.00

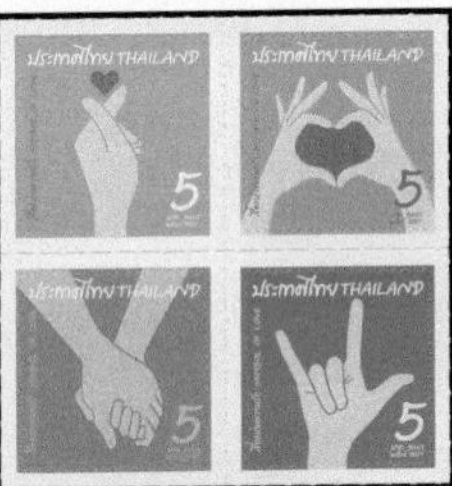

Love A1412

No. 3132: a, Hand with crossed thumb and index finger (pink background). b, Hands making heart with thumbs and index fingers (lt. blue background). c, People holding hands (turquoise blue background). d, Hand with thumb, index finger and pinkie extended (magenta background).

Die Cut Perf. 11½

2021, Feb. 8 **Litho.**

Self-Adhesive

3132 A1412 Block of 4 —
a.-d. 5b Any single — —

Ordination Hall, Wat Ratchabophit Sathitmahasimaram
A1413

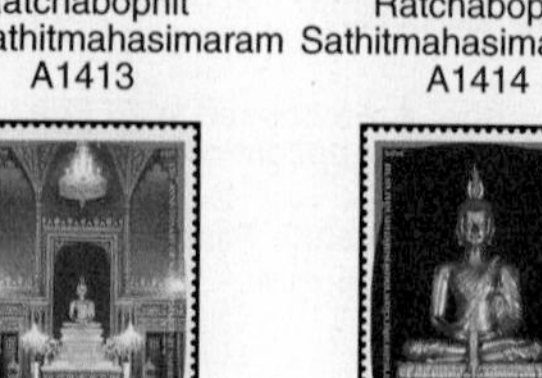

Main Stupa, Wat Ratchabophit Sathitmahasimaram
A1414

Ordination Hall Interior, Wat Ratchabophit Sathitmahasimaram
A1415

Phra Buddha Ankiros, Wat Ratchabophit Sathitmahasimaram
A1416

Supreme Patriarch Somdet Phra Ariyavongsagatanana IX — A1417

Supreme Patriarch Somdet Phra Ariyavongsagatanana IX — A1418

2021, Jan. 22 **Litho.** ***Perf. 13¼***

Granite Paper

3133 A1413 5b multi — —
3134 A1414 5b multi — —
3135 A1415 5b multi — —
3136 A1416 5b multi — —
3137 A1417 10b multi — —

Souvenir Sheet

3138 A1418 10b multi — —

Wat Ratchabophit Sathitmahasimaram, 150th anniv. No. 3138 sold for 20b.

A1419

A1420

A1421

Thai Massage, UNESCO Intangible Cultural Heritage
A1422

Litho. With Foil Application

2021, Apr. 2 ***Perf. 13¼***

Granite Paper

3142 A1419 3b gold & multi — —
3143 A1420 3b gold & multi — —
3144 A1421 3b gold & multi — —
3145 A1422 3b gold & multi — —

Thai heritage conservation. No. 3142 exists in a souvenir sheet that sold for 15b.

SEMI-POSTAL STAMPS

Nos. 164-175 Overprinted in Red

1918, Jan. 11 **Unwmk.** ***Perf. 14***

B1 A21 2s orange brown 1.75 1.00
B2 A21 3s emerald 1.75 1.00
B3 A21 5s rose red 6.00 4.25
B4 A21 10s black & olive 16.00 6.00
B5 A21 15s blue 10.00 6.00
B6 A22 1b blue & gray blk 45.00 24.00
B7 A22 2b car rose & brn 60.00 30.00
B8 A22 3b yel grn & blk 120.00 50.00
B9 A22 5b dp vio & blk 350.00 175.00
a. Double overprint 775.00 400.00
B10 A22 10b ol grn & vio brn 575.00 300.00
B11 A22 20b sea grn & brn 2,100. 1,500.
Nos. B1-B11 (11) 3,286. 2,097.

Excellent counterfeit overprints are known.

These stamps were sold at an advance over face value, the excess being given to the Siamese Red Cross Society.

Stamps of 1905-19 Handstamp Overprinted

1920, Feb.

On Nos. 164, 146, 168

B12 A21 2s (+ 3s) org brn 42.50 28.00
B13 A21 3s (+ 2s) green 42.50 28.00
B14 A21 15s (+ 5s) blue 120.00 85.00

On No. 105

B15 A15 1t (+ 25s) 340.00 340.00

On Nos. 185-186

B16 A21 5s on 6s (+ 5s) 57.50 42.50
a. Overprint inverted
B17 A21 10s on 12s (+ 5s) 57.50 42.50
Nos. B12-B17 (6) 660.00 566.00
Set, never hinged 1,150.

Sold at an advance over face value, the excess being for the benefit of the Wild Tiger Corps. Counterfeits exist.

Stamps of 1905-20 Handstamp Overprinted

On Nos. 164, 146, 168

B18 A21 2s (+ 3s) org brn 32.50 24.00
B19 A21 3s (+ 2s) green 32.50 24.00
a. Pair, one without ovpt.
B20 A21 15s (+ 5s) blue 60.00 50.00

On No. 105

B21 A15 1t (+ 25s) 275.00 250.00

On No. 186

B22 A21 10s on 12s (+ 5s) 60.00 42.50

On No. 190

B23 A23 5s (+ 5s) 65.00 47.50
Nos. B18-B23 (6) 525.00 438.00
Set, never hinged 850.00

Sold at an advance over face value, the excess being for the benefit of the Wild Tiger Corps. Counterfeits exist.

No. B23 was issued in late April or May 1920.

Nos. 187-188, 190, 193-194, 196, 198 Overprinted in Blue or Red

1920, Dec. 17

B24 A23 2s brown, *yel* 13.50 13.50
B25 A23 3s grn, *grn* (R) 13.50 13.50
B26 A23 5s rose, *pale rose* 13.50 13.50
B27 A23 10s blk & org (R) 13.50 13.50
B28 A23 15s bl, *bluish* (R) 26.00 26.00
B29 A23 25s chocolate 90.00 90.00
B30 A23 50s ocher & blk (R) 210.00 210.00
Nos. B24-B30 (7) 380.00 380.00
Set, never hinged 575.00

Nos. B12-B30 were sold at an advance over face value, the excess being for the benefit of the Wild Tiger Corps. Counterfeits exist.

Nos. 170-172 Surcharged in Red

1939, Apr. 6 **Unwmk.** ***Perf. 14***

B31 A22 5s + 5s on 1b 20.00 16.00
B32 A22 10s + 5s on 2b 25.00 24.00
B33 A22 15s + 5s on 3b 25.00 24.00
Nos. B31-B33 (3) 70.00 64.00
Set, never hinged 120.00

Founding of the Intl. Red Cross Soc., 75th anniv.

Bottom line of overprint is different on Nos. B32-B33.

Catalogue values for unused stamps in this section, from this point to the end of the section, are for Never Hinged items.

No. 214 Surcharged in Carmine

1952 **Unwmk.** ***Perf. 12½***

B34 A25 80s + 20s blue & blk 20.00 15.00

New constitution.

Red Cross and Dancer — SP1

Lithographed, Cross Typographed

1953, Apr. 6 **Wmk. 299** ***Perf. 11***

Cross in Red, Dancer Dark Blue

B35 SP1 25s + 25s yellow grn 5.00 4.50
B36 SP1 50s + 50s brt rose 16.00 8.00
B37 SP1 1b + 1b lt blue 19.00 12.50
Nos. B35-B37 (3) 40.00 25.00

60th anniv. of the founding of the Siamese Red Cross Society.

Nos. B35-B37 Overprinted in Black

1955, Apr. 3

Cross in Red, Dancer Dark Blue

B38 SP1 25s + 25s yel grn 30.00 16.00
B39 SP1 50s + 50s brt rose 120.00 100.00
B40 SP1 1b + 1b lt blue 175.00 150.00
Nos. B38-B40 (3) 325.00 266.00

Counterfeits exist.

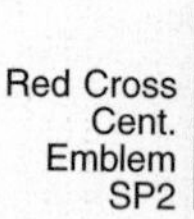

Red Cross Cent. Emblem
SP2

1963 **Wmk. 334** **Litho.** ***Perf. 13½***

B41 50s + 10s cross at right .80 .40
B42 50s + 10s cross at left .80 .40
a. SP2 Pair, #B41-B42 2.40 1.60

Cent. of the Intl. Red Cross.

Nos. B41-B42 Surcharged

1973, Feb. 15

B43 SP2 75s + 25s on 50s + 10s 1.40 1.20
B44 SP3 75s + 25s on 50s + 10s 1.40 1.20
a. Pair, #B43-B44 3.00 2.40

Red Cross Fair, Feb. 15-19.

Nos. B41-B42 Surcharged

1974, Feb. 2

B45 SP2 75s + 25s on 50s + 10s 1.40 1.40
B46 SP3 75s + 25s on 50s + 10s 1.40 1.40
a. Pair, #B45-B46 2.90 2.90

Red Cross Fair, Feb. 1974. Position of surcharge reversed on No. B46.

Nos. B41-B42 Surcharged

1975, Feb 11 52

B47 SP2 75s + 25s on 50s + 10s 1.40 1.40
B48 SP3 75s + 25s on 50s + 10s 1.40 1.40
a. Pair, #B47-B48 2.90 2.90

Red Cross Fair, Feb. 1975. Position of surcharge reversed on No. B48.

Nos. B41-B42 Surcharged

1976, Feb. 26

B49 SP2 75s + 25s on 50s + 10s 1.40 1.40
B50 SP3 75s + 25s on 50s + 10s 1.40 1.40
a. Pair, #B49-B50 2.90 2.90

Red Cross Fair, Feb. 16-Mar. 1. Position of surcharge reversed on #B50.

Nos. B41-B42 Surcharged

1977, Apr. 6 Wmk. 334 Perf. 13½
B51 SP2 75s + 25s on 50s + 10s 1.40 .65
B52 SP3 75s + 25s on 50s + 10s 1.40 .65
a. Pair, #B51-B52 2.90 2.90

Red Cross Fair 1977.

Red Cross Blood Collection — SP4

Wmk. 329
1978, Apr. 6 Photo. Perf. 13
B53 SP4 2.75b + 25s multi 2.00 2.00

"Give blood, save life."
For surcharge see No. B58.

Eye and Blind People — SP5

Perf. 14x13½
1979, Apr. 6 Litho. Wmk. 368
B54 SP5 75s + 25s multi .95 .50

"Give an eye, save new life." Red Cross Fair. Surtax was for Thai Red Cross.
For surcharge see No. B59.

Extracting Snake Venom, Red Cross — SP6

1980, Apr. Perf. 11x13
B55 SP6 75s + 25s multi 1.20 .95
Complete booklet, 10 #B55 20.00

Red Cross Fair. Surtax was for Thai Red Cross.
For surcharge see No. B60.

Nurse Helping Victim — SP7

1981, Apr. 6 Wmk. 377 Perf. 12½
B56 SP7 75 + 25s red & gray grn 1.50 1.40

Red Cross Fair (canceled). Surtax was for Thai Red Cross.
For surcharge see No. B65.

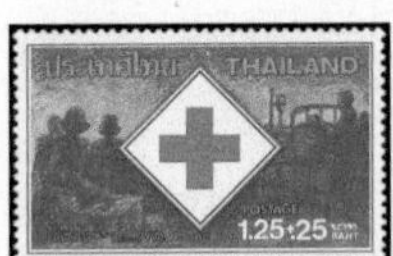
Red Cross Fair — SP8

Perf. 13x13½
1983, Apr. 6 Litho. Wmk. 329
B57 SP8 1.25b + 25s multi 1.20 1.00

Surtax was for Thai Red Cross.

No. B53 Surcharged

1984, Apr. 6 Photo. Perf. 13
B58 SP4 3.25b + 25s on 2.75b + 25s 2.25 4.50

Red Cross Fair. Surtax was for Thai Red Cross. Overprint translates: Red Cross Donation.

No. B54 Surcharged

Wmk. 368
1985, Mar. 30 Litho. Perf. 13
B59 SP5 2b + 25c on 75s + 25s 1.90 1.90

Surtax for the Thai Red Cross.

No. B55 Overprinted and Surcharged

1986, Apr. 6 Wmk. 368 Perf. 11x13
B60 SP6 2b + 25s on 75s + 25s 2.25 2.00

Natl. Children's Day. Surtax for Natl. Red Cross Society. Overprint translates "Red Cross Donation."

Natl. Scouting Movement, 75th Anniv., 15th Asia-Pacific Conference, Thailand SP9

#B61, Scouts, saluting, community service. #B62, Scout activities. #B63, King & queen at ceremony. #B64, 15th Asia-Pacific conf.

1986, Nov. 7 Wmk. 385 Perf. 13½
B61 SP9 2b + 50s multi .50 .25
B62 SP9 2b + 50s multi .50 .25
B63 SP9 2b + 50s multi .50 .25
B64 SP9 2b + 50s multi .50 .25
Nos. B61-B64 (4) 2.00 1.00

Surtax for the Natl. Scouting Fund.

No. B56 Surcharged
1987, Apr. Wmk. 377 Perf. 12½
B65 SP7 2b + 50s on 75s + 25s 2.00 1.60

Sports — SP10

Designs: No. B66, Hurdles, medal winners. No. B67, Race, nurse treating injured cyclist. No. B68, Boxers training. No. B69, Soccer.

1989, Dec. 16 Wmk. 387 Perf. 13½
B66 SP10 2b +1b multi .40 .30
B67 SP10 2b +1b multi .40 .30
B68 SP10 2b +1b multi .40 .30
B69 SP10 2b +1b multi .40 .30
Nos. B66-B69 (4) 1.60 1.20

Surtax for sports welfare organizations.

Sports — SP11

1990, Dec. 16
B70 SP11 2b +1b Judo .45 .30
B71 SP11 2b +1b Archery .45 .30
B72 SP11 2b +1b High jump .45 .30
B73 SP11 2b +1b Windsurfing .45 .30
Nos. B70-B73 (4) 1.80 1.20

Surtax for sports welfare organization.

Sports — SP12

Wmk. 387
1991, Dec. 16 Litho. Perf. 13½
B74 SP12 2b +1b Jogging .40 .30
B75 SP12 2b +1b Cycling .40 .30
B76 SP12 2b +1b Soccer, jump-ing rope .40 .30
B77 SP12 2b +1b Swimming .40 .30
Nos. B74-B77 (4) 1.60 1.20

Surtax for sports welfare organizations.

18th South East Asian Games, Chiang Mai — SP13

No. B78: a, Water polo. b, Tennis. c, Hurdles. d, Gymnastics.
No. B79: a, Fencing. b, Pool. c, Diving. d, Pole vault.

1994, Dec. 16 Wmk. 340
B78 SP13 2b +1b Strip of 4, #a.-d. 2.25 1.75
e. Souvenir sheet, #B78 2.25 2.25

Wmk. 387
B79 SP13 2b +1b Strip of 4, #a.-d. 1.60 1.40
e. Souvenir sheet, #B79 2.40 2.40

Nos. B78e, B79e sold for 15b.
Issued: #B78, 12/16/94; #B79, 12/9/95.
For surcharges see Nos. 2338-2339, 2347-2348.

13th Asian Games, Bangkok SP14

1998, Mar. 27 Perf. 14½x14
B80 SP14 2b +1b Shooting .25 .25
B81 SP14 3b +1b Rhythmic gymnastics .35 .25
B82 SP14 4b +1b Swimming .45 .35
B83 SP14 7b +1b Wind-surfing .70 .55
Nos. B80-B83 (4) 1.75 1.40

13th Asian Games, Bangkok SP15

Perf. 14½x14
1998, Dec. 6 Litho. Unwmk.
Granite Paper
B84 SP15 2b +1b Field hockey .35 .25
B85 SP15 3b +1b Wrestling .40 .25
B86 SP15 4b +1b Rowing .50 .30
B87 SP15 7b +1b Equestrian .80 .45
Nos. B84-B87 (4) 2.05 1.25

AIR POST STAMPS

Garuda — AP1

1925 Unwmk. Engr. Perf. 14, 14½
C1 AP1 2s brown, *yel* 2.25 .50
C2 AP1 3s dark brown 2.25 .50
C3 AP1 5s green 11.00 .55
C4 AP1 10s black & org 20.00 .60
C5 AP1 15s carmine 18.50 1.00
C6 AP1 25s dark blue 12.50 1.20
C7 AP1 50s brown org & blk 40.00 7.50
C8 AP1 1b blue & brown 40.00 9.00
Nos. C1-C8 (8) 146.50 20.85
Set, never hinged 200.00

Issue dates: 2s, 50s, Apr. 21; others, Jan. 3.

Nos. C1-C8 received this overprint ("Government Museum 2468") in 1925, but were never issued. The death of King Vajiravudh caused cancellation of the fair at which this set was to have been released.

They were used during 1928 only in the interdepartmental service for accounting purposes of the money-order sections of various Bangkok post offices, and were never sold to the public. Values for set: unused, $1,400; used, $40.

1930-37 Perf. 12½
C9 AP1 2s brown, *yel* 7.50 .60
C10 AP1 5s green 1.75 .30
C11 AP1 10s black & org 6.00 .30
C12 AP1 15s carmine 24.00 6.00
C13 AP1 25s dark blue ('37) 3.00 .90
a. Vert. pair, imperf. btwn. 600.00
C14 AP1 50s brn org & blk ('37) 3.00 2.00
Nos. C9-C14 (6) 45.25 10.10
Set, never hinged 70.00

Monument of Democracy, Bangkok — AP2

1942-43 Engr. Perf. 11
C15 AP2 2s dk org brn ('43) 3.25 2.40
C16 AP2 3s dk grn ('43) 32.50 24.00
a. Vert. pair, imperf. btwn. 275.00 275.00
C17 AP2 5s deep claret 3.25 1.20
a. Horiz. pair, imperf. btwn. 150.00 150.00
b. Vert. pair, imperf. btwn. 150.00 150.00
C18 AP2 10s carmine ('43) 15.00 1.20
a. Vert. pair, imperf. btwn. 150.00 150.00
C19 AP2 15s dark blue 5.25 2.00
a. Vert. pair, imperf. btwn. 175.00 175.00
Nos. C15-C19 (5) 59.25 30.80
Set, never hinged 90.00

Catalogue values for unused stamps in this section, from this point to the end of the section, are for Never Hinged items.

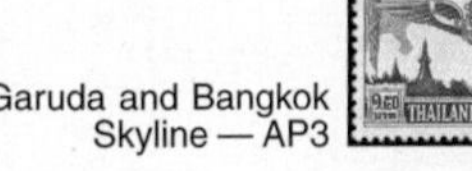
Garuda and Bangkok Skyline — AP3

1952-53 Perf. 13x12½
C20 AP3 1.50b red violet ('53) 4.75 1.00
C21 AP3 2b dark blue 13.00 2.00
C22 AP3 3b gray ('53) 17.50 1.25
Nos. C20-C22 (3) 35.25 4.25

Issue dates: June 15, 1952. Sept. 15, 1953.

OFFICIAL STAMPS

Catalogue values for unused stamps in this section are for Never Hinged items.

O1

O2

Perf. 10½ Rough
1963, Oct. 1 Typo. Unwmk.
Without Gum
O1 O1 10s pink & dp car .25 .25
O2 O1 20s brt grn & car rose .25 .25
O3 O1 25s blue & dp car .30 *.35*
O4 O1 50s deep carmine 1.10 *2.00*
O5 O2 1b silver & car rose 1.25 *3.00*
O6 O2 2b bronze & car rose 2.25 2.25
Nos. O1-O6 (6) 5.40 8.10

Issued as an official test from Oct. 1, 1963, to Jan. 31, 1964, to determine the amount of mail sent out by various government departments.
Nos. O5, O9, O10 exist with oval frame of type O1.

1964 Without Gum
O7 O1 20s green .50 .50
O8 O1 25s blue .50 .50
O9 O2 1b silver 1.00 1.00
O10 O2 2b bister 2.50 2.50
Nos. O7-O10 (4) 4.50 4.50

Others values exist printed in one color.

THRACE

'thrās

LOCATION — In southeastern Europe between the Black and Aegean Seas
GOVT. — Former Turkish Province
AREA — 89,361 sq. mi. (approx.)

Thrace underwent many political changes during the Balkan Wars and World War I. It was finally divided among Turkey, Greece and Bulgaria.

100 Lepta = 1 Drachma
40 Paras = 1 Piaster
100 Stotinki = 1 Leva (1919)

A large number of minor overprint errors exist on most issues of Thrace. See the *Scott Classic Specialized Catalogue of Stamps and Covers 1840-1940* for much more specialized listings.

Giumulzina District Issue

Turkish Stamps of 1909 Surcharged in Blue or Red

1913 Unwmk. *Perf. 12, 13½*

1 A21 10 l on 20pa rose (Bl) 45.00 *50.00*
a. Inverted overprint 170.00
b. Double overprint 170.00
2 A21 25 l on 10pa bl grn 67.50 *75.00*
a. Inverted overprint 175.00
b. Double overprint 175.00
3 A21 25 l on 20pa rose (Bl) 67.50 *75.00*
a. Inverted overprint 170.00
b. Double overprint 170.00
c. Béhié ovpt. (#162) 200.00
4 A21 25 l on 1pi ultra 110.00 *125.00*
a. Inverted overprint 220.00
b. Double overprint 220.00
Nos. 1-4 (4) 290.00 325.00

Counterfeits exist of Nos. 1-4.

Eight other values exist, bearing surcharges differing in color or denomination from Nos. 1-4. These stamps were not issued. Values, each: unused $175; never hinged $350.

Turkish Inscriptions
A1 A2

Type 1

Type 2

1913 Litho. *Imperf.*

Laid Paper

Control Mark in Rose

Without Gum

5 A1 1pi blue, type 1 17.50 17.50
a. Double print 250.00
b. Type 2 85.00 75.00
6 A1 2pi violet 17.50 17.50
a. Double print 500.00 200.00
b. Type 2 200.00

Wove Paper

7 A2 10pa vermilion 35.00 30.00
8 A2 20pa blue 35.00 30.00
9 A2 1pi violet 37.50 30.00
Nos. 5-9 (5) 142.50 125.00

Turkish Stamps of 1913 Surcharged in Red or Black

1913 *Perf. 12*

10 A22 1pi on 2pa ol grn (R) 30.00 27.50
10A A22 1pi on 2pa ol grn 30.00 27.50
11 A22 1pi on 5pa ocher 30.00 27.50
11A A22 1pi on 5pa ocher (R) 30.00 27.50
12 A22 1pi on 20pa rose 35.00 35.00
13 A22 1pi on 5pi dk vio (R) 70.00 70.00
13A A22 1pi on 5pi dk vio 70.00 70.00
14 A22 1pi on 10pi dl red 125.00 *125.00*
15 A22 1pi on 25pi dk grn 500.00 *500.00*
Nos. 10-15 (9) 920.00 910.00

On Nos. 13-15 the surcharge is vertical, reading up. No. 15 exists with double surcharge, one black, one red.

Nos. 10-15 exist with forged surcharges.

Bulgarian Stamps of 1911 Handstamped Surcharged in Red or Blue

1913

16 A20 10pa on 1s myr grn (R) 25.00 25.00
a. Top ovpt. inverted 100.00
b. Top ovpt. double 100.00
c. Top ovpt. omitted 150.00
d. Bottom ovpt. omitted 150.00
e. Bottom ovpt. inverted 100.00
17 A21 20pa on 2s car & blk 25.00 25.00
a. Inverted overprint 60.00
18 A23 1pi on 5s grn & blk (R) 25.00 25.00
a. Inverted overprint 125.00 125.00
c. Double ovpt., one at top, one at bottom
19 A22 2pi on 3s lake & blk 28.00 28.00
a. Inverted overprint & surcharge 80.00 80.00
20 A24 2½pi on 10s dp red & blk 40.00 40.00
b. 2½pi on 2s 265.00
21 A25 5pi on 15s brn bis 70.00 70.00
a. Inverted overprint & surcharge 260.00
Nos. 16-21 (6) 213.00 213.00

Same Surcharges on Greek Stamps

On Issue of 1911

1913 *Serrate Roulette 13½*

22 A24 10pa on 1 l grn (R) 25.00 25.00
23 A24 10pa on 1 l grn 25.00 25.00
24 A26 10pa on 5 l grn 125.00 125.00
25 A25 10pa on 25 l ultra (R) 35.00 35,00
26 A25 20pa on 2 l car rose 25.00 25.00
27 A24 1pi on 3 l ver 25.00 25,00
a. Value omitted 65.00 65.00
b. Red overprint 25.00 25.00
27C A24 1pi on 10 l car rose 550.00
28 A26 2pi on 5 l grn (R) 65.00 65.00
29 A24 2½pi on 10 l car rose 65.00 65.00
30 A25 5pi on 40 l dp bl (R) 125.00 125.00
Nos. 22-30 (9) 515.00 455.60

On Occupation Stamps of 1912

31 O1 10pa on 1 l brn 25.00 20.00
a. Value omitted 125.00
b. Value srch. inverted 65.00
32 O1 20pa on 1 l brn 25.00 20.00
33 O1 1pi on 1 l brn 25.00 20.00
Nos. 31-33 (3) 75.00 60.00

These surcharges were made with handstamps, two of which were required for each surcharge. The upper handstamp, reads "Administration of Autonomous Western Thrace" in old Turkish. The lower handstamp expresses the new value. On horizontal designs, the text appears on the right, and the value appears on the left. On inverted overprints on horizontal stamps, this is reversed. One or both parts may be found inverted or omitted.

Nos. 16-33 exist with forged surcharges.

OCCUPATION STAMPS

Issued under Allied Occupation

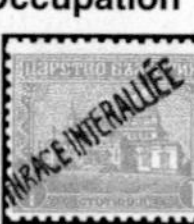

Bulgarian Stamps of 1915-19 Handstamped in Violet Blue

Perf. 11½, 11½x12, 14

1919 Unwmk.

N1b A43 1s black 2.50 2.00
N2 A43 2s olive green 2.50 2.00
N3 A44 5s green .85 .85
N4 A44 10s rose .85 .85
N5 A44 15s violet .85 .85
N6 A26 25s indigo & black .85 .85

The overprint on Nos. N1-N6 exists applied both ascending and descending, as well as inverted in both positions. On the 1s value, the usual position of the overprint is upright, reading from lower left to upper right; on the rest of the set, the overprint is usually inverted, reading from lower right to upper left. See the *Scott Classic Specialized Catalogue of Stamps and Covers* for detailed listings.

Bulgarian Stamps of 1911-19 Overprinted in Red or Black

1919

N7 A43 1s black (R) .25 .25
N8 A43 2s olive green .25 .25
c. Inverted ovpt. 40.00
d. Pair, one without ovpt. —
N9 A44 5s green .25 .25
c. Inverted ovpt.
d. Pair, one without ovpt.
e. Double ovpt. 50.00
N10 A44 10s rose .25 .25
d. Pair, one without ovpt.
e. Double ovpt. 35.00
f. Imperf., pair —
N11 A44 15s violet .25 .25
c. Imperf., pair —
N12 A26 25s indigo & black .25 .25
N13 A29 1 l chocolate 5.00 5.00
N14 A37a 2 l brown orange 9.00 9.00
N15 A38 3 l claret 12.50 12.50
Nos. N7-N15 (9) 28.00 28.00

Overprint is vertical, reading up, on Nos. N9-N13.

The following varieties are found in the setting of "INTERALLIEE": Inverted "V" for "A," second "L" inverted, "F" instead of final "E."

Bulgarian Stamps of 1919 Overprinted

1920

N16 A44 5s green .25 .25
d. Imperf, pair 75.00
N17 A44 10s rose .25 .25
N18 A44 15s violet .25 .25
N19 A44 50s yel brn, ovpt. reading up 1.50 1.50
d. Ovpt. reading down 25.00 *30.00*
h. As "d," imperf, pair 140.00
Nos. N16-N19 (4) 2.25 2.25

Various typographical errors in the overprint are found on all values.

Bulgarian Stamps of 1919 Overprinted

1920 *Perf. 12x11½*

N20 A44 5s green .25 .25
a. Inverted overprint 35.00 *50.00*
b. Pair, one without ovpt. 42.50 *65.00*
c. Imperf, pair 45.00 *65.00*
d. As "c," inverted overprint 55.00 *75.00*
N21 A44 10s rose .25 .25
a. Inverted overprint 30.00 *40.00*
b. Double ovpt., one on gum side 45.00 *65.00*
c. Imperf, pair 45.00 *65.00*
d. As "c," inverted overprint 55.00 *75.00*
N22 A44 15s violet .25 .25
a. Inverted overprint 30.00 *40.00*
b. Imperf, pair 45.00 *65.00*
c. As "b," inverted overprint 55.00 *75.00*
N23 A44 25s deep blue .25 .25
a. Inverted overprint 30.00 *40.00*
b. Imperf, pair 45.00 *65.00*
c. As "b," inverted overprint 55.00 *75.00*
d. Double ovpt., one on gummed side 45.00
N24 A44 50s ocher .25 .25
a. Inverted overprint 35.00 *50.00*
b. Imperf, pair 45.00 65.00
c. As "b," inverted ovpt. 55.00 80.00

Imperf

N25 A44 30s chocolate 1.50 1.50
a. Inverted overprint 35.00 *55.00*
b. Perforated 22.50
Nos. N20-N25 (6) 2.75 2.75

No. N25 is not known without overprint.

ISSUED UNDER GREEK OCCUPATION

Counterfeits exist of Nos. N26-N84.

For Use in Western Thrace

Greek Stamps of 1911-19 Overprinted "Administration Western Thrace" in Greek

Serrate Roulette 13½

1920 Litho. Unwmk.

N26 A24 1 l green .25 *.25*
a. Inverted overprint 20.00
b. Double overprint 20.00
c. Double overprint, one inverted 75.00
N27 A25 2 l rose .25 *.25*
N28 A24 3 l vermilion .25 *.25*
a. Inverted overprint 32.50
N29 A26 5 l green .25 *.25*
a. Inverted overprint 25.00
b. Double overprint 25.00
N30 A24 10 l rose .40 *.85*
N31 A25 15 l dull blue .40 *.75*
a. Inverted overprint 20.00
b. Double overprint 20.00
c. Dbl. ovpt., one inverted 30.00
N32 A25 25 l blue .40 *.85*
N34 A25 40 l indigo 2.00 *4.00*
N35 A26 50 l violet brn 2.50 *6.50*
N36 A27 1d ultra 9.00 *15.00*
N37 A27 2d vermilion 30.00 *35.00*
a. Double overprint 75.00
Nos. N26-N37 (11) 45.70 *63.95*

The 20 l value with this overprint was not issued. Values: unused $25; never hinged $65.

Engr.

N38 A25 2 l car rose 1.25 *1.00*
N39 A24 3 l vermilion 1.25 *1.00*
N39A A25 20 l slate 32.50
N39B A25 25 l blue 35.00
N39C A26 30 l rose 45.00
N40 A27 1d ultra 30.00 *25.00*
N41 A27 2d vermilion 45.00 *35.00*
N42 A27 3d car rose 62.50 *80.00*
N43 A27 5d ultra 25.00 *30.00*
N44 A27 10d deep blue 25.00 *30.00*
Nos. N38-N44 (10) 302.50

Nos. N38-N44 were not issued. Values for used examples of Nos. N38-N39 and N40-N44 are for cancelled-to-order stamps.

Nos. N42-N44 are overprinted on the reissues of Greece Nos. 210-212. See footnote below Greece No. 213.

Overprinted

N45 A28 25d deep blue 62.50 35.00

This overprint reads: "Administration Western Thrace."

With Additional Overprint

Litho.

N46 A24 1 l green 5.00 3.50
N47 A25 2 l rose .25 *.50*
a. Inverted overprint 65.00
N47B A26 5 l green 27.50
N48 A24 10 l rose .65 *.85*
a. Inverted overprint 19.00
N49 A25 20 l slate .65 *.85*
a. Inverted overprint 19.00
N49B A25 25 l blue 45.00
N50 A26 30 l rose (#240) .65 *1.25*

Engr.

N50A	A26	30 l rose (#244)	75.00	
N51	A27	2d vermilion	35.00	*30.00*
N52	A27	3d car rose	47.50	*35.00*
N53	A27	5d ultra	42.50	*32.50*
N54	A27	10d deep blue	35.00	*22.50*
		Nos. N46-N54 (12)	314.70	*126.95*

Nos. N46, N47B, N49B, N50A, N51, N53 and N54 were not issued. Used values for Nos. N46, N51, N53 and N54 are for canceled-to-order stamps.

For Use in Eastern and Western Thrace

Greek Stamps of 1911-19 Overprinted "Administration Thrace" in Greek

1920 **Litho.**

N55	A24	1 l green	.25	*1.00*
a.		Inverted overprint	15.00	
b.		Double overprint	15.00	
N56	A25	2 l rose	.25	*.50*
a.		Inverted overprint	12.50	
b.		Double overprint	15.00	
c.		Triple overprint	25.00	
N57	A24	3 l vermilion	.25	*.50*
a.		Inverted overprint	12.50	
b.		Double overprint	15.00	
c.		Double overprint, one inverted	17.50	
N58	A26	5 l green	.25	*.50*
a.		Inverted overprint	20.00	
b.		Double overprint	35.00	
N59	A24	10 l rose	.50	*.75*
a.		Double overprint	85.00	
N59B	A25	15 l dull blue	60.00	
a.		Inverted overprint	62.50	
N60	A25	20 l slate	.65	*1.50*
a.		Inverted overprint	17.50	
b.		Double overprint	15.00	
N61	A25	25 l blue	1.75	*2.50*
N62	A25	40 l indigo	2.50	*7.00*
N63	A26	50 l violet brn	3.00	*6.50*
N64	A27	1d ultra	15.00	*30.00*
N65	A27	2d vermilion	32.50	*45.00*

Engr.

N65A	A25	2 l rose	2.50	*4.00*
N66	A24	3 l vermilion	3.00	*4.00*
N67	A25	20 l gray lilac	8.50	*22.50*
N68	A28	25d deep blue	75.00	*100.00*
		Nos. N55-N68 (16)	205.90	*226.25*

Nos. N59B and N65A-N68 were not issued. Used values for Nos. N65A-N68 are for canceled-to-order stamps.

With Additional Overprint

Litho.

N68A	A24	1 l green	12.50	*6.00*
N69	A25	2 l car rose	.25	*.50*
a.		Inverted overprint	35.00	
b.		Double overprint	30.00	
N70	A26	5 l green	7.50	*8.00*
N71	A25	20 l slate	.25	*.50*
a.		Double overprint	350.00	325.00
N72	A26	30 l rose	.25	*.50*

Engr.

N73	A27	3d car rose	17.50	*25.00*
a.		Inverted overprint	—	
N74	A27	5d ultra	27.50	*45.00*
N75	A27	10d deep blue	45.00	*60.00*
a.		Double overprint	125.00	
		Nos. N68A-N75 (8)	110.75	*145.50*

Nos. N68A, N70 and N74-N75 were not issued. Used values are for canceled-to-order stamps.

Turkish Stamps of 1916-20 Srchd. in Blue, Black or Red

1920 ***Perf. 11½, 12½***

N76	A43	1 l on 5pa org (Bl)	.40	*.50*
a.		Inverted overprint	35.00	35.00
b.		Double overprint	30.00	30.00
c.		Double overprint, one inverted	50.00	50.00
d.		Double overprint, one on gummed side	35.00	
N77	A32	5 l on 3pi blue	.40	*.50*
a.		Inverted overprint	100.00	100.00
b.		Double overprint	70.00	70.00
N78	A30	20 l on 1pi bl grn	.65	*.75*
a.		Inverted overprint	27.50	27.50
b.		Double overprint	27.50	27.50
c.		Double overprint, one inverted	40.00	40.00
d.		Double overprint, one on gummed side	37.50	
N79	A53	25 l on 5pi on 2pa Prus bl (R)	.85	*1.00*
a.		Inverted overprint	50.00	50.00
b.		Double overprint	50.00	50.00
N80	A49	50 l on 5pi bl & blk (R)	6.50	*7.50*
N81	A45	1d on 20pa dp rose (Bl)	1.75	1.75
a.		Double overprint	40.00	40.00
N82	A22	2d on 10pa on 2pa ol grn (R)	2.50	*3.00*
a.		Double overprint	60.00	60.00
N83	A57	3d on 1pi dp bl (R)	12.50	12.50
a.		Inverted overprint	60.00	60.00
b.		Double overprint	65.00	65.00
N84	A23	5d on 20pa rose	12.50	12.50
a.		Inverted overprint	75.00	75.00
b.		Double overprint, one inverted	75.00	75.00
		Nos. N76-N84 (9)	38.05	40.00

On Nos. N83 and N84, the normal overprint is reading down. On the inverted overprints, it is reading up.

Nos. N77, N78 and N84 are on the 1920 issue with designs modified. Nos. N81, N82 and N83 are on stamps with the 1919 overprints.

POSTAGE DUE STAMPS

Issued under Allied Occupation

1919 Bulgarian Postage Due Stamps Overprinted, Reading Vertically Up

1919 **Unwmk.** ***Perf. 12x11½***

NJ1	D6	5s emerald	.50	.50
c.		Imperf. pair	—	—
NJ2	D6	10s purple	1.00	1.25
c.		Imperf. pair	—	—
NJ3	D6	50s blue	2.75	3.50
c.		Imperf. pair	—	—
		Nos. NJ1-NJ3 (3)	4.25	5.25

Type of Bulgarian Postage Due Stamps of 1919-22 Overprinted

1920 ***Imperf.***

NJ4	D6	5s emerald	.25	.50
a.		Inverted overprint	40.00	
NJ5	D6	10s deep violet	2.00	2.00
a.		Inverted overprint	40.00	
NJ6	D6	20s salmon	1.00	1.00
NJ7	D6	50s blue	1.50	1.50

Perf. 12x11½

NJ8	D6	10s deep violet	1.25	1.25
		Nos. NJ4-NJ8 (5)	6.00	6.25

No. NJ6 issued without gum.

TIBET

tə-'bet

LOCATION — A high tableland in Central Asia

GOVT. — A semi-independent state, nominally under control of China (under Communist China since 1950-51). In 1965 Tibet became a nominally autonomous region of the People's Republic of China.

AREA — 463,200 sq. mi.

POP. — 1,500,000 (approx.)

CAPITAL — Lhasa

Tibet's postage stamps were valid only within its borders.

6 ⅔ Trangka = 1 Sang

"Stamps" produced by the "Tibetan Government in Exile" have no postal value. These include four-value sets for Himalayan animals and the UPU that were put on sale in the early 1970s.

Excellent counterfeits of Nos. 1-18 exist. Numerous shades of all values.

All stamps issued without gum.

Small bits of foreign matter (inclusions) are to be expected in Native Paper. These do not reduce the value of the stamp unless they have caused serious damage to the design or paper.

A1

1912-50 **Unwmk.** **Typo.** ***Imperf.***

Native Paper

1	A1	⅙t green	40.00	*45.00*
2	A1	⅓t blue	40.00	*55.00*
a.		⅓t ultramarine	50.00	*60.00*
3	A1	½t violet	40.00	*55.00*
4	A1	⅔t carmine	50.00	*60.00*
a.		"POTSAGE"	150.00	*175.00*
5	A1	1t vermilion	55.00	*75.00*
6	A1	1s sage green ('50)	100.00	*110.00*
		Nos. 1-6 (6)	325.00	*400.00*

The "POTSAGE" error is found on all shades of the ⅔t (positions 6 and 7).

Pin-perf. examples of Nos. 1 and 3 exist.

Issued in sheets of 12.

Beware of private reproductions of #1-5 that were printed in the US around 1986. Sheets of 12 bear "J. Crow Co." imprint. The set of 5 sheets was sold for $5.

Printed Using Shiny Enamel Paint

1920

1a	A1	⅙t green	60.00	40.00
2b	A1	⅓t blue	500.00	500.00
3d	A1	½t purple	100.00	*110.00*
4h	A1	⅔t carmine	100.00	*110.00*
i.		"POTSAGE"	*225.00*	*250.00*
5c	A1	1t carmine	350.00	400.00

In some 1920-30 printings, European enamel paint was used instead of ink. It has a glossy surface.

Lion — A2

1914

7	A2	4t milky blue	750.	*850.*
a.		4t dark blue	1,100.	1,100.
8	A2	8t carmine rose	165.	175.
a.		8t carmine	1,100.	*1,100.*

Issued in sheets of 6.

Printed Using Shiny Enamel Paint

1920

7b	A2	4t blue	1,350.	*1,500.*
8b	A2	8t carmine	1,350.	*1,500.*

See note following No. 5c.

A3

Thin White Native Paper

1933 ***Pin-perf.***

9	A3	½t orange	95.00	*100.00*
10	A3	⅔t dark blue	95.00	*120.00*
11	A3	1t rose carmine	95.00	*120.00*
12	A3	2t scarlet	95.00	*120.00*
13	A3	4t emerald	95.00	*120.00*
		Nos. 9-13 (5)	475.00	*580.00*

Issued in sheets of 12.

Exist imperf.

Heavy Toned Native Paper

1934 ***Imperf.***

14	A3	½t yellow	16.00	*18.00*
15	A3	⅔t blue	14.00	*15.00*
16	A3	1t orange ver	14.00	*15.00*
a.		1t carmine	16.00	*18.00*
17	A3	2t red	14.00	*15.00*
a.		2t orange vermilion	14.00	*15.00*
18	A3	4t green	14.00	*15.00*
a.		25x25mm instead of 24x24mm	55.00	*65.00*
		Nos. 14-18 (5)	72.00	*78.00*

Nos. 14-18 are also known with a private pin-perf.

The ½t and 1t exist printed on both sides.

Issued in sheets of 12.

OFFICIAL STAMPS

O1

O2

Sizes: No. O1, 32½x32½mm. No. O2, 38x28½mm. No. O3, 34x33mm. No. O4, 44x44mm. No. O5, 66x66mm.

Various Designs and Sizes Inscribed "STAMP"

1945 **Unwmk.** **Typo.** ***Imperf.***

Native Paper

O1	O1	⅓t bronze green	
O2	O2	⅓t slate black	
O3	O1	⅔t reddish brown	
O4	O1	1⅓t olive green	
O5	O1	1s dark gray blue	

The status of Nos. O1-O5 is in question. Other values exist.

TIMOR

'tē-,mor

LOCATION — The eastern part of Timor island, Malay archipelago
GOVT. — Former Portuguese Overseas Territory
AREA — 7,330 sq. mi.
POP. — 660,000 (est. 1974)
CAPITAL — Dili

The Portuguese territory of Timor was annexed by Indonesia May 3, 1976. Timor-Leste achieved independent statehood status on May 20, 2002.

1000 Reis = 1 Milreis
78 Avos = 1 Rupee (1895)
100 Avos = 1 Pataca
100 Centavos = 1 Escudo (1960)
100Cents = 1 Dollar (2000)

Catalogue values for unused stamps in this country are for Never Hinged items, beginning with Scott 256 in the regular postage section, Scott J31 in the postage due section, and Scott RA11 in the postal tax section.

Watermark

Wmk. 232 — Maltese Cross

Stamps of Macao Overprinted in Black or Carmine

1885	**Unwmk.**	*Perf. 12½, 13½*		
1	A1	5r black (C)	2.50	2.00
a.		Double overprint	85.00	85.00
b.		Triple overprint	200.00	
c.		Perf. 13½	3.25	2.25
2	A1	10r green	6.75	4.50
a.		Overprint on Mozambique stamp	*20.00*	*20.00*
b.		Overprinted on Portuguese India stamp	*150.00*	*150.00*
c.		Perf. 13½	6.50	4.50
3	A1	20r rose, perf. 13½	9.00	3.75
a.		Double overprint	35.00	
b.		Perf. 12½	11.50	7.00
4	A1	25r violet	2.75	1.50
a.		Perf. 13½	27.50	12.50
5	A1	40r yellow	5.50	4.00
a.		Double overprint	25.00	
b.		Inverted overprint	*42.50*	*27.50*
c.		Perf. 13½	15.75	14.50
6	A1	50r blue	2.75	2.00
a.		Perf. 13½	16.75	14.50
7	A1	80r slate, perf. 13½	7.50	5.50
a.		Perf. 12½	7.75	5.75
8	A1	100r lilac	3.00	2.25
a.		Double overprint	30.00	
b.		Perf. 13½	14.00	5.25
9	A1	200r org, perf. 13½	6.00	5.00
a.		Perf. 12½	10.50	5.50
10	A1	300r brown, perf. 13½	6.00	4.25
a.		Perf. 12½	6.75	4.25
		Nos. 1-10 (10)	51.75	34.75

The 20r bister, 25r rose and 50r green were prepared for use but not issued.

The reprints are printed on a smooth white chalky paper, ungummed, with rough perforation 13½, and on thin white paper with shiny white gum and clean-cut perforation 13½.

King Luiz — A2

1887	**Embossed**	*Perf. 12½*		
11	A2	5r black	3.50	2.25
12	A2	10r green	4.00	3.25
13	A2	20r bright rose	5.75	3.25
14	A2	25r violet	7.75	4.00
15	A2	40r chocolate	13.50	5.25
16	A2	50r blue	14.00	6.00
17	A2	80r gray	16.00	6.50
18	A2	100r yellow brown	18.00	8.00
19	A2	200r gray lilac	35.00	17.50
20	A2	300r orange	40.00	21.00
		Nos. 11-20 (10)	157.50	77.00

Reprints of Nos. 11, 16, 18 and 19 have clean-cut perforation 13½.

For surcharges see Nos. 34-43, 83-91.

Macao No. 44 Surcharged in Black

1892	**Without Gum**	*Perf. 13½*		
21	A7	30r on 300r orange	7.25	5.00
a.		Perf. 12½	10.50	5.00
b.		As "a," double surcharge	110.00	55.00

For surcharge see No. 44.

King Carlos — A3

1894	**Typo.**	*Perf. 11½*		
22	A3	5r yellow	2.25	1.00
23	A3	10r red violet	2.25	1.00
24	A3	15r chocolate	3.25	1.25
25	A3	20r lavender	3.50	1.40
26	A3	25r green	4.50	2.00
27	A3	50r light blue	6.00	4.25
a.		Perf. 13½	*175.00*	*160.00*
28	A3	75r rose	7.50	5.50
29	A3	80r light green	8.00	5.50
30	A3	100r brown, *buff*	6.00	4.75
31	A3	150r car, *rose*	23.00	11.00
32	A3	200r dk bl, *lt bl*	23.00	11.00
33	A3	300r dk bl, *salmon*	27.50	12.50
		Nos. 22-33 (12)	116.75	61.15

For surcharges and overprints see Nos. 92-102, 120-122, 124-128, 131-133, 183-193, 199.

Stamps of 1887 Surcharged in Red, Green or Black

1895	**Without Gum**	*Perf. 12½*		
34	A2	1a on 5r black (R)	2.75	1.50
35	A2	2a on 10r green	3.00	2.25
a.		Double surcharge	25.00	
36	A2	3a on 20r brt rose (G)	4.25	2.25
37	A2	4a on 25r violet	4.25	2.25
38	A2	6a on 40r choc	7.00	3.25
39	A2	8a on 50r blue (R)	8.50	4.50
40	A2	13a on 80r gray	15.50	15.00
41	A2	16a on 100r yellow brn	15.75	14.00
42	A2	31a on 200r gray lilac	43.00	28.00
43	A2	47a on 300r org (G)	45.00	32.50
		Nos. 34-43 (10)	149.00	105.50

No. 21 Surcharged

1895	**Without Gum**	*Perf. 12½, 13½*		
44	A7	5a on 30r on 300r org	11.00	7.50
a.		Double surcharge	70.00	60.00

Common Design Types pictured following the introduction.

Vasco da Gama Issue

Common Design Types

1898	**Engr.**	*Perf. 14 to 15*		
45	CD20	½a blue green	2.50	2.00
46	CD21	1a red	2.50	2.00
47	CD22	2a red violet	2.50	2.00
48	CD23	4a yellow green	2.50	2.00
49	CD24	8a dark blue	4.00	2.50
50	CD25	12a violet brown	5.50	3.50
51	CD26	16a bister brown	5.50	3.75
52	CD27	24a bister	8.50	5.50
		Nos. 45-52 (8)	33.50	23.25

400th anniversary of Vasco da Gama's discovery of the route to India.

For overprints and surcharge see Nos. 148-155.

King Carlos — A5

1898-1903 Typo. *Perf. 11½*

Name & Value in Black Except #79

No.	Type	Description	Unused	Used
53	A5	½a gray	.85	.70
a.		Perf. 12½	3.75	3.50
54	A5	1a orange	.85	.70
a.		Perf. 12½	3.75	3.50
55	A5	2a light green	.85	.70
56	A5	2½a brown	2.25	1.50
57	A5	3a gray violet	2.25	1.50
58	A5	3a gray green ('03)	3.50	1.90
59	A5	4a sea green	2.25	1.50
60	A5	5a rose ('03)	2.50	1.90
61	A5	6a pale yel brn ('03)	2.50	1.90
62	A5	8a blue	2.25	1.50
63	A5	9a red brown ('03)	2.50	1.90
64	A5	10a slate blue ('00)	2.25	1.50
65	A5	10a gray brown ('03)	2.50	1.90
66	A5	12a rose	6.00	5.00
67	A5	12a dull blue ('03)	16.00	12.00
68	A5	13a violet	6.00	5.00
69	A5	13a red lilac ('03)	4.25	2.50
70	A5	15a gray lilac ('03)	6.50	4.00
71	A5	16a dark bl, *bl*	6.00	5.00
72	A5	20a brn, *yelsh* ('00)	6.00	5.00
73	A5	22a brn org, *pink* ('03)	7.00	4.75
74	A5	24a brown, *buff*	6.00	5.00
75	A5	31a red lil, *pinkish*	6.00	5.00
76	A5	31a brn, *straw* ('03)	7.50	4.75
77	A5	47a dk blue, *rose*	12.00	8.00
78	A5	47a red vio, *pink* ('03)	7.50	4.75
79	A5	78a blk & red, *bl* ('00)	15.00	10.50
80	A5	78a dl bl, *straw* ('03)	17.50	10.25
		Nos. 53-80 (28)	156.55	110.60

Most of Nos. 53-80 were issued without gum.

For surcharges & overprints see #81-82, 104-119, 129-130, 134-147, 195-196.

King Carlos — A6

1899		**Black Surcharge**		
81	A6	10a on 16a dk bl, *bl*	4.50	3.75
82	A6	20a on 31a red lil, *pnksh*	4.50	3.75

Surcharged in Black

1902		**On Issue of 1887**		
83	A2	5a on 25r violet	3.50	2.25
84	A2	5a on 200r gray lil	5.50	3.50
85	A2	6a on 10r blue grn	225.00	175.00
86	A2	6a on 300r orange	5.00	4.50
87	A2	9a on 40r choc	6.50	4.75
88	A2	9a on 100r yel brn	6.50	4.75
89	A2	15a on 20r rose	6.50	4.75
90	A2	15a on 50r blue	200.00	165.00
91	A2	22a on 80r gray	13.50	10.00
		Nos. 83-91 (9)	472.00	374.50

Reprints of Nos. 83-88, 90-91, 104A have clean-cut perf. 13½.

On Issue of 1894

No.	Type	Description	Unused	Used
92	A3	5a on 5r yellow	2.25	1.50
a.		Inverted surcharge	32.50	29.00
93	A3	5a on 25r green	2.50	1.50
94	A3	5a on 50r lt blue	3.00	1.75
a.		Perf. 13½	3.00	1.75
95	A3	6a on 20r lavender	3.00	2.25
96	A3	9a on 15r choc	3.00	2.25
97	A3	9a on 75r rose	3.00	2.25
98	A3	15a on 10r red vio	4.00	3.25
99	A3	15a on 100r brn, *buff*	4.00	3.25
100	A3	15a on 300r bl, *sal*	4.00	3.25
101	A3	22a on 80r lt green	6.75	5.50
102	A3	22a on 200r bl, *blue*	7.25	5.50

On Newspaper Stamp of 1893

No.	Type	Description	Unused	Used
103	N2	6a on 2½r brn	1.50	1.25
a.		Inverted surcharge	30.00	30.00
b.		Perf. 12½	250.00	250.00
c.		Perf. 13½	1.50	1.25
		Nos. 92-103 (12)	44.25	33.50

Nos. 93-97, 99-102 issued without gum.

Stamps of 1898 Overprinted in Black

No.	Type	Description	Unused	Used
104	A5	3a gray violet	3.50	2.40
104A	A5	12a rose	7.50	5.50

Reprint noted after No. 91.

No. 67 Surcharged in Black

1905				
105	A5	10a on 12a dull blue	5.00	3.75

Stamps of 1898-1903 Overprinted in Carmine or Green

1911				
106	A5	½a gray	.70	.70
a.		Inverted overprint	*20.00*	*20.00*
107	A5	1a orange	.70	.70
a.		Perf. 12½	*7.00*	*7.00*
108	A5	2a light green	.70	.60
109	A5	3a gray green	.70	.60
110	A5	5a rose (G)	1.40	.80
111	A5	6a yel brown	1.40	.80
112	A5	9a red brown	1.40	.80
113	A5	10a gray brown	2.00	1.75
114	A5	13a red lilac	2.00	1.75
115	A5	15a gray lilac	2.00	1.75
116	A5	22a brn org, *pink*	2.00	1.75
117	A5	31a brown, *straw*	2.00	1.75
118	A5	47a red vio, *pink*	4.25	3.50
119	A5	78a dl bl, *straw*	6.00	4.75
		Nos. 106-119 (14)	27.25	22.00

Preceding Issues Overprinted in Red

1913		**Without Gum**		

On Provisional Issue of 1902

No.	Type	Description	Unused	Used
120	A3	5a on 5r yellow	2.25	2.00
121	A3	5a on 25r green	2.25	2.00
122	A3	5a on 50r lt bl	5.75	4.50
a.		Perf. 13½	5.75	4.50
123	N2	6a on 2½r brn	5.00	3.00
a.		Perf. 13½	5.00	3.00
124	A3	6a on 20r lavender	3.00	2.25
125	A3	9a on 15r choc	3.00	2.25
126	A3	15a on 100r brn, *buff*	3.75	3.25
127	A3	22a on 80r lt grn	6.50	4.00
128	A3	22a on 200r bl, *bl*	6.25	4.00

On Issue of 1903

No.	Type	Description	Unused	Used
129	A5	3a gray green	6.25	*4.75*

On Issue of 1905

No.	Type	Description	Unused	Used
130	A5	10a on 12a dull bl	3.00	2.25
		Nos. 120-130 (11)	47.00	*34.25*

Overprinted in Green or Red

On Provisional Issue of 1902

1913				
131	A3	9a on 75r rose (G)	3.50	3.25
132	A3	15a on 10r red vio (G)	3.50	3.25
a.		Inverted overprint	*35.00*	*35.00*
133	A3	15a on 300r bl, *sal* (R)	5.50	4.75
a.		"REUBPLICA"	25.00	25.00
b.		"REPBLICAU"	25.00	25.00

On Issue of 1903

No.	Type	Description	Unused	Used
134	A5	5a rose (G)	3.50	3.25
		Nos. 131-134 (4)	16.00	14.50

Stamps of 1898-1903 Overprinted in Red

1913				
135	A5	6a yellow brown	2.50	2.00
136	A5	9a red brown	2.50	2.00
137	A5	10a gray brown	2.50	2.00

138 A5 13a violet 2.50 2.00
a. Inverted overprint 40.00 40.00
139 A5 13a red lilac 2.50 2.00
140 A5 15a gray lilac 4.50 3.50
141 A5 22a brn org, *pnksh* 5.00 3.75
142 A5 31a red lil, *pnksh* 5.25 3.75
143 A5 31a brown, *straw* 5.50 3.75
144 A5 47a blue, *pink* 7.50 6.00
145 A5 47a red vio, *pink* 8.00 6.00
146 A5 78a dl bl, *straw* 10.00 8.50

No. 79 Overprinted in Red

147 A5 78a blk & red, *bl* 10.00 6.50
Nos. 135-147 (13) 68.25 51.75

Vasco da Gama Issue of 1898 Overprinted or Surcharged in Black

1913
148 CD20 ½a blue green 1.00 .70
149 CD21 1a red 1.00 .70
150 CD22 2a red violet 1.00 .70
151 CD23 4a yellow green 1.00 .70
152 CD24 8a dark blue 2.00 1.40
153 CD25 10a on 12a vio brn 3.50 2.75
154 CD26 16a bister brown 3.00 2.10
155 CD27 24a bister 4.00 3.25
Nos. 148-155 (8) 16.50 12.30

Ceres — A7

Name and Value in Black
Chalky Paper

1914 Typo. *Perf. 15x14*
156 A7 ½a olive brown .85 .60
157 A7 1a black .85 .60
158 A7 2a blue green .85 .60
159 A7 3a lilac brown 1.50 1.00
160 A7 4a carmine 1.50 1.00
161 A7 6a light violet 1.75 1.00
162 A7 10a deep blue 1.75 1.00
163 A7 12a yellow brown 2.25 1.75
164 A7 16a slate 3.00 2.25
165 A7 20a org brown 25.00 8.50
166 A7 40a plum 15.00 7.00
167 A7 58a brown, *grn* 15.00 7.50
168 A7 76a brown, *rose* 15.00 9.50
169 A7 1p org, *salmon* 25.00 16.50
170 A7 3p green, *blue* 57.50 31.00
Nos. 156-170 (15) 166.80 89.80

For surcharges see Nos. 200-201, MR1.

1920 Ordinary Paper
171 A7 1a black 1.75 1.25
172 A7 2a blue green 1.75 1.25

1922-26 *Perf. 12x11½*
173 A7 ½a olive brown 1.25 1.15
174 A7 1a black 1.25 1.15
175 A7 1½a yel grn ('23) 1.25 *1.25*
176 A7 2a blue green 1.60 1.50
177 A7 4a carmine 4.00 3.00
178 A7 7a lt green ('23) 2.50 *1.75*
179 A7 7½a ultra ('23) 2.50 *1.75*
180 A7 9a blue ('23) 2.50 *1.75*
181 A7 11a gray ('23) 3.75 *3.25*
182 A7 12a yellow brown 4.00 3.00
182A A7 15a lilac ('23) 10.50 *7.00*
182B A7 18a dp blue ('23) 11.00 7.00
182C A7 19a gray grn ('23) 11.00 6.00
182D A7 36a turq blue ('23) 10.50 6.00
182E A7 54a choc ('23) 11.00 6.00
182F A7 72a brt rose ('23) 22.50 12.50

Glazed Paper
182G A7 5p car rose ('23) 92.50 45.00
Nos. 173-182G (17) 193.60 109.05

Preceding Issues Overprinted in Carmine

1915 *Perf. 11½*
On Provisional Issue of 1902
183 A3 5a on 5r yellow 1.25 .75
184 A3 5a on 25r green 1.25 .75
185 A3 5a on 50r lt blue 1.25 .75
a. Perf. 13½ 1.25 .75
186 A3 6a on 20r lavender 1.25 .75
187 A3 9a on 15r chocolate 1.25 .75
188 A3 9a on 75r rose 1.50 .75
189 A3 15a on 10r red vio 1.50 1.00
190 A3 15a on 100r brn, *buff* 1.90 1.00
191 A3 15a on 300r bl, *sal* 1.90 1.50
192 A3 22a on 80r lt grn 4.50 2.75
193 A3 22a on 200r bl, *bl* 6.50 4.75

On No. 103
194 N2 6a on 2½r, perf. 13½ 1.40 .75
a. Perf. 12½ 1.75 1.50
b. Perf. 11½ 1.40 .75

On No. 104
195 A5 3a gray violet 1.25 .75

On No. 105
196 A5 10a on 12a dull bl 1.25 .75
Nos. 183-196 (14) 27.95 17.75

Type of 1915 with Additional Surcharge in Black

Perf. 11½
199 A3 ½a on 5a on 50r lt bl 25.00 17.50
a. Perf. 13½ 29.50 27.50

Nos. 178 and 169 Surcharged

1932 *Perf. 12x11½*
200 A7 6a on 72a brt rose 2.10 1.75
201 A7 12a on 15a lilac 2.10 1.75

"Portugal" and Vasco da Gama's Flagship "San Gabriel" — A8

Perf. 11½x12
1935 Typo. Wmk. 232
202 A8 ½a bister .45 .30
203 A8 1a olive brown .45 .30
204 A8 2a blue green .45 .30
205 A8 3a red violet .55 .50
206 A8 4a black .80 .50
207 A8 5a gray .80 .65
208 A8 6a brown .90 .60
209 A8 7a bright rose .90 .75
210 A8 8a bright blue 1.40 .80
211 A8 10a red orange 1.40 .80
212 A8 12a dark blue 1.60 .90
213 A8 14a olive green 1.60 .90
214 A8 15a maroon 1.60 .90
215 A8 20a orange 1.75 .90
216 A8 30a apple green 2.00 1.10
217 A8 40a violet 5.75 3.00
218 A8 50a olive bister 5.75 3.00
219 A8 1p light blue 16.00 9.00
220 A8 2p brn orange 35.00 14.50
221 A8 3p emerald 57.50 22.50
222 A8 5p dark violet 80.00 40.00
Nos. 202-222 (21) 216.65 102.20

Common Design Types
1938 Unwmk. Engr. *Perf. 13½x13*
Name and Value in Black
223 CD34 1a gray green .55 .45
224 CD34 2a orange brown .55 .45
225 CD34 3a dk violet brn .55 .45
226 CD34 4a brt green .55 .45
227 CD35 5a dk carmine .70 *.55*
228 CD35 6a slate .70 .55
229 CD35 8a rose violet .70 .55
230 CD37 10a brt red violet .70 .55
231 CD37 12a red .95 .70
232 CD37 15a orange 1.75 1.10
233 CD36 20a blue 1.85 1.15
234 CD36 40a gray black 2.50 1.50
235 CD36 50a brown 4.00 2.25
236 CD38 1p brown carmine 11.00 6.25
237 CD38 2p olive green 30.00 8.00
238 CD38 3p blue violet 35.00 16.00
239 CD38 5p red brown 70.00 32.50
Nos. 223-239 (17) 162.05 73.45

For overprints see Nos. 245A-245K.

Mozambique Nos. 273, 276, 278, 280, 282 and 283 Surcharged in Black

1946 *Perf. 13½x13*
240 CD34 1a on 15c dk vio brn 7.00 5.50
241 CD35 4a on 35c brt grn 7.00 5.50
242 CD35 8a on 50c brt red vio 7.00 5.50
243 CD36 10a on 70c brn vio 7.00 5.50
244 CD36 12a on 1e red 7.00 5.50
245 CD37 20a on 1.75e blue 7.00 5.50
Nos. 240-245 (6) 42.00 33.00

Nos. 223-227 and 229-234 Overprinted

1947
245A CD34 1a gray green 20.00 13.00
245B CD34 2a org brown 42.50 26.00
245C CD34 3a dk vio brn 17.50 8.50
245D CD34 4a brt green 17.50 8.50
245E CD35 5a dark car 7.50 3.50
245F CD35 8a rose violet 2.00 1.25
245G CD37 10a brt red vio 7.50 3.50
245H CD37 12a red 7.50 3.50
245I CD37 15a orange 7.50 3.50
245J CD36 20a blue 90.00 60.00
m. Inverted overprint *250.00* *275.00*
245K CD36 40a gray black 20.00 15.00
Nos. 245A-245K (11) 239.50 146.25

Timor Woman — A9

Designs: 3a, Gong ringer. 4a, Girl with basket. 8a, Aleixo de Ainaro. 10a, 1p, 3p, Heads of various chieftains. 20a, Warrior and horse.

1948 Litho. *Perf. 14*
246 A9 1a aqua & dk brn 1.25 .70
247 A9 3a gray & dk brn 2.25 1.30
248 A9 4a pink & dk grn 3.00 3.00
249 A9 8a red & blue blk 2.00 .80
250 A9 10a blue grn & org 2.00 .80
251 A9 20a ultra, aqua & bl 1.40 1.10
252 A9 1p org, bl & ultra 32.50 9.50
253 A9 3p vio & dk brn 35.00 17.50
a. Sheet of 8, #246-253 105.00 140.00
Nos. 246-253 (8) 79.40 34.70

No. 253a sold for 5p.

Lady of Fatima Issue
Common Design Type
1948, Oct.
254 CD40 8a slate gray 6.00 12.50

UPU Issue

UPU Symbols — A10

1949 Unwmk. *Perf. 14.*
255 A10 16a brown & buff 20.00 *20.00*

UPU, 75th anniversary.

Catalogue values for unused stamps in this section, from this point to the end of the section, are for Never Hinged items.

Craftsman A11

Timor Woman A12

1950 *Perf. 14½*
256 A11 20a dull vio blue 1.75 1.50
257 A12 50a dull brown 4.75 2.25

Holy Year Issue
Common Design Types
1950, May *Perf. 13x13½*
258 CD41 40a green 3.75 2.00
259 CD42 70a black brown 5.00 3.00

Blackberry Lily — A13

Designs: Various flowers.

1950 Unwmk. Litho. *Perf. 14½*
260 A13 1a multicolored 1.20 .60
261 A13 3a multicolored 4.75 3.25
262 A13 10a multicolored 5.25 3.50
263 A13 16a multicolored 10.00 4.75
264 A13 20a multicolored 4.75 3.25
265 A13 30a multicolored 5.25 3.50
266 A13 70a multicolored 6.75 4.00
267 A13 1p multicolored 11.50 6.75
268 A13 2p multicolored 17.00 12.00
269 A13 5p multicolored 27.50 22.50
Nos. 260-269 (10) 93.95 64.10

Holy Year Extension Issue
Common Design Type
1951 *Perf. 14*
270 CD43 86a bl & pale bl + label 3.75 2.75

Stamp without label attached sells for much less.

Medical Congress Issue
Common Design Type
Design: Weighing baby.
1952 Litho. *Perf. 13½*
271 CD44 10a ol blk & brn 2.00 1.60

St. Francis Xavier Issue

Statue of St. Francis Xavier — A14

Designs: 16a, Miraculous Arm of St. Francis. 1p, Tomb of St. Francis.

1952, Oct. 25 *Perf. 14*
272 A14 1a black .50 .25
273 A14 16a blk brn & brn 1.90 1.00
274 A14 1p dk car & gray 6.50 3.00
Nos. 272-274 (3) 8.90 4.25

400th death anniv. of St. Francis Xavier.

Madonna and Child — A15

1953 *Perf. 13x13½*
275 A15 3a dk brn & dull gray .50 .25
276 A15 16a dk brown & cream 1.40 .80
277 A15 50a dk bl & dull gray 3.50 2.25
Nos. 275-277 (3) 5.40 3.30

Exhibition of Sacred Missionary Art, Lisbon, 1951.

Stamp Centenary Issue

Stamp of Portugal and Arms of Colonies — A16

1953 Photo. *Perf. 13*
278 A16 10a multicolored 3.00 2.00

Sao Paulo Issue
Common Design Type

1954 Litho. *Perf. 13½*
279 CD46 16a dk brn red, bl & blk 2.00 1.40

Map of Timor — A17

1956 Unwmk. *Perf. 14x12½*
Inscription and design in brown, red, green, ultramarine & yellow

280 A17 1a pale salmon .40 .25
281 A17 3a pale gray blue .50 .25
282 A17 8a buff .80 .50
283 A17 24a pale green .85 .50
284 A17 32a lemon 1.25 .60
285 A17 40a pale gray 1.50 .75
286 A17 1p yellow 4.00 1.10
287 A17 3p pale blue 10.75 5.50
Nos. 280-287 (8) 20.05 9.45

For surcharges see Nos. 291-300.

Brussels Fair Issue

Exhibition Emblems and View — A18

1958 *Perf. 14½*
288 A18 40a multicolored 1.50 .75

Tropical Medicine Congress Issue
Common Design Type

Design: Calophyllum inophyllum.

1958 *Perf. 13½*
289 CD47 32a multicolored 5.50 4.25

Symbolical Globe — A19

1960 Unwmk. Litho. *Perf. 13½*
290 A19 4.50e multicolored 1.40 .75

500th death anniv. of Prince Henry the Navigator.

Nos. 280-287 Surcharged with New Value and Bars
Inscription and design in brown, red, green, ultramarine & yellow

1960 Unwmk. *Perf. 14x12½*
291 A17 5c on 1a pale salmon .45 .25
292 A17 10c on 3a pale gray bl .45 .25
293 A17 20c on 8a buff .45 .25
294 A17 30c on 24a pale grn .45 .25
295 A17 50c on 32a lemon .45 .25
296 A17 1e on 40a pale gray .50 .40
297 A17 2e on 40a pale gray .85 .45
298 A17 5e on 1p yellow 1.50 1.00
299 A17 10e on 3p pale blue 5.00 2.50
300 A17 15e on 3p pale blue 5.75 3.50
Nos. 291-300 (10) 15.85 9.10

Carved Elephant Jar — A20

Native Art: 10c, House on stilts. 20c, Madonna and Child. 30c, Silver rosary. 50c, Two men in boat, horiz. 1e, Silver box in shape of temple. 2.50e, Archer. 4.50e, Elephant. 5e, Man climbing tree. 10e, Woman carrying pot on head. 20e, Cockfight. 50e, House on stilts and animals.

Multicolored Designs

1961 Litho. *Perf. 11½x12*
301 A20 5c pale violet .35 .25
302 A20 10c pale green .35 .25
a. Value & legend inverted *45.00 45.00*
303 A20 20c pale blue .45 .30
304 A20 30c rose .70 .50
305 A20 50c pale grnsh bl .80 .55
306 A20 1e bister 1.30 .60
307 A20 2.50e pale ol bis 1.50 .60
308 A20 4.50e lt salmon 1.75 .60
309 A20 5e lt gray 2.25 .60
310 A20 10e gray 5.25 1.50
311 A20 20e yellow 12.50 4.00
312 A20 50e lt bluish gray 15.00 5.25
Nos. 301-312 (12) 42.20 15.00

Sports Issue
Common Design Type

Sports: 50c, Duck hunting. 1e, Horseback riding. 1.50e, Swimming. 2e, Gymnastics. 2.50e, Soccer. 15e, Big game hunting.

1962, Mar. 22 Unwmk. *Perf. 13½*
Multicolored Designs

313 CD48 50c gray & bis .50 .25
314 CD48 1e olive bister 1.75 .45
315 CD48 1.50e gray & bl grn 1.40 .70
316 CD48 2e buff 1.75 .80
317 CD48 2.50e gray 2.00 1.20
318 CD48 15e salmon 4.25 2.50
Nos. 313-318 (6) 11.655.90

Anti-Malaria Issue
Common Design Type

Design: Anopheles sundaicus.

1962 Litho. *Perf. 13½*
319 CD49 2.50e multicolored 2.25 1.40

National Overseas Bank Issue
Common Design Type

Design: 2.50e, Manuel Pinheiro Chagas.

1964, May 16 Unwmk. *Perf. 13½*
320 CD51 2.50e grn, gray, yel, lt bl & blk 1.50 1.30

ITU Issue
Common Design Type

1965, May 17 Litho. *Perf. 14½*
321 CD52 1.50e multicolored 2.20 1.40

National Revolution Issue
Common Design Type

Design: 4.50e, Dr. Vieira Machado Academy and Dili Health Center.

1966, May 28 Litho. *Perf. 11½*
322 CD53 4.50e multicolored 2.40 1.40

Navy Club Issue
Common Design Type

10c, Capt. Gago Coutinho and gunboat Patria. 4.50e, Capt. Sacadura Cabral and seaplane Lusitania.

1967, Jan. 31 Litho. *Perf. 13*
323 CD54 10c multicolored .75 .50
324 CD54 4.50e multicolored 3.50 1.90

Sepoy Officer, 1792 — A21

Designs: 1e, Officer, 1815. 1.50e, Infantry soldier, 1879. 2e, Infantry soldier, 1890. 2.50e, Infantry officer, 1903. 3e, Sapper, 1918. 4.50e, Special forces soldier, 1964. 10e, Paratrooper, 1964.

1967, Feb. 12 Photo. *Perf. 13½*
325 A21 35c multicolored .40 .30
326 A21 1e multicolored 2.50 1.00
327 A21 1.50e multicolored .70 .40
328 A21 2e multicolored .70 .40
329 A21 2.50e multicolored .90 .40
330 A21 3e multicolored 1.25 .60
331 A21 4.50e multicolored 2.00 .70
332 A21 10e multicolored 3.00 1.75
Nos. 325-332 (8) 11.45 5.55

Our Lady of Fatima — A22

1967, May 13 Litho. *Perf. 12½x13*
333 A22 3e multicolored .95 .50

Apparition of the Virgin Mary to three shepherd children at Fatima, Portugal, 50th anniv.

Cabral Issue

Map of Brazil, by Lopo Homem-Reinéis, 1519 — A23

1968, Apr. 22 Litho. *Perf. 14*
334 A23 4.50e multicolored 2.00 1.00

See note after Macao No. 416.

Admiral Coutinho Issue
Common Design Type

Design: 4.50e, Adm. Coutinho and frigate Adm. Gago Coutinho.

1969, Feb. 17 Litho. *Perf. 14*
335 CD55 4.50e multicolored 2.50 1.40

View of Dili, 1834 — A24

1969, July 25 Litho. *Perf. 14*
336 A24 1e multicolored 1.00 .80

Bicentenary of Dili as capital of Timor.

Vasco da Gama Issue

da Gama Medal in St. Jerome's Convent — A25

1969, Aug. 29 Litho. *Perf. 14*
337 A25 5e multicolored 1.15 .70

Vasco da Gama (1469-1524), navigator.

Administration Reform Issue
Common Design Type

1969, Sept. 25 Litho. *Perf. 14*
338 CD56 5e multicolored 1.40 .70

King Manuel I Issue

Emblem of King Manuel, St. Jerome's Convent — A26

1969, Dec. 1 Litho. *Perf. 14*
339 A26 4e multicolored 1.10 .70

King Manuel I, 500th birth anniv.

Capt. Ross Smith, Arms of Great Britain, Portugal and Australia, and Map of Timor — A27

Design: Capt. Ross Smith, arms of Great Britain, Portugal and Australia, and map of Timor.

1969, Dec. 9
340 A27 2e multicolored 1.40 .80

50th anniv. of the first England to Australia flight of Capt. Ross Smith and Lt. Keith Smith.

Marshal Carmona Issue
Common Design Type

Antonio Oscar Carmona in civilian clothes.

1970, Nov. 15 Litho. *Perf. 14*
341 CD57 1.50e multicolored 1.00 .50

Lusiads Issue

Sailing Ship and Monks Preaching to Islanders — A28

1972, May 25 Litho. *Perf. 13*
342 A28 1e brown & multi 1.00 *.50*

4th centenary of publication of The Lusiads by Luiz Camoens.

Olympic Games Issue
Common Design Type

Design: 4.50e, Soccer, Olympic emblem.

1972, June 20 *Perf. 14x13½*
343 CD59 4.50e multicolored 1.60 .80

Lisbon-Rio de Janeiro Flight Issue
Common Design Type

Design: 1e, Sacadura Cabral and Gago Coutinho in cockpit of "Lusitania."

1972, Sept. 20 Litho. *Perf. 13½*
344 CD60 1e multicolored 1.25 *.90*

WMO Centenary Issue
Common Design Type

1973, Dec. 15 Litho. *Perf. 13*
345 CD61 20e multicolored 3.75 *2.75*

United Nations Transitional Authority in East Timor

A30

2000, Apr. 29 Litho. *Perf. 12x11¾*
350 A30 Dom. red & multi *6.50 6.50*
351 A30 Int. blue & multi *20.00 20.00*

No. 350 sold for 10c and No. 351 sold for 50c on day of issue.

INDEPENDENT STATE OF TIMOR-LESTE

Independence A31

Designs: 25c, Crocodile. 50c, Palm fronds. $1, Coffee beans and picker. $2, Flag.

2002, May 20 Litho. *Perf. 14½x14*
352-355 A31 Set of 4 *17.50 35.00*

A32

Flag and: 10c, Pres. Xanana Gusmao. 50c, Map of country.

2002 Litho. *Perf. 13x13¼*
356-357 A32 Set of 2 *19.00 25.00*

A33

Independence From Portugal, 30th Anniv. — A34

Designs: 15c, Timorese flag, old man. 25c, Timorese flag, child. 50c, Timorese coin, rooster. 75c, Timorese flag, Pres. Nicolau Lobato.

2005, Nov. 28 Litho. *Perf. 12x12½*
358 A33 15c multi *2.00* *3.00*
359 A33 25c multi *4.00* *3.00*
360 A33 50c multi *4.00* *4.00*
361 A34 75c multi *9.00* *8.00*
Nos. 358-361 (4) *19.00* *18.00*

1996 Nobel Peace Laureates — A35

Designs: 25c, Pres. José Ramos-Horta. 50c, Bishop Carlos Filipe Ximenes Belo.

2008, June 20 Litho. *Perf. 13x12½*
362-363 A35 Set of 2 — —

Reptiles and Amphibians A36

Designs: No. 364, 50c, Timor river frog. No. 365, 50c, Timor snake-necked turtle. No. 366, 75c, Island tree viper. No. 367, 75c, Timor monitor. No. 368, $1, Saltwater crocodile. No. 369, $1, Timor bronzeback.

2010, Nov. 28 Litho. *Perf. 12½x13*
364-369 A36 Set of 6 — —
369a Souvenir sheet of 6, #364-369 — —

Association of Postal and Telecommunications Operators of Portuguese-Speaking Countries and Territories, 20th Anniv. — A37

2011, Feb. 14 Litho. *Perf. 12½x13*
370 A37 75c multi — —

Arrival of Portuguese in Timor, 500th Anniv. — A38

Designs: $1, Settlement near hills, cross, woman. $1.50, Cross, Dom Aleixo Corte-Real (1886-1943), leader of revolt against Japanese occupation, Timorese sash.

2016, Oct. 31 Litho. *Perf. 12x11¾*
371-372 A38 Set of 2 — —

AIR POST STAMPS

Common Design Type

1938 Unwmk. Engr. *Perf. 13½x13*
Name and Value in Black

C1 CD39 1a scarlet 1.20 1.00
C2 CD39 2a purple 1.20 .80
C3 CD39 3a orange 1.40 .80
C4 CD39 5a ultra 1.50 1.10
C5 CD39 10a lilac brown 2.00 1.50
C6 CD39 20a dark green 4.25 2.25
C7 CD39 50a red brown 7.75 5.25
C8 CD39 70a rose carmine 10.00 7.75
C9 CD39 1p magenta 22.50 11.00
Nos. C1-C9 (9) 51.80 31.45

No. C7 exists with overprint "Exposicao Internacional de Nova York, 1939-1940" and Trylon and Perisphere. Counterfeits exist.
For overprints see Nos. C15-C23.

Mozambique Nos. C3, C4, C6, C7 and C9 Surcharged in Black

1946 Unwmk. *Perf. 13½x13*
C10 CD39 8a on 50c orange 7.00 5.50
C11 CD39 12a on 1e ultra 7.00 5.50
C12 CD39 40a on 3e dk green 7.00 5.50
C13 CD39 50a on 5e red brn 7.00 5.50
C14 CD39 1p on 10e mag 7.00 5.50
Nos. C10-C14 (5) 35.00 27.50

Nos. C1-C9 Overprinted "Libertacao"

1947
C15 CD39 1a scarlet 25.00 9.00
C16 CD39 2a purple 25.00 9.00
C17 CD39 3a orange 25.00 9.00
C18 CD39 5a ultra 25.00 9.00
C19 CD39 10a lilac brown 7.50 3.25
C20 CD39 20a dark green 7.50 3.25
C21 CD39 50a red brown 7.50 3.25
C22 CD39 70a rose carmine 17.50 10.00
C23 CD39 1p magenta 15.00 4.75
Nos. C15-C23 (9) 155.00 60.50

POSTAGE DUE STAMPS

D1

1904 Unwmk. Typo. *Perf. 12*
Without Gum
Name and Value in Black

J1 D1 1a yellow green .85 .65
J2 D1 2a slate .85 .65
J3 D1 5a yellow brown 2.10 1.50
J4 D1 6a red orange 2.20 1.50
J5 D1 10a gray brown 2.25 1.50
J6 D1 15a red brown 4.00 3.25
J7 D1 24a dull blue 11.00 6.75
J8 D1 40a carmine 12.00 7.50
J9 D1 50a orange 16.00 8.00
J10 D1 1p dull violet 32.50 17.00
Nos. J1-J10 (10) 83.75 48.30

Overprinted in Carmine or Green

1911 Without Gum
J11 D1 1a yellow green .50 .45
J12 D1 2a slate .50 .45
a. Inverted overprint
J13 D1 5a yellow brown .75 .85
J14 D1 6a deep orange .95 .90
J15 D1 10a gray brown 1.50 1.15
J16 D1 15a brown 1.75 1.50
J17 D1 24a dull blue 2.50 2.00
J18 D1 40a carmine (G) 3.25 2.50
J19 D1 50a orange 5.75 3.50
J20 D1 1p dull violet 14.50 9.00
Nos. J11-J20 (10) 31.95 22.30

Nos. J1-J10 Overprinted in Red or Green

1913 Without Gum
J21 D1 1a yellow green 13.50 *10.00*
J22 D1 2a slate 13.50 *10.00*
J23 D1 5a yellow brown 6.50 *4.50*
J24 D1 6a deep orange 6.50 *4.50*
a. Inverted surcharge 45.00
J25 D1 10a gray brown 6.50 *5.00*
J26 D1 15a red brown 6.50 *5.00*
J27 D1 24a dull blue 7.25 *5.25*
J28 D1 40a carmine (G) 7.25 *5.25*
J29 D1 50a orange 15.00 *7.75*
J30 D1 1p gray violet 17.00 *7.75*
Nos. J21-J30 (10) 99.50 65.00

Catalogue values for unused stamps in this section, from this point to the end of the section, are for Never Hinged items.

Common Design Type

1952 Photo. & Typo. *Perf. 14*
Numeral in Red, Frame Multicolored

J31 CD45 1a chocolate .45 .25
J32 CD45 3a brown .45 .25
J33 CD45 5a dark green .45 .25
J34 CD45 10a green .45 .25
J35 CD45 30a purple .60 .35
J36 CD45 1p brown carmine 1.60 1.00
Nos. J31-J36 (6) 4.00 2.35

WAR TAX STAMP

Regular Issue of 1914 Surcharged in Red

1919 Unwmk. *Perf. 15x14*
Without Gum

MR1 A7 2a on ½a ol brn 10.00 5.50
a. Inverted surcharge 150.00 115.00

See note after Macao No. MR2.

NEWSPAPER STAMPS

Macao Nos. 37, 39, 41 Surcharged in Black

1892 Unwmk. *Perf. 12½*
Without Gum

P1 A7 2½r on 20r rose 2.75 1.80
a. "TIMOR" inverted 20.00 18.00
P2 A7 2½r on 40r chocolate 2.75 1.80
a. "TIMOR" inverted 20.00 18.00
b. Perf. 13½ 8.50 6.25
c. As "a," perf. 13½ 20.00 18.00
P3 A7 2½r on 80r gray 2.75 1.80
a. "TIMOR" inverted 20.00 18.00
b. Perf. 13½ 17.50 14.00
c. Double surcharge 85.00 70.00
Nos. P1-P3 (3) 8.25 5.40

N2

No. P4 Surcharged

1893-95 Typo. *Perf. 11½x12*
P4 N2 2½r brown 1.15 .95
a. Perf. 12½ 4.25 2.75
b. Perf. 13½ 1.15 .95
P5 N2 ½a on 2½r brn ('95) .95 .85

For surcharges see Nos. 103, 123, 194.

POSTAL TAX STAMPS

Pombal Issue
Common Design Types

1925 Unwmk. *Perf. 12½*
RA1 CD28 2a lake & black .65 .45
RA2 CD29 2a lake & black .65 .45
RA3 CD30 2a lake & black .65 .45
Nos. RA1-RA3 (3) 1.95 1.35

Type of War Tax Stamp of Portuguese India Overprinted in Red

1934-35 *Perf. 12*
RA4 WT1 2a green & blk 5.25 *4.50*
RA5 WT1 5a green & blk 8.00 4.50

Surcharged in Black

RA6 WT1 7a on ½a rose & blk ('35) 9.00 5.75
Nos. RA4-RA6 (3) 22.25 *14.75*

The tax was for local education.

Type of War Tax Stamp of Portuguese India Overprinted in Black

1936 *Perf. 12x11½*
RA7 WT1 10a rose & black 6.00 *5.00*

1937 *Perf. 11½*
RA8 WT1 10a green & blk 5.00 *4.50*

PT1

1948 Unwmk. Typo. *Perf. 11½*
Without Gum

RA9 PT1 10a blue 3.00 2.50
RA10 PT1 20a green 3.50 3.50

The 20a bears a different emblem.

Catalogue values for unused stamps in this section, from this point to the end of the section, are for Never Hinged items.

PT2

1960 Without Gum *Perf. 11½*
RA11 PT2 70c dark blue 2.00 1.75
RA12 PT2 1.30e dk gray grn 3.00 3.00

See Nos. RA13-RA16. For surcharges see Nos. RA20-RA25.

Type of 1960 Redrawn

1967 Typo. *Perf. 10½*
Without Gum

RA13 PT2 70c deep blue 5.50 *7.00*
RA14 PT2 1.30e emerald 7.50 7.50

The denominations of Nos. RA13-RA14 are 2mm high. They are 2½mm high on Nos. RA11-RA12. Other differences exist. The printed area of No. RA13 measures 18x31mm; "Republica" 16mm.

Type of 1960

1967 Serif Type Face

RA14A PT2 70c deep blue 16.00 13.00

Type of 1960, 2nd Redrawing

1967-68 Typo. *Perf. 10½*

Without Gum

RA15 PT2 70c violet blue 1.25 1.25
RA16 PT2 1.30e bluish grn ('68) 2.50 2.50

The printed area measures 13x30mm on Nos. RA15-RA16; "Republica" measures 10½mm.

Woman and Star — PT3

1969-70 Litho. *Perf. 13½*

RA17 PT3 30c vio bl & lt bl ('70) .50 .45
RA18 PT3 50c dl org & maroon .50 .45
RA19 PT3 1e yellow & brown .50 .45
Nos. RA17-RA19 (3) 1.50 1.35

The 2.50e and 10e in design PT3 were revenue stamps. Value $1.50 each.

Nos. RA15-RA16 Surcharged in Red or Carmine

1970 Typo. *Perf. 10½*

Without Gum

RA20 PT2 30c on 70c 12.50 12.50
RA21 PT2 30c on 1.30e 12.50 12.50
RA22 PT2 50c on 70c *45.00 45.00*
RA23 PT2 50c on 1.30e 12.50 12.50
RA24 PT2 1e on 70c (C) *25.00 25.00*
RA25 PT2 1e on 1.30e 13.00 13.00
Nos. RA20-RA25 (6) 120.50 120.50

POSTAL TAX DUE STAMPS

Pombal Issue

Common Design Types

1925 Unwmk. *Perf. 12½*

RAJ1 CD28 4a lake & black .65 *.70*
RAJ2 CD29 4a lake & black .65 *.70*
RAJ3 CD30 4a lake & black .65 *.70*
Nos. RAJ1-RAJ3 (3) 1.95 *2.10*

TOBAGO

tə-ˈbā-ˌgō

LOCATION — An island in the West Indies lying off the Venezuelan coast north of Trinidad
GOVT. — British Colony
AREA — 116 sq. mi.
POP. — 25,358
CAPITAL — Scarborough (Port Louis)

In 1889 Tobago, then an independent colony, was united with Trinidad under the name of Colony of Trinidad and Tobago. It became a ward of that colony January 1, 1899.

12 Pence = 1 Shilling
20 Shillings = 1 Pound

Queen Victoria — A1

Wmk. Crown and C C (1)

1879 Typo. *Perf. 14*

1 A1 1p rose 145.00 110.00
2 A1 3p blue 145.00 87.50
3 A1 6p orange 67.50 *82.50*
4 A1 1sh green 425.00 82.50
a. Half used as 6p on cover
5 A1 5sh slate 925.00 825.00
6 A1 £1 violet *4,500.*

Stamps of the above set with revenue cancellations sell for a small fraction of the price of postally used examples.

Stamps of Type A1, watermarked Crown and C A, are revenue stamps.

1880 Manuscript Surcharge

7 A1 1p on half of 6p org *6,250. 875.*

Queen Victoria — A2

1880

8 A2 ½p brown violet 77.50 *115.00*
9 A2 1p red brown 145.00 72.50
a. Half used as ½p on cover *2,250.*
10 A2 4p yellow green 325.00 40.00
a. Half used as 2p on cover *2,250.*
11 A2 6p bister brown 425.00 125.00
12 A2 1sh bister 115.00 *145.00*
a. Imperf.
Nos. 8-12 (5) 1,088. 497.50

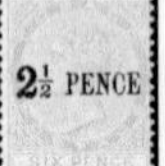

No. 11 Surcharged in Black

1883

13 A2 2½p on 6p bister brn 110.00 110.00
a. Double surcharge 4,000. 2,250.

1882-96 Wmk. Crown and C A (2)

14 A2 ½p brown vio ('82) 3.50 *21.00*
15 A2 ½p dull green ('86) 6.00 2.25
16 A2 1p red brown ('82) 14.50 3.75
a. Diagonal half used as ½p on cover —
17 A2 1p rose ('89) 9.50 2.50
18 A2 2½p ultra ('83) 16.50 1.60
a. 2½p dull blue ('83) 67.50 3.75
b. 2½p bright blue 17.50 1.60
19 A2 4p yel grn ('82) 230.00 100.00
20 A2 4p gray ('85) 9.50 4.25
a. Imperf., pair 2,250.
21 A2 6p bis brn ('84) 625.00 550.00
a. Imperf.
22 A2 6p brn org ('86) 2.75 *9.50*
23 A2 1sh olive bis ('94) 5.00 *32.50*
24 A2 1sh brn org ('96) 29.00 *145.00*

Stamps of 1882-96 Surcharged in Black

Nos. 25-29 — No. 30

1886-92

25 A2 ½p on 2½p ultra 12.00 *27.50*
a. Inverted surcharge
b. Pair, one without surcharge 16,000.
c. Space between "½" and "PENNY" 3mm 42.50 *82.50*
d. Double surcharge 2,800. 2,600.
26 A2 ½p on 4p gray 32.50 *87.50*
a. Space between "½" and "PENNY" 3mm 75.00
b. Double surcharge 3,500.
27 A2 ½p on 6p bis brn 4.25 *29.00*
a. Inverted surcharge 3,250.
b. Space between "½" and "PENNY" 3mm 30.00 *125.00*
c. Double surcharge 3,750.
28 A2 ½p on 6p brn org 160.00 210.00
a. Space between "½" and "PENNY" 3mm 375.00 *450.00*
b. Double surcharge *2,750.*
29 A2 1p on 2½ ultra 110.00 25.00
a. Space between "1" and "PENNY" 4mm 300.00 *90.00*
b. Half used as ½p on cover *1,650.*
30 A2 2½p on 4p gray 25.00 *11.00*
a. Double surcharge 3,500. 3,500.
Nos. 25-30 (6) 343.75 *390.00*

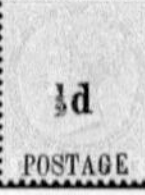

Revenue Stamp Type A1 Surcharged in Black

1896

31 A1 ½p on 4p lilac & rose 110.00 57.50
a. Space between "½" and "d" 1½ to 2½mm 150.00 82.50

Tobago stamps were replaced by those of Trinidad or Trinidad and Tobago.

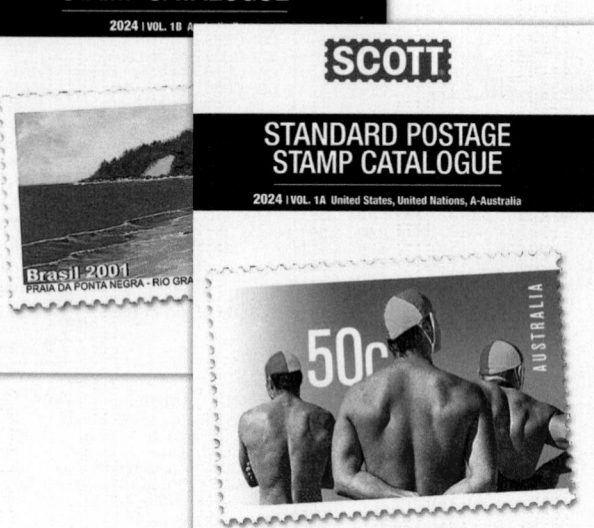

TOGO

'tō-ˌgō

LOCATION — Western Africa, bordering on the Gulf of Guinea
GOVT. — Republic
AREA — 20,400 sq. mi.
POP. — 4,320,000 (1997 est.)
CAPITAL — Lome

The German Protectorate of Togo was occupied by Great Britain and France in World War I, and later mandated to them. The British area became part of Ghana. The French area was granted internal autonomy in 1956 and achieved independence in 1958.

100 Pfennig = 1 Mark
12 Pence = 1 Shilling
100 Centimes = 1 Franc

Catalogue values for unused stamps in this country are for Never Hinged items, beginning with Scott 309 in the regular postage section, Scott B11 in the semi-postal section, Scott C14 in the airpost section, Scott J32 in the postage due section, and Scott O1 in the official section.

Watermark

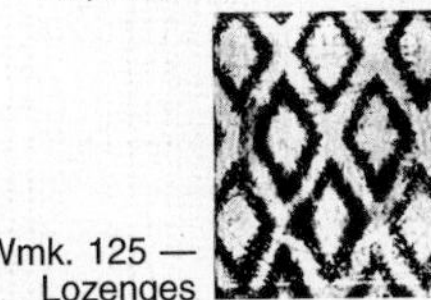

Wmk. 125 — Lozenges

German Protectorate

AREA — 34,934 sq. mi.
POP. — 1,000,368 (1913)

Stamps of Germany Overprinted in Black

1897 Unwmk. *Perf. 13½x14½*

No.	Type	Denom.	Color	Unused	Used
1	A9	3pf	dark brown	5.00	*6.25*
a.			3pf yellow brown	8.25	*22.50*
b.			3pf reddish brown	45.00	*120.00*
c.			3pf pale gray brown	1,500.	*1,150.*
2	A9	5pf	green	4.50	*2.60*
3	A10	10pf	carmine	5.25	*2.90*
4	A10	20pf	ultra	5.25	*12.00*
5	A10	25pf	orange	35.00	*52.50*
6	A10	50pf	red brown	35.00	*52.50*
			Nos. 1-6 (6)	90.00	*128.75*

A3

Kaiser's Yacht, the "Hohenzollern"
A4

1900 Typo. *Perf. 14*

No.	Type	Denom.	Color	Unused	Used
7	A3	3pf	brown	.90	*1.10*
8	A3	5pf	green	11.00	*1.80*
9	A3	10pf	carmine	20.00	1.50
10	A3	20pf	ultra	.90	*1.40*
11	A3	25pf	org & blk, *yel*	.90	*9.00*
12	A3	30pf	org & blk, *sal*	1.25	*9.00*
13	A3	40pf	lake & blk	.90	*9.00*
14	A3	50pf	pur & blk, *sal*	1.25	*6.75*
15	A3	80pf	lake & blk, *rose*	2.25	*15.00*

Engr.

Perf. 14½x14

No.	Type	Denom.	Color	Unused	Used
16	A4	1m	carmine	3.00	*50.00*
17	A4	2m	blue	5.00	*75.00*
18	A4	3m	black vio	6.50	*135.00*
19	A4	5m	slate & car	150.00	*450.00*
			Nos. 7-19 (13)	203.85	*764.55*

Counterfeit cancellations are found on Nos. 10-19 and 22.

1909-19 Wmk. 125 Typo. *Perf. 14*

No.	Type	Denom.	Color	Unused	Used
20	A3	3pf	brown ('19)	.75	
21	A3	5pf	green	1.10	*2.00*
22	A3	10pf	carmine ('14)	1.50	*110.00*

Engr.

Perf. 14½x14

No.	Type	Denom.	Color	Unused	Used
23	A4	5m	slate & carmine ('19)	30.00	
			Nos. 20-23 (4)	33.35	

Nos. 20 and 23 were never placed in use.

British Protectorate

Nos. 7, 10-19, 21-22 Overprinted or Surcharged

First (Wide) Setting
3mm between Lines
2mm between "Anglo" & "French"

Wmk. 125 (5pf, 10pf); Unwmkd.

1914, Oct. 1 *Perf. 14, 14½*

No.	Type	Denom.	Color	Unused	Used
33	A3	½p	on 3pf brn	160.00	140.00
a.			Thin "y" in "penny"	*400.00*	*350.00*
34	A3	1p	on 5pf grn	*160.00*	*140.00*
a.			Thin "y" in "penny"	*400.00*	*350.00*
35	A3	3pf	brown	*130.00*	*100.00*
36	A3	5pf	green	*130.00*	*100.00*
37	A3	10pf	carmine	*130.00*	*100.00*
a.			Inverted overprint	*10,000.*	*3,000.*
b.			Unwmk.		*5,500.*
38	A3	20pf	ultra	*42.50*	*50.00*
39	A3	25pf	org & blk, *yel*	*40.00*	*47.50*
40	A3	30pf	org & blk, *sal*	*47.50*	*60.00*
41	A3	40pf	lake & blk	*225.00*	*250.00*
42	A3	50pf	pur & blk, *sal*	*12,000.*	*10,000.*
43	A3	80pf	lake & blk, *rose*	*275.00*	*275.00*
44	A4	1m	carmine	*5,000.*	*2,750.*
45	A4	2m	blue	*13,500.*	*15,000.*
a.			Inverted overprint	*16,000.*	
b.			"Occupation" double	*24,500.*	*16,000.*

On Nos. 33-34, the surcharge line ("Half penny" or "One penny") was printed separately and its position varies in relation to the 3-line overprint. On Nos. 46-47, the surcharge and overprint lines were printed simultaneously.

Second (Narrow) Setting
2mm between Lines
2mm between "Anglo" & "French"

1914, Oct.

No.	Type	Denom.	Color	Unused	Used
46	A3	½p	on 3pf brown	*47.50*	*26.00*
a.			Thin "y" in "penny"	*75.00*	*60.00*
b.			"TOG"	*425.00*	*300.00*
47	A3	1p	on 5pf green	*8.00*	*4.25*
a.			Thin "y" in "penny"	*12.00*	*15.00*
b.			"TOG"	*130.00*	110.00
48	A3	3pf	brown	*6,500.*	*1,100*
a.			"Occupation" omitted		
49	A3	5pf	green	*1,500.*	*750.00*
50	A3	10pf	carmine		*3,000.*
51	A3	20pf	ultra	*30.00*	*12.00*
a.			"TOG"	*3,500.*	*2,500.*
b.			Vert. pair, #51 & #38	*9,000.*	
52	A3	25pf	org & blk, *yel*	40.00	*32.50*
a.			"TOG"	*12,000.*	
53	A3	30pf	org & blk, *sal*	20.00	*29.00*
54	A3	40pf	lake & blk	*6,000.*	*1,600.*
55	A3	50pf	pur & blk, *sal*		*9,000.*
56	A3	80pf	lake & blk, *rose*	*3,250.*	*2,250.*
57	A4	1m	carmine	*8,000.*	*4,250.*
58	A4	2m	blue		*14,500.*
59	A4	3m	black violet		110,000.
60	A4	5m	slate & car		110,000.

Third Setting
1¼mm btwn. "Anglo" & "French"
2mm between Lines
"Anglo-French" 15mm Wide

1915, Jan. 7

No.	Type	Denom.	Color	Unused	Used
61	A3	3pf	brown	*9,000.*	*2,500.*
62	A3	5pf	green	*225.*	*130.*
63	A3	10pf	carmine	*200.*	*130.*
64	A3	20pf	ultra	*1,400.*	*400.*
64A	A3	40pf	lake & blk		*9,000.*
65	A3	50pf	pur & blk, *sal*	*16,000.*	*11,000.*

Stamps of Gold Coast Overprinted Locally

"OCCUPATION" 14½-14¾mm Long

1915, May Wmk. 3 *Perf. 14*

No.	Type	Denom.	Color	Unused	Used
66	A7	½p	green	.35	*3.75*
a.			Double overprint		
67	A8	1p	scarlet	.35	*.60*
a.			Double ovpt.	*350.00*	*475.00*
b.			Inverted ovpt.	*175.00*	*250.00*
c.			As "b," "Togo" omitted	*8,000.*	
68	A7	2p	gray	.35	1.50
69	A7	2½p	ultra	4.00	*7.00*

Chalky Paper

No.	Type	Denom.	Color	Unused	Used
70	A7	3p	violet, *yel*	3.50	*6.00*
71	A7	6p	dl vio & red vio	2.75	*2.00*
72	A7	1sh	black, *grn*	2.50	*11.00*
a.			Double overprint	*1,500.*	
73	A7	2sh	vio & bl, *bl*	15.00	*22.50*
74	A7	2sh6p	blk & red, *bl*	5.50	*30.00*
75	A7	10sh	grn & red, *grn*	50.00	*60.00*
76	A7	20sh	vio & blk, *red*	150.00	*160.00*

Surfaced-Colored Paper

No.	Type	Denom.	Color	Unused	Used
77	A7	3p	violet, *yel*	4.00	*24.00*
78	A7	5sh	grn & red, *yel*	9.50	*15.00*
			Nos. 66-78 (13)	247.80	*343.35*

Nos. 66-78 exist with small "F" in "French" and thin "G" in "Togo." Value, set $450.

Eight denominations are known without the hyphen between "Anglo-French." Value, set of eight $1,500. All denominations but No. 77 without the first "O" in "Occupation."

Stamps of Gold Coast Overprinted in London

"OCCUPATION" 15mm Long

1916, Apr. Ordinary Paper

No.	Type	Denom.	Color	Unused	Used
80	A7	½p	green	.35	*2.75*
81	A8	1p	scarlet	.35	*.85*
a.			Inverted overprint		
82	A7	2p	gray	.60	*3.00*
83	A7	2½p	ultra	.70	*1.50*

Chalky Paper

No.	Type	Denom.	Color	Unused	Used
84	A7	3p	violet, *yel*	6.00	1.25
85	A7	6p	dl vio & red vio	2.50	2.00
86	A7	1sh	black, *grn*	8.00	*13.00*
a.			1sh black, *emerald*	400.00	*850.00*
b.			1sh black, *bl grn,* ol back	12.00	*18.00*
87	A7	2sh	vio & ultra, *bl*	4.50	8.50
88	A7	2sh6p	blk & red, *bl*	4.50	*7.00*
89	A7	5sh	grn & red, *yel*	37.50	*27.50*
90	A7	10sh	grn & red, *bl grn,* ol back ('20)	21.00	*75.00*
a.			10sh green & red, *grn*	27.50	*65.00*
91	A7	20sh	vio & blk, *red*	160.00	*190.00*
			Nos. 80-91 (12)	246.00	*332.35*

The overprint on Nos. 80-91 is in heavier letters than on Nos. 66-78 and the 2nd and 3rd lines are each ½mm longer. The letter "O" on Nos. 80-91 is narrower and more oval.

Issued under French Occupation

Stamps of German Togo Surcharged

c

d

e

f

g

h

i

Wmk. Lozenges (5pf and 10pf) (125), Unwmk. (other values)

1914 *Perf. 14, 14½*

No.	Type	Denom.	Color	Unused	Used
151	A3(c+d)	5c	on 3pf brn	70.00	70.00
152	A3(c+e)	5c	on 3pf brn	67.50	67.50
153	A3(c+f)	5c	on 3pf brn	77.50	77.50
154	A3(c+g)	10c	on 5pf grn	25.00	25.00
a.			Double surcharge	1,200.	1,200.
155	A3(c+h)	10c	on 5pf grn	25.00	25.00
156	A3(c+i)	10c	on 5pf grn	50.00	50.00
158	A3(c)	20pf	ultra	55.00	55.00
a.			3½mm between "TOGO" and "Occupation"	875.00	*875.00*
159	A3(c)	25pf	org & blk, *yel*	80.00	80.00
160	A3(c)	30pf	org & blk, *sal*	100.00	100.00
161	A3(c)	40pf	lake & black	600.00	625.00
162	A3(c)	80pf	lake & blk, *rose*	600.00	625.00
			Nos. 151-162 (11)	1,750.	1,800.

Surcharged or Overprinted in Sans-Serif Type

1915

No.	Type	Denom.	Color	Unused	Used
164	A3	5c	on 3pf brown	*21,000.*	*4,500.*
165	A3	5pf	green	1,050.	450.
166	A3	10pf	carmine	1,150.	450.
a.			Inverted overprint	*27,000.*	*16,500.*
167	A3	20pf	ultra	*1,400.*	1,050.
168	A3	25pf	org & blk, *yel*	*15,000.*	*7,000.*
169	A3	30pf	org & blk, *sal*	*15,000.*	*7,000.*
170	A3	40pf	lake & blk	*15,000.*	*7,000.*
171	A3	50pf	pur & blk, *sal*	*21,000.*	*12,500.*
171A	A3	80pf	red & blk, *rose*		—
172	A4	1m	carmine		—
173	A4	2m	blue	—	—
174	A4	3m	black vio		—
175	A4	5m	slate & car	—	—

Stamps of Dahomey, 1913-17, Overprinted

1916-17 Unwmk. *Perf. 13½x14*

No.	Type	Denom.	Color	Unused	Used
176	A5	1c	violet & blk	.35	*.50*
177	A5	2c	choc & rose	.35	*.50*
178	A5	4c	black & brn	.35	.80
a.			Double overprint	500.00	500.00
179	A5	5c	yel grn & bl grn	.70	.70
180	A5	10c	org red & rose	.70	.70
181	A5	15c	brn org & dk vio ('17)	1.75	1.75
182	A5	20c	gray & choc	.70	1.10
183	A5	25c	ultra & dp bl	1.10	*1.10*
184	A5	30c	choc & vio	1.10	*1.40*
185	A5	35c	brown & blk	1.75	*2.10*
186	A5	40c	blk & red org	1.40	*1.75*
187	A5	45c	gray & ultra	1.75	2.10
188	A5	50c	choc & brn	1.75	*2.10*
189	A5	75c	blue & vio	7.00	*8.00*
190	A5	1fr	bl grn & blk	8.50	*10.50*
191	A5	2fr	buff & choc	12.00	*14.00*
192	A5	5fr	vio & do bl	14.00	*16.00*
			Nos. 176-192 (17)	55.25	*65.10*

All values of the 1916-17 issue exist on chalky paper and all but the 15c, 25c and 35c on ordinary paper. See the *Scott Classic Specialized Catalogue of Stamps & Covers* for detailed listings.

French Mandate

AREA — 21,893 sq. mi.
POP. — 780,497 (1938)

Type of Dahomey, 1913-39, Overprinted

1921

193 A5 1c gray & yel grn .35 *.35*
a. Overprint omitted 125.00 125.00
194 A5 2c blue & org .35 *.35*
195 A5 4c ol grn & org .35 *.35*
196 A5 5c dull red & blk .35 .35
a. Overprint omitted 410.00 425.00
197 A5 10c bl grn & yel grn .35 *.70*
198 A5 15c brown & car .70 *.70*
199 A5 20c bl grn & org 1.10 1.10
200 A5 25c slate & org 1.10 1.10
201 A5 30c dp rose & ver 1.40 *1.75*
202 A5 35c red brn & yel grn 1.10 *1.40*
203 A5 40c bl grn & ol 2.10 1.75
204 A5 45c red brn & ol 2.10 *2.10*
205 A5 50c deep blue 2.10 *1.40*
206 A5 75c dl red & ultra 2.10 *2.10*
207 A5 1fr gray & ultra 2.10 *2.10*
208 A5 2fr ol grn & rose 7.00 *7.00*
209 A5 5fr orange & blk 10.50 *10.50*
Nos. 193-209 (17) 35.15 *35.10*

Stamps and Type of 1921 Surcharged

No. 210

No. 213

1922-25

210 A5 25c on 15c ol brn & rose red .35 *.55*
211 A5 25c on 2fr ol grn & rose .70 *.80*
212 A5 25c on 5fr org & blk .70 *.80*
a. "TOGO" omitted 275.00 275.00
213 A5 60c on 75c vio, *pnksh* 1.10 *1.40*
a. "60" omitted 200.00 210.00
214 A5 65c on 45c red brn & ol 1.40 *1.75*
a. "TOGO" omitted 190.00 200.00
215 A5 85c on 75c dull red & ultra 2.10 *2.75*
Nos. 210-215 (6) 6.35 *8.05*

Issue years: #213, 1922; #211-212, 1924; others, 1925.

Coconut Grove — A6

Cacao Trees — A7

Oil Palms — A8

1924-38 **Typo.**

216 A6 1c yellow & blk .25 *.35*
217 A6 2c dp rose & blk .25 *.35*
218 A6 4c dk blue & blk .25 *.35*
219 A6 5c dp org & blk .25 *.35*
220 A6 10c red vio & blk .25 .35
221 A6 15c green & blk .25 .35
222 A7 20c gray & blk .30 .50
223 A7 25c grn & blk, *yel* .70 .70
224 A7 30c gray grn & blk .35 .35
225 A7 30c dl grn & lt grn ('27) .70 *.70*
226 A7 35c lt brown & blk .70 .70
227 A7 35c dp bl grn & grn ('38) .70 .70
228 A7 40c red org & blk .35 .35
229 A7 45c carmine & blk .35 .35
230 A7 50c ocher & blk, *bluish* .35 .70
231 A7 55c vio bl & car rose ('38) 1.10 1.10
232 A7 60c vio brn & blk, *pnksh* .35 .35
233 A7 60c dp red ('26) .35 *.70*
234 A7 65c gray lil & brn .70 .70
235 A7 75c blue & black .70 *.70*
236 A7 80c ind & dl vio ('38) 1.75 1.75
237 A7 85c brn org & brn 1.10 1.10
238 A7 90c brn red & cer ('27) 1.10 *1.10*
239 A8 1fr red brn & blk, *bluish* 1.10 *1.10*
240 A8 1fr blue ('26) .70 *.70*
241 A8 1fr gray lil & grn ('28) 2.75 2.75
242 A8 1fr dk red & red org ('38) 1.10 1.10
243 A8 1.10fr vio & dk brn ('28) 4.25 *5.50*
244 A8 1.25fr mag & rose ('33) 1.40 *1.75*
245 A8 1.50fr bl & lt bl ('27) .70 *1.10*
246 A8 1.75fr bis & pink ('33) 8.50 5.25
247 A8 1.75fr vio bl & ultra ('38) 1.40 1.40
248 A8 2fr bl blk & blk, *bluish* 1.10 1.40
249 A8 3fr bl grn & red org ('27) 1.40 *1.75*
250 A8 5fr red org & blk, *bluish* 2.10 *3.50*
251 A8 10fr ol brn & rose ('26) 2.50 *2.75*
252 A8 20fr brn red & blk, *yel* ('26) 3.50 *3.50*
Nos. 216-252 (37) 45.65 *48.20*

For surcharges see Nos. 253, 301-302, B8-B9.

No. 240 Surcharged with New Value and Bars in Red

1926

253 A8 1.25fr on 1fr lt bl .70 .70

Common Design Types pictured following the introduction.

Colonial Exposition Issue
Common Design Types
Engr., "TOGO" Typo. in Black

1931, Apr. 13 ***Perf. 12½***

254 CD70 40c deep green 5.50 5.50
255 CD71 50c violet 5.50 5.50
256 CD72 90c red orange 5.50 5.50
257 CD73 1.50fr dull blue 5.50 5.50
Nos. 254-257 (4) 22.00 22.00
Set, never hinged 42.00

Paris International Exposition Issue
Common Design Types

1937 ***Perf. 13***

258 CD74 20c deep violet 1.60 1.60
259 CD75 30c dark green 1.60 1.60
260 CD76 40c car rose 1.60 1.60
261 CD77 50c dark brown 1.60 1.60
262 CD78 90c red 1.75 1.75
263 CD79 1.50fr ultra 1.75 1.75
Nos. 258-263 (6) 9.90 9.90
Set, never hinged 17.50

Colonial Arts Exhibition Issue
Souvenir Sheet
Common Design Type

1937 ***Imperf.***

264 CD77 3fr Prus bl & blk 10.50 *10.50*
Never hinged 14.00

Caillié Issue
Common Design Type

1939, Apr. 5 ***Perf. 12½x12***

265 CD81 90c org brn & org .35 1.10
266 CD81 2fr brt violet .35 1.10
267 CD81 2.25fr ultra & dk bl .35 1.10
Nos. 265-267 (3) 1.05 3.30
Set, never hinged 2.10

New York World's Fair Issue
Common Design Type

1939, May 10

268 CD82 1.25fr carmine lake .70 1.40
Never hinged 1.10
269 CD82 2.25fr ultra .70 1.40
Never hinged 1.10

Togolese Women
A9 A12

Mono River Bank — A10

Hunters — A11

1941 **Engr.** ***Perf. 12½***

270 A9 2c brown vio .25 *.30*
271 A9 3c yellow grn .35 *.35*
272 A9 4c brown blk .25 *.30*
273 A9 5c lilac rose .25 *.30*
274 A9 10c light blue .25 *.30*
275 A9 15c chestnut .25 .25
276 A10 20c plum .25 .25
277 A10 25c violet blue .25 .25
278 A10 30c brown blk .25 .25
279 A10 40c dk carmine .35 *.35*
280 A10 45c dk green .35 *.35*
281 A10 50c chestnut .35 .35
282 A10 60c red violet .35 *.70*
283 A11 70c black .70 *1.10*
284 A11 90c lt violet 1.40 *1.40*
285 A11 1fr yellow grn .35 *.70*
286 A11 1.25fr cerise 1.10 *1.40*
287 A11 1.40fr orange brn .70 *.70*
288 A11 1.60fr orange .70 *1.10*
289 A11 2fr lt ultra .70 *.70*
290 A12 2.25fr ultra 1.40 *2.10*
291 A12 2.50fr lilac rose 1.10 1.10
292 A12 3fr brown vio 1.10 *1.10*
293 A12 5fr vermilion 1.10 *1.10*
294 A12 10fr rose violet 1.75 *1.75*
295 A12 20fr brown blk 2.50 *2.50*
Nos. 270-295 (26) 18.35 21.05
Set, never hinged 26.00

For surcharges see Nos. 303-308, B7, B10.

Mono River Bank and Marshal Pétain — A12a

1941 **Engr.** ***Perf. 12½x12***

296 A12a 1fr green .35
297 A12a 2.50fr blue .35
Set, never hinged 1.40

Nos. 296-297 were issued by the Vichy government in France, but were not placed on sale in Togo.

For surcharges, see Nos. B10D-B10E.

Types of 1941 Without "RF"

1942-44 ***Perf. 12½***

298 A9 10c blue green .35
299 A9 15c yel brn & black .70
300 A10 20c lil brn & blk .70
300A A11 1fr yellow grn 1.10
300B A11 1.50fr lilac & green .70
300C A12 3fr brown violet 1.10
300D A12 5fr red brown 1.10
300E A12 10fr rose violet 1.40
300F A12 20fr black 1.40
Nos. 298-300F (9) 8.55
Set, never hinged 12.00

Nos. 298-300F were issued by the Vichy government in France, but were not placed on sale in Togo.

Nos. 231, 238, 284 Surcharged in Various Colors

a

b

Perf. 14x13½, 12½

1943-44 **Unwmk.**

301 A7(a) 1.50fr on 55c (Bk) 1.10 1.10
302 A7(a) 1.50fr on 90c (Bk) 1.10 1.10
303 A11(b) 3.50fr on 90c (Bk) .70 .70
304 A11(b) 4fr on 90c (R) 1.40 1.40
305 A11(b) 5fr on 90c (Bl) 2.10 2.10
306 A11(b) 5.50fr on 90c (Br) 2.10 2.10
307 A11(b) 10fr on 90c (G) ('44) 2.10 2.10
308 A11(b) 20fr on 90c (R) 3.50 3.50
Nos. 301-308 (8) 14.10 14.10
Set, never hinged 17.50

Catalogue values for unused stamps in this section, from this point to the end of the section, are for Never Hinged items.

Extracting Palm Oil
A13

Hunter
A14

Cotton Spinners
A15

Village of Atakpamé
A16

Red-fronted Gazelles — A17

Houses of the Cabrais — A18

1947, Oct. 6 **Engr.** ***Perf. 12½***

309 A13 10c dark red .70 .35
310 A13 30c brt ultra .70 .35
311 A13 50c bluish green .70 .35
312 A14 60c lilac rose .70 .35
313 A14 1fr chocolate .70 .35
314 A14 1.20fr yellow grn 1.10 .70
315 A15 1.50fr brown org 1.10 .70
316 A15 2fr olive 1.10 .70
317 A15 2.50fr gray blk 1.75 1.40
318 A16 3fr slate 1.10 .70
319 A16 3.60fr rose car 1.10 1.10
320 A16 4fr Prus green 1.10 .35
321 A17 5fr black brn 2.10 .70
322 A17 6fr ultra 2.10 1.40
323 A17 10fr orange red 2.75 .70
324 A18 15fr dp yel grn 2.75 .70
325 A18 20fr grnsh black 2.10 .70
326 A18 25fr lilac rose 2.75 1.10
Nos. 309-326 (18) 26.40 12.70

Military Medal Issue
Common Design Type
Engr. & Typo.

1952, Dec. 1 ***Perf. 13***

327 CD101 15fr multicolored 5.50 4.75

Gathering Palm Nuts — A19

1954, Nov. 29 **Engr.**

328 A19 8fr vio & vio brn 1.40 .70
329 A19 15fr indigo & dk brn 1.75 .70

Goliath Beetle — A20

1955, May 2

330 A20 8fr black & green 3.25 1.40

Intl. Exhibition for Wildlife Protection, Paris, May 1955.

FIDES Issue
Common Design Type

Design: 15fr, Teacher and children planting tree.

1956 Unwmk. *Perf. 13x12½*
331 CD103 15fr dk vio brn & org brn 4.25 2.10

Republic

Woman Holding Flag — A21

1957, June 8 Engr. *Perf. 13*
332 A21 15fr dk bl grn, sepia & red .70 .25

Konkomba Helmet A22

Teak Forest A23

Design: 4fr, 5fr, 6fr, 8fr, 10fr, Buffon's kob.

1957, Oct. Unwmk.
333 A22 30c violet & claret .25 .25
334 A22 50c indigo & blue .25 .25
335 A22 1fr pur & lil rose .25 .25
336 A22 2fr dk brn & olive .25 .25
337 A22 3fr black & green .25 .25
338 A22 4fr blue & gray .60 .25
339 A22 5fr bluish gray & mag .60 .25
340 A22 6fr crim rose & bl gray .75 .25
341 A22 8fr bluish gray & vio .75 .25
342 A22 10fr grn & red brn .75 .25
343 A23 15fr multicolored .50 .25
344 A23 20fr violet, mar & org .60 .25
345 A23 25fr indigo & bis brn .75 .25
346 A23 40fr dk brn, ol & dk grn 1.10 .35
Nos. 333-346 (14) 7.65 3.60

See Nos. 350-363.

Flags, Dove and UN Emblem — A24

1958, Dec. 10 Engr. *Perf. 13*
347 A24 20fr dk grn & rose red .65 .25

Universal Declaration of Human Rights, 10th anniversary.

Flower Issue
Common Design Type

Designs: 5fr, Flower of Bombax tree (kapok). 20fr, Tectona grandis (teakwood) flower, horiz.

Perf. 12x12½, 12½x12
1959, Jan. 15 Photo. Unwmk.
348 CD104 5fr dp bl, rose & grn .55 .25
349 CD104 20fr black, yel & grn .55 .25

Types of 1957
Inscribed:"Republique du Togo"

1959, Jan. 15 Engr. *Perf. 13*
Designs as Before
350 A22 30c ultra & gray .45 .25
351 A22 50c org & brt grn .45 .25
352 A22 1fr red lil & lt ol grn .45 .25
353 A22 2fr olive & bl grn .45 .25
354 A22 3fr vio & rose car .45 .25
355 A22 4fr lil rose & pale pur .45 .25
356 A22 5fr green & brown .45 .25
357 A22 6fr ultra & gray bl .45 .25
358 A22 8fr sl grn & bis .45 .25
359 A22 10fr vio & lt brn .45 .25
360 A23 15fr dk brn, bis & cl .45 .25
361 A23 20fr blk, bl grn & brn .45 .25
362 A23 25fr sep, red brn, ol & vio .60 .25
363 A23 40fr dk grn, org brn & bl .60 .25
Nos. 350-363 (14) 6.60 3.50

"Five Continents," Ceiling Painting, Palais des Nations, Geneva — A25

1959, Oct. 24 Engr. *Perf. 12½*
Centers in Dark Ultramarine
364 A25 15fr brown .35 .25
365 A25 20fr purple .35 .25
366 A25 25fr dark orange .35 .25
367 A25 40fr dark green .55 .25
368 A25 60fr carmine rose .60 .30
Nos. 364-368 (5) 2.20 1.30

Issued for United Nations Day, Oct. 24.

Skier — A26

Bicyclist — A27

Sports: 50c, Ice Hockey. 1fr, Tobogganing. 15fr, Discus thrower, vert. 20fr, Boxing, vert. 25fr, Runner.

1960 Unwmk. *Perf. 13*
369 A26 30c sl grn, car & bl grn .45 .25
370 A26 50c red & black .45 .25
371 A26 1fr red, blk & emer .45 .25
372 A27 10fr brown, ultra & sl .45 .25
373 A27 15fr dk red brn & grn .45 .25
374 A27 20fr dk grn, gldn brn & brn .55 .25
375 A27 25fr orange, mag & brn .65 .25
Nos. 369-375 (7) 3.45 1.75

8th Winter Olympic Games, Squaw Valley, Calif. (Nos. 369-371); 17th Olympic Games, Rome (Nos. 372-375).

Prime Minister Sylvanus Olympio and Togo Flag — A28

1960, Apr. 27 Litho.
Center in Green, Red, Yellow & Brown
376 A28 30c black & buff .25 .25
377 A28 50c brown & buff .25 .25
378 A28 1fr lilac & buff .25 .25
379 A28 10fr blue & buff .25 .25
380 A28 20fr red & buff .25 .25
381 A28 25fr green & buff .25 .25
Nos. 376-381 (6) 1.50 1.50

Proclamation of Togo's full independence, Apr. 27, 1960.
See Nos. C31-C33.

Flags of "Big Four," and British Flag — A29

1960, May 21 *Perf. 14x14½*
382 A29 50c shown .35 .25
383 A29 1fr USSR .35 .25
384 A29 20fr France .35 .25
385 A29 25fr US .35 .25
Nos. 382-385 (4) 1.40 1.00

Summit Conference of France, Great Britain, United States and USSR, Paris, May 16.

Flag of Togo and UN Emblem — A30

1961, Jan. 6 *Perf. 14½x15*
Flag in red, olive green & yellow
386 A30 30c red .30 .25
387 A30 50c brown .30 .25
388 A30 1fr ultramarine .30 .25
389 A30 10fr maroon .30 .25
390 A30 25fr black .30 .25
391 A30 30fr violet .30 .25
Nos. 386-391 (6) 1.80 1.50

Togo's admission to United Nations.

Crowned Cranes over Map — A31

1961, Apr. 1 *Perf. 14½x15*
392 A31 1fr multicolored .40 .25
393 A31 10fr multicolored .40 .25
394 A31 25fr multicolored .50 .25
395 A31 30fr multicolored .70 .25
Nos. 392-395 (4) 2.00 1.00

Augustino de Souza — A32

1961, Apr. 27 Litho. *Perf. 15*
396 A32 50c yellow, red & blk .35 .25
397 A32 1fr emerald, brn & blk .35 .25
398 A32 10fr grnsh bl, vio & blk .35 .25
399 A32 25fr salmon, grn & blk .35 .25
400 A32 30fr rose lil, bl & blk .35 .25
Nos. 396-400 (5) 1.75 1.25

1st anniv. of independence; "Papa" Augustino de Souza, leader of the independence movement.

Daniel C. Beard — A33

Designs: 1fr, Lord Baden-Powell. 10fr, Togolese Scout and emblems. 25fr, Togolese Scout and flag, vert. 30fr, Symbolic tents and fire, vert. 100fr, Three hands of different races giving Scout sign.

1961, Oct. 7 Photo. *Perf. 13*
401 A33 50c brt rose & grn .45 .25
402 A33 1fr dp violet & car .45 .25
403 A33 10fr dk gray & brn .45 .25
404 A33 25fr multicolored .45 .25
405 A33 30fr grn, red & org brn .55 .25
406 A33 100fr rose car & bl 1.25 .25
Nos. 401-406 (6) 3.60 1.50

Togolese Boy Scouts; 20th anniv. of the deaths of Daniel C. Beard and Lord Baden-Powell.

Four imperf. souvenir sheets each contain the six stamps, Nos. 401-406. Two sheets have a solid background of bright yellow, two a background of pale grayish brown. One yellow and one brown sheet have simulated perforations around the stamps. Size: 120x145mm. "REPUBLIQUE DU TOGO" is inscribed in white on bottom sheet margin. Value, each $4.

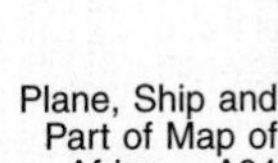

Plane, Ship and Part of Map of Africa — A34

Part of Map of Africa and: 25fr, Electric train and power mast. 30fr, Tractor and oil derricks. 85fr, Microscope and atomic symbol.

1961, Oct. 24 Litho.
Black Inscriptions; Map in Ocher
407 A34 20fr vio bl, org & yel .50 .25
408 A34 25fr gray, org & yel .50 .25
409 A34 30fr dk red, yel & org .60 .25
410 A34 85fr blue, yel & org 1.10 .25
a. Souvenir sheet of 4 4.00 2.75
Nos. 407-410 (4) 2.70 1.00

UN Economic Commission for Africa. No. 410a contains one each of Nos. 407-410, imperf., printed without separating margin between the individual stamps to show a complete map of Africa.

Children Dancing around Globe — A35

UNICEF Emblem, children and globe.

1961, Dec. 9 Unwmk. *Perf. 13½*
Black Inscription; Multicolored Design
411 A35 1fr ultra .40 .25
412 A35 10fr red brown .40 .25
413 A35 20fr lilac .40 .25
414 A35 25fr gray .40 .25
415 A35 30fr bright blue .45 .25
416 A35 85fr deep lilac .85 .25
a. Souvenir sheet of 6 5.00 3.50
Nos. 411-416 (6) 2.90 1.50

UNICEF, 15th anniv.

Nos. 411-416a assembled in two rows show the globe and children of various races dancing around it.

Cmdr. Alan B. Shepard — A36

Designs: 1fr, 30fr, Yuri A. Gagarin. 25fr, Shepherd.

1962, Feb. 24 *Perf. 15x14*
417 A36 50c green .25 .25
418 A36 1fr carmine rose .25 .25
419 A36 25fr blue .30 .25
420 A36 30fr purple .45 .25
Nos. 417-420 (4) 1.25 1.00

Astronauts of 1961.

Issued in sheets of 50 and in miniature sheets of 12 stamps plus four central labels showing photographs of Alan B. Shepard (US), Virgil I. Grissom (US), Yuri A. Gagarin (USSR), Gherman S. Titov (USSR).

No. 417 Surcharged in Black

1962, Apr. 7
421 A36 100fr on 50c green 2.00 .50
a. Carmine surcharge 2.00 .50

Orbital flight of Lt. Col. John H. Glenn, Jr., US, Feb. 20, 1962.

Independence Monument, Lomé — A37

Woman Carrying Fruit Basket — A38

1962, Apr. 27 Litho. *Perf. 13½x14*
422 A37 50c multicolored .25 .25
423 A38 1fr green & pink .25 .25
424 A37 5fr multicolored .25 .25
425 A38 20fr purple & yel .35 .25
426 A37 25fr multicolored .40 .25
427 A38 30fr red & yellow .40 .25
a. Souv. sheet of 3, #424-425, 427, imperf. 2.40 1.75
Nos. 422-427 (6) 1.90 1.50

2nd anniversary of Togo's independence.

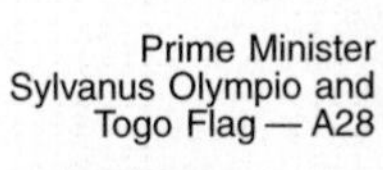

Malaria Eradication Emblem — A39

1962, June 2 ***Perf. 13½x13***

Multicolored Design

428	A39	10fr	yellow green	.35	.25
429	A39	25fr	pale lilac	.50	.25
430	A39	30fr	ocher	.55	.25
431	A39	85fr	light blue	1.10	.25
			Nos. 428-431 (4)	2.50	1.00

WHO drive to eradicate malaria.

Capitol, Pres. John F. Kennedy and Pres. Sylvanus Olympio — A40

1962, July 4 **Unwmk.** ***Perf. 13***

Inscription and Portraits in Slate Green

432	A40	50c	yellow	.25	.25
433	A40	1fr	blue	.25	.25
434	A40	2fr	vermilion	.25	.25
435	A40	5fr	lilac	.25	.25
436	A40	25fr	pale violet	.45	.25
437	A40	100fr	brt green	1.75	.80
a.			Souvenir sheet, imperf.	5.50	5.75
			Nos. 432-437 (6)	3.20	2.05

Visit of Pres. Sylvanus Olympio of Togo to the US, Mar. 1962.

Mail Coach and Stamps of 1897 — A41

50c, Mail ship, stamps of 1900. 1fr, Mail train, stamps of 1915. 10fr, Motorcycle truck, stamp of 1924. 25fr, Mail truck, stamp of 1941. 30fr, DC-3, stamp of 1947.

1963, Jan. 12 **Photo.** ***Perf. 13***

438	A41	30c	multicolored	.25	.25
439	A41	50c	multicolored	.25	.25
440	A41	1fr	multicolored	.35	.25
441	A41	10fr	vio, dp org & blk	.40	.25
442	A41	25fr	dk red brn, blk & yel grn	.75	.25
443	A41	30fr	ol brn & lil rose	.75	.25
			Nos. 438-443,C34 (7)	4.35	1.95

65th anniv. of Togolese mail service.
For souvenir sheet see No. C34a.

Hands Reaching for FAO Emblem — A42

1963, Mar. 21 ***Perf. 14***

444	A42	50c	bl, org & dk brn	.25	.25
445	A42	1fr	ol grn, org & dk brn	.25	.25
446	A42	25fr	brn, dk brn & org	.75	.25
447	A42	30fr	vio, dk brn & org	1.10	.25
			Nos. 444-447 (4)	2.35	1.00

FAO "Freedom from Hunger" campaign.

Togolese Flag and Lomé Harbor — A43

1963, Apr. 27 **Litho.** ***Perf. 13x12½***

Flag in Red, Green and Yellow

448	A43	50c	red brn & blk	.25	.25
449	A43	1fr	dk car rose & blk	.25	.25
450	A43	25fr	dull bl & blk	.35	.25
451	A43	50fr	bister & blk	.40	.25
			Nos. 448-451 (4)	1.25	1.00

3rd anniversary of independence.

Centenary Emblem — A44

1963, June 1 **Photo.** ***Perf. 14***

Flag in Red, Olive Green, Yellow

452	A44	25fr	blue, blk & red	1.00	.25
453	A44	30fr	dull grn, blk & red	1.20	.25

International Red Cross centenary.

Lincoln, Broken Fetters, Maps of Africa and US. — A45

1963, Oct. **Unwmk.** ***Perf. 13x14***

454	A45	50c	multicolored	.25	.25
455	A45	1fr	multicolored	.25	.25
456	A45	25fr	multicolored	.35	.25
			Nos. 454-456,C35 (4)	2.35	1.20

Centenary of the emancipation of the American slaves. See souvenir sheet No. C35a.
For overprints see Nos. 473-475, C41.

UN Emblem and "15" — A46

1963, Dec. 10 **Photo.** ***Perf. 14x13***

457	A46	50c	ultra, dk bl & rose red	.25	.25
458	A46	1fr	yel grn, dk bl & rose red	.25	.25
459	A46	25fr	lil, dk bl & rose red	.50	.25
460	A46	85fr	gold, dk bl & rose red	1.10	.30
			Nos. 457-460 (4)	2.10	1.05

15th anniv. of the Universal Declaration of Human Rights.

Hibiscus — A47

Designs: 50c, Orchid. 2fr, Butterfly. 5fr, Hinged tortoise. 8fr, Ball python. 10fr, Bunea alcinoe (moth). 20fr, Octopus. 25fr, John Dory (fish). 30fr, French angelfish. 40fr, Hippopotamus. 60fr, Bohor reedbuck. 85fr, Anubius baboon.

1964 **Size: 22½x31mm** ***Perf. 14***

461	A47	50c	multicolored	.25	.25
462	A47	1fr	yellow, car & grn	.25	.25
463	A47	2fr	lilac, yel & blk	.35	.25
464	A47	5fr	gray & multi	.25	.25
465	A47	8fr	cit, red brn & blk	.45	.25
466	A47	10fr	multicolored	1.20	.25
467	A47	20fr	dl bl, yel & brn	1.40	.25
468	A47	25fr	dl bl, grn & yel	1.40	.25
469	A47	30fr	multicolored	1.55	.25
470	A47	40fr	grn, red brn & blk	2.10	.25
471	A47	60fr	grnsh bl & red brn	4.50	.25
472	A47	85fr	lt grn, brn & org	5.50	.25
			Nos. 461-472 (12)	19.20	3.00

See Nos. 511-515, C36-C40, J56-J63.

Nos. 454-456 Overprinted Diagonally

1964, Mar. 7 ***Perf. 13x14***

473	A45	50c	multicolored	.25	.25
474	A45	1fr	multicolored	.25	.25
475	A45	25fr	multicolored	.50	.25
			Nos. 473-475,C41 (4)	2.75	1.05

Issued in memory of John F. Kennedy.

See No. C41 and note on souvenir sheets following it.

Isis of Kalabsha — A48

Designs: 25fr, Head of Ramses II. 30fr, Colonnade of Birth House at Philae.

1964, Mar. 8 **Litho.** ***Perf. 14***

476	A48	20fr	blk, pale grn & red	.35	.25
477	A48	25fr	black & lil rose	.45	.25
478	A48	30fr	black & citron	.70	.25
a.			Souvenir sheet of 3	2.75	2.50
			Nos. 476-478 (3)	1.50	.75

UNESCO world campaign to save historic monuments in Nubia. No. 478a contains three imperf. stamps similar to Nos. 476-478 with simulated perforations.

Phosphate Mine, Kpeme — A49

25fr, Phosphate plant, Kpeme. 60fr, Phosphate train. 85fr, Loading ship with phosphate.

1964, Apr. 27 **Unwmk.** ***Perf. 14***

479	A49	5fr	brown & bis brn	.30	.25
480	A49	25fr	dk pur & brn car	.30	.25
481	A49	60fr	dk green & olive	.70	.25
482	A49	85fr	vio blk & Prus bl	1.00	.25
			Nos. 479-482 (4)	2.30	1.00

Fourth anniversary of independence.

African Breaking Slavery Chain, and Map — A50

1964, May 25 **Photo.** ***Perf. 14x13***

483	A50	5fr	dp orange & brn	.25	.25
484	A50	25fr	olive grn & brn	.40	.25
485	A50	85fr	rose car & brn	1.00	.25
			Nos. 483-485,C42 (4)	3.15	1.05

1st anniv. of the meeting of African heads of state at Addis Ababa.

Pres. Nicolas Grunitzky and Butterfly — A51

1964, Aug. 18 **Litho.** ***Perf. 14***

486	A51	1fr	shown	.55	.25
487	A51	5fr	Dove	.55	.25
488	A51	25fr	Flower	.55	.25
489	A51	45fr	as 1fr	.90	.25
490	A51	85fr	Flower	1.75	.25
			Nos. 486-490 (5)	4.30	1.25

National Union and Reconciliation.

Soccer — A52

1964, Oct. **Photo.** ***Perf. 14***

491	A52	1fr	shown	.25	.25
492	A52	5fr	Runner	.30	.25
493	A52	25fr	Discus	.50	.25
494	A52	45fr	as 1fr	.65	.25
			Nos. 491-494,C43 (5)	2.95	1.30

18th Olympic Games, Tokyo, Oct. 10-25.
For souvenir sheet see No. C43a.

Cooperation Issue

Common Design Type

1964, Nov. 7 **Engr.** ***Perf. 13***

495	CD119 25fr	mag, dk brn & ol bis	.70	.25

Dirigible and Balloons A53

25fr, 45fr, Otto Lilienthal's glider, 1894; Wright Brothers' plane, 1903; Boeing 707.

1964, Dec. 5 **Photo.** ***Perf. 14x13***

496	A53	5fr	org lil & grn	.25	.25
497	A53	10fr	brt grn, dl bl & dk red	.30	.25
498	A53	25fr	bl, vio bl & org	.50	.25
499	A53	45fr	brt pink, vio bl & grn	1.10	.25
a.			Souv. sheet of 4	8.75	7.25
			Nos. 496-499,C44 (5)	3.65	1.50

Inauguration of the national airline, Air Togo. #499a contains 4 imperf. stamps similar to #497-499 and #C44 with simulated perfs.

International Quiet Sun Year — A54

Space Satellites: 10fr, 45fr, Orbiting Geophysical Observatory and Mariner, 15fr, 25fr, Tiros, Telstar and Orbiting Solar Observatory. 20fr, 50fr, Nimbus, Syncom and Relay.

1964, Dec. 12 **Litho.** ***Perf. 14***

500	A54	10fr	dp rose, bl & yel	.40	.25
501	A54	15fr	multi	.40	.25
502	A54	20fr	yel, grn & vio	.40	.25
503	A54	25fr	multi	.40	.25
504	A54	45fr	brt grn, dk bl & yel	.55	.25
505	A54	50fr	yel, grn & org	.75	.25
a.			Souv. sheet, #502-505, imperf.	3.00	2.50
			Nos. 500-505 (6)	2.90	1.50

Togo Olympic Stamps Printed in Israel — A55

Arms of Israel and Togo — A56

Pres. Nicolas Grunitzky of Togo and: 20fr, Church of the Mount of Beatitudes. 45fr, Ruins of Synagogue at Capernaum.

Perf. 13½x14½, 14x13½

1964, Dec. 26 **Photo.**

506	A55	5fr	rose violet	.40	.25
507	A56	20fr	grnsh bl, grn & dl pur	.40	.25
508	A56	25fr	red & bluish grn	.40	.25
509	A56	45fr	dl yel, ol & dl pur	.85	.25
510	A56	85fr	mag & bluish grn	.65	.25
a.			Souv. sheet of 4, imperf.	4.50	3.50
			Nos. 506-510 (5)	2.70	1.25

Israel-Togo friendship.

Type of Regular Issue, 1964

Designs: 3fr, Morpho aega butterfly. 4fr, Scorpion. 6fr, Bird-of-paradise flower. 15fr, Flap-necked chameleon. 45fr, Ring-tailed palm civet.

1965, June **Unwmk.** ***Perf. 14***

Size: 23x31mm

511	A47	3fr	bister & multi	1.20	.25
512	A47	4fr	org & bluish blk	.30	.25
513	A47	6fr	multi	.45	.25
514	A47	15fr	brt pink, yel & brn	1.75	.25
515	A47	45fr	dl grn, org & brn	3.50	.25
			Nos. 511-515 (5)	7.20	1.25

Syncom Satellite, Radar Station and ITU Emblem
A57

1965, June *Perf. 13x14*

516 A57 10fr Prus blue .45 .25
517 A57 20fr olive bister .45 .25
518 A57 25fr bright blue .45 .25
519 A57 45fr crimson .65 .25
520 A57 50fr green .75 .25
Nos. 516-520 (5) 2.75 1.25

ITU, centenary.

Abraham Lincoln — A58

1965, June 26 Photo. *Perf. 13x14*

521 A58 1fr magenta .25 .25
522 A58 5fr dull green .25 .25
523 A58 20fr brown .40 .25
524 A58 25fr slate .40 .25
Nos. 521-524,C45 (5) 3.30 1.35

Death cent. of Abraham Lincoln. For souvenir sheet see No. C45a.

Discus Thrower, Flags of Togo and Congo — A59

Flags and: 10fr, Javelin thrower. 15fr, Handball player. 25fr, Runner.

1965, July Unwmk. *Perf. 14x13*

Flags in Red, Yellow and Green

525 A59 5fr deep magenta .25 .25
526 A59 10fr dark blue .25 .25
527 A59 15fr brown .35 .25
528 A59 25fr dark purple .90 .25
Nos. 525-528,C46 (5) 3.50 1.35

1st African Games, Brazzaville, July 18-25.

Winston Churchill and "V" — A60

Stalin, Roosevelt and Churchill at Yalta — A61

Perf. 13½x14, 14x13½

1965, Aug. 7 **Photo.**

529 A60 5fr dull green .25 .25
530 A61 10fr brt vio & gray .25 .25
531 A60 20fr brown .50 .25
532 A61 45fr Prus bl & gray .85 .25
Nos. 529-532,C47 (5) 3.35 1.40

Sir Winston Spencer Churchill (1874-1965), British statesman and World War II leader.

Unisphere and New York Skyline — A62

10fr, Togolese dancers & drummer, Unisphere. 50fr, Michelangelo's Pieta & Unisphere.

1965, Aug. 28 Photo. *Perf. 14*

533 A62 5fr grnsh bl & vio blk .35 .25
534 A62 10fr yel grn & dk brn .35 .25
535 A62 25fr brn org & dk grn .35 .25
536 A62 50fr vio & sl grn .50 .25
537 A62 85fr rose red & brn 1.10 .30
a. Souvenir sheet of 2 2.75 1.75
Nos. 533-537 (5) 2.65 1.30

New York World's Fair, 1964-65. No. 537a contains two imperf. stamps similar to Nos. 536-537 with simulated perforations.

"Constructive Cooperation" and Olive Branch — A63

Designs: 25fr, 40fr, Hands of various races holding globe and olive branch. 85fr, Handclasp, olive branch and globe.

1965, Sept. 25 Unwmk. *Perf. 14*

538 A63 5fr violet, lt bl & org .35 .25
539 A63 15fr brn, org & gray .35 .25
540 A63 25fr blue & orange .35 .25
541 A63 40fr dp car, gray & org .55 .25
542 A63 85fr green & org 1.00 .30
Nos. 538-542 (5) 2.60 1.30

International Cooperation Year.

Major White and Gemini 4 — A64

25fr, Lt. Col. Alexei Leonov and Voskhod 2.

1965, Nov. 25 Photo. *Perf. 13½x14*

543 A64 25fr dp bl & brt car rose .60 .25
544 A64 50fr green & brown 1.00 .25

"Walks in Space" of Lt. Col. Alexei Leonov (USSR), and Major Edward H. White (US). Printed in sheets of 12 with ornamental borders.

For overprints and surcharges see Nos. 563-566.

Adlai E. Stevenson and UN Headquarters — A65

5fr, "ONU" and doves. 10fr, UN emblem and headquarters. 20fr, "ONU" and orchids.

1965, Dec. 15 *Perf. 14x13½*

545 A65 5fr dk brn, yel & lt bl .40 .25
546 A65 10fr org, dk bl & grn .40 .25
547 A65 20fr dk grn, yel grn & org brn .40 .25
548 A65 25fr brt yel, dk bl & bluish grn .40 .25
Nos. 545-548,C48 (5) 3.35 1.40

UN, 20th anniv.; Adlai E. Stevenson (1900-1965), US ambassador to the UN.

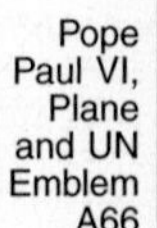

Pope Paul VI, Plane and UN Emblem A66

15fr, 30fr, Pope addressing UN General Assembly & UN emblem, vert. 20fr, Pope, NYC skyline with UN Headquarters.

1966, Mar. 5 Litho. *Perf. 12*

549 A66 5fr blue & multi .25 .25
550 A66 15fr lt violet & multi .25 .25
551 A66 20fr bister & multi .35 .25
552 A66 30fr lt ultra & multi .50 .25
Nos. 549-552,C49-C50 (6) 3.90 1.50

Visit of Pope Paul VI to the UN, New York City, Oct. 4, 1965.

Surgical Operation and Togolese Flag — A67

Togolese Flag and: 10fr, 30fr, Blood transfusion. 45fr, Profiles of African man and woman.

1966, May 7 Litho. *Perf. 12*

553 A67 5fr multicolored .40 .25
554 A67 10fr multicolored .40 .25
555 A67 15fr multicolored .40 .25
556 A67 30fr multicolored .40 .25
557 A67 45fr multicolored .60 .25
Nos. 553-557,C51 (6) 4.45 1.60

Togolese Red Cross, 7th anniversary.

Talisman Roses and WHO Headquarters, Geneva — A68

Various flowers & WHO Headquarters.

1966, May Litho. *Perf. 12*

558 A68 5fr lt yel grn & multi .25 .25
559 A68 10fr pale pink & multi .35 .25
560 A68 15fr dull yel & multi .45 .25
561 A68 20fr pale gray & multi .55 .25
562 A68 30fr tan & multi .70 .25
Nos. 558-562,C52-C53 (7) 4.70 1.75

Inauguration of WHO Headquarters, Geneva.

Nos. 543-544 Overprinted or Surcharged in Red

No. 563, Envolée Surveyor 1. No. 564, Envolée Gemini 9. No. 565, Envolée Luna 9. No. 566, Envolée Venus 3.

1966, July 11 Photo. *Perf. 13½x14*

563 A64 50fr multi .70 .25
564 A64 50fr multi .70 .25
a. Pair, #563-564 1.50 .60
565 A64 100fr on 25fr multi 1.60 .25
566 A64 100fr on 25fr multi 1.60 .25
a. Pair, #565-566 3.50 .90
Nos. 563-566 (4) 4.60 1.00

US and USSR achievements in Space.

Wood Carver — A69

Arts and Crafts: 10fr, Basket maker. 15fr, Woman weaver. 30fr, Woman potter.

1966, Sept. Photo. *Perf. 13x14*

567 A69 5fr blue, yel & dk brn .25 .25
568 A69 10fr emer, org & dk brn .25 .25
569 A69 15fr ver, yel & dk brn .30 .25
570 A69 30fr lilac, dk brn & yel .40 .25
Nos. 567-570,C55-C56 (6) 4.00 1.50

Togolese Dancer — A70

Designs: 5fr, Togolese man. 20fr, Woman dancer from North Togo holding branches. 25fr, Male dancer. 30fr, Male dancer from North Togo with horned helmet. 45fr, Drummer.

1966, Nov. Photo. *Perf. 13x14*

571 A70 5fr emerald & multi .25 .25
572 A70 10fr dl yel & multi .25 .25
573 A70 20fr lt ultra & multi .40 .25
574 A70 25fr dp orange & multi .50 .25
575 A70 30fr red violet & multi .55 .25
576 A70 45fr blue & multi .95 .25
Nos. 571-576,C57-C58 (8) 5.10 2.00

Soccer Players and Jules Rimet Cup — A71

Various Soccer Scenes.

1966, Dec. 14 Photo. *Perf. 14x13*

577 A71 5fr blue, brn & red .25 .25
578 A71 10fr brick red & multi .30 .25
579 A71 20fr ol, brn & dk grn .40 .25
580 A71 25fr vio, brn & org .40 .25
581 A71 30fr ocher & multi .50 .25
582 A71 45fr emerald, brn & mag .85 .25
Nos. 577-582,C59-C60 (8) 4.95 2.00

England's victory in the World Soccer Cup Championship, Wembley, July 30. For souvenir sheet see No. C60a.

African Mouthbreeder and Sailboat — A72

Designs: 10fr, Yellow jack and trawler. 15fr, Banded distichodus and seiner. 25fr, Jewelfish and galley. 30fr, like 5fr.

1967, Jan. 14 Photo. *Perf. 14*

Fish in Natural Colors

583 A72 5fr lt ultra & blk .25 .25
584 A72 10fr brn org & brn .40 .25
585 A72 15fr brt rose & dk bl .45 .25
586 A72 25fr olive & blk .70 .25
587 A72 30fr grnsh bl & blk .85 .25
Nos. 583-587,C61-C62 (7) 5.90 1.85

African Boy and Greyhound A73

UNICEF Emblem and: 10fr, Boy and Irish setter. 20fr, Girl and doberman.

1967, Feb. 11 Photo. ***Perf. 14x13½***

588 A73 5fr orange, plum & blk .25 .25
589 A73 10fr yel grn, red brn & dk grn .35 .25
590 A73 15fr brt rose, brn & blk .50 .25
591 A73 20fr bl, vio bl & blk .60 .25
592 A73 30fr ol, sl grn & blk 1.10 .25
Nos. 588-592,C63-C64 (7) 5.95 1.85

UNICEF, 20th anniv. (in 1966).

French A-1 Satellite A74

5fr, Diamant rocket, vert. 15fr, Fr-1 satellite, vert. 20fr, 40fr, D-1 satellite. 25fr, A-1 satellite.

Perf. 14x13½, 13½x14

1967, Mar. 18 Photo.

593 A74 5fr multi .25 .25
594 A74 10fr multi .25 .25
595 A74 15fr multi .35 .25
596 A74 20fr multi .40 .25
597 A74 25fr multi .55 .25
598 A74 40fr multi .75 .25
Nos. 593-598,C65-C66 (8) 5.30 2.05

French achievements in space.

Johann Sebastian Bach and Organ A75

UNESCO Emblem and: 10fr, Ludwig van Beethoven, violin and oboe. 15f, Duke Ellington, saxophone, trumpet, drums. 20fr, Claude A. Debussy, piano and harp. 30fr, like 15fr.

1967, Apr. 15 Photo. ***Perf. 14x13½***

599 A75 5fr org & multi .25 .25
600 A75 10fr multi .50 .25
601 A75 15fr multi .70 .25
602 A75 20fr lt bl & multi 1.10 .25
603 A75 30fr lil & multi 1.50 .25
Nos. 599-603,C67-C68 (7) 6.05 1.75

20th anniv. (in 1966) of UNESCO.

EXPO Emblem, British Pavilion and Day Lilies A76

10fr, French pavilion, roses. 30fr, African village, bird-of-paradise flower.

1967, May 30 Photo. ***Perf. 14***

604 A76 5fr brt pink & multi .25 .25
605 A76 10fr dull org & multi .25 .25
606 A76 30fr blue & multi .55 .25
Nos. 604-606,C69-C72 (7) 5.65 2.05

EXPO '67 Intl. Exhibition, Montreal, Apr. 28-Oct. 27.

For overprints see Nos. 628-630, C86-C89.

Lions Emblem — A77

20fr, 45fr, Lions emblem and flowers.

1967, July 29 Photo. ***Perf. 13x14***

607 A77 10fr yellow & multi .45 .25
608 A77 20fr multicolored .45 .25
609 A77 30fr green & multi .55 .25
610 A77 45fr blue & multi .80 .25
Nos. 607-610 (4) 2.25 1.00

50th anniversary of Lions International.

Montagu's Harriers A78

5fr, Bohor reedbucks. 15fr, Zebras. 20fr, 30fr, Marsh harriers. 25fr, Leopard.

1967, Aug. 19 Photo. ***Perf. 14x13½***

611 A78 5fr lilac & org brn .55 .25
612 A78 10fr dk red, yel & dl bl .55 .25
613 A78 15fr grn, blk & lil .55 .25
614 A78 20fr dk brn, yel & dl bl .55 .25
615 A78 25fr brn, ol & yel .55 .25
616 A78 30fr vio, yel & dl bl .65 .25
Nos. 611-616,C79-C80 (8) 6.10 2.00

Stamp Auction and Togo Nos. 16 and C42 — A79

10fr, 45fr, Exhibition, #67 (British) & 520. 15fr, 30fr, Stamp store, #230. 20fr, Stamp packet vending machine, #545.

Stamps on Stamps in Original Colors

1967, Oct. 14 Photo. ***Perf. 14x13***

617 A79 5fr purple .30 .25
618 A79 10fr dk brown .30 .25
619 A79 15fr deep blue .30 .25
620 A79 20fr slate green .35 .25
621 A79 30fr red brown .50 .25
622 A79 45fr Prus blue .80 .25
Nos. 617-622,C82-C83 (8) 5.80 2.15

70th anniv. of the 1st Togolese stamps. For souvenir sheet see No. C82a.

See Nos. 853-855, C205.

Monetary Union Issue

Common Design Type

1967, Nov. 4 Engr. ***Perf. 13***

623 CD125 30fr dk bl, vio bl & brt grn .60 .25

Broad Jump, Summer Olympics Emblem and View of Mexico City A80

15fr, Ski jump, Winter Olympics emblem, ski lift. 30fr, Runners, Summer Olympics emblem, view of Mexico City. 45fr, Bobsledding, Winter Olympics emblem, ski lift.

1967, Dec. 2 Photo. ***Perf. 13x14***

624 A80 5fr orange & multi .50 .25
625 A80 15fr multicolored .50 .25
626 A80 30fr multicolored .50 .25
627 A80 45fr multicolored .65 .25
Nos. 624-627,C84-C85 (6) 5.15 1.95

1968 Olympic Games. For souvenir sheet see No. C85a.

Nos. 604-606 Overprinted: "JOURNÉE NATIONALE / DU TOGO / 29 SEPTEMBRE 1967"

1967, Dec. ***Perf. 14***

628 A76 5fr multicolored .30 .25
629 A76 10fr multicolored .30 .25
630 A76 30fr blue & multi .40 .25
Nos. 628-630,C86-C89 (7) 5.40 1.85

National Day, Sept. 29, 1967.

The Gleaners, by François Millet and Phosphate Works, Benin — A81

Industrialization of Togo: 20fr, 45fr, 90fr, The Weaver at the Loom, by Vincent van Gogh, and textile plant, Dadia.

1968, Jan. Photo. ***Perf. 14***

631 A81 10fr olive & multi .45 .25
632 A81 20fr multicolored .45 .25
633 A81 30fr brown & multi .55 .25
634 A81 45fr multicolored .65 .25
635 A81 60fr dk blue & multi .95 .25
636 A81 90fr multicolored 1.60 .25
Nos. 631-636 (6) 4.65 1.50

Togolese Women Brewing Beer — A82

The Beer Drinkers, by Edouard Manet — A83

Design: 45fr, Modern beer bottling plant.

1968, Mar. 26 Litho. ***Perf. 14***

637 A82 20fr emerald & multi .55 .25
638 A83 30fr dk car & multi .70 .25
639 A82 45fr orange & multi .85 .25
Nos. 637-639 (3) 2.10 .75

Publicity for local beer industry.

Symbolic Water Cycle, Flower and Cogwheels — A84

1968, Apr. 6

640 A84 30fr multicolored .65 .25

Hydrological Decade (UNESCO), 1965-74. See No. C90.

Viking Ship and Portuguese Brigantine A85

10fr, Fulton's steamship and modern steamship. 20fr, Harbor activities and map of Africa.

1968, Apr. 26 Photo. ***Perf. 14x13½***

641 A85 5fr brt green & multi .25 .25
642 A85 10fr dp orange & multi .25 .25
643 A85 20fr green & multi .40 .25
644 A85 30fr yel grn & multi .85 .25
Nos. 641-644,C91-C92 (6) 4.85 1.50

Inauguration of Lomé Harbor.

See Nos. C91-C92.

Adenauer and 1968 Europa Emblem — A86

1968, May 25 Photo. ***Perf. 14***

645 A86 90fr olive grn & brn org 1.90 .25

Konrad Adenauer (1876-1967), chancellor of West Germany (1949-63).

Adam and Eve Expelled from Paradise, by Michelangelo — A87

Paintings: 20fr, The Anatomy Lesson of Dr. Tulp, by Rembrandt. 30fr, The Anatomy Lesson, by Rembrandt (detail). 45fr, Jesus Healing the Sick, by Raphael.

1968, June 22 Photo. ***Perf. 14***

646 A87 15fr crimson & multi .35 .25
647 A87 20fr multicolored .40 .25
648 A87 30fr green & multi .70 .25
649 A87 45fr multicolored 1.00 .25
Nos. 646-649,C93-C94 (6) 4.70 1.50

WHO, 20th anniv.

Olympic Monument, San Salvador Island, Bahamas A88

1968, July 27 ***Perf. 14x13½***

650 A88 15fr Wrestling .25 .25
651 A88 20fr Boxing .40 .25
652 A88 30fr Judo .60 .25
653 A88 45fr Running .75 .25
Nos. 650-653,C95-C96 (6) 4.10 1.50

19th Olympic Games, Mexico City, 10/12-27.

Chick Holding Lottery Ticket — A89

45fr, Lottery ticket, horseshoe & 4-leaf clover.

1968, Oct. 5 Litho. ***Perf. 14***

654 A89 30fr dk green & multi .65 .25
655 A89 45fr multicolored .75 .25

2nd anniversary of National Lottery.

Scout Before Tent — A90

10fr, 45fr, Scout leader training cub scouts, horiz. 20fr, First aid practice, horiz. 30fr, Scout game.

1968, Nov. 23

656 A90 5fr dp org & multi .25 .25
657 A90 10fr emerald & multi .25 .25
658 A90 20fr multicolored .40 .25
659 A90 30fr multicolored .50 .25
660 A90 45fr blue & multi .70 .25
Nos. 656-660,C97-C98 (7) 4.50 1.85

Issued to honor the Togolese Boy Scouts.

Adoration of the Shepherds, by Giorgione A91

Paintings: 20f, Adoration of the Magi, by Pieter Brueghel. 30fr, Adoration of the Magi, by Botticelli. 45fr, Adoration of the Magi, by Durer.

1968, Dec. 28 Litho. *Perf. 14*

661 A91 15fr green & multi .35 .25
662 A91 20fr multicolored .40 .25
663 A91 30fr multicolored .55 .25
664 A91 45fr multicolored .90 .25
Nos. 661-664,C100-C101 (6) 4.80 1.60

Christmas.

Martin Luther King, Jr. — A92

Portraits and Human Rights Flame: 20fr, Professor René Cassin (author of Declaration of Human Rights). 45fr, Pope John XXIII.

1969, Feb. 1 Photo. *Perf. 13½x14*

665 A92 15fr brn org & sl grn .25 .25
666 A92 20fr grnsh bl & vio .40 .25
667 A92 30fr ver & slate bl .60 .25
668 A92 45fr olive & car rose 1.25 .25
Nos. 665-668,C102-C103 (6) 4.90 1.65

International Human Rights Year.
For overprints see Nos. 683-686, C110-C111.

Omnisport Stadium and Soccer A93

Stadium and: 15fr, Handball. 20fr, Volleyball. 30fr, Basketball. 45fr, Tennis.

1969, Apr. 26 Photo. *Perf. 14x13½*

669 A93 10fr emer, dp car & dk brn .25 .25
670 A93 15fr org, ultra & dk brn .35 .25
671 A93 20fr yel, ol & dk brn .40 .25
672 A93 30fr dl grn, bl & dk brn .55 .25
673 A93 45fr org, lil & dk brn .70 .25
Nos. 669-673,C105-C106 (7) 4.60 1.80

Opening of Omnisport Stadium, Lomé.

Astronaut and Eagle on Moon, Earth and Stars in Sky — A94

Designs: 1f, 30f, Lunar Module Eagle Landing on Moon. 45fr, Astronaut and Eagle on moon, earth and stars in sky.

1969, July 21 Litho. *Perf. 14*

674 A94 1fr green & multi .25 .25
675 A94 20fr brown & multi .25 .25
676 A94 30fr scarlet & multi .40 .25
677 A94 45fr ultra & multi .70 .25
Nos. 674-677,C107-C108 (6) 4.00 1.75

Man's 1st landing on the moon, 7/20/69. US astronauts Neil A. Armstrong & Col. Edwin E. Aldrin, Jr., with Lieut. Col. Michael Collins piloting Apollo 11.
For overprints see #710-712, C120-C121.

Christ at Emmaus, by Velazquez — A95

Paintings: 5fr, The Last Supper, by Tintoretto. 20fr, Pentecost, by El Greco. 30fr, The Annunciation, by Botticelli. 45fr, Like 10fr.

1969, Aug. 16 Litho. *Perf. 14*

678 A95 5fr red, gold & multi .25 .25
679 A95 10fr multicolored .35 .25
680 A95 20fr grn, gold & multi .55 .25
681 A95 30fr multicolored .75 .25
682 A95 45fr pur, gold & multi 1.25 .25
Nos. 678-682,C109 (6) 5.25 1.75

Nos. 665-668 Overprinted

1969, Sept. 1 Photo. *Perf. 13½x14*

683 A92 15fr brn org & sl grn .30 .25
684 A92 20fr grnsh bl & vio .50 .25
685 A92 30fr ver & slate bl .55 .25
686 A92 45fr olive & car rose 1.00 .25
Nos. 683-686,C110-C111 (6) 4.50 1.55

Gen. Dwight D. Eisenhower (1890-1969), 34th President of the US.

African Development Bank and Emblem — A96

Designs: 45fr, Bank emblem and hand holding railroad bridge and engine.

1969, Sept. 10 Photo. *Perf. 13x14*

687 A96 30fr ultra, blk gold & grn .65 .25
688 A96 45fr grn, dk bl, gold & dk red 2.00 .35

5th anniv. of the African Development Bank.
See No. C112.

Louis Pasteur and Help for 1968 Flood Victims A97

Designs: 15fr, Henri Dunant and Red Cross workers meeting Biafra refugees at airport. 30fr, Alexander Fleming and help for flood victims. 45fr, Wilhelm C. Roentgen and Red Cross workers with children in front of Headquarters.

1969, Sept. 27 Litho. *Perf. 14*

689 A97 15fr red & multi .35 .25
690 A97 20fr emerald & multi .40 .25
691 A97 30fr purple & multi .75 .25
692 A97 45fr brt blue & multi .90 .25
Nos. 689-692,C113-C114 (6) 4.50 1.70

League of Red Cross Societies, 50th anniv.

Glidji Agricultural Center — A98

Designs (Emblem of Young Pioneer and Agricultural Organization and): 1fr, Corn harvest. 3fr, Founding meeting of Agricultural Pioneer Youths, Mar. 7, 1967. 4fr, Class at Glidji Agricultural School. 5fr, Boys forming human pyramid. 7fr, Farm students threshing. 8fr, Instruction in gardening. 10fr, 50fr, Cooperative village. 15fr, Gardening School. 20fr, Cattle breeding. 25fr, Chicken farm. 30fr, Independence parade. 40fr, Boys riding high wire. 45fr, Tractor and trailer. 60fr, Instruction in tractor driving.

1969-70 Litho. *Perf. 14*

693 A98 1fr multi ('70) .25 .25
694 A98 2fr multi .25 .25
695 A98 3fr multi ('70) .25 .25
696 A98 4fr multi ('70) .25 .25
697 A98 5fr ultra & multi .25 .25
698 A98 7fr multi ('70) .25 .25
699 A98 8fr red & multi .25 .25
700 A98 10fr bl & multi ('70) .25 .25
701 A98 15fr red & multi ('70) .30 .25
702 A98 20fr lilac & multi .35 .25
703 A98 25fr multi ('70) .50 .25
704 A98 30fr brt bl & multi .50 .25
705 A98 40fr brt yel & multi .70 .25
706 A98 45fr rose lil & multi .75 .25
707 A98 50fr blue & multi .85 .25
708 A98 60fr orange & multi .85 .25
Nos. 693-708,C115-C119 (21) 25.40 6.55

Books and Map of Africa — A99

1969, Nov. 27 Litho. *Perf. 14*

709 A99 30fr lt blue & multi .60 .25

12th anniv. of the Intl. Assoc. for the Development of Libraries in Africa.

Christmas Issue

Nos. 674-675, 677 Overprinted "JOYEUX NOEL"

1969, Dec. Litho. *Perf. 14*

710 A94 1fr green & multi .60 .25
711 A94 20fr brown & multi 1.90 .35
712 A94 45fr ultra & multi 2.60 .65
Nos. 710-712,C120-C121 (5) 13.85 2.35

George Washington — A100

Portraits: 20fr, Albert Luthuli. 30fr, Mahatma Gandhi. 45fr, Simon Bolivar.

1969, Dec. 27 Photo. *Perf. 14x13½*

713 A100 15fr dk brn, emer & buff .35 .25
714 A100 20fr dk brn, org & buff .35 .25
715 A100 30fr dk brn, grnsh bl & ocher .60 .25
716 A100 45fr dk brn, sl grn & dl yel 1.00 .25
Nos. 713-716,C122-C123 (6) 4.70 1.60

Issued to honor leaders for world peace.
For overprint & surcharges see #764-766, C143.

Plower, by M.K. Klodt and ILO Emblem — A101

Paintings and ILO Emblem: 10fr, Gardening, by Camille Pissarro. 20fr, Fruit Harvest, by Diego Rivera. 30fr, Spring Sowing, by Vincent van Gogh. 45fr, Workers, by Rivera.

1970, Jan. 24 Litho. *Perf. 12½x13*

717 A101 5fr gold & multi .25 .25
718 A101 10fr gold & multi .35 .25
719 A101 20fr gold & multi .60 .25
720 A101 30fr gold & multi 1.40 .25
721 A101 45fr gold & multi 1.40 .25
Nos. 717-721,C124-C125 (7) 8.50 1.75

ILO, 50th anniversary.

Togolese Hair Styles A102

Various hair styles. 20fr, 30fr, vertical.

1970, Feb. 21 *Perf. 13x12½, 12½x13*

722 A102 5fr multicolored .25 .25
723 A102 10fr ver & multi .35 .25
724 A102 20fr purple & multi .50 .25
725 A102 30fr yellow grn & multi 1.25 .25
Nos. 722-725,C126-C127 (6) 5.00 1.65

Togo No. C127 and Independence Monument, Lomé — A103

30fr, Pres. Etienne G. Eyadéma, Presidential Palace and Independence Monument. 50fr, Map of Togo, dove and Independence Monument, vert.

Perf. 13x12½, 12½x13

1970, Apr. 27 Litho.

726 A103 20fr multicolored .50 .25
727 A103 30fr multicolored .70 .25
728 A103 50fr multicolored 1.20 .25
Nos. 726-728,C128 (4) 3.25 1.00

10th anniv. of independence.

Inauguration of UPU Headquarters, Bern — A104

1970, May 30 Photo. *Perf. 14x13½*

729 A104 30fr orange & pur 1.20 .25

See No. C129.

Soccer, Jules Rimet Cup and Flags of Italy and Uruguay A105

Designs (Various Scenes from Soccer, Rimet Cup and Flags of): 10fr, Great Britain and Brazil. 15fr, USSR and Mexico. 20fr, Germany and Morocco. 30fr, Romania and Czechoslovakia.

1970, June 27 Litho. *Perf. 13x14*

730 A105 5fr olive & multi .25 .25
731 A105 10fr pink & multi .30 .25
732 A105 15fr yellow & multi .50 .25
733 A105 20fr multicolored .60 .25
734 A105 30fr emerald 1.20 .25
Nos. 730-734,C130-C132 (8) 6.40 2.10

Soccer Championships for the Jules Rimet Cup, Mexico City, May 30-June 21, 1970.

Lenin and UNESCO Emblem — A106

1970, July 25 Litho. *Perf. 12½*

735 A106 30fr fawn & multi 1.75 .25

Lenin (1870-1924), Russian communist leader. See No. C133.
For surcharge see No. C179.

EXPO '70 Emblem and View of US Pavilion A107

Designs: 2fr, Paper carp flying over Sanyo pavilion. 30fr, Russian pavilion. 50fr, Tower of the Sun pavilion. 60fr, French and Japanese pavilions.

1970, Aug. 8 Litho. *Perf. 13*

Size: 56½x35mm

736 A107 2fr gray & multi .25 .25

Size: 50x33mm

737 A107 20fr blue & multi .30 .25
738 A107 30fr blue & multi .50 .25
739 A107 50fr blue & multi 1.00 .25
740 A107 60fr blue & multi 1.25 .25
a. Strip of 4, #737-740 3.50 1.90
Nos. 736-740 (5) 3.30 1.25

EXPO '70 Intl. Exhibition, Osaka, Japan, Mar. 15-Sept. 13. No. 740a has continuous view of EXPO. See No. C134.

Neil A. Armstrong, Michael Collins and Edwin E. Aldrin, Jr. — A108

Designs: 2fr, US flag, moon rocks and Apollo 11 emblem. 20fr, Astronaut checking Surveyor 3 on moon, and Apollo 12 emblem. 30fr, Charles Conrad, Jr., Richard F. Gordon, Jr., Alan L. Bean and Apollo 12 emblem. 50fr, US flag, moon rocks and Apollo 12 emblem.

1970, Sept. 26

741 A108 1fr multi .25 .25
742 A108 2fr multi .25 .25
743 A108 20fr multi .40 .25
744 A108 30fr multi .75 .25
745 A108 50fr multi 1.20 .25
Nos. 741-745,C135 (6) 5.75 2.00

Moon landings of Apollo 11 and 12. For overprints see Nos. 746-750, C136.

Nos. 741-745 Inscribed: "FELICITATIONS / BON RETOUR APOLLO XIII"

1970, Sept. 26

746 A108 1fr multi .25 .25
747 A108 2fr multi .25 .25
748 A108 20fr multi .40 .25
749 A108 30fr multi .75 .25
750 A108 50fr multi 1.20 .25
Nos. 746-750,C136 (6) 5.60 1.85

Safe return of the crew of Apollo 13.

Forge of Vulcan, by Velazquez, and ILO Emblem A109

Paintings and Emblems of UN Agencies: 15fr, Still Life, by Delacroix, and FAO emblem. 20fr, Portrait of Nicholas Kratzer, by Holbein, and UNESCO emblem. 30fr, UN Headquarters, New York, and UN emblem. 50fr, Portrait of a Little Girl, by Renoir, and UNICEF emblem.

1970, Oct. 24 Litho. *Perf. 13x12½*

751 A109 1fr car, gold & dk brn .65 .25
752 A109 15fr ultra, gold & blk .65 .25
753 A109 20fr grnsh bl, gold & dk grn .65 .25
754 A109 30fr lil & multi .80 .25
755 A109 50fr org brn, gold & sepia 1.25 .25
Nos. 751-755,C137-C138 (7) 6.85 1.80

United Nations, 25th anniversary.

Euchloron Megaera — A110

Butterflies and Moths: 2fr, Cymothoe chrysippus. 30fr, Danaus chrysippus. 50fr, Morpho.

1970, Nov. 21 Litho. *Perf. 13x14*

756 A110 1fr yellow & multi 2.00 .25
757 A110 2fr lt vio & multi 2.00 .25
758 A110 30fr multicolored 2.00 .25
759 A110 50fr orange & multi 3.75 .25
Nos. 756-759,C139-C140 (6) 20.25 1.50

For surcharge see No. 859.

Nativity, by Botticelli A111

Paintings: 20fr, Adoration of the Shepherds, by Veronese. 30fr, Adoration of the Shepherds, by El Greco. 50fr, Adoration of the Kings, by Fra Angelico.

1970, Dec. 26 Litho. *Perf. 12½x13*

760 A111 15fr gold & multi .65 .25
761 A111 20fr gold & multi .65 .25
762 A111 30fr gold & multi .65 .25
763 A111 50fr gold & multi 1.10 .25
Nos. 760-763,C141-C142 (6) 6.80 1.55

Christmas.

No. 715 Overprinted

No. C123 Surcharged

No. 714 Surcharged

1971, Jan. 9 Photo. *Perf. 14x13½*

764 A100 30fr multicolored 2.00 .25
765 A100 30fr on 90fr multi 2.00 .25
766 A100 150fr on 20fr multi 8.50 .35
Nos. 764-766,C143 (4) 24.00 1.45

"Aerienne" obliterated with heavy bar on No. 765.

De Gaulle and Churchill — A112

De Gaulle and: 30fr, Dwight D. Eisenhower. 40fr, John F. Kennedy. 50fr, Konrad Adenauer.

1971, Feb. 20 Photo. *Perf. 13x14*

767 A112 20fr blk & brt blue .90 .25
768 A112 30fr blk & crimson .90 .25
769 A112 40fr blk & dp green 1.40 .25
770 A112 50fr blk & brown 1.60 .25
Nos. 767-770,C144-C145 (6) 10.00 1.50

Nos. 764-770 issued in memory of Charles de Gaulle (1890-1970), President of France.

Resurrection, by Raphael — A113

Easter: 30fr, Resurrection, by Master of Trebon. 40fr, like 1fr.

1971, Apr. 10 Litho. *Perf. 10½x11½*

771 A113 1fr gold & multi .50 .25
772 A113 30fr gold & multi .50 .25
773 A113 40fr gold & multi .50 .25
Nos. 771-773,C146-C148 (6) 5.20 1.55

Cmdr. Alan B. Shepard, Jr. — A114

Designs: 10fr, Edgar D. Mitchell and astronaut on moon. 30fr, Stuart A. Roosa, module on moon. 40fr, Take-off from moon, and spaceship.

1971, May Litho. *Perf. 12½*

774 A114 1fr blue & multi .40 .25
775 A114 10fr green & multi .40 .25
776 A114 30fr dull red & multi .40 .25
777 A114 40fr dk green & multi .45 .25
Nos. 774-777,C149-C151 (7) 5.90 2.55

Apollo 14 moon landing, Jan. 31-Feb. 9. For overprints see Nos. 788, C162-C164.

Cacao Tree and Pods A115

Designs: 40fr, Sorting and separating beans and pods. 50fr, Drying cacao beans.

1971, June 6 Litho. *Perf. 14*

778 A115 30fr multicolored .40 .25
779 A115 40fr ultra & multi .60 .25
780 A115 50fr multicolored .75 .25
Nos. 778-780,C152-C154 (6) 4.85 1.85

International Cacao Day, June 6.

Napoleon, Death Sesquicentennial — A115a

Die Cut Perf. 12

1971, June 11 Embossed

780A A115a 1000fr gold 37.50 37.50
b. Sheet of 1, imperf. 27.50 27.50

No. 780Ab contains one 48x69mm stamp.

Control Tower and Plane — A116

1971, June 26 Litho. *Perf. 14*

781 A116 30fr multicolored 1.00 .25

10th anniv. of the Agency for the Security of Aerial Navigation in Africa and Madagascar (ASECNA). See No. C155.

Great Market, Lomé A117

Tourist publicity: 30fr, Bird-of-paradise flower and sculpture of a man. 40fr, Aledjo Gorge and anubius baboon.

1971, July 17

782 A117 20fr multicolored .35 .25
783 A117 30fr multicolored .55 .25
784 A117 40fr multicolored .85 .25
Nos. 782-784,C156-C158 (6) 4.05 1.65

For surcharge and overprint see Nos. 804, C172.

Great Fetish of Gbatchoume A118

Religions of Togo: 30fr, Chief Priest in front of Atta Sakuma Temple. 40fr, Annual ceremony of the sacred stone.

1971, July 31 Litho. *Perf. 14½*

785 A118 20fr multicolored .30 .25
786 A118 30fr multicolored .40 .25
787 A118 40fr multicolored .70 .25
Nos. 785-787,C159-C161 (6) 3.65 1.50

No. 777 Overprinted in Silver "EN MEMOIRE / DOBROVOLSKY — VOLKOV — PATSAYEV / SOYUZ 11"

1971, Aug. *Perf. 12½*

788 A114 40fr multicolored 1.10 .25
Nos. 788,C162-C164 (4) 5.40 1.65

Russian astronauts Lt. Col. Georgi T. Dobrovolsky, Vladislav N. Volkov and Victor I. Patsayev, who died during the Soyuz 11 space mission, June 6-30, 1971.

Sapporo '72 Emblem and Speed Skating A119

Sapporo '72 Emblem and: 10fr, Slalom skiing. 20fr, Figure skating, pairs. 30fr, Bobsledding. 50fr, Ice hockey.

1971, Oct. 30 *Perf. 14*

789 A119 1fr multicolored .25 .25
790 A119 10fr multicolored .25 .25
791 A119 20fr multicolored .35 .25
792 A119 30fr multicolored .50 .25
793 A119 50fr multicolored 1.00 .25
Nos. 789-793,C165 (6) 4.45 1.75

11th Winter Olympic Games, Sapporo, Japan, Feb. 3-13, 1972.

Toy Crocodile and UNICEF Emblem A120

Toys and UNICEF Emblem: 30fr, Fawn and butterfly. 40fr, Monkey. 50fr, Elephants.

1971, Nov. 27

794 A120 20fr multicolored .35 .25
795 A120 30fr violet & multi .35 .25
796 A120 40fr green & multi .45 .25
797 A120 50fr bister & multi .65 .25
Nos. 794-797,C167-C168 (6) 3.20 1.50

UNICEF, 25th anniv.
For overprints see Nos. 918, C263-C264.

Virgin and Child, by Botticelli — A121

Virgin and Child by: 30fr, Master of the Life of Mary. 40fr, Dürer. 50fr, Veronese.

1971, Dec. 24 ***Perf. 14x13***

798 A121 10fr purple & multi .25 .25
799 A121 30fr green & multi .40 .25
800 A121 40fr brown & multi .85 .25
801 A121 50fr dk blue & multi .95 .25
Nos. 798-801,C169-C170 (6) 5.20 1.80

Christmas.

St. Mark's Basilica A122

Design: 40fr, Rialto Bridge.

1972, Feb. 26 **Litho.** ***Perf. 14***

802 A122 30fr multicolored .90 .25
803 A122 40fr multicolored 1.40 .25
Nos. 802-803,C171 (3) 4.05 1.05

UNESCO campaign to save Venice.

No. 784 Surcharged

1972, Mar. **Litho.** ***Perf. 14***

804 A117 300fr on 40fr multi 3.25 1.60

Visit of Pres. Richard M. Nixon to the People's Republic of China, Feb. 20-27.
See No. C172.

Easter — A123

Paintings: 25s, Crucifixion, by Master MS. 30fr, Pietà, by Botticelli. 40fr, Like 25fr.

1972, Mar. 31

805 A123 25fr gold & multi .60 .25
806 A123 30fr gold & multi .95 .25
807 A123 40fr gold & multi 1.20 .25
Nos. 805-807,C173-C174 (5) 5.95 1.25

Heart, Smith, WHO Emblem — A124

Heart, WHO Emblem and: 40fr, Typist. 60fr, Athlete with javelin.

1972, Apr. 4

808 A124 30fr multicolored .50 .25
809 A124 40fr multicolored .55 .25
810 A124 60fr multicolored .90 .25
Nos. 808-810,C175 (4) 3.20 1.20

"Your heart is your health," World Health Day.

Org. of African and Malagasy Union Conf. — A124a

Die Cut Perf. 12x12½

1972, Apr. 24 **Litho. & Embossed**
Self-adhesive

810A A124a 1000fr gold, red & grn 9.00 9.00

On No. 810A embossing may cut through stamp and embossed backing paper may not adhere well to the unused stamps.
For overprint see No. 893A.

Video Telephone — A125

1972, June 24 **Litho.** ***Perf. 14***

811 A125 40fr violet & multi 1.00 .25

4th World Telecommunications Day. See No. C176.
For overprints see Nos. 880, C229.

Cassava Production — A126

25fr, Cassava collection by truck, horiz. 40fr, Grating Cassava.

1972, June 30

812 A126 25fr yellow & multi .45 .25
813 A126 40fr multicolored .60 .25
Nos. 812-813,C177-C178 (4) 3.40 1.00

For overprint & surcharge see #866-867.

Basketball — A127

1972, Aug. 26 **Litho.** ***Perf. 14***

814 A127 30fr shown .40 .25
815 A127 40fr Running .65 .25
816 A127 50fr Discus .85 .25
Nos. 814-816,C180-C181 (5) 4.30 1.90

20th Olympic Games, Munich, 8/26-9/11.
See Nos. C180-C181. For overprints see Nos. C234-C235.

Pin-tailed Whydah — A128

Birds: 30fr, Broad-tailed widowbird. 40fr, Yellow-shouldered widowbird. 60fr, Yellow-tailed widowbird.

1972, Sept. 9

817 A128 25fr citron & multi .55 .25
818 A128 30fr lt blue & multi .75 .25
819 A128 40fr multicolored 1.10 .25
820 A128 60fr lt green & multi 2.10 .25
Nos. 817-820,C182 (5) 7.25 1.45

Paul P. Harris, Rotary Emblem — A129

50fr, Flags of Togo and Rotary Club.

1972, Oct. 7 **Litho.** ***Perf. 14***

821 A129 40fr green & multi .40 .25
822 A129 50fr multicolored .45 .25
a. Souvenir sheet of 2 2.10 1.25
Nos. 821-822,C183-C185 (5) 3.65 1.60

Rotary International, Lomé. No. 822a contains 2 stamps with simulated perforations similar to Nos. 821-822.
For overprints see Nos. 862, 898, C212-C213, C244-C235.

Mona Lisa, by Leonardo da Vinci — A130

40fr, Virgin and Child, by Giovanni Bellini.

1972, Oct. 21

823 A130 25fr gold & multi 1.50 .25
824 A130 40fr gold & multi 1.60 .25
Nos. 823-824,C186-C188 (5) 8.50 1.50

West African Monetary Union Issue
Common Design Type

Design: 40fr, African couple, city, village and commemorative coin.

1972, Nov. 2 **Engr.** ***Perf. 13***

825 CD136 40fr red brn, rose red & gray .60 .25

Presidents Pompidou and Eyadema, Party Headquarters — A131

1972, Nov. 23 **Litho.** ***Perf. 14***

826 A131 40fr purple & multi 1.60 .25

Visit of Pres. Georges Pompidou of France to Togo, Nov. 1972. See No. C189.

Christmas A132

Paintings: 25fr, Anunciation, Painter Unknown. 30fr, Nativity, Master of Vyshchibrod. 40fr, Like 25fr.

1972, Dec. 23

827 A132 25fr gold & multi .40 .25
828 A132 30fr gold & multi .65 .25
829 A132 40fr gold & multi 1.00 .25
Nos. 827-829,C191-C193 (6) 5.65 1.80

Raoul Follereau and Lepers A133

1973, Jan. 23 **Photo.** ***Perf. 14x13½***

830 A133 40fr violet & green 1.75 .25

World Leprosy Day and 20th anniv. of the Raoul Follereau Foundation. See No. C194.

WHO Emblem — A134

1973, Apr. 7 **Photo.** ***Perf. 14x13***

831 A134 30fr blue & multi .50 .25
832 A134 40fr dp yellow & multi .65 .25

WHO, 25th anniv.

Christ on the Cross — A135

1973, Apr. 21 **Litho.** ***Perf. 14***

833 A135 25fr shown .50 .25
834 A135 30fr Pietá .50 .25
835 A135 40fr Ascension .60 .25
Nos. 833-835,C195 (4) 3.00 1.15

Easter.

Eugene Cernan, Ronald Evans, Harrison Schmitt, Apollo 17 Badge A136

Design: 40fr, Lunar rover on moon.

1973, June 2 **Litho.** ***Perf. 14***

836 A136 30fr multicolored .50 .25
837 A136 40fr multicolored .60 .25
Nos. 836-837,C196-C197 (4) 5.95 1.60

Apollo 17 moon mission, Dec. 7-19, 1972.

Scouts Pitching Tent — A137

20fr, Campfire, horiz. 30fr, Rope climbing.

1973, June 30

838 A137 10fr multicolored .25 .25
839 A137 20fr multicolored .40 .25
840 A137 30fr violet & multi .65 .25
841 A137 40fr ocher & multi .90 .25
Nos. 838-841,C198-C199 (6) 5.95 2.15

24th Boy Scout World Conference (1st in Africa), Nairobi, Kenya, July 16-21.
For overprints see Nos. C265-C266.

Nicolaus Copernicus, 500th Anniv. Birth — A138

Designs: 10fr, Heliocentric system. 20fr, Nicolaus Copernicus. 30fr, Seated figure of Astronomy and spacecrafts around earth and moon. 40fr, Astrolabe.

1973, July 18

842	A138 10fr multicolored	.25	.25
843	A138 20fr multicolored	.40	.25
844	A138 30fr multicolored	.85	.25
845	A138 40fr lilac & multi	1.10	.25
	Nos. 842-845,C200-C201 (6)	6.10	1.80

Red Cross Ambulance Crew — A139

1973, Aug. 4

846	A139 40fr multicolored	1.40	.25

Togolese Red Cross. See No. C202.
For overprints see Nos. 942, C294.

Teacher and Students A140

40fr, Hut and man reading under tree, vert.

1973, Aug. 18 Litho. *Perf. 14*

847	A140 30fr multicolored	.50	.25
848	A140 40fr multicolored	.65	.25
	Nos. 847-848,C203 (3)	2.65	.85

Literacy campaign.

African Postal Union Issue
Common Design Type

1973, Sept. 12 Engr. *Perf. 13*

849	CD137 100fr yel, red & claret	1.00	.35

INTERPOL Emblem and Headquarters — A141

1973, Sept. 29 Photo. *Perf. 13½x14*

850	A141 30fr yel, brn & gray grn	.55	.25
851	A141 40fr yel grn, bl & mag	.65	.25

50th anniv. of Intl. Criminal Police Org.

Weather Vane and WMO Emblem — A142

1973, Oct. 4 *Perf. 14x13*

852	A142 40fr yel, dp brn & grn	1.00	.25

Intl. meteorological cooperation, cent. See No. C204.

Type of 1967

Designs: 25fr, Old and new locomotives, No. 795. 30fr, Mail coach and bus, No. 613. 90fr, Mail boat and ship, Nos. C61 and 469.

1973, Oct. 20 Photo. *Perf. 14x13*

853	A79 25fr multicolored	.60	.25
854	A79 30fr purple & green	.80	.25
855	A79 90fr dk blue & multi	2.10	.35
	Nos. 853-855,C205 (4)	6.00	1.20

Togolese postal service, 75th anniv.

John F. Kennedy and Adolf Schaerf — A143

Designs: 30fr, Kennedy and Harold MacMillan. 40fr, Kennedy and Konrad Adenauer.

1973, Nov. 22 Litho. *Perf. 14*

856	A143 20fr blk, gray & vio	.55	.25
857	A143 30fr blk, rose & brn	.55	.25
858	A143 40fr blk, lt grn & grn	.65	.25
	Nos. 856-858,C206-C208 (6)	9.10	2.55

John F. Kennedy (1917-1963).

No. 758 Surcharged with New Value, 2 Bars and Overprinted in Ultramarine: "SECHERESSE SOLIDARITE AFRICAINE"

1973, Dec. Photo. *Perf. 13x14*

859	A110 100fr on 30fr multi	1.40	.50

African solidarity in drought emergency.

Virgin and Child, Italy, 15th Century — A144

30fr, Adoration of the Kings, Italy, 15th cent.

1973, Dec. 22 Litho. *Perf. 14*

860	A144 25fr gold & multi	.60	.25
861	A144 30fr gold & multi	.70	.25
	Nos. 860-861,C210-C211 (4)	3.90	1.30

Christmas.

No. 821 Overprinted: "PREMIERE CONVENTION / 210eme DISTRICT / FEVRIER 1974 / LOME"

1974, Feb. 21 Litho. *Perf. 14*

862	A129 40fr green & multi	.40	.25
	Nos. 862,C212-C213 (3)	2.05	.85

First convention of Rotary Intl., District 210, Lomé, Feb. 22-24.

Soccer and Games' Cup — A145

Various soccer scenes and games' cup.

1974, Mar. 2 Litho. *Perf. 14*

863	A145 20fr lt blue & multi	.35	.25
864	A145 30fr yellow & multi	.50	.25
865	A145 40fr lilac & multi	.55	.25
	Nos. 863-865,C214-C216 (6)	5.30	2.65

World Soccer Championships, Munich, Germany, June 13-July 7.

Nos. 812-813 Overprinted and Surcharged: "10e ANNIVERSAIRE DU P.A.M."

1974, Mar. 25 Litho. *Perf. 14*

866	A126 40fr multicolored	.65	.25
867	A126 100fr on 25fr multi	1.40	.50

10th anniv. of World Food Program. Overprint on No. 866 is in one line; 2 lines on No. 867 and 2 bars through old denomination.

Girl Before Mirror, by Picasso — A146

Paintings by Picasso: 30fr, The Turkish Shawl. 40fr, Mandolin and Guitar.

1974, Apr. 6

868	A146 20fr vio blue & multi	.40	.25
869	A146 30fr maroon & multi	.65	.25
870	A146 40fr multicolored	.85	.25
	Nos. 868-870,C217-C219 (6)	9.50	2.45

Pablo Picasso (1881-1973), Spanish painter.

Kpeme Village and Wharf — A147

Design: 40fr, Tropicana tourist village.

1974, Apr. 20

871	A147 30fr multicolored	.45	.25
872	A147 40fr multicolored	.45	.25
	Nos. 871-872,C220-C221 (4)	3.25	1.10

Mailman, UPU Emblem — A148

Design: 40fr, Mailman, different uniform.

1974, May 10 Litho. *Perf. 14*

873	A148 30fr salmon & multi	.45	.25
874	A148 40fr multicolored	.50	.25
	Nos. 873-874,C222-C223 (4)	2.90	1.10

UPU, centenary.

Map and Flags of Members — A148a

1974, May 29 Litho. *Perf. 13x12½*

875	A148a 40fr blue & multi	.60	.25

15th anniversary of the Council of Accord.

Fisherman with Net — A149

40fr, Fisherman casting net from canoe.

1974, June 22 Litho. *Perf. 14*

876	A149 30fr multicolored	.55	.25
877	A149 40fr multicolored	.65	.25
	Nos. 876-877,C224-C226 (5)	5.70	1.65

Lagoon fishing.

Pioneer Communicating with Earth — A150

30fr, Radar station and satellite, vert.

1974, July 6 *Perf. 14*

878	A150 30fr multicolored	.35	.25
879	A150 40fr multicolored	.40	.25
	Nos. 878-879,C227-C228 (4)	3.65	1.50

US Jupiter space probe.

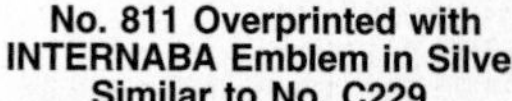

No. 811 Overprinted with INTERNABA Emblem in Silver Similar to No. C229

1974, July

880	A125 40fr multicolored	3.00	.55

INTERNABA 1974 Intl. Philatelic Exhibition, Basel, June 7-16. See No. C229.

No. 880 exists overprint in black. Value, unused $10.

Tympanotomus Radula — A151

Designs: Seashells.

1974, July 13 Litho. *Perf. 14*

881	A151 10fr shown	.85	.25
882	A151 20fr Tonna galea	.85	.25
883	A151 30fr Conus mercator	1.00	.25
884	A151 40fr Cardium costatum	1.40	.25
	Nos. 881-884,C230-C231 (6)	8.10	1.70

Groom with Horses — A152

Design: 40fr, Trotting horses.

1974, Aug. 3 Litho. *Perf. 14*

885	A152 30fr multicolored	.90	.25
886	A152 40fr multicolored	1.10	.25
	Nos. 885-886,C232-C233 (4)	6.50	1.20

Horse racing.

Leopard — A153

1974, Sept. 7 Litho. *Perf. 14*

887	A153 20fr shown	.70	.25
888	A153 30fr Giraffes	.70	.25
889	A153 40fr Elephants	.95	.25
	Nos. 887-889,C236-C237 (5)	6.70	1.50

Wild animals of West Africa.

1974, Oct. 14

890	A153 30fr Herding cattle	.40	.25
891	A153 40fr Milking cow	.55	.25
	Nos. 890-891,C238-C239 (4)	3.30	1.10

Domestic animals.

Churchill and Frigate F390 — A154

Design: 40fr, Churchill and fighter planes.

1974, Nov. 1 Photo. *Perf. 13x13½*

892	A154 30fr multicolored	.55	.25
893	A154 40fr multicolored	.70	.25
	Nos. 892-893,C240-C241 (4)	5.25	1.55

Winston Churchill (1874-1965).

No. 810A Ovptd. "Inauguration de l'hotel de la Paix 9-1-75"

Litho. & Embossed

1975, Jan. 9 *Perf. 12½*

Self-adhesive

893A	A124a 1000fr gold, red & grn	10.00	10.00

On No. 893A embossing may cut through stamp and embossed backing paper may not adhere well to the unused stamps.

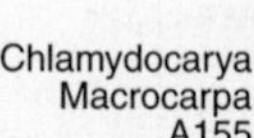

Chlamydocarya Macrocarpa A155

Flowers of Togo: 25fr, Strelitzia reginae, vert. 30fr, Storphanthus sarmentosus, vert. 60fr, Clerodendrum scandens.

1975, Feb. 15 Litho. *Perf. 14*

894 A155 25fr multicolored .35 .25
895 A155 30fr multicolored .50 .25
896 A155 40fr multicolored .80 .25
897 A155 60fr multicolored 1.10 .25
Nos. 894-897,C242-C243 (6) 7.25 1.80

No. 821 Overprinted: "70e ANNIVERSAIRE / 23 FEVRIER 1975"

1975, Feb. 23 Litho. *Perf. 14*

898 A129 40fr green & multi .55 .25
Nos. 898,C244-C245 (3) 2.45 .85

Rotary Intl., 70th anniv.

Radio Station, Kamina — A156

30fr, Benedictine Monastery, Zogbegan. 40fr, Causeway, Atchinedji. 60fr, Ayome Waterfalls.

1975, Mar. 1 Photo. *Perf. 13x14*

899 A156 25fr multicolored .35 .25
900 A156 30fr multicolored .35 .25
901 A156 40fr multicolored .45 .25
902 A156 60fr multicolored .65 .25
Nos. 899-902 (4) 1.80 1.00

Jesus Mocked, by El Greco — A157

Paintings: 30fr, Crucifixion, by Master Janoslet. 40fr, Descent from the Cross, by Bellini. 90fr, Pietà, painter unknown.

1975, Apr. 19 Litho. *Perf. 14*

903 A157 25fr black & multi .35 .25
904 A157 30fr black & multi .45 .25
905 A157 40fr black & multi .55 .25
906 A157 90fr black & multi 1.10 .30
Nos. 903-906,C246-C247 (6) 5.45 1.85

Easter.

Stilt Walking, Togolese Flag — A158

Design: 30fr, Flag and dancers.

1975, Apr. 26 Litho. *Perf. 14*

907 A158 25fr multicolored .40 .25
908 A158 30fr multicolored .40 .25
Nos. 907-908,C248-C249 (4) 2.00 1.00

15th anniv. of independence.

Rabbit Hunter with Club — A159

40fr, Beaver hunter with bow and arrow.

1975, May 24 Photo. *Perf. 13x13½*

909 A159 30fr multicolored .75 .25
910 A159 40fr multicolored .95 .25
Nos. 909-910,C250-C251 (4) 5.55 1.10

Pounding Palm Nuts — A160

Design: 40fr, Man extracting palm oil, vert.

1975, June 28 Litho. *Perf. 14*

911 A160 30fr multicolored .95 .25
912 A160 40fr multicolored .95 .25
Nos. 911-912,C252-C253 (4) 5.65 1.50

Palm oil production.

Apollo-Soyuz Link-up — A161

1975, July 15

913 A161 30fr multicolored .40 .25
Nos. 913,C254-C258 (6) 5.80 1.85

Apollo Soyuz space test project (Russo-American cooperation), launching July 15; link-up July 17.

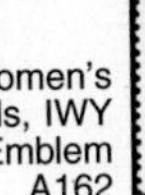

Women's Heads, IWY Emblem A162

1975, July 26 Litho. *Perf. 12½*

914 A162 30fr blue & multi .50 .25
915 A162 40fr multicolored .60 .25

International Women's Year.

Dr. Schweitzer and Children A163

1975, Aug. 23 Litho. *Perf. 14x13½*

916 A163 40fr multicolored .75 .25
Nos. 916,C259-C261 (4) 4.50 1.30

Dr. Albert Schweitzer (1875-1965), medical missionary and musician.

Merchant Writing Letter, by Vittore Carpaccio — A164

1975, Oct. 9 Litho. *Perf. 14*

917 A164 40fr multicolored .60 .25

Intl. Letter Writing Week. See No. C262.

No. 797 Overprinted: "30ème Anniversaire / des Nations-Unies"

1975, Oct. 24 Litho. *Perf. 14*

918 A120 50fr multi .50 .25
Nos. 918,C263-C264 (3) 1.85 .75

UN, 30th anniv.

Virgin and Child, by Mantegna — A165

Paintings of the Virgin and Child: 30fr, El Greco. 40fr, Barend van Orley.

1975, Dec. 20 Litho. *Perf. 14*

919 A165 20fr red & multi .35 .25
920 A165 30fr bl & multi .40 .25
921 A165 40fr red & multi .50 .25
Nos. 919-921,C267-C269 (6) 4.70 1.75

Christmas.

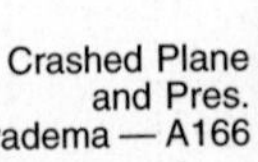

Crashed Plane and Pres. Eyadema — A166

1976, Jan. 24 Photo. *Perf. 13*

922 A166 50fr multi 11.00 .45
923 A166 60fr multi 26.00 .50

Airplane crash at Sara-kawa, Jan. 24, 1974, in which Pres. Eyadema escaped injury.

1976 Summer Olympics, Montreal — A166a

Litho. & Embossed

1976, Feb. 24 *Perf. 11*

923A A166a 1000fr Diving 15.00 —
923B A166a 1000fr Track 15.00 —
923C A166a 1000fr Pole vault 15.00 —
923D A166a 1000fr Equestrian 15.00 —
923E A166a 1000fr Cycling 15.00 —
Nos. 923A-923E (5) 75.00

Exist imperf.

Frigates on the Hudson A167

American Bicentennial: 50fr, George Washington, by Gilbert Stuart, and Bicentennial emblem, vert.

1976, Mar. 3 Litho. *Perf. 14*

924 A167 35fr multicolored .45 .25
925 A167 50fr multicolored .65 .25
Nos. 924-925,C270-C273 (6) 5.50 1.80

For overprints see Nos. C280-C283.

ACP and CEE Emblems — A168

50fr, Map of Africa, Europe and Asia.

1976, Apr. 24 Photo. *Perf. 13x14*

926 A168 10fr orange & multi .30 .25
927 A168 50fr pink & multi .50 .30
Nos. 926-927,C274-C275 (4) 2.00 1.05

First anniv. of signing of treaty between Togo and European Common Market, Lomé, Feb. 28, 1975.

Cable-laying Ship — A169

30fr, Telephone, tape recorder, speaker.

1976, Mar. 10 Photo. *Perf. 13x14*

928 A169 25fr ultra & multi .25 .25
929 A169 30fr pink & multi .35 .25
Nos. 928-929,C276-C277 (4) 1.70 1.15

Centenary of first telephone call by Alexander Graham Bell, Mar. 10, 1876.

Blind Man and Insect — A170

1976, Apr. 8 *Perf. 14x13*

930 A170 50fr brt grn & multi .75 .25

World Health Day: "Foresight prevents blindness." See No. C278.

Air Post Type, 1976, and

Marine Exhibition Hall — A171

10fr, Pylon, flags of Ghana, Togo and Dahomey.

1976 Litho. *Perf. 14*

931 A171 5fr multicolored .25 .25
932 AP19 10fr multicolored .50 .25
933 A171 50fr multicolored .70 .45
Nos. 931-933,C279 (4) 2.45 1.20

Marine Exhibition, 10th anniv. (5fr, 50fr). Ghana-Togo-Dahomey electric power grid, 1st anniversary (10fr).

Issue dates: 50fr, May 8; 5fr, 10fr, August.

Running A172

Montreal Olympic Emblem and: 30fr, Kayak. 50fr, High jump.

1976, June 15 Photo. *Perf. 14x13*

934 A172 25fr multicolored .30 .25
935 A172 30fr multicolored .30 .25
936 A172 50fr multicolored .45 .25
Nos. 934-936,C284-C286 (6) 4.10 2.05

21st Olympic Games, Montreal, Canada, July 17-Aug. 1.

For overprints see Nos. 947, C298-C299.

Titan 3 and Viking Emblem A173

50fr, Viking trajectory, Earth to Mars.

1976, July 15 Litho. *Perf. 14*

937 A173 30fr blue & multi .35 .25
938 A173 50fr rose & multi .50 .25
Nos. 937-938,C287-C290 (6) 4.70 2.00

US Viking Mars missions.

Young Routy at Celeyran, by Toulouse-Lautrec A174

Paintings by Toulouse-Lautrec: 20fr, Model in Studio. 35fr, Louis Pascal, portrait.

1976, Aug. 7 Litho. *Perf. 14*

939 A174 10fr black & multi .25 .25
940 A174 20fr black & multi .50 .25
941 A174 35fr black & multi .65 .25
Nos. 939-941,C291-C293 (6) 5.80 1.80

Henri Toulouse-Lautrec (1864-1901), French painter, 75th death anniversary.

No. 846 Overprinted: "Journée / Internationale / de l'Enfance"

1976, Nov. 27 **Litho.** ***Perf. 14***

942 A139 40fr multi .40 .25

Intl. Children's Day. See No. C294.

Adoration of the Shepherds, by Pontormo A175

Paintings: 30fr, Nativity, by Carlo Crivelli. 50fr, Virgin and Child, by Jacopo da Pontormo.

1976, Dec. 18

943 A175 25fr multi .35 .25
944 A175 30fr multi .50 .25
945 A175 50fr multi .85 .25
Nos. 943-945,C295-C297 (6) 5.10 2.35

Christmas.

Mohammed Ali Jinnah, Flags of Togo and Pakistan — A176

1976, Dec. 24 **Litho.** ***Perf. 13***

946 A176 50fr multi .60 .25

Jinnah (1876-1948), first Governor General of Pakistan.

No. 936 Overprinted: "CHAMPIONS OLYMPIQUES / SAUT EN HAUTEUR / POLOGNE"

1976, Dec. **Photo.** ***Perf. 14x13***

947 A172 50fr multi .55 .25
Nos. 947,C298-C299 (3) 2.95 1.15

Olympic winners.

Queen Elizabeth II, Silver Jubilee — A176a

Designs: No. 947A, Portrait. No. 947B, Wearing coronation regalia.

Litho. & Embossed

1977, Jan. 10 ***Perf. 11***

947A A176a 1000fr silver & multi 7.00

Souvenir Sheet

947B A176a 1000fr silver & multi 8.50

Exist imperf.

Kpeme Phosphate Mine, Sara-kawa Crash — A177

1977, Jan. 13 **Photo.** ***Perf. 13x14***

948 A177 50fr multi .55 .25
Nos. 948,C300-C301 (3) 1.95 .85

Presidency of Etienne Eyadema, 10th anniv.

Musical Instruments A178

1977, Feb. 7 **Litho.** ***Perf. 14***

949 A178 5fr Gongophone .25 .25
950 A178 10fr Tamtam, vert. .25 .25
951 A178 25fr Dondon .60 .25
Nos. 949-951,C302-C304 (6) 4.40 1.55

Victor Hugo and his Home — A179

1977, Feb. 26 ***Perf. 13x14***

952 A179 50fr multi .65 .25

Victor Hugo (1802-1885), French writer, 175th birth anniversary. See No. C305.

For overprints see Nos. 959, C316.

Beethoven and Birthplace, Bonn — A180

50fr, Bronze bust, 1812, & Heiligenstadt home.

1977, Mar. 7 ***Perf. 14***

953 A180 30fr multi .50 .25
954 A180 50fr multi .75 .25
Nos. 953-954,C306-C307 (4) 4.60 1.45

Benz, 1894, Germany A181

Early Automobiles: 50fr, De Dion Bouton, 1903, France.

1977, Apr. 11 **Litho.** ***Perf. 14***

955 A181 35fr multi .65 .25
956 A181 50fr multi .90 .25
Nos. 955-956,C308-C311 (6) 6.05 2.10

Lindbergh, Ground Crew and Spirit of St. Louis A182

50fr, Lindbergh and Spirit of St. Louis.

1977, May 9

957 A182 25fr multi .35 .25
958 A182 50fr multi .70 .25
Nos. 957-958,C312-C315 (6) 4.15 1.55

Charles A. Lindbergh's solo transatlantic flight from New York to Paris, 50th anniv.

No. 952 Overprinted: "10ème ANNIVERSAIRE DU / CONSEIL INTERNATIONAL / DE LA LANGUE FRANCAISE"

1977, May 17 **Litho.** ***Perf. 14***

959 A179 50fr multi .70 .25

Intl. French Language Council, 10th anniv. See No. C316.

African Slender-snouted Crocodile — A183

Endangered wildlife: 15fr, Nile crocodile.

1977, June 13

960 A183 5fr multi .35 .25
961 A183 15fr multi .35 .25
Nos. 960-961,C317-C320 (6) 5.90 1.60

Agriculture School, Tove — A184

1977, July 11 **Litho.** ***Perf. 14***

962 A184 50fr multi .50 .25
Nos. 962,C321-C323 (4) 3.60 1.20

Agricultural development.

Landscape with Cart, by Peter Paul Rubens (1577-1640) A185

Rubens Painting: 35fr, Exchange of the Princesses at Hendaye, 1623.

1977, Aug. 8

963 A185 15fr multi .45 .25
964 A185 35fr multi .60 .25
Nos. 963-964,C324-C325 (4) 3.35 1.00

Orbiter 101 on Ground A186

Designs: 30fr, Launching of Orbiter, vert. 50fr, Ejection of propellant tanks at take-off.

1977, Oct. 4 **Litho.** ***Perf. 14***

965 A186 20fr multi .30 .25
966 A186 30fr multi .40 .25
967 A186 50fr multi .50 .25
Nos. 965-967,C326-C328 (6) 4.50 1.60

Space shuttle trials in the US.

Lafayette Arriving in Montpelier, Vt. — A187

Design: 25fr, Lafayette, age 19, vert.

1977, Nov. 7 ***Perf. 14x13, 13x14***

968 A187 25fr multi .35 .25
969 A187 50fr multi .60 .25
Nos. 968-969,C329-C330 (4) 2.70 1.00

Arrival of the Marquis de Lafayette in North America, 200th anniv.

Lenin, Cruiser Aurora, Red Flag — A188

1977, Nov. 7 **Litho.** ***Perf. 12***

970 A188 50fr multi 1.20 .25

Russian October Revolution, 60th anniv.

Virgin and Child, by Lorenzo Lotto — A189

Virgin and Child by: 30fr, Carlo Crivelli. 50fr, Cosimo Tura.

1977, Dec. 19 ***Perf. 14***

971 A189 20fr multi .25 .25
972 A189 30fr multi .35 .25
973 A189 50fr multi .50 .25
Nos. 971-973,C331-C333 (6) 4.20 1.65

Christmas.

Edward Jenner — A190

Design: 20fr, Vaccination clinic, horiz.

Perf. 14x13, 13x14

1978, Jan. 9 **Litho.**

974 A190 5fr multi .25 .25
975 A190 20fr multi .25 .25
Nos. 974-975,C334-C335 (4) 1.25 1.00

Worldwide eradication of smallpox.

Orville and Wilbur Wright A191

Design: 50fr, Wilbur Wright flying at Kill Devil Hill, 1902.

1978, Feb. 6 **Litho.** ***Perf. 14***

976 A191 35fr multi .40 .25
977 A191 50fr multi .55 .25
Nos. 976-977,C336-C339 (6) 6.55 1.95

75th anniversary of first motorized flight.

Anniversaries and Events — A192

Designs: No. 978, High jump. No. 979, Westminster Abbey. No. 980, Soccer players, World Cup. No. 981, Apollo 8. No. 982, Duke of Wellington, by Goya. No. 983, Hurdles. No. 984, Coronation coach. No. 985, Soccer players. No. 986, Apollo launch. No. 987, Dona Isabel Cobos de Porcel, by Goya.

1978, Mar. 13 **Litho.** ***Perf. 11***

978 A192 1000fr gold & multi *9.00*
979 A192 1000fr gold & multi *9.00*
980 A192 1000fr gold & multi *9.00*
981 A192 1000fr gold & multi *9.00*
982 A192 1000fr gold & multi *9.00*

Souvenir Sheets

983 A192 1000fr gold & multi *12.00*
984 A192 1000fr gold & multi *12.00*
985 A192 1000fr gold & multi *12.00*
986 A192 1000fr gold & multi *12.00*
987 A192 1000fr gold & multi *12.00*

Nos. 978, 983, 1980 Summer Olympics, Moscow. Nos. 979, 984, Coronation of Queen Elizabeth II, 25th anniv. Nos. 980, 985, 1978 World Cup Soccer Championships, Argentina. Nos. 981, 986, 1st manned lunar orbit, 10th anniv. Nos. 982, 987, Death sesquicent. of Francisco Goya.

For overprints see Nos. 1056A-1056B, 1094A-1094B.

Exist imperf.

John, the Evangelist and Eagle — A197

Evangelists: 10fr, Luke and ox. 25fr, Mark and lion. 30fr, Matthew and angel.

1978, Mar. 20 **Litho.** ***Perf. 13½x14***

988 A197 5fr multi .25 .25
989 A197 10fr multi .25 .25
990 A197 25fr multi .25 .25
991 A197 30fr multi .35 .25
a. Souvenir sheet of 4 1.25 .60
Nos. 988-991 (4) 1.10 1.00

No. 991a contains one each of Nos. 988-991 with simulated perforations.

Anchor, Fishing Harbor, Lomé — A199

1978, Apr. 26 **Photo.** ***Perf. 13***

997 A199 25fr multi .25 .25
Nos. 997,C340-C342 (4) 3.05 1.15

Venera I, USSR — A200

Designs: 30fr, Pioneer, US, horiz. 50fr, Venera, fuel base and antenna.

1978, May 8 **Litho.** ***Perf. 14***

998 A200 20fr multi	.25	.25
999 A200 30fr multi	.30	.25
1000 A200 50fr multi	.40	.25
Nos. 998-1000,C343-C345 (6)	3.90	1.60

US Pioneer and USSR Venera space missions.

Soccer — A201

50fr, Soccer players and Argentina '78 emblem.

1978, June 5 ***Perf. 14***

1001 A201 30fr multi	.30	.25
1002 A201 50fr multi	.45	.25
Nos. 1001-1002,C346-C349 (6)	5.40	1.95

11th World Cup Soccer Championship, Argentina, June 1-25.

Celerifère, 1818 — A202

History of the Bicycle: 50fr, First bicycle sidecar, c. 1870, vert.

Perf. 13x14, 14x13

1978, July 10 **Photo.**

1003 A202 25fr multi	.35	.25
1004 A202 50fr multi	.75	.25
Nos. 1003-1004,C350-C353 (6)	4.25	1.70

Thomas A. Edison, Sound Waves — A203

Design: 50fr, Victor's His Master's Voice phonograph, 1905, and dancing couple.

1978, July 8 **Photo.** ***Perf. 14x13***

1005 A203 30fr multicolored	.30	.25
1006 A203 50fr multicolored	.40	.25
Nos. 1005-1006,C354-C357 (6)	5.35	1.85

Centenary of the phonograph, invented by Thomas Alva Edison.

Dunant's Birthplace, Geneva — A204

Designs: 10fr, Henri Dunant and red cross. 25fr, Help on battlefield, 1864, and red cross.

1978, Sept. 4 **Photo.** ***Perf. 14x13***

1007 A204 5fr Prus bl & red	.25	.25
1008 A204 10fr red brn & red	.25	.25
1009 A204 25fr grn & red	.25	.25
Nos. 1007-1009,C358 (4)	1.20	1.00

Dunant (1828-1910), founder of Red Cross.

Threshing, by Raoul Dufy A205

50fr, Horsemen on Seashore, by Paul Gauguin.

1978, Nov. 6 **Litho.** ***Perf. 14***

1010 A205 25fr multi	.30	.25
1011 A205 50fr multi	.50	.25
Nos. 1010-1011,C359-C362 (6)	4.70	2.15

Eiffel Tower, Paris — A206

1978, Nov. 27 **Photo.** ***Perf. 14x13***

1012 A206 50fr multi	.60	.25
Nos. 1012,C365-C367 (4)	3.45	1.70

Centenary of the Congress of Paris.

Virgin and Child, by Antonello da Messina — A207

Paintings (Virgin and Child): 30fr, by Cario Crivelli. 50fr, by Francesco del Cossa.

1978, Dec. 18 **Litho.** ***Perf. 14***

1013 A207 20fr multi	.30	.25
1014 A207 30fr multi	.40	.25
1015 A207 50fr multi	.50	.25
Nos. 1013-1015,C368-C370 (6)	4.65	2.20

Christmas.

Capt. Cook's Ship off New Zealand — A208

Design: 50fr, Endeavour in drydock, N.E. Coast of Australia, horiz.

1979, Feb. 12 **Litho.** ***Perf. 14***

1016 A208 25fr multi	.25	.25
1017 A208 50fr multi	.45	.25
Nos. 1016-1017,C371-C374 (6)	4.25	2.55

200th death anniv. of Capt. James Cook.

Entry into Jerusalem — A209

Easter: 40fr, The Last Supper, horiz. 50fr, Descent from the Cross, horiz.

1979, Apr. 9

1018 A209 30fr multi	.30	.25
1019 A209 40fr multi	.35	.25
1020 A209 50fr multi	.40	.25
Nos. 1018-1020,C375-C377 (6)	3.70	2.10

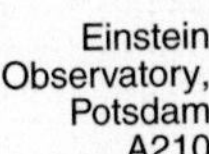

Einstein Observatory, Potsdam A210

Design: 50fr, Einstein and James Ramsay MacDonald, Berlin, 1931.

1979, July 2 **Photo.** ***Perf. 14x13***

1021 A210 35fr multi	.30	.25
1022 A210 50fr multi	.45	.25
Nos. 1021-1022,C380-C383 (6)	4.65	2.45

Albert Einstein (1879-1955), theoretical physicist.

Children and Children's Village Emblem — A211

IYC: 10fr, Mother and children. 15fr, Map of Africa, Children's Village emblem, horiz. 20fr, Woman and children walking to Children's Village, horiz. 25fr, Children sitting under African fan palm. 30fr, Map of Togo with location of Children's Villages.

1979, July 30 **Photo.** ***Perf. 14x13***

1023 A211 5fr multi	.25	.25
1024 A211 10fr multi	.25	.25
1025 A211 15fr multi	.25	.25
1026 A211 20fr multi	.25	.25
1027 A211 25fr multi	.25	.25
1028 A211 30fr multi	.25	.25
a. Souv. sheet of 2, #1027-1028	.75	.45
Nos. 1023-1028 (6)	1.50	1.50

Man Planting Tree — A212

1979, Aug. 13 ***Perf. 14x13***

1029 A212 50fr lilac & green	.60	.25

Second Arbor Day. See No. C384.

Sir Rowland Hill (1795-1879), Originator of Penny Postage — A213

30fr, French mail-sorting office, 18th cent., horiz. 50fr, Mailbox, Paris, 1850.

1979, Aug. 27

1030 A213 20fr multi	.25	.25
1031 A213 30fr multi	.30	.25
1032 A213 50fr multi	.40	.25
Nos. 1030-1032,C385-C387 (6)	3.80	2.05

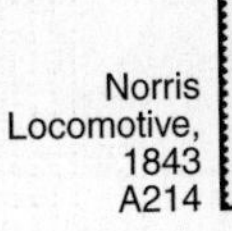

Norris Locomotive, 1843 A214

35fr, Stephenson's "Rocket," 1829, vert.

1979, Oct. 1 **Litho.** ***Perf. 14***

1033 A214 35fr multi	.50	.25
1034 A214 50fr multi	.55	.25
Nos. 1033-1034,C388-C391 (6)	4.90	2.60

Olympic Flame, Lake Placid 80 Emblem, Slalom — A215

1980 Olympic Emblems, Olympic Flame and: 30fr, Yachting 50fr, Discus.

1979, Oct. 18 **Litho.** ***Perf. 13½***

1035 A215 20fr multi	.25	.25
1036 A215 30fr multi	.25	.25
1037 A215 50fr multi	.55	.25
Nos. 1035-1037,C392-C394 (6)	3.90	2.05

13th Winter Olympic Games, Lake Placid, NY, 2/12-24/80 (90fr); 22nd Summer Olympic Games, Moscow, 7/19-8/3/80.

Catholic Priests — A216

Design: 30fr, Native praying, vert.

1979, Oct. 29 ***Perf. 13x14***

1038 A216 30fr multi	.25	.25
1039 A216 50fr multi	.40	.25
Nos. 1038-1039,C396-C397 (4)	1.70	1.05

Religions in Togo.

Astronaut Walking on Moon — A217

Design: 50fr, Space capsule orbiting moon.

1979, Nov. 5

1040 A217 35fr multi	.30	.25
1041 A217 50fr multi	.40	.25
Nos. 1040-1041,C398-C401 (6)	5.25	2.65

Apollo 11 moon landing, 10th anniversary.

Telecom 79 — A218

1979, Nov. 26 **Photo.** ***Perf. 13x14***

1042 A218 50fr multi	.35	.25

3rd World Telecommunications Exhibition, Geneva, Sept. 20-26. See No. C402.

Holy Family — A219

Christmas: 30fr, Virgin and Child. 50fr, Adoration of the Kings.

1979, Dec. 17 **Litho.** ***Perf. 14***

1043 A219 20fr multi	.25	.25
1044 A219 30fr multi	.30	.25
1045 A219 50fr multi	.50	.25
Nos. 1043-1045,C403-C405 (6)	4.15	2.20

Rotary Emblem — A220

Rotary Emblem and: 30fr, Anniversary emblem. 40fr, Paul P. Harris, Rotary founder.

1980, Jan. 14
1046 A220 25fr multi .25 .25
1047 A220 30fr multi .35 .25
1048 A220 40fr multi .40 .25
Nos. 1046-1048,C406-C408 (6) 4.25 2.45

Rotary International, 75th anniversary.

Biathlon, Lake Placid '80 Emblem — A221

1980, Jan. 31 Litho. *Perf. 13½*
1049 A221 50fr multi .40 .25
Nos. 1049,C409-C411 (4) 3.00 1.50

13th Winter Olympic Games, Lake Placid, NY, Feb. 12-24. See No. C412.

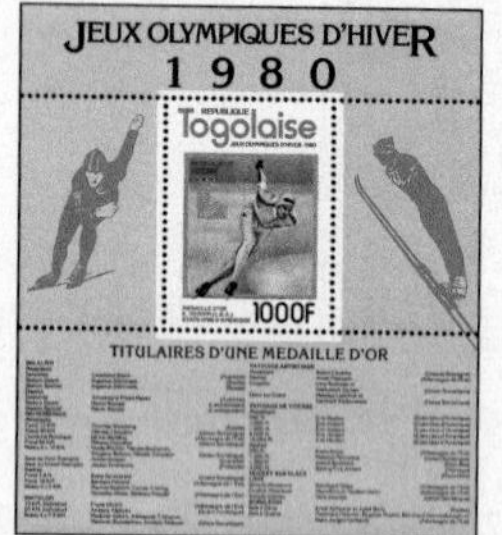

1980 Winter Olympics, Lake Placid — A221a

Gold medalist: No. 1049F, Hanni Wenzel, Liechtenstein, women's slalom. No. 1049G, Eric Heiden, US, men's speed skating. No. 1049H, Jouko Tormanen, Finland, 90-meter ski jumping. No. 1049I, Erich Schaerer, Josef Benz, Switzerland, 2-man bobsled. No. 1049J, US, ice hockey.

1980 Litho. *Perf. 11*
1049A A221a 1000fr multi 20.00 4.50
1049B A221a 1000fr multi 20.00 4.50
1049C A221a 1000fr multi 20.00 4.50
1049D A221a 1000fr multi 20.00 4.50
1049E A221a 1000fr multi 20.00 4.50
Nos. 1049A-1049E (5) 100.00 22.50

Souvenir Sheets
1049F A221a 1000fr gold & multi —
1049G A221a 1000fr gold & multi —
1049H A221a 1000fr gold & multi —
1049I A221a 1000fr gold & multi —
1049J A221a 1000fr gold & multi —

Exist imperf.

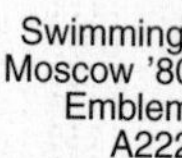

Swimming, Moscow '80 Emblem A222

1980, Feb. 29 Litho. *Perf. 13½*
1050 A222 20fr shown .25 .25
1051 A222 30fr Gymnastics .30 .25
1052 A222 50fr Running .50 .25
Nos. 1050-1052,C413-C415 (6) 5.20 3.25

22nd Summer Olympic Games, Moscow, July 19-Aug. 3.

Christ and the Angels, by Andrea Mantegna — A223

Easter 1980 (Paintings by): 40fr, Carlo Crivelli. 50fr, Jacopo Pontormo.

1980, Mar. 31 *Perf. 14*
1053 A223 30fr multi .30 .25
1054 A223 40fr multi .55 .25
1055 A223 50fr multi .55 .25
Nos. 1053-1055,C416-C418 (6) 4.05 2.00

Jet over Map of Africa — A224

1980, Mar. 24 Litho. *Perf. 12½*
1056 A224 50fr multi .60 .25

ASECNA (Air Safety Board), 20th anniv. See No. C419.

Nos. 979, 984 Ovptd. "Londres / 1980"

Litho. & Embossed

1980, May 6 *Perf. 11*
1056A A192 1000fr gold & multi 6.50 —

Souvenir Sheet
1056B A192 1000fr gold & multi 7.25 —

12th World Telecommunications Day — A225

1980, May 17 Photo. *Perf. 14x13½*
1057 A225 50fr multi .50 .25

See No. C420.

Red Cross over Globe Showing Lomé, Togo — A226

1980, June 16 Photo. *Perf. 14x13*
1058 A226 50fr multi .60 .25

Togolese Red Cross. See No. C421.

Jules Verne (1828-1905), French Science Fiction Writer — A227

50fr, Shark (20,000 Leagues Under the Sea).

1980, July 14 Litho. *Perf. 14*
1059 A227 30fr multi .30 .25
1060 A227 50fr multi .55 .25
Nos. 1059-1060,C422-C425 (6) 4.05 2.00

Baroness James de Rothschild, by Ingres — A228

Paintings by Jean Auguste Dominique Ingres (1780-1867): 30fr, Napoleon I on Imperial Throne. 40fr, Don Pedro of Toledo and Henri IV.

1980, Aug. 29 Litho. *Perf. 14*
1061 A228 25fr multi .25 .25
1062 A228 30fr multi .35 .25
1063 A228 40fr multi .40 .25
Nos. 1061-1063,C426-C428 (6) 4.25 2.05

Minnie Holding Mirror for Leopard — A229

Disney Characters and Animals from Fazao Reserve: 2fr, Goofy (Dingo) cleaning teethof hippopotamus. 3fr, Donald holding snout of crocodile. 4fr, Donald dangling over clifffrom horn of rhinoceros. 5fr, Goofy riding water buffalo. 10fr, Monkey taking picture of Mickey. 100fr, Mickey as doctor examining giraffe with sore throat. 200fr, Pluto in party hat. No. 1071, Elephant giving shower to Goofy. No. 1072, Lion carrying Goofy by seat of his pants. No. 1072A, Pluto.

1980, Sept. 15 *Perf. 11*
1064 A229 1fr multi .25 .25
1065 A229 2fr multi .25 .25
1066 A229 3fr multi .25 .25
1067 A229 4fr multi .25 .25
1068 A229 5fr multi .25 .25
1069 A229 10fr multi .25 .25
1070 A229 100fr multi .75 .35
1070A A229 200fr multi 1.50 .75
1071 A229 300fr multi 2.25 1.10
Nos. 1064-1071 (9) 6.00 3.70

Souvenir Sheets
1072 A229 300fr multi 8.00 3.00
1072A A229 300fr multi 4.00 1.50

50th anniv. of the Disney character Pluto.

Market Activities, Women Preparing Meat — A230

1fr, Grinding savo. 3fr, Truck going to market. 4fr, Unloading produce. 5fr, Sugar cane vendor. 6fr, Barber curling child's hair, vert. 7fr, Vegetable vendor. 8fr, Sampling mangos, vert. 9fr, Grain vendor. 10fr, Spiced fish vendor. 15fr, Clay pot vendor. 20fr, Straw baskets. 25fr, Selling lemons and onions, vert. 30fr, Straw baskets, diff. 40fr, Shore market. 45fr, Vegetable stall. 50fr, Women carrying produce, vert. 60fr, Rice wine.

1980-81 *Perf. 14*
1073 A230 1fr multicolored .25 .25
1074 A230 2fr shown .25 .25
1075 A230 3fr multicolored .25 .25
1076 A230 4fr multicolored .25 .25
1077 A230 5fr multicolored .25 .25
1078 A230 6fr multicolored .25 .25
1079 A230 7fr multicolored .25 .25
1080 A230 8fr multicolored .25 .25
1081 A230 9fr multicolored .25 .25
1082 A230 10fr multicolored .25 .25
1083 A230 15fr multicolored .25 .25
1084 A230 20fr multicolored .25 .25
1085 A230 25fr multicolored .25 .25
1086 A230 30fr multicolored .25 .25
1087 A230 40fr multicolored .30 .25
1087A A230 45fr multicolored .30 .25
1088 A230 50fr multicolored .40 .25
1088A A230 60fr multicolored .40 .25
Nos. 1073-1088A (18) 4.90 4.50

Issued: 45fr, 60fr, 3/8/81; others, 3/17/80.
Nos. 1087A, 1088A dated 1980.
See Nos. C440-C445, J68-J71. For overprints see Nos. C486-C487.

Commemorative Wreath — A231

Famous Men of the Decade: 40fr, Mao Tse-tung, vert.

1980, Feb. 11 *Perf. 14x13*
1089 A231 25fr multi .40 .25
1090 A231 40fr emer grn & dk grn .60 .25
Nos. 1089-1090,C429-C431 (5) 5.10 1.80

World Tourism Conference, Manila, Sept. 27 — A232

1980, Sept. 15 Litho. *Perf. 14*
1091 A232 50fr Hotel tourism emblem, vert. .35 .25
1092 A232 150fr shown 1.10 .75

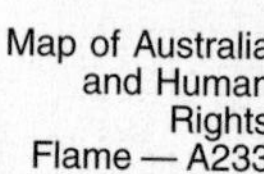

Map of Australia and Human Rights Flame — A233

1980, Oct. 13 Photo. *Perf. 13x14*
1093 A233 30fr shown .30 .25
1094 A233 50fr Europe and Asia map .50 .25
Nos. 1093-1094,C432-C433 (4) 2.20 1.25

Declaration of Human Rights, 30th anniv.

Nos. 980, 985 Ovptd. in Gold & Black

Litho. & Embossed

1980, Nov. 24 *Perf. 11*
1094A A192 1000fr gold & multi 8.50 —

Souvenir Sheet
1094B A192 1000fr gold & multi 7.00 —

No. 1094B ovptd. with additional text and black bars in sheet margin.

Melk Monastery, Austria, 18th Century — A234

30fr, Tarragon Cathedral, Spain, 12th cent. 50fr, St. John the Baptist, Florence, 1964.

Perf. 14½x13½

1980, Dec. 22 Litho.
1095 A234 20fr shown .25 .25
1096 A234 30fr multicolored .35 .25
1097 A234 50fr multicolored .55 .25
Nos. 1095-1097,C435-C437 (6) 4.35 2.25

Christmas.

African Postal Union, 5th Anniversary — A235

1980, Dec. 24 Photo. *Perf. 13½*
1098 A235 100fr multi .75 .35

February 2nd Hotel Opening — A236

1981, Feb. 2 Litho. *Perf. 12½x13*
1099 A236 50fr multi .60 .25

See No. C437B.

A236a

1981, Dec. 21 Litho. *Perf. 12½*
1100 A236a 70fr lt grn & multi .70 .35

West African Rice Development Assoc.
See No. C461.

A237

Easter (Rembrandt Paintings): 30fr, Rembrandt's Father. 40fr, Self-portrait. 50fr, Artist's father as an old man. 60fr, Rider on Horseback.

1981, Apr. 13 *Perf. 14½x13½*
1101 A237 30fr multi .35 .25
1102 A237 40fr multi .40 .25
1103 A237 50fr multi .50 .25
1104 A237 60fr multi .60 .30
Nos. 1101-1104,C438-C439 (6) 4.50 2.15

Wedding of Prince Charles and Lady Diana Spencer — A237a
1105

1981, July 29 Litho. *Perf. 11*
1105 A237a 1000fr gold & multi 4.00 2.50

Souvenir Sheet
Litho. & Embossed
1106 A237a 1000fr Charles & Diana, diff. 5.00 3.00

No. 1105 printed with embossed se-tenant label.
For overprints see Nos. 1143A-1143B.

Red-headed Rock Fowl — A238

40fr, Splendid sunbird. 60fr, Violet-backed starling. 90fr, Red-collared widowbird.

1981, Aug. 10 *Perf. 13½x14½*
1107 A238 30fr shown .45 .25
1108 A238 40fr multicolored .55 .25
1109 A238 60fr multicolored .90 .25
1110 A238 90fr multicolored 1.40 .30
Nos. 1107-1110,C446-C447 (6) 5.60 1.65

1982 World Soccer Championships, Spain — A238a

Flags (Nos. 1110A-1110E) or Players (Nos. 1110F-1110J) and stadiums; 1000fr: Nos. 1110A, 1110F, Athletico de Madrid. Nos. 1110B, 1110G, Real Madrid C.F. Nos. 1110C, 1110H, R.C.D. Espanol. Nos. 1110D, 1110I, Real Zaragoza. Nos. 1110E, 1110J, Valencia.

Litho. & Embossed
1981, Aug. 17 *Perf. 11*
1110A-1110E A238a Set of 5 40.00 10.00

Souvenir Sheets
1110F-1110J A238a Set of 2 35.00 10.00

African Postal Union Ministers, 6th Council Meeting, July 28-20 — A239

1981, Aug. 31 Litho. *Perf. 12½*
1111 A239 70fr Dish antenna .50 .25
1112 A239 90fr Computer operator, vert. .70 .35
1113 A239 105fr Map .80 .40
Nos. 1111-1113 (3) 2.00 1.00

Intl. Year of the Disabled — A240

1981, Aug. 31 *Perf. 14*
1114 A240 70fr Blind man .85 .45
Nos. 1114,C448-C449 (3) 3.25 1.70

See No. C449A.

Woman with Hat, by Picasso, 1961 — A241

Picasso Birth Centenary: Sculptures.

1981, Sept. 14 *Perf. 14½x13½*
1116 A241 25fr shown .30 .25
1117 A241 50fr She-goat .50 .25
1118 A241 60fr Violin, 1915 .55 .25
Nos. 1116-1118,C450-C452 (6) 5.75 2.55

Aix-la-Chapelle Cathedral, Germany — A242

World Heritage Year: 40fr, Geyser, Yellowstone Natl. Park. 50fr, Nahanni Natl. Park, Canada. 60fr, Stone churches, Ethiopia.

1981, Sept. 28 *Perf. 13½x14½*
1119 A242 30fr multi .25 .25
1120 A242 40fr multi .30 .25
1121 A242 50fr multi .40 .25
1122 A242 60fr multi .50 .35
Nos. 1119-1122,C453-C454 (6) 4.00 2.35

Yuri Gagarin's Vostok I, 20th. A243

Space Anniversaries: 50fr, 20th Anniv. of Alan Shepard's Flight. 60fr, Lunar Orbiter I, 15th.

1981, Nov. *Perf. 14*
1123 A243 25fr multi .25 .25
1124 A243 50fr multi .45 .25
1125 A243 60fr multi .55 .25
Nos. 1123-1125,C455-C456 (5) 2.60 1.25

Christmas — A244

Rubens Paintings: 20fr, Adoration of the Kings. 30fr, Adoration of the Shepherds. 50fr, St. Catherine.

Perf. 14½x13½
1981, Dec. 10 Litho.
1126 A244 20fr multi .25 .25
1127 A244 30fr multi .25 .25
1128 A244 50fr multi .40 .25
Nos. 1126-1128,C457-C459 (6) 5.20 2.75

15th Anniv. of Natl. Liberation A245

1982, Jan. 13 Litho. *Perf. 12½*
1129 A245 70fr Dove, flag .70 .35
1130 A245 90fr Citizens, Pres. Eyadema, vert. .90 .45
Nos. 1129-1130,C462-C463 (4) 3.20 1.55

Scouting Year — A246

1982, Feb. 25 Litho. *Perf. 14*
1131 A246 70fr Pitching tent .55 .25
Nos. 1131,C464-C467 (5) 4.50 1.80

Easter — A247

Designs: The Ten Commandments.

1982, Mar. 15 *Perf. 14x14½*
1132 A247 10fr multi .25 .25
1133 A247 25fr multi .25 .25
1134 A247 30fr multi .25 .25
1135 A247 45fr multi .30 .25
1136 A247 50fr multi .35 .25
1137 A247 70fr multi .45 .25
1138 A247 90fr multi .60 .30
Nos. 1132-1138,C469-C470 (9) 3.95 2.55

Papilio Dardanus — A248

1982, July 15 Litho. *Perf. 14½x14*
1139 A248 15fr shown .35 .25
1140 A248 20fr Belenois calypso .55 .25
1141 A248 25fr Palla decius .55 .25
Nos. 1139-1141,C474-C475 (5) 4.80 1.60

1982 World Cup — A249

Designs: Various soccer players.

1982, July 26 *Perf. 14x14½*
1142 A249 25fr multi .25 .25
1143 A249 45fr multi .35 .25
Nos. 1142-1143,C477-C479 (5) 4.90 2.50

For overprints see Nos. 1150-1155.

Nos. 1105-1106 Overprinted on one or two lines

1982, Oct. 28 Litho. *Perf. 11*
1143A A237a 1000fr gold & multi 8.00 4.00

Souvenir Sheet
Litho. & Embossed
1143B A237a 1000fr gold & multi 9.25 3.50

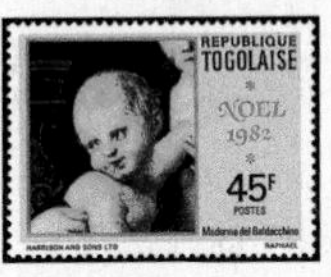

Christmas A250

Madonna of Baldacchino, by Raphael. #1144-1148 show details; #1149 entire painting.

1982, Dec. 24 Litho. *Perf. 14½x14*
1144 A250 45fr multi .45 .25
1145 A250 70fr multi .65 .25
1146 A250 105fr multi .85 .25
1147 A250 130fr multi 1.20 .30
1148 A250 150fr multi 1.40 .35
Nos. 1144-1148 (5) 4.55 1.40

Souvenir Sheet
Perf. 14x14½
1149 A250 500fr multi, vert. 3.75 1.75

Nos. 1142-1143, C477-C480 Overprinted: VAINQUER / COUPE DU MONDE / FOOTBALL 82 / "ITALIE"

1983, Jan. 31 Litho. *Perf. 14x14½*
1150 A249 25fr multi .25 .25
1151 A249 45fr multi .35 .25
1152 A249 105fr multi .75 .35
1153 A249 200fr multi 1.40 .55
1154 A249 300fr multi 2.10 .85
Nos. 1150-1154 (5) 4.85 2.25

Souvenir Sheet
1155 A249 500fr multi 4.25 2.50

Italy's victory in 1982 World Cup. Nos. 1152-1155 airmail.

20th Anniv. of West African Monetary Union (1982) — A251

1983, May Litho. *Perf. 12½x12*
1156 A251 70fr Map .60 .25
1157 A251 90fr Emblem .80 .30

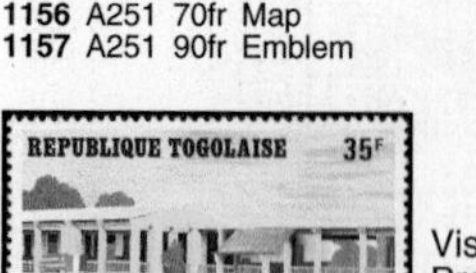

Visit of Pres. Mitterand of France, Jan. 13-15 A252

35fr, Sokode Regional Hospital. 45fr, Citizens joining hands. 70fr, Soldiers, vert. 90fr, Pres. Mitterand, vert. 105fr, Pres. Eyadema, Mitterand, vert. 130fr, Greeting crowd.

1983, Jan. 13 Litho. *Perf. 13*
1158 A252 35fr multicolored .25 .25
a. Souvenir sheet, imperf. 1.00 .55
1159 A252 45fr multicolored .40 .25
a. Souvenir sheet, imperf. 1.00 .55
1160 A252 70fr multicolored .60 .25
a. Souvenir sheet, imperf. 1.00 .55
1161 A252 90fr multicolored .70 .30
a. Souvenir sheet, imperf. 1.00 .55
1162 A252 105fr multicolored .90 .35
a. Souvenir sheet, imperf. 1.00 .55
1163 A252 130fr multicolored 1.25 .45
a. Souvenir sheet, imperf. 1.00 .55
Nos. 1158-1163 (6) 4.10 1.85

Nos. 1161-1163 airmail.

Easter A253

Paintings: 35fr, Mourners at the Death of Christ, by Bellini. 70fr, Crucifixion, by Raphael. 90fr, Descent from the Cross, by Carracci. 500fr Christ, by Reni.

1983 Litho. *Perf. 13½x14½*
1164 A253 35fr multi .35 .25
1165 A253 70fr multi, vert. .55 .25
1166 A253 90fr multi .85 .25
Nos. 1164-1166 (3) 1.75 .75

Souvenir Sheet
Perf. 14½x13½
1167 A253 500fr multi 3.75 1.75

90fr, 500fr airmail.

Folkdances A254

1983, Dec. 1 *Perf. 14½x14*
1168 A254 70fr Kondona .55 .25
1169 A254 90fr Kondona, diff. .65 .25
1170 A254 105fr Toubole .85 .30
1171 A254 130fr Adjogbo 1.00 .25
Nos. 1168-1171 (4) 3.05 1.05

90fr, 105fr, 130fr airmail.

World Communications Year — A255

1983, June 20 Litho. *Perf. 14x14½*
1172 A255 70fr Drummer .60 .25
1173 A255 90fr Modern communication .70 .25

90fr airmail.

Christmas A256

70fr, Catholic Church, Kante. 90fr, Altar, Dapaong Cathedral. 105fr, Protestant Church, Dapaong.
500fr, Ecumenical Church, Pya.

1983, Dec. *Perf. 13½x14½*
1174 A256 70fr multicolored .55 .25
1175 A256 90fr multicolored .65 .25
1176 A256 105fr multicolored .80 .25
Nos. 1174-1176 (3) 2.00 .75

Souvenir Sheet
1177 A256 500fr multicolored 4.50 1.75

90fr, 105fr, 500fr airmail.

Sarakawa Presidential Assassination Attempt, 10th Anniv. — A257

70fr, Wrecked plane. 90fr, Plane, diff. 120fr, Memorial Hall. 270fr, Pres. Eyadema statue, vert.

1984, Jan. 24 Litho. *Perf. 13*
1178 A257 70fr multicolored .60 .25
1179 A257 90fr multicolored .70 .25
1180 A257 120fr multicolored 1.00 .25
1181 A257 270fr multicolored 2.25 .45
Nos. 1178-1181 (4) 4.55 1.20

120fr, 270fr airmail.

20th Anniv. of World Food Program (1983) — A258

1984, May 2 Litho. *Perf. 13*
1182 A258 35fr Orchard .25 .25
1183 A258 70fr Fruit tree .50 .25
1184 A258 90fr Rice paddy .65 .25
Nos. 1182-1184 (3) 1.40 .75

Souvenir Sheet
1185 A258 300fr Village, horiz. 3.00 1.90

25th Anniv. of Council of Unity — A259

1984, May 29 *Perf. 12*
1186 A259 70fr multi .55 .25
1187 A259 90fr multi .70 .25

Easter 1984 — A260

Various stained-glass windows.

1984 Litho. *Perf. 14x14½*
1188 A260 70fr multi .55 .25
1189 A260 90fr multi .65 .25
1190 A260 120fr multi .85 .25
1191 A260 270fr multi 1.90 .50
1192 A260 300fr multi 2.10 .55
Nos. 1188-1192 (5) 6.05 1.80

Souvenir Sheet
1193 A260 500fr multi 4.50 3.50

Nos. 1189-1193 airmail.

Centenary of German-Togolese Friendship — A261

#1194, Degbenou Catholic Mission, 1893. #1195, Kara Bridge, 1911. #1196, Treaty Site, Baguida, 1884. #1197, Degbenou Students, 1893. #1198, Sansane Administrative Post, 1908. #1199, Adjido Official School.
#1200, Sokode Cotton Market, 1910. #1201, William Fountain, Atakpame, 1906. #1202, Lome Main Street, 1895, No. 19. #1203, Police, 1905. #1204, Lome Railroad Construction. #1205, Governor's Palace, Lome, 1905. #1206, No. 9, Commerce Street, Lome.
#1207, Nos. 10, 17. #1208, Lome Wharf, 1903. #1209, G. Nachtigal. #1210, Wilhelm II. #1211, O.F. de Bismark. #1212, J. de Puttkamer. #1213, A. Koehler. #1214, W. Horn. #1215, J.G. de Zech. #1216, E. Bruckner. #1217, A.F. de Mecklenburg. #1218, H.G. de Doering. #1219, Land Development, 1908.
#1220, Postal Courier, No. 8. #1221, Treaty Signers, 1885. 150fr, German & Togolese Children, Flags. #1223, Aneho Line Locomotive, 1905. #1224, Mallet Locomotive, 1907. #1225, German Ship "Mowe," 1884. #1226, "La Sophie," 1884. 300fr, Pres. Eyadema, Helmut Kohl.

1984, July 5 Litho. *Perf. 13*
1194 A261 35fr multi .50 .25
1195 A261 35fr multi .50 .25
1196 A261 35fr multi, vert. .50 .25
1197 A261 35fr multi .50 .25
1198 A261 35fr multi .50 .25
1199 A261 35fr multi .50 .25
1200 A261 35fr multi .50 .25
1201 A261 45fr multi, vert. .50 .25
1202 A261 45fr multi .50 .25
1203 A261 45fr multi .50 .25
1204 A261 45fr multi .50 .25
1205 A261 45fr multi .50 .25
1206 A261 45fr multi .50 .25
1207 A261 70fr multi .60 .25
1208 A261 70fr multi .60 .25
1209 A261 90fr multi, vert. .75 .25
1210 A261 90fr multi, vert. .75 .25
1211 A261 90fr multi, vert. .75 .25
1212 A261 90fr multi, vert. .75 .25
1213 A261 90fr multi, vert. .75 .25
1214 A261 90fr multi, vert. .75 .25
1215 A261 90fr multi, vert. .75 .25
1216 A261 90fr multi, vert. .75 .25
1217 A261 90fr multi, vert. .75 .25
1218 A261 90fr multi, vert. .75 .25
1219 A261 90fr multi .75 .25
1220 A261 120fr multi, vert. 1.00 .25
1221 A261 120fr multi 1.00 .25
1222 A261 150fr multi, vert. 1.25 .25
1223 A261 270fr multi 2.25 .45
1224 A261 270fr multi 2.25 .45
1225 A261 270fr multi 2.25 .45
1226 A261 270fr multi 2.25 .45
1227 A261 300fr multi 2.40 .50
Nos. 1194-1227 (34) 30.60 9.55

Souvenir sheets of one exist for each design. Stamp size: 65x80mm. Value, set of 34, $35.

Donald Duck, 50th Anniv. — A262

1fr, Donald, Chip. 2fr, Donald, Chip and Dale. 3fr, Louie, Chip and Dale. 5fr, Donald, Chip. 10fr, Daisy Duck, Donald. 15fr, Goofy, Donald. 105fr, Huey, Dewey and Louie. 500fr, Nephews, Donald. No. 1238, 1000fr, Nephews, Donald.
No. 1239, Surprised Donald. No. 1240, Perplexed Donald.

1984, Sept. 21 Litho. *Perf. 11*
1230 A262 1fr multi .55 .25
1231 A262 2fr multi .55 .25
1232 A262 3fr multi .55 .25
1233 A262 5fr multi .55 .25
1234 A262 10fr multi .55 .25
1235 A262 15fr multi .55 .25
1236 A262 105fr multi .80 .25
1237 A262 500fr multi 3.75 .70
1238 A262 1000fr multi 8.25 1.40
Nos. 1230-1238 (9) 16.10 3.85

Souvenir Sheets
Perf. 14
1239 A262 1000fr multi 7.50 7.50
1240 A262 1000fr multi 7.50 7.50

Nos. 1236-1240 airmail.
For overprints see Nos. C551-C554.

Endangered Mammals — A263

45fr, Manatee swimming. 70fr, Manatee eating. 90fr, Manatees floating. 105fr, Young manatee, mother.
No. 1245, Olive Colobus monkey, vert. No. 1246, Galago (Bushbaby)

1984, Oct. 1 Litho. *Perf. 15x14½*
1241 A263 45fr multi 1.60 .50
1242 A263 70fr multi 2.25 .50
1243 A263 90fr multi 2.25 1.00
1244 A263 105fr multi 2.75 1.00
Nos. 1241-1244 (4) 8.85 3.00

Souvenir Sheets
Perf. 14x15, 15x14
1245 A263 1000fr multi 10.00 6.00
1246 A263 1000fr multi 10.00 6.00

Nos. 1243-1246 airmail. See #1444-1447.

Birth Centenary of Eleanor Roosevelt A264

90fr, Mrs. Roosevelt, Statue of Liberty.

1984, Oct. 10 Litho. *Perf. 13½*
1247 A264 70fr shown .55 .25
1248 A264 90fr multicolored .70 .25

No. 1248 airmail.

Classic Automobiles A265

1984, Nov. 15 Litho. *Perf. 15*
1249 A265 1fr 1947 Bristol .25 .25
1250 A265 2fr 1925 Frazer Nash .25 .25
1251 A265 3fr 1950 Healey .25 .25
1252 A265 4fr 1925 Kissell .25 .25
1253 A265 50fr 1927 La Salle .80 .25
1254 A265 90fr 1921 Minerva .65 .25
1255 A265 500fr 1950 Morgan 4.00 .70
1256 A265 1000fr 1921 Napier 8.00 1.40
Nos. 1249-1256 (8) 14.45 3.60

Souvenir Sheets
1257 A265 1000fr 1941 Nash 8.00 2.00
1258 A265 1000fr 1903 Peugeot 8.00 2.00

Nos. 1254-1258 airmail.
For overprints see Nos. 1328-1331, C542-C544, C564-C565.

Christmas — A266

70fr, Connetable Madonna. 290fr, Cowper Madonna. 300fr, Alba Madonna. 500fr, Madonna of the Curtain.
1000fr, Madonna with Child.

Perf. 14½x13½
1984, Nov. 23 Litho.
1259 A266 70fr multi .50 .25
1260 A266 290fr multi 2.00 .50
1261 A266 300fr multi 2.10 .55
1262 A266 500fr multi 3.50 .85
Nos. 1259-1262 (4) 8.10 2.15

Souvenir Sheet
1263 A266 1000fr multi 7.00 6.75

Nos. 1260-1263 airmail.

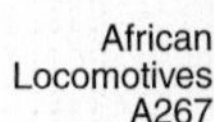

African Locomotives A267

1fr, Decapotable, Madeira. 2fr, 2-6-0, Egypt. 3fr, 4-8-2+2-8-4, Algeria. 4fr, Congo-Ocean diesel. 50fr, 0-4-0+0-4-0, Libya. 90fr, #49, Malawi. 105fr, 1907 Mallet, Togo. 500fr, 4-8-2, Rhodesia. 1000fr, Beyer-Garratt, East Africa.
No. 1273, 2-8-2, Ghana. No. 1274, Locomotive, Senegal.

1984, Nov. 30 Litho. *Perf. 15*

No.	Type	Denomination	Mint	Used
1264	A267	1fr multi	.25	.25
1265	A267	2fr multi	.25	.25
1266	A267	3fr multi	.25	.25
1267	A267	4fr multi	.25	.25
1268	A267	50fr multi	.25	.25
1269	A267	90fr multi	.75	.25
1270	A267	105fr multi	.90	.25
1271	A267	500fr multi	3.75	.80
1272	A267	1000fr multi	6.50	1.60
		Nos. 1264-1272 (9)	13.15	4.15

Souvenir Sheets

No.	Type	Denomination	Mint	Used
1273	A267	1000fr multi	9.00	6.00
1274	A267	1000fr multi	9.00	6.00

Nos. 1269-1274 airmail.
For overprints see Nos. 1343-1346, 1356-1360, C541, C566.

Economic Convention, Lome — A268

100fr, Map of the Americas. 130fr, Map of Eurasia, Africa. 270fr, Map of Asia, Australia. 500fr, President Eyadema.

1984, Dec. 8 Litho. *Perf. 12½*

No.	Type	Denomination	Mint	Used
1275		100fr multicolored	.70	.25
1276		130fr multicolored	1.00	.25
1277		270fr multicolored	1.90	.50
a.	A268	Strip of 3, #1275-1277	3.75	3.75

Souvenir Sheet

No.	Type	Denomination	Mint	Used
1278	A268	500fr multicolored	3.75	3.25

No. 1277a has continuous design.

Intl. Civil Aviation Org., 40th Anniv. — A269

Map of Togo, ICAO emblem and: 70fr, Lockheed Constellation, 1944. 105fr, Boeing 707, 1954. 200fr, Doublas DC-8-61, 1966. 500fr, Bac/Sud Concorde, 1966. 1000fr, Icarus, by Hans Erni.

1984, Oct. 15 Litho. *Perf. 15x14*

No.	Type	Denomination	Mint	Used
1279	A269	70fr multi	.65	.25
1280	A269	105fr multi	.85	.25
1281	A269	200fr multi	1.40	.25
1282	A269	500fr multi	3.75	.75
		Nos. 1279-1282 (4)	6.65	1.50

Souvenir Sheet

No.	Type	Denomination	Mint	Used
1283	A269	1000fr multi	6.50	6.00

Nos. 1280-1283 airmail.

Mosaic of the 12 Apostles, Baptistry of the Aryans, Ravenna, Italy, — A270

Designs: 1fr, St. Paul. 2fr, St. Thomas. 3fr, St. Matthew. 4fr, St. James the Younger. 5fr, St. Simon. 70fr, St. Thaddeaus Judas. 90fr, St. Bartholomew. 105fr, St. Philip. 200fr, St. John. 270fr, St. James the Greater. 400fr, St. Andrew. 500fr, St. Peter. No. 1296, The Last Supper, by Andrea del Castagno, c. 1421-1457, horiz. No, 1297, Coronation of the Virgin, by Raphael, 1483-1520, horiz.

1984, Dec. 14 *Perf. 15*

No.	Type	Denomination	Mint	Used
1284	A270	1fr multi	.25	.25
1285	A270	2fr multi	.25	.25
1286	A270	3fr multi	.25	.25
1287	A270	4fr multi	.25	.25
1288	A270	5fr multi	.25	.25
1289	A270	70fr multi	1.20	.25
1290	A270	90fr multi	.80	.25
1291	A270	105fr multi	.95	.25
1292	A270	200fr multi	1.75	.25
1293	A270	270fr multi	2.25	.35
1294	A270	400fr multi	3.50	.45
1295	A270	500fr multi	4.75	.55
		Nos. 1284-1295 (12)	16.45	3.60

Souvenir Sheets

No.	Type	Denomination	Mint	Used
1296-1297	A270	1000fr each	10.00	4.50

Nos. 1290-1297 airmail.
For overprints see Nos. C545-C547.

Race Horses — A271

1fr, Allez France. 2fr, Arkle, vert. 3fr, Tingle Creek, vert. 4fr, Interco. 50fr, Dawn Run. 90fr, Seattle Slew, vert. 500fr, Nijinsky. No. 1305, 1000fr, Politician.
No. 1306, Shergar. No. 1307, Red Rum.

1985, Jan. 10

No.	Type	Denomination	Mint	Used
1298	A271	1fr multi	.25	.25
1299	A271	2fr multi	.25	.25
1300	A271	3fr multi	.25	.25
1301	A271	4fr multi	.25	.25
1302	A271	50fr multi	.75	.25
1303	A271	90fr multi	.75	.25
1304	A271	500fr multi	3.75	.60
1305	A271	1000fr multi	6.00	1.25
		Nos. 1298-1305 (8)	12.25	3.35

Souvenir Sheets

No.	Type	Denomination	Mint	Used
1306	A271	1000fr multi	7.00	5.50
1307	A271	1000fr multi	7.00	5.50

Nos. 1303-1307 airmail.
For overprints see Nos. 1353-1355A.

Easter A272

Paintings by Raphael (1483-1520) — 70fr, Christ and His Flock. 90fr, Christ and the Fishermen. 135fr, The Blessed Christ, vert. 150fr, The Entombment, vert. 250fr, The Resurrection, vert.
1000fr, The Transfiguration.

Perf. 13½x14½, 14½x13½

1985, Mar. 7

No.	Type	Denomination	Mint	Used
1308	A272	70fr multi	.65	.25
1309	A272	90fr multi	.70	.25
1310	A272	135fr multi	1.20	.25
1311	A272	150fr multi	1.25	.25
1312	A272	250fr multi	2.10	.35
		Nos. 1308-1312 (5)	5.90	1.35

Souvenir Sheet

No.	Type	Denomination	Mint	Used
1313	A272	1000fr multi	8.50	6.50

Nos. 1309-1313 airmail.

Technical & Cultural Cooperation Agency, 15th Anniv. A273

1985, Mar. 20 *Perf. 12½*

No.	Type	Denomination	Mint	Used
1314	A273	70fr multi	.60	.25
1315	A273	90fr multi	.60	.25

Philexafrica '85, Lome A274

No. 1316, Woman carrying fruit basket. No. 1317, Man plowing field.

1985, May 9 *Perf. 13*

No.	Type	Denomination	Mint	Used
1316	A274	200fr multi	1.75	.25
1317	A274	200fr multi	1.75	.25
a.		Pair, #1316-1317 + label	4.00	4.00

Scarification Ritual — A275

25fr, Kabye (Pya). 70fr, Mollah (Kotokoli). 90fr, Maba (Dapaong). 105fr, Kabye (Pagouda). 270fr, Peda.

1985, May 14 *Perf. 14x15*

No.	Type	Denomination	Mint	Used
1318	A275	25fr multi	.60	.25
1319	A275	70fr multi	.60	.25
1320	A275	90fr multi	.60	.25
1321	A275	105fr multi	.75	.25
1322	A275	270fr multi	1.75	.30
		Nos. 1318-1322 (5)	4.30	1.30

Nos. 1320-1322 airmail.

Seashells A276

70fr, Clavatula muricata. 90fr, Marginella desjardini. 120fr, Clavatula nifat. 135fr, Cypraea stercoraria. 270fr, Conus genuanus. 1000fr, Dancers wearing traditional shell decorations.

1985, June 1 *Perf. 15x14*

No.	Type	Denomination	Mint	Used
1323	A276	70fr multi	.85	.25
1324	A276	90fr multi	.90	.25
1325	A276	120fr multi	1.10	.25
1326	A276	135fr multi	1.40	.25
1327	A276	270fr multi	2.75	.35
		Nos. 1323-1327 (5)	7.00	1.35

Souvenir Sheet

No.	Type	Denomination	Mint	Used
1327A	A276	1000fr multi	8.50	6.00

Nos. 1324-1327A airmail.

Nos. 1253, 1256-1258 Overprinted "Exposition Mondiale 1985 / Tsukuba, Japon"

1985, June *Perf. 15*

No.	Type	Denomination	Mint	Used
1328	A265	50fr #1253	1.50	.25
1329	A265	1000fr #1256	11.50	3.50

Souvenir Sheets

No.	Type	Denomination	Mint	Used
1330	A265	1000fr #1257	9.75	3.75
1331	A265	1000fr #1258	9.75	3.75

EXPO '85.

Audubon Birth Bicent. — A277

Illustrations by artist-naturalist J.J. Audubon (1785-1851) — 90fr, Larus bonapartii. 120fr, Pelecanus occidentalis. 135fr, Cassidix mexicanus. 270fr, Aquila chrysaetos. 500fr, Picus erythrocephalus.
1000fr, Dendroica petechia.

1985, Aug. 13 *Perf. 13*

No.	Type	Denomination	Mint	Used
1332	A277	90fr multi	.95	.25
1333	A277	120fr multi	1.25	.25
1334	A277	135fr multi	1.25	.25
1335	A277	270fr multi	2.50	.35
1336	A277	500fr multi	4.50	.60
		Nos. 1332-1336 (5)	10.45	1.70

Souvenir Sheet

No.	Type	Denomination	Mint	Used
1337	A277	1000fr multi	9.50	7.50

Nos. 1332, 1334 and 1336-1337 airmail.

Dove, UN Emblem A278

Kara Port Construction A279

Designs: 115fr, Hands, UN emblem. 250fr, Millet crop, Atalote Research Facility. 500fr, UN, Togo flags, statesmen.

1985, Oct. 24 Litho. *Perf. 13*

No.	Type	Denomination	Mint	Used
1338	A278	90fr multi	.70	.25
1339	A278	115fr multi	.95	.25
1340	A279	150fr multi	1.25	.25
1341	A279	250fr multi	1.60	.35
1342	A279	500fr multi	3.50	.65
		Nos. 1338-1342 (5)	8.00	1.75

UN, 40th anniv. Nos. 1340-1342 are airmail.

Nos. 1267, 1270, 1272, 1273 Ovptd. with Rotary Emblem and "80e ANNIVERSAIRE DU / ROTARY INTERNATIONAL"

1985 Litho. *Perf. 15*

No.	Type	Denomination	Mint	Used
1343	A267	4fr multi	.60	.40
1344	A267	105fr multi	1.10	1.00
1345	A267	1000fr multi	11.00	5.00
		Nos. 1343-1345 (3)	12.70	6.40

Souvenir Sheet

No.	Type	Denomination	Mint	Used
1346	A267	1000fr multi	12.50	6.50

Nos. 1344-1346 are airmail.

Christmas — A280

Religious paintings and statuary: 90fr, The Garden of Roses Madonna. 115fr, Madonna and Child, Byzantine, 11th cent. 150fr, Rest During the Flight to Egypt, by Gerard David (1450-1523). 160fr, African Madonna, 16th cent. 250fr, African Madonna, c. 1900. 500fr, Mystic Madonna, by Sandro Botticelli (1444-1510).

Perf. 14½x13½

1985, Dec. 10 Litho.

No.	Type	Denomination	Mint	Used
1347	A280	90fr multi	.70	.25
1348	A280	115fr multi	.90	.25
1349	A280	150fr multi	1.10	.25
1350	A280	160fr multi	1.10	.25
1351	A280	250fr multi	2.00	.40
		Nos. 1347-1351 (5)	5.80	1.40

Souvenir Sheet

No.	Type	Denomination	Mint	Used
1352	A280	500fr multi	4.50	3.50

Nos. 1348-1352 air airmail. No. 1352 contains one stamp 36x51mm.

Nos. 1302, 1305-1307 Ovptd. "75e Anniversaire / du Scoutisme Feminin"

1986, Jan. *Perf. 15*

No.	Type	Denomination	Mint	Used
1353	A271	50fr multi	1.60	.30
1354	A271	1000fr multi	15.00	3.50

Souvenir Sheet

No.	Type	Denomination	Mint	Used
1355	A271	1000fr multi	9.50	7.50
1355A	A271	1000fr multi	9.50	7.50

Nos. 1354-1355A airmail.

Nos. 1268-1269, 1271, 1273-1274 Ovptd. "150e ANNIVERSAIRE / DE CHEMIN FER 'LUDWIG'"

1985, Dec. 27 Litho. *Perf. 15*

No.	Type	Denomination	Mint	Used
1356	A267	50fr multi	1.25	.35
1357	A267	90fr multi	1.25	.60
1358	A267	500fr multi	8.00	3.50
		Nos. 1356-1358 (3)	10.50	4.45

Souvenir Sheets

No.	Type	Denomination	Mint	Used
1359	A267	1000fr No. 1273	9.00	6.50
1360	A267	1000fr No. 1274	9.00	6.50

Halley's Comet — A281

Designs: 70fr, Suisei space probe, comets. 90fr, Vega-1 probe. 150fr, Space telescope. 200fr, Giotto probe, comet over Togo. 1000fr, Edmond Halley, Sir Isaac Newton.

1986, Mar. 27 *Perf. 13*

1361 A281 70fr multi .70 .25
1362 A281 90fr multi .70 .30
1363 A281 150fr multi 1.20 .45
1364 A281 200fr multi 1.75 .60
Nos. 1361-1364 (4) 4.35 1.60

Souvenir Sheet

1365 A281 1000fr multi 7.00 6.50

Nos. 1362-1365 are airmail.
For overprints see Nos. 1405-1409.

Flowering and Fruit-bearing Plants — A282

70fr, Anacardium occidentale. 90fr, Ananas comosus. 120fr, Persea americana. 135fr, Carica papaya. 290fr, Mangifera indica, vert.

1986, June *Perf. 14*

1366 A282 70fr multi .55 .25
1367 A282 90fr multi .80 .30
1368 A282 120fr multi .90 .40
1369 A282 135fr multi 1.10 .45
1370 A282 290fr multi 2.25 .90
Nos. 1366-1370 (5) 5.60 2.30

Nos. 1368-1370 airmail.

1986 World Cup Soccer Championships, Mexico — A283

Various soccer plays.

1986, May 5 **Litho.** *Perf. 15x14*

1371 A283 70fr multi .55 .25
1372 A283 90fr multi .55 .30
1373 A283 130fr multi .85 .40
1374 A283 300fr multi 2.00 .90
Nos. 1371-1374 (4) 3.95 1.85

Souvenir Sheet

1375 A283 1000fr multi 7.00 5.50

Nos. 1372-1375 are airmail.
For overprints see Nos. 1394-1397.

Mushrooms — A284

70fr, Ramaria moelleriana. 90fr, Hygrocybe firma. 150fr, Kalchbrennera corallocephala. 200fr, Cookeina tricholoma.

1986, June 9 *Perf. 13x12½*

1376 A284 70fr multi 1.10 .25
1377 A284 90fr multi 1.40 .30
1378 A284 150fr multi 2.25 .45
1379 A284 200fr multi 3.00 .60
Nos. 1376-1379 (4) 7.75 1.60

Intl. Youth Year — A285

1986, June *Perf. 13½x14½*

1380 A285 25fr shown .80 .25
1381 A285 90fr Youths, doves 2.10 .30

Dated 1985.

Wrestling — A286

15fr, Single-leg takedown move. 20fr, Completing takedown. 70fr, Pinning combination. 90fr, Riding.

1986, July 16 *Perf. 14x15, 15x14*

1382 A286 15fr multicolored .40 .25
1383 A286 20fr multicolored .40 .25
1384 A286 70fr multicolored .65 .25
1385 A286 90fr multicolored .95 .35
Nos. 1382-1385 (4) 2.40 1.10

Nos. 1384-1385 horiz. No. 1385 is airmail.

Wedding of Prince Andrew and Sarah Ferguson — A287

No. 1386, Sarah Ferguson. No. 1387, Prince Andrew.
No. 1388, Couple.

1986, July 23 *Perf. 14*

1386 A287 10fr multi .50 .25
1387 A287 1000fr multi 6.50 2.75

Souvenir Sheet

1388 A287 1000fr multi 7.50 6.00

Nos. 1387-1388 are airmail.

Easter — A288

Paintings (details): 25fr, 1000fr, The Resurrection, by Andrea Mantegna (1431-1506), vert. 70fr, The Calvary, by Paolo Veronese (1528-1588), vert. 90fr, The Last Supper, by Jacopo Tintoretto (1518-1594). 200fr, Christ at the Tomb, by Alonso Berruguette (1486-1561).

Perf. 14x15, 15x14

1986, Mar. 24 **Litho.**

1389 A288 25fr multi .25 .25
1390 A288 70fr multi .50 .25
1391 A288 90fr multi .75 .30
1392 A288 200fr multi 1.60 .60
Nos. 1389-1392 (4) 3.10 1.40

Souvenir Sheet

1393 A288 1000fr multi 7.50 5.00

Nos. 1391-1393 are airmail.

Nos. 1371-1374 Overprinted

No. 1394

No. 1395

No. 1396

No. 1397

1986, Aug. 4 **Litho.** *Perf. 15x14*

1394 A283 70fr multi .60 .25
1395 A283 90fr multi .75 .30
1396 A283 130fr multi 1.00 .40
1397 A283 300fr multi 2.40 .90
Nos. 1394-1397 (4) 4.75 1.85

Nos. 1395-1397 are airmail.

Hotels A289

1986, Aug. 18 *Perf. 12½*

1398 A289 70fr Fazao .55 .25
1399 A289 90fr Sarakawa .60 .35
1400 A289 120fr Le Lac 1.00 .40
Nos. 1398-1400 (3) 2.15 1.00

Nos. 1399-1400 are airmail.

Keran Natl. Park — A290

1986, Sept. 15 **Litho.** *Perf. 14½*

1401 A290 70fr Wild ducks .95 .25
1402 A290 90fr Antelope 1.10 .25
1403 A290 100fr Elephant 1.25 .30
1404 A290 130fr Waterbuck 1.75 .35
Nos. 1401-1404 (4) 5.05 1.15

Nos. 1402-1404 are airmail.

Nos. 1361-1365 Ovptd. with Halley's Comet Emblem in Silver

1986, Oct. 9 *Perf. 13*

1405 A281 70fr multi 1.60 .25
1406 A281 90fr multi 1.90 .30
1407 A281 150fr multi 3.25 .50
1408 A281 200fr multi 4.25 .65
Nos. 1405-1408 (4) 11.00 1.70

Souvenir Sheet

1409 A281 1000fr multi 21.00 7.25

Nos. 1406-1409 are airmail.

Frescoes from Togoville Church — A291

Togoville Church A292

45fr, Annunciation. 120fr, Nativity. 130fr, Adoration of the Magi. 200fr, Flight into Egypt.

1986, Dec. 22 **Litho.** *Perf. 14½x15*

1410 A291 45fr multicolored .40 .25
1411 A291 120fr multicolored .90 .30
1412 A291 130fr multicolored 1.10 .35
1413 A291 200fr multicolored 1.50 .55
Nos. 1410-1413 (4) 3.90 1.45

Souvenir Sheet

1414 A292 1000fr multicolored 7.00 5.50

Christmas. Nos. 1411-1414 are airmail.

Phosphate Mining A293

Natl. Liberation, 20th Anniv. — A294

50fr, Sugar refinery, Anie. 70fr, Nangbeto Dam. 90fr, Hotel, post office in Lome. 100fr, Post office, Kara. 120fr, Peace monument. 130fr, Youth vaccination campaign.

1987, Jan. 13 **Litho.** *Perf. 12½*

1415 A293 35fr shown .30 .25
1416 A293 50fr multicolored .40 .25
1417 A293 70fr multicolored .50 .25
1418 A293 90fr multicolored .70 .40
1419 A293 100fr multicolored .80 .40
1420 A293 120fr multicolored .90 .45
1421 A293 130fr multicolored 1.00 .60
Nos. 1415-1421 (7) 4.60 2.60

Souvenir Sheet

Perf. 13

1422 A294 500fr shown 3.50 3.25

Nos. 1419-1422 are airmail.

Easter — A295

Paintings in Nadoba Church, Keran: 90fr, The Last Supper. 130fr, Christ on the Cross. 300fr, The Resurrection. 500fr, Evangelization in Tamberma, fresco, horiz.

1987, Apr. 13 **Litho.** *Perf. 14½x15*

1423 A295 90fr multi .65 .35
1424 A295 130fr multi .95 .45
1425 A295 300fr multi 2.10 1.00
Nos. 1423-1425 (3) 3.70 1.80

Souvenir Sheet

Perf. 15x14½

1426 A295 500fr multi 4.00 3.75

Nos. 1424-1426 are airmail.

World Rugby Cup — A296

70fr, Dive. 130fr, Running with the ball. 300fr, Scrimmage.
1000fr, Stands, goal, vert.

1987, May 11 *Perf. 15x14½*

1427 A296 70fr multicolored .75 .25
1428 A296 130fr multicolored 1.50 .45
1429 A296 300fr multicolored 3.00 1.10
Nos. 1427-1429 (3) 5.25 1.80

Souvenir Sheet

Perf. 14½x15

1430 A296 1000fr multicolored 9.50 9.50

Nos. 1427-1429 are horiz. Nos. 1428-1430 are airmail.

Indigenous Flowers — A297

70fr, Adenium obesum. 90fr, Amorphophallus abyssinicus, vert. 100fr, Ipomoea mauritana. 120fr, Salacia togoica, vert.

1987, June 22 **Litho.** *Perf. 13*

1431 A297 70fr multi .70 .25
1432 A297 90fr multi .85 .25
1433 A297 100fr multi .95 .30
1434 A297 120fr multi 1.25 .35
Nos. 1431-1434 (4) 3.75 1.15

Nos. 1432-1434 are airmail.

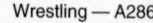

Fish — A298

70fr, Chaetodon hoefleri. 90fr, Tetraodon lineatus. 120fr, Chaetodipterus goreensis. 130fr, Labeo parvus.

1987, Sept. 8 Litho. *Perf. 13*

1435 A298 70fr multi .75 .30
1436 A298 90fr multi .85 .35
1437 A298 120fr multi 1.10 .50
1438 A298 130fr multi 1.25 .55
Nos. 1435-1438 (4) 3.95 1.70

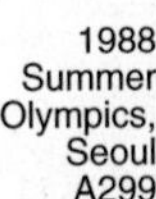

1988 Summer Olympics, Seoul A299

Buddha and athletes

1987, Sept. 14 *Perf. 12½*

1439 A299 70fr Long jump .60 .30
1440 A299 90fr Relay .75 .35
1441 A299 200fr Cycling 1.75 .80
1442 A299 250fr Javelin 2.25 .85
Nos. 1439-1442 (4) 5.35 2.30

Souvenir Sheet

1443 A299 1000fr Tennis 7.50 5.50

Nos. 1440-1443 are airmail.

World Wildlife Fund Type of 1984

1987, Dec. 15 Litho. *Perf. 14*

Size: 32x24mm

1444 A263 60fr like 45fr 1.10 .30
1445 A263 75fr like 70fr 1.25 .30
1446 A263 80fr like 90fr 1.75 .30
1447 A263 100fr like 105fr 2.75 .50
Nos. 1444-1447 (4) 6.85 1.40

No. 1447 is airmail.

Christmas — A300

Paintings: 40fr, Springtime in Paradise, horiz. 45fr, Creation of Man, Sistine Chapel, by Michelangelo, horiz. 105fr, Presentation in the Temple. 270fr, Original Sin. 500fr, Nativity, horiz.

Perf. 15x14, 14x15

1987, Dec. 15 Litho.

1448 A300 40fr multi .40 .25
1449 A300 45fr multi .45 .25
1450 A300 105fr multi 1.10 .45
1451 A300 270fr multi 2.75 1.00
Nos. 1448-1451 (4) 4.70 1.95

Souvenir Sheet

1452 A300 500fr multi 4.50 4.00

Nos. 1450-1452 are airmail.

Eradication of Tuberculosis — A301

80fr, Inoculation, horiz. 90fr, Family under umbrella. 115fr, Hospital, horiz.

1987, Dec. 28 *Perf. 12½x13, 13x12½*

1453 A301 80fr multicolored .55 .30
1454 A301 90fr multicolored .65 .30
1455 A301 115fr multicolored .80 .40
Nos. 1453-1455 (3) 2.00 1.00

Health for all by the year 2000. Nos. 1454-1455 are airmail.

Intl. Fund for Agricultural Development (IFAD), 10th Anniv. — A302

1988, Feb. 25 Litho. *Perf. 13½*

1456 A302 90fr multi .75 .30

Easter 1988 — A303

Stained-glass windows: 70fr, Jesus and the Disciples at Emmaus. 90fr, Mary at the Foot of the Cross. 120fr, The Crucifixion. 200fr, St. Thomas Touching the Resurrected Christ. 500fr, The Agony of Jesus on the Mount of Olives.

1988, June 6 Litho. *Perf. 14x15*

1457 A303 70fr multi .55 .25
1458 A303 90fr multi .85 .35
1459 A303 120fr multi .85 .50
1460 A303 200fr multi 1.60 .85
Nos. 1457-1460 (4) 3.85 1.95

Souvenir Sheet

1461 A303 500fr multi 3.50 2.75

Nos. 1459-1461 are airmail.

Paintings by Picasso (1881-1973) A304

Designs: 45fr, The Dance. 160fr, Portrait of a Young Girl. No. 1464, Gueridon. No. 1465, Mandolin and Guitar.

1988, Apr. 25 Litho. *Perf. 12½x13*

1462 A304 45fr multi .50 .25
1463 A304 160fr multi 1.60 .75
1464 A304 300fr multi 3.00 1.50
Nos. 1462-1464 (3) 5.10 2.50

Souvenir Sheet

1465 A304 300fr multi 2.75 2.00

Nos. 1464-1465 are airmail.

1988 Summer Olympics, Seoul — A305

1988, Aug. 30 *Perf. 14x15*

1466 A305 70fr Basketball .55 .30
1467 A305 90fr Tennis .70 .35
1468 A305 120fr Archery .90 .50
1469 A305 200fr Discus 1.75 .80
Nos. 1466-1469 (4) 3.90 1.95

Souvenir Sheet

1470 A305 500fr Marathon 3.50 2.75

Nos. 1468-1470 are airmail.

WHO, 40th Anniv. — A306

1988, Oct. 28 Litho. *Perf. 13*

1471 A306 80fr shown .65 .35
1472 A306 125fr Emblems .95 .45

Traditional Costumes — A307

1988, July 25 Litho. *Perf. 13½*

1473 A307 80fr Watchi chief .55 .25
1474 A307 125fr Watchi woman .85 .40
1475 A307 165fr Kotokoli 1.25 .60
1476 A307 175fr Ewe 1.25 .60
Nos. 1473-1476 (4) 3.90 1.85

Souvenir Sheet

1477 A307 500fr Moba 3.50 2.75

PHILTOGO 3, Aug. 11-12 — A308

Children's drawings by: 10fr, B. Gossner. 35fr, K. Ekoue-Kouvahey. 70fr, A. Abbey. 90fr, T.D. Lawson. 120fr, A. Tazzar.

1988, Dec. 3

1478 A308 10fr multi .25 .25
1479 A308 35fr multi .25 .25
1480 A308 70fr multi .75 .30
1481 A308 90fr multi .90 .35
1482 A308 120fr multi 1.10 .50
Nos. 1478-1482 (5) 3.25 1.65

Christmas — A309

Paintings: 80fr, Adoration of the Magi, by Brueghel. 150fr, The Virgin, Infant Jesus, Sts. Jerome and Dominic, by Lippi. 175fr, Madonna, Infant Jesus, St. Joseph and Infant John the Baptist, by Barocci. 195fr, Virgin and Child, by Bellini. 750fr, The Holy Family and a Shepherd, by Titian.

1988, Dec. 15 *Perf. 14½x15*

1483 A309 80fr multi .55 .35
1484 A309 150fr multi 1.25 .60
1485 A309 175fr multi 1.40 .70
1486 A309 195fr multi 1.75 .80
Nos. 1483-1486 (4) 4.95 2.45

Souvenir Sheet

1487 A309 750fr multi 5.25 4.25

Nos. 1484-1487 are airmail.

Natl. Industries — A310

1988, May 28 Litho. *Perf. 13*

1488 A310 125fr Cement factory .80 .40
1489 A310 165fr Bottling plant 1.20 .60
1490 A310 195fr Phosphate mine 1.40 .70
1491 A310 200fr Plastics factory 1.40 .70
1492 A310 300fr Manufacturing plant 2.10 1.10
Nos. 1488-1492 (5) 6.90 3.50

John F. Kennedy — A311

Designs: 125fr, Arrival in Paris, 1961. 155fr, At Hotel de Ville, vert. 165fr, With De Gaulle at Elysee Palace, vert. 180fr, Boarding Air Force One with Jackie at Orly, France. 750fr, Kennedy and De Gaulle, natl. colors, vert.

1988, July 30 Litho. *Perf. 14*

1493 A311 125fr multi 1.90 .40
1494 A311 155fr multi 1.25 .55
1495 A311 165fr multi 1.40 .60
1496 A311 180fr multi 1.50 .65
Nos. 1493-1496 (4) 6.05 2.20

Souvenir Sheet

Perf. 13½x13

1497 A311 750fr multi 5.25 4.25

Hairstyles A312

1988, Nov. 20 *Perf. 13*

1498 A312 80fr shown .45 .25
1499 A312 125fr multi, diff. .85 .40
1500 A312 170fr multi, diff. 1.25 .55
1501 A312 180fr multi, diff., vert. 1.40 .60
Nos. 1498-1501 (4) 3.95 1.80

Souvenir Sheet

Perf. 14

1502 A312 500fr multi, diff. 3.50 2.75

Sarakawa Plane Crash, 15th Anniv. — A313

Portrait and various views of the wreckage.

1989, Jan. 24 *Perf. 13½*

1503 A313 10fr multi .25 .25
1504 A313 80fr multi, vert. .70 .35
1505 A313 125fr multi 1.10 .55
Nos. 1503-1505 (3) 2.05 1.15

1990 World Cup Soccer Championships, Italy — A314

ITALIA '90 emblem, flag of Togo, athletes and architecture: 80fr, Cathedral of St. Januarius, Naples. 125fr, Milan Cathedral. 165fr, Bevilacqua Palace, Verona. 175fr, Baptistery of San Giovanni, Florence. 380fr, Madama Palace, Turin. 425fr, Cathedral of San Lorenzo, Genoa. 650fr, The Colosseum, Rome.

1989, Jan. 10 Litho. *Perf. 13½*

1506 A314 80fr multi .55 .30
1507 A314 125fr multi .90 .45
1508 A314 165fr multi 1.25 .60
1509 A314 175fr multi 1.25 .65
1510 A314 380fr multi 2.75 1.50
1511 A314 425fr multi 3.00 1.50
Nos. 1506-1511 (6) 9.70 5.00

Souvenir Sheet

1512 A314 650fr multi 5.25 5.25

Nos. 1510-1512 are airmail.

A316

Prince Emanuel of Liechtenstein Foundation — A316a

1988 Summer Olympics, Seoul: Flags of Liechtenstein, Togo, athletes, Pres. Eyadema. No. 1522A, Olympic rings. No. 1522B, Tennis players Miroslav Mecir, Steffi Graf, vert.

1989, May 25 Litho. *Perf. 13½*

1520 A316 80fr Boxing 1.10 .30
1521 A316 125fr Long jump 1.25 .45
1522 A316 165fr Running 2.10 .55
Nos. 1520-1522 (3) 4.45 1.30

Litho. & Embossed

1522A A316a 1500fr gold & multi 10.00
1522B A316a 1500fr gold & multi 10.00

Nos. 1522A-1522B are airmail and exist imperf. and in souvenir sheets of 1 both perf. and imperf.

Federal Republic of Germany, 40th Anniv. — A317

1989, June 1

1523 A317 90fr Palace .65 .30
1524 A317 125fr Statesmen, vert. 1.00 .40
1525 A317 180fr Natl. flag, crest 1.50 .60
Nos. 1523-1525 (3) 3.15 1.30

Council for Rural Development, 30th Anniv. — A318

75fr, Flags, well, tractor, field.

1989, June 19 ***Perf. 15x14***

1526 A318 75fr multicolored .70 .35

See Ivory Coast No. 874.

Intl. Red Cross, 125th Anniv. — A319

1989, June 30 ***Perf. 13½***

1527 A319 90fr shown .70 .35
1528 A319 125fr Geneva Convention, 1864 .90 .50

French Revolution, Bicent. — A320

Designs: 90fr, Storming of the Bastille, vert. 125fr, Tennis Court Oath. 180fr, Abolition of privileges. 1000fr, Declaration of Human Rights and Citizenship, vert.

1989, July 15

1529 A320 90fr multi .70 .30
1530 A320 125fr multi 1.10 .45
1531 A320 180fr multi 1.40 .65
Nos. 1529-1531 (3) 3.20 1.40

Souvenir Sheet

1532 A320 1000fr multi 8.50 2.75

Electric Corp. of Benin, 20th Anniv. — A321

1989, July 15

1533 A321 80fr multi .65 .30
1534 A321 125fr multi 1.10 .45

A322

PHILEXFRANCE '89, French Revolution, Bicent. — A322a

Figures and scenes from the revolution: 90fr, Jacques Necker (1732-1804), financier, statesman, and The Three Estates. 190fr, Guy Le Chapelier (1754-1794), politician, and abolition of feudalism (seigniorial privileges), Aug. 4, 1789. 425fr, Talleyrand-Perigord (1754-1838), statesman, and Lafayette's Oath at the Festival of Federation, July 14, 1790. 480fr, Paul Barras (1755-1829), revolutionary, and overthrowing of Robespierre during the Revolution of 9th Thermidor, July 27, 1794. 750fr, Georges Jacques Danton (1759-1794), revolutionary leader, and arrest of Louis XVI at Varennes, June 21, 1791, horiz. Nos. 1537-1539 are airmail.

No. 1539A, Assassination of Jean-Paul Marat (1743-93). No. 1539B, Fabré d'Eglantine (1750-94), making of the calendar of the republic.

1989 **Litho.** ***Perf. 13½***

1535 A322 90fr multi .70 .25
1536 A322 190fr multi 1.40 .40
1537 A322 425fr multi 3.25 .60
1538 A322 480fr multi 3.75 .60
Nos. 1535-1538 (4) 9.10 1.85

Souvenir Sheet

1539 A322 750fr multi 8.00 2.00

Litho. & Embossed

1539A A322a 1500fr gold & multi 10.00 2.00

Souvenir Sheet

1539B A322a 1500fr gold & multi 8.00

#1539A-1539B are airmail and exist imperf.

Nos. 1535-1538 exist in souvenir sheets of 1, No. 1539A in souvenir sheets of 1, perf. and imperf.

Issued: 90fr-750fr, 6/12; 1500fr, 7/15.

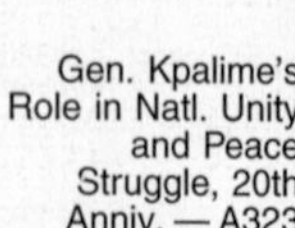

Gen. Kpalime's Role in Natl. Unity and Peace Struggle, 20th Anniv. — A323

1989, Aug. 21

1540 A323 90fr shown .70 .30
1541 A323 125fr Giving speech 1.00 .40

A324

Butterflies — 5fr, Danaus chrysippus. 10fr, Morpho aega. 15fr, Papilio demodocus. 90fr, Papilio dardanus.

500fr, Papilio zalmoxis.

1990, Apr. 30 **Litho.** ***Perf. 13½***

1542 A324 5fr multicolored .60 .25
1543 A324 10fr multicolored .60 .25
1544 A324 15fr multicolored .60 .25
1545 A324 90fr multicolored 2.10 .60
Nos. 1542-1545 (4) 3.90 1.35

Souvenir Sheet

1545A A324 500fr multicolored 5.50 2.75

No. 1545A is airmail.

A325

1989, Dec. 1 **Litho.** ***Perf. 13½***

1546 A325 40fr Apollo 11 liftoff .25 .25
1547 A325 90fr Module transposition .55 .30
1548 A325 150fr *Eagle* 1.25 .45
1549 A325 250fr Splashdown 1.90 .80
Nos. 1546-1549 (4) 3.95 1.80

Souvenir Sheet

1550 A325 500fr Astronaut on Moon 3.50 2.75

1st Moon Landing, 20th anniv.

Lome IV Conference, Dec. 1989 A326

1989, Dec. 15 **Litho.** ***Perf. 13***

1551 A326 100fr "Dec. 89" .70 .30
1552 A326 100fr "15 Dec. 89" .70 .30

A327

Boy Scouts, Flora and Fauna — A327a

80fr, Myrina silenus. 90fr, Phlebobus silvaticus. 125fr, Volvariella esculenta. 165fr, Hypolicaena antifaunus. 380fr, Termitomyces striatus. 425fr, Axiocerces harpax.

750fr, Cupidopsis jobates. No. 1559A, Kalchbrennera corallocephala. No. 1559B, Spindasis mozambica.

1990, Jan. 8 **Litho.** ***Perf. 13½***

1553 A327 80fr multicolored .65 .25
1554 A327 90fr multicolored .65 .25
1555 A327 125fr multicolored .90 .25
1556 A327 165fr multicolored 1.10 .35
1557 A327 380fr multicolored 2.50 .50
1558 A327 425fr multicolored 3.25 .50
Nos. 1553-1558 (6) 9.05 2.10

Souvenir Sheet

1559 A327 750fr multicolored 6.00 1.10

Litho. & Embossed

1559A A327a 1500fr gold & multi 12.00

Souvenir Sheet

1559B A327a 1500fr gold & multi 6.50

Nos. 1557-1559B are airmail. Nos. 1559A-1559B exist imperf. No. 1559A exists in souvenir sheet of 1 both perf. and imperf.

People's Republic of Togo, 20th Anniv. A328

45fr, Government House, Kara. 90fr, Pres. Eyadema, House.

1990, Jan. 8

1560 A328 45fr multicolored .45 .25
1561 A328 90fr multicolored .80 .40

Pan-African Postal Union, 10th Anniv. — A329

1990, Jan. 1 ***Perf. 13½***

1562 A329 125fr bronze, blk & bl 1.10 .30

Ninth Convention of Lions Club International Multidistrict 403, Lome — A329a

Frame color: 90fr, Blue. 125fr, Rose. 165fr, Yellow.

1990, May 5 **Litho.** ***Perf. 13½***

1562A-1562C A329a Set of 3 3.00 1.50

US-Togo Relations — A330

180fr, Pres. Bush, Pres. Eyadema, horiz.

1990, July 20 **Litho.** ***Perf. 13½***

1563 A330 125fr multicolored .85 .40
1564 A330 180fr multicolored 1.20 .40

Size: 90 x 75mm

1565 A330 125fr multicolored .85 .50
1566 A330 180fr multicolored 1.10 .70
Nos. 1563-1566 (4) 4.00 2.00

Nos. 1565-1566 printed in sheets of 1.

Reptiles — A331

1fr, Varanus niloticus. 25fr, Vipere bitis arietans. 60fr, Naja melaneuloca. 90fr, Python de sebae.

1990, May 22

1567 A331 1fr multicolored .25 .25
1568 A331 25fr multicolored .25 .25
1569 A331 60fr multicolored .65 .25
1570 A331 90fr multicolored .70 .30
Nos. 1567-1570 (4) 1.85 1.05

Cowrie Shell Ornaments — A332

1990, July, 20 **Litho.** ***Perf. 13½***

1571 A332 90fr shown .65 .35
1572 A332 125fr Shell necklace 1.10 .45
1573 A332 180fr Shells on horned helmet 1.40 .60
Nos. 1571-1573 (3) 3.15 1.40

Stamp Day — A333

1990, Aug. 23

1574 A333 90fr multicolored .70 .40

Traditional Homes — A334

1990, Sept. 9

1575 A334 90fr shown .65 .35
1576 A334 125fr multi, diff. .90 .45
1577 A334 190fr multi, diff. 1.40 .70
Nos. 1575-1577 (3) 2.95 1.50

Charles de Gaulle (1890-1970), Speech at Brazzaville, 1944 — A335

1990, Aug. 30 **Litho.** ***Perf. 14***

1578 A335 125fr multicolored 1.10 .45

New Lome Airport — A336

1990, Sept. 17 *Perf. 13½*

1579 A336 90fr multicolored	.70	.30

Children's Art — A337

1990, Sept. 28 Litho. *Perf. 13½*

1580 A337 90fr multicolored	.70	.40

Forest Wildlife A342

1991, June 5 Litho. *Perf. 13½x14*

1593 A342 90fr Chimpanzee	.55	.35
1594 A342 170fr Green parrot	1.25	.60
1595 A342 185fr White parrot	1.40	.80
Nos. 1593-1595 (3)	3.20	1.75

Python Regius — A343

Various snakes emerging from eggs.

1992, Aug. 24 Litho. *Perf. 13½*

1596 A343 90fr multicolored	.65	.30
1597 A343 125fr multicolored	.85	.30
1598 A343 190fr multicolored	1.25	.60
1599 A343 300fr multicolored	1.90	.80
Nos. 1596-1599 (4)	4.65	2.00

Dated 1991.

Voodoo Dances — A344

Various women dancing.

1992, Aug. 24

1600 A344 90fr multicolored	.70	.30
1601 A344 125fr multicolored	.90	.45
1602 A344 190fr multicolored	1.40	.65
Nos. 1600-1602 (3)	3.00	1.40

Dated 1991.

A345

1994 World Cup Soccer Championships, US — A346

Various soccer players in action: 5fr, 10fr, 25fr, 60fr, 90fr, 100fr, 200fr, 1000fr.

1500fr, Player in white & green uniform. 3000fr, Two players in air, horiz.

1994, Nov. 15 Litho. *Perf. 14*

1603-1610 A345 Set of 8	6.75	3.50

Souvenir Sheets

1611 A346 1500fr multicolored	7.50	3.50
1612 A346 3000fr multicolored	12.50	6.25

UPU, 120th Anniv. — A347

1994, July 29 *Perf. 13½*

1613 A347 180fr multicolored	.70	.35

A miniature sheet may exist.

Stamp Day — A348

1994, Oct. 9

1614 A348 90fr pale bl & multi	.60	.25
1615 A348 125fr pale yel & multi	.75	.40

Intl. Olympic Committee, Cent. — A348a

Designs, each 300fr: b, Pierre de Coubertin, Olympic Hymn. c, Original members of IOC. d, Olympic flame.

900fr, Pierre de Coubertin holding document.

1994, Oct. Litho. *Perf. 13½*

1615A A348a Strip of 3, #b.-d.	4.25	4.25

Souvenir Sheet

1615E A348a 900fr multicolored	4.25	2.10

Nos. 1615A, 1615E exist imperf. No. 1615c is 60x51mm. No. 1615E is airmail and contains one 36x51mm stamp.

Birds — A349

Designs: #1616, 5fr, Secretary bird, vert. #1617, 10fr, Paradise flycather, vert. #1618, 25fr, African spoonbill. #1619, 60fr, Cordon bleu waxbill. #1620, 90fr, Orange-breasted sunbird, vert. #1621, 100fr, Yellow-billed hornbill, vert. #1621A, 180fr, Barn owl. #1622, 200fr, African hoopoe. #1622A, 300fr, Fire-crowned bishop, vert. #1623, 1000fr, Red-throated bee eater, vert.

1995 Litho. *Perf. 14*

1616-1623 A349 Set of 10	7.75	3.75

Souvenir Sheet

1624 A349 1500fr Vulture	7.50	3.50

Issued: 180fr, 300fr, 8/7; others, 1/23.

A350

Motion Picture, Alien: a, Alien creature. b, Humans in combat with creature. c, Sigourney Weaver.

1994 Litho. *Perf. 13½*

1625 A350 600fr Strip of 3, #a.-c.	7.50	3.75

No. 1625b is 60x48mm. No. 1625 is a continuous design and exists in souvenir sheets of 1.

First Manned Moon Landing, 25th Anniv. — A351

No. 1626, each 600fr: a, Edwin "Buzz" Aldrin. b, Eagle, olive branch, Neil Armstrong. c, Michael Collins.

No. 1627, each 600fr: a, Apollo emblem, footprint. b, Crew of Apollo 11. c, Moon rock, NASA emblem.

1994 **Strips of 3, #a.-c.**

1626-1627 A351 Set of 2	15.00	7.50

Nos. 1626b, 1627b are each 60x47mm. Nos. 1626-1627 are continuous designs and exist in souvenir sheets of 1.

Dinosaurs — A352

125fr, Polacanthus. 180fr, Pachycephalosaurus. 425fr, Coelophysis. 480fr, Brachiosaurus. 500fr, Dilophosaurus. 1500fr, Scutellosaurus.

No. 1634, Velociraptor, vert.

1994

1628-1633 A352 Set of 6	13.00	6.50

Souvenir Sheet

1634 A352 1500fr multicolored	6.25	3.00

No. 1634 is airmail.

Flowers — A353

Designs: 15fr, Belvache de Madagascar. 90fr, Oeuillets. 125fr, Agave, horiz.

1995, May 12

1635-1637 A353 Set of 3	1.10	.55

Easter — A354

Details or entire paintings: 90fr, The Resurrection, by A. Mantegna. 180fr, Calvary, by Veronese. 190fr, The Last Supper, by Tintoretto, horiz.

1995, May 12

1638-1640 A354 Set of 3	2.10	1.10

Fish — A355

10fr, Pike. 90fr, Capitaine. 180fr, Carp.

1995, May 12

1641-1643 A355 Set of 3	2.10	1.10

Miniature Sheets of 6 and 8

VJ Day, 50th Anniv. — A356

Japanese leaders: No. 1644a, Adm. Isoroko Yamamoto. b, Gen. Hideki Tojo. c, Vice Adm. Shigeru Fukudome. d, Adm. Shigetaro Shimada. e, Contre-Adm. Chuichi Nagumo. f, Gen. Shizu Ichi Tanaka.

VE Day: No. 1645a, 200fr, German fighter planes making final attacks. b, 200fr, Allies win Battle of the Atlantic. c, 200fr, Ludendorf Bridge at Remagen is taken intact. d, 200fr, Russian rockets fired at Berlin. e, 45fr, Hostilities suspended in Italy. f, 90fr, Russians capture devastated Warsaw. g, 125fr, Russian tanks enter Berlin. h, 500fr, UN flag.

No. 1646, Japanese signing peace agreement. No. 1647, German U-236 surrenders.

1995, July 20 Litho. *Perf. 14*

1644 A356 200fr #a.-f.	4.75	2.50
1645 A356 #a.-h.	6.25	3.25

Souvenir Sheets

1646 A356 1500fr multicolored	6.00	3.00
1647 A356 1500fr multicolored	10.00	5.00

UN, 50th Anniv. A357

No. 1648: a, 25fr, Doves, earth from space. b, 90fr, Doves, UN headquarters. c, 400fr, Doves, earth from space.

1000fr, Earth, dove.

1995, June 26

1648 A357 Strip of 3, #a.-c.	2.40	1.25

Souvenir Sheet

1649 A357 1000fr multicolored	6.25	3.00

1995 Boy Scout Jamboree, Holland — A358

Designs: 90fr, Nat. flag. 190fr, Scout oath. 300fr, Lord Baden-Powell.

1500fr, Scout salute.

1995, July 20

1650-1652 A358 Set of 3	2.75	1.40

Souvenir Sheet

1653 A358 1500fr multicolored	6.00	3.00

Queen Mother, 95th Birthday — A359

No. 1654: a, Formal portrait. b, Cutting cake. c, As younger woman wearing jewels, waving. d, Drawing.

No. 1654E, Holding umbrella. No. 1654F, Formal portrait as young woman.

No. 1655, Royal attire, pearls.

No. 1655A, Early picture of King George VI, Queen Mother.

1995, July 20 *Perf. 13½x14*

1654 A359 250fr Strip of 4, #a.-d.	5.00	2.50
1654E A359 250fr multicolored	1.25	.65

1654F A359 250fr multicolored 1.25 .65
g. Block or strip of 4, #1654a, 1654d, 1654E, 1654F 5.00 2.50
Nos. 1654-1654F (3) 7.50 3.80

Souvenir Sheets

1655 A359 1000fr multicolored 4.00 2.00
1655A A359 1000fr multicolored 4.00 2.00

Nos. 1654, 1654Fg were issued in sheets of 8 stamps.
Issued: #1654, 1655, 7/20; # 1654E, 1654F, 1655A, 11/22.

FAO, 50th Anniv. A360

No. 1656: a, 45fr, Cattle. b, 125fr, Water buffalo. c, 200fr, Boy, man with water buffaloes.
1000fr, Woman milking cow.

1995, Mar. 3 Litho. *Perf. 14*
1656 A360 Strip of 3, #a.-c. 2.25 1.10

Souvenir Sheet

1657 A360 1000fr multicolored 4.50 2.10

No. 1656 is a continuous design.

Nobel Prize Winners — A361

No. 1658, each 200fr: a, Elihu Root, peace, 1912. b, Alfred Fried, peace, 1911. c, Henri Moissan, chemistry, 1906. d, Charles Barkla, physics, 1917. e, Rudolf Eucken, literature, 1908. f, Carl von Ossietzky, peace, 1935. g, Sir Edward Appleton, physics. 1947. h, Camillo Golgi, physiology, 1906. i, Wilhelm Roentgen, physics, 1901.
No. 1659, each 200fr: a, Manfred Eigen, chemistry, 1967. b, Donald J. Cram, chemistry, 1987. c, Paul J. Flory, chemistry, 1974. d, Johann Deisenhofer, chemistry, 1988. e, P.W. Bridgman, physics, 1946. f, Otto Stern, physics, 1943. g, Arne Tiselius, chemistry, 1948. h, J. Georg Bednorz, physics, 1987. i, Albert Claude, medicine, 1974.
Each 1500fr: No. 1660, Albert Einstein, physics, 1921. No. 1661, Woodrow Wilson, peace, 1919.

1995, Aug. 21

Miniature Sheets of 9, a-i

1658-1659 A361 Set of 2 25.00 12.00

Souvenir Sheets

1660-1661 A361 Set of 2 12.50 6.50

Rotary Intl., 90th Anniv. — A362

No. 1663, Natl. flag, Rotary emblem.

1995, July 20
1662 A362 1000fr shown 4.25 2.00

Souvenir Sheet

1663 A362 1000fr multi 4.25 2.00

Miniature Sheets

Fauna — A363

Primates, each 200fr, vert: No. 1664a, Black-faced monkey in tree. b, Brown monkey in tree. c, Black monkey. d, Baboon.
Wild animals, each 200fr: No. 1665a, Hyena. b, Hyrax. c, Mongoose. d, Elephant. e, Mandrill. f, Okapi. g, Hippopotamus. h, Flamingo. i, Wild boar.
1500fr, Potto.

1995, Oct. 2 Litho. *Perf. 14*
1664 A363 Sheet of 4, #a.-d. 3.25 1.60
1665 A363 Sheet of 9, #a.-i. 7.25 3.50

Souvenir Sheet

1666 A363 1500fr multicolored 6.00 3.00

FAO, 50th Anniv. — A364

1995, Mar. 3 Litho. *Perf. 14*
1667 A364 125fr shown .50 .25

Souvenir Sheet

1668 A364 300fr like No. 1667 1.50 .75

Sir Rowland Hill (1795-1879) — A365

1995, June 3 *Perf. 13½*
1669 A365 125fr multicolored .75 .40

UN, 50th Anniv. — A366

1995, June 26
1670 A366 180fr multicolored .90 .50

Mushrooms — A367

No. 1671: a, Cortinarius violaceus. b, Hygrocybe flavescens. c, Mycena haematopus. d, Coprinus micaceus. e, Helvella lacunosa. f, Flammulina velutipes. g, Aleuria aurantia. h, Geastrum triplex.
No. 1672: a, Russula laurocerasi. b, Phyllotopsis nidulans. c, Xeromphalina campanella. d, Psathyrella hydrophila. e, Entoloma murraii. f, Hygrophorus speciosus. g, Mycena leaiana. h, Cystoderma amianthinum.
No. 1673, each 200fr: a, Amanita muscaria. b, Amanita virosa. c, Galerina autumnalis. d, Omphalotus illudens. e, Naematoloma fasciculare. f, Paxillus involutus. g, Russula emetica. h, Scleroderma citrinum.
No. 1674, each 200fr: a, Armillaria ponderosa. b, Agaricus augustus. c, Gomphidius subroseus. d, Morchella esculenta. e, Stropharia rugoso. f, Boletus edulis. g, Clitocybe nuda. h, Lactarius deliciosus.
Each 1500fr: No. 1675, Trametes versicolor. No. 1676, Collybia iocephala.

1995, Nov. 1 *Perf. 14*
1671 A367 180fr Sheet of 8, #a.-h. 9.00 4.50
1672 A367 195fr Sheet of 8, #a.-h. 10.00 4.75
1673-1674 A367 Set of 2 Sheets, #a.-h. 21.00 10.50

Souvenir Sheets

1675-1676 A367 Set of 2 20.00 10.00

Miniature Sheets

History of Transportation A368

Steam locomotives: No. 1677, each 200fr: a, SNCF Class 231 D Le Havre-Paris Express. b, Princess Royal Class Pacific, England. c, Class 52 2-10-0, German Railroad. d, Class "15A" 4-6-4+4-6-4 Beyer-Garratt, Rhodesia. e, Japanese 2-8-0. f, Class 940, 2-8-2 engine, Italy.
Various vehicles: No. 1678, each 200fr: a, Semi truck. b, Roman chariot. c, Motorcycle. d, Hummer 4-wheel drive. e, Bicycle. f, London autobus. g, Lunar rover. h, 1954 Jaguar XK 140. i, Ski-doo.
No. 1679, First land vehicle to break sound barrier.

1995, Dec. 1 Litho. *Perf. 14*
1677 A368 Sheet of 6, #a.-f. 5.50 2.75
1678 A368 Sheet of 9, #a.-i. 8.00 3.75

Souvenir Sheet

1679 A368 1500fr multicolored 6.50 3.50

No. 1679 contains one 85x28mm stamp.

World Post Day — A369

Designs: 220fr, Selling stamps. 315fr, Sorting stamps. 335fr, Post office workers handling large sacks of mail.

1995 Litho. *Perf. 13½*
1680-1682 A369 Set of 3 4.50 2.25

Christmas A370

Paintings: 90fr, Nativity scene, vert. 325fr, Adoration of the Magi, vert. 340fr, 500fr, Adoration of the shepherds.

1995, Sept. 13 Litho. *Perf. 13½*
1683-1685 A370 Set of 3 4.00 2.00

Souvenir Sheet

Perf. 12½

1686 A370 500fr multi, vert. 3.75 1.90

Sheets of 6

Wildlife of Africa — A371

No. 1687: a, Gorilla. b, Uroota suraka. c, Pan troglodytes. d, Panthera pardus. e, Crocodylus niloticus. f, Leptailurus serval.
No. 1688a, Papilio tynderaeus. b, Bongo taurotragus. c, Epiphora aldiba. d, Cephalophus zebra. e, Cercopithecus cephus. f, Arctocebus calabarensis.

1996, May 10 Litho. *Perf. 14*
1687 A371 150fr #a.-f. 3.75 1.90
1688 A371 180fr #a.-f. 4.75 2.50

China '96, 9th Asian Intl. Philatelic Exhibition.

A372

Designs: 50fr, Olympic Stadium, Mexico, 1968, horiz. 90fr, Yevgeny Petrov, skeet shooter, Mexico, 1968, horiz. 220fr, Lia Manoliu, women's discus, Mexico, 1968, horiz. 325fr, Dumb-bell lifting, discontinued sport.
Medal winners from past games: No. 1693, each 200fr: a, China, Women's Volleyball, 1984. b, Wayne Wells, wrestling, 1972. c, Bob Beaman, long jump, 1968. d, Victor Kurentsov, weight lifting, 1968. e, Shirley Strong, 100m hurdles, 1984. f, Nadia Comaneci, balance beam, 1976. g, Giovanni Parisi, boxing, 1988. h, Emil Zatopek, 10,000m, 1948. i, USSR, Brazil, Germany, soccer, 1988.
1000fr, Helen Mayer, fencing, 1936.

1996, July 8 Litho. *Perf. 14*
1689-1692 A372 Set of 4 2.75 1.40
1693 A372 Sheet of 9, #a.-i. 7.25 3.50

Souvenir Sheet

1694 A372 1000fr multicolored 4.00 2.00

1996 Summer Olympics, Atlanta — A373

100fr, Women's gymnastics. 150fr, Women's tennis. 200fr, Javelin. 300fr, Men's field hockey. 400fr, Weight lifting. 500fr, Men's soccer.
1000fr, Synchronized swimming.

1996, Mar. 25 *Perf. 12½*
1695-1700 A373 Set of 6 7.50 3.75

Souvenir Sheet

1701 A373 1000fr multicolored 5.50 2.75

Butterflies — A374

Designs: 40fr, Euphaedra eleus, vert. 90fr, Papilio dardanus, vert. 220fr, Iolaus timon. 315fr, Charaxes cynthia.

1996, June 17 Litho. *Perf. 13*
1702-1705 A374 Set of 4 2.75 1.50

Beetles — A375

Designs: 100fr, Purpuricenus kaehleri. 150fr, Carabus auronitens. 200fr, Semanotus rassicus. 300fr, Rosalia alpina. 400fr, Mylabris variabilis. 500fr, Odontolabis cuvera.
1000fr, Psalidognathus atys.

1996, May 5
1706-1711 A375 Set of 6 7.75 3.75

Souvenir Sheet

Perf. 12½

1712 A375 1000fr multicolored 5.50 2.75

No. 1712 contains one 40x32mm stamp.

1998 World Cup Soccer Championships, France — A376

French flag, various action scenes: 100fr, 150fr, 200fr, 300fr, 400fr, 500fr.

1996, Apr. 10 *Perf. 12½*
1713-1718 A376 Set of 6 7.75 3.75

Souvenir Sheet

1719 A376 1000fr multicolored 5.50 2.75

World Wildlife Fund A377

Designs: a, 325fr, Cephalophus drosalis. b, 220fr, Cephalophus maxwelli. c, 180fr, Cephalophus rufilatus. d, 370fr, Cephalophus syvicultor.
1500fr, Cephalophus dorsalis, diff.

1996, July 30 ***Perf. 14***
1720 A377 Block of 4, #a.-d. 7.00 3.00

Souvenir Sheet

1721 A377 1500fr multicolored 8.25 4.00

No. 1720 was issued in sheets of 16 stamps.

Endangered Species A378

Designs, vert: 220fr, Zebra. 315fr, Cheetah. 325fr, Antelope. 335fr, Madoqua Kirki.
No. 1726, each 200fr: a, African elephants. b, Toucan (c, d, e, f.) c, Mamba (f). d, Lionesses. e, Impala. f, Nyala. g, Hippoppotamus. h, Crocodile. i, Kingfisher.
Each 1500 fr: No. 1727, Buphagus erythyrorhynchus, vert. No. 1728, Leopard, vert.

1996, July 30
1722-1725 A378 Set of 4 8.50 4.00
1726 A378 Sheet of 9, #a.-i. 9.50 4.75

Souvenir Sheets

1727-1728 A378 Set of 2 17.00 9.25

Endangered Species — A379

75fr, Elephant. 90fr, Crocodile. 315fr, Deer.

1996, July 30 **Litho.** ***Perf. 13***
1729-1731 A379 Set of 3 5.50 3.00

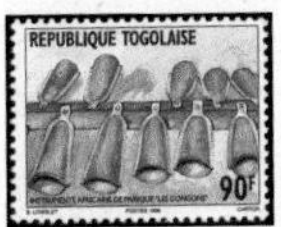
Traditional Musical Instruments — A380

90fr, Gongs. 220fr, Cymbals (balafon). 325fr, String instrument. 500fr, Drums.

1996, July 15
1732-1735 A380 Set of 4 5.00 2.50

Traditional Dances — A381

Designs: 10fr, Kamou dance, Kabyes. 90fr, Kondona dance, Kabyes. 220fr, Bassar. 315fr, Kloto. 335fr, Voudoussis.

1996, June 30
1736-1740 A381 Set of 5 8.00 4.00

New Year 1997 (Year of the Ox) — A382

Paintings, by Ren Bonian (1840-95): No. 1741: a, Herdboy on Buffalo. b, Return from the Pasture. c, Grazing by the Pond.
500fr, Reading Beside an Ox.

1997, Jan. 2 **Litho.** ***Perf. 14***
1741 A382 180fr Strip of 3, #a.-c. 2.50 2.50
d. Souvenir sheet of 6, 2 each #a-c 5.00 5.00

Souvenir Sheet
Perf. 13½x14

1742 A382 500fr multicolored 2.75 2.75

No. 1741 was issued in sheets of 6 stamps. No. 1742 contains one 34x46mm stamp.

Fruits — A383

100fr, Mango. 150fr, Bananas. 200fr, Peaches. 300fr, Papaya. 400fr, Lemon. 500fr, Coconuts.
1000fr, Various fruits.

1996, June 2 **Litho.** ***Perf. 12½***
1743-1748 A383 Set of 6 7.25 7.25

Souvenir Sheet
Perf. 13

1749 A383 1000fr multicolored 5.25 5.25

No. 1749 contains one 40x32mm stamp.

Souvenir Sheet

Chinese Stone Carving — A384

1996, May 10 **Litho.** ***Perf. 12***
1750 A384 370fr multicolored 1.50 1.50

China '96. No. 1750 was not available until March 1997.

Jaffar Ballogou, Boxer — A384a

1996 **Litho.** ***Perf. 13***
1750A A384a 90fr red & multi —
1750B A384a 220fr blk & multi —
1750C A384a 315fr red & multi —

World Telecommunications Day.

UNESCO, 50th Anniv. — A385

World Heritage Sites: No. 1751, each 235fr: a, Axum archaeological site, Ethiopia. b, Victoria Falls, Zambia. c, Archaeological site, Zimbabwe. d, Nature reserve, Niger. e, Arguin Natl. Park, Mauritania. f, Goree Island, Senegal. g, Timgad Ruins, Algeria. h, Ait Ben-Haddou, Morocco.
No. 1752, each 235fr: a, Kyoto, Japan. b, Waterfalls, Colombia. c, Necropolis, Egypt. d, Old Rama Church, Finland. e, Palladian villa, Vicenza, Italy. f, Rock paintings, China. g, Church, Ouro Preto, Brazil. h, Rhodes, Greece.
No. 1753, each 235fr: a, Exterior of Cistercian Abbey, Fontenay, France. b, Dubrovnik, Croatia. c, Interior of Cistercian Abbey, Fontenay. d, e, Quedlinberg, Germany. f, Ironbridge Gorge, England. g, Grand Canyon, US. h, Village, Ironbridge Gorge, England.
Each 1000fr: No. 1754, Kyoto, Japan, horiz. No. 1755, Mt. Huangshan, China, horiz. No. 1756, Village, Ironbridge, England, horiz.

1997, Mar. 24 **Litho.** ***Perf. 14***
Sheets of 8, a-h, + Label
1751-1753 A385 Set of 3 25.00 25.00

Souvenir Sheets

1754-1756 A385 Set of 3 12.50 12.50

Cats — A386

150fr, American shorthair. 200fr, Siamese, vert. 300fr, Java. 400fr, "Ocicat," vert. 500fr, Scottish fold. No. 1762, 1000fr, Persian, vert.
No. 1763, Colorpoint shorthair, vert.

1997 **Litho.** ***Perf. 12½***
1757-1762 A386 Set of 6 12.00 12.00

Souvenir Sheet

1763 A386 1000fr multicolored 4.50 4.50

No. 1763 contains one 32x40mm stamp.

Military Uniforms — A387

Designs: 150fr, Officer of cuirassiers. 200fr, Norman regiment officer. 300fr, Volunteer battalion foot soldier. 400fr, Berlin Campaign Militiaman. 500fr, Foot soldier. No. 1769, 1000fr, Musketeer.
No. 1770, Belling Regiment Hussar.

1997 ***Perf. 13x12½***
1764-1769 A387 Set of 6 12.00 12.00

Souvenir Sheet

1770 A387 1000fr multicolored 4.50 4.50

No. 1770 contains one 40x32mm stamp.

Return of Hong Kong to China — A388

Deng Xiaoping (1904-97) — A388a

Views of city: 220fr, Chinese flag as inscription, skyscraper. 315fr, Chinese flag as inscription, night scene. 325fr, Circular stair railing, skyscraper at night. 340fr, Chinese flag, view of city through inscription. 370fr, Deng Xiaoping (1904-97), fireworks over city.
#1775A: a, shown. b, Looking left.

1997, June 2 ***Perf. 14***
1771-1775 A388 Set of 5 7.50 7.50

Sheet of 2
Perf. 13½

1775A A388a 500fr #a.-b. 4.50 4.50

Nos. 1771-1773 are 28x44mm and were each issued in sheets of 4. Nos. 1774-1775 were each issued in sheets of 3.

Queen Elizabeth II and Prince Philip, 50th Wedding Anniv. — A389

No. 1776: a, Queen. b, Royal arms. c, Queen in yellow hat, Prince in military uniform. d, Queen in white hat, Prince. e, Windsor Castle. f, Prince.
1000fr, Portrait of Queen, Prince.

1997, June 25
1776 A389 315fr Sheet of 6, #a.-f. 7.50 7.50

Souvenir Sheet

1777 A389 1000fr multicolored 4.50 4.50

Locomotives A390

150fr, Light locomotive, Adams Bridges. 200fr, Norris Type, England 1866. 300fr, Jones and Ports locomotive with long boiler, 1848. 400fr, Cargo and passenger locomotive, Ansaldo, 1850. 500fr, Birkenhead, Italy, 1863. #1783, 1000fr, Quarter locomotive, New York, 1890.
#1783A, Six-wheeled locomotive, Robert Stephenson, 1830, vert.

1996, Dec. 5 **Litho.** ***Perf. 12½x12***
1778-1783 A390 Set of 6 12.00 12.00

Souvenir Sheet
Perf. 12½

1783A A390 1000fr multi 4.50 4.50

Birds — A391

150fr, Poephila guttata. 200fr, Lonchura malacca. 300fr, Acanthis cannabina. 400fr, Fringilla coelebs. 500fr, Emblema guttata. #1789, 1000fr, Passerina amoena.
#1789A, Chloebia gouldiae.

1996, Nov. 27 ***Perf. 13***
1784-1789 A391 Set of 6 11.00 11.00

Souvenir Sheet

1789A A391 1000fr multi 4.50 4.50

Nos. 1784-1789 are dated 1996.
No. 1789A contains one 32x40mm stamp.

Turtles — A392

Designs: 150fr, Asterochelys yniphora. 200fr, Staurotypus triporcatus. 300fr, Puxidea mouhoti. 400fr, Geomyda spengleri. 500fr, Cuora galbinifrons. #1795, 1000fr, Malaclemys terrapin.
#1795A, Asterochelys radiata.

1996, Nov. 30
1790-1795 A392 Set of 6 11.00 11.00

Souvenir Sheet

1795A A392 1000fr multi 4.50 4.50

Nos. 1790-1795 are dated 1996.
No. 1795A contains one 40x32mm stamp.

Natl. Liberation, 30th Anniv. — A393

1997 **Litho.** ***Perf. 13½***
1796 A393 90fr yellow & multi .30 .30
1797 A393 220fr green & multi .75 .75

Diana, Princess of Wales (1961-97) — A394

Nos. 1798a-1798i: Various portraits of Princess Diana in designer gowns, each 180fr.
Views up close, each 180fr: No. 1799, like #1798a. No. 1799A, Like #1798b. No. 1800, like #1798c. No. 1801, like #1798d. No. 1802, like #1798e. No. 1802A, Like #1798f. No. 1802B, Like #1798g. No. 1803, like #1798h. No. 1804, like #1798i.

1997
1798 A394 Sheet of 9, #a.-i. 7.50 7.50

Souvenir Sheets

1799-1804 A394 Set of 9 50.00 50.00

Diana, Princess of Wales (1961-97) — A395

Nos. 1805-1807, Various pictures of Diana during her lifetime as Princess of Wales.
Each 1000fr: Pictures of Diana with (in margin): No. 1808, French Pres. Giscard d'Estaing. No. 1809, Mother Teresa. No. 1810, US First Lady Hillary Clinton.

1998, Jan. 2 Sheets of 6 *Perf. 14*

1805 A395 240fr #a.-f. 5.00 5.00
1806 A395 315fr #a.-f. 6.50 6.50
1807 A395 340fr #a.-f. 7.25 7.25

Souvenir Sheets

1808-1810 A395 Set of 3 10.50 10.50

Souvenir Sheet

Marilyn Monroe (1926-62) — A396

1997 Litho. *Perf. 13½*

1811 A396 2000fr multicolored 8.50 8.50

New Year 1998 (Year of the Tiger) — A397

Various paintings of tigers, by Liu Jiyou (1918-83): No. 1812: a, 180fr. b, 200fr. No. 1813: a, 90fr. b, 100fr, c, 180fr. d, 200fr.

1998, Jan. 5 Litho. *Perf. 14*

1812 A397 Sheet of 2, #a.-b. 1.25 1.25
1813 A397 Sheet of 4, #a.-d. 2.00 2.00

No. 1812 contains two 26x65mm stamps.

Hiroshige (1797-1858), Painter A398

Paintings: No. 1814: a, Sixty-Nine Stations of the Kisokaido Road: Mochizuki. b, Eight Views of Lake Biwa Evening Snow at Mt. Hira. c, Kinkizan Temple on Enoshima Island, Sagami Provence. d, Cherry Blossoms. e, Evening Snow at Asakusa. f, Miyanokoshi.
No. 1815: a, Two Terrapins (Fan print). b, Swimming Carp. c, Takanawa by Moonlight. d, Night Rain at Karasaki. e, Chiryu: The Summer Horse Fair. f, Shower over the Nihonbashi.
No. 1816, vert: a, Takata Riding Grounds. b, Sugatami & Omokage Bridges & Jariba at Takata. c, Dam on the Otonashi River at Oji. d, Basho's Hermitage and Camellia Hill. e, Fudo Falls, Oji. f, Takinogawa Oji.
Each 1000fr: No. 1817, Bird in a Tree. No. 1818, Title Page for Hiroshige's One Hundred Views of Edo, by Baisotei. No. 1819, Memorial Portrait of Hiroshige, by Utagawa. No. 1820, Street Stalls and Tradesmen in Jouricho. No. 1821, Cherry Blossom, Morning Glory, Cranes and Rabbits. No. 1822, Three Wild Geese Flying Across the Moon. No. 1823, Suwa Bluff, Nippori. Nos. 1817-1823 are vert.

Perf. 14x13½, 13½x14

1998, Mar. 2 Sheets of 6 Litho.

1814 A398 220fr #a.-f. 5.50 5.50
1815 A398 315fr #a.-f. 7.50 7.50
1816 A398 370fr #a.-f. 8.50 8.50

Souvenir Sheets

Perf. 13½x14

1817-1823 A398 Set of 7 30.00 30.00

Nos. 1817-1823 each contain one 26x72mm stamp.

Fauna, Flora, Minerals A399

Dolphins and whales: No. 1824: a, Souffleur nesarnack. b, Lagenorhynque. c, Sotalie du cameroun. d, Petit rorqual. e, Rorqual commun. f, Faux orque.
Insects and spiders: No. 1825: a, Lasius niger. b, Sceliphron spirifex. c, Peucetia. d, Mygale. e, Theraphoside. f, Dynaste hercule.
Precious stones, minerals: No. 1826: a, Ruby. b, Diamond in kimberlite. c, Cut diamond. d, Rock salt. e, Tiger's eye. f, Uraninite.
Moths and butterflies: No. 1827: a, Pirate. b, Euchromie des liserons. c, Asterope. d, Psalis de kiriakoff. e, Sphinx de fabricius. f, Pensee bleue.
Mushrooms: No. 1828: a, Lepiote. b, Hypholome. c, Lactaire. d, Russule fetide. e, Russule doree. f, Strophaire.
Each 2000fr: No. 1829, Tricholome a odeur de savon. No. 1830, Potto.

1998(?) Litho. *Perf. 13½*

Sheets of 6

1824 A399 180fr #a.-f. 4.00 4.00
1825 A399 250fr #a.-f. 5.75 5.75
1826 A399 300fr #a.-f. 6.75 6.75
1827 A399 400fr #a.-f. 9.00 9.00
1828 A399 450fr #a.-f. 10.25 10.25

Souvenir Sheets

1829-1830 A399 Set of 2 15.50 15.50

Intl. Scouting, 90th Anniv. (#1825, 1827-1830). Nos. 1829-1830 each contain one 41x60mm stamp.

Jerry Garcia (1942-95) — A400

Various portraits.

1998 Litho. *Perf. 13½*

1831 A400 250fr Sheet of 9, #a.-i. 7.75 7.75

Souvenir Sheet

1832 A400 2000fr multicolored 7.00 7.00

No. 1832 contains one 42x51mm stamp.

Dinosaurs — A401

Various unidentified dinosaurs.

1998

1833 A401 290fr Sheet of 9, #a.-i. 10.00 10.00

Souvenir Sheet

1834 A401 2000fr multicolored 7.50 7.50

No. 1834 contains one 42x51mm stamp.

1998 Winter Olympic Games, Nagano A402

No. 1835: a, Hockey. b, Speed skating. c, Pairs figure skating. d, Luge. e, Curling. f, Bobsledding.
No. 1836: a, Downhill skiing. b, Freestyle ski jumping (blue skis). c, Ski jumping. d, Downhill skiier in tuck. e, Snow boarding. f, Freestyle skiing (red skis).

1998 Sheets of 6

1835 A402 250fr #a.-f. 5.75 5.75
1836 A402 300fr #a.-f. 6.75 6.75

Nos. 1835-1836 each have 3 labels.

1998 World Cup Soccer Championships, France — A403

Player, country, vert: No. 1837, Kluivert, Netherlands. No. 1838, Asprilla, Colombia. No. 1839, Bergkamp, Netherlands. No. 1840, Gascoigne, England. No. 1841, Ravanelli, Italy. No. 1842, Sheringham, England.
No. 1843: a, Paul Gascoigne, England, diff. b, Ryan Giggs, Wales. c, Roy Keane, Ireland. d, Stuart Pearce, England. e, Tony Adams, England. f, Teddy Sheringham, England, diff. g, Paul Ince, England. h, Steve McManaman, England.
No. 1844: a, Rossi, Italy. b, Lineker, England. c, Lato, Poland. d, Futre, Poland. e, Klinsmann, Germany. f, Hurst, England. g, Kempes, Argentina. h, McCoist, Scotland.
World Cup Champions, year, vert. — #1845: a, Argentina, 1978. b, Italy, 1982. c, England, 1966. d, Uruguay, 1930. e, Germany, 1954. f, Argentina, 1986. g, Brazil, 1994.
Each 1500fr: No. 1846, Ronaldo, Brazil, vert. No. 1847, Gary Lineker, England, vert. No. 1848, Shearer, England, vert.

Perf. 13½x14, 14x13½

1998, July 10 Litho.

1837-1842 A403 370fr Set of 6 10.00 10.00

Sheets of 8 + Label

1843 A403 220fr #a.-h. 6.50 7.75
1844 A403 315fr #a.-h. 11.00 11.00

Sheet of 7 + 2 Labels

1845 A403 325fr #a.-g. 10.00 10.00

Souvenir Sheets

1846-1848 A403 Set of 3 18.00 18.00

Bella Bellow (d. 1973), Singer — A403a

1998-2004 Litho. *Perf. 13½*

1848A A403a 5fr yel orange
1848B A403a 10fr ol grn
1848C A403a 25fr emerald
1848D A403a 40fr violet
1848E A403a 50fr grnsh blk
s. gray green, dated "2002" —
1848F A403a 75fr yel orange
t. Dated "2002" — —
1848G A403a 100fr orange
1848H A403a 125fr blue
v. Dated "2002" — —
1848I A403a 200fr brt purple
x. Dated "2002" — —
1848J A403a 240fr red violet
1848K A403a 280fr green
1848L A403a 300fr Prus blue
y. Dated "2002" — —
1848M A403a 320fr red org
1848N A403a 340fr car lake
1848O A403a 390fr car rose
1848P A403a 450fr brt blue ('02) — —
1848Q A403a 470fr rose — —
1848R A403a 500fr gray ol ('02) — —
1848T A403a 1000fr gray —
1848W A403a 5000fr vio, dated "2004" — —

Nso. 1848E-1848F, 1848H are dated "1998." Two additional stamps were issued in this set. The editors would like to examine any examples.
See Nos. 1990A-1990O.

Star Wars Movies A404

Return of the Jedi — #1849: a, Princess Leia. b, Darth Vader. c, Han Solo. d, R2-D2, C-3PO. e, Emperor Palpatine. f, Chewbacca. g, Leia on speeder. h, Luke Skywalker. i, Storm trooper on speeder.
Empire Strikes Back — #1850: a, Lando Calrissian. b, Yoda. c, Chewbacca. d, C-3PO, R2-D2. e, Luke Skywalker. f, Darth Vader. g, Battle on snow planet. h, Leia. i, Rider on snow planet.
2000fr, Han Solo, Luke Skywalker, Princess Leia, R2-D2.

1997 Litho. *Perf. 13½*

Sheets of 9

1849 A404 190fr #a.-i. 6.50 6.50
1850 A404 350fr #a.-i. 11.50 11.50

Souvenir Sheet

1851 A404 2000fr multicolored 8.00 8.00

No. 1851 contains one 42x60mm.

Jacqueline Kennedy Onassis (1929-94) — A405

No. 1852: Various portraits.
No. 1853: Various portraits of John F. Kennedy (1917-63).

1997 Sheets of 9

1852 A405 250fr #a.-i. 10.00 10.00
1853 A405 400fr #a.-i. 12.00 12.00

Diana, Princess of Wales (1961-97) — A406

No. 1854: Various portraits.
2000fr, Diana in black (Mother Teresa in sheet margin).

1997 **Sheet of 8 + Label**
1854 A406 500fr #a.-h. 16.00 16.00

Souvenir Sheet
1854I A406 2000fr multicolored 10.00 10.00

Marilyn Monroe (1926-62) — A407

Various portraits, each 300fr.

1997 **Litho.** ***Perf. 13½***
1855 A407 Sheet of 9, #a.-i. 11.00 11.00

Minerals A408

Designs: 100fr, Calcite. 150fr, Turquoise, vert. 200fr, Pyrite, vert. 300fr, Tourmaline, vert. 400fr, Pyrargirite, vert. 500fr, Malachite.
1000fr, Beryl, vert.

1999 **Litho.** ***Perf. 12¾***
1856-1861 A408 Set of 6 6.00 6.00

Souvenir Sheet
Perf. 13
1861A A408 1000fr multicolored 4.00 4.00

No. 1861A contains one 32x40mm stamp.

Butterflies — A408a

Designs: 100fr, Quercusia quercus. 150fr, Pseudacraea boisduvali. 200fr, Argynnis paphia. 300fr, Erebia pandrose. 400fr, Euphydryas maturna. 500fr, Pyronia tithonus.
1000fr, Charaxes pollux.

1999, June 7 **Litho.** ***Perf. 12¾***
1861B-1861G A408a Set of 6 5.75 5.75

Souvenir Sheet
Perf. 13
1861H A408a 1000fr multi 3.75 3.75

No. 1861H contains one 40x32mm stamp.

Flowers — A409

Designs: No. 1862, Caralluma burchardii. No. 1863, Dimorphotheca barberiae. No. 1864, Hoya carnosa. No. 1865, Amaryllis belladonna. No. 1866, Watsonia beatricis. No. 1867, Anthurium schezerianum. No. 1868, Thumbergia alata. No. 1869, Arctotis breviscapa. No. 1870, Glauciun flavum. No. 1871, Impatiens petersiana. No. 1872, Chrysanthemum segetum. No. 1873, Zantedeschia aethiopica, horiz.

1999 ***Perf. 12¼***
1862 A409 100fr brown .30 .30
1863 A409 100fr violet .30 .30
1864 A409 100fr pale red .30 .30
1865 A409 150fr dark grn bl .55 .55
1866 A409 150fr red brown .55 .55
1867 A409 150fr violet blue .55 .55
1868 A409 200fr orange .75 .75
1869 A409 200fr bright grn bl .75 .75
1870 A409 300fr olive 1.10 1.10
1871 A409 300fr blue 1.10 1.10
1872 A409 500fr brown 1.75 1.75
1873 A409 1000fr bright pink 3.75 3.75
Nos. 1862-1873 (12) 11.75 11.75

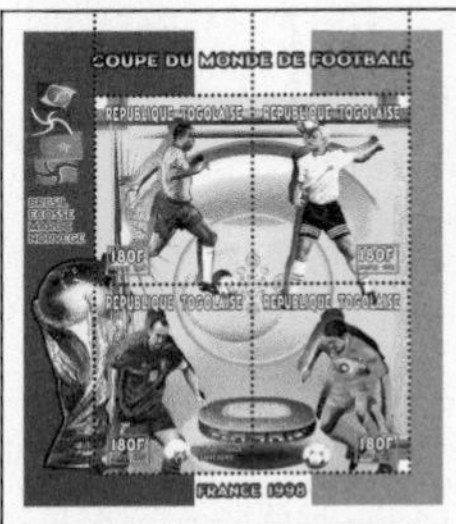

1998 World Cup Soccer Championship, France — A410

Predominant colors of player's shirts. No. 1874: a, Yellow. b, White. c, Blue. d, Red.
No. 1875: a, White. b, Blue. c, Red. d, Green.
No. 1876: a, White, with black shorts. b, Yellow, with blue shorts. c, Yellow, with yellow shorts. d, White, with white shorts.
No. 1877: a, Red. b, Green. c, White. d, Red & white striped.
No. 1878: a, Blue. b, Yellow. c, Red. d, White.
No. 1879: a, Orange. b, White. c, Red. d, Multicolored diamonds.
No. 1880: a, White, with black shorts. b, White, with blue and red chest stripes. c, White, with green trim. d, White, with red and blue arm stripes.
No. 1881: a, Blue & white stripes. b, Red & white checks. c, Yellow & green, d, Blue.
2000fr, Player, map of France.

1998 **Litho.** ***Perf. 13¼***
Sheets of 4
1874 A410 180fr #a.-d. 3.25 3.25
1875 A410 200fr #a.-d. 3.50 3.50
1876 A410 250fr #a.-d. 4.25 4.25
1877 A410 290fr #a.-d. 5.00 5.00
1878 A410 300fr #a.-d. 5.25 5.25
1879 A410 350fr #a.-d. 6.25 6.25
1880 A410 400fr #a.-d. 6.75 6.75
1881 A410 425fr #a.-d. 7.25 7.25
Nos. 1874-1881 (8) 41.50 41.50

Souvenir Sheet
1882 A410 2000fr multicolored 7.50 7.50

Birds — 1882A

Designs: 100fr, Luscinia svecica. 150fr, Oriolus oriolus. 200fr, Carduelis carduelis. 300fr, Parus caeruleus. 400fr, Fringilla coelebs. 500fr, Parus montanus.
1000fr, Regulus ignicapillus.

1999 **Litho.** ***Perf. 12¾***
1882A-1882F A410a Set of 6 6.00 6.00

Souvenir Sheet
Perf. 13x13¼
1882G A410a 1000fr multi 4.00 4.00

No. 1882G contains one 40x32mm stamp.

Antique Automobiles A410b

Designs: 100fr, 1913 Peugeot Bebe. 150fr, 1950 Rolls-Royce. 200fr, 1921 Stutz Bearcat. 300fr, 1923 Ford Model T. 400fr, 1907 Packard. 500fr, 1950 Citroen II Legere sedan.
1000fr, 1929 Ford Model A Tudor sedan.

1999 ***Perf. 12¾***
1882H-1882M A410b Set of 6 6.00 6.00

Souvenir Sheet
Perf. 13
1882N A410b 1000fr multi 4.00 4.00

No. 1882N contains one 40x32mm stamp.

Mushrooms — A410c

Designs: 100fr, Ganoderma lucidum. 150fr, Cantharellus lutescens. 200fr, Lactarius deliciosus. 300fr, Amanita caesarea. 400fr, Cortinarius violaceus. 500fr, Amanita rubescens.
1000fr, Clitopilus prunulus.

1999, Feb. 23 **Litho.** ***Perf. 12¾***
1882O-1882T A410c Set of 6 — —

Souvenir Sheet
Perf. 13¼
1882U A410c 1000fr multi — —

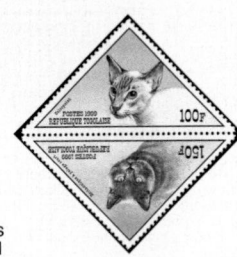

Cats A411

No. 1883: a, 100fr, Colorpoint. b, 150fr, British shorthair.
No. 1884: a, 200fr, Ocicat. b, 300fr, Ragdoll.
No. 1885: a, 400fr, Balinese. b, 500fr, California Spangled.
1000fr, Somali.

1999 **Litho.** ***Perf. 12½***
1883 A411 Pair, #a.-b. .85 .85
1884 A411 Pair, #a.-b. 1.90 1.90
1885 A411 Pair, #a.-b. 3.50 3.50
Nos. 1883-1885 (3) 6.25 6.25

Souvenir Sheet
1886 A411 1000fr multicolored 4.00 4.00

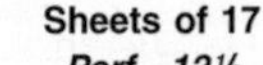

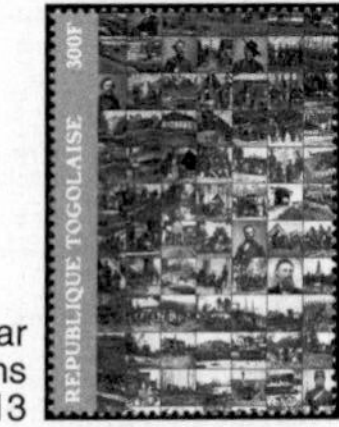

Millennium — A412

No. 1886A, Invention of Paper by Chinese (with millennium emblem).
No. 1887 — Chinese Science & Technology: a, Lacquerware. b, Counting rods. c, Sericulture. d, Acupuncture. e, "Tuned chime bell." f, Piston bellows. g, Compass. h, Manufacture of steel. i. Crossbow. j, Spinning wheel. k, Water conservancy. l, Pulse taking. m, Multi-tube seed drill. n, Rotary winnowing fan. o, Like #1886A (no millennium emblem). p, Silk loom (60x40mm). q, Wheelbarrow.
No. 1888 — Highlights of the 11th Century: a, Chinese invent gunpowder. b, Islamic bronze griffin. c, Battle of Clontarf. d, William becomes Duke of Normandy. e, Norman knight. f, Spinning wheels in use in China. g, Yaroslav becomes Grand Prince of Kiev. h, Polyphonic singing introduced. i, Macbeth becomes King of Scotland. j, Edward the Confessor becomes King of England. k, Astrolabe. l, Harp introduced in Europe. m, Trier Cathedral. n, Mandingo Empire founded in Africa. o, Toltecs invade Yucatan. p, Vikings reach North Americam (60x40mm). q, Movable type used in China.
No. 1889 — Western Paintings of the 20th century by: a, Henri Matisse. b, Pablo Picasso. c, Marc Chagall. d, Wassily Kandinsky. e, Fernand Léger. f, Piet Mondrian. g, George Bellows. h, Georgia O'Keeffe. i, Salvador Dali. j, Francis Bacon. k, Edward Hopper. l, Andy Warhol. m, Helen Frankenthaler. n, Richard Anuszkiewicz. o, Audrey Flack. p, Jackson Pollack, Lee Krasner (60x40mm). q, Jean-Michel Basquiat.

1999 **Litho.** ***Perf. 13¼x13***
1886A A412 120fr multi .70 .70

Sheets of 17
Perf. 12½
1887 A412 120fr #a.-q. + label 9.00 9.00
1888 A412 130fr #a.-q. + label 9.00 9.00
1889 A412 140fr #a.-q. + label 11.00 11.00

Inscriptions on Nos. 1887b, 1887e, 1888i, and perhaps others, are incorrect or misspelled.
Issued: 130fr, 7/20.

US Civil War Photographs A413

Various Civil War photographs making up a photomosaic of Abraham Lincoln, each 300fr.

1999, July 20 **Litho.** ***Perf. 13½***
1890 A413 Sheet of 8, #a.-h. 10.00 10.00

See Nos. 1939-1940.

Free Trade Zone, 10th Anniv. — A414

Symbol and: 125fr, Map. 240fr, Clouds. 340fr, Wall.

1999 **Litho.** ***Perf. 12¾***
1891 A414 125fr multi .45 .45
1892 A414 240fr multi .85 .85
1893 A414 340fr multi 1.25 1.25
Nos. 1891-1893 (3) 2.55 2.55

Rural Development Council, 40th Anniv. — A414a

1999 **Litho.** ***Perf. 13x13¼***
1893A A414a 100fr grn & multi —
1893B A414a 125fr blue & multi —
1893C A414a 240fr red & multi
1893D A414a 380fr vio & multi
1893E A414a 390fr blk & multi

Other stamps for this subject may exist. The editors would like to examine any examples. Numbers may change.

Goldfish A415

Various depictions of Carassius auratus auratus: 100fr, 150fr, 200fr, 300fr, 400fr, 500fr.

1999
1894-1899 A415 Set of 6 6.00 6.00

Souvenir Sheet
Perf. 13
1899A A415 1000fr multi 4.00 4.00

No. 1899A contains one 40x31mm stamp.

SOS Children's Villages, 50th Anniv. — A416

1999 Litho. *Perf. 13¼x13*

1900 A416 125fr multi ('01) .70 .70
1901 A416 240fr multi
1902 A416 340fr multi

Additional stamps may have been issued in this set. The editors would like to examine any examples.

Sailing Vessels — A417

Designs: 100fr, Phoenician boat. 150fr Roman cargo boat. 200fr, New Guinea fishing boat. 300fr, Caravel, vert. 400fr, 16th cent. English ship, vert. 500fr, 17th cent. English ship, vert.
1000fr, Steamship with sails.

1999 Litho. *Perf. 12½*

1905-1910 A417 Set of 6 6.00 6.00

Souvenir Sheet

Perf. 12¼x12

1911 A417 1000fr multi 4.00 4.00

No. 1911 contains one 42x30mm stamp.

Dogs — A417a

Designs: 100fr, St. Bernard. 150fr, Teckel. 200fr, German shepherd. 300fr, Italian hound. 400fr, Yorkshire terrier. 500fr, Schnauzer.
1000fr, Afghan hound.

1999 Litho. *Perf. 12¾*

1911A-1911F A417a Set of 6 6.00 6.00

Souvenir Sheet

Perf. 12½

1911G A417a 1000fr multi 4.00 4.00

No. 1911G contains one 40x31mm stamp.

Trains — A417b

Designs: 100fr, Baldwin 0-4-0. 150fr, Baldwin 2-6-2. 200fr, Baldwin gasoline locomotive. 300fr, H.K. Porter 0-4-0. 400fr, H.K. Porter 2-6-2. 500fr, Vulcan 0-4-0.
1000fr, Jordanian locomotive.

1999 Litho. *Perf. 12¾*

1911H-1911M A417b Set of 6 6.00 6.00

Souvenir Sheet

1911N A417b 1000fr multi 4.00 4.00

No. 1911N contains one 40x31mm stamp.

Orchids — A417c

Designs: 100fr, Gramangis ellisii. 150fr, Habenaria columbae. 200fr, Epidendrum atropurpureum. 300fr, Odontoglossum majale. 400fr, Oncidium splendidum. 500fr, Zygopetalum mackai.
1000fr, Paphiopedilum pairieanum.

1999, Nov. 8 Litho. *Perf. 12x12¼*

1911O-1911T A417c Set of 6 7.25 7.25

Souvenir Sheet

Perf. 12½

1911U A417c 1000fr multi 4.00 4.00

No. 1911U contains one 31x39mm stamp.

New Year 2000 (Year of the Dragon) — A418

Various views of dragon: 100fr, 150fr, 200fr, 300fr, 400fr, 500fr.
1000fr, Head of dragon, horiz.

2000 *Perf. 12¾x12*

1912-1917 A418 Set of 6 6.25 6.25

Souvenir Sheet

Perf. 13¼

1918 A418 1000fr multi 3.50 3.50

No. 1918 contains one 40x32mm stamp.

Wild Cats — A419

Designs: 100fr, Panthera tigris. 150fr, Acinonyx jubatus. 200fr, Felis concolor. 300fr, Panthera leo, female. 400fr, Felis pardalis. 500fr, Panthera leo, male.
1000fr, Panthera tigris, diff.

2000 *Perf. 13*

1919-1924 A419 Set of 6 6.25 6.25

Souvenir Sheet

1925 A419 1000fr multi 3.50 3.50

No. 1925 contains one 40x32mm stamp.

Flowers A420

No. 1926, 290fr: a, Cyrtanthus contractus. b, Sandersonia aurantiaca. c, Anomateca grandiflora. d, Helichrysum ecklonis. e, Striga elegans. f, Nymphaea odorata.
No. 1927, 290fr: a, Leomotis leonii. b, Strelitzia reginae. c, Freesia refracta. d, Garzania nivea. e, Dimophotheca sinuata. f, Pelargonium domesticum.
No. 1928, 290fr: a, Gloriosa rothchiliana. b, Clematis vitalba. c, Rochea falcato. d, Plumbago capensis. e, Thunbergia alata. f, Lampranthus coccineus.
No. 1929, 1500fr, Epiphyllum hybrid. No. 1930, 1500fr, Agapanthus africanus.
Illustration reduced.

2000, July 28 Litho. *Perf. 14*

Sheets of 6, #a-f

1926-1928 A420 Set of 3 24.00 24.00

Souvenir Sheets

1929-1930 A420 Set of 2 13.50 13.50

Wildlife — A421

Designs: 200fr, Thompson's gazelle. 300fr, Felis margarita. 400fr, Blesbok. 500fr, Kob.
No. 1935, 290fr, vert.: a, Hoopoe. b, Harpactira spider. c, Marabou. d, Bee-eater. e, Oryx. f, Okapi. g, Wart hog. h, Baboon.
No. 1936, 290fr, vert.: a, Hornbill. b, Pygmy kingfisher. c, Vulture. d, Bataleur eagle. e, Kudu. f, Hyena. g, Gorilla. h, Lizard.
No. 1937, 1500fr, Eland, vert. No. 1938, 1500fr, Mongoose, vert.

2000, July 28

1931-1934 A421 Set of 4 6.75 6.75

Sheets of 8, #a-h

1935-1936 A421 Set of 2 22.50 22.50

Souvenir Sheets

1937-1938 A421 Set of 2 13.50 13.50

Mushrooms — A421a

Designs: 100fr, Hebeloma crustuliniforme. 150fr, Polyporellus squamosus, horiz. 200fr, Morchella deliciosa. 300fr, Disciotis venosa, horiz. 400fr, Cantharellus tubiformis. 500fr, Otidea onotica, horiz.
1000fr, Ixocomus granulatus, horiz.

2000, July 30 Litho. *Perf. 12¾*

1938A-1938F A421a Set of 6 6.25 6.25

Souvenir Sheet

Perf. 13

1938G A421a 1000fr multi 3.50 3.50

No. 1938G contains one 39x31mm stamp.

Civil War Photographs Type of 1999

No. 1939, 290fr: Various photographs with a science theme making up a photomosaic of Albert Einstein.
No. 1940, 290fr: Various photographs with an Oriental theme making up a photomosaic of Mao Zedong.

2000, Sept. 5 *Perf. 13¾*

Sheets of 8, #a-h

1939-1940 A413 Set of 2 24.00 24.00

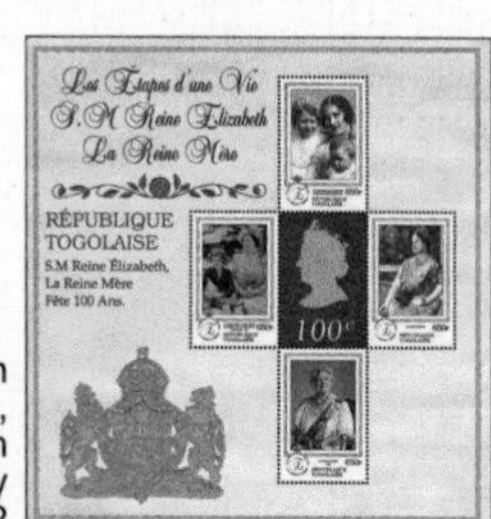

Queen Mother, 100th Birthday A422

No. 1941: a, With Princesses Elizabeth and Margaret, 1931. b, With daughter, 1940. c, Black and white photo. d, In 1990.
1500fr, With Princess Margaret, 1939.

2000, Sept. 5 *Perf. 14*

1941 A422 650fr Sheet of 4, #a-d, + label 12.50 12.50

Souvenir Sheet

Perf. 13¾

1942 A422 1500fr multi 7.25 7.25

No. 1942 contains one 38x51mm stamp.

Popes A423

No. 1943, 400fr: a, Anastasius I, 399-401. b, Boniface I, 418-22. c, Gaius, 283-96. d, Hilarius, 461-68. e, Hyginus, 136-40. f, Innocent I, 402-17.
No. 1944, 400fr: a, Martin I, 649-55. b, Nicholas I, 858-67. c, Paschal I, 817-24. d, Paul I, 757-67. e, Pelagius, 556-61. f, Pelagius II, 579-90.
No. 1945, 400fr: a, Sergius, 687-701. b, Sergius II, 844-47. c, Severinus, 640. d, Sisinnius, 708. e, Stephen II, 752-57. f, Stephen IV, 816-17.
No. 1946, 1500fr, Pontian, 230-35. No. 1947, 1500fr, Pelagius II, diff. No. 1948, 1500fr, Stephen V, 885-91.
Illustration reduced.

2000, Sept. 5 *Perf. 12x12¼*

Sheets of 6, #a-f

1943-1945 A423 Set of 3 32.50 32.50

Souvenir Sheets

1946-1948 A423 Set of 3 20.00 20.00

British Monarchs — A424

No. 1949, 400fr: a, Charles II, 1660-85. b, Anne, 1702-14. c, George I, 1714-27. d, George IV, 1820-30. e, James II, 1685-88. f, George II, 1727-60.
No. 1950, 400fr: a, Elizabeth II, 1952-present. b, Edward VIII, 1936. c, George VI, 1936-52. d, George V, 1910-36. e, Edward VII, 1901-10. f, William IV, 1830-37.
No. 1951, 1500fr, William III and Mary, 1689-1702. No. 1952, 1500fr, Victoria, 1837-1901.

2000, Sept. 5 Sheets of 6, #a-f

1949-1950 A424 Set of 2 22.50 22.50

Souvenir Sheets

1951-1952 A424 Set of 2 13.50 13.50

Millennium Type of 1999

Highlights of 1950-59: a, US sends troops to defend South Korea. b, Rock and roll hits the air waves. c, Death of Eva Peron. d, Structure of DNA revealed by Watson and Crick. e, Sir Edmund Hillary and Tenzing Norgay reach peak of Mt. Everest. f, John F. Kennedy marries Jacqueline Bouvier. g, Coronation of Queen Elizabeth II. h, Millionth Volkswagen produced. i, German soccer team wins World Cup. j, Roger Bannister runs 1st 4-minute mile. k, Dr. Jonas Salk develops polio vaccine. l, 1st McDonald's franchise. m, New phone lines cross Atlantic. n, Soviet Union launches Sputnik. o, Jack Kerouac writes "On the Road." p, China begins "Great Leap Forward." q, Communist revolution in Cuba. r, Computer chip patented.

2000 *Perf. 12¾x12½*

1953 A412 200fr Sheet of 18, #a-r, + label 17.50 17.50

36th Organization of African Unity Summit, Lomé — A425

OAU emblem, map of Africa, doves and panel color of: 10fr, Bright yellow. 25fr, Green. 100fr, Dull yellow. 125fr, Blue violet. 250fr, Red violet. 375fr, Red. 400fr, Brown. 425fr, Orange.
No. 1954: a, Peace dove statue. b, Hotel du 2 Février. c, Congress building, Lomé. d, Alédjo Fault. e, Temberma hut. f, Cacao plantation.
No. 1955: a, Pres. Gnassingbé Eyadema, map of Europe and Africa, handshakes. b, Algerian Pres. Abdelazir Bouteflika, Pres. Eyadema, and map of Africa. c, Pres. Eyadema and OAU emblem. d, Map of Africa, doves, OAU emblem.
Illustration reduced.

2000 Litho. *Perf. 14x13¾*

1953S-1953Z A425 Set of 8 7.25 7.25

Sheets of 6 and 4

1954 A425 350fr #a-f 7.50 7.50
1955 A425 550fr #a-d 7.75 7.75

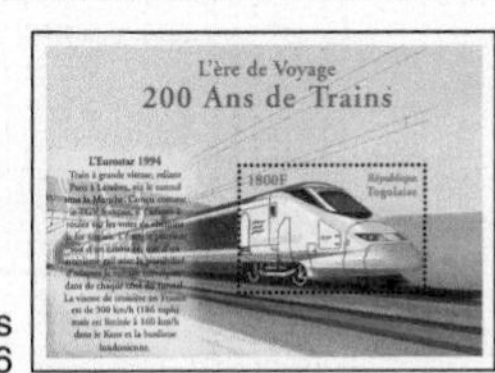

Trains A426

No. 1956, 425fr: a, Richard Trevethick's engine. b, Stephenson's Adler. c, Crampton Continent. d, Atlantic Coastlines 4-4-2. e, Great Northern Railway Ivatt Atlantic. f, Great Western Railway City of Truro 4-4-0.

No. 1957, 425fr: a, Paris-Lyon-Mediterranean Railway, compound 4-8-2. b, Canadian Pacific Railway Royal Hudson 4-6-4. c, London-Midland Railway Duchess. d, New York Central Twentieth Century Limited. e, New Zealand Government Railway J class 4-8-4. f, British Railways Evening Star 5-10-0.

No. 1958, 1800fr, Eurostar. No. 1959, 1800fr, TGV Atlantique.

2000, Sept. 8 Litho. *Perf. 14*

Sheets of 6, #a-f

1956-1957 A426 Set of 2 22.50 22.50

Souvenir Sheets

1958-1959 A426 Set of 2 16.00 16.00

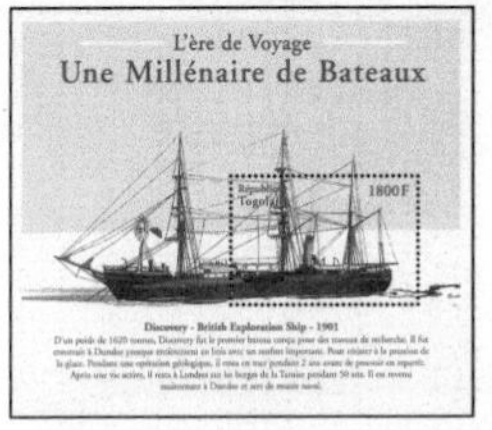

Ships A427

No. 1960, 425fr: a, Norse knaar. b, Hanseatic cog. c, Iberian caravel. d, Henri Grace à Dieu. e, Ark Royal. f, Dutch Hooker.

No. 1961, 425fr: a, HMS Victory. b, HMS Warrior. c, Cutty Sark. d, USS Olympia. e, Empress of Canada. f, James Clark Ross.

No. 1962, 1800fr, Discovery. No. 1963, 1800fr, Sea Cat ferry.

2000, Sept. 8 Litho. *Perf. 14*

Sheets of 6, #a-f

1960-1961 A427 Set of 2 22.50 22.50

Souvenir Sheets

1962-1963 A427 Set of 2 16.00 16.00

Dogs and Cats — A428

Designs: 275fr, Bloodhound. 300fr, Sphinx cat. 325fr, Basset hound. 350fr, Cocker spaniel. No. 1968, 375fr, American curl cat. 400fr, Scottish fold cat.

No. 1970, 375fr, horiz. — Dogs: a, Bearded collie. b, Chow chow. c, Boxer. d, Irish setter. e, Bracco Italiano. f, Pointer.

No. 1971, 375fr, horiz. — Cats: a, Devon Rex. b, Cornish Rex. c, Siamese. d, Balinese. e, Birman. f, Korat.

No. 1972, 1500fr, Yorkshire terrier. No. 1973, 1500fr, Chinchilla cat.

Perf. 13½x13¼, 13¼x13½

2001, Dec. 17 Litho.

1964-1969 A428 Set of 6 10.00 10.00

Sheets of 6, #a-f

1970-1971 A428 Set of 2 22.50 22.50

Souvenir Sheets

1972-1973 A428 Set of 2 15.00 15.00

Marine Life A429

No. 1974, 200fr (31x31mm): a, Priacanthus arenatus. b, Diplodus annularis. c, Lithognathus mormyrus. d, Selene vomer. e, Penaeus duorarum. f, Arbacia lixula. g, Serranus scriba. h, Trachurus trachurus. i, Lepas anatifera. j, Octopus vulgaris. k, Scorpaena scrofa. l, Dardanus arrosor.

No. 1975, 250fr (31x31mm): a, Porcupine fish. b, Blue shark. c, Sting ray. d, Physalia physalis. e, Turtles. f, Coryphaena hippurus. g, Caranx hippos. h, Sawfish. i, Todaropsis eblanae. j, Pompano. k, Diplodus cervinus. l, Barracuda.

No. 1976, 1500fr, Octopus vulgaris, diff. No. 1977, 1500fr, Blue shark, diff.

2001, Dec. 17 *Perf. 12½*

Sheets of 12, #a-l

1974-1975 A429 Set of 2 26.00 26.00

Souvenir Sheets

Perf. 13¼x13½

1976-1977 A429 Set of 2 15.00 15.00

African Wildlife — A430

Designs: 150fr, Okapia johnstoni, vert. 200fr, Sagittarius serpentarius. 250fr, Lemur catta, vert. 300fr, Gorilla gorilla. 350fr, Genetta genetta, vert. 400fr, Fennecus zerda.

No. 1984, 380fr: a, Papio hamadryas. b, Felis serval. c, Suricata suricatta. d, Orycteropus afer. e, Connochataetes taurinus. f, Tragelaphus strepsiceros.

No. 1985, 380fr: a, Panthera pardus. b, Loxodonta africana. c, Cercopithecus hamlyni. d, Ephippiorhynchuus senegalensis. e, Hippopotamus amphibius. f, Hippotragus niger.

No. 1986, 415fr: a, Equus burchelli boehmi. b, Ceratotherium simum. c, Achionyx jubatus. d, Gazella dama. e, Crocuta crocuta. f, Lyacon pictus.

No. 1987, 1500fr, Crocodylus niloticus. No. 1988, 1500fr, Panthera leo, vert. No. 1989, 1500fr, Giraffa camelopardalis.

Perf. 13½x13¼, 13¼x13½

2001, Dec. 17

1978-1983 A430 Set of 6 8.00 8.00

Sheets of 6, #a-f

1984-1986 A430 Set of 3 35.00 35.00

Souvenir Sheets

1987-1989 A430 Set of 3 22.50 22.50

United We Stand — A431

2002, Mar. 18 Litho. *Perf. 14*

1990 A431 400fr multi 2.00 2.00

Bella Bellow Type of 1998-2004

2002-04 Litho. *Perf. 13½*

1990A	A403a	20fr yel green	—	—
1990B	A403a	30fr brown	—	—
1990C	A403a	110fr blue green	—	—
1990D	A403a	150fr aquamarine		—
1990E	A403a	175fr brt pur ('04)	—	—
1990F	A403a	250fr red		—
1990G	A403a	350fr lilac ('04)		—
1990H	A403a	400fr yellow green		—
1990I	A403a	550fr pale orange		—
1990J	A403a	600fr brown ('04)	—	—
1990K	A403a	650fr black		—
1990L	A403a	750fr brt blue ('04)	—	—
1990M	A403a	1000fr rose		—
1990N	A403a	2000fr dull brn ('04)	—	—
1990O	A403a	3000fr light blue		—

The editors suspect that additional stamps were issued in this set and would like to examine any examples.

Numbers may change.

2004 Summer Olympics, Athens A432

Designs: 150fr, Chariot rider and horses. 300fr, Pin from 1960 Rome Olympics, vert. 450fr, Emblem of 1960 Squaw Valley Winter Olympics, vert. 500fr, Diver, vert.

2004, Aug. 25 Litho. *Perf. 13¼*

1991-1994 A432 Set of 4 6.50 6.50

Pres. Gnassingbé Eyadema (1935-2005) — A433

2004 *Perf. 13½x13¼*

Panel Color

1995	A433	25fr dark blue	.25	.25
1996	A433	50fr yel green	.25	.25
1997	A433	150fr olive green	.60	.60
1998	A433	400fr dull brown	1.60	1.60
1999	A433	550fr green	2.25	2.25
2000	A433	650fr brt blue	2.75	2.75
2001	A433	1000fr lilac	4.25	4.25
2002	A433	2000fr salmon pink	8.25	8.25
2003	A433	3000fr blue green	12.50	12.50
		Nos. 1995-2003 (9)	32.70	32.70

Cooperation Between Togo and People's Republic of China, 30th Anniv. (in 2002) — A434

2004, Mar. 1 *Perf. 12*

Frame Color

2003A	A434	150fr org yellow	—
2004	A434	300fr gray	—
2005	A434	450fr green	—
2006	A434	500fr red brown	—

Pope John Paul II (1920-2005) — A435

2006, Jan. 24 *Perf. 13½*

2007 A435 550fr multi 2.50 2.50

Printed in sheets of 4.

Jules Verne (1828-1905), Writer — A436

No. 2008: a, Home of Verne from 1882-1900. b, Monument to Verne, Amiens, France. c, Sculpture of Verne, Amiens. d, Mysterious Island.

2006, Jan. 24 Litho. *Perf. 13½*

2008 A436 550fr Sheet of 4, #a-d 10.00 10.00

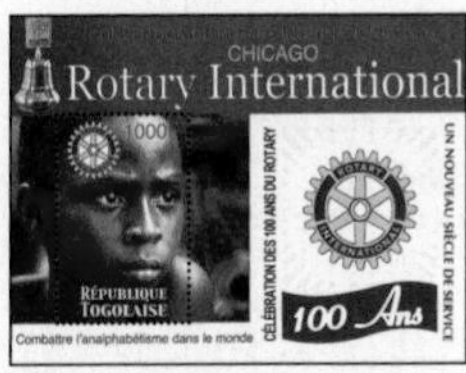

Rotary International, Cent. (in 2005) — A437

No. 2009 — Children and denomination in: a, Yellow in upper right. b, Red. c, Yellow in upper left.

1000fr, Child.

2006, Jan. 24

2009 A437 700fr Sheet of 3, #a-c 10.00 10.00

Souvenir Sheet

2010 A437 1000fr multi 4.50 4.50

Friedrich von Schiller (1759-1805), Writer — A438

No. 2011, vert. — Schiller: a, Monument. b, Bust. c, Portrait.

1000fr, Birthplace of Schiller.

2006, Jan. 24

2011 A438 700fr Sheet of 3, #a-c 10.00 10.00

Souvenir Sheet

2012 A438 1000fr multi 4.50 4.50

World Cup Soccer Championships, 75th Anniv. (in 2005) — A439

No. 2013: a, David Beckham. b, Ronaldo Nazario. c, Fernando Hierro.

1000fr, Eusebio.

2006, Jan. 24

2013 A439 700fr Sheet of 3, #a-c 10.00 10.00

Souvenir Sheet

2014 A439 1000fr multi 4.50 4.50

V-E Day, 50th Anniv. (in 2005) A440

No. 2015, vert.: a, Monument to victory. b, New York Times front page with war reports. c, Soldiers at Battle of the Bulge, 1944. d, Airplanes. e, Sculpture of Holocaust victim.

1000fr, DUKW.

2006, Jan. 24 Litho. *Perf. 13¼*

2015 A440 400fr Sheet of 5, #a-e 7.50 7.50

Souvenir Sheet

2016 A440 1000fr multi 3.75 3.75

V-J Day, 50th Anniv. (in 2005) A441

No. 2017: a, USS Charles Carroll. b, BB-35. c, LCT-515. d, LST-388. e, Destroyer Thompson DD-627. f, USS Thomas Jefferson.

1000fr, Battle of Iwo Jima.

2006, Jan. 24

2017 A441 350fr Sheet of 6, #a-f 7.75 7.75

Souvenir Sheet

2018 A441 1000fr multi 3.75 3.75

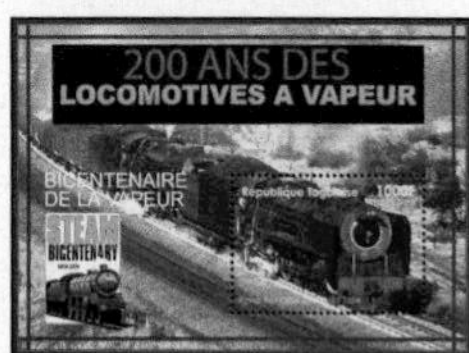

Railroads, Bicent. — A442

No. 2019: a, DX5287. b, W192. c, Central Pacific Jupiter. d, LWDHAM.
No. 2020, 1000fr, Rovos Ralf Class 25NC. No. 2021, 1000fr, Class 242 streamlined tank locomotive.

2006, Jan. 24

2019 A442 550fr Sheet of 4, #a-d 8.25 8.25

Souvenir Sheets

2020-2021 A442 Set of 2 7.50 7.50

Léopold Sédar Senghor Year — A443

2006, July 28

2022	A443	150fr multi	.60	.60
2023	A443	550fr multi	2.25	2.25
2024	A443	650fr multi	2.60	2.60
2025	A443	1000fr multi	4.00	4.00
2026	A443	2000fr multi, horiz.	8.00	8.00
2027	A443	3000fr multi, horiz.	12.00	12.00
2028	A443	5000fr multi, horiz.	20.00	20.00
2029	A443	10,000fr multi, horiz.	40.00	40.00
		Nos. 2022-2029 (8)	89.45	89.45

Souvenir Sheet

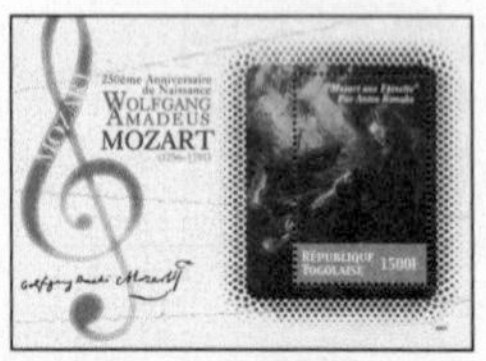

Wolfgang Amadeus Mozart (1756-91), Composer — A444

2006, Dec. 21 ***Perf. 14***

2030 A444 1500fr multi 6.00 6.00

Space Achievements A445

Designs: 150fr, Luna 9. 300fr, Hayabusa probe. 450fr, Venus Express. 500fr, Space Shuttle Discovery, vert.
No. 2035: a, Intl. Space Station. b, Deep Impact probe. c, Muse Asteroid. d, Artist's view of L1 spacecraft. e, Odyssey. f, Calipso.
No. 2036: a, Viking 1 in oribit around Mars. b, Viking 1. c, Phobos. d, Viking Lander 1.
No. 2037, 1500fr, Mars Reconnaissance Orbiter. No. 2038, 1500fr, Apollo 11, vert.

2006, Dec. 21 ***Perf. 13¼***

2031-2034	A445	Set of 4	5.75	5.75
2035	A445	400fr Sheet of 6, #a-f	9.50	9.50
2036	A445	550fr Sheet of 4, #a-d	8.75	8.75

Souvenir Sheets

2037-2038 A445 Set of 2 12.00 12.00

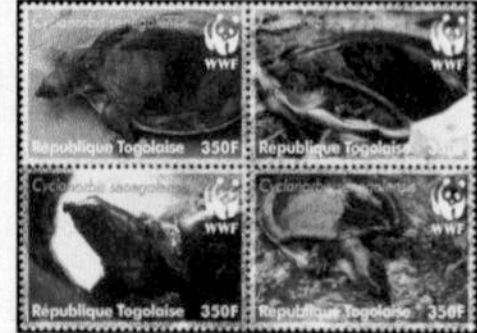

Worldwide Fund for Nature (WWF) — A446

No. 2039 — Cyclanorbis senegalensis: a, On sand, facing left. b, With foliage, facing left. c, Head. d, With foliage, facing right.

2006, Dec. 28

2039 A446 350fr Block or strip of 4, #a-d 5.75 5.75
e. Minature sheet, 2 each #a-d 11.50 11.50

Birds A447

No. 2040: a, Platnea alba. b, Ceryle rudis. c, Ardea alba. d, Ephipphorhynchus senegalensis.
1500fr, Ephipphorhynchus senegalensis, diff.

2006,Dec. 28 ***Perf. 14***

2040 A447 450fr Sheet of 4, #a-d 7.25 7.25

Souvenir Sheet

2041 A447 1500fr multi 6.00 6.00

Mushrooms — A448

No. 2042: a, Coprinus micaceus. b, Cookeina sulcipes. c, Hygrocybe firma. d, Chlorophyllum molybdites.
1500fr, Volvariella esculenta.

2006,Dec. 28

2042 A448 450fr Sheet of 4, #a-d 7.25 7.25

Souvenir Sheet

2043 A448 1500fr multi 6.00 6.00

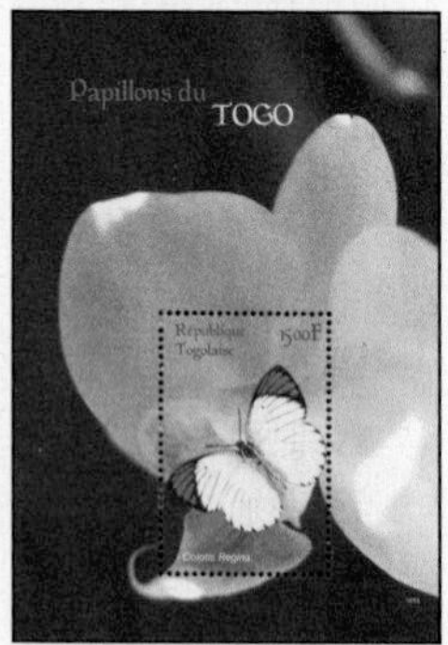

Butterflies — A449

No. 2044, horiz.: a, Papilio nobilis. b, Colotis celimene. c, Salamis anacardii. d, Eronia cleodora.
1500fr, Colotis regina.

2006,Dec. 28 ***Perf. 14***

2044 A449 450fr Sheet of 4, #a-d 7.25 7.25

Souvenir Sheet

2045 A449 1500fr multi 6.00 6.00

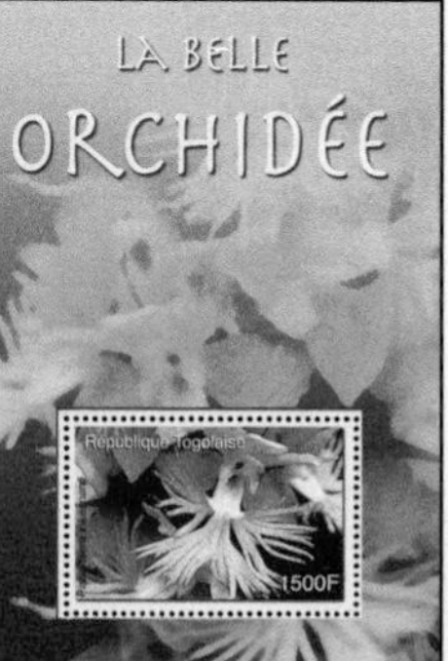

Orchids A450

No. 2046, vert.: a, Triphora trianthophora. b, Amerorchis rotundifolia. c, Cypripedium x andrewsii. d, Pogonia ophioglossoides.
1500fr, Platanthera x keenanii.

2006,Dec. 28 ***Perf. 14***

2046 A450 450fr Sheet of 4, #a-d 7.25 7.25

Souvenir Sheet

2047 A450 1500fr multi 6.00 6.00

Rembrandt (1606-69), Painter — A451

Designs: 50fr, Three Oriental Figures (Jacob and Laban). 100fr, The Pancake Woman. 150fr, The Goldsmith. 250fr, The Golf Player. 325fr, The Persian. 350fr, Jacob and Rachel Listening to an Account of Joseph's Dreams.
1250fr, The Conspiracy of Julius Civilis, horiz.

2006 ***Perf. 14¼***

2048-2053 A451 Set of 6 5.00 5.00

Imperf

Size: 106x76mm

2054 A451 1250fr multi 5.00 5.00

Souvenir Sheets

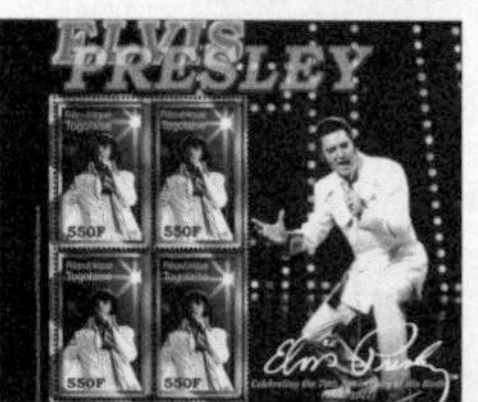

A452

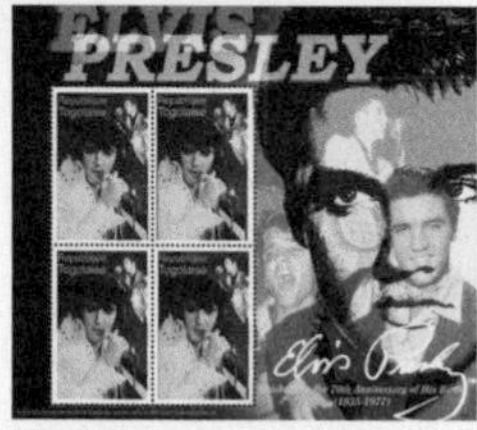

Elvis Presley (1935-77) — A453

No. 2055 — Country name in: a, Pale blue. b, Pale yellow. c, Pink. d, Pale green.
No. 2056 — Country name in: a, Pale blue. b, Pale yellow. c, Pink. d, Pale green.

2006, Dec. 21 **Litho.** ***Perf. 14***

2055 A452 550fr Sheet of 4, #a-d 8.75 8.75
2056 A453 550fr Sheet of 4, #a-d 8.75 8.75

New Year 2007 (Year of the Pig) — A454

2008, Jan. 21 **Litho.** ***Perf. 13½***

2057 A454 275fr multi 1.25 1.25

Printed in sheets of 4.

Pope Benedict XVI — A455

2008, Jan. 21 ***Perf. 12½x12¾***

2058 A455 300fr multi 1.40 1.40

Printed in sheets of 8.

Miniature Sheet

Inauguration of Pres. John F. Kennedy, 47th Anniv. — A456

No. 2059: a, Band passing reviewing stand. b, Kennedy taking oath of office. c, Capitol. d, Kennedy giving inaugural address.

2008, Jan. 21 ***Perf. 13¼***

2059 A456 450fr Sheet of 4, #a-d 8.00 8.00

Wedding of Queen Elizabeth II and Prince Philip, 60th Anniv. A457

No. 2060: a, Couple, white frame. b, Queen, pink frame. c, Couple, light blue frame. d, Queen, light blue frame. e, Couple, pink frame. f, Queen, white frame.
1250fr, Couple, diff., green frame.

2008, Jan. 21 ***Perf. 12¾***

2060 A457 400fr Sheet of 6, #a-f 11.00 11.00

Souvenir Sheet

2061 A457 1250fr multi 5.75 5.75

Princess Diana (1961-97) — A458

No. 2062, vert.: a, Wearing double-stranded pearl necklace, large photo. b, Wearing white hat, cropped photo. c, Wearing black and white houndstooth dress, large photo. d, Wearing double-stranded pearl necklace, cropped photo. e, Wearing white hat, large photo. f, Wearing black and white houndstooth dress, cropped photo.
1500fr, Wearing black jacket.

2008, Jan. 21
2062 A458 400fr Sheet of 6, #a-f 11.00 11.00

Souvenir Sheet

2063 A458 1500fr multi 6.75 6.75

Campaign to Prevent AIDS — A459

Red AIDS ribbon and: 200fr, Colored squares. 550fr, Hand, horiz. 650fr, Man and woman carrying Togo flags, horiz.

2008, Feb. 8 ***Perf. 11½***
2064-2066 A459 Set of 3 5.75 5.75

Dated 2007.

Miniature Sheet

2008 Summer Olympics, Beijing — A460

No. 2067: a, Swimming. b, Running. c, Soccer. d, Sailing.

2008, Aug. 18 **Litho.** ***Perf. 12***
2067 A460 240fr Sheet of 4, #a-d 4.50 4.50

Peony — A461

2009, Apr. 10 **Litho.** ***Perf. 13¼***
2068 A461 200fr multi .80 .80

Printed in sheets of 8.

Miniature Sheet

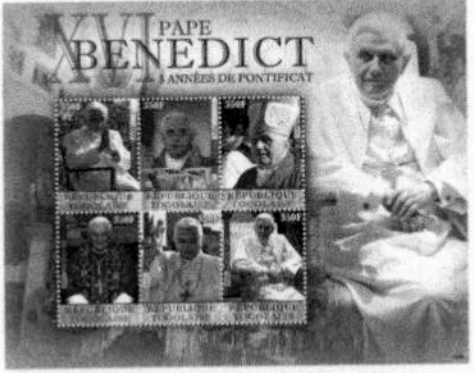

Pope Benedict XVI A462

No. 2069 — Pope Benedict XVI: a, Seated, with hands in prayer. b, With covered chalices. c, Wearing miter. d, Wearing red vestments and red and gold stole. e, Wearing white vestments, hand raised. f, Seated with hands crossed.

2010, Feb. 11 ***Perf. 11½***
2069 A462 350fr Sheet of 6, #a-f 8.75 8.75

Miniature Sheet

U.S. Pres. Barack Obama A463

No. 2070 — Pres. Obama: a, With people in background. b, With blue sky in background. c, On telehone. d, Wearing suit, with hand raised.

2010, Feb. 11 ***Perf. 12x11½***
2070 A463 450fr Sheet of 4, #a-d 7.50 7.50

A464

A465

Michael Jackson (1958-2009), Singer — A466

No. 2071 — Jackson with microphone: a, Near mouth, gray area at top. b, Near eyes, black area behind head. c, Near eyes, tan area behind head. d, Near mouth, black area behind head.

No. 2072 — Jackson wearing: a, White costume with pearls. b, Black costume with sequins. c, Sunglasses, with hands together. d, Sunglasses, hands not visible.

2010, Feb. 11 ***Perf. 11½x12***
2071 A464 450fr Sheet of 4, #a-d 7.50 7.50

Perf. 11½

2072 A465 450fr Sheet of 4, #a-d 7.50 7.50

Souvenir Sheet

2073 A466 1000fr black & gray 4.25 4.25

A467

A468

A469

Phataginus Tricuspis — A470

2010, Mar. 6 ***Perf. 13x13¼***

2074	Horiz. strip of 4	9.00	9.00
a.	A467 550fr multi	2.25	2.25
b.	A468 550fr multi	2.25	2.25
c.	A469 550fr multi	2.25	2.25
d.	A470 550fr multi	2.25	2.25
e.	Sheet of 8, 2 each #2074a-2074d, + 2 labels	18.00	18.00

Pan-African Postal Union, 30th Anniv. — A471

Pan-African Postal Union emblem and various Tamberma dwellings.

2010 **Litho.** ***Perf. 13x13½***
2075 A471 50fr multi —
2076 A471 200fr multi — —
2077 A471 500fr multi —

Independence, 50th Anniv. — A472

2010 **Litho.** ***Perf. 13***
2079 A472 550fr yel & multi —

Two additional items were issued in this set. The editors would like to examine any examples.

Granary — A472b

2011 **Litho.** ***Perf. 13***
2081 A472b 200fr red & multi —
2082 A472b 550fr brt blue & multi — —

Lomé Cathedral — A472c

2011 **Litho.** ***Perf. 13***
2082A A472c 200fr blue & multi —
2083 A472c 550fr multi —

King Mensah, Musician, 15th Anniv. of Performing — A472d

2011 **Litho.** ***Perf. 13***
2084 A472d 550fr multi —

Post Bus — A473

2011 **Litho.** ***Perf. 13***
2085 A473 200fr yel grn & multi —

An additional stamp was issued in this set. The editors would like to examine any example.

A474

A475

Diplomatic Relations Between Togo and People's Republic of China, 40th Anniv. A476

2012 **Litho.** ***Perf. 12***
2087 A474 200fr multi —
2088 A475 550fr multi —
2089 A476 700fr multi —

The editors suspect that additional stamps may have been issued in this set and would like to examine any examples.

SEMI-POSTAL STAMPS

Curie Issue
Common Design Type

1938 **Unwmk.** **Engr.** ***Perf. 13***
B1 CD80 1.75fr + 50c brt ultra 20.00 20.00
Never hinged 32.50

French Revolution Issue
Common Design Type

Photo., Name and Value Typo. in Black

1939

B2	CD83	45c + 25c green	8.50	8.50
B3	CD83	70c + 30c brown	8.50	8.50
B4	CD83	90c + 35c red org	8.50	8.50
B5	CD83	1.25fr + 1fr rose pink	8.50	8.50
B6	CD83	2.25fr + 2fr blue	8.50	8.50
		Nos. B2-B6 (5)	42.50	42.50
		Set, never hinged	70.00	

French Revolution, 150th anniv. Surtax for defense of the colonies.

Nos. 281, 236, 245, 289 Srchd. in Red or Black

1941 ***Perf. 14 x 13½, 12½***

B7	A10	50c + 1fr	3.50	3.50
B8	A7	80c + 2fr	7.00	7.00
B9	A8	1.50fr + 2fr	7.00	7.00
B10	A11	2fr + 3fr (R)	7.00	7.00
		Nos. B7-B10 (4)	24.50	24.50
		Set, never hinged	50.00	

Catalogue values for unused stamps in this section, from this point to the end of the section, are for Never Hinged items.

Common Design Type and

Togolese Militiaman — SP1

Military Infirmary — SP2

1941 **Photo.** ***Perf. 13½***
B10A SP1 1fr + 1fr red 1.10
B10B CD86 1.50fr + 3fr maroon 1.10
B10C SP2 2.50fr + 1fr blue 1.10
Nos. B10A-B10C (3) 3.30

Nos. B10A-B10C were issued by the Vichy government in France, but were not placed on sale in Togo.

Nos. 296-297 Surcharged in Black or Red

1944 Engr. *Perf. 12x12½*
B10D 50c + 1.50fr on 2.50fr deep blue (R) .70
B10E + 2.50fr on 1fr green .70

Colonial Development Fund.
Nos. B10D-B10E were issued by the Vichy government in France, but were not placed on sale in Togo.

Tropical Medicine Issue
Common Design Type

1950 Engr. *Perf. 13*
B11 CD100 10fr + 2fr indigo & dk bl 5.00 3.50

The surtax was for charitable work.

Republic

Patient on Stretcher — SP3

Designs: 30fr+5fr, Feeding infant. 50fr+10fr, Blood transfusion.

1959 Engr. *Perf. 13*
B12 SP3 20fr + 5fr multicolored .75 .75
a. Souvenir sheet of 4 5.00 5.00
B13 SP3 30fr + 5fr bl, car & brn .75 .75
a. Souvenir sheet of 4 5.00 5.00
B14 SP3 50fr + 10fr emer, brn & car .75 .75
a. Souvenir sheet of 4 5.00 5.00
Nos. B12-B14 (3) 2.25 2.25

Issued for the Red Cross.
Nos. B12a, B13a, B14a exist imperf.; same values.

Uprooted Oak Emblem — SP4

No. B16 similar to No. B15, with emblem on top.

1960 Unwmk. *Perf. 13*
B15 SP4 25fr + 5fr dk bl, brn & yel grn .45 .45
B16 SP4 45fr + 5fr dk bl, brn & ol .80 .80

World Refugee Year, July 1, 1959-June 30, 1960. The surtax was for aid to refugees.

AIR POST STAMPS

Common Design Type

1940 Unwmk. Engr. *Perf. 12½x12*
C1 CD85 1.90fr ultra .35 .35
C2 CD85 2.90fr dark red .35 .35
C3 CD85 4.50fr dk gray grn .35 .35
C4 CD85 4.90fr yellow bister .70 .70
C5 CD85 6.90fr deep orange 1.40 1.40
Nos. C1-C5 (5) 3.15 3.15
Set, never hinged 5.00

Common Design Type
Inscribed "Togo" across top

1942
C6 CD88 50c car & bl .25
C7 CD88 1fr brn & blk .35
C8 CD88 2fr grn & red brn .50
C9 CD88 3fr dk bl & scar .65
C10 CD88 5fr vio & brn red .70

Frame Engraved, Center Typographed
C11 CD89 10fr ultra, ind & org 1.10
C12 CD89 20fr rose car, mag & gray blk 1.10
C13 CD89 50fr yel grn, dl grn & lt vio 2.10 —
Nos. C6-C13 (8) 6.75
Set, never hinged 10.50

There is doubt whether Nos. C6-C12 were officially placed in use.

Catalogue values for unused stamps in this section, from this point to the end of the section, are for Never Hinged items.

Elephants AP1

Plane AP2

Plane AP3

Post Runner and Plane AP4

1947, Oct. 6 Engr. *Perf. 12½*
C14 AP1 40fr blue 8.50 3.50
C15 AP2 50fr lt ultra, & red vio 4.25 1.40
C16 AP3 100fr emer & dk brn 8.50 2.10
C17 AP4 200fr lilac rose 13.00 3.50
Nos. C14-C17 (4) 34.25 10.50

UPU Issue
Common Design Type

1949, July 4 *Perf. 13*
C18 CD99 25fr multi 8.50 7.00

Liberation Issue
Common Design Type

1954, June 6
C19 CD102 15fr indigo & pur 7.00 5.50

Freight Highway — AP5

1954, Nov. 29
C20 AP5 500fr indigo & dk grn 52.50 42.50

Republic

Independence Allegory — AP6

Unwmk.
1957, Oct. 29 Engr. *Perf. 13*
C21 AP6 25fr bl, brn & ver .60 .30

1st anniv. of Togo's autonomy.

Flag and Torch AP7

Great White Egret AP8

1957, Oct. 29
C22 AP7 50fr multi .65 .35
C23 AP7 100fr multi 1.10 .60
C24 AP7 200fr multi 2.25 1.00
C25 AP8 500fr ind, lt bl & grn 18.00 6.75
Nos. C22-C25 (4) 22.00 8.70

Types of 1957 Inscribed "Republique du Togo" and

Flag, Plane and Map — AP9

1959, Jan. 15 Engr. *Perf. 13*
C26 AP9 25fr ultra, emer & vio brn .40 .25
C27 AP7 50fr dk bl, dl grn & red .60 .35
C28 AP7 100fr multi 1.40 .60
C29 AP7 200fr dk grn, red & ultra 3.50 1.25
C30 AP8 500fr blk brn, rose lil & grn 14.00 3.50
Nos. C26-C30 (5) 19.90 5.95

Hotel Le Benin AP10

Eagle and Map of Togo AP11

Perf. 14½x15, 15x14½
1960, Apr. 27 Litho. Unwmk.
C31 AP10 100fr crim, emer & yel 1.75 .25
C32 AP10 200fr multi 4.00 .40
C33 AP11 500fr grn & gldn brn 8.50 1.00
Nos. C31-C33 (3) 14.25 1.65

Proclamation of Togo's full independence, Apr. 27, 1960.

Mail Service Type

100fr, Boeing 707 and stamps of 1960.

1963, Jan. 12 Photo. *Perf. 13*
C34 A41 100fr multi 1.60 .45
a. Souvenir sheet of 4 4.50 3.50

No. C34a contains 4 stamps similar to Nos. 441-443 and C34, with simulated perforations.

Emancipation Type

1963, Oct. Unwmk. *Perf. 13x14*
C35 A45 100fr multi 1.50 .45
a. Souv. sheet of 4, #454-456, C35, imperf. 2.50 2.00

For overprint see No. C41.

Type of 1964 Regular Issue

50fr, Pirenestes ostrinus. 100fr, Spermestes bicolor. 200fr, Agapornis pullaria. 250fr, Psittacus erithacus. 500fr, Trachyphonus margaritaceus.

1964-65 Photo. *Perf. 14*
Size: 22½x31mm
Birds in Natural Colors
C36 A47 50fr yel grn 3.00 .30
C37 A47 100fr ocher 6.00 .35
C38 A47 200fr dl bl grn 11.50 .90
C39 A47 250fr dl rose ('65) 15.50 1.10
C40 A47 500fr violet 30.00 1.60
Nos. C36-C40 (5) 66.00 4.25

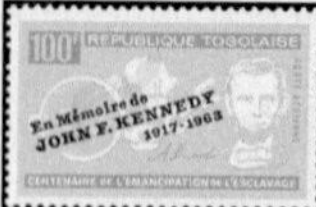

No. C35 Ovptd. Diagonally

1964, Feb. *Perf. 13x14*
C41 A45 100fr multi 1.75 .30

Issued in memory of John F. Kennedy.
Same overprint was applied to stamps of No. C35a, with black border and commemorative inscription added. Two sheets exist: with and without gray silhouetted head of Kennedy covering all four stamps. Value: without silhouette, $15; with silhouette, $25.

Liberation Type

1964, May 25 *Perf. 14x13*
C42 A50 100fr dl bl grn & dk brn 1.50 .30

Olympic Games Type

1964, Oct. Photo. *Perf. 14*
C43 A52 100fr Tennis 1.25 .30
a. Souv. sheet of 3, #493-494, C43, imperf. 2.50 2.00

Flag of Togo and Jet — AP12

1964, Dec. 5 Unwmk. *Perf. 14x13*
C44 AP12 100fr multi 1.50 .50

Inauguration of the national airline "Air Togo." For souvenir sheet see No. 499a.

Lincoln Type

1965, June Photo. *Perf. 13½x14*
C45 A58 100fr ol gray 2.00 .35
a. Souv. sheet, #545, C45, imperf 3.00 2.25

Sports Type

100fr, Soccer player, flags of Togo and Congo.

1965, July Unwmk. *Perf. 14x13*
C46 A59 100fr multi 1.75 .35

Churchill Type

1965, Aug. 7 Photo. *Perf. 13½x14*
C47 A60 85fr car rose 1.50 .40
a. Souv. sheet, #532, C47, imperf 2.50 2.00

UN Type

100fr, Apple, grapes, wheat and "ONU."

1965, Dec. 15 *Perf. 14x13½*
C48 A65 100fr dk bl & bis 1.75 .40
a. Souvenir sheet of 2 2.40 1.75

No. C48a contains two imperf. stamps similar to Nos. 548 and C48 with simulated perforations.

Pope Type

Designs: 45fr, Pope speaking at UN rostrum, world map and UN emblem. 90fr, Pope, plane and UN emblem.

1966, Mar. 5 Litho. *Perf. 12*
C49 A66 45fr emer & multi .80 .25
C50 A66 90fr gray & multi 1.75 .25
a. Souvenir sheet of 2, #C49-C50 3.00 2.00

Red Cross Type

Jean Henri Dunant and Togolese Flag.

1966, May 7 Litho. *Perf. 12*
C51 A67 100fr multi 2.25 .35

WHO Type

Flowers: 50fr, Daisies and WHO Headquarters. 90fr, Talisman roses and WHO Headquarters.

1966, May Litho. *Perf. 12*
C52 A68 50fr lt bl & multi .90 .25
C53 A68 90fr gray & multi 1.50 .25
a. Souvenir sheet of 2, #C52-C53 3.00 2.00

Air Afrique Issue
Common Design Type

1966, Aug. 31 Photo. *Perf. 13*
C54 CD123 30fr brt grn, blk & lem .80 .25

Arts and Crafts Type

60fr, Basket maker. 90fr, Wood carver.

1966, Sept. *Perf. 13x14*
C55 A69 60fr ultra, org & blk 1.40 .25
C56 A69 90fr brt rose, yel & blk 1.40 .25

Dancer Type

50fr, Woman from North Togo holding branches. 60fr, Man from North Togo with horned helmet.

1966, Nov. Photo. *Perf. 13x14*
C57 A70 50fr multi .95 .25
C58 A70 60fr olive & multi 1.25 .25

Soccer Type

Designs: Different Soccer Scenes.

1966, Dec. 14 Photo. *Perf. 14x13*
C59 A71 50fr org, brn & pur .85 .25
C60 A71 60fr ultra, brn & org 1.40 .25
a. Souv. sheet of 3, #582, C59-C60, imperf. 3.25 2.40

Fish Type

Designs: 45fr, Yellow jack and trawler. 90fr, Banded distichodus and seiner.

1967, Jan. 14 Photo. *Perf. 14*
Fish in Natural Colors
C61 A72 45fr org & brn 1.25 .25
C62 A72 90fr emer & dk bl 2.00 .35

UNICEF Type

UNICEF Emblem and: 45fr, Girl and miniature poodle. 90fr, African boy and greyhound.

1967, Feb. 11 Photo. *Perf. 14x13½*
C63 A73 45fr yel, red brn & blk 1.25 .25
C64 A73 90fr ultra, dk grn & blk 1.90 .35
a. Souvenir sheet of 2 4.00 2.25

No. C64a contains 2 imperf., lithographed stamps with simulated perforations similar to Nos. C63-C64.

Satellite Type

50fr, Diamant rocket. 90fr, Fr-1 satellite.

1967, Mar. 18 Photo. *Perf. 13½x14*
C65 A74 50fr multi, vert. 1.00 .25
C66 A74 90fr multi, vert. 1.75 .30
a. Souvenir sheet of 2 3.00 1.75

No. C66a contains 2 imperf. stamps similar to Nos. C65-C66 with simulated perforations.

Musician Type

UNESCO Emblem and: 45fr, Johann Sebastian Bach and organ. 90fr, Ludwig van Beethoven, violin and oboe.

1967, Apr. 15 Photo. *Perf. 14x13½*
C67 A75 45fr multi .75 .25
C68 A75 90fr pink & multi 1.25 .25
a. Souvenir sheet of 2 3.50 1.40

No. C68a contains 2 imperf. stamps similar to Nos. C67-C68 with simulated perforations.

EXPO '67 Type

EXPO '67 Emblem and: 45fr, French pavilion, roses. 60fr, British pavilion, day lilies. 90fr, African village, bird-of-paradise flower. 105fr, US pavilion, daisies.

1967, May 30 Photo. *Perf. 14*
C69 A76 45fr multi .75 .25
C70 A76 60fr multi .85 .25
C71 A76 90fr yel & multi 1.25 .30
a. Souv. sheet, #C69-C71, imperf 3.50 2.50
C72 A76 105fr multi 1.75 .50
Nos. C69-C72 (4) 4.60 1.30

For overprints see Nos. C86-C89.

Mural by José Vela Zanetti
AP13

The designs are from a mural in the lobby of the UN Conf. Building, NYC. The mural depicting mankind's struggle for a lasting peace is shown across 3 stamps twice in the set: on the 5fr, 15fr, 30fr and 45fr, 60fr, 90fr.

1967, July 15 Litho. *Perf. 14*
C73 AP13 5fr multi .40 .25
C74 AP13 15fr org & multi .40 .25
C75 AP13 30fr multi .45 .25
C76 AP13 45fr multi .70 .25
C77 AP13 60fr car & multi 1.10 .25
C78 AP13 90fr ind & multi 1.75 .30
a. Souvenir sheet of 3, #C76-C78 3.50 2.50
Nos. C73-C78 (6) 4.80 1.55

Issued to publicize general disarmament.

Animal Type

1967, Aug. 19 Photo. *Perf. 14x13½*
C79 A78 45fr Lion 1.10 .25
C80 A78 60fr Elephant 1.60 .25

African Postal Union Issue, 1967

Common Design Type

1967, Sept. 9 Engr. *Perf. 13*
C81 CD124 100fr bl, brt grn & ol brn 1.90 .30

Stamp Anniversary Type

Designs: 90fr, Stamp auction and Togo Nos. 16 and C42. 105fr, Father and son with stamp album and No. 474.

1967, Oct. 14 Photo. *Perf. 14x13*
Stamps on Stamps in Original Colors
C82 A79 90fr olive 1.25 .25
a. Souvenir sheet of 3 3.00 2.50
C83 A79 105fr dk car rose 2.00 .40

No. C82a contains 3 imperf. stamps similar to Nos. 621-622 and C82 with simulated perforations.

Pre-Olympics Type

View of Mexico City, Summer Olympics emblem and: 60fr, Runners. 90fr, Broad jump.

1967, Dec. 2 *Perf. 13x14*
C84 A80 60fr pink & multi 1.50 .45
C85 A80 90fr multi 1.50 .50
a. Souv. sheet of 3, #627, C84-C85, imperf. 5.00 3.00

Nos. C69-C72 Overprinted

1967, Dec. Photo. *Perf. 14*
C86 A76 45fr multi .60 .25
C87 A76 60fr multi .90 .25
C88 A76 90fr yel & multi 1.40 .25
C89 A76 105fr multi 1.50 .35
Nos. C86-C89 (4) 4.40 1.10

Issued for National Day, Sept. 29, 1967.

Hydrological Decade Type

1968, Apr. 6 Litho. *Perf. 14*
C90 A84 60fr multi 1.75 .25

Ship Type

Designs: 45fr, Fulton's and modern steamships. 90fr, US atomic ship Savannah and atom symbol.

1968, Apr. 26 Photo. *Perf. 14x14½*
C91 A85 45fr yel & multi 1.10 .25
C92 A85 90fr bl & multi 2.00 .25
a. Souvenir sheet of 2 3.75 1.75

No. C92a contains 2 imperf. stamps similar to Nos. C91-C92 with simulated perforations.

WHO Type

Paintings: 60fr, The Anatomy Lesson, by Rembrandt (detail). 90fr, Jesus Healing the Sick, by Raphael.

1968, June 22 Photo. *Perf. 14*
C93 A87 60fr multi 1.00 .25
C94 A87 90fr pur & multi 1.25 .25
a. Souvenir sheet of 2 3.50 2.50

No. C94a contains 2 imperf. stamps similar to Nos. C93-C94 with simulated perforations.

Olympic Games Type

1968, July 27 *Perf. 14x13½*
C95 A88 60fr Wrestling .85 .25
C96 A88 90fr Running 1.25 .25
a. Souvenir sheet of 2 2.50 2.10

No. C96a contains 2 imperf. stamps similar to Nos. C95-C96 with simulated perforations.

Boy Scout Type

60fr, First aid practice, horiz. 90fr, Scout game.

1968, Nov. 23 Litho. *Perf. 14*
C97 A90 60fr ol & multi 1.00 .25
C98 A90 90fr org & multi 1.40 .35
a. Souvenir sheet of 2 3.00 1.75

No. C98a contains 2 imperf. stamps with simulated perforations similar to Nos. C97-C98.

PHILEXAFRIQUE Issue

The Letter, by Jean Auguste Franquelin
AP14

1968, Nov. 9 Photo. *Perf. 12½x12*
C99 AP14 100fr multi 2.75 1.75

PHILEXAFRIQUE Philatelic Exhibition in Abidjan, Feb. 14-23. Printed with alternating light ultramarine label.

Christmas Type

Paintings: 60fr, Adoration of the Magi, by Pieter Brueghel. 90fr, Adoration of the Magi, by Dürer.

1968, Dec. 28 Litho. *Perf. 14*
C100 A91 60fr red & multi 1.10 .25
C101 A91 90fr multi 1.50 .35
a. Souvenir sheet 3.75 1.75

No. C101a contains 2 imperf. stamps similar to Nos. C100-C101 with simulated perforations.

Human Rights Type

Human Rights Flame and: 60fr, Robert F. Kennedy. 90fr, Martin Luther King, Jr.

1969, Feb. 1 Photo. *Perf. 13½x14*
C102 A92 60fr brt rose lil & vio bl 1.00 .25
C103 A92 90fr emer & brn 1.40 .40
a. Souvenir sheet 2.50 1.75

No. C103a contains 2 imperf. stamps similar to Nos. C102-C103 with simulated perforations.

For overprints see Nos. C110-C111.

2nd PHILEXAFRIQUE Issue

Common Design Type

Design: 50fr, Togo #16 and Aledjo Fault.

1969, Feb. 14 Engr. *Perf. 13*
C104 CD128 50fr red brn, grn & car rose 2.25 .45

Sports Type

Stadium and: 60fr, Boxing. 90fr, Bicycling.

1969, Apr. 26 Photo. *Perf. 14x13½*
C105 A93 60fr bl, red & dk brn .95 .25
C106 A93 90fr ultra, brt pink & dk brn 1.40 .30
a. Souvenir sheet 2.50 1.75

No. C106a contains 2 imperf. stamps similar to Nos. C105-C106 with simulated perforations.

Lunar Type

Designs: 60fr, Astronaut exploring moon surface. 100fr, Astronaut gathering rocks.

1969, July 21 Litho. *Perf. 14*
C107 A94 60fr dk bl & multi .90 .25
C108 A94 100fr multi 1.50 .50
a. Souvenir sheet 14.00 5.00

No. C108a contains 4 imperf. stamps with simulated perforations similar to Nos. 676-677 and C107-C108, magenta margin. No. C108a also exists with colors of 30fr and 100fr stamps changed, and margin in orange. Value, unused $6, used $2.

For overprints see Nos. C120-C121.

Painting Type

Painting: 90fr, Pentecost, by El Greco.

1969, Aug. 16 Litho. *Perf. 14*
C109 A95 90fr multi 2.10 .50
a. Souvenir sheet 2.75 1.50

No. C109a contains two imperf. stamps with simulated perforations similar to Nos. 682 and C109.

Nos. C102-C103 Overprinted Like Nos. 683-686

1969, Sept. 1 Photo. *Perf. 13½x14*
C110 A92 60fr brt rose lil & vio bl .90 .25
C111 A92 90fr emer & brn 1.25 .30
a. Souv. sheet of 2 3.00 2.00

#C111a is #C103a with Eisenhower overprint.

Bank Type

Design: 100fr, Bank emblem and hand holding cattle and farmer.

1969, Sept. 10 Photo. *Perf. 13x14*
C112 A96 100fr multi 1.10 .40

Red Cross Type

60fr, Wilhelm C. Roentgen & Red Cross workers with children in front of Togo Headquarters. 90fr, Henri Dunant & Red Cross workers meeting Biafra refugees at airport.

1969, Sept. 27 Litho. *Perf. 14*
C113 A97 60fr brn & multi .85 .30
C114 A97 90fr ol & multi 1.25 .40
a. Souv. sheet of 2 2.75 2.10

No. C114a contains 2 imperf. stamps with simulated perforations similar to Nos. C113-C114.

Agricultural Center Type

Emblem of Young Pioneer and Agricultural Organization and: 90fr, Manioc harvest. 100fr, Instruction in gardening. 200fr, Corn harvest. 250fr, Marching drum corps. 500fr, Parade of Young Pioneers.

1969-70 Litho. *Perf. 14*
C115 A98 90fr multi 1.20 .25
C116 A98 100fr org & multi 1.40 .30
C117 A98 200fr multi ('70) 2.75 .40
C118 A98 250fr ol & multi 4.25 .70
C119 A98 500fr multi ('70) 9.00 .90
Nos. C115-C119 (5) 18.60 2.55

Christmas Issue

Nos. C107-C108, C108a Overprinted: "JOYEUX NOEL"

1969, Dec. Litho. *Perf. 14*
C120 A94 60fr multi 3.50 .45
C121 A94 100fr multi 5.25 .65
a. Souvenir sheet of 4 60.00 60.00

Peace Leaders Type

60fr, Friedrich Ebert. 90fr, Mahatma Gandhi.

1969, Dec. 27 Litho. *Perf. 14x13½*
C122 A100 60fr dk brn, dk red & yel 1.00 .25
C123 A100 90fr dk brn, vio bl & ocher 1.40 .35

For surcharges see Nos. 765, C143.

ILO Type

Paintings and ILO Emblem: 60fr, Spring Sowing, by Vincent van Gogh. 90fr, Workers, by Diego de Rivera.

1970, Jan. 24 Litho. *Perf. 12½x13*
C124 A101 60fr gold & multi 1.75 .25
C125 A101 90fr gold & multi 2.75 .25
a. Souvenir sheet of 2 3.50 1.40

No. C125a contains two stamps similar to Nos. C124-C125, with simulated perforations.

Hair Styles Type

Various hair styles. 45fr, vert. 90fr, horiz.

1970, Feb. 21 *Perf. 12½x13, 13x12½*
C126 A102 45fr car & multi .90 .25
C127 A102 90fr multi 1.75 .40

Independence Type

Design: 60fr, Togo No. C33 and Independence Monument, Lomé.

1970, Apr. 27 Litho. *Perf. 13x12½*
C128 A103 60fr yel & multi .85 .25

UPU Type

1970, May 30 Photo. *Perf. 14x13½*
C129 A104 50fr grnsh bl & dk car .90 .25

Soccer Type

Various Scenes from Soccer, Rimet Cup and Flags of: 50fr, Sweden and Israel. 60fr, Bulgaria and Peru. 90fr, Belgium and Salvador.

1970, June 27 Litho. *Perf. 13x14*
C130 A105 50fr multi .75 .25
C131 A105 60fr lil & multi .90 .25
C132 A105 90fr multi 1.90 .35
a. Souvenir sheet of 4 4.00 4.00
Nos. C130-C132 (3) 3.55 .85

No. C132a contains 4 stamps similar to Nos. 734, C130-C132, but imperf. with simulated perforations.

Lenin Type

Design: 50fr, Lenin Meeting Peasant Delegation, by V. A. Serov, and UNESCO emblem.

1970, July 25 Litho. *Perf. 12½*
C133 A106 50fr multi 1.95 .25

For overprint see No. C179.

EXPO '70 Type
Souvenir Sheet

150fr, Mitsubishi pavilion, EXPO '70 emblem.

1970, Aug. 8 Litho. *Perf. 13*
C134 A107 150fr yel & multi 5.00 3.50
a. Inscribed "AERINNE"

No. C134 contains one stamp 86x33mm.

Astronaut Type

Design: 200fr, James A. Lovell, Fred W. Haise, Jr. and Tom Mattingly (replaced by John L. Swigert, Jr.) and Apollo 13 emblem.

1970, Sept. 26
C135 A108 200fr multi 2.90 .75
a. Souv. sheet of 3 3.75 2.50

Space flight of Apollo 13. No. C135a contains 3 stamps similar to Nos. 741, 744 and C135, with simulated perforations.
For overprint see No. C136.

Nos. C135, C135a Inscribed: "FELICITATIONS / BON RETOUR APOLLO XIII"

1970, Sept. 26
C136 A108 200fr multi 2.75 .60
a. Souvenir sheet of 3 3.75 2.50

Safe return of the crew of Apollo 13.

UN Type

Paintings and Emblems of UN Agencies: 60fr, The Mailman Roulin, by van Gogh, and UPU emblem. 90fr, The Birth of the Virgin, by Vittore Carpaccio, and WHO emblem.

1970, Oct. 24 Litho. *Perf. 13x12½*
C137 A109 60fr grn, gold & blk 1.10 .25
C138 A109 90fr red org, gold & brn 1.75 .30
a. Souvenir sheet of 4 3.50 2.50

No. C138a contains one each of Nos. 754-755 and C137-C138 with simulated perforations.

Moth Type

Moths: 60fr, Euchloron megaera. 90fr, Pseudacraea boisduvali.

1970, Nov. 21 Photo. *Perf. 13x14*
C139 A110 60fr multi 5.25 .25
C140 A110 90fr multi 5.25 .25

Christmas Type

Paintings: 60fr, Adoration of the Magi, by Botticelli. 90fr, Adoration of the Kings, by Tiepolo.

1970, Dec. 26 Litho. *Perf. 12½x13*
C141 A111 60fr gold & multi 1.50 .25
C142 A111 90fr gold & multi 2.25 .30
a. Souv. sheet of 2, #C141-C142 3.50 1.75

No. C122 Surcharged and Overprinted

1971, Jan. 9 Photo. *Perf. 14x13½*
C143 A100 200fr on 60fr 11.50 .60

De Gaulle Type

Designs: 60fr, De Gaulle and Pope Paul VI. 90fr, De Gaulle and satellite.

1971, Feb. 20 Photo. *Perf. 13x14*
C144 A112 60fr blk & dp vio 2.20 .25
C145 A112 90fr blk & bl grn 3.00 .25
a. Souvenir sheet of 4 8.50 3.00

Nos. C143-C145 issued in memory of Charles De Gaulle (1890-1970), President of France. No. C145a contains 4 imperf. stamps similar to Nos. 769-770, C144-C145.

Easter Type

Paintings: 50fr, Resurrection, by Matthias Grunewald. 60fr, Resurrection, by Master of Trebon. 90fr, Resurrection, by El Greco.

1971, Apr. 10 Litho. *Perf. 10½x11½*
C146 A113 50fr gold & multi .85 .25
C147 A113 60fr gold & multi 1.25 .25
C148 A113 90fr gold & multi 1.60 .30
a. Souvenir sheet of 4, #773, C146-C148 4.50 2.50
Nos. C146-C148 (3) 3.70 .80

Apollo 14 Type

Designs: 50fr, 200fr, Apollo 14 badge. 100fr, Take-off from moon, and spaceship.

1971, May Litho. *Perf. 12½*
C149 A114 50fr grn & multi .65 .25
C150 A114 100fr multi 1.10 .45
C151 A114 200fr org & multi 2.50 .85
a. Souv. sheet of 4 5.75 5.50
Nos. C149-C151 (3) 4.25 1.55

No. C151a contains 4 stamps similar to Nos. 777 and C149-C151 with simulated perforations.
For surcharge and overprints see Nos. C162-C164.

Cacao Type

60fr, Ministry of Agriculture. 90fr, Cacao tree and & pods. 100fr, Sorting & separating beans from pods.

1971, June 6 Litho. *Perf. 14*
C152 A115 60fr multi .75 .25
C153 A115 90fr multi 1.10 .40
C154 A115 100fr multi 1.25 .45
Nos. C152-C154 (3) 3.10 1.10

ASECNA Type

1971, June 26
C155 A116 100fr multi 1.60 .35

Tourist Type

Designs: 50fr, Château Viale and antelope. 60fr, Lake Togo and crocodile. 100fr, Old lime furnace, Tokpli, and hippopotamus.

1971, July 17
C156 A117 50fr multi .55 .25
C157 A117 60fr multi .75 .25
C158 A117 100fr multi 1.00 .40
Nos. C156-C158 (3) 2.30 .90

For overprint see No. C172.

Religions Type

Designs: 50fr, Mohammedans praying in front of Lomé Mosque. 60fr, Protestant service. 90fr, Catholic bishop and priests.

1971, July 31 Litho. *Perf. 14½*
C159 A118 50fr multi .55 .25
C160 A118 60fr multi .75 .25
C161 A118 90fr multi .95 .25
a. Souvenir sheet of 4, #787, C159-C161 4.25 2.50
Nos. C159-C161 (3) 2.25 .75

Nos. C149-C151 Overprinted and Surcharged in Black or Silver: "EN MEMOIRE / DOBROVOLSKY — VOLKOV — PATSAYEV / SOYUZ 11"

1971, Aug. *Perf. 12½*
C162 A114 90fr on 50fr multi 1.00 .35
C163 A114 100fr multi (S) 1.20 .40
C164 A114 200fr multi 2.10 .65
a. Souvenir sheet of 4, #788, C162-C164 7.00 7.00
Nos. C162-C164 (3) 4.30 1.40

See note after No. 788.

Olympic Type

200fr, Sapporo '72 emblem and Ski jump.

1971, Oct. 30 Litho. *Perf. 14*
C165 A119 200fr multi 2.10 .50
a. Souvenir sheet of 4 4.25 3.50

No. C165 contains 4 stamps with simulated perforations similar to Nos. 791-793 and C165 printed on glazed paper.

African Postal Union Issue
Common Design Type

Design: 100fr, Adjogbó dancers and UAMPT Building, Brazzaville, Congo.

1971, Nov. 13 Photo. *Perf. 13x13½*
C166 CD135 100fr bl & multi 1.25 .40

Intl. Organization for the Protection of Children (U.I.P.E.) — AP14a

Die Cut Perf. 10½

1971, Nov. 13 Embossed
C166A AP14a 1500fr gold 20.00

UNICEF Type

Toys: 60fr, Turtle. 90fr, Parrot.

1971, Nov. 27 Litho. *Perf. 14*
C167 A120 60fr lt bl & multi .55 .25
C168 A120 90fr multi .85 .25
a. Souvenir sheet of 4 2.75 2.50

No. C168a contains 4 stamps with simulated perforations similar to Nos. 796-797 and C167-C168.
For overprints see Nos. C263-C264.

Christmas Type

Virgin and Child by: 60fr, Giorgione. 100fr, Raphael.

1971, Dec. 24 *Perf. 14x13*
C169 A121 60fr olive & multi 1.00 .30
C170 A121 100fr multi 1.75 .50
a. Souvenir sheet of 4 5.25 2.25

No. C170a contains 4 stamps with simulated perforations similar to Nos. 800-801, C169-C170.

Venice Type

Design: 100fr, Ca' d'Oro, Venice.

1972, Feb. 26 Litho. *Perf. 14*
C171 A122 100fr multi 1.75 .55
a. Souvenir sheet of 3 5.75 2.50

No. C171a contains 3 stamps similar to Nos. 802-803, C171 with simulated perforations.

No. C156 Overprinted

1972, Mar. Litho. *Perf. 14*
C172 A117 50fr multi .90 .25

Visit of Pres. Richard M. Nixon to the People's Republic of China, Feb. 20-27.

Easter Type

Paintings: 50fr, Resurrection, by Thomas de Coloswa. 100fr, Ascension by Andrea Mantegna.

1972, Mar. 31
C173 A123 50fr gold & multi 1.10 .25
C174 A123 100fr gold & multi 2.10 .25
a. Souvenir sheet of 4 3.00 1.50

No. C174a contains 4 stamps similar to Nos. 806-807, C173-C174 with simulated perforations.

Heart Type

100fr, Heart, WHO emblem and smith.

1972, Apr. 4
C175 A124 100fr multi 1.25 .45
a. Souvenir sheet of 2 3.25 1.40

No. C175a contains 2 stamps similar to Nos. 810 and C175 with simulated perforations.

Telecommunications Type

Design: 100fr, Intelsat 4 over Africa.

1972, June 24 *Perf. 14*
C176 A125 100fr multi 1.60 .30

For overprint see No. C229.

Cassava Type

60fr, Truck and cassava processing factory, horiz. 80fr, Children, mother holding tapioca cake.
Stamps inscribed "POSTE AERIENNE".

1972, June 30
C177 A126 60fr multi 1.10 .25
C178 A126 80fr multi 1.25 .25

No. C133 Srchd. in Deep Carmine

1972, July 15 Litho. *Perf. 12½*
C179 A106 300fr on 50fr multi 4.75 1.40

President Nixon's visit to the USSR, May 1972. Old denomination obliterated with 6x5mm rectangle.

Olympic Type

1972, Aug. 26 Litho. *Perf. 14*
C180 A127 90fr Gymnastics .65 .40
a. Souv. sheet of 2 3.25 1.60
C181 A127 200fr Basketball 1.75 .75

No. C180a contains 2 stamps with simulated perforations similar to Nos. 816 and C180.
For overprints see Nos. C234-C235.

Bird Type

Bird: 90fr, Rose-ringed parakeet.

1972, Sept. 9
C182 A128 90fr multi 2.75 .45
a. Souvenir sheet of 4 13.00 2.60

No. C182a contains 4 stamps similar to Nos. 818-820, C182 with simulated perforations.

Rotary Type

Rotary Emblem and: 60fr, Map of Togo, olive branch. 90fr, Flags of Togo and Rotary Club. 100fr, Paul P. Harris.

1972, Oct. 7 Litho. *Perf. 14*
C183 A129 60fr brn & multi .65 .25
C184 A129 90fr multi .90 .40
C185 A129 100fr multi 1.25 .45
Nos. C183-C185 (3) 2.80 1.10

For overprints see Nos. C212-C213, C244-C245.

Type of 1972 Painting

Designs: 60fr, Mystical Marriage of St. Catherine, by Assistant to the P. M. Master. 80fr, Self-portrait, by Leonardo da Vinci. 100fr, Sts. Mary and Agnes by Botticelli.

1972, Oct. 21
C186 A130 60fr gold & multi 1.40 .25
C187 A130 80fr gold & multi 1.75 .30
C188 A130 100fr gold & multi 2.25 .45
a. Souvenir sheet of 4 4.50 2.00
Nos. C186-C188 (3) 5.40 1.00

No. C188a contains 4 stamps with simulated perforations similar to Nos. 824, C186-188.

Presidential Visit Type

Design: 100fr, Pres. Pompidou and Col. Etienne Eyadema, front view of party headquarters.

1972, Nov. 23 Litho. *Perf. 14*
C189 A131 100fr multi 2.40 .40

Johann Wolfgang von Goethe (1749-1832), German Poet and Dramatist — AP15

1972, Dec. 2 Photo. *Perf. 13x14*
C190 AP15 100fr grn & multi 1.40 .40

Christmas Type

Paintings: 60fr, Nativity, by Master Vyshchibrod. 80fr, Adoration of the Kings, anonymous. 100fr, Flight into Egypt, by Giotto.

1972, Dec. 23 Litho. *Perf. 14*

C191 A132 60fr gold & multi 1.00 .25
C192 A132 80fr gold & multi 1.20 .35
C193 A132 100fr gold & multi 1.40 .45
a. Souvenir sheet of 4 5.00 2.75
Nos. C191-C193 (3) 3.60 1.05

No. C193a contains 4 stamps with simulated perforations similar to Nos. 829, C191-C193.

Leprosy Day Type

Design: 100fr, Dr. Armauer G. Hansen, apparatus, microscope and Petri dish.

1973, Jan. 23 Photo. *Perf. 14x13½*

C194 A133 100fr rose car & bl 2.75 .40

World Leprosy Day and centenary of the discovery of the Hansen bacillus, the cause of leprosy.

Miniature Sheets

1972 Summer Olympics, Munich — AP15a

Medalists, each 1500fr: #C194A, Mark Spitz, US, swimming. #C194B, L. Linsenhoff, West Germany, equestrian. #C194C, D. Morelon, France, cycling.

Litho. & Embossed

1973, Jan. *Perf. 13½*

C194A-C194C AP15a Set of 3 375.00

Exist imperf.

Miniature Sheet

Apollo 17 Moon Landing — AP15b

1973, Jan.

C194D AP15b 1500fr gold & multi 55.00

Exists imperf.

Easter Type

1973, Apr. 21 Litho. *Perf. 14*

C195 A135 90fr Christ in Glory 1.40 .40
a. Souvenir sheet of 2 2.75 1.75

No. C195a contains one each of Nos. 835 and C195 with simulated perforations.

Apollo 17 Type

Designs: 100fr, Astronauts on moon and orange rock. 200fr, Rocket lift-off at Cape Kennedy and John F. Kennedy.

1973, June 2 Litho. *Perf. 14*

C196 A136 100fr multi 1.60 .45
C197 A136 200fr multi 3.25 .65
a. Souvenir sheet of 2 4.25 3.00

No. C197a contains 2 stamps similar to Nos. C196-C197 with simulated perforations.

Boy Scout Type

100fr, Canoeing, horiz. 200fr, Campfire, horiz.

1973, June 30 Litho. *Perf. 14*

C198 A137 100fr bl & multi 1.25 .45
C199 A137 200fr bl & multi 2.50 .70
a. Souvenir sheet of 2 3.50 2.10

No. C199a contains 2 stamps similar to Nos. C198-C199 with simulated perforations.

For overprints see Nos. C265-C266.

Copernicus Type

Designs: 90fr, Heliocentric system. 100fr, Nicolaus Copernicus.

1973, July 18

C200 A138 90fr multi 1.60 .35
C201 A138 100fr bis & multi 1.90 .45
a. Souv. sheet of 2, #C200-C201 3.00 1.60

Red Cross Type

Design: 100fr, Dove carrying Red Cross letter, sun, map of Togo.

1973, Aug. 4

C202 A139 100fr multi 3.00 .35

For overprint see No. C294.

Literacy Type

Design: 90fr, Woman teacher in classroom.

1973, Aug. 18 Litho. *Perf. 14*

C203 A140 90fr multi 1.50 .35

WMO Type

1973, Oct. 4 Photo. *Perf. 14x13*

C204 A142 200fr dl bl, pur & brn 2.00 .60

Type 1967

Early & contemporary planes, #758, C36.

1973, Oct. 20 Photo. *Perf. 14x13*

C205 A79 100fr multi 2.50 .35
a. Souvenir sheet of 2 3.00 1.75

75th anniversary of Togolese postal service. No. C205a contains 2 stamps similar to Nos. 855 and C205 with simulated perforations.

Kennedy Type

Designs: 90fr, Kennedy and Charles De Gaulle. 100fr, Kennedy and Nikita Khrushchev. 200fr, Kennedy and model of Apollo spacecraft.

1973, Nov. 22 Litho. *Perf. 14*

C206 A143 90fr blk & pink 1.60 .45
C207 A143 100fr blk, lt bl & bl 1.75 .60
C208 A143 200fr blk, buff & brn 4.00 .75
a. Souvenir sheet of 2 4.00 2.00
Nos. C206-C208 (3) 7.35 1.80

No. C208a contains 2 stamps similar to Nos. C207-208 with simulated perforations.

Human Rights Flame and People — AP16

1973, Dec. 8 Photo. *Perf. 13x14*

C209 AP16 250fr lt bl & multi 2.75 .80

25th anniversary of the Universal Declaration of Human Rights.

Christmas Type

Paintings: 90fr, Virgin and Child. 100fr, Adoration of the Kings. Both after 15th century Italian paintings.

1973, Dec. 22 Litho. *Perf. 14*

C210 A144 90fr gold & multi 1.10 .35
C211 A144 100fr gold & multi 1.50 .45
a. Souvenir sheet of 2 2.75 1.50

No. C211a contains 2 stamps with simulated perforations similar to Nos. C210-C211.

Nos. C183 and C185 Overprinted: "PREMIERE CONVENTION / 210eme DISTRICT / FEVRIER 1974 / LOME"

1974, Feb. 21 Litho. *Perf. 14*

C212 A129 60fr brn & multi .65 .25
C213 A129 100fr multi 1.00 .35

First convention of Rotary International, District 210, Lomé, Feb. 22-24.

Soccer Type

Various soccer scenes and games' cup.

1974, Mar. 2 Litho. *Perf. 14*

C214 A145 90fr multi .90 .45
C215 A145 100fr multi 1.00 .50
C216 A145 200fr multi 2.00 .95
a. Souvenir sheet of 2 3.75 2.10
Nos. C214-C216 (3) 3.90 1.90

No. C216a contains 2 stamps with simulated perforations similar to Nos. C215-C216.

Picasso Type

Paintings: 90fr, The Muse. 100fr, Les Demoiselles d'Avignon. 200fr, Sitting Nude.

1974, Apr. 6 Litho. *Perf. 14*

C217 A146 90fr brn & multi 1.60 .40
C218 A146 100fr pur & multi 2.00 .45
C219 A146 200fr multi 4.00 .85
a. Souvenir sheet of 3 7.00 4.00
Nos. C217-C219 (3) 7.60 1.70

No. C219a contains 3 stamps similar to Nos. C217-C219 with simulated perforations.

Coastal Views Type

Designs: 90fr, Fishermen on Lake Togo. 100fr, Mouth of Anecho River.

1974, Apr. 20

C220 A147 90fr multi 1.10 .25
C221 A147 100fr multi 1.25 .35
a. Souvenir sheet of 2 2.50 1.25

No. C221a contains 2 stamps similar to Nos. C220-C221 with simulated perforations.

UPU Type

Designs: Old mailmen's uniforms.

1974, May 10 Litho. *Perf. 14*

C222 A148 50fr multi .70 .25
C223 A148 100fr multi 1.25 .35
a. Souvenir sheet of 2 40.00 17.00

No. C223a contains 2 stamps similar to Nos. C222-C223, rouletted.

Fishing Type

Designs: 90fr, Fishermen bringing in net with catch. 100fr, Fishing with rod and line. 200fr, Fishing with basket, vert.

1974, June 22 Litho. *Perf. 14*

C224 A149 90fr multi 1.00 .25
C225 A149 100fr multi 1.10 .25
C226 A149 200fr multi 2.40 .65
a. Souvenir sheet of 3 5.25 2.50
Nos. C224-C226 (3) 4.50 1.15

No. C226a contains 3 stamps with simulated perforations similar to Nos. C224-C226.

Jupiter Probe Type

Designs: 100fr, Rocket take-off, vert. 200fr, Satellite in space.

1974, July 6 *Perf. 14*

C227 A150 100fr multi .90 .35
C228 A150 200fr multi 2.00 .65
a. Souvenir sheet of 2 5.50 4.00

No. C228a contains 2 stamps similar to Nos. C227-C228 with simulated perforations; imperf. or rouletted.

No. C176 Overprinted in Black

1974, July *Perf. 14*

C229 A125 100fr multi 3.50 1.20

INTERNABA 1974 Intl. Philatelic Exhibition, Basel, June 7-16.

No. C229 exists overprinted in silver. Value, unused $11.

Seashell Type

1974, July 13 Litho. *Perf. 14*

C230 A151 90fr Alcithoe ponsonbyi 1.75 .30
C231 A151 100fr Casmaria iredalei 2.25 .40
a. Souvenir sheet of 2 4.50 1.40

No. C231a contains 2 stamps similar to Nos. C230-C231 with simulated perforations.

Horse Racing Type

90fr, Steeplechase. 100fr, Galloping horses.

1974, Aug. 3 Litho. *Perf. 14*

C232 A152 90fr multi 2.10 .30
C233 A152 100fr multi 2.40 .40
a. Souvenir sheet of 2 6.50 2.25

No. C233a contains one each of Nos. C232-C233 with simulated perforations.

Nos. C180, C180a and C181 Overprinted

1974, Aug. 19

C234 A127 90fr multi .75 .25
a. Souvenir sheet of 2 18.00 —
C235 A127 200fr multi 1.50 .65

World Cup Soccer Championship, Munich, 1974, victory of German Federal Republic. For description of No. C234a see note after No. C181.

Animal Type

1974, Sept. 7 Litho. *Perf. 14*

C236 A153 90fr Lions 2.10 .35
C237 A153 100fr Rhinoceroses 2.25 .40
a. Souvenir sheet of 3 3.75 1.90

Wild animals of West Africa. No. C237a contains 3 stamps similar to Nos. 889, C236-C237 with simulated perforations.

1974, Oct. 14

C238 A153 90fr Herd at waterhole 1.10 .25
C239 A153 100fr Village and cows 1.25 .35
a. Souvenir sheet of 2 2.50 1.25

Domestic animals. No. C239a contains 2 stamps with simulated perforations similar to Nos. C238-C239.

Churchill Type

Designs: 100fr, Churchill and frigate. 200fr, Churchill and fighter planes.

1974, Nov. 1 Photo. *Perf. 13x13½*

C240 A154 100fr multi 1.25 .35
C241 A154 200fr org & multi 2.75 .70
a. Souvenir sheet of 2 4.50 2.10

No. C241a contains 2 stamps similar to Nos. C240-C241; perf. or imperf.

Flower Type

Flowers of Togo: 100fr, Clerodendrum thosonae. 200fr, Gloriosa superba.

1975, Feb. 15 Litho. *Perf. 14*

C242 A155 100fr multi 1.75 .30
C243 A155 200fr multi 2.75 .50
a. Souvenir sheet of 2 7.00 1.90

No. C243a contains one each of Nos. C242-C243, perf. 13x14 or imperf.

Nos. C184-C185 Overprinted: "70e ANNIVERSAIRE / 23 FEVRIER 1975"

1975, Feb. 23 Litho. *Perf. 14*

C244 A129 90fr multi .90 .25
C245 A129 100fr multi 1.00 .35

Rotary International, 70th anniversary.

Easter Type

Paintings: 100fr, Christ Rising from the Tomb, by Master MS. 200fr, Holy Trinity (detail), by Dürer.

1975, Apr. 19 Litho. *Perf. 14*

C246 A157 100fr multi 1.00 .25
C247 A157 200fr multi 2.00 .55
a. Souvenir sheet of 2 3.50 2.00

No. C247a contains 2 stamps similar to Nos. C246-C247 with simulated perforations.

Independence Type

50fr, National Day parade, flag and map of Togo. 60fr, Warriors' dance and flag of Togo.

1975, Apr. 26 Litho. *Perf. 14*

C248 A158 50fr multi, vert. .50 .25
C249 A158 60fr multi .70 .25
a. Souvenir sheet of 2 1.50 .75

No. C249a contains 2 stamps similar to Nos. C248-C249 with simulated perforations.

Hunt Type

Designs: 90fr, Running deer. 100fr, Wild boar hunter with shotgun.

1975, May 24 Photo. *Perf. 13x13½*
C250 A159 90fr multi 1.75 .30
C251 A159 100fr multi 2.10 .30

Palm Oil Type

Designs: 85fr, Selling palm oil in market, vert. 100fr, Oil processing plant, Alokoegbe.

1975, June 28 Litho. *Perf. 14*
C252 A160 85fr multi 1.75 .50
C253 A160 100fr multi 2.00 .50

Apollo-Soyuz Type and

Soyuz Spacecraft — AP17

Designs: 60fr, Donald K. Slayton, Vance D. Brand and Thomas P. Stafford. 90fr, Aleksei A. Leonov and Valery N. Kubasov. 100fr, Apollo-Soyuz link-up, American and Russian flags. 200fr, Apollo-Soyuz emblem and globe.

1975, July 15
C254 AP17 50fr yel & multi .50 .25
C255 A161 60fr lil & multi .70 .25
C256 A161 90fr bl & multi .85 .25
C257 A161 100fr grn & multi 1.25 .40
C258 A161 200fr yel & multi 2.10 .45
a. Souv. sheet of 4, #C255-C258 6.00 3.50
Nos. C254-C258 (5) 5.40 1.60

See note after No. 913.

Schweitzer Type

Dr. Schweitzer: 80fr, playing organ, vert. 90fr, with pelican, vert. 100fr, and Lambarene Hospital.

1975, Aug. 23 Litho. *Perf. 14x13½*
C259 A163 80fr multi 1.10 .30
C260 A163 90fr multi 1.25 .35
C261 A163 100fr multi 1.40 .40
Nos. C259-C261 (3) 3.75 1.05

Letter Writing Type

80fr, Erasmus Writing Letter, by Hans Holbein.

1975, Oct. 9 Litho. *Perf. 14*
C262 A164 80fr multi 1.00 .25

Nos. C167-C168a Overprinted: "30ème Anniversaire / des Nations-Unies"

1975, Oct. 24 Litho. *Perf. 14*
C263 A120 60fr multi .60 .25
C264 A120 90fr multi .75 .25
a. Souvenir sheet of 4 3.00 1.90

UN, 30th anniv. #C264a contains Nos. 796 (with overprint), 918, C263-C264.

Nos. C198-C199 Overprinted: "14ème JAMBORÉE / MONDIAL / DES ÉCLAIREURS"

1975, Nov. 7
C265 A137 100fr multi .90 .25
C266 A137 200fr multi 1.75 .50
a. Souvenir sheet of 2 3.25 2.00

14th World Boy Scout Jamboree, Lillehammer, Norway, July 29-Aug. 7. No. C266a contains one each of Nos. C265-C266 with simulated perforations.

Christmas Type

Paintings of the Virgin and Child: 90fr, Nativity, by Federico Barocci. 100fr, Bellini. 200fr, Correggio.

1975, Dec. 20 Litho. *Perf. 14*
C267 A165 90fr bl & multi .80 .25
C268 A165 100fr red & multi .90 .25
C269 A165 200fr bl & multi 1.75 .50
a. Souv. sheet of 2, #C268-C269 3.50 2.00
Nos. C267-C269 (3) 3.45 1.00

Bicentennial Type

Paintings (and Bicentennial Emblem): 60fr, Surrender of Gen. Burgoyne, by John Trumbull. 70fr, Surrender at Trenton, by Trumbull, vert. 100fr, Signing of Declaration of Independence, by Trumbull. 200fr, Washington Crossing the Delaware, by Emanuel Leutze.

1976, Mar. 3 Litho. *Perf. 14*
C270 A167 60fr multi .65 .25
C271 A167 70fr multi .75 .25
C272 A167 100fr multi 1.00 .25
C273 A167 200fr multi 2.00 .55
a. Souv. sheet of 2, #C272-C273 4.00 2.00
Nos. C270-C273 (4) 4.40 1.30

No. C273a also exists imperf. Value $22.50.
For overprints see Nos. C280-C283.

Common Market Type

Designs: 60fr, ACP and CEE emblems. 70fr, Map of Africa, Europe and Asia.

1976, Apr. 24 Photo. *Perf. 13x14*
C274 A168 60fr lt bl & multi .55 .25
C275 A168 70fr yel & multi .65 .25

Telephone Type

Designs: 70fr, Thomas A. Edison, old and new communications equipment. 105fr, Alexander Graham Bell, old and new telephones.

1976, Mar. 10 Photo. *Perf. 13x14*
C276 A169 70fr multi .50 .25
C277 A169 105fr multi .60 .40
a. Souv. sheet of 2, #C276-C277 2.25 1.40

No. C277a exists imperf. Value $10.00.

Eye Examination — AP18

1976, Apr. 8 *Perf. 14x13*
C278 AP18 60fr dk red & multi .60 .25

World Health Day: "Foresight prevents blindness."

Pylon, Flags of Ghana, Togo, Dahomey — AP19

1976, May 8 Litho. *Perf. 14*
C279 AP19 60fr multi 1.00 .25

Ghana-Togo-Dahomey electric power grid, 1st anniv. See No. 932.

Nos. C270-C273, C273a, Overprinted: "INTERPHIL / MAI 29-JUIN 6, 1976"

1976, May 29
C280 A167 60fr multi .50 .25
C281 A167 70fr multi .55 .25
C282 A167 100fr multi .80 .25
C283 A167 200fr multi 1.60 .55
a. Souvenir sheet of 2 3.00 3.00
Nos. C280-C283 (4) 3.45 1.30

Interphil 76 Intl. Philatelic Exhibition, Philadelphia, Pa., May 29-June 6. Overprint on No. C281 in 3 lines; overprint on No. C283a applied to each stamp.

Olympic Games Type

Montreal Olympic Emblem and: 70fr, Yachting. 105fr, Motorcycling. 200fr, Fencing.

1976, June 15 Photo. *Perf. 14x13*
C284 A172 70fr multi .60 .25
C285 A172 105fr multi .85 .40
C286 A172 200fr multi 1.60 .65
a. Souvenir sheet of 2, #C285-C286, perf. 14 3.00 2.25
Nos. C284-C286 (3) 3.05 1.30

For overprints see Nos. C298-C299.

Viking Type

60fr, Viking landing on Mars. 70fr, Nodus Gordii (view on Mars). 105fr, Lander over Mare Tyrrhenum. 200fr, Landing on Mars.

1976, July 15 Litho. *Perf. 14*
C287 A173 60fr bis & multi .55 .25
C288 A173 70fr multi .65 .25
C289 A173 105fr bl & multi .90 .40
C290 A173 200fr multi 1.75 .60
a. Souv. sheet of 2, #C289-C290, perf. 14x13½ 3.50 2.25
Nos. C287-C290 (4) 3.85 1.50

Toulouse-Lautrec Type, 1976

Paintings: 60fr, Carmen, portrait. 70fr, Maurice at the Somme. 200fr, "Messalina."

1976, Aug. 7 Litho. *Perf. 14*
C291 A174 60fr blk & multi 1.00 .25
C292 A174 70fr blk & multi 1.00 .25
C293 A174 200fr blk & multi 2.40 .55
a. Souv. sheet of 2, #C292-C293, perf. 13½x14 5.00 2.25
Nos. C291-C293 (3) 4.40 1.05

No. C202 Overprinted: "Journeé / Internationale / de l'Enfance"

1976, Nov. 27 Litho. *Perf. 14*
C294 A139 100fr multi .55 .35

International Children's Day.

Christmas Type

Paintings: 70fr, Holy Family, by Lorenzo Lotto. 105fr, Virgin and Child with Saints, by Jacopo da Pontormo. 200fr, Virgin and Child with Saints, by Lotto.

1976, Dec. 18
C295 A175 70fr multi .55 .25
C296 A175 105fr multi 1.10 .45
C297 A175 200fr multi 1.75 .90
a. Souv. sheet of 2, #C296-C297 1.75 2.00
Nos. C295-C297 (3) 3.40 1.60

No. C284 Overprinted

No. C286 Overprinted

1976, Dec. Photo. *Perf. 14x13*
C298 A172 70fr multi .65 .25
C299 A172 200fr multi 1.75 .65
a. Souvenir sheet of 2 3.50 2.50

Olympic winners. No. C299a (on No. C286a) contains Nos. C285 and C299.

Eyadema Anniversary Type

60fr, National Assembly Building. 100fr, Pres. Eyadema greeting people at Aug. 30th meeting.

1977, Jan. 13 Photo. *Perf. 13x14*
C300 A177 60fr multi .55 .25
C301 A177 100fr multi .85 .35
a. Souv. sheet of 2, #C300-C301 1.75 1.10

Musical Instrument Type

Musical Instruments: 60fr, Atopani. 80fr, African violin, vert. 105fr, African flutes, vert.

1977, Feb. 7 Litho. *Perf. 14*
C302 A178 60fr multi .80 .25
C303 A178 80fr multi 1.00 .25
C304 A178 105fr multi 1.50 .30
a. Souv. sheet of 2, #C303-C304 2.75 1.50
Nos. C302-C304 (3) 3.30 .80

Victor Hugo Type

Victor Hugo in exile on Guernsey Island.

1977, Feb. 26 *Perf. 13x14*
C305 A179 60fr multi .70 .25
a. Souvenir sheet of 2, #952, C305 1.25 .75

For overprint see No. C316.

Beethoven Type

Designs: 100fr, Beethoven's piano and 1818 portrait. 200fr, Beethoven on his deathbed and Holy Trinity Church, Vienna.

1977, Mar. 7 *Perf. 14*
C306 A180 100fr multi 1.25 .35
C307 A180 200fr multi 2.10 .60
a. Souv. sheet of 2, #C306-C307 3.25 1.50

Automobile Type

Early Automobiles: 60fr, Cannstatt-Daimler, 1899, Germany. 70fr, Sunbeam, 1904, England. 100fr, Renault, 1908, France. 200fr, Rolls Royce, 1909, England.

1977, Apr. 11 Litho. *Perf. 14*
C308 A181 60fr multi .80 .25
C309 A181 70fr multi .85 .25
C310 A181 100fr multi 1.10 .35
C311 A181 200fr multi 1.75 .75
a. Souv. sheet of 2, #C310-C311 5.00 1.75
Nos. C308-C311 (4) 4.50 1.60

Lindbergh Type

Designs: 60fr, Lindbergh and son Jon, birds in flight. 85fr, Lindbergh home in Kent, England. 90fr, Spirit of St. Louis over Atlantic Ocean. 100fr, Concorde over NYC.

1977, May 9
C312 A182 60fr multi .50 .25
C313 A182 85fr multi .75 .25
C314 A182 90fr multi .75 .25
C315 A182 100fr multi 1.10 .30
a. Souv. sheet of 2, #C314-C315 2.40 1.20
Nos. C312-C315 (4) 3.10 1.05

No. C305 Overprinted: "10ème ANNIVERSAIRE DU / CONSEIL INTERNATIONAL / DE LA LANGUE FRANCAISE"

1977, May 17 Litho. *Perf. 14*
C316 A179 60fr multi .70 .25

10th anniv. of the French Language Council.

Wildlife Type

60fr, Colobus monkeys. 90fr, Chimpanzee, vert. 100fr, Leopard. 200fr, West African manatee.

1977, June 13
C317 A183 60fr multi .70 .25
C318 A183 90fr multi 1.00 .25
C319 A183 100fr multi 1.10 .25
C320 A183 200fr multi 2.40 .35
a. Souv. sheet of 2, #C319-C320 4.00 1.75
Nos. C317-C320 (4) 5.20 1.10

Agriculture Type

Designs: 60fr, Corn silo. 100fr, Hoeing and planting by hand. 200fr, Tractor on field.

1977, July 11 Litho. *Perf. 14*
C321 A184 60fr multi .50 .25
C322 A184 100fr multi .85 .25
C323 A184 200fr multi 1.75 .45
a. Souv. sheet of 2, #C322-C323, perf. 13x14 3.40 1.60
Nos. C321-C323 (3) 3.10 .95

Rubens Type

Paintings: 60fr, Heads of Black Men, 1620. 100fr, Anne of Austria, 1624.

1977, Aug. 8
C324 A185 60fr multi .90 .25
C325 A185 100fr multi 1.40 .25
a. Souv. sheet of 2, #C324-C325, perf. 14x13 2.10 1.25

Orbiter Type

90fr, Retrieval of unmanned satellite in space. 100fr, Satellite's return to space after repairs. 200fr, Manned landing of Orbiter.

1977, Oct. 4 Litho. *Perf. 14*
C326 A186 90fr multi, vert. .75 .25
C327 A186 100fr multi .80 .25
C328 A186 200fr multi 1.75 .35
a. Souv. sheet of 2, #C327-C328 3.00 1.50
Nos. C326-C328 (3) 3.30 .85

Lafayette Type

60fr, Lafayette landing in New York, 1824. 105fr, Lafayette and Washington at Valley Forge.

1977, Nov. 7 *Perf. 13x14*
C329 A187 60fr multi .65 .25
C330 A187 105fr multi 1.10 .25
a. Souv. sheet of 2, #C329-C330 1.75 1.00

Christmas Type

Virgin & Child by: 90fr, 200fr, Carlo Crivelli, diff. 1 00fr, Bellini.

1977, Dec. 19 *Perf. 14*
C331 A189 90fr multi .70 .25
C332 A189 100fr multi .90 .25
C333 A189 200fr multi 1.50 .40
a. Souv. sheet of 2, #C332-C333 3.25 1.75
Nos. C331-C333 (3) 3.10 .90

Jenner Type

Designs: 50fr, Edward Jenner. 60fr, Smallpox vaccination clinic, horiz.

1978, Jan. 9 *Perf. 14x13, 13x14*
C334 A190 50fr multi .35 .25
C335 A190 60fr multi .40 .25
a. Souvenir sheet of 2 1.40 .65

No. C335a contains 2 stamps with simulated perforations similar to Nos. C334-C335.

Wright Brothers Type

Designs: 60fr, Orville Wright's 7½-minute flight. 70fr, Orville Wright injured in first aircraft accident, 1908. 200fr, Wrights' bicycle shop, Dearborn, Mich. 300fr, First flight, 1903.

1978, Feb. 6 Litho. *Perf. 14*

C336	A191	60fr multi	1.00	.25
C337	A191	70fr multi	1.10	.25
C338	A191	200fr multi	1.40	.35
C339	A191	300fr multi	2.10	.60
a.		Souvenir sheet of 2	9.25	5.25
		Nos. C336-C339 (4)	5.60	1.45

No. C339a contains one each of Nos. C338-C339 with simulated perforations.

Port of Lomé Type, 1978

Anchor and: 60fr, Industrial harbor. 100fr, Merchant marine harbor. 200fr, Bird's-eye view of entire harbor.

1978, Apr. 26 Photo. *Perf. 13*

C340	A199	60fr multi	.45	.25
C341	A199	100fr multi	.75	.25
C342	A199	200fr multi	1.60	.40
a.		Souv. sheet of 2, #C341-C342	3.00	1.50
		Nos. C340-C342 (3)	2.80	.90

Space Type

Designs: 90fr, Module camera, horiz. 100fr, Module antenna. 200fr, Pioneer, US, in orbit.

1978, May 8 Litho. *Perf. 14*

C343	A200	90fr multi	.70	.25
C344	A200	100fr multi	.75	.25
C345	A200	200fr multi	1.50	.35
a.		Souv. sheet of 2, #C344-C345, perf. 13½x14	2.50	1.50
		Nos. C343-C345 (3)	2.95	.85

Soccer Type

Various soccer scenes & Argentina '78 emblem.

1978, June 5 *Perf. 14*

C346	A201	60fr multi	.50	.25
C347	A201	80fr multi	.65	.25
C348	A201	200fr multi	1.40	.40
C349	A201	300fr multi	2.10	.55
a.		Souvenir sheet of 2, #C348-C349, perf. 13½x14	3.25	1.90
		Nos. C346-C349 (4)	4.65	1.45

Bicycle Type

History of Bicycle: 60fr, Bantam, 1896, vert. 85fr, Fold-up bicycle for military use, 1897. 90fr, Draisienne, 1816, vert. 100fr, Penny-farthing, 1884, vert.

Perf. 14x13, 13x14

1978, July 10 Photo.

C350	A202	60fr multi	.50	.25
C351	A202	85fr multi	.70	.25
C352	A202	90fr multi	.85	.35
C353	A202	100fr multi	1.10	.35
a.		Souv. sheet of 2, #C352-C353	2.75	1.10
		Nos. C350-C353 (4)	3.15	1.20

Phonograph Type

60fr, Edison's original phonograph, horiz. 80fr, Emile Berliner's phonograph, 1888. 200fr, Berliner's improved phonograph, 1894, horiz. 300fr, His Master's Voice phonograph, 1900, horiz.

Perf. 13x14, 14x13

1978, July 8 Photo.

C354	A203	60fr multi	.45	.25
C355	A203	80fr multi	.60	.25
C356	A203	200fr multi	1.40	.35
C357	A203	300fr multi	2.20	.50
a.		Souv. sheet of 2, #C356-C357	3.50	2.00
		Nos. C354-C357 (4)	4.65	1.35

Red Cross Type

Design: 60fr, Red Cross and other pavilions at Paris Exhibition, 1867.

1978, Sept. 4 Photo. *Perf. 14x13*

C358	A204	60fr pur & red	.45	.25
a.		Souv. sheet, #1009, C358	1.10	.55

Paintings Type

60fr, Langlois Bridge, by Vincent van Gogh. 70fr, Witches' Sabbath, by Francisco Goya. 90fr, Jesus among the Doctors, by Albrecht Dürer. 200fr, View of Arco, by Dürer.

1978, Nov. 6 Litho. *Perf. 14*

C359	A205	60fr multi	.60	.25
C360	A205	70fr multi	.65	.30
C361	A205	90fr multi	.90	.40
C362	A205	200fr multi	1.75	.70
a.		Souv. sheet of 2, #C361-C362	3.25	1.40
		Nos. C359-C362 (4)	3.90	1.65

Birth and death anniversaries of famous painters.

Philexafrique II — Essen Issue

Common Design Types

#C363, Warthog and Togo No. C36. #C364, Firecrest and Thurn and Taxis No. 1.

1978, Nov. 1 Litho. *Perf. 13x12½*

C363	CD138	100fr multi	1.40	.50
C364	CD139	100fr multi	1.40	1.00
a.		Pair, #C363-C364 + label	3.00	1.50

Congress of Paris Type

60fr, Mail ship "Slieve Roe" 1877, post horn. 105fr, Congress of Paris medal. 200fr, Locomotive, 1870. All horizontal.

1978, Nov. 27 Photo. *Perf. 14x13*

C365	A206	60fr multi	.55	.25
C366	A206	105fr multi	.90	.45
C367	A206	200fr multi	1.40	.75
a.		Souv. sheet of 2, #C366-C367	2.50	1.20
		Nos. C365-C367 (3)	2.85	1.45

Christmas Type

Paintings (Virgin and Child): 90fr, 200fr, by Carlo Crivelli, diff. 100fr, by Cosimo Tura.

1978, Dec. 18

C368	A207	90fr multi	.75	.35
C369	A207	100fr multi	.95	.40
C370	A207	200fr multi	1.75	.70
a.		Souv. sheet of 2, #C369-C370	3.25	1.40
		Nos. C368-C370 (3)	3.45	1.45

Capt. Cook Type

Designs: 60fr, "Freelove," Whitby Harbor, horiz. 70fr, Trip to Antarctica, 1773, horiz. 90fr, Capt. Cook. 200fr, Sails of Endeavour.

1979, Feb. 12 Litho. *Perf. 14*

C371	A208	60fr multi	.50	.25
C372	A208	70fr multi	.55	.25
C373	A208	90fr multi	.75	.30
C374	A208	200fr multi	1.75	1.25
a.		Souv. sheet of 2, #C373-C374	3.00	1.75
		Nos. C371-C374 (4)	3.55	2.05

Easter Type

60fr, Resurrection. 100fr, Ascension. 200fr, Jesus appearing to Mary Magdalene.

1979, Apr. 9

C375	A209	60fr multi	.45	.25
C376	A209	100fr multi	.70	.40
C377	A209	200fr multi	1.50	.70
a.		Souv. sheet of 2, #C376-C377	2.75	1.40
		Nos. C375-C377 (3)	2.65	1.35

UPU Emblem, Drummer AP20

Design: 100fr, UPU emblem, hands passing letter, satellites.

1979, June 8 Engr. *Perf. 13*

C378	AP20	60fr multi	1.40	.50
C379	AP20	100fr multi	1.20	1.00

Philexafrique II, Libreville, Gabon, June 8-17.

Einstein Type

Designs: 60fr, Sights and actuality diagram. 85fr, Einstein playing violin, vert. 100fr, Atom symbol and formula of relativity, vert. 200fr, Einstein portrait, vert.

Perf. 14x13, 13x14

1979, July 2 Photo.

C380	A210	60fr multi	.50	.25
C381	A210	85fr multi	.80	.40
C382	A210	100fr multi	.85	.45
C383	A210	200fr multi	1.75	.85
a.		Souv. sheet of 2, #C382-C383	3.00	1.50
		Nos. C380-C383 (4)	3.90	1.95

Tree Type

Design: 60fr, Man watering tree.

1979, Aug. 13 *Perf. 14x13*

C384	A212	60fr blk & brn	.40	.25

Rowland Hill Type

Designs: 90fr, Bellman, England, 1820. 100fr, "Centercycles" used for parcel delivery, 1883, horiz. 200fr, French P.O. railroad car, 1848, horiz.

1979, Aug. 27 Photo.

C385	A213	90fr multi	.65	.30
C386	A213	100fr multi	.70	.35
C387	A213	200fr multi	1.50	.65
a.		Souv. sheet of 2, #C386-C387	2.50	1.25
		Nos. C385-C387 (3)	2.85	1.30

Train Type

Historic Locomotives: 60fr, "Le General," 1862. 85fr, Stephenson's, 1843. 100fr, "De Witt Clinton," 1831. 200fr, Joy's "Jenny Lind," 1847.

1979, Oct. 1 Litho. *Perf. 14*

C388	A214	60fr multi	.55	.25
C389	A214	85fr multi	.70	.45
C390	A214	100fr multi	.85	.50
C391	A214	200fr multi	1.75	.90
a.		Souv. sheet of 2, #C390-C391	6.00	3.00
		Nos. C388-C391 (4)	3.85	2.10

Olympic Type

1980 Olympic Emblems and: 90fr, Ski jump. No. C393, Doubles canoeing, Olympic flame. No. C394, Rings. No. C395a, Bobsledding, horiz. No. C395b, Gymnast, horiz.

1979, Oct. 18 Litho. *Perf. 13½*

C392	A215	90fr multi	.70	.30
C393	A215	100fr multi	.75	.35
C394	A215	200fr multi	1.40	.65
		Nos. C392-C394 (3)	2.85	1.30

Souvenir Sheet

C395		Sheet of 2	2.50	1.25
a.		A215 100fr multi	.65	.35
b.		A215 200fr multi	1.40	.65

Religion Type

Designs: 60fr, Moslems praying. 70fr, Protestant ministers.

1979, Oct. 29 *Perf. 13x14*

C396	A216	60fr multi	.50	.25
C397	A216	70fr multi	.55	.30
a.		Souv. sheet, #C396-C397	1.40	.50

Apollo 11 Type

60fr, Astronaut leaving Apollo 11. 70fr, US flag. 200fr, Sun shield. 300fr, Lunar take-off.

1979, Nov. 5

C398	A217	60fr multi	.45	.25
C399	A217	70fr multi	.50	.25
C400	A217	200fr multi	1.50	.65
C401	A217	300fr multi	2.10	1.00
a.		Souv. sheet of 2, #C400-C401	4.00	1.75
		Nos. C398-C401 (4)	4.55	2.15

Telecom Type

Design: 60fr, Telecom 79, dish antenna.

1979, Nov. 26 Photo. *Perf. 14x13*

C402	A218	60fr multi	.55	.25

Miniature Sheets

President Eyadema, 10th Anniv. of the People's Republic AP21

Litho. & Embossed

1979, Nov. 30 *Perf. 13½*

C402A	AP21	1000fr In uniform	6.00	—

Imperf

C402B	AP21	1000fr In suit, vert.	6.00	—

Exist imperf.

Christmas Type

90fr, Adoration of the Kings. 100fr, Presentation of Infant Jesus. 200fr, Flight into Egypt.

1979, Dec. 17 Litho. *Perf. 14*

C403	A219	90fr multi	.55	.35
C404	A219	100fr multi	.80	.40
C405	A219	200fr multi	1.75	.70
a.		Souv. sheet of 2, #C404-C405	3.50	1.50
		Nos. C403-C405 (3)	3.10	1.45

Rotary Type

3-H Emblem and: 90fr, Man reaching for sun. 100fr, Fish, grain. 200fr, Family, globe.

1980, Jan. 14

C406	A220	90fr multi	.80	.40
C407	A220	100fr multi	.85	.45
C408	A220	200fr multi	1.60	.85
a.		Souv. sheet of 2, C407-C408	3.25	1.60
		Nos. C406-C408 (3)	3.25	1.70

Rotary Intl., 75th anniv.; 3-H program (health, hunger, humanity).

Winter Olympic Type, 1980

1980, Jan. 31 Litho. *Perf. 13½*

C409	A221	60fr Downhill skiing	.45	.25
C410	A221	100fr Speed skating	.75	.35
C411	A221	200fr Cross-country skiing	1.40	.65
		Nos. C409-C411 (3)	2.60	1.25

Souvenir Sheet

C412		Sheet of 2	2.50	1.25
a.		A221 100fr Ski jump, horiz.	.65	.35
b.		A221 200fr Hockey, horiz.	1.25	.65

Olympic Type

1980, Feb. 29 Litho. *Perf. 13½*

C413	A222	100fr Fencing	.65	.45
C414	A222	200fr Pole vault	1.40	.80
C415	A222	300fr Hurdles	2.10	1.25
a.		Souv. sheet of 2, #C414-C415	3.75	1.75
		Nos. C413-C415 (3)	4.15	2.50

Easter Type

Easter 1980 (Paintings by): 60fr, Lorenzo Lotto. 100fr, El Greco. 200fr, Carlo Crivelli.

1980, Mar. 31 *Perf. 14*

C416	A223	60fr multi	.50	.25
C417	A223	100fr multi	.75	.35
C418	A223	200fr multi	1.40	.65
a.		Souv. sheet of 2, #C417-C418	2.50	1.25
		Nos. C416-C418 (3)	2.65	1.25

ASECNA Type

1980, Mar. 24 Litho. *Perf. 12½*

C419	A224	60fr multi	.60	.25

Telecommunications Type

1980, May 17 Photo. *Perf. 13½x14*

C420	A225	60fr "17 MAI", vert.	.60	.25

Red Cross Type

1980, June 16 Photo. *Perf. 14x13*

C421	A226	60fr Nurses, patient	.60	.25

Jules Verne Type

Designs: 60fr, Rocket (From Earth to Moon). 80fr, Around the World in 80 Days. 100fr, Rocket and moon (From Earth to Moon). 200fr, Octopus (20,000 Leagues Under the Sea).

1980, July 14 Litho. *Perf. 14*

C422	A227	60fr multi	.45	.25
C423	A227	80fr multi	.55	.25
C424	A227	100fr multi	.80	.35
C425	A227	200fr multi	1.40	.65
a.		Souv. sheet of 2, #C424-C425, perf. 13½x14	2.50	1.25
		Nos. C422-C425 (4)	3.20	1.50

Ingres Type

Ingres Paintings: 90fr, Jupiter and Thetis. 100fr, Countess d'Haussonville. 200fr, "Tu Marcellus Eris."

1980, Aug. 29 Litho. *Perf. 14*

C426	A228	90fr multi	.80	.30
C427	A228	100fr multi	.85	.35
C428	A228	200fr multi	1.60	.65
a.		Souv. sheet of 2, #C427-C428	3.00	1.25
		Nos. C426-C428 (3)	3.25	1.30

Famous Men Type

90fr, Salvador Allende, vert. 100fr, Pope Paul VI, vert. 200fr, Jomo Kenyatta, vert.

1980, Feb. 11 Litho. *Perf. 14x13*

C429	A231	90fr ultra & lt bl grn	1.00	.30
C430	A231	100fr pur & pink	1.10	.35
C431	A231	200fr brn & yel bis	2.00	.65
a.		Souv. sheet of 2, #C430-C431	2.50	1.25
		Nos. C429-C431 (3)	4.10	1.30

Human Rights Type

1980, Oct. 13 *Perf. 13x14*

C432	A233	60fr Map of Americas	.40	.25
C433	A233	150fr Map of Africa	1.00	.50
a.		Souv. sheet of 2, #C432-C433	1.75	1.25

American Order of Rosicrucians Emblem — AP22

1980, Nov. 17 Litho. *Perf. 13*

C434	AP22	60fr multi	.60	.25

General Conclave of the American Order of Rosicrucians, meeting of French-speaking countries, Lome, Aug.

Christmas Type

Designs: 100fr, Cologne Cathedral, Germany, 13th cent. 150fr, Notre Dame, Paris, 12th cent. 200fr, Canterbury Cathedral, England, 11th cent.

1980, Dec. 22 *Perf. 14½x13½*

C435 A234 100fr multi .70 .35
C436 A234 150fr multi 1.10 .50
C437 A234 200fr multi 1.40 .65
a. Souv. sheet of 2, #C436-C437 3.00 1.40
Nos. C435-C437 (3) 3.20 1.50

Hotel Type of 1981

1981, Feb. 2 **Litho.** *Perf. 12½x13*

C437B A236 60fr multi .60 .25

Easter Type of 1981

Rembrandt Paintings: 100fr, Artist's Mother. 200fr, Man in a Ruff.

1981, Apr. 13 **Litho.** *Perf. 14½x13½*

C438 A237 100fr multi .90 .40
C439 A237 200fr multi 1.75 .70
a. Souv. sheet of 2, #C438-C439 3.50 1.50

Market Type

1981, Mar. 8 **Litho.** *Perf. 14*

C440 A230 90fr Fabric dealer .60 .30
C441 A230 100fr Bananas .65 .35
C442 A230 200fr Clay pottery 1.40 .65
C443 A230 250fr Setting up 1.60 .80
C444 A230 500fr Selling 3.50 1.60
C445 A230 1000fr Measuring grain 6.50 3.50
Nos. C440-C445 (6) 14.25 7.20

For overprints see Nos. C486-C487.

Bird Type

50fr, Violet-backed sunbird. 100fr, Red bishop.

Perf. 13½x14½

1981, Aug. 10 **Litho.**

C446 A238 50fr multi .80 .25
C447 A238 100fr multi 1.50 .35
a. Souv. sheet, #1110, C447 5.50 2.50

IYD Type

90fr, Carpenter. 200fr, Basketball players. 300fr, Weaver.

1981, Aug. 31 *Perf. 14*

C448 A240 90fr multi .80 .40
C449 A240 200fr multi 1.60 .85

Souvenir Sheet

C449A A240 300fr multi 2.75 1.60

Picasso Type

90fr, Violin and Bottle on Table, 1916. 100fr, Baboon and Young. 200fr, Mandolin and Clarinet, 1914.

1981, Sept. 14 *Perf. 14½x13½*

C450 A241 90fr multi .90 .40
C451 A241 100fr multi 1.10 .50
C452 A241 200fr multi 2.40 .90
a. Souv. sheet of 2, #C451-C452 3.50 1.40
Nos. C450-C452 (3) 4.40 1.80

World Heritage Year Type

100fr, Cracow Museum, Poland. 200fr, Goree Isld., Senegal.

1981, Sept. 28 *Perf. 13½x14½*

C453 A242 100fr multi .80 .40
C454 A242 200fr multi 1.75 .85
a. Souv. sheet of 2, #C453-C454 2.75 1.25

Space Type

1981, Nov. *Perf. 14*

C455 A243 90fr multi .65 .25
C456 A243 100fr multi .70 .25

Souvenir Sheet

Perf. 13x14

C456A A243 300fr multi, vert. 2.25 1.25

10th anniv. of Soyuz 10 (90fr) and Apollo 14 (100fr).

Christmas Type

Rubens Paintings: 100fr, Adoration of the Kings. 200fr, Virgin and Child. 300fr, Virgin giving Chasuble to St. Idefonse.

Perf. 14½x13½

1981, Dec. 10 **Litho.**

C457 A244 100fr multi .70 .35
C458 A244 200fr multi 1.50 .65
C459 A244 300fr multi 2.10 1.00
a. Souv. sheet of 2, #C458-C459 4.00 1.90
Nos. C457-C459 (3) 4.30 2.00

West African Rice Development Assoc. Type

1981, Dec. 21 **Litho.** *Perf. 12½*

C461 A236a 105fr yel & multi .70 .35

Liberation Type

Designs: 105fr, Citizens holding hands, Pres. Eyadema, vert. 130fr, Hotel.

1982, Jan. 13 **Litho.** *Perf. 12½*

C462 A245 105fr multi .70 .35
C463 A245 130fr multi .90 .40

Scouting Year Type

1982, Feb. 25 **Litho.** *Perf. 14*

C464 A246 90fr Semaphore .75 .30
C465 A246 120fr Tower 1.00 .40
C466 A246 130fr Scouts, canoe 1.10 .40
C467 A246 135fr Scouts, tent 1.10 .45
Nos. C464-C467 (4) 3.95 1.55

Souvenir Sheet

Perf. 13x14

C468 A246 500fr Baden-Powell 4.25 1.60

Easter Type

1982, Apr. *Perf. 14x14½*

C469 A247 105fr multi .70 .35
C470 A247 120fr multi .80 .40

Souvenir Sheet

C471 A247 500fr multi 4.00 1.60

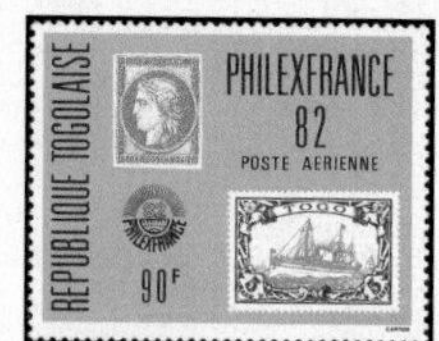

PHILEXFRANCE '82 Intl. Stamp Exhibition, Paris, June 11-21 — AP23

1982 **Litho.** *Perf. 13*

C472 AP23 90fr shown .70 .30
C473 AP23 105fr ROMOLYMPHIL '82, vert. .90 .35

Issue dates: 90fr, June 11; 105fr, May 19.

Butterfly Type

90fr, Euxanthe eurionome. 105fr, Mylothris rhodope.
500fr, Papilio zalmoxis.

1982, July 15 *Perf. 14½x14*

C474 A248 90fr multi 1.60 .40
C475 A248 105fr multi 1.75 .45

Souvenir Sheet

C476 A248 500fr multi 4.25 1.60

World Cup Type

1982, July 26 *Perf. 14x14½*

C477 A249 105fr multi .80 .35
C478 A249 200fr multi 1.40 .65
C479 A249 300fr multi 2.10 1.00
Nos. C477-C479 (3) 4.30 2.00

Souvenir Sheet

C480 A249 500fr multi 3.75 1.65

For overprints see Nos. 1152-1155.

Pre-Olympics, 1984 Los Angeles — AP24

1983, Oct. 3 **Photo.** *Perf. 12½*

C481 AP24 70fr Boxing .55 .25
C482 AP24 90fr Hurdles .70 .25
C483 AP24 105fr Pole vault .80 .25
C484 AP24 130fr Runner .90 .25
Nos. C481-C484 (4) 2.95 1.00

Souvenir Sheet

C485 AP24 500fr Runner, diff. 4.00 1.50

Nos. C443-C444 Overprinted: "19E CONGRES UPU HAMBOURG 1984"

1984, June **Litho.** *Perf. 14*

C486 A230 250fr multi 1.75 1.00
C487 A230 500fr multi 3.75 2.00

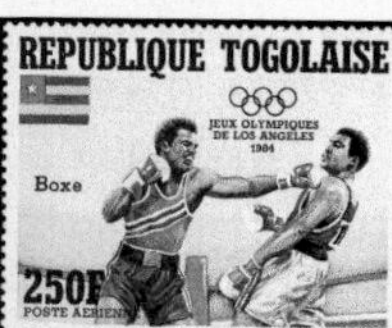

1984 Summer Olympics AP25

1984, July 27 *Perf. 13*

C488 AP25 70fr Pole vault .45 .25
C489 AP25 90fr Bicycling .45 .25
C490 AP25 120fr Soccer .75 .25
C491 AP25 250fr Boxing 1.50 .40
C492 AP25 400fr Running 2.25 .65
Nos. C488-C492 (5) 5.40 1.80

Souvenir Sheet

C493 AP25 1000fr like 120fr, without flag 7.50 6.50

Nos. C488-C490, C493 vert.

Olympic Champions — AP26

No. C494, Jim Thorpe, US. No. C495, Jesse Owens, US. No. C496, Muhammad Ali, US. No. C497, Bob Beamon, US.
No. C498, Bill Steinkraus, US. No. C499, New Zealand rowing team. No. C500, Pakistani hockey team. No. C501, Yukio Endo, Japan.

1984, Nov. 15 **Litho.** *Perf. 15*

C494 AP26 500fr multi 7.25 3.25
C495 AP26 500fr multi 7.25 3.25
C496 AP26 500fr multi 40.00 3.25
C497 AP26 500fr multi 7.25 3.25
Nos. C494-C497 (4) 61.75 13.00

Souvenir Sheets

C498 AP26 500fr multi 7.25 3.25
C499 AP26 500fr multi 7.25 3.25
C500 AP26 500fr multi 7.25 3.25
C501 AP26 500fr multi 7.25 3.25

West German Olympians

No. C502, Dietmar Mogenburg. No. C503, Fredy Schmidtke. No. C504, Matthias Behr. No. C505, Sabine Everts.
No. C506, Karl-Heinz Radschinsky. No. C507, Pasquale Passarelli. No. C508, Michale Gross. No. C509, Jurgen Hingsen.

1984, Nov. 15

C502 AP26 500fr multi 7.25 3.25
C503 AP26 500fr multi 7.25 3.25
C504 AP26 500fr multi 7.25 3.25
C505 AP26 500fr multi 7.25 3.25
Nos. C502-C505 (4) 29.00 13.00

Souvenir Sheets

C506 AP26 500fr multi 7.25 3.25
C507 AP26 500fr multi 7.25 3.25
C508 AP26 500fr multi 7.25 3.25
C509 AP26 500fr multi 7.25 3.25

For overprints see Nos. C521-C536, C563.

Peace and Human Rights — AP28

230fr, Map of Togo, globe, doves. 270fr, Palm tree, emblem. 500fr, Opencast mining operation. 1000fr, Human Rights Monument, UN, NYC.

1985, Jan. 14 **Litho.** *Perf. 13½x14*

C510 AP28 230fr multi 1.50 .25
C511 AP28 270fr multi 1.90 .30
C512 AP28 500fr multi 3.50 .50
C513 AP28 1000fr multi 7.00 1.00
Nos. C510-C513 (4) 13.90 2.05

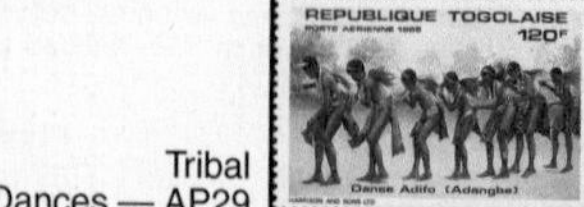

Tribal Dances — AP29

120fr, Adifo, Adangbe. 135fr, Fouet (whip), Kente. 290fr, Idjombi, Pagouda. 500fr, Moba, Dapaong.

1985, July *Perf. 15x14*

C514 AP29 120fr multicolored .85 .25
C515 AP29 135fr multicolored .85 .25
C516 AP29 290fr multicolored 2.00 .30
C517 AP29 500fr multicolored 3.50 .50
Nos. C514-C517 (4) 7.20 1.30

Visit of Pope John Paul II — AP30

90fr, The Pope outside Lome Cathedral. 130fr, Blessing crowd in St. Peter's Square. 500fr, Greeting Pres. Eyadema.

1985, Aug. 9 *Perf. 13*

C518 AP30 90fr multi .75 .25
C519 AP30 130fr multi, vert. 1.25 .25
C520 AP30 500fr multi 3.50 .50
Nos. C518-C520 (3) 5.50 1.00

Nos. C495, C497, C499, C502, C505-508 Overprinted with Winners Names, Country and Type of Olympic Medal

No. C521, Kirk Baptiste, US. No. C522, Carl Lewis, US. No. C523, Patrik Sjoberg, Sweden. No. C524, Glynis Nunn, Australia.
No. C525, Rowing eights, Canada. No. C526, Rolf Milser, W. Germany. No. C527, Takashi Irie, Japan. No. C528, Frederic Delcourt, France.

1985, Aug. *Perf. 15*

C521 AP26 500fr multicolored 6.50 1.50
C522 AP26 500fr multicolored 6.50 1.50
C523 AP26 500fr multicolored 6.50 1.50
C524 AP26 500fr multicolored 6.50 1.50
Nos. C521-C524 (4) 26.00 6.00

Souvenir Sheets

C525 AP26 500fr multicolored 3.50 3.00
C526 AP26 500fr multicolored 3.50 3.00
C527 AP26 500fr multicolored 3.50 3.00
C528 AP26 500fr multicolored 3.50 3.00

Nos. C494, C496, C503-C504, C498, C500, C501, C509 Ovptd. with Winners Names, Country and Type of Olympic Medal

No. C529, Italy. No. C530, Kevin Barry. No. C531, Rolf Golz. No. C532, Philippe Boisse.
No. C533, Karen Stives. No. C534, R.F.A. (West Germany). No. C535, Koji Gushiken. No. C536, Daley Thompson.

1985, Sept. 19 **Litho.** *Perf. 15*

C529 AP26 500fr multicolored 6.50 1.50
C530 AP26 500fr multicolored 6.50 1.50
C531 AP26 500fr multicolored 6.50 1.50
C532 AP26 500fr multicolored 6.50 1.50
Nos. C529-C532 (4) 26.00 6.00

Souvenir Sheets

C533 AP26 500fr multicolored 3.50 3.00
C534 AP26 500fr multicolored 3.50 3.00
C535 AP26 500fr multicolored 3.50 3.00
C536 AP26 500fr multicolored 3.50 3.00

Traditional Instruments AP31

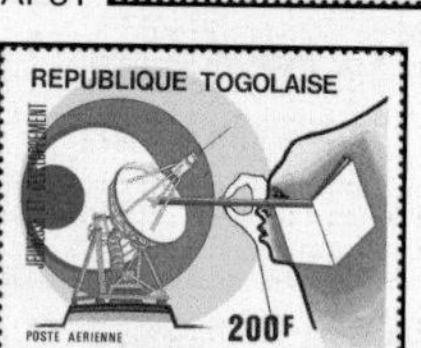

Youth and Development — AP32

Designs: No. C537, Xylophone, Kante horn, tambour. No. C538, Bongo drums, castanets, bassar horn. No. C539, Communications. No. C540, Agriculture and industry.

1985 **Litho.** *Perf. 13*

C537 AP31 100fr multi .90 .60
C538 AP31 100fr multi .90 .60
a. Pair, #C537-C538 3.00 3.00

C539 AP32 200fr multi 1.75 1.25
C540 AP32 200fr multi 1.75 1.25
a. Pair, #C539-C540 7.50 7.50
Nos. C537-C540 (4) 5.30 3.70

PHILEXAFRICA '85, Lome, Togo, 11/16-24. Issued: 100fr, Nov. 4; 200fr, Nov. 16.

No. 1274 Ovptd. with Organization Emblem and "80e Anniversaire du Rotary International."

1985, Nov. 15 Litho. *Perf. 15*

Souvenir Sheet

C541 A267 1000fr multi 20.00 6.50

Nos. 1254-1255, 1258 Ovptd. "10e ANNIVERSAIRE DE APOLLO-SOYUZ" in 1 or 2 lines

1985, Dec. 27 Litho. *Perf. 15*

C542 A265 90fr multi 1.25 .40
C543 A265 500fr multi 6.75 2.00

Souvenir Sheet

C544 A265 1000fr multi 8.50 2.90

Nos. 1294-1295, 1297 Ovptd. "75e ANNIVERSAIRE DE LA MORT DE HENRI DUNANT FONDATEUR DE LA CROIX ROUGE" in 2 or 4 lines

1985, Dec. 27

C545 A270 400fr multi 4.75 1.50
C546 A270 500fr multi 6.25 2.00

Souvenir Sheet

C547 A270 1000fr multi 7.50 6.00

Statue of Liberty, Cent. — AP33

70fr, Eiffel Tower. 90fr, Statue of Liberty. 500fr, Empire State Building.

1986, Apr. 10 *Perf. 13*

C548 AP33 70fr multicolored .55 .25
C549 AP33 90fr multicolored .65 .25
C550 AP33 500fr multicolored 3.75 1.40
Nos. C548-C550 (3) 4.95 1.90

Nos. 1237-1240 Ovptd. with AMERIPEX '86 Emblem

1986, May 22 *Perf. 11*

C551 A262 500fr multi 6.50 1.40
C552 A262 1000fr multi 12.50 2.75

Souvenir Sheets

Perf. 14

C553 A262 1000fr No. 1239 8.50 3.50
C554 A262 1000fr No. 1240 8.50 3.50

Air Africa, 25th Anniv. — AP34

1986, Dec. 29 Litho. *Perf. 12½x13*

C555 AP34 90fr multi .75 .25

Konrad Adenauer (1876-1967) West German Chancellor AP35

120fr, At podium. No. C557, 500fr, With Pres. Kennedy, 1962.
No. C558, 500fr, Portrait, vert.

1987, July 15 Litho. *Perf. 12½x13*

C556 AP35 120fr multi .90 .60
C557 AP35 500fr multi 3.50 3.00

Souvenir Sheet

Perf. 13x12½

C558 AP35 500fr multi 3.50 3.00

Berlin, 750th Anniv. — AP36

Designs: 90fr, Wilhelm I (1781-1864) coin, Victory statue. 150fr, Frederick III (1831-1888) coin, Brandenburg Gate. 300fr, Wilhelm II (1882-1951) coin, Reichstag building. 750fr, Otto Leopold von Bismarck (1815-1898), first chancellor of the German empire, and Charlottenburg Palace.

1987, Aug. 31 Litho. *Perf. 13½*

C559 AP36 90fr multi .60 .30
C560 AP36 150fr multi 1.00 .50
C561 AP36 300fr multi 2.00 1.00
Nos. C559-C561 (3) 3.60 1.80

Souvenir Sheet

C562 AP36 750fr multi 5.50 4.25

Nos. C506, 1258, 1273 and 1274 Overprinted in Black for Philatelic Exhibitions

a

b

c

d

1988, Apr. 25 Litho. *Perf. 15*

Souvenir Sheets

C563 AP26 (a) 500fr #C506 9.50 3.00
C564 A265 (b) 1000fr #1258 10.00 5.50
C565 A265 (c) 1000fr #1273 10.00 5.50
C566 A267 (d) 1000fr #1274 10.00 5.50
Nos. C563-C566 (4) 39.50 19.50

Additional overprints appear on souvenir sheets away from stamps.

AIR POST SEMI-POSTAL STAMPS

Nursery SPAP1

Perf. 13½x12½

1942, June 22 Unwmk. Photo.

CB1 SPAP1 1.50fr + 3.50fr green .55 5.50
CB2 SPAP1 2fr + 6fr brown .55 5.50
Set, never hinged 1.40

Native children's welfare fund.

Nos. CB1-CB2 were issued by the Vichy government in France, but were not placed on sale in Togo.

Colonial Education Fund

Common Design Type

1942, June 22 Engr.

CB3 CD86a 1.20fr + 1.80fr blue & red .35 5.50
Set, never hinged .70

No. CB3 was issued by the Vichy government in France, but was not placed on sale in Togo.

POSTAGE DUE STAMPS

Postage Due Stamps of Dahomey, 1914 Overprinted

1921 Unwmk. *Perf. 14x13½*

J1 D2 5c green .65 .85
J2 D2 10c rose .65 .90
J3 D2 15c gray 1.25 1.75
J4 D2 20c brown 2.50 2.50
J5 D2 30c blue 2.50 2.75
J6 D2 50c black 2.10 2.50
J7 D2 60c orange 2.10 2.50
J8 D2 1fr violet 3.75 4.50
Nos. J1-J8 (8) 15.50 18.25

Cotton Field — D3

1925 Typo. Unwmk.

J9 D3 2c blue & blk .25 .35
J10 D3 4c dl red & blk .25 .35
J11 D3 5c ol grn & blk .25 .35
J12 D3 10c cerise & blk .35 .45
J13 D3 15c orange & blk .70 .85
J14 D3 20c red vio & blk .35 .55
J15 D3 25c gray & blk 1.10 1.10
J16 D3 30c ocher & blk .35 .55
J17 D3 50c brown & blk 1.10 1.10
J18 D3 60c green & blk 1.10 1.10
J19 D3 1fr dk vio & blk 1.10 1.10
Nos. J9-J19 (11) 6.90 7.85

Type of 1925 Issue Surcharged

1927

J20 D3 2fr on 1fr rose red & vio 7.00 7.00
J21 D3 3fr on 1fr org brn, blk & ultra 7.00 7.00

Mask — D4

1941 Engr. *Perf. 13*

J22 D4 5c brown black .25 .30
J23 D4 10c yellow green .25 .30
J24 D4 15c carmine .25 .30
J25 D4 20c ultra .30 .35
J26 D4 30c chestnut .55 .65
J27 D4 50c olive green 1.40 1.75
J28 D4 60c violet .70 .85
J29 D4 1fr light blue .90 1.00
J30 D4 2fr orange vermilion .85 .90
J31 D4 3fr rose violet .85 1.10
Nos. J22-J31 (10) 6.30 7.50
Set, never hinged 8.00

For type D4 without "RF," see Nos. J31A-J31F.

Type of 1941 Without "RF"

1942-44

J31A D4 5c brown black .25
J31B D4 10c green & violet .30
J31C D4 15c car rose & brn .35
J31D D4 30c brown & black .55
J31E D4 2fr brn org & brn vio .70
J31F D4 3fr violet & green .70
Nos. J31A-J31F (6) 2.85
Set, never hinged 3.50

Nos. J31A-J31F were issued by the Vichy government in France, but were not placed on sale in Togo.

Catalogue values for unused stamps in this section, from this point to the end of the section, are for Never Hinged items.

Carved Figures — D5

1947

J32 D5 10c brt ultra .30 .30
J33 D5 30c red .30 .30
J34 D5 50c dp yellow grn .30 .30
J35 D5 1fr chocolate .50 .50
J36 D5 2fr carmine .50 .50
J37 D5 3fr gray blk .50 .50
J38 D5 4fr ultra .80 .80
J39 D5 5fr sepia 1.10 .90
J40 D5 10fr dp orange 1.10 1.00
J41 D5 20fr dk blue vio 1.50 1.40
Nos. J32-J41 (10) 6.90 6.50

Republic

Konkomba Helmet — D6

1957 Engr. *Perf. 14x13*

J42 D6 1fr brt violet .25 .25
J43 D6 2fr brt orange .25 .25
J44 D6 3fr dk gray .25 .25
J45 D6 4fr brt red .25 .25
J46 D6 5fr ultra .25 .25
J47 D6 10fr dp green .35 .35
J48 D6 20fr dp claret .50 .50
Nos. J42-J48 (7) 2.10 2.10

Konkomba Helmet — D7

1959 *Perf. 14x13*

J49 D7 1fr orange brn .25 .35
J50 D7 2fr lt blue grn .25 .35
J51 D7 3fr orange .25 .35
J52 D7 4fr blue .25 .45
J53 D7 5fr lilac rose .25 .45
J54 D7 10fr violet blue .45 .65
J55 D7 20fr black .80 .85
Nos. J49-J55 (7) 2.50 3.45

Type of Regular Issue

Shells: 1fr, Conus papilionaceus. 2fr, Marginella faba. 3fr, Cypraea stercoraria. 4fr, Strombus latus. 5fr, Costate cockle (sea shell). 10fr, Cancellaria cancellata. 15fr, Cymbium pepo. 20fr, Tympanotomus radula.

1964-65 Unwmk. Photo. *Perf. 14*

Size: 20x25½mm

J56 A47 1fr gray grn & red brn ('65) .25 .25
J57 A47 2fr tan & ol grn ('65) .25 .25
J58 A47 3fr gray, brn & yel ('65) .25 .25
J59 A47 4fr tan & multi ('65) .30 .25
J60 A47 5fr sep, org & grn .70 .30
J61 A47 10fr sl bl, brn & bis .95 .40
J62 A47 15fr grn & brn 2.75 1.00
J63 A47 20fr sl, dk brn & yel 3.25 1.25
Nos. J56-J63 (8) 8.70 3.95

Tomatoes — D8

1969-70 Litho. *Perf. 14*

J64 D8 5fr yellow & multi .25 .25
J65 D8 10fr blue & multi .45 .25
J66 D8 15fr multi ('70) .70 .30
J67 D8 20fr multi ('70) 1.00 .40
Nos. J64-J67 (4) 2.40 1.20

Market Type

1981, Mar. 8 Litho. *Perf. 14*

Size: 23x32mm, 32x23mm

J68 A230 5fr Millet, vert. .25 .25
J69 A230 10fr Packaged goods .25 .25
J70 A230 25fr Chickens .25 .25
J71 A230 50fr Ivory vendor .50 .25
Nos. J68-J71 (4) 1.25 1.00

OFFICIAL STAMPS

Catalogue values for unused stamps in this section are for never hinged items.

O1

1991? Litho. *Perf. 13½*

O1 O1 15fr multicolored — —
O2 O1 100fr multicolored — —
O3 O1 125fr multicolored — —
O4 O1 500fr multicolored — —

1991?

O5 O1 10fr multicolored — —
O6 O1 90fr yellow & multi — —

1991?

O7 O1 180fr ap grn & multi — —

1991

O8 O1 50fr yellow & multi — —
O9 O1 300fr ap grn & multi — —

The editors would like information on dates of issue and stamps of other denominations. The catalogue numbers will change.

TOKELAU

'tō-kə-,lau

(Union Islands)

LOCATION — Pacific Ocean 300 miles north of Apia, Western Samoa
GOVT. — A dependency of New Zealand
AREA — 4 sq. mi.
POP. — 1,487 (1996)

The Tokelau islands consist of three atolls: Atafu, Nukunono and Fakaofo, which span 100 miles of ocean.

12 Pence = 1 Shilling
100 Cents = 1 Dollar (1967)

Catalogue values for all unused stamps in this country are for Never Hinged items.

Map and Scene on Atafu — A1

Nukunono Dwelling and Map — A2

Fakaofo Shore Line and Map — A3

Perf. 13½x13

1948, June 22 Wmk. 253 Engr.

1 A1 ½p red brown & rose lilac .25 .45
2 A2 1p dp green & orange brn .25 .50
3 A3 2p deep ultra & green .25 .50
Nos. 1-3 (3) .75 1.45

For surcharges see Nos. 5, 9-11.

Coronation Issue

Queen Elizabeth II — A3a

1953, May 25 Photo. ***Perf. 14x14½***

4 A3a 3p brown 2.75 2.75

No. 1 Srchd. in Black

Perf. 13½x13

1956, Mar. 27 Engr. Wmk. 253

5 A1 1sh on ½p 1.30 3.25

Postal-Fiscal Type of New Zealand, 1950, Surcharged

Wmk. 253

1966, Nov. Typo. ***Perf. 14***

6 A109 6p light blue .50 1.00
7 A109 8p light green .50 1.00
8 A109 2sh pink .75 1.25
Nos. 6-8 (3) 1.75 3.25

Nos. 1-3 Surcharged with New Value and Dots Obliterating Old Denomination

1967, July 10 Engr. ***Perf. 13½x13***

9 A2 1c on 1p .45 .45
10 A3 2c on 2p .85 .85
11 A1 10c on ½p 2.25 2.25
Nos. 9-11 (3) 3.55 3.55

The 1c and 2c surcharges include two dots, the 10c surcharge has only one.

Postal Fiscal Type of New Zealand, 1950, Surcharged

1967, July 10 Typo. ***Perf. 14***

12 A109 3c light lilac .25 .25
13 A109 5c light blue .40 .40
14 A109 7c light green .40 .40
15 A109 20c pink .75 .75
Nos. 12-15 (4) 1.80 1.80

1877, British Protectorate — A4

History of Tokelau: 10c, 1916, part of Gilbert and Ellice Islands Colony. 15c, 1925, administration transferred to New Zealand. 20c, 1948, New Zealand Territory.

Perf. 13x12½

1969, Aug. 8 Litho. Wmk. 253

16 A4 5c ultra, yellow & blk .75 .45
17 A4 10c rose red, yel & blk .85 .75
18 A4 15c dull grn, yel & blk 1.00 .90
19 A4 20c brown, yel & blk 1.25 1.75
Nos. 16-19 (4) 3.85 3.85

Nativity, by Federico Fiori — A4a

1969, Oct. 1 Photo. ***Perf. 13½x14***

20 A4a 2c multicolored .30 .30

Christmas.

Adoration, by Correggio — A4b

Perf. 12½

1970, Oct. 1 Unwmk. Litho.

21 A4b 2c multicolored .30 .30

Christmas.

"Dolphin," 1765, Map of Atafu — A5

Designs: 10c, "Pandora," 1791, and map of Nukunono. 25c, "General Jackson," 1835, and map of Fakaofo, horiz.

1970, Dec. 9 Unwmk. ***Perf. 13½***

22 A5 5c yellow & multi .75 .50
23 A5 10c multicolored 1.75 1.00
24 A5 25c pink & multi 3.50 2.50
Nos. 22-24 (3) 6.00 4.00

Discovery of Tokelau Islands.

Fan — A6

Native Handicrafts: 2c, Round vessel. 3c, Hexagonal box. 5c, Shoulder bag. 10c, Handbag. 15c, Jewelry box with beads. 20c, Outrigger canoe model. 25c, Fish hooks.

1971, Oct. 20 Litho. ***Perf. 14***

25 A6 1c olive & multi .25 .25
26 A6 2c red & multi .25 .30
27 A6 3c dk violet & multi .35 .45
28 A6 5c dull blue & multi .40 .50
29 A6 10c dp orange & multi .50 .60
30 A6 15c emerald & multi .70 .90
31 A6 20c multicolored .90 1.00
32 A6 25c violet blue & multi 1.00 1.00
Nos. 25-32 (8) 4.35 5.00

Windmill Pump, Map of Atafu — A7

South Pacific Commission Emblem and: 10c, Community well, map of Fakaofo. 15c, Eradication of rhinoceros beetle, map of Nukunono. 20c, members.

1972, Sept. 6 Litho. ***Perf. 14x13½***

33 A7 5c lt blue grn & multi .75 .70
34 A7 10c grnsh blue & multi .85 .85
35 A7 15c lilac & multi 1.00 1.00
36 A7 20c violet bl & multi 1.50 1.40
Nos. 33-36 (4) 4.10 3.95

South Pacific Commission, 25th anniversary. On 15c, "PACIFIC" reads "PACFIC."

Horny Coral — A8

1973, Sept. 12 Litho. ***Perf. 13x13½***

37 A8 3c shown 1.00 .75
38 A8 5c Soft coral 1.00 .75
39 A8 15c Mushroom coral 1.60 1.15
40 A8 25c Staghorn coral 2.00 1.35
Nos. 37-40 (4) 5.60 4.00

Cowrie (Cypraea Mauritiana) — A9

Cowrie shells: 5c, Cypraea tigris. 15c, Cypraea talpa. 25c, Cypraea argus.

1974, Nov. 13 Litho. ***Perf. 14***

41 A9 3c apple grn & multi 1.05 .75
42 A9 5c dk blue & multi 1.40 1.00
43 A9 15c blue & multi 1.90 1.35
44 A9 25c green & multi 2.10 1.50
Nos. 41-44 (4) 6.45 4.60

Moorish Idol — A10

Fish: 10c, Long-nosed butterflyfish. 15c, Lined butterflyfish. 25c, Red firefish.

1975, Nov. 19 Litho. ***Perf. 14***

45 A10 5c blue & multi .50 .50
46 A10 10c brown & multi .90 .90
47 A10 15c lilac & multi 1.35 1.35
48 A10 25c multicolored 2.25 2.25
Nos. 45-48 (4) 5.00 5.00

Canoe Making — A11

Designs: 2c, Reef fishing. 3c, Woman preparing pandanus leaves for weaving. 5c, Communal kitchen (umu). 9c, Wood carving. 20c, Husking coconuts. 50c, Wash day. $1, Meal time. 9c, 20c, 50c, $1, vertical.

1976, Oct. 27 Litho. ***Perf. 14***

49 A11 1c pink & multi .55 *.55*
50 A11 2c multicolored .40 *1.40*
51 A11 3c lt blue & multi .35 *.50*
52 A11 5c yellow & multi .40 *.50*
53 A11 9c bister & multi .25 *.50*
54 A11 20c multicolored .25 *.50*
55 A11 50c tan & multi .35 *.70*
56 A11 $1 multicolored .70 *1.00*
Nos. 49-56 (8) 3.25 *5.65*

1981, July 17 ***Perf. 15***

49a A11 1c .50 .40
51a A11 3c .50 .40
52a A11 5c .50 .40
53a A11 9c .90 .75
54a A11 20c .90 .75
55a A11 50c 1.75 1.00
56a A11 $1 3.00 3.00
Nos. 49a-56a (7) 8.05 6.70

White Tern — A12

Birds of Tokelau: 10c, Turnstone. 15c, White-capped noddy. 30c, Brown noddy.

1977, Nov. 16 Litho. ***Perf. 14½x15***

57 A12 8c multicolored .45 .35
58 A12 10c multicolored .60 .40
59 A12 15c multicolored .70 .65
60 A12 30c multicolored 1.50 1.40
Nos. 57-60 (4) 3.25 2.80

Westminster Abbey — A13

10c, King Edward's Chair. 15c, Scepter, Crown, Orb, Bible and Staff of State. 30c, Elizabeth II.

1978, June 28 Litho. ***Perf. 14***

61 A13 8c multicolored .25 .25
62 A13 10c multicolored .30 .25
63 A13 15c multicolored .45 .45
64 A13 30c multicolored .80 .80
Nos. 61-64 (4) 1.80 1.75

25th anniv. of coronation of Elizabeth II.

Canoe Racing — A14

Designs: Various canoe races.

1978, Nov. 8 Litho. ***Perf. 13½x14***

65 A14 8c multicolored .30 .35
66 A14 12c multicolored .45 .50
67 A14 15c multicolored .50 .60
68 A14 30c multicolored .85 .90
Nos. 65-68 (4) 2.10 2.35

1979, Nov. 7 Photo. ***Perf. 14***

69 A14 10c Rugby .35 .35
70 A14 15c Cricket .70 .70
71 A14 20c Rugby, diff. .70 .70
72 A14 30c Cricket, diff. .75 .75
Nos. 69-72 (4) 2.50 2.50

1980, Nov. 5 Litho. *Perf. 13½*

73	A14 10c Surfing	.25	.25
74	A14 20c Surfing, diff.	.25	.25
75	A14 30c Swimming	.35	.40
76	A14 50c Swimming, diff.	.50	.55
	Nos. 73-76 (4)	1.35	1.45

1981, Nov. 4 Photo. *Perf. 14*

77	A14 10c Pole vaulting, vert.	.25	.25
78	A14 20c Volleyball, vert.	.30	.25
79	A14 30c Running, vert.	.40	.35
80	A14 50c Volleyball, vert., diff.	.50	.55
	Nos. 77-80 (4)	1.45	1.40

Wood Carving — A15

1982, May 5 Litho. *Perf. 13½x13*

81	A15 10s shown	.30	.30
82	A15 22s Bow-drilling sea shells	.30	.30
83	A15 34s Bowl finishing	.40	.40
84	A15 60s Basket weaving	.80	.80
	Nos. 81-84 (4)	1.80	1.80

Octopus Lure Fishing — A16

Designs: Fishing Methods.

1982, Nov. 3 Litho. *Perf. 14*

85	A16 5s shown	.25	.25
86	A16 18s Multiple-hook	.25	.25
87	A16 23s Ruvettus	.25	.25
88	A16 34s Netting flying fish	.30	.30
89	A16 63s Noose	.50	.50
90	A16 75s Bonito	.65	.65
	Nos. 85-90 (6)	2.20	2.20

Outrigger Canoe — A17

1983, May 4 Litho. *Perf. 13½x14*

91	A17 5s shown	.25	.25
92	A17 18s Whale boat	.25	.25
93	A17 23s Aluminium whale boat	.25	.25
94	A17 34s Alia fishing boat	.25	.25
95	A17 63s Cargo ship	.45	.45
96	A17 75s Seaplane	.75	.75
	Nos. 91-96 (6)	2.20	2.20

Traditional Games — A18

1983, Nov. 2 Litho. *Perf. 14*

97	A18 5s Javelin throwing	.25	.25
98	A18 18s Tifaga string game	.25	.25
99	A18 23s Fire making	.25	.25
100	A18 34s Shell throwing	.25	.25
101	A18 63s Handball	.30	.30
102	A18 75s Mass wrestling	.50	.50
	Nos. 97-102 (6)	1.80	1.80

Planting, Harvesting Copra — A19

Copra Industry: b, Husking, splitting. c, Drying, cutting. d, Bagging, weighing. e, Shipping. Continuous design.

1984, May 2 Litho. *Perf. 13½x13*

103	Strip of 5	2.50	2.50
a.-e.	A19 48s any single	.45	.45

Local Fish — A20

1984, Dec. 5 Litho. *Perf. 14½x14*

104	A20 1c Manini	.25	.25
105	A20 2c Hahave	.25	.25
106	A20 5c Uloulo	.25	.25
107	A20 9c Ume Ihu	.25	.25
108	A20 23c Lifilafi	.25	.25
109	A20 34c Fagamea	.30	.30
110	A20 50c Kakahi	.40	.40
111	A20 75c Palu Po	.80	.80
112	A20 $1 Mokoha	1.00	1.00
113	A20 $2 Hakula	1.75	1.75
	Nos. 104-113 (10)	5.50	5.50

No. 110 exists overprinted "STAMPEX 86 / 4-10 AUGUST / 1986." These overprinted stamps were not available at post offices in Tokelau. Used examples were sent to the islands for cancellation.

Trees, Fruits and Herbs — A21

1985, June 26 Litho. *Perf. 13½*

114	A21 5c Mati	.25	.25
115	A21 18c Nonu	.25	.25
116	A21 32c Ulu	.30	.30
117	A21 48c Fala	.35	.35
118	A21 60c Kanava	.50	.50
119	A21 75c Niu	.75	.75
	Nos. 114-119 (6)	2.40	2.40

Public Buildings and Churches — A22

Designs: 5c, Administration Center, Atafu. 18c, Administration Center, Nukunonu. 32c, Administration Center, Fakaofo. 48c, Congregational Church, Atafu. 60c, Catholic Church, Nukunonu. 75c, Congregational Church, Fakaofo.

1985, Dec. 4

120	A22 5c multicolored	.25	.25
121	A22 18c multicolored	.25	.25
122	A22 32c multicolored	.30	.30
123	A22 48c multicolored	.35	.35
124	A22 60c multicolored	.50	.50
125	A22 75c multicolored	.75	.75
	Nos. 120-125 (6)	2.40	2.40

Hospitals and Schools — A23

Designs: 5c, Atafu Hospital. 18c, St. Joseph's Hospital, Nukunonu. 32c, Fenuafala Hospital, Fakaofo. 48c, Matauala School, Atafu. 60c, Matiti School, Nukunonu. 75c, Fenuafala School, Fakaofo.

1986, May 7 *Perf. 13½*

126	A23 5c multicolored	.25	.25
127	A23 18c multicolored	.25	.25
128	A23 32c multicolored	.30	.30
129	A23 48c multicolored	.35	.35
130	A23 60c multicolored	.50	.50
131	A23 75c multicolored	.75	.75
	Nos. 126-131 (6)	2.40	2.40

Fauna — A24

1986, Dec. 3 Litho. *Perf. 14*

132	A24 5c Coconut crab	.25	.25
133	A24 18c Pigs	.25	.25
134	A24 32c Chickens	.40	.40
135	A24 48c Turtles	.65	.65
136	A24 60c Goats	.80	.80
137	A24 75c Ducks	.95	.95
	Nos. 132-137 (6)	3.30	3.30

Flora — A25

1987, May 6

138	A25 5c Gahu	.40	.50
139	A25 18c Puka	.60	.75
140	A25 32c Higano	.75	.95
141	A25 48c Tialetiale	1.00	1.30
142	A25 60c Gagie	1.25	1.50
143	A25 75c Puapua	1.50	1.60
	Nos. 138-143 (6)	5.50	6.60

Olympic Sports — A26

1987, Dec. 2 Litho. *Perf. 14x14½*

144	A26 5c Javelin	.25	.35
145	A26 18c Shot put	.50	.60
146	A26 32c Long jump	.65	.75
147	A26 48c Hurdles	.75	.85
148	A26 60c Running	1.00	1.05
149	A26 75c Wrestling	1.35	1.45
	Nos. 144-149 (6)	4.50	5.05

Australia Bicentennial, SYDPEX '88 — A27

Re-enactment of the arrival of the First Fleet in Sydney Harbor, Jan. 26, 1988 (in a continuous design): a, Ships in harbor, building (LL). b, Ships in harbor, tall ship (LR). c, Ships in harbor, Sydney Opera House. d, Bridge. e, North Sydney.

1988, July 30 Litho. *Perf. 13½x13*

150	Strip of 5	10.00	10.00
a.-e.	A27 50c any single	1.90	1.90

Political Development — A28

Designs: 5c, Transfer of administration from the New Zealand Department of Maori and Island Affairs to the Ministry of Foreign Affairs, 1975. 18c, The General Fono empowered as the decision-making body of Tokelau, 1977. 32c, 1st Visit of New Zealand's prime minister, 1985. 48c, 1st Visit of UN representatives, 1976. 60c, 1st Tokelau delegation to go to the UN, 1987. 75c, 1st Tokelau appointed to the office of Official Secretary, 1987.

1988, Aug. 10 *Perf. 14½*

151	A28 5c multicolored	.25	.25
152	A28 18c multicolored	.25	.25
153	A28 32c multicolored	.65	.65
154	A28 48c multicolored	1.00	1.00
155	A28 60c multicolored	1.10	1.10
156	A28 75c multicolored	1.60	1.60
	Nos. 151-156 (6)	4.85	4.85

Island Christmas — A29

Designs: 5c, Three Wise Men *(Na Makoi)*. 20c, Holy family *(He Tala)*. 40c, Escape into Egypt *(Fakagagalo ki Aikupito)*. 60c, Christmas presents *(Meaalofa Kilihimahi)*. 70c, Christ child *(Pepe ko Iesu)*. $1, Christmas parade *(Holo Tamilo)*.

1988, Dec. 7 Litho. *Perf. 13½*

157	A29 5c multicolored	.25	.25
158	A29 20c multicolored	.25	.25
159	A29 40c multicolored	.50	.50
160	A29 60c multicolored	.80	.80
161	A29 70c multicolored	.90	.90
162	A29 $1 multicolored	1.25	1.25
	Nos. 157-162 (6)	3.95	3.95

Food Gathering — A30

Fishing and gathering coconuts. Printed se-tenant in continuous designs.

No. 163: a, Launching outrigger canoe. b, Outrigger canoe and sailboat starboard side. c, Outrigger canoe and sailboat stern.

No. 164: a, Outrigger and sailboat port side. b, Islander carrying baskets of coconuts. c, Gathering coconuts from palm trees.

1989, June 28 Litho. *Perf. 14x14½*

163	A30 Strip of 3	4.00	4.25
a.-c.	50c any single	1.30	1.30
164	A30 Strip of 3	4.00	4.25
a.-c.	50c any single	1.30	1.30

Women's Work and Leisure — A31

1990, May 2 Litho. *Perf. 14½*

165	A31 5c Weavers	.50	.50
166	A31 20c Washing clothes	.75	.75
167	A31 40c Resting among palm trees	1.25	1.25
168	A31 60c Weaving mat	1.60	1.60
169	A31 80c Weaving, diff.	2.50	2.50
170	A31 $1 Basket weaver	2.75	2.75
	Nos. 165-170 (6)	9.35	9.35

Souvenir Sheet

Penny Black, 150th Anniv. A32

1990, May 3 Litho. *Perf. 11½*

171	A32 $3 multicolored	15.00	15.00

Men's Handicrafts A33

1990, Aug. 1 Photo. *Perf. 13*

172	A33 50c shown	1.30	1.10
173	A33 50c Carving pots	1.30	1.10
174	A33 50c Tying rope on pot	1.30	1.10
a.	Strip of 3, #172-174	5.00	5.00
175	A33 50c Finishing pots	1.30	1.10
176	A33 50c Shaping a canoe	1.30	1.10
177	A33 50c Three men working	1.30	1.10
a.	Strip of 3, #175-177	5.00	5.00

1992 Summer Olympics, Barcelona — A34

1992, July 8 Litho. *Perf. 13½*

178	A34 40c Swimming	.50	.50
179	A34 60c Long jump	1.75	.75
180	A34 $1 Volleyball	2.25	2.25
181	A34 $1.80 Running	3.00	3.00
	Nos. 178-181 (4)	7.50	6.50

Discovery of America, 500th Anniv. — A35

1992, Dec. 18

182	A35 40c Santa Maria	.50	.50
183	A35 60c Columbus	.75	.75
184	A35 $1.20 Columbus' fleet	2.25	2.25
185	A35 $1.80 Landfall	3.50	3.50
	Nos. 182-185 (4)	7.00	7.00

Coronation of Queen Elizabeth II, 40th Anniv. — A36

25c, Queen, early portrait. 40c, Prince Philip. $1, Queen, recent portrait. $2, Queen & Prince Philip.

1993, July 8 Litho. *Perf. 13½*

186 A36 25c multicolored .55 .55
187 A36 40c multicolored 1.00 1.00
188 A36 $1 multicolored 1.75 1.75
189 A36 $2 multicolored 3.00 3.00
Nos. 186-189 (4) 6.30 6.30

Birds — A37

25c, Numenius tahitiensis. 40c, Phaethon rubricauda. $1, Egretta sacra. $2, Pluvialis fulva.

1993-94 Litho. *Perf. 13½*

190 A37 25c multicolored .75 .75
191 A37 40c multicolored 1.00 1.00
192 A37 $1 multicolored 2.00 2.00
193 A37 $2 multicolored 2.75 2.75
a. Souvenir sheet of 4, #190-193, perf. 14x14½ 8.00 8.00
Nos. 190-193 (4) 6.50 6.50

No. 193a contains Hong Kong '94 emblem, inscription in Chinese and English in sheet margin and sold for $20 HK at the show.
Issued: #190-193, 12/15/93; #193a, 2/1/94.

PHILAKOREA '94 — A38

1994, Aug. 16 Litho. *Perf. 12*

194 A38 $2 White heron 3.25 3.25
a. Souvenir sheet of 1 4.75 4.75

No. 194a has a continuous design.

Handicrafts — A39

1995 Litho. *Perf. 13½*

195 A39 5c Outrigger canoe .25 .25
196 A39 25c Plaited fan .30 .30
197 A39 40c Plaited baskets .45 .45
198 A39 50c Fishing box .60 .60
199 A39 80c Water bottle .85 .85
200 A39 $1 Fishing hook 1.00 1.00
201 A39 $2 Coconut gourds 2.00 2.00
202 A39 $5 Shell necklace 4.50 4.50
Nos. 195-202 (8) 9.95 9.95

Souvenir Sheet

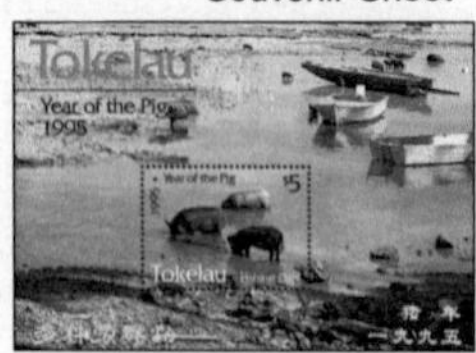

New Year 1995 (Year of the Boar) A40

1995, Feb. 3 Litho. *Perf. 14*

203 A40 $5 multicolored 7.50 7.50
a. Ovptd. in sheet margin 14.00 14.00
b. Ovptd. in sheet margin 9.00 9.00

No. 203a ovptd. in red in sheet margin "POST'X 95 / 3-6 February / 1995 / AUCKLAND" surrounded by simulated perforations.
No. 203b ovptd. in red in sheet margin with Singapore '95 exhibition emblem.

Pacific Imperial Pigeon — A41

1995, Apr. 27 Litho. *Perf. 13½*

204 A41 25c shown .50 .50
205 A41 40c Full view 1.00 1.00
206 A41 $1 In tree, red berries 1.75 1.75
207 A41 $2 Nesting 3.25 3.25
Nos. 204-207 (4) 6.50 6.50

World Wildlife Fund.

Reef Fish — A42

Designs: 25c, Long nosed butterfly fish. 40c, Emperor angelfish. $1, Moorish idol. $2, Lined butterfly fish.
$3, Red fire fish.

1995, Sept. 1 Litho. *Perf. 12*

208 A42 25c multicolored .30 .30
209 A42 40c multicolored .50 .50
210 A42 $1 multicolored 1.45 1.45
211 A42 $2 multicolored 3.25 3.25
Nos. 208-211 (4) 5.50 5.50

Souvenir Sheet

212 A42 $3 multicolored 4.25 4.25

No. 212 contains one 40x35mm stamp and is inscribed in sheet margin for Singapore '95.

Butterflies — A43

Designs: 25c, Danaus plexippus. 40c, Precis villida samoensis. $1, Hypolimnas bolina. $2, Euploea lewenii.

1995, Oct. 16 Litho. *Perf. 12*

213 A43 25c multicolored .50 .50
214 A43 40c multicolored .75 .75
215 A43 $1 multicolored 2.25 2.25
216 A43 $2 multicolored 3.00 3.00
Nos. 213-216 (4) 6.50 6.50

Sea Turtles — A44

1995, Nov. 27 Litho. *Perf. 12*

217 A44 25c Hawksbill .50 .50
218 A44 40c Leatherback .75 .75
219 A44 $1 Green 2.25 2.25
220 A44 $2 Loggerhead 3.25 3.25
Nos. 217-220 (4) 6.75 6.75

Souvenir Sheet

221 A44 $3 like #220 4.75 4.75

No. 221 contains one 50x40mm stamp and is a continuous design.

Souvenir Sheet

New Year 1996 (Year of the Rat) A45

1996, Feb. 19 Litho. *Perf. 12*

222 A45 $3 Pacific rat 4.25 4.25
a. Ovptd. in sheet margin 4.25 4.25
b. Ovptd. in sheet margin 4.25 4.25

Overprinted in sheet margin with red exhibition emblem: No. 222a, CHINA '96; No. 222b, TAIPEI '96.

Common Design Types pictured following the introduction.

Queen Elizabeth II, 70th Birthday

Common Design Type

Various portraits of Queen, scenes of Tokelau: 40c, Nukunonu. $1, Atafu, silhouette of island, boat. $1.25, Atafu, building on island, boat. $2, Atafu, huts.
$3, Queen wearing tiara, formal dress.

1996, Apr. 22 Litho. *Perf. 13½*

223 CD354 40c multicolored .50 .50
224 CD354 $1 multicolored 1.50 1.50
225 CD354 $1.25 multicolored 1.75 1.75
226 CD354 $2 multicolored 2.50 2.50
Nos. 223-226 (4) 6.25 6.25

Souvenir Sheet

227 CD354 $3 multicolored 4.25 4.25

Dolphins A46

1996, July 15 Litho. *Perf. 14*

228 A46 40c Fraser's 1.00 1.00
229 A46 $1 Common 2.25 2.25
230 A46 $1.25 Striped 2.50 2.50
231 A46 $2 Spotted 3.50 3.50
Nos. 228-231 (4) 9.25 9.25

Shells — A47

Designs: 40c, Cypraea talpa. $1, Cypraea mauritiana. $1.25, Cypraea argus. $2, Cypraea tigris.
$3, Cypraea mauritana, diff.

1996, Oct. 16 Litho. *Perf. 12*

232 A47 40c multicolored .50 .50
233 A47 $1 multicolored 1.25 1.25
234 A47 $1.25 multicolored 1.75 1.75
235 A47 $2 multicolored 2.75 2.75
Nos. 232-235 (4) 6.25 6.25

Souvenir Sheet

236 A47 $3 multicolored 4.25 4.25

No. 236 contains one 50x40mm stamp with a continuous design.

Souvenir Sheet

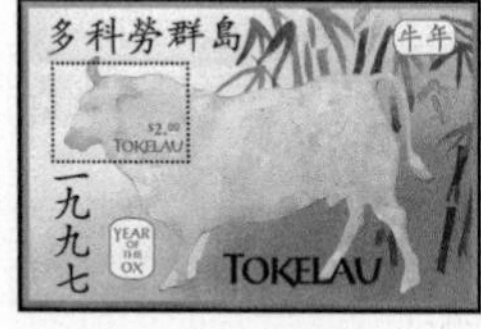

New Year 1997 (Year of the Ox) A48

1997, Feb. 12 Litho. *Perf. 15x14*

237 A48 $2 multicolored 3.50 3.50
a. Overprinted in gold 4.00 4.00
b. Overprinted in red 6.00 6.00

No. 237a ovptd. in sheet margin HONG KONG '97 / STAMP EXHIBITION" in English and Chinese.
No. 237b overprinted in sheet margin with Pacific 97 emblem. Issued 5/29.

Humpback Whale — A49

Designs: 40c, With school of fish. $1, Calf, adult, young adult. $1.25, With mouth open, school of fish. $2, Adult, calf.
$3, Mouth, head of whale.

1997, May 29 Litho. *Perf. 12*

238 A49 40c multicolored .50 .50
239 A49 $1 multicolored 1.25 1.25
240 A49 $1.25 multicolored 2.00 2.00
241 A49 $2 multicolored 2.75 2.75
Nos. 238-241 (4) 6.50 6.50

Souvenir Sheet

242 A49 $3 multicolored 4.25 4.25
a. Ovptd. in sheet margin 4.50 4.50

No. 242a ovptd. in sheet margin, "AUPEX '97 / 13-16 NOVEMBER / NZ NATIONAL / STAMP EXHIBITION." Issued: 11/13.

South Pacific Commission, 50th Anniv. — A50

1997, Sept. 17 Litho. *Perf. 14*

243 A50 40c Church, waterfront .50 .50
244 A50 $1 Beach, child 1.25 1.25
245 A50 $1.25 Island 1.75 1.75
246 A50 $2 Atoll 3.75 3.75
Nos. 243-246 (4) 7.25 7.25

Year of the Coral Reef — A51

Designs: No. 247, Gorgonian coral, emperor angelfish. No. 248, Soft coral. No. 249, Mushroom coral. No. 250, Staghorn coral. No. 251, Staghorn coral, Moorish idol.

1997, Oct. 20 Litho. *Perf. 13½*

247 A51 $1 multicolored 1.20 1.20
248 A51 $1 multicolored 1.20 1.20
249 A51 $1 multicolored 1.20 1.20
250 A51 $1 multicolored 1.20 1.20
251 A51 $1 multicolored 1.20 1.20
a. Strip of 5, #247-251 6.00 6.00

Souvenir Sheet

New Year 1998 (Year of the Tiger) A52

1998, Jan. 28 Litho. *Perf. 14x14½*

252 A52 $2 multicolored 2.75 2.75
a. Ovptd. in sheet margin 4.00 4.00

No. 252a overprinted in sheet margin with emblem of Singpex '98 Stamp Exhibition, Singapore.

Diana, Princess of Wales (1961-97)

Common Design Type

Designs: No. 252B, Holding yellow flowers. No. 253: a, Wearing high-collared ruffled blouse. b, Wearing red beret. c, Wearing pink and yellow jacket.

1998, May 15 Litho. *Perf. 14½x14*

252B CD355 $1 multi 1.75 1.75

Souvenir Sheet

253 CD355 $1 Sheet of 4, #252B, 253a-253c 4.25 4.25

No. 253 sold for $4 + 50c, with surtax from international sales being donated to the Princess Diana Memorial Fund and surtax from national sales being donated to designated local charity.

Souvenir Sheet

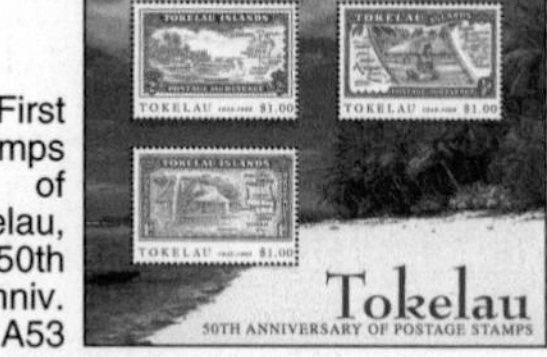

First Stamps of Tokelau, 50th Anniv. A53

Designs: a, #3. b. #1. c, #2.

1998, June 22 Litho. *Perf. 14½*

254 A53 $1 Sheet of 3, #a.-c. 4.00 4.00

Beetles — A54

Designs: 40c, Oryctes rhinoceros. $1, Tribolium castaneum. $1.25, Coccinella repanda. $2, Amarygmus hyorophiloides.
$3, Coccinella repanda, diff.

1998, Aug. 24 Litho. *Perf. 14*

255	A54	40c multicolored	.50	.50
256	A54	$1 multicolored	1.50	1.50
257	A54	$1.25 multicolored	1.75	1.75
258	A54	$2 multicolored	2.50	2.50
		Nos. 255-258 (4)	6.25	6.25

Souvenir Sheet

259	A54	$3 multicolored	3.75	3.75

Tropical Flowers — A55

40c, Ipomoea pes-caprae. $1, Ipomoea littoralis. $1.25, Scaevola taccada. $2, Thespesia populnea.

1998, Nov. 19 Litho. *Perf. 14*

260	A55	40c multicolored	.55	.55
261	A55	$1 multicolored	1.20	1.20
262	A55	$1.25 multicolored	1.60	1.60
263	A55	$2 multicolored	2.40	2.40
		Nos. 260-263 (4)	5.75	5.75

Souvenir Sheet

New Year 1999 (Year of the Rabbit) A56

1999, Feb. 16 Litho. *Perf. 14*

264	A56	$3 multicolored	4.00	4.00
a.		Ovptd. in sheet margin	4.00	4.00

No. 264a overprinted in sheet margin with emblem of IBRA '99 Intl. Stamp Exhibtion, Nuremburg. Issued: 4/27.

Souvenir Sheet

Australia '99, World Stamp Exhibition — A57

1999, Mar. 19

265	A57	$3 HMS Pandora	4.50	4.50

First Manned Moon Landing, 30th Anniv. — A58

Designs: 25c, Lift-off. 50c, Separation of stages. 75c, Aldrin deploying instruments on moon. $1, Planting flag. $1.25, Returning to Earth. $2, Splashdown.
$3, Apollo 11, Moon, Earth.

Perf. 13½x13¼

1999, Aug. 31 Litho.

266	A58	25c multicolored	.25	.25
267	A58	50c multicolored	.50	.50
268	A58	75c multicolored	.75	.75
269	A58	$1 multicolored	1.10	1.10
270	A58	$1.25 multicolored	1.50	1.50
271	A58	$2 multicolored	2.25	2.25
		Nos. 266-271 (6)	6.35	6.35

Souvenir Sheet

272	A58	$3 multicolored	3.50	3.50
a.		Ovptd. in silver "World Stamp Expo 2000 7-16 July Anaheim - U.S.A." on sheet margin	7.50	*7.50*

Crabs — A59

1999 Litho. *Perf. 14¼x14½*

273	A59	40c Coconut	.50	.50
274	A59	$1 Ghost	1.25	1.25
275	A59	$1.25 Land hermit	1.50	1.50
276	A59	$2 Purple hermit	2.50	2.50
		Nos. 273-276 (4)	5.75	5.75

Souvenir Sheet

277	A59	$3 Ghost, diff.	3.50	3.50

Black-naped Tern — A60

Designs: 40c, Chick and egg. $1, On nest. $1.25, Pair near water. $2, Pair in flight.

Perf. 13½x14

1999, Dec. 31 Litho. Unwmk.

278-281	A60	Set of 4	5.25	5.25

Souvenir Sheet

New Year 2000 (Year of the Dragon) A61

2000 Litho. *Perf. 14x14¼*

282	A61	$3 multi	4.50	4.50
a.		Overprinted in sheet margin	4.50	4.50

No. 282a overprinted in sheet margin with emblem "Bangkok 2000," "World Youth Stamp Exhibition" and Thai text.

Souvenir Sheet

The Stamp Show 2000, London A62

Unwmk.

2000, May 22 Litho. *Perf. 14*

283	A62	$6 multi	6.25	6.25

Queen Mother, 100th Birthday — A63

Various photos. Denominations 40c, $1.20, $1.80, $3.

Perf. 14½x14¼

2000, Aug. 4 Wmk. 373

284-287	A63	Set of 4	6.75	6.75

Lizards — A64

Designs: 40c, Gehyra oceanica. $1, Lepidodactylus lugubris. $1.25, Gehyra mutilata. $2, Emoia cyanura.

2001, Feb. 1 Litho. *Perf. 14*

288-291	A64	Set of 4	7.25	7.25

Souvenir Sheet

New Year 2001 (Year of the Snake) A65

2001, Feb. 1

292	A65	$3 multi	4.75	4.75
a.		With gold ovpt. in margin	5.00	5.00

Overprint in margin on No. 292a is for Hong Kong 2001 Stamp Exhibition.

Hippocampus Histrix — A66

Various views of seahorses. Denominations: 40c, $1, $1.25, $2.

2001, Aug. 23 Litho. *Perf. 14*

293-296	A66	Set of 4	5.50	5.50

Souvenir Sheet

297	A66	$3 multi	4.00	4.00

Island Scenery — A67

Designs: 40c, Sky over Atafu. $1, Waters of Fakaofo. $2, Sunrise over Nukunonu village. $2.50, Ocean, Nukunonu.

Unwmk.

2001, Dec. 17 Litho. *Perf. 14*

298-301	A67	Set of 4	7.50	7.50
a.		Souvenir sheet, #298-301	13.00	13.00

Issued: No. 301a issued 5/27/06 for Washington 2006 World Philatelic Exhibition.

Reign Of Queen Elizabeth II, 50th Anniv. Issue

Common Design Type

Designs: Nos. 302, 306a, 40c, Princess Elizabeth, Prince Philip on honeymoon, 1947. Nos. 303, 306b, $1, Wearing purple hat. Nos. 304, 306c, $1.25, Holding Prince Charles, 1948. Nos. 305, 306d, $2, In 1996. No. 306e, $3, 1955 portrait by Annigoni (38x50mm).

Perf. 14¼x14½, 13¾ (#306e)

2002, Feb. 6 Litho. Wmk. 373

With Gold Frames

302	CD360	40c multicolored	.50	.50
303	CD360	$1 multicolored	1.25	1.25
304	CD360	$1.25 multicolored	1.50	1.50
305	CD360	$2 multicolored	2.25	2.25
		Nos. 302-305 (4)	5.50	5.50

Souvenir Sheet

Without Gold Frames

306	CD360	Sheet of 5, #a-e	9.00	9.00

Souvenir Sheet

New Year 2002 (Year of the Horse) A68

2002, Feb. 12 Litho. *Perf. 14*

307	A68	$4 multi	5.25	5.25
a.		As #307, with gold ovpt. in margin	5.75	5.75

No. 307a was issued 2/22 and has overprint reading "STAMPEX 2002 / HONG KONG / 22-24 FEBRUARY 2002."

Worldwide Fund for Nature (WWF) — A69

Various views of Pelagic thresher shark: 40c, $1, $2, $2.50.

2002, July 2 Litho. *Perf. 14¼*

308-311	A69	Set of 4	7.25	7.25

Queen Mother Elizabeth (1900-2002)

Common Design Type

Designs: 40c, Wearing broad-brimmed hat (black and white photograph). $2, Wearing blue hat.

No. 314: a, $2.50, Wearing hat (black and white photograph). b, $4, Wearing purple hat.

Wmk. 373

2002, Aug. 5 Litho. *Perf. 14¼*

With Purple Frames

312	CD361	40c multicolored	.60	.60
313	CD361	$2 multicolored	3.25	3.25

Souvenir Sheet

Without Purple Frames

Perf. 14½x14¼

314	CD361	Sheet of 2, #a-b	8.00	8.00

New Zealand Navy Ships That Have Stopped at Tokelau — A70

Designs: 40c, HMNZS Kaniere. $1, HMNZS Endeavour. $2, HMNZS Wellington. $2.50, HMNZS Monowai.

2002, Dec. Litho. Unwmk. *Perf. 14*

315-318	A70	Set of 4	8.50	8.50

Souvenir Sheet

New Year 2003 (Year of the Ram) A71

2003, Feb. 3

319	A71	$4 multi	5.50	5.50
a.		With Bangkok 2003 overprint in gold in margin	5.50	5.50

Issued: No. 319a, 10/13.

Coronation of Queen Elizabeth II, 50th Anniv.

Common Design Type

Designs: Nos. 320, 322a, $2.50, Queen with maids of honor. Nos. 321, 322b, $4, Queen with Prince Philip.

Perf. 14¼x14½

2003, June 2 Litho. Wmk. 373

Vignettes Framed, Red Background

320	CD363	$2.50 multicolored	3.25	3.25
321	CD363	$4 multicolored	5.25	5.25

Souvenir Sheet

Vignettes Without Frame, Purple Panel

322	CD363	Sheet of 2, #a-b	8.75	8.75

Prince William, 21st Birthday

Common Design Type

No. 323: a, Color photograph at right. b, Color photograph at left.

Wmk. 373

2003, June 21 Litho. *Perf. 14¼*

323		Horiz. pair	7.25	7.25
a.		CD364 $1.50 multi	2.25	2.25
b.		CD364 $3 multi	5.00	5.00

Souvenir Sheet

Welpex 2003 Stamp Show, Wellington, New Zealand — A72

Unwmk.

2003, Nov. 7 Litho. *Perf. 14*
324 A72 $4 multi 6.00 6.00

Souvenir Sheet

New Year 2004 (Year of the Monkey) A73

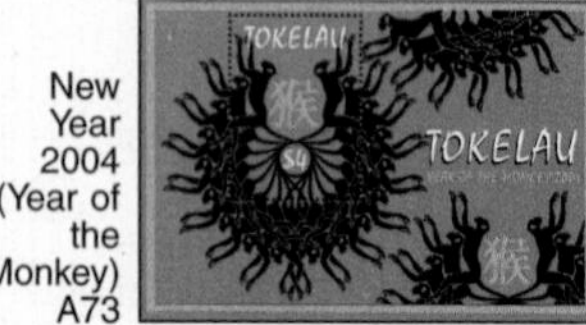

2004 Litho. with Foil Application
325 A73 $4 multi 5.50 5.50
a. With 2004 Hong Kong Stamp Expo emblem in gold in margin 5.50 5.50

Issued: No. 325, 1/22; No. 325a, 1/28.

Island Scenes — A74

Designs: 40c, Atafu dawn. $1, Return of the fishermen, Nukunonu. $2, A Fakaofo calm evening glow. $2.50, Solitude in Atafu.

2004, June 30 Litho. *Perf. 14¼x14*
326-329 A74 Set of 4 7.75 7.75

No. 324 Overprinted in Silver

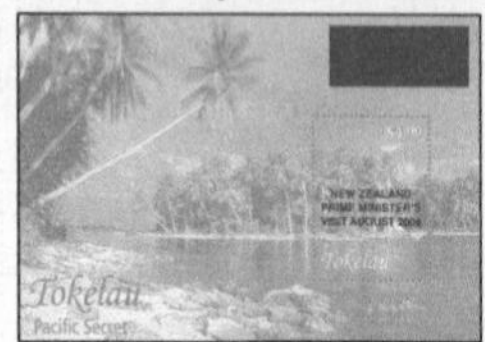

2004, Aug. 8 Litho. *Perf. 14*
330 A72 $4 multi 6.50 6.50

Fregata Ariel — A75

Designs: 40c, Bird on nest. $1, Birds in flight. $2, Birds on nest and in flight. $2.50, Bird on nest, diff.

2004, Dec. 20 Litho. *Perf. 14*
331-334 A75 Set of 4 9.25 9.25

Souvenir Sheet

New Year 2005 (Year of the Rooster) A76

2005, Feb. 9
335 A76 $4 multi 7.25 7.25
a. Ovptd. in gold in margin with Pacific Explorer 2005 emblem 7.25 7.25

No. 335a issued 4/21/05.

Pope John Paul II (1920-2005) — A77

2005, Aug. 18 Litho. *Perf. 14*
336 A77 $1 multi 1.80 1.80

Visit of HMNZS Te Kaha — A78

Various views of ship: 40c, $1, $2, $2.50.

2005, Dec. 15 Litho. *Perf. 14*
337-340 A78 Set of 4 10.00 10.00

Souvenir Sheet

New Year 2006 (Year of the Dog) A79

2006, Jan. 29
341 A79 $4 multi 7.25 7.25

Queen Elizabeth II, 80th Birthday — A80

Queen: 40c, With head on hands. $1, In wedding gown. No. 344, $2, Wearing tiara. No. 345, $2.50, Wearing blue hat.
No. 346: a, $2, Like $1. b, $2.50, Like #344.
No. 347: a, #346a overprinted "KIWIPEX." b, #346b overprinted "2006"

2006 Litho. *Perf. 14*
With White Frames
342-345 A80 Set of 4 9.00 9.00

Souvenir Sheets
Without White Frames
346 A80 Sheet of 2, #a-b 7.00 7.00

Overprinted in Metallic Blue
347 A80 Sheet of 2, #a-b 7.75 7.75

Issued: Nos. 342-346, 4/21; No. 347, 11/2. No. 347 is also overprinted in sheet margin "National Stamp Exhibition, Christchurch, New Zealand."

Souvenir Sheet

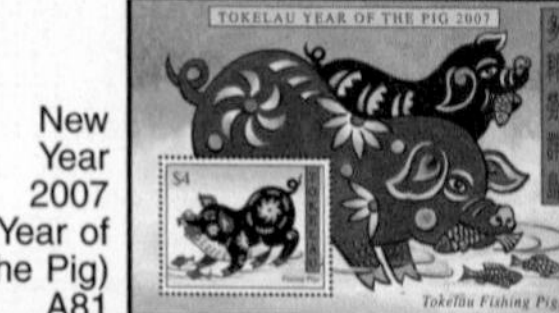

New Year 2007 (Year of the Pig) A81

2007, Feb. 18 Litho. *Perf. 14*
348 A81 $4 multi 8.00 8.00

Worldwide Fund for Nature (WWF) — A82

Pacific golden plover: 40c, Flock of birds. $1, Head. $2, Bird standing on one leg. $2.50, Birds and driftwood.

2007, Oct. 19 Litho. *Perf. 14*
349-352 A82 Set of 4 8.00 8.00
a. Miniature sheet of 16, 4 each #349-352 40.00 40.00

Marine Life — A83

Designs: 10c, Bicolor angelfish. 20c, Staghorn coral. 40c, Black-tipped reef sharks. 50c, Sea star. $1, Porcupine fish. $1.50, Thorny seahorses. $2, Spotted eagle rays. $2.50, Small giant clams. $5, Green turtles. $10, Slate pencil urchin.

2007, Dec. 19 *Perf. 14½x14¼*
353 A83 10c multi .25 .25
354 A83 20c multi .30 .30
355 A83 40c multi .65 .65
356 A83 50c multi .80 .80
357 A83 $1 multi 1.60 1.60
358 A83 $1.50 multi 2.40 2.40
359 A83 $2 multi 3.25 3.25
360 A83 $2.50 multi 4.00 4.00
361 A83 $5 multi 7.75 7.75
362 A83 $10 multi 15.50 15.50
a. Miniature sheet, #353-362 42.50 42.50
Nos. 353-362 (10) 36.50 36.50

Souvenir Sheet

New Year 2008 (Year of the Rat) A84

2008, Feb. 7 *Perf. 14*
363 A84 $4 multi 8.00 8.00

Sir Edmund Hillary (1919-2008), Mountaineer — A85

Hillary: 50c, As young man. $1, Wearing plaid shirt. $2, Wearing hat and glasses. $2.50, Wearing blue jacket.
$5, On mountain, horiz.

2008, Nov. 5 Litho. *Perf. 14¼*
364-367 A85 Set of 4 10.00 10.00

Souvenir Sheet
Perf. 13¾x13¼
368 A85 $5 multi 8.50 8.50

Local Scenes — A86

Designs: 50c, Buildings near seashore. $1, Boats on beach. $2, Trees. $2.50, Boat anchored near buildings.
$5, Islets.

2008, Nov. 7 *Perf. 14¼*
369-372 A86 Set of 4 10.00 10.00

Souvenir Sheet
Perf. 13¾x13¼
373 A86 $5 multi 7.50 7.50

Tarapex National Exhibition, New Plymouth, New Zealand (#373).

Souvenir Sheet

New Year 2009 (Year of the Ox) A87

2009, Jan. 26 Litho. *Perf. 14*
374 A87 $4 multi 7.25 7.25

Coins of the Pacific Area — A88

Obverse and reverse of: 50c, Chile 1875 one-peso. $1, Great Britain 1911 one-sovereign. $2, New Zealand 1950 half-crown. $2.50, Tokelau 1997 ten-dollar.

2009, Dec. 22 Litho. *Perf. 14x14¼*
375-378 A88 Set of 4 9.00 9.00
a. Souvenir sheet of 4, #375-378 9.00 9.00

For overprint, see No. 380.

Souvenir Sheet

New Year 2010 (Year of the Tiger) A89

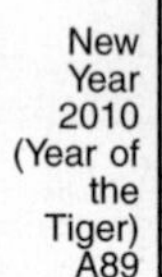

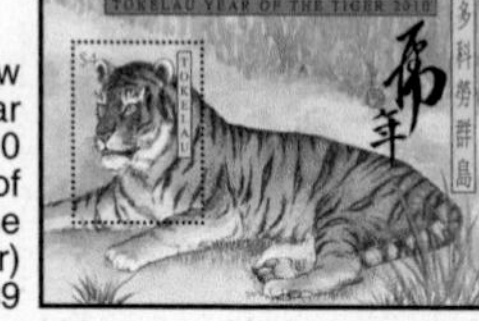

2010, Feb. 12 *Perf. 13¼x13½*
379 A89 $4 multi 6.50 6.50

No. 378a Overprinted in Gold

Designs as before.

Method and Perf. As Before

2010, May 8
380 A88 Sheet of 4, #a-d 10.00 10.00

London 2010 Festival of Stamps.

2009 Tokelauan Bible Translation — A90

Open Bible and: 50c, Atafu Church. $1, Fakaofo Church. $2, Nukunonu Church. $2.50, Closed Tokelauan Bibles.

Perf. 13½x13¼

2010, Sept. 21 Litho.
381-384 A90 Set of 4 9.00 9.00

Souvenir Sheet

New Year 2011 (Year of the Rabbit) A91

Perf. 13¼x13¾

2011, Feb. 3 Unwmk.
385 A91 $5 multi 7.75 7.75

Worldwide Fund for Nature (WWF) — A92

Yellow-bellied sea snake: 50c, On rocks. $1, On beach. $2, In sea. $2.50, Three in sea.

2011, Mar. 25 Unwmk. *Perf. 13½*
386-389 A92 Set of 4 9.50 9.50
a. Miniature sheet of 16, 4 each #386-389 40.00 40.00

Souvenir Sheet

Wedding of Prince William and Catherine Middleton — A93

Perf. 14¾x14¼

2011, Apr. 29 Wmk. 406
390 A93 $6 multi 9.50 9.50

Christmas — A94

Designs: 40c, Christmas tree. 45c, Ornament. $1.40, Stocking. $2, Angel.

2011, Nov. 16 Unwmk. *Perf. 13½*
391-394 A94 Set of 4 6.75 6.75

Island Scenes — A95

Designs: 10c, Man in coconut palm. 20c, Clouds over island. 25c, Small inhabited island. 40c, Snorkelers. 45c, Sailboat. 50c, House and boats. $1, Beach and trees. $1.40, Fisherman. $2, Beach and trees, diff.

2012, Apr. 11 *Perf. 13½x13¼*

395	A95	10c multi	.25	.25
396	A95	20c multi	.35	.35
397	A95	25c multi	.40	.40
398	A95	40c multi	.65	.65
399	A95	45c multi	.75	.75
400	A95	50c multi	.80	.80
401	A95	$1 multi	1.60	1.60
402	A95	$1.40 multi	2.25	2.25
403	A95	$2 multi	3.25	3.25
		Nos. 395-403 (9)	10.30	10.30

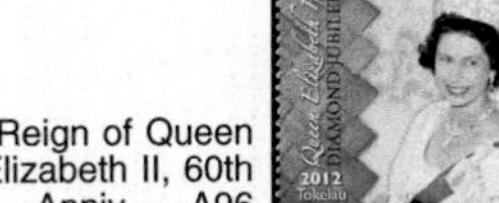

Reign of Queen Elizabeth II, 60th Anniv. — A96

Photograph of Queen Elizabeth II from: $2, 1963. $3, 2012.

2012, May 23
404-405 A96 Set of 2 7.75 7.75
a. Souvenir sheet of 2, #404-405 7.75 7.75

Fish — A97

Designs: 40c, Yellowfin tuna. 45c, Ruby snapper. $1.40, Wahoo. $2, Common dolphinfish.

2012, Oct. 3
406-409 A97 Set of 4 7.00 7.00
a. Souvenir sheet of 4, #406-409 7.00 7.00

Christmas — A98

Designs: 45c, Santa Claus, sleigh, reindeer over Atafu. $2, Reindeer over Nukunonu. $3, Reindeer over Fakaofo.

2012, Nov. 21 *Perf. 13¼x13½*
410-412 A98 Set of 3 9.25 9.25
a. Horiz. strip of 3, #410-412 9.25 9.25
b. Souvenir sheet of 3, #410-412 9.25 9.25

Coronation of Queen Elizabeth II, 60th Anniv. — A99

Designs: $2, Queen Elizabeth II and Prince Philip waving from Buckingham Palace balcony. $3, Queen Elizabeth II and family.

2013, May 8 *Perf. 13½x13¼*
413-414 A99 Set of 2 8.00 8.00
a. Souvenir sheet of 2, #413-414 8.00 8.00

Butterflies A100

Designs: 45c, Female Blue moon butterfly. $1, Male Blue moon butterfly. $1.40, Common crow butterfly. $3, Meadow argus butterfly.

2013, Aug. 7 *Perf. 13½*
415-418 A100 Set of 4 9.50 9.50
a. Souvenir sheet of 4, #415-418 9.50 9.50

Christmas — A101

Designs: 45c, Journey to Bethlehem. $1.40, Nativity. $2, Shepherds. $3, Magi.

Perf. 13¼x13½

2013, Nov. 20 Litho.
419-422 A101 Set of 4 10.00 10.00
a. Souvenir sheet of 4, #419-422 10.00 10.00

Woven Items — A102

Designs: 45c, Taulima (bracelets). $1.40, Pupu (water containers). $2, Tapili (fan). $3, Ato (basket).

2014, Apr. 23 Litho. *Perf. 13½x13¼*
423-426 A102 Set of 4 10.00 10.00
a. Souvenir sheet of 4, #423-426 10.00 10.00

Vakas — A103

Designs: 45c, Vakas in water. $1.40, Men building vaka. $2, Men rowing vaka. $3, Men bringing vaka ashore.

Perf. 13¼x13½

2014, June 14 Litho.
427-430 A103 Set of 4 10.00 10.00
a. Souvenir sheet of 4, #427-430 10.00 10.00

Tokelau Language Week — A104

Stylized people and speech balloons with English and Tokelauan words for: 45c, "Hello." $1.40, "How are you?" $2, "What is your name?" $3, "Farewell then."

2014, Oct. 15 Litho. *Perf. 13½x13¼*
431-434 A104 Set of 4 10.00 10.00
a. Souvenir sheet of 4, #431-434 10.00 10.00

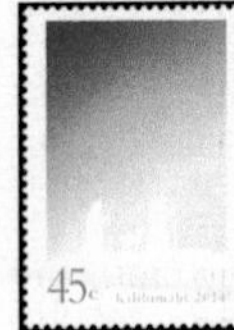

Christmas — A105

Designs: 45c, Shepherds. $2, Holy Family. $3, Magi.

Perf. 13¼x13½

2014, Dec. 10 Litho.
435-437 A105 Set of 3 8.50 8.50
a. Souvenir sheet of 3, #435-437 8.50 8.50

Fishing — A106

Fishing gear and: 45c, Atu (skipjack tuna). $1.40, Manini (convict tang). $2, Laulaufau (Moorish idols). $3, Pala (wahoos).

2015, Apr. 7 Litho. *Perf. 13½x13¼*
438-441 A106 Set of 4 9.00 9.00
a. Souvenir sheet of 4, #438-441 9.00 9.00

Crabs — A107

Designs: 45c, Birgus latro. $1.40, Cardisoma sp. $2, Ocypode sp. $3, Grapsus sp.

2015, June 3 Litho. *Perf. 13½x13¼*
442-445 A107 Set of 4 9.25 9.25
a. Souvenir sheet of 4, #442-445 9.25 9.25

Miniature Sheets

Tokelau Language Week — A108

No. 446: a, One pandanus tree. b, Two tackle boxes. c, Three atolls. d, Four wickets. e, Five crabs.

No. 447: a, Six butterflies. b, Seven fish. c, Eight fans. d, Nine canoes. e, Ten fish hooks.

2015, Oct. 13 Litho. *Perf. 13¼x13½*
446 A108 45c Sheet of 5, #a-e 3.25 3.25
447 A108 $1.40 Sheet of 5, #a-e 9.50 9.50

Christmas — A109

Designs: 45c, Tropical snowman. $1.40, Palm tree decorated as Christmas tree. $2, Reindeer making sand angels. $3, Santa Claus on beach.

Perf. 13¼x13½

2015, Nov. 25 Litho.
448-451 A109 Set of 4 9.25 9.25
a. Souvenir sheet of 4, #448-451 9.25 9.25

Miniature Sheet

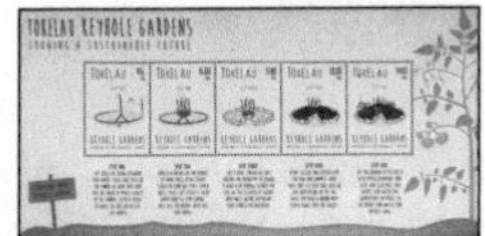

Keyhole Gardening — A110

No. 452 — Construction of a keyhole garden with inscriptions of: a, 45c, Step one. b, $1, Step two. c, $1.40, Step three. d, $2, Step four. e, $3, Step five.

2016, Apr. 6 Litho. *Perf. 13¼x13½*
452 A110 Sheet of 5, #a-e 11.00 11.00
f. Like #452, 180x48mm sheet size 11.00 11.00

Queen Elizabeth II, 90th Birthday — A111

Queen Elizabeth II: 45c, As child, with mother. $1.40, With Princes Philip and Charles. $2, With Prince Philip. $3, Wearing yellow dress.

2016, May 4 Litho. *Perf. 13¼x13½*
453-456 A111 Set of 4 9.50 9.50

MV Matliki — A112

Designs: 45c, Deck, flags and anchor. $1.40, Ship and dinghy. $2, Two ships. $3, Ship and passengers on barge.

2016, Aug. 3 Litho. *Perf. 14x14¼*
457-460 A112 Set of 4 10.00 10.00
a. Souvenir sheet of 4, #457-460 10.00 10.00

Tokelau Language Week — A113

English and Tokelauan words for foods: 45c, Coconut. $1.40, Coconut crab. $2, Fish. $3, Breadfruit.

2016, Oct. 5 Litho. *Perf. 13½x13¼*
461-464 A113 Set of 4 10.00 10.00
a. Souvenir sheet of 4, #461-464 10.00 10.00

Christmas — A114

Designs: 45c, Shepherd. $1.40, Holy Family. $2, Magi. $3, Angel.

2016, Dec. 7 Litho. *Perf. 13¼x13½*
465-468 A114 Set of 4 9.50 9.50
a. Souvenir sheet of 4, #465-468 9.50 9.50

Birds — A115

Designs: 45c, Bristle-thighed curlew. $1.40, Black noddy. $2, Great frigatebird. $3, Brown booby.

2017, Mar. 1 Litho. *Perf. 14x14¼*
469-472 A115 Set of 4 9.75 9.75
a. Souvenir sheet of 4, #469-472 9.75 9.75

Worldwide Fund for Nature (WWF) — A116

Corals: 45c, Common mushroom coral, open. $1.40, Common mushroom coral, closed. $2, Brain coral, up close view. $3, Brain coral, not up close.

2017, Aug. 2 Litho. ***Perf. 13½x13¼***
473-476 A116 Set of 4 10.00 10.00
a. Souvenir sheet of 4, #473-476 10.00 10.00

Reptiles — A117

Designs: 45c, Moth skink. $1.40, Pelagic gecko. $2, Copper-tailed skink. $3, Black skink.

Perf. 13½x13¼

2017, Sept. 20 Litho.
477-480 A117 Set of 4 10.00 10.00
a. Souvenir sheet of 4, #477-480 10.00 10.00

70th Wedding Anniversary of Queen Elizabeth II and Prince Philip — A118

Designs: 45c, Engagement photograph, 1947. $1.40, Family photograph, 1972. $2, Queen and Prince Philip on tour of Pacific, 1977. $3, Queen Elizabeth II, Princes Philip, Charles and William, 2003.

Perf. 13¼x13½

2017, Nov. 20 Litho.
481-484 A118 Set of 4 9.50 9.50
a. Souvenir sheet of 4, #481-484 9.50 9.50

Christmas — A119

Designs: 45c, Angel. $1.40, Madonna and Child. $2, Adoration of the Magi. $3, Infant Jesus in manger.

2017, Dec. 6 Litho. ***Perf. 13¼x13½***
485-488 A119 Set of 4 9.75 9.75
a. Souvenir sheet of 4, #485-488 9.75 9.75

Sea Walls — A120

Various buildings near sea walls: 45c, $1.40, $2, $3.

2018, May 2 Litho. ***Perf. 13½x13¼***
489-492 A120 Set of 4 9.75 9.75
a. Souvenir sheet of 4, #489-492 9.75 9.75

Wedding of Prince Harry and Meghan Markle — A121

Various photographs of the couple: 45c, $1.40, $2, $3.

2018, May 21 Litho. ***Perf. 13¼x13½***
493-496 A121 Set of 4 9.75 9.75
a. Souvenir sheet of 4, #493-496 9.75 9.75

Aerial Photographs A122

Photographs of: 45c, Atafu Atoll. $1.40, Fakaofo Atoll. $2, Atafu Atoll, diff. $3, Nukunonu Atoll.

2018, Sept. 5 Litho. ***Perf. 13½x13¼***
497-500 A122 Set of 4 9.25 9.25
a. Souvenir sheet of 4, #497-500 9.25 9.25

Tradition of Sharing Foods — A123

Designs: 45c, Taro leaves. $1.40, Breadfruit leaves. $2, Fish. $3, Coconuts.

2019, May 1 Litho. ***Perf. 13¼x13½***
501-504 A123 Set of 4 9.25 9.25
504a Souvenir sheet of 4, #501-504 9.25 9.25

First Man on the Moon, 50th Anniv. — A124

Designs: 45c, Apollo 11 on launch pad. $1.40, Lift-off. $2, Astronaut and Lunar Module on Moon. $3, Apollo 11 capsule in ocean.

2019, July 3 Litho. ***Perf. 13¼x13½***
505-508 A124 Set of 4 9.00 9.00
508a Souvenir sheet of 4, #505-508 9.00 9.00

Queen Victoria (1819-1901) — A125

Designs: 45c, Queen Victoria. $1.40, Queen Victoria, diff. $2, Queen Victoria and Prince Albert. $3, Queen Victoria, diff.

2019, Oct. 16 Litho. ***Perf. 13¼x13½***
509-512 A125 Set of 4 9.00 9.00
512a Souvenir sheet of 4, #509-512 9.00 9.00

Christmas — A126

Designs: 45c, Hand holding fisherman's box with cross. $1.40, Person holding two fisherman's boxes. $2, Person giving small fisherman's box to child. $3, Person opening fisherman's box.

2019, Dec. 4 Litho. ***Perf. 13¼x13½***
513-516 A126 Set of 4 9.25 9.25
516a Souvenir sheet of 4, #513-516 9.25 9.25

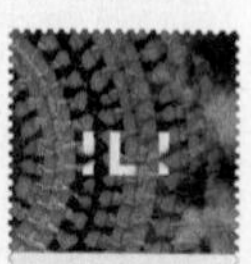

Weaving — A127

Designs: 45c, Ili (fan). $1.40, Ato (basket). $2, Pupu (wrapping for coconut shell container). $3, Titi (woman's garment).

2020, Apr. 16 Litho. ***Perf. 13¼x13½***
517-520 A127 Set of 4 8.50 8.50
520a Souvenir sheet of 4, #517-520 8.50 8.50

Christmas — A128

Designs: 45c, Angel Gabriel. $1.40, Manger of Jesus. $2, Shepherds. $3, Three Wise Men.

2020, Nov. 4 Litho. ***Perf. 13¼x13½***
521-524 A128 Set of 4 9.75 9.75
524a Souvenir sheet of 4, #521-524 9.75 9.75

TONGA

'täŋ-gə

LOCATION — A group of islands in the south Pacific Ocean, south of Samoa
GOVT. — Kingdom in British Commonwealth
AREA — 289 sq. mi.
POP. — 109,082 (1999 est.)
CAPITAL — Nuku'alofa

This group, also known as the Friendly Islands, became a British Protectorate in 1900 under the Anglo-German Agreement of 1899. On June 4, 1970, the United Kingdom ceased to have any responsibility for the external relations of Tonga.

12 Pence = 1 Shilling
20 Shillings = 1 Pound
100 Seniti = 1 Pa'anga (1967)

Catalogue values for unused stamps in this country are for Never Hinged items, beginning with Scott 87 in the regular postage section, Scott B1 in the semi-postal section, Scott C1 in the air post section Scott CE1 in the air post special delivery section, Scott CO1 in the air post official section, and Scott O11 in the officials section.

Watermarks

Wmk. 62 — NZ and Small Star Wide Apart

Wmk. 79 — Turtles

King George I — A1

Perf. 12x11½

1886-92 Typo. Wmk. 62
1 A1 1p car rose ('87) 13.00 4.00
a. Perf. 12½ 525.00 7.00
b. Perf. 12½x10
2 A1 2p violet ('87) 50.00 3.50
a. Perf. 12½ 57.50 14.00
3 A1 6p ultra ('88) 57.50 3.25
a. Perf. 12½ 75.00 3.25
4 A1 6p org yel ('92) 20.00 *45.00*
5 A1 1sh blue grn ('88) 75.00 8.00
a. Perf. 12½ 120.00 4.50
b. Half used as 6p on cover
Nos. 1-5 (5) 215.50 *63.75*

Stamps with Perf. 11½ to 12 on 4 sides are made on the same machine as the Perf. 12x11½.

For surcharges and overprints see #6-9, 24.

Nos. 1 and 2 Surcharged in Black

a

1891, Nov. 10 ***Perf. 12x11½***
6 A1(a) 4p on 1p car rose 5.00 *16.00*
a. No period after "PENCE" 57.50 *135.00*
7 A1(a) 8p on 2p violet 45.00 *110.00*

Nos. 1 and 2 Overprinted in Black

b

Type I Type II

Two types of overprint:
I — Solid stars, rays pointed and short.
II — Open-center stars, rays blunt and long.

1891, Nov. 23 ***Perf. 12½***
8 A1(b) 1p car rose (I) 55.00 *75.00*
a. Overprinted with 3 stars (I) 400.00
b. Overprinted with 4 stars (I) 600.00
c. Overprinted with 5 stars (I) 850.00
d. Type II 55.00 *75.00*
e. Perf. 12x11½ (I or II) 350.00
9 A1(b) 2p violet (I) 95.00 *42.50*
a. Type II 95.00 *42.50*
b. Perf. 12x11½ (I or II) 425.00

Coat of Arms A4

George I A5

1892, Nov. 10 Typo. ***Perf. 12x11½***
10 A4 1p rose 25.00 *40.00*
a. Diagonal half used as ½p on cover 975.00
11 A5 2p olive gray 45.00 *20.00*
12 A4 4p red brown 55.00 *90.00*
13 A5 8p violet 75.00 *225.00*
14 A5 1sh brown 90.00 *150.00*
Nos. 10-14 (5) 290.00 *525.00*

For surcharges and overprints see Nos. 15-23, 25-28, 36-37, O1-O10.

Types A4 and A5 Surcharged in Carmine or Black

c

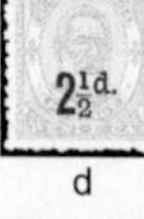

d

e

f

1893
15 A4(c) ½p on 1p ultra (C) 26.00 *30.00*
a. Surcharge omitted
16 A4(c) ½p on 1p ultra 50.00 *60.00*
17 A5(d) 2½p on 2p blue grn (C) 27.50 *15.00*
18 A5(d) 2½p on 2p blue grn 25.00 25.00
a. Double surcharge 2,250. 2,000.
19 A4(e) 5p on 4p org yel (C) 4.50 *9.00*
20 A5(f) 7½p on 8p rose (C) 35.00 *90.00*
Nos. 15-20 (6) 168.00 *229.00*

Stamps of 1886-92 Surcharged in Blue or Black

g

h

1894

21 A4 ½p on 4p red brn (Bl) 2.25 *8.00*
 a. "SURCHARCE" 10.00 *25.00*
 b. Pair, one without surcharge
 c. "HALF PENNY" omitted
22 A5 ½p on 1sh brn (Bk) 2.75 *12.50*
 a. Double surcharge 310.00
 b. "SURCHARCE" 11.50 45.00
 c. As "b," double surcharge 1,000.
23 A5 2½p on 8p vio (Bk) 15.00 *10.00*
 a. No period after "SURCHARGE" 55.00 *62.50*
24 A1 2½p on 1sh blue grn (Bk), perf. 12½ 65.00 *30.00*
 a. No period after "SURCHARGE" 250.00
 b. Perf. 12x11½ 20.00 50.00
 Nos. 21-24 (4) 85.00 *60.50*

Type A5 with Same Surcharges in Carmine

1895 **Unwmk.**

25 A5(g) 1p on 2p lt blue 60.00 45.00
26 A5(h) 1½p on 2p lt bl, perf. 12x11 65.00 55.00
 a. Perf. 12 75.00 55.00
27 A5(h) 2½p on 2p lt blue 50.00 55.00
 b. Without period 250.00 250.00
28 A5(h) 7½p on 2p lt bl, perf. 12x11 75.00 60.00
 a. Perf. 12 550.00
 Nos. 25-28 (4) 250.00 215.00

King George II — A13

1895, Aug. 16 ***Perf. 12***

29 A13 1p gray green 35.00 *40.00*
 a. Diagonal half used as ½p on cover *850.00*
 b. Horiz. pair, imperf. btwn. — *7,500.*
30 A13 2½p dull rose 32.50 11.00
31 A13 5p brt blue, perf. 12x11 30.00 *70.00*
 a. Perf. 12 45.00 *75.00*
 b. Perf. 11 400.00
32 A13 7½p yellow 50.00 *60.00*
 Nos. 29-32 (4) 147.50 *181.00*

Type A13 Redrawn and Surcharged "g" or "h" in Black

33 A13(g) ½p on 2½p red 55.00 *37.50*
 a. "SURCHARCE" 100.00 75.00
 b. Period after "Postage" 150.00 75.00
34 A13(g) 1p on 2½p red 115.00 50.00
 a. Period after "Postage" 170.00 110.00
35 A13(h) 7½p on 2½p red 65.00 *80.00*
 a. Period after "Postage" 180.00 *225.00*
 Nos. 33-35 (3) 235.00 *167.50*

Nos. 26 and 28 with Additional Surcharge in Violet and Black

1896, May ***Perf. 12x11***

36 A5 ½p on 1½p on 2p 500.00
 a. Tongan surch. reading up 475.00 475.00
 b. Perf. 12 450.00 *450.00*
 c. As "a," perf. 12 500.00 *500.00*
 d. As "a," "Haalf" 3,500.
 e. "Halef" 7,250.
37 A5 ½p on 7½p on 2p 95.00 *125.00*
 a. "Half penny" inverted 3,250.
 b. "Half penny" double
 c. Tongan surch. reading up 97.50 *125.00*
 d. Tongan surcharge as "c" and double
 e. "Hafl Penny" 2,500. *2,750.*
 f. "Hafl" only 5,500.
 g. "Hwlf"
 h. Periods instead of hyphens after words 1,100.
 j. Perf. 12 925.00

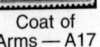

Coat of Arms — A17

Ovava Tree — A18

George II A19

Prehistoric Trilithon, Tongatabu A20

Breadfruit A21

Coral Formations A22

View of Haabai — A23

Red-breasted Musk Parrot — A24

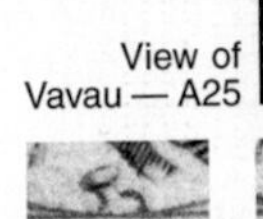
View of Vavau — A25

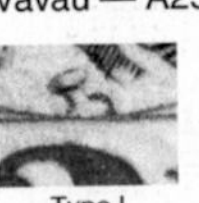
Type I

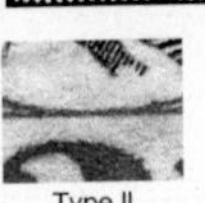
Type II

Two types of 2p:
I — Top of sword hilt shows above "2."
II — No hilt shows.

1897-1934 Engr. Wmk. 79 ***Perf. 14***

38 A17 ½p dark blue .70 3.00
39 A17 ½p green ('34) 1.10 *1.40*
40 A18 1p dp red & blk .90 .90
41 A19 2p bis & sep (I) 20.00 3.50
 a. bister & gray, type II 50.00 11.00
42 A19 2½p lt blue & blk 13.00 1.60
 a. "½" without fraction bar 140.00 75.00
43 A20 3p ol grn & blk 4.00 *18.00*
44 A21 4p dull vio & grn 5.00 *4.50*
45 A19 5p orange & blk 35.00 16.00
46 A22 6p red 14.00 *10.00*
47 A19 7½p green & blk 20.00 *26.00*
 a. Center inverted 9,250.
48 A19 10p carmine & blk 50.00 55.00
49 A19 1sh red brn & blk 16.00 14.00
 a. "SILENI-E-TAHA" missing second hyphen *175.00* 150.00
50 A23 2sh dk ultra & blk 37.50 *32.50*
51 A24 2sh6p dk violet 60.00 45.00
52 A25 5sh dull red & blk 32.50 40.00
 Nos. 38-52 (15) 309.70 271.40

See Nos. 73-74, 77-78, 80-81. For surcharges see Nos. 63-69.

Stamp of 1897 Overprinted in Black

1899, June 1

53 A18 1p red & black 45.00 *72.50*
 a. "1889" instead of "1899" 250.00 *400.00*
 b. Comma omitted after June
 c. Double overprint

Marriage of George II to Lavinia, June 1, 1899. The letters "T L" are the initials of Taufa'ahau, the King's family name, and Lavinia.

No. 53 exists with serifed "T" and "L". Some specialists consider it to be an essay or proof.

Queen Salote — A26

Die I

Die II

Dies of 2p:
Die I — Ball of "2" smaller.
Die II — Ball of "2" larger. "U" has spur at left.

1920-35 Engr. Wmk. 79

54 A26 1½p gray blk ('35) 2.25 *3.50*
55 A26 2p violet & sepia 12.00 *15.00*
56 A26 2p dl vio & blk (I) ('24) 25.00 2.50
 a. Die II 11.00 *11.00*
57 A26 2½p blue & black 9.00 *50.00*
58 A26 2½p ultra ('34) 12.50 1.10
59 A26 5p red org & blk 3.75 *9.00*
60 A26 7½p green & blk 2.00 2.50
61 A26 10p carmine & blk 3.00 *5.50*
62 A26 1sh red brown & blk 1.60 2.90
 Nos. 54-62 (9) 71.10 *92.00*

See Nos. 75-76, 79.

Stamps of 1897 Srchd. in Dark Blue or Red

1923

63 A19 2p on 5p org & blk 1.10 1.40
64 A19 2p on 7½p grn & blk 42.50 55.00
65 A19 2p on 10p car & blk 25.00 *80.00*
66 A19 2p on 1sh red brn & blk 75.00 30.00
 a. "SILENI-E-TAHA" missing second hyphen *400.00* 225.00
67 A23 2p on 2sh ultra & blk (R) 15.00 20.00
68 A24 2p on 2sh6p dk vio (R) 45.00 10.00
69 A25 2p on 5sh dull red & blk (R) 5.00 3.00
 Nos. 63-69 (7) 208.60 199.40

Queen Salote — A27

Inscribed "1918-1938"

1938, Oct. 12 ***Perf. 14***

70 A27 1p carmine & blk .65 *4.00*
71 A27 2p violet & blk 8.00 3.00
72 A27 2½p ultra & blk 8.00 3.75
 Nos. 70-72 (3) 16.65 *10.75*
 Set, never hinged 32.00

Accession of Queen Salote Tupou, 20th anniv.
See Nos. 82-86.

Types of 1897-1920

Die III of 2p:
Foot of "2" longer than in Die II, extending beyond curve of loop.

1942 Engr. Wmk. 4

73 A17 ½p green .30 *2.75*
74 A18 1p scarlet & blk 1.75 *2.75*
75 A26 2p dull vio & blk (II) 4.50 *3.00*
 a. Die III 5.50 *10.00*
76 A26 2½p ultra 1.10 *2.00*
77 A20 3p green & black .40 *4.25*
78 A22 6p orange red 2.00 *2.25*
79 A26 1sh red brown & gray blk 3.00 *3.50*
80 A24 2sh6p dk violet 25.00 *30.00*

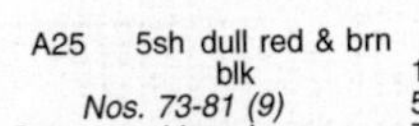

81 A25 5sh dull red & brn blk 12.00 *60.00*
 Nos. 73-81 (9) 50.05 *110.50*
 Set, never hinged 70.00

Type of 1938, Inscribed "1918-1943"

1944, Jan. 25

82 A27 1p rose car & blk .25 *1.10*
83 A27 2p purple & blk .25 *1.10*
84 A27 3p dk yel grn & blk .25 *1.10*
85 A27 6p red orange & blk .40 *2.00*
86 A27 1sh dk red brn & blk .25 *2.00*
 Nos. 82-86 (5) 1.40 *7.30*
 Set, never hinged 2.00

25th anniv. of the accession of Queen Salote.

Catalogue values for unused stamps in this section, from this point to the end of the section, are for Never Hinged items.

UPU Issue

Common Design Types

Engr.; Name Typo. on 3p, 6p
Perf. 13½, 11x11½

1949, Oct. 10 **Wmk. 4**

87 CD306 2½p ultra .25 *.90*
88 CD307 3p deep olive 2.00 *3.25*
89 CD308 6p deep carmine .30 .55
90 CD309 1sh red brown .45 .55
 Nos. 87-90 (4) 3.00 *5.25*

Common Design Types pictured following the introduction.

A28

A29

Queen Salote — A30

1950, Nov. 1 Photo. ***Perf. 12½***

91 A28 1p cerise 1.00 *5.00*
92 A29 5p green 1.00 *5.00*
93 A30 1sh violet 1.00 *5.00*
 Nos. 91-93 (3) 3.00 *15.00*

50th anniv. of the birth of Queen Salote.

Map and Island Scene A31

Badges and Royal Palace A32

2½p, Queen Salote & coastal scene. 3p, Queen Salote & ship "Bellona." 5p, Flag of Tonga, island view. 1sh, Arms of Tonga & Great Britain.

Perf. 13x13½ (1p), 13½x13, 12½ (3p)

1951, July 2 Engr. Wmk. 4

94 A31 ½p deep green .40 3.25
95 A32 1p carmine & black .40 *3.25*
96 A32 2½p choc & dp grn .75 *3.25*
97 A31 3p ultra & org yel 2.25 *3.25*
98 A32 5p dp green & car 2.25 1.50
99 A32 1sh purple & orange 2.25 1.50
 Nos. 94-99 (6) 8.30 *16.00*

50th anniv. of the treaty of friendship between Tonga and Great Britain.

Royal Palace, Nukualofa — A33

Fisherman — A33a

Canoe and Schooners — A33b

Swallows' Cave, Vavau — A34

Map of Tongatabu — A34a

Vavau Harbor — A34b

Post Office, Nukualofa — A34c

Fuaamotu Airport — A34d

Map of Tonga Islands — A34f

Wharf, Nukualofa — A34e

Beach at Lifuka, Haapai — A34g

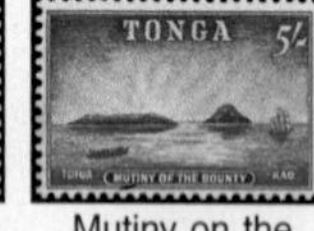

Mutiny on the Bounty — A34h

Queen Salote — A34i

Arms of Tonga — A34j

Perf. 11½x11, 11x11½

1953, July 1 — Wmk. 79

No.	Type	Value / Description	Unused	Used
100	A33	1p chocolate & blk	.25	.25
101	A33a	1½p emerald & ultra	.25	.25
102	A33b	2p black & aqua	1.00	.25
103	A34	3p dk grn & ultra	2.00	.25
104	A34a	3½p carmine & yel	1.40	.60
105	A34b	4p rose car & yel	2.00	.25
106	A34c	5p choc & ultra	.80	.25
107	A34d	6p black & dp ultra	1.25	.25
108	A34e	8p purple & pale grn	1.25	1.75
109	A34f	1sh black & ultra	1.80	.25
110	A34g	2sh choc & ol grn	8.00	.80
111	A34h	5sh dp vio & yel	18.00	7.75
112	A34i	10sh black & yellow	11.00	7.75
113	A34j	£1 ultra, car & yel	11.00	5.00
		Nos. 100-113 (14)	60.00	25.65

For surcharges and overprints see Nos. 119-126, 158-174, 182-202, 210-215, 218-221, 237, 269-273, C34-C39, C47-C54, C87-C91, CO4-CO6, CO11-CO20, CO27-CO43.

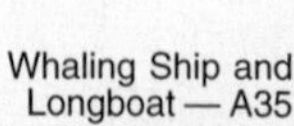

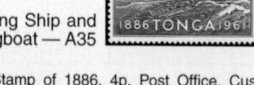

Whaling Ship and Longboat — A35

1p, Stamp of 1886. 4p, Post Office, Customs & Treasury Building & Queen Salote. 5p, Diesel-driven ship Aoniu. 1sh, Plane over Tongatabu.

1961, Dec. 1 — Photo. — *Perf. 14½x13½*

No.	Type	Value / Description	Unused	Used
114	A35	1p brn org & car rose	.30	.25
115	A35	2p ultra	.90	.30
116	A35	4p bright green	.30	.30
117	A35	5p purple	.90	.30
118	A35	1sh red brown	1.00	.60
		Nos. 114-118 (5)	3.40	1.75

75th anniversary of postal service.

For surcharges & overprints see #146-151, 216-221, C16-C21, C55-C57, CO1-CO3, CO9-CO10.

Stamps of 1953 & 1961 Overprinted in Red

No. 119

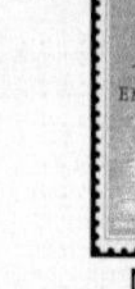

No. 125

Perf. 11½x11, 11x11½, 14½x13

Engr.; Photo. (4p)

1962, Feb. 7 — Wmk. 79

No.	Type	Value / Description	Unused	Used
119	A33	1p choc & blk	.25	*.60*
120	A35	4p brt green	.25	*.65*
121	A34c	5p choc & ultra	.25	*.65*
122	A34d	6p black & dp ultra	.25	*1.10*
123	A34e	8p purple & emer	.50	*1.60*
124	A34f	1sh black & ultra	.35	*.80*
125	A34	2sh on 3p dk grn & ultra	.60	*3.75*
126	A34h	5sh purple & yellow	6.25	3.75
		Nos. 119-126 (8)	8.70	12.90

Cent. of emancipation. See Nos. CO1-CO6.

Nos. 119-126 were overprinted locally. Nos. 124-125 exist with inverted overprint. No. 125 exists surcharged "2/" instead of "2/-".

Freedom from Hunger Issue

Common Design Type with Portrait of Queen Salote

Perf. 14x14½

1963, June 4 — Wmk. 79 — Photo.

No.	Type	Value / Description	Unused	Used
127	CD314	11p ultra	.60	.35

Coat of Arms, ¼ Koula Coin, Reverse — A36

Designs: 2p, 9p, 2sh, Queen Salote (head), ¼-koula coin, obverse.

Litho.; Embossed on Gilt Foil

1963, July 15 — Unwmk. — *Die Cut*

Diameter: 40mm

No.	Type	Value / Description	Unused	Used
128	A36	1p dp carmine	.50	.40
129	A36	2p violet blue	.50	.40
130	A36	6p dp green	.50	.40
131	A36	9p magenta	.50	.40
132	A36	1sh6p violet	.70	.70
133	A36	2sh emerald	.75	.75
		Nos. 128-133,C1-C6,CO7 (13)	12.45	12.05

1st gold coinage of Polynesia. Backed with paper inscribed in salmon-colored alternating rows: "TONGA" and "THE FRIENDLY ISLANDS" in multiple.

For surcharges see #140-145, C11-C15, CO8.

Red Cross Centenary Issue

Common Design Type with Portrait of Queen Salote

Wmk. 79

1963, Sept. 2 — Litho. — *Perf. 13*

No.	Type	Value / Description	Unused	Used
134	CD315	2p black & red	.25	.25
135	CD315	11p ultra & red	.75	1.00

Queen Salote on ¼- Koula Coin — A37

Litho.; Embossed on Gilt Foil

1964, Oct. 19 — Unwmk. — *Die Cut*

No.	Type	Value / Description	Unused	Used
136	A37	3p pink	.45	.40
137	A37	9p light blue	.45	.40
138	A37	2sh yellow green	.45	.50
139	A37	5sh pale lilac	1.40	1.40
		Nos. 136-139,C7-C10 (8)	5.90	5.85

Pan-Pacific and Southeast Asia Women's Association Conf., Nukualofa, Aug. 1964. See note on paper backing after No. 133.

For surcharges & overprints see #152-157, 263-268.

Nos. 128-133 Surcharged in Red, White or Black

1965, Mar. 18

No.	Type	Value / Description	Unused	Used
140	A36	1sh3p on 1sh6p (R)	.70	.30
141	A36	1sh9p on 9p (W)	.70	.30
142	A36	2sh6p on 6p (R)	.70	.30
143	A36	5sh on 1p	20.00	30.00
144	A36	5sh on 2p	3.50	5.00
145	A36	5sh on 2sh	.75	1.50
		Nos. 140-145,C11-C15,CO8 (12)	78.50	99.40

Nos. 114-115 Overprinted and Surcharged in Purple or Red

Perf. 14½x13½

1966, June 18 — Photo. — Wmk. 79

No.	Type	Value / Description	Unused	Used
146	A35	1p (P)	.25	.25
147	A35	3p on 1p (P)	.25	.25
148	A35	6p on 2p (R)	.25	.25
149	A35	1sh2p on 2p (R)	.25	.25
150	A35	2sh on 2p (R)	.35	.25
151	A35	3sh on 2p (R)	.35	.30
		Nos. 146-151,C16-C21,CO9-CO10 (14)	4.55	4.00

Centenary of Tupou College and of secondary eucation.

Nos. 136-137 Ovptd. and Srchd. in Silver on Black or Ultramarine

Litho.; Embossed on Gilt Foil

1966, Dec. 16 — Unwmk. — *Die Cut*

No.	Type	Value / Description	Unused	Used
152	A37	3p pink (U)	.50	.40
153	A37	5p on 9p lt blue	.50	.40
154	A37	9p lt bl	.50	.40
155	A37	1sh7p on 3p pink (U)	1.25	.65
156	A37	3sh6p on 9p lt blue	1.50	1.00
157	A37	6sh6p on 3p pink (U)	2.00	1.25
		Nos. 152-157,C22-C26 (11)	15.55	11.80

Nos. 100-110, 147 and 151 Srchd. in Black or Red

No. 158-165 Surcharged

Nos. 166-167 Surcharged

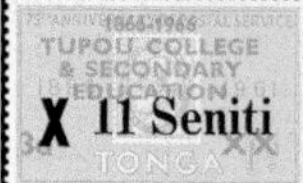

No. 168 Surcharged

No. 169 Surcharged

Nos. 170-171, 173 Surcharged

Nos. 172, 174 Surcharged

Perf. 11½x11, 11x11½, 14½x13½

1967, Mar. 25 — Wmk. 79

No.	Type	Value / Description	Unused	Used
158	A33	1s on 1p	.25	.25
159	A34b	2s on 4p	.25	.25
160	A34c	3s on 5p	.25	.25
161	A34c	4s on 5p	.25	.25
162	A34a	5s on 3½p	.25	.25
163	A34e	6s on 8p	.25	.25
164	A33a	7s on 1½p	.25	.25
165	A34d	8s on 6p	.25	.25
166	A34	9s on 3p	.25	.25
167	A34f	10s on 1sh	.30	.30
168	A35	11s on 3p on 1p	.40	.40
169	A35	21s on 3sh on 2p	.60	.60
170	A33	23s on 1p	.65	.65
171	A34g	30s on 2sh (R) (1-line surcharge)	1.40	1.40
172	A34g	30s on 2sh (R) (3-line surcharge)	1.50	1.50
173	A34d	50s on 6p (R)	1.75	1.75
174	A33b	60s on 2p (R)	2.25	2.25
		Nos. 158-174 (17)	11.10	11.10

The size, typeface and arrangement of surcharge vary on the different denominations.

King Taufa'ahau IV — A38

Designs: 1s, 4s, 28s, 1pa, Coat of Arms, reverse of new palladium coins.

Diameter: 1s, 44mm; 2s, 50s, 52mm; 4s, 59mm; 15s, 68mm; 28s, 40mm; 1pa, 74mm

Litho.; Embossed on Palladium Foil

1967, July 4 — Unwmk. — *Die Cut*

No.	Type	Value / Description	Unused	Used
175	A38	1s orange & brt bl	.50	.40
176	A38	2s brt bl & dp mag	.50	.40
177	A38	4s emerald & mag	.50	.40
178	A38	15s blue grn & vio	.50	.40
179	A38	28s blk & brt red lil	.60	.60
180	A38	50s red & vio bl	1.10	1.10
181	A38	1pa ultra & brt rose	2.75	2.75
		Nos. 175-181,C27-C33 (14)	14.40	12.25

Coronation of King Taufa'ahau IV, July 4, 1967. Backed with paper inscribed in yellow alternating rows: "Tonga The Friendly Islands" and "Historically The First Palladium Coinage."

For surcharges and overprints see Nos. 203-209, C40-C46, CO21-CO24,

Types of Regular Issue, 1953, Surcharged

Wmk. 79

1967, Dec. 15 — Engr. — *Die Cut*

No.	Type	Value / Description	Unused	Used
182	A33	1s on 1p yellow & blk	.25	.25
183	A33b	2s on 2p car & ultra	.25	.25
184	A34	3s on 3p brn org & yel	.25	.25
185	A34b	4s on 4p purple & yel	.25	.25
186	A34c	5s on 5p green & yel	.25	.25
187	A34f	10s on 1sh rose red & yel	.25	.25
188	A34g	20s on 2sh car & ultra	.25	.25

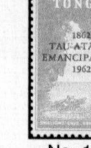

189 A34h 50s on 5sh sepia & yel .55 2.25
190 A34i 1pa on 10sh org yel .55 2.50
Nos. 182-190,C34-C36,CO12-CO14 (15) 5.55 12.90

Arrival of US Peace Corps.

Nos. 100-111 Surcharged in Red, Black or Ultra

No. 191

No. 193

Perf. 11½x11, 11x11½

1968, Apr. 6 Engr. Wmk. 79

191 A33 1s on 1p (R) .25 .25
192 A34b 2s on 4p .25 .25
193 A34 3s on 3p (U) .25 .25
194 A34c 4s on 5p (R) .25 .25
195 A33b 5s on 2p (R) .25 .25
196 A34d 6s on 6p (R) .25 .25
197 A33a 7s on 1½p (R) .35 .25
198 A34e 8s on 8p (R) .25 .25
199 A34a 9s on 3½p .25 .25
200 A34f 10s on 1sh (R) .25 .25
201 A34h 20s on 5sh (R) 1.75 .80
202 A34g 2pa on 2sh (R) 1.60 3.00
Nos. 191-202,C37-C39,CO15-CO18 (19) 10.50 15.50

Surcharge on 3s and 10s is vertical.

Nos. 175-181 Overprinted: "H.M'S BIRTHDAY / 4 July 1968" in Gold on Red Panel on 1s, 4s, 28s and 1pa. "HIS MAJESTY'S 50th BIRTHDAY" in Silver on Blue Panel on 2s, 15s and 50s

Litho.; Embossed on Palladium Foil

1968, July 4 Unwmk. *Die Cut*

203 A38 1s orange & brt bl .25 .25
204 A38 2s brt bl & dp mag .25 .25
205 A38 4s emerald & mag .25 .25
206 A38 15s blue grn & vio 1.40 .45
207 A38 28s blk & brt red lil 2.00 .40
208 A38 50s red & vio bl 2.75 1.90
209 A38 1pa ultra & brt rose 5.25 7.00
Nos. 203-209,C40-C46,CO21-CO24 (18) 44.10 42.00

Types of 1953 Surcharged in Red, Black or Green

No. 210

No. 211

No. 212

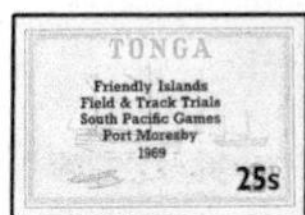
No. 213

No. 214
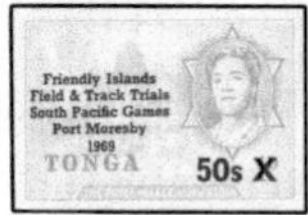

Designs as before.

Wmk. 79

1968, Dec. 19 Engr. *Die Cut*

210 A34c 5s on 5p grn & yel (R) .25 .25
211 A34f 10s on 1sh cer & buff .25 .25
212 A34g 15s on 2sh rose car & bl .25 .25
213 A33b 25s on 2p rose car & bl .55 .55
214 A33 50s on 1p yel & blk .75 .75
215 A34i 75s on 10sh org (G) 1.10 1.10
Nos. 210-215,C47-C54,CO19-CO20 (16) 9.95 8.45

Issued to publicize the field and track trials for the third South Pacific Games, Port Moresby, 1969. The overprint is in 5 lines on the horizontal stamps, in 7 lines on vertical stamps. On the vertical stamps "Trial" is printed on the line ahead of "Field & Track." On #215 the denomination is spelled out.

Nos. 149-150 and Types of 1953 Surcharged

Nos. 216-217 Surcharged

Nos. 218, 221 Surcharged

No. 219 Surcharged

No. 220 Surcharged

Perf. 14½x13½

1968 Photo. Wmk. 79

216 A35 1s on 1sh2p on 2p 1.60 1.60
217 A35 1s on 2sh on 2p 1.60 1.60

Engr. *Die Cut*

218 A34d 1s on 6p yel & blk .90 .90
219 A34a 2s on 3½p dk blue 1.00 1.00
220 A33a 3s on 1½p lt green 1.00 1.00
221 A34e 4s on 8p blk & pale grn 1.10 1.10
Nos. 216-221,C55-C57 (9) 16.95 16.95

Banana A39

Unwmk.

1969, Apr. 21 Typo. *Die Cut*

Self-adhesive

222 A39 1s yellow, black & red 1.00 .85
223 A39 2s yel, black & emer 1.10 1.00
224 A39 3s yellow, black & lil 1.25 1.10
225 A39 4s yellow, black & ultra 1.40 1.10
226 A39 5s yel, blk & ol grn 1.75 1.75
Nos. 222-226 (5) 6.50 5.80

Packed in boxes of 200. See Nos. 248-252, 297-301, O11-O15, design A75.

Peelable Backing Inscribed

Starting in 1969, self-adhesive stamps are attached to peelable paper backing printed with "TONGA where time begins" in multiple rows and various colors, unless otherwise stated.

Shot-putter — A40

1969, Aug. 13 Litho. *Die Cut*

Self-adhesive

227 A40 1s bister, red & blk .25 .25
228 A40 3s bis, red & emer .25 .25
229 A40 6s bister, red & bl .25 .25
230 A40 10s bister, red & pur .25 .25
231 A40 30s bister, red & bl .30 .30
Nos. 227-231,C58-C62,CO25-CO26 (12) 7.30 7.30

3rd Pacific Games, Port Moresby, Papua and New Guinea, Aug. 13-23.

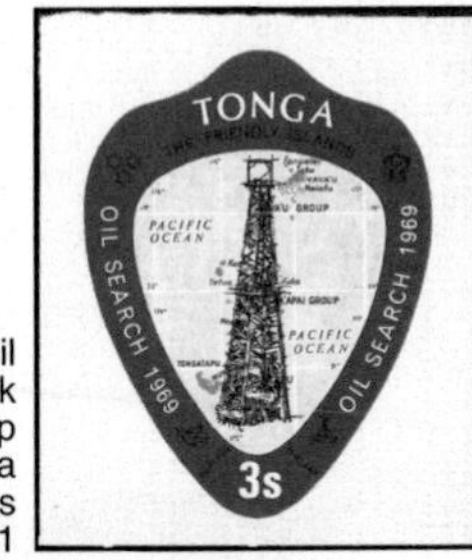

Oil Derrick and Map of Tonga Islands A41

1969, Dec. 23 Litho. *Die Cut*

Self-adhesive

232 A41 3s brown & multi .40 .40
233 A41 7s brt blue & multi .45 .45
234 A41 20s multicolored .75 .75
235 A41 25s orange & multi .85 .85
236 A41 35s henna brn & multi 1.10 1.10

Type of 1953 Regular Issue Surcharged in Red

Wmk. 79 *Die Cut*

237 A34j 1.10pa on £1 grn & multi 3.50 3.50
Nos. 232-237,C63-C67,CO27 (12) 14.05 14.05

First scientific search for oil in Tonga.

British and Tongan Royal Families — A42

Litho.; Gold Embossed

1970, Mar. 7 Self-adhesive *Die Cut*

238 A42 3s multicolored .25 .25
239 A42 5s multicolored .25 .25
240 A42 10s multicolored .55 .40
241 A42 25s multicolored 1.25 .90
242 A42 50s multicolored 2.75 2.00
Nos. 238-242,C68-C72,CO28-CO30 (13) 30.60 16.95

Visit of Elizabeth II, Prince Philip and Princess Anne, Mar. 1970.

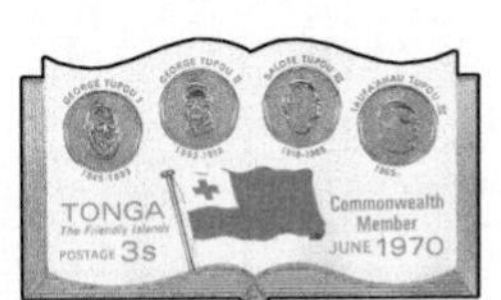

Open Book, George Tupou I and II, Salote Tupou III, Taufa'ahau Tupou IV and Tonga Flag — A43

Litho.; Gold Embossed

1970, June 4 *Die Cut*

Self-adhesive

243 A43 3s multicolored .40 .40
244 A43 7s multicolored .55 .55
245 A43 15s multicolored .80 .80
246 A43 25s multicolored 1.00 1.00
247 A43 50s multicolored 1.60 1.60
Nos. 243-247,C73-C77,CO31-CO33 (13) 20.00 20.00

Tonga's independence and entry into the British Commonwealth of Nations.

For surcharges see Nos. CO49-CO51, CO71.

Banana Type of 1969 redrawn and

Coconut — A44

1970, June 9 Typo.

Self-adhesive

248 A39 1s yellow, blk & mag .40 .40
249 A39 2s yellow, blk & bl .50 .50
250 A39 3s yellow, blk & brn .50 .50
251 A39 4s yellow, blk & grn .50 .50
252 A39 5s yellow, blk & org .55 .55

Typo.; Embossed on Gilt Foil

Coconut Brown

253 A44 6s blue, grn & mag .65 .65
254 A44 7s purple & green .70 .70
255 A44 8s gold, grn & vio bl .75 .75
256 A44 9s carmine & green .85 .85
257 A44 10s gold, grn & org .85 .85
Nos. 248-257,O11-O20 (20) 16.00 16.00

Nos. 248-252 have no white shading in upper part of the banana, Nos. 222-226 have white shading. Nos. 253-256 have self-adhesive control numbers in lower left corner of paper backing. Paper backing is green on Nos. 253-257.

See Nos. 302-306, O26-O30.

Red Cross and Arms of Tonga — A45

1970, Oct. 17 Litho. *Die Cut*

Self-adhesive

258 A45 3s red, black & grn .25 .25
259 A45 7s red, blk & vio bl .25 .25
260 A45 15s red, blk & red lil .55 .55
261 A45 25s red, black & brt grn .90 .90
262 A45 75s red, black & brn 4.50 4.50
Nos. 258-262,C78-C82,CO34-CO36 (13) 30.05 29.90

Centenary of the British Red Cross.

See Nos. C78-C82.

Nos. 153, 152 Surcharged

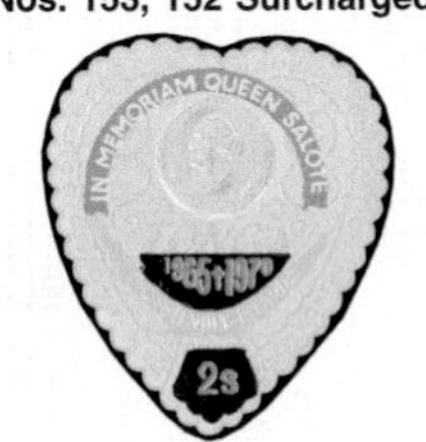

Litho.; Embossed on Gilt Foil

1971, Jan. 31 *Die Cut*

263 A37 2s on 9p lt blue .25 .25
264 A37 3s on 9p lt blue .25 .25
265 A37 5s on 3p pink .35 .25
266 A37 15s on 9p lt blue 1.10 .65
267 A37 25s on 3p pink 1.50 1.00
268 A37 50s on 3p pink 3.50 2.10
Nos. 263-268,C83-C86,CO37-CO40 (14) 35.55 24.40

In memory of Queen Salote (1900-65). The "In Memoriam" inscription is in silver on black panel on the 2s, 3s and 15s; in silver on ultramarine panel on the 5s, 25s and 50s. The dates and denominations are all on black panels in silver and metallic red, green, bronze, magenta or gold respectively.

Type of Regular Issue, 1953, Surcharged in Red and Black

No. 269

Nos. 270-272

1971 Engr. Wmk. 79 *Imperf*

269 A34e 3s on 8p blk & pale grn .25 .25
270 A34b 7s on 4p pur & yel .25 .25
271 A33 25s on 1p yel & blk .55 .40
272 A34g 75s on 2sh rose car & blue 3.25 2.10
Nos. 269-272,C87-C89,CO41-CO43 (10) 13.75 9.40

Philatokyo 71, Philatelic Exposition, Tokyo, Apr. 19-29.

Type of Regular Issue, 1971, Surcharged

1971

273 A34f 15s on 1sh car & buff .50 .50
Nos. 273,C90-C91 (3) 2.90 2.75

Centenary of Japanese postal service.

Self-adhesive & Die Cut

Starting with Nos. 274-278, all issues are self-adhesive and die cut, unless otherwise stated.

Pole Vault — A46

1971, July Litho. Unwmk. *Die Cut*

274 A46 3s green, blk & brn .25 .25
275 A46 7s red, blk & brn .25 .25
276 A46 15s green, blk & brn .25 .25
277 A46 25s rose lil, blk & brn .30 .30
278 A46 50s dk bl, blk & brn .55 .55
Nos. 274-278,C92-C96,CO44-CO46 (13) 8.80 8.80

4th South Pacific Games, Papeete, French Polynesia, Sept. 8-19.
For surcharges see Nos. 332, C140.

Gold Medal of Merit — A47

24s, Silver Medal of Merit. 38s, Bronze Medal of Merit, obverse (King Taufa'ahau IV).

Litho; Embossed

1971, Oct. 30 *Imperf.*

279 A47 3s gold & multi .25 .25
280 A47 24s silver & multi .35 .35
281 A47 38s bronze & multi .65 .65
Nos. 279-281,C99-C101,CO49-CO51 (9) 8.50 8.50

First investiture of Tongan Medal of Merit.
For surcharges see Nos. 333-336.

Juggler, UNICEF Emblem — A48

1971, Dec. Litho. *Die Cut*

282 A48 2s violet & multi .25 .25
283 A48 4s multicolored .25 .25
284 A48 8s blue & multi .25 .25
285 A48 16s emerald & multi .35 .35
286 A48 30s lil rose & multi .50 .50
Nos. 282-286,C102-C106,CO52-CO54 (13) 12.60 12.60

25th anniv. of UNICEF.

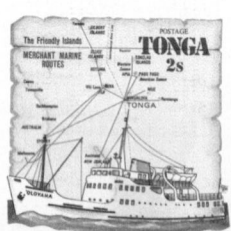

Merchant Marine Routes from Tonga and "Olovaha" A49

1972, Apr. 14

287 A49 2s blue & multi .30 .30
288 A49 10s magenta & multi .70 .70
289 A49 17s brown & multi 1.00 .35
290 A49 21s dk green & multi 1.10 .50
291 A49 60s multicolored 5.25 3.25
Nos. 287-291,C107-C111,CO55-CO57 (13) 33.70 23.85

Togan Merchant Marine publicity
For surcharges see Nos. C124, CO66-CO69.

King Taufa'ahau IV Coronation Coin, ¼ Hau — A50

Litho.; Embossed on Metallic Foil

1972, July 15

292 A50 5s silver & multi .25 .25
293 A50 7s silver & multi .25 .25
294 A50 10s silver & multi .25 .25
295 A50 17s silver & multi .30 .30
296 A50 60s silver & multi 1.00 1.00
Nos. 292-296,C112-C116,CO58-CO60 (13) 11.55 11.55

Coronation of King Taufa'ahau IV, 5th anniv.

Coconut Type of 1970 and

Banana — A51

Watermelon A52

1972, Sept. 30 Typo.

297 A51 1s brt yel, red & blk .35 .25
298 A51 2s brt yel, bl & blk .40 .25
299 A51 3s brt yel, emer & blk .45 .25
300 A51 4s brt yel & blk .45 .25
301 A51 5s brt yel & brn blk .45 .25
302 A44 6s brn, org & grn .50 .25
303 A44 7s brn, ultra & grn .55 .30
304 A44 8s brn, mag & grn .55 .30
305 A44 9s brn, red & grn .55 .30
306 A44 10s brn, bl & grn .65 .35
307 A52 15s green, org brn & ultra 1.40 .50
308 A52 20s grn, bl & red 1.50 .70
309 A52 25s grn, red & brn 1.75 .80
310 A52 40s grn, bl & org 3.00 1.75
311 A52 50s grn, dk bl & yel 3.00 2.00
Nos. 297-311,O21-O35 (30) 28.85 17.35

Paper backing is brown on Nos. 302-311. Nos. 302-306 have self-adhesive control number in lower left corner of paper backing.

Flag Raising, Minerva Reef A53

1972, Dec. 9 Litho.

312 A53 5s black & multi .25 .25
313 A53 7s green & multi .25 .25
314 A53 10s purple & multi .25 .25
315 A53 15s orange & multi .30 .30
316 A53 40s ultra & multi 1.10 1.10
Nos. 312-316,C119-C123,CO63-CO65 (13) 10.55 10.55

Tonga's proclamation of sovereignty over the Minerva Reefs, June 1972.

Tongan Coins and Bank Building A54

1973, Mar. 30 Litho.

317 A54 5s silver & multi .25 .25
318 A54 7s silver & multi .25 .25
319 A54 10s silver & multi .25 .25
320 A54 20s silver & multi .35 .25
321 A54 30s silver & multi .50 .30
Nos. 317-321,C125-C129,CO66-CO68 (13) 14.80 14.15

Establishment of Bank of Tonga.

Handshake, Outrigger Canoe — A55

1973, June 29

322 A55 5s silver & multi .25 .25
323 A55 7s silver & multi .35 .25
324 A55 15s silver & multi 1.10 .40
325 A55 21s silver & multi 1.40 .55
326 A55 50s silver & multi 5.00 2.50
Nos. 322-326,C130-C134,CO69-CO71 (13) 101.35 52.75

Tongan Boy Scout Movement, 25th anniv.

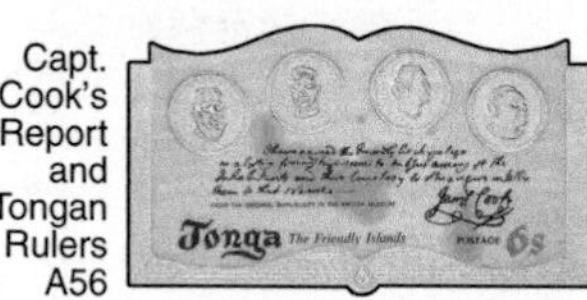

Capt. Cook's Report and Tongan Rulers A56

Litho.; Embossed on Gilt Foil

1973, Oct. 2

327 A56 6s multicolored .50 .45
328 A56 8s multicolored .50 .45
329 A56 11s multicolored .70 .55
330 A56 35s multicolored 4.75 1.90
331 A56 40s multicolored 4.75 2.25
Nos. 327-331,C135-C139,CO72-CO74 (13) 52.45 31.10

Bicentenary of Capt. Cook's arrival. Design is from the manuscript in British Museum.

Nos. 278, 281, C100-C101 and 280 Srchd. & Ovptd. in Silver or Gold on Red (12s, 14s) or Black Panels (5s, 20s, 50s): "Commonwealth Games Christchurch 1974"

1973, Dec. 19 Litho.

332 A46 5s on 50s (G) .25 .25

Litho.; Embossed

333 A47 12s on 38s (S) .35 .35
334 A47 14s on 75s (G) .35 .35
335 A47 20s on 1pa (G) .60 .60
336 A47 50s on 24s (S) 1.10 1.10
Nos. 332-336,C140-C144,CO75-CO77 (13) 12.20 11.75

10th British Commonwealth Games, Christchurch, N.Z., Jan. 24-Feb. 2, 1974.

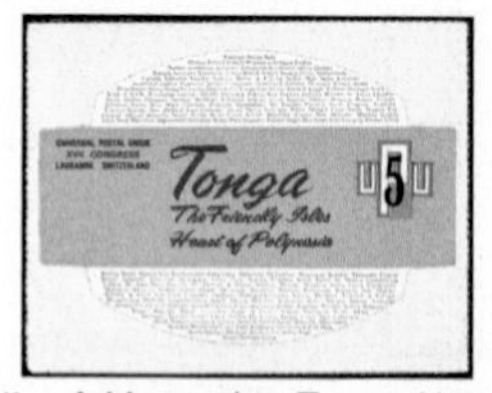

Letter Addressed to Tonga, Names of UPU Members — A57

1974, June 20 Typo.

337 A57 5s tan & multi .25 .25
338 A57 10s tan & multi .25 .25
339 A57 15s tan & multi .35 .35
340 A57 20s tan & multi .40 .40
341 A57 50s tan & multi 1.25 1.25
Nos. 337-341,C154-C158,CO87-CO89 (13) 11.65 11.65

Centenary of Universal Postal Union.

Girl Guide Badges A58

1974, Sept. 11 Litho.

342 A58 5s multicolored .45 .30
343 A58 10s multicolored .85 .50
344 A58 20s multicolored 2.00 1.25
345 A58 40s multicolored 4.00 2.40
346 A58 60s multicolored 5.50 3.25
Nos. 342-346,C159-C163,CO90-CO92 (13) 45.80 28.55

Girl Guides of Tonga.
For surcharges see Nos. C189, C192.

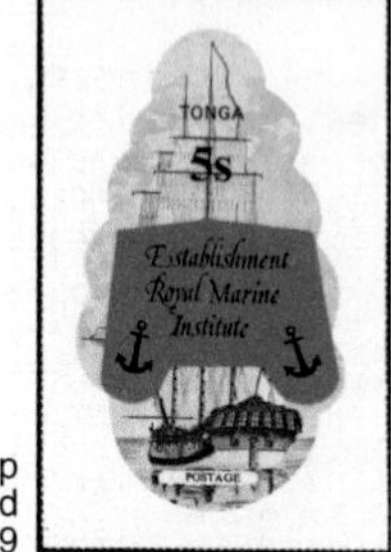

Sailing Ship and Anchors — A59

1974, Dec. 11

347 A59 5s blue & multi .40 .35
348 A59 10s blue & multi .90 .45
349 A59 25s blue & multi 2.00 .80
350 A59 50s blue & multi 4.00 2.75
351 A59 75s blue & multi 6.00 4.50
Nos. 347-351,C164-C168,CO93-CO95 (13) 41.30 27.75

Establishment of Royal Marine Institute.

Dateline Hotel, Nukualofa — A60

1975, Mar. 11

352 A60 5s blue & multi .25 .25
353 A60 10s green & multi .25 .25
354 A60 15s scarlet & multi .30 .30
355 A60 30s purple & multi .65 .65
356 A60 1pa orange & multi 2.40 2.40
Nos. 352-356,C169-C173,CO96-CO98 (13) 13.30 13.30

First meeting of South Pacific area Prime Ministers. See note after No. 226.

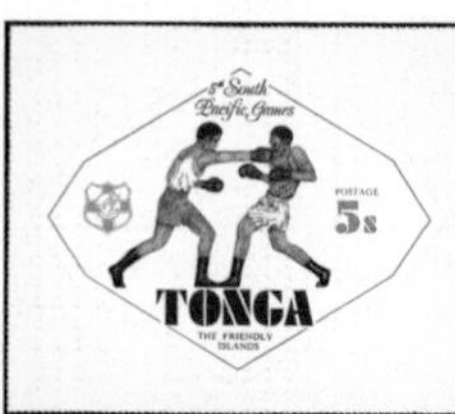

Boxing and Games' Emblem A61

1975, June 11 Litho.

357 A61 5s black & multi .25 .25
358 A61 10s green & multi .35 .35
359 A61 20s brown & multi .55 .55
360 A61 25s orange & multi .65 .65
361 A61 65s violet & multi 1.40 1.40
Nos. 357-361,C174-C178,CO99-CO101 (13) 10.65 10.50

5th South Pacific Games, Guam, Aug. 1-10. See note after No. 226.
For surcharges see Nos. 412, 482.

King Taufa'ahau IV Coin — A62

Designs (FAO Coins): 5s, Chicken. 20s, like 1pa, (small coin, 27mm). 50s, School of fish. 2pa, Animals and plants on reverse, King on obverse (large coin, 42mm).

1975, Sept. 3

362	A62	5s red, sil & blk	.25	.25
363	A62	20s ultra, grn, sil & blk	.50	.50
364	A62	50s blue, sil & blk	.95	.95
365	A62	1pa silver & black	2.00	2.00
366	A62	2pa silver & black	3.25	3.25
		Nos. 362-366,C179-C183 (10)	11.70	11.70

Coinage issued for the benefit of the FAO. Size of paper backing of 2pa: 82x50mm; others 45x45mm. See note after No. 226.

For surcharge see Nos. 413.

Coat of Arms, 5pa Coin, Reverse A63

George Tupou I Coin, Reverse and Obverse A64

Coins: 20s, King Taufa'ahau IV. 50s, King George Tupou II, 50pa obverse and reverse. 75s, 20pa reverse.

Litho.; Embossed on Gilt Foil

1975, Nov. 4 Pink Background

367	A63	5s black, sil & vio bl	.30	.30
368	A64	10s gold, blk & red	.40	.40
369	A63	20s black, sil & grn	.75	.75
370	A64	50s gold, blk & vio	1.75	1.75
371	A63	75s black, sil & red lil	2.75	2.75
		Nos. 367-371,C184-C188,CO102-CO104 (13)	19.05	17.75

Centenary of Constitution of Tonga. Size of paper backing of Nos. 367 and 369: 65x60mm; of No. 371, 87x78mm. See note after No. 226.

For surcharges see Nos. C232, C296.

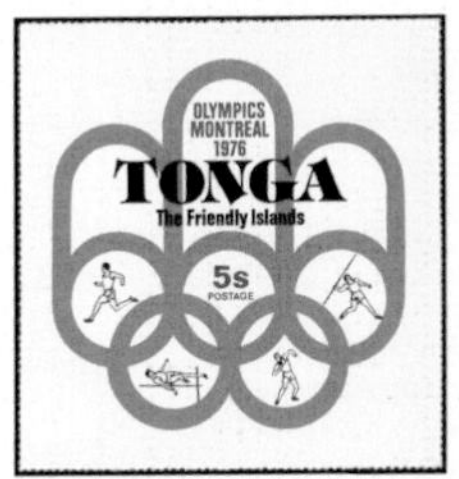

Montreal Olympic Games Emblem A65

1976, Feb. 24 Litho.

372	A65	5s red, ultra & blk	.40	.35
373	A65	10s red, green & blk	.60	.35
374	A65	25s red, lt brown & blk	1.40	.80
375	A65	35s red, lilac & blk	1.75	1.10
376	A65	70s red, bister & blk	3.50	2.75
		Nos. 372-376,C189-C193,CO105-CO107 (13)	36.65	23.45

21st Olympic Games, Montreal, Canada, July 17-Aug. 1. See note after No. 226.

For surcharges see Nos. 414, 478.

William Hooper, William Floyd, John Penn, Francis Lightfoot Lee A66

Signers of Declaration of Independence, Flags of US and Tonga: 10s, Benjamin Franklin, Thomas Nelson, Jr., Benjamin Harrison, William Ellery. 15s, Oliver Wolcott, Lyman Hall, William Whipple, Carter Braxton. 25s, George Taylor, Thomas Stone, Arthur Middleton, Richard Stockton. 75s, Stephen Hopkins, Elbridge Gerry, James Wilson, Francis Hopkinson.

1976, May 26 Litho.

377	A66	9s buff & multi	.25	.25
378	A66	10s buff & multi	.25	.25
379	A66	15s buff & multi	.35	.30
380	A66	25s buff & multi	.50	.50
381	A66	75s buff & multi	3.00	2.25
		Nos. 377-381,C194-C198,CO108-CO110 (13)	17.15	15.10

American Bicentennial. Printed on peelable buff paper backing, inscribed in carmine with facsimile of Declaration of Independence.

For surcharges see #481, C233, C236-C237, C297.

Nathaniel Turner and John Thomas — A67

1976, Aug. 25

382	A67	5s yellow & multi	.25	.25
383	A67	10s multicolored	.40	.25
384	A67	20s multicolored	.90	.50
385	A67	25s multicolored	1.00	.55
386	A67	85s multicolored	2.75	2.75
		Nos. 382-386,C199-C203,CO111-CO113 (13)	20.45	17.15

Sesquicentennial of the arrival of Methodist missionaries and establishment of Christianity in Tonga. Printed on peelable paper backing inscribed in manuscript with segments of John Thomas's Tonga diary.

For surcharges see Nos. 415-416, 479-480.

Wilhelm I and George Tupou I A68

1976, Nov. 1

387	A68	9s yellow & multi	.35	.35
388	A68	15s yellow & multi	.55	.50
389	A68	22s yellow & multi	.85	.85
390	A68	50s yellow & multi	1.50	1.50
391	A68	73s yellow & multi	2.00	2.00
		Nos. 387-391,C204-C208,CO114-CO116 (13)	15.70	16.10

Tonga-Germany Friendship Treaty, centenary. Printed on peelable paper backing showing reproduction of original treaty.

Queen Salote in Coronation Procession, 1953 — A69

1977, Feb. 7 Litho.

392	A69	11s blue & multi	.40	.40
393	A69	20s green & multi	.30	.30
394	A69	30s vio blue & multi	.30	.30
395	A69	50s lt green & multi	.45	.45
396	A69	75s violet & multi	.65	.65
		Nos. 392-396,C209-C213,CO117-CO119 (13)	7.95	6.60

25th anniv. of the reign of Elizabeth II. Printed on peelable paper backing showing replica of handwritten Proclamation of Accession.

For surcharge see No. 417.

Various Coins A70

1977, July 4

397	A70	10s multicolored	.25	.25
398	A70	15s multicolored	.25	.25
399	A70	25s multicolored	.30	.30
400	A70	50s multicolored	.70	.70
401	A70	75s multicolored	1.20	1.20
		Nos. 397-401,C214-C218,CO120-CO122 (13)	10.90	10.90

10th anniversary of coronation of King Taufa'ahau IV. Printed on peelable paper backing showing multicolored replicas of Tongan stamps.

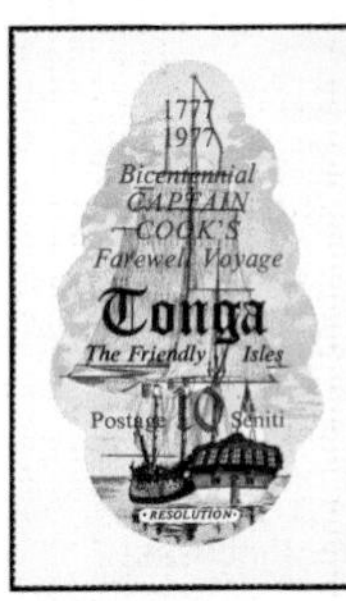

Capt. Cook's Resolution A71

1977, Sept. 27 Litho.

402	A71	10s multicolored	1.25	.75
403	A71	17s multicolored	2.25	1.10
404	A71	25s multicolored	3.75	2.00
405	A71	30s multicolored	3.75	2.75
406	A71	40s multicolored	4.50	4.50
		Nos. 402-406,C219-C223,CO123-CO125 (13)	55.00	49.60

Bicentenary of Capt. Cook's farewell voyage.

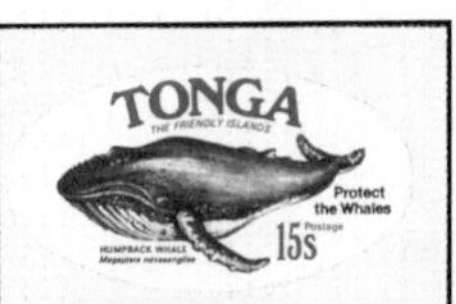

Humpback Whale — A72

1977, Dec. 16

407	A72	15s ultra & black	4.25	.85
408	A72	22s green & black	4.50	1.50
409	A72	31s orange & black	5.25	2.00
410	A72	38s lilac & black	5.50	5.25
411	A72	64s red & black	9.25	5.50
		Nos. 407-411,C224-C228,CO126-CO128 (13)	86.00	40.00

Whale protection.

Stamps of 1975-77 Surcharged in Black, Green, Brown or Black on Silver

1978, Feb. 17

412	A61	15s on 20s (#359;B)	2.00	1.75
413	A62	15s on 5s (#362;B)	2.00	1.75
414	A65	15s on 10s (#373;G)	2.00	1.75
415	A67	15s on 5s (#382;Br)	2.00	1.75
416	A67	15s on 10s (#383;B)	2.00	1.75
417	A69	15s on 11s (#392;B on S)	*2.00*	*3.00*
418	OA11	15s on 38s (#CO99;B)	2.00	1.75
		Nos. 412-418,C229-C238 (17)	*64.25*	*63.75*

The surcharge on No. 413 is only the "1," and on No. 418 includes "postage."

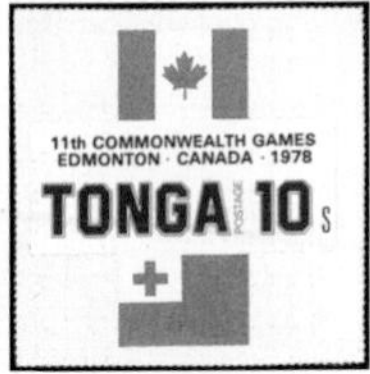

Flags of Canada and Tonga — A73

1978, May 5 Litho.

419	A73	10s red & multi	.25	.25
420	A73	15s red & multi	.35	.35
421	A73	20s red & multi	.45	.45
422	A73	25s red & multi	.60	.60
423	A73	45s red & multi	2.00	2.00
		Nos. 419-423,C239-C243,CO129-CO131 (13)	13.15	12.90

11th Commonwealth Games, Edmonton, Canada, Aug. 3-12. See note after No. 226.

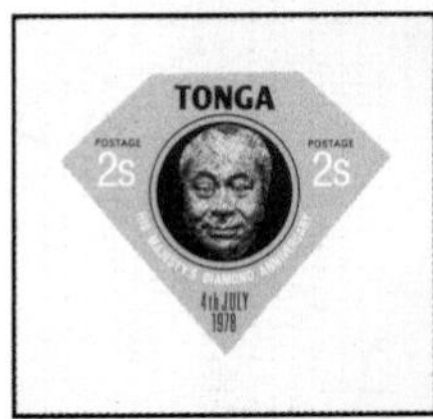

King Taufa'ahau IV — A74

1978, July 4

424	A74	2s multicolored	.25	.25
425	A74	5s multicolored	.25	.25
426	A74	10s multicolored	.25	.25
427	A74	25s multicolored	.60	.60
428	A74	75s multicolored	1.90	2.00
		Nos. 424-428,C244-C248,CO132-CO134 (13)	12.15	12.25

60th birthday of King Taufa'ahau IV. See note after No. 226.

Two Bananas A75

Coconut A76

Designs: 1s to 5s, Bananas. 6s to 10s, Coconuts. 15s to 1pa, Pineapples.

1978, Sept. 29 Typo.

429	A75	1s yellow & black	.30	.30
430	A75	2s yellow & dk blue	.30	.30
431	A75	3s multicolored	.40	.40
432	A75	4s multicolored	.40	.40
433	A75	5s multicolored	.40	.40
434	A76	6s multicolored	.60	.60
435	A76	7s multicolored	.60	.60
436	A76	8s multicolored	.60	.60
437	A76	9s multicolored	.60	.60
438	A76	10s brown & green	.60	.60
439	A76	15s green & lt brown	1.75	1.75
440	A76	20s multicolored	2.00	2.00
441	A76	30s multicolored	2.25	2.25
442	A76	50s multicolored	2.75	2.75
443	A76	1pa multicolored	3.25	3.25
		Nos. 429-443,O36-O50 (30)	31.95	31.95

Nos. 429-443 issued in coils; self-adhesive control numbers on paper backing, except on 1s and 5s. See note after No. 226.

See No. 529.

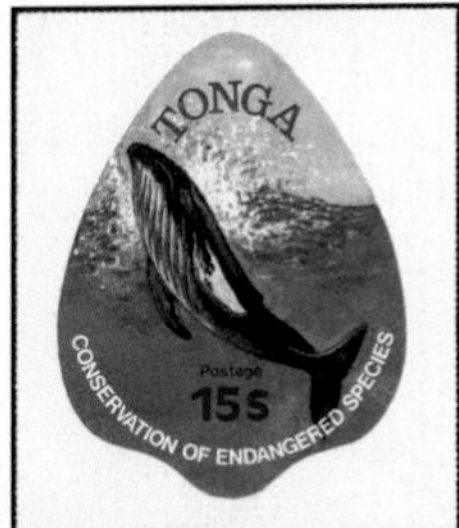

Whale A77

1978, Dec. 15 **Litho. & Typo.**

444	A77 15s shown	3.75	2.00
445	A77 18s Bat	3.75	2.00
446	A77 25s Turtle	3.75	2.00
447	A77 28s Parrot	4.25	3.00
448	A77 60s like 15s	10.00	6.00
	Nos. 444-448,C249-C253,CO150-CO152 (13)	79.00	45.50

Wildlife conservation. See note after No. 226.

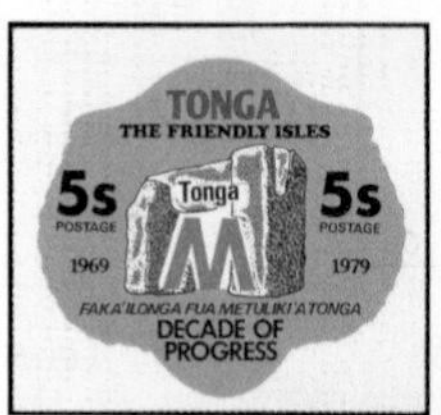

Introduction of Metric System A78

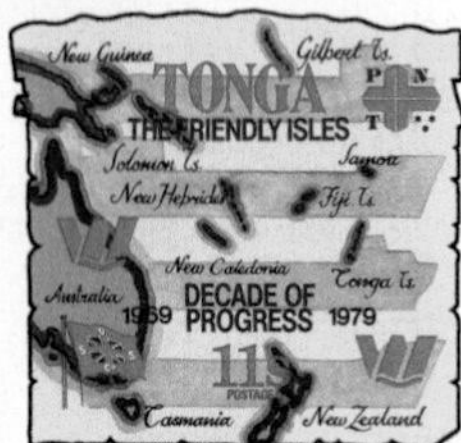

Shipping Routes, South Pacific Map A79

Peace Corps — A80

22s, New church buildings. 50s, Air routes to Auckland, Suva, Apia & Pago Pago.

1979, Feb. 16 **Litho.**

449	A78 5s multicolored	.25	.25
450	A79 11s multicolored	.60	.60
451	A80 18s multicolored	.60	.60
452	A79 22s multicolored	.60	.60
453	A79 50s multicolored	2.25	2.25
	Nos. 449-453,C254-C258,CO153-CO155 (13)	22.80	18.00

Decade of Progress. Paper backing shows map of Tonga.

Tongan First Day Covers A81

1979, June 1

454	A81 5s multicolored	.30	.25
455	A81 10s multicolored	.40	.30
456	A81 25s multicolored	.70	.60
457	A81 50s multicolored	1.25	1.25
458	A81 1pa multicolored	1.75	1.75
	Nos. 454-458,C259-C263,CO156-CO158 (13)	13.40	11.60

10th anniversary of introduction of self-adhesive stamps and for Bernard Mechanick, inventor of self-adhesive, free-form stamps; death centenary of Sir Rowland Hill.

Printed on peelable paper backing showing advertisement.

For surcharges and overprints see Nos. 469-473.

Eua Island through Camera Lens A82

1979, Nov. 23 **Litho.**

459	A82 10s multicolored	.30	.30
460	A82 18s multicolored	.35	.35
461	A82 31s multicolored	.60	.60
462	A82 50s multicolored	.95	.95
463	A82 60s multicolored	1.10	1.10
	Nos. 459-463,C275-C279,CO170-CO172 (13)	10.50	10.50

Printed on peelable paper backing showing film and camera.

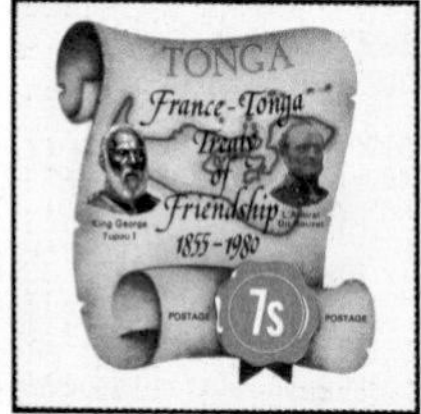

King George Tupou I, Admiral du Bouzet, Map of Tonga A83

1980, Jan. 9 **Litho.**

464	A83 7s multicolored	.30	.30
465	A83 10s multicolored	.40	.40
466	A83 14s multicolored	.50	.50
467	A83 50s multicolored	1.50	1.50
468	A83 75s multicolored	2.00	2.00
	Nos. 464-468,C280-C284,CO173-CO175 (13)	16.40	14.40

Tongan-French Friendship Treaty, 125th anniversary. Printed on peelable paper; multicolored backing shows map of Tonga.

Nos. 454-458 Surcharged and Overprinted in Black on Silver: "1980 OLYMPIC GAMES," Moscow '80 and Bear Emblems

1980, Apr. 30 **Litho.**

469	A81 13s on 5s multi	.50	.50
470	A81 20s on 10s multi	.75	.75
471	A81 25s multicolored	.90	.90
472	A81 33s on 50s multi	1.10	1.10
473	A81 1pa multicolored	3.50	3.50
	Nos. 469-473,C285-C289,CO176-CO178 (13)	17.75	17.75

Boy Scout Cooking over Campfire A84

1980, Sept. 30 **Litho.**

474	A84 9s multicolored	.25	.25
475	A84 13s multicolored	.35	.35
476	A84 15s multicolored	.40	.40
477	A84 30s multicolored	.75	.75
	Nos. 474-477,C290-C293,CO179-CO180 (10)	14.45	14.45

Boy Scout Jamboree; Rotary Intl., 75th anniv. Peelable backing shows map of Tonga.

Nos. 361, 375, 380, 384-385 Surcharged

1980, Dec. 3 **Litho.**

478	A65 9s on 35s multi	.50	.50
479	A67 13s on 20s multi	.75	.75
480	A67 13s on 25s multi	.75	.75
481	A66 19s on 25s multi	1.10	1.10
482	A61 1pa on 65s multi	6.25	6.25
	Nos. 478-482,C294-C299,CO181 (12)	22.85	22.85

Intl. Year of the Disabled A85

1981, Sept. 9 **Litho.**

483	A85 2pa multicolored	2.50	2.50
484	A85 3pa multicolored	3.75	3.75
	Nos. 483-484,C300-C302 (5)	7.95	7.95

Prince Charles and Lady Diana — A86

Designs: 13s, Charles, King Taufa'ahau. 47s, 1.50pa, Couple, diff.

1981, Oct. 21 **Litho.**

485	A86 13s multicolored	.75	.50
486	A86 47s multicolored	1.00	.50
487	A86 1.50pa multicolored	1.50	1.75
488	A86 3pa multicolored	2.00	3.25
	Nos. 485-488 (4)	5.25	6.00

Royal Wedding and Gt. Britain-Tonga Friendship Treaty centenary. Issued in sheets of 20 (2x10) and 5 labels in vert. center row.

For surcharge see No. B1.

Bicentenary of Discovery of Vavau by Francisco Maurelle — A87

18th century Spanish engravings and maps.

1981, Nov. 25 **Litho.**

489	A87 9s multicolored	.60	.50
490	A87 13s multicolored	.90	.60
491	A87 47s multicolored	2.75	1.40
492	A87 1pa multicolored	3.75	3.75
a.	Souvenir sheet, imperf.	9.00	9.00
	Nos. 489-492 (4)	8.00	6.25

No. 492a contains one No. 492 (32x25mm).

Bible Class, 1830 Print — A88

1981, Nov. 25

493	A88 9s Open book	.25	.25
494	A88 13s Book, diff.	.50	.40
495	A88 32s Type	.90	.90
496	A88 47s shown	1.60	1.60
	Nos. 493-496 (4)	3.25	3.15

Christmas 1981 and sesquicentennial of books printed in Tonga.

175th Anniv. of Capture of The Port-au-Prince — A89

1981, Dec. 16 **Litho.**

497	A89 29s Battle	1.00	.75
498	A89 32s Battle, diff.	1.25	.90
499	A89 47s Map	1.60	1.50
500	A89 47s Sinking ship	1.60	1.50
a.	Pair, #499-500	3.25	
501	A89 1pa Ship	3.50	3.50
	Nos. 497-501 (5)	8.95	8.15

Nos. CO179-CO180 Surcharged

1982, Jan. 4 **Litho.**

502	OA19 5pa on 25s multi	17.50	17.50
503	OA19 5pa on 2pa multi	17.50	17.50

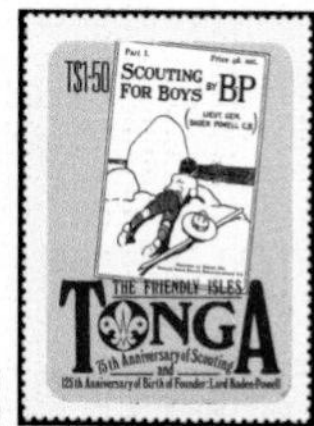

Scouting Year — A90

29s, Brownsea Isld. Camp, 1907. 32s, Baden-Powell, horse. 47s, Imperial Jamboree, 1924. 1.50pa, "Scouting for Boys". 2.50pa, Mafeking stamp.

1982, Feb. 22 **Litho.**

504	A90 29s multicolored	1.00	.60
505	A90 32s multicolored	1.00	.65
506	A90 47s multicolored	1.50	1.00
507	A90 1.50pa multicolored	4.00	4.00
508	A90 2.50pa multicolored	5.50	*6.00*
	Nos. 504-508 (5)	13.00	12.25

1982 World Cup — A91

Designs: Various soccer players, map showing match sites.

1982, July 7 **Litho.**

509	A91 32s multicolored	.85	.60
510	A91 47s multicolored	1.25	.85
511	A91 75s multicolored	1.40	1.40
512	A91 1.50pa multicolored	3.00	2.50
	Nos. 509-512 (4)	6.50	5.35

Inter-island Transport — A92

9s, 13s, Ferry Olovaha. 47s, 1pa SPIA Twin Otter (Niuatoputapu Airport opening).

1982, Aug. 11

513	A92 9s multicolored	.50	.25
514	A92 13s multicolored	.60	.30
515	A92 47s multicolored	2.00	1.00
516	A92 1pa multicolored	3.25	2.75
	Nos. 513-516 (4)	6.35	4.30

Tin Can Mail Centenary — A93

13s, 32s, 47s, Collecting mail. 2pa, Map. Nos. 517-519 form continuous design.

1982, Sept. 29 **Litho.**

517	A93 13s multicolored	.25	.25
518	A93 32s multicolored	.55	.55
519	A93 47s multicolored	.90	.90
a.	Souv. sheet of 3 (13s, 32s, 47s)	2.00	2.00
520	A93 2pa multicolored	2.00	2.00
a.	Souvenir sheet of 1	3.00	3.00
	Nos. 517-520 (4)	3.70	3.70

No. 520 comes with different labels. For surcharges see Nos. 526-528.

Tonga College Centenary A94

Inscribed in English

1982, Oct. 25 **Size: 42x30mm (5s)**

521 A94 5s Students .60 .60
522 A94 29s King George Tupou I 2.50 2.50
523 A94 29s Monument 2.50 2.50
b. Pair, #522-523 5.00
Nos. 521-523 (3) 5.60 5.60

Inscribed in Tongan

521A A94 5s Students .60 .60
522A A94 29s King George Tupou I 2.50 2.50
523A A94 29s Monument 2.50 2.50
c. Pair, #522A-523A 5.00
Nos. 521A-523A (3) 5.60 5.60

Nos. 521-523 inscribed in English or Tongan.

12th Commonwealth Games, Brisbane, Australia, Sept. 30-Oct. 9 — A95

1982, Oct. 25

524 A95 32s Decathlon, vert. 1.00 .75
525 A95 1.50pa Opening ceremony 8.00 8.00

Nos. 517-519 Overprinted in Red or Silver in 1 or 2 Lines: "Christmas / Greetings / 1982"

1982, Nov. 17

526 A93 13s multicolored .30 .30
527 A93 32s multicolored .70 .70
528 A93 47s multicolored .75 .75
Nos. 526-528 (3) 1.75 1.75

Pineapple Type of 1978 and

Fruit A96

1982, Nov. 17

529 A76 13s multicolored 5.50 5.50
530 A96 2pa multicolored 12.00 12.00
531 A96 3pa multicolored 15.00 15.00
Nos. 529-531 (3) 32.50 32.50

Capt. Cook's Resolution, 1777 and Canberra, 1983 — A96a

32s, like 29s. 47s, 1.50pa, Montgolfier Bros. balloon, 1783, Concorde. 2.50pa, Concorde, Canberra. 29s se-tenant with label showing Resolution.

1983, Feb. 22 **Litho.**

532 A96a 29s multicolored 2.25 1.50
533 A96a 32s multicolored 3.00 1.50
534 A96a 47s multicolored 4.25 2.50
535 A96a 1.50pa multicolored 11.00 11.00
Nos. 532-535 (4) 20.50 16.50

Souvenir Sheet

536 A96a 2.50pa multicolored 5.25 5.25

Pacific Forum of Sea and Air Transport (29s, 32s, 2.50pa); manned flight bicentenary (47s, 1.50pa).

For overprints see Nos. O68-O70.

A96b

29s, Map. 32s, Dancers. 47s, Fishermen. 1.50pa, King Taufa'ahau IV, flag.

1983, Mar. 14

537 A96b 29s multi 1.00 1.00
538 A96b 32s multi 5.00 5.00
539 A96b 47s multi 2.00 2.00
540 A96b 1.50pa multi 2.00 2.00
Nos. 537-540 (4) 10.00 10.00

Commonwealth Day.

Niuafo'ou Airport Opening — A97

1983, May 11 **Litho.**

541 A97 32s De Havilland Otter .90 .50
542 A97 47s like 32s 1.25 .50
543 A97 1pa Boeing 707 2.10 1.40
544 A97 1.50pa like 1pa 3.25 2.10
Nos. 541-544 (4) 7.50 4.50

World Communications Year — A98

1983, June 22 **Litho.**

545 A98 29s Intelsat IV .50 .50
546 A98 32s Intelsat IV-A .60 .60
547 A98 75s Intelsat V 1.40 1.40

Size: 45x32mm

548 A98 2pa Apollo 15 Moon post cover 3.00 3.00
Nos. 545-548 (4) 5.50 5.50

10th Anniv. of Bank of Tonga — A99

Various banknotes.

1983, Aug. 3 **Litho.**

549 A99 1pa multicolored 2.25 2.25
550 A99 2pa multicolored 3.75 3.75

Printing Press, 1830 — A100

1983, Sept. 22 **Litho.**

551 A100 13s shown .30 .30
552 A100 32s Woon's arrival, 1831 .75 .75
553 A100 1pa Print 1.75 1.75
554 A100 2pa Tonga Chronicle 2.40 2.40
Nos. 551-554 (4) 5.20 5.20

Sesquicentennial of printing in Tonga (by missionary William Woon).

Christmas 1983 — A101

Designs: Various sailboats off Vava'u.

1983, Nov. 17 **Litho.**

555 A101 29s multicolored .50 .40
556 A101 32s multicolored .60 .50
557 A101 1.50pa multicolored 2.40 2.40
558 A101 2.50pa multicolored 4.00 4.00
Nos. 555-558 (4) 7.50 7.30

Abel Tasman, Discoverer of Tonga, and his Zeehan — A102

Navigators and Explorers of the Pacific and their Ships — 47s, Samuel Wallis, Dolphin. 90s, William Bligh, Bounty. 1.50pa, James Cook, Resolution.

1984, Mar. 12 **Litho.**

559 A102 32s shown 2.00 2.00
560 A102 47s multi 2.75 2.75
561 A102 90s multi 5.00 5.00
562 A102 1.50pa multi 7.00 7.00
Nos. 559-562 (4) 16.75 16.75

See Nos. 593-596.

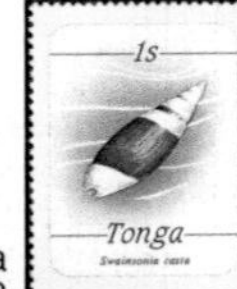

Swainsonia Casta — A103

Shells, Fish — 2s, Porites (coral). 3s, Holocentrus ruber. 5s, Cypraea mappa viridis. 6s, Dardanus megistos (crab). 9s, Stegostoma fasciatum. 10s, Conus bullatus. 13s, Pterois volitans. 15s, Conus textile. 20s, Dascyllus aruanus. 29s, Conus aulicus. 32s, Acanthurus leucosternon. 47s, Lambis truncata. 1pa, Millepora dichotama (coral). 2pa, Birgus latro (crab). 3pa, Chicoreus palma-rosae. 5pa, Thunnus albacares.

1984-85 **Litho.**

563 A103 1s shown .50 *1.90*
564 A103 2s multi 1.25 *1.90*
565 A103 3s multi 1.60 *2.25*
566 A103 5s multi .60 *1.90*
567 A103 6s multi 1.60 *2.25*
568 A103 9s multi 1.60 .90
a. Perf. 14½ ('85) 1.60 .90
569 A103 10s multi 1.25 *.95*
570 A103 13s multi 1.90 .95
571 A103 15s multi 1.25 *2.25*
572 A103 20s multi 2.75 2.75
573 A103 29s multi 2.25 1.25
574 A103 32s multi 4.00 1.25
575 A103 47s multi 4.00 2.00

Size: 39x25mm

576 A103 1pa multi 12.00 12.00
577 A103 2pa multi 17.50 *19.00*
578 A103 3pa multi 11.00 *19.00*
579 A103 5pa multi 13.50 *22.50*
Nos. 563-579 (17) 78.55 *95.00*

See Nos. 682-692, 701-709, 756-759. For surcharges and overprints see Nos. 618-625, 808-810, O52-O67, O71-O77.

Tonga Chronicle, 20th Anniv. — A104

1984, June 26

580 A104 3s multicolored .25 .25
a. Sheet of 12 .75
581 A104 32s multicolored .60 .60
a. Sheet of 12 7.00

Nos. 580-581 issued in sheets of 12; sheet backgrounds show pages of Chronicle, giving each stamp different background.

1984 Summer Olympics — A105

1984, July 23

582 A105 29s Running .25 .25
583 A105 47s Javelin .35 .35
584 A105 1.50pa Shot put .85 .85
585 A105 3pa Torch 1.50 1.50
Nos. 582-585 (4) 2.95 2.95

Intl. Dateline Centenary A106

47s, George Airy, Greenwich Meridian pioneer. 2pa, Sandford Fleming, time zone pioneer.

1984, Aug. 20

586 A106 47s multicolored 1.50 1.50
587 A106 2pa multicolored 6.00 5.50

Ausipex '84 — A107

1984, Sept. 17

588 A107 32s Australia #18 1.25 .85
589 A107 1.50pa Tonga #51 4.50 3.75

Souvenir Sheet

589A Sheet of 2, #588-589 4.75 4.75

Nos. 588-589 each printed se-tenant with label showing exhibition emblem.

No. 589A contains two imperf. stamps similar to Nos. 588-589, but with denomination replacing logo. No. 589A without denominations was not valid for postage.

Christmas 1984 — A108

Christmas Carols in local settings.

1984, Nov. 12 **Litho.**

590 A108 32s Silent Night .90 .50
591 A108 47s Away in a Manger 1.35 .80
592 A108 1pa I Saw Three Ships 2.50 2.50
Nos. 590-592 (3) 4.75 3.80

Explorers Type of 1984

Designs: 32s, Willem Schouten (c. 1580-1625), The Eendracht, 1616. 47s, Jakob Le Maire (1585-1616), The Hoorn, 1615. 90s, Lt. Fletcher Christian, The Bounty, 1789. 1.50pa, Francisco Maurelle, La Princessa, 1781.

1985, Feb. 27 **Litho.** ***Die Cut***

593 A102 32s multicolored 2.50 1.50
a. Perf. 14 *35.00 35.00*
594 A102 47s multicolored 3.75 1.75
595 A102 90s multicolored 6.75 5.00
596 A102 1.50pa multicolored 10.00 7.75
Nos. 593-596 (4) 23.00 16.00

Nos. 593-596 each printed se-tenant with self-adhesive label picturing anchor.

Geological Survey of Tonga Trench for Oil — A110

Designs: 29s, Tonga Trench and islands. 32s, Marine exploration, seismic surveying. 47s, Search for oil off Tongatapu, vert. No. 600, Exploration of sea bed, vert. No. 601, Angler fish.

1985, Apr. 10

597 A110 29s multicolored 1.25 1.00
598 A110 32s multicolored 1.30 1.00
599 A110 47s multicolored 2.10 1.25
600 A110 1.50pa multicolored 7.00 7.00
Nos. 597-600 (4) 11.65 10.25

Souvenir Sheet

601 A110 1.50pa multicolored 10.00 5.00
a. Perf. 14 10.00 5.00

Nos. 597-600 printed in sheets of 40, 2 panes of 20 separated by labels inscribed "Proof 1," etc.

Adventures of Will Mariner — A111

29s, Readying Port au Prince for sail, Gravesend, 1805. 32s, Captured & set afire, 1806. 47s, Mariner taken prisoner by Chief Finow, Tonga. 1.50pa, Passage to China aboard brig Favourite. 2.50pa, Returning to England aboard East Indiaman Cuffnells, 1810.

1985, June 18 ***Die Cut***

602 A111 29s multicolored .55 .45
a. Perf. 14 .55 .45

603 A111 32s multicolored .60 .50
a. Perf. 14 .60 .50
604 A111 47s multicolored .90 .70
a. Perf. 14 .90 .70
605 A111 1.50pa multicolored 3.25 3.25
a. Perf. 14 3.25 3.25
606 A111 2.50pa multicolored 5.50 5.50
a. Perf. 14 5.50 5.50
Nos. 602-606 (5) 10.80 10.40
Nos. 602a-606a (5) 10.80 10.40

Mutiny on the Bounty, Film 50th Anniv. — A112

Designs: a, Byron Russell (Quintal), Stanley Fields (Muspratt) and Charles Laughton (Capt. Bligh). b, Laughton, Donald Crisp (Burkitt), Eddie Quillon (Ellison) and David Thursby (Maxwell). c, Clark Gable (Fletcher Christian). d, Russell, Alec Craig (McCoy), Laughton and Fields. e, Laughton and Franchot Tone (Roger Byam).

1985, July 16 ***Perf. 14***
607 Strip of 5 52.50 52.50
a.-e. A112 47s, any single 9.50 9.50

Sheets consist of four strips of 5 and a central strip of labels showing film credits.

Queen Mother, 85th Birthday — A113

Designs: 32s, Age 10. 47s, At Hadfield Girl Guides rally, 1931. 1.50pa, In Guide uniform. 2.50pa, Portrait by Norman Parkinson, 1985.

1985, Aug. 20 ***Imperf.***
608 A113 32s multicolored 1.10 .80
a. Perf. 14 1.75 1.25
609 A113 47s multicolored 1.75 1.25
a. Perf. 14 3.00 2.10
610 A113 1.50pa multicolored 5.50 5.50
a. Perf. 14 8.25 8.25
611 A113 2.50pa multicolored 8.75 8.75
a. Perf. 14 13.50 13.50
Nos. 608-611 (4) 17.10 16.30
Nos. 608a-611a (4) 26.50 25.10

Girl Guides movement, 75th anniv.

Christmas — A114

32s, No room at the inn. 42s, Shepherds follow star. 1.50pa, The three kings. 2.50pa, Holy family.

1985, Nov. 12
612 A114 32s multicolored .50 .35
613 A114 42s multicolored .75 .50
614 A114 1.50pa multicolored 2.50 2.50
615 A114 2.50pa multicolored 3.50 3.50
Nos. 612-615 (4) 7.25 6.85

Self-adhesive Discontinued
In 1986, die cut self-adhesive stamps attached to peelable paper backing were no longer issued, unless otherwise stated.

Halley's Comet — A115

Designs: Nos. 616a, 617a, Comet. Nos. 616b, 617b, Edmond Halley. Nos. 616c, 617c, Solar system. Nos. 616d, 617d, Telescope. Nos. 616e, 617e, Giotto space probe.

1986, Mar. 26 ***Perf. 14***
616 Strip of 5 15.00 15.00
a.-e. A115 42s, any single 2.50 2.50
617 Strip of 5 15.00 15.00
a.-e. A115 57s, any single 2.50 2.50

Nos. 564, 570, 565, 568, 567, 572, 577 and 579 Surcharged

1986, Apr. 16 Litho. ***Die Cut***
Self-adhesive
618 A103 4s on 2s, #564 1.00 *2.25*
619 A103 4s on 13s, #570 1.00 *2.25*
620 A103 42s on 3s, #565 2.60 1.75
621 A103 42s on 9s, #568 2.60 1.75
622 A103 57s on 6s, #567 3.25 2.50
623 A103 57s on 20s, #572 3.25 2.50
624 A103 2.50pa on 2pa, #577 10.00 10.00
625 A103 2.50pa on 5pa, #579 10.00 10.00
Nos. 618-625 (8) 33.70 33.00

For overprints see Nos. O71-O77.

Royal Links with the United Kingdom — A116

1986, May 22 ***Perf. 14***
626 57s Taufa'ahau IV 1.50 1.50
627 57s Elizabeth II 1.50 1.50
a. A116 Pair, #626-627 3.50 3.50
Size: 40x40mm
628 A116 2.50pa King and queen 6.00 6.00
Nos. 626-628 (3) 9.00 9.00

Queen Elizabeth II, 60th birthday. No. 628 printed in sheets of 5 + one label.

AMERIPEX '86, Chicago, May 22-June 1 — A117

Peace Corps activities: No. 629, Health care. No. 630, Education.

1986, May 22
629 A117 57s multicolored .85 .85
630 A117 1.50pa multicolored 2.25 2.25
a. Souv. sheet, #629, 630, imperf 4.50 4.50
b. Pair, #629-630 4.50 4.50

Peace Corps in Tonga, 20th anniv.

Intl. Sporting Events — A118

Designs: 42s, 1986 Field Hockey World Cup, London. 57s, Women's basketball, 13th Commonwealth Games, Scotland. 1pa, Boxing, Commonwealth Games. 2.50pa, 1986 World Cup Soccer Championships, Mexico.

1986, July 23 Litho. ***Perf. 14***
631 A118 42s multicolored 1.25 1.25
632 A118 57s multicolored 2.00 2.00
633 A118 1pa multicolored 3.25 3.25
634 A118 2.50pa multicolored 6.00 6.00
Nos. 631-634 (4) 12.50 12.50

Postage Stamp Cent. — A119

Stamps on stamps: No. 635, #1. No. 636, #47a. No. 637, #91. No. 638, #628. No. 639a, #40, UL portion of #C29. No. 639b, UR portion of #C29, left side #245. No. 639c, Center of #245, Type AP10. No. 639d, Left side #245, #C148. No. 639e, LL portion of #C29, #429, #440. No. 639f, LR portion of #C29, #C135. No. 639g, #507. No. 639h, #514. Nos. 639a-639h, vert.

1986, Aug. 27
635 A119 32s multi 2.50 1.75
636 A119 42s multi 2.75 2.00
637 A119 57s multi 3.00 2.00
638 A119 2.50pa multi 5.00 5.75
Nos. 635-638 (4) 13.25 11.50

Souvenir Sheet
639 Sheet of 8 13.50 13.50
a.-h. A119 50s, any single 1.50 1.50

Christmas A120

Designs: 32s, Girls wearing shell jewelry. 42s, Boy, totem poles, vert. 57s, Folk dancers, vert. 2pa, outrigger canoe.

1986, Nov. 12 Litho. ***Perf. 14***
640 A120 32s multicolored 2.50 .75
641 A120 42s multicolored 2.75 1.00
642 A120 57s multicolored 3.00 1.50
643 A120 2pa multicolored 7.50 7.50
Nos. 640-643 (4) 15.75 10.75

Nos. 641-642 Ovptd. with Jamboree Emblem and "BOY SCOUT / JAMBOREE / 5th-10th DEC '86" in Silver

1986, Dec. 2 Litho. ***Perf. 14***
644 A120 42s multicolored 3.50 3.50
645 A120 57s multicolored 3.75 3.75

Dumont d'Urville's Second Voyage — A121

Designs: 32s, D'Urville and ship Astrolabe. 42s, Four Tongan girls, detail fron D'Urville's engraving, Voyage au Pole et dans l'Oceanie. 1pa, Map of voyage. 2.50pa, Wreck of the Astrolabe.

1987, Feb. 24
646 A121 32s multicolored 4.25 2.00
647 A121 42s multicolored 4.25 2.00
648 A121 1pa multicolored 10.00 6.00
649 A121 2.50pa multicolored 16.00 16.00
Nos. 646-649 (4) 34.50 26.00

Dumont d'Urville (1790-1842), explorer and admiral.

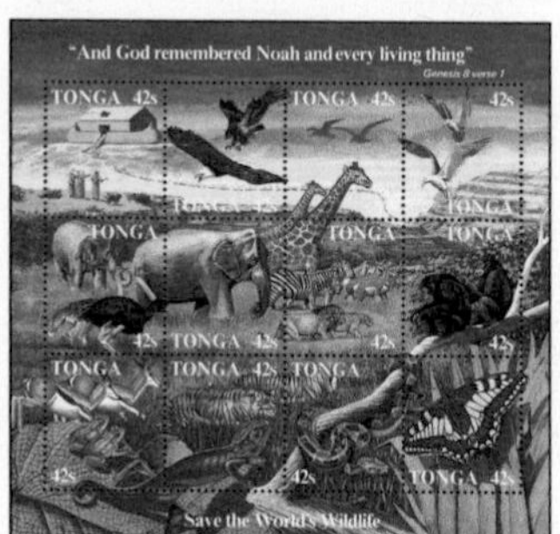

Wildlife Conservation — A122

Fauna: a, Noah's Ark. b, Eagles. c, Giraffes, birds. d, Seagulls. e, Elephants, ostriches. f, Elephant. g, Lions, zebras, antelopes. h, Chimpanzees. i, Antelope, frogs. j, Tigers, lizard. k, Tiger, snake. l, Butterfly.

1987, May 6 ***Perf. 13½***
650 A122 Sheet of 12 55.00 55.00
a.-l. 42s any single 4.00 4.00

1st Inter-island Canoe Race, Tonga to Samoa — A123

1987, July 1 ***Perf. 14***
651 A123 32s Two paddlers .55 .45
652 A123 42s Five paddlers .85 .70
653 A123 57s Three paddlers 1.10 .90
654 A123 1.50pa Two, diff. 2.50 2.50
a. Souvenir sheet of 4, #651-654 7.75 7.75
Nos. 651-654 (4) 5.00 4.55

Coronation of King Taufa'ahau IV, 20th Anniv. — A124

Booklet Stamps
1987-88 Self-Adhesive ***Imperf.***
655 A124 1s green & yel grn .35 *.85*
655A A124 2s blk & pale yel org 4.00 4.00
656 A124 5s black & brt pink .35 *.85*
a. Bklt. pane of 12 (6 5s plus 1 5s, 2 10s, 3 15s with gutter between) 5.00
657 A124 10s black & bluish lil .45 *.95*
658 A124 15s brn blk & org ver .60 *.95*
a. Bklt. pane of 12 (1s, 2 2s, 3 10s, plus 2 5s, 10s, 3 15s with gutter between) ('88) 14.00
659 A124 32s Prus bl & aqua .70 *1.00*
a. Bklt. pane, 4 32s, 2 15s + 4 10s, 2 1s with gutter between) 7.00
b. Bklt. pane, 6 32s + 2 2s, 4 1s with gutter btwn. ('88) 14.00
Nos. 655-659 (6) 6.45 8.60

Issued: 2s, 7/4/88; others, 7/1/87.

Parliament, 125th Anniv. — A125

1987, Sept. 2 Litho. ***Perf. 14½***
660 A125 32s multicolored .50 .50
661 A125 42s multicolored .75 .75
662 A125 75s multicolored 1.25 1.25
663 A125 2pa multicolored 2.75 2.75
Nos. 660-663 (4) 5.25 5.25

Christmas 1987 — A126

Cartoons featuring Octopus as Santa Claus and mouse as his helper: 42s, Sack of gifts. 57s, Delivering them by canoe. 1pa, By automobile. 3pa, Sipping tropical drinks.

1987, Nov. 18 Litho. ***Perf. 14***
664 A126 42s multicolored 1.25 .80
665 A126 57s multicolored 1.50 1.50
666 A126 1pa multicolored 3.00 3.00
667 A126 3pa multicolored 6.50 6.50
Nos. 664-667 (4) 12.25 11.80

King Taufa'ahau Tupou IV, 70th Birthday — A127

Portrait and: 32s, M.V. *Olovaha* inter-island ship, athlete pole vaulting and offshore oil derrick. 42s, Banknote and coins, Ha'Amonga Trilithon and traditional craftsman. 57s, Rowing, Red Cross nurse and communications satellite. 2.50pa, Tonga Scouts emblem, No. 506 and Friendly Islands Airways passenger plane.

1988, July 4 Litho. ***Perf. 11½***
668 A127 32s multicolored 2.50 1.00
669 A127 42s multicolored 1.75 1.10
670 A127 57s multicolored 1.90 1.10
671 A127 2.50pa multicolored 8.75 8.00
Nos. 668-671 (4) 14.90 11.20

See Nos. 744-747 for stamps inscribed for the silver jubilee.

Souvenir Sheet

Australia Bicentennial — A128

Designs: a, Cook and his journal. b, List of stores shipped aboard the *Lady Juliana,* the ship, Arthur Philip, 1st gov. of New South Wales, 1788, and left half of the list of sentences of all the prisoners tried at Glo'ster Assizes. c, Right half of list of sentences, Australia Type A59 redrawn and aerial view of an early settlement. d, Robert O'Hara Burke (1820-61) and W.J. Wills (1834-61), the 1st explorers to cross Australia from south to north. e, Emu pictured on a Player's cigarette card, U.R. Stuart's (gold) prospecting license and opals. f, Australian Commonwealth Military Forces emblem, WW I recruit on cigarette card, and war poster. g, Souv. card commemorating 1st overland mail delivery by transcontinental railway, and Australia Type A4 on cover. h, Hand-canceled cover commemorating the 1st England-Australia transcontinental airmail flight, Nov. 12-Dec.10, 1919, aviator Capt. Ross Smith (1892-1922) and Great Britain #588. i, Don Bradman and Harold Larwood, cricket champions of the 1930s, on cigarette cards, and era newspaper frontispiece. j, Frontispiece of Hulton's natl. weekly *Picture Post* Victory Special issue, and WW II campaign medals. k, Australia #676 and a sheep station. l, Sydney Harbor Bridge, Opera House and theater tickets to *The Bartered Bride.*

1988, July 11 Litho. *Perf. 13½*
672 A128 Sheet of 12 45.00 45.00
a.-l. 42s any single 3.00 3.00

1988 Summer Olympics, Seoul — A129

57s, Running. 75s, Yachting. 2pa, Cycling. 3pa, Women's tennis.

1988, Aug. 11 *Perf. 14*
673 A129 57s multicolored .90 .90
674 A129 75s multicolored 1.10 1.10
675 A129 2pa multicolored 7.00 7.00
676 A129 3pa multicolored 6.50 6.50
Nos. 673-676 (4) 15.50 15.50

Music of Tonga — A130

42s, Choir. 57s, Tonga Police Band. 2.50pa, The Jets.
No. 681b, Olympic eternal flame.

1988, Sept. 9 Litho. *Perf. 14*
677 A130 32s shown .40 .40
678 A130 42s multi .50 .50
679 A130 57s multi 1.25 1.00
680 A130 2.50pa multi 3.00 3.00
Nos. 677-680 (4) 5.15 4.90

Souvenir Sheet

681 Sheet of 2 3.00 3.00
a. A130 57s like 2.50pa 1.25 1.25
b. A130 57s multicolored 1.25 1.25

SPORT AID '88.

Marine Type of 1984

Two types of background shading on No. 690:
Type I: Shading at top and sides extends to vert. & horiz. edges of design.
Type II: Shading is oval shaped.

1988 Litho. *Perf. 14½*
Size: 27x34mm
682 A103 1s like No. 563 .30 .30
683 A103 2s like No. 564 .40 .40
684 A103 5s like No. 566 .55 .55
685 A103 6s like No. 567 1.10 1.10
686 A103 10s like No. 569 .65 .65
687 A103 15s like No. 571 .65 .65
688 A103 20s like No. 572 .95 .95
689 A103 32s like No. 574 1.10 1.10
690 A103 42s Fregata ariel, type I 4.00 .95
a. Type II 35.00
691 A103 57s Sula leucogaster 4.75 1.25
Size: 41x27mm
Perf. 14
692 A103 3pa Like No. 578 3.00 *9.00*
Nos. 682-692 (11) 17.45 16.90

Issued: 1s, 5s, 10s, 20s, 32s, Oct. 4; 2s, 6s, 15s, 42s, 57s, 3pa, Oct. 18.
Nos. 683-684, 686, 689 exist inscribed "1990."

See #701-709. For surcharge see #808.

Tonga-US Treaty, Cent. — A131

42s, Resolution. 57s, Santa Maria. 2pa, Capt. Cook, Columbus.

1988, Oct. 20 *Perf. 14*
693 A131 42s multicolored 1.00 .75
694 A131 57s multicolored 1.50 1.10
695 A131 2pa multicolored 4.50 4.50
a. Souvenir sheet of 3, #693-695 6.50 6.50
Nos. 693-695 (3) 7.00 6.35

Christmas — A132

Designs (a, Intl. Red Cross, b, Natl. Red Cross): 15s, Girl, teddy bear. 32s, Nurse reading to child. 42s, Checking pulse. 57s, Tucking child into bed. 1.50pa, Boy in wheelchair.

1988, Nov. 17 Litho. *Perf. 14½*
696 A132 15s Pair, #a.-b. .50 .50
697 A132 32s Pair, #a.-b. 1.00 1.00
698 A132 42s Pair, #a.-b. 1.10 1.10
699 A132 57s Pair, #a.-b. 1.90 1.90
700 A132 1.50pa Pair, #a.-b. 3.75 3.75
Nos. 696-700 (5) 8.25 8.25

Intl. Red Cross 125th anniv. and 25th anniv. of the natl. Red Cross.

Marine Type of 1984

7s, Diomedea exulans. 35s, Hippocampus. 1pa, Chelonia mydas. 1.50pa, Megaptera novaeangliae.

1989, Mar. 2 Litho.
Size: 27x34mm
701 A103 4s like No. 570 1.90 1.90
702 A103 7s multicolored 4.50 3.00
703 A103 35s multicolored 4.00 3.25
704 A103 50s like No. 573 4.50 2.40
Size: 41x27mm
Perf. 14
705 A103 1pa multicolored 7.25 5.50
706 A103 1.50pa multicolored 14.50 9.00
707 A103 2pa like No. 577 10.50 10.50
709 A103 5pa like No. 579 17.00 *20.00*
Nos. 701-709 (8) 64.15 55.55

Mutiny on the *Bounty,* Bicent. A133

32s, Map of Tofua & Kao Isls., breadfruit. 42s, *Bounty,* chronometer. 57s, William Bligh & castaways in longboat. 2pa, Mutineers on the *Bounty,* vert. 3pa, Castaways.

Perf. 13½x14, 14x13½
1989, Apr. 28 Photo.
710 A133 32s multicolored 4.50 2.50
711 A133 42s multicolored 6.50 3.25
712 A133 57s multicolored 8.00 4.75
Nos. 710-712 (3) 19.00 10.50

Souvenir Sheet

713 Sheet of 2 15.00 15.00
a. A133 2pa multicolored 5.00 5.00
b. A133 3pa multicolored 7.50 7.50

Butterflies — A134

42s, Hypolimnas bolina. 57s, Jamides bochus. 1.20pa, Melanitis leda solandra. 2.50pa, Danaus plexippus.

1989, May 15 Litho. *Perf. 14½*
714 A134 42s multi 1.25 .85
715 A134 57s multi 1.50 1.10
716 A134 1.20pa multi 3.75 2.75
717 A134 2.50pa multi 5.50 5.50
Nos. 714-717 (4) 12.00 10.20

A135

Rugby (No. 718): a, Rugby Public School, 1870. b, Dave Gallaher and the Springboks vs. East Midlands, 1906. c, King George V inspecting Cambridge team of 1922 and Wavell Wakefield, captain of England. d, Ernie Crawford, captain of Ireland, Danie Craven demonstrating the dive pass and cigarette cards from the 1930's. e, Sioni Mafi, captain of Tonga, and match scene.
Tennis (No. 719): a, Royal tennis, 1659. b, Walter Clopton Wingfield and game of lawn tennis, 1873. c, Oxford and Cambridge teams of 1884. d, Bunny Ryan in 1910 and cigarette cards. e, Tennis players, 1980's.
Cricket (No. 720): a, Match in 1743 and bronze memorial to Fuller Pilch. b, W.G. Grace, 19th cent. c, *The Boys Own Paper,* 1909. d, Australian team of 1909 and cigarette cards. e, The Ashes trophy and modern match scene.

1989, Aug. 22 Litho. *Perf. 14*
718 Strip of 5 6.25 6.25
a.-e. A135 32s any single 1.00 1.00
719 Strip of 5 9.50 9.50
a.-e. A135 42s any single 1.50 1.50
720 Strip of 5 14.50 14.50
a.-e. A135 57s any single 2.50 2.50
Nos. 718-720 (3) 30.25 30.25

Opening of the Natl. Sports Stadium and the South Pacific Mini Games, Aug. 22.
Printed in sheets of 10 containing descriptions and emblem.

Natl. Aviation History — A136

Designs: 42s, Short S30. 57s, Vought F4U Corsair. 90s, Boeing 737. 3pa, Montgolfier brothers' hot-air balloon, the Wright Flyer, Concorde jet and space shuttle.

1989, Oct. 23 Litho. *Perf. 14½x14*
721 A136 42s multicolored 3.25 1.60
722 A136 57s multicolored 3.75 2.00
723 A136 90s multicolored 6.50 6.00
Size: 97x126½mm
724 A136 3pa multicolored 16.00 16.00
Nos. 721-724 (4) 29.50 25.60

1st Flight to Tonga, 1939 (42s); military base on the island, 1943 (57s); civil aviation, Fua'amotu Airport (90s); aviation through the ages (3pa).

Flying Home for Christmas — A137

32s, Aircraft landing. 42s, Islanders waving, aircraft. 57s, Tongan in outrigger canoe, aircraft. 3pa, Islanders waving, aircraft, diff.

1989, Nov. 9 *Perf. 14x13½*
725 A137 32s multi 2.40 1.10
726 A137 42s multi 2.75 1.10
727 A137 57s multi 3.00 1.50
728 A137 3pa multi 8.00 8.00
Nos. 725-728 (4) 16.15 11.70

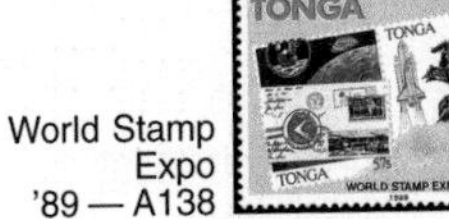

World Stamp Expo '89 — A138

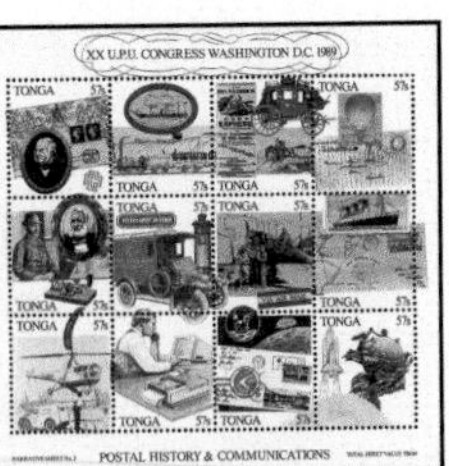
20th UPU Congress, Washington, DC — A139

Postal history and communications (No. 730): a, Sir Rowland Hill, penny blacks on Mulready envelope. b, Clipper ship, early train. c, Pony Express advertisement, stagecoach, post rider. d, Hot-air balloon and flight cover. e, Samuel Morse, miniature, telegraph key. f, Early Royal Mail truck, mailbox. g, Biplane and early aviators. h, Zeppelin flight cover, HMS *Queen Mary.* i, Helicopter, truck. j, Computer operator, facsimile machine. k, Apollo 11 mission emblem, flight cover, planetary bodies. l, American space shuttle, UPU monument.

1989, Nov. 17 Litho. *Perf. 14*
729 A138 57s #730k-730l 3.50 3.50

Souvenir Sheet
Perf. 13½
730 A139 Sheet of 12 47.50 47.50
a.-l. A139 57s any single 2.75 2.75

A140

1990, Feb. 14 Litho. *Perf. 14*
731 A140 42s Boxing 1.25 .75
732 A140 57s Archery 2.25 1.50
733 A140 1pa Bowls 2.50 2.50
734 A140 2pa Swimming 4.50 4.50
Nos. 731-734 (4) 10.50 9.25

1990 Commonwealth Games.

Protect the Environment — A141

32s, Wave power, ocean pollution. 57s, Wind power, acid rain. $1.20, Solar power, ozone layer. $2.50, Green earth, rain forests.

1990, Apr. 11 Litho. *Perf. 14*
735 A141 32s multicolored 2.00 .90
736 A141 57s multicolored 3.00 1.50
737 A141 1.20pa multicolored 6.00 6.00
Nos. 735-737 (3) 11.00 8.40

Souvenir Sheet

738 A141 2.50pa multicolored 11.00 11.00

First Postage Stamps, 150th Anniv. — A142

1990 Litho. *Perf. 14*
739 A142 42s G. B. #1 2.10 1.50
740 A142 42s G. B. #2 2.10 1.50
a. Pair, #739-740 3.75 3.75
741 A142 57s Tonga #1 2.50 1.50
742 A142 1.50pa Tonga #CO180 5.00 5.00
743 A142 2.50pa Tonga #736 7.00 7.00
Nos. 739-743 (5) 18.70 16.50

King's Birthday Type of 1988 Inscribed "Silver Jubilee of His Majesty King Taufa'ahau Tupou IV 1965-1990"

1990, July 4 Litho. *Perf. 11½*
744 A127 32s like No. 668 1.50 1.00
745 A127 42s like No. 669 1.50 1.00
746 A127 57s like No. 670 2.25 1.25
747 A127 2.50pa like No. 671 7.75 7.75
Nos. 744-747 (4) 13.00 11.00

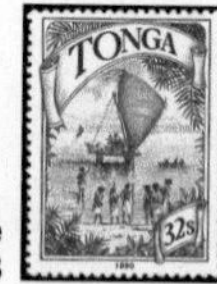

Native Catamaran — A143

1990, June 6 *Perf. 14½*

No.	Type	Denom.	Description	Unused	Used
748	A143	32s	buff & green	1.60	.75
749	A143	42s	buff & bl, diff.	1.60	.85
750	A143	1.20pa	buff & brn, diff.	3.75	3.75
751	A143	3pa	buff & vio, diff.	7.00	7.00
			Nos. 748-751 (4)	13.95	12.35

Banded Iguana — A144

1990, Sept. 12 Litho. *Perf. 14*

No.	Type	Denom.	Description	Unused	Used
752	A144	32s	multicolored	2.00	1.25
753	A144	42s	multi, diff.	2.50	1.75
754	A144	57s	multi, diff.	3.25	2.25
755	A144	1.20pa	multi, diff.	6.25	4.75
			Nos. 752-755 (4)	14.00	10.00

Marine Type of 1984

1990, July 6 Litho. *Perf. 14*

Size: 20x22mm

No.	Type	Denom.	Description	Unused	Used
756	A103	2s	like No. 564	1.25	.85
a.			Booklet pane of 10	12.50	12.50
757	A103	5s	like No. 566	1.25	.85
a.			Booklet pane of 10	12.50	12.50
758	A103	10s	like No. 569	1.25	.85
a.			Booklet pane of 10	12.50	12.50
759	A103	32s	like No. 574	2.25	2.25
a.			Booklet pane of 10	22.50	22.50
			Nos. 756-759 (4)	6.00	4.80

Nos. 756-758 exist inscribed "1992."
For surcharges see Nos. 809-810.
Issue date: #756a-759a, Sept. 4.

UN Development Program, 40th Anniv. A145

No. 760, Tourism. No. 761, Agriculture, fisheries. No. 762, Education. No. 763, Healthcare.

1990, Oct. 25 Litho. *Perf. 14*

No.	Type	Denom.	Description	Unused	Used
760	A145	57s	multicolored	2.00	2.00
761	A145	57s	multicolored	2.00	2.00
a.			Pair, #760-761	4.50	4.50
762	A145	3pa	multicolored	8.00	8.00
763	A145	3pa	multicolored	8.00	8.00
a.			Pair, #762-763	18.50	18.50
			Nos. 760-763 (4)	20.00	20.00

Rotary Intl. — A146

1990, Nov. 28

No.	Type	Denom.	Description	Unused	Used
764	A146	32s	shown	1.00	.55
765	A146	42s	Two boys	1.50	.80
766	A146	2pa	Three children	4.00	4.00
767	A146	3pa	Two girls	5.50	5.50
			Nos. 764-767 (4)	12.00	10.85

Accident Prevention — A147

No. 768: a, d, Care at work; hard hats save lives. b, c, Keep matches and medicines out of children's reach. e, as "d," corrected inscription

No. 769: a, d, Don't drink and drive. b, c, Crash helmets save lives; mind cyclists and children.

No. 770: a, d, Listen to forecasts; learn to swim. b, c, Swim from safe beaches; beware of broken glass.

"a" and "b" have English inscriptions, denominations at top; "c" and "d" have Tongan inscriptions, denominations at bottom.

Strips of 4 + Label

1991, Apr. 10 Litho. *Perf. 14½*

No.	Type	Denom.	Description	Unused	Used
768	A147	32s	#a.-d.	4.50	4.50
f.			Strip of 4, #a.-c., e.	35.00	
769	A147	42s	#a.-d.	7.50	7.50
770	A147	57s	#a.-d.	8.50	8.50
			Nos. 768-770 (3)	20.50	20.50

Center label is a progressive proof.

No. 768d was incorrectly inscribed, "Ngauo tokanga." No. 768e was issued 8/11/91 with correct inscription, "Ngaue tokanga."

For surcharges see No. 811, 1124.

Heilala Week — A148

1991, July 2 Litho. *Perf. 14½*

No.	Type	Denom.	Description	Unused	Used
771	A148	42s	Fish	.75	.65
772	A148	57s	Island, boat	.90	.80
773	A148	2pa	Fruit, island	3.25	3.25
774	A148	3pa	Turtle, beach	5.75	5.75
			Nos. 771-774 (4)	10.65	10.45

Around the World Yacht Race — A149

Racing yachts: a, Red spinnaker. b, Yellow spinnaker. c, Green striped spinnaker. d, Yacht at sunset. e, Yacht, moon.

Miniature Sheet of 5 + Label

1991, July 2

No.	Type	Denom.	Description	Unused	Used
775	A149	1pa	#775a-775e	11.00	11.00

Church of Jesus Christ of Latter Day Saints in Tonga, Cent. — A150

1991, Aug. 19

No.	Type	Denom.	Description	Unused	Used
776	A150	42s	Tonga Temple	1.25	1.25
777	A150	57s	Temple at night	2.00	2.00

Rowing Festival — A151

42s, Women's coxed eight. 57s, Men's longboat. 1pa, Outrigger. No. 781, Bow of large canoe. No. 782, Stern of large canoe.

1991, Oct. 29 Litho. *Perf. 14*

No.	Type	Denom.	Description	Unused	Used
778	A151	42s	multicolored	1.00	1.00
779	A151	57s	multicolored	1.50	1.50
780	A151	1pa	multicolored	2.75	2.75
781	A151	2pa	multicolored	4.50	4.50
782	A151	2pa	multicolored	4.50	4.50
a.			Pair, #781-782	9.00	9.00
			Nos. 778-782 (5)	14.25	14.25

For surcharges see Nos. 898-899C.

Telecommunications — A152

No. 783: a, Recording television program. b, Communications Satellite. c, Watching television program.

No. 784: a, Man on telephone, woman at computer. b, Communications satellite, diff. c, Man in city on telephone.

No. 785: a, Seaman on sinking ship broadcasting SOS. b, Man on telephone, satellite relay station. c, Rescue missions.

No. 786: a, Weather satelite. b, Men at computers. c, Television weather report, storm.

1991, Oct. 15 Litho. *Perf. 14½*

No.	Type	Denom.	Description	Unused	Used
783	A152	15s	Strip of 3, #a.-c.	1.25	1.25
784	A152	32s	Strip of 3, #a.-c.	2.75	2.75
785	A152	42s	Strip of 3, #a.-c.	4.00	4.00
786	A152	57s	Strip of 3, #a.-c.	5.50	5.50
			Nos. 783-786 (4)	13.50	13.50

For surcharges, see 1095-1098.

Christmas A153

Designs: 32s, Turtles pulling Santa's sleigh. 42s, Santa on roof. 57s, Family with presents. 3.50pa, Waving goodbye to Santa.

1991, Nov. 11 *Perf. 14*

No.	Type	Denom.	Description	Unused	Used
787	A153	32s	multicolored	1.00	.70
788	A153	42s	multicolored	1.25	.90
789	A153	57s	multicolored	1.75	1.75
790	A153	3.50pa	multicolored	8.25	8.25
			Nos. 787-790 (4)	12.25	11.60

For surcharges, see 1120-1122.

Armed Forces A154

1991, Dec. 15

No.	Type	Denom.	Description	Unused	Used
791		42s	Royal Tonga Marine	1.00	1.00
792		42s	Patrol boat Pangai	1.00	1.00
a.	A154		Pair, #791-792	2.50	2.50
793		57s	Patrol boat Neiafu	1.50	1.50
794		57s	Tonga Royal Guards	1.50	1.50
a.	A154		Pair, #793-794	3.50	3.50
795		2pa	King Tupou IV, military parade	5.25	5.25
796		2pa	Patrol boat Savea	5.25	5.25
a.	A154		Pair, #795-796	11.00	11.00
			Nos. 791-796 (6)	15.50	15.50

Miniature Sheet

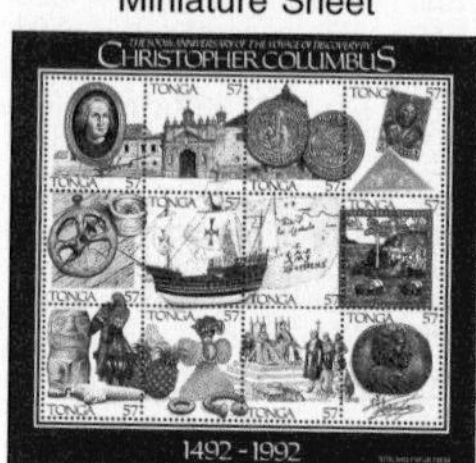

Discovery of America, 500th Anniv. — A155

Designs: a, Columbus. b, Monastery of Santa Maria de la Chevas. c, Obverse and reverse of coin of Ferdinand and Isabella. d, Spain #C48, #426. e, Compass, astrolabe. f, Santa Maria. g, Map, Columbus' signature. h, Columbus arriving in New World. i, Lucayan artifacts, parrot. j, Pineapple, artifacts. k, Columbus announcing his discovery. l, Medal of Columbus, signature.

1992, Apr. 28 Litho. *Perf. 13½*

No.	Type	Denom.	Description	Unused	Used
797	A155	57s	Sheet of 12, #a.-l.	42.50	42.50

Marine Type of 1984 and

A155a

1s, Swainsonia casta. 3s, Holocentrus ruber. 5s, Cypraea mappa viridis. 10s, Conus bullatus. 20s, Dascyllus aruanus. 45s, Lambis truncata. 60s, Conus aulicus. 80s, Pterois volitans.

Perf. 13x13½, 14 (15s, 20s, 10pa)

1992-93 Litho.

No.	Type	Denom.	Description	Unused	Used
798	A155a	1s	multicolored	.25	.25
799	A155a	3s	multicolored	.25	.25
800	A155a	5s	multicolored	.25	.25
801	A155a	10s	multicolored	.25	.25
802	A103	15s	like #567	.30	.30
803	A155a	20s	multicolored	.35	.35
804	A155a	45s	multicolored	.75	.75
805	A155a	60s	multicolored	1.00	1.00
806	A155a	80s	multicolored	1.40	1.40

Size: 27x41mm

No.	Type	Denom.	Description	Unused	Used
807	A103	10pa	like #568	20.00	20.00
			Nos. 798-807 (10)	24.80	24.80

Issued: 1s, 3s, 5s, 10s, 20s, 45s, 60s, 80s, May 12, 1993. 15s, 10pa, May 5, 1992.

See Nos. 874-884. Area covered by background colors on Nos. 874, 876-879 has been reduced in size. See Nos. 920-924.

For inscribed stamps see Nos. O78-O87.

Surcharges

On #688

On #756 in Blue

On #759

On #769 in Red and Black

1992-93 Litho. *Perf. 14½, 14*

No.	Type	Denom.	Description	Unused	Used
808	A103	1s	on 20s #688	.25	.25
809	A103	10s	on 2s #756	65.00	65.00
810	A103	45s	on 32s #759	4.00	4.00
811	A147	60s	on 42s Strip of 4, #a.-d. + label	16.00	16.00

Issued: 1s, 5/19; 45s, 60s, 8/11; 10s, 3/29/93.

Miniature Sheet

World War II in Pacific, 50th Anniv. — A156

Designs: a, Newspaper headline, Japanese attack on Pearl Harbor. b, Map of Bataan, Corregidor, and Manila, pilot's wings, airplanes. c, Newspaper headline, troops landing in Gilbert Islands, Marine Corps emblem, dogtags. d, Uniform patch, B-29 "Enola Gay," troops landing on Iwo Jima. e, Map of Battle of Midway, Admiral Nimitz. f, Southwest Pacific campaign map, Gen. MacArthur. g, Map of Saipan and Tinian, Lt. Gen. Holland Smith. h, Map outling bombing of Japan, Maj. Gen. Curtis Lemay. i, Mitsubishi A6M Zero. j, Douglas SBD Dauntless. k, Grumman F4F Wildcat. l, Supermarine Seafire.

1992, May 26 Litho. *Perf. 14*

No.	Type	Denom.	Description	Unused	Used
814	A156	42s	Sheet of 12, #a.-l.	30.00	30.00

1992 Summer Olympics, Barcelona — A157

1992, June 16

No.	Type	Denom.	Description	Unused	Used
815	A157	42s	Boxing	1.10	.85
816	A157	57s	Diving	1.50	1.10
817	A157	1.50pa	Tennis	4.00	4.00
818	A157	3pa	Cycling	8.50	8.50
			Nos. 815-818 (4)	15.10	14.45

For surcharges, see 1123, 1125.

King Taufa'ahau IV, 25th Anniv. of Coronation — A158

Designs: 45s, 2pa, King, Queen Halaevalu. No. 820a, King, crown. b, Extract from investiture ceremony. c, King, #C33.

1992, July 4 *Perf. 13½x13*

No.	Type	Denom.	Description	Unused	Used
819	A158	45s	multicolored	1.25	.90

Size: 51x38mm
Perf. 12½x12

820 A158 80s Strip of 3, #a.-c. 6.00 6.00
821 A158 2pa multicolored 5.00 5.00
Nos. 819-821 (3) 12.25 11.90

Sacred Bats of Kolovai A159

Designs: No. 822a, Bats in flight. b, Close-up of flying bat. c, Flying bats, tree. d, Bats hanging in tree. e, Bat hanging from tree limb.
Origin of sacred bats: No. 823a, 45s, Kula leaving for Upolu to be tattooed as Tongan chief. b, 45s, Kula looking through path of fires. c, 2pa, Kula walking down path, Hina. d, 2pa, Hina waving, Kula leaving with pet fruit bats.
Nos. 823a-823d are horiz.

1992, Oct. 20 Litho. *Perf. 14*
822 A159 60s Strip of 5, #a.-e. 12.00 12.00

Souvenir Sheet
Perf. 14½

823 A159 Sheet of 4, #a.-d. 13.00 13.00

Christmas A160

1992, Nov. 10 *Perf. 14*
824 A160 60s Pearls 1.25 1.10
825 A160 80s Reef fish 1.50 1.40
826 A160 2pa Pacific orchids 4.75 4.75
827 A160 3pa Eua parrots 6.50 6.50
Nos. 824-827 (4) 14.00 13.75

For surcharges see Nos. 894-897.

Anniversaries and Events — A161

Designs: 60s, Tonga flag, Rotary emblem. 80sh, John F. Kennedy, Peace Corps emblem. 1.50pa, FAO, WHO emblems. 3.50pa, Globe, Rotary Foundation emblem.

1992, Dec. 15 *Perf. 14½*
828 A161 60s multicolored 1.40 1.00
829 A161 80s multicolored 1.90 1.40
830 A161 1.50pa multicolored 3.50 3.50
831 A161 3.50pa multicolored 6.50 6.50
Nos. 828-831 (4) 13.30 12.40

Rotary Intl. in Tonga, 25th anniv. (#828). Peace Corps in Tonga, 25th anniv. (#829). Intl. Conference of FAO and WHO (#830). Rotary Foundation of Rotary Intl., 75th anniv. (#831).
For overprint see No. 869.

Family Planning A163

Outdoor silhouette scenes: No. 832, Mother, girl, butterflies. No. 833, Child on tricycle pulling kite. No. 834, Girl, kittens. No. 835, Adult, child playing chess.

1993, Jan. 26 *Perf. 14x13½*
832 A163 15s Pair, #a.-b. 2.50 2.50
833 A163 45s Pair, #a.-b. 3.50 3.50
834 A163 60s Pair, #a.-b. 5.00 5.00
835 A163 2pa Pair, #a.-b. 15.00 15.00
Nos. 832-835 (4) 26.00 26.00

Nos. 832a-835a have Tongan inscriptions. Nos. 832b-835b have English inscriptions and are mirror images of Nos. 832a-835a.

Health and Fitness A164

Designs: 60s, Fresh fruit, fish, anti-smoking and anti-drug symbols. 80s, Anti-smoking symbol, weight training. 1.50pa, Anti-drug symbol, water sports. 2.50pa, Fresh fruit, fish, cyclist, jogger.

1993, Mar. 16 Litho. *Perf. 14*
836 A164 60s multicolored 2.00 2.00
837 A164 80s multicolored 2.75 2.75
838 A164 1.50pa multicolored 3.50 3.50
839 A164 2.50pa multicolored 6.50 6.50
Nos. 836-839 (4) 14.75 14.75

Tonga Fire Service, 25th Anniv. A165

No. 840, Fireman's badge. No. 841, Police van, badge. No. 842, Police band. No. 843, Putting out fire. No. 844, Fire truck at station. No. 845, Policeman, police dog.

1993, May 18 Litho. *Perf. 14*
840 45s multi 2.00 2.00
841 45s multi 2.00 2.00
a. A165 Pair, #840-841 4.50 3.50
842 60s multi 2.50 2.50
843 60s multi 2.50 2.50
a. A165 Pair, #842-843 5.50 4.50
844 2pa multi 7.00 7.00
845 2pa multi 7.00 7.00
a. A165 Pair, #844-845 16.00 14.00
Nos. 840-845 (6) 23.00 23.00

Tonga Police Training College, 25th anniv. (#841-842, 845).
For surcharges see Nos. 943-948.

A166

Abel Tasman's Voyage to Eua, 350th Anniv.: 30s, Map of islands. 60s, Sailing ships, Heemskirk and Zeehaen. 80s, Sailing ships, natives in canoes. 3.50pa, Landing on Eua.

1993, June 21
846 A166 30s multicolored .80 .50
847 A166 60s multicolored 1.75 1.10
848 A166 80s multicolored 2.00 2.00
849 A166 3.50pa multicolored 8.25 8.25
Nos. 846-849 (4) 12.80 11.85

A167

King Taufa'ahau IV, 75th Birthday: 45s, 2pa, Musical instruments.
No. 851a, Sporting events. b, Ancient landmarks. c, Royal Palace.

1993, July 1 Litho. *Perf. 13x13½*
850 A167 45s multicolored .65 .65

Perf. 12x12½
Size: 37x48mm

851 A167 80s Strip of 3, #a.-c. 4.50 4.50
852 A167 2pa multicolored 3.00 3.00
Nos. 850-852 (3) 8.15 8.15

A168

Children's Stamp Designs: Nos. 853a, 854a, Beach scene. Nos. 853b, 854b, "Maui-The Fisher of the Islands." Nos. 853c, 854c, Raft on ocean. Nos. 853d, 854d, Woman with hands in mixing bowl. Nos. 853e, 854e, "Maui and his Hook." Nos. 853f, 854f, "Communication in the South Pacific."

1993, Dec. 1 Litho. *Perf. 14*
853 A168 10s Strip of 6, #a.-f. 2.50 2.50
854 A168 80s Strip of 6, #a.-f. 12.50 12.50

A168a

Christmas traditions: 60s, Festive dinner. 80s, Shooting cannon. 1.50pa, Musicians. 3pa, Going to church.

1993, Nov. 10 Litho. *Perf. 14*
855 A168a 60s multicolored 1.50 1.25
856 A168a 80s multicolored 2.00 1.50
857 A168a 1.50pa multicolored 3.25 3.25
858 A168a 3pa multicolored 6.00 6.00
Nos. 855-858 (4) 12.75 12.00

Miniature Sheet

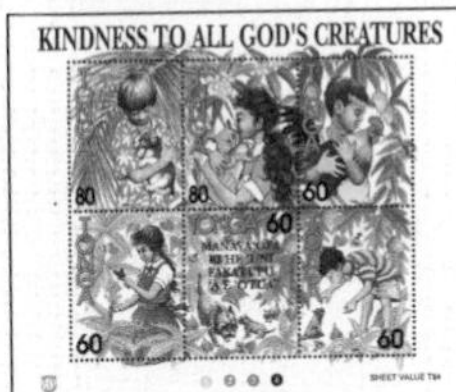

Kindness to Animals A169

Designs: a, 80s, Boy holding puppy. b, 80s, Girl holding kitten. c, 60s, Boy holding rooster (b). d, 60s, Girl with butterfly. e, 60s, Three dogs. f, 60s, Boy, puppy.

1994, Jan. 14 *Perf. 14½*
859 A169 Sheet of 6, #a.-f. 15.00 15.00

For overprint see No. 868.

Game Fishing A170

60s, Tiger shark. 80s, Dolphin fish. 1.50pa, Yellow fin tuna. 2.50pa, Pacific blue marlin.

1994, Feb. 28 Litho. *Perf. 12*
860 A170 60s multicolored 1.50 1.00
861 A170 80s multicolored 2.00 1.40
862 A170 1.50pa multicolored 3.50 3.50
863 A170 2.50pa multicolored 5.00 5.00
Nos. 860-863 (4) 12.00 10.90

1994 World Cup Soccer Championships, US — A171

Designs: No. 864a, Player's legs. No. 864b, World Cup trophy. No. 865a, American player in red, white, & blue. No. 865b, German player in black shorts, white shirt.

1994, June 1 *Perf. 14x14½*
864 A171 80s Pair, #a.-b. 4.00 4.00
865 A171 2pa Pair, #a.-b. 8.00 8.00

Pan Pacific & South East Asia Women's Assoc. Conference — A172

Career women: No. 866a, Lawyer. No. 866b, Policewoman. No. 867a, Doctor. No. 867b. Nurse.

1994, Aug. 18 Litho. *Perf. 14*
866 A172 45s Pair, #a.-b. 3.50 3.50
867 A172 2.50pa Pair, #a.-b. 9.00 9.00

No. 859 Overprinted

1994, Nov. 10 Litho. *Perf. 14½*
868 A169 Sheet of 6, #a.-f. 7.00 7.00

No. 831 Ovptd. in Dark Blue

1994, Nov. 17 Litho. *Perf. 14½*
869 A161 60s on 3.50pa multi 3.00 3.00

Types of 1969-85 and

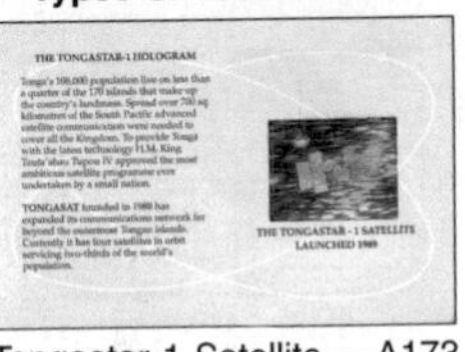

Tongastar 1 Satellite — A173

Design: a, 10s, Type A39 banana, size 22x11mm. b, 25s, Type AP12. c, Booklet pane, 12 #870a, 3 #870b. d, 45s, like #608. e, 45s, like #609. f, 45s, like #610. g, 45s, like #611. h, Booklet pane of 3 each #870d-870e, 2 #870f, 1 #870g. i, 60s, Type A72. j, 60s, Type OA19. k, 80s, Type OA17. l, Booklet pane, #870i-870k. m, 2pa, Tongastar 1. n, Booklet pane of 1 #870m.

Unwmk.
1994, Dec. 14 Litho. *Die Cut*
Self-adhesive

870 A173 Souvenir booklet 27.50

First full-scale production of self-adhesive stamps by Tonga, 25th anniv. (#870). Satellite communications network for Tongan Islands (#870m).
No. 870b is airmail. Nos. 870j-870k are air post official stamps.
No. 870m contains a holographic image. Soaking in water may affect the hologram.

Marine Type of 1992-93 Redrawn

1994-95 Litho. *Perf. 14*
874 A155a 10s like #801 .25 .25
876 A155a 20s like #803 .35 .35
877 A155a 45s like #804 .80 .80
878 A155a 60s like #805 1.10 1.10
879 A155a 80s like #806 1.75 1.75

Size: 41x27mm, 27x41mm

880 A155a 1pa like #705, horiz. 3.00 3.00
881 A155a 2pa like #577, horiz. 5.00 5.00
882 A155a 3pa like #578, horiz. 7.00 7.00
883 A155a 5pa like #706 10.00 10.00
884 A155a 10pa like #568 22.00 22.00
Nos. 874-884 (10) 51.25 51.25

Area covered by background colors on Nos. 874, 876-879 has been reduced in size.
Issued: 1pa, 2pa, 3pa, 6/21/94; 5pa, 9/21/94; 10pa, 1/18/95; 10s, 20s, 45s, 60s, 80s, 9/25/95.
For overprints, see Nos. O78-O87.

FAO, 50th Anniv. — A174

1995, May 16 Litho. *Perf. 14*
886 A174 5pa multicolored 15.00 15.00

Tonga's Entry into British Commonwealth, 25th Anniv. — A175

Children with bicycles from parts of Commonwealth.

1995, June 6

887	A175	45s Polynesia	1.10	.90
888	A175	60s Asia	1.50	1.25
889	A175	80s Africa	1.75	1.75
890	A175	2pa India	3.75	3.75
891	A175	2.50pa Europe	4.75	4.75
		Nos. 887-891 (5)	12.85	12.40

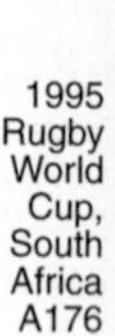

1995 Rugby World Cup, South Africa A176

Designs: No. 892a, Player running right with ball, two others. b, Two players. No. 893a, Three players. b, Player ready to catch ball.

1995, June 20 ***Perf. 14½***

892	A176	80s Pair, #a.-b.	5.00	5.00
893	A176	2pa Pair, #a.-b.	12.50	12.50

Nos. 892-893 were each issued in sheets of 4 stamps.

For surcharges see Nos. 954A, 956A.

Nos. 824-827 Surcharged

i

j

1995, June 30 **Litho.** ***Perf. 14***

894	60s Pair	4.50	4.50
a.	A160(i) on #824	2.00	2.00
b.	A160(j) on #824	2.00	2.00
895	60s Pair	4.50	4.50
a.	A160(i) on 80s #825	2.00	2.00
b.	A160(j) on 80s #825	2.00	2.00
896	60s Pair	4.50	4.50
a.	A160(i) on 2pa #826	2.00	2.00
b.	A160(j) on 2pa #826	2.00	2.00
897	60s Pair	4.50	4.50
a.	A160(i) on 3pa #827	2.00	2.00
b.	A160(j) on 3pa #827	2.00	2.00
	Nos. 894-897 (4)	18.00	18.00

Nos. 779-782 Surcharged

1995, June 30 **Litho.** ***Perf. 14***

898	A151	60s on 57s #779	1.50	1.50
899	A151	80s on 2pa #781	1.75	1.75
899A	A151	80s on 2pa #782	1.75	1.75
b.		Pair, #899-899A	4.00	4.00
899C	A151	1pa on #780	2.00	2.00
		Nos. 898-899C (4)	7.00	7.00

Victory in the Pacific, 50th Anniv. — A177

Nos. 900, 901: a, Soldier climbing from rope ladder. b, Ship, soldiers. c, Ship, landing craft with troops, soldiers up close. d, Ship, landing craft with troops. e, Map.

1995, Aug. 1 **Litho.** ***Perf. 14x14½***

900	A177	60s Strip of 5, #a.-e.	10.00	10.00
901	A177	80s Strip of 5, #a.-e.	10.00	10.00

Nos. 900-901 are continuous designs and were issued together in sheet containing ten stamps.

Singapore '95 — A178

Designs: No. 902a, 45s, #887. b, 60s, #888. 2pa, Boy cycling in Singapore.

1995, Sept. 1 **Litho.** ***Perf. 12***

902	A178	Pair, #a.-b.	3.25	3.25

Souvenir Sheet

903	A178	2pa multicolored	4.50	4.50

Souvenir Sheet

Beijing Intl. Coin & Stamp Show '95 A179

Design: 1.40pa, Mount Song, Henan Province, China.

1995, Sept. 14 ***Perf. 14½***

904	A179	1.40pa multicolored	4.25	4.25

End of World War II, UN, 50th Anniv. A180

No. 905a, Holocaust survivors. b, UN emblem, "50." c, Children of Holocaust survivors in celebration.

No. 906a, Mushroom cloud from atom bomb explosion. b, Like #905b. c, Space shuttle.

1995, Oct. 20 **Litho.** ***Perf. 13***

905	A180	60s Strip of 3, #a.-c.	4.00	4.00
906	A180	80s Strip of 3, #a.-c.	6.00	6.00

Nos. 905b, 906b are 23x31mm.

Christmas and New Year — A181

Orchids: 20s, Calanthe triplicata. Nos. 908, Spathoglottis plicata, inscribed "MERRY CHRISTMAS." No. 909, like #908, inscribed "A HAPPY 1996." No. 910, Dendrobium platygastrium, inscribed "MERRY CHRISTMAS". No. 911, like #910, inscribed "A HAPPY 1996." 80s, Goodyera rubicunda. 2pa, Dendrobium toki. 2.50pa, Phaius tankervilliae.

1995, Nov. 15 **Litho.** ***Perf. 14x14½***

907	A181	20s multicolored	.75	.75
908	A181	45s multicolored	1.00	1.00
909	A181	45s multicolored	1.00	1.00
910	A181	60s multicolored	1.25	1.25
911	A181	60s multicolored	1.25	1.25
912	A181	80s multicolored	1.75	1.75
913	A181	2pa multicolored	4.00	4.00
914	A181	2.50pa multicolored	5.00	5.00
		Nos. 907-914 (8)	16.00	16.00

Humpback Whale — A182

1996, Jan. 7 ***Perf. 14***

915	A182	45s In water	2.00	2.00
916	A182	60s With calf	3.00	3.00
917	A182	1.50pa Sounding	4.50	4.50
918	A182	2.50pa Breaching	7.00	7.00
		Nos. 915-918 (4)	16.50	16.50

World Wildlife Fund.

Miniature Sheet

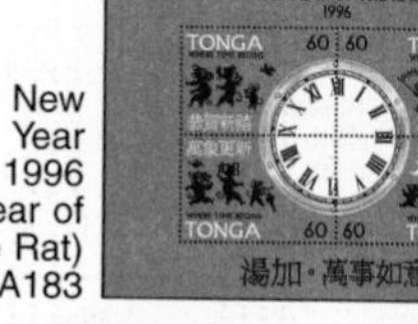

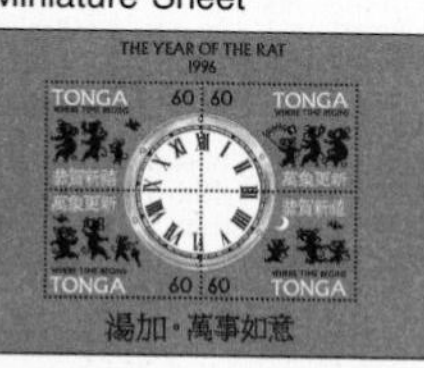

New Year 1996 (Year of the Rat) A183

Denomination: a, UR. b, UL. c, LR. d, LL.

1996, Feb. 23

919	A183	60s Sheet of 4, #a.-d.	7.00	7.00

No. 919 is a continuous design.

See Nos. 930-932, 932E, 942, 986.

Marine Type of 1992-93 Redrawn

1996, May 31 **Litho.** ***Perf. 14***

Size: 40x26mm

920	A155a	1pa like #880	3.00	3.00
921	A155a	2pa like #881	5.50	5.50
922	A155a	3pa like #882	8.00	8.00
923	A155a	5pa like #883	15.00	15.00
924	A155a	10pa like #884	27.50	27.50
		Nos. 920-924 (5)	59.00	59.00

Size of "TONGA" on Nos. 920-923 is smaller than on Nos. 880-883. Name of species appears at top instead of bottom on Nos. 920-924. Background colors vary. Inscribed "1996."

1996 Summer Olympic Games, Atlanta — A184

Statues of classical Greek figures, modern athletes: 45s, Zeus, runner. 80s, The Discus Thrower. 2pa, The Javelin Thrower. 3pa, The Horseman, dressage competitor.

1996, July 2 **Litho.** ***Perf. 14***

925	A184	45s multicolored	1.25	.80
926	A184	80s multicolored	2.00	1.90
927	A184	2pa multicolored	5.00	5.00
928	A184	3pa multicolored	6.00	6.00
		Nos. 925-928 (4)	14.25	13.70

For surcharges & overprint see Nos. 949-952.

13th Congress of Intl. Union of Preshistoric and Protohistoric Sciences — A185

a, Prehistoric man using fire, knife, bow & arrow, animals. b, Ancient Egyptians, Greeks, Romans.

1996, Sept. 5 **Litho.** ***Perf. 12***

929	A185	1pa Pair, #a.-b.	5.00	5.00

No. 929 was issued in sheets of 6 stamps.

New Year 1996 (Year of the Rat) Type

Denomination: a, UR. b, UL. c, LR. d, LL.

1996, June 27 **Litho.** ***Perf. 14***

Sheets of 4

930	A183	10s #a.-d.	1.40	1.40
931	A183	20s #a.-d.	2.75	2.75
932	A183	45s #a.-d.	6.75	6.75
932E	A183	60s #a.-d.	10.00	10.00

The denominations are larger on No. 932E than those on No. 919.

Christmas A186

Paintings: 20s, Virgin and Child, by Sassoferrato. 60s, Adoration of the Shepherds, by Murillo. 80s, Virgin and Child, by Delaroche. 1pa, Adoration of the Shepherds, by Champaigne.

1996, Oct. 29 **Litho.** ***Perf. 14***

933	A186	20s multicolored	.75	.50
934	A186	60s multicolored	2.00	1.50
935	A186	80s multicolored	2.50	2.50
936	A186	1pa multicolored	7.50	7.50
		Nos. 933-936 (4)	12.75	12.00

UNICEF, 50th Anniv. A187

Children in sports activities: a, Running, playing rugby. b, Tennis. c, Cycling.

1996, Oct. 29

937	A187	80s Strip of 3, #a.-c.	8.00	8.00

No. 937 is a continuous design.

Queen Halaevalu Mata'aho, 70th Birthday A188

Designs: 60s, Queen, natl. flag. No. 939a, Queen, coin with portrait. No. 939b, Coin with natl. arms, Queen.

1996, Nov. 27 **Litho.** ***Perf. 12***

938	A188	60s multicolored	2.50	2.50
939	A188	2pa Pair, #a.-b.	9.50	9.50

Towards the Year 2000 — A189

Year "2000" rising out of Pacific, Tonga landmarks: Nos. 940a, 941a, The Ha'amonga stone monument, globe, Kao Island. Nos. 940b, 941b, Mount Talau overlooking Port of Reguge, Royal Palance, Tongatapu, communication satellite.

1996, Dec. 9

940	A189	80s Pair, #a.-b.	4.00	4.00
941	A189	2pa Pair, #a.-b.	8.00	8.00

New Year Type of 1996 Redrawn with Ox

Denomination located: a, 60s, UR. b, 60s, UL. c, 80s, LR. d, 2pa, LL.

1997, Jan. 24 **Litho.** ***Perf. 14***

942	A183	Sheet of 4, #a.-d.	9.50	9.50

New Year 1997 (Year of the Ox).

Nos. 840-845 Surcharged

1997, Mar. 3 **Litho.** ***Perf. 14***

943	A165	10s on 45s #840	2.75	2.50
944	A165	10s on 45s #841	2.75	2.50
a.		Pair, #943-944	5.50	5.00
945	A165	10s on 60s #842	2.75	2.50
946	A165	10s on 60s #843	2.75	2.50
a.		Pair, #945-946	5.50	5.00
947	A165	20s on 2pa #844	3.50	3.00
948	A165	20s on 2pa #845	3.50	3.00
a.		Pair, #947-948	7.00	6.00
		Nos. 943-948 (6)	18.00	16.00

Nos. 925-928 Surcharged & Overprinted.

1997, Mar. 24 Litho. *Perf. 14*

949 A184 10s on 45s #925 .90 .90
950 A184 10s on 80s #926 .90 .90
951 A184 10s on 2pa #927 .90 .90
952 A184 3pa #928 9.25 9.25
Nos. 949-952 (4) 11.95 11.95

Size and location of surcharge varies.

Nos. 892-893 Surcharged

a

b

1997, Mar. 24 *Perf. 14½*
Sheets of 4

954A A176 10s on 80s 2.00 2.00
956A A176 1pa on 2pa 14.00 14.00

No. 954A contains Nos. 892a (a), 892b (a), 892b (b), 892a (b). No. 956A contains Nos. 893a (a), 893b (a), 893b (b), 893a (b).

Christianity in Tonga, Birth of King George Tupou I, Bicent. — A190

Nos. 957, 961a, 962a, Arrival of missionary ship, Duff, Captain James Wilson. No. 958, King George Tupou I, village. Nos. 959, 961b, 962b, People in water, rowboats coming ashore from Duff. No. 960, 961c, 962c, Natives, missionaries, Duff.

1997, Apr. 28 *Perf. 14*

957 A190 10s multicolored 2.00 2.00
958 A190 10s multicolored .65 .65
959 A190 10s multicolored 2.00 2.00
960 A190 10s multicolored 2.00 2.00
a. Sheet of 6, #957, 959-960, 3 #958 7.50 7.50
961 A190 60s Strip of 3, #a.-c. 6.00 6.00
962 A190 80s Strip of 3, #a.-c. 7.00 7.00

Nos. 961-962 were each issued in sheets of 9 stamps.
See Nos. 972-975.

Souvenir Sheet

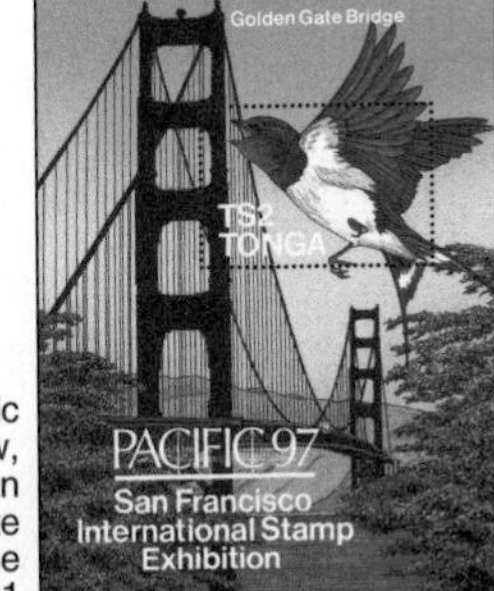

Pacific Swallow, Golden Gate Bridge A191

1997, May 30

963 A191 2pa multicolored 4.00 4.00

Pacific '97.

Tonga High School, 50th Anniv. — A192

Designs: 20s, Students in uniforms outside of school. 60s, Dressed for sports. 80s, Brass band. 3.50pa, Running competition.

1997, June 4

964 A192 20s multicolored .75 .40
965 A192 60s multicolored 1.75 1.10
966 A192 80s multicolored 2.00 1.50
967 A192 3.50pa multicolored 6.00 6.00
Nos. 964-967 (4) 10.50 9.00

A193

Nos. 968, 970: a, Queen, King with bowed heads, royal escorts. b, Coronation ceremony. c, Queen, King. 45s, 2pa, King's crown.

1997, June 30 Litho. *Perf. 13x13½*

968 A193 10s Strip of 3, #a.-c. 4.00 4.00
969 A193 45s multicolored 1.75 1.75

Size: 34x47mm
Perf. 12

970 A193 60s Strip of 3, #a.-c. 6.00 6.00
971 A193 2pa multicolored 4.75 4.75

King Taufa'ahau IV, Queen Halaevalu Mata'aho, 50th wedding anniv., coronation, 30th anniv.

Christianity in Tonga Type of 1997

1997, Aug. 27 *Perf. 14*
Size: 27x18mm

972 A190 10s like #957 .25 .25
973 A190 10s like #958 .25 .25
974 A190 10s like #959 .25 .25
975 A190 10s like #960 .25 .25
a. Sheet of 12, 6 #973, 2 each #972, #974-975 5.50 5.50

A194

Mushrooms: Nos. 976a, 977a, Lenzites elegans. Nos. 976b, 977b, Marasmiellus semiustus. No. 976c, 978a, Aseroe rubra. Nos. 976d, 978b, Podoscypha involuta. Nos. 976e, 979a, Microporus xanthopus. Nos. 976f, 979b, Lentinus tuberregium.

1997, Oct. 1 Litho. *Perf. 14*

976 A194 10s Strip of 6, #a.-f. 13.50 13.50

Size: 26x40mm

977 A194 20s Pair, #a.-b. 5.00 5.00
978 A194 60s Pair, #a.-b. 6.00 6.00
979 A194 2pa Pair, #a.-b. 8.00 8.00
c. Sheet of 6, #977-979 35.00 35.00

No. 976 is a continuous design.

Diana, Princess of Wales (1961-97)
Common Design Type

Various portraits: a, 10s. b, 80s, c, 1pa. d, 2.50pa.

Perf. 13½x14

1998, May 29 Litho. Unwmk.

980 CD355 Sheet of 4, #a.-d 4.00 4.00

No. 980 sold for 4.40pa + 50s with surtax from international sales going to the Princess Diana Memorial Fund and surtax from local sales going to designated local charity.
For surcharge, see No. 1192.

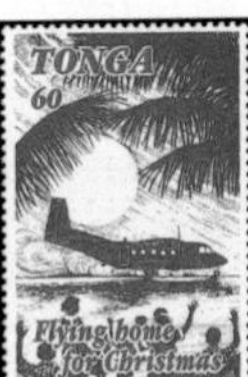

Flying Home for Christmas — A195

Designs: 60s, Airplane on ground, people waving. 80s, People waving, house, plane overhead. 1.50pa, Man in outrigger canoe waving to airplane. 3.50pa, Man, woman, people in boat on lake waving, airplane overhead.

1997, Oct. 20 Litho. *Perf. 14x13½*

981 A195 60s bister & red .85 .85
982 A195 80s bister & red 1.10 1.10
983 A195 1.50pa bister & red 2.00 2.00
984 A195 3.50pa bister & red 4.75 4.75
Nos. 981-984 (4) 8.70 8.70

King Taufa'ahau Tupou IV, 80th Birthday — A196

1998, July 4 Litho. *Perf. 14*

985 A196 2.70pa multicolored 6.50 6.50
a. Souv. sheet, #985, Niuafo'ou #207 9.00 9.00

New Year 1998 (Year of the Tiger)

Tiger: a, 55s, Leaping down. b, 80s, Lying down. c, 1pa, Leaping upward. d, 1pa, Stalking.

1998, July 23

986 A183 Sheet of 4, #a.-d. 6.00 6.00

No. 986 is a continuous design. Singpex '98.
For surcharges, see No. 1098.

Birds — A197

5s, Fairy tern, vert. 10s, Tongan whistler, vert. 15s, Common barn owl, vert. 20s, Purple swamp hen, vert. 30s, Red-footed booby, vert. 40s, Banded rail. 50s, Swamp harrier. 55s, Blue-crowned lorikeet, vert. 60s, Great frigate bird, vert. 70s, Friendly ground dove. 80s, Red-tailed tropic bird, vert. 1pa, Red shining parrot, vert. 2pa, Pacific pigeon, vert. 3pa, Pacific golden plover. 5pa, Tongan megapode.

Perf. 14x14½, 14½x14

1998, Aug. 26 Litho.

992 A197 5s multicolored .25 .25
993 A197 10s multicolored .25 .25
994 A197 15s multicolored .25 .25
995 A197 20s multicolored .30 .30
996 A197 30s multicolored .45 .45
997 A197 40s multicolored .60 .60
998 A197 50s multicolored .70 .70
999 A197 55s multicolored .80 .80
1000 A197 60s multicolored .85 .85
1001 A197 70s multicolored 1.00 1.00
1002 A197 80s multicolored 1.10 1.10
1003 A197 1pa multicolored 1.50 1.50
1004 A197 2pa multicolored 2.75 2.75
1005 A197 3pa multicolored 4.50 4.50
1006 A197 5pa multicolored 7.25 7.25
Nos. 992-1006 (15) 22.55 22.55

For surcharges, see Nos. 1077A, 1077B, 1099-1114, 1126, 1147.

Fish — A198

Designs: a, 10s, Chaetodon pelewensis. b, 55s, Chaetodon lunula. c, 1pa, Chaetodon ephippium.

1998, Sept. 23 Litho. *Perf. 14*

1008 A198 Strip of 3, #a.-c. 4.00 4.00

Intl. Year of the Ocean. No. 1008 was issued in sheets of 9 stamps.

Christmas — A199

Designs: 10s, Angel, "Kilisimasi Fiefia." 80s, Angel, "Merry Christmas." 1pa, Children, candle, "Ta'u Fo'ou Monu'ia." 1.60pa, Children, candle, "Happy New Year."

1998, Nov. 12 Litho. *Perf. 14x14½*

1009 A199 10s multicolored .60 .40
1010 A199 80s multicolored 2.25 1.00
1011 A199 1pa multicolored 2.50 2.00
1012 A199 1.60pa multicolored 3.50 3.50
Nos. 1009-1012 (4) 8.85 6.90

New Year 1999 (Year of the Rabbit) — A200

a, 10s, Three rabbits. b, 55s, Rabbit eating. c, 80s, Rabbit looking upward. d, 1pa, Rabbit hopping.

1999, Feb. 16 *Perf. 14*

1013 A200 Sheet of 4, #a.-d. 4.00 4.00

Explorers A201

Explorer, ship: 55s, Tasman, Heemskerck, 1643. 80s, La Perouse, Astrolabe, 1788. 1pa, William Bligh, Bounty, 1789. 2.50pa, James Cook, Resolution, 1777.

1999, Mar. 19 Litho. *Perf. 14*

1014 A201 55s multicolored 1.40 .65
1015 A201 80s multicolored 1.75 1.00
1016 A201 1pa multicolored 2.50 2.00
1017 A201 2.50pa multicolored 4.00 4.00
a. Souvenir sheet of 1 5.25 5.25
Nos. 1014-1017 (4) 9.65 7.65

Australia '99 World Stamp Expo (#1017a).

Scenic Views, Vava'u — A202

Designs: 10s, Neiafu. 55s, Boats on water, Port of Refuge. 80s, Aerial view, Port of Refuge. 1pa, Sunset, Neiafu. 2.50pa, Mounu Island.

1999, May 19 *Perf. 14½*

1018 A202 10s multicolored .75 .40
1019 A202 55s multicolored 1.00 .60
1020 A202 80s multicolored 1.75 .80
1021 A202 1pa multicolored 2.00 2.00
1022 A202 2.50pa multicolored 3.50 3.50
Nos. 1018-1022 (5) 9.00 7.30

For surcharge see No. 1148.

Flowers A203

Designs: 10s, Fagraea berteroana. 80s, Garcinia pseudoguttifera. 1pa, Phlaeria disperma, vert. 2.50pa, Gardenia taitensis, vert.

Perf. 13¼x13, 13x13¼

1999, Sept. 29 Litho.

1023 A203 10s multicolored .30 .30
1024 A203 80s multicolored 1.40 1.40
1025 A203 1pa multicolored 1.75 1.75
1026 A203 2.50pa multicolored 2.80 2.80
Nos. 1023-1026 (4) 6.25 6.25

Millennium — A204

Designs: a, 55s, Ha'amonga monument, people, clocks at 11:15 to 11:25. b, 80s, Monument, people, clocks at 11:30 to 11:40. c, 1pa, People, clocks at 11:45 to 11:55. d, 2.50pa, King Taufa'ahau IV, clocks at 12:00, 12:05.

1999, Dec. 1
1027 A204 Strip of 4, #a.-d. 6.50 6.50

Millennium A205

Clock, dove and: 10s, Flowers. 1pa, Ha'amonga Monument. 2.50pa, Native boat. 2.70pa, Crown.

Litho. & Embossed
2000, Jan. 1 *Perf. and Die Cut*
1028 A205 10s multi .25 .25
1029 A205 1pa multi 1.50 1.50
1030 A205 2.50pa multi 3.50 3.50
1031 A205 2.70pa multi 3.75 3.75
a. Souv. sheet, #1030-1031 7.50 7.50
Nos. 1028-1031 (4) 9.00 9.00

Values are for stamps with attached selvage.

Souvenir Sheet

New Year 2000 (Year of the Dragon) A206

Various dragons; a, 10s. b, 55s, c, 80s. d, 1pa.

Litho. with Foil Application
2000, Feb. 4 *Perf. 14½*
1032 A206 Sheet of 4, #a.-d. 4.50 4.50

Souvenir Sheet

The Stamp Show 2000, London A207

Litho. with Foil Application
2000, May 22 *Perf. 13x13¼*
1033 A207 Sheet of 2 5.00 5.00
a. 1pa Queen Mother 1.50 1.50
b. 2.50pa Queen Salote Tupou III 3.50 3.50

Geostationary Orbital Slot Program — A208

Designs: 10s, Proton RU500 lauch vehicle, vert. 1pa, LM3 launch vehicle. 2.50pa, Apstar 1. 2.70pa, Gorizont.

Litho. with Foil Application
2000, July 5 *Perf. 14½x15, 15x14½*
1034-1037 A208 Set of 4 8.50 8.50
a. Souvenir sheet, #1036-1037 7.50 7.50

World Stamp Expo 2000, Anaheim.

2000 Summer Olympics, Sydney — A209

No. 1038: a, Runner, koalas, sailboats. b, Boxers, kangaroos, Ayers Rock. c, Torchbearers, Ayers Rock, Sydney Opera House (60x45mm). d, Discus thrower, Sydney Harbour Bridge, flower. e, Weight lifter, kookaburra, fish.

2000, Sept. 15 **Litho.** *Perf. 14*
1038 A209 Horiz. strip of 5 5.50 5.50
a.-e. 80s Any single 1.00 1.00

Commonwealth Membership, 30th Anniv. — A210

Designs: 10s, Education. 55s, Arts. 80s, Health. 2.70pa, Agriculture.

2000, Oct. 25
1039-1042 A210 Set of 4 5.50 5.50

For surcharge see No. 1149.

Souvenir Sheet

New Year 2001 (Year of the Snake) A211

No. 1043 — Various snakes: a, 10s. b, 55s, c, 80s, d, 1pa.

Litho. with Foil Application
2001, Feb. 1 *Perf. 14¼*
1043 A211 Sheet of 4, #a-d 4.50 4.50

Hong Kong 2001 Stamp Exhibition.

Dance — A212

Designs: 10s, Ma'ulu'ulu. 55s, Me'etupaki. 80s, Tau'olunga. 2.70pa, Faha'iula.

2001, Apr. 4 **Litho.** *Perf. 13¼*
1044-1047 A212 Set of 4 5.25 5.25

For surcharge see No. 1151.

Year of the Mangrove — A213

Designs: 10s, Fiddler crab. 55s, Black duck, gray mullet, vert. 80s, Red mangrove, emperor fish, vert. 1pa, Reef heron, mangrove. 2.70pa, Mangrove crab.

2001, May 5 **Litho.** *Perf. 13¾*
1048-1052 A213 Set of 5 6.00 6.00
a. Souvenir sheet, #1048-1052, perf. 13½ 6.50 6.50

For surcharge see No. 1150.

Sport Fishing — A214

2001, July 31 *Perf. 14¾x14*
1053 A214 Horiz. strip of 4 with central label 8.25 8.25
a. 45s Sailfish .50 .50
b. 80s Blue marlin 1.00 1.00
c. 2.40pa Wahoo 3.00 3.00
d. 2.60pa Dorado 3.25 3.25

Fruit — A215

2001, Sept. 19 *Serpentine Die Cut*
Self-Adhesive
1054 Horiz. strip of 5 6.75 6.75
a. A215 10s Banana .50 .50
b. A215 45s Coconut .90 .90
c. A215 60s Pineapple 1.00 1.00
d. A215 80s Watermelon 1.10 1.10
e. A215 2.40pa Passion fruit 2.40 2.40

Shells — A216

Designs: 10s, Haliotis ovina. 80s, Turbo petholatus. 1pa, Trochus niloticus. 2.70pa, Turbo marmoratus.

Perf. 12¾
2001, Dec. 13 **Litho.** **Unwmk.**
1055-1058 A216 Set of 4 6.50 6.50

Values are for stamps with surrounding selvage.

Reign Of Queen Elizabeth II, 50th Anniv. Issue
Common Design Type
Souvenir Sheet

No. 1059: a, 15s, Princess Elizabeth as child. b, 90s, Wearing yellow hat. c, 1.20pa, With Princess Anne and Prince Charles. d, 1.40pa, Wearing crown. e, 2.25pa, 1955 portrait by Annigoni (38x50mm).

Perf. 14¼x14½, 13¾ (2.25pa)
2002, Feb. 6 **Litho.** **Wmk. 373**
1059 CD360 Sheet of 5, #a-e 8.00 8.00

Souvenir Sheet

New Year 2002 (Year of the Horse) A217

Various horses: a, 65s. b, 80s. c, 1pa. d, 2.50pa.

Litho. With Foil Application
2002, Feb. 12 **Unwmk.** *Perf. 14*
1060 A217 Sheet of 4, #a-d 7.50 7.50

Intl. Year of Ecotourism A218

Designs: 5s, Whale, surfer. 15s, Woman, shoreline. 70s, Beach, fish. 1.40pa, Arch, man. 2.25pa, Boats, man.

2002, Apr. 9 **Litho.** *Perf. 13¼x13¾*
1061-1065 A218 Set of 5 6.75 6.75

Pearls — A219

Pearls and: 90s, Workers preparing oysters for pearl cultivation. 1pa, Diver checking strung oysters. 1.20pa, Woman, pearl on necklace. 2.50pa, Islands.

2002, June 12 **Litho.** *Perf. 13½*
1066-1069 A219 Set of 4 7.50 7.50
a. Souvenir sheet, #1068-1069 6.25 6.25

Values are for stamps with surrounding selvage.

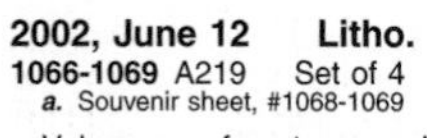

Participation of Tongan Team in Rugby Sevens Tournament A220

Designs: 15s, Player leaping for ball. 30s, Players ready for scrum. 90s, Player attempting tackle. 4pa, Players on ground.

2002, July 27
1070-1073 A220 Set of 4 11.00 11.00

Values are for stamps with surrounding selvage.

Weaving — A221

Designs: 30s, Woman and young girl. 90s, Woman with work hanging on line, boy with baskets. 1.40pa, Women weaving baskets. 2.50pa, Woman weaving basket lid.

2002, Sept. 17 *Perf. 12¼*
1074-1077 A221 Set of 4 6.50 6.50

No. 999 Surcharged

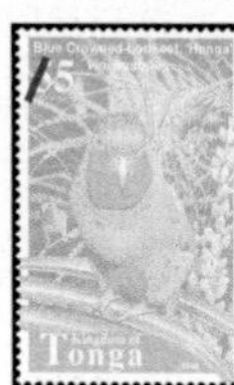

Type 1 — Slash Over First "5"

No. 1003 Surcharged

Methods and Perfs As Before
2002, Sept.
1077A A197 5s on 55s #999, Type 1 *65.00* —
1077B A197 15(s) on 1pa #1003 *75.00* —

See Nos. 1099-1114 for additional surcharges on No. 999.

'Eua National Park, 10th Anniv. — A222

Various depictions of red shining parrots 45s, 1pa, 1.50pa, 2.50pa.

2002, Nov. 27 **Litho.** *Perf. 12¼*
1078-1081 A222 Set of 4 7.00 7.00

New Year 2003 (Year of the Ram) A223

No. 1082: a, 65s, One ram. 80s, Three sheep. 1pa, Three sheep, diff. 2.50pa, Two sheep.

2003, Apr. 14 **Litho.** *Perf. 13¼*
1082 A223 Sheet of 4, #a-d 7.00 7.00

Coronation of Queen Elizabeth II, 50th Anniv. — A224

Designs: 90s, Queen Elizabeth II in coach. 1.20pa, Queen Salote of Tonga. 1.40pa, Queen Salote in coach. 2.50pa, Queen Elizabeth II.

Litho. With Foil Application

2003, June 2

1083-1086 A224 Set of 4 8.50 8.50

Boats of Abel Tasman — A225

Various boats: 15s, 75s, 90s, 2.50pa.

2003, Aug. 7 Litho. *Perf. 13¼*

1087-1090 A225 Set of 4 10.00 10.00
a. Souvenir sheet, #1087-1090 10.00 10.00

Beaches A226

Flower and: 15s, Euakafa Beach. 90s, Pangaimotu Beach. 1.40pa, Fafa Beach. 2.25pa, Nuku Beach.

2003, Sept. 11

1091-1094 A226 Set of 4 8.00 8.00

Nos. 784, 785a, 785b, 785c, 786 Surcharged

Methods and Perfs As Before

2003, Sept.

1095 A152 10s on 32s Horiz. strip of 3, #784a-784c *150.00* —
1096 A152 10s on 42s #785a —
1097 A152 10s on 42s #785b —
1097A A152 10s on 42s #785c —
1098 A152 10s on 57s Horiz. strip of 3, #786a-786c *150.00* —

No. 999 Surcharged

Type 2 — Small numerals and cent sign

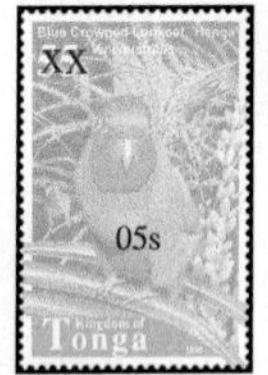

Type 3 — Small numerals and "s"

Type 4 — Thin numerals and "s"

Type 5 — Large numerals and "s"

Type 6 — Medium-sized numerals and "s"

Type 7 — Very large, bold numerals and "c"

Methods and Perfs As Before

2003-04

1099 A197 05s on 55s, Type 3 *150.00* —
a. Obliterators 2x1½mm —
1100 A197 05s on 55s, Type 4 *350.00* —
1101 A197 5s on 55s, Type 5 *20.00* —
1102 A197 5c on 55s, Type 7 *10.00* —
1103 A197 10s on 55s, Type 4 *50.00* —
1104 A197 10s on 55s, Type 5 *45.00* —
1105 A197 10c on 55s, Type 7 *25.00* —
1106 A197 15c on 55s, Type 2 *75.00* —
1107 A197 15s on 55s, Type 4 *350.00* —
1108 A197 15s on 55s, Type 5 *20.00* —
1109 A197 15c on 55s, Type 7 *25.00* —
1110 A197 20c on 55s, Type 2 *65.00* —
1111 A197 20s on 55s, Type 4 *25.00* —
1112 A197 20s on 55s, Type 5 *50.00* —
1113 A197 45c on 55s, Type 2 *50.00* —
1114 A197 45s on 55s, Type 6 *75.00* —

Earliest known uses: Nos. 1099, 1106, 1110, 10/03; Nos. 1100, 1103, 1107, 1111, 12/03; Nos. 1101, 1108, 2/04; Nos. 1113, 4/04; Nos. 1104, 1112, 1114, 6/04; Nos. 1105, 1109, 8/04; No. 1102, 9/04.

Churches A227

Designs: 15s, Catholic Church, Neiafu, Vava'u. 90s, Wesleyan Church, Uiha, Ha'apai. 1.40pa, Cathedral of the Immaculate Conception of Mary. 2.25pa, Free Wesleyan Church, Nuku'alofa.

2003, Nov. 10

1115-1118 A227 Set of 4 8.25 8.25

Christmas.

New Year 2004 (Year of the Monkey) A228

No. 1119: a, 60s, Spider monkey. b, 80s, Ring-tailed lemur. c, 1pa, Cotton-top tamarin. d, 2.50pa, White-cheeked gibbon.

2004, Feb. 12 Litho. *Perf. 13¼*

1119 A228 Sheet of 4, #a-d 6.25 6.25

Nos. 770, 787, 788, 815, 816, 1001, Niuafo'ou Nos. 140, 141 and 145 Surcharged

Type 1 — Small denomination and obliterator

Type 2 — Large denomination and obliterator

Methods and Perfs As Before

2004

1120 A153 10s on 32s #787 *50.00* —
1121 A153 10s on 42s #788, Type 1 — —
1122 A153 10s on 42s #788, Type 2 *150.00* —
1123 A157 10s on 42s #815 *350.00* —
1124 A147 10s on 57s Horiz. strip of 4, + central label, #770a-770d *350.00* —
1125 A157 10s on 57s #816 *90.00* —
1126 A197 60s on 70s #1001 *30.00* —

On Stamps of Niuafo'ou

1127 A25 10s on 42s #140 *350.00* —
1128 A26 10s on 42s #145 *110.00* —
1129 A25 10s on 57s #141 *350.00* —

Size and location of obliterators and new denominations varies. Earliest known use: No. 1126, 3/04; Nos. 1120, 1121, 4/04; Nos. 1122, 1123, 1124, 1125, 1127, 1128, 1129, 6/04. The surcharged Niuafo'ou stamps were not necessarily sent only to Niuafo'ou for sale there.

Fruit Plants — A229

Designs: 45s, Mango. 60s, Pineapple. 80s, Coconut. 1.80pa, Banana.

2004, Sept. 21 Litho. *Perf. 14¼x14*

1130-1133 A229 Set of 4 5.00 5.00

Christmas A230

Designs: 65s, Madonna and Child. 80s, Journey to Bethlehem. 1.20pa, Annunciation to the Shepherds. 2.50pa, Magi.

2004, Dec. *Perf. 14*

1134-1137 A230 Set of 4 8.25 8.25

Royalty — A231

Designs: 65s, King George Tupou I. 90s, King George Tupou II. 1.40pa, Queen Salote Tupou III. 3.05pa, King Taufa'ahau Tupou IV.

2004, July 7 Litho. *Perf. 14*

1138-1141 A231 Set of 4 6.50 6.50
a. Souvenir sheet of 4, #1138-1141 6.50 6.50

Souvenir Sheet

New Year 2005 (Year of the Rooster) A232

No. 1142 — Various roosters with panel color of: a, 65s, Yellow orange. b, 80s, Light green. c, 1pa, Tan. d, 2.50pa, Gray blue.

2005, Feb. 12

1142 A232 Sheet of 4, #a-d 8.50 8.50

Souvenir Sheet

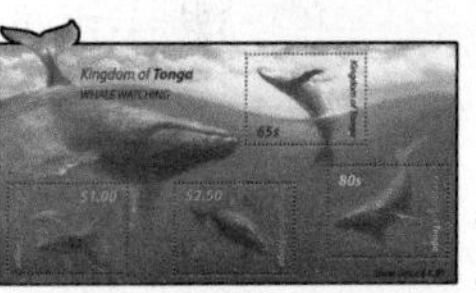

Whales A233

No. 1143 — Various whales with denominations in: a, 65s, Purple. b, 80s, Yellow. c, 1pa, Green. d, 2.50pa, Pink.

2005, May 4 *Perf. 13¼*

1143 A233 Sheet of 4, #a-d 8.25 8.25

Coronation of King Siaosi Tupou V — A234

King Siaosi Tupou V wearing: 30s, Uniform and sash. 1pa, Tuxedo and sash. 5pa, Robe and crown.

Litho. With Foil Application

2008, Aug. 1 *Perf. 14*

1144-1145 A234 Set of 2 1.50 1.50

Souvenir Sheet

1146 A234 5pa multi 5.50 5.50

No. 1146 contains one 30x60mm stamp.

Tonga Nos. 999, 1019, 1040, 1045, 1049, and Niuafo'ou Nos. 203, 211, 225 and 235 Surcharged

Type 1 — Serifed Surcharge

Type 2 — Unserifed Surcharge

Methods and Perfs As Before

2008-10 On Stamps of Tonga

1147 A197 30s on 55s #999, type 1 — —
1148 A202 30s on 55s #1019, type 1 *60.00* —
a. Surcharge double 120.00
1149 A210 30s on 55s #1040, type 2 *40.00 900.00*
1150 A213 30s on 55s #1049, type 2 *40.00* —
1151 A212 70s on 55s #1045, type 1 *50.00* —

On Stamps of Niuafo'ou

1152 A41 30s on 55s #203, type 2 — —
1153 A44 30s on 55s #211, type 2 —
1154 A52 30s on 55s #225, type 2 —
1155 A41 70s on 55s #203, type 2 *90.00* —
1156 A56 70s on 55s #235, type 2 — —

Size, location and obliterators of surcharges vary. Surcharged Niuafo'ou stamps were used in Tonga.

Issued: No. 1147, Nov. 2009; No. 1148, Nov. 2008; Nos. 1149, 1153, July 2008; No. 1150, Feb. 2010; No. 1151, June 2010; Nos. 1152, 1154, 2008; Nos. 1155, 1156, May 2010.

No. 1149 used is valued on cover.

Christmas — A235

No. 1157: a, 3pa, Lighthouse ornament on Christmas tree. b, 5pa, Christmas lights and Free Church of Tonga Cathedral.

2011, Dec. 24 Litho. *Perf. 14*
1157 A235 Horiz. pair, #a-b 9.25 9.25

Birds — A236

Designs: 60s, Prosopeia tabuensis. 2.25pa, Anas superciliosa. 2.40pa, Halcyon chloris. 2.50pa, Egretta novaehollandiae. 2.70pa, Aplonis tabuensis. 3pa, Megapodius pritchardii. 3.40pa, Megapodius pritchardii, diff. 4pa, Lalage maculosa. 5pa, Tyto alba. 6.60pa, Halcyon chloris, diff. 7.30pa, Prosopeia tabuensis, diff. 10pa, Swamp harrier.

2012, Feb. 6 *Perf. 14*

Stamps With White Frames

1158	A236	60s multi	.75	.75
1159	A236	2.25pa multi	2.75	2.75
1160	A236	2.40pa multi	3.00	3.00
1161	A236	2.50pa multi	3.00	3.00
1162	A236	2.70pa multi	3.25	3.25
1163	A236	3pa multi	3.75	3.75
1164	A236	3.40pa multi	4.00	4.00
1165	A236	4pa multi	4.75	4.75
1166	A236	5pa multi	6.00	6.00
1167	A236	6.60pa multi	8.00	8.00
1168	A236	7.30pa multi	8.75	8.75
1169	A236	10pa multi	12.00	12.00
		Nos. 1158-1169 (12)	60.00	60.00

Stamps Without White Frames

1170		Sheet of 12	60.00	60.00
a.	A236	60s multi	.75	.75
b.	A236	2.25pa multi	2.75	2.75
c.	A236	2.40pa multi	3.00	3.00
d.	A236	2.50pa multi	3.00	3.00
e.	A236	2.70pa multi	3.25	3.25
f.	A236	3pa multi	3.75	3.75
g.	A236	3.40pa multi	4.00	4.00
h.	A236	4pa multi	4.75	4.75
i.	A236	5pa multi	6.00	6.00
j.	A236	6.60pa multi	8.00	8.00
k.	A236	7.30pa multi	8.75	8.75
l.	A236	10pa multi	12.00	12.00

Reign of Queen Elizabeth II, 60th Anniv. — A237

2012, Mar. 6 *Perf. 14¾x14*
1171 A237 3.40pa multi 4.00 4.00

Souvenir Sheet

1172 A237 10pa multi 12.00 12.00

Worldwide Fund for Nature (WWF) — A238

Various depictions of Thorny seahorse: 45s, 2pa, 2.40pa, 3.40pa.

2012, Mar. 12 *Perf. 14¼x14*
1173-1176 A238 Set of 4 9.75 9.75
a. Sheet of 16, 4 each #1173-1176 39.00 39.00

For surcharges, see Nos. 1262-1265.

Miniature Sheet

Reconstruction and Development Porjects — A239

No. 1177: a, 45s, Nuku'alofa construction. b, 85s, Vuna Wharf. c, 2.70pa, Vaiola Hospital. d, 5pa, New construction. e, 8pa, New Vuna Wharf. f, 10pa, Nuku'alofa sidewalks.

2012, May 30 *Perf. 12½*
1177 A239 Sheet of 6, #a-f 30.00 30.00

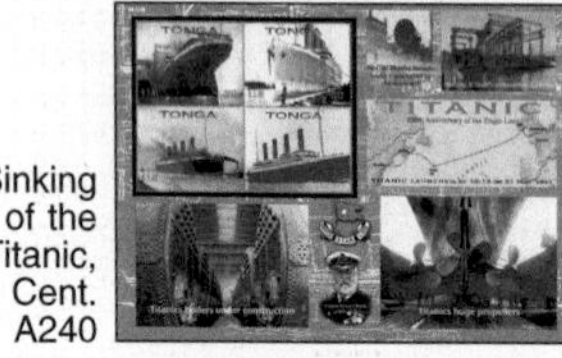

Sinking of the Titanic, Cent. A240

No. 1178: a, Titanic under construction with ship under gantries. b, Titanic at dock, ropes at right. c, Titanic and tuboat. d, Titanic at sea.

No. 1179a, Like #1178a.

2012, June 6 *Perf. 12½*
1178 A240 3.40pa Sheet of 4, #a-d 16.00 16.00

Souvenir Sheet

1179 A240 Sheet of 2, #1178c, 1179a 4.50 4.50
a. 45s multi .50 .50

ANZAC Day — A241

Designs: 45s, Council of the South Pacific Scout Association emblem. 1pa, Flag of Tonga. 2.40pa, Tonga Girl Guides Emblem. 3.40pa, Rotary International emblem.

No. 1184: a, 3.40pa, Scouts and leaders. b, 5pa, Scouts and leaders, diff.

2012, June 25 *Perf. 13½*
1180-1183 A241 Set of 4 8.25 8.25

Souvenir Sheet

1184 A241 Sheet of 2, #a-b 9.50 9.50

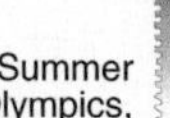

2012 Summer Olympics, London — A242

Designs: 45s, Boxing. 1.40pa, Track. 3.40pa, Swimming.

2012, June 25 *Perf. 13¾*
1185-1187 A242 Set of 3 6.00 6.00
a. Souvenir sheet of 3, #1185-1187 6.00 6.00
b. Souvenir sheet of 6, 2 each #1185-1187 12.00 12.00

Personalizable Stamp — A243

2012, Aug. 8 *Perf. 13¼*
1188 A243 3pa multi 3.50 3.50

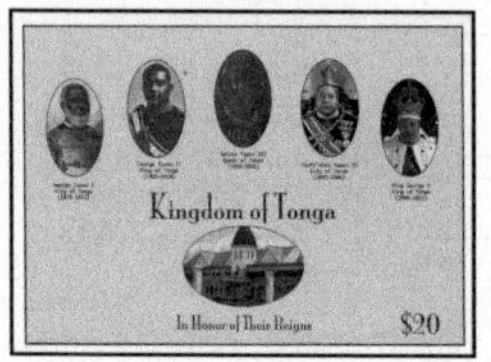

Tongan Monarchs — A244

2012, Aug. 20 *Imperf.*
1189 A244 20pa multi 23.00 23.00

Miniature Sheets

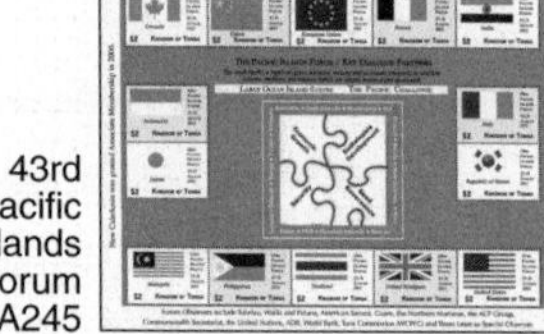

43rd Pacific Islands Forum A245

No. 1190 — Flags of: a, Canada. b, People's Republic of China. c, European Union. d, France. e, India. f, Indonesia. g, Italy. h, Japan. i, Republic of Korea. j, Malaysia. k, Philippines. l, Thailand. m, United Kingdom. n, United States.

No. 1191 — Flags of: a, Australia. b, Cook Islands. c, Fiji. d, Kiribati. e, Micronesia. f, Nauru. g, New Zealand. h, Niue. i, Palau. j, Papua New Guinea. k, Marshall Islands. l, Samoa. m, Solomon Islands. n, Tonga. o, Tuvalu. p, Vanuatu.

2012, Aug. 31 *Perf. 14*
1190 A245 2pa Sheet of 14, #a-n 32.50 32.50
1191 A245 2pa Sheet of 16, #a-p 37.50 37.50

No. 980 Surcharged in Gold and Black

No. 1192: a, 5pa on 10s. b, 5pa on 80s. c, 5pa on 1pa. d, 5pa on 2.50pa.

2012, Sept. 4 Litho.
1192 CD355 Sheet of 4, #a-d 23.00 23.00

Overprint is printed across the four stamps of the sheet. It reads "In Loving Memory of Diana, Princess of Wales / 31 August 1997 / Her Legacy will live on forever. / William and Kate, Duke and Duchess of Cambridge / 1st Anniversary of their Royal Wedding 2011".

Miniature Sheet

Christmas — A246

No. 1193 — Mystical Nativity, by Sandro Botticelli: a, Angel in red robe at left, angels with white and brown robes at center. b, White angel's robe at UL, angels in brown and red robes at center. c, Parts of five angels, with angel with red robe at right. d, Angels and manger roof. e, Virgin Mary, heads of cow and donkey. f, Angel with green robe to left of manger post. g, Infant Jesus. h, Angels to right of manger post. i, Angel in green robe embracing man. j, Angel in white robe embracing man. k, Angel in red robe embracing man.

2012, Nov. 21 *Perf. 14¾x14¼*
1193 A246 1pa Sheet of 11, #a-k, + 2 labels 13.00 13.00

Wedding of Crown Prince Tupouto'a 'Ulukulala and Sinaitakala Fakafanua — A247

Designs: No. 1194, Photograph of bride, groom and families.

No. 1195: a, King Tupou VI and Queen Nanasipau'u (36x36mm). b, Like No. 1194, without top panel. c, Procession of dignitaries (36x36mm). d, Bride and groom in robes (36x36mm). e, Limousine (36x36mm).

2012, Dec. 14 *Perf. 13¼*
1194 A247 3pa multi 3.50 3.50
1195 A247 3pa Sheet of 5, #a-e 17.50 17.50

Miniature Sheet

New Year 2013 (Year of the Snake) A248

No. 1196: a, Olive green snake with yellow green underside. b, Red brown snake with green underside. c, Yellow green snake with orange red underside. d, Purple snake with yellow green underside.

2013, Feb. 20 *Perf. 14¾x14¼*
1196 A248 2.45pa Sheet of 4, #a-d 11.50 11.50

A249

A250

A251

A252

A253

A254

A255

Turtles — A256

2013, Feb. 21 ***Perf. 14***

Stamps With White Backgrounds

1197		Horiz. strip of 4	19.00	19.00
a.	A249	4pa multi	4.75	4.75
b.	A250	4pa multi	4.75	4.75
c.	A251	4pa multi	4.75	4.75
d.	A252	4pa multi	4.75	4.75
1198		Horiz. strip of 4	23.00	23.00
a.	A253	5pa multi	5.75	5.75
b.	A254	5pa multi	5.75	5.75
c.	A255	5pa multi	5.75	5.75
d.	A256	5pa multi	5.75	5.75

Miniature Sheets

Stamps With Colored Backgrounds

1199		Sheet of 4	19.00	19.00
a.	A249	4pa multi	4.75	4.75
b.	A250	4pa multi	4.75	4.75
c.	A251	4pa multi	4.75	4.75
d.	A252	4pa multi	4.75	4.75
1200		Sheet of 4	23.00	23.00
a.	A253	5pa multi	5.75	5.75
b.	A254	5pa multi	5.75	5.75
c.	A255	5pa multi	5.75	5.75
d.	A256	5pa multi	5.75	5.75

Souvenir Sheet

Australia 2013 World Stamp Expo, Melbourne — A257

No. 1201: a, Koala. b, Royal Exhibition Building, Melbourne. c, Red kangaroo.

2013, May 10 ***Perf. 13¼***

1201 A257 3pa Sheet of 3, #a-c 10.00 10.00

Miniature Sheet

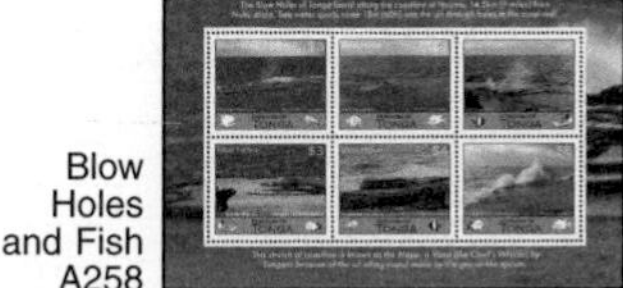

Blow Holes and Fish A258

No. 1202 — Fish: a, 3pa, Chaetodon flavirostris, Pseudanthias pleurotaenia. b, 3pa, Pygoplites diacathus, Amblyglyphidodon melanopterus. c, 4pa, Acanthurus guttatus, Myripristis hexagona. d, 4pa, Pseudanthias pleurotaenia, Zanclus comutus. e, 5pa, Zanclus comutus, Pygoplites diacanthus. f, 5pa, Amblyglyphidodon melanopterus, Myripristis hexagona.

2013, June 4 ***Perf. 13¾***

1202 A258 Sheet of 6, #a-f 27.00 27.00

Birds and Flora — A259

Designs: 10s, Halcyon chloris, Adenanthera pavonina. 20s, Aplonis tabuensis, Myristica hypagyraea. 30s, Vini australis, Artocarpus altilis. 40s, Fregata minor, Hibiscus tiliaceus. 50s, Sula sula, Terminalia catappa. 80s, Phaeton rubricauda, Cocos nucifera. 90s, Anous minutus, Elattostachys falcata. 1.10pa, Lalage maculosa, Tarenina sambucina. 1.20pa, Porzana tabuensis, Mimosa pigra. 2pa, Foulehaio carunculatus, Solanum mauritianum. 12.50pa, Prosopeia tabuensis, Adenanthera pavonina. 20pa, Ptilinopus perousil, Psidium guajava.

2013, June 6 ***Perf. 14***

Stamps With White Frames

1203	A259	10s	multi	.25	.25
1204	A259	20s	multi	.25	.25
1205	A259	30s	multi	.35	.35
1206	A259	40s	multi	.45	.45
1207	A259	50s	multi	.55	.55
1208	A259	80s	multi	.90	.90
1209	A259	90s	multi	1.00	1.00
1210	A259	1.10pa	multi	1.25	1.25
1211	A259	1.20pa	multi	1.40	1.40
1212	A259	2pa	multi	2.25	2.25
1213	A259	12.50pa	multi	14.00	14.00
1214	A259	20pa	multi	22.50	22.50
	Nos. 1203-1214 (12)			45.15	45.15

Miniature Sheet

Stamps Without White Frames

1215		Sheet of 12	46.00	46.00
a.	A259	10s multi	.25	.25
b.	A259	20s multi	.25	.25
c.	A259	30s multi	.35	.35
d.	A259	40s multi	.45	.45
e.	A259	50s multi	.55	.55
f.	A259	80s multi	.90	.90
g.	A259	90s multi	1.00	1.00
h.	A259	1.10pa multi	1.25	1.25
i.	A259	1.20pa multi	1.40	1.40
j.	A259	2pa multi	2.25	2.25
k.	A259	12.50pa multi	14.00	14.00
l.	A259	20pa multi	22.50	22.50

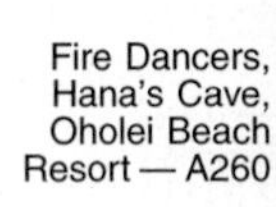

Fire Dancers, Hana's Cave, Oholei Beach Resort — A260

Designs: 15s, Girl clapping. 1.75pa, Dancers. 4.70pa, Dancers with three torches.

No. 1219, vert.: a, 5.25pa, Dancer with torch burining on both ends. b, 7.85pa, Dancer holding torch well above head. c, 8.65pa, Dancer holding torch close to mouth.

2013, Aug. 14 **Litho.** ***Perf. 13¾***

1216-1218 A260 Set of 3 7.25 7.25

Souvenir Sheet

Perf. 13¾x13½

1219 A260 Sheet of 3, #a-c 23.50 23.50

Birth of Prince George of Cambridge — A261

Designs: 1.75pa, Baby's feet on adult's hands. 2.40pa, Adult's hands touching baby's feet. 2.60pa, Baby's hand holding adult's finger. 3.40pa, Baby's hand holding adult's finger, diff.

11.30pa, Baby's hand in adult's hand.

2013, Aug. 30 **Litho.** ***Perf. 13¾***

1220-1223 A261 Set of 4 11.00 11.00

Souvenir Sheet

1224 A261 11.30pa multi 12.50 12.50

Miniature Sheet

Giant Pandas A262

No. 1225 — Panda: a, Sitting under tree. b, In snow. c, Chewing on long stick. d, Face. e, Eating bamboo leaves.

2013, Sept. 26 **Litho.** ***Perf. 12***

1225 A262 2.50pa Sheet of 5, #a-e 14.00 14.00

Souvenir Sheet

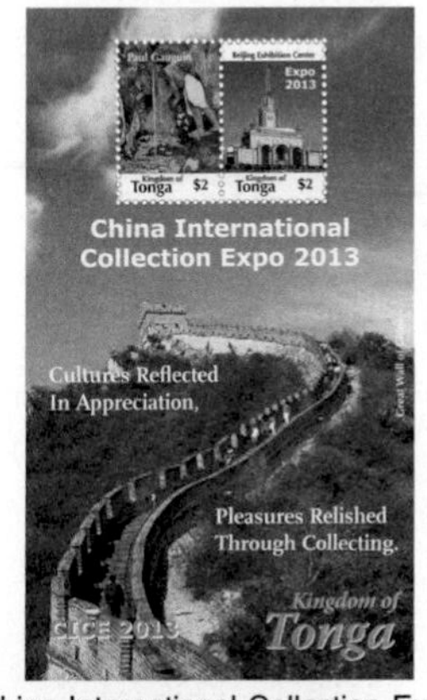

China International Collection Expo 2013, Beijing — A263

No. 1226: a, Painting by Paul Gauguin. b, Beijing Exhibition Center.

2013, Sept. 26 **Litho.** ***Perf. 12***

1226 A263 2pa multi 4.50 4.50

Watercraft and Tin Can Island Mail Cans A264

Design: 2.25pa, Ship and mail can at sea. 5.40pa, Canoe, mail can on shore.

2013, Sept. 27 **Litho.** ***Perf. 14¼***

1227 A264 2.25pa multi 2.50 2.50

Souvenir Sheet

1228 A264 5.40pa multi 6.00 6.00

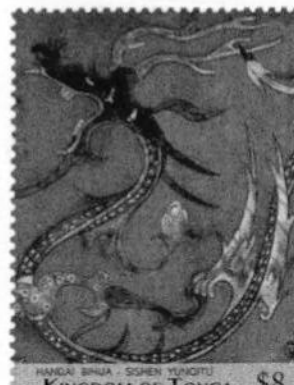

Dragon — A265

2013, Oct. 15 **Litho.** ***Perf. 12***

1229 A265 8pa multi 8.75 8.75

No. 1229 was printed in sheets of 2.

Souvenir Sheets

A266

Diplomatic Relations Between Tonga and People's Republic of China, 15th Anniv. — A267

No. 1230: a, Vaipua Bridge, Tonga. b, MA60 airplane.

No. 1231: a, Great Wall of China. b, Haamonga Trilithon, Tonga.

2013, Nov. 2 **Litho.** ***Perf. 13½x13¾***

1230 A266 3pa Sheet of 2, #a-b 6.75 6.75

Perf. 13x13¼

1231 A267 3pa Sheet of 2, #a-b 6.75 6.75

King Tupou VI — A268

2013, Nov. 12 **Litho.** ***Perf. 14¼***

Panel Color

1232	A268	45s	blue gray	.50	.50
1233	A268	50s	dull org	.55	.55
1234	A268	75s	yel bister	.80	.80
1235	A268	1.05pa	dull yel grn	1.10	1.10
1236	A268	2.40pa	brown	2.60	2.60
1237	A268	2.60pa	dull yel org	2.75	2.75
1238	A268	3.40pa	dull brn	3.75	3.75
	Nos. 1232-1238 (7)			12.05	12.05

Christmas — A269

Paintings by: 1.75pa, Simon Vouet. 2.35pa, Giotto di Bondone. 2.60pa, Jan van Eyck.

2013, Nov. 13 **Litho.** ***Perf. 13½***

1239-1241 A269 Set of 3 7.25 7.25

Miniature Sheets

Cruise Ships and Wharves A270

No. 1242: a, 1.75pa, Ocean Princess at New Vuna Wharf. b, 1.75pa, MS Amadea. c, 1.75pa, Seabourne Quest. d, 2.40pa, MS Columbus. e, 2.40pa, MS Europa. f, 2.40pa, New Vuna Wharf.

No. 1243: a, 2.60pa, Pacific Jewel. b, 2.60pa, MS Dawn Princess. c, 2.60pa, MS Artania. d, 3.40pa, Sea Princess. e, 3.40pa, MS Regatta. f, 3.40pa, New Vuna Wharf, diff.

2013, Dec. 11 **Litho.** ***Perf. 14***

1242 A270 Sheet of 6, #a-f 13.50 13.50

1243 A270 Sheet of 6, #a-f 19.50 19.50

Souvenir Sheet

Christening of Prince George of Cambridge — A271

2014, Jan. 3 **Litho.** ***Perf. 13¼***

1244 A271 10pa multi 11.00 11.00

Miniature Sheet

New Year 2014 (Year of the Horse) A272

No. 1245: a, Horse's head. b, Horse facing left, leaping. c, Horse facing right, walking. d, Horse facing right, leaping.

2014, Jan. 6 **Litho.** ***Perf. 13¾***

1245 A272 2.45pa Sheet of 4, #a-d 10.50 10.50

Chinese Space Program — A273

Spacecraft and: 1.75pa, Astronaut Liu Yang. 2.40pa, Map of People's Republic of China. 2.60pa, Astronaut Jing Haipeng. 3.40pa, Jing Haipeng, diff.

2014, Feb. 3 Litho. *Perf. 14¾x14¼*

1246-1249 A273 Set of 4 11.00 11.00

Miniature Sheet

Easter A274

No. 1250 — Various paintings of the resurrected Christ by Tiziano Vecellio (Titian): a, 2.35pa. b, 3pa. c, 4.60pa. d, 6.95pa.

2014, Apr. 7 Litho. *Perf. 13¼*

1250 A274 Sheet of 4, #a-d 18.50 18.50

Bactrian Camels, by Wu Zuoren (1908-97) A275

2014, Apr. 9 Litho. *Perf. 14¾x14¼*

1251 A275 5pa multi 5.50 5.50

No. 1251 was printed in sheets of 4.

Souvenir Sheet

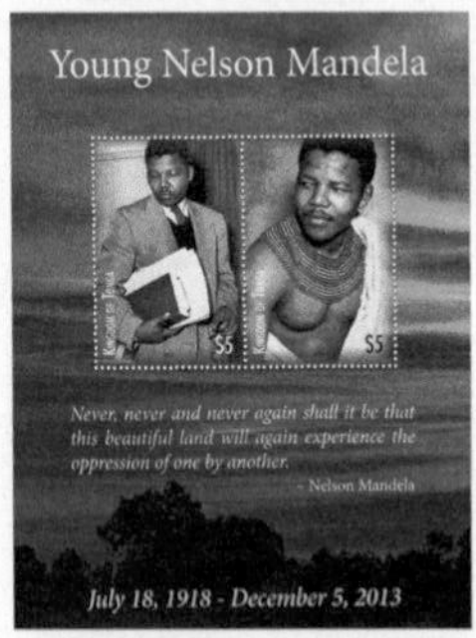

Nelson Mandela (1918-2013), President of South Africa — A276

No. 1252 — Mandela: a, Carrying book and papers. b, Wearing necklace.

2014, May 13 Litho. *Perf. 14¾x14¼*

1252 A276 5pa Sheet of 2, #a-b 11.00 11.00

Pacific Small Island Developing States — A277

No. 1253: a, Rising sea levels. b, Tropical Cyclone Ian. c, Emblem of Pacific Small Island Developing States. d, Map of Tonga and Fiji. e, Island Voices Global Choices emblem. f, Sailboat. g, Cruise ship. h, USS Cleveland. i, Fishing boat. j, Landing Craft Utility 1665. k, Tubastraea micranthus. l, Pseudanthias squamipinnis. m, Amphiprion ocellaris. n, Rhincodon typus. o, Laticauda colubrina, p, Flag of Tonga.

No. 1254: a, Like #1253a. b, Like #1253p, c, Like #1253b. d, Like #1253c. e, Like #1253d. f, Like #1253e.

No. 1255: a, Like #1253f. b, Like #1253p. c, Like #1253g. d, Like #1253h. e, Like #1253i. f, Like #1253j.

No. 1256: a, Like #1253k. b, Like #1253p. c, Like #1253l. d, Like #1253m. e, Like #1253n. f, Like #1253o.

2014, May 20 Litho. *Perf. 13¼*

1253 Block of 18, #1253a-1253o, 3 #1253p 9.00 9.00
a.-p. A277 45s Any single .50 .50

Miniature Sheets

1254 Sheet of 6 11.50 11.50
a.-f. A277 1.75pa Any single 1.90 1.90
1255 Sheet of 6 15.00 15.00
a.-f. A277 2.35pa Any single 2.50 2.50
1256 Sheet of 6 15.00 15.00
a.-f. A277 2.60pa Any single 2.75 2.75
Nos. 1254-1256 (3) 41.50 41.50

No. 1253 was printed in sheets containing 3 blocks of 18. The frame on each stamp in the sheet, depicting a map of the Pacific Ocean, differs.

Birds A278

No. 1257: a, 11.30pa, Barn owl. b, 16.90pa, Blue-crowned lorikeet. c, 28pa, Buff-banded rail.

2014, Sept. 15 Litho. *Perf. 13¼*

1257 A278 Horiz. strip of 3, #a-c, + 3 labels 57.50 57.50

Miniature Sheet

Tongan Participation in the Commonwealth Games, 40th Anniv. — A279

No. 1258: a, 1.75pa, Boxing. b, 2.35pa, Pole vault. c, 2.40pa, Rugby sevens. d, 2.60pa, Judo. e, 3.40pa, Weight lifting.

2014, Sept. 17 Litho. *Perf. 14*

1258 A279 Sheet of 5, #a-e, + label 13.00 13.00

Miniature Sheet

Christmas — A280

Bells and: a, Musical score with five staffs, denomination in white. b, Musical score with five staffs, denomination in black. c, Musical score with three staffs, denomination in black. d, Curving staff with G clef and notes, denomination in white.

2014, Dec. 15 Litho. *Perf. 13¾*

1259 A280 2.25pa Sheet of 4, #a-d 9.25 9.25

A281

New Year 2015 (Year of the Sheep) A282

No. 1261 — Sheep with background colors of: a, 11.30pa, Yellow green and green. b, 16.90pa, Yellow brown and brown.

2015, Jan. 5 Litho. *Perf. 13¼*

1260 A281 8pa multi 7.75 7.75

Souvenir Sheet

Self-Adhesive

Die Cut Perf. 13½

1261 A282 Sheet of 2, #a-b 27.00 27.00

No. 1261 has rouletting in sheet margin allowing the entire sheet to be folded into a hangable lantern.

Nos. 1173-1176 Surcharged

Methods and Perfs. As Before

2015, Apr. 1

1262 A238 90s on 2.40pa #1175 .90 .90
1263 A238 1pa on 3.40pa #1176 1.00 1.00
1264 A238 1.10pa on 45s #1173 1.10 1.10
1265 A238 1.20pa on 2pa #1174 1.25 1.25
Nos. 1262-1265 (4) 4.25 4.25

Appointment of Soane Patita Paini Mafi as Cardinal of Tonga — A283

Cardina Mafi: 2.25pa, Holding scroll. 2.70pa, Smiling. 5pa, Pope Francis. 8.50pa, Cardinal Mafi and Pope Francis.

2015, Apr. 1 Litho. *Perf. 13¼*

1266-1268 A283 Set of 3 10.00 10.00

Souvenir Sheet

1269 A283 8.50pa multi 8.50 8.50

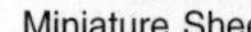

Miniature Sheet

Easter A284

No. 1270 — Details of painting by Rembrandt: a, Christ and another man on cross. b, Another man on cross. c, People at base of Christ's cross. d, Foliage and mourning women.

2015, Apr. 3 Litho. *Perf. 14¼*

1270 A284 2.25pa Sheet of 4, #a-d 9.00 9.00

Souvenir Sheet

Birth of Princess Charlotte of Cambridge — A285

No. 1271: a, Duchess of Cambridge holding Princess Charlotte. b, Duke of Cambridge holding Prince George.

2015, June 30 Litho. *Perf. 14¾x14*

1271 A285 5pa Sheet of 2, #a-b 9.75 9.75

Coronation of King Tupou VI — A286

Designs: No. 1272, 2.25pa, King Tupou VI. $5, King Tupou VI and Queen Nanasipau'u.

No. 1274, 2.25pa: a, Throne (30x30mm). b, King Tupou VI and Queen Nanasipau'u, diff. (40x30mm). c, Crown (40x30mm).

2015, July 4 Litho. *Perf. 14¼x14¾*

1272-1273 A286 Set of 2 7.00 7.00

Souvenir Sheet

Perf. 14¾ (#1274a), 14¾x14¼

1274 A286 2.25pa Sheet of 3, #a-c 6.50 6.50

Magna Carta, 800th Anniv. A287

Designs: 2pa, Medallion depicting King John. 2.25pa, Statue of Justice. 2.70pa, King John. 5pa, Arms of England and Tonga.

2015, July 20 Litho. *Perf. 14x14¾*

1275-1278 A287 Set of 4 11.50 11.50

New Year 2016 (Year of the Monkey) — A288

Designs: 8pa, Monkey with peach. 11.70pa, Monkey.

No. 1281: a, 11.30pa, Monkey with peach, diff. b, 16.90pa, Monkey, diff.

2015, Sept. 25 Litho. *Perf. 13¼*

1279-1280 A288 Set of 2 18.00 18.00

Souvenir Sheet
Self-Adhesive
Die Cut Perf. 11

1281 A288 Sheet of 2, #a-b 26.00 26.00

No. 1281 has rouletting in the sheet margin allowing the entire sheet to be folded into a lantern and contains two 51x51 diamond-shaped stamps.

Miniature Sheet

Queen Elizabeth II, Longest-Reigning British Monarch — A289

No, 1282 — Queen Elizabeth II in Tonga: a, Laying wreath at War Memorial. b, Approaching feast house. c, Holding plate at feast house. d, With Tongan Queen Salote Tupou III and Prince Philip.

2015, Nov. 23 Litho. *Perf. 14*

1282 A289 2pa Sheet of 4, #a-d 7.00 7.00

Miniature Sheet

Christmas — A290

No. 1283 — Religious paintings by: a, Pietro Perugino. b, Sandro Botticelli. c, Martin Schongauer. d, Fra Diamante.

2015, Dec. 7 Litho. *Perf. 13¾*

1283 A290 1.50pa Sheet of 4, #a-d 5.25 5.25

A291

Mohandas K. Gandhi, Garcinia sessilis, lotus flower and: 2.25pa, Red pandas. 4.20pa, Bengal tigers. 5pa, Indian cobras. 6.50pa, Indian leopards.

2016, Jan. 14 Litho. *Perf. 13¼*

1284-1287 A291 Set of 4 15.50 15.50

a. Souvenir sheet of 4, #1284-1287 15.00 15.00

Second summit of the forum for India-Pacific Islands Cooperation, Jaipur, India.

Miniature Sheets

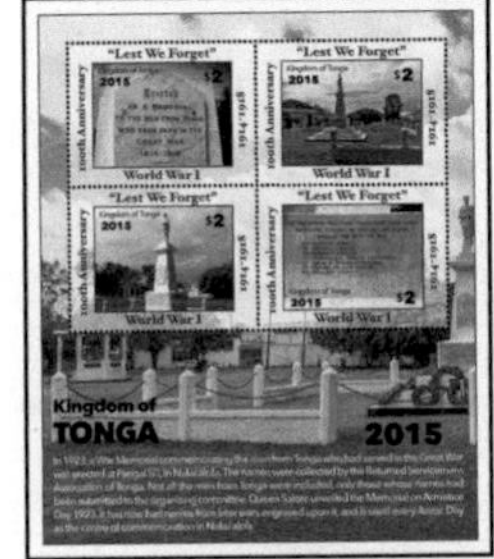

World War I, Cent. A292

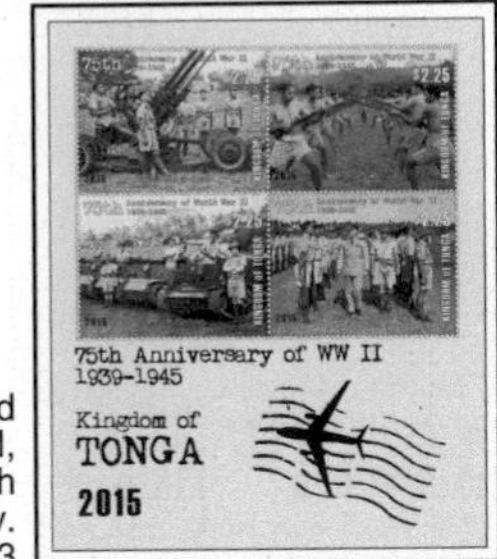

World War II, 75th Anniv. A293

No. 1288: a, Inscription on Tonga World War I Memorial. b, View of World War I Memorial from side. c, View of World War I Memorial from front. d, Inscription of war casualties.

No. 1289 — Inscription: a, Aircraft front. b, Bayonet drill. c, Carrier platoon. d, Governor General inspecting Guard of Honor.

2016, Feb. 2 Litho. *Perf. 14¼*

1288 A292 2pa Sheet of 4, #a-d 7.00 7.00

1289 A293 2.25pa Sheet of 4, #a-d 7.75 7.75

Worldwide Fund for Nature (WWF) — A294

Banded iguana: Nos. 1290, 1294a, 1.20pa, On rock with head raised. Nos. 1291, 1294b, 2pa, On rock. Nos. 1292, 1294c, 2.25pa, On heliconia flower. Nos. 1293, 1294d, 2.70pa, On branch.

2016, Mar. 14 Litho. *Perf. 14¾x14*

Stamps With White Frames

1290-1293 A294 Set of 4 7.50 7.50

Stamps Without White Frames

1294 Strip of 4 7.50 7.50
a. A294 1.20pa multi 1.10 1.10
b. A294 2pa multi 1.75 1.75
c. A294 2.25pa multi 2.10 2.10
d. A294 2.70pa multi 2.50 2.50

For surcharges, see Nos. 1443-1445.

Miniature Sheet

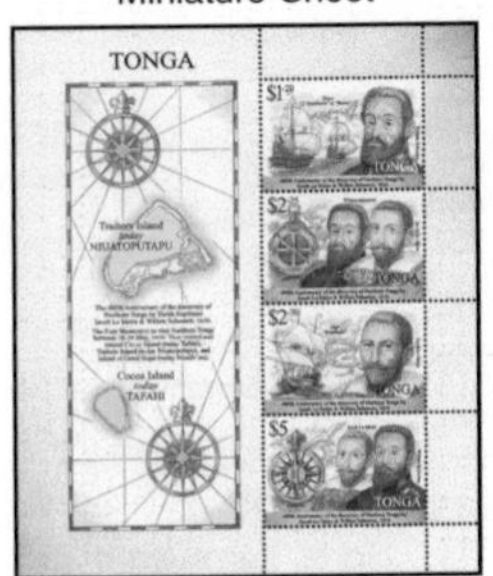

Landing of Dutch Explorers in Tonga, 400th Anniv. — A295

No. 1295: a, 1.20pa, Willem Schouten, ships Eendracht and Hoorn. b, 2.25pa, Schouten and Jacob Le Maire, astrolabe. c, 2.70pa, Le Maire and Eendracht. d, 5pa, Le Maire, Schouten and compass.

2016, Apr. 25 Litho. *Perf. 14*

1295 A295 Sheet of 4, #a-d 10.00 10.00

Souvenir Sheet

Queen Elizabeth II, 90th Birthday A296

No. 1296 — Queen Elizabeth II: a, Wearing military cap. b, Holding baby.

2016, May 3 Litho. *Perf. 13*

1296 A296 2pa Sheet of 2, #a-b 3.50 3.50

Souvenir Sheet

Tupou College, Toloa, 150th Anniv. A297

No. 1297: a, 2.25pa, Students. b, 5pa, University building.

2016, June 10 Litho. *Perf. 13*

1297 A297 Sheet of 2, #a-b 6.75 6.75

2016 Summer Olympics, Rio de Janeiro — A298

Nos. 1298 and 1299: a, Swimming. b, Athletics. c, Archery. d, Taekwondo.

2016, Sept. 5 Litho. *Perf. 13¼*

1298 Horiz. strip of 4 7.00 7.00
a.-d. A298 2pa Any single 1.75 1.75
1299 Horiz. strip of 4 8.00 8.00
a.-d. A298 2.25pa Any single 2.00 2.00

Marine Life and Birds — A299

Designs: 90s, Stony coral. 1pa, Black noddy. 1.10pa, Brown booby. 1.20pa, Bryde's whale. 2pa, Yellowfin goatfish. 2.25pa, Short-beaked common dolphin. 2.70pa, Fairy terns. 4.20pa, Whale shark. 5pa, Blue-footed booby. 6.70pa, Freckled hawkfish. 9.20pa, Spinner dolphin. 11.70pa, Tiger shark.

2016, Mar. 2 Litho. *Perf. 14x14¾*

1300 A299 90s multi .80 .80
1301 A299 1pa multi .90 .90
1302 A299 1.10pa multi 1.00 1.00
1303 A299 1.20pa multi 1.10 1.10
1304 A299 2pa multi 1.75 1.75
1305 A299 2.25pa multi 2.00 2.00
1306 A299 2.70pa multi 2.40 2.40
1307 A299 4.20pa multi 3.75 3.75
1308 A299 5pa multi 4.50 4.50
1309 A299 6.70pa multi 6.00 6.00
1310 A299 9.20pa multi 8.25 8.25
1311 A299 11.70pa multi 10.50 10.50
Nos. 1300-1311 (12) 42.95 42.95

New Year 2017 (Year of the Rooster) — A300

Designs: No. 1312, 5pa, No. 1314a, 15pa, One rooster. No. 1313, 5.50pa, No. 1314b, 16.90pa, Two roosters.

2016, Aug. 10 Litho. *Perf. 13½*

1312-1313 A300 Set of 2 9.75 9.75

Souvenir Sheet
Self-Adhesive
Die Cut Perf. 11

1314 A300 Sheet of 2, #a-b 29.50 29.50

No. 1314 contains two 50x50mm diamond-shaped stamps, and sheet could be folded into a lantern.

Miniature Sheet

Queen Mother Halaevalu Mata'aho, 90th Birthday — A301

No. 1315 — Queen Mother and: a, Girls at play, "Education" at right. b, Girls and infant, "Empowerment of women" at left. c, Woman with fishing net, "Empowerment of women" at right. d, Girl and boy, "Education" at left.

2016, Dec. 2 Litho. *Perf. 13¾*

1315 A301 2.25pa Sheet of 4, #a-d 8.25 8.25

Christmas — A302

No. 1316 — Various churches with "Christmas" at: a, 2pa, Left. b, 2pa, Right. c, 2.70pa, Left. d, 2.70pa, Right.

2016, Dec. 19 Litho. *Perf. 13¼*

1316 A302 Block of 4, #a-d 8.25 8.25

Miniature Sheet

Easter A303

No. 1317 — Paintings depicting the resurrection of Christ by: a, Jean François de Troy. b, Carl Bloch. c, Benjamin West. d, Rembrandt van Rijn.

2017, Apr. 10 Litho. *Perf. 12¾*

1317 A303 2.25pa Sheet of 4, #a-d 8.00 8.00

Miniature Sheet

Reign of Queen Elizabeth II, 65th Anniv. A304

No. 1318 — Queen Elizabeth II wearing: a, Blue jacket and hat. b, Red jacket and hat. c, Pink and white dress and pink hat. d, Bright yellow green jacket and hat.

2017, June 7 Litho. *Perf. 12¾*

1318 A304 3pa Sheet of 4, #a-d 11.00 11.00

Miniature Sheet

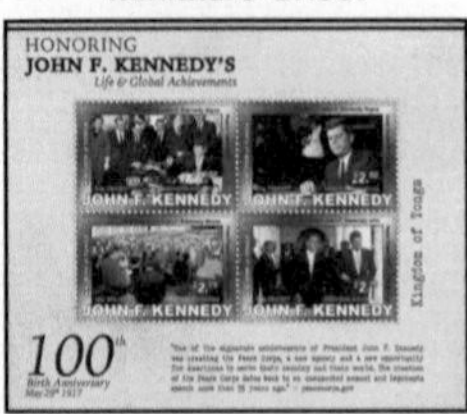

Pres. John F. Kennedy (1917-63) — A305

No. 1319 — Pres. Kennedy: a, 2.50pa, Signing Peace Corps Act. b, 2.50pa, Signing Cuba quarantine order. c, 2.75pa, Meeting first Peace Corps volunteers. d, 2.75pa, With Peace Corps director Sargent Shriver.

2017, June 21 Litho. *Perf. 12¾*

1319 A305 Sheet of 4, #a-d 9.75 9.75

'Eua National Park A306

No. 1320: a, Red shining parrot facing left. b, 'Eua National Park lookout. c, Coastline as seen from overlook. d, Red shining parrot facing right.

7.50pa, Red shining parrot, horiz.

2017, July 10 Litho. *Perf. 13x13¼*

1320 A306 5pa Block of 4, #a-d 19.00 19.00

Souvenir Sheet

Perf. 13¼x13

1321 A306 7.50pa multi 7.00 7.00

Halley's Comet A307

No. 1322: a, People viewing comet. b, Comet and squares. c, Comet appearance on Bayeux Tapestry. d, Man holding string of comet model.

5pa, Cross-sections of meteorites.

2017, July 12 Litho. *Perf. 13¼x13*

1322 A307 2.25pa Block of 4, #a-d 8.50 8.50

Souvenir Sheet

1323 A307 5pa multi 4.75 4.75

Miniature Sheet

Cheongsams With Seasonal Designs — A308

No. 1324 — Background color of cheongsam: a, 5pa, Apple green. b, 6.50pa, Light blue. c, 9pa, Light brown. d, 11.50pa, Salmon pink.

2017, July 14 Litho. *Die Cut*

Self-Adhesive

1324 A308 Sheet of 4, #a-d 30.00 30.00

e. Souvenir sheet of 4, #1324a-1324d, 269x163mm sheet 30.00 30.00

Nos. 1324a-1324d have simulated perforations.

Miniature Sheet

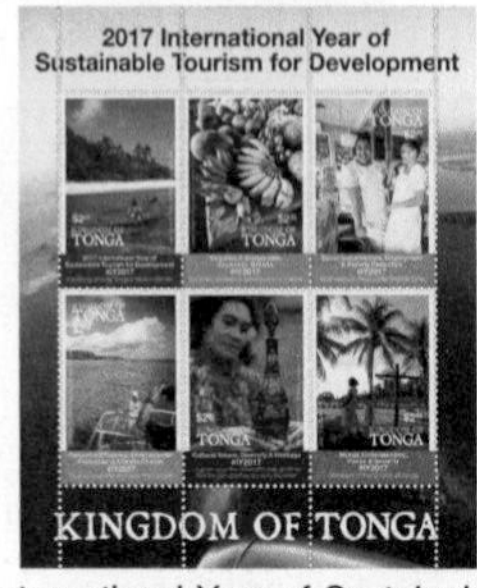

International Year of Sustainable Tourism for Development — A309

No. 1325: a, Kayaker near Vava'u Islands. b, Bananas, papayas and breadfruit. c, Waitresses at Friends Café. d, Tourists viewing Mounu Island from boat. e, Woman holding decanter. f, Members of Church of Tonga.

2017, July 18 Litho. *Perf. 12¾*

1325 A309 2.25pa Sheet of 6, #a-f 13.00 13.00

Peace Corps in Tonga, 50th Anniv. — A310

Designs: No. 1326, 2.25pa, Scarlet dove in white emblem. No. 1327, 6.50pa, Scarlet dove in black emblem. No. 1328, 6.50pa, White dove in black emblem. No. 1329, 8pa. White dove in scarlet emblem.

2017, Aug. 31 Litho. *Perf. 13*

1326-1329 A310 Set of 4 21.50 21.50

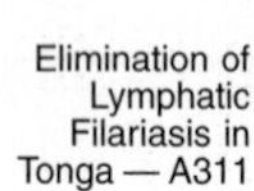

Elimination of Lymphatic Filariasis in Tonga — A311

2017, Sept. 9 Litho. *Perf. 13*

1330 A311 10pa multi 9.00 9.00

New Year 2018 (Year of the Dog) — A312

Designs; 6.50pa, One dog. 6.70pa, Two stylized dogs.

2017, Nov. 1 Litho. *Perf. 13¼*

1331-1332 A312 Set of 2 12.00 12.00

a. Souvenir sheet of 2, #1331-1332 12.00 12.00

Christmas — A313

No. 1333: a, Shell. b, Birds, palm trees and Christmas ornament. c, Bat. d, Whale.

2017, Dec. 4 Litho. *Perf. 12½*

1333 A313 2.25pa Block of 4, #a-d 8.25 8.25

Miniature Sheet

Easter A314

No. 1334: a, Purple flowers and butterfly. b, Church and palm trees. c, Flowers, shells and Easter eggs. d, Palm fronds.

2018, Mar. 15 Litho. *Perf. 12¾*

1334 A314 2.25pa Sheet of 4, #a-d 8.25 8.25

Birdpex 2018, Mondorf-les-Bains, Luxembourg — A315

No. 1335 — Orange-footed scrubfowl facing: a, Left. b, Right.

2018, May 3 Litho. *Perf. 13¼*

1335 A315 5pa Horiz. pair, #a-b 9.00 9.00

Souvenir Sheet

Birth of Prince Louis of Cambridge — A316

No. 1336: a, Duke and Duchess of Cambridge with Prince Louis. b, Public birth announcement. c, Duke of Cambridge with Prince George and Princess Charlotte.

2018, May 25 Litho. *Perf. 13*

1336 A316 2.50pa Sheet of 3, #a-c 6.75 6.75

Wedding of Prince Harry and Meghan Markle A317

No. 1337: a, Bride and page boys. b, Couple kissing.

9.20pa, Couple in coach, waving.

2018, July 27 Litho. *Perf. 13*

1337 A317 5pa Sheet of 2, #a-b 8.75 8.75

Souvenir Sheet

1338 A317 9.20pa multi 8.25 8.25

Animals of the World A318

No. 1339, 2.50pa: a, Mini lop-eared rabbit. b, Fennec fox.

No. 1340, 5pa: a, Derbyana flower beetle. b, Big-eyed tree frog.

10pa, Tiger swallowtail butterfly.

2018-19 Litho. *Perf. 13*

Horiz. Pairs, #a-b

1339-1340 A318 Set of 2 13.50 13.50

Souvenir Sheet

1341 A318 10pa multi 9.00 9.00

Issued: Nos. 1339-1340, 2/8/19; No. 1341, 9/10.

New Year 2019 (Year of the Pig) — A319

Designs: 6.50pa, Two pigs. 6.70pa, Two pigs, diff.

2018, Dec. 10 Litho. *Perf. 13¼*

1342-1343 A319 Set of 2 11.50 11.50

Miniature Sheets

A320

Christmas — A321

No. 1344 — Madonna and Child paintings by: a, Hugo van der Goes. b, Sandro Botticelli (hands of Jesus on Mary's breasts). c, Hans Memling. d, Peter Paul Rubens. e, Botticelli (hand of Jesus on book). f, Master of the Legend of St. Catherine.

No. 1345 — Madonna and Child paintings by: a, Raphael (two angels in foreground). b, Rubens (Jesus held by Mary and Joseph). c, Giovanni Battista Tiepolo. d, Rubens (Jesus in swaddling cloth). e, Rubens (Jesus held by Mary). f, Raphael (halo above Mary).

2018, Dec. 17 Litho. *Perf. 13*

1344 A320 50s Sheet of 6, #a-f 2.75 2.75

1345 A321 2.30pa Sheet of 6, #a-f 12.00 12.00

Birds — A322

Designs: 5s, Bat hawk. 10s, White-tailed kite. 1.40pa, Black-winged kite. 2.30pa, Madagascar fish eagle. 2.50pa, Gray-headed kite. 2.80pa, Lesser fish eagle. 4.30pa, Besra. 5.20pa, Jerdon's baza. 6.90pa, Black baza. 9.30pa, African cuckoo-hawk. 9.50pa, Dark chanting goshawk. 11.50pa, Scissor-tailed kite.

2018, Dec. 18 Litho. *Perf. 13*

Stamps With White Frames

1346 A322 5s multi .25 .25

1347 A322 10s multi .25 .25

1348 A322 1.40pa multi 1.25 1.25

1349 A322 2.30pa multi 2.00 2.00

1350 A322 2.50pa multi 2.25 2.25

1351 A322 2.80pa multi 2.50 2.50

a. Souvenir sheet of 6, #1346-1351 8.50 8.50

1352 A322 4.30pa multi 3.75 3.75

1353 A322 5.20pa multi 4.75 4.75

1354 A322 6.90pa multi 6.00 6.00

1355 A322 9.30pa multi 8.25 8.25

1356 A322 9.50pa multi 8.50 8.50

1357 A322 11.50pa multi 10.00 10.00

a. Souvenir sheet of 6, #1352-1357 41.50 41.50

Nos. 1346-1357 (12) 49.75 49.75

Miniature Sheet

Stamps Without White Frame

1358 Sheet of 12 50.00 50.00

a. A322 5s multi .25 .25

b. A322 10s multi .25 .25

c. A322 1.40pa multi 1.25 1.25

d. A322 2.30pa multi 2.00 2.00
e. A322 2.50pa multi 2.25 2.25
f. A322 2.80pa multi 2.50 2.50
g. A322 4.30pa multi 3.75 3.75
h. A322 5.20pa multi 4.75 4.75
i. A322 6.90pa multi 6.00 6.00
j. A322 9.30pa multi 8.25 8.25
k. A322 9.50pa multi 8.50 8.50
l. A322 11.50pa multi 10.00 10.00

Stamps on Nos. 1351a and 1357a have white frames on one or two sides. See Nos. 1376-1380, 1381-1385, 1398-1402, 1403-1407.

Gardens of the World A323

No. 1359: a, Kirstenbosch Garden, South Africa. b, Keukenhof, Netherlands. c, Butchart Gardens, Canada. d, Botanical Gården on Curitiba, Brazil. e, Nong Nooch Garden, Thailand. f, Kenrokuen Garden, Japan.
$9.50 Monet's Garden, France.

2019, June 14 Litho. *Perf. 13*
1359 A323 2.30pa Sheet of 6, #a-f 12.50 12.50

Souvenir Sheet
Perf. 13¼x13
1360 A323 9.50pa multi 8.50 8.50

No. 1360 contains one 48x40mm stamp.

Miniature Sheets

Apollo 11 Mission, 50th Anniv. A324

No. 1361: a, 1.10pa, Pres. John F. Kennedy. b, 2.30pa, U.S. flag and rocket launch. c, 2.50pa, Commemorative plaque on Apollo 11 Lunar Module. d, 6.90pa, Stopwatch.
No. 1362: a, 1.20pa, Landing pad of Lunar Module and bag on Moon. b, 2.70pa, Control panel of Lunar Module. c, 2.80pa, Lunar Module. d, 4.30pa, Lunar Module and bag on Moon.
No. 1363: a, 1.40pa, Rocket being assembled. b, 2.25pa, Rocket on launch pad. c, 4.20pa, Top of rocket on launch pad. d, 5.20pa, Rocket lifting off.

2019, July 6 Litho. *Perf. 13*
1361 A324 Sheet of 4, #a-d 11.50 11.50
1362 A324 Sheet of 4, #a-d 9.75 9.75

Perf. 13¼x13
1363 A324 Sheet of 4, #a-d 11.50 11.50
Nos. 1361-1363 (3) 32.75 32.75

No. 1363 contains four 30x40mm stamps.

Activities in Tonga — A325

Designs: 5s, Diving. 10s, Bird watching. 20s, Swimming with whales. 30s, Snorkeling. 45s, Exploring. 50s, Fishing. 75s, Kayaking. 1pa, Relaxing. 2pa, Sailing. 5pa, Surfing.

2019, Aug. 12 Litho. *Perf. 13*
1364-1373 A325 Set of 10 9.00 9.00

New Year 2020 (Year of the Rat) — A326

Different depictions of two rats: 6.50pa, 6.70pa.

2019, Oct. 11 Litho. *Perf. 13¼*
1374-1375 A326 Set of 2 11.50 11.50

Birds Type of 2018

Designs: 2.25pa, Harpy eagle, horiz. 2.70pa, Rough-legged hawk, horiz. 4.20pa, African fish eagle, horiz. 9.20pa, Black-and-chestnut eagles, horiz.

2019, Nov. 18 Litho. *Perf. 13*
Stamps With White Frames
1376 A322 2.25pa multi 2.00 2.00
1377 A322 2.70pa multi 2.40 2.40
1378 A322 4.20pa multi 3.75 3.75
1379 A322 9.20pa multi 8.00 8.00
Nos. 1376-1379 (4) 16.15 16.15

Stamps Without White Frames
Size: 48x40mm
Perf. 13¼x13
1380 Block or vert. strip of 4 16.50 16.50
a. A322 2.25pa multi 2.00 2.00
b. A322 2.70pa multi 2.40 2.40
c. A322 4.20pa multi 3.75 3.75
d. A322 9.20pa multi 8.00 8.00
e. Sheet of 4, #1380a-1380d 16.50 16.50

Stamps on No. 1380e have white frames on two sides.

Birds Type of 2018

Designs: 14.40pa, Eastern screech owl, horiz. 20.60pa, Long-eared owl, horiz. 25pa, Northern hawk owl, horiz. 30pa, Tawny owl, horiz.

2019, Nov. 25 Litho. *Perf. 13*
Stamps With White Frames
1381 A322 14.40pa multi 12.50 12.50
1382 A322 20.60pa multi 17.50 17.50
1383 A322 25pa multi 21.50 21.50
1384 A322 30pa multi 25.50 25.50
Nos. 1381-1384 (4) 77.00 77.00

Stamps Without White Frames
Size: 48x40mm
Perf. 13¼x13
1385 Block or vert. strip of 4 77.00 77.00
a. A322 14.40pa multi 12.50 12.50
b. A322 20.60pa multi 17.50 17.50
c. A322 25pa multi 21.50 21.50
d. A322 30pa multi 25.50 25.50
e. Sheet of 4, #1385a-1385d 77.00 77.00

Stamps on No. 1385e have white frames on two adjacent sides.

Christmas — A327

Stocking cap and: 1pa, Beach chair. 2pa, Suitcase, palm trees, sandals, and passport.

2019, Dec. 12 Litho. *Perf. 13¼*
1386-1387 A327 Set of 2 2.60 2.60

Compare with types A243 and A325.

Whales and Dolphins — A328

Designs: 75s, Spinner dolphins. 1pa, Humpback whale. 5pa, Killer whale. 11.80pa, Striped dolphin. 12.10pa, Hector's dolphin. 20pa, Minke whale. 50pa, Sperm whale. 60pa, Long-beaked common dolphins.

2020, Jan. 28 Litho. *Perf. 13*
Stamps With White Frames
1388 A328 75s multi .65 .65
1389 A328 1pa multi .85 .85
1390 A328 5pa multi 4.50 4.50
1391 A328 11.80pa multi 10.50 10.50
1392 A328 12.10pa multi 10.50 10.50
1393 A328 20pa multi 17.50 17.50
1394 A328 50pa multi 43.00 43.00
1395 A328 60pa multi 52.00 52.00
Nos. 1388-1395 (8) 139.50 139.50

Stamps Without White Frames
Size: 48x40mm
Perf. 13¼x13
1396 Block or vert. strip of 4 16.50 16.50
a. A328 75s multi .65 .65
b. A328 1pa multi .85 .85
c. A328 5pa multi 4.50 4.50
d. A328 11.80pa multi 10.50 10.50
e. Sheet of 4, #1396a-1396d 16.50 16.50
1397 Block or vert. strip of 4 125.00 125.00
a. A328 12.10pa multi 10.50 10.50
b. A328 20pa multi 17.50 17.50
c. A328 50pa multi 43.00 43.00
d. A328 60pa multi 52.00 52.00
e. Sheet of 4, #1397a-1397d 125.00 125.00

Stamps on Nos. 1396e and 1397e have white frames on two adjacent sides.

Birds Type of 2018

Parrots: 2.25pa, Green-winged macaw. 2.70pa, Bronze-winged parrots. 4.20pa, Galahs. 9.20pa, Eclectus parrot.

2020, May 4 Litho. *Perf. 13*
Stamps With White Frames
1398 A322 2.25pa multi 2.00 2.00
1399 A322 2.70pa multi 2.40 2.40
1400 A322 4.20pa multi 3.75 3.75
1401 A322 9.20pa multi 8.00 8.00
Nos. 1398-1401 (4) 16.15 16.15

Stamps Without White Frames
Size: 48x40mm
Perf. 13¼x13
1402 Block or vert. strip of 4 16.50 16.50
a. A322 2.25pa multi 2.00 2.00
b. A322 2.70pa multi 2.40 2.40
c. A322 4.20pa multi 3.75 3.75
d. A322 9.20pa multi 8.00 8.00
e. Sheet of 4, #1402a-1402d 16.50 16.50

Stamps on No. 1402e have white frames on two adjacent sides.

Birds Type of 2018

Ibises: 14.40pa, Australian white ibis. 20.60pa, Crested ibises. 25pa, Scarlet ibises. 30pa, Straw-necked ibis.

2020, May 18 Litho. *Perf. 13*
Stamps With White Frames
1403 A322 14.40pa multi 12.50 12.50
1404 A322 20.60pa multi 18.00 18.00
1405 A322 25pa multi 22.00 22.00
1406 A322 30pa multi 26.00 26.00
Nos. 1403-1406 (4) 78.50 78.50

Stamps Without White Frames
Size: 48x40mm
Perf. 13¼x13
1407 Block or vert. strip of 4 78.50 78.50
a. A322 14.40pa multi 12.50 12.50
b. A322 20.60pa multi 18.00 18.00
c. A322 25pa multi 22.00 22.00
d. A322 30pa multi 26.00 26.00
e. Sheet of 4, #1407a-1407d 78.50 78.50

Stamps on No. 1407e have white frames on two adjacent sides.

Butterflies A329

Designs: 75s, Large blue butterfly. 1pa, Gatekeeper butterfly. 5pa, High brwon fritillary butterfly. 11.80pa, Clouded yellow butterfly. 12.10pa, White admiral butterfly. 20pa, Eros blue butterfly. 50pa, Dark green fritillary butterfly. 60pa, Green-veined white butterfly.

2020, June 22 Litho. *Perf. 13*
Stamps With White Frames
1408 A329 75s multi .65 .65
1409 A329 1pa multi .85 .85
1410 A329 5pa multi 4.50 4.50
1411 A329 11.80pa multi 10.50 10.50
1412 A329 12.10pa multi 10.50 10.50
1413 A329 20pa multi 17.50 17.50
1414 A329 50pa multi 43.00 43.00
1415 A329 60pa multi 52.00 52.00
Nos. 1408-1415 (8) 139.50 139.50

Stamps Without White Frames
Size: 48x40mm
Perf. 13¼x13
1416 Block or vert. strip of 4 16.50 16.50
a. A329 75s multi .65 .65
b. A329 1pa multi .85 .85
c. A329 5pa multi 4.50 4.50
d. A329 11.80pa multi 10.50 10.50
e. Sheet of 4, #1416a-1416d 16.50 16.50
1417 Block or vert. strip of 4 125.00 125.00
a. A329 12.10pa multi 10.50 10.50
b. A329 20pa multi 17.50 17.50
c. A329 50pa multi 43.00 43.00
d. A329 60pa multi 52.00 52.00
e. Sheet of 4, #1397a-1397d 125.00 125.00

Stamps on Nos. 1416e and 1417e have white frames on two adjacent sides.

A330

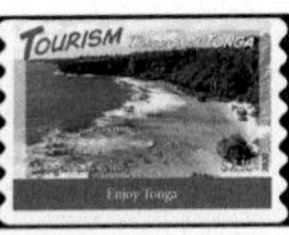

Tourism — A331

Designs: 40s, Kayaking. 60s, Tongan feast. 70s, Tongatapu Church. 80s, Underwater flora and fauna. 90s, Tongan shoreline. 1.10pa, Tongan tapa. 1.20pa, Diving. 1.50pa, Cruise ship. 1.60pa, Frangipani plumeria flower. 1.75pa, Vav'au Swallows Cave. 1.80pa, Taro crop. 1.95pa, Sailing. 2.10pa, Tongan shoreline, diff. 2.15pa, Tongan dancers. 2.20pa, Coral reef and fish. 2.40pa, Humpback whale. 2.60pa, Aerial view. 3.40pa, Horseback riding in Ha'apai. 3.50pa, Diving with sea turtles. 4pa, Tonga shoreline, diff. 4.70pa, Tonga flora. 5.20pa, Neiafu Harbor, Vava'u. 5.50pa, Fafa Island. 11.70pa, Tongatapu surfing.

Serpentine Die Cut 6¼ Horiz.
2020, Oct. 7 Litho.
Self-Adhesive
1418 A330 40s multi .35 .35
1419 A330 60s multi .50 .50
1420 A330 70s multi .60 .60
1421 A330 80s multi .70 .70
1422 A330 90s multi .80 .80
1423 A330 1.10pa multi .95 .95
1424 A330 1.20pa multi 1.10 1.10
1425 A330 1.50pa multi 1.30 1.30
1426 A330 1.60pa multi 1.40 1.40
1427 A330 1.75pa multi 1.50 1.50
1428 A330 1.80pa multi 1.60 1.60
1429 A330 1.95pa multi 1.75 1.75

Serpentine Die Cut 6¼ Vert.
1430 A331 2.10pa multi 1.90 1.90
1431 A331 2.15pa multi 1.90 1.90
1432 A331 2.20pa multi 1.90 1.90
1433 A331 2.40pa multi 2.10 2.10
1434 A331 2.60pa multi 2.25 2.25
1435 A331 3.40pa multi 3.00 3.00
1436 A331 3.50pa multi 3.00 3.00
1437 A331 4pa multi 3.50 3.50
1438 A331 4.70pa multi 4.25 4.25
1439 A331 5.20pa multi 4.50 4.50
1440 A331 5.50pa multi 4.75 4.75
1441 A331 11.70pa multi 10.00 10.00
Nos. 1418-1441 (24) 55.60 55.60

Souvenir Sheet

New Year 2021 (Year of the Ox) A332

2021, Apr. 7 Litho. *Perf. 13¼x13*
1442 A332 8pa multi 7.25 7.25

Nos. 1291-1293 Surcharged

Methods and Perfs. As Before
2021, May 18
1443 A294 6.90pa on 2.70pa #1293 6.25 6.25
1444 A294 11.50pa on 2pa #1291 10.50 10.50
1445 A294 12.50pa on 2.25pa #1292 11.50 11.50
Nos. 1443-1445 (3) 28.25 28.25

Giant Panda — A333

Giant panda: 50s, In snow. 1pa, In water. 2.80pa, In tree. 6.90pa, Eating.
12.50pa, Giant panda on log, vert.

2021, May 24 Litho. *Perf. 13*

1446-1449 A333 Set of 4 10.00 10.00

Souvenir Sheet

Perf. 13x13¼

1450 A333 12.50pa multi 11.50 11.50

No. 1450 contains one 40x48mm stamp.

A334

A335

A336

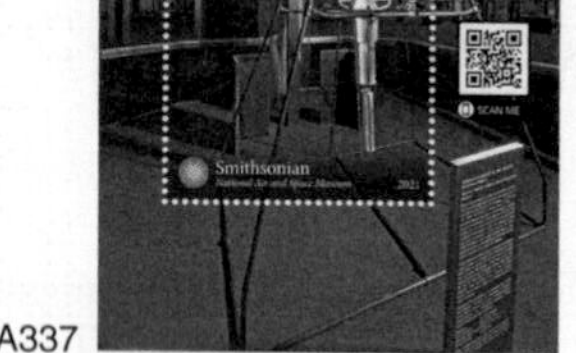

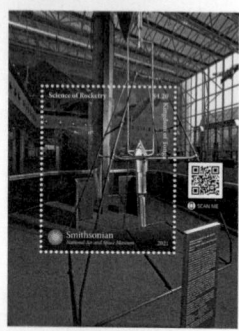

A337

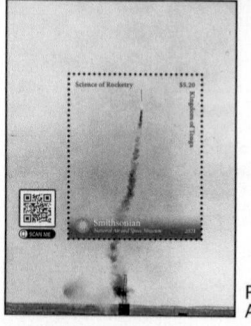

Rocketry
A338

No. 1451: a, Wernher von Braun (1912-77), space engineer standing near rocket display. b, Von Braun holding model of rocket with tip at left (mirrored image). c, Von Braun inspecting rocket parts with another man. d, Von Braun with pen and paper. e, Von Braun looking at rocket display with another man. f, Von Braun holding rocket model with tip at right.

No. 1452: a, Robert Goddard (1882-1945), builder of first liquid-fueled rocket, wearing lab coat. b, Goddard with his first liquid-fueled rocket, 1926. c, Head of Goddard. d, Goddard and rocket on sawhorse.

2.80pa, Von Braun meeting with government and military leaders, 1954. 4.20pa, Goddard's first liquid-fueled rocket. 5.20pa, Rocket launch.

2021, May 24 Litho. *Perf. 13*

1451 A334 2.25pa Sheet of 6, #a-f 12.50 12.50

1452 A335 2.50pa Sheet of 4, #a-d 9.00 9.00

Souvenir Sheets

Perf. 13¼x13

1453 A336 2.80pa multi 2.60 2.60

Perf. 13x13¼

1454 A337 4.20pa multi 3.75 3.75
1455 A338 5.20pa multi 4.75 4.75
Nos. 1453-1455 (3) 11.10 11.10

Miniature Sheets

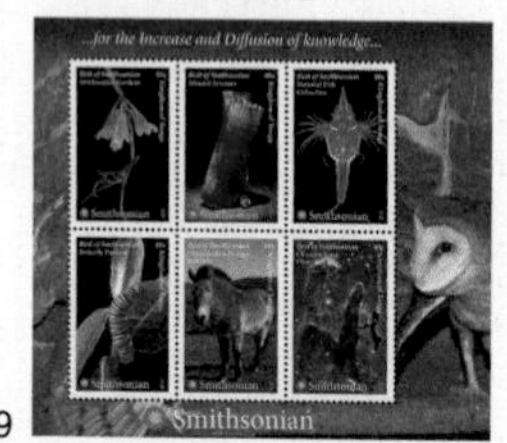

A339

Items in Smithsonian Institution Museums and Collections — A340

No. 1456: a, Flower. b, Mineral crystal. c, Fish. d, Caterpillar. e, Przewalski's horse. f, Image of "Pillars of Creation" of the Eagle Nebula.

No. 1457: a, Trumpet. b, Locomotive and tender. c, Book illustration. d, Gauges in airplane cockpit. e, Telegraph key. f, Quilt.

2021, May 24 Litho. *Perf. 13*

1456 A339 40s Sheet of 6, #a-f 2.25 2.25
1457 A340 50s Sheet of 6, #a-f 2.75 2.75

A341

A342

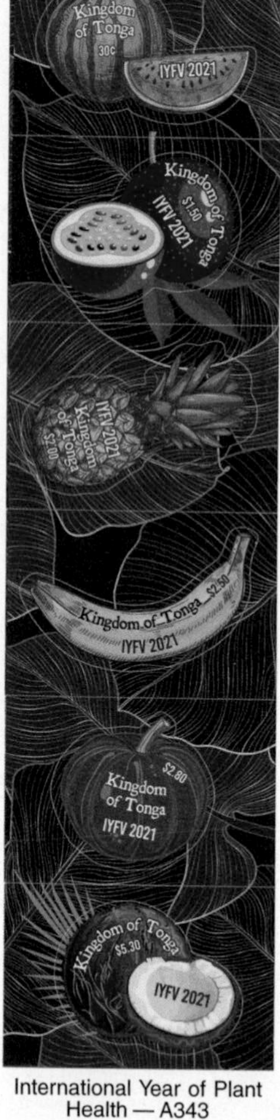

International Year of Plant Health — A343

No. 1460: a, 30s, Watermelons. b, 1.50pa, Passion fruits. c, 2pa, Pineapple. d, 2.50pa, Banana. e, 2.80pa, Pumpkin. f, 5.30pa, Coconuts.

Serpentine Die Cut 6¼ Horiz.

2021, June 10 Litho.

Self-Adhesive

1458 A341 2.50pa multi 2.25 2.25
1459 A342 20.60pa multi 18.50 18.50

Miniature Sheet

Die Cut

1460	A343	Sheet of 6	12.50	
a.		30s multi	.30	.30
b.		1.50pa multi	1.40	1.40
c.		2pa multi	1.90	1.90
d.		2.50pa multi	2.25	2.25
e.		2.80pa multi	2.60	2.60
f.		5.30pa multi	4.75	4.75

SEMI-POSTAL STAMP

Catalogue values for unused stamps in this section are for Never Hinged items.

No. 488 Surcharged in Silver

1982, Apr. 14 Litho.

B1 A86 1pa +50s on 3pa multi 4.50 4.50

AIR POST STAMPS

Catalogue values for unused stamps in this section are for Never Hinged items.

Type of Regular Gold Coin Issue

Designs: 10p, 1sh1p, Queen Salote standing, ½-koula coin, obverse. 11p, Coat of arms, ½-koula coin, reverse. 2sh1p, 2sh9p, Queen Salote standing, 1-koula coin, obverse. 2sh4p, Coat of arms, 1-koula coin, reverse.

Litho.; Embossed on Gilt Foil

1963, July 15 Unwmk. *Die Cut*

Diameter: 54mm

C1	A36	10p dp carmine	.25	.25
C2	A36	11p green	.35	.35
C3	A36	1sh1p violet blue	.35	.35

Diameter: 80mm

C4	A36	2sh1p magenta	.50	.50
C5	A36	2sh4p emerald	.65	.65
C6	A36	2sh9p violet	.65	.65
		Nos. C1-C6 (6)	2.75	2.75

See note after No. 133.

Map of Tongatabu and ¼-Koula Coin — AP1

Litho.; Embossed on Gilt Foil

1964, Oct. 19

C7	AP1	10p deep green	.30	.30
C8	AP1	1sh2p black	.40	.40
C9	AP1	3sh6p carmine	.85	.85
C10	AP1	6sh6p purple	1.60	1.60
		Nos. C7-C10 (4)	3.15	3.15

Pan-Pacific and Southeast Asia Women's Association Conf., Nukualofa, Aug. 1964. See note after No. 133.

For overprints and surcharges see Nos. C22-C26, C83-C86.

Nos. C1-C2, C4-C6 Srchd. like Regular Issue, 1965, in Black, White or Red

1965, Mar. 18

C11	A36	2sh3p on 10p (B)	1.40	.50
C12	A36	2sh9p on 11p (W)	2.50	1.25
C13	A36	4sh6p on 2sh1p	16.00	20.00
C14	A36	4sh6p on 2sh4p	16.00	20.00
C15	A36	4sh6p on 2sh9p	9.50	13.50
		Nos. C11-C15 (5)	45.40	55.25

Nos. 114-115, 117-118 Ovptd. or Srchd.

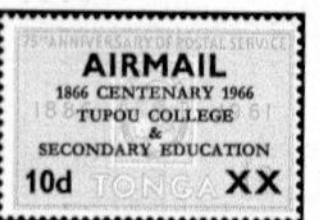

Perf. 14½x13½

1966, June 18 Wmk. 79

C16	A35	5p purple	.25	.25
C17	A35	10p on 1p brn org & car rose	.25	.25
C18	A35	1sh red brown	.25	.25
C19	A35	2sh9p on 2p ultra	.30	.25
C20	A35	3sh6p on 5p purple	.30	.25
C21	A35	4sh6p on 1sh red brn	.40	.25
		Nos. C16-C21 (6)	1.75	1.50

Centenary of Tupou College and secondary education. The overprint or surcharge is spaced differently on other values.

For Surcharges see Nos. C55-C57.

Nos. C7-C8 Ovptd. and Srchd. in Silver or Gold on Black, or in Black on Gold

Litho.; Embossed on Gilt Foil

1966, Dec. 16 Unwmk. *Die Cut*

C22 AP1 10p (S on B) .75 .25
C23 AP1 1sh2p (B on G) .80 .45
C24 AP1 4sh on 10p (S on B) 2.25 1.50
C25 AP1 5sh6p on 1sh2p (B on G) 2.50 2.50
C26 AP1 10sh6p on 1sh2p (G on B) 3.00 3.00
Nos. C22-C26 (5) 9.30 7.70

In memory of Queen Salote (1900-65). See Nos. C83-C86.

King Taufa'ahau Type of Regular Issue, 1967

Designs: 7s, 11s, 23s, 2pa, Taufa'ahau IV, obverse of new palladium coins. 9s, 21s, 29s, Coat of Arms, reverse.

Litho.; Embossed on Palladium Foil

1967, July 4

Diameter: 7s, 44mm; 9s, 29s, 52mm; 11s, 59mm; 21s, 68mm; 23s, 40mm; 2pa, 74mm.

C27 A38 7s red & black .25 .25
C28 A38 9s maroon & emer .35 .25
C29 A38 11s brt blue & org .45 .25
C30 A38 21s black & emer .80 .30
C31 A38 23s magenta & emer .90 .50
C32 A38 29s vio blue & emer 1.20 .65
C33 A38 2pa magenta & orange 4.00 4.00
Nos. C27-C33 (7) 7.95 6.20

See note after No. 181.

Regular Issues of 1953 Srchd. in Red or Black

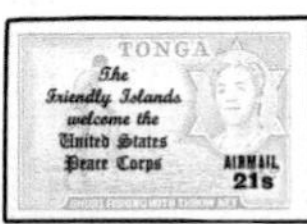

Wmk. 79

1967, Dec. 15 Engr. *Die Cut*

C34 A34a 11s on 3½p ultra (R) .25 .25
C35 A33a 21s on 1½p emerald .25 .25
C36 A34a 23s on 3½p ultra (R) .25 .30
Nos. C34-C36 (3) .75 .80

Arrival of the United States Peace Corps.

No. 112 Surcharged in Red

1968, Apr. 6 Engr. *Perf. 11x11½*

C37 A34i 11s on 10sh blk & yel .35 .35
C38 A34i 21s on 10sh blk & yel .35 .55
C39 A34i 23s on 10sh blk & yel .35 .55
Nos. C37-C39 (3) 1.05 1.45

Nos. C27-C33 Overprinted "HIS MAJESTY'S 50th BIRTHDAY" in Silver on Blue Panel on 7s, 11s, 23s and 2pa. "H.M.'s BIRTHDAY / 4. JULY. 1968" in Gold on Red Panel on 9s, 21s and 29s

Litho.; Embossed on Palladium Foil

1968, July 4 Unwmk. *Die Cut*

C40 A38 7s red & black .65 .25
C41 A38 9s maroon & emer .70 .25
C42 A38 11s brt blue & org .80 .25
C43 A38 21s black & emerald 1.90 .35
C44 A38 23s mag & emerald 1.90 .35
C45 A38 29s vio blue & emer 2.00 .40
C46 A38 2pa magenta & org 8.25 12.50
Nos. C40-C46 (7) 16.20 14.35

50th birthday of King Taufa'ahau IV.

Types of 1953 Surcharged

No. C47

No. C48

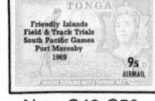

Nos. C49-C50, C52-C53

No. C51

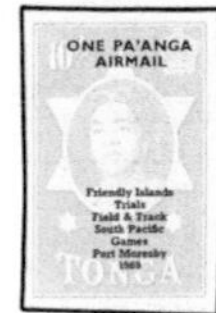

No. C54

Designs as before.

1968, Dec. 19 Engr. Wmk. 79

C47 A34d 6s on 6p yel & blk .25 .25
C48 A34b 7s on 4p purple & yel .25 .25
C49 A34e 8s on 8p blk & lt grn .25 .25
C50 A33a 9s on 1½p emerald .25 .25
C51 A34 11s on 3p brn org & yel .25 .25
C52 A34a 21s on 3½p dk blue .25 .25
C53 A34h 38s on 5sh sepia & yel 3.00 1.50
C54 A34i 1pa on 10sh orange yel .80 .80
Nos. C47-C54 (8) 5.30 3.80

Issued to publicize the field and track trials for the third South Pacific Games, Port Moresby, 1969. The overprint is in 5 lines on the horizontal stamps, in 7 lines on the vertical stamps. On the vertical stamps "Trial" is printed on the line ahead of "Field & Track." On No. C54 the denomination is spelled out.

Nos. C19-C21 Srchd.

Perf. 14½x13½

1968 Photo. Wmk. 79

C55 A35 1s on 2sh9p on 2p ultra 3.25 3.25
C56 A35 1s on 3sh6p on 5p pur 3.25 3.25
C57 A35 1s on 4sh6p on 1sh red brown 3.25 3.25
Nos. C55-C57 (3) 9.75 9.75

Pacific Games Type of Regular Issue

Design: Boxer.

1969, Aug. 13 Litho. *Die Cut*

Self-adhesive

C58 A40 9s orange, blk & pur .30 .30
C59 A40 11s orange, blk & dk bl .30 .30
C60 A40 20s org, blk & yel grn .45 .45
C61 A40 60s orange, blk & scar 1.10 1.10
C62 A40 1pa orange, blk & grn 1.50 1.50
Nos. C58-C62 (5) 3.65 3.65

See note after No. 231.

Oil Derrick on Map of Tongatabu and King Taufa'ahau IV — AP2

Litho.; Gold Embossed

1969, Dec. 23 Self-adhesive

C63 AP2 9s multicolored .40 .40
C64 AP2 10s multicolored .40 .40
C65 AP2 24s multicolored .75 .75
C66 AP2 29s multicolored .85 .85
C67 AP2 38s multicolored 1.10 1.10
Nos. C63-C67 (5) 3.50 3.50

1st scientific search for oil in Tonga.

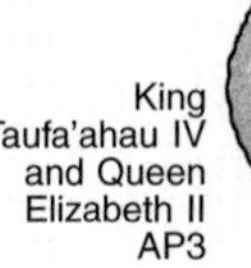

King Taufa'ahau IV and Queen Elizabeth II AP3

Litho.; Gold Embossed

1970, Mar. 7 Self-adhesive

C68 AP3 7s multicolored .75 .25
C69 AP3 9s multicolored .80 .35
C70 AP3 24s multicolored 2.00 .75
C71 AP3 29s multicolored 2.25 .80
C72 AP3 38s multicolored 3.00 1.25
Nos. C68-C72 (5) 8.80 3.40

See note after No. 242.

King Taufa'ahau Tupou IV Medal — AP4

Litho.; Gold Embossed

1970, June 4 Self-adhesive

C73 AP4 9s grnsh bl, ver & gold .30 .30
C74 AP4 10s lilac, bl & gold .30 .30
C75 AP4 24s yel, grn & gold .65 .65
C76 AP4 29s ultra, org & gold .90 .90
C77 AP4 38s ocher, emer & gold 1.25 1.25
Nos. C73-C77 (5) 3.40 3.40

See note after No. 247.

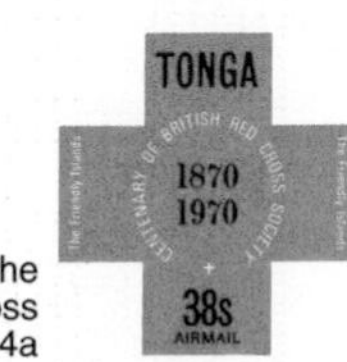

Centenary of the British Red Cross — AP4a

1970, Oct. 17 Litho. *Die Cut*

Self-adhesive

C78 AP4a 9s red & silver .35 .30
C79 AP4a 10s red & magenta .35 .25
C80 AP4a 18s red & brt green .75 .75
C81 AP4a 38s red & blue 2.75 2.75
C82 AP4a 1pa red & turq blue 6.50 6.50
Nos. C78-C82 (5) 10.70 10.55

See Nos. 258-262.

Nos. C22-C24 Surcharged

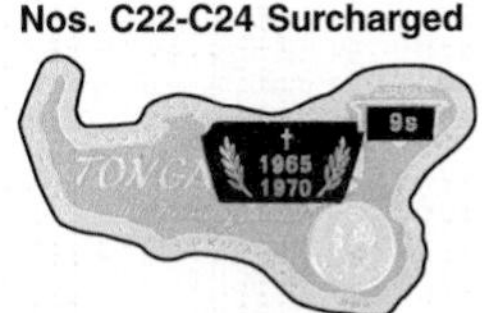

Lithographed; Embossed on Gilt Foil

1971, Jan. 31 *Die Cut*

C83 AP1 9s on #C22 (S on B) 1.00 .35
C84 AP1 24s on #C24 (G on B) 2.50 .75
C85 AP1 29s on #C23 (R on B) 2.75 1.25
C86 AP1 38s on #C23 (G on B) 1.75 1.60
Nos. C83-C86 (4) 8.00 3.95

In memory of Queen Salote (1900-1965).

Regular Issues of 1953, Srchd. in Red and Black

1971 Engr. Wmk. 79 *Imperf*

C87 A33a 9s on 1½p green .25 .25
C88 A34b 10s on 4p purple & yel .25 .25
C89 A33 38s on 1p yellow & blk .80 .60
Nos. C87-C89 (3) 1.30 1.10

See note after No. 272.

Types of Regular Issue Srchd. in Purple or Black "AIRMAIL," New Denomination and "HONOURING JAPANESE POSTAL CENTENARY 1871-1971"

1971

C90 A34f 18s on 1sh car & buff (P) .40 .25
C91 A34g 1pa on 2sh car & ultra 2.00 2.00

Surcharge on #C90 in 6 lines, on #C91 in 4.

Self-adhesive & Die Cut

Starting with Nos. C92-C96, all airmail issues are self-adhesive and die cut, unless otherwise stated.

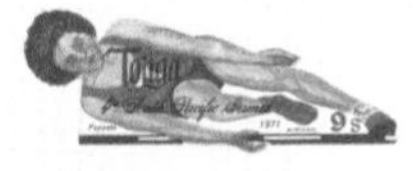

High Jump — AP5

1971, July Litho. Unwmk.

C92 AP5 9s brown, mag & blk .25 .25
C93 AP5 10s brown, blue & blk .25 .25
C94 AP5 24s brn, dk grn & blk .25 .25
C95 AP5 29s brown, vio & blk .40 .40
C96 AP5 38s brown, red & blk .55 .55
Nos. C92-C96 (5) 1.70 1.70

4th South Pacific Games, Papeete, French Polynesia, Sept. 8-19.

For surcharges see Nos. C141-C142.

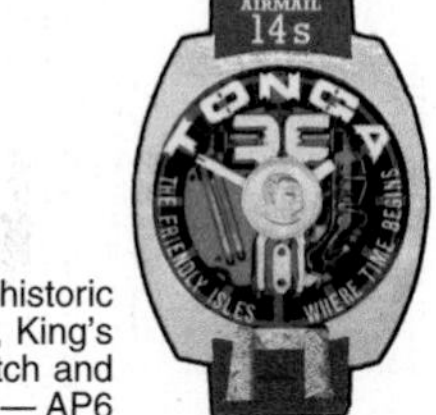

Prehistoric Trilithon, King's Watch and Portrait — AP6

Litho. and Embossed

1971, July 20

C97 AP6 14s dk brown & multi .75 .75
C98 AP6 21s ocher & multi 1.10 1.10

2nd anniversary of man's first landing on the moon and the placement of a Bulova Accutron there. See Nos. C117-118, CO47-CO48, CO61-CO62. Advertisement on peelable paper backing.

Medal Type of Regular Issue

Designs: 10s, Gold Medal of Merit, obverse (King Taufa'ahau IV). 75s, Silver Medal of Merit, obverse (King Taufa'ahau IV). 1pa, Bronze Medal of Merit, reverse.

1971, Oct. 30 Litho. & Embossed

C99 A47 10s gold & multi .25 .25
C100 A47 75s silver & multi 1.25 1.25
C101 A47 1pa bronze & multi 1.40 1.40
Nos. C99-C101 (3) 2.90 2.90

Girl with Blocks and UNICEF Emblem — AP7

1971, Dec. Litho.

C102 AP7 10s multicolored .25 .25
C103 AP7 15s multicolored .35 .35
C104 AP7 25s multicolored .55 .55
C105 AP7 50s multicolored 1.20 1.20
C106 AP7 1pa multicolored 2.25 2.25
Nos. C102-C106 (5) 4.60 4.60

25th anniversary of UNICEF.

Ship Type of Regular Issue

Design: Map of Merchant Marine routes from Tonga and cargo ship "Niuvakai."

1972, Apr. 14

C107 A49 9s ver & multi .70 .35
C108 A49 12s multicolored .90 .35
C109 A49 14s dk pur & multi 1.00 .35
C110 A49 75s olive & multi 5.50 4.00
C111 A49 90s black & multi 5.50 5.25
Nos. C107-C111 (5) 13.60 10.30

For surcharge and overprint see No. C124.

Coin Type of Regular Issue

Design: Coins on top; panel at bottom inscribed "5th anniversary world's first palladium coinage."

Litho.; Embossed on Metallic Foil

1972, July 15

C112 A50 9s silver & multi .25 .25
C113 A50 12s silver & multi .25 .25
C114 A50 14s silver & multi .40 .40
C115 A50 21s silver & multi .55 .55
C116 A50 75s silver & multi 1.60 1.60
Nos. C112-C116 (5) 3.05 3.05

Watch Type of 1971

Litho. and Embossed

1972, July 20

C117 AP6 17s multicolored 2.50 2.50
C118 AP6 38s multicolored 3.50 3.50

Advertisement on peelable paper backing.

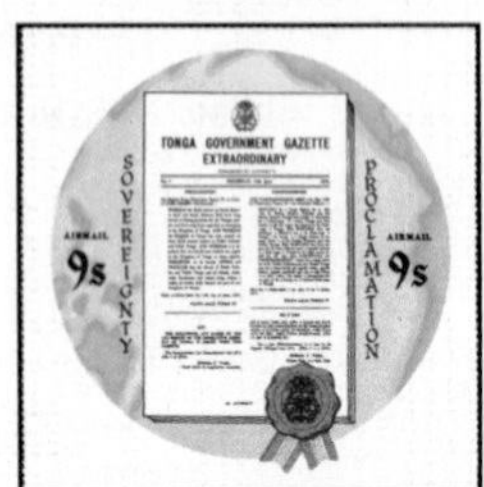

Proclamation of Sovereignty — AP8

1972, Dec. 9 **Litho.**

C119 AP8 9s ultra & multi .25 .25
C120 AP8 12s red brown & multi .25 .25
C121 AP8 14s magenta & multi .30 .30
C122 AP8 38s brn org & multi .85 .85
C123 AP8 1pa olive & multi 2.25 2.25
Nos. C119-C123 (5) 3.90 3.90

Tonga's proclamation of sovereignty over the Minerva Reefs, June 1972.

No. C107 Surcharged

1972, Nov. **Litho.**

C124 A49 7s on 9s multicolored 1.50 1.50

Inauguration of internal airmail service Nukualofa-Vavau, Nov. 1972.

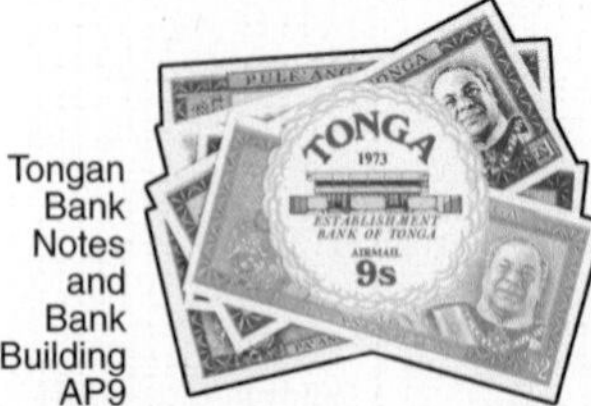

Tongan Bank Notes and Bank Building AP9

1973, Mar. 30 **Litho.**

C125 AP9 9s multicolored .25 .25
C126 AP9 12s ultra & multi .25 .25
C127 AP9 17s dp car & multi .35 .25
C128 AP9 50s lt blue & multi 1.25 1.00
C129 AP9 90s multicolored 2.25 2.25
Nos. C125-C129 (5) 4.35 4.00

Establishment of Bank of Tonga.

Boy Scout Emblem AP10

1973, June 29 **Litho.**

C130 AP10 9s silver & multi .55 .25
C131 AP10 12s silver & multi .65 .35
C132 AP10 14s silver & multi .95 .55
C133 AP10 17s silver & multi 1.10 .65
C134 AP10 1pa silver & multi 11.00 7.00
Nos. C130-C134 (5) 14.25 8.80

See note after No. 326.
For surcharges see Nos. C143-C144.

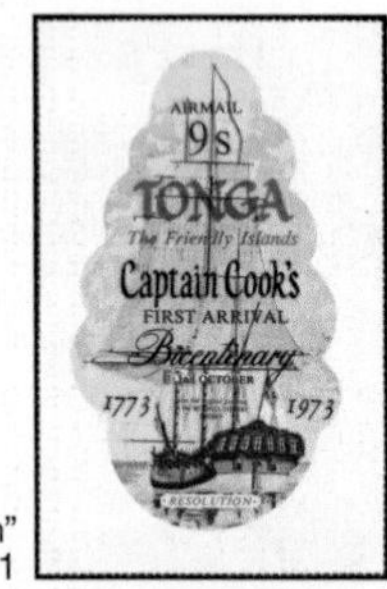

"Resolution" AP11

1973, Oct. 2 **Litho.**

C135 AP11 9s multicolored .75 .30
C136 AP11 14s multicolored 1.50 .60
C137 AP11 29s multicolored 4.50 2.25
C138 AP11 38s multicolored 5.00 3.00
C139 AP11 75s multicolored 9.50 4.50
Nos. C135-C139 (5) 21.25 10.65

Bicentenary of Capt. Cook's arrival.

Nos. 277, C96, C94, C130 and C132 Surcharged in Silver, Violet or Black: "Commonwealth Games Christchurch 1974"

1973, Dec. 19

C140 A46 7s on 25s multi (S) .25 .25
C141 AP5 9s on 38s multi (V) .25 .25
C142 AP5 24s multicolored (B) .70 .45
C143 AP10 29s on 9s multi (V) .90 .80
C144 AP10 40s on 14s multi (B) 1.10 1.00
Nos. C140-C144 (5) 3.20 2.75

10th British Commonwealth Games, Christchurch, New Zealand, Jan. 24-Feb. 2, 1974. No. C140 is overprinted "AIRMAIL" in black; the silver surcharge and overprint are on black panels.

Parrot of Eua — AP12

1974, Mar. 20 **Litho.**

C145 AP12 7s multicolored 1.20 .75
C146 AP12 9s multicolored 1.25 .85
C147 AP12 12s multicolored 1.50 .85
C148 AP12 14s multicolored 1.60 .85
C149 AP12 17s multicolored 1.60 1.25
C150 AP12 29s multicolored 2.75 1.60
C151 AP12 38s multicolored 3.25 1.60
C152 AP12 50s multicolored 3.75 3.75
C153 AP12 75s multicolored 5.00 5.00
Nos. C145-C153 (9) 21.90 16.50

Printed in rolls of 500. Self-adhesive rose red control number in upper left corner.

Carrier Pigeon Scattering Letters over Tonga AP13

1974, June 20 **Typo.**

C154 AP13 14s lt blue & multi .35 .35
C155 AP13 21s lt blue & multi .45 .45
C156 AP13 60s lt blue & multi 1.40 1.40
C157 AP13 75s lt blue & multi 1.50 1.50
C158 AP13 1pa lt blue & multi 2.00 2.00
Nos. C154-C158 (5) 5.70 5.70

Centenary of Universal Postal Union.

Girl Guide Leaders AP14

1974, Sept. 11 **Litho.**

C159 AP14 14s blue & multi 1.00 .55
C160 AP14 16s blue & multi 1.00 .55
C161 AP14 29s blue & multi 2.25 1.25
C162 AP14 31s blue & multi 2.50 1.50
C163 AP14 75s blue & multi 6.00 5.00
Nos. C159-C163 (5) 12.75 8.85

Girl Guides of Tonga.
For surcharges and overprints see Nos. C190-C191, C193.

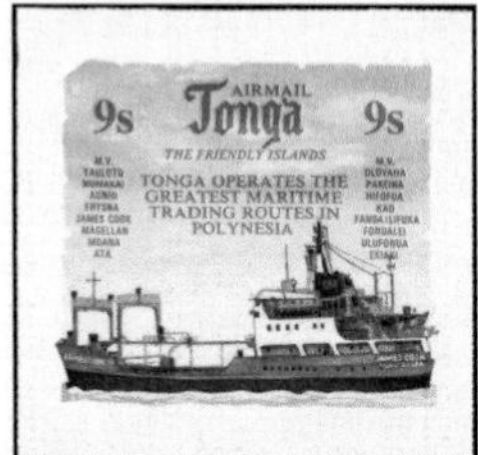

Freighter "James Cook" and List of Tongan Merchantmen — AP15

1974, Dec. 11

C164 AP15 9s blue & multi 1.25 .30
C165 AP15 14s blue & multi 1.75 .55
C166 AP15 17s blue & multi 2.00 .60
C167 AP15 60s blue & multi 4.50 3.75
C168 AP15 90s blue & multi 6.00 5.50
Nos. C164-C168 (5) 15.50 10.70

Establishment of Royal Marine Institute.

Beach — AP16

Designs: 12s, 14s, like 9s. 17s, 38s, Surf.

1975, Mar. 11 **Litho.**

C169 AP16 9s gold & multi .25 .25
C170 AP16 12s gold & multi .25 .25
C171 AP16 14s gold & multi .25 .25
C172 AP16 17s gold & multi .25 .25
C173 AP16 38s gold & multi .85 .85
Nos. C169-C173 (5) 1.85 1.85

First meeting of South Pacific area Prime Ministers. See note after No. 226.
For surcharges see Nos. C229, C298.

Women's Discus and Games' Emblem AP17

1975, June 11

C174 AP17 9s multicolored .25 .25
C175 AP17 12s multicolored .30 .25
C176 AP17 14s multicolored .30 .25
C177 AP17 17s black & multi .35 .30
C178 AP17 90s olive & multi 1.50 1.50
Nos. C174-C178 (5) 2.70 2.55

5th South Pacific Games, Guam, Aug. 1-10. See note after No. 226.
For surcharges see Nos. C230-C231.

FAO Type of 1975

Designs (FAO Coins): 12s, Coins showing cattle, corn and pig. 14s, Cornucopias; coins showing king, family planning emblem and melons. 25s, Bananas and treasure chest. 50s, King Taufa'ahau. 1pa, Palms.

1975, Sept. 3

C179 A62 12s multicolored .40 .40
C180 A62 14s blue & multi .40 .40
C181 A62 25s silver, blk & org .60 .60
C182 A62 50s car, sil & blk 1.10 1.10
C183 A62 1pa silver & black 2.25 2.25
Nos. C179-C183 (5) 4.75 4.75

Size of paper backing of 14s: 82x50mm; others 45x45mm. See note after No. 226.

Coin Type of 1975

Coins: 9s, King Taufa'ahau IV, obverse. 12s, Queen Salote III, 75pa reverse and obverse. 14s, 10pa reverse. 38s, King Taufa'ahau IV, 10pa reverse and observe. 1pa, Heads of four constitutional monarchs.

1975, Nov. 4 **Lt. Blue Background**

C184 A63 9s black, sil & red .50 .35
C185 A63 12s gold, blk & grn .55 .35
C186 A63 14s black, sil & ol .55 .35
C187 A63 38s gold, blk & org 1.50 .75
C188 A63 1pa black, sil & blue 3.50 3.50
Nos. C184-C188 (5) 6.60 5.30

Size of paper backing of 1pa: 87x78mm, others 65x60mm. See note after No. 226.

Nos. 344-345, C160, C163 Srchd. and Ovptd. in Carmine on Silver, Green or Gold

a

b

1976, Feb. 24 **Litho.**

C189 A58 (a) 12s on 20s (S) 1.75 .70
C190 AP14 (b) 14s on 16s (Gr) 1.75 .70
C191 AP14 (b) 16s (G) 1.75 .70
C192 A58 (a) 38s on 40s (G) 3.50 .75
C193 AP14 (b) 75s (S) 6.50 5.50
Nos. C189-C193 (5) 15.25 8.35

21st Olympic Games, Montreal, Canada, July 17-Aug. 1. See note after No. 226.

Bicentennial Type of 1976

Signers of Declaration of Independence, Flags of US and Tonga: 12s, Abraham Clark, George Ross, Thomas Lynch, Jr., Charles Carroll, Roger Sherman (no flags). 14s, Robert Treat Paine, Thomas Jefferson, Thomas McKean, John Adams. 17s, Button Gwinnett, Lewis Morris, Caesar Rodney, Richard Henry Lee. 38s, John Hart, Samuel Huntington, Philip Livingston, John Morton. 1pa, John Hancock, Joseph Hewes, Josiah Bartlett, John Witherspoon.

1976, May 26

C194 A66 12s buff & multi .35 .25
C195 A66 14s buff & multi .40 .25
C196 A66 17s buff & multi .40 .30
C197 A66 38s buff & multi 1.75 .75
C198 A66 1pa buff & multi 3.25 4.25
Nos. C194-C198 (5) 6.15 5.80

See note after No. 381.

Missionary Ship "Triton" — AP18

1976, Aug. 25 **Litho.**

C199	AP18	9s pink & multi	.65	.40
C200	AP18	12s multicolored	.70	.45
C201	AP18	14s multicolored	.80	.55
C202	AP18	17s buff & multi	1.00	.60
C203	AP18	38s multicolored	2.25	1.10
		Nos. C199-C203 (5)	5.40	3.10

See note after No. 386.

For surcharges see Nos. C234, C294, C299.

Treaty Signing Ceremony, Nukualofa — AP19

1976, Nov. 1

C204	AP19	11s multicolored	.25	.25
C205	AP19	17s multicolored	.45	.45
C206	AP19	18s multicolored	.45	.45
C207	AP19	31s multicolored	.65	.85
C208	AP19	39s multicolored	.75	1.00
		Nos. C204-C208 (5)	2.55	3.00

See note after No. 391.

For surcharges see Nos. C235, C295.

Elizabeth II and Taufa'ahau IV — AP20

1977, Feb. 7

C209	AP20	15s gray & multi	.35	.35
C210	AP20	17s gray & multi	.35	.35
C211	AP20	22s gray & multi	3.00	1.50
C212	AP20	31s gray & multi	.35	.45
C213	AP20	39s gray & multi	.35	.45
		Nos. C209-C213 (5)	*4.40*	*3.10*

See note after No. 396.

Coronation Coin — AP21

1977, July 4 **Litho.**

C214	AP21	11s multicolored	.30	.30
C215	AP21	17s multicolored	.40	.40
C216	AP21	18s multicolored	.40	.40
C217	AP21	39s multicolored	.65	.65
C218	AP21	1pa multicolored	2.25	2.25
		Nos. C214-C218 (5)	4.00	4.00

See note after No. 401.

See Nos. CO120-CO122.

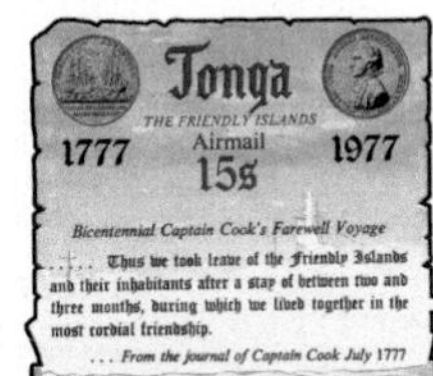

Capt. Cook Medal and Journal Quotation AP22

1977, Sept. 27

C219	AP22	15s multicolored	1.75	1.25
C220	AP22	22s multicolored	2.75	2.75
C221	AP22	31s multicolored	3.25	2.75
C222	AP22	50s multicolored	4.50	4.75
C223	AP22	1pa multicolored	8.00	9.00
		Nos. C219-C223 (5)	20.25	20.50

Bicentenary of Capt. Cook's farewell voyage.

See Nos. CO123-CO125.

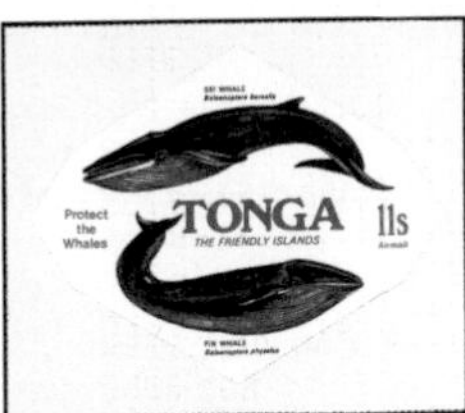

Sei and Fin Whales AP23

1977, Dec. 16

C224	AP23	11s blk, vio & bl	3.50	.90
C225	AP23	17s blk, red & bl	4.50	1.00
C226	AP23	18s blk, grn & bl	4.50	1.25
C227	AP23	39s blk, brn & bl	5.75	2.25
C228	AP23	50s blk, mag & bl	7.25	5.00
		Nos. C224-C228 (5)	25.50	10.40

Whale protection.

See Nos. CO126-CO128.

Stamps of 1975-77 Surcharged in Various Colors

1978

C229	AP16	17s on 38s (#C173;Gr)	1.75	1.75
C230	AP17	17s on 9s (#C174;B)	1.75	1.75
C231	AP17	17s on 12s (#C175;DBl)	1.75	1.75
C232	A63	17s on 38s (#C187;B)	1.75	1.75
C233	A66	17s on 12s (#C194; R on G)	1.75	1.75
C234	AP18	17s on 9s (#C199; B)	1.75	1.75
C235	AP19	17s on 18s (#C206; G on Brn)	1.75	1.75
C236	A66	1pa on 75s (#381; Gr on S)	*20.00*	*20.00*
C237	A66	1pa on 38s (#C197; DBl on G)	*9.00*	*9.00*
C238	OA15	1pa on 1.10pa (#CO119; S on DBl)	*9.00*	*9.00*

Edmonton Games Type of 1978

Canadian Maple leaf and Tongan coat of arms.

1978, May 5 **Litho.**

C239	A73	17s red & multi	.45	.30
C240	A73	35s red & multi	.75	.65
C241	A73	38s red & multi	.95	.95
C242	A73	40s red & multi	1.00	1.00
C243	A73	65s red & multi	1.75	1.75
		Nos. C239-C243 (5)	4.90	4.65

See note after No. 423.

King Type of 1978

Design: Head of King Taufa'ahau IV within 6-pointed star.

1978, July 4

C244	A74	11s multicolored	.25	.25
C245	A74	15s multicolored	.35	.35
C246	A74	17s multicolored	.40	.40
C247	A74	39s multicolored	.90	.90
C248	A74	1pa multicolored	2.25	2.25
		Nos. C244-C248 (5)	4.15	4.15

See note after No. 226.

Wildlife Type of 1978

1978, Dec. 15 **Litho. & Typo.**

C249	A77	17s Whale	3.75	2.00
C250	A77	22s Bat	3.75	2.00
C251	A77	31s Turtle	3.75	2.00
C252	A77	39s Parrot	8.00	3.50
C253	A77	45s like 17s	8.25	4.00
		Nos. C249-C253 (5)	27.50	13.50

Wildlife conservation. See note after No. 226.

Types of 1979

Designs: 15s, like No. 453. 17s, like No. 450. 31s, Rotary emblem. 39s, Ministry and tourism buildings, Bank of Tonga, GPO. 1pa, Dish antenna and map of Tonga.

1979, Feb. 16 **Litho.**

C254	A79	15s multicolored	2.00	.60
C255	A79	17s multicolored	2.00	.60
C256	A78	31s vio blue & gold	2.00	1.00
C257	A79	39s multicolored	1.50	1.00
C258	A79	1pa multicolored	4.50	4.50
		Nos. C254-C258 (5)	12.00	7.70

Decade of Progress. Paper backing shows map of Tonga.

Type of 1979

Tongan self-adhesive, free-form stamps.

1979, June 1

C259	A81	15s multicolored	.45	.35
C260	A81	17s multicolored	.45	.35
C261	A81	18s multicolored	.45	.35
C262	A81	31s multicolored	.65	.55
C263	A81	39s multicolored	.75	.60
		Nos. C259-C263 (5)	2.75	2.20

See note after No. 458.

Jet — AP24

1979, Aug. 17

C264	AP24	5s multicolored	.60	.60
C265	AP24	11s multicolored	.65	.65
C266	AP24	14s multicolored	.65	.65
C267	AP24	15s multicolored	.70	.70
C268	AP24	17s multicolored	.70	.70
C269	AP24	18s multicolored	.75	.75
C270	AP24	22s multicolored	.90	.90
C271	AP24	31s multicolored	1.25	1.25
C272	AP24	39s multicolored	1.50	1.50
C273	AP24	75s multicolored	2.50	1.75
C274	AP24	1pa multicolored	3.50	2.50
		Nos. C264-C274 (11)	13.70	11.95

Nos. C264-C274 issued in coils; self-adhesive control number in lower left corner of paper backing except on 14s, 18s, 22s, 75s. See note after No. 226.

See Nos. C303-C305.

View Type of 1979

Design: Kao Island. See note after No. 463.

1979, Nov. 23

C275	A82	5s multicolored	.25	.25
C276	A82	15s multicolored	.40	.40
C277	A82	17s multicolored	.40	.40
C278	A82	39s multicolored	1.00	1.00
C279	A82	75s multicolored	1.40	1.40
		Nos. C275-C279 (5)	3.45	3.45

Friendship Treaty Type of 1980

George Tupou I, Napoleon III, Adventure. See notes over #464 & after #468.

1980, Jan. 9 **Litho.**

C280	A83	15s multicolored	.65	.30
C281	A83	17s multicolored	.70	.35
C282	A83	22s multicolored	.85	.55
C283	A83	31s multicolored	1.50	1.00
C284	A83	39s multicolored	1.50	1.00
		Nos. C280-C284 (5)	5.20	3.20

Nos. C259-C263 Surcharged and Overprinted in Black on Silver "1980 OLYMPIC GAMES," Moscow '80 and Bear Emblems

1980, Apr. 30 **Litho.**

C285	A81	9s on 15s multi	.30	.30
C286	A81	16s on 17s multi	.50	.50
C287	A81	29s on 18s multi	.85	.85
C288	A81	32s on 31s multi	1.00	1.00
C289	A81	47s on 39s multi	1.75	1.75
		Nos. C285-C289 (5)	4.40	4.40

22nd Summer Olympic Games, Moscow, July 19-Aug. 3.

Scouting Activities in Rotary Emblem AP25

1980, Sept. 30 **Litho.**

C290	AP25	29s multicolored	.85	.85
C291	AP25	32s multicolored	.85	.85
C292	AP25	47s multicolored	1.25	1.25
C293	AP25	1pa multicolored	2.50	2.50
		Nos. C290-C293 (4)	5.45	5.45

Boy Scout Jamboree; Rotary International, 75th anniversary. Peelable backing shows map of Tonga.

Nos. C170, C185, C195, C200-C201, C208 Surcharged

1980, Dec. 3 **Litho.**

C294	AP18	29s on 14s multi	1.00	1.00
C295	AP19	29s on 39s multi	1.00	1.00
C296	A63	32s on 12s multi	1.25	1.25
C297	A66	32s on 14s multi	1.25	1.25
C298	AP16	47s on 12s multi	1.75	1.75
C299	AP18	47s on 12s multi	1.75	1.75
		Nos. C294-C299 (6)	8.00	8.00

IYD Type of 1981

1981, Sept. 9 **Litho.**

Size: 25x32mm

C300	A85	29s multicolored	.40	.40
C301	A85	32s multicolored	.45	.45
C302	A85	47s multicolored	.85	.85
		Nos. C300-C302 (3)	1.70	1.70

Jet Type of 1979

1982, Nov. 17 **Litho.**

C303	AP24	29s pink & black	*12.00*	*5.00*
C304	AP24	32s pale yel & blk	*12.00*	*5.00*
C305	AP24	47s lt brown & blk	*12.00*	*5.00*
		Nos. C303-C305 (3)	*36.00*	*15.00*

AIR POST SPECIAL DELIVERY STAMPS

Catalogue values for unused stamps in this section are for Never Hinged items.

Owl APSD1

1990, Feb. 21 **Litho.** ***Perf. 11½***

CE1	APSD1	10pa multi	12.50	12.50

APSD2

APSD3

APSD4

Short-eared Owl APSD5

2012, Aug. 30 *Perf. 14¼*

Stamps With White Frame All Around

CE2	APSD2 25pa multi	25.00	25.00
CE3	APSD3 25pa multi	25.00	25.00
CE4	APSD4 25pa multi	25.00	25.00
CE5	APSD5 25pa multi	25.00	25.00
	Nos. CE2-CE5 (4)	100.00	100.00

Stamps With White Frame on Two Sides

CE6	Sheet of 4	100.00	100.00
a.	APSD2 25pa multi	25.00	25.00
b.	APSD3 25pa multi	25.00	25.00
c.	APSD4 25pa multi	25.00	25.00
d.	APSD5 25pa multi	25.00	25.00

A sheet of 16 ontaining four of each of types APSD2-APSD5 without white frames on the stamps was produced in a limited printing.

Butterflies APSD6

Designs: 15pa, Scarlet Mormon butterfly. 50pa, Eggfly butterfly. 53pa, Great Mormon butterfly. 71pa, Dark cerulean butterfly. 83pa, Common lime butterfly. 89pa, Old world swallowtail butterfly.

2015-16 **Litho.** *Perf. 14¼*

Stamps With White Frames

CE7	APSD6 15pa multi	14.00	14.00
CE8	APSD6 50pa multi	47.00	47.00
CE9	APSD6 53pa multi	49.00	49.00
CE10	APSD6 71pa multi	65.00	65.00
a.	Souvenir sheet of 4, #CE7-CE10	175.00	175.00
CE11	APSD6 83pa multi	72.50	72.50
CE12	APSD6 89pa multi	77.50	77.50
a.	Souvenir sheet of 2, #CE11-CE12	150.00	150.00
	Nos. CE7-CE12 (6)	325.00	325.00

Souvenir Sheets

Stamps Without White Frame

CE13	APSD6 15pa multi	14.00	14.00
CE14	APSD6 50pa multi	47.00	47.00
CE15	APSD6 53pa multi	49.00	49.00
CE16	APSD6 71pa multi	65.00	65.00
CE17	APSD6 83pa multi	72.50	72.50
CE18	APSD6 89pa multi	77.50	77.50
	Nos. CE13-CE18 (6)	325.00	325.00

Issued: 15pa, 50pa, 9/1; 53pa, 71pa, No. CE10a, 11/2; 83pa, 89pa, No. CE12a, 1/4/16. Stamps on No. CE10a have white frames on 2 sides. Stamps on No. CE12a have white frames on 3 sides.

AIR POST OFFICIAL STAMPS

Catalogue values for unused stamps in this section are for Never Hinged items.

Nos. 115, 117-118, 111-113 Overprinted in Red

Engr.; Photo. (A35)

1962, Feb. 7 **Wmk. 79**

CO1	A35	2p ultra	16.00	7.50
CO2	A35	5p purple	16.00	8.00
CO3	A35	1sh red brown	9.00	4.00
CO4	A34h	5sh pur & yel	90.00	55.00
CO5	A34i	10sh black & yel	42.50	22.50
CO6	A34j	£1 ultra, car & yel	75.00	37.50
		Nos. CO1-CO6 (6)	248.50	134.50

Centenary of emancipation.

Nos. CO1-CO6 were overprinted locally. Overprint varieties of nos. CO1-CO6 exist with "OFFICIAl" instead of "OFFICIAL" and "MAIl" instead of "MAIL".

Type of Regular Gold Coin Issue

Design: 15sh, Queen Salote standing, 1-koula coin, obverse.

Litho.; Embossed on Gilt Foil

1963, July 15 **Unwmk.** *Die Cut*

Diameter: 80mm

CO7	A36 15sh black	6.25	6.25

Note after No. 133 also applies to No. CO7.

No. CO7 Surcharged like Regular Issue of 1965 in Black

1965, Mar. 18

CO8	A36 30sh on 15sh black	6.75	6.75

No. 116 Surcharged in Italic Letters Similarly to Nos. C16-C21

Perf. 14½x13½

1966, June 18 **Wmk. 79**

CO9	A35 10sh on 4p brt green	.45	.40
CO10	A35 20sh on 4p brt green	.65	.55

Centenary of Tupou College and secondary education.

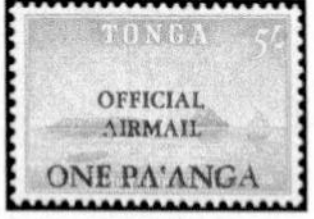

No. 111 Srchd. in Red

1967, Mar. 25 **Engr.** *Perf. 11½x11*

CO11	A34h 1p on 5sh pur & yel	3.00	3.00

Type of Regular Issue Surcharged

1967, Dec. 15 **Wmk. 79** *Die Cut*

CO12	A34j	30s on £1 multi	.45	.45
CO13	A34j	70s on £1 multi	.65	1.90
CO14	A34j	1.50pa on £1 multi	.85	3.25
		Nos. CO12-CO14 (3)	1.95	5.60

Arrival of US Peace Corps.

No. 113 Surcharged

Nos. CO15-CO16 Nos. CO17-CO18

1968, Apr. 6 **Engr.** *Perf. 11x11½*

CO15	A34j 40s on £1 multi	.55	.75
CO16	A34j 60s on £1 multi	.65	1.25
CO17	A34j 1pa on £1 multi	.90	2.50
CO18	A34j 2pa on £1 multi	1.40	3.25
	Nos. CO15-CO18 (4)	3.50	7.75

Type of 1953 Surcharged: "Friendly Islands / Trials / Field & Track / South Pacific / Games / Port Moresby / 1969 / OFFICIAL AIRMAIL"

Wmk. 79

1968, Dec. 19 **Engr.** *Die Cut*

CO19	A34j 20s on £1 grn & multi	.40	.40
CO20	A34j 1pa on £1 grn & multi	1.10	1.10

No. 176 Overprinted and Surcharged in Gold on Colored Panels (Green, Emerald, Violet or Lilac) like Nos. 203-209

Litho.; Embossed on Palladium Foil

1968 **Unwmk.**

CO21	A38 40s on 2s (G)	2.25	.75
CO22	A38 60s on 2s (E)	2.50	1.40
CO23	A38 1pa on 2s (V)	3.50	4.50
CO24	A38 2pa on 2s (L)	7.50	10.50
	Nos. CO21-CO24 (4)	15.75	17.15

50th birthday of King Taufa'ahau IV.

Pacific Games Type of Regular Issue

Design: Boxer.

1969, Aug. 13 **Litho.** *Die Cut*

Self-adhesive

CO25	A40 70s gray, red & grn	1.10	1.10
CO26	A40 80s gray, red & org	1.25	1.25

See note after No. 231.

Type of 1953 Regular Issue Surcharged

1969, Dec. 23 *Die Cut* **Wmk. 79**

CO27	A34j 90s on £1 grn & multi	3.50	3.50

First scientific search for oil in Tonga.

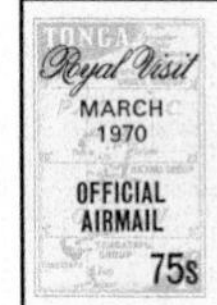

Type of 1953 Regular Issue Surcharged in Black, Violet Blue or Emerald

1970, Mar. 7 **Engr.** **Wmk. 79**

CO28	A34f 75s on 1sh red & yel	4.25	2.25
CO29	A34f 1pa on 1sh (VBl)	5.50	3.25
CO30	A34f 1.25pa on 1sh (E)	7.00	4.25
	Nos. CO28-CO30 (3)	16.75	9.75

See note after No. 242.

Regular Issue Srchd. in Black, Red or Emerald

1970, June 4 **Wmk. 79** *Die Cut*

CO31	A34h	50s on 5sh (B)	3.25	3.25
CO32	A34h	90s on 5sh (R)	4.00	4.00
CO33	A34h	1.50pa on 5sh (E)	5.00	5.00
		Nos. CO31-CO33 (3)	12.25	12.25

See note after No. 247.

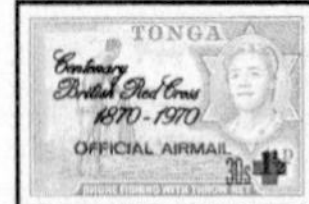

Regular Issue of 1953, Srchd. in Red and Purple or Black

1970, Oct. 17 **Engr.** *Die Cut*

CO34	A33a 30s on 1½p (B & R)	1.90	1.90
CO35	A34h 80s on 5sh (P & R)	5.00	5.00
CO36	A34h 90s on 5sh (P & R)	6.00	6.00
	Nos. CO34-CO36 (3)	12.90	12.90

Centenary of the British Red Cross.

Type of Regular Issue, 1953, Surcharged in Black, Purple, Blue or Green

1971, Jan. 31 **Engr.** *Die Cut*

CO37	A34i 20s on 10sh (Bk)	1.25	.85
CO38	A34i 30s on 10sh (P)	2.10	1.25
CO39	A34i 50s on 10sh (Bl)	3.50	2.10
CO40	A34i 2pa on 10sh (G)	13.75	11.75
	Nos. CO37-CO40 (4)	20.60	15.95

In memory of Queen Salote (1900-1965).

Type of Regular Issue, 1953, Surcharged in Red and Blue, Black or Purple

1971 **Engr.** **Wmk. 79** *Imperf*

Colors: Green & Yellow

CO41	A34c 30s on 5p (R & Bl)	1.40	.80
CO42	A34c 80s on 5p (R & Bk)	3.25	2.10
CO43	A34c 90s on 5p (R & P)	3.50	2.40
	Nos. CO41-CO43 (3)	8.15	5.30

See note after No. 272.

Self-adhesive & Die Cut

Starting with Nos. CO44-CO46, all airmail official issues are self-adhesive and die cut, unless otherwise stated.

Soccer Ball — OA1

1971, July **Litho.** **Unwmk.**

CO44	OA1	50s multi	1.00	1.00
CO45	OA1	90s multi	1.50	1.50
CO46	OA1	1.50pa multi	3.00	3.00
		Nos. CO44-CO46 (3)	5.50	5.50

4th South Pacific Games, Papeete, French Polynesia, Sept. 8-19.

For overprints see Nos. CO75-CO77.

Watch Type of Air Post Issues

Litho. and Embossed

1971, July 20

CO47	AP6 14s brown & multi	1.25	1.25
CO48	AP6 21s brn red & multi	1.75	1.75

Advertisement on peelable paper backing.

Nos. 243-244, 246 Surcharged

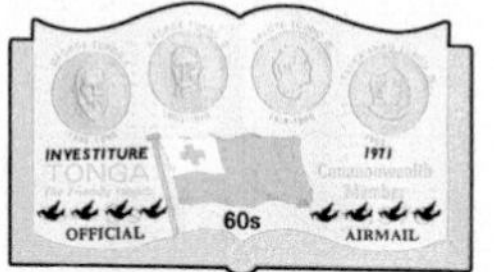

Litho.; Gold Embossed

1971, Oct. 30

CO49	A43	60s on 3s multi	1.20	1.20
CO50	A43	80s on 25s multi	1.40	1.40
CO51	A43	1.10pa on 7s multi	1.75	1.75
		Nos. CO49-CO51 (3)	4.35	4.35

First investiture of Tongan Medal of Honor.

"UNICEF" OA2

1971, Dec. **Litho.**
CO52 OA2 70s black & multi 1.75 1.75
CO53 OA2 80s multicolored 2.25 2.25
CO54 OA2 90s multicolored 2.40 2.40
Nos. CO52-CO54 (3) 6.40 6.40

25th anniversary of UNICEF.
For overprint see No. CO70.

Ship Type of Regular Issue

Design: Map of Merchant Marine routes from Tonga and tanker "Aoniu."

1972, Apr. 14
CO55 A49 20s multi 1.50 .70
CO56 A49 50s multi 3.25 2.25
CO57 A49 1.20pa multi 7.00 5.50
Nos. CO55-CO57 (3) 11.75 8.45

Coin Type of Regular Issue

Design: Coins in center, inscription panel above, date below coins.

Litho.; Embossed on Metallic Foil

1972, July 15
CO58 A50 50s silver & multi 1.30 1.30
CO59 A50 70s silver & multi 1.90 1.90
CO60 A50 1.50pa silver & multi 3.25 3.25
Nos. CO58-CO60 (3) 6.45 6.45

Watch Type of Air Post Issue

1972, July 20 **Litho.; Embossed**
CO61 AP6 17s multicolored 1.25 1.25
CO62 AP6 38s ocher & multi 2.50 2.50

Advertisement on peelable paper backing.

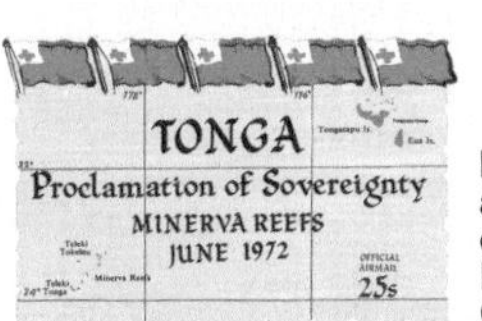

Flags and Map of Tonga Islands
OA3

1972, Dec. 9 **Litho.**
CO63 OA3 25s black & multi .45 .45
CO64 OA3 75s multicolored 1.30 1.30
CO65 OA3 1.50pa multicolored 2.75 2.75
Nos. CO63-CO65 (3) 4.50 4.50

Tonga's proclamation of sovereignty over the Minerva Reefs, June 1972.

No. 290 Surcharged in Black, Ultramarine or Green

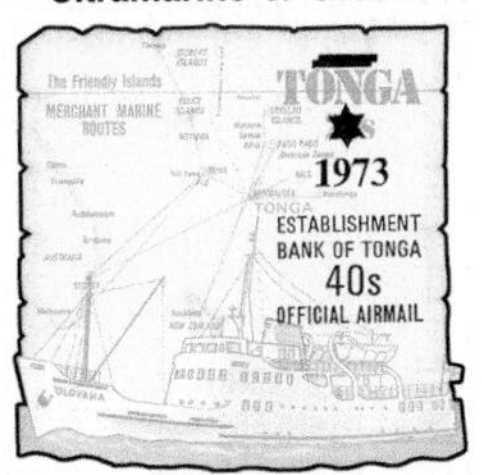

1973, Mar. 30 **Litho.**
CO66 A49 40s on 21s (B) 1.60 1.60
CO67 A49 85s on 21s (U) 3.25 3.25
CO68 A49 1.25pa on 21s (G) 4.00 4.00
Nos. CO66-CO68 (3) 8.85 8.85

Establishment of Bank of Tonga.

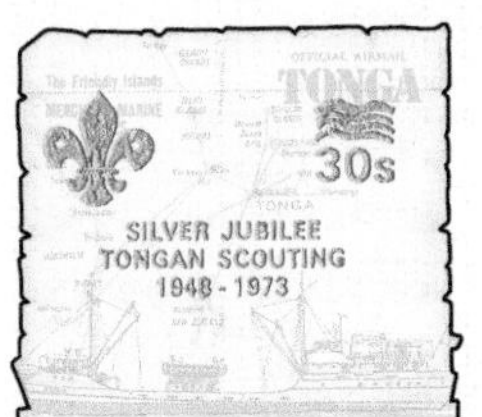

Nos. CO55 Ovptd. & Srchd. in Silver

No. CO53 Ovptd. in Silver

No. 247 Srchd. & Ovptd. in Silver on Dark Blue Panels

1973, June 29
CO69 A49 30s on 20s 11.00 3.00
CO70 OA2 80s multi 28.00 11.00
CO71 A43 1.40pa on 50s 40.00 26.00
Nos. CO69-CO71 (3) 79.00 40.00

25th anniv. of Tongan Boy Scout movement.

Tanker James Cook and Cook Medal
OA4

1973, Oct. 2 **Litho.**
CO72 OA4 25s multi 3.00 1.60
CO73 OA4 80s multi 7.50 5.00
CO74 OA4 1.30pa multi 9.50 8.25
Nos. CO72-CO74 (3) 20.00 14.85

Bicentenary of Capt. Cook's arrival.

Nos. CO44-CO46 Ovptd. in Dark Blue, Black or Green

1973, Dec. 19
CO75 OA1 50s multi (DBl) 1.25 1.25
CO76 OA1 90s multi (B) 2.10 2.10
CO77 OA1 1.50pa multi (G) 3.00 3.00
Nos. CO75-CO77 (3) 6.35 6.35

10th British Commonwealth Games, Christchurch, N.Z., Jan. 24-Feb. 2, 1974.

Peace Dove — OA5

1974, Mar. 20 **Litho.**
CO78 OA5 7s multicolored .50 .25
CO79 OA5 9s multicolored .65 .35
CO80 OA5 12s multicolored .65 .35
CO81 OA5 14s multicolored .90 .50
CO82 OA5 17s multicolored 1.00 .65
CO83 OA5 29s multicolored 1.75 1.10
CO84 OA5 38s multicolored 2.50 1.40
CO85 OA5 50s multicolored 3.00 3.00
CO86 OA5 75s multicolored 4.25 4.25
Nos. CO78-CO86 (9) 15.20 11.85

Printed in rolls of 500. Self-adhesive lilac control number in upper left corner.

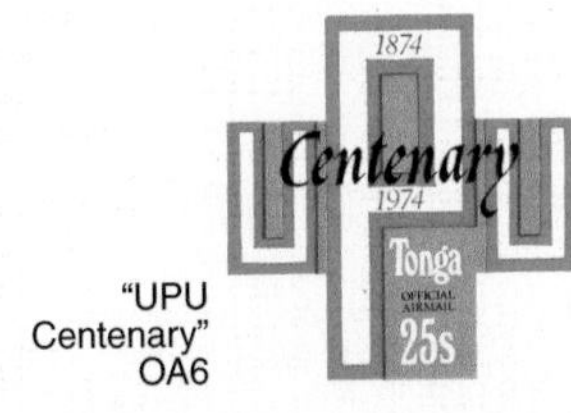

"UPU Centenary"
OA6

1974, June 20 **Typo.**
CO87 OA6 25s red, green & blk .80 .80
CO88 OA6 35s yel, red lil & blk .90 .90
CO89 OA6 70s dp org, bl & blk 1.75 1.75
Nos. CO87-CO89 (3) 3.45 3.45

Centenary of Universal Postal Union.

Lady Baden-Powell
OA7

1974, Sept. 11 **Litho.**
CO90 OA7 45s emer & multi 4.50 2.75
CO91 OA7 55s emer & multi 6.50 3.75
CO92 OA7 1pa emer & multi 9.25 5.50
Nos. CO90-CO92 (3) 20.25 12.00

Girl Guides of Tonga.
For overprints see Nos. CO105-CO107.

Handshake and Institute's Emblem — OA8

Institute's Emblem and Banknotes — OA9

1974, Dec. 11
CO93 OA8 30s multicolored 2.75 1.60
CO94 OA8 35s multicolored 3.25 2.10
CO95 OA9 80s red & multi 6.50 4.50
Nos. CO93-CO95 (3) 12.50 8.20

Establishment of Royal Marine Institute.

Arch and Palms
OA10

Designs: 75s, 1.25pa, Dawn over lagoon.

1975, Mar. 11 **Litho.**
CO96 OA10 50s multi 1.50 1.50
CO97 OA10 75s multi 2.60 2.60
CO98 OA10 1.25pa multi 3.50 3.50
Nos. CO96-CO98 (3) 7.60 7.60

First meeting of South Pacific area Prime Ministers. See note after No. 226.

Track and Games' Emblem
OA11

1975, June 11
CO99 OA11 38s multi .75 .75
CO100 OA11 75s multi 1.50 1.50
CO101 OA11 1.20pa multi 2.50 2.50
Nos. CO99-CO101 (3) 4.75 4.75

5th South Pacific Games, Guam, Aug. 1-10. See note after No. 226.
For surcharge see No. 418.

Four Constitutional Monarchs — OA12

Litho.; Embossed on Gilt Foil

1975, Nov. 4
CO102 OA12 17s multicolored 1.00 1.00
CO103 OA12 60s multicolored 2.50 2.50
CO104 OA12 90s multicolored 3.00 3.00
Nos. CO102-CO104 (3) 5.40 5.00

No. CO90-CO92 Ovptd. in Carmine on Blue, Silver or Gold

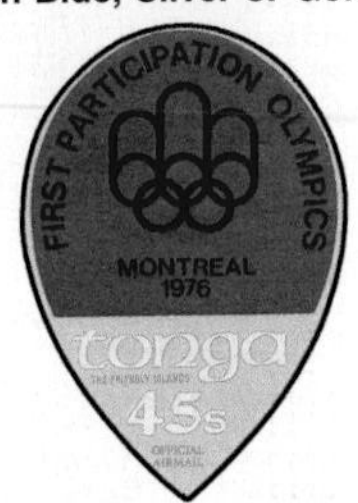

1976, Feb. 24 **Litho.**
CO105 OA7 45s multi (B) 3.50 1.40
CO106 OA7 55s multi (S) 3.50 1.60
CO107 OA7 1pa multi (G) 6.75 6.75
Nos. CO105-CO107 (3) 13.75 9.75

21st Olympic Games, Montreal, Canada, July 17-Aug. 1. See note after No. 226.

Bicentennial Type of 1976

Signers of Declaration of Independence: 20s, William Paca, Francis Lewis, George Read, Edward Rutledge, Thomas Heyward, Jr. 50s, George Walton, Matthew Thornton, Robert Morris, William Williams, James Smith. 1.15pa, Benjamin Rush, Samuel Adams, Samuel Chase, George Wythe, George Clymer.

1976, May 26
CO108 A66 20s buff & multi .65 .50
CO109 A66 50s buff & multi 2.00 1.25
CO110 A66 1.15pa buff & multi 4.00 4.00
Nos. CO108-CO110 (3) 6.65 5.75

See note after No. 381.

Inside View of Lifuka Chapel
OA13

1976, Aug. 25 **Litho.**
CO111 OA13 65s multi 2.75 2.75
CO112 OA13 85s multi 3.00 3.00
CO113 OA13 1.15pa multi 4.00 4.00
Nos. CO111-CO113 (3) 9.75 9.75

See note after No. 386.
For surcharge see No. CO181.

OA14

1976, Nov. 1
CO114 OA14 30s silver & multi .90 .90
CO115 OA14 60s silver & multi 2.25 2.25
CO116 OA14 1.25pa silver & multi 4.75 4.75
Nos. CO114-CO116 (3) 7.35 7.35

See note after No. 391.

Flags of Great Britain and Tonga OA15

1977, Feb. 7 **Litho.**

No.	Type	Description	Unused	Used
CO117	OA15	35s multi	.70	.45
CO118	OA15	45s multi	.30	.35
CO119	OA15	1.10pa multi	.45	.60
		Nos. CO117-CO119 (3)	1.45	1.40

See note after No. 396.
For surcharge see No. C238.

Coin Type of Air Post Stamps 1977

Design: Coronation coin, inscriptions in round upper panel.

1977, July 4

No.	Type	Description	Unused	Used
CO120	AP21	20s multicolored	.60	.60
CO121	AP21	40s multicolored	1.20	1.20
CO122	AP21	80s multicolored	2.40	2.40
		Nos. CO120-CO122 (3)	4.20	4.20

See note after No. 401.

Capt. Cook Type of Air Post Stamps 1977

Design: Inscription and flying dove.

1977, Sept. 27

No.	Type	Description	Unused	Used
CO123	AP22	20s gold & multi	2.75	2.50
CO124	AP22	55s on 20s multi	8.00	6.50
CO125	AP22	85s on 20s multi	8.50	9.00
		Nos. CO123-CO125 (3)	19.25	18.00

Printed on peelable paper backing showing dark brown replica of entry in Capt. Cook's diary.

Whale Type of Air Post Stamps 1977

Design: Blue whale.

1977, Dec. 16

No.	Type	Description	Unused	Used
CO126	AP23	45s multicolored	7.75	3.50
CO127	AP23	65s multicolored	11.00	5.00
CO128	AP23	85s multicolored	13.00	6.00
		Nos. CO126-CO128 (3)	31.75	14.50

Whale protection.

Games' Emblem and Athletes — OA16

1978, May 5 **Litho.**

No.	Type	Description	Unused	Used
CO129	OA16	30s red & multi	.70	.70
CO130	OA16	60s red & multi	1.40	1.40
CO131	OA16	1pa red & multi	2.50	2.50
		Nos. CO129-CO131 (3)	4.60	4.60

See note after No. 423.

King Type of 1978

Head of King Taufa'ahau IV on medal.

1978, July 4

No.	Type	Description	Unused	Used
CO132	A74	26s multicolored	.60	.60
CO133	A74	85s multicolored	1.90	1.90
CO134	A74	90s multicolored	2.25	2.25
		Nos. CO132-CO134 (3)	4.75	4.75

See note after No. 226.

Wildlife Type of 1978

1978, Dec. 15 **Litho. & Typo.**

No.	Type	Description	Unused	Used
CO150	A77	40s Whale	7.75	4.00
CO151	A77	50s Bat	7.75	4.00
CO152	A77	1.10pa Turtle	10.50	9.00
		Nos. CO150-CO152 (3)	26.00	17.00

Wildlife conservation. See note after No. 226.

Types of 1979

Designs: 38s, Red Cross and star. 74s, like No. 451. 80s, like No. 450.

1979, Feb. 16 **Litho.**

No.	Type	Description	Unused	Used
CO153	A78	38s multicolored	1.50	1.00
CO154	A80	74s multicolored	2.00	2.00
CO155	A79	80s multicolored	3.00	3.00
		Nos. CO153-CO155 (3)	5.60	3.70

Decade of Progress. Paper backing shows map of Tonga.

Hands Peeling off No. CO118 OA17

1979, June 1

No.	Type	Description	Unused	Used
CO156	OA17	45s multicolored	1.50	1.25
CO157	OA17	65s multicolored	2.00	1.75
CO158	OA17	80s multicolored	2.75	2.25
		Nos. CO156-CO158 (3)	5.25	5.25

See note after No. 458.
For surcharges see Nos. CO176-CO178.

Parrot — OA18

1979, Aug. 1

No.	Type	Description	Unused	Used
CO159	OA18	5s multicolored	.60	.60
CO160	OA18	11s multicolored	.65	.65
CO161	OA18	14s multicolored	.65	.65
CO162	OA18	15s multicolored	.70	.70
CO163	OA18	17s multicolored	.70	.70
CO164	OA18	18s multicolored	.70	.70
CO165	OA18	22s multicolored	.80	.80
CO166	OA18	31s multicolored	1.10	1.10
CO167	OA18	39s multicolored	1.50	1.50
CO168	OA18	75s multicolored	2.25	2.25
CO169	OA18	1pa multicolored	2.75	2.75
		Nos. CO159-CO169 (11)	12.40	12.40

Nos. CO159-CO169 issued in coils. See note after No. 226.

The 5s exists with denomination in magenta and the leaves behind the bird missing. This seems to be a special printing that was not available for postal purposes.

View Type of 1979

Design: Niuatoputapu and Tafahi Islands. See note after No. 463.

1979, Nov. 23 **Litho.**

No.	Type	Description	Unused	Used
CO170	A82	35s multicolored	.75	.75
CO171	A82	45s multicolored	1.00	1.00
CO172	A82	1pa multicolored	2.00	2.00
		Nos. CO170-CO172 (3)	3.75	3.75

Friendship Treaty Type of 1980

Design: Church. See note after No. 468.

1980, Jan. 9 **Litho.**

No.	Type	Description	Unused	Used
CO173	A83	40s multicolored	1.25	1.25
CO174	A83	55s multicolored	1.75	1.75
CO175	A83	1.25pa multicolored	3.50	3.50
		Nos. CO173-CO175 (3)	5.75	5.75

Nos. CO156-CO158 Srchd. & Ovptd. in Black on Silver "1980 OLYMPIC GAMES," Moscow '80 and Bear Emblems

1980, Apr. 30 **Litho.**

No.	Type	Description	Unused	Used
CO176	OA17	26s on 45s	1.00	1.00
CO177	OA17	40s on 65s	1.60	1.60
CO178	OA17	1.10pa on 80s	4.00	4.00
		Nos. CO176-CO178 (3)	6.60	6.60

22nd Summer Olympic Games, Moscow, July 19-Aug. 3.

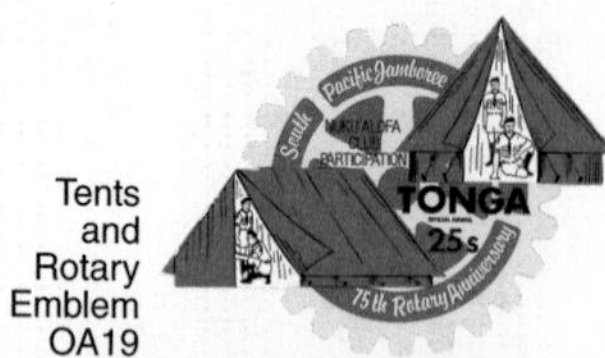

Tents and Rotary Emblem OA19

1980, Sept. 30 **Litho.**

No.	Type	Description	Unused	Used
CO179	OA19	25s multicolored	1.50	1.50
CO180	OA19	2pa multicolored	5.75	5.75

Boy Scout Jamboree; Rotary Intl., 75th anniv. Peelable backing shows map of Tonga.

For surcharges see Nos. 502-503.

No. CO111 Surcharged

1980, Dec. 3 **Litho.**

No.	Type	Description	Unused	Used
CO181	OA13	2pa on 65s multi	5.50	5.50

REGISTRATION STAMPS

Souvenir Sheets

Common Eggfly Butterfly R1

Inscriptions: No. F1, Domestic Registered Mail. No. F2, International Registered Mail.

2018, Sept. 6 **Litho.** ***Perf. 13***

No.	Type	Description	Unused	Used
F1	R1	8pa multi	7.00	7.00
F2	R1	20.60pa multi	18.50	18.50

OFFICIAL STAMPS

Types of Postage Issue of 1892 Overprinted in Carmine

Perf. 12x11½

1893, Feb. 13 **Wmk. 62**

No.	Type	Description	Unused	Used
O1	A4	1p ultra	11.50	*55.00*
a.		Half used as ½p on cover		
O2	A5	2p ultra	30.00	*62.50*
O3	A4	4p ultra	55.00	*110.00*
O4	A5	8p ultra	100.00	*200.00*
O5	A5	1sh ultra	110.00	*210.00*
		Nos. O1-O5 (5)	306.50	*637.50*

Values are for stamps of good color. Faded and discolored stamps sell for much less.

The overprinted initials stand for "Gaue Faka Buleaga" (On Government Service).

Nos. O1-O5 with Additional Surcharge Handstamped in Black

1893

No.	Type	Description	Unused	Used
O6	A4	½p on 1p ultra	20.00	*57.50*
O7	A5	2½p on 2p ultra	27.50	*50.00*
O8	A4	5p on 4p ultra	27.50	*50.00*
O9	A5	7½p on 8p ultra	27.50	*92.50*
O10	A5	10p on 1sh ultra	32.50	*95.00*
		Nos. O6-O10 (5)	135.00	*345.00*

Catalogue values for unused stamps in this section, from this point to the end of the section, are for Never Hinged items.

Redrawn Banana and Coconut Types of Regular Issue, 1970, Inscribed "Official Post"

1970, June 9 **Typo.** ***Die Cut***

Self-adhesive

No.	Type	Description	Unused	Used
O11	A39	1s yel, blk & dp car	.55	.55
O12	A39	2s yel, blk & blue	.70	.70
O13	A39	3s yel, blk & brn	.70	.70
O14	A39	4s yel, blk & emer	.70	.70
O15	A39	5s yel, blk & org	.80	.80

Litho.; Embossed on Gilt Foil

No.	Type	Description	Unused	Used
O16	A44	6s brown & multi	.95	.95
O17	A44	7s brown & multi	1.00	1.00
O18	A44	8s brown & multi	1.10	1.10
O19	A44	9s brown & multi	1.50	1.50
O20	A44	10s brown & multi	1.75	1.75
		Nos. O11-O20 (10)	9.75	9.75

Nos. O13, O17-O18 and O20 have self-adhesive control numbers in lower left corner of paper backing.

Types of Regular Issue 1970-72

1972, Sept. 30 **Typo.** ***Die Cut***

Self-adhesive

No.	Type	Description	Unused	Used
O21	A51	1s yel, red & brn	.25	.25
O22	A51	2s yel, grn & brn	.30	.25
O23	A51	3s yel, emer & brn	.35	.25
O24	A51	4s yel, blk & brn	.35	.25
O25	A51	5s yellow & brn	.35	.25
O26	A44	6s brown & green	.45	.25
O27	A44	7s brown & green	.50	.30
O28	A44	8s brown & green	.50	.30
O29	A44	9s brown & green	.50	.30
O30	A44	10s brown & green	.60	.35
O31	A52	15s green & ultra	1.00	.50
O32	A52	20s green & ver	1.25	.70
O33	A52	25s green & dk brn	1.40	.90
O34	A52	40s green & org	2.50	1.75
O35	A52	50s green & vio bl	3.00	2.25
		Nos. O21-O35 (15)	13.30	8.70

Paper backing is brown on Nos. O26-O35. Nos. O30-O35 have self-adhesive control number in lower left corner, Nos. O21-O29 lower right corner.

Types of Regular Issue 1978

Designs: 1s-5s, Bananas (similar to type A75). 6s-10s, Coconuts. 15s-1pa, Pineapples.

1978, Sept. 29 **Typo.** ***Die Cut***

Self-Adhesive

No.	Type	Description	Unused	Used
O36	A75	1s yellow & lilac	.30	.30
O37	A75	2s yellow & brown	.30	.30
O38	A75	3s multicolored	.40	.40
O39	A75	4s multicolored	.40	.40
O40	A75	5s multicolored	.40	.40
O41	A76	6s multicolored	.60	.60
O42	A76	7s multicolored	.60	.60
O43	A76	8s multicolored	.60	.60
O44	A76	9s multicolored	.60	.60
O45	A76	10s multicolored	.60	.60
O46	A76	15s multicolored	1.50	1.50
O47	A76	20s multicolored	1.60	1.60
O48	A76	30s multicolored	1.75	1.75
O49	A76	50s multicolored	2.25	2.25
O50	A76	1pa multicolored	3.25	3.25
		Nos. O36-O50 (15)	15.15	15.15

Nos. O36-O50 issued in coils; self-adhesive control numbers on paper backing except on 1s. See note after No. 226.

Nos. 563-577, 579 Ovptd.

1984-85 **Litho.** ***Die Cut***

Self-Adhesive

No.	Type	Description	Unused	Used
O52	A103	1s multicolored	.50	.50
O53	A103	2s multicolored	.50	.50
O54	A103	3s multicolored	.50	.50
O55	A103	5s multicolored	.50	.50
O56	A103	6s multicolored	.50	.50
O57	A103	9s multicolored	.75	.75
a.		Perf. 14½ ('85)	.75	.75
O58	A103	10s multicolored	.75	.75
O59	A103	13s multicolored	1.25	1.25
O60	A103	15s multicolored	1.25	1.25
O61	A103	20s multicolored	1.50	1.50
O62	A103	29s multicolored	1.75	1.75
O63	A103	32s multicolored	1.75	1.75
O64	A103	47s multicolored	2.00	2.00
O65	A103	1pa multicolored	4.00	4.00
O66	A103	2pa multicolored	7.00	7.00
O67	A103	5pa multicolored ('85)	12.00	12.00
		Nos. O52-O67 (16)	36.50	36.50

Nos. 532-534 Overprinted

1983, Feb. 22 **Litho.** ***Die Cut***

Self-Adhesive

No.	Type	Description	Unused	Used
O68	A96a	29s multicolored	4.75	4.75
O69	A96a	32s multicolored	4.75	4.75
O70	A96a	47s multicolored	10.00	10.00
		Nos. O68-O70 (3)	19.50	19.50

O68-O70 handstamped.

Nos. 618-624 Overprinted

1986, Apr. 16 Litho. *Die Cut*

Self-adhesive

O71	A103	4s on 2s, #618	1.00	1.00
O72	A103	4s on 13s, #619	1.00	1.00
O73	A103	42s on 3s, #620	3.25	3.25
O74	A103	42s on 9s, #621	3.25	3.25
O75	A103	57s on 6s, #622	3.50	3.50
O76	A103	57s on 20s, #623	3.50	3.50
O77	A103	2.50pa on 2pa, #624	12.00	12.00
		Nos. O71-O77 (7)	27.50	27.50

Marine Type Inscribed "POSTAGE & REVENUE" and "OFFICIAL"

1995-96 Litho. *Perf. 14*

O78	A155a	10s multicolored	.60	.60
O79	A155a	20s multicolored	.90	.40
O80	A155a	45s multicolored	1.10	.70
O81	A155a	60s multicolored	1.40	.95
O82	A155a	80s multicolored	1.75	1.25
O83	A155a	1pa multicolored	2.25	1.75
O84	A155a	2pa multicolored	4.00	4.00
O85	A155a	3pa multicolored	5.00	5.00
O86	A155a	5pa multicolored	9.75	9.75
O87	A155a	10pa multicolored	14.00	14.00
		Nos. O78-O87 (10)	40.75	38.40

Issued: 10s-80s, 9/25/95; 1pa-10pa, 5/31/96.

Nos. 1158-1169 Overprinted

2014, May 9 Litho. *Perf. 14*

Stamps With White Frames

O88	A236	60s multi	.65	.65
O89	A236	2.25pa multi	2.40	2.40
O90	A236	2.40pa multi	2.60	2.60
O91	A236	2.50pa multi	2.75	2.75
O92	A236	2.70pa multi	3.00	3.00
O93	A236	3pa multi	3.25	3.25
O94	A236	3.40pa multi	3.75	3.75
O95	A236	4pa multi	4.25	4.25
O96	A236	5pa multi	5.50	5.50
O97	A236	6.60pa multi	7.00	7.00
O98	A236	7.30pa multi	7.75	7.75
O99	A236	10pa multi	11.00	11.00
		Nos. O88-O99 (12)	53.90	53.90

Nos. 1203-1214 Overprinted

2014, May 9 Litho. *Perf. 14*

Stamps With White Frames

O100	A259	10s multi	.25	.25
O101	A259	20s multi	.25	.25
O102	A259	30s multi	.35	.35
O103	A259	40s multi	.45	.45
O104	A259	50s multi	.55	.55
O105	A259	80s multi	.85	.85
O106	A259	90s multi	.95	.95
O107	A259	1.10pa multi	1.25	1.25
O108	A259	1.20pa multi	1.40	1.40
O109	A259	2pa multi	2.25	2.25
O110	A259	12.50pa multi	13.50	13.50
O111	A259	20pa multi	21.50	21.50
		Nos. O100-O111 (12)	43.55	43.55

NIUAFO'OU

Tin Can Island

Catalogue values for all unused stamps in this country are for Never Hinged items.

Nos. 1-63 are die cut self-adhesive stamps on peelable inscribed backing paper.

Niuafo'ou Airport Type of Tonga

1983, May 11 Litho. *Die Cut*

1	A97	29s multicolored	1.75	1.75
2	A97	1pa multicolored	3.75	3.75

Map of Niuafo'ou — A1

1983, May 11

3	A1	1s buff, blk & red	.45	.45
4	A1	2s buff, blk & brt green	.45	.45
5	A1	3s buff, blk & brt blue	.45	.45
6	A1	3s buff, blk & brn org	.45	.45
7	A1	5s buff, blk & deep rose lil	.45	.45
8	A1	6s buff, blk & grnsh blue	.45	.45
9	A1	9s buff, blk & lt ol grn	.45	.45
10	A1	10s buff, blk & brt bl	.45	.45
11	A1	13s buff, blk & brt grn	.50	.50
12	A1	15s buff, blk & brn org	.60	.60
13	A1	20s buff, blk & grnsh blue	.75	.75
14	A1	29s buff, blk & deep rose lil	1.25	1.25
15	A1	32s buff, blk & lt ol grn	1.40	1.40
16	A1	47s buff, blk & red	1.90	1.90
		Nos. 3-16 (14)	10.00	10.00

See Nos. 19-22.

Tonga No. 520 Surcharged or Ovptd. in Purple or Gold "NIUAFO'OU / Kingdom of Tonga"

1983, May 11

17	A93	1pa on 2pa multi (P)	3.25	3.25
18	A93	2pa multicolored (G)	4.50	4.50

Nos. 17-18 each exist se-tenant with label.

Map Type of 1983

Value Typo. in Violet Blue

1983, May 30

19	A1	3s buff & black	.25	.25
20	A1	5s buff & black	.25	.25
21	A1	32s buff & black	1.50	1.50
22	A1	2pa buff & black	8.00	8.00
		Nos. 19-22 (4)	10.00	10.00

The denomination on Nos. 19-22 added like a surcharge and is larger than on Nos. 5-7, 15, covering part of the design.

Nos. 19-22 each exist se-tenant with label.

Eruption of Niuafo'ou, Sept. 9, 1946 — A2

29s, Lava flow. 32s, Moving to high ground. 1.50pa, Evacuation to Eua.

1983, Sept. 29

23	A2	5s shown	.75	.70
24	A2	29s multicolored	1.50	1.25
25	A2	32s multicolored	1.75	1.25
26	A2	1.50pa multicolored	5.00	*6.00*
		Nos. 23-26 (4)	9.00	9.20

Birds — A3

1s, Purple swamphen. 2s, White-collared kingfisher. 3s, Red-headed parrotfinch. 5s, Banded rail. 6s, Niuafo'ou megapode. 9s, Giant forest honeyeater. 10s, Purple swamphen, drinking. 13s, Banded rail, diff. 15s, Niuafo'ou megapode, diff. 29s, Red-headed parrotfinch, diff. 32s, White-collared kingfisher, diff.

1983, Nov. 15

27	A3	1s multicolored	1.00	1.00
28	A3	2s multicolored	1.00	1.00
29	A3	3s multicolored	1.00	1.00
30	A3	5s multicolored	1.25	1.25
31	A3	6s multicolored	1.60	1.60
32	A3	9s multicolored	2.50	2.50
33	A3	10s multicolored	2.50	2.50
34	A3	13s multicolored	2.75	2.75
35	A3	15s multicolored	2.75	2.75

Size: 25x39mm

36	A3	20s like #34	3.25	3.25
37	A3	29s multicolored	3.50	3.50
38	A3	32s multicolored	3.50	3.50
39	A3	47s like #35	4.25	4.25

Size: 32x42mm

40	A3	1pa like #33	8.00	*9.75*
41	A3	2pa like #35	11.00	*14.00*
		Nos. 27-41 (15)	49.85	*54.60*

Nos. 34-36, 39 and 41 horiz.

For surcharges see Nos. 66-73.

Wildlife — A4

29s, Green turtle. 32s, Flying fox, vert. 47s, Humpback whale. 1.50pa, Niuafo'ou megapode, vert.

1984, Mar. 7

42	A4	29s multicolored	.75	.75
43	A4	32s multicolored	.75	.75
44	A4	47s multicolored	3.00	2.10
45	A4	1.50pa multicolored	5.50	*8.25*
		Nos. 42-45 (4)	10.00	*11.85*

Map — A5

47s, Intl. Date Line, Cent.

1984, Aug. 20

46	A5	47s multicolored	1.00	1.00
47	A5	2pa shown	3.50	3.50

AUSIPEX '84 — A6

1984, Sept. 17

48	A6	32s Australia No. 15	.90	.90
49	A6	1.50pa No. 10	3.75	3.75

Souvenir Sheet

50	Sheet of 2	4.75	4.75

No. 50 contains two imperf. stamps similar to Nos. 48-49, but with denomination replacing logo. No. 50 without denominations was not valid for postage.

A7

Jacob Le Maire, 400th Birth Anniv.: 13s, Dutch band entertaining natives. 32s, Natives preparing kava. 47s, Native outrigger canoes. 1.50pa, Le Maire's ship at anchor.

1985, Feb. 20

51	A7	13s multicolored	.40	.40
52	A7	32s multicolored	.85	.85
53	A7	47s multicolored	1.15	1.15
54	A7	1.50pa multicolor	3.50	*3.50*
		Nos. 51-54 (4)	5.90	5.90

Souvenir Sheet

55	A7	1.50pa multicolored	3.50	3.50

Mail Ships — A8

1985, May 22 *Die Cut*

56	A8	9s Ysabel, 1902	.75	.75
a.		Perf. 14	.90	.90
57	A8	13s Tofua I, 1908	.85	.85
a.		Perf. 14	1.25	1.25
58	A8	47s Mariposa, 1934	1.75	1.75
a.		Perf. 14	2.00	2.00
59	A8	1.50pa Matua, 1936	3.50	3.50
a.		Perf. 14	4.50	*6.50*
		Nos. 56-59 (4)	6.85	6.85
		Nos. 56a-59a (4)	8.65	*10.65*

Rocket Mail — A9

Designs: 32s, Preparing to fire rocket. 42s, Rocket airborne. 57s, Captain watching rocket's progress. 1.50pa, Islanders reading mail.

1985, Nov. 5

60	A9	32s multicolored	1.50	.90
61	A9	42s multicolored	1.75	1.10
62	A9	57s multicolored	2.00	1.60
63	A9	1.50pa multicolored	4.25	*6.25*
		Nos. 60-63 (4)	9.50	9.85

Self-adhesive stamps discontinued.

Halley's Comet — A10

Nos. 64, 65: a, Drawing of Comet in 684. b, Comet shown in Bayeux Tapestry, 1066. c, Edmond Halley. d, Comet, 1910. e, Infrared photography, 1986.

1986, Mar. 26 *Perf. 14*

64	A10	42s Strip of #a.-e.	30.00	20.00
65	A10	57s Strip of #a.-e.	30.00	20.00

Nos. 32-39 Surcharged in Blue

1986, Apr. 16 *Die Cut*

Self-Adhesive

66	A3	4s on 9s #32	1.00	*2.75*
67	A3	4s on 10s #33	1.00	*2.75*
68	A3	42s on 13s #34	3.25	2.75
69	A3	42s on 15s #35	3.25	2.75
70	A3	57s on 29s #37	4.25	3.25
71	A3	57s on 32s #38	4.25	3.25
72	A3	2.50pa on 20s #36	12.50	*14.00*
73	A3	2.50pa on 47s #39	12.50	*14.00*
		Nos. 66-73 (8)	42.00	*45.50*

Placement of surcharge varies.

AMERIPEX '86 Type of Tonga

1986, May 22 *Perf. 14*

74	A117	57s Surveying	2.25	2.25
75	A117	1.50pa Agriculture	4.00	4.00
a.		Souv. sheet of 2, #74-75, imperf.	7.00	7.00

Peace Corps in Tonga, 25th anniv.

First Tongan Postage Stamps, Cent. — A11

42s, Swimmers with mail. 57s, Loading tin can mail into canoe. 1pa, Rocket mail. 2.50pa, Outrigger canoe.
No. 80, Outrigger canoe, diff.

1986, Aug. 27

76 A11 42s multicolored 1.25 1.25
77 A11 57s multicolored 1.50 1.50
78 A11 1pa multicolored 3.25 3.25
79 A11 2.50pa multicolored 4.25 4.25
Nos. 76-79 (4) 10.25 10.25

Souvenir Sheet

80 A11 2.50pa multicolored 9.50 9.50

Red Cross — A12

15s, Balanced diet. 42s, Post-natal care. 1pa, Insects spread disease. 2.50pa, Fight against drugs, alcohol, smoking.

1987, Mar. 11 ***Perf. 14x14½***

81 A12 15s multicolored 1.00 1.00
82 A12 42s multicolored 2.00 2.00
83 A12 1pa multicolored 3.75 3.75
84 A12 2.50pa multicolored 6.25 6.25
Nos. 81-84 (4) 13.00 13.00

Sharks — A13

1987, Apr. 29 ***Perf. 14***

85 A13 29s Hammerhead 2.50 2.25
86 A13 32s Tiger 2.50 2.25
87 A13 47s Gray nurse 3.00 2.75
88 A13 1pa Great white 5.25 *7.00*
Nos. 85-88 (4) 13.25 *14.25*

Souvenir Sheet

89 A13 2pa Shark attack 15.50 15.50

Aviators and Aircraft — A14

Designs: 42s, Capt. E. C. Musick and Sikorsky S-42. 57s, Capt. J.W. Burgess and Shorts S-30. 1.50pa, Sir Charles Kingsford Smith and Fokker F.VIIb-3m. 2pa, Amelia Earhart and Lockheed Electra 10A.

1987, Sept. 2

90 A14 42s multicolored 2.50 1.75
91 A14 57s multicolored 3.00 2.00
92 A14 1.50pa multicolored 5.00 5.00
93 A14 2pa multicolored 5.25 5.25
Nos. 90-93 (4) 15.75 14.00

First Niuafo'ou Postage Stamps, 5th Anniv. — A15

Designs: 42s, 57s, Niuafo'ou megapode, No. 15. 1pa, 2pa, Concorde, No. 1.

1988, May 18

94 A15 42s multicolored 1.00 .75
95 A15 57s multicolored 1.00 .95
96 A15 1pa multicolored 5.00 3.25
97 A15 2pa multicolored 6.00 4.50
Nos. 94-97 (4) 13.00 9.45

#96-97, Niuafo'ou Airport Inauguration, 5th anniv.

Settlement of Australia, Bicent. Type of Tonga

Miniature Sheet

Designs: a, Arrival of First Fleet, Sydney Cove, Jan. 1788. b, Aborigines. c, Early settlement. d, Soldier on guard. e, Herd of sheep. f, Horseman. g, Locomotive, kangaroos. h, Train, kangaroos. i, Flying doctor service. j, Cricket players. k, Stadium, batsman guarding wicket. l, Sydney Harbor Bridge, Opera House.

1988, July 11 ***Perf. 13½***

98 A128 42s Sheet of 12, #98a-98 l 45.00 45.00

Polynesian Islands — A16

Birds and landmarks: 42s, Audubon's shearwater, blowholes at Houma, Tonga. 57s, Kiwi, Akaroa Harbor, New Zealand. 90s, Red-tailed tropicbird, Rainmaker Mountain, Samoa. 2.50pa, Laysan albatross, Kapoho Volcano, Hawaii.

1988, Aug. 18 ***Perf. 14***

99 A16 42s multicolored 1.50 1.00
100 A16 57s multicolored 2.25 1.40
101 A16 90s multicolored 2.50 2.50
102 A16 2.50pa multicolored 4.75 4.75
Nos. 99-102 (4) 11.00 9.65

Miniature Sheet

Mutiny on the Bounty, Bicent. — A17

Designs: a, Sextant. b, William Bligh. c, Royal Navy lieutenant. d, Midshipman. e, Contemporary newspaper, Tahitian girl. f, Breadfruit. g, *Mutiny on the Bounty* excerpt, pistol grip. h, Pistol barrel, illustration of Bounty castaways. i, Tahitian girl, newsprint. j, Bligh's and Fletcher Christian's signatures. k, Christian, Pitcairn Island. l, Tombstone of John Adams.

1989, Apr. 28 ***Perf. 13½***

103 A17 42s Sheet of 12, #a.-l. 25.00 25.00

Marine Conservation A18

1989, June 2 ***Perf. 14***

104 A18 32s Hatchet fish 1.40 1.40
105 A18 42s Snipe eel 1.60 1.60
106 A18 57s Viper fish 2.00 2.00
107 A18 1.50pa Angler fish 5.00 5.00
Nos. 104-107 (4) 10.00 10.00

Evolution of the Earth — A19

Designs: 1s, Formation of the crust. 2s, Cross-section of crust. 5s, Volcanism. 10s, Surface cools. 13s, Gem stones. 15s, Oceans form. 20s, Mountains develop. 32s, River valley. 42s, Silurian Era plant life. 45s, Early marine life. 50s, Trilobites, Cambrian Era marine life. 57s, Carboniferous Era forest, coal seams. 60s, Dinosaurs feeding. 80s, Dinosaurs fighting. 1pa, Carboniferous Era insect, amphibians. 1.50pa, Stegosaurus, Jurassic Era. 2pa, Birds and mammals, Jurassic Era. 5pa, Hominid family, Pleistocene Era. 10pa, Mammoth, saber tooth tiger.

1989-93 ***Perf. 14½***

108 A19 1s multicolored .70 .70
109 A19 2s multicolored .70 .70
110 A19 5s multicolored .90 .90
111 A19 10s multicolored .90 .90
111A A19 13s multicolored 1.10 1.10
112 A19 15s multicolored .90 .90
113 A19 20s multicolored .90 .90
114 A19 32s multicolored 1.10 1.10
115 A19 42s multicolored 1.50 1.50
115A A19 45s multicolored 1.50 1.50
116 A19 50s multicolored 1.60 1.60
117 A19 57s multicolored 1.60 1.60
117A A19 60s multicolored 1.75 1.75
117B A19 80s multicolored 2.10 2.10

Size: 26x40mm

Perf. 14

118 A19 1pa multicolored 3.00 3.00
119 A19 1.50pa multicolored 4.75 4.75
120 A19 2pa multicolored 4.75 4.75
121 A19 5pa multicolored 9.25 9.25

Perf. 14

121A A19 10pa multicolored 16.00 16.00
Nos. 108-121A (19) 55.00 55.00

Issued: 1s-10s, 15s-42s, 50s-57s, 6/6/89; 13s, 45s, 60s, 80s, 5/3/93; 10pa, 9/14/93; others, 8/1/89.

A20

1989, Nov. 17 ***Perf. 14***

122 A20 57s multicolored 1.90 1.90

Miniature Sheet

UPU emblem on: Nos. 123a-123d, stamps like #108-111, Nos. 123e-123h, stamps like #112-115, Nos. 123i-123j, stamps like #116-117, Nos. 123k-123n, stamps like #118-121, No. 123o, stamp like No. 122.

123 Sheet of 15, #a.-o. 27.50 27.50
a.-e. A19 32s any single, perf. 14½ 1.00 1.00
f.-j. A19 42s any single, perf. 14½ 1.50 1.50
k.-n. A19 57s any single, perf. 14 2.00 2.00
o. A20 57s multi 2.00 2.00

Miniature Sheet

Lake Vai Lahi, Niuafo'ou — A21

a, d, Left part of lake. b, e, Small islands in center of lake. c, f, Small islet in right side of lake.

1990, Apr. 4 ***Perf. 14***

124 A21 Sheet of 6 8.75 8.75
a.-c. 42s any single .75 .75
d.-f. 1pa any single 2.00 2.00

Nos. 124a-124c and 124d-124f printed in continuous designs.

Penny Black, 150th Anniv. — A22

Tin Can Mail and: 42s, Penny Black. 57s, US #2. 75s, Western Australia #1. 2.50pa, Cape of Good Hope #178.

1990, May 1

125 A22 42s multicolored 1.50 1.00
126 A22 57s multicolored 1.75 1.25
127 A22 75s multicolored 2.00 2.00
128 A22 2.50pa multicolored 5.25 5.50
Nos. 125-128 (4) 10.50 9.75

Polynesian Whaling — A23

Designs: 15s, Whale surfacing. 42s, Whale diving beneath outrigger canoe. 57s, Tail flukes. 1pa, 2pa, Old man, two whales.

1990 ***Perf. 11½***

129 A23 15s multicolored 2.25 2.25
130 A23 42s multicolored 3.25 3.25
131 A23 57s multicolored 3.50 3.50
132 A23 2pa multicolored 9.50 9.50
Nos. 129-132 (4) 18.50 18.50

Souvenir Sheet

Perf. 14x14½

133 A23 1pa multicolored 19.00 19.00

Issue dates: #133, Sept. 4, others, June 6.
The entire souvenir sheet, No. 133, shows a modified No. 132. The 37½x30½mm stamp shows the two whales.
For surcharges see Nos. 139, 174-178.

UN Development Program, 40th Anniv. — A24

Designs: No. 134a, Agriculture and fisheries. No. 134b, Education. No. 135a, Health care. No. 135b, Communications.

1990, Oct. 25 ***Perf. 14***

134 A24 57s Pair, #a.-b. 2.75 2.75
135 A24 2.50pa Pair, #a.-b. 11.50 11.50

Charting of Niuafo'ou, Bicent. — A24a

Designs: No. 136a, 32s, The Bounty. b, 42s, Chart showing location of Niuafo'ou and Tonga. c, 57s, The Pandora.
No. 137a, 2pa, Capt. Edwards of the Pandora. b, 3pa, Capt. Bligh of the Bounty.

1991, July 25 Litho. ***Perf. 14½***

136 A24a Strip of 3, #a.-c. 5.25 5.25

Souvenir Sheet

137 A24a Sheet of 2, #a.-b. 15.50 15.50

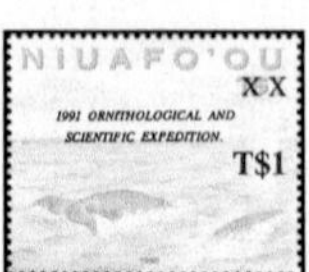

No. 133 Surcharged in Dark Blue Violet

1991, July 31 Litho. ***Perf. 14x14½***

139 A23 1pa on 1pa #133 13.00 13.00

"1991 Ornithological and Scientic Expedition" overprint appears on souvenir sheet at top center.

Ceresium Unicolor — A25

42s, Larva stage. 57s, Mature beetle. 1.50pa, Larva stage, diff. 2.50pa, Mature beetle on tree limb.

1991, Sept. 11 ***Perf. 14½x14***

140 A25 42s multicolored 1.25 1.25
141 A25 57s multicolored 1.50 1.50
142 A25 1.50pa multicolored 3.25 3.25
143 A25 2.50pa multicolored 6.00 6.00
Nos. 140-143 (4) 12.00 12.00

For surcharges, see Tonga Nos. 1127, 1129.

Christmas — A26

Legend of the origin of the coconut tree: 15s, No. 146a, Heina bathing in lake being watched by eel. 42s, No. 146b, Heina weeping over plant growing from eel's grave. No. 146c, 1.50pa, Heina's boy climbing coconut tree. No. 146d, 3pa, "Eel's face" on coconut.

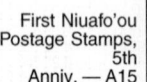

1991, Nov. 12 Litho. *Perf. 14½*
144 A26 15s multicolored .75 .75
145 A26 42s multicolored 2.00 2.00
146 A26 Sheet of 4, #a.-d. 14.00 14.00
Nos. 144-146 (3) 16.75 16.75

For surcharge, see Tonga No. 1128.

Nos. 144-145 inscribed "Christmas Greetings 1991." No. 146 contains Nos. 144-145, 146a-146d inscribed "A Love Story."

Miniature Sheet

Discovery of America, 500th Anniv. — A27

Designs: a, Columbus. b, Queen Isabella, King Ferdinand. c, Columbus being blessed by Abbot of Palos. d, Men in boat, 15th century compass. e, Wooden traverse, wind rose, Nina. f, Bow of Santa Maria. g, Stern of Santa Maria. h, Pinta. i, Two men raising cross. j, Explorers, natives. k, Columbus kneeling before King and Queen. l, Columbus' second coat of arms.

1992, Apr. 28 Litho. *Perf. 13½*
147 A27 57s Sheet of 12, #a.-l. 30.00 30.00

Miniature Sheet

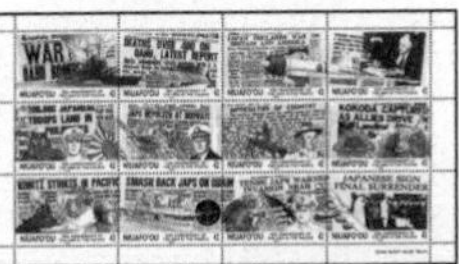
World War II in Pacific, 50th Anniv. — A28

Newspaper headline and: a, Battleship ablaze at Pearl Harbor. b, Destroyed aircraft. c, Japanese A6M Zero fighter. d, Declaration of war, Pres. Franklin D. Roosevelt. e, Japanese T95 tank, Gen. MacArthur, Japanese naval ensign. f, Douglas SBD Dauntless dive bomber, Admiral Nimitz. g, Bren gun, Gen. Sir Thomas Blamey. h, Australian mortar crew, Kokoda Trail. i, US battleship, Maj. Gen. Julian C. Smith. j, Aircraft carrier USS Enterprise. k, American soldier, flag, Maj. Gen. Curtis Lemay. l, B-29 bomber, surrender ceremony on USS Missouri in Tokyo bay.

1992, May 12 Litho. *Perf. 14*
148 A28 42s Sheet of 12, #a.-l. 25.00 25.00

King Taufa'ahau IV, 25th Anniv. of Coronation — A29

45s, 2pa, King, Queen Halaevalu during coronation. No. 150a, King, Tongan national anthem. b, Extract from investiture ceremony. c, Tongan national anthem, singers.

1992, July 4 *Perf. 13½x13*
149 A29 45s multicolored 1.10 1.10

Size: 51x38mm

Perf. 12½x12
150 A29 80s Strip of 3, #a.-c. 5.00 5.00
151 A29 2pa multicolored 4.00 4.00
Nos. 149-151 (3) 10.10 10.10

Megapodius Pritchardii A30

1992, Sept. 15 Litho. *Perf. 14*
152 A30 45s Female & male 1.50 1.75
153 A30 60s Female with egg 2.00 2.10
154 A30 80s Chick 2.75 3.00
155 A30 1.50pa Head of male 5.00 6.00
Nos. 152-155 (4) 11.25 12.85

World Wildlife Fund.

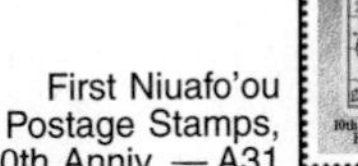

First Niuafo'ou Postage Stamps, 10th Anniv. — A31

1993, May 3 Litho. *Perf. 14x14½*
156 A31 60s Nos. 4, 117A 1.90 1.90
157 A31 80s Nos. 7, 117B 2.10 2.10

Aviation in Niuafo'ou, 10th Anniv. — A32

Airplanes of: 1pa, South Pacific Island Airways. 2.50pa, Friendly Islands Airways.

1993, May 3
158 A32 1pa multicolored 2.50 2.50
159 A32 2.50pa multicolored 5.50 5.50

King's 75th Birthday Type of Tonga

King and: 45s, 2pa, Patrol boat Pangai. No. 161a, Sporting events. b, Aircraft and communications. c, Musical instruments.

1993, July 1 *Perf. 13x13½*
160 A167 45s multicolored 1.00 1.00

Perf. 12x12½

Size: 37x48mm
161 A167 80s Strip of 3, #a.-c. 5.00 5.00
162 A167 2pa multicolored 3.75 3.75
Nos. 160-162 (3) 9.75 9.75

Wildlife — A33

Designs: a, Two parrots. b, Bird with fish. c, Butterfly, beetle. d, Birds, dragonfly, butterfly. e, Bird in flight, two on ground.

1993, Aug. 10 Litho. *Perf. 14*
163 A33 60s Strip of 5, #a.-e. 6.50 6.50

No. 163 is a continuous design.

Winners of Children's Painting Competition — A34

Designs: Nos. 164a, 165a, Ofato Beetle Grubbs of Niuafo'ou, by Peni Finau. Nos. 164b, 165b, Crater Lake Megapode, Volcano, by Paea Puletau.

1993, Dec. 1 Litho. *Perf. 14*
164 A34 10s Pair, #a.-b. .75 .75
165 A34 1pa Pair, #a.-b. 6.75 6.75

Beetles — A35

1994, Mar. 15 Litho. *Perf. 14*
168 A35 60s Scarabaeidea 1.25 1.25
169 A35 80s Coccinellidea 1.75 1.75
170 A35 1.50pa Cerambycidea 3.00 3.00
171 A35 2.50pa Pentatomidae 5.50 5.50
Nos. 168-171 (4) 11.50 11.50

A36

Sailing Ships: a, Stern of HMS Bounty. b, Bow of HMS Bounty. c, HMS Pandora. d, Whaling ship. e, Trading schooner.

1994, June 21 Litho. *Perf. 14*
172 A36 80s Strip of 5, #a.-e. 12.50 12.50

No. 172 is a continuous design.

A37

1946 Volcanic Eruption: a, Blue-crowned lorikeet, lava flow. b, Black Pacific ducks, lava flow. c, Megapodes, palm trees (b). d, White-tailed tropic birds, people evacuating island (c). e, People wading out to sailboats, Pacific reef heron.

1994, Sept. 21 Litho. *Perf. 14½*
173 A37 80s Strip of 5, #a.-e. 8.50 8.50

No. 173 is a continuous design.

Nos. 129-133 Surcharged in Blue

1995, June 30 Litho. *Perf. 11½*
174 A23 60s on 42s #130 2.25 2.25
175 A23 80s on 15s #129 3.00 3.00
176 A23 80s on 57s #131 4.00 4.00
177 A23 2pa on #132 7.50 7.50
Nos. 174-177 (4) 16.75 16.75

Souvenir Sheet

178 A23 1.50pa on 1pa #133 8.50 8.50

Size and location of surcharge varies. Surcharge on No. 178 includes "COME WHALE WATCHING / IN THE SOUTH PACIFIC."

Victory in the Pacific Type of Tonga

Nos. 179, 180: a, Soldier holding rifle. b, Soldier aiming rifle, tank. c, Front of tank. d, Troops coming off boat, firing weapons. e, Troops on beach.

1995, Aug. 1 Litho. *Perf. 14x14½*
179 A177 60s Strip of 5, #a.-e. 9.50 9.50
180 A177 80s Strip of 5, #a.-e. 12.50 12.50

Nos. 179-180 are continuous designs and were issued together in sheets containing 10 stamps.

Singapore '95 Type of Tonga

Designs, vert: No. 181a, 45s, like #117A. b, 60s, like #117B.
2pa, Plesiosaurus.

1995, Sept. 1 Litho. *Perf. 12*
181 A178 Pair, #a.-b. 4.50 4.50

Souvenir Sheet

182 A178 2pa multicolored 5.50 5.50

Beijing Intl. Coin & Stamp Show '95 Type of Tonga

Souvenir Sheet

Design: 1.40pa, The Great Wall of China.

1995, Sept. 14 *Perf. 14½*
183 A179 1.40pa multicolored 4.00 4.00

End of World War II, UN, 50th Anniv. Type of Tonga

No. 184: a, London blitz. b, UN emblem, "50." c, Concorde.
No. 185: a, Building of Siam-Burma Railway by Allied prisoners of war. b, Like #184b. c, Japanese bullet train.

1995, Oct. 20 Litho. *Perf. 14*
184 A180 60s Strip of 3, #a.-c. 5.50 5.50
185 A180 80s Strip of 3, #a.-c. 6.50 6.50

Nos. 184b, 185b are 23x31mm.

Mailmen of Niuafo'ou — A38

Portrait, illustration of postal history: 45s, Charles Stuart Ramsey, companions, floating with poles. 60s, Ramsey with can of mail encountering shark. 1pa, Walter George Quensell, mail being lowered from ship to canoes. 3pa, Quensell, original "tin can" mail cancels.

1996, Aug. 21 Litho. *Perf. 14*
186 A38 45s multicolored .75 .75
187 A38 60s multicolored 1.25 1.25
188 A38 1pa multicolored 2.00 2.00
189 A38 3pa multicolored 8.00 8.00
Nos. 186-189 (4) 12.00 12.00

Congress of Preshistoric and Protohistoric Sciences Type of Tonga

a, Prehistoric man making drawings, fire, living in huts, animals. b, Ancient Egyptians, Romans.

1996, Sept. 5 *Perf. 12*
190 A185 1pa Pair, #a.-b. 6.25 6.25

Evacuation of Niuafo'ou, 50th Anniv. — A39

a, Island, two canoes. b, Volcano, four canoes. c, Edge of island, canoe. d, Canoe. e, People boarding MV Matua.

1996, Dec. 2 *Perf. 14*
191 A39 45s Strip of 5, #a.-e. 6.00 6.00
192 A39 60s Strip of 5, #a.-e. 8.00 8.00

Nos. 191-192 are continuous designs and were issued together in sheet containing 10 stamps.

UNICEF, 50th Anniv. Type of Tonga

Children's toys on checkerboard: a, Dolls, truck, balls on pegs. b, Tricycle, car, balls on pegs, teddy bear, train. c, Car, helicopter, roller skates, books, blocks.

1996, Oct. 29 Litho. *Perf. 14*
193 A187 80s Strip of 3, #a.-c. 6.50 6.50

No. 193 is a continuous design.

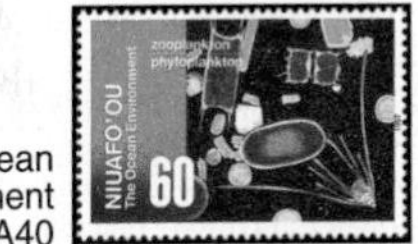

Ocean Environment A40

Various zooplankton and phytoplankton.

1997, May 19 Litho. *Perf. 14*
194 A40 60s red & multi 1.50 1.50
195 A40 80s brown & multi 2.00 2.00
196 A40 1.50pa blue & multi 3.00 3.00
197 A40 2.50pa green & multi 4.25 4.25
Nos. 194-197 (4) 10.75 10.75

Pacific '97 Type of Tonga

Souvenir Sheet

Design: Oakland Bay Bridge, back-naped tern.

1997, May 30
198 A191 2pa multicolored 5.25 5.25

1997 Wedding Anniv., Coronation Anniv. Type of Tonga

No. 199: a, King Taufa'ahau, Queen Halaevalu Mata'aho on wedding day. b, King in coronation regalia.
5pa, King in coronation procession, horiz.

1997, June 30 Litho. *Perf. 12*

Size: 34x47mm
199 A193 80s vert. pair, #a.-b. 4.50 4.50

Souvenir Sheet

200 A193 5pa multicolored 10.00 10.00

No. 199 was issued in sheets of 6 stamps.

Diana, Princess of Wales (1961-97)
Common Design Type

Various portraits: a, 10s. b, 80s, c, 1pa. d, 2.50pa.

Perf. 13½x14

1998, May 29 Litho. Unwmk.
201 CD355 Sheet of 4, #a.-d. 6.50 6.50

No. 201 sold for 4.40pa + 50s with surtax from international sales going to the Princess Diana Memorial Fund and surtax from local sales going to designated local charity.
For surcharge, see No. 291.

Blue Crowned Lorikeet — A41

World Wildlife Fund: 10s, Young birds in nest. 55s, Adult on branch of flower. 80s, Adult on branch of bush. 3pa, Two adults on tree branch.

1998, May 15 Litho. *Perf. 14½x15*

202	A41	10s multicolored	1.00	1.00
203	A41	55s multicolored	2.50	1.00
204	A41	80s multicolored	3.50	2.00
205	A41	3pa multicolored	7.50	7.50
a.		Sheet, 2 each #202-205	*32.50*	*32.50*
		Nos. 202-205 (4)	14.50	11.50

For surcharges see Tonga Nos. 1152, 1155.

King Taufa'ahau Tupou IV Type of Tonga

1998, July 4 Litho. *Perf. 14*
207 A196 2.70pa multicolored 4.00 4.00

See Tonga #985a for souvenir sheet containing one #207.

Fish A43

a, 10s, Amphipiron melanopus. b, 55s, Amphipiron perideraion. c, 80s, Amphipiron chrysopterus.

1998, Sept. 23 Litho. *Perf. 14*
208 A43 Strip of 3, #a.-c. 2.25 2.25

Intl. Year of the Ocean. No. 208 was issued in sheets of 9 stamps.

Year of the Tiger Type of Tonga

Designs: a, 55s, Head of tiger with mouth open. b, 80s, Two tigers standing. c, 1pa, Two tigers lying down. 1pa, Head of tiger.

1998, July 23 Litho. *Perf. 14*
209 A183 Sheet of 4, #a.-d. 5.75 5.75

No. 209 is a continuous design. Singpex '98.

Christmas — A44

Designs: 20s, Angel playing mandolin. 55s, Angel playing violin. 1pa, Children singing, bells. 1.60pa, Children singing, candles.

1998, Nov. 12 *Perf. 14x14½*

210	A44	20s multicolored	.80	.80
211	A44	55s multicolored	1.35	1.35
212	A44	1pa multicolored	1.75	1.75
213	A44	1.60pa multicolored	2.50	2.50
		Nos. 210-213 (4)	6.40	6.40

For surcharge see Tonga No. 1153.

New Year 1999 (Year of the Rabbit) — A45

Stylized rabbits: a, 10s. b, 55s. c, 80s. d, 1pa.

1999, Feb. 16 *Perf. 14*
214 A45 Sheet of 4, #a.-d. 4.00 4.00

Jakob le Maire (1585-1616), Explorer — A46

1999, Mar. 19 Litho. *Perf. 14*

215	A46	80s shown	1.80	1.80
216	A46	2.70pa Tongiaki canoe	4.50	4.50
a.		Souvenir sheet, #215-216	7.00	7.00

Australia '99 World Stamp Expo (#216a).

Flowers — A47

55s, Cananga odorata. 80s, Gardenia tannaensis, vert. 1pa, Coleus amboinicus, vert. 2.50pa, Hernandia moerenhoutiana.

Perf. 13x13¼, 13¼x13

1999, Sept. 29 Litho.

217	A47	55s multicolored	.75	.75
218	A47	80s multicolored	1.25	1.25
219	A47	1pa multicolored	1.50	1.50
220	A47	2.50pa multicolored	3.00	3.00
		Nos. 217-220 (4)	6.50	6.50

Souvenir Sheet

Millennium — A48

a, 1pa, Dove. b, 2.50pa, Native boat.

2000, Jan. 1 Litho. *Perf. 14½x15*
221 A48 Sheet of 2, #a.-b. 4.50 4.50

Souvenir Sheet

New Year 2000 (Year of the Dragon) A49

Various dragons; a, 10s. b, 55s, c, 80s. d, 1pa.

Litho. with Foil Application

2000, Feb. 4 *Perf. 14½*
222 A49 Sheet of 4, #a.-d. 3.75 3.75

Souvenir Sheet

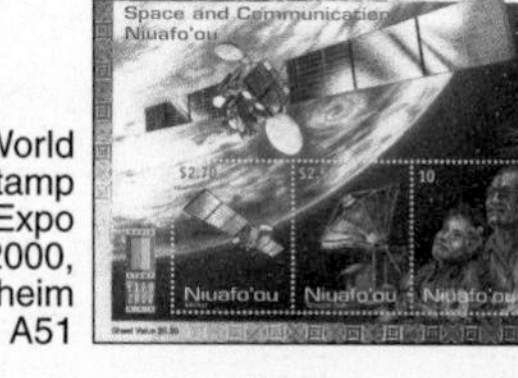

The Stamp Show 2000, London A50

Litho. with Foil Application

2000, May 22 *Perf. 13x13¼*

223	A50	Sheet of 2	5.00	5.00
a.		$1.50 Queen Mother	2.00	2.00
b.		$2.50 Queen Salote Tupou III	3.00	3.00

Souvenir Sheet

World Stamp Expo 2000, Anaheim A51

No. 224: a, 10s, Man and woman. b, 2.50pa, Satellite dish. c, 2.70pa, Intelsat.

2000, July 7 Litho. *Perf. 13x13¼*
224 A51 Sheet of 3, #a-c 6.75 6.75

Butterflies A52

Designs: 55s, Jamides bochus. 80s, Blue moon. 1pa, Eurema hecabe aprica. 2.70pa, Monarch.

2000, Oct. 25 *Perf. 14*
225-228 A52 Set of 4 8.25 8.25

For surcharge see Tonga No. 1154.

Souvenir Sheet

New Year 2001 (Year of the Snake) A53

No. 229 — Various snakes: a, 10s. b, 55s, c, 80s, d, 1pa.

Litho. with Foil Application

2001, Feb. 1 *Perf. 14¼*
229 A53 Sheet of 4, #a-d 4.00 4.00

Hong Kong 2001 Stamp Exhibition.

Fish — A54

Designs: 80s, Prognichthys sealei. 1pa, Xiphias gladius. 2.50pa, Katsuwonus pelamis.

2001, June 5 Litho. *Perf. 13¾*

230-232	A54	Set of 3	8.50	8.50
232a		Souvenir sheet, #230-232	9.00	9.00

Souvenir Sheet

Fruit A55

No. 233: a, 55s, Papaya. b, 80s, Limes. c, 1pa, Mangos. d, 2.50pa, Bananas.

Perf. 14¼x14

2001, Sept. 19 Litho. Unwmk.
233 A55 Sheet of 4, #a-d 7.00 7.00

Barn Owl — A56

Designs: Nos. 234, 238a, 10s, Owl in flight. Nos. 235, 238b, 55s, Adult feeding young. Nos. 236, 238c, 2.50pa, Four owls. Nos. 237, 238d, 2.70pa, Owl's head.

2001, Nov. 21 *Perf. 12¾x13¼*

Without Vertical Bister Line Separating Panels

234-237 A56 Set of 4 8.50 8.50

Souvenir Sheet

With Vertical Bister Line Separating Panels

238 A56 Sheet of 4, #a-d 8.75 8.75

For surcharge see Tonga No. 1156.

Reign Of Queen Elizabeth II, 50th Anniv. Issue
Common Design Type
Souvenir Sheet

No. 239: a, 15s, Princess Elizabeth with Queen Mother. b, 90s, Wearing purple hat. c, 1.20pa, As young woman. d, 1.40pa, Wearing red hat. e, 2.25pa, 1955 portrait by Annigoni (38x50mm).

Perf. 14¼x14½, 13¾ (2.25pa)

2002, Feb. 6 Litho. Wmk. 373
239 CD360 Sheet of 5, #a-e 8.75 8.75

Souvenir Sheet

New Year 2002 (Year of the Horse) A57

Various horses: a, 65s. b, 80s. c, 1pa. d, 2.50pa.

Litho. With Foil Application

2002, Feb. 12 Unwmk. *Perf. 14*
240 A57 Sheet of 4, #a-d 7.25 7.25

Megapodius Pritchardii — A58

Designs: 15s, Bird, eggs. 70s, Two birds. 90s, Bird, vert. 2.50pa, Two birds, vert.

Perf. 14x13½, 13½x14

2002, Apr. 9 Litho.

241-244	A58	Set of 4	5.75	5.75
244a		Souvenir sheet, #243-244	6.75	6.75

Nos. 243-244 lack white frame around stamp.

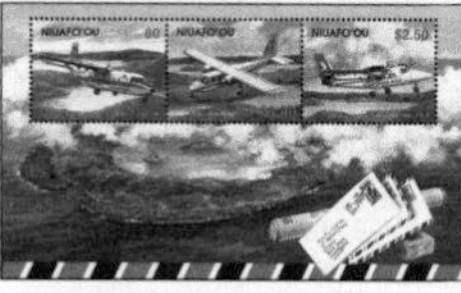

Cephalopods A59

Designs: 80s, Octopus vulgaris. 1pa, Sepioteuthis lessoniana. 2.50pa, Nautilus belauensis.

2002, July 25 Litho. *Perf. 13¾*

245-247	A59	Set of 3	7.50	7.50
247a		Souvenir sheet, #245-247	8.50	8.50

Souvenir Sheet

Mail Planes A60

No. 248: a, 80c, Casa C-212 Aviocar. b, 1.40pa, Britten-Norman Islander. c, 2.50pa, DHC 6-300 Twin Otter.

2002, Nov. 27 Litho. *Perf. 12¾*
248 A60 Sheet of 3, #a-c 7.00 7.00

New Year 2003 (Year of the Ram) Type of Tonga

No. 249: a, 65s, One ram. 80s, Three sheep. 1pa, Three sheep, diff. 2.50pa, Two sheep.

2003, Apr. 14 Litho. *Perf. 13¼*
249 A223 Sheet of 4, #a-d 8.00 8.00

Coronation of Queen Elizabeth II, 50th Anniv. Type of Tonga

Designs: 90s, Queen Elizabeth II. 1.20pa, Queen Elizabeth II seated. 1.40pa, Queen Salote of Tonga in coach. 2.50pa, Queen Salote.

2003, June 2 **Litho.**
250-253 A224 Set of 4 10.00 10.00

New Year (Year of the Monkey) Type of Tonga

No. 254: a, 60s, Spider monkey. b, 80s, Ring-tailed lemur. c, 1pa, Cotton-top tamarin. d, 2.50pa, White-cheeked gibbon.

2004, Feb. 12 **Litho.** ***Perf. 13¼***
254 A228 Sheet of 4, #a-d 6.00 6.00

Trees Type of Tonga

Designs: 45s, Pawpaw (papaya). 60s, Banana. 80s, Coconut. 1.80pa, Lime.

2004 **Litho.** ***Perf. 14¼x14***
255-258 A229 Set of 4 5.50 5.50

Christmas Type of Tonga

Designs: 15s, Madonna and Child. 90s, Journey to Bethlehem. 1.20pa, Annunciation to the Shepherds. 2.60pa, Magi.

2004, Dec. ***Perf. 14***
259-262 A230 Set of 4 5.75 5.75

Royalty Type of Tonga

Designs: 30s, King George Tupou I. 65s, King George Tupou II. 80s, Queen Salote Tupou III. 3.05pa, King Taufa'ahau Tupou IV.

2004, July 7 **Litho.** ***Perf. 14***
263-266 A231 Set of 4 5.25 5.25
266a Souvenir sheet, #263-266 5.75 5.75

New Year 2005 (Year of the Rooster) Type of Tonga

Souvenir Sheet

No. 267 — Various roosters with panel color of: a, 65s, Gray. b, 80s, Grayish tan. c, 1pa, Gray. d, 2.50pa, Yellow green.

2005, Feb. 12
267 A232 Sheet of 4, #a-d 6.75 6.75

Christmas — A61

No. 268: a, 3.40pa, Palm frond and Christmas lights. b, 5pa, Grass and snowflakes.

2011, Dec. 24
268 A61 Horiz. pair, #a-b 9.00 9.00

Miniature Sheets

Megaptera Novaeangliae — A62

No. 269 — Various depictions of humpback whale: a, 1pa. b, 1.40pa. c, 1.60pa.
No. 270 — Various depictions of humpback whale: a, 2pa. b, 2.25pa. c, 2.40pa.

2012, Jan. 16
269 A62 Sheet of 3, #a-c, + label 4.00 4.00
270 A62 Sheet of 3, #a-c, + label 6.00 6.00

Worldwide Fund for Nature (WWF) — A63

Various depictions of Zebra shark: 45s, 2pa, 2.40pa, 3.40pa.

2012, Mar. 12 ***Perf. 14¼x14***
271-274 A63 Set of 4 8.25 8.25
274a Sheet of 16, 4 each #271-274 35.00 35.00

For surcharges, see Nos. 324-327.

Butterflies A64

Designs: 45s, Australian meadow-argus. 1.95pa, Crow butterfly. 2pa, Monarch butterfly. 2.40pa, Monarch butterfly, diff. 2.50pa, Blue moon butterfly. 3pa, Australian meadow-argus, diff. 3.40pa, Crow butterfly, diff. 4pa, Blue moon butterfly, diff. 5pa, Monarch butterfly, diff. 6pa, Blue moon butterfly, diff. 7.30pa, Crow butterfly, diff. 8pa, Australian meadow-argus, diff.

2012, Apr. 20 ***Perf. 12¾x12½***

Stamps With White Backgrounds

275 A64 45s multi .55 .55
276 A64 1.95pa multi 2.25 2.25
277 A64 2pa multi 2.40 2.40
278 A64 2.40pa multi 2.75 2.75
279 A64 2.50pa multi 3.00 3.00
280 A64 3pa multi 3.50 3.50
281 A64 3.40pa multi 4.00 4.00
282 A64 4pa multi 4.75 4.75
283 A64 5pa multi 6.00 6.00
284 A64 6pa multi 7.00 7.00
285 A64 7.30pa multi 8.50 8.50
286 A64 8pa multi 9.50 9.50
Nos. 275-286 (12) 54.20 54.20

Stamps With Light Blue Background

287 Sheet of 12 55.00 55.00
a. A64 45s multi .55 .55
b. A64 1.95pa multi 2.25 2.25
c. A64 2pa multi 2.40 2.40
d. A64 2.40pa multi 2.75 2.75
e. A64 2.50pa multi 3.00 3.00
f. A64 3pa multi 3.50 3.50
g. A64 3.40pa multi 4.00 4.00
h. A64 4pa multi 4.75 4.75
i. A64 5pa multi 6.00 6.00
j. A64 6pa multi 7.00 7.00
k. A64 7.30pa multi 8.50 8.50
l. A64 8pa multi 9.50 9.50

Titanic Type of Tonga

No. 288: a, Titanic facing left at dock. b, Photograph of Titanic facing right. c, Titanic facing left at sea. d, Color painting of Titanic at sea.
No. 289a, Like #288d.

2012, June 6 ***Perf. 12½***
288 A240 3.40pa Sheet of 4, #a-d 16.00 16.00

Souvenir Sheet

289 A240 Sheet of 2, #288a, 289a 4.50 4.50
a. 45s multi .50 .50

Personalizable Stamp — A65

2012, Aug. 8 ***Perf. 14x14¾***
290 A65 3pa multi 3.00 3.00

No. 201 Surcharged in Gold and Black

No. 1192: a, 4pa on 10s. b, 4pa on 80s. c, 4pa on 1pa. d, 4pa on 2.50pa.

2012, Sept. 4 **Litho.**
291 CD355 Sheet of 4, #a-d 18.50 18.50

Overprint is printed across the four stamps of the sheet. It reads "In Loving Memory of Diana, Princess of Wales / 31 August 1997 / Her Legacy will live on forever. / William and Kate, Duke and Duchess of Cambridge / 1st Anniversary of their Royal Wedding 2011".

Miniature Sheet

Christmas — A66

No. 292 — Nativity, by Giotto di Bondone: a, Angels, manger roof at LR, denomination at UL. b, Angels, manger roof at LL, denomination at LL. c, Angels in sky, no roof visible. d, Angels, manger post at right. e, Angels, manger post at left. f, Angel and tree. g, Madonna and Child, cow and donkey. h, Two shepherds. i, Joseph. j, Attendant holding infant Jesus. k, Attendant and sheep. l, Sheep and legs of shepherds.

2012, Nov. 21 ***Perf. 14¾x14¼***
292 A66 1pa Sheet of 12, #a-l, + 2 labels 12.50 12.50

New Year 2013 (Year of Snake) Type of Tonga

No. 293: a, Red snake with yellow green spots. b, Dark green snake with blue spots. c, Purple snake with green spots. d, Yellow green snake with green spots.

2013, Feb. 20
293 A248 2.45pa Sheet of 4, #a-d 10.50 10.50

Tin Can Island Mail Cans — A67

Designs: 2.25pa, Can on beach, ship at sea. 5.40pa, Can on beach, ship at sea, diff.

2013, Aug. 21 **Litho.** ***Perf. 14x14¾***
294-295 A67 Set of 2 7.00 7.00

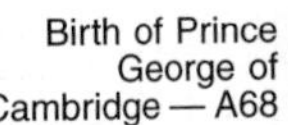
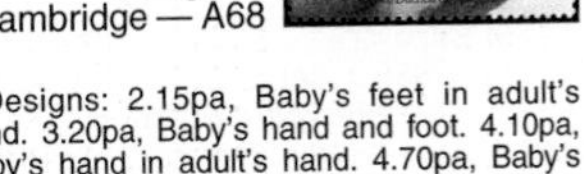

Birth of Prince George of Cambridge — A68

Designs: 2.15pa, Baby's feet in adult's hand. 3.20pa, Baby's hand and foot. 4.10pa, Baby's hand in adult's hand. 4.70pa, Baby's hand.
16.90pa, Baby's feet in adult's hand, diff.

2013, Aug. 30 **Litho.** ***Perf. 13¾***
296-299 A68 Set of 4 13.00 13.00

Souvenir Sheet

300 A68 16.90pa multi 16.00 16.00

Butterflies and Flowers — A69

Designs: 20s, Blue moon butterfly, Jasmine. 30s, Monarch butterfly, Hibiscus. 40s, Meadow argus butterfly, Elder. 50s, Crow butterfly, Heilala. 60s, Blue moon butterfly, Blue wild indigo. 80s, Monarch butterfly, Purple coneflowers. 90s, Meadow argus butterfly, Yellow bell. 1.10pa, Crow butterfly, Frangipani. 1.20pa, Blue moon butterfly, Tahitian gardenia. 10pa, Blue moon butterfly, Frangipani. 12.50pa, Monarch butterfly, Hibiscus, diff. 20pa, Meadow argus butterfly, Tahitian vanilla orchid.

2013, Sept. 6 **Litho.** ***Perf. 14***

Stamps With White Frames

301 A69 20s multi .25 .25
302 A69 30s multi .35 .35
303 A69 40s multi .45 .45
304 A69 50s multi .55 .55
305 A69 60s multi .65 .65
306 A69 80s multi .90 .90
307 A69 90s multi 1.00 1.00
308 A69 1.10pa multi 1.25 1.25
309 A69 1.20pa multi 1.40 1.40
310 A69 10pa multi 11.00 11.00
311 A69 12.50pa multi 13.50 13.50
312 A69 20pa multi 22.00 22.00
Nos. 301-312 (12) 53.30 53.30

Miniature Sheet

Stamps With Blue Frames

313 Sheet of 12 54.00 54.00
a. A69 20s multi .25 .25
b. A69 30s multi .35 .35
c. A69 40s multi .45 .45
d. A69 50s multi .55 .55
e. A69 60s multi .65 .65
f. A69 80s multi .90 .90
g. A69 90s multi 1.00 1.00
h. A69 1.10pa multi 1.25 1.25
i. A69 1.20pa multi 1.40 1.40
j. A69 10pa multi 11.00 11.00
k. A69 12.50pa multi 13.50 13.50
l. A69 20pa multi 22.00 22.00

China International Collection Expo Type of Tonga of 2013

Souvenir Sheet

No. 314: a, 2.35pa, Painting by Paul Gauguin. b, 2.60pa, Beijing Exhibition Center.

2013, Sept. 26 **Litho.** ***Perf. 12***
314 A263 Sheet of 2, #a-b 5.00 5.00

Christmas Type of Tonga of 2013

Paintings of angels by: 1.75pa, Pietro Perugino. 2.35pa, Melozzo da Forli. 2.60pa, Sandro Botticelli.

2013, Nov. 13 **Litho.** ***Perf. 13½***
315-317 A269 Set of 3 6.50 6.50

Miniature Sheet

New Year 2014 (Year of the Horse) A70

No. 318: a, Brown horse, black denomination at UL. b, White horse, white denomination at UR. c, Two horses. d, White horse, white denomination at UL.

2014, Jan. 6 **Litho.** ***Perf. 13¾***
318 A70 $1.50 Sheet of 4, #a-d 5.50 5.50

Miniature Sheet

Easter A71

No. 319 — Various paintings depicting the resurrected Christ by Pietro Perugino: a, 1.75pa. b, 2.25pa. c, 2.75pa. d, 4.55pa.

2014, Apr. 7 **Litho.** ***Perf. 13¼***
319 A71 Sheet of 4, #a-d 12.50 12.50

Souvenir Sheet

Nelson Mandela (1918-2013), President of South Africa — A72

No. 320 — Mandela's: a, 2.25pa, Head. b, 5.40pa, Head and hands.

2014, May 13 Litho. *Perf. 14¾x14¼*

320	A72	Sheet of 2, #a-b	8.25 8.25

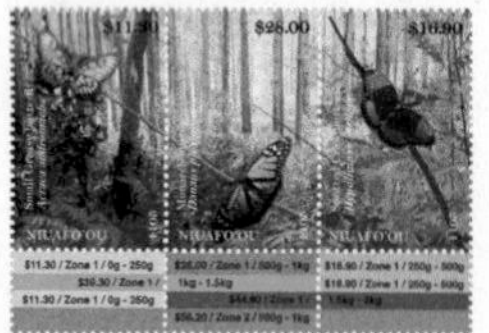

Butterflies — A73

No. 321: a, 11.30pa, Small greasy butterfly. b, 16.90pa, Spotted crow butterfly. c, 28pa, Monarch butterfly.

2014, May 22 Litho. *Perf. 13¼*

321	A73	Horiz. strip of 3, #a-c, + 3 labels	60.00 60.00

Miniature Sheet

Christmas — A74

Bells and: a, Curved staff and notes in foreground, slanted musical score in background. b, Faint musical score with three staffs in background. c, G clef and musical notes, faint musical score with six staffs. d, Curving staff with G clef and notes, faint musical score with four staffs in background.

2014, Dec. 15 Litho. *Perf. 13¾*

322	A74	2.25pa Sheet of 4, #a-d	9.25 9.25

Souvenir Sheet

New Year 2015 (Year of the Sheep) A75

Sheep with background color of: a, 3.40pa, Blue. b, 4.60pa, Purple.

2015, Jan. 5 Litho. *Perf. 13¼*

323	A75	Sheet of 2, #a-b	7.75 7.75

Nos. 271-274 Surcharged

Methods and Perfs. As Before

2015, Apr. 1

324	A63	90s on 2.40pa #273	.90	.90
325	A63	1pa on 3.40pa #274	1.00	1.00
326	A63	1.10pa on 45s #271	1.10	1.10
327	A63	1.20pa on 2pa #272	1.25	1.25
		Nos. 324-327 (4)	4.25	4.25

Miniature Sheet

Easter A76

No. 328 — Details of painting of the Holy Trinity: a, UL quadrant. b, UR quadrant. c, LL quadrant. d, LR quadrant.

2015, Apr. 3 Litho. *Perf. 14¼*

328	A76	2.25pa Sheet of 4, #a-d	9.00 9.00

Birth of Princess Charlotte Type of Tonga of 2015

Souvenir Sheet

No. 329: a, Duke and Duchess of Cambridge with Princess Charlotte. b, Duke of Cambridge holding Prince George.

2015, June 30 Litho. *Perf. 14¾x14*

329	A285	5pa Sheet of 2, #a-b	9.75 9.75

Year of the Monkey Type of Tonga of 2015

Designs: 2.25pa, Monkey. 3.60pa, Monkey holding flower.

No. 332: a, 3.40pa, Monkey, diff. b, 4.60pa, Monkey holding flower, diff.

2015, Sept. 25 Litho. *Perf. 13¼*

330-331	A288	Set of 2	5.50 5.50

Souvenir Sheet

332	A288	Sheet of 2, #a-b	7.50 7.50

No. 332 contains two 51x51 diamond-shaped stamps.

Queen Elizabeth II Type of Tonga of 2015

Miniature Sheet

No, 333 — Queen Elizabeth II in Tonga: a, With Queen Salote Tupou III and her granddaughter Mele Siuilikutapu. b, Arriving at Wesleyan Church, Nukulofa. c, On path with Queen Salote Tupou III. d, With Queen Salote Tupou III, wearing flower garland.

2015, Nov. 23 Litho. *Perf. 14*

333	A289	2pa Sheet of 4, #a-d	7.00 7.00

Christmas Type of Tonga of 2015

Miniature Sheet

No. 334 — Religious paintings with inscription: a, Altar. b, Ghirlandaio. c, Hey. d, Diamante.

2015, Dec. 9 Litho. *Perf. 13¾*

334	A290	1.50pa Sheet of 4, #a-d	5.25 5.25

Second Summit of the Forum for India-Pacific Islands Cooperation Type of Tonga of 2016

Mohandas K. Gandhi, Garcinia sessilis, lotus flower and: 2.25pa, Indian elephants. 4.20pa, Indian rhinoceroses. 5pa, Asiatic lions. 6.50pa, Indian peafowl.

2016, Jan. 14 Litho. *Perf. 13¼*

335-338	A291	Set of 4	15.50 15.50
338a		Souvenir sheet of 4, #335-338	15.50 15.50

World Wildlife Fund (WWF) — A77

Various depictions of black petrel: 50s, 2pa, 2.25pa. 3.50pa.

2016, Feb. 26 Litho. *Perf. 14¾x14*

Stamps With White Frames

339-342	A77	Set of 4	7.25 7.25

Stamps Without White Frames

343		Strip of 4	7.25	7.25
a.	A77	50s multi	.45	.45
b.	A77	2pa multi	1.75	1.75
c.	A77	2.25pa multi	2.00	2.00
d.	A77	3.50pa multi	3.00	3.00

Landing of Dutch Explorers in Tonga, 400th Anniv. — A78

No. 344: a, 2pa, Jacob Le Maire. b, 2.25pa, Ship Eendracht off Tafahi Island. c, 2.50pa, Birds, Tongan natives in boats. d, 2.70pa, Willem Schouten.

2016, Apr. 25 Litho. *Perf. 14*

344	A78	Sheet of 4, #a-d	8.50 8.50

Queen Elizabeth II, 90th Birthday Type of Tonga of 2016

Souvenir Sheet

No. 345 — Queen Elizabeth II: a, Waving. b, Wearing strapless gown and tiara.

2016, May 3 Litho. *Perf. 13*

345	A296	2pa Sheet of 2, #a-b	3.50 3.50

Tupou College Type of Tonga of 2016

Souvenir Sheet

No. 346: a, 2.25pa, Building and trees. b, 5pa, Building and students.

2016, June 10 Litho. *Perf. 13*

346	A297	Sheet of 2, #a-b	6.75 6.75

Marine Life and Birds Type of Tonga of 2016

Designs: 90s, Masked booby. 1pa, Gray reef shark. 1.10pa, Hard coral. 1.20pa, Bottlenose dolphins. 2pa, Humpback whale. 2.25pa, Atlantic spotted dolphin. 2.70pa, Red-tailed tropicbird. 4.20pa, Whale shark. 5pa, Tiger shark. 6.70pa, Fairy tern. 9.20pa, Killer whales. 11.70pa, Black noddies.

2016, Mar. 2 Litho. *Perf. 14x14¾*

347	A299	90s multi	.80	.80
348	A299	1pa multi	.90	.90
349	A299	1.10pa multi	1.00	1.00
350	A299	1.20pa multi	1.10	1.10
351	A299	2pa multi	1.75	1.75
352	A299	2.25pa multi	2.00	2.00
353	A299	2.70pa multi	2.40	2.40
354	A299	4.20pa multi	3.75	3.75
355	A299	5pa multi	4.50	4.50
356	A299	6.70pa multi	6.00	6.00
357	A299	9.20pa multi	8.25	8.25
358	A299	11.70pa multi	10.50	10.50
		Nos. 347-358 (12)	42.95	42.95

Year of the Rooster Type of Tonga of 2016

Designs: 5pa, Rooster. 5.50pa, Rooster and chicks.

2016, Aug. 10 Litho. *Perf. 13½*

359-360	A300	Set of 2	9.75 9.75
360a		Souvenir sheet of 2, #359-360	9.75 9.75

Christmas Type of Tonga of 2016

No. 361, vert.: a, 2pa, Church and railing. b, 2pa, Blue church with white steeple. c, 2.70pa, Church. d, 2.70pa, Church doors.

2016, Dec. 19 Litho. *Perf. 13¼*

361	A302	Block of 4, #a-d	8.25 8.25

Easter Type of Tonga of 2017

Miniature Sheet

No. 362 — Paintings depicting the resurrection of Christ by: a, Pietro Perugino. b, Carl Bloch (incorrectly identified as Mantegna). c, Titian. d, Sandro Botticelli.

2017, Apr. 10 Litho. *Perf. 12¾*

362	A3032pa	Sheet of 4, #a-d	7.00 7.00

Reign of Queen Elizabeth II Type of Tonga of 2017

Miniature Sheet

No. 363 — Queen Elizabeth II wearing: a, Turquoise green jacket and hat. b, White jacket and hat. c, Magenta jacket and hat. d, White and Turquoise blue jacket and hat.

2017, June 7 Litho. *Perf. 12¾*

363	A304	3pa Sheet of 4, #a-d	11.00 11.00

Kennedy Type of Tonga of 2017

Miniature Sheet

No. 364: a, 2.50pa, Pres. Kennedy signing Peace Corps Act. b, 2.50pa, Women's Strike for Peace in Cuban Missile Crisis. c, 2.75pa, Pres. Kennedy at desk in White House. d, 2.75pa, Sargent Shriver speaking to Peace Corps volunteers at White House.

2017, June 21 Litho. *Perf. 12¾*

364	A305	Sheet of 4, #a-d	9.75 9.75

Halley's Comet Type of Tonga of 2017

No. 365, vert.: a, Director of probe to Halley's Comet wearing Halley's Comet shirt. b, Man holding comet dust collector. c, Material streaming from Halley's Comet. d, Man holding good luck charm from Halley's Comet space mission.

6pa, Spacecraft.

2017, July 12 Litho. *Perf. 13x13¼*

365	A307	2.25pa Block of 4, #a-d	8.50 8.50

Souvenir Sheet

Perf. 13¼x13

366	A307	6pa multi	5.75 5.75

Year of the Dog Type of 2017

Designs; 6.50pa, Dog facing right. 6.70pa, Dog facing left.

2017, Nov. 1 Litho. *Perf. 13¼*

367-368	A312	Set of 2	12.00 12.00
368a		Souvenir sheet of 2, #367-368	12.00 12.00

Christmas Type of 2017

No. 369: a, Sailboat. b, Parrot. c, Hibiscus flowers. d, Starfish.

2017, Dec. 4 Litho. *Perf. 12½*

369	A313	2.25pa Block of 4, #a-d	8.25 8.25

Easter Type of Tonga of 2018

Miniature Sheet

No. 370: a, Jesus. b, Easter eggs, shell and butterflies. c, Church and palmtree. d, Cross and flowers.

2018, Mar. 15 Litho. *Perf. 12¾*

370	A314	2.25pa Sheet of 4, #a-d	8.25 8.25

Birdpex Type of Tonga of 2018

No. 371: a, New Zealand dotterel. b, Red-capped plover. c, Antipodes parakeet. d, Shore plover.

2018, May 3 Litho. *Perf. 13¼*

371	A315	2.25pa Block of 4, #a-d	8.00 8.00

Wedding of Prince Harry and Meghan Markle Type of Tonga of 2018

No. 372: a, Couple walking down aisle in chapel. b, Couple seated in coach.

9.20pa, Couple and automobile.

2018, July 27 Litho. *Perf. 13*

372	A317	5pa Sheet of 2, #a-b	8.75 8.75

Souvenir Sheet

373	A317	9.20pa multi	8.25 8.25

Souvenir Sheets

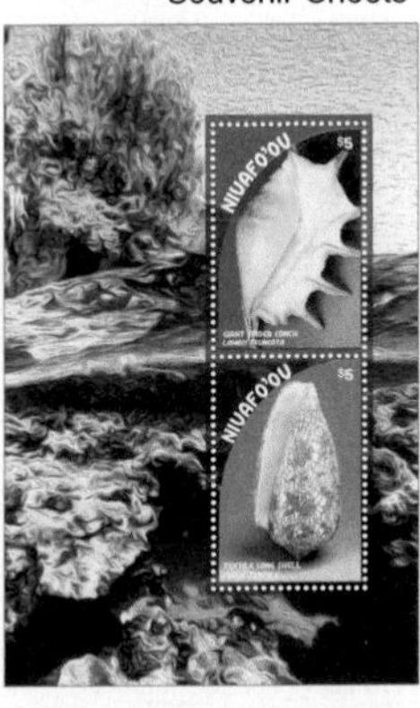

Shells A79

No. 374, 5pa: a, Giant spider conch. b, Textile cone shell.
No. 375, 5pa: a, Venus comb murex shell. b, Emperor nautilus shell.

2018, Sept. 7 Litho. *Perf. 13*
Sheets of 2, #a-b

374-375 A79 Set of 2 18.00 18.00

Animals of the World Type of Tonga of 2018-19

No. 376, 2.80pa: a, Cobalt blue tarantula. b, Veiled chameleon.
No. 377, 4.30pa: a, Sugar glider. b, Rowley's palm pit viper.
10pa, Jandaya conure.

2018-19 Litho. *Perf. 13*
Horiz. Pairs, #a-b

376-377 A318 Set of 2 13.00 13.00

Souvenir Sheet

378 A318 10pa multi 9.00 9.00

Issued: Nos. 376-377, 2/8/19; No. 378, 9/10.

Year of the Pig Type of Tonga of 2018

Designs: 6.50pa, Pig facing right. 6.70pa, Pig facing forward.

2018, Dec. 10 Litho. *Perf. 13¼*

379-380 A319 Set of 2 11.50 11.50

Birds of Prey Type of Tonga of 2018

Designs: 5s, Black-and-white owl and Band-bellied owl hybrid. 10s, Powerful owl. 1.40pa, Martial eagle. 2.30pa, Great gray owl. 2.50pa, Crested goshawk. 2.80pa, Jungle owlet. 4.30pa, Short-toed snake eagle. 5.20pa, Minahasa masked owl. 6.90pa, Gray-headed fish eagle. 9.30pa, White-eyed buzzard. 9.50pa, Western marsh harrier. 11.50pa, African hawk eagle.

2018, Dec. 18 Litho. *Perf. 13*
Stamps With White Frames

381 A322 5s multi .25 .25
382 A322 10s multi .25 .25
383 A322 1.40pa multi 1.25 1.25
384 A322 2.30pa multi 2.00 2.00
385 A322 2.50pa multi 2.25 2.25
386 A322 2.80pa multi 2.50 2.50
a. Souvenir sheet of 6, #381-386 8.50 8.50
387 A322 4.30pa multi 3.75 3.75
388 A322 5.20pa multi 4.75 4.75
389 A322 6.90pa multi 6.00 6.00
390 A322 9.30pa multi 8.25 8.25
391 A322 9.50pa multi 8.50 8.50
392 A322 11.50pa multi 10.00 10.00
a. Souvenir sheet of 6, #387-392 41.50 41.50
Nos. 381-392 (12) 49.75 49.75

Miniature Sheet
Stamps Without White Frame

393 Sheet of 12 50.00 50.00
a. A322 5s multi .25 .25
b. A322 10s multi .25 .25
c. A322 1.40pa multi 1.25 1.25
d. A322 2.30pa multi 2.00 2.00
e. A322 2.50pa multi 2.25 2.25
f. A322 2.80pa multi 2.50 2.50
g. A322 4.30pa multi 3.75 3.75
h. A322 5.20pa multi 4.75 4.75
i. A322 6.90pa multi 6.00 6.00
j. A322 9.30pa multi 8.25 8.25
k. A322 9.50pa multi 8.50 8.50
l. A322 11.50pa multi 10.00 10.00

Stamps on Nos. 386a and 392a have white frames on one or two sides. See Nos. 398-402, 403-407.

Sharks A80

No. 394: a, Thresher shark. b, Zebra shark. c, Blacktip reef shark. d, Whale shark. e, Hammerhead shark. f, Mako shark.
9.30pa, Great white shark.

2019, June 21 Litho. *Perf. 13*

394 A80 2.80pa Sheet of 6, #a-f 15.00 15.00

Souvenir Sheet
Perf. 13¼x13

395 A80 9.30pa multi 8.25 8.25

No. 395 contains one 48x40mm stamp.

Year of the Rat Type of Tonga of 2019

Different depictions of rat: 6.50pa, 6.70pa.

2019, Oct. 11 Litho. *Perf. 13¼*

396-397 A326 Set of 2 11.50 11.50

Birds Type of Tonga of 2018

Designs: 2.25pa, Sharp-shinned hawk, horiz. 2.70pa, Philippine eagle, horiz. 4.20pa, Palm-nut vulture, horiz. 9.20pa, Crested serpent-eagle, horiz.

2019, Nov. 18 Litho. *Perf. 13*
Stamps With White Frames

398 A322 2.25pa multi 2.00 2.00
399 A322 2.70pa multi 2.40 2.40
400 A322 4.20pa multi 3.75 3.75
401 A322 9.20pa multi 8.00 8.00
Nos. 398-401 (4) 16.15 16.15

Stamps Without White Frames
Size: 48x40mm
Perf. 13¼x13

402 Block or vert. strip of 4 16.50 16.50
a. A322 2.25pa multi 2.00 2.00
b. A322 2.70pa multi 2.40 2.40
c. A322 4.20pa multi 3.75 3.75
d. A322 9.20pa multi 8.00 8.00
e. Sheet of 4, #402a-402d 16.50 16.50

Stamps on No. 402e have white frames on two sides.

Birds Type of Tonga of 2018

Designs: 14.40pa, Victoria's riflebird, horiz. 20.60pa, Ribbon-tailed astrapia, horiz. 25pa, Raggiana bird-of-paradise, horiz. 30pa, Wilson's bird-of-paradise, horiz.

2019, Nov. 25 Litho. *Perf. 13*
Stamps With White Frames

403 A322 14.40pa multi 12.50 12.50
404 A322 20.60pa multi 17.50 17.50
405 A322 25pa multi 21.50 21.50
406 A322 30pa multi 25.50 25.50
Nos. 403-406 (4) 77.00 77.00

Stamps Without White Frames
Size: 48x40mm
Perf. 13¼x13

407 Block or vert. strip of 4 77.00 77.00
a. A322 14.40pa multi 12.50 12.50
b. A322 20.60pa multi 17.50 17.50
c. A322 25pa multi 21.50 21.50
d. A322 30pa multi 25.50 25.50
e. Sheet of 4, #407a-407d 77.00 77.00

Stamps on No. 407e have white frames on two sides.

Christmas — A81

Designs: 1pa, Palm trees with Christmas lights, gifts, stocking hat, star and candy cane. 2pa, Santa Claus, reindeer, surfboard, beach ball and beach umbrella.

2019, Dec. 12 Litho. *Perf. 14x14¾*

408-409 A81 Set of 2 2.60 2.60

Compare with type A65.

Whales and Dolphins Type of Tonga of 2020

Designs: 75s, Atlantic spotted dolphins. 1pa, Bryde's whale. 5pa, Short-beaked common dolphin. 11.80pa, False killer whales. 12.10pa, Short-finned pilot whales. 20pa, Bottlenose dolphin. 50pa, Pacific white-sided dolphin. 60pa, Blue whale.

2020, Jan. 28 Litho. *Perf. 13*
Stamps With White Frames

410 A328 75s multi .65 .65
411 A328 1pa multi .85 .85
412 A328 5pa multi 4.50 4.50
413 A328 11.80pa multi 10.50 10.50
414 A328 12.10pa multi 10.50 10.50
415 A328 20pa multi 17.50 17.50
416 A328 50pa multi 43.00 43.00
417 A328 60pa multi 52.00 52.00
Nos. 410-417 (8) 139.50 139.50

Stamps Without White Frames
Size: 48x40mm
Perf. 13¼x13

418 Block or vert. strip of 4 16.50 16.50
a. A328 75s multi .65 .65
b. A328 1pa multi .85 .85
c. A328 5pa multi 4.50 4.50
d. A328 11.80pa multi 10.50 10.50
e. Sheet of 4, #418a-418d 16.50 16.50
419 Block or vert. strip of 4 125.00 125.00
a. A328 12.10pa multi 10.50 10.50
b. A328 20pa multi 17.50 17.50
c. A328 50pa multi 43.00 43.00
d. A328 60pa multi 52.00 52.00
e. Sheet of 4, #419a-419d 125.00 125.00

Stamps on Nos. 418e and 419e have white frames on two adjacent sides.

Birds Type of Tonga of 2018

Hummingbirds: 2.25pa, Tufted coquette. 2.70pa, Rufous-crested coquette. 4.20pa, White-booted racket-tail. 9.20pa, Chestnut-breasted coronet.

2020, May 4 Litho. *Perf. 13*
Stamps With White Frames

420 A322 2.25pa multi 2.00 2.00
421 A322 2.70pa multi 2.40 2.40
422 A322 4.20pa multi 3.75 3.75
423 A322 9.20pa multi 8.00 8.00
Nos. 420-423 (4) 16.15 16.15

Stamps Without White Frames
Size: 48x40mm
Perf. 13¼x13

424 Block or vert. strip of 4 16.50 16.50
a. A322 2.25pa multi 2.00 2.00
b. A322 2.70pa multi 2.40 2.40
c. A322 4.20pa multi 3.75 3.75
d. A322 9.20pa multi 8.00 8.00
e. Sheet of 4, #424a-424d 16.50 16.50

Stamps on No. 424e have white frames on two adjacent sides.

Birds Type of Tonga of 2018

Frigatebirds: 14.40pa, Magnificent frigatebird. 20.60pa, Lesser frigatebird. 25pa, Ascension frigatebird. 30pa, Christmas frigatebird.

2020, May 18 Litho. *Perf. 13*
Stamps With White Frames

425 A322 14.40pa multi 12.50 12.50
426 A322 20.60pa multi 18.00 18.00
427 A322 25pa multi 22.00 22.00
428 A322 30pa multi 26.00 26.00
Nos. 425-428 (4) 78.50 78.50

Stamps Without White Frames
Size: 48x40mm
Perf. 13¼x13

429 Block or vert. strip of 4 78.50 78.50
a. A322 14.40pa multi 12.50 12.50
b. A322 20.60pa multi 18.00 18.00
c. A322 25pa multi 22.00 22.00
d. A322 30pa multi 26.00 26.00
e. Sheet of 4, #429a-429d 78.50 78.50

Stamps on No. 429e have white frames on two adjacent sides.

Butterflies Type of Tonga of 2020

Designs: 75s, Glanville fritillary butterfly. 1pa, Grizzled skipper butterfly. 5pa, Brown argus butterfly. 11.80pa, Common brimstone butterfly. 12.10pa, Peacock butterfly. 20pa, Chalkhill blue butterfly. 50pa, Green hairstreak butterfly. 60pa, Comma butterfly.

2020, June 22 Litho. *Perf. 13*
Stamps With White Frames

430 A329 75s multi .65 .65
431 A329 1pa multi .85 .85
432 A329 5pa multi 4.50 4.50
433 A329 11.80pa multi 10.50 10.50
434 A329 12.10pa multi 10.50 10.50
435 A329 20pa multi 17.50 17.50
436 A329 50pa multi 43.00 43.00
437 A329 60pa multi 52.00 52.00
Nos. 430-437 (8) 139.50 139.50

Stamps Without White Frames
Size: 48x40mm
Perf. 13¼x13

438 Block or vert. strip of 4 16.50 16.50
a. A329 75s multi .65 .65
b. A329 1pa multi .85 .85
c. A329 5pa multi 4.50 4.50
d. A329 11.80pa multi 10.50 10.50
e. Sheet of 4, #438a-438d 16.50 16.50
439 Block or vert. strip of 4 125.00 125.00
a. A329 12.10pa multi 10.50 10.50
b. A329 20pa multi 17.50 17.50
c. A329 50pa multi 43.00 43.00
d. A329 60pa multi 52.00 52.00
e. Sheet of 4, #439a-439d 125.00 125.00

Stamps on Nos. 438e and 439e have white frames on two adjacent sides.

New Year 2021 (Year of the Ox) Type of Tonga of 2021

Souvenir Sheet

2021, Apr. 7 Litho. *Perf. 13¼x13*

440 A332 6.90pa Ox, diff. 6.25 6.25

Clouded Leopard — A82

Clouded leopard: 10s, On branch. 2pa, Two juveniles. 2.70pa, On its back. 7pa, With mouth open.
11.70pa, Head of Clouded leopard, vert.

2021, May 24 Litho. *Perf. 13*

441-444 A82 Set of 4 11.00 11.00

Souvenir Sheet
Perf. 13x13¼

445 A82 11.70pa multi 10.50 10.50

No. 445 contains one 40x48mm stamp.

Miniature Sheet

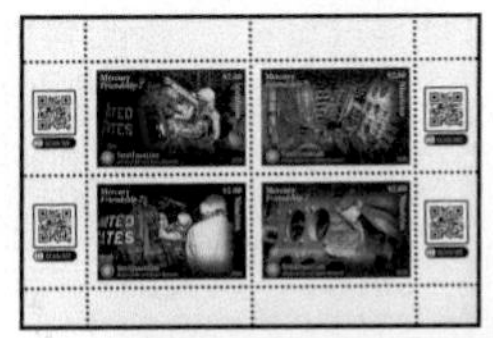
A83

Spaceflight of Friendship 7 — A84

No. 446: a, Color photograph of technicians assisting John Glenn enter capsule. b, Friendship 7 control panel. c, Black-and-white photograph of technician assisting Glenn enter capsule. d, Reminder note on Friendship 7 control panel.
5.20pa, Elephant at Colombo, Ceylon parade showing Friendship 7,

2021, May 24 Litho. *Perf. 13*

446 A83 2.80pa Sheet of 4, #a-d 10.00 10.00

Souvenir Sheet
Perf. 13¼x13

447 A84 5.20pa multi 4.75 4.75

Souvenir Sheets

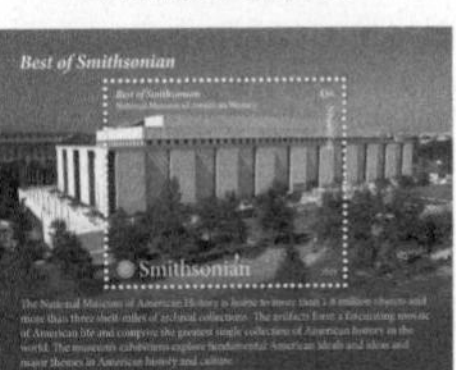

Smithsonian Institution Venues — A85

Designs: 45s, National Museum of American History. 50s, National Museum of Natural History. 70s, Enid A. Haupt Garden. 90s, National Museum of African-American History and Culture. 1pa, Folger Rose Garden, vert.

Perf. 13¼x13, 13x13¼ (1pa)

2021, May 24 **Litho.**

448-452 A85 Set of 5 3.25 3.25

AIR POST SPECIAL DELIVERY STAMPS

APSD1

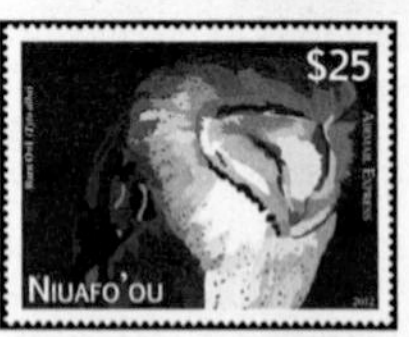

APSD2

APSD3

Barn Owl APSD4

2012, Aug. 30 **Litho.** ***Perf. 14¼***

Stamps With White Frame All Around

CE1 APSD1 25pa multi 21.00 21.00
CE2 APSD2 25pa multi 21.00 21.00
CE3 APSD3 25pa multi 21.00 21.00
CE4 APSD4 25pa multi 21.00 21.00
Nos. CE1-CE4 (4) 84.00 84.00

Stamps With White Frame on Two Sides

CE5 Sheet of 4 84.00 84.00
a. APSD1 25pa multi 21.00 21.00
b. APSD2 25pa multi 21.00 21.00
c. APSD3 25pa multi 21.00 21.00
d. APSD4 25pa multi 21.00 21.00

A sheet of 16 ontaining four of each of types APSD1-APSD4 without white frames on the stamps was produced in a limited printing.

Butterflies APSD5

Designs: 15pa, Common crow butterfly. 50pa, Peablue butterfly. 53pa, Monarch butterfly. 71pa, Meadow argus butterfly. 83pa, Chinese yellow swallowtail butterfly. 89pa, Clipper butterfly.

2015-16 **Litho.** ***Perf. 14¼***

Stamps With White Frames

CE6 APSD5 15pa multi 14.00 14.00
CE7 APSD5 50pa multi 47.00 47.00
CE8 APSD5 53pa multi 49.00 49.00
CE9 APSD5 71pa multi 65.00 65.00
a. Souvenir sheet of 4, #CE6-CE9 175.00 175.00
CE10 APSD5 83pa multi 72.50 72.50
CE11 APSD5 89pa multi 77.50 77.50
a. Souvenir sheet of 2, #CE10-CE11 150.00 150.00
Nos. CE6-CE11 (6) 325.00 325.00

Souvenir Sheets
Stamps Without White Frame

CE12 APSD5 15pa multi 14.00 14.00
CE13 APSD5 50pa multi 47.00 47.00
CE14 APSD5 53pa multi 49.00 49.00
CE15 APSD5 71pa multi 65.00 65.00
CE16 APSD5 83pa multi 72.50 72.50
CE17 APSD5 89pa multi 77.50 77.50
Nos. CE12-CE17 (6) 325.00 325.00

Issued: 15pa, 50pa, 9/1; 53pa, 71pa, No. CE9a, 11/2; 83pa, 89pa, No. CE11a, 1/4/16.

Stamps on No. CE9a have white frames on 2 sides. Stamps on No. CE11a have white frames on 3 sides.

TRANSCAUCASIAN FEDERATED REPUBLIC

ˌtranˌt͟s-ko-ˈkā-zhən ˈfe-də-rāted ri-ˈpə-blik

LOCATION — In southeastern Europe, south of the Caucasus Mountains between the Black and Caspian Seas
GOVT. — Former republic
AREA — 71,255 sq. mi.
POP. — 5,851,000 (approx.)
CAPITAL — Tiflis

The Transcaucasian Federation was made up of the former autonomies of Armenia, Georgia and Azerbaijan. Its stamps were replaced by those of Russia.

100 Kopecks = 1 Ruble

Russian Stamps of 1909-17 Overprinted in Black or Red

1923 **Unwmk.** ***Perf. 14½x15***

1 A15 10k dark blue 3.00 5.00
2 A14 10k on 7k lt bl 4.00 5.00
3 A11 25k grn & gray vio 10.00 5.00
4 A11 35k red brn & grn (R) 4.00 5.00
a. Double overprint 75.00 75.00
5 A8 50k brn red & grn 4.00 5.00
6 A9 1r pale brn, brn & org 12.00 12.00
7 A12 3½r mar & lt grn 50.00

Imperf

8 A9 1r pale brn, brn & red org 10.00 12.00
Nos. 1-8 (8) 97.00
Nos. 1-6,8 (7) 49.00

No. 7 was prepared but not issued.

Overprinted on Stamps of Armenia Previously Handstamped

a c

Perf. 14½x15

9 A11(c) 25k grn & gray vio 250.00 250.00
10 A8(c) 50k vio & grn 250.00 150.00

Perf. 13½

11 A9(a) 1r pale brn, brn & org 100.00 50.00
12 A9(c) 1r pale brn, brn & org 150.00 50.00

Imperf

13 A9(c) 1r pale brn, brn & red org 35.00 35.00
Nos. 9-13 (5) 785.00 535.00

Counterfeit overprints exist.

Oil Fields — A1

Soviet Symbols — A2

1923 ***Perf. 11½***

14 A1 40,000r red violet 3.00 2.25
15 A1 75,000r dark grn 3.00 2.25
16 A1 100,000r blk vio 3.00 2.25
17 A1 150,000r red 3.00 2.25
18 A2 200,000r dull grn 3.00 2.25
19 A2 300,000r blue 3.00 2.25
20 A2 350,000r dark brn 3.00 2.25
21 A2 500,000r rose 3.00 2.25
Nos. 14-21 (8) 24.00 18.00

Nos. 14-21 exist imperf. but are not known to have been issued in that condition. Values, set $125.

Nos. 14-15 Srchd. in Brown

1923

22 A1 700,000r on 40,000r 2.50 5.00
a. Imperf., pair 30.00
23 A1 700,000r on 75,000r 2.50 5.00
a. Imperf., pair 30.00

Types of Preceding Issue with Values in Gold Kopecks

1923, Oct. 24

25 A2 1k orange 2.25 1.90
26 A2 2k blue green 2.25 1.90
27 A2 3k rose 2.25 1.90
28 A2 4k gray brown 2.25 1.90
29 A1 5k dark violet 2.25 1.90
30 A1 9k deep blue 2.25 1.90
31 A1 18k slate 2.25 1.90
Nos. 25-31 (7) 15.75 13.30

Nos. 25-31 exist imperf. but are not known to have been issued in that condition. Values, set $100.

TRANSVAAL

tranˌt͟s-ˈväl

(South African Republic)

LOCATION — Southern Africa
GOVT. — A former British Colony
AREA — 110,450 sq. mi.
POP. — 1,261,736 (1904)
CAPITAL — Pretoria

Transvaal was known as the South African Republic until 1877 when it was occupied by the British. The republic was restored in 1884 and continued until 1900 when it was annexed to Great Britain and named "The Transvaal."

12 Pence = 1 Shilling
20 Shillings = 1 Pound

Most unused stamps between Nos. 1-96, 119-122 and 136-137 were issued with gum, but do not expect gum on scarcer stamps as few examples retain their original gum. In many cases removal of the remaining gum may enhance the preservation of the stamps. Otherwise, values for unused stamps are for examples with original gum as defined in the catalogue introduction.

Very fine imperforate stamps will have adequate to large margins. However, rouletted stamps are valued as partly rouletted, with straight edges, and rouletted just into the design, as the rouletting methods were quite inaccurate.

First Republic

Coat of Arms — A1

A1 has spread wings on eagle.

Mecklenburg Printings
By Adolph Otto, Gustrow
Fine Impressions
Thin Paper

1869 **Unwmk.** ***Imperf.***

1 A1 1p brown lake 575.00
a. 1p red 725.00 725.00
2 A1 6p ultra 325.00 325.00
3 A1 1sh dark green 875.00 875.00
a. Tete beche pair —

Rouletted 15½, 16

4 A1 1p red 185.00
5 A1 6p ultra 165.00 160.00
6 A1 1sh blue green 210.00 200.00
a. 1sh yellow green 285.00 250.00
b. 1sh deep green 350.00 375.00

Nos. 1-6 were printed from 2 sets of plates, differing in the spacing between the stamps.

The only known example of No. 3a is in a museum.

See Nos. 9-24, 26-33, 35-36, 38-39, 41-42, 43-49, 119, 122. For overprints see Nos. 53-61, 63-66, 68-72, 75-78, 81-83, 86-87, 90-91, 94.

Coat of Arms — A2

1871-74

7 A2 3p lilac 92.50 100.00
a. 3p violet 110.00 125.00
8 A2 6p brt ultra ('74) 87.50 32.50
a. Half used as 3p on cover 1,850.

Many forgeries exist in colors duller or lighter than the genuine stamps.

In forgeries of type A1, all values, the "D" of "EENDRAGT" is not noticeably larger than the other letters and does not touch the top of the ribbon. In type A1 genuine stamps, the "D" is large and touches the ribbon top. The eagle's eye is a dot and its face white on the genuine stamps; the eye is a loop or blob attached to the beak, and the beak is strongly hooked, on the forgeries. Many forgeries of the 1sh have the top line of the ribbon broken above "EENDRAGT."

Forgeries of type A2 usually can be detected only by color.

A sharply struck cancellation of a numeral in three rings is found on many of these forgeries. The similar genuine cancellation is always roughly or heavily struck.

See Nos. 25, 34, 437, 40, 42B, 120-121. For overprints see Nos. 50-52, 62, 67, 73-74, 79-80, 84-85, 88-89, 92-93, 95-96.

Local Printings
(A) By M. J. Viljoen, Pretoria
Poor Impressions,
Overinked and Spotted

1870 **Thin Soft Paper** ***Imperf.***

9 A1 1p pink 125.00
a. 1p rose red 135.00
b. 1p carmine 110.00 125.00
10 A1 6p dull ultra 425.00 100.00
a. Tete beche pair —

The only known examples of No. 10a are in museums.

Rouletted 15½, 16

11 A1 1p carmine 875.00 375.00
a. Rouletted 6½ 1,100.
12 A1 6p dull ultra 325.00 135.00

Hard Paper, Thick to Medium

Imperf

13 A1 1p carmine 115.00 125.00
14 A1 6p ultra —
15 A1 1sh gray green 210.00 175.00
a. 1sh dark green —
b. Tete beche pair 29,000.
c. Half used as 6p on cover 2,800.

The existence of No. 14 is questionable.

Rouletted 15½, 16

16 A1 1p light carmine 125.00 130.00
a. 1p carmine 87.50 92.50
17 A1 6p ultra 145.00 125.00
a. Tete beche pair 35,000. 25,000.
18 A1 1sh dark green 260.00 125.00
a. 1sh gray green 850.00 850.00

Examples of Nos. 16-18 are sometimes so heavily inked as to be little more than blots of color.

(B) By J. P. Borrius, Potchefstroom
Clearer Impressions Though Often Overinked

1870 **Thick Porous Paper** ***Imperf.***

19 A1 1p black 200.00 175.00
20 A1 6p indigo —

Rouletted 15½, 16

21 A1 1p black 32.50 42.50
22 A1 6p gray blue 210.00 87.50
a. 6p indigo 145.00 115.00
b. 6p bright ultra —

Thin Transparent Paper

23 A1 1p black 325.00 750.00
24 A1 1p brt carmine 260.00 87.50
a. 1p deep carmine 110.00 67.50
25 A2 3p gray lilac 160.00 72.50
26 A1 6p ultra 110.00 42.50
27 A1 1sh yellow green 135.00 72.50
a. 1sh deep green 135.00 72.50
b. Half used as 6p on cover — 2,900.

Thick Soft Paper

28 A1 1p dull rose 525.00 115.00
a. 1p brown rose 675.00 155.00
b. Printed on both sides —

29 A1 6p dull blue 135.00 57.50
a. 6p bright blue 325.00 87.50
b. 6p ultramarine 300.00 87.50
c. Rouletted 6½ —
30 A1 1sh yellow green 1,400. 875.00

The paper of Nos. 28 to 30 varies considerably in thickness.

(C) By P. Davis & Son, Natal

Thin to Medium Paper

1874 ***Perf. 12½***

31 A1 1p red 180.00 60.00
a. 1p brownish red 180.00 60.00
32 A1 6p deep blue 225.00 75.00
a. 6p blue 225.00 75.00
b. Horiz. pair, imperf. between —

(D) By the Stamp Commission, Pretoria

Pelure Paper

1875-76 ***Imperf.***

33 A1 1p pale red 75.00 65.00
a. 1p orange red 75.00 35.00
b. 1p brown red 80.00 42.50
c. Pin perf. 775.00 475.00
34 A2 3p gray lilac 80.00 55.00
a. 3p dull violet 90.00 55.00
b. Pin perf. — 500.00
35 A1 6p blue 80.00 55.00
a. 6p pale blue 80.00 70.00
b. 6p dark blue 85.00 60.00
c. Tete beche pair, thin opaque paper 21,000.
d. Tete beche pair, pelure, transparent paper —
e. Pin perf. — 450.00

The only known examples of No. 35c are in museums.

Rouletted 15½, 16

36 A1 1p orange red 450.00 155.00
a. Rouletted 6½ 1,250. 250.00
37 A2 3p dull violet 500.00 180.00
a. Rouletted 6½ 1,100. 320.00
38 A1 6p blue 250.00 130.00
a. Rouletted 6½ 1,275. 145.00

The paper of this group varies slightly in thickness and is sometimes divided into pelure and semipelure. We believe there was only one lot of the paper and that the separation is not warranted.

Thick Hard Paper

Imperf

39 A1 1p org red ('76) 37.50 30.00
40 A2 3p lilac 475.00 160.00
41 A1 6p deep blue 85.00 27.50
a. 6p blue 140.00 32.50
b. Tete beche pair 21,500.

Rouletted 15½, 16

42 A1 1p org red ('76) 550.00 200.00
a. Rouletted 6½ ('75) 750.00 200.00
42B A2 3p lilac 500.00
43 A1 6p deep blue 750.00 350.00
a. 6p blue 950.00 135.00
b. Rouletted 6½ ('75) 800.00 350.00

Soft Porous Paper

Imperf

44 A1 1p orange red 250.00 75.00
45 A1 6p deep blue 300.00 650.00
a. 6p dull blue 450.00 140.00
46 A1 1sh yellow green 600.00 175.00
a. Half used as 6p on cover 2,200.

Rouletted 15½, 16

47 A1 1p orange red — 500.00
a. Rouletted 6½ — 550.00
48 A1 6p deep blue — 250.00
a. Rouletted 6½ — 1,275.
49 A1 1sh yellow grn 1,000. 450.00
a. Rouletted 6½ — 1,400.
b. Rouletted 15½-16x16½ 1,000. 500.00

First British Occupation

Stamps and Types of 1875 Overprinted

Red Overprint

Pelure Paper

1877 **Unwmk.** ***Imperf.***

50 A2 3p lilac 1,675. 275.00
a. Overprinted on back 4,000. 3,750.
b. Double ovpt., red and black 7,500.

Rouletted 15½, 16

51 A2 3p lilac — 1,850.
a. Rouletted 6½ — 2,750.

Thin Hard Paper

Imperf

52 A2 3p lilac 1,650. 400.00

Soft Porous Paper

53 A1 6p blue 2,250. 275.00
a. 6p deep blue — 350.00
b. Inverted overprint 6,000.
c. Double overprint 5,250. 1,250.
54 A1 1sh yellow grn 900.00 300.00
a. Inverted overprint 5,250.
b. Half used as 6p on cover 3,000.

Rouletted 15½, 16

55 A1 6p blue 2,000.
a. Rouletted 6½ 2,750.
56 A1 1sh yellow grn 20,000. 900.00
a. Rouletted 6½ 4,750. 2,750.
b. As "a.", overprint inverted 7,500.

Black Overprint

Pelure Paper

Imperf

57 A1 1p red 400.00 200.00

Rouletted 15½, 16

58 A1 1p red — 1,350.

Thick Hard Paper

Imperf

59 A1 1p red 40.00 27.50
a. Inverted overprint 650.00 575.00

Rouletted 15½, 16

60 A1 1p red 250.00 57.50
a. Rouletted 6½ 800.00 350.00
b. Inverted overprint —
c. Double overprint 1,275.

Soft Porous Paper

Imperf

61 A1 1p red 40.00 40.00
a. Double overprint 1,400.
62 A2 3p lilac 140.00 52.50
a. 3p deep lilac 250.00 125.00
b. Inverted overprint —
63 A1 6p dull blue 200.00 100.00
a. 6p bright blue — 575.00
b. 6p dark blue 275.00 250.00
d. Inverted overprint 1,650. 225.00
e. Double overprint 4,000. 2,400.
64 A1 6p blue, *rose* 150.00 75.00
a. Tete beche pair —
b. Inverted overprint 160.00 75.00
c. Overprint omitted 4,000. 2,900.
d. Half used as 3p on cover
65 A1 1sh yellow grn 225.00 85.00
a. Tete beche pair 27,500. 27,500.
b. Inverted overprint 1,550. 500.00
c. Half used as 6p on cover 2,100.

The only known examples of No. 64a are in museums.

Rouletted 15½, 16

66 A1 1p red 125.00 125.00
a. Rouletted 6½ 850.00 200.00
67 A2 3p lilac 340.00 95.00
a. Rouletted 6½ 950.00
68 A1 6p dull blue 400.00 85.00
a. Inverted overprint — 875.00
b. Rouletted 6½ — 1,550.
c. As "a," rouletted 6½ 5,000.
69 A1 6p blue, *rose* 400.00 87.50
a. Inverted overprint 750.00 87.50
b. Rouletted 6½
c. Tete beche pair
d. Overprint omitted
e. As "a," rouletted 6½ 850.00
f. As "d," rouletted 6½
70 A1 1sh yellow grn 400.00 135.00
a. Inverted overprint 1,600. 625.00
b. Rouletted 6½ 725.00 190.00
c. As "a," rouletted 6½ 2,350. 775.00

In this issue the space between "V. R." and "TRANSVAAL" is normally 8½mm but in position 11 it is 12mm. In this and the following issues there are numerous minor varieties of the overprint, missing periods, etc.

The only known examples of No. 69c are in museums.

Types A1 and A2 Overprinted

1877-79 ***Imperf.***

71 A1 1p red, *blue* 85.00 42.50
a. "Transvral" 6,500. 2,900.
b. Inverted overprint 975.00 475.00
c. Double overprint 4,750.
d. Overprint omitted —
72 A1 1p red, *org* ('78) 37.50 30.00
a. Printed on both sides —
b. Pin perf. —
73 A2 3p lilac, *buff* 85.00 50.00
a. Inverted overprint 875.00
b. Pin perf. —
74 A2 3p lilac, *grn* ('79) 300.00 70.00
a. Inverted overprint 2,450.
b. Double overprint —
c. Pin perf. —
75 A1 6p blue, *grn* 160.00 50.00
a. Tete beche pair 22,500.
b. Inverted overprint 1,375.
c. Half used as 3p on cover —
d. Pin perf. —
76 A1 6p blue, *bl* ('78) 115.00 40.00
a. Tete beche pair —
b. Overprint omitted 2,750.
c. Inverted overprint 1,450.
d. Half used as 3p on cover 1,150.
e. Double overprint 3,750.
f. Pin perf. —
Nos. 71-76 (6) 782.50 282.50

The only known examples of No. 76a are in museums.

Rouletted 15½, 16

77 A1 1p red, *blue* 150.00 50.00
a. "Transvral" 3,500.
b. Inverted overprint —
c. Double overprint —
78 A1 1p red, *org* ('78) 55.00 40.00
a. Horiz. pair, imperf. vert.
b. Rouletted 6½ 375.00 135.00
79 A2 3p lilac, *buff* 155.00 40.00
a. Inverted overprint 3,500.
b. Vert. pair, imperf. horiz. 875.00
c. Rouletted 6½ 135.00
80 A2 3p lilac, *grn* ('79) 900.00 240.00
a. Inverted overprint
b. Rouletted 6½ 900.00 375.00
81 A1 6p blue, *green* 135.00 40.00
a. Inverted overprint 800.00
b. Overprint omitted 4,750.
c. Tete beche pair —
d. Half used at 3p on cover 950.00
e. Rouletted 6½ — 1,450.
82 A1 6p blue, *bl* ('78) 400.00 75.00
a. Inverted overprint — 1,100.
b. Overprint omitted — 4,000.
c. Tete beche pair —
d. Horiz. pair, imperf. vert. —
e. Half used as 3p on cover 1,050.
f. Double overprint —
g. Rouletted 6½ 400.00
h. As "a," rouletted 6½ —
Nos. 77-82 (6) 1,795. 485.00

The only known examples of No. 81c are in museums. The existence of No. 82c is questioned.

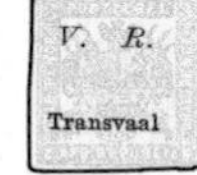

Types A1 and A2 Overprinted

Imperf

83 A1 1p red, *org* ('78) 95.00 52.50
84 A2 3p lilac, *buff* ('78) 110.00 40.00
a. Pin perf. 875.00 875.00
85 A2 3p lilac, *grn* ('79) 240.00 40.00
a. Inverted overprint 2,300.
b. Overprint omitted —
c. Printed on both sides 1,150.
86 A1 6p blue, *bl* ('78) 240.00 50.00
a. Tete beche pair 19,500.
b. Inverted overprint 800.00
Nos. 83-86 (4) 685.00 182.50

Rouletted 15½, 16

87 A1 1p red, *org* ('78) 240.00 160.00
a. Rouletted 6½ 375.00
88 A2 3p lilac, *buff* ('78) 300.00 150.00
a. Vert. pair, imperf. horiz. —
b. Rouletted 6½ 450.00
89 A2 3p lilac, *grn* ('79) 875.00 240.00
a. Inverted overprint —
b. Overprint omitted —
c. Rouletted 6½ ('97) 900.00 375.00
90 A1 6p blue, *bl* ('78) 650.00 150.00
a. Tete beche pair —
b. Inverted overprint — 1,450.
d. Rouletted 6½ 450.00
e. As "b," rouletted 6½

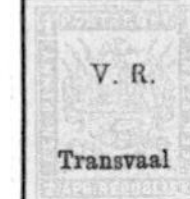

Types A1 and A2 Overprinted

1879 ***Imperf.***

91 A1 1p red, *orange* 75.00 50.00
a. 1p red, *yellow* 75.00 55.00
b. Small capital "T" 375.00 200.00
92 A2 3p lilac, *green* 65.00 40.00
a. Small capital "T" 325.00 135.00
93 A2 3p lilac, *blue* 75.00 40.00
a. Small capital "T" 375.00 135.00
Nos. 91-93 (3) 215.00 130.00

Rouletted 15½, 16

94 A1 1p red, *yellow* 450.00 300.00
a. 1p red, *orange* 1,000. 450.00
b. Small capital "T" 1,350. 825.00
c. Rouletted 6½ 900.00 775.00
d. Pin perf. 875.00
95 A2 3p lilac, *green* 925.00 350.00
a. Small capital "T" 1,050.
b. Rouletted 6½ 1,325. 750.00
96 A2 3p lilac, *blue* 275.00
a. Small capital "T" 850.00
b. Rouletted 6½ 950.00
c. Pin perf. 1,500.

Queen Victoria — A3

1878-80 **Engr.** ***Perf. 14, 14½***

97 A3 ½p vermilion ('80) 30.00 100.00
98 A3 1p red brown 22.50 7.00
99 A3 3p claret 42.50 12.00
100 A3 4p olive green 45.00 12.25
101 A3 6p slate 20.00 10.00
a. Half used as 3p on cover —
102 A3 1sh green 180.00 57.50
103 A3 2sh blue 325.00 105.00
Nos. 97-103 (7) 665.00 303.75

For surcharges see Nos. 104-118, 138-139.

No. 101 Surcharged in Red or Black

(a) Surcharged

Surcharge distinction: "PENNY" in gothic capitals.

1879

104 A3 1p on 6p slate (R) 200.00 95.00
105 A3 1p on 6p slate (Bk) 67.50 27.50

(b) Surcharged

Surcharge distinction: "1" has heavy serif at base; "P," thin serif at base.

106 A3 1p on 6p slate (R) 800.00 400.00
107 A3 1p on 6p slate (Bk) 310.00 95.00

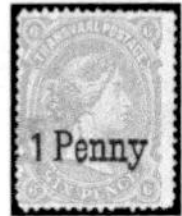

(c) Surcharged

Surcharge distinction: No serif at base of "1."

108 A3 1p on 6p slate (R) 825.00 425.00
109 A3 1p on 6p slate (Bk) 325.00 95.00

(d) Surcharged

Surcharge distinction: Heavy serifs at base of "1" and "p."

110 A3 1p on 6p slate (R) 425.00 210.00
111 A3 1p on 6p slate (Bk) 140.00 65.00
a. Pair, one without surcharge —

(e) Surcharged

Surcharge distinction: Italics.

112 A3 1p on 6p slate (R) 775.00 375.00
113 A3 1p on 6p slate (Bk) 290.00 87.50

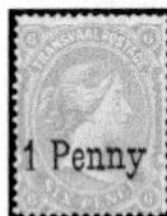

(f) Surcharged

Surcharge distinction: "1" has long, sloping serif at top, thin serif at base.

114 A3 1p on 6p slate (R) 375.00 185.00
115 A3 1p on 6p slate (Bk) 120.00 50.00

(g) Surcharged

Surcharge distinction: Tail of "y" missing.

116 A3 1p on 6p slate (R) 7,000. 1,850.
117 A3 1p on 6p slate (Bk) 775.00 190.00

Second Republic

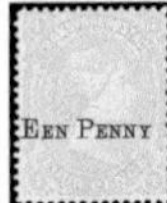

No. 100 Surcharged

1882 **Unwmk.** ***Perf. 14, 14½***

118 A3 1p on 4p olive grn 25.00 9.00
a. Inverted surcharge 375.00 250.00

1883 ***Perf. 12***

119 A1 1p black 9.50 3.50
a. Imperf. —
b. Vert. pair, imperf. horiz. 675.00 500.00
c. Horiz. pair, imperf. vert. 375.00
120 A2 3p red 19.00 4.00
a. Horiz. pair, imperf. vert. — *1,000.*
b. Half used as 1p on cover *825.00*
121 A2 3p black, *rose* 40.00 9.00
a. Half used as 1p on cover *825.00*
122 A1 1sh green 90.00 9.00
a. Tete beche pair 1,325. 185.00
b. Half used as 6p on cover *625.00*
Nos. 119-122 (4) 158.50 25.50

The so-called reprints of this issue are forgeries. They were made from the counterfeit plates described in the note following No. 8, plus a new false plate for the 3p. The false 3p plate has many small flaws and defects.

Forgeries of No. 120 are in dull orange red, clearly printed on whitish paper, and those of No. 121 in brownish or grayish black on bright rose. Genuine examples of No. 120 lack the orange tint and the paper is yellowish; genuine examples of No. 121 are in black without gray or brown shade, on dull lilac rose paper.

A 6p in slate on white, apparently of this issue, is a late print from the counterfeit plate.

A4

Perf. 13½, 11½x12, 12½, 12½x12

1885-93 **Typo.**

123 A4 ½p gray 2.50 .25
a. Imperf. at top and bottom (used strip of 4) —
124 A4 1p rose 10.00 2.00
125 A4 2p brown 3.50 *5.00*
126 A4 2p olive bis ('87) 3.50 .25
127 A4 2½p purple ('93) 4.50 .65
128 A4 3p lilac 5.00 3.25
129 A4 4p bronze green 7.00 2.25
130 A4 6p blue 5.00 4.50
a. Imperf.
131 A4 1sh green 4.75 2.50
132 A4 2sh6p yellow 17.50 4.50
133 A4 5sh steel blue 10.00 7.50
134 A4 10sh pale brown 45.00 17.50
135 A4 £5 dk grn ('92) 4,000. 225.00
Nos. 123-134 (12) 118.25 50.15

Reprints of Nos. 123-137, 140-163, 166-174 closely resemble the originals. Paper is whiter; perf. 12½, large holes.

Excellent counterfeits of No. 135 exist.

For overprint and surcharges see Nos. 140-147, 163, 213.

Nos. 120, 122 Surcharged

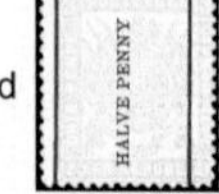

1885 ***Perf. 12***

136 A2 ½p on 3p red 10.00 *15.00*
a. Surcharge reading down 11.00 *16.00*
137 A1 ½p on 1sh green 42.50 70.00
a. Surcharge reading down 45.00 72.50
b. Tete beche pair 1,000. 450.00

Almost all examples of No. 137b have telegraph cancellations. Postally used examples are rare.

Nos. 101, 128 Surcharged in Red or Black

Perf. 14

138 A3 ½p on 6p slate 85.00 *125.00*
139 A3 2p on 6p slate 17.50 *21.00*
a. Horiz. pair, imperf. vert. —

Perf. 11½x12, 12½x12

140 A4 ½p on 3p lil (Bk) 10.00 9.50
a. "PRNNY" 65.00 *85.00*
b. 2nd "N" of "PENNY" invtd. 115.00 *130.00*

No. 128 Surcharged

No. 141

No. 142

1887

141 A4 2p on 3p violet 3.25 *6.00*
a. Double surcharge 230.00 225.00
142 A4 2p on 3p violet 15.00 13.25
a. Double surcharge — *425.00*

Nos. 126, 130, 131 Surcharged

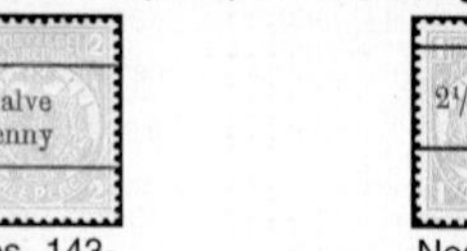

Nos. 143-144

Nos. 145-146

No. 147

1893 **Red Surcharge**

143 A4 ½p on 2p olive bis 1.75 *3.00*
a. Inverted surcharge 3.75 4.00
b. Bars 14mm apart 2.50 *4.25*
c. As "b," inverted 7.00 *13.50*

Black Surcharge

144 A4 ½p on 2p olive bis 2.00 *3.75*
a. Inverted surcharge 5.25 *6.00*
b. Bars 14mm apart 2.75 *4.50*
c. As "b," inverted 23.00 20.00
145 A4 1p on 6p blue 3.00 2.50
a. Inverted surcharge 3.25 *3.75*
b. Double surcharge 65.00 52.50
c. Pair, one without surcharge 325.00
d. Bars 14mm apart 3.50 3.50
e. As "d," inverted 7.25 5.75
f. As "d," double 95.00
146 A4 2½p on 1sh green 3.00 *8.00*
a. Inverted surcharge 8.75 *9.00*
b. Fraction line misplaced "2/½" 50.00 *92.50*
c. As "b," inverted 400.00 350.00
d. Bars 14mm apart 4.00 *10.00*
e. As "d," inverted 11.00 *21.00*
147 A4 2½p on 1sh green 12.50 10.00
a. Inverted surcharge 12.50 12.50
b. Bars 14mm apart 15.00 15.00
c. As "b," inverted 25.00 25.00
d. Double surcharge 92.50 *105.00*
Nos. 143-147 (5) 22.25 27.25

A13

Wagon with Two Shafts

1894 **Typo.** ***Perf. 12½***

148 A13 ½p gray 2.50 1.50
149 A13 1p rose 4.00 .25
150 A13 2p olive bister 4.00 .30
151 A13 6p blue 5.00 1.00
152 A13 1sh yellow grn 22.50 *30.00*
Nos. 148-152 (5) 38.00 33.05

Counterfeits of Nos.148-152 are plentiful.
See note following No. 135 for reprints.

1895-96 **Wagon with Pole**

153 A13 ½p gray 2.25 .25
154 A13 1p rose 2.50 .25
155 A13 2p olive bister 2.75 .35
156 A13 3p violet 4.00 1.25
157 A13 4p slate 4.00 1.00
158 A13 6p blue 4.00 1.00
159 A13 1sh green 5.00 1.75
160 A13 5sh slate blue ('96) 25.00 *42.50*
161 A13 10sh red brown ('96) 25.00 10.00
Nos. 153-161 (9) 74.50 58.35

Most of the unused examples of Nos. 153-161 now on the market are reprints.

See Nos. 166-174. For surcharge see No. 162.

See note following No. 135 for reprints.

Nos. 159, 127 Surcharged in Red or Green

1895

162 A13 ½p on 1sh green (R) 2.50 .25
a. Inverted surcharge 5.50 5.25
b. "Pennij" instead of "Penny" 70.00 *80.00*
c. Double surcharge 75.00 *105.00*
163 A4 1p on 2½p pur (G) .60 .30
a. Inverted surcharge 25.00 20.00
b. Surcharge sideways — —
c. Surcharge on back 100.00 —
d. Space between "1" and "d" 2.00 *1.75*

A16

1895 ***Perf. 11½***

164 A16 6p rose (G) 3.50 3.00
a. Vertical pair, imperf. between —

Counterfeits of No. 164 are on the 6p dark red revenue stamp of 1898, and have a shiny green ink for the overprint. The false overprint is also found on other revenue denominations, though only the 6p rose was converted to postal use.

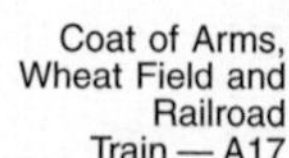

Coat of Arms, Wheat Field and Railroad Train — A17

1895, Sept. 6 **Litho.**

165 A17 1p red 3.00 *3.50*
a. Imperf. —
b. Vertical pair, imperf. between 240.00 *260.00*

Penny Postage in Transvaal. Horiz. pair, imperf. between also exists.

For overprint see No. 245.

Arms Type of 1894 With Pole

1896 **Typo.** ***Perf. 12½***

166 A13 ½p green 1.75 .25
167 A13 1p rose & grn 2.00 .25
168 A13 2p brown & grn 2.00 .25
169 A13 2½p ultra & grn 3.00 .35
170 A13 3p red vio & grn 3.25 3.00
171 A13 4p olive & grn 3.25 *4.00*
172 A13 6p violet & grn 3.00 3.00
173 A13 1sh bister & grn 2.60 1.50
174 A13 2sh6p lilac & grn 4.00 *4.50*
Nos. 166-174 (9) 24.85 17.10

See note following No. 135 for reprints.

For overprints and surcharges see Nos. 202-212, 214-235, 237-244, 246-251, Cape of Good Hope Nos. N5-N8.

Pietersburg Issue

Date large; "P" in Postzegel large — A18

Date small; "P" in Postzegel large — A19

Date small; "P" in Postzegel small — A20

1901 **Typeset** ***Imperf.***

Initials in Red

175 A18 ½p black, *green* 37.50
a. Initials omitted 125.00
b. Initials in black 45.00
176 A19 ½p black, *green* 50.00
a. Initials omitted 125.00
b. Initials in black 52.50
177 A20 ½p black, *green* 50.00
a. Initials omitted 125.00
b. Initials in black 52.50

Initials in Black

178 A18 1p black, *rose* 5.00
179 A19 1p black, *rose* 6.50
180 A20 1p black, *rose* 8.00
181 A18 2p black, *orange* 7.50
182 A19 2p black, *orange* 20.00
183 A20 2p black, *orange* 25.00
184 A18 4p black, *dull blue* 12.50
185 A19 4p black, *dull blue* 15.00
186 A20 4p black, *dull blue* 40.00
187 A18 6p black, *green* 17.00
188 A19 6p black, *green* 20.00
189 A20 6p black, *green* 55.00
190 A18 1sh black, *yellow* 12.50
191 A19 1sh black, *yellow* 20.00
192 A20 1sh black, *yellow* 30.00

Perf. 11½

Initials in Red

193 A18 ½p black, *green* 6.50
194 A19 ½p black, *green* 20.00
195 A20 ½p black, *green* 15.00

Initials in Black

196 A18 1p black, *rose* 3.00
a. Horiz. pair, imperf. vert. 65.00
197 A19 1p black, *rose* 3.50
a. Horiz. pair, imperf. vert. 100.00
198 A20 1p black, *rose* 6.50
a. Horiz. pair, imperf. vert. 100.00
199 A18 2p black, *orange* 7.50
200 A19 2p black, *orange* 9.50
201 A20 2p black, *orange* 17.00

Nos. 193-201 inclusive are always imperforate on one side.

The setting consisted of 12 stamps of type A18, 6 of type A19, and 6 of type A20. Numerous type-setting varieties exist. The perforated stamps are from the first printing and were put into use first. Used stamps are not valued because all seem to show evidence of having been canceled to order.

Second British Occupation Issued under Military Authority

Nos. 166-174, 160-161, 135 Overprinted

1900 **Unwmk.** ***Perf. 12½***

202 A13 ½p green .40 1.50
a. "V.I.R." 850.00
203 A13 1p rose & grn .75 1.50
204 A13 2p brown & grn 4.50 4.00
a. "V.I.R." 900.00 *1,000.*
205 A13 2½p ultra & grn 1.25 *3.50*
206 A13 3p red vio & grn 1.50 *3.50*
207 A13 4p olive & grn 3.75 4.50
a. "V.I.R." 900.00 —
208 A13 6p violet & grn 4.00 3.00
209 A13 1sh bister & grn 4.00 *5.00*
210 A13 2sh6p hel & grn 5.00 *17.50*
211 A13 5sh slate blue 10.00 25.00
212 A13 10sh red brown 13.00 27.50
213 A4 £5 dark green 2,500. 925.00
Nos. 202-212 (11) 48.15 96.50

Nos. 202-213 have been extensively counterfeited. The overprint on the forgeries is clear and clean, with small periods and letters showing completely. In the genuine, letters are worn and lack many or all serifs; the periods are large and oval.

The genuine overprint exists inverted; double; with period missing after "V," after "R," after "I," etc.

Issued in Lydenburg

Nos. 166-169, 171-173 Overprinted in Black

1900

214 A13 ½p green 200.00 200.00
215 A13 1p rose & grn 200.00 190.00
216 A13 2p brown & grn 1,500. 1,000.
217 A13 2½p ultra & grn 2,600. 1,150.
218 A13 4p olive & grn 3,750. 1,150.
219 A13 6p violet & grn 4,000. 1,100.
220 A13 1sh bister & grn 5,500. 3,750.

Beware of counterfeits.

No. 167 Surcharged

221 A13 3p on 1p rose & grn 175.00 150.00

Issued in Rustenburg

Nos. 166-170, 172-174 Handstamped in Violet

1900 ***Perf. 12½***

223 A13 ½p green 200.00 150.00
224 A13 1p rose & grn 150.00 110.00
225 A13 2p brown & grn 425.00 190.00
226 A13 2½p ultra & grn 275.00 150.00
227 A13 3p red vio & grn 350.00 200.00
229 A13 6p violet & grn 1,475. 600.00

230 A13 1sh bister & grn 2,200. 1,375.
231 A13 2sh6p hel & grn 9,000. *4,400.*
a. Handstamped in black *8,000.*

Issued in Schweizer Reneke
Nos. 166-168 and 172 Handstamped "BESIEGED" in Black

1900 Typo. *Perf. 12½*
232 A13 ½p green 350.00
233 A13 1p rose & green 350.00
234 A13 2p brown & green 475.00
235 A13 6p violet & green 1,275.
Nos. 232-235 (4) 2,450.

Same Overprint on Cape of Good Hope No. 59 and Type of 1893
Perf. 14
236 A15 ½p green 600.00
236A A15 1p carmine 600.00

In 1902 five revenue stamps overprinted "V.R.I." are said to have been used postally in Volksrust. There seems to be some doubt that this issue was properly authorized for postal use.

Issued in Wolmaransstad

Nos. 166-173 Handstamped in Blue or Red

1900
237 A13 ½p green 375.00 *500.00*
238 A13 1p rose & grn 250.00 *400.00*
239 A13 2p brown & grn 2,250. 2,250.
240 A13 2½p ultra & grn (R) 2,250.
241 A13 3p red vio & grn 3,500. *3,750.*
242 A13 4p olive & grn 5,000. *5,250.*
243 A13 6p violet & grn 6,000. *6,400.*
244 A13 1sh bister & grn *12,750.*

No. 165 Overprinted in Blue

245 A17 1p red 260.00 *475.00*

Regular Issues
No. 166-168, 170-171, 174 Surcharged or Overprinted

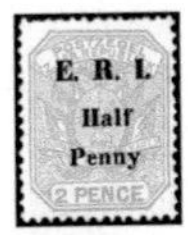

1901-02
246 A13 ½p on 2p brn & grn .80 2.00
247 A13 ½p green .60 *3.00*
248 A13 1p rose & grn .60 .25
a. Overprint "E" omitted 87.50
249 A13 3p red vio & grn 2.60 *4.75*
250 A13 4p olive & grn 2.75 *11.00*
251 A13 2sh6p hel & grn 10.50 *40.00*
Nos. 246-251 (6) 17.85 61.00

Excellent counterfeits of Nos. 246-251 are plentiful. See note after No. 213 for the recognition marks of the counterfeits.

Edward VII — A27

Nos. 260, 262 to 267 and 275 to 280 have "POSTAGE" at each side; the other stamps of type A27 have "REVENUE" at the right.

Wmk. Crown and C A (2)

1902-03 Typo. *Perf. 14*
252 A27 ½p gray grn & blk 3.00 .25
253 A27 1p rose & blk 1.50 .25
254 A27 2p violet & blk 8.50 1.20
255 A27 2½p ultra & blk 16.00 2.25
256 A27 3p ol grn & blk 18.00 2.00
257 A27 4p choc & blk 18.00 3.25
258 A27 6p brn org & blk 5.00 1.50
259 A27 1sh ol grn & blk 21.00 *26.00*
260 A27 1sh red brn & blk 19.00 6.00
261 A27 2sh brown & blk 75.00 *85.00*
262 A27 2sh yel & blk 22.50 *25.00*
263 A27 2sh6p black & vio 18.50 19.00
264 A27 5sh vio & blk, *yel* 42.50 *50.00*
265 A27 10sh vio & blk, *red* 80.00 50.00
266 A27 £1 violet & grn 375.00 225.00
267 A27 £5 violet & org 2,250. 950.00
Nos. 252-266 (15) 723.50 496.70

Issue dates: 3p, 4p, Nos. 260, 262, £1, £5, 1903. Others, Apr. 1, 1902.

1904-09 Wmk. 3
268 A27 ½p gray grn & blk 13.00 3.50
269 A27 1p rose & blk 12.00 2.00
270 A27 2p violet & blk 27.50 2.40
271 A27 2½p ultra & blk 32.50 14.00
272 A27 3p ol grn & blk 4.50 .60
273 A27 4p choc & blk 6.50 .80
274 A27 6p brn org & blk 19.00 2.40
275 A27 1sh red brn & blk 15.00 .60
276 A27 2sh yellow & blk 35.00 16.00
277 A27 2sh6p blk & red vio 60.00 12.50
278 A27 5sh vio & blk, *yel* 35.00 1.75
279 A27 10sh vio & blk, *red* 90.00 5.00
280 A27 £1 violet & grn 425.00 52.50
Nos. 268-280 (13) 775.00 114.05

The 2p and 3p are on chalky paper, the 2½p, 4p, 6p and £1 on both chalky and ordinary, and the other values on ordinary paper only.

Issue years: ½p, 1p, 5sh, 1904. 2½p, 6p, 1sh, 1905. 2p, 3p, 4p, 2sh, 1906. 10sh, 1907. £1, 1908. 2sh6p, 1909.

1905-10
281 A27 ½p green 4.00 .25
a. Booklet pane of 6 —
282 A27 1p carmine 1.50 .25
a. Wmk. 16 (anchor) ('07) — *375.00*
b. Booklet pane of 6 — —
283 A27 2p dull vio ('10) 4.00 1.50
284 A27 2½p ultra ('10) 30.00 15.00
Nos. 281-284 (4) 39.50 17.00

Wmk. 16 is illustrated in the Cape of Good Hope.

Some of the above stamps are found with the overprint "C. S. A. R." for use by the Central South African Railway, the control mark being applied after the stamps had left the post office.

POSTAGE DUE STAMPS

D1

Wmk. Multiple Crown and C A (3)

1907 Typo. *Perf. 14*
J1 D1 ½p green & blk 4.00 1.50
J2 D1 1p carmine & blk 4.75 1.00
J3 D1 2p brown org 5.75 1.50
J4 D1 3p blue & blk 8.75 5.00
J5 D1 5p violet & blk 2.75 *14.00*
J6 D1 6p red brown & blk 5.00 *14.00*
J7 D1 1sh black & car 14.00 10.00
Nos. J1-J7 (7) 45.00 47.00

Most canceled stamps of #J1-J7 were used outside the Transvaal under the Union of South Africa administration in 1910-16.

The stamps of Transvaal were replaced by those of South Africa.

TRINIDAD

'tri-nə-,dad

LOCATION — West Indies, off the Venezuelan coast
GOVT. — British Colony which became part of the Colony of Trinidad and Tobago in 1889
AREA — 1,864 sq. mi.
POP. — 387,000
CAPITAL — Port of Spain

12 Pence = 1 Shilling
20 Shillings = 1 Pound

In 1847 David Bryce, owner of the "Lady McLeod," issued a blue, lithographed, imperf. stamp to prepay his 5-cent rate for carrying letters on his sail-equipped steamer between Port of Spain and San Fernando, another Trinidad port. The stamp pictures the "Lady McLeod" above the monogram "LMcL," expressing no denomination. Value, unused, $50,000, used (pen canceled), $12,500. Used stamps canceled by having a corner skinned off are worth less.

Values for unused stamps are for examples with original gum as defined in the catalogue introduction. However, Nos. 9-12 are seldom found with gum, and these are valued without gum.

Values for Nos. 18-26 are for stamps with pin perforations on two or three sides. Stamps with pin perforations on all four sides are not often seen and command large premiums.

Very fine examples of Nos. 27-47 will have perforations touching the design on one or more sides due to the narrow spacing of the stamps on the plates and imperfect perforating methods. These stamps with perfs clear of the design on all four sides are scarce and command substantially higher prices.

"Britannia" — A1

1851-56 Unwmk. Engr. *Imperf.*
Blued Paper
1 A1 (1p) brick red ('56) 200.00 85.00
a. (1p) brown red ('53) 360.00 77.50
2 A1 (1p) purple brown 22.50 *90.00*
3 A1 (1p) blue 24.00 *72.50*
a. (1p) deep blue, deeply blued paper 175.00 95.00
4 A1 (1p) gray brn ('53) 57.50 *90.00*
a. (1p) gray ('52) 90.00 77.50
Nos. 1-4 (4) 304.00 *337.50*

1854-57 White Paper
6 A1 (1p) brown red ('57) 3,250. 77.50
7 A1 (1p) gray 55.00 *95.00*
8 A1 (1p) black violet 32.50 *100.00*

See Nos. 14, 18, 22, 27, 33, 39, 43, 45, 48, 58. For surcharges see Nos. 62-64.

"Britannia" — A2

1852 Litho.
Fine Impressions
Yellowish Paper
9 A2 (1p) blue *11,500.* 1,950.
a. (1p) deep blue *11,500.* 1,950.
b. White paper 1,950.

1853 Bluish Paper
10 A2 (1p) blue *10,000.* 2,400.

Same, Lines of Background More or Less Worn

1855-60 Thin Paper
11 A2 (1p) slate blue *5,500.* 800.00
12 A2 (1p) blue *5,000.* 500.00
a. (1p) greenish blue 800.00
13 A2 (1p) rose 17.50 *750.00*
a. (1p) dull red 17.50 *725.00*

A3

1859 Engr. *Imperf.*
White Paper
14 A1 (1p) dull rose — —
15 A3 4p gray lilac 125.00 *400.00*
a. 4p dull lilac —
16 A3 6p green *15,000.* 525.00
17 A3 1sh slate blue 125.00 *425.00*

Pin-perf. 12½
18 A1 (1p) dull rose red *2,000.* 70.00
a. (1p) lake *2,250.* 70.00
19 A3 4p brown lilac — 1,250.
a. 4p dull purple 7,500. 1,250.
20 A3 6p deep green *3,500.* 250.00
a. 6p yellow green 3,500. 250.00
21 A3 1sh black violet *9,000.* 1,750.

Pin-perf. 14
22 A1 (1p) rose red 275.00 42.50
a. (1p) carmine 325.00 40.00
23 A3 4p brown lilac 250.00 *150.00*
a. 4p violet 600.00 160.00
b. 4p dull violet 1,650. 125.00
24 A3 6p deep green 800.00 100.00
25 A3 6p yellow green 200.00 160.00
a. Vert. pair, imperf. between *8,000.*
26 A3 1sh black violet *9,000.* *1,150.*

1860 *Clean-cut Perf. 14 to 15½*
27 A1 (1p) dull rose 190.00 67.50
a. (1p) lake 100.00 40.00
b. Horiz. pair, imperf. vert. *3,000.*
29 A3 4p violet brown 210.00 95.00
a. 4p dull violet 375.00
30 A3 6p deep green 300.00 175.00
31 A3 6p yellow green 550.00 115.00
32 A3 1sh black violet *5,000.*

1861 *Rough Perf. 14 to 16½*
33 A1 (1p) dull rose 170.00 37.50
34 A3 4p gray lilac 750.00 100.00
35 A3 4p brown lilac 325.00 85.00
a. 4p dull violet 750.00 115.00
36 A3 6p green 475.00 85.00
a. 6p blue green 325.00 95.00
37 A3 1sh indigo 1,000. 350.00
a. 1sh purplish blue 1,675. 550.00
b. Unwatermarked —

Thick Paper

1863 *Perf. 11½ to 12*
39 A1 (1p) carmine 160.00 29.00
a. Perf. 11½-12x11 2,000. *600.00*
40 A3 4p dull violet 225.00 72.50
41 A3 6p dp blue green *1,350.* 100.00
a. Perf. 11½-12x11 *8,000.*
42 A3 1sh indigo 2,750. 110.00

Perf. 12½
43 A1 (1p) lake 62.50 29.00

Perf. 13
45 A1 (1p) lake 52.50 29.00
46 A3 6p emerald 525.00 62.50
47 A3 1sh brt violet 4,500. 300.00

1864-72 Wmk. 1 *Perf. 12½*
48 A1 (1p) red 65.00 3.50
a. (1p) lake 65.00 8.25
b. (1p) rose 65.00 3.00
c. (1p) carmine 70.00 3.75
d. Imperf., pair *800.00* *800.00*
49 A3 4p brt violet 150.00 21.00
a. 4p pale violet 250.00 24.00
b. Imperf. *600.00*
50 A3 4p lilac 200.00 21.00
a. 4p gray lilac
51 A3 4p gray ('72) 160.00 8.50
52 A3 6p blue green 190.00 10.00
a. 6p emerald 125.00 19.00
53 A3 6p yellow grn 115.00 8.00
a. 6p dp grn 500.00 10.00
b. Imperf., pair *800.00*
54 A3 1sh purple 200.00 12.00
a. 1sh lilac 150.00 12.00
b. 1sh violet 150.00 12.00
c. 1sh red lilac 160.00 13.00
d. Imperf. *750.00*
55 A3 1sh orange yel ('72) 175.00 2.50
Nos. 48-55 (8) 1,255. 86.50

See Nos. 59-61A, 65. For surcharge see No. 67.

Queen Victoria — A4

1869-94 Typo. *Perf. 12½*
56 A4 5sh dull lake 200.00 90.00
a. Imperf., pair *1,250.*

Perf. 14
57 A4 5sh claret ('94) 67.50 *115.00*

For overprint see No. O7.

1876 Engr. *Perf. 14*
58 A1 (1p) carmine 52.50 3.00
a. (1p) red 82.50 3.00
b. (1p) lake 55.00 3.00
c. Half used as ½p on cover 750.00

59 A3 4p gray 140.00 2.25
60 A3 6p yellow green 120.00 4.00
a. 6p deep green 150.00 3.25
61 A3 1sh orange yellow 165.00 5.00
Nos. 58-61 (4) 477.50 14.25

Perf. 14x12½

61A A3 6p yel grn ('80) *6,750.*

Value for No. 61A is for stamp with perfs barely touching the design.

Type A1 Surcharged in Black

1879 **Wmk. 1** ***Perf. 14***
62 A1 ½p lilac 22.50 14.00

Same Surcharge

1882 **Wmk. Crown and C A (2)**
63 A1 ½p lilac *250.00* 90.00
64 A1 1p carmine 77.50 2.75
a. Half used as ½p on cover 675.00

Type of 1859

1882 **Wmk. 2**
65 A3 4p gray 215.00 17.50

No. 60 Surcharged by pen and ink in Black or Red

1882 **Wmk. 1**
67 A3 1p on 6p green (R) 16.00 10.00
a. Half used as ½p on cover 400.00
b. Black surcharge *1,900.*

Counterfeits of No. 67b are plentiful. Various handwriting exists on both 60 and 60a.

A7

1883-84 **Typo.** **Wmk. 2**
68 A7 ½p green 12.00 1.50
69 A7 1p rose 25.00 .60
a. Half used as ½p on cover 950.00
70 A7 2½p ultra 29.00 .70
a. 2½p blue 27.50 .75
71 A7 4p slate 5.00 .70
72 A7 6p olive brn ('84) 9.00 *7.00*
73 A7 1sh orange brn ('84) 16.00 7.00
Nos. 68-73 (6) 96.00 17.50

For overprints see Nos. O1-O6.

A8 A9

ONE ONE
Type I Type II

ONE PENNY:
Type I — Round "O" in "ONE."
Type II — Oval "O" in "ONE."

1896-1904 ***Perf. 14***
74 A8 ½p lilac & green 4.00 .35
75 A8 ½p gray grn ('02) 1.25 *2.40*
76 A8 1p lil & car, type I 4.25 .25
77 A8 1p lil & car, type II ('00) 400.00 4.75
78 A8 1p blk, *red,* type II ('01) 5.50 .25
a. Value omitted *36,000.*
79 A8 2½p lilac & ultra 7.25 .25
80 A8 2½p vio & bl, *bl* ('02) 27.50 .75
81 A8 4p lilac & orange 9.00 *27.50*
82 A8 4p grn & ultra, *buff* ('02) 4.00 *24.00*
83 A8 5p lilac & violet 11.00 *17.50*
84 A8 6p lilac & black 9.00 6.50
85 A8 1sh grn & org brn 8.25 7.75
86 A8 1sh blk & bl, *yel* ('04) 22.50 6.50

Wmk. C A over Crown (46)

87 A9 5sh green & org 65.00 90.00
88 A9 5sh lil & red vio ('02) 90.00 110.00
89 A9 10sh grn & ultra 350.00 *575.00*
Revenue cancel 30.00
90 A9 £1 grn & car 210.00 350.00
Nos. 74-90 (17) 1,229. 1,224.

No. 82 also exists on chalky paper. Values: unused $3.50, used $14. Nos. 88 and 90 exist on both ordinary and chalky paper.

Circular "Registrar General" cancels are revenue usage and of minimal value.

See Nos. 92-104.

Landing of Columbus — A10

1898 **Engr.** **Wmk. 1**
91 A10 2p gray vio & yel brn 3.25 1.40
Overprinted "SPECIMEN" 60.00

400th anniv. of the discovery of the island of Trinidad by Columbus, July 31, 1498.

1904-09 **Wmk. 3** **Chalky Paper**
92 A8 ½p gray green 13.00 2.50
a. Ordinary paper 10.00 1.25
93 A8 1p blk, *red,* type II 15.00 .25
a. Ordinary paper 15.00 .25
94 A8 2½p vio & bl, *bl* 27.50 1.10
95 A8 4p blk & car, *yel* ('06) 5.00 *17.50*
96 A8 6p lilac & blk ('05) 24.00 18.00
97 A8 6p vio & dp vio ('06) 12.00 *17.50*
98 A8 1sh blk & bl, *yel* 26.00 12.00
99 A8 1sh vio & bl, *yel* 18.00 28.00
100 A8 1sh blk, *grn* ('06) 3.00 1.50
101 A9 5sh lil & red vio ('07) 85.00 115.00
102 A9 £1 grn & car ('07) 325.00 *400.00*
Nos. 92-102 (11) 553.50 613.35

For overprints see Nos. O8-O9.

1906-07
103 A8 1p carmine ('07) 4.00 .25
104 A8 2½p ultramarine 12.00 .25

A11 A12

1909 **Ordinary Paper**
105 A11 ½p gray green 11.00 .25
106 A12 1p carmine 14.00 .25
107 A11 2½p ultramarine 29.00 4.75
Nos. 105-107 (3) 54.00 5.25

For overprint see No. O10.

POSTAGE DUE STAMPS

D1

Wmk. Crown and C A (2)

1885, Jan. 1 **Typo.** ***Perf. 14***
J1 D1 ½p black 22.50 55.00
J2 D1 1p black 11.00 .25
J3 D1 2p black 52.50 .25
J4 D1 3p black 62.50 .50
J5 D1 4p black 52.50 7.50
J6 D1 5p black 27.50 .70
J7 D1 6p black 55.00 14.00
J8 D1 8p black 65.00 6.00
J9 D1 1sh black 82.50 9.00
Nos. J1-J9 (9) 431.00 93.20

1906-07 **Wmk. 3**
J10 D1 1p black 9.50 .25
J11 D1 2p black 42.50 .25
J12 D1 3p black 15.00 3.75
J13 D1 4p black 15.00 *22.50*
J14 D1 5p black 21.00 *24.00*
J15 D1 6p black 7.25 *18.00*
J16 D1 8p black 21.00 *24.00*
J17 D1 1sh black 30.00 *47.50*
Nos. J10-J17 (8) 161.25 140.25

See Trinidad and Tobago Nos. J1-J16.

OFFICIAL STAMPS

Postage Stamps of 1869-84 Overprinted in Black

1893-94 **Wmk. 2** ***Perf. 14***
O1 A7 ½p green 50.00 *65.00*
O2 A7 1p rose 52.50 *72.50*
O3 A7 2½p ultra 57.50 *110.00*
O4 A7 4p slate 62.50 *135.00*
O5 A7 6p olive brown 62.50 *145.00*
O6 A7 1sh orange brown 82.50 *200.00*

Wmk. Crown and C C (1)

Perf. 12½

O7 A4 5sh dull lake 190.00 *875.00*
Nos. O1-O7 (7) 557.50 *1,603.*

Nos. 92 and 103 Overprinted

1909-10 **Wmk. 3** ***Perf. 14***
O8 A8 ½p gray green 3.75 12.00
O9 A8 1p carmine 3.50 13.00
a. Double overprint 375.00
b. Inverted overprint 900.00 275.00
c. Vertical overprint 140.00 160.00

Same Overprint on No. 105

1910
O10 A11 ½p gray green 13.00 *17.50*

Stamps of Trinidad have been superseded by those inscribed "Trinidad and Tobago."

TRINIDAD & TOBAGO

ˈtri-nə-ˌdad and tə-ˈbā-ˌgō

LOCATION — West Indies off the coast of Venezuela
GOVT. — Republic
AREA — 1,980 sq. mi.
POP. — 1,102,096 (1999 est.)
CAPITAL — Port-of-Spain

The two British colonies of Trinidad and Tobago were united from 1889 until 1899, when Tobago became a ward of the united colony. From 1899 until 1913 postage stamps of Trinidad were used. The two islands became a state in August 1962, and the independent Republic of Trinidad and Tobago on August 1, 1976.

12 Pence = 1 Shilling
20 Shillings = 1 Pound
100 Cents = 1 Dollar (1935)

Catalogue values for unused stamps in this country are for Never Hinged items, beginning with Scott 62 in the regular postage section and Scott J9 in the postage due section.

"Britannia" — A1

1913 **Typo.** **Wmk. 3** ***Perf. 14***

Ordinary Paper

1 A1 ½p green 3.50 .25
2 A1 1p scarlet 1.75 .25
a. 1p carmine 2.75 .25
4 A1 2½p ultra 8.00 .50

Chalky Paper

5 A1 4p scar & blk, *yel* .80 *7.00*
6 A1 6p red vio & dull vio 11.00 8.00
7 A1 1sh black, *emerald* back 1.75 *3.50*
a. 1sh black, *green* 2.00 *5.00*
b. 1sh black, *bl grn,* ol back 22.00 *10.00*
Nos. 1-2,4-7 (6) 26.80 19.50

"Britannia" — A2

1914

Surface-colored Paper (White Back)

8 A1 4p scar & blk, *yel* 2.00 *11.50*
9 A1 1sh black, *green* 1.60 *17.50*

Chalky Paper

10 A2 5sh dull vio & red vio 85.00 *125.00*
11 A2 £1 green & car 325.00 *375.00*
Nos. 8-11 (4) 413.60 *529.00*

1921-22 **Ordinary Paper** **Wmk. 4**
12 A1 ½p green 3.50 2.50
13 A1 1p scarlet .65 .30
14 A1 1p brown ('22) .65 *1.50*
15 A1 2p gray ('22) 1.00 *1.25*
16 A1 2½p ultra 1.00 *27.50*
17 A1 3p ultra ('22) 10.00 3.25

Chalky Paper

18 A1 6p red vio & dull vio 5.75 *16.75*
19 A2 5sh dull vio & red vio 80.00 *175.00*
20 A2 £1 green & car 190.00 *390.00*
Nos. 12-20 (9) 292.55 *618.05*

For overprints see Nos. B2-B3, MR1-MR13, O1-O5.

"Britannia" and King George V — A3

1922-28 **Ordinary Paper**
21 A3 ½p green .80 .25
22 A3 1p brown .80 .25
23 A3 1½p rose red 2.60 .45
24 A3 2p gray .85 *1.30*
25 A3 3p ultra 1.30 *1.30*

Chalky Paper

26 A3 4p red & blk, *yel* ('28) 3.75 3.50
27 A3 6p red vio & dl vio 4.25 *29.00*
28 A3 6p red & grn, *emer* ('24) 1.60 .80
29 A3 1sh blk, *emer* ('25) 5.75 1.85
30 A3 5sh vio & dull vio 40.00 *42.50*
31 A3 £1 rose & green 170.00 *290.00*

Wmk. Multiple Crown and C A (3)

Chalky Paper

32 A3 4p red & blk, *yel* 6.25 *22.00*
33 A3 1sh blk, *emerald* 8.50 *10.00*
Nos. 21-33 (13) 246.45 *403.20*

First Boca — A4

Designs: 2c, Agricultural College. 3c, Mt. Irvine Bay, Tobago. 6c, Discovery of Lake Asphalt. 8c, Queen's Park, Savannah. 12c, Town Hall, San Fernando. 24c, Government House. 48c, Memorial Park. 72c, Blue Basin.

1935-37 **Engr.** **Wmk. 4** ***Perf. 12***
34 A4 1c emer & bl, perf. 12½ ('36) .30 .25
a. Perf. 12 .40 *.90*
35 A4 2c lt brn & ultra, perf. 12 3.00 *1.05*
a. Perf. 12½ ('36) 3.00 .25
36 A4 3c red & blk, perf. 12½ ('36) 4.00 .30
a. Perf. 12 2.10 .30
37 A4 6c bl & brn, perf. 12 4.50 2.60
a. Perf. 12½ ('37) 21.00 16.00
38 A4 8c red org & yel grn 3.90 3.65
39 A4 12c dk violet & blk 4.75 1.85
a. Perf. 12½ ('37) 22.00 15.75
40 A4 24c ol grn & blk 10.00 3.00
a. Perf. 12½ ('37) 33.50 25.00
41 A4 48c slate green 12.50 *19.00*
42 A4 72c mag & sl grn 47.50 *33.50*
Nos. 34-42 (9) 90.45 65.20

Common Design Types pictured following the introduction.

Silver Jubilee Issue
Common Design Type

1935, May 6 *Perf. 11x12*

43 CD301 2c black & ultra .30 *.80*
44 CD301 3c car & blue .30 *2.60*
45 CD301 6c ultra & brn 3.25 *2.60*
46 CD301 24c brn vio & ind 14.75 *31.50*
Nos. 43-46 (4) 18.60 37.50
Set, never hinged 34.00

Coronation Issue
Common Design Type

1937, May 12 *Perf. 13½x14*

47 CD302 1c deep green .30 .60
48 CD302 2c yellow brown .30 .25
49 CD302 8c deep orange .50 2.35
Nos. 47-49 (3) 1.10 3.20
Set, never hinged 1.85

First Boca A13 — George VI A14

Various Frames and: 2c, Agricultural College. 3c, Mt. Irvine Bay, Tobago. 4c, Memorial Park. 5c, General Post Office and Treasury. 6c, Discovery of Lake Asphalt. 8c, Queen's Park, Savannah. 12c, Town Hall, San Fernando. 24c, Government House. 60c, Blue Basin.

Perf. 11½x11

1938-41 **Wmk. 4** **Engr.**

50 A13 1c emer & blue .60 .30
51 A13 2c lt brn & ultra .75 .25
52 A13 3c dk car & blk 6.75 1.00
52A A13 3c vio brn & bl grn ('41) .30 .25
53 A13 4c brown 19.00 3.00
53A A13 4c red ('41) .30 1.05
54 A13 5c mag ('41) .30 .25
55 A13 6c brt bl & sep 1.60 .85
56 A13 8c red org & yel grn 1.75 1.05
57 A13 12c dk vio & blk 3.50 .25
58 A13 24c dk ol grn & blk 5.00 .25
59 A13 60c mag & sl grn 9.00 1.15

Perf. 12

60 A14 $1.20 dk grn ('40) 8.50 2.60
61 A14 $4.80 rose pink ('40) 24.00 *57.50*
Nos. 50-61 (14) 81.35 69.75
Set, never hinged 135.00

Watermark sideways on Nos. 50-59.

Catalogue values for unused stamps in this section, from this point to the end of the section, are for Never Hinged items.

Peace Issue
Common Design Type
Perf. 13½x14

1946, Oct. 1 **Engr.** **Wmk. 4**

62 CD303 3c brown .30 .25
63 CD303 6c deep blue .45 1.60

Silver Wedding Issue
Common Design Types

1948, Nov. 22 **Photo.** *Perf. 14x14½*

64 CD304 3c red brown .30 .25

Perf. 11½x11
Engr.

65 CD305 $4.80 rose car 31.50 *50.00*

UPU Issue
Common Design Types
Engr.; Name Typo. on 6c, 12c
Perf. 13½, 11x11½

1949, Oct. 10 **Wmk. 4**

66 CD306 5c red violet .35 1.05
67 CD307 6c indigo 2.10 2.60
68 CD308 12c rose violet .55 1.85
69 CD309 24c olive .55 1.30
Nos. 66-69 (4) 3.55 6.80

University Issue
Common Design Types
Inscribed: "Trinidad"

1951, Feb. 16 **Engr.** *Perf. 14x14½*

70 CD310 3c choc & grn .50 2.10
71 CD311 12c purple & blk .50 2.10

Types of 1938 with Portrait of Queen Elizabeth II

1953, Apr. 20 *Perf. 11½x11*

72 A13 1c yel grn & dp blue .30 .40
73 A13 2c org brn & sl blue .30 .40
74 A13 3c vio brn & blue grn .30 .25
75 A13 4c red .30 .40
76 A13 5c magenta .40 .25
77 A13 6c blue & brown .60 .30
78 A13 8c red org & dp grn 2.50 .30
79 A13 12c dk violet & blk .50 .25
80 A13 24c dk ol grn & blk 3.00 .30
81 A13 60c rose car & grnsh blk 28.50 1.85

Perf. 11½

82 A14 $1.20 dark green 4.25 .35
a. Perf. 12 1.55 2.60
83 A14 $4.80 rose pink 19.00 *23.00*
a. Perf. 12 15.75 *29.50*
Nos. 72-83 (12) 59.95 28.05

For surcharge see No. 85.

Coronation Issue
Common Design Type

1953, June 3 *Perf. 13½x13*

84 CD312 3c dark green & blk .30 .25

No. 73 Surcharged "ONE CENT"
Perf. 11½x11

1956, Dec. 20 **Wmk. 4**

85 A13 1c on 2c org brn & sl blue 1.30 *2.40*

West Indies Federation
Common Design Type
Perf. 11½x11

1958, Apr. 22 **Engr.** **Wmk. 314**

86 CD313 5c green .75 .25
87 CD313 6c blue .80 *1.85*
88 CD313 12c carmine rose .85 .25
Nos. 86-88 (3) 2.40 2.35

Cipriani Memorial, Port-of-Spain A27

Queen's Hall, Port-of-Spain A28

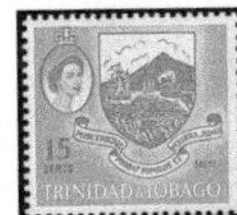

Crest of Colony — A28a

Copper-rumped Hummingbird and Hibiscus — A28b

Designs: 5c, Whitehall. 6c, Treasury Building. 8c, Governor General's House. 10c, General Hospital, San Fernando. 12c, Oil refinery. 25c, Scarlet ibis. 35c, Lake Asphalt (Pitch). 50c, Jinnah Memorial Mosque. 60c, Anthurium lilies. $4.80, Map.

Perf. 13½x14, 14x13½

1960, Sept. 24 **Photo.** **Wmk. 314**
Size: 22½x25mm, 25x22½mm

89 A27 1c dark gray & buff 1.30 .25
a. Wmkd. sideways ('66) .30 2.10
90 A28 2c ultra .75 .25
91 A28 5c dark blue .30 .25
92 A28 6c lt red brown 1.30 1.05
93 A28 8c yellow green .30 *1.60*
94 A28 10c light purple .30 .25
95 A28 12c bright red .30 1.30
96 A28a 15c orange 3.90 1.65
97 A28 25c dk blue & crim .85 .25
98 A28 35c green & black 4.00 .25
99 A28 50c blue, yel & olive .40 *1.60*
100 A27 60c multicolored .55 .30
a. Perf. 14 ('65) 145.00 52.50

Size: 48x25mm

101 A28b $1.20 multicolored 15.75 4.25
102 A28b $4.80 lt bl & lt yel grn 23.00 22.00
Nos. 89-102 (14) 53.00 35.25

See No. 116. For overprints see Nos. 123-124, 126.

Scouts and Map of Trinidad and Tobago A29

Perf. 13½x14

1961, Apr. 4

103 A29 8c multicolored .30 .25
104 A29 25c multicolored .30 .25

2nd Caribbean Scout Jamboree, Valsayn Park, Trinidad, Apr. 4-14.

Independent State

Underwater Scene from Painting by Carlisle Chang — A30

Designs: 8c, Elizabeth II and new Terminal Building, Piarco Airport. 25c, Elizabeth II and Hilton Hotel. 35c, Map and greater bird of paradise. 60c, Map and scarlet ibis.

1962, Aug. 31 **Photo.** *Perf. 14½*

105 A30 5c blue green .30 .25
106 A30 8c slate .40 *1.05*
107 A30 25c purple .30 .25
108 A30 35c emer, yel, brn & blk 2.35 .25
109 A30 60c ultra, black & ver 2.90 *3.90*
Nos. 105-109 (5) 6.25 5.70

Issued to mark Trinidad and Tobago's independence, Aug. 31, 1962.

Freedom from Hunger Issue

Protein Food — A31

1963, June 1 *Perf. 14x13½*

110 A31 5c henna brown .40 .25
111 A31 8c citron .70 .90
112 A31 25c violet blue .95 .25
Nos. 110-112 (3) 2.05 1.40

See note in Common Design section.

Girl Guide Emblem — A32

Perf. 14½x14

1964, Sept. 15 **Wmk. 314**

113 A32 6c red, dk blue & yel .30 .25
114 A32 25c brt blue, dk bl & yel .30 .25
115 A32 35c lt green, dk bl & yel .30 .25
Nos. 113-115 (3) .90 .75

50th anniv. of the Trinidad and Tobago Girl Guide Association.

Arms of Independent State — A33

1964, Sept. 15 *Perf. 14x13½*

116 A33 15c orange 15.75 .25

For overprint see No. 125.

ICY Emblem — A34

Unwmk.

1965, Nov. 15 **Litho.** *Perf. 12*
Granite Paper

117 A34 35c dull yel, red brn & grn .70 .25

International Cooperation Year, 1965.

Eleanor Roosevelt A35

Perf. 13½x14

1965, Dec. 10 **Wmk. 314**

118 A35 25c vio blue, red & blk .30 .25

Issued to honor Eleanor Roosevelt and to publicize the Eleanor Roosevelt Memorial Foundation.

"Redhouse," Parliament Building A36

8c, Map of Trinidad & Tobago, royal yacht "Britannia," arms of State. 25c, Flag, map. 35c, Flag, Trinity Hills, General Post Office, sugar cane, coconut palms, derricks.

1966, Feb. 8 **Photo.** **Wmk. 314**

119 A36 5c ultra, red, blk & grn 1.15 .25
120 A36 8c ultra, sil, blk & yel brn 2.35 1.05
121 A36 25c red, blk & emerald 2.35 .60
122 A36 35c ultra, red, blk & grn 2.35 .75
Nos. 119-122 (4) 8.20 2.65

Visit of Elizabeth II and Prince Philip.

Nos. 93-94, 116 Overprinted

No. 100 Overprinted

Perf. 14x13½, 13½x14

1967, Aug. 31 **Photo.** **Wmk. 314**

123 A28 8c yellow green .30 .25
124 A28 10c lt purple .30 .25
125 A33 15c orange .30 .25
126 A27 60c multicolored .30 .25
Nos. 123-126 (4) 1.20 1.00

Carnival Symbols — A37

Designs: 10c, Calypso King, vert. 15c, Steel band. 25c, Chinese masks. 35c, Carnival King, vert. 60c, Carnival Queen, vert.

Unwmk.

1968, Feb. 16 **Litho.** *Perf. 12*

127 A37 5c pink & multi .30 .25
128 A37 10c vio blue & multi .30 .25
129 A37 15c multicolored .30 .25
130 A37 25c multicolored .30 .25
131 A37 35c dk purple & multi .30 .25
132 A37 60c brown ol & multi .40 1.05
Nos. 127-132 (6) 1.90 2.30

Issued to publicize the Trinidad Carnival.

WHO Emblem and Eye Examination — A38

Wmk. 314

1968, May 7 **Photo.** *Perf. 14*

133 A38 5c rose red, gold & blk .30 .25
134 A38 25c orange, gold & blk .30 .25
135 A38 35c brt blue, gold & blk .40 .30
Nos. 133-135 (3) 1.00 .80

Dancing Children and Human Rights Flame — A39

1968, Aug. 5 *Perf. 14*

136 A39 5c carmine, yel & blk .30 .25
137 A39 10c brt blue, yel, & blk .30 .25
138 A39 25c yel grn, yel & blk .30 .25
Nos. 136-138 (3) .90 .75

International Human Rights Year.

Bicycling and Map — A40

Designs (Olympic Rings, Map of Trinidad and Tobago and): 15c, Weight lifting. 25c, Relay race. 35c, Running. $1.20, Map of Mexico and flags of Mexico and Trinidad and Tobago.

Photo.; Gold Impressed (except $1.20)

1968, Oct. 12 *Perf. 14*

139 A40 5c vio, gold & multi .85 .25
140 A40 15c red, gold & multi .30 .25
141 A40 25c org, gold & multi .30 .25
142 A40 35c brt grn, gold & multi .30 .25
143 A40 $1.20 blue, gold & multi 1.70 1.90
Nos. 139-143 (5) 3.45 2.90

19th Olympic Games, Mexico City, 10/12-27.

Cacao — A41

Designs: 3c, Sugar refinery. 5c, Redtailed chachalaca. 6c, Oil refinery. 8c, Fertilizer plant. 10c, Green hermit (hummingbird) vert. 12c, Citrus fruit, vert. 15c, Coat of arms, vert. 20c, 25c, Flag and map of islands, vert. 30c, Wild poinsettia, vert. 40c, Scarlet ibis. 50c, Maracas Bay. $1, Blooming tabebuia (tree) vert. $2.50, Fishermen hauling in net. $5, Red House, Port-of-Spain.

Photo.; Silver or Gold Impressed

1969, Apr. 1 **Wmk. 314** *Perf. 14*

144 A41 1c sliver & multi .30 *.45*
a. Silver omitted *200.00* —
145 A41 3c gold & multi .30 .25
a. Wmk. upright ('74) 4.00 *9.50*
146 A41 5c gold & multi 2.10 .25
a. Wmk. upright ('73) 8.00 3.50
b. Gold omitted *300.00* —
c. Imperf. pair *325.00* —
d. Imperf. pair, gold omitted *475.00* —
147 A41 6c gold & multi .30 .25
a. Wmk. upright ('74) 3.00 *4.00*
b. Gold omitted *350.00* —
c. Imperf. pair *425.00* —
148 A41 8c silver & multi 5.25 3.50
149 A41 10c gold & multi 2.90 .25
b. Wmk. 373 ('76) 1.50 1.50
150 A41 12c silver & multi .30 3.90
151 A41 15c silver & multi .30 .25
a. Silver omitted *575.00* —
152 A41 20c gold & multi .30 .25
153 A41 25c silver & multi .30 1.05
a. Silver omitted *400.00* —
154 A41 30c silver & multi .30 .25
155 A41 40c gold & multi 4.75 .25
156 A41 50c silver & multi .30 *4.50*
157 A41 $1 gold & multi .65 .25
a. Gold omitted *325.00* —

Perf. 14x14½

158 A41 $2.50 gold & multi 1.05 *5.75*
a. Perf. 14 ('72) 6.00 14.00
159 A41 $5 gold & multi 1.05 *5.75*
a. Perf. 14 ('72) *6.00* *30.00*
b. Gold omitted *525.00* —
Nos. 144-159 (16) 20.45 27.15

Nos. 144-157 exists on two paper types.
For overprint see No. 187. For surcharges see Nos. 903-904.

Capt. A. A. Cipriani, ILO Emblem and Gate — A42

ILO, 50th Anniv.: 15c, Industrial Court's & ILO emblems, & Woodford Square gate.

Unwmk.

1969, May 1 **Photo.** *Perf. 12*

160 A42 6c dp car, gold & blk .30 .25
161 A42 15c brt blue, gold & blk .30 .25

Union Jack and Flags of CARIFTA Members — A43

Designs: 6c, Cornucopia, vert. 30c, Map of Caribbean, vert. 40c, Jet plane and "Strength through Unity" emblem.

1969, Aug. 1 *Perf. 14x13½, 13½x14*

162 A43 6c lilac, gold & multi .30 .25
163 A43 10c multicolored .30 .25
164 A43 30c red, emer, blk & gold .30 .25
165 A43 40c blue, blk, grn & gold .40 .95
Nos. 162-165 (4) 1.30 1.70

Caribbean Free Trade Area (CARIFTA).

Moon Landing and Earth — A44

40c, Lunar landing module & astronauts on moon. $1, Astronauts Aldrin at control panel, Armstrong collecting rocks.

1969, Sept. 1 **Litho.** *Perf. 14*

166 A44 6c multi .30 .30
167 A44 40c multi, vert. .30 .50
168 A44 $1 multi .60 .80
Nos. 166-168 (3) 1.20 1.60

See note after US No. C76.

Maces of Senate and House of Representatives A45

10c, Chamber of Parliament. 15c, View of Kennedy Complex, University of the West Indies at St. Augustine. 40c, Cannon & view of Scarborough from Fort King George.

Perf. 14x13½

1969, Oct. 23 **Photo.** **Wmk. 314**

169 A45 10c multicolored .30 .25
170 A45 15c multicolored .30 .25
171 A45 30c lt blue & multi .30 .50
172 A45 40c multicolored .30 .50
Nos. 169-172 (4) 1.20 1.50

15th Conf. of the Commonwealth Parliamentary Assoc., Port-of-Spain, Oct. 4-19.

Congress Emblem and Landscape — A46

6c, Congress emblem (steel drum and bird). 30c, Palms, landscape and emblem, horiz.

Perf. 14x13½, 13½x14

1969, Nov. 2 **Litho.** **Unwmk.**

173 A46 6c red, black & gold .30 .25
174 A46 30c lt blue, plum & gold .30 .40
175 A46 40c ultra, black & gold .30 .40
Nos. 173-175 (3) .90 1.05

24th Cong. of the Intl. Junior Chamber of Commerce.

Carnival King as "Man in the Moon" — A47

Designs: 6c, Carnival Queen as "City Beneath the Sea." 15c, Bambara god (antelope) from the Band of the Year. 30c, Pheasant Queen (Chanticleer) of Malaya. 40c, Steel Band of the Year with 1969 Calypso and Road March Kings, horiz.

1970, Feb. 2 **Wmk. 314** *Perf. 14*

176 A47 5c dk brown & multi .30 .25
177 A47 6c dk blue & multi .30 .25
178 A47 15c violet bl & multi .30 .25
179 A47 30c dk green & multi .30 .25
180 A47 40c green & multi .30 .25
Nos. 176-180 (5) 1.50 1.25

Issued to publicize the Trinidad Carnival.

Mahatma Gandhi and Indian Flag — A48

Design: 10c, Gandhi monument, vert.

Unwmk.

1970, Mar. 2 **Photo.** *Perf. 12*

181 A48 10c ultra & multi .70 .80
182 A48 30c crimson & multi 1.05 .80

Mohandas K. Gandhi (1869-1948), leader in India's fight for independence.

A49

A49a

UN, 25th Anniv. — A49b

Designs: 5c, Culture, Science, Arts andTechnology. 10c, Children of various races, map of Trinidad and Tobago and "UNICEF." 20c, Noah's ark, rainbow, dove and UN emblem.

1970, June 26 **Photo.** *Perf. 13½*

183 A49 5c multicolored .30 .25
184 A49a 10c multicolored .30 .25
185 A49b 20c multicolored .30 .45
Nos. 183-185 (3) .90 .95

UPU Headquarters, Bern — A50

1970, June 26 **Unwmk.** *Perf. 12*

186 A50 30c ultra & multi .30 .30

Opening of new UPU Headquarters in Bern.

No. 146 Overprinted "NATIONAL / COMMERCIAL / BANK / ESTABLISHED / 1.7.70"

Photo.; Gold Embossed

1970, July 1 **Wmk. 314** *Perf. 14*

187 A41 5c gold & multi .30 .30

San Fernando Town Hall — A51

Designs: 3c, East Indian Immigrants, 1820, after painting by Cazabon, vert. 40c, Ships in San Fernando Harbor, 1860, after painting by Michel J. Cazabon.

Perf. 14x13½, 13½x14

1970, Nov. **Litho.** **Wmk. 314**

188 A51 3c bister & multi .30 .95
189 A51 5c lemon & multi .30 .25
190 A51 40c lemon & multi 1.00 .25
Nos. 188-190 (3) 1.60 1.45

Municipality of San Fernando, 125th anniv.

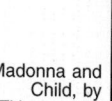

Madonna and Child, by Titian — A52

Paintings: 3c, Adoration of the Shepherds, School of Saville. 30c, Adoration of the Shepherds, by Louis Le Nain. 40c, Virgin and Child with St. John and Angel, by Morando. $1, Adoration of the Magi, by Paolo Veronese.

Perf. 13½

1970, Dec. 8 **Unwmk.** **Litho.**

191 A52 3c dull org & multi .30 .25
a. Booklet pane of 2 .30
192 A52 5c brt pink & multi .30 .25
a. Booklet pane of 2 .30
193 A52 30c lt utra & multi .30 .25
a. Booklet pane of 2 .60
194 A52 40c yellow grn & multi .30 .25
a. Booklet pane of 2 .75
b. Souvenir sheet of 4, #191-194 1.05 5.25
195 A52 $1 pale lilac & multi .40 *2.60*
Nos. 191-195 (5) 1.60 3.60

Brocket Deer — A53

Perf. 14x13½

1971, Aug. 9 **Litho.** **Wmk. 314**

196 A53 3c shown .35 .25
197 A53 5c Collared peccary .40 .25
198 A53 6c Paca .50 .40
199 A53 30c Agouti 1.60 *3.00*
200 A53 40c Ocelot 1.60 *2.25*
Nos. 196-200 (5) 4.45 6.15

Capt. A. A. Cipriani — A54

Design: 30c, Chaconia medal (for distinction in social field).

1971, Aug. 31 *Perf. 14*

201 A54 5c multicolored .30 .25
202 A54 30c multicolored .30 .30

9th anniversary of independence. Capt. Arthur Andrew Cipriani (died 1945) was mayor of Port of Spain and member of First Executive Council.

Virgin and Child with St. John, by Bartolommeo — A55

Christmas: 5c, Local creche. 10c, Virgin and Child with Sts. Jerome and Dominic, by Filippino Lippi. 15c, Virgin and Child with St. Anne, by Gerolamo dai Libri.

1971, Oct. 25 **Litho.** *Perf. 14x14½*

203 A55 3c yellow & multi .30 .25
204 A55 5c dull blue & multi .30 .25
205 A55 10c red & multi .30 .25
206 A55 15c orange & multi .30 .30
Nos. 203-206 (4) 1.20 1.05

Satellite Earth Station, Matura — A56

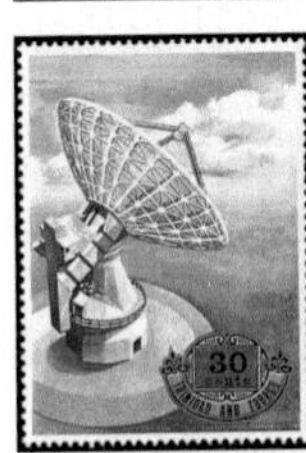

Dish Antenna — A57

Design: 40c, Satellite over earth (Africa).

1971, Nov. 18 *Perf. 14*

207 A56 10c ultra & multi .30 .25
208 A57 30c green & multi .30 .25
209 A57 40c black & multi .35 .35
a. Souvenir sheet of 3 1.90 1.90
Nos. 207-209 (3) .95 .85

Opening of Satellite Earth Station at Matura. No. 209a contains 3 imperf. stamps with simulated perforations similar to Nos. 207-209.

Morpho Hybrid — A58

Butterflies: 5c, Purple mort bleu. 6c, Jaune d'abricot. 10c, Purple king shoemaker. 20c, Southern white pape. 30c, Little jaune.

1972, Feb. 18 **Photo.** **Wmk. 314**

210 A58 3c olive & multi .85 .80
211 A58 5c ocher & multi 1.10 .25
212 A58 6c yellow & multi 1.50 1.00
213 A58 10c yel grn & multi 1.75 .30
214 A58 20c lilac & multi 2.25 2.25
215 A58 30c dull grn & multi 3.00 2.75
Nos. 210-215 (6) 10.45 7.35

S.S. Lady McLeod and Stamp — A59

10c, Map of Trinidad and Tobago. 30c, Commemorative inscription.

1972, Apr. 12 **Litho.** *Perf. 14½x14*

216 A59 5c blue & multi .30 .25
217 A59 10c blue & multi .30 .25
218 A59 30c blue & multi .65 .65
a. Souvenir sheet of 3, #216-218 1.50 1.50
Nos. 216-218 (3) 1.25 1.15

125th anniv. of the Lady McLeod stamp.

Trinity Cross — A60

Medals: 10c, Chaconia medal. 20c, Hummingbird medal. 30c, Medal of Merit.

1972, Aug. 28 **Photo.** *Perf. 13½x13*

219 A60 5c blue & multi .30 .25
220 A60 10c multicolored .30 .25
221 A60 20c yellow grn & multi .30 .30
222 A60 30c brt rose & multi .30 .40
a. Souvenir sheet of 4, #219-222 1.10 1.10
Nos. 219-222 (4) 1.20 1.20

10th anniversary of independence. See Nos. 235-238.

Olympic Rings, Relay Race Medal, 1964 — A61

Olympic Rings and: 20c, Bronze medal, 200-meters, 1964. 30c, Bronze medals, weight lifting, 1952. 40c, Silver medal, 400-meters, 1964. 50c, Silver medal, weight lifting, 1948.

1972, Sept. 7 **Litho.** *Perf. 14*

223 A61 10c yellow & multi .30 .25
224 A61 20c multicolored .30 .25
225 A61 30c lilac & multi .30 .30
226 A61 40c lt blue & multi .35 .35
227 A61 50c orange & multi .45 *1.25*
a. Souv. sheet, #223-227 + label 2.00 2.00
Nos. 223-227 (5) 1.70 2.40

20th Olympic Games, Munich, 8/26-9/11.

Holy Family, by Titian — A62

Christmas: 3c, Adoration of the Kings, by Dosso Dossi. 30c, Like 5c.

1972, Nov. 9 **Photo.** **Wmk. 314**

228 A62 3c blue & multi .30 .25
229 A62 5c rose lilac & multi .30 .25
230 A62 30c lt green & multi .50 .50
a. Souvenir sheet of 3, #228-230 1.50 1.50
Nos. 228-230 (3) 1.10 1.00

ECLA Headquarters, Santiago, Chile — A63

Designs: 20c, INTERPOL emblem. 30c, WMO emblem. 40c, University of West Indies Administration Building.

1973, Aug. 15 **Litho.** **Wmk. 314**

231 A63 10c orange & multi .30 .25
232 A63 20c multicolored .30 .25
233 A63 30c ultra & multi .35 .35
234 A63 40c lilac & multi .40 .40
a. Souvenir sheet of 4, #231-234 1.40 1.40
Nos. 231-234 (4) 1.35 1.25

Economic Commission for Latin America, 25th anniv. (10c); Intl. Criminal Police Organization, 50th anniv. (20c); Intl. Meteorological cooperation, cent. (30c); Admission of 1st students to the University of West Indies, 25th anniv. (40c).

Medal Type of 1972 Redrawn

Medals: 10c, Trinity Cross. 20c, Medal of Merit. 30c, Chaconia medal. 40c, Hummingbird medal.

1973, Aug. 30 **Photo.** *Perf. 14½x14*

235 A60 10c dark green & multi .30 .25
236 A60 20c dark brown & multi .30 .25
237 A60 30c dark blue & multi .30 .25
238 A60 40c deep violet & multi .30 .30
a. Souv. sheet, #235-238, perf. 14 1.10 1.10
Nos. 235-238 (4) 1.20 1.05

11th anniv. of independence. "Trinidad and Tobago" in one line on #235-238.

General Post Office, Port of Spain — A64

40c, Conference Hall & flags, Chagaramas.

1973, Oct. 8 **Photo.** *Perf. 14*

239 A64 30c multicolored .30 .25
240 A64 40c multicolored .30 .30
a. Souvenir sheet of 2, #239-240 1.00 1.00

2nd Commonwealth Conf. of Postal Administrations, Trinidad, Oct. 8-20. On #240a the perforations extend through margin and divide map.

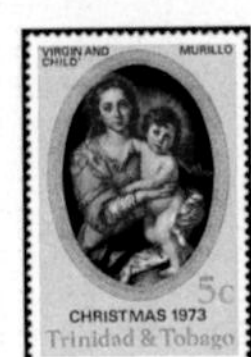

Virgin and Child, by Murillo — A65

1973, Oct. 22 *Perf. 14½x14*

241 A65 5c pink & multi .30 .25
242 A65 $1 lt blue & multi .60 .60
a. Souv. sheet, #241-242, perf. 14 1.00 1.00

Christmas 1973.

Post Office and UPU Emblem A66

UPU, Cent.: 50c, Map of Islands, UPU emblem, means of transportation.

1974, Nov. 18 **Photo.** *Perf. 13½x14*

243 A66 40c brt purple & multi .35 .30
244 A66 50c blue gray & multi .60 .55
a. Souvenir sheet of 2, #243-244 16.00 *16.00*

Humming Bird I, Transatlantic Crossing, 1960 — A67

Design: 50c, Globe, Humming Bird II, Harold and Kwailan La Borde.

1974, Dec. 2 *Perf. 14½*

245 A67 40c multicolored .60 .60
246 A67 50c multicolored .75 .75
a. Souvenir sheet of 2, #245-246 2.50 2.50

First anniversary of the voyage around the world by Harold and Kwailan La Borde aboard Humming Bird II, 1969-1973.

"Equality" and IWY Emblem — A68

1975, June 23 **Litho.** **Wmk. 314**

247 A68 15c multicolored .30 .25
248 A68 30c multicolored .40 .40

International Women's Year 1975.

Dr. Pawan and Laboratory Equipment A69

25c, Vampire bat, microscope, syringe, bat's head.

Perf. 14x14½

1975, Sept. 23 **Photo.** **Wmk. 373**

249 A69 25c yellow & multi .45 .45
250 A69 30c lt blue & multi .55 .55

Isolation of rabies virus by Dr. Joseph Lennox Pawan (1887-1957).

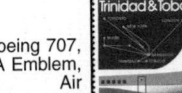

Boeing 707, BWIA Emblem, Air Routes — A70

Designs: 30c, Boeing 707 on ground. 40c, Boeing 707 in the air.

Wmk. 373

1975, Nov. 27 **Litho.** *Perf. 14½*

251 A70 20c dark blue & multi .45 .45
252 A70 30c deep ultra & multi .60 .60
253 A70 40c dull green & multi .75 .75
a. Souvenir sheet of 3, #251-253 2.25 2.25
Nos. 251-253 (3) 1.80 1.80

British West Indian Airways, 35th anniv.

Land of the Hummingbird Costume — A71

Carnival 1976: $1, Carib Prince riding pink ibis. Designs show prize-winning costumes from 1974 carnival.

1976, Jan. 12 **Photo.** *Perf. 14½*

254 A71 30c multicolored .30 .25
255 A71 $1 multicolored .80 .80
a. Souvenir sheet of 2, #254-255 1.40 1.40

Angostura Building, Port of Spain — A72

Designs (Exposition Medals, obverse and reverse): 35c, New Orleans, 1885-86. 45c, Sydney, 1879. 50c, Brussels, 1897.

1976, July 14 **Litho.** *Perf. 13*

256 A72 5c bister & multi .30 .25
257 A72 35c yellow grn & multi .30 .25
258 A72 45c blue & multi .30 .25
259 A72 50c violet & multi .30 .25
a. Souv. sheet, #256-259, perf. 14 1.10 1.10
Nos. 256-259 (4) 1.20 1.00

Sesquicentennial of the manufacture of Angostura Bitters.

Map of West Indies, Bats, Wicket and Ball — A72a

Prudential Cup — A72b

1976, Oct. 4 **Unwmk.** *Perf. 14*

260 A72a 35c lt blue & multi .40 .40
261 A72b 45c lilac rose & blk .60 .60
a. Souvenir sheet of 2, #260-261 2.25 2.25

World Cricket Cup, won by West Indies Team, 1975.

Columbus Sailing through the Bocas, by A. Camps-Campins A73

Paintings: 10c, View, by Jean Michael Cazabon. 20c, Landscape, by Cazabon. 35c, Los Gallos Point, by Cazabon. 45c, Corbeaux Town, by Cazabon.

1976, Nov. 1 **Litho.** **Wmk. 373**

262 A73 5c ocher & multi .75 .30
263 A73 10c lilac & multi .30 .25
264 A73 20c green & multi .50 .25
265 A73 35c red orange & multi .60 .25
266 A73 45c blue & multi .65 .25
a. Souvenir sheet of 5, #262-266 2.25 2.25
Nos. 262-266 (5) 2.80 1.30

For overprints see Nos. 325, 327.

Hasely Crawford and Gold Medal — A74

1977, Jan. 4 **Litho.** *Perf. 12½*

267 A74 25c multicolored .35 .35
a. Souvenir sheet of 1 .70 .70

Hasely Crawford, winner of 100-meter dash at Montreal Olympic Games.

Sikorsky S-38 (Lindbergh's Plane) — A75

Designs: 35c, Charles Lindbergh delivering first airmail to Port of Spain, 1927. 45c, Boeing 707, British West Indies Airways. 50c, Boeing 747, British Airways.

1977, Apr. **Wmk. 373** *Perf. 13*

268 A75 20c lt blue & multi .35 .25
269 A75 35c lt blue & multi .50 .35
270 A75 45c lt blue & multi .60 .60
271 A75 50c lt blue & multi 1.00 *2.00*
a. Souv. sheet, #268-271, perf. 14 4.50 4.50
Nos. 268-271 (4) 2.45 3.20

Airmail to Trinidad & Tobago, 50th anniv.

Trinidad and Tobago Flag — A76

35c, Coat of arms. 45c, Government House.

1977, July 26 Litho. *Perf. 13½x13*

272	A76	20c yellow & multi	.40	.40
273	A76	35c red & multi	.65	.65
274	A76	45c lt blue & multi	.80	.80
a.		Souv. sheet, #272-274, perf. 14	1.75	1.75
		Nos. 272-274 (3)	1.85	1.85

Inauguration of the Republic, Aug. 1, 1976.

White Poinsettia — A77

Christmas: 45c, 50c, Red poinsettia.

1977, Oct. 11 Litho. *Perf. 14½*

275	A77	10c multicolored	.30	.25
276	A77	35c multicolored	.35	.35
277	A77	45c multicolored	.40	.40
278	A77	50c multicolored	.45	.45
a.		Souvenir sheet of 4, #275-278	1.60	1.60
		Nos. 275-278 (4)	1.50	1.45

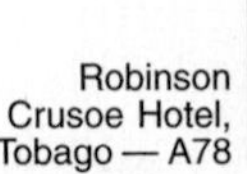

Robinson Crusoe Hotel, Tobago — A78

15c, Turtle Beach Hotel, Tobago. 25c, Mount Irvine Hotel, Tobago. 70c, Mount Irvine beach, Tobago. $5, Holiday Inn, Trinidad.

Wmk. 373

1978, Jan. 17 Litho. *Perf. 14*

279	A78	6c multicolored	.30	*1.75*
280	A78	15c multicolored	.40	*2.00*
281	A78	25c multicolored	.50	.25
282	A78	70c multicolored	.60	*.70*
283	A78	$5 multicolored	1.75	*4.00*
a.		Souvenir sheet of 5, #279-283	3.50	3.50
		Nos. 279-283 (5)	3.55	8.70

For overprint see No. 326.

Paphinia Cristata — A79

Orchids: 30c, Caularthron bicornutum. 40c, Miltassia. 50c, Oncidium ampiliatum. $2.50, Oncidium papilio.

1978, June 7 Wmk. 373 *Perf. 14*

284	A79	12c multicolored	1.50	*1.75*
285	A79	30c multicolored	1.50	*1.75*
286	A79	40c multicolored	2.00	.25
287	A79	50c multicolored	1.50	.25
288	A79	$2.50 multicolored	2.25	*5.50*
a.		Souvenir sheet of 5, #284-288	6.00	6.00
		Nos. 284-288 (5)	8.75	9.50

Miss Universe and Trophy — A80

Designs: 35c, Portrait with crown. 45c, Miss Universe in evening dress.

1978, Aug. 2 Litho. *Perf. 14½*

289	A80	10c multicolored	.35	.35
290	A80	35c multicolored	.60	.60
291	A80	45c multicolored	.75	.75
a.		Souvenir sheet of 3, #289-291	1.50	1.50
		Nos. 289-291 (3)	1.70	1.70

Janelle (Penny) Commissiong, Miss Universe, 1977.

Tayra — A81

1978, Nov. 7 *Perf. 13½x14*

292	A81	15c shown	.30	.25
293	A81	25c Ocelot	.35	.35
294	A81	40c Porcupine	.55	.55
295	A81	70c Yellow anteater	.75	*1.50*
a.		Souvenir sheet of 4, #292-295	2.00	2.00
		Nos. 292-295 (4)	1.95	2.65

"Burst of Beauty" — A82

Costumes: 10c, Rain worshipper. 35c, Zodiac. 45c, Praying mantis. 50c, Eye of the hurricane. $1, Steel orchestra.

1979, Feb. 1 Litho. *Perf. 13½*

296	A82	5c multicolored	.30	.25
297	A82	10c multicolored	.30	.25
298	A82	35c multicolored	.30	.25
299	A82	45c multicolored	.30	.25
300	A82	50c multicolored	.30	.25
301	A82	$1 multicolored	.30	.25
		Nos. 296-301 (6)	1.80	1.50

Day Care Center — A83

IYC Emblem and: 10c, School lunch program. 35c, Dental care. 45c, Nursery school. 50c, Free school bus. $1, Medical care.

Unwmk.

1979, June 5 Litho. *Perf. 13*

302	A83	5c multicolored	.30	.25
303	A83	10c multicolored	.30	.25
304	A83	35c multicolored	.30	.25
305	A83	45c multicolored	.30	.25
306	A83	50c multicolored	.30	.25
307	A83	$1 multicolored	.45	.45
a.		Souvenir sheet of 6, #302-307	1.50	1.50
		Nos. 302-307 (6)	1.95	1.70

International Year of the Child.

Geothermal Exploration — A84

Designs: 35c, Hydrogeology. 45c, Petroleum exploration. 70c, Preservation of the environment.

1979, July 3 Wmk. 373

308	A84	10c multicolored	.30	.25
309	A84	35c multicolored	.35	.35
310	A84	45c multicolored	.40	.40
311	A84	70c multicolored	.55	.55
a.		Souvenir sheet of 4, #308-311	1.90	1.90
		Nos. 308-311 (4)	1.60	1.55

4th Latin American Geological Cong., July 7-15.

Map of Tobago and Tobago No. 1 — A85

15c, Tobago #2, 7. 35c, Tobago #28, 11. 45c, Tobago #25, 4. 70c, Great Britain #28 used in Scarborough and Tobago #5. $1, General Post Office, Scarborough and Tobago #6.

Perf. 13½x14

1979, Aug. 1 Litho. Wmk. 373

312	A85	10c multicolored	.30	.25
313	A85	15c multicolored	.30	.25
314	A85	35c multicolored	.30	.25
315	A85	45c multicolored	.30	.25
316	A85	70c multicolored	.30	*1.00*
317	A85	$1 multicolored	.35	*1.25*
a.		Souvenir sheet of 6, #312-317	1.90	1.90
		Nos. 312-317 (6)	1.85	3.25

Centenary of Tobago's postage stamps.

Rowland Hill, Trinidad and Tobago No. 109 — A86

Hill and: 45c, Trinidad and Tobago #273. $1, Trinidad #62, Tobago #10.

1979, Oct. 4 *Perf. 13*

318	A86	25c multicolored	.30	.25
319	A86	45c multicolored	.35	.35
320	A86	$1 multicolored	.55	*1.00*
a.		Souvenir sheet of 3, #318-320	1.50	1.50
		Nos. 318-320 (3)	1.20	1.60

Sir Rowland Hill (1795-1879), originator of penny postage.

Poui Tree — A87

Designs: 10c, Court House. 50c, Royal Train locomotive. $1.50, HMS Bacchante.

Wmk. 373

1980, Jan. 21 Litho. *Perf. 14½*

321	A87	5c multicolored	.30	.25
322	A87	10c multicolored	.30	.25
323	A87	50c multicolored	.40	.40
324	A87	$1.50 multicolored	.95	*1.50*
a.		Souvenir sheet of 4, #321-324	2.25	2.25
		Nos. 321-324 (4)	1.95	2.40

Princes Town centenary.

Nos. 262, 279, 263 Overprinted in 3 or 5 Lines "1844-1980 POPULATION CENSUS 12th MAY 1980"

1980, Apr. 8 Litho. *Perf. 14*

325	A73	5c multicolored	.30	.25
326	A78	6c multicolored	.30	.25
327	A73	10c multicolored	.30	.25
		Nos. 325-327 (3)	.90	.75

Scarlet Ibis Hen and Nest — A88

Scarlet Ibis: b, Nest and eggs. c, Chick in nest. d, Male. e, Male and female.

Wmk. 373

1980, May 6 Litho. *Perf. 14½*

328		Strip of 5, multi	4.00	*6.75*
a.-e.		A88 single stamp	.70	.70

Bronze and Silver Medals, 1948, 1952 — A89

15c, Hasely Crawford, 1976 gold medal. 70c, 1964 silver, bronze medals. $2.50, Moscow '80 emblem, vert.

Wmk. 373

1980, July 22 Litho. *Perf. 14*

329	A89	10c shown	.30	.25
330	A89	15c multicolored	.30	.25
331	A89	70c multicolored	.30	.30
		Nos. 329-331 (3)	.90	.80

Souvenir Sheet

332	A89	$2.50 multicolored	2.25	2.25

22nd Summer Olympic Games, Moscow, July 19-Aug. 3.

Charcoal Production A90

Wmk. 373

1980, Sept. 8 Litho. *Perf. 14*

333	A90	10c shown	.30	.25
334	A90	55c Logging	.30	.25
335	A90	70c Teak plantation	.35	.35
336	A90	$2.50 Watershed management	.75	.75
a.		Souvenir sheet of 4, #333-336	2.25	2.25
		Nos. 333-336 (4)	1.70	1.60

11th Commonwealth Forestry Conference.

Elizabeth Bourne, Judiciary and Isabella Tesbier, Government A91

Decade for Women: No. 338, Beryl McBurnie, dance and culture; Audrey Jeffers, social work. No. 339, Dr. Stella Abidh, public health; Louise Horne, nutrition.

1980, Sept. 29

337	A91	$1 multicolored	.45	*.55*
338	A91	$1 multicolored	.45	*.55*
339	A91	$1 multicolored	.45	*.55*
		Nos. 337-339 (3)	1.35	*1.65*

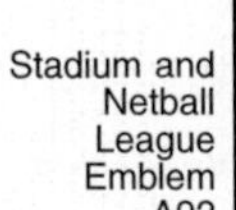

Stadium and Netball League Emblem A92

1980, Oct. 21

340	A92	70c multicolored	.40	.40

1979 World Netball Tournament, Port-of-Spain.

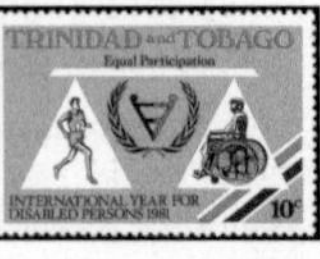

Athlete, Man in Wheelchair, IYD Emblem — A93

Wmk. 373

1981, Apr. 6 Litho. *Perf. 14½*

341	A93	10c shown	.30	.25
342	A93	70c Amputee with crutch	.30	*.50*
343	A93	$1.50 Blind people	.55	*1.00*
344	A93	$2 IYD emblem	.55	*1.25*
		Nos. 341-344 (4)	1.70	*3.00*

International Year of the Disabled.

Marine Preservation A94

1981, July 7 Litho. *Perf. 13x13½*

345	A94	10c Land	.30	.25
346	A94	55c shown	.40	.40
347	A94	$3 Sky	1.50	1.50
a.		Souvenir sheet of 3, #345-347	4.00	4.00
		Nos. 345-347 (3)	2.20	2.15

World Food Day — A95

1981, Oct. 16 Litho. *Perf. 14½x14*

348 A95 10c Produce .30 .25
349 A95 15c Rice threshing, mill .30 .25
350 A95 45c Bigeye .30 .30
351 A95 55c Cow, pig, goats .40 .40
352 A95 $1.50 Poultry .80 .80
353 A95 $2 Smallmouth grunt 1.25 1.25
a. Souvenir sheet of 6, #348-353 3.50 3.50
Nos. 348-353 (6) 3.35 3.25

President Awards — A96

1981, Nov. 30 *Perf. 14*

354 A96 10c First aid .30 .25
355 A96 70c Motor mechanics .35 .40
356 A96 $1 Hiking .55 .60
357 A96 $2 President giving award .95 *1.50*
Nos. 354-357 (4) 2.15 2.75

Commonwealth Pharmaceutical Conference — A97

1982, Feb. 12 Litho. *Perf. 14½x14*

358 A97 10c Pharmacist .50 .50
359 A97 $1 Pluchea symphitfolia 2.00 2.00
360 A97 $2 Nopalea cochenilifera 3.50 3.50
Nos. 358-360 (3) 6.00 6.00

Scouting Year — A98

1982, June 28 Litho. *Perf. 14*

361 A98 15c Production .60 .25
362 A98 55c Tolerance 1.35 .50
363 A98 $5 Discipline 4.75 *7.00*
Nos. 361-363 (3) 6.70 7.75

25th Anniv. of Tourist Board — A99

Perf. 13½x14

1982, Oct. 18 Litho. Wmk. 373

364 A99 55c Charlotteville .35 .35
365 A99 $1 Boating .55 .55
366 A99 $3 Fort George 1.60 *2.25*
Nos. 364-366 (3) 2.50 3.15

Pa Pa Bois — A100

Designs: Various folklore characters.

1982, Nov. 8

367 A100 10c multicolored .30 .25
368 A100 15c multicolored .30 .25
369 A100 65c multicolored .40 .40
370 A100 $5 multicolored 2.60 2.60
a. Souvenir sheet of 4, #367-370 6.25 6.25
Nos. 367-370 (4) 3.60 3.50

Canefarmers' Centenary A101

1982, Dec. 13 Litho. *Perf. 14*

371 A101 30c Harvest .30 .25
372 A101 70c Loading bullock cart .55 .75
373 A101 $1.50 Field 1.00 *2.00*
a. Souvenir sheet of 3, #371-373, perf. 14½ 2.25 2.25
Nos. 371-373 (3) 1.85 3.00

20th Anniv. of Independence A102

10c, Natl. Stadium. 35c, Caroni Arena Water Treatment Plant. 50c, Mount Hope Maternity Hospital. $2, Natl. Insurance Board Mall, Tobago.

1982, Dec. 28 *Perf. 13½x14*

374 A102 10c multicolored .35 .55
375 A102 35c multicolored .45 .70
376 A102 50c multicolored .90 1.40
377 A102 $2 multicolored 1.25 2.00
Nos. 374-377 (4) 2.95 4.65

Commonwealth Day — A103

1983, Mar. 14 *Perf. 14*

378 A103 10c Flags .30 .25
379 A103 55c Satellite view .35 .35
380 A103 $1 Oil industry, vert. .45 *.60*
381 A103 $2 Maps, vert. .85 *1.10*
Nos. 378-381 (4) 1.95 2.30

10th Anniv. of CARICOM A104

1983, July 11 Litho. *Perf. 14*

382 A104 35c Jet, map 1.50 1.50

World Communications Year — A105

15c, Operator. 55c, Scarborough PO, Tobago. $1, Textel Building. $3, Morne Bleu Receiving Station.

1983, Aug. 5 *Perf. 14½*

383 A105 15c multicolored .30 .25
384 A105 55c multicolored .30 .30
385 A105 $1 multicolored .60 .75
386 A105 $3 multicolored 1.60 *2.60*
Nos. 383-386 (4) 2.80 3.90

Commonwealth Finance Ministers Conference A106

Wmk. 373

1983, Sept. 19 Litho. *Perf. 14*

387 A106 $2 multicolored .70 .70

World Food Day — A107

1983, Oct. 17 *Perf. 14x13½*

388 A107 10c Kingfish .30 .30
389 A107 55c Flying fish .85 .85
390 A107 70c Queen conch 1.10 1.10
391 A107 $4 Red shrimp 4.25 4.25
Nos. 388-391 (4) 6.50 6.50

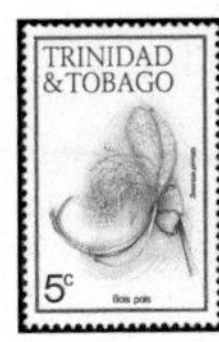

Flowers — A108

5c, Bois pois. 10c, Maraval Lily. 15c, Star grass. 20c, Bois caco. 25c, Strangling fig. 30c, Cassia moschata. 50c, Chalice flower. 65c, Black stick. 80c, Columnea scandens. 95c, Cats Claws. $1, Bois l'agli. $1.50, Eustoma exeltatum. $2, Chaconia, horiz. $2.50, Chysothemis pulchella, horiz. $5, Centratherum punctatum, horiz. $10, Savanna flower, horiz.

1983, Dec. 14 Wmk. 373 *Perf. 14*

No Year Imprint Below Design

392 A108 5c multicolored .60 .90
b. Imprint "1989" .90 .25
393 A108 10c multicolored .45 .35
b. Imprint "1985" .40 .25
c. Imprint "1986" .40 .25
d. Imprint "1987" .40 .25
e. Imprint "1989" .40 .25
394 A108 15c multicolored .50 .30
395 A108 20c multicolored .30 .25
396 A108 25c multicolored 1.00 *1.10*
397 A108 30c multicolored .40 .25
398 A108 50c multicolored .50 .50
399 A108 65c multicolored .70 *.90*
400 A108 80c multicolored .90 *1.25*
401 A108 95c multicolored .95 *1.25*
402 A108 $1 multicolored 1.00 .75
403 A108 $1.50 multicolored 1.50 *2.25*

Size: 38½x26mm

404 A108 $2 multicolored 2.00 *2.50*
405 A108 $2.50 multicolored 2.00 *3.00*
406 A108 $5 multicolored 4.00 *7.00*
407 A108 $10 multicolored 8.00 *9.00*
Nos. 392-407 (16) 24.80 31.55

1984, Oct.

"1984" Imprint Below Design

392a A108 5c multicolored 3.00 *4.00*
393a A108 10c multicolored 1.50 *2.00*
394a A108 15c multicolored 2.50 *3.00*
396a A108 25c multicolored 4.25 *5.00*
Nos. 392a-396a (4) 11.25 *14.00*

1985-89 Wmk. 384

"1985" Imprint Below Design

392f A108 5c multicolored 1.50 1.25
401f A108 95c multicolored .90 .80
402f A108 $1 multicolored .85 .85
406f A108 $5 multicolored 4.00 3.25
407f A108 $10 multicolored 9.00 6.50
Nos. 392f-407f (5) 16.25 12.65

"1986" Imprint Below Design

393g A108 10c multicolored .40 .25

"1987" Imprint Below Design

393h A108 10c multicolored .40 .25
397h A108 30c multicolored .40 .25
399h A108 65c multicolored .80 .60
400h A108 80c multicolored 1.20 .75
401h A108 95c multicolored 1.50 1.00
402h A108 $1 multicolored 1.75 .60
403h A108 $1.50 multicolored 2.75 2.00
404h A108 $2 multicolored 2.00 2.00
406h A108 $5 multicolored 8.00 6.00
407h A108 $10 multicolored 15.00 10.00
Nos. 393h-407h (10) 33.80 23.45

"1988" Imprint Below Design

393i A108 10c multicolored .85 .85
395i A108 20c multicolored .40 .25
396i A108 25c multicolored .85 .85
397i A108 30c multicolored .40 .25
399i A108 65c multicolored 1.10 .40
400i A108 80c multicolored 1.60 .75
401i A108 95c multicolored 1.75 .95
402i A108 $1 multicolored 10.00 —
406i A108 $5 multicolored 12.00 5.00
407i A108 $10 multicolored 20.00 10.00
Nos. 393i-407i (9) 38.95 19.30

"1989" Imprint Below Design

393j A108 10c multicolored .40 .25
395j A108 20c multicolored .40 .25
396j A108 25c multicolored .85 .85
397j A108 30c multicolored .85 .25
399j A108 65c multicolored 1.60 .40
402j A108 $1 multicolored 2.25 .60
403j A108 $1.50 multicolored 3.50 1.50
404j A108 $2 multicolored 4.75 1.90
405j A108 $2.50 multicolored 5.50 2.50
406j A108 $5 multicolored 12.00 6.50
407j A108 $10 multicolored 20.00 10.00
Nos. 393j-407j (11) 52.10 25.00

For surcharges see Nos. 906-907, 979-980.

Castles on Chess Board — A109

World Chess Federationn, 60th Anniv.: Various chess pieces.

Wmk. 373

1984, Sept. 12 Litho. *Perf. 14*

408 A109 50c multicolored 2.00 .75
409 A109 70c multicolored 2.75 2.75
410 A109 $1.50 multicolored 3.50 3.50
411 A109 $2 multicolored 5.75 5.75
Nos. 408-411 (4) 14.00 12.75

1984 Summer Olympics — A110

1984, Sept. 21 *Perf. 14x14½*

412 A110 15c Swimming .30 .30
413 A110 55c Running .45 .45
414 A110 $1.50 Yachting 1.25 1.25
415 A110 $4 Bicycling 4.50 4.50
a. Souvenir sheet of 4, #412-415 6.75 6.75
Nos. 412-415 (4) 6.50 6.50

St. Mary's Children's Home, 125th Anniv. — A111

1984, Nov. 13 Litho. *Perf. 13½*

416 A111 10c Children's band .30 .25
417 A111 70c St. Mary's Home .75 .75
418 A111 $3 Group scene 3.00 *3.75*
Nos. 416-418 (3) 4.05 4.75

Christmas 1984 — A112

10c, Parang Band. 30c, Musical notes, Poinsettia. $1, Bandola, Cuatro, Bandolin. $3, Fiddle, Guitar, Double Bass.

1984, Nov. Litho. *Perf. 14*

419 A112 10c multicolored .30 .25
420 A112 30c multicolored .60 .25
421 A112 $1 multicolored 1.50 1.00
422 A112 $3 multicolored 2.60 *5.00*
Nos. 419-422 (4) 5.00 6.50

Emancipation, 150th Anniv. — A113

35c, Slave ship. 55c, Map, Slave Triangle. $1, Book by Eric Williams. $2, Toussaint L'Ouverture.

1984, Oct. 22 Litho. *Perf. 13½x13*

423 A113 35c multicolored 1.00 1.00
424 A113 55c multicolored 1.50 1.50
425 A113 $1 multicolored 2.75 2.75
426 A113 $2 multicolored 3.75 3.75
a. Souvenir sheet of 4, #423-426 9.50 9.50
Nos. 423-426 (4) 9.00 9.00

Labor Day — A114

Labor leaders: No. 427, A.A. Cipriani and T.U.B. Butler. No. 428, A. Cola Rienzi and C.T.W.E. Worrell. No. 429, C.P. Alexander and Q. O'Connor.

Wmk. 373

1985, June 17 Litho. *Perf. 14*

427	A114	55c dull rose & blk	1.75	1.75
428	A114	55c brt green & blk	1.75	1.75
429	A114	55c lt orange & blk	1.75	1.75
		Nos. 427-429 (3)	5.25	5.25

Ships — A115

Wmk. 373

1985, Aug 20 Litho. *Perf. 14½*

430	A115	30c Lady Nelson	.90	.30
431	A115	95c Lady Drake	1.50	1.50
432	A115	$1.50 Federal Palm	1.60	*2.50*
433	A115	$2 Federal Maple	3.00	*3.25*
		Nos. 430-433 (4)	7.00	7.55

UN Decade for Women — A116

Women in the arts, public service and education: No. 434, Sybil Atteck, Marjorie Padmore. No. 435, May Cherrie, Evelyn Tracey. No. 436, Jessica Smith-Phillips, Irene Omilta McShine.

1985, Oct. 30 Wmk. 384 *Perf. 14*

434	A116	$1.50 multicolored	2.10	2.10
435	A116	$1.50 multicolored	2.10	2.10
436	A116	$1.50 multicolored	2.10	2.10
		Nos. 434-436 (3)	6.30	6.30

Intl. Youth Year — A117

Anniversaries and events: 10c, Natl. Cadet Force, 75th anniv. 65c, Girl Guides, 75th anniv.

1985, Nov. 27 *Perf. 14x14½*

437	A117	10c Cadet emblem	.55	.25
438	A117	65c Badges, anniv. emblem	2.25	2.25
439	A117	95c shown	2.75	2.75
		Nos. 437-439 (3)	5.55	5.25

A118

Sisters of St. Joseph de Cluny in Trinidad, 150th Anniv.: 10c, Sister Anne-Marie Javouhey, founder. 65c, St. Joseph's Convent, Port-of-Spain. 95c, Statue of Sr. Anne-Marie.

Perf. 14x14½

1986, Mar. 19 Litho. Wmk. 384

440	A118	10c multicolored	.30	.25
441	A118	65c multicolored	.50	*1.00*
442	A118	95c multicolored	.75	*1.25*
		Nos. 440-442 (3)	1.55	*2.50*

A119

10c, At the Cenotaph. 15c, Aboard HMY Britannia. 30c, With Pres. Clarke. $5, Receiving bouquet.

Wmk. 384

1986, Apr. 21 Litho. *Perf. 14½*

443	A119	10c multicolored	.35	.25
444	A119	15c multicolored	.75	.30
445	A119	30c multicolored	.50	.30
446	A119	$5 multicolored	3.00	*6.00*
		Nos. 443-446 (4)	4.60	6.85

Queen Elizabeth II, 60th birthday.

Locomotives, AMERIPEX '86 — A120

65c, Arma tank locomotive. 95c, Canadian-built No. 22. $1.10, Tender engine. $1.50, Saddle tank.

Perf. 14½x14

1986, May 26 Wmk. 373

447	A120	65c multicolored	.30	.30
448	A120	95c multicolored	.45	.45
449	A120	$1.10 multicolored	.55	*1.00*
450	A120	$1.50 multicolored	.75	*1.50*
a.		Souvenir sheet of 4, #447-450	3.00	3.00
		Nos. 447-450 (4)	2.05	3.25

Boy Scouts, 75th Anniv. — A121

$1.70, Campsite. $2, Uniforms, 1911, 1986.

1986, July 21 Wmk. 384 *Perf. 14*

451	A121	$1.70 multicolored	1.25	*1.75*
452	A121	$2 multicolored	1.75	*2.25*

Dr. Eric Williams (1911-1981), First Prime Minister — A122

10c, Graduating college, 1935. 30c, Wearing red tie. 95c, Pro-Chancellor of UWI. $5, Williams, prime minister's residence.

Wmk. 373

1986, Sept. 25 Litho. *Perf. 14*

453	A122	10c multicolored	.80	.25
454	A122	30c multicolored	1.25	.30
a.		Black tie	1.40	.40
455	A122	95c multicolored	2.25	1.00
456	A122	$5 multicolored	4.00	*7.00*
a.		Souvenir sheet of 4, #453-456	8.50	8.50
		Nos. 453-456 (4)	8.30	8.55

Nos. 453-454 vert.

Intl. Peace Year — A123

1986, Oct. 30 Wmk. 384

457	A123	95c shown	.60	.50
458	A123	$3 Dove	1.50	*2.50*

Giselle LaRonde, Miss World 1986 — A124

10c, Wearing folk costume. 30c, Bathing suit. 95c, Crown. $1.65, Crown and sash.

Wmk. 384

1987, July 27 Litho. *Perf. 14*

459	A124	10c multi	1.10	.30
460	A124	30c multi	1.75	.50
461	A124	95c multi	3.50	2.00
462	A124	$1.65 multi	4.50	*7.00*
		Nos. 459-462 (4)	10.85	9.80

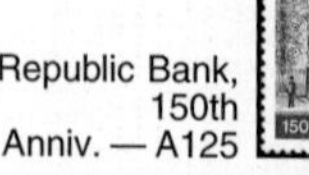

Republic Bank, 150th Anniv. — A125

Designs: 10c, Colonial Bank, Port of Spain. 65c, Cocoa plantation. 95c, Oil fields. $1.10, Tramcar, Belmont Tramway Co.

Wmk. 373

1987, Dec. 21 Litho. *Perf. 14*

463	A125	10c buff, red brn & blk	.35	.35
464	A125	65c buff, red brn & blk	.70	.70
465	A125	95c buff, red brn & blk	2.50	2.50
466	A125	$1.10 buff, red brn & blk	2.75	2.75
		Nos. 463-466 (4)	6.30	6.30

Defense Force, 25th Anniv. — A126

Various army, coast guard and navy uniforms: 10c, Army. 30c, Army (women). $1.10, Navy, army, coast guard. $1.50, Navy.

Wmk. 384

1988, Feb. 29 Litho. *Perf. 14*

467	A126	10c multicolored	1.25	.30
468	A126	30c multicolored	2.75	.50
469	A126	$1.10 multicolored	3.75	3.75
470	A126	$1.50 multicolored	5.00	5.00
		Nos. 467-470 (4)	12.75	9.55

Cricket — A127

Bat, wicket posts, ball, 18th cent. belt buckle and batters: 30c, George John. 65c, Learie Constantine. 95c, Sonny Ramadhin. $1.50, Gerry Gomez. $2.50, Jeffrey Stollmeyer.

Wmk. 373

1988, June 6 Litho. *Perf. 14*

471	A127	30c multicolored	1.70	.50
472	A127	65c multicolored	2.35	1.00
473	A127	95c multicolored	2.75	1.75
474	A127	$1.50 multicolored	3.25	3.75
475	A127	$2.50 multicolored	4.00	*6.00*
		Nos. 471-475 (5)	14.05	13.00

Oilfield Workers' Trade Union, 50th Anniv. — A128

50, Star, oil well and: 10c, Uriah Buzz Butler, labor leader. 30c, Adrian C. Rienzi, pres. from 1937-42. 65c, John Rojas, pres. from 1943-62. $5, George Weekes, pres. from 1962-87.

Wmk. 384

1988, July 11 Litho. *Perf. 14½*

476	A128	10c multicolored	.30	.25
477	A128	30c multicolored	.30	.25
478	A128	65c multicolored	.40	.40
479	A128	$5 multicolored	2.60	2.60
		Nos. 476-479 (4)	3.60	3.50

Borough of Arima, Cent. — A129

20c, Mary Werges, Santa Rosa Church. 30c, Gov. W. Robinson, royal charter. $1.10, Mayor C.P. Lopez greeting Gov. Robinson at train station. $1.50, Mayor J.F. Wallen, centennial emblem.

Wmk. 384

1988, Aug. 22 Litho. *Perf. 14½*

480	A129	20c multicolored	.30	.35
481	A129	30c multicolored	.30	.35
482	A129	$1.10 multicolored	1.25	1.60
483	A129	$1.50 multicolored	1.25	1.60
		Nos. 480-483 (4)	3.10	3.90

Lloyds of London, 300th Anniv.

Common Design Type

Designs: 30c, Queen Mother at the "Topping Out" ceremony of new Lloyds's building, 1984. $1.10, BWIA Tristar 500, horiz. $1.55, ISCOTT iron and steel mill, horiz. $2, *Atlantic Empress* on fire off Tobago.

1988, Nov. 21 Litho. *Perf. 14*

484	CD341	30c multicolored	1.25	.35
485	CD341	$1.10 multicolored	2.75	1.00
486	CD341	$1.55 multicolored	1.75	2.00
487	CD341	$2 multicolored	4.50	3.00
		Nos. 484-487 (4)	10.25	6.35

Unification of the Islands, Cent. — A130

Torch and: 40c, Natl. arms, 1889, and 1p Type A1. $1, Badge from Tobago flag and Tobago No. 31. $1.50, Badge from Trinidad flag and Trinidad No. 71. $2.25, Natl. arms, 1989, and No. 274.

Wmk. 384

1989, Mar. 20 Litho. *Perf. 14½*

488	A130	40c multicolored	1.75	.25
489	A130	$1 multicolored	3.00	1.00
490	A130	$1.50 multicolored	3.25	3.50
491	A130	$2.25 multicolored	3.75	*7.00*
		Nos. 488-491 (4)	11.75	11.75

Rare Species — A131

Designs: a, Pipile pipile. b, Phyllodytes auratus. c, Cebus albifrons trinitatis. d, Tamandua tetradactyla. e, Lutra longicaudis. Printed in a continuous design.

Perf. 14x14½

1989, July 31 Wmk. 373

492		Strip of 5	20.00	20.00
a.-e.	A131	$1 any single	2.50	2.50

A132

10c, Men using walking sticks. 40c, City Hall. $1, Guides and leader. $2.25, Volunteers, anniv. emblem.

1989, Oct. 2 *Perf. 14½*

493	A132	10c multi	1.50	.35
494	A132	40c multi	.50	.25
495	A132	$1 multi	3.00	.75
496	A132	$2.25 multi	4.25	3.00
		Nos. 493-496 (4)	9.25	4.35

Blind Welfare, 75th anniv. (10c), Port-of-Spain City Hall, 75th anniv. (40c), Girl Guides, 75th anniv. ($1), and Red Cross, 50th anniv. ($2.25).

A133

Drum instruments played in a steel band.

Perf. 14½x14

1989, Nov. 30 Wmk. 384

497	A133	10c Tenor	.35	.35
498	A133	40c Guitar	.40	.40
499	A133	$1 Cello	.75	.75
500	A133	$2.25 Bass	1.50	1.50
		Nos. 497-500 (4)	3.00	3.00

Mushrooms A134

10c, Xeromphalina tenuipes. 40c, Dictyophora indusiata. $1, Leucocoprinus birnbaumii. $2.25, Crinipellis perniciosa.

1990, May 3 *Perf. 14x13½*
501 A134 10c multicolored .45 .45
502 A134 40c multicolored .70 .70
503 A134 $1 multicolored 1.50 1.50
504 A134 $2.25 multicolored 3.00 3.00
Nos. 501-504 (4) 5.65 5.65

Stamp World London '90.

Scarlet Ibis — A135

1990, Sept. 7 *Perf. 14*
505 A135 40c Immature bird *1.75 1.75*
506 A135 80c Mating display *2.00 2.00*
507 A135 $1 Adult male *2.50 2.50*
508 A135 $2.25 Adult, egg & young *4.25 4.25*
Nos. 505-508 (4) 10.50 10.50

World Wildlife Fund.

Yellow Oriole — A136

No. 510, Green rumped parrotlet. No. 511, Fork-tailed flycatcher. No. 512, Copper rumped hummingbird. No. 513, Bananaquit. No. 514, Semp. No. 515, Channel-billed toucan. No. 516, Bay headed tanager. No. 517, Green honeycreeper. No. 518, Cattle egret. No. 519, Golden olive woodpecker. No. 520, Peregrine falcon.

1990, Dec. 17 Litho. Wmk. 384
509 A136 20c shown 1.00 .50
510 A136 25c multicolored 1.25 .30
511 A136 40c multicolored 1.40 .25
512 A136 50c multicolored 1.50 .50
513 A136 $1 multicolored 1.60 .50
514 A136 $2 multicolored 2.50 1.50
515 A136 $2.25 multicolored 2.50 2.00
516 A136 $2.50 multicolored 2.00 1.25
517 A136 $5 multicolored 3.50 3.25
518 A136 $10 multicolored 4.25 3.50
519 A136 $20 multicolored 6.00 *7.00*
520 A136 $50 multicolored 12.00 *17.50*
Nos. 509-520 (12) 39.50 38.05

1994-98 Wmk. 373
510a A136 25c 2.60 .40
511a A136 40c — —
512a A136 50c .55 .35
513a A136 $1 3.25 .65
514a A136 $2 4.00 1.75
516a A136 $2.50 3.00 2.50
517a A136 $5 3.75 2.75
b. Souvenir sheet of 1, wmk. 373, dated "1997" 4.75 4.75
518a A136 $10 4.00 *5.00*
519a A136 $20 7.00 *10.00*

Issued: #510a, 8/94; #512a, 4/95; #513a, 514a, 3/3/97; #516a, 518a, 519a, 10/14/98; #517a, 6/1996.

#510a, 511a, 512a, 513a, 514a, 516a, 517a, 518a, 519a are dated 1990. No. 517b issued 2/3/97 for Hong Kong '97.

For overprints & surcharges see Nos. 565-568, 597A, 609, 888A, 889, 897, 898, 919, 936, 949.

Two additional items were issued in this set. The editors would like to examine any examples of them.

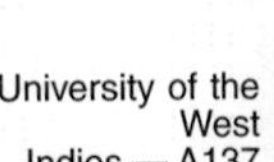

University of the West Indies — A137

Chancellors and Campus Buildings: 40c, HRH Princess Alice, Administration Building. 80c, Sir Hugh Wooding, Main Library. $1, Sir Allen Lewis, Faculty of Engineering. $2.25, Sir Shridath Ramphal, Faculty of Medical Studies.

Perf. 13½x14
1990, Oct. 15 Litho. Wmk. 373
521 A137 40c multicolored .75 .25
522 A137 80c multicolored 1.00 1.00
523 A137 $1 multicolored 1.50 1.25
524 A137 $2.25 multicolored 3.75 *4.50*
Nos. 521-524 (4) 7.00 7.00

Britsh West Indies Airways, 50th Anniv. — A138

Airplanes: 40c, Lockheed Lodestar. 80c, Vickers Viking 1A. $1, Vickers Viscount 702. $2.25, Boeing 707. $5, Lockheed TriStar 500.

1990, Nov. 27 *Perf. 14*
525 A138 40c multicolored 1.30 .50
526 A138 80c multicolored 1.70 1.00
527 A138 $1 multicolored 1.85 1.25
528 A138 $2.25 multicolored 3.25 *5.50*
Nos. 525-528 (4) 8.10 8.25

Souvenir Sheet

529 A138 $5 multicolored 5.00 5.00

Ferns — A139

40c, Lygodium volubile. 80c, Blechnum occidentale. $1, Gleichenia bifida. $2.25, Polypodium lycopodiodes.

1991, July 1 *Perf. 13½*
530 A139 40c multicolored .35 .35
531 A139 80c multicolored .75 .75
532 A139 $1 multicolored .90 .90
533 A139 $2.25 multicolored 2.00 2.00
Nos. 530-533 (4) 4.00 4.00

Trinidad & Tobago in World War II — A140

Designs: 40c, Firing practice by Trinidad & Tobago regiment. 80c, Fairey Barracuda surprises U-boat. $1, Avro Lancaster returns from bombing raid. $2.25, River class frigate on convoy duty. No. 538a, Supermarine Spitfire. b, Vickers Wellington.

Perf. 13½x14
1991, Dec. 7 Litho. Wmk. 384
534 A140 40c multicolored 1.75 .40
535 A140 80c multicolored 2.50 1.10
536 A140 $1 multicolored 3.25 1.25
537 A140 $2.25 multicolored 5.00 *6.50*
Nos. 534-537 (4) 12.50 9.25

Souvenir Sheet of 2

538 A140 $2.50 #a.-b. 17.50 17.50

H. E. Rapsey A141

Inca Clathrata Quesneli A142

Holy Name Convent — A143

1992, Mar. 30 Wmk. 373 *Perf. 14*
539 A141 40c multicolored .50 .25
540 A142 80c multicolored 1.25 1.25
541 A143 $1 multicolored 1.75 1.75
Nos. 539-541 (3) 3.50 3.25

#539, Building and Loan Assoc., cent. #540, Trinidad & Tobago Field Naturalists' Club. #541, Holy Name Convent, cent.

Religions of Trinidad and Tobago — A145

No. 544, Baptist, baptism by immersion. No. 545, Muslim, minaret. No. 546, Hindu, Brahman..the source of all. No. 547, Christianity, cross. No. 548, Baha'i, slogan.

1992, Apr. 21 Litho. *Perf. 14*
544 A145 40c multicolored 1.40 *1.60*
545 A145 40c multicolored 1.40 *1.60*
546 A145 40c multicolored 1.40 *1.60*
547 A145 40c multicolored 1.40 *1.60*
548 A145 40c multicolored 1.40 *1.60*
Nos. 544-548 (5) 7.00 *8.00*

BWIA Aircraft — A146

Wmk. 373
1992, Aug. 6 Litho. *Perf. 14*
549 A146 $2.25 MD83 3.50 3.50
550 A146 $2.25 L1011 3.50 3.50

Natl. Museum and Art Gallery, Cent. — A147

Wmk. 384
1992, Dec. 7 Litho. *Perf. 14½*
551 A147 $1 multicolored .60 .60

Christmas — A148

1992, Dec. 21
552 A148 40c multicolored .45 .45

Trinidad Guardian, 75th Anniv. — A149

1992, Dec. 23
553 A149 40c multicolored .45 .45

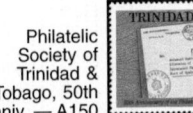

Philatelic Society of Trinidad & Tobago, 50th Anniv. — A150

1992, Dec. 30
554 A150 $2.25 multicolored 1.40 1.40

CARICOM (Caribbean Economic Community), 20th Anniv. — A151

Map of CARICOM nations, portraits of West Indian men: 50c, $1.50, $2.75, $3, Derek Walcott, Sir Shridath Ramphal, William Demas.

$6, Order of the Caribbean Community.

Perf. 13x13½
1994, Jan. 31 Litho. Wmk. 373
555 A151 50c pink & multi .40 .25
556 A151 $1.50 green & multi .70 .70
557 A151 $2.75 gray & multi 1.10 1.10
558 A151 $3 violet & multi 1.25 1.25
Nos. 555-558 (4) 3.45 3.30

Souvenir Sheet
Perf. 13½x13

559 A151 $6 multicolored 3.00 3.00

No. 559 contains one 34x56mm stamp.

Drum Instruments Played in a Steel Band — A152

Perf. 14x15
1994, Feb. 11 Wmk. 384
560 A152 50c Quadrophonic pan .30 .30
561 A152 $1 Tenor base pan .55 .50
562 A152 $2.25 Six pan 1.00 *2.00*
563 A152 $2.50 Rocket pan 1.15 *2.25*
Nos. 560-563 (4) 3.00 5.05

Aldwyn Roberts Kitchener, Calypso Singer — A153

1994, Feb. 11 Wmk. 373 *Perf. 14*
564 A153 50c multicolored 3.00 1.00

Nos. 510-511, 514, 518 Ovptd. with Hong Kong '94 Exhibition Emblem

Wmk. 384
1994, Feb. 18 Litho. *Perf. 14*
565 A136 25c multicolored .45 .30
566 A136 40c multicolored .50 .30
567 A136 $2 multicolored 1.50 1.25
568 A136 $10 multicolored 5.50 *6.25*
Nos. 565-568 (4) 7.95 8.10

Hotels & Lodges — A154

#569, Trinidad Hilton. #570, Sandy Point Village, Tobago. #571, Asa Wright Nature Center and Lodge. #572, ML's Bed and Breakfast.

Wmk. 373
1994, Aug. 10 Litho. *Perf. 14*
569 A154 $3 multicolored 1.20 *1.40*
570 A154 $3 multicolored 1.20 *1.40*
571 A154 $3 multicolored 1.20 *1.40*
572 A154 $3 multicolored 1.20 *1.40*
Nos. 569-572 (4) 4.80 *5.60*

Snakes — A155

50c, Boa constrictor. $1.25, Horse whip or vine snake. $2.50, Bushmaster. $3, Large coral snake.

Wmk. 373
1994, Sept. 19 Litho. *Perf. 14*
573 A155 50c multicolored .45 .30
574 A155 $1.25 multicolored .90 .75
575 A155 $2.50 multicolored 1.60 *1.75*
576 A155 $3 multicolored 1.75 *2.25*
Nos. 573-576 (4) 4.70 5.05

Trinidad Art Society, 50th Anniv. — A156

Artworks: No. 577, Copper sculpture, by Ken Morris. No. 578, Fisherman, by Sybil Atteck. No. 579, Snowballman, by Mahmoud P. Alladin.

1995, Mar. 6 **Wmk. 384**
577 A156 50c multicolored .70 *.90*
578 A156 50c multicolored .70 *.90*
579 A156 50c multicolored .70 *.90*
Nos. 577-579 (3) 2.10 *2.70*

Conservation A157

Designs: $1.25, Leatherback turtle. $2.50, POS Lighthouse, vert. $3, "Knowsley" Ministry of Foreign Affairs.

1995, Aug. 7
580 A157 $1.25 multicolored .75 .75
581 A157 $2.50 multicolored 1.75 1.75
582 A157 $3 multicolored 1.50 1.50
Nos. 580-582 (3) 4.00 4.00

Brian Lara, Cricket Hero — A158

Designs: $1.25, Batting. $2.50, In batting stance. $3, Batting, diff.
No. 587: a, $3.75, With arms raised at crowd. b, $5.01, Down on one knee with bat.

Perf. 13x13½
1996, May 15 **Litho.** **Wmk. 373**
583 A158 50c multicolored .40 .40
584 A158 $1.25 multicolored .75 .75
585 A158 $2.50 multicolored 1.40 1.40
586 A158 $3 multicolored 1.75 1.75
Nos. 583-586 (4) 4.30 4.30

Souvenir Sheet
587 A158 Sheet of 2, #a.-b. 5.00 5.00

Trinidad & Tobago Remembers World War II — A159

50c, Red Cross Economy Label. $1.25, Battleship USS Missouri. $2.50, US servicemen playing baseball, Queen's Park, Savannah, 1942. $3, Fulmar 1, Royal Naval Air Station.
No. 592: a, Grumman Goose seaplane. b, US Navy Airship.

Wmk. 373
1996, June 7 **Litho.** ***Perf. 14***
588 A159 50c multicolored .60 .30
589 A159 $1.25 multicolored 1.50 .75
590 A159 $2.50 multicolored 1.75 1.75
591 A159 $3 multicolored 2.50 2.50
Nos. 588-591 (4) 6.35 5.30

Souvenir Sheet of 2
592 A159 $3 #a.-b. 7.00 7.00

A160

Wendy Fitzwilliam, 1998 Miss Universe: $1.25, Lying on beach. $2.50, In traditional costume. $3, Wearing evening gown.
$5, After coronation.

1999, May 3 **Litho.** ***Perf. 14***
593 A160 50c multicolored .75 .75
594 A160 $1.25 multicolored 1.50 1.50
595 A160 $2.50 multicolored 2.25 2.25
596 A160 $3 multicolored 2.75 2.75
Nos. 593-596 (4) 7.25 7.25

Souvenir Sheet
597 A160 $5 multicolored 7.50 7.50

No. 511 Surcharged

Method, Perf. & Watermark As Before
1999, May 24
597A A136 75c on 40c multi *13.00 3.00*

A161

Angostura Bitters, 175th Anniv.: 75c, Angostura Bitters bottle. $3, Distillery. $4.50, Bitters bottle, cocktails.

Serpentine Die Cut
2000, Jan. 27 **Litho.** **Unwmk.**
Self-Adhesive
598 A161 75c multi .50 .50
599 A161 $3 multi 2.00 2.00
600 A161 $4.50 multi 3.25 2.25
a. Souvenir sheet, #598-600 5.25 5.25
Nos. 598-600 (3) 5.75 4.75

Tourism — A162

Shoreline scenes: 75c, Maracas Bay. $1, Pirates Bay. $3.75, Pigeon Point. $5, Toco, North Coast.

2000, July 25 **Litho.** ***Perf. 14¼x14½***
601 A162 75c multi 1.00 .30
602 A162 $1 multi 1.25 .40
603 A162 $3.75 multi 2.50 2.50
604 A162 $5 multi 3.25 3.25
Nos. 601-604 (4) 8.00 6.45

For surcharge, see No. 890.

Christmas — A163

Design: 75c, Caroni landscape. $3.75, Pastelles, sorrel and ginger beer. $4.50, Musicians under palm trees. $5.25, Angels with steel drums.

Perf. 14¼x14½
2000, Nov. 14 **Litho.**
605 A163 75c multi .75 .30
606 A163 $3.75 multi 2.25 1.75
607 A163 $4.50 multi 2.50 2.50
608 A163 $5.25 multi 3.25 3.25
Nos. 605-608 (4) 8.75 7.80

For surcharge, see No. 923.

No. 515 Surcharged

Method, Perf. & Watermark As Before
2001, Jan. 26
609 A136 75c on $2.25 multi *13.00 5.00*

National Mail Center — A164

Designs: $3, Building entrance. $10, Side of building.

Perf. 14¼x14½
2000, Nov. 20 **Litho.** **Unwmk.**
610-611 A164 Set of 2 6.75 6.75

Endangered Fauna — A165

Designs: 25c, Paca, 50c, Prehensile-tailed porcupine. 75c, Iguana. $1, Leatherback turtle. $2, Golden tegu. $2, Red howler monkey. $4, Weeping capuchin monkey, vert. $5, River otter. $10, Ocelot. $20, Trinidad piping guan, vert.

Perf. 14¼x14½, 14½x14¼
2001, Feb. 6 **Litho.**
612 A165 25c multi .60 .30
613 A165 50c multi 1.00 .40
614 A165 75c multi 1.25 .45
615 A165 $1 multi 1.50 .50
616 A165 $2 multi 2.00 1.00
617 A165 $3 multi 2.50 1.25
618 A165 $4 multi 2.50 1.50
619 A165 $5 multi 2.75 1.75
620 A165 $10 multi 5.75 5.75
621 A165 $20 multi 15.00 15.00
Nos. 612-621 (10) 34.85 27.90

For surcharge, see No. 932.

Salvation Army in Trinidad & Tobago, Cent. — A166

Designs: 75c, Emblem. $2, William Booth Memorial Hall.

2001, Aug. 9 ***Perf. 14½x14¼***
622-623 A166 Set of 2 2.50 2.50
623a Souvenir sheet, #622-623, perf. 13¾x14¼ 2.50 2.50

For surcharge, see No. 916.

Natl. Library, 150th Anniv. — A167

Designs: 75c, Port of Spain Public Library, Carnegie Free Library. $3.25, New National Library building.

2001, Aug. 9 ***Perf. 14¼x14½***
624-625 A167 Set of 2 3.50 3.50
625a Souvenir sheet, #624-625 3.50 3.50

For surcharge, see No. 917.

Under 17 World Soccer Championships A168

Designs: $2, Emblem of Soca Warriors. $3.25, National flag. $4.50, Lion holding flag. $5.25, Stadiums.

2001, Sept. 6 ***Perf. 14½x14***
626-629 A168 Set of 4 8.25 8.25
629a Souvenir sheet, #626-629 8.25 8.25

For surcharge, see No. 934.

Flowers — A169

Designs: $1, Pachystachys coccinea. $2.50, Heliconia psittacorum. $3.25, Brownea latifolia, horiz. $3.75, Oncidium papilio.

Perf. 14½x14¼, 14¼x14½
2001, Nov. 1
630-633 A169 Set of 4 8.00 8.00

Christmas — A170

People and: $1, Boats, church. $3.75, Flowers. $4.50, House, flowers. $5.25, Church, post office.

2001, Nov. 15 ***Perf. 14½x14¼***
634-637 A170 Set of 4 8.00 8.00
637a Souvenir sheet, #634-637 8.25 8.25

For surcharge, see No. 924.

Butterflies — A171

Designs: $1, Cracker. $3.75, Tiger. $4.50, Four continent. $5.25, "89."

2002, June 19 **Litho.** ***Perf. 13¼x13***
638-641 A171 Set of 4 11.00 11.00

For surcharges, see Nos. 920-922.

Hummingbirds A172

Designs: $1, Rufous-breasted hermit. $2.50, Black-throated mango. $3.25, Tufted coquette. $3.75, White-chested emerald.

2002, Apr. 17 ***Perf. 13x13¼***
642-645 A172 Set of 4 9.00 9.00

For surcharges, see Nos. 918, 928.

Historic Forts — A173

Designs: $1, Fort Picton. $3.75, Fort George. $4.50, Fort King George. $5.25, Fort James.

2002, July 31 ***Perf. 13¼x13***
646-649 A173 Set of 4 10.50 10.50
649a Souvenir sheet, #646-649 10.50 10.50

For surcharges, see Nos. 913-915.

Reign of Queen Elizabeth II, 50th Anniv. — A174

Queen: $3.75, At Governor General's House. $4.50, With Mayor E. Taylor of Port of

Spain. $5.25, At Red House, addressing Parliament, #119, and former personal flag of the Queen.
$10, In limousine, waving to crowd.

2002, Sept. 23 Litho. *Perf. 13¾*
650-652 A174 Set of 3 7.50 7.50

Souvenir Sheet

653 A174 $10 multi 10.00 10.00

For overprints and surcharges, see Nos. 975-978.

Independence, 40th Anniv. — A175

2002, Sept. 23
654 A175 $1 multi 1.25 1.25

Christmas — A176

Designs: $1, Child opening gift of steel drum, vert. $2.50, People, musicians, house. $3.75, Houses. $5.25, Santa Claus on horse-drawn cart, vert.

Perf. 14½x14¼, 14¼x14½
2002, Nov. 20 Litho.
655-658 A176 Set of 4 8.50 8.50

For surcharges, see Nos. 925-926.

Pan-American Health Organization, Cent. — A177

Designs: $1, Emblem. $2.50, National headquarters, Port of Spain. $3.25, Steel drum with symbols. $4.50, Joseph L. Pawan (1887-1957), discoverer of vampire bat rabies.

2002, Dec. 2 *Perf. 14½x14¼*
659-662 A177 Set of 4 8.00 8.00

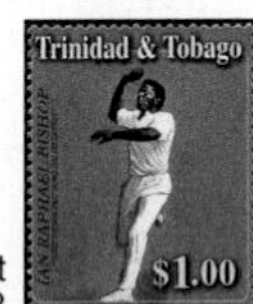

Cricket Players — A178

Designs: $1, Ian Raphael Bishop. $2.50, Deryck Lance Murray. $4.50, Augustine Lawrence Logie. $5.25, Ann Browne John.

2003, Feb. 7 *Perf. 13*
663-666 A178 Set of 4 10.00 10.00

For surcharge, see No. 933.

Carnival — A179

Various costumed participants: $1, $2.50, $3.75, vert., $4.50, vert., $5.25, vert.

Perf. 14¼x14½, 14½x14¼
2003, Feb. 25 Litho.
667-671 A179 Set of 5 8.50 8.50
671a Souvenir sheet of 1 4.25 4.25

For surcharge, see No. 930.

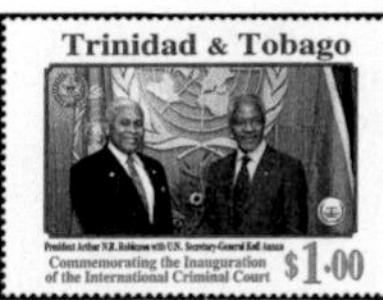

Inauguration of Intl. Criminal Court A180

Designs: $1, Trinidad & Tobago Pres. Arthur N. R. Robinson and UN Secretary General Kofi Annan. $2.50, Robinson, Prof. Benjamin Ferencz, Prof. Cherif Bassiouni, Philippe Kirsch, UN Undersecretary for Legal Affairs Hans Corell. $3.75, Robinson and Corell. $4.50, Robinson, Emma Bonino, and Italian Pres. Carlo Ciampi.
$6, Robinson, vert.

Perf. 14¾x14½, 14½x14¾
2003, Feb. 25
672-675 A180 Set of 4 8.00 8.00

Souvenir Sheet

676 A180 $6 multi 4.75 4.75

Rainforest Flora & Fauna — A181

No. 677: a, Mountain immortelle. b, Blue-crowned motmot. c, Red howler monkey. d, Butterfly orchid. e, Channel-billed toucan. f, Ocelot. g, Bromeliads. h, Lineated woodpecker. i, Tamandua. j, Emperor butterfly.

Serpentine Die Cut 12½
2003, Feb. 24 Litho.

Self-Adhesive

677 Booklet pane of 10 12.00 —
a.-j. A181 $1 Any single .85 .85

Lighthouses — A182

Designs: $1, Port-of-Spain. $3.75, Chacachacare. $4.50, Port-of-Spain, diff. $5.25, Chacachacare, diff.
No. 681B, Like No. 679, spelled "Chacacharie." No. 681C, Like No. 681, spelled "Chacacharie."

2002-03 *Perf. 14½x14¼*
678-681 A182 Set of 4 11.50 11.50
681a Souvenir sheet, #678-681 11.50 11.50
681B A182 $3.75 multi — —
681C A182 $5.25 multi — —

Nos. 678, 680, 681B and 681C were issued on 11/6/02 and all were withdrawn from sale later that day when the incorrect spelling of the lighthouse was discovered. Nos. 678 and 680 were put back on sale, along with new stamps with the corrected spelling of the lighthouse, Nos. 679 and 681, and the souvenir sheet with the stamps with the corrected spelling, No. 681a, on 5/26/03. The editors would like to examine any examples of the souvenir sheet with stamps with the incorrect spelling.

Scenes of Village Life — A183

Designs: $1, Dancing the cocoa. $2.50, Dirt oven. $3.75, River washing. $4.50, Box cart racing. $5.25, Pitching marbles.

2003, Oct. 28
682-686 A183 Set of 5 8.50 8.50

For surcharge, see No. 931.

Marine Life — A184

Designs: $1, Boulder brain coral. $2.50, Hawksbill turtle. $3.75, Green moray eel. $4.50, Creole wrasse. $5.25, Black-spotted sea goddess.
$10, Queen angelfish.

2003, Oct. 28 *Perf. 14¼x14½*
687-691 A184 Set of 5 10.00 10.00

Souvenir Sheet

692 A184 $10 multi 9.00 9.00

Christmas A185

Paintings by Jean Michel Cazabon (1813-88): $1, View of Port-of-Spain from Laventille Hill. $2.50, View of Diego Martin from Fort George. $3.75, Corbeaux Town, Trinidad. $4.50, Rain Clouds over Cedros. $5.25, Los Galos, Icacos Bay.
No. 698: a, $5, River at St. Ann's. b, $6.50, House in Trinidad.

2003, Nov. 17 *Perf. 13¾*
693-697 A185 Set of 5 9.50 9.50

Souvenir Sheet

698 A185 Sheet of 2, #a-b 9.50 9.50

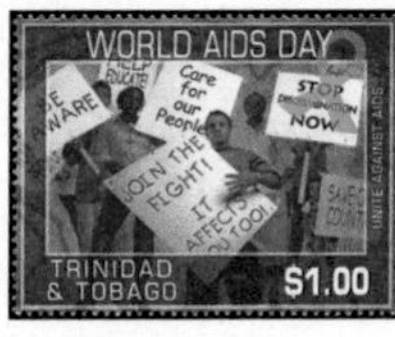

World AIDS Day — A186

Designs: $1, Unite against AIDS. $2.50, Stigma isolates. $3.75, Care stops AIDS, vert. $4.50, Family protects, vert.
$10, People and AIDS ribbon.

2003, Nov. 21
699-702 A186 Set of 4 7.50 7.50

Souvenir Sheet

703 A186 $10 multi 7.25 7.25

2004 Carnival — A187

Calypso musicians: $1, Aldric Farrel, "The Lord Pretender." $2.50, Roy Lewis, "The Mystic Prowler." $3.75, Lord Kitchener, The Mighty Sparrow and The Roaring Lion. $4.50, McArthur Linda Sandy-Rose, "Calypso Rose." $5.25, Nap Hepburne, Lord Brynner and The Mighty Sparrow.
$10, McArthur Linda Sandy-Rose, diff.

2004, Feb. 18
704-708 A187 Set of 5 7.50 7.50

Souvenir Sheet

709 A187 $10 multi 7.00 7.00

2004 Summer Olympics, Athens — A188

Designs: $1, Track and field. $2.50, Boxing. $3.75, Taekwondo. $4.50, Swimming.

2004, July 19 Litho. *Perf. 13*
710-713 A188 Set of 4 7.00 7.00

Intl. Year Commemorating the Struggle Against Slavery and Its Abolition — A189

Designs: $1, Slave ship. $2.50, Rada community, Belmont. $3.75, Daaga, Prince of Popo. $4.50, Slaves singing freedom songs, horiz. $5.25, Providence Estate Aqueduct, Tobago, horiz.
$15, Sandy's escape, horiz.

2004, Sept. 23 Litho. *Perf. 13*
714-718 A189 Set of 5 8.00 8.00

Souvenir Sheet

719 A189 $15 multi 6.50 6.50

Christmas — A190

Paintings by Arthur Aldwin "Boscoe" Holder: $1, Lady with Ginger Lilies. $2.50, View from Maracas Lookout. $3.75, Lady in Peacock Chair. $4.50, Caribbean Beauty in White, horiz. $5.25, Teteron Bay, Chaguaramas, horiz.
$10, Creole Ladies in Straw Hats, horiz.

2004, Nov. 22
720-724 A190 Set of 5 7.75 7.75

Souvenir Sheet

725 A190 $10 multi 5.25 5.25

Fruits — A191

Designs: $1, Mango. $2.50, Lime. $3.75, Pineapple. $4.50, Coconut, horiz. $5.25, Orange, horiz.
$10, Guava, horiz.

2004, June 7
726-730 A191 Set of 5 8.00 8.00

Souvenir Sheet

731 A191 $10 multi 6.50 6.50

Carnival — A192

Designs: $1, Dame Lorraine. $2.50, Jab Jab. $3.25, Burrokeet, horiz. $3.75, Midnight Robber. $4.50, Fancy Indian.
$15, Fancy Sailor.

2005, Jan. 18 Litho. *Perf. 13*
732-736 A192 Set of 5 7.25 7.25

Souvenir Sheet

737 A192 $15 multi 7.50 7.50

Brian Lara, Cricket Player — A193

Various photos of Lara in action: $1, $2.50, $3.75, $4.50, $5.25.
$15, Lara walking under raised cricket bats.

2005, Apr. 12 Litho. *Perf. 13*
738-742 A193 Set of 5 11.00 11.00

Souvenir Sheet

743 A193 $15 multi 11.00 11.00

Tobago Heritage Festival — A194

Designs: $1, Belé. $2.50, Dancing the jig. $3.75, Goat race, horiz. $4.50, Harvest Festival, horiz. $5.25, Drumming Festival, horiz.
$15, Traditional Tobago wedding.

Perf. 13½x13¼, 13¼x13½

2005, Aug. 15
744-748 A194 Set of 5 7.50 7.50

Souvenir Sheet

Perf. 13¼

749 A194 $15 multi 7.50 7.50

Medicinal Herbs — A195

Designs: 25c, Rachet. 50c, Chandelier. 75c, Worm grass. $1, Black sage. $3, Wonder of the world. $3.25, Vervine. $4, Aloe vera. $5, Senna. $10, Bois bande. $20, Herbal garden.

2005, May 18 *Perf. 13¼x13*
750 A195 25c multi .40 .25
751 A195 50c multi .75 .35
752 A195 75c multi .90 .40
753 A195 $1 multi 1.00 .40
754 A195 $3 multi 1.50 1.25
755 A195 $3.25 multi 2.00 1.50
756 A195 $4 multi 2.25 1.75
757 A195 $5 multi 2.25 2.25
758 A195 $10 multi 3.50 3.50
759 A195 $20 multi 7.00 10.00
Nos. 750-759 (10) 21.55 21.65

For surcharges see Nos. 905, 935, 961.

Fish and Marine Life — A196

No. 760: a, Foureye butterfly fish. b, Caribbean reef squid. c, Hawksbill turtle. d, Southern sting ray. e, Queen angelfish. f, Giant anemone. g, Peppermint shrimp. h, Rough file clam. i, White-speckled hermit crab. j, Christmas tree worm.

Serpentine Die Cut 12½

2005, May 1 Self-Adhesive Litho.
760 Booklet of 10 11.00 —
a.-j. A196 $1 Any single .75 .75

Sir Solomon Hochoy (1905-83), First Governor-General A197

Hochoy and: $1, Prime Minister Dr. Eric E. Williams. $2.50, Haile Selassie. $3.75, His wife, Thelma. $4.50, Queen Elizabeth II. $5.25, Honor Guard.
$15, Hochoy in uniform.

2005, Aug. 22 *Perf. 13½x13*
761-765 A197 Set of 5 7.50 7.50

Souvenir Sheet

Perf. 13½x13¼

766 A197 $15 multi 7.50 7.50

For surcharge, see No. 891.

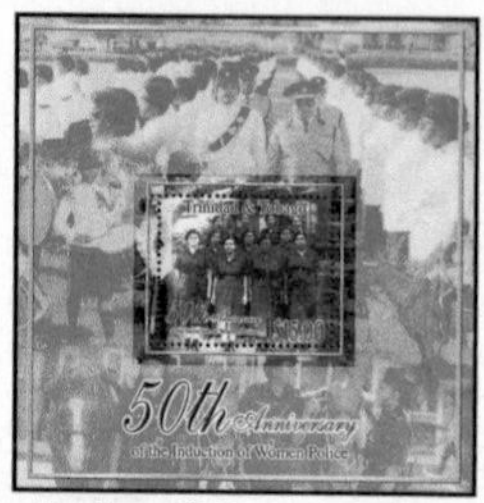

Introduction of Women Police, 50th Anniv. — A198

2005, Sept. 30 *Perf. 12¾*
767 A198 $15 black 7.50 7.50

Souvenir Sheet

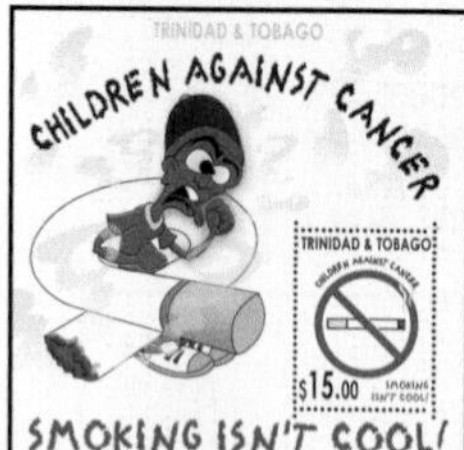

Children Against Cancer A199

2005, Nov. 7 *Perf. 13½x13¼*
768 A199 $15 multi 8.50 8.50

No. 768 sold for $20.

Anansi and the Cricket Match — A200

Anansi: $1, And friends reading cricket brochure. $2.50, And friends hiding in bathroom. $3.75, And friends under umbrella. $4.50, Holding bag, talking to woman. $5.25, Laughing at friends paying woman.
$15, Anansi rubbing stomach.

2005, Dec. 12 *Perf. 13½x13*
769-773 A200 Set of 5 7.50 7.50

Souvenir Sheet

774 A200 $15 multi 7.00 7.00

Pope John Paul II (1920-2005) — A201

Scenes from Pope's 1985 visit to Trinidad & Tobago: $1, Leaving airplane. $2.50, Kissing ground. $3.75, Shaking hands with priest. $4.50, With bishop, waving. $5.25, Celebrating mass.
$15, Waving to crowd from police vehicle.

2006, Apr. 10 Litho. *Perf. 13½x13¼*
775-779 A201 Set of 5 6.50 6.50

Souvenir Sheet

780 A201 $15 multi 5.75 5.75

2006 World Cup Soccer Championships, Germany — A202

Various images of Trinidad & Tobago soccer players in action: $1, $2.50, $3.75, $4.50.

Perf. 13¼x13½

2006, June 28 **Litho.**
781-784 A202 Set of 4 *10.00 10.00*

Initial reports said this set was available only with the purchase of a first day cover for $50, but the stamps have been made available individually at face value.

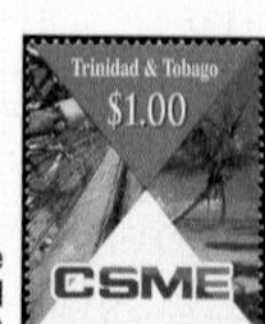

CARICOM Single Market and Economy — A203

Designs: $1, Cables, palm tree. $2.50, Lighthouse, check. $3.75, Cell phone, diver. $4.50, Sprinter's hands, beach, horiz. $5.25, Hands on computer keyboard, globe, horiz.
$15, Map of Caribbean, horiz.

Perf. 13½x13¼, 13¼x13½

2006, July 3
785-789 A203 Set of 5 8.25 8.25

Souvenir Sheet

790 A203 $15 multi 7.50 7.50

Souvenir Sheet

Orchid Society, 50th Anniv. A204

2006, Sept. 5 *Perf. 13½x13¼*
791 A204 $15 multi 8.00 8.00

Arrival of Chinese to Trinidad and Tobago, Bicent. — A205

Art: $1, Guayaguayare Beach, by Ou Hing Wan. $2.50, Hosay, by Carlisle Chang. $3.75, Saddle Road, by Amy Leong Pang, vert. $4.50, Mother & Child, sculpture by Patrick Chu Foon, vert. $5.25, Still Life, by Sybil Atteck, vert.
$15, Inherent Nobility of Man, by Chang, vert.

Perf. 14¼x14½, 14½x14¼

2006, Oct. 11
792-796 A205 Set of 5 9.50 9.50

Souvenir Sheet

Perf. 13x13¼

797 A205 $15 multi 7.50 7.50

Children's Games — A206

Designs: $1, Rim driving. $2.50, Top spinning. $3.75, Playing 3A. $4.50, Farmer in the Den.
$15, Tire swing.

2006, Nov. 29 *Perf. 13¼*
798-801 A206 Set of 4 6.25 6.25

Souvenir Sheet

802 A206 $15 multi 6.25 6.25

2007 Cricket World Cup, West Indies — A207

2007 Cricket World Cup emblem, Cricket World Cup and: $1, Batsman. $2, Bowler. $2.50, Bowler, diff. $3.75, Batsman, diff. $4.50, Wicketkeeper.
$15, Cricket World Cup.

2007, Mar. 15 Litho. *Perf. 13*
803-807 A207 Set of 5 5.50 5.50

Souvenir Sheet

Perf. 13½

808 A207 $15 multi 5.50 5.50

No. 808 contains one 27x45mm stamp.

Reopening of Red House, Cent. — A208

Designs: $1, Red House, c. 1907. $2.50, Parliament Chamber. $3.75, Cenotaph and Eternal Flame. $5.25, Rotunda and fountain.
$15, Dome.

2007, Sept. 14 *Perf. 13½x13¼*
809-812 A208 Set of 4 4.50 4.50

Souvenir Sheet

813 A208 $15 multi 5.00 5.00

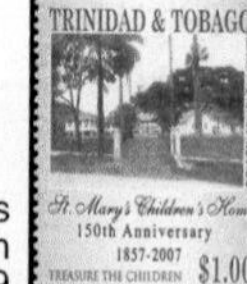

St. Mary's Children's Home, 150th Anniv. — A209

Designs: $1, Main entrance, c. 1930. $2.50, Fountain. $3.75, St. Mary's Anglican Church. $4.50, St. Mary's Children's Home Cub Scout pack.

2007, Sept. 21
814-817 A209 Set of 4 4.00 4.00

Historic Buildings — A210

Designs: $1, Roomor. $2, Killarney. $2.50, Queen's Royal College. $3.25, Hayes Court. $3.75, Knowsley. $4.50, Mille Fleurs. $10, Boissiere House. $20, Archbishop's House. $50, White Hall.

2007, Dec. 14 Litho. *Perf. 13*
818 A210 $1 multi .30 .30
819 A210 $2 multi .90 .65
820 A210 $2.50 multi 1.00 .75
821 A210 $3.25 multi 1.10 1.10
822 A210 $3.75 multi 1.25 1.25
823 A210 $4.50 multi 1.50 1.50
824 A210 $10 multi 3.25 3.25
825 A210 $20 multi 6.50 6.50
826 A210 $50 multi 16.00 16.00
Nos. 818-826 (9) 31.80 31.30

Souvenir Sheet

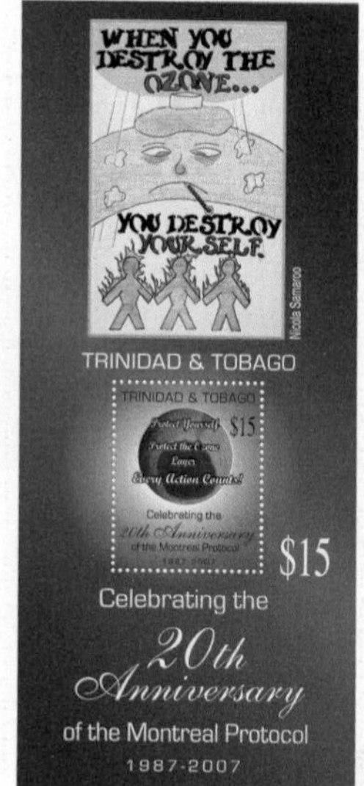

Ozone Layer Protection — A211

2008, Jan. 24 Litho. *Perf. 13x13¼*
827 A211 $15 multi 5.50 5.50

Miniature Sheet

2008 Summer Olympics, Beijing — A212

No. 828: a, Running. b, Table tennis. c, Cycling. d, Swimming.

2008, June 16 ***Perf. 12***
828 A212 $3.50 Sheet of 4, #a-d 5.25 5.25

Scouting, Cent. (in 2007) — A213

Designs: $1, Cub scouts. $2.50, Scouts. $3.75, Venturers. $4.50, Leaders.
$15, Lord Robert Baden-Powell, vert.

2008, July 29 Litho. ***Perf. 13¼x13½***
829-832 A213 Set of 4 4.00 4.00

Souvenir Sheet

Perf. 13½x13¼

833 A213 $15 multi 5.00 5.00

University of the West Indies, 60th Anniv. — A214

Designs: $1, Sir Arthur Lewis, first West Indian principal. $2.50, Princess Alice, Countess of Athlone, first Chancellor. $3.75, Sir Philip Sherlock, first principal of St. Augustine Campus. $4.50, Administration Building, St. Augustine Campus, horiz. $5.25, Samaan tree, St. Augustine Campus, horiz.
$15, Administration Building, St. Augustine Campus, at night.

Perf. 13½x13¼, 13¼x13½

2008, Oct. 3
834-838 A214 Set of 5 5.50 5.50

Souvenir Sheet

839 A214 $15 multi 5.00 5.00

For surcharge, see No. 892.

Worldwide Fund for Nature (WWF) — A215

No. 840 — Brazilian porcupine: a, Adult on branch (shown). b, Head. c, Adult and juvenile. d, Juvenile on branch.

2008, Nov. 3 ***Perf. 13½x13¼***
840 Strip or block of 4 5.00 5.00
a.-d. A215 $3.75 Any single 1.25 1.25
e. Miniature sheet, 2 each #840a-840d 10.00 10.00

Commonwealth Heads of Government Meeting, Port of Spain — A216

Designs: $1, International Finance Center, Waterfront Complex, Port of Spain. $2.50, Steel drums. $3.75, Pigeon Point, Tobago. $4.50, Queen Elizabeth II and Commonwealth Secretaries-General chief Emeka Anyaoku, Kamalesh Sharma, Sir Shridath Ramphal, and Sir Donald McKinnon. $5.25, Scarlet ibis.
$15, Emblem of Commonwealth Heads of Government Meeting.

2009, Nov. 16 ***Perf. 13¼***
841-845 A216 Set of 5 5.50 5.50

Souvenir Sheet

Perf. 14x13¾

846 A216 $15 multi 4.75 4.75
a. As No. 846, with Twelfth Conference of Defense Ministers of the Americas emblem overprinted in sheet margin 4.50 4.50

No. 846 contains one 33x45mm stamp. For surcharges, see Nos. 893, 929.
Issued: No. 846a, 10/10/16.

Souvenir Sheet

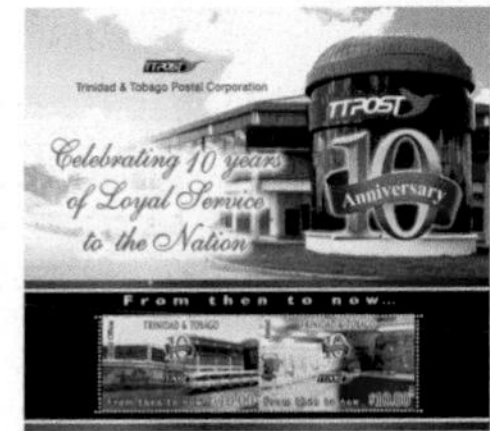
Trinidad & Tobago Postal Corporation, 10th Anniv. — A217

No. 847: a, Head office. b, Retail counter.

Litho. & Embossed

2009, Dec. 18 ***Perf. 13¾x13¼***
847 A217 $10 Sheet of 2, #a-b 6.50 6.50

Miniature Sheets

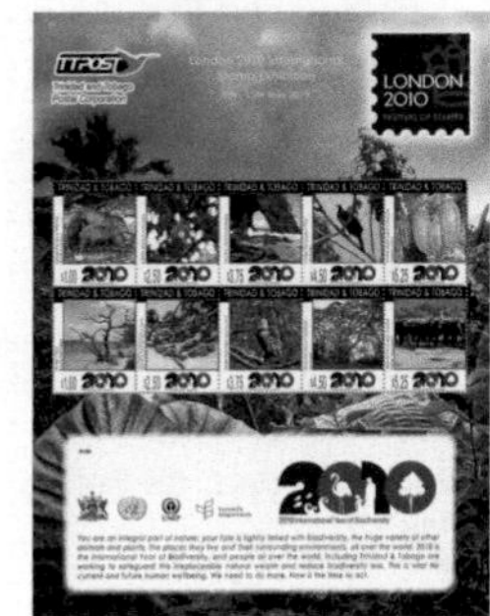
Intl. Year of Biodiversity — A218

No. 848: a, $1, Collared peccary. b, $1, No Man's Land, Bon Accord, Tobago. c, $2.50, Butterfly orchid. d, $2.50, Hot peppers. e, $3.75, Paria Bay, Trinidad. f, $3.75, Ornate hawk eagle. g, $4.50, Trinidad piping-guan. h, $4.50, Royal poinciana tree. i, $5.25, Trinidad select hybrid cocoa pods. j, $5.25, Water buffalos, Aripo Livestock Station.
No. 849: a, $1, Agouti. b, $1, Fishermen at Grafton Beach, Tobago. c, $2.50, Caroni Swamp and Bird Sanctuary, Trinidad. d, $2.50, Red brocket deer. e, $3.75, Turkey vulture. f, $3.75, White-chested emerald hummingbird. g, $4.50, Leatherback turtle. h, $4.50, Nariva Swamp, Trinidad. i, $5.25, Soldado Rock, Gulf of Paria. j, $5.25, Orchid.

2010, May 26 Litho. ***Perf. 13¼x12½***

Sheets of 10, #a-j

848-849 A218 Set of 2 22.50 22.50

London 2010 Festival of Stamps. For surcharges, see Nos. 951-952.

Syrians and Lebanese in Trinidad & Tobago, Cent. — A219

Designs: $1, Rahme Sabga, peddler. $2.50, Kashish, peddler. $3.75, Grand Bazaar Shopping Center. $4.50, Nicholas Tower.
$15, Woman wearing traditional Arab head covering.

2010, July 20 ***Perf. 13¼x13***
850-853 A219 Set of 4 5.50 4.00

Souvenir Sheet

854 A219 $15 multi 6.00 6.00

Trinidad & Tobago Cadet Force, Cent. — A220

Various photographs of cadets: $1, $2.50, $3.75, $4.50, $5.25.
$15, Rifles, Sir George Ruthven Le Hunte, Cadet Force founder, and Pres. George Maxwell Richards.

2010, Dec. 1 ***Perf. 13x13¼***
855-859 A220 Set of 5 6.00 6.00

Souvenir Sheet

860 A220 $15 multi 6.00 6.00

Tobago House of Assembly, 30th Anniv. — A221

Designs: $1, Tobago House of Assembly. $2.50, Englishman's Bay. $3.75, St. Patrick's Anglican Church. $4.50, Fort King George. $5.25, Buccoo Goat Race.
$15, Pigeon Point Heritage Park.

2010, Dec. 4 ***Perf. 13x13¼***
861-865 A221 Set of 5 6.00 6.00

Souvenir Sheet

Perf. 13¼

866 A221 $15 multi 6.00 6.00

Festivities — A222

Designs: $1, Spiritual Baptist Liberation Day. $2.50, Eid ul-Fitr. $3.75, Christmas. $4.50, Diwali.
$15, Parang.

2010, Dec. 10 ***Perf. 13¼x13***
867-870 A222 Set of 4 5.50 5.50

Souvenir Sheet

Perf. 13¼

871 A222 $15 multi 6.00 6.00

Carnival — A223

Designs: $1, Participant in Sky People costume designed by Peter Minshall. $2.50, Children portraying Pierrot Grenade. $3.75, Junior Carnival Queen on Broadway. $4.50, Children's Carnival on Frederick Street. $5.25, Participant in Black Indian Chief costume designed by Larrie Approo.
$15, Participant in Pan Woman costume designed by Wendy Kallicharan.

2011, Mar. 1 ***Perf. 12***
872-876 A223 Set of 5 6.00 6.00

Souvenir Sheet

877 A223 $15 multi 6.00 6.00

Dr. Eric Williams (1911-81), Prime Minister — A224

Designs: $1, Williams with Sir V. S. Naipaul, Michael Anthony, and Andre Deutsch. $1.50, Williams playing cricket with C. L. R. James and Sir Learie Constantine. $2.50, Williams and Kwame Nkrumah. $3.75, Painting of Williams by Georgia M. Cordner. $4.50, Williams with John Lennon and Ringo Starr. $5.25, Williams and Jawaharlal Nehru.
$15, Williams with Sir Winston Churchill.

2011, Apr. 5 Litho. ***Perf. 13¼x13***
878-883 A224 Set of 6 7.00 7.00

Souvenir Sheet

884 A224 $15 multi 6.00 6.00

Independence, 50th Anniv. — A225

Designs: No. 885, $1, Flag of Trinidad & Tobago. No. 886, $1, Arms of colonial and independent Trinidad & Tobago. No. 887, $1, Sir Solomon Hochoy, first Governor-General and Dr. Eric E. Williams, first Prime Minister. No. 888, $1, 50th anniversary emblem, vert.

2012, Aug. 8 ***Perf. 13¼***
885-888 A225 Set of 4 1.40 1.40

No. 515 Surcharged

No. 888A No. 889

Method, Perf. and Watermark As Before

2012 ?
888A A136 $1 on $2.25 #515 — —
889 A136 $1 on $2.25 #515 *3.00* —
a. Inverted surcharge *150.00* —
b. Surcharge with decimal point omitted — —

Issued: No. 889, 4/2/12.

Nos. 604, 765, 838 & 845 Srchd. in Blue

Methods and Perfs As Before

2013, July 4
890 A162 $1 on $5 #604 *2.00 2.00*
891 A197 $1 on $5.25 #765 *2.00 2.00*
892 A214 $1 on $5.25 #838 *2.00 2.00*
893 A216 $1 on $5.25 #845 *2.00 2.00*
Nos. 890-893 (4) 8.00 8.00

The new denomination on Nos. 890-893 obliterates the old denomination.

A226

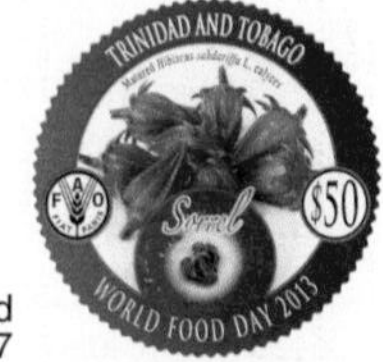
World Food Day — A227

Designs: $1, Sorrel drink. $2.50, Sorrel plant. $3.75, Capsular fruit of Hibiscus sabdariffa. $4.50, Biodiversity of sorrel in Trinidad & Tobago. $5.25, Flower of Hibiscus sabdariffa. $50, Mature Hibiscus sabdariffa calyces.

Perf. 13¾

2013, Dec. 4 Litho. Unwmk.
894 A226 $1 multi .40 .40

Self-Adhesive

Serpentine Die Cut

895 A227 $50 multi *14.00 14.00*

Miniature Sheet

Serpentine Die Cut 12¼

896 Sheet of 5 *8.50*
a. A226 $1 multi .50 .50
b. A226 $2.50 multi 1.00 1.00

c. A226 $3.75 multi 1.40 1.40
d. A226 $4.50 multi 1.60 1.60
e. A226 $5.25 multi 2.00 2.00

Sorrel seeds were placed under a circle of plastic affixed to Nos. 895 and 896a-896e.

No. 516 Surcharged — 897srch

Method, Perf. and Watermark As Before

2013, July

897 A136 $1 on $2.50 #516 *3.50 3.50*
a. Wmk. 373 (on #516a) — —

No. 516 Surcharged

Method and Perf. As Before

2014, Dec. Wmk. 384

898 A136 $1 on $2.50 #516 *2.00 5.00*
a. Wmk. 373 (on #516a) .90 .90
b. As "a," inverted surcharge — —

No. 516 Surcharged

Method, Perf. and Watermark As Before

2014, July

899 A136 $1 on $2.50 #516 *3.50* —
a. Wmk. 373 (on #516a) — —
b. As No. 899a, with two obliterators — —

A228

Designs: $1, Chaconia flower. $3, Henan Luoyang peony. $3.25, Red-crowned crane. $4, Scarlet ibis.

Unwmk.

2014, June 20 Litho. *Perf. 12*

901 A228 $1 multi .30 .30
901A A228 $3 multi .95 .95
b. Souvenir sheet of 2, #901-901A *30.00 30.00*
902 A228 $3.25 multi 1.00 1.00
902A A228 $4 multi 1.25 1.25
b. Souvenir sheet of 2, #902-902A *60.00 60.00*
Nos. 901-902A (4) 3.50 3.50

Diplomatic Relations Between Trinidad & Tobago and People's Republic of China, 40th Anniv.

In 2015, Trinidad & Tobago postal authorities declared as illegal sheets of 6 and 9 stamps depicting Cats, Butterflies and Moths dated 2010 and 2011.

Nos. 144, 145, 401h, 401i and 750 Surcharged in Black or Red

No. 903

No. 904

No. 905

Nos. 906-907

Methods, Perfs and Watermarks As Before

2015-16

903 A41 $1 on 1c #144 .35 .35
904 A41 $1 on 3c #145 — —
905 A195 $2 on 25c #750 .65 .65
906 A108 $3.25 on 95c #401h (dated 1987) (R) — —
907 A108 $3.25 on 95c #401i (dated 1988) (R) 1.00 1.00

Issued: No. 903, 1/7/16; No. 904, 2/25/16. No. 905, 11/30/15, Nos. 906-907, 9/1/15.

Indigenous Banking, Cent. — A229

Emblem of First Citizens Bank and: $1, Trinidad Cooperative Bank, 1914. $2, Workers' Bank and National Commercial Bank, 1970-71. $2.50, First Citizens Bank, 1993.

No. 911 — Emblem of First Citizens Bank and: a, $4, People and bank building. b, $6.50, Men and women on balance. c, $7.50, Automatic teller machine, banking by computer and smartphone.

Perf. 13x13¼ Syncopated

2015, Sept. 16 Litho. Unwmk.

908-910 A229 Set of 3 1.75 1.75

Souvenir Sheet

911 A229 Sheet of 3, #a-c *50.00 50.00*

Souvenir Sheet

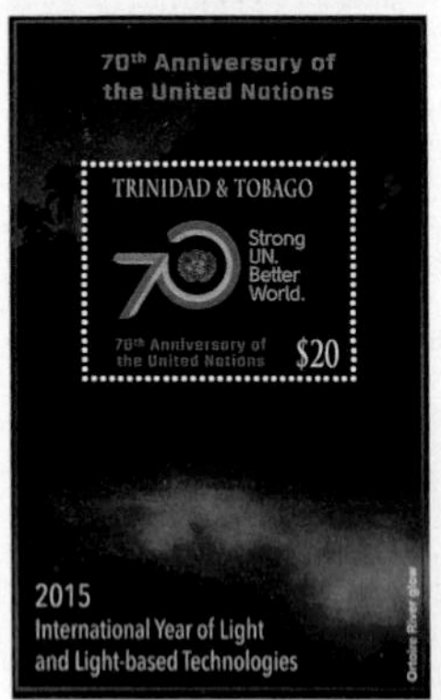

United Nations, 70th Anniv. A230

Litho, Sheet Margin Litho. With Foil Application

2015, Oct. 24 *Perf. 13¼*

912 A230 $20 gold & multi 6.50 6.50

Nos. 647-649 Surcharged

Methods and Perfs. As Before

2016, Oct. 10

913 A173 $1 on $3.75 #647 .30 .30
a. Inverted surcharge — —
914 A173 $1 on $4.50 #648 .30 .30
a. Inverted surcharge — —
915 A173 $1 on $5.25 #649 .30 .30
Nos. 913-915 (3) .90 .90

No. 622 Surcharged

2017 Method and Perf. As Before

916 A166 $1 on 75c #622 .30 .30

No. 624 Surcharged

2017 Method and Perf. As Before

917 A167 $1 on 75c #624 .30 .30

No. 643 Surcharged

Method and Perf. As Before

2017, May 25

918 A172 $1 on $2.50 #643 .30 .30

No. 516a Surcharged

Method, Perf. and Watermark As Before

2017

919 A136 $3 on $2.50 #516a .90 .90

No. 639-641 Surcharged in Silver or Black

No. 920 No. 921

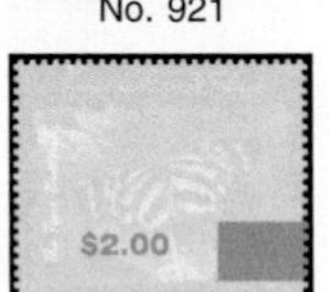

No. 922

2017 Method and Perf. As Before

920 A171 $1 on $4.50 #640 (S) .30 .30
921 A171 $1 on $5.25 #641 .30 .30
922 A171 $2 on $3.75 #639 (S) .60 .60
Nos. 920-922 (3) 1.20 1.20

No. 608 Surcharged

2017 Method and Perf. As Before

923 A163 $1 on $5.25 #608 .30 .30

No. 637 Surcharged

2017 Method and Perf. As Before

924 A170 $1 on $5.25 #637 .30 .30

Nos. 656, 658 Surcharged

No. 925

No. 926

2017 Method and Perf. As Before

925 A176 $1 on $2.50 #656 .30 .30
926 A176 $1 on $5.25 #658 .30 .30

Creole Harvest — A231

No. 927: a, Woman with cocoa knife. b, Mortar and pestle. c, Creole dancers. d, Cocoa house. e, Jar of cocoa. f, Woman carrying cake. g, Creole dancer with dwiyet. h, Man playing bongo drum. i, Man with bamboo kwa-kwa. j, Tapia house.

Serpentine Die Cut14x13½

2018, Jan. 22 Litho. Unwmk.

Self-Adhesive

927 Booklet pane of 10 3.00
a.-j. A231 $1 Any single .30 .30

No. 645 Surcharged in Silver

Method and Perf. As Before

2017, July 28

928 A172 $1 on $3.75 #645 .30 .30

No. 843 Surcharged

Method and Perf. As Before

2018, Aug. 17

929 A216 $1 on $3.75 #843 .30 .30

No. 671 Surcharged

Method and Perf. As Before

2018, Aug. 17

930 A179 $1 on $5.25 #671 .30 .30

Nos. 517a, 614, 629, 664, 683, and 750 Surcharged

No. 931

No. 932

No. 933

No. 934

No. 935

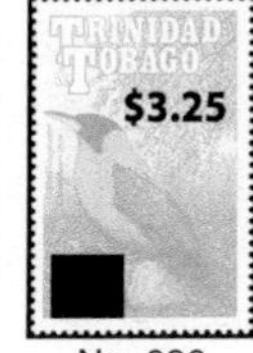
No. 936

Methods, Perfs. and Watermarks As Before

2018

931	A183	50c on $2.50 #683	.30	.25
932	A165	$1 on 75c #614	.30	.30
933	A178	$1 on $2.50 #664	.30	.30
934	A168	$1 on $5.25 #629	.30	.30
935	A195	$2 on 25c #750	.60	.60
936	A136	$3.25 on $5 #517a	1.00	1.00
		Nos. 931-936 (6)	2.80	2.75

Miniature Sheet

Trinidad & Tobago Philatelic Society, 75th Anniv. (in 2017) A232

No. 937: a, $1, Ambulance bought by Red Cross Fund, Trinidad & Tobago #B1 on cover. b, $2, Trinidad & Tobago #52 with Plymouth cancel, old Plymouth Post Office. c, $3.75, Ships in 1797 Battle of Trinidad, sailor's letter describing battle. d, $4.50, Immigrants from India, Indian postal stationery used in Trinidad & Tobago with additional stamps, Trinidad #75 and 91. e, $5.25, Picture postcard from sailor on USS Missouri franked with trinidad #76, and 1907 picture post depicting sailors visiting Trinidad. f, $6.50, Dornier Do X flying boat, 1931 cover flown on Dornier flight.

Unwmk.

2018, Sept. 27 Litho. *Perf. 12*

937 A232 Sheet of 6, #a-f 7.00 7.00

Gas Exporting Countries Forum, 10th Anniv. — A233

Drilling platform, bird, flower and: $1, Marine production facilities. $2, Natural gas transmission system. $3, Point Lisas Industrial Estate. $3.25, Liquid natural gas production and export. $5.25, Bus at compressed natural gas filling station.

2018, Nov. 13 Litho. *Perf. 13x13¼*

938-942 A233 Set of 5 4.25 4.25

Royal Botanic Gardens, Trinidad, 200th Anniv. A234

Flowers: $1, Ixora sp. (59x46mm). $2, Buttercup flower (69x37mm). $3.25, Thunbergia sp. (36x64mm). $4, Flamboyant (55x52mm). $6.50, Croton (64x42mm).
$30, Double chaconia.

2018, Dec. 6 Litho. *Die Cut*

Self-Adhesive

943-947 A234 Set of 5 5.00 5.00

Souvenir Sheet

948 A234 $30 multi 9.00 9.00

No. 948 contains one 65x42mm stamp.

No. 511 Surcharged

Method, Perf. and Watermark As Before

2018

949 A136 $1 on 40c #511 .30 .30
a. Wmk. 373 (# 511a) — —

Diplomatic Relations Between Trinidad & Tobago and People's Republic of China, 45th Anniv. — A235

No. 950: a, Chinese peony. b, Double chaconia. c, West Indian manatee. d, Giant panda. e, Ocelot.

Serpentine Die Cut

2019, June Litho. Unwmk.

Self-Adhesive

950	Sheet of 5	22.50	
a.	A235 $5 multi	1.50	1.50
b.	A235 $10 multi	3.00	3.00
c.	A235 $15 multi	4.50	4.50
d.	A235 $20 multi	6.00	6.00
e.	A235 $25 multi	7.50	7.50

Cut Down Sheets of Nos. 848-849 Surcharged

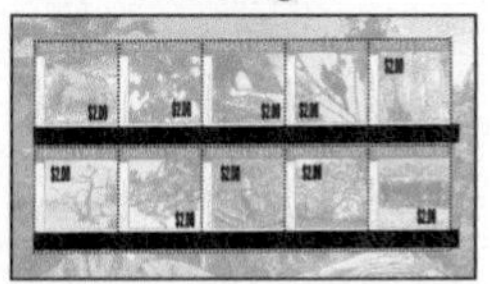

No. 951: a, Collared peccary. b, No Man's Land, Bon Accord, Tobago. c, Butterfly orchid. d, Hot peppers. e, Paria Bay, Trinidad. f, Ornate hawk eagle. g, Trinidad piping-guan. h, Royal poinciana tree. i, Trinidad select hybrid cocoa pods. j, Water buffalos, Aripo Livestock Station.

No. 952: a, Agouti. b, Fishermen at Grafton Beach, Tobago. c, Caroni Swamp and Bird Sanctuary, Trinidad. d, Red brocket deer. e, Turkey vulture. f, White-chested emerald hummingbird. g, Leatherback turtle. h, Nariva Swamp, Trinidad. i, Soldado Rock, Gulf of Paria. j, Orchid.

Methods and Perfs. As Before

2019

951 A218	Cut down sheet of 10 (#848)	6.00	6.00
a.-b.	$2 on $1 either single (#848a-848b)	.60	.60
c.-d.	$2 on $2.50 either single (#848c-848d)	.60	.60
e.-f.	$2 on $3.75 either single (#848e-848f)	.60	.60
g.-h.	$2 on $4.50 either single (#848g-848h)	.60	.60
i.-j.	$2 on $5.25 either single (#848i-848j)	.60	.60
k.	As #951, with inverted surcharge frame	—	—
952 A218	Cut down sheet of 10 (#849)	6.00	6.00
a.-b.	$2 on $1 either single (#849a-849b)	.60	.60
c.-d.	$2 on $2.50 either single (#849c-849d)	.60	.60
e.-f.	$2 on $3.75 either single (#849e-849f)	.60	.60
g.-h.	$2 on $4.50 either single (#849g-849h)	.60	.60
i.-j.	$2 on $5.25 either single (#849i-849j)	.60	.60
k.	As #952, with inverted surcharge frame	—	—

Some stamps on Nos. 951k and 952k lack revised denomination, but all show obliterator bar.

TTPost, 20th Anniv. A236

2019, July 1 Litho. *Perf. 13¼*

953 A236 $1 multi .30 .30

Express Mail Service, 20th Anniv. — A237

2019, Oct. 9 Litho. *Perf. 13½*

954 A237 $1 multi .30 .30

Arrival of East Indians in Trinidad, 175th Anniv. — A238

Designs: $1, East Indian sweets. $6.50, Tassa band. $7.50, East Indian dancers. $8.50, Man cooking on chulha near river. $9, Temple in the Sea.

No. 960: a, Phawga (holi). b, Hosay. c, Divali.

2020, July 1 Litho. *Perf. 13x13¼*

955-959 A238 Set of 5 9.75 9.75

Souvenir Sheet

960 A238 $10 Sheet of 3, #a-c 9.00 9.00

No. 752 Surcharged

2021 Method and Perf. As Before

961 A195 $2 on 75c #752 .60 .60

Landscapes A239

Designs: $1, Batteaux Bay. $2, Galera Point, Toco. $3, Cumana Bay. $3.75, Ricon Waterfalls. $4, Gasparee Caves. $5, Roxborough Beach. $6, Bamboo Cathedral, Chaguaramas. $10, Caroni River Swamp. $15, Parlatuvier Bay. $25, Pitch Lake, La Brea. $30, Argyle Waterfalls. $50, Salt Pond, Chacachacare.

2021, June Litho. *Perf. 13x13¼*

962	A239	$1 multi	.30	.30
963	A239	$2 multi	.60	.60
964	A239	$3 multi	.90	.90
965	A239	$3.75 multi	1.10	1.10
966	A239	$4 multi	1.25	1.25
967	A239	$5 multi	1.50	1.50
968	A239	$6 multi	1.75	1.75
969	A239	$10 multi	3.00	3.00
970	A239	$15 multi	4.50	4.50
971	A239	$25 multi	7.50	7.50
972	A239	$30 multi	9.00	9.00
973	A239	$50 multi	15.00	15.00
		Nos. 962-973 (12)	46.40	46.40

Cuisine of Trinidad & Tobago — A240

No. 974: a, Chicken Pelau. b, Salt fish and provision. c, Roast corn. d, Cow heel soup. e, Crab and dumpling. f, Chicken Roti. g, Shark and bake. h, Black pudding. i, Doubles. j, Sunday lunch.

2021, June Litho. *Die Cut*

Self-Adhesive

974 Booklet pane of 10 3.00
a.-j. A240 $1 Any single .30 .30

Horizontal Pairs of Nos. 650-652 Surcharged

Methods and Perfs. As Before

2021, May 6

975	A174	$1 on $3.75 pair of #650	.30	.30
976	A174	$1 on $4.50 pair of #651	.30	.30
977	A174	$1 on $5.25 pair of #652	.30	.30
		Nos. 975-977 (3)	.90	.90

No. 653 Overprinted

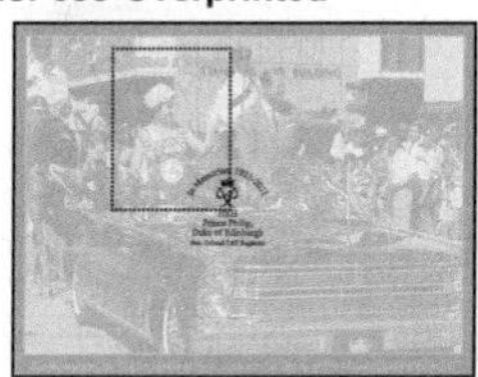

Method and Perf. As Before

2021, May 6

978 A174 $10 on #653 3.00 3.00

Prince Philip (1921-2021).

No. 394a Surcharged

No. 400i Surcharged

Methods, Perfs. and Watermarks As Before

2022, July

979 A108 50c on 15c #394a .30 .30
980 A108 50c on 80c #400i .30 .30

Lady McLeod stamp, 175th anniv. (No. 979), Reign of Queen Elizabeth II, 70th anniv. (No. 980).

KC Candy Company, Cent. — A241

Centenary emblem, QR code and wrapped: $1, Dinner Mint. $2.50, Ginger Mint. $3.75, Red Tongue Pop.

$30, Delivery bicycle, scissors and vessel with grate.

Litho. With Foil Application
Serpentine Die Cut 11½
2022, Nov. 26 Unwmk.
Self-Adhesive

981-983 A241 Set of 3 2.25 2.25

Souvenir Sheet

984 A241 $30 multi 9.00 9.00

Nos. 981-984 have a scratch-and-sniff panel with a mint aroma.

Independence, 60th Anniv. — A242

Diamond jubilee emblem and: $1, Scales of justice, gavel and law books. $2.50, Mortarboard, diploma, school books and apple. $3.75, Medical equipment. $5.25, Fruits and vegetables.

Perf. 11½x11¼
2022, Dec. 6 Litho. Unwmk.

985-988 A242 Set of 4 3.75 3.75

SEMI-POSTAL STAMPS

Emblem of Red Cross — SP1

Perf. 11, 12
1914, Sept. 18 Typo. Unwmk.

B1 SP1 (½p) red (on cover) 250.00

This stamp was allowed to pay ½p postage on one day, Sept. 18, 1914, on circulars distributed by the Red Cross. Value on cover is for proper Red Cross usage. Value unused, $35.

No. 2 Overprinted in Red (Cross) and Black (Date)

a

b

1915, Oct. 21 Wmk. 3 *Perf. 14*

B2 A1 (a) 1p scarlet 4.25 *6.75*

1916, Oct. 19

B3 A1 (b) 1p scarlet 1.00 *2.25*
 a. Date omitted

POSTAGE DUE STAMPS

D1

1923-45 Typo. Wmk. 4 *Perf. 14*

J1 D1 1p black 4.25 *4.25*
J2 D1 2p black 8.75 1.90
J3 D1 3p black ('25) 13.00 *6.50*
J4 D1 4p black ('29) 8.75 *30.00*
J5 D1 5p black ('45) 42.50 *140.00*
J6 D1 6p black ('45) 77.50 55.00
J7 D1 8p black ('45) 52.50 *200.00*
J8 D1 1sh black ('45) 90.00 *160.00*
 Nos. J1-J8 (8) 297.25 597.65

Catalogue values for unused stamps in this section, from this point to the end of the section, are for Never Hinged items.

Denominations in Cents

1947, Sept. 1

J9 D1 2c black 5.50 *8.50*
J10 D1 4c black 2.75 *3.00*
J11 D1 6c black 5.00 *7.50*
J12 D1 8c black 1.25 *42.50*
J13 D1 10c black 3.25 *9.50*
J14 D1 12c black 4.00 *30.00*
J15 D1 16c black 2.00 *57.50*
J16 D1 24c black 13.00 *15.00*
 Nos. J9-J16 (8) 36.75 173.50

Nos. J9-J16 also exist on chalky paper.

Wmk. 4a (error)

J9a D1 2c 60.00
J11a D1 6c 125.00
J14a D1 12c 175.00

D2

1970 Unwmk. Litho. *Perf. 14x13½*
Size: 18x23mm

J17 D2 2c green .25 *2.75*
J18 D2 4c carmine rose .25 *8.50*
J19 D2 6c brown .55 *5.50*
J20 D2 8c lt violet .75 *5.75*
J21 D2 10c brick red 1.10 *6.25*
J22 D2 12c dull orange 1.00 *6.25*
J23 D2 16c brt yellow grn 1.00 *6.75*
J24 D2 24c gray 1.00 *11.00*
J25 D2 50c blue 1.00 *5.00*
J26 D2 60c olive green 1.00 *5.00*
 Nos. J17-J26 (10) 7.90 *62.75*

Perf. 13½x14
1976-77 Litho. Unwmk.
Size: 17x21mm

J27 D2 2c green .25 *2.00*
J28 D2 4c carmine rose .25 *1.50*
J29 D2 6c brown .25 *2.40*
J30 D2 8c lt violet .30 *2.40*
J31 D2 10c brick red .30 *1.75*
J32 D2 12c dull orange .50 *2.00*
 Nos. J27-J32 (6) 1.85 *12.05*

Issued: 4c, 12c, 4/1/76; 2c, 6c, 8c, 10, 1977.

The letters in the top label on Nos. J27-J32 are larger with D's and O's more squarish than the oval letters on Nos. J17-J26. "Postage Due" is 13mm long and is composed of finer letters than on Nos. J17-J26, which have a 14mm inscription.

WAR TAX STAMPS

Nos. 1-2 Overprinted

1917 Wmk. 3 *Perf. 14*

MR1 A1 1p scarlet 6.00 3.75
 a. Invtd. overprint 250.00 *300.00*

Overprinted

MR2 A1 ½p green 2.00 .40
 a. Overprinted on face and back 425.00
 b. Pair, one without overprint *1,000.* *1,650.*
MR3 A1 1p scarlet 5.50 *2.25*
 a. Pair, one without overprint *1,000.* *1,750.*
 b. Double overprint 175.00

Overprinted

MR4 A1 ½p green 2.00 *19.00*
MR5 A1 1p scarlet .90 *.90*
 a. Pair, one without overprint

Overprinted

MR6 A1 ½p green .30 *5.00*
MR7 A1 1p scarlet 10.00 1.00

Overprinted

MR8 A1 ½p green 1.00 *3.25*
MR9 A1 1p scarlet 80.00 67.50

Overprinted

MR10 A1 1p scarlet 1.00 *1.00*
 a. Inverted overprint 175.00 *175.00*

Overprinted

MR11 A1 1p scarlet 2.50 .25
 a. Double overprint 250.00 *250.00*
 b. Inverted overprint 160.00 *175.00*

Overprinted

1918

MR12 A1 ½p green 1.00 *4.00*
 a. Pair, one without overprint 1,750.
MR13 A1 1p scarlet .90 .60
 a. Double overprint 175.00
 b. Horiz. pair, one without overprint *2,000.*

The War Tax Stamps show considerable variations in the colors, thickness of the paper, distinctness of the watermark, and the gum. Counterfeits exist of the errors of Nos. MR1-MR13.

OFFICIAL STAMPS

Regular Issue of 1913 Overprinted

1913 Wmk. 3 *Perf. 14*

O1 A1 ½p green 2.90 *20.00*

Same Overprinted

1914

O2 A1 ½p green 6.25 *27.50*

Same Overprinted

1916

O3 A1 ½p green 6.75 *11.50*
 a. Double overprint 57.50

Same Overprint without Period

1917

O4 A1 ½p green 1.30 *11.50*

Same Overprinted

1917, Aug. 22

O5 A1 ½p green 3.40 *33.50*

The official stamps are found in several shades of green and on paper of varying thickness.

TRIPOLITANIA

tri-,pä-lə-'tā-nyə

LOCATION — In northern Africa, bordering on Mediterranean Sea
GOVT. — A former Italian Colony
AREA — 350,000 sq. mi. (approx.)
POP. — 570,716 (1921)
CAPITAL — Tripoli

Formerly a Turkish province, Tripolitania became part of Italian Libya. See Libya.

100 Centesimi = 1 Lira

Used values in italics are for postally used stamps. CTO's or stamps with fake cancels sell for about the same as unused, hinged stamps.

Watermark

Wmk. 140 — Crowns

Propagation of the Faith Issue
Italian Stamps Overprinted

1923, Oct. 24 Wmk. 140 *Perf. 14*

1 A68 20c ol grn & brn org 9.00 *40.00*
2 A68 30c claret & brn org 9.00 *40.00*
 a. Double overprint 2,000.
 b. Vert. pair, imperf. btwn and at bottom 1,000. 1,400.
3 A68 50c vio & brn org 6.00 *45.00*
4 A68 1 l blue & brn org 6.00 *70.00*
 Nos. 1-4 (4) 30.00 *195.00*
 Set, never hinged 75.00

Fascisti Issue

Italian Stamps Overprinted in Red or Black

1923, Oct. 29 Unwmk.

5 A69 10c dk green (R) 12.00 *15.00*
6 A69 30c dk violet (R) 12.00 *15.00*
7 A69 50c brown car 12.00 *15.00*

Wmk. 140

8 A70 1 l blue 12.00 *40.00*
9 A70 2 l brown 12.00 *50.00*
 a. Double overprint 1,350.
10 A71 5 l blk & bl (R) 12.00 *72.50*
 Nos. 5-10 (6) 72.00 *207.50*
 Set, never hinged 180.00

Manzoni Issue

Stamps of Italy, 1923, Overprinted in Red

1924, Apr. 1 Wmk. 140 *Perf. 14*

11 A72 10c brown red & blk 9.75 *60.00*
12 A72 15c blue grn & blk 9.75 *60.00*
13 A72 30c black & slate 9.75 *60.00*
 a. Imperf. —

14 A72 50c org brn & blk 9.75 *60.00*
15 A72 1 l blue & blk 60.00 *350.00*
16 A72 5 l violet & blk 400.00 *2,400.*
Nos. 11-16 (6) 499.00 *2,990.*
Set, never hinged 1,250.

On Nos. 15 and 16 the overprint is placed vertically at the left side.

Victor Emmanuel Issue

Italy Nos. 175-177 Overprinted

1925-26 Unwmk. *Perf. 11*
17 A78 60c brown car 1.75 *11.00*
18 A78 1 l dark blue 2.40 *11.00*
a. Perf. 13½ 8.50 *34.00*

Perf. 13½
19 A78 1.25 l dk bl ('26) 3.00 *30.00*
a. Perf. 11 1,600. *2,100.*
Nos. 17-19 (3) 7.15 *52.00*
Set, #17-19, 18a, 19a, never hinged 3,200.

Saint Francis of Assisi Issue

Italy Nos. 178-180 Overprinted

1926, Apr. 12 Wmk. 140 *Perf. 14*
20 A79 20c gray green 1.75 *11.00*
a. Vert. pair, one without ovpt. *4,250.*
21 A80 40c dark violet 1.75 *11.00*
22 A81 60c red brown 1.75 *21.00*

Italy No. 182 and Type of A83 Overprinted in Red

Unwmk.
23 A82 1.25 l dark blue 1.75 *28.00*
24 A83 5 l + 2.50 l ol grn 6.00 *55.00*
a. Horiz. pair, imperf. btwn. *1,800.*
Nos. 20-24 (5) 13.00 *126.00*
Set, never hinged 20.00

Volta Issue

Type of Italy Overprinted

1927, Oct. 10 Wmk. 140 *Perf. 14*
25 A84 20c purple 3.75 *30.00*
26 A84 50c deep orange 6.00 *21.00*
a. Double overprint 155.00
27 A84 1.25 l brt blue 11.00 *50.00*
Nos. 25-27 (3) 20.75 *101.00*
Set, never hinged 50.00

Monte Cassino Issue

Types of Italy Overprinted in Red or Blue

1929, Oct. 14
28 A96 20c dk green (R) 5.00 *17.00*
29 A96 25c red org (Bl) 5.00 *17.00*
30 A98 50c + 10c crim (Bl) 5.00 *18.00*
31 A98 75c + 15c ol brn (R) 5.00 *18.00*
32 A96 1.25 l + 25c dk vio (R) 11.00 *34.00*
33 A98 5 l + 1 l saph (R) 11.00 *35.00*

Overprinted in Red

Unwmk.
34 A100 10 l + 2 l gray brn 11.00 *55.00*
Nos. 28-34 (7) 53.00 *194.00*
Set, never hinged 130.00

Royal Wedding Issue

Type of Italy Overprinted

1930, Mar. 17 Wmk. 140
35 A101 20c yellow green 2.40 *7.25*
36 A101 50c + 10c dp org 1.75 *7.25*
37 A101 1.25 l + 25c rose red 1.75 *14.50*
Nos. 35-37 (3) 5.90 *29.00*
Set, never hinged 15.50

Ferrucci Issue

Types of Italy Overprinted in Red or Blue

1930, July 26
38 A102 20c violet (R) 5.00 *5.00*
39 A103 25c dk green (R) 5.00 *5.00*
40 A103 50c black (R) 5.00 *9.00*
41 A103 1.25 l dp bl (R) 5.00 *17.00*
42 A104 5 l + 2 l dp car (Bl) 11.00 *35.00*
Nos. 38-42,C1-C3 (8) 60.50 157.00
Set, never hinged 145.00

Virgil Issue

Types of Italy Overprinted in Red or Blue

1930, Dec. 4 Photo.
43 A106 15c violet black .90 *9.25*
44 A106 20c orange brown .90 *3.75*
45 A106 25c dark green .90 *3.75*
46 A106 30c lt brown .90 *3.75*
47 A106 50c dull violet .90 *3.75*
48 A106 75c rose red .90 *7.25*
49 A106 1.25 l gray blue .90 *9.25*

Unwmk.
Engr.
50 A106 5 l + 1.50 l dk vio 3.75 *35.00*
51 A106 10 l + 2.50 l ol brn 3.75 *55.00*
Nos. 43-51,C4-C7 (13) 30.80 250.25
Set, never hinged 72.50

Saint Anthony of Padua Issue

Types of Italy Overprinted in Blue or Red

1931, May 7 Photo. Wmk. 140
52 A116 20c brown (Bl) 1.20 *17.00*
53 A116 25c green (R) 1.20 *6.00*
54 A118 30c gray brn (Bl) 1.20 *6.00*
55 A118 50c dull vio (Bl) 1.20 *6.00*
56 A120 1.25 l slate bl (R) 1.20 *30.00*

Overprinted in Red or Black

Unwmk. Engr.
57 A121 75c black (R) 1.20 *17.00*
58 A122 5 l + 2.50 l dk brn (Bk) 8.50 *60.00*
Nos. 52-58 (7) 15.70 *142.00*
Set, never hinged 40.00

Native Village Scene — A14

1934, Oct. 16 Wmk. 140
73 A14 5c ol grn & brn 4.25 *17.00*
74 A14 10c brown & black 4.25 *17.00*
75 A14 20c scar & indigo 4.25 *15.50*
76 A14 50c pur & brn 4.25 *15.50*
77 A14 60c org brn & ind 4.25 *21.00*
78 A14 1.25 l dk bl & grn 4.25 *35.00*
Nos. 73-78,C43-C48 (12) 51.00 242.00
Set, never hinged 125.00

2nd Colonial Arts Exhibition, Naples.

SEMI-POSTAL STAMPS

Many issues of Italy and Italian Colonies include one or more semipostal denominations. To avoid splitting sets, these issues are generally listed as regular postage, airmail, etc., unless all values carry a surtax.

Holy Year Issue

Italian Stamps of 1924 Overprinted in Black or Red

1925 Wmk. 140 *Perf. 12*
B1 SP4 20c+ 10c dk grn & brn 3.00 *18.00*
B2 SP4 30c+ 15c dk brn & brn 3.00 *19.50*
B3 SP4 50c+ 25c vio & brn 3.00 *18.00*
B4 SP4 60c+ 30c dp rose & brn 3.00 *24.00*
B5 SP8 1 l + 50c dp bl & vio (R) 3.00 *30.00*
B6 SP8 5 l + 2.50 l org brn & vio (R) 3.00 *47.50*
Nos. B1-B6 (6) 18.00 *157.00*
Set, never hinged 45.00

Colonial Institute Issue

Peace Substituting Spade for Sword — SP1

1926, June 1 Typo. *Perf. 14*
B7 SP1 5c + 5c brown .90 *7.75*
B8 SP1 10c + 5c ol brn .90 *7.75*
B9 SP1 20c + 5c bl grn .90 *7.75*
B10 SP1 40c + 5c brn red .90 *7.75*
B11 SP1 60c + 5c orange .90 *7.75*
B12 SP1 1 l + 5c blue .90 *16.00*
Nos. B7-B12 (6) 5.40 *54.75*
Set, never hinged 13.50

The surtax was for the Italian Colonial Institute.

> Fiera Campionaria Tripoli
> See Libya for stamps with this inscription.

Types of Italian Semi-Postal Stamps of 1926 Overprinted like Nos. 17-19

1927, Apr. 21 Unwmk. *Perf. 11*
B19 SP10 40c + 20c dk brn & blk 3.00 *32.00*
B20 SP10 60c + 30c brn red & ol brn 3.00 *32.00*
B21 SP10 1.25 l + 60c dp bl & blk 3.00 *50.00*
B22 SP10 5 l + 2.50 l dk grn & blk 5.00 *75.00*
Nos. B19-B22 (4) 14.00 *189.00*
Set, never hinged 34.00

The surtax was for the charitable work of the Voluntary Militia for Italian National Defense.

Allegory of Fascism and Victory — SP2

1928, Oct. 15 Wmk. 140
B29 SP2 20c + 5c bl grn 2.60 *11.00*
B30 SP2 30c + 5c red 2.60 *11.00*
B31 SP2 50c + 10c pur 2.60 *18.00*
B32 SP2 1.25 l + 20c dk bl 3.25 *24.00*
Nos. B29-B32 (4) 11.05 *64.00*
Set, never hinged 26.00

46th anniv. of the Societa Africana d'Italia. The surtax aided that society.

Types of Italian Semi-Postal Stamps of 1928 Ovptd.

1929, Mar. 4 Unwmk. *Perf. 11*
B33 SP10 30c + 10c red & blk 3.75 *21.00*
B34 SP10 50c + 20c vio & blk 3.75 *22.50*
B35 SP10 1.25 l + 50c brn & bl 5.50 *40.00*
B36 SP10 5 l + 2 l ol grn & blk 5.50 *80.00*
Nos. B33-B36 (4) 18.50 *163.50*
Set, never hinged 45.00

The surtax on these stamps was for the charitable work of the Voluntary Militia for Italian National Defense.

Types of Italian Semi-Postal Stamps of 1926, Overprinted in Black or Red Like Nos. B33-B36

1930, Oct. 20
B50 SP10 30c + 10c dp grn & bl grn (Bk) 28.00 *42.50*
B51 SP10 50c + 10c dk grn & vio (R) 28.00 *80.00*
B52 SP10 1.25 l + 30c blk brn & red brn (R) 28.00 *80.00*
B53 SP10 5 l + 1.50 l ind & grn (R) 90.00 *210.00*
Nos. B50-B53 (4) 174.00 *412.50*
Set, never hinged 425.00

Ancient Arch — SP3

1930, Nov. 27 Photo. Wmk. 140
B54 SP3 50c + 20c ol brn 3.00 *19.50*
B55 SP3 1.25 l + 20c dp bl 3.00 *19.50*
B56 SP3 1.75 l + 20c green 3.00 *26.00*
B57 SP3 2.55 l + 50c purple 7.25 *35.00*
B58 SP3 5 l + 1 l deep car 7.25 *75.00*
Nos. B54-B58 (5) 23.50 *175.00*
Set, never hinged 60.00

25th anniv. of the Italian Colonial Agricultural Institute. The surtax was for the benefit of that institution.

AIR POST STAMPS

Ferrucci Issue

Type of Italian Air Post Stamps Overprinted in Blue or Red like #38-42

1930, July 26 Wmk. 140 *Perf. 14*
C1 AP7 50c brown vio (Bl) 5.00 *11.00*
C2 AP7 1 l dk blue (R) 5.00 *15.00*
C3 AP7 5 l + 2 l dp car (Bl) 19.50 *60.00*
Nos. C1-C3 (3) 29.50 *86.00*
Set, never hinged 72.50

Virgil Issue

Types of Italian Air Post Stamps Overprinted in Red or Blue like #43-51

1930, Dec. 4 Photo.
C4 AP8 50c deep green 1.75 *9.75*
C5 AP8 1 l rose red 1.75 *9.75*

Unwmk.

Engr.

No.	Type	Description	Unused	Used
C6	AP8	7.70 l + 1.30 l dk brn	6.75	50.00
C7	AP8	9 l + 2 l gray	6.75	50.00
		Nos. C4-C7 (4)	17.00	119.50
		Set, never hinged	40.00	

Airplane over Columns of the Basilica, Leptis AP1

Arab Horseman Pointing at Airplane AP2

1931-32 Photo. Wmk. 140

No.	Type	Description	Unused	Used
C8	AP1	50c rose car	.60	.25
C9	AP1	60c red org	1.75	8.50
C10	AP1	75c dp bl ('32)	1.75	7.25
C11	AP1	80c dull violet	9.75	13.50
C12	AP2	1 l deep blue	1.20	.25
C13	AP2	1.20 l dk brown	24.00	18.00
C14	AP2	1.50 l org red	11.00	18.00
C15	AP2	5 l green	28.00	28.00
		Nos. C8-C15 (8)	78.05	93.75
		Set, never hinged	170.00	

For surcharges and overprint see Nos. C29-C32.

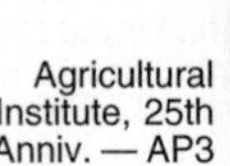

Agricultural Institute, 25th Anniv. — AP3

1931, Dec. 7

No.	Type	Description	Unused	Used
C16	AP3	50c dp blue	2.40	19.50
C17	AP3	80c violet	2.40	19.50
C18	AP3	1 l gray black	2.40	28.00
C19	AP3	2 l deep green	7.25	35.00
C20	AP3	5 l + 2 l rose red	11.00	75.00
		Nos. C16-C20 (5)	25.45	177.00
		Set, never hinged	65.00	

Graf Zeppelin Issue

Mercury, by Giovanni da Bologna, and Zeppelin — AP4

Designs: 3 l, 12 l, Mercury. 10 l, 20 l, Guido Reni's "Aurora." 5 l, 15 l, Arch of Marcus Aurelius.

1933, May 5

No.	Type	Description	Unused	Used
C21	AP4	3 l dark brown	9.75	97.50
C22	AP4	5 l purple	9.75	97.50
C23	AP4	10 l deep green	9.75	180.00
C24	AP4	12 l deep blue	9.75	190.00
C25	AP4	15 l carmine	9.75	210.00
C26	AP4	20 l gray black	9.75	280.00
		Nos. C21-C26 (6)	58.50	1,055.
		Set, never hinged	145.00	

For overprints and surcharges see Nos. C38-C42.

North Atlantic Flight Issue

Airplane, Lion of St. Mark — AP7

1933, June 1

No.	Type	Description	Unused	Used
C27	AP7	19.75 l blk & ol brn	16.00	525.00
C28	AP7	44.75 l dk bl & lt grn	16.00	525.00
		Set, never hinged	77.50	

Type of 1931 Ovptd. or Srchd.

1934, Jan. 20

No.	Type	Description	Unused	Used
C29	AP2	2 l on 5 l org brn	3.75	72.50
C30	AP2	3 l on 5 l grn	3.75	72.50
C31	AP2	5 l ocher	3.75	85.00
C32	AP2	10 l on 5 l rose	5.00	85.00
		Nos. C29-C32 (4)	16.25	315.00
		Set, never hinged	42.50	

For use on mail to be carried on a special flight from Rome to Buenos Aires.

Types of Libya Airmail Issue Overprinted in Black or Red

1934, May 1 Wmk. 140

No.	Type	Description	Unused	Used
C38	AP4	50c rose red	11.00	130.00
C39	AP4	75c lemon	11.00	130.00
C40	AP4	5 l + 1 l brn	11.00	130.00
C41	AP4	10 l + 2 l dk bl	190.00	700.00
C42	AP5	25 l + 3 l pur	190.00	700.00
		Nos. C38-C42,CE1-CE2 (7)	435.00	2,050.
		Set, never hinged	1,050.	

"Circuit of the Oases."

Plane Shadow on Desert — AP11

Designs: 25c, 50c, 75c, Plane shadow on desert. 80c, 1 l, 2 l, Camel corps.

1934, Oct. 16 Photo.

No.	Type	Description	Unused	Used
C43	AP11	25c sl bl & org red	4.25	17.00
C44	AP11	50c dk grn & ind	4.25	15.50
C45	AP11	75c dk brn & org red	4.25	15.50
C46	AP11	80c org brn & ol grn	4.25	17.00
C47	AP11	1 l scar & ol grn	4.25	21.00
C48	AP11	2 l dk bl & brn	4.25	35.00
		Nos. C43-C48 (6)	25.50	121.00
		Set, never hinged	62.50	

Second Colonial Arts Exhibition, Naples.

AIR POST SEMI-POSTAL STAMPS

King Victor Emmanuel III — SPAP1

1934, Nov. 5 Wmk. 140 *Perf. 14*

No.	Type	Description	Unused	Used
CB1	SPAP1	25c + 10c gray grn	7.25	20.00
CB2	SPAP1	50c + 10c brn	7.25	20.00
CB3	SPAP1	75c + 15c rose red	7.25	20.00
CB4	SPAP1	80c + 15c blk brn	7.25	20.00
CB5	SPAP1	1 l + 20c red brn	7.25	20.00
CB6	SPAP1	2 l + 20c brt bl	7.25	20.00
CB7	SPAP1	3 l + 25c pur	20.00	100.00
CB8	SPAP1	5 l + 25c org	20.00	100.00
CB9	SPAP1	10 l + 30c rose vio	20.00	100.00
CB10	SPAP1	25 l + 2 l dp grn	20.00	100.00
		Nos. CB1-CB10 (10)	123.50	520.00
		Set, never hinged	390.00	

65th birthday of King Victor Emmanuel III; non-stop flight from Rome to Mogadiscio.

For overprint see No. CBO1.

AIR POST SEMI-POSTAL OFFICIAL STAMP

Type of Air Post Semi-Postal Stamps Ovptd. Crown and "SERVIZIO DI STATO" in Black

1934 Wmk. 140 *Perf. 14*

No.	Type	Description	Unused	Used
CBO1	SPAP1	25 l + 2 l cop red	1,950.	4,800.
		Never hinged	3,900.	

AIR POST SPECIAL DELIVERY STAMPS

Type of Libya Overprinted in Black Like Nos. C38-C42

1934, May 1 Wmk. 140 *Perf. 14*

No.	Type	Description	Unused	Used
CE1	APSD1	2.25 l red orange	11.00	130.00
CE2	APSD1	4.50 l + 1 l dp rose	11.00	130.00
		Set, never hinged	52.00	

AUTHORIZED DELIVERY STAMP

Authorized Delivery Stamp of Italy 1930, Overprinted like Nos. 38-42

1931, Mar. Wmk. 140 *Perf. 14*

No.	Type	Description	Unused	Used
EY1	AD2	10c reddish brown	15.00	36.00
		Never hinged	36.00	

TRISTAN DA CUNHA

ˌtris-tən-də-ˈkü-nə

LOCATION — Group of islands in the south Atlantic Ocean midway between the Cape of Good Hope and South America

GOVT. — A dependency of St. Helena

AREA — 40 sq. mi.

POP. — 313 (1988)

12 Pence = 1 Shilling
100 Cents = 1 Rand (1961)
12 Pence = 1 Shilling (1963)
20 Shillings = 1 Pound
100 Pence = 1 Pound (1971)

Catalogue values for all unused stamps in this country are for Never Hinged items.

Stamps of St. Helena, 1938-49, Overprinted in Black

1952, Jan. 1 Wmk. 4 *Perf. 12½*

No.	Type	Description	Unused	Used
1	A24	½p purple	.25	2.75
2	A24	1p blue grn & blk	1.00	1.50
3	A24	1½p car rose & blk	1.00	1.50
4	A24	2p carmine & blk	1.00	1.50
5	A24	3p gray	1.25	1.50
6	A24	4p ultra	6.50	2.50
7	A24	6p gray blue	6.50	2.50
8	A24	8p olive	6.50	7.50
9	A24	1sh sepia	5.50	2.00
10	A24	2sh6p deep claret	18.00	16.00
11	A24	5sh brown	30.00	20.00
12	A24	10sh violet	45.00	32.50
		Nos. 1-12 (12)	122.50	91.75
		Set, hinged	85.00	

Common Design Types pictured following the introduction.

Coronation Issue

Common Design Type

1953, June 2 Engr. *Perf. 13½x13*

No.	Type	Description	Unused	Used
13	CD312	3p dk green & black	1.00	1.75

Tristan Crayfish A1

Carting Flax A2

Designs: 1½p, Rockhopper penguin. 2p, Factory. 2½p, Mollymauk. 3p, Island boat. 4p, View of Tristan. 5p, Potato patches. 6p, Inaccessible Island. 9p, Nightingale Island. 1sh, St. Mary's Church. 2sh 6p, Elephant seal. 5sh, Flightless rail. 10sh, Island spinning wheel.

1954-58 *Perf. 12½*

No.	Type	Description	Unused	Used
14	A1	½p choc & red	.25	.25
a.		Bklt. pane of 4 ('58)	2.50	
15	A2	1p green & choc	.25	.60
a.		Bklt. pane of 4 ('58)	4.00	
16	A1	1½p dp plum & blk	2.00	1.40
a.		Bklt. pane of 4 ('58)	7.00	
17	A2	2p org & vio blue	.35	.25
18	A2	2½p carmine & blk	1.75	.70
19	A1	3p ol grn & ultra	.80	1.40
a.		Bklt. pane of 4 ('58)	10.50	
20	A2	4p dp bl & aqua	.80	.75
a.		Bklt. pane of 4 ('58)	13.00	
21	A2	5p gray & bl grn	.80	.75
22	A2	6p vio & dk ol grn	.80	.75
23	A2	9p henna brn & rose lil	.80	.45
24	A2	1sh choc & ol grn	.80	.45
25	A2	2sh6p blue & choc	17.50	10.00
26	A2	5sh red org & blk	47.50	15.00
27	A2	10sh red vio & org	22.50	14.00
		Nos. 14-27 (14)	96.90	46.75
		Set, hinged	57.50	

Starfish — A3

Fish: 1p, Concha. 1½p, Klipfish. 2p, Heron fish (saury). 2½p, Snipefish ("swordfish"). 3d, Tristan crawfish. 4p, Soldier fish. 5p, Five finger fish. 6p, Mackeral scad. 9p, Stumpnose. 1sh, Bluefish. 2sh6p, Snoek (snake mackerel). 5sh, Shark. 10sh, Atlantic right whale.

Perf. 12½x13

1960, Feb. 1 Engr. Wmk. 314

No.	Type	Description	Unused	Used
28	A3	½p org & blk	.25	.25
a.		Booklet pane of 4	1.50	
29	A3	1p rose lil & blk	.25	.25
a.		Booklet pane of 4	2.50	
30	A3	1½p grnsh bl & blk	.30	.25
a.		Booklet pane of 4	2.60	
31	A3	2p green & black	.40	.35
32	A3	2½p brown & black	.45	.35
33	A3	3p rose red & blk	1.20	1.40
a.		Booklet pane of 4	7.25	
34	A3	4p gray ol & blk	1.10	.65
a.		Booklet pane of 4	6.50	
35	A3	5p org yel & blk	1.40	.70
36	A3	6p blue & black	1.40	.80
37	A3	9p rose car & blk	1.60	.70
38	A3	1sh brn org & blk	2.40	.60
39	A3	2sh6p vio blue & blk	11.00	11.00
40	A3	5sh emerald & blk	12.00	12.00
41	A3	10sh violet & blk	42.50	30.00
		Nos. 28-41 (14)	76.25	59.30

1961, Apr. 15 *Perf. 12½x13*

No.	Type	Description	Unused	Used
42	A3	½c like No. 28	.25	.25
43	A3	1c like No. 29	.25	.25
44	A3	1½c like No. 30	.40	.40
45	A3	2c like No. 32	.75	.75
46	A3	2½c like No. 33	1.00	1.10
47	A3	3c like No. 34	1.00	1.10
48	A3	4c like No. 35	1.25	1.25
49	A3	5c like No. 36	1.25	1.25
50	A3	7½c like No. 37	1.25	1.25
51	A3	10c like No. 38	1.60	1.60
52	A3	25c like No. 39	7.00	7.00
53	A3	50c like No. 40	16.00	17.00
54	A3	1r like No. 41	37.50	35.00
		Nos. 42-54 (13)	69.50	68.20

Nos. 46, 49-51 surcharged for "Tristan Relief" are listed as St. Helena Nos. B1-B4.

Types of St. Helena, 1961 Overprinted

Perf. 11½x12, 12x11½

1963, Apr. 12 Photo. Wmk. 4

No.	Type	Description	Unused	Used
55	A29	1p rose, ultra, yel & grn	.25	1.00
56	A29	1½p bis, sep, yel & grn	.25	.40
57	A29	2p gray & red	.25	1.00
58	A30	3p dk bl, rose & grnsh bl	.30	1.00
a.		Double overprint		
59	A29	4½p slate, brn & grn	.55	.70
60	A29	6p cit, brn & dp car	.80	.40
61	A29	7p vio, blk & red brn	.55	.40
62	A29	10p bl & dp claret	.55	.40
63	A29	1sh red brn, grn & yel	.55	.40
64	A29	1sh6p gray bl & blk	5.00	1.10
65	A29	2sh6p grnsh bl, yel & red	1.25	.75
66	A29	5sh grn, brn & yel	5.00	1.25
67	A29	10sh gray bl, blk & sal	6.00	1.25
		Nos. 55-67 (13)	21.30	10.05

Freedom from Hunger Issue

Common Design Type

Perf. 14x14½

1963, Oct. 2 Photo. Wmk. 314

No.	Type	Description	Unused	Used
68	CD314	1sh6p rose carmine	.75	.35

Red Cross Centenary Issue

Common Design Type

1964, Jan. 2 Litho. *Perf. 13*

No.	Type	Description	Unused	Used
69	CD315	3p black & red	.40	.30
70	CD315	1sh6p ultra & red	.75	.50

Flagship of Tristáo da Cunha, 1506 A4

Queen Elizabeth II A5

½p, Map of South Atlantic Ocean. 1½p, Dutch ship Heemstede, first landing, 1643. 2p, New England whaler. 3p, Confederate ship Shenandoah. 4½p, H.M.S. Galatea, 1867. 6p, H.M.S. Cilicia, 1942. 7p, H.M. Royal Yacht Britannia, 1957. 10p, H.M.S. Leopard, Evacuation, 1961. 1sh, Dutch ship Tjisadane, 1961. 1sh6p, M.V. Tristania. 2sh6p, M.V. Boissevain, returning islanders, 1963. 5sh, M.S. Bornholm, returning islanders, 1963.

Perf. 11x11½

1965, Feb. 17 Engr. Wmk. 314

No.	Type	Description	Unused	Used
71	A4	½p black & dk blue	.25	.25
a.		Booklet pane of 4	.25	
72	A4	1p black & emerald	.85	.25
a.		Booklet pane of 4	4.25	
73	A4	1½p black & ultra	.85	.25
a.		Booklet pane of 4	4.25	
74	A4	2p black & lilac	.85	.25
75	A4	3p blk & grnsh bl	.85	.25
a.		Booklet pane of 4	4.25	
76	A4	4½p black & brown	.85	.25
77	A4	6p black & green	.70	.30
a.		Booklet pane of 4	4.25	
78	A4	7p black & ver	.85	.40
79	A4	10p black & dk brn	.85	.40
80	A4	1sh black & lil rose	.85	.50
81	A4	1sh6p black & olive	7.00	2.75
82	A4	2sh6p black & brn org	3.00	3.00
83	A4	5sh black & violet	9.00	8.00

Perf. 11½x11

No.	Type	Description	Unused	Used
84	A5	10sh lil rose & dk bl	1.75	1.50
		Nos. 71-84 (14)	28.50	18.35

See Nos. 113-115. For surcharges see Nos. 108, 141-152. For overprints see Nos. 132.

ITU Issue

Common Design Type

1965, May 11 Litho. *Perf. 11x11½*

No.	Type	Description	Unused	Used
85	CD317	3p vermilion & gray	.40	.25
86	CD317	6p purple & orange	.60	.40

Intl. Cooperation Year Issue

Common Design Type

1965, Oct. 25 Wmk. 314 *Perf. 14½*

No.	Type	Description	Unused	Used
87	CD318	1p blue grn & claret	.25	.25
88	CD318	6p lt violet & green	.80	.40

Churchill Memorial Issue

Common Design Type

Wmk. 314

1966, Jan. 24 Photo. *Perf. 14*

Design in Black, Gold and Carmine Rose

No.	Type	Description	Unused	Used
89	CD319	1p bright blue	.25	.25
90	CD319	3p green	.35	.25
91	CD319	6p brown	1.35	.70
92	CD319	1sh6p violet	4.00	1.50
		Nos. 89-92 (4)	5.95	2.70

World Cup Soccer Issue

Common Design Type

1966 Litho. *Perf. 14*

No.	Type	Description	Unused	Used
93	CD320	3p multicolored	.25	.25
94	CD321	2sh6p multicolored	1.00	.55

Nos. 93-94 were issued Oct. 1 in Tristan da Cunha, but on July 1 in St. Helena.

Light Dragoon of 19th Century and Sailing Ship — A6

Wmk. 314

1966, Aug. 15 Litho. *Perf. 14½*

No.	Type	Description	Unused	Used
95	A6	3p pale green & multi	.25	.25
96	A6	6p tan & multi	.25	.25
97	A6	1sh6p gray & multi	.40	.30
98	A6	2sh6p multicolored	.55	.45
		Nos. 95-98 (4)	1.45	1.25

150th anniv. of the establishment of a garrison on Tristan da Cunha.

WHO Headquarters Issue

Common Design Type

1966, Oct. 1 Litho. *Perf. 14*

No.	Type	Description	Unused	Used
99	CD322	6p multicolored	.30	.25
100	CD322	5sh multicolored	1.60	1.00

UNESCO Anniversary Issue

Common Design Type

1966, Dec. 1 Litho. *Perf. 14*

No.	Type	Description	Unused	Used
101	CD323	10p "Education"	.30	.25
102	CD323	1sh6p "Science"	.60	.40
103	CD323	2sh6p "Culture"	1.10	.75
		Nos. 101-103 (3)	2.00	1.40

Calshot Harbor — A7

Perf. 14x14½

1967, Jan. 2 Litho. Unwmk.

No.	Type	Description	Unused	Used
104	A7	6p dull green & multi	.25	.25
105	A7	10p brown & multi	.25	.25
106	A7	1sh6p dull blue & multi	.25	.25
107	A7	2sh6p orange brn & multi	.25	.30
		Nos. 104-107 (4)	1.00	1.05

Opening of the artificial Calshot Harbor.

No. 76 Surcharged with New Value and Three Bars

Perf. 11x11½

1967, May 10 Engr. Wmk. 314

No.	Type	Description	Unused	Used
108	A4	4p on 4½p blk & brn	.45	.30

Tristan da Cunha, Prince Alfred, Queen Elizabeth II and Prince Philip — A8

1967, July 10 Litho. *Perf. 14x14½*

No.	Type	Description	Unused	Used
109	A8	3p blue grn, dk grn & blk	.25	.25
110	A8	6p dk carmine & blk	.25	.25
111	A8	1sh6p brt grn, gray grn & blk	.25	.25
112	A8	2sh6p dull ultra, sep & blk	.25	.30
		Nos. 109-112 (4)	1.00	1.05

Cent. of the visit of Prince Alfred, First Duke of Edinburgh, to Tristan da Cunha.

Types of 1965

Designs: 4p, H.M.S. Challenger, 1870. 10sh, South African research vessel, R.S.A. £1, Queen Elizabeth II.

Perf. 11x11½

1967, Sept. 1 Engr. Wmk. 314

No.	Type	Description	Unused	Used
113	A4	4p black & orange	4.00	3.75
114	A4	10sh black & dull grn	14.00	12.00

Perf. 11½x11

No.	Type	Description	Unused	Used
115	A5	£1 brn org & dk blue	10.00	*12.00*
		Nos. 113-115 (3)	28.00	27.75

Wandering Albatross Nest — A9

Birds: 1sh, Big-billed buntings. 1sh6p, Tristan thrushes. 2sh6p, Great shearwaters.

Perf. 14x14½

1968, May 15 Photo. Wmk. 314

No.	Type	Description	Unused	Used
116	A9	4p multicolored	.25	.25
117	A9	1sh multicolored	.50	.30
118	A9	1sh6p multicolored	.85	.50
119	A9	2sh6p multicolored	1.20	.85
		Nos. 116-119 (4)	2.80	1.90

Union Jack and St. Helena Flag — A10

Design: 9p, 2sh6p, Map showing locations of St. Helena and Tristan da Cunha.

1968, Nov. 1 Litho. Wmk. 314

No.	Type	Description	Unused	Used
120	A10	6p violet & multi	.25	.25
121	A10	9p brn, bl grn & vio bl	.25	.25
122	A10	1sh6p green & multi	.25	.25
123	A10	2sh6p dp car, bl grn & vio bl	.25	*.35*
		Nos. 120-123 (4)	1.00	1.10

30th anniv. of Tristan da Cunha as a Dependency of St. Helena.

Frigate — A11

Designs: 1sh, Cape Horner. 1sh6p, Barque. 2sh6p, Tea Clipper.

Perf. 11x11½

1969, June 1 Engr. Wmk. 314

No.	Type	Description	Unused	Used
124	A11	4p brt blue	.25	.25
125	A11	1sh rose carmine	.40	.40
126	A11	1sh6p green	.55	.50
127	A11	2sh6p sepia	.95	.90
		Nos. 124-127 (4)	2.15	2.05

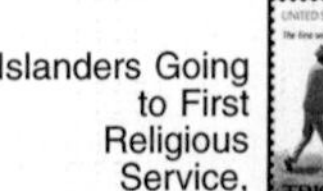

Islanders Going to First Religious Service, 1851 — A12

Designs: 4p, Tristan da Cunha, birds and ship. 1sh6p, Landing at the beach. 2sh6p, St. Mary's Church, 1969, and procession.

Perf. 14½x14

1969, Nov. 1 Litho. Wmk. 314

No.	Type	Description	Unused	Used
128	A12	4p multicolored	.25	*.40*
129	A12	9p multicolored	.25	*.40*
130	A12	1sh6p multicolored	.30	*.55*
131	A12	2sh6p multicolored	.40	*.55*
		Nos. 128-131 (4)	1.20	1.90

Issued to honor the work of the United Society for the Propagation of the Faith.

No. 77 Overprinted in Deep Orange: "NATIONAL / SAVINGS"

Perf. 11x11½

1970, May 15 Engr. Wmk. 314

No.	Type	Description	Unused	Used
132	A4	6p black & green	.45	.25

Issued to promote national savings. No. 132 also used as savings stamp.

In 1971, No. 132 was locally surcharged "2½p" and 3 short bars by means of a rubber handstamp. Value $7.

Globe and Red Cross — A13

1sh9p, 2sh6p, British & Red Cross flags, vert.

Perf. 13½x13, 13x13½

1970, June 1 Litho.

No.	Type	Description	Unused	Used
133	A13	4p emer, red & grnsh bl	.25	.25
134	A13	9p bister, red & grnsh bl	.35	.25
135	A13	1sh9p gray, vio bl & red	.55	.35
136	A13	2sh6p rose cl, vio bl & red	.75	.60
		Nos. 133-136 (4)	1.90	1.45

Centenary of the British Red Cross Society.

Rock Lobster and Lobster Men Placing Trap — A14

10p, 2sh6p, Workers in processing plant and side view of rock lobster (jasus tristani).

Perf. 12½x13

1970, Nov. 1 Litho. Wmk. 314

No.	Type	Description	Unused	Used
137	A14	4p lilac rose & multi	.25	*.30*
138	A14	10p dull yel & multi	.25	*.35*
139	A14	1sh6p brown org & multi	.60	.60
140	A14	2sh6p olive & multi	.90	.75
		Nos. 137-140 (4)	2.00	2.00

Tristan da Cunha rock lobster (crawfish) industry.

Nos. 72-74, 77-83, 113-114 Surcharged with New Value and Three Bars

Perf. 11x11½

1971, Feb. 15 Engr. Wmk. 314

No.	Type	Description	Unused	Used
141	A4	½p on 1p	.25	.25
142	A4	1p on 2p	.25	.25
143	A4	1½p on 4p	.30	.25
144	A4	2½p on 6p	.30	.25
145	A4	3p on 7p	.30	.25
146	A4	4p on 10p	.30	.25
147	A4	5p on 1sh	.30	.25
148	A4	7½p on 1sh6p	1.90	2.10
149	A4	12½p on 2sh6p	2.50	3.00
150	A4	15p on 1½p	2.50	3.50
151	A4	25p on 5sh	2.50	*6.25*
152	A4	50p on 10sh	3.75	*12.50*
		Nos. 141-152 (12)	15.15	29.10

"Quest" A15

4p, Presentation of Scout Troop flag in front of Tristan school. 7½p, Great Britain #167a with Tristan da Cunha cancellation. 12½p, Sir Ernest Henry Shackleton, boat & expedition cancellations.

Perf. 13½x14

1971, June 1 Litho. Wmk. 314

No.	Type	Description	Unused	Used
153	A15	1½p lt blue & multi	.95	.25
154	A15	4p buff, yel grn & blk	.95	.45
155	A15	7½p pale grn, rose lil & blk	.95	1.00
156	A15	12½p buff & multi	1.60	2.00
		Nos. 153-156 (4)	4.45	3.70

50th anniversary of the Shackleton-Rowett South Atlantic expedition.

"Victory" at Trafalgar and Thomas Swain Catching Nelson A16

Ships and Island Families: 2½p, "Emily of Stonington" and inscribed P. W. Green, 1836. 4p, "Italia" and inscribed Gaetano Lavarello, 1892, and Andrea Repetto. 7½p, "Falmouth" and Corp. William Glass, 1816. 12½p, American Whaler and inscribed 1836 Joshua Rogers, 1849, Capt. Andrew Hangan.

1971, Nov. 1

157	A16	1½p bister & multi	.25	.25
158	A16	2½p multicolored	.25	.25
159	A16	4p gray & multi	.40	.55
160	A16	7½p multicolored	.65	.85
161	A16	12½p blue & multi	1.00	1.40
		Nos. 157-161 (5)	2.55	3.30

Cow Pudding — A17

Native Flora: 1p, Peak berry and crater lake. 1½p, Sand flower, horiz. 2½p, New Zealand flax, horiz. 3p, Island tree. 4p, Bog fern and snow-capped mountain. 5p, Dog catcher and albatrosses. 7½p, Celery and terns. 12½p, Pepper tree and waterfall. 25p, Foul berry, horiz. 50p, Tussock and penguins. £1, Tussac and islands, horiz.

Perf. 13½x13, 13x13½

1972, Feb. 26 **Wmk. 314**

162	A17	½p gray & multi	.25	.25
163	A17	1p salmon & multi	.25	.25
164	A17	1½p green & multi	.25	.25
165	A17	2½p multicolored	.25	.25
166	A17	3p multicolored	.25	.25
167	A17	4p lemon & multi	.30	.30
168	A17	5p yel grn & multi	.45	.30
169	A17	7½p dull yel & multi	1.90	1.75
170	A17	12½p multicolored	1.25	1.00
171	A17	25p gray & multi	2.50	2.40

Litho. and Engr.

172	A17	50p multicolored	6.00	4.50
173	A17	£1 lt blue & multi	11.00	4.50
		Nos. 162-173 (12)	24.65	16.00

Coxswain — A18

2½p, Launching longboat. 4p, Men rowing longboat. 12½p, Longboat under sail.

1972, June 1 **Litho.** ***Perf. 14***

174	A18	2½p multi, horiz.	.25	.25
175	A18	4p multi, horiz.	.25	.25
176	A18	7½p multi	.50	.40
177	A18	12½p multi	.85	.50
		Nos. 174-177 (4)	1.85	1.40

Silver Wedding Issue, 1972

Common Design Type

Design: Queen Elizabeth II, Prince Philip, thrush and wandering albatrosses.

Perf. 14x14½

1972, Nov. 20 **Photo.** **Wmk. 314**

178	CD324	2½p multicolored	.25	.25
179	CD324	7½p ultra & multi	.45	.45

Altar, St. Mary's Church — A19

1973, July 8 **Litho.** ***Perf. 13½***

180	A19	25p dk blue & multi	1.10	1.10

St. Mary's Church, Tristan da Cunha, 50th anniv.

"Challenger" off Tristan, Steil's Sounding Instrument A20

Designs: 4p, Challenger's laboratory. 7½p, Challenger off Nightingale Island. 12½p, Map of Challenger's voyage. Each stamp shows an instrument for deep sea soundings.

Perf. 13½x14

1973, Oct. 15 **Wmk. 314**

181	A20	4p multicolored	.25	.25
182	A20	5p multicolored	.25	.25
183	A20	7½p multicolored	.40	.40
184	A20	12½p multicolored	.80	.80
a.		Souv. sheet, #181-184, perf. 13½	2.25	2.25
		Nos. 181-184 (4)	1.70	1.70

Centenary of "Challenger's" visit to Tristan da Cunha during oceanographic exploration world trip, 1872-76.

View of English Port from Shipboard A21

5p, Inspectors at volcano rim. 7½p, Islanders disembarking from "Bornholm." 12½p, Islanders on board ship approaching Tristan da Cunha.

1973, Nov. 10 ***Perf. 14½***

185	A21	4p yellow, blk & gold	.25	.25
186	A21	5p multicolored	.25	.25
187	A21	7½p multicolored	.40	.30
188	A21	12½p multicolored	.50	.40
		Nos. 185-188 (4)	1.40	1.20

10th anniversary of return of islanders to Tristan da Cunha.

Princess Anne's Wedding Issue

Common Design Type

1973, Nov. 14 **Wmk. 314** ***Perf. 14***

189	CD325	7½p multicolored	.25	.25
190	CD325	12½p bl grn & multi	.25	.25

Rockhopper Penguin — A22

Designs: Rockhopper penguins.

1974, May 1 **Litho.**

191	A22	2½p shown	2.60	1.25
192	A22	5p Colony	3.00	1.65
193	A22	7½p Penguins fishing	3.25	2.00
194	A22	25p Penguin and fledgling	6.50	5.00
		Nos. 191-194 (4)	15.35	9.90

Souvenir Sheet

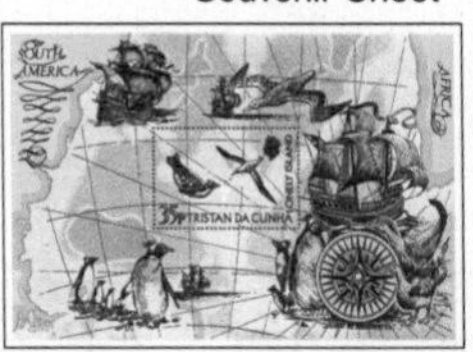

Map of Tristan da Cunha, Penguin and Sea Gull A23

1974, Oct. 1 **Wmk. 314** ***Perf. 13½***

195	A23	35p multicolored	5.25	5.25

Blenheim Palace — A24

25p, Churchill and Queen Elizabeth II.

Wmk. 373

1974, Nov. 30 **Litho.** ***Perf. 14***

196	A24	7½p black & yellow	.25	.25
197	A24	25p black & brown	.40	.40
a.		Souvenir sheet of 2, #196-197	.90	.90

Sir Winston Churchill (1874-1965).

Plocamium Fuscorubrum A25

Aquatic Plants: 5p, Ulva lactuca. 10p, Epymenia flabellata. 20p, Macrocystis pyrifera.

Perf. 13x14

1975, Apr. 16 **Wmk. 314**

198	A25	4p lilac & multi	.25	.25
199	A25	5p ultra & multi	.25	.25
200	A25	10p yellow & multi	.30	.30
201	A25	20p lt green & multi	.65	.65
		Nos. 198-201 (4)	1.45	1.45

Killer Whales A26

Wmk. 314

1975, Nov. 1 **Litho.** ***Perf. 13½***

202	A26	2p shown	.30	.25
203	A26	3p Rough-toothed dolphins	.55	.25
204	A26	5p Atlantic right whale	1.50	.85
205	A26	20p Finback whales	3.75	1.90
		Nos. 202-205 (4)	6.10	3.25

Tristan da Cunha No. 1 — A27

Designs: 9p, Tristan da Cunha #13, vert. 25p, Freighter Tristania II.

Perf. 13½x14, 14x13½

1976, May 6 **Litho.** **Wmk. 373**

206	A27	5p lilac, vio & blk	.25	.25
207	A27	9p bluish gray, grn & blk	.25	.25
208	A27	25p multicolored	.60	.60
a.		Souvenir sheet of 3	3.25	3.25
		Nos. 206-208 (3)	1.10	1.10

Festival of Stamps 1976. #208a contains one each of Ascension #214, St. Helena #297 and Tristan da Cunha #208.

The Patches — A28

Views, by Roland Svensson: 3p, Tristan house, vert. 10p, Tristan Settlement and Cliffs. 20p, Huts at Nightingale, vert.

1976, Oct. 4 **Litho.** ***Perf. 14***

209	A28	3p multicolored	.25	.25
210	A28	5p multicolored	.25	.25
211	A28	10p multicolored	.30	.30
212	A28	20p multicolored	.45	.45
a.		Souvenir sheet of 4, #209-211	1.60	1.60
		Nos. 209-212 (4)	1.25	1.25

An artist's view of Tristan da Cunha. See Nos. 234-237, 268-271.

Royal Yacht Britannia A29

15p, Royal standard. 25p, Royal family.

1977, Feb. 7 **Wmk. 373** ***Perf. 13***

213	A29	10p multicolored	.25	.25
214	A29	15p multicolored	.25	.25
215	A29	25p multicolored	.25	.25
		Nos. 213-215 (3)	.75	.75

25th anniv. of the reign of Elizabeth II. For surcharges see Nos. 220-221.

H.M.S. Eskimo, Sept. 1970 — A30

Royal Naval Ships and Arms: 10p, Naiad, Nov. 1968. 15p, Jaguar, Mar. 1964. 20p, London, Dec. 1964. Dates of visits to island.

1977, Oct. 1 **Litho.** ***Perf. 14½***

216	A30	5p multicolored	.25	.25
217	A30	10p multicolored	.25	.25
218	A30	15p multicolored	.25	.25
219	A30	20p multicolored	.30	.30
a.		Souvenir sheet of 4, #216-219	1.75	1.75
		Nos. 216-219 (4)	1.05	1.05

Nos. 214-215 Surcharged with New Value and Bar

1977, Oct. 13 **Wmk. 373** ***Perf. 13***

220	A29	4p on 15p multi	2.50	*6.50*
221	A29	7½p on 25p multi	2.50	*6.50*

Giant Fulmars A31

1p, Pterodroma macroptera, horiz. 2p, Fregetta marina, horiz. 3p, Macronectes giganteus. 4p, Pterodroma mollis. 5p, Diomedea exulans. 10p, Pterodroma brevirostris. 15p, Sterna vittata. 20p, Puffinus gravis. 25p, Pachyptila vittata. 50p, Catharacta skua. £1, Pelecanoides urinatrix. £2, Diomedea chlororynchos.

Perf. 13½x14, 14x13½

1977, Dec. 1 **Litho.**

222	A31	1p multicolored	.25	*.45*
223	A31	2p multicolored	.25	*.75*
224	A31	3p multicolored	.25	*.75*
225	A31	4p multicolored	.25	*.85*
226	A31	5p multicolored	.25	*.85*
227	A31	10p multicolored	.30	*.85*
228	A31	15p multicolored	.50	*1.25*
229	A31	20p multicolored	.65	*1.25*
230	A31	25p multicolored	.80	*1.25*
231	A31	50p multicolored	1.75	1.25
232	A31	£1 multicolored	2.50	2.25
233	A31	£2 multicolored	5.25	3.00
		Nos. 222-233 (12)	13.00	14.75

Nos. 224-233 are vertical. For overprints see Nos. 318-319.

Painting Type of 1976

Views by Roland Svensson: 5p, St. Mary's Church. 10p, Longboats. 15p, A Tristan home. 20p, Harbor, 1970.

Wmk. 373

1978, Mar. 1 **Litho.** ***Perf. 14½***

234	A28	5p multicolored	.25	.25
235	A28	10p multicolored	.25	.25
236	A28	15p multicolored	.30	.30
237	A28	20p multicolored	.45	.45
a.		Souvenir sheet of 4, #234-237	1.75	1.75
		Nos. 234-237 (4)	1.25	1.25

An artist's view of Tristan da Cunha.

Elizabeth II Coronation Anniversary

Common Design Types

Souvenir Sheet

1978, Apr. 21 **Unwmk.** ***Perf. 15***

238		Sheet of 6	1.50	1.50
a.		CD326 25p King's Bull	.30	.30
b.		CD327 25p Elizabeth II	.30	.30
c.		CD328 25p Tristan crawfish	.30	.30

No. 238 contains 2 se-tenant strips of Nos. 238a-238c, separated by horizontal gutter with commemorative and descriptive inscriptions and showing central part of coronation procession with coach.

Sodalite A32

Local Minerals: 5p, Aragonite. 10p, Sulphur. 20p, Lava containing pyroxene crystal.

Perf. 13½x14

1978, June 9 **Litho.** **Wmk. 373**

239	A32	3p multicolored	.40	.40
240	A32	5p multicolored	.45	.45
241	A32	10p multicolored	.70	.70
242	A32	20p multicolored	1.10	1.10
		Nos. 239-242 (4)	2.65	2.65

Fish — A33

1978, Sept. 29 Litho. *Perf. 14*

243 A33 5p Klipfish .30 .30
244 A33 10p Fivefinger .30 .30
245 A33 15p Concha .35 .35
246 A33 20p Soldier .40 .40
Nos. 243-246 (4) 1.35 1.35

Orangeleaf and Navy Flag — A34

Royal Fleet Auxiliary Vessels: 10p, Tarbatness. 20p, Tidereach. 25p, Reliant.

1978, Nov. 24 Litho. *Perf. 12½*

247 A34 5p multicolored .25 .25
248 A34 10p multicolored .25 .25
249 A34 20p multicolored .25 .25
250 A34 25p multicolored .30 .30
a. Souvenir sheet of 4, #247-250 1.40 *2.75*
Nos. 247-250 (4) 1.05 1.05

Fur Seals — A35

Wildlife conservation: 5p, Elephant seal. 15p, Tristan thrush. 20p, Tristan buntings.

Wmk. 373

1979, Jan. 3 Litho. *Perf. 14*

251 A35 5p multicolored .25 .25
252 A35 10p multicolored .25 .25
253 A35 15p multicolored .30 .30
254 A35 20p multicolored .35 .35
Nos. 251-254 (4) 1.15 1.15

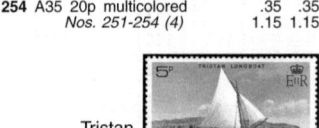

Tristan Longboat A36

Ships: 10p, Queen Mary. 15p, Queen Elizabeth. 20p, QE II. 25p, QE II, longboat, view of Tristan.

1979, Feb. 8 *Perf. 14½*

255 A36 5p multicolored .25 .25
256 A36 10p multicolored .25 .25
257 A36 15p multicolored .25 .25
258 A36 20p multicolored .35 .35
Nos. 255-258 (4) 1.10 1.10

Souvenir Sheet

259 A36 25p multicolored 1.00 *1.50*

Visit of cruise ship QE II, Feb. 8.
No. 259 contains one 132x28mm stamp.

Tristan da Cunha No. 12 — A37

Tristan da Cunha Stamps: 10p, No. 26. 25p, No. 58, vert. 50p, 1p-local "potatoe" stamp.

Perf. 14½x14, 14x14½

1979, Aug. 27 Litho. Wmk. 373

260 A37 5p multicolored .25 .25
261 A37 10p multicolored .25 .25
262 A37 25p multicolored .40 .40
Nos. 260-262 (3) .90 .90

Souvenir Sheet

263 A37 50p multicolored .75 .75

Sir Rowland Hill (1795-1879), originator of penny postage.

The Padre's House, IYC Emblem — A38

IYC Emblem, Children's Drawings: 10p, "Houses in the Village." 15p, "St. Mary's Church." 20p, "Rockhopper Penguins."

1979, Nov. 26 Litho. *Perf. 14*

264 A38 5p multicolored .25 .25
265 A38 10p multicolored .25 .25
266 A38 15p multicolored .25 .25
267 A38 20p multicolored .25 .25
Nos. 264-267 (4) 1.00 1.00

International Year of the Child.

Painting Type of 1976

Views (Sketches by Roland Svensson): 5p, Stoltenhoff Island. 10p, Nightingale from the East. 15p, The Administrator's abode, vert. 20p, "Ridge where the goat jumped off," vert.

1980, Feb. Litho. *Perf. 14*

268 A28 5p multicolored .25 .25
269 A28 10p multicolored .25 .25
270 A28 15p multicolored .25 .25
271 A28 20p multicolored .25 .25
a. Souvenir sheet of 4, #268-271 1.00 1.00
Nos. 268-271 (4) 1.00 1.00

Mail Pickup Boat — A40

1980, May 6 Litho. *Perf. 14*

272 A40 5p shown .25 .25
273 A40 10p Unloading mail .25 .25
274 A40 15p Truck transport .25 .25
275 A40 20p Delivery bell .25 .25
276 A40 25p Distribution .25 .25
Nos. 272-276 (5) 1.25 1.25

London 80 Intl. Stamp Exhib., May 6-14.

Queen Mother Elizabeth Birthday
Common Design Type

1980, Aug. 11 Litho. *Perf. 14*

277 CD330 14p multicolored .45 .45

Golden Hinde — A41

1980, Sept. 6 *Perf. 14½*

278 A41 5p shown .25 .25
279 A41 10p Drake's route .25 .25
280 A41 20p Sir Francis Drake .25 .25
281 A41 25p Queen Elizabeth I .25 .25
Nos. 278-281 (4) 1.00 1.00

Sir Francis Drake's circumnavigation, 400th anniversary.

Humpty Dumpty — A42

Wmk. 373

1980, Oct. 31 Litho. *Perf. 13½*

282 Sheet of 9 1.90 1.90
a. A42 15p shown .25 .25
b. A42 15p Mary had a Little Lamb .25 .25
c. A42 15p Little Jack Horner .25 .25
d. A42 15p Hey Diddle Diddle .25 .25
e. A42 15p London Bridge .25 .25
f. A42 15p Old King Cole .25 .25
g. A42 15p Sing a Song of Sixpence .25 .25
h. A42 15p Tom Tom the Piper's Son .25 .25
i. A42 25p Owl and the Pussy Cat .25 .25

Christmas 1980.

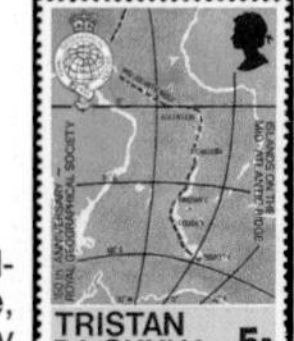

Islands on Mid-Atlantic Ridge, Society Emblem — A43

Royal Geographical Soc., 150th Anniv. (Maps and Expeditions): 10p, Tristan da Cunha, Francis Beaufort, 1806. 15p, Tristan Island, Norwegian expedition, 1937-1938. 20p, Gough Island, scientific survey, 1955-1956.

1980, Dec. 15

283 A43 5p multicolored .25 .25
284 A43 10p multicolored .25 .25
285 A43 15p multicolored .25 .25
286 A43 20p multicolored .25 .25
Nos. 283-286 (4) 1.00 1.00

Rev. Edwin Dodgson — A44

Wmk. 373

1981, Mar. 23 Litho. *Perf. 14*

287 A44 10p portrait, vert. .25 .25
288 A44 20p shown .30 .30
289 A44 30p Dodgson preaching, vert. .40 .40
a. Souvenir sheet of 3, #287-289 .90 .90
Nos. 287-289 (3) .95 .95

Centenary of arrival of Rev. Edwin H. Dodgson, who saved population from starvation.

Map of Tristan da Cunha showing L'heure du Berger Route, 1767 (Dalrymple's Map, 1781) — A45

Early Maps and Charts By: 5p, 21p, Capt. Denham, 1853 (diff.). 35p, Ivan Keulen, 1700.

1981, May 22

290 A45 5p multicolored .25 .25
291 A45 14p multicolored .30 .30
292 A45 21p multicolored .45 .45
Nos. 290-292 (3) 1.00 1.00

Souvenir Sheet

293 A45 35p multicolored .65 *.85*

Royal Wedding Issue
Common Design Type
Wmk. 373

1981, July 22 Litho. *Perf. 14*

294 CD331 5p Bouquet .25 .25
295 CD331 20p Charles .25 .25
296 CD331 50p Couple .40 .40
Nos. 294-296 (3) .90 .90

Hiking — A46

1981, Sept. 14

297 A46 5p shown .25 .25
298 A46 10p Camping .25 .25
299 A46 20p Map reading .25 .25
300 A46 25p Prince Philip .25 .25
Nos. 297-300 (4) 1.00 1.00

Duke of Edinburgh's Awards, 25th anniv.

Inaccessible Island Rail — A47

1981, Nov. 1 Litho. *Perf. 13½x14*

301 Strip of 4 1.20 1.20
a. A47 10p Nest .30 .30
b. A47 10p Eggs .30 .30
c. A47 10p Chicks .30 .30
d. A47 10p Adult rail .30 .30

Six-gilled Shark — A48

1982, Feb. 8 Litho. *Perf. 13½x14*

302 A48 5p shown .25 .25
303 A48 14p Porbeagle shark .40 .30
304 A48 21p Blue shark .65 .55
305 A48 35p Hammerhead shark .90 .85
Nos. 302-305 (4) 2.20 1.95

Marcella A49

1982, Apr. 5 Litho. *Perf. 14*

306 A49 5p shown .35 .35
307 A49 15p Eliza Adams .35 .35
308 A49 30p Corinthian .50 .50
309 A49 50p Samuel & Thomas .80 .80
Nos. 306-309 (4) 2.00 2.00

See Nos. 324-327.

Princess Diana Issue
Common Design Type
Perf. 14½x14

1982, July 1 Litho. Wmk. 373

310 CD333 5p Arms .25 .25
311 CD333 15p Diana .55 .25
312 CD333 30p Wedding 1.10 .35
313 CD333 50p Portrait 1.75 .60
Nos. 310-313 (4) 3.65 1.45

Scouting Year — A50

5p, Baden-Powell, vert. 20p, Brownsea Isld. camp, 1907, vert. No. 316, 50p, Saluting. No. 317, 50p, Tree illustration, vert.

Perf. 13½x13, 13x13½

1982, Aug. 23 Litho.

314 A50 5p multicolored .25 .25
315 A50 20p multicolored .30 .30
316 A50 50p multicolored .75 .75
Nos. 314-316 (3) 1.30 1.30

Souvenir Sheet
Perf. 14

317 A50 50p multicolored 1.40 1.25

Nos. 226, 230 Overprinted: "1st PARTICIPATION / COMMONWEALTH / GAMES 1982"
Perf. 13½x14

1982, Sept. 28 Litho. Wmk. 373

318 A31 5p multicolored .25 .25
319 A31 25p multicolored .40 .40

12th Commonwealth Games, Brisbane, Australia, Sept. 30-Oct. 9.

Formation of Volcanic Island — A51

1982, Nov. 1 *Perf. 14x14½*

320 A51 5p shown .30 .30
321 A51 15p Surface cinder cones .40 .40
322 A51 25p Eruption .50 .50
323 A51 35p 1961 eruption .60 .60
Nos. 320-323 (4) 1.80 1.80

Ship Type of 1982

1983, Feb. 1 Litho. *Perf. 14*

324 A49 5p Islander, vert. .25 .25
325 A49 20p Roscoe .40 .40
326 A49 35p Columbia .75 .60
327 A49 50p Emeline, vert. 1.00 .90
Nos. 324-327 (4) 2.40 2.15

Tractor Pulling Trailer — A52

1983, May 2 Litho. *Perf. 14*

328 A52 5p shown .25 .25
329 A52 15p Pack mules .25 .25
330 A52 30p Oxen pulling cart .40 .40
331 A52 50p Jeep .60 .60
Nos. 328-331 (4) 1.50 1.50

Map of South Atlantic — A53

Island History — 3p, Tristao d'Acunha's flagship. 4p, Landing, 1643. 5p, 17th cent. views. 10p, Landing party, 1815. 15p, Settlement. 18p, Governor Glass's house. 20p, Rev. W.F. Taylor, Peter Green. 25p, Three-master John and Elizabeth. 50p, Dependency declaration of St. Helena, 1938. £1, Commissioning ceremony. £2, Evacuation, 1961.

Wmk. 373

1983, Aug. 1 Litho. *Perf. 14*

332 A53 1p multicolored .25 .25
333 A53 3p multicolored .25 .25
334 A53 4p multicolored .25 .25
335 A53 5p multicolored .25 .25
336 A53 10p multicolored .25 .25
337 A53 15p multicolored .35 .45
338 A53 18p multicolored .40 .50
339 A53 20p multicolored .45 .60
340 A53 25p multicolored .70 .90
341 A53 50p multicolored 1.25 1.75
342 A53 £1 multicolored 2.50 3.50
343 A53 £2 multicolored 5.25 7.25
Nos. 332-343 (12) 12.15 16.20

Raphael, 500th Birth Anniv. — A54

1983, Oct. 27 Litho. *Perf. 14½*

344 A54 10p multicolored .25 .25
345 A54 25p multicolored .50 .50
346 A54 40p multicolored .90 .90
Nos. 344-346 (3) 1.65 1.65

Souvenir Sheet

347 A54 50p multi, horiz. 1.50 1.25

Details from Christ's Charge to St. Peter.

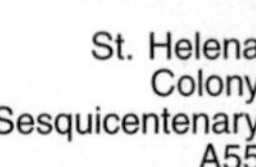

St. Helena Colony Sesquicentenary A55

1984, Jan. 3 Litho. *Perf. 14*

348 A55 10p No. 7 .25 .25
349 A55 15p No. 9 .25 .25
350 A55 25p No. 10 .40 .40
351 A55 60p No. 12 1.10 1.00
Nos. 348-351 (4) 2.00 1.90

Local Fungi — A56

10p, Agrocybe praecox, vert. 20p, Laccaria tetraspora, vert. 30p, Agrocybe cylindracea. 50p, Sarcoscypha coccinea.

1984, Mar. 26

352 A56 10p multicolored .50 .75
353 A56 20p multicolored .85 .85
354 A56 30p multicolored 1.35 1.35
355 A56 50p multicolored 2.10 2.10
Nos. 352-355 (4) 4.80 5.05

Constellations — A57

1984, July 30 *Perf. 14½*

356 A57 10p Orion .25 .25
357 A57 20p Scorpius .55 .45
358 A57 25p Canis Major .60 .55
359 A57 50p Crux 1.20 1.10
Nos. 356-359 (4) 2.60 2.35

Sheep Shearing — A58

1984, Oct. 1

360 A58 9p shown .25 .25
361 A58 17p Carding wool .35 .30
362 A58 29p Spinning .60 .50
363 A58 45p Knitting .95 .85
a. Souvenir sheet of 4, #360-363 2.25 2.25
Nos. 360-363 (4) 2.15 1.90

Stamps from No. 363a do not have white border around the design.

Christmas 1984 — A59

1984, Dec. 3 *Perf. 14*

364 A59 10p Three angels, Christmas dinner .25 .25
365 A59 20p Two angels, cart .40 .35
366 A59 30p Candles, sailboat .65 .55
367 A59 50p Trees, Nativity 1.00 .85
Nos. 364-367 (4) 2.30 2.00

Shipwrecks A60

10p, HMS Julia, 1817, vert. 25p, Bell from Mabel Clark, 1878, vert. 35p, Barque Glenhuntley, 1898.
60p, Map of shipwreck sites.

1985, Feb. 4 *Perf. 14x13½, 13½x14*

368 A60 10p multicolored .70 .45
369 A60 25p multicolored 1.10 1.10
370 A60 35p multicolored 1.60 1.50
Nos. 368-370 (3) 3.40 3.05

Souvenir Sheet

371 A60 60p multicolored 2.25 2.00

No. 371 contains one 48x32mm stamp.
See Nos. 393-396, 412-415.

Queen Mother 85th Birthday
Common Design Type

10p, With Prince Charles, 1954. 20p, With Margaret at Ascot. 30p, Queen Mother. 50p, Holding Prince Henry.
80p, With Anne.

Perf. 14½x14

1985, June 7 Litho. Wmk. 384

372 CD336 10p multicolored .25 .25
373 CD336 20p multicolored .45 .45
374 CD336 30p multicolored .70 .70
375 CD336 50p multicolored .85 .85
Nos. 372-375 (4) 2.25 2.25

Souvenir Sheet

376 CD336 80p multicolored 2.75 2.75

Flags — A61

10p, Jonathan Lambert & flag of 1811, Isles of Refreshment. 15p, Cannon & flag of 21st Light Dragoons, 1816-17, Fort Malcolm. 25p, HMS Falmouth, 1816, & flag of HMS Atlantic Isle, HMS JOB 9, 1942-46. 60p, View of Tristan & Union Jack, 1816 to date.

1985, Sept. 30 Wmk. 373 *Perf. 14*

377 A61 10p multicolored .45 .45
378 A61 15p multicolored .60 .60
379 A61 25p multicolored 1.05 1.05
380 A61 60p multicolored 2.75 2.40
Nos. 377-380 (4) 4.85 4.50

Nos. 378-380 vert.

Loss of The Lifeboat, Cent. — A62

1985, Nov. 28

381 A62 10p Lifeboat, barque West Riding .25 .25
382 A62 30p Map .75 .75
383 A62 50p Death toll 1.25 1.25
Nos. 381-383 (3) 2.25 2.25

Halley's Comet — A63

10p, Bayeux Tapestry, c. 1092. 20p, Trajectory around Earth. 30p, Comet over Inaccessible Is. 50p, Ship Paramour.

1986, Mar. 3 Wmk. 384

384 A63 10p multicolored .50 .50
385 A63 20p multicolored .80 .80
386 A63 30p multicolored 1.10 1.10
387 A63 50p multicolored 1.75 1.75
Nos. 384-387 (4) 4.15 4.15

Queen Elizabeth II 60th Birthday
Common Design Type

Designs: 10p, With Prince Charles, 1950. 15p, Birthday Parade, wearing uniform of Scots Guards, 1976. 25p, At Westminster Abbey, London, 1972, wearing mantle and robes of the Most Noble Order of Bath. 45p, Silver Jubilee Tour, Canada, 1977. 65p, Visiting Crown Agents' offices, 1983.

1986, Apr. 21 *Perf. 14½*

388 CD337 10p scarlet, blk & sil .25 .25
389 CD337 15p ultra & multi .30 .30
390 CD337 25p green & multi .50 .50
391 CD337 45p violet & multi .80 .80
392 CD337 65p rose vio & multi 1.15 1.15
Nos. 388-392 (5) 3.00 3.00

For overprints see Nos. 429-433.

Shipwrecks Type of 1985

9p, SV Allanshaw, 1893. 20p, Church font from Edward Vittery, 1881. 40p, Figurehead, 1940.
65p, Barque Italia, 1892.

1986, June 2 *Perf. 13½*

393 A60 9p multicolored .45 .45
394 A60 20p multicolored .90 .90
395 A60 40p multicolored 1.75 1.75
Nos. 393-395 (3) 3.10 3.10

Souvenir Sheet

Perf. 13½x13

396 A60 65p multicolored 3.25 3.25

Nos. 394-395 vert.

Royal Wedding Issue, 1986
Common Design Type

Designs: 10p, Informal portrait. 40p, Andrew operating helicopter.

1986, July 23 *Perf. 14*

397 CD338 10p multicolored .25 .25
398 CD338 40p multicolored 1.15 1.15

A64

5p, Wandering albatross. 10p, Daisy. 20p, Vanessa butterfly. 25p, Wilkins's bunting. 50p, Ring-eye.

1986, Sept. 30

399 A64 5p multicolored .25 .25
400 A64 10p multicolored .50 .50
401 A64 20p multicolored 1.00 1.00
402 A64 25p multicolored 1.25 1.25
403 A64 50p multicolored 2.40 2.40
Nos. 399-403 (5) 5.40 5.40

Flora & fauna of Inaccessible Island.

A65

Indigenous Flightless Species and Habitats: 10p, Flightless moth, Edinburgh Settlement. 25p, Strap-winged fly, Crater Lake. 35p, Flightless rail, Inaccessible Island. 50p, Gough Island moorhen, Gough Island.

1987, Jan. 23 *Perf. 14½*

404 A65 10p multicolored .45 .45
405 A65 25p multicolored 1.10 1.10
406 A65 35p multicolored 1.50 1.50
407 A65 50p multicolored 2.25 2.25
Nos. 404-407 (4) 5.30 5.30

Rockhopper Penguins — A66

1987, June 22

408 A66 10p Swimming .60 .60
409 A66 20p Nesting 1.30 1.30
410 A66 30p Adult and young 1.90 1.90
411 A66 50p Adult's head 3.50 3.50
Nos. 408-411 (4) 7.30 7.30

Shipwrecks Type of 1985

Designs: 11p, Castaways attacking sea elephant, vert. 17p, Henry A. Paull, 1879, Sandy Point. 45p, Gustav Stoltenhoff, Stoltenhoff Is., vert. 70p, Map of wrecks off Inaccessible Is.

1987, Apr. 2 *Perf. 14*

412 A60 11p olive gray & blk .55 .55
413 A60 17p dark violet & blk .90 .90
414 A60 45p myrtle green & blk 2.60 2.60
Nos. 412-414 (3) 4.05 4.05

Souvenir Sheet

415 A60 70p lt bl, royal bl & apple grn 4.50 4.50

Norwegian Scientific Expedition, 50th Anniv. — A67

10p, Microscope and textbooks symbolic of expedition results. 20p, Scientists tagging a mollymawk. 30p, Expedition headquarters on the island. 50p, S.S. Thorshammer.

Wmk. 384

1987, Dec. 7 Litho. *Perf. 14*

416 A67 10p multicolored .95 .90
417 A67 20p multicolored 1.90 1.50

Wmk. 373

418 A67 30p multicolored 2.75 2.10
419 A67 50p multicolored 4.00 3.50
Nos. 416-419 (4) 9.60 8.00

Fauna of Nightingale Island — A68

1988, Mar. 21 Wmk. 384 *Perf. 14*

420 A68 5p Tristan bunting .30 .30
421 A68 10p Tristan thrush .55 .55
422 A68 20p Yellow-nosed albatross .90 .90
423 A68 25p Great shearwater 1.10 1.10
424 A68 50p Elephant seal 2.50 2.50
Nos. 420-424 (5) 5.35 5.35

Handicrafts — A69

1988, May 30 ***Perf. 14½***

425 A69 10p Painted penguin eggs .35 .35
426 A69 15p Moccasins .50 .50
427 A69 35p Woolen clothing 1.25 1.25
428 A69 50p Model canvas boats 1.75 1.75
Nos. 425-428 (4) 3.85 3.85

Nos. 388-392 Ovptd. "40TH WEDDING ANNIVERSARY" in Silver

1988, Mar. 9

429 CD337 10p scar, blk & sil .25 .25
430 CD337 15p ultra & multi .35 .35
431 CD337 25p green & multi .50 .50
432 CD337 45p violet & multi .90 .90
433 CD337 65p rose vio & multi 1.40 1.40
Nos. 429-433 (5) 3.40 3.40

19th Cent. Whaling — A70

1988, Oct. 6 ***Perf. 14x14½***

434 A70 10p "Trying out" blubber .70 .70
435 A70 20p Harpoon guns 1.25 1.25
436 A70 30p Scrimshaw 2.10 2.10
437 A70 50p Ships 3.25 3.25
Nos. 434-437 (4) 7.30 7.30

Souvenir Sheet

438 A70 £1 Right whale 5.00 5.00

Lloyds of London, 300th Anniv.
Common Design Type

10p, Lloyds's new building, 1988. 25p, Cargo ship *Tristania II*, horiz. 35p, Supply ship *St. Helena*, horiz. 50p, Square-rigger *Kobenhavn*, lost at sea.

1988, Nov. 7 ***Perf. 14***

439 CD341 10p multicolored .60 .60
440 CD341 25p multicolored 1.75 1.75
441 CD341 35p multicolored 2.25 2.25
442 CD341 50p multicolored 3.00 3.00
Nos. 439-442 (4) 7.60 7.60

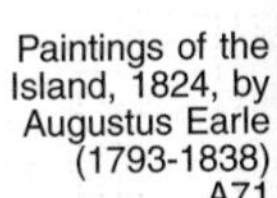

Paintings of the Island, 1824, by Augustus Earle (1793-1838) A71

Designs: 1p, Government House. 3p, Squall off Tristan. 4p, Rafting Blubber. 5p, Tristan. 10p, Man Killing an Albatross. 15p, View on the Summit. 20p, Nightingale Island. 25p, Tristan, diff. 35p, "Solitude," Watching the Horizon. 50p, North Eastern. £1, Tristan, diff. £2, Governor Glass and His Companions.

1988, Dec. 10

443 A71 1p multicolored .25 .25
444 A71 3p multicolored .25 .25
445 A71 4p multicolored .25 .25
446 A71 5p multicolored .25 .25
447 A71 10p multicolored .35 .35
448 A71 15p multicolored .45 .60
449 A71 20p multicolored .60 1.10
450 A71 25p multicolored .80 1.25
451 A71 35p multicolored 1.10 2.00
452 A71 50p multicolored 1.40 2.75
453 A71 £1 multicolored 3.00 5.50
454 A71 £2 multicolored 6.00 10.50
Nos. 443-454 (12) 14.70 25.05

Gough Is. Fauna — A72

1989, Feb. 6 **Litho.** **Wmk. 384**

455 A72 5p Giant petrel .45 .45
456 A72 10p Gough moorhen .80 .80
457 A72 20p Gough bunting 1.50 1.50
458 A72 25p Sooty albatross 1.75 1.75
459 A72 50p Amsterdam fur seal 3.50 3.50
Nos. 455-459 (5) 8.00 8.00

Ferns — A73

10p, Eriosorus cheilanthoides. 25p, Asplenium alvarezense. 35p, Elaphoglossum hybridum. 50p, Ophioglossum opacum.

1989, May 22 **Wmk. 373** ***Perf. 14***

460 A73 10p multicolored .55 .55
461 A73 25p multicolored 1.40 1.40
462 A73 35p multicolored 2.10 2.10
463 A73 50p multicolored 2.60 2.60
Nos. 460-463 (4) 6.65 6.65

A74

1989, Nov. 20 **Wmk. 384**

464 A74 10p Cattle egret 1.30 1.10
465 A74 25p Spotted sandpiper 2.75 2.50
466 A74 35p Purple gallinule 4.00 3.50
467 A74 50p Barn swallow 5.25 4.75
Nos. 464-467 (4) 13.30 11.85

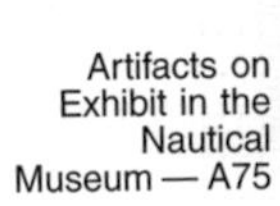

Artifacts on Exhibit in the Nautical Museum — A75

10p, Surgeon's mortar. 20p, Parts of a harpoon. 30p, Compass with binnacle hood. 60p, Rope-twisting device.

1989, Sept. 25

468 A75 10p multicolored .55 .55
469 A75 20p multicolored 1.10 1.10
470 A75 30p multicolored 1.75 1.75
471 A75 60p multicolored 3.50 3.50
Nos. 468-471 (4) 6.90 6.90

Moths — A76

10p, Peridroma saucia. 15p, Ascalapha odorata. 35p, Agrius cingulata. 60p, Eumorpha labruscae.

1990, Feb. 1 ***Perf. 14***

472 A76 10p multicolored .70 .70
473 A76 15p multicolored 1.10 1.10
474 A76 35p multicolored 2.75 2.75
475 A76 60p multicolored 5.00 5.00
Nos. 472-475 (4) 9.55 9.55

Starfish (Echinoderms) — A77

1990, June 12 ***Perf. 14x13½***

476 A77 10p shown .80 .80
477 A77 20p multi, diff. 1.10 1.50
478 A77 30p multi, diff. 2.60 2.25
479 A77 60p multi, diff. 4.50 4.50
Nos. 476-479 (4) 9.00 9.05

Queen Mother, 90th Birthday
Common Design Types

25p, Queen Mother at the Coliseum. £1, Broadcasting to women of the empire, 1939.

1990, Aug. 4 **Wmk. 384** ***Perf. 14x15***

480 CD343 25p multicolored 1.10 1.10

Perf. 14½

481 CD344 £1 multicolored 4.50 4.50

Dunnottar Castle, 1942 — A78

Designs: 15p, RMS St. Helena, 1977-1990. 35p, Launching new RMS St. Helena, 1989. 60p, Duke of York launching new RMS St. Helena. £1, New RMS St. Helena.

1990, Sept. 13 **Wmk. 373** ***Perf. 14½***

482 A78 10p multicolored .95 .95
483 A78 15p multicolored 1.50 1.50
484 A78 35p multicolored 4.00 3.25
485 A78 60p multicolored 6.25 5.50
Nos. 482-485 (4) 12.70 11.20

Souvenir Sheet

486 A78 £1 multicolored 8.75 8.75

See Ascension Nos. 493-497, St. Helena Nos. 535-539.

Royal Navy Warships — A79

Perf. 14½x14

1990, Nov. 30 **Litho.** **Wmk. 373**

487 A79 10p Pyramus, 1829 1.25 1.25
488 A79 25p Penguin, 1815 3.00 3.00
489 A79 35p Thalia, 1886 4.25 4.25
490 A79 50p Sidon, 1858 6.00 6.00
Nos. 487-490 (4) 14.50 14.50

See Nos. 547-550.

1991, Feb. 4

491 A79 10p Milford, 1938 2.10 1.60
492 A79 25p Dublin, 1923 3.25 2.75
493 A79 35p Yarmouth, 1919 4.50 4.00
494 A79 50p Carlisle, 1938 5.00 *6.00*
Nos. 491-494 (4) 14.85 14.35

Souvenir Sheet

Royal Viking Sun A80

Wmk. 384

1991, Apr. 1 **Litho.** ***Perf. 14***

495 A80 £1 multicolored 10.00 10.00

Prince Philip, 70th Birthday — A81

Designs: 10p, HMS Galatea, Prince Alfred. 25p, Royal Visit, 1957. 30p, HMY Britannia, Prince Philip. 50p, Settlement of Edinburgh, Prince Philip.

1991, June 10 **Wmk. 373**

496 A81 10p multicolored 1.50 1.25
497 A81 25p multicolored 3.25 3.00
498 A81 30p multicolored 4.00 3.50
499 A81 50p multicolored 6.25 6.00
Nos. 496-499 (4) 15.00 13.75

Birds — A82

8p, Gough moorhens. 10p, Gough bunting. 12p, Gough moorhen in nest. 15p, Gough bunting with chicks.

1991, Oct. 1

500 A82 8p multicolored 2.50 1.60
501 A82 10p multicolored 2.50 1.90
502 A82 12p multicolored 2.75 1.90
503 A82 15p multicolored 3.00 2.25
Nos. 500-503 (4) 10.75 7.65

World Wildlife Fund.

Discovery of America, 500th Anniv. — A83

10p, STV Eye of the Wind. 15p, STV Soren Larsen. 35p, STV Pinta, Nina, Santa Maria. 60p, Columbus, Santa Maria.

1992, Jan. 23

504 A83 10p multicolored .95 .75
505 A83 15p multicolored 1.25 1.10
506 A83 35p multicolored 3.00 2.75
507 A83 60p multicolored 5.50 4.75
Nos. 504-507 (4) 10.70 9.35

World Columbian Stamp Expo '92, Chicago and Genoa '92 Intl. Philatelic Exhibitions.

Queen Elizabeth II's Accession to the Throne, 40th Anniv.
Common Design Type

1992, Feb. 6

508 CD349 10p multicolored .55 .55
509 CD349 20p multicolored 1.15 1.10
510 CD349 25p multicolored 1.40 1.25
511 CD349 35p multicolored 1.90 1.90
512 CD349 65p multicolored 3.75 3.50
Nos. 508-512 (5) 8.75 8.30

Fish — A84

Designs: 10p, Caesioperca coatsii. 15p, Mendosoma lineatum. 35p, Physiculus karrerae. 60p, Decapterus longimanus.

1992, June 1

513 A84 10p multicolored .80 .55
514 A84 15p multicolored 1.50 1.10
515 A84 35p multicolored 2.75 2.40
516 A84 60p multicolored 5.00 4.25
Nos. 513-516 (4) 10.05 8.30

Wreck of the Italia, Cent. — A85

Designs: 10p, Italia leaving Greenock. 45p, In mid-Atlantic. 65p, Driving ashore on Stony Beach. £1, Italia in peaceful waters.

1992, Sept. 18 ***Perf. 13½x14***

517 A85 10p multicolored .85 .80
518 A85 45p multicolored 3.50 3.50
519 A85 65p multicolored 5.25 5.25
Nos. 517-519 (3) 9.60 9.55

Souvenir Sheet

520 A85 £1 multicolored 9.75 9.75

Genoa '92 Intl. Philatelic Exhibition (#520).

Insects — A86

15p, Stenoscelis hylastoides. 45p, Trogloscaptomyza brevilamellata. 60p, Senilites tristanicola.

Perf. 14x13½

1993, Feb. 2 **Litho.** **Wmk. 384**

521 A86 15p multicolored 1.25 1.25
522 A86 45p multicolored 3.50 3.50
523 A86 60p multicolored 4.00 4.00
Nos. 521-523 (3) 8.75 8.75

Coronation of Queen Elizabeth II, 40th Anniv. — A87

Designs: 10p, Ampulla, spoon. 15p, Orb. 35p, Imperial State Crown. 60p, St. Edward's Crown.

1993, June 14 *Perf. 14½*

524 A87 10p green & black .70 .70
525 A87 15p red vio & black 1.10 1.10
526 A87 35p purple & black 2.40 2.40
527 A87 60p blue & black 4.25 4.25
Nos. 524-527 (4) 8.45 8.45

Resettlement to Tristan, 30th Anniv. — A88

Ships: No. 528, Tristania, Frances Repetto. No. 529, Boissevain. 50p, Bornholm.

1993, Nov. 10 *Perf. 13½x14*

528 A88 35p multicolored 2.75 2.50
529 A88 35p multicolored 2.75 2.50
a. Pair, #528-529 6.50 6.00
530 A88 50p multicolored 4.50 4.25
Nos. 528-530 (3) 10.00 9.25

Christmas — A89

Entire paintings or details: 5p, Madonna with Child, School of Botticelli. 15p, The Holy Family, by Daniel Gran. 35p, The Holy Virgin and Child, by Rubens. 65p, The Mystical Marriage of St. Catherine with the Holy Child, by Jan Van Balen.

1993, Nov. 30 **Wmk. 373** *Perf. 13*

531 A89 5p multicolored .60 .60
532 A89 15p multicolored 1.75 1.25
533 A89 35p multicolored 3.75 2.75
534 A89 65p multicolored 6.00 5.25
Nos. 531-534 (4) 12.10 9.85

Ships — A90

Designs: 1p, Duchess of Atholl, 1929. 3p, Empress of Australia, 1935. 5p, Anatolia, 1937. 8p, Viceroy of India, 1939. 10p, Rangitata, 1943. 15p, Caronia, 1950. 20p, Rotterdam, 1960. 25p, Leonardo da Vinci, 1972. 35p, Vistafjord, 1974. £1, World Discoverer, 1984. £2, Astor, 1984. £5, RMS St. Helena, 1992.

1994, Feb. 3 **Wmk. 384** *Perf. 14*

535 A90 1p multicolored .30 .35
536 A90 3p multicolored .30 .35
537 A90 5p multicolored .30 .35
538 A90 8p multicolored .30 .35
539 A90 10p multicolored .40 .50
540 A90 15p multicolored .60 .70
541 A90 20p multicolored .80 .90
542 A90 25p multicolored 1.00 1.10
543 A90 35p multicolored 1.50 1.75
544 A90 £1 multicolored 3.75 4.50
545 A90 £2 multicolored 7.75 9.00
546 A90 £5 multicolored 20.00 17.00
Nos. 535-546 (12) 37.00 36.85

Royal Navy Warships Type of 1990

10p, HMS Nigeria, 1948. 25p, HMS Phoebe, 1949. 35p, HMS Liverpool, 1949. 50p, HMS Magpie, 1955.

1994, May 2 **Wmk. 373**

547 A79 10p multicolored 1.00 1.00
548 A79 25p multicolored 2.50 2.50
549 A79 35p multicolored 3.25 3.25
550 A79 50p multicolored 5.25 5.25
Nos. 547-550 (4) 12.00 12.00

Sharks — A91

1994, Aug. **Wmk. 384**

551 A91 10p Blue shark .95 .95
552 A91 45p Seven-gill shark 3.75 3.75
553 A91 65p Mako shark 5.25 5.25
Nos. 551-553 (3) 9.95 9.95

Farm Animals A92

1994, Nov. **Wmk. 373**

554 A92 10p Donkeys .75 .75
555 A92 20p Cattle 1.75 1.75
556 A92 35p Ducks, geese 3.25 3.25
557 A92 60p Girl feeding lamb 5.75 5.75
Nos. 554-557 (4) 11.50 11.50

See Nos. 601-604.

Local Transport — A93

Designs: 15p, Pick-up truck. 20p, Leyland Daf Sherpa van. 45p, Yamaha motorcycle, scooter. 60p, Administrator's Landrover.

Wmk. 384

1995, Feb. 27 **Litho.** *Perf. 14*

558 A93 15p multicolored 1.15 1.15
559 A93 20p multicolored 1.35 1.35
560 A93 45p multicolored 3.25 3.25
561 A93 60p multicolored 4.50 4.50
Nos. 558-561 (4) 10.25 10.25

End of World War II, 50th Anniv.

Common Design Types

Designs: 15p, Lewis gun instruction, 1943. 20p, Tristan defense volunteers, 1943-46. 45p, Radio, weather stations. 60p, HNS Birmingham, 1942.

£1, Reverse of War Medal, 1939-45.

Perf. 13x13½

1995, June 19 **Litho.** **Wmk. 373**

562 CD351 15p multicolored 1.50 1.50
563 CD351 20p multicolored 2.10 2.10
564 CD351 45p multicolored 4.00 4.00
565 CD351 60p multicolored 5.75 5.75
Nos. 562-565 (4) 13.35 13.35

Souvenir Sheet

Perf. 14

566 CD352 £1 multicolored 6.75 6.75

Souvenir Sheet

Queen Mother, 95th Birthday A94

1995, Aug. 4 **Litho.** *Perf. 14½x14*

567 A94 £1.50 multicolored 9.00 9.00

UN, 50th Anniv.

Common Design Type

20p, Bedford 4-ton truck. 30p, Saxon armored personnel carrier. 45p, Mi26 heavy lift helicopter. 50p, RFA Sir Tristram transporting UN vehicles.

1995, Oct. 24 *Perf. 13½x13*

568 CD353 20p multicolored 1.75 1.75
569 CD353 30p multicolored 3.00 3.00
570 CD353 45p multicolored 4.00 4.00
571 CD353 50p multicolored 4.75 4.75
Nos. 568-571 (4) 13.50 13.50

Seals — A95

Sub Antarctic fur seal: 10p, On rock. 35p, Coming out of water with young.

Southern elephant seal: 45p, On beach with young. 50p, In water.

1995, Nov. 3 *Perf. 13½*

572 A95 10p multicolored .70 .70
573 A95 35p multicolored 2.75 2.75
574 A95 45p multicolored 4.00 4.00
575 A95 50p multicolored 4.25 4.25
Nos. 572-575 (4) 11.70 11.70

Queen Elizabeth II, 70th Birthday

Common Design Type

Various portraits of Queen, island scenes: 15p, Tristan from sea. 20p, Traditional cottage. 45p, The Residency. 60p, With Prince Philip.

1996, Apr. 22 **Litho.** *Perf. 13½*

576 CD354 15p multicolored .90 .90
577 CD354 20p multicolored 1.20 1.20
578 CD354 45p multicolored 2.75 2.75
579 CD354 60p multicolored 3.50 3.50
Nos. 576-579 (4) 8.35 8.35

New Harbor A96

15p, View of Old Harbor. 20p, Earthmoving, New Harbor construction. 45p, Crane, new construction. 60p, View of New Harbor. Nos. 581-582 are 45x28mm.

1996, July 5 **Wmk. 373** *Perf. 13*

580 A96 15p multicolored 1.75 1.75
581 A96 20p multicolored 2.75 2.75
582 A96 45p multicolored 3.50 3.50
583 A96 60p multicolored 4.50 4.50
Nos. 580-583 (4) 12.50 12.50

Nos. 581-582 are 45x28mm.

A97

Gough Island Birds: 15p, Gough moorhen. 20p, Wandering albatross. 45p, Sooty albatross. 60p, Gough bunting.

1996, Oct. 1 *Perf. 14*

584 A97 15p multicolored .90 .90
585 A97 20p multicolored 1.35 1.35
586 A97 45p multicolored 3.25 3.25
587 A97 60p multicolored 4.50 4.50
a. Souvenir sheet of 1 5.00 5.00
Nos. 584-587 (4) 10.00 10.00

No. 587a for return of Hong Kong to China, July 1, 1997. Issued 6/20/97.

A98

Presentation of Portrait of Queen Victoria, Cent.: 20p, 19th cent. map of Trista da Cunha. 30p, HMS Magpie. 45p, Peter Green, former governor. 50p, Detail of portrait of Queen Victoria, by Heinrich Von Angell.

1996, Dec. 18 *Perf. 13½*

588 A98 20p multicolored 1.40 1.40
589 A98 30p multicolored 2.25 2.25
590 A98 45p multicolored 3.25 3.25
591 A98 50p multicolored 3.50 3.50
Nos. 588-591 (4) 10.40 10.40

Atlantic Marine Fauna of the Cretaceous — A99

Designs: a, Archelon. b, Trinacromerum. c, Platecarpus. d, Clidastes.

1997, Feb. 10 **Wmk. 384** *Perf. 14*

592 A99 35p Sheet of 4, #a.-d. 10.50 10.50

See No. 619.

Visual Communications — A100

Designs: No. 593, Smoke signals. No. 594, HMS Eurydice. No. 595, HMS Challenger. No. 596, Flag hoists. No. 597, Semaphore. No. 598, HMS Carlisle. No. 599, Light signals. No. 600, HMS Cilicia.

1997 **Litho.** **Wmk. 384** *Perf. 14½*

593 10p multicolored .65 .65
594 10p multicolored .65 .65
a. A100 Pair, #593-594 1.50 1.50
595 15p multicolored .90 .90
596 15p multicolored .90 .90
a. A100 Pair, #595-596 2.40 2.40
597 20p multicolored 1.10 1.10
598 20p multicolored 1.10 1.10
a. A100 Pair, #597-598 3.00 3.00
599 35p multicolored 1.90 1.90
600 35p multicolored 1.90 1.90
a. A100 Pair, #599-600 5.00 5.00
Nos. 593-600 (8) 9.10 9.10

Farm Animals Type of 1994

1997, Aug. 26 **Litho.** *Perf. 14*

601 A92 20p Chickens 1.30 1.30
602 A92 30p Cattle 2.25 2.25
603 A92 45p Sheep 3.25 3.25
604 A92 50p Dogs 3.25 3.25
Nos. 601-604 (4) 10.05 10.05

Queen Elizabeth II and Prince Philip, 50th Wedding Anniv. A101

Designs: No. 605, Queen up close. No. 606, Prince riding polo pony. No. 607, Queen with horse. No. 608, Prince up close. No. 609, Prince in military attire, Queen in green coat. No. 610, Princess Anne riding horse.

£1.50, Queen, Prince riding in open carriage, horiz.

1997, Nov. 20 **Wmk. 373** *Perf. 14*

605 15p multicolored .90 .90
606 15p multicolored .90 .90
a. A101 Pair, #605-606 2.40 2.40
607 20p multicolored 1.30 1.30
608 20p multicolored 1.30 1.30
a. A101 Pair, #607-608 4.25 4.25
609 45p multicolored 2.75 2.75
610 45p multicolored 2.75 2.75
a. A101 Pair, #609-610 8.75 8.75
Nos. 605-610 (6) 9.90 9.90

Souvenir Sheet

611 A101 £1.50 multicolored 12.50 12.50

First Lobster Survey, 50th Anniv. — A102

Ships: 15p, Hilary, Melodie. 20p, Tristania II, Hekla. 30p, Pequena, Frances Repetto. 45p, Tristania, Gillian Gaggins. 50p, MFV. Kelso, MV. Edinburgh.

£1.20, Fr. C.P. Lawrence, lobster.

1998, Feb. 6 ***Perf. 14½***

612	A102	15p multicolored	.75	.75
613	A102	20p multicolored	1.10	1.10
614	A102	30p multicolored	1.60	1.60
615	A102	45p multicolored	2.75	2.75
616	A102	50p multicolored	2.75	2.75
		Nos. 612-616 (5)	8.95	8.95

Souvenir Sheet

617	A102	£1.20 multicolored	10.50	10.50

Diana, Princess of Wales (1961-97)

Common Design Type

a, In beige dress. b, In white top with black collar. c, In striped top. d, In lilac & white print dress.

1998, May 15 ***Perf. 14½x14***

618	CD355	35p Strip of 4, #a.-d.	5.00	5.00

No. 618 sold for £1.40 + 20p with surtax from international sales going to the Princess Diana Memorial Fund and surtax from local sales going to a designated local charity.

Atlantic Marine Fauna Type of 1997

Fauna of the Miocene Epoch: a, Carcharodon. b, Orycterocetus. c, Eurhinodelphis. d, Hexanchus (six gilled shark), myliobatis.

1998, July 8 ***Perf. 14***

619	A99	45p Sheet of 4, #a.-d.	16.00	16.00

Visiting Cruise Ships — A103

1998, Sept. 15 ***Perf. 14***

620	A103	15p Livonia	1.35	1.35
621	A103	20p Professor Molchanov	1.90	1.90
622	A103	45p Explorer	4.25	4.25
623	A103	60p Hanseatic	5.50	5.50
		Nos. 620-623 (4)	13.00	13.00

Sailing Ships — A104

15p, H.G. Johnson, 1892. 35p, Theodore, 1893. 45p, Hesperides, 1893. 50p, Bessfield, 1894.

1998, Nov. 23 **Wmk. 373** ***Perf. 14½***

624	A104	15p multicolored	1.40	1.40
625	A104	35p multicolored	3.00	3.00
626	A104	45p multicolored	4.25	4.25
627	A104	50p multicolored	4.50	4.50
		Nos. 624-627 (4)	13.15	13.15

1999, Mar. 19

20p, Derwent, 1895. 30p, Strathgryffe, 1898. 50p, Celestial Empire, 1898. 60p, Lamorna, 1902.

628	A104	20p multicolored	2.00	2.00
629	A104	30p multicolored	2.75	2.75
630	A104	50p multicolored	4.25	4.25
631	A104	60p multicolored	4.50	4.50
		Nos. 628-631 (4)	13.50	13.50

Wandering Albatross A105

World Wildlife Fund: 5p, Two adults. 8p, Adult, juvenile in nest. 12p, Adult spreading wings. 15p, Two in flight.

1999, Apr. 27 **Wmk. 373** ***Perf. 14***

632	A105	5p multicolored	.60	.60
633	A105	8p multicolored	.65	.65
634	A105	12p multicolored	.70	.70
635	A105	15p multicolored	.80	.80
a.		Strip of 4, #632-635	3.00	3.00
		Nos. 632-635 (4)	2.75	2.75

Issued in sheets of 16.

Wedding of Prince Edward and Sophie Rhys-Jones

Common Design Type

Perf. 13¾x14

1999, June 18 **Litho.** **Wmk. 384**

636	CD356	45c Separate portraits	2.25	2.25
637	CD356	£1.20 Couple	5.25	5.25

Queen Mother's Century

Common Design Type

Queen Mother: 20p, With Princess Elizabeth on her 18th birthday. 30p, With King George VI at Balmoral. 50p, With Royal Family, 94th birthday. 60p, As colonel-in-chief of Black Watch.

£1.50, Age 5 photo, airplanes from Battle of Britain, 1940.

1999, Aug. 18 **Wmk. 384** ***Perf. 13½***

638	CD358	20p multi	1.00	1.00
639	CD358	30p multi	1.75	1.75
640	CD358	50p multi	2.75	2.75
641	CD358	60p multi	3.50	3.50
		Nos. 638-641 (4)	9.00	9.00

Souvenir Sheet

642	CD358	£1.50 black	9.00	9.00

Millennium A106

Various birds.

2000, Jan. 1 **Wmk. 373** ***Perf. 14***

Color of Queen's Head

643	A106	20p bister	1.25	1.25
644	A106	30p green	2.10	2.10
645	A106	50p blue	4.00	4.00
646	A106	60p brown	4.75	4.75
		Nos. 643-646 (4)	12.10	12.10

Royalty — A107

British monarchs on 8p-£5: 1p, King Manuel I of Portugal. 3p, Frederick Henry, Prince of Orange. 5p, Empress Maria Theresa of Austria. 8p, King George III. 10p, King George IV. 15p, King Willian IV. 20p, Queen Victoria. 25p, Edward VII. 35p, George V. £1, Edward VIII. £2, George VI. £5, Elizabeth II.

2000, Feb. 1 **Wmk. 384** ***Perf. 14***

647	A107	1p multi	.25	.25
648	A107	3p multi	.25	.25
649	A107	5p multi	.25	.25
650	A107	8p multi	.30	.30
651	A107	10p multi	.40	.40
652	A107	15p multi	.55	.80
653	A107	20p multi	.70	1.00
654	A107	25p multi	.90	1.10
655	A107	35p multi	1.40	1.90
656	A107	£1 multi	3.50	5.25
657	A107	£2 multi	7.50	10.00
658	A107	£5 multi	18.00	24.50
		Nos. 647-658 (12)	34.00	46.00

The Stamp Show 2000, London — A108

Designs: 15p, Longboat under oars. 45p, Longboat under sail. 50p, Cutty Sark, 1876. 60p, Cutty Sark, 2000.

£1.50, Cutty Sark visiting Tristan da Cunha, 1876.

Wmk. 373

2000, May 22 **Litho.** ***Perf. 14***

659	A108	15p multi	1.50	1.50
660	A108	45p multi	3.50	3.50
661	A108	50p multi	4.00	4.00
662	A108	60p multi	4.75	4.75
		Nos. 659-662 (4)	13.75	13.75

Souvenir Sheet

663	A108	£1.50 multi	13.00	13.00

Prince William, 18th Birthday

Common Design Type

William: Nos. 664, 668a, As toddler, with Princes Charles and Harry, vert. Nos. 665, 668b, Holding paper, vert. Nos. 666, 668c, Wearing scarf. Nos. 667, 668d, Wearing suit and wearing sweater. No. 668e, As child, with Shetland pony.

Perf. 13¾x14¼, 14¼x13¾

2000, June 21 **Litho.** **Wmk. 373**

Stamps With White Border

664	CD359	45p multi	2.25	2.25
665	CD359	45p multi	2.25	2.25
666	CD359	45p multi	2.25	2.25
667	CD359	45p multi	2.25	2.25
		Nos. 664-667 (4)	9.00	9.00

Souvenir Sheet

Stamps Without White Border

Perf. 14¼

668	CD359	45p Sheet of 5, #a-e	12.50	12.50

Ships and Helicopters — A109

No. 669, 10p: a, SA Agulhas. b, SA 330J Puma, 1999.

No. 670, 15p: a, HMS London. b, Westland Wessex HAS 1, 1964.

No. 671, 20p: a, HMS Endurance. b, Westland Lynx HAS 3, 1996.

No. 672, 50p: a, USS Spiegel Grove. b, Sikorsky UH-19F, 1963.

Wmk. 373

2000, Sept. 4 **Litho.** ***Perf. 14***

Pairs, #a-b

669-672	A109	Set of 4	14.50	14.50

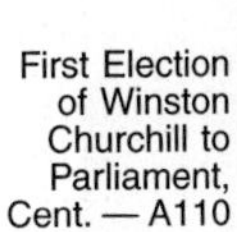

First Election of Winston Churchill to Parliament, Cent. — A110

Designs: 20p, During siege of Sidney Street, 1911. 30p, With Franklin D. Roosevelt, 1941. 50p, VE Day broadcast, 1945. 60p, Greeting Queen Elizabeth, 1955.

Perf. 13¾x14

2000, Oct. 2 **Wmk. 373**

673-676	A110	Set of 4	10.00	10.00

Souvenir Sheet

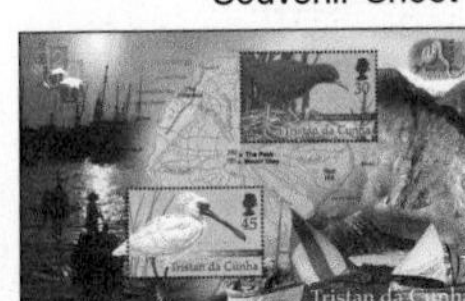

New Year 2001 (Year of the Snake) A111

No. 677: a, 30p, Inaccessible Island rail. b, 45p, Black-faced spoonbill.

Wmk. 373

2001, Feb. 1 **Litho.** ***Perf. 14½***

677	A111	Sheet of 2, #a-b	10.00	10.00

Hong Kong 2001 Stamp Exhibition.

Age of Victoria — A112

Designs: 15p, Letter, 1846. 20p, Prince Alfred, Duke of Edinburgh, vert. 30p, HMS Galatea. 35p, Queen Victoria, vert. 50p, Charles Dickens, vert. 60p, Resupplying ships.

£1.50, Jubilee celebrations.

Wmk. 373

2001, May 24 **Litho.** ***Perf. 14***

678-683	A112	Set of 6	10.50	10.50

Souvenir Sheet

684	A112	£1.50 multi	8.00	8.00

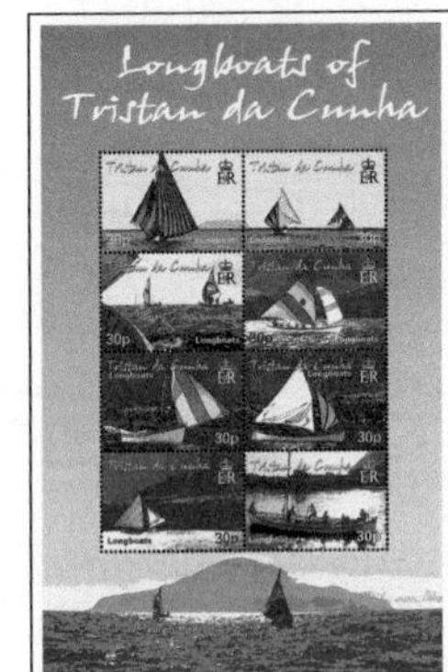

Longboats — A113

No. 685: a, Boat with dark and light blue striped sails, island in distance. b, Boat with red and blue striped and white sails, boat with blue, red and yellow striped and blue and white striped sails. c, Prow and sail of boat, two boats in distance. d, Boat with blue red and yellow striped and blue and white striped sails. e, Boat with dark and light blue sails near shore. f, Boat with red and blue striped and white sails. g, Boat with gray, red and white sails. h, Boat with sails down.

2001, July 12

685	A113	30p Sheet of 8, #a-h	12.00	12.00

Nos. 669-672 Overprinted in Blue Violet

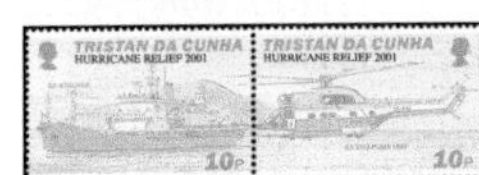

Wmk. 373

2001, Sept. 17 **Litho.** ***Perf. 14***

686	A109	10p Pair, #a-b	2.00	2.00
687	A109	15p Pair, #a-b	2.75	2.75
688	A109	20p Pair, #a-b	3.50	3.50
689	A109	50p Pair, #a-b	9.00	9.00
		Nos. 686-689 (4)	17.25	17.25

Souvenir Sheet

Birdlife International World Bird Festival — A114

Spectacled petrel: a, Head. b, Diving (island in background). c, In flight with legs extended. d, Diving (sea in background). e, Chick.

Wmk. 373

2001, Oct. 1 **Litho.** ***Perf. 14½***

690	A114	35p Sheet of 5, #a-e	14.00	14.00

Royal Navy Ships — A115

Designs: No. 691, 20p, HMS Penguin, 1815. No. 692, 20p, HMS Julia, 1817. No. 693, 35p, HMS Beagle, 1901. No. 694, 35p, HMS Puma, 1962. No. 695, 60p, HMS Monmouth, 1997. No. 696, 60p, HMS Somerset, 1999.

Wmk. 373

2001, Oct. 31 **Litho.** ***Perf. 14***

691-696	A115	Set of 6	14.00	14.00

Churches A116

Designs: No. 697, 35p, Exterior, St. Joseph's Catholic Church. No. 698, 35p, Exterior, St. Mary's Anglican Church. No. 699, 60p, Stained glass window, St. Joseph's. No. 700, 60p, Altar, St. Mary's.

Perf. 13¼x13½, 13½x13¼

2001, Nov. 27

697-700 A116 Set of 4 13.00 13.00

Christmas, Arrival of first USPG missionary, 150th anniv.

Tristan da Cunha Postage Stamps, 50th Anniv. — A117

Designs: Nos. 701, 45p, 705a, 45p, #5, 6, 9, 10 canceled. Nos. 702, 20p, 705, 45p, #7, 8, 11, 12 canceled. Nos. 703, 50p, 705c, 45p, #1-4 canceled. Nos. 704, 60p, 705d, 45p, Men at post office, 1952.

2002, Jan. 1 ***Perf. 13½***

Without "Tristan da Cunha" in Script

701-704 A117 Set of 4 12.00 12.00

Souvenir Sheet

With "Tristan da Cunha" in Script at Top or Bottom of Stamps

705 A117 45p Sheet of 4, #a-d 11.50 11.50

Reign Of Queen Elizabeth II, 50th Anniv. Issue

Common Design Type

Designs: Nos. 706, 710a, 15p, Princess Elizabeth, 1947. Nos. 707, 710b, 30p, Wearing tiara, 1991. Nos. 708, 710c, 45p, Wearing red coat. Nos. 709, 710d, 50p, Wearing purple hat, 1997. No. 710e, 60p, 1955 portrait by Annigoni (38x50mm).

Perf. 14¼x14½, 13¾ (#710e)

2002, Feb. 6 Litho. Wmk. 373

With Gold Frames

706 CD360 15p multicolored .95 .95
707 CD360 30p multicolored 1.80 1.80
708 CD360 45p multicolored 2.50 2.50
709 CD360 50p multicolored 2.75 2.75
Nos. 706-709 (4) 8.00 8.00

Souvenir Sheet

Without Gold Frames

710 CD360 Sheet of 5, #a-e 10.50 10.50

Fishing Industry — A118

Designs: 20p, Pelagic armorhead. 35p, Yellowtail. 50p, Splendid alfonsino. 60p, Ship San Liberatore.

Wmk. 373

2002, May Litho. ***Perf. 14***

711-713 A118 Set of 3 6.75 6.75
714 Souvenir sheet, #711-713, 714a 8.50 8.50
a. A118 60p multi 1.75 1.75

Queen Mother Elizabeth (1900-2002)

Common Design Type

Designs: 20p, Wearing hat (black and white photograph). £1.50, Wearing blue green hat.

No. 717: a, 75p, Holding baby (black and white photograph). b, 75p, Wearing dark blue hat.

Wmk. 373

2002, Aug. 5 Litho. ***Perf. 14¼***

With Purple Frames

715 CD361 20p multicolored 1.00 1.00
716 CD361 £1.50 multicolored 6.25 6.25

Souvenir Sheet

Without Purple Frames

Perf. 14½x14¼

717 CD361 Sheet of 2, #a-b 9.00 9.00

Marine Mammals — A119

No. 718: a, Gray's beaked whale. b, Dusky dolphin. c, False killer whale. d, Long-finned pilot whale. e, Sperm whale. f, Shepherd's beaked whale.

£2, Humpback whale.

Wmk. 373

2002, Sept. 24 Litho. ***Perf. 13¼***

718 A119 30p Sheet of 6, #a-f 13.50 13.50

Souvenir Sheet

719 A119 £2 multi 16.00 16.00

HMS Herald Survey, 150th Anniv. — A120

Designs: 20p, Captain Denham and officers. 35p, HMS Herald in Bay of Biscay. 50p, Surveying, Oct. 30, 1852. 60p, HMS Herald and Torch at sunset, 1852.

2002, Nov. 11 ***Perf. 14x14¾***

720-723 A120 Set of 4 8.75 8.75

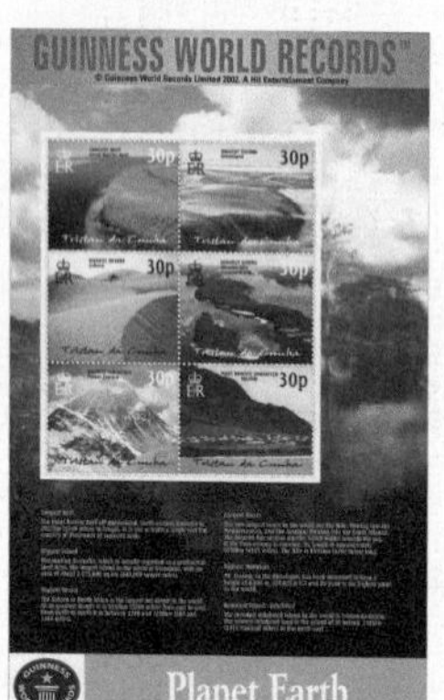

Guinness Book of World Records — A121

No. 724: a, Great Barrier Reef (longest reef). b, Greenland (biggest island). c, Sahara Desert (biggest desert). d, Amazon and Nile Rivers (longest rivers). e, Mt. Everest (biggest mountain). f, Tristan da Cunha (most remote inhabited island).

£2, Like No. 724f.

Wmk. 373

2003, Jan. 10 Litho. ***Perf. 13¾***

724 A121 30p Sheet of 6, #a-f 9.50 9.50

Souvenir Sheet

725 A121 £2 multi 11.00 11.00

Atlantic Yellow-nosed Albatross — A122

Designs: Nos. 726, 730a, 15p, Heads of two birds. Nos. 727, 730b, 30p, Bird on nest, vert. Nos. 728, 730c, 45p, Bird in flight, vert. Nos. 729, 730d, Two birds in flight. No. 730e, £1, Two birds in flight, diff.

Perf. 14¼x13¾, 13¾x14¼

2003, May 7 Litho.

Stamps With White Frames

726-729 A122 Set of 4 7.50 7.50

Souvenir Sheet

Stamps Without Frames

Perf. 14¼x14½

730 A122 Sheet of 5, #a-e 11.00 11.00

Birdlife International.

Head of Queen Elizabeth II

Common Design Type

Wmk. 373

2003, June 2 Litho. ***Perf. 13¾***

731 CD362 £2.80 multi 10.00 10.00

Coronation of Queen Elizabeth II, 50th Anniv.

Common Design Type

Designs: Nos. 732, 20p, 734a, Queen and extended family. Nos. 733, £1.50, 734b, Bishops paying homage to Queen at coronation.

Perf. 14¼x14½

2003, June 2 Litho. Wmk. 373

Vignettes Framed, Red Background

732 CD363 20p multicolored 1.00 1.00
733 CD363 £1.50 multicolored 7.00 7.00

Souvenir Sheet

Vignettes Without Frame, Purple Panel

734 CD363 75p Sheet of 2, #a-b 8.75 8.75

Prince William, 21st Birthday

Common Design Type

No. 735: a, William in polo uniform at right. b, In sweater at left.

Wmk. 373

2003, June 21 Litho. ***Perf. 14¼***

735 Horiz. pair 6.00 6.00
a.-b. CD364 50p Either single 2.60 2.60

William Glass (1787-1853), Governor — A123

No. 736: a, Arrival of Glass on HMS Falmouth, 1816. b, As corporal, stationed on Tristan da Cunha. c, Glass and family onshore, 1817. d, Glass family with dog. e, Gov. Glass conducting daughter's marriage ceremony, 1833. f, Glass as old man.

Perf. 14¼x14½

2003, Nov. 24 Litho. Wmk. 373

736 A123 30p Sheet of 6, #a-f, + 6 labels 9.00 9.00

Royal Navy Ships A124

No. 737, 20p: a, RFA Tideflow. b, RFA Tidespring.

No. 738, 35p: a, RFA Gold Rover. b, RFA Diligence.

No. 739, 60p: a, RFA Wave Chief. b, HMY Britannia.

Wmk. 373

2003, Dec. 8 Litho. ***Perf. 14***

Horiz. pairs, #a-b

737-739 A124 Set of 3 12.00 12.00

History of Writing Implements A125

Designs: 15p, Cave paintings and pigment blocks. 20p, Clay tablet. 35p, Egyptian writing palette. 45p, Goose quill pen. 50p, Fountain pen. 60p, Ballpoint pen.

£1.50, Word processing.

2004, Jan. 8 ***Perf. 13¾***

740-745 A125 Set of 6 9.25 9.25

Souvenir Sheet

Litho. with Margin Embossed

746 A125 £1.50 multi 8.00 8.00

Worldwide Fund for Nature (WWF) — A126

Subantarctic fur seal: No. 747, 35p, Underwater. No. 748, 35p, Pair on rocks. No. 749, 35p, Seal on rock. No. 750, 35p, Head.

Wmk. 373

2004, July 12 Litho. ***Perf. 14***

747-750 A126 Set of 4 6.00 6.00
a. Sheet, 4 each #747-750 26.00 26.00

New Flag — A127

2004, July 27 Unwmk. ***Die Cut***

Self-Adhesive

Booklet Stamp

751 A127 30p multi 1.35 1.35
a. Booklet pane of 6 8.25
Complete booklet, 2 #751a 16.50

Merchant Ships — A128

Designs: No. 752, 20p, RMS Dunnottar Castle. No. 753, 20p, RMS Caronia. No. 754, 35p, SA Agulhas. No. 755, 35p, MV Edinburgh. No. 756, 60p, MV Explorer. No. 757, 60p, MV Hanseatic.

Wmk. 373

2004, Nov. 9 Litho. ***Perf. 13¼***

752-757 A128 Set of 6 11.00 11.00

Battle of Trafalgar, Bicent. — A129

Designs: 15p, Admiral Horatio Nelson's quadrant. 20p, HMS Royal Sovereign breaks the line, horiz. 25p, Thomas Swain aids the wounded Nelson, horiz. 35p, HMS Victory breaks the line, horiz. 50p, Nelson. 60p, HMS Victory, horiz.

No. 764: a, Capt. Thomas Masterman Hardy. b, HMS Victory.

Perf. 13¼

2005, Jan. 20 Litho. Unwmk.

758-763 A129 Set of 6 11.50 11.50

Souvenir Sheet

764 A129 75p Sheet of 2, #a-b 9.50 9.50

No. 763 has particles of wood from the HMS Victory embedded in the areas covered by a thermographic process that produces a shiny, raised effect.

Island Flora, Fauna and Scenes — A130

No. 765 — Tristan da Cunha: a, Rockhopper penguins. b, Southern elephant seals. c, Tristan rock lobster. d, Crowberry. e, Tristan da Cunha island settlement and volcano.

No. 766 — Gough Island: a, Gough moorhen. b, Subantarctic fur seal. c, Bluefish. d,

Gough tree fern. e, South African Weather Station.

No. 767 — Inaccessible Island: a, Inaccessible rail. b, Dusky dolphins. c, Sebastes capensis. d, Pepper tree. e, Inaccessible Island Waterfall.

No. 768 — Nightingale Island: a, Tristan thrush. b, Southern right whale. c, Fivefinger fish. d, Tussock grass. e, Nightingale Island.

No. 769 — Middle Island: a, Broad-billed prion. b, False killer whale. c, Wreckfih. d, Fern. e, Middle Island.

No. 770 — Stoltenhoff Island: a, Brown skua. b, Shepherd's beaked whales. c, Snoeks. d, Sea bind weed. e, Stoltenhoff Island.

2005 **Wmk. 373** ***Perf. 13¾***

765	Horiz. strip of 5	11.00	11.00
a.-e.	A130 50p Any single	2.25	2.25
766	Horiz. strip of 5	11.00	11.00
a.-e.	A130 50p Any single	2.25	2.25
767	Horiz. strip of 5	11.00	11.00
a.-e.	A130 50p Any single	2.25	2.25
768	Horiz. strip of 5	11.00	11.00
a.-e.	A130 50p Any single	2.25	2.25
769	Horiz. strip of 5	11.00	11.00
a.-e.	A130 50p Any single	2.25	2.25
770	Horiz. strip of 5	11.00	11.00
a.-e.	A130 50p Any single	2.25	2.25

Issued: No. 765, 2/21; No. 766, 3/28; No. 767, 4/18; No. 768, 2/7/06; No. 769, 3/30/06; No. 770, 9/27/06.

See No. 796.

Birds — A131

Designs: 1p, Kerguelen petrel. 3p, Sooty albatross. 5p, Antarctic tern. 8p, Tristan bunting. 10p, Cape petrel. 15p, Tristan moorhen. 20p, Giant fulmar. 25p, Brown skua. 35p, Great-winged petrel. £1, Broad-billed prion. £2, Soft-plumaged petrel. £5, Rockhopper penguin.

Perf. 14¼x14¾

2005, June 1 **Litho.** **Wmk. 373**

771	A131	1p multi	.25	.25
772	A131	3p multi	.25	.25
773	A131	5p multi	.25	.25
774	A131	8p multi	.30	.30
775	A131	10p multi	.35	.35
776	A131	15p multi	.55	.55
777	A131	20p multi	.75	.75
778	A131	25p multi	.90	.90
779	A131	35p multi	1.25	1.25
780	A131	£1 multi	4.00	4.00
781	A131	£2 multi	7.25	8.75
782	A131	£5 multi	18.00	21.00
	Nos. 771-782 (12)		34.10	38.60

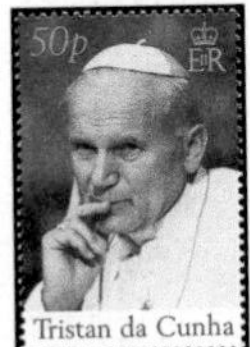

Pope John Paul II (1920-2005) — A132

Wmk. 373

2005, Aug. 18 **Litho.** ***Perf. 14***

783 A132 50p multi 3.00 3.00

Battle of Trafalgar, Bicent. — A133

Designs: 20p, HMS Victory. 70p, Ships in battle, horiz. £1, Admiral Horatio Nelson.

Perf. 13¼

2005, Oct. 18 **Litho.** **Unwmk.**

784-786 A133 Set of 3 12.00 12.00

Discovery of Tristan da Cunha, 500th Anniv. — A134

No. 787: a, 30p, Discovery by Tristao d'Acunha, 1506. b, 30p, First survey, 1767. c, 30p, Jonathan Lambert of Salem, 1810. d, 50p, William Glass, 1816. e, 50p, Duke of Gloucester (ship), 1824. f, 80p, Wreck of the Emily, 1836.

No. 788: a, 30p, Thomas Swain (1774-1862). b, 30p, HMS Challenger, 1873. c, 30p, Rev. Edwin Dodgson arrives, 1881. d, 50p, Wreck of the Italia, 1892. e, 50p, HMS Milford, 1938. f, 80p, Norwegian Expedition, 1937-38.

No. 789: a, 30p, World War II TDV training. b, 30p, HMS Atlantic Isle, 1944. c, 30p, Hands holding potatoes, 1946 potato stamp. d, 50p, Tristan da Cunha #5. e, 50p, Volcano eruption and evacuation, 1961. f, 80p, Gough Island Scientific Expedition, 1955.

No. 790: a, 30p, Royal Society Expedition, 1962. b, 30p, Resettlement, 1963. c, 30p, Denstone Expedition to Inaccessible Island, 1982. d, 50p, RMS St. Helena, 1992. e, 50p, New coat of arms, 2002. f, 80p, Hurricane disaster, 2001.

Perf. 14¼x14½

2006 **Litho.** **Wmk. 373**

787 A134 Sheet of 6, #a-f 15.00 15.00
788 A134 Sheet of 6, #a-f 15.00 15.00

Perf. 14¼x14¾

789 A134 Sheet of 6, #a-f 16.00 16.00
790 A134 Sheet of 6, #a-f 16.00 16.00

Issued: Nos. 787-788, 2/2; Nos. 789-790, 6/1.

Queen Elizabeth II, 80th Birthday — A135

Queen: No. 791, 60p, As child. No. 792, 60p, Wearing feathered hat. No. 793, 60p, Wearing red hat. No. 794, 60p, Wearing sunglasses.

No. 795: a, 50p, Like No. 792. b, 50p, Like No. 793.

2006, Apr. 21 ***Perf. 14***

791-794 A135 Set of 4 12.00 12.00

Souvenir Sheet

795 A135 50p Sheet of 2, #a-b 5.25 5.25

Island Flora, Fauna and Scenes Type of 2005-06

Miniature Sheet

No. 796: a, Map of Tristan da Cunha, flag. b, Map of Inaccessible Island, wandering albatross. c, Map of Nightingale Island, humpback whale. d, Map of Middle Island, traditional longboats. e, Map of Stoltenhoff Island, mackerel. f, Map of Gough Island, sub-antarctic fur seal.

Wmk. 373

2007, Jan. 22 **Litho.** ***Perf. 13¾***

796 Sheet of 6 15.00 15.00
a.-f. A130 50p Any single 2.40 2.40

Local Vehicles — A136

Designs: 15p, Wave Dancer fishery patrol boat. 20p, Ambulance. 30p, Inshore rescue craft. 45p, Police Land Rover. 50p, Fire engine. 85p, Administrator's Land Rover.

Perf. 12½x13

2007, Apr. 17 **Litho.** **Unwmk.**

797-802 A136 Set of 6 13.00 13.00

Wedding of Queen Elizabeth II and Prince Philip, 60th Anniv. — A137

Designs: No. 803, 50p, Shown. No. 804, 50p, Queen waving. No. 805, 50p, Queen and Prince (black and white photograph). No. 806, 50p, Queen and Prince (color photograph). £2, Queen in wedding gown.

2007, June 1 **Wmk. 373** ***Perf. 13¾***

803-806 A137 Set of 4 9.50 9.50

Souvenir Sheet

Perf. 14

807 A137 £2 multi 9.50 9.50

No. 807 contains one 42x57mm stamp.

Miniature Sheet

BirdLife International — A138

No. 808 — Great shearwater: a, In flight, facing right. b, In flight, facing left, showing land and sky. c, On ground, showing land and sky. d, In flight facing left, showing land and water. e, On ground, showing land only. f, Chick.

2007, July 1 **Unwmk.** ***Perf. 13¾***

808 A138 50p Sheet of 6, #a-f 16.00 16.00

Scouting, Cent. — A139

Designs: 15p, Scout J. W. S. Marr and his book, *Into the Frozen South,* hands tying knot. 20p, The Quest frozen in, Marr, hands tightening rope. £1.25, Flag raising ceremony, hand with compass. £1.40, Children of Tristan da Cunha, trumpeter.

No. 813, vert.: a, Marr and Questie, the ship's cat. b, Lord Robert Baden-Powell.

2007, July 9 **Wmk. 373**

809-812 A139 Set of 4 15.00 15.00

Souvenir Sheet

813 A139 £1.50 Sheet of 2, #a-b 15.00 15.00

A140

A141

A142

A143

A144

Princess Diana (1961-97) — A145

Perf. 13x12½

2007, Nov. 30 **Litho.** **Unwmk.**

814	A140	50p multi	2.40	2.40
815	A141	50p multi	2.40	2.40
816	A142	50p multi	2.40	2.40
817	A143	50p multi	2.40	2.40
818	A144	50p multi	2.40	2.40
819	A145	50p multi	2.40	2.40
	Nos. 814-819 (6)		14.40	14.40

Military Uniforms — A146

Designs: No. 820, 15p, Officer, 21st Light Dragoon. No. 821, 15p, Corporal, Royal Artillery. No. 822, 20p, Privates, Royal Artillery. No. 823, 20p, Lieutenant, Royal Artillery. No. 824, £1, Soldiers from Cape Regiment. No. 825, £1, Soldiers from South Africa Army Engineering Corps.

Unwmk.

2007, Dec. 10 **Litho.** ***Perf. 14***

820-825 A146 Set of 6 15.00 15.00

Marine Invertebrates A147

Designs: 15p, Tristan rock lobster. 20p, Trumpet anemone. 35p, Starfish. No. 829, 60p, Tristan urchin. No. 830, 60p, Sponge. 85p, Strawberry anemone.

2007, Dec. 10 **Unwmk.** ***Perf. 13¼***

826-831 A147 Set of 6 12.50 12.50

A148

Royal Air Force, 90th Anniv. A149

Designs: No. 832, 30p, Royal Aircraft Factory S. E. 5a. No. 833, 30p, Hawker Hart. No. 834, 30p, Hawker Typhoon. No. 835, 30p, Avro Vulcan. No. 836, 30p, SEPECAT Jaguar. £1.50, Sir Hugh Trenchard reviewing troops.

Wmk. 373

2008, Apr. 1 **Litho.** ***Perf. 14***

832-836 A148 Set of 5 8.00 8.00

Souvenir Sheet

837 A149 £1.50 black 8.00 8.00

Nos. 832-836 each were printed in sheets of 8 + central label.

Tristan Fisheries, 60th Anniv. — A150

Designs: 15p, Fishing boats in harbor. 20p, Fishing boats. 30p, Offloading and loading fish. 70p, Sorting tails. 80p, Wrapping and packaging of rock lobster tails. £1.25, Shipping for export.

Perf. 13¼x13

2008, July 1 Litho. Unwmk.

838-843	A150	Set of 6	15.00	15.00

Allan B. Crawford (1912-2007), Writer — A151

Designs: 15p, Crawford. 20p, Local Tristan da Cunha stamp. 50p, First map of Tristan da Cunha. 60p, Members of 1937-38 Norwegian Scientific Expedition, Crawford's book, *I Went to Tristan,* horiz. 85p, Men at opening of Marion Island Meteorological Office, Crawford's book, *Tristan da Cunha and the Roaring Forties,* horiz. £1.20, Crawford and his book, *Penguins, Potatoes and Postage Stamps,* horiz.

Perf. 13x13¼, 13¼x13

2008, Aug. 1 Litho. Unwmk.

844-849	A151	Set of 6	15.00	15.00

End of World War I, 90th Anniv. — A152

Paintings: No. 850, 50p, End of Richthofen, by Charles H. Hubbell. No. 851, 50p, Lion Leads in Jutland, by W. L. Wyllie. No. 852, 50p, Oppy Wod, by John Nash. No. 853, 50p, A Battery Shelled, by Percy Wyndham Lewis. No. 854, 50p, Somme Tank, by Louis Dauphin. No. 855, 50p, The Angels of Mons, by R. Crowhurst, vert.

£1, Wreath of Remembrance, vert.

Wmk. 406

2008, Sept. 16 Litho. *Perf. 14*

850-855	A152	Set of 6	12.50	12.50

Souvenir Sheet

856	A152	£1 multi	4.50	4.50

Ships — A153

Tristao da Cunha (1460-1540), Explorer — A154

Designs: No. 857, 50p, Mary Rose. No. 858, 50p, Endurance. No. 859, 50p, Cutty Sark. No. 860, 50p, Suomen Joutsen. No. 861, 50p, RFA Lyme Bay. No. 862, 50p, MS Explorer.

Wmk. 406

2009, Mar. 9 Litho. *Perf. 14*

857-862	A153	Set of 6	11.50	11.50

Souvenir Sheet

863	A154	£1 multi	4.00	4.00

Naval Aviation, Cent. — A155

Designs: 25p, Felixstowe F.2A. 35p, Short S.27. No. 866, 50p, Blackburn Dart. No. 867, 50p, Sikorsky Hoverfly helicopter.

£1.50, Lieutenant Commander C. R. Samson in Short S.27 taking off from HMS Hibernia, 1912.

Wmk. 406

2009, Apr. 17 Litho. *Perf. 14*

864-867	A155	Set of 4	9.25	9.25

Souvenir Sheet

868	A155	£1.50 multi	6.50	6.50

Nos. 864-867 each were printed in sheets of 8 + central label.

Space Exploration — A156

Designs: 25p, Goddard Rocket, 1936. 35p, X-24B Spaceplane, 1972. 60p, Launch of Apollo 11, 1969. 90p, Space Shuttle Discovery ferried by Boeing 747, 2005. £1, X-43C experimental hypersonic aircraft.

£1.50, Astronauts on Moon, painting by Capt. Alan Bean, vert.

Wmk. 406

2009, July 20 Litho. *Perf. 13¼*

869-873	A156	Set of 5	12.50	12.50

Souvenir Sheet

Perf. 13x13½

874	A156	£1.50 multi	6.50	6.50

First man on the Moon, 40th anniv. No. 874 contains one 40x60mm stamp.

Potato Production — A157

No. 875, 25p: a, Preparing seed potatoes. b, Planting.

No. 876, 35p: a, Digging out. b, Harvesting.

No. 877, £1.10: a, Potato blossoms. b, Potato fields.

Unwmk.

2009, Aug. 3 Litho. *Perf. 13*

Horiz. Pairs, #a-b

875-877	A157	Set of 3	13.50	13.50

Island Traditions A158

Designs: 25p, Sheep shearing. 35p, Ratting Day. 70p, Longboats to Nightingale. £1.60, Old Year's Night Okalolies.

2009, Sept. 28

878-881	A158	Set of 4	10.50	10.50

See Nos. 927-930.

Mail Delivery on Tristan da Cunha — A159

Designs: 25p, Mail arriving by ship. 35p, Transporting mail to post office. £1, Hitting the gong. £1.60, Giving out the mail.

Unwmk.

2009, Nov. 23 Litho. *Perf. 13*

882-885	A159	Set of 4	12.50	12.50

British History — A160

Designs: No. 886, 35p, Battle of Hastings. No. 887, 35p, Peasants' Revolt. No. 888, 35p, King Henry VIII. No. 889, 35p, English Reformation. No. 890, 35p, Elizabethan era. No. 891, 35p, English Civil War. No. 892, 35p, Scientific innovation. No. 893, 35p, Bonnie Prince Charlie.

Wmk. 406

2010, Jan. 15 Litho. *Perf. 13¼*

886-893	A160	Set of 8	11.00	11.00

See Nos. 902-909, 944-951.

A161

A162

A163

A164

A165

Battle of Britain, 70th Anniv. — A166

Design: £1.50, Sir Douglas Bader, vert.

Wmk. 406

2010, Mar. 18 Litho. *Perf. 13*

894	A161	25p black & gray	1.05	1.05
895	A162	25p black & gray	1.05	1.05
896	A163	50p black & gray	2.10	2.10
897	A164	50p black & gray	2.10	2.10
898	A165	70p black & gray	2.75	2.75
899	A166	70p black & gray	2.75	2.75
		Nos. 894-899 (6)	11.80	11.80

Souvenir Sheet

900	A166	£1.50 black & gray	5.75	5.75

Souvenir Sheet

Great Britain No. 159 A167

2010, May 8 *Perf. 14x14¼*

901	A167	£1.50 multi	5.50	5.50

London 2010 Festival of Stamps.

British History Type of 2010

Designs: No. 902, 35p, Thomas Becket. No. 903, 35p, Battle of Agincourt. No. 904, 35p, Battle of Trafalgar. No. 905, 35p, Engineering & transportation. No. 906, 35p, Wireless age. No. 907, 35p, Votes for women. No. 908, 35p, The Great Depression. No. 909, 35p, Second World War.

Wmk. 406

2010, July 16 Litho. *Perf. 13¼*

902-909	A160	Set of 8	11.00	11.00

Surnames of Island Families — A168

Surnames of island families, flags and birds: No. 910, 50p, Hagan and Rogers, US flag, bald eagle. No. 911, 50p, Repetto and Lavaretto, Italian flag, hoopoe. No. 912, 50p, Glass, Scottish flag, golden eagle. No. 913, 50p, Green, Netherlands flag, oystercatcher. No. 914, 50p, Swain, English flag, avocet.

Perf. 12½x13

2010, Sept. 6 Unwmk.

910-914	A168	Set of 5	10.50	10.50

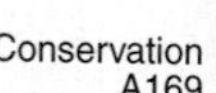

Conservation A169

Designs: 1p, New Conservation R1 boat. 3p, Eradication of New Zealand flax on Nightingale Island. 5p, Banding Tristan albatross. 8p, Hag's Tooth, Gough Island UNESCO World Heritage Site. 10p, Inaccessible rail. 15p, Inaccessible Island UNESCO World Heritage Site. 25p, Counting seals. 35p, Eradication of Sagina plant on Gough Island. 70p, Eradication of Loganberry plants at Sandy Point. £1, Banding Yellow-nosed albatross. £2, Gough bunting. £5, Counting penguins.

2010, Nov. 1 Litho. *Perf. 13*

915	A169	1p multi	.30	.30
916	A169	3p multi	.30	.30
917	A169	5p multi	.30	.30
918	A169	8p multi	.30	.30
919	A169	10p multi	.40	.40
920	A169	15p multi	.55	.55
921	A169	25p multi	.90	.90
922	A169	35p multi	1.30	1.30
923	A169	70p multi	2.60	2.60
924	A169	£1 multi	3.75	3.75
925	A169	£2 multi	7.50	7.50
926	A169	£5 multi	19.00	19.00
		Nos. 915-926 (12)	37.20	37.20

Island Traditions Type of 2009

Designs: 25p, Thatching a roof. 35p, Bullock cart. 70p, Music. £1.60, Pillow dance.

2010, Nov. 24

927-930	A158	Set of 4	11.00	11.00

Service of Queen Elizabeth II and Prince Philip A170

Designs: 25p, Queen Elizabeth II. 35p, Queen and Prince Philip. No. 933, 50p, Queen and Prince Philip, diff. No. 934, 50p, Queen (wearing hat) and Prince Philip. No. 935, 70p, Queen and Prince Philip, diff. No. 936, 70p, Prince Philip.

£1.50, Queen and Prince Philip, diff.

2011, Mar. 14 *Perf. 13¼*

931-936	A170	Set of 6	11.00	11.00
a.		Souvneir sheet of 6, #931-936, + 3 labels	11.00	11.00

Souvenir Sheet

937	A170	£1.50 multi	5.50	5.50

Cruise Ships — A171

Designs: 25p, MV Professor Multanovskiy. 35p, MV Aleksey Maryshev. 70p, MV Professor Molchanov. £1.10, MV Plancius.

£1.50, MV Plancius.

Perf. 14x14¾

2011, Apr. 12 Unwmk.

938-941	A171	Set of 4	8.50	8.50

Souvenir Sheet

942	A171	£1.50 multi	5.50	5.50

Souvenir Sheet

Wedding of Prince William and Catherine Middleton — A172

Perf. 14¾x14¼

2011, Apr. 29 **Wmk. 406**

943 A172 £3 multi 11.00 11.00

British History Type of 2010

Designs: No. 944, 35p, Magna Carta. No. 945, 35p, Wars of the Roses. No. 946, 35p, The Gunpowder Plot. No. 947, 35p, Great Fire of London. No. 948, 35p, Battle of Waterloo. No. 949, 35p, Age of Empire. No. 950, 35p, Industry and Commerce. No. 951, 35p, First World War.

2011, May 24 **Wmk. 406** ***Perf. 13¼***

944-951 A160 Set of 8 9.25 9.25

Photographs of Wedding of Prince William and Catherine Middleton — A173

Couple: No. 952, 70p, Standing, holding hands. No. 953, 70p, Kissing. No. 954, 70p, In coach, waving, horiz. No. 955. 70p, In car, waving, horiz.

2011, Sept. 1 **Unwmk.** ***Perf. 12½***

952-955 A173 Set of 4 9.00 9.00

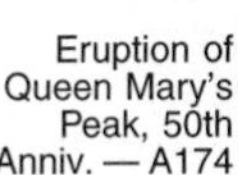

Eruption of Queen Mary's Peak, 50th Anniv. — A174

Queen Mary's Peak and: No. 956, 25p, Tholoid. No. 957, 35p, October 1961 eruption. No. 958, 95p, Islanders leave aboard the MV Tjisadane. No. 959, £1.10, Islanders arrive in Cape Town.
No. 960, MV Tjisadane.

2011, Oct. 10 **Unwmk.** ***Perf. 14***

956-959 A174 Set of 4 8.50 8.50

Souvenir Sheet

960 A174 £2 multi 6.25 6.25

See Nos. 961-965, 999-1003, 1006-1010.

Volcano Eruption Type of 2011

Queen Mary's Peak and: No. 961, 25p, Returning with the report. No. 962, 35p, Resettlement survey team. No. 963, 95p, HMS Protector Whirlwind helicopter. No. 964, £1.10, Royal Society members.
No. 965, £2, Landing party.

2012, Jan. 30 **Unwmk.** ***Perf. 14***

961-964 A174 Set of 4 8.50 8.50

Souvenir Sheet

965 A174 £2 multi 6.50 6.50

Reign of Queen Elizabeth II, 60th Anniv. A175

Queen Elizabeth II: 25p, Color photograph. 35p, Color photograph, diff. No. 968, 50p, Black-and-white photograph. No. 969, 50p, Color photograph, diff. No. 970, 70p, Color photograph, diff. No. 971, 70p, Black-and-white photograph, diff.
£1.50, Queen Elizabeth II wearing crown.

2012, Feb. 6 **Unwmk.** ***Perf. 13¼***

966-971 A175 Set of 6 9.50 9.50
a. Sheet of 6, #966-971, + 3 labels 9.50 9.50

Souvenir Sheet

972 A175 £1.50 multi 4.75 4.75

Miniature Sheet

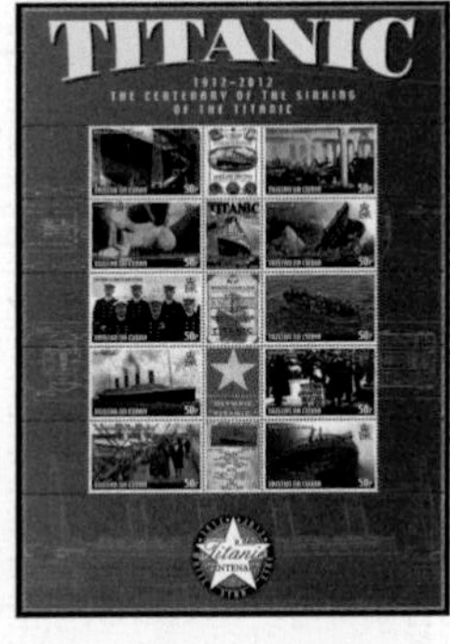

Sinking of the Titanic, Cent. A176

No. 973: a, Titanic being built in Harland & Wolff Shipyard. b, First class dining room. c, Titanic's propellers. d, Sinking of the ship. e, Captain. E. J. Smith and crew. f, Survivors in lifeboat. g, Titanic setting sail. h, Newspaper reports. i, Passengers strolling on board. j, Discovery of the wreck.

2012, Feb. 27 **Unwmk.** ***Perf. 13¼***

973 A176 50p Sheet of 10, #a-j, + 5 labels 16.00 16.00

Ships — A177

Designs: No. 974, 35p, Agulhas I at sea. No. 975, 35p, Agulhas II at sea. 70p, Agulhas I near land. £1.10, Agulhas II near land.

2012, Sept. 17 ***Perf. 14***

974-977 A177 Set of 4 8.00 8.00

Miniature Sheet

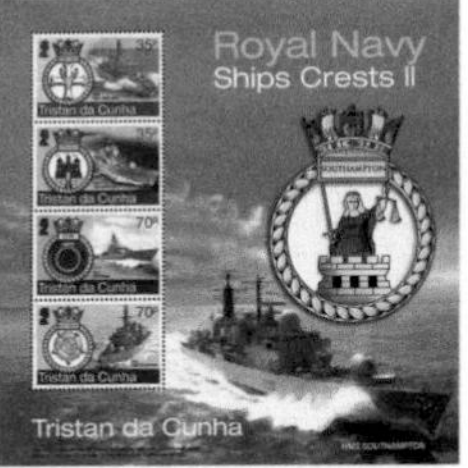

Royal Navy Ships and Their Crests — A178

No. 978: a, 35p, HMS Portland, 2005. b, 35p, HMS Edinburgh, 2006. c, 70p, HMS Clyde, 2011. d, 70p, HMS Montrose, 2012.

2012, Oct. 15 ***Perf. 13¼x13½***

978 A178 Sheet of 4, #a-d 6.75 6.75

Members of Shackleton-Rowett Antarctic Expedition — A179

Designs: No. 979, 70p, Frank Wild, Inaccessible Island. No.980, 70p, Hubert Wilkins, Gough Island. No. 981, 70p, James Marr, Tristan da Cunha. No. 982, 70p, Frank Worsley, Nightingale Island.

2012, Nov. 28 ***Perf. 14***

979-982 A179 Set of 4 9.00 9.00

Worldwide Fund for Nature (WWF) — A180

Tristan albatross: Nos. 983, 987a, 35p, Bird on nest. Nos. 984, 987b, 45p, Two birds. Nos. 985, 987c, 70p, Two birds, diff. Nos. 986, 987d, £1.10, Bird in flight.
£3, Bird landing.

2013, Jan. 28 **Litho.** ***Perf. 13¼x13½***

Stamps With White Frames

983-986 A180 Set of 4 8.25 8.25

Stamps Without White Frames

987 A180 Horiz. strip of 4, #a-d 8.25 8.25

Souvenir Sheet

988 A180 £3 multi 9.50 9.50

No. 988 contains one 48x30mm stamp.

Tristan Song Project — A181

Designs: 35p, Recorder and lyrics of "When Fish Get the Flu." 45p, Violin and lyrics of "Rockhopper Penguins." 70p, Guitar and lyrics of "The Volcano's Black." £1.10, Accordion and lyrics to "The Molly."

2013, Feb. 14 ***Perf. 13¼x13½***

989-992 A181 Set of 4 8.25 8.25

Items Produced for Coronations A182

Coronation of Queen Elizabeth II, 60th Anniv. — A183

Items produced for coronation of: 35p, Queen Victoria. 45p, King Edward VII. 70p, King George V. £1.10, King George VI. £1.50, Queen Elizabeth II.

2013, Apr. 15 ***Perf. 14***

993-997 A182 Set of 5 13.00 13.00

Souvenir Sheet

Perf. 14¾x14

998 A183 £2 multi 6.25 6.25

Nos. 993-997 each were printed in sheets of 8 + label.

Volcano Eruption Type of 2011

Queen Mary's Peak and: 25p, Returning islanders sitting near their possessions. 35p, Returning islanders walking toward possessions. 95p, Islanders on shore waiting for ships transporting their possessions. £1.10, Islanders returning to their homes in a tractor-pulled wagon.
£2, Islanders pulling longboat over rocks on shore.

2013, Nov. 11 **Litho.** ***Perf. 14***

999-1002 A174 Set of 4 8.50 8.50

Souvenir Sheet

1003 A174 £2 multi 6.50 6.50

Christmas A184

No. 1004: a, St. Mary's Anglican Church, Tristan da Cunha. b, Canterbury Cathedral, Canterbury, England.
No. 1005: a, St. Joseph's Catholic Church, Tristan da Cunha. b, St. Peter's Basilica, Vatican City.

Perf. 13¼x13½

2013, Nov. 18 **Litho.**

1004 Horiz. pair + central label 5.00 5.00
a. A184 35p multi 1.25 1.25
b. A184 £1.10 multi 3.75 3.75

1005 Horiz. pair + central label 5.00 5.00
a. A184 35p multi 1.25 1.25
b. A184 £1.10 multi 3.75 3.75

Volcano Eruption Type of 2011

Queen Mary's Peak and: 25p, HMS Puma. 35p, HMS Jaguar. 95p, MV Tristania. £1.10, MV Stirling Castle.
£2, MV Bornholm.

2013, Dec. 9 **Litho.** ***Perf. 14***

1006-1009 A174 Set of 4 8.75 8.75

Souvenir Sheet

1010 A174 £2 multi 6.50 6.50

Polar Explorers and Their Ships — A185

Designs: 35p, James Weddell (1787-1834) and Jane. 45p, George Nares (1831-1915) and HMS Challenger. 70p, Carsten Borchgrevink (1864-1934) and SS Antarctic. £1.50, Dr. Alexander Macklin (1889-1967) and Quest.

2014, Apr. 7 **Litho.** ***Perf. 13¼x13½***

1011-1014 A185 Set of 4 10.00 10.00

Royal Christenings A186

Photographs of British royalty with christened infants: 35p, Queen Elizabeth II, 1926. 45p, Prince Charles, 1948. £1.10, Prince William, 1982. £1.50, Prince George, 2013.

2014, May 21 **Litho.** ***Perf. 13¼***

1015-1018 A186 Set of 4 11.50 11.50

Finches — A187

Designs: 35p, Gough finch, Gough Island. 45p, Dunn's finch, Inaccessible Island. 50p, Nightingale finch, Nightingale Island Group. £1.50, Wilkin's finch, Nightingale Island.
£2, Inaccessible finch, Inaccessible Island.

2014, June 18 **Litho.** ***Perf. 14***

1019-1022 A187 Set of 4 9.75 9.75

Souvenir Sheet

1023 A187 £2 multi 7.00 7.00

Paintings by Augustus Earle (1793-1838) A188

Designs: No. 1024, 50p, Scudding Before a Heavy Westerly Gale Off the Cape, Latitude 44 Degrees (brown panel). No. 1025, 50p, On Board the Duke of Gloucester, Margate Hoy, Between Rio de Janeiro and Tristan de Acunha (olive green panel). No. 1026, 70p, Tristan da Cunha (blue panel). No. 1027, 70p, Solitude, Watching the Horizon at Sunset, in the Hopes of Seeing a Vessel, Tristan de Acunha in the South Atlantic (brown panel).

2014, July 10 **Litho.** ***Perf. 13¾***

1024-1027 A188 Set of 4 8.25 8.25

World War I, Cent. — A189

Poppies and war posters inscribed: No. 1028, £1, "Rally Round the Flag / We Must Have More Men." No. 1029, £1, "Join the Royal Marines." No. 1030, £1, "The Empire Needs Men." No. 1031, £1, "National Service / Women's Land Army."

2014, Aug. 4 **Litho.** ***Perf. 13¼***

1028-1031 A189 Set of 4 13.50 13.50

Royal Marines, 350th Anniv. — A190

Designs: 25p, Battle of Landguard Fort, 1667. 35p, Capture of Gibraltar, 1704. 40p, Zeebrugge Raid, 1918. 60p, Normandy Invasion, 1944. 80p, Falklands Conflict, 1982. £1.10, Marines in Afghanistan, 2013.

2014, Oct. 28 Litho. *Perf. 14*

1032-1037 A190 Set of 6 11.50 11.50

Miniature Sheet

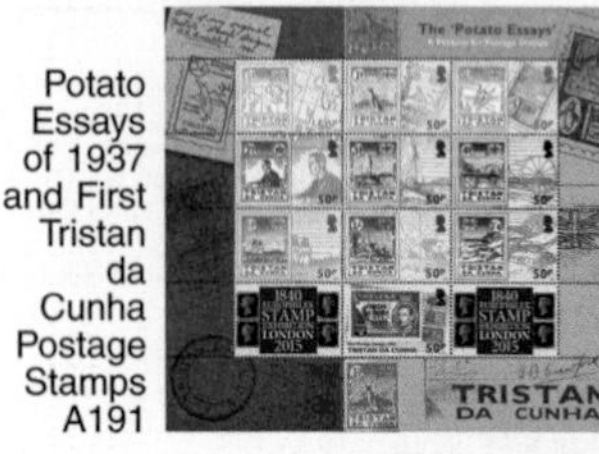

Potato Essays of 1937 and First Tristan da Cunha Postage Stamps A191

No. 1038: a, Essay for ½p stamp. b, Essay for 1p stamp. c, Essay for 1½p stamp. d, Essay for 2p stamp. e, Essay for 3p stamp. f, Essay for 4p stamp. g, Essay for 6p stamp. h, Essay for 1sh stamp. i, Essay for 2sh6p stamp. j, Tristan da Cunha #1-3.

2015, Apr. 8 Litho. *Perf. 13¼x13½*

1038 A191 50p Sheet of 10, #a-j, + 2 labels 15.50 15.50

Last Battle of War of 1812, 200th Anniv. — A192

Designs: No. 1039, £1.10, USS Hornet. No. 1040, £1.10, HMS Penguin.

£2.50, Battle between USS Hornet and HMS Penguin off Tristan da Cunha, horiz.

2015, June 1 Litho. *Perf. 13¾*

1039-1040 A192 Set of 2 6.75 6.75

Souvenir Sheet

Perf. 14¼x14¾

1041 A193 £2.50 multi 7.75 7.75

No. 1041 contains one 48x33mm stamp.

Magna Carta, 800th Anniv. — A193

Designs: 35p, King John, barons with Magna Carta. 80p, Administrator's Residency, Tristan da Cunha. 90p, Administration Building, Tristan da Cunha. £1.50, Arms of Tristan da Cunha, King John.

2015, June 15 Litho. *Perf. 12¾*

1042-1045 A193 Set of 4 11.00 11.00

Queen Elizabeth II, Longest-Reigning British Monarch — A194

Queen Elizabeth II and: 35p, Publications reporting on her coronation, 1953. 45p, Royal yacht Britannia. £1.10, Order of the Garter, Windsor Castle. £2, Trooping of the Color.

2015, Sept. 9 Litho. *Perf. 14*

1046-1049 A194 Set of 4 12.00 12.00

1885 Lifeboat Disaster — A195

Designs: 35p, Sighting the SV West Riding. 70p, Launching the lifeboat. 90p, Lifeboat in rough seas. £1.20, SV West Riding.

2015, Nov. 27 Litho. *Perf. 13*

1050-1053 A195 Set of 4 9.50 9.50

Publication of *Alice's Adventures in Wonderland,* by Lewis Carroll, 150th Anniv. — A196

Designs: No. 1054, 50p, White Rabbit. No. 1055, 50p, Alice and Caterpillar smoking hookah. No. 1056, 60p, Alice holding pig. No. 1057, 60p, Alice and Cheshire Cat. No. 1058, 70p, Hatter, March Hare and Cheshire Cat. No. 1059, 70p, Queen of Hearts.

2015, Dec. 1 Litho. *Perf. 14*

1054-1059 A196 Set of 6 11.00 11.00

a. Souvenir sheet of 6, #1054-1059 11.00 11.00

Early Mail Ships — A197

Designs: 1p, HMS Odin, 1904. 2p, RMS Asturias, 1927. 5p, SS Empress of France, 1928. 10p, HMS Carlisle, 1932, 1937. 25p, Barque Ponape, 1934. 35p, RMS Atlantis, 1934. 45p, Sailing Ship Cap Pilar, 1937. 60p, RMS Franconia, 1939. £1, HMS Queen of Bermuda, 1940. £1.50, HMS Carnarvon Castle, 1940. £2, RMS Darro, 1945. £5, MV Pequena, 1948-53.

2015, Dec. 8 Litho. *Perf. 14*

1060	A197	1p multi	.25	.25
1061	A197	2p multi	.25	.25
1062	A197	5p multi	.25	.25
1063	A197	10p multi	.30	.30
1064	A197	25p multi	.75	.75
1065	A197	35p multi	1.00	1.00
1066	A197	45p multi	1.40	1.40
1067	A197	60p multi	1.75	1.75
1068	A197	£1 multi	3.00	3.00
1069	A197	£1.50 multi	4.50	4.50
1070	A197	£2 multi	6.00	6.00
1071	A197	£5 multi	15.00	15.00
	Nos. 1060-1071 (12)		34.45	34.45

Queen Elizabeth II, 90th Birthday — A198

Photograph of Queen Elizabeth II from: 35p, 1954. 40p, 1952. 90p, 1979. £1.10, 2011. £3, Queen Elizabeth II, 1962.

2016, Apr. 21 Litho. *Perf. 14*

1072-1075 A198 Set of 4 8.25 8.25

Souvenir Sheet

1076 A198 £3 multi 9.00 9.00

William Shakespeare (1564-1616), Writer — A199

Characters from Shakespeare plays: 35p, Bottom, Titania and Puck from *A Midsummer Night's Dream.* 50p, Three witches from *Macbeth.* £1, Ophelia from *Hamlet.* £1.20, Falstaff from *The Merry Wives of Windsor.*

2016, July 4 Litho. *Perf. 14*

1077-1080 A199 Set of 4 8.00 8.00

British Garrison on Tristan da Cunha, 200th Anniv. — A200

Designs: 25p, Carronade with Royal Artillery crew. 35p, Thomas Currie and Bastiano Camilla greet Lieutenant David Rice and garrison members. £1, Captain A. Josias Cloete relieves Rice. £2, Arrival of Corporal William Glass and his family.

Perf. 13½x13¼

2016, Aug. 14 Litho.

1081-1084 A200 Set of 4 9.75 9.75

Peter Green (1808-1902), Headman of Tristan da Cunha — A201

Designs: 35p, Green's birthplace, Katwijk aan Zee, Netherlands. 50p, Wreck of the Emily, £1, Green's house, Tristan da Cunha. £1.60, Green.

Perf. 13¼x13¾

2016, Nov. 10 Litho.

1085-1088 A201 Set of 4 8.75 8.75

Biodiversity A202

Designs: No. 1089, Bog fern. No. 1090, Devil's fingers. No. 1091, Tristan rock lobster. No. 1092, Orange starfish. No. 1093, Klipfish. No. 1094, Gough brass buttons. No. 1095, Antarctic tern. No. 1096, Gough flightless moth. No. 1097, Tristan thrush. No. 1098, Inaccessible rail. No. 1099, Sub-Antarctic fur seal. No. 1100, Spectacled petrel.

2016 Litho. *Perf. 13¼x13¾*

1089	A202	25p multi	.65	.65
1090	A202	25p multi	.65	.65
1091	A202	35p multi	.90	.90
1092	A202	35p multi	.90	.90
1093	A202	45p multi	1.25	1.25
1094	A202	45p multi	1.25	1.25
1095	A202	60p multi	1.50	1.50
1096	A202	60p multi	1.50	1.50
1097	A202	70p multi	1.75	1.75
1098	A202	70p multi	1.75	1.75
1099	A202	£2 multi	5.00	5.00
1100	A202	£2 multi	5.00	5.00
	Nos. 1089-1100 (12)		22.10	22.10

Issued: Nos. 1089, 1091, 1093, 1095, 1097, 1099, 11/30; Nos. 1090, 1092, 1094, 1096, 1098, 1100, 12/7.

Visit of Prince Philip to Tristan da Cunha, 60th Anniv. — A203

No. 1101, 50p: a, Prince Philip with Sidney and Alice Glass and daughters Pamela and Trina. b, Three longboats at sea.

No. 1102, 50p: a, Edinburgh of the Seven Seas in 1957. b, Prince Philip, Dilys Bell and another woman.

No. 1103, 50p: a, Prince Philip with Martha Rogers, Willie Repetto, Pat and Forsyth Thompson. b, Islanders near longboats on shore.

2017, Jan. 24 Litho. *Perf. 13¼x13½*

Horiz. pairs, #a-b

1101-1103 A203 Set of 3 7.75 7.75

c. Souvenir sheet of 6, #1101a-1101b, 1102a-1102b, 1103a-1103b 7.75 7.75

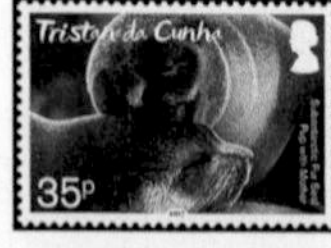

Subantarctic Fur Seals — A204

Designs: No. 1104, 35p, Mother and pup, resting head on each other. No. 1105, 35p, Pup, with tongue out. No. 1106, 70p, Mother and pup, looking forward. No. 1107, 70p, Adult male, near rocks. No. 1108, £1, Head of adult male. No. 1109, £1, Pup, without tongue out.

2017, Apr. 12 Litho. *Perf. 12¾*

1104-1109 A204 Set of 6 11.00 11.00

Visit of Prince Alfred to Tristan da Cunha, 150th Anniv. — A205

Designs: 40p, Prince Alfred (1844-1900). 80p, HMS Galatea. £1.10, Edinburgh of the Seven Seas, Tristan da Cunha, horiz. £1.50, Tristan da Cunha #110, horiz.

Perf. 13x12¾, 12¾x13

2017, Aug. 5 Litho.

1110-1113 A205 Set of 4 10.00 10.00

Worldwide Fund for Nature (WWF) — A206

Northern rockhopper penguins: 35p, Chicks. 50p, Juveniles. £1.50, Adult. £2, Mother and chick.

2017, Oct. 13 Litho. *Perf. 13x13¼*

1114-1117 A206 Set of 4 10.00 10.00

a. Souvenir sheet of 4, #1114-1117 10.00 10.00

70th Wedding Anniversary of Queen Elizabeth II and Prince Philip — A207

Photograph of Queen Elizabeth II and Prince Philip from: 25p, 1961. 60p, 1968. £1, 1970s. £2, 2015.

2017, Nov. 20 Litho. *Perf. 13¼x13*

1118-1121 A207 Set of 4 10.50 10.50

Norwegian Scientific Expedition to Tristan da Cunha, 80th Anniv. — A208

Designs: 35p, Dr. Sverre Dick Henriksen and Per Oeding in laboratory. 70p, Surveyor Allan Crawford. £1, Dr. Henriksen testing Tristan residents for tuberculosis. £1.50, Expedition members Egil Baardseth, Erling Sivertsen, and Yngvar Hagen on Nightingale Island.

2017, Dec. 7 Litho. *Perf. 13¼x13½*

1122-1125 A208 Set of 4 9.75 9.75

Visiting Royal Navy Ships — A209

Designs: 45p, HMS Portland, 2017. 55p, HMS Lancaster, 2015. 80p, HMS Protector, 2017. £1.60, RFA Gold Rover, 2017.

2018, Feb. 20 Litho. *Perf. 13*

1126-1129 A209 Set of 4 9.50 9.50

Tristan Venture, 70th Anniv. — A210

Designs: 45p, Captain L. E. Pettit and Reverend C. P. Lawrence. 70p, Tristan da Cunha #1, vert. £1.10, Cover of *The South African Shipping News and Fishing Industry Review,* vert. £1.60, Minesweeper M.V. Pequena.

Perf. 13¼ Syncopated (horiz. stamps), 13½x13¼ Syncopated (vert. stamps)

2018, Mar. 12 **Litho.**
1130-1133 A210 Set of 4 11.00 11.00
a. Souvenir sheet of 4, #1130-1133 11.00 11.00

Royal Air Force, Cent. — A211

Designs: 45p, Felixstowe F.5. 55p, Supermarine Southampton I. £1.60, Supermarine S.6B. £2, Short Sunderland Mk V.

2018, July 2 **Litho.** ***Perf. 13¼x13½***
1134-1137 A211 Set of 4 12.00 12.00

Wedding of Prince Harry and Meghan Markle — A212

Designs: 45p, Engagement photograph. 55p, Couple on trip to Scotland. £1.30, Couple at altar. £2, Couple leaving Windsor Castle.
£3, Couple kissing, vert.

Perf. 13¼x13½

2018, Aug. 20 **Litho.**
1138-1141 A212 Set of 4 11.00 11.00

Souvenir Sheet

Perf. 13½x13¼

1142 A212 £3 multi 7.75 7.75

Wreck of the Mabel Clark, 140th Anniv. — A213

Designs: 45p, Mabel Clark foundering off Molly Gulch. 70p, Arrival of USS Essex to repatriate crew members. £1.15, Gold watch awarded to Tristan da Cunha by Pres. Rutherford B. Hayes. £1.50, HMS Comus delivering messages and gifts of appreciation.

2018, Sept. 3 **Litho.** ***Perf. 13¼x13½***
1143-1146 A213 Set of 4 9.75 9.75

Migratory Birds — A214

No. 1147, 85p — Map of migration and Atlantic yellow-nosed albatross: a, In flight. b, On nest.
No. 1148, 95p — Map of migration and Great shearwater: a, In flight. b, On water.

2018, Oct. 18 **Litho.** ***Perf. 13¼x13½***

Vert. Pairs, #a-b

1147-1148 A214 Set of 2 9.00 9.00

Whales — A215

Designs: 45c, Shepherd's beaked whale. 70p, Southern right whale. £1, Fin whale. £1.50, Killer whale.

Perf. 13¼x13½

2019, Feb. 11 **Litho.**
1149-1152 A215 Set of 4 9.75 9.75

Tristan da Cunha Lobster Fisheries — A216

Designs: 35p, Lobster boats. 50p, Lobster packaging factory and boxes of packaged lobsters. £1, Small lobster boat and factory freezer vessel, Geo Searcher. £2, Tristan lobster.

2019, Apr. 10 **Litho.** ***Perf. 13x13¼***
1153-1156 A216 Set of 4 10.00 10.00

D-Day, 75th Anniv. — A217

Designs: 45p, Royal Marines exiting landing craft near Juno Beach. 85p, Soldiers bringing a survivor of landing craft sinking on shore. £1.30, Soldiers marching with gear. £2, Soldiers in trench and climbing hill.

2019, June 19 **Litho.** ***Perf. 13x13½***
1157-1160 A217 Set of 4 12.00 12.00

Children's Art — A218

Designs: 45p, MFV Edinburgh at Anchor, by Shannon Swain. 70p, Fishing off Tristan Island, by Calvin Green. £1.10, Nightingale Island and the Great Shearwater, by Deanna Rogers. £1.60, Old Year's Night Okalolies, by Chantelle Repetto.

2019, Oct. 1 **Litho.** ***Perf. 13¼x13½***
1161-1164 A218 Set of 4 9.50 9.50

Vagrant Species — A219

Designs: 45p, Yellow-billed cuckoo. 60p, Leopard seal. £1, Loggerhead turtle. £2, Indian yellow-nosed albatross.

2019, Nov. 19 **Litho.** ***Perf. 13¼x13***
1165-1168 A219 Set of 4 10.50 10.50

See Nos. 1190-1193, 1254-1257.

Whaling and Sealing Ships — A220

Designs: 45p, Franklin, seal. 70p, Francis Allyn, seal. £1.15, Stafford, whale. £1.50, Eliza Adams, whale.

2019, Dec. 2 **Litho.** ***Perf. 13¼x13***
1169-1172 A220 Set of 4 10.00 10.00

Birds of Gough and Inaccessible Islands UNESCO World Heritage Site — A221

Designs: 35p, Tristan albatrosses. 55p, Gough bunting. £1.60, Speckled petrel. £1.80, Rockhopper penguin.
£3.50, Inaccessible Island rail.

Perf. 13¼x13½

2020, Mar. 24 **Litho.**
1173-1176 A221 Set of 4 10.50 10.50

Souvenir Sheet

1177 A221 £3.50 multi 8.75 8.75

Gough and Inaccessible Islands UNESCO World Heritage Site, 25th anniv.

Women of Tristan da Cunha — A222

Designs: 45p, Maria Leenders (1801-58), settler who arrived in 1816. 50p, Two unnamed women who arrived in 1827. £1, Susannah Philips (1843-1932), settler who arrived in 1867. £2, Elizabeth (1876-1917) and Agnes Smith (1887-1970), who arrived in 1908.

2020, May 7 **Litho.** ***Perf. 13½x13¼***
1178-1181 A222 Set of 4 9.75 9.75

Sharks — A223

Designs: 45p, Broadnose seven-gill shark. 70p, Porbeagle shark. £1.10, Great hammerhead sharks. £1.50, Blue shark.

2020, Sept. 29 **Litho.** ***Perf. 11½***
1182-1185 A223 Set of 4 9.75 9.75

See Nos. 1219-1222.

Health Care — A224

Designs: 45p, Ship's surgeon inspecting patient's teeth at Mission House. 70p, Doctor giving immunization to infant, Station Hospital. £1.10, Doctor examining patient, Camogli Hospital. £1.50, Medical personnel, Camogli Healthcare Center.

2020, Oct. 20 **Litho.** ***Perf. 11½***
1186-1189 A224 Set of 4 9.75 9.75

Vagrant Species Type of 2019

Designs: 45p, Leatherback sea turtle. 60p, Purple gallinule. £1, Black witch moth. £2, King penguin.

2020, Nov. 9 **Litho.** ***Perf. 13¼x13***
1190-1193 A219 Set of 4 11.00 11.00

Ships Awarded the Sword of Peace — A225

Designs: £1.50, SAS Simon Van Der Stel. £2.50, RFA Ennerdale.

2020, Dec. 8 **Litho.** ***Perf. 13¼x13¾***
1194-1195 A225 Set of 2 11.00 11.00

Modern Mail Ships — A226

Designs: 1p, RRS John Biscoe, 1957. 2p, SS Brasil, 1960-65. 5p, Gillian Gaggins, 1965-73. 10p, MV RSA, 1963-77. 25p, RMS Queen Elizabeth 2, 1979. 35p, SS Rotterdam, 1960-80. 45p, HMS Endurance, 1983. 60p, MV Tristania II, 1973-96. £1, MV Hekla, 1984-96. £1.50, RMS St. Helena, 1992-2018. £2, RRS James Clark Ross, 2013 and 2018. £3, MFV Geo Searcher, 2017-20. £5, Bark Europa, 2005-19.

2020, Dec. 14 **Litho.** ***Perf. 11½***

1196	A226	1p multi	.25	.25
1197	A226	2p multi	.25	.25
1198	A226	5p multi	.25	.25
1199	A226	10p multi	.30	.30
1200	A226	25p multi	.70	.70
1201	A226	35p multi	.95	.95
1202	A226	45p multi	1.25	1.25
1203	A226	60p multi	1.75	1.75
1204	A226	£1 multi	2.75	2.75
1205	A226	£1.50 multi	4.25	4.25
1206	A226	£2 multi	5.50	5.50
1207	A226	£3 multi	8.25	8.25
1208	A226	£5 multi	13.50	13.50
		Nos. 1196-1208 (13)	39.95	39.95

Queen Elizabeth II, 95th Birthday — A227

Designs: 35p, Princess Elizabeth, 1946. 45p, Queen Elizabeth II at coronation, 1953. 50p, Queen Elizabeth II and Prince Philip, 2017. 70p, Queen Elizabeth II, 2009. £1.10, Queen Elizabeth II, 2002. £1.50, Queen Elizabeth II, 2009, diff.

2021, Apr. 21 **Litho.** ***Perf. 13¼***
1209-1214 A227 Set of 6 13.00 13.00

See Isle of Man No. 2150a.

Currencies and Trade of Tristan da Cunha — A228

Designs: 50p, Ship, 1880 British gold one-pound coin, reverse of United States Seated Liberty silver dollar. 90p, Island buildings, potatoes, Royal Navy typed paper chit, South African one-pound note. £1.15, Island buildings, South African coins and banknotes. £2, Island buildings, British one-pound banknote, two-shilling coin, two ten-pence coins.

2021, May 26 **Litho.** ***Perf. 13½***
1215-1218 A228 Set of 4 13.00 13.00

Sharks Type of 2020

Designs: 45p, Bluntnose sixgill shark. 70p, Great lanternshark. £1.10, Shortfin mako shark. £1.50, Great white shark.

2021, July 14 **Litho.** ***Perf. 13¼x13¾***
1219-1222 A223 Set of 4 10.50 10.50

Prince Philip (1921-2021) — A229

Various photographs of Prince Philip: 45p, 80p, £1.05, £2.30.

Perf. 13¾x13¼

2021, Sept. 23 **Litho.**
1223-1226 A229 Set of 4 12.50 12.50

Eruption of Queen Mary's Peak, 60th Anniv. — A230

Designs: 45p, Ship Frances Repetto offloading Tristan da Cunha evacuees in longboat. 60p, Volcano and ship Tristania. £1.10, Evacuees Sophie Green and Edith Repetto. £1.80, Evacuees at Pendell Camp, Great Britain.

2021, Nov. 3 **Litho.** ***Perf. 13¼x13¾***
1227-1230 A230 Set of 4 10.50 10.50

See Nos. 1236-1239.

Blue Belt Program — A231

Portion of map of Tristan da Cunha and other islands: Nos. 1231, 1235a, 45p, Tristan lobster. Nos. 1232, 1235b, 80p, FPS Wave Dancer. Nos. 1233, 1235c, £1, Blue shark. Nos. 1234, 1235d, £2.10, Coral.

Perf. 13¼x13¾

2021, Nov. 29 Litho.

Stamps With White Frames

1231-1234	A231	Set of 4	11.50	11.50

Miniature Sheet

Stamps Without White Frames

1235	A231	Sheet of 4, #a-d	11.50	11.50

Eruption of Queen Mary's Peak, 60th Anniv. Type of 2021

Designs: 45p, HMS Jaguar and members of 1962 Royal Society Expedition. 60p, HMSAS Transvaal and volcano surveyor. £1.10, MV Tristania and dinghy, Vulcan, expedition members. £1.80, HMS Protector, helicopter with expedition members.

Perf. 13¼x13¾

2022, Mar. 21 Litho.

1236-1239	A230	Set of 4	10.50	10.50

1962 Royal Society Expedition to Tristan da Cunha, 60th anniv.

Reign of Queen Elizabeth II, 70th Anniv. — A232

Photograph of Queen Elizabeth II from: No. 1240, £2, c. 1947. No. 1241, £2, 2021.

£3.50, Queen Elizabeth II wearing tiara, 1956, vert.

2022, Mar. 24 Litho. *Perf. 13¼x13*

1240-1241	A232	Set of 2	10.50	10.50

Souvenir Sheet

Perf. 13¼

1242	A232	£3.50 multi	9.25	9.25

No. 1242 contains one 29x48mm stamp.

Liberation of the Falkland Islands, 40th Anniv. — A233

Tristan da Cunha tugboats used in Falkland Islands War: No. 1243, £1.50, Yorkshireman. No. 1244, £1.50, Salvageman. No. 1245, £1.50, Irishman.

2022, May 16 Litho. *Perf. 13¼x13*

1243-1245	A233	Set of 3	11.50	11.50

Sir Ernest Shackleton (1874-1922), Polar Explorer — A234

Designs: 35p, Shackleton's ship, Quest, on the River Thames, 1921. 70p, Shackleton leaning out of ship's window. £1.60, Shackleton's coffin, Montevideo, Uruguay. £2, Shackleton's cairn, Grytviken, South Georgia Island.

2022, May 25 Litho. *Perf. 13¼x13*

1246-1249	A234	Set of 4	12.00	12.00

Jacques Cousteau (1910-97), Oceanographer and Film Maker — A235

Cousteau and: 50p, "Diving saucer" submarine. 90p, Scuba equipment. £1.30, Underwater camera. £1.60, RV Calypso.

2022, Oct. 3 Litho. *Perf. 13¼x13½*

1250-1253	A235	Set of 4	9.75	9.75

Vagrant Species Type of 2019

Designs: 45p, Salvin's albatross. 60p, Eastern kingbird. £1, Great egret. £2, Spotted sandpiper.

2022, Oct. 6 Litho. *Perf. 13¼x13*

1254-1257	A219	Set of 4	9.50	9.50

Queen Elizabeth II (1926-2022) — A236

Photograph of Queen Elizabeth II from: No. 1258, £3, 1951 (denomination at UR). No. 1259, £3, 2017 (denomination at UL).

2023, Feb. 15 Litho. *Perf. 13x13¼*

1258-1259	A236	Set of 2	14.50	14.50
1259a		Souvenir sheet of 2, #1258-1259	14.50	14.50

United States Liberty Ships of World War II and Their Namesakes — A237

No. 1260: a, 85p, Clara Barton (1821-1912), nurse and founder of American Red Cross. b, £1.15, USS Clara Barton.

No. 1261: a, 85p, Louis D. Brandeis (1856-1941), Supreme Court justice. £1.15, USS Louis D. Brandeis.

No. 1262: a, 85p, William Moultrie (1730-1805), Revolutionary War general and governor of South Carolina. b, £1.15, USS William Moultrie.

No. 1263: a, 85p, James McHenry (1753-1816), military surgeon and Secretary of War. b, £1.15, USS James McHenry.

2023, Apr. 6 Litho. *Perf. 13¼x13*

Horiz. pairs, #a-b

1260-1263	A237	Set of 4	20.00	20.00

POSTAGE DUE STAMPS

Type of Barbados 1934-47

Perf. 14

1957, Feb. 1 Wmk. 4 Typo.

Chalky Paper

J1	D1	1p rose red	3.50	*7.00*
J2	D1	2p orange yellow	4.25	*9.25*
J3	D1	3p green	4.50	*11.50*
J4	D1	4p ultramarine	5.25	*13.50*
J5	D1	5p deep claret	6.50	*16.00*
		Nos. J1-J5 (5)	24.00	*57.25*

Numeral — D2

Perf. 13½x14

1976, Sept. 3 Litho. Wmk. 373

J6	D2	1p lilac rose	.25	*.70*
J7	D2	2p grayish green	.25	*1.00*
J8	D2	4p violet	.25	*1.00*
J9	D2	5p light blue	.25	*1.00*
J10	D2	10p brown	.65	*1.50*
		Nos. J6-J10 (5)	1.65	*5.20*

1976, May 31 Wmk. 314

J6a	D2	1p lilac rose	.35	*.70*
J7a	D2	2p grayish green	.35	*1.00*
J8a	D2	4p violet	.35	*1.00*
J9a	D2	5p light blue	.35	*1.00*
J10a	D2	10p brown	.75	*1.50*
		Nos. J6a-J10a (5)	2.15	*5.20*

Outline Map of Tristan da Cunha — D3

Perf. 15x14

1986, Nov. 20 Litho. Wmk. 384

J11	D3	1p pale yel brn & brn	.25	*.45*
J12	D3	2p orange & brown	.25	*.45*
J13	D3	5p crimson rose & brn	.25	*.45*
J14	D3	7p lt lilac & black	.25	*.45*
J15	D3	10p pale ultra & blk	.30	*.55*
J16	D3	25p lt green & blk	.75	*1.60*
		Nos. J11-J16 (6)	2.05	*3.95*

TRUCIAL STATES

'trü-shəl 'stāts

LOCATION — Qatar Peninsula, Persian Gulf

GOVT. — Sheikdoms under British Protection

AREA — 32,300 sq. mi.

POP. — 86,000

CAPITAL — Dubai

The Trucial States are: Abu Dhabi, Ajman, Dubai, Fujeira, Ras al Khaima, Sharjah and Kalba, and Umm al Qiwain.

Stamps inscribed "Trucial States" were issued and used only in Dubai. Beginning Aug. 1972 all Trucial States used the stamps of United Arab Emirates.

100 Naye Paise = 1 Rupee

Catalogue values for all unused stamps in this country are for Never Hinged items.

7 Palm Trees A1

Dhow A2

Perf. 14½x14

1961, Jan. 7 Photo. Unwmk.

1	A1	5np emerald	1.75	1.40
2	A1	15np red brown	.75	*1.10*
3	A1	20np ultra	1.60	1.60
4	A1	30np orange	.75	.35
5	A1	40np purple	.75	.40
6	A1	50np brown olive	.75	.60
7	A1	75np gray	.75	*1.00*

Engr. *Perf. 13x12½*

8	A2	1r emerald	9.00	4.00
9	A2	2r black	9.00	*24.00*
10	A2	5r rose red	11.00	*26.50*
11	A2	10r violet blue	17.50	*27.50*
		Nos. 1-11 (11)	53.60	*88.45*

Stamps inscribed "Trucial States" were withdrawn in June, 1963, when the individual states began issuing their own stamps.

TUNISIA

tü-'nē-zh,ē,ə

LOCATION — Northern Africa, bordering on the Mediterranean Sea

GOVT. — Republic

AREA — 63,362 sq. mi.

POP. — 9,513,603 (1999 est.)

CAPITAL — Tunis

The former French protectorate became a sovereign state in 1956 and a republic in 1957.

100 Centimes = 1 Franc

1000 Millimes = 1 Dinar (1959)

Catalogue values for unused stamps in this country are for Never Hinged items, beginning with Scott 163 in the regular postage section, Scott B78 in the semi-postal section, Scott C13 in the airpost section, Scott CB1 in the airpost semi-postal section, and Scott J33 in the postage due section.

Coat of Arms — A1

Perf. 14x13½

1888-97 Typo. Unwmk.

1	A1	1c black, *blue*	5.50	3.50
2	A1	2c pur brn, *buff*	7.00	3.50
3	A1	5c green, *grnsh*	35.00	17.50
4	A1	15c blue, *grysh*	55.00	27.50
5	A1	25c black, *rose*	110.00	70.00
6	A1	40c red, *straw*	110.00	77.50
7	A1	75c car, *rose*	110.00	85.00
8	A1	5fr gray vio, *grysh*	510.00	275.00
		Nos. 1-8 (8)	942.50	559.50

All values exist imperforate.

Reprints were made in 1893 and some values have been reprinted twice since then. The shades usually differ from those of the originals. Stamps from the 1897 printing are on thicker paper, with white gum instead of grayish, and have a background of horizontal ruled lines.

A2

A3

1888-1902

9	A2	1c blk, *lil bl*	1.75	1.10
10	A2	2c pur brn, *buff*	1.75	1.10
11	A2	5c grn, *grnsh*	7.00	1.10
12	A2	5c yellow grn ('99)	7.00	1.10
13	A2	10c blk, *lav* ('93)	14.00	2.10
14	A2	10c red ('01)	7.00	1.10
15	A2	15c blue, *grysh*	50.00	1.10
16	A2	15c gray ('01)	11.00	2.10
17	A2	20c red, *grn* ('99)	21.00	2.10
18	A2	25c blk, *rose*	25.00	2.10
19	A2	25c blue ('01)	21.00	2.75
20	A2	35c brown ('02)	55.00	3.50
21	A2	40c red, *straw*	21.00	2.10
22	A2	75c car, *rose*	170.00	80.00
23	A2	75c dp vio, *org* ('93)	35.00	11.00
24	A3	1fr olive, *cream*	35.00	9.00
25	A3	2fr dull violet ('02)	175.00	130.00
26	A3	5fr red lil, *lav*	200.00	77.50
		Bar cancellation		1.00

Quadrille Paper

27	A2	15c bl, *grysh* ('93)	50.00	1.40
		Nos. 9-27 (19)	907.50	332.25

For surcharges see Nos. 28, 58-61.

No. 27 Surcharged in Red

1902

28	A2	25c on 15c blue	3.50	3.50

Ordinary Paper

Mosque at Kairouan A4

Plowing A5

Ruins of Hadrian's Aqueduct — A6

Carthaginian Galley — A7

1906-26 Typo.

29	A4	1c blk, *yel*	.25	.25
30	A4	2c red brn, *straw*	.25	.25
31	A4	3c lt red ('19)	.25	.25
32	A4	5c grn, *grnsh*	.35	.25
33	A4	5c orange ('21)	.35	.25
34	A5	10c red	.35	.30
35	A5	10c green ('21)	.35	.35
36	A5	15c vio, *pnksh*	1.40	.30
a.		Imperf., pair	160.00	
37	A5	15c brn, *org* ('23)	.35	.35
38	A5	20c brn, *pnksh*	.35	.30
39	A5	25c deep blue	2.10	.70
a.		Imperf., pair		
40	A5	25c violet ('21)	.35	.35
41	A6	30c red brn & vio ('19)	1.10	.70
42	A5	30c pale red ('21)	1.10	.70
43	A6	35c ol grn & brn	10.50	2.10

44 A6 40c blk brn & red brn 5.50 .70
45 A5 40c blk, *pnksh* ('23) 1.10 .70
46 A5 40c gray grn ('26) .25 .25
47 A5 50c blue ('21) 1.10 .70
48 A6 60c ol grn & vio ('21) 1.10 1.10
49 A6 60c ver & rose ('25) .70 .35
50 A6 75c red brn & red 1.10 .70
51 A6 75c ver & dl red ('26) .50 .50
52 A7 1fr red & dk brn 1.10 .70
53 A7 1fr ind & ultra ('25) .35 .35
54 A7 2fr brn & ol grn 6.50 2.00
55 A7 2fr grn & red, *pink* ('25) 1.10 .35
56 A7 5fr violet & blue 12.50 5.50
57 A7 5fr gray vio & grn ('25) 1.10 .70
Nos. 29-57 (29) 53.40 22.00

For surcharges and overprints see Nos. 62-64, 70-73115-116, B1-B23, B25-B27, B29-B30, B32-B36, C1-C6.

Stamps and Type of 1888-1902 Surcharged

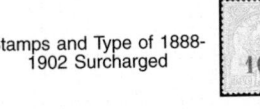

1908, Sept.
58 A2 10c on 15c gray, *lt gray* (R) 2.10 2.10
59 A3 35c on 1fr ol, *ol* (R) 5.50 5.50
60 A3 40c on 2fr dl vio (Bl) 10.50 10.50
61 A3 75c on 5fr red lil, *lav* (Bl) 7.00 7.00
Nos. 58-61 (4) 25.10 25.10

No. 36 Surcharged

1911
62 A5 10c on 15c vio, *pinkish* 1.75 .70
a. Inverted surcharge 2,100.

No. 34 Surcharged

1917, Mar. 16
63 A5 15c on 10c red 1.10 .35
a. "15c" omitted 40.00
b. Double surcharge 87.50

No. 36 Surcharged

1921
64 A5 20c on 15c vio, *pinkish* 1.10 .35
a. Grayish paper (#36b) 1.40 .45

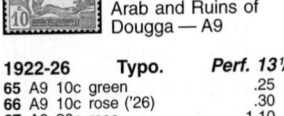

Arab and Ruins of Dougga — A9

1922-26 Typo. *Perf. 13½x14*
65 A9 10c green .25 .25
66 A9 10c rose ('26) .30 .30
67 A9 30c rose 1.10 1.10
68 A9 30c lilac ('26) .45 .45
69 A9 50c blue .70 .70
Nos. 65-69 (5) 2.80 2.80

For surcharges see Nos. 117, B24, B28, B31.

Stamps and Type of 1906 Surcharged in Red or Black

a

b

1923-25
70 A4(a) 10c on 5c grn, *grnsh* (R) .35 .35
a. Double surcharge 80.00
b. Inverted surcharge 115.00
c. Double surcharge, one inverted 115.00
71 A5(b) 20c on 15c vio (Bk) 1.10 .35
a. Double surcharge 115.00
72 A5(b) 30c on 20c yel brn (Bk) ('25) .35 .35
73 A5(b) 50c on 25c blue (R) 1.10 .35
a. Double surcharge 110.00
b. Inverted surcharge 110.00
Nos. 70-73 (4) 2.90 1.40

Arab Woman Carrying Water A10

Grand Mosque at Tunis A11

Mosque, Tunis A12

Roman Amphitheater, El Djem (Thysdrus) A13

1926-46 Typo. *Perf. 14x13½*
74 A10 1c lt red .25 .25
75 A10 2c olive grn .25 .25
76 A10 3c slate blue .25 .25
77 A10 5c yellow grn .25 .25
78 A10 10c rose .25 .25
78A A12 10c brown ('46) .25 .25
79 A11 15c gray lilac .25 .25
80 A11 20c deep red .30 .25
81 A11 25c gray green .45 .30
82 A11 25c lt violet ('28) .70 .30
83 A11 30c lt violet .45 .35
84 A11 30c bl grn ('28) .35 .30
84A A12 30c dk ol grn ('46) .25 .25
85 A11 40c deep brown .25 .25
85A A12 40c lil rose ('46) .30 .30
86 A11 45c emer ('40) 1.10 1.10
87 A12 50c black .25 .25
88 A12 50c ultra ('34) .70 .35
88B A12 50c emer ('40) .25 .25
88C A12 50c lt blue ('46) .30 .30
89 A12 60c red org ('40) .25 .25
89A A12 60c ultra ('45) .25 .25
90 A12 65c ultra ('38) .70 .35
91 A12 70c dk red ('40) .25 .25
92 A12 75c vermilion .35 .70
93 A12 75c lil rose ('28) 1.10 .35
94 A12 80c blue green 1.10 .70
94A A12 80c blk brn ('40) .30 .30
94B A12 80c emer ('45) .45 .30
95 A12 90c org red ('28) .35 .35
96 A12 90c ultra ('39) 10.00 10.00
97 A12 1fr brown violet .70 .70
97A A12 1fr rose ('40) .25 .25
98 A13 1.05fr dl bl & mag .70 .70
98A A12 1.20fr blk brn ('45) .35 .30
99 A13 1.25fr gray bl & dk bl .70 .70
100 A13 1.25fr car rose ('40) 1.10 1.10
100A A13 1.30fr bl & vio bl ('42) .35 .30
101 A13 1.40fr brt red vio ('40) 1.20 1.20
102 A13 1.50fr bl & dp bl ('28) 1.40 .50
102A A13 1.50fr rose red & red org ('42) .35 .50
102B A12 1.50fr rose lil ('46) .25 .25
103 A13 2fr rose & ol brn 1.40 .35
104 A13 2fr red org ('39) .35 .35
104A A12 2fr Prus grn ('45) .35 .25
105 A13 2.25fr ultra ('39) .70 .90
105A A13 2.40fr red ('46) .65 .50
106 A13 2.50fr green ('40) .80 .80
107 A13 3fr dl bl & org 1.75 .70
108 A13 3fr violet ('39) .35 .35
108A A13 3fr blk brn ('46) .35 .25
108B A13 4fr ultra ('45) 1.10 .55
109 A13 5fr red & grn, *grnsh* 2.75 1.40
110 A13 5fr dp red brn ('40) 1.25 1.25
110A A13 5fr dk grn ('46) .45 .45
110B A13 6fr dp ultra ('45) .70 .45
111 A13 10fr brn red & blk, *bluish* 11.00 3.50
112 A13 10fr rose pink ('40) .80 .80
112A A13 10fr ver ('46) .70 .45
112B A13 10fr ultra ('46) .65 .35
112C A13 15fr rose lil ('45) .35 .25
113 A13 20fr lil & red, *pnksh* ('28) 2.50 1.10
113A A13 20fr dk grn ('45) .70 .45
113B A13 25fr violet ('45) .70 .65
113C A13 50fr carmine ('45) 1.75 .85
113D A13 100fr car rose ('45) 2.10 1.10
Nos. 74-113D (66) 64.05 44.65

See Nos. 152A-162, 185-189, 199-206.

For surcharges and overprints see Nos. 114, 118-121, 143-152, B74-B77, B87-B88, B91-B95, B98, C7-C12.

No. 99 Surcharged with New Value and Bars in Red

1927, Mar. 24
114 A13 1.50fr on 1.25fr .80 .30

Stamps of 1921-26 Surcharged

1928, May 1
115 A4 3c on 5c orange .35 .25
116 A5 10c on 15c brn, *org* .70 .30
c. Double surcharge 125.00
117 A9 25c on 30c lilac .70 .70
118 A12 40c on 80c bl grn .70 .45
119 A12 50c on 75c ver 1.10 .50
Nos. 115-119 (5) 3.55 2.20

No. 83 Surcharged

1929
120 A11 10c on 30c lt violet 1.75 1.10

No. 120 exists precanceled only. The value in first column is for a stamp which has not been through the post and has original gum. The value in the second column is for a postally used, gumless stamp. See No. 199a.

No. 85 Surcharged with New Value and Bars

1930
121 A11 50c on 40c dp brn 5.50 .70

A14 A15

A16

A17

Perf. 11, 12½, 12½x13

1931-34 Engr.
122 A14 1c deep blue .25 .25
123 A14 2c yellow brn .25 .25
124 A14 3c black .35 .35
125 A14 5c yellow grn .25 .25
126 A14 10c red .25 .25
127 A15 15c dull violet .70 .70
128 A15 20c dull brown .25 .25
129 A15 25c rose red .35 .35
130 A15 30c deep green .35 .70
131 A15 40c red orange .35 .35
132 A16 50c ultra .35 .35
133 A16 75c yellow 2.10 2.10
134 A16 90c red .70 .70
135 A16 1fr olive black .35 .70
136 A16 1fr dk brn ('34) .50 .45
137 A17 1.50fr brt ultra 1.00 .70
138 A17 2fr deep brown .70 1.00
139 A17 3fr blue green 10.50 10.50
140 A17 5fr car rose 28.00 21.00
a. Perf. 12½ 37.50 35.00
141 A17 10fr black 50.00 35.00
142 A17 20fr dark brown 62.50 45.00
Nos. 122-142 (21) 160.05 121.20

For surcharges see Nos. B54-B73.

Nos. 88, 102 Surcharged in Red or Black

1937 *Perf. 14x13½*
143 A12 65c on 50c (R) .70 .35
b. Double surcharge 105.00 87.50
144 A13 1.75fr on 1.50fr (R) 5.50 1.40
a. Double surcharge 95.00 95.00
b. In pair with unsurcharged stamp 250.00

1938
145 A12 65c on 50c (Bk) .70 .35
a. Double surcharge, one inverted 175.00 175.00
146 A13 1.75fr on 1.50fr (R) 10.50 7.00

Stamps of 1938-39 Surcharged in Red or Carmine

1940
147 A12 25c on 65c ultra (C) .25 .25
148 A12 1fr on 90c ultra (R) .50 .50
a. Double surcharge 120.00

Stamps of 1938-40 Surcharged in Red or Black

1941
149 A12 25c on 65c ultra (R) .35 .35
150 A13 1fr on 1.25fr car rose .70 .35
151 A13 1fr on 1.40fr brt red vio .70 .70
152 A13 1fr on 2.25fr ultra (R) .70 .70
Nos. 149-152 (4) 2.45 2.10

Types of 1926 Without RF

1941-45 Typo. *Perf. 14x13½*
152A A11 30c carmine ('45) .25 .25
152B A12 1.20fr int blue ('45) .25 .25
153 A12 1.50fr brn red ('42) .35 .45
154 A13 2.40fr car & brt pink ('42) .45 .45
155 A13 2.50fr dk bl & lt bl .35 .45
156 A13 3fr lt violet ('42) .30 .30
157 A13 4fr blk & bl vio ('42) .35 .45
158 A13 4.50fr ol grn & brn ('42) .70 .70
159 A13 5fr brown blk ('42) .70 .55
160 A13 10fr lil & dull vio .35 .50
161 A13 15fr henna brn ('42) 5.50 4.50
162 A13 20fr lt vio & car 2.75 1.50
Nos. 152A-162 (12) 12.30 10.35

Catalogue values for unused stamps in this section, from this point to the end of the section, are for Never Hinged items.

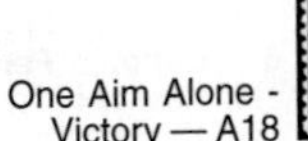

One Aim Alone - Victory — A18

1943 Litho. *Perf. 12*
163 A18 1.50fr rose .35 .25

Mosque and Olive Tree — A19

1944-45 Unwmk. ***Perf. 11½***

Size: 15½x19mm

165 A19 30c yellow ('45) .35 .25
166 A19 40c org brn ('45) .35 .25
168 A19 60c red org ('45) .70 .45
169 A19 70c rose pink ('45) .35 .25
170 A19 80c Prus grn ('45) .35 .30
171 A19 90c violet ('45) .35 .30
172 A19 1fr red ('45) .35 .30
173 A19 1.50fr dp bl ('45) .35 .30

Size: 21¼x26½mm

175 A19 2.40fr red .70 .45
176 A19 2.50fr red brn .70 .45
177 A19 3fr lt vio 1.10 .65
178 A19 4fr brt bl vio .70 .45
179 A19 4.50fr apple grn .70 .45
180 A19 5fr gray 1.10 .65
181 A19 6fr choc ('45) .70 .45
182 A19 10fr brn lake ('45) 1.10 .70
183 A19 15fr copper brn 1.10 .70
184 A19 20fr lilac 1.10 .80
Nos. 165-184 (18) 12.15 8.15

For surcharge see No. B79.

Types of 1926

1946-47 Typo. ***Perf. 14x13½***

185 A12 2fr emerald ('47) .70 .45
186 A12 3fr rose pink .35 .25
187 A12 4fr violet ('47) .85 .45
188 A13 4fr violet ('47) 1.10 .50
189 A12 6fr carmine ('47) .35 .25
Nos. 185-189 (5) 3.35 1.90

Neptune, Bardo Museum — A20

1947-49 Engr. ***Perf. 13***

190 A20 5fr dk grn & bluish blk 1.10 .90
191 A20 10fr blk brn & bluish blk .55 .30
192 A20 18fr dk bl gray & Prus bl ('48) 1.75 1.00
193 A20 25fr dk bl & bl grn ('49) 2.10 1.10
Nos. 190-193 (4) 5.50 3.30

For surcharge see No. B108.

Detail from Great Mosque at Kairouan — A21

1948-49

194 A21 3fr dk bl grn & bl grn 1.10 .55
195 A21 4fr dk red vio & red vio .70 .45
196 A21 6fr red brn & red .35 .25
197 A21 10fr purple ('49) .65 .35
198 A21 12fr henna brn 1.10 .65
198A A21 12fr dk brn & org brn ('49) .90 .55
198B A21 15fr dk red ('49) .80 .55
Nos. 194-198B (7) 5.60 3.35

See No. 225. For surcharge see No. B103.

Types of 1926

1947-49 Typo. ***Perf. 14x13½***

199 A12 2.50fr brown orange .70 .45
a. 2.50fr brown 1.50 .80
200 A12 4fr brown org ('49) 1.20 .45
201 A12 4.50fr lt ultra 1.10 .45
202 A12 5fr blue ('48) .70 .55
203 A12 5fr lt bl grn ('49) 1.20 .25
204 A13 6fr rose red .35 .25
205 A12 15fr rose red 1.20 .65
206 A13 25fr red orange 2.10 .90
Nos. 199-206 (8) 8.55 3.95

No. 199a is known only precanceled. See note after No. 120.

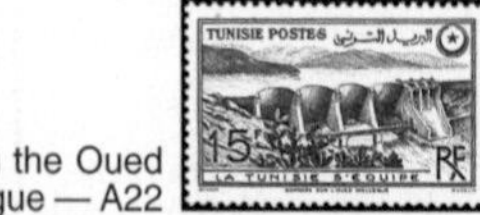

Dam on the Oued Mellegue — A22

1949, Sept. 1 Engr. ***Perf. 13***

207 A22 15fr grnsh black 3.50 .70

UPU Symbols and Tunisian Post Rider — A23

1949, Oct. 28 Bluish Paper

208 A23 5fr dark green 1.75 1.40
209 A23 15fr red brown 1.75 1.40
Nos. 208-209,C13 (3) 6.00 4.55

UPU, 75th anniversary.
Nos. 208-209 exist imperf.

Berber Hermes at Carthage — A24

1950-51

210 A24 15fr red brown 1.10 .70
211 A24 25fr indigo ('51) 1.10 .70
212 A24 50fr dark green ('51) 2.50 .70
Nos. 210-212 (3) 4.70 2.10

Horse, Carthage Museum — A25

1950, Dec. 26 Typo. ***Perf. 13½x14***

Size: 21½x17½mm

213 A25 10c aquamarine .30 .25
214 A25 50c brown .30 .25
215 A25 1fr rose lilac .30 .25
216 A25 2fr gray .35 .30
217 A25 4fr vermilion .55 .45
218 A25 5fr blue green .35 .25
219 A25 8fr deep blue .55 .35
220 A25 12fr red 1.40 .65
221 A25 15fr carmine rose ('50) .55 .45
Nos. 213-221 (9) 4.65 3.20

See Nos. 222-224, 226-228.

1951-53 Engr. ***Perf. 13x14***

Size: 22x18mm

222 A25 15fr carmine rose 1.20 .65
223 A25 15fr ultra ('53) 1.40 .55
224 A25 30fr deep ultra 2.50 .70
Nos. 222-224 (3) 5.10 1.90

Type of 1948-49

1951, Aug. 1 ***Perf. 13***

225 A21 30fr dark blue 1.40 1.10

Horse Type of 1950

1952 Typo. ***Perf. 13½x14***

226 A25 3fr brown orange .70 .45
227 A25 12fr carmine rose 1.40 .45
228 A25 15fr ultra .70 .25
Nos. 226-228 (3) 2.80 1.15

Charles Nicolle — A26

1952, Aug. 4 Engr. ***Perf. 13***

229 A26 15fr black brown 2.10 .90
230 A26 30fr deep blue 2.10 .90

Founding of the Society of Medical Sciences of Tunisia, 50th anniv.

Flags, Pennants and Minaret — A27

1953, Oct. 18

231 A27 8fr black brn & choc 1.40 1.10
232 A27 12fr dk green & emer 1.40 1.10
233 A27 15fr indigo & ultra 1.40 1.10
234 A27 18fr dk pur & pur 1.40 1.10
235 A27 30fr dk car & car 2.10 1.40
Nos. 231-235 (5) 7.70 5.80

First International Fair of Tunis.

Courtyard at Sousse A28

Sidi Bou Maklouf Mosque A29

Designs: 1fr, Courtyard at Sousse. 2fr, 4fr, Citadel, Takrouna. 5fr, 8fr, View of Tatahouine. 10fr, 12fr, Oasis of Matmata. 15fr, Street Corner, Sidi Bou Said. 20fr, 25fr, Genoese fort, Tabarka. 30fr, 40fr, Bab-El-Khadra gate. 50fr, 75fr, Four-story building, Medenine.

Perf. 13½x13 (A28), 13

1954, May 29

236 A28 50c emerald .30 .25
237 A28 1fr carmine rose .30 .25
238 A28 2fr violet brown .35 .30
239 A28 4fr turq blue .55 .30
240 A28 5fr violet .55 .25
241 A28 8fr black brown .55 .30
242 A28 10fr dk blue grn .55 .25
243 A28 12fr rose brown .55 .30
244 A28 15fr dp ultra 2.25 .35
245 A29 18fr chocolate 2.00 .65
246 A29 20fr dp ultra 1.25 .30
247 A29 25fr indigo 1.25 .30
248 A29 30fr dp claret 1.40 .30
249 A29 40fr dk Prus grn 1.50 .65
250 A29 50fr dk violet 2.50 .30
251 A29 75fr carmine rose 5.50 2.10

Typo.

Perf. 14x13½

252 A28 15fr ultra .80 .25
Nos. 236-252 (17) 22.15 7.40

Imperforates exist. Value $50. See Nos. 271-287. For surcharge see No. B125.

Mohammed al-Amin, Bey of Tunis — A30

1954, Oct. ***Perf. 13***

253 A30 8fr bl & dk bl 1.10 .85
254 A30 12fr lil gray & indigo 1.10 .85
255 A30 15fr dp car & brn lake 1.20 .90
256 A30 18fr red brn & blk brn 1.20 .90
257 A30 30fr bl grn & dk bl grn 1.75 1.40
Nos. 253-257 (5) 6.35 4.90

Theater Drapes, Dove and Sun — A31

1955

258 A31 15fr dk red brn, bl & org 1.10 .85

Essor, Tunisian amateur theatrical society.

Rotary Emblem, Map and Symbols of Punic, Roman, Arab and French Civilizations A32

1955, May 14 Unwmk.

259 A32 12fr vio brn & blk brn 1.10 .85
260 A32 15fr vio gray & dk brn 1.10 .85
261 A32 18fr rose vio & dk pur 1.20 .90
262 A32 25fr blue & dp ultra 1.20 .90
263 A32 30fr dk Prus grn & ind 1.75 1.40
Nos. 259-263 (5) 6.35 4.90

Rotary International, 50th anniv.

Bey of Tunis — A33

1955 Engr. ***Perf. 13½x13***

264 A33 15fr dark blue .70 .25

Embroiderers — A34

15fr, 18fr, Potters. 20fr, 30fr, Florists.

1955, July 25 ***Perf. 13***

265 A34 5fr rose brown 1.10 .85
266 A34 12fr ultra 1.10 .85
267 A34 15fr Prussian green 1.10 .90
268 A34 18fr red 1.10 .90
269 A34 20fr dark violet 1.40 1.10
270 A34 30fr violet brown 1.40 1.10
Nos. 265-270 (6) 7.20 5.70

For surcharge see No. B126.

Independent Kingdom

Types of 1954 Redrawn with "RF" Omitted

1956, Mar. 1 ***Perf. 13½x13, 13 (A29)***

271 A28 50c emerald .25 .25
272 A28 1fr carmine rose .25 .25
273 A28 2fr violet brown .25 .25
274 A28 4fr turquoise blue .30 .25
275 A28 5fr violet .30 .25
276 A28 8fr black brown .30 .25
277 A28 10fr dk blue grn .30 .25
278 A28 12fr rose brown .30 .25
279 A28 15fr deep ultra 1.10 .25
280 A29 18fr chocolate .35 .25
281 A29 20fr deep ultra .30 .25
282 A29 25fr indigo .30 .25
283 A29 30fr deep claret 1.10 .25
284 A29 40fr dk Prus grn 1.10 .25
285 A29 50fr dark violet 1.00 .25
286 A29 75fr carmine rose 1.75 1.10

Perf. 14x13

Typo.

287 A28 15fr ultra .70 .25
Nos. 271-287 (17) 9.95 5.10

Mohammed al-Amin Bey of Tunis — A35

Designs: 12fr, 18fr, 30fr, Woman and Dove. 5fr, 20fr, Bey of Tunis.

1956 Unwmk. Engr. ***Perf. 13***

288 A35 5fr deep blue .25 .25
289 A35 12fr brown violet .30 .35
290 A35 15fr red .30 .35
291 A35 18fr dk blue gray .45 .40
292 A35 20fr dark green .45 .40
293 A35 30fr copper brown .85 .50
Nos. 288-293 (6) 2.60 2.25

Issued to commemorate Tunisian autonomy.

Farhat Hached — A36

1956, May 1

294 A36 15fr rose brown .30 .30
295 A36 30fr indigo .35 .35

Farhat Hached (1914-1952), nationalist leader.

Grapes — A37

Fruit Market — A38

Designs: 15fr, Hand holding olive branch. 18fr, Wheat harvest. 20fr, Man carrying food basket ("Gifts for the wedding").

1956-57 Unwmk. Engr. *Perf. 13*

296	A37 12fr lil, vio & vio brn	.55	.25
297	A37 15fr ind, dk ol grn & red brn	.65	.25
298	A37 18fr brt violet blue	.90	.40
299	A37 20fr brown orange	.90	.40
300	A38 25fr chocolate	1.25	.80
301	A38 30fr deep ultra	1.40	.65
	Nos. 296-301 (6)	5.65	2.75

Habib Bourguiba A39

Farmers and Workers A40

Perf. 14 (A39), 11½x11 (A40)

1957, Mar. 20

302	A39 5fr dark blue	.25	.25
303	A40 12fr magenta	.25	.25
304	A39 20fr ultra	.30	.30
305	A40 25fr green	.35	.25
306	A39 30fr chocolate	.45	.35
307	A40 50fr crimson rose	.80	.55
	Nos. 302-307 (6)	2.40	1.95

First anniversary of independence.

Dove and Handclasp — A41

Labor Bourse, Tunis — A42

1957, July 5 Engr. *Perf. 13*

308	A41 18fr dk red violet	.30	.30
309	A42 20fr crimson	.35	.35
310	A41 25fr green	.35	.35
311	A42 30fr dark blue	.45	.45
	Nos. 308-311 (4)	1.45	1.45

5th World Congress of the Intl. Federation of Trade Unions, Tunis, July 5-13.

Republic

Officer and Soldier — A43

1957, Aug. 8 Typo. *Perf. 11*

312	A43 20fr rose pink	14.00	20.00
313	A43 25fr light violet	14.00	19.00
314	A43 30fr brown orange	14.00	19.00
	Nos. 312-314 (3)	42.00	58.00

Proclamation of the Republic.

Bourguiba in Exile, Ile de la Galité — A44

1958, Jan. 18 Engr. *Perf. 13*

315	A44 20fr blue & dk brn	.55	.40
316	A44 25fr lt blue & vio	.55	.40

6th anniv. of Bourguiba's deportation.

Map of Tunisia — A45

25fr, Woman & child. 30fr, Hand holding flag.

1958, Mar. 20 *Perf. 13*

317	A45 20fr dk brown & emer	.40	.25
318	A45 25fr blue & sepia	.40	.25
319	A45 30fr red brown & red	.55	.25
	Nos. 317-319 (3)	1.35	.75

2nd anniv. of independence. See No. 321.

Andreas Vesalius and Abderrahman ibn Khaldoun — A46

1958, Apr. 17 Unwmk.

320	A46 30fr bister & slate grn	.65	.25

World's Fair, Brussels, Apr. 17-Oct. 19.

Redrawn Type of 1958

1958, June 1 Engr. *Perf. 13*

321	A45 20fr brt bl & ocher	.65	.25

Date has been changed to "1 Juin 1955-1958."

3rd anniv. of the return of Pres. Habib Bourguiba.

Gardener — A47

1958, May 1

322	A47 20fr multicolored	.65	.30

Labor Day, May 1.

A48

1958, July 25 Unwmk. *Perf. 13*
Blue Paper

323	A48 5fr dk vio brn & ol	.45	.25
324	A48 10fr dk grn & yel grn	.45	.25
325	A48 15fr org red & brn lake	.45	.25
326	A48 20fr vio, ol grn & yel	.45	.25
327	A48 25fr red lilac	.45	.25
	Nos. 323-327 (5)	2.25	1.25

First anniversary of the Republic.

Pres. Habib Bourguiba — A49

1958, Aug. 3 Unwmk. *Perf. 13*

328	A49 20fr vio & brn lake	.65	.25

Pres. Bourguiba's 55th birthday.

Fishermen Casting Net — A50

1958, Oct. 18 Engr. *Perf. 13*

329	A50 25fr dk brn, grn & red	.65	.30

6th International Fair, Tunis.

UNESCO Building, Paris — A51

1958, Nov. 3

330	A51 25fr grnsh black	.65	.30

Opening of UNESCO Headquarters, Nov. 3.

Woman Opening Veil — A52

1959, Jan. 1 Engr. *Perf. 13*

331	A52 20m greenish blue	.65	.25

Emancipation of Tunisian women.

Hand Planting Symbolic Tree — A53

Habib Bourguiba at Borj le Boeuf — A54

10m, Shield with flag and people holding torch. 20m, Habib Bourguiba at Borj le Boeuf, Sahara.

1959, Mar. 2 Unwmk. *Perf. 13*

332	A53 5m vio brn, car & sal	.25	.25
333	A53 10m multicolored	.30	.25
334	A53 20m blue	.40	.25
335	A54 30m grnsh bl, ind & org brn	.70	.40
	Nos. 332-335 (4)	1.65	1.15

25th anniv. of the founding of the Neo-Destour Party at Kasr Helal, Mar. 2, 1934.

"Independence" A55

1959, Mar. 20

336	A55 50m olive, blk & red	.85	.40

3rd anniversary of independence.

Map of Africa and Drawings — A56

1959, Apr. 15 Litho. *Perf. 13*

337	A56 40m lt bl & red brn	.85	.40

Africa Freedom Day, Apr. 15.

Camel Camp and Mosque, Kairouan — A57

Horseback Rider — A58

Olive Picker A59

Open Window A58a

Designs: ½m, Woodcock in Ain-Draham forest. 2m, Camel rider. 3m, Saddler's shop. 4m, Old houses of Medenine, gazelle and youth. 6m, Weavers. 8m, Woman of Gafsa. 10m, Unveiled woman holding fruit. 12m, Ivory craftsman. 15m, Skanes Beach, Monastir, and mermaid. 16m, Minaret of Ez-Zitouna University, Tunis. 20m, Oasis of Gabès. 25m, Oil, flowers and fish of Sfax. 30m, Modern and Roman aqueducts. 40m, Festival at Kairouan (drummer and camel). 45m, Octagonal minaret, Bizerte (boatman). 50m, Three women of Djerba island. 60m, Date palms, Djerid. 70m, Tapestry weaver. 75m, Pottery of Nabeul. 90m, Le Kef (man on horse). 100m, Road to Sidi-bou-Said. 200m, Old port of Sfax. ½d, Roman temple, Sbeitla. 1d, Farmer plowing with oxen, Beja.

1959-61 Unwmk. Engr. *Perf. 13*

338	A58	½m	emer, brn & bl grn ('60)	.25	.25
339	A57	1m	lt bl & ocher	.25	.25
340	A58	2m	multicolored	.25	.25
341	A58	3m	slate green	.25	.25
342	A57	4m	red brn ('60)	.25	.25
343	A58	5m	gray green	.25	.25
344	A58	6m	rose violet	.25	.25
345	A58	8m	vio brn ('60)	.75	.30
346	A58	10m	ol, dk grn & car	.25	.25
347	A58	12m	vio bl & ol bis ('61)	.60	.25
348	A57	15m	brt blue ('60)	.30	.25
349	A57	16m	grnsh blk ('60)	.35	.25
350	A58a	20m	grnsh blue	1.10	.30
351	A58	20m	grnsh blk, ol & mar ('60)	2.00	.25
352	A57	25m	multi ('60)	.30	.25
353	A58a	30m	brn, grnsh bl & ol	.45	.25
354	A59	40m	dp grn ('60)	1.80	.25
355	A58a	45m	brt grn ('60)	.75	.30
356	A58a	50m	Prus grn, dk bl & rose ('60)	1.10	.25
357	A58a	60m	grn & red brn ('60)	1.10	.40
358	A59	70m	multi ('60)	1.60	.55
359	A59	75m	ol gray ('60)	1.50	.60
360	A58a	90m	brt grn, ultra & choc ('60)	1.50	.60
361	A59	95m	multicolored	2.00	1.10
362	A58a	100m	dk bl, ol & brn	2.10	1.00
363	A58a	200m	brt bl, bis & car	5.25	2.40
363A	A59	½d	lt brn ('60)	12.00	6.75
363B	A58a	1d	sl grn & bis ('60)	22.50	13.50
			Nos. 338-363B (28)	61.05	31.80

UN Emblem and Clasped Hands — A60

1959, Oct. 24

364	A60 80m org brn, brn & ultra	.75	.60

UN Day, Oct. 24.

Dancer and Coin — A61

1959, Nov. 4

365 A61 50m grnsh bl & blk .75 .60

Central Bank of Tunisia, first anniversary.

Uprooted Oak Emblem A62

Doves and WRY Emblem A63

1960, Apr. 7 Engr. *Perf. 13*

366 A62 20m blue black .60 .35
367 A63 40m red lil & dk grn .75 .50

World Refugee Year, 7/1/59-6/30/60.

Girl, Boy and Scout Badge — A64

Designs: 25m, Hand giving Scout sign. 30m, Bugler and tent. 40m, Peacock and Scout emblem. 60m, Scout and campfire.

1960, Aug. 9

368 A64 10m lt blue green .30 .30
369 A64 25m green, red & brn .45 .35
370 A64 30m vio bl, grn & mar .50 .35
371 A64 40m black, car & bl .75 .45
372 A64 60m dk brn, vio blk & lake 1.10 .60
Nos. 368-372 (5) 3.10 2.05

4th Arab Boy Scout Jamboree, Tunis, Aug.

Cyclist — A65

Designs: 10m, Olympic rings forming flower. 15m, Girl tennis player and minaret. 25m, Runner and minaret. 50m, Handball player and minaret.

1960, Aug. 25

373 A65 5m dk brown & olive .30 .30
374 A65 10m sl, red vio & emer .30 .30
375 A65 15m rose red & rose car .30 .30
376 A65 25m grnsh bl & gray bl .45 .45
377 A65 50m brt green & ultra .80 .85
Nos. 373-377 (5) 2.15 2.20

17th Olympic Games, Rome, 8/25-9/11.

Symbolic Forest Design — A66

Designs: 15m, Man working in forest. 25m, Tree superimposed on leaf. 50m, Symbolic tree and bird.

1960, Aug. 29

378 A66 8m multicolored .30 .25
379 A66 15m dark green .45 .25
380 A66 25m dk pur, crim & brt grn .60 .30
381 A66 50m Prus grn, yel grn & rose lake 1.10 .55
Nos. 378-381 (4) 2.45 1.35

5th World Forestry Congress, Seattle, Wash., Aug. 29-Sept. 10.

National Fair Emblems — A67

1960, June 1

382 A67 100m black & green .60 .50

5th Natl. Fair, Sousse, May 27-June 12.

Pres. Bourguiba Signing Constitution A68

Pres. Bourguiba A69

1960, June 1

383 A68 20m choc, red & emer .30 .25
384 A69 20m grayish blk .25 .25
385 A69 30m blue, dl red & blk .35 .25
386 A69 40m grn, dl red & blk .50 .25
Nos. 383-386 (4) 1.40 1.00

Promulgation of the Constitution (No. 383).

UN Emblem and Arms — A70

1960, Oct. 24 Engr. *Perf. 13*

387 A70 40m mag, ultra & gray grn .60 .50

15th anniversary of the United Nations.

Dove and "Liberated Tunisia" — A71

Design: 75m, Globe and arms.

1961, Mar. 20 *Perf. 13*

388 A71 20m maroon, bis & bl .25 .25
389 A71 30m blue, vio & brn .35 .25
390 A71 40m yel grn & ultra .65 .45
391 A71 75m bis, red lil & Prus bl .80 .55
Nos. 388-391 (4) 2.05 1.50

5th anniversary of independence.

Map of Africa, Woman and Animals — A72

Map of Africa: 60m, Negro woman and Arab. 100m, Arabic inscription and Guinea masque. 200m, Hands of Negro and Arab.

1961, Apr. 15 Engr. Unwmk.

392 A72 40m bis brn, red brn & dk grn .30 .25
393 A72 60m sl grn, blk & org brn .35 .30
394 A72 100m sl grn, emer & vio .75 .45
395 A72 200m dk brn & org brn 1.40 1.10
Nos. 392-395 (4) 2.80 2.10

Africa Freedom Day, Apr. 15.

Mother and Child with Flags — A73

Designs: 50m, Tunisians. 95m, Girl with wings and half-moon.

1961, June 1 Unwmk. *Perf. 13*

396 A73 25m pale vio, red & brn .30 .25
397 A73 50m bl grn, sep & brn .45 .25
398 A73 95m pale vio, rose lil & ocher .70 .35
Nos. 396-398 (3) 1.45 .85

National Feast Day, June 1.

Dag Hammarskjold — A74

1961, Oct. 24 Photo. *Perf. 14*

399 A74 40m ultramarine .60 .30

UN Day; Dag Hammarskjold (1905-1961), Secretary General of the UN, 1953-61.

Arms of Tunisia — A75

1962, Jan. 18 *Perf. 11½*

Arms in Original Colors

400 A75 1m black & yellow .25 .25
401 A75 2m black & pink .25 .25
402 A75 3m black & lt blue .25 .25
403 A75 6m black & gray .30 .25
Nos. 400-403 (4) 1.05 1.00

Tunisia's campaign for independence, 10th anniv.

Mosquito in Spider Web and WHO Emblem — A76

Designs: 30m, Symbolic horseback rider spearing mosquito. 40m, Hands crushing mosquito, horiz.

1962, Apr. 7 Engr. *Perf. 13*

404 A76 20m chocolate .50 .30
405 A76 30m red brn & slate grn .50 .30
406 A76 40m dk brn, mar & grn .90 .35
Nos. 404-406 (3) 1.90 .95

WHO drive to eradicate malaria.

Boy and Map of Africa A77

African Holding "Africa" A78

1962, Apr. 15 Photo. *Perf. 14*

407 A77 50m brown & orange .50 .35
408 A78 100m blue, blk & org .75 .50

Africa Freedom Day, Apr. 15.

Farm Worker A79

Industrial Worker A80

1962, May 1 Unwmk.

409 A79 40m multicolored .50 .25
410 A80 60m dark red brown .60 .35

Labor Day.

"Liberated Tunisia" — A81

1962, June 1 Typo. *Perf. 13½x14*

411 A81 20m salmon & blk .65 .35

National Feast Day, June 1.

Woman of Gabès — A82

Women in costume of various localities: 10m, 30m, Mahdia. 15m, Kairouan. 20m, 40m, Hammamet. 25m, Djerba. 55m, Ksar Hellal. 60m, Tunis.

1962-63 Photo. *Perf. 11½*

412 A82 5m multi .65 .25
413 A82 10m multi .75 .35
414 A82 15m multi ('63) 1.20 .50
415 A82 20m multi 1.20 .65
416 A82 25m multi ('63) 1.20 .65
417 A82 30m multi 1.40 .75
418 A82 40m multi 1.40 .75
419 A82 50m multi 1.40 .85
420 A82 55m multi ('63) 2.10 1.10
421 A82 60m multi ('63) 2.90 1.40
Nos. 412-421 (10) 14.20 7.25

6 stamps issued July 25, 1962 (July 25) for the 6th anniv. of Tunisia's independence. 4 issued June 1, 1963 for Natl. Feast Day. See Nos. 470-471.

UN Emblem, Flag and Dove — A83

30m, Leaves, globe, horiz. 40m, Dove, globe.

1962, Oct. 24 Unwmk.

422 A83 20m gray, blk & scar .30 .25
423 A83 30m multicolored .45 .25
424 A83 40m claret brn, blk & bl .70 .35
Nos. 422-424 (3) 1.45 .85

Issued for United Nations Day, Oct. 24.

Aboul-Qasim Chabbi — A84

1962, Nov. 20 Engr. *Perf. 13*

425 A84 15m purple .65 .25

Aboul-Qasim Chabbi (1904-34), Arab poet.

Pres. Habib Bourguiba — A85

1962, Dec. 7 Photo. *Perf. 12½x13½*

426	A85	20m bright blue	.25	.25
427	A85	30m rose claret	.25	.25
428	A85	40m green	.25	.25
		Nos. 426-428 (3)	.75	.75

Hached Telephone Exchange — A86

Designs: 10m, Carthage Exchange. 15m, Sfax telecommunications center. 50m, Telephone operators. 100m, Symbol of automatization. 200m, Belvedere Central Exchange.

1962, Dec. 7 Litho.

429	A86	5m multicolored	.30	.25
430	A86	10m multicolored	.35	.25
431	A86	15m multicolored	.50	.35
432	A86	50m multicolored	.80	.50
433	A86	100m multicolored	1.90	1.00
434	A86	200m multicolored	2.75	1.60
		Nos. 429-434 (6)	6.60	3.95

1st Afro-Asian Philatelic Exhibition; automation of the telephone system.

Dove over Globe A87

"Hunger" A88

1963, Mar. 21 Engr. *Perf. 13*

435	A87	20m brt bl & brn	.35	.25
436	A88	40m bis brn & dk brn	.65	.25

FAO "Freedom from Hunger" campaign.

Runner and Walker — A89

1963, Feb. 17 Litho. *Perf. 13*

437	A89	30m brn, blk & grn	.45	.50

Army Sports Day; 13th C.I.S.M. cross country championships.

Centenary Emblem — A90

1963, May 8 Engr. *Perf. 13*

438	A90	20m brn, gray & red	1.10	.30

Centenary of International Red Cross.

"Human Rights" — A91

1963, Dec. 10 Unwmk. *Perf. 13*

439	A91	30m grn & dk brn	.60	.30

15th anniv. of the Universal Declaration of Human Rights.

Hand Raising Gateway of Great Temple of Philae — A92

1964, Mar. 8 Engr.

440	A92	50m red brn, bis & bluish blk	.55	.30

UNESCO world campaign to save historic monuments in Nubia.

Sunshine, Rain and Barometer — A93

1964, Mar. 8 Unwmk. *Perf. 13*

441	A93	40m brn, red lil & slate	.55	.25

4th World Meteorological Day, Mar. 23.

Mohammed Ali — A94

1964, May 15 Engr.

442	A94	50m sepia	.60	.35

Mohammed Ali (1894-1928), labor leader.

Map of Africa and Symbolic Flower — A95

1964, May 25 Photo. *Perf. 13x14*

443	A95	60m multicolored	.60	.30

Addis Ababa charter on African Unity, 1st anniv.

Pres. Habib Bourguiba — A96

1964, June 1 Engr. *Perf. 12½x13½*

444	A96	20m vio bl	.30	.25
445	A96	30m black	.30	.25

"Ship and Torch" — A97

1964, Oct. 19 Photo. *Perf. 11½x11*

446	A97	50m blk & blue grn	.60	.30

Neo-Destour Congress, Bizerte. "Bizerte" in Arabic forms the ship and "Neo-Destour Congress 1964" the torch of the design.

Communication Equipment and ITU Emblem — A98

1965, May 17 Engr. *Perf. 13*

447	A98	55m gray & blue	.60	.30

ITU, centenary.

Carthaginian Coin — A99

Perf. 12½x14

1965, July 9 Photo. Unwmk.

448	A99	5m turq grn & blk brn	.25	.25
449	A99	10m bis & blk brn	.30	.25
450	A99	75m bl & blk brn	.75	.25
		Nos. 448-450 (3)	1.30	.75

Festival of Popular Arts, Carthage.

Girl with Book — A100

1965, Oct. 1 Engr. *Perf. 13*

451	A100	25m brt bl, blk & red	.30	.25
452	A100	40m blk, bl & red	.35	.25
453	A100	50m red, bl & blk	.45	.35
	a.	Souvenir sheet of 3, #451-453	5.00	5.00
		Nos. 451-453 (3)	1.10	.85

Girl Students' Center; education for women. No. 453a sold for 200m. Issued perf. and imperf.; same value.

Links and ICY Emblem — A101

1965, Oct. 24

454	A101	40m blk, brt bl & rose lil	.60	.25

International Cooperation Year.

Man Pouring Water — A102

Symbolic Designs: 10m, Woman and pool. 30m, Woman pouring water. 100m, Mountain and branches.

Inscribed "Eaux Minerales"

1966, Jan. 18 Photo. *Perf. 13x14*

455	A102	10m gray, ocher & dk red	.30	.25
456	A102	20m multicolored	.45	.35
457	A102	30m yel, bl & red	.45	.35
458	A102	100m ol, bl & yel	1.20	.70
		Nos. 455-458 (4)	2.40	1.65

Mineral waters of Tunisia.

President Bourguiba and Hands A103

"Promotion of Culture" A104

25m, "Independence" (arms raised), flag and doves. 40m, "Development."

1966, June 1 Engr. *Perf. 13*

459	A103	5m dl pur & vio	.25	.25
460	A103	10m gray grn & sl grn	.25	.25

Perf. 11½

Photo.

461	A104	25m multi	.25	.25
462	A104	40m multi, horiz.	.55	.25
463	A104	60m multi	.85	.35
		Nos. 459-463 (5)	2.15	1.35

10th anniversary of independence.

Map of Africa through View Finder, Plane and UN Emblem — A105

1966, Sept. 12 Engr. *Perf. 13*

464	A105	15m lilac & multi	.30	.25
465	A105	35m blue & multi	.35	.25
466	A105	40m multicolored	.50	.35
	a.	Souvenir sheet, #464-466	10.00	10.00
		Nos. 464-466 (3)	1.15	.85

2nd UN Regional Cartographic Conference for Africa, held in Tunisia, Sept. 12-24.

No. 466a sold for 150m. Issued perf. and imperf.; same value.

UNESCO Emblem and Nine Muses — A106

1966, Nov. 4 *Perf. 13*

467	A106	100m blk & brn	1.10	.35

UNESCO, 20th anniv.

Runners and Mediterranean Map — A107

1967, Mar. 20 Engr. *Perf. 13*

468	A107	20m dk red, brn ol & bl	.30	.25
469	A107	30m brt bl & blk	.60	.35

Mediterranean Games, Sept. 8-17.

Types of 1962-63 and 1965-66 with EXPO '67 Emblem, Inscription and

Symbols of Various Activities — A108

Designs: 50m, Woman of Djerba. 75m, Woman of Gabes. 155m, Pink flamingoes.

Photo.; Engr. (A108)

1967, Apr. 28 *Perf. 11½, 13 (A108)*

470 A82	50m multicolored	.45	.25
471 A82	75m multicolored	.70	.30
472 A108	100m dk grn, sl bl & blk	1.10	.30
473 A108	110m dk brn, ultra & red	1.40	.55
474 AP6	155m multicolored	2.10	.75
	Nos. 470-474 (5)	5.75	2.15

EXPO '67, Intl. Exhibition, Montreal, Apr. 28-Oct. 27.

Tunisian Pavilion, Pres. Bourguiba and Map of Tunisia A109

Designs: 105m, 200m, Tunisian Pavilion and bust of Pres. Bourguiba.

1967, June 13 **Engr.** *Perf. 13*

475 A109	65m red lil & dp org	.45	.35
476 A109	105m multicolored	.50	.35
477 A109	120m brt bl	.65	.40
478 A109	200m red, lil & blk	1.10	.50
	Nos. 475-478 (4)	2.70	1.60

Tunisia Day at EXPO '67.

"Tunisia" Holding 4-leaf Clovers A110

Woman Freeing Doves A111

1967, July 25 **Litho.** *Perf. 13½*

479 A110	25m multicolored	.30	.25
480 A111	40m multicolored	.45	.25

10th anniversary of the Republic.

Tennis Courts, Players and Games' Emblem A112

10m, Games' emblem & sports emblems, vert. 15m, Swimming pool & swimmers. 35m, Sports Palace & athletes. 75m, Stadium & athletes.

1967, Sept. 8 **Engr.** *Perf. 13*

481 A112	5m sl grn & hn brn	.25	.25
482 A112	10m brn red & multi	.25	.25
483 A112	15m black	.30	.25
484 A112	35m dk brn & Prus bl	.45	.25
485 A112	75m dk car rose, vio & bl grn	.80	.45
	Nos. 481-485 (5)	2.05	1.45

Mediterranean Games, Tunis, Sept. 8-17.

Bird, Punic Period — A113

History of Tunisia: 20m, Sea horse, medallion from Kerkouane. 25m, Hannibal, bronze bust, Volubilis. 30m, Stele, Carthage. 40m, Hamilcar, coin. 60m, Mask, funereal pendant.

1967, Dec. 1 **Litho.** *Perf. 13½*

486 A113	15m gray grn, pink & blk	.30	.25
487 A113	20m dp bl, red & blk	.30	.25
488 A113	25m dk grn & org brn	.45	.25
489 A113	30m grnsh gray, pink & blk	.45	.25
490 A113	40m red brn, yel & blk	.55	.25
491 A113	60m multicolored	.65	.35
	Nos. 486-491 (6)	2.70	1.60

"Mankind" and Human Rights Flame — A114

1968, Jan. 18 **Engr.** *Perf. 13*

492 A114	25m brick red	.55	.35
493 A114	60m deep blue	.55	.25

International Human Rights Year.

Computer Fantasy — A115

1968, Mar. 20 **Engr.** *Perf. 13*

494 A115	25m mag, bl vio & ol	.40	.35
495 A115	40m ol grn, red brn & brn	.40	.35
496 A115	60m ultra, slate & brn	.50	.40
	Nos. 494-496 (3)	1.30	1.10

Introduction of electronic equipment for postal service.

Physician and Patient — A116

1968, Apr. 7 **Engr.** *Perf. 13*

497 A116	25m dp grn & brt grn	.45	.35
498 A116	60m magenta & carmine	.65	.35

WHO, 20th anniversary.

Arabian Jasmine — A117

Flowers: 5m, Flax. 6m, Canna indica. 10m, Pomegranate. 15m, Rhaponticum acaule. 20m, Geranium. 25m, Madonna lily. 40m, Peach blossoms. 50m, Caper. 60m, Ariana rose. 100m, Jasmine.

Granite Paper

1968-69 **Photo.** *Perf. 11½*

499 A117	5m multicolored	.25	.25
500 A117	6m multicolored	.25	.25
501 A117	10m multicolored	.30	.25
502 A117	12m multicolored	.30	.25
503 A117	15m multicolored	.35	.25
504 A117	20m multicolored	.45	.25
505 A117	25m multicolored	.45	.30
506 A117	40m multicolored	.65	.30
507 A117	50m multicolored	.80	.35
508 A117	60m multicolored	1.20	.60
509 A117	100m multicolored	1.75	.80
	Nos. 499-509 (11)	6.75	3.85

Issued: 12, 50, 60, 100m, 4/9/68; others, 3/20/69.

Flower with Red Crescent and Globe — A118

25m, Dove with Red Crescent and globe.

1968, May 8 **Engr.** *Perf. 13*

510 A118	15m Prus bl, grn & red	.40	.35
511 A118	25m brt rose lil & red	.50	.35

Red Crescent Society.

Flutist — A119

1968, June 1 **Litho.** *Perf. 13*

512 A119	20m vio & multi	.50	.25
513 A119	50m multicolored	.55	.35

Stamp Day.

Jackal — A120

Animals: 8m, Porcupine. 10m, Dromedary. 15m, Dorcas gazelle. 20m, Desert fox (fennec). 25m, Desert hedgehog. 40m, Arabian horse. 60m, Boar.

1968-69 **Photo.** *Perf. 11½*

514 A120	5m dk brn, lt bl & bis	.30	.25
515 A120	8m dk vio brn & yel grn	.45	.25
516 A120	10m dk brn, lt bl & ocher	.65	.25
517 A120	15m dk brn, ocher & yel grn	.70	.25
518 A120	20m dl yel & dk brn	1.10	.45
519 A120	25m blk, tan & brt grn	1.40	.60
520 A120	40m blk, lil & pale grn	1.75	.90
521 A120	60m dk brn, buff & yel grn	2.75	1.20
	Nos. 514-521 (8)	9.10	4.15

Issued: 5, 8, 20, 60m, 9/15/68; others, 1/18/69.

Worker and ILO Emblem — A121

60m, Young man & woman holding banner.

1969, May 1 **Engr.** *Perf. 13*

522 A121	25m Prus bl, blk & bis	.45	.35
523 A121	60m rose car, bl & yel	.65	.40

ILO, 50th anniversary.

Veiled Women and Musicians with Flute and Drum — A122

1969, June 20 **Litho.** *Perf. 14x13½*

524 A122	100m dp yel grn & multi	1.25	.35

Stamp Day.

Tunisian Coat of Arms — A123

1969, July 25 **Photo.** *Perf. 11½*

525 A123	15m yel & multi	.30	.25
526 A123	25m pink & multi	.45	.25
527 A123	40m gray & multi	.60	.25
528 A123	60m lt bl & multi	.75	.25
	Nos. 525-528 (4)	2.10	1.00

Symbols of Industry — A124

1969, Sept. 10 *Perf. 13x12*

529 A124	60m blk, red & yel	.60	.30

African Development Bank, 5th anniv.

Lute — A125

Musical Instruments: 50m, Zither, horiz. 70m, Rebab (2-strings). 90m, Drums and flute, horiz.

1970, Mar. 20 **Photo.** *Perf. 11½*

Granite Paper

530 A125	25m multicolored	.45	.35
531 A125	50m multicolored	.60	.35
532 A125	70m multicolored	.80	.35
533 A125	90m multicolored	1.20	.35
	Nos. 530-533 (4)	3.05	1.40

Nurse and Maghrib Flags — A126

1970, May 4 **Photo.** *Perf. 11½*

534 A126	25m lilac & multi	.60	.25

6th Medical Seminar of Maghrib Countries (Morocco, Algeria, Tunisia and Libya), Tunis, May 4-10.

Common Design Types pictured following the introduction.

UPU Headquarters Issue

Common Design Type

1970, May 20 **Engr.** *Perf. 13*

535 CD133	25m dl red & dk ol bis	.60	.25

Mail Service Symbol — A127

35m, Mailmen of yesterday and today, vert.

1970, Oct. 15 **Litho.** *Perf. 12½x13*

Size: 37x31½mm

536 A127	25m pink & multi	.30	.25

Size: 22x37½mm

Perf. 13x12½

537 A127	35m blk & multi	.45	.25

Stamp Day.

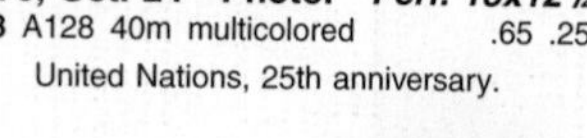

Dove, Laurel and UN Emblem — A128

1970, Oct. 24 **Photo.** *Perf. 13x12½*

538 A128	40m multicolored	.65	.25

United Nations, 25th anniversary.

Jasmine Vendor and Veiled Woman — A129

Scenes from Tunisian Life: 25m, "The 3rd Day of the Wedding." 35m, Perfume vendor. 40m, Fish vendor. 85m, Waiter in coffeehouse.

1970, Nov. 9 **Photo.** *Perf. 14*

539 A129	20m dk grn & multi	.25	.25
540 A129	25m multicolored	.30	.25
541 A129	35m multicolored	.45	.35
542 A129	40m dp car & multi	.50	.35

543 A129 85m brt bl & multi .85 .35
a. Souvenir sheet of 5, #539-543 7.00 7.00
Nos. 539-543 (5) 2.35 1.55

No. 543a sold for 500m. Issued perf. and imperf.; same value.

Lenin, after N.N. Joukov — A130

1970, Dec. 28 Engr. *Perf. 13*
544 A130 60m dk car rose 2.10 .30

Lenin (1870-1924), Russian communist leader.

Radar, Flags and Carrier Pigeon — A131

1971, May 17 Litho. *Perf. 13x12½*
545 A131 25m lt bl & multi .60 .35

Coordinating Committee for Post and Telecommunications Administrations of Maghrib Countries.

UN Headquarters, Symbolic Flower — A132

1971, May 10 Photo. *Perf. 12½x13*
546 A132 80m brt rose lil, blk & yel .50 .30

Intl. year against racial discrimination.

"Telecommunications" — A133

1971, May 17 *Perf. 13x12½*
547 A133 70m sil, blk & lt grn .50 .25

3rd World Telecommunications Day.

Earth, Moon, Satellites — A134

Design: 90m, Abstract composition.

1971, June 21 Photo. *Perf. 13x12½*
548 A134 15m brt bl & blk .40 .25
549 A134 90m scar & blk .75 .30

Conquest of space.

"Pottery Merchant" — A135

Life in Tunisia (stylized drawings): 30m, Esparto weaver selling hats and mats. 40m, Poultry man. 50m, Dyer.

1971, July 24 Photo. *Perf. 14x13½*
550 A135 25m gold & multi .50 .25
551 A135 30m gold & multi .60 .25
552 A135 40m gold & multi .70 .25
553 A135 50m gold & multi .80 .25
a. Sheet of 4, #550-553, perf. 13½ 7.50 7.50
Nos. 550-553 (4) 2.60 1.00

No. 553a sold for 500m. Issued perf. and imperf.; same value.

Pres. Bourguiba Sick in 1938 — A136

Designs: 25m, Bourguiba and "8," vert. 50m, Bourguiba carried in triumph, vert. 80m, Bourguiba and irrigation dam.

1971, Oct. 11 *Perf. 13½x13, 13x13½*
554 A136 25m multicolored .30 .25
555 A136 30m multicolored .35 .25
556 A136 50m multicolored .35 .30
557 A136 80m blk, ultra & grn .50 .30
Nos. 554-557 (4) 1.50 1.10

8th Congress of the Neo-Destour Party.

Shah Mohammed Riza Pahlavi and Stone Head 6th Century B.C. — A137

50m, King Bahram-Gur hunting, 4th cent. 100m, Coronation, from Persian miniature, 1614.

1971, Oct. 17 *Perf. 11½*
Granite Paper
558 A137 25m multicolored .30 .30
559 A137 50m multicolored .35 .25
560 A137 100m multicolored .70 .30
a. Souvenir sheet of 3, #558-560 4.25 4.25
Nos. 558-560 (3) 1.35 .85

2500th anniv. of the founding of the Persian empire by Cyrus the Great. No. 560a sold for 500m. Issued perf. and imperf.; same value.

Pimento and Warrior — A138

2m, Mint & farmer. 5m, Pear & 2 men under pear tree. 25m, Oleander & girl. 60m, Pear & sheep. 100m, Grapefruit & fruit vendor.

1971, Nov. 15 Litho. *Perf. 13*
561 A138 1m lt bl & multi .25 .25
562 A138 2m gray & multi .30 .30
563 A138 5m citron & multi .35 .30
564 A138 25m lilac & multi .60 .35
565 A138 60m multicolored 1.20 .30
566 A138 100m buff & multi 1.75 .45
a. Souvenir sheet of 6, #561-566 7.50 7.50
Nos. 561-566 (6) 4.45 1.95

Fruit, flowers and folklore. No. 566a sold for 500m. Exists imperf.; same value.

Dancer and Musician — A139

1971, Nov. 22 Photo. *Perf. 11½*
567 A139 50m blue & multi .60 .25

Stamp Day.

Map of Africa, Communication Symbols — A139a

Perf. 13½x12½
1971, Nov. 30 Litho.
568 A139a 95m multicolored .60 .45

Pan-African telecommunications system.

UNICEF Emblem, Mother and Child — A140

1971, Dec. 6 Photo. *Perf. 11½*
569 A140 110m multicolored .60 .45

UNICEF, 25th anniv.

Symbolic Olive Tree and Oil Vat — A141

1972, Jan. 9 Litho. *Perf. 13½*
570 A141 60m multicolored .60 .25

International Olive Year.

Gondolier in Flood Waters — A142

Designs: 30m, Young man and Doge's Palace. 50m, Gondola's prow and flood. 80m, Rialto Bridge and hand holding gondolier's hat, horiz.

1972, Feb. 7 Photo. *Perf. 11½*
571 A142 25m lt bl & multi .30 .25
572 A142 30m blk & multi .50 .25
573 A142 50m yel grn, gray & blk .50 .40
574 A142 80m bl & multi .95 .40
Nos. 571-574 (4) 2.25 1.30

UNESCO campaign to save Venice.

Man Reading and Book Year Emblem — A143

1972, Mar. 27 Photo. *Perf. 11½*
Granite Paper
575 A143 90m brn & multi .60 .45

International Book Year.

"Your Heart is Your Health" — A144

World Health Day: 60m, Smiling man pointing to heart.

1972, Apr. 7 *Perf. 13x13½*
576 A144 25m grn & multi .50 .25
577 A144 60m red & multi .70 .35

"Only One Earth" Environment Emblem — A145

1972, June 5 Engr. *Perf. 13*
578 A145 60m lemon & slate green .75 .25

UN Conference on Human Environment, Stockholm, June 5-16.

Hurdler, Olympic Emblems — A146

1972, Aug. 26 Photo. *Perf. 11½*
579 A146 5m Volleyball .25 .25
580 A146 15m shown .30 .25
581 A146 20m Athletes .30 .25
582 A146 25m Soccer .30 .25
583 A146 60m Swimming, women's .50 .25
584 A146 80m Running .65 .30
a. Souv. sheet of 6 4.50 4.50
Nos. 579-584 (6) 2.30 1.55

20th Olympic Games, Munich, Aug. 26-Sept. 11. No. 584a contains 6 imperf. stamps similar to Nos. 579-584. Sold for 500m.

Chessboard and Pieces — A147

1972, Sept. 25 Photo. *Perf. 11½*
585 A147 60m grn & multi 3.00 1.00

20th Men's Chess Olympiad, Skopje, Yugoslavia, Sept.-Oct.

Fisherman — A148

1972, Oct. 23 Litho. *Perf. 13½*
586 A148 5m shown .25 .25
587 A148 10m Basket maker .25 .25
588 A148 25m Musician .35 .25
589 A148 50m Married Berber woman .75 .25
590 A148 60m Flower merchant 1.00 .25
591 A148 80m Festival 1.20 .45
a. Souvenir sheet of 6, #586-591 4.50 4.50
Nos. 586-591 (6) 3.80 1.70

Life in Tunisia. No. 591a sold for 500m; exists imperf.

Post Office, Tunis — A149

Litho. & Engr.
1972, Dec. 8 *Perf. 13*
592 A149 25m ver, org & blk .50 .25

Stamp Day.

Dome of the Rock, Jerusalem A150

1973, Jan. 22 Photo. *Perf. 13½*
593 A150 25m multicolored .60 .35

Globe, Pen and Quill — A151

Design: 60m, Lyre and minaret.

1973, Mar. 19 Photo. *Perf. 14x13½*
594 A151 25m gold, brt mag & brn .30 .25
595 A151 60m bl & multi .45 .25

9th Congress of Arab Writers.

Family — A152

Family Planning: 25m, profiles and dove.

1973, Apr. 2 *Perf. 11½*
596 A152 20m grn & multi .30 .25
597 A152 25m lil & multi .50 .35

"10" and Bird Feeding Young — A153

Design: 60m, "10" made of grain and bread, and hand holding spoon.

1973, Apr. 26 Photo. *Perf. 11½*
598 A153 25m multicolored .60 .25
599 A153 60m multicolored .60 .25

World Food Program, 10th anniversary.

Roman Head and Ship — A154

Drawings of Tools and: 25m, Mosaic with ostriches and camel. 30m, Mosaic with 4 heads and 4 emblems. 40m, Punic stele to the sun, vert. 60m, Outstretched hand & arm of Christian preacher; symbols of 4 Evangelists. 75m, 17th cent. potsherd with Arabic inscription, vert.

1973, May 6
600 A154 5m multicolored .50 .25
601 A154 25m multicolored .75 .40
602 A154 30m multicolored .75 .40
603 A154 40m multicolored 1.10 .40
604 A154 60m multicolored 1.40 .40
605 A154 75m multicolored 1.50 .50
a. Souvenir sheet of 6 12.00 12.00
Nos. 600-605 (6) 6.00 2.35

UNESCO campaign to save Carthage. No. 605a contains 6 imperf. stamps similar to Nos. 600-605. Sold for 500m.

Overlapping Circles — A155

Design: 75m, Printed circuit board.

1973, May 17 Photo. *Perf. 14x13½*
606 A155 60m yel & multi .75 .25
607 A155 75m vio & multi .90 .25

5th Intl. Telecommunications Day.

Map of Africa as Festival Emblem — A156

40m, African heads, festival emblem in eye.

1973, July 15 Photo. *Perf. 13½x13*
608 A156 25m multicolored .40 .35
609 A156 40m multicolored .50 .35

Pan-African Youth Festival, Tunis.

Scout Emblem and Pennants — A157

1973, July 23 Litho. *Perf. 13½x13*
610 A157 25m multicolored .60 .35

International Boy Scout Organization.

Crescent-shaped Racing Cars — A158

1973, July 30 *Perf. 13x13½*
611 A158 60m multicolored .65 .40

2nd Pan-Arab auto race.

Highway Cloverleaf A159

Traffic Lights and Signs A160

Perf. 12½x13, 13x12½
1973, Sept. 28 Litho.
612 A159 25m lt bl & multi .65 .40
613 A160 30m multicolored .75 .35

Highway safety campaign.

Stylized Camel — A161

Stamp Day: 10m, Stylized bird and philatelic symbols, horiz.

1973, Oct. 8 Photo. *Perf. 13½*
614 A161 10m multicolored .50 .25
615 A161 65m multicolored .60 .40

Copernicus — A162

Lithographed and Engraved
1973, Oct. 16 *Perf. 13x12½*
616 A162 60m blk & multi 2.50 .30

African Unity — A163

1973, Nov. 4 Photo. *Perf. 14x13½*
617 A163 25m blk & multi .65 .25

10th anniv. of the OAU.

Handshake and Emblems — A164

1973, Nov. 15 Litho. *Perf. 14½x14*
618 A164 65m yel & multi .65 .40

25th anniv. of Intl. Criminal Police Org.

Globe, Hand Holding Carnation — A165

1973, Dec. 10 Photo. *Perf. 11½*
619 A165 60m blk & multi .75 .35

25th anniv. of Universal Declaration of Human Rights.

National Meteorological Institute and World Meteorological Organization Emblem A166

Design: 60m, Globe and emblem.

1973, Dec. 24 Litho. *Perf. 14x14½*
620 A166 25m multicolored .55 .25
621 A166 60m multicolored .75 .30

Intl. meteorological cooperation, cent.

Bourguiba in the Desert, 1945 — A167

Portraits of Pres. Habib Bourguiba: 25m, Exile transfer from Galite Island to Ile de la Groix, France, 1954. 60m, Addressing crowd, 1974. 75m, In Victory Parade, 1955. 100m, In 1934.

1974, Mar. 2 Photo. *Perf. 11½*
622 A167 15m plum & multi .45 .25
623 A167 25m multicolored .45 .25
624 A167 60m multicolored .45 .25
625 A167 75m multicolored .60 .25
626 A167 100m multicolored .75 .40
a. Souvenir sheet of 5, #622-626 3.00 3.00
Nos. 622-626 (5) 2.70 1.40

40th anniv. of the Neo-Destour Party. No. 626a sold for 500m. Issued perf. and imperf.; same value.

Scientist with Microscope — A168

1974, Mar. 21 *Perf. 14*
627 A168 60m multicolored 1.10 .50

6th African Congress of Micropaleontology, Mar. 21-Apr. 3.

Woman with Telephones and Globe — A169

60m, Telephone dial, telephones, wires.

1974, July 1 Photo. *Perf. 11½*
628 A169 15m multicolored .50 .40
629 A169 60m multicolored .80 .50

Introduction of international automatic telephone dialing system.

WPY Emblem and Symbolic Design — A170

1974, Aug. 19 Photo. *Perf. 11½*
630 A170 110m multicolored .75 .40

World Population Year.

Pres. Bourguiba and Sun Flower Emblem — A171

60m, Bourguiba and cactus flower, horiz. 200m, Bourguiba and verbena, horiz.

1974, Sept. 12 Photo. *Perf. 11½*
631 A171 25m blk, ultra & grnsh bl .35 .25
632 A171 60m red, car & yel .40 .25
633 A171 200m blk, brt lil & grn 1.50 .60
a. Souv. sheet, #631-633, imperf. 3.75 3.75
Nos. 631-633 (3) 2.25 1.10

Congress of the Socialist Destour Party.

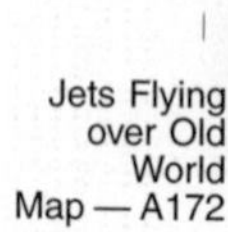

Jets Flying over Old World Map — A172

1974, Sept. 23 Litho. *Perf. 12½*
634 A172 60m brn & multi .65 .40

25th anniversary of Tunisian aviation.

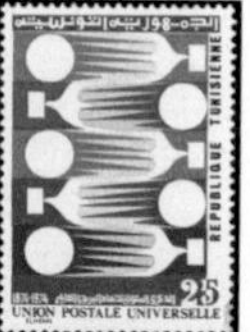
Symbolic Carrier Pigeons A173

Handshake, Letter, UPU Emblem A174

1974, Oct. 9 Photo. *Perf. 13*
635 A173 25m multicolored .40 .25
636 A174 60m multicolored .75 .35

Centenary of Universal Postal Union.

Le Bardo, National Assembly A175

Pres. Bourguiba Ballot A176

1974, Nov. 3 Photo. *Perf. 11½*

637 A175 25m grn, bl & blk .40 .30
638 A176 100m org & blk 1.00 .40

Legislative (25m) and presidential elections (100m), Nov. 1974.

Mailman with Letters and Bird — A177

1974, Dec. 5 Litho. *Perf. 14½x14*

639 A177 75m lt vio & multi .65 .25

Stamp Day.

Water Carrier — A178

1975, Feb. 17 Photo. *Perf. 13½*

640 A178 5m shown .30 .25
641 A178 15m Perfume vendor .30 .25
642 A178 25m Laundresses .30 .25
643 A178 60m Potter .65 .25
644 A178 110m Fruit vendor 1.40 .65
a. Souvenir sheet of 5, #640-644 7.00 7.00
Nos. 640-644 (5) 2.95 1.65

Life in Tunisia. No. 644a sold for 500m. Issued perf. and imperf.; same value.

Steel Tower, Skyscraper A179

Geometric Designs and Arrow A180

Perf. 14x13½, 13½x14

1975, Mar. 17 Photo.

645 A179 25m yel, org & blk .30 .25
646 A180 65m ultra & multi .80 .35

Union of Arab Engineers, 13th Conference, Tunis, Mar. 17-21.

Brass Coffeepot and Plate — A181

15m, Horse and rider. 25m, Still life. 30m, Bird cage. 40m, Woman with earrings. 60m, Design patterns.

1975, Apr. 14 *Perf. 13x14, 14x13*

647 A181 10m blk & multi .25 .25
648 A181 15m blk & multi .25 .25
649 A181 25m blk & multi .45 .25
650 A181 30m blk & multi, vert. .50 .25
651 A181 40m blk & multi, vert. .50 .25
652 A181 60m blk & multi .95 .30
Nos. 647-652 (6) 2.90 1.55

Artisans and their works.

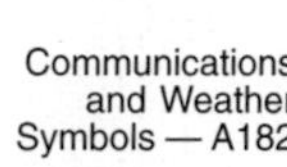

Communications and Weather Symbols — A182

1975, May 17 Photo. *Perf. 11½*

653 A182 50m lt bl & multi .50 .25

World Telecommunications Day (communications serving meteorology).

Youth and Hope — A183

65m, Bourguiba arriving at La Goulette, Tunis.

1975, June 1 Photo. *Perf. 11½*

654 A183 25m multi .25 .25
655 A183 65m multi, horiz. .50 .25

Victory (independence), 20th anniversary.

Tunisian Woman, IWY Emblem — A184

1975, June 19 Litho. *Perf. 14x13½*

656 A184 110m multicolored .75 .35

International Women's Year.

Children Crossing Street — A185

1975, July 5 Photo. *Perf. 13½x14*

657 A185 25m multicolored .60 .25

Highway safety campaign, July 1-Sept. 30.

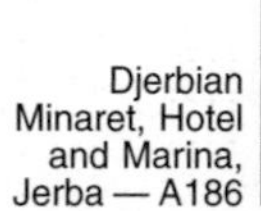

Djerbian Minaret, Hotel and Marina, Jerba — A186

Old & new Tunisia: 15m, 17th cent. minaret & modern hotel, Tunis. 20m, Fortress, earring & hotel, Monastir. 65m, View of Sousse, hotel & pendant. 500m, Town wall, mosque & palms, Tozeur. 1d, Mosques & Arab ornaments, Kairouan.

1975, July 12 Litho. *Perf. 14x14½*

658 A186 10m multicolored .25 .25
659 A186 15m multicolored .25 .25
660 A186 20m multicolored .25 .25
661 A186 65m multicolored .75 .40
662 A186 500m multicolored 4.75 1.75
663 A186 1d multicolored 7.50 2.50
Nos. 658-663 (6) 13.75 5.40

Victors A187

Symbolic Ship A188

1975, Aug. 23 Photo. *Perf. 13½*

664 A187 25m olive & multi .25 .25
665 A188 50m blue & multi .50 .25

7th Mediterranean Games, Algiers, 8/23-9/6.

Flowers in Vase, Birds Holding Letters — A189

1975, Sept. 29 Litho. *Perf. 13½x13*

666 A189 100m blue & multi .65 .25

Stamp Day.

Sadiki College, Young Bourguiba A190

Engr. & Litho.

1975, Nov. 17 *Perf. 13*

667 A190 25m sepia, orange & olive .50 .25

Sadiki College, centenary.

Duck — A191

Vergil — A192

Mosaics: 10m, Fish. 25m, Lioness, horiz. 60m, Head of Medusa, horiz. 75m, Circus spectators.

1976, Feb. 16 Photo. *Perf. 13*

668 A191 5m multicolored .30 .25
669 A191 10m multicolored .45 .25
670 A192 25m multicolored .75 .50
671 A192 60m multicolored 1.00 .50
672 A192 75m multicolored 1.10 .50
673 A192 100m multicolored 1.40 .50
a. Souvenir sheet of 6, #668-673 6.50 6.50
Nos. 668-673 (6) 5.00 2.50

Tunisian mosaics, 2nd-5th centuries.
No. 673a sold for 500m. Issued perf. and imperf.; same value.

Telephone — A193

1976, Mar. 10 Litho. *Perf. 14x13½*

674 A193 150m blue & multi .70 .35

Centenary of first telephone call by Alexander Graham Bell, Mar. 10, 1876.

Pres. Bourguiba and "20" — A194

Pres. Bourguiba and: 100m, "20" and symbolic Tunisian flag. 150m, "Tunisia" rising from darkness, and 20 flowers.

1976, Mar. 20 Photo. *Perf. 11½*

675 A194 40m multicolored .25 .25
676 A194 100m multicolored .55 .25
677 A194 150m multicolored .80 .35
Nos. 675-677 (3) 1.60 .85

Souvenir Sheets

Perf. 11½, Imperf.

678 Sheet of 3 3.50 3.50
a. A194 50m like 40m .50 .50
b. A194 200m like 100m 1.00 1.00
c. A194 250m like 150m 1.50 1.50

20th anniversary of independence.

Blind Man with Cane — A195

1976, Apr. 7 Engr. *Perf. 13*

679 A195 100m black & red .60 .25

World Health Day: "Foresight prevents blindness."

Procession and Buildings — A196

1976, May 31 Photo. *Perf. 12x11½*

680 A196 40m multicolored .60 .25

Habitat, UN Conf. on Human Settlements, Vancouver, Canada, May 31-June 11.

Face and Hands Decorated with Henna — A197

Old and new Tunisia: 50m, Sponge fishing at Jerba. 65m, Textile industry. 110m, Pottery of Guellala.

1976, June 15 Photo. *Perf. 13x13½*

681 A197 40m multicolored .25 .25
682 A197 50m multicolored .55 .25
683 A197 65m multicolored .55 .25
684 A197 110m multicolored .75 .50
Nos. 681-684 (4) 2.10 1.25

The Spirit of '76, by Archibald M. Willard — A198

1976, July 4 *Perf. 13x14*

685 A198 200m multicolored 1.75 .85

Souvenir Sheets

Perf. 13x14, Imperf.

686 A198 500m multicolored 5.00 5.00

American Bicentennial.

Running — A199

Montreal Olympic Games Emblem and: 75m, Bicycling. 120m, Peace dove.

1976, July 17 Photo. *Perf. 11½*

687 A199 50m gray, red & blk .25 .25
688 A199 75m red, yel & blk .45 .25
689 A199 120m orange & multi .70 .35
Nos. 687-689 (3) 1.40 .85

21st Olympic Games, Montreal, Canada, July 17-Aug. 1.

Child Reading — A200

1976, Aug. 23 Litho. *Perf. 13*

690 A200 100m brown & multi .60 .25

Books for children.

Heads and Bird — A201

1976, Sept. 30 Litho. *Perf. 13*

691 A201 150m orange & multi .75 .25

Non-aligned Countries, 15th anniv. of 1st Conference.

Mouradite Mausoleum, 17th Century — A202

Cultural Heritage: 100m, Minaret, Kairouan Great Mosque and psalmodist. 150m, Monastir Ribat monastery and Alboracq (sphinx). 200m, Barber's Mosque, Kairouan and man's bust.

1976, Oct. 25 Photo. *Perf. 14*

692 A202 85m multicolored .40 .25
693 A202 100m multicolored .50 .25
694 A202 150m multicolored .75 .25
695 A202 200m multicolored 1.10 .40
Nos. 692-695 (4) 2.75 1.15

Globe and Emblem A203

1976, Dec. 24 Photo. *Perf. 13x14*

696 A203 150m multicolored .95 .35

25th anniv. of UN Postal Administration.

Electronic Tree and ITU Emblem — A204

1977, May 17 Photo. *Perf. 14x13½*

697 A204 150m multicolored 1.25 .50

9th World Telecommunications Day.

"Communication," Sassenage Castle, Grenoble — A205

1977, May 19 Litho. *Perf. 13½x13*

698 A205 100m multicolored 1.50 .40

10th anniv. of Intl. French Language Council.

Soccer — A206

1977, June 27 Photo. *Perf. 13½*

699 A206 150m multicolored 1.25 .50

Junior World Soccer Tournament, Tunisia, June 27-July 10.

Gold Coin, 10th Century — A207

Cultural Heritage: 15m, Stele, Gorjani Cemetery, Tunis, 13th century. 20m, Floral design, 17th century illumination. 30m, Bird and flowers, glass painting, 1922. 40m, Antelope, from 11th century clay pot. 50m, Gate, Sidi Bou Said, 20th century.

1977, July 9 Photo. *Perf. 13*

700 A207 10m multicolored .25 .25
701 A207 15m multicolored .25 .25
702 A207 20m multicolored .25 .25
703 A207 30m multicolored .40 .25
704 A207 40m multicolored .50 .25
705 A207 50m multicolored .50 .25
a. Miniature sheet of 6, #700-705 3.75 3.75
Nos. 700-705 (6) 2.15 1.50

"The Young Republic" and Bourguiba — A208

Habib Bourguiba and: 100m, "The Confident Republic" and 20 doves. 150m, "The Determined Republic" and 20 roses.

1977, July 25 Photo. *Perf. 13x13½*

706 A208 40m multicolored .40 .25
707 A208 100m multicolored .50 .25
708 A208 150m multicolored .85 .35
a. Souvenir sheet of 3, #706-708 2.75 2.75
Nos. 706-708 (3) 1.75 .85

20th anniv. of the Republic. No. 708a sold for 500m. Exists imperf., same value.

Symbolic Cancellation, APU Emblem — A209

1977, Aug. 16 Litho. *Perf. 13x12½*

709 A209 40m multicolored .50 .25

Arab Postal Union, 25th anniversary.

Diseased Knee, Gears and Globe — A210

1977, Sept. 26 Photo. *Perf. 14x13½*

710 A210 120m multicolored .95 .35

World Rheumatism Year.

Farmer, Road, Water and Electricity A211

1977, Dec. 15 Photo. *Perf. 13½*

711 A211 40m multicolored .60 .25

Rural development.

Factory Workers — A212

Designs: 20m, Bus driver and trains, horiz. 40m, Farmer driving tractor, horiz.

1978, Mar. 6 *Perf. 13x14, 14x13*

712 A212 20m rose red & multi .25 .25
713 A212 40m black & green .35 .25
714 A212 100m multicolored .75 .35
Nos. 712-714 (3) 1.35 .85

5th development plan, creation of new jobs.

Pres. Bourguiba, Torch and "9" — A213

Bourguiba and "9" — A213a

1978, Apr. 9 Engr. *Perf. 13*

715 A213 40m multicolored .30 .25
716 A213a 60m multicolored .30 .25

40th anniv. of 1st fight for independence, 4/9/38.

A214

1978, May 2 Photo. *Perf. 13x13½*

717 A214 150m Policeman 1.10 .35

6th Regional African Interpol Conference, Tunis, May 2-5.

A215

Designs: 40m, Tunisian Goalkeeper. 150m., Soccer player, maps of South America and Africa, flags.

1978, June 1 Photo. *Perf. 13x14*

718 A215 40m multicolored .35 .25
719 A215 150m multicolored 1.00 .40

11th World Cup Soccer Championship, Argentina, June 1-25.

Destruction of Apartheid, Map of South Africa — A216

Fight Against Apartheid: 100m, White and black doves flying in unison.

1978, Aug. 30 Litho. *Perf. 13½x14*

720 A216 50m multicolored .25 .25
721 A216 100m multicolored .60 .35

"Pollution is a Plague" — A217

Designs: 50m, "The Sea, mankind's patrimony." 120m, "Greening of the desert."

1978, Sept. 11 Photo. *Perf. 14x13*

722 A217 10m multicolored .25 .25
723 A217 50m multicolored .60 .25
724 A217 120m multicolored 1.25 .35
Nos. 722-724 (3) 2.10 .85

Protection of the environment.

"Eradication of Smallpox" — A218

1978, Oct. 16 Litho. *Perf. 12½*

725 A218 150m multicolored .95 .40

Global eradication of smallpox.

Jerba Wedding A219

5m, Horseman from Zlass. 75m, Women potters from the Mogods. 100m, Dove over Marabout Sidi Mahrez cupolas, Tunis. 500m, Plowing in Jenduba. 1d, Spring Festival in Tozeur (man on swing).

1978, Nov. 1 Photo. *Perf. 13*

726 A219 5m multi, vert. .25 .25
727 A219 60m multi .35 .25
728 A219 75m multi .50 .25
729 A219 100m multi .50 .25
730 A219 500m multi 3.75 1.25
731 A219 1d multi 6.00 2.50
Nos. 726-731 (6) 11.35 4.75

Traditional Arab calligraphy.

Lenin and Red Banner over Kremlin — A220

1978, Nov. 7 *Perf. 13½*

732 A220 150m multicolored 1.60 .50

Russian October Revolution, 60th anniv.

Farhat Hached, Union Emblem — A221

1978, Dec. 5 Photo. *Perf. 14*

733 A221 50m multicolored .60 .25

Farhat Hached (1914-1952), founder of General Union of Tunisian Workers.

Family — A222

1978, Dec. 15 Photo. *Perf. 13½*

734 A222 50m multicolored .60 .25

Tunisian Family Planning Assoc., 10th anniv.

Sun with Man's Face — A223

1978, Dec. 25 *Perf. 14*

735 A223 100m multicolored .75 .25

Sun as a source of light and energy.

Plane, Weather Map and Instruments A224

1978, Dec. 29

736 A224 50m multicolored .60 .25

Tunisian civil aviation and meteorology, 20th anniv.

Habib Bourguiba and Constitution — A225

1979, May 31 Photo. *Perf. 14x13½*

737 A225 50m multicolored .60 .25

20th anniversary of Constitution.

El Kantaoui Port — A226

1979, June 3 *Perf. 13½x14*

738 A226 150m multicolored 1.25 .35

Development of El Kantaoui as a resort area.

Landscapes — A227

1979, July 14 *Perf. 12½x13½*

739 A227 50m Korbous .25 .25
740 A227 100m Mides .50 .25

Bow Net Weaving — A228

1979, Aug. 15 Photo. *Perf. 11½*

741 A228 10m shown .30 .25
742 A228 50m Beekeeping .70 .25

Pres. Bourguiba, "10" and Hands — A229

1979, Sept. 5

743 A229 50m multicolored .50 .25

Socialist Destour Party, 10th Congress.

Modes of Communication, ITU Emblem — A230

1979, Sept. 20 Litho. *Perf. 11½*

744 A230 150m multicolored 1.00 .50

3rd World Telecommunications Exhibition, Geneva, Sept. 20-26.

Arab Achievements A231

1979, Oct. 1 *Perf. 14½*

745 A231 50m multicolored .50 .25

Children Crossing Street, IYC Emblem — A232

1979, Oct. 16 *Perf. 14x13½*

746 A232 50m shown .30 .25
747 A232 100m Child and birds .75 .25

International Year of the Child.

Dove, Olive Tree, Map of Tunisia — A233

1979, Nov. 1 Litho. *Perf. 12*

748 A233 150m multicolored 1.10 .40

2nd International Olive Oil Year.

Woman Wearing Crown — A234

1979, Nov. 3 *Perf. 14½*

749 A234 50m multicolored .50 .25

Central Bank of Tunisia, 20th anniversary.

Children and Jujube Tree — A235

1979, Dec. 25 Litho. *Perf. 15x14½*

750 A235 20m shown .30 .25
751 A235 30m Peacocks .60 .25
752 A235 70m Goats 1.10 .35
753 A235 85m Girl, date palm 1.10 .40
Nos. 750-753 (4) 3.10 1.25

Postal Code Introduction A236

1980, Mar. 20 Photo. *Perf. 14*

754 A236 50m multicolored .55 .25

Fight Against Cigarette Smoking — A237

1980, Apr. 7

755 A237 150m multicolored .85 .25

Pres. Bourguiba in Flower, Open Book — A238

1980, June 1 Photo. *Perf. 11½*

756 A238 50m shown .25 .25
757 A238 100m Dove, Bourguiba, mosque 1.00 .40

Victory (independence), 25th anniversary.

Butterfly and Gymnast — A239

1980, June 3 Photo. *Perf. 12x11½*
Granite Paper

758 A239 100m multicolored .60 .25

Turin Gymnastic Games, June 1-7.

Artisans
A240 A241

1980, July 21 Photo. *Perf. 13½*

759 A240 30m multicolored .35 .25
760 A241 75m multicolored .75 .25

ibn-Khaldun (1332-1406), Historian — A242

1980, July 28 *Perf. 14*

761 A242 50m multicolored .60 .25

Avicenna (Arab Physician), Birth Millenium — A243

1980, Aug. 18 Engr. *Perf. 12½x13*

762 A243 100m redsh brn & sepia .75 .30

Arab Achievements A244

1980, Aug. 25 Photo. *Perf. 13½x14*

763 A244 50m multicolored .85 .25

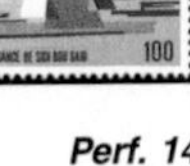
Port Sidi bou Said — A245

1980, Sept. 4 *Perf. 14*

764 A245 100m multicolored .50 .30

World Tourism Conference, Manila, Sept. 27 — A246

1980, Sept. 27 Photo. *Perf. 14*

765 A246 150m multicolored .75 .25

Wedding in Jerba, by Yahia (1903-1969) A247

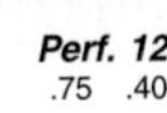

1980, Oct. 1 *Perf. 12*

766 A247 50m multicolored .75 .40

Tozeur-Nefta International Airport Opening — A248

1980, Oct. 13 Photo. *Perf. 13x13½*

767 A248 85m multicolored .60 .25

Eye and Text — A249

1980, Oct. 26 Litho. *Perf. 13½x14*

768 A249 100m multicolored 1.00 .50

7th Afro-Asian Ophthalmologic Congress.

Hegira, 1500th Anniv. — A250

1980, Nov. 9

769 A250 50m Spiderweb .25 .25
770 A250 80m City skyline .50 .25

Film Strip and Woman's Head — A251

1980, Nov. 15 Photo. *Perf. 14x13½*

771 A251 100m multicolored .75 .35

Carthage Film Festival.

Orchid — A252

1980, Nov. 17 *Perf. 13½x14*
772 A252 20m shown .55 .30
773 A252 25m Wild cyclamen .70 .30

Size: 39x27mm

Perf. 14

774 A252 50m Mouflon 1.40 .30
775 A252 100m Golden eagle 3.00 .40
Nos. 772-775 (4) 5.65 1.30

Campaign to Save Kairouan Mosque — A253

1980, Dec. 29 Photo. *Perf. 12*
Granite Paper
776 A253 85m multicolored .55 .25

Heinrich von Stephan (1831-1897), Founder of UPU — A254

1981, Jan. 7
777 A254 150m multicolored .90 .40

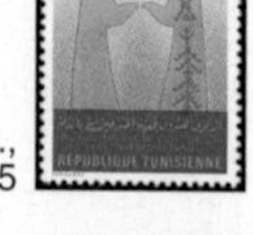
Blood Donors' Assoc., 20th Anniv. — A255

1981, Mar. 5 Litho. *Perf. 14x13½*
778 A255 75m multicolored .90 .50

Pres. Bourguiba and Flag — A256

1981, Mar. 20 Photo. *Perf. 12x11½*
Granite Paper
779 A256 50m shown .25 .25
780 A256 60m Stork, "25" .50 .25
781 A256 85m Doves .75 .40
782 A256 120m Victory on winged horse .75 .40
a. Souvenir sheet of 4, #779-782 4.00 4.00
Nos. 779-782 (4) 2.25 1.30

25th anniversary of independence. No. 782 sold for 500m. Exists imperf., same value.

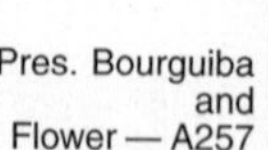

Pres. Bourguiba and Flower — A257

1981, Apr. 10 Photo. *Perf. 12x11½*
783 A257 50m shown .25 .25
784 A257 75m Bourguiba, flower, diff. .50 .25

Destourien Socialist Party Congress.

Mosque Entrance, Mahdia — A258

1981, Apr. 20 *Perf. 13½*
785 A258 50m shown .35 .25
786 A258 85m Tozeur Great Mosque, vert. .50 .35
787 A258 100m Needle Rocks, Tabarka .60 .25
Nos. 785-787 (3) 1.45 .85

A259

1981, May 17 Litho. *Perf. 14x15*
788 A259 150m multicolored .95 .35

13th World Telecommunications Day.

Youth Festival — A260

1981, June 2 Photo. *Perf. 11½*
Granite Paper
789 A260 100m multicolored .65 .25

A261

1981, June 15 Photo. *Perf. 14*
790 A261 150m multicolored .95 .35

Kemal Ataturk (1881-1938), 1st president of Turkey.

A262

1981, July 15 Photo. *Perf. 11½x12*
791 A262 150m Skifa, Mahdia .80 .40

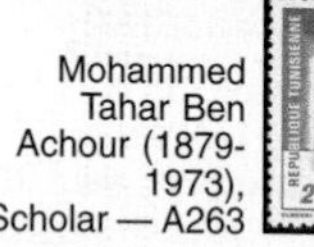

Mohammed Tahar Ben Achour (1879-1973), Scholar — A263

1981, Aug. 6 *Perf. 13*
792 A263 200m multicolored 1.50 .50

25th Anniv. of Personal Status Code (Women's Liberation) A264

1981, Aug. 13
793 A264 50m Woman .25 .25
794 A264 100m shown .75 .35

Intl. Year of the Disabled — A265

1981, Sept. 21 Photo. *Perf. 13½*
795 A265 250m multicolored 1.50 .65

Pilgrimage to Mecca — A266

1981, Oct. 7 Photo. *Perf. 13½*
796 A266 50m multicolored .60 .25

World Food Day — A267

1981, Oct. 16 Litho. *Perf. 12*
Granite Paper
797 A267 200m multicolored 1.50 .65

Traditional Jewelry — A268

150m, Mneguech silver earrings. 180m Mahfdha (silver medallion worn by married women). 200m, Essalta gold headdress.

1981, Dec. 7 Photo. *Perf. 14*
798 A268 150m multi, vert. .75 .35
799 A268 180m multi .90 .40
800 A268 200m multi, vert. 1.10 .50
Nos. 798-800 (3) 2.75 1.25

Bizerta Bridge — A269

1981, Dec. 14 Litho. *Perf. 12x11½*
Granite Paper
801 A269 230m multicolored 1.25 .50

A270

Chemist compounding honey mixture, manuscript miniature, 1224.

1982, Apr. 3 Photo. *Perf. 13*
802 A270 80m multicolored .95 .35

Arab Chemists' Union, 16th anniv.

A271

1982, May 12 Photo. *Perf. 13½*
803 A271 150m multicolored 1.25 .60

Oceanic Enterprise Symposium, Tunis, 5/12-14.

A272

1982, June 26 *Perf. 12½*
Granite Paper
804 A272 80m multicolored .60 .25

The Productive Family Employment campaign.

A273

25th Anniv. of Republic: Pres. Bourguiba and Various Women.

1982, July 25 Litho. *Perf. 14x13½*
805 A273 80m multicolored .40 .25
806 A273 100m multicolored .60 .35
807 A273 200m multicolored 1.00 .40
Nos. 805-807 (3) 2.00 1.00

Scouting Year — A274

Perf. 14½x14, 14x14½

1982, Aug. 23
808 A274 80m multicolored .50 .25
809 A274 200m multicolored 1.10 .25

75th anniv. of scouting and 50th anniv. of scouting in Tunisia (80m, horiz.).

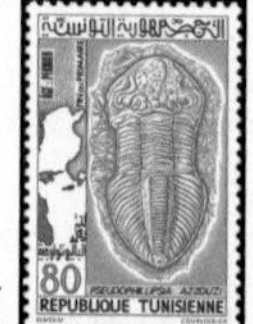
Tunisian Fossils — A274a

Designs: 80m, Pseudophillipsia azzouzi, vert. 200m, Mediterraneotrigonia cherahilensis, vert. 280m, Numidiopleura enigmatica. 300m, Micreschara tunisiensis, vert. 500m, Mantelliceras pervinquieri, vert. 1000m, Elephas africanavus.

1982, Sept. 20 Photo. *Perf. 11½x12*
809A A274a 80m multi .90 .40
809B A274a 200m multi 1.80 .50
809C A274a 280m multi 2.10 .65
809D A274a 300m multi 2.75 .90
809E A274a 500m multi 5.25 1.40
809F A274a 1000m multi 11.00 2.75
Nos. 809A-809F (6) 23.80 6.60

A275

1982, Sept. 29 ***Perf. 14x13½***
810 A275 80m shown .60 .25

Size: 23x40mm

811 A275 200m Woman, buildings 1.00 .50

30th Anniv. of Arab Postal Union.

A276

1982, Oct. 1 **Photo.** ***Perf. 12***
Granite Paper
812 A276 200m multicolored 1.00 .25

ITU Plenipotentiaries Conf., Nairobi.

World Food Day — A277

1982, Oct. 16 **Litho.** ***Perf. 13***
813 A277 200m multicolored 1.00 .35

Tahar Haddad (1899-1935), Social Reformer — A278

1982, Oct. 25 **Engr.**
814 A278 200m brnish black 1.00 .25

TB Bacillus Centenary — A279

1982, Nov. 16 **Litho.** ***Perf. 13½***
815 A279 100m multicolored 1.25 .25

Folk Songs and Stories — A280

20m, Dancing in the Rain. 30m, Woman Sweeping. 70m, Fisherman and the Child. 80m, Rooster and the Oranges, horiz. 100m, Woman and the Mirror, horiz. 120m, The Two Girls, horiz.

1982, Nov. 22 **Photo.** ***Perf. 14***
816 A280 20m multi .30 .25
817 A280 30m multi .30 .25
818 A280 70m multi .30 .25
819 A280 80m multi .40 .25
820 A280 100m multi .60 .25
821 A280 120m multi .85 .30
Nos. 816-821 (6) 2.75 1.55

Intl. Palestinian Solidarity Day — A281

1982, Nov. 30 **Litho.** ***Perf. 13x12***
822 A281 80m multicolored .60 .25

Farhat Hached (1914-1952) — A282

1982, Dec. 6 **Engr.** ***Perf. 13***
823 A282 80m brown red .60 .25

Bourguiba Dam Opening — A283

1982, Dec. 20 **Litho.** ***Perf. 13½***
824 A283 80m multicolored .75 .25

Environmental Training College Opening — A284

1982, Dec. 29 **Photo.** ***Perf. 11½***
Granite Paper
825 A284 80m multicolored .60 .25

World Communications Year — A285

1983, May 17 **Litho.** ***Perf. 13½x14***
826 A285 200m multicolored .80 .35

20th Anniv. of Org. of African Unity — A286

1983, May 25 **Photo.** ***Perf. 12***
Granite Paper
827 A286 230m ultra & grnsh bl .90 .50

30th Anniv. of Customs Cooperation Council — A287

1983, May 30 **Litho.** ***Perf. 13½***
828 A287 100m multicolored .60 .25

Aly Ben Ayed (1930-1972), Actor — A288

1983, Aug. 15 **Engr.** ***Perf. 13***
829 A288 80m dk car, dl red & gray .60 .35

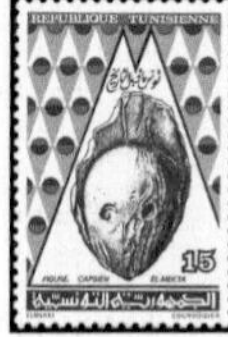

Stone-carved Face, El-Mekta — A289

Pre-historic artifacts: 20m, Neolithic necklace, Kel el-Agab. 30m, Mill and grindstone, Redeyef. 40m, Orynx head rock carving, Gafsa. 80m, Dolmen Mactar. 100m, Acheulian Bi-face flint, El-Mekta.

1983, Aug. 20 **Photo.** ***Perf. 11½x12***
830 A289 15m multicolored .25 .25
831 A289 20m multicolored .45 .25
832 A289 30m multicolored .45 .25
833 A289 40m multicolored .45 .25
834 A289 80m multicolored .60 .40
835 A289 100m multicolored .75 .40
Nos. 830-835 (6) 2.95 1.80

Sports for All — A290

1983, Sept. 27 **Litho.** ***Perf. 12½***
836 A290 40m multicolored .45 .25

World Fishing Day — A291

1983, Oct. 17 ***Perf. 14½***
837 A291 200m multicolored 1.25 .25

Evacuation of French Troops, 20th Anniv. — A292

1983, Oct. 17 **Litho.** ***Perf. 14x13½***
838 A292 80m multicolored .50 .25

Tapestry Weaver, by Hedi Khayachi (1882-1948) A293

1983, Nov. 22 **Photo.** ***Perf. 11½***
Granite Paper
839 A293 80m multicolored .90 .40

Natl. Allegiance — A294

1983, Nov. 30 **Litho.** ***Perf. 14½***
840 A294 100m Children, flag .50 .25

Jet, Woman's Head, Emblem — A295

1983, Dec. 21 ***Perf. 13½***
841 A295 150m multicolored .80 .25

Pres. Bourguiba — A296

Destourien Socialist Party, 50th Anniv.: Portraits of Bourguiba. 200m, 230m horiz.

Perf. 12½x12, 12x12½
1984, Mar. 2 **Photo.**
Granite Paper
842 A296 40m multicolored .25 .25
843 A296 70m multicolored .25 .25
844 A296 80m multicolored .40 .25
a. Pair, #843-844 .75 .75
845 A296 150m multicolored .65 .40
a. Pair, #842, 845 1.00 1.00
846 A296 200m multicolored .85 .40
847 A296 230m multicolored .90 .60
a. Pair, #846-847 2.00 2.00
Nos. 842-847 (6) 3.30 2.15

Nos. 844a, 845a and 847a were printed checkerwise in sheets of ten.

4th Molecular Biology Symposium — A297

1984, Apr. 3 ***Perf. 13½x13***
848 A297 100m Map, diagram .80 .35

Ibn El Jazzar, Physician — A298

1984, May 15 **Photo.** ***Perf. 14x13***
849 A298 80m multicolored .70 .40

Economic Development Program, 20th Anniv. — A299

230m, Merchant, worker.

1984, June 15 ***Perf. 11½***
Granite Paper
850 A299 230m multicolored 1.25 .40

Coquette, The Sorceress and the Fairy Carabosse A300

80m, Counting with fingers. 100m, Boy riding horse, vert.

Perf. 13½x14, 14x13½
1984, Aug. 27 **Photo.**
851 A300 20m shown .30 .25
852 A300 80m multicolored .50 .25
853 A300 100m multicolored .65 .25
Nos. 851-853 (3) 1.45 .75

Legends and folk tales.

Family and Education Org., 20th Anniv. — A301

80m, Family looking into future.

1984, Sept. 4 *Perf. 13x14*
854 A301 80m multicolored .50 .25

Natl. Heritage Protection — A302

100m, Medina Mosque Minaret, hand.

1984, Sept. 13 *Perf. 14*
855 A302 100m multicolored .60 .35

Aboul-Qasim Chabbi, Poet (1909-1934) — A303

1984, Oct. 9 **Engr.** *Perf. 12½x13*
856 A303 100m multicolored — .25

40th Anniv., ICAO — A304

1984, Oct. 25 **Photo.** *Perf. 13*
857 A304 200m Aircraft tail, bird 1.00 .60

Sahara Festival — A305

1984, Dec. 3 **Litho.** *Perf. 14½*
858 A305 20m Musicians .80 .25

20th Anniv., Intelsat — A306

100m, Tunisian Earth Station.

Perf. 13½x14½

1984, Dec. 25 **Photo.**
859 A306 100m multicolored .70 .25

Mediterranean Landscape, by Jilani Abdelwaheb (Abdul) — A307

1984, Dec. 31 **Photo.** *Perf. 14½*
860 A307 100m multicolored .80 .40

EXPO '85, Tsukuba, Japan — A308

1985, Mar. 20 **Photo.** *Perf. 12*
861 A308 200m multicolored 1.00 .50

Civil Protection Week — A309

100m, Hands, water and fire.

1985, May 13 **Litho.** *Perf. 14*
862 A309 100m multicolored .75 .40

Pres. Habib Bourguiba, Crowded Pier — A310

Pres. Bourguiba: 75m, On horseback, vert. 200m, Wearing hat, vert. 230m, Waving to crowd.

1985, June 1 *Perf. 12½*
863 A310 75m multicolored .50 .50
864 A310 100m multicolored .80 .80
865 A310 200m multicolored 1.10 1.10
866 A310 230m multicolored 1.40 1.40
Nos. 863-866 (4) 3.80 3.80

Natl. independence, 30th anniv.

Head of a Statue, Carthage and Pres. Bourguiba A311

1985, June 4 *Perf. 14*
867 A311 250m multicolored 1.00 .65

EXPO '85.

Intl. Amateur Film Festival, Kelibia — A312

1985, July 20 *Perf. 14½x13*
868 A312 250m multicolored 1.40 .65

Natl. Folk Tales — A313

25m, Sun, Sun Shine Again, horiz. 50m, I Met a Man With Seven Wives. 100m, Uncle Shisbene.

1985, July 29 *Perf. 14*
869 A313 25m multi .25 .25
870 A313 50m multi .25 .25
871 A313 100m multi .40 .25
Nos. 869-871 (3) .90 .75

Intl. Youth Year — A314

1985, Sept. 30 *Perf. 14½x13½*
872 A314 250m multicolored 1.10 .60

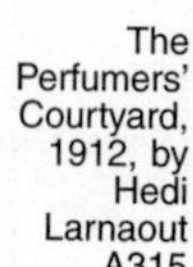

The Perfumers' Courtyard, 1912, by Hedi Larnaout A315

1985, Oct. 4 *Perf. 14*
873 A315 100m multicolored .65 .25

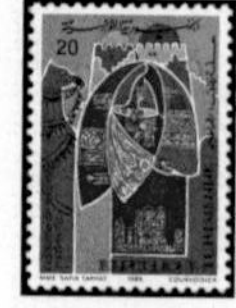

Regional Bridal Costumes — A316

1985, Oct. 22 *Perf. 12*
874 A316 20m Matmata .30 .25
875 A316 50m Moknine .30 .25
876 A316 100m Tunis .75 .25
Nos. 874-876 (3) 1.35 .75

UN, 40th Anniv. — A317

1985, Oct. 24 *Perf. 14x13½*
877 A317 250m multicolored 1.00 .60

Self-Sufficiency in Food Production A318

100m, Makhtar stele of feast.

Perf. 13½x14½

1985, Nov. 26 **Photo.**
878 A318 100m multicolored .60 .25

League of Arab States, 40th Anniv. — A319

1985, Nov. 29 **Litho.** *Perf. 13½x14*
879 A319 100m multicolored .50 .25

Aziza Othmana (d. 1669) — A320

1985, Dec. 16 **Engr.** *Perf. 12½x13*
880 A320 100m dk grn, hn brn & brn .75 .25

Land Law, Cent. — A321

1985, Dec. 25 **Litho.** *Perf. 13½*
881 A321 100m multicolored .65 .25

Natl. Independence, 30th Anniv. — A322

Perf. 13x13½, 13½x13

1986, Mar. 20 **Photo.**
882 A322 100m Dove, vert. .45 .25
883 A322 120m Rocket .50 .25
884 A322 280m Horse and rider 1.40 .65
885 A322 300m Balloons, vert. 1.60 .75
a. Souvenir sheet of 4, #882-885 4.00 4.00
Nos. 882-885 (4) 3.95 1.90

No. 885a exists imperf. Same value.

A323

A324

1986, Apr. 30 **Litho.** *Perf. 14x13½*
886 A323 300m multicolored 1.50 .40
887 A324 380m multicolored 2.00 .50

Prof. Hulusi Behcet (1889-1948), discovered virus causing Behcet's Disease affecting eyes and joints. 3rd Mediterranean Rheumatology Day (#886). Intl. Geographical Ophtalmological Soc. Cong. (#887).

12th Destourian Socialist Party Congress — A325

1986, June 19 **Photo.** *Perf. 12*
888 A325 120m shown .50 .25
889 A325 300m Torchbearer 1.50 .75

A326

Regional bridal costumes.

1986, Aug. 25 **Litho.** *Perf. 14*
890 A326 40m Homi-Souk .25 .25
891 A326 280m Mahdia 1.00 .60
892 A326 300m Nabeul 1.40 .65
Nos. 890-892 (3) 2.65 1.50

A327

1986, Sept. 20 **Engr.** *Perf. 13*
893 A327 160m dark red .80 .25

Hassen Husni Abdul-Wahab (1883-1968), historian, archaeologist

Founding of Carthage, 2800th Anniv. A328

1986, Oct. 18 **Engr.** *Perf. 13*
894 A328 2d dark violet 9.00 3.00

Protohistoric Artifacts — A329

Design: 10m, Flint arrowhead, El Borma, c. 3000 B.C. 20m, Rock cut-out dwelling, Sejnane, c. 1000 B.C. 50m, Lintel bas-relief from a cult site in Tunis, c. 1000 B.C., horiz. 120m, Base of a Neolithic vase, Kesra. 160m, Phoenician trireme, petroglyph, c. 800 B.C., horiz. 250m, Ceramic pot, c. 700 B.C., found at Sejnane, vert.

1986, Oct. 30 Litho. *Perf. 13½*

895 A329 10m multicolored .35 .25
896 A329 20m multicolored .35 .25
897 A329 50m multicolored .60 .25
898 A329 120m multicolored .95 .25
899 A329 160m multicolored 1.25 .40
900 A329 250m multicolored 2.40 .60
Nos. 895-900 (6) 5.90 2.00

Bedouins, by Ammar Farhat — A330

1986, Nov. 20 Photo. *Perf. 13½*

901 A330 250m multicolored 1.60 .40

Intl. Peace Year — A331

1986, Nov. 24 *Perf. 13½x13*

902 A331 300m multicolored 1.25 .40

FAO, 40th Anniv. — A332

1986, Nov. 27 *Perf. 13x13½*

903 A332 280m multicolored 1.25 .60

Computer Education Inauguration — A333

1986, Dec. 8 *Perf. 13½*

904 A333 2d multicolored 9.50 2.75

Breast-feeding for Child Survival — A334

1986, Dec. 22 Photo. *Perf. 14*

905 A334 120m multicolored .50 .25

Wildlife, Natl. Parks — A335

Designs: 60m, Mountain gazelle, Chambi Natl. Park. 120m, Addax, Bou. Hedma. 350m, Seal, Zembretta. 380m, Greylag goose, Ichkeul.

Granite Paper

1986, Dec. 29 *Perf. 12*

906 A335 60m multicolored .25 .25
907 A335 120m multicolored .55 .35
908 A335 350m multicolored 1.60 1.00
909 A335 380m multicolored 1.90 1.10
Nos. 906-909 (4) 4.30 2.70

City of Monastir, Cent. — A336

120m, Pres. Bourguiba, city arms.

1987, Jan. 24 Litho. *Perf. 12x11½*
Granite Paper

910 A336 120m multicolored .60 .25

Invention of the Telegraph by Samuel F.B. Morse, 150th Anniv. — A337

1987, June 15 Litho. *Perf. 13½x14*

911 A337 500m multicolored 2.25 1.00

30th Anniv. of the Republic — A338

Pres. Bourguiba and women of various sects.

1987, July 25 Photo. *Perf. 13½*

912 A338 150m multi .45 .25
913 A338 250m multi .80 .35
914 A338 350m multi, diff. 1.10 .55
915 A338 500m multi, diff. 1.60 .75
a. Souvenir sheet of 4, #912-915 5.00 5.00
Nos. 912-915 (4) 3.95 1.90

No. 915a sold for 1.50d. Exists imperf.

UN Universal Vaccination by 1990 Campaign — A339

1987, Sept. 14 *Perf. 12*
Granite Paper

916 A339 250m multicolored 1.00 .50

The Street, by Azouz ben Raiz (1902-1962) A340

1987, Sept. 22 Granite Paper

917 A340 250m multicolored 1.25 .50

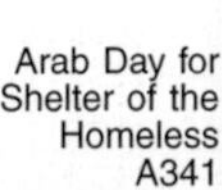

Arab Day for Shelter of the Homeless A341

1987, Oct. 5 Photo. *Perf. 12x11½*
Granite Paper

918 A341 150m multicolored .65 .25

Advisory Council for Postal Research, 30th Anniv. — A342

1987, Oct. 9 *Perf. 14*

919 A342 150m Express mail .65 .25
920 A342 350m Use postal code 1.50 .60

The Arabs, by Ibn-Mandhour (1233-1312), Lexicographer — A343

1987, Oct. 26 Engr. *Perf. 13*

921 A343 250m plum 1.10 .50

Pasteur Institute, Tunis — A344

1987, Nov. 21 *Perf. 13x12½*

922 A344 250m blk, grn & rose lake 2.50 .50

Pasteur Institute, Paris, cent.

Intl. Year of the Vine (Wine) — A345

1987, Nov. 27 Photo. *Perf. 14*

923 A345 250m multicolored 1.50 .50

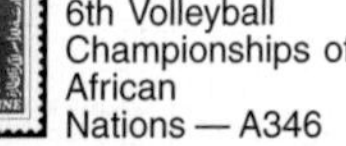

6th Volleyball Championships of African Nations — A346

1987, Dec. 2 Litho. *Perf. 14x13½*

924 A346 350m multicolored 1.60 .70

African Basketball Championships A347

1987, Dec. 15

925 A347 350m multicolored 1.60 .70

Folk Costumes — A348

1987, Dec. 25 Photo.

926 A348 20m Midoun .25 .25
927 A348 30m Tozeur .25 .25
928 A348 150m Sfax .75 .40
Nos. 926-928 (3) 1.25 .90

Flowering Plants — A349

30m, Narcissus tazetta. 150m, Gladiolus communis. 400m, Iris xiphium. 500m, Tulipa sylvestris.

1987, Dec. 29 *Perf. 14½*

929 A349 30m multicolored .25 .25
930 A349 150m multicolored .60 .30
931 A349 400m multicolored 1.50 .80
932 A349 500m multicolored 1.90 1.00
Nos. 929-932 (4) 4.25 2.35

Declaration of Nov. 7, 1987 — A350

Cameo portrait of Pres. Zine el Abidine Ben Ali and: 150m, Scales of Justice. 200m, Girl with flowers (party badges) in her hair, vert. 350m, Mermaid, doves, natl. coat of arms. 370m, "CMA," emblem of the Maghreb states (Tunisia, Mauritania, Morocco, Algeria and Libya), vert.

1988, Mar. 21 Photo. *Perf. 12*
Granite Paper

933 A350 150m multicolored .60 .25
934 A350 200m multicolored .70 .30
935 A350 350m multicolored 1.25 .55
936 A350 370m multicolored 1.25 .60
Nos. 933-936 (4) 3.80 1.70

Youth and Change — A351

1988, Mar. 22 Litho. *Perf. 14x14½*

937 A351 75m shown .25 .25
938 A351 150m Happy family .55 .25

Martyr's Day, 50th Anniv. — A352

Perf. 13x13½, 13½x13

1988, Apr. 9 Photo.

939 A352 150m shown .65 .25
940 A352 500m Monument, vert. 1.75 .75

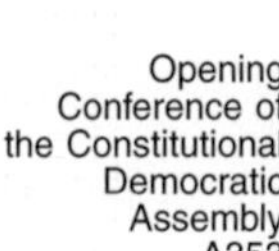

Opening Conference of the Constitutional Democratic Assembly A353

150m, Flag, Pres. Ben Ali.

1988, July 30 *Perf. 12x11½*
Granite Paper

941 A353 150m multicolored .60 .25

1988 Summer Olympics, Seoul — A354

430m, Running, boxing, weight lifting, wrestling.

1988, Sept. 20 Photo. *Perf. 13½*

942 A354 150m shown .60 .25
943 A354 430m multicolored 1.60 1.00

A355

1988, Sept. 21

944 A355 200m multicolored .75 .35

Restoration of the City of San'a, Yemen.

A356

1988, Nov. 7 Photo. *Perf. 14*
945 A356 150m multicolored .50 .30

Appointment of Pres. Zine El Abidine Ben Ali, 1st anniv.

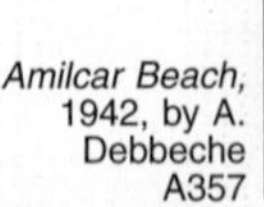

Amilcar Beach, 1942, by A. Debbeche A357

1988, Nov. 21 Photo. *Perf. 13½x13*
946 A357 100m multicolored .75 .25

Tunis Air, 40th Anniv. — A358

1988, Nov. 28 Photo. *Perf. 12x11½*
Granite Paper
947 A358 500m multicolored 1.60 .80

UN Declaration of Human Rights, 40th Anniv. — A359

1988, Dec. 10 *Perf. 12*
Granite Paper
948 A359 370m black 1.25 .60

Tunisian Postage Stamp Cent. A360

1988, Dec. 16 *Perf. 12½*
Granite Paper
949 A360 150m multicolored .75 .40

Decorative Doorways — A361

1988, Dec. 26 *Perf. 14x13½*

950	A361	50m multi	.30	.25
951	A361	70m multi, diff.	.30	.25
952	A361	100m multi, diff.	.30	.25
953	A361	150m multi, diff.	.50	.25
954	A361	370m multi, diff.	1.00	.40
955	A361	400m multi, diff.	1.25	.40
		Nos. 950-955 (6)	3.65	1.80

Ali Douagi (1909-49) — A362

1989, Mar. 7 Engr. *Perf. 13½x13*
956 A362 1000m dark blue 3.25 1.60

Natl. Day for the Handicapped — A363

1989, May 30 Photo. *Perf. 13½*
957 A363 150m multicolored .65 .25

Education A364

1989, July 10 *Perf. 14*
958 A364 180m multicolored .65 .25

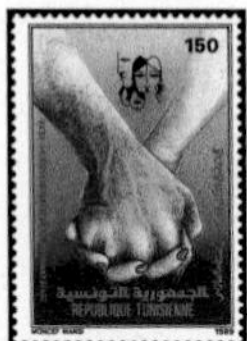
Family Planning Assoc., 20th Anniv. — A365

1989, Aug. 14 Litho. *Perf. 14*
959 A365 150m multicolored .65 .25

Family Care — A366

1989, Aug. 14 Litho. *Perf. 14*
960 A366 150m multicolored .65 .25

Fauna — A367

1989, Aug. 28 Photo. *Perf. 13½x14*
961 A367 250m Tortoise 1.10 .50
962 A367 350m Oryx 1.50 .65

Intl. Fair, Tunis — A368

1989, Oct. 16 Photo. *Perf. 14*
963 A368 150m shown .50 .25
964 A368 370m Pavilion, horiz. 1.25 .60

Mohamed Beyram V (1840-1889) — A369

1989, Oct. 28 Engr. *Perf. 13*
965 A369 150m blk & dp rose lil .65 .25

Theater, Carthage — A370

1989, Nov. 3 Photo. *Perf. 14*
966 A370 300m multicolored 1.00 .40

Monument — A371

1989, Nov. 7 *Perf. 11½x12*
Granite Paper
967 A371 150m multicolored .65 .25

Appointment of Pres. Zine El Abidine Ben Ali, 2nd Anniv.

Nehru — A372

1989, Nov. 29 Engr. *Perf. 13*
968 A372 300m dark brown 1.25 .35

Jawaharlal Nehru, 1st prime minister of independent India.

Flags — A373

1990, Jan. 15 Photo. *Perf. 12x11½*
Granite Paper
969 A373 200m multicolored .75 .35

Maghreb Union summit, Tunis.

Museum of Bardo, Cent. — A374

1990, Feb. 20 Litho. *Perf. 13½*
970 A374 300m multicolored 1.00 .50

Pottery — A375

1990, Mar. 22 *Perf. 14*
971 A375 75m multicolored .35 .25
972 A375 100m multi, diff. .50 .35

Sheep Museum A376

1990, Apr. 13 Litho. *Perf. 13½*
973 A376 400m Sheep 1.25 .75
974 A376 450m Ram's head 1.75 .85
a. Souvenir sheet of 2, #973-974 4.50 4.50

No. 974a sold for 1000m, exists imperf. Nos. 973-974 inscribed 1989.

Tunisian Olympic Movement A377

1990, May 27
975 A377 150m multicolored .65 .25

Child's Drawing — A378

1990, June 5 *Perf. 14*
976 A378 150m multicolored .65 .25

Traditional Costumes — A379

1990, July 13 Photo. *Perf. 14x14½*
977 A379 150m Sbiba .75 .35
978 A379 500m Bou Omrane 2.00 .85

A380

Relic from Punic city of Dougga.

1990, Aug. 1 Litho. *Perf. 14*
979 A380 300m multicolored 1.00 .50

Intl. Literacy Year — A381

1990, Sept. 8 Photo. *Perf. 12x11½*
Granite Paper
980 A381 120m multicolored .65 .25

Water Preservation — A382

1990, Oct. 15 *Perf. 11½x12*
Granite Paper
981 A382 150m multicolored .75 .25

A383

1990, Nov. 7 Granite Paper
982 A383 150m shown .50 .25
983 A383 150m Clock tower .50 .25

Appointment of Pres. Zine El Abidine Ben Ali, 3rd anniv.

A384

1990, Nov. 16 Engr. *Perf. 13½x13*
984 A384 150m green .65 .25

Kheireddine Et-Tounsi (1822-1889), politician.

Fauna and Flora — A385

150m, Cervus elaphus barbarus. 200m, Cynara cardenculus. 300m, Bubalus bubalis. 600m, Ophris lutea.

1990, Dec. 17 Photo. *Perf. 13½*
985 A385 150m multicolored .50 .25
986 A385 200m multicolored .80 .35
987 A385 300m multicolored 1.25 .40
988 A385 600m multicolored 2.60 .85
Nos. 985-988 (4) 5.15 1.85

Maghreb Arab Union, 2nd Anniv. — A386

1991, Jan. 21 Photo. *Perf. 13½*
989 A386 180m multicolored .75 .25

Harbor of Tabarka — A387

1991, Mar. 17
990 A387 450m multicolored 1.50 .50

Fish — A388

1991, Sept. 10 Photo. *Perf. 14x13*
991 A388 180m Pagre .70 .25
992 A388 350m Rouget de roche 1.40 .40
993 A388 450m Maquereau 1.40 .60
994 A388 550m Pageot commun 2.40 .90
Nos. 991-994 (4) 5.90 2.15

Child Welfare — A389

1991, Sept. 29 *Perf. 14*
995 A389 450m multicolored 2.10 .85

A390

1991, Oct. 9 *Perf. 13½x14*
996 A390 400m multicolored 1.75 .50

Jewelry — A391

120m, Ring, bracelets, horiz. 180m, Necklace. 220m, Earrings. 730m, Belt ring.

Perf. 14x13, 13x14

1991, Oct. 22 Litho.
997 A391 120m multi .45 .25
998 A391 180m multi .55 .25
999 A391 220m multi .70 .35
1000 A391 730m multi 2.75 1.10
Nos. 997-1000 (4) 4.45 1.95

A392

1991, Nov. 7 *Perf. 11½*
1001 A392 180m multicolored .65 .25

Appointment of Pres. Zine El Abidine Ben Ali, 4th anniv.

Tunis-Carthage Center — A393

1991, Nov. 22 Engr. *Perf. 13*
1002 A393 80m red, blue & grn 1.00 .40

World Day of Human Rights — A394

1991, Dec. 12 Photo. *Perf. 14*
1003 A394 450m bright blue 1.60 .55

A395

1991, Dec. 26 Engr. *Perf. 12½x13*
1004 A395 200m blue .65 .35

Mahmoud Bayram Et Tounsi (1893-1960), poet.

Expo '92, Seville — A396

1992, Apr. 20 Photo. *Perf. 13½*
1005 A396 180m multicolored .65 .25

A397

General Post Office, Tunis, Cent. — A397a

Perf. 13x12½, 12½x13

1992, June 15 Engr.
1006 A397 180m red brn, horiz. .60 .25
1007 A397a 450m dark brown 1.60 .45

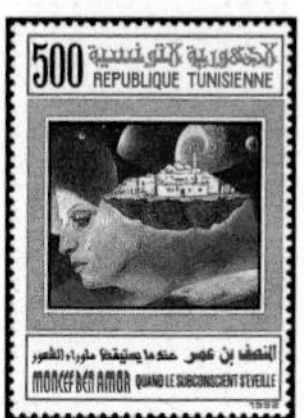
"When the Subconscious Awakes," by Moncef ben Amor — A398

1992, July 21 Litho. *Perf. 13½*
1008 A398 500m multicolored 1.90 .50

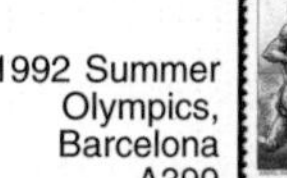
1992 Summer Olympics, Barcelona A399

1992, Aug. 4
1009 A399 180m Running 1.00 .40
1010 A399 450m Judo, vert. 2.25 .65

Birds — A400

100m, Merops apiaster. 180m, Carduelis carduelis. 200m, Serinus serinus. 500m, Carduelis chloris.

1992, Sept. 22 Photo. *Perf. 11½*
Granite Paper
1011 A400 100m multicolored .75 .25
1012 A400 180m multicolored 1.25 .40
1013 A400 200m multicolored 1.50 .50
1014 A400 500m multicolored 3.00 1.00
Nos. 1011-1014 (4) 6.50 2.15

A401

1992, Oct. 21 *Perf. 11½x12*
Granite Paper
1015 A401 180m multicolored .85 .40

UN Conference on Rights of the Child.

African Human Rights Conference, Tunis — A402

1992, Nov. 2 Photo. *Perf. 11½*
Granite Paper
1016 A402 480m multicolored 2.00 .85

A403

A404

1992, Nov. 7 Granite Paper
1017 A403 180m multicolored .95 .40
1018 A404 730m multicolored 3.00 1.10

Appointment of Pres. Zine El Abidine Ben Ali, 5th anniv.

Arbor Day — A405

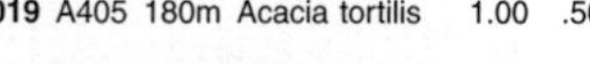

1992, Nov. 8 *Perf. 11½x12*
Granite Paper
1019 A405 180m Acacia tortilis 1.00 .50

Intl. Conference on Nutrition, Rome A406

1992, Dec. 15 Litho. *Perf. 13½*
1020 A406 450m multicolored 2.00 .65

Traditional Costumes — A407

1992, Dec. 23
1021 A407 100m Chemesse .60 .25
1022 A407 350m Hanifites 1.60 .50

Mosaics — A408

1992, Dec. 29
1023 A408 100m Goat .40 .25
1024 A408 180m Duck .85 .35
1025 A408 350m Horse 1.40 .50
1026 A408 450m Gazelle 1.50 .90
Nos. 1023-1026 (4) 4.15 2.00

World Conference on Human Rights, Vienna A409

1993, June 8 Litho. *Perf. 13½*
1027 A409 450m multi — —

Arab-African Fair of Tunisia — A410

1993, July 10 Litho. *Perf. 13½x14*
1028 A410 450m multicolored 1.75 .50

Relaxation in the Patio, by Ali Guermassi — A411

1993, July 20 Litho. *Perf. 13½*

1029 A411 450m multicolored 1.75 .50

Reassembly of the Democratic Congress — A412

1993, July 29 *Perf. 13½*

1030 A412 180m multicolored .65 .25

A413 A414

1993 *Perf. 13*

1031 A413 20m Wolf 1.25 .25
1032 A414 60m Hoya carnosa .75 .25

Appointment of Pres. Zine El Abidine, 6th Anniv.
A414a A415

1993, Nov. 7 *Perf. 13½*

1033 A414a 180m multicolored .75 .25
1034 A415 450m multicolored 1.75 .50

Kairouan Tapestries — A416

Designs: Various ornate patterns.

1993, Dec. 13 *Perf. 13½*

1035 A416 100m multicolored .40 .25
1036 A416 120m multicolored .75 .25
1037 A416 180m multicolored 1.25 .35
1038 A416 350m multicolored 1.40 .75
Nos. 1035-1038 (4) 3.80 1.60

Pasteur Institute of Tunis, Cent. — A417

Design: 450m, Charles Nicolle (1866-1936), bacteriologist, 1928 Nobel medal.

1993, Oct. 12 Litho. *Perf. 13½*

1039 A417 450m multicolored 2.00 .65

A418 School Activities — A419

1993, Dec. 30 Litho. *Perf. 13½*

1040 A418 180m Music .75 .25
1041 A419 180m Art, reading .75 .25

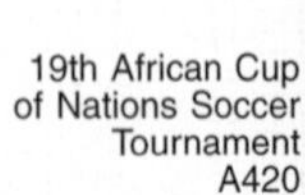

19th African Cup of Nations Soccer Tournament A420

350m, Two players, one in blue, red and gray long sleeve shirt. 450m, Map, player.

1994, Mar. 26

1042 A420 180m shown 1.00 .25
1043 A420 350m multi 2.00 .35
1044 A420 450m multi 2.75 .65
Nos. 1042-1044 (3) 5.75 1.25

Presidential and Legislative Elections — A421

1994, Mar. 20

1045 A421 180m multicolored .80 .25

Election of Pres. Zine El Abidine ben Ali — A422

1994, May 15 Photo. *Perf. 11½*
Granite Paper

1046 A422 180m multicolored .75 .35
1047 A422 350m multicolored 1.25 .75
a. Souvenir sheet, #1046-1047 3.50 3.50

No. 1047a exists imperf.

ILO, 75th Anniv. — A423

1994, May 12 *Perf. 13½x14*

1048 A423 350m multicolored 1.75 .35

Intl. Year of the Family — A424

1994, May 15 Litho. *Perf. 14x13½*

1049 A424 180m multicolored .85 .50

Plants — A425

50m, Prunus spinosa. 100m, Xeranthemum inapertum. 200m, Orchis simia. 1d, Scilla peruviana.

1994, June 2

1050 A425 50m multicolored .35 .25
1051 A425 100m multicolored .35 .25
1052 A425 200m multicolored 1.00 .30
1053 A425 1d multicolored 4.50 1.50
Nos. 1050-1053 (4) 6.20 2.30

Organization of African Unity Summit Meeting, Tunis — A426

1994, June 3 *Perf. 13½*

1054 A426 480m multicolored 2.00 .75

Intl. Olympic Committee, Cent. — A427

1994, July 7 Litho. *Perf. 13½*

1055 A427 450m multicolored 1.75 .65

Philakorea '94 — A428

1994, Aug 18 Litho. *Perf. 13¼x13½*

1056 A428 450m multi 3.00 .65

A429

Butterflies: 100m, Colias croceus, horiz. 180m, Vanessa atalanta, horiz. 300m, Papilio podalirius. 350m, Danaus chrysippus, horiz. 450m, Vanessa cardui. 500m, Papilio machaon.

Perf. 13½x14, 14x13½

1994, Oct. 13 Litho.

1057 A429 100m multicolored .45 .25
1058 A429 180m multicolored .70 .35
1059 A429 300m multicolored 1.00 .50
1060 A429 350m multicolored 1.40 .65
1061 A429 450m multicolored 1.75 .85
1062 A429 500m multicolored 2.10 .90
Nos. 1057-1062 (6) 7.40 3.50

A430 A430a

350m, Pres. Ali, "7," horiz. 730m, "7," Emblem.

1994, Nov. 16 *Perf. 13½*

1063 A430 350m multi 1.25 .50
1064 A430a 730m multi 2.75 1.00

Pres. Zine El Abidine, 7th anniv. of taking office.

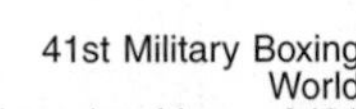

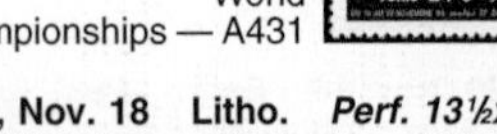

41st Military Boxing World Championships — A431

1994, Nov. 18 Litho. *Perf. 13½x14*

1065 A431 450m multicolored 1.75 .70

Intl. Civil Aviation Organization, 50th Anniv. — A432

1994, Dec. 7 Litho. *Perf. 13¾x14*

1066 A432 450m multi 1.25 .50

Wildlife — A433

180m, Anser anser. 350m, Aythya ferina, Aythya fuligula. 500m, Bubalus bubalis. 1d, Lutra lutra, horiz.

1994, Dec. 27 Litho. *Perf. 13½*

1067 A433 180m multi .65 .40
1068 A433 350m multi 1.10 .85
1069 A433 500m multi 1.60 1.25
1070 A433 1d multi 3.00 2.75
Nos. 1067-1070 (4) 6.35 5.25

"Composition," by Ridha Bettaieb — A434

1994, Dec. 29 Litho. *Perf. 13*

1071 A434 500m multicolored 1.50 .85

Arab League, 50th Anniv. — A435

1995, May 29 Litho. *Perf. 13½*

1072 A435 180m multicolored 1.00 .40

Art of Glass Blowing — A436

1995, June 29

1073 A436 450m Water bottle 1.50 .90
1074 A436 730m Incense burner 2.25 1.50

Aboulkacem Chebbi (1909-34), Poet — A437

1995, Aug. 12 Litho. *Perf. 13½*

1075 A437 180m multicolored .85 .40

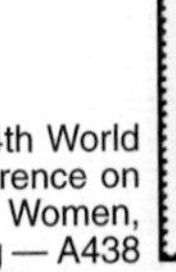
4th World Conference on Women, Beijing — A438

1995, Sept. 6 Litho. *Perf. 13½*
1076 A438 180m multicolored 1.40 .40

FAO, 50th Anniv. — A439

1995, Oct. 2 Litho. *Perf. 13½x13*
1077 A439 350m multicolored 1.40 .65

Hannibal (247-183BC), Carthaginian General — A440

1995, Nov. 14 Engr. *Perf. 14x13½*
1078 A440 180m maroon *.65* .40
a. Souvenir sheet of 1 *2.50* 2.50

No. 1078a sold for 1d and exists imperf.

United Nations, 50th Anniv. — A441

1995, Oct. 24 Litho. *Perf. 14x13½*
1079 A441 350m multicolored 1.50 .65

A442 A443

1995, Nov. 7 Litho. *Perf. 13x13½*
1080 A442 180m multicolored .65 .35
1081 A443 350m multicolored 1.25 .65

Appointment of Pres. Zine El Abidine ben Ali, 8th anniv.

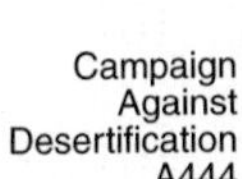

Campaign Against Desertification A444

1995, Oct. 31 Litho. *Perf. 13¼*
1082 A444 180m multi .75 .35

Human Rights Day — A445

1995, Dec. 10 Litho. *Perf. 13x13½*
1083 A445 350m multicolored 1.40 .65

Pedestrian Security — A446

1995, Dec. 19 *Perf. 13½x13*
1084 A446 350m multicolored 1.10 .65

Flora and Fauna — A447

Designs: 50m, Ophrys lapethica. 180m, Gazella dorcas. 300m, Scupellaria cypria. 350m, Chlamydotis undulata.

1995, Dec. 28 *Perf. 13½*
1085 A447 50m multicolored .35 .25
1086 A447 180m multicolored .70 .25
1087 A447 300m multicolored 1.10 .55
1088 A447 350m multicolored 1.25 .75
Nos. 1085-1088 (4) 3.40 1.80

Traditional Costumes — A448

170m, Jebra, Khamri. 200m, Kaftan brode, Hammamet.

1996, Mar.16 *Perf. 14x13½*
1089 A448 170m multi .85 .40
1090 A448 200m multi .85 .40

Independence, 40th Anniv. — A449

390m, Dove, rainbow, "20, 40."

1996, Mar. 20 *Perf. 13x13½*
1091 A449 200m multicolored .75 .30
1092 A449 390m multicolored 1.25 .75

Natl. Trade Union, 50th Anniv. — A450

1996, Jan. 20 Litho. *Perf. 13x13½*
1093 A450 440m multicolored 1.75 .85

Painting, "Hannana," by Noureddine Khayachi (1917-87) A451

1996, Apr. 25 Litho. *Perf. 13½*
1094 A451 810m multicolored 2.50 1.60

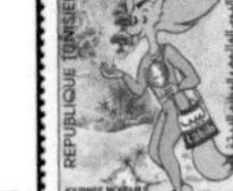
Environment Day — A451a

1996, June 5 Litho. *Perf. 13x13½*
1094A A451a 390m multicolored 1.50 .75

CAPEX '96 — A452

1996, June 8 Litho. *Perf. 13x13½*
1095 A452 200m multicolored 1.10 .35

Insects — A453

200m, Coccinella septempunctata. 810m, Apis mellifica.

1996, May 23 Litho. *Perf. 14x13½*
1096 A453 200m multicolored 1.00 .40
1097 A453 810m multicolored 5.00 2.00

1996 Summer Olympic Games, Atlanta — A455

Olympic emblem, and: 20m, Flags, Olympic rings, athletic field. 200m, Torch bearer, fireworks, "100," globe, vert. 390m, Early Olympic wrestlers.

1996, July 19 Litho. *Perf. 13*
1099 A455 20m multicolored .40 .25
1100 A455 200m multicolored .90 .35
1101 A455 390m multicolored 1.75 .85
Nos. 1099-1101 (3) 3.05 1.45

Code of Personal Status (Women's Liberation), 40th Anniv. — A456

1996, Aug. 13 *Perf. 14*
1102 A456 200m multicolored .80 .35

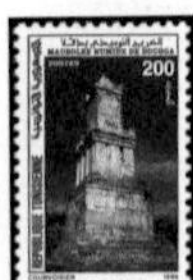
Landmarks — A457

Designs: 20m, Ramparts of Sousse, horiz. 200m, Numidian Mausoleum, Dougga. 390m, Arch of Trajan, Makthar, horiz.

1996, Sept. 16 Photo. *Perf. 11½*
Granite Paper
1103 A457 20m multicolored .35 .25
1104 A457 200m multicolored .65 .35
1105 A457 390m multicolored 1.50 .85
Nos. 1103-1105 (3) 2.50 1.45

Intl. Year to Fight Poverty — A458

1996, Oct. 17 Litho. *Perf. 13x13½*
1106 A458 390m multicolored 1.50 .65

Appointment of Pres. Zine El Abidine, 9th Anniv.
A459 A460

1996, Nov. 7
1107 A459 200m multicolored .75 .35
1108 A460 390m multicolored 1.00 .75

National Day of Saharan Tourism A461

Designs: No. 1109, Camels, oasis, balloon. No. 1110, Decorative designs.

1996, Nov. 12 Litho. *Perf. 13¼x13*
1109 200m multi .85 .35
1110 200m multi .85 .35
a. A461 Horiz. pair, #1109-1110 1.75 1.75

Ezzitouna Mosque, 1300th Anniv. — A462

1996, Nov. 25 Litho. *Perf. 14x13½*
1111 A462 250m multicolored .85 .40

Natl. Solidarity Day
A463 A464

1996, Dec. 8 *Perf. 13x13½*
1112 A463 500m multicolored 1.50 .95
1113 A464 500m multicolored 1.50 .95

World Human Rights Day — A465

1996, Dec. 10
1114 A465 500m multicolored 1.75 .90

UNICEF, 50th Anniv. — A466

1996, Dec. 11
1115 A466 810m multicolored 2.75 1.50

Musical Instruments A467

1996, Dec. 26 Litho. *Perf. 13½*

1116	A467 250m Mezoued	.85	.50
1117	A467 300m Gombri	1.00	.60
1118	A467 350m Tabla	1.60	.65
1119	A467 500m Tar Tounsi (Riq)	2.50	.90
	Nos. 1116-1119 (4)	5.95	2.65

Perf. 13½x13¼

Size: 38x25mm

1119A	Vert. strip of 4	—	—
b.	A467 20m Tabla	—	—
c.	A467 30m Mezoued	—	—
d.	A467 50m Gombri	—	—
e.	A467 100m Tar Tounsi	—	—

World Book and Copyright Day — A468

1997, Apr. 23 Litho. *Perf. 13½*

1120 A468 1d multicolored 3.25 1.75

Marine Life — A469

Designs: 50m, Mytilus galloprovincialis. 70m, Tapes decussatus. 350m, Octopus vulgaris. 500m, Sepia officinalis.

1997, May 13

1121	A469 50m multicolored	.30	.25
1122	A469 70m multicolored	.30	.25
1123	A469 350m multicolored	1.10	.65
1124	A469 500m multicolored	1.90	1.25
	Nos. 1121-1124 (4)	3.60	2.40

PACIFIC 97, Intl. Stamp Exhibition, San Francisco — A470

1997, May 29 Photo. *Perf. 11½x12*

Granite Paper

1125 A470 250m multicolored .85 .40

A471

1997, June 16 Litho. *Perf. 13½*

1126 A471 350m multicolored 1.40 .65

Mediterranean Games, Bari.

A472

1997, July 15

1127 A472 250m multicolored .85 .40

Tunis, 1997 Cultural Capital.

A473

Republic, 40th Anniv. — A474

1997, July 25

1128	A473 130m multicolored	.50	.25
1129	A474 500m multicolored	1.50	1.00

Reptiles — A475

100m, Uromastix acanthinurus. 350m, Chamaeleo chamaeleon, vert. 500m, Varanus griseus.

1997, Sept. 9 Litho. *Perf. 13½*

1130	A475 100m multicolored	.25	.25
1131	A475 350m multicolored	1.00	.65
1132	A475 500m multicolored	1.25	1.10
	Nos. 1130-1132 (3)	2.50	2.00

Rosa Gallica Flore Pleno A476

1997, Sept. 23 Litho. *Perf. 13½*

1134 A476 350m multicolored 1.40 .85

Intl. Day for Protection of the Elderly — A477

1997, Oct. 1 Litho. *Perf. 13½*

1135 A477 250m multicolored .85 .40

Tunisian Works of Art — A478

#1136, "L'Automne," by Ammar Farhat. #1137, Sculpture, "Pecheur D'Hommes," by Hedi Selmi. #1138, "Au Cafe-Maure," by Farhat. #1139, "Le Viellard au Kanoun," by Farhat. #1140, "Cafe Des Nattes-Sidi Bou Said," by Hedi Khayachi. #1141, "Le Kouttab," by Yahia Turki. 1000d, "La Fileuse," by Farhat.

1997, Nov. 5

1136	A478 250m multi, vert.	.80	.55
1137	A478 250m multi, vert.	.80	.55
1138	A478 250m multi, vert.	.80	.55
1139	A478 250m multi, vert.	.80	.55
1140	A478 500m multi	1.60	1.10
1141	A478 500m multi	1.60	1.10
1142	A478 1000m multi, vert.	3.50	2.25
a.	Sheet of 7, #1136-1142, + 3 labels	*10.00*	*10.00*
	Nos. 1136-1142 (7)	9.90	6.65

No. 1142a issued 11/7.

A479

A480

1997, Nov. 7

1143	A479 250m multicolored	.75	.40
1144	A480 500m multicolored	1.75	1.10

Pres. Zine El Abdine, 10th anniv. of taking office.

Desert Rose — A481

1997, Nov. 29

1145 A481 250m multicolored 1.10 .40

Intl. Human Rights Day — A482

1997, Dec. 10 Litho. *Perf. 13½*

1146 A482 500m multicolored 1.50 .90

Horses — A483

Designs: 50m, Arabian. 70m, Barb. 250m, Arabian barb, vert. 500m, Arabian, vert.

1997, Dec. 18 *Perf. 12½x13*

1147	A483 50m multicolored	.35	.25
1148	A483 70m multicolored	.35	.25
1149	A483 250m multicolored	1.00	.40
1150	A483 500m multicolored	2.00	.75
	Nos. 1147-1150 (4)	3.70	1.65

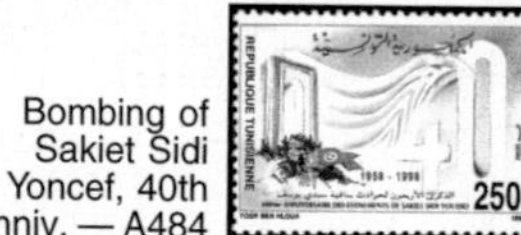

Bombing of Sakiet Sidi Yoncef, 40th Anniv. — A484

1998, Feb. 8

1151 A484 250m multicolored .85 .30

School Health Week — A485

1998, Feb. 16 Litho. *Perf. 12½x13*

1152 A485 250m multicolored .85 .30

Bar Assoc. of Tunisia, Cent. — A486

1998, Mar. 27 *Perf. 13x12½*

1153 A486 250m multicolored .85 .30

Martyr's Day, 60th Anniv.
A487 A488

1998, Apr. 9

1154	A487 250m multicolored	.75	.30
1155	A488 520m multicolored	1.60	.55

Okba Ibn Nafaa Mosque, Kairouan A489

1998, May 28 Litho. *Perf. 13*

1156 A489 500m multicolored 1.75 .60

1998 World Cup Soccer Championships, France — A490

250m, Tunisian team. 500m Player, trophy.

1998, June 10 Litho. *Perf. 13*

1157	A490 250m multi	.85	.30
1158	A490 500m multi, vert.	1.90	.60

Crustaceans A491

1998, July 8 *Perf. 12½x13*

1159	A491 110m Crab	.30	.25
1160	A491 250m Shrimp	.75	.30
1161	A491 1000m Lobster	3.00	1.10
	Nos. 1159-1161 (3)	4.05	1.65

21st Reassembly of the Democratic Congress (RCD) A492

#1162, Pres. Zine El Abidine ben Ali, flag, emblems. #1163, People holding torches, flag, dove.

1998, July 30 *Perf. 13*

1162	A492 250m multi	.85	.30
1163	A492 250m multi, vert.	.85	.30

36th Intl. Congress on the History of Medicine A493

1998, Sept. 6 Litho. *Perf. 13*

1164 A493 500m multicolored 1.75 .60

Paintings A494

#1165, "The Weaver," by Ali Guermassi (1923-92). #1166, "Woman Musician," by

Noureddine Khayachi (1917-87). 500m, Still life by Ali Khouja (1947-91).

1998, Oct. 8

1165 A494 250m multi .90 .30
1166 A494 250m multi, vert. .90 .30
1167 A494 500m multi, vert. 1.75 .60
Nos. 1165-1167 (3) 3.55 1.20

Central Bank of Tunisia, 40th Anniv. — A495

1998, Nov. 10 Litho. *Perf. 13*

1168 A495 250m multicolored .85 .30

A496

1998, Nov. 7

1169 A496 250m multicolored .85 .30

Appointment of Pres. Zine El Abidine ben Ali, 11th anniv.

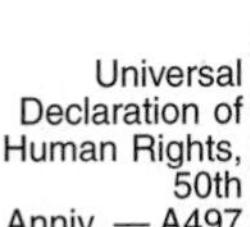

Universal Declaration of Human Rights, 50th Anniv. — A497

1998, Dec. 10 Litho. *Perf. 12½x13*

1170 A497 250m multicolored .85 .35

Averroes (Ibn Rushd) (1126-1198), Philosopher A498

1998, Dec. 12

1171 A498 500m multicolored 1.75 .60

Musicians A499

1998, Dec. 21 *Perf. 12½x13, 13x12½*

1172 A499 250m Kaddour Srarfi .85 .30
1173 A499 250m Saliha, vert. .85 .30
1174 A499 500m Ali Riahi, vert. 1.75 .60
Nos. 1172-1174 (3) 3.45 1.20

Boukornine Natl. Park — A500

1998, Dec. 29 Litho. *Perf. 13*

1175 A500 70m Gazelles .35 .25
1176 A500 110m Rabbit .35 .25
1177 A500 250m Eagles .85 .30
1178 A500 500m Cyclamens 1.75 .60
Nos. 1175-1178 (4) 3.30 1.40

Fruit Trees — A501

1999, Feb. 27 Litho. *Perf. 13*

1179 A501 250m Orange 1.00 .30
1180 A501 250m Date, vert. 1.00 .30
1181 A501 500m Olive 2.00 .60
Nos. 1179-1181 (3) 4.00 1.20

Archaeological Sites — A502

50m, Gate, Thuburbo Majus. 250m, Thermal baths, Bulla Regia. 500m, Zaghouan Aqueduct.

1999, Mar. 31 Litho. *Perf. 13*

1182 A502 50m multi, vert. .40 .25
1183 A502 250m multi .95 .30
1184 A502 500m multi 2.10 .60
Nos. 1182-1184 (3) 3.45 1.15

Paintings by Tunisian Artists — A503

Designs: No. 1185, "L'Intemporel," by Moncef Ben Amor. No. 1186, "Fiancailles," by Ali Guermassi. No. 1187, "La Poterie," by Ammar Farhat. No. 1188, "Vendeur d'ombrelles et d'eventails," by Yahia Turki.

1999, May 6 Litho. *Perf. 13*

1185 A503 250m multicolored .85 .30
1186 A503 250m multicolored .85 .30
1187 A503 500m multicolored 1.60 .55
1188 A503 500m multicolored 1.60 .55
Nos. 1185-1188 (4) 4.90 1.70

Constitution, 40th Anniv. A504

1999, June 1 Litho. *Perf. 13*

1189 A504 250m multicolored .85 .40

Flowers — A505

70m, Acacia cyanophilla. #1191, Bougainvillea spectabilis. #1192, Papaver rhoeas. 500m, Dianthus caryophylius.

1999, June 25 Litho. *Perf. 12¾*

1190 A505 70m multicolored .35 .25
1191 A505 250m multicolored .85 .30
1192 A505 250m multicolored .85 .30
1193 A505 500m multicolored 1.90 .70
a. Souvenir sheet, #1190-1193, imperf. 8.25 8.25
Nos. 1190-1193 (4) 3.95 1.55

No. 1193a sold for 1.50d.

Philex France 99 — A506

1999, July 2 *Perf. 13x12¾*

1194 A506 500m multicolored 2.50 .85

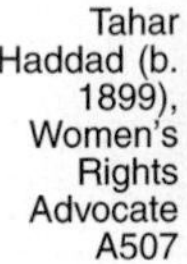

Tahar Haddad (b. 1899), Women's Rights Advocate A507

1999, Aug. 13 Litho.

1195 A507 500m multicolored 2.50 .85

Marine Life — A508

250m, Caretta caretta. 500m, Epinephelus marginatus.

1999, Sept. 22 *Perf. 12¾*

1196 A508 250m multi *.90 .90*
1197 A508 500m multi *1.75 1.75*

National Organ Donation Day — A509

1999, Oct. 2 *Perf. 13x12¾*

1198 A509 250m multicolored 1.10 .45

UPU, 125th Anniv. — A510

1999, Oct. 9 *Perf. 12¾*

1199 A510 500m multicolored 2.00 .75

Elections — A511

1999, Oct. 10 Litho.

1200 A511 500m multicolored 2.25 .85

Tamarisk — A512

1999, Oct. 28 Litho. *Perf. 12¾x13*

1201 A512 250m shown 1.10 .35
1202 A512 500m Dromedary 2.25 .75

Appointment of Pres. Zine El Abidine Ben Ali, 12th Anniv. — A513

1999, Nov. 7 *Perf. 13x12¾*

1203 A513 250m multi 1.00 .45

Human Rights Day — A514

1999, Dec. 10 Litho. *Perf. 13x12¾*

1204 A514 250m multi 1.75 .45

Famous Tunisians — A515

No. 1205, Ahmed Ibn Abi Dhiaf (1802-74), historian. No. 1206, Abdelaziz Thaalbi (1876-1944), anti-colonial leader. 500m, Khemaies Tarnane (1894-1964), musician.

1999, Dec. 28 *Perf. 13x12¾, 12¾x13*

1205 A515 250m multi .85 .35
1206 A515 250m multi .85 .35
1207 A515 500m multi, horiz. 1.60 .75
Nos. 1205-1207 (3) 3.30 1.45

Millennium A516

1999, Dec. 31 *Perf. 13*

1208 A516 250m multi .90 .45

A517

A518

Archaeology A519

Design: 100m, Methred cup. 110m, Aghlabide plate. 250m, Zaghouan water temple. 500m, Ulysses and the Sirens mosaic.

2000, Apr. 22 Litho. *Perf. 13x13¼*

1209 A517 100m multi .40 .35
1210 A517 110m multi .50 .45

Perf. 13¼

1211 A518 250m multi 1.20 1.00
1212 A519 500m multi 2.40 2.00
Nos. 1209-1212 (4) 4.50 3.80

Ferry Carthage A520

2000, Apr. 29 *Perf. 13¼x13*

1213 A520 500m multi 1.90 .80
a. Souvenir sheet, imperf. 6.00 3.00

No. 1213a sold for 2d.

Expo 2000, Hanover — A521

2000, June 1 *Perf. 13¼x13*
1214 A521 1d multi 3.50 1.75

Trees — A522

Designs: 50m, Carob. 100m, Apricot. 250m, Avocado, vert. 400m, Apple.

2000, July 5 **Litho.** *Perf. 12¾*
1215-1218 A522 Set of 4 3.00 1.50

2001 Mediterranean Games, Tunis — A523

2000, Sept. 2 **Litho.** *Perf. 13*
1219 A523 500m multi 1.75 .80
a. Souvenir sheet of 1, imperf. 3.75 1.90

No. 1219a sold for 1500m.

2000 Summer Olympics, Sydney — A524

2000, Sept. 22 *Perf. 12¾*
1220 A524 500m multi 1.75 .80

Souvenir Sheet

Imperf

1221 A524 1500m multi 6.00 1.90

Flowers — A525

Designs: 110m, Freesias. 200m, Chrysanthemums. No. 1224, 250m, "Golden Times" roses. No. 1225, 250m, Vase with flowers (33x49mm). 500m, "Calibra" roses.

2000, Oct. 21 *Perf. 12¾, 13 (#1225)*
1222-1226 A525 Set of 5 4.75 2.40

Appointment of Pres. Zine El Abidine Ben Ali, 13th Anniv. — A526

2000, Nov. 7 *Perf. 13*
1227 A526 250m multi 1.00 .50

Art — A527

Designs: 100m, Still Life, by Hédi Khayachi. No. 1229, 250m, Landscape, by Abdelaziz Berraies. No. 1230, 250m, The Knife Sharpener, by Ali Guermassi. 400m, Date and Milk Seller, by Yahia Turki, vert.

2000, Nov. 18
1228-1231 A527 Set of 4 3.50 1.50

Intl. Human Rights Day — A528

2000, Dec. 10
1232 A528 500m multi 1.75 .85

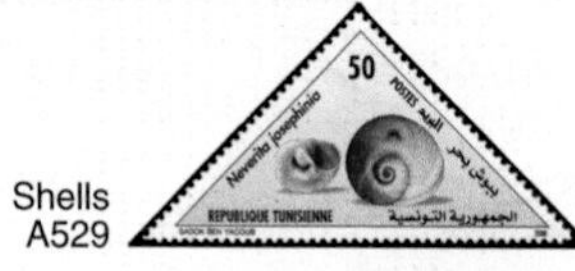

Shells A529

Designs: 50m, Neverita josephinia. No. 1234, 250m, Phyllonotus trunculus. No. 1235, 250m, Columbella rustica. 1d, Arca noe.

2000, Dec. 29 *Perf. 13x13¼*
1233-1236 A529 Set of 4 8.00 2.50

A530

Famous Tunisians — A531

Designs: No. 1237, 250m, Imam Sahnoun. No. 1238, 250m, Imam Ibn Arafa. No. 1239, 250m, Ali Belhaouane (1909-58), vert. 1d, Mohamed Jamoussi (1910-82), musician.

2000, Dec. 30 *Perf. 12¾*
1237 A530 250m shown .85 .35
1238 A530 250m multi .85 .35
1239 A531 250m multi .85 .35
1240 A531 1d shown 3.50 1.50
Nos. 1237-1240 (4) 6.05 2.55

Tunisian Presidency of UN Security Council A532

2001, Feb. 19 **Litho.** *Perf. 13*
1241 A532 250m multi 1.10 .55

World Fund of Solidarity — A533

2001, Mar. 29
1242 A533 500m multi 1.75 .80

Year of Digital Culture — A534

2001, May 17 *Perf. 12¾*
1243 A534 250m multi 1.10 .55

Mohamed Dorra, Child Killed in Israeli-Palestinian Violence — A535

2001, May 30
1244 A535 600m multi 2.25 1.10

A536 A537

Designs: No. 1245, 19th cent. ceramic tile, Qallaline. No. 1246, Gigthis, horiz. No. 1247, Tunis City Hall, horiz. 500m, Needles of Tabarka.

2001, Aug. 24
1245 A536 250m multi .60 .25
1246 A537 250m multi .60 .25
1247 A537 250m multi .60 .25
1248 A537 500m multi 1.20 .50
Nos. 1245-1248 (4) 3.00 1.25

2001 Mediterranean Games, Tunis — A538

Desings: No. 1249, 250m, No. 1251b, Track, stadium. No. 1250, 500m, No. 1251a, Runners, medal.

2001, Sept. 2 *Perf. 12¾*
1249-1250 A538 Set of 2 1.75 .75

Souvenir Sheet

Imperf

1251 A538 750m Sheet of 2, #a-b 3.00 1.50

Paintings A539

Designs: No. 1252, 250m, Sidi Bou Said, by Pierre Boucherle. No. 1253, 250m, Still Life, by Boucherle. No. 1254, 250m, Dream in Traditional Space, by Aly Ben Salem, vert. 500m, Traditional Open-air Marriage, by Ben Salem.

2001, Sept. 29 **Litho.** *Perf. 13*
1252-1255 A539 Set of 4 3.00 1.40

Year of Dialogue Among Civilizations A540

2001, Oct. 9 *Perf. 12¾x13*
1256 A540 500m multi *2.00* .55

National Employment Fund — A541

2001, Oct. 10
1257 A541 250m multi .60 .30

Appointment of Pres. Zine El Abidine Ben Ali, 14th Anniv. — A542

2001, Nov. 7 *Perf. 13x12¾*
1258 A542 250m multi .60 .30

Butterflies — A543

Designs: Nos. 1259, 1263a, 250m, Ariane. No. 1260, 250m, No. 1263c, 500m, Pacha à deux queues. Nos. 1261, 1263b, 250m, Demi-deuil. Nos. 1262, 1263d, 500m, Grand paon de nuit.

2001, Nov. 15 *Perf. 13x13¼*
1259-1262 A543 Set of 4 *3.00* 1.50

Souvenir Sheet

Imperf

1263 A543 Sheet of 4, #a-d *3.50* 1.75

Birds — A544

Designs: No. 1264, 250m, No. 1268a, 300m, Bec-croise des sapins. 500m, Mesange charbonnière. No. 1266, 600m, Cigogne blanche. No. 1267, 600m, Geai des chenes.

2001, Nov. 22 *Perf. 13*
1264-1267 A544 Set of 4 4.50 2.25

Souvenir Sheet

1268 A544 Sheet, #1265-1267, 1268a 5.50 2.50

Intl. Human Rights Day — A545

2001, Dec. 10 *Perf. 13x12¾*
1269 A545 250m multi .60 .30

Famous Men — A546

Designs: No. 1270, 250m, Ibrahim ibn al-Aghlab (757-812), founder of Aghlabid dynasty. No. 1271, 250m, Ibn Rachiq al Kairaouani (1000-71). 350m, Abdelaziz Laroui (1898-1971). 650m, Assad ibn al-Fourat (759-828).

2001, Dec. 29 *Perf. 12¾x13*
1270-1273 A546 Set of 4 3.25 1.60

Arabic Calligraphy A547

Designs: No. 1274, 350m, Shown. No. 1275, 350m, Calligraphy, vert.

2001, Dec. 31 ***Perf. 12¾x13, 13x12¾***

1274-1275 A547 Set of 2 2.00 1.10

Archaeology
A548 A549

Designs: 250m, Kef casbah. 390m, Amphitheater, Oudhna, horiz. No. 1278, Baron of Erlanger Palace. No. 1279, Mosaic of Virgil.

Perf. 13x12¾, 12¾x13

2002, Mar. 26 **Litho.**

1276 A548 250m multi .60 .25

1277 A548 390m multi .95 .40

1278 A549 600m multi 1.40 .60

1279 A549 600m multi 1.40 .60

Nos. 1276-1279 (4) 4.35 1.85

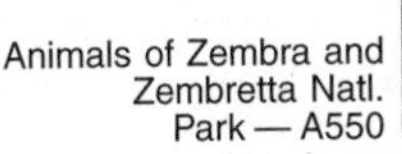

Animals of Zembra and Zembretta Natl. Park — A550

Designs: No. 1280, 250m, No. 1284a, 400m, Ovis musimon. No. 1281, 250m, No. 1284b, 400m, Oryctolagus cuniculus. No. 1282, 600m, Falco peregrinus brookei. No. 1283, 600m, Larus audouinii.

2002, Apr. 10 ***Perf. 13***

1280-1283 A550 Set of 4 4.50 1.75

Souvenir Sheet

1284 A550 Sheet, #1282-1283, 1284a-1284b 5.50 1.90

Sahara Desert Tourism — A551

Designs: No. 1285, 250m, No. 1289a, 400m, Gazella leptoceros. No. 1286, 390m, No. 1289b, 400m, Sahara village. No. 1287, 600m, Horseman. No. 1288, 600m, Tamaghza.

2002, May 22 ***Perf. 13¼***

1285-1288 A551 Set of 4 4.00 1.90

Souvenir Sheet

1289 A551 Sheet, #1287-1288, 1289a-1289b, imperf. 5.00 2.00

2002 World Cup Soccer Championships, Japan and Korea — A552

World Cup, Emblem of Tunisia and World Cup tournament and: No. 1290, 390m, No. 1292a, 500m, Player, map of Japan and Korea. No. 1291, 600m, 1292b, 1000m, Ball in goal net.

2002, May 29 ***Perf. 13***

1290-1291 A552 Set of 2 2.50 1.00

Souvenir Sheet

1292 A552 Sheet of 2, #a-b 4.00 1.50

Famous Men — A553

Designs: 100m, Sheikh Mohamed Senoussi (1851-1900). No. 1294, 250m, Mosbah Jarbou (1914-58). No. 1295, 250m, Mohamed Daghbaji (1885-1924). 1.10d, Abou al-Hassen al-Housri (1029-95).

2002, July 18 ***Perf. 12¾***

1293-1296 A553 Set of 4 4.00 1.75

World Handicapped Games — A554

Tunisian flag and: 100m, Wheelchair racer. 700m, Discus thrower, vert.

2002, July 20

1297-1298 A554 Set of 2 1.75 .85

27th World Veterinary Congress, Tunis — A555

2002, Sept. 25 **Litho.** ***Perf. 12¾***

1299 A555 600m multi 1.50 .60

Travel International Club, 20th Anniv. — A556

2002, Oct. 25 **Litho.** ***Perf. 13x13¼***

1300 A556 600m multi 1.50 .60

Appointment of Pres. Zine El Abidine Ben Ali, 15th Anniv. — A557

2002, Nov. 7 ***Perf. 13x12¾***

1301 A557 390m multi .95 .40

Assassination of Farhat Hached (1914-52) — A558

2002, Dec. 3 **Litho.** ***Perf. 13x12¾***

1302 A558 390m multi .95 .40

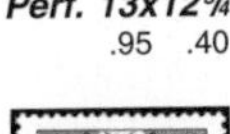

Intl. Human Rights Day — A559

2002, Dec. 10

1303 A559 700m multi 1.75 .75

Art Type of 2001

Designs: No. 1304, 250m, Space for Gazelles, by Aly Ben Salem. No. 1305, 250m, Popular Arts, by Ammar Farhat, vert. No. 1306, 250m, Marriage, by Habib Bouabana, vert. 900m, Still Life, by Pierre Boucherle, vert.

2002, Dec. 28 ***Perf. 13***

1304-1307 A539 Set of 4 4.00 1.75

Mosaics — A560

Designs: 390m, Spinner. 600m, Africa.

2003, Feb. 28

1308-1309 A560 Set of 2 2.40 1.00

Scouting in Tunisia, 70th Anniv. A561

"70" and scouts: 250m, Reading map, at computer, planting tree. 600m, Saluting flag, at computer, vert.

2003, Mar. 29 **Litho.** ***Perf. 13***

1310-1311 A561 Set of 2 1.90 .85

National Book Year — A562

2003, Apr. 23

1312 A562 390m multi .95 .40

The Washerwoman, by Yahia Turki — A563

2003, June 13

1313 A563 1d multi 2.40 1.00

National Tourism Day — A564

2003, June 28 ***Perf. 13¼***

1314 A564 600m multi 1.50 .60

Parks A565

Designs: 200m, Farhat Hached Park, Rades. 250m, Friguia Animal Park. 390m, La Marsa Park. 1d, Ennahli Park.

2003, June 28 ***Perf. 13***

1315-1318 A565 Set of 4 *4.00* 2.00

Congress of Ambition — A566

2003, July 28 **Litho.** ***Perf. 13x12¾***

1319 A566 250m multi .70 .35

A567

2003, Aug. 3

1320 A567 390m multi .95 .45

Pres. Habib Bourguiba (1903-2000).

A568

Flora and Fauna — A569

Designs: Nos. 1321a, 50m, 1326, 600m, Oryx dammah. Nos. 1321b, 50m, 1324, 250m, Nyctanthes sambac. Nos. 1321c, 100m, 1323, 250m, Aries. Nos. 1321d, 100m, 1327, 1d, Myrtus communis. Nos. 1321e, 200m, 1325, 390m, Struthio camelus. Nos. 1321f, 200m, 1322, 100m, Rosa canina.

2003, Sept. 25 ***Perf. 12¾***

1321 Strip of 6 *3.50* .80

a.-b. A568 50m Either single *.50* .25

c.-d. A568 100m Either single *.50* .25

e.-f. A568 200m Either single *.90* .25

1322-1327 A569 Set of 6 5.75 2.75

No. 1321 was issued in a sheet of 6 strips that sold for 4500m.

Appointment of Pres. Zine El Abidine Ben Ali, 16th Anniv. — A570

2003, Nov. 7 **Litho.** ***Perf. 13x12¾***

1328 A570 250m multi .60 .30

First 5+5 Dialogue Summit, Tunis — A571

2003, Dec. 5 ***Perf. 13¼***

1329 A571 600m multi 1.40 .60

Universal Declaration of Human Rights — A572

2003, Dec. 10 ***Perf. 13x12¾***

1330 A572 350m multi .85 .35

Silver Items — A573

Designs: No. 1331, 600m, Machmoum. No. 1332, 600m, Jewelry.

2003, Dec. 18 ***Perf. 12¾x13***

1331-1332 A573 Set of 2 2.75 1.25
a. Souvenir sheet, #1331-1332 4.50 2.50

No. 1332a sold for 1.50d.

African Soccer Championships A574

Designs: 250m, Stylized soccer players, African cup, map. 600m, Map of Africa as soccer player.

2004, Jan. 24 ***Perf. 13***

1333-1334 A574 Set of 2 1.90 .95

Values are for stamps with surrounding selvage.

Ksar Helal Congress, 70th Anniv. — A575

2004, Mar. 2 Litho. ***Perf. 13x12¾***

1335 A575 250m multi .60 .30

Arab League Conference, Tunis — A576

2004, May 22 ***Perf. 13***

1336 A576 600m multi 2.50 .60

Copper Handicrafts — A577

Designs: 100m, Water jar, 18th cent. 200m, Ewer, 18th cent. 250m, Bucket, 19th cent. 600m, Brazier, 18th cent. 700m, Amphora, 18th cent. 1000m, Ewer, 19th cent.

2004, June 5 ***Perf. 13x13¼***

1337-1342 A577 Set of 6 6.25 3.00
1343 Sheet, 3 each #1337, 1338, 1343a-1343d 7.50 3.75
a. A577 50m Like #1340 .25 .25
b. A577 150m Like #1342 .30 .25
c. A577 250m Like #1341 .60 .30
d. A577 300m Like #1339 .70 .35

No. 1343 sold for 3500m.

Coins and Banknotes — A578

Designs: No. 1344, 250m, Gold coin, 706. No. 1345, 250m, Gold coin, 1767. No. 1346, 600m, Punic silver coin, 300 B.C. No. 1347, 600m, Punic gold coin, 310-290 B.C. 1000m, Banknote, 1847 (65x30mm).

2004, July 23 ***Perf. 13¼***

1344-1348 A578 Set of 5 5.75 2.75
a. Souvenir sheet, #1344-1348 + label 5.75 2.75

No. 1348a sold for 3000m.

African Development Bank, 40th Anniv. — A579

2004, Sept. 10 Litho. ***Perf. 13***

1349 A579 700m multi 1.50 .75

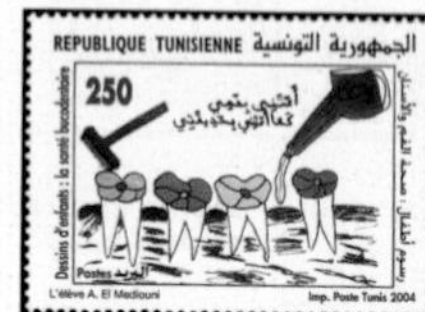

Children's Art — A580

2004, Oct. 20

1350 A580 250m multi .60 .30

Presidential and Legislative Elections — A581

2004, Oct. 24

1351 A581 250m multi .60 .30

Appointment of Pres. Zine El Abidine Ben Ali, 17th Anniv. — A582

2004, Nov. 7

1352 A582 250m multi .60 .30

El Abidine Mosque, Carthage A583

2004, Nov. 11

1353 A583 250m multi .60 .30

Birds — A584

Designs: 100m, Oxyura leucocephala. No. 1355, 600m, Phoenicurus moussieri. No. 1356, 600m, Aythya nyroca. 1000m, Marmaronetta angustirostris.

2004, Nov. 20 ***Perf. 13¼***

1354-1357 A584 Set of 4 6.00 2.50

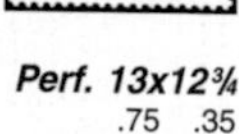

Universal Declaration of Human Rights — A585

2004, Dec. 10 ***Perf. 13x12¾***

1358 A585 350m multi .75 .35

Famous People — A586

Designs: 250m, Ibn Chabbat (1221-85), writer. 500m, Ibn Charaf (1000-67), writer. No. 1361, 600m, Princess Elyssa. No. 1362, 600m, Hatem El Mekki (1918-2003), stamp designer, and #580, 619. No. 1363, 600m, Dr. Mongi Ben Hmida (1928-2002), neurologist.

2004, Dec. 18 ***Perf. 12¾x13***

1359-1363 A586 Set of 5 6.00 2.75

World Handball Championships A587

2005, Jan. 23 ***Perf. 13***

1364 A587 600m multi 1.40 .60

Native Costumes — A588

Designs: 250m, Takhlila, Hammam Sousse. No. 1366, 390m, Tarf-Ras ceremonial costume, Kerkennah. No. 1367, 390m, Karmassoud jebba. 600m, Traditional bridal costume, Matmata.

2005, Mar. 16 ***Perf. 13x12¾***

1365-1368 A588 Set of 4 3.75 1.75

World Summit on the Information Society, Tunis — A589

2005, Apr. 7 Litho. ***Perf. 13***

1369 A589 600m multi 1.40 .60

Sculptures of the Punic and Roman Eras — A590

Designs: No. 1370, 250m, Victory, 2nd cent. No. 1371, 250m, Aesculapius, 2nd-3rd cent. 600m, Pottery mask of a woman's face, 4th-5th cent. B.C. 1000m, Baal Ammon, 1st cent.

2005, May 18 ***Perf. 13¼***

1370-1373 A590 Set of 4 5.00 2.25

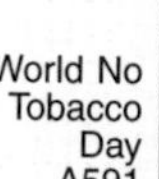

World No Tobacco Day A591

2005, May 31 ***Perf. 13¼x13***

1374 A591 250m multi .60 .30

Rotary International, Cent. — A592

2005, June 22 ***Perf. 13x12¾***

1375 A592 600m multi 1.50 .60

Intl. Year of Sport and Physical Education — A593

2005, July 1

1376 A593 600m multi 1.50 .60

World Scout Conference — A594

2005, Sept. 5

1377 A594 600m multi 1.50 .60

Intl. Year of Physics — A595

2005, Oct. 15 Litho. ***Perf. 13***

1378 A595 2d multi 5.00 2.00

Appointment of Pres. Zine El Abidine Ben Ali, 18th Anniv. — A596

2005, Nov. 8

1379 A596 250m multi .60 .25

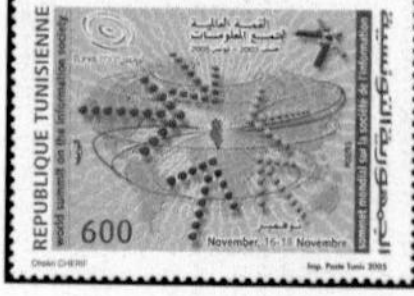

World Summit on the Information Society, Tunis A597

2005, Nov. 12 Litho. ***Perf. 13¼x13***

1380 A597 600m multi .90 .45

Universal Declaration of the Rights of Man, 57th Anniv. — A598

2005, Dec. 10 Litho. *Perf. 13*
1381 A598 350m multi 1.10 .55

Medicinal Plants — A599

Designs: 250m, Foeniculum. No. 1383, 600m, Mentha aquatica. No. 1384, 600m, Lavandula angustifloia. 1000m, Origanum majorana.

2005, Dec. 22
1382-1385 A599 Set of 4 5.50 2.50
1386 Booklet pane, 2 each #1383-1384, 1386a, 1386b 9.75 —
a. A599 600m Like #1382 1.40 .60
b. A599 600m Like #1385 1.40 .60
Complete booklet, #1386 11.00

Ibn Khaldun (1332-1406), Philosopher — A600

2006, Mar. 15 Litho. *Perf. 13x12¾*
1387 A600 390m multi 1.00 .45

A601

Independence, 50th Anniv. — A602

Designs: No. 1390, Stylized map and flag, doctor examining child. No. 1391, Bridge and ship. No. 1392, Stylized woman holding torch. No. 1393, Woman and book. No. 1394, Computer, man, woman, "@," and stylized dove.

2006, Mar. 18 *Perf. 13x12¾, 12¾x13*
1388 A601 250m shown .65 .30
1389 A602 250m shown .65 .30
1390 A601 250m multi .65 .30
1391 A601 250m multi .65 .30
1392 A601 390m multi .85 .40
1393 A601 390m multi .85 .40
1394 A601 390m multi .85 .40
a. Souvenir sheet, #1388-1394, + 2 labels 6.00 6.00
Nos. 1388-1394 (7) 5.15 2.40

No. 1394a sold for 2.50d.

Dialogue Among Civilizations and Religions — A603

2006, Apr. 26 Litho. *Perf. 13½*
1395 A603 1.35d multi 3.00 1.40

Punic and Roman Era Jewelry — A604

Designs: No. 1396, 250m, Gold and garnet vestment clasps. No. 1397, 250m, Gold-plated bronze earrings. No. 1398, 600m, Ring depicting god Baal Hammon. No. 1399, 600m, Gold and amethyst pendants.

2006, May 18 Litho. *Perf. 13¼*
1396-1399 A604 Set of 4 4.25 1.90

Special Handicapped Employment Program — A605

2006, May 29 *Perf. 13*
1400 A605 2.35d multi 5.50 2.25

National Cleanliness and Environmental Protection Program — A606

2006, June 11
1401 A606 250m multi .85 .30

2006 World Cup Soccer Championships, Germany — A607

Map, flags of Germany and Tunisia and: 250m, Feet of soccer players. 600m, Soccer player.

2006, June 14
1402-1403 A607 Set of 2 2.10 .95

Tunisian Army, 50th Anniv. — A608

2006, June 24
1404 A608 250m multi .65 .30

Diplomatic Relations Between Tunisia and Japan, 50th Anniv. — A609

2006, July 7
1405 A609 700m multi 1.60 .70

Vacation Safety Program A610

2006, July 31
1406 A610 250m multi .65 .30

Personal Status Code, 50th Anniv. — A611

2006, Aug. 8
1407 A611 2.35d multi 5.25 2.25

Appointment of Pres. Zine El Abidine Ben Ali, 19th Anniv. — A612

2006, Nov. 7
1408 A612 250m multi .75 .30

Universal Declaration of Human Rights A613

2006, Dec. 10
1409 A613 700m multi 1.60 .70

Traditional Clothing and Textiles — A614

Designs: No. 1410, 250m, Jelwa (wedding dress). No. 1411, 250m, Silk jebba. 1.10d, Klim. 1.35d, Woolen blanket from Gafsa.

2007, Mar. 16 Litho. *Perf. 13*
1410-1413 A614 Set of 4 8.00 3.25

Independence, 51st Anniv. — A615

2007, Mar. 20
1414 A615 250m multi .75 .30

Youth and Digital Culture — A616

2007, Mar. 21
1415 A616 250m multi 1.25 .30

Natl. Energy Conservation Program — A617

2007, Apr. 7
1416 A617 1d multi 3.00 1.00

Dialogue Between Cultures, Civilizations and Religions — A618

2007, May 7 Litho. *Perf. 13*
1417 A618 600m multi 1.75 .60

Archaeological Sites — A619

Designs: No. 1418, 250m, Baths of Caracalla, Dougga. No. 1419, 250m, Punic city of Kerkouane. No. 1420, 600m, Baths, Makthar. No. 1421, 600m, Capitol, Sbeitla.

2007, May 18 *Perf. 13½*
1418-1421 A619 Set of 4 4.50 1.90

Carthage Investment Forum A620

2007, June 21 *Perf. 13*
1422 A620 600m multi 1.60 .60

National Tourism Day — A621

Designs: No. 1423, 250m, Sahara tourism. No. 1424, 250m, Beach tourism. No. 1425, 600m, Tabarka Jazz Festival. No. 1426, 600m, Golf tourism.

2007, June 28
1423-1426 A621 Set of 4 5.00 1.90

A622

Republic of Tunisia, 50th Anniv. — A623

2007, July 25 Litho. *Perf. 13*
1427 A622 250m multi .75 .30
1428 A623 250m multi .75 .30

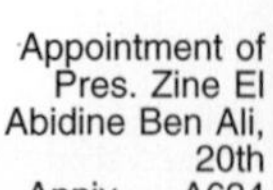

Appointment of Pres. Zine El Abidine Ben Ali, 20th Anniv. — A624

2007, Nov. 7 Litho. *Perf. 13*
1429 A624 250m multi .75 .30

Friendship Between Germany and Tunisia, 50th Anniv. — A625

2007, Dec. 17
1430 A625 600m multi 1.75 .60

Intl. Human Solidarity Day — A626

2007, Dec. 20
1431 A626 1.35d multi 3.50 1.50

French Air Raid on Sakiet Sidi Youssef, 50th Anniv. — A627

2008, Feb. 8 Litho. *Perf. 13*
1432 A627 250m multi .75 .30

Government Accounting Board, 40th Anniv. A628

2008, Mar. 8 Litho. *Perf. 13*
1433 A628 250m multi .60 .25

Universal Declaration of Human Rights, 60th Anniv. A629

2008, Mar. 10
1434 A629 600m multi 1.25 .55

World Meteorological Day — A630

2008, Mar. 23
1435 A630 250m multi .75 .25

Terra Cotta Objects — A631

Designs: 250m, Water jug, 19th cent. No. 1437, 600m, Goblet, 3rd cent. B.C. No. 1438, 600m, Plate, 10th cent. B.C. 1.10d, Lamp, 1st cent. B.C.

2008, May 18 *Perf. 13x12¾*
1436-1439 A631 Set of 4 6.00 3.00

National Day of the Disabled — A632

2008, May 29 *Perf. 13*
1440 A632 250m multi .65 .25

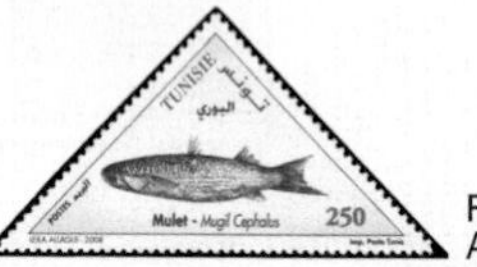

Fish A633

Designs: No. 1441, 250m, Mugil cephalus. No. 1442, 250m, Thunnus thynnus. No. 1443, 600m, Sparus aurata. No. 1444, 600m, Dicentrarchus labrax.

2008, June 5 Litho. *Perf. 13x13¼*
1441-1444 A633 Set of 4 4.00 2.00
a. As #1444, with incomplete frame lines 3.00 .55
b. As #1444, with incomplete frame lines 3.00 .55

No. 1444b sold for 1.800d.

Democratic Constitutional Rally — A634

2008, July 30 *Perf. 13*
1445 A634 250m multi .60 .25

Souvenir Sheet

Arab Post Day A635

No. 1446 — Emblem and: a, World map, pigeon. b, Camel caravan.

2008, Aug. 3 *Perf. 12¾*
1446 A635 600m Sheet of 2, #a-b 3.50 1.00

2008 Summer Olympics, Beijing — A636

Olympic rings, star and crescent, emblem of 2008 Summer Olympics, symbols of athletic events and: No. 1447, 250m, Colored dots and ribbons. No. 1448, 600m, Starbursts.

2008, Aug. 8 *Perf. 13½*
1447-1448 A636 Set of 2 2.00 1.00
a. Souvenir sheet of 2 #1447-1448 2.00 2.00

No. 1448a sold for 900m.

Dialogue With Youth — A637

2008, Sept. 20 Litho. *Perf. 13¼*
1449 A637 250m multi .75 .40

Appointment of Pres. Zine El Abidine Ben Ali, 21st Anniv. — A638

2008, Nov. 7 *Perf. 13x13¼*
1450 A638 250m multi .60 .30

University of Tunisia, 50th Anniv. A639

2008, Nov. 11 *Perf. 13¼x13*
1451 A639 250m multi .70 .35

Famous Men — A640

Designs: No. 1452, 250m, Ridha El Kalai (1931-2004), musician. No. 1453, 250m, Ammar Farhat (1911-87), painter. No. 1454, 600m, Mahmoud Messadi (1911-2004), writer. No. 1455, 600m, Hedi Jouini (1909-90), musician.

2008, Dec. 20 *Perf. 12¾x13, 13x12¾*
1452-1455 A640 Set of 4 3.50 1.75

Arab Maghreb Union, 20th Anniv. A641

2009, Feb. 17 Litho. *Perf. 13*
1456 A641 250m multi .50 .25

Aboul Qasem Chebbi (1909-34), Poet — A642

2009, Feb. 24 *Perf. 12¾*
1457 A642 250m multi .50 .25

Kairouan, 2009 Islamic Cultural Capital — A643

Designs: No. 1458, 250m, Mausoleum of Abi Zamaa al-Balawi. No. 1459, 250m, Okba Ibn Nafaa Mosque. 1000m, Emblem.

2009, Mar. 8
1458-1460 A643 Set of 3 3.00 1.50
a. Souvenir sheet, #1458-1460 3.00 3.00

Woven Fiber Crafts — A644

Designs: No. 1461, 250m, Esparto basket and jug holder. No. 1462, 250m, Rattan mat. No. 1463, 600m, Palm fiber fan. No. 1464, 600m, Rattan basket.

2009, Mar. 16 *Perf. 13¼*
1461-1464 A644 Set of 4 2.50 1.25

Intl. Society for Military Law and the Law of War, 18th Congress — A645

2009, May 5 Litho. *Perf. 13*
1465 A645 700m multi 1.25 .65

Constitution, 50th Anniv. A646

2009, June 1
1466 A646 250m multi .90 .45

Fruit — A647

Designs: 250m, Eryobotrica japonica. No. 1468, 600m, Cerasus spp. No. 1469, 600m, Ficus carica. No. 1470, 600m, Prunus persica.

2009, June 5 *Perf. 13¼*
1467-1470 A647 Set of 4 3.50 1.75
a. Sheet of 4, #1467-1470 3.50 3.50

No. 1470a sold for 2.10d.

16th Mediterranean Games, Pescara, Italy — A648

2009, June 26 Litho. *Perf. 13*
1471 A648 600m multi 1.00 .50

Presidential and Legislative Elections — A649

2009, Oct. 25 Litho. *Perf. 13x13¼*
1472 A649 250m multi .90 .45

Appointment of Pres. Zine El Abidine Ben Ali, 22nd Anniv. — A650

2009, Nov. 7
1473 A650 390m multi .90 .45

Universal Declaration of Human Rights, 61st Anniv. — A651

2009, Dec. 10
1474 A651 1.35d multi 2.50 1.25

Tunisian Cuisine — A652

Designs: 250m, Tajine à la viande (meat tagine). 700m, Salade mechouia (grilled vegetable salad). 1000m, Poisson grillé (grilled fish). 1100m, Couscous à la viande (couscous with meat).

2009, Dec. 26 *Perf. 13¼*
1475-1478 A652 Set of 4 6.00 3.00
a. Souvenir sheet of 4, #1475-1478 7.00 7.00

Arab Women's Day — A653

2010, Feb. 1 *Perf. 13¼x13*
1479 A653 1350m multi 3.00 1.50

Intl. Year of Rapprochement of Cultures — A654

2010, Feb. 6 *Perf. 13x13¼*
1480 A654 2350m multi 5.00 2.50

Intl. Youth Year A655

2010, Mar. 21 *Perf. 13¼x13*
1481 A655 390m multi .90 .45

Expo 2010, Shanghai — A656

2010, May 1 *Perf. 13¼*
1482 A656 390m multi .90 .45

Organic Foods and Food Products — A657

Designs: No. 1483, 250m, Cynara scolymus. No. 1484, 250m, Prunus dulcis. No. 1485, 250m, Punica granatum. No. 1486, 600m, Capsicum annuum. No. 1487, 600m, Opuntia ficus-indica. No. 1488, 600m, Solanum lycopersicum. No. 1489, 600m, Olea europaea and picher of olive oil. No. 1490, 600m, Phoenix dactylifera.

2010, May 12
1483-1490 A657 Set of 8 7.00 3.50
a. Souvenir sheet, #1483-1490 7.00 7.00

Tunisia, a Technological Pole — A658

2010, May 17 *Perf. 13*
1491 A658 390m multi .90 .45

Year of Peace and Security in Africa — A659

2010, June 25
1492 A659 250m multi .90 .45

Landmarks in Medina of Tunis — A660

Designs: No. 1493, 250m, Bab El Khadra. No. 1494, 250m, Bab Jedid. No. 1495, 250m, Dar Hsine. No. 1496, 250m, Dar Ben Abdallah. 600m, Bab Bhar. 1000m, Bab Saâdoun.

2010, July 2 *Perf. 12¾*
1493-1498 A660 Set of 6 4.00 2.00

2010 Youth Olympics, Singapore — A661

2010, Aug. 4 *Perf. 13*
1499 A661 700m multi 1.10 .55

Famous Men — A662

Designs: 250m, Zoubeir Turki (1924-2009), painter. 600m, Jaâfar Majed (1940-2009), poet. 1000m, Ali Ben Salem (1910-2001), painter. 1100m, Mustapha Khraief (1910-67), poet.

2010, Oct. 10 *Perf. 12¾*
1500-1503 A662 Set of 4 4.50 2.25

Third Congress of Organization of Arab Women, Tunis — A663

2010, Oct. 28 *Perf. 13*
1504 A663 1350m multi 2.25 1.00

Appointment of Pres. Zine El Abidine Ben Ali, 23rd Anniv. — A664

2010, Nov. 7
1505 A664 390m multi .90 .45

National Year of Tunisian Cinema — A665

2010, Nov. 27 Litho.
1506 A665 390m multi .90 .45

Universal Declaration of Human Rights, 62nd Anniv. — A666

2010, Dec. 10
1507 A666 390m multi .90 .45

A667

A668

A669

Revolution of 2010-11 — A670

2011, Mar. 25 Litho. *Perf. 13*

1508	A667	250m multi	.65	.35
1509	A668	390m multi	.90	.45
1510	A669	600m multi	1.40	.70
1511	A670	1350m multi	3.00	1.50
		Nos. 1508-1511 (4)	5.95	3.00

World Book and Copyright Day — A671

2011, Apr. 23
1512 A671 2350m multi 4.50 2.25

World Press Freedom Day — A672

2011, May 3
1513 A672 250m multi 1.25 .40

Children's Art — A673

Designs: 700m, I Love My Country, by Syrine Zouari. 1350m, Spring, by Mustapha Gader, vert.

2011, May 20 ***Perf. 13***
1514-1515 A673 Set of 2 4.75 2.50

Medicinal Plants — A674

Designs: No. 1516, 250m, Allium sativum. No. 1517, 250m, Pimpinella anisum. 600m, Lippia tryphilla. 1000m, Rosemarinus officinalis.

2011, June 28 ***Perf. 13¼***
1516-1519 A674 Set of 4 5.25 2.75

Phila Nippon 2011 Intl. Philatelic Exhibition, Yokahama, Japan — A675

2011, July 28
1520 A675 250m multi .65 .30

Human Rights Day — A676

2011, Dec. 10 ***Perf. 13***
1521 A676 390m multi .80 .40

January 14 Revolution, 1st Anniv. — A677

2012, Jan. 14
1522 A677 390m multi 1.60 .80

Pottery — A678

Designs: Nos. 1523, 1527a, 250m, Maajina plate. Nos. 1524, 1527b, 600m, Borniya jar. Nos. 1525, 1527c, 900m, Charbiya jug. Nos. 1526, 1527d, 1000m, Quallaline receptacle.

2012, Mar. 23 ***Perf. 13¼***
Stamps With White Backgrounds
1523-1526 A678 Set of 4 6.75 3.50
Souvenir Sheet
Stamps With Buff Backgrounds
1527 A678 Sheet of 4, #a-d 6.75 3.50

Organic Farming — A679

Organic: No. 1528, 250m, Melons. No. 1529, 250m, Strawberries. 600m, Grapes. 1350m, Honey.

2012, May 12 **Litho.** ***Perf. 13¼***
1528-1531 A679 Set of 4 5.50 2.75
a. Souvenir sheet of 4, #1528-1531 5.50 2.75

National Army, 56th Anniv. — A680

2012, June 24 ***Perf. 13***
1532 A680 700m multi 1.40 .70

Fish — A681

Designs: No. 1533, 250m, Saupe (Sarpa salpa). No. 1534, 250m, Marbré (Lithognathus mormyrus). 600m, Sardine (Sardina pilchardus). 1100m, Sparaillon (Diplodus sargus).

2012, Sept. 15 ***Perf. 13¼***
1533-1536 A681 Set of 4 5.50 2.75

Arab Post Day — A682

2012, Aug. 3 ***Perf. 13***
1537 A682 600m multi 1.40 .70

25th Universal Postal Congress, Doha, Qatar — A683

2012, Sept. 24
1538 A683 1000m multi 2.50 1.25

Values are for stamps with surrounding selvage.

Famous Tunisians — A684

Designs: No. 1539, 250m, Sheikh Salem Bouhajeb (1827-1926). No. 1540, 250m, Hamda Ben Tijani (1901-83), actor. 390m, Mohamed Bechrouch (1911-44), writer. 600m, Salah Khemissi (1912-58), singer. 900m, Sheikh Mohamed El Fadhel Ben Achour (1909-70), theologian. 1350m, Tawhida Ben Cheikh (1909-2010), physician.

2012, Oct. 16 ***Perf. 12¾x13***
1539-1544 A684 Set of 6 9.00 4.50

Intl. Anti-Corruption Day — A685

2012, Dec. 9 ***Perf. 13***
1545 A685 700m multi 1.60 .80

World Water Day — A686

2013, Mar. 22 ***Perf. 12¾***
1546 A686 2350m multi 4.75 2.50

Train Station, Tozeur A687

Medina, Tozeur A688

2013, Apr. 26
1547 A687 250m multi .50 .25
1548 A688 600m multi 1.20 .60

Kairouani Kufic Calligraphy A689

2013, May 18 ***Perf. 13***
1549 A689 250m multi .50 .25

African Union, 50th Anniv. — A690

2013, May 25 ***Perf. 13¼***
1550 A690 1100m multi 2.25 1.10

Handcrafted Wood Items — A691

Designs: No. 1551, 250m, Cooking utensils and spice rack (denomination in green). No. 1552, 250m, Rack (denomination in black). 600m, Mortar and pestle. 900m, Clothing box.

2013, June 28 **Litho.** ***Perf. 13¼***
1551-1554 A691 Set of 4 4.00 2.00

Traffic Accident Prevention — A692

2013, Aug. 7 **Litho.** ***Perf. 13***
1555 A692 1350m multi 2.75 1.50

Lighthouses A693

Designs: 250m, Cani Island Lighthouse. 600m, Galite Island Lighthouse. 700m, Borj Khadija Lighthouse. 1000m, Borj Jlij Lighthouse.

2013, Sept. 20 **Litho.** ***Perf. 12¾***
1556-1559 A693 Set of 4 4.75 2.50

See No. 1598A.

Parental Love — A694

2013, Oct. 18 **Litho.** ***Perf. 13***
1560 A694 250m multi .50 .25

Intl. Day Against Violence Towards Women — A695

2013, Nov. 25 **Litho.** ***Perf. 12¾***
1561 A695 600m multi 1.10 .55

Universal Declaration of Human Rights, 65th Anniv. — A696

2013, Dec. 10 **Litho.** ***Perf. 12¾***
1562 A696 600m multi 1.10 .55

Famous People — A697

Designs: No. 1563, 250m, Youssef Rekik (1940-2012), glass painter and playwright. No. 1564, 250m, Ibrahim Dhahhak (1931-2004), painter, vert. 600m, Taher Cheriaa (1927-2010), film maker. 1000m, Zoubeida Bechir (1938-2011), poet.

2013, Dec. 27 **Litho.** ***Perf. 12¾***
1563-1566 A697 Set of 4 3.50 1.75

Diplomatic Relations Between Tunisia and People's Republic of China, 50th Anniv. — A698

2014, Jan. 10 **Litho.** ***Perf. 13¼***
1567 A698 700m multi 1.25 .60

Adoption of New Constitution A699

2014, Feb. 7 **Litho.** ***Perf. 13***
1568 A699 1350m multi 2.25 1.10

Mediterranean Diet — A700

2014, Mar. 25 Litho. *Perf. 13*
1569 A700 2350m multi 4.00 2.00

Cities A701

Designs: 250m, Sfax. 600m, Djerba.

2014, Apr. 23 Litho. *Perf. 13*
1570-1571 A701 Set of 2 1.50 .75
a. Souvenir sheet of 2, #1570-1571 1.75 1.75

No. 1571a sold for 1d.

Labor Day — A702

Designs: 250m, Woman's hand, handicrafts. 390m, Books, chemical flasks and beakers.

2014, May 1 Litho. *Perf. 13*
1572-1573 A702 Set of 2 1.00 .50

A703

National Cleanliness and Environmental Maintenance Day — A704

2014, June 11 Litho. *Perf. 12¾*
1574 A703 250m multi .40 .25
1575 A704 1000m multi 1.50 .75

Postal Forum on Electronic Commerce, Hammamet A705

2014, Sept. 22 Litho. *Perf. 13*
1576 A705 600m multi .70 .35
a. Souvenir sheet of 1 1.10 1.10

No. 1576a sold for 1d.

Stamp Day — A706

2014, Oct. 9 Litho. *Perf. 13*
1577 A706 250m multi .30 .25

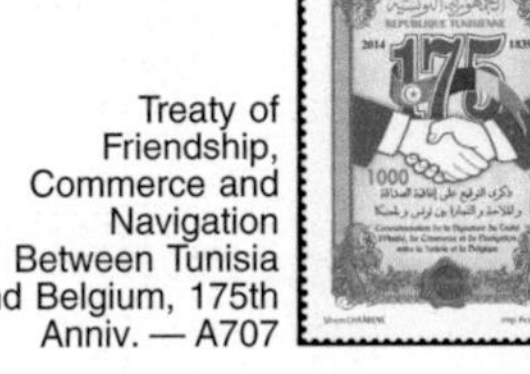
Treaty of Friendship, Commerce and Navigation Between Tunisia and Belgium, 175th Anniv. — A707

2014, Oct. 14 Litho. *Perf. 13*
1578 A707 1000m multi 1.10 .55

World Rural Women's Day — A708

2014, Oct. 15 Litho. *Perf. 13*
1579 A708 2350m multi 2.60 1.40

Lighthouses A709

Designs: 900m, Taguermess Lighthouse. 1350m, Sidi Bou Said Lighthouse.

2014, Nov. 18 Litho. *Perf. 12¾*
1580-1581 A709 Set of 2 2.50 1.25

See No. 1598A.

Butterflies A710

Designs: No. 1582, 250m, Pyronia cecilia. No. 1583, 250m, Zegris eupheme. No. 1584, 250m, Spialia sertorius. 600m. Pieris brassicae.

2014, Dec. 19 Litho. *Perf. 13*
1582-1585 A710 Set of 4 1.50 .75
a. Souvenir sheet of 4, #1582-1585 1.90 1.90

No. 1585a sold for 1750m.

Traditional Pottery — A711

Designs: Nos. 1586, 1590a, 250m, Djerba jar. Nos. 1587, 1590b, 600m, Sejnane couscous pot. Nos. 1588, 1590c, 700m, Jars without decoration. Nos. 1589, 1590d, 1000m, Qalllaline two-handled jar.

2015, Mar. 16 Litho. *Perf. 13x13¼*
Stamps With White Frames
1586-1589 A711 Set of 4 2.75 1.40

Souvenir Sheet
Stamps With Colored Frames
Imperf
1590 A711 Sheet of 4, #a-d 3.25 3.25

No. 1590 sold for 3d. Stamps on No. 1590 have simulated perforations.

Room in Palace of the Beys — A712

2015, Apr. 18 Litho. *Perf. 12¾*
1591 A712 600m multi .65 .30

A713

Youth Training — A714

2015, May 1 Litho. *Perf. 12¾*
1592 A713 250m multi .30 .25
1593 A714 250m multi .30 .25

Fauna — A715

Designs: 700m, Houbara bustard. 1000m, Arabian horse, horiz.

2015, June 2 Litho. *Perf. 12¾*
1594-1595 A715 Set of 2 1.75 .85

Homage to Tunisian Army Martyrs A716

2015, June 15 Litho. *Perf. 13*
1596 A716 2350m multi 2.40 1.25

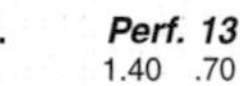
Ship A717

2015, July 9 Litho. *Perf. 13*
1597 A717 1350m multi 1.40 .70

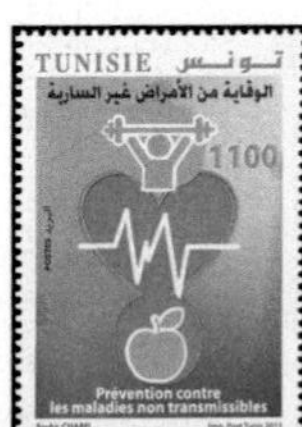
Disease Prevention — A718

2015, July 28 Litho. *Perf. 13*
1598 A718 1100m multi 1.10 .55

Lighthouse Types of 2013-14
Miniature Sheet

2015, Sept. 1 Litho. *Perf. 12¾*
1598A Sheet of 5 2.00 1.25
a. A693 390m Like #1557 .40 .25
b. A693 390m Like #1556 .40 .25
c. A693 390m Like #1558 .40 .25
d. A709 390m Like #1580 .40 .25
e. A709 390m Like #1581 .40 .25

Campaign Against Sports Doping — A719

2015, Sept. 10 Litho. *Perf. 13*
1599 A719 900m multi .95 .45

International Year of Soils — A720

2015, Oct. 16 Litho. *Perf. 13*
1600 A720 250m multi .25 .25

United Nations, 70th Anniv. — A721

2015, Oct. 24 Litho. *Perf. 13*
1601 A721 1000m multi 1.00 .50

Awarding of 2015 Nobel Peace Prize to the Tunisian National Dialogue Quartet — A722

2015, Dec. 10 Litho. *Perf. 13*
1602 A722 2000m multi 2.00 1.00
a. Souvenir sheet of 1 3.00 3.00

No, 1602a sold for 3d.

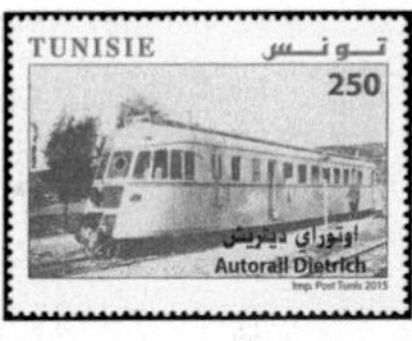
Old Trains A723

Designs: No. 1603, 250m, Dietrich rail cars. No. 1604, 250m, Tunis trams. 390m, Decauville rail cars. 600m, Lezard Rouge train.

2015, Dec. 22 Litho. *Perf. 13*
1603-1606 A723 Set of 4 1.50 .75

Tunisian General Labor Union, 70th Anniv. — A724

2016, Jan. 20 Litho. *Perf. 13*
1607 A724 250m multi .25 .25

World Day of Civil Protection A725

2016, Mar. 1 Litho. *Perf. 13*
1608 A725 250m multi .25 .25

Independence, 60th Anniv. — A726

2016, Mar. 20 Litho. *Perf. 13*
1609 A726 1000m multi 1.00 .50

First Cooperation Agreement Between Tunisia and the European Union, 40th Anniv. — A727

2016, Apr. 25 Litho. *Perf. 13*
1610 A727 2350m multi 2.40 1.25

A728

A729

Sfax, 2016 Capital of Arab Culture — A730

2016, May 20 Litho. *Perf. 12¾*
1611 A728 250m multi .25 .25
1612 A729 600m multi .60 .30
1613 A730 1350m multi 1.25 .65
Nos. 1611-1613 (3) 2.10 1.20

Tunisian Television, 50th Anniv. A731

2016, May 31 Litho. *Perf. 13*
1614 A731 250m multi .25 .25

Tunisian Army, 60th Anniv. — A732

2016, June 24 Litho. *Perf. 13*
1615 A732 250m multi .25 .25

Diplomatic Relations Between Tunisia and Japan, 60th Anniv. — A733

2016, July 7 Litho. *Perf. 13*
1616 A733 1000m multi .90 .45

Ministry of Foreign Affairs, 60th Anniv. A734

2016, Aug. 1 Litho. *Perf. 13*
1617 A734 900m multi .85 .40

Arab Postal Day A735

No. 1618: a, Blue background, denomination at left. b, Green background, denomination at right.

2016, Aug. 3 Litho. *Perf. 12¾*
1618 A735 600m Horiz. pair, #a-b 1.10 .55

National Postal Savings, 60th Anniv. — A736

2016, Aug. 28 Litho. *Perf. 13*
1619 A736 500m multi .45 .25

Conifers — A737

Designs: 50m, Pinus pinea branch, cones and nuts, jar with nuts. 900m, Pinus halepensis tree, branch and cones. 1000d, Pinus halepensis branch, cones, and nuts, bowl. 2000d, Pinus pinea tree and cones.

2016, Sept. 20 Litho. *Perf. 13¼*
1620-1623 A737 Set of 4 3.75 1.90
1622a Without "Pin d'Alep" inscription .95 .45
1623a Souvenir sheet of 4, #1620, 1621, 1622a, 1623 3.75 1.90

No. 1623a sold for 4d.

National Family Planning Program, 50th Anniv. — A738

2016, Oct. 13 Litho. *Perf. 13*
1624 A738 500m multi .45 .25

Ahmed Tlili (1916-67), Labor Union Leader — A739

2016, Oct. 16 Litho. *Perf. 13¼x13*
1625 A739 1200m multi 1.10 .55

World Telecommunication Standardization Assembly, Yasmine Hammamet A740

2016, Oct. 25 Litho. *Perf. 13*
1626 A740 2000m multi 1.90 .95

Miniature Sheet

United Nations Sustainable Development Goals — A741

No. 1627: a, Heart and "3." b, Steaming bowl and "2." c, Stylized men, women, children and "1." d, United Nations Headquarters, New York. e, United Nations Headquarters, United Nations emblem and Tunisian flag. f, Arrow on graph and "8." g, Power button in sun and "7." h, Water drop in glass, arrow and "6." i, Combined male and female symbols and "5." j, Book, pencil and "4." k, Globe in eye and "13." l, Arrow in shape of infinity symbol and "12." m, Buildings and "11." n, Equal sign in circle and "10." o, Cubes and "9." p, Sustainable Development Goals emblem and Arabic text. q, Five linked circles and "17." r, Dove on gavel and "16." s, Tree, birds and "15." t, Fish in water and "14."

2016, Nov. 12 Litho. *Perf. 13¼*
1627 A741 500m Sheet of 20, #a-t 8.75 4.50

Tunisia's admission to United Nations, 60th anniv.

Famous People — A742

Designs: 500m, Bchira Ben Mrad (1913-93), founder of Muslim Women's Union of Tunisia. 1000m, Tahar Ben Ammar (1889-1985), Prime Minister.

2016, Dec. 15 Litho. *Perf. 12¾*
1628-1629 A742 Set of 2 1.50 .75

Tunisian Union of Industry, Commerce and Handicrafts, 70th Anniv. A743

2017, Jan. 17 Litho. *Perf. 13*
1630 A743 2000m multi 2.00 1.00

National Internet Freedom Day — A744

Designs: 900m, Zouhair Yahyaoui (1967-2005), convicted cyber-dissident. 1200m, Birds and network.

2017, Mar. 13 Litho. *Perf. 12¾*
1631-1632 A744 Set of 2 2.10 1.10

Mohamed Sghaier Ouled Ahmed (1955-2016), Poet — A745

2017, Apr. 5 Litho. *Perf. 13*
1633 A745 1000m multi .85 .40

Support for Investment in Tunisia A746

2017, Apr. 20 Litho. *Perf. 13*
1634 A746 2000m multi 1.75 .85

Rouis Primary School, Médenine A747

2017, Apr. 24 Litho. *Perf. 13x13¼*
1635 A747 500m multi .40 .25

Monastir — A748

2017, May 24 Litho. *Perf. 12¾*
1636 A748 500m multi .45 .25

Mosques — A749

Designs: No. 1637, 500m, Al Baji Mosque, Sidi Bou Said. No. 1638, 500m, Chenini Mosque, Tataouine.

2017, June 15 Litho. *Perf. 13¼*
1637-1638 A749 Set of 2 .85 .40

Olive Trees — A750

Designs: 900m, Lakarit olive tree, Doiret. 3000m, Zarrazi olive tree.

2017, July 9 Litho. *Perf. 13x13¼*
1639-1640 A750 Set of 2 3.25 1.60

53rd Carthage International Festival — A751

2017, July 13 Litho. *Perf. 13*
1641 A751 1000m multi .85 .40

Republic of Tunisia, 60th Anniv. — A752

2017, July 25 **Litho.** ***Perf. 13***
1642 A752 500m multi .45 .25

Habib Achour (1913-99), Founder of Tunisian General Labor Union — A753

2017, Aug. 5 **Litho.** ***Perf. 12¾***
1643 A753 1200m multi 1.00 .50

Victory in 2016 Battle of Ben Guerdane A754

2017, Sept. 11 **Litho.** ***Perf. 12¾***
1644 A754 2000m multi 1.60 .80

A755

Transitional Justice Process — A756

Design: 500m, The public open session. 2000m, Logo of the Instance.

2017, Sept. 26 **Litho.** ***Perf. 12¾***
1645 A755 500m multi .40 .25
1646 A756 2000m multi 1.60 .80

Archaeology A757

Designs: No. 1647, 500m, Amphitheater, Oudhna. No. 1648, 500m, Arches, Great Baths of Makthar. 1000m, Artifact from Chimtou Archaeological Museum. 1200m, Lion mosaic, Salakta.

2017, Oct. 20 **Litho.** ***Perf. 12¾***
1647-1650 A757 Set of 4 2.60 1.40
a. Souvenir sheet of 4, #1647-1650 2.60 1.40

Taher Cheriaa (1927-2010), Film Critic and Founder of Carthage Film Festival — A757a

National Year of Tunisian Cinema — A757b

2017 **Litho.** ***Perf. 12¾***
1650B A757a 1d multi .80 .40
Perf. 13
1650C A757b 1.20d multi 1.00 .50

Citrus Fruits — A758

Designs: 50m, Mandarin oranges. No. 1652, 500m, Eureka lemons. No. 1653, 500m, Maltese oranges. 4d, Sweet lemons.

2017, Nov. 22 **Litho.** ***Perf. 13¼***
1651-1654 A758 Set of 4 4.25 2.10

National Archives Day — A759

2017, Dec. 9 **Litho.** ***Perf. 12¾***
1655 A759 2d multi 1.75 .85

Tunisia Post Stamp Printing Plant, 20th Anniv. — A760

2017, Dec. 18 **Litho.** ***Perf. 13***
1656 A760 1.20d multi 1.00 .50

Tourism — A761

Designs: No. 1657, 1d, Midès Oasis. No. 1658, 1d, Cap Blanc. No. 1659, 1.20d, Jugurtha Tableland. No. 1660, 1.20d, El Haouaria.

2018, Feb. 14 **Litho.** ***Perf. 12¾***
1657-1660 A761 Set of 4 3.75 1.90

Holiday Colonies and Patronage National Childhood Organization, 70th Anniv. — A762

2018, Mar. 1 **Litho.** ***Perf. 13x13¼***
1661 A762 500m multi .45 .25

Court of Accounts, 50th Anniv. — A763

2018, Mar. 8 **Litho.** ***Perf. 12¾***
1662 A763 500m multi .45 .25

Handicrafts From Sejnane — A764

Designs: 500m. Pottery. 2d, Clay dolls.

2018, Mar. 16 **Litho.** ***Perf. 13½***
1663-1664 A764 Set of 2 2.10 1.10
a. Souvenir sheet of 2, #1663-1664 2.10 1.10

Amnesty International in Tunisia, 30th Anniv. — A765

2018, Apr. 12 **Litho.** ***Perf. 12¾***
1665 A765 110m multi .25 .25

Taoufik Baccar (1927-2017), Literary Critic — A766

2018, Apr. 24 **Litho.** ***Perf. 13***
1666 A766 900m multi .75 .35

Mohamed Ezzedine Mili (1917-2013), Secretary General of International Telecommunication Union — A767

2018, May 10 **Litho.** ***Perf. 13***
1667 A767 500m multi .40 .25

Postal Current Accounts, Cent. — A768

2018, May 27 **Litho.** ***Perf. 13***
1668 A768 4d multi 3.25 1.60

2018 World Cup Soccer Championships, Russia — A769

2018, June 14 **Litho.** ***Perf. 13***
1669 A769 500m multi .40 .25

Values are for stamps with surrounding selvage.

Houses of the Mediterranean Area — A770

Various houses with denomination in: No. 1670, 1.20d, Red. No. 1671, 1.20d, Dark violet.

2018, July 9 **Litho.** ***Perf. 12¾***
1670-1671 A770 Set of 2 1.90 .95
a. Souvenir sheet of 2, #1670-1671 1.90 .95

60th International Festival of Sousse — A771

2018, July 15 **Litho.** ***Perf. 13***
1672 A771 900m multi .70 .35

Souvenir Sheet

Nelson Mandela (1918-2013), President of South Africa — A772

2018, July 18 **Litho.** ***Perf. 13¼***
1673 A772 500m multi .40 .25

Habib Bourguiba (1903-2000), First Minister of Foreign Affairs and First President — A773

2018, July 31 **Litho.** ***Perf. 13***
1674 A773 500m multi .40 .25

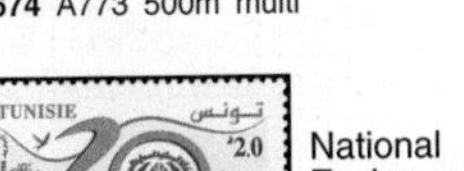

National Environmental Protection Agency, 30th Anniv. — A774

2018, Aug. 2 **Litho.** ***Perf. 12¾***
1675 A774 2d multi 1.50 .75

National Real Estate Company of Tunisia — A775

2018, Sept. 2 **Litho.** ***Perf. 12¾***
1676 A775 500m multi .40 .25

Hédi Chaker (1908-53), Assassinated Politician — A776

2018, Sept. 13 **Litho.** ***Perf. 13***
1677 A776 2d multi 1.50 .75

Tunisia No. 1 — A777

2018, Oct. 9 **Litho.** ***Perf. 13***
1678 A777 2d multi 1.40 .70

Tunisian postage stamps, 130th anniv.

Tunisair, 70th Anniv. A778

2018, Oct. 21 **Litho.** ***Perf. 13***
1679 A778 1.20d multi .85 .40

Mohandas K. Gandhi (1869-1948), Indian Nationalist Leader — A779

2018, Nov. 5 Litho. *Perf. 12¾*
1680 A779 1d multi .70 .35

Calligraphy by Mohamed Salah Khammassi (1910-92) A780

2018, Nov. 10 Litho. *Perf. 13*
1681 A780 2d multi 1.40 .70

Homage to Killed Presidential Security Team Members — A781

2018, Nov. 24 Litho. *Perf. 13*
1682 A781 500m multi .35 .25

Campaign Against Corruption — A782

2018, Dec. 8 Litho. *Perf. 13*
1683 A782 1d multi .70 .35

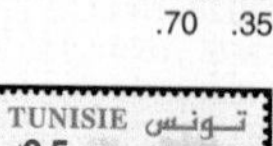

Fauna — A783

Inscriptions: 500m, Orphie (garfish). 900m, Chacal doré (golden jackal). 1d, Pica pica. 2d, Cervus elaphus barbarus.

2018, Dec. 18 Litho. *Perf. 13¼*
1684-1687 A783 Set of 4 3.00 1.50
1687a Souvenir sheet of 4, #1684-1687 3.50 1.75

No. 1687a sold for 5d.

Espérance Sportive de Tunis Sports Club, Cent. — A784

2019, Jan. 15 Litho. *Perf. 12¾*
1688 A784 500m multi .35 .25

Size: 40x40mm
Denomination at Upper Left
Perf. 13

1689 A784 2d multi 1.40 .70

Souvenir Sheet
Denomination at Upper Right

1690 A784 5d multi 3.50 1.75

No. 1690 contains one 37x52mm stamp.

Tunis Stock Exchange, 50th Anniv. — A785

2019, Mar. 6 Litho. *Perf. 13*
1691 A785 250m multi .25 .25

2019 Arab Summit, Tunis — A786

2019, Mar. 31 Litho. *Perf. 12¾*
1692 A786 500m multi .35 .25

Tunis, 2019 Capital of Islamic Culture — A787

2019, May 5 Litho. *Perf. 13*
1693 A787 1.50d multi 1.00 .50

Ghriba Synagogue, Djerba A788

2019, May 15 Litho. *Perf. 13*
1694 A788 1.50d multi 1.00 .50

Endangered Animals — A789

Designs: 250m, Mogod pony. 500m, Addax. 1d, Oryx.

2019, May 22 Litho. *Perf. 13*
1695-1697 A789 Set of 3 1.25 .60
1697a Souvenir sheet of 3, #1695-1697 1.40 .70

No. 1697a sold for 2d.

International Labor Organization, Cent. — A790

2019, June 1 Litho. *Perf. 13*
1698 A790 2d multi 1.40 .70

Husainid Beys — A791

Designs: 50m, Al-Husayn I ibn Ali (1669-1740). 500m, Ahmed I ibn Mustafa (1805-55). 750m, Muhammad VII al-Munsif (1881-1948). 900m, Hammuda ibn Ali (1759-1814).

2019, June 10 Litho. *Perf. 12¾*
1699-1702 A791 Set of 4 1.60 .80
1702a Souvenir sheet of 4, #1699-1702 — —

No. 1702a sold for 3d.

Palais de la Rose National Military Museum, Manouba A792

Patrol Vessel Istiklal A793

2019, June 25 Litho. *Perf. 13*
1703 A792 750m multi .55 .25
1704 A793 3d multi 2.10 1.10

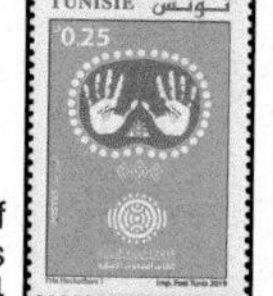

International Year of Indigenous Languages — A794

No. 1705 — Country name in red with background in: a, Pale orange. b, Deep violet blue. c, Orange brown. d, Blue.

2019, July 18 Litho. *Perf. 12¾*
1705 Horiz strip of 4 + flanking label — —
a.-d. A794 250m Any single — —

Traditional Costumes — A795

Euromed Postal emblem and: 750m, Woman. 1d, Man.

2019, Sept. 5 Litho. *Perf. 12¾*
1706-1707 A795 Set of 2 1.25 .65

Express Mail Service, 20th Anniv. — A796

2019, Sept. 10 Litho. *Perf. 12¾*
1708 A796 2d multi 1.40 .70

Seed and Food Sovereignty — A797

Designs: 750m, Children and farm field. 1.50d, Hands and grain.

2019, Oct. 4 Litho. *Perf. 13*
1709-1710 A797 Set of 2 1.60 .80

Rafik El Kamel, Painter — A798

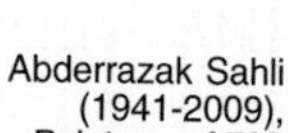

Abderrazak Sahli (1941-2009), Painter — A799

2019, Nov. 8 Litho. *Perf. 12¾*
1711 A798 750m multi .55 .25
1712 A799 1d multi .70 .35

Flag of Palestinian Authority, Doves, Dome of the Rock, Jerusalem A800

2019, Nov. 20 Litho. *Perf. 12¾*
1713 A800 1.50d multi 1.10 .55
a. Souvenir sheet of 1 2.10 1.10

Jerusalem, capital of the Palestinian Authority. No. 1713a sold for 3d.

Tunisia as Member of United Nations Security Council in 2020-21 — A801

2019, Dec. 16 Litho. *Perf. 14¼x14*
1714 A801 2d multi — —

Elimination of Racial Discrimination A802

2019, Dec. 20 Litho. *Perf. 14x14¼*
1715 A802 250m multi .25 .25

Pope Victor I (d. 199) — A803

Pope Gelasius I (d. 496) — A804

Pope Miltiades (d. 314) — A805

2019, Dec. 25 Litho. *Perf. 14x14¼*
1716 A803 750m multi .55 .25

Perf. 14¼x14

1717 A804 1d multi .75 .35
1718 A805 2d multi 1.50 .75
Nos. 1716-1718 (3) 2.80 1.35

Popes from Africa.

Architectural Sites, Monuments and Tourist Attractions A806

Designs: 750m, Ghar El Mleh Fort. 1d, Ruins, Althiburos. 1.50d, Haidra Archaeological Site. 2d, Ain Dhab Cave of Djebel Serj.

2019, Dec. 29 Litho. *Perf. 14x14¼*
1719-1722 A806 Set of 4 3.75 1.90

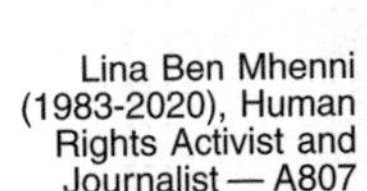

Lina Ben Mhenni (1983-2020), Human Rights Activist and Journalist — A807

2020, Mar. 5 Litho. *Perf. 14¼x14*
1723 A807 3d multi 2.10 1.10

Chokri Belaid (1964-2013), Lawyer A808

Mohamed Brahmi (1955-2013), Politician A809

2020, Apr. 9 Litho. *Perf. 14¼x14*
1724 A808 750m multi .55 .25
1725 A809 750m multi .55 .25

Kantaoui Dahmane, Postal Official — A810

2020, Apr. 11 Litho. *Perf. 14¼x14*
1726 A810 1.50d multi 1.10 .55

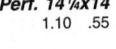

International Year of Plant Health — A811

2020, May 12 Litho. *Perf. 14¼x14*
1727 A811 750m multi .55 .25

Djebel Bliji Rock Painting — A812

Djebel Ousselet Rock Painting — A813

2020, June 2 Litho. *Perf. 14x14¼*
1728 A812 750m multi .55 .25
1729 A813 2d multi 1.40 .70

Dams — A814

Designs: 750m, Sidi El-Barraq Dam, Béja. 1d, Beni Mtir Dam, Jendouba. 1.50d, Oued Mellègue Dam, Le Kef. 2d, Nebhana Dam, Kairouan.

2020, June 24 Litho. *Perf. 14x14¼*
1730-1733 A814 Set of 4 3.75 1.90

Traditional Dishes — A815

Designs: 750m, Chakchouka (tomato stew). 2d, Borzguène (lamb with couscous, nuts and dried fruits).

2020, July 15 Litho. *Perf. 14x14¼*
1734-1735 A815 Set fo 2 2.00 1.00

Arab Postal Day — A816

2020, Aug. 3 Litho. *Perf. 14¼x14*
1736 A816 1.50d multi 1.10 .55

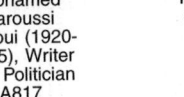

Mohamed Laroussi Metoui (1920-2005), Writer and Politician A817

Hedi Labidi (1911-85), Journalist A818

2020, Sept. 27 Litho. *Perf. 14¼x14*
1737 A817 1d multi — —
1738 A818 1.50d multi — —

Emblem of Club Africain Soccer Team A819

Béchir Ben Mustapha, Founder and First President of Club Africain A820

2020, Oct. 4 Litho. *Perf. 14x14¼*
1739 A819 750m red & black — —

Perf. 14¼x14
1740 A820 2d multi — —

Club Africain, cent.

United Nations, 75th Anniv. — A821

2020, Oct. 24 Litho. *Perf. 14x14¼*
1741 A821 750m multi .55 .30

Ouled Soltane Fortified Granary, Tataouine — A822

2020, Nov. 5 Litho. *Perf. 14¼x14*
1742 A822 1d multi — —

Ficus Macrophylla A823

2020, Nov. 24 Litho. *Perf. 14x14¼*
1743 A823 750m multi — —

A souvenir sheet containing an imperforate example of No. 1743 with simulated perfs sold for 2d.

National Social Security Fund, 60th Anniv. A824

2020, Dec. 14 Litho. *Perf. 13*
1744 A824 750m multi — —

Campaign Against the COVID-19 Pandemic A825

2020, Dec. 17 Litho. *Perf. 14x14¼*
1745 A825 3d multi — —
a. Souvenir sheet of 1, imperf. — —

No. 1745a sold for 3.50d.

Tunis-Afrique-Presse News Agency, 60th Anniv. — A826

2021, Jan. 12 Litho. *Perf. 13*
1746 A826 750m multi .55 .30

Abolition of Slavery in Tunisia, 175th Anniv. A827

2021, Jan. 23 Litho. *Perf. 13*
1747 A827 2d multi 1.50 .75

Assabah Newspaper, 70th Anniv. — A828

2021, Feb. 9 Litho. *Perf. 13*
1748 A828 750m multi .55 .30

Tapestries by Safia Farhat (1924-2004) — A829

No. 1749: a, 750m, Gafsa and Elsewhere (detail, 20x30mm). b, 900m, The Couple (20x30mm). c, 4d, Gafsa and Elsewhere, (detail, 40x30mm).

2021, Mar. 16 Litho. *Perf. 13x13¼*
1749 A829 Horiz. strip of 3, #a-c 4.25 2.10

Military and Commercial Port of Carthage A830

2021, Apr. 20 Litho. *Perf. 13*
1750 A830 750m multi — —

A831

A832

A833

Street Art — A834

2021, May 20 Litho. *Perf. 13*
1751 A831 750m multi — —
1752 A832 900m multi — —
1753 A833 3d multi — —
1754 A834 4d multi — —

Marine Life — A835

No. 1755: a, Serranus scriba. b, Octopus vulgaris. c, Cratena peregrina. d, Loligo vulgaris.

2021, June 1 Litho. *Perf. 13*
1755 Strip of 4 — —
a. A835 250m multi — —
b. A835 750m multi — —
c. A835 900m multi — —
d. A835 1d multi — —
e. Souvenir sheet of 4, #1755a-1755d — —

No. 1755e sold for 3.50d.

Idarti Service Houses Project — A836

2021, June 21 Litho. *Perf. 13*
1756 A836 1.20d multi — —

Jewelry — A837

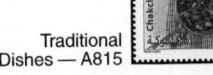

Designs: 900m, Khomsa necklace. 4d, Tlila necklace.

2021, July 15 Litho. *Perf. 13*
1757-1758 A837 Set of 2 — —

Values are for stamps with surrounding selvage.

Hamadi Agrebi (1951-2020), Soccer Player — A838

2021, Aug. 21 **Litho.** ***Perf. 13***
1759 A838 1.20d multi — —

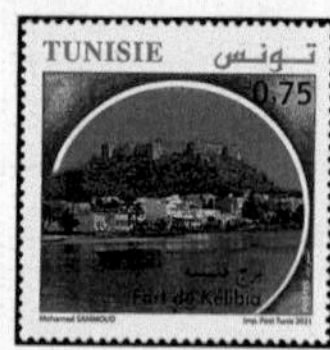

Forts — A839

Designs: 750m, Kélibia Fort. 900m, Mahdia Fort. 1d, Hammamet Fort. 3d, Tabarka Fort.

2021, Sept. 10 **Litho.** ***Perf. 13***
1760-1763 A839 Set of 4 — —

Mathematics — A840

Physics — A841

Robotics A842

Coding — A843

2021, Sept. 30 **Litho.** ***Perf. 13***
1764 A840 750m multi — —
1765 A841 1.20d multi — —
1766 A842 2.50d multi — —
1767 A843 4d multi — —

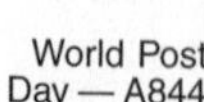

World Post Day — A844

2021, Oct. 9 **Litho.** ***Perf. 13***
1768 A844 750m multi — —

Medjerda River — A845

2021, Oct. 24 **Litho.** ***Perf. 12¾x13***
1769 A845 1.20d multi — —

Joint issue between Tunisia and Algeria. See Algeria No. 1826.

Musicians — A846

No. 1770: a, 2d, Gnaoua musicians, Morocco. b, 3d, Stambali musicians, Tunisia.

2021, Dec. 2 **Litho.** ***Perf. 13***
1770 A846 Horiz. pair, #a-b — —

Joint issue between Tunisia and Morocco. See Morocco No. 1310.

Transfer of Control of Customs Department to Tunisian Officials, 65th Anniv. A847

2021, Dec. 6 **Litho.** ***Perf. 13***
1771 A847 750m multi — —

Famous Men — A848

Designs: 750m, Gilbert Naccache (1939-2020), writer. 1.20d, Chedli Klibi (1925-2020), Minister of Culture.

2021, Dec. 15 **Litho.** ***Perf. 13***
1772-1773 A848 Set of 2 — —

Aerial View of Tataouine Land Formations A849

2022, Mar. 7 **Litho.** ***Perf. 13¾***
1774 A849 750m multi — —

Values are for stamps with surrounding selvage.

Independence Day — A850

Perf. 14 Syncopated

2022, Mar. 20 **Litho.**
1775 A850 900m multi — —

Tunisian Company of Electricity and Gas, 60th Anniv. — A851

Perf. 14x13¾ Syncopated

2022, Apr. 3 **Litho.**
1776 A851 4d multi — —

Flowers — A852

Designs: 750m, Thymbra capitata. 900m, Globularia alypum. 1d, Chamaemelum nobile. 1.20d, Salvia officinalis.

Perf. 14x13½ Syncopated

2022, Apr. 15 **Litho.**
1777-1780 A852 Set of 4 — —
1780a Souvenir sheet of 4, #1777-1780 — —

No. 1780a sold for 5d.

Ecotourism A853

Designs: 750m, Kesra. 1.20d, Dahar.

Perf. 14x13¼ Syncopated

2022, June 1 **Litho.**
1781-1782 A853 Set of 2 — —

Ships From Military Museum, Manouba — A854

Designs: 750m, Carthaginian military vessel. 4d, Chebec.

Perf. 14x13¼ Syncopated

2022, June 24 **Litho.**
1783-1784 A854 Set of 2 — —

Tunisian-Egyptian Cultural Year — A855

Perf. 13¼x14 Syncopated

2022, June 30 **Litho.**
1785 A855 900m multi — —

See Egypt No. 2271.

Takrouna A856

Testour A857

Perf. 14x13¼ Syncopated

2022, July 11 **Litho.**
1786 A856 750m multi — —

Perf. 13¼x14 Syncopated

1787 A857 750m multi — —

Miniature Sheet

Tunisian Women A858

No. 1788: a, Fatima Haddad (1936-2013), philosopher. b, Maya Jribi (1960-2018), politician. c, Agricultural worker (Les ouvrières agricoles). d, Zaara Soltani (1955-2020), mother of two sons murdered by Jihadists. e, Moufida Tlatli (1947-2021), movie director. f, Zohra Faiza (1919-99), actress. g, Naama (1934-2020), singer. h, Raja Ben Ammar (c. 1954-2017), actress. i, Azza Hammou (1950-2017), pediatric radiologist. j, Fattouma Namla (1935-94), labor union activist. k, Cherifa Messaidi (1908-90), teacher and labor union activist. l. Semia Akrout (1955-2015), architect. m, Sophonisba (235 B.C.-203 B.C.) Carthaginian princess. n, Zeineb Farhat (1957-2021), human rights activist and theater manager. o, Gladys Adda (1921-95), women's rights activist. p, Saida Jallali (1934-2014), fishing boat captain. q, Kahina (Dihya) (fl. 7th cent.), Berber queen. r, Aicha Mannoubia (1198-1267), Muslim saint. s, Arwa Kairounaise (c.735-c. 764), wife of Caliph of Baghdad who kept husband from taking more wives. t, Zazia Hlalia (fl. 10th cent.), wife of Sharif of Mecca. u, Ons Jabeur, tennis player. v, Aroussia Nalouti, writer.

2022, Aug. 13 **Litho.** ***Perf. 14x13¼***
1788 A858 250m Sheet of 22, #a-v, + 2 labels — —

Birds — A859

Designs: No. 1789, 750m, Circaète Jean le Blanc (short-toed eagle). No. 1790, 750m, Grande duc Ascalaphe (pharaoh eagle owl). 900m, Effraie des clochers (barn owl). 4d, Vautour percnoptère (Egyptian vulture).

Perf. 14x13¼ Syncopated

2022, Sept. 26 **Litho.**
1789-1792 A859 Set of 4 4.00 2.00
1792a Souvenir sheet of 4, #1789-1792 4.75 4.75

No. 1792a sold for 7.50d.

World Teachers Day — A860

Perf. 14x13¼ Syncopated

2022, Oct. 5 **Litho.**
1793 A860 750m multi .50 .30

World Post Day — A861

Perf. 13¼x14 Syncopated

2022, Oct. 9 **Litho.**

1794 A861 1d multi .65 .30

Campaign for Breast Cancer Examinations A862

Perf. 13¼x14¼ Syncopated

2022, Oct. 14 **Litho.**

1795 A862 3d multi 1.90 .95

Arab League Summit, Algiers — A863

2022, Oct. 25 **Litho.** *Perf. 14*

1796 A863 900m multi .55 .30

Values are for stamps with surrounding selvage.

SEMI-POSTAL STAMPS

No. 36 Overprinted in Red

1915, Feb. **Unwmk.** *Perf. 14x13½*

B1 A5 15c vio, *pnksh* 1.40 1.40

No. 32 Overprinted in Red

1916, Feb. 15

B2 A4 5c grn, *grnsh* 2.10 2.10

Types of Regular Issue of 1906 in New Colors and Surcharged

1916, Aug.

B3 A5 10c on 15c brn vio, *bl* 1.40 1.10
B4 A5 10c on 20c brn, *org* 2.10 1.40
B5 A5 10c on 25c bl, *grn* 3.50 3.50
B6 A6 10c on 35c ol grn & vio 10.50 7.00
B7 A6 10c on 40c bis & blk 7.00 4.50
B8 A6 10c on 75c vio brn & grn 14.00 10.50
B9 A7 10c on 1fr red & grn 7.00 7.00
B10 A7 10c on 2fr bis & bl 110.00 110.00
B11 A7 10c on 5fr vio & red 125.00 125.00
Nos. B3-B11 (9) 280.50 270.00

Nos. B3-B11 were sold at their face value but had a postal value of 10c only. The excess was applied to the relief of prisoners of war in Germany.

Types of Regular Issue of 1906 in New Colors and Surcharged in Carmine

1918

B12 A5 15c on 20c blk, *grn* 2.75 2.75
B13 A5 15c on 25c dk bl, *buff* 2.75 2.75
B14 A6 15c on 35c gray grn & red 3.75 3.75
B15 A6 15c on 40c brn & lt bl 5.00 5.00
B16 A6 15c on 75c red brn & blk 14.00 14.00
B17 A7 15c on 1fr red & vio 32.50 32.50
B18 A7 15c on 2fr bis brn & red 110.00 110.00
B19 A7 15c on 5fr vio & blk 175.00 175.00
Nos. B12-B19 (8) 345.75 345.75

The different parts of the surcharge are more widely spaced on the stamps of types A6 and A7. These stamps were sold at their face value but had a postal value of 15c only. The excess was intended for the relief of prisoners of war in Germany.

Types of 1906-22 Surcharged

1923

B20 A4 0c on 1c blue 1.10 1.10
B21 A4 0c on 2c ol brn 1.10 1.10
B22 A4 1c on 3c green 1.10 1.10
B23 A4 2c on 5c red lilac 1.10 1.10
B24 A9 3c on 10c vio 1.10 1.10
B25 A5 5c on 15c ol grn 1.10 1.10
B26 A5 5c on 20c bl, *pink* 2.10 2.10
B27 A5 5c on 25c vio, *bluish* 2.10 2.10
B28 A9 5c on 30c orange 2.10 2.10
B29 A6 5c on 35c bl & vio 4.25 4.25
B30 A6 5c on 40c bl & brn 4.25 4.25
B31 A9 10c on 50c blk, *bluish* 7.00 5.50
B32 A6 10c on 60c ol brn & bl 10.50 7.75
B33 A6 10c on 75c vio & lt grn 9.00 8.50
B34 A7 25c on 1fr mar & vio 10.50 8.50
B35 A7 25c on 2fr bl & rose 27.50 26.00
B36 A7 25c on 5fr grn & ol brn 70.00 70.00
Nos. B20-B36 (17) 155.90 147.65

These stamps were sold at their original values but had postal franking values only to the amounts surcharged on them. The difference was intended to be used for the benefit of wounded soldiers.

This issue was entirely speculative. Before the announced date of sale most of the stamps were taken by postal employees and practically none of them were offered to the public.

Type of 1906 Parcel Post Stamps Surcharged in Black

1925, June 7 *Perf. 13½x14*

B37 PP1 1c on 5c brn & red, *pink* .70 .70
a. Surcharge omitted 140.00 140.00
B38 PP1 2c on 10c brn & bl, *yel* .70 .70
B39 PP1 3c on 20c red vio & rose, *lav* 1.40 1.40
B40 PP1 5c on 25c sl grn & rose, *bluish* 1.40 1.40
B41 PP1 5c on 40c rose & grn, *yel* 1.40 1.40
B42 PP1 10c on 50c vio & bl, *lav* 2.75 2.75
B43 PP1 10c on 75c grn & ol, *grnsh* 2.75 2.75
B44 PP1 25c on 1fr bl & grn, *bluish* 2.75 2.75
B45 PP1 25c on 2fr rose & vio, *pnksh* 14.00 14.00
B46 PP1 25c on 5fr red & brn, *lem* 50.00 50.00
Nos. B37-B46 (10) 77.85 77.85

These stamps were sold at their original values but paid postage only to the amount of the surcharged values. The difference was given to Child Welfare societies.

Tunis-Chad Motor Caravan — SP2

1928, Feb. **Engr.** *Perf. 13½*

B47 SP2 40c + 40c org brn 1.40 1.40
B48 SP2 50c + 50c dp vio 1.75 1.75
B49 SP2 75c + 75c dk bl 1.75 1.75
B50 SP2 1fr + 1fr carmine 1.75 1.75
B51 SP2 1.50fr + 1.50fr brt bl 1.75 1.75
B52 SP2 2fr + 2fr dk grn 2.10 2.10
B53 SP2 5fr + 5fr red brn 2.10 2.10
Nos. B47-B53 (7) 12.60 12.60

The surtax on these stamps was for the benefit of Child Welfare societies.

Nos. 122-135, 137-142 Surcharged in Black

a

b

1938 *Perf. 11, 12½, 12½x13*

B54 A14(a) 1c + 1c 2.75 2.75
B55 A14(a) 2c + 2c 2.75 2.75
B56 A14(a) 3c + 3c 2.75 2.75
B57 A14(a) 5c + 5c 2.75 2.75
B58 A14(a) 10c + 10c 2.75 2.75
B59 A15(a) 15c + 15c 2.75 2.75
B60 A15(a) 20c + 20c 2.75 2.75
B61 A15(a) 25c + 25c 2.75 2.75
B62 A15(a) 30c + 30c 2.75 2.75
B63 A15(a) 40c + 40c 2.75 2.75
B64 A16(a) 50c + 50c 2.75 2.75
B65 A16(a) 75c + 75c 2.75 2.75
B66 A16(a) 90c + 90c 2.75 2.75
B67 A16(a) 1fr + 1fr 2.75 2.75
B68 A17(b) 1.50fr + 1fr 2.75 2.75
B69 A17(b) 2fr + 1.50fr 5.00 5.00
B70 A17(b) 3fr + 2fr 5.50 5.50
B71 A17(b) 5fr + 3fr 21.00 21.00
a. Perf. 12½ 110.00 110.00
B72 A17(b) 10fr + 5fr 45.00 45.00
B73 A17(b) 20fr + 10fr 70.00 70.00
Nos. B54-B73 (20) 187.75 187.75

50th anniversary of the post office.

Nos. 86, 100-101, 105 Surcharged in Black, Blue or Red

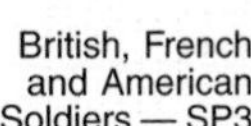

1941 *Perf. 14x13½*

B74 A11 1fr on 45c (Bk) .55 .55
B75 A13 1.30fr on 1.25fr (Bl) .55 .55
B76 A13 1.50fr on 1.40fr (Bk) .55 .55
B77 A13 2fr on 2.25fr (R) .80 .80
Nos. B74-B77 (4) 2.45 2.45

The surcharge measures 11x14mm on #B74.

Catalogue values for unused stamps in this section, from this point to the end of the section, are for Never Hinged items.

British, French and American Soldiers — SP3

1943 **Litho.** *Perf. 12*

B78 SP3 1.50fr + 8.50fr rose red .55 .25

Liberation of Tunisia.

Children — SP3a

1944 **Engr.** *Perf. 13½*

B78A SP3a 1.20fr + 1.30fr brown 1.10
B78B SP3a 1.50fr + 2fr black brown 1.10
B78C SP3a 2fr + 3fr dark green 1.10
B78D SP3a 3fr + 4fr red orange 1.10
Nos. B78A-B78D (4) 4.40

National welfare fund.

Nos. B78A-B78D were issued by the Vichy government in France, but were not issued in Tunisia.

Native Scene — SP4

Surcharged in Black

1944 *Perf. 11½*

B79 SP4 2fr + 48fr red 1.40 1.10

The surtax was for soldiers.

Sidi Mahrez Mosque — SP5

Ramparts of Sfax — SP6

Fort Saint SP7

Sidi-bou-Said — SP8

1945 **Unwmk.** **Litho.** *Perf. 11½*

B80 SP5 1.50fr + 8.50fr choc & red 1.40 1.10
B81 SP6 3fr + 12fr dk bl grn & red 1.40 1.10
B82 SP7 4fr + 21fr brn org & red 1.40 1.10
B83 SP8 10fr + 40fr red & blk 1.40 1.10
Nos. B80-B83 (4) 5.60 4.40

The surtax was for soldiers.

France No. B193 Overprinted in Black — c

1945 *Perf. 14x13½*

B84 SP147 2fr + 1fr red org .70 .50

The surtax was for the aid of tuberculosis victims.

Same Overprint on Type of France, 1945

1945 **Engr.** *Perf. 13*

B85 SP150 2fr + 3fr dk grn 1.10 .55

Stamp Day.

Same Overprint on France No. B192

1945

B86 SP146 4fr + 6fr dk vio brn .70 .55

The surtax was for war victims of the P.T.T.

Types of 1926 Surcharged in Carmine

1945 **Typo.** *Perf. 14x13½*

B87 A10 4fr + 6fr on 10c ultra .70 .35
B88 A12 10fr + 30fr on 80c dk grn .70 .35

The design of type A12 is redrawn, omitting "RF." The surtax was for war veterans.

Tunisian Soldier — SP9

1946 Unwmk. Engr. *Perf. 13*

B89 SP9 20fr + 30fr grn, red & blk 1.75 1.40

The surtax aided Tunisian soldiers in Indo-China.

Type of France Overprinted Type "c" in Carmine

1946

B90 SP160 3fr + 2fr dk bl 1.40 1.10

Stamp Day.

Stamps and Types of 1926-46 Surcharged in Carmine and Black

1946 *Perf. 14x13½*

B91 A12	80c + 50c emerald	1.40	1.10
B92 A12	1.50fr + 1.50fr rose lil	1.40	1.10
B93 A12	2fr + 2fr Prus grn	1.40	1.10
B94 A13	2.40fr + 2fr sal pink	1.40	1.10
B95 A13	4fr + 4fr ultra	2.10	1.40
	Nos. B91-B95 (5)	7.70	5.80

The two parts of the surcharge are more widely spaced on stamps of type A13.

Type of France Overprinted in Carmine

1947 *Perf. 13*

B96 SP172 4.50fr + 5.50fr sepia 1.40 1.10

On Type of France Surcharged in Carmine

B97 SP158 10fr + 15fr on 2fr + 3fr brt ultra 1.40 1.10

Type of 1926 Surcharged in Carmine

1947 Typo. *Perf. 14x13½*

B98 A13 10fr + 40fr black 1.40 1.10

Feeding Young Bird — SP10

1947 Engr. *Perf. 13*

B99 SP10	4.50fr + 5.50fr dk bl grn	1.75	1.40
B100 SP10	6fr + 9fr brt ultra	1.75	1.40
B101 SP10	8fr + 17fr dp car	1.75	1.40
B102 SP10	10fr + 40fr dk pur	1.75	1.40
	Nos. B99-B102 (4)	7.00	5.60

The surtax was for child welfare.

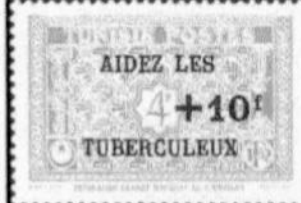

Type of Regular Issue of 1948 Surcharged in Blue

1948

B103 A21 4fr + 10fr ol grn & org 1.40 1.10

The surtax was for anti-tuberculosis work.

Arch of Triumph, Sbeitla — SP11

1948

B104 SP11 10fr + 40fr ol grn & olive 1.75 1.40

B105 SP11 18fr + 42fr dk bl & indigo 1.75 1.40

Surtax for charitable works of the army.

Arago Type of France Overprinted in Carmine

1948

B106 SP176 6fr + 4fr brt car 1.40 1.10

Stamp Day, Mar. 6-7.

Sleeping Child — SP12

1949, June 1

B107 SP12 25fr + 50fr dk grn 2.75 2.10

The surtax was for child welfare.

Neptune Type of 1947 Srchd. in Black

1949, Dec. 8

B108 A20 10fr + 15fr dp ultra & car 1.75 1.40

The surtax was for the Tunisian section of the Association of Free French.

Type of France Overprinted in Carmine — e

1949, Mar. 26

B109 SP180 15fr + 5fr indigo 2.10 1.40

Stamp Days, Mar. 26-27.

Type of France, 1950, Ovptd. Like No. B106 in Ultramarine

1950, Mar. 11 Unwmk. *Perf. 13*

B110 SP183 12fr + 3fr greenish black 2.75 2.10

Stamp Days, Mar. 11-12.

Tunisian and French Woman Shaking Hands — SP13

1950, June 5

B111 SP13 15fr + 35fr red 1.75 1.40

B112 SP13 25fr + 45fr dp ultra 1.75 1.40

The surtax was for Franco-Tunisian Mutual Assistance.

Arab Soldier — SP14

1950, Aug. 21 Engr.

B113 SP14 25fr + 25fr dp bl 2.75 2.10

The surtax was for old soldiers.

Type of France Overprinted Type "c" in Black

1951, Mar. 10

B114 SP186 12fr + 3fr brnsh gray 2.10 1.40

Stamp Days, Mar. 10-11.

Mother Carrying Child — SP15

1951, June 19 Engr. *Perf. 13*

B115 SP15 30fr + 15fr dp ultra 3.50 2.75

The surtax was for child welfare.

National Cemetery of Gammarth SP16

1952, June 15

B116 SP16 30fr + 10fr blue 2.75 2.10

Surtax aided orphans of the military services.

Type of France Overprinted Type "e" in Lilac

1952, Mar. 8 Unwmk.

B117 SP190 12fr + 3fr purple 1.75 1.40

Stamp Day, Mar. 8.

Stucco Work, Bardo — SP17

1952, May 5 Engr. *Perf. 13*

B118 SP17 15fr + 1fr ultra & indigo 1.40 1.10

Surtax for charitable works of the army.

Boy Campers — SP18

1952, June 15

B119 SP18 30fr + 10fr dp bl grn 3.50 2.10

The surtax was for the Educational League vacation camps.

Type of France Surcharged Type "c" and Surtax

1952, Oct. 15

B120 A226 15fr + 5fr bl grn 3.50 2.10

Creation of the French Military Medal, cent.

Type of France Overprinted Type "c"

1953, Mar. 14

B121 SP193 12fr + 3fr vermilion 2.10 1.75

"Day of the Stamp."

Type of France Overprinted Type "c"

1954, Mar. 20

B122 SP196 12fr + 3fr indigo 2.10 1.75

Stamp Day.

Balloon Post, 1870 — SP19

1955, Mar. 19

B123 SP19 12fr + 3fr red brown 2.10 1.75

Stamp Days, Mar. 19-20.

Independent Kingdom

Franz von Taxis — SP20

1956, Mar. 17

B124 SP20 12fr + 3fr dark green 1.25 1.25

Stamp Days, Mar. 17-18

Republic

No. 246 Surcharged in Red

1957, Aug. 8 Engr.

B125 A29 20fr + 10fr dp ultra .70 .70

15th anniversary of the army.

Florist Type of 1955 with Added Inscriptions, Surcharged in Red

1957, Oct. 19 *Perf. 13*

B126 A34 20fr + 10fr dk vio .70 .70

No. B126 is inscribed "5e. Foire Internationale" at bottom and lines of Arabic at either side.

Mailman Delivering Mail — SP21

1959, May 1 Engr. *Perf. 13*

B127 SP21 20fr + 5fr dk brn & org brn .70 .70

Day of the Stamp. The surtax was for the Post Office Mutual Fund.

Ornamental Cock — SP22

1959, Oct. 24 Litho. *Perf. 13*

B128 SP22 10m + 5m yel, lt bl & red .75 .35

Surtax for the Red Crescent Society.

Mailman on Camel Phoning — SP23

1960, Apr. 16 **Engr.** ***Perf. 13***

B129 SP23 60m + 5m ol, org & ultra	1.25	.75

Day of the Stamp.

Dancer of Kerkennah Holding Stamp — SP24

Stamp Day: 15m+5m, Mail truck, horiz. 20m+6m, Hand holding magnifying glass and stamps. 50m+5m, Running boy, symbols of mail.

1961, May 6 **Unwmk.** ***Perf. 13***

B130 SP24 12m + 4m multi	.60	.60
B131 SP24 15m + 5m multi	.75	.75
B132 SP24 20m + 6m multi	.85	.85
B133 SP24 50m + 5m multi	.95	.95
Nos. B130-B133 (4)	3.15	3.15

Nos. B130-B133 Overprinted

1963, Oct. 24

B134 SP24 12m + 4m cl, vio & ol	.35	.35
B135 SP24 15m + 5m ol, cl & vio bl	.40	.40
B136 SP24 20m + 6m multi	.50	.50
B137 SP24 50m + 5m multi	.85	.85
Nos. B134-B137 (4)	2.10	2.10

United Nations Day.

Old Man, Red Crescent — SP25

Tunisian Red Crescent: 75m+10m, Mother, child and Red Crescent.

1972, May 8 **Engr.** ***Perf. 13***

B138 SP25 10m + 10m pur & dk red	.50	.35
B139 SP25 75m + 10m bis brn & dl red	.75	.40

SP26

SP26a

Design: 25m+10m, Nurse Holding Bottle of Blood. 60m+10m, Red Crescent and blood donors' arms, horiz.

1973, May 10 **Engr.** ***Perf. 13***

B140 SP26 25m + 10m multi	.60	.40
B141 SP26a 60m + 10m gray & car	1.00	.40

Red Crescent appeal for blood donors.

Blood Donors — SP27

Red Crescent Society: 75m+10m, Blood transfusion, symbolic design.

1974, May 8 **Photo.** ***Perf. 14x13***

B142 SP27 25m + 10m multi	.50	.40
B143 SP27 75m + 10m multi	.75	.50

Man Holding Scales with Balanced Diet — SP28

1975, May 8 **Photo.** ***Perf. 11½***

B144 SP28 50m + 10m multi	.65	.40

Tunisian Red Crescent fighting malnutrition.

Blood Donation, Woman and Man — SP29

1976, May 8 **Photo.** ***Perf. 11½***

B145 SP29 40m + 10m multi	1.20	.35

Tunisian Red Crescent Society.

Litter Bearers and Red Crescent SP30

1977, May 8 **Photo.** ***Perf. 13½x14***

B146 SP30 50m + 10m multi	.65	.40

Tunisian Red Crescent Society.

Blood Donors — SP31

1978, May 8 **Photo.** ***Perf. 13x14***

B147 SP31 50m + 10m multi	.65	.40

Blood drive of Tunisian Red Crescent Society.

Hand and Red Crescent — SP32

1979, May 8 **Photo.** ***Perf. 13½***

B148 SP32 50m + 10m multi	.65	.40

Tunisian Red Crescent Society.

Red Crescent Society — SP33

1980, May 8 **Photo.** ***Perf. 13½***

B149 SP33 50m + 10m multi	.65	.40

Red Crescent Society — SP34

1981, May 8 ***Perf. 14½x13½***

B150 SP34 50m + 10m multi	.55	.35

Dome of the Rock, Jerusalem SP35

1981, Nov. 29 **Photo.** ***Perf. 13½***

B151 SP35 50m + 5m multi	.55	.35
B152 SP35 150m + 5m multi	1.00	.60
B153 SP35 200m + 5m multi	1.60	.70
Nos. B151-B153 (3)	3.15	1.65

Intl. Palestinian Solidarity Day.

Red Crescent Society — SP36

1982, May 8 **Photo.** ***Perf. 13½***

B154 SP36 80m + 10m multi	.65	.40

Red Crescent Society — SP37

1983, May 8 **Litho.** ***Perf. 14x13½***

B155 SP37 80m + 10m multi	.75	.35

Sabra and Chatilla Massacre SP38

1983, Sept. 20 **Photo.** ***Perf. 13***

B156 SP38 80m + 5m multi	.75	.50

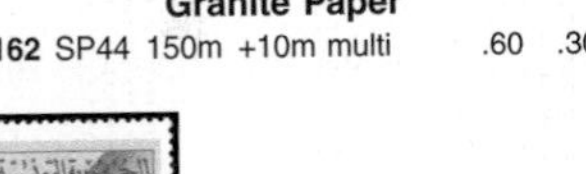
Red Crescent Society SP39

80m + 10m, First aid.

1984, May 8 **Litho.** ***Perf. 12½***

B157 SP39 80m + 10m multi	.65	.40

Red Crescent Society — SP40

1985, May 8 **Litho.** ***Perf. 14***

B158 SP40 100m + 10m multi	.50	.25

Red Crescent Society — SP41

120m + 10m, Map of Tunisia.

1986, May 9 **Litho.** ***Perf. 14½x13½***

B159 SP41 120m + 10m multi	1.10	.40

Red Crescent Society — SP42

1987, May 8 **Litho.** ***Perf. 13x13½***

B160 SP42 150m + 10m multi	.75	.45

Intl. Red Cross and Red Crescent Organizations, 125th Annivs. — SP43

1988, May 9 **Photo.** ***Perf. 14***

B161 SP43 150m + 10m multi	.75	.40

Red Crescent Society — SP44

1989, May 8 **Photo.** ***Perf. 11½***
Granite Paper

B162 SP44 150m +10m multi	.60	.30

Red Crescent Society — SP45

1990, May 8 **Litho.** ***Perf. 14x13½***

B163 SP45 150m +10m multi	.60	.25

Red Crescent Society — SP46

1991, May 8 **Litho.** ***Perf. 13½***

B164 SP46 180m +10m multi	.85	.45

Red Crescent Society — SP47

1993, Aug. 17 Litho. *Perf. 14x13½*
B165 SP47 120m +30m multi .85 .30

AIR POST STAMPS

No. 43 Surcharged in Red

1919, Apr. Unwmk. *Perf. 14x13½*
C1 A6 30c on 35c ol grn & brn 1.40 1.40
a. Inverted surcharge 160.00
b. Double surcharge 160.00
c. Double inverted surcharge 190.00
d. Double surcharge, one inverted 160.00

Type A6, Overprinted in Rose

1920, Apr.
C2 A6 30c ol grn, bl 1.10 1.10

Nos. 53 and 55 Overprinted in Red

1927, Mar. 24
C3 A7 1fr indigo & ultra 1.10 .70
C4 A7 2fr grn & red org, *pink* 3.50 2.10

Nos. 51 and 57 Srchd. in Black or Red

C5 A6 1.75fr on 75c (Bk) 1.10 .70
C6 A7 1.75fr on 5fr (R) 3.50 2.10

Type A13 Ovptd. like #C3-C4 in Blue

1928, Feb.
C7 A13 1.30fr org & lt vio 3.50 1.40
C8 A13 1.80fr gray grn & red 4.25 1.10
C9 A13 2.55fr lil & ol brn 3.50 1.10
Nos. C7-C9 (3) 11.25 3.60

Type A13 Surcharged like #C5-C6 in Blue

1930, Aug.
C10 A13 1.50fr on 1.30fr org & lt vio 2.75 .85
C11 A13 1.50fr on 1.80fr gray grn & red 4.25 .70
C12 A13 1.50fr on 2.55fr lil & ol brn 8.50 2.10
Nos. C10-C12 (3) 15.50 3.65

Catalogue values for unused stamps in this section, from this point to the end of the section, are for Never Hinged items.

UPU Type of Regular Issue

1949, Oct. 28 Engr. *Perf. 13*
C13 A23 25fr dk bl, *bluish* 2.50 1.75

UPU, 75th anniv. Exists imperf.; value $40.

Bird from Antique Mosaic, Museum of Sousse — AP2

1949 Unwmk.
C14 AP2 200fr blue & indigo 8.00 2.10

(Arabic on one line) — AP3

1950-51
C15 AP3 100fr bl grn & brn 5.00 1.40
C16 AP3 200fr dk bl & ind ('51) 10.50 3.50

Monastir — AP4

Coast at Korbous — AP5

Design: 1000fr, Air view of Tozeur mosque.

1953-54
C17 AP4 100fr dk bl, ind & dk grn ('54) 4.50 1.10
C18 AP4 200fr cl, blk brn & red brn ('54) 6.25 1.75
C19 AP5 500fr dk brn & ultra 35.00 12.50
C20 AP5 1000fr dk green 60.00 25.00
Nos. C17-C20 (4) 105.75 40.35

Imperforates exist.

Independent Kingdom

Types of 1953-54 Redrawn with "RF" Omitted

1956, Mar. 1
C21 AP4 100fr slate bl, indigo & dk grn 1.50 .70
C22 AP4 200fr multi 3.00 1.40
C23 AP5 500fr dk brn & ultra 6.00 6.00
C24 AP5 1000fr dk green 12.00 12.00
Nos. C21-C24 (4) 22.50 20.10

Republic

Desert Swallows — AP6

Birds: #C26, Butcherbird. #C27, Cream-colored courser. 100m, European chaffinch. 150m, Pink flamingoes. 200m, Barbary partridges. 300m, European roller. 500m, Bustard.

1965-66 Photo. *Perf. 12½*

Size: 23x31mm

C25 AP6 25m multi .75 .30
C26 AP6 55m blk & lt bl 1.10 .75
C27 AP6 55m multi ('66) .90 .55

Size: 22½x33mm

Perf. 11½

C28 AP6 100m multi 1.50 .90
C29 AP6 150m multi ('66) 4.75 2.25
C30 AP6 200m multi ('66) 5.75 2.40
C31 AP6 300m multi ('66) 7.50 5.00
C32 AP6 500m multi 11.00 6.00
Nos. C25-C32 (8) 33.25 18.15

See No. 474.

AIR POST SEMI-POSTAL STAMP

Catalogue value for the unused stamp in this section is for a Never Hinged item.

Window, Great Mosque of Kairouan — SPAP1

Unwmk.

1952, May 5 Engr. *Perf. 13*
CB1 SPAP1 50fr + 10fr blk & gray grn 4.25 3.25

Surtax for charitable works of the army.

POSTAGE DUE STAMPS

Regular postage stamps perforated with holes in the form of a "T," the holes varying in size and number, were used as postage due stamps from 1888 to 1901.

For listings, see the *Scott Classic Specialized Catalogue of Stamps and Covers.*

D1

Perf. 14x13½

1901-03 Unwmk. Typo.
J1 D1 1c black .35 .45
J2 D1 2c orange .70 .55
J3 D1 5c blue .70 .45
J4 D1 10c brown .70 .55
J5 D1 20c blue green 4.25 .85
J6 D1 30c carmine 3.50 .80
J7 D1 50c brown violet 1.75 .85
J8 D1 1fr olive green 1.40 .85
J9 D1 2fr carmine, *grn* 4.25 1.75
J10 D1 5fr blk, *yellow* 52.50 35.00
Nos. J1-J10 (10) 70.10 42.10

No. J10 Surcharged in Blue

1914, Nov.
J11 D1 2fr on 5fr blk, *yellow* 3.50 3.50

In Jan. 1917 regular 5c postage stamps were overprinted "T" in an inverted triangle and used as postage due stamps.

D2

1922-49
J12 D2 1c black .35 .30
J13 D2 2c black, *yellow* .35 .30
J14 D2 5c violet brown .70 .30
J15 D2 10c blue .35 .45
J16 D2 10c yel green ('45) .25 .25
J17 D2 20c orange, *yel* .35 .45
J18 D2 30c brown ('23) .35 .30
J19 D2 50c rose red 1.05 .50
J20 D2 50c blue vio ('45) .25 .25
J21 D2 60c violet ('28) 1.05 .50
J22 D2 80c bister ('28) .70 .35
J23 D2 90c orange red ('28) 1.10 .65
J24 D2 1fr green .70 .30
J25 D2 2fr olive grn, *straw* 1.40 .55
J26 D2 2fr car rose ('45) .30 .30
J27 D2 3fr vio, *pink* ('29) .35 .30
J28 D2 4fr grnsh bl ('45) .35 .45
J29 D2 5fr violet .70 .55
J30 D2 10fr cerise ('49) .35 .35
J31 D2 20fr olive gray ('49) 1.40 1.10
Nos. J12-J31 (20) 12.40 8.50

Inscribed: "Timbre Taxe"

1950 Unwmk. *Perf. 14x13½*
J32 D2 30fr blue 1.75 1.50

Catalogue values for unused stamps in this section, from this point to the end of the section, are for Never Hinged items.

Independent Kingdom

Grain and Fruit — D3

1957, Apr. 1 Engr. *Perf. 14x13*
J33 D3 1fr bright green .25 .25
J34 D3 2fr orange brown .25 .25
J35 D3 3fr bluish green .65 .50
J36 D3 4fr indigo .65 .50
J37 D3 5fr lilac .65 .50
J38 D3 10fr carmine .65 .50
J39 D3 20fr chocolate 2.10 1.60
J40 D3 30fr blue 2.75 2.10
Nos. J33-J40 (8) 7.95 6.20

Republic

Inscribed "Republique Tunisienne"

1960-77
J41 D3 1m emerald .50 .25
J42 D3 2m red brown .50 .25
J43 D3 3m bluish green .50 .25
J44 D3 4m indigo .50 .25
J45 D3 5m lilac .50 .25
J46 D3 10m carmine rose 1.00 .50
J47 D3 20m violet brown 1.50 .75
J48 D3 30m blue 1.75 .90
J49 D3 40m lake ('77) .50 .25
J50 D3 100m blue green ('77) 1.00 .50
Nos. J41-J50 (10) 8.25 4.15

PARCEL POST STAMPS

Mail Delivery — PP1

1906 Unwmk. Typo. *Perf. 13½x14*
Q1 PP1 5c grn & vio brn .70 .55
Q2 PP1 10c org & red 1.10 .70
Q3 PP1 20c dk brn & org 1.75 .70
a. Center double 450.00 *5,000.*
Q4 PP1 25c blue & brn 2.50 .70
Q5 PP1 40c gray & rose 2.75 .70
Q6 PP1 50c vio brn & vio 2.75 .70
Q7 PP1 75c bis brn & bl 3.50 .70
Q8 PP1 1fr red brn & red 2.75 .50
Q9 PP1 2fr carmine & bl 8.50 1.10
Q10 PP1 5fr vio & vio brn 23.00 1.40
Nos. Q1-Q10 (10) 49.30 7.75

For surcharges see Nos. B37-B46.

Gathering Dates — PP2

1926
Q11 PP2 5c pale brn & dk bl .45 .45
Q12 PP2 10c rose & vio .55 .45
Q13 PP2 20c yel grn & blk .55 .45
Q14 PP2 25c org brn & blk .55 .45
Q15 PP2 40c dp rose & dp grn 2.75 .55
Q16 PP2 50c lt vio & blk 1.75 .80
Q17 PP2 60c ol & brn red 1.75 .70
Q18 PP2 75c gray vio & bl grn 1.75 .70
Q19 PP2 80c ver & ol brn 1.75 .70
Q20 PP2 1fr Prus bl & dp rose 2.10 .70
Q21 PP2 2fr vio & mag 4.25 .70
Q22 PP2 4fr red & blk 4.50 .70
Q23 PP2 5fr red brn & dp vio 7.00 1.10
Q24 PP2 10fr dl red & grn, *grnsh* 14.00 1.10
Q25 PP2 20fr yel grn & dp vio, *lav* 27.00 1.75
Nos. Q11-Q25 (15) 70.70 11.30

Parcel post stamps were discontinued July 1, 1940.

TURKEY

'tər-kē

LOCATION — Southeastern Europe and Asia Minor, between the Mediterranean and Black Seas
GOVT. — Republic
AREA — 300,947 sq. mi.
POP. — 65,599,206 (1999 est.)
CAPITAL — Ankara

The Ottoman Empire ceased to exist in 1922, and the Republic of Turkey was inaugurated in 1923.

40 Paras = 1 Piaster
40 Paras = 1 Ghurush (1926)
40 Paras = 1 Kurush (1926)
100 Kurush = 1 Lira

Catalogue values for unused stamps in this country are for Never Hinged items, beginning with Scott 817 in the regular postage section, Scott B69 in the semi-postal section, Scott C1 in the airpost section, Scott J97 in the postage due section, Scott O1 in the official section, Scott P175 in the newspaper section, and Scott RA139 in the postal tax section.

Watermarks

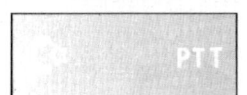

Wmk. 394 — "PTT," Crescent and Star

Wmk. 405

Turkish Numerals

١ ٢ ٣ ٤ ٥
1 2 3 4 5
٦ ٧ ٨ ٩ ٠
6 7 8 9 0

"Tughra," Monogram of Sultan Abdul-Aziz
A1 A2

A3

A4

1863 Unwmk. Litho. *Imperf.*
Red Band: 20pa, 1pi, 2pi
Blue Band: 5pi
Thin Paper

1 A1 20pa blk, *yellow* 75.00 20.00
a. Tête bêche pair 250.00 250.00
b. Without band 100.00
c. Green band
2 A2 1pi blk, *dl vio* 125.00 20.00
a. 1pi black, *gray* 125.00 21.50
b. Tête bêche pair 400.00 300.00
c. Without band 140.00
d. Design reversed *175.00*
e. 1pi blk, *yel* (error) 250.00 150.00
4 A3 2pi blk, *grnsh bl* 115.00 20.00
a. 2pi black, *ind* 115.00 21.50
b. Tête bêche pair 400.00 300.00
c. Without band 140.00
5 A4 5pi blk, *rose* 225.00 45.00
a. Tête bêche pair 500.00 400.00
b. Without band 250.00
c. Green band *275.00*
d. Red band *275.00*

Thick, Surface Colored Paper

6 A1 20pa blk, *yellow* 250.00 37.50
a. Tête bêche pair 450.00 450.00
b. Design reversed 325.00 325.00
c. Without band 225.00 225.00
d. Paper colored through 225.00 225.00
7 A2 1pi blk, *gray* 300.00 35.00
a. Tête bêche pair 900.00 900.00
b. Design reversed
c. Without band
d. Paper colored through 350.00 225.00
Nos. 1-7 (6) 1,090. 177.50

The 2pi and 5pi had two printings. In the common printing, the stamps are more widely spaced and alternate horizontal rows of 12 are inverted. In the first and rare printing, the stamps are more closely spaced and no rows are tête bêche.
See Nos. J1-J4.

Crescent and Star, Symbols of Turkish Caliphate — A5

Surcharged

The bottom characters of this and the following surcharges denote the denomination. The characters at top and sides translate, "Ottoman Empire Posts."

1865 Typo. *Perf. 12½*

8 A5 10pa deep green 11.00 *35.00*
c. "1" instead of "10" in each corner *300.00 300.00*
9 A5 20pa yellow 7.00 6.00
a. Star without rays 9.00 *6.00*
10 A5 1pi lilac 12.50 4.00
a. Star without rays 25.00 10.00
11 A5 2pi blue 6.50 4.00
12 A5 5pi carmine 5.50 4.50
d. Inverted surcharge
13 A5 25pi red orange 325.00 250.00

Imperf., Pairs

8b A5 10pa 125.00 125.00
9b A5 20pa 125.00 125.00
10b A5 1pi *100.00 90.00*
11a A5 2pi *100.00 90.00*
12b A5 5pi *150.00 110.00*
13a A5 25pi *900.00 900.00*

See Nos. J6-J35. For overprints and surcharges see Nos. 14-52, 64-65, 446-461, 467-468, J71-J77, Eastern Rumelia 1.

Surcharged

1867

14 A5 10pa gray green 9.50
a. Imperf., pair 55.00
15 A5 20pa yellow 15.00
a. Imperf., pair 75.00
16 A5 1pi lilac 20.00
a. Imperf., pair 110.00
b. Imperf., with surcharge of 5pi 200.00
17 A5 2pi blue 5.50 *45.00*
a. Imperf. 50.00
18 A5 5pi rose 4.50 *45.00*
a. Imperf. 50.00
19 A5 25pi orange *3,600.*
Nos. 14-18 (5) 54.50

Nos. 14, 15, 16 and 19 were never placed in use.

Surcharged

1869 *Perf. 13½*

20 A5 10pa dull violet 100.00 12.00
a. Printed on both sides
b. Imperf., pair *90.00 80.00*
c. Inverted surcharge *90.00*
d. Double surcharge
e. 10pa yellow (error) *300.00*
21 A5 20pa pale green 400.00 14.00
a. Printed on both sides *450.00 275.00*
22 A5 1pi yellow 10.00 2.50
c. Inverted surcharge *100.00*
d. Double surcharge
e. Surcharged on both sides
f. Printed on both sides
23 A5 2pi orange red 200.00 10.00
b. Imperf., pair 125.00 125.00
c. Printed on both sides 125.00
d. Inverted surcharge 70.00 70.00
e. Surcharged on both sides 140.00
24 A5 5pi blue 5.00 *10.00*
25 A5 5pi gray 30.00 37.50
26 A5 25pi dull rose 37.50 125.00
Nos. 20-26 (7) 782.50 *211.00*

Pin-perf., Perf. 5 to 11 and Compound

1870-71

27 A5 10pa lilac *550.00 25.00*
28 A5 10pa brown *500.00 15.00*
29 A5 20pa gray green 75.00 *10.00*
a. Printed on both sides
30 A5 1pi yellow *550.00 10.00*
a. Inverted surcharge *500.00 80.00*
b. Without surcharge
31 A5 2pi red 8.00 5.00
a. Imperf. 40.00 40.00
b. Printed on both sides *40.00*
c. Surcharged on both sides
32 A5 5pi blue 5.00 *12.50*
a. 5pi greenish blue 6.00 *8.00*
33 A5 5pi slate 40.00 50.00
a. Printed on both sides
b. Surcharged on both sides *80.00*
34 A5 25pi dull rose 40.00 *75.00*
Nos. 27-34 (8) 1,768. *202.50*

1873 *Perf. 12, 12½*

35 A5 10pa dark lilac 475.00 25.00
a. Inverted surcharge 90.00
36 A5 10pa olive brown 110.00 17.50
a. 10pa bister 110.00 11.00
37 A5 2pi vermilion 3.50 4.50
a. Surcharged on both sides 22.50 22.50
Nos. 35-37 (3) 588.50 *47.00*

Surcharged

1874-75 *Perf. 13½*

38 A5 10pa red violet 52.50 7.50
a. Imperf., pair 210.00 50.00
39 A5 20pa yellow green 15.00 5.00
b. Inverted surcharge 30.00 13.00
c. Double surcharge
40 A5 1pi yellow 210.00 30.00
a. Imperf., pair 100.00 80.00

Perf. 12, 12½

41 A5 10pa red violet 25.00 10.00
a. Inverted surcharge 45.00 60.00
Nos. 38-41 (4) 302.50 52.50

Surcharged

1876, Apr. *Perf. 13½*

42 A5 10pa red lilac 2.00 .50
a. Inverted surcharge 70.00
b. Imperf., pair 60.00 60.00
43 A5 20pa pale green 2.00 .50
b. Inverted surcharge 70.00
c. Imperf., pair 60.00 60.00
44 A5 1pi yellow 2.00 .50
a. Imperf., pair 60.00 60.00
46 A5 5pi gray blue *1,700.*
47 A5 25pi dull rose *1,700.*
Nos. 42-44 (3) 6.00

Nos. 46 and 47 were never placed in use.
See Nos. 64-65.

Surcharged

1876, Jan.

48 A5 ¼pi on 10pa violet 3.00 2.50
49 A5 ½pi on 20pa yel grn 6.25 2.50
50 A5 1¼pi on 50pa rose 2.25 2.50
a. Imperf., pair 80.00
51 A5 2pi on 2pi redsh brn 40.00 7.50
52 A5 5pi on 5pi gray blue *10.00 85.00*
Nos. 48-52 (5) 61.50 *100.00*

The surcharge on Nos. 48-52 restates in French the value originally expressed in Turkish characters.
The vast majority of No. 51 unused are without gum.

A7

1876, Sept. Typo. *Perf. 13½*

53 A7 10pa black & rose lil 2.00 6.25
54 A7 20pa red vio & grn 62.50 5.00
55 A7 50pa blue & yellow 1.50 *10.00*
56 A7 2pi black & redsh brn 1.60 *5.00*
57 A7 5pi red & blue 3.00 *12.50*
b. Cliché of 25pi in plate of 5pi 400.00 375.00
58 A7 25pi claret & rose 15.00 85.00
a. Imperf. 160.00
Nos. 53-58 (6) 85.60 123.75

Nos. 56-58 exist perf. 11½, but were not regularly issued.
See Nos. 59-63, 66-91, J36-J38. For overprints see Nos. 462-466, 469-476, J78-J79, P10-P14, Eastern Rumelia 2-40.

1880-84 *Perf. 13½*

59 A7 5pa black & ol ('81) 3.00 6.50
a. Imperf. 60.00
60 A7 10pa black & grn ('84) 3.00 3.50
61 A7 20pa black & rose 55.00 2.00
62 A7 1pi blk & bl *(piastres)* 75.00 3.00
a. 1pi black & gray blue 85.00
b. Imperf. 90.00
63 A7 1pi blk & bl *(piastre)* ('81) 110.00 5.00
Nos. 59-63 (5) 246.00 20.00

A cliché of No. 63 was inserted in a plate of the Eastern Rumelia 1pi (No. 13). This was found in the remainder stock.
Nos. 60-61 and 63 exist perf. 11½, but were not regularly issued.
See Nos. J36-J38.

1881-82
Surcharged like Apr., 1876 Issue

64 A5 20pa gray 4.25 6.25
a. Inverted surcharge 30.00
b. Imperf., pair 60.00
65 A5 2pi pale salmon 3.00 1.00
a. Inverted surcharge 30.00

1884-86 *Perf. 11½, 13½*

66 A7 5pa lil & pale lil ('86) 200.00 *150.00*
67 A7 10pa grn & pale grn 1.60 1.25
68 A7 20pa rose & pale rose 2.00 1.25
69 A7 1pi blue & lt blue 2.00 1.25

Perf. 11½

70	A7	2pi ocher & pale ocher	2.25	1.25
71	A7	5pi red brn & pale brn	20.00	25.00
c.		5pi ocher & pale ocher (error)	40.00	40.00

Perf. 11½, 13½

73	A7	25pi blk & pale gray ('86)	300.00	*425.00*
		Nos. 66-73 (7)	527.85	*605.00*

Imperf

66a	A7	5pa	60.00
67a	A7	10pa	40.00
68b	A7	20pa	40.00
69b	A7	1pi	40.00
73a	A7	25pi	150.00

1886 *Perf. 13½*

74	A7	5pa black & pale gray	2.00	2.50
75	A7	2pi orange & lt bl	2.00	2.00
76	A7	5pi grn & pale grn	3.00	25.00
77	A7	25pi bis & pale bis	45.00	*150.00*
		Nos. 74-77 (4)	52.00	*179.50*

Imperf

74a	A7	5pa	30.00
75b	A7	2pi	40.00
76b	A7	5pi	40.00
77a	A7	25pi	40.00

Stamps of 1884-86, bisected and surcharged as above, 10pa, 20pa, 1pi and 2pi or surcharged "2" in red are stated to have been made privately and without authority. With the aid of employees of the post office, stamps were passed through the mails.

1888 *Perf. 13½*

83	A7	5pa green & yellow	2.50	5.00
84	A7	2pi red lilac & bl	1.50	1.50
85	A7	5pi dk brown & gray	5.00	*20.00*
86	A7	25pi red & yellow	30.00	*150.00*
		Nos. 83-86 (4)	39.00	*176.50*

Imperf

83a	A7	5pa	40.00
84a	A7	2pi	40.00
85a	A7	5pi	40.00
86a	A7	25pi	40.00

Nos. 74-86 exist perf. 11½, but were not regularly issued.

1890 *Perf. 11½, 13½*

87	A7	10pa green & gray	8.00	1.00
88	A7	20pa rose & gray	1.60	1.00
89	A7	1pi blue & gray	125.00	1.00
90	A7	2pi yellow & gray	2.25	*7.50*
91	A7	5pi buff & gray	5.00	*22.50*
		Nos. 87-91 (5)	141.85	*33.00*

Imperf

87a	A7	10pa	40.00
88a	A7	20pa	40.00
89a	A7	1pi	100.00
90b	A7	2pi	100.00
91a	A7	5pi	40.00

Arms and Tughra of "El Gazi" (The Conqueror) Sultan Abdul Hamid
A10 A11

A12

A13

A14

1892-98 **Typo.** *Perf. 13½*

95	A10	10pa gray green	2.00	.50
96	A11	20pa violet brn ('98)	1.25	.50
a.		20pa dark pink	7.50	1.00
b.		20pa pink	40.00	1.00
97	A12	1pi pale blue	90.00	.50
98	A13	2pi brown org	4.50	.50
a.		Tête bêche pair	*120.00*	*75.00*
99	A14	5pi dull violet	2.25	*13.00*
a.		Turkish numeral in upper right corner reads "50" instead of "5"	50.00	45.00
		Nos. 95-99 (5)	100.00	*15.00*

See Nos. J39-J42. For surcharges and overprints see Nos. 100, 288-291, 350, 355-359, 477-478, B38, B41, J80-J82, P25-P34, P36, P121-P122, P134-P137, P153-P154.

No. 95 Surcharged in Red

1897

100	A10	5pa on 10pa gray grn	3.00	1.00
a.		"Cniq" instead of "Cinq"	30.00	25.00

Turkish stamps of types A11, A17-A18, A21-A24, A26, A28-A39, A41 with or without Turkish overprints and English surcharges with "Baghdad" or "Iraq" are listed under Mesopotamia in Vol. 4.

Turkish stamps of types A19 and A21 with Double-headed Eagle and "Shqipenia" handstamp are listed under Albania in Vol. 1.

A16

1901 **Typo.** *Perf. 13¼*

For Foreign Postage

102	A16	5pa bister	1.25	.60
103	A16	10pa yellow green	1.25	.60
104	A16	20pa magenta	1.25	.60
a.		Perf. 12	2.50	1.00
105	A16	1pi violet blue	1.50	1.00
106	A16	2pi gray blue	2.50	1.00
107	A16	5pi ocher	8.50	3.50
108	A16	25pi dark green	100.00	30.00
109	A16	50pi yellow	250.00	100.00
		Nos. 102-109 (8)	366.25	137.30

A17

For Domestic Postage
Perf. 12, 13¼

110	A17	5pa purple	1.25	.35
111	A17	10pa green	1.25	.35
112	A17	20pa carmine	1.25	.35
113	A17	1pi blue	1.25	.35
a.		Imperf.	40.00	
114	A17	2pi orange	2.00	.50
115	A17	5pi lilac rose	6.00	.50

Perf. 13½

116	A17	25pi brown	12.00	2.25
a.		Perf. 12	25.00	8.50
117	A17	50pi yellow brown	60.00	6.00
a.		Perf. 12	55.00	17.00
		Nos. 110-117 (8)	85.00	10.65

Nos. 110-113 exist perf. 12x13½.
See Nos. J43-J46.
For overprints and surcharges see Nos. 165-180, 292-303, 340-341, 361-377, 479-493, B19-B20, B37, P37-P48, P69-P80, P123-P126, P138-P146, P155-P164.

A18

1905 *Perf. 12, 13½ and Compound*

118	A18	5pa ocher	1.00	.35
119	A18	10pa dull green	1.25	.50
a.		Imperf.	40.00	40.00
120	A18	20pa carmine	1.00	.50
a.		Imperf.	40.00	40.00
121	A18	1pi blue	1.00	.50
122	A18	2pi slate	1.50	.90
123	A18	2½pi red violet	1.50	.90
a.		Imperf.	40.00	40.00
124	A18	5pi brown	2.00	1.25
125	A18	10pi orange brn	5.00	1.50
126	A18	25pi olive green	15.00	12.00
127	A18	50pi deep violet	50.00	25.00

See Nos. J47-J48. For overprints and surcharges see Nos. 128-131, 181-182, 304-314, 351-354, 378-389, 494-508, B1-B3, B21-B23, B39-B40, P49-P54, P127-P129, P147-P150, P165-P171.

Large "Discount" Overprint in Carmine or Blue

1906

128	A18	10pa dull green (C)	2.50	1.00
129	A18	20pa carmine (Bl)	4.00	1.00
130	A18	1pi blue (C)	4.00	1.50
131	A18	2pi slate (C)	22.50	8.00
		Nos. 118-131 (14)	112.25	54.90

Stamps bearing this overprint were sold to merchants at a discount from face value to encourage the use of Turkish stamps on foreign correspondence, instead of those of the various European powers which maintained post offices in Turkey. The overprint is the Arab "B," for "Béhié," meaning "discount."

Tughra and 'Reshad' of Sultan Abdülhamid — A19

Tughra is upright and there is no space between the script and the frame.

1908

132	A19	5pa ocher	1.25	.50
133	A19	10pa blue green	1.75	.50
134	A19	20pa carmine	45.00	1.50
135	A19	1pi bright blue	13.00	1.50
a.		1pi ultramarine	50.00	10.00
136	A19	2pi blue black	6.50	1.00
137	A19	2½pi violet brown	2.00	1.00
138	A19	5pi dark violet	14.00	1.50
139	A19	10pi red	35.00	2.00
140	A19	25pi dark green	6.50	5.00
141	A19	50pi red brown	30.00	32.50

See Nos. J49-J50. For overprints and surcharges see Nos. 142-145, 314B-316B, 390-396, 509-516A, B4-B6, B17, B24-B27, P55-P60, P130-P131, P151, P172, Thrace 15.

Small "Discount" Overprint in Carmine or Blue

142	A19	10pa blue green (C)	7.50	1.75
143	A19	20pa carmine (Bl)	7.50	1.75
144	A19	1pi brt blue (C)	19.00	1.75
145	A19	2pi blue black (C)	30.00	8.00
		Nos. 132-145 (14)	219.00	60.25

A20

Perf. 12, 13½ & Compound

1908, Dec. 17

146	A20	5pa ocher	1.00	1.25
147	A20	10pa blue green	1.50	1.25
148	A20	20pa carmine	1.50	1.25
149	A20	1pi ultra	4.50	1.50
150	A20	2pi gray black	20.00	15.00
		Nos. 146-150 (5)	28.50	20.25

Imperf

146a	A20	5pa	30.00	30.00
147a	A20	10pa	30.00	30.00
148a	A20	20pa	30.00	30.00
149a	A20	1pi	45.00	45.00

Granting of a Constitution, the date of which is inscribed on the banderol: "324 Temuz 10" (July 24, 1908).

For overprints see Nos. 397, 517.

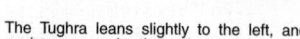

Tughra and "Reshad" of Sultan Mohammed V — A21

The Tughra leans slightly to the left, and there is space under the script.

1909, Dec.

151	A21	5pa ocher	1.00	.35
152	A21	10pa blue green	1.00	.35
a.		Imperf.	30.00	30.00
153	A21	20pa carmine rose	1.00	.35
154	A21	1pi ultra	8.00	.50
a.		1pi bright blue	12.50	.50
155	A21	2pi blue black	2.00	.50
156	A21	2½pi dark brown	70.00	14.00
157	A21	5pi dark violet	2.00	1.00
158	A21	10pi dull red	25.00	1.00
159	A21	25pi dark green	325.00	75.00
160	A21	50pi red brown	125.00	75.00

The 2pa olive green, type A21, is a newspaper stamp, No. P68.

Two types exist for the 10pa, 20pa and 1pi. In the second type, the damaged crescent is restored.

See Nos. J51-J52. For overprints and surcharges see Nos. 161-164, 317-327, 342-343, 398-406, 518-528, 567, B7-B14, B18, B28-B32, P61-P68, P81, P132-P133, P152, P173, Turkey in Asia 67, 72, Thrace 1-4, 13, 13A, 14.

Overprinted in Carmine or Blue

161	A21	10pa blue grn (C)	5.00	1.25
a.		Imperf.	40.00	
162	A21	20pa car rose (Bl)	5.00	1.50
a.		Imperf.	40.00	
163	A21	1pi ultra (C)	8.00	2.00
a.		Imperf.	40.00	
b.		1pi bright blue	6.50	3.00
164	A21	2pi blue black (C)	75.00	25.00
a.		Imperf.		
		Nos. 151-164 (14)	653.00	197.80

Stamps of 1901-05 Overprinted in Carmine or Blue

The overprint was applied to 18 denominations in four settings with change of city name, producing individual sets for each city: "MONASTIR," "PRISTINA," "SALONIQUE" and "USKUB."

1911, June 26 *Perf. 12, 13½*

165	A16	5pa bister	4.50	*5.00*
166	A16	10pa yel grn	4.50	*5.00*
167	A16	20pa magenta	9.50	*10.00*
168	A16	1pi violet blue	9.50	*10.00*
169	A16	2pi gray blue	9.50	*10.00*
170	A16	5pi ocher	50.00	*80.00*
171	A16	25pi dark green	70.00	*100.00*
172	A16	50pi yellow	100.00	*150.00*
173	A17	5pa purple	5.50	4.50
174	A17	10pa green	6.25	4.50
175	A17	20pa carmine	8.50	9.00
176	A17	1pi blue	8.50	9.00
177	A17	2pi orange	8.50	9.00
178	A17	5pi lilac rose	47.50	*70.00*
179	A17	25pi chocolate	150.00	*200.00*
d.		Perf. 12	150.00	200.00
180	A17	50pi yel brn	120.00	*145.00*
d.		Perf. 12	150.00	200.00
181	A18	2½pi red violet	65.00	*110.00*
182	A18	10pi org brn	65.00	*90.00*
		Nos. 165-182 (18)	742.25	*1,021.*

Sultan's visit to Macedonia. The Arabic overprint reads: "Souvenir of the Sultan's Journey, 1329." See Nos. P69-P81.

General Post Office, Constantinople — A22

1913, Mar. 14 ***Perf. 12***

237 A22 2pa olive green .65 .50
238 A22 5pa ocher .65 .50
239 A22 10pa blue green .80 .50
240 A22 20pa carmine rose .80 .50
241 A22 1pi ultra .80 .50
242 A22 2pi indigo 1.50 .50
243 A22 5pi dull violet 12.00 .50
244 A22 10pi dull red 8.00 1.00
245 A22 25pi gray green 22.50 22.50
246 A22 50pi orange brown 85.00 100.00

See Nos. J53-J58. For overprints and surcharges see Nos. 247-250, 328-339, 344, 407-414, 529-538, 568, B14-B16, B33-B36. Mesopotamia Nos. N6, N16-N19, N24-N25. Turkey in Asia 68, Thrace 10, 10A, 11, 11A, 12, N82.

Overprinted in Carmine or Blue

247 A22 10pa blue green (C) 1.50 .50
248 A22 20pa car rose (Bl) 1.75 .50
249 A22 1pi ultra (C) 2.00 .50
250 A22 2pi indigo (C) 25.00 7.50
Nos. 237-250 (14) 162.95 136.00

Mosque of Selim, Adrianople A23

1913, Oct. 23 **Engr.**

251 A23 10pa green 1.50 1.75
252 A23 20pa red 2.50 1.75
253 A23 40pa blue 12.00 2.50
Nos. 251-253 (3) 16.00 6.00

Recapture of Adrianople (Edirne) by the Turks.

See Nos. 592, J59-J62. For overprints and surcharge see Nos. 415-417, 539-540, J59-J62, J67-J70, J83-J86, Mesopotamia No. N7, Thrace N84.

Obelisk of Theodosius in the Hippodrome A24

Column of Constantine A25

Leander's Tower A26

One of the Seven Towers A27

Fener Bahçe (Garden Lighthouse) A28

The Castle of Europe on the Bosporus A29

Mosque of Sultan Ahmed — A30

Monument to the Martyrs of Liberty — A31

Fountains of Suleiman — A32

Cruiser "Hamidie" — A33

View of Kandili on the Bosporus — A34

War Ministry (Later Istanbul University) — A35

Sweet Waters of Europe Park — A36

Mosque of Suleiman — A37

The Bosporus — A38

Sultan Ahmed's Fountain — A39

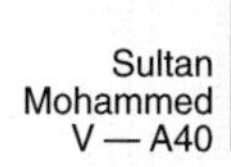

Sultan Mohammed V — A40

Designs A24-A39: Views of Constantinople.

1914, Jan. 14 **Litho.**

254 A24 2pa red lilac 1.00 .50
255 A25 4pa dark brown 1.00 .50
256 A26 5pa violet brown 1.00 .50
257 A27 6pa dark blue 1.00 .50

Engr.

258 A28 10pa green 2.25 .50
259 A29 20pa red 2.00 .50
260 A30 1pi blue 1.00 .50
b. Booklet pane of 2+2 labels
261 A31 1½pi car & blk 1.25 .50
262 A32 1¾pi sl & red brn 1.50 1.00
263 A33 2pi green & blk 2.00 .50
264 A34 2½pi org & ol grn 2.00 .50
265 A35 5pi dull violet 3.50 .60
266 A36 10pi red brown 5.50 1.00
267 A37 25pi olive green 125.00 18.00
268 A38 50pi carmine 5.50 4.50
269 A39 100pi deep blue 75.00 40.00
Cut cancellation 14.00
270 A40 200pi green & blk 550.00 *300.00*
Cut cancellation 50.00
Nos. 254-270 (17) 780.50 370.10

See Nos. 590-591, 593-598.

For overprints and surcharges see Nos. 271-287, 419, 541, 552-553, 574A, 601, 603-604, P174, Mesopotamia Nos. N1-N5, N28-N41, N50-N53, NO1-NO22, Turkey in Asia 1-3, 5-9, 73-74, Thrace N77, N78.

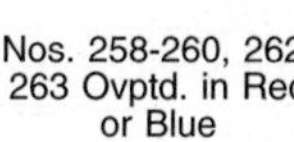

Nos. 258-260, 262-263 Ovptd. in Red or Blue

271 A28 10pa green (R) 4.00 1.00
272 A29 20pa red (Bl) 8.00 1.25
273 A30 1pi blue (R) 2.00 .50
275 A32 1¾pi sl & red brn (Bl) 2.00 1.50
276 A33 2pi green & blk (R) 50.00 5.50
Nos. 271-276 (5) 66.00 9.75

No. 261 Surcharged

1914, July 23

277 A31 1pi on 1½pi car & blk 7.00 1.50
a. "1330" omitted 15.00 15.00
b. Double surcharge 30.00 30.00
c. Triple surcharge 30.00 30.00

7th anniv. of the Constitution. The surcharge reads "10 July, 1330, National fête" and has also the numeral "1" at each side, over the original value of the stamp.

Stamps of 1914 Overprinted in Black or Red

278 A26 5pa violet brn (Bk) 2.00 .60
279 A28 10pa green (R) 5.00 .60
280 A29 20pa red (Bk) 5.00 .60
281 A30 1pi blue (R) 10.00 1.50
282 A33 2pi grn & blk (R) 11.00 1.50
283 A35 5pi dull violet (R) 60.00 3.00
284 A36 10pi red brown (R) 190.00 55.00
Nos. 278-284 (7) 283.00 62.80

This overprint reads "Abolition of the Capitulations, 1330".

No. 269 Surcharged

1915

286 A39 10pi on 100pi 70.00 20.00
a. Inverted surcharge 90.00 —

No. 270 Surcharged

287 A40 25pi on 200pi 25.00 8.00

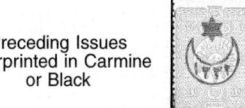

Preceding Issues Overprinted in Carmine or Black

1915 **On Stamps of 1892**

288 A10 10pa gray green 1.00 .50
a. Inverted overprint 15.00 15.00
289 A13 2pi brown orange 1.50 .50
a. Inverted overprint 15.00 15.00
290 A14 5pi dull violet 4.00 .50
a. On No. 99a 17.00 17.00

On Stamp of 1897

291 A10 5pa on 10pa gray grn 1.00 .50
a. Inverted overprint 15.00 15.00
b. On No. 100a 10.00 10.00

On Stamps of 1901

292 A16 5pa bister 1.00 .50
293 A16 1pi violet blue 3.00 .50
294 A16 2pi gray blue 2.50 .50
295 A16 5pi ocher 20.00 .50
296 A16 25pi dark green 50.00 20.00
297 A17 5pa purple 1.00 .50
298 A17 10pa green 1.50 .50
299 A17 20pa carmine 1.50 .50
a. Inverted overprint 15.00 15.00
300 A17 1pi blue 1.50 .50
a. Inverted overprint 15.00 15.00
301 A17 2pi orange 2.00 .50
a. Inverted overprint 15.00 15.00
b. Double ovpt. (R and Bk) 5.00 5.00
302 A17 5pi lilac rose 2.50 .50
303 A17 25pi brown 12.50 2.00

On Stamps of 1905

304 A18 5pa ocher 1.00 .50
305 A18 10pa dull green 1.00 .50
a. Inverted overprint 15.00 15.00
306 A18 20pa carmine 1.00 .50
a. Inverted overprint 15.00 15.00
307 A18 1pi brt blue 1.50 .50
a. Inverted overprint 15.00 15.00
308 A18 2pi slate 2.50 .50
a. Inverted overprint 20.00 20.00
309 A18 2½pi red violet 1.50 .50
310 A18 5pi brown 2.00 .50
a. Inverted overprint 20.00 20.00
311 A18 10pi orange brown 12.50 .50
312 A18 25pi olive green 50.00 8.00

With Additional Overprint On Nos. 313-314

On Stamps of 1906

313 A18 10pa dull green 2.00 .50
314 A18 2pi slate 5.00 .50
a. Inverted overprint 15.00 15.00

On Stamps of 1908

314B A19 2pi blue black 225.00 50.00
315 A19 2½pi violet brown 5.00 1.50
315A A19 5pi dark violet 100.00 35.00
315B A19 10pi red 15.00 7.50
316 A19 25pi dark green 30.00 5.00
a. Inverted overprint 50.00 50.00

For surcharges see Mesopotamia Nos. N13-N15.

With Additional Overprint on No. 316B

316B A19 2pi blue black 15.00 5.00

On Stamps of 1909

317 A21 5pa ocher 1.00 .50
a. Inverted overprint 15.00 15.00
b. Double overprint 15.00 15.00
318 A21 20pa car rose 1.25 .75
a. Inverted overprint 15.00 15.00
319 A21 1pi ultra 2.00 .50
a. Inverted overprint 15.00 15.00
320 A21 2pi blue blk 2.50 .75
a. Inverted overprint 15.00 15.00
321 A21 2½pi dark brn 67.50 25.00
322 A21 5pi dark violet 1.00 .50
a. Inverted overprint 15.00 15.00
323 A21 10pi dull red 10.00 .50
324 A21 25pi dark green 1,750. 1,200.

With Additional Overprint On Nos. 325, 326, and 327

325 A21 20pa carmine rose 2.00 .50
a. Inverted overprint 20.00 20.00
326 A21 1pi ultra 2.00 .50
327 A21 2pi blue black 3.50 .50

On Stamps of 1913

328 A22 5pa ocher 1.00 .50
a. Inverted overprint 15.00 14.00
329 A22 10pa blue green 1.00 .50
a. Inverted overprint 20.00 18.00
330 A22 20pa carmine rose 1.00 .50
a. Inverted overprint 15.00 14.00
331 A22 1pi ultra 1.50 .50
a. Inverted overprint 15.00 15.00
332 A22 2pi indigo 2.00 .50
a. Inverted overprint 15.00 13.00
333 A22 5pi dull violet 3.00 .50
334 A22 10pi dull red 10.00 .50
a. Inverted overprint 20.00 18.00
335 A22 25pi gray green 30.00 20.00

With Additional Overprint

336 A22 10pa blue green 1.00 .50
337 A22 20pa carmine rose 1.00 .50
338 A22 1pi ultra 2.00 .50
339 A22 2pi indigo 7.50 3.00
a. Inverted overprint 15.00 15.00

See Nos. P121-P133.

Stamps of 1901-13 Overprinted

1916

340 A17 5pa purple 1.00 .50
a. 5pa purple, #P43 80.00 80.00

341 A17 10pa green 1.50 .50
a. Double overprint 6.50 6.50
b. 10pa yellow green, #103 80.00 80.00
342 A21 20pa car rose, #153 2.00 .75
a. 20pa carmine rose, #162 110.00 110.00
343 A21 1pi ultra 5.50 1.00
344 A22 5pi dull violet 10.00 3.00
Nos. 340-344 (5) 20.00 5.75

Occupation of the Sinai Peninsula.

Old General Post Office of Constantinople — A41

1916, May 29 Litho. ***Perf. 12½, 13½***

345 A41 5pa green 1.00 .90
346 A41 10pa carmine 1.00 .50
347 A41 20pa ultra 1.00 .50
348 A41 1pi violet & blk 2.00 .50
349 A41 5pi yel brn & blk 30.00 2.50
Nos. 345-349 (5) 35.00 4.90

Introduction of postage in Turkey, 50th anniv.
For overprints see Nos. 418, B42-B45.

Stamps of 1892-1905 Overprinted

1916

350 A10 10pa gray grn (R) 1.50 1.50
351 A18 20pa carmine (Bl) 2.50 1.50
352 A18 1pi blue (R) 12.00 6.00
353 A18 2pi slate (Bk) 15.00 1.00
354 A18 2½pi red violet (Bk) 25.00 3.00
Nos. 350-354 (5) 56.00 13.00

National Fête Day. Overprint reads "10 Temuz 1332" (July 23, 1916).

Preceding Issues Overprinted or Surcharged in Red or Black

a

b

1916 On Stamps of 1892-98

355 A10(a) 10pa gray green 1.00 .50
355A A11(a) 20pa vio brn 1.00 .50
b. Inverted overprint 15.00 15.00
356 A12(a) 1pi gray blue 50.00 50.00
357 A13(a) 2pi brown org 5.00 1.50
358 A14(a) 5pi dull violet 50.00 50.00

On Stamp of 1897

359 A15(b) 5pa on 10pa gray grn .75 .50

On Stamps of 1901

361 A16(a) 5pa bister 1.00 .75
a. Double overprint 15.00 7.50
362 A16(a) 10pa yel grn 1.00 .50
363 A16(a) 20pa magenta .75 .50
364 A16(a) 1pi violet blue 1.00 .50
a. Inverted overprint 15.00 15.00
365 A16(a) 2pi gray blue 5.00 1.00
366 A16(b) 5pi on 25pi dk grn 55.00 55.00
367 A16(b) 10pi on 25pi dk grn 55.00 55.00
368 A16(a) 25pi dark green 55.00 55.00
369 A17(a) 5pa purple 75.00 50.00
370 A17(a) 10pa green 2.00 1.50
371 A17(a) 20pa carmine .75 .50
a. Inverted overprint 15.00 15.00
372 A17(a) 1pi blue 1.00 .50
a. Inverted overprint 30.00 30.00
373 A17(a) 2pi orange 1.50 .50
374 A17(b) 10pi on 25pi brown 5.00 1.50
375 A17(b) 10pi on 50pi yel brn 7.50 1.50
376 A17(a) 25pi brown 7.50 1.50
377 A17(a) 50pi yel brn 10.00 2.50

On Stamps of 1905

378 A18(a) 5pa ocher .75 .50
379 A18(a) 20pa carmine 1.00 .50
a. Inverted overprint 30.00 30.00
380 A18(a) 1pi brt blue 2.00 .50
a. Inverted overprint 30.00 30.00
381 A18(a) 2pi slate 1.50 1.00
382 A18(a) 2½pi red violet 7.50 1.50
383 A18(b) 10pi on 25pi ol grn 10.00 3.00
384 A18(b) 10pi on 50pi dp vio 10.00 4.00
385 A18(a) 25pi olive green 10.00 5.00
386 A18(a) 50pi deep violet 7.50 5.00

On Stamps of 1906

387 A18(a) 10pa dull green 1.50 .60
388 A18(a) 20pa carmine 1.50 1.00
389 A18(a) 1pi brt blue 1.50 1.00

On Stamps of 1908

390 A19(a) 2½pi violet brown 67.50 67.50
391 A19(b) 10pi on 25pi dk grn 20.00 12.50
392 A19(b) 10pi on 50pi red brn 67.50 67.50
393 A19(b) 25pi on 50pi red brn 67.50 67.50
394 A19(a) 25pi dark green 15.00 5.00
395 A19(a) 50pi red brown 50.00 50.00

With Additional Overprint

396 A19(a) 2pi blue black 67.50 67.50

On Stamps of 1908-09

397 A20(a) 5pa ocher 67.50 67.50
398 A21(a) 5pa ocher 1.00 2.50
399 A21(a) 10pa blue green 50.00 50.00
400 A21(a) 20pa carmine rose 50.00 50.00
401 A21(a) 1pi ultra 2.00 1.00
402 A21(a) 2pi blue black 4.00 2.00
403 A21(a) 2½pi dark brown 50.00 50.00
404 A21(a) 5pi dark violet 50.00 50.00

With Additional Overprint

405 A21(a) 1pi ultra 67.50 67.50
406 A21(a) 2pi blue black 50.00 50.00

On Stamps of 1913

407 A22(a) 5pa ocher 1.00 .75
408 A22(a) 20pa carmine rose 1.50 .50
409 A22(a) 1pi ultra 1.50 .50
410 A22(a) 2pi indigo 3.00 1.00
411 A22(b) 10pi on 50pi org brn 12.50 10.00
412 A22(a) 25pi gray green 7.50 5.00
413 A22(a) 50pi orange brown 15.00 12.50

With Additional Overprint

414 A22(a) 1pi ultra 2.00 1.00

On Commemorative Stamps of 1913

415 A23(a) 10pa green 1.25 .50
416 A23(a) 20pa red 2.00 .75
417 A23(a) 40pa blue 6.00 2.50

On Commemorative Stamp of 1916

418 A41(a) 5pi yel brn & blk 1.00 .50

No. 277 Surcharged in Blue

419 A31 60pa on 1pi on 1½pi 3.25 3.50
a. "1330" omitted 40.00 40.00

See Nos. P134-P152, J67-J70.

Turkish Artillery A42

Mosque at Orta Köy, Constantinople A43

Lighthouse on Bosporus A44

Monument to Martyrs of Liberty A45

Map of the Dardanelles; Sultan Mohammed V — A46

Map of the Dardanelles A47

Istanbul Across the Golden Horn A48

Pyramids of Egypt — A49

Dolma Bahçe Palace and Mohammed V — A50

Sentry and Shell — A51

Sultan Mohammed V — A52

1916-18 Typo. ***Perf. 11½, 12½***

420 A42 2pa violet 1.10 1.10
421 A43 5pa orange 1.00 .50
424 A44 10pa green 1.00 .50

Engr.

425 A45 20pa deep rose 1.00 .50
426 A46 1pi dull violet 2.00 .50

Typo.

428 A47 50pa ultra 1.00 .50
429 A48 2pi org brn & ind 2.00 .50
430 A49 5pi pale blue & blk 25.00 2.25

Engr.

431 A50 10pi dark green 10.00 3.50
432 A50 10pi dark violet 55.00 1.50
433 A50 10pi dark brown 14.00 1.50
434 A51 25pi carmine, *straw* 8.00 3.00
437 A52 50pi carmine 3.50 1.50
438 A52 50pi indigo 3.00 1.50
439 A52 50pi green, *straw* 3.00 10.00
Nos. 420-439 (15) 130.60 28.85

For overprints and surcharges see Nos. 541B-541E, 554-560, 565-566, 569-574, 575, 577-578, 579A-580, Turkey in Asia 4, 10, 64-66, Thrace N76, N80, N81. Compare designs A42-A43 with A53-A54.

Forgeries of Nos. 446-545 abound.

Preceding Issues Overprinted or Surcharged in Red, Black or Blue

d

e

1917 On Stamps of 1865

446 A5(d) 20pa yellow (R) 45.00 67.50
a. Star without rays (R) 50.00 57.50
447 A5(d) 1pi pearl gray (R) 45.00 67.50
a. Star without rays (R) 50.00 57.50
448 A5(d) 2pi blue (R) 45.00 67.50
449 A5(d) 5pi car (Bk) 45.00 67.50

On Stamp of 1867

450 A5(d) 5pi rose (Bk) 45.00 67.50

On Stamps of 1870-71

451 A5(d) 2pi red (Bl) 45.00 67.50
452 A5(d) 5pi blue (Bk) 45.00 67.50
453 A5(d) 25pi dl rose (Bl) 45.00 67.50

On Stamp of 1874-75

454 A5(d) 10pa red vio (Bl) 45.00 67.50

On Stamps of April, 1876

455 A5(d) 10pa red lilac (Bl) 45.00 67.50
a. 10pa red violet (Bl) 50.00 67.50
457 A5(d) 20pa pale grn (R) 45.00 67.50
458 A5(d) 1pi yellow (Bl) 45.00 67.50

On Stamps of January, 1876

459 A5(d) ¼pi on 10pa rose lil (Bl) 45.00 67.50
460 A5(d) ½pi on 20pa yel grn (R) 45.00 67.50
461 A5(d) 1¼pi on 50pa rose (Bl) 45.00 67.50

On Stamps of September, 1876

462 A7(d) 50pa blue & yel (R) 45.00 67.50
463 A7(d) 2pi blk & redsh brn (R) 45.00 67.50
464 A7(d) 25pi clar & rose (Bk) 45.00 67.50

On Stamps of 1880-84

465 A7(d) 5pa blk & ol (R) 45.00 67.50
466 A7(d) 10pa blk & grn (R) 45.00 67.50

On Stamps of 1881-82

467 A5(d) 20pa gray (Bl) 45.00 67.50
468 A5(d) 2pi pale sal (Bl) 45.00 67.50

On Stamps of 1884-86

469 A7(d) 10pa grn & pale grn (Bk) 45.00 67.50
470 A7(d) 2pi ocher & pale ocher (Bk) 45.00 67.50
471 A7(d) 5pi red brn & pale brn (Bk) 45.00 67.50

On Stamps of 1886

472 A7(d) 5pa blk & pale gray (R) 4.00 2.25
a. Inverted overprint 30.00 30.00
473 A7(d) 2pi org & bl (Bk) 4.50 2.50
a. Inverted overprint 35.00 35.00
474 A7(d) 5pi grn & pale grn (R) 45.00 67.50
475 A7(d) 25pi bis & pale bis (Bk) 45.00 67.50

On Stamp of 1888

476 A7(d) 5pi dk brn & gray (Bk) 45.00 67.50

On Stamps of 1892-98

477 A11(d) 20pa vio brn (R) 4.00 3.00
478 A13(d) 2pi brn org (R) 4.00 3.50
a. Tête bêche pair 13.50 13.50

On Stamps of 1901

479 A16(d) 5pa bister (R) 3.00 3.00
a. Inverted overprint 20.00 20.00
480 A16(d) 20pa mag (Bk) 2.00 1.50
a. Inverted overprint 25.00 25.00
481 A16(d) 1pi vio bl (R) 3.00 3.00
a. Inverted overprint 20.00 20.00
482 A16(d) 2pi gray bl (R) 5.00 5.00
483 A16(d) 5pi ocher (R) 32.50 50.00
484 A16(e) 10pi on 50pi yel (R) 32.50 50.00
485 A16(d) 25pi dk grn (R) 100.00 50.00
486 A17(d) 5pa pur (Bk) 32.50 50.00
487 A17(d) 10pa green (R) 5.00 5.00
488 A17(d) 20pa car (Bk) 2.00 1.50
a. Inverted overprint 35.00 35.00
489 A17(d) 1pi blue (R) 1.00 .90
490 A17(d) 2pi org (Bk) 3.00 3.00
a. Inverted overprint 20.00 20.00
491 A17(d) 5pi lil rose (R) 32.50 50.00
492 A17(e) 10pi on 50pi yel brn (R) 45.00 50.00
493 A17(d) 25pi brown (R) 25.00 5.00

On Stamps of 1905

494 A18(d) 5pa ocher (R) 2.00 1.00
a. Inverted overprint 20.00 20.00
495 A18(d) 10pa dl grn (R) 32.50 50.00
496 A18(d) 20pa car (Bk) 1.00 1.00
a. Double ovpt., one invtd. 35.00 35.00
b. Inverted overprint 35.00 35.00
497 A18(d) 1pi blue (R) 1.50 1.00
a. Inverted overprint 35.00 35.00
498 A18(d) 2pi slate (R) 5.00 5.00
499 A18(d) 2½pi red vio (Bk) 5.00 5.00
a. Inverted overprint 35.00 35.00

500 A18(d) 5pi brown (R) 35.00 45.00
501 A18(d) 10pi org brn (R) 35.00 50.00
502 A18(e) 10pi on 50pi dp vio (R) 35.00 50.00
503 A18(d) 25pi ol grn (R) 35.00 50.00

On Nos. 128-131

504 A18(d) 10pa dl grn (R) 1.50 1.00
a. Inverted overprint 20.00 20.00
505 A18(d) 20pa car (Bk) 1.00 .75
a. Double ovpt., one invtd. 20.00 20.00
b. Inverted overprint 35.00 35.00
506 A18(d) 1pi brt bl (Bk) 1.00 .75
a. Inverted overprint 35.00 35.00
507 A18(d) 1pi brt bl (R) 1.50 1.25
a. Inverted overprint 35.00 35.00
508 A18(d) 2pi slate (Bk) 35.00 50.00
Nos. 494-508 (15) 227.00 311.75

On Stamps of 1908

509 A19(d) 5pa ocher (R) 1.50 1.25
510 A19(d) 10pa bl grn (R) 20.00 20.00
510A A19(d) 1pi brt blue (R) *125.00* 140.00
511 A19(d) 2pi bl blk (R) 35.00 50.00
512 A19(d) 2½pi vio brn (Bk) 35.00 35.00
512A A19(d) 10pi red (R) *150.00* 225.00
513 A19(e) 10pi on 50pi red brn (R) 35.00 50.00
514 A19(d) 25pi dk grn (R) 35.00 50.00

With Additional Overprint

514A A19(d) 10pa bl grn (Bk) 150.00 225.00
515 A19(d) 1pi brt bl (Bk) 35.00 50.00
516 A19(d) 2pi bl blk (R) 5.00 5.00
516A A19(d) 2pi bl blk (Bk) 65.00 67.50

On Stamps of 1908-09

517 A20(d) 5pa ocher (R) 3.00 3.00
518 A21(d) 5pa ocher (R) 2.00 1.50
a. Double overprint 20.00 20.00
b. Dbl. ovpt., one inverted 20.00 20.00
519 A21(d) 10pa bl grn (R) 2.00 1.50
520 A21(d) 20pa car rose (Bk) 2.00 1.50
a. Double overprint 35.00 35.00
521 A21(d) 1pi ultra (R) 1.50 1.00
a. 1p bright blue (R) 30.00 30.00
522 A21(d) 2pi bl blk (R) 5.00 5.00
523 A21(d) 2½pi dk brn (Bk) 35.00 50.00
524 A21(d) 5pi dk vio (R) 35.00 50.00
525 A21(d) 10pi dull red (R) 35.00 50.00

With Additional Overprint

525A A21(d) 10pa bl grn (Bk) 175.00 225.00
526 A21(d) 1pi ultra (Bk) 125.00 190.00
527 A21(d) 1pi ultra (R) 5.00 4.00
a. 1pi bright blue (R) 125.00 140.00
528 A21(d) 2pi bl blk (Bk) 35.00 50.00

On Stamps of 1913

529 A22(d) 5pa ocher (R) 2.50 2.00
530 A22(d) 10pa bl grn (R) 35.00 50.00
531 A22(d) 20pa car rose (Bk) 2.50 2.50
532 A22(d) 1pi ultra (R) 2.50 3.50
533 A22(d) 2pi indigo (R) 3.50 3.50
534 A22(d) 5pi dl vio (R) 35.00 50.00
535 A22(d) 10pi dl red (Bk) 45.00 50.00

With Additional Overprint

536 A22(d) 10pa bl grn (Bk) 1.50 1.50
a. Inverted overprint 35.00 35.00
537 A22(d) 1pi ultra (Bk) 3.00 3.00
a. Inverted overprint 35.00 35.00
538 A22(d) 2pi indigo (Bk) 35.00 100.00

On Commemorative Stamps of 1913

539 A23(d) 10pa green (R) 5.00 5.00
a. Inverted overprint 35.00 35.00
540 A23(d) 40pa blue (R) 7.00 7.00
a. Inverted overprint 20.00 20.00

On No. 277, with Addition of New Value

541 A31 60pa on 1pi on 1½pi (Bk) 8.00 5.00
a. "1330" omitted 45.00 45.00

On Stamps of 1916-18

f g

541B A51(f) 25pi car, *straw* 5.00 5.00
541C A52(g) 50pi carmine 17.50 17.50
541D A52(g) 50pi indigo 35.00 50.00
541E A52(g) 50pi grn, *straw* 15.00 27.50

Ovptd. on Eastern Rumelia No. 12

542 A4(d) 20pa blk & rose (Bl) 35.00 35.00

Ovptd. in Black on Eastern Rumelia #15-17

543 A4(d) 5pa lil & pale lil 45.00 45.00
544 A4(d) 10pa grn & pale grn 45.00 45.00
545 A4(d) 20pa car & pale rose 45.00 45.00

Some experts question the status of Nos. 510A, 512A and 525A.

See Nos. J71-J86, P153-P172.

Soldiers in Trench — A52a

1917

545A A52a 5pa on 1pi red 1.50 .75

It is stated that No. 545A was never issued without surcharge.

See Nos. 548A, 548Af, 602.

Turkish Artillery — A53

1917 Typo. *Perf. 11½, 12½*

546 A53 2pa Prussian blue 125.00

In type A42 the Turkish inscription at the top is in one group, in type A53 it is in two groups. It is stated that No. 546 was never placed in use. Examples were distributed through the Universal Postal Union at Bern.

For surcharges see Nos. 547-548, Turkey in Asia 69-70.

Surcharged

547 A53 5pi on 2pa Prus blue 12.50 .75
a. Inverted surcharge 35.00 15.00
b. Turkish "5" omitted at lower left

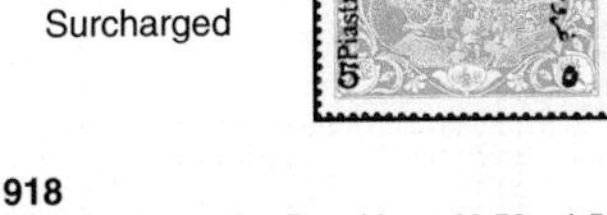

Surcharged

1918

548 A53 5pi on 2pa Prus blue 12.50 1.50
g. Inverted surcharge 35.00 20.00

Top line of surcharge on Nos. 547-548 reads "Ottoman Posts."

For surcharge see Thrace No. N79.

No. 545A Surcharged

1918

548A A52a 2pa on 5pa on 1pi red 2.50 1.75
b. Double surcharge 20.00 20.00
c. Inverted surcharge 30.00 30.00
d. Double surcharge inverted 30.00 30.00
e. Dbl. surch., one inverted 30.00 30.00
f. In pair with No. 545A 30.00 30.00

Enver Pasha and Kaiser Wilhelm II on Battlefield A54

St. Sophia and Obelisk of the Hippodrome A55

1918 Typo. *Perf. 12, 12½*

549 A54 5pa brown red 125.00
550 A55 10pa gray green 90.00

The stamps, of which very few saw postal use, were converted into paper money by pasting on thick yellow paper and reperforating.

Values are for stamps with original gum. Examples removed from the yellow paper are worth $10 each.

Armistice Issue

Overprinted in Black or Red

1919, Nov. 30

On Stamps of 1913

552 A34 2½pi org & ol grn 125.00 200.00
553 A38 50pi carmine 125.00 200.00

On Stamps of 1916-18

554 A46 1pi dl vio (R) 6.50 11.00
555 A47 50pa ultra (R), perf 11½ 1.50 1.00
556 A48 2pi org brn & ind 1.50 1.00
557 A49 5pi pale bl & blk (R), perf 11½ 1.50 1.00
558 A50 10pi dk grn (R) 11.00 12.00
559 A51 25pi car, *straw* 6.25 12.00
560 A52 50pi grn, *straw* (R) 11.00 12.50

Fountain in Desert near Sinai A56

Sentry at Beersheba A57

Turkish Troops at Sinai — A58

Typo.

562 A56 20pa claret 1.50 *1.10*
563 A57 1pi blue (R) 125.00 160.00
564 A58 25pi slate blue (R) 125.00 160.00
Nos. 552-564 (12) 540.75 771.60

The overprint reads: "Souvenir of the Armistice, 30th October 1334." Nos. 562-564 are not known to have been regularly issued without overprint.

See No. J87. For overprints and surcharges see Nos. 576, 579, 582, 583-584, 586, Turkey in Asia 71, Thrace N83.

Stamps of 1911-19 Overprinted in Turkish

"Accession to the Throne of His Majesty, 3rd July 1334-1918," the Tughra of Sultan Mohammed VI and sometimes Ornaments and New Values

Dome of the Rock, Jerusalem — A59

No. 565 No. 566

No. 567 No. 568

No. 569 No. 570

No. 571 No. 572

No. 573

No. 574

No. 575

No. 576

1919

565 A42 2pa violet 1.00 *2.00*
566 A43 5pa orange .50 .50
567 A21 5pa on 2pa ol grn .75 .50
a. Inverted surcharge 30.00 30.00
568 A22 10pa on 2pa ol grn .50 .50
569 A44 10pa green 1.50 1.50
a. Inverted overprint 50.00 —
570 A45 20pa deep rose 1.25 1.00
a. Inverted overprint 30.00 30.00
571 A46 1pi dull violet 1.25 1.00
572 A47 60pa on 50pa ultra 1.25 1.00
573 A48 60pa on 2pi org brn & ind .75 .50
574 A48 2pi org brn & ind .50 1.00
574A A34 2½pi org & ol grn 35.00 *50.00*
575 A49 5pi pale blue & blk .50 1.00
576 A56 10pi on 20pa clar .50 1.00
577 A50 10pi dark brown 2.00 2.00
578 A51 25pi car, *straw* 1.75 1.75
579 A57 35pi on 1pi blue 1.00 2.00
579A A52 50pi carmine 35.00 *50.00*
580 A52 50pi grn, *straw* 4.00 4.00
581 A59 100pi on 10pa grn 4.00 4.00
582 A58 250pi on 25pi sl bl 4.00 4.00
Nos. 565-582 (20) 97.00 129.25

See note after #586. See #J88-J91.

For overprint and surcharge see Nos. 585, Thrace N82.

Surcharged with Ornaments, New Values

No. 583

No. 584

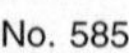

No. 585

No. 586

Perf. 11½, 12½

583 A56 20pa claret 1.50 8.00
584 A57 1pi deep blue 1.75 13.00
585 A59 60pa on 10pa green 1.00 6.50
586 A58 25pi slate blue 15.00 60.00
a. Inverted overprint 250.00 —
Nos. 583-586 (4) 19.25 87.50

#576, 579, 581, 582, 583-586 were prepared in anticipation of the invasion and conquest of Egypt by the Turks. They were not issued at that time but subsequently received various overprints in commemoration of Sultan Mehmet Sadi's accession to the throne (#565-582) and of the 1st anniv. of this event (#583-586).

For surcharge see Thrace No. N83.

Designs of 1913 Modified

1920 Litho. *Perf. 11, 12*
590 A26 5pa brown orange 1.25 .60

Engr.

591 A28 10pa green 1.25 .60
592 A23 20pa rose 1.25 .60
593 A30 1pi blue green 4.75 .60
594 A32 3pi blue 1.25 .60
595 A34 5pi gray 65.00 6.00
596 A36 10pi gray violet 8.00 .60
597 A37 25pi maroon 4.00 2.00
598 A38 50pi yel brn 4.00 10.00
Nos. 590-598 (9) 90.75 21.60

On most stamps of this issue the designs have been modified by removing the small Turkish word at right of the tughra of the Sultan. In the 3pi and 5pi the values have been altered, while for the 25pi the color has been changed.

For surcharges see Thrace Nos. N77, N78, N84.

No. B46 Surcharged

No. 258 Surcharged

No. 594 Surcharged

1921-22 Black Surcharge
600 SP1 30pa on 10pa red vio 1.50 .50
a. Double surcharge 37.50 37.50
b. Imperf. 40.00 40.00
601 A28 60pa on 10pa green 1.50 .50
a. Double surcharge 22.50 22.50
602 A52a 4½pi on 1pi red 2.50 .50
a. Inverted surcharge 75.00 —
603 A32 7½pi on 3pi blue 20.00 2.00
604 A32 7½pi on 3pi bl (R) ('22) 25.00 2.00
a. Double surcharge 35.00 30.00
Nos. 600-604 (5) 50.50 5.50

Turkish Stamps of 1916-21 with Greek surcharge as above in blue or black are of private origin.

Issues of the Republic

Crescent and Star — A64

TWO PIASTERS:
Type I — "2" measures 3¼x1¾mm
Type II — "2" measures 2¾x1½mm

FIVE PIASTERS:
Type I — "5" measures 3½x2¼mm
Type II — "5" measures 3x1¾mm

Printed by Ahmed Nazmi, Istanbul

Perf. 13¼x12¾-13¼

1923 Litho. Thin Paper
605 A64 10pa gray black .30 .25
606 A64 20pa olive yel .30 .25
607 A64 1pi deep violet .30 .25
a. Slanting numeral in lower left corner .50 .25
608 A64 1½pi emerald .90 .25
609 A64 2pi bluish grn (I) .90 .25
a. 2pi deep green (II) .90 .25
610 A64 3pi yel brn .90 .60
611 A64 3¾pi lilac brown 3.00 3.00
612 A64 4½pi carmine .90 1.20
613 A64 5pi dp pur (I) 4.50 1.75
a. 5pi purple (II) 21.00 1.25
614 A64 7½pi blue 3.00 .60
615 A64 10pi slate 12.00 1.25
a. 10pi blue 16.00 1.25
616 A64 11¼pi dull rose 3.00 2.50
617 A64 15pi brown 15.00 1.25
618 A64 18¾pi myr grn 4.25 3.75
619 A64 22½pi orange 12.00 2.50
620 A64 25pi blk brn 50.00 3.00
621 A64 50pi gray 125.00 5.00
622 A64 100pi dark violet 250.00 11.00
623 A64 500pi dp grn 950.00 275.00
Cut cancellation 15.00
Nos. 605-623 (19) 1,436. 313.65
Set, never hinged 4,250.

Nos. 605-610, 612-617 exist imperf. & part perf.

Printed by Ikdam, Istanbul

1924 Thick Paper *Perf. 11*
605b A64 10pa greenish gray .90 .25
606b A64 20pa olive yellow .90 .25
607b A64 1pi deep violet 1.75 .25
d. Slanting numeral in lower left corner 2.00 .25
609b A64 2pi bluish green (I) 6.00 .90
d. 2pi bluish green (II) 175.00 2.00
610b A64 3pi yellow brown 150.00 7.50
612b A64 4½pi carmine 1.50 .60
613b A64 5pi purple (II) 3.50 .25
614b A64 7½pi blue 3.50 .60
615b A64 10pi slate 11.00 12.00
617b A64 15pi yellow brown 11.00 12.00
Set, never hinged 555.00

Printed by Ottoman Public Debt Administration, Istanbul

1924-26 Thick Paper *Perf. 12*
605c A64 10pa black .30 .25
606c A64 20pa olive yellow .30 .25
607c A64 1pi violet .60 .60
609c A64 2pi green (II) 3.00 .60
610c A64 3pi yellow brown 3.50 .60
613c A64 5pi violet 3.50 1.00
615c A64 10pi dark blue 60.00 12.00
d. 10pi perf. 13¼x12 60.00 12.00
Set, never hinged 285.00

Bridge of Sakarya and Mustafa Kemal — A65

1924, Jan. 1 *Perf. 12*
625 A65 1½pi emerald 1.50 1.00
626 A65 3pi purple 1.50 1.25
627 A65 4½pi pale rose 2.00 2.25
628 A65 5pi yellow brown 2.00 5.00
629 A65 7½pi deep blue 2.00 3.00
630 A65 50pi orange 50.00 40.00
631 A65 100pi brown violet 70.00 50.00
632 A65 200pi olive brown 125.00 75.00
Nos. 625-632 (8) 254.00 177.50
Set, never hinged 850.00

Signing of Treaty of Peace at Lausanne.

The Legendary Blacksmith and his Gray Wolf A66

Fortress of Ankara A68

Sakarya Gorge A67

Mustafa Kemal Pasha A69

1926 Engr.
634 A66 10pa slate .40 .25
635 A66 20pa orange .40 .25
636 A66 1g brt rose .40 .25
637 A67 2g green 1.10 .25
638 A67 2½g gray black 1.40 .25
639 A67 3g copper red 1.75 .25
640 A68 5g deep blue 1.75 .40
641 A68 6g red 1.00 .25
642 A68 10g blue 6.00 .40
643 A68 15g deep orange 7.50 .40
644 A69 25g dk grn & blk 12.00 1.10
645 A69 50g car & blk 15.00 1.25
646 A69 100g ol grn & blk 55.00 5.00
647 A69 200g brown & blk 120.00 12.00
Nos. 634-647 (14) 223.70 22.30
Set, never hinged 1,300.

For surcharges see Nos. 648-675.

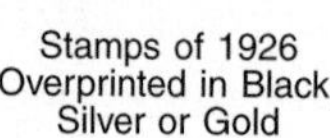

Stamps of 1926 Overprinted in Black, Silver or Gold

1927, Sept. 9
648 A66 1g brt rose .50 .50
649 A67 2g green .50 1.00
650 A67 2½g gray black 1.25 1.25
651 A67 3g copper red 1.60 1.75
652 A68 5g lilac gray 2.00 2.25
653 A68 6g red 1.25 1.25
654 A68 10g deep blue 2.00 2.50
655 A68 15g deep orange 5.00 3.25
656 A69 25g dk grn & blk (S) 20.00 15.00
657 A69 50g car & blk (S) 60.00 30.00
658 A69 100g ol grn & blk (G) 150.00 65.00
Nos. 648-658 (11) 244.10 123.75
Set, never hinged 700.00

Agricultural and industrial exhibition at Izmir, Sept. 9-20, 1927.

The overprint reads: "1927" and the initials of "Izmir Dokuz Eylul Sergisi" (Izmir Exhibition, September 9).

Second Izmir Exhibition Issue

Nos. 634-647 Overprinted in Red or Black

On A66-A68

On A69

1928, Sept. 9
659 A66 10pa slate (R) .50 .25
660 A66 20pa orange .50 .25
661 A66 1g brt rose 1.00 .50
662 A67 2g green (R) 1.50 1.10
663 A67 2½g gray blk (R) 1.50 1.10
664 A67 3g copper red 1.50 1.10
665 A68 5g lilac gray (R) 1.60 2.40
666 A68 6g red 2.40 2.40
667 A68 10g deep blue 3.50 2.40
668 A68 15g deep orange 5.00 1.60
669 A69 25g dk grn & blk (R) 12.00 6.00
670 A69 50g car & blk 21.00 20.00
671 A69 100g ol grn & blk (R) 60.00 50.00
672 A69 200g brn & blk (R) 160.00 95.00
Nos. 659-672 (14) 272.00 184.10
Set, never hinged 900.00

The overprint reads "Izmir, September 9, 1928."

No. 636 Surcharged in Black

No. 640 Surcharged in Red

1929
673 A66 20pa on 1g brt rose .50 .25
a. Inverted surcharge 25.00 12.50
674 A68 2½k on 5g deep blue 1.00 .80
a. Inverted surcharge 50.00 35.00

No. 642 Surcharged in Red

675 A68 6k on 10g blue 6.00 .75
Nos. 673-675 (3) 7.50 1.80
Set, never hinged 40.00

Railroad Bridge over Kizil Irmak — A70

A71

A72

A73

Latin Inscriptions

Without umlaut over first "U" of "CUMHURIYETI"

1929 Engr.
676 A70 2k gray black 4.50 .80
677 A70 2½k green 2.00 .80
678 A70 3k violet brown 3.25 1.10
679 A71 6k dark violet 22.50 .80
680 A72 12½k deep blue 27.50 3.25
681 A73 50k carmine & blk 90.00 8.75
Nos. 676-681 (6) 149.75 15.50
Set, never hinged 500.00

See Nos. 682-691, 694-695, 697, 699. For surcharges & overprints see #705-714, 716-717, 719, 721, 727, 765-766, 770-771, 777, C2, C7.

Sakarya Gorge A74

Mustafa Kemal Pasha A75

With umlaut over first "U" of "CUMHURIYETI"

1930
682 A71 10pa green .50 .25
683 A70 20pa gray violet .50 .25
684 A70 1k olive green .75 .50
685 A71 1½k olive black .75 .50
686 A70 2k dull violet 1.75 .50
687 A70 2½k deep green 1.60 .50
688 A70 3k brown orange 20.00 1.50
689 A71 4k deep rose 11.00 .40

690 A72 5k rose lake 12.50 .40
691 A71 6k indigo 15.00 .25
692 A74 7½k red brown .50 .35
694 A72 12½k deep ultra .75 .25
695 A72 15k deep orange .75 .40
696 A74 17½k dark gray .75 .40
697 A72 20k black brown 60.00 1.60
698 A74 25k olive brown 2.40 1.00
699 A72 30k yellow brown 1.25 1.00
700 A74 40k red violet 1.10 1.00
701 A75 50k red & black 1.75 1.00
702 A75 100k olive grn & blk 1.75 1.00
703 A75 200k dk green & blk 1.75 1.25
704 A75 500k chocolate & blk 17.50 27.50
Nos. 682-704 (22) 154.60 41.80
Set, never hinged 600.00

For surcharges and overprints see Nos. 715, 718, 720, 722-726, 767-769, 772-773, 775-776, 778-780, 823-828, 848-850, C1, C3-C6, C8-C11.

Nos. 682-704 Surcharged in Red or Black

a

b

c

1930, Aug. 30
705 A71(a) 10pa on 10pa (R) 1.00 1.25
706 A70(b) 10pa on 20pa 1.00 1.50
707 A70(b) 20pa on 1ku 1.00 1.25
708 A71(a) 1k on 1½k (R) 1.00 1.25
709 A70(b) 1½k on 2k 1.00 1.25
710 A70(b) 2k on 2½k (R) 1.75 1.60
711 A70(b) 2½k on 3k 1.75 1.50
712 A71(a) 3k on 4k 1.75 1.00
713 A72(a) 4k on 5k 1.75 1.00
714 A71(a) 5k on 6k (R) 3.50 3.50
715 A74(a) 6k on 7½k .75 .50
716 A72(a) 7½k on 12½k (R) 1.25 1.00
717 A72(a) 12½k on 15k 1.25 1.00
718 A74(b) 15k on 17½k (R) 5.00 4.75
719 A72(b) 17½k on 20k (R) 5.00 4.75
720 A74(b) 20k on 25k (R) 5.50 2.25
721 A72(b) 25k on 30k 5.00 2.50
722 A74(b) 30k on 40k 6.50 2.50
723 A75(c) 40k on 50k 12.50 6.25
724 A75(c) 50k on 100k (R) 80.00 17.00
725 A75(c) 100k on 200k (R) 160.00 30.00
726 A75(c) 250k on 500k (R) 95.00 60.00
Nos. 705-726 (22) 393.25 147.60
Set, never hinged 1,200.

Inauguration of the railroad between Ankara and Sivas.
There are numerous varieties in these settings as: "309," "390," "930" inverted, no period after "D," no period after "Y" and raised period before "Y."

No. 685 Surcharged in Red

1931, Apr. 1
727 A71 1k on 1½k olive blk 1.75 1.00

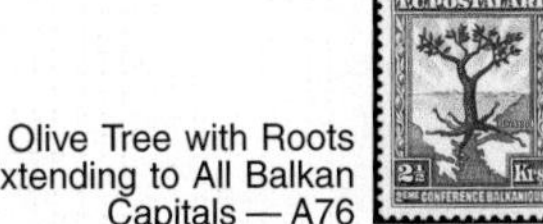
Olive Tree with Roots Extending to All Balkan Capitals — A76

1931, Oct. 20 Engr. *Perf. 12*
728 A76 2½k dark green .50 .40
729 A76 4k carmine .50 .40
730 A76 6k steel blue .50 .40
731 A76 7½k dull red .50 .40
732 A76 12k deep orange .75 .40
733 A76 12½k dark blue .75 .40
734 A76 30k dark violet 1.25 1.25
735 A76 50k dark brown 1.25 1.25
736 A76 100k brown violet 5.50 3.00
Nos. 728-736 (9) 11.50 7.90
Set, never hinged 35.00

Second Balkan Conference.

A77

A78

Mustafa Kemal Pasha (Kemal Atatürk) — A79

1931-42 Typo. *Perf. 11½, 12*
737 A77 10pa blue green .50 .25
738 A77 20pa deep orange .50 .25
739 A77 30pa brt violet ('38) .50 .25
740 A78 1k dk slate green .50 .25
740A A77 1½k magenta ('42) .65 .25
741 A78 2k dark violet .50 .25
741A A78 2k yel grn ('40) .50 .25
742 A77 2½k green .50 .25
743 A78 3k brn org ('38) 1.00 .25
744 A78 4k slate 2.00 .25
745 A78 5k rose red .75 .50
745A A78 5k brown blk ('40) 2.00 .50
746 A78 6k deep blue 3.00 .25
746A A78 6k rose ('40) 1.00 .30
747 A77 7½k deep rose ('32) .75 .25
747A A78 8k brt blue ('38) 1.50 1.00
b. 8k dark blue ('36) 2.75 2.50
748 A77 10k black brn ('32) 1.00 .25
748A A77 10k deep blue ('40) 7.00 .60
749 A77 12k bister ('32) .75 .25
750 A79 12½k indigo ('32) .75 .25
751 A77 15k org yel ('32) .75 .25
752 A77 20k olive grn ('32) 1.25 .50
753 A77 25k Prus blue ('32) 2.00 .25
754 A77 30k magenta ('32) 8.50 .25
755 A79 100k maroon ('32) 100.00 8.00
756 A79 200k purple ('32) 5.50 2.25
757 A79 250k chocolate ('32) 125.00 20.00
Nos. 737-757 (27) 268.65 38.15
Set, never hinged 1,200.

See Nos. 1015-1033, 1117B-1126. For overprints see Nos. 811-816.

Symbolizing 10th Anniversary of Republic — A80

President Atatürk A81

1933, Oct. 29 *Perf. 10*
758 A80 1½k blue green .50 .65
759 A80 2k olive brown .50 1.00
760 A81 3k dull red .65 1.00
761 A81 6k deep blue .65 1.00
762 A80 12½k dark blue 2.00 2.00
763 A80 25k dark brown 14.00 8.00
764 A81 50k orange brown 15.00 20.00
Nos. 758-764 (7) 33.30 33.65
Set, never hinged 80.00

10th year of the Turkish Republic. The stamps were in use for three days only.

Nos. 682, 685, 692, 694, 696-698, 702 Overprinted or Surcharged in Red

1934, Aug. 26 *Perf. 12*
765 A71 10pa green .50 1.00
766 A71 1k on 1½k 1.00 .50
767 A74 2k on 25k 1.50 1.00
768 A74 5k on 7½k 5.00 3.25
769 A74 6k on 17½k 2.00 1.60
770 A72 12½k deep ultra 5.50 5.00
771 A72 15k on 20k 100.00 45.00
772 A74 20k on 25k 40.00 37.50
773 A75 50k on 100k 55.00 37.50
Nos. 765-773 (9) 210.50 132.35
Set, never hinged 675.00

Izmir Fair, 1934.

Nos. 696, 698, 701-704 Surcharged in Black

1936, Oct. 26
775 A74 4k on 17½k 1.00 1.00
776 A74 5k on 25k 1.10 1.00
777 A73 6k on 50k .50 .50
778 A75 10k on 100k 1.75 2.00
779 A75 20k on 200k 8.50 6.00
780 A75 50k on 500k 10.00 6.00
Nos. 775-780 (6) 22.85 16.50
Set, never hinged 90.00

"1926" in Overprint
775a A74 4k on 17½k 6.50 3.75
776a A74 5k on 25k 7.00 3.75
777a A73 6k on 50k 7.00 3.75
778a A75 10k on 100k 9.00 4.50
779a A75 20k on 200k 20.00 10.00
780a A75 50k on 500k 55.00 27.50
Nos. 775a-780a (6) 104.50 53.25
Set, never hinged 250.00

Re-militarization of the Dardanelles.

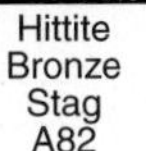
Hittite Bronze Stag A82

Thorak's Bust of Kemal Atatürk A83

1937, Sept. 20 Litho. *Perf. 12*
781 A82 3k light violet 1.10 1.10
782 A83 6k blue 1.60 1.60
783 A82 7½k bright pink 2.00 3.25
784 A83 12½k indigo 9.00 8.00
Nos. 781-784 (4) 13.70 13.95
Set, never hinged 40.00

2nd Turkish Historical Congress, Istanbul, Sept. 20-30.

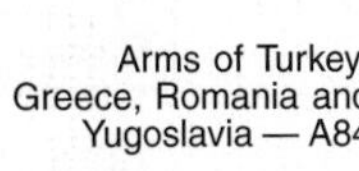

Arms of Turkey, Greece, Romania and Yugoslavia — A84

1937, Oct. 29 *Perf. 11½*
785 A84 8k carmine 8.00 3.25
786 A84 12½k dark blue 11.00 6.50
Set, never hinged 60.00

The Balkan Entente.

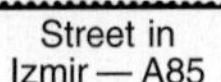
Street in Izmir — A85

Fig Tree — A87

30pa, View of Fair Buildings. 3k, Tower, Government Square. 5k, Olive branch. 6k, Woman with grapes. 7½k, Woman picking grapes. 8k, Izmir Harbor through arch. 12k, Statue of Pres. Ataturk. 12½k, Pres. Ataturk.

1938, Aug. 20 Photo. *Perf. 11½*
Inscribed: "Izmir Enternasyonal Fuari 1938"
789 A85 10pa dark brown .40 .50
790 A85 30pa purple .60 .40
791 A87 2½k brt green 1.00 .80
792 A87 3k brown orange 1.00 .40
793 A87 5k olive green 1.75 .60
794 A85 6k brown 4.00 .35
795 A87 7½k scarlet 4.00 2.25
796 A87 8k brown lake 2.75 1.25
797 A87 12k rose violet 5.00 2.75
798 A87 12½k deep blue 8.00 7.00
Nos. 789-798 (10) 28.50 16.30
Set, never hinged 75.00

Izmir International Fair.

President Atatürk Teaching Reformed Turkish Alphabet — A95

1938, Nov. 2
799 A95 2½k brt green .65 .55
800 A95 3k orange .85 .55
801 A95 6k rose violet 1.00 .65
802 A95 7½k deep rose 1.25 1.00
803 A95 8k red brown 1.40 1.10
804 A95 12½k brt ultra 1.75 1.25
Nos. 799-804 (6) 6.90 5.10
Set, never hinged 25.00

Reform of the Turkish alphabet, 10th anniv.

Army and Air Force A96

Atatürk Driving Tractor A98

3k, View of Kayseri. 7½k, Railway bridge. 8k, Scout buglers. 12½k, President Ataturk.

Inscribed: "Cumhuriyetin 15 inc yil donumu hatirasi"

1938, Oct. 29
805 A96 2½k dark green .50 .35
806 A96 3k red brown .50 .35
807 A98 6k bister .80 .35
808 A96 7½k red 1.75 .90
809 A96 8k rose violet 4.50 2.50
810 A98 12½k deep blue 3.50 1.75
Nos. 805-810 (6) 11.55 6.20
Set, never hinged 32.50

15th anniversary of the Republic.

Stamps of 1931-38 Overprinted in Black

1938, Nov. 21 *Perf. 11½x12*
811 A78 3k brown orange .75 .35
812 A78 5k rose red .75 .35
813 A78 6k deep blue 1.00 .50
814 A77 7½k deep rose 1.25 .55
815 A78 8k dark blue 3.00 .75
a. 8k bright blue 225.00 150.00
816 A79 12½k indigo 3.75 1.75
Nos. 811-816 (6) 10.50 4.25
Set, never hinged 35.00

President Kemal Atatürk (1881-1938). The date is that of his funeral.

Catalogue values for unused stamps in this section, from this point to the end of the section, are for Never Hinged items.

Turkish and American Flags
A102

Presidents Inönü and F. D. Roosevelt and Map of North America
A103

Designs: 3k, 8k, Inonu and Roosevelt. 7½k, 12½k, Kemal Ataturk and Washington.

1939, July 15 Photo. Perf. 14

817	A102	2½k	ol grn, red & bl	.45	.25
818	A103	3k	dk brn & bl grn	.90	.25
819	A102	6k	purple, red & bl	.90	.25
820	A103	7½k	org ver & bl grn	1.75	.40
821	A103	8k	dp cl & bl grn	1.40	.40
822	A103	12½k	brt bl & bl grn	3.25	1.60
			Nos. 817-822 (6)	8.65	3.15

US constitution, 150th anniversary.

Nos. 698, 702-704 Surcharged in Black

1939, July 23 Unwmk. Perf. 13

823	A74	3k	on 25k	.60	.35
824	A75	6k	on 200k	.95	.75
825	A74	7½k	on 25k	1.10	.75
826	A75	12k	on 100k	1.50	.75
827	A75	12½k	on 200k	3.00	.75
828	A75	17½k	on 500k	4.50	2.25
			Nos. 823-828 (6)	11.65	5.60

Annexation of Hatay.

Railroad Bridge
A105

Locomotive
A106

Track Through Mountain Pass — A107

Design: 12½k, Railroad tunnel, Atma Pass.

1939, Oct. 20 Typo. Perf. 11½

829	A105	3k	lt orange red	3.50	3.00
830	A106	6k	chestnut	4.00	3.50
831	A107	7½k	rose pink	6.00	5.50
832	A107	12½k	dark blue	9.00	8.00
			Nos. 829-832 (4)	22.50	20.00

Completion of the Sivas to Erzerum link of the Ankara-Erzerum Railroad.

Atatürk Residence in Ankara
A109

Kemal Atatürk
A110

A111

Designs: 5k, 6k, 7½k, 8k, 12½k, 17½k, Various portraits of Ataturk, "1880-1938."

1939-40 Photo.

833	A109	2½k	brt green	1.10	.50
834	A110	3k	dk blue gray	1.10	.50
835	A110	5k	chocolate	1.40	.75
836	A110	6k	chestnut	1.40	.75
837	A110	7½k	rose red	4.00	1.25
838	A110	8k	gray green	1.90	1.25
839	A110	12½k	brt blue	2.25	1.60
840	A110	17½k	brt rose	7.00	3.50
			Nos. 833-840 (8)	20.15	10.10

Souvenir Sheet

841	A111	100k	blue black	75.00	75.00

Death of Kemal Ataturk, first anniversary. Size of No. 841: 90x120mm.

Issued: 2½k, 6k, 12½k, 11/11/39; others, 1/3/40.

Namik Kemal — A118

1940, Jan. 3

842	A118	6k	chestnut	2.00	.60
843	A118	8k	dk olive grn	3.25	1.50
844	A118	12k	brt rose red	4.00	2.00
845	A118	12½k	brt blue	8.00	3.00
			Nos. 842-845 (4)	17.25	7.10

Birth cent. of Namik Kemal, poet and patriot.

Arms of Turkey, Greece, Romania and Yugoslavia — A119

Perf. 11½

1940, Jan. 1 Typo. Unwmk.

846	A119	8k	light blue	4.50	1.00
847	A119	10k	deep blue	10.00	2.25

The Balkan Entente.

Nos. 703-704 Surcharged in Red or Black

1940, Aug. 20 Perf. 12

848	A75	6k	on 200k dk grn & blk (R)	1.00	1.00
849	A75	10k	on 200k dk grn & blk	1.50	1.50
850	A75	12k	on 500k choc & blk	2.50	2.50
			Nos. 848-850 (3)	5.00	5.00

13th International Izmir Fair.

Map of Turkey and Census Figures — A120

1940, Oct. 1 Typo. Perf. 11½

851	A120	10pa	dark blue green	.50	.25
852	A120	3k	orange	1.50	1.25
853	A120	6k	carmine rose	2.00	1.50
854	A120	10k	dark blue	3.00	2.50
			Nos. 851-854 (4)	7.00	5.50

Census of Oct. 20, 1940.

Runner
A121

Pole Vaulter
A122

Hurdler
A123

Discus Thrower
A124

1940, Oct. 5

855	A121	3k	olive green	3.00	3.00
856	A122	6k	rose	9.00	3.50
857	A123	8k	chestnut brown	4.25	4.00
858	A124	10k	dark blue	6.50	10.00
			Nos. 855-858 (4)	22.75	20.50

11th Balkan Olympics.

Mail Carriers on Horseback
A125

Postman of 1840 and 1940
A126

Old Sailing Vessel and Modern Mailboat — A127

Design: 12k, Post Office, Istanbul.

1940, Dec. 31 Typo. Perf. 10

859	A125	3k	gray green	.85	.50
860	A126	6k	rose	1.10	.75
861	A127	10k	dark blue	1.75	1.00
862	A127	12k	olive brown	2.25	1.50
			Nos. 859-862 (4)	5.95	3.75

Centenary of the Turkish post.

Harbor Scene
A129

Statue of Atatürk
A132

Designs: 3k, 6k, 17½k, Various Izmir Fair buildings. 12k, Girl picking grapes.

Inscribed: "Izmir Enternasyonal Fuari 1941"

1941, Aug. 20 Litho. Perf. 11½

863	A129	30pa	dull green	.35	.25
864	A129	3k	olive gray	.75	.35
865	A129	6k	salmon rose	.90	.35
866	A132	10k	blue	.95	.30
867	A129	12k	dull brown vio	1.10	.45
868	A129	17½k	dull brown	1.75	1.25
			Nos. 863-868 (6)	5.80	2.95

Izmir International Fair, 1941.

Tomb of Barbarossa II — A135

Barbarossa's Fleet in Battle — A136

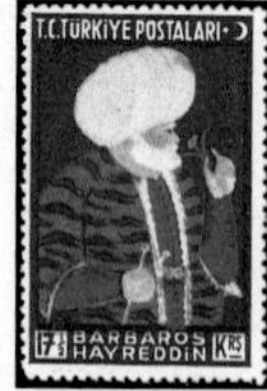

Barbarossa II (Khair ed-Din) — A137

1941

869	A135	20pa	dark violet	.55	.25
870	A136	3k	light blue	.85	.75
871	A136	6k	rose red	1.40	1.25
872	A136	10k	deep ultra	1.60	1.50
873	A136	12k	dull brn & bis	1.90	1.75
874	A137	17½k	multicolored	3.25	2.25
			Nos. 869-874 (6)	9.55	7.75

400th death anniv. of Barbarossa II.

President Inönü
A138 A138a

1942-45 Perf. 11½x11, 11

875	A138	0.25k	yellow bis	.25	.25
876	A138	0.50k	lt yellow grn	.25	.25
877	A138	1k	gray green	.25	.25
877A	A138	1½k	brt vio ('45)	.25	.25
878	A138	2k	bluish green	.30	.25
879	A138	4k	fawn	.30	.30
880	A138	4½k	slate	.30	.30
881	A138	5k	light blue	.35	.25
882	A138	6k	sal rose	.30	.25
883	A138	6¾k	ultra	.25	.25
884	A138	9k	blue violet	.90	.25
885	A138	10k	dark blue	.30	.25
886	A138	13½k	brt pink	.30	.25
887	A138	16k	Prus green	.60	.25
888	A138	17½k	rose lake	.30	.25
889	A138	20k	brown violet	.60	.50
890	A138	27½k	orange	.60	.50
891	A138	37k	buff	.60	.50
892	A138	50k	purple	2.25	.25
893	A138	100k	olive bister	6.00	3.00
894	A138a	200k	brown	19.00	2.50
			Nos. 875-894 (21)	34.25	11.10

Ankara
A139

Antioch
A141

0.50k, Mohair goats. 1½k, Ankara Dam. 2k, Oranges. 4k, Merino sheep. 4½k, Train. 5k, Tile decorating. 6k, Atatürk statue, Ankara. 6¾k, 10k, Pres. Ismet Inonu. 13½k, Grand National Assembly. 16k, Arnavutkoy, Istanbul. 17½k, Republic monument, Istanbul. 20k, Safety monument, Ankara. 27½k, Post Office, Istanbul. 37k, Monument at Afyon. 50k, "People's House," Ankara. 100k, Atatürk & Inonu. 200k, Pres. Inonu.

1943, Apr. 1 Perf. 11

896	A139	0.25k	citron	.50	.25
897	A139	0.50k	brt green	.75	.25
898	A141	1k	yellow olive	.50	.25
899	A141	1½k	deep violet	.50	.25
900	A139	2k	brt blue green	.75	.25
901	A139	4k	copper red	4.00	1.00
902	A139	4½k	black	6.00	2.00
903	A141	5k	sapphire	1.25	.50
904	A139	6k	carmine rose	.50	.50
905	A139	6¾k	brt ultra	.50	.50
906	A139	10k	dark blue	.50	.50

907 A141 13½k brt red violet .60 .50
908 A141 16k myrtle green 3.50 .50
909 A139 17½k brown orange 2.00 .50
910 A139 20k sepia 2.00 .50
911 A139 27½k dk orange 1.50 1.00
912 A139 37k lt yellow brn 2.50 .50
913 A141 50k purple 10.00 .25
914 A139 100k dk olive grn 12.50 2.50
915 A139 200k dark brown 9.00 2.00
a. Souvenir sheet 70.00 100.00
Nos. 896-915 (20) 59.35 14.50

No. 915a contains one stamp similar to No. 915, perf. 13½ and printed in sepia. Issued Apr. 20.

For surcharge see No. 928.

Girl with Grapes
A158

Entrance to Izmir Fair
A159

Fair Building — A160

1943, Aug. 20 Litho. *Perf. 11½*

916 A158 4½k dull olive .25 .25
917 A159 6k carmine rose .60 .25
918 A160 6¾k blue .60 .25
919 A159 10k dark blue .80 .50
920 A158 13½k sepia 1.25 1.00
921 A160 27½k dull gray 1.75 1.75
Nos. 916-921 (6) 5.25 4.00

Izmir International Fair.

Soccer Team on Parade
A161

Turkish Flag and Soldier
A162

Designs: 6¾k, Bridge. 10k, Hospital. 13½k, View of Ankara. 27½k, President Inonu.

Inscribed: "Cumhuriyetin 20 nci Yildonomu Hatirasi"

1943, Oct. 29 *Perf. 11x11½, 11½x11*

922 A161 4½k lt olive grn 1.50 1.75
923 A162 6k rose red .75 .25
924 A161 6¾k ultra .75 .50
925 A161 10k violet blue .75 .50
926 A161 13½k olive .75 .25
927 A162 27½k lt brown .95 .75
Nos. 922-927 (6) 5.45 4.00

Republic, 20th anniv. Nos. 922-927 exist imperf. Value, $50.

No. 905 Surcharged with New Value in Red

1945 *Perf. 11*

928 A139 4½k on 6¾k brt ultra .65 .40

Recording Census Data — A167

1945, Oct. 21 Litho. *Perf. 11½*

929 A167 4½k olive black .70 .25
930 A167 9k violet .85 .25
931 A167 10k violet blue .85 .25
932 A167 18k dark red 1.75 .60
Nos. 929-932 (4) 4.15 1.35

Souvenir Sheet

Imperf

933 A167 1 l chocolate 65.00 50.00

Census of 1945.

President Ismet Inönü — A169

Perf. 11½ to 12½

1946, Apr. 1 Unwmk.

934 A169 0.25k brown red .50 .25
935 A169 1k dk slate grn .50 .25
936 A169 1½k plum 1.00 .25
937 A169 9k purple 1.75 .25
938 A169 10k deep blue 2.00 .75
939 A169 50k chocolate 8.50 .75
Nos. 934-939 (6) 14.25 2.50

U.S.S. Missouri — A170

1946, Apr. 5 *Perf. 11½*

940 A170 9k dark purple .75 .30
941 A170 10k dk chalky blue .85 .40
942 A170 27½k olive green 2.25 2.00
a. Imperf., pair 75.00
Nos. 940-942 (3) 3.85 2.70

Visit of the USS Missouri to Istanbul, 4/5.

Sower — A171

1946, June 16 *Perf. 11½ to 12½*

943 A171 9k violet .50 .25
944 A171 10k dark blue .75 .25
945 A171 18k olive green 1.00 .75
946 A171 27½k red orange 1.75 1.50
Nos. 943-946 (4) 4.00 2.75

Passing of legislation to distribute state lands to poor farmers.

Dove and Flag-Decorated Banderol — A172

1947, Aug. 20 Photo. *Perf. 12*

947 A172 15k violet & dp violet .40 .25
948 A172 20k blue & dk blue 1.00 .50
949 A172 30k brown & gray blk .40 .25
950 A172 1 l ol grn & dk grn .50 .50
Nos. 947-950 (4) 2.30 1.50

Izmir International Fair.

Victory Monument, Afyon Karahisar
A173

Ismet Inönü as General
A174

Kemal Atatürk as General — A175

1947, Aug. 30

951 A173 10k dk brn & pale brn .60 .30
952 A174 15k brt violet & gray .50 .30
953 A175 20k dp blue & gray .60 .25
954 A173 30k grnsh blk & gray 1.25 .70
955 A174 60k ol gray & pale brn 1.75 .90
956 A175 1 l dk green & gray 2.75 1.75
Nos. 951-956 (6) 7.45 4.20

25th anniv. of the Battle of Dumlupinar, Aug. 30, 1922.

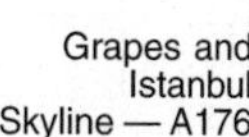

Grapes and Istanbul Skyline — A176

1947, Sept. 22

957 A176 15k rose violet .40 .25
958 A176 20k deep blue .80 .40
959 A176 60k dark brown 1.00 .60
Nos. 957-959 (3) 2.20 1.25

International Vintners' Congress, Istanbul.

Approaching Train, Istanbul Skyline and Sirkeci Terminus — A177

1947, Oct. 9

960 A177 15k reddish violet .60 .30
961 A177 20k brt blue 1.00 .75
962 A177 60k olive green 2.40 1.90
Nos. 960-962 (3) 4.00 2.95

International Railroad Congress, Istanbul.

President Ismet Inönü
A178 A179

1948 Unwmk. Engr. *Perf. 12, 14*

963 A178 0.25k dark red .30 .25
964 A178 1k olive black .30 .25
965 A178 2k brt rose lilac .30 .25
966 A178 3k red orange .30 .25
967 A178 4k dark green .30 .25
968 A178 5k blue .30 .25
969 A178 10k chocolate .75 .25
970 A178 12k deep red 1.25 .30
971 A178 15k violet .75 .25
972 A178 20k deep blue 1.00 .50
973 A178 30k brown 1.50 .30
974 A178 60k black 4.00 .50
975 A179 1 l olive green 8.00 .50
976 A179 2 l dark brown 30.00 5.00
977 A179 5 l deep plum 17.50 27.50
Nos. 963-977 (15) 66.55 36.60

For overprints see Nos. O13-O42.

President Ismet Inönü and Lausanne Conference
A180

Conference Building — A180a

1948, July 23 Photo. *Perf. 11½*

978 A180 15k rose lilac .75 .75
979 A180a 20k blue 1.00 1.00
980 A180a 40k gray green 1.25 1.25
981 A180 1 l brown 2.00 2.00
Nos. 978-981 (4) 5.00 5.00

25th anniversary of Lausanne Treaty.

Statue of Kemal Atatürk, Ankara — A181

1948, Oct. 29

982 A181 15k violet .60 .40
983 A181 20k blue .75 .50
984 A181 40k gray green 1.50 1.10
985 A181 1 l brown 3.25 3.00
Nos. 982-985 (4) 6.10 5.00

25th anniv. of the proclamation of the republic.

A182

A183

A184

Wrestlers — A185

1949, June 3

986 A182 15k rose lilac 2.40 .60
987 A183 20k blue 2.75 1.25
988 A184 30k brown 2.75 .60
989 A185 60k green 4.00 3.50
Nos. 986-989 (4) 11.90 5.95

5th European Wrestling Championships, Istanbul, June 3-5, 1949.

Ancient Galley
A186

Galleon Mahmudiye
A187

Monument to Khizr Barbarossa — A188

Designs: 15k, Cruiser Hamidiye. 20k, Submarine Sakarya. 30k, Cruiser Yavuz.

1949, July 1

990 A186 5k violet 1.00 1.00
991 A187 10k brown 1.00 1.00
992 A186 15k lilac rose 1.00 1.00
993 A186 20k gray blue 2.50 1.00
994 A186 30k gray 2.50 1.00
995 A188 40k olive gray 4.00 1.75
Nos. 990-995 (6) 12.00 6.75

Fleet Day, July 1, 1949.

A189

UPU Monument, Bern — A190

Perf. 11½

1949, Oct. 9 Unwmk. Photo.

996 A189 15k violet .55 .30
997 A189 20k blue .55 .30
998 A190 30k dull rose .55 .30
999 A190 40k green 1.10 .55
Nos. 996-999 (4) 2.75 1.45

UPU, 75th anniversary.

Istanbul Fair Building — A191

1949, Oct. 1 Litho. *Perf. 10*

1000 A191 15k brown .60 .30
1001 A191 20k blue .60 .30
1002 A191 30k olive .80 .60
Nos. 1000-1002 (3) 2.00 1.20

Istanbul Fair, Oct. 1-31.

Boy and Girl and Globe — A192

1950, Aug. 13 *Perf. 11½*

1003 A192 15k purple .35 .25
1004 A192 20k deep blue .75 .50

2nd World Youth Council Meeting, 1950. No. 1004 exists imperf. Value $12.

Aged Woman Casting Ballot A193

Kemal Atatürk and Map A194

1950, Aug. 30

1005 A193 15k dark brown .50 .25
1006 A193 20k dark blue .50 .25
1007 A194 30k dk blue & gray 1.00 .50
Nos. 1005-1007 (3) 2.00 1.00

Election of May 14, 1950.

Hazel Nuts — A195

Designs: 12k, Acorns. 15k, Cotton. 20k, Symbolical of the fair. 30k, Tobacco.

1950, Sept. 9

1008 A195 8k gray grn & buff .60 .60
1009 A195 12k magenta 1.25 1.25
1010 A195 15k brn blk & lt brn .60 .60
1011 A195 20k dk blue & aqua 1.75 1.75
1012 A195 30k brn blk & dull org 1.75 1.75
Nos. 1008-1012 (5) 5.95 5.95

Izmir International Fair, Aug. 20-Sept. 20.

Symbolical of 1950 Census — A196

1950, Oct. 9 Litho. *Perf. 11½*

1013 A196 15k dark brown .40 .25
1014 A196 20k violet blue 1.00 .25

General census of 1950.

Atatürk Types of 1931-42

Perf. 10x11½, 11½x12

1950-51 Typo.

1015 A77 10p dull red brn .50 .25
1016 A77 10p vermilion ('51) .60 .50
1017 A77 20p blue green 1.50 .35
1018 A78 1k olive green .50 .25
1019 A78 2k plum .50 .25
1020 A78 2k dp yellow ('51) .90 .30
1021 A78 3k yellow orange 1.25 .45
1022 A78 3k gray ('51) .90 .25
1023 A78 4k green ('51) .90 .25
1024 A78 5k blue 1.25 .45
1025 A78 5k plum ('51) 6.50 .45
1026 A77 10k brown orange 2.25 .25
1027 A77 15k purple 2.75 .45

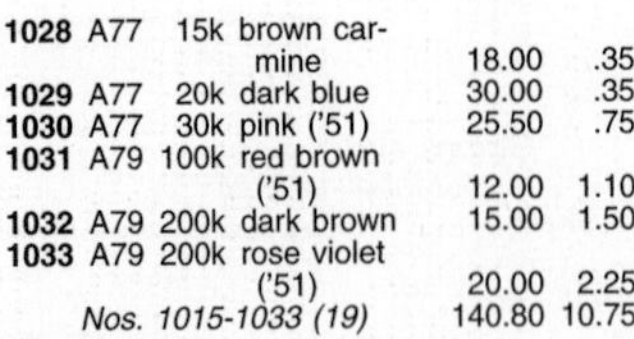

1028 A77 15k brown carmine 18.00 .35
1029 A77 20k dark blue 30.00 .35
1030 A77 30k pink ('51) 25.50 .75
1031 A79 100k red brown ('51) 12.00 1.10
1032 A79 200k dark brown 15.00 1.50
1033 A79 200k rose violet ('51) 20.00 2.25
Nos. 1015-1033 (19) 140.80 10.75

16th Century Flight of Hezarfen Ahmet Celebi A197

Plane over Istanbul A198

40k, Biplane over Taurus Mountains.

1950, Oct. 17 Litho. *Perf. 11*

1034 A197 20k dk green & blue .50 .35
1035 A197 40k dk brown & blue .75 .75
1036 A198 60k purple & blue 1.25 .90
Nos. 1034-1036 (3) 2.50 2.00

Regional meeting of the ICAO, Istanbul, Oct. 17.

Farabi — A199

1950, Dec. 1 Unwmk. *Perf. 11½*

Multicolored Center

1037 A199 15k blue .75 .75
1038 A199 20k blue violet .75 .75
1039 A199 60k red brown 4.25 2.75
1040 A199 1 l gold & bl vio 4.75 4.25
Nos. 1037-1040 (4) 10.50 8.50

Death millenary of Farabi, Arab philosopher.

Mithat Pasha and Security Bank Building A200

Design: 20k, Agricultural Bank.

1950, Dec. 21 Photo.

1041 A200 15k rose violet 2.00 2.00
1042 A200 20k blue 2.00 2.00

3rd Congress of Turkish Cooperatives, Istanbul, Dec. 25, 1950.

Floating a Ship A201

Lighthouse A202

1951, July 1

1043 A201 15k shown .75 .75
1044 A201 20k Steamship .75 .75
1045 A201 30k Diver rising 1.50 1.50
1046 A202 1 l shown 2.75 2.75
Nos. 1043-1046 (4) 5.75 5.75

25th anniv. of the recognition of coastal rights in Turkish waters to ships under the Turkish flag.

Mosque of Sultan Ahmed A203

Henry Carton de Wiart A204

Designs: 20k, Dolma Bahce Palace. 60k, Rumeli Hisari Fortress.

1951, Aug. 31 Photo. *Perf. 13½*

1047 A203 15k dark green .35 .25
1048 A203 20k deep ultra .60 .25
1049 A204 30k brown .75 .35
1050 A203 60k purple brown 1.40 1.40
Nos. 1047-1050 (4) 3.10 2.25

40th Interparliamentary Conf., Istanbul.

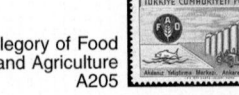

Allegory of Food and Agriculture A205

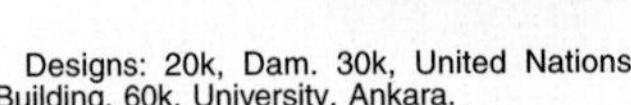

Designs: 20k, Dam. 30k, United Nations Building. 60k, University, Ankara.

Inscribed: "Akdeniz Yetistirme Merkezi. Ankara 1951."

1952, Jan. 3 Unwmk. *Perf. 14*

1051 A205 15k green 1.00 .65
1052 A205 20k blue violet 1.10 .75
1053 A205 30k blue 2.50 2.00
1054 A205 60k red 3.75 3.25
a. Souvenir sheet of 4 95.00 85.00
Nos. 1051-1054 (4) 8.35 6.65

UN Mediterranean Economic Instruction Center.

No. 1054a contains one each of Nos. 1051-1054, imperf., with inscriptions in dark blue gray.

Abdulhak Hamid Tarhan, Poet, Birth Cent. — A206

1952, Feb. 5 Photo. *Perf. 13½*

1055 A206 15k dark purple 1.00 1.00
1056 A206 20k dark blue 1.00 1.00
1057 A206 30k brown 1.00 1.00
1058 A206 60k dark olive grn 2.75 1.75
Nos. 1055-1058 (4) 5.75 4.75

Ruins, Bergama A207

Pavilion, Istanbul A208

Designs: 1k, Ruins, Bergama. 2k, Ruins, Milas. 3k, Karatay Gate, Konya. 4k, Kozak plateau. 5k, Urgup. 10k, 12k, 15k, 20k, Kemal Ataturk. 30k, Mosque, Bursa. 40k, Mosque, Istanbul. 50, Tarsus Cataract. 75k, Rocks, Urgup. 1 l, Palace, Istanbul. 5 l, Museum interior, Istanbul.

1952, Mar. 15 *Perf. 13½*

1059 A207 1k brown orange .25 .25
1060 A207 2k olive green .25 .25
1061 A207 3k rose brown .35 .25
1062 A207 4k blue green .55 .40
1063 A207 5k brown .35 .25
1064 A207 10k dark brown .25 .25
1065 A207 12k brt rose car .75 .50
1066 A207 15k purple .50 .25
1067 A207 20k chalky blue .90 .25
1068 A207 30k grnsh gray .75 .25
1069 A207 40k slate blue 4.50 .75
1070 A208 50k olive .75 .25
1071 A208 75k slate .75 .30
1072 A208 1 l deep purple .55 .25
1073 A208 2 l brt ultra 2.50 .50
1074 A208 5 l sepia 35.00 9.00
Nos. 1059-1074 (16) 48.95 13.95

Imperfs, value, set $90.

For surcharge & overprint see #1075, 1255.

No. 1059 Surcharged

1952, June 1

1075 A207 0.50k on 1k brn org .50 .25

Technical Faculty Building — A209

1952, Aug. 20 *Perf. 12x12½*

1076 A209 15k violet .65 .65
1077 A209 20k blue .95 .95
1078 A209 60k brown 1.60 1.60
Nos. 1076-1078 (3) 3.20 3.20

8th Intl. Congress of Theoretic and Applied Mechanics.

Turkish Soldier — A210

20k, Soldier with Turkish flag. 30k, Soldier & child with comic book. 60k, Raising Turkish flag.

1952, Sept. 25 *Perf. 14*

1079 A210 15k Prus blue .40 .40
1080 A210 20k deep blue .60 .60
1081 A210 30k brown .85 .85
1082 A210 60k olive blk & car 1.75 1.75
Nos. 1079-1082 (4) 3.60 3.60

Turkey's participation in the Korean war.

Pigeons Bandaging Wounded Hand — A212

20k, Flag, rainbow and ruined homes.

Dated "1877-1952"

1952, Oct. 29 *Perf. 12½x12*

1085 A212 15k dk green & red .80 .40
1086 A212 20k blue & red 2.00 .70

Turkish Red Crescent Society, 75th anniv.

Relief From Panel of Aziziye Monument A213

Aziziye Monument A214

Design: 40k, View of Erzerum.

1952, Nov. 9 *Perf. 11*

1087 A213 15k purple .50 .30
1088 A214 20k blue .60 .50
1089 A214 40k olive gray 1.00 .70
Nos. 1087-1089 (3) 2.10 1.50

75th anniv. of the Battle of Aziziye at Erzerum.

Rumeli Hisari Fortress A215

Troops Entering Constantinople A216

Sultan Mohammed II — A217

Designs: 8k, Soldiers moving cannon. 10k, Mohammed II riding into sea, and Turkish armada. 12k, Landing of Turkish army. 15k, Ancient wall, Constantinople. 30k, Mosque of Faith. 40k, Presenting mace to Patriarch Yenadios. 60k, Map of Constantinople, c. 1574. 1 l, Tomb of Mohammed II. 2.50 l, Portrait of Mohammed II.

Inscribed: "Istanbulun Fethi 1453-1953"

1953, May 29 Photo. *Perf. 11½*

1090 A215 5k brt blue 1.25 .60
1091 A215 8k gray 1.90 .60
1092 A215 10k blue .60 .60
1093 A215 12k rose lilac 1.25 .60
1094 A215 15k brown .90 .30
1095 A216 20k vermilion 1.25 .30
1096 A216 30k dull green 2.40 1.25
1097 A215 40k violet blue 4.25 1.50
1098 A215 60k chocolate 3.00 1.50
1099 A215 1 l blue green 7.25 2.10

Perf. 12

1100 A217 2 l multi 15.00 6.00
1101 A217 2.50 l multi 9.00 9.00
a. Souvenir sheet 125.00 95.00
Nos. 1090-1101 (12) 48.05 24.35

Conquest of Constantinople by Sultan Mohammed II, 500th anniv.

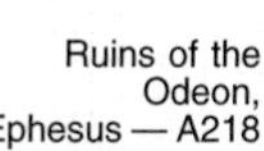

Ruins of the Odeon, Ephesus — A218

15k, Church of St. John the Apostle. 20k, Shrine of Virgin Mary, Panaya Kapulu. 40k, Ruins of the Double Church. 60k, Shrine of the Seven Sleepers. 1 l, Restored house of the Virgin Mary.

1953, Aug. 16 Litho. *Perf. 13½*
Multicolored Center

1102 A218 12k sage green .40 .25
1103 A218 15k lilac .40 .25
1104 A218 20k dk slate blue .50 .35
1105 A218 40k light green .75 .60
1106 A218 60k violet blue 1.00 .75
1107 A218 1 l brown red 2.75 2.00
Nos. 1102-1107 (6) 5.80 4.20

Pres. Celal Bayar, Mithat Pasha. Herman Schulze-Delitzsch and People's Bank — A219

Design: 20k, Pres. Bayar, Mithat Pasha and University of Ankara.

1953, Sept. 2 Photo. *Perf. 10½*

1108 A219 15k orange brown 1.00 .50
1109 A219 20k Prus green 1.00 .50

5th Intl. People's Credit Congress, Istanbul, Sept.

Combined Harvester A220

Kemal Atatürk A221

Designs: 15k, Berdan dam. 20k, Military parade. 30k, Diesel train. 35k, Yesilkoy airport.

1953, Oct. 29 *Perf. 14*

1110 A220 10k olive bister .90 .25
1111 A220 15k dark gray .90 .25
1112 A220 20k rose red .90 .75
1113 A220 30k olive green 1.50 1.25
1114 A220 35k dull blue 1.00 .75
1115 A221 55k dull purple 2.25 1.75
Nos. 1110-1115 (6) 7.45 5.00

Turkish Republic, 30th anniv.

Kemal Atatürk and Mausoleum at Ankara — A222

1953, Nov. 10

1116 A222 15k gray black 1.00 .50
1117 A222 20k violet brown 1.25 .75

15th death anniv. of Kemal Ataturk.

Type of 1931-42
Without umlaut over first "U" of "CUMHURIYETI"
Perf. 11½x12, 10x11½

1953-56 Typo. Unwmk.

1117B A77 20p yellow .30 .25
1118 A78 1k brown orange .30 .25
1119 A78 2k rose pink ('53) .50 .25
1120 A78 3k yel brn ('53) .50 .25
1120A A78 4k slate ('56) 1.50 .40
1121 A78 5k blue 2.00 .25
1121A A78 8k violet ('56) .50 .25
1122 A77 10k dark olive ('53) .50 .25
1123 A77 12k brt car rose ('53) .50 .25
1124 A77 15k fawn .60 .25
1125 A77 20k rose lilac 3.50 .40
1126 A77 30k lt blue grn ('54) 1.25 .25
Nos. 1117B-1126 (12) 11.95 3.30

Compass and Map — A223

Designs: 20k, Globe, crescent and stars. 40k, Tree symbolical of 14 NATO members.

1954, Apr. 4 Photo. *Perf. 14*

1127 A223 15k brown 1.75 1.25
1128 A223 20k violet blue 2.25 1.75
1129 A223 40k dark green 15.50 13.00
Nos. 1127-1129 (3) 19.50 16.00

NATO, 5th anniv.

Industry, Engineering and Agriculture A224

Justice and Council of Europe Flag A225

1954, Aug. 8 Litho. *Perf. 10½*

1130 A224 10k brown 3.25 2.40
1131 A225 15k dark green 3.00 1.25
1132 A225 20k blue 3.25 1.25
1133 A224 30k brt violet 14.50 10.00
Nos. 1130-1133 (4) 24.00 14.90

Council of Europe, 5th anniv.

Flag Signals to Plane A226

Amaury de La Grange and Plane A227

Design: 45k, Kemal Ataturk and air fleet.

1954, Sept. 20 *Perf. 12½*

1134 A226 20k black brown .55 .25
1135 A227 35k dull violet .85 .25
1136 A227 45k deep blue 1.25 .30
Nos. 1134-1136 (3) 2.65 .80

47th Congress of the Intl. Aeronautical Federation, Istanbul, 1954.

Souvenir Sheet

A228

1954, Oct. 18 *Imperf.*

1137 A228 Sheet of 3 16.00 14.00
a. 20k aquamarine 1.25 .85
b. 30k violet blue 1.50 .85
c. 1 l red violet 3.00 1.90

First anniv. of Law of Oct. 17, 1953, reorganizing the Department of Post, Telephone and Telegraph.

Ziya Gokalp — A229

1954, Oct. 25 *Perf. 11*

1138 A229 15k rose lilac .50 .50
1139 A229 20k dark green .60 .60
1140 A229 30k crimson .90 .90
Nos. 1138-1140 (3) 2.00 2.00

30th death anniv. of Ziya Gokalp, author and historian.

Kemal Atatürk — A230

1955, Mar. 1 *Perf. 12½*

1141 A230 15k carmine rose .60 .60
1142 A230 20k blue .75 .75
1143 A230 40k dark gray .90 .90
1144 A230 50k blue green 1.25 1.25
1145 A230 75k orange brown 1.50 1.50
Nos. 1141-1145 (5) 5.00 5.00

Relief Map of Dardanelles A231

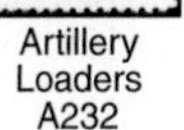

Artillery Loaders A232

30k, Minelayer Nusrat. 60k, Col. Kemal Atatürk.

1955, Mar. 18 *Perf. 10½*

1146 A231 15k green .60 .25
1147 A232 20k orange brown .60 .25
1148 A231 30k ultra .90 .45
1149 A232 60k olive gray 1.50 .65
Nos. 1146-1149 (4) 3.60 1.60

Battle of Gallipoli, 40th anniversary.

Aerial Map — A233

1955, Apr. 14 *Perf. 11*

1150 A233 15k gray .35 .25
1151 A233 20k aquamarine .35 .25
1152 A233 50k brown .60 .25
1153 A233 1 l purple 1.10 .50
Nos. 1150-1153 (4) 2.40 1.25

City Planning Congress, Ankara, 1955.

Carnation — A234

1955, May 19 Litho. *Perf. 10*

1154 A234 10k shown .55 .55
1155 A234 15k Tulip .55 .55
1156 A234 20k Rose .85 .55
1157 A234 50k Lily 2.00 1.10
Nos. 1154-1157 (4) 3.95 2.75

National Flower Show, Istanbul, May 20-Aug. 20.

Battle First Aid Station — A235

30k, Gulhane Military Hospital, Ankara.

1955, Aug. 28 Unwmk. *Perf. 12*

1158 A235 20k red, lake & gray .75 .50
1159 A235 30k dp grn & yel grn 1.25 .75

XVIII Intl. Congress of Military Medicine, Aug. 8-Sept. 1, Istanbul.

Soccer Game — A236

Emblem and Soccer Ball — A237

1 l, Emblem with oak & olive branches.

1955, Aug. 30 *Perf. 10*

1160 A236 15k light ultra .70 .25
1161 A237 20k crimson rose .85 .25
1162 A236 1 l light green 1.75 1.10
Nos. 1160-1162 (3) 3.30 1.60

Intl. Military Soccer Championship games, Istanbul, Aug. 30.

Sureté Monument, Ankara — A238

20k, Dolma Bahce Palace. 30k, Police College, Ankara. 45k, Police Martyrs' Monument, Istanbul.

Inscribed: "Enterpol Istanbul 1955"

1955, Sept. 5 ***Perf. 10***
1163 A238 15k blue green .30 .30
1164 A238 20k brt violet .45 .45
1165 A238 30k gray black .55 .40
1166 A238 45k lt brown 1.10 .65
Nos. 1163-1166 (4) 2.40 1.80

24th general assembly of the Intl. Criminal Police, Istanbul, Sept. 5-9.

Early Telegraph Transmitter A239

Modern Transmitter A240

Perf. 13½x14, 14x13½
1955, Sept. 10 **Photo.**
1167 A239 15k olive .40 .25
1168 A240 20k crimson rose .40 .25
1169 A239 45k fawn .80 .25
1170 A240 60k ultra .90 .75
Nos. 1167-1170 (4) 2.50 1.50

Centenary of telecommunication.

Academy of Science, Istanbul — A241

Designs: 20k, University. 60k, Hilton Hotel. 1 l, Kiz Kulesi (Leander's Tower).

1955, Sept. 12 ***Perf. 13½x14***
1171 A241 15k yellow orange .45 .35
1172 A241 20k crimson rose .45 .35
1173 A241 60k purple .60 .35
1174 A241 1 l deep blue .95 .60
Nos. 1171-1174 (4) 2.45 1.65

10th meeting of the governors of the Intl. Bank of Reconstruction and Development and the Intl. Monetary Fund, Istanbul, Sept. 12-16.

Surlari, Istanbul A242

Mosque of Sultan Ahmed A243

Designs: 30k, Haghia Sophia. 75k, Map of Constantinople, by Christoforo Buondelmonti, 1422.

1955, Sept. 15 **Litho.** ***Perf. 11½***
1175 A242 15k grnsh blk & Prus grn .75 .25
1176 A243 20k vermilion & org .60 .25
1177 A242 30k sepia & vio brn .60 .25
1178 A243 75k ultramarine 1.60 .75
Nos. 1175-1178 (4) 3.55 1.50

10th Intl. Congress of Byzantine Research, Istanbul, Sept. 15-21, 1955.

Congress Emblem — A244

30k, Chalet in Istanbul. 55k, Bridges.

Inscribed: "Beynelmiel X. Vol Kongresi Istanbul 1955"

1955, Sept. 26 ***Perf. 10½x11***
1179 A244 20k red violet .30 .25
1180 A244 30k dk grn & yel grn .30 .25
1181 A244 55k dp bl & brt bl 1.00 .75
Nos. 1179-1181 (3) 1.60 1.25

10th International Transportation Congress.

Map of Turkey, Showing Population Increase — A245

1955, Oct. 22 **Unwmk.** ***Perf. 10***
Map in Rose
1182 A245 15k lt & dk gray & red .50 .25
1183 A245 20k lt & dk vio & red .40 .25
1184 A245 30k lt & dk ultra & red .45 .25
1185 A245 60k lt & dk bl grn & red 1.00 .30
Nos. 1182-1185 (4) 2.35 1.05

Census of 1955.

Waterfall, Antalya A246

Alanya and Seljukide Dockyards A247

Designs: 30k, Theater at Aspendos. 45k, Ruins at Side. 50k, View of Antalya. 65k, St. Nicholas Church at Myra (Demre) and St. Nicholas.

Perf. 14x13½, 13½x14
1955, Dec. 10 **Photo.** **Unwmk.**
1186 A246 18k bl, ol grn & ultra .50 .25
1187 A247 20k blue, ultra & brn .50 .25
1188 A247 30k dl grn, ol bis & grn .50 .25
1189 A246 45k yel grn & brn 2.25 1.00
1190 A246 50k Prus grn & ol bis .60 .30
1191 A247 65k orange ver & blk .80 .40
Nos. 1186-1191 (6) 5.15 2.45

Kemal Atatürk — A248

1955-56 **Litho.** ***Perf. 12½***
1192 A248 0.50k carmine .60 .25
1193 A248 1k yellow orange .90 .25
1194 A248 2k brt blue .60 .25
1195 A248 3k scarlet .60 .25
1196 A248 5k lt brown .60 .25
1197 A248 6k lt blue grn .70 .25
1198 A248 10k blue green .70 .25
1199 A248 18k rose violet .80 .25
1200 A248 20k lt violet bl .95 .25
1201 A248 25k olive green .95 .45
1202 A248 30k violet .95 .25
1203 A248 40k fawn 1.00 .40
1204 A248 75k slate blue 3.00 1.25
Nos. 1192-1204 (13) 12.35 4.60

Issue dates: 3k, 1955. Others, 1956.

Tomb at Nigde — A249

1956, Apr. 12 ***Perf. 10½***
1205 A249 40k violet bl & bl .50 .45

25th anniv. of the Turkish History Society. The tomb of Hüdavent Hatun, a sultan's daughter, exemplifies Seljukian architecture of the 14th century.

Zubeyde Hanum — A250

1956, May 13 ***Perf. 11***
1206 A250 20k pale brn & dk brn .65 .50
Imperf
1207 A250 20k lt grn & dk grn 1.00 *.60*

Mother's Day; Zubeyde Hanum, mother of Kemal Ataturk.

Shah and Queen of Iran — A251

1956, May 15 **Unwmk.** ***Perf. 11***
1208 A251 100k grn & pale grn 1.25 .50
Imperf
1209 A251 100k red & pale grn 6.00 4.50

Visit of the Shah and Queen of Iran to Turkey, May 15.

Erenkoy Sanitarium A252

1956, July 31 ***Perf. 11***
1210 A252 50k dk bl grn & pink .60 .50

Anti-Tuberculosis work among PTT employees.

Symbol of Izmir Fair — A253

A254

1956, Aug. 20 ***Perf. 11***
1211 A253 45k brt green .50 .35

Souvenir Sheet
Imperf
1212 A254 Sheet of 2 4.00 3.00
a. 50k rose red 1.25 .45
b. 50k bright ultramarine 1.25 .45

25th Intl. Fair, Izmir, 8/20-9/20. See #C28.

Hands Holding Bottled Serpent — A255

1956, Sept. 10 **Litho.** ***Perf. 10½***
1213 A255 25k multicolored .30 .30
a. Tete beche pair 1.00 1.00

25th Intl. Anti-Alcoholism Congress, Istanbul Sept. 10-15.

Printed both in regular sheets and in sheets with alternate vertical rows inverted.

Medical Center at Kayseri — A256

1956, Nov. 1 ***Perf. 12½x12***
1214 A256 60k violet & yel .40 .30

750th anniv. of the first medical school and clinic in Anatolia.

Sariyar Dam — A257

1956, Dec. 2 **Litho.** ***Perf. 10½***
1215 A257 20k vermilion .50 .30
1216 A257 20k bright blue .50 .30

Inauguration of Sariyar Dam.

Freestyle Wrestling — A258

Design: 65k, Greco-Roman wrestling.

1956, Dec. 8 **Unwmk.** ***Perf. 10½***
1217 A258 40k brt yel grn & brn 1.00 .40
1218 A258 65k lt bluish gray & dp car 1.25 .40

16th Olympic Games, Melbourne, Nov. 22-Dec. 8, 1956.

Mehmet Akif Ersoy — A259

1956, Dec. 26
1219 A259 20k brn & brt yel grn .40 .25
1220 A259 20k rose car & lt gray .40 .25
1221 A259 20k vio bl & brt pink .40 .25
Nos. 1219-1221 (3) 1.20 .75

20th death anniv. of Mehmet Akif Ersoy, author of the Turkish National Anthem.

Each value bears a different verse of the anthem.

Theater in Troy — A260

Trojan Vase — A261

Design: 30k, Trojan Horse.

Perf. 13½x14, 14x13½
1956, Dec. 31 **Photo.** **Unwmk.**
1222 A260 15k green 1.60 .85
1223 A261 20k red violet 1.60 .85
1224 A260 30k chestnut 2.50 .85
Nos. 1222-1224 (3) 5.70 2.55

Excavations at Troy.

Mobile Chest X-Ray Unit — A262

1957, Jan. 1 **Litho.** ***Perf. 12***
1225 A262 25k ol brn & red .35 .25

Fight against tuberculsois.

Kemal Atatürk — A263

1956-57 ***Perf. 12½***
1226 A263 ½k blue green .25 .25
1227 A263 1k yellow orange .40 .25
1228 A263 3k gray olive .40 .25
1229 A263 5k violet .40 .25
1230 A263 6k rose car ('57) .50 .25
1231 A263 10k rose violet .50 .25
1232 A263 12k fawn ('57) .60 .25

1233 A263 15k lt violet bl .50 .25
1234 A263 18k carmine ('57) .60 .25
1235 A263 20k lt brown .50 .25
1236 A263 25k lt blue green .50 .25
1237 A263 30k slate blue .50 .25
1238 A263 40k olive ('57) .75 .25
1239 A263 50k orange .60 .25
1240 A263 60k brt blue ('57) .90 .35
1241 A263 70k Prus green ('57) 2.50 1.25
1242 A263 75k brown 1.75 .90
Nos. 1226-1242 (17) 12.15 6.00

Pres. Heuss of Germany — A264

1957, May 5 Unwmk. *Perf. 10½*
1243 A264 40k yellow & brown .25 .25

Visit of Pres. Theodor Heuss of Germany to Turkey, May 5. See No. C29.

View of Bergama and Ruin — A265

40k, Dancers in kermis at Bergama.

1957, May 24
1244 A265 30k brown .30 .25
1245 A265 40k green .30 .25

20th anniv. of the kermis at Bergama (Pergamus).

Symbols of Industry and Flags — A266

1957, July 1 Photo. *Perf. 13½x14*
1246 A266 25k violet .40 .40
1247 A266 40k gray blue .40 .40

Turkish-American collaboration, 10th anniv.

Osman Hamdi Bey — A267

Hittite Sun Course from Alaça Höyük A268

1957, July 6 *Perf. 10½*
1248 A267 20k beige, pale brn & blk .35 .25
1249 A268 30k Prussian green .40 .25

75th anniv. of the Academy of Art. The 20k exists with "cancellation" omitted.

King of Afghanistan — A269

1957, Sept. 1 Litho. *Perf. 10½*
1250 A269 45k car lake & pink .25 .25

Visit of Mohammed Zahir Shah, King of Afghanistan, to Turkey. See No. C30.

Medical Center, Amasya — A270

Design: 65k, Suleiman Medical Center.

1957, Sept. 29 Unwmk. *Perf. 10½*
1251 A270 25k vermilion & yellow .25 .25
1252 A270 65k brt grnsh bl & cit .30 .25

11th general meeting of the World Medical Assoc.

Mosque of Suleiman A271

Architect Mimar Koca Sinan (1489-1587) A272

1957, Oct. 18 *Perf. 11*
1253 A271 20k gray green .25 .25
1254 A272 100k brown .45 .30

400th anniv. of the opening of the Mosque of Suleiman, Istanbul.

No. 1073 Surcharged with New Value and "ISTANBUL Filatelik n. Sergisi 1957"

1957, Nov. 11 Photo. *Perf. 13½*
1255 A208 50k on 2 l brt ultra .30 .25

1957 Istanbul Philatelic Exhibition.

Forestation Map of Turkey — A273

25k, Forest & hand planting tree, vert.

1957, Nov. 18 Litho. *Perf. 10½*
1256 A273 20k green & brown .25 .25
1257 A273 25k emerald & bl grn .25 .25

Centenary of forestry in Turkey.

Nos. 1256-1257 each come with two different tabs attached (four tabs in all) bearing various quotations.

A274

1957, Nov. 23
1258 A274 50k pink, vio, red & yel .40 .25

400th death anniv. of Fuzuli (Mehmet Suleiman Ogiou), poet.

A275

1957, Nov. 28 Photo. *Perf. 14x13½*
1259 A275 65k dk Prus blue .40 .25
1260 A275 65k rose violet .40 .25

Benjamin Franklin (1706-1790).

Green Dome, Tomb of Mevlana, at Konya A276

Konya Museum A277

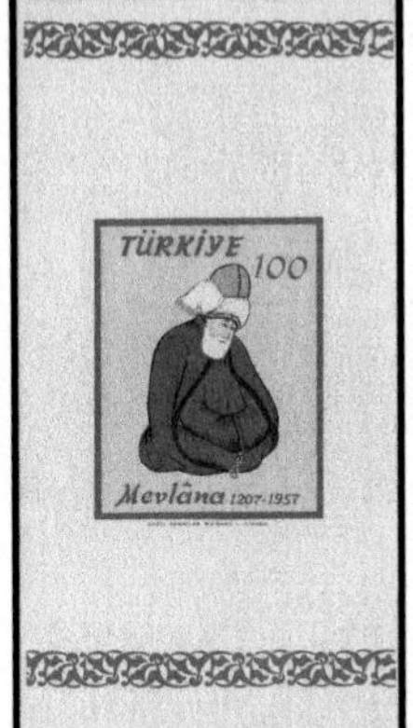

Mevlana A278

Perf. 11x10½, 10½x11

1957, Dec. 17 Litho. Unwmk.
1261 A276 50k green, bl & vio .25 .25
1262 A277 100k dark blue .50 .25

Miniature Sheet

Imperf

1263 A278 100k multicolored 1.75 1.40

Jalal-udin Mevlana (1207-1273), Persian poet and founder of the Mevlevie dervish order. No. 1263 contains one stamp 32x42mm.

Kemal Atatürk (Double Frame; Serifs) — A279

1957 Unwmk. *Perf. 11½*
Size: 18x22mm

1264 A279 ½k lt brown .60 .25
1265 A279 1k lt violet bl .50 .25
1266 A279 2k black violet .50 .25
1267 A279 3k orange .50 .25
1268 A279 5k blue green .50 .25
1269 A279 6k dk slate grn .50 .25
1270 A279 10k violet .50 .25
1271 A279 12k brt green .50 .25
1272 A279 15k dk blue grn .60 .25
1273 A279 18k rose carmine .60 .25
1274 A279 20k brown .60 .25
1275 A279 25k brown red .60 .25
1276 A279 30k brt blue .60 .25
1277 A279 40k slate blue .80 .25
1278 A279 50k yellow orange .80 .25
1279 A279 60k black .80 .25
1280 A279 70k rose violet .90 .25
1281 A279 75k gray olive 1.25 .30

Size: 21x29mm

1282 A279 100k carmine 1.50 .40
1283 A279 250k olive 3.50 .90
Nos. 1264-1283 (20) 16.65 5.85

College Emblem — A280

1958, Jan. 16 Litho. *Perf. 10½x11*
1288 A280 20k bister, ind & org .25 .25
1289 A280 25k dk blue, bis & org .25 .25

"Turkiye" on top of 25k. 75th anniv. of the College of Economics and Commerce, Istanbul.

View of Adana — A281

1958 Photo. *Perf. 11½*
Size: 26x20½mm

1290 A281 5k Adana .25 .25
1291 A281 5k Adapazari .25 .25
1292 A281 5k Adiyaman .25 .25
1293 A281 5k Afyon .25 .25
1294 A281 5k Amasya .25 .25
1295 A281 5k Ankara .25 .25
1296 A281 5k Antakya .25 .25
1297 A281 5k Antalya .25 .25
1298 A281 5k Artvin .25 .25
1299 A281 5k Aydin .25 .25
1300 A281 5k Balikesir .25 .25
1301 A281 5k Bilecik .25 .25
1302 A281 5k Bingol .25 .25
1303 A281 5k Bitlis .25 .25
1304 A281 5k Bolu .25 .25
1305 A281 5k Burdur .25 .25
1306 A281 5k Bursa .25 .25
1307 A281 5k Canakkale .25 .25
1308 A281 5k Cankiri .25 .25
1309 A281 5k Corum .25 .25
1310 A281 5k Denizli .25 .25
1311 A281 5k Diyarbakir .25 .25

Size: 32½x22mm

1312 A281 20k Adana .25 .25
1313 A281 20k Adapazari .25 .25
1314 A281 20k Adiyaman .25 .25
1315 A281 20k Afyon .25 .25
1316 A281 20k Amasya .25 .25
1317 A281 20k Ankara .25 .25
1318 A281 20k Antakya .25 .25
1319 A281 20k Antalya .25 .25
1320 A281 20k Artvin .25 .25
1321 A281 20k Aydin .25 .25
1322 A281 20k Balikesir .25 .25
1323 A281 20k Bilecik .25 .25
1324 A281 20k Bingol .25 .25
1325 A281 20k Bitlis .25 .25
1326 A281 20k Bolu .25 .25
1327 A281 20k Burdur .25 .25
1328 A281 20k Bursa .25 .25
1329 A281 20k Canakkale .25 .25
1330 A281 20k Cankiri .25 .25
1331 A281 20k Corum .25 .25
1332 A281 20k Denizli .25 .25
1333 A281 20k Diyarbakir .25 .25
Nos. 1290-1333 (44) 11.00 11.00

1959 Size: 26x20½mm

1334 A281 5k Edirne .25 .25
1335 A281 5k Elazig .25 .25
1336 A281 5k Erzincan .25 .25
1337 A281 5k Erzurum .25 .25
1338 A281 5k Eskisehir .25 .25
1339 A281 5k Gaziantep .25 .25
1340 A281 5k Giresun .25 .25
1341 A281 5k Gumusane .25 .25
1342 A281 5k Hakkari .25 .25
1343 A281 5k Isparta .25 .25
1344 A281 5k Istanbul .25 .25
1345 A281 5k Izmir .25 .25
1346 A281 5k Izmit .25 .25
1347 A281 5k Karakose .25 .25
1348 A281 5k Kars .25 .25
1349 A281 5k Kastamonu .25 .25
1350 A281 5k Kayseri .25 .25
1351 A281 5k Kirklareli .25 .25
1352 A281 5k Kirsehir .25 .25
1353 A281 5k Konya .25 .25
1354 A281 5k Kutahya .25 .25
1355 A281 5k Malatya .25 .25

Size: 32½x22mm

1356 A281 20k Edirne .25 .25
1357 A281 20k Elazig .25 .25
1358 A281 20k Erzincan .25 .25
1359 A281 20k Erzurum .25 .25
1360 A281 20k Eskisehir .25 .25
1361 A281 20k Gaziantep .25 .25
1362 A281 20k Giresun .25 .25
1363 A281 20k Gumusane .25 .25
1364 A281 20k Hakkari .25 .25
1365 A281 20k Isparta .25 .25
1366 A281 20k Istanbul .25 .25
1367 A281 20k Izmir .25 .25
1368 A281 20k Izmit .25 .25
1369 A281 20k Karakose .25 .25
1370 A281 20k Kars .25 .25
1371 A281 20k Kastamonu .25 .25
1372 A281 20k Kayseri .25 .25
1373 A281 20k Kirklareli .25 .25
1374 A281 20k Kirsehir .25 .25
1375 A281 20k Konya .25 .25
1376 A281 20k Kutahya .25 .25
1377 A281 20k Malatya .25 .25
Nos. 1334-1377 (44) 11.00 11.00

1960 Size: 26x20½mm

1378 A281 5k Manisa .25 .25
1379 A281 5k Maras .25 .25
1380 A281 5k Mardin .25 .25
1381 A281 5k Mersin .25 .25
1382 A281 5k Mugla .25 .25
1383 A281 5k Mus .25 .25
1384 A281 5k Nevsehir .25 .25
1385 A281 5k Nigde .25 .25
1386 A281 5k Ordu .25 .25
1387 A281 5k Rize .25 .25
1388 A281 5k Samsun .25 .25

1389 A281 5k Siirt .25 .25
1390 A281 5k Sinop .25 .25
1391 A281 5k Sivas .25 .25
1392 A281 5k Tekirdag .25 .25
1393 A281 5k Tokat .25 .25
1394 A281 5k Trabzon .25 .25
1395 A281 5k Tunceli .25 .25
1396 A281 5k Urfa .25 .25
1397 A281 5k Usak .25 .25
1398 A281 5k Van .25 .25
1399 A281 5k Yozgat .25 .25
1400 A281 5k Zonguldak .25 .25

Size: 32½x22mm

1401 A281 20k Manisa .25 .25
1402 A281 20k Maras .25 .25
1403 A281 20k Mardin .25 .25
1404 A281 20k Mersin .25 .25
1405 A281 20k Mugla .25 .25
1406 A281 20k Mus .25 .25
1407 A281 20k Nevsehir .25 .25
1408 A281 20k Nigde .25 .25
1409 A281 20k Ordu .25 .25
1410 A281 20k Rize .25 .25
1411 A281 20k Samsun .25 .25
1412 A281 20k Siirt .25 .25
1413 A281 20k Sinop .25 .25
1414 A281 20k Sivas .25 .25
1415 A281 20k Tekirdag .25 .25
1416 A281 20k Tokat .25 .25
1417 A281 20k Trabzon .25 .25
1418 A281 20k Tunceli .25 .25
1419 A281 20k Urfa .25 .25
1420 A281 20k Usak .25 .25
1421 A281 20k Van .25 .25
1422 A281 20k Yozgat .25 .25
1423 A281 20k Zonguldak .25 .25
Nos. 1378-1423 (46) 11.50 11.50
Nos. 1290-1423 (134) 33.50 33.50

Ruins at Pamukkale
A282

Designs: 25k, Travertines at Pamukkale.

1958, May 18 Litho. *Perf. 12*
1424 A282 20k brown .40 .25
1425 A282 25k blue .40 .25

"Industry" — A283

1958, Oct. 10 Unwmk. *Perf. 10½*
1426 A283 40k slate blue .40 .25

National Industry Exhibition.

Europa Issue

Symbolizing New Europe — A284

1958, Oct. 10
1427 A284 25k vio & dull pink *.40* .25
1428 A284 40k brt ultra *.40* .25

Letters — A285

1958, Oct. 5
1429 A285 20k orange & blk .40 .25

Intl. Letter Writing Week, Oct. 5-11.

Atatürk 20th Anniv. Death
A286

1958, Nov. 10 *Perf. 12*
1430 25k Flame and mausoleum .25 .25
1431 75k Atatürk .25 .25
a. A286 Pair, #1430-1431 .65 .60

20th death anniv. of Kemal Ataturk.

Emblem — A288

1959, Jan. 10 Litho. *Perf. 10*
1432 A288 25k dk violet & yel .40 .25

25th anniv. of the Agricultural Faculty of Ankara University.

Blackboard and School Emblem — A289

1959, Jan. 15 *Perf. 10½*
1433 A289 75k black & yellow .60 .30

75th anniv. of the establishment of a secondary boys' school in Istanbul.

State Theater, Ankara — A290

Design: 25k, Portrait of Sinasi.

1959, Mar. 30 Unwmk. *Perf. 10½*
1434 A290 20k red brn & emer .25 .25
1435 A290 25k Prus grn & org .25 .25

Centenary of the Turkish theater; Sinasi, writer of the first Turkish play in 1859.

Globe and Stars — A291

1959, Apr. 4 *Perf. 10*
1436 A291 105k red .25 .25
1437 A291 195k green 1.00 .50

10th anniversary of NATO.

Aspendos Theater — A292

1959, May 1 Litho. *Perf. 10½*
1438 A292 20k bis brn & vio .40 .25
1439 A292 20k grn & ol bis .40 .25

Aspendos (Belkins) Festival.

No. B70 Surcharged in Ultramarine

1959, May 5
1440 SP25 105k on 15k + 5k org .55 .25

Council of Europe, 10th anniversary.

Basketball — A293

1959, May 21 *Perf. 10*
1441 A293 25k red org & dk bl .45 .25

11th European and Mediterranean Basketball Championship.

"Karadeniz" — A294

Telegraph Mast
A295

Kemal Atatürk
A296

Designs: 1k, Turkish Airlines' SES plane. 10k, Grain elevator, Ankara. 15k, Iron and Steel Works, Karabück. 20k, Euphrates Bridge, Birecik. 25k, Zonguldak Harbor. 30k, Gasoline refinery, Batman. 40k, Rumeli Hisari Fortress. 45k, Sugar factory, Konya. 55k, Coal mine, Zonguldak. 75k, Railway. 90k, Crane loading ships. 100k, Cement factory, Ankara. 120k, Highway. 150k, Harvester. 200k, Electric transformer.

Perf. 10½, 11, 11½, 12½, 13½
1959-60 Litho. Unwmk.
1442 A294 1k indigo .25 .25
1443 A294 5k brt blue ('59) .25 .25
1444 A294 10k blue .25 .25
1445 A294 15k brown .70 .25
1446 A294 20k slate green .25 .25
1447 A294 25k violet .25 .25
1448 A294 30k lilac .45 .35
1449 A294 40k blue .70 .25
1450 A294 45k dull violet .70 .25
1451 A294 55k olive brown .70 .25
1452 A295 60k green .95 .25
1453 A295 75k gray olive 3.50 .25
1454 A295 90k dark blue 7.75 .25
1455 A295 100k gray 10.50 .25
1456 A295 120k magenta 3.50 .35
1457 A294 150k orange 3.50 .45
1458 A295 200k yellow green 4.25 .45
1459 A296 250k black brown 4.25 .55
1460 A296 500k dark blue 7.00 .85
Nos. 1442-1460 (19) 49.70 6.25

Postage Due Stamps of 1936 Surcharged

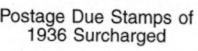

1959, June 1 *Perf. 11½*
1461 D6 20k on 20pa brown .85 .25
1462 D6 20k on 2k lt blue .35 .25
1463 D6 20k on 3k brt vio .45 .25
1464 D6 20k on 5k Prus bl .55 .25
1465 D6 20k on 12k brt rose .55 .25
Nos. 1461-1465 (5) 2.75 1.25

Anchor Emblem — A297

Design: 40k, Sea Horse emblem.

1959, July 4 *Perf. 11*
1466 A297 30k multicolored .40 .25
1467 A297 40k multicolored .40 .25

50th anniv. of the Merchant Marine College.

11th Century Warrior — A298

1959, Aug. 26 Litho. *Perf. 11*
1468 A298 2½ l rose lil & lt bl .60 .35

Battle of Malazkirt, 888th anniversary.

A299

Ornament — A300

Design: 40k, Mosque.

1959, Oct. 19 Unwmk. *Perf. 12½*
1469 A299 30k black & red .25 .25
1470 A299 40k lt blue, blk & ocher .25 .25
1471 A300 75k dp blue, yel & red .50 .25
Nos. 1469-1471 (3) 1.00 .75

Turkish Artists Congress, Ankara.

Kemal Atatürk — A301

Litho.; Center Embossed
1959, Nov. 10 *Perf. 14*
1472 A301 500k dark blue 2.50 1.75
a. Min. sheet of 1, red, imperf. 4.00 4.00

School of Political Science, Ankara
A302

Emblem
A303

1959, Dec. 4 Photo. *Perf. 13½*
1473 A302 40k green & brown .25 .25
1474 A302 40k red brown & bl .25 .25
1475 A303 1 l lt & dk vio & buff .50 .25
Nos. 1473-1475 (3) 1.00 .75

Political Science School, Ankara, cent.

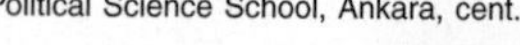

Window on World and WRY Emblem — A305

Crossed Swords Emblem — A304

Design: 40k, Bayonet and flame.

Inscribed: "Kara Harbokulunum 125 Yili"

1960, Feb. 28 Litho. *Perf. 10½*
1476 A304 30k vermilion & org .25 .25
1477 A304 40k brown, car & yel .25 .25

125th anniv. of the Territorial War College.

150k, Symbolic shanties & uprooted oak emblem.

1960, Apr. 7

1478 A305 90k brt grnsh bl & blk .25 .25
1479 A305 105k yellow & blk .30 .25

World Refugee Year, 7/1/59-6/30/60.

Spring Flower Festival — A306

1960, June 4 Photo. *Perf. 11½*
Granite Paper

1480 A306 30k Carnations .50 .25
1481 A306 40k Jasmine .70 .25
1482 A306 75k Rose 1.00 .25
1483 A306 105k Tulip 1.40 .50
Nos. 1480-1483 (4) 3.60 1.25

Atatürk Square, Nicosia — A307

Design: 105k, Map of Cyprus.

1960, Aug. 16 Litho. *Perf. 10½*

1484 A307 40k blue & pink .25 .25
1485 A307 105k blue & yellow .35 .25

Independence of the Republic of Cyprus.

Women and Nest — A308

Design: 30k, Globe and emblem.

1960, Aug. 22 Photo. *Perf. 11½*

1486 A308 30k lt vio & yel .25 .25
1487 A308 75k grnsh bl & gray .35 .25

16th meeting of the Women's Intl. Council.

Soccer — A309

#1489, Basketball. #1490, Wrestling. #1491, Hurdling. #1492, Steeplechase.

1960, Aug. 25

1488 A309 30k yellow green .55 .45
1489 A309 30k black .55 .45
1490 A309 30k slate blue .55 .45
1491 A309 30k purple .55 .45
1492 A309 30k brown .55 .45
a. Sheet of 25, #1488-1492 20.00 11.50
Nos. 1488-1492 (5) 2.75 2.25

17th Olympic Games, Rome, 8/25-9/11.
Printed in sheets of 25 (5x5) with every horizontal and every vertical row containing one of each design. Also printed in normal sheets of 100.

Common Design Types pictured following the introduction.

Europa Issue
Common Design Type

1960, Sept. 19 Size: 33x22mm

1493 CD3 75k green & bl grn *.85* .50
1494 CD3 105k dp bl & lt bl *1.25* .85

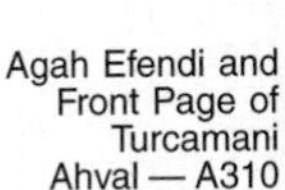

Agah Efendi and Front Page of Turcamani Ahval — A310

1960, Oct. 21 Photo. *Perf. 11½*

1495 A310 40k brown blk & sl .50 .25
1496 A310 60k brn blk & bis brn .50 .25

Centenary of Turkish journalism.

UN Emblem and Torch — A311

Design: 105k, UN headquarters building and UN emblem forming "15," horiz.

1960, Oct. 24 Unwmk.

1497 A311 90k brt bl & dk bl .30 .30
1498 A311 105k lt bl grn & brn .30 .30

15th anniversary of the United Nations.

Army Emblem — A312

Tribunal — A313

Design: 195k, "Justice," vert.

1960, Oct. 14 Litho. *Perf. 13*

1499 A312 40k violet & bister .25 .25
1500 A313 105k red, gray & brn .25 .25
1501 A313 195k grn, rose red & brn .45 .25
Nos. 1499-1501 (3) .95 .75

Trial of ex-President Celal Bayar and ex-Premier Adnan Menderes.

Revolutionaries and Statue — A314

Prancing Horse, Broken Chain — A315

Designs: 30k, Ataturk and hand holding torch. 105k, Youth, soldier and broken chain.

1960, Dec. 1 Photo. *Perf. 14½*

1502 A314 10k gray & blk .25 .25
1503 A314 30k purple .25 .25
1504 A315 40k brt red & blk .25 .25
1505 A314 105k blue blk & red .40 .25
Nos. 1502-1505 (4) 1.15 1.00

Revolution of May 27, 1960.

Faculty Building A316

Sculptured Head of Atatürk A317

Designs: 40k, Map of Turkey and sun disk.

1961, Jan. 9 Litho. *Perf. 13*

1506 A316 30k slate grn & gray .50 .25
1507 A316 40k brn blk & bis brn .65 .25
1508 A317 60k dk green & buff .80 .25
Nos. 1506-1508 (3) 1.95 .75

25th anniv. of the Faculty of Languages, History and Geography, University of Ankara.

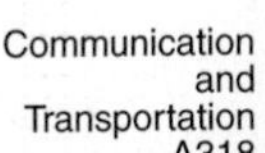

Communication and Transportation A318

40k, Highway construction, telephone & telegraph. 75k, New parliament building, Ankara.

1961, Apr. 27 Unwmk. *Perf. 13*

1509 A318 30k dull vio & blk .25 .25
1510 A318 40k green & black .35 .25
1511 A318 75k dull blue & blk .45 .25
Nos. 1509-1511 (3) 1.05 .75

9th conference of ministers of the Central Treaty Org. (CENTO), Ankara.

Flag and People A319

Legendary Wolf and Osman Warriors A320

Design: 60k, "Progress" (Atatürk showing youth the way).

1961, May 27 Litho.

1512 A319 30k multicolored .30 .25
1513 A320 40k sl grn & yel .30 .25
1514 A319 60k grn, pink & dk red .60 .25
Nos. 1512-1514 (3) 1.20 .75

First anniversary of May 27 revolution.

Rockets — A321

Designs: 40k, Crescent and star emblem, "50" and Jet. 75k, Atatürk, eagle and jets, vert.

1961, June 1

1515 A321 30k brn, org yel & blk .30 .25
1516 A321 40k violet & red .45 .25
1517 A321 75k slate blk & bis .60 .25
Nos. 1515-1517 (3) 1.35 .75

50th anniversary of Turkey's air force.

Europa Issue
Common Design Type

1961, Sept. 18 *Perf. 13*
Size: 32x22mm

1518 CD4 30k dk violet bl *.35* .25
1519 CD4 40k gray *.45* .30
1520 CD4 75k vermilion *.75* .35
Nos. 1518-1520 (3) 1.55 .90

Tulip and Cogwheel A322

Torch, Hand and Cogwheel A323

1961, Oct. 21 Unwmk. Litho.

1521 A322 30k slate, pink & sil .25 .25
1522 A323 75k ultra, org & blk .25 .25

Technical and professional schools, cent.

Open Book and Olive Branch — A324

1961, Oct. 29

1523 A324 30k red, blk & olive .60 .25
1524 A324 75k brt blue, blk & grn .85 .25

Inauguration of the new Parliament.

Kemal Atatürk
A325 A326

1961-62 Litho. *Perf. 10x10½*
Size: 20x25mm

1525 A325 1k brown org ('62) .90 .25
1526 A325 5k blue 1.50 .25
1527 A325 10k sepia 2.40 .25
1528 A326 10k car rose 2.40 .25
1529 A325 30k dull grn ('62) 3.50 .30

Size: 21½x31mm

1530 A325 10 l violet ('62) 18.00 1.90
Nos. 1525-1530 (6) 28.70 3.20

NATO Emblem and Dove — A327

Design: 105k, NATO emblem, horiz.

1962, Feb. 18 Unwmk. *Perf. 13*

1545 A327 75k dl bl, blk & sil .25 .25
1546 A327 105k crimson, blk & sil .60 .25

10th anniv. of Turkey's admission to NATO.

Scouts at Campfire — A328

60k, Scouts with flag. 105k, Scouts saluting.

1962, July 22 Litho.

1547 A328 30k lt grn, blk & red .25 .25
1548 A328 60k gray, blk & red .60 .25
1549 A328 105k tan, blk & red .80 .25
Nos. 1547-1549 (3) 1.65 .75

Turkish Boy Scouts, 50th anniversary.

Soldier Statue A329

Oxcart from Victory Monument, Ankara A330

Design: 75k, Atatürk.

1962, Aug. 30 Unwmk. *Perf. 13*

1550 A329 30k slate green .25 .25
1551 A330 40k gray & sepia .25 .25
1552 A329 75k gray blk & lt gray .80 .25
Nos. 1550-1552 (3) 1.30 .75

40th anniv. of Battle of Dumlupinar.

Europa Issue
Common Design Type

1962, Sept. 17 Size: 37x23mm

1553 CD5 75k emerald & blk *.45* .25
1554 CD5 105k red & blk *.60* .40
1555 CD5 195k blue & blk *1.00* .45
Nos. 1553-1555 (3) *2.05* 1.10

Brown imprint.

Virgin Mary's House, Ephesus — A331

40k, Inside view after restoration, horiz. 75k, Outside view, horiz. 105k, Statue of Virgin Mary.

1962, Dec. 8 Photo. *Perf. 13½*

1556 A331 30k multicolored .25 .25
1557 A331 40k multicolored .25 .25
1558 A331 75k multicolored .35 .25
1559 A331 105k multicolored .45 .25
Nos. 1556-1559 (4) 1.30 1.00

20pa Stamp of 1863 — A332

Issue of 1863: 30k, 1pi. 40k, 2pi. 75k, 5pi.

1963, Jan. 13 *Perf. 13x13½*

1560 A332 10k yellow, brn & blk .25 .25
1561 A332 30k rose, lil & blk .25 .25
1562 A332 40k lt bl, bluish grn & blk .25 .25
1563 A332 75k red brn, rose & blk .45 .25
Nos. 1560-1563 (4) 1.20 1.00

Centenary of Turkish postage stamps. See No. 1601, souvenir sheet.

Starving People — A333

Designs: 40k, Sowers. 75k, Hands protecting Wheat Emblem, and globe.

1963, Mar. 21 Unwmk. *Perf. 13*

1564 A333 30k dp bl & dk bl .25 .25
1565 A333 40k brn org & brn .25 .25
1566 A333 75k grn & dk grn .55 .25
Nos. 1564-1566 (3) 1.05 .75

FAO "Freedom from Hunger" campaign.

Julian's Column, Ankara A334

Ethnographic Museum A335

10k, Ankara Citadel. 30k, Gazi Institute of Education. 50k, Atatürk's mausoleum. 60k, President's residence. 100k, Ataturk's home, Cankaya. 150k, Parliament building.

1963 Litho. *Perf. 13*

1568 A334 1k sl grn & yel grn .65 .65
1569 A334 1k purple .25 .25
1570 A335 5k sepia & buff .65 .65
1571 A335 10k lil rose & pale bl .65 .25
1573 A335 30k black & violet .65 .25
1574 A335 50k blue & yellow .65 .25
1575 A335 60k dk blue gray 4.00 .65
1576 A335 100k olive brown 2.40 .55
1577 A335 150k dull green 12.00 1.60
Nos. 1568-1577 (9) 21.90 5.10

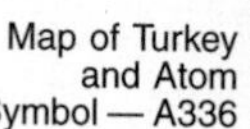

Map of Turkey and Atom Symbol — A336

Designs: 60k, Symbols of medicine, agriculture, industry and atom. 100k, Emblem of Turkish Atomic Energy Commission.

1963, May 27 Unwmk. *Perf. 13*

1584 A336 50k red brn & blk .25 .25
1585 A336 60k grn, dk grn, yel & red .25 .25
1586 A336 100k violet bl & bl .55 .30
Nos. 1584-1586 (3) 1.05 .80

Turkish nuclear research center, 1st anniv.

Meric Bridge A337

Sultan Murad I A338

Designs: 10k, Üçserefeli Mosque. 60k, Summerhouse, Edirne Palace.

1963, June 17

1587 A338 10k dp bl & yel grn .25 .25
1588 A337 30k red org & ultra .25 .25
1589 A337 60k dk bl, red & brn .25 .25
1590 A338 100k multicolored 1.10 .35
Nos. 1587-1590 (4) 1.85 1.10

600th anniv. of the conquest of Edirne (Adrianople).

Soldier and Rising Sun — A339

1963, June 28

1591 A339 50k red, blk & gray .25 .25
1592 A339 100k red, blk & ol .45 .25

600th anniversary of the Turkish army.

Plowing A340

Mithat Pasha A341

Design: 50k, Agriculture Bank, Ankara.

Perf. 13x13½, 13½x13

1963, Aug. 27 Photo. Unwmk.

1593 A340 30k brt yel grn, red brn & grn .25 .25
1594 A340 50k pale vio & Prus bl .25 .25
1595 A341 60k gray & green .30 .25
Nos. 1593-1595 (3) .80 .75

Centenary of Agriculture Bank, Ankara.

Sports and Exhibition Palace, Istanbul and #5 — A342

Designs: 50k, Sultan Ahmed Mosque & Turkey in Asia #22. 60k, View of Istanbul & Turkey in Asia #83. 100k, Rumeli Hisari Fortress & #679. 130k, Ankara Fortress & #C2.

1963, Sept. 7 Litho. *Perf. 13*

1596 A342 10k blk, yel & rose .25 .25
a. Rose omitted *37.50 37.50*
1597 A342 50k blk, grn & rose lil .30 .25
1598 A342 60k dk brn, dk bl & blk .35 .25
1599 A342 100k dk vio & lil rose .50 .25
1600 A342 130k brn, tan & dp org .75 .25
Nos. 1596-1600 (5) 2.15 1.25

"Istanbul 63" Intl. Stamp Exhibition.

Type of 1963 Inscribed: "F.I.P. GÜNÜ"

Souvenir Sheet

Issues of 1863: 10k, 20pa. 50k, 1pi. 60k, 2pi. 130k, 5pi.

Unwmk.

1963, Sept. 13 Litho. *Imperf.*

1601 Sheet of 4 2.00 1.50
a. A332 10k yel, brown & blk .25 .25
b. A332 50k lilac, pink & blk .25 .25
c. A332 60k bluish grn, lt bl & blk .40 .25
d. A332 130k red brn, pink & blk .50 .25

Intl. Philatelic Federation.

Europa Issue

Common Design Type

1963, Sept. 16 Size: 32x24mm

1602 CD6 50k red & black *.50* .25
1603 CD6 130k bl grn, blk & bl *.70* .25

Atatürk and First Parliament Building — A343

Atatürk and: 50k, Turkish flag. 60k, New Parliament building.

1963, Oct. 29 Photo. *Perf. 13½*

1604 A343 30k blk, gold, yel & mar .50 .25
1605 A343 50k dk grn, gold, yel & red .60 .25
1606 A343 60k dk brn, gold & yel .80 .25
Nos. 1604-1606 (3) 1.90 .75

40th anniversary of Turkish Republic.

Atatürk, 25th Death Anniv. — A344

1963, Nov. 10

1607 A344 50k red, gold, grn & brn .50 .25
1608 A344 60k red, gold, bl & brn .75 .25

NATO, 15th Anniv. — A346

130k, NATO emblem and olive branch.

1964, Apr. 4 Litho. *Perf. 13*

1610 A346 50k grnsh bl, vio bl & red .45 .25
1611 A346 130k red & black .75 .70

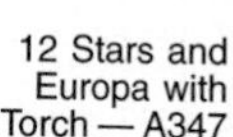

12 Stars and Europa with Torch — A347

Design: 130k, Torch and stars.

1964, May 5 Litho. *Perf. 12*

1612 A347 50k red brn, yel & dk ultra .30 .25
1613 A347 130k ultra, lt bl & org .50 .35

15th anniversary of Council of Europe.

Hüseyin Rahmi Gürpinar, novelist — A348

Portraits: 1k, Hüseyin Rahmi Gürpinar, novelist. 5k, Ismail Hakki Izmirli, scientist. 10k, Sevket Dag, painter. 50k, Recaizade Mahmut Ekrem, Writer. 60k, Gazi Ahmet Muhtar Pasha, commander. 100k, Ahmet Rasim, writer. 130k, Salih Zeki, mathematician.

1964 Litho. *Perf. 13½x13*

1614 A348 1k red & blk .25 .25
1615 A348 5k dull grn & blk .25 .25
1616 A348 10k tan & blk .25 .25
1617 A348 50k ultra & dk bl 1.25 .25
1618 A348 60k gray & blk 1.40 .25
1619 A348 100k grnsh bl & dk bl 1.50 .25
1620 A348 130k brt grn & dk grn 6.50 .65
Nos. 1614-1620 (7) 11.40 2.15

Mosque of Sultan Ahmed A349

Kiz Kulesi, Mersin A350

Designs: No. 1622, Zeus Temple, Silifke. No. 1623, View of Amasra. No. 1625, Augustus' Gate and minaret, Ankara.

1964, June 11 Unwmk. *Perf. 13*

1621 A349 50k gray ol & yel grn .25 .25
1622 A349 50k claret & car .35 .25
1623 A349 50k dk bl & vio bl .35 .25
1624 A350 60k sl grn & dk gray .50 .25
1625 A350 60k dk brn & org brn .60 .25
Nos. 1621-1625 (5) 2.05 1.25

Kars Castle A351

Alp Arslan, Conqueror of Kars, 1064 A352

1964, Aug. 16 Unwmk. *Perf. 13*

1626 A351 50k blk & pale vio .40 .30
1627 A352 130k blk, gold, sal & pale vio 1.10 .50

900th anniversary of conquest of Kars.

Europa Issue

Common Design Type

1964, Sept. 14 Litho. *Perf. 13*
Size: 22x33mm

1628 CD7 50k org, ind & sil *.50* .30
1629 CD7 130k lt bl, mag & cit *1.50* .50

Fuat, Resit and Ali Pashas A353

Design: 60k, Mustafa Resit Pasha, vert.

1964, Nov. 3 *Perf. 13*
Sizes: 48x33mm (50k, 100k); 22x33mm (60k)

1630 A353 50k multicolored .50 .25
1631 A353 60k multicolored .65 .25
1632 A353 100k multicolored .90 .45
Nos. 1630-1632 (3) 2.05 .95

125th anniversary of reform decrees.

Parachutist — A354

Designs: 90k, Glider, horiz. 130k, Ataturk watching squadron in flight.

1965, Feb. 16 Litho. *Perf. 13*

1633 A354 60k lt bl, blk, red & yel .25 .25
1634 A354 90k bister & multi .50 .25
1635 A354 130k lt blue & multi .80 .25
Nos. 1633-1635 (3) 1.55 .75

Turkish Aviation League, 40th anniv.

Emblem — A355

Designs: 50k, Radio mast and waves, vert. 75k, Hand pressing button.

1965, Feb. 24 Unwmk. *Perf. 13*
1636 A355 30k multicolored .25 .25
1637 A355 50k multicolored .25 .25
1638 A355 75k multicolored .55 .25
Nos. 1636-1638 (3) 1.05 .75

Telecommunications meeting of the Central Treaty Org., CENTO.

Coast of Ordu — A356

50k, Manavgat Waterfall, Antalya. 60k, Sultan Ahmed Mosque, Istanbul. 100k, Hali Rahman Mosque, Urfa. 130k, Red Tower, Alanya.

1965, Apr. 5 Litho.
1639 A356 30k multicolored .25 .25
1640 A356 50k multicolored .35 .25
1641 A356 60k multicolored .35 .25
1642 A356 100k multicolored .65 .25
1643 A356 130k multicolored .95 .25
Nos. 1639-1643 (5) 2.55 1.25

ITU Emblem, Old and New Communication Equipment A357

1965, May 17 *Perf. 13*
1644 A357 50k multicolored .30 .25
1645 A357 130k multicolored .55 .25

ITU, centenary.

ICY Emblem — A358

1965, June 26 Litho. Unwmk.
1646 A358 100k red org, red brn & brt grn .40 .25
1647 A358 130k gray, lil & ol grn .65 .35

International Cooperation Year.

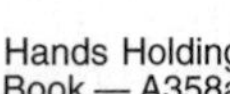
Hands Holding Book — A358a

Map and Flags of Turkey, Iran and Pakistan A358b

1965, July 21 Unwmk. *Perf. 13*
1648 A358a 50k org brn, yel & dk brn .30 .25
1649 A358b 75k dl bl, red, grn blk & org .45 .25

1st anniv. of the signing of the Regional Cooperation Development Pact by Turkey, Iran and Pakistan.

See Iran 1327-1328, Pakistan 217-218.

Kemal Ataturk — A359

1965 Litho. *Perf. 12½*
1650 A359 1k brt green .40 .25
1651 A359 5k violet blue .80 .25
1652 A359 10k blue 1.25 .25
1653 A359 25k gray 2.75 .25
1654 A359 30k magenta 2.00 .25
1655 A359 50k brown 3.25 .30
1656 A359 150k orange 11.50 .75
Nos. 1650-1656 (7) 21.95 2.30

Europa Issue
Common Design Type

1965, Sept. 27 *Perf. 13*
Size: 32x23mm
1665 CD8 50k gray, ultra & grn *.75* .50
1666 CD8 130k tan, blk & grn *1.25* .75

Map of Turkey and People — A360

Designs: 50k, "1965." 100k, "1965," symbolic eye and man, vert.

Unwmk.
1965, Oct. 24 Litho. *Perf. 13*
1667 A360 10k multicolored .25 .25
1668 A360 50k grn, blk & lt yel grn .30 .25
1669 A360 100k orange, sl & blk .65 .25
Nos. 1667-1669 (3) 1.20 .75

Issued to publicize the 1965 census.

Plane over Ankara Castle — A361

Designs: 30k, Archer and Ankara castle. 50k, Horsemen with spears (ancient game). 100k, Three stamps and medal. 150k, Hands holding book, vert.

1965, Oct. 25
1670 A361 10k brt vio, yel & red .25 .25
1671 A361 30k multicolored .25 .25
1672 A361 50k lt gray ol, ind & red .25 .25
1673 A361 100k gray & multi .60 .30
Nos. 1670-1673 (4) 1.35 1.05

Souvenir Sheet
Imperf
1674 A361 150k multicolored 2.50 2.50

1st Natl. Postage Stamp Exhibition "Ankara 65."

Resat Nuri Guntekin, Novelist — A362

Portraits: 5k, Besim Omer Akalin, M.D. 10k, Tevfik Fikret, poet. 25k, Tanburi Cemil, composer. 30k, Ahmet Vefik Pasha, playwright. 50k, Omer Seyfettin, novelist. 60k, Kemalettin Mimaroglu, architect. 150k, Halit Ziya Usakligil, novelist. 220k, Yahya Kemal Beyatli, poet.

1965 Litho. *Perf. 13½x13*
Black Portrait and Inscriptions
1675 A362 1k rose .25 .25
1676 A362 5k blue .45 .25
1677 A362 10k buff .45 .25
1678 A362 25k dull red brn .75 .25
1679 A362 30k gray .75 .25
1680 A362 50k orange 1.10 .25
1681 A362 60k red lilac 1.25 .25
1682 A362 150k lt green 1.75 .25
1683 A362 220k tan 3.00 .45
Nos. 1675-1683 (9) 9.75 2.45

Training Ship Savarona — A363

Designs: 60k, Submarine "Piri Reis." 100k, Cruiser "Alpaslan." 130k, Destroyer "Gelibolu." 220k, Destroyer "Gemlik."

1965, Dec. 6 Photo. *Perf. 11½*
1684 A363 50k blue & brown .40 .25
1685 A363 60k blue & black .55 .25
1686 A363 100k blue & black .90 .25
1687 A363 130k blue & vio blk 1.40 .40
1688 A363 220k blue & indigo 2.10 .65
Nos. 1684-1688 (5) 5.35 1.80

First Congress of Turkish Naval Society.

Kemal Ataturk — A364

Imprint: "Apa Ofset Basimevi"
Black Portrait and Inscriptions

1965 Litho. *Perf. 13½*
1689 A364 1k rose lilac .90 .25
1690 A364 5k lt green .90 .25
1691 A364 10k blue gray 1.40 .40
1692 A364 50k olive bister 1.60 .40
1693 A364 150k silver 2.75 .90
Nos. 1689-1693 (5) 7.55 2.20

See Nos. 1724-1728.

Halide Edip Adivar, Writer — A365

Portraits: 25k, Huseyin Sadettin Arel, writer and composer. 30k, Kamil Akdik, graphic artist. 60k, Abdurrahman Seref, historian. 130k, Naima, historian.

1966 Litho. *Perf. 13½*
1694 A365 25k gray & brn blk .90 .25
1695 A365 30k rose vio & blk brn 1.10 .25
1696 A365 50k blue & black 1.25 .25
1697 A365 60k lt grn & blk brn 1.40 .25
1698 A365 130k lt vio bl & blk 1.90 .25
Nos. 1694-1698 (5) 6.55 1.25

Tiles, Green Mausoleum, Bursa — A366

Tiles: 60k, Spring flowers, Hurrem Sultan Mausoleum, Istanbul. 130k, Stylized flowers, 16th century.

1966, May 15 Litho. *Perf. 13½x13*
1699 A366 50k multicolored .85 .25
1700 A366 60k multicolored 1.40 .50
1701 A366 130k multicolored 2.10 .60
Nos. 1699-1701 (3) 4.35 1.35

On No. 1700 the black ink was applied by a thermographic process and varnished, producing a shiny, raised effect to imitate the embossed tiles of the design source.

Volleyball — A367

1966, May 20 *Perf. 13x13½*
1702 A367 50k tan & multi .60 .25

4th Intl. Military Volleyball Championship.

View of Bodrum — A368

Views: 30k, Kusadasi. 50k, Anadolu Hisari, Istanbul. 90k, Marmaris. 100k, Izmir.

1966, May 25 *Perf. 13x13½, 13½x13*
1703 A368 10k multi .25 .25
1704 A368 30k multi .65 .25
1705 A368 50k multi, horiz. .35 .25
1706 A368 90k multi .35 .25
1707 A368 100k multi, horiz. .45 .25
Nos. 1703-1707 (5) 2.05 1.25

Inauguration of Keban Dam — A369

Design: 60k, View of Keban Dam area.

1966, June 10 *Perf. 13½*
1708 A369 50k multicolored .35 .25
1709 A369 60k multicolored .65 .40

Visit of King Faisal of Saudi Arabia — A370

1966, Aug. 29 Litho. *Perf. 13½x13*
1710 A370 100k car rose & dk car .90 .30

Symbolic Postmark and Stamp — A371

Designs: 60k, Flower made of stamps. 75k, Stamps forming display frames. 100k, Map of Balkan states, magnifying glass and stamp.

1966, Sept. 3 *Perf. 13½x13*
1711 A371 50k multicolored .25 .25
1712 A371 60k multicolored .25 .25
1713 A371 75k multicolored .55 .25
Nos. 1711-1713 (3) 1.05 .75

Souvenir Sheet
Imperf
1714 A371 100k multicolored 2.50 1.50

2nd "Balkanfila" stamp exhibition, Istanbul.

Sultan Suleiman on Horseback — A372

90k, Mausoleum, Istanbul. 130k, Suleiman.

1966, Sept. 6 *Perf. 13½x13*
1715 A372 60k multicolored .65 .25
1716 A372 90k multicolored 1.10 .40
1717 A372 130k multicolored 2.25 .65
Nos. 1715-1717 (3) 4.00 1.30

Sultan Suleiman the Magnificent (1496?-1566). On No. 1717 a gold frame was applied by raised thermographic process.

Europa Issue
Common Design Type

1966, Sept. 26 Litho. *Perf. 13x13½*
Size: 22x33mm
1718 CD9 50k lt bl, vio bl & blk *1.10* .65
a. Black (inscriptions & imprint) omitted *65.00*
1719 CD9 130k lil, dk red lil & blk *2.25* 1.10

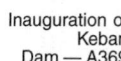

Symbols of Education, Science and Culture — A373

1966, Nov. 4 Litho. *Perf. 13*
1720 A373 130k brn, bis brn & yel .50 .25

UNESCO, 20th anniversary.

Middle East University of Technology A374

Designs: 100k, Atom symbol. 130k, design symbolizing sciences.

1966, Nov. 15

1721 A374 50k multicolored .25 .25
1722 A374 100k multicolored .55 .25
1723 A374 130k multicolored .85 .55
Nos. 1721-1723 (3) 1.65 1.05

10th anniv. of the Middle East University of Technology.

Ataturk Type of 1965
Imprint: "Kiral Matbaasi — Ist"

1966 Litho. *Perf. 12½*
Black Portrait and Inscriptions

1724 A364 25k yellow .35 .25
1725 A364 30k pink .50 .25
1726 A364 50k rose lilac 1.50 .25
1727 A364 90k pale brown 1.25 .25
1728 A364 100k gray 1.50 .25
Nos. 1724-1728 (5) 5.10 1.25

Statue of Ataturk, Ankara — A375

Equestrian Statues of Ataturk: No. 1729A, Statue in Izmir. No. 1729B, Statue in Samsun.

Without Imprint
1967 Litho. *Perf. 13x12½*
Size: 23x16mm

1729 A375 10k black & yellow .50 .25

Inscribed "1967"
Imprint: Kiral Matbaasi
Size: 22x15mm

1729A A375 10k black & salmon .50 .25
1729B A375 10k black & lt grn .50 .25
Nos. 1729-1729B (3) 1.50 .75

Issued for use on greeting cards. See Nos. 1790-1791A, 1911.

Puppets Karagöz and Hacivat A376

Intl. Tourist Year Emblem and: 60k, Sword and shield game. 90k, Traditional military band. 100k, raised effect.

Perf. 13x13½, 13½x13
1967, Mar. 30 Litho.

1730 A376 50k multicolored .90 .25
1731 A376 60k multicolored 1.25 .25
1732 A376 90k multicolored 1.60 .45
1733 A376 100k multicolored 2.50 .65
Nos. 1730-1733 (4) 6.25 1.60

Intl. Tourist Year. On No. 1733 the black ink was applied by a thermographic process and varnished, producing a shiny, raised effect.

Woman Vaccinating Child, Knife and Lancet — A377

1967, Apr. 1 *Perf. 13x13½*

1734 A377 100k multicolored .50 .25

250th anniv. of smallpox vaccination (variolation) in Turkey. The gold was applied by a thermographic process and varnished, producing a shiny, raised effect.

Fallow Deer — A378

1967, Apr. 23 Litho. *Perf. 13x13½*

1735 A378 50k shown .50 .25
1736 A378 60k Wild goat .65 .25
1737 A378 100k Brown bear .90 .25
1738 A378 130k Wild boar 1.25 .40
Nos. 1735-1738 (4) 3.30 1.15

Soccer Players and Emblem with Map of Europe — A379

130k, Players at left, smaller emblem.

1967, May 1 *Perf. 13*

1739 A379 50k multicolored .75 .25
1740 A379 130k yellow & multi 1.25 .50

20th Intl. Youth Soccer Championships.

Sivas Hospital — A380

1967, July 1 Litho. *Perf. 13*

1741 A380 50k multicolored .40 .25

750th anniversary of Sivas Hospital.

Selim Sirri Tarcan — A381

60k, Olympic Rings, Baron Pierre de Coubertin.

1967, July 20

1742 A381 50k lt blue & multi .40 .25
1743 A381 60k lilac & multi .60 .40
a. Pair, #1742-1743 1.25 1.00

1st Turkish Olympic competitions.

Ahmed Mithat, Writer — A382

Portraits: 5k, Admiral Turgut Reis. 50k, Sokullu Mehmet, statesman. 100k, Nedim, poet. 150k, Osman Hamdi, painter.

1967 Litho. *Perf. 12½*

1744 A382 1k green & blk .65 .25
1745 A382 5k dp bister & blk 1.00 .25
1746 A382 50k brt violet & blk 1.40 .25
1747 A382 100k citron & blk 2.50 .40
1748 A382 150k yellow & blk 4.00 .40
Nos. 1744-1748 (5) 9.55 1.55

Ruins of St. John's Church, Ephesus — A383

Design: 130k, Inside view of Virgin Mary's House, Ephesus.

1967, July 26 *Perf. 13*

1749 A383 130k multicolored .40 .25
1750 A383 220k multicolored .85 .40

Visit of Pope Paul VI to the House of the Virgin Mary in Ephesus, July 26.

Plate on Firing Grid and Ornaments — A384

1967, Sept. 1

1751 A384 50k pale lil, blk, ind & bl .50 .25

5th International Ceramics Exhibition.

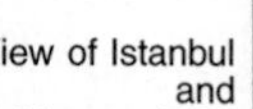

View of Istanbul and Emblem — A385

1967, Sept. 4 Litho. *Perf. 13*

1752 A385 130k dk blue & gray .95 .25

9th Congress of the Intl. Commission of Large Dams.

Stamps, Ornament and Map of Turkey — A386

Design: 60k, Grapes and stamps.

1967

1753 A386 50k multicolored .35 .25
1754 A386 60k multicolored .45 .25
a. Souvenir sheet, #1753-1754 2.50 2.50

Intl. Trade Fair, Izmir.

Kemal Ataturk — A387

1967 Litho. *Perf. 11½x12*
Booklet Stamps

1755 A387 10k blk & lt ol grn 3.25 .80
a. Booklet pane of 10 100.00
b. Booklet pane of 25 250.00
1756 A387 50k blk & pale rose 3.25 .80
a. Booklet pane of 2 40.00
b. Bklt. pane, 5 #1755, 4 #1756 + label 35.00

Symbolic Water Cycle — A388

1967, Dec. 1 Litho. *Perf. 13*

1757 A388 90k lt grn, blk & org .60 .25
1758 A388 130k lilac, blk & org .70 .60

Hydrological Decade (UNESCO), 1965-74.

Child and Angora Cat, Man with Microscope A389

60k, Horse and man with microscope.

1967, Dec. 23 *Perf. 13*

1759 A389 50k multicolored .50 .25
1760 A389 60k multicolored .70 .40

125th anniv. of Turkish veterinary medicine.

Human Rights Flame — A390

1968, Jan. 1 *Perf. 13x13½*

1761 A390 50k rose lil, dk bl & org .40 .25
1762 A390 130k lt bl, dk bl & red org .75 .25

International Human Rights Year.

Archer on Horseback A391

Miniatures, 16th Century: 50k, Investiture. 60k, Sultan Suleiman the Magnificent receiving an ambassador, vert. 100k, Musicians.

Perf. 13x13½, 13½x13
1968, Mar. 1 Litho.

1763 A391 50k multicolored .60 .50
1764 A391 60k multicolored 1.10 .90
1765 A391 90k multicolored 1.50 1.25
1766 A391 100k multicolored 1.75 1.50
Nos. 1763-1766 (4) 4.95 4.15

Kemal Ataturk — A392

1968 Litho. *Perf. 12½*

1767 A392 1k dk & lt blue .35 .25
1768 A392 5k dk & lt green .55 .25
1769 A392 50k org brn & yel 2.10 .25
1770 A392 200k dk brown & pink 6.50 .30
Nos. 1767-1770 (4) 9.50 1.05

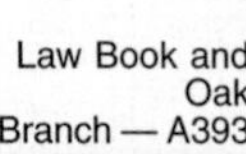

Law Book and Oak Branch — A393

Mithat Pasha and Scroll — A394

1968, Apr. 1 *Perf. 13*

1771 A393 50k multicolored .35 .35
1772 A394 60k multicolored .40 .40

Centenary of the Court of Appeal.

Court Type of 1968

Designs: 50k, Scales of Justice. 60k, Ahmet Cevdet Pasha and scroll.

1968, Apr. 1

1773 A393 50k multicolored .40 .25
1774 A394 60k multicolored .60 .25

Centenary of the Supreme Court.

Europa Issue
Common Design Type

1968, May 6 Litho. *Perf. 13*
Size: 31½x23mm

1775 CD11 100k pck bl, yel & red *1.00* .50
1776 CD11 130k green, yel & red *1.50* .75

Yacht Kismet — A395

1968, June 15 Litho. *Perf. 13*

1777 A395 50k lt ultra & multi .85 .65

Round-the-world trip of the yacht Kismet, Aug. 22, 1965-June 14, 1968.

"Fight Usury" — A396

1968, June 19

1778 A396 50k multicolored 1.00 .60

Centenary of the Pawn Office, Istanbul.

Sakarya Battle and Independence Medal — A397

130k, Natl. anthem & reverse of medal.

1968, Aug. 30 *Perf. 13x13½*
1779 A397 50k gold & multi .75 .40
1780 A397 130k gold & multi 1.25 .60

Turkish Independence medal. The gold on Nos. 1779-1780 was applied by a thermographic process and varnished, producing a shiny, raised effect.

Ataturk and Galatasaray High School A398

50k, "100" and old and new school emblems. 60k, Portraits of Beyazit II and Gulbaba.

1968, Sept. 1 **Litho.**
1781 A398 50k gray & multi .25 .25
1782 A398 60k tan & multi .50 .50
1783 A398 100k lt blue & multi .75 .75
Nos. 1781-1783 (3) 1.50 1.50

Centenary of Galatasaray High School.

Charles de Gaulle — A399

1968, Oct. 25 **Litho.** *Perf. 13*
1784 A399 130k multicolored 1.25 .70

Visit of President Charles de Gaulle of France to Turkey.

Kemal Ataturk A400

Ataturk and his Speech to Youth A401

50k, Ataturk's tomb and Citadel of Ankara. 60k, Ataturk looking out a train window. 250k, Framed portrait of Ataturk in military uniform.

1968, Nov. 10
1785 A400 30k orange & blk .50 .25
1786 A400 50k brt grn & sl grn .50 .25
1787 A400 60k bl grn & blk .60 .25
1788 A401 100k blk, gray & brt grn .90 .25
1789 A401 250k multicolored 1.75 .40
Nos. 1785-1789 (5) 4.25 1.40

30th death anniv. of Kemal Ataturk.

Ataturk Statue Type of 1967

Equestrian Statues of Ataturk: No. 1790, Statue in Zonguldak. No. 1791, Statue in Antakya. No. 1791A, Statue in Bursa.

Imprint: Kiral Matbaasi 1968

1968-69 **Litho.** *Perf. 13x12½*

Size: 22x15mm

1790 A375 10k black & lt blue .75 .25
1791 A375 10k blk & brt rose lil .75 .25

Perf. 13½

Imprint: Tifdruk Matbaacilik Sanayii A. S. 1969

Size: 21x16½mm

1791A A375 10k dk grn & tan ('69) .75 .25
Nos. 1790-1791A (3) 2.25 .75

Ince Minare Mosque, Konya — A402

Historic Buildings: 10k, Doner Kumbet (tomb), Kayseri. 50k, Karatay Medresse (University Gate), Konya. 100k, Ortakoy Mosque, Istanbul. 200k, Ulu Mosque, Divriki.

1968-69 **Photo.** *Perf. 13x13½*
1792 A402 1k dk brn & buff ('69) .25 .25
1793 A402 10k plum & dl rose ('69) .75 .25
1794 A402 50k dk ol grn & gray .90 .35
1795 A402 100k dk & lt grn ('69) 2.25 .40
1796 A402 200k dp bl & lt bl ('69) 3.25 .90
Nos. 1792-1796 (5) 7.40 2.15

ILO Emblem — A403

1969, Apr. 15 **Litho.** *Perf. 13*
1797 A403 130k dk red & black .80 .25

ILO, 50th anniv.

Sultana Hafsa, Medical Pioneer — A404

1969, Apr. 26 **Litho.** *Perf. 13½x13*
1798 A404 60k multicolored 1.25 1.00

Europa Issue

Common Design Type

1969, Apr. 28 *Perf. 13*

Size: 32x23mm

1799 CD12 100k dull vio & multi *1.00* .65
1800 CD12 130k gray grn & multi *1.50* 1.00

Kemal Ataturk A405

Ataturk and S.S. Bandirma A406

1969, May 19 **Litho.** *Perf. 13*
1801 A405 50k multicolored .60 .25
1802 A406 60k multicolored .90 .35

50th anniv. of the landing of Kemal Ataturk at Samsun.

Map of Istanbul — A407

1969, May 31
1803 A407 130k vio bl, lt bl, gold & red .60 .25

22nd Congress of the Intl. Chamber of Commerce, Istanbul.

Educational Progress — A408

Agricultural Progress — A409

Designs: 90k, Pouring ladle and industrial symbols. 100k, Road sign (highway construction). 180k, Oil industry chart and symbols.

1969 **Litho.** *Perf. 13½x13*
1804 A408 1k black & gray .25 .25
1805 A408 1k black & bis brn .25 .25
1806 A408 1k black & lt grn .25 .25
1807 A408 1k black & lt vio .25 .25
1808 A408 1k black & org red .25 .25
1809 A409 50k brown & ocher .65 .25
1810 A409 90k blk & grnsh gray 1.10 .25
1811 A408 100k black & org red 1.50 .25
1812 A408 180k violet & orange 2.50 .25
Nos. 1804-1812 (9) 7.00 2.25

Issued: 1, 100k, 4/8; 50k, 6/11; 90, 180k, 8/15.

Sultan Suleiman Receiving Sheik Abdul Latif — A410

Designs: 80k, Lady Serving Wine, Safavi miniature, Iran. 130k, Lady on Balcony, Mogul miniature, Pakistan.

1969, July 21 **Litho.** *Perf. 13*
1813 A410 50k yellow & multi .45 .25
1814 A410 80k yellow & multi .75 .25
1815 A410 130k yellow & multi 1.25 .50
Nos. 1813-1815 (3) 2.45 1.00

5th anniv. of the signing of the Regional Cooperation for Development Pact by Turkey, Iran and Pakistan.

See Iran 1513-1515, Pakistan 274-276.

Kemal Ataturk — A411

Design: 60k, Ataturk monument and bas-relief showing congress.

1969, July 23
1816 A411 50k black & gray .90 .25
1817 A411 60k black & grnsh gray 1.75 .50

50th anniversary, Congress of Erzerum.

Sivas Congress Delegates A412

Design: 50k, Congress Hall.

1969, Sept. 4 **Litho.** *Perf. 13*
1818 A412 50k dk brn & dp rose .35 .35
1819 A412 60k olive blk & yel .45 .45

50th anniv. of the Congress of Sivas (preparation for the Turkish war of independence).

Bar Dance A413

Folk Dances: 50k, Candle dance (çaydaçira). 60k, Scarf dance (halay). 100k, Sword dance (kiliç-kalkan). 130k, Two male dancers (zeybek), vert.

1969, Sept. 9
1820 A413 30k brown & multi .40 .25
1821 A413 50k multicolored .50 .25
1822 A413 60k multicolored .80 .25
1823 A413 100k yellow & multi .90 .90
1824 A413 130k multicolored 1.40 .55
Nos. 1820-1824 (5) 4.00 2.20

1914 Airplane "Prince Celaleddin" A414

75k, First Turkish letter carried by air.

1969, Oct. 18 **Litho.** *Perf. 13*
1825 A414 60k dk blue & blue .40 .25
1826 A414 75k black & bister .65 .25

55th anniv. of the first Turkish mail transported by air.

"Kutadgu Bilig" — A415

1969, Nov. 20 **Litho.** *Perf. 13*
1827 A415 130k ol bis, brn & gold .55 .25

900th anniv. of "Kutadgu Bilig," a book about the function of the state, compiled by Jusuf of Balasagun in Tashkent, 1069.

Ataturk's Arrival in Ankara, after a Painting A416

Design: 60k, Ataturk and his coworkers in automobiles arriving in Ankara, after a photograph.

1969, Dec. 27 **Litho.** *Perf. 13*
1828 A416 50k multicolored .75 .25
1829 A416 60k multicolored 1.25 .30

50th anniv. of Kemal Ataturk's arrival in Ankara, Dec. 27, 1919.

Bosporus Bridge, Map of Europe and Asia — A417

Design: 60k, View of proposed Bosporus Bridge and shore lines.

1970, Feb. 20 **Litho.** *Perf. 13*
1830 A417 60k gold & multi .75 .30
1831 A417 130k gold & multi 1.50 .65

Foundation ceremonies for the bridge across the Bosporus linking Europe and Asia.

Kemal Ataturk and Signature A418

Kemal Ataturk A419

1970 **Litho.** *Perf. 13*
1832 A418 1k dp orange & brn .25 .25
1833 A419 5k silver & blk .25 .25
1834 A418 30k citron & blk .35 .25
1835 A418 50k lt olive & blk .40 .25
1836 A419 50k pink & blk .70 .25
1837 A419 75k lilac & blk 1.40 .25
1838 A419 100k blue & blk .90 .25
Nos. 1832-1838 (7) 4.25 1.75

For surcharge see No. 2078.

Education Year Emblem — A420

1970, Mar. 16

1839 A420 130k ultra, pink & rose lil .80 .25

International Education Year.

Turkish EXPO '70 Emblem — A421

100k, EXPO '70 emblem & Turkish pavilion.

1970, Mar. 27

1840 A421 50k gold & multi .25 .25
1841 A421 100k gold & multi .60 .25

EXPO '70 International Exhibition, Osaka, Japan, Mar. 15-Sept. 13.

Opening of Grand National Assembly A422

Design: 60k, Session of First Grand National Assembly, 1920.

1970, Apr. 23

1842 A422 50k multicolored .35 .25
1843 A422 60k multicolored .55 .25

Turkish Grand National Assembly, 50th anniv.

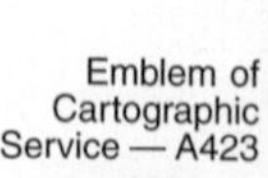

Emblem of Cartographic Service — A423

Turkish Cartographic Service, 75th Anniv. — A424

Designs: 60k, Plane and aerial mapping survey diagram. 100k, Triangulation point in mountainous landscape. 130k, Map of Turkey and Gen. Mehmet Sevki Pasha.

Perf. 13½x13 (A423), 13x13½ (A424)

1970, May 2 Litho.

1844 A423 50k blue & multi .40 .25
1845 A424 60k blk, gray grn & brick red .40 .25
1846 A423 100k multicolored .60 .35
1847 A424 130k multicolored 1.00 .50
Nos. 1844-1847 (4) 2.40 1.35

Europa Issue
Common Design Type

1970, May 4 ***Perf. 13***
Size: 37x23mm

1848 CD13 100k ver, blk & org *1.00* .50
1849 CD13 130k dk bl grn, blk & org *1.50* 1.00

Inauguration of UPU Headquarters, Bern — A425

1970, May 20

1850 A425 60k blk & dull blue .40 .25
1851 A425 130k blk & dl ol grn .75 .35

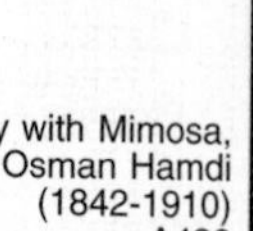

Lady with Mimosa, by Osman Hamdi (1842-1910) A426

Paintings: No. 1853, Deer, by Seker Ahmet (1841-1907). No. 1854, Portrait of Fevzi Cakmak, by Avni Lifij (d. 1927). No. 1855, Sailboats, by Nazmi Ziya (1881-1937); horiz.

1970 Litho. ***Perf. 13***
Size: 29x49mm

1852 A426 250k multicolored 1.00 .35
1853 A426 250k multicolored 1.00 .35

Size: 32x49mm

1854 A426 250k multicolored 1.25 .35

Size: 73½x33mm

1855 A426 250k multicolored 1.25 .35
Nos. 1852-1855 (4) 4.50 1.40

Issued: #1852-1853, 6/15; #1854-1855, 12/15.

Turkish Folk Art — A427

1970, June 15

1856 A427 50k multicolored .75 .25

3rd National Stamp Exhibition, ANKARA 70, Oct. 28-Nov. 4. Pane of 50, each stamp se-tenant with label. This 50k, in pane of 50 without labels, was re-issued Oct. 28 with Nos. 1867-1869.

View of Fethiye — A428

80k, Seeyo-Se-Pol Bridge, Esfahan, Iran. 130k, Saiful Malook Lake, Pakistan.

1970, July 21 Litho. ***Perf. 13***

1857 A428 60k multicolored .35 .25
1858 A428 80k multicolored .50 .25
1859 A428 130k multicolored .75 .35
Nos. 1857-1859 (3) 1.60 .85

6th anniv. of the signing of the Regional Cooperation for Development Pact by Turkey, Iran and Pakistan.
See Iran 1558-1560, Pakistan 290-292.

Sultan Balim's Tomb A429

Haci Bektas Veli A430

30k, Tomb of Haci Bektas Veli, horiz.

1970, Aug. 16 Litho. ***Perf. 13***

1860 A429 30k multicolored .25 .25
1861 A429 100k multicolored .60 .25
1862 A430 180k multicolored 1.25 .25
Nos. 1860-1862 (3) 2.10 .75

700th death anniv. of Haci Bektas Veli, mystic.

Hittite Sun Disk and "ISO" — A431

1970, Sept. 15

1863 A431 110k car rose, gold & blk .35 .25
1864 A431 150k ultra, gold & blk .65 .35

8th General Council Meeting of the Intl. Standardization Org., Ankara.

UN Emblem, People and Globe — A432

100k, UN emblem and propeller, horiz.

1970, Oct. 24 Litho. ***Perf. 13***

1865 A432 100k gray & multi .60 .25
1866 A432 220k multicolored .90 .35

25th anniversary of the United Nations.

Stamp "Flower" and Book — A433

Designs: 60k, Ataturk monument and stamps, horiz. 130k, Abstract flower.

1970, Oct. 28

1867 A433 10k multicolored .50 .25
1868 A433 60k blue & multi .90 .25

Souvenir Sheet

1869 A433 130k dk green & org 2.50 1.90

3rd National Stamp Exhibition, ANKARA 70, Oct. 28-Nov. 4. See note below No. 1856.

InönüBattle Scene A434

Design: No. 1871, Second Battle of Inönü.

1971 Litho. ***Perf. 13***

1870 A434 100k multicolored .80 .25
1871 A434 100k multicolored .80 .25

1st and 2nd Battles of Inönü, 50th anniv. Issue dates: #1870, Jan. 10; #1871, Apr. 1.

Village on River Bank, by Ahmet Sekür A435

Painting: No. 1872, Landscape, Yildiz Palace Garden, by Ahmet Ragip Bicakcilar.

1971, Mar. 15 Litho. ***Perf. 13***

1872 A435 250k multicolored 1.00 .40
1873 A435 250k multicolored 1.00 .40

See #1901-1902, 1909-1910, 1937-1938.

Campaign Against Discrimination A436

1971, Mar. 21 Litho. ***Perf. 13***

1874 A436 100k multicolored .50 .25
1875 A436 250k gray & multi 1.00 .35

Intl. Year against Racial Discrimination.

Europa Issue
Common Design Type

1971, May 3 Litho. ***Perf. 13***
Size: 31½x22½mm

1876 CD14 100k lt bl, cl & mag *1.00* .50
1877 CD14 150k dp org, grn & red *1.50* .75

Kemal Ataturk
A437 A438

1971

1878 A437 5k gray & ultra .60 .25
1879 A437 25k gray & dk red .90 .25
1880 A438 25k brown & pink .60 .25
1881 A437 100k gray & violet 1.25 .25
1882 A438 100k grn & sal 1.25 .35
1883 A438 250k blue & gray 3.00 .60
1884 A437 400k tan & ol grn 5.00 .70
Nos. 1878-1884 (7) 12.60 2.65

Pres. Kemal Gürsel — A439

1971, May 27 Litho. ***Perf. 13***

1885 A439 100k multicolored .75 .25

Revolution of May 27, 1960; Kemal Gürsel (1895-1966), president.

Mosque of Selim, Edirne — A440

150k, Religious School, Chaharbagh, Iran. 200k, Badshahi Mosque, Pakistan.

1971, July 21 Litho. ***Perf. 13***

1886 A440 100k multi .40 .25
1887 A440 150k multi .55 .25
1888 A440 200k multi, horiz. .80 .25
Nos. 1886-1888 (3) 1.75 .75

Regional Cooperation by Turkey, Iran and Pakistan, 7th anniversary.
See Iran 1599-1601, Pakistan 305-307.

Alp Arslan and Battle of Malazkirt A441

Design: 250k, Archers on horseback.

1971, Aug. 26 Litho. ***Perf. 13x13½***

1889 A441 100k multicolored .65 .25
1890 A441 250k red, org & blk 1.00 .40

900th anniversary of the Battle of Malazkirt, which established the Seljuk Dynasty in Asia Minor.

Battle of Sakarya A442

1971, Sept. 13

1891 A442 100k slate lil & multi 1.00 .45

50th anniversary of the victory of Sakarya.

Turkey-Bulgaria Railroad — A443

Designs: 110k, Ferry and map of Lake Van. 250k, Turkey-Iran railroad.

1971

1892 A443 100k multicolored .60 .25
1893 A443 110k multicolored .60 .25
1894 A443 250k yellow & multi 1.40 .60
Nos. 1892-1894 (3) 2.60 1.10

Turkish railroad connections with Bulgaria &Iran. Issued: 110, 250k, 9/27; 100k, 10/4.

Soccer and Map of Mediterranean A444

200k, Runner and stadium, vert. 250k, Shot put and map of Mediterranean, vert.

1971, Oct. 6

1895 A444 100k redsh lil & blk .45 .25
1896 A444 200k brn, blk & emer .80 .35

Souvenir Sheet

Imperf

1897 A444 250k ol bis & slate grn 2.00 1.75

Mediterranean Games, Izmir.

Tomb of Cyrus the Great A445

Designs: 100k, Harpist, Persian mosaic, vert. 150k, Ataturk and Riza Shah Pahlavi.

1971, Oct. 13

1898 A445 25k lt blue & multi .30 .25
1899 A445 100k multicolored .70 .25
1900 A445 150k dk brown & buff 1.00 .35
Nos. 1898-1900 (3) 2.00 .85

2500th anniversary of the founding of the Persian empire by Cyrus the Great.

Painting Type of 1971

No. 1901, Sultan Mohammed I and his Staff. No. 1902, Palace with tiled walls.

1971, Nov. 15 Litho. *Perf. 13*

1901 A435 250k multicolored 1.00 .40
1902 A435 250k multicolored 1.00 .40

Yunus Emre — A446

1971, Dec. 27 Litho. *Perf. 13*

1903 A446 100k brown & multi .60 .25

650th death anniv. of Yunus Emre, Turkish folk poet.

First Turkish World Map and Book Year Emblem A447

1972, Jan. 3 *Perf. 13*

1904 A447 100k buff & multi .75 .25

International Book Year.

Doves and NATO Emblem — A448

1972, Feb. 18 Litho. *Perf. 13*

1905 A448 100k dull grn, blk & gray 1.25 .40
1906 A448 250k dull bl, blk & gray 1.50 1.00

Turkey's membership in NATO, 20th anniv.

Europa Issue

Common Design Type

1972, May 2 Litho. *Perf. 13*

Size: 22x33mm

1907 CD15 110k blue & multi *1.50* .75
1908 CD15 250k brown & multi *2.50* 1.25

Painting Type of 1971

No. 1909, Forest, Seker Ahmet. No. 1910, View of Gebze, Anatolia, by Osman Hamdi.

1972, May 15 Litho.

1909 A435 250k multicolored 1.00 .35
1910 A435 250k multicolored 1.00 .35

Ataturk Statue Type of 1967

Imprint: Ajans - Turk/Ankara 1972

Design: 25k, Ataturk Statue in front of Ethnographic Museum, Ankara.

Perf. 12½x11½

1972, June 12 Litho.

Size: 22x15½mm

1911 A375 25k black & buff .60 .25

Fisherman, by Cevat Dereli — A449

Paintings: 125k, Young Man, by Abdur Rehman Chughtai (Pakistan). 150k, Persian Woman, by Behzad.

1972, July 21 Litho. *Perf. 13*

1912 A449 100k gold & multi .70 .25
1913 A449 125k gold & multi 1.20 .40
1914 A449 150k gold & multi 1.40 .45
Nos. 1912-1914 (3) 3.30 1.10

Regional Cooperation for Development Pact among Turkey, Iran and Pakistan, 8th anniv. See Iran 1647-1649, Pakistan 322-324.

Ataturk and Commanders at Mt. Koca — A450

Designs: No. 1916, Battle of the Commander-in-chief. No. 1917, Turkish army entering Izmir. 110k, Artillery and cavalry.

1972 Litho. *Perf. 13x13½*

1915 A450 100k lt ultra & blk 1.00 .25
1916 A450 100k pink & multi 1.00 .25
1917 A450 100k yellow & multi 1.00 .25
1918 A450 110k orange & multi 1.00 .25
Nos. 1915-1918 (4) 4.00 1.00

50th anniv. of fight for establishment of independent Turkish republic. Issued: #1915, 1918, 8/26; #1916, 8/30; #1917, 9/9.

"Cancer is Curable" — A451

1972, Oct. 10 Litho. *Perf. 12½x13*

1919 A451 100k blk, brt bl & red .50 .25

Fight against cancer.

International Railroad Union Emblem — A452

1972, Dec. 31 Litho. *Perf. 13*

1920 A452 100k sl grn, ocher & red .60 .25

Intl. Railroad Union, 50th anniv.

Kemal Ataturk — A453

1972-76 Litho. *Perf. 13½x13*

Size: 21x26mm

1921 A453 5k gray & blue .45 .25
1922 A453 25k orange ('75) .60 .25
1923 A453 100k buff & red brn ('73) 1.75 .25
1924 A453 100k lt gray & gray ('75) .60 .25
1925 A453 110k lt bl & vio bl 1.25 .35
1926 A453 125k dull grn ('73) 1.60 .25
1927 A453 150k tan & brown 1.75 .25
1928 A453 150k lt grn & grn ('75) .45 .25
1929 A453 175k yel & lil ('73) 2.50 .35
1930 A453 200k buff & red 2.00 .25
1931 A453 250k pink & pur ('75) .60 .25
1931A A453 400k gray & Prus bl ('76) .60 .25
1932 A453 500k pink & violet 3.25 .65
1933 A453 500k gray & ultra ('75) 2.00 .30

Size: 22x33mm

Perf. 13

1934 A453 10 l pink & car rose ('75) 3.25 .30
Nos. 1921-1934 (15) 22.65 4.45

See Nos. 2060-2061. For surcharges see Nos. 2180-2181.

Europa Issue

Common Design Type

1973, Apr. 4 Litho. *Perf. 13*

Size: 32x23mm

1935 CD16 110k gray & multi *1.40* .75
1936 CD16 250k multicolored *2.75* 1.50

Painting Type of 1971

Paintings: No. 1937, Beyazit Almshouse, Istanbul, by Ahmet Ziya Akbulut. No. 1938, Flowers, by Suleyman Seyyit, vert.

1973, June 15 Litho. *Perf. 13*

1937 A435 250k multicolored 1.25 .50
1938 A435 250k multicolored 1.25 .50

Army Day — A454

Designs: 90k, Helmet, sword and oak leaves. 100k, Helmet, sword and laurel.

1973, June 28 *Perf. 13x12½*

1939 A454 90k brn, gray & grn .35 .25
1940 A454 100k brn, lem & grn .35 .25

Mausoleum of Antiochus I — A455

Designs: 100k, Colossal heads, mausoleum of Antiochus I (69-34 B.C.), Commagene, Turkey. 150k, Statue, Shahdad Kerman, Persia, 3000 B.C. 200k, Street, Mohenjo-daro, Pakistan.

1973, July 21 Litho. *Perf. 13*

1941 A455 100k lt blue & multi .35 .25
1942 A455 150k olive & multi .50 .25
1943 A455 200k brown & multi .75 .95
Nos. 1941-1943 (3) 1.60 1.45

Regional Cooperation for Development Pact among Turkey, Iran and Pakistan, 9th anniv. See Iran 1714-1716, Pakistan 343-345.

Minelayer Nusret — A456

Designs: 25k, Destroyer Istanbul. 100k, Speedboat Simsek and Naval College. 250k, Two-masted training ship Nuvid-i Futuh.

1973, Aug. 1 Size: 31½x22mm

1944 A456 5k Prus bl & multi .25 .25
1945 A456 25k Prus bl & multi .25 .25
1946 A456 100k Prus bl & multi 1.10 .25

Size: 48x32mm

1947 A456 250k blue & multi 2.50 .40
Nos. 1944-1947 (4) 4.10 1.15

abu-al-Rayhan al-Biruni — A457

1973, Sept. 4 Litho. *Perf. 13x12½*

1948 A457 250k multicolored .60 .40

abu-al-Rayhan al-Biruni (973-1048), philosopher and mathematician.

Emblem of Darussafaka Foundation — A458

1973, Sept. 15 *Perf. 13*

1949 A458 100k silver & multi .50 .25

Centenary of the educational and philanthropic Darussafaka Foundation.

BALKANFILA IV Emblem — A459

Designs: 110k, Symbolic view and stamps. 250k, "Balkanfila 4."

1973 Litho. *Perf. 13*

1950 A459 100k gray & multi .35 .25
1951 A459 110k multicolored .25 .25
1952 A459 250k multicolored .45 .25
Nos. 1950-1952 (3) 1.05 .75

BALKANFILA IV, Philatelic Exhibition of Balkan Countries, Izmir, Oct. 26-Nov. 5. Issued: 100k, Sept. 26; 110k, 250k, Oct. 26.

Sivas Shepherd Dog — A460

1973, Oct. 4

1953 A460 25k shown .35 .25
1954 A460 100k Angora cat .90 .25

Kemal Ataturk — A461

1973, Oct. 10 Litho. *Perf. 13*

1955 A461 100k gold & blk brn .75 .25

35th death anniv. of Kemal Ataturk.

Flower and "50" — A462

Ataturk A463

250k, Torch & "50." 475k, Grain & cogwheel.

1973, Oct. 29

1956 A462 100k purple, red & bl .25 .25
1957 A462 250k multicolored .70 .25
1958 A462 475k brt blue & org 1.10 .50
Nos. 1956-1958 (3) 2.05 1.00

Souvenir Sheet

Imperf

1959 A463 500k multicolored 3.00 2.00

50th anniv. of the Turkish Republic. #1959 contains one stamp with simulated perforations.

Bosporus Bridge — A464

150k, Istanbul & Bosporus Bridge. 200k, Bosporus Bridge, children & UNICEF emblem, vert.

1973, Oct. 30 *Perf. 13*

1960 A464 100k multicolored .35 .25
1961 A464 150k multicolored .55 .35
1962 A464 200k multicolored .60 .35
Nos. 1960-1962 (3) 1.50 .95

Inauguration of the Bosporus Bridge from Istanbul to Üsküdar, Oct. 30, 1973; UNICEF; children from East and West brought closer through Bosporus Bridge (No. 1962).

Mevlana's Tomb and Dancers A465

Jalal-udin Mevlana A466

1973, Dec. 1 *Perf. 13x12½*

1963 A465 100k blk, lt ultra & grn .45 .25
1964 A466 250k blue & multi .65 .35

Jalal-udin Mevlana (1207-1273), poet and founder of the Mevlevie dervish order.

Cotton and Ship — A467

Export Products: 90k, Grapes. 100k, Figs. 250k, Citrus fruits. 325k, Tobacco. 475k, Hazelnuts.

1973, Dec. 10 Litho. *Perf. 13*

1965 A467 75k black, gray & bl .25 .25
1966 A467 90k black, olive & bl .40 .25
1967 A467 100k black, emer & bl .55 .25
1968 A467 250k blk, brt yel & bl 1.40 .35
1969 A467 325k blk, yel & bl 1.40 .35
1970 A467 475k blk, org brn & bl 2.10 .55
Nos. 1965-1970 (6) 6.10 2.00

Pres. Inönü — A468

1973, Dec. 25 Litho. *Perf. 13*

1971 A468 100k sepia & buff .60 .25

Ismet Inönü, (1884-1973), first Prime Minister and second President of Turkey.

Hittite King, 8th Century B.C. — A469

Europa: 250k, Statuette of a Boy, (2nd millenium B.C.).

1974, Apr. 29 Litho. *Perf. 13*

1972 A469 110k multicolored *2.50 1.00*
1973 A469 250k lt blue & multi *4.00 2.00*

Silver and Gold Figure, 3000 B.C. — A470

Archaeological Finds: 175k, Painted jar, 5000 B.C., horiz. 200k, Vessels in bull form, 1700-1600 B.C., horiz. 250k, Pitcher, 700 B.C.

1974, May 24 Litho. *Perf. 13*

1974 A470 125k multicolored .30 .25
1975 A470 175k multicolored .55 .25
1976 A470 200k multicolored .65 .25
1977 A470 250k multicolored 1.00 .40
Nos. 1974-1977 (4) 2.50 1.15

Child Care — A471

1974, May 24

1978 A471 110k gray blue & blk .60 .25

Sisli Children's Hospital, Istanbul, 75th anniv.

Anatolian Rug, 15th Century — A472

Designs: 150k, Persian rug, late 16th century. 200k, Kashan rug, Lahore.

1974, July 21 Litho. *Perf. 12½x13*

1979 A472 100k blue & multi .90 .25
1980 A472 150k brown & multi 1.40 .25
1981 A472 200k red & multi 2.75 .25
Nos. 1979-1981 (3) 5.05 .75

10th anniversary of the Regional Cooperation for Development Pact among Turkey, Iran and Pakistan.

See Iran 1806-1808, Pakistan 365-367.

Dove with Turkish Flag over Cyprus — A473

1974, Aug. 26 Litho. *Perf. 13*

1982 A473 250k multicolored .95 .45

Cyprus Peace Operation.

Wrestling — A474

90k, 250k, various wrestling holds, horiz.

1974, Aug. 29

1983 A474 90k multicolored .25 .25
1984 A474 100k multicolored .40 .25
1985 A474 250k multicolored .70 .25
Nos. 1983-1985 (3) 1.35 .75

World Freestyle Wrestling Championships.

Arrows Circling Globe — A475

UPU Emblem and: 110k, "UPU" in form of dove. 200k, Dove.

1974, Oct. 9 Litho. *Perf. 13*

1986 A475 110k bl, gold & dk bl .25 .25
1987 A475 200k green & brown .30 .25
1988 A475 250k multicolored .55 .30
Nos. 1986-1988 (3) 1.10 .80

Centenary of Universal Postal Union.

"Law Reforms" A476

"National Economy" A477

"Education" — A478

1974, Oct. 29

1989 A476 50k blue & black .30 .25
1990 A477 150k red & multi .45 .25
1991 A478 400k multicolored .75 .40
Nos. 1989-1991 (3) 1.50 .90

Works and reforms of Kemal Ataturk.

Arrows Pointing Up — A479

Cogwheel and Map of Turkey — A480

1974, Nov. 29 Litho. *Perf. 13*

1992 A479 25k brown & black .40 .25
1993 A480 100k brown & gray .60 .25

3rd 5-year Development Program (#1992), and industrialization progress (#1993).

Volleyball — A481

1974, Dec. 30

1994 A481 125k shown .35 .25
1995 A481 175k Basketball .70 .25
1996 A481 250k Soccer 1.10 .25
Nos. 1994-1996 (3) 2.15 .75

Automatic Telex Network — A482

Postal Check — A483

Radio Transmitter and Waves — A484

1975, Feb. 5 Litho. *Perf. 13*

1997 A482 5k black & yellow .30 .25
1998 A483 50k ol grn & org .30 .25
1999 A484 100k blue & black .40 .25
Nos. 1997-1999 (3) 1.00 .75

Post and telecommunications.

Child Entering Classroom A485

Children's paintings: 50k, View of village. 100k, Dancing children.

1975, Apr. 23 Litho. *Perf. 13*

2000 A485 25k multicolored .25 .25
2001 A485 50k multicolored .25 .25
2002 A485 100k multicolored .30 .25
Nos. 2000-2002 (3) .80 .75

Karacaoglan Monument in Mut, by Huseyin Gezer — A486

1975, Apr. 25

2003 A486 110k dk grn, bis & red .75 .30

Karacaoglan (1606-1697), musician.

Orange Harvest in Hatay, by Cemal Tollu A487

Europa: 250k, Yoruk Family on Plateau, by Turgut Zaim.

1975, Apr. 28

2004 A487 110k bister & multi *1.75 .75*
2005 A487 250k bister & multi *2.25 1.00*

Porcelain Vase, Turkey — A488

Designs: 200k, Ceramic plate, Iran, horiz. 250k, Camel leather vase, Pakistan.

Perf. 13½x13, 13x13½

1975, July 21 Litho.

2006 A488 110k multicolored 1.25 .35
2007 A488 200k multicolored 1.75 .60
2008 A488 250k ultra & multi 1.75 .95
Nos. 2006-2008 (3) 4.75 1.90

Regional Cooperation for Development Pact among Turkey, Iran and Pakistan.
See Iran 1871-1873, Pakistan 383-385.

Horon Folk Dance A489

Regional Folk Dances: 125k, Kasik. 175k, Bengi. 250k, Kasap. 325k, Kafkas, vert.

1975, Aug. 30 Litho. *Perf. 13*

2009 A489 100k blue & multi .50 .25
2010 A489 125k green & multi .70 .25
2011 A489 175k rose & multi .80 .25
2012 A489 250k multicolored 1.00 .25
2013 A489 325k orange & multi 1.50 .40
Nos. 2009-2013 (5) 4.50 1.40

Knight Slaying Dragon A490

The Plunder of Salur Kazan's House A491

Design: 175k, Two Wanderers, horiz.

1975, Oct. 15 Litho. *Perf. 13*

2014 A490 90k multicolored .60 .25
2015 A490 175k multicolored .60 .30
2016 A491 200k multicolored .90 .40
Nos. 2014-2016 (3) 2.10 .95

Illustrations for tales by Dede Korkut.

Common Carp — A492

1975, Nov. 27 Litho. *Perf. 12½x13*

2017 A492 75k Turbot 1.00 .65
2018 A492 90k shown 1.25 .75
2019 A492 175k Trout 2.00 1.00
2020 A492 250k Red mullet 3.75 1.00
2021 A492 475k Red bream 6.00 2.00
Nos. 2017-2021 (5) 14.00 5.40

Women's Participation A493

Insurance Nationalization A494

Fine Arts — A495

1975, Dec. 5 *Perf. 12½x13, 13x12½*

2022 A493 100k bis, blk & red .25 .25
2023 A494 110k violet & multi .30 .25
2024 A495 250k multicolored .40 .25
Nos. 2022-2024 (3) .95 .75

Works and reforms of Ataturk.

Ceramic Plate — A496

Europa: 400k, Decorated pitcher.

1976, May 3 Litho. *Perf. 13*

2025 A496 200k purple & multi *3.25 1.50*
2026 A496 400k multicolored *6.50 2.50*

Sultan Ahmed Mosque — A497

1976, May 10

2027 A497 500k gray & multi .95 .45

7th Islamic Conference, Istanbul.

Lunch in the Field — A498

Children's Drawings: 200k, Boats on the Bosporus, vert. 400k, Winter landscape.

1976, May 19 Litho. *Perf. 13*

2028 A498 50k multicolored .35 .25
2029 A498 200k multicolored .35 .25
2030 A498 400k multicolored .55 .25
Nos. 2028-2030 (3) 1.25 .75

Samsun 76, First National Junior Philatelic Exhibition, Samsun.

Storks, Sultan Marsh — A499

Conservation Emblem and: 200k, Horses, Manyas Lake. 250k, Borabay Lake. 400k, Manavgat Waterfall.

1976, June 5

2031 A499 150k multicolored 2.10 .65
2032 A499 200k multicolored .75 .25
2033 A499 250k multicolored 1.20 .25
2034 A499 400k multicolored 1.40 .35
Nos. 2031-2034 (4) 5.45 1.50

European Wetland Conservation Year.

Nasreddin Hodja Carrying Liver — A500

Turkish Folklore: 250k, Friend giving recipe for cooking liver. 600k, Hawk carrying off liver and Hodja telling hawk he cannot enjoy liver without recipe.

1976, July 5 Litho. *Perf. 13*

2035 A500 150k multicolored .40 .25
2036 A500 250k multicolored .60 .25
2037 A500 600k multicolored 1.40 .50
Nos. 2035-2037 (3) 2.40 1.00

Montreal Olympic Emblem and Flame — A501

Designs: 400k, "76," Montreal Olympic emblem, horiz. 600k, Montreal Olympic emblem and ribbons.

1976, July 17

2038 A501 100k red & multi .25 .25
2039 A501 400k red & multi .75 .40
2040 A501 600k red & multi 1.40 .60
Nos. 2038-2040 (3) 2.40 1.25

21st Olympic Games, Montreal, Canada, 7/17-8/1.

Kemal Ataturk — A502

Designs: 200k, Riza Shah Pahlavi. 250k, Mohammed Ali Jinnah.

1976, July 21 Litho. *Perf. 13½*

2041 A502 100k multicolored .30 .25
2042 A502 200k multicolored .40 .25
2043 A502 250k multicolored .70 .35
Nos. 2041-2043 (3) 1.40 .85

Regional Cooperation for Development Pact among Turkey, Pakistan and Iran, 12th anniversary.
See Iran 1903-1905, Pakistan 412-414.

"Ataturk's Army" A503

Ataturk's Speeches A504

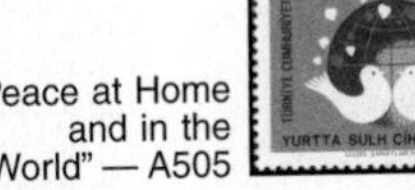

"Peace at Home and in the World" — A505

1976, Oct. 29 Litho. *Perf. 13*

2044 A503 100k black & red .25 .25
2045 A504 200k gray grn & multi .30 .25
2046 A505 400k blue & multi .70 .30
Nos. 2044-2046 (3) 1.25 .80

Works and reforms of Ataturk.

Hora — A506

1977, Jan. 19 Litho. *Perf. 13*

2047 A506 400k multicolored .95 .30

MTA Sismik 1 "Hora" geophysical exploration ship.

Keyboard and Violin Sound Hole — A507

1977, Feb. 24 Litho. *Perf. 13x13½*

2048 A507 200k multicolored .75 .25

Turkish State Symphony Orchestra, sesquicentennial.

Ataturk and "100" — A508

Design: 400k, Hand holding ballot.

1977, Mar. 21 Litho. *Perf. 13*

2049 A508 200k black & red .50 .25
2050 A508 400k black & brown .85 .40

Centenary of Turkish Parliament.

Hierapolis (Pamukkale) A509

Europa: 400k, Zelve (mountains and poppies).

1977, May 2 Litho. *Perf. 13½x13*

2051 A509 200k multicolored *3.00 1.00*
2052 A509 400k multicolored *5.00 1.50*

Terra Cotta Pot, Turkey — A510

Designs: 225k, Terra cotta jug, Iran. 675k, Terra cotta bullock cart, Pakistan.

1977, July 21 Litho. *Perf. 13*

2053 A510 100k multicolored .35 .25
2054 A510 225k multicolored 1.10 .35
2055 A510 675k multicolored 2.10 .75
a. Souv. sheet, #2053-2055 *8.00 8.00*
Nos. 2053-2055 (3) 3.55 1.35

Regional Cooperation for Development Pact among Turkey, Iran and Pakistan, 13th anniv.
See Iran 1946-1948, Pakistan 431-433.

Finn-class Yacht — A511

200k, Three yachts. 250k, Symbolic yacht.

1977, July 28

2056 A511 150k lt bl, bl & blk .30 .25
2057 A511 200k ultra & blue .55 .25
2058 A511 250k ultra & black .75 .25
Nos. 2056-2058 (3) 1.60 .75

European Finn Class Sailing Championships, Istanbul, July 28.

Ataturk Type of 1972

1977, June 13 Litho. *Perf. 13½x13*

2060 A453 100k olive .45 .25
2061 A453 200k brown .65 .25

Kemal Ataturk — A512

Imprint: "GUZEL SANATLAR MATBAASI A.S. 1977"

1977, Sept. 23 Litho. *Perf. 13*

Size: 20½x22mm

2062 A512 200k blue 1.25 .25
2063 A512 250k Prussian blue 1.75 .25

Imprint: "TIFDRUK-ISTANBUL 1978"

1978, June 28 Photo. *Perf. 13*

Size: 20x25mm

2065	A512	10k brown	.35	.25
2066	A512	50k grnsh gray	.50	.25
2067	A512	1 l fawn	.50	.25
2068	A512	2½ l purple	.65	.25
2069	A512	5 l blue	.80	.25
2072	A512	25 l dl grn & lt bl	2.00	.25
2073	A512	50 l dp org & tan	2.50	.50
		Nos. 2065-2073 (7)	7.30	2.00

No. 1832 Surcharged with New Value and Wavy Lines

1977, Aug. 17

2078	A418	10k on 1k dp org & brn	.30	.25

"Rationalism" A513

"National Sovereignty" A514

"Liberation of Nations" — A515

1977, Oct. 29 Litho. *Perf. 13*

2079	A513	100k multicolored	.25	.25
2080	A514	200k multicolored	.25	.25
2081	A515	400k multicolored	.70	.25
		Nos. 2079-2081 (3)	1.20	.75

Works and reforms of Ataturk.

Mohammad Allama Iqbal — A516

1977, Nov. 9 *Perf. 13x12½*

2082	A516	400k multicolored	.65	.25

Mohammad Allama Iqbal (1877-1938), Pakistani poet and philosopher.

Trees and Burning Match — A517

Design: 250k, Sign showing growing tree.

1977, Dec. 15 Litho. *Perf. 13*

2083	A517	50k green, blk & red	.30	.25
2084	A517	250k gray, grn & blk	.60	.25

Forest conservation. See type A542.

Wrecked Car — A518

Passing on Wrong Side — A519

Traffic Sign, "Slow!" — A520

Type I

Type II

Two types of 50k:
I — Number on license plate.
II — No number on plate.

Traffic Safety: 250k, Tractor drawing overloaded farm cart. 800k, Accident caused by incorrect passing. 10 l, "Use striped crossings."

1977-78 *Perf. 13½x13, 13x13½*

2085	A518	50k ultra, blk & red, II	.60	.55
a.		Type I	.70	.55
2086	A519	150k red, gray & blk	.25	.25
2087	A518	250k ocher, blk & red	.50	.25
2088	A520	500k gray, red & blk	.50	.25
2089	A520	800k multicolored	1.10	.25
2090	A520	10 l dl grn, blk & brn	1.75	.35
		Nos. 2085-2090 (6)	4.70	1.90

Issued: 500k, 1977; others, 1978.
For No. 2089 surcharged, see No. 2182.

Ishak Palace, Dogubeyazit A521

Europa: 5 l, Anamur Castle.

1978, May 2 Litho. *Perf. 13*

2091	A521	2½ l multicolored	*4.25*	*1.50*
2092	A521	5 l multicolored	*7.50*	*2.50*

Riza Shah Pahlavi — A522

1978, June 16 Litho. *Perf. 13x13½*

2093	A522	5 l multicolored	.65	.40

Riza Shah Pahlavi (1877-1944) of Iran, birth centenary.

Yellow Rose, Turkey — A523

3½ l, Pink roses, Iran. 8 l, Red roses, Pakistan.

1978, July 21 Litho. *Perf. 13*

2094	A523	2½ l multi	.30	.25
2095	A523	3½ l multi	.60	.25
2096	A523	8 l multi	1.60	.35
		Nos. 2094-2096 (3)	2.50	.85

Regional Cooperation for Development Pact among Turkey, Iran and Pakistan.
See Iran 1984-1986, Pakistan 449-451.

Anti-Apartheid Emblem — A524

1978, Aug. 14 Litho. *Perf. 13½x13*

2097	A524	10 l multicolored	.85	.25

Anti-Apartheid Year.

View of Ankara — A525

Design: 5 l, View of Tripoli, horiz.

Perf. 13x12½, 12½x13

1978, Aug. 17

2098	A525	2½ l multi	.35	.25
2099	A525	5 l multi	.75	.25

Turkish-Libyan friendship.

Souvenir Sheet

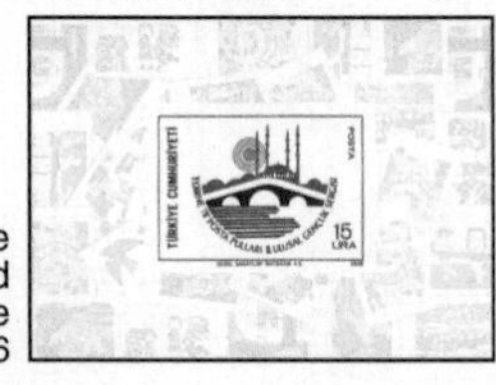

Bridge and Mosque A526

1978, Oct. 25 *Imperf.*

2100	A526	15 l multicolored	1.50	1.00

Edirne '78, 2nd Natl. Phil. Youth Exhib.

Independence Medal A527

Latin Alphabet A529

Speech Reform — A528

1978, Oct. 29 *Perf. 13x13½, 13½x13*

2101	A527	2½ l multi	.25	.25
2102	A528	3½ l multi	.30	.25
2103	A529	5 l multi	.45	.25
		Nos. 2101-2103 (3)	1.00	.75

Ataturk's works and reforms.

House on Bosporus, 1699 A530

Turkish Houses: 2½ l, Izmit, 1774, vert. 3½ l, Kula, 17th cent., vert. 5 l, Milas, 18th-19th cent., vert. 8 l, Safranbolu, 18th-19th cent.

Perf. 13x12½, 12½x13

1978, Nov. 22

2104	A530	1 l multi	.40	.25
2105	A530	2½ l multi	.60	.25
2106	A530	3½ l multi	.60	.40
2107	A530	5 l multi	.90	.40
2108	A530	8 l multi	1.50	.45
		Nos. 2104-2108 (5)	4.00	1.75

Carrier Pigeon, Plane, Horseback Rider, Train — A531

Europa: 5 l, Morse key, telegraph and Telex machine. 7½ l, Telephone dial and satellite.

1979, Apr. 30 Litho. *Perf. 13*

2109	A531	2½ l multicolored	*1.50*	*.75*
2110	A531	5 l org brn & blk	*2.75*	*.75*
2111	A531	7½ l brt blue & blk	*3.25*	*1.00*
		Nos. 2109-2111 (3)	*7.50*	*2.50*

Plowing, by Namik Ismail — A532

Paintings: 7½ l, Potters, by Kamalel Molk, Iran. 10 l, At the Well, by Allah Baksh, Pakistan.

1979, Sept. 5 Litho. *Perf. 13½x13*

2112	A532	5 l multi	.25	.25
2113	A532	7½ l multi	.50	.25
2114	A532	10 l multi	.75	.35
		Nos. 2112-2114 (3)	1.50	.85

Regional Cooperation for Development Pact among Turkey, Pakistan and Iran, 15th anniversary.
See Iran 2020-2022, Pakistan 486-488.

A533

1979, Sept. 17 *Perf. 13*

2115	A533	5 l Colemanite	.35	.25
2116	A533	7½ l Chromite	.50	.25
2117	A533	10 l Antimonite	.80	.25
2118	A533	15 l Sulphur	1.00	.30
		Nos. 2115-2118 (4)	2.65	1.05

10th World Mining Congress.

A534

8-shaped road, train tunnel, plane and emblem.

1979, Sept. 24

2119	A534	5 l multicolored	.50	.25

European Ministers of Communications, 8th Symposium.

Youth A535

Secularization A536

Design: 5 l, National oath.

1979, Oct. 29 *Perf. 13x12½, 12½x13*

2120	A535	2½ l multi	.40	.25
2121	A536	3½ l multi	.40	.25
2122	A535	5 l black & orange	.60	.25
		Nos. 2120-2122 (3)	1.40	.75

Ataturk's works and reforms.

Poppies — A537

7½ l, Oleander. 10 l, Late spider orchid. 15 l, Mandrake.

1979, Nov. 26 Litho. *Perf. 13x13½*

2123	A537	5 l shown	.25	.25
2124	A537	7½ l multicolored	.45	.25
2125	A537	10 l multicolored	.70	.25
2126	A537	15 l multicolored	1.10	.25
		Nos. 2123-2126 (4)	2.50	1.00

See Nos. 2154-2157.

Kemal Ataturk — A538

Perf. 12½x11½, 13x12½(No. 2131)

1979-81 Litho.

2127 A538 50k olive ('80) .25 .25
2128 A538 1 l grn & lt grn .30 .25
2129 A538 2½ l purple .35 .25
2130 A538 2½ l bl grn & lt bl ('80) .30 .25
2131 A538 2½ l orange ('81) .35 .25
2132 A538 5 l ultra & gray .55 .25
a. Sheet of 8 3.25 3.25
2133 A538 7½ l brown .55 .25
2134 A538 7½ l red ('80) .75 .25
2135 A538 10 l rose carmine 1.00 .30
2136 A538 20 l gray ('80) 1.40 .40
Nos. 2127-2136 (10) 5.80 2.70

No. 2132a for Ankara '79 Philatelic Exhibition, Oct. 14-20.

For surcharge see No. 2261.

Kemal Ataturk — A538a

1980-82 Photo. *Perf. 13½*

2137 A538a 7½ l red brown .45 .25
c. Sheet of 4 4.00 2.50
2137A A538a 10 l brown .90 .25
2138 A538a 20 l lilac .90 .25
2138A A538a 30 l gray 1.10 .30
2139 A538a 50 l orange red 2.00 .30
2140 A538a 75 l brt green 2.75 .75
2141 A538a 100 l blue 3.50 1.00
Nos. 2137-2141 (7) 11.60 3.10

No. 2137c for ANTALYA '82 4th Natl. Junior Stamp Show. Exists both perf 13½ and imperf. Same value.

Issued: #2137, 7/15/81; #2137c, 10/3/82; 30 l, 9/23/81; others, 12/10/80.

See Nos. 2164-2169.

Turkish Printing, 250th Anniversary A539

1979, Nov. 30 Litho. *Perf. 13*

2142 A539 10 l multicolored .75 .40

2nd International Olive Oil Year — A540

10 l, Globe, oil drop, vert.

Perf. 12½x13, 13x12½

1979, Dec. 20 Litho.

2143 A540 5 l shown .25 .25
2144 A540 10 l multicolored .45 .25

Uskudarli Hoca Ali Riza Bey (1857-1930), Painter — A541

Europa: 15 l, Ali Sami Boyar (1880-1967), painter. 20 l, Dr. Hulusi Behcet (1889-1948), physician, discovered Behcet skin disease.

1980, Apr. 28 *Perf. 13*

2145 A541 7½ l multi *1.10* .50
2146 A541 15 l multi *1.50* .75
2147 A541 20 l multi *2.00* .75
Nos. 2145-2147 (3) 4.60 2.00

Forest Conservation — A542

1980, July 3 *Perf. 13½x13*

2148 A542 50k ol grn & red org .35 .25

See type A517. For surcharge see No. 2262.

Earthquake Destruction — A543

1980, Sept. 8 *Perf. 13*

2149 A543 7½ l shown .30 .25
2150 A543 20 l Seismograph .70 .50

7th World Conference on Earthquake Engineering, Istanbul.

Games' Emblem, Sports — A544

20 l, Emblem, sports, diff.

1980, Sept. 26 *Perf. 13x13½*

2151 A544 7½ l shown .30 .25
2152 A544 20 l multicolored .70 .25

First Islamic Games, Izmir.

Hegira — A545

1980, Nov. 9

2153 A545 20 l multicolored .80 .40

Plant Type of 1979

2½ l, Manisa tulip. 7½ l, Ephesian bellflower. 15 l, Angora crocus. 20 l, Anatolian orchid.

1980, Nov. 26 *Perf. 13*

2154 A537 2½ l multicolored .25 .25
2155 A537 7½ l multicolored .50 .25
2156 A537 15 l multicolored .75 .25
2157 A537 20 l multicolored 1.25 .25
Nos. 2154-2157 (4) 2.75 1.00

Avicenna Treating Patient — A546

Avicenna (Arab Physician), Birth Millenium: 20 l, Portrait, vert.

1980, Dec. 15

2158 A546 7½ l multi .45 .25
2159 A546 20 l multi .55 .30

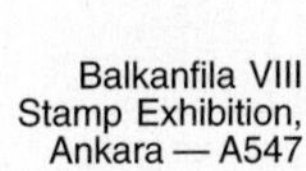

Balkanfila VIII Stamp Exhibition, Ankara — A547

1981, Jan. 1 Litho. *Perf. 13*

2160 A547 10 l red & black .85 .25

Kemal Ataturk — A548

1981, Feb. 4 *Perf. 13*

2163 A548 10 l lilac rose .65 .25

Ataturk Type of 1980

1983-84 *Perf. 13x13½*

2164 A538a 15 l grnsh blue .35 .25
2165 A538a 20 l orange ('84) .45 .25
2167 A538a 65 l bluish grn 1.25 .25
2169 A538a 90 l lilac rose 1.60 .25
Nos. 2164-2169 (4) 3.65 1.00

Issued: #2164, 2167, 2169, 11/30; #2165, 7/25.

Sultan Mehmet the Conqueror (1432-1481) — A549

1981, May 3 Litho. *Perf. 13x12½*

2173 A549 10 l multicolored .45 .25
2174 A549 20 l multicolored .95 .50

Gaziantep (Folk Dance) — A550

Antalya — A551

1981, May 4 Litho. *Perf. 13*

2175 A550 7½ l shown .25 .25
2176 A550 10 l Balikesir .30 .25
2177 A550 15 l Kahramanmaras 1.40 .60
2178 A551 35 l shown *1.50* .50
2179 A551 70 l Burdur *2.00* 1.00
Nos. 2175-2179 (5) 5.45 2.60

Nos. 2178-2179 show CEPT (Europa) emblem.

Nos. C40, 1925, 1931A, 2089 Surcharged in Black with New Value and Wavy Lines

1981, June 3 *Perf. 13½x13*

2179A AP7 10 l on 60k .90 .25
2180 A453 10 l on 110k .90 .25
2181 A453 10 l on 400k .90 .25
2182 A520 10 l on 800k .90 .25
Nos. 2179A-2182 (4) 3.60 1.00

A552

7½ l, Rug, Bilecik. 10 l, Embroidery. 15 l, Drum, zurna players. 20 l, Embroidered napkin. 30 l, Yellow, red & black rug.

1981, June 22 *Perf. 13x12½*

2183 A552 7½ l multicolored .25 .25
2184 A552 10 l multicolored .30 .25
2185 A552 15 l multicolored .50 .25
2186 A552 20 l multicolored .50 .25
2187 A552 30 l multicolored 1.00 .25
Nos. 2183-2187 (5) 2.55 1.25

22nd Intl. Turkish Folklore Congress.

Kemal Ataturk — A553

1981, May 19 Litho. *Perf. 14x15*

2188 A553 2½ l No. 1801 .25 .25
2189 A553 7½ l No. 1816 .25 .25
2190 A553 10 l No. 1604 .30 .25
2191 A553 20 l No. 804 .60 .25
2192 A553 25 l No. 777 .75 .30
2193 A553 35 l No. 1959 1.00 .40
Nos. 2188-2193 (6) 3.15 1.70

Souvenir Sheet

2194 Sheet of 6 15.00 12.50
a. A553 2½ l like 2½ l .25 .25
b. A553 37½ l like 7½ l .35 .25
c. A553 50 l like 10 l .50 .25
d. A553 100 l like 20 l 1.00 .30
e. A553 125 l like 25 l 1.40 .50
f. A553 175 l like 35 l 2.00 .70

Souvenir Sheet

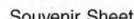

Balkanfila VIII Stamp Exhibition, Ankara — A554

1981, Aug. 8 Litho. *Perf. 13*

2195 A554 Sheet of 2 3.50 3.00
a. 50 l No. B68 1.00 .60
b. 50 l No. 733 1.00 .60

5th General Congress of European Physics Society — A555

1981, Sept. 7 *Perf. 12½x13*

2196 A555 10 l red & multi .50 .25
2197 A555 30 l blue & multi 1.00 .40

World Food Day — A556

1981, Oct. 16

2198 A556 10 l multicolored .45 .25
2199 A556 30 l multicolored 1.00 .25

Constituent Assembly Inauguration A557

1981, Oct. 23 *Perf. 13*

2200 A557 10 l multicolored .40 .25
2201 A557 30 l multicolored 1.10 .25

Ataturk — A558

Portraits of Ataturk.

1981-82 *Perf. 11½x12½, 13 (#2204)*

2202 A558 1 l green .25 .25
2203 A558 2½ l purple .25 .25
2204 A558 2½ l gray & org *.50* *.25*
2205 A558 5 l blue .25 .25
2206 A558 10 l orange .25 .25
2207 A558 35 l brown .70 .25
Nos. 2202-2207 (6) 2.20 1.50

Issued: #2204, 12/10/81; others, 1/27/82.

Literacy Campaign — A559

1981, Dec. 24 *Perf. 13½*

2217 A559 2½ l Procession .55 .25

Energy Conservation — A560

1982, Jan. 11 *Perf. 13*

2218 A560 10 l multicolored .55 .25

Magnolias, by Ibrahim Calli (b. 1882) — A561

1982, Mar. 17 ***Perf. 13x13½, 13½x13***

2219 A561 10 l shown .45 .25
2220 A561 20 l Fishermen, horiz. .90 .25
2221 A561 30 l Sewing Woman 1.10 .25
Nos. 2219-2221 (3) 2.45 .75

Europa Issue

Sultanhan Caravanserai — A562

1982, Apr. 26 ***Perf. 13x12½***

2222 A562 30 l shown .50 .25
2223 A562 70 l Silk Route .75 .35
a. Min. sheet, 2 each #2222-2223 3.50 3.50
b. Pair, #2222-2223 1.25 .75

1250th Anniv. of Kul-Tigin Monument, Kosu Saydam, Mongolia — A563

10 l, Monument. 30 l, Kul-Tigin (685-732), Gok-Turkish commander.

1982, June 9 ***Perf. 13***

2224 A563 10 l multicolored .25 .25
2225 A563 30 l multicolored .60 .25

Pendik Shipyard Opening — A564

1982, July 1 ***Perf. 12½x13***

2226 A564 30 l Ship, emblem .65 .25

Mountains of Anatolia — A565

7½ l, Agri Dagi, vert. 10 l, Buzul Dagi. 15 l, Demirkazik, vert. 20 l, Erciyes. 30 l, Kackar Dagi, vert. 35 l, Uludag.

1982, July 17 ***Perf. 13***

2227 A565 7½ l multicolored .30 .25
2228 A565 10 l multicolored .55 .25
2229 A565 15 l multicolored .85 .25
2230 A565 20 l multicolored 1.10 .25
2231 A565 30 l multicolored 1.75 .25
2232 A565 35 l multicolored 2.25 .25
Nos. 2227-2232 (6) 6.80 1.50

Beyazit State Library Centenary A566

1982, Sept. 27

2233 A566 30 l multicolored .70 .35

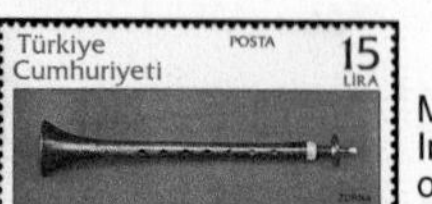

Musical Instruments of Anatolia A567

1982, Oct. 13

2234 A567 7½ l Davul .60 .25
2235 A567 10 l Baglama .60 .25
2236 A567 15 l shown .90 .25
2237 A567 20 l Kemence 1.10 .25
2238 A567 30 l Ney 1.50 .25
Nos. 2234-2238 (5) 4.70 1.25

Roman Temple Columns, Sardis — A568

1982, Nov. 3

2239 A568 30 l multi 1.25 .40

Family Planning and Mother-Child Health — A569

1983, Jan. 12 **Litho.** ***Perf. 13***

2240 A569 10 l Family on map .25 .25
2241 A569 35 l Mother and child .75 .25

30th Anniv. of Customs Cooperation Council — A570

1983, Jan. 26

2242 A570 45 l multi 1.00 .25

1982 Constitution A571

1983, Jan. 27

2243 A571 10 l Ballot box .40 .25
2244 A571 30 l Open book, scale .60 .25

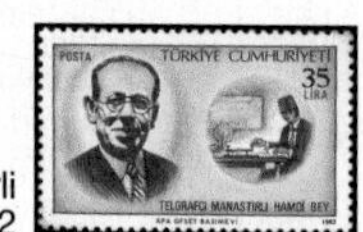

Manastirli Bey — A572

1983, Mar. 16 **Litho.**

2245 A572 35 l multi 1.00 .25

Manastirli Hamdi Bey (1890-1945), telegrapher of news of Istanbul's occupation to Ataturk, 1920.

Europa Issue

Piri Reis, Geographer A573

100 l, Ulugh Beg (1394-1449), astronomer.

1983, May 5 **Litho.** ***Perf. 12½x13***

2246 A573 50 l shown *6.00 1.50*
2247 A573 100 l multi *15.00 5.00*

Youth Week — A574

1983, May 16

2248 A574 15 l multi .65 .25

World Communications Year — A575

15 l, Carrier pigeon, vert. 50 l, Phone lines. 70 l, Emblem, vert.

1983, May 16 ***Perf. 13***

2249 A575 15 l multicolored .40 .25
2250 A575 50 l multicolored .80 .25
2251 A575 70 l multicolored 1.50 .25
Nos. 2249-2251 (3) 2.70 .75

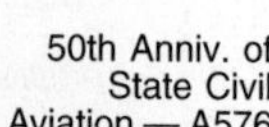

50th Anniv. of State Civil Aviation — A576

1983, May 20 **Litho.** ***Perf. 13***

2252 A576 50 l Plane, jet 1.10 .25
2253 A576 70 l Airport 1.50 .45

18th Council of Europe Art Exhibition A577

15 l, Eros, 2nd cent. BC, vert. 35 l, Two-headed duck, Hittite, 14th cent BC. 50 l, Zinc jugs, plate, 16th cent., vert. 70 l, Marcus Aurelius and his wife Faustina the Young, 2nd cent.

1983, May 22 ***Perf. 13***

2254 A577 15 l multi .50 .25
2255 A577 35 l multi 1.25 .25
2256 A577 50 l multi 1.25 .25
2257 A577 70 l multi 1.40 .25
Nos. 2254-2257 (4) 4.40 1.00

Council of Europe's "The Water's Edge" Campaign — A578

Coastal Views.

1983, June 1 **Litho.** ***Perf. 13x12½***

2258 A578 10 l Olodeniz .60 .35
2259 A578 25 l Olympus .60 .35
2260 A578 35 l Kekova 1.25 .65
Nos. 2258-2260 (3) 2.45 1.35

Nos. 2127, 2148 Surcharged

Perf. 12½x11½, 13½x13

1983, June 8

2261 A538 5 l on 50k olive .50 .25
2262 A542 5 l on 50k ol grn & red org .50 .25

Kemal Ataturk — A579

1983, June 22 ***Perf. 13***

2263 A579 15 l bl grn & bl .35 .25
a. Sheet of 5 + label 2.50 2.00
2264 A579 50 l green & blue 1.40 .25
2265 A579 100 l orange & blue 2.75 .45
Nos. 2263-2265 (3) 4.50 .95

For surcharge see No. 2432.

Aga Khan Architecture Award — A580

1983, Sept. 4 **Photo.** ***Perf. 11½***

2266 A580 50 l View of Istanbul .95 .25

60th Anniv. of the Republic — A582

1983, Oct. 29 ***Perf. 13½x13***

2268 A582 15 l multi .30 .25
2269 A582 50 l multi .95 .25

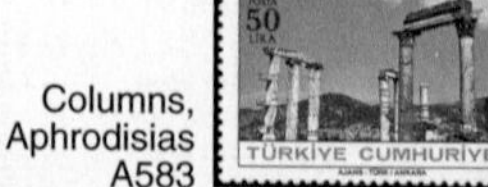

Columns, Aphrodisias A583

1983, Nov. 2 ***Perf. 13***

2270 A583 50 l multi 1.10 .85

UNESCO Campaign for Istanbul and Goreme — A584

25 l, St. Sophia Basilica. 35 l, Goreme. 50 l, Istanbul.

1984, Feb. 15 **Litho.** ***Perf. 13***

2271 A584 25 l multicolored .50 .25
2272 A584 35 l multicolored .75 .25
2273 A584 50 l multicolored 1.00 .25
Nos. 2271-2273 (3) 2.25 .75

Natl. Police Org. Emblem — A585

1984, Apr. 10 **Litho.** ***Perf. 13***

2274 A585 15 l multi .75 .30

Europa (1959-84) — A586

1984, Apr. 30 ***Perf. 13½x13***

2275 A586 50 l blue & multi *6.00 1.00*
2276 A586 100 l gray & multi *10.00 2.00*

Mete Khan, Hun Ruler, 204 BC, Flag — A587

Sixteen States (Hun Rulers and Flags): 20 l, Panu, Western Hun empire (48-216). 50 l, Attila, 375-454. 70 l, Aksunvar, Ak Hun empire, 420-562.

1984, June 20 **Litho.** ***Perf. 13***

2277 A587 10 l multi .70 .25
2278 A587 20 l multi .90 .35
2279 A587 50 l multi 1.75 .45
2280 A587 70 l multi 3.00 .45
Nos. 2277-2280 (4) 6.35 1.50

See Nos. 2315-2318, 2349-2352, 2382-2385.

Occupation of Cyprus, 10th Anniv. — A588

70 l, Dove, olive branch.

1984, July 20 **Litho.** ***Perf. 13***

2281 A588 70 l multicolored 1.40 .60

Wild Flowers — A589

10 l, Marshmallow flower. 20 l, Red poppy. 70 l, Sowbread. 200 l, Snowdrop. 300 l, Tulip.

1984, Aug. 1 ***Perf. 11½x12½***

2282 A589 10 l multicolored .25 .25
2283 A589 20 l multicolored .30 .25
2284 A589 70 l multicolored .90 .25
2285 A589 200 l multicolored 2.50 .35
2286 A589 300 l multicolored 4.00 .45
Nos. 2282-2286 (5) 7.95 1.55

See Nos. 2301-2308. For surcharges see Nos. 2467, 2479-2480.

Armed Forces Day — A590

20 l, Soldier, dove, flag. 50 l, Sword. 70 l, Arms, soldier, flag. 90 l, Map, soldier.

1984, Aug. 26 *Perf. 13½x13*

2287	A590	20 l multicolored	.45	.25
2288	A590	50 l multicolored	.90	.25
2289	A590	70 l multicolored	1.40	.25
2290	A590	90 l multicolored	1.75	.25
		Nos. 2287-2290 (4)	4.50	1.00

Trees and Wood Products — A591

Seed, Tree and Product: 10 l, Liquidambar, liquidambar grease. 20 l, Oriental spruce, stringed instrument. 70 l, Oriental beech, chair. 90 l, Cedar of Lebanon, ship.

1984, Sept. 19 Litho. *Perf. 13x12½*

2291	A591	10 l multi	.55	.25
2292	A591	20 l multi	.55	.25
2293	A591	70 l multi	1.40	.25
2294	A591	90 l multi	2.00	.25
		Nos. 2291-2294 (4)	4.50	1.00

Pres. Ismet Inonu (1884-1973), — A592

1984, Sept. 24 *Perf. 13*

2295 A592 20 l Portrait 1.10 .25

First Intl. Turkish Carpet Congress — A593

70 l, Seljukian carpet, 13th cent.

1984, Oct. 7 *Perf. 13x13½*

2296 A593 70 l multicolored 1.10 .75

Ruins of Ancient City of Harran — A594

1984, Nov. 7 *Perf. 13½x13*

2297 A594 70 l Columns, arch 1.75 1.25

Turkish Women's Suffrage, 50th Anniv. — A595

1984, Dec. 5 Litho. *Perf. 13*

2298 A595 20 l Women voting .65 .25

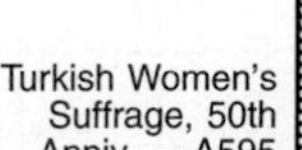

40th Anniv., ICAO — A596

100 l, Icarus, ICAO emblem.

1984, Dec. 7 Litho. *Perf. 13*

2299 A596 100 l multicolored 1.50 1.25

Souvenir Sheet

No. 1047 A597

1985, Jan. 13 Litho. *Imperf.*

2300	A597	Sheet of 4, 2 each #a.-b.	3.75	2.50
a.-b.		70 l, any single	.45	.45

Istanbul '87. No. 2300b has denomination in lower right.

Flower Type of 1984

1985 *Perf. 11½x12½*

2301 A589 5 l Narcissus .65 .25

Perf. 12½x13

2308 A589 100 l Daisy 1.40 .25

Issue dates: #2301, Feb. 6; #2308, July 31.
For surcharge see No. 2465.

Turkish Aviation League, 60th Anniv. — A598

10 l, Parachutist, glider. 20 l, Hot air balloon, vert.

1985, Feb. 16 *Perf. 13*

2310	A598	10 l multicolored	.50	.25
2311	A598	20 l multicolored	1.25	.55

INTELSAT, 20th Anniv. — A599

1985, Apr. 3

2312 A599 100 l multi 1.50 .75

Europa Issue

Ulvi Cemal Erkin (1906-1972) and Kosekce — A600

Composers and music: 200 l, Mithat Fenmen (1916-1982) and Concertina.

1985, Apr. 29 *Perf. 13½x13*

2313	A600	100 l multi	*10.00*	*1.50*
2314	A600	200 l multi	*15.00*	*2.50*

States Type of 1984

Sixteen States (Kagan rulers and flags): 10 l, Bilge, Gokturk Empire (552-743) and Orhon-Turkish alphabet. 20 l, Bayan, Avar Empire (565-803). 70 l, Hazar, Hazar Empire (651-983). 100 l, Kutlug Kul Bilge, Uygur State (774-1335).

1985, June 20

2315	A587	10 l multi	.60	.25
2316	A587	20 l multi	1.25	.25
2317	A587	70 l multi	2.40	.25
2318	A587	100 l multi	4.75	.25
		Nos. 2315-2318 (4)	9.00	1.00

Intl. Youth Year — A601

1985, Aug. 8

2319	A601	100 l multi	1.00	.75
2320	A601	120 l multi	1.50	1.00

Postal Code Inauguration — A602

1985, Sept. 4 *Perf. 13*

Background Color

2321	A602	10 l pale yel brn	.35	.25
2322	A602	20 l fawn	.55	.25
2323	A602	20 l gray green	.55	.25
2324	A602	20 l brt blue	.55	.25
2325	A602	70 l rose lilac	1.25	.25
2326	A602	100 l gray	1.75	.45
		Nos. 2321-2326 (6)	5.00	1.70

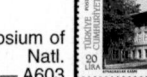

Symposium of Natl. Palaces — A603

20 l, Aynalikavak, c. 1703. 100 l, Beylerbeyi, 1865.

1985, Sept. 25 *Perf. 13½x13*

2327	A603	20 l multicolored	.40	.25
2328	A603	100 l multicolored	1.60	.25

UN, 40th Anniv. — A604

1985, Oct. 24

2329 A604 100 l multi 1.00 .75

Alanya Fortress and City — A605

1985, Nov. 7

2330 A605 100 l multi 1.50 .75

A606

1985, Nov. 12 *Perf. 13x13½*

2331 A606 100 l multi 1.50 .75

Turkish Meteorological Service, 60th anniv.

Isik Lyceum, Istanbul, Cent. — A607

1985, Dec. 14

2332 A607 20 l multi .75 .25

Ataturk — A608

Perf. 11½x12½

1985, Dec. 18 Litho.

2334	A608	10 l pale bl & ultra	.30	.25
2335	A608	20 l beige & brn	.40	.25
2336	A608	100 l lt pink & claret	1.50	.25
		Nos. 2334-2336 (3)	2.20	.75

For surcharges see Nos. 2433-2434, 2449.

7th Intl. Children's Festival, Ankara — A609

Various children's drawings.

1986, Apr. 23 Litho. *Perf. 12½x13*

2342	A609	20 l multi	.40	.30
2343	A609	100 l multi	1.20	.30
2344	A609	120 l multi	1.40	1.40
		Nos. 2342-2344 (3)	3.00	2.00

Europa Issue

Pollution — A610

200 l, Bandaged leaf.

1986, Apr. 28 *Perf. 13*

2345	A610	100 l shown	*6.50*	*1.50*
2346	A610	200 l multi	*8.50*	*2.50*

1st Ataturk Intl. Peace Prize — A611

1986, May 19 Litho. *Perf. 13*

2347	A611	20 l gold & multi	.55	.55
2348	A611	100 l silver & multi	1.40	.75

States Type of 1984

Sixteen States (Devleti rulers and flags): 10 l, Bilge Kul Kadir Khan, Kara Khanids State (840-1212). 20 l, Alp-Tekin, Ghaznavids State (963-1183). 100 l, Seldjuk Bey, Seldjuks State (1040-1157). 120 l, Muhammed Harezmsah, Khwarizm-Shahs State (1157-1231).

1986, June 20

2349	A587	10 l multi	.45	.25
2350	A587	20 l multi	1.25	.40
2351	A587	100 l multi	1.90	.70
2352	A587	120 l multi	4.50	1.40
		Nos. 2349-2352 (4)	8.10	2.75

1st Turkish Submarine, Cent. — A612

20 l, Torpedo sub Abdulhamid.

1986, June 16 Litho. *Perf. 13*

2353 A612 20 l multi 1.25 .50

Kirkpinar Wrestling Matches, Edirne — A613

1986, June 30

2354	A613	10 l Oiling bodies	.65	.65
2355	A613	20 l Five wrestlers	.65	.65
2356	A613	100 l Two wrestlers	1.90	1.25
		Nos. 2354-2356 (3)	3.20	2.55

Organization for Economic Cooperation and Development, 25th Anniv. — A614

1986, Sept. 30 Litho. *Perf. 13½x13*

2357 A614 100 l multi 1.40 .45

Automobile, Cent. — A615

10 l, Benz Velocipede, 1886. 20 l, Rolls-Royce Silver Ghost, 1906. 100 l, Mercedes Touring Car, 1928. 200 l, Abstract speeding car.

1986, Oct. 15

2358	A615	10 l multi	.75	.50
2359	A615	20 l multi	1.00	.50
2360	A615	100 l multi	2.00	1.00
2361	A615	200 l multi	2.75	1.40
		Nos. 2358-2361 (4)	6.50	3.40

Paintings — A616

Designs: 100 l, Bouquet with Tulip, by Feyhaman Duran (1886-1970). 120 l, Landscape with Fountain, by H. Avni Lifij (1886-1927), horiz.

1986, Oct. 22 *Perf. 13½x13, 13x13½*

2362 A616 100 l multi 1.50 .50
2363 A616 120 l multi 3.75 .75

Celal Bayar (1883-1986), 3rd President — A617

1986, Oct. 27 *Perf. 13*

2364 A617 20 l shown .60 .25
2365 A617 100 l Profile 1.00 .25

Kubad-Abad Ruins, Beysehir Lake — A618

1986, Nov. 7 *Perf. 13½x13*

2366 A618 100 l multi 1.40 .50

Mehmet Akif Ersoy (1873-1936), Composer of the Turkish National Anthem — A619

1986, Dec. 27 Litho. *Perf. 13½x13*

2367 A619 20 l multi .75 .25

Road Safety — A620

10 l, Use seatbelts. 20 l, Don't drink alcohol and drive. 150 l, Observe speed limit.

1987, Feb. 4 Litho. *Perf. 13x13½*

2368 A620 10 l multi .25 .25
2369 A620 20 l multi .45 .25
2370 A620 150 l multi 1.60 .25
Nos. 2368-2370 (3) 2.30 .75

For surcharges see Nos. 2466, 2477-2478.

Butterflies A621

10 l, Celerio euphorbiae. 20 l, Vanessa atalanta. 100 l, Euplagia quadripunctaria. 120 l, Colias crocea.

1987, Feb. 25 *Perf. 13½x13*

2371 A621 10 l multi .80 .25
2372 A621 20 l multi 1.20 .40
2373 A621 100 l multi 4.00 1.40
2374 A621 120 l multi 5.00 2.00
Nos. 2371-2374 (4) 11.00 4.05

Intl. Year of Shelter for the Homeless — A622

1987, Mar. 18 Litho. *Perf. 13x13½*

2375 A622 200 l multi 1.25 .75

Karabuk Iron and Steel Works, 50th Anniv. — A623

1987, Apr. 3 Litho. *Perf. 13½x13*

2376 A623 50 l Interior .55 .25
2377 A623 200 l Exterior 1.40 .25

Natl. Sovereignty A624

1987, Apr. 23 *Perf. 13½x13*

2378 A624 50 l multi .90 .25

Founding of the Turkish state, 67th anniv.

Architecture A625

Europa: 50 l, Turkish History Institute, 1951-67, designed by Turgut Cansever with Ertur Yener. 200 l, Social Insurance Institute, 1963, designed by Sedad Hakki Eldem.

1987, Apr. 28 *Perf. 13*

2379 A625 50 l multi *5.00 1.00*
2380 A625 200 l multi *12.50 2.00*

92nd Session, Intl. Olympic Committee, Istanbul, May 9-12 — A626

1987, May 9 Litho. *Perf. 13x13½*

2381 A626 200 l multi 1.75 1.00

States Type of 1984

Sixteen states (Devleti and Imparatorlugu rulers and flags): 10 l, Batu Khan, Golden Horde State (1227-1502). 20 l, Kutlug Timur Khan, Great Timur Empire (1368-1507). 50 l, Babur Shah, Babur Empire (1526-1858). 200 l, Osman Bey Gasi, Ottoman Empire (1299-1923).

1987, June 20 *Perf. 12½x13*

2382 A587 10 l multi .50 .25
2383 A587 20 l multi 1.00 .30
2384 A587 50 l multi 1.50 .30
2385 A587 200 l multi 3.00 1.00
Nos. 2382-2385 (4) 6.00 1.85

Album of the Conqueror, Mehmet II, 15th Cent., Topkapi Palace Museum A627

Untitled paintings by Mehmet Siyah Kalem: 10 l, Two warriors, vert. 20 l, Three men, donkey. 50 l, Blackamoor whipping horse. 200 l, Demon, vert.

Perf. 13½x13, 13x13½

1987, July 1 Litho.

2386 A627 10 l multi .75 .40
2387 A627 20 l multi 1.00 .40
2388 A627 50 l multi 1.25 .40
2389 A627 200 l multi 2.00 1.00
Nos. 2386-2389 (4) 5.00 2.20

Natl. Palaces — A628

50 l, Ihlamur, c. 1850. 200 l, Kucuksu Pavilion, 1857.

1987, Sept. 25 *Perf. 13½x13*

2390 A628 50 l multicolored 1.00 .60
2391 A628 200 l multicolored 2.00 .75

See Nos. 2425-2426.

"Tughra," Suleiman's Calligraphic Signature A629

Designs: 30 l, Portrait, vert. 200 l, Suleiman Receiving a Foreign Minister, contemporary miniature, vert. 270 l, Bust, detail of bas-relief, The Twenty-Three Law-Givers, entrance to the gallery of the US House of Representatives.

Litho., Litho. & Engr. (270 l)

1987, Oct. 1 *Perf. 13½x13, 13x13½*

2392 A629 30 l multi .50 .35
2393 A629 50 l shown .75 .45
2394 A629 200 l multi 2.25 .90
2395 A629 270 l multi 2.75 1.25
Nos. 2392-2395 (4) 6.25 2.95

Suleiman the Magnificent (1494-1566), sultan of the Turkish Empire (1520-1566). On No. 2395, the gold ink was applied by a thermographic process producing a shiny, raised effect.

A630

Presidents: a, Cemal Gursel (1961-1966). b, Cevdet Sunay (1966-1973). c, Fahri S. Koruturk (1973-1980). d, Kenan Evren (1982-). e, Ismet Inonu (1938-1950). f, Celal Bayar (1950-1960). g, Mustafa Kemal Ataturk (1923-1938).

1987, Oct. 29 Litho. *Imperf.*

Souvenir Sheet

2396 A630 Sheet of 7 6.00 6.00
a.-f. 50 l any single .55 .55
g. 100 l multi, 26x37mm .75 .75

A631

200 l, Mosque, architectural elements.

1988, Apr. 9 Litho. *Perf. 13*

2397 A631 50 l shown *.65 .40*
2398 A631 200 l multi *2.00 .80*

Joseph (Mimar) Sinan (1489-1588), architect.

Health — A632

50 l, Immunization, horiz. 200 l, Fight drug abuse. 300 l, Safe work conditions, horiz. 600 l, Organ donation.

1988, May 4

2399 A632 50 l multicolored .25 .25
2400 A632 200 l multicolored .65 .25
2401 A632 300 l multicolored .95 .25
2402 A632 600 l multicolored 2.10 .55
Nos. 2399-2402 (4) 3.95 1.30

Europa Issue

Telecommunications — A633

Transport and communication: 200 l, Modes of transportation, vert.

1988, May 2 Litho. *Perf. 13, 12½*

2403 A633 200 l multi *3.50 1.25*
2404 A633 600 l multi *11.00 1.50*

Steam, Electric and Diesel Locomotives A634

50 l, American Standard steam engine, c. 1850. 100 l, Steam engine produced in Esslingen for Turkish railways, 1913. 200 l, Henschel Krupp steam engine, 1926. 300 l, E 43001 Toshiba electric engine produced in Japan, 1987. 600 l, MTE-Tulomsas #24361 diesel-electric high-speed engine, 1984.

1988, May 24 *Perf. 13*

2405 A634 50 l buff, brn & blk 1.10 .45
2406 A634 100 l buff, brn & blk 2.25 .90
2407 A634 200 l buff, brn & blk 3.50 1.50
2408 A634 300 l buff, brn & blk 4.50 1.75
2409 A634 600 l buff, brn & blk 6.25 2.75
Nos. 2405-2409 (5) 17.60 7.35

Court of Cassation (Supreme Court), 120th Anniv. — A635

1988, July 1 Litho. *Perf. 13½x13*

2410 A635 50 l multi .75 .35

Bridge Openings A636

Designs: 200 l, Fatih Sultan Mehmet Bridge, Kavacik-Hisarustu. 300 l, Seto Ohashi (Friendship) Bridges, the Minami and Kita.

1988, July 3 Litho. *Perf. 13x13½*

2411 A636 200 l multi 1.90 1.10
2412 A636 300 l multi 3.00 1.50

Telephone System — A637

1988, Aug. 24 Litho. *Perf. 13½x13*

2413 A637 100 l multi .65 .25

1988 Summer Olympics, Seoul — A638

Perf. 12½x13, 13x12½

1988, Sept. 17 **Litho.**

2414 A638 100 l Running .50 .25
2415 A638 200 l Archery .80 .25
2416 A638 400 l Weight lifting 1.10 .35
2417 A638 600 l Gymnastics, vert. 1.60 .45
Nos. 2414-2417 (4) 4.00 1.30

Naim Suleymanoglu, 1988 Olympic Gold Medalist, Weight Lifting — A639

1988, Oct. 5 **Litho.** *Perf. 13x12½*

2418 A639 1000 l multi 7.00 3.50

Aerospace Industries A640

50 l, Gear, aircraft, vert.

1988, Oct. 28 *Perf. 13½x13, 13x13½*

2419 A640 50 l multicolored .35 .25
2420 A640 200 l shown .90 .25

Butterflies A641

100 l, Gonepteryx rhamni. 200 l, Chazara briseis. 400 l, Allancastria cerisyi godart. 600 l, Nymphalis antiopa.

1988, Oct. 28 *Perf. 13½x13*

2421 A641 100 l multi 1.25 .65
2422 A641 200 l multi 3.00 1.10
2423 A641 400 l multi 5.00 1.75
2424 A641 600 l multi 6.25 3.00
a. Souvenir sheet of 4, #2421-2424 20.00 20.00
Nos. 2421-2424 (4) 15.50 6.50

ANTALYA '88.

Natl. Palaces Type of 1987

100 l, Maslak Royal Lodge, c. 1890. 400 l, Yildiz Sale Pavilion, 1889.

1988, Nov. 3 **Litho.** *Perf. 13*

2425 A628 100 l multicolored .45 .35
2426 A628 400 l multicolored 1.00 .85

Souvenir Sheet

Kemal Ataturk A642

1988, Nov. 10 *Perf. 13x13½*

2427 A642 400 l multi 1.60 1.60

Medicinal Plants of Anatolia — A643

150 l, Tilia rubra. 300 l, Malva silvestris. 600 l, Hyoscyamus niger. 900 l, Atropa belladonna.

1988, Dec. 14 **Litho.** *Perf. 13*

2428 A643 150 l multicolored .50 .25
2429 A643 300 l multicolored .60 .25
2430 A643 600 l multicolored 1.25 .25
2431 A643 900 l multicolored 2.50 .45
Nos. 2428-2431 (4) 4.85 1.20

Stamps of 1983-85 Surcharged

Perf. 13, 11½x12½

1989, Feb. 8 **Litho.**

2432 A579 50 l on 15 l No. 2263 .50 .25
2433 A608 75 l on 10 l No. 2334 .75 .25
2434 A608 150 l on 20 l No. 2336 1.40 .25
Nos. 2432-2434 (3) 2.65 .75

Surcharge on No. 2432 is slightly different.

Artifacts in the Museum of Anatolian Civilizations, Ankara — A644

Designs: 150 l, Seated Goddess with Child, neolithic bisque figurine, Hacilar, 6th millennium B.C. 300 l, Lead figurine, Alisar Huyuk, Assyrian Trading Colonies Era, c. 19th cent. B.C. 600 l, Human-shaped vase, Kultepe, Assyrian Trading Colonies Era, 18th cent. B.C. 1000 l, Ivory mountain god, Bogazkoy, Hittite Empire, 14th cent. B.C.

1989, Feb. 8 **Litho.** *Perf. 13½x13*

2435 A644 150 l multi .75 .25
2436 A644 300 l multi 1.10 .70
2437 A644 600 l multi 1.75 1.40
2438 A644 1000 l multi 3.75 2.00
Nos. 2435-2438 (4) 7.35 4.35

See Nos. 2458-2461, 2495-2498, 2520-2523, 2617-2620.

NATO, 40th Anniv. — A645

Wmk. 394

1989, Apr. 4 **Litho.** *Perf. 13½*

2439 A645 600 l multi 1.50 .25

Europa Issue

Children's Games — A646

600 l, Leapfrog. 1000 l, Open the door, Headbezirgan.

Perf. 13x12½

1989, Apr. 23 **Wmk. 394**

2440 A646 600 l multi *10.00 1.75*
2441 A646 1000 l multi *15.00 2.50*

Steamships A647

Perf. 13½x13

1989, July 1 **Litho.** **Wmk. 394**

2442 A647 150 l Sahilbent 2.75 1.50
2443 A647 300 l Ragbet 4.00 2.10
2444 A647 600 l Tari 5.50 2.50
2445 A647 1000 l Guzelhisar 8.00 4.00
Nos. 2442-2445 (4) 20.25 10.10

French Revolution, Bicent. — A648

Wmk. 394

1989, July 14 **Litho.** *Perf. 14*

2446 A648 600 l multi 1.75 .25

Kemal Ataturk — A649

1989, Aug. 16 *Perf. 13x13½*

2447 A649 2000 l gray & bluish gray 2.50 .50
2448 A649 5000 l gray & deep red brn 5.00 1.50

See Nos. 2485-2486, 2538-2541. For surcharge see No. 2656.

No. 2336 Surcharged in Bright Blue

Perf. 11½x12½

1989, Aug. 31 **Litho.** **Unwmk.**

2449 A608 500 l on 20 l .80 .25

Photography, 150th Anniv. — A650

1989, Oct. 17 *Perf. 13½x13*

2450 A650 175 l Camera .40 .25
2451 A650 700 l Shutter 1.40 .25

State Exhibition of Paintings and Sculpture A651

Designs: 200 l, *Manzara,* by Hikmet Onat. 700 l, *Sari Saz,* by Bedri Rahmi Eyuboglu. 1000 l, *Kadin,* by Zuhtu Muridoglu.

Perf. 13½x13

1989, Oct. 30 **Litho.** **Wmk. 394**

2452 A651 200 l multicolored .30 .25
2453 A651 700 l multicolored 1.10 .25
2454 A651 1000 l multicolored 1.40 .35
Nos. 2452-2454 (3) 2.80 .85

Jawaharlal Nehru, 1st Prime Minister of Independent India — A652

1989, Nov. 14 *Perf. 13½x12½*

2455 A652 700 l multicolored 1.65 .25

Sea Turtles — A653

700 l, Caretta caretta. 1000 l, Chelonia mydas.

1989, Nov. 16 *Perf. 13½x13*

2456 A653 700 l multi 3.00 1.00
2457 A653 1000 l multi 6.00 2.00
a. Souv. sheet of 2, #2456-2457 17.50 17.50

Artifacts Type of 1989

100 l, Ivory female deity. 200 l, Ceremonial vessel. 500 l, Seated goddess pendant. 700 l, Carved lion.

Perf. 13x12½, 12½x13

1990, Feb. 8 **Litho.** **Wmk. 394**

2458 A644 100 l multi .30 .30
2459 A644 200 l multi .50 .50
2460 A644 500 l multi 1.00 .75
2461 A644 700 l multi 1.75 1.25
Nos. 2458-2461 (4) 3.55 2.80

Nos. 2458 and 2460 vert.

Wars of Dardanelles, 1915 — A654

1990, Mar. 18 *Perf. 13*

2462 A654 1000 l multicolored 1.10 .25

EXPO '90 Intl. Garden and Greenery Exposition, Osaka — A655

Perf. 12½x13

1990, Apr. 1 **Litho.** **Wmk. 394**

2463 1000 l Bridge at left 1.40 .35
2464 1000 l Pavilion at left 1.40 .35
a. A655 Pair, #2463-2464 3.00 3.00

Nos. 2301, 2368 and 2284 Surcharged

Perfs. as Before

1990, Apr. 4 **Litho.**

2465 A589 50 l on 5 l #2301 .85 .25
2466 A620 100 l on 10 l #2368 2.25 .25
2467 A589 200 l on 70 l #2284 5.00 .30
Nos. 2465-2467 (3) 8.10 .80

Grand Natl. Assembly, 70th Anniv. — A657

1990, Apr. 23 *Perf. 13*

2468 A657 300 l multicolored .95 .50

Europa 1990 — A658

Post offices — 700 l, Ulus, Ankara. 1000 l, Sirkeci, Istanbul, horiz.

1990, May 2

2469 A658 700 l multicolored *5.00 1.50*
2470 A658 1000 l multicolored *6.50 2.00*

8th European Supreme Courts Conf. — A659

1990, May 7 **Litho.** *Perf. 12½x13*

2471 A659 1000 l multicolored 2.00 .75

Salamandra Salamandra A660

World Environment Day: No. 2473, Triturus vittatus. No. 2474, Bombina bombina. No. 2475, Hyla arborea, vert.

1990, June 5 *Perf. 13½x13*

2472 A660 300 l multicolored .70 .70
2473 A660 500 l multicolored .70 .70
2474 A660 1000 l multicolored 1.50 1.50
2475 A660 1500 l multicolored 2.50 2.50
Nos. 2472-2475 (4) 5.40 5.40

Turkey-Japan Relations, Cent. — A661

1990, June 13 *Perf. 12½x13*
2476 A661 1000 l multicolored 1.75 1.10

Traffic Types of 1987 and Nos. 2283-2284 Surcharged

1990, June 20 *Perf. 14*
2477 A620 150 l on 10 l 7.00 1.75
2478 A620 300 l on 20 l 11.00 1.75

Perf. 11½x12½
2479 A589 300 l on 70 l #2284 3.00 .75
2480 A589 1500 l on 20 l #2283 8.75 .75
Nos. 2477-2480 (4) 29.75 5.00

Boats in Saintes Marines A662

Paintings by Vincent Van Gogh (1853-1890): 300 l, Self-portrait, vert. 1000 l, Vase with Sunflowers, vert. 1500 l, Road of Cypress and Stars.

Wmk. 394
1990, July 29 **Litho.** *Perf. 13*
2481 A662 300 l multicolored 2.00 1.40
2482 A662 700 l multicolored 3.50 2.00
2483 A662 1000 l multicolored 4.50 3.00
2484 A662 1500 l multicolored 5.00 4.00
Nos. 2481-2484 (4) 15.00 10.40

Ataturk Type of 1989

1990, Aug. 1 **Unwmk.** *Perf. 14*
2485 A649 500 l gray & ol grn 1.40 .25
2486 A649 1000 l gray & rose vio 1.75 .70

Intl. Literacy Year — A664

Perf. 13x13½
1990, Aug. 22 **Wmk. 394**
2487 A664 300 l multicolored .50 .50

A665

State exhibition of paintings and sculpture by: 300 l, Nurullah Berk. 700 l, Cevat Dereli. 1000 l, Nijad Sirel.

1990, Oct. 17 **Litho.** *Perf. 13x13½*
2488 A665 300 l multicolored .45 .25
2489 A665 700 l multicolored .90 .35
2490 A665 1000 l multicolored 1.40 .50
Nos. 2488-2490 (3) 2.75 1.10

PTT, 150th Anniv. — A666

Past and present communication methods: 200 l, Post rider, truck, train, airplane, ship. 250 l, Telegraph key, computer terminal. 400 l, Telephone switchboard, computerized telephone exchange. 1500 l, Power lines, satellite.

1990, Oct. 23 *Perf. 14*
2491 A666 200 l multicolored .25 .25
2492 A666 250 l multicolored .25 .25
2493 A666 400 l multicolored .70 .25
2494 A666 1500 l multicolored 2.75 1.50
a. Souv. sheet of 4, #2491-2494 4.00 4.00
Nos. 2491-2494 (4) 3.95 2.25

For surcharges see Nos. 2657-2659.

Artifacts Type of 1989

300 l, Figurine of a woman, c. 5000-4500 BC. 500 l, Sistrum, c. 2100-2000 BC. 1000 l, Spouted vessel with 3-footed pedestal, c. 2000-1750 BC. 1500 l, Ceremonial vessel, 1900-1700 BC.

1991, Feb. 8 **Litho.** *Perf. 13x12½*
2495 A644 300 l multi .35 .25
2496 A644 500 l multi .70 .40
2497 A644 1000 l multi 1.00 .70
2498 A644 1500 l multi 2.00 1.00
Nos. 2495-2498 (4) 4.05 2.35

Nos. 2495-2498 are vert.

Lakes of Turkey — A667

Wmk. 394
1991, Apr. 24 **Litho.** *Perf. 13*
2499 A667 250 l Abant .25 .25
2500 A667 500 l Egridir .60 .25
2501 A667 1500 l Van 1.75 .90
Nos. 2499-2501 (3) 2.60 1.40

Europa — A668

Unwmk.
1991, May 6 **Litho.** *Perf. 13*
2502 A668 1000 l multicolored *9.00* *2.00*
2503 A668 1500 l multi, diff. *13.50* *3.00*

Natl. Statistics Day — A669

1991, May 9 *Perf. 13½x13*
2504 A669 500 l multicolored .75 .25

Eastern Mediterranean Fiber Optic Cable System — A670

1991, May 13
2505 A670 500 l multicolored .55 .25

European Conf. of Transportation Ministers — A671

1991, May 22 *Perf. 13*
2506 A671 500 l multicolored .90 .60

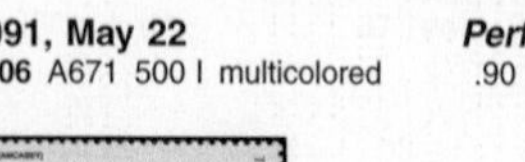

Caricature Art — A672

500 l, "Amcabey" by Cemal Nadir Guler. 1000 l, "Abdulcanbaz" by Turhan Selcuk, vert.

Wmk. 394
1991, Sept. 11 **Litho.** *Perf. 13*
2507 A672 500 l multicolored .70 .25
2508 A672 1000 l multicolored 1.10 .60

Ceramics — A673

Wall facings: 500 l, 13th cent. Seljuk bird. 1500 l, 16th cent. Ottoman floral pattern.

1991, Sept. 23 *Perf. 13½x13*
2509 A673 500 l multicolored .40 .25
2510 A673 1500 l multicolored 1.40 .65

Symposium on Intl. Protection of Human Rights, Antalya — A674

1991, Oct. 4 *Perf. 13x12½*
2511 A674 500 l multicolored .75 .25

Southeastern Anatolia Irrigation and Power Project — A675

1991, Oct. 6 **Unwmk.** *Perf. 13½x13*
2512 A675 500 l multicolored .75 .25

Turkish Fairy Tales — A676

Baldboy: 500 l, With genie. 1000 l, At party. 1500 l, Plowing field.

1991, Oct. 9 *Perf. 13x13½*
2513 A676 500 l multicolored .40 .25
2514 A676 1000 l multicolored .90 .45
2515 A676 1500 l multicolored 1.40 .65
Nos. 2513-2515 (3) 2.70 1.35

Snakes — A677

250 l, Eryx jaculus. 500 l, Elaphe quatuorlineata. 1000 l, Vipera xanthina. 1500 l, Vipera kaznakovi.

Perf. 12½x13
1991, Oct. 23 **Wmk. 394**
2516 A677 250 l multi 2.40 .60
2517 A677 500 l multi 3.50 1.25
2518 A677 1000 l multi 7.25 2.40
2519 A677 1500 l multi 9.50 4.25
Nos. 2516-2519 (4) 22.65 8.50

World Environment Day.

Antiquities Type of 1989

300 l, Statuette of Mother Goddess, Neolithic, 6000 B.C., vert. 500 l, Hasanoglan statuette, Early Bronze Age, 3000 B.C., vert. 1000 l, Inandik vase, Old Hittite, 18th cent. B.C., vert. 1500 l, Lion statuette, Urartian, 8th cent. B.C., vert.

Wmk. 394
1992, Feb. 12 **Litho.** *Perf. 13*
2520 A644 300 l multicolored .30 .25
2521 A644 500 l multicolored .40 .25
2522 A644 1000 l multicolored .80 .40
2523 A644 1500 l multicolored 1.25 .50
Nos. 2520-2523 (4) 2.75 1.40

Discovery of America, 500th Anniv. — A678

2000 l, Balloons, vert.

Wmk. 394
1992, May 4 **Litho.** *Perf. 13*
2524 A678 1500 l shown *4.50* *1.00*
2525 A678 2000 l multicolored *7.50* *1.50*

Europa.

Settlement of Jews in Turkey, 500th Anniv. — A679

1992, May 15 *Perf. 12½x13*
2526 A679 1500 l multicolored 1.00 1.00

A681

Wmk. 394
1992, June 1 **Litho.** *Perf. 13*
2529 A681 500 l multicolored .45 .45

Turkish Court of Accounts, 130th anniv.

Economics Congress, Izmir — A682

1992, June 4
2530 A682 1500 l multicolored .90 .90

World Environment Day — A683

500 l, Vanellus vanellus. 1000 l, Oriolus oriolus. 1500 l, Tadorna tadorna. 2000 l, Halcyon smyrnensis, vert.

1992, June 5 **Litho.** *Perf. 13*
2531 A683 500 l multi .60 .60
2532 A683 1000 l multi .90 .60
2533 A683 1500 l multi 1.25 .60
2534 A683 2000 l multi 1.75 1.25
Nos. 2531-2534 (4) 4.50 3.05

Ataturk Type of 1989 and

Kemal Ataturk — A683a

A683b

10,000 l, Full face. 100,000 l, Facing left.

Perf. 13, 14 (#2539, 2541, 2543-2544)
1992-96 **Litho.** **Unwmk.**
2538 A649 250 l gold, brn & org 1.50 .25
2539 A649 5000 l gold & vio 2.00 .40
2540 A649 10,000 l gold & blue 4.50 1.90
2541 A649 20,000 l gold & lil rose 8.00 1.60
2542 A683a 50,000 l multi 4.50 1.75
2543 A683b 50,000 l lake & pink 3.50 .90
2544 A683b 100,000 l grn bl & yel org 4.50 1.75
Nos. 2538-2544 (7) 28.50 8.55

Issued: 250 l, 10,000 l, 5/28/92; 5000 l, 20,000 l, 9/29/93; #2542, 11/10/94; #2543, 100,000 l, 6/1/96.

For surcharges see Nos. 2655, 2732.

Black Sea Economic Cooperation Summit — A684

Wmk. 394

1992, June 25 Litho. *Perf. 13*

2545 A684 1500 l multicolored 1.00 .45

1992 Summer Olympics, Barcelona A685

1992, July 25 Wmk. 394

2546 A685 500 l Doves .45 .25
2547 A685 1000 l Boxing .60 .35
2548 A685 1500 l Weight lifting 1.10 .45
2549 A685 2000 l Wrestling 2.25 .65
Nos. 2546-2549 (4) 4.40 1.70

Anatolian Folktales — A686

Scenes: 500 l, Woman carrying milk to soldiers. 1000 l, Pouring milk into trough. 1500 l, Soldiers dipping into trough.

Perf. 13x12½

1992, Sept. 23 Litho. Wmk. 394

2550 A686 500 l multicolored .25 .25
2551 A686 1000 l multicolored .60 .25
2552 A686 1500 l multicolored 1.00 .45
Nos. 2550-2552 (3) 1.85 .95

Turkish Handicrafts A687

500 l, Embroidered flowers. 1000 l, Dolls in traditional costumes, vert. 3000 l, Saddlebags.

1992, Oct. 21 *Perf. 13½x13, 13x13½*

2553 A687 500 l multicolored .25 .25
2554 A687 1000 l multicolored .55 .25
2555 A687 3000 l multicolored 1.50 .80
Nos. 2553-2555 (3) 2.30 1.30

See Nos. 2585-2588, 2611-2612.

Fruits — A688

Wmk. 394

1992, Nov. 25 Litho. *Perf. 13*

2556 A688 500 l Cherries .30 .25
2557 A688 1000 l Peaches .55 .25
2558 A688 3000 l Grapes 1.10 .50
2559 A688 5000 l Apples 2.50 .80
Nos. 2556-2559 (4) 4.45 1.80

See Nos. 2565-2568.

Famous Men — A689

Designs: No. 2560, Sait Faik Abasiyanik (1906-54), writer. No. 2561, Fikret Mualla Saygi (1904-67), artist. No. 2562, Cevat Sakir Kabaagacli (1886-1973), author. No. 2563, Muhsin Ertugrul (1892-1979), actor and producer. No. 2564, Asik Veysel Satiroglu (1894-1973), composer.

Perf. 14, 13½x13 (#2561, 2564)

1992, Dec. 30 Litho.

2560 A689 T multicolored 1.10 .25
2561 A689 T multicolored 1.10 .25
2562 A689 M multicolored 1.50 .25
2563 A689 M multicolored 1.50 .25
2564 A689 M multicolored 1.50 .25
Nos. 2560-2564 (5) 6.70 1.25

Value on day of issue: Nos. 2560-2561, 500 l. Nos. 2562-2564, 1000 l.

See Nos. 2577-2581.

Fruit Type of 1992

Wmk. 394

1993, Apr. 28 Litho. *Perf. 13*

2565 A688 500 l Bananas .50 .30
2566 A688 1000 l Oranges .50 .50
2567 A688 3000 l Pears 1.00 .75
2568 A688 5000 l Pomegranates 2.00 1.40
Nos. 2565-2568 (4) 4.00 2.95

Europa — A690

Sculptures by: 1000 l, Hadi Bara. 3000 l, Zuhtu Muridoglu.

1993, May 3

2569 A690 1000 l multicolored *1.00 .50*
2570 A690 3000 l multicolored *2.25 .75*

A691

Wmk. 394

1993, July 6 Litho. *Perf. 13*

2571 A691 2500 l lt bl, dk bl & gold .90 .60

Economic Cooperation Organization Meeting, Istanbul.

Houses — A692

Various houses from Black Sea region.

1993, July 7

2572 A692 1000 l multicolored .65 .25
2573 A692 2500 l multi, horiz. .65 .50
2574 A692 3000 l multicolored 1.25 .80
2575 A692 5000 l multi, horiz. 1.40 1.00
Nos. 2572-2575 (4) 3.95 2.55

See Nos. 2604-2607, 2631-2634, 2647-2650, 2676-2679.

Hodja Ahmet Yesevi (1093-1166), Poet — A693

Design: Yesevi Mausoleum.

1993, July 28

2576 A693 3000 l lt bl, dk bl & gold .85 .35

Famous Men Type of 1992

Designs: No. 2577, Haci Arif Bey (1831-84), composer. No. 2578, Neyzen Tevfik Kolayli (1878-1953), poet. No. 2579, Munir Nurettin Selcuk (1900-81), composer, musician. No. 2580, Cahit Sitki Taranci (1910-56), poet. No. 2581, Orhan Veli Kanik (1914-50), writer.

Perf. 14, 13½x13 (2578-2580)

1993, Aug. 4 Litho. Unwmk.

2577 A689 T brown & red brown 1.10 .25
2578 A689 T brown & red brown 1.10 .25
2579 A689 M brown & red brown 1.50 .25
2580 A689 M brown & red brown 1.50 .25
2581 A689 M brown & red brown 1.50 .25
Nos. 2577-2581 (5) 6.70 1.25

Value on day of issue: Nos. 2577-2578, 500 l. Nos. 2579-2581, 1000 l.

Istanbul, Proposed Site for 2000 Olympics — A694

1993, Aug. 11 *Perf. 12½x13*

2582 A694 2500 l multicolored .90 .45

Protection of Mediterranean Sea Against Pollution — A695

1000 l, Amphora on sea floor. 3000 l, Dolphin jumping.

Unwmk.

1993, Oct. 12 Litho. *Perf. 13*

2583 A695 1000 l multicolored .25 .25
2584 A695 3000 l multicolored 1.60 .65

Handicrafts Type of 1992

Perf. 12½x13, 13x12½

1993, Oct. 21 Wmk. 394

2585 A687 1000 l Painted rug .25 .25
2586 A687 2500 l Earrings .75 .25
2587 A687 5000 l Money purse, vert. 1.60 .75
Nos. 2585-2587 (3) 2.60 1.25

Republic, 70th Anniv. — A696

1993, Oct. 29 Wmk. 394 *Perf. 13*

2588 A696 1000 l multicolored .50 .35

Civil Defence Organization A697

Perf. 12½x13

1993, Nov. 25 Unwmk.

2589 A697 1000 l multicolored .50 .35

Turksat Satellite — A698

Designs: 1500 l, Satellite, globe, map of Turkey. 5000 l, Satellite transmissions to areas in Europe and Asia.

Perf. 13x13½

1994, Jan. 21 Litho. Wmk. 394

2590 A698 1500 l multicolored .25 .25
2591 A698 5000 l multicolored 1.10 .25

Natl. Water Project — A699

1994, Feb. 28 *Perf. 13x12½*

2592 A699 1500 l multicolored .60 .35

Native Cuisine — A700

1000 l, Ezogel in corbasi. 1500 l, Mixed dolma. 3500 l, Shish kebabs. 5000 l, Baklava.

Perf. 12½x13

1994, Mar. 23 Litho. Wmk. 394

2593 A700 1000 l multi .65 .65
2594 A700 1500 l multi .65 .65
2595 A700 3500 l multi .65 .65
2596 A700 5000 l multi 1.25 .65
Nos. 2593-2596 (4) 3.20 2.60

Europa — A701

1500 l, Marie Curie (1867-1934), chemist, vert. 5000 l, Albert Einstein (1879-1955), physicist.

Unwmk.

1994, May 2 Litho. *Perf. 13*

2597 A701 1500 l multicolored *.50 .50*
2598 A701 5000 l multicolored *1.50 1.50*

World Environment Day — A703

Views of: 6000 l, Antalya. 8500 l, Mugla, vert.

Wmk. 394

1994, June 5 Litho. *Perf. 13*

2602 A703 6000 l multicolored 1.00 .75
2603 A703 8500 l multicolored 1.75 1.10

Houses Type of 1993

2500 l, 2-story housing complex. 3500 l, 3-story home with balconies. 6000 l, Tri-level country home. 8500 l, 2-story home.

1994, July 7

2604 A692 2500 l multi, horiz. .60 .60
2605 A692 3500 l multi, horiz. .60 .60
2606 A692 6000 l multi, horiz. .60 .60
2607 A692 8500 l multi, horiz. 1.75 .60
Nos. 2604-2607 (4) 3.55 2.40

Tourism — A704

1994, Aug. 3

2608 A704 5000 l Hiking .75 .45
2609 A704 10,000 l Rafting 1.50 .75

Project of the Year 2001 — A705

1994, Aug. 27

2610 A705 2500 l multicolored .65 .50

Handicrafts Type of 1992

Designs: 7500 l, Kusak pattern used on 18th cent. clothing, vert. 12,000 l, Pacalik pattern used on 19th cent. clothing.

1994, Oct. 21

2611 A687 7500 l multicolored .90 .50
2612 A687 12,500 l multicolored 1.60 1.60

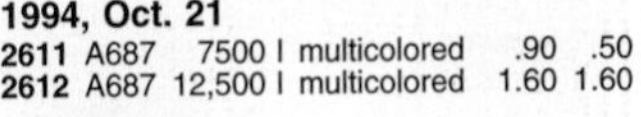

Mushrooms — A706

2500 l, Morchella conica. 5000 l, Agaricus bernardii. 7500 l, Lactarius deliciosus. 12,500 l, Macrolepiota procera.

1994, Nov. 16

2613 A706 2500 l multi .50 .50
2614 A706 5000 l multi .90 .90
2615 A706 7500 l multi 1.60 1.60
2616 A706 12,500 l multi 3.25 3.25
Nos. 2613-2616 (4) 6.25 6.25

See Nos. 2637-2640.

Antiquities Type of 1989

Lydian Treasures, 6th cent. B.C.: 2500 l, Silver pitcher, vert. 5000 l, Silver incense burner, vert. 7500 l, Gold, glass necklace. 12,500 l, Gold brooch.

1994, Dec. 7

2617 A644 2500 l multicolored .50 .40
2618 A644 5000 l multicolored .75 .45
2619 A644 7500 l multicolored 1.10 .65
2620 A644 12,500 l multicolored 2.00 .85
Nos. 2617-2620 (4) 4.35 2.35

Nevruz, New Day — A707

1995, Mar. 21

2621 A707 3500 l multicolored .65 .45

Europa — A708

1995, May 5

2622 A708 3500 l Flowers *1.00 1.00*
2623 A708 15,000 l Olive branch *2.00 2.00*

Istanbul '96 World Stamp Exhibition — A709

a, 7000 l, Buildings. b, 25,000 l, Tower, buildings. c, 7000 l, Mosque, city along harbor. c, 25,000 l, Residential area, mosque, harbor.

1995, May 24

2624 A709 Block of 4, #a.-d. 6.00 4.50

Nos. 2624a-2624b and 2624c-2624d are each continuous designs.

European Nature Conservation Year — A710

5000 l, Field of poppies. 15,000 l, Trees. 25,000 l, Mountain valley.

1995, June 5

2625 A710 5000 l multi .40 .25
2626 A710 15,000 l multi 1.25 .60
2627 A710 25,000 l multi 2.00 1.00
Nos. 2625-2627 (3) 3.65 1.85

Motion Pictures, Cent. — A711

1995, Feb. 1

2628 A711 15,000 l red & blue 1.75 1.25

A712

1995, Apr. 23

2629 A712 5000 l multicolored .65 .45

1sh Conference of the Moslem Women Parliamentaries, Pakistan.

Houses Type of 1993

5000 l, 2-story block house. 10,000 l, Tower of part-stone house. 15,000 l, Interior view of 2-story house, horiz. 20,000 l, Three unit-connecting apartment, horiz.

1995, July 7

2631 A692 5000 l multicolored .75 .35
2632 A692 10,000 l multicolored 1.10 .40
2633 A692 15,000 l multicolored 1.25 .55
2634 A692 20,000 l multicolored 1.40 1.10
Nos. 2631-2634 (4) 4.50 2.40

UN, 50th Anniv. — A713

1995, Oct. 24

2635 A713 15,000 l shown .75 .40
2636 A713 30,000 l UN emblem, "50" 1.50 .80

Mushroom Type of 1994

Designs: 5000 l, Amanita phalloides. 10,000 l, Lepiota helveola. 20,000 l, Gyromitra esculenta. 30,000 l, Amanita gemmata.

1995, Nov. 16

2637 A706 5000 l multicolored .65 .65
2638 A706 10,000 l multicolored 1.10 1.10
2639 A706 20,000 l multicolored 2.25 2.25
2640 A706 30,000 l multicolored 2.50 2.50
Nos. 2637-2640 (4) 6.50 6.50

Children's Rights — A714

6,000 l, Rainbow, hearts, flower, sun in sky. 10,000 l, Child's hand drawing letter "A."

1996, Mar. 13

2641 A714 6,000 l multicolored .35 .25
2642 A714 10,000 l multicolored .90 .65

Fauna A715

Designs: a, 5,000 l, Bee. b, 10,000 l, Dog. c, 15,000 l, Rooster. d, 30,000 l, Fish.

1996, Apr. 10 **Unwmk.**

2643 A715 Sheet of 4, #a.-d. 4.50 4.50

ISTANBUL '96.

Famous Women — A716

10,000 l, Nene Hatun. 40,000 l, Halide Edip Adivar.

Perf. 12½x13

1996, May 5 **Litho.** **Unwmk.**

2644 A716 10,000 l multi 1.25 .75
2645 A716 40,000 l multi 2.00 1.50

Europa.

World Environment Day — A717

Unwmk.

1996, June 3 **Litho.** ***Perf. 13***

2646 A717 50,000 l multicolored 1.60 .80

Houses Type of 1993

Designs: 10,000 l, Tri-level block house, horiz. 15,000 l, Two story with bay window, gate at entrance to side courtyard, horiz. 25,000 l, Two story townhouse, double wooden doors at bottom. 50,000 l, Flat-roofed, two-story townhouse.

1996, July 7 ***Perf. 13***

2647 A692 10,000 l multicolored .45 .25
2648 A692 15,000 l multicolored .75 .35
2649 A692 25,000 l multicolored 1.00 .55
2650 A692 50,000 l multicolored 2.10 1.10
Nos. 2647-2650 (4) 4.30 2.25

1996 Summer Olympic Games, Atlanta A718

a, 10,000 l, Archery. b, 15,000 l, Wrestling. c, 25,000 l, Weight lifting. d, 50,000 l, Hurdles.

1996, July 19

2651 A718 Sheet of 4, #a.-d. 6.00 6.00

ISTANBUL '96.

Turkish Press, 50th Anniv. — A719

1996, July 24 ***Perf. 12½x13***

2652 A719 15,000 l multicolored .60 .30

Euro '96, European Soccer Championships, Great Britain — A720

15,000 l, Player, vert. 50,000 l, Soccer ball, flags.

1996, June 8 ***Perf. 13***

2653 A720 15,000 l multi 1.10 .45
2654 A720 50,000 l multi 2.50 1.25

Nos. 2447, 2491, 2493-2494, 2538 Surcharged in Orange or Deep Violet Blue

or

Perfs., Printing Methods as Before

1996, July 22

2655 A649 T on 250 l #2538 (O) 1.25 .25
2656 A649 T on 2000 l #2447 1.25 .25
2657 A666 M on 200 l #2491 2.00 .25
2658 A666 M on 400 l #2493 2.00 .25
2659 A666 M on 1500 l #2494 2.00 .25
Nos. 2655-2659 (5) 8.50 1.25

Nos. 2655-2656 and 2657-2659 had face values of 10,000 l and 15,000 l on day of issue.

See No. 2732.

Methods of Transportation — A721

a, 25,000 l, Airplane (b). b, 50,000 l, Helicopter, ship (d). c, 75,000 l, Train. d, 100,000 l, Bus (c).

Unwmk.

1996, Sept. 27 **Litho.** ***Perf. 13***

2660 A721 Sheet of 4, #a.-d. 12.00 12.00

ISTANBUL '96. Exists imperf. Value, $85.

New Year — A722

Unwmk.

1996, Oct. 23 **Litho.** ***Perf. 13***

2661 A722 15,000 l multicolored .55 .30

Social and Cultural Heritage — A723

10,000 l, Public Library, Bayezit, Amasya. 15,000 l, Mosque and hospital, Divrigi.

1996, Dec. 17 **Litho.** ***Perf. 13***

2662 A723 10,000 l multicolored .35 .35
2663 A723 15,000 l multicolored .55 .55

Stories and Legends A724

Europa: 25,000 l, Little children dressed in flowers and leaves riding a giant peacock. 70,000 l, Genie, man being riding a giant bird.

1997, May 5 **Litho.** ***Perf. 13***

2664 A724 25,000 l multicolored *1.25 1.25*
2665 A724 70,000 l multicolored *2.50 2.50*

White Cat A725

Designs: a, 25,000 l, Tail, hindquarters. b, 50,000 l, Back legs. c, 75,000 l, Front legs. d, 150,000 l, Face.

1997, Apr. 23

2666 A725 Sheet of 4, #a.-d. 8.00 8.00

Language Day — A726

1997, May 13 **Litho.** ***Perf. 13***

2667 A726 25,000 l multicolored .50 .50

World Environment Day — A727

1997, June 5

2668 A727 35,000 l multicolored 1.00 .90

Orchids — A728

Designs: 25,000 l, Ophrys tenthredinifera. 70,000 l, Ophrys apifera.

1997, May 28
2669 A728 25,000 l multicolored .80 .25
2670 A728 70,000 l multicolored 1.90 .55

25th Intl. Istanbul Festival — A729

1997, June 13 *Perf. 13½*
Background Color
2671 A729 15,000 l blue .25 .25
2672 A729 25,000 l pink .55 .45
2673 A729 70,000 l blue green 1.40 1.20
2674 A729 75,000 l purple 1.75 1.50
2675 A729 100,000 l green blue 2.40 2.00
Nos. 2671-2675 (5) 6.35 5.40

House Type of 1993

Inscribed: 25,000 l, Bir Urfa Evi, vert. 40,000 l, Bir Mardin Evi. 80,000 l, Bir Diyarbakir Evi. 100,000 l, Kemaliye'de Bir Ev, vert.

1997, July 7 **Litho.** *Perf. 13*
2676 A692 25,000 l multicolored .50 .50
2677 A692 40,000 l multicolored .90 .90
2678 A692 80,000 l multicolored 1.75 1.75
2679 A692 100,000 l multicolored 2.25 2.25
Nos. 2676-2679 (4) 5.40 5.40

A730

Flowers: 40,000 l, Lilium candidum. 100,000 l, Euphorbia pulcherima.

1997, Sept. 8 **Litho.** *Perf. 13*
2680 A730 40,000 l multicolored .75 .25
2681 A730 100,000 l multicolored 2.00 .65

A731

World Air Games: No. 2682, Hang gliding. No. 2683, Sailplane. No. 2684, Man pointing up at biplanes. No. 2685, Hot air balloon.

1997, Sept. 13
2682 A731 40,000 l multi 1.00 .65
2683 A731 40,000 l multi 1.00 .65
2684 A731 100,000 l multi 3.00 2.00
2685 A731 100,000 l multi 4.00 3.00
Nos. 2682-2685 (4) 9.00 6.30

Forestry Congress A732

1997, Oct. 13 **Litho.** *Perf. 13*
2686 A732 50,000 l multicolored 1.00 .80

15th European Gymnastics Congress — A733

1997, Oct. 13
2687 A733 100,000 l multicolored 2.25 1.90

Traditional Women's Headcovers A734

1997, Nov. 19 **Litho.** *Perf. 13*
2688 A734 50,000 l Gaziantep 1.40 .70
2689 A734 50,000 l Canakkale 1.40 .70
2690 A734 100,000 l Isparta 2.25 1.25
2691 A734 100,000 l Bursa 2.25 1.25
Nos. 2688-2691 (4) 7.30 3.90

See Nos. 2711-2714, 2748-2751, 2765-2768, 2790-2793.

1998 Winter Olympic Games, Nagano A735

Slalom skiers: No. 2692, #1 on bib. No. 2693, #119 on bib.

1998, Feb. 7 **Litho.** *Perf. 13*
2692 125,000 l multicolored 1.75 1.50
2693 125,000 l multicolored 1.75 1.50
a. A735 Pair, #2692-2693 4.00 4.00

Intl. Year of the Ocean A736

Designs: a, 50,000 l, Turtle, jellyfish. b, 75,000 l, Fish, octopus. c, 125,000 l, Coral, crab. d, 125,000 l, Fish, coral, starfish.

1998, Apr. 18 **Litho.** *Perf. 13*
2694 A736 Sheet of 4, #a.-d. 6.00 6.00

Dardenelles Campaign — A737

Memorial Statues: #2695, "Mother with Children," Natl. War Memorial, Wellington. #2696, "With Great Respect to the Mehmetcik, Gallipoli" (Turkish soldier carrying wounded ANZAC).

1998, Mar. 18 **Litho.** *Perf. 13*
2695 A737 125,000 l multicolored 1.75 1.75
2696 A737 125,000 l multicolored 1.75 1.75

See New Zealand Nos. 1490-1491.

A738

Europa (National Festivals and Holidays): 100,000 l, Kemal Ataturk, natl. flag, people celebrating. 150,000 l, Ataturk, natl. flag, children of different races celebrating together.

1998, May 5
2697 A738 100,000 l multicolored *1.25 1.25*
2698 A738 150,000 l multicolored *2.25 2.25*

A739

Tulips: 50,000 l, Sylvestris. 75,000 l, Armena (pink). 100,000 l, Armena (violet). 125,000 l, Saxatilis.

1998, May 1 **Litho.** *Perf. 13*
2699 A739 50,000 l multicolored .75 .75
2700 A739 75,000 l multicolored 1.60 1.60
2701 A739 100,000 l multicolored 1.90 1.90
2702 A739 125,000 l multicolored 3.00 3.00
Nos. 2699-2702 (4) 7.25 7.25

Souvenir Sheet

World Environment Day — A740

Owls: a, Two on branches. b, One flying, one standing.

1998, June 5 **Litho.** *Perf. 13½*
2703 A740 150,000 l Sheet of 2, #a.-b. 6.25 4.00

Contemporary Arts — A741

75,000 l, Couple dancing. 100,000 l, Man playing cello. 150,000 l, Ballerina.

1998, Aug. 14 **Litho.** *Perf. 13*
2704 A741 75,000 l multi 1.00 .50
2705 A741 100,000 l multi, vert. 1.25 .70
2706 A741 150,000 l multi, vert. 1.90 1.10
Nos. 2704-2706 (3) 4.15 2.30

Kemal Ataturk — A742

1998, Aug. 20 **Litho.** *Perf. 13*
2707 A742 150,000 l cl & brn 1.60 .65
2708 A742 175,000 l bl & rose brn 2.25 .85
2709 A742 250,000 l brn & cl 3.00 1.25
2710 A742 500,000 l brn & dk bl 6.50 2.50
Nos. 2707-2710 (4) 13.35 5.25

Women's Headcovers Type of 1997

1998, Nov. 24 **Litho.** *Perf. 13*
2711 A734 75,000 l Afyon .85 .40
2712 A734 75,000 l Ankara .85 .40
2713 A734 175,000 l Mus 1.90 .95
2714 A734 175,000 l Mugla 1.90 .95
Nos. 2711-2714 (4) 5.50 2.70

Turkish Republic, 75th Anniv. A743

275,000 l, Flag, silhouette of Ataturk.

1998, Oct. 29 **Litho.** *Perf. 13*
2715 A743 175,000 l shown 1.75 .90
a. Souvenir sheet of 1, imperf. 1.75 1.25
2716 A743 275,000 l red & blk 2.75 1.40
a. Souvenir sheet of 1, imperf. 3.75 2.00

Nos. 2715a, 2716a have simulated perforations.

Famous People — A744

#2717, Ihap Hulusi Görey (1898-1986). #2718, Bedia Muvahhit (1897-1993). No. 2719, Feza Gürsey (1921-92). #2720, Haldun Taner (1915-86). #2721, Vasfi Riza Zobu (1902-92).

1998, Dec. 31 **Photo.** *Perf. 13*
2717 A744 M gray bl, bl & plum 1.40 .30
2718 A744 M lil, dp lil & plum 1.40 .30
2719 A744 T org, brn & plum 1.75 .50
2720 A744 T gray vio, vio & plum 1.75 .50
2721 A744 T grn, blk & plum 1.75 .50
Nos. 2717-2721 (5) 8.05 2.10

On day of issue, Nos. 2717-2718 were valued at 50,000 l each, and Nos. 2719-2721 were valued at 75,000 l each.

NATO, 50th Anniv. — A745

1999, Apr. 4 **Litho.** *Perf. 13*
2722 A745 200,000 l multicolored 2.00 1.50

Ottoman Empire, 700th Anniv. — A746

Designs: No. 2723, Man on horse surrounded by people in buildings. No. 2724, Man on horse, three men in foreground. No. 2725, Men seated.

No. 2726, Man on white horse, castle. No. 2727, Group of women, horiz.

1999, Apr. 12
2723 A746 175,000 l multicolored 1.75 1.25
2724 A746 175,000 l multicolored 1.75 1.25
2725 A746 175,000 l multicolored 1.75 1.25
Nos. 2723-2725 (3) 5.25 3.75

Size: 79x119mm, 119x79mm
Imperf
2726 A746 200,000 l multicolored 3.00 2.75
2727 A746 200,000 l multicolored 3.00 2.75

Europa — A747

Natl. Parks: 175,000 l, Köprülü Canyon, vert. 200,000 l, Kackarlar.

Perf. 13¼x13, 13x13¼
1999, May 5 **Litho.**
2728 A747 175,000 l multicolored 2.00 2.00
2729 A747 200,000 l multicolored 2.00 2.00

World Environment Day — A748

No. 2730: a, 100,000 l, Tetrax tetrax. 200,000 l, Hoplopterus spinosus.

No. 2731: a, 100,000 l, Marbled duck. b, 200,000 l, Sitta kruperi.

1999, June 3 **Litho.** *Perf. 13¼*
2730 A748 Sheet of 2, #a.-b. 5.00 2.50
2731 A748 Sheet of 2, #a.-b. 5.00 2.50

See Nos. 2763-2764, 2800-2801.

No. 2538 Surcharged in Violet Blue

1999 Litho. *Perf. 13*
2732 A649 T on 250 l #2537 .75 .40

No. 2732 sold for 50,000 l on day of issue.

Souvenir Sheet

National Congress During the War for Independence — A749

Designs: a, 100,000 l, Ataturk, two other men, building. b, 100,000 l, Ataturk, two other men seated. c, 200,000 l, Two men standing in front of building. d, 200,000 l, Ataturk standing in front of building.

Perf. 13¼x13
1999, June 22 Litho. Unwmk.
2733 A749 Sheet of 4, #a.-d. 6.25 6.25

Art — A750

1999, July 8 Litho. *Perf. 13x13¼*
2734 A750 250,000 l shown 2.25 1.10
2735 A750 250,000 l multi, diff. 2.25 1.10

Tourism — A751

No. 2736, Temple to Zeus. No. 2737, Antakya Archaeological Museum, horiz. No. 2738, Golf course, Antalya. No. 2739, Sailboat off Bodrum.

Perf. 13x13¼, 13¼x13
1999, Sept. 19 Litho.
2736 A751 125,000 l multi 1.40 1.40
2737 A751 125,000 l multi 1.40 1.40
2738 A751 225,000 l multi 2.10 2.10
2739 A751 225,000 l multi 2.10 2.10
Nos. 2736-2739 (4) 7.00 7.00

Dams — A752

225,000 l, Cubuk 1. 250,000 l, Atatürk.

1999, Sept. 19 Litho. *Perf. 13¼x13*
2740 A752 225,000 l multi 2.25 2.25
2741 A752 250,000 l multi 2.25 2.25

Kemal Atatürk — A753

1999, Sept. 27 Litho. *Perf. 13¾*
2742 A753 225,000 l grn & brn 2.50 .55
2743 A753 250,000 l brn & lil 2.50 .65
2744 A753 500,000 l pink & grn 3.75 1.40
2745 A753 1,000,000 l bl & red 9.00 4.00
Nos. 2742-2745 (4) 17.75 6.60

Thanks for Earthquake Rescue Efforts A754

Designs: 225,000 l, Hands holding wreckage, flowers, vert. 250,000 l, Rescuers, handclasp.

Perf. 13¼x13, 13x13¼
1999, Oct. 15 Litho.
2746 A754 225,000 l multi 1.25 .65
2747 A754 250,000 l multi 1.50 .75

Women's Headcovers Type of 1997

1999, Nov. 24 Litho. *Perf. 13¼*
2748 A734 150,000 l Manisa 1.10 .55
2749 A734 150,000 l Nigde 1.10 .55
2750 A734 250,000 l Antalya 2.00 .90
2751 A734 250,000 l Amasya 2.00 .90
Nos. 2748-2751 (4) 6.20 2.90

Caravansaries A755

1999, Dec. 24 Litho. *Perf. 13¼x13*
2752 A755 150,000 l Sarapsa .85 .25
2753 A755 250,000 l Obruk 1.75 .45

Millennium — A756

Designs: 275,000 l, Earth, brain, satellite. 300,000 l, Monachus monachus.

2000, Feb. 1 Litho. *Perf. 13¼*
2754 A756 275,000 l multi 2.00 2.00
2755 A756 300,000 l multi 2.00 2.00

Merchant Ships — A757

125,000 l, Bug. 150,000 l, Gülcemal. 275,000 l, Nusret. 300,000 l, Bandirma.

2000, Mar. 16
2756 A757 125,000 l multi .65 .65
2757 A757 150,000 l multi .90 .90
2758 A757 275,000 l multi 2.40 2.40
2759 A757 300,000 l multi 2.75 2.75
Nos. 2756-2759 (4) 6.70 6.70

See Nos. 2813-2816, 2840-2843.

Grand National Assembly, 80th Anniv. — A758

300,000 l, Sprouts, horiz.

Perf. 13x13¼, 13¼x13
2000, Apr. 23 Litho.
2760 A758 275,000 l shown 2.00 1.00
2761 A758 300,000 l multi 2.25 1.10

Europa, 2000
Common Design Type

2000, May 9 *Perf. 13x13¼*
2762 CD17 300,000 l multi 2.75 2.00

World Environment Day Type of 1999
Souvenir Sheets

No. 2763, 275,000 l: a, Aquila heliaca. b, Picus viridis.
No. 2764, 275,000 l: a, Oxyura leucocephala. b, Recurvirostra avosetta.

2000, June 5 Litho. *Perf. 13¼*
Sheets of 2, #a-b
2763-2764 A748 Set of 2 14.00 14.00

Women's Headcover Type of 1997

Designs: No. 2765, 275,000 l, Trabzon. No. 2766, 275,000 l, Tunceli. No. 2767, 275,000 l, Corum. No. 2768, 275,000 l, Izmir.

2000, July 15
2765-2768 A734 Set of 4 6.50 6.50

Souvenir Sheet

Nomadic Life — A759

a, Woman at loom, woman seated. b, Women & containers. c, Women, 2 goats, carpet on tent rope. d, Woman, children, 6 goats, carpet on rope.

2000
2769 A759 Sheet of 4 9.00 9.00
a.-d. 300,000 l Any single 1.60 1.60

Military Leaders — A760

Designs: 100,000 l, Gen. Yakup Sevki Subasi. 200,000 l, Lt. Gen. Musa Kazim Karabekir (c. 1882-1948). 275,000 l, Marshal Mustafa Fevzi Cakmak (1876-1950). 300,000 l, Gen. Cevat Cobanli (1871-1938).

2000
2770-2773 A760 Set of 4 5.50 5.50

2000 Summer Olympics, Sydney — A761

Designs: 125,000 l, Rhythmic gymnastics. 150,000 l, Swimming. 275,000 l, High jump. 300,000 l, Archery.

2000
2774-2777 A761 Set of 4 5.50 5.50

Crocuses — A762

Designs: 250,000 l, Crocus chrysanthus. 275,000 l, Crocus olivieri. 300,000 l, Crocus biflorus. 1,250,000 l, Crocus sativus.

2000, Oct. 9 Litho. *Perf. 13¾x14*
2778-2781 A762 Set of 4 12.00 5.50

Architecture A763

Designs: 200,000 l, Arslan Baba. 275,000 l, Karasaç Ana. 300,000 l, Hoca Ahmet Yesevi.

2000, Oct. 19 Litho. *Perf. 13¼x13*
2782-2784 A763 Set of 3 8.00 8.00

Turksat 2A — A764

2001, Jan. 25 Litho. *Perf. 13x13¾*
2785 A764 200,000 l multi 1.25 1.25

Women's Clothing — A765

Designs: No. 2786, 200,000 l, Afyon. No. 2787, 200,000 l, Balikesir. No. 2788, 325,000 l, Kars. No. 2789, 325,000 l, Tokat.

2001, Mar. 19
2786-2789 A765 Set of 4 6.25 6.25

See Nos. 2822-2825, 2757-2760, 2880-2883.

Women's Headcovers Type of 1997

Designs: 200,000 l, Mersin-Silifke. 250,000 l, Sivas. 425,000 l, Aydin. 450,000 l, Hakkari.

2001, Apr. 16 Litho. *Perf. 13¼*
2790-2793 A734 Set of 4 7.25 7.25

Europa — A766

Waterfalls: 450,000 l, Düdenbasi. 500,000 l, Yerköprü.

2001, May 5 *Perf. 13*
2794-2795 A766 Set of 2 4.00 3.00

Aviators — A767

Designs: 250,000 l, Capt. Ismail Hakki Bey. 300,000 l, Lieut. Nuri Bey. 450,000 l, Lieut. Sadik Bey. 500,000 l, Capt. Fethi Bey.

2001, May 15
2796-2799 A767 Set of 4 6.00 5.00

World Environment Day Type of 1999

No. 2800, 300,000 l: a, Turdus pilaris. b, Carduelis carduelis.
No. 2801, 450,000 l: a, Merops apiaster. b, Upupa epops.

2001, June 5 *Perf. 13¼*
Sheets of 2, #a-b
2800-2801 A748 Set of 2 7.00 7.00

Kemal Ataturk — A768

Ataturk (1881-1938) and: 300,000 l, Turkish flag. 450,000 l, Birthplace

2001, May 19 Litho. *Perf. 13*
2802-2803 A768 Set of 2 3.25 3.25

Medicinal Plants — A769

Designs: 250,000 l, Myrtus communis. 300,000 l, Achillea millefolium. 450,000 l, Hypericum perforatum. 500,000 l, Rosa moyesii. 1,750,000 l, Crataegus oxyacantha.

2001, June 27 *Perf. 13¾*
2804-2808 A769 Set of 5 11.00 2.50

Horses — A770

Designs: 300,000 l, Horse and foal. No. 2810, 450,000 l, Three horses. No. 2811, 450,000 l, Two horses galloping. 500,000 l, Horse, vert.

2001, July 16 *Perf. 13*
2809-2812 A770 Set of 4 5.50 5.50

Merchant Ships Type of 2000

Designs: 250,000 l, Resitpasa. No. 2814, 300,000 l, Mithatpasa. No. 2815, 300,000 l, Gülnihal, 500,000 l, Aydin.

2001, Sept. 3 *Perf. 13¼*
2813-2816 A757 Set of 4 5.00 5.00

Architecture A771

Designs: No. 2817, 300,000 l, Sirvansahlar Palace, Baku, Azerbaijan. No. 2818, 300,000 l, Sultan Tekes Mausoleum, Urgench, Uzbekistan. 450,000 l, Timur Mausoleum, Samarkand, Uzbekistan. 500,000 l, White Tlightning Mausoleum, Bursa.

2001, Oct. 15
2817-2820 A771 Set of 4 6.25 6.25

Sultan Nevruz — A772

2002, Mar. 21 **Litho.** *Perf. 13¼*
2821 A772 400,000 l multi 2.25 2.25

Women's Clothing Type of 2001

Designs: 350,000 l, Kastamonu. 400,000 l, Canakkale. 500,000 l, Amasya-Ilisu. 600,000 l, Elazig.

2002, Apr. 16 *Perf. 13x13¼*
2822-2825 A765 Set of 4 7.25 7.25

Europa — A773

2002, May 5 **Litho.** *Perf. 13x13¼*
2826 A773 500,000 l multi 2.50 1.50

2002 World Cup Soccer Championships, Japan and Korea — A774

Designs: 400,000 l, Players, referee. 600,000 l, Crowd, player making scissors kick.

2002, May 31 **Litho.** *Perf. 13¼x13*
2827-2828 A774 Set of 2 4.50 4.50

Famous Men — A775

Designs: 100,000 l, Muzaffer Sarisözen (1898-1963), musician. 400,000 l, Arif Nihat Asya (1904-75), writer. 500,000 l, Vedat Tek (1873-1942), architect. 600,000 l, Hilmi Ziya Ulken (1901-74), philosopher. 2,500,000 l, Ibrahim Calli (1882-1960), painter.

2002, June 3 *Perf. 13¾x14*
2829-2833 A775 Set of 5 16.00 5.50

Souvenir Sheet

Wild Cats A776

No. 2834: a, Panthera pardus tulliana. b, Lynx lynx. c, Panthera tigris. d, Caracal caracal.

2002, June 20 *Perf. 13¼x13*
2834 A776 400,000 l Sheet of 4, #a-d 9.00 9.00

Souvenir Sheet

Shells A777

Various shells: a, 400,000 l. b, 500,000 l. c, 600,000 l. d, 750,000 l.

2002, June 25
2835 A777 Sheet of 4, #a-d 9.00 9.00

Third Place Finish of Turkish Team in World Cup Soccer Championships — A778

Designs: 400,000 l, Players in action. 700,000 l, Team photo.

2002, July 29 *Perf. 13x13¼*
2836-2837 A778 Set of 2 4.50 4.50

String Instruments — A779

Designs: 450,000 l, Violin. 700,000 l, Bass.

2002, Oct. 10 *Perf. 13¼x13*
2838-2839 A779 Set of 2 4.50 4.50

Merchant Ships Type of 2000

Designs: 450,000 l, Ege. 500,000 l, Ayvalik. No. 2842, 700,000 l, Karadeniz. No. 2843, 700,000 l, Marakaz.

2002, Nov. 4 **Litho.** *Perf. 13*
2840-2843 A757 Set of 4 8.00 8.00

Souvenir Sheet

Turkish and Hungarian Buildings — A780

No. 2844: a, 450,000 l, Gazi Kassim Pasha Mosque, Pécs, Hungary. b, 700,000 l, Rakoczi House, Tekirdag, Turkey.

2002, Dec. 2 **Litho.** *Perf. 13¼*
2844 A780 Sheet of 2, #a-b 4.50 4.50

See Hungary Nos. 3819-3820.

BJK Soccer Team, Cent. A781

Team emblem and: 500,000 l, Eagle, Turkish and team flags. 700,000 l, Eagle, stadium. 750,000 l, Soccer players. 1,000,000 l, Eagle's head.

2003, Mar. 3 *Perf. 13x13¼*
2845-2848 A781 Set of 4 8.00 8.00

A782

Europa: 500,000 l, Travel poster. 700,000 l, Ankara State Theater poster.

2003, May 9 **Litho.** *Perf. 13*
2849-2850 A782 Set of 2 3.00 3.00

A783

Conquest of Constantinople, 550th Anniv.: No. 2851, 500,000 l, Leaders at table. No. 2852, 500,000 l, Sultan Mehmet II seated. 700,000 l, Robe. 1,500,000 l, Sultan Mehmet II and cartouche.

2003, May 29
2851-2854 A783 Set of 4 7.25 7.25

Souvenir Sheet

World Environment Day — A784

No. 2855: a, Gazella subgutturosa. b, Cervus elaphus. c, Capreolus capreolus. d, Cervus dama.

2003, June 5
2855 A784 500,000 l Sheet of 4, #a-d 6.25 6.25

Zodiac — A785

2003, June 19 *Perf. 13¼*
2856 A785 500,000 l multi 1.40 1.40

Women's Clothing Type of 2001

Designs: No. 2857, 500,000 l, Sivas. No. 2858, 500,000 l, Gaziantep. No. 2859, 700,000 l, Erzincan. No. 2860, 700,000 l, Ankara-Beypazari.

2003, July 8 *Perf. 13*
2857-2860 A765 Set of 4 7.25 7.25

Fruit Blossoms — A786

Blossoms: 500,000 l, Ayva cicegi (quince). 700,000 l, Erik cicegi (plum). 750,000 l, Kiraz cicegi (cherry) . 1,000,000 l, Nar cicegi (pomegranate). 3,000,000 l, Portakal cicegi (orange).

2003, July 25 *Perf. 13¾x14*
2861-2865 A786 Set of 5 13.50 7.25

Brass Instruments A787

Designs: 600,000 l, French horn. 800,000 l, Trumpet.

2003, Sept. 23 **Litho.** *Perf. 13¼x13*
2866-2867 A787 Set of 2 4.50 4.50

Republic of Turkey, 80th Anniv. — A788

Kemal Ataturk, flag and: No. 2868, 600,000 l, Cavalry. No. 2869, 600,000 l, Buildings.

2003, Oct. 29 **Litho.** *Perf. 13¼x13*
2868-2869 A788 Set of 2 3.50 3.50

Navy Ships — A789

Designs: No. 2870, 600,000 l, Karadeniz. No. 2871, 600,000 l, Gediz. No. 2872, 700,000 l, Salihreis. No. 2873, 700,000 l, Kocatepe.

2003, Nov. 14
2870-2873 A789 Set of 4 9.00 9.00

Agriculture Bank, 140th Anniv. A790

2003, Nov. 20 *Perf. 13x13¼*
2874 A790 600,000 l multi 1.75 1.75

Buildings Associated with Kemal Ataturk — A791

Designs: 600,000 l, House, Trabzon. 700,000 l, Museum, Sakarya. 800,000 l, House, Selanik. 1,000,000 l, Museum, Ankara.

2003, Dec. 12
2875-2878 A791 Set of 4 7.25 7.25

PTT Bank — A792

2004, Mar. 3 ***Perf. 14***
2879 A792 600,000 l multi 1.75 .80

Women's Clothing Type of 2001

Designs: 600,000 l, Edirne. No. 2881, 700,000 l, Tunceli. No. 2882, 700,000 l, Burdur. 800,000 l, Trabzon.

2004, Apr. 30 ***Perf. 13x13¼***
2880-2883 A765 Set of 4 7.25 7.25

Europa — A793

Designs: 700,000 l, Skier, windsurfer. 800,000 l, Tourist at archaeological ruins, ships.

2004, May 9
2884-2885 A793 Set of 2 3.00 3.00

Souvenir Sheet

World Environment Day — A794

No. 2886: a, Falco tinnunculus. b, Buteo buteo. c, Aquila chrysaetos. d, Milvus migrans.

2004, June 5 ***Perf. 13¼x13***
2886 A794 700,000 l Sheet of 4, #a-d 7.00 6.25

Caravansaries A795

Designs: 600,000 l, Mamahatun Caravansary, Erzincan. 700,000 l, Cardak Caravasary, Denizli.

2004, June 7
2887-2888 A795 Set of 2 3.50 3.50

Gendarmerie, 165th Anniv. — A796

2004, June 14 ***Perf. 13x13¼***
2889 A796 600,000 l multi 1.40 .70

Birds — A797

Designs: 100,000 l, Regulus regulus. 250,000 l, Sylvia rueppelli. 600,000 l, Hippolais polyglotta. 700,000 l, Passer domesticus. 800,000 l, Emberiza bruniceps. 1,000,000 l, Fringilla coelebs. 1,500,000 l, Phoenicurus phoenicurus. 3,500,000 l, Erithacus rubecula.

2004, July 23 ***Perf. 14***

2890	A797	100,000 l multi	.25	.25
2891	A797	250,000 l multi	.35	.25
2892	A797	600,000 l multi	.80	.40
2893	A797	700,000 l multi	1.40	.70
2894	A797	800,000 l multi	1.50	.75
2895	A797	1,000,000 l multi	2.00	1.00
2896	A797	1,500,000 l multi	3.00	1.40
2897	A797	3,500,000 l multi	6.75	3.25
		Nos. 2890-2897 (8)	16.05	8.00

2004 Summer Olympics, Athens — A798

Designs: 600,000 l, Wrestling. No. 2899, 700,000 l, Weight lifting. No. 2900, 700,000 l, Women's track and field, vert. 800,000 l, Wrestling, diff.

Perf. 13¼x13, 13x13¼
2004, Aug. 13
2898-2901 A798 Set of 4 6.25 6.25

Souvenir Sheet

Navy Submarines — A799

No. 2902: a, 600,000 l, 18 Mart. b, 700,000 l, Preveze. c, 700,000 l, Anafartalar. d, 800,000 l, Atilay.

2004, Sept. 14 ***Perf. 13x13¼***
2902 A799 Sheet of 4, #a-d 7.00 6.25

Piri Reis (1465-1554), Admiral and Map Compiler — A800

2004, Sept. 20
2903 A800 600,000 l multi 1.40 1.40

Waterfalls A801

Designs: 600,000 l, Kapuzbasi Waterfall. 700,000 l, Sudüsen Waterfall, vert.

2004, Oct. 19 ***Perf. 13x13¼, 13¼x13***
2904-2905 A801 Set of 2 3.50 3.50

Buildings Associated With Kemal Ataturk — A802

Designs: 600,000 l, Ataturk Summer House, Bursa. No. 2907, 700,000 l, Ataturk House Museum, Erzurum. No. 2908, 700,000 l, Ataturk House, Havza. 800,000 l, State Railways Director's Building, Ankara.

2004, Nov. 8 Litho. ***Perf. 13¼x13***
2906-2909 A802 Set of 4 6.25 6.25

Souvenir Sheet

Turkish Stars Aerobatics Team — A803

No. 2910: a, 600,000 l, Two airplanes. b, 700,000 l, Five airplanes. c, 800,000 l, Seven airplanes flying upwards. d, 900,000 l, Seven airplanes flying left.

2004, Dec. 7 Litho. ***Perf. 13¼x13***
2910 A803 Sheet of 4, #a-d 9.00 9.00

Provinces — A804

2005, Jan. 1 Litho. ***Perf. 14***

2914	A804	1k	Adana	.25	.25
2915	A804	5k	Adiyaman	.25	.25
2916	A804	10k	Afyon	.25	.25
2917	A804	25k	Agri	.35	.25
2918	A804	50k	Amasya	.75	.35
2919	A804	60k	Ankara	.90	.40
2920	A804	60k	Bitlis	.90	.40
2921	A804	70k	Antalya	1.10	.50
2922	A804	70k	Bolu	1.10	.50
2923	A804	80k	Artvin	1.20	.55
2924	A804	80k	Burdur	1.20	.55
2925	A804	90k	Aydin	1.40	.60
2926	A804	1 l	Balikesir	1.60	.75
2927	A804	1.50 l	Bilecik	2.50	1.10
2928	A804	3.50 l	Bingol	5.50	2.50
2929	A804	3.50 l	Bursa	5.50	2.50
			Nos. 2914-2929 (16)	24.75	11.70

A805

Designs: 60k, Batiburnu Lighthouse, Canakkale. 70k, Zonguldak Lighthouse, Zonguldak.

2005, Mar. 18 Litho. ***Perf. 13x13¼***
2930-2931 A805 Set of 2 2.75 1.40

A806

Marmaris Intl. Maritime Festival: 70k, Sailboat. 80k, Sailboat, sun on horizon.

2005, Apr. 1
2932-2933 A806 Set of 2 2.75 1.40

A807

2005, Apr. 10
2934 A807 70k multi 1.40 .70

Turkish Police, 160th anniv.

A808

Grand National Assembly, 85th anniv.: 60k, Torch, star and crescent. 70k, Crescent and fireworks over Grand National Assembly.

2005, Apr. 23
2935-2936 A808 Set of 2 2.25 1.10

Europa A809

2005, May 9
2937 A809 70k multi 1.50 .55

Caftans of Sultans — A810

Caftan of Sultan: No. 2938, 70k, Ahmed I (shown). No. 2939, 70k, Ahmed I, diff. No. 2940, 70k, Murad III. No. 2941, 70k, Selim.

2005, May 20
2938-2941 A810 Set of 4 5.00 2.50

Souvenir Sheet

World Environment Day — A811

No. 2942: a, 60k, Pagellus bogaraveo. b, 70k, Epinephelus guaza. c, 70k, Merlanyus euxinus. d, 80k, Maena smaris.

2005, June 5 Litho. ***Perf. 13¼x13***
2942 A811 Sheet of 4, #a-d 5.50 2.75

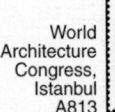

Tapestries & Carpets A812

Designs: 60k, Carpet from Hereke region, Turkey. 70k, L'humanité Assaillie par les Sept Pechés Capitaux tapestry, Belgium.

2005, June 22 Litho. ***Perf. 13x13¼***
2943-2944 A812 Set of 2 3.00 1.10

See Belgium Nos. 2098-2099.

World Architecture Congress, Istanbul A813

2005, July 3
2945 A813 70k multi 1.50 .70

Mosaics — A814

Designs: 60k, Akelos. No. 2947, 70k, Oceanos and Tethys. No. 2948, 70k, Achilles. 80k, Menad.

2005, July 5 *Perf. 13¼x13*
2946-2949 A814 Set of 4 5.50 2.75

Clocks — A815

Designs: 60k, Musical clock, 1770. 70k, Clock, 1867.

2005, July 20 *Perf. 13x13¼*
2950-2951 A815 Set of 2 2.50 1.25

Turkish Grand Prix, Istanbul A816

2005, Aug. 19 **Litho.** *Perf. 13x13¼*
2952 A816 70k multi 1.50 .65

Philanthropic Businessmen A817

Designs: 60k, Sakip Sabanci (1933-2004). 70k, Vehbi Koç (1901-96).

2005, Sept. 21 **Litho.** *Perf. 13¼x13*
2953-2954 A817 Set of 2 2.50 1.25

Provinces — A818

2005, Sept. 28 *Perf. 13¾*

2955	A818	50k	Canakkale	.75	.35
2956	A818	60k	Cankiri	1.00	.50
2957	A818	60k	Corum	1.00	.50
2958	A818	60k	Denizli	1.00	.50
2959	A818	60k	Diyarbakir	1.00	.50
2960	A818	60k	Edirne	1.00	.50
2961	A818	60k	Elazig	1.00	.50
2962	A818	70k	Erzincan	1.25	.60
2963	A818	70k	Erzurum	1.25	.60
2964	A818	70k	Eskisehir	1.25	.60
2965	A818	70k	Gaziantep	1.25	.60
2966	A818	70k	Giresun	1.25	.60
2967	A818	70k	Gumushane	1.25	.60
2968	A818	1 l	Hakkari	1.75	.80
2969	A818	1.50 l	Hatay	2.50	1.25
2970	A818	2.50 l	Isparta	4.25	2.10
	Nos. 2955-2970 (16)			22.75	11.10

Mevlana Jalal ad-Din ar-Rumi (1207-73), Islamic Philosopher — A819

2005, Sept. 30 *Perf. 13x13¼*
2971 A819 70k multi 1.50 .65

See Afghanistan Nos. 1449-1451, Iran No. 2911 and Syria No. 1574.

Galatasaray Sports Club, Cent. A820

Club emblem and: No. 2972, 60k, Soccer stadium crowd, lion and "100." No. 2973, 70k, Soccer stadium, trophy.

No. 2974: a, 60k, Man, lion and "100." b, 70k, Club emblem, building. c, 80k, Soccer players. d, 1 l, Soccer players with trophy.

2005, Oct. 11 *Perf. 13x13¼*
2972-2973 A820 Set of 2 2.25 1.10

Souvenir Sheet

Perf. 13¼x13

2974 A820 Sheet of 4, #a-d 6.00 3.00

No. 2974 contains four 41x26mm stamps. Exist imperf. Value, $40.

Start of Negotiations for Turkish Admission to European Union — A821

2005, Nov. 3 *Perf. 13¼x13*
2975 A821 70k multi 1.40 .65

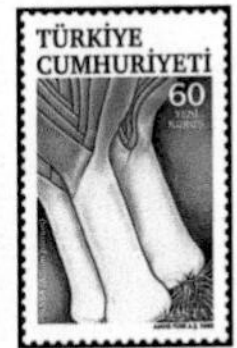

Vegetables — A824

Designs, 60k, Allium porrum (leeks). 70k, Allium sativum (garlic). 80k, Allium cepa (onions).

2005, Nov. 21 **Litho.** *Perf. 13x13¼*
2978-2980 A824 Set of 3 3.50 1.75

Europa Stamps, 50th Anniv. (in 2006) — A825

Designs: No. 2981, 60k, Vignette of #1907. No. 2982, 70k, Vignette of #1628. 80k, Vignette of #B120. 1 l, Vignette of #1719.

No. 2985, horiz.: a, 10k, #1520. b, 25k, #1800. c, 60k, #1553. d, 70k, #1775.

No. 2986, horiz.: a, 10k, #1493. b, 25k, #1936. c, 60k, #1602. d, 70k, #1876.

2005, Dec. 15 **Litho.** *Perf. 13x13¼*
2981-2984 A825 Set of 4 8.00 4.00

Souvenir Sheets

Perf. 13¼x13

2985 A825 Sheet of 4, #a-d 9.00 4.50

Imperf

2986 A825 Sheet of 4, #a-d 13.50 6.75

2006 Winter Olympics, Turin — A826

Designs: 60k, Speed skating. 70k, Skiing.

2006, Feb. 10 *Perf. 13¼x13*
2987-2988 A826 Set of 2 2.00 1.00

March 29 Total Solar Eclipse — A827

2006, Mar. 29 **Litho.** *Perf. 13¼x13*
2989 A827 70k multi 1.10 .55

Support for Education A828

2006, Apr. 10
2990 A828 60k multi .95 .45

Karaoglan, Cartoon Hero — A829

Karaoglan: 60k, With bow and arrow. No. 2992, 70k, Attacking swordsman. No. 2993, 70k, On horseback. 80k, On horseback, diff.

2006, Apr. 20 *Perf. 13x13¼*
2991-2994 A829 Set of 4 4.25 2.10

Izzet Baysal (1907-2000), Architect — A830

2006, May 11 **Litho.** *Perf. 13¼x13*
2995 A830 60k multi .85 .45

A831

A832

A833

A834

A835

A836

A837

A838

A839

Kemal Ataturk (1881-1938) A840

2006, May 19

2996	Block of 10	8.00	3.75
a.	A831 60k multi	.75	.35
b.	A832 60k multi	.75	.35
c.	A833 60k multi	.75	.35
d.	A834 60k multi	.75	.35
e.	A835 60k multi	.75	.35
f.	A836 60k multi	.75	.35
g.	A837 60k multi	.75	.35
h.	A838 60k multi	.75	.35
i.	A839 60k multi	.75	.35
j.	A840 60k multi	.75	.35

Europa A841

2006, May 30 *Perf. 13x13¼*
2997 A841 70k multi 1.25 .45

Miniature Sheet

World Environment Day — A842

No. 2998: a, 25k, Parched earth. b, 50k, Tree. c, 60k, Tree, diff. d, 70k, Forest.

2006, June 5
2998 A842 Sheet of 4, #a-d 3.50 3.00

Intl. Year of Deserts and Desertification.

2006 World Cup Soccer Championships, Germany — A843

Designs: No. 2999, 70k, Player dribbling ball. No. 3000, 70k, Player kicking ball, horiz.

2006, June 9 *Perf. 13x13¼, 13¼x13*
2999-3000 A843 Set of 2 2.25 .95

Airplanes A844

Designs: 60k, Deperdussin monoplane. No. 3002, 70k, Bleriot monoplane. No. 3003, 70k, R. E. P. monoplane.

2006, June 22 *Perf. 13¼x13*
3001-3003 A844 Set of 3 3.25 1.40

See Nos. 3034-3036.

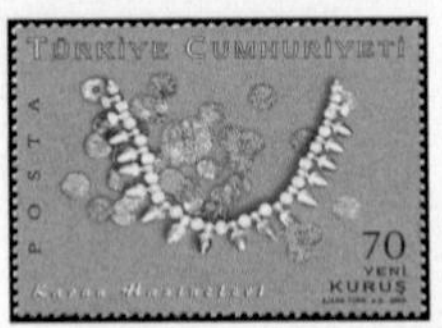

Treasures of Karun A845

Designs: No. 3004, 70k, Bracelet and coins. No. 3005, 70k, Winged sun disc pectoral and bracelet. 80k, Lion's head bracelets.

2006, July 10 *Perf. 13x13¼*
3004-3006 A845 Set of 3 3.25 1.40

Provinces — A846

2006, Sept. 11 *Perf. 13¼x13*

3007	A846	10k	Kahramanmaras	.25	.25
3008	A846	10k	Manisa	.25	.25
3009	A846	50k	Kirsehir	.70	.35
3010	A846	50k	Kocaeli	.70	.35
3011	A846	60k	Izmir	.80	.40
3012	A846	60k	Konya	.80	.40
3013	A846	60k	Mardin	.80	.40
3014	A846	60k	Mugla	.80	.40
3015	A846	70k	Istanbul	.95	.50
3016	A846	70k	Mersin	.95	.50
3017	A846	1 l	Kastamonu	1.40	.70
3018	A846	1 l	Kirklareli	1.40	.70
3019	A846	1.60 l	Kayseri	2.25	1.10
3020	A846	2 l	Malatya	2.75	1.40
3021	A846	4 l	Kars	5.50	2.75
3022	A846	4 l	Kutahya	5.50	2.75
	Nos. 3007-3022 (16)			25.80	13.20

See nos. 3055-3062.

Scenes From Movie, "Selvi Boylum Al Yazmalim" A847

Various scenes: 60k, 70k.

2006, Sept. 16 *Perf. 13x13¼*
3023-3024 A847 Set of 2 1.75 .85

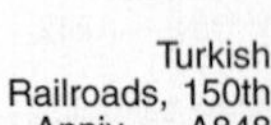
Turkish Railroads, 150th Anniv. — A848

Designs: 60k, Steam locomotive. 70k, Electric train.

2006, Sept. 23 *Perf. 13¼x13*
3025-3026 A848 Set of 2 1.75 .85

Central Bank, 75th Anniv. — A849

2006, Oct. 3
3027 A849 60k multi 1.00 .40

Intl. Telecommunications Union Conference, Antalya — A850

Conference emblem and: 60k, Globe with spotlight on Turkey. 70k, Map with lines drawn to Turkey.

2006, Nov. 6 *Perf. 13x13¼*
3028-3029 A850 Set of 2 1.90 .95

Middle East Technical University, Ankara, 50th Anniv. A851

2006, Nov. 15 Litho. *Perf. 13x13¼*
3030 A851 60k multi .85 .40

Turkish Atomic Energy Authority, 50th Anniv. — A852

2006, Nov. 22 Litho. *Perf. 13¼x13*
3031 A852 60k multi .85 .40

Geothermal Resources A853

Designs: 60k, Four steam clouds. 70k, Steam leaving smokestack.

2006, Dec. 11
3032-3033 A853 Set of 2 1.90 .95

Airplanes Type of 2006

Designs: 60k, Breguet XIV B-2. No. 3035, 70k, Albatros C-XV. No. 3036, 70k, Fiat R2.

2007, Mar. 15 Litho. *Perf. 13¼x13*
3034-3036 A844 Set of 3 3.00 1.50

A854

A855

A856

Hittite Artifacts — A857

2007, Mar. 30

3037	A854	60k	multi	1.00	.45
3038	A855	60k	multi	1.00	.45
3039	A856	60k	multi	1.00	.45
3040	A857	60k	multi	1.00	.45
	Nos. 3037-3040 (4)			4.00	1.80

Third Meeting of Economic Cooperation Organization Postal Authorities, Tehran — A858

2007, Apr. 5 *Perf. 13x13¼*
3041 A858 60k multi 1.00 .45

See Iran No. 2917, Kazakhstan No. 526 and Pakistan No. 1101.

Tekirdag as Part of Turkey, 650th Anniv. — A859

2007, Apr. 14 *Perf. 13¼x13*
3042 A859 60k multi 1.00 .45

Fenerbahce Sports Club, Cent. A860

Club emblem and: No. 3043, 60k, Men witnessing signing ceremony. No. 3044, 70k, Quotation and Arabic text.

No. 3045 — Club emblem and: a, 60k, Lighthouse. b, 70k, Three men seated at table. c, 80k, Building, stadium interior. d, 90k, Stadium exterior.

2007, May 3 *Perf. 13x13¼*
3043-3044 A860 Set of 2 2.00 1.00

Souvenir Sheet

Perf. 13¼x13

3045 A860 Sheet of 4, #a-d 4.50 4.50

No. 3045 contains four 38x23mm stamps. No. 3045 exists affixed to a booklet cover which was only sold in a set with an imperforate sheet of eight 41x31mm stamps depicting various athletes, two first day covers, and a folder, for 25 l. Value $15.

Souvenir Sheet

Mevlana Jalal ad-Din ar-Rumi (1207-73), Islamic Philosopher — A861

No. 3046: a, 25k, Portrait. b, 50k, Arabic calligraphy. c, 60k, Dervishes. d, 70k, Mausoleum.

2007, May 8 *Perf. 13x13¼*
3046 A861 Sheet of 4, #a-d 3.50 2.50

Europa — A862

Designs: 60k, Turkish Scouting emblem, Scout at campfire. 70k, Scouts saluting.

2007, May 9 *Perf. 13¼*
3047-3048 A862 Set of 2 2.00 1.00

Scouting, cent.

Mehmetcik Foundation, 25th Anniv. — A863

2007, May 17 Litho. *Perf. 13¼x13*
3049 A863 60k multi .95 .45

Souvenir Sheet

World Environment Day — A864

No. 3050: a, 25k, Goats. b, 50k, Cattle. c, 60k, Sheep. d, 70k, Chickens.

2007, June 5 Litho. *Perf. 13¼x13*
3050 A864 Sheet of 4, #a-d 4.50 2.50

Turkish Cuisine A865

Designs: No. 3051, 1 l, Nohutlu Bulgur Pilavi (chick pea and bulgur pilaf). No. 3052, 1 l, Yüksük Corbasi (soup). 2 l, Asure (vegetables).

2007, June 20 Litho. *Perf. 13x13¼*
3051-3053 A865 Set of 3 6.25 3.25

Black Sea Economic Cooperation Organization, 15th Anniversary Summit — A866

2007, June 25 *Perf. 13¼*
3054 A866 60k multi .95 .95

Provinces Type of 2006

2007, July 10 *Perf. 13¼x13*

3055	A846	10k	Siirt	.25	.25
3056	A846	50k	Ordu	.80	.40
3057	A846	60k	Rize	.95	.45
3058	A846	1 l	Nigde	1.60	.80
3059	A846	2 l	Nevsehir	3.25	1.60
3060	A846	2 l	Samsun	3.25	1.60
3061	A846	4 l	Mus	6.25	3.25
3062	A846	4 l	Sakarya	6.25	3.25
	Nos. 3055-3062 (8)			22.60	11.60

Turkish Language Association, 75th Anniv. A867

2007, July 12 *Perf. 13x13¼*
3063 A867 70k multi 1.10 .55

Roses — A869

Color of rose: No. 3065, 60k, White. No. 3066, 60k, Red. No. 3067, 60k, Yellow.

2007, Aug. 16 Litho. *Perf. 13¼*
3065-3067 A869 Set of 3 2.75 1.40

Shadow Play Characters — A870

Designs: 60k, Tuzsuz Deli Bekir and Efe. 70k, Hacivat and Karagöz. 80k, Tiryaki and Celebi.

2007, Sept. 13 Litho. *Perf. 13¼x13*
3068-3070 A870 Set of 3 3.75 1.90

Miniature Sheet

Balkanfila XIV Intl. Philatelic Exhibition, Istanbul — A871

No. 3071: a, 60k, Blue Mosque, Galata Tower. b, 70k, Hagia Sophia. c, 80k, City walls and painting. d, 1 l, Bosporus Bridge.

2007, Oct. 28
3071 A871 Sheet of 4, #a-d 5.50 3.50

An imperforate sheet containing a 60k dove and flags stamp, a 70k bridge stamp, 80k flags stamp and a 1 l flags and map of Turkey stamp exists. It sold for considerably above face value. Value, $25.

Mimar Sinan (1489-1588), Architect — A873

Sinan and: 60k, Büyükcekmece Bridge. No. 3074, 70k, Bath of Roxelana (Haseki Hürrem Sultan Hamami Ayasofya). No. 3075, 70k, Selimye Mosque, Edirne. 80k, Suleiman Mosque, Istanbul.

2007, Nov. 14 *Perf. 13¼*
3073-3076 A873 Set of 4 4.75 2.40

World Philosophy Day — A874

2007, Nov. 22 *Perf. 13x13¼*
3077 A874 60k multi 1.00 .50

Cartoon Character "Keloglan" A875

Designs: 60k, Keloglan in giant's hand. No. 3079, 70k, Keloglan leaving house. No. 3080, 70k, Keloglan on horse. 80k, Keloglan with carpet and birds.

2007, Nov. 28
3078-3081 A875 Set of 4 4.75 2.40

Provinces Type of 2006

2007, Dec. 4 *Perf. 13¼x13*

3082	A846	5k	Tunceli	.25	.25
3083	A846	10k	Tokat	.25	.25
3084	A846	65k	Sanliurfa	1.10	.55
3085	A846	65k	Trabzon	1.10	.55
3086	A846	80k	Sivas	1.40	.70
3087	A846	85k	Usak	1.50	.75
3088	A846	1 l	Tekirdag	1.75	.90
3089	A846	4.50 l	Sinop	7.75	4.00
			Nos. 3082-3089 (8)	15.10	7.95

TRT Television, 40th Anniv. — A876

Designs: 65k, Emblem. 80k, Emblem and headquarters.

2008, Jan. 31 Litho. *Perf. 12¾x13*
3090-3091 A876 Set of 2 2.50 1.25

Nasreddin Hoca Fables, 800th Anniv. A877

Hoca: 25k, And two men at table. 65k, Sitting backward on horse. 80k, Showing two pots to man. 85k, Spooning water into lake.

2008, Feb. 7 *Perf. 13x13¼*
3092-3095 A877 Set of 4 4.25 2.10

A878

St. Valentine's Day — A879

2008, Feb. 14 *Perf. 13*
3096 A878 65k multi 1.10 .55
3097 A879 80k multi 1.40 .70

Miniature Sheet

Amasya Medical Center, 700th Anniv. A880

No. 3098: a, 50k, Building. b, 65k, Six musicians. c, 80k, Seven people. d, 85k, Four people.

2008, Mar. 13 *Perf. 13x13¼*
3098 A880 Sheet of 4, #a-d 4.50 2.25

Urartian Cultural Artifacts — A881

Designs: No. 3099, 65k, Carved ivory spirit figure (Fildisi Kanati Cin). No. 3100, 65k, Gold earring, bronze pin and necklace (Altin küpe, Tunc igne, Boncuk kolye). No. 3101, 80k, Bronze cauldron (Uc ayak uzerinde tunc kazan). No. 3102, 80k, Harput Castle (Harput Kalesi).

2008, Mar. 27 *Perf. 13¼x13*
3099-3102 A881 Set of 4 4.50 2.25

Military Aircraft — A882

Designs: 65k, Consolidated B24 D. 80k, Curtiss Hawk. 85k, PZL XXIV.

2008, Apr. 25
3103-3105 A882 Set of 3 3.75 1.90

See Nos. 3148-3150.

Europa — A883

Designs: 65k, Letter, fingers making heart. 80k, Pen, inkwell.

2008, May 9 Litho. *Perf. 13¼*
3106-3107 A883 Set of 2 2.40 1.25

Diplomatic Relations Between Turkey and Thailand, 50th Anniv. — A884

Designs: 65k, Loha Prasat, Bangkok, Thailand. 80k, Sultan Ahmed Mosque, Istanbul.

2008, May 12 Litho. *Perf. 13¼x13*
3108-3109 A884 Set of 2 2.40 1.25

See Thailand No. 2359.

National Olympic Committee, Cent. A885

Olympic Committee emblem and: 65k, Dove and Olympic flag. 80k, Parading athletes. 85k, Stadium. 1 l, Athlete and Olympic flag.

2008, May 26 *Perf. 13x13¼*
3110-3113 A885 Set of 4 5.25 2.60

Provinces — A886

2008, May 28 *Perf. 13¼x13*

3114	A886	5k	Zonguldak	.25	.25
3115	A886	50k	Yozgat	.80	.40
3116	A886	65k	Aksaray	1.10	.55
3117	A886	65k	Kirikkale	1.10	.55
3118	A886	80k	Karaman	1.40	.70
3119	A886	85k	Van	1.40	.70
3120	A886	1 l	Bayburt	1.60	.80
3121	A886	4.50 l	Batman	7.25	3.75
			Nos. 3114-3121 (8)	14.90	7.70

See Nos. 3129-3137.

Miniature Sheet

World Environment Day — A887

No. 3122: a, 25k, Boy and polar bears. b, 65k, Sea ice. c, 80k, Mountains and stream. d, 85k, Girl, flower, parched earth.

2008, June 5 *Perf. 13x12¾*
3122 A887 Sheet of 4, #a-d 4.25 2.10

Turkish Diplomats Who Saved Jews During World War II — A888

Birds and: 65k, Selehattin Ulkümen (1914-2003). 80k, Necdet Kent (1911-2002).

2008, July 17 *Perf. 12¾x13*
3123-3124 A888 Set of 2 2.50 1.25

2008 Summer Olympics, Beijing A889

Designs: 25k, Archery. 65k, Taekwondo, vert. No. 3127, 80k, Weight lifting. No. 3128, 80k, Wrestling.

Perf. 13x13¼, 13¼x13
2008, Aug. 8 Litho.
3125-3128 A889 Set of 4 4.25 2.10

Provinces Type of 2008

Perf. 13¼x13, 13x13¼

2008, Aug. 29

3129	A886	50k	Kilis	.85	.40
3130	A886	65k	Bartin, vert.	1.10	.55
3131	A886	1 l	Ardahan	1.75	.85
3132	A886	1 l	Igdir	1.75	.85
3133	A886	1.50 l	Yalova	2.60	1.25
3134	A886	2 l	Karabuk	3.50	1.75
3135	A886	2 l	Osmaniye	3.50	1.75
3136	A886	4.50 l	Düzce	7.75	3.75
3137	A886	4.50 l	Sirnak	7.75	3.75
			Nos. 3129-3137 (9)	30.55	14.90

Glassware — A890

Designs: 65k, Bowl. 80k, Vase.

2008, Sept. 11 *Perf. 13x12¾*
3138-3139 A890 Set of 2 2.25 1.10

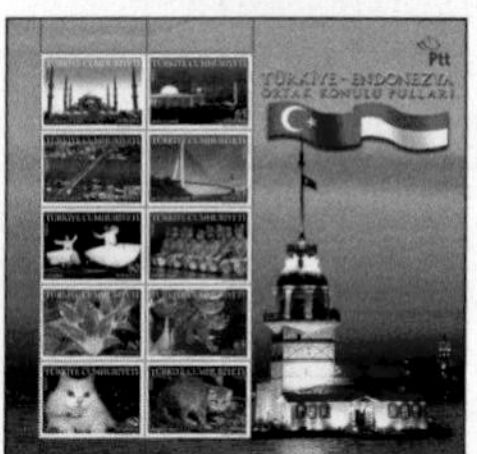

Battle of Preveza, 470th Anniv. A891

Designs: 65k, Khair ed-Din (Barbarossa), battle, map. 80k, Kemal Ataturk, ships.

2008, Sept. 27 *Perf. 13x13¼*
3140-3141 A891 Set of 2 2.25 1.10

Miniature Sheet

Friendship Between Turkey and Indonesia — A892

No. 3142: a, 80k Blue Mosque, Turkey. b, 65k Istiqlal Mosque, Indonesia. c, 80k Bosporus Bridge, Turkey. d, 65k Barelang Bridge, Indonesia. e, 80k Whirling dervishes. f, 65k Saman dance. g, 80k Turkish tulip (ters lale). h, 65k Flame of Irian (Mucuna bennettii). i, 80k Turkish Van cat. j, 65k Flat-headed cat (Yassibas kedi).

2008, Oct. 24 *Perf. 13x13¼*
3142 A892 Sheet of 10, #a-j 9.50 4.75

See Indonesia No. 2167.

Republic of Turkey, 85th Anniv. — A893

Kemal Ataturk, Turkish flag and: No. 3143, 80k, Airplane, ship, truck and train. No. 3144, 80k, Computer keyboard, satellite, dish antenna.

2008, Oct. 29 Litho. ***Perf. 12¾x13***
3143-3144 A893 Set of 2 2.10 1.10

Turkish Maritime Enterprises, 160th Anniv. — A894

Designs: 65k, Docked ship. No. 3146, 80k, Emblem. No. 3147, 80k, Ship at sea, horiz.

Perf. 13½x13¼, 13¼x13½
2008, Nov. 29 Litho.
3145-3147 A894 Set of 3 3.00 1.50

Military Aircraft Type of 2008

Designs: 65k, C-47 Dakota. 80k, F-100 D Super Sabre. 1 l, F-86 E Sabre.

2009, Mar. 12 Litho. ***Perf. 13¼x13***
3148-3150 A882 Set of 3 3.25 1.60

Miniature Sheet

Fifth World Water Forum, Istanbul A895

No. 3151 — Emblem and: a, 25k, Head, Earth, water. b, 65k, Bosporus Bridge, water drop. c, 80k, Bosporus Bridge, waterfall. d, 80k, Waterfall, parched land, clay jug pouring water.

2009, Mar. 16 ***Perf. 13x13¼***
3151 A895 Sheet of 4, #a-d 3.25 1.60

Sultan's Boats A896

Boats from Istanbul Sea Museum: No. 3152, 80k, Boat with yellow hull and short bowsprit, gray green sky. No. 3153, 80k, Boat with brown hull, long bowsprit, blue gray sky.

2009, Apr. 2
3152-3153 A896 Set of 2 2.10 1.10

Council of Europe, 60th Anniv. — A897

European Court for Human Rights, 50th Anniv. — A898

2009, May 5 ***Perf. 13¼x13***
3154 A897 80k multi 1.10 .55
3155 A898 80k multi 1.10 .55

Mother's Day — A899

Designs: 65k, Bird, hatchlings in nest shaped like heart. 80k, Mother's hands holding infant, hearts. No. 3158, 1 l, Mother and child. No. 3159, 1 l, Hands of mother and baby, flower.

2009, May 10 ***Perf. 13¾***
3156-3159 A899 Set of 4 4.50 2.25

Nos. 3156-3159 each have perforations in a heart shape in the vignette.

Ceramics A900

Designs: 80k, Ceramic pot, Portugal. 85k, Faience mosque lamp, Turkey.

2009, May 12 ***Perf. 13x13¼***
3160-3161 A900 Set of 2 2.25 1.10

See Portugal Nos. 3111-3112.

Miniature Sheet

Arrival of Kemal Ataturk at Samsun, 90th Anniv. A901

No. 3162: a, 25k, Congress Building, Sivas. b, 65k, Congress Building, Erzurum. c, 65k, Government building, Amasya. d, 80k, Statue of Ataturk, Samsun.

2009, May 19 Litho.
3162 A901 Sheet of 4, #a-d 3.25 1.60

Ministry of Transport and Communication, 70th Anniv. — A902

Designs: 50k, Ship, map. 65k, Bridge, highway interchange, bus. 80k, Earth, satellite, dish antenna, envelopes, computer, cellular phone. No. 3166, 1 l, Map, train. No. 3167, 1 l, Postal worker delivering parcel, envelope, airplane, globe.

2009, May 27 ***Perf. 13¼x13***
3163-3167 A902 Set of 5 5.25 2.60

Miniature Sheet

World Environment Day — A903

No. 3168 — Butterflies: a, 25k, Aporia crataegi. b, 65k, Lasiommate megera. c, 80k, Plebeius agestis. d, 80k, Gonepteryx rhamni.

2009, June 5 ***Perf. 13x13¼***
3168 A903 Sheet of 4, #a-d 3.25 1.60

Kemal Ataturk — A904

Various photographs of Ataturk.

2009, June 5 ***Perf. 13½ Syncopated***
3169 A904 5k multi .25 .25
3170 A904 10k multi .25 .25
3171 A904 25k multi .35 .25
3172 A904 50k multi .65 .35
3173 A904 65k multi .85 .40
3174 A904 80k multi 1.10 .55
3175 A904 85k multi 1.10 .55
3176 A904 1 l multi 1.40 .70
3177 A904 2 l multi 2.60 1.40
3178 A904 4.50 l multi 6.00 3.00
Nos. 3169-3178 (10) 14.55 7.70

Europa — A905

Designs: 80k, Cacabey Astronomy Madrassa, Kirsehir. 1 l, Ali Kuscu (1403-74), astronomer.

2009, June 16 ***Perf. 13¼x13***
3179-3180 A905 Set of 2 2.40 1.25

Items of the Phrygians — A906

Designs: 65k, Pitcher. 80k, Clay ceremonial cup with birds. No. 3183, 1 l, Goose-shaped clay ceremonial cup. No. 3184, 1 l, Cauldron.

2009, June 25 ***Perf. 13x13¼***
3181-3184 A906 Set of 4 4.50 2.25

Embroidery A907

Various embroidered pieces with background color of: 75k, Blue. 90k, Pink.

2009, July 2 ***Perf. 13¼x13***
3185-3186 A907 Set of 2 2.25 1.10

Kemal Ataturk — A908

Various photographs of Ataturk.

2009, July 16 ***Perf. 13½ Syncopated***
3187 A908 75k multi 1.10 .55
3188 A908 90k multi 1.25 .60
3189 A908 5 l multi 7.00 3.50
Nos. 3187-3189 (3) 9.35 4.65

Miniature Sheet

Haci Bektas Veli (1209-71), Mystic — A909

No. 3190: a, 75k, Haci Bektas Veli, birds. b, 75k, Birds over town. c, 90k, Dancers. d, 90k, Haci Bektas Veli, deer, lion, birds.

2009, Aug. 12 ***Perf. 13x13¼***
3190 A909 Sheet of 4, #a-d 4.50 2.25

Postal Cooperation Between Turkey and Bosnia and Herzegovina A910

2009, Oct. 9 Litho.
3191 A910 90k multi 1.25 .60

See Bosnia and Herzegovina No. 656.

Namik Kemal Yolga (1914-2001), Diplomat Who Rescued Jews in World War II — A911

2009, Oct. 20 ***Perf. 13¼x13***
3192 A911 75k multi 1.00 .50

Castles — A912

Designs: 25k, Kolan Castle, Adana. 75k, Afyon Castle. 90k, Amasya Castle. 1 l, Ankara Castle.

2009, Nov. 5
3193-3196 A912 Set of 4 4.00 2.00

Mekteb-i Mülkiye Political Science Faculty, 150th Anniv. — A913

Designs: 75k, Political Science Faculty Building, anniversary emblem. 90k, Anniversary emblem.

2009, Dec. 4 ***Perf. 13¼x13***
3197-3198 A913 Set of 2 2.25 1.10

Süleyman Celebi (1351-1422), Writer — A914

Cengiz Aytmatov (1928-2008), Writer — A915

2009, Dec. 17
3199 A914 75k multi 1.00 .50
3200 A915 90k multi 1.25 .60

Miniature Sheets

A916

Istanbul, 2010 Capital of European Culture — A917

No. 3201: a, Silhouette of Hagia Sophia, red sky. b, Sculpture. c, Artwork of main dome of Blue Mosque. d, Blue Mosque, blue sky. e, Tower on coastline, blue sky. f, Bread. g, Tram. h, Haydarpasa Station, cloudy sky.

No. 3202: a, Silhouettes of buildings, pink sky. b, Religious painting. c, Fishermen. d, Man in boat, Bosporus Bridge. e, Ship. f, Birds over Bosporus. g, Topkapi Palace. h, Silhouettes of Hagia Sophia and Blue Mosque, orange red sky.

2010, Jan. 7 ***Perf. 13x13x¼***
3201 A916 75k Sheet of 8, #a-h 8.00 4.00

Perf. 13¼x13
3202 A917 90k Sheet of 8, #a-h 8.00 4.00

2010 Winter Olympics, Vancouver — A918

Designs: 25k, Slalom skier. 75k, Snowboarder. No. 3205, 90k, Cross-country skier. No. 3206, 90k, Speed skater.

2010, Feb. 12 ***Perf. 13¼***
3203-3206 A918 Set of 4 3.75 1.90

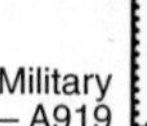

Military Aircraft — A919

Designs: 75k, F-4. 90k, F-16. 1 l, CN-235.

2010, Mar. 18 *Perf. 13x13¼*
3207-3209 A919 Set of 3 3.50 1.75

Early Bronse Age Items A920

Designs: 75k, Twinned figures. 90k, Ceremonial symbol. No. 3212, 1 l, Necklace. No. 3213, 1 l, Sculpture of nursing woman, vert.

Perf. 13¼x13½, 13½x13¼
2010, Mar. 31
3210-3213 A920 Set of 4 5.00 2.50

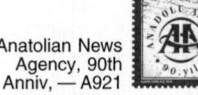

Anatolian News Agency, 90th Anniv, — A921

2010, Apr. 6 *Perf. 13¼x13*
3214 A921 75k multi 1.00 .50

A922

National Assembly, 90th Anniv. — A923

2010, Apr. 23 *Perf. 13x13¼*
3215 A922 75k multi 1.00 .50
3216 A923 90k multi 1.25 .60

Sile Lighthouse, 150th Anniv. — A924

2010, May 1
3217 A924 75k multi 1.00 .50

Labor Day — A925

Designs: No. 3218, 80k, Dove with olive branch. No. 3219, 80k, Hands holding globe. No. 3220, 110k, Dove with banner. No. 3221, 110k, Worker.

2010, May 1 *Perf. 13x12¾*
3218-3221 A925 Set of 4 5.00 2.50

Yunus Emre (c. 1240-c. 1321), Poet — A926

Emre and: 75k, Tomb, Eskisehir. 90k, Poem, vert.

2010, May 3 *Perf. 13¼x13, 13x13¼*
3222-3223 A926 Set of 2 2.10 1.10

Europe Day — A927

2010, May 9 *Perf. 12¾x13*
3224 A927 75k multi .95 .45

Europa — A928

Children's stories: 80k, Balik Cobani (The Fish and the Shepherd). 110k, Book of Dede Korkut.

2010, May 9 *Perf. 13¼x13*
3225-3226 A928 Set of 2 2.40 1.25

RASAT Observational Satellite — A929

2010, May 17 *Perf. 13x13¼*
3227 A929 75k multi .95 .45

Miniature Sheet

World Environment Day — A930

No. 3228 — Flowers: a, Crocus stevenii. b, Crocus mathewii. c, Astragalus lineatus. d, Erica bocquetii.

2010, June 5
3228 A930 110k Sheet of 4, #a-d 5.75 3.00

Sultan's Boats A931

Boats from Istanbul Sea Museum: 80k, Boat with red orange and white hull. 110k, Boat with white and gold hull with bird figurehead.

2010, June 14 *Perf. 13x13¼*
3229-3230 A931 Set of 2 2.50 1.25

Kemal Atatürk — A932

Various portraits.

Perf. 13½ Syncopated
2010, June 24
3231 A932 25k multi .35 .25
3232 A932 80k multi 1.10 .55
3233 A932 110k multi 1.40 .70
3234 A932 355k multi 4.50 2.25
Nos. 3231-3234 (4) 7.35 3.75

2010 World Men's Basketball Championships, Turkey
A933 A934

2010, Aug. 28 *Perf. 13x12¾*
Background Color
3235 A933 80k blue 1.10 .55
3236 A934 80k brown 1.10 .55
3237 A933 110k yellow brown 1.50 .75
3238 A934 110k red 1.50 .75
Nos. 3235-3238 (4) 5.20 2.60

Miniature Sheet

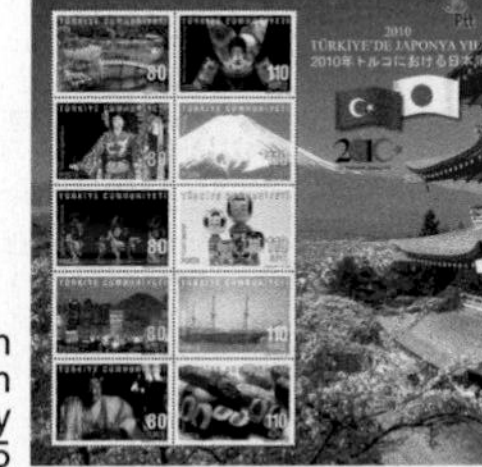

Japan Year in Turkey A935

No. 3239: a, 80k, Bridge in Ritsurin Garden, Takamatsu, Japan. b, 80k, Traditional Japanese dancer. c, 80k, Japanese dancers with drums. d, 80k, Tokyo skyline. e, 80k, Noh theater. f, 110k, Samurai headgear. g, 110k, Mt. Fuji. h, 110k, Kokeshi dolls. i, 110k, Turkish frigate Ertugrul. j, 110k, Sushi.

2010, Sept. 2 *Perf. 13x13¼*
3239 A935 Sheet of 10, #a-j 13.00 6.50

Souvenir Sheet

Religious Buildings in Spain and Turkey A936

No. 3240: a, 80k, Santa María de la Mayor Collegiate Church, Toro, Spain. b, 110k, Ortaköy Mosque, Istanbul.

2010, Oct. 18 *Perf. 12¾x13*
3240 A936 Sheet of 2, #a-b 2.75 1.40

See Spain No. 3755.

Miniature Sheet

11th Economic Cooperation Orgaization Summit, Istanbul — A937

No. 3241 — Emblem with background color of: a, 90k, Blue. b, 100k, Lilac. c, 130k, Rose. d, 150k, Green

2010, Dec. 20 *Perf. 13x12¾*
3241 A937 Sheet of 4, #a-d 6.25 3.00

Miniature Sheet

2011 Winter Universiade, Erzurum — A938

No. 3242 — Emblems and: a, 90k, Twin Minaret Madrasa, Erzurum. b, 90k, Ice hockey player. c, 1.30 l, Mascot. d, 1.30 l, Ski jumper.

2011, Jan. 27 *Perf. 13¼x13*
3242 A938 Sheet of 4, #a-d 5.75 2.75

A sheet of four imperforate 1.30 l stamps sold for 30 l.

Lilies — A939

Various lilies.

2011, Feb. 4 *Perf. 13¾*
3243 A939 25k multi .35 .25
3244 A939 1 l multi 1.25 .65
3245 A939 3.65 l multi 4.75 2.40
3246 A939 6 l multi 7.75 3.75
Nos. 3243-3246 (4) 14.10 7.05

Values are for stamps with surrounding selvage.

Souvenir Sheet

Treaty of Moscow, 90th Anniv. A940

No. 3247: a, Turkish flag, building. b, Treaty negotiators.

2011, Feb. 4 *Perf. 13¼x13*
3247 A940 90k Sheet of 2, #a-b 2.40 1.25

Evliya Celebi (1611-82), Travel Writer A941

Map and: 90k, Celebi writing, silhouette of Celebi on horse. 1.30 l, Celebi on horse.

2011, Mar. 25 *Perf. 13x13¼*
3248-3249 A941 Set of 2 3.00 1.50

Fish — A942

Designs: No. 3250, 1.30 l, Trigla lucerna. No. 3251, 1.30 l, Diplodus vulgaris. No. 3252, 1.30 l, Xiphias gladius.

2011, Apr. 28 *Perf. 13¼x13*
3250-3252 A942 Set of 3 5.25 2.60

Organization for Economic Cooperation and Development, 50th Anniv. — A943

2011, May 5 *Perf. 13x13¼*
3253 A943 1.30 l multi 1.75 .85

Europa — A944

Forest and: 90k, Woodpecker. 1.30 l, Deer.

2011, May 9 *Perf. 13¼x13*
3254-3255 A944 Set of 2 2.75 1.40

Intl. Year of Forests.

Week of the Disabled — A945

Week of the Disabled emblem, stylized person in wheelchair, Turkish text, and: 90k, Stylized person walking. 1.30 l, Hand with blackboard eraser.

2011, May 10 **Litho.**
3256-3257 A945 Set of 2 2.75 1.40

Souvenir Sheet

Kemal Atatürk (1881-1938) — A946

2011, May 19 ***Perf. 13x13¼***
3258 A946 90k multi 1.25 .60

Miniature Sheet

Turkish Air Force, Cent. A947

No. 3259: a, Jet on ground, blue skies. b, Jets over bridge. c, Jet in flight. d, Jet on runway, gray skies.

2011, June 1 ***Perf. 13¼x13***
3259 A947 1.30 l Sheet of 4 #a-d 6.75 3.50

A sheet of four imperforate 1.30 l vertical stamps depicting jets in flight sold for 30 l.

Miniature Sheet

World Environment Day — A948

No. 3260: a, 25k, Anas acuta. b, 90k, Streptopelia turtur. c, 1.30 l, Phasianus colchicus. d, 1.30 l, Alectoris chukar.

2011, June 5 ***Perf. 13¾***
3260 A948 Sheet of 4, #a-d 4.75 2.40

Korean War, 60th Anniv. — A949

2011, June 25 ***Perf. 13¼x13***
3261 A949 1.30 l multi 1.60 .80

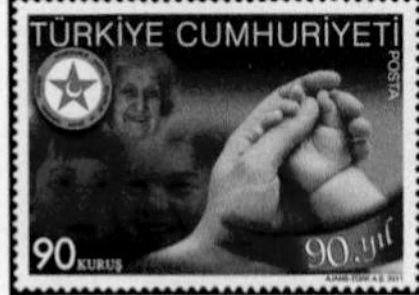

Social Services and Child Protection Agency, 90th Anniv. A950

2011, June 30 ***Perf. 13x13¼***
3262 A950 90k multi 1.10 .55

Miniature Sheet

Kirkpinar Oil Wrestling Festival, 650th Anniv. A951

No. 3263: a, 90k, Two wrestlers, both heads visible. b, 90k, Two wrestlers, heads not visible. c, 1.30 l, Two wrestlers. d, 1.30 l, Two wrestlers and referee.

2011, July 8 ***Perf. 13¼x13***
3263 A951 Sheet of 4, #a-d 5.50 2.75

Miniature Sheet

Tourist Attractions of Van — A952

No. 3264: a, 25k, Van Castle. b, 90k, Hüsrev Pasha Mosque. c, 1.30 l, Bridge and fish. d, 1.30 l, Akdamar Church, Van cat.

2011, July 12 ***Perf. 13x13¼***
3264 A952 Sheet of 4, #a-d 4.25 2.10

A953

Festival mascot and: 25k, Festival emblem. 90k, Festival emblem, diff. No. 3267, 1.30 l, Festival flag and balloons. No. 3268, 1.30 l, Festival emblem, vert.

2011, July 23 ***Perf. 13¼x13, 13x13¼***
3265-3268 A953 Set of 4 4.25 2.10

2011 European Youth Summer Olympic Festival, Trabzon.

Yildiz Technical University, Cent. — A954

Centenary emblem and: 90k, University building. 1.30 l, Star, University building.

2011, Aug. 22 ***Perf. 13¼x13***
3269-3270 A954 Set of 2 2.50 1.25

Fruit — A955

Designs: 10k, Pyracantha coccinea. 1 l, Prunus persica. 1.30 l, Prunus avium. 3.65 l, Rubus fruticosus.

Perf. 13½ Syncopated

2011, Aug. 26

3271	A955	10k multi	.25	.25
3272	A955	1 l multi	1.10	.55
3273	A955	1.30 l multi	1.50	.75
3274	A955	3.65 l multi	4.25	2.10
		Nos. 3271-3274 (4)	7.10	3.65

39th Mechanized Infantry Brigade — A956

Designs: 50k, Turkish flag and soldiers carrying flag. 90k, Turkish flag and soldiers. 1.30 l, Soldiers on ship, horiz.

2011, Oct. 6 **Litho.**
3275-3277 A956 Set of 3 3.00 1.50

Sultan's Boats A957

Designs: 90k, Boat with pointed tip. 1.30 l, Boat with white hull and eagle figurehead.

2011, Nov. 28 ***Perf. 13x13¼***
3278-3279 A957 Set of 2 2.40 1.25

Photographs of Turkish People and Agriculture — A958

Designs: No. 3280, 50k, Woman and string of pepers. No. 3281, 50k, Workers in field of protected plants. No. 3282, 1 l, Boy swimming in water with livestock, horiz. No. 3283, 1 l, Farm worker in field of plants under protective tents, horiz.

2011, Dec. 28 ***Perf. 13x13¼, 13¼x13***
3280-3283 A958 Set of 4 3.25 1.60

Istanbul, 2012 European Capital of Sports — A959

Emblem, Istanbul landmarks and: 50k, Runners, wheelchair racer. No. 3285, 1 l, Sailing. No. 3286, 1 l, Tennis. 2 l, Cycling.

Perf. 13¾ Syncopated

2012, Feb. 15
3284-3287 A959 Set of 4 5.25 2.60

Stylized Man and Woman Holding Up Globe — A960

Woman and Flower — A961

2012, Mar. 8 ***Perf. 13½***

3288	A960	10k multi + label	.25	.25
3289	A961	1 l multi + label	1.10	.55
3290	A960	2 l multi + label	2.25	1.10
		Nos. 3288-3290 (3)	3.60	1.90

Equality of opportunities for men and women.

Miniature Sheet

2012 World Track and Field Championships, Istanbul — A962

No. 3291 — Bridge and: a, 50k, Female hurdler. b, 1 l, Female long jumper. c, 1 l, Male high jumper. d, 2 l, Male hurdler.

2012, Mar. 9 ***Perf. 13¾***
3291 A962 Sheet of 4, #a-d 5.00 2.50

National History Society Building, Cent. A963

Perf. 13¾ Syncopated

2012, Mar. 25
3292 A963 1 l multi 1.10 .55

Pertevniyal High School, 140th Anniv. A964

2012, Apr. 6
3293 A964 1 l multi 1.10 .55

Souvenir Sheet

Morality and Rights — A965

No. 3294: a, Hands and emblem. b, Rose, Arabic inscription.

2012, Apr. 14 ***Perf. 14 Syncopated***
3294 A965 1 l Sheet of 2, #a-b 2.25 1.10

Constitutional Court, 50th Anniv. — A966

Designs: 1 l, 50th anniversary emblem. 2 l, Court and 50th anniversary emblem.

2012, Apr. 25 ***Perf. 13¾ Syncopated***
3295-3296 A966 Set of 2 3.50 1.75

Tourism — A967

Hands and: No. 3297, 2 l, Aspendos (Amphitheater), Antalya. No. 3298, 2 l, Yat Limani (Harbor), Antalya. No. 3299, 2 l, Kiz Kulesi (Leander's Tower), Istanbul. No. 3300, 2 l, Ortaköy, Istanbul. No. 3301, 2 l, Efes (Ephesus), Izmir. No. 3302, 2 l, Saat Kulesi (Clock tower), Izmir. No. 3303, 2 l, Göreme, Nevsehir. No. 3304, 2 l, Zelve Monastery and balloon, Nevsehir.

2012, Apr. 30 ***Perf. 14 Syncopated***
3297-3304 A967 Set of 8 18.50 9.25

Europa — A968

Designs: No. 3305, 2 l, Skier and parachute skier. No. 3306, 2 l, Whirling dervishes, sea turtle, tourist attractions.

2012, May 9 ***Perf. 13¾ Syncopated***
3305-3306 A968 Set of 2 4.50 2.25

Union of Chambers and Commodity Excahnges of Turkey, 60th Anniv. — A969

2012, May 17
3307 A969 1 l multi 1.10 .55

Treasury and Audit Department, 150th Anniv. A970

Designs: 1 l, Building and 150th anniversary emblem. 2 l, 150th anniversary emblem.

2012, May 29
3308-3309 A970 Set of 2 3.25 1.60

Miniature Sheet

10th Turkish Olympics A971

No. 3310: a, 50k, "10 Yasinda." b, 1 l, Globe tethered to map of Turkey with crescent and star. c, 1 l, Flags of various nations around flag of Turkey in oval. d, 2 l, Stylized faces of people of various cultures.

2012, May 30 ***Perf. 13***
3310 A971 Sheet of 4, #a-d 5.00 2.50

Miniature Sheet

World Environment Day — A980

No. 3312 — Dinosaurs: a, 50k, Carnotaurus. b, 1 l, Pteranodon. c, 1 l, Tyrannosaurus rex. d, 2 l, Triceratops.

2012, June 5 Litho. ***Perf. 13¼x13***
3312 A980 Sheet of 4, #a-d 5.00 2.50

A 46x46mm 3-dimensional 2 l stamp was sold only with a booklet to which the stamp was not attached.

Intl. Year of Cooperatives A981

Designs: 1 l, Ants carrying Earth. 2 l, Stylized people carrying Turkey.

2012, June 6
3313-3314 A981 Set of 2 3.25 1.60

Istanbul Shopping Festival A982

Designs: 1 l, Istanbul skyline, woman in red dress. 2 l, Folding fan.

2012, June 9 ***Perf. 13¾ Syncopated***
3315-3316 A982 Set of 2 3.50 1.75

Miniature Sheet

2012 Summer Olympics, London — A983

No. 3317: a, 50k, Volleyball, London Eye. b, 1 l, Hurdles, Tower Bridge. c, 1 l, Wrestling, Regent Street buildings. d, 2 l, Basketball, Buckingham Palace.

2012, July 27 ***Perf. 13½x14***
3317 A983 Sheet of 4, #a-d 5.00 2.50

Souvenir Sheet

European Kick Boxing Championships, Ankara — A984

No. 3318 — Kick boxers and map of: a, Western Europe. b, Central and Eastern Europe.

2012, Oct. 27 ***Perf. 13¼x13½***
3318 A984 1 l Sheet of 2, #a-b 2.25 1.10

Souvenir Sheet

Bridges A985

No. 3319: a, Bosporus Bridge, Istanbul. b, Yangtze River Bridge, Taizhou, People's Republic of China.

2012, Nov. 26 ***Perf. 14x13½***
3319 A985 1 l Sheet of 2, #a-b 2.25 1.10

See People's Republic of China Nos. 4056-4057.

Souvenir Sheet

Cultural Heritage of Kütahya A986

No. 3320: a, 1 l, Shaft of light on altar. b, 2 l, Temple of Zeus.

2012, Nov. 29 ***Perf. 13¼***
3320 A986 Sheet of 2, #a-b 3.50 1.75

Photographs of Everyday Life — A987

Designs: No. 3321, 50k, Fishermen tending nets. No. 3322, 50k, Hands of goat herder and goat. No. 3323, 1 l, Fisherman casting net. No. 3324, 1 l, Sheep grazing in field. No. 3325, 2 l, Woman with harvesting basket. No. 3326, 2 l, Horses in corral.

2012, Dec. 26 ***Perf. 13½x14***
3321-3326 A987 Set of 6 8.00 4.00

A988

Black line and: 20k Flowers. 1.10 l, Tulips. 2.20 l, Flowers, diff. 3.85 l, Decorative circles. 8 l, Flowers, diff.

2013, Jan. 7 ***Perf. 13x12½***
3327 A988 20k multi .25 .25
3328 A988 1.10 l multi 1.25 .65
3329 A988 2.20 l multi 2.50 1.25
3330 A988 3.85 l multi 4.50 2.25
3331 A988 8 l multi 9.25 4.50
Nos. 3327-3331 (5) 17.75 8.90

Miniature Sheet

Turkish Postage Stamps, 150th Anniv. A989

No. 3332: a, Emblem of Turkish PTT. b, Leaves, star and crescent. c, Tughra of Sultan Abdul-Aziz. d, Stamp inscribed "150 Yil."

Litho. & Embossed With Foil Application

2013, Jan. 14 ***Perf. 14¼***
3332 A989 1.10 l Sheet of 4, #a-d, + label 5.00 2.50

Souvenir Sheet

Yildiz Palace, Istanbul A990

No. 3333: a, Palace and fountain. b, Palace, photograph and tughra of Sultan Abdul Hamid II.

2013, Feb. 27 ***Perf. 13½x13¼***
3333 A990 1.10 l Sheet of 2, #a-b 2.50 1.25

Miniature Sheet

Eskisehir, 2013 UNESCO Intangible Culture Capital — A991

No. 3334: a, 1.10 l, Train. b, 1.10 l, Meerschaum pipe, spa pool. c, 2.20 l, Porsuk River. d, 2.20 l, Houses in Odupazari District.

2013, Mar. 21 Litho. ***Perf. 13¾x14***
3334 A991 Sheet of 4, #a-d 7.50 3.75

Souvenir Sheet

World Down Syndrome Day — A992

No. 3335 — Face of child with Down Syndrome and: a, 50k, Chromosomes, strand of DNA, heart (40x30mm). b, 1.10 l, Heart (40x30mm). c, 2.20 l, Children in field of flowers, hearts (80x30mm).

Perf. 13½x13¼

2013, Mar. 21 **Litho.**
3335 A992 Sheet of 3, #a-c 4.25 2.10

Souvenir Sheet

Expo 2020, Izmir A993

No. 3336: a, 1.10 l, Izmir tourist attractions, emblem of Expo 2020. b, 1.10 l, Man and woman jogging on waterside path. c, 2.20 l, Emblem of Expo 2020.

2013, Apr. 4 Litho. ***Perf. 13½***
3336 A993 Sheet of 3, #a-c 5.00 2.50

Tourist Attractions in Antalya — A994

Designs: No. 3337, 2.20 l, Alanya Kalesi (Alanya Castle). No. 3338, 2.20 l, Apollon Tapinagi (Temple of Apollo), Side. No. 3339, 2.20 l, Hadrian Kapisi (Hadrian's Gate). No. 3340, 2.20 l, Kaleiçi (historic city center). No. 3341, 2.20 l, Manavgat Selalesi (Manavgat Waterfalls). No. 3342, 2.20 l, Saat Kulesi ve Yivli Minare (Clock Tower and Yivli Minaret).

Perf. 13¾ Syncopated

2013, Apr. 12 **Litho.**
3337-3342 A994 Set of 6 15.00 7.50

Miniature Sheet

Piri Reis Map, 500th Anniv. A995

No. 3343 — Part of map with: a, 1.10 l, Ship and compass rose. b, 1.10 l, Ship, birds, monkeys. c, 2.20 l, Ships and compass rose. d, 2.20 l, Text and Piri Reis (c.1464-1553).

2013, Apr. 18 Litho. ***Perf. 13½***
3343 A995 Sheet of 4, #a-d, + label 7.50 3.75

Europa A996

Designs: 1.10 l, Mailbox, envelope, postal vans and motorcycle. 2.20 l, Postrider, sealed scroll, horse-drawn carrialge, postal trucks, mailbox.

2013, May 9 Litho. ***Perf. 13½x13¼***
3344-3345 A996 Set of 2 3.50 1.75

Miniature Sheet

Istanbul Technical University, 240th Anniv. — A997

No. 3346: a, Building with eight short pillars. b, Doors and windows. c, Building without pillars. d, Building with four tall pillars.

2013, May 24 Litho. ***Perf. 13¾x14***
3346 A997 1.10 l Sheet of 4, #a-d 4.75 2.40

Miniature Sheet

World Environment Day — A998

No. 3347: a, Head and neck with water and dry earth. b, House, stylized globe, flower and trees. c, Farm, tractor, polar bears, map of Northern Africa. d, Family, foxes, rabbit, seal.

2013, June 5 Litho. ***Perf. 14x13¾***
3347 A998 1.10 l Sheet of 4, #a-d 4.75 2.40

Miniature Sheet

17th Mediterranean Games, Mersin — A999

No. 3348: a, Shell, track and field athletes, boxer. b, Boxer, weight lifter, yacht. c, Yacht, archer, gymnast. d, Volleyball player, cyclist.

2013, June 10 Litho. ***Perf. 14x13¾***
3348 A999 1.10 l Sheet of 4, #a-d 4.75 2.40

A 5 l self-adhesive three-dimensional plastic stamp depicting turtles and the turtle mascot of the Mediterranean Games was produced in a limited quantity and sold only in a folder that also contained No. 3348 and a first day cover of No. 3348.

Public Administration Institute for Turkey and the Middle East, 60th Anniv. — A1000

Perf. 13¾ Syncopated

2013, June 28 Litho.
3349 A1000 1.10 l multi 1.10 .55

Expo 2016, Antalya — A1001

Designs: No. 3350, 2.20 l, Children, flowers, Yivli Minaret. No. 3351, 2.20 l, Emblem of Expo 2016.

Perf. 13¾ Syncopated

2013, July 25 Litho.
3350-3351 A1001 Set of 2 4.75 2.40

Miniature Sheet

Cuisine of Central Anatolia A1002

No. 3352: a, Tomato, bread, meat dish, bowl of vegetables and sauce. b, Wheat stalk, three plates of food. c, Scallions, radishes, food in clay pots, rolls. d, Grapes, two plates of food.

2013, Aug. 16 Litho. ***Perf. 14x13¾***
3352 A1002 1.10 l Sheet of 4, #a-d 4.50 2.25

Calligraphy — A1003

Various depictions of Arabic "w."

Perf. 13¾ Syncopated

2013, Aug. 27 Litho.

3353	A1003	10k lilac & blk	.25	.25
3354	A1003	1 l gray & blk	1.00	.50
3355	A1003	1.10 l blue & blk	1.10	.55
3356	A1003	8 l multi	8.00	4.00
		Nos. 3353-3356 (4)	10.35	5.30

Council of State Building — A1004

Council of State 145th Anniv. Emblem — A1005

2013, Sept. 2 Litho. ***Perf. 13¾x14***
3357 A1004 1.10 l multi 1.10 .55
3358 A1005 1.10 l multi 1.10 .55

11th Transportation, Maritime Affairs and Communication Forum, Istanbul — A1006

Forum emblem and: No. 3359, 1.10 l, Satellite above Earth. No. 3360, 1.10 l, Airplane over new Istanbul Airport. No. 3361, 2.20 l, Train, Marmaray Tunnel, map of Istanbul. No. 3362, 2.20 l, Yavuz Sultan Selim Bridge, Istanbul.

2013, Sept. 5 Litho. ***Perf. 13¾***
3359-3362 A1006 Set of 4 6.50 3.25

A sheet of four 1.10 l stamps depicting parts of the Izmit Bay Bridge was only offered in a presentation folder that sold for 30 l.

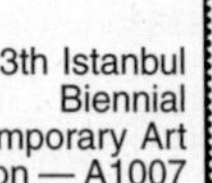

13th Istanbul Biennial Contemporary Art Exhibition — A1007

2013, Sept. 14 Litho. ***Perf. 13¾***
3363 A1007 1.10 l black 1.10 .55

Turkish Language Festival — A1008

2013, Sept. 26 Litho. ***Perf. 13¾***
3364 A1008 1.10 l multi 1.10 .55

Souvenir Sheet

King Carol I Mosque, Constanta, Romania — A1009

2013, Oct. 10 Litho. ***Perf. 13½***
3365 A1009 3.85 l multi 4.00 2.00

Diplomatic relations between Turkey and Romania, 135th anniv. See Romania No. 5492.

Turkish Postage Stamp Museum — A1010

Designs: 1.10 l, Turkey #3094-3095. 2.20 l, Museum displays.

2013, Oct. 22 Litho. ***Perf. 13¾***
3366-3367 A1010 Set of 2 3.25 1.60

Values for Nos. 3366-3367 are for stamps with surrounding selvage. A 8 l souvenir sheet depicting postal workers, buildings and equipment was only offered in a presentation folder that sold for 30 l.

Souvenir Sheet

Republic of Turkey, 90th Anniv. A1011

No. 3368 — Bridge and; a, Tank, military jet and helicopter, map of Europe. b, Satellite, train, Kemal Ataturk.

2013, Oct. 29 Litho. ***Perf. 13¼***
3368 A1011 1.10 l Sheet of 2, #a-b 2.25 1.10

Souvenir Sheet

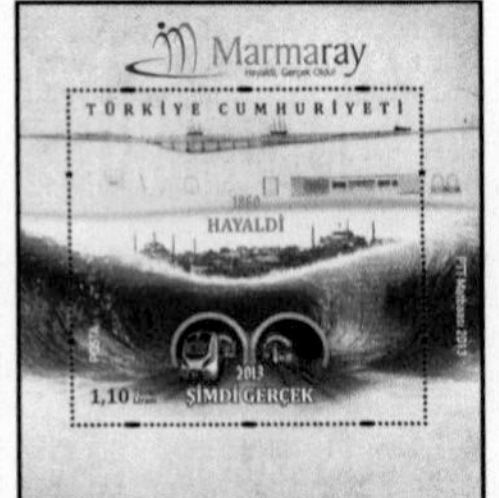

Completion of Marmaray Tunnel Project — A1012

Perf. 13¾ Syncopated

2013, Oct. 29 Litho.
3369 A1012 1.10 l multi 1.10 .55

No. 3369 exists imperforate in a limited printing.

Fifth Izmir Economic Congress A1013

2013, Oct. 30 Litho. ***Perf. 13¾x14***
3370 A1013 1.10 l multi 1.10 .55

Souvenir Sheet

Mosques A1014

No. 3371: a, 1.10 l, Sultan Ahmed Mosque, Istanbul. b, 2.20 l, Al-Aqsa Mosque, Jerusalem.

Perf. 13½x13¾

2013, Dec. 12 Litho.
3371 A1014 Sheet of 2, #a-b 3.25 1.60

See Palestinian Authority No. 245.

University of Ankara Faculty of Dentistry, 50th Anniv. A1015

2013, Dec. 14 Litho. ***Perf. 13½***
3372 A1015 1.10 l multi 1.00 .50

Yasar Dogu (1913-61), Wrestler — A1016

Perf. 13¾ Syncopated

2013, Dec. 23 Litho.
3373 A1016 50k multi .45 .25

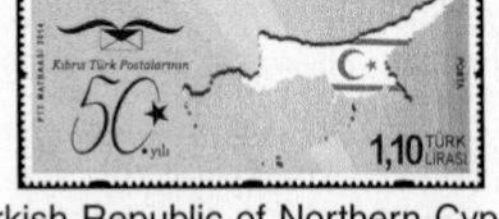

Turkish Republic of Northern Cyprus Postal Service, 50th Anniv. A1017

Perf. 14x13¾ Syncopated

2014, Jan. 6 Litho.
3374 A1017 1.10 l multi 1.00 .50

Altay Sports Club, Cent. — A1018

Designs: No. 3375, 1.10 l, Basketball. No. 3376, 1.10 l, Soccer. No. 3377, 2.20 l, Swimming. No. 3378, 2.20 l, Handball.

2014, Jan. 16 Litho. ***Perf. 13¾***
3375-3378 A1018 Set of 4 6.00 3.00

Values are for stamps with surrounding selvage.

2014 Winter Olympics, Sochi, Russia — A1019

Designs: No. 3379, 1.10 l, Ski jumping. No. 3380, 1.10 l, Pairs figure skating. No. 3381,

2.20 l, Alpine skiing. No. 3382, 2.20 l, Speed skating.

2014, Feb. 7 **Litho.** ***Perf. 13¾***
3379-3382 A1019 Set of 4 6.00 3.00

Turkish Radio and Television, 50th Anniv. — A1020

50th anniv. emblem and: 1.10 l, Text. 2.20 l, Building.

2014, Feb. 20 **Litho.** ***Perf. 13¾***
3383-3384 A1020 Set of 2 3.00 1.50

Souvenir Sheet

Topkapi Palace A1021

No. 3385: a, Tower of Justice and Gate of Salutation, b, Palace interior, Sultan Mehmed II (1432-81) and his monogram.

Litho. With Foil Application
2014, Feb. 27 ***Perf. 13½x13¼***
3385 A1021 1.10 l Sheet of 2, #a-b 2.00 1.00

Miniature Sheet

First Deaths of Turkish Military Aviators, Cent. A1022

No. 3386: a, 50k, Lieutenant Selim Saiq Bey and Captain Mehmet Fethi Bey. b, 1.10 l, Fethi Bey and airplane. c, 1.10 l, Memorial, Haon, Israel. d, 2.20 l, Building and Fethi Bey Monument, Istanbul.

Perf. 13½x13¼
2014, Feb. 27 **Litho.**
3386 A1022 Sheet of 4, #a-d 4.50 2.25

General Directorate of Hydraulic Works, 60th Anniv. — A1023

2014, Mar. 22 **Litho.** ***Perf. 13¾***
3387 A1023 1.10 l multi + label 1.10 .55

Souvenir Sheet

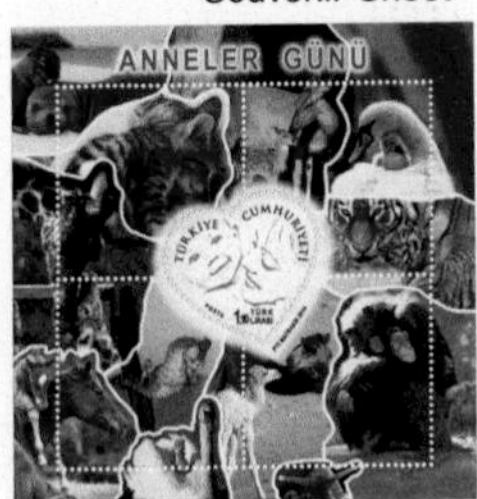
Mother's Day A1024

2014, Apr. 17 **Litho.** ***Perf.***
3388 A1024 1.10 l multi + 4 labels 1.10 .55

Tour of Turkey Bicycle Race, 50th Anniv. A1025

2014, Apr. 27 **Litho.** ***Perf. 13½x13¼***
3389 A1025 1.10 l multi 1.10 .55

A folder containing No. 3389, a first day cover of No. 3389, and a souvenir sheet containing a 2.20 l stamp was produced in limited quantities.

Europa A1026

Musical instruments: 1.25 l, Kabak kemane. 2.50 l, Ud.

2014, May 9 **Litho.** ***Perf. 13½x13¼***
3390-3391 A1026 Set of 2 3.75 1.90

Tourist Attractions — A1027

Attractions in: No. 3392, Erzurum Province. No. 3393, Sanliurfa Province. No. 3394, Izmir Province. No. 3395, Konya Province. No. 3396, Antalya Province. No. 3397, Istanbul Province. 4 l, Trabzon Province. 9 l, Ankara Province.

Perf. 13¾ Syncopated
2014, May 22 **Litho.**

3392	A1027	35k multi	.35	.25
3393	A1027	35k multi	.35	.25
3394	A1027	1.25 l multi	1.25	.60
3395	A1027	1.25 l multi	1.25	.60
3396	A1027	2.50 l multi	2.40	1.25
3397	A1027	2.50 l multi	2.40	1.25
3398	A1027	4 l multi	3.75	1.90
3399	A1027	9 l multi	8.50	4.25
		Nos. 3392-3399 (8)	20.25	10.35

Souvenir Sheet

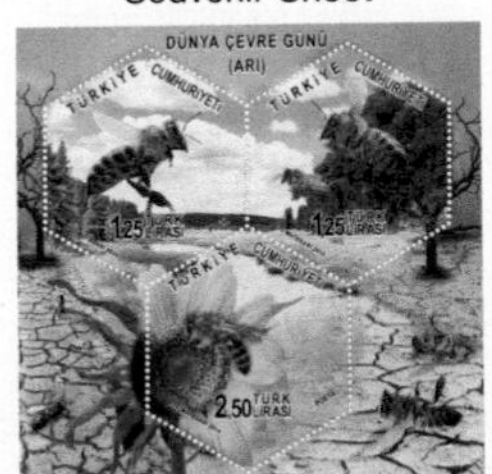
World Environment Day — A1028

No. 3400: a, 1.25 l, Bee in flight. b, 1.25 l, Two bees in flight. c, 2.50 l, Bee on flower.

2014, June 5 **Litho.** ***Perf. 13½***
3400 A1028 Sheet of 3, #a-c 4.75 2.40

Turkish Gendarmerie, 175th Anniv. — A1030

Perf. 13½x13¼
2014, June 14 **Litho.**
3405 A1030 1.25 l multi 1.25 .60

Souvenir Sheet

Deer and Mushrooms in National Park — A1031

2014, July 9 **Litho.** ***Perf. 13¼***
3406 A1031 2.50 l multi 2.40 1.25

2014 World Cup Soccer Championships, Brazil — A1032

Designs: 1.25 l, World Cup trophy. 2.50 l, Mascot of 2014 World Cup, horiz.

Perf. 14x13¾, 13¾x14
2014, Aug. 6 **Litho.**
3407-3408 A1032 Set of 2 3.50 1.75

Miniature Sheet

Local Cuisine A1033

No. 3409: a, 1.25 l, Agzi açik (lamb pies), Sanliurfa Province. b, 1.25 l, Sihilmahsi (stuffed zucchini), Kilis Province. c, 2.50 l, Sogan kebabi (stuffed onions), Mardin Province. d, 2.50 l, Saçma tavasi (stew), Gaziantep Province.

2014, Aug. 15 **Litho.** ***Perf. 14x13¾***
3409 A1033 Sheet of 4, #a-d 7.00 3.50

Ottoman Navy Galleon Mahmudiya — A1034

Various depictions of the Mahmudiya, 1.25 l, 2.50 l.

Litho. With Foil Application
Perf. 13¾ Syncopated
2014, Sept. 10
3410-3411 A1034 Set of 2 3.50 1.75

2014 Women's World Basketball Championships, Istanbul and Ankara — A1035

Design: 1.25 l, Emblem. 2.50 l, Emblem and stylized basketball (38x38mm).

Perf. 13¼x13½, 13¼
2014, Sept. 29 **Litho.**
3412-3413 A1035 Set of 2 3.50 1.75

Souvenir Sheet

Presidential Palace, Ankara — A1036

Litho., Sheet Margin Litho & Embossed With Foil Application
2014, Oct. 29 ***Perf. 13½x13¼***
3414 A1036 1.25 l multi 1.10 .55

Republic of Turkey, 91st anniv. A limited edition packet contained three imperforate souvenir sheets showing different images of the Presidential Palace, with denominations of 1.25 l, 2.50 l, and 4 l, along with first day covers of these items.

Turkish Cinema, Cent. A1037

Perf. 13½x13¼
2014, Nov. 14 **Litho.**
3415 A1037 1.25 l multi 1.10 .55

A souvenir sheet of 3 containing two 1.25 l and one 2.50 l stamp was produced in limited quantities and sold for 12.50 l.

Souvenir Sheet

Diplomatic Relations Between Turkey and Poland, 600th Anniv. — A1038

Perf. 13½x13¼
2014, Nov. 28 **Litho.**
3416 A1038 4 l multi 3.75 1.90

See Poland No. 4155.

Safranbolu Tourist Attractions A1039

Antalya Tourist Attractions A1040

Antalya Tourist Attractions A1041

Izmir Tourist Attractions A1042

Izmir Tourist Attractions A1043

Izmir Tourist Attractions A1044

Perf. 13¾ Syncopated
2014-15 **Litho.**

3417	A1039	50k multi	.40	.25
3418	A1040	2.50 l multi	2.10	1.10
3419	A1041	2.50 l multi	2.00	1.00
3420	A1042	2.50 l multi	2.00	1.00
3421	A1043	2.50 l multi	2.00	1.00
3422	A1044	2.50 l multi	2.00	1.00
		Nos. 3417-3422 (6)	10.50	5.35

Issued: No. 3418, 12/10; others, 3/20/15.
Compare Nos. 3418-3419 with No. 3396.

Battle of Sarikamish, Cent. A1045

Perf. 13½x13¼

2014, Dec. 22 **Litho.**
3423 A1045 1.25 l multi 1.10 .55

A souvenir sheet containing one 2.50 l stamp was printed in limited quantities and sold for 12.50 l.

Campaign to Prevent Waste of Bread — A1046

2015, Jan. 19 **Litho.** ***Perf. 13x13¼***
3424 A1046 1.25 l multi + label 1.10 .55

Mosques A1047

No. 3425: a, Green Mosque, Bursa, Turkey. b, Kabood Mosque, Tabriz, Iran.

Perf. 13½x13¼

2015, Feb. 18 **Litho.**
3425 Sheet of 2 2.00 1.00
a.-b. A1047 1.25 l Either single 1.00 .50

See Iran No. 3135.

Souvenir Sheet

Dolmabahce Palace, Istanbul — A1048

No. 3426: a, Palace exterior, Gate to the Bosporus. b, Gate of the Treasury, portrait and monogram of Sultan Abdülmecid I.

Litho. With Foil Application

2015, Feb. 27 ***Perf. 13½x13¼***
3426 A1048 1.25 l Sheet of 2, #a-b 2.00 1.00

Battle of Gallipoli, Cent. — A1049

Designs: 1.10 l, Statue of soldier carrying fallen comrade, Gallipoli. 1.35 l, Soldiers, Turkish flag. 2.50 l, Battle scene.

2015, Mar. 18 **Litho.** ***Perf. 13¼***
3427-3429 A1049 Set of 3 3.75 1.90

A 2.50 l imperforate souvenir sheet and a 4 l perforated souvenir sheet were produced in limited quantities and were sold with a first day cover for 25 l.

Frigate "Ertugrul," 125th Anniv. A1050

Designs: 1.25 l, Frigate "Ertugrul." 2.50 l, Crew members.

2015, Apr. 1 **Litho.** ***Perf. 13½x13¼***
3430-3431 A1050 Set of 2 3.00 1.50

Court of Military Appeals, Cent. A1051

2015, Apr. 6 **Litho.** ***Perf. 13½x13¼***
3432 A1051 1.25 l multi 1.00 .50

Grand National Assembly, 95th Anniv. A1052

Designs: 1.25 l, Old Assembly Building. 2.50 l, Current Assembly Building, Assembly Room.

2015, Apr. 23 **Litho.** ***Perf. 13½x13¼***
3433-3434 A1052 Set of 2 2.75 1.40

Peace Summit A1053

Designs: 1.25 l, Turkish flag, soldiers, women. 2.50 l, Statue of soldier carrying fallen comrade, Gallipoli, soldiers with artillery.

Perf. 13¾ Syncopated

2015, Apr. 23 **Litho.**
3435-3436 A1053 Set of 2 2.75 1.40

A 2.50 l imperforate souvenir sheet and a 4 l perforated souvenir sheet were produced in limited quantities and were sold with a first day cover for 25 l.

Jewelry — A1054

Jewelry made from: 1.25 l, Sepiolite (lüle tasi). 2.50 l, Black amber (oltu tasi).

Litho. & Thermography

2015, Apr. 29 ***Perf. 13¼***
3437-3438 A1054 Set of 2 2.75 1.40

Europa A1055

Children and: 1.25 l, Doll in cradle. 2.50 l, Pull toy with hammers.

2015, May 9 **Litho.** ***Perf. 13½x13¼***
3439-3440 A1055 Set of 2 3.00 1.50

Miniature Sheet

Historic Areas of Istanbul UNESCO World Heritage Site — A1056

No. 3441: a, 1.25 l, Sultanahmet Mosque Archaeological Park. b, 1.25 l, Süleymaniye Quarter. c, 2.50 l, Zeyrek Quarter. d, 2.50 l, Walls of Istanbul.

2015, May 21 **Litho.** ***Perf. 14x13¾***
3441 A1056 Sheet of 4, #a-d 5.75 3.00

Miniature Sheet

World Environment Day — A1057

No. 3442 — Mushrooms: a, 1.25 l, Auricularia auricula-judae. b, 1.25 l, Coprinopsis picacea. c, 2.50 l, Morchella deliciosa. d, 2.50 l, Mucidula mucida.

Perf. 13¾ Syncopated

2015, June 5 **Litho.**
3442 A1057 Sheet of 4, #a-d 5.75 3.00

2015 Women's World Cup Soccer Championships, Canada — A1058

Designs: No. 3443, 1.25 l, Trophy. No. 3444, 1.25 l, Mascot holding soccer ball. No. 3445, 2.50 l, Mascot preparing to kick soccer ball, horiz. No. 3446, 2.50 l, Emblem, horiz.

Perf. 14x13¾, 13¾x14

2015, June 6 **Litho.**
3443-3446 A1058 Set of 4 5.75 3.00

Fire Fighting — A1059

Designs: 50k, Fire station, fire fighters battling blaze. 1 l, Fire fighters and trucks, vert. 9 l, Rescue crews, fire trucks, vert.

Perf. 13¾ Syncopated

2015, June 26 **Litho.**
3447-3449 A1059 Set of 3 7.75 4.00

Souvenir Sheet

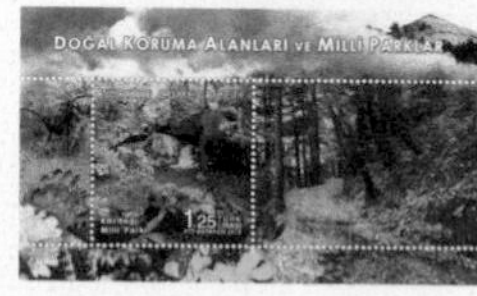

Kazdagi National Park A1060

2015, July 9 **Litho.** ***Perf. 13¼***
3450 A1060 1.25 l multi .90 .45

Tapestries — A1061

Tapestries depicing: 30k, Ducks in pond. 1.40 l, Swans and flowers. 2.80 l, Birds, nest, flowers, vert. 4.50 l, House, fence, ducks, vert. 10 l, Chickens, feeder, fence, vert.

Perf. 13¼ Syncopated

2015, Aug. 6 **Litho.**
3451-3455 A1061 Set of 5 13.00 6.50

Miniature Sheet

Turkish Cuisine A1062

No. 3456: a, 60k, Börülce. b, 60k, Sevket-i-Bostan. c, 2.80 l, Sinkonta. d, 2.80 l, Cökertme Kebabi.

2015, Aug. 17 **Litho.** ***Perf. 14x13¾***
3456 A1062 Sheet of 4, #a-d 4.75 2.40

Occupations of the Past — A1063

Designs: No. 3457, 1.40 l. Saddle maker (semerci). No. 3458, 1.40 l, Blacksmith (demirci). No. 3459, 2.80 l, Cobbler (kösker). No. 3460, 2.80 l, Street vendor (macuncu).

2015, Sept. 3 **Litho.** ***Perf. 13¼x13½***
3457-3460 A1063 Set of 4 5.75 3.00

Souvenir Sheet

Water Conservation — A1064

No. 3461: a, 60k, Dead trees, dry creek bed. b, 1.40 l, Water drop, healthy tree, c, 2.80 l, Trees, bird.

2015, Oct. 7 **Litho.** ***Perf. 14x13¾***
3461 A1064 Sheet of 3, #a-c 3.50 1.75

Turkish Posts, Telegraph and Telephone, 175th Anniv. A1065

Designs: No. 3462, 1.40 l, Postal sorting boxes and machinery. No. 3463, 1.40 l, Exteriors of post offices. No. 3464, 1.40 l, Telegraph, computer, dove. 2.80 l, Turkey #2, envelope and "@" symbol.

2015, Oct. 23 **Litho.** ***Perf. 13½x13¼***
3462-3465 A1065 Set of 4 5.00 2.50

An imperforate 2.80 l souvenir sheet was produced in limited quantities and sold with a first day cover for 25 l.

Postmen — A1066

Inscriptions at left: No. 3466, Tatar Agasi. No. 3467, Müjdecibasi. No. 3468, Peyk (sword hilt close to body). No. 3469, Peyk (sword hilt away from body). No. 3470, Posta Tatari. No. 3471, Posta Tatari (coat with red piping). No. 3472, Posta Memuru (Postaci) (wearing red fez). No. 3473, Posta Memuru (wearing cap, holding mail bag). No. 3474, Posta Dagiticisi (wearing red scarves). No. 3475, Posta Dagiticisi (man at right with yellow and black uniform).

Litho. With Foil Application
Perf. 13¾ Syncopated

2015, Oct. 23 **Booklet Panes of 1**

3466 A1066 60k multi .60 .60
3467 A1066 60k multi .60 .60
3468 A1066 1.40 l multi 1.40 1.40
3469 A1066 1.40 l multi 1.40 1.40
3470 A1066 1.40 l multi 1.40 1.40
3471 A1066 1.40 l multi 1.40 1.40
3472 A1066 2.80 l multi 2.75 2.75
3473 A1066 2.80 l multi 2.75 2.75
3474 A1066 2.80 l multi 2.75 2.75
3475 A1066 2.80 l multi 2.75 2.75
Complete booklet, #3466-3475 18.00
Nos. 3466-3475 (10) 17.80 17.80

Complete booklet sold for 25 l.

Souvenir Sheet

Republic of Turkey, 92nd Anniv. A1067

Perf. 13¾ Syncopated

2015, Oct. 29 **Litho.**
3476 A1067 1.40 l multi 1.00 .50

G20 Summit, Antalya — A1068

2015, Nov. 15 **Litho.** ***Perf. 13¼***
3477 A1068 2.80 l multi 2.00 1.00

Dr. Aziz Sancar, 2015 Nobel Chemistry Laureate A1069

Perf. 13½x13¼

2015, Dec. 10 **Litho.**
3478 A1069 2.80 l multi 1.90 .95

Souvenir Sheet

Haliç Shipyards — A1070

No. 3479: a, 1.40 l, Buildings, boats and crane. b, 1.40 l, Buildings and boats. c, 2.80 l, Buildings, ships and boats

Perf. 13¾ Syncopated

2015, Dec. 11 **Litho.**
3479 A1070 Sheet of 3, #a-c 4.00 2.00

Animals — A1071

Designs: No. 3480, 1.40 l, Lepus cuniculus angorensis. No. 3481, 1.40 l, Capra hircus angorensis. 2.80 l, Felis catus angolensis.

2015, Dec. 31 **Litho.** ***Perf. 14x13¾***
3480-3482 A1071 Set of 3 4.00 2.00

Post Offices — A1072

Buildings: 30k, Meram Post Office. 50k, Kozlu Post Office. 1 l, PTT Museum, Ankara. 1.40 l, Sirkeci Post Office. 4.50 l, Artuklu Post Office. 10 l, Old Parcel Building, Izmir.

Perf. 13¾ Syncopated

2016, Feb. 22 **Litho.**
3483-3488 A1072 Set of 6 12.00 6.00

Souvenir Sheet

Ishak Pasha Palace A1073

No. 3489 — Palace and: a, Gate at right. b, Minaret at right.

Litho. With Foil Application

2016, Feb. 26 ***Perf. 13¾x14***
3489 A1073 1.40 l Sheet of 2, #a-b 1.90 .95

Souvenir Sheets

Grand Bazaar, Istanbul A1074

Egyptian Bazaar, Istanbul A1075

No. 3490 — "Kapali Carsi" and: a, 1.40 l, Shoppers, drinking fountain in aisle. b, 2.80 l, Shoppers.

No. 3491 — "Misir Carsisi" and: a, 1.40 l, Building exterior. b, 2.80 l, Building ceiling.

Litho., Sheet Margin Litho. With Foil Application

2016, Mar. 22 ***Perf. 13½x13¾***
3490 A1074 Sheet of 2, #a-b 3.00 1.50
3491 A1075 Sheet of 2, #a-b 3.00 1.50

13th Islamic Summit, Istanbul — A1076

2016, Apr. 14 **Litho.** ***Perf. 13¼x13½***
3492 A1076 2.80 l multi 2.00 1.00

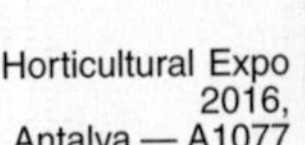

Horticultural Expo 2016, Antalya — A1077

Emblem and: No. 3493, 1.40 l, Girls, flowers, pillars. No. 3494, 1.40 l, Turkcell Expo Tower, boy and girl. 2.80 l, Paeonia turcia.

2016, Apr. 23 **Litho.** ***Perf. 13¾x14***
3493-3495 A1077 Set of 3 4.00 2.00

A1078

End of Siege of Kut Al Amara, Cent. — A1079

2016, Apr. 29 **Litho.** ***Perf. 13¾x14***
3496 A1078 1.40 l multi 1.00 .50
3497 A1079 2.80 l multi 2.00 1.00

World Humanitarian Summit, Istanbul — A1080

2016, May 23 **Litho.** ***Perf. 13¾x14***
3498 A1080 2.80 l multi 1.90 .95

Souvenir Sheet

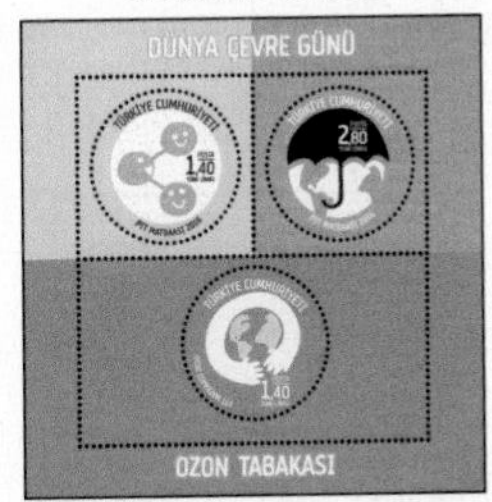

World Environment Day — A1081

No. 3499: a, 1.40 l, Water molecule. b, 1.40 l, Arms wrapped around Earth. c, 2.80 l, Umbrella over Earth.

2016, June 5 **Litho.** ***Perf. 13¾***
3499 A1081 Sheet of 3, #a-c 4.00 2.00

2016 European Soccer Championships, France — A1082

Emblem and: No. 3500, 1.40 l, Player on knees celebrating goal, orange background. No. 3501, 1.40 l, Player kicking ball, blue background. No. 3502, 2.80 l, Player holding trophy, green background. No. 3503, 2.80 l, Trophy, red background.

2016, June 10 **Litho.** ***Perf. 14x13¾***
3500-3503 A1082 Set of 4 6.00 3.00

UNESCO World Heritage Committee, 40th Meeting, Istanbul — A1083

Perf. 13¾ Syncopated

2016, July 10 **Litho.**
3504 A1083 3.20 l blk & blue 2.25 1.10

A souvenir sheet containing a 3.20 l stamp was printed in limited quantities and sold for 15 l.

Souvenir Sheet

Sarikamis-Allahuekber Mountains National Park — A1084

2016, July 12 **Litho.** ***Perf. 13***
3505 A1084 3.20 l multi 2.25 1.10

Ahmed Yesevi (1083-1166), Poet — A1085

Mausoleum of Ahmed Yesevi, Turkistan, Kazakhstan — A1086

2016, July 26 **Litho.** ***Perf. 13¼***
3506 A1085 1.60 l multi 1.10 .55
3507 A1086 3.20 l multi 2.25 1.10

Tourist Attractions — A1087

Attractions in: 20k, Ordu. 40k, Erzincan. 1.60 l, Denizli, horiz. 3.20 l, Nevsehir, horiz. 5.10 l, Izmir, horiz. 11 l, Kars, horiz.

Perf. 13¾ Syncopated

2016, July 27 **Litho.**
3508 A1087 20k multi .25 .25
3509 A1087 40k multi .25 .25
3510 A1087 1.60 l multi 1.10 .55
3511 A1087 3.20 l multi 2.25 1.10
3512 A1087 5.10 l multi 3.50 1.75
3513 A1087 11 l multi 7.50 3.75
Nos. 3508-3513 (6) 14.85 7.65

A1088

A1089

A1090

Konya, 2016 Islamic Capital of Tourism — A1091

2016, Aug. 4 **Litho.** ***Perf. 13***
3514 A1088 1.60 l multi 1.10 .55
3515 A1089 1.60 l multi 1.10 .55
3516 A1090 1.60 l multi 1.10 .55
3517 A1091 3.20 l multi 2.25 1.10
Nos. 3514-3517 (4) 5.55 2.75

Martyr's Day A1092

2016, Aug. 5 **Litho.** ***Perf. 13¼***
3518 A1092 1.60 l multi 1.10 .55

Miniature Sheet

Eastern Anatolian Dishes A1093

No. 3519: a, 1.60 l, Kete (butter pastry). b, 1.60 l, Kaz eti (goose). c, 1.60 l, Jagli yumurta (scrambled eggs). d, 3.20 l, Kadayif dolmasi (filled pastry).

2016, Aug. 8 **Litho.** ***Perf. 14x13¾***
3519 A1093 Sheet of 4, #a-d 5.50 2.75

Justice and Development Party, 15th Anniv. — A1094

2016, Aug. 14 Litho. *Perf. 13¼*
3520 A1094 1.60 l multi 1.10 .55

An imperforate 1.60 l stamp with a different design was produced in limited quantities and sold with No. 3520 and a first day cover for 15 l.

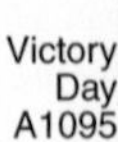

Victory Day A1095

Perf. 13¾ Syncopated

2016, Aug. 30 Litho.
3521 A1095 1.60 l multi 1.10 .55

A 1.60 l souvenir sheet with a different design was produced in limited quantities and sold with No. 3521 and a first day cover for 12.50 l.

Souvenir Sheet

Leaders of the Battle of Szigetvár A1096

No. 3522: a, Nikola Zrinski (1508-66). b, Suleiman the Magnificent (1495-1566).

2016, Sept. 7 Litho. *Perf. 13¼*
3522 A1096 3.20 l Sheet of 2, #a-b 4.25 2.10

See Hungary No. 4403.

26th Universal Postal Union Congress, Istanbul — A1097

Perf. 13¾ Syncopated

2016, Sept. 20 Litho.
3523 A1097 3.20 l multi 2.10 1.10

A miniature sheet containing five 1.60 l stamps with different designs was produced in limited quantities and sold with No. 3523 and a first day cover for 25 l.

23rd World Energy Council Congres, Istanbul — A1098

2016, Oct. 9 Litho. *Perf. 13*
3524 A1098 3.20 l multi 2.10 1.10

Miniature Sheet

Gaziantep, 2015 UNESCO Creative City of Gastronomy — A1099

No. 3525 — Various foods: a, Three plates. b, Bowl, two plates, tray and spoon. c, Three plates and lid. d, Two plates.

2016, Oct. 12 Litho. *Perf. 13*
3525 A1099 1.60 l Sheet of 4, #a-d 4.25 2.10

Turkey to Turkish Republic of Northern Cyprus Water Pipeline Project A1100

2016, Oct. 17 Litho. *Imperf.*
3526 A1100 1.60 l multi 1.10 .55

See Turkish Republic of Northern Cyprus No. 800.

South Eastern Europe Defense Ministerial Process, 20th Anniv. A1101

2016, Oct. 18 Litho. *Perf. 13¼*
3527 A1101 3.20 l multi 2.10 1.10

Republic Day — A1102

2016, Oct. 29 Litho. *Perf. 13*
3528 A1102 1.60 l multi 1.10 .55

A 3.20 l souvenir sheet with a different design was produced in limited quantities and sold with No. 3528 and a first day cover for 12.50 l.

A1103 A1104

A1105 A1106

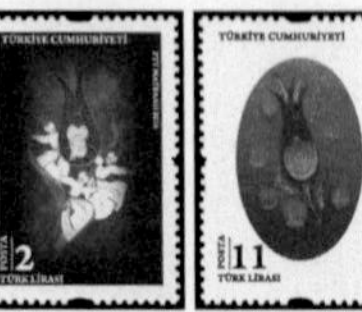

Art

A1107 A1108

Perf. 13¾ Syncopated

2016, Nov. 28 Litho.

3529	A1103	10k multi	.25	.25
3530	A1104	20k multi	.25	.25
3531	A1105	1 l multi	.60	.30
3532	A1106	1.60 l multi	.90	.45
3533	A1107	2 l multi	1.25	.60
3534	A1108	11 l multi	6.25	3.25
		Nos. 3529-3534 (6)	9.50	5.10

Women's Right to Vote, 82nd Anniv. — A1109

2016, Dec. 5 Litho. *Perf. 13*
3535 A1109 1 l multi + label .55 .30

Souvenir Sheet

Opening of Eurasia Tunnel (in 2016) A1110

Perf. 13¾x13½ Syncopated

2017, Jan. 30 Litho.
3536 A1110 1.60 l multi .85 .40

European Youth Olympic Winter Festival, Erzurum A1111

European Olympic Committees emblem and: No. 3537, 1.60 l, Festival emblem. No. 3538, 1.60 l, Festival mascot. 3.70 l, Skiers and mosques.

2017, Feb. 12 Litho. *Perf. 13*
3537-3539 A1111 Set of 3 3.75 1.90

Tombs, Myra A1112

Temple of Apollo, Side A1113

Alanya Harbor A1114

Clock Tower and Yivliminare Mosque Minaret, Antalya A1115

Perf. 13¼ Syncopated

2017, Apr. 4 Litho.

3540	A1112	3.70 l multi	2.10	1.10
3541	A1113	3.70 l multi	2.10	1.10
3542	A1114	3.70 l multi	2.10	1.10
3543	A1115	3.70 l multi	2.10	1.10
		Nos. 3540-3543 (4)	8.40	4.40

Antalya Province tourist attractions.

Souvenir Sheet

Kemeralti Bazaar, Izmir A1116

Litho. & Silk-Screened

2017, Apr. 4 *Perf. 13½x14*
3544 A1116 1.60 l multi .90 .45

Slogans A1117

Designs: No. 3545, 3.70 l, Turkish slogan "Gücü Keşfet." No. 3546, 3.70 l, English slogan "Discover the potential."

Perf. 13¼ Syncopated

2017, Apr. 17 Litho.
3545-3546 A1117 Set of 2 4.25 2.10

Souvenir Sheet

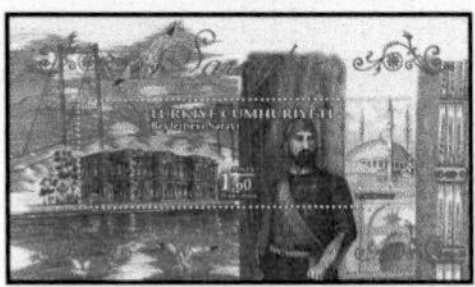

Beylerbeyi Palace, Istanbul — A1118

Litho., Sheet Margin Litho. With Foil Application

2017, Apr. 21 *Perf. 13½x14*
3547 A1118 1.60 l multi .90 .45

Europa A1119

Designs: 1.60 l, Bayburt Castle. 3.70 l, Kars Castle.

2017, May 9 Litho. *Perf. 13½x13¼*
3548-3549 A1119 Set of 2 3.00 1.50

A1120

2017, May 30 Litho. *Perf. 13¼*
3550 A1120 3.70 l multi 2.10 1.10

Diplomatic Relations Between Turkey and Azerbaijan, Belarus, Georgia, Kazakhstan, Kyrgyzstan, Moldova, Tajikistan, Turkmenistan, Ukraine, and Uzbekistan, 25th Anniv.

World Environment Day — A1121

2017, June 5 Litho. *Imperf.*
Self-Adhesive
3551 A1121 1.60 l multi .90 .45

Souvenir Sheet

Ankapark Amusement Park, Ankara — A1122

No. 3552: a, Dinosaur statue. b, Door in archway, vert.

Perf. 13¼ (#3552a), 14x13½ (#3552b)

2017, June 15 Litho.

3552 A1122 1.60 l Sheet of 2, #a-b 1.90 .95

Fountain of Sultan Ahmed III, Istanbul A1123

2017, June 20 Litho. *Perf. 13¼*

3553 A1123 1.60 l multi .90 .45

22nd World Petroleum Congress, Istanbul A1124

2017, July 9 Litho. *Perf. 13¼*

3554 A1124 1.60 l multi .90 .45

A1125

Democracy and National Unity Day — A1126

2017, July 15 Litho. *Perf. 13¼*

3555 A1125 1.60 l multi .90 .45
3556 A1126 1.60 l multi .90 .45

A souvenir sheet of four 60k stamps was printed in limited quantities and sold with Nos. 3555-3556 and a first day cover for 17.50 l.

A1127 A1128

A1129 Turkish Language Year — A1130

Perf. 13½x13¾ Syncopated

2017, July 31 Litho.

3557 A1127 1.50 l multi .85 .45
3558 A1128 1.80 l multi 1.10 .55
3559 A1129 5.80 l multi 3.25 1.60
3560 A1130 12.50 l multi 7.25 3.75
Nos. 3557-3560 (4) 12.45 6.35

Ismir Clock Tower — A1131

Perf. 13½x13¾ Syncopated

2017, Sept. 9 Litho.

3561 A1131 1.80 l multi 1.00 .50

Souvenir Sheet

Spil Dagi National Park A1132

2017, Sept. 15 Litho. *Perf. 13¼*

3562 A1132 3.70 l multi 2.10 1.10

Miniature Sheet

Turkish Cuisine A1133

No. 3563: a, 75k, Adana kebap and salgam (lamb kebabs and turnip juice). b, 75k, Banak and bicibici, vert. c, 1.80 l, Burdur sis and hibes (shishkebab and garlic dip), vert. d, 3.70 l, Maras dondurmasi, tantuni, and künefe (ice cream, meat wrap, and cheese pastry).

2017, Sept. 29 Litho. *Perf. 13¾*

3563 A1133 Sheet of 4, #a-d 4.00 2.00

World Post Day — A1134

Birds, UPU emblem and: 75k, Man making smoke signals. No. 3565, 1.80 l, Man, quill pen. No. 3566, 1.80 l, Postal workers, horse-drawn cart, telephone poles and wires. 3.70 l, Postman on scooter, mail sorting equipment.

2017, Oct. 9 Litho. *Perf. 13¼*

3564-3567 A1134 Set of 4 4.25 2.10

A souvenir sheet with a self-adhesive 3.70 l stamp printed on silk and a souvenir sheet of four stamps (1.80 l, 3.70 l and two 75k stamps) were printed in limited quantities and sold together with Nos. 3564-3567 for 40 l.

Republic of Turkey, 94th Anniv. — A1135

Inscription: No. 3568, 75k, "Tek Devlet" (one state). No. 3569, 75k, "Tek Vatan" (one homeland). No. 3570, 1.80 l, "Tek Millet" (one nation). No. 3571, 3.70 l, "Tek Bayrak" (one flag).

2017, Oct. 29 Litho. *Perf. 13¼*

3568-3571 A1135 Set of 4 3.75 3.75

A souvenir sheet containing one 1.80 l stamp of a different design was printed in limited quantities and was sold with a first day cover for 20 l.

Souvenir Sheet

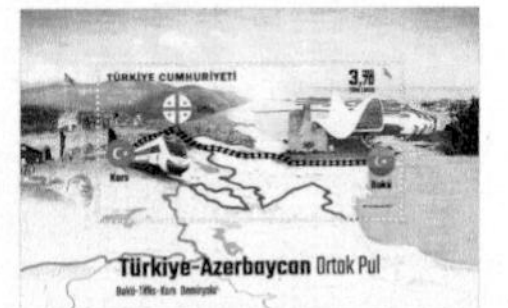

Baku-Tbilisi-Kars Railway — A1136

2017, Oct. 30 Litho. *Perf. 13¼x13*

3572 A1136 3.70 l multi 2.00 1.00

See Azerbaijan No. 1141.

Turkish Animal Breeds — A1137

Designs: No. 3573, 75k, Anatolian shepherd. No. 3574, 75k, Van cat, vert. 1.80 l, Turkish horses. 3.70 l, Turkish mastiff.

Perf. 13½x13¾, 13¾x13½

2017, Nov. 7 Litho.

3573-3576 A1137 Set of 4 3.75 1.90

Souvenir Sheet

Diplomatic Relations Between Turkey and Pakistan, 70th Anniv. — A1138

No. 3577: a, Mehmet Akif Ersoy (1873-1936),Turkish poet. b, Allama Muhammed Iqbal (1877-1938), Pakistani poet.

2017, Nov. 9 Litho. *Perf. 13¼*

3577 A1138 3.70 l Sheet of 2, #a-b 3.75 1.90

See Pakistan No. 1254.

Hieropolis-Pamukkale UNESCO World Heritage Sites, Denizli — A1139

2017, Dec. 8 Litho. *Perf. 13¼*

3578 A1139 1.80 l multi .95 .50

A souvenir sheet of five stamps (3.70 l, two 75k, and two 1.80 l) was printed in limited quantities and sold for 15 l.

Lakes — A1140

Designs: No. 3579, 1.80 l, Lake Van. No. 3580, 1.80 l, Flamingo at Lake Tuz.

2017, Dec. 12 Litho. *Perf. 13¼*

3579-3580 A1140 Set of 2 1.90 .95

Legumes — A1141

Designs: 20k, Lens culinaris. 2 l, Vigna sinensis. 3 l, Phaseolus vulgaris (fasulye). 4 l, Phaseolus vulgaris (barbunya). 6.50 l, Vicia faba. 14 l, Cicer arietinum.

Perf. 13¾x13½ Syncopated

2018, Jan. 5 Litho.

3581 A1141 20k multi .25 .25
3582 A1141 2 l multi 1.10 .55
3583 A1141 3 l multi 1.60 .80
3584 A1141 4 l multi 2.10 1.10
3585 A1141 6.50 l multi 3.50 1.75
3586 A1141 14 l multi 7.50 3.75
Nos. 3581-3586 (6) 16.05 8.20

Sultan Süleyman Fountain, Istanbul A1142

2018, Jan. 31 Litho. *Perf. 13¼*

3587 A1142 2 l multi 1.10 .55

Souvenir Sheet

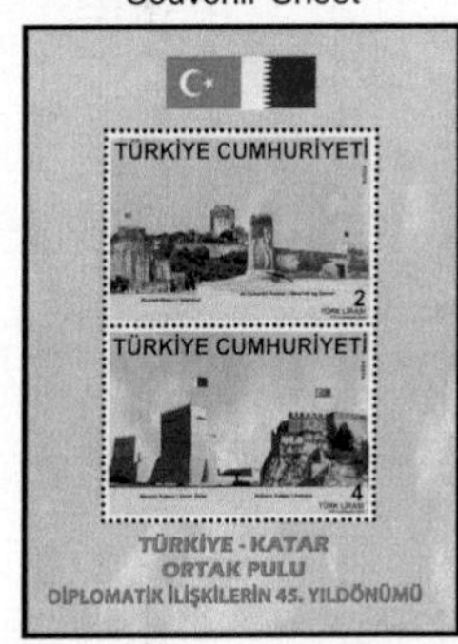

Diplomatic Relations Between Turkey and Qatar, 45th Anniv. — A1143

No. 3588: a, 2 l, Rumeli Fortress, Istanbul, Al Zubara Fort, Qatar. b, 4 l, Barzan Towers, Qatar, Ankara Castle, Ankara.

Litho., Sheet Margin Litho. With Foil Application

2018, Feb. 21 *Perf. 13¼*

3588 A1143 Sheet of 2, #a-b 3.25 1.60

See Qatar No. 1143.

Court of Cassation, 150th Anniv. — A1144

Perf. 13½x13¾ Syncopated

2018, Mar. 6 Litho.

3589 A1144 2 l multi 1.00 .50

Liberation of Erzurum, Cent. — A1145

Perf. 13½x13¾ Syncopated

2018, Mar. 12 Litho.

3590 A1145 2 l multi 1.00 .50

Flora — A1146

Designs: No. 3591, 2 l, Fritillaria imperialis. No. 3592, 2 l, Olea europaea. No. 3593, 2 l, Tulipa. No. 3594, 2 l, Centaurea tchihatcheffii. No. 3595, 2 l, Rhododendron ponticum. No. 3596, 2 l, Crocus antalyensis subsp. antalyensis. No. 3597, 2 l, Centaurea cyanus.

Perf. 13¾x13½

2018, Mar. 21 **Litho.**
3591-3597 A1146 Set of 7 7.00 3.50

Liberation of Van, Cent. — A1147

2018, Apr. 2 **Litho.** ***Perf. 13½x13¾***
3598 A1147 2 l multi 1.00 .50

Dolmabahçe Clock Tower, Istanbul — A1148

Perf. 13½x13¾ Syncopated

2018, Apr. 5 **Litho.**
3599 A1148 2 l multi 1.00 .50

Spices — A1149

Designs: 20k, Mentha. 50k, Piper nigrum. 2.30 l, Capsicum annum. 6.50 l, Cuminum cyminum.

Perf. 13¾x13½ Syncopated

2018, Apr. 18 **Litho.**
3600-3603 A1149 Set of 4 4.75 2.40

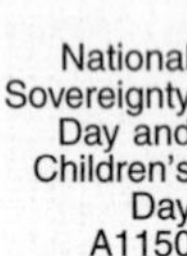

National Sovereignty Day and Children's Day A1150

2018, Apr. 23 **Litho.** ***Perf. 13¼***
3604 A1150 2 l multi 1.00 .50

A souvenir sheet containing one 78x36mm 2 l stamp was produced in limited quantities.

Europa A1151

Designs: 2 l, Twin bridges, Artvin. 4 l, Meriç Bridge, Edirne.

2018, May 9 **Litho.** ***Perf. 13¼***
3605-3606 A1151 Set of 2 2.60 1.40

Universal Postal Union World Chief Executive Officer Forum, Istanbul — A1152

Perf. 14 Syncopated

2018, May 9 **Litho.**
3607 A1152 4 l multi 1.75 .85

Council of State (Administrative Court), 150th Anniv. — A1153

Designs: 1 l, Modern building. 2 l, Drawing of old building and street scene.

Perf. 13¾ Syncopated

2018, May 10 **Litho.**
3608-3609 A1153 Set of 2 1.40 .70

Diplomatic Relations Between Turkey and Thailand, 60th Anniv. — A1154

No. 3610: a, Wrestlers (denomination at LL). b, Kick boxers (denomination at LR).

2018, May 12 **Litho.** ***Perf. 13¼x13½***
3610 A1154 2 l Sheet of 2, #a-b 1.75 .85

See Thailand No. 3005.

Perge Archaeological Site, Antalya Province — A1155

Perf. 13½x13¾ Syncopated

2018, May 22 **Litho.**
3611 A1155 4 l multi 1.75 .85

Souvenir Sheet

World Environment Day — A1156

No. 3612 — Wind generator and: a, Tanks and house. b, Solar panels and domed tanks.

2018, June 5 **Litho.** ***Perf. 13¼***
3612 A1156 2 l Sheet of 2, #a-b 1.75 .85

Camlica Mosque, Istanbul A1157

2018, June 10 **Litho.** ***Perf. 13¼***
3613 A1157 2 l multi .90 .45

2018 World Cup Soccer Championships, Russia — A1158

Designs: No. 3614, 2 l, Mascot holding soccer ball. No. 3615, 2 l, Emblerm. No. 3616, 4 l, Mascot kicking soccer ball. No. 3617, 4 l, Poster.

2018, June 14 **Litho.** ***Perf. 14x13¾***
3614-3617 A1158 Set of 4 5.25 2.60

Houses of the Mediterranean Area — A1159

Various houses: 2 l, 4 l.

2018, July 9 **Litho.** ***Perf. 13¼***
3618-3619 A1159 Set of 2 2.50 1.25

Democracy and National Unity Day — A1160

Perf. 13½x13¾ Syncopated

2018, July 15 **Litho.**
3620 A1160 2 l multi .85 .40

A souvenir sheet containing one 38x38mm 2 l stamp was printed in limited quantities.

Souvenir Sheet

Troy UNESCO World Heritage Site — A1161

No. 3621: a, Buildings (26x26mm octagonal). b, Trojan Horse (18x24mm). c, Amphitheater (18x24mm octagonal).

2018, Aug. 1 **Litho.** ***Perf. 13¼***
3621 A1161 2 l Sheet of 3, #a-c 2.50 1.25

Mosque, Milodraz, Bosnia and Herzegovina A1162

2018, Aug. 10 **Litho.** ***Perf. 13¼***
3622 A1162 4 l multi 1.25 .60

Jee Bosnia and Herzegovina No. 802.

Miniature Sheet

Cuisine of Marmara Region A1163

No. 3623: a, 1 l, Edirne Tava Ciger, Boza (fried livers and fermented bulgur wheat drink). b, 2 l, Peynir Helvasi, Tekirdag Köftesi (cheese halvah and meatballs), vert. c, 2 l, Iskender Kebabi, Mustafakemalpasa Peynir Tatlisi (lamb kebab and cheese-filled biscuits), vert. d, 4 l, Kestane Sekeri, Islama Köfte (chestnut candy and meatballs).

2018, Aug. 16 **Litho.** ***Perf. 13¾***
3623 A1163 Sheet of 4, #a-d 2.75 1.40

Victory Day A1164

Perf. 13¾ Syncopated

2018, Aug. 30 **Litho.**
3624 A1164 2 l multi .60 .30

An imperforate 111x62mm 2 l sheet was printed in limited quantities.

Souvenir Sheet

Islamic Army of the Caucasus, Cent. — A1165

2018, Sept. 15 **Litho.** ***Perf. 13¾***
3625 A1165 2 l multi .70 .35

Souvenir Sheet

Flamingos, Sultan Marshes National Park — A1166

2018, Sept. 26 **Litho.** ***Perf. 13¼***
3626 A1166 2 l multi .70 .35

Opening of New Istanbul Airport A1167

2018, Oct. 29 **Litho.** ***Perf. 13¼***
3627 A1167 2 l multi .75 .35

Kastamonu, 2018 Cultural Capital of the Turkic World — A1168

Emblem and various tourist attractions: 2 l, 4 l.

2018, Nov. 26 **Litho.** ***Perf. 13¼***
3628-3629 A1168 Set of 2 2.25 1.10

An imperforate 75x75mm 2 l stamp was printed in limited quantities.

World Map by Erzurumlu ibrahim Hakki's (1705-72) in his Marifetname Book — A1169

2018, Nov. 27 **Litho.** ***Perf. 13¾***
3630 A1169 4 l multi 1.50 .75

Joint Issue between Turkey and Slovakia. See Slovakia No. 807.

Houses Connected to Kemal Atatürk — A1170

Designs: 50k, Atatürk's Headquarters for Battle of Dumlupinar, Dumlupinar. 2 l, Atatürk Museum, Istanbul, vert. 14 l, Atatürk House Museum, Kayseri.

Perf. 12¾x13, 13x12¾

2018, Dec. 26 **Litho.**

3631 A1170 50k multi .25 .25
3632 A1170 2 l multi .75 .35
3633 A1170 14 l multi 5.25 2.60
Nos. 3631-3633 (3) 6.25 3.20

Valuable Stones — A1171

Designs: 2 l, Striped agate. 4 l, Blue chalcedony.

Litho. & Silk-Screened

2019, Jan. 9 *Perf. 13¼*

3634-3635 A1171 Set of 2 2.40 1.25

Souvenir Sheet

Train Stations A1172

No. 3636: a, 2 l, Main Ankara Station. b, 4 l, Ankara YHT (high-speed train) Station.

2019, Jan. 24 **Litho.** *Perf. 13½x13¼*

3636 A1172 Sheet of 2, #a-b 2.40 1.25

Folk Dances — A1173

Designs: No. 3637, 2 l, Zeybek. No. 3638, 2 l, Segmen.

2019, Feb. 5 **Litho.** *Perf. 13¼*

3637-3638 A1173 Set of 2 1.50 .75

Pottery From Baksi Museum A1174

Aerial View of Baksi Museum, Bayburt A1175

2019, Feb. 25 **Litho.** *Perf. 13¼*

3639 A1174 2 l multi .75 .35
3640 A1175 2 l multi .75 .35

Four additional 2 l stamps with serial numbers were printed in limited quantities, and sold together along with Nos. 3639-3640 and a first day cover for 35 l.

Carved Stone A1176

Megaliths A1177

2019, Feb. 28 **Litho.** *Perf. 13¼*

3641 A1176 2 l multi .75 .35
3642 A1177 2 l multi .75 .35

Göbekli Tepe Archaeological Site.

This 4 l stamp with serial number, released Feb. 28, 2019, was printed in limited quantities and sold together along with Nos. 3641-3642, a first day cover and postal stationery for 28 l.

Musical Instruments A1178

Designs: No. 3643, 2 l, Agiz kopuzu (mouth harp). No. 3644, 2 l, Tar (stringed instrument), vert. No. 3645, 2 l, Ersurum defi (tambourine), vert.

2019, Mar. 19 **Litho.** *Perf. 13¾*

3643-3645 A1178 Set of 3 2.25 1.10

World Meteorology Day — A1179

2019, Mar. 23 **Litho.** *Perf. 13¼*

3646 A1179 2 l multi .75 .35

Clock Tower, Adana — A1180

Perf. 13¼x13¾ Syncopated

2019, Apr. 2 **Litho.**

3647 A1180 2 l multi .75 .35

Children's Games A1181

Designs: No. 3648, 2 l, Hide and seek. No. 3649, 2 l, Marbles. No. 3650, 2 l, Hopscotch.

2019, Apr. 11 **Litho.** *Perf. 13½x13¼*

3648-3650 A1181 Set of 3 2.00 1.00

Dancers — A1182

Designs: No. 3651, 2 l, Tango dancers. No. 3652, 2 l, Waltz dancers.

2019, Apr. 29 **Litho.** *Perf. 13¼x13½*

3651-3652 A1182 Set of 2 1.40 .70

Europa — A1183

Birds: 2 l, Otus brucei. 4 l, Sitta krueperi, horiz.

Perf. 13¼x13½, 13½x13¼

2019, May 9 **Litho.**

3653-3654 A1183 Set of 2 2.10 1.10

Fuat Sezgin (1924-2018), Historian — A1184

Litho. With Foil Application

2019, May 14 *Perf. 13¼x13½*

3655 A1184 2 l copper .70 .35

Souvenir Sheets

1919 Travels of Kemal Atatürk (1881-1938) in Turkish War of Independence — A1185

Statue of Kemal Atatürk on Horse, Samsun A1186

Perf. 13¼ Syncopated

2019, May 19 **Litho.**

3656 A1185 2 l multi .70 .35

Litho. & Embossed With Foil Application

3657 A1186 4 l blue & silver 1.40 .70

Start of Turkish War of Independence, cent.

Kemal Atatürk (1881-1938) and His Signature A1187

Atatürk's House in Sisil A1188

Instructions Regarding Dispatch of Atatürk to Ninth Army A1189

Steamer "Bandirma" Which Carried Atatürk to Samsun A1190

Minhka Palace, Residence of Atatürk in Samsun A1191

Atatürk House, Havza A1192

Atatürk and Havza Circular — A1193

Atatürk and Telegram Recalling Him to Istanbul — A1194

Atatürk and Delegates Issuing Amasya Circular — A1195

Saraydüzü Casern, Site of Signing of Amasya Circular — A1196

Telegraph Key and Amasya Circular A1197

Atatürk House, Erzurum A1198

Atatürk and His Military Resignation Letter — A1199

Erzurum Congress Building — A1200

Delegates of Erzurum Congress and Their Declaration A1201

Press Used to Print Erzurum Congress Declarations A1202

Erzurum Congress Delegates at Table A1203

Erzurum Congress Delegates A1204

Sivas Congress Building A1205

Atatürk and Sivas Congress Declaration A1206

Press Used to Print Newspaper *Irade-i Milliye* A1207

Delegates to Sivas Congress A1208

Members of Sivas Anatolian Women's Defense of the Country Society — A1209

Members of the Association for the Defense of Rights — A1210

2019, May 19 Litho. *Die Cut*
Self-Adhesive

3658	Booklet pane of 24	19.50	
a.	A1187 2 l multi	.80	.40
b.	A1188 2 l multi	.80	.40
c.	A1189 2 l multi	.80	.40
d.	A1190 2 l multi	.80	.40
e.	A1191 2 l multi	.80	.40
f.	A1192 2 l multi	.80	.40
g.	A1193 2 l multi	.80	.40
h.	A1194 2 l multi	.80	.40
i.	A1195 2 l multi	.80	.40
j.	A1196 2 l multi	.80	.40
k.	A1197 2 l multi	.80	.40
l.	A1198 2 l multi	.80	.40
m.	A1199 2 l multi	.80	.40
n.	A1200 2 l multi	.80	.40
o.	A1201 2 l multi	.80	.40
p.	A1202 2 l multi	.80	.40
q.	A1203 2 l multi	.80	.40
r.	A1204 2 l multi	.80	.40
s.	A1205 2 l multi	.80	.40
t.	A1206 2 l multi	.80	.40
u.	A1207 2 l multi	.80	.40
v.	A1208 2 l multi	.80	.40
w.	A1209 2 l multi	.80	.40
x.	A1210 2 l multi	.80	.40

Start of Turkish War of Independence, cent. No. 3658 sold for 55 l.

Tourist Attractions A1211

Designs: 2 l, Atakum District, Samsun. 4 l, Manavgat Waterfall, Antalya. 16.20 l, Semsi Pasha Mosque, Istanbul.

2019, May 24 Litho. *Perf. 13¼x13½*
3659-3661 A1211 Set of 3 7.75 4.00

Souvenir Sheet

World Environment Day — A1212

2019, June 10 Litho. *Die Cut*
Self-Adhesive
3662 A1212 2 l multi .70 .35

Souvenir Sheet

Diplomatic Relations Between Turkey and Mongolia, 50th Anniv. — A1213

No. 3663: a, Tulip, Mongolian Airlines jet over Bosporus Bridge. b, Scabiosa comosa flower, Turkish Airlines jet, Mongolian woman.

2019, June 14 Litho. *Perf. 13¼*
3663 A1213 2 l Sheet of 2, #a-b, + central label 1.40 .70

Souvenir Sheet

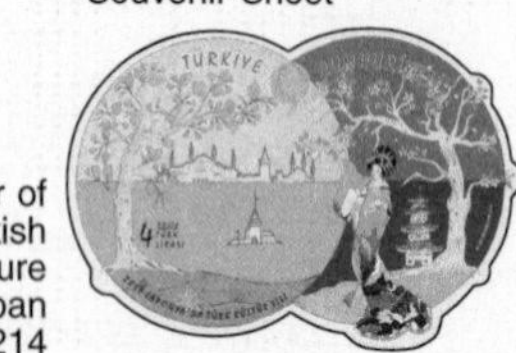

Year of Turkish Culture in Japan A1214

2019, June 27 Litho. *Imperf.*
Self-Adhesive
3664 A1214 4 l multi 1.40 .70

A1215

Traditional Women's Clothing — A1216

2019, July 8 Litho. *Perf. 13¼*
3665 A1215 2 l multi .75 .35
3666 A1216 2 l multi .75 .35

Life of Pres. Kemal Atatürk (1881-1938) — A1217

Various photographs of Atatürk with other people.

2019, July 16 Litho. *Perf. 13½x13¼*
Panel Color

3667	A1217	50k	Turq blue	.25	.25
3668	A1217	1 l	orange	.35	.25
3669	A1217	1.20 l	brt blue	.45	.25
3670	A1217	2.30 l	pink	.85	.40
3671	A1217	4.60 l	red	1.75	.85
3672	A1217	7.50 l	green	2.75	.85
3673	A1217	16.20 l	violet	5.75	3.00
	Nos. 3667-3673 (7)			12.15	5.85

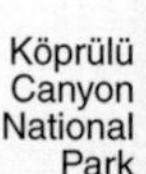

Köprülü Canyon National Park A1218

Mount Nemrut National Park A1219

2019, Sept. 6 Litho. *Perf. 13*
3674 A1218 2 l multi .70 .35
3675 A1219 2 l multi .70 .35

Express Mail Service, 20th Anniv. — A1220

2019, Sept. 10 Litho. *Perf. 13¼*
3676 A1220 4.60 l multi 1.60 .80

Mohandas K. Gandhi (1869-1948), Indian Nationalist Leader — A1221

2019, Sept. 24 Litho. *Perf. 13¼*
3677 A1221 2.30 l multi .80 .40

Gallus Gallus Domesticus A1222

Various roosters: 2.40 l, 5.50 l.

2019, Oct. 24 Litho. *Perf. 13¼*
3678-3679 A1222 Set of 2 2.75 1.40

Slow Cities — A1223

Snail and: 10k, Akyaka. 20k, Gerze. 50k, Savsat. No. 3683, Seferihisar. No. 3684, Gökçeada. No. 3685, Göynük. No. 3686, Mudurnu. No. 3687, Egirdir. No. 3688, Persembe. No. 3689, Tarakli. No. 3690, Köycegiz.

2019 Litho. *Perf. 13½x13¾*

3680	A1223	10k	multi	.25	.25
3681	A1223	20k	multi	.25	.25
3682	A1223	50k	multi	.25	.25
3683	A1223	2.40 l	multi	.85	.40
3684	A1223	2.40 l	multi	.85	.40
3685	A1223	5.50 l	multi	2.00	1.00
3686	A1223	5.50 l	multi	2.00	1.00
3687	A1223	8.40 l	multi	3.00	1.50
3688	A1223	8.40 l	multi	3.00	1.50
3689	A1223	19 l	multi	6.75	3.50
3690	A1223	19 l	multi	6.75	3.50
	Nos. 3680-3690 (11)			25.95	13.55

Issued: Nos. 3681, 3683, 3685, 3687, 3689, 10/25; others, 12/23.

Souvenir Sheet

Arslantepe Archaeological Site Museum — A1224

2019, Nov. 6 Litho. *Perf. 14¼*
3691 A1224 2.40 l multi .85 .40

A1225

A1226

Arrival of Kemal Atatürk in Ankara, Cent. A1227

No. 3692: a, Atatürk (32mm diameter). b, Heyet-i Temsiliye (members of the Board of Representatives, 39x30mm). c, Heyet-i Temsiliye/Ankara Vilayet Binasi (members of the Board of Representatives at Ankara Province Building, 39x30mm). d, Ziraat Mektebi (School of Agriculture, 39x30mm).

Perf. (#3692a), Perf. 13¼ (#3692b-3692d)

2019, Dec. 27 Litho.
3692 A1225 2.40 l Sheet of 4, #a-d 3.25 1.60

Souvenir Sheets
Perf. 13¾x13½ Syncopated
3693 A1226 2.40 l multi .80 .40

Litho. With Foil Application
Perf. 13¼x13 Syncopated
3694 A1227 5.50 l gold 1.90 .95

Souvenir Sheet

National Sovereignty, Cent. — A1228

Perf. 13¾x13 Syncopated
2020, Jan. 28 Litho.
3695 A1228 2.40 l multi .80 .40

Souvenir Sheet

Kemal Ataturk A1229

Perf. 13¾x13 Syncopated
Litho. & Silk-screened

2020, Jan. 28
3696 A1229 5.50 l multi 1.90 .95

Adoption of National Pact, cent.

A1230

A1231

Service Dogs — A1232

2020, Mar. 4 Litho. *Perf. 13¼*

3697 A1230 2.40 l multi	.75	.35
3698 A1231 2.40 l multi	.75	.35
3699 A1232 2.40 l multi	.75	.35
Nos. 3697-3699 (3)	2.25	1.05

A1233

A1234

A1235

Mosaics at Archaeology and Mosaic Museum, Sanliurfa — A1236

2020, Apr. 10 Litho. *Perf. 13¼*

3700 A1233 3 l multi	.85	.45
3701 A1234 3 l multi	.85	.45
3702 A1235 3 l multi	.85	.45
3703 A1236 3 l multi	.85	.45
Nos. 3700-3703 (4)	3.40	1.80

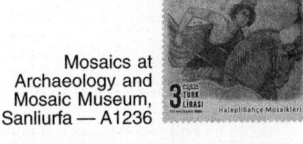

Grand National Assembly, Cent. — A1237

2020, Apr. 23 Litho. *Perf. 13½*
3704 A1237 3 l multi + label .85 .45

War of Independence Museum, Ankara — A1238

Republic Museum, Ankara A1239

Grand National Assembly Building, Ankara — A1240

2020, Apr. 23 Litho. *Perf. 13¾x13½*

3705 A1238 10 l multi + label	4.75	4.75
3706 A1239 10 l multi + label	4.75	4.75
3707 A1240 10 l multi + label	4.75	4.75
Nos. 3705-3707 (3)	14.25	14.25

Nos. 3705-3707 were sold in a folder that sold for 50 l.

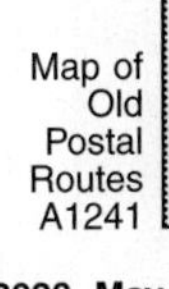

Map of Old Postal Routes A1241

2020, May 9 Litho. *Perf. 13¼*
3708 A1241 5.50 l multi 1.60 .80

Europa.

Patara — A1242

Designs: 20k, Roman amphitheater and Bouleuterion. 60k, City gate. 1 l, Lighthouse ruins and image of reconstructed lighthouse. 3 l, Pillars. 5 l, Beach and sea turtle. 9 l, Old telegraph station towers.

2020, May 12 Litho. *Perf. 13½x13¾*

3709 A1242 20k muilti	.25	.25
3710 A1242 60k muilti	.25	.25
3711 A1242 1 l muilti	.30	.25
3712 A1242 3 l muilti	.90	.45
3713 A1242 5 l muilti	1.50	.75
3714 A1242 9 l muilti	2.75	1.40
Nos. 3709-3714 (6)	5.95	3.35

Souvenir Sheet

World Environment Day — A1243

2020, June 5 Litho. *Perf. 13*
3715 A1243 3 l multi .90 .45

Souvenir Sheet

Turkish Cuisine A1244

No. 3716: a, 3 l, Asure in bowl, baklava in covered dish. b, 3 l, Plate of pastries and cup of coffee. c, 5.50 l, Bread rings and cup of tea, vert.

2020, July 11 Litho. *Perf. 13½x13¾*
3716 A1244 Sheet of 3, #a-c 3.25 1.60

Opuntia Cactus A1245

Cacti A1246

No. 3718: a, 1.40 l, Echinopsis Peach Monarch. b, 3 l, Echinopsis. c, 3 l, Mammillaria spinosissima, horiz. d, 5.50 l, Matucana haynei, horiz. e, 5.50 l, Astrophytum myriostigma.

2020, July 24 Litho. *Perf. 13½x13¼*
3717 A1245 3 l multi .85 .40

Miniature Sheet
Perf. 13¾

3718 A1246 Sheet of 5, #a-e 5.25 2.60

Reopening of Hagia Sophia as a Mosque A1247

Designs: 3 l, Ground-level view. 5.50 l, Aerial view.

2020, July 24 Litho. *Perf. 13¼*
3719-3720 A1247 Set of 2 2.50 1.25

Birds — A1248

Designs: No. 3721, 3 l, Ciconia ciconia. No. 3722, 3 l, Mycteria ibis. No. 3723, 3 l, Ciconia nigra.

Perf. 13¼x13½
2020, Aug. 20 Litho.
3721-3723 A1248 Set of 3 2.50 1.25

Solar System A1249

No. 3725: a, Mercury. b, Venus. c, Earth. d, Mars. e, Jupiter. f, Saturn. g, Uranus. h, Neptune.

2020, Sept. 8 Litho. *Perf. 13½x13¼*

3724 A1249 3 l multi	.80	.40
3725 Booklet of 8	9.00	
a.-h. A1249 3 l Any booklet pane of 1	1.10	—

No. 3725 sold for 35 l. A metal grommet fastens the booklet panes within the booklet cover.

International Year of Plant Health — A1250

2020, Sept. 24 Litho. *Perf. 13¼*
3726 A1250 3 l multi .80 .40

Fractals in Nature A1251

Mathematical formula and: No. 3727, 3 l, Fern, magnifying glass. No. 3728, 3 l, Snail, golden spiral diagram. No. 3729, 6.50 l, Snowflakes. No. 3730, 6.50 l, Peacock and its feathers.

2020, Oct. 15 Litho. *Perf. 13½x13¼*
3727-3730 A1251 Set of 4 4.50 2.25

Souvenir Sheet

2020 Mountain Bike Marathon World Championships, Sakarya — A1252

No. 3731: a, 3 l, Cyclist on bicycle. b, 6.50 l, Cyclist going downhill.

2020, Oct. 22 Litho. *Perf.*
3731 A1252 Sheet of 2, #a-b 2.25 1.10

United Nations, 75th Anniv. A1253

2020, Oct. 24 Litho. *Perf. 13x13¼*
3732 A1253 3 l multi .75 .35

Souvenir Sheet

Diplomatic Relations Between Turkey and Russia, Cent. — A1254

No. 3733: a, Mosque of Suleiman the Magnificent, Istanbul (denomination at UR). b, Moscow Cathedral Mosque (denomination at UL).

2020, Nov. 3 Litho. *Perf. 13½x13¼*
3733 A1254 6.50 l Sheet of 2, #a-b 3.50 1.75

See Russia No. 8214.

Istanbul Tourism — A1255

Designs: 50k, Tulips, poppies, Hagia Sophia. 6.50 l, Maiden's Tower.

Perf. 13¼x13½

2020, Nov. 24 Litho.

3734-3735 A1255 Set of 2 1.75 .90

Turkish Scientific Research Station in Antarctica A1256

2020, Dec. 1 Litho. *Perf. 13¾*

3736 A1256 3 l multi .80 .40

Souvenir Sheet

Opening of Central Mosque of Imam Al-Sarakhsi, Bishkek, Kyrgyzstan — A1257

2020, Dec. 21 Litho. *Perf. 13*

3737 A1257 6.50 l multi 1.75 .90

See Kyrgyz Express Post No. 144.

Souvenir Sheets

National Independence, Cent. — A1258

Pres. Kemal Atatürk (1881-1938) — A1259

Perf. 13¾x13 Syncopated

2021, Jan. 6 Litho.

3738 A1258 3 l multi .85 .40

Litho. With Foil Application

3739 A1259 6.50 l copper & multi 1.90 .95

Birdhouse on Topkapi Palace Imperial Mint Building A1260

Birdhouse on Ayazma Mosque A1261

2021, Feb. 19 Litho. *Perf. 13¼*

3740 A1260 3 l multi .85 .40
3741 A1261 3 l multi .85 .40

National Anthem, Cent. A1262

Perf. 13¾x13¼

2021, Mar. 12 Litho.

3742 A1262 3 l multi .75 .35

A1263

A1264

A1265

Paintings by Devrim Erbil — A1266

2021, Mar. 19 Litho. *Perf. 13¼*

3743 A1263 3 l multi .75 .35
3744 A1264 3 l multi .75 .35
3745 A1265 3 l multi .75 .35
3746 A1266 3 l multi .75 .35
Nos. 3743-3746 (4) 3.00 1.40

Globe on Heart — A1267

Globe on Dove — A1268

2021, Mar. 25 Litho. *Perf. 13¼*

3747 A1267 2 l multi .50 .25
3748 A1268 3 l multi .75 .35

A1269

Dara Archaeological Site — A1270

2021, Apr. 20 Litho. *Perf. 13¼*

3749 A1269 3 l multi .75 .35
3750 A1270 3 l multi .75 .35

Souvenir Sheet

Turksat Satellites A1271

No. 3751: a, Turksat 5A above Europe. b, Turksat 5A and Turksat 5B over Earth.

Perf. 14x13¾ Syncopated

2021, May 5 Litho.

3751 A1271 3 l Sheet of 2, #a-b 1.50 .75

Souvenir Sheet

Archery A1272

No. 3752: a, Arrow and shooting technique. b, Diagram of bow and arrow.

2021, May 6 Litho. *Perf. 13½x13¾*

3752 A1272 3 l Sheet of 2, #a-b 1.40 .70

Europa A1273

Endangered animals: 3 l, Monachus monachus. 6.50 l, Circus pygargus

2021, May 9 Litho. *Perf. 13¼*

3753-3754 A1273 Set of 2 2.25 1.10

Souvenir Sheet

Zeki Müren (1931-96), Singer — A1274

No. 3755 — Müren: a, With flower in lapel of jacket. b, Standing behind microphone. c, Wearing necklace.

2021, May 26 Litho. *Perf. 14x13¾*

3755 A1274 3 l Sheet of 3, #a-c 2.10 1.10

These souvenir sheets depicting Müren and the bottom item, a self-adhesive stamp produced in a booklet pane of 6 stamps depicting various images of Müren, were produced in limited quantities and sold only in a folder, which also included three post-cards, for 125 l.

Souvenir Sheet

World Environment Day — A1275

2021, June 5 Litho. *Die Cut*

Self-Adhesive

3756 A1275 3 l multi .70 .35

2020 European Soccer Championships A1276

Mascot: No. 3757, 3 l, Holding trophy. No. 3758, 3 l, Dribbling soccer ball. No. 3759, 6.50 l, Balancing soccer ball on side of head. No. 3760, 6.50 l, Celebrating goal.

2021, June 11 Litho. *Perf. 14¼*

3757-3760 A1276 Set of 4 4.50 2.25

The 2020 European Soccer Championships were postponed until 2021 because of the COVID-19 pandemic.

Souvenir Sheet

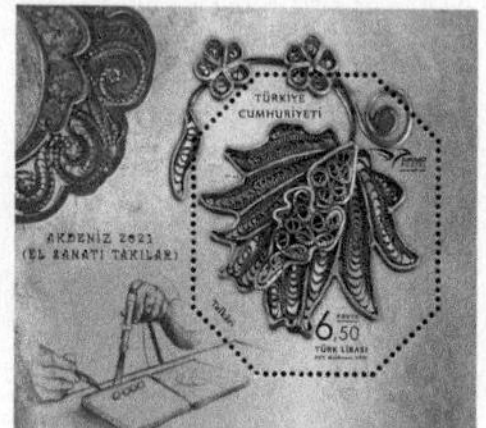

Traditional Mediterranean Jewelry — A1277

2021, July 12 Litho. *Perf. 14¼*

3761 A1277 6.50 l multi 1.60 .80

2020 Summer Olympics, Tokyo — A1278

Designs: 3 l, Pole vaulter, volleyball player, wrestlers. 6.50 l, Shooter, karateka, cyclist.

2021, July 23 Litho. *Perf. 13¼*

3762-3763 A1278 Set of 2 2.25 1.10

The 2020 Summer Olympics were postponed until 2021 because of the COVID-19 pandemic.

Fruits and Vegetables A1279

Designs: No. 3764, 3 l, Citrillus lanatus. No. 3765, 3 l, Cucumis sativus. No. 3766, 3 l, Momordica charantia.

2021, July 30 Litho. *Perf. 13¼x13½*
3764-3766 A1279 Set of 3 2.25 1.10

Battle of the Sakarya, Cent. A1280

2021, Aug. 23 Litho. *Perf. 13¼*
3767 A1280 3 l multi .75 .35

Battle of Malazgirt, 950th Anniv. — A1281

2021, Aug. 26 Litho. *Perf. 13¾*
3768 A1281 3 l multi .75 .35

High-speed Train — A1282

Container Ship Passing Under Yavuz Sultan Selim Bridge — A1283

Control Tower, Istanbul Airport — A1284

Camlica Telecommunications Tower, Istanbul, and Flag of Turkey — A1285

2021, Oct. 6 Litho. *Perf. 13¼*
3769 A1282 4 l multi .85 .40
3770 A1283 4 l multi .85 .40
3771 A1284 4 l multi .85 .40
3772 A1285 4 l multi .85 .40
Nos. 3769-3772 (4) 3.40 1.60

12th International Transport and Communications Forum, Istanbul.

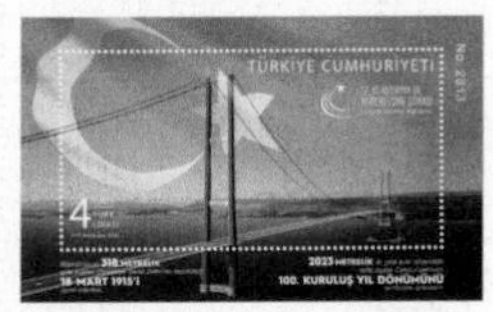

This souvenir sheet issued to commemorate the 12th International Transport and Communications Forum was produced in limited quantities.

Sharks — A1286

Designs: No. 3773, 4 l, Sphyrna zygaena. No. 3774, 4 l, Cetorhinus maximus. No. 3775, 4 l, Carcharodon carcharias. No. 3776, 4 l, Carcharias taurus.

2021, Oct. 22 Litho. *Perf. 13¼*
3773-3776 A1286 Set of 4 3.50 1.75

Pres. Kemal Atatürk (1881-1938) — A1287

Perf. 13¾ Syncopated
2021, Nov. 5 Litho.

Background Color

3777 A1287 4 l pink .60 .30
3778 A1287 7 l light blue 1.10 .55
3779 A1287 12 l light org brn 1.90 .95
3780 A1287 26 l dull green 4.00 2.00
Nos. 3777-3780 (4) 7.60 3.80

Old Means of Transportation — A1288

Designs: No. 3781, 4 l, Electric commuter train. No. 3782, 4 l, Tram. No. 3783, 4 l, Trolleybus. No. 3784, 4 l, Ferry.

2022, Jan. 7 Litho. *Perf. 13½x13¼*
3781-3784 A1288 Set of 4 2.40 1.25

Hillside Village and its Reflection in Water — A1289

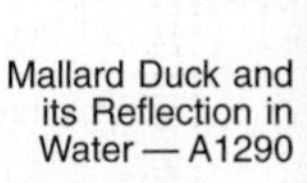

Mallard Duck and its Reflection in Water — A1290

2022, Feb. 24 Litho. *Perf. 13¼*
3785 A1289 5 l multi .75 .35
3786 A1290 5 l multi .75 .35

Alaeddin Yavasca (1926-2021), Gynecologist and Musician — A1291

2022, Mar. 1 Litho. *Perf. 13¾*
3787 A1291 5 l multi .75 .35

Opening of 1915 Canakkale Bridge — A1292

Perf. 13¼x13½
2022, Mar. 18 Litho.
3788 A1292 5 l multi .75 .35

Turkish Cities with Cittaslow Membership A1293

Designs: 1 l, Uzundere. 2 l, Vize. 5 l, Iznik. 15 l, Güdül. 20 l, Foça. 31 l, Halfeti.

2022, Mar. 24 Litho. *Perf. 13¾*
3789-3794 A1293 Set of 6 10.00 5.00

Souvenir Sheet

Opening of Expo 2021, Hatay Province A1294

2022, Apr. 1 Litho. *Perf. 13½x13¼*
3795 A1294 5 l multi .70 .35

The opening of Expo 2021 was postponed until Apr. 1, 2022 because of the COVID-19 pandemic.

Pres. Kemal Atatürk (1881-1938)
A1295 A1296

Perf. 13¾ Syncopated
2022, Apr. 7 Litho.
3796 A1295 1 l multi .30 .30
3797 A1296 5 l multi .70 .35

Kites — A1297

Designs: No. 3798, 5 l, Three kites. No. 3799, 5 l, Box kite.

2022, Apr. 23 Litho. *Perf. 13¼*
3798-3799 A1297 Set of 2 1.40 .70

A1298

Scenes From the Epic of Köroglu — A1299

2022, May 9 Litho. *Perf. 13¼*
3800 A1298 5 l multi .60 .30
3801 A1299 5 l multi .60 .30

Europa.

Turkish Cheeses A1300

No. 3802 — Various cheeses with denomination at: a, Left. b, Right.

2022, May 17 Litho. *Perf. 13¼*
3802 A1300 5 l Horiz. pair, #a-b 1.25 .60

World Environment Day — A1301

No. 3803 — Turtle carrying: a, Water bottle. b, Thermometer.

2022, June 5 Litho. *Perf. 13¼*
3803 A1301 5 l Horiz. pair, #a-b 1.25 .60

Crabs A1302

No. 3804: a, Atergatis roseus. b, Callinectes sapidus.

2022, June 21 Litho. *Perf. 13¼*
3804 A1302 5 l Horiz. pair, #a-b 1.25 .60

Archaeologists Researching 14th Cent. B.C. Uluburun Shipwreck — A1303

2022, July 19 Litho. *Perf. 13½x13¼*
3805 A1303 5 l multi .55 .30

Dr. Mahmut Gazi Yasargil, Microneurosurgeon — A1304

2022, July 29 Litho. *Perf. 13¼*
3806 A1304 5 l multi .55 .30

Canyons A1305

Designs: No. 3807, 7.50 l, Karaleylek Canyon. No. 3808, 7.50 l, Incesu Canyon.

Perf. 13½x13¼
2022, Aug. 18 Litho.
3807-3808 A1305 Set of 2 1.75 .85

Souvenir Sheet

Battle of Dumlupinar (Victory Day), Cent. — A1306

Perf. 13¾x13 Syncopated
2022, Aug. 30 Litho.
3809 A1306 7.50 l multi .85 .40

This souvenir sheet issued to commemorate Victory Day was produced in limited quantities.

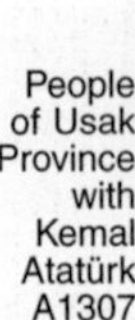

People of Usak Province with Kemal Atatürk
A1307

2022, Sept. 1 Litho. ***Perf. 13¼***
3810 A1307 7.50 l multi .85 .40

A1308

Neset Ertas (1938-2012), Folk Musician — A1309

2022, Sept. 25 Litho. ***Perf. 13¼***
3811 A1308 7.50 l multi .80 .40

Perf. 13¼x13½
3812 A1309 7.50 l multi .80 .40

These souvenir sheets issued to commemorate Neset Ertas were produced in limited quantities.

World Post Day — A1310

2022, Oct. 9 Litho. ***Perf. 13¼***
3813 A1310 7.50 l multi .80 .40

Souvenir Sheet

Armistice of Mudanya, Cent. — A1311

Perf. 13¾x13 Syncopated
2022, Oct. 11 Litho.
3814 A1311 7.50 l multi .80 .40

Birds on Impala
A1312

Hummingbird and Flowers — A1313

Perf. 13½x13¼
2022, Dec. 14 Litho.
3815 A1312 7.50 l multi .80 .40

Perf. 13¼
3816 A1313 7.50 l multi .80 .40

Trees
A1314

Designs: No. 3817, 10 l, Oleae europaе. No. 3818, 10 l, Juniperus foetidissima.

2023, Jan. 26 Litho. ***Perf. 13½x13¼***
3817-3818 A1314 Set of 2 2.10 1.10

Pres. Kemal Atatürk (1881-1938) — A1315

Various portraits of Atatürk.

Perf. 13½ Syncopated
2023, Feb. 6 Litho.
3819 A1315 10 l multi 1.10 .55
3820 A1315 28 l multi 3.00 1.50
3821 A1315 58 l multi 6.25 3.25
Nos. 3819-3821 (3) 10.35 5.30

Cross-Stitched Flowers
A1316

2023, Feb. 22 Litho. ***Perf. 13¼***
3822 A1316 10 l multi 1.10 .55

SEMI-POSTAL STAMPS

Regular Issues Overprinted in Carmine or Black

Overprint reads: "For War Orphans"

Perf. 12, 13½ and Compound
1915 Unwmk.

On Stamps of 1905
B1 A18 10pa dull grn (#119) 2.00 .75
B2 A18 10pi orange brown 12.50 .80

On Stamp of 1906
B3 A18 10pa dull grn (#128) 40.00 25.00

On Stamps of 1908
B4 A19 10pa blue green 1.50 .75
B5 A19 5pi dark violet 75.00 12.50
Nos. B1-B5 (5) 131.00 39.80

No. B6 with Additional "Discount" Overprint on No. B4

B6 A19 10pa blue green 240.00 175.00

On Stamps of 1909
B7 A21 10pa blue green 2.00 .75
a. Inverted overprint 30.00 30.00
b. Double overprint, one invtd. 30.00 30.00
B8 A21 20pa carmine rose 2.00 .75
a. Inverted overprint 30.00 30.00
B9 A21 1pi ultra 2.00 .75
B10 A21 5pi dark violet 8.75 1.50
Nos. B7-B10 (4) 14.75 3.75

See note after No. 131.

Nos. B11-B13 with Additional Overprint on Nos. B7-B9

B11 A21 10pa blue green 2.00 .75
b. Double overprint, one inverted 30.00 30.00
B12 A21 20pa carmine rose 1.50 .75
B13 A21 1pi ultra 2.00 .75

On Stamps of 1913
B14 A22 10pa blue green 2.00 .75
a. Inverted overprint 35.00 35.00
B15 A22 1pi ultra 2.00 .75
a. Double overprint 20.00 20.00
Nos. B11-B15 (5) 9.50 3.75

No. B16 with Additional Overprint on No. B14

B16 A22 10pa blue green 1.75 .75
a. Inverted overprint 30.00 30.00

On Newspaper Stamp of 1908
B17 A19 10pa blue green 360.00 175.00

On Newspaper Stamp of 1909
B18 A21 10pa blue green 1.75 1.00

Regular Issues Overprinted in Carmine or Black

1916 On Stamps of 1901
B19 A17 1pi blue 2.00 .50
B20 A17 5pi lilac rose 10.00 1.50

On Stamps of 1905
B21 A18 1pi brt blue 7.50 2.00
B22 A18 5pi brown 7.50 5.00

On Stamp of 1906
B23 A18 1pi brt blue 1.00 .75

On Stamps of 1908
B24 A19 20pa carmine (Bk) *300.00*
B25 A19 10pi red 500.00 200.00

Nos. B26-B27 with Additional Overprints

B26 A19 20pa carmine 8.00 8.00
B27 A19 1pi brt blue (C) 20.00 5.00

On Stamps of 1909
B28 A21 20pa carmine rose 2.00 1.25
B29 A21 1pi ultra 1.50 1.00
B30 A21 10pi dull red 175.00 100.00

No. B26 is No. B24 with an additional overprint. No. B27 is the design of 1908, with two overprints. Its was not issued with one.

Nos. B31-B32 with Additional Overprint on Nos. B28-B29

B31 A21 20pa carmine rose 1.50 .75
B32 A21 1pi ultra 2.00 1.00

On Stamps of 1913
B33 A22 20pa carmine rose 2.00 1.50
B34 A22 1pi ultra 2.00 1.00
a. Inverted overprint 30.00 30.00
B35 A22 10pi dull red 22.50 15.00

No. B36 with Additional Overprint on No. B33

B36 A22 20pa carmine rose 2.00 1.25

On Newspaper Stamps of 1901
B37 A16 5pi ocher 11.50 6.00
a. 5pa bister, No. P37 150.00 150.00

Regular Issues Surcharged in Black

On Stamp of 1898
B38 A11 10pa on 20pa vio brn 2.00 1.50

On Stamp of 1905
B39 A18 10pa on 20pa carmine 2.00 1.50

On Stamp of 1906
B40 A18 10pa on 20pa carmine 1.50 1.25

On Newspaper Stamp of 1893-99
B41 A11 10pa on 20pa violet brn 2.00 1.50
Nos. B38-B41 (4) 7.50 5.75

Nos. 346-349 Overprinted

B42 A41 10pa carmine 1.50 .75
a. Inverted overprint 20.00 20.00
B43 A41 20pa ultra 1.50 .75
a. Inverted overprint 20.00 20.00
B44 A41 1pi violet & blk 1.50 .90
a. Inverted overprint 20.00 20.00
B45 A41 5pi yel brn & blk 2.00 1.50
a. Inverted overprint 30.00 30.00
Nos. B42-B45 (4) 6.50 3.90

Nos. B42-B45 formed part of the Postage Commemoration issue of 1916.

A Soldier's Farewell — SP1

1917, Feb. 20 Engr. ***Perf. 12½***
B46 SP1 10pa red violet 1.25 .50

For surcharges see Nos. 600, B47.

Stamp of Same Design Surcharged

B47 SP1 10pa on 20pa car rose 2.00 .50

Badge of the Society
SP9

School Teacher
SP10

Marie Sklodowska Curie SP16

Kemal Atatürk SP23

Designs: 2k+2k, Woman farmer. 2½k+2½k, Typist. 4k+4k, Aviatrix and policewoman. 5k+5k, Women voters. 7½k+7½k, Yildiz Palace, Istanbul. 10k+10k, Carrie Chapman Catt. 12½k+12½k, Jane Addams. 15k+15k, Grazia Deledda. 20k+20k, Selma Lagerlof. 25k+25k, Bertha von Suttner. 30k+30k, Sigrid Undset.

1935, Apr. 17 Photo. *Perf. 11½*

Inscribed: "XII Congres Suffragiste International"

B54	SP9	20pa + 20pa brn	.50	.50
B55	SP10	1k + 1k rose car	.75	.50
B56	SP10	2k + 2k sl bl	1.00	.75
B57	SP10	2½k + 2½k yel grn	1.00	.75
B58	SP10	4k + 4k blue	1.50	1.00
B59	SP10	5k + 5k dl vio	2.50	2.00
B60	SP10	7½k + 7½k org red	2.50	2.00
B61	SP16	10k + 10k org	2.50	2.50
B62	SP16	12½k + 12½k dk bl	2.50	2.50
B63	SP16	15k + 15k violet	5.00	5.00
B64	SP16	20k + 20k red org	7.50	6.25
B65	SP16	25k + 25k grn	15.00	14.00
B66	SP16	30k + 30k ultra	90.00	100.00
B67	SP16	50k + 50k dk sl grn	175.00	150.00
B68	SP23	100k + 100k brn car	125.00	140.00
		Nos. B54-B68 (15)	432.25	427.75
		Set, never hinged	750.00	

12th Congress of the Women's Intl. Alliance.

Catalogue values for unused stamps in this section, from this point to the end of the section, are for Never Hinged items.

Katip Chelebi — SP24

Perf. 10½

1958, Sept. 24 Litho. Unwmk.

B69	SP24	50k + 10k gray	.50	.25

Mustafa ibn 'Abdallah Katip Chelebi Hajji Khalifa (1608-1657), Turkish author.

Road Building Machine SP25

Kemal Atatürk SP26

Design: 25k+5k, Tanks and planes.

1958, Oct. 29

B70	SP25	15k + 5k orange	.40	.25
B71	SP26	20k + 5k lt red brn	.40	.25
B72	SP25	25k + 5k brt grn	.40	.25
		Nos. B70-B72 (3)	1.20	.75

The surtax went to the Red Crescent Society and to the Society for the Protection of Children.

For surcharge see No. 1440.

Ruins, Göreme — SP27

1959, July 8 Litho. *Perf. 10*

B73	SP27	105k + 10k pur & buff	.50	.25

Issued for tourist publicity.

Istanbul — SP28

1959, Sept. 11

B74	SP28	105k + 10k lt bl & red	.50	.25

15th International Tuberculosis Congress.

Manisa Asylum SP29

Merkez Muslihiddin SP30

Kermis at Manisa: 90k+5k, Sultan Camil Mosque, Manisa, vert.

1960, Apr. 17 Unwmk. *Perf. 13*

B75	SP29	40k + 5k grn & lt bl	.25	.25
B76	SP29	40k + 5k vio & rose lil	.25	.25
B77	SP29	90k + 5k dp cl & car rose	.50	.25
B78	SP30	105k + 10k multi	.65	.25
		Nos. B75-B78 (4)	1.65	1.00

Census Chart SP31

Census Symbol SP32

1960, Sept. 23 Photo. *Perf. 11½*

Granite Paper

B79	SP31	30k + 5k bl & rose pink	.25	.25
B80	SP32	50k + 5k grn, dk bl & ultra	.35	.25

Issued for the 1960 Census.

Old Observatory SP33

Fatin Gökmen SP34

Designs: 30k+5k, Observatory emblem. 75k+5k, Building housing telescope.

1961, July 1 Litho. *Perf. 13*

B81	SP33	10k + 5k grnsh bl & grn	.25	.25
B82	SP33	30k + 5k vio & blk	.60	.60
B83	SP34	40k + 5k brown	.25	.25
B84	SP33	75k + 5k olive grn	.60	.60
		Nos. B81-B84 (4)	1.70	1.70

Kandili Observatory, 50th anniversary.

Anti-Malaria Work — SP35

UNICEF, 10th anniv.: 30k+5k, Mother and infant, horiz. 75k+5k, Woman distributing pasteurized milk.

1961, Dec. 11 Unwmk. *Perf. 13*

B85	SP35	10k + 5k Prus green	.25	.25
B86	SP35	30k + 5k dull violet	.30	.25
B87	SP35	75k + 5k dk olive bis	.60	.25
		Nos. B85-B87 (3)	1.15	.75

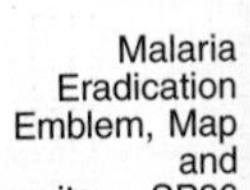

Malaria Eradication Emblem, Map and Mosquito — SP36

1962, Apr. 7 Litho.

B88	SP36	30k + 5k dk & lt brn	.25	.25
B89	SP36	75k + 5k blk & lil	.50	.25

WHO drive to eradicate malaria.

Poinsettia — SP37

Flowers: 40k+10k, Bird of paradise flower. 75k+10k, Water lily.

1962, May 19 *Perf. 12½x13½*

Flowers in Natural Colors

B90	SP37	30k + 10k lt bl & blk	.25	.25
B91	SP37	40k + 10k lt bl & blk	.45	.25
B92	SP37	75k + 10k lt bl & blk	.95	.40
		Nos. B90-B92 (3)	1.65	.90

Wheat and Census Chart — SP38

Design: 60k+5k, Wheat and chart, horiz.

Inscribed: "Umumi Ziraat Sayimi"

1963, Apr. 14 Photo. *Perf. 11½*

B93	SP38	40k + 5k gray grn & yel	.35	.25
B94	SP38	60k + 5k org yel & blk	.35	.25

1961 agricultural census. Two black bars obliterate "Kasim 1960" inscription.

Red Lion and Sun, Red Crescent, Red Cross and Globe — SP39

Designs: 60k+10k, Emblems in flowers, vert. 100k+10k, Emblems on flags.

1963, Aug. 1 *Perf. 13*

B95	SP39	50k + 10k multi	.25	.25
B96	SP39	60k + 10k multi	.40	.25
B97	SP39	100k + 10k multi	.60	.45
		Nos. B95-B97 (3)	1.25	.95

Centenary of International Red Cross.

Angora Goat — SP40

Animals: 10k+5k, Steppe cattle, horiz. 50k+5k. Arabian horses, horiz. 60k+5k, Three Angora goats. 100k+5k, Montofon cattle, horiz.

1964, Oct. 4 Litho. *Perf. 13*

B98	SP40	10k + 5k multi	.35	.25
B99	SP40	30k + 5k multi	.35	.25
B100	SP40	50k + 5k multi	.60	.25
B101	SP40	60k + 5k multi	.85	.25
B102	SP40	100k + 5k multi	1.10	.25
		Nos. B98-B102 (5)	3.25	1.25

Issued for Animal Protection Day.

Olympic Torch Bearer — SP41

Designs: 10k+5k, Running, horiz. 60k+5k, Wrestling. 100k+5k, Discus.

1964, Oct. 10 Unwmk.

B103	SP41	10k + 5k org brn, blk & red	.40	.25
B104	SP41	50k + 5k ol, blk & red	.40	.25
B105	SP41	60k + 5k bl, blk & red	1.00	.25
B106	SP41	100k + 5k vio, blk, red & sil	1.40	.40
		Nos. B103-B106 (4)	3.20	1.15

18th Olympic Games, Tokyo, Oct. 10-25.

Map of Dardanelles and Laurel — SP42

Designs: 90k+10k, Soldiers and war memorial, Canakkale. 130k+10k, Turkish flag and arch, vert.

1965, Mar. 18 Litho. *Perf. 13*

B107	SP42	50k + 10k vio, yel & gold	.25	.25
B108	SP42	90k + 10k vio bl, bl, yel & grn	.60	.25
B109	SP42	130k + 10k dk brn, red & yel	1.10	.90
		Nos. B107-B109 (3)	1.95	1.40

50th anniversary of Battle of Gallipoli.

Tobacco Plant — SP43

50k+5k, Tobacco leaves and Leander's tower, horiz. 100k+5k, Tobacco leaf.

1965, Sept. 16 Unwmk. *Perf. 13*

B110	SP43	30k + 5k brn, lt brn & grn	.25	.25
B111	SP43	50k + 5k vio bl, ocher & pur	.60	.25
B112	SP43	100k + 5k blk, ol grn & ocher	1.00	.50
		Nos. B110-B112 (3)	1.85	1.00

Second International Tobacco Congress.

Goddess, Basalt Carving — SP44

Archaeological Museum, Ankara: 30k+5k, Eagle and rabbit, ivory carving, horiz. 60k+5k, Bronze bull. 90k+5k, Gold pitcher.

Perf. 13½x13, 13x13½

1966, June 6 Litho.

B113	SP44	30k + 5k multi	.25	.25
B114	SP44	50k + 5k multi	.55	.25
B115	SP44	60k + 5k multi	.85	.45
B116	SP44	90k + 5k multi	1.10	.60
		Nos. B113-B116 (4)	2.75	1.55

Grand Hotel Ephesus — SP45

Designs: 60k+5k, Konak Square, Izmir, vert. 130k+5k, Izmir Fair Grounds.

1966, Oct. 18 Litho. *Perf. 12*

B117 SP45 50k + 5k multi .25 .25
B118 SP45 60k + 5k multi .45 .25
B119 SP45 130k + 5k multi .95 .55
Nos. B117-B119 (3) 1.65 1.05

33rd Congress of the Intl. Fair Assoc.

Europa Issue, 1967

Common Design Type

1967, May 2 Litho. *Perf. 13x13½*

Size: 22x33mm

B120 CD10 100k + 10k multi .75 .75
B121 CD10 130k + 10k multi 1.75 1.25
Nos. B120-B121 (2) 2.50 2.00

Cloverleaf Crossing, Map of Turkey — SP46

130k+5k, Highway E5 & map of Turkey.

1967, June 30 Litho. *Perf. 13*

B122 SP46 60k + 5k multi .60 .25
B123 SP46 130k + 5k multi, vert. 1.00 .60

Inter-European Express Highway, E5.

WHO Emblem — SP47

1968, Apr. 7 Litho. *Perf. 13*

B124 SP47 130k + 10k lt ultra, blk & yel .80 .25

WHO, 20th anniversary.

Efem Pasha, Dr. Marko Pasha and View of Istanbul SP48

60k+10k, Omer Pasha, Dr. Abdullah Bey & wounded soldiers. 100k+10k, Ataturk & Dr. Refik Saydam in front of Red Crescent headquarters, vert.

1968, June 11 Litho. *Perf. 13*

B125 SP48 50k + 10k multi .45 .25
B126 SP48 60k + 10k multi .60 .30
B127 SP48 100k + 10k multi .95 .45
Nos. B125-B127 (3) 2.00 1.00

Centenary of Turkish Red Crescent Society.

NATO Emblem and Dove — SP49

NATO, 20th anniv.: 130k+10k, NATO emblem and globe surrounded by 15 stars, symbols of the 15 NATO members.

1969, Apr. 4 Litho. *Perf. 13*

B128 SP49 50k + 10k brt grn, blk & lt bl .45 .25
B129 SP49 130k + 10k bluish blk, bl & gold .75 .35

Red Cross, Crescent, Lion and Sun Emblems — SP50

Design: 130k+10k, Conference emblem and Istanbul skyline.

1969, Aug. 29 Litho. *Perf. 13*

B130 SP50 100k + 10k dk & lt bl & red .50 .25
B131 SP50 130k + 10k red, lt bl & blk .65 .40

21st Intl. Red Cross Conf., Istanbul.

Erosion Control — SP51

60k+10k, Protection of flora (dead tree). 130k+10k, Protection of wildlife (bird of prey).

1970, Feb. 9 Litho. *Perf. 13*

B132 SP51 50k + 10k multi .40 .40
B133 SP51 60k + 10k multi .60 .60
B134 SP51 130k + 10k multi 1.40 1.40
Nos. B132-B134 (3) 2.40 2.40

1970 European Nature Conservation Year.

Globe and Fencer — SP52

Design: 130k+10k, Globe, fencer and folk dancer with sword and shield.

1970, Sept. 13 Litho. *Perf. 13*

B135 SP52 90k + 10k bl & blk .50 .25
B136 SP52 130k + 10k ultra, lt bl, blk & org .70 .25

International Fencing Championships.

"Children's Protection" — SP53

Designs: 100k+15k, Hand supporting child, vert. 110k+15k, Mother and child.

1971, June 30 Litho. *Perf. 13*

Star and Crescent Emblem in Red

B137 SP53 50k + 10k lil rose & blk .25 .25
B138 SP53 100k + 15k brn, rose & blk .35 .25
B139 SP53 110k + 15k org brn, bis & blk .45 .25
Nos. B137-B139 (3) 1.05 .75

50th anniv. of the Child Protection Assoc.

UNICEF, 25th Anniv. — SP54

1971, Dec. 11

B140 SP54 100k + 10k multi .35 .25
B141 SP54 250k + 15k multi .90 .70

"Your Heart is your Health" — SP55

1972, Apr. 7 Litho. *Perf. 13*

B142 SP55 250k + 25k gray, blk & red .80 .65

World Health Day.

Olympic Emblems, Runners — SP56

100k+15k, Olympic rings & motion emblem. 250k+25k, Olympic rings & symbolic track ('72).

1972, Aug. 26

B143 SP56 100k + 15k multi .40 .25
B144 SP56 110k + 25k multi .50 .25
B145 SP56 250k + 25k multi .70 .45
Nos. B143-B145 (3) 1.60 .95

20th Olympic Games, Munich, 8/26-9/11.

Emblem of Istanbul Technical University — SP57

1973, Apr. 21 Litho. *Perf. 13*

B146 SP57 100k + 25k multi .65 .25

Istanbul Technical University, 200th anniv.

Dove and "50" — SP58

1973, July 24 Litho. *Perf. 12½x13*

B147 SP58 100k + 25k multi .75 .35

Peace Treaty of Lausanne, 50th anniversary.

World Population Year — SP59

1974, June 15 Litho. *Perf. 13*

B148 SP59 250k + 25k multi .75 .35

Guglielmo Marconi (1874-1937), Italian Electrical Engineer and Inventor — SP60

1974, Nov. 15 Litho. *Perf. 13½*

B149 SP60 250k + 25k multi .75 .35

Dr. Albert Schweitzer — SP61

1975, Jan 14 Litho. *Perf. 13*

B150 SP61 250k + 50k multi .90 .45

Dr. Albert Schweitzer (1875-1965), medical missionary and music scholar.

Africa with South-West Africa — SP62

1975, Aug. 26 Litho. *Perf. 13x12½*

B151 SP62 250k + 50k multi .70 .35

Namibia Day (independence for South-West Africa).

Ziya Gökalp — SP63

1976, Mar. 23 Litho. *Perf. 13*

B152 SP63 200k + 25k multi .60 .30

Ziya Gökalp (1876-1924), philosopher.

Spoonbill — SP64

Birds: 150k+25k, European roller. 200k+25k, Flamingo. 400k+25k, Hermit ibis, horiz.

1976, Nov. 19 Litho. *Perf. 13*

B153 SP64 100k + 25k multi .65 .25
B154 SP64 150k + 25k multi .80 .25
B155 SP64 200k + 25k multi 1.25 .35
B156 SP64 400k + 25k multi 2.25 .45
Nos. B153-B156 (4) 4.95 1.30

Decree by Mehmet Bey, and Ongun Holy Bird — SP65

1977, May 13 Litho. *Perf. 13*

B157 SP65 200k + 25k grn & blk .60 .25

700th anniv. of Turkish as official language.

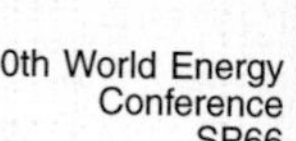

10th World Energy Conference SP66

Design: 600k+50k, Conference emblem and globe with circles.

1977, Sept. 19 Litho. *Perf. 12½*

B158 SP66 100k + 25k multi .25 .25
B159 SP66 600k + 50k multi 1.00 .40

Running — SP67

Designs: 2½ l+50k, Gymnastics. 5 l+ 50k, Table tennis. 8 l+50k, Swimming.

1978, July 18 Litho. *Perf. 13*

B160 SP67 1 l + 50k multi .25 .25
B161 SP67 2½ l + 50k multi .30 .25
B162 SP67 5 l + 50k multi .55 .25
B163 SP67 8 l + 50k multi 1.00 .30
Nos. B160-B163 (4) 2.10 1.05

GYMNASIADE '78, World School Games, Izmir.

Ribbon and Chain — SP68

Design: 5 l+50k, Ribbon and flower, vert.

Perf. 12½x13, 13x12½

1978, Sept. 3 Litho.

B164 SP68 2½ l + 50k multi .65 .25
B165 SP68 5 l + 50k multi 1.10 .25

European Declaration of Human Rights, 25th anniversary.

Children, Head of Ataturk — SP69

IYC Emblem and: 5 l+50k, Children with globe as balloon. 8 l+50k, Kneeling person and child, globe.

1979, Apr. 23 Litho. *Perf. 13x13½*

B166 SP69 2½ l + 50k multi .35 .25
B167 SP69 5 l + 50k multi .55 .25
B168 SP69 8 l + 50k multi .85 .35
Nos. B166-B168 (3) 1.75 .85

International Year of the Child.

Black Francolin — SP70

No. B170, Great bustard. No. B171, Crane. No. B172, Gazelle. No. B173, Mouflon muffelwild.

1979, Dec. 3 Litho. *Perf. 13x13½*

B169 SP70 5 l + 1 l multi .55 .25
B170 SP70 5 l + 1 l multi .55 .25
B171 SP70 5 l + 1 l multi .55 .25
B172 SP70 5 l + 1 l multi .55 .25
B173 SP70 5 l + 1 l multi .55 .25
a. Strip of 5, #B169-B173 3.00 3.00

European Wildlife Conservation Year. No. B173a has continuous design.

Flowers, Trees and Sun — SP71

Environment Protection: 7½ l+ 1 l Sun, water. 15 l+1 l, Industrial pollution, globe. 20 l+1 l, Flower in oil puddle.

1980, June 4 Litho. *Perf. 13*

B174 SP71 2½ l + 1 l multi .25 .25
B175 SP71 7½ l + 1 l multi .25 .25
B176 SP71 15 l + 1 l multi .45 .25
B177 SP71 20 l + 1 l multi .50 .35
Nos. B174-B177 (4) 1.45 1.10

Rodolia Cardinalis — SP72

Useful Insects: 7½ l+1 l, Bracon hebetor; 15 l+1 l, Calosoma sycophanta; 20 l+1 l, Deraeocoris rutilus.

1980, Dec. 3 Litho. *Perf. 13*

B178 SP72 2½ l + 1 l multi .25 .25
B179 SP72 7½ l + 1 l multi .45 .25
B180 SP72 15 l + 1 l multi .80 .25
B181 SP72 20 l + 1 l multi 1.00 .25
Nos. B178-B181 (4) 2.50 1.00

Intl. Year of the Disabled — SP73

1981, Mar. 25 Litho. *Perf. 13*

B182 SP73 10 l + 2½ l multi .50 .25
B183 SP73 20 l + 2½ l multi .75 .25

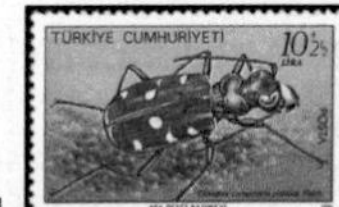

Insects — SP74

Useful Insects: No. B184, Cicindela campestris. No. B185, Syrphus vitripennis. No. B186, Ascalaphus macaronius. No. B187, Empusa fasciata.

1981, Dec. 16 Litho. *Perf. 13*

B184 SP74 10 l + 2½ l multi .50 .25
B185 SP74 20 l + 2½ l multi .85 .25
B186 SP74 30 l + 2½ l multi 1.40 .45
B187 SP74 40 l + 2½ l multi 1.75 .60
Nos. B184-B187 (4) 4.50 1.55

See Nos. B190-B194, B196-B200.

TB Bacillus Centenary — SP75

Portraits: #B188, Dr. Tevfik Saglam (1882-1963). #B189, Robert Koch.

1982, Mar. 24 *Perf. 13x12½*

B188 SP75 10 l + 2½ l multi .35 .25
B189 SP75 30 l + 2½ l multi .65 .25

Insect Type of 1981

Useful Insects: 10 l+2½ l, Eurydema spectabile. 15 l+2½ l, Dacus oleae. 20 l+2½ l, Klapperichicen viridissima. 30 l+2½ l, Leptinotarsa decemlineata. 35 l+2½ l, Rhynchites auratus.

1982, Aug. 18 Litho. *Perf. 13*

B190 SP74 10 l + 2½ l multi .55 .25
B191 SP74 15 l + 2½ l multi .80 .25
B192 SP74 20 l + 2½ l multi .80 .25
B193 SP74 30 l + 2½ l multi .90 .25
B194 SP74 35 l + 2½ l multi 1.00 .25
Nos. B190-B194 (5) 4.05 1.25

Richard Wagner (1813-1883), Composer SP76

1983, Feb. 13

B195 SP76 30 l + 5 l multi 1.00 .65

Insect Type of 1981

Harmful Insects: 15 l+5 l, Eurygaster Intergriceps Put. 25 l+5 l, Phyllobius nigrofasciatus Pes. 35 l+5 l, Cercopis intermedia Kbm. 50 l+10 l, Graphosoma lineatum (L). 75 l+10 l, Capnodis miliaris (King).

1983, Sept. 14 Litho. *Perf. 13*

B196 SP74 15 l + 5 l multi .40 .25
B197 SP74 25 l + 5 l multi .55 .25
B198 SP74 35 l + 5 l multi .65 .25
B199 SP74 50 l + 10 l multi 1.00 .25
B200 SP74 75 l + 10 l multi 1.40 .40
Nos. B196-B200 (5) 4.00 1.40

Topkapi Museum Artifacts — SP77

1984, May 30 Litho. *Perf. 13*

B201 SP77 20 l + 5 l Kaftan, 16th cent. .50 .25
B202 SP77 70 l + 15 l Ewer 1.60 .75
B203 SP77 90 l + 20 l Swords 2.50 .85
B204 SP77 100 l + 25 l Lock, key 3.00 1.00
Nos. B201-B204 (4) 7.60 2.85

Surtax was for museum. See Nos. B208-B211, B213-B216, B218-B221.

1984 Summer Olympics — SP78

Designs: 20 l+5 l, Banners, horiz. 70 l+15 l, Medalist. 100 l+20 l, Running, horiz.

1984, July 28

B205 SP78 20 l + 5 l multi 1.25 .70
B206 SP78 70 l + 15 l multi 1.50 1.10
B207 SP78 100 l + 20 l multi 2.25 1.40
Nos. B205-B207 (3) 5.00 3.20

Artifacts Type of 1984

Ceramicware: 10 l+5 l, Iznik plate. 20 l+10 l, Iznik boza pitcher and mug, 16th cent. 100 l+15 l, Du Paquier ewer and basin, 1730. 120 l+20 l, Ching dynasty plate, 1522-1566.

1985, May 30 Litho. *Perf. 13*

B208 SP77 10 l + 5 l multi .50 .25
B209 SP77 20 l + 10 l multi .85 .40
B210 SP77 100 l + 15 l multi 1.75 1.10
B211 SP77 120 l + 20 l multi 2.50 1.25
Nos. B208-B211 (4) 5.60 3.00

Rabies Vaccine, Cent. — SP79

1985, July 16 *Perf. 13x13½*

B212 SP79 100 l + 15 l Pasteur 1.25 .90

Artifacts Type of 1984

20 l+5 l, Metal and ceramic incense burner, c. 17th cent. 100 l+10 l, Jade lidded mug decorated with precious gems, 16th cent. 120 l+15 l, Dagger designed by Mahmut I, 1714. 200 l+30 l, Willow buckler, defensive shield, undated.

1986, May 30 Litho. *Perf. 13x12½*

B213 SP77 20 l + 5 l multi .70 .45
B214 SP77 100 l + 10 l multi 1.40 .70
B215 SP77 120 l + 15 l multi 1.60 .90
B216 SP77 200 l + 30 l multi 3.25 1.40
Nos. B213-B216 (4) 6.95 3.45

General Assembly of NATO — SP80

1986, Nov. 13 Litho. *Perf. 13½x13*

B217 SP80 100 l + 20 l multi 1.50 .85

Artifacts Type of 1984

Designs: 20 l+5 l, Crystal and gold ewer, 16th cent., vert. 50 l+10 l, Emerald and gold pendant, 17th cent. 200 l+15 l, Sherbet jug, 19th cent., vert. 250 l+30 l, Crystal and gold pen box, 16th cent.

1987, May 30 Litho. *Perf. 13*

B218 SP77 20 l + 5 l multi .60 .25
B219 SP77 50 l + 10 l multi .90 .45
B220 SP77 200 l + 15 l multi 1.10 1.10
B221 SP77 250 l + 30 l multi 1.75 1.40
Nos. B218-B221 (4) 4.35 3.20

15th Intl. Chemotherapy Congress, Istanbul — SP81

1987, July 19 Litho. *Perf. 13*

B222 SP81 200 l + 25 l multi 1.50 .25

Intl. Road Transport Union (IRU) 21st World Congress SP82

1988, June 13 Litho. *Perf. 12½x13*

B223 SP82 200 l +25 l multi .65 .25

European Environmental Campaign Balancing Nature and Development SP83

Designs: 100 l+25 l, Hands, desert reclamation. 400 l+50 l, Eye, road, planted field.

1988, Oct. 19 Litho. *Perf. 12½x13*

B224 SP83 100 l +25 l multi .35 .25
B225 SP83 400 l +50 l multi 1.40 .40

Silkworm Industry — SP84

No. B226, Silkworm. No. B227, Cocoon, strands.

Perf. 13½x13

1989, Apr. 15 Litho. Wmk. 394

B226 SP84 150 l +50 l multi .40 .25
B227 SP84 600 l +100 l multi 1.50 .40

Council of Europe, 40th Anniv. — SP85

1989, May 5 Litho. *Perf. 13*

B228 SP85 600 l +100 l multi 1.50 .45

European Tourism Year — SP86

1990, Apr. 26 Wmk. 394

B229 SP86 300 l +50 l Antalya .50 .25
B230 SP86 1000 l +100 l Istanbul 1.25 .40

Fight Against Addictions — SP87

Fight Against: No. B231, Smoking. No. B232, Drugs, horiz.

1990, June 26 Litho. *Perf. 13*

B231 SP87 300 l +50 l multi .50 .25
B232 SP87 1000 l +100 l multi 1.40 .65

Yunus Emre (died c.1321), Poet
SP88 SP89

1991, June 26 Litho. *Perf. 13*

B233 SP88 500 l +100 l multi .50 .35
B234 SP89 1500 l +100 l multi 1.40 .65

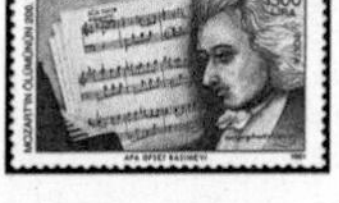

Wolfgang Amadeus Mozart (1756-1791), Composer SP90

1991, July 24

B235 SP90 1500 l +100 l multi 1.75 .90

Turkish Supreme Court, 30th Anniv. — SP91

1992, Apr. 25

B236 SP91 500 l + 100 l multi .65 .25

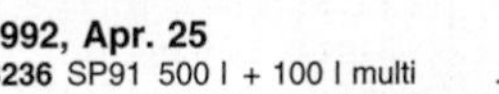

Scouts Planting Tree — SP92

No. B238 Mountain climber on rope, vert.

1992, Dec. 18

B237 SP92 1000 l +200 l multi 1.00 .60
B238 SP92 3000 l +200 l multi 1.75 1.00

Travertine, Pamukkale — SP93

Different views of rock formations.

1993, June 6

B239 SP93 1000 l +200 l multi .75 .25
B240 SP93 3000 l +500 l multi 1.50 .55

Intl. Day for Natural Disaster Reduction SP94

1993, Oct. 13 ***Perf. 12½x13***

B241 SP94 3000 l + 500 l multi 1.25 .75

Intl. Olympic Committee, Cent. — SP95

1994, Aug. 17 ***Perf. 13***

B242 SP95 12,500 l +500 l multi 1.75 1.10

Trees — SP96

Designs: No. B243, Platanus orientalis. No. B244, Cupressus sempervirens, vert.

1994, Nov. 30

B243 SP96 7500 l +500 l multi .75 .50
B244 SP96 12,500 l +500 l multi 1.75 .75

TBMM (Great Natl. Assembly), 75th Anniv. — SP97

1995, Apr. 23

B245 SP97 3500 l +500 l multi .65 .25

The Epic of Manas — SP98

Designs: No. B246, Lancers charging. No. B247, Abay Kunanbay (1845-1904), poet, vert.

1995, June 28

B246 SP98 3500 l +500 l multi .75 .25
B247 SP98 3500 l +500 l multi .75 .25

For the People of Bosnia-Herzegovina — SP99

1996, Feb. 28

B248 SP99 10,000 l +2500 l multi .65 .65

Ankara University, 50th Anniv. — SP100

Unwmk.

1996, Nov. 20 **Litho.** ***Perf. 13***

B249 15,000 l +2500 l multi .65 .30

Fight Against Cancer, 50th Anniv. — SP101

1997, Feb. 18 **Litho.** ***Perf. 12½x13***

B250 SP101 25,000 l +5000 l multi .65 .30

Pakistan Independence, 50th Anniv. — SP102

Mohammed Ali Jinnah (1876-1948).

1997, Mar. 23 **Litho.** ***Perf. 13***

B251 SP102 25,000 l +5000 l multi .65 .30

Universal Declaration of Human Rights — SP103

Stylized designs: 75,000 l, Puzzle piece with outlines of people's faces. 175,000 l, Heart-shaped kite with people as tail.

1998, Dec. 10 **Litho.** ***Perf. 13½***

B252 SP103 75,000 l +25,000 l .80 .40
B253 SP103 175,000 l +25,000 l 1.60 .80

GATA (Gulhane Military Medical Academy), Cent. — SP104

1998, Dec. 30 **Litho.** ***Perf. 13***

B254 SP104 75,000 l +10,000 l multi .80 .40

Kemal Ataturk's Entry Into War College, Cent. — SP105

1999, Mar. 13 **Litho.** ***Perf. 13***

B255 SP105 75,000 l +5,000 l multi 1.00 .25

Council of Europe, 50th Anniv. — SP106

1999, Apr. 30 **Litho.** ***Perf. 13¼***

B256 SP106 175,000 l +10,000 l 2.00 1.10

Church, Mosque and Synagogue SP107

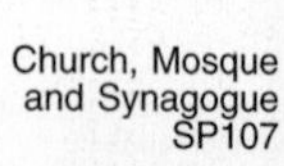

Dancers SP108

2000, May 25 **Litho.** ***Perf. 13¼***

B257 SP107 275,000 l +10,000 l 2.00 2.00
B258 SP108 300,000 l +10,000 l 2.00 2.00

Tombs and Mausoleums — SP109

150,000 l+25,000 l, Usta Sagirt Kumbeti Ahlat, vert. 200,000 l+25,000 l, Kocbasli Mezar Tasi Tunceli. 275,000 l+25,000 l, Isabey Turbesi, Uskup, vert. 300,000 l+25,000 l, Yusuf bin Kuseyr Turbesi, Nahcivan, vert.

2000

B259-B262 SP109 Set of 4 7.25 7.25

Coins — SP110

Various coins with background colors of: No. B263, 300,000 l + 25,000 l, Red. No. B264, 300,000 l + 25,000 l, Blue green. 450,000 l + 25,000 l, Dark carmine. 500,000 l + 25,000 l, Blue violet.

2001, Oct. 1 **Litho.** ***Perf. 13***

B263-B266 SP110 Set of 4 7.25 7.25

Caravansaries SP111

Designs: 300,000 l + 25,000 l, Ashab i Kehf Han, Afsin. 500,000 l + 25,000 l, Horozlu Han, Konya.

2001, Nov. 19 **Litho.** ***Perf. 13***

B267-B268 SP111 Set of 2 4.50 4.50

Turkey's Admission to NATO, 50th Anniv. — SP112

2002, Feb. 18

B269 SP112 400,000 l + 25,000 l 2.25 1.90

Trains — SP113

Designs: 500,000 l + 25,000 l, Steam locomotive. 700,000 l + 25,000 l, Electric locomotive.

2002, Sept. 16 **Litho.** ***Perf. 13¼x13***

B270-B271 SP113 Set of 2 7.25 5.50

Trains — SP114

Designs: 600,000 l+50,000 l, Trolley. 800,000 l+50,000 l, Subway.

2003, Sept. 9 **Litho.** ***Perf. 13¼x13***

B272-B273 SP114 Set of 2 3.50 3.50

Ibrahim Hakki Erzurumlu (1703-72), Writer — SP115

2003, Dec. 24 **Litho.** ***Perf. 13x13¼***

B274 SP115 600,000 l +50,000 l multi 2.00 1.40

Lighthouses — SP116

Designs: 600,000 l + 50,000 l, Kerempe Lighthouse, Kastamonu. 700,000 l + 50,000 l, Taslikburnu Lighthouse, Antalya.

2004, Apr. 5

B275-B276 SP116 Set of 2 4.50 4.50

Scouting — SP117

Designs: 600,000 l + 50,000 l, Girl Scout in foreground. 700,000 l + 50,000 l, Boy Scout in foreground.

2004, Sept. 30

B277-B278 SP117 Set of 2 3.50 3.50

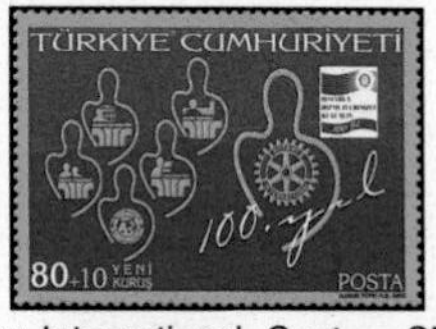

Rotary International, Cent. — SP118

2005, Feb. 23 **Litho.** ***Perf. 13x13¼***

B279 SP118 80k +10k multi 1.50 1.50

Intl. Year of Physics — SP119

2005, Sept. 13 **Litho.** ***Perf. 13¼x13***

B280 SP119 70k +10k multi 1.25 1.25

World Forests Day — SP120

2006, Mar. 21 **Litho.** ***Perf. 13¼x13***

B281 SP120 60k +10k multi 1.10 1.10

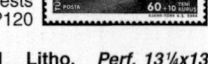

Mehmet Akif Ersoy (1873-1936), Poet — SP121

Ersoy at: 60k+10k, Left. 70k+10k, Right.

2006, Oct. 13 **Litho.** ***Perf. 13¼x13***

B282-B283 SP121 Set of 2 2.10 2.10

Coast Guard Command, 25th Anniv. SP122

2007, July 13 **Litho.** ***Perf. 13x13¼***

B284 SP122 60k + 10k multi 1.10 1.10

Marbled Art — SP123

Designs: 60k+10k, White flowers. 70k+10k, Red tulips.

2007, Dec. 6 ***Perf. 13¼x13***
B285-B286 SP123 Set of 2 2.60 2.60

Kasgarli Mahmut (1008-1105), Lexicographer SP124

Kasgarli: 65k+10k, On horseback. 80k+10k, Holding book.

2008, Apr. 10 Litho. ***Perf. 13¼x13***
B287-B288 SP124 Set of 2 2.60 2.60

Railway Terminals in Istanbul — SP125

Designs: 65k+10k, Haydarpasa Terminal. 80k+10k, Sirkeci Terminal.

2008, Oct. 15 Litho. ***Perf. 13x13¼***
B289-B290 SP125 Set of 2 2.25 2.25

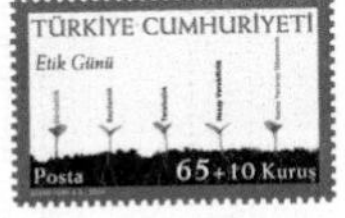
Ethics Day — SP126

2009, May 25 ***Perf. 13¼x13***
B291 SP126 65k +10k multi 1.00 1.00

Katip Celebi (1609-57), Historian — SP127

Celebi, book and: 75k+10k, Quill pen. 90k+10k, Ships.

2009, July 16
B292-B293 SP127 Set of 2 2.60 2.60

Locomotives SP128

Various locomotives: 80k+10k, 110k+10k.

2010, Aug. 4 ***Perf. 12¾x13***
B294-B295 SP128 Set of 2 3.00 3.00

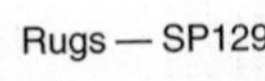
Rugs — SP129

Various rugs: 80k+10k, 110k+10k.

2010, Nov. 17
B296-B297 SP129 Set of 2 3.00 3.00

Hasankeyf SP130

2011, Sept. 21 ***Perf. 13x13¼***
B298 SP130 130k +10k multi 1.60 1.60

State Personnel Department, 50th Anniv. — SP131

2011, Dec. 17 ***Perf. 13¼x13***
B299 SP131 100k +10k multi 1.25 1.25

Souvenir Sheet

Turkish Cuisine SP132

No. B300: a, 50k+10k, Tursu Kavurma (roasted pickles). b, 1 l+10k, Kara Lahana Dolmasi (stuffed collard greens). c, 1 l+10k, Mihlama (corn meal and cheese fondue). d, 2 l+10k, Hamsi Tava (fried anchovies).

2012, Aug. 16 ***Perf. 14¼***
B300 SP132 Sheet of 4, #a-d + label 5.50 5.50

Karsiyaka Sporting Club, Cent. — SP133

Designs: 50k+10k, Bowling, motorcycling, billiards. 1 l+10k, Volleyball, swimming, tennis. 2 l+10k, Basketball, sailing, soccer.

2012, Nov. 1 Litho. ***Perf. 13¼x13½***
B301-B303 SP133 Set of 3 4.25 4.25

Souvenir Sheet

Eurasian Social Business Forum, Erzincan SP134

No. B304: a, Bridge, roads, wind generators, buildings, power lines. b, Earth in droplet.

Perf. 13¾ Syncopated
2013, May 23 **Litho.**
B304 SP134 1.10 l +10k Sheet of 2, #a-b 2.60 2.60

Beypazari District, 130th Anniv. SP135

Designs: No. B305, 1.10 l+10k, Plates of food, carrots, bottle and decorative butterflies. No. B306, 1.10 l+10k, House, vert.

Perf. 13½x13¼, 13¼x13½
2013, May 29 **Litho.**
B305-B306 SP135 Set of 2 2.60 2.60

Historic Bridges SP136

Designs: No. B307, 1.10 l +10k, Kesik Bridge, Sivas. No. B308, 1.10 l + 10k, Clandiras Bridge, Usak.

2014, Apr. 10 Litho. ***Perf. 13½x13¼***
B307-B308 SP136 Set of 2 2.25 2.25

Souvenir Sheet

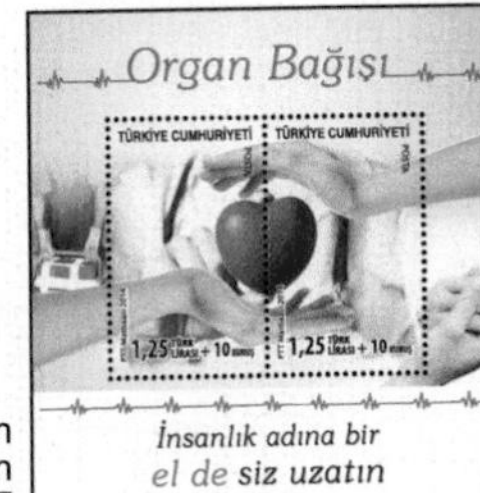
Organ Donation SP137

Hands and: a, Heart at right. b, Heart at left.

2014, Nov. 3 Litho. ***Perf. 14x13¾***
B309 SP137 1.25 l +10k Sheet of 2, #a-b 2.40 2.40

Bridges SP138

Designs: No. B310, 1.25 l +10k, Malabadi Bridge. No. B311, 1.25 l + 10k, On Gozlu Bridge (Dicle Bridge).

2015, Apr. 10 Litho. ***Perf. 13½x13¼***
B310-B311 SP138 Set of 2 2.00 2.00

Campaign Against Obesity — SP139

2015, Nov. 12 Litho. ***Perf. 13¼x13***
B312 SP139 1.40 l +10k multi + label 1.10 1.10

Bridges SP140

Designs: No. B313, 1.40 l+10k, Varda Railroad Bridge. No. B314, 1.40 l+10k, Irgandi Bridge.

2016, Mar. 9 Litho. ***Perf. 13½x13¼***
B313-B314 SP140 Set of 2 2.25 2.25

Think Green — SP141

Designs: No. B315, 1.40 l+10k, Umbrella over Earth and animals. No. B316, 1.40 l+10k, Tree in head.

2016, May 9 Litho. ***Perf. 13¼***
B315-B316 SP141 Set of 2 2.10 2.10

Bitlis Tourist Attractions SP142

Designs: 75k+10k, Seljuk Cemetery. No. B318, 1.80 l+10k, Narlidere (Kasrik) Bridge, Ihlasiye Madrasa. No. B319, 1.80 l+10k, Tomb of Emir Bayindir.

2017, Aug. 10 Litho. ***Perf. 13¼***
B317-B319 SP142 Set of 3 2.75 2.75

Military Equipment SP143

Designs: No. B320, 75k+10k, Anka drone. No. B321, 75k+10k, ATAK helicopter. No. B322, 1.80 l+10k, Bayraktar TB2 drone. No. B323, 1.80 l+10k, Hürkus airplane. No. B324, 3.70 l+10k, Milgem combat ship. No. B325, 3.70 l+10k, Altay tank.

2017, Nov. 23 Litho. ***Perf. 13¼***
B320-B325 SP143 Set of 6 6.75 6.75

Souvenir Sheet

Safranbolu Bazaar — SP144

No. B326: a, Table and chairs under tree and booths, denomination at LL. b, Bazaar booths, denomination at LR.

Litho., Sheet Margin Litho. With Foil Application
2018, Mar. 30 ***Perf. 13½x13¾***
B326 SP144 2 l + 10k Sheet of 2, #a-b 2.10 1.10

SP145

Health Tourism SP146

2018, Sept. 12 Litho. ***Perf. 13¼***
B327 SP145 2 l +10k multi .70 .70
B328 SP146 2 l +10k multi .70 .70

Week of Disabled People
SP147

Litho. & Embossed

2019, May 10 *Perf. 13¼*

B329 SP147 2 l +10k multi .75 .75

SP148

Turkish Red Crescent, 150th Anniv. — SP149

Perf. 13½x13¾

2019, June 11 **Litho.**

B330 SP148 2 l +10k multi .75 .75
B331 SP149 2 l +10k multi .75 .75

Ramadan Traditions — SP150

2020, Apr. 30 **Litho.** *Perf. 13x13¼*

B332 SP150 3 l+10k multi .90 .90

Turkish Coffee Culture and Traditions
SP151

2020, Aug. 14 **Litho.** *Perf. 13¼*

B333 SP151 3 l+10k multi .85 .85

Souvenir Sheet

Museum of Anatolian Civilizations, Ankara, Cent. — SP152

2021, Jan. 21 **Litho.** *Perf. 13¼*

B334 SP152 3 l+10k multi .90 .90

Antique Stove — SP153

Perf. 13¼x13½

2021, Dec. 16 **Litho.**

B335 SP153 4 l+10k multi .65 .65

Campaign Against COVID-19 Pandemic
SP154

Perf. 13½x13¼

2022, Mar. 11 **Litho.**

B336 SP154 5 l+10k multi .70 .70

5th Islamic Solidarity Games, Konya
SP155

2022, Aug. 9 **Litho.** *Perf. 13½x13¼*

B337 SP155 7.50 l +10k multi .85 .85

AIR POST STAMPS

Catalogue values for unused stamps in this section are for Never Hinged items.

Nos. 692, 695, 698, 700 Overprinted or Surcharged in Brown or Blue

1934, July 15 **Unwmk.** *Perf. 12*

C1 A74 7½k (Br) 1.25 .25
C2 A72 12½k on 15k (Br) 1.25 .25
C3 A74 20k on 25k (Br) 1.50 .25
C4 A74 25k (Bl) 1.75 .40
C5 A74 40k (Br) 3.00 1.25
Nos. C1-C5 (5) 8.75 2.40

Regular Stamps of 1930 Surcharged in Brown

1937

C6 A74 4½k on 7½k red brn 6.00 1.00
C7 A72 9k on 15k dp org 47.50 20.00
C8 A74 35k on 40k red vio 12.00 6.50
Nos. C6-C8 (3) 65.50 27.50

Nos. 698, 703-704 Surcharged in Black

1941, Dec. 18

C9 A74 4½k on 25k 2.25 1.50
C10 A75 9k on 200k 10.50 8.25
C11 A75 35k on 500k 6.75 5.25
Nos. C9-C11 (3) 19.50 15.00

Plane over Izmir — AP1

Planes over: 5k, 40k, Izmir. 20k, 50k, Ankara. 30k, 1 l, Istanbul.

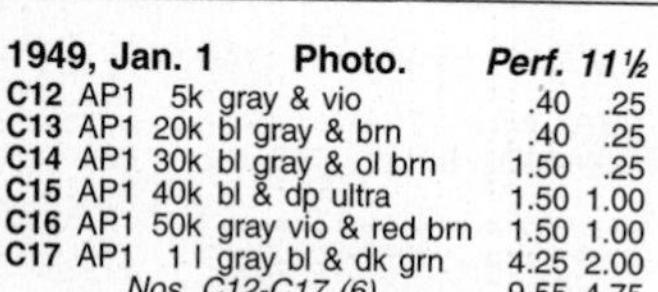

1949, Jan. 1 **Photo.** *Perf. 11½*

C12 AP1 5k gray & vio .40 .25
C13 AP1 20k bl gray & brn .40 .25
C14 AP1 30k bl gray & ol brn 1.50 .25
C15 AP1 40k bl & dp ultra 1.50 1.00
C16 AP1 50k gray vio & red brn 1.50 1.00
C17 AP1 1 l gray bl & dk grn 4.25 2.00
Nos. C12-C17 (6) 9.55 4.75

For overprints see Nos. C19-C21.

Plane Over Rumeli Hisari Fortress — AP2

1950, May 19 **Unwmk.**

C18 AP2 2½ l gray bl & dk grn 22.50 18.00

Nos. C12, C14 and C16 Overprinted in Red

1951, Apr. 9 *Perf. 11½*

C19 AP1 5k gray & vio 1.50 .50
C20 AP1 30k bl gray & ol brn 2.00 .60
C21 AP1 50k gray vio & red brn 2.50 .70
Nos. C19-C21 (3) 6.00 1.80

Industrial Congress, Ankara, Apr. 9.

Yesilkoy Airport and Plane — AP3

Designs: 20k, 45k, Yesilkoy Airport and plane in flight. 35k, 55k, Ankara Airport and plane. 40k, as No. C22.

1954, Nov. 1 *Perf. 14*

C22 AP3 5k red brn & bl 1.25 .25
C23 AP3 20k brn org & bl .85 .25
C24 AP3 35k dk grn & bl .85 .25
C25 AP3 40k dp car & bl .85 .25
C26 AP3 45k violet & bl .95 .25
C27 AP3 55k black & bl 1.90 1.00
Nos. C22-C27 (6) 6.65 2.25

Symbol of Izmir Fair — AP4

1956, Aug. 20 **Litho.** *Perf. 10½*

C28 AP4 25k reddish brown .75 .30

25th Intl. Fair at Izmir, Aug. 20-Sept. 20.

Heuss Type of Regular Issue, 1957

1957, May 5

C29 A264 40k sal pink & magenta .75 .30

Zahir Shah Type of Regular Issue, 1957

1957, Sept. 1

C30 A269 25k grn & lt grn .75 .30

Hawk
AP5

Crane
AP6

Birds: 40k, 125k, Swallows. 65k, Cranes. 85k, 195k, Gulls. 245k, Hawk.

1959, Aug. 13 **Litho.** *Perf. 10½*

C31 AP5 40k bright lilac .50 .25
C32 AP5 65k blue green 3.00 .40
C33 AP5 85k bright blue 1.00 .40
C34 AP5 105k yel & sepia .75 .40
C35 AP6 125k brt violet 1.00 .40
C36 AP6 155k yel green 1.25 .40
C37 AP6 195k violet blue 1.50 .40
C38 AP6 245k brn & brn org 3.50 1.00
Nos. C31-C38 (8) 12.50 3.65

De Havilland Rapide Biplane — AP7

Designs: 60k, Fokker Friendship transport plane. 130k, DC9-30. 220k, DC-3. 270k, Viscount 794.

1967, July 13 **Litho.** *Perf. 13½x13*

C39 AP7 10k pink & blk .65 .25
C40 AP7 60k lt grn, red & blk .95 .25
C41 AP7 130k bl, blk & red 1.15 .25
C42 AP7 220k lt brn, blk & red 1.75 .35
C43 AP7 270k org, blk & red 2.75 .45
Nos. C39-C43 (5) 7.25 1.55

For surcharge see No. 2179A.

Kestrel — AP8

Birds: 60k, Golden eagle. 130k, Falcon. 220k, Sparrow hawk. 270k, Buzzard.

1967, Oct. 10 **Litho.** *Perf. 13*

C44 AP8 10k brown & salmon 1.10 .25
C45 AP8 60k brown & yellow .85 .25
C46 AP8 130k brown & lt bl 2.10 .25
C47 AP8 220k brown & lt grn 3.25 .45
C48 AP8 270k org brn & gray 4.75 .65
Nos. C44-C48 (5) 12.05 1.85

F-104 Jet Plane
AP9

Turkish Air Force Emblem and Jets
AP10

Designs: 200k, Victory monument, Afyon, and Jets. 325k, F-104 jets and pilot. 400k, Bleriot XI plane with Turkish flag. 475k, Flight of Hezarfen Ahmet Celebi from Galata Tower to Usküdar.

1971, June 1 **Litho.** *Perf. 13*

C49 AP9 110k multi .90 .25
C50 AP9 200k multi 2.00 .25
C51 AP10 250k multi 2.00 .45
C52 AP9 325k multi 3.10 .45
C53 AP10 400k multi 3.50 .55
C54 AP10 475k multi 4.50 .65
Nos. C49-C54 (6) 16.00 2.60

The gold ink on No. C51 is applied by a thermographic process which gives a raised and shiny effect.

F-28 Plane — AP11

1973, Dec. 11 **Litho.** *Perf. 13*

C55 AP11 110k shown .95 .25
C56 AP11 250k DC-10 1.25 .45

POSTAGE DUE STAMPS

Same Types as Regular Issues of Corresponding Dates

1863 **Unwmk.** *Imperf.*

Blue Band

J1 A1 20pa blk, *red brn* 100.00 32.50
a. Tête bêche pair 225.00 225.00
b. Without band 50.00
c. Red band 90.00 45.00

J2 A2 1pi blk, *red brn* 150.00 22.50
a. Tête bêche pair 225.00 225.00
b. Without band 50.00
J3 A3 2pi blk, *red brn* 500.00 70.00
a. Tête bêche pair 650.00 450.00
J4 A4 5pi blk, *red brn* 300.00 80.00
a. Tête bêche pair 425.00 425.00
b. Without band 100.00
c. Red band 150.00
Nos. J1-J4 (4) 1,050. 205.00

1865 ***Perf. 12½***
J6 A5 20pa brown 4.00 5.00
J7 A5 1pi brown 4.00 5.00
b. Half used as 20pa on cover
c. Printed on both sides 25.00
J8 A5 2pi brown 12.50 25.00
a. Half used as 1pi on cover
J9 A5 5pi brown 5.00 30.00
a. Half used as 2½pi on cover
J10 A5 25pi brown 45.00 100.00
Nos. J6-J10 (5) 70.50 165.00

Exist imperf. Values, $60 to $100 each.
The 10pa brown is an essay. Value about $2,750.

1867
J11 A5 20pa bister brn 9.00 100.00
J12 A5 1pi bister brn 9.00
a. With surcharge of 5pi 13.50
b. Imperf., pair 65.00
J13 A5 2pi fawn 75.00
J14 A5 5pi fawn 17.50
J15 A5 25pi bister brn *21,250.*
Nos. J11-J14 (4) 110.50

Nos. J12-J15 were not placed in use.

1869 ***Perf. 13½***
With Yellow-Brown Border
J16 A5 20pa bister brn 10.00 10.00
a. Without surcharge
J17 A5 1pi bister brn 550.00 20.00
a. Without surcharge
J18 A5 2pi bister brn 800.00 20.00
J19 A5 5pi bister brn 2.25 12.50
b. Without border
c. Printed on both sides 15.00
J20 A5 25pi bister brn — —
Nos. J16-J19 (4) 1,362. 62.50

With Brown Border

Color of border ranges from brown to reddish brown and black brown.

J21 A5 20pa bister brn 125.00 20.00
a. Inverted surcharge
b. Without surcharge
J22 A5 1pi bister brn 550.00 12.50
a. Without surcharge
J23 A5 2pi bister brn 450.00 12.50
b. Inverted surcharge
J24 A5 5pi bister brn 2.50 15.00
b. Without surcharge
J25 A5 25pi bister brn 37.50 100.00
Nos. J21-J25 (5) 1,165. 160.00

Pin-perf., Perf. 5 to 11½ and Compound
1871 **With Bright Red Border**
J26 A5 20pa bister brn 1,250. 50.00
J27 A5 1pi bister brn *5,000.*
J28 A5 2pi bister brn 110.00 140.00

With Orange Brown Border
J29 A5 5pi bister brn 7.50 25.00

With Brown to Deep Brown Border
J31 A5 20pa bister brn 150.00 3.50
a. Half used as 10pa on cover
b. Imperf., pair 16.50
c. Printed on both sides 40.00 40.00
J32 A5 1pi bister brn 225.00 2.50
a. Half used as 20pa on cover
c. Inverted surcharge 50.00 35.00
d. Printed on both sides
J33 A5 2pi bister brn 6.00 9.00
a. Half used as 1pi on cover
c. Imperf., pair 16.50
J34 A5 5pi bister brn 2.50 20.00
a. Half used as 2½pi on cover
c. Printed on both sides
J35 A5 25pi bister brn 40.00 125.00
a. Inverted surcharge
Nos. J31-J35 (5) 423.50 *160.00*

1888 ***Perf. 11½ and 13½***
J36 A7 20pa black 3.00 10.00
J37 A7 1pi black 3.00 10.00
J38 A7 2pi black 3.00 10.00
b. Diagonal half used as 1pi
Nos. J36-J38 (3) 9.00 30.00

Imperf
J36a A7 20pa 17.50
J37a A7 1pi 17.50
J38a A7 2pi 17.50

1892 ***Perf. 13½***
J39 A11 20pa black 7.00 12.50
J40 A12 1pi black 25.00 12.50
a. Printed on both sides
J41 A13 2pi black 17.50 12.50
Nos. J39-J41 (3) 49.50 *37.50*

1901
J42 A11 20pa black, *deep rose* 2.50 20.00

1901
J43 A17 10pa black, *deep rose* 4.00 6.00
J44 A17 20pa black, *deep rose* 3.75 8.75
J45 A17 1pi black, *deep rose* 3.00 10.00
J46 A17 2pi black, *deep rose* 2.50 15.00
Nos. J43-J46 (4) 13.25 39.75

1905 ***Perf. 12***
J47 A18 1pi black, *deep rose* 3.00 10.00
J48 A18 2pi black, *deep rose* 4.50 20.00

1908, ***Perf. 12, 13½ and Compound***
J49 A19 1pi black, *deep rose* 80.00 7.50
J50 A19 2pi black, *deep rose* 12.50 45.00

1909
J51 A21 1pi black, *deep rose* 15.00 *50.00*
J52 A21 2pi black, *deep rose* *150.00 175.00*
a. Imperf. 65.00

1913 ***Perf. 12***
J53 A22 2pa black, *deep rose* 2.00 .50
J54 A22 5pa black, *deep rose* 2.00 .50
J55 A22 10pa black, *deep rose* 2.00 .50
J56 A22 20pa black, *deep rose* 2.00 .50
J57 A22 1pi black, *deep rose* 6.00 10.00
J58 A22 2pi black, *deep rose* 9.00 17.50
Nos. J53-J58 (6) 23.00 29.50

Adrianople Issue
Nos. 251-253 Surcharged in Black, Blue or Red

1913
J59 A23 2pa on 10pa green (Bk) 3.25 .35
J60 A23 5pa on 20pa red (Bl) 3.25 .35
J61 A23 10pa on 40pa blue (R) 10.00 .80
J62 A23 20pa on 40pa blue (Bk) 32.50 11.00
Nos. J59-J62 (4) 49.00 12.50

For surcharges see Nos. J67-J70, J83-J86.

D1
D2

D3
D4

1914 **Engr.**
J63 D1 5pa claret 2.00 10.00
J64 D2 20pa red 2.00 10.00
J65 D3 1pi dark blue 2.00 10.00
J66 D4 2pi slate 2.00 10.00
Nos. J63-J66 (4) 8.00 40.00

For surcharges and overprints see Nos. J87-J91.

Nos. J59 to J62 Surcharged in Red or Black

1916
J67 A23 10pa on 2pa on 10pa (R) 55.00 55.00
J68 A23 20pa on 5pa on 20pa 55.00 55.00
J69 A23 40pa on 10pa on 40pa 55.00 55.00
J70 A23 40pa on 20pa on 40pa (R) 55.00 55.00
Nos. J67-J70 (4) 220.00 220.00

Preceding Issues Overprinted in Red, Black or Blue

1917 **On Stamps of 1865**
J71 A5 20pa red brn (Bl) 45.00 67.50
J72 A5 1pi red brn (Bl) 45.00 67.50
J73 A5 2pi bis brn (Bl) 45.00 67.50
J74 A5 5pi bis brn (Bl) 45.00 67.50
J75 A5 25pi dk brn (Bl) 45.00 67.50
Nos. J71-J75 (5) 225.00 337.50

On Stamp of 1869
Red Brown Border
J76 A5 5pi bis brn (R) 45.00 67.50

On Stamp of 1871
Black Brown Border
J77 A5 5pi bis brn 75.00 50.00

On Stamps of 1888
J78 A7 1pi black (R) 45.00 67.50
J79 A7 2pi black (R) 45.00 67.50

On Stamps of 1892
J80 A11 20pa black (R) 2.50 2.50
J81 A12 1pi black (R) 2.50 2.50
J82 A13 2pi black (R) 2.50 2.50
Nos. J80-J82 (3) 7.50 7.50

Adrianople Issue
On Nos. J59 to J62 with Addition of New Value

J83 A23 10pa on 2pa on 10pa (R) 1.95 1.00
J84 A23 20pa on 5pa on 20pa (Bk) 2.50 1.00
J85 A23 40pa on 10pa on 40pa (Bk) 3.00 1.50
a. "40pa" double
J86 A23 40pa on 20pa on 40pa (R) 5.25 3.50
Nos. J83-J86 (4) 12.70 7.00

Nos. J71-J86 were used as regular postage stamps.

Armistice Issue

No. J65 Overprinted

1919, Nov. 30
J87 D3 1pi dark blue 125.00 150.00

Accession to the Throne Issue
Postage Due Stamps of 1914 Overprinted in Turkish "Accession to the Throne of His Majesty. 3rd July, 1334-1918"

1919
J88 D1 10pa on 5pa claret 25.00 37.50
J89 D2 20pa red 25.00 37.50
J90 D3 1pi dark blue 25.00 37.50
J91 D4 2pi slate 25.00 37.50
Nos. J88-J91 (4) 100.00 150.00

Railroad Bridge over Kizil Irmak — D5

1926 **Engr.**
J92 D5 20pa ocher 1.25 2.50
J93 D5 1g red 2.00 5.00
J94 D5 2g blue green 3.00 5.00
J95 D5 3g lilac brown 3.50 12.50
J96 D5 5g lilac 6.00 20.00
Nos. J92-J96 (5) 15.75 45.00
Set, never hinged 40.00

Catalogue values for unused stamps in this section, from this point to the end of the section, are for Never Hinged items.

Kemal Atatürk — D6

1936 **Litho.** ***Perf. 11½***
J97 D6 20pa brown .40 .25
J98 D6 2k light blue .40 .25
J99 D6 3k bright violet .40 .25
J100 D6 5k Prussian blue .40 .25
J101 D6 12k bright rose .50 .25
Nos. J97-J101 (5) 2.10 1.25

For surcharges see Nos. 1461-1465.

LOCAL ISSUES

Type I

Type II

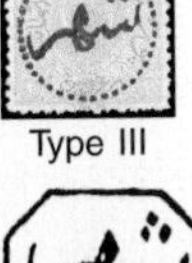
Type III

Type IV

Type V

Type VI

During 1873//1882 Turkish stamps with the above overprints were used for local postage in Constantinople (types 1-5) and Mount Athos (type 6).

MILITARY STAMPS

For the Army in Thessaly

Tughra and Bridge at Larissa — M1

1898, Apr. 21 **Unwmk.** ***Perf. 13***
M1 M1 10pa yellow green 10.00 7.50
M2 M1 20pa rose 10.00 7.50
M3 M1 1pi dark blue 10.00 7.50
M4 M1 2pi orange 10.00 7.50
M5 M1 5pi violet 10.00 7.50
Nos. M1-M5 (5) 50.00 37.50
Set, never hinged 75.00

Issued for Turkish occupation forces to use in Thessaly during the Greco-Turkish War of 1897-98.
Forgeries of Nos. M1-M5 are perf. 11½.

OFFICIAL STAMPS

Catalogue values for unused stamps in this section are for Never Hinged items.

O1

Perf. 10 to 12 and Compound
1948 **Typo.** **Unwmk.**
O1 O1 10pa rose brown .50 .25
O2 O1 1k gray green .50 .25
O3 O1 2k rose violet .50 .25
O4 O1 3k orange .50 .25
O5 O1 5k blue 25.00 .90
O6 O1 10k brown org 7.50 .25
O7 O1 15k violet 2.50 .25
O8 O1 20k dk blue 3.00 .25
O9 O1 30k olive bister 5.00 .80

O10 O1 50k black 5.00 .80
O11 O1 1 l bluish grn 5.00 .80
O12 O1 2 l lilac rose 10.00 1.00
Nos. O1-O12 (12) 65.00 6.05

Regular Issue of 1948 Overprinted Type "a" in Black

1951
O13 A178 5k blue .50 .25
O14 A178 10k chocolate .60 .25
O15 A178 20k deep blue .90 .25
O16 A178 30k brown 1.50 .25
Nos. O13-O16 (4) 3.50 1.00

Overprint "a" is 15½mm wide. Points of crescent do not touch star. The 0.25k (No. 963) exists with overprint "a" but its status is questionable.

b

Overprinted Type "b" in Dark Brown

1953
O17 A178 0.25k dk red .50 .25
O18 A178 5k blue .60 .25
O19 A178 10k chocolate .80 .25
O20 A178 15k violet 1.50 .25
O21 A178 20k deep blue 7.00 1.00
O22 A178 30k brown 2.00 .30
O23 A178 60k black 2.50 .25
Nos. O17-O23 (7) 14.90 2.55

Overprint "b" is 14mm wide. Lettering thin with sharp, clean corners.

c

Overprinted Type "c" in Black or Green Black

1953-54
O23A A178 0.25k dk red (G Bk) ('53) .25 .25
f. Black overprint 4.00 4.00
g. Violet overprint ('53) 4.00 4.00
O23B A178 10k chocolate 12.50 .65
O23C A178 15k violet 15.00 1.00
O23D A178 30k brown 6.50 .65
O23E A178 60k black 8.00 1.00
Nos. O23A-O23E (5) 42.25 3.55

Lettering of type "c" heavy with rounded corners.

Small Star — d

Overprinted or Surcharged Type "d" in Black

1955
O24 A178 0.25k dark red .30 .25
O25 A178 1k olive black .30 .25
O26 A178 2k brt rose lil .30 .25
O27 A178 3k red orange .40 .25
O28 A178 4k dk green .50 .25
O29 A178 5k on 15k vio .50 .25
O31 A178 10k on 15k vio .60 .25
O32 A178 15k violet .60 .25
O33 A178 20k deep blue .70 .25
O35 A179 40k on 1 l ol grn .80 .35
O36 A179 75k on 2 l dk brn 1.10 .80
O37 A179 75k on 5 l dp plum 8.00 8.00
Nos. O24-O37 (12) 14.10 11.40

Type "d" measures 15x16mm. Overprint on Nos. O35-O37 measures 19x22mm. Nos. O29, O31, O35-O37 have two bars and new value added.

Large Star — e

Overprinted or Surcharged Type "e" in Black

1955
O25a A178 1k olive black .60 .25
O29a A178 5k on 15k violet 1.60 .25
O30 A178 5k blue 3.00 .25
O31a A178 10k on 15k violet *3.00 1.00*
c. "10" without serif .90 .30
O33a A178 20k deep blue 1.20 .30
O34 A178 30k brown .90 .30

Heavy crescent — f

Overprinted or Surcharged Type "f" in Black

1957
O24b A178 0.25k dark red .75 .25
O25b A178 1k olive black .60 .30
O31b A178 10k on 15k violet 1.10 .30
O35b A179 75k on 1 l olive grn *1.90 .50*
O38b A178 ½k on 1k ol blk .85 .25
Nos. O24b-O38b (5) *5.20 1.60*

Type "f" crescent is larger and does not touch wavy line. The surcharged "10" on No. O31b exists only without serifs. The overprint on O35b measures 17x22½mm.

Thin crescent — g

Overprinted or Surcharged Type "g" in Black

1957
O38 A178 ½k on 1k ol blk .90 .30
O39 A178 1k ol blk .90 .30
O40 A178 2k on 4k dk grn .90 .30
O41 A178 3k on 4k dk grn .90 .30
O42 A178 10k on 12k dp red .90 .30
Nos. O38-O42 (5) 4.50 1.50

The shape of crescent and star on type "g" varies on each value. Overprint measures 14x18mm. The surcharged stamps have two bars and new value added.

O2

1957 Litho. *Perf. 10½*
O43 O2 5k blue .25 .25
O44 O2 10k orange brn .25 .25
O45 O2 15k lt violet .25 .25
O46 O2 20k red .25 .25
O47 O2 30k gray olive .25 .25
O48 O2 40k brown vio .25 .25
O49 O2 50k grnsh blk .25 .25
O50 O2 60k lt yel grn .30 .25
O51 O2 75k yellow org .50 .25
O52 O2 100k green .75 .25
O53 O2 200k deep rose 1.25 .50
Nos. O43-O53 (11) 4.55 3.00

1959 Unwmk. *Perf. 10*
O54 O2 5k rose .25 .25
O55 O2 10k ol grn .25 .25
O56 O2 15k car rose .25 .25
O57 O2 20k lilac .25 .25
O58 O2 40k blue .25 .25
O59 O2 60k orange .25 .25
O60 O2 75k gray .50 .25
O61 O2 100k violet .65 .25
O62 O2 200k red brn 1.10 .65
Nos. O54-O62 (9) 3.75 2.65

O3

1960 Litho. *Perf. 10½*
O63 O3 1k orange .25 .25
O64 O3 5k vermilion .25 .25
O65 O3 10k gray grn .75 .25
O67 O3 30k red brn .25 .25
O70 O3 60k green .25 .25
O71 O3 1 l rose lilac .65 .25
O72 O3 1½ l brt ultra 2.00 .25
O74 O3 2½ l violet 3.00 .35
O75 O3 5 l blue 7.50 .85
Nos. O63-O75 (9) 14.90 2.95

For surcharge see No. O83.

O4

1962 Typo. *Perf. 13*
O76 O4 1k olive bister .30 .25
O77 O4 5k brt green .30 .25
O78 O4 10k red brown .30 .25
O79 O4 15k dk blue .30 .25
O80 O4 25k carmine .30 .25
O81 O4 30k ultra .30 .25
Nos. O76-O81 (6) 1.80 1.50

For surcharge see No. O82.

Nos. O81 and O70 Surcharged

1963
O82 O4 50k on 30k ultra .35 .25

Perf. 10½
Litho.
O83 O3 100k on 60k green .50 .25

O5

1963 Litho. *Perf. 12½*
O84 O5 1k gray .50 .25
O85 O5 5k salmon .50 .25
O86 O5 10k green .50 .25
O87 O5 50k car rose .50 .25
O88 O5 100k ultra 1.00 .50
Nos. O84-O88 (5) 3.00 1.50

For surcharge see No. O139.

O6

1964 Unwmk. *Perf. 12½*
O89 O6 1k gray .25 .25
O90 O6 5k blue .25 .25
O91 O6 10k yellow .25 .25
O92 O6 30k red .40 .25
O93 O6 50k lt green .50 .25
O94 O6 60k brown 1.50 .25
O95 O6 80k pale grnsh bl 3.50 .40
O96 O6 130k indigo 3.00 .60
O97 O6 200k lilac 7.50 .80
Nos. O89-O97 (9) 17.15 3.30

For surcharge see No. O140.

O7

1965 Litho. *Perf. 13*
O98 O7 1k emerald .40 .25
O99 O7 10k ultra .40 .25
O100 O7 50k orange .50 .25
Nos. O98-O100 (3) 1.30 .75

For surcharge see No. O141.

Carpet Designs — O8

1k, Usak. 50k, Bergama. 100k, Ladik. 150k, Seljuk. 200k, Nomad. 500k, Anatolia.

1966 Litho. *Perf. 13*
O101 O8 1k orange .25 .25
O102 O8 50k green .25 .25
O103 O8 100k brt pink .45 .25
O104 O8 150k violet blue .85 .25
O105 O8 200k olive bister 1.00 .25
O106 O8 500k lilac 4.00 .40
Nos. O101-O106 (6) 6.80 1.65

For surcharge see No. O142.

Seljuk Tile, 13th Century — O9

1967 Litho. *Perf. 11½x12*
O107 O9 1k dk bl & lt bl .50 .25
O108 O9 50k org & dk bl .50 .25
O109 O9 100k lil & dk bl .50 .25
Nos. O107-O109 (3) 1.50 .75

For surcharge see No. O143.

Leaf Design — O10

1968 Litho. *Perf. 13*
O110 O10 50k brn & lt grn .35 .25
O111 O10 150k blk & dl yel 1.00 .25
O112 O10 500k red brn & lt bl 3.00 .25
Nos. O110-O112 (3) 4.35 .75

O11

1969, Aug. 25 Litho. *Perf. 13*
O113 O11 1k lt grn & red .30 .25
O114 O11 10k lt grn & bl .35 .25
O115 O11 50k lt grn & brn .40 .25
O116 O11 100k lt grn & red vio 1.00 .25
Nos. O113-O116 (4) 2.05 1.00

O12

1971, Mar. 1 Litho. *Perf. 11½x12*
O117 O12 5k brown & blue .25 .25
O118 O12 10k vio bl & ver .25 .25
O119 O12 30k org & vio bl .35 .25
O120 O12 50k Prus bl & sepia .60 .25
O121 O12 75k yellow & green 1.00 .25
Nos. O117-O121 (5) 2.45 1.25

O13

1971, Nov. 15 Litho. *Perf. 11½x12*
O122 O13 5k lt bl & gray .25 .25
O123 O13 25k cit & lt brn .35 .25
O124 O13 100k org & olive .45 .25
O125 O13 200k dk brn & bis 1.00 .25
O126 O13 250k rose lil & vio 1.25 .25
O127 O13 500k dk bl & brt bl 2.00 .45
Nos. O122-O127 (6) 5.30 1.70

O14

1972, Apr. 7 Litho. *Perf. 13*
O128 O14 5k buff & blue .45 .25
O129 O14 100k buff & olive .55 .25
O130 O14 200k buff & carmine 1.25 .25
Nos. O128-O130 (3) 2.25 .75

O15

1973, Sept 20 Litho. *Perf. 13*
O131 O15 100k violet & buff .65 .25

O16

1974, June 17 Litho. *Perf. 13½x13*
O132 O16 10k sal pink & brn .25 .25
O133 O16 25k blue & dk brn .25 .25
O134 O16 50k brt pink & brn .25 .25
O135 O16 150k lt grn & brn .50 .25
O136 O16 250k rose & brn .75 .25
O137 O16 500k yellow & brn 1.50 .25
Nos. O132-O137 (6) 3.50 1.50

O17

1975, Nov. 5 Litho. *Perf. 12½x13*
O138 O17 100k lt blue & maroon .25 .25

Nos. O84, O89, O98, O101, O107 Surcharged in Red or Black
Perf. 12½, 13, 11½x12

1977, Aug. 17 Litho.
O139 O5 5k on 1k gray .25 .25
O140 O6 5k on 1k gray .25 .25
O141 O7 5k on 1k emer .25 .25
O142 O8 5k on 1k org (B) .25 .25
O143 O9 5k on 1k dk & lt bl .25 .25
Nos. O139-O143 (5) 1.25 1.25

O18

1977, Dec. 29 Litho. *Perf. 13½x13*
O144 O18 250k lt bl & grn .50 .25

O19

1978 Photo. *Perf. 13½*
O145 O19 50k pink & rose .25 .25
O146 O19 2½ l buff & grnsh blk .25 .25
O147 O19 4½ l lil rose & sl grn .40 .25
O148 O19 5 l lt blue & pur .40 .25
O149 O19 10 l lt grn & grn .85 .25
O150 O19 25 l yellow & red 2.25 .25
Nos. O145-O150 (6) 4.40 1.50

O20

1979 Litho. *Perf. 13½*
O151 O20 50k dp org & brn .25 .25
O152 O20 2½ l bl & dk bl .25 .25

O21

1979, Dec. 20 Litho. *Perf. 13½*
O153 O21 50k sal & dk bl .40 .25
O154 O21 1 l lt grn & red .40 .25
O155 O21 2½ l lil rose & red .50 .25
O156 O21 5 l lt bl & mag .40 .25
O157 O21 7½ l lt lil & dk bl .40 .25
O158 O21 10 l yel & dk bl .50 .40
O159 O21 35 l gray & rose ('81) 1.65 .45
O160 O21 50 l pnksh & dk bl ('81) 2.90 .55
Nos. O153-O160 (8) 7.15 2.65

O22

1981, Oct. 23 Litho. *Perf. 13½*
O161 O22 5 l yel & red 2.75 .25
O162 O22 10 l salmon & red 3.50 .25
O163 O22 35 l gray & rose 4.25 .25
O164 O22 50 l pink & dk bl 5.00 .25
O165 O22 75 l pale grn & grn 8.50 .25
O166 O22 100 l lt bl & dk bl 11.00 .45
Nos. O161-O166 (6) 35.00 1.70

O23

1983-84 Litho. *Perf. 12½x13*
Background Color
O167 O23 5 l yellow 1.00 .25
O168 O23 15 l yellow 1.25 .25
O169 O23 20 l gray ('84) .50 .25
O170 O23 50 l sky blue 3.00 .25
O171 O23 65 l pink 3.75 .25
O172 O23 70 l pale rose ('84) .75 .25
O173 O23 90 l bister brn 5.50 .25
O174 O23 90 l bl gray ('84) 1.10 .25
O175 O23 100 l lt green ('84) 1.75 .25
O176 O23 125 l lt green 6.00 .50
O177 O23 230 l pale salmon ('84) 3.00 .40
Nos. O167-O177 (11) 27.60 3.15

For surcharges see Nos. O184, O186-O190.

O24

1986-87
O178 O24 5 l yel & vio .45 .25
O179 O24 10 l org & vio .45 .25
O180 O24 20 l gray & vio .45 .25
O180A O24 50 l pale blue & dp ultra ('87) .55 .25
O181 O24 100 l lt yel grn & vio 2.25 .25
O182 O24 300 l pale vio & vio blue ('87) 2.75 .25
Nos. O178-O182 (6) 6.90 1.50

For surcharges see Nos. O183, O185.

Nos. O179, O168, O180, O172-O173, O177 Surcharged in Dark Orange

1989
O183 O24 500 l on 10 l 2.25 .25
O184 O23 500 l on 15 l 2.25 .25
O185 O24 500 l on 20 l 2.25 .25
O186 O23 1000 l on 70 l 3.25 .25
O187 O23 1000 l on 90 l 3.25 .25
O188 O23 1250 l on 230 l 4.50 .50
Nos. O183-O188 (6) 17.75 1.75

Issued: #O183, O185-O188, 8/9; #O184, 6/7.

Nos. O171, O173 & O174 Surcharged in Black

1991, Mar. 27
O189 O23 100 l on 65 l 1.20 .30
O189A O23 250 l on 90l (#O173) —
O190 O23 250 l on 90 l(#O174) 1.90 .30

O25

Perf. 11½x12½
1992, Mar. 24 Litho.
O191 O25 3000 l lt brn & dk brn 2.00 .30
O192 O25 5000 l lt grn & dk grn 6.00 .50

O26

1992, Dec. 2 Litho. *Perf. 12½x13*
O193 O26 1000 l bl grn & vio bl .75 .25
O194 O26 10,000 l vio bl & bl grn 6.00 .50

O27

1993, Sept. 27 Litho. *Perf. 12½x13*
O195 O27 1000 l brown & green 1.25 .25
O196 O27 1500 l brown & green 1.75 .25
O197 O27 5000 l green & claret 4.50 .40
Nos. O195-O197 (3) 7.50 .90

O28

1994, May 9 Litho. *Perf. 11½x12*
O198 O28 2500 l pink & violet 2.00 .25
O199 O28 25,000 l yel & brn 5.00 .50

O29

1995, Jan. 25
O200 O29 3500 l violet & lt vio 1.50 .25
O201 O29 17,500 l bl grn & lt grn 6.00 .45

O30

1995, May 17
O202 O30 50,000 l ol & apple grn 3.50 1.60

O31

1995, Nov. 8 Litho. *Perf. 12½x13*
O203 O31 5000 l salmon & org 1.25 .25

O32 O32a

O32b O32c

1996, July 10 Litho. *Perf. 11½x12¼*
O204 O32 15,000 l bl & red 1.00 .25
O205 O32a 20,000 l grn & pur 1.50 .25
O206 O32b 50,000 l pur & grn 2.00 .40
O207 O32c 100,000 l red & bl 3.00 .75
Nos. O204-O207 (4) 7.50 1.65

O33

1997, Feb. 5 Litho. *Perf. 12½x13*
O208 O33 25,000 l red & blue 1.50 .30

O34 O35

1997, Aug. 4 Litho. *Perf. 12½x13*
O209 O34 40,000 l multicolored 1.00 .30
O210 O35 250,000 l multicolored 6.00 1.75

O36 O37

O38 O39

1998, June 10 Litho. *Perf. 12½x13*
O211 O36 40,000 l dk bl & lt bl .75 .25
O212 O37 100,000 l purple 2.00 .50
O213 O38 200,000 l brn & pale bl grn 3.75 1.00
O214 O39 500,000 l brn & pale bl grn 9.00 2.50
Nos. O211-O214 (4) 15.50 4.25

O40

1998, July 29 Litho. *Perf. 12½x13*
O215 O40 75,000 l multicolored 1.25 .30

O41 O42

1999 Litho. *Perf. 11½x12¼*
O216 O41 (R) vio & blue grn 3.00 .45
O217 O42 (RT) black & pink 7.00 .45

On day of issue, No. O216 sold for 75,000 l; No. O217, 275,000 l.

O43 O44

O45 O46

2000, Apr. 3 Litho. *Perf. 11½x12¼*
O218 O43 50,000 l blue & pink .60 .25
O219 O44 75,000 l brn & gray .75 .25
O220 O45 500,000 l red brn & lt bl 4.50 .40
O221 O46 1,250,000 l dk bl & buff 7.50 1.00
Nos. O218-O221 (4) 13.35 1.90

O46a O46b

Perf. 11½x12¼
2000, Nov. 20 Litho.
O221A O46a R blue & yel grn 4.00 .25
O221B O46b RT dk bl & lt bl 6.00 .75

No. O221A sold for 300,000 l on day of issue. No. O221B sold for 500,000 l on day of issue.

O47

Perf. 11½x12¼
2001, Dec. 13 Litho.
O222 O47 R blue & yel org 3.00 .25

Sold for 300,000 l on day of issue.

O48 O49

O50 O51

O52

Perf. 11½x12¼

2002, Dec. 10 **Litho.**

O223	O48	50,000 l multi	.35	.25
O224	O49	100,000 l multi	.35	.25
O225	O50	250,000 l multi	.75	.30
O226	O51	500,000 l multi	1.50	.60
O227	O52	1,500,000 l multi	5.50	1.75
		Nos. O223-O227 (5)	8.45	3.15

O53 O54

O55 O56

Perf. 11½x12¼

2003, Aug. 18 **Litho.**

O228	O53	500,000 l bl & red	2.00	.70
O229	O54	750,000 l bl & yel	3.00	.80
O230	O55	1,000,000 l bl & grn	3.00	1.00
O231	O56	3,000,000 l bl & yel	10.00	2.10
		Nos. O228-O231 (4)	18.00	4.60

O57

2003, Oct. 13 **Litho.** *Perf. 11½x12¼*

O232	O57	R pink & purple	1.25	.85

Sold for 600,000 l on day of issue.

Buildings — O58

Designs: 100,000 l, Hamidiye Etfal Children's Sanitorium. 500,000 l, Heating Plant, Silahtaraga. 600,000 l, PTT Headquarters, Ankara, vert. 1,000,000 l, Finance Ministry building, Ankara, vert. 3,500,000 l, Old Post and Telegraph Ministry building, Istanbul.

2004, Oct. 15 *Perf. 13¼x13, 13x13¼*

O233	O58	100,000 l multi	.25	.25
O234	O58	500,000 l multi	.75	.50
O235	O58	600,000 l multi	.80	.60
O236	O58	1,000,000 l multi	1.50	1.00
O237	O58	3,500,000 l multi	5.50	2.00
		Nos. O233-O237 (5)	8.80	4.35

Building Type of 2004

Design: 60k, Prime Minister's Building, Ankara.

2005, Jan. 1 **Litho.** *Perf. 14*

O238	O58	60k multi	.90	.90

Buildings — O59

Designs: 10k, Museum of the Republic, Ankara. 25k, Culture and Tourism Ministry, Ankara. 50k, State Guest House, Ankara. 60k, Sculpture Museum, Ankara. 1 l, Ethnographic Museum, Ankara. 3.50 l, National Library, Ankara.

2005, July 4 **Litho.** *Perf. 13¼x13*

Frame Color

O239	O59	10k orange	.25	.25
O240	O59	25k orange	.35	.35
O241	O59	50k yel green	.75	.75
O242	O59	60k blue	.90	.90
O243	O59	1 l yellow	1.50	1.50
O244	O59	3.50 l dull org	5.25	5.25
		Nos. O239-O244 (6)	9.00	9.00

Kemal Ataturk — O60

Various portraits.

2006, Apr. 21 **Litho.** *Perf. 13x13¼*

Background Color

O245	O60	10k blue	.25	.25
O246	O60	50k brown	.75	.75
O247	O60	60k dark red	.95	.95
O248	O60	1 l blue green	1.50	1.50
O249	O60	3.50 l red	5.50	5.50
		Nos. O245-O249 (5)	8.95	8.95

Kemal Ataturk — O61

Various portraits.

Perf. 13x13½

2007, Feb. 26 **Wmk. 405**

O250	O61	10k multi	.25	.25
O251	O61	50k multi	.70	.70
O252	O61	60k multi	.85	.85
O253	O61	1 l multi	1.40	1.40
O254	O61	4 l multi	5.75	5.75
		Nos. O250-O254 (5)	8.95	8.95

Kemal Ataturk — O62

2007, Dec. 4 **Wmk. 405**

O255	O62	65k multi	1.10	1.10

Kemal Ataturk

O63 O64

Various portraits.

Perf. 13x13¼

2008, Feb. 29 **Wmk. 405**

O256	O63	5k multi	.25	.25
O257	O64	65k multi	1.10	1.10
O258	O64	85k multi	1.40	1.40
O259	O64	1 l multi	1.75	1.75
O260	O64	3.35 l multi	5.50	5.50
O261	O64	4.50 l multi	7.50	7.50
		Nos. O256-O261 (6)	17.50	17.50

O65

O66

Kemal Ataturk

O67 O68

Perf. 13x13¼, 13¼x13

2008, Dec. 4 **Wmk. 405**

O262	O65	5k multi	.25	.25
O263	O66	50k multi	.65	.65
O264	O67	65k multi	.85	.85
O265	O68	1 l multi	1.25	1.25
		Nos. O262-O265 (4)	3.00	3.00

Flowers — O69

Designs: 5k, Nergis (daffodils). 10k, Nilüfer (water lily). 25k, Papatya (daisies). 50k, Cigdem (crocuses). 65k, Zambak (lilies). 75k, Yildiz (dahlia). 1 l, Kardelen (snowdrops). 3.35 l, Menekse (violet). 4.50 l, Ortanca (hydrangea). 5 l, Sardunya (geraniums).

2009 **Wmk. 405** *Perf. 13¾*

O266	O69	5k multi	.25	.25
O267	O69	10k multi	.25	.25
O268	O69	25k multi	.35	.35
O269	O69	50k multi	.65	.65
O270	O69	65k multi	.85	.85
O271	O69	75k multi	1.10	1.10
O272	O69	1 l multi	1.25	1.25
O273	O69	3.35 l multi	4.25	4.25
O274	O69	4.50 l multi	5.75	5.75
O275	O69	5 l multi	7.00	7.00
		Nos. O266-O275 (10)	21.70	21.70

Issued: 75k, 5 l, 7/16; others, 3/26.

Flowers — O70

Designs: 5k, Ayçiçegi (sunflowers). 10k, Gelincik (poppies). 25k, Carkifelek (passion flower). 80k, Zinya (zinnia). 1 l Gül (rose).

Perf. 13x13¼

2010, Aug. 26 **Wmk. 405**

O276	O70	5k multi	.25	.25
O277	O70	10k multi	.25	.25
O278	O70	25k multi	.35	.35
O279	O70	80k multi	1.10	1.10
O280	O70	1 l multi	1.40	1.40
		Nos. O276-O280 (5)	3.35	3.35

Stylized Flowers — O71

Various stylized flowers.

2010, Dec. 10 **Wmk. 405**

O281	O71	5k multi	.25	.25
O282	O71	50k multi	.70	.70
O283	O71	80k multi	1.10	1.10
O284	O71	90k multi	1.25	1.25
O285	O71	1 l multi	1.40	1.40
		Nos. O281-O285 (5)	4.70	4.70

Stylized Flowers Type of 2010

Various stylized flowers.

Perf. 13½ Syncopated

2011, Apr. 18 **Wmk. 405**

Inscribed "2011"

O286	O71	10k multi	.25	.25
O287	O71	1 l multi	1.40	1.40
O288	O71	2.80 l multi	3.75	3.75
O289	O71	6 l multi	7.75	7.75
		Nos. O286-O289 (4)	13.15	13.15

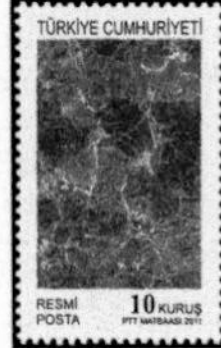

Abstract Art — O72

Various abstract designs.

Perf. 13x13¼

2011, Dec. 19 **Wmk. 405**

O290	O72	10k multi	.25	.25
O291	O72	1 l multi	1.10	1.10
O292	O72	2 l multi	2.25	2.25
O293	O72	7 l multi	7.50	7.50
		Nos. O290-O293 (4)	11.10	11.10

Flowers — O73

Various flowers.

2012, May 2 *Perf. 13¾ Syncopated*

Background Color

O294	O73	25k dull orange	.30	.30
O295	O73	50k buff	.60	.60
O296	O73	1 l pink	1.10	1.10
O297	O73	3.75 l lilac	4.25	4.25
O298	O73	7 l light blue	8.00	8.00
		Nos. O294-O298 (5)	14.25	14.25

Four Seasons — O74

Designs: 10k, Evergreen branch in winter. 25k, Blossoms on tree in spring. 50k, Cherries on branch in summer. 1k, Brown leaves on tree in autumn.

2012, Sept. 11 *Perf. 14x13¾*

O299	O74	10k multi	.25	.25
O300	O74	25k multi	.30	.30
O301	O74	50k multi	.55	.55
O302	O74	1 l multi	1.10	1.10
		Nos. O299-O302 (4)	2.20	2.20

Carpets — O75

Carpet from: 10k, Balikesir. 25k Kayseri. 1.10 l, Aksaray. 3.85 l, Mugla.

Perf. 13x12½

2013, Feb. 14 **Wmk. 405**

O303	O75	10k multi	.25	.25
O304	O75	25k multi	.30	.30
O305	O75	1.10 l multi	1.25	1.25
O306	O75	3.85 l multi	4.25	4.25
		Nos. O303-O306 (4)	6.05	6.05

Kemal Ataturk — O76

Various portraits.

Perf. 13¾ Syncopated

2013, Sept. 19 Litho. Unwmk.

O307	O76	10k multi	.25	.25
O308	O76	25k multi	.25	.25
O309	O76	1 l multi	1.00	1.00
O310	O76	1.10 l multi	1.10	1.10
O311	O76	8 l multi	8.00	8.00
		Nos. O307-O311 (5)	10.60	10.60

Kemal Ataturk — O77

Various portraits.

Perf. 13¾ Syncopated

2014, Apr. 16 Litho. Unwmk.

O312	O77	10k multi	.25	.25
O313	O77	1 l multi	.95	.95
O314	O77	1.10 l multi	1.10	1.10
		Nos. O312-O314 (3)	2.30	2.30

Carpets — O78

Carpet from: 15k, Manisa Province. 1.25 l, Kocaeli Province. 9 l, Konya Province.

Perf. 13¾ Syncopated

2014, May 7 Litho.

O315	O78	15k multi	.25	.25
O316	O78	1.25 l multi	1.25	1.25
O317	O78	9 l multi	8.50	8.50
		Nos. O315-O317 (3)	10.00	10.00

Tourist Attractions — O79

Various tourist attractions.

Perf. 13¾ Syncopated

2014, June 18 Litho.

O318	O79	15k multi	.25	.25
O319	O79	25k multi	.25	.25
O320	O79	1.25 l multi	1.25	1.25
O321	O79	9 l multi	8.50	8.50
		Nos. O318-O321 (4)	10.25	10.25

Museum of Anatolian Civilizations, Ankara — O80

Atatürk Mausoleum and Museum, Ankara — O81

Ethnographic Museum, Ankara — O82

Perf. 13¾ Syncopated

2015, Mar. 10 Litho. Unwmk.

O322	O80	15k multi	.25	.25
O323	O81	1.25 l multi	1.00	1.00
O324	O82	9 l multi	7.00	7.00
		Nos. O322-O324 (3)	8.25	8.25

Painting and Sculpture Museum, Ankara — O83

Perf. 13¾ Syncopated

2015, June 8 Litho. Wmk. 405

O325	O83	1 l multi	.75	.75

O84

Zeugma Mosaic Museum, Gaziantep — O85

Perf. 13¾ Syncopated

2015, June 19 Litho. Unwmk.

O326	O84	25k multi	.25	.25
O327	O85	50k multi	.40	.40

Turkish and Islamic Arts Museum, Istanbul — O86

Hagia Sophia Museum, Istanbul — O87

Rumeli Hisari Museum, Istanbul O88

Galata Tower Museum, Istanbul O89

Archaeological Museum, Istanbul — O90

Perf. 13¾ Syncopated

2015, Aug. 7 Litho. Unwmk.

O328	O86	15k multi	.25	.25
O329	O87	30k multi	.25	.25
O330	O88	1.40 l multi	.95	.95
O331	O89	4.50 l multi	3.00	3.00
O332	O90	10 l multi	6.75	6.75
		Nos. O328-O332 (5)	11.20	11.20

O91

O92

O93

Miniatures by Nusret Colpan (1952-2008) — O94

Perf. 13¾ Syncopated

2015, Dec. 14 Litho. Unwmk.

O333	O91	50k multi	.35	.35
O334	O92	1 l multi	.70	.70
O335	O93	4.50 l multi	3.00	3.00
O336	O94	10 l multi	6.75	6.75
		Nos. O333-O336 (4)	10.80	10.80

Stylized Flowers — O95

Various flowers.

Perf. 13¾ Syncopated

2016, Jan. 15 Litho. Unwmk.

O337	O95	1 l multi	.70	.70
O338	O95	1.40 l multi	.95	.95
O339	O95	10 l multi	6.75	6.75
		Nos. O337-O339 (3)	8.40	8.40

Miniature Roses — O96

Various roses with background colors of: 20k, Gray brown. 60k, Light blue. 65k, Dull orange and pink. 1.60 l, Yellow and lavender. 5.10 l, Mauve and pale green. 11 l, Lavender gray and pale green.

Perf. 13¾ Syncopated

2016, July 25 Litho. Unwmk.

O340	O96	20k multi	.25	.25
O341	O96	60k multi	.40	.40
O342	O96	65k multi	.45	.45
O343	O96	1.60 l multi	1.10	1.10
O344	O96	5.10 l multi	3.50	3.50
O345	O96	11 l multi	7.50	7.50
		Nos. O340-O345 (6)	13.20	13.20

Glazed Pottery Vessels — O97

Various vessels: 10k, Short wide neck, wide opening. 20k, Long skinny neck. 50k, Short wide neck with handles. 60k, Long skinny neck with lid.

Perf. 13¾ Syncopated

2016, Dec. 8 Litho. Unwmk.

O346	O97	10k multi	.25	.25
O347	O97	20k multi	.25	.25
O348	O97	50k multi	.30	.30
O349	O97	60k multi	.35	.35
		Nos. O346-O349 (4)	1.15	1.15

Flower — O98

Perf. 12½x13

2017, May 23 Litho. Unwmk.

Background Color

O350	O98	10k turq blue	.25	.25
O351	O98	20k org yellow	.25	.25
O352	O98	50k red violet	.30	.30
O353	O98	1 l yel grn	.60	.60
O354	O98	5.10 l brt blue	3.00	3.00
		Nos. O350-O354 (5)	4.40	4.40

Flowers

O99 O100

Perf. 12½x13

2017, July 31 Litho. Unwmk.

Flower Color

O355	O99	10k dk grn	.25	.25
O356	O99	20k orange	.25	.25
O357	O99	50k ultra	.30	.30
O358	O99	75k pink	.30	.30
O359	O100	1 l reddish pur	.60	.60
O360	O100	1.50 l yellow	.85	.85
O361	O100	1.80 l black	1.10	1.10
O362	O100	5.80 l brt grn	3.25	3.25
O363	O100	12.50 l vermilion	7.25	7.25
		Nos. O355-O363 (9)	14.15	14.15

O101 O102

O103

O104

O105 O106

O107 O108

Anatolian Rug Design Elements — O109

Perf. 13½x13¾

2017, Dec. 13 Litho. Unwmk.

O364	O101	20k multi	.25	.25
O365	O102	70k multi	.40	.40
O366	O103	1 l multi	.55	.55
O367	O104	1.50 l multi	.80	.80
O368	O105	2 l multi	1.10	1.10
O369	O106	2.75 l multi	1.50	1.50
O370	O107	4 l multi	2.10	2.10
O371	O108	6.50 l multi	3.50	3.50
O372	O109	14 l multi	7.50	7.50
		Nos. O364-O372 (9)	17.70	17.70

President Mustafa Kemal Atatürk — O110

Various portraits.

Perf. 13¾ Syncopated

2018, May 23 Litho. Unwmk.

O373	O110	10k multi	.25	.25
O374	O110	20k multi	.25	.25
O375	O110	50k multi	.25	.25
O376	O110	1 l multi	.45	.45
O377	O110	2 l multi	.90	.90
		Nos. O373-O377 (5)	2.10	2.10

Museums — O111

Designs: 50k, National Struggle Museum, Kayseri. 1 l, Liberation Museum, Eskisehir. 2 l, Western Front Headquarters Museum, Aksehir. 4 l, Victory Museum, Afyon.

2018, Dec. 26 Litho. *Perf. 13x12½*

O378	O111	50k multi	.25	.25
O379	O111	1 l multi	.40	.40
O380	O111	2 l multi	.75	.75
O381	O111	4 l multi	1.50	1.50
		Nos. O378-O381 (4)	2.90	2.90

Flowers — O112

Various flowers.

2019, May 27 Litho. *Perf. 13*

O382	O112	10k multi	.25	.25
O383	O112	20k multi	.25	.25
O384	O112	50k multi	.25	.25
O385	O112	1 l multi	.35	.35
O386	O112	2 l multi	.70	.70
O387	O112	16.20 l multi	5.75	5.75
		Nos. O382-O387 (6)	7.55	7.55

O113 O114

O115 O116

O117 O118

Anatolian Rug Design Elements
O119 O120

2019, July 17 Litho. *Perf. 13*

O388 O113 10k multi .25 .25
O389 O114 20k multi .25 .25
O390 O115 50k multi .25 .25
O391 O116 1 l multi .35 .35
O392 O117 2.30 l multi .85 .85
O393 O118 4.60 l multi 1.75 1.75
O394 O119 7.50 l multi 2.75 2.75
O395 O120 16.20 l multi 5.75 5.75
Nos. O388-O395 (8) 12.20 12.20

O121

Paper Marbling — O122

2019, Oct. 23 Litho. *Perf. 13¾*

O396 O121 2.40 l multi .85 .85
O397 O122 8.40 l multi 3.00 3.00

Floral Fabric Designs — O123

Various floral fabric designs.

2019, Dec. 16 Litho. *Perf. 12¾x13*

O398 O123 10k multi .25 .25
O399 O123 50k multi .25 .25
O400 O123 1 l multi .35 .35
O401 O123 2.40 l multi .80 .80
O402 O123 8.40 l multi 3.00 3.00
O403 O123 19 l multi 6.50 6.50
Nos. O398-O403 (6) 11.15 11.15

O124 O125

O126 O127

Anatolian Rug Design Elements — O128

2020, Apr. 17 Litho. *Perf. 12¾x13*

O404 O124 20k multi .25 .25
O405 O125 60k multi .25 .25
O406 O126 1 l multi .30 .30
O407 O127 3 l multi .85 .85
O408 O128 9 l multi 2.60 2.60
Nos. O404-O408 (5) 4.25 4.25

O129

O130

O131

Crocheted Flowers — O132

2021, Mar. 23 Litho. *Perf. 13¾*

O409 O129 50k multi .30 .30
O410 O130 1 l multi .30 .30
O411 O131 2 l multi .50 .50
O412 O132 5 l multi 1.25 1.25
Nos. O409-O412 (4) 2.35 2.35

Wildflowers — O133

Designs: 1 l, Potentilla sp. 2 l, Aquilegia vulgaris. 4 l, Myosotis scorpioides. 12 l, Dianthus carthusianorum. 26 l, Papaver commutatum.

2021, Oct. 27 Litho. *Perf. 12½x13*

O413 O133 1 l multi .30 .30
O414 O133 2 l multi .45 .45
O415 O133 4 l multi .85 .85
O416 O133 12 l multi 2.50 2.50
O417 O133 26 l multi 5.50 5.50
Nos. O413-O417 (5) 9.60 9.60

Wildflowers — O134

Designs: 1 l, Geum rivale. 3 l, Campanula rotundifolia alba. 5 l, Scilla chionodoxa. 15 l, Pyrrhopappus carolinianus. 31 l, Aster alpinus.

2022, Mar. 21 Litho. *Perf. 12½x13*
Inscribed "Kir Cicekleri-2"

O418 O134 1 l multi .30 .30
O419 O134 3 l multi .40 .40
O420 O134 5 l multi .70 .70
O421 O134 15 l multi 2.10 2.10
O422 O134 31 l multi 4.25 4.25
Nos. O418-O422 (5) 7.75 7.75

NEWSPAPER STAMPS

N1

Black Overprint

1879 Unwmk. *Perf. 11½ and 13½*

P1 N1 10pa blk & rose lilac 225.00 225.00

Other stamps found with this "IMPRIMES" overprint were prepared on private order and have no official status as newspaper stamps.
Counterfeits exist of No. P1.

The 10pa surcharge, on half of 20pa rose and pale rose was made privately. See note after No. 77.

Regular Issue of 1890 Handstamped in Black, Blue or Red

Nos. P10-P29 were overprinted with a single wooden handstamp. Variations in size are due to inking and pressure.

The handstamps on Nos. P10-P29 are found double, inverted and sideways. Counterfeit overprints comprise most of the examples offered for sale in the marketplace.

1891 *Perf. 13½, 11½*

P10 A7 10pa grn & gray 40.00 12.50
a. Imperf. 22.50 12.50
P11 A7 20pa rose & gray 75.00 15.00
P12 A7 1pi blue & gray 210.00 150.00
P13 A7 2pi yel & gray *525.00 400.00*
P14 A7 5pi buff & gray *1,050. 750.00*
Nos. P10-P14 (5) *1,900. 1,328.*

Blue Handstamp

P10b A7 10pa green & gray 210.00 *125.00*
P11a A7 20pa rose & gray 340.00 *250.00*
P12a A7 1pi blue & gray 425.00 *375.00*
Nos. P10b-P12a (3) *975.00 750.00*

This overprint on 2pi and 5pi in blue is considered bogus.

Red Handstamp

P10c A7 10pa green & gray *400.00 325.00*
P11b A7 20pa rose & gray *600.00 450.00*
P12b A7 1pi blue & gray *900.00 1,000.*
Nos. P10c-P12b (3) 1,900. 1,775.

This overprint in red on 2pi and 5pi is considered bogus.

Excellent forgeries of Nos. P10-P14 exist. Certification by a competant authority is suggested.

Same Handstamp on Regular Issue of 1892

1892 *Perf. 13½*

P25 A10 10pa gray green *500.00 100.00*
P26 A11 20pa rose *1,250. 375.00*
P27 A12 1pi pale blue *110.00 150.00*
P28 A13 2pi brown org *200.00 175.00*
P29 A14 5pi pale violet *1,800. 1,250.*
a. On No. 99a *500.00*
Nos. P25-P29 (5) 3,860. 2,050.

Regular Issues of 1892-98 Overprinted in Black

1893-98

P30 A10 10pa gray grn 3.75 2.50
P31 A11 20pa vio brn ('98) 3.00 1.50
a. 20pa dark pink 3.50 2.00
b. 20pa pink 325.00 22.50
P32 A12 1pi pale blue 3.75 2.00
P33 A13 2pi brown org 27.50 12.50
a. Tete beche pair 90.00 22.50
P34 A14 5pi pale violet 85.00 75.00
a. On No. 99a 140.00 65.00
Nos. P30-P34 (5) 123.00 93.50

For surcharge and overprints see Nos. B41, P121-P122, P134-P136, P153-P154.

No. 95 Surcharged

1897

P36 A10 5pa on 10pa gray grn 5.00 3.00
a. "Cniq" instead of "Cinq" 15.00 15.00

For overprint see No. P137.

Nos. 102-107 Overprinted in Black

1901 *Perf. 12, 13½ and Compound*

P37 A16 5pa bister 1.75 1.00
a. Inverted overprint
P38 A16 10pa yellow grn 6.25 6.25
P39 A16 20pa magenta 32.50 7.50
P40 A16 1pi violet blue 60.00 22.50
P41 A16 2pi gray blue 125.00 37.50
P42 A16 5pi ocher 300.00 90.00
Nos. P37-P42 (6) 525.50 164.75

For overprints see Nos. B37, P69-P74, P123, P138-P141, P155-P158.

Same Overprint on Nos. 110-115

1901

P43 A17 5pa purple 8.75 2.00
a. Inverted overprint 55.00
P44 A17 10pa green 32.50 2.50
P45 A17 20pa carmine 8.75 1.50
a. Overprinted on back
P46 A17 1pi blue 25.00 2.00
P47 A17 2pi orange 87.50 4.00
a. Inverted overprint
P48 A17 5pi lilac rose 160.00 27.50
Nos. P43-P48 (6) 322.50 39.50

For overprints see Nos. P75-P80, P124-P126, P142-P146, P159-P164.

Same Overprint on Regular Issue of 1905

1905

P49 A18 5pa ocher 2.50 1.00
P50 A18 10pa dull green 30.00 1.50
P51 A18 20pa carmine 2.50 1.25
P52 A18 1pi pale blue 2.50 1.25
P53 A18 2pi slate 70.00 10.00
P54 A18 5pi brown 175.00 20.00
Nos. P49-P54 (6) 282.50 35.00

For overprints see Nos. P127-P129, P147-P150, P165-P171.

Regular Issue of 1908 Overprinted in Carmine or Blue

1908

P55 A19 5pa ocher (Bl) 10.00 .50
P56 A19 10pa blue grn (C) 17.50 .50
P57 A19 20pa carmine (Bl) 22.50 1.00
P58 A19 1pi brt blue (C) 100.00 2.50
P59 A19 2pi blue blk (C) 150.00 7.50
P60 A19 5pi dk violet (C) 200.00 17.50
Nos. P55-P60 (6) 500.00 29.50

For overprints see Nos. B17, P130-P131, P151, P172.

Same Overprint on Regular Issue of 1909

1909

P61 A21 5pa ocher (Bl) 3.50 1.25
a. Imperf. *30.00 30.00*
P62 A21 10pa blue grn (C) 8.75 1.50
P63 A21 20pa car rose (Bl) 60.00 1.75
a. Imperf. *80.00 80.00*
P64 A21 1pi brt blue (C) 100.00 5.00
P65 A21 2pi blue blk (C) 250.00 30.00
P66 A21 5pi dk violet (C) 500.00 65.00
Nos. P61-P66 (6) 922.25 104.50

For surcharge and overprints see Nos. B18, P67-P68, P81, P132-P133, P152.

No. 151 Surcharged in Blue

1910 *Perf. 12, 13½ and Compound*

P67 A21 2pa on 5pa ocher .75 .75

Type of 1909 Tughra and "Reshad" of Sultan Mohammed V

1911 *Perf. 12*

P68 A21 2pa olive green 1.00 .50

For overprints see Nos. 567, P173.

Newspaper Stamps of 1901-11 Overprinted in Carmine or Blue

The overprint was applied to 13 denominations in four settings with change of city name, producing individual sets for each city: "MONASTIR," "PRISTINA," "SALONIQUE" and "USKUB."

1911, June 26 *Perf. 12, 13½*

P69 A16 5pa bister 16.50 *20.00*
P70 A16 10pa yellow grn 16.50 *20.00*
P71 A16 20pa magenta 16.50 *20.00*
P72 A16 1pi violet blue 16.50 *20.00*
P73 A16 2pi gray blue 22.50 *30.00*
P74 A16 5pi ocher 45.00 *60.00*
P75 A17 5pa purple 8.75 *11.50*
P76 A17 10pa green 8.75 *11.50*
P77 A17 20pa carmine 8.75 *11.50*
P78 A17 1pi blue 8.75 *11.50*
P79 A17 2pi orange 11.00 *14.50*
P80 A17 5pi lilac rose 30.00 32.50
P81 A21 2pa olive green 3.00 *3.75*
Nos. P69-P81 (13) 212.50 *266.75*

Values for each of the 4 city sets of 13 are the same.

The note after No. 182 will also apply to Nos. P69-P81.

Newspaper Stamps of 1901-11 Overprinted in Carmine or Black

1915 **On Stamps of 1893-98**

P121 A10 10pa gray green 6.00 .50
a. Inverted overprint 20.00 20.00
P122 A13 2pi yellow brn 1.50 1.00
a. Inverted overprint 20.00 20.00

On Stamps of 1901

P123 A16 10pa yellow grn 2.00 .50
P124 A17 5pa purple 2.00 1.00
P125 A17 20pa carmine 2.00 1.00
P126 A17 5pi lilac rose 20.00 5.00

On Stamps of 1905

P127 A18 5pa ocher 2.00 1.00
a. Inverted overprint 20.00 20.00
P128 A18 2pi slate 17.50 5.00
P129 A18 5pi brown 10.00 .60

On Stamps of 1908

P130 A19 2pi blue blk *1,375.* *550.00*
P131 A19 5pi dk violet 10.00 1.25

On Stamps of 1909

P132 A21 5pa ocher 3.00 1.00
P133 A21 5pi dk violet 100.00 35.00
Nos. P121-P129,P131-P133 (12) 176.00 52.85

Preceding Newspaper Issues with additional Overprint in Red or Black

1916 **On Stamps of 1893-98**

P134 A10 10pa gray green 2.00 .75
P135 A11 20pa violet brn 2.00 .75
P136 A14 5pi dull violet 50.00 50.00

On Stamp of 1897

P137 A10 5pa on 10pa gray grn .60 .50

On Stamps of 1901

P138 A16 5pa bister 1.00 .30
P139 A16 10pa yellow grn 1.50 .90
P140 A16 20pa magenta 1.50 .90
a. Inverted overprint 20.00 20.00
P141 A16 1pi violet blue 1.00 1.00
P142 A17 5pa purple 50.00 50.00
P143 A17 10pa green 50.00 50.00
P144 A17 20pa carmine 1.50 .90
P145 A17 1pi blue 1.50 .90
P146 A17 2pi orange 1.50 .90

On Stamps of 1905

P147 A18 5pa ocher 1.50 .75
P148 A18 10pa dull green 50.00 50.00
P149 A18 20pa carmine 50.00 50.00
P150 A18 1pi pale blue 1.75 1.00

On Stamp of 1908

P151 A19 5pa ocher 62.50 62.50

On Stamp of 1909

P152 A21 5pa ocher 62.50 62.50
Nos. P134-P152 (19) 392.35 384.55

Preceding Newspaper Issues with additional Overprint in Red or Black

1917 **On Stamps of 1893-98**

P153 A12 1pi gray (R) 2.50 2.00
P154 A11 20pa vio brn (R) 3.75 3.75

On Stamps of 1901

P155 A16 5pa bister (Bk) 2.00 1.50
a. Inverted overprint 20.00 20.00
P156 A16 10pa yellow grn (R) 1.50 1.25
P157 A16 20pa magenta (Bk) 1.50 1.25
P158 A16 2pi gray blue (R) 40.00 30.00
P159 A17 5pa purple (Bk) 2.25 2.25
a. Inverted overprint 20.00 20.00
b. Double overprint 20.00 20.00
c. Double ovpt., one inverted 25.00 25.00
P160 A17 10pa green (R) 22.50 35.00
P161 A17 20pa carmine (Bk) 1.50 1.25
P162 A17 1pi blue (R) 3.00 3.00
P163 A17 2pi orange (Bk) 2.50 2.50
P164 A17 5pi lilac rose (R) 32.50 50.00

On Stamps of 1905

P165 A18 5pa ocher (R) 2.50 2.00
a. Inverted overprint 20.00 20.00
P166 A18 5pa ocher (Bk) 3.00 2.50
a. Inverted overprint 20.00 20.00
P167 A18 10pa dull green (R) 2.50 2.00
P168 A18 20pa carmine (Bk) 2.50 2.00
a. Double overprint 20.00 20.00
P169 A18 1pi blue (R) 2.50 2.00
a. Inverted overprint 25.00 25.00
P170 A18 2pi slate (R) 32.50 50.00
P171 A18 5pi brown (R) 32.50 50.00

On Stamp of 1908

P172 A19 5pa ocher (R) 32.50 50.00
Nos. P153-P172 (20) *226.00* *294.25*

Nos. P153-P172 were used as regular postage stamps.

Type of 1909 Surcharged in Blue and Overprinted in Red

1919

P173 A21 5pa on 2pa ol grn 1.25 1.00
a. Red overprint double 20.00 10.00
b. Blue surcharge double 20.00 10.00

No. 255 Surcharged in Red

1920

P174 A25 5pa on 4pa brn 1.25 .50

Catalogue values for unused stamps in this section, from this point to the end of the section, are for Never Hinged items.

Dove and Citadel of Ankara — N6

1952-55 **Litho.** *Perf. 12½*

P175 N6 0.50k grnsh gray .25 .25
P176 N6 0.50k violet ('53) .25 .25

Perf. 10½, 10

P177 N6 0.50k red org ('54) .25 .25
P178 N6 0.50k brown ('55) .25 .25
Nos. P175-P178 (4) 1.00 1.00

POSTAL TAX STAMPS

Map of Turkey and Red Crescent — PT1

1928 **Unwmk.** **Typo.** *Perf. 14*

Crescent in Red

RA1 PT1 ½pi lt brown .90 .35
RA2 PT1 1pi red violet .90 .35
RA3 PT1 2½pi orange .95 .35

Engr.

Various Frames

RA4 PT1 5pi dk brown .90 .45
RA5 PT1 10pi yellow green 1.10 .60
RA6 PT1 20pi slate 1.60 .80
RA7 PT1 50pi dark violet 6.25 1.75
Nos. RA1-RA7 (7) 12.60 4.65
Set, never hinged 13.00

The use of these stamps on letters, parcels, etc. in addition to the regular postage, was obligatory on certain days in each year.

For surcharges see Nos. RA16, RA21-RA22.

Cherubs Upholding Star — PT2

1932

RA8 PT2 1k ol bis & red 1.00 .30
RA9 PT2 2½k dk brn & red 1.25 .30
RA10 PT2 5k green & red 1.50 .30
RA11 PT2 25k black & red 3.00 1.00
Nos. RA8-RA11 (4) 6.75 1.90
Set, never hinged 9.00

For surcharges and overprints see Nos. RA12-RA15, RA28-RA29, RA36-RA38.

No. RA8 Surcharged

RA12 PT2 20pa on 1k 2.00 .50
RA13 PT2 3k on 1k 3.50 2.00
a. 3 "kruus" 2.50 2.50

By a law of Parliament the use of these stamps on letters and telegraph forms, in addition to the regular fees, was obligatory from Apr. 20-30 of each year. The inscription in the tablet at the bottom of the design states that the money derived from the sale of the stamps is devoted to child welfare work.

No. RA8 Surcharged

1933

RA14 PT2 20pa on 1k ol bis & red 1.00 .50
RA15 PT2 3k on 1k ol bis & red 1.75 1.00

No. RA5 Surcharged

RA16 PT1 5k on 10pi yel grn & red 1.50 .75
Nos. RA14-RA16 (3) 4.25 2.25

PT3 PT4

1933 *Perf. 11, 11½*

RA17 PT3 20pa gray vio & red 1.00 .50
RA18 PT4 1k violet & red 1.00 .50
RA19 PT4 5k dk brown & red 4.00 2.00
RA20 PT3 15k green & red 5.00 2.00
Nos. RA17-RA20 (4) 11.00 5.00
Set, never hinged 12.00

Nos. RA17 and RA20 were issued in Ankara; Nos. RA18 and RA19 in Izmir.

For overprint see No. RA27.

Nos. RA3, RA1 Surcharged in Black

1933-34

RA21 PT1 1k on 2½pi orange .75 .30
RA22 PT1 5k on ½pi lt brown 2.25 .50

Map of Turkey — PT5

1934-35 **Crescent in Red** *Perf. 12*

RA23 PT5 ½k blue ('35) .40 .25
RA24 PT5 1k red brown .40 .25
RA25 PT5 2½k brown ('35) .60 .25
RA26 PT5 5k blue green ('35) 1.50 .25
Nos. RA23-RA26 (4) 2.90 1.00
Set, never hinged 5.00

Frame differs on No. RA26.

See Nos. RA30-RA35B.

Nos. RA17, RA8-RA9 Overprinted in Roman Capitals

1936 *Perf. 11, 14*

RA27 PT3 20pa gray vio & red .75 .25
RA28 PT2 1k ol bis & red .75 .25
RA29 PT2 3k on 2½k dk brn & red 1.50 .30
Nos. RA27-RA29 (3) 3.00
Set, never hinged 12.00

Type of 1934-35, Inscribed "Türkiye Kizilay Cemiyeti"

1938-46 *Perf. 8½-11½*

Type I — Imprint, "Devlet Basimevi". Crescent red.

Type II — Imprint, "Alaeddin Kiral Basimevi". Crescent carmine.

Type III — Imprint, "Damga Matbaasi". Crescent red.

Crescent in Red or Carmine

RA30 PT5 ½k blue (I) 1.25 .50
a. Type II 4.00 1.00
b. Type III 1.75 .50
RA31 PT5 1k red vio (I) .75 .25
a. Type II 6.50 2.00
b. Type III .75 .25
RA32 PT5 2½k orange (I) .90 .30
a. Type III 2.00 1.00
RA33 PT5 5k blue grn (I) .75 .25
RA33A PT5 5k choc (III) ('42) 1.25 .25
RA34 PT5 10k pale grn (I) 1.50 .30
a. Type III 2.00 1.00
RA35 PT5 20k black (I) 3.50 1.50
RA35A PT5 50k pur (III) ('46) 7.50 1.00
RA35B PT5 1 l blue (III) ('44) 30.00 2.50
Nos. RA30-RA35B (9) 47.40 6.85
Set, never hinged 75.00

For surcharge see No. RA63.

No. RA9 Surcharged in Black

1938 *Perf. 14*

RA36 PT2 20pa on 2½k 1.00 .50
RA37 PT2 1k on 2½k 1.00 .50

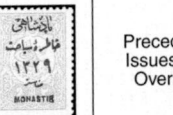

No. RA9 Surcharged in Black

1938 Unwmk. *Perf. 14*

RA37A	PT2	20pa on 2½k	1.25	.60
RA37B	PT2	1k on 2½k	1.50	.75

No. RA9 Surcharged "1 Kurus" in Black

1939 *Perf. 14*

RA38	PT2	1k on 2½k dk brn & red	.90	.90

Child
PT6

Nurse with Child
PT7

1940 Typo. *Perf. 12*

Star in Carmine

RA39	PT6	20pa bluish grn	.30	.25
RA40	PT6	1k violet	.30	.25
RA41	PT7	1k lt blue	.30	.25
RA42	PT7	2½k pale red lil	.30	.25
RA43	PT6	3k black	.35	.25
RA44	PT7	5k pale violet	.30	.25
RA45	PT7	10k blue green	1.00	.40
RA46	PT6	15k dark blue	.75	.30
RA47	PT7	25k olive bister	2.50	1.25
RA48	PT7	50k olive gray	6.00	2.50
		Nos. RA39-RA48 (10)	12.10	5.95
		Set, never hinged	30.00	

Soldier and Map of Turkey — PT8

1941-44 *Perf. 11½*

RA49	PT8	1k purple	.40	.25
RA50	PT8	2k light blue	2.50	.25
RA51	PT8	3k chestnut	2.75	.50
RA51A	PT8	4k mag ('44)	12.00	1.25
RA52	PT8	5k brt rose	7.75	2.50
RA53	PT8	10k dk blue	11.00	4.00
		Nos. RA49-RA53 (6)	36.40	8.75
		Set, never hinged	75.00	

The tax was used for national defense.

Baby
PT9

Nurse and Baby
PT13

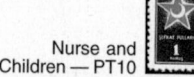

Nurse and Children — PT10

Nurse Feeding Child — PT11

Nurse and Child
PT12

Nurse and Child
PT14

President Inonu Holding Child
PT15

Children
PT16

1942 Unwmk. Typo. *Perf. 11½*

Star in Red

RA54	PT9	20pa brt violet	.75	.25
RA55	PT9	20pa chocolate	.75	.25
RA56	PT10	1k dk slate grn	.75	.25
RA57	PT11	2½k yellow grn	.75	.30
RA58	PT12	3k dark blue	.75	.30
RA59	PT13	5k brt pink	.90	.30
RA60	PT14	10k lt blue	1.20	.40
RA61	PT15	15k dk red brn	1.60	.70
RA62	PT16	25k brown	3.00	1.00
		Nos. RA54-RA62 (9)	10.45	3.75

See Nos. RA175, RA179-RA180.

No. RA32 Surcharged with New Value in Brown

1942 *Perf. 10*

RA63	PT5	1k on 2½k org & red (I)	.25	.25

Child Eating
PT17

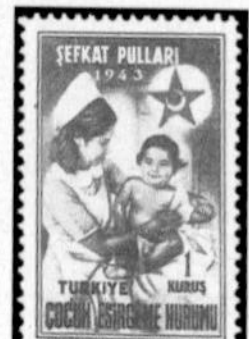

Nurse and Child
PT18

Nurse and Child — PT19

Child and Red Star — PT20

President Inönü and Child — PT21

Inscribed: "Sefcat Pullari 23 Nisan 1943 Cocuk Esirgeme Kurumu."

1943 Star in Red *Perf. 11*

RA64	PT17	50pa dp lilac	.65	.25
RA65	PT17	50pa gray green	.65	.25
RA66	PT18	1k lt ultra	.65	.25
RA67	PT19	3k dark red	.65	.25
RA68	PT20	15k cream & blk	2.50	.40
RA69	PT21	100k brt violet blue	3.75	1.60
	a.	Souvenir sheet, #RA64-RA69, imperf.	5.50	5.50
		Nos. RA64-RA69 (6)	8.85	3.00

Star and Crescent
PT23

Hospital
PT24

Nurse and Children
PT25

Baby
PT26

Nurse Bathing Baby
PT27

Nurse Feeding Child
PT28

Baby with Bottle
PT29

Child
PT30

Hospital — PT31

Perf. 10 to 12 and Compound

1943-44 Star in Red

RA71	PT23	20pa deep blue	.50	.30
RA72	PT24	1k gray green	.50	.25
RA73	PT25	3k pale gray brn	.50	.25
RA74	PT26	5k yellow orange	.90	.30
RA75	PT26	5k violet brn	.50	.25
RA76	PT27	10k red	.50	.30
RA77	PT28	15k red violet	.75	.40
RA78	PT29	25k pale violet	1.10	.50
RA79	PT30	50k lt blue	2.50	1.00
RA80	PT31	100k lt green	6.50	4.00
		Nos. RA71-RA80 (10)	14.25	7.55
		Set, never hinged	27.50	

For surcharge see No. RA156.

Nurse Holding Baby
PT32

Nurse Feeding Child
PT33

Child
PT34

Star and Crescent
PT35

1945-47 Unwmk. Litho. *Perf. 11½*

Star in Red

RA81	PT32	1k lilac brn	.40	.25
	a.	1k rose violet	.50	.25
RA82	PT33	5k yellow grn	.70	.25
	a.	5k green	.70	.25
RA83	PT34	10k red brown	.50	.25
RA84	PT35	250k gray black	9.50	3.50
RA84A	PT35	500k dull vio ('47)	37.50	12.50
		Nos. RA81-RA84A (5)	48.60	16.75
		Set, never hinged	90.00	

Imprint on No. RA82: "Kagit ve Basim isleri A.S. ist." On No. RA82a: "Guzel Sanatlar Matbaasi — Ankara."

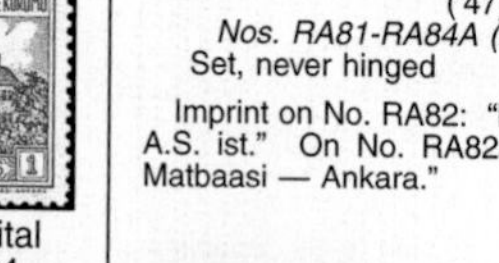

Nurse and Wounded Soldier
PT36

President Inönü and Victim of Earthquake
PT37

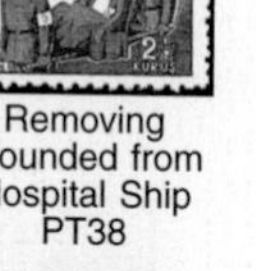

Removing Wounded from Hospital Ship
PT38

Nurse and Soldier
PT39

Feeding the Poor — PT40

Wounded Soldiers on Landing Raft — PT41

Symbolical of Red Crescent Relief — PT42

1945 *Perf. 12x10, 10x12*

Crescent in Red

RA85	PT36	20pa dp bl & brn org	.50	.25
RA86	PT37	1k ol grn & ol bis	.50	.25
RA87	PT38	2½k dp bl & red	1.00	.50
RA88	PT39	5k dp bl & red	2.00	1.00
RA89	PT40	10k dp bl & lt grn	2.00	1.00
RA90	PT41	50k blk & gray grn	4.50	2.00
RA91	PT42	1 l black & yel	15.00	7.50
		Nos. RA85-RA91 (7)	25.50	12.50
		Set, never hinged	45.00	

See Nos. RA181-RA182.

Ankara Sanatorium — PT43

1946 *Perf. 12*

RA92	PT43	20k red & lt bl	.65	.30

See No. RA210. For surcharge see No. RA186.

Covering Sleeping Child — PT44

Designs: 1k, Mother and child. 2½k, Nurse at playground. 5k, Doctor examining infant. 15k, Feeding child. 25k, Bathing child. 50k, Weighing baby. 150k, Feeding baby.

Inscribed: "25ci Yil Hatirasi 1946" Star in Carmine

1946 **Litho.** *Perf. 12½*

No.	Type	Description	Unused	Used
RA93	PT44	20pa brown	.50	.25
RA94	PT44	1k blue	.50	.25
RA95	PT44	2½k carmine	.50	.25
RA96	PT44	5k vio brn	.75	.25
RA97	PT44	15k violet	1.15	.50
RA98	PT44	25k gray grn	1.50	.60
RA99	PT44	50k bl grn	1.75	1.50
RA100	PT44	150k gray brn	4.00	1.75
		Nos. RA93-RA100 (8)	10.65	5.35
		Set, never hinged	20.00	

For surcharge see No. RA155.

Hospital Ship — PT52

Ambulance Plane — PT53

Hospital Train PT54

Ambulance PT55

Boy Scout and Red Crescent Flag PT56

Stretcher Bearers and Wounded Soldier PT57

Nurse and Hospital PT58

Sanatorium PT59

1946 *Perf. 11½*

No.	Type	Description	Unused	Used
RA101	PT52	1k multi	1.75	1.75
RA102	PT53	4k multi	1.75	1.75
RA103	PT54	10k multi	6.00	6.00
RA104	PT55	25k multi	6.25	6.25
RA105	PT56	40k multi	9.50	9.50
RA106	PT57	70k multi	8.00	8.00
RA107	PT58	1 l multi	6.50	6.50
RA108	PT59	2½ l multi	14.00	14.00
		Nos. RA101-RA108 (8)	53.75	53.75

For overprints see Nos. RA139-RA146.

Souvenir Sheet

Pres. Inönü and Child PT60

1946 **Unwmk.** **Typo.** *Imperf.*

Without Gum

No.	Type	Description	Unused	Used
RA109	PT60	250k slate blk, pink & red	20.00	17.50

Turkish Society for the Prevention of Cruelty to Children, 25th anniv.

Nurse and Wounded Soldier PT61

Pres. Inönü and Victim of Earthquake PT62

Nurse and Soldier PT64

Symbolical of Red Crescent Relief PT67

1946-47 **Litho.** *Perf. 11½*

Crescent in Red

No.	Type	Description	Unused	Used
RA113	PT61	20pa dk bl vio & ol ('47)	.60	.25
RA114	PT62	1k dk brn & yel	.90	.25
RA115	PT64	5k dp bl & red	1.00	.90
RA116	PT67	1 l brn blk & yel	3.50	2.50
		Nos. RA113-RA116 (4)	6.00	3.90

PT68

Nurse and Wounded Soldier PT69

Victory and Soldier PT70

1947 **Crescent in Red**

No.	Type	Description	Unused	Used
RA117	PT68	250k brn blk & grn	5.25	2.00
RA118	PT69	5 l sl gray & org	8.75	3.50

Booklet Pane of One

Perf. 11½ (top) x Imperf.

No.	Type	Description	Unused	Used
RA119	PT70	10 l deep blue	22.50	—

Black numerals above No. RA119 indicate position in booklet.

President Inönü and Victim of Earthquake PT71

Nurse and Child PT72

1947 *Perf. 11½*

No.	Type	Description	Unused	Used
RA120	PT71	1k dk brn, pale bl & red	.65	.25
RA121	PT72	2½k bl vio & car	.65	.25

See Nos. RA221-RA223. For surcharge see No. RA154.

Nurse Offering Encouragement PT73

Plant with Broken Stem PT74

Perf. 8½, 11½x10, 11x10½

1948-49 **Typo.** **Unwmk.**

Crescent in Red

No.	Type	Description	Unused	Used
RA122	PT73	½k ultra ('49)	.75	.25
RA123	PT73	1k indigo	.50	.25
RA124	PT73	2k lilac rose	.50	.25
RA125	PT73	2½k org ('49)	.50	.25
RA126	PT73	3k bl grn	.50	.25
RA127	PT73	4k gray ('49)	.60	.25
RA128	PT73	5k blue	.90	.25
RA129	PT73	10k pink	1.50	.25
RA130	PT73	25k chocolate	1.75	.25

Perf. 10

No.	Type	Description	Unused	Used
RA130A	PT74	50k ultra & bl gray ('49)	2.25	.75
RA130B	PT74	100k grn & pale grn ('49)	5.25	1.00
		Nos. RA122-RA130B (11)	15.00	4.00
		Set, never hinged	30.00	

For surcharges see Nos. RA151-RA153, RA187.

Nurse and Children — PT75

Various Scenes with Children.

Inscribed: "1948 Cocuk Yili Hatirasi"

1948 **Litho.** *Perf. 11*

Star in Red

No.	Type	Description	Unused	Used
RA131	PT75	20pa dp ultra	.50	.25
RA132	PT75	20pa rose lilac	.50	.25
RA133	PT75	1k dp Prus bl	.60	.30
RA134	PT75	3k dk brn vio	.90	.50
RA135	PT75	15k slate black	3.25	1.25
RA136	PT75	30k orange	4.00	3.00
RA137	PT75	150k yellow grn	5.25	4.00
RA138	PT75	300k brown red	8.25	6.50
		Nos. RA131-RA138 (8)	23.25	16.05
		Set, never hinged	30.00	

No. RA136 is arranged horizontally. For overprints and surcharges see Nos. RA199-RA206.

Catalogue values for unused stamps in this section, from this point to the end of the section, are for Never Hinged items.

Nos. RA101 to RA108 Overprinted in Carmine

1949 *Perf. 11½*

No.	Type	Description	Unused	Used
RA139	PT52	1k multi	10.00	10.00
RA140	PT53	4k multi	10.00	10.00
RA141	PT54	10k multi	10.00	10.00
RA142	PT55	25k multi	10.00	10.00
RA143	PT56	40k multi	20.00	20.00
RA144	PT57	70k multi	10.00	10.00
RA145	PT58	1 l multi	10.00	10.00
RA146	PT59	2½ l multi	10.00	10.00
		Nos. RA139-RA146 (8)	90.00	90.00

Ruins and Tent — PT76

Booklet Panes of One

1949 *Perf. 10 (top) x Imperf.*

No.	Type	Description	Unused	Used
RA149	PT76	5k gray, vio gray & red	4.00	3.00
RA150	PT76	10k red vio, sal & red	4.00	3.00

Black numerals above each stamp indicate its position in the booklet.

No. RA124 Surcharged in Black

1950 **Unwmk.** *Perf. 8½*

No.	Type	Description	Unused	Used
RA151	PT73	20pa on 2k	1.25	1.00

Postal Tax Stamps of 1944-48 Surcharged with New Value in Black or Carmine

Perf. 8½ to 12½ and Compound

1952

No.	Type	Description	Unused	Used
RA152	PT73	20pa on 3k bl grn	.50	.25
RA153	PT73	20pa on 4k gray	.75	.25
RA154	PT72	1k on 2½k bl vio & car (C)	1.00	1.50
RA155	PT44	1k on 2½k car	2.00	1.00
RA156	PT25	1k on 3k pale gray brn	2.00	1.00
		Nos. RA152-RA156 (5)	6.25	4.00

"Protection" — PT77

Various Symbolical Designs Inscribed "75 iNCi" etc.

1952 **Typo.** *Perf. 10*

Crescent in Carmine

No.	Type	Description	Unused	Used
RA157	PT77	5k bl grn & bl	2.00	1.50
RA158	PT77	15k yel grn, bl & cr	2.00	1.50
RA159	PT77	30k bl, grn & brn	2.00	1.50
RA160	PT77	1 l blk, lt bl & yel	2.00	1.50
a.		Souvenir sheet, #RA157-RA160, imperf.	30.00	30.00
		Nos. RA157-RA160 (4)	8.00	6.00

Printed in sheets of 20 containing one horizontal row of each value.

Nurse and Children — PT78

Design: 1k, Nurse and baby.

1954 **Litho.** *Perf. 10½*

Star in Red

No.	Type	Description	Unused	Used
RA161	PT78	20pa aqua	.60	.35
RA162	PT78	20pa yellow	.90	.35
RA163	PT12	1k deep blue	1.50	.80
		Nos. RA161-RA163 (3)	3.00	1.50

Globe and Flag — PT79

Designs: 5k, Winged nurse in clouds. 10k, Protecting arm of Red Crescent.

1954

No.	Type	Description	Unused	Used
RA164	PT79	1k multi	.50	.25
RA165	PT79	5k multi	.75	.25
RA166	PT79	10k car, grn & gray	1.25	.25
		Nos. RA164-RA166 (3)	2.50	.75

See Nos. RA208, RA211-RA213. For surcharges see Nos. RA187A-RA187B.

Florence Nightingale PT80

Selimiye Barracks PT81

30k, Florence Nightingale, full-face.

Crescent in Carmine

1954, Nov. 4

No.	Type	Description	Unused	Used
RA167	PT80	20k gray grn & dk brn	.60	.50
RA168	PT80	30k dl brn & blk	.90	.50
RA169	PT81	50k buff & blk	1.40	.50
		Nos. RA167-RA169 (3)	2.90	1.50

Arrival of Florence Nightingale at Scutari, cent.

Type of 1942 and

Children Kissing
PT82

Nurse Holding Baby
PT83

1955, Apr. 23 — Star in Red

RA170 PT82 20pa chalky bl .25 .25
RA171 PT82 20pa org brn .25 .25
RA172 PT82 1k lilac .25 .25
RA173 PT82 3k gray bis .25 .25
RA174 PT82 5k orange .25 .25
RA175 PT12 10k green 2.50 .75
RA176 PT82 15k dk blue .25 .25
RA177 PT83 25k brn car 1.50 1.40
RA178 PT83 50k dk gray grn 2.00 1.50
RA179 PT12 2½ l dull brn 375.00 125.00
RA180 PT12 10 l rose lil 875.00 250.00
Nos. RA170-RA180 (11) 1,258. 380.15

Types of 1945

Inscribed: "Turkiye Kizilay Dernegi"

1955 Litho. *Perf. 10½x11½, 10½*

Crescent in Red

RA181 PT36 20pa vio brn & lem .50 .25
RA182 PT41 1k blk & gray grn .50 .25

Nurse
PT85

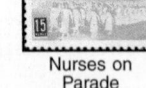

Nurses on Parade
PT86

Design: 100k, Two nurses under Red Cross and Red Crescent flags and UN emblem.

Perf. 10½

1955, Sept. 5 Unwmk. Litho.

Crescent and Cross in Red

RA183 PT85 10k blk & pale brn .75 .35
RA184 PT86 15k dk grn & pale yel grn .75 .45
RA185 PT85 100k lt ultra 3.50 1.75
Nos. RA183-RA185 (3) 5.00 2.55

Meeting of the board of directors of the Intl. Council of Nurses, Istanbul, Aug. 29-Sept. 5, 1955.

Nos. RA92 and RA130B Surcharged "20 Para"

1955

RA186 PT43 20p on 20k .75 .40

Typo.

RA187 PT74 20p on 100k (surch. 11½x2mm) .90 .40
c. Surcharge 13½x2½mm 2.00 .75

No. RA164 Surcharged with New Value and Two Bars

1956 Litho. *Perf. 10½*

RA187A PT79 20p on 1k multi .25 .25
RA187B PT79 2.50k on 1k multi .25 .25

Woman and Children — PT87

Designs: 10k, 25k, 50k, Flag and building. 250k, 5 l, 10 l, Mother nursing baby.

1956 Litho. *Perf. 10½*

Star in Red

RA188 PT87 20pa red org .75 .75
RA189 PT87 20pa gray grn .75 .75
RA190 PT87 1k purple .75 .75
RA191 PT87 1k grnsh bl .75 .75
RA192 PT87 3k lt red brn 1.25 1.25
RA193 PT87 10k rose car 2.25 2.25
RA194 PT87 25k brt grn 5.00 5.00
RA195 PT87 50k brt ultra 6.50 6.50
RA196 PT87 250k red lilac 17.00 17.00
RA197 PT87 5 l sepia 35.00 15.00
RA198 PT87 10 l dk sl grn 57.50 30.00
Nos. RA188-RA198 (11) 127.50 80.00

Nos. RA131-RA138 Ovptd. and Srchd. in Black or Red

1956, Oct. 1 Unwmk. *Perf. 11*

RA199 PT75 20pa (R) 12.00 12.00
RA200 PT75 20pa 12.00 12.00
RA201 PT75 1k (R) 12.00 12.00
RA202 PT75 3k (R) 12.00 12.00
RA203 PT75 15k (R) 12.00 12.00
RA204 PT75 25k on 30k 12.00 12.00
RA205 PT75 100k on 150k (R) 12.00 12.00
RA206 PT75 250k on 300k 18.00 18.00
Nos. RA199-RA206 (8) 102.00 102.00

The tax was for child welfare.

Type of 1954, Redrawn Type of 1946, and

Flower — PT88

Crescent in Red

1957 Unwmk. *Perf. 10½*

RA207 PT88 ½k lt ol gray & brn .50 .25
RA208 PT79 1k ol bis, blk & grn .50 .25
RA209 PT88 2½k yel grn & bl grn .50 .25
RA210 PT43 20k red & lt bl 2.75 1.25
RA211 PT79 25k lt gray, blk & grn 2.75 1.25
RA212 PT79 50k bl, dk grn & grn 8.00 1.50
RA213 PT79 100k vio, blk & grn 8.75 3.00
Nos. RA207-RA213 (7) 23.75 7.75

No. RA210 inscribed "Turkiye Kizilay Cemiyeti." No. RA92 inscribed ". . . . Dernegi."

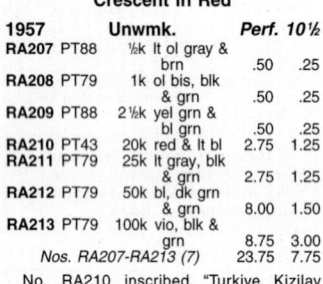

Children — PT89

1957 Unwmk. *Perf. 10½*

RA214 PT89 20pa car & red .50 .25
RA215 PT89 20pa grn & red .50 .25
RA216 PT89 1k ultra & car .50 .25
RA217 PT89 3k red org & car 2.25 1.50
Nos. RA214-RA217 (4) 3.75 2.25

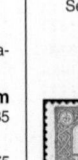

"Blood Donor and Recipient" — PT90

Designs: 75k, Figure showing blood circulation. 150k, Blood transfusion symbolism.

1957, May 22 Size: 24x40mm

RA218 PT90 25k gray, blk & red .50 .35

Size: 22½x37½mm

RA219 PT90 75k grn, blk & red .90 .75
RA220 PT90 150k yel grn & red 2.25 2.00
Nos. RA218-RA220 (3) 3.65 3.10

Redrawn Type of 1947

Inscribed: "V Dunya Cocuk Gunu"

1957 Star in Red *Perf. 10½*

RA221 PT72 100k blk & bis brn 1.25 .75
RA222 PT72 150k blk & yel grn 1.25 .75
RA223 PT72 250k blk & vio 2.50 1.00
Nos. RA221-RA223 (3) 5.00 2.50

The tax was for child welfare.

Child and Butterfly — PT91

Various Butterflies. 50k, 75k horiz.

1958 Litho. Unwmk.

RA224 PT91 20k gray & red .75 .75
RA225 PT91 25k multi .75 .75
RA226 PT91 50k multi 1.50 1.50
RA227 PT91 75k grn, yel & blk 2.00 2.00
RA228 PT91 150k multi 2.50 2.50
Nos. RA224-RA228 (5) 7.50 7.50

Florence Nightingale — PT92

1958 Crescent in Red

RA229 PT92 1 l bluish green .75 .25
RA230 PT92 1½ l gray .90 .50
RA231 PT92 2½ l blue 1.25 .60
Nos. RA229-RA231 (3) 2.90 1.35

Turkey stopped issuing postal tax stamps in June, 1958. Similar stamps of later date are private charity stamps issued by the Red Crescent Society and the Society for the Protection of Children.

POSTAL TAX AIR POST STAMPS

Air Fund Issues

These stamps were obligatory on all air mail for 21 days a year. Tax for the Turkish Aviation Society: 20pa for a postcard, 1k for a regular letter, 2 1/2k for a registered letter, 3k for a telegram, 5k-50k for a package, higher values for air freight. Postal tax air post stamps were withdrawn Aug. 21, 1934 and remainders destroyed later that year.

Biplane — PTAP1

Type PTAP1

Perf. 11, Pin Perf.

1926 Unwmk. Litho.

Size: 35x25mm

RAC1 20pa brn & pale grn 3.00 .30
RAC2 1g blue grn & buff 2.00 .30

Size: 40x29mm

RAC3 5g vio & pale grn 8.00 1.00
RAC4 5g car lake & pale grn 35.00 15.00
Nos. RAC1-RAC4 (4) 48.00 16.60
Set, never hinged 275.00

PTAP2

PTAP3

1927-29 Type PTAP2

RAC5 20pa dl red & pale grn 1.75 .50
RAC6 1k green & yel 1.50 .50

Type PTAP3

Perf. 11½

RAC7 2k dp cl & yel grn 1.75 .50
RAC8 2½k red & yel grn 11.00 2.50
RAC9 5k dk bl gray & org 2.75 1.00
RAC10 10k dk grn & rose 5.00 1.25
RAC11 15k green & yel 5.00 1.00
RAC12 20k ol brn & yel 7.00 2.00
RAC13 50k dk bl & cob bl 10.00 4.50
RAC14 100k car & lt bl 110.00 80.00
Nos. RAC5-RAC14 (10) 155.75 93.75
Set, never hinged 825.00

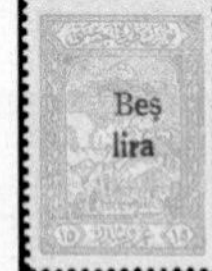

Nos. RAC1, RAC5, RAC7 and RAC11 Surcharged in Black or Red

1930-31

RAC15 1k ("Bir kurus") on RAC1 200.00 125.00
RAC16 1k ("Bir Kurus") on RAC5 1.50 .50
RAC17 100pa ("Yuz Para") on RAC7 2.00 .75
RAC18 5k ("Bes Kurus") on RAC5 8.00 1.50
RAC19 5k ("5 Kurus") on RAC5 3.00 .75
RAC20 10k ("On kurus") on RAC7 4.00 1.25
RAC21 50k ("Elli kurus") on RAC7 12.00 4.00
RAC22 1 l ("Bir lira") on RAC7 *37.50* *9.00*
RAC23 5 l ("Bes lira") on RAC11 *2,000.* *400.00*
Nos. RAC15-RAC23 (9) *2,268.* *542.75*
Set, never hinged 5,000.

PTAP4

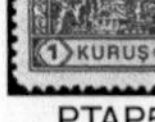
PTAP5

1931-32 Litho. *Perf. 11½*

RAC24 PTAP4 20pa black 5.00 1.75

Typo.

RAC25 PTAP5 1k brown car ('32) 2.00 .50
RAC26 PTAP5 5k red ('32) 4.00 .75
RAC27 PTAP5 10k green ('32) 6.00 1.50
Nos. RAC24-RAC27 (4) 17.00 4.50
Set, never hinged 65.00

PTAP6

1933 Type PTAP6

RAC28 10pa ("On Para") grn 3.50 2.00
RAC29 1k ("Bir Kurus") red 8.00 2.75
RAC30 5k ("Bes Kurus") lil 12.00 3.00
Nos. RAC28-RAC30 (3) 23.50 7.75
Set, never hinged 70.00

TURKEY IN ASIA

'tər-kē in 'ā-zhə

(Anatolia)

40 Paras = 1 Piaster

This designation, which includes all of Turkey in Asia Minor, came into existence during the uprising of 1919, led by Mustafa Kemal Pasha. Actually there was no separation of territory, the Sultan's sovereignty being almost immediately reduced to a small area surrounding Constantinople. The formation of the Turkish Republic and the expulsion of the Sultan followed in 1923. Subsequent issues of postage stamps are listed under Turkey (Republic).

Issues of the Nationalist Government

Turkish Stamps of 1913-18 Surcharged in Black or Red

(The Surcharge reads "Angora 3 Piastres")

1920 Unwmk. *Perf. 12*

On Stamps of 1913

No.	Type	Description	Unused	Used
1	A24	3pi on 2pa red lilac	4.00	*6.00*
2	A25	3pi on 4pa dk brn	50.00	*85.00*
3	A27	3pi on 6pa dk bl	325.00	*250.00*

On Stamp of 1916-18

No.	Type	Description	Unused	Used
4	A42	3pi on 2pa vio (Bk)	40.00	40.00
		Nos. 1-4 (4)	419.00	381.00

Turkish Stamps of 1913-18 Hstmpd. in Black or Red

(The Srch. reads "Post, Piastre 3")

1921 On Stamps of 1913 *Perf. 12*

No.	Type	Description	Unused	Used
5	A24	3pi on 2pa red lilac	30.00	45.00
a.		On No. 1	60.00	85.00
6	A25	3pi on 4pa dk brown	47.50	70.00
a.		On No. 2	225.00	300.00
7	A25	3pi on 4pa dk brn (R)	225.00	300.00
a.		On No. 2	250.00	350.00
8	A27	3pi on 6pa dk blue	250.00	350.00
a.		On No. 3	475.00	600.00
9	A27	3pi on 6pa dk bl (R)	60.00	85.00
a.		On No. 3	120.00	75.00

On Stamps of 1916-18

No.	Type	Description	Unused	Used
10	A42	3pi on 2pa vio (R)	125.00	200.00
a.		On No. 4	125.00	175.00
		Nos. 5-10 (6)	737.50	1,050.

Turkish Revenue Stamps Handstamped in Turkish "Osmanli Postalari, 1336" (Ottoman Post, 1920).

Type a

Dash at upper left is set high. Bottom (date) line is 8½mm long.

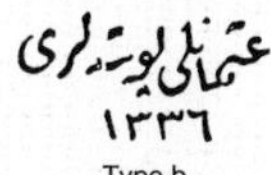

Type b

Dash at upper left is set lower. Bottom (date) line is 10mm long.

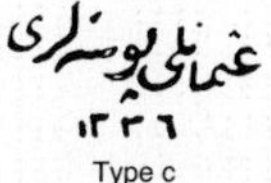

Type c

Dash at upper left is set lower. Bottom (date) line is 9mm long.

Religious Tribunals Revenue — R1

No.	Type	Description	Unused	Used
12	R1	1pi grn (a, b, c)	*1,000.*	500.00
13	R1	5pi ultra (a, b)	*16,000.*	*15,500.*
14	R1	50pi gray grn (a, b, c)	40.00	60.00
		Cut cancellation		2.00
15	R1	100pi buff (a)	160.00	170.00
a.		100pi yellow (a)	95.00	100.00
		Cut cancellation		8.50
16	R1	500pi org (a)	300.00	240.00
		Cut cancellation		22.00
17	R1	1000pi brn (a)	3,500.	2,100.
		Cut cancellation		190.00

See Nos. 29-32.

Court Costs Revenue — R2

Black Overprint

No.	Type	Description	Unused	Used
18	R2	10pa grn (b, c)	110.00	100.00
19	R2	1pi ultra (a, c)	—	*19,000.*
20	R2	5pi rose (c)	*17,500.*	—
21	R2	50pi ocher (a, b, c)	50.00	50.00
a.		50pi yellow (a, b, c)	30.00	40.00
		Cut cancellation, #21, 21a		2.00
22	R2	100pi brown (a)	110.00	100.00
		Cut cancellation		20.00
23	R2	500pi slate (a)	325.00	315.00
		Cut cancellation		20.00

See Nos. 24, 33-39.

Notary Public Revenue — R3

Design R2 Overprinted "Katibi Adliye Masus dur" in Red

No.	Type	Description	Unused	Used
24	R3	50pi ocher (a)	1,225.	145.00
		Cut cancellation		30.00

Laborer's Passport Tax Stamp — R4

Notary Public Revenue — R5

Black Overprint

No.	Type	Description	Unused	Used
25	R4	2pi emerald (a, c)	—	*22,000.*
26	R5	100pi yellow brn (a)	1,200.	145.00
		Cut cancellation		30.00

See Nos. 46-48.

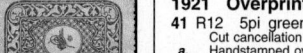

Theater Tax Stamp — R6

Land Registry Revenue — R7

No.	Type	Description	Unused	Used
27	R6	20pa black	*5,000.*	*5,000.*
28	R7	2pi blue black	*6,250.*	*6,250.*

See Nos. 40, 45.

Hejaz Railway Tax Stamp — R8

Black Overprint

Perf. 11½

No.	Type	Description	Unused	Used
28A	R8	2pi dk red & bl (b)	1,700.	*1,700.*

See Nos. 53-57.

Turkish Revenue Stamps Overprinted in Turkish "Osmanli Postalari, 1337" (Ottoman Post, 1921)

On #29-63

Perf. 12

No.	Type	Description	Unused	Used
29	R1	10pa slate	25.00	*17.50*
a.		Handstamped overprint	100.00	*50.00*
b.		Double overprint		
30	R1	1pi green	30.00	20.00
a.		Inverted overprint	35.00	22.50
b.		Handstamped overprint	*3,500.*	*3,250.*
31	R1	5pi ultra	29.00	20.00
a.		"1337" inverted	100.00	90.00
b.		Half used as 2½pi on cover		
c.		Handstamped overprint	850.00	850.00
		Nos. 29-31 (3)	84.00	57.50

Handstamped Overprint

No.	Type	Description	Unused	Used
32	R1	50pi green	*7,250.*	*7,250.*

Design R2 Overprinted

No.	Type	Description	Unused	Used
33	R2	10pa green	30.00	35.00
a.		Handstamped overprint	3,500.	*3,500.*
34	R2	1pi ultra	50.00	25.00
a.		Handstamped overprint	850.00	850.00
35	R2	5pi red	24.50	25.00
a.		Inverted overprint		
b.		"1337" inverted	*100.00*	100.00
c.		Half used as 2½pi on cover		
d.		Handstamped overprint	7,500	*7,500.*
36	R2	50pi ocher, handstamped ovpt.	500.00	100.00
		Cut cancellation		20.00
		Nos. 33-36 (4)	604.50	185.00

Design R3 Overprinted

Additional Turkish Overprint in Red or Black

No.	Type	Description	Unused	Used
37	R3	10pa green (R)	*100.00*	60.00
38	R3	1pi ultra (R)	72.50	50.00
39	R3	5pi rose (Bk)	72.50	50.00
a.		"1337" inverted	*200.00*	*200.00*
b.		Handstamped overprint	*7,000.*	*7,000.*
		Nos. 37-39 (3)	245.00	160.00

Design R7 Overprinted

No.	Type	Description	Unused	Used
40	R7	2pi blue black	120.00	110.00
a.		Handstamped overprint	*5,500.*	*5,500.*

R12

1921 Overprinted in Black *Perf. 12*

No.	Type	Description	Unused	Used
41	R12	5pi green	145.00	120.00
		Cut cancellation		17.50
a.		Handstamped overprint	*5,500.*	*5,000.*

Museum Tax Stamp — R13

Overprinted in Black

No.	Type	Description	Unused	Used
42	R13	1pi ultra	400.00	400.00
a.		Handstamped overprint	*5,500.*	*5,500.*
43	R13	5pi deep green	450.00	450.00
a.		Handstamped overprint	*5,500.*	*5,500.*

Handstamped Overprint

No.	Type	Description	Unused	Used
44	R13	5pi dark vio	*7,000.*	*7,000.*

The overprint variety "337" for "1337" exists on Nos. 42-43.

Design R6 Overprinted

Perf. 12, 12½

No.	Type	Description	Unused	Used
45	R6	20pa black	12.50	5.50
a.		Date 4½mm high	15.00	
b.		"337" for "1337"	25.00	

Design R5 Overprinted

No.	Type	Description	Unused	Used
46	R5	10pa green	25.00	25.00
a.		Overprint 21mm long		
b.		"131" for "1337"		
47	R5	1pi ultra	37.50	25.00
a.		"13" for "1337"	*50.00*	*50.00*
b.		"131" for "1337"	*50.00*	*50.00*
c.		Inverted overprint	*90.00*	*90.00*
d.		Handstamped overprint	*4,500.*	*4,500.*
48	R5	5pi red	62.50	25.00
a.		Inverted overprint	*90.00*	*90.00*
b.		"131" for "1337"	*85.00*	*85.00*
c.		Handstamped overprint	*4,500.*	*4,400.*
		Nos. 46-48 (3)	125.00	75.00

R16

Perf. 11½, 11½x11

Overprinted in Black

No.	Type	Description	Unused	Used
49	R16	10pa pink	5.00	1.80
a.		Imperf.		
b.		Date "1237"	5.00	2.50
d.		Inverted overprint	17.50	
e.		Handstamped overprint	*1,950.*	*1,950.*
50	R16	1pi yellow	10.00	5.00
a.		Overprint 18mm long	10.00	5.00
b.		Date "1332"	12.00	
c.		Date "1317"		
d.		Inverted overprint	30.00	
e.		Handstamped overprint	*1,950.*	*1,950.*
51	R16	2pi yellow grn	12.50	5.50
a.		Date "1237"	15.00	
b.		Date "1317"		
c.		Imperf.		
d.		Inverted overprint	40.00	10.00
e.		Handstamped overprint	—	—
52	R16	5pi red	20.00	1.25
a.		Horiz. pair, imperf. vert.		
b.		Inverted overprint	25.00	8.00

c.	Double overprint	30.00	12.50
d.	Date "1332"	45.00	
e.	Half used as 2½pi on cover		
f.	Overprint 18mm long	20.00	8.00
g.	Handstamped overprint	*1,950.*	*1,950.*
	Nos. 49-52 (4)	47.50	13.55

Design R8 Overprinted
Turkish Inscriptions

20 Paras

1 Piaster

2 Piasters

5 Piasters

1921	**Dark Red & Blue**	***Perf. 11½***	
53 R8	20pa on 1pi	95.00	100.00
54 R8	1pi on 1pi	4.00	3.00
55 R8	2pi on 1pi	4.00	3.00
a.	Inverted surcharge	27.50	
56 R8	5pi on 1pi	6.00	5.00
	Nos. 53-56 (4)	109.00	111.00

See No. 57.

No. 54 Overprinted

57 R8 1pi on 1pi dk red & bl	90.00	50.00

Hejaz Railway Tax Stamp — R19

Overprinted in Black

58 R19 1pi grn & brn red	4.00	3.00
a. Double overprint		
b. Handstamped overprint		

The errors "1307," "1331" and "2337" occur once in each sheet of Nos. 53-58.

Naval League Labels — R20

Overprinted in Black

1921		***Perf. 12x11½***	
59 R20	1pa orange	10.00	15.00
a.	Date "1327"	45.00	45.00
60 R20	2pa indigo	10.00	15.00
61 R20	5pa green	12.00	17.00
62 R20	10pa brown	24.50	29.00
63 R20	40pa red brown	300.00	180.00
	Nos. 59-63 (5)	356.50	256.00
	Set, never hinged	1,100.	

The error "2337" occurs on all values of this issue.

The Naval League stamps have pictures of three Turkish warships. They were sold for the benefit of sailors of the fleet but did not pay postage until they were overprinted in 1921.

Turkish Stamps of 1915-20 Overprinted

a

b

The overprints on Nos. 64-77 read "Adana December 1st, 1921." This issue commemorated the withdrawal of the French from Cilicia.

On No. 71 the lines of the overprint are further apart than on Nos. 68-70 and 73-74.

1921		***Perf. 12***	
64 A44 (a)	10pa grn (424)	6.00	6.00
65 A45 (a)	20pa deep rose (425)	6.00	6.00
a.	Inverted overprint	17.00	
66 A51 (a)	25pi car, *straw* (434)	15.00	*20.00*
a.	Double overprint		
b.	Inverted overprint	37.50	37.50
	Nos. 64-66 (3)	27.00	32.00

On Newspaper Stamp of 1915

67 A21 (a)	5pa och (P132)	87.50	*145.00*

On Stamp of 1915

68 A22 (b)	5pa och (328)	350.00	*400.00*

On Stamps of 1917-18

69 A53 (b)	5pi on 2pa (547)	12.00	*14.50*
70 A53 (b)	5pi on 2pa (548)	12.00	*14.50*

On Stamp of 1919

71 A57 (b)	35pi on 1pi bl (Bk; 579)	42.50	*50.00*
a.	Inverted surcharge	100.00	

On Newspaper Stamp of 1915

72 A21 (b)	5pa och (P132)	*200.00*	*200.00*

On No. 72 the overprint is vertical, half reading up and half reading down.

On Stamps of 1920

73 A32 (b)	3pi blue (594)	10.00	10.00
74 A36 (b)	10pi gray vio (596)	12.00	14.50

On Postage Due Stamps of 1914

75 D1 (a)	5pa claret (J63)	340.00	340.00
76 D2 (a)	20pa red (J64)	340.00	400.00
a.	Inverted overprint	750.00	
77 D3 (b)	1pi dk bl (J65)	340.00	400.00
a.	Inverted overprint	*750.00*	*750.00*
	Nos. 75-77 (3)	1,020.	1,140.

Withdrawal of the French from Cilicia. Forged overprints exist.

Pact of Revenge, Burning Village at Top — A21

Izmir Harbor — A22

Mosque of Selim, Adrianople A23

Mosque of Selim, Konya A24

Soldier A25

Legendary Gray Wolf A26

Snake Castle and Seyhan River, Adana — A27

Parliament Building at Sivas — A28

A29

Mosque at Urfa — A30

Map of Anatolia A31

Declaration of Faith from the Koran A32

1922	**Litho.**	***Perf. 11½***	
78 A21	10pa violet brn	.50	.25
79 A22	20pa blue grn	.50	.25
80 A23	1pi dp blue	1.00	.35
81 A24	2pi red brown	3.00	.50
82 A25	5pi dk blue	3.00	.50
83 A26	10pi dk brown	13.00	3.50
a.	Vert. pair, imperf between	*100.00*	
b.	Vert. strip of 3, imperf between	*300.00*	
84 A27	25pi rose	14.50	3.00
85 A28	50pi indigo	1.00	14.50
86 A29	50pi dk gray	3.00	1.20
87 A30	100pi violet	72.50	5.00
	Cut cancellation		1.25
88 A31	200pi slate	195.00	80.00
	Cut cancellation		1.50
89 A32	500pi green	110.00	65.00
	Cut cancellation		3.00
	Nos. 78-89 (12)	417.00	174.05
	Set, never hinged	2,070.	

Imperf

79a	A22	20pa	25.00	*30.00*
80a	A23	1pi	20.00	*20.00*
82a	A25	5pi	20.00	*20.00*
84a	A27	25pi	35.00	*30.00*
85a	A28	50pi	27.50	*30.00*

Stamps of Type A23 Overprinted

1922			
90 A23	1pi deep blue	7.25	14.50
91 A23	5pi deep blue	7.25	20.00
92 A23	10pi brown	7.25	20.00
93 A23	25pi rose	7.25	24.00
94 A23	50pi slate	12.50	24.00
95 A23	100pi violet	17.50	37.50
96 A23	200pi black vio	17.50	50.00
97 A23	500pi blue green	25.00	75.00
	Nos. 90-97 (8)	101.50	265.00
	Set, never hinged	200.00	

Withdrawal of the French from Cilicia and the return of the Kemalist Natl. army. The overprint reads: "Adana, Jan. 5, 1922."

No. 90-97 without overprint were presented to some high government officials.

First Parliament House, Ankara — A33

1922		**Litho.**	
98 A33	5pa violet	1.00	2.50
99 A33	10pa green	1.00	2.50
100 A33	20pa pale red	1.50	2.00
101 A33	1pi brown org	10.00	1.50
102 A33	2pi red brown	25.00	4.25
103 A33	3pi rose	2.50	.50
a.	Arabic "13" in right corner	10.00	7.50
b.	Thin grayish paper	55.00	7.25
	Nos. 98-103 (6)	41.00	13.25
	Set, never hinged	157.00	

Nos. 98-103, 103b exist imperf. In 1923 several stamps of Turkey and Turkey in Asia were overprinted in Turkish for advertising purposes. The overprint reads: "Izmir Economic Congress, 17 Feb., 1339."

POSTAGE DUE STAMPS

D1

1922	**Litho.**	***Perf. 11½***	
J1 D1	20pa dull green	1.00	5.00
a.	Imperf.	35.00	*25.00*
J2 D1	1pi gray green	1.00	4.50
J3 D1	2pi red brown	1.50	16.00
J4 D1	3pi rose	11.50	22.50
J5 D1	5pi dark blue	12.50	50.00
	Nos. J1-J5 (5)	27.50	
	Set, never hinged	75.00	

TURKISH REPUBLIC OF NORTHERN CYPRUS

'tər-kish ri-'pə-blik of 'nor-thə(r)n 'sī-prəs

LOCATION — Northern 40% of the Island of Cyprus in the Mediterranean Sea off the coast of Turkey.

Established following Turkish invasion of Cyprus in 1974. On Nov. 15, 1983 Turkey declared the Turkish Republic of Northern Cyprus to be independent. No other country has recognized this country.

1000 Milliemes = 1 Pound

100 Kurus = 1 Turkish Lira (1978)

Catalogue values for all unused stamps in this country are for Never Hinged items.

Letters bearing these stamps enter international mail via the Turkish Post Office.

Watermark

Wmk. 390

Republic of Turkey, 50th Anniv.

A1 A2

Designs: 3m, Woman sentry. 5m, Military parade. 10m, Flag bearers. 15m, Anniversary emblem. 20m, Ataturk statue. 50m, Painting, "The Fallen." 70m, Turkish flag, map of Cyprus.

Perf. 12x11½, 11½x12

1974, July 27 Litho. Unwmk.

No.	Type	Description	Unused	Used
1	A1	3m multicolored	45.00	37.50
2	A2	5m multicolored	1.00	.50
3	A1	10m multicolored	2.00	.50
4	A2	15m multicolored	1.50	.90
5	A1	20m multicolored	1.25	.70
6	A1	50m multicolored	4.00	2.75
7	A2	70m multicolored	35.00	15.00
		Nos. 1-7 (7)	89.75	57.85

First day covers are dated 10/29/73.

Nos. 5, 3 Surcharged

1975, Mar. 3 *Perf. 12x11½*

No.	Type	Description	Unused	Used
8	A1	30m on 20m, #5	*1.50*	*1.00*
9	A1	100m on 10m, #3	*3.00*	*2.25*

Surcharge appears in different positions.

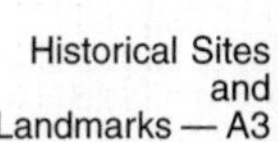

Historical Sites and Landmarks — A3

Designs: 3m, Namik Kemal's bust, Famagusta. 5m, 30m, Kyrenia Harbor. 10m, Ataturk Statue, Nicosia. 15m, St. Hilarion Castle. 20m, Ataturk Square, Nicosia. 25m, Coastline, Famagusta. 50m, Lala Mustafa Pasha Mosque, Famagusta vert. 100m, Kyrenia Castle. 250m, Kyrenia Castle, exterior walls. 500m, Othello Tower, Famagusta vert.

1975-76 *Perf. 13*

No.	Type	Description	Unused	Used
10	A3	3m pink & multi	.40	.30
11	A3	5m bl & multi	.40	.30
12	A3	10m pink & multi	.45	.40
13	A3	15m pink & multi	.50	.40
14	A3	15m bl & multi	.50	.40
15	A3	20m pink & multi	3.00	.40
16	A3	20m bl & multi	.50	.40
17	A3	25m pink & multi	.70	.50
18	A3	30m pink & multi	1.00	.75
19	A3	50m pink & multi	1.50	1.00
20	A3	100m pink & multi	1.75	1.25
21	A3	250m pink & multi	2.50	1.75
22	A3	500m pink & multi	3.50	3.00
		Nos. 10-22 (13)	16.70	10.85

Issued: #10, 12-13, 15, 17-22, 4/21; #11, 14, 16, 8/2/76. #1, 14, 16 have different inscriptions and "1976."

For surcharges see Nos. 28-29.

Peace in Cyprus — A4

Map, Olive Branch, Severed Chain — A4a

Map, Globe, Olive Branch — A4b

1975, July 20 *Perf. 13½x13, 13x13½*

No.	Type	Description	Unused	Used
23	A4	30m multicolored	.40	.25
24	A4a	50m multicolored	.50	.35
25	A4b	150m multicolored	1.10	1.00
		Nos. 23-25 (3)	2.00	1.60

Freedom of Cyprus.

Europa A5

Paintings: 90m, Pomegranates by I.V. Guney. 100m, Harvest Time by F. Direkoglu.

1975, Dec. 29 *Perf. 13*

No.	Type	Description	Unused	Used
26	A5	90m multicolored	*2.00*	*1.00*
27	A5	100m multicolored	*3.00*	*1.50*

Nos. 19, 20 Surcharged

1976, Apr. 28 *Perf. 13*

No.	Type	Description	Unused	Used
28	A3	10m on 50m, #19	.75	.50
29	A3	30m on 100m, #20	1.25	1.25

Europa — A6

1976, May 3

No.	Type	Description	Unused	Used
30	A6	60m Expectation	*1.00*	*.30*
31	A6	120m Man in Meditation	*1.25*	*.65*

Fruits — A7

1976, June 28

No.	Type	Description	Unused	Used
32	A7	10m Ceratonia siliqua	.35	.25
33	A7	25m Citrus nobilis	.40	.25
34	A7	40m Fragaria vesca	.50	.25
35	A7	60m Citrus sinensis	.60	.30
36	A7	80m Citrus limon	.90	.45
		Nos. 32-36 (5)	2.75	1.50

For surcharges see Nos. 66-69.

Olympic Games, Montreal — A8

Design: 100m, Olympic rings, doves, horiz.

1976, July 17

No.	Type	Description	Unused	Used
37	A8	60m multicolored	.75	.25
38	A8	100m multicolored	1.00	.35

Liberation Monument — A9

1976, Nov. 1 *Perf. 13x13½*

No.	Type	Description	Unused	Used
39	A9	30m multi	.35	.25
40	A9	150m multi, diff.	.75	.45

Europa A10

1977, May 2 *Perf. 13*

No.	Type	Description	Unused	Used
41	A10	80m Salamis Bay	*2.00*	*.75*
42	A10	100m Kyrenia Port	*3.00*	*1.25*

Handicrafts A11

1977, June 27

No.	Type	Description	Unused	Used
43	A11	15m Pottery	.45	.25
44	A11	30m Gourds, vert.	.65	.25
45	A11	125m Baskets	1.25	.30
		Nos. 43-45 (3)	2.35	.80

Landmarks — A12

Designs: 20m, Arap Ahmet Pasha Mosque, Nicosia, vert. 40m, Paphos Castle. 70m, Bekir Pasha aqueduct, Larnaca. 80m, Sultan Mahmut library, Nicosia.

1977, Dec. 2 *Perf. 13x13½, 13½x13*

No.	Type	Description	Unused	Used
46	A12	20m multicolored	.25	.25
47	A12	40m multicolored	.30	.25
48	A12	70m multicolored	.40	.25
49	A12	80m multicolored	.60	.40
		Nos. 46-49 (4)	1.55	1.15

Namik Kemal (1840-1888), Writer — A13

1977, Dec. 21 *Perf. 13*

No.	Type	Description	Unused	Used
50	A13	30m Bust, home	.45	.25
51	A13	140m Portrait, vert.	1.00	.50

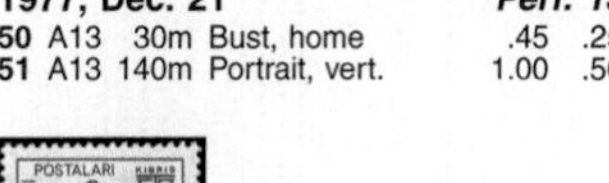

Social Security — A14

Designs: 275k, Man with sling, crutch. 375k, Woman with children.

1978, Apr. 17 *Perf. 13x13½*

No.	Type	Description	Unused	Used
52	A14	150k blk, bl & yel	.30	.25
53	A14	275k blk, grn & red org	.40	.25
54	A14	375k blk, red org & bl	.70	.25
		Nos. 52-54 (3)	1.40	.75

Europa — A15

225k, Oratory in Buyuk Han, Nicosia. 450k, Reservoir, Selimiye Mosque, Nicosia.

1978, May 2 *Perf. 13x13½, 13½x13*

No.	Type	Description	Unused	Used
55	A15	225k multi	*3.25*	*1.00*
56	A15	450k multi, horiz.	*6.50*	*1.50*

Transportation A16

1978, July 10 *Perf. 13½x13*

No.	Type	Description	Unused	Used
57	A16	75k Roadway	.50	.25
58	A16	100k Hydrofoil	.60	.25
59	A16	650k Airplane	.90	.70
		Nos. 57-59 (3)	2.00	1.20

National Oath — A17

1978, Sept. 13

No.	Type	Description	Unused	Used
60	A17	150k Dove, olive branch	.35	.25
61	A17	225k Stylized pen, vert.	.50	.25
62	A17	725k Stylized dove	.90	.65
		Nos. 60-62 (3)	1.75	1.15

Kemal Ataturk — A18

1978, Nov. 10

No.	Type	Description	Unused	Used
63	A18	75k bl grn & lt grn	.50	.25
64	A18	450k brn & buff	.50	.25
65	A18	650k Prus bl & lt bl	.50	.30
		Nos. 63-65 (3)	1.50	.80

Nos. 33-36 Surcharged

1979, June 4

No.	Type	Description	Unused	Used
66	A7	50k on 25m	.40	.25
67	A7	1 l on 40m	.50	.25
68	A7	3 l on 60m	.75	.25
69	A7	5 l on 80m	.90	.25
		Nos. 66-69 (4)	2.55	1.00

Souvenir Sheet

Turkish Invasion of Cyprus, 5th Anniv. A19

1979, July 2 *Imperf.*

No.	Type	Description	Unused	Used
70	A19	15 l multicolored	4.00	3.25

Europa — A20

Communications: 3 l, Stamps, building, map. 8 l, Early and modern telephones, globe, satellite.

1979, Aug. 20 Litho. *Perf. 13*

71 A20 2 l multicolored *1.50* *.40*
72 A20 3 l multicolored *2.00* *.65*
73 A20 8 l multicolored *4.25* *1.00*
Nos. 71-73 (3) 7.75 2.05

Intl. Consultative Radio Committee, 50th Anniv. — A21

1979, Sept. 24

74 A21 2 l blue & multi .25 .25
75 A21 5 l gray & multi .25 .25
76 A21 6 l green & multi .35 .30
Nos. 74-76 (3) .85 .80

Intl. Year of the Child — A22

Childrens' drawings of children.

1979, Oct. 29

77 A22 1½ l multi, vert. .35 .25
78 A22 4½ l multicolored .45 .30
79 A22 6 l multi, vert. .60 .40
Nos. 77-79 (3) 1.40 .95

Press reports in Jan. 1980 state that the 1979 UPU Congress declared Turkish Cyprus stamps invalid for international mail.

A23

Anniv. and events: 2½ l, Lala Mustafa Pasha Mosque, Famagusta. 10 l, Arap Ahmet Pasha Mosque, Lefkosa. 20 l, Holy Kaaba, Mosque.

1980, Mar. 23

80 A23 2½ l multicolored .25 .25
81 A23 10 l multicolored .45 .25
82 A23 20 l multicolored .70 .70
Nos. 80-82 (3) 1.40 1.20

1st Islamic Conference in Turkish Cyprus (2½ l). General Assembly of World Islam Congress (10 l). Moslem year 1400 AH (20 l).

Europa — A24

1980, May 23

83 A24 5 l Ebu-Suud Efendi *.75* *.40*
84 A24 30 l Sultan Selim II *2.50* *.80*

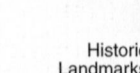

Historic Landmarks A25

Designs: 2½ l, Omer's Shrine, Kyrenia. 3½ l, Entrance gate, Famagusta. 5 l, Funerary monuments, Famagusta. 10 l, Bella Paise Abbey, Kyrenia. 20 l, Selimiye Mosque, Nicosia.

1980, June 25 Blue Paper

85 A25 2½ l buff & Prus bl .30 .25
86 A25 3½ l pale pink & dk grn .30 .25
87 A25 5 l pale bl grn & dk car .30 .25
88 A25 10 l lt grn & red lil .30 .25
89 A25 20 l buff & dk bl .50 .35
Nos. 85-89 (5) 1.70 1.35

For overprints and surcharges see Nos. 198-200.

Cyprus Postage Stamps, Cent. — A26

7½ l, No. 5, vert. 15 l, No. 199. 50 l, Social welfare, vert.

1980, Aug. 16

90 A26 7½ l multicolored .25 .25
91 A26 15 l multicolored .35 .25
92 A26 50 l multicolored .90 .80
Nos. 90-92 (3) 1.50 1.30

Palestinian Solidarity — A27

15 l, Dome of the Rock, entrance, vert.

1980, Mar. 24

93 A27 15 l multicolored .50 .25
94 A27 35 l multicolored 1.25 .60

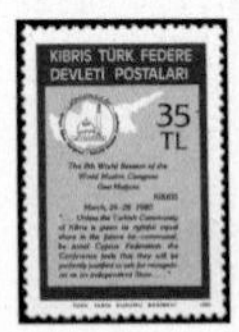

World Muslim Congress Statement — A28

1981, Mar. 24

95 A28 1 l In Turkish .35 .25
96 A28 35 l In English .90 .65

Ataturk by Feyhaman Duran A29

1981, May 19

97 A29 20 l multicolored 1.50 .75

Printed with se-tenant label promoting Ataturk Stamp Exhibition.

Europa — A30

Folk dances.

1981, June 29

98 A30 10 l multicolored *.90* *.40*
99 A30 30 l multi, diff. *2.25* *1.00*

Souvenir Sheet

Ataturk, Birth Cent. A31

1981, July 23 *Imperf.*

100 A31 150 l multicolored 3.00 1.75

No. 100 has simulated perfs.

Flowers — A32

Designs: 1 l, Convolvulus althaeoides, vert. 5 l, Cyclamen persicum. 10 l, Mandragora officinarum. 25 l, Papaver rhoeas, vert. 30 l, Arum dioscoridis, vert. 50 l, Chrysanthemum segetum. 100 l, Cistus salyiaefolius, vert. 150 l, Ferula communis.

1981-82 *Perf. 13*

101 A32 1 l multicolored .25 .25
102 A32 5 l multicolored .25 .25
103 A32 10 l multicolored .25 .25
104 A32 25 l multicolored .40 .40
105 A32 30 l multicolored .45 .45
106 A32 50 l multicolored .75 .75
107 A32 100 l multicolored 1.50 1.50
108 A32 150 l multicolored 2.25 2.25
Nos. 101-108 (8) 6.10 6.10

Issue dates: 1 l, 10 l, 25 l, 150 l, Sept. 28; 5 l, 30 l, 50 l, 100 l, Jan. 22, 1982.

For surcharge & overprints see #138-141, 201.

Intl. Year for Disabled Persons A33

Fight Against Apartheid A34

World Food Day — A35

1981, Oct. 16

109 A33 7½ l multicolored .25 .25
110 A34 10 l multicolored .35 .30
111 A35 20 l multicolored .65 .50
Nos. 109-111 (3) 1.25 1.05

Palestinian Solidarity — A36

1981, Nov. 29

112 A36 10 l multicolored .35 .25

Royal Wedding of Prince Charles and Lady Diana Spencer — A37

1981, Nov. 30

113 A37 50 l multicolored 1.00 .70

Charter of Cyprus, 1865 — A38

Turkish Forces Landing in Tuzla — A39

1982, July 30

114 Sheet of 4 *5.00* *5.00*
a. A38 30 l multicolored *1.00* *1.00*
b. A39 70 l multicolored *1.00* *1.00*

Europa. #114 contains 2 each #114a, 114b.

Buffavento Castle A40

Windsurfing A41

Kantara Castle — A42

Tourism: 30 l, Shipwreck museum.

Perf. 12½x12, 12x12½

1982, Aug. 20

116 A40 5 l multicolored .25 .25
117 A41 10 l multicolored .30 .25
118 A42 15 l multicolored .35 .30
119 A42 30 l multicolored .60 .40
Nos. 116-119 (4) 1.50 1.20

Art Treasures A43

Designs: 30 l, The Wedding by Aylin Orek. 50 l, Carob Pickers by Ozden Nazim, vert.

1982, Dec. 3 *Perf. 13x13½, 13½x13*

120 A43 30 l multicolored 1.00 .30
121 A43 50 l multicolored 1.25 .50

Robert Koch, TB Bacillus — A44

World Cup Soccer Championships, Spain — A45

Scouting, 75th Anniv. — A46

1982, Dec. 15 *Perf. 12½*

122 A44 10 l multicolored .25 .25
123 A45 30 l multicolored .75 .60
124 A46 70 l multicolored 2.00 1.50
Nos. 122-124 (3) 3.00 2.35

Paintings — A47

30 l, Calloused Hands by Salih Oral. 35 l, Malya-Limassol Bus by Emin Cizenel.

1983, May 16 *Perf. 13½x13*

125 A47 30 l multicolored .90 .75
126 A47 35 l multicolored 1.25 1.00

Miniature Sheet

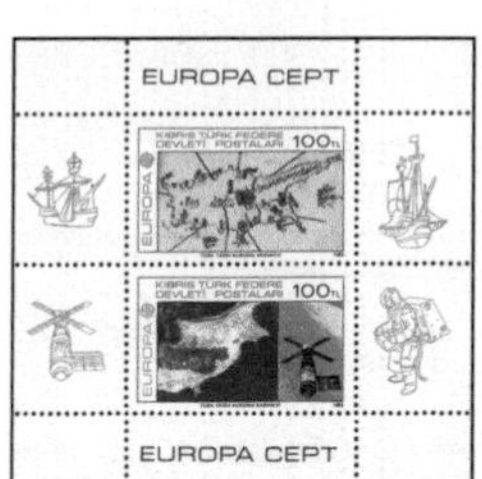

Europa A48

a, Map by Piri Reis. b, Cyprus seen from Skylab.

1983, June 30 *Perf. 13*

127	A48	Sheet of 2	*60.00*	*30.00*
a.-b.		100 l any single	*15.00*	*15.00*

25th Anniv. of Turkish Resistance A49

Designs: 15 l, No. 3. 20 l, Exploitation, Suppression & Resurrection by Aziz Hasan. 25 l, Resistance by Guner Pir.

1983, Aug. 1 *Perf. 13*

129	A49	15 l multi, vert.	.30	.30
130	A49	20 l multi	.45	.45
131	A49	25 l multi, vert.	.50	.50
		Nos. 129-131 (3)	1.25	1.25

World Communications Year — A50

1983, Aug. 1

132	A50	30 l shown	.90	.60
133	A50	50 l Letters	1.50	1.00

Birds — A51

10 l, Merops apiaster. 15 l, Carduelis carduelis. 50 l, Erithacus rubecula. 65 l, Oriolus oriolus.

1983, Oct. 10

134	A51	10 l multicolored	.40	.25
135	A51	15 l multicolored	.55	.25
136	A51	50 l multicolored	1.25	.70
137	A51	65 l multicolored	1.50	1.00
a.		Block of 4, #134-137	4.25	4.25
		Nos. 134-137 (4)	3.70	2.20

Nos. 103, 108 Ovptd.

Nos. 101, 104 Ovptd. or Srchd.

1983, Dec. 7

138	A32	10 l multicolored	.25	.25
139	A32	15 l on 1 l multi	.25	.25
140	A32	25 l multicolored	.35	.35
141	A32	150 l multicolored	2.00	2.00
		Nos. 138-141 (4)	2.85	2.85

Europa, 25th Anniv. — A52

1984, May 30 *Perf. 12x12½*

142	A52	50 l blk, yel & brn	*1.00*	*.50*
143	A52	100 l blk, bl & ultra	*2.00*	*1.00*
a.		Pair, #142-143	*3.25*	*2.75*

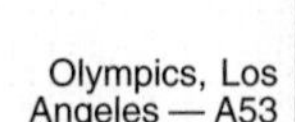

Olympics, Los Angeles — A53

Perf. 12½x12, 12x12½

1984, June 19

144	A53	10 l Olympic flame, vert.	.30	.25
145	A53	20 l Olympic rings	.40	.25
146	A53	70 l Judo	.80	.60
		Nos. 144-146 (3)	1.50	1.10

Ataturk Cultural Center — A54

Perf. 12x12½

1984, July 20 **Wmk. 390**

147	A54	120 l blk, yel & brn	1.00	.90

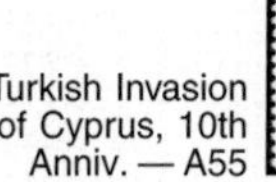

Turkish Invasion of Cyprus, 10th Anniv. — A55

70 l, Map, flag, olive branch.

1984, July 20

148	A55	20 l shown	.40	.40
149	A55	70 l multicolored	.70	.70

Forest Conservation A56

1984, Aug. 20

150	A56	90 l multicolored	1.25	.75

Paintings A57

20 l, Old Turkish Houses in Nicosia by Cevdet Cagdas. 70 l, Scenery by Olga Rauf.

1984, Sept. 21 *Perf. 13*

151	A57	20 l multicolored	.40	.40
152	A57	70 l multicolored	1.10	1.10

Proclamation of Turkish Republic of Northern Cyprus A58

Unanimous Vote by Legislative Assembly A59

Perf. 12½x12, 12x12½

1984, Nov. 15

153	A58	20 l multicolored	.75	.30
154	A59	70 l multicolored	1.40	.70

Independence, 1st Anniv.

European Taekwondo Championship, Kyrenia — A60

1984, Dec. 10

155	A60	10 l Competitors	.30	.25
156	A60	70 l Flags	.60	.55

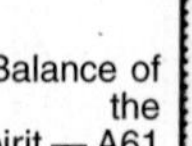

Balance of the Spirit — A61

Paintings by Saulo Mercader: 20 l, The Look, vert.

1984, Dec. 10 ***Perf. 12½x13, 13x12½***

157	A61	20 l multicolored	.25	.25
158	A61	70 l multicolored	.50	.50

Visit by Nuremburg Chamber Orchestra — A62

1984, Dec. 10 *Perf. 12½*

159	A62	70 l multicolored	1.00	.50

Dr. Fazil Kucuk (1906-1984), Politician — A63

70 l, Kucuk reading newspaper, c. 1970.

1985, Jan.

160	A63	20 l multicolored	.50	.25
161	A63	70 l multicolored	.70	.50

Domestic Animals — A64

1985, May 29 *Perf. 12x12½*

162	A64	100 l Capra	.55	.55
163	A64	200 l Bos taurus	1.10	1.10
164	A64	300 l Ovis aries	1.60	1.60
165	A64	500 l Equus asinus	2.75	2.75
		Nos. 162-165 (4)	6.00	6.00

Europa — A65

Composers: No. 166, George Frideric Handel (1685-1759). No. 167, Domenico Scarlatti (1685-1757). No. 168, Johann Sebastian Bach (1685-1750). No. 169, Buhurizade Mustafa Itri (1640-1712).

1985, June 26 *Perf. 12½x12*

166	A65	20 l grn & multi	*.30*	*.25*
167	A65	20 l brn lake & multi	*.30*	*.25*
168	A65	100 l bl & multi	*1.25*	*.80*
169	A65	100 l brn & multi	*1.25*	*.80*
a.		Block of 4, #166-169	*3.75*	*3.75*

Printed in sheets of 16, containing 4 No. 169a.

Paintings — A66

Paintings: 20 l, Pastoral Life by Ali Atakan. 50 l, Woman Carrying Water by Ismet V. Guney.

1985, Aug. *Perf. 12½x13*

170	A66	20 l multicolored	.35	.35
171	A66	50 l multicolored	.55	.55

Intl. Youth Year — A67

Wmk. 390

1985, Oct. 29 **Litho.** *Perf. 12½*

172	A67	20 l shown	.40	.25
173	A67	100 l Globe, dove	.90	.60

Northern Cyprus Air League — A68

Development of Rabies Vaccine, Cent. — A69

Ismet Inonu (1884-1973), Turkish Pres. — A70

UN, 40th Anniv. — A71

Blood Donor Services — A72

1985, Nov. 29

174	A68	20 l multicolored	.25	.25
175	A69	50 l Pasteur	.30	.30
176	A70	100 l brown	.60	.60
177	A71	100 l multicolored	.60	.60
178	A72	100 l multicolored	.60	.60
		Nos. 174-178 (5)	2.35	2.35

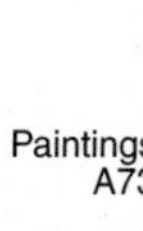

Paintings A73

20 l, House with Arches by Gonen Atakol. 100 l, Ataturk Square by Yalkin Muhtaroglu.

1986, June 20 *Perf. 13*

179	A73	20 l multicolored	.40	.25
180	A73	100 l multicolored	.75	.40

Miniature Sheet

Europa A74

1986, June 20 *Perf. 12x12½*

181	A74	Sheet of 2	*16.00*	*16.00*
a.		100 l Gyps fulvus	*4.00*	*2.00*
b.		200 l Roadside litter	*8.00*	*4.00*

Karagoz Puppets — A75

1986, July 25 *Perf. 12½x13*

182	A75	100 l multicolored	.90	.40

Anatolian Artifacts — A76

Designs: 10 l, Ring-shaped composite pottery, Kernos, Old Bronze Age (2300-1050 B.C.). 20 l, Bird-shaped lidded pot, Skuru Hill tomb, Morphou, late Bronze Age (1600-1500 B.C.), vert. 50 l, Earthenware jug, Vryse, Kyrenia, Neolithic Age (4000 B.C.). 100 l, Terra sigillata statue of Artemis, Sea of Salamis, Roman Period (200 B.C.), vert.

1986, Sept. 15 *Perf. 12½*

183	A76	10 l multicolored	.25	.25
184	A76	20 l multicolored	.25	.25
185	A76	50 l multicolored	.25	.25
186	A76	100 l multicolored	.50	.50
		Nos. 183-186 (4)	1.25	1.25

For surcharge see No. 295A.

Defense Forces, 10th Anniv. A77

World Food Day A78

World Cup Soccer Championships, Mexico — A79

Halley's Comet — A80

1986, Oct. 13

187	A77	20 l multicolored	.25	.25
188	A78	50 l multicolored	.30	.30
189	A79	100 l multicolored	.35	.35
190	A80	100 l multicolored	.40	.40
		Nos. 187-190 (4)	1.30	1.30

Development Projects — A81

1986, Nov. 17

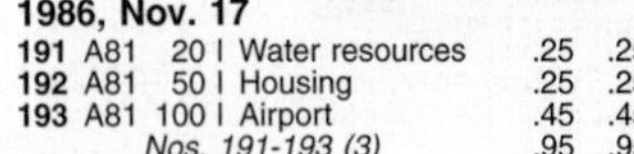

191	A81	20 l Water resources	.25	.25
192	A81	50 l Housing	.25	.25
193	A81	100 l Airport	.45	.45
		Nos. 191-193 (3)	.95	.95

Royal Wedding of Prince Andrew and Sarah Ferguson — A82

Anniv. and events: No. 195, Queen Elizabeth II, 60th birthday.

Perf. 12½x13

1986, Nov. 20 **Wmk. 390**

194	A82	100 l multicolored	.50	.35
195	A82	100 l multicolored	.50	.35
a.		Pair, #194-195	1.00	.70

Trakhoni Station, 1904 — A83

100 l, Locomotive #1, 1904.

1986, Dec. 31

196	A83	50 l shown	.40	.25
197	A83	100 l	1.00	.60

Rail transport, 1904-1951.

Nos. 86, 88-89, 105 Overprinted or Surcharged

a

b

1987, May 18 **Unwmk.** *Perf. 13*

198	A25(a)	10 l on #89	.40	.25
199	A25(a)	15 l on 3½ l, #86	.40	.25
200	A25(a)	20 l on #88	.50	.25
201	A32(b)	30 l on #105	.80	.35
		Nos. 198-201 (4)	2.10	1.10

Paintings — A84

Designs: 50 l, Shepherd by Feridun Isiman. 125 l, Pear Woman by Mehmet Uluhan.

Perf. 12½x13

1987, May 27 **Wmk. 390**

202	A84	50 l multicolored	.45	.25
203	A84	125 l multicolored	1.10	.40

Europa — A85

Modern architecture: 50 l, Bauhaus-style house, designed by A. Vural Behaeddin, 1973. 200 l, House, designed by Necdet Turgay, 1979.

1987, June 30 *Perf. 12½*

204	A85	50 l multicolored	*3.00*	.40
205	A85	200 l multicolored	*6.00*	*1.75*
a.		Bklt. pane, 2 each #204-205	*20.00*	

No. 205a contains two copies each of Nos. 204-205, printed alternately, with unprinted selvage at each end of the pane, perf between stamps and selvage and imperf on outside edges. Thus, singles from the pane gauge 12½ by imperf.

Folk Dancers — A86

1987, Aug. 20

206	A86	20 l multicolored	.25	.25
207	A86	50 l multi, diff.	.25	.25
208	A86	200 l multi, diff.	.50	.50
209	A86	1000 l multi, diff.	2.50	2.50
		Nos. 206-209 (4)	3.50	3.50

For surcharge see No. 295B.

Infantry Regiment, 1st Anniv. A87

5th Islamic Summit Conf., Kuwait A88

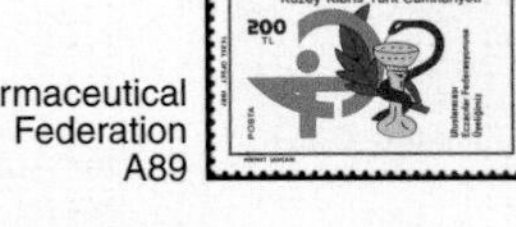

Pharmaceutical Federation A89

1987, Sept. 30

210	A87	50 l multicolored	.25	.25
211	A88	200 l multicolored	.50	.50
212	A89	200 l multicolored	.50	.50
		Nos. 210-212 (3)	1.25	1.25

Ahmet Belig Pasha (1851-1924), Egyptian Judge A90

Mehmet Emin Pasha (1813-1871), Turkish Grand Vizier A91

Famous men: 125 l, Mehmet Kamil Pasha (1832-1913), grand vizier.

1987, Oct. 22

213	A90	50 l brn & yel	.25	.25
214	A91	50 l multicolored	.25	.25
215	A91	125 l multicolored	.35	.30
		Nos. 213-215 (3)	.85	.80

A92

Design: Pres. Rauf Denktash, Turkish Prime Minister Turgut Ozal.

1987, Nov. 2

216	A92	50 l multi	.45	.25

New Kyrenia Harbor — A93

200 l, Eastern Mediterranean University.

Wmk. 390

1987, Nov. 20 **Litho.** *Perf. 12½*

217	A93	150 l shown	.40	.40
218	A93	200 l multicolored	.55	.55

Chair Weaver, by Osman Guvenir A94

Paintings: 20 l, Woman Making Pastry, by Ayhan Mentes, vert. 150 l, Woman Weaving a Rug, by Zekai Yesiladali, vert.

Wmk. 390

1988, May 2 **Litho.** *Perf. 13*

219	A94	20 l multi	.25	.25
220	A94	50 l multi	.45	.25
221	A94	150 l multi	.85	.35
		Nos. 219-221 (3)	1.55	.85

Europa — A95

200 l, Tugboat Piyale Pasha. 500 l, Satellite dish, broadcast tower, vert.

1988, May 31 *Perf. 12½*

222	A95	200 l multicolored	*2.75*	*1.00*
223	A95	500 l multicolored	*4.00*	*1.25*

Bayrak Radio and Television Corporation, 25th anniv. (500 l).

Tourism — A96

Photographs: 150 l, Nicosia, by Aysel Erduran. 200 l, Famagusta, by Sonia Halliday and Laura Lushington. 300 l, Kyrenia, by Halliday and Lushington.

1988, June 17

224	A96	150 l multi	.25	.25
225	A96	200 l multi	.35	.35
226	A96	300 l multi	.50	.50
		Nos. 224-226 (3)	1.10	1.10

Turkish Prime Ministers — A97

No. 227, Bulent Ecevit, 1970's. No. 228, Bulent Ulusu, Sept. 21, 1980-Dec. 13, 1983. No. 229, Turgut Ozal, from Dec. 13, 1983.

1988, July 20

227	A97	50 l shown	.25	.25
228	A97	50 l multi	.25	.25
229	A97	50 l multi	.25	.25
		Nos. 227-229 (3)	.75	.75

Civil Defense — A98

1988, Aug. 8 *Perf. 12x12½*

230	A98	150 l multicolored	.35	.35

Summer Olympics, Seoul — A99

1988, Sept. 17 *Perf. 12½*

231	A99	200 l shown	.30	.30
232	A99	250 l Women's running	.40	.40
233	A99	400 l Seoul	.65	.65
		Nos. 231-233 (3)	1.35	1.35

Sedat Simavi (1896-1953), Turkish Journalist A100

Intl. Conferences, Kyrenia A101

North Cyprus Intl. Industrial Fair A102

Intl. Red. Cross and Red Crescent Organizations, 125th Anniv. A103

US-USSR Summit Meeting on Nuclear Arms Reduction A104

WHO, 40th Anniv. A105

No. 238, Gorbachev and Reagan.

1988, Oct. 17 *Perf. 12½x12, 12x12½*

234 A100 50 l olive grn .25 .25
235 A101 100 l multi .25 .25
236 A102 300 l multi .55 .55
237 A103 400 l multi .85 .85
238 A104 400 l multi .85 .85
239 A105 600 l multi 1.10 1.10
Nos. 234-239 (6) 3.85 3.85

Miniature Sheet

Portraits and Photographs of Kemal Ataturk — A106

b, Holding canteen. c, In uniform. d, Facing left.

1988, Nov. 10 *Perf. 12½*

240 A106 Sheet of 4 3.00 3.00
a.-d. 250 l any single .50 .40

Souvenir Sheet

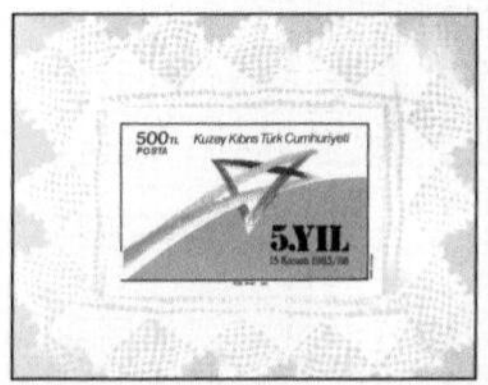

Turkish Republic of Northern Cyprus, 5th Anniv. A107

1988, Nov. 15 *Imperf.*

241 A107 500 l multicolored 3.25 1.75

A108

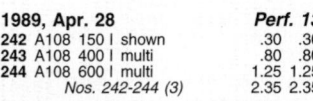

Designs: 400 l, Gamblers' Inn, 17th cent., Asmaalti Meydani. 600 l, Camii Cedit Mosque, 1902, Paphos, vert.

1989, Apr. 28 *Perf. 13*

242 A108 150 l shown .30 .30
243 A108 400 l multi .80 .80
244 A108 600 l multi 1.25 1.25
Nos. 242-244 (3) 2.35 2.35

Dervis Pasha Mansion, 19th Cent., Nicosia.

Europa — A109

1989, May 31 *Perf. 12½x12*

245 A109 600 l Girl, doll *3.00* *1.00*
246 A109 1000 l Flying kite *4.00* *1.25*
a. Bklt. pane, 2 each #245-246, perf. 12½ *16.00*

Geneva Peace Summit, Aug. 24, 1988 — A110

1989, June 30 *Perf. 12½*

247 A110 500 l blk & dark red 1.00 1.00

Wildlife — A111

100 l, Alectoris chukar. 200 l, Lepus cyprius. 700 l, Francolinus francolinus. 2000 l, Vulpes vulpes.

1989, July 31

248 A111 100 l multicolored .25 .25
249 A111 200 l multicolored .40 .40
250 A111 700 l multicolored 1.40 1.40
251 A111 2000 l multicolored 4.00 4.00
Nos. 248-251 (4) 6.05 6.05

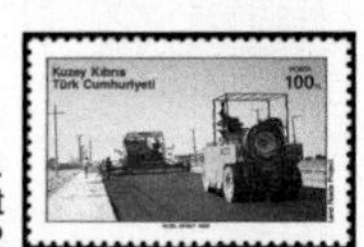

Natl. Development Projects — A112

100 l, Road construction. 150 l, Sanitary water supply. 200 l, Afforestation. 450 l, Telecommunications. 650 l, Power station. 700 l, Irrigation ponds.

Perf. 12½x12, 12x12½

1989, Sept. 29

252 A112 100 l multicolored .30 .25
253 A112 150 l multicolored .40 .30
254 A112 200 l multicolored .45 .40
255 A112 450 l multicolored 1.00 .90
256 A112 650 l multicolored 1.40 1.25
257 A112 700 l multicolored 1.50 1.40
Nos. 252-257 (6) 5.05 4.50

Nos. 253-256 vert.

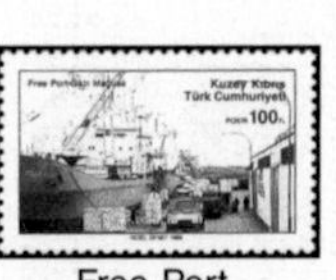

Free Port, Famagusta, 15th Anniv. — A113

Turkish Cypriot Post, 25th Anniv. — A114

Saded Newspaper, Cent. — A115

Intl. Marine Organization, 30th Anniv. — A116

Erenkoy Uprising, 25th Anniv. — A117

Perf. 12x12½, 12½x13 (450 l)

1989, Nov. 17

258 A113 100 l multicolored .25 .25
259 A114 450 l multicolored .90 .90
260 A115 500 l multicolored 1.00 1.00
261 A116 600 l multicolored 1.25 1.25
262 A117 1000 l multicolored 2.00 2.00
Nos. 258-262 (5) 5.40 5.40

Erdal Inonu — A118

1989, Dec. 15 *Perf. 12½x12*

263 A118 700 l multicolored 1.60 1.40

Visit of Inonu, Turkish politician, to northern Cyprus.

Agriculture — A119

150 l, Mule drawn. 450 l, Ox drawn. 550 l, Millstone, olive press.

1989, Dec. 25 *Perf. 12x12½, 12½x12*

264 A119 150 l multicolored .30 .30
265 A119 450 l multicolored .90 .90
266 A119 550 l multicolored 1.10 1.10
Nos. 264-266 (3) 2.30 2.30

Nos. 264-265 horiz.

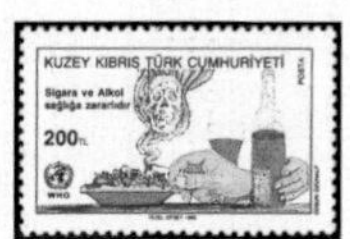

World Health Day — A120

Perf. 12x12½

1990, Apr. 19 **Litho.** **Wmk. 390**

267 A120 200 l shown .40 .25
268 A120 700 l Cigarette, heart 1.50 .40

Europa — A121

Post offices: 1000 l, Yenierenkoy. 1500 l, Ataturk Meydani.

Perf. 12x12½

1990, May 31 **Litho.** **Wmk. 390**

269 A121 1000 l multicolored *3.00* *1.50*
270 A121 1500 l multicolored *4.50* *2.00*
a. Souv. sheet, 2 #269, 2 #270 *18.00* *16.00*

A122

300 l, Turkish Cypriot team. 1000 l, Ball, emblem, globe.

1990, June 8

271 A122 300 l multicolored .65 .65
272 A122 1000 l multicolored 2.00 2.00

World Cup Soccer Championships, Italy.

A123

World Environment Day: Birds: 150 l, Turdus philomelos. 300 l, Sylvia atricapilla. 900 l, Phoenicurus ochruros. 1000 l, Phyllosopus collybita.

1990, June 5 *Perf. 12*

273 A123 150 l multicolored *4.00* .75
274 A123 300 l multicolored *5.75* 1.25
275 A123 900 l multicolored *12.00* 2.75
276 A123 1000 l multicolored *15.00* 5.00
Nos. 273-276 (4) 36.75 9.75

World Wildlife Fund. For surcharge see No. 386.

A125

Designs: 300 l, Painting by Filiz Ankac. 1000 l, Sculpture by Sinasi Tekman, vert.

1990, July 31 *Perf. 13x12½, 12½x13*

279 A125 300 l multicolored .65 .65
280 A125 1000 l multicolored 2.00 2.00

European Tourism Year — A126

150 l, Amphitheater, Soli. 1000 l, Mosaic, Soli.

Wmk. 390

1990, Aug. 24 **Litho.** *Perf. 12½*

281 A126 150 l multicolored .35 .35
282 A126 1000 l multicolored 2.00 2.00

Visit by Turkish President Kenan Evren — A127

1990, Sept. 19

283 A127 500 l multicolored 1.00 1.00

Traffic Safety — A128

150 l, Wear seat belts. 300 l, Obey the speed limit. 1000 l, Obey traffic signals.

1990, Sept. 21

284 A128 150 l multicolored .35 .35
285 A128 300 l multicolored .65 .65
286 A128 1000 l multicolored 2.00 2.00
Nos. 284-286 (3) 3.00 3.00

A129

1990, Oct. 1

287 A129 1000 l multicolored 2.00 2.00

Visit by Turkish Prime Minister Yildirim Akbulut.

Flowers — A130

150 l, Rosularia cypria. 200 l, Silene fraudratrix. 300 l, Scutellaria sibthorpii. 600 l, Sedum lampusae. 1000 l, Onosma caespitosum. 1500 l, Arabis cypria.

Perf. 12½x12

1990, Oct. 31 Litho. Wmk. 390

288	A130	150 l multicolored	.35	.25
289	A130	200 l multicolored	.40	.25
290	A130	300 l multicolored	.65	.25
291	A130	600 l multicolored	1.25	.30
292	A130	1000 l multicolored	2.00	.50
293	A130	1500 l multicolored	3.25	.80
		Nos. 288-293 (6)	7.90	2.35

For surcharges see Nos. 295C, 387.

Intl. Literacy Year — A131

300 l, Ataturk as teacher. 750 l, A, b, c, books, map.

1990, Nov. 24 ***Perf. 12x12½***

294	A131	300 l multicolored	.65	.25
295	A131	750 l multicolored	1.60	.40

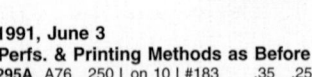

Nos. 183, 206, 288 Surcharged

1991, June 3

Perfs. & Printing Methods as Before

295A	A76	250 l on 10 l #183	.35	.25
295B	A86	250 l on 20 l #206	.35	.25
295C	A130	500 l on 150 l #288	.45	.25
		Nos. 295A-295C (3)	1.15	.75

Shape of obliterator varies.

Orchids — A132

Wmk. 390

1991, July 8 Litho. ***Perf. 14***

296	A132	250 l Ophrys lapethica	.55	.55
297	A132	500 l Ophrys kotschyi	1.60	1.60

See Nos. 303-306.

A133

Europa: a, Hermes space shuttle. b, Ulysses probe.

Perf. 12½x12

1991, July 29 Litho. Wmk. 390

Miniature Sheet

298	A133	2000 l Sheet of 2, #a.-b.	*10.00*	*8.00*

Public Fountains A134

250 l, Kuchuk Medrese. 500 l, Djafer Pasha. 1500 l, Sarayonu Square. 5000 l, Arabahmet Mosque.

Wmk. 390

1991, Sept. 9 Litho. ***Perf. 12***

299	A134	250 l multicolored	.25	.25
300	A134	500 l multicolored	.35	.35
301	A134	1500 l multicolored	1.10	1.10
302	A134	5000 l multicolored	3.50	3.50
		Nos. 299-302 (4)	5.20	5.20

Orchid Type of 1991

100 l, Serapias levantina. 500 l, Dactylorhiza romana. 2000 l, Orchis simia. 3000 l, Orchis sancta.

1991, Oct. 10 ***Perf. 14***

303	A132	100 l multicolored	.25	.25
304	A132	500 l multicolored	.40	.40
305	A132	2000 l multicolored	1.40	1.40
306	A132	3000 l multicolored	2.00	2.00
		Nos. 303-306 (4)	4.05	4.05

Hindiler by Salih M. Cizel — A135

Painting: 500 l, Dusme by Asik Mene.

Wmk. 390

1991, Nov. 5 Litho. ***Perf. 13***

307	A135	250 l multicolored	.25	.25
308	A135	500 l multicolored	.25	.25

See type A143. For surcharge see No. 381.

World Food Day A136

Basbakan Mustafa Cagatay (1937-1989) A137

Eastern Mediterranean University A138

Wolfgang Amadeus Mozart, Death Bicent. A139

1991, Nov. 20 ***Perf. 12***

309	A136	250 l multicolored	.25	.25
310	A137	500 l multicolored	.30	.30
311	A138	500 l multicolored	.30	.30
312	A139	1500 l multicolored	.85	.85
		Nos. 309-312 (4)	1.70	1.70

For surcharge see No. 380.

World AIDS Day — A140

1991, Dec. 13 ***Perf. 12***

313	A140	1000 l multicolored	.55	.55

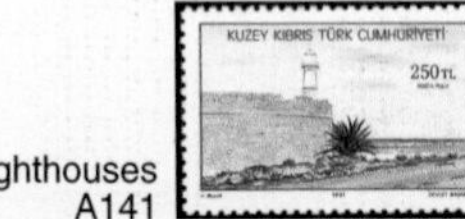

Lighthouses A141

250 l, Canbulat Burcu, Famagusta. 500 l, Yat Limani, Kyrenia. 1500 l, Turizm Limani, Kyrenia.

1991, Dec. 16 ***Perf. 12x12½***

314	A141	250 l multicolored	.25	.25
315	A141	500 l multicolored	.30	.30
316	A141	1500 l multicolored	.85	.85
		Nos. 314-316 (3)	1.40	1.40

Tourism — A142

Designs: 250 l, Elephant and hippopotamus fossils, Kyrenia. 500 l, Roman fish ponds, Lambusa (58 BC-398 AD). 1500 l, Roman tomb and church, Lambusa (58 BC-1192 AD).

1991, Dec. 27

317	A142	250 l multicolored	.25	.25
318	A142	500 l multicolored	.30	.30
319	A142	1500 l multicolored	.85	.85
		Nos. 317-319 (3)	1.40	1.40

Paintings — A143

Designs: 500 l, Ebru, by Arife Kandulu. 3500 l, Nicosia, by Ismet Tartar.

Wmk. 390

1992, Mar. 31 Litho. ***Perf. 14***

320	A143	500 l multicolored	.25	.25
321	A143	3500 l multicolored	1.75	1.75

See type A135.

Tourism — A144

No. 322, Ancient building, Famagusta. No. 323, Trap shooting range, Nicosia. 1000 l, Salamis Bay resort, Famagusta. 1500 l, Casino, Kyrenia.

1992, Apr. 21 ***Perf. 13½x14, 14x13½***

322	A144	500 l multicolored	.25	.25
323	A144	500 l multicolored	.25	.25
324	A144	1000 l multicolored	.50	.50
325	A144	1500 l multi, vert.	.75	.75
		Nos. 322-325 (4)	1.75	1.75

Souvenir Sheet

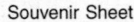

Discovery of America, 500th Anniv. — A145

Europa: a, 1500 l, Santa Maria, Nina and Pinta. b, 3500 l, Columbus.

1992, May 29 ***Perf. 13½x14***

326	A145	Sheet of 2, #a.-b.	*10.00*	*10.00*

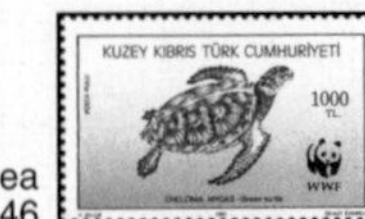

Sea Turtles — A146

Perf. 13½x14

1992, June 30 Litho. Wmk. 390

327	A146	1000 l Green turtle	*3.00*	*3.00*
328	A146	1500 l Loggerhead turtle	*3.50*	*3.50*
a.		Souv. sheet, 2 ea #327-328	*14.00*	*14.00*

World Wildlife Fund.

1992 Summer Olympics, Barcelona A147

#329: a, Women's gymnastics, vert. b, Tennis, vert. 1000 l, High jump. 1500 l, Cycling.

1992, July 25 ***Perf. 14x13½***

329	A147	500 l Pair, #a-b.	.75	.75

Perf. 13½x14

330	A147	1000 l multicolored	.50	.50
331	A147	1500 l multicolored	.75	.75
		Nos. 329-331 (3)	2.00	2.00

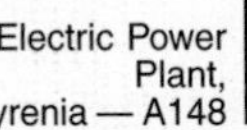

Electric Power Plant, Kyrenia — A148

Social Insurance, 15th Anniv. — A149

Intl. Federation of Women Artists — A150

Veterinary Services — A151

Perf. 13½x14

1992, Sept. 30 Litho. Wmk. 390

332	A148	500 l multicolored	.25	.25
333	A149	500 l multicolored	.25	.25
334	A150	1500 l multicolored	.75	.75
335	A151	1500 l multicolored	.75	.75
		Nos. 332-335 (4)	2.00	2.00

Civil Aviation Office, 17th Anniv. — A152

Meteorology Office, 18th Anniv. — A153

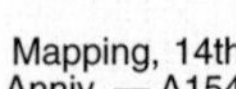

Mapping, 14th Anniv. — A154

Perf. 13½x14

1992, Nov. 20 Litho. Wmk. 390

336	A152	1000 l multicolored	.50	.50
337	A153	1000 l multicolored	.50	.50
338	A154	1200 l multicolored	.60	.60
		Nos. 336-338 (3)	1.60	1.60

Native Cuisine — A155

Food: 2000 l, Zulbiye (pastry). 2500 l, Cicek Dolmasi (stuffed squash flowers). 3000 l, Tatar Boregi (flaky pastry dish). 4000 l, Seftali kebab (meat dish).

1992, Dec. 14

339 A155 2000 l multicolored 1.00 1.00
340 A155 2500 l multicolored 1.25 1.25
341 A155 3000 l multicolored 1.50 1.50
342 A155 4000 l multicolored 2.00 2.00
Nos. 339-342 (4) 5.75 5.75

Intl. Conference on Nutrition, Rome. See Nos. 388-390.

Tourism — A156

Designs: 500 l, Church and Monastery of St. Barnabas. 10,000 l, Bowl.

Perf. 13½x14

1993, Apr. 1 Litho. Wmk. 390

343 A156 500 l multi .25 .25
344 A156 10,000 l multi 5.00 5.00

Souvenir Sheet

Europa A157

Contemporary paintings by: a, 2000 l, Turksal Ince. b, 3000 l, Ilkay Onsoy.

Perf. 14x13½

1993, May 5 Litho. Wmk. 390

345 A157 Sheet of 2, #a.-b. *3.00 3.00*

Trees — A158

500 l, Olea europea. 1000 l, Eucalyptus camaldulensis. 3000 l, Platanus orientalis. 4000 l, Pinus brutia tenore.

1993, June 11 ***Perf. 14x13½***

346 A158 500 l multicolored .25 .25
347 A158 1000 l multicolored .50 .50
348 A158 3000 l multicolored 1.50 1.50
349 A158 4000 l multicolored 2.00 2.00
Nos. 346-349 (4) 4.25 4.25

Arabahmet Rehabilitation Project — A159

Perf. 13½x14

1993, Sept. 20 Litho. Wmk. 390

350 A159 1000 l shown .25 .25
351 A159 3000 l Homes, diff. .50 .50

Creation of Turkish Republic of Northern Cyprus, 10th Anniv. — A160

Designs: No. 353, Flags changing to dove, vert. 1000 l, Dove flying from flag. 5000 l, Flowers forming "10," map.

Perf. 13½x14, 14x13½

1993, Nov. 15 Litho. Wmk. 390

352 A160 500 l multicolored .25 .25
353 A160 500 l multicolored .25 .25
354 A160 1000 l multicolored .25 .25
355 A160 5000 l multicolored .80 .80
Nos. 352-355 (4) 1.55 1.55

Ataturk, 55th Death Anniv. A161

State Theaters, 30th Anniv. A162

Turkish Resistance Organization, 35th Anniv. — A163

Turkish News Agency, 20th Anniv. — A164

Tchaikovsky, Death Cent. — A165

Perf. 14x13½, 13½x14

1993, Dec. 27 Litho. Wmk. 390

356 A161 500 l multicolored .25 .25
357 A162 500 l multicolored .25 .25
358 A163 1500 l multicolored .30 .30
359 A164 2000 l multicolored .40 .40
360 A165 5000 l multicolored 1.10 1.10
Nos. 356-360 (5) 2.30 2.30

Soyle Falci, by Goral Ozkan — A166

Design: 6500 l, Sculpture, IV Hareket, by Senol Özdevrim.

1994, Mar. 31 ***Perf. 14***

361 A166 1000 l multicolored .25 .25
362 A166 6500 l multicolored 1.40 1.40

Fazil Kucuk (1906-84), Physician and Political Leader A167

1994, Apr. 1

363 A167 1500 l multicolored .45 .30

Souvenir Sheet

Archaeological Discoveries — A168

Europa: a, Neolithic village, Ayios Epectitos Vrysi. b, Neolithic man, early tools found in excavation.

1994, May 16 ***Perf. 13½***

364 A168 8500 l Sheet of 2, #a.-b. *4.00 4.00*

1994 World Cup Soccer Championships, US — A169

1994, June 30

365 A169 2500 l Trophy, vert. .25 .25
366 A169 10,000 l US map .80 .80

Turkish Postal Service in Northern Cyprus, 30th Anniv. — A170

1994, June 30

367 A170 50,000 l multicolored 4.00 4.00

A171

A172

Turkish Peace Operation, 20th Anniv. — A173

1994, July 20 ***Perf. 14***

368 A171 2500 l shown .25 .25
369 A172 5000 l Monument .40 .40
370 A172 7000 l Monument, diff. .50 .50
371 A173 8500 l shown .65 .65
Nos. 368-371 (4) 1.80 1.80

First Rural Postal Cancellations, Cent. — A174

Postmarks, stamps: 1500 l, Karpas, Cyprus #131. 2500 l, Gazi Magusa (Famagusta), #71. 5000 l, Bey Keuy, Cyprus #150. 7000 l, Aloa, Cyprus, #179. 8500 l, Pyla, Cyprus #152.

1994, Aug. 15 ***Perf. 13½***

372 A174 1500 l multicolored .25 .25
373 A174 2500 l multicolored .25 .25
374 A174 5000 l multicolored .35 .35
375 A174 7000 l multicolored .55 .55
376 A174 8500 l multicolored .70 .70
Nos. 372-376 (5) 2.10 2.10

Sea Shells — A175

No. 377, Charonia tritonis. No. 378, Tonna galea. No. 379, Cypraea talpa.

1994, Nov. 15 ***Perf. 14***

377 A175 2500 l multi .25 .25
378 A175 12,500 l multi .70 .35
379 A175 12,500 l multi .70 .35
Nos. 377-379 (3) 1.65 .95

Nos. 307, 309 Surcharged

1994, Dec. 12 ***Perfs., etc. as Before***

380 A136 1500 l on 250 l multi .25 .25
381 A135 2500 l on 250 l multi .25 .25

Size and location of surcharge varies.

European Nature Conservation Year — A176

Designs: 2000 l, Donkeys on mountain top. 3500 l, Shoreline. 15,000 l, Donkeys in field.

1995, Feb. 10 Wmk. 390 ***Perf. 14***

382 A176 2000 l multicolored .25 .25
383 A176 3500 l multicolored .25 .25
384 A176 15,000 l multicolored 1.00 1.00
Nos. 382-384 (3) 1.50 1.50

Souvenir Sheet

Peace and Freedom A177

Europa: a, Globe, dove. b, Doves over Europe.

1995, Apr. 20 ***Perf. 13½x14***

385 A177 15,000 l Sheet of 2, #a.-b. *3.50 3.50*

Nos. 275 & 290 Surcharged

1995, Apr. 21 ***Perfs., etc. as Before***

386 A123 2000 l on 900 l #275 1.75 1.50
387 A130 3500 l on 300 l #290 3.50 3.50

Size and location of surcharge varies.

Native Cusine Type of 1992

Food: 3500 l, Sini katmeri. 10,000 l, Kolokas musakka, Bullez kizartma. 14,000 l, Enginar dolmasi.

Perf. 13½x14

1995, May 29 Litho. Wmk. 390

388 A155 3500 l multicolored .25 .25
389 A155 10,000 l multicolored .55 .55
390 A155 14,000 l multicolored .80 .80
Nos. 388-390 (3) 1.60 1.60

Butterflies A178

3500 l, Papilio machaon. 4500 l, Charaxes jasius. 15,000 l, Cynthia cardui. 30,000 l, Vanessa atalanta.

1995, June 30

391 A178 3500 l multicolored .25 .25
392 A178 4500 l multicolored .25 .25
393 A178 15,000 l multicolored .70 .70
394 A178 30,000 l multicolored 1.40 1.40
Nos. 391-394 (4) 2.60 2.60

Visit by Turkish Pres. Suleyman Demirel — A179

1995, Aug. 21 ***Perf. 13½***

395 A179 5000 l multicolored .25 .25

Tourism — A180

Designs: 3500 l, Beach scene, Kyrenia. 7500 l, Sailboats. 15,000 l, Ruins, Famagusta, vert. 20,000 l, St. George Cathedral, Famagusta, vert.

1995, Aug. 21

396 A180 3500 l multicolored .25 .25
397 A180 7500 l multicolored .40 .40
398 A180 15,000 l multicolored .80 .80
399 A180 20,000 l multicolored 1.00 1.00
Nos. 396-399 (4) 2.45 2.45

State Printing Office, 20th Anniv. — A181

Turkish Natl. Assembly, 75th Anniv. — A182

Louis Pasteur (1822-95) A183

UN, 50th Anniv. — A184

G. Marconi (1874-1937), Radio, Cent. A185

Motion Pictures, Cent. A186

Perf. 13½x14, 14x13½

1995, Nov. 7 Litho. Wmk. 390

400 A181 3000 l multicolored .25 .25
401 A182 3000 l multicolored .25 .25
402 A183 5000 l multicolored .25 .25
403 A184 22,000 l multicolored 1.25 1.25
404 A185 30,000 l multicolored 1.60 1.60
405 A186 30,000 l multicolored 1.60 1.60
Nos. 400-405 (6) 5.20 5.20

A187

Tombstone inscriptions, Orhon and Yenisey river region: 5000 l, Kültigin Heykelinin Basi. 10,000 l, Kültigin Yaziti.

1995, Dec. 28 ***Perf. 14x13½***

406 A187 5000 l multicolored .25 .25
407 A187 10,000 l multicolored .55 .55

Reading of Orhon Epitaphs, cent.

Tribute to Bosnia-Herzegovina A188

1996, Jan. 31

408 A188 10,000 l multicolored .55 .55

Fish — A189

Designs: 6,000 l, Mullus surmuletus. 10,000 l, Thalassoma pavo. 28,000 l, Diplodus vulgaris. 40,000 l, Epinephelus guaza.

1996, Mar. 29 ***Perf. 14***

409 A189 6,000 l multicolored .25 .25
410 A189 10,000 l multicolored .30 .30
411 A189 28,000 l multicolored .80 .80
412 A189 40,000 l multicolored 1.10 1.10
Nos. 409-412 (4) 2.45 2.45

For surcharge see no. 506.

Tourism — A190

Designs: 100,000 l, Palm trees, vert. 150,000 l, Pomegranate fruit, vert. 250,000 l, Bellapais Monastery. 500,000 l, Folk dancing.

Perf. 14x13½, 13½x14

1996, Apr. 26 Litho. Wmk. 390

413 A190 100,000 l multi 3.00 3.00
414 A190 150,000 l multi 5.00 5.00
415 A190 250,000 l multi 7.00 7.00
416 A190 500,000 l multi 15.00 15.00
Nos. 413-416 (4) 30.00 30.00

Famous Women — A191

Europa: 15,000 l, Beria Remzi Ozoran. 50,000 l, Kadriye Hulusi Hacibulgur.

1996, May 31 ***Perf. 13½x14***

417 A191 15,000 l multicolored *.50 .50*
418 A191 50,000 l multicolored *2.00 2.00*

World Environment Day — A192

Designs: a, Older, dying trees in mountainous area. b, Newly-planted trees.

1996, June 28 ***Perf. 13½***

419 A192 50,000 l Sheet of 2, #a.-b. 2.00 2.00

1996 Summer Olympic Games, Atlanta A193

a, 15,000 l, Basketball. b, 50,000 l, Javelin. c, 15,000 l, Discus. d, 50,000 l, Volleyball.

1996, July 31

420 A193 Sheet of 4, #a.-d. 3.00 3.00

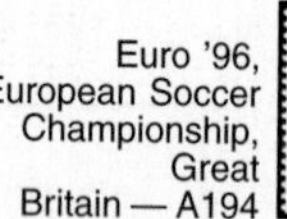

Euro '96, European Soccer Championship, Great Britain — A194

35,000 l, Flags, soccer ball.

1996, Oct. 31 ***Perf. 13½x14***

421 A194 15,000 l shown .40 .40
422 A194 35,000 l multi 1.40 1.40
a. Pair, #421-422 2.00 2.00

Civil Defense A195

Security Forces A196

Nasreddin Hodja — A197

Children's Rights — A198

Perf. 13½x14, 14x13½

1996, Dec. 23 Litho. Wmk. 390

423 A195 10,000 l multicolored .25 .25
424 A196 20,000 l multicolored .50 .50
425 A197 50,000 l multicolored 1.25 1.25
426 A198 75,000 l multicolored 1.90 1.90
Nos. 423-426 (4) 3.90 3.90

Paintings A199

Designs: 25,000 l, Buildings, people, by Lebibe Sonuc. 70,000 l, Woman seated beside plant, by Ruzen Atakan.

1997, Jan. 31 ***Perf. 14***

427 A199 25,000 l multicolored .65 .65
428 A199 70,000 l multicolored 1.75 1.75

Mushrooms — A200

Designs: 15,000 l, Amanita phallioides. No. 430, Morchella esculenta. No. 431, Pleurotus eryngii. 70,0000 l, Amanita muscaria.

1997, Mar. 31

429 A200 15,000 l multicolored .45 .45
430 A200 25,000 l multicolored .65 .65
431 A200 25,000 l multicolored .65 .65
432 A200 70,000 l multicolored 1.75 1.75
Nos. 429-432 (4) 3.50 3.50

Natl. Flag on Mountainside — A201

1997, Apr. 23

433 A201 60,000 l multicolored 1.50 1.50

Stories and Legends — A202

Europa: 25,000 l, Woman with broom, children playing, man with donkey. 70,000 l, Well, apple tree, man behind bushes.

1997, May 30 ***Perf. 13½x14***

434 A202 25,000 l multicolored .75 .75
435 A202 70,000 l multicolored 1.75 1.75

Visit by Turkish Leaders — A203

Designs: 15,000 l, Prime Minister Necmeddin Erbakan, vert. 80,000 l, Pres. Süleyman Demirel.

Perf. 14x13½, 13½x14

1997, June 20

436 A203 15,000 l multicolored .30 .30
437 A203 80,000 l multicolored 1.50 1.50

A204

Raptors: No. 438, Aquila chrysaetos. No. 439, Falco eleanorae. 75,000 l, Falco tinnunculus. 100,000 l, Pernis apivorus.

1997, July 31 ***Perf. 14x13½***

438 A204 40,000 l multicolored .55 .55
439 A204 40,000 l multicolored .55 .55
440 A204 75,000 l multicolored 1.00 1.00
441 A204 100,000 l multicolored 1.40 1.40
Nos. 438-441 (4) 3.50 3.50

A205

Old Coins Used in Cyprus: 25,000 l, 1861 Abdül Aziz gold lira. 40,000 l, 1808 Mahmud II gold rumi. 75,000 l, 1566 Selim II gold lira. 100,000 l, 1909 Mehmed V gold besibirlik.

1997, Oct. 28

442 A205 25,000 l multicolored .35 .35
443 A205 40,000 l multicolored .55 .55
444 A205 75,000 l multicolored 1.00 1.00
445 A205 100,000 l multicolored 1.40 1.40
Nos. 442-445 (4) 3.30 3.30

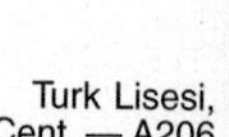

Turk Lisesi, Cent. — A206

Scouting, 90th Anniv. A207

Fight Against AIDS A208

Diesel Engine, Cent. — A209

Perf. 13½x14, 14x13½

1997, Dec. 22 Litho. Wmk. 390

446 A206 25,000 l multicolored .30 .30
447 A207 40,000 l multicolored .50 .50
448 A208 100,000 l multicolored 1.25 1.25
449 A209 150,000 l multicolored 1.75 1.75
Nos. 446-449 (4) 3.80 3.80

Ismet Sevki (1884-1957) and Ahmet Sevki (1874-1959), Photographers A210

105, 000 l, Ahmet Sevki, vert.

1998, Jan. 28 *Perf. 13½x14*
450 A210 40,000 l brn, *cream* .50 .50
451 A210 105,000 l brn, *cream* 1.25 1.25

Insects — A211

Designs: 40,000 l, Agrion splendens. 65,000 l, Ascalaphus macaronius. 125,000 l, Podalonia hirsuta. 150,000 l, Rhyssa persuasoria.

1998, Mar. 30
452 A211 40,000 l multicolored .40 .40
453 A211 65,000 l multicolored .65 .65
454 A211 125,000 l multicolored 1.25 1.25
455 A211 150,000 l multicolored 1.50 1.50
Nos. 452-455 (4) 3.80 3.80

For surcharge, see No. 766.

Doors — A212

1998, Apr. 30 *Perf. 14x13½*
456 A212 115,000 l shown 1.10 1.10
457 A212 140,000 l Door, steps 1.40 1.40

Natl. Festival — A213

Europa: 150,000 l, Globe, map of Cyprus, flags, vert.

1998, May 30 *Perf. 13½x14, 14x13½*
458 A213 40,000 l multicolored .65 .65
459 A213 150,000 l multicolored 2.10 2.10

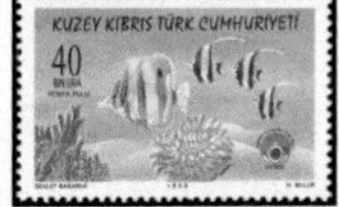

Intl. Year of the Ocean — A214

Various marine life.

1998, June 30 *Perf. 13½x14*
460 A214 40,000 l multicolored .30 .30
461 A214 90,000 l multicolored .65 .65

For surcharge, see No. 767.

Visit by Turkish Prime Minister Mesut Yilmaz — A215

1998, July 20
462 A215 75,000 l multicolored .55 .55

Turkish Pres. Süleyman Demirel — A216

Design: 175,000 l, Pres. Demirel, Pres. Rauf R. Denktash, view of ocean, horiz.

1998, July 25 *Perf. 13½x14, 14x13½*
463 A216 75,000 l multicolored .55 .55
464 A216 175,000 l multicolored 1.25 1.25

Establishment of Yaylacik water program.

1998 World Cup Soccer Championships, France — A217

75,000 l, Team coming across field, fans in stadium. 175,000 l, Holding up World Cup trophy.

1998, July 31 *Perf. 13½x14, 13x13½*
465 A217 75,000 l multi, horiz. .55 .55
466 A217 175,000 l multi 1.25 1.25

Visit of Turkish Deputy Prime Minister Bülent Ecevit — A218

1998, Sept. 5 *Perf. 14*
467 A218 200,000 l multicolored 1.50 1.50

Traditional Crafts — A219

No. 468, Kalayci, horiz. No. 469, Sepetci. No. 470, Bileyici. No. 471, Oymaci, horiz.

1998, Oct. 26 *Perf. 13½x14, 14x13½*
468 A219 50,000 l multi .40 .40
469 A219 75,000 l multi .60 .60
470 A219 130,000 l multi 1.00 1.00
471 A219 400,000 l multi 3.00 3.00
Nos. 468-471 (4) 5.00 5.00

Bayrak Radio & Television, 35th Anniv. — A220

Turkish Cyprus, 15th Anniv. — A221

Turkish Republic, 75th Anniv. A222

Universal Declaration of Human Rights, 50th Anniv. A223

No. 476a, 75,000 l, Natl. flag, map of Turkish Cyprus.

1998, Nov. 15
472 A220 50,000 l multicolored .40 .40
473 A221 75,000 l multicolored .55 .55
474 A222 75,000 l multicolored .55 .55
475 A223 175,000 l multicolored 1.25 .65
Nos. 472-475 (4) 2.75 2.15

Souvenir Sheet

476 Sheet of 2, #473, #476a 1.10 1.10

A224

1999, Jan. 15 *Perf. 14*
477 A224 75,000 l multicolored .55 .55

Dr. Fazil Kücük (1906-84), politician.

A225

Scene from "Othello," by Verdi: a, Singers standing. b, Singer on floor.

1999, Jan. 30
478 A225 200,000 l Sheet of 2, #a.-b. 2.00 2.00

Snakes — A226

Designs: 50,000 l, Malpolon monspessulanus insignitus. 75,000 l, Hierophis jugularis. 195,000 l, Vipera lebetina. 220,000 l, Natrix natrix.

1999, Mar. 26 *Perf. 13½x14*
479 A226 50,000 l multicolored .40 .40
480 A226 75,000 l multicolored .60 .60
481 A226 195,000 l multicolored 1.60 1.60
482 A226 220,000 l multicolored 1.75 1.75
Nos. 479-482 (4) 4.35 4.35

Europa — A227

No. 483, Sütunlu Cave. No. 484, Incirli Cave, vert.

1999, May 17 *Perf. 14*
483 A227 75,000 l multi 1.00 1.00
484 A227 200,000 l multi 2.25 2.25

Turkish Peace Operation, 25th Anniv. — A228

No. 486, Dove, map, sun.

Wmk. 390

1999, July 20 **Litho.** *Perf. 13¾*
485 A228 150,000 l multi 1.25 1.25
486 A228 250,000 l multi 2.00 2.00

Turkish Postal Administration in Cyprus, 35th Anniv. — A229

1999, Nov. 12 **Litho.** *Perf. 13¾*
487 A229 75,000 l multicolored .50 .50

UPU, 125th Anniv. — A230

1999, Nov. 12
488 A230 225,000 l multicolored .80 .80

Total Solar Eclipse, Aug. 11 — A231

1999, Nov. 12
489 A231 250,000 l multicolored .90 .90

Destruction of Turkish Heritage in Southern Cyprus — A232

Photos of: 75,000 l, Building, Limassol. 150,000 l, Mosque, Evdim. 210,000 l, Bayraktar Mosque, Nicosia (Lefkosa). 1,000,000 l, Cami-i Kebir Mosque, Paphos (Baf), vert.

1999, Dec. 3
490 A232 75,000 l multi .25 .25
491 A232 150,000 l multi .55 .55
492 A232 210,000 l multi .75 .75
493 A232 1,000,000 l multi 3.75 3.75
Nos. 490-493 (4) 5.30 5.30

Millennium A233

Designs: 75,000 l, Cellular phone. 150,000 l, "Welcome 2000." 275,000 l, Computer. 300,000 l, Satellite.

2000, Mar. 3 **Litho.** *Perf. 13¾*
494 A233 75,000 l multi .25 .25
495 A233 150,000 l multi .50 .50
496 A233 275,000 l multi .95 .95
497 A233 300,000 l multi 1.00 1.00
Nos. 494-497 (4) 2.70 2.70

Beach Scenes — A234

Designs: 300,000 l, Umbrella, pail, shovel, beach ball, sailboats. 340,000 l, Beach chair.

2000, Apr. 29 **Litho.** *Perf. 13¾*
498 A234 300,000 l multi 1.00 1.00
499 A234 340,000 l multi 1.10 1.10

Europa Issue

Common Design Type and

A235

2000, May 31 **Wmk. 390** *Perf. 14*
500 Sheet of 2 2.50 2.50
a. CD17 300,000 l multi 1.10 .95
b. A235 300,000 l multi 1.10 .95

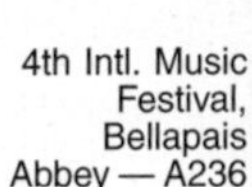

4th Intl. Music Festival, Bellapais Abbey — A236

Designs: 150,000 l, Bellapais Abbey. 350,000 l, Blended colors, vert.

2000, June 21 *Perf. 13¾*
501 A236 150,000 l multi .45 .45
502 A236 350,000 l multi 1.10 1.10

Visit of Turkish Pres. Ahmet N. Sezer — A237

2000, June 22
503 A237 150,000 l multi .45 .45

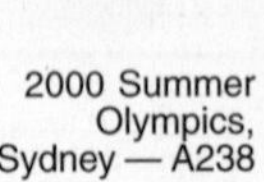

2000 Summer Olympics, Sydney — A238

125,000 l, Torch and Olympic rings, vert. 200,000 l, Runner.

2000, July 25
504-505 A238 Set of 2 .90 .90

No. 409 Surcharged

Method & Perf. as Before

2000, Sept. 28 Wmk. 390
506 A189 50,000 l on 6000 l .25 .25

Flora and Fauna — A239

Designs: 125,000 l, Praying mantis on flower. 200,000 l, Butterfly on flower. 275,000 l, Bee on flower. 600,000 l, Snail on flower stem.

Wmk. 390

2000, Oct. 16 Litho. *Perf. 13¾*
507-510 A239 Set of 4 3.75 3.75

Kerchief Borders — A240

Background colors: 125,000 l, Yellow. 200,000 l, Lilac. 265,000 l, Green. 350,000 l, Brown.

2000, Nov. 28
511-514 A240 Set of 4 3.00 3.00

Restored Buildings, Nicosia (Lefkosa) — A241

Designs: 125,000 l, Lusignan House. 200,000 l, Eaved House.

Wmk. 390

2001, Mar. 28 Litho. *Perf. 13¾*
515-516 A241 Set of 2 .75 .75

Art — A242

Works by: 125,000 l, Inci Kansu. 200,000 l, Emel Samioglu. 350,000 l, Ozden Selenge, vert. 400,000 l, Ayhatun Atesin.

2001, Mar. 30
517-520 A242 Set of 4 2.50 2.50

Europa — A243

Designs: 200,000 l, Degirmenlik Reservoir. 500,000 l, Waterfall, Sinar.

2001, May 31
521-522 A243 Set of 2 1.60 1.60

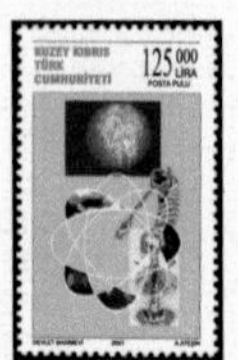

World Environment Day — A244

Designs: 125,000 l, Atomic model, x-ray images. 450,000 l, X-ray images, radiation symbol.

2001, June 22
523-524 A244 Set of 2 1.10 1.10

Police Uniforms — A245

Uniforms from: 125,000 l, 1885. 200,000 l, 1933. 500,000 l, 1934. 750,000 l, 1983.

2001, Aug. 24
525-528 A245 Set of 4 2.75 2.75

Automobiles A246

Designs: 175,000 l, 1954 MG TF. 300,000 l, 1948 Vauxhall 14. 475,000 l, 1922 Bentley. 600,000 l, 1955 Jaguar XK 120.

Wmk. 390

2001, Nov. 2 Litho. *Perf. 13¾*
529-532 A246 Set of 4 1.90 1.90

Publication of The Genocide Files, by Harry Scott Gibbons — A247

2001, Dec. 24
533 A247 200,000 l multi .30 .30

July 20th Technical School, Cent. — A248

2001, Dec. 24
534 A248 200,000 l multi .30 .30

Cartoon Art — A249

Designs: 250,000 l, Chef with grinder and book, by Utku Karsu, vert. 300,000 l, People singing "We Are the World," malnourished Africans, by Musa Kayra. 475,000 l, Can of diet cola airdropped for a malnourished African, by Serhan Gazi, vert. 850,000 l, Child viewing city and painting a country scene, by Mustafa Tozaki, vert.

Wmk. 390

2002, Feb. 28 Litho. *Perf. 13¾*
535-538 A249 Set of 4 2.60 2.60

Tourism — A250

Underwater photographs: 250,000 l, Turtle swimming. 300,000 l, Starfish on coral. 500,000 l, Fish. 750,000 l, Shipwreck.

2002, Mar. 27
539-542 A250 Set of 4 2.50 2.50

Souvenir Sheet

Europa A251

No. 543: a, Man on stilts. b, Tightrope walker.

Wmk. 390

2002, May 27 Litho. *Perf. 13¾*
543 A251 600,000 l Sheet of 2, #a-b 1.50 1.50

A252

Designs: 300,000 l, Soccer team. 1,000,000 l, "Lift Embargo on Sports."

2002, June 24
544-545 A252 Set of 2 1.60 1.60

2002 World Cup Soccer Championships, Japan and Korea.

Native Costumes — A253

Designs: 250,000 l, Woman. 300,000 l, Man. 425,000 l, Man, diff. 700,000 l, Woman, diff.

2002, Aug. 8
546-549 A253 Set of 4 2.00 2.00

Children's Art — A254

Art by: 300,000 l, M. A. Alpdogan. 600,000 l, S. Avci, vert.

Wmk. 390

2002, Sept. 30 Litho. *Perf. 13¾*
550-551 A254 Set of 2 .90 .90

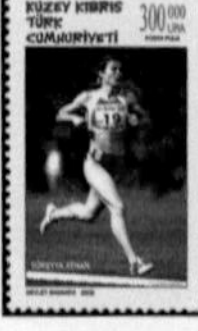

Sports Personalities — A255

Designs: 300,000 l, Sureyya Ayhan, winner of women's 1500m race at 2002 European Track and Field Championships. 1,000,000 l, Park Jung-tae (1944-2002), father of modern taekwondo.

2002, Oct. 28
552-553 A255 Set of 2 1.60 1.60

Famous Men — A256

Designs: 100,000 l, Oguz Karayel (1933-96), soccer player. 175,000 l, Mete Adanir (1961-89), soccer player. 300,000 l, M. Necati Ozkan (1899-1970). 575,000 l, Osman Turkay (1927-2001), poet, horiz.

2002, Dec. 3
554-557 A256 Set of 4 1.40 1.40

Art — A257

Paintings by: 250,000 l, S. Bayraktar. 1,000,000 l, F. Sükan.

Wmk. 390

2003, Feb. 21 Litho. *Perf. 13¾*
558-559 A257 Set of 2 1.50 1.50

Souvenir Sheet

Europa A258

Poster art: a, Tree. b, Question mark.

2003, May 8
560 A258 600,000 l Sheet of 2, #a-b 1.60 1.60

Birds — A259

Designs: 100,000 l, Oenanthe cypriaca. 300,000 l, Sylvia melanothorax. 500,000 l, Phalacrocorax pygmeus, vert. 600,000 l, Phoenicopterus ruber, vert.

2003, June 3
561-564 A259 Set of 4 2.10 2.10

Chests — A260

Chest from: 250,000 l, Seher. 300,000 l, Lapta. 525,000 l, Baf. 1,000,000 l, Karpaz ve Akatu.

Perf. 13¾x14

2003, July 25 Litho. Wmk. 390
565-568 A260 Set of 4 3.00 3.00

Flowers — A261

Designs: 150,000 l, Gladiolus triphyllus. 175,000 l, Tulipa cypria. 500,000 l, Ranunculus asiaticus. 525,000 l, Narcissus tazetta.

2003, Oct. 21 ***Perf. 14x13¾***
569-572 A261 Set of 4 1.75 1.75

National Anniversaries — A262

No. 573 — Kemal Ataturk and flag of: a, Turkey. b, Turkish Republic of Northern Cyprus.

2003, Nov. 14 ***Perf. 13¾x14***
573 A262 3,000,000 l Horiz. pair, #a-b 8.50 8.50

Republic of Turkey, 80th anniv. (#573a), Turkish Republic of Northern Cyprus, 20th anniv. (#573b).

Federation of Agricultural Producers, 60th Anniv. — A263

2003, Dec. 12
574 A263 300,000 l multi .45 .45

Lions International in Turkish Republic of Northern Cyprus, 40th Anniv. — A263a

2003, Dec. 12
575 A263a 500,000 l multi .70 .70

Turkish Postal Service in Northern Cyprus, 40th Anniv. — A264

Emblem and: 250,000 l, Mailbox and Nicosia Post Office. 1,500,000 l, Globe, winged envelopes.

Perf. 13¾x14
2004, Apr. 30 **Litho.** **Wmk. 390**
576-577 A264 Set of 2 2.40 2.40

Souvenir Sheet

Europa A265

No. 578: a, Beach, sailboat. b, Woman holding drink, beach.

2004, May 25
578 A265 600,000 l Sheet of 2, #a-b 1.60 1.60

Exists imperf.

Eurasia Postal Union — A266

2004, June 7
579 A266 300,000 l multi .40 .40

Flowers — A267

Designs: 250,000 l, Salvia veneris. 300,000 l, Phlomis cypria. 500,000 l, Pimpinella cypria. 600,000 l, Rosularia cypria.

2004, July 9 ***Perf. 14x13¾***
580-583 A267 Set of 4 2.40 2.40

Soccer Stadiums — A268

Stadium and: 300,000 l, European Soccer Championships emblem. 1,000,000 l, UEFA (European Football Union) 50th anniv. emblem.

2004, Aug. 20 ***Perf. 13¾x14***
584-585 A268 Set of 2 1.75 1.75

2004 Summer Olympics, Athens A269

No. 586, 300,000 l: a, Sailing, handball. b, Boxing, equestrian.
No. 587, 500,000 l: a, Weight lifting, gymnastics. b, Canoeing, tennis.

2004, Sept. 24 ***Perf. 14x13¾***
Horiz. pairs, #a-b
586-587 A269 Set of 2 2.25 2.25

Eastern Mediterranean University, 25th Anniv. (in 2004) — A270

2005, Feb. 15 **Litho.** ***Perf. 13¾x14***
588 A270 15k multi .25 .25

Cyprus Turkish Philatelic Association, 25th Anniv. (in 2004) — A271

2005, Feb. 15
589 A271 30k multi .50 .50

Website for Universities in Turkish Republic of Northern Cyprus — A272

2005, Feb. 15
590 A272 50k multi .80 .80

A273

Tourism — A274

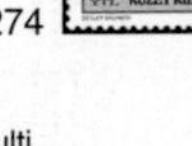

2005, Mar. 9
591 A273 10k multi .25 .25
592 A274 1 l multi 1.60 1.60

Children's Drawings — A275

Drawings of men and women by: 25k, E. Demirci. 50k, E. Oztemiz.

2005, Apr. 22 ***Perf. 14x13¾***
593-594 A275 Set of 2 1.10 1.10

Europa A276

No. 595: a, Woman at left, round table. b, Oven, square table, woman at right.

2005, May 30 ***Perf. 13¾x14***
595 A276 60k Pair, #a-b 1.75 1.75
c. Souvenir sheet, 2 #595 3.50 3.50

Flowers — A277

Designs: 15k, Fianthus cyprius. 25k, Delphinium caseyi. 30k, Brassica hilarionis. 50k, Limonium albidum.

2005, July 8 ***Perf. 14x13¾***
596-599 A277 Set of 4 1.90 1.90

See Nos. 608-613.

Arts in Towns — A278

Designs, 10k, Beach, umbrellas, musical symbols, artist's palette, olive branches, Kyrenia (Girne). 25k, Musical symbols, mosque, Famagusta (Gazimagusa). 50k, Dancers, building, Nicosia (Lefkosa). 1 l, Theater and masks, Kyrenia, Famagusta and Nicosia.

Perf. 13½x13¾
2005, Sept. 9 **Litho.** **Wmk. 390**
600-603 A278 Set of 4 2.75 2.75

Ercan Airport — A279

2005, Nov. 23 ***Perf. 13¾x13½***
604 A279 50k multi .75 .75

University of Northern Cyprus — A280

2005, Nov. 23 ***Perf. 13½x13¾***
605 A280 1 l multi 1.50 1.50

Europa Stamps, 50th Anniv. — A281

Designs: No. 606, 1.40 l, Map of Cyprus. No. 607, 1.40 l, Photo of Cyprus from space, satellite.

2006, Jan. 6
606-607 A281 Set of 2 4.25 4.25
607a Souvenir sheet, #606-607 4.25 4.25

No. 607a exists imperf.

Flowers Type of 2005

Designs: 15k, Helianthemum obtusifolium. 25k, Iris sisyrhinchium, horiz. 40k, Ranunculus asiaticus, horiz. 50k, Crocus veneris, horiz. 60k, Anemone coronaria, horiz. 70k, Cyclamen persicum.

Perf. 14x13¾, 13¾x14
2006 **Litho.** **Wmk. 390**
608-613 A277 Set of 6 3.75 3.75

Art — A282

Design: 55k, Sculpture by S. Oztan. 60k, Painting by M. Hastürk.

Perf. 13¾x13½
2006, Apr. 7 **Litho.** **Wmk. 390**
614-615 A282 Set of 2 1.75 1.75

Dr. Fazil Kucuk (1906-84), Politician — A283

2006, May 18
616 A283 40k multi .50 .50

Kemal Ataturk (1881-1938) — A284

2006, May 18
617 A284 1 l multi 1.25 1.25

Europa — A286

Designs: No. 618, 70k, Birds and stars. No. 619, 70k, Pregnant woman, fetus, flags of European countries.

2006, May 18
618-619 A286 Set of 2 1.75 1.75
619a Souvenir sheet, #618-619 1.75 1.75

No. 619a exists imperf.

2006 World Cup Soccer Championships, Germany — A287

No. 620: a, 50k, World Cup trophy, map of Germany, mascots, soccer ball and field. b, 1 l, Soccer ball, player, Brandenburg Gate.

2006, July 7 ***Perf. 13¾x13½***
620 A287 Pair, #a-b 2.00 2.00

Birds — A288

Designs: 40k, Vanellus vanellus. 50k, Anas platyrhynchos. 60k, Alcedo atthis. 1 l, Himantopus himantopus.

2006, Sept. 22
621-624 A288 Set of 4 3.50 3.50

Forest Fire Prevention — A289

2006, Oct. 10 *Perf. 14x13¾*
625 A289 50k multi .70 .70

Naci Talat (1945-91), Politician — A290

2006, Oct. 10 *Perf. 14*
626 A290 70k multi .95 .95

Eastern Mediterranean Intl. Regatta — A291

2006, Oct. 10 *Perf. 14x13¾*
627 A291 1.50 l multi 2.10 2.10

Environmental Conference — A292

Designs: 50k, Leaf. 80k, Globe, plant and drought-stricken ground.

Wmk. 390
2007, Feb. 19 **Litho.** *Perf. 14*
628-629 A292 Set of 2 1.90 1.90

Antique Household Items — A293

Designs: 70k, Pitcher. 80k, Iron. 1.50 l, Oil lamp, vert. 2 l, Gas burner and pot, vert.

2007, Apr. 6 *Perf. 13¾x14, 14x13¾*
630-633 A293 Set of 4 7.50 7.50

Europa — A294

Emblems, tent, campfire, hand giving Scout sign, dove and: No. 634, 80k, One Scout. No. 635, 80k, Three Scouts playing musical instruments.

2007, May 4 *Perf. 14x13¾*
634-635 A294 Set of 2 2.40 2.40
635a Souvenir sheet, #634-635, imperf. 2.40 2.40

Scouting, cent.

Painting by O. Keten A295

Painting by S. Cavusoglu A296

2007, July 12 *Perf. 14x13¾, 13¾x14*
636 A295 50k multi .80 .80
637 A296 70k multi 1.10 1.10

Occupations of the Past — A297

Designs: 40k, Rattan weaver. 65k, Fruit peddler. 70k, Shoemaker. 1 l, Shoeshiner.

2007, Sept. 14 *Perf. 13¾x14*
638-641 A297 Set of 4 4.75 4.75

Methods of Postal Transport — A298

Designs: 50k, Carrier pigeons. 60k, Mounted postman, coach, automobile. 1 l, Postman on bicycle, horiz. 1.25 l, Postman on motor scooter, horiz.

Perf. 14x13¾, 13¾x14
2007, Nov. 16
642-645 A298 Set of 4 5.75 5.75

Flowers — A299

Designs: 25k, Asphodelus aestivus. 50k, Ophrys fusca. 60k, Bellis perennis. 70k, Ophrys sphegodes. 80k, Dianthus strictus. 1.60 l, Ophrys argolica. 2.20 l, Crocus cyprius. 3 l, Limodorum abortivum. 5 l, Carlina pygmaea. 10 l, Ophrys kotschyi.

Wmk. 390
2008, Mar. 20 **Litho.** *Perf. 14*

646	A299	25k multi	.40	.40
647	A299	50k multi	.80	.80
648	A299	60k multi	.95	.95
649	A299	70k multi	1.10	1.10
650	A299	80k multi	1.25	1.25
651	A299	1.60 l multi	2.50	2.50
652	A299	2.20 l multi	3.50	3.50
653	A299	3 l multi	4.75	4.75
654	A299	5 l multi	7.75	7.75
655	A299	10 l multi	15.50	15.50
		Nos. 646-655 (10)	38.50	38.50

Europa — A300

Designs: No. 656, 80k, Woman writing letter. No. 657, 80k, Quill pen, world map.

2008, May 8 *Perf. 14x13¾*
656-657 A300 Set of 2 2.60 2.60

Souvenir Sheet

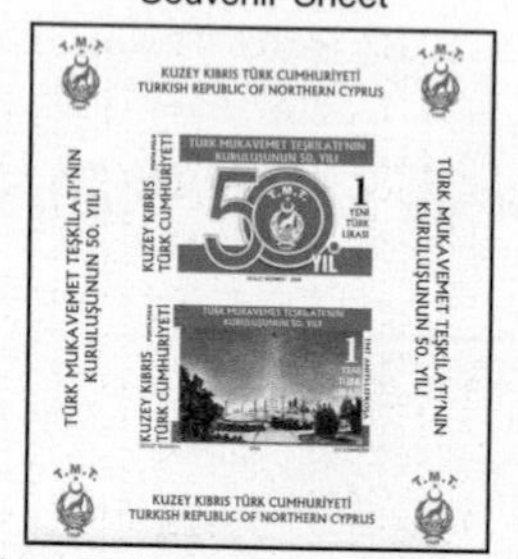

2008 Summer Olympics, Beijing — A301

No. 658: a, Diving. b, Gymnastics.

2008, July 24
658 A301 65k Sheet of 2, #a-b 2.25 2.25

Exists imperf.

Souvenir Sheet

Turkish Resistance Organization, 50th Anniv. — A302

No. 659: a, Emblem and "50." b, Monument, Lefkosa.

2008, Aug. 1 *Imperf.*
659 A302 1 l Sheet of 2, #a-b 3.50 3.50

Nicosia (Lefkosa) Municipal Government, 50th Anniv. A303

Inner Wheel International A304

Cyprus Turkish Airlines Jet A305

Civil Defense Organization A306

Perf. 14x13¾, 13¾x14
2008, Sept. 18

660	A303	55k multi	.85	.85
661	A304	80k multi	1.25	1.25
662	A305	1 l multi	1.60	1.60
663	A306	1.50 l multi	2.40	2.40
		Nos. 660-663 (4)	6.10	6.10

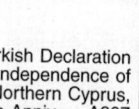

Turkish Declaration of Independence of Northern Cyprus, 25th Anniv. — A307

2008, Nov. 15 *Perf. 14*
664 A307 1 l multi 1.25 1.25

Tradesmen A308

Designs: 60k, Upholsterer. 70k, Miller. 80k, Bicycle mechanic. 2 l, Circumcisor.

2008, Nov. 20 *Perf. 13¾x14*
665-668 A308 Set of 4 5.25 5.25

Archaeology A309

Items from Soli archaeological site: 60k, Gold ring. 2 l, Gold crown.

Perf. 13¾x14
2009, Mar. 23 **Litho.** **Wmk. 390**
669-670 A309 Set of 2 3.25 3.25

Europa A310

No. 671: a, Solar system. b, Galaxy and comet.

2009, May 5
671 A310 80k Pair, #a-b 2.10 2.10

Intl. Year of Astronomy.

Medicinal Plants — A311

Designs: 50k, Cistus creticus. 60k, Capparis spinosa. 70k, Pancratium maritimum. 1 l, Passiflora caerulea.

2009, July 9 *Perf. 14x13¾*
672-675 A311 Set of 4 3.75 3.75

Reptiles and Amphibians A312

Designs: 80k, Agama stellio. 1.50 l, Bufo viridis.

2009, Sept. 14 *Perf. 13¼*
676-677 A312 Set of 2 3.25 3.25

Turkish Cypriot Air Traffic Controllers Association
A313

Turkish Cypriot Chamber of Commerce
A314

Ziya Rizki (1919-94), Politician — A315

2009, Nov. 12 ***Perf. 13¾x14***
678 A313 65k multi .90 .90

Perf. 14x13¾

679 A314 1 l multi 1.40 1.40
680 A315 1.50 l multi 2.00 2.00
Nos. 678-680 (3) 4.30 4.30

Turkish Cypriot Representation at Organization of the Islamic Conference, 34th Anniv. — A316

Emblem and: 70k, Map of Islamic Conference countries, flag, mosque, arch. 1 l, Mosque, flag, arch.

2010, Mar. 17 ***Perf. 14x13¾***
681-682 A316 Set of 2 2.25 2.25

Europa — A317

2010, May 28 ***Perf. 13¾x14***
683 A317 Pair 2.00 2.00

- *a.* 80k Two faces 1.00 1.00
- *b.* 80k Girl reading book 1.00 1.00
- *c.* As "a," perf. 13¾ horiz. 1.00 1.00
- *d.* As "b," perf. 13¾ horiz. 1.00 1.00
- *e.* Vert. pair, #683c-683d 2.00 2.00
- *f.* Booklet pane, 2 #683e 4.00 —
- Complete booklet, #683f 4.00

Worldwide Fund for Nature (WWF) — A318

Designs: No. 684, 25k, Larus melanocephalus. No. 685, 25k, Larus audouinii. No. 686, 30k, Larus ridibundus. No. 687, 30k, Larus genei.

2010, June 4 ***Perf. 14***
684-687 A318 Set of 4 1.40 1.40

2010 World Cup Soccer Championships, South Africa — A319

2010 World Cup Soccer Championships emblem and: 50k, World Cup trophy, crowd. 2 l, Flag of South Africa, elephants, soccer player, mascot.

2010, July 8 ***Perf. 14x13¾***
688-689 A319 Set of 2 3.25 3.25

Foreign Press Association — A320

Journalists: 60k, Kemal Asik (1925-89). 70k, Abdi Ipekçi (1929-79). 80k, Adem Yavuz (1943-74). 1 l, Sedat Simavi (1896-1953).

2010, Sept. 1 ***Perf. 14***
690-693 A320 Set of 4 4.25 4.25

Cruise Ships and Tourist Attractions
A321

Various ships and attractions: 1.50 l, 2 l.

2010, Oct. 20 ***Perf. 13¾x14***
694-695 A321 Set of 2 5.00 5.00

Workers for Turkish Cypriot Society — A322

Designs: 50k, Ozdemir Sennaroglu (1931-85). 60k, Osman Orek (1925-99). 70k, Salih Miroglu (1953-2005). 80k, Ozker Özgür (1940-2005).

2010, Dec. 24 ***Perf. 14x13¾***
696-699 A322 Set of 4 3.50 3.50

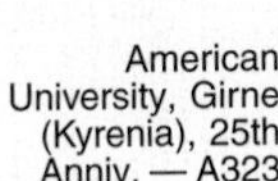

American University, Girne (Kyrenia), 25th Anniv. — A323

2010, Dec. 24 ***Perf. 13¾x14***
700 A323 1 l multi 1.40 1.40

Politicians — A324

Designs: 80k, Dr. Niyazi Manyera (1911-99), Republic of Cyprus Minister of Health. 1.10 l, Mustafa Fazil Plümer (1914-2001), Republic of Cyprus Agriculture Minister. 2 l, Osman Orek (1925-99), Prime Minister of Turkish Republic of Northern Cyprus. 2.20 l, Dr. Fazil Küçük (1906-84), Vice-president of Republic of Cyprus.

2011, Mar. 9 ***Perf. 14x13¾***
701-704 A324 Set of 4 7.75 7.75

Tourism — A325

Designs: 50k, Ayios Philon Church. 80k, Ayios Trias Basilica, vert. 1.10 l, Aphendrika. 2 l, Apostolos Andreas Monastery, vert.

2011, Apr. 18 ***Perf. 13¾x14, 14x13¾***
705-708 A325 Set of 4 5.75 5.75

Europa — A326

Designs: No. 709, 1.50 l, Ladybug, forest on hillside. No. 710, 1.50 l, Pinecone, forest.

Perf. 14x13¾

2011, May 16 **Wmk. 390**
709-710 A326 Set of 2 4.00 4.00
710a Souvenir sheet of 2, #709-710 4.00 4.00

Intl. Year of Forests.

Wedding of Prince William and Catherine Middleton — A327

2011, May 27
711 A327 1 l multi 1.25 1.25

Trees — A328

Designs: 1 l, Quercus infectoria. 2.50 l, Olea europaea.

2011, July 18
712-713 A328 Set of 2 4.00 4.00

Art — A329

Design: 60k, Drawing by Birol Ruhi. 70k, Painting by Kemal Ankaç. 80k, Sculpture by Baki Bogaç. 1 l, Painting by Salih Bayraktar, horiz.

Perf. 14x13¾, 13¾x14

2011, Sept. 14
714-717 A329 Set of 4 3.50 3.50

Flora — A330

Designs: 25k, Ziziphus lotus. 50k, Cynara cardunculus. 60k, Oxalis pes-caprae. 70k, Malva sylvestris. 80k, Rubus sanctus. 1.50 l, Crataegus monogyna.

2011, Nov. 25 ***Perf. 13¾***
718-723 A330 Set of 6 4.75 4.75

Miniature Sheet

Rauf Denktash (1924-2012), First President of Turkish Republic of Northern Cyprus — A331

No. 724 — Denktash: a, 60k, With dove on arm, flag in background. b, 60k, With flag in background. c, 1 l, At microphone. d, 1 l, Wearing striped tie.

2012, Mar. 16 ***Perf. 14***
724 A331 Sheet of 4, #a-d 3.75 3.75

Europa
A332

No. 725 — Birds and various tourist attractions with denomination at: a, Left. b, Right.

Perf. 13¾x14

2012, May 8 **Litho.** **Wmk. 390**
725 A332 80k Horiz. pair, #a-b 1.75 1.75

Reign of Queen Elizabeth II, 60th Anniv.
A333

2012, June 1
726 A333 80k multi .90 .90

2012 European Soccer Championships, Poland and Ukraine — A334

Emblem of Euro 2012, legs of soccer players, soccer balls and: 70k, Clock tower. 1 l, Stadium.

2012, June 29 ***Perf. 14x13¾***
727-728 A334 Set of 2 1.90 1.90

2012 Summer Olympics, London — A335

Sites in London and: 2 l, Track. 2.20 l, Sailing.

2012, July 27 ***Perf. 13¾***
729-730 A335 Set of 2 4.75 4.75

Motorcycles and Buses — A336

Designs: 60k, 1952 Triumph Tiger Twin motorcycle. 70k, 1948 Ariel Army W110 motorcycle. 80k, 1963 Bedford bus. 1 l, 1960 Fagor bus.

2012, Nov. 22 ***Perf. 13¾x14***
731-734 A336 Set of 4 3.50 3.50

Politicians — A337

Designs: 60k, Ahmet Mithat Berberoglu (1921-2002). 70k, Faiz Kaymak (1904-82). 80k, Dr. Mehmet Dervis Manizade (1903-2003). 1 l, Mehmet Zeka (1903-84).

2013, Mar. 12 **Wmk. 390** ***Perf. 14***
735-738 A337 Set of 4 3.50 3.50

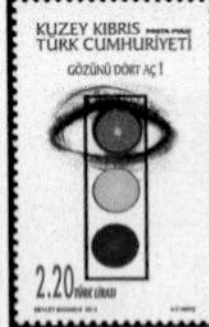

Traffic Safety
A338 A339

2013, Apr. 18 ***Perf. 14x13¾***

739 A338 1 l multi 1.10 1.10
740 A339 2.20 l multi 2.50 2.50

Europa — A340

Postal vehicles: Nos. 741, 743, Bicycle. Nos. 742, 744, Van.

Thick Lettering in Country Name and Bottom Inscriptions

Perf. 13¾x14

2013, May 6 Litho. Wmk. 390

741 A340 80k multi .85 .85
742 A340 80k multi .85 .85

Thin Lettering in Country Name and Bottom Inscriptions

743 A340 80k multi .85 .85
744 A340 80k multi .85 .85
Nos. 741-744 (4) 3.40 3.40

Nos. 741 and 742 were each printed in sheets of 15 stamps + label. Each of the 15 stamps on the sheet of No. 741 and 13 of the 15 stamps on the sheet of No. 742 have a gray background design that reproduces the building shown on the label. Values for Nos. 741 and 742 are for any single stamp from the sheets of 15 + label. Nos. 743 and 744 were each printed in sheets of 40 having no gray background design.

A341

Flora and Fauna
A342

Designs: 25k, Polyommatus icarus, Iris oratoria. 50k, Upupa epops. 60k, Teucrinum divaricatum ssp.canescens.

Perf. 13¾x14

2013, July 8 Litho. Wmk. 390

745 A341 25k multi .25 .25

Perf. 13½

746 A342 50k multi .55 .55
747 A342 60k multi .65 .65
Nos. 745-747 (3) 1.45 1.45

Islamic Art — A343

Designs: 60k, 18th cent.ceremonial leather shield. 70k, 19th cent. prayer rug. 2 l, 16th cent. candlestick.

Wmk. 390

2013, Sept. 10 Litho. *Perf. 14*

748-750 A343 Set of 3 3.25 3.25

Conflict Between Greek and Turkish Cypriots, 50th Anniv.
A344

Turkish Republic of Northern Cyprus, 30th Anniv.
A345

Republic of Turkey, 90th Anniv. — A346

Perf. 14x13¾

2013, Nov. 20 Litho. Wmk. 390

751 A344 60k black & gray .60 .60
752 A345 70k multi .70 .70

Perf. 13¾x14

753 A346 80k red & black .80 .80
Nos. 751-753 (3) 2.10 2.10

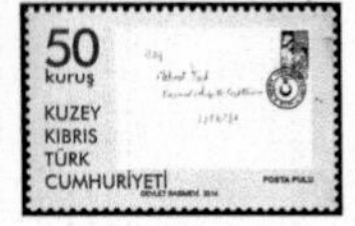

Turkish Cypriot Post, 50th Anniv. — A347

Designs: 50k, Cover bearing Cyprus #227. 60k, Cover bearing Cyprus #230. 1 l, Cover bearing Cyprus #223 and three U.S. #1213.

Perf. 13¾x14

2014, Jan. 6 Litho. Wmk. 390

754-756 A347 Set of 3 1.90 1.90

Turkish Education College, 50th Anniv.
A348

Perf. 14x13¾

2014, Jan. 27 Litho. Wmk. 390

757 A348 2.20 l multi 2.00 2.00

2014 World Cup Soccer Championships, Brazil — A349

2014 World Cup emblem and various soccer players: 70k, 2 l.

Wmk. 390

2014, Feb. 17 Litho. *Perf. 13¾*

758-759 A349 Set of 2 2.50 2.50

Scenes From *The Only Witness Was the Fig Tree,* Play by Abdullah Oztoprak — A350

Various scenes: 25k, 60k, 70k, 1 l.

Perf. 14x13¾

2014, Mar. 10 Litho. Wmk. 390

760-763 A350 Set of 4 2.40 2.40

Europa — A351

Musicians and instruments: 80k, Tef (tambourine). 1.80 l, Davul and zurna (drum and reed pipe).

2014, May 23 Litho. *Perf. 13¾*

764-765 A351 Set of 2 2.50 2.50
765a Souvenir sheet of 2, #764-765 2.50 2.50

Nos. 452 and 461 Surcharged

Methods, Perfs. And Watermarks As Before

2014, July 4

766 A211 30k on 40,000 l #452 .30 .30
767 A214 40k on 90,000 l #461 .40 .40

Erenköy Uprising, 50th Anniv.
A352

Perf. 14x13¾

2014, Aug. 8 Litho. Wmk. 390

768 A352 1 l multi .95 .95

Fruit Blossoms — A353

Designs: 60k, Apple blossom. 70k, Orange blossom. 80k, Pomegranate blossom. 1 l, Peach blossom.

Wmk. 390

2014, Sept. 19 Litho. *Perf. 13¾*

769-772 A353 Set of 4 2.75 2.75

Adjacent stamps in the sheet are rotated 90 degrees.

St. Valentine's Day — A354

Perf. 13¾x14

2015, Feb. 9 Litho. Wmk. 390

773 A354 2.20 l multi 1.75 1.75

Naval Battle of the Dardanelles, Cent.
A355

Perf. 14x13¾

2015, Mar. 18 Litho. Wmk. 390

774 A355 2 l multi 1.60 1.60

Road Safety — A356

Designs: 1 l, Stylized man. 2.20 l, Motorcyclist and caution sign.

Wmk. 390

2015, May 14 Litho. *Perf. 13¼*

775-776 A356 Set of 2 2.40 2.40

Europa — A357

Designs: 70k, Toy cars. 80k, Dolls.

Perf. 14x13¾

2015, June 25 Litho. Wmk. 390

777-778 A357 Set of 2 1.10 1.10
778a Souvenir sheet of 2, #777-778, imperf. 1.10 1.10

Cats and Dogs — A358

Designs: No. 779, 60k, Cat. No. 780, 60k, Dog. No. 781, 70k, Cat, diff. No. 782, 79k, Dog, diff.

Perf. 14x13¾

2015, Aug. 5 Litho. Wmk. 390

779-782 A358 Set of 4 1.75 1.75

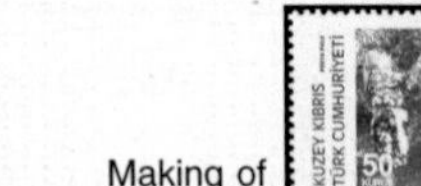

Archaeological Artifacts in World Museums — A359

Designs: 60k, Sculpture from Istanbul museum. 70k, Coin from New York museum. 80k, Sculpture from Stockholm museum, horiz. 1 l, Bust from Stockholm museum.

Perf. 14x13¾, 13¾x14

2015, Oct. 12 Litho. Wmk. 390

783-786 A359 Set of 4 2.25 2.25

Making of Marzipan — A360

Designs: 50k, Harvesting of almonds. 70k, Shelling of almonds. 1 l, Drying of almond paste. 2 l, Cooking equipment and marzipan.

Perf. 13¾x14

2015, Nov. 23 Litho. Wmk. 390

787-790 A360 Set of 4 3.00 3.00

2016 European Soccer Championships, France — A361

Emblem, soccer player, stadium and: 40k, French flag, Eiffel Tower. 6 l, Louvre Museum.

Wmk. 390

2016, Feb. 25 Litho. *Perf. 13¾*

791-792 A361 Set of 2 4.50 4.50

2016 Summer Olympics, Rio de Janeiro — A362

Olympic rings, Rio landmarks and: 1.30 l, Long jumper. 2.20 l, Gymnast on rings. 3.05 l, Swimmer.

Perf. 13¾x14

2016, Apr. 28 Litho. Wmk. 390
793-795 A362 Set of 3 4.75 4.75

A363

Europa — A364

Perf. 13¾x14

2016, May 12 Litho. Wmk. 390
796 A363 2.80 l multi 1.90 1.90
797 A364 2.80 l multi 1.90 1.90

Think Green Issue.

Traditional Household Furnishings — A365

Designs: 1.60 l, Kitchen. 2 l, Bedroom.

Wmk. 390

2016, Sept. 22 Litho. *Perf. 14*
798-799 A365 Set of 2 2.40 2.40

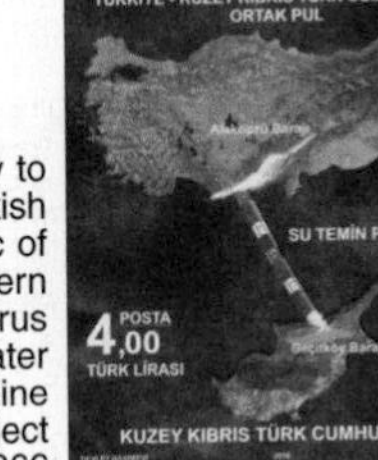

Turkey to Turkish Republic of Northern Cyprus Water Pipeline Project A366

Wmk. 390

2016, Oct. 17 Litho. *Imperf.*
800 A366 4 l multi 2.60 2.60

See Turkey No. 3526.

Bees — A367

Designs: 1 l, Apis mellifera on purple flower. 1.50 l, Apis mellifera on pink flower. 20 l, Apis mellifera cypria.

Wmk. 390

2016, Nov. 24 Litho. *Perf. 13¾*
801-803 A367 Set of 3 13.00 13.00

Delphinus Delphis — A368

Perf. 13¾x14

2017, Feb. 23 Litho. Wmk. 390
804 A368 1 l multi .55 .55

Towns — A369

Cittaslow emblem and: 60k, Grapes, beach, Mehmetçik (Galateia). 1 l, Ruins, Yenibogaziçi (Agios Sergios). 2 l, Oranges, arch, Lefke (Lefka).

Perf. 13¾x14

2017, Mar. 23 Litho. Wmk. 390
805-807 A369 Set of 3 2.00 2.00

Europa — A370

Designs: 1.50 l, St. Hilarion Castle. 3.30 l, Kyrenia (Girne) Castle.

Perf. 13¾x14

2017, May 11 Litho. Wmk. 390
808-809 A370 Set of 2 2.75 2.75

Flowers — A371

Designs: 1 l, Teucrium divaricatum subsp. canescens. 1.50 l, Dianthus strictus subsp. troodi. 1.65 l, Teucrium salaminium, vert. 1.80 l, Sideritis cypria, vert.

Perf. 13¾x14, 14x13¾

2017, July 31 Litho. Wmk. 390
810-813 A371 Set of 4 3.50 3.50

Hakan Asik, Food Vendor A372

Hasan Eminaga, Potter A373

Wmk. 390

2017, Oct. 5 Litho. *Perf. 14*
814 A372 1 l multi .55 .55
815 A373 1.50 l multi .80 .80

No. B1 Surcharged

No. B2 Surcharged

Methods, Perfs., and Watermarks As Before

2018, Apr. 6
816 SP1 1.50 l on 80k+10k #B1 .75 .75
817 SP2 2 l on 1 l + 10k #B2 1.00 1.00

Europa — A374

Bridge in: 1.50 l, Degirmenlik (Kythrea). 2 l, Ortaköy.

Perf. 13¾x14

2018, May 18 Litho. Wmk. 390
818-819 A374 Set of 2 1.60 1.60
a. Souvenir sheet of 4, 2 each #818-819 3.25 3.25

2018 World Cup Soccer Championships, Russia — A375

No. 820 — Emblem, mascot, soccer ball, stadium, nesting doll, with denomination at: a, LL. b, LR.

Wmk. 390

2018, June 14 Litho. *Perf. 13¾*
820 A375 1.50 l Horiz. pair, #a-b 1.40 1.40

Reptiles — A376

Designs: 1.50 l, Mauremys rivulata. 1.65 l, Phoenicolacerta troodica.

Wmk. 390

2018, July 31 Litho. *Perf. 14*
821-822 A376 Set of 2 1.25 1.25
822a Souvenir sheet of 4, 2 each #821-822 2.50 2.50

Occupational Health and Safety — A377

Wmk. 390

2018, Sept. 25 Litho. *Perf. 14*
823 A377 2 l multi .70 .70

Outdoor Activities — A378

Designs: 2.50 l, Kayaking and diving. 4 l, Rock climbing and cycling.

Perf. 14x13½

2018, Dec. 13 Litho. Wmk. 390
824-825 A378 Set of 2 2.50 2.50

National Stamp Exhibition — A379

Cyprus Turkish Philatelic Association, 40th Anniv. A380

Wmk. 390

2019, Apr. 15 Litho. *Perf. 14*
826 A379 2.50 l multi .85 .85
827 A380 4 l multi 1.40 1.40

Nos. 826-827 were each printed in sheets of 8 + central label.

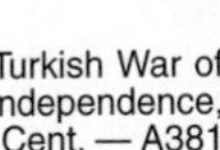

Turkish War of Independence, Cent. — A381

Perf. 13¾x14

2019, May 19 Litho. Wmk. 390
828 A381 2.50 l multi .90 .90

A382

A383

Children's Art — A384

Perf. 14x13¾

2019, May 31 Litho. Wmk. 390
829 Horiz. strip of 3 + flanking label 2.70 2.70
a. A382 2.50 l multi .90 .90
b. A383 2.50 l multi .90 .90
c. A384 2.50 l multi .90 .90

Children's Day.

National Birds A385

No. 830: a, Aquila fasciata. b, Tyto alba.

Perf. 14x13¾

2019, June 20 Litho. Wmk. 390
830 A385 5.25 l Horiz. pair, #a-b 3.75 3.75

Europa.

Cactus Flowers A386

No. 831: a, Echinocereus metornii. b, Hamatocactus setispinus brevispinus.

Wmk. 390

2019, Sept. 24 Litho. *Perf. 13¾*
831 A386 2.50 l Pair, #a-b 1.75 1.75

2020 European Soccer Championships — A387

Digitally Printed

2020, Mar. 13 Wmk. 390 *Perf. 13¾*
832 A387 6.25 l multi 1.90 1.90

The 2020 European Soccer Championships were postponed until 2021 because of the COVID-19 pandemic.

Europa — A388

Horse-drawn mail coach, ship, cancellation, and map of old postal routes of Cyprus with background color of: 1.25 l, Light yellow green. 12.50 l, Yellow.

Digitally Printed
Perf. 13½x14

2020, Sept. 10 **Wmk. 390**
833-834 A388 Set of 2 3.75 3.75

Social Insurance Stamps, 50th Anniv. — A389

Digitally Printed
Perf. 13½x14

2020, Nov. 19 **Wmk. 390**
835 A389 2 l black & red .50 .50

Campaign Against COVID-19 A390

Digitally Printed
Perf. 13½x14

2020, Nov. 19 **Wmk. 390**
836 A390 8 l multi 2.10 2.10

Europa — A391

Endangered species: 6 l, Aythya ferina in flight. 6.50 l, Aythya ferina in water.

Digitally Printed
Perf. 13½x14

2021, July 15 **Wmk. 390**
837-838 A391 Set of 2 3.00 3.00
838a Souvenir sheet of 2, #837-838 3.00 3.00

Ibrahim Yavuz, Wheelchair Basketball Player Competing in 2016 Summer Paralympics A392

Meliz Redif, Sprinter Competing in 2012 Summer Olympics — A393

Digitally Printed
Perf. 13½x14

2021, Sept. 9 **Wmk. 390**
839 A392 2 l multi .45 .45
840 A393 3 l multi .70 .70

2020, Summer Olympics and Paralympics, Tokyo, which were postponed until 2021 because of the COVID-19 pandemic.

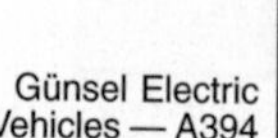

Günsel Electric Vehicles — A394

Günsel emblem and: 3.50 l, Vehicle dashboard and interior. 6.25 l, Five vehicles.

Digitally Printed
Perf. 13½x14

2021, Oct. 7 **Wmk. 390**
841-842 A394 Set of 2 2.10 2.10

Nos. 841-842 were each printed in sheets containing 8 stamps at top of sheet and 8 labels at the bottom of the sheet.

Bottled Beverages — A395

Designs: 1.50 l, Bottles of 14 beverages. 2.75 l, Bottle and donkey cart.

Digitally Printed

2021, Nov. 4 **Wmk. 390** ***Perf. 13¾***
843-844 A395 Set of 2 .65 .65

Reopening of Maras (Varosha) A396

Digitally Printed

2021, Dec. 9 **Wmk. 390** ***Perf. 13¾***
845 A396 2.25 l multi .35 .35

Adoption of "Independence March" as Turkish National Anthem, Cent. — A397

Digitally Printed

2021, Dec. 9 **Wmk. 390** ***Perf. 13¾***
846 A397 3 l multi .45 .45

Myths and Legends — A398

Legend of: 6 l, Karakix. 10.75 l, Pygmalion and Galatea, vert.

Digitally Printed

2022, May 9 **Wmk. 390** ***Perf. 13¾***
847-848 A398 Set of 2 2.10 2.10

Europa.

Architecture — A399

Various unnamed buildings: 9 l, 9.25 l.

Digitally Printed

2022, Sept. 19 **Wmk. 390** ***Perf. 13¾***
849-850 A399 Set of 2 2.00 2.00

2022 World Cup Soccer Championships, Qatar — A400

Emblem, mascot, soccer ball, World Cup trophy, flag of Qatar and: 1.75 l, Stadium. 6.75 l, Soccer player.

Digitally Printed

2022, Oct. 13 **Wmk. 390** ***Perf. 13¾***
851-852 A400 Set of 2 .95 .95

A401

Battle of Dumlupinar (Victory Day), Cent. — A402

Digitally Printed

2022, Dec. 6 **Wmk. 390** ***Perf. 13¾***
853 A401 2.25 l multi .30 .30
854 A402 4.50 l multi .50 .50

Flags of Members of Organization of Turkic States — A403

Digitally Printed

2022, Dec. 6 **Wmk. 390** ***Perf. 13¾***
855 A403 10.75 l multi 1.25 1.25

Acceptance of Turkish Republic of Northern Cyprus as observer member of Organization of Turkic States.

SEMI-POSTAL STAMPS

Campaign Against Cancer
SP1 SP2

Perf. 14x13¾

2015, Apr. 1 **Litho.** **Wmk. 390**
B1 SP1 80k+10k multi .70 .70
B2 SP2 1 l+10k multi .85 .85

For surcharges, see Nos. 816-817.

POSTAL TAX STAMP

Trees — PT1

1995, July 24 **Litho.** ***Perf. 14***
RA1 PT1 1000 l black & green 9.00 2.00

TURKMENISTAN

ˌtərk-ˌme-nə-ˈstan

LOCATION — Southern Asia, bounded by Kazakhstan, Uzbekistan, Iran and Afghanistan
GOVT. — Independent republic, member of the Commonwealth of Independent States
AREA — 188,417 sq. mi.
POP. — 4,366,383 (1999 est.)
CAPITAL — Ashgabat

With the breakup of the Soviet Union on Dec. 26, 1991, Turkmenistan and ten former Soviet republics established the Commonwealth of Independent States.

100 Kopecks = 1 Ruble
100 Tenge = 1 Manat (1994)

Catalogue values for all unused stamps in this country are for Never Hinged items.

Dagdan Necklace, 19th Century — A1

Designs: No. 3, Girl in traditional costume, horiz. No. 4, Akhaltekin horse and rider in native riding dress. No. 5, Mollanepes Theater, horiz. 15r, National arms. No. 7, Pres. Saparmurad Niyazov at left, national flag, horiz. No. 8, Niyazov at right, flag, horiz. No. 9, Map of Turkmenistan.

1992 **Litho.** ***Perf. 12x12½***
1 A1 50k multicolored .35 .35

Perf. 12½

2	A1	10r multicolored	.40	.40
3	A1	10r multicolored	.55	.55
4	A1	10r multicolored	.55	.55
5	A1	10r multicolored	.55	.55
6	A1	15r multicolored	1.10	1.10
7	A1	25r multicolored	1.35	1.35
8	A1	25r multicolored	1.35	1.35
		Nos. 1-8 (8)	6.20	6.20

Size: 112x79mm
Imperf

9 A1 10r multicolored 6.25 6.25

Issued: 50k, 1992; No. 8, 12/8; others, 8/27.
Nos. 2-7 exist imperf. Value, set *$75*.

Nos. 4, 6 Overprinted

1992, Dec. 12		**Color of Overprint**		
10	A1	10r black	*4.50*	*4.50*
11	A1	10r brown	*4.50*	*4.50*
12	A1	10r red	*4.50*	*4.50*
13	A1	10r vermilion	*25.00*	—
14	A1	10r carmine	*4.50*	*4.50*
15	A1	10r green	*4.50*	*4.50*
16	A1	15r black	*4.50*	*4.50*
17	A1	15r brown	*4.50*	*4.50*
18	A1	15r red	*4.50*	*4.50*
19	A1	15r pink	—	—
20	A1	15r blue	*4.50*	*4.50*
21	A1	15r yellow	*6.00*	—
		Nos. 10-21 (12)	*71.50*	*40.50*

1992 Summer Olympics, Barcelona — A2

Designs: a, 1r, Weight lifting. b, 3r, Equestrian. c, 5r, Wrestling. d, 10r, Rowing. e, 15r, Emblem of Turkmenistan Olympic Committee.
No. 23, Flags, symbols for modern pentathlon, weight lifting, rowing, gymnastics.

1992, Dec. 15 **Photo.** ***Perf. 10½x10***
22 A2 Strip of 5, #a.-e. 7.00 7.00

Imperf
Size: 108x82mm

23 A2 15r multicolored 7.50 7.50

For surcharge see No. 33.

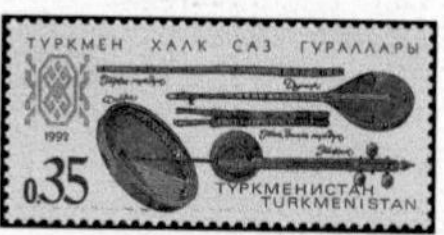

Musical Instruments — A3

Photo. & Engr.

1992, Sept. 13 ***Perf. 12x11½***
28 A3 35k buff, red brn, gold & black .40 .40

Horse — A4

1992, Aug. 9 **Photo.** ***Perf. 12***
29 A4 20k shown .25 .25
30 A4 40k Snake, vert. .25 .25

A5

1992, Nov. 29 **Litho.** ***Perf. 12x11½***
31 A5 1r multicolored .35 .35

US Pres. Bill Clinton, Pres. Saparmurad Niyazov — A6

Designs dated: a. 21.30.93. b. 22.03.93. c, 23.03.93. d, 24.03.93. e, 25.03.93.

1993, Mar. 21 Litho. *Perf. 10½*

32	A6	100r Strip of 5, #a.-e.	10.00	10.00

Pres. Niyazov's visit to New York City & Washington DC.
Exists imperf. Value, $25.

No. 22 Surcharged

1993, Apr. 1 Photo. *Perf. 10½x10*

33	A2	Strip of 5	7.00	7.00
a.		25r on 1r	1.40	1.40
b.		10r on 3r	.65	.65
c.		15r on 5r	.75	.75
d.		15r on 10r	.75	.75
e.		50r on 15r	2.40	2.40

Size of surcharge varies.

Phoca Caspica A7

World Wildlife Fund — A8

Phoca caspica: No. 34a, 25r, Facing right. No. 34b, 50r, Facing left. 15r, Lying in snow. 50r, On rocks. 100r, Mother and young. 150r, Swimming.

1993, Oct. 11 Litho. *Perf. 13½*

34	A7	Pair #a.-b.	4.00	4.00
35	A8	15r multicolored	.50	.50
36	A8	50r multicolored	.80	.80
37	A8	100r multicolored	1.05	1.05
38	A8	150r multicolored	2.40	2.40
a.		Bklt. pane, 2 ea #34-38	24.00	24.00
		Booklet, #38a	28.00	
		Nos. 34-38 (5)	8.75	8.75

Exists Imperf. Value, set $350.

Formation of Tovarishch Society for Exploitation of Turkmen Oil Fields, 115th Anniv. — A9

Designs: 1m, Two men viewing oil field. 1.5m, Early tanker Turkmen. 2m, Oil well. 3m, Alfred Nobel, Ludwig Nobel, Robert Nobel, Petr Bilderling, vert. 5m, Early oil field.

1994, June 26 Litho. *Perf. 13*

39	A9	1m multicolored	.65	.65
40	A9	1.5m multicolored	1.00	1.00
41	A9	2m multicolored	1.40	1.40
42	A9	3m multicolored	2.10	2.10
a.		Miniature sheet of 8 + label	19.00	19.00
		Nos. 39-42 (4)	5.15	5.15

Souvenir Sheet

43	A9	5m multicolored	4.75	4.75

See Azerbaijan Nos. 415-418a.

Repetek Natl. Park — A10

Designs: 3m, Repetek Institute. No. 45, Desert, camels. No. 46, Echis carinatus. No. 47, Varanus griseus. 20m, Testudo horsfieldi. No. 49, Haloxylon ammodendron.

1994, Dec. 11 Litho. *Perf. 13*

44	A10	3m multicolored	.50	.50
45	A10	5m multicolored	.55	.55
46	A10	5m multicolored	.55	.55
a.		Miniature sheet of 8 + label	10.00	10.00
47	A10	10m multicolored	1.10	1.10
48	A10	20m multicolored	2.00	2.00
		Nos. 44-48 (5)	4.70	4.70

Souvenir Sheet

49	A10	10m multicolored	3.25	3.25

Intl. Olympic Committee, Cent. — A11

1994, Dec. 30 Litho. *Perf. 14*

50	A11	11.25m multicolored	2.75	2.75

Souvenir Sheet

51	A11	20m multicolored	5.00	5.00

Miniature Sheet

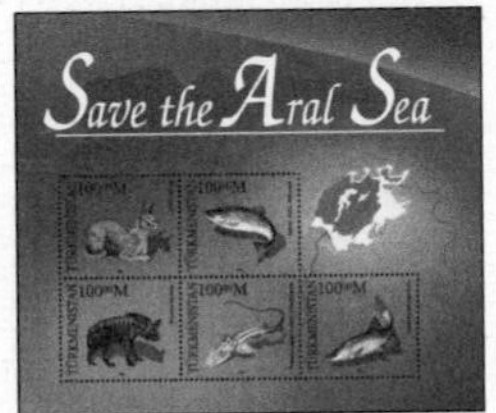

Save the Aral Sea A12

Designs: a, Feis caracal. b, Salmo trutta aralensis. c, Hyaena hyaena. d, Pseudoscaphirhynchus kaufmanni. e, Aspiolucius esocinus.

1996, Apr. 29 Litho. *Perf. 14*

52	A12	100m Sheet of 5, #a.-e.	7.00	7.00

Independence, 5th Anniv. — A13

No. 53, Map of Turkmenistan on globe, vert. No. 54, Train pulling into station. No. 55, Natl. Airport, vert. No. 56, Iranian Pres. Rafsanjani, Turkmenistan Pres. Saparmurad Niyazov, Turkish Pres. Demirel. 500m, UN Secretary-General Boutros Boutros-Gali, Pres. Niyazov, vert. 1000m, Natl. flag, arms.

1996, Oct. 27 Litho. *Perf. 14*

53	A13	100m multicolored	.40	.40
54	A13	100m multicolored	.50	.50
55	A13	300m multicolored	1.25	1.25
56	A13	300m multicolored	1.60	1.60
57	A13	500m multicolored	1.75	1.75
58	A13	1000m multicolored	3.75	3.75
		Nos. 53-58 (6)	9.25	9.25

1996 Summer Olympic Games, Atlanta — A14

1997, May 5 Litho. *Perf. 14x14½*

59	A14	100m Judo	.70	.70
60	A14	300m Boxing	1.60	1.60
61	A14	300m Track & field	1.60	1.60
62	A14	300m Wrestling	1.60	1.60
63	A14	500m Shooting	3.25	3.25
		Nos. 59-63 (5)	8.75	8.75

Souvenir Sheet

64	A14	1000m Olympic torch	6.25	6.25

Items inscribed "Turkmenistan" that were not authorized by Turkmenistan postal officials but which have appeared on the market include:

Single stamps of 100m depicting Princess Diana (3 different stamps), Mother Teresa, Pope John Paul II and Mother Teresa, 50th Anniv. of India, and 50th Anniv. of Pakistan.

Sheets of 4 stamps with denominations of 100m depicting JAPEX 98 / Cats.

Sheets of 9 stamps with denominations of 100m depicting the Titanic, Trains, Golfers, Japanese Armor, Japanese Paper Dolls, and Japanese Art.

Sheets of 6 stamps with denominations of 120m depicting Millennium (8 different sheets).

Sheets of 6 stamps with denominations of 120m depicting Pokémon, and Brad Pitt.

Sheets of 4 stamps with denominations of 195m depicting Greenpeace, Elvis Presley, Birds, Orchids, and Japanese Fashion.

Sheets of 6 stamps with denominations of 195m depicting Marilyn Monroe.

Sheets of 9 stamps with denominations of 195m depicting Cacti, and Minerals.

Sheets of 4 stamps with denominations of 250m depicting Akira Kurosawa.

Sheets of 2 stamps with denominations of 390m depicting Brazilian soccer players from 1998 World Cup.

Sheets of 9 stamps with denominations of 1000m depicting IBRA / Mushrooms (2 different sheets).

Souvenir sheets of 1 stamp with various denominations depicting Hokusai Artwork (2 different sheets), Pope John Paul II (2 different sheets), the Titanic (2 different sheets), 1998 Winter Olympics (2 sheets), Year of the Tiger (2 sheets), 50th Anniv. of Israel, Princess Diana, Queen Mother, Che Guevara, Frank Sinatra, Marilyn Monroe, Elvis Presley, International Year of Older Persons / Bob Hope, 1998 World Cup Soccer Championships, Severiano Ballasteros, Jacques Villeneuve, Leaders of the World / Automobiles, and Maria de Medici / Millennium.

Women's Traditional Clothing — A15

Various costumes.

1999, July 5 Litho. *Perf. 14*

65	A15	500m multi	.80	.80
66	A15	1000m multi	1.35	1.35
67	A15	1200m multi	1.90	1.90
68	A15	2500m multi	2.50	2.50
69	A15	3000m multi	3.25	3.25
		Nos. 65-69 (5)	9.80	9.80

Falcons A16

a, 1000m, Falco tinnunculus. b, 1000m, Falco peregrinus, looking left. c, 1000m, Falco peregrinus, looking right. d, 2500m, Falco tinnunculus, diff. e, 3000m, Falco peregrinus, diff.

2000, Mar. 30 Litho. *Perf. 14*

70	A16	Sheet of 5, #a-e	13.00	13.00

Horn — A17

2000, Oct. Litho. *Imperf.*

Self-Adhesive

71	A17	A multi	1.50	1.50

Sold for 5000m on day of issue.

UN Resolution on the Permanent Neutrality of Turkmenistan, 5th Anniv. — A18

UN emblem, "5," and flags of Turkmenistan and resolution co-sponsors: a, Afghanistan. b, Armenia. c, Azerbaijan. d, Bangladesh. e, Belarus. f, Colombia. g, Czech Republic. h, Egypt. i, France. j, Georgia. k, India. l, Indonesia. m, Iran. n, Kenya. o, Kyrgyzstan. p, Malaysia. q, Mauritius. r, Pakistan. s, Moldova. t, Russia. u, Senegal. v, Tajikistan. w, Turkey. x, Ukraine.

2000, Dec. Litho. *Perf. 14*

72		Sheet of 24 + label	65.00	65.00
a.-x.	A18	3000m Any single	2.40	2.40

Trade Center Building A19

Flag and Arms A20

2001, Apr. 24 Litho. *Imperf.*

Self-Adhesive

73	A19	B multi	.75	.75
74	A20	U multi	1.75	1.75

No. 73 sold for 1,200m, No. 74 sold for 3,000m on day of issue.

Horses A21

No. 75, horiz.: a, Perenli. b, Garader. c, Pyyada. d, Tyllanur. e, Arkadas. f, Yanardag.
No. 76, 5000m, Yanardag, diff., horiz. (denomination at LR). No. 77, 5000m, Yanardag, diff., horiz. (denomination at UR).
No. 78: a, Bitarap. b, Yanardag, diff.

2001, Aug. 20 Litho. *Perf. 14½x14*

75	A21	3000m Sheet of 6, #a-f	8.75	8.75

Size: 116x90mm

Imperf

76-77	A21	Set of 2	8.75	8.75

Souvenir Sheet

Perf. 14x14½

78	A21	5000m Sheet of 2, #a-b	8.75	8.75

Items inscribed "Turkmenistan" that were not authorized by Turkmenistan postal officials but which have appeared on the market include:

Sheets of 9 stamps with denominations of 50m depicting Kim Basinger, Matt Damon, and Pope John Paul II.

Sheets of 9 stamps with denominations of 100m depicting Leading Personalities of the 20th Century.

Sheets of 6 stamps with denominations of 120m depicting Leonardo DiCaprio, and Princess Diana.

Sheets of 8 stamps with denominations of 120m and one label depicting scenes and people from the 20th Century (3 different sheets).

Sheets of 9 stamps with denominations of 120m depicting Princess Diana, Musical group V.I.P., Television show "Xena, Warrior Princess," Elizabeth Taylor, Bruce Lee, Jackie Chan, Tiger Woods, Muhammad Ali, Monaco Grand Prix race cars, Auto racer David Coulthard, Soccer player David Beckham, Euro 2000 European Football Championships, Rugby players, Tennis Stars of the Millennium, Sportsmen of the Millennium, Elephants, Cats, Butterflies, and Pokémon.

Sheets of 2 stamps with denominations of 390m depicting Soccer players from the 1998 World Cup (2 different sheets depicting French and Japanese players).

Souvenir sheets of 1 with denominations of 975m depicting the Mona Lisa, Marilyn Monroe, and Lucille Ball.

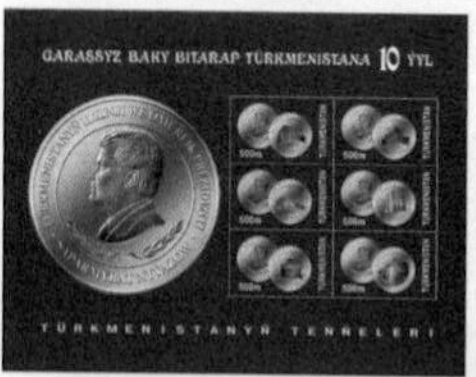

A22

Independence, 10th Anniv. — A23

No. 79 — 500m coins with reverses showing: a, Building with domed roof, coin denomination at right. b, Building with domed roof and tower, coin denomination at left. c, Building with pointed, conical roof. d, Building with archway. e, Building with domed roof on cubic base. f, Statue.

No. 80 — Archaeological sites: a, Soltan Sanjar. b, Nusay. c, Gyz Gala. d, Urgenç. e, Anew. f, Köne Urgenç.

No. 81 — Items in National museum: a, Horn. b, 19th cent. carpet. c, Musical instrument. d, Statue of nude woman. e, Vase. f, 20th cent. decoration.

No. 82, horiz. — Hotels: a, Ahal. b, Gara Altyn. c, Demiryolçy. d, Altyn Suw. e, Köpetdag. f, Aziya.

No. 83 — Buildings: a, Altyn Asyryn Yasayys Jaylary. b, Bitaraplyk Binasy (Arch of Neutrality). c, Türkmendöwletätiyaçlandyrys. d, Random Tower. e, Türkmenbasy Bank. f, Altyn Asyr Söwda Merkezi (Trade Center Building).

No. 84 — Monuments to: a, Oguz Han. b, Seljuk Bay. c, Bayram Han. d, Soltan Sanjar. e, Gorkut Ata. f, Görogly Beg.

No. 85 — Monuments to: a, Sahyrlary Bayram Han. b, Sahyrlary Kemine. c, Sahyrlary Zelili. d, Sahyrlary Seydi. e, Sahyrlary Mollanepes. f, Sahyrlary Mätäji.

2001 Litho. *Imperf.*

79 A22 500m Sheet of 6, #a-f 50.00 50.00
80 A23 1000m Sheet of 6, #a-f 50.00 50.00
81 A23 1200m Sheet of 6, #a-f 125.00 125.00
82 A23 1250m Sheet of 6, #a-f 125.00 125.00
83 A23 1250m Sheet of 6, #a-f 50.00 50.00
84 A23 3000m Sheet of 6, #a-f 50.00 50.00
85 A23 3000m Sheet of 6, #a-f 50.00 50.00
Nos. 79-85 (7) 500.00 500.00

Issued: Nos. 79-80, 10/17; No. 81, 10/19; Nos. 82-83, 10/23; Nos. 84-85, 10/21.

Mohammed Ali Jinnah (1876-1948), First Governor General of Pakistan — A24

2001, Dec. 25 Litho. *Perf. 13*

86 A24 500m multi 1.25 1.25

Birds A25

No. 87, 3000m: a, Motacilla flava. b, Lanius isabellinus. c, Oenanthe oenanthe. d, Corvus monedula. e, Corvus cornix. f, Upupa pyrrhocorax.

No. 88, 3000m: a, Sylvia communis. b, Cuculus canorus. c, Sylvia curruca. d, Corvus pica. e, Corvus frugilegus. f, Corvus corax.

No. 89, 5000m, Anas crecca. No. 90, 5000m, Riparia riparia.

2002, Dec. 1 Litho. *Perf. 14*

Sheets of 6, #a-f

87-88 A25 Set of 2 21.00 21.00

Souvenir Sheets

89-90 A25 Set of 2 6.50 6.50

Butterflies — A26

No. 91, 3000m, vert.: a, Vanessa indica. b, Cynthia cardui. c, Pararge aegeria. d, Pieris rapae. e, Lysandra bellargus. f, Anthocharis cardamines.

No. 92, 3000m, vert.: a, Pandoriana pandora. b, Chazara briseis. c, Aphantopus hyperantus. d, Iolana iolas. e, Pararge schakra. f, Maniola jurtina.

No. 93, 5000m, Hamearis lucina. No. 94, 5000m, Quercusia quercus.

2002, Dec. 1 Sheets of 6, #a-f

91-92 A26 Set of 2 21.00 21.00

Souvenir Sheets

93-94 A26 Set of 2 6.50 6.50

Mosque — A27

2003, Feb. Litho. *Imperf.*

Self-Adhesive

95 A27 B multi 1.25 1.25

Independence and Peace Monument, Ashkhabad — A28

2003, July 25 Self-Adhesive

96 A28 G multi *1.50 1.50*

Building and Flags — A29

2004, Feb. 25 Self-Adhesive

97 A29 B multi *1.25 1.25*

Dog — A30

2004, Aug. 13 Self-Adhesive

98 A30 A multi *1.75 1.75*

Building — A31

2005 Self-Adhesive *Perf. 11¼*

99 A31 M multi *1.25 1.25*

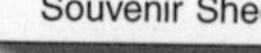

Souvenir Sheet

Permanent Neutrality of Turkmenistan, 10th Anniv. — A32

No. 100: a, UN Secretary General Kofi Annan and Turkmenistan Pres. Saparmurad Niyazov. b, Sculpture on building, UN emblem.

2005, Dec. 1 Litho. *Perf. 11½*

100 A32 5000m Sheet of 2, #a-b *20.00 20.00*

Souvenir Sheets

A33

A34

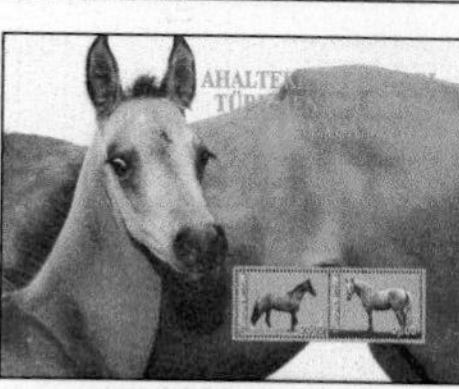

A35

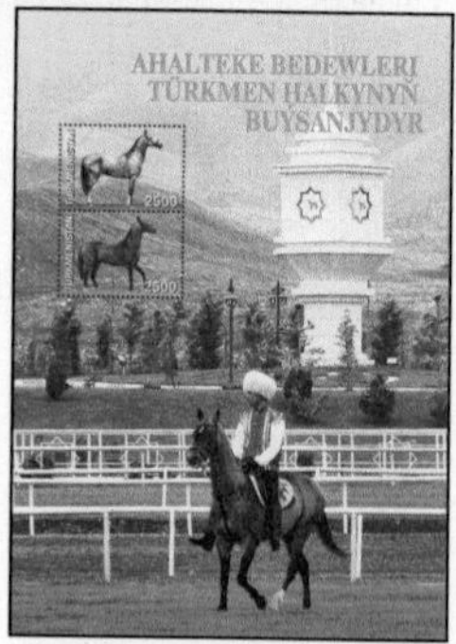

Akhal-Teke Horses — A36

No. 101: a, Horse's head. b, Horse rearing up.

No. 102: a, Pony nursing. b, Horse walking left.

No. 103: a, Horse facing right. b, Horse facing left.

No. 104: a, Gray horse and mountain. b, Brown horse and mountain.

2005, Dec. 1

101 A33 2500m Sheet of 2, #a-b *5.75 5.75*
102 A34 2500m Sheet of 2, #a-b *5.75 5.75*
103 A35 2500m Sheet of 2, #a-b *5.75 5.75*
104 A36 2500m Sheet of 2, #a-b *5.75 5.75*
Nos. 101-104 (4) *23.00 23.00*

Miniature Sheet

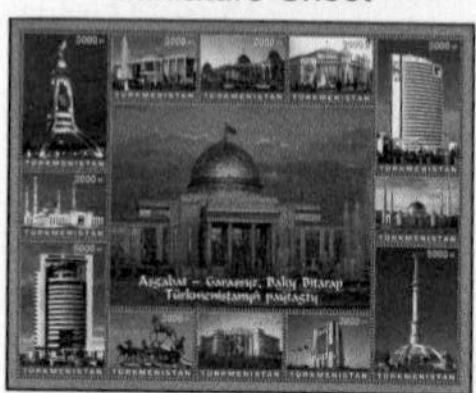

Ashgabat Architecture — A37

No. 105: a, 3000m, Building with dome, fountain at left. b, 3000m, Rukhiyet Palace (building with three green domes, automobiles). c, 3000m, Building with three golden domes and fountain. d, 3000m, Goktepe Mosque (green domes). e, 3000m, Mosque with golden domes. f, 3000m, Statue of Akhal-Teke horses. g, 3000m, Domed building with fence. h, 3000m, Central Bank and flags. i, 5000m, Neutrality Arch at night, vert. j, 5000m, Oil and Gas Ministry Building with flagpoles at right, vert. k, 5000m, President Hotel with flagpoles at left, vert. l, Independence Monument with statues at left and right, vert. Sizes: Nos. 105a-105h, 40x30mm; Nos. 105i-105l, 40x60mm.

2006 Litho. *Perf. 13x12¾*

105 A37 Sheet of 12, #a-l, + label *21.00 21.00*

Independence, 15th Anniv. — A38

2006 Litho. *Imperf.*

Self-Adhesive

106 A38 multi *1.00 1.00*

Miniature Sheets

Pres. Saparmurat Niyazov (1940-2006) — A39

Nos. 108 and 109 — Pres. Niyazov: a, On reviewing stand, tank in background (34x47mm). b, At airplane's door, waving (34x47mm). c, Walking past women in red costumes (34x24mm). d, Wearing suit, seated in chair (34x24mm). e, Lifting girl, helicopter in background (34x24mm). f, Standing with children in front of helicopter (34x24mm). g, Turning key on box on table (34x24mm). h, Waving at crowd (34x24mm). i, Walking from under canopy (34x47mm). j, Seated in front of microphones (34x24mm). k, Standing in farm field (50x24mm). l, Cutting ribbon (34x24mm). m, Standing on red carpet, holding bowl (34x47mm).

Litho. with Foil Application

2007 ***Perf. 11½***

Stamps With Light Blue Panels

107	A39	A Sheet of 13, #a-m	32.50	32.50

Stamps With Green Panels

108	A39	A Sheet of 13, #a-m	32.50	32.50

Leopard — A40

2007 **Litho.** ***Rouletted 8***

Self-Adhesive

109	A40	A multi	2.00	2.00

TURKS & CAICOS ISLANDS

'tərks ən‚d‚ ' kā-kəs 'ī-lənds

LOCATION — A group of islands in the West Indies, at the southern extremity of the Bahamas
GOVT. — British colony; a dependency of Jamaica until 1959
AREA — 192 sq. mi.
POP. — 16,863 (1999 est.)
CAPITAL — Grand Turk

12 Pence = 1 Shilling
20 Shillings = 1 Pound
100 Cents = 1 US Dollar (1969)

Catalogue values for unused stamps in this country are for Never Hinged items, beginning with Scott 90.

Dependency's Badge
A6 A7

1900-04 **Engr.** **Wmk. 2** ***Perf. 14***

1	A6	½p green	3.00	4.50
2	A6	1p rose	4.00	.85
3	A6	2p black brown	1.10	1.40
4	A6	2½p gray blue ('04)	2.00	1.10
a.		2½p blue ('00)	11.50	17.50
5	A6	4p orange	4.25	8.00
6	A6	6p violet	2.75	7.50
7	A6	1sh purple brn	3.75	24.00

Wmk. 1

8	A7	2sh violet	50.00	80.00
9	A7	3sh brown lake	80.00	110.00
		Nos. 1-9 (9)	150.85	237.35

1905-08 **Wmk. 3**

10	A6	½p green	7.00	.40
11	A6	1p carmine	20.00	.60
12	A6	3p violet, *yel* ('08)	2.50	7.00
		Nos. 10-12 (3)	29.50	8.00

King Edward VII — A8

1909, Sept. 2 ***Perf. 14***

13	A8	½p yellow green	.85	.45
14	A8	1p carmine	1.40	.45
15	A8	2p gray	6.50	1.60
16	A8	2½p ultra	9.00	2.00
17	A8	3p violet, *yel*	2.75	2.50
18	A8	4p red, *yel*	3.75	4.75
19	A8	6p violet	8.00	2.75
20	A8	1sh black, *green*	8.00	4.25
21	A8	2sh red, *grn*	45.00	75.00
22	A8	3sh black, *red*	47.50	45.00
		Nos. 13-22 (10)	132.75	138.75

Turk's-Head Cactus — A9

1910-11 **Wmk. 3**

23	A9	¼p claret	2.00	1.10
24	A9	¼p red ('11)	.70	.50

See Nos. 36, 44.

George V — A10

1913-16

25	A10	½p yellow green	.55	2.00
26	A10	1p carmine	1.10	2.50
27	A10	2p gray	2.50	4.00
28	A10	2½p ultra	2.50	3.50
29	A10	3p violet, *yel*	2.50	12.50
30	A10	4p scarlet, *yel*	1.10	11.00
31	A10	5p olive grn ('16)	7.50	25.00
32	A10	6p dull violet	2.75	4.00
33	A10	1sh orange	1.75	5.75
34	A10	2sh red, *bl grn*	30.00	60.00
a.		2sh red, *grnsh white* ('19)	33.00	80.00
b.		2sh red, *emerald* ('21)	55.00	80.00
35	A10	3sh black, *red*	17.50	30.00
		Nos. 25-35 (11)	69.75	160.25

Issued: 5p, 5/18/16; others, 4/1/13.
For overprints see Nos. MR1-MR13.

1921, Apr. 23 **Wmk. 4**

36	A9	¼p red	4.75	32.50
37	A10	½p green	3.50	9.00
38	A10	1p scarlet	1.10	7.00
39	A10	2p gray	1.10	25.00
40	A10	2½p ultra	2.00	9.50
41	A10	5p olive green	12.00	90.00
42	A10	6p dull violet	7.50	90.00
43	A10	1sh brown orange	14.00	65.00
		Nos. 36-43 (8)	45.95	328.00

A11

1922-26 **Inscribed "Postage"**

44	A9	¼p gray black ('26)	1.50	1.10
45	A11	½p green	5.50	5.00
46	A11	1p brown	.65	3.75
47	A11	1½p rose red ('25)	9.00	21.00
48	A11	2p gray	.65	6.50
49	A11	2½p violet, *yel*	.65	2.25
50	A11	3p ultra	.65	6.50
51	A11	4p red, *yel*	1.25	25.00
52	A11	5p yellow grn	1.25	27.50
53	A11	6p dull violet	.95	14.00
54	A11	1sh orange	1.10	25.00
55	A11	2sh red, *green*	2.50	12.50

Wmk. 3

56	A11	2sh red, *green* ('25)	27.50	115.00
57	A11	3sh black, *red* ('25)	6.50	50.00
		Nos. 44-57 (14)	59.65	315.10

Issued: Nos. 47, 56-57, 11/24; No. 44, 10/11; others, 11/20.

A12

Inscribed "Postage and Revenue"

1928, Mar. 1 **Wmk. 4**

60	A12	½p green	.95	.60
61	A12	1p brown	.95	.90
62	A12	1½p red	.95	4.50
63	A12	2p dk gray	.95	.60
64	A12	2½p vio, *yel*	.95	5.25
65	A12	3p ultra	.95	11.00
66	A12	6p brown vio	.95	7.50
67	A12	1sh brown org	4.50	7.50
68	A12	2sh red, *grn*	8.50	37.50
69	A12	5sh green, *yel*	13.50	35.00
70	A12	10sh violet, *bl*	65.00	125.00
		Nos. 60-70 (11)	98.15	235.35

Common Design Types pictured following the introduction.

Silver Jubilee Issue

Common Design Type

1935, May 6 ***Perf. 11x12***

71	CD301	½p green & blk	.40	1.00
72	CD301	3p ultra & brn	5.50	4.00
73	CD301	6p ol grn & lt bl	2.00	5.50
74	CD301	1sh brn vio & ind	2.00	4.00
		Nos. 71-74 (4)	9.90	14.50
		Set, never hinged	15.00	

Coronation Issue

Common Design Type

1937, May 12 ***Perf. 13½x14***

75	CD302	½p deep green	.25	.25
76	CD302	2p gray	.50	.35
77	CD302	3p brt ultra	.50	.35
		Nos. 75-77 (3)	1.25	.95
		Set, never hinged	2.00	

Raking Salt A13

Salt Industry A14

1938-45 **Wmk. 4** ***Perf. 12½***

78	A13	¼p black	.25	.25
79	A13	½p green	3.50	.25
80	A13	1p brown	.35	.25
81	A13	1½p carmine	.35	.25
82	A13	2p gray	.50	.25
83	A13	2½p orange	5.00	1.00
84	A13	3p ultra	.40	.25
85	A13	6p rose violet	8.25	3.00
85A	A13	6p blk brn ('45)	.25	.25
86	A13	1sh bister	2.00	11.00
86A	A13	1sh dk ol grn ('45)	.25	.25
87	A14	2sh rose car	18.00	17.50
88	A14	5sh green	30.00	21.00
89	A14	10sh dp violet	22.50	6.50
		Nos. 78-89 (14)	91.60	62.00
		Set, never hinged	135.00	

Catalogue values for unused stamps in this section, from this point to the end of the section, are for Never Hinged items.

Peace Issue

Common Design Type

1946, Nov. 4 **Engr.** ***Perf. 13½x14***

90	CD303	2p gray black	.25	.25
91	CD303	3p deep blue	.25	.25

Silver Wedding Issue

Common Design Types

1948, Sept. 13 **Photo.** ***Perf. 14x14½***

92	CD304	1p red brown	.25	.25

Perf. 11½x11

Engr.; Name Typo.

93	CD305	10sh purple	16.00	22.50

Dependency's Badge — A17

Flag and Merchant Ship — A18

Map of the Islands — A19

Victoria and George VI — A20

1948, Dec. 14 **Engr.** ***Perf. 12½***

94	A17	½p green	2.25	.25
95	A17	2p carmine	2.25	.25
96	A18	3p deep blue	1.75	.25
97	A19	6p violet	1.75	.30
98	A20	2sh ultra & blk	1.25	2.25
99	A20	5sh blue grn & blk	2.00	8.00
100	A20	10sh chocolate & blk	4.25	8.00
		Nos. 94-100 (7)	15.50	19.30

Cent. of political separation from the Bahamas.

UPU Issue

Common Design Types

Engr.; Name Typo. on 3p, 6p

Perf. 13½, 11x11½

1949, Oct. 10 **Wmk. 4**

101	CD306	2½p red orange	.25	2.50
102	CD307	3p indigo	2.25	2.40
103	CD308	6p chocolate	.30	3.50
104	CD309	1sh olive	.25	.50
		Nos. 101-104 (4)	3.05	8.90

Loading Bulk Salt — A21

Dependency's Badge — A22

Designs: 1p, Salt Cay. 1½p, Caicos mail. 2p, Grand Turk. 2½p, Sponge diving. 3p, South Creek. 4p, Map. 6p, Grand Turk Light. 1sh, Government House. 1sh6p, Cockburn Harbor. 2sh, Government offices. 5sh, Salt Loading.

1950, Aug. 2 **Engr.** ***Perf. 12½***

105	A21	½p deep green	.90	.40
106	A21	1p chocolate	1.25	.75
107	A21	1½p carmine	1.25	.55
108	A21	2p red orange	1.50	.40
109	A21	2½p olive green	1.25	.50
110	A21	3p ultra	1.25	.40
111	A21	4p rose car & blk	4.00	.70
112	A21	6p ultra & blk	3.50	.50
113	A21	1sh bl gray & blk	3.00	.40
114	A21	1sh6p red & blk	16.00	3.25
115	A21	2sh ultra & emer	7.00	4.50
116	A21	5sh black & ultra	27.50	8.50
117	A22	10sh purple & blk	29.00	32.50
		Nos. 105-117 (13)	97.40	53.35

Coronation Issue

Common Design Type

1953, June 2 ***Perf. 13½x13***

118	CD312	2p red orange & blk	.40	1.10

M. S. Kirksons — A23

Design: 8p, Flamingos in flight.

1955, Feb. 1 **Wmk. 4** ***Perf. 12½***

119	A23	5p emerald & blk	2.00	1.25
120	A23	8p yellow brn & blk	3.00	.90

Queen Elizabeth II
A24

Bonefish
A25

Pelican and Salinas — A26

Designs: 2p, Red grouper. 2½p, Spiny lobster. 3p, Albacore. 4p, Muttonfish snapper. 5p, Permit. 6p, Conch. 8p, Flamingos. 1sh, Spanish mackerel. 1sh6p, Salt Cay. 2sh, Caicos sloop. 5sh, Cable office. 10sh, Dependency's badge.

Perf. 13½x14 (1p), 13½x13

1957-60 Engr. Wmk. 314

121 A24 1p lil rose & dk bl .75 .25
122 A25 1½p orange & slate .40 .25
123 A25 2p ol & brn red .40 .25
124 A25 2½p brt grn & car .40 .25
125 A25 3p purple & blue .40 .25
126 A25 4p blk & dp rose 1.50 .25
127 A25 5p brown & grn 1.75 .40
128 A25 6p ultra & car 2.25 .55
129 A25 8p black & ver 3.25 .25
130 A25 1sh blk & dk blue 1.25 .25
131 A25 1sh6p vio bl & dk brn 20.00 2.50
132 A25 2sh lt brn & vio bl 16.00 3.00
133 A25 5sh brt car & blk 12.50 2.75

Perf. 14

134 A26 10sh purple & blk 25.00 7.50

Perf. 14x14½

Photo.

135 A26 £1 dk red & brn 52.50 20.00
Nos. 121-135 (15) 138.35 38.70

Issued: £1, 11/1/60; others, 11/25/57.

Map of Islands — A27

Perf. 13½x14

1959, July 4 Wmk. 4 Photo.

136 A27 6p ol grn & salmon .75 .70
137 A27 8p violet & salmon .75 .40

Granting of a new constitution.

Freedom from Hunger Issue
Common Design Type

Perf. 14x14½

1963, June 4 Wmk. 314

138 CD314 8p carmine rose .30 .25

Red Cross Centenary Issue
Common Design Type

1963, Sept. 2 Litho. *Perf. 13*

139 CD315 2p black & red .25 .50
140 CD315 8p ultra & red .30 .50

Shakespeare Issue
Common Design Type

1964, Apr. 23 Photo. *Perf. 14x14½*

141 CD316 8p green .30 .25

ITU Issue
Common Design Type

Perf. 11x11½

1965, May 17 Litho. Wmk. 314

142 CD317 1p ver & brown .25 .25
143 CD317 2sh emer & lt blue .25 .25

Intl. Cooperation Year Issue
Common Design Type

1965, Oct. 25 Wmk. 314 *Perf. 14½*

144 CD318 1p blue grn & claret .25 .25
145 CD318 8p lt violet & green .25 .25

Churchill Memorial Issue
Common Design Type

1966, Jan. 24 Photo. *Perf. 14*

Design in Black, Gold and Carmine Rose

146 CD319 1p bright blue .25 .25
147 CD319 2p green .25 .25
148 CD319 8p brown .35 .25
a. Gold impression double 200.00
149 CD319 1sh6p violet .75 1.00
Nos. 146-149 (4) 1.60 1.75

Royal Visit Issue
Common Design Type

1966, Feb. 4 Litho. *Perf. 11x12*

Portraits in Black

150 CD320 8p violet blue .40 .25
151 CD320 1sh6p dk car rose .60 .25

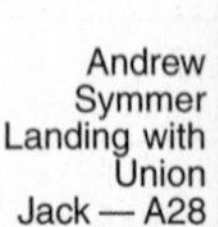

Andrew Symmer Landing with Union Jack — A28

Designs: 8p, Andrew Symmer, his signature, Royal Warrant and Union Jack. 1sh6p, New coat of arms, Royal Cypher and St. Edward's crown.

Perf. 13½

1966, Oct. 1 Unwmk. Photo.

152 A28 1p dk blue & dp org .25 .25
153 A28 8p dk blue, dl yel & car .25 .25
154 A28 1sh6p multicolored .25 .25
Nos. 152-154 (3) .75 .75

200th anniv. of the landing of Andrew Symmer, British agent, establishing the ties with Great Britain.

UNESCO Anniversary Issue
Common Design Type

Wmk. 314

1966, Dec. 1 Litho. *Perf. 14*

155 CD323 1p "Education" .25 .25
156 CD323 8p "Science" .30 .25
157 CD323 1sh6p "Culture" .60 .70
Nos. 155-157 (3) 1.15 1.20

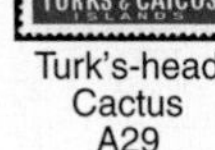

Turk's-head Cactus
A29

Boat Building
A30

Designs: 2p, Donkey cart. 3p, Sisal industry. 4p, Conch industry. 6p, Salt industry. 8p, Skin diving. 1sh, Fishing. 1sh6p, Water skiing. 2sh, Crawfish industry. 3sh, Map of Islands. 5sh, Fishing industry. 10sh, Coat of arms. £1, Queen Elizabeth II.

Perf. 14½x14, 14x14½

1967, Feb. 1 Photo. Wmk. 314

158 A29 1p vio, red & yel .25 .25
159 A30 1½p choc & org yel 1.30 .25
160 A29 2p gray, yel & sl .25 .25
161 A29 3p green & dk brn .25 .25
162 A30 4p grnsh bl, blk & pink 2.50 .25
163 A29 6p blue & dk brn 2.00 .25
164 A29 8p aqua, dk bl & yel .55 .25
165 A30 1sh grnsh bl & red brn .25 .25
166 A29 1sh6p brt grnsh bl, yel & brn .40 .25
167 A30 2sh multicolored 1.10 *1.75*
168 A30 3sh grnsh bl & mar 3.00 .50
169 A30 5sh sky bl, dk bl & yel 2.00 *2.50*
170 A30 10sh multicolored 4.50 *3.75*
171 A29 £1 dk car rose, sil & dk bl 5.00 *11.50*
Nos. 158-171 (14) 23.35 22.25

See #181, 217-230. For surcharges see #182-195.

Turks Islands No. 1 — A31

Designs: 6p, Turks Islands No. 2 and portrait of Queen Elizabeth on simulated stamp. 1sh, Turks Islands No. 3 (like 1p).

1967, May 1 Photo. *Perf. 14½*

172 A31 1p lilac rose & blk .25 .25
173 A31 6p gray & black .25 .25
174 A31 1sh Prus blue & blk .25 .25
Nos. 172-174 (3) .75 .75

Centenary of Turks Islands stamps.

Human Rights Flame — A32

1968, Apr. 1 *Perf. 14x14½*

175 A32 1p lt green & multi .25 .25
176 A32 8p lt blue & multi .25 .25
177 A32 1sh6p multicolored .25 .25
Nos. 175-177 (3) .75 .75

International Human Rights Year.

Martin Luther King, Jr. and Protest March of 1968 — A33

1968, Oct. 1 Photo. Wmk. 314

178 A33 2p dk blue, dk & lt brn .25 .25
179 A33 8p dk car rose, dk & lt brn .25 .25
180 A33 1sh6p dp vio, dk & lt brn .25 .25
Nos. 178-180 (3) .75 .75

Martin Luther King, Jr. (1929-68), American civil rights leader.

Nos. 158-171 Surcharged

Designs as before and: ¼c, Coat of arms like 10sh.

Perf. 14x14½, 14½x14

1969, Sept. 8 Photo. Wmk. 314

181 A30 ¼c lt gray & multi .25 .25
182 A29 1c on 1p multi .25 .25
183 A29 2c on 2p multi .25 .25
184 A29 3c on 3p multi .25 .25
185 A30 4c on 4p multi .25 .25
186 A29 5c on 6p multi .25 .25
187 A29 7c on 8p multi .25 .25
188 A30 8c on 1½p multi .25 .25
189 A30 10c on 1sh multi .25 .25
190 A29 15c on 1sh6p multi .25 .25
191 A30 20c on 2sh multi .30 .25
192 A30 30c on 3sh multi .70 .30
193 A30 50c on 5sh multi 1.25 .40
194 A30 $1 on 10sh multi 2.50 3.00
195 A29 $2 on £1 multi 3.50 17.50
Nos. 181-195 (15) 10.75 23.95

The surcharge is differently arranged on each denomination to fit the design; the old denomination is obliterated with a rectangle on the 8c and 15c.

See Nos. 217-230.

1969 Wmk. 314 Sideways

182a A29 1c on 1p .25 *.25*
183a A29 2c on 2p .25 *.25*
184a A29 3c on 3p .25 *.25*
186a A29 5c on 6p .25 *.50*
187a A29 7c on 8p .25 *.40*
190a A29 15c on 1sh6p .25 *.30*
195a A29 $2 on £1 2.50 *8.00*
Nos. 182a-195a (7) 4.00 9.95

Nativity with John the Baptist — A34

Designs from the Book of Hours of Eleanora, Duchess of Tuscany: 3c, 30c, Flight into Egypt.

Perf. 13x12½

1969, Oct. 20 Litho. Wmk. 314

196 A34 1c plum & multi .25 .25
197 A34 3c dk blue & multi .25 .25
198 A34 15c olive & multi .25 .25
199 A34 30c yellow brn & multi .25 .25
Nos. 196-199 (4) 1.00 1.00

Christmas.

Coat of Arms — A35

1970, Feb. 2 Litho. *Perf. 13x12½*

200 A35 7c brown & multi .25 .25
201 A35 35c violet blue & multi .55 .25

New Constitution, inaugurated 6/16/69. See No. 769.

Christ Bearing the Cross, by Dürer — A36

Albrecht Dürer Engravings: 7c, Christ on the Cross. 50c, The Lamentation for Christ.

Perf. 13½x14

1970, Mar. 17 Engr. Wmk. 314

202 A36 5c dp blue & blk .25 .25
203 A36 7c vermilion & blk .25 .25
204 A36 50c dk brown & multi .50 1.00
Nos. 202-204 (3) 1.00 1.50

Easter.

Dickens and "Oliver Twist" Scene — A37

Charles Dickens and Scene from: 3c, "A Christmas Carol." 15c, "Pickwick Papers." 30c, "The Old Curiosity Shop."

Litho. & Engr.

1970, June 17 *Perf. 13½x13*

205 A37 1c yel, red brn & blk .25 .40
206 A37 3c sal pink, sl & blk .25 .35
207 A37 15c salmon, bl & blk .60 .25
208 A37 30c lt blue, ol & blk 1.00 .40
Nos. 205-208 (4) 2.10 1.40

Charles Dickens (1812-70), English novelist.

Red Cross Ambulance, 1870 — A38

5c, 30c, Red Cross ambulance, 1970.

1970, Aug. 4 Litho. *Perf. 13½x14*

209 A38 1c orange & multi .25 .25
210 A38 5c ocher & multi .25 .25
211 A38 15c brt pink & multi .25 .25
212 A38 30c multicolored .50 .40
Nos. 209-212 (4) 1.25 1.15

Centenary of British Red Cross Society.

Gen. George Monck, Duke of Albemarle, and his Coat of Arms — A39

Designs: 8c, 35c, Coats of arms of Charles II and Queen Elizabeth II.

1970, Dec. 1 Litho. ***Perf. 12½x13½***
213 A39 1c multicolored .25 *.30*
214 A39 8c multicolored .30 *.40*
215 A39 10c multicolored .30 .25
216 A39 35c multicolored .60 *.80*
Nos. 213-216 (4) 1.45 *1.75*

Tercentenary of the issue of Letters Patent to the Six Lords Proprietors.

Types of 1967

Values in Cents and Dollars

Designs: 1c, Turk's-head cactus. 2c, Donkey cart. 3c, Sisal industry. 4c, Conch industry. 5c, Salt industry. 7c, Skin diving. 8c, Boat building. 10c, Fishing. 15c, Water skiing. 20c, Crawfish industry. 30c, Map of Islands. 50c, Fishing industry. $1, Arms of Colony. $2, Queen Elizabeth II.

Perf. 14x14½, 14½x14
1971, Feb. 2 Photo. Wmk. 314
217 A29 1c violet, red & yel .25 .25
218 A29 2c gray, yel & slate .25 .25
219 A29 3c green & dk brn .25 .25
220 A30 4c grnsh bl, blk & pink 1.25 .25
221 A29 5c blue & dk brown .40 .25
222 A29 7c aqua, dk bl & yel .30 .25
223 A30 8c choc & org yel 1.25 .25
224 A30 10c grnsh bl & red brn .75 .25
225 A29 15c brt grnsh bl, yel & brn 1.00 .65
226 A30 20c multicolored 1.50 2.50
227 A30 30c grnsh bl & mar 2.75 1.25
228 A30 50c sky bl, dk bl & yel 3.50 2.00
229 A30 $1 blue & multi 3.00 3.00
230 A29 $2 dk car rose, sil & dk blue 4.00 8.00
Nos. 217-230 (14) 20.45 19.40

The ¼c, released with this set is a shade of No. 181, the background being a greenish, slightly darker gray.

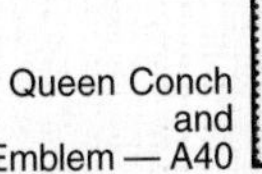

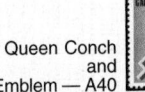

Queen Conch and Emblem — A40

Tourist publicity (Sun, Sea and Sand Emblem and): 1c, Seahorse, vert. 15c, American oyster catcher. 30c, Blue Marlin.

Perf. 14½x14, 14x14½
1971, May 2 Litho. Wmk. 314
232 A40 1c multicolored .25 .25
233 A40 3c multicolored .25 .25
234 A40 15c multicolored .45 .30
235 A40 30c multicolored .90 .55
Nos. 232-235 (4) 1.85 1.35

Pirate Sloop — A41

Designs: 3c, Pirates burying treasure. 15c, Marooned pirate. 30c, Buccaneers.

1971, July 17 ***Perf. 14½x14***
236 A41 2c multicolored .25 .25
237 A41 3c multicolored .25 .25
238 A41 15c multicolored .60 .40
239 A41 30c multicolored 1.25 .90
Nos. 236-239 (4) 2.35 1.80

A42

Adoration of the Virgin and Child, from Wilton Diptych, French School, c. 1395 — A43

1971, Oct. 12 Litho. ***Perf. 14x13½***
240 A42 2c dull brn & multi .25 .25
241 A43 2c dull brn & multi .25 .25
242 A42 8c green & multi .25 .25
243 A43 8c green & multi .25 .25
244 A42 15c dk blue gray & multi .25 .25
245 A43 15c dk blue gray & multi .25 .25
Nos. 240-245 (6) 1.50 1.50

Christmas.

Rocket Launch, Cape Canaveral A44

10c, Space capsule in orbit around earth. 15c, Map of Turks & Caicos Islands & splashdown. 20c, Distinguished Service Medal, vert.

1972, Feb. 21 ***Perf. 13½***
246 A44 5c multicolored .25 .25
247 A44 10c multicolored .25 .25
248 A44 15c lt green & multi .25 .25
249 A44 20c blue & multi .25 .25
Nos. 246-249 (4) 1.00 1.00

First orbital flight by US astronaut Lt. Col. John H. Glenn, Jr., and splashdown off Turks and Caicos Islands, 10th anniversary.

The Three Crosses, by Rembrandt A45

Details from Etchings by Rembrandt: 2c, Christ Before Pilate, vert. 30c, Descent from the Cross, vert.

1972, Mar. 17 ***Perf. 14x13½, 13½x14***
250 A45 2c lilac & black .25 .25
251 A45 15c pink & black .25 .25
252 A45 30c yellow & black .25 .25
Nos. 250-252 (3) .75 .75

Easter.

Discoverers and Explorers of the Americas — A46

Designs: ¼c, Christopher Columbus, Niña, Pinta and Santa Maria. 8c, Richard Grenville and "Revenge," horiz. 10c, Capt. John Smith and three-master. 30c, Juan Ponce de León and three-master, horiz.

1972, July 4
253 A46 ¼c multicolored .25 .75
254 A46 8c multicolored 1.00 .25
255 A46 10c multicolored 1.00 .25
256 A46 30c multicolored 2.00 .90
Nos. 253-256 (4) 4.25 2.15

Silver Wedding Issue

Common Design Type

Design: Queen Elizabeth II, Prince Philip, turk's-head cactus and spiny lobster.

Perf. 14x14½
1972, Nov. 20 Photo. Wmk. 314
257 CD324 10c ultra & multi .25 .25
258 CD324 20c multicolored .25 .25

Treasure Hunting, c. 1700 — A47

Designs: 5c, Replica of silver bank medallion, 1687, obverse. 10c, Same, reverse. 30c, Scuba diver, 1973.

Perf. 14x14½
1973, Jan. 18 Litho. Wmk. 314
259 A47 3c Prus blue & multi .25 .25
260 A47 5c plum, silver & blk .25 .25
261 A47 10c brt rose, silver & blk .25 .25
262 A47 30c violet blue & multi .50 .50
a. Souvenir sheet of 4, #259-262 2.00 2.25
Nos. 259-262 (4) 1.25 1.25

Treasure hunting.

Arms of Jamaica, Turks and Caicos Islands — A48

1973, Apr. 16 Litho. ***Perf. 13½x14***
263 A48 15c buff & multi .30 .25
264 A48 35c lt green & multi .75 .25

Centenary of annexation to Jamaica.

Sooty Tern — A49

Birds: 1c, Magnificent frigate bird. 2c, Noddy tern. 3c, Blue gray gnatcatcher. 4c, Little blue heron. 5c, Catbird. 7c, Black-whiskered vireo. 8c, Osprey. 10c, Flamingo. 15c, Brown pelican. 20c, Parula warbler. 30c, Northern mockingbird. 50c, Ruby-throated hummingbird. $1, Bahama bananaquit. $2, Cedar waxwing. $5, Painted bunting.

Wmk. 314 Sideways
1973, Aug. 1 Litho. ***Perf. 14***
265 A49 ¼c yellow & multi .25 .40
266 A49 1c pink & multi .25 .60
267 A49 2c orange & multi .25 .60
268 A49 3c lilac rose & multi .55 .50
269 A49 4c lt blue & multi .25 1.50
270 A49 5c lt green & multi .40 .30
271 A49 7c salmon & multi 5.50 .30
272 A49 8c blue & multi 6.25 3.25
273 A49 10c brt blue & multi .65 1.25
274 A49 15c tan & multi 3.00 .50
275 A49 20c brt yel & multi 2.00 1.25
276 A49 30c yellow & multi 3.50 1.00
277 A49 50c yellow & multi 3.50 3.75
278 A49 $1 blue & multi 4.00 4.00
279 A49 $2 gray & multi 5.00 7.00
Nos. 265-279 (15) 35.35 26.20

1974-75 Wmk. 314 Upright
266a A49 1c pink & multi ('75) .75 *2.50*
267a A49 2c orange & multi 1.50 *1.60*
268a A49 3c lil rose & multi ('75) 2.50 *2.50*
275a A49 20c brt yel & multi ('75) 2.75 *4.00*
Nos. 266a-275a (4) 7.50 10.60

1976-77 Wmk. 373
265a A49 ¼c yellow & multi ('77) .25 .25
266b A49 1c pink & multi ('77) .25 .25
267b A49 2c orange & multi ('77) .25 .25
268b A49 3c lilac rose & multi .25 .25
269a A49 4c lt bl & multi ('77) .25 .25
270a A49 5c lt grn & multi ('77) .25 .25
273a A49 10c brt bl & multi ('77) .25 .25
274a A49 15c tan & multi ('77) .40 .75
275b A49 20c brt yel & multi .50 .90
276a A49 30c yel & multi ('77) .75 1.45
277a A49 50c yel & multi ('77) 1.25 2.25
278a A49 $1 blue & multi ('77) 2.50 4.50
279b A49 $2 gray & multi ('77) 5.25 9.25
279A A49 $5 yel grn & multi 8.50 16.00
Nos. 265a-279A (14) 20.90 36.85

Bermuda Sloop — A50

Old Sailing Ships: 5c, HMS Blanche. 8c, US privateer Grand Turk and packet Hinchinbrooke. 10c, HMS Endymion. 15c, RMS Medina. 20c, HMS Daring.

1973, July 19 Litho. ***Perf. 13½***
280 A50 2c multicolored .25 1.00
281 A50 5c multicolored .25 .25
282 A50 8c multicolored .25 .75
283 A50 10c multicolored .25 .25
284 A50 15c multicolored .25 .35
285 A50 20c multicolored .40 1.00
a. Souvenir sheet of 6, #280-285 2.50 3.75
Nos. 280-285 (6) 1.65 3.60

Princess Anne's Wedding Issue

Common Design Type

1973, Nov. 14 Wmk. 314 ***Perf. 14***
286 CD325 12c blue grn & multi .25 .25
287 CD325 18c slate & multi .25 .25
Nos. 286-287 (2) .50 .50

Lucayan Stool — A51

Lucayan artifacts: 10c, Broken wood bowl. 12c, Greenstone axe. 18c, Wood bowl. 35c, Animal head, fragment of stool.

1974, July 17 Litho. ***Perf. 14½***
288 A51 6c brt rose & multi .25 .25
289 A51 10c ol grn & multi .25 .25
290 A51 12c brt lil & multi .25 .25
291 A51 18c turq & multi .25 .25
292 A51 35c buff & multi .25 .25
a. Souvenir sheet of 5, #288-292 1.75 1.75
Nos. 288-292 (5) 1.25 1.25

Carvings made by Lucayan Indians, first inhabitants of the islands.

Grand Turk G.P.O. — A52

UPU Emblem and: 12c, Map of Turks and Caicos Islands and local mail sloop. 18c, "United Service" (globe and "UPU"). 55c, Design symbolic of the Islands joining the UPU in 1881.

1974, Oct. 9 Wmk. 314 ***Perf. 14***
293 A52 4c yellow & multi .25 .25
294 A52 12c blue & multi .25 .25
295 A52 18c violet & multi .25 .25
296 A52 55c lt blue & multi .35 .35
Nos. 293-296 (4) 1.10 1.10

Centenary of Universal Postal Union.

"His Finest Hour" — A53

12c, Churchill and Franklin D. Roosevelt.

1974, Nov. 30 Wmk. 373
297 A53 12c multicolored .25 .25
298 A53 18c multicolored .25 .25
a. Souvenir sheet of 2, #297-298 .70 .70

Sir Winston Churchill (1874-1965).

Spanish Captain, c. 1492 — A54

Uniforms: 20c, Officer, Royal Artillery, 1783. 25c, Officer, 67th Foot, 1798. 35c, Private, First West India Regiment, 1833.

1975, Mar. 26 Wmk. 314 ***Perf. 14½***
299 A54 5c blue & multi .25 .25
300 A54 20c blue & multi .25 .25
301 A54 25c blue & multi .35 .25
302 A54 35c blue & multi .50 .50
a. Souvenir sheet of 4, #299-302 1.50 1.60
Nos. 299-302 (4) 1.35 1.25

Old Windmill, Salt Cay — A55

Salt industry: 10c, Pink salt pans, horiz. 20c, Salt raking at Salt Cay, horiz. 25c, Unprocessed salt ready for shipment.

1975, Oct. 16 Litho. Wmk. 373

303	A55	6c violet & multi	.25	.25
304	A55	10c lt brown & multi	.25	.25
305	A55	20c red & multi	.35	.25
306	A55	25c magenta & multi	.45	.35
		Nos. 303-306 (4)	1.30	1.10

Star Coral — A56

1975, Dec. 4 Litho. Wmk. 373

307	A56	6c shown	.25	.25
308	A56	10c Elkhorn coral	.25	.25
309	A56	20c Brain coral	.70	.25
310	A56	25c Staghorn coral	.75	.25
		Nos. 307-310 (4)	1.95	1.00

Schooner — A57

American Bicentennial: 20c, Ship of the line. 25c, Frigate Grand Turk. 55c, Ketch.

1976, May 28 *Perf. 14x13½*

311	A57	6c orange & multi	.25	.25
312	A57	20c violet blue & multi	.35	.25
313	A57	25c brown & multi	.45	.35
314	A57	55c multicolored	.55	.80
a.		Souvenir sheet of 4, #311-314	2.00	4.00
		Nos. 311-314 (4)	1.60	1.65

Turks and Caicos Islands No. 151 — A58

25c, Turks and Caicos Islands No. 150.

1976, July 14 Wmk. 373 *Perf. 14½*

315	A58	20c carmine & multi	.50	.45
316	A58	25c violet blue & multi	.60	.55

Visit of Queen Elizabeth II and Prince Philip to the Caribbean, 10th anniversary.

Virgin and Child, by Carlo Dolci — A59

Christmas: 10c, Virgin and Child with St. John, by Botticelli. 20c, Adoration of the Kings, from Retable by the Master of Paradise. 25c, Adoration of the Kings, illuminated page, French, 15th century.

1976, Nov. 10 Litho. *Perf. 14x13½*

317	A59	6c turq grn & multi	.25	.25
318	A59	10c orange & multi	.25	.25
319	A59	20c red lilac & multi	.25	.25
320	A59	25c ol yel & multi	.25	.25
		Nos. 317-320 (4)	1.00	1.00

Queen with Regalia — A60

Designs: 6c, Queen presenting Order of British Empire to E. T. Wood, Grand Turk, 1966. 55c, Royal family on balcony of Buckingham Palace. $5, Portrait of Queen from photograph taken during her 1966 visit to Grand Turk.

1977 Litho. *Perf. 14x13½*

321	A60	6c multicolored	.25	.25
322	A60	25c multicolored	.25	.25
323	A60	55c multicolored	.30	.25
		Nos. 321-323 (3)	.80	.75

Souvenir Sheet

Perf. 14

324	A60	$5 multicolored	2.00	2.00

25th anniv. of the reign of Elizabeth II.

Nos. 322 and 323 were also issued in booklet panes of 2.

Issued: #321-323, Feb. 7; #324, Dec. 6.

Friendship 7 Capsule — A61

Designs: 3c, Lunar rover, vert. 6c, Tracking Station on Grand Turk. 20c, Moon landing craft, vert. 25c, Col. Glenn's rocket leaving launching pad, vert. 50c, Telstar 1 satellite.

Wmk. 373

1977, June 20 Litho. *Perf. 13½*

325	A61	1c multicolored	.25	.25
326	A61	3c multicolored	.25	.25
327	A61	6c multicolored	.25	.25
328	A61	20c multicolored	.25	.25
329	A61	25c multicolored	.25	.25
330	A61	50c multicolored	.50	.50
		Nos. 325-330 (6)	1.75	1.75

US Tracking Station on Grand Turk, 25th anniversary.

Adoration of the Kings, 1634 by Rubens — A63

Rubens Paintings: ¼c, Flight into Egypt. 1c, Adoration of the Kings, 1624. 6c, Madonna with Garland. 20c, $1, Virgin and Child Adored by Angels. $2, Adoration of the Kings, 1618.

1977, Dec. 23

331	A63	¼c multicolored	.25	.25
332	A63	½c multicolored	.25	.25
333	A63	1c multicolored	.25	.25
334	A63	6c multicolored	.25	.25
335	A63	20c multicolored	.25	.25
336	A63	$2 multicolored	1.25	1.25
		Nos. 331-336 (6)	2.50	2.50

Souvenir Sheet

337	A63	$1 multicolored	1.50	1.60

Christmas and 400th birth anniversary of Peter Paul Rubens (1577-1640).

Map of Turks Island Passage — A64

Designs: 20c, Grand Turk lighthouse and sailboat (LUG cargo vessel). 25c, Deepsea fishing yacht. 55c, S.S. Jamaica Planter.

Wmk. 373, Unwmkd.

1978, Feb. 2 Litho. *Perf. 13½*

338	A64	6c multicolored	.25	.30
339	A64	20c multicolored	.40	.40
340	A64	25c multicolored	.40	.50
341	A64	55c multicolored	1.25	1.25
a.		Souv. sheet of 4, #338-341, unwmkd.	2.50	2.75
		Nos. 338-341 (4)	2.30	2.45

Turks Island Passage, a major Caribbean shipping route.

No. 341a exists watermarked. Value $50.

Queen Victoria in Coronation Regalia — A65

British Monarchs in Coronation Regalia: 10c, Edward VII. 25c, George V. $2, George VI. $2.50, Elizabeth II.

1978, June 2 Litho. *Perf. 14*

342	A65	6c multicolored	.25	.25
343	A65	10c multicolored	.25	.25
344	A65	25c multicolored	.25	.25
345	A65	$2 multicolored	.65	.75
		Nos. 342-345 (4)	1.40	1.50

Souvenir Sheet

346	A65	$2.50 multicolored	1.50	1.50

25th anniversary of coronation of Queen Elizabeth II. Nos. 342-345 also issued in sheets of 3 plus label, perf. 12.

Wilbur Wright and Flyer 3 — A66

Aviation Progress: 6c, Cessna 337 and Wright brothers. 10c, Southeast Airlines' Electra and Orville Wright. 15c, C47 cargo plane on South Caicos runway. 35c, Norman-Britten Islander at Grand Turk airport. $1, Orville Wright and Flyer, 1902. $2, Wilbur Wright and Flyer.

1978, June 29 Litho. *Perf. 14½*

347	A66	1c multicolored	.25	.25
348	A66	6c multicolored	.25	.25
349	A66	10c multicolored	.25	.25
350	A66	15c multicolored	.25	.25
351	A66	35c multicolored	.50	.30
352	A66	$2 multicolored	1.60	1.90
		Nos. 347-352 (6)	3.10	3.20

Souvenir Sheet

353	A66	$1 multicolored	1.25	1.60

Coronation of Queen Elizabeth II, 25th Anniv. — A67

Designs: 15c, Ampulla and anointing spoon. 25c, St. Edward's crown. $2 Queen Elizabeth II

Imperf. x Roulette 5

1978, July 24 Litho.

Self-adhesive

354		Souvenir booklet	3.75
a.		A67 Bklt. pane of 3, 15c, 25c, $2	2.40
b.		15c value from #354a	.25
c.		25c value from #354a	.25
d.		$2 value from #354a	1.90
e.		A67 Bklt. pane, 3 each, 15c, 25c	1.35

No. 354 contains #354a-354b printed on peelable paper backing with music and text of hymns.

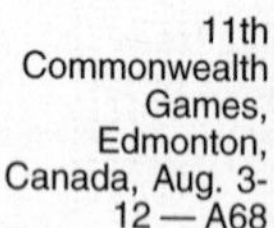
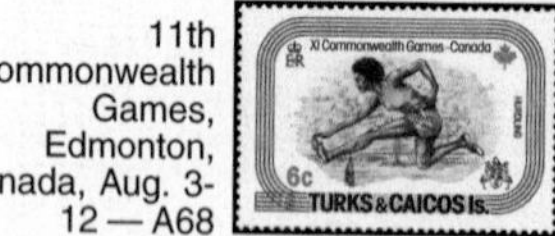

11th Commonwealth Games, Edmonton, Canada, Aug. 3-12 — A68

1978, Aug. 3 Litho. *Perf. 15*

355	A68	6c shown	.25	.25
356	A68	20c Weight lifting	.25	.25
357	A68	55c Boxing	.45	.45
358	A68	$2 Bicycling	.80	1.25
		Nos. 355-358 (4)	1.75	2.20

Souvenir Sheet

359	A68	$1 Sprinting	1.40	1.50

Fish — A69

1c, Indigo hamlet. 2c, Tobacco fish. 3c, Passing Jack. 4c, Porkfish. 5c, Spanish grunt. 7c, Yellowtail snapper. 8c, Foureye butterflyfish. 10c, Yellow fin grouper. 15c, Beau Gregory. 20c, Queen angelfish. 30c, Hogfish. 50c, Fairy Basslet. $1, Clown wrasse. $2, Stoplight parrotfish. $5, Queen triggerfish.

No Year Imprint Below Design

1978-79 Litho. *Perf. 14¼*

360	A69	1c multi	.25	.25
361	A69	2c multi	.60	.80
362	A69	3c multi	.40	.25
363	A69	4c multi	.60	.80
364	A69	5c multi	.40	.30
365	A69	7c multi	.90	1.50
366	A69	8c multi	.90	.25
367	A69	10c multi	.40	.25
368	A69	15c multi	1.00	.30
369	A69	20c multi	.80	1.00
370	A69	30c multi	1.50	.60
371	A69	50c multi	1.00	1.00
372	A69	$1 multi	1.90	1.90
373	A69	$2 multi	2.50	4.25
374	A69	$5 multi	4.50	6.00
		Nos. 360-374 (15)	17.65	19.45

Issue dates: 1c, 3c, 5c, 10c, 15c, 20c, Nov. 17, 1978; others Feb. 6, 1979.

1981, Dec. 15 *Perf. 12½x12*

"1981" Imprint Below Design

360a	A69	1c multicolored	2.00	2.25
364a	A69	5c multicolored	2.25	2.75
367a	A69	10c multicolored	2.25	2.75
369a	A69	20c multicolored	2.25	2.50
371a	A69	50c multicolored	1.25	1.00
372a	A69	$1 multicolored	.80	1.25
373a	A69	$2 multicolored	4.50	5.00
374a	A69	$5 multicolored	8.00	9.00
		Nos. 360a-374a (8)	23.30	26.50

1983, Jan. 25 *Perf. 14¼x12*

"1983" Imprint Below Design

368b	A69	15c multicolored	1.75	1.00
369b	A69	20c multicolored	2.25	1.25
372b	A69	$1 multicolored	3.50	3.00
373b	A69	$2 multicolored	4.75	4.25
374b	A69	$5 multicolored	5.25	9.00
		Nos. 368b-374b (5)	17.50	18.50

Virgin with the Goldfinch, by Dürer — A70

Dürer Paintings: 20c, Virgin and Child with St. Anne. 35c, Nativity, horiz. $1, Adoration of the Kings, horiz. $2, Praying Hands.

1978, Dec. 11 Litho. *Perf. 14*

375	A70	6c multicolored	.25	.25
376	A70	20c multicolored	.25	.25
377	A70	35c multicolored	.35	.25
378	A70	$2 multicolored	1.25	1.75
		Nos. 375-378 (4)	2.10	2.50

Souvenir Sheet

379	A70	$1 multicolored	1.90	2.75

Christmas and 450th death anniversary of Albrecht Dürer (1471-1528), German painter.

Ospreys — A71

Endangered Species: 20c, Green turtle. 25c, Queen conch. 55c, Rough-toothed dolphin. $1, Humpback whale. $2, Iguana.

1979, May 17 Litho. *Perf. 14*

380	A71	6c multicolored	.60	.25
381	A71	20c multicolored	.50	.25
382	A71	25c multicolored	.60	.50
383	A71	55c multicolored	1.60	1.20
384	A71	$1 multicolored	3.25	3.00
		Nos. 380-384 (5)	6.55	5.20

Souvenir Sheet

385	A71	$2 multicolored	3.50	4.50

The Beloved, by Dante Gabriel Rossetti — A72

Paintings and IYC Emblem: 25c, Tahitian Girl, by Paul Gauguin. 55c, Calmady Children, by Sir Thomas Lawrence. $1, Mother and Daughter (detail), by Gauguin. $2, Marchesa Elena Grimaldi, by Van Dyck.

1979, July 2 Litho. *Perf. 14*
386 A72 6c multicolored .25 .25
387 A72 25c multicolored .25 .25
388 A72 55c multicolored .35 .35
389 A72 $1 multicolored .55 .50
Nos. 386-389 (4) 1.40 1.35

Souvenir Sheet

390 A72 $2 multicolored .80 1.50

International Year of the Child.

Stampless Cover and "Medina" — A73

Designs: 20c, Map of Islands and Rowland Hill. 45c, Stamped envelope and "Orinoco." 75c, Paddlewheeler "Shannon" and letter. $1, Royal Packet "Trent," map of Islands. $2, New and old seals.

1979, Sep. 10 Litho. *Perf. 14*
391 A73 6c multicolored .25 .25
392 A73 20c multicolored .25 .25
393 A73 45c multicolored .25 .25
394 A73 75c multicolored .30 .30
395 A73 $1 multicolored .50 .50

Perf. 12

396 A73 $2 multicolored ('80) 3.25 4.00
a. Souv. sheet of 1, perf. 14 ('79) 1.00 1.75
Nos. 391-396 (6) 4.80 5.55

Nos. 391-395 were issued in sheets of 40, and in sheets of 5 stamps plus label, in changed colors, perf. 12.

No. 396 issued May 6, 1980 in sheet of 5 plus label picturing signal flags and map.

No. 396a Overprinted
Souvenir Sheet

1979, Sept. 10 Litho. *Perf. 14*
397 A73 $2 multicolored 1.00 1.50

Brasiliana 79 Intl. Philatelic Exhibition, Rio de Janeiro, Sept. 15-23.

Cuneiform Script — A74

Designs: 5c, Egyptian papyrus; Chinese writing. 15c, Greek runner; Roman post horse; Roman ship. 25c, Pigeon post; railway post; steamship postal packet. 40c, Balloon post; first airmail plane; supersonic airmail jet. $1, Original stamp press (3 designs each of 5c, 15c, 25c, 40).

Imperf. x Roulette 5, Imperf. ($1)
1979, Sept. 27 Litho.
Self-adhesive

398 Souvenir booklet *6.00*
a. A74 Bklt. pane of 1 ($1)
b. A74 Bklt. pane, 3 each 5c, 15c
c. A74 Bklt. pane, 3 each 25c, 40c

Sir Rowland Hill (1795-1879), originator of penny postage. No. 398 contains 3 booklet panes on peelable paper backing with descriptions of stamp designs.

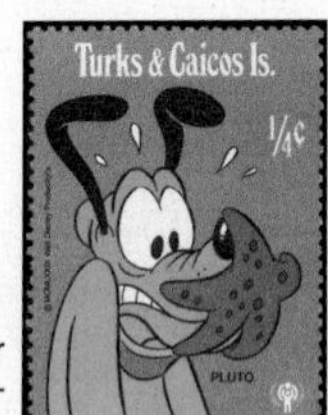

International Year of the Child — A74a

Designs: Aquatic scenes — ¼c, Pluto and starfish. ½c, Minnie Mouse. 1c, Mickey Mouse skin-diving. 2c, Goofy riding turtle. 3c, Donald and dolphin. 4c, Mickey Mouse and fish. 5c, Goofy surfing. 25c, Pluto and lobster. $1, Daisy Duck waterskiing.
$1.50, Goofy.

1979, Nov. 2 Litho. *Perf. 11*
399 A74a ¼c multicolored .25 .25
400 A74a ½c multicolored .25 .25
401 A74a 1c multicolored .25 .25
402 A74a 2c multicolored .25 .25
403 A74a 3c multicolored .25 .25
404 A74a 4c multicolored .25 .25
405 A74a 5c multicolored .25 .25
406 A74a 25c multicolored .45 .25
407 A74a $1 multicolored 1.25 2.50
Nos. 399-407 (9) 3.45 4.50

Souvenir Sheet
Perf. 13½x14

408 A74a $1.50 multicolored 1.75 1.80

St. Nicholas, Icon, 17th Century — A75

Icons or Illuminations: 3c, Emperor Otto II, 10th century. 6c, St. John, Book of Lindisfarne. 15c, Christ and angels. 20c, Christ attended by angels, Book of Kells, 9th century. 25c, St. John the Evangelist. 65c, Christ enthroned, 17th century. $1, St. John, 8th century. $2, St. Matthew, Book of Lindisfarne.

1979, Nov. 26
409 A75 1c multicolored .25 .25
410 A75 3c multicolored .25 .25
411 A75 6c multicolored .25 .25
412 A75 15c multicolored .25 .25
413 A75 20c multicolored .25 .25
414 A75 25c multicolored .25 .25
415 A75 65c multicolored .25 .25
416 A75 $1 multicolored .25 .25
Nos. 409-416 (8) 2.00 2.00

Souvenir Sheet

417 A75 $2 multicolored 1.00 1.50

Christina's World, by Andrew Wyeth A76

Art Treasures: 10c, Ivory leopards, Benin, 19th century. 20c, The Kiss, by Gustav Klimt, vert. 25c, Portrait of a Lady, by Rogier van der Weyden, vert. 80c, Sumerian bull's head harp, 2600 B.C., vert. $1, The Wave, by Hokusai. $2, Holy Family, by Rembrandt, vert.

1979, Dec. 19 Litho. *Perf. 13½*
418 A76 6c multicolored .25 .25
419 A76 10c multicolored .25 .25
420 A76 20c multicolored .25 .25
421 A76 25c multicolored .25 .25
422 A76 80c multicolored .25 .30
423 A76 $1 multicolored .30 .50
Nos. 418-423 (6) 1.55 1.80

Souvenir Sheet

424 A76 $2 multicolored 1.40 1.50

Pied-billed Grebe — A77

25c, Ovenbirds. 35c, Marsh hawks. 55c, Yellow-bellied sapsucker. $1, Blue-winged teals.
$2, Glossy ibis.

1980, Feb. 20 Litho. *Perf. 14*
425 A77 20c shown .75 .55
426 A77 25c multicolored .90 .55
427 A77 35c multicolored 1.25 .65
428 A77 55c multicolored 1.75 .65
429 A77 $1 multicolored 2.50 3.00
Nos. 425-429 (5) 7.15 5.40

Souvenir Sheet

430 A77 $2 multicolored 3.50 3.50

Stamp Under Magnifier, Perforation Gauge, London 1980 Emblem — A78

40c, Stamp in tongs, gauge.
$2, Exhibition Hall.

1980, May 6 Litho. *Perf. 14x14½*
431 A78 25c shown .25 .25
432 A78 40c multicolored .25 .25

Souvenir Sheet

433 A78 $2 multicolored 1.00 1.10

London 1980 International Stamp Exhibition, May 6-14.

Trumpet Triton — A79

1980, June 26 Litho. *Perf. 14*
434 A79 15c shown .25 .25
435 A79 20c Measled cowry .25 .25
436 A79 30c True tulip .25 .40
437 A79 45c Lion's paw .50 .60
438 A79 55c Sunrise tellin .60 .75
439 A79 70c Grown cone .70 1.00
Nos. 434-439 (6) 2.55 3.25

Queen Mother Elizabeth, 80th Birthday — A80

1980, Aug. 4 Litho. *Perf. 14*
440 A80 80c multicolored .60 1.40

Souvenir Sheet
Perf. 12

441 A80 $1.50 multicolored 1.20 2.00

Pinocchio A81

Christmas: Scenes from Walt Disney's Pinocchio.

1980, Sept. 25 *Perf. 11*
442 A81 ¼c multicolored .25 .25
443 A81 ½c multicolored .25 .25
444 A81 1c multicolored .25 .25
445 A81 2c multicolored .25 .25
446 A81 3c multicolored .25 .25
447 A81 4c multicolored .25 .25
448 A81 5c multicolored .25 .25
449 A81 75c multicolored 1.00 .90
450 A81 $1 multicolored 1.25 1.00
Nos. 442-450 (9) 4.00 3.65

Souvenir Sheet

451 A81 $2 multi, vert. 3.50 3.50

Medical Examination, Lions — A82

15c, Scholarships, Kiwanis. 45c, Education, Soroptimists. $1, Lobster boat, Rotary.
$2, Funds for schools, Rotary.

1980, Oct. 8 Litho. *Perf. 14*
452 A82 10c shown .25 .25
453 A82 15c multicolored .25 .25
454 A82 45c multicolored .45 .35
455 A82 $1 multicolored .75 .80
Nos. 452-455 (4) 1.70 1.65

Souvenir Sheet

456 A82 $2 multicolored 1.75 2.25

Lions, Rotary, Kiwanis and Soroptimists service organizations; 75th anniv. of Rotary Intl.

Martin Luther King, Jr. (1929-68) A83

Human Rights Leaders: 30c, John F. Kennedy. 45c, Roberto Clemente (1934-72), baseball player. 70c, Frank Worrel (1927-67), cricket player. $1, Harriet Tubman (1823-1913), born slave, helped others escape to freedom. $2, Marcus Garvey (1887-1940), Jamaican black nationalist leader.

1980, Dec. 22 Litho. *Perf. 14*
457 A83 20c multicolored .25 .25
458 A83 30c multicolored .30 .25
459 A83 45c multicolored .45 .35
460 A83 70c multicolored 1.50 1.40
461 A83 $1 multicolored 1.00 1.25
Nos. 457-461 (5) 3.50 3.50

Souvenir Sheet

462 A83 $2 multicolored 1.60 1.75

Racing Yachts — A84

Designs: Racing yachts.

1981, Jan. 29 Litho. *Perf. 14*
463 A84 6c multicolored .25 .25
464 A84 15c multicolored .25 .25
465 A84 35c multicolored .25 .25
466 A84 $1 multicolored .75 .85
Nos. 463-466 (4) 1.50 1.60

Souvenir Sheet

467 A84 $2 multicolored 1.40 1.75

South Caicos Regatta. No. 467 contains one 28x42mm stamp.

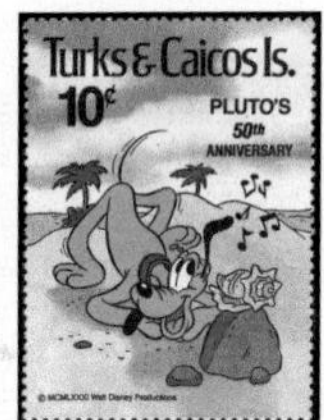

Pluto Listening to Sea Shell — A85

75c, Pluto on raft, dolphin
$1.50, Pluto.

1981, Feb. 16 *Perf. 13½x14*
468 A85 10c shown .25 .25
469 A85 75c multicolored 1.50 1.60

Souvenir Sheet

470 A85 $1.50 multicolored 3.00 3.00

50th anniversary of Walt Disney's Pluto.

Night Queen Cactus — A86

35c, Ripsaw cactus. 55c, Royal strawberry cactus. 80c, Caicos cactus.
$2, Turks head cactus.

1981, Feb. 10 *Perf. 14*
471 A86 25c shown .25 .25
472 A86 35c multicolored .30 .35
473 A86 55c multicolored .50 .60
474 A86 80c multicolored .85 1.00
Nos. 471-474 (4) 1.90 2.20

Souvenir Sheet

475 A86 $2 multicolored 1.75 2.25

Donald Duck and Louie with Easter Egg — A87

Easter: Various Disney characters with Easter eggs.

1981, Mar. 20 Litho. *Perf. 11*

476 A87 10c multicolored .60 .60
477 A87 25c multicolored .75 .75
478 A87 60c multicolored .90 1.60
479 A87 80c multicolored 1.00 2.00
Nos. 476-479 (4) 3.25 4.95

Souvenir Sheet

480 A87 $4 multicolored 6.00 6.50

Pablo Picasso (1881-1973) — A88

20c, Woman with Fan, 1909. 45c, Woman with Pears, 1909. 80c, The Accordionist, 1911. $1, The Aficionado, 1912.
$2, Girl with a Mandolin, 1910.

1981, May 28 Litho. *Perf. 14*

481 A88 20c shown .25 .25
482 A88 45c multicolored .50 .25
483 A88 80c multicolored .75 .85
484 A88 $1 multicolored 1.00 1.20
Nos. 481-484 (4) 2.50 2.55

Souvenir Sheet

485 A88 $2 multicolored 2.30 2.30

Royal Wedding Issue
Common Design Type and

A88a

65c, Kensington Palace. 90c, Charles. No. 489, Glass coach.

1981, June 23 Litho. *Perf. 14*

486 CD331a 35c Couple .25 .25
487 CD331a 65c multi .30 .30
488 CD331a 90c multi .40 .40
Nos. 486-488 (3) .95 .95

Souvenir Sheet

489 CD331 $2 multi 1.25 1.25

Imperf. x Roulette 5 (20c, $1), Imperf. ($2)

1981, July 7 Self-adhesive

490 Booklet 4.00
a. A88a Pane of 6 (3x20c, Lady Diana, 3x$1, Charles) 2.25
b. A88a Pane of 1, $2, Couple 1.75

Nos. 486-488 also printed in sheets of 5 plus label, perf. 12, in changed colors.

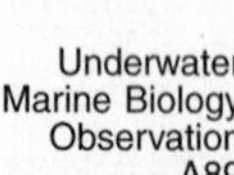

Underwater Marine Biology Observation A89

40c, Underwater photography. 75c, Diving for wreckage. $1, Diver, dolphins.
$2, Diving flag.

1981, Aug. 21 Litho. *Perf. 14*

491 A89 15c shown .30 .30
492 A89 40c multicolored .50 .50
493 A89 75c multicolored 1.00 1.10
494 A89 $1 multicolored 1.25 1.50
Nos. 491-494 (4) 3.05 3.40

Souvenir Sheet

495 A89 $2 multicolored 3.00 3.00

Br'er Rabbit Barricading his Door — A90

Christmas: Scenes from Walt Disney's Uncle Remus.

1981, Nov. 2 Litho. *Perf. 14x13½*

496 A90 ¼c multicolored .25 .25
497 A90 ½c multicolored .25 .25
498 A90 1c multicolored .25 .25
499 A90 2c multicolored .25 .25
500 A90 3c multicolored .25 .25
501 A90 4c multicolored .25 .25
502 A90 5c multicolored .25 .25
503 A90 75c multicolored 1.00 1.00
504 A90 $1 multicolored 1.50 1.25
Nos. 496-504 (9) 4.25 4.00

Souvenir Sheet

505 A90 $2 multicolored 3.50 3.50

Flags of Turks and Caicos Islands — A91

Maps of Various Islands: a, Grand Turk. b, Salt Cay. c, South Caicos. d, East Caicos. e, Middle Caicos. f, North Caicos. g, Caicos Cays. h, Providenciales. i, West Caicos.

1981, Dec. 1 *Perf. 14*

506 Strip of 10 5.75 5.50
a.-j. A91 20c any single .55 .55

Caribbean Buckeyes — A92

35c, Clench's hairstreaks. 65c, Gulf fritillarys. $1, Bush sulphurs.
$2, Turk Island leaf butterfly.

1982, Jan. 21 Litho. *Perf. 14*

507 A92 20c shown .40 .40
508 A92 35c multicolored .75 .75
509 A92 65c multicolored 1.00 1.25
510 A92 $1 multicolored 1.50 2.00
Nos. 507-510 (4) 3.65 4.40

Souvenir Sheet

511 A92 $2 multicolored 3.25 3.75

Scouting Year — A93

40c, Flag ceremony. 50c, Building raft. 75c, Cricket match. $1, Nature study.
$2, Baden-Powell, salute.

1982, Feb. 17 Litho. *Perf. 14*

512 A93 40c multicolored .60 .60
513 A93 50c multicolored .75 1.00
514 A93 75c multicolored 1.50 1.60
515 A93 $1 multicolored 1.75 2.00
Nos. 512-515 (4) 4.60 5.20

Souvenir Sheet

516 A93 $2 multicolored 3.50 4.50

1982 World Cup Soccer — A94

Designs: Various soccer players.

1982, Apr. 30 Litho. *Perf. 14*

517 A94 10c multicolored .25 .25
518 A94 25c multicolored .35 .25
519 A94 45c multicolored .60 .45
520 A94 $1 multicolored 1.00 1.25
Nos. 517-520 (4) 2.20 2.20

Souvenir Sheet

521 A94 $2 multi, horiz. 2.00 2.25

#517-520 issued in sheets of 5 + label.

Phillis Wheatley (1753-1784), Poet, and Washington Crossing Delaware — A95

Washington's 250th Birth Anniv. and F.D. Roosevelt's Birth Centenary: 35c, Washington, Benjamin Banneker (1731-1806), astronomer and mathematician, map. 65c, FDR, George Washington Carver (1864-1943). 80c, FDR with stamp collection. $2, FDR examining Washington stamp.

1982, May 3 Litho. *Perf. 14*

522 A95 20c multicolored .35 .35
523 A95 35c multicolored .70 .70
524 A95 65c multicolored .90 1.25
525 A95 80c multicolored 1.00 1.50
Nos. 522-525 (4) 2.95 3.80

Souvenir Sheet

526 A95 $2 multicolored 2.50 3.00

Second Thoughts, by Norman Rockwell — A96

1982, June 23 Litho. *Perf. 14x13½*

527 A96 8c shown .30 .30
528 A96 15c The Proper Gratuity .30 .30
529 A96 20c Before the Shot .35 .35
530 A96 25c The Three Umpires .35 .35
Nos. 527-530 (4) 1.30 1.30

Princess Diana Issue
Common Design Type

1982 Litho. *Perf. 14½x14*

530A CD332 8c Sandringham .30 .35
530B CD332 35c Wedding 1.40 1.40
530C CD332 $1.10 Diana 2.50 2.50
Nos. 530A-530C (3) 4.20 4.25

1982, July 1 *Perf. 14½x14*

531 CD332 55c Sandringham .75 1.00
532 CD332 70c Wedding 1.25 1.00
533 CD332 $1 Diana 2.00 1.75
Nos. 531-533 (3) 4.00 3.75

Also issued in sheetlets of 5 + label.

Souvenir Sheet

534 CD332 $2 Diana, diff. 3.50 4.00

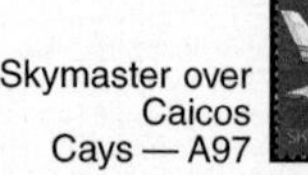

Skymaster over Caicos Cays — A97

15c, Jetstar, Grand Turk. 65c, Helicopter, South Caicos. $1.10, Seaplane, Providenciales.
$2, Boeing 727.

1982, Aug. 26 Litho. *Perf. 14*

535 A97 8c shown .25 .25
536 A97 15c multicolored .35 .35
537 A97 65c multicolored .85 1.00
538 A97 $1.10 multicolored 1.50 1.60
Nos. 535-538 (4) 2.95 3.20

Souvenir Sheet

539 A97 $2 multicolored 3.00 3.25

Christmas A98

Christmas: Scenes from Walt Disney's Mickey's Christmas Carol.

1982, Dec. 1 Litho. *Perf. 13½*

540 A98 1c multicolored .25 .25
541 A98 1c multicolored .25 .25
542 A98 2c multicolored .25 .25
543 A98 2c multicolored .25 .25
544 A98 3c multicolored .25 .25
545 A98 3c multicolored .25 .25
546 A98 4c multicolored .25 .25
547 A98 65c multicolored 1.10 1.10
548 A98 $1.10 multicolored 1.50 1.40
Nos. 540-548 (9) 4.35 4.25

Souvenir Sheet

549 A98 $2 multicolored 3.75 3.75

Trams and Locomotives A99

15c, West Caicos trolley tram. 55c, West Caicos steam locomotive. 90c, Mule-drawn tram, East Caicos. $1.60, Sisal locomotive, East Caicos.
$2.50, Steam engine.

1983, Jan. 18 Litho. *Perf. 14*

550 A99 15c multicolored .30 .30
551 A99 55c multicolored 1.00 1.10
552 A99 90c multicolored 1.5 1.50
553 A99 $1.60 multicolored 2.25 2.50
Nos. 550-553 (4) 5.05 5.40

Souvenir Sheet

554 A99 $2.50 multicolored 3.75 3.75

Commonwealth Day — A99a

1c, Woman crossing guard. 8c, Wind and solar energy sources. 65c, Sailing. $1, Cricket game.

1983, Mar. 14

555 A99a 1c multicolored .85 .50
556 A99a 8c multicolored .35 .25
557 A99a 65c multicolored 1.25 1.25
558 A99a $1 multicolored 2.50 2.50
a. Block or strip of 4, #555-558 4.95 4.50

Easter — A100

Crucifixion, by Raphael: 35c, Mary Magdalene, St. John. 50c, Mary. 95c, Angel looking to heaven. $1.10, Angel looking to earth.
$2.50 shows entire painting.

1983, Apr. 7 Litho. *Perf. 14*

559 A100 35c multicolored .40 .40
560 A100 50c multicolored .60 .60
561 A100 95c multicolored .90 .90
562 A100 $1.10 multicolored 1.00 1.00
Nos. 559-562 (4) 2.90 2.90

Souvenir Sheet

563 A100 $2.50 multicolored 3.75 3.75

Piked Whale A101

65c, Right whale. 70c, Killer whale. 95c, Sperm whale. $1.10, Gooseback whale. $2, Blue whale. $2.20, Humpback whale. No. 571, Longfin pilot whale.
No. 572, Fin whale.

1983 Litho. *Perf. 14*

564 A101 50c shown 1.75 1.75
565 A101 65c multi 2.00 2.00
566 A101 70c multi 2.25 2.25
567 A101 95c multi 2.50 2.50
568 A101 $1.10 multi 2.75 2.75
569 A101 $2 multi 4.00 4.00
570 A101 $2.20 multi 5.25 5.25
571 A101 $3 multi 6.00 6.00
Nos. 564-571 (8) 26.50 26.50

Souvenir Sheet

572 A101 $3 multi 7.50 7.50

Issued: 50c, $2.20, #571, 5/16; 70c, 95c, $2, 6/13; others 7/11. Issued in sheets of 4.
For overprints see Nos. 637-639.

Manned Flight Bicentenary — A102

25c, 1st hydrogen balloon, 1783. 35c, Friendship 7, 1962. 70c, Montgolfiere, 1783. 95c, Columbia space shuttle.
$2, Montgolfiere, Columbia.

1983, Aug. 30 Litho. *Perf. 14*

573 A102 25c multicolored .35 .35
574 A102 35c multicolored .50 .50
575 A102 70c multicolored .75 .90
576 A102 95c multicolored 1.00 1.25
Nos. 573-576 (4) 2.60 3.00

Souvenir Sheet

577 A102 $2 multicolored 2.50 3.00

Ships — A103

4c, Dug-out canoe. 5c, Santa Maria. 8c, Spanish treasure galleons. 10c, Bermuda sloop. 20c, Privateer Grand Turk. 25c, Nelson's Frigate Boreas. 30c, Warship Endymion. 35c, Bark Caesar. 50c, Schooner Grapeshot. 65c, Invincible. 95c, Magicienne. $1.10, Durban. $2, Sentinel. $3, Minerva. $5, Caicos sloop.

1983 Litho. *Perf. 12½x12*

578 A103 4c multicolored 2.75 4.00
579 A103 5c multicolored 1.00 3.00
580 A103 8c multicolored 3.75 3.50
581 A103 10c multicolored 2.75 2.00
582 A103 20c multicolored .50 3.50
583 A103 25c multicolored .50 3.50
584 A103 30c multicolored 2.75 2.00
585 A103 35c multicolored .50 3.50
586 A103 50c multicolored .50 2.00
587 A103 65c multicolored 2.50 4.00
588 A103 95c multicolored 2.50 4.25
589 A103 $1.10 multicolored 11.00 6.00
590 A103 $2 multicolored 2.50 7.00
591 A103 $3 multicolored 8.50 16.00
592 A103 $5 multicolored 17.00 18.00
Nos. 578-592 (15) 59.00 82.25

Issued: 4c, 8c, 10c, 30c, 65c, $1.10, $5, Mar.; 5c, 20c, 25c, 35c, 50c, 95c, $2, Aug. 12; $3, Dec.

1983-84 *Perf. 14*

578a A103 4c 1.50 4.00
579a A103 5c 2.00 4.00
580a A103 8c 2.50 4.00
581a A103 10c 2.25 1.50
582a A103 20c 1.75 2.50
583a A103 25c 3.50 1.75
584a A103 30c 3.00 1.50
585a A103 35c 2.00 3.50
586a A103 50c 3.50 1.25
587a A103 65c 4.50 2.50
588a A103 95c 4.50 2.50
589a A103 $1.10 6.00 3.75
590a A103 $2 7.00 4.00
591a A103 $3 7.50 7.50
592a A103 $5 8.50 14.00
Nos. 578a-592a (15) 60.00 58.25

Issued: 10c, 30c, 65c, $1.10-$3, 10/5/83; 8c, 25c, 50c, 95c, 12/16/83; 4c, 5c, 20c, 35c, $5, 1/9/84.

For overprints see Nos. 744-746.

Christmas — A104

Scenes from Walt Disney's *Oh Christmas Tree* — No. 593, Fifer Pig. No. 594, Fiddler Pig. No. 595, Practical Pig. No. 596, Pluto. No. 597, Goofy. No. 598, Mickey Mouse. No. 599, Gyro Gearloose. No. 600, Ludwig Von Drake. No. 601, Huey, Dewey and Louie.
No. 602, Around the tree.

1983, Nov. *Perf. 11*

593 A104 1c multi .25 .25
594 A104 1c multi .25 .25
595 A104 2c multi .25 .25
596 A104 2c multi .25 .25
597 A104 3c multi .25 .25
598 A104 3c multi .25 .25
599 A104 35c multi .75 .35
600 A104 50c multi .75 .60
601 A104 $1.10 multi 1.50 1.25
Nos. 593-601 (9) 4.50 3.70

Souvenir Sheet

Perf. 13½

602 A104 $2.50 multi 5.50 6.00

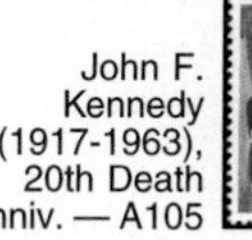

John F. Kennedy (1917-1963), 20th Death Anniv. — A105

1983, Dec. 22 Litho. *Perf. 14*

603 A105 20c multicolored .35 .25
604 A105 $1 multicolored 1.25 1.50

Classic Cars — A106

4c, Cadillac V-16, 1933. 8c, Rolls Royce Phantom III, 1937. 10c, Saab 99, 1969. 25c, Maserati Bora, 1973. 40c, Datsun 260Z, 1970. 55c, Porsche 917, 1971. 80c, Lincoln Continental, 1939 . $1, Triumph TR3A, 1957.
$2, Daimler, 1886.

1984, Mar. 15 Litho. *Perf. 14*

605 A106 4c multi + label .25 .25
606 A106 8c multi + label .25 .25
607 A106 10c multi + label .25 .25
608 A106 25c multi + label .75 .50
609 A106 40c multi + label 1.25 1.00
610 A106 55c multi + label 1.75 1.25
611 A106 80c multi + label 2.25 1.50
612 A106 $1 multi + label 2.50 2.00
Nos. 605-612 (8) 9.25 7.00

Souvenir Sheet

613 A106 $2 multicolored 3.50 3.75

125th anniv. of first commercially productive oil well, Drake's Rig, Titusville, Pa. Nos. 605-612 se-tenant with labels showing flags and auto museum names. No. 613 for 150th birth anniv. of Gotlieb Daimler, inventor of high-speed internal combustion engine.

Easter — A107

450th death anniv. of Antonio Allegri Correggio (Various cameo portraits of Correggio, paintings): 15c, Rest on the Flight to Egypt with St. Francis. 40c, St. Luke and St. Ambrose. 60c, Diana and her Chariot. 95c, Deposition of Christ. $2, Nativity with St. Elizabeth and the Infant St. John.

1984, Apr. 9

614 A107 15c multicolored .30 .30
615 A107 40c multicolored .75 .50
616 A107 60c multicolored 1.00 1.00
617 A107 95c multicolored 1.50 1.50
Nos. 614-617 (4) 3.55 3.30

Souvenir Sheet

618 A107 $2 multi, horiz. 2.75 2.75

1984 Los Angeles Olympics A108

Various Disney characters participating in Olympic sports: No. 619, 500-meter. No. 620, Diving. No. 621, Single kayak. No. 622, 1000-meter kayak. No. 623, Highboard diving. No. 624, Kayak slalom. No. 625, Freestyle swimming. No. 626, Water polo. No. 627, Yachting.
No. 628, Platform diving.

1984, Feb. 21 Litho. *Perf. 14*

619 A108 1c multi .25 .25
620 A108 1c multi .25 .25
621 A108 2c multi .25 .25
622 A108 2c multi .25 .25
623 A108 3c multi .25 .25
624 A108 3c multi .25 .25
625 A108 25c multi .80 .80
626 A108 75c multi 2.25 2.00
627 A108 $1 multi 2.25 2.25
Nos. 619-627 (9) 6.80 6.55

Souvenir Sheet

628 A108 $2 multi 5.50 5.50

1984, Apr. *Perf. 12½x12*

Same Designs

619a A108 1c .25 .25
620a A108 1c .25 .25
621a A108 2c .25 .25
622a A108 2c .25 .25
623a A108 3c .25 .25
624a A108 3c .25 .25
625a A108 25c .50 .50
626a A108 75c 1.75 1.75
627a A108 $1 1.75 1.75
Nos. 619a-627a (9) 5.50 5.50

Souvenir Sheet

628a A108 $2 5.50 6.50

Nos. 619a-628a inscribed with Olympic rings emblem. Printed in sheets of 5.

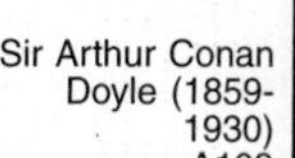

Sir Arthur Conan Doyle (1859-1930) A109

Scenes from the Adventures of Sherlock Holmes: 25c, Second Stain. 45c, Final Problem. 70c, Empty House. 85c, Greek Interpreter.
$2, Doyle, vert.

1984, July 16 Litho. *Perf. 14*

629 A109 25c multi 3.00 2.10
630 A109 45c multi 4.00 3.50
631 A109 70c multi 6.00 5.25
632 A109 85c multi 7.00 6.75
Nos. 629-632 (4) 20.00 17.60

Souvenir Sheet

633 A109 $2 multi 16.00 16.00

Nos. 567-568, 572 Overprinted

1984 Litho. *Perf. 14*

637 A101 95c multicolored 3.00 2.50
638 A101 $1.10 multicolored 3.00 3.00

Souvenir Sheet

639 A101 $3 multicolored 6.50 6.50

AUSIPEX '84 — A110

Darwin, Ship, Map of Australia, Fauna and: 5c, Clown fish. 35c, Monitor lizard. 50c, Rainbow lorikeets. $1.10, Koalas.
$2, Grey kangaroo.

1984, Aug. 22 *Perf. 14x13½*

640 A110 5c multi 1.05 .85
641 A110 35c multi 3.00 3.00
642 A110 50c multi 4.00 4.00
643 A110 $1.10 multi 4.50 5.00
Nos. 640-643 (4) 12.55 12.85

Souvenir Sheet

644 A110 $2 multi 5.00 5.75

Christmas A111

Scenes from Walt Disney's The Toy Tinkers.

1984 Litho. *Perf. 14*

645 A111 20c multicolored .80 .50
646 A111 35c multicolored 1.15 .75
647 A111 50c multicolored 1.45 1.25
648 A111 75c multicolored 1.85 1.75
649 A111 $1.10 multicolored 2.50 2.50
Nos. 645-649 (5) 7.75 6.75

Souvenir Sheet

650 A111 $2 multicolored 4.50 5.00

No. 648 issued in sheets of 8. Issue dates: 75c, Nov. 26, others, Oct. 8.

Audubon Birth Bicentenary — A112

Cameo portrait of Audubon, signature and illustrations from Birds of North America: 25c, Dendroica magnoliae. 45c, Asio flammeus. 70c, Zenaida macroura. 85c, Progne subis.
$2, Haematopus ostralegus.

1985, Jan. 28 Litho. *Perf. 14*

651 A112 25c multicolored 2.00 1.00
652 A112 45c multicolored 3.00 2.00
653 A112 70c multicolored 3.25 3.25
654 A112 85c multicolored 3.25 3.50
Nos. 651-654 (4) 11.50 9.75

Souvenir Sheet

655 A112 $2 multicolored 5.25 5.25

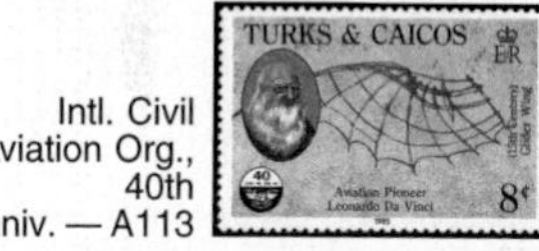

Intl. Civil Aviation Org., 40th Anniv. — A113

Pioneers & inventions: 8c, Leonardo da Vinci, 15th century glider wing. 25c, Sir Alliott Verdon Roe, 1949 C. 102 Jet. 65c, Robert H. Goddard, first liquid fuel rocket launch, 1926. $1, Igor Sikorsky, 1939 Sikorsky VS300. $2, Aviator Amelia Earhart, 1937 Lockheed 10E Electra.

1985, Feb. 21

656 A113 8c multicolored .55 .45
657 A113 25c multicolored 1.50 .60
658 A113 65c multicolored 2.25 2.25
659 A113 $1 multicolored 4.75 5.25
Nos. 656-659 (4) 9.05 8.55

Souvenir Sheet

660 A113 $2 multicolored 4.00 4.25

Arrival of the Statue of Liberty in New York, Cent. — A114

Designs: 20c, Flags of US, France, Franklin, Lafayette. 30c, Designer Frederic A. Bartholdi, engineer Gustave Eiffel, Statue, Eiffel Tower. 65c, Isere, arriving in New York with Statue, 1885. $1.10, Fund raisers Louis Agassiz, H. W. Longfellow, Charles Sumner, Joseph Pulitzer. $2, Dedication day, Oct. 28, 1886.

1985, Mar. 28

661 A114 20c multicolored 1.00 .80
662 A114 30c multicolored 1.50 .95
663 A114 65c multicolored 3.00 2.10
664 A114 $1.10 multicolored 3.25 2.50
Nos. 661-664 (4) 8.75 6.35

Souvenir Sheet

665 A114 $2 multicolored 5.00 5.50

Royal Navy — A115

Designs: 20c, Sir Edward Hawke, Royal George. 30c, Lord Nelson, H.M.S. Victory. 65c, Adm. Sir George Cockburn, H.M.S. Albion. 95c, Adm. Sir David Beatty, H.M.S. Indefatigable. $2, 18th century naval gunner, cannons.

1985, Apr. 17

666	A115	20c multicolored	3.00	2.25
667	A115	30c multicolored	3.50	3.25
668	A115	65c multicolored	4.75	4.25
669	A115	95c multicolored	5.75	5.75
		Nos. 666-669 (4)	17.00	15.50

Souvenir Sheet

670	A115	$2 multicolored	5.50	6.00

Intl. Youth Year — A116

Anniversaries: 25c, Return of Halley's Comet, 1986. 35c, Mark Twain (1835-1910), Mississippi river boat. 50c, Jakob Grimm (1785-1863), Hansel & Gretel, vert. 95c, Grimm, Rumpelstiltskin, vert. $2, Twain, Grimm, portraits.

1985, May 17

671	A116	25c multicolored	1.50	.65
672	A116	35c multicolored	2.50	.90
673	A116	50c multicolored	2.50	1.75
674	A116	95c multicolored	3.50	3.25
		Nos. 671-674 (4)	10.00	6.55

Souvenir Sheet

675	A116	$2 multicolored	5.25	6.00

Queen Mother, 85th Birthday — A117

Designs: 30c, Queen Mother outside Clarence House, vert. 50c, Visiting Biggin Hill Airfield by helicopter. $1.10, 80th birthday portrait, vert. $2, With Prince Charles at the 1968 Garter Ceremony, Windsor Castle, vert.

1985, July 15

676	A117	30c multicolored	1.00	.50
677	A117	50c multicolored	2.25	1.00
678	A117	$1.10 multicolored	2.25	2.50
		Nos. 676-678 (3)	5.50	4.00

Souvenir Sheet

679	A117	$2 multicolored	4.25	4.25

George Frideric Handel A118

Johann Sebastian Bach A119

Handel or Bach and: 4c, King George II, Zadok the Priest music, 1727. 10c, Queen Caroline, Funeral Anthem, 1737. 15c, Bassoon, Invention No. 3 in D Major. 40c, Natural horn, Invention No. 3 in D Major. 50c, King George I, Water Music, 1714. 60c, Viola d'amore, Invention No. 3 . . . 95c, Clavichord, Invention No. 3 . . . $1.10, Queen Anne, Or la Tromba from Rinaldo. No. 688, Handel, portrait. No. 689, Bach, portrait.

1985, July 17 ***Perf. 15***

680	A118	4c multicolored	.70	.55
681	A118	10c multicolored	1.25	.55
682	A119	15c multicolored	1.25	.50
683	A119	40c multicolored	2.25	1.00
684	A118	50c multicolored	2.75	2.50
685	A119	60c multicolored	2.50	1.25
686	A119	95c multicolored	2.75	2.50
687	A118	$1.10 multicolored	3.50	5.50
		Nos. 680-687 (8)	16.95	14.35

Souvenir Sheets

688	A118	$2 multicolored	6.00	7.50
689	A119	$2 multicolored	5.00	5.00

Motorcycle Centenary A120

Flag of US, UK, Fed. Rep. of Germany or Japan and: 8c, 1915 dual cylinder Harley-Davidson. 25c, 1950 Thunderbird Triumph. 55c, 1985 BMW K100RS. $1.20, 1985 Honda 1100 Shadow. $2, 1885 Daimler Single Track, vert.

1985, Sept. 4 ***Perf. 14***

690	A120	8c multicolored	1.00	.40
691	A120	25c multicolored	2.10	1.00
692	A120	55c multicolored	3.25	2.25
693	A120	$1.20 multicolored	4.50	*7.75*
		Nos. 690-693 (4)	10.85	11.40

Souvenir Sheet

694	A120	$2 multicolored	5.50	5.50

Pirates of the Caribbean A121

Disneyland, 30th Anniv.: No. 695, Fate of Capt. Kidd. No. 696, Pirates imprisoned. No. 697, Bartholomew Roberts, church-going pirate. No. 698, Buccaneers in battle. No. 699, Bride auction. No. 700, Plunder. No. 701, Singing pirates. No. 702, Blackbeard. No. 703, Henry Morgan. No. 704, Mary Read, Anne Bonney.

1985, Oct. 4 **Litho.** ***Perf. 14***

695	A121	1c multicolored	.25	.25
696	A121	1c multicolored	.25	.25
697	A121	2c multicolored	.25	.25
698	A121	2c multicolored	.25	.25
699	A121	3c multicolored	.25	.25
700	A121	3c multicolored	.25	.25
701	A121	35c multicolored	1.75	1.00
702	A121	75c multicolored	3.75	*4.00*
703	A121	$1.10 multicolored	4.50	*5.00*
		Nos. 695-703 (9)	11.50	11.50

Souvenir Sheet

704	A121	$2.50 multicolored	7.75	7.75

Girl Guides, 75th Anniv. — A122

Uniforms of Turks and Caicos and: 10c, Papua New Guinea and China brownies. 40c, Surinam and Korea brownies. 70c, Australia and Canada girl guides. 80c, West Germany and Israel girl guides.

1985, Nov. 4

705	A122	10c multicolored	.75	.50
706	A122	40c multicolored	1.75	2.00
707	A122	70c multicolored	2.50	*3.75*
708	A122	80c multicolored	2.75	*3.75*
		Nos. 705-708 (4)	7.75	10.00

Souvenir Sheet

709	A122	$2 Anniv. emblem	4.25	4.25

Grand Turk Chapter, 35th anniv.

World Wildlife Fund — A123

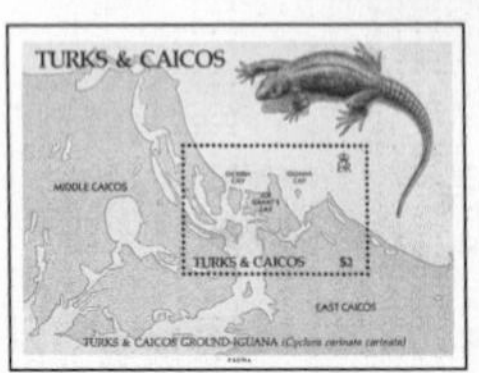

Map of the Islands A124

Turks & Caicos ground iguanas.

1986, Nov. 20 ***Perf. 14***

710	A123	8c multicolored	*1.90*	*1.25*
711	A123	10c multicolored	*1.90*	*1.25*
712	A123	20c multicolored	*3.00*	*2.50*
713	A123	35c multicolored	*5.75*	*5.00*
		Nos. 710-713 (4)	*12.55*	*10.00*

Souvenir Sheet

714	A124	$2 multicolored	16.00	*16.00*

A125

Wedding pictures: 35c, Couple. 65c, Sarah in coach. $1.10, Couple, close-up. $2, In Westminster Abbey.

1986, Dec. 19 **Litho.** ***Perf. 14***

715	A125	35c multi	1.25	.85
716	A125	65c multi	2.25	1.40
717	A125	$1.10 multi	3.00	2.75
		Nos. 715-717 (3)	6.50	5.00

Souvenir Sheet

718	A125	$2 multi	6.00	6.00

Wedding of Prince Andrew and Sarah Ferguson.

Christmas — A126

Illuminations by miniaturist Giorgio Giulio Clovio (1498-1578) from the Farnese Book of Hours: 35c, Prophecy of the Birth of Christ to King Achaz. 50c, The Annunciation. 65c, The Circumcision. 95c, Adoration of the Kings. $2, The Nativity, from the Townley Lectionary.

1987, Dec. 9 **Litho.** ***Perf. 14***

719	A126	35c multicolored	1.05	.75
720	A126	50c multicolored	1.40	2.00
721	A126	65c multicolored	1.75	2.50
722	A126	95c multicolored	2.50	*4.00*
		Nos. 719-722 (4)	6.70	9.25

Souvenir Sheet

723	A126	$2 multicolored	5.25	*6.50*

Accession of Queen Victoria to the Throne of England, 150th Anniv. — A127

Ships and memorials: 8c, HMS Victoria, Victoria Cross. 35c, SS Victoria, coin. 55c, Victoria & Albert I, Great Britain No. 1. 95c, Victoria & Albert II, Victoria Public Library, Turks & Caicos. $2, Bark Victoria.

1987, Dec. 24

724	A127	8c multicolored	1.40	.90
725	A127	35c multicolored	2.60	2.25
726	A127	55c multicolored	2.75	2.75
727	A127	95c multicolored	3.75	3.75
		Nos. 724-727 (4)	10.50	9.65

Souvenir Sheet

728	A127	$2 multicolored	7.50	7.50

US Constitution Bicentennial A128

Designs: 10c, NJ state flag. 35c, Freedom of Worship, vert. 65c, US Supreme Court, vert. 80c, John Adams, vert. $2, George Mason, vert.

1987, Dec. 31

729	A128	10c multicolored	.25	.25
730	A128	35c multicolored	.55	.55
731	A128	65c multicolored	1.30	1.40
732	A128	80c multicolored	1.75	2.25
		Nos. 729-732 (4)	3.85	4.45

Souvenir Sheet

733	A128	$2 multicolored	3.50	*4.50*

Discovery of America, 500th Anniv. (in 1992) — A129

4c, Caravel, first sighting of land, Oct. 12, 1492. 25c, Columbus meets with Indians, Oct. 14. 70c, Fleet anchored in harbor, Oct. 15. $1, Landing, Oct. 16. $2, Nina, Pinta and Santa Maria.

1988, Jan. 20

734	A129	4c multicolored	.50	.30
735	A129	25c multicolored	1.15	.60
736	A129	70c multicolored	3.25	*3.50*
737	A129	$1 multicolored	3.25	*3.50*
		Nos. 734-737 (4)	8.15	7.90

Souvenir Sheet

738	A129	$2 multicolored	6.50	6.50

Sea Scouts Salute Jamboree and Australia A130

Australia Bicent.: 8c, Arawak artifact, scouts exploring cave on Middle Caicos, vert. 35c, Santa Maria, scouts rowing to Hawks Nest. 65c, Scouts diving to explore a sunken Spanish galleon, vert. 95c, Plantation worker cutting sisal, scouts exploring plantation ruins. $2, Splashdown of Friendship 7, piloted by John Glenn, Feb. 20, 1962, vert.

1988, Feb. 12 **Litho.** ***Perf. 14***

739	A130	8c multicolored	.35	.35
740	A130	35c shown	.80	.80
741	A130	65c multicolored	1.50	1.90
742	A130	95c multicolored	2.00	2.25
		Nos. 739-742 (4)	4.65	5.30

Souvenir Sheet

743	A130	$2 multicolored	4.50	5.75

Nos. 581, 583 and 590 Ovptd. "40th WEDDING ANNIVERSARY / H.M. QUEEN ELIZABETH II / H.R.H. THE DUKE OF EDINBURGH"

1988, Mar. 14 **Litho.** ***Perf. 14***

744	A103	10c multicolored	.75	.50
745	A103	25c multicolored	1.25	.50
746	A103	$2 multicolored	4.00	5.00
		Nos. 744-746 (3)	6.00	6.00

A131

1988, Aug. 29 **Litho.**

747	A131	8c Soccer	.60	.25
748	A131	30c Yachting	1.00	.75
749	A131	70c Cycling	5.50	2.50
750	A131	$1 Running	2.25	*3.00*
		Nos. 747-750 (4)	9.35	6.50

Souvenir Sheet

751	A131	$2 Swimming	4.50	4.50

1988 Summer Olympics, Seoul.

A132

Billfish Tournament: 8c, Passenger jet, fishing boat and fisherman reeling-in giant swordfish. 10c, Photographing prize catch. 70c, Fishing boat, lighthouse. $1, Blue marlin. $2, Sailfish.

1988, Sept. 5 **Litho.**

752	A132	8c multicolored	.70	.35
753	A132	10c multicolored	.70	.35
754	A132	70c multicolored	2.75	*3.25*
755	A132	$1 multicolored	3.50	*4.25*
		Nos. 752-755 (4)	7.65	8.20

Souvenir Sheet

756	A132	$2 multicolored	5.25	6.00

Christmas — A133

Paintings by Titian: 15c, Madonna and Child with St. Catherine and the Infant John the Baptist, c. 1530. 25c, Madonna with a Rabbit, c. 1526. 35c, Virgin and Child with Sts. Stephen, Jerome and Mauritius, c. 1520. 40c, The Gypsy Madonna, c. 1510. 50c, The Holy Family and a Shepherd, c. 1510. 65c, Madonna and Child, c. 1510. $3, Madonna and Child with St. John the Baptist and St. Catherine, c. 1530. No. 764, Adoration of the Magi, c. 1560. No. 765, The Annunciation, c. 1560.

1988, Oct. 24 **Litho.**

757	A133	15c	multicolored	.40	.40
758	A133	25c	multicolored	.60	.60
759	A133	35c	multicolored	.85	.85
760	A133	40c	multicolored	.95	.95
761	A133	50c	multicolored	1.00	1.00
762	A133	65c	multicolored	1.25	1.10
763	A133	$3	multicolored	5.50	7.00
			Nos. 757-763 (7)	10.55	11.90

Souvenir Sheets

764	A133	$2	multicolored	4.25	4.50
765	A133	$2	multicolored	4.25	4.50

Visit of Princess Alexandra, 1st Cousin of Queen Elizabeth II A134

Various portraits and: 70c, Government House. $1.40, Map. $2, Flora, vert.

1988, Nov. 14 **Litho.** ***Perf. 14***

766	A134	70c	multicolored	3.25	2.00
767	A134	$1.40	multicolored	9.25	5.75

Souvenir Sheet

768	A134	$2	multicolored	10.00	8.00

Arms Type of 1970 Without Inscription

Perf. 14½x15

1988, Dec. 15 **Litho.** **Unwmk.**

769	A35	$10	multicolored	17.50	18.00

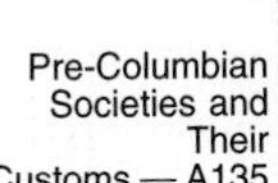

Pre-Columbian Societies and Their Customs — A135

UPAE and discovery of America anniv. emblems and: 10c, Hollowing-out tree to make a canoe, vert. 50c, Body painting and statue. 65c, Three islanders with body paint. $1, Canoeing, vert. $2, Petroglyph.

1989, May 15 **Litho.** ***Perf. 14***

770	A135	10c	multicolored	.40	.40
771	A135	50c	multicolored	1.25	1.25
772	A135	65c	multicolored	1.50	1.50
773	A135	$1	multicolored	2.75	2.75
			Nos. 770-773 (4)	5.90	5.90

Souvenir Sheet

774	A135	$2	multicolored	6.50	*7.50*

Discovery of America 500th anniv. (in 1992).

Souvenir Sheet

Lincoln Memorial, Washington, D.C. — A136

1989, Nov. 17 **Litho.** ***Perf. 14***

775	A136	$1.50	multicolored	4.50	5.25

World Stamp Expo '89.

Miniature Sheets

American Presidential Office, 200th Anniv. — A137

US presidents, historic events and monuments.

No. 776: a, Jackson, early train. b, Van Buren, origins of baseball and Moses Fleetwood Walker, 1st black to play professional baseball. c, Harrison, Harrison's "Keep the Ball Rollin'" slogan and parade. d, Tyler, annexation of Texas, 1845. e, Polk, 1st US postage stamps (#2), 1847, and discovery of gold in California, 1849. f, Taylor, Mexican-American War, 1847.

No. 777: a, Hayes, end of Civil War reconstruction. b, Garfield, Garfield leading Union soldiers in the Battle of Shiloh. c, Arthur, opening of the Brooklyn Bridge, 1883. d, Cleveland, Columbian Exposition, 1893 (US #245). e, Benjamin Harrison, Pan-American Union building, map. f, McKinley, Spanish-American War (Rough Riders Monument, by Solon Borglum).

No. 778: a, Hoover, 1933 Olympic Games, Los Angeles and Lake Placid (American sprinter Ralph Metcalf and Norwegian figure skater Sonja Henie). b, Franklin Delano Roosevelt, Roosevelt's support of the March of Dimes (dime, 1946). c, 150th anniv. of inauguration of Washington, New York World's Fair, 1939. d, Truman, founding of the U.N., 1945. e, Eisenhower, invasion of Normandy, 1944. f, Kennedy, Apollo 11 mission, 1969.

1989, Nov. 19 ***Perf. 14***

776	Sheet of 6		13.50	13.50
a.-f.	50c any single		2.25	2.25
777	A137	Sheet of 6	13.50	13.50
a.-f.	50c any single		2.25	2.25
778	A137	Sheet of 6	13.50	13.50
a.-f.	50c any single		2.25	2.25

Fraser is incorrectly spelled "Frazer" on No. 778c.

Christmas — A138

Religious paintings by Giovanni Bellini: 15c, Madonna and Child. 25c, The Madonna of the Shrubs. 35c, The Virgin and Child. 40c, The Virgin and Child with a Greek Inscription. 50c, The Madonna of the Meadow. 65c, The Madonna of the Pear. 70c, The Virgin and Child, diff. $1, Madonna and Child, diff. No. 787, The Madonna with John the Baptist and Another Saint. No. 788, The Virgin and Child Enthroned.

1989, Dec. 18

779	A138	15c	multicolored	.85	.60
780	A138	25c	multicolored	1.00	.60
781	A138	35c	multicolored	1.25	.75
782	A138	40c	multicolored	1.50	.90
783	A138	50c	multicolored	1.75	1.00
784	A138	65c	multicolored	2.25	2.25
785	A138	70c	multicolored	2.50	2.50
786	A138	$1	multicolored	4.25	3.50
			Nos. 779-786 (8)	15.35	12.10

Souvenir Sheets

787	A138	$2	multicolored	7.00	8.00
788	A138	$2	multicolored	7.00	8.00

Souvenir Sheet

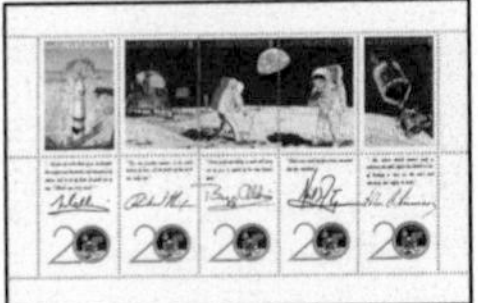

1st Moon Landing, 20th Anniv. — A139

Designs: a, Liftoff. b, Eagle lunar module on Moon's surface. c, Aldrin obtaining soil samples. d, Neil Armstrong walking on Moon. e, Columbia and Eagle in space.

1990, Jan. 8

789	A139	Sheet of 5	7.50	7.50
a.-e.		50c any single	1.50	1.50

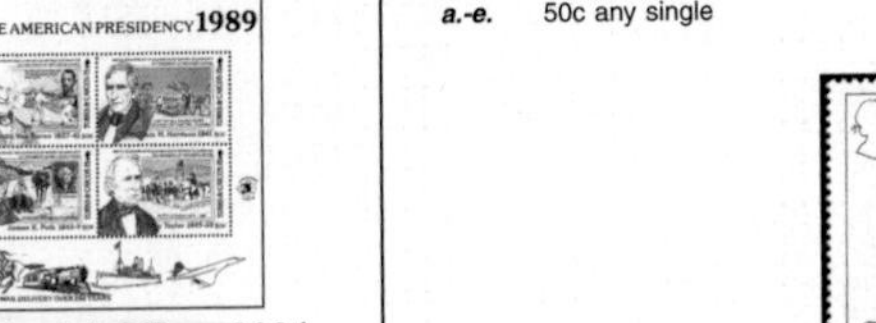

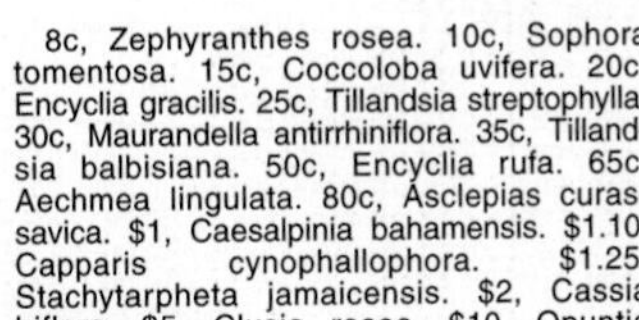

Flowers — A140

8c, Zephyranthes rosea. 10c, Sophora tomentosa. 15c, Coccoloba uvifera. 20c, Encyclia gracilis. 25c, Tillandsia streptophylla. 30c, Maurandella antirrhiniflora. 35c, Tillandsia balbisiana. 50c, Encyclia rufa. 65c, Aechmea lingulata. 80c, Asclepias curassavica. $1, Caesalpinia bahamensis. $1.10, Capparis cynophallophora. $1.25, Stachytarpheta jamaicensis. $2, Cassia biflora. $5, Clusia rosea. $10, Opuntia bahamana.

1990, Jan. 11 **Litho.** ***Perf. 14***

790	A140	8c	multicolored	1.00	.25
791	A140	10c	multicolored	1.00	.25
792	A140	15c	multicolored	1.25	.25
793	A140	20c	multicolored	1.25	.30
794	A140	25c	multicolored	1.25	.35
795	A140	30c	multicolored	1.50	.70
796	A140	35c	multicolored	1.50	.50
797	A140	50c	multicolored	2.00	1.25
798	A140	65c	multicolored	2.25	1.50
799	A140	80c	multicolored	2.50	1.50
800	A140	$1	multicolored	2.75	1.60
801	A140	$1.10	multicolored	3.50	2.75
802	A140	$1.25	multicolored	3.50	3.25
803	A140	$2	multicolored	4.25	4.50
804	A140	$5	multicolored	8.00	11.00
805	A140	$10	multicolored	18.00	20.00
			Nos. 790-805 (16)	55.50	49.95

1994 ***Perf. 12***

790a	A140	8c	1.00	.25
791a	A140	10c	1.00	.25
792a	A140	15c	1.00	.25
793a	A140	20c	1.00	.30
794a	A140	25c	1.00	.35
795a	A140	30c	1.25	.70
796a	A140	35c	1.25	.50
797a	A140	50c	1.50	1.25
798a	A140	65c	1.75	1.50
799a	A140	80c	2.00	1.75
800a	A140	$1	2.25	1.75
801a	A140	$1.10	3.00	3.25
802a	A140	$1.25	3.25	4.25
803a	A140	$2	4.00	5.50
804a	A140	$5	8.50	13.00
805a	A140	$10 ('95)	21.00	24.00
		Nos. 790a-805a (16)	54.75	58.85

Birds — A141

10c, Yellow-billed cuckoo. 15c, White-tailed tropic bird. 20c, Kirtland's warbler. 30c, Yellow-crowned night heron. 50c, West Indian tree duck. 80c, Yellow-bellied sapsucker. $1, American kestrel. $1.40, Mockingbird.

No. 814, Osprey. No. 815, Yellow warbler.

1990, Feb. 19

806	A141	10c	multicolored	1.40	.80
807	A141	15c	multicolored	1.60	.80
808	A141	20c	multicolored	2.00	1.10
809	A141	30c	multicolored	2.50	1.10
810	A141	50c	multicolored	3.50	1.60
811	A141	80c	multicolored	4.25	3.50
812	A141	$1	multicolored	5.75	*6.50*
813	A141	$1.40	multicolored	5.50	4.25
			Nos. 806-813 (8)	26.50	19.65

Souvenir Sheets

814	A141	$2	multicolored	12.50	8.00
815	A141	$2	multicolored	12.50	8.00

Fish — A142

8c, Queen parrotfish. 10c, Queen triggerfish. 25c, Sergeant major. 40c, Spotted goatfish. 50c, Neon goby. 75c, Nassau grouper. 80c, Jawfish. $1, Blue tang.

No. 824, Butter hamlet. No. 825, Queen angelfish.

1990, Feb. 12 **Litho.** ***Perf. 14***

816	A142	8c	multicolored	.30	.25
817	A142	10c	multicolored	.30	.25
818	A142	25c	multicolored	.70	.65
819	A142	40c	multicolored	1.00	1.00
820	A142	50c	multicolored	1.25	1.25
821	A142	75c	multicolored	1.75	1.75
822	A142	80c	multicolored	2.25	2.50
823	A142	$1	multicolored	2.25	2.50
			Nos. 816-823 (8)	9.80	10.15

Souvenir Sheets

824	A142	$2	multicolored	8.00	8.50
825	A142	$2	multicolored	8.00	8.50

Butterflies A143

15c, White peacock. 25c, Cloudless sulphur. 35c, Mexican fritillary. 40c, Fiery skipper. 50c, Chamberlain's sulphur. 60c, Pygmy blue. 90c, Dusky swallowtail. $1, Antillean dagger wing.

No. 834, Thomas's blue. No. 835, 9 Queen species.

1990, Mar. 19

826	A143	15c	multicolored	1.00	.45
827	A143	25c	multicolored	1.25	.60
828	A143	35c	multicolored	1.40	.75
829	A143	40c	multicolored	1.50	.80
830	A143	50c	multicolored	1.50	1.00
831	A143	60c	multicolored	1.75	1.50
832	A143	90c	multicolored	3.00	*3.25*
833	A143	$1	multicolored	3.00	*3.25*
			Nos. 826-833 (8)	14.40	11.60

Souvenir Sheets

834	A143	$2	multicolored	6.25	6.25
835	A143	$2	multicolored	6.25	6.25

Nos. 826, 831 and 833 vert.

America Issue — A144

Fish, UPAE and discovery of America 500th anniv. emblems: 10c, Rock beauty. 15c, Coney. 25c, Red hind. 50c, Banded butterflyfish. 60c, French angelfish. 75c, Blackbar soldierfish. 90c, Stoplight parrotfish. $1, French grunt.

No. 844, Gray angelfish. No. 845, Blue chromis.

1990, Apr. 2

836	A144	10c	multicolored	.60	.40
837	A144	15c	multicolored	.70	.45
838	A144	25c	multicolored	1.00	.60
839	A144	50c	multicolored	1.60	1.40
840	A144	60c	multicolored	1.90	1.75
841	A144	75c	multicolored	2.25	2.25
842	A144	90c	multicolored	2.50	2.50
843	A144	$1	multicolored	2.50	2.75
			Nos. 836-843 (8)	13.05	12.10

Souvenir Sheets

844	A144	$2	multicolored	4.50	5.00
845	A144	$2	multicolored	4.50	5.00

Penny Black, 150th Anniv. — A145

British Pillar Boxes — A146

25c, 1p essay in blue, without letters. 35c, Letter Box #1, 1855. 50c, Penfold Box, 1866. 75c, Great Britain #3, essay. $1, 2p blue essay. $1.25, Air mail box, 1935. #852, Great Britain #1. #853, K type box, 1979.

1990, May 3 **Litho.** ***Perf. 14***

846	A145	25c	bluish blk	1.25	.60
847	A146	35c	gray & pale brn	1.00	1.00
848	A146	50c	gray & dk blue	1.25	1.00
849	A145	75c	red brown	3.00	2.25
850	A145	$1	dk blue	3.50	3.75
851	A146	$1.25	gray & blue	3.00	*4.00*
			Nos. 846-851 (6)	13.00	12.60

Souvenir Sheets

852	A145	$2	black	5.75	5.75
853	A146	$2	blk & red brn	6.25	6.25

Stamp World London '90.

Queen Mother, 90th Birthday — A147

1990, Aug. 20 **Litho.** ***Perf. 14***

854	A147	10c multicolored	.50	.25
855	A147	25c multi, diff.	1.00	.65
856	A147	75c multi, diff.	1.75	2.00
857	A147	$1.25 multi, diff.	2.50	*3.00*
		Nos. 854-857 (4)	5.75	5.90

Souvenir Sheet

858	A147	$2 multi, diff.	6.00	6.50

Birds — A148

8c, Stripe-headed tanager, vert. 10c, Black-whiskered vireo. 25c, Blue-grey gnatcatcher. 40c, Lesser scaup. 50c, White-cheeked pintail. 75c, Common stilt. 80c, Common oystercatcher, vert. $1, Tricolored heron.

No. 867, Bahama woodstar. No. 868, American coot.

1990, Sept. 24 **Litho.** ***Perf. 14***

859	A148	8c multicolored	1.25	.55
860	A148	10c multicolored	1.25	.55
861	A148	25c multicolored	2.00	.55
862	A148	40c multicolored	2.50	1.25
863	A148	50c multicolored	2.50	1.25
864	A148	75c multicolored	3.00	2.00
865	A148	80c multicolored	3.00	*3.25*
866	A148	$1 multicolored	3.75	*4.25*
		Nos. 859-866 (8)	19.25	13.65

Souvenir Sheets

867	A148	$2 multicolored	5.25	5.50
868	A148	$2 multicolored	5.25	5.50

Christmas — A149

Different details from paintings by Rubens: 10c, 50c, 75c, No. 876, Triumph of Christ over Sin and Death. 35c, 45c, 65c, $1.25, No. 877, St. Theresa Praying for the Souls in Purgatory. Nos. 876-877 show entire painting.

1990, Dec. 17 **Litho.** ***Perf. 14***

869	A149	10c multicolored	.45	.25
870	A149	35c multicolored	1.00	.45
871	A149	45c multicolored	1.05	.60
872	A149	50c multicolored	1.25	.70
873	A149	65c multicolored	1.75	1.05
874	A149	75c multicolored	2.00	2.50
875	A149	$1.25 multicolored	2.50	3.75
		Nos. 869-875 (7)	10.00	9.30

Souvenir Sheets

876	A149	$2 multicolored	7.50	8.00
877	A149	$2 multicolored	7.50	8.00

1992 Summer Olympics, Barcelona — A150

1991, Jan. 17

878	A150	10c Kayaking	.45	.25
879	A150	25c Track	.90	.60
880	A150	75c Pole vault	2.00	2.00
881	A150	$1.25 Javelin	2.75	3.75
		Nos. 878-881 (4)	6.10	6.60

Souvenir Sheet

882	A150	$2 Baseball	9.00	10.00

No. 878 inscribed Canoeing.

Voyages of Discovery A151

Designs: 5c, Henry Hudson, 1611. 10c, Roald Amundsen (airship), 1926. 15c, Amundsen (ship), 1906. 50c, USS Nautilus, 1958. 75c, Robert Scott, 1911. $1, Richard Byrd, Floyd Bennett, 1926. $1.25, Lincoln Ellsworth, 1935. $1.50, Cook, 1772-75. No. 891, The Nina. No. 892, The search for land.

1991, Apr. 15 **Litho.** ***Perf. 14***

883	A151	5c multicolored	1.00	.75
884	A151	10c multicolored	1.00	.75
885	A151	15c multicolored	1.25	.90
886	A151	50c multicolored	2.25	1.10
887	A151	75c multicolored	3.50	1.75
888	A151	$1 multicolored	3.75	2.50
889	A151	$1.25 multicolored	4.00	*3.75*
890	A151	$1.50 multicolored	5.00	*5.50*
		Nos. 883-890 (8)	21.75	17.00

Souvenir Sheets

891	A151	$2 multicolored	5.50	6.00
892	A151	$2 multicolored	5.50	6.00

Discovery of America, 500th anniv. (in 1992).

Butterflies A152

5c, White peacock. 25c, Orion. 35c, Gulf fritillary. 45c, Caribbean buckeye. 55c, Flambeau. 65c, Malachite. 70c, Florida white. $1, Great southern white.

No. 901, Giant hairstreak. No. 902, Orange-barred sulphur.

1991, May 13 **Litho.** ***Perf. 14***

893	A152	5c multicolored	.45	.50
894	A152	25c multicolored	1.05	.65
895	A152	35c multicolored	1.15	.85
896	A152	45c multicolored	1.45	1.15
897	A152	55c multicolored	1.60	1.60
898	A152	65c multicolored	2.10	2.10
899	A152	70c multicolored	2.25	2.25
900	A152	$1 multicolored	2.50	2.60
		Nos. 893-900 (8)	12.55	11.70

Souvenir Sheets

901	A152	$2 multicolored	5.75	6.25
902	A152	$2 multicolored	5.75	6.25

Extinct Animals — A153

5c, Protohy- drochoerus. 10c, Phororhacos. 15c, Prothylacynus. 50c, Borhyaena. 75c, Smilodon. $1, Thoatherium. $1.25, Cuvieronius. $1.50, Toxodon.

No. 911, Mesosaurus. No. 912, Astrapotherium.

1991, June 3

903	A153	5c multi	.80	.60
904	A153	10c multi	.80	.60
905	A153	15c multi	.95	.60
906	A153	50c multi	2.50	1.10
907	A153	75c multi	3.00	1.75
908	A153	$1 multi	3.25	2.00
909	A153	$1.25 multi	3.25	3.75
910	A153	$1.50 multi	3.25	4.00
		Nos. 903-910 (8)	17.80	14.40

Souvenir Sheets

911	A153	$2 multi	6.50	6.75
912	A153	$2 multi	6.50	6.75

Royal Family Birthday, Anniversary

Common Design Type

No. 921, Elizabeth, Philip. No. 922, Diana, sons, Charles.

1991 **Litho.** ***Perf. 14***

913	CD347	10c multicolored	.80	.30
914	CD347	25c multicolored	.70	.50
915	CD347	35c multicolored	1.00	.75
916	CD347	45c multicolored	2.50	1.00
917	CD347	50c multicolored	3.50	1.50
918	CD347	65c multicolored	1.50	1.50
919	CD347	80c multicolored	1.75	*3.00*
920	CD347	$1 multicolored	3.25	*3.00*
		Nos. 913-920 (8)	15.00	11.55

Souvenir Sheets

921	CD347	$2 multicolored	5.00	*6.25*
922	CD347	$2 multicolored	7.50	7.50

10c, 45c, 50c, $1, No. 922, Charles and Diana, 10th wedding anniv., issued: July 29. Others, Queen Elizabeth II, 65th birthday, issued: June 8.

For overprints see Nos. 1020-1022.

Mushrooms A154

10c, Pluteus chrysophlebius. 15c, Leucopaxillus gracillimus. 20c, Marasmius haematocephalus. 35c, Collybia subpruinosa. 50c, Marasmius atrorubens, vert. 65c, Leucocoprinus birnbaumii, vert. $1.10, Trogia cantharelloides, vert. $1.25, Boletellus cubensis, vert. No. 931, Gerronema citrinum. No. 932, Pyrrhoglossum pyrrhum, vert.

1991, June 24 **Litho.** ***Perf. 14***

923	A154	10c multicolored	.55	.40
924	A154	15c multicolored	.75	.40
925	A154	20c multicolored	.90	.55
926	A154	35c multicolored	1.25	.60
927	A154	50c multicolored	1.75	1.00
928	A154	65c multicolored	2.25	1.75
929	A154	$1.10 multicolored	2.75	3.50
930	A154	$1.25 multicolored	2.75	3.75
		Nos. 923-930 (8)	12.95	11.95

Miniature Sheets

931	A154	$2 multicolored	6.50	*7.00*
932	A154	$2 multicolored	6.50	*7.00*

Paintings by Vincent Van Gogh A155

Paintings: 15c, Weaver Facing Left, with Spinning Wheel. 25c, Head of a Young Peasant with Pipe, vert. 35c, The Old Cemetery Tower at Nuenen, vert. 45c, Cottage at Nightfall. 50c, Still Life with Open Bible. 65c, Lane at the Jardin du Luxembourg. 80c, The Pont du Carrousel and the Louvre. $1, Vase with Poppies, Cornflowers, Peonies and Chrysanthemums, vert. No. 941, Entrance to the Public Park. No. 942, Plowed Field.

1991, Aug. 26 ***Perf. 13***

933	A155	15c multicolored	1.25	.60
934	A155	25c multicolored	1.50	.60
935	A155	35c multicolored	1.75	.60
936	A155	45c multicolored	1.75	.70
937	A155	50c multicolored	1.75	.75
938	A155	65c multicolored	2.25	1.60
939	A155	80c multicolored	2.75	3.25
940	A155	$1 multicolored	3.00	3.25
		Nos. 933-940 (8)	16.00	11.35

Size: 107x80mm

Imperf

941	A155	$2 multicolored	7.50	7.75
942	A155	$2 multicolored	7.50	7.75

Phila Nippon '91 — A156

Japanese steam locomotives.

1991, Nov. 4 **Litho.** ***Perf. 14***

943	A156	8c Series 8550	.80	.70
944	A156	10c C 57	.80	.60
945	A156	45c Series 4110	1.75	.80
946	A156	50c C 55	1.75	.80
947	A156	65c Series 6250	2.25	1.60
948	A156	80c E 10	2.60	2.60
949	A156	$1 Series 4500	2.60	2.75
950	A156	$1.25 C 11	4.00	6.25
		Nos. 943-950 (8)	16.55	16.10

Souvenir Sheets

951	A156	$2 C 62	6.00	6.00
952	A156	$2 C 58	6.00	6.00

Christmas — A157

Details or entire paintings by Gerard David: 8c, Adoration of the Shepherds. 15c, Virgin and Child Enthroned with Two Angels. 35c, The Annunciation (outside wings). 45c, The Rest on the Flight into Egypt. 50c, The Rest on the Flight into Egypt, diff. 65c, Virgin and Child with Angels. 80c, The Adoration of the Shepherds, diff. $1.25, The Perussis Altarpiece. No. 961, The Adoration of the Kings. No. 962, The Nativity.

1991, Dec. 23 ***Perf. 12***

953	A157	8c multicolored	.75	.25
954	A157	15c multicolored	.95	.25
955	A157	35c multicolored	1.75	.50
956	A157	45c multicolored	1.75	.75
957	A157	50c multicolored	1.75	.90
958	A157	65c multicolored	2.25	1.25
959	A157	80c multicolored	2.75	3.00
960	A157	$1.25 multicolored	3.50	5.50
		Nos. 953-960 (8)	15.45	12.40

Souvenir Sheets

Perf. 14½

961	A157	$2 multicolored	6.50	6.50
962	A157	$2 multicolored	6.50	6.50

Boy Scouts — A160

No. 968, Member of Boy Scout Service Corps at New York World's Fair, 1964-65. No. 969, Lord Robert Baden-Powell, vert. $2, Silver Buffalo Award.

1992, July 6 **Litho.** ***Perf. 14***

968	A160	$1 multicolored	3.75	4.00
969	A160	$1 multicolored	3.75	4.00

Souvenir Sheet

970	A160	$2 multicolored	8.00	9.50

17th World Scout Jamboree, Korea.

Anniversaries and Events — A161

Designs: 25c, Astronaut releasing communications satellite. 50c, Tree with dead side, healthy side. 65c, Emblems, globe, food products. 80c, Fish in polluted, clean water. $1, Runners, Lions Intl. emblem. $1.25, Orbiting quarantine facility modules. No. 977, Planned orbital transfer vehicle for Mars. No. 977A, Industrial pollution, clean beach.

1992-93 **Litho.** ***Perf. 14***

971	A161	25c multicolored	2.50	.80
972	A161	50c multicolored	2.75	1.00
973	A161	65c multicolored	2.25	1.75
974	A161	80c multicolored	3.75	3.50
975	A161	$1 multicolored	3.75	3.50
976	A161	$1.25 multicolored	4.00	5.00
		Nos. 971-976 (6)	19.00	15.55

Souvenir Sheets

977	A161	$2 multicolored	8.50	9.00
977A	A161	$2 multicolored	8.50	9.00

Intl. Space Year (#971, 976-977). Earth Summit, Rio de Janeiro (#972, 974, 977A). Intl. Conf. on Nutrition, Rome (#973). Lions Intl., 75th anniv. (#975).

Issued: #972, 974, 977A, 1/93; others, 12/92.

Queen Elizabeth II's Accession to the Throne, 40th Anniv.

Common Design Type

1992, Feb. 6 **Litho.** ***Perf. 14***

978	CD348	10c multicolored	.80	.50
979	CD348	20c multicolored	1.25	.70
980	CD348	25c multicolored	1.40	.75
981	CD348	35c multicolored	1.50	.90
982	CD348	50c multicolored	2.00	1.25
983	CD348	65c multicolored	2.25	2.00
984	CD348	80c multicolored	2.50	2.50
985	CD348	$1.10 multicolored	2.75	2.75
		Nos. 978-985 (8)	14.45	11.35

Souvenir Sheets

986	CD348	$2 Queen at left, boat dock	6.50	6.50
987	CD348	$2 Queen at right, shoreline	6.50	6.50

Spanish Art — A162

Paintings: 8c, St. Monica, by Luis Tristan. 20c, 45c, The Vision of Ezekiel: The Resurrection of the Flesh (different details) by Francisco Collantes. 50c, The Martyrdom of St. Philip, by Jose de Ribera. 65c, St. John the Evangelist, by Juan Ribalta. 80c, Archimedes by Jose de Ribera. $1, St. John the Baptist in the Desert by de Ribera. $1.25, The Martyrdom of St. Philip (detail), by de Ribera. No. 996, The Baptism of Christ by Juan Fernandez Navarrete. No. 997, Battle between Christians and Moors at El Sotillo, by Francisco de Zurbaran.

1992, May 26 Litho. *Perf. 13*

988	A162	8c multicolored	.80	.25
989	A162	20c multicolored	1.25	.30
990	A162	45c multicolored	1.75	.65
991	A162	50c multicolored	1.75	.65
992	A162	65c multicolored	2.25	1.25
993	A162	80c multicolored	2.50	2.50
994	A162	$1 multicolored	2.50	2.75
995	A162	$1.25 multicolored	2.75	3.25
		Nos. 988-995 (8)	15.55	11.60

Size: 95x120mm

Imperf

996	A162	$2 multicolored	7.25	7.25
997	A162	$2 multicolored	7.25	7.25

Granada '92.

Discovery of America, 500th Anniv. — A163

Commemorative coins, scenes of first voyage: 10c, Nina, ship. 15c, Pinta, ship. 20c, Santa Maria, Columbus' second coat of arms. 25c, Fleet at sea, ships. 30c, Landfall, sailing ship. 35c, Setting sail, Columbus departing. 50c, Columbus sighting New World, Columbus. 65c, Columbus exploring Caribbean, ship. 80c, Claiming land for Spain, Columbus, priest and cross. $1.10, Columbus exchanging gifts with native, Columbus, native.

No. 1008, Coins like #998-1000. No. 1009, Coins like #1004, 1006-1007.

1992, Oct. Litho. *Perf. 14*

998	A163	10c multicolored	1.00	.65
999	A164	15c multicolored	1.10	.65
1000	A164	20c multicolored	1.10	.80
1001	A164	25c multicolored	1.75	.80
1002	A164	30c multicolored	1.75	.80
1003	A164	35c multicolored	1.75	.85
1004	A164	50c multicolored	2.00	1.25
1005	A164	65c multicolored	2.25	1.50
1006	A164	80c multicolored	2.25	2.50
1007	A164	$1.10 multicolored	2.50	3.50
		Nos. 998-1007 (10)	17.45	13.30

Souvenir Sheets

1008	A164	$2 multicolored	7.25	7.25
1009	A164	$2 multicolored	7.25	7.25

Christmas — A164

Details or entire paintings by Simon Bening: 8c, Nativity. 15c, Circumcision. 35c, Flight to Egypt. 50c, Massacre of the Innocents.

By Dirk Bouts: 65c, The Annunciation. 80c, The Visitation. $1.10, The Adoration of the Angels. $1.25, The Adoration of the Wise Men. No. 1018, The Virgin and Child. No. 1019, The Virgin Seated with the Child.

1992, Nov. Litho. *Perf. 13½x14*

1010	A164	8c multicolored	.35	.35
1011	A164	15c multicolored	.70	.70
1012	A164	35c multicolored	1.05	1.05
1013	A164	50c multicolored	1.35	1.35
1014	A164	65c multicolored	1.75	1.75
1015	A164	80c multicolored	2.10	2.10
1016	A164	$1.10 multicolored	2.10	2.10
1017	A164	$1.25 multicolored	2.10	2.10
		Nos. 1010-1017 (8)	11.50	11.50

Souvenir Sheets

1018	A164	$2 multicolored	5.75	5.75
1019	A164	$2 multicolored	5.75	5.75

Nos. 915, 918 & 921 Ovptd. in Red or Black

1993, Mar. 20 Litho. *Perf. 14*

1020	CD347	35c on #915	3.00	1.50
1021	CD347	65c on #918	4.50	2.50

Souvenir Sheet

1022	CD347	$2 on #921 (Bk)	8.50	8.50

Miniature Sheet

Coronation of Queen Elizabeth II, 40th Anniv. — A165

Designs: a, 15c, Chalice and paten from royal collection. b, 50c, Official coronation photograph. c, $1, Coronation ceremony. d, $1.25, Queen, Prince Philip.

$2, New Portrait.

1993, June 2 Litho. *Perf. 13½x14*

1023	A165	Sheet, 2 ea #a.-d.	13.50	14.50

Souvenir Sheet

Perf. 14

1024	A165	$2 multicolored	8.00	8.25

No. 1024 contains one 28x42mm stamp.

Christmas — A166

Details or entire woodcut, Mary, Queen of the Angels, by Durer: 8c, 20c, 35c, $1.25.

Details or entire paintings by Raphael: 50c, $1, Virgin and Child with St. John the Baptist. 65c, The Canagiani Holy Family. 80c, The Holy Family with the Lamb.

Each $2: No. 1033, Mary, Queen of the Angels, by Durer. No. 1034, The Canagiani Holy Family, diff., by Raphael.

Perf. 13½x14, 14x13½

1993, Dec. Litho.

1025-1032	A166	Set of 8	16.00	16.00

Souvenir Sheets

1033-1034	A166	Set of 2	11.00	12.00

Dinosaurs A167

8c, Omphalosaurus. 15c, Coelophysis. 20c, $2 (#1043), Triceratops. 35c, $2 (#1044), Dilophosaurus. 50c, Pterodactylus. 65c, Elasmosaurus. 80c, Stegosaurus. $1.25, Euoplocephalus.

1993, Nov. 15 Litho. *Perf. 14*

1035-1042	A167	Set of 8	8.50	8.50

Souvenir Sheets

1043-1044	A167	Set of 2	13.00	13.00

Birds — A168

Designs: 10c, Killdeer. 15c, Yellow-crowned night heron, vert. 35c, Northern mockingbird. 50c, Eastern kingbird, vert. 65c, Magnolia warbler. 80c, Cedar waxwing, vert. $1.10, Ruby-throated hummingbird. $1.25, Painted bunting, vert. No. 1053, American kestrel. No. 1054, Ruddy duck.

1993, Dec.

1045	A168	10c multicolored	1.40	.80
1046	A168	15c multicolored	1.75	.80
1047	A168	35c multicolored	2.50	.80
1048	A168	50c multicolored	2.75	1.10
1049	A168	65c multicolored	3.00	1.75
1050	A168	80c multicolored	3.25	3.25
1051	A168	$1.10 multicolored	3.50	3.50
1052	A168	$1.25 multicolored	3.50	*4.50*
		Nos. 1045-1052 (8)	21.65	16.50

Souvenir Sheets

1053	A168	$2 multicolored	7.50	7.50
1054	A168	$2 multicolored	7.50	7.50

Fish — A169

Designs: 10c, Bluehead wrasse. 20c, Honeycomb cowfish. 25c, Glasseye snapper. 35c, Spotted drum. 50c, Jolthead porgy. 65, Smallmouth grunt. 80c, Peppermint bass. $1.10, Indigo hamlet.

Each $2: No. 1063, Bonnethead shark. No. 1064, Sharpnose shark.

1993, Dec. 15

1055-1062	A169	Set of 8	8.50	8.50

Souvenir Sheets

1063-1064	A169	Set of 2	8.75	9.75

1994 World Cup Soccer Championships, US — A170

Designs: 8c, Segrio Goycochea, Argentina. 10c, Bodo Illgner, Germany. 50c, Nico Claesen, Belgium. 65c, West German team. 80c, Cameroun team. $1, Santin, Francescoli, Uruguay; Cuciuffo, Argentina. $1.10, Sanchez, Mexico.

Each $2: No. 1072, Imre Garaba, Hungary, vert. No. 1073, Pontiac Silverdome.

1994, Sept. 26 Litho. *Perf. 14*

1065-1071	A170	Set of 7	11.50	10.00

Souvenir Sheets

1072-1073	A170	Set of 2	8.00	8.50

Mushrooms A171

Designs: 5c, Xerocomus guadelupae, vert. 10c, Volvariella volvacea, vert. 35c, Hygrocybe atrosquamosa. 50c, Pleurotus ostreatus. 65c, Marasmius pallescens. 80c, Coprinus plicatilis, vert. $1.10, Bolbitius vitellinus. $1.50, Pyroglossum lilaceipes, vert.

Each $2: No. 1082, Lentinus edodes. No. 1083, Russula cremeolilacina, vert.

1994, Oct. 10

1074-1081	A171	Set of 8	10.50	10.50

Souvenir Sheets

1082-1083	A171	Set of 2	10.00	10.00

Christmas — A172

Illustrations from French Book of Hours: 25c, The Annunciation. 50c, The Visitation. 65c, Annunciation to the Shepherds. 80c, The Nativity. $1, Flight into Egypt.

$2, The Adoration of the Magi.

1994, Dec. 5 Litho. *Perf. 14*

1084-1088	A172	Set of 5	11.50	8.75

Souvenir Sheet

1089	A172	$2 multicolored	7.00	7.00

Butterflies A173

Designs: 15c, Dryas julia. 20c, Urbanus proteus. 25c, Colobura dirce. 50c, Papilio homerus. 65c, Chiodes catillus. 80c, Eurytides zonaria. $1, Hypolymnas misippus. $1.25, Phoebis avellaneda.

Each $2: No. 1098, Eurema adamsi. No. 1099, Morpho peleides.

1994, Dec. 12

1090-1097	A173	Set of 8	11.50	11.50

Souvenir Sheets

1098-1099	A173	Set of 2	8.25	8.75

D-Day, 50th Anniv. — A174

Designs: 10c, Gen. Montgomery, British landing on Juno Beach. 15c, Adm. Sir Bertram Ramsay, British commandos at Sword Beach. 35c, Gun crew aboard HMS Belfast. 50c, Montgomery, Eisenhower, Tedder review battle scene. 65c, Gen. Eisenhower, 101st Airborne Div. paratroopers. 80c, Gen. Omar Bradley, US landings on Omaha Beach. $1.10, Second wave of US troops on D-Day. $1.25, Supreme Commander Eisenhower presents Operation Overload.

Each $2: No. 1108, Eisenhower, Montgomery seated at table. No. 1109, Beachhead secured.

1994, Dec. 19

1100-1107	A174	Set of 8	10.00	10.00

Souvenir Sheets

1108-1109	A174	Set of 2	8.50	8.50

Orchids — A175

Designs: 8c, Cattleya deckeri. 20c, Epidendrum carpophorum. 25c, Epidendrum ciliare. 50c, Encyclia phoenicea. 65c, Bletia patula. 80c, Brassia caudata. $1, Brassavola nodosa. $1.25, Bletia purpurea.

Each $2: No. 1118, Ionopsis utricularioides. No. 1119, Vanilla planifolia.

1995, Jan. 5

1110-1117	A175	Set of 8	10.00	9.50

Souvenir Sheets

1118-1119	A175	Set of 2	9.50	9.50

Miniature Sheet of 12

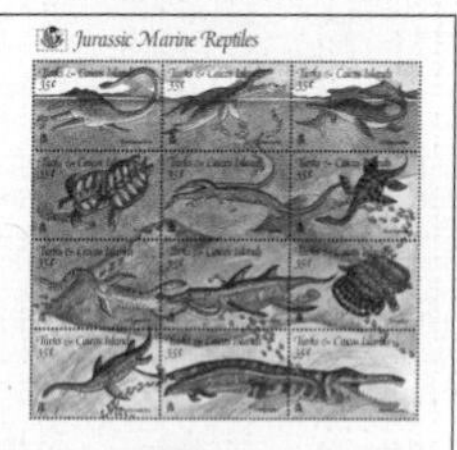

PHILAKOREA '94 — A176

Jurassic marine reptiles: a, Elasmosaurus. b, Plesiosaurus. c, Ichthyosaurus. d, Arcfielon. e, Askeptosaurus. f, Macroplata. g, Ceresiosaurus. h, Lipoleurodon. i, Henodus. j, Muraenosaurus. k, Placodus. l, Kronosaurus.

1995, Jan. 23

1120	A176	35c #1120a-1120 l	9.50	9.50

First Manned Moon Landing, 25th Anniv. — A177

Designs: 10c, Apollo XI in flight. 20c, Simulated moon landing. 25c, Painting, Astronauts on the Moon, by Kovales. 35c, First foot, footprint on moon. 50c, Aldrin, solar wind experiment. 65c, Armstrong, Aldrin setting up flag on moon. 80c, Command module Columbia in Lunar orbit. $1.10, Recovery of Apollo XI in Pacific.

Each $2: No. 1129, Lift-off at Cape Canaveral, vert. No. 1130, Moon rock on display in Houston.

1995, Jan. 9 Litho. *Perf. 14*

1121-1128 A177 Set of 8 9.00 9.00

Souvenir Sheets

1129-1130 A177 Set of 2 9.00 9.00

Intl. Olympic Committee, Cent. — A178

Summer, Winter Olympic events: 8c, Fencing. 10c, Speed skating. 15c, Diving. 20c, Cycling. 25c, Ice hockey. 35c, Figure skating. 50c, Soccer. 65c, Bobsled. 80c, Super giant slalom. $1.25, Equestrian.

Each $2: #1141, Gymnastics. #1142, Downhill skiing.

1995, Feb. 6

1131-1140 A178 Set of 10 15.00 11.00

Souvenir Sheets

1141-1142 A178 Set of 2 9.50 9.50

Domestic Cats — A179

Various cats, kittens: 15c, 20c, 35c, 50c, 65c, 80c, $1, $1.25.

Each $2: No. 1151, Two sleeping. No. 1152, Kitten, ladybugs in flowers.

1995, July 3 Litho. *Perf. 14*

1143-1150 A179 Set of 8 15.00 11.00

Souvenir Sheets

1151-1152 A179 Set of 2 10.00 10.00

Birds — A180

A180a

10c, Belted kingfisher. 15c, Clapper rail. 20c, American redstart. 25c, Roseate tern. 35c, Purple gallinule. 45c, Ruddy turnstone. 50c, Barn owl. 60c, Brown booby. 80c, Great blue heron. $1, Antillean nighthawk. $1.25, Thick-billed vireo. $1.40, American flamingo. $2, Wilson's plover. $5, Blue-winged teal. $10, Reddish egret.

1995, Aug. 2 Litho. *Perf. 13*

1153	A180	10c multi	1.50	1.00
1154	A180	15c multi	1.50	1.00
1155	A180	20c multi	1.50	1.00
1156	A180	25c multi	1.75	1.00
1157	A180	35c multi	1.75	1.00
1158	A180	45c multi	2.25	1.25
1159	A180	50c multi	3.75	2.25
1160	A180	60c multi	2.50	1.50
1161	A180	80c multi	3.00	1.50
1162	A180	$1 multi	3.75	2.50
1163	A180	$1.25 multi	4.25	2.75
1164	A180	$1.40 multi	4.75	4.00
1165	A180	$2 multi	5.25	6.75
1166	A180	$5 multi	8.00	12.00
1166A	A180a	$10 multi	14.00	20.00
		Nos. 1153-1166A (15)	59.50	59.50

Queen Mother, 95th Birthday A181

No. 1167: a, Drawing. b, Wearing crown jewels. c, Formal portrait. d, Blue dress with pearls.

$2, Green blue outfit.

1995, Aug. 4 *Perf. 13½x14*

1167 A181 50c Block or strip of 4, #a.-d. 7.00 7.00

Souvenir Sheet

1168 A181 $2 multicolored 7.00 7.00

No. 1167 was issued in sheets of 8 stamps.

VE Day, 50th Anniv. — A182

Designs: 10c, "Big Three" meet at Yalta. 15c, Allied war prisoners released. 20c, American, Soviets meet at Elbe River. 25c, Death of Franklin D. Roosevelt. 60c, US 9th Army confirms cease fire. 80c, New York City celebrates VE Day. $1, Nuremberg War Crimes trials begin.

$2, Big Ben, US Capitol, St. Basil's Cathedral.

1995, Aug. 14 Litho. *Perf. 14*

1169-1175 A182 Set of 7 9.50 9.50

Souvenir Sheet

1176 A182 $2 multicolored *8.00 8.00*

Miniature Sheet of 9

Singapore '95 — A183

Diving equipment, each 60c: No. 1177a, Wm. James, scuba, 1825. b, Rouquayrol apparatus, 1864. c, Fluess oxygen rebreathing apparatus, 1878. d, Armored diving suit, 1900. e, Jim Janett explores sunken Lusitania in Peress armored diving suit, 1935. f, Cousteau-Gagnan aqualung, 1943. g, Underwater camera, 1955. h, Sylvia Earle dives to 1,520 ft. in Jim suit, 1979. i, Spider propeller-driven rigid suit, 1984.

Each $2: No. 1178, Helmet diver, 1935. No. 1179, Jacques-Yves Cousteau.

1995, Sept. 1 *Perf. 14½*

1177 A183 Sheet of 9, #a.-i. 13.00 13.00

Souvenir Sheets

1178-1179 A183 Set of 2 8.50 8.50

Christmas — A184

Details or entire paintings, by Piero di Cosimo (1462-1521): 20c, Madonna and Child with Young St. John. 25c, Adoration of the Child. 60c, Madonna and Child with Young St. John, St. Margaret, and An Angel. $1, Madonna and Child with An Angel.

$2, Madonna and Child with Angels and Saints.

1995, Dec. 29 Litho. *Perf. 14*

1180-1183 A184 Set of 4 7.00 6.25

Souvenir Sheet

1184 A184 $2 multicolored 9.00 10.00

UN, 50th Anniv. A185

Designs: 15c, Rights of women and children. 60c, Peace. 80c, Human rights. $1, Education.

Each $2: No. 1189, Flags of nations forming "50." No. 1190, Tractor, portions of UN, FAO emblems.

1996, Feb. 26 Litho. *Perf. 14*

1185-1188 A185 Set of 4 5.50 5.50

Souvenir Sheets

1189-1190 A185 Set of 2 8.75 10.00

Queen Elizabeth II, 70th Birthday — A186

No. 1191: a, Portrait. b, Wearing blue hat. c, In uniform, on horseback.

$2, As younger woman wearing white and yellow hat.

1996, Apr. 21 Litho. *Perf. 13½x14*

1191 A186 80c Strip of 3, #a.-c. 4.75 4.75

Souvenir Sheet

1192 A186 $2 multicolored 4.25 4.75

No. 1191 was issued in sheets of 9 stamps.

History of Underwater Exploration A187

No. 1193, each 55c: a, Glaucus, God of Divers, 2500BC. b, Alexander the Great decends to ocean bottom, 332BC. c, Salvage diver, 1430. d, Borelli's rebreathing device, 1680. e, Edmond Halley's diving bell, 1690. f, John Lethbridge's diving machine, 1715. g, Klingert's diving apparatus, 1789. h, Drieberg's triton, 1808. i, Seibe's diving helmet, 1819.

No. 1194, each 60c: a, Jim Jarrat in "Iron Man" armored diving suit explores Lusitania, 1935. b, Cousteau, team excavate first shipwreck using scuba gear, 1952. c, Oldest shipwreck ever found, coast of Turkey, 1959. d, Swedish warship Vasa raised, 1961. e, Mel Fisher discovers Spanish galleon Atocha, 1971. f, Whydah, first pirate ship found, is discovered by Barry Clifford, 1984. g, Dr. Robert Ballard, using robot sub Argo finds battleship Bismarck, 1989. h, Radeau "Land Tortoise" scuttled in 1758 during French and Indian War found in Lake George, NY, 1991. i, Deep-diving nuclear submarine recovers ancient Roman shipwreck cargo, 1994.

Each $2: No. 1195, Arab diver Issa, 12th cent. No. 1196, Pearl diver in Caribbean, 1498. No. 1197, Diver in Newtsuit investigates Edmund Fitzgerald. No. 1198, Submarine Alvin explores Titanic, 1985.

1996, May 13 Litho. *Perf. 14*

1193 A187 Sheet of 9, #a.-i. 15.00 15.00

1194 A187 Sheet of 9, #a.-i. 11.00 11.00

Souvenir Sheets

1195-1198 A187 Set of 4 17.75 17.75

CHINA '96 (Nos. 1193, 1195-1196). CAPEX '96 (Nos. 1194, 1197-1198).

1996 Summer Olympics, Atlanta — A188

Olympic gold medals for: No. 1199, Equestrian. No. 1200, Cycling. No. 1201, Fencing. No. 1202, Gymnastics. No. 1203, Hurdles. No. 1204, Pole vault. No. 1205, Sprints. No. 1206, Swimming. No. 1207, Diving. No. 1208, Running.

1996, May 27 *Perf. 13½*

1199-1208 A188 55c Set of 10 10.00 11.00

1208a Sheet of 10, #1199-1208 10.00

Nos. 1199-1208 issued in sheets as well as in No. 1208a.

A189

James A.G.S. McCartney (1945-80), 1st Chief Minister of Turks & Caicos Islands.

1996, July 8 Litho. *Perf. 14*

1209 A189 60c multicolored 1.00 1.00

Ministerial Government, 20th anniv.

No. 1209 was issued in sheets of 9.

A190

Working Dogs: No. 1210: a, Space research. b, Racing. c, Rescue. d, Military. e, Sporting. f, Companion. g, Hearing ear. h, Sled. i, Police. j, Guarding. k, Watch. l, Security.

Each $2: No. 1211, Guide. No. 1212, Sheep dog.

1996, Sept. 8 Litho. *Perf. 14*

1210 A190 25c Sheet of 12, #a.-l. 11.00 11.00

Souvenir Sheets

1211-1212 A190 Set of 2 11.00 11.00

Winnie the Pooh, Christmas — A191

Designs: 15c, Pooh trying to stay awake. 20c, Piglet, star. 35c, Ribbons and bows. 50c, Jingle bells. 60c, "Pooh loves Christmas." 80c, "Big hearts come in bouncy packages." $1, Santa Pooh. $1.25, "My most favorite."

No. 1221, Piglet, cookie. No. 1222, Piglet placing star atop tree.

1996, Nov. 25 Litho. *Perf. 13½x14*

1213-1220 A191 Set of 8 13.00 10.50

Souvenir Sheets

1221 A191 $2 multicolored 6.50 6.50

1222 A191 $2.60 multicolored 6.50 6.50

Flowers — A192

No. 1223: a, Giant milkweed. b, Geiger tree. c, Passion flower. d, Hibiscus.
No. 1224: a, Yellow elder. b, Prickly poppy. c, Frangipani. d, Seaside mahoe.
Each $2: No. 1225, Chain of love. No. 1226, Firecracker.

1997, Feb. 10 Litho. *Perf. 14*

1223 A192 20c Strip or block of 4, #a.-d. 3.25 3.25
1224 A192 60c Strip or block of 4, #a.-d. 3.50 3.50

Souvenir Sheets

1225-1226 A192 Set of 2 8.00 8.00

Nos. 1223-1224 were each issued in sheets of 8 stamps.

UNICEF, 50th Anniv. — A193

a, Dove flying right. b, Three children. c, Dove flying left. d, Boy with dog, girl holding cat.

1997, Mar. 24 Litho. *Perf. 14*

1227 A193 60c Sheet of 4, #a.-d. 7.25 8.00

Souvenir Sheets

UNESCO, 50th Anniv. — A194

Canterbury Cathedral: No. 1228, View from rear. No. 1229, Interior view.

1997, Mar. 24 Litho. *Perf. 14*

1228 A194 $2 multicolored 4.25 4.25
1229 A194 $2 multicolored 4.25 4.25

Queen Elizabeth II, Prince Philip, 50th Wedding Anniv. — A195

Designs: a, Queen waving. b, Royal arms. c, Queen, Prince riding in car. d, Prince, Queen seated. e, Windsor Castle. f, Prince Philip.
$2, Wedding portrait.

1997, Apr. 21 Litho. *Perf. 14*

1230 A195 60c Sheet of 6, #a.-f. 11.00 10.00

Souvenir Sheet

1231 A195 $2 multicolored 7.50 7.50

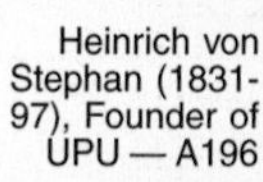

Heinrich von Stephan (1831-97), Founder of UPU — A196

Portrait of Von Stephan and: No. 1232: a, British mail coach, 1700's. b, UPU emblem. c, Space shuttle, future transport.
$2, Von Stephan, Hemerodrome, messenger of ancient Greece.

1997, July 1 Litho. *Perf. 14*

1232 A196 50c Sheet of 3, #a.-c. 5.00 5.00

Souvenir Sheet

1233 A196 $2 multicolored 5.00 5.00

PACIFIC 97.

Underwater Exploration A197

No. 1234: a, Edgerton camera taking photos at 6,000 ft., 1954. b, Conshelf Habitat, 1963. c, Sealab II, 1965. d, Research Habitat, Tektite, 1970. e, Discovery of Galapagos Volcanic Rift, 1974. f, Epaulard, robot survey craft, 1979. g, Sea life discovered thriving in undersea oil field, 1995. h, Deep flight, 1996, one-man research vessel. i, Sea ice is studied from above, under sea, Okhotsk Tower, off Japan, 1996.
Each $2: No. 1235, Coelacanth. No. 1236, John Williamson makes first underwater movies, 1914.

1997, Aug. 21 Litho. *Perf. 14*

1234 A197 20c Sheet of 9, #a.-i. 7.50 7.50

Souvenir Sheets

1235-1236 A197 Set of 2 8.50 9.00

Stampshow 97.

Christmas — A198

Entire paintings or details: 15c, Adoration of an Angel, by Studio of Fra Angelico. 20c, Scenes from the Life of St. John the Baptist, by Master of Saint Severin. 35c, Archangel Gabriel, by Masolino de Panicale. 50c, 60c, Jeremiah with Two Angels, by Gherardo Starnina (diff. angels). 80c, The Annunciation, by Giovanni di Palo di Grazia. $1, The Annunciation, by Carlo di Bracceso. $1.25, The Nativity, by Benvenuto di Giovanni Guasta.
Each $2: No. 1245, The Wilton Diptych (right panel), by unknown English or French artist, c. 1395. No. 1246, Adoring Angels, from The Journey of the Magi, by Benozzo Gozzoli.

1997, Dec. 8 Litho. *Perf. 14*

1237-1244 A198 Set of 8 10.00 10.00

Souvenir Sheets

1245-1246 A198 Set of 2 9.00 9.00

World Wildlife Fund A199

Snapper: a, Blackfin. b, Dog. c, Cubera. d, Mahogany.

1998, Feb. 24 Litho. *Perf. 14*

1247 A199 25c Block of 4, #a.-d. 3.00 3.00

No. 1247 was issued in sheets of 16 stamps.
Intl. Year of the Reef.

Marine Life — A200

Underwater photographs: 20c, Spotted flamingo tongue. 50c, Feather duster. 60c, Squirrel fish. 80c, Queen angelfish. $1, Barracuda. $1.25, Fairy basslet.
Each $2: No. 1254, Rough file clam. No. 1255, Spotted cleaning shrimp.

1998, May 1 Litho. *Perf. 14*

1248-1253 A200 Set of 6 11.00 11.00

Souvenir Sheets

1254-1255 A200 Set of 2 8.75 8.75

A201

Stylized designs showing symbol for earth, water, and — No. 1256: a, Dove. b, Crab. c, Fish. d, Clover leaf.
$2, Symbol for earth and water.

1998, July 30 Litho. *Perf. 14*

1256 A201 50c Sheet of 4, #a.-d. 6.00 6.00

Souvenir Sheet

1257 A201 $2 multicolored 5.50 5.50

Intl. Year of the Ocean.

Royal Air Force, 80th Anniv.

Common Design Type Re-Inscribed

Designs: 20c, SE 5A. 50c, Sopwith Camel. 60c, Supermarine Spitfire. 80c, Avro Lancaster. $1, Panavia Tornado. $1.25, Hawker Hurricane.
Each $2: No. 1264, Hawker Siddeley Harrier. No. 1265, Avro Vulcan.

1998, Aug. 18 Litho. *Perf. 14*

1258-1263 CD350 Set of 6 14.00 14.00

Souvenir Sheets

1264-1265 CD350 Set of 2 13.50 13.50

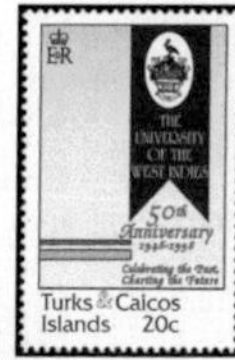

A202

Anniversaries and Events: 20c, University of the West Indies, 50th anniv. 60c, UNESCO, World Summit Program. 80c, Universal Declaration of Human Rights. $1, John Glenn's return to space.
$2, NASA Space Shuttle leaving launching pad.

1998, July 30 Litho. *Perf. 14*

1266-1269 A202 Set of 4 5.50 5.50

Souvenir Sheet

1270 A202 $2 multicolored 4.75 4.75

A203

1998, Aug. 31

1271 A203 60c multicolored 2.00 1.75

Diana, Princess of Wales (1961-97). No. 1271 was issued in sheets of 6.

Paintings by Sister Thomasita Fessler — A204

a, Magi's Visit. b, Flight Into Egypt. c, Wedding Feast. d, Maria. e, Annunciation & Visitation. f, Nativity.
$2, Queen of Mothers.

1998, Nov. 30 Litho. *Perf. 14*

1272 A204 50c Sheet of 6, #a.-f. 8.00 8.00

Souvenir Sheet

1273 A204 $2 multicolored 4.75 4.75

Christmas. Nos. 1272e-1272f are each 58x48mm.

Coral Gardens — A205

No. 1274: a, Flamingos in flight. b, Sailboats. c, Seagulls, lighthouse. d, House along shore, seagulls. e, Pillar coral, yellowtail snapper (f). f, Eliptical star coral. g, Porkfish. h, Spotted eagle ray. i, Large ivory coral. j, Mustard hill coral, shy hamlet. k, Blue crust coral. l. Fused staghorn coral. m, Queen angelfish, massive starlet coral. n, Pinnate spiny sea fan. o, Knobby star coral, squirrelfish. p, Lowridge cactus coral, juvenile porkfish. q, Orange telesto coral. r, Spanish hogfish (q), Knobby ten-ray star coral. s, Boulder brain coral, clown wrasse. t, Rainbow parrotfish, regal sea fan. u, Great star coral, bluestriped grunt. v, Stinging coral, blue tang. w, Lavender thin finger coral. x, Juvenile french grunt (w), brilliant sea fingers.
Each $2: No. 1275, Sea fan. No. 1276, Elkhorn coral.

1999, June 7 Litho. *Perf. 14¼x14½*

1274 A205 20c Sheet of 24, #a.-x. 21.00 21.00

Souvenir Sheets

1275-1276 A205 Set of 2 18.00 18.00

Wedding of Prince Edward and Sophie Rhys-Jones — A206

Portraits — #1277: a, Couple facing forward. b, Edward. c, Sophie. d, Couple walking arm in arm.
Each $2: No. 1278, Couple facing forward. No. 1279, Couple facing each other.

1999, June 19 Litho. *Perf. 14*

1277 A206 60c Sheet of 4, #a.-d. 6.00 6.00

Souvenir Sheets

1278-1279 A206 Set of 2 10.00 10.00

Queen Mother (b. 1900) — A207

Designs: a, At age 7. b, At age 19. c, At wedding. d, With daughters. e, With King George VI during World War II. f, In 1958. g, At age 60. h, In 1970. i, With Princes Charles and William, 1983. j, Current photograph.

1999, Aug. 4 Litho. *Perf. 13½x13¾*

1280 A207 50c Sheet of 10, #a.-j. 15.00 15.00

Stamp inscription on No. 1280f is incorrect.
No. 1280 was reissued in 2002 with added inscription in margin, "Good Health and Happiness to her Majesty The Queen Mother on her 101st Birthday." Value, $19.

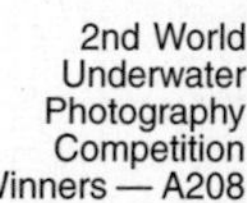

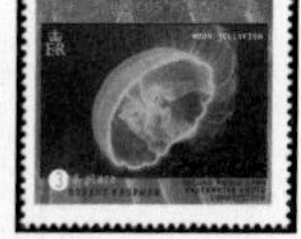

2nd World Underwater Photography Competition Winners — A208

No. 1281: a, 10c, Painted tunicates (8th place). b, 20c, Peacock flounder (7th). c, 50c,

Squirt anemone shrimps (6th). d, 60c, Juvenile drum (5th). e, 80c, Batwing coral crab (4th). f, $1, Moon jellyfish (3rd).
Each $2: No. 1282, Christmas tree worms (2nd). No. 1283, Longhorn nudibranch (1st).

1999, Oct. 11 Litho. *Perf. 14¼x13¾*
1281 A208 Sheet of 6, #a.-f. 9.75 10.00
g. As No. 1281, with corrected pictures 9.75 10.00

Issued: No. 1281g, 11/6/00.
On No. 1281, the illustrations for the 10c and 20c stamps are incorrect, with the 10c stamp inscribed "Painted tunicates," but depicting a peacock flounder, and the 20c stamp inscribed "Peacock flounder," but depicting painted tunicates. The pictures were switched on No. 1281g, making the inscriptions match the pictures.

Souvenir Sheets
Perf. 13¾
1282-1283 A208 Set of 2 14.00 14.00

Nos. 1282-1283 each contain one 50x38mm stamp.

Christmas — A209

Paintings by Anthony Van Dyck: 20c, The Mystic Marriage of Saint Catherine. 50c, Rest on the Flight into Egypt. No. 1286, $2, Holy Family with Saints John and Elizabeth.
No. 1287, The Madonna of the Rosary.

1999, Dec. 7 *Perf. 13¾*
1284-1286 A209 Set of 3 8.00 8.00
Souvenir Sheet
1287 A209 $2 multicolored 7.50 7.50

Millennium — A210

Perf. 14½x14¼
1999, Nov. 15 Litho.
1288 A210 20c silver & multi .80 .80
1289 A210 $1 gold & multi 3.75 3.75

Millennium — A211

Globe, clock and: No. 1290: a, London. b, Turks & Caicos Islands. c, New York. d, Rome. e, Jerusalem. f, Paris.
Each $2: No. 1291, Flag of Islands. No. 1292, Arms of Islands.

2000, Jan. 18 Litho. *Perf. 14x13¾*
1290 A211 50c Sheet of 6, #a.-f. 12.00 12.00
Souvenir Sheets
1291-1292 A211 Set of 2 17.00 17.00

Mushrooms — A212

No. 1293, vert.: a, Pholiota squarroides. b, Psilocybe squamosa. c, Spathularia velutipes. d, Russula. e, Clitocybe clavipes. f, Boletus frostii.
No. 1294, Strobilurus conigenoides. No. 1295, Stereum ostrea.

2000, July 6 Litho. *Perf. 14*
1293 A212 50c Sheet of 6, #a-f 9.00 9.00
Souvenir Sheets
1294-1295 A212 $2 Set of 2 11.00 11.00

Souvenir Sheet

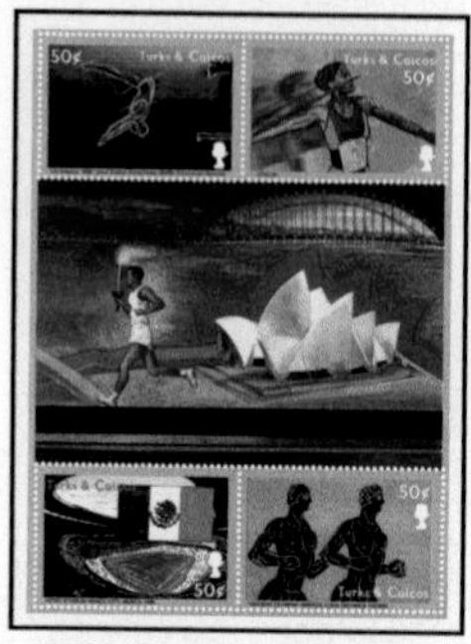
2000 Summer Olympics, Sydney — A213

No. 1296: a, Johan Gabriel Oxenstierna. b, Javelin. c, Aztec Stadium, Mexico City and Mexican flag. d, Ancient Greek runners.

2000, Sept. 25
1296 A213 50c Sheet of 4, #a-d 7.00 7.00

Birds — A214

Designs: No. 1297, Chickadee. No. 1298, Scrub turkey. No. 1299, Sickle-bill gull.
No. 1300: a, Egret. b, Tern. c, Osprey. d, Great blue heron. e, Pelican. f, Bahama pintail.
No. 1301, Flamingo, vert. No. 1302, Macaw, vert.

2000, Oct. 2
1297-1299 A214 50c Set of 3 5.25 5.25
1300 A214 60c Sheet of 6, #a-f 11.00 11.00
Souvenir Sheets
1301-1302 A214 $2 Set of 2 12.50 12.50

Dogs and Cats A215

No. 1303, 60c: a, Airedale terrier. b, Beagle. c, Dalmatian. d, Chow chow. e, Chihuahua. f, Pug.
No. 1304, 80c: a, Egyptian mau. b, Manx. c, Burmese. d, Korat. e, Maine coon cat. f, American shorthair.
No. 1305, $2, Collie. No. 1306, $2, Devon rex.

2000, Nov. 13 Litho. *Perf. 14*
Sheets of 6, #a-f
1303-1304 A215 Set of 2 22.00 22.00
Souvenir Sheets
1305-1306 A215 Set of 2 11.00 12.00

Battle of Britain, 60th Anniv. — A216

Designs: No. 1307, 50c, Douglas Robert Stewart Bader. No. 1308, 50c, Alan Christopher "Al" Deere. No. 1309, 50c, James Edgar "Johnny" Johnson. No. 1310, 50c, Edgar James "Cobber" Kain. No. 1311, 50c, James Harry "Ginger" Lacey. No. 1312, 50c, Air Vice-marshal Trafford Leigh Mallory. No. 1313, 50c, Adolph Gysbert "Sailor" Malan. No. 1314, Air Vice-marshal Keith Park.

No. 1315, each 50c: a, Winston Churchill. b, Barrage balloon. c, Heinkel He-111 Casa 2 111E. d, Soldier's farewell kiss to son. e, Hawker Hurricane. f, Dr, Jocelyn Henry Temple Perkins, clergyman in Home Guard. g, RAF fighter pilots scramble after an alert. h, Civilian volunteers scan the skies.
No. 1316, $2, Churchill, British flag. No. 1317, $2, London children.

2000, Dec. 4 *Perf. 14*
Stamps + labels
1307-1314 A216 Set of 8 12.00 12.00
1315 A216 Sheet of 8, #a-h 12.00 12.00
Souvenir Sheets
1316-1317 A216 Set of 2 10.00 10.00

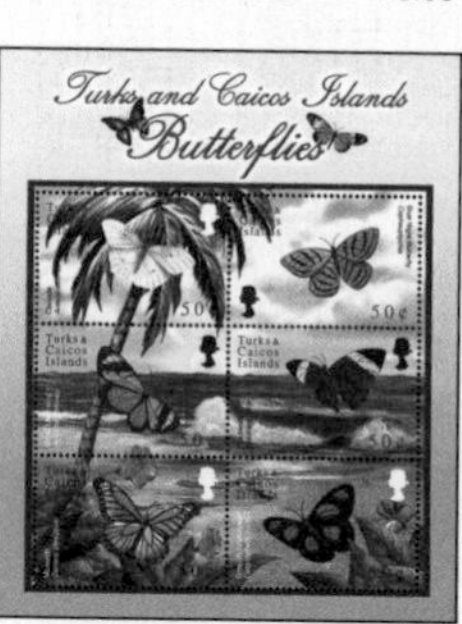
Butterflies — A217

No. 1318, 50c: a, Clorinde. b, Blue night. c, Small lace-wing. d, Mosaic. e, Monarch. f, Grecian shoemaker.
No. 1319, 50c: a, Giant swallowtail. b, Common morpho. c, Tiger pierid. d, Banded king shoemaker. e, Figure-of-eight. f, Polydamas swallowtail.
No. 1320, $2, Orange-barred sulphur. No. 1321, $2, White peacock.

2000, Dec. 11 Litho.
Sheets of 6, #a-f
1318-1319 A217 Set of 2 21.00 21.00
Souvenir Sheets
1320-1321 A217 Set of 2 12.00 12.00

Ships — A218

Designs: No. 1322, 60c, Neptune. No. 1323, 60c, Eagle. No. 1324, 60c, Gloria. No. 1325, 60c, Clipper ship, vert.
No. 1326, 60c: a, Viking long ship. b, Henri Grace à Dieu. c, Golden Hind. d, Endeavor. e, Anglo-Norman. f, Libertad.
No. 1327, 60c: a, Northern European cog. b, Carrack. c, Mayflower. d, Queen Anne's Revenge. e, Holkar. f, Amerigo Vespucci.
No. 1328, $2, USS Constitution, vert. No. 1329, $2, Denmark, vert.

2001, May 15 Litho. *Perf. 14*
1322-1325 A218 Set of 4 8.75 8.75
Sheets of 6, #a-f
1326-1327 A218 Set of 2 24.00 24.00
Souvenir Sheets
1328-1329 A218 Set of 2 16.00 16.00

Whales — A219

Designs: No. 1330, 50c, Beluga. No. 1331, 50c, Killer. No. 1332, 50c, Dwarf sperm. No. 1333, 50c, Shortfin pilot.
No. 1334, 50c: a, Bowhead. b, Two killer. c, Pygmy sperm. d, Right. e, Sperm. f, California gray.
No. 1335, 50c: a, Narwhal. b, One killer (in air). c, Bryde's. d, Belugas. e, Sperm (and starfish). f, Pilot.
No. 1336, $2, Cuvier's beaked. No. 1337, $2, Humpback (with calf).

2001, May 15
1330-1333 A219 Set of 4 8.25 8.25
Sheets of 6, #a-f
1334-1335 A219 Set of 2 25.00 25.00
Souvenir Sheets
1336-1337 A219 Set of 2 14.00 14.00

UN Women's Human Rights Campaign — A220

Designs: 60c, Woman. 80c, Woman, bird, torch.

2001, June 18 Litho. *Perf. 14*
1338-1339 A220 Set of 2 6.00 6.00

Phila Nippon '01 — A221

Designs: No. 1340, 60c, Autumn Moon in Mirror, by Suzuki Harunobu. No. 1341, 60c, Rikaku II as a Fisherman, by Hirosada. No. 1342, 60c, Musical Party, by Hishikawa Moronobu. No. 1343, 60c, Kannon and Four Farmers, by H. Gatto. No. 1344, 60c, Rain in Fifth Month, by Kunisada I. No. 1345, 60c, The Lives of Women, by Kuniyoshi Utagawa.

2001, July 30 *Perf. 12x12¼*
1340-1345 A221 Set of 6 10.00 10.00

Queen Victoria (1819-1901) — A222

No. 1346, 60c, oval frames: a, Wearing white headcovering. b, Wearing crown as young woman. c, Wearing black hat. d, Wearing crown as old woman.
No. 1347, 60c, rectangular frames: a, Wearing white headcovering. b, Holding flowers. c, Wearing white dress. d, Wearing crown, white dress with blue sash.
No. 1348, $2, Brown orange background. No. 1349, $2, Holding umbrella.

2001, July 2 *Perf. 14*
Sheets of 4, #a-d
1346-1347 A222 Set of 2 16.00 16.00
Souvenir Sheets
1348-1349 A222 Set of 2 12.00 12.00

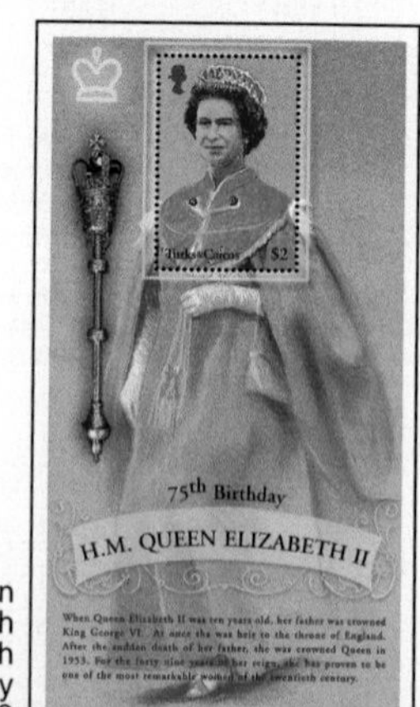
Queen Elizabeth II, 75th Birthday A223

No. 1350: a, In pink hat. b, With crown looking left. c, In green hat. d, With crown looking forward. e, In red orange hat. f, With crown and veil.
$2, Wearing robe.

2001, July 2

1350 A223 60c Sheet of 6, #a-f 12.00 12.00

Souvenir Sheet

1351 A223 $2 multi 6.50 6.50

Butterflies — A224

Designs: 10c, Cuban mimic. 15c, Gundlach's swallowtail, vert. 20c, Graphium androcles. 25c, Eastern black swallowtail. 35c, Papilio velvois, vert. 45c, Schaus swallowtail, vert. 50c, Pipevine swallowtail, vert. 60c, Euploea mniszecki, vert. 80c, Poey's black swallowtail, vert. $1, Graphium encelades, vert. $1.25, Jamaican ringlet. $1.40, Eastern tiger swallowtail. $2, Graphium milon, vert. $5, Palamedes swallowtail. $10, Zebra swallowtail.

Perf. 14x14¾, 14¾x14

2001, Sept. 27

1352	A224	10c multi	.40	.40
1353	A224	15c multi	.50	.50
1354	A224	20c multi	.75	.75
1355	A224	25c multi	2.25	.75
1356	A224	35c multi	2.25	.75
1357	A224	45c multi	1.00	.80
1358	A224	50c multi	1.00	.80
1359	A224	60c multi	1.25	1.00
1360	A224	80c multi	1.50	1.25
1361	A224	$1 multi	2.00	1.75
1362	A224	$1.25 multi	2.50	2.25
1363	A224	$1.40 multi	2.75	3.00
1364	A224	$2 multi	4.50	5.00
1365	A224	$5 multi	10.00	12.00
1366	A224	$10 multi	18.00	20.00
		Nos. 1352-1366 (15)	50.65	51.00

25c, 35c, $5, $10 exist dated "2003." Value, set $32.50.

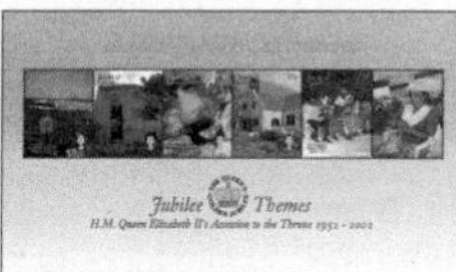

Reign of Queen Elizabeth II, 50th Anniv. A225

No. 1367: a, Crossing Place Trail, Middle Caicos. b, Wades Green Plantation, North Caicos. c, Underwater scenery, Grand Turk. d, St. Thomas Anglican Church, Grand Turk. e, Ripsaw band, Grand Turk. f, Basketweaving.
No. 1368: a, Visit of Princess Royal, 1960. b, Visit of Queen Elizabeth II, 1966. c, Visit of Princess Alexandra, 1988. d, Visit of Duke of Edinburgh, 1993. e, Visit of Prince Andrew, 2000.
No. 1369: a, Salt Industry, 1952-62. b, Space splashdown, 1962-72. c, Ministerial government system, 1972-82. d, Quincentennial of Columbus' landfall, 1982-92. e, National Museum, 1992-2002.

2002, June 1 **Litho.** ***Perf. 14¼***

1367 A225 Sheet of 6 3.50 3.50
a.-f. 25c Any single .60 .60

Perf. 13¾

1368 A225 Sheet of 5 7.50 7.50
a.-e. 60c Any single 1.50 1.50

Perf. 13¾x14¼

1369 A225 Sheet of 5 9.00 9.00
a.-e 80c Any single 1.80 1.80

No. 1368 contains five 31x31mm stamps; No. 1369 contains five 30x34mm stamps.

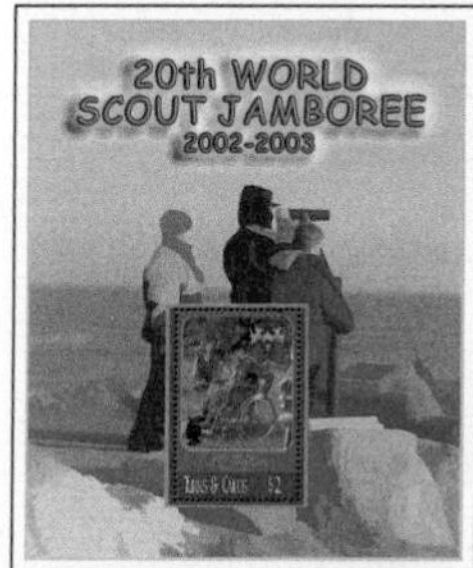

20th World Scout Jamboree, Thailand — A226

No. 1370: a, Scout with mallet and chisel. b, Scout with rifle. c, Scout hanging on rope above water. d, Scouts and lantern.
$2, Handicapped Scouts.

2002, July 15 ***Perf. 14***

1370 A226 80c Sheet of 4, #a-d 8.00 8.00

Souvenir Sheet

1371 A226 $2 multi 5.00 5.00

Intl. Year of Ecotourism — A227

No. 1372, vert.: a, Humpback whale. b, Water sports. c, Regattas. d, Queen angelfish. e, Manta ray. f, Turtle.
$2, Jojo dolphin.

2002, July 15

1372 A227 60c Sheet of 6, #a-f 10.00 10.00

Souvenir Sheet

1373 A227 $2 multi 5.25 5.50

No. 1372 contains six 28x42mm stamps.

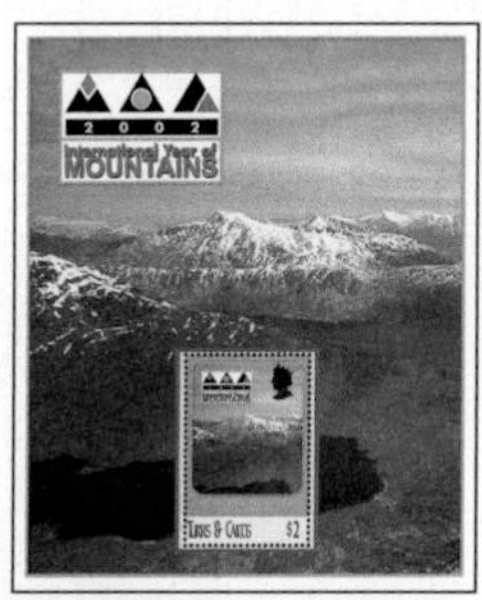

Intl. Year of Mountains — A228

No. 1374: a, Devil's Peak, South Africa. b, Mt. Drakensburg, South Africa. c, Mt. Blanc, France. d, Roan Mountain, US. e, Mt. Sefton, New Zealand. f, Mt. Cook, New Zealand.
$2, Northwest Highlands, Scotland.

2002, July 22

1374 A228 80c Sheet of 6, #a-f 11.50 11.50

Souvenir Sheet

1375 A228 $2 multi 5.25 5.50

United We Stand — A229

2002, Aug. 5

1376 A229 50c multi 1.50 1.50

Printed in sheets of 4.

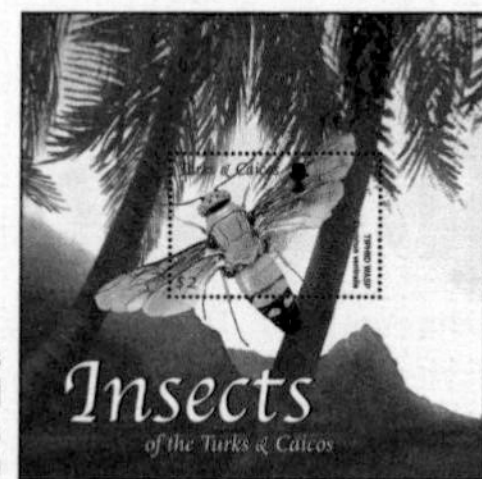

Insects and Birds A230

No. 1377, 60c: a, Hawk moth. b, Burnet moth. c, Mammoth wasp. d, Branch-boring beetle. e, Flower mantid, Pseudocrebotra species. f, Flower mantid, Creobroter species.
No. 1378, 60c: a, Sooty tern. b, Magnificent frigatebird. c, American white pelican. d, Northern shoveler. e, Baltimore oriole. f, Roseate spoonbill.
No. 1379, $2, Tiphiid wasp. No. 1380, $2, Greater flamingo, vert.

2002, Aug. 12 ***Perf. 14***

Sheets of 6, #a-f

1377-1378 A230 Set of 2 22.50 20.00

Souvenir Sheets

1379-1380 A230 Set of 2 10.00 10.00

Queen Mother Elizabeth (1900-2002) — A231

No. 1381: a, Without hat. b, With hat.

2002, Oct. 21

1381 A231 80c Sheet, 2 each #a-b 8.00 8.00

First Nonstop Solo Transatlantic Flight, 75th Anniv. — A232

No. 1382: a, Charles Lindbergh's early exploits as a barnstormer. b, Lindbergh standing in front of Spirit of St. Louis. c, Spirit of St. Louis. d, Take-off from Roosevelt Field. e, Crossing the Atlantic. f, Arrival and welcome in Paris.

2002, Nov. 18 **Litho.** ***Perf. 14***

1382 A232 60c Sheet of 6, #a-f 11.50 10.00

Pres. John F. Kennedy (1917-63) — A233

No. 1383 — Portrait color: a, Orange brown. b, Red violet. c, Greenish gray. d, Blue violet. e, Purple. f, Dull brown.

2002, Nov. 18

1383 A233 60c Sheet of 6, #a.-f. 10.00 10.00

Christmas — A234

Designs: 20c, Madonna and Child, by Giovanni Bellini, vert. 25c, Adoration of the Magi, by Correggio. 60c, Transfiguration of Christ, by Bellini, vert. 80c, Polyptych of St. Vincent Ferrer, by Bellini, vert. $1, Miraculous Mass, by Simone Martini, vert.
$2, Christ in Heaven with Four Saints, by Domenico Ghirlandaio.

2002, Nov. 25

1384-1388 A234 Set of 5 7.00 7.00

Souvenir Sheet

1389 A234 $2 multi 5.50 6.00

Japanese Art — A235

Designs: 25c, Nagata no Taro Nagamune, by Kuniyoshi Utagawa. 35c, Danjuro Ichikawa VII, by Kunisada Utagawa. 60c, Nagata no Taro Nagamune, by Kuniyoshi Utagawa, diff. $1, Nagata no Taro Nagamune, by Kuniyoshi Utagawa, diff.
No. 1394 — Scroll of Actors, by Chikanobu Toyohara and others: a, Smiling man holding fan. b, Man holding sword at mouth. c, Man holding sword vertically. d, Man with tree branch above head.
$2, Two Women by a River, by Chikanobu Hashimoto.

2003, June 17 **Litho.** ***Perf. 14¼***

1390-1393 A235 Set of 4 4.50 4.50
1394 A235 80c Sheet of 4, #a-d 7.00 7.00

Souvenir Sheet

1395 A235 $2 multi 4.00 4.00

Rembrandt Paintings — A236

Designs: 25c, Portrait of a Young Man Resting His Chin on His Hand. 50c, A Woman at an Open Door. No. 1398, $1, The Return of the Prodigal Son. No. 1399, $1, Portrait of an Elderly Man.
No. 1400: a, Nicolaas van Bambeeck. b, Agatha Bas, Wife of Nicolaas van Bambeeck. c, Portrait of a Man Holding His Hat. d, Saskia in a Red Hat.
$2, Christ Driving the Money Changers from the Temple.

Perf. 14¼, 13¼ (#1400)

2003, June 17

1396-1399 A236 Set of 4 6.00 6.00
1400 A236 60c Sheet of 4, #a-d 5.00 5.00

Souvenir Sheet

1401 A236 $2 multi 4.50 4.50

Paintings by Joan Miró — A237

Designs: 25c, Portrait of a Young Girl. 50c, Table with Glove. 60c, Self-portrait, 1917. $1, The Farmer's Wife.
No. 1406: a, Portrait of Ramon Sunyer. b, Self-portrait, 1919. c, Portrait of a Spanish Dancer. d, Portrait of Joana Obrador.
No. 1407, Flowers and Butterfly. No. 1408, Still Life of the Coffee Grinder, horiz.

2003, June 17 ***Perf. 14¼***

1402-1405 A237 Set of 4 4.75 4.75
1406 A237 80c Sheet of 4, #a-d 6.50 6.50

Imperf

Size: 104x83mm

1407 A237 $2 multi 4.25 4.25

Size: 83x104mm

1408 A237 $2 multi 4.25 4.25

Caribbean Community, 30th Anniv. — A238

2003, July 4 ***Perf. 14***

1409 A238 60c multi 2.75 1.50

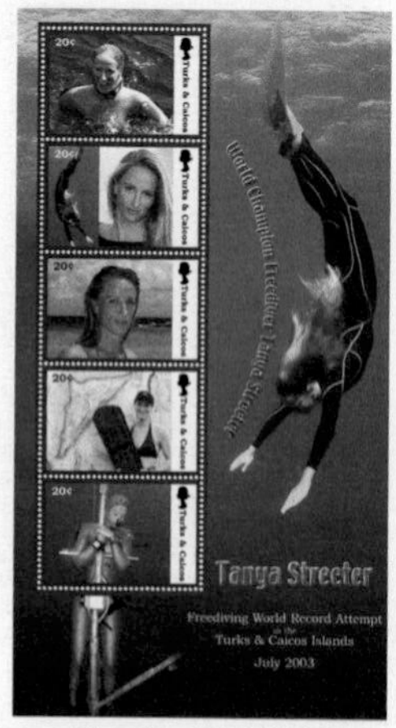

Tanya Streeter, World Champion Freediver — A239

No. 1410: a, Wearing wetsuit in water. b, Diving underwater, portrait. c, Wearing bathing suit at shore. d, Standing in front of map. e, Holding on to diving apparatus.

2003, July 15

1410 A239 20c Sheet of 5, #a-e 3.25 3.50

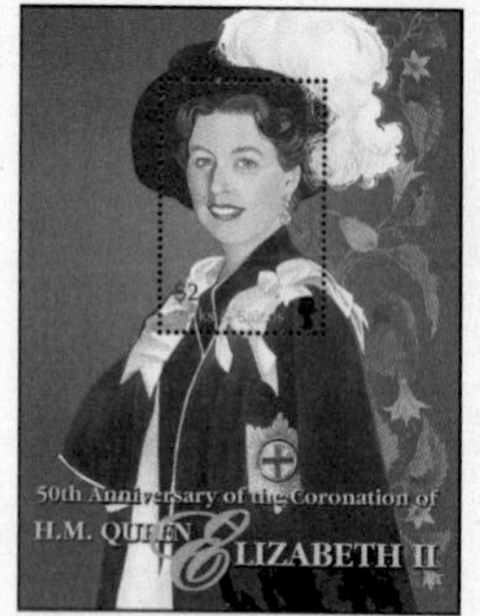

Coronation of Queen Elizabeth II, 50th Anniv. — A240

No. 1411: a, Wearing crown and white robe. b, Wearing lilac dress. c, Wearing tiara and red dress.

$2, Wearing hat and blue cape. $5, Profile portrait.

2003, Aug. 25

1411 A240 80c Sheet of 3, #a-c 6.50 6.50

Souvenir Sheets

1412-1413 A240 Set of 2 16.00 16.00

Prince William, 21st Birthday A241

No. 1414: a, Portrait in blue. b, Pink background. c, Purple background.

$2, Dark blue background.

2003, Aug. 25

1414 A241 $1 Sheet of 3, #a-c 7.00 7.50

Souvenir Sheet

1415 A241 $2 multi 5.00 5.50

Tour de France Bicycle Race, Cent. A242

No. 1416: a, Eddy Merckx, 1974. b, Bernard Thévenet, 1975. c, Lucien Van Impe, 1976. d, Thévenet, 1977.

$2, Bernard Hinault, 1979.

2003, Aug. 25 ***Perf. 13¾x14¼***

1416 A242 $1 Sheet of 4, #a-d 10.00 11.00

Souvenir Sheet

1417 A242 $2 multi 6.50 7.00

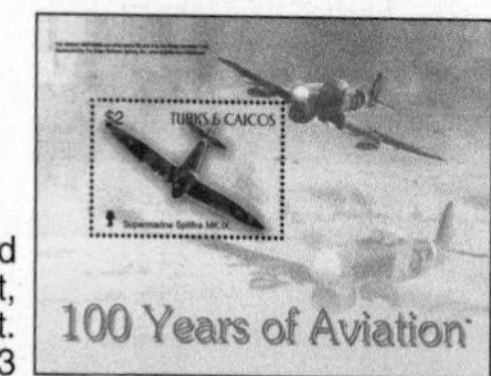

Powered Flight, Cent. A243

No. 1418: a, Vought F4U Corsair. b, Messerschmidt Me 262. c, A6M. d, Hawker Hurricane.

$2, Supermarine Spitfire Mk IX.

2003, Aug. 25 ***Perf. 14***

1418 A243 60c Sheet of 4, #a-d 7.00 7.00

Souvenir Sheet

1419 A243 $2 multi 6.00 7.00

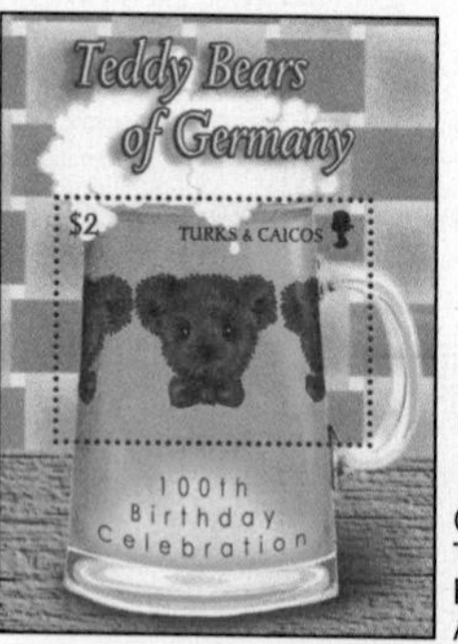

German Teddy Bears A244

No. 1420, vert.: a, Bear with red and yellow uniform. b, Bear with dress. c, Bear with violin case. d, Bear with sword.

$2, Bear on beer mug.

2003, Aug. 25 ***Perf. 12x12¼***

1420 A244 50c Sheet of 4, #a-d 5.50 5.50

Souvenir Sheet

Perf. 12¼x12

1421 A244 $2 multi 5.50 5.50

Butterflies A245

Designs: 50c, Papilio thersites. 60c, Papilio andraemon. 80c, Papilio pelaus. $1, Consul hippona.

$2, Papilio pelaus, diff.

2003, Nov. 17 ***Perf. 14***

1422-1425 A245 Set of 4 11.00 9.00

Souvenir Sheet

1426 A245 $2 multi 7.00 8.00

Orchids — A246

Designs: 50c, Laelia anceps. 60c, Laelia briegeri. 80c, Laelia fidelensis. $1, Laelia cinnabarina.

$2, Laelia rubescens.

2003, Nov. 17

1427-1430 A246 Set of 4 11.00 9.00

Souvenir Sheet

1431 A246 $2 multi 7.50 8.50

Dogs — A247

Designs: 50c, Beagle. 60c, Sabueso Espanol, vert. 80c, Basset hound, vert. $1, Jack Russell terrier, vert.

$2, Dachshund.

2003, Nov. 17

1432-1435 A247 Set of 4 8.00 8.00

Souvenir Sheet

1436 A247 $2 multi 6.00 6.00

Cats — A248

Designs: 50c, Persian. 60c, Cymric. 80c, Main Coon, vert. $1, Tiffany.

$2, Kurile Island bobtail.

2003, Nov. 17

1437-1440 A248 Set of 4 8.00 8.00

Souvenir Sheet

1441 A248 $2 multi 6.00 6.00

Christmas — A249

Paintings: 25c, Madonna of the Harpies, by Andrea del Sarto. 60c, Madonna and Child with St. John, by del Sarto. 80c, Madonna and Child with St. Joseph and St. Peter Martyr, by del Sarto. $1, Madonna and Child with the Angels, by del Sarto.

$2, Montefeltro Altarpiece, by Piero della Francesca.

2003, Nov. 24 ***Perf. 14¼***

1442-1445 A249 Set of 4 5.50 5.50

Souvenir Sheet

1446 A249 $2 multi 5.00 5.00

Marine Life — A250

Photographs from underwater photography contest: Nos. 1447, 1452a, 25c, Golden Rough Head Blennie, by Rand McMeins. Nos. 1448, 1452b, 50c, Octopus at Night, by Marc Van Driessche. Nos. 1449, 1452c, 60c, Sea Turtle, by Mike Nebel. Nos. 1450, 1452d, 80c, Juvenile Octopus, by Amber Blecker. Nos. 1451, 1452e, $1, School of Horse Eye Jacks, by Blecker.

$2, Coral Reef, by Keith Kaplan, vert.

Perf. 12, 12¾ (#1452)

2006, June 1 **Litho.**

Stamps With Thin "Shadow" Frame

1447-1451 A250 Set of 5 6.50 6.50

Miniature Sheet

Stamps With Thick "Shadow" Frame

1452 A250 Sheet of 5, #a-e 6.50 6.50

Souvenir Sheet

1453 A250 $2 multi 4.75 5.00

Washington 2006 World Philatelic Exhibition. (Nos. 1452-1453). The perforation tips at the tops of the stamps on Nos. 1452a-1452e are all white, gradiating to blue on the lower halves of the stamps, while the perforation tips on Nos. 1447-1451 show other colors. The shadow frames at the bottom of Nos 1452a-1452e are 1mm thick and about ½mm thick on Nos. 1447-1451. The distances between the bottom of the denomination and the top of the country name differ on Nos. 1452a-1452e from those found on Nos. 1447-1451. No. 1447 has incorrect spelling, "Ruogh," in inscription, while No. 1452a has word correctly spelled as "Rough."

Queen Elizabeth II, 80th Birthday A251

No. 1454 — Various depictions of Queen Elizabeth II: a, 50c. b, 60c. c, 80c. d, $1.

$6, Wearing crown.

2006, Sept. 12 **Litho.** ***Perf. 13½***

1454 A251 Sheet of 4, #a-d 8.25 8.25

Souvenir Sheet

1455 A251 $6 multi 12.50 12.50

Christmas A252

The Birth of Christ and Adoration of the Shepherds, by Peter Paul Rubens: Nos. 1456, 1460a, 25c, Praying shepherd. Nos. 1457, 1460b, 60c, Infant Jesus. Nos. 1458, 1460c, 80c, Heads of two shepherds. Nos. 1459, 1460d, $1, Virgin Mary.

$6, Our Lady, The Christ Child and Saints, by Rubens, vert.

2006, Dec. 27 ***Perf. 13¼x13½***

Stamps With Painting Title

1456-1459 A252 Set of 4 5.50 5.50

Stamps Without Painting Title

1460 A252 Sheet of 4, #a-d 6.50 6.50

Souvenir Sheet

Perf. 13½x13¼

1461 A252 $6 multi 12.00 12.00

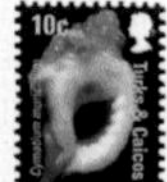

Shells — A253

Designs: 10c, Cymatium muricinum. 15c, Tellina radiata. 20c, Tonna maculosa. 25c, Leucozonia nassa. 35c, Trachycardium magnum. 45c, Papyridea soleniformis. 50c, Epitonium lamellosum. 60c, Astraea brevispina. 80c, Bulla striata. $1, Murex margaritensis. $1.25, Chama macerophylla. $1.40, Vasum capitellum. $2, Coralliophila abbreviata. $5, Trachycardium isocardia. $10, Oliva reticularis.

2007, June 11 **Litho.** ***Perf. 12¾***

1462	A253	10c multi	.70	.80
1463	A253	15c multi	1.00	.80
1464	A253	20c multi	1.25	1.00
1465	A253	25c multi	1.25	.50
1466	A253	35c multi	1.50	.70
1467	A253	45c multi	2.00	1.25
1468	A253	50c multi	2.00	1.25
1469	A253	60c multi	2.50	1.50
1470	A253	80c multi	3.00	2.00
1471	A253	$1 multi	3.50	2.75
1472	A253	$1.25 multi	4.00	3.25
1473	A253	$1.40 multi	4.25	4.00
1474	A253	$2 multi	5.00	6.00
1475	A253	$5 multi	9.00	10.00
1476	A253	$10 multi	16.00	20.00
	Nos. 1462-1476 (15)		56.95	55.80

Christmas — A254

Paintings: 25c, The Virgin and Child, by Carlo Maratta. 60c, The Adoration of the Magi, by Vincent Malo, horiz. 80c, The Annunciation, by Robert Campin, horiz. $1, The Adoration of the Magi, by Giovanni di Paolo, horiz.
$6, The Adoration of the Magi, by Quentin Massys.

Perf. 14¼x14¾, 14¾x14¼

2007, Dec. 10
1477-1480 A254 Set of 4 7.50 6.50

Souvenir Sheet
Perf. 14

1481 A254 $6 multi 14.00 15.00

No. 1481 contains one 28x42mm stamp.

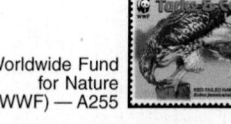

Worldwide Fund for Nature (WWF) — A255

No. 1482 — Red-tailed hawk: a, Pair on fenceposts. b, Adults and chicks at nest. c, Adults on hill and in flight. d, Head of hawk.

2007, Dec. 24 *Perf. 13¼*
1482 Horiz. strip of 4 5.50 5.50
a.-d A255 50c Any single 1.35 1.35
e. Souvenir sheet, 2 each #a-d 13.50 13.50

Wedding of Queen Elizabeth II and Prince Philip, 60th Anniv. A256

No. 1483, vert.: a, Couple, country name in purple. b, Queen, country name in purple. c, Queen, country name in blue. d, Couple, country name in blue. e, Couple, country name in black. f, Queen, country name in black.
$6, Couple on balcony.

2007, Dec. 28 *Perf. 13¼*
1483 A256 $1 Sheet of 6, #a-f 12.75 12.75

Souvenir Sheet

1484 A256 $6 multi 12.00 12.00

Princess Diana (1961-97) — A257

No. 1485 — Various photographs as shown.
$6, Princess Diana wearing hat.

2007, Dec. 28
1485 A257 $1 Sheet of 4, #a-d 8.00 8.00

Souvenir Sheet

1486 A257 $6 multi 12.00 12.00

Pope Benedict XVI — A258

2008, Sept. 15 Litho. *Perf. 13¼*
1487 A258 75c multi 2.00 2.00

Printed in sheets of 8.

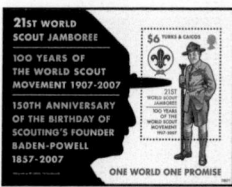

Scouting, Cent. (in 2007) A259

No. 1488, horiz.: a, Fleur-de-lis, silhouette of Lord Robert Baden-Powell and flags of Tanzania, United States and Colombia on top row. b, Dove, silhouette of fleur-de-lis and green, light green and red national Scouting emblem at UL. c, As "b," with orange, brown and dark green national Scouting emblem at UL. d, As "a," with flags of Israel, Canada, Chile and Macedonia on second row. e, As "a," with flags of Taiwan, Luxembourg and Philippines on top row. f, As "b," with Israel Scouting emblem at UL.
$6, Lord Baden-Powell.

2008, Sept. 23
1488 A259 80c Sheet of 6, #a-f 10.00 10.00

Souvenir Sheet

1489 A259 $6 multi 13.75 13.75

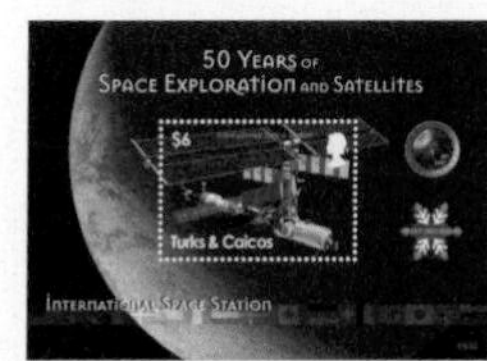

Space Exploration, 50th Anniv. (in 2007) — A260

No. 1490 — International Space Station: a, With solar panels under silhouette of Queen. b, With solar panels touching nose of Queen. c, With solar panels spread horizontally. d, With solar panels running to UL from Queen's chest.
$6, International Space Station, diff.

2008, Sept. 23
1490 A260 $1 Sheet of 4, #a-d 10.00 10.00

Souvenir Sheet

1491 A260 $6 multi 17.50 18.50

Marine Life — A261

Photographs from underwater photography contest: 25c, Arrow Crab, by Garin Bescoby. 60c, Trumpet Fish, by Karin Nargis. 80c, Sting Ray, by Barbara Shively. $1, Giant Anemone, by Roddy Mcleod.
$6, Red Banded Lobster, by Jayne Baker.

2008, Nov. 25 Litho. *Perf. 13¼*
1492-1495 A261 Set of 4 5.50 6.00
1495a Souvenir sheet, #1492-1495 5.50 6.00

Souvenir Sheet

1496 A261 $6 multi 16.00 17.50

Christmas — A262

Paintings: 25c, The Nativity, by Philippe de Champaigne. 60c, Mystic Nativity, by Sandro Botticelli. 80c, The Virgin in a Rose Arbor, by Stefan Lochner. $1, The Adoration of the Shepherds, by Francisco Zurbaran.
$6, The Virgin with Angels, by William Bouguereau.

2008, Nov. 25 *Perf. 14x14¾*
1497-1500 A262 Set of 4 7.25 6.50

Souvenir Sheet

1501 A262 $6 multi 14.00 15.00

Souvenir Sheet

New Year 2012 (Year of the Dragon) — A263

2012, July 12 *Perf.*
1502 A263 $3 multi 6.00 6.00

Charles Dickens (1812-70), Writer — A264

No. 1503: a, Dickens in 1858. b, Illustration from "A Tale of Two Cities." c, Dickens, c. 1860. d, Statue of Dickens in Philadelphia. e, Illustration from "Oliver Twist." f, Illustration from "A Christmas Carol."
$5, Dickens in his study, horiz.

2012, July 12 *Perf. 14*
1503 A264 30c Sheet of 6, #a-f 5.50 5.50

Souvenir Sheet
Perf. 12½

1504 A264 $5 multi 11.00 11.00

No. 1504 contains one 51x38mm stamp.

Flight of John Glenn in Friendship 7, 50th Anniv. — A265

No. 1505: a, Glenn in space helmet. b, Launch of Friendship 7. c, Launch of Space Shuttle (incorrectly identified as launch of Friendship 7). d, Friendship 7 capsule in ocean.
$6, Glenn in space suit, U.S. flags.

2012, July 12 *Perf. 14*
1505 A265 $1.25 Sheet of 4, #a-d 10.00 10.00

Souvenir Sheet
Perf. 12

1506 A265 $6 multi 12.00 12.00

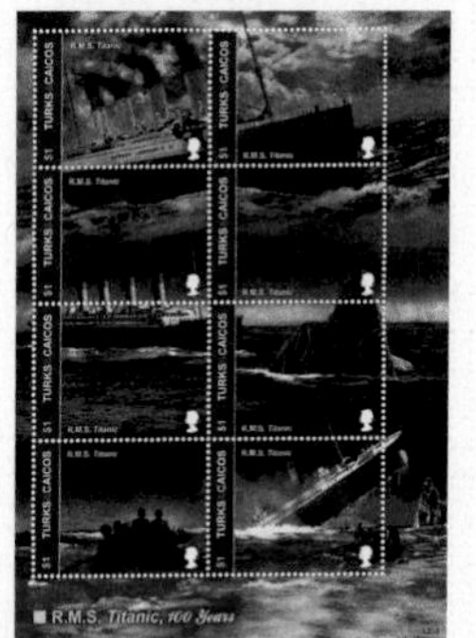

Sinking of the Titanic, Cent. — A266

No. 1507: a, Sky, smokestacks of the Titanic. b, Sky, bow of the Titanic. c, Hull of Titanic at top, waves, smokestacks of Titanic at bottom. d, Hull of Titanic, waves, top of iceberg. e, Titanic at top. f, Prow of Titanic, iceberg. g, Passengers on lifeboat. h, Titanic sinking, lifeboat.
No. 1508, Titanic approaching iceberg. No. 1509, Titanic sinking, lifeboat, diff.

2012, July 12 *Perf. 14*
1507 A266 $1 Sheet of 8, #a-h 16.00 16.00

Souvenir Sheets

1508 A266 $5 multi 11.50 11.50
1509 A266 $5 multi 11.50 11.50

Reign of Queen Elizabeth II, 60th Anniv. A267

Roses and Queen Elizabeth II wearing: $3.50, Crown. $9, Tiara.

2012, Oct. 10 *Perf. 13¾*
1510 A267 $3.50 multi 7.00 7.00

Souvenir Sheet

1511 A267 $9 multi 18.50 18.50

No. 1510 was printed in sheets of 4.

Souvenir Sheet

Replica of Slave Cabin, Cheshire Hall Plantation Ruins — A268

2013, Mar. 7 *Perf. 12½x13¼*
1512 A268 $3.50 multi 7.50 8.00

Turks & Caicos National Trust, 20th anniv.

New Year 2013 (Year of the Snake) A269

No. 1513: a, Tail of snake. b, Head of snake.
$3.50, Entire snake.

2013, July 12 *Perf. 13¾*
1513 A269 $1.25 Horiz. pair, #a-b 5.00 5.00

Souvenir Sheet

1514 A269 $3.50 multi 7.00 7.00

No. 1513 was printed in sheets containing two pairs.

Birth of Prince George of Cambridge — A270

No. 1515 — Illustrations of characters from *Alice's Adventures in Wonderland,* by Lewis Carroll: a, White Rabbit. b, Knave of Hearts carrying crown. c, Alice.
$2.50, Playing Card Gardeners and rose bush.

2013, Oct. 1 Litho. *Perf. 12¾*
1515 A270 $1 Sheet of 3, #a-c 6.00 6.00

Souvenir Sheet

1516 A270 $2.50 multi 8.50 8.50

A271

Nelson Mandela (1918-2013), President of South Africa — A272

No. 1517: a, Mandela without hat. b, Mandela with hat.
No. 1518: a, Mandela casting ballot. b, Mandela in stadium.
No. 1519, $3.50, Mandela seated, black-and-white photograph. No. 1520, $3.50, Mandela seated, color photograph.

2014, Mar. 3 Litho. *Perf. 13¾*

1517 A271 $1 Pair, #a-b 4.00 4.00
1518 A272 $1 Pair, #a-b 4.00 4.00

Souvenir Sheets

1519-1520 A272 Set of 2 15.00 15.00

Nos. 1517-1518 each were printed in sheets containing two pairs.

Tang Sancai Glazed Horses A273

No. 1521: a, Brown horse with blue green saddle. b, Brown horse with white saddle with gray trim and straps, two ornaments on hindquarters. c, Brown horse with white saddle with black trim and straps, three ornaments on hindquarters. d, Light brown horse with red saddle. e, Brown horse with light brown saddle and blue pads. f, Black horse with blue green saddle.
$2.50, Black horse with black saddle, vert.

2014, Mar. 3 Litho. *Perf. 14*

1521 A273 75c Sheet of 6, #a-f 8.75 8.75

Souvenir Sheet

Perf. 12½

1522 A273 $2.50 multi 4.75 4.75

New Year 2014 (Year of the Horse). No. 1522 contains one 38x51mm stamp.

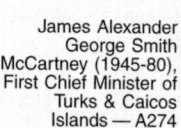

James Alexander George Smith McCartney (1945-80), First Chief Minister of Turks & Caicos Islands — A274

Frame color: 25c, Purple. $10, Red.

2014, May 1 Litho. *Perf. 12x12½*

1523 A274 25c multi .50 .50

Souvenir Sheet

1524 A274 $10 multi 20.00 20.00

No. 1523 was printed in sheets of 4.

Shells A275

No. 1525: a, Junonia. b, Channeled duck clam. c, Zigzag scallop. d, Scotch bonnet.
$4, Queen conch.

2014, Nov. 3 Litho. *Perf. 14*

1525 A275 $1.20 Sheet of 4, #a-d 9.75 9.75

Souvenir Sheet

Perf. 12¾

1526 A275 $4 multi 9.50 9.50

No. 1526 contains one 51x38mm stamp.

Orchids A276

No. 1527: a, Oncidium auriferum. b, Oncidium excavatum. c, Oncidium graminifolium. d, Oncidium altissimum.
No. 1527E: f, Cypripedium dickinsonianum. g, Cattleya gaskelliana. h, Cattleya dowiana. i, Oncidium cheirophorum.
No. 1528: a, Oncidium citrinum. b, Oncidium wentworthianum.
No. 1528C: d, Brassavola nodosa. e, Cypripedium irapeanum.

2014, Nov. 3 Litho. *Perf. 12¾*

1527 A276 $1.20 Sheet of 4, #a-d 12.50 12.50

Perf. 12½

1527E A276 $1.20 Sheet of 4 #f-i 9.75 9.75

Souvenir Sheet

1528 A276 $2 Sheet of 2, #a-b 10.00 10.00

Perf. 12½

1528C A276 $2 Sheet of 2 #d-e 8.00 8.00

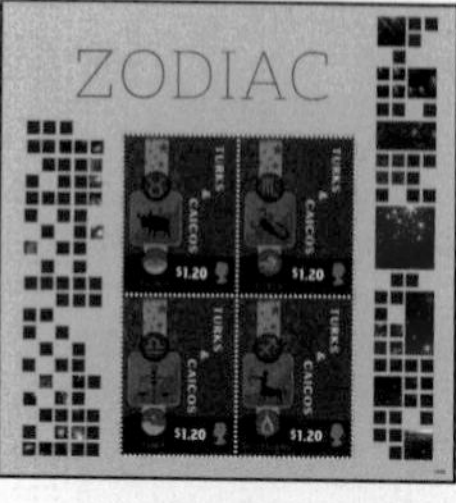

Signs of the Zodiac A277

No. 1529, $1.20: a, Taurus. b, Scorpio. c, Libra. d, Sagittarius.
No. 1530, $1.20: a, Aquarius. b, Cancer. c, Capricorn. d, Leo.
No. 1531, $2: a, Gemini. b, Aries.
No. 1532, $2: a, Virgo. b, Pisces.

2014, Nov. 3 Litho. *Perf. 12½*

Sheets of 4, #a-d

1529-1530 A277 Set of 2 22.50 22.50

Souvenir Sheets of 2, #a-b

1531-1532 A277 Set of 2 16.00 16.00

Miniature Sheets

A278

New Year 2015 (Year of the Ram) A279

No. 1533 — Chinese character for "ram" on ram in: a, Green. b, Red. c, Blue. d, Bister.
No. 1534: a, Chinese character for "happiness." b, "Happy New Year." c, Flower and ram, denomination at right. d, Ram and flower, denomination at left. e, "2015 Year of the Ram." f, Chinese character for "ram."

2014, Nov. 24 Litho. *Perf. 14*

1533 A278 $1.20 Sheet of 4, #a-d 12.00 12.00

Perf. 13¾

1534 A279 $1.20 Sheet of 6, #a-f, + central label 18.00 18.00

Christmas — A280

Paintings by Titian: 34c, Madonna and Child, 1528. 49c, Madonna and Child, 1511. $1.50, Madonna and Child in an Evening Landscape, 1562-65. $3.50, Madonna and Child, 1560-65.

2015, Dec. 1 Litho. *Perf. 12¾*

1535-1538 A280 Set of 4 15.00 15.00

Miniature Sheet

New Year 2016 (Year of the Monkey) A281

No. 1539 — Various monkeys with denomination color of: a, Magenta. b, Green. c, Red. d, Blue.

2015, Dec. 1 Litho. *Perf. 14*

1539 A281 75c Sheet of 4, #a-d 8.00 8.00

Travels of Queen Elizabeth II A282

No. 1540 — Queen Elizabeth visiting: a, South Africa, 1947. b, Australia, 1954. c, Rome, Italy, 1961. d, India, 1961 (attendant with red coat in background). e, India, 1961 (attendant with white coat in background). f, Pakistan, 1961. g, Nepal, 1961. h, Sri Lanka, 1981. i, New Zealand, 1981. j, United States, 1983 (bearded man in background). k, United States, 1983, (with park ranger). l, Kathmandu, Nepal, 1986. m, Germany, 1992.
$4, Queen Elizabeth II and Prince Philip in Ireland, 2011.

2015, Dec. 7 Litho. *Perf. 12*

1540 A282 50c Sheet of 13, #a-m, + label 17.25 17.25

Souvenir Sheet

1541 A282 $4 multi 10.50 10.50

Queen Elizabeth II, longest-reigning British monarch.

Fish — A283

Designs: 10c, Yellow goatfish. 15c, Queen triggerfish. 20c, Royal gramma. 25c, Bonefish. 35c, Bicolor damselfish. 45c, Honeycomb cowfish. 50c, Marlin. 60c, Squirrelfish. 80c, Queen angelfish. $1, Tuna. $1.25, Spotted drum. $1.40, Nassau grouper. $2, Mutton snapper. $5, Atlantic spadefish. $10, Stoplight parrotfish.

2022, Oct. 1 Litho. *Perf. 13¾*

1542	A283	10c	multi	.30	.30
1543	A283	15c	multi	.30	.30
1544	A283	20c	multi	.40	.40
1545	A283	25c	multi	.50	.50
1546	A283	35c	multi	.70	.70
1547	A283	45c	multi	.90	.90
1548	A283	50c	multi	1.00	1.00
1549	A283	60c	multi	1.25	1.25
1550	A283	80c	multi	1.60	1.60
1551	A283	$1	multi	2.00	2.00
1552	A283	$1.25	multi	2.50	2.50
1553	A283	$1.40	multi	3.00	3.00
1554	A283	$2	multi	4.00	4.00
1555	A283	$5	multi	10.00	10.00
1556	A283	$10	multi	20.00	20.00
	Nos. 1542-1556 (15)			48.45	48.45

WAR TAX STAMPS

Regular Issue of 1913-16 Overprinted

Black Overprint at Bottom of Stamp

1917 Wmk. 3 *Perf. 14*

MR1 A10 1p carmine .25 *1.75*
a. Double overprint 200.00 *275.00*
b. "TAX" omitted
c. Pair, one without ovpt. 700.00
d. Inverted overprint 65.00 *85.00*
e. Double overprint, one inverted 110.00
MR2 A10 3p violet, *yel* 2.50 *10.00*
a. Double overprint 110.00

Black Overprint at Top or Middle of Stamp

1917

MR3 A10 1p carmine .25 *1.40*
a. Inverted overprint 65.00
b. Double overprint 65.00 *77.50*
c. Pair, one without overprint 650.00
MR4 A10 3p violet, *yel* .70 *3.00*
a. Double overprint 50.00 *55.00*
b. Dbl. ovpt., one inverted 375.00

Same Overprint in Violet or Red

1918-19

MR5 A10 1p car (V) ('19) 2.00 *8.00*
a. Double overprint 24.00 22.00
b. "WAR" omitted 200.00
MR6 A10 3p violet, *yel* (R) 24.00 *65.00*
a. Double overprint 375.00

Regular Issue of 1913-16 Overprinted in Black

1918

MR7 A10 1p carmine .25 *3.75*
MR8 A10 3p violet, *yel* 7.50 *12.00*

Same Overprint in Red

1919

MR9 A10 3p violet, *yel* .25 *7.50*

Regular Issue of 1913-16 Overprinted in Black

MR10 A10 1p carmine .35 *2.75*
a. Double overprint 160.00 *190.00*
MR11 A10 3p violet, *yel* .75 *3.25*

Regular Issue of 1913-16 Overprinted

MR12 A10 1p carmine .35 4.50
a. Double overprint *100.00*
MR13 A10 3p violet, *yel* 2.50 4.50

The bottom two rows of this setting show the words "War" and "Tax" about 1mm farther apart.

CAICOS

Catalogue values for all unused stamps in this country are for Never Hinged items.

Turks & Caicos Nos. 360, 364, 366, 369, 371-373 Ovptd.

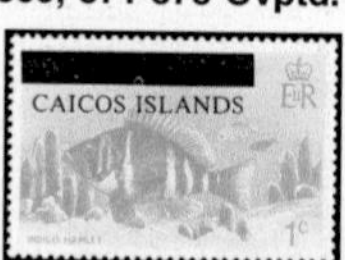

1c, Indigo hamlet. 5c, Spanish grunt. 8c, Foureye butterflyfish. 20c, Queen angelfish. 50c, Fairy basslet. $1, Clown wrasse. $2, Stoplight parrotfish.

Unwmk.

1981, July 24 Litho. *Perf. 14*

1	A69	1c multi	.25	.25
2	A69	5c multi	.25	.25
3	A69	8c multi	.25	.25
4	A69	20c multi	.40	.40
5	A69	50c multi	.85	.85
6	A69	$1 multi	1.00	1.75
7	A69	$2 multi	2.00	3.25
		Nos. 1-7 (7)	5.00	7.00

Common Design Types pictured following the introduction.

Royal Wedding Issue

Common Design Type

Turks & Caicos Nos. 486-489 Overprinted

35c, Charles & Diana. 65c, Kensington Palace. 90c, Prince Charles.
$2, Glass coach.

1981, July 24

8	CD331a	35c multicolored	.25	.25
9	CD331a	65c multicolored	.50	.50
10	CD331a	90c multicolored	.75	.75
		Nos. 8-10 (3)	1.50	1.50

Souvenir Sheet

11	CD331	$2 multicolored	3.50	3.50

Roulette x Imperf. (#12a), Imperf. (#12b)

1981, Oct. 29 Self-Adhesive

12 Souvenir booklet 13.00
- *a.* A88a Pane, 3 each 20c, Diana, $1, Charles 4.00
- *b.* A88a Pane of 1 $2, Couple 5.00

No. 12 is similar to Turks & Caicos No. 490. No. 12 has Caicos Islands instead of Turks & Caicos Islands.

Hawksbill turtle — C1

8c, Diver with lobster and conch shell. 20c, Stone idol, Arawak Indians. 35c, Sloop construction. 50c, Marine biology. 95c, 707 Jetliner. $1.10, 15th cent. Spanish ship. $2, British soldier, Fort St. George. $3, Pirates Anne Bonny, Calico Jack.

1983-84 *Perf. 14*

13	C1	8c multicolored	1.60	.80
14	C1	10c shown	1.80	1.40
15	C1	20c multicolored	1.80	1.40
16	C1	35c multicolored	1.80	1.80
17	C1	50c multicolored	2.60	2.75
18	C1	95c multicolored	4.75	2.75
19	C1	$1.10 multicolored	4.75	2.75
20	C1	$2 multicolored	3.50	4.00
21	C1	$3 multicolored	4.75	4.00
		Nos. 13-21 (9)	27.35	21.65

Issued: Nos. 13-19, 6/6/83; Nos. 20-21, 5/18/84.
For overprints see Nos. 47-49.

Christmas Type of Turks and Caicos

Walt Disney characters in Santa Claus is Coming to Town: No. 22, Chip 'n Dale. No. 23, Goofy & Patch. No. 24, Morty, Ferdie & Pluto. No. 25, Morty. No. 26, Donald, Huey, Dewey & Louie. No. 27, Goofy & Louie. No. 28, Uncle Scrooge. No. 29, Mickey Mouse & Ferdie. No. 30, Pinocchio, Jiminy Cricket and Figaro.
No. 31, Morty & Ferdie, fireplace.

1983, Nov. 7 *Perf. 11*

22	A104	1c multicolored	.25	.30
23	A104	1c multicolored	.25	.30
24	A104	2c multicolored	.25	.30
25	A104	2c multicolored	.25	.30
26	A104	3c multicolored	.25	.30
27	A104	3c multicolored	.25	.30
28	A104	50c multicolored	4.00	3.25
29	A104	70c multicolored	4.25	3.75
30	A104	$1.10 multicolored	5.00	4.50
		Nos. 22-30 (9)	14.75	13.30

Souvenir Sheet

Perf. 13½x14

31	A104	$2 multicolored	4.75	4.50

Drawings by Raphael — C2

Designs: 35c, Leda and the Swan. 50c, Study of Apollo for Parnassus. 95c, Study of two figures for The Battle of Ostia. $1.10, Study for the Madonna of the Goldfinch. $2.50, The Garvagh Madonna.

1983, Dec. 15 *Perf. 14*

32	C2	35c multicolored	1.00	.65
33	C2	50c multicolored	1.25	.90
34	C2	95c multicolored	2.50	1.60
35	C2	$1.10 multicolored	2.50	1.90
		Nos. 32-35 (4)	7.25	5.05

Souvenir Sheet

36	C2	$2.50 multicolored	5.75	5.75

500th birth anniv. of Raphael.

1984 Summer Olympics, Los Angeles — C3

4c, High jump. 25c, Archery. 65c, Cycling. $1.10, Soccer.
$2, Show jumping, horiz.

1984, Mar. 1

37	C3	4c multicolored	.25	.25
38	C3	25c multicolored	.30	.25
39	C3	65c multicolored	2.25	.75
40	C3	$1.10 multicolored	1.25	.90
		Nos. 37-40 (4)	4.05	2.15

Souvenir Sheet

41	C3	$2 multicolored	4.00	4.00

Easter — C4

Walt Disney characters: 35c, Horace Horsecollar, Clarabelle Cow. 45c, Mickey, Minnie & Chip. 75c, Gyro Gearloose, Chip 'n Dale. 85c, Mickey, Chip 'n Dale. $2.20, Donald sailing with nephews.

1984, Apr. 15 *Perf. 14x13½*

42	C4	35c multicolored	1.00	.75
43	C4	45c multicolored	1.15	1.00
44	C4	75c multicolored	1.75	1.50
45	C4	85c multicolored	1.75	1.75
		Nos. 42-45 (4)	5.65	5.00

Souvenir Sheet

46	C4	$2.20 mulitcolored	5.50	4.00

Nos. 18-19 Ovptd. in Black

Universal Postal Union 1874-1984

1984, June 19 *Perf. 14*

47	C1	95c multicolored	1.50	1.75
48	C1	$1.10 multicolored	1.75	2.00

No. 20 Overprinted

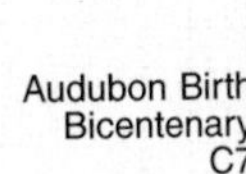

Ausipex 1984

1984, Aug. 22

49	C1	$2 multicolored	3.50	3.75

Columbus' First Landfall — C5

1984, Sept. 21

50	C5	10c Sighting manatees	1.00	.80
51	C5	70c Fleet	3.75	3.25
52	C5	$1 West Indies landing	4.25	3.25
		Nos. 50-52 (3)	9.00	7.30

Souvenir Sheet

53	C5	$2 Fleet, map	3.50	3.75

Columbus' first landing, 492nd anniv.

Christmas — C6

Walt Disney characters: 20c, Santa Claus, Donald and Mickey. 35c, Donald at refrigerator. 50c, Donald, Micky riding toy train. 75c, Donald carrying presents. $1.10, Huey, Louie, Dewey and Donald singing carols. $2, Donald as Christmas tree.

Perf. 13½x14, 12x12½ (75c)

1984, Nov. 26

54	C6	20c multicolored	1.15	.85
55	C6	35c multicolored	1.30	1.00
56	C6	50c multicolored	1.90	2.25
57	C6	75c multicolored	2.25	3.00
58	C6	$1.10 multicolored	2.50	3.25
		Nos. 54-58 (5)	9.10	10.35

Souvenir Sheet

Perf. 13½x14

59	C6	$2 multicolored	3.75	4.00

No. 57 printed in sheets of 8.

Audubon Birth Bicentenary C7

20c, Thick-billed vireo. 35c, Black-faced grassquit. 50c, Pearly-eyed thrasher. $1, Greater Antillean bullfinch.
$2, Stripe-headed tanagers.

1985, Feb. 12 *Perf. 14*

60	C7	20c multicolored	2.25	.65
61	C7	35c multicolored	2.60	1.25
62	C7	50c multicolored	3.00	2.00
63	C7	$1 multicolored	3.50	3.25
		Nos. 60-63 (4)	11.35	7.15

Souvenir Sheet

64	C7	$2 multicolored	4.75	5.25

No. 64 exists imperf.

Intl. Youth Year — C8

1985, May 8

65	C8	16c Education	.25	.30
66	C8	35c Health	.65	.70
67	C8	70c Love	1.25	1.40
68	C8	90c Peace	1.50	1.75
		Nos. 65-68 (4)	3.65	4.15

Souvenir Sheet

69	C8	$2 Peace dove, child	3.50	4.50

UN 40th anniv.

Intl. Civil Aviation Org., 40th Anniv. — C9

1985, May 26

70	C9	35c DC-3	3.50	.55
71	C9	75c Convair 440	4.50	1.40
72	C9	90c TCNA Islander	4.50	1.60
		Nos. 70-72 (3)	12.50	3.55

Souvenir Sheet

73	C9	$2.20 Hang glider	3.50	4.50

Queen Mother, 85th Birthday Type of Turks & Caicos

35c, Wearing green hat. 65c, With Princess Anne, horiz. 95c, Wearing white hat.
$2, Inspecting guardsmen.

1985, July 7

74	A117	35c sal pink & multi	1.25	.55
75	A117	65c yel & multi	1.75	.95
76	A117	95c lt blue & multi	2.25	1.60
		Nos. 74-76 (3)	5.25	3.10

Souvenir Sheet

77	A117	$2 sage grn & multi	6.00	4.00

Mark Twain, 150th Birth Anniv. — C10

Walt Disney characters in Tom Sawyer, Detective (Intl. Youth Year): 8c, Mickey and Goofy as Tom and Huck reading reward poster. 35c, Meeting Jake Dunlap. 95c, Spying on Jubiter Dunlap. $1.10, With Pluto finding body. No. 86, Unmasking Jubiter Dunlap.
Walt Disney characters portraying Six Soldiers of Fortune (The Brothers Grimm, Bicent.): 16c, Donald receiving his meager pay. 25c, Donald meets Horace Horsecollar as strong man. 65c, Donald meets Mickey the marksman. $1.35, Goofy wins footrace against Princess Daisy. No. 87, Soldiers with sack of gold.

1985, Dec. 5 *Perf. 14x13½*

78	C10	8c multicolored	.25	.25
79	C10	16c multicolored	.35	.35
80	C10	25c multicolored	.55	.55
81	C10	35c multicolored	.80	.80
82	C10	65c multicolored	1.45	1.45
83	C10	95c multicolored	2.15	2.15
84	C10	$1.10 multicolored	2.65	2.65
85	C10	$1.35 multicolored	3.25	3.25
		Nos. 78-85 (8)	11.45	11.45

Souvenir Sheet

86	C10	$2 multicolored	6.00	6.00
87	C10	$2 multicolored	6.00	6.00

Stamps are no longer being produced for Caicos.

TURKS ISLANDS

'tərks 'ī-ləndz

LOCATION — West Indies, at the southern extremity of the Bahamas
GOVT. — Former dependency of Jamaica
POP. — 2,000 (approx.)
CAPITAL — Grand Turk

In 1848 the Turks Islands together with the Caicos group, lying to the northwest, were made a British colony. In 1873 the Colony became a dependency under the government of Jamaica although separate stamp issues were continued. Postage stamps inscribed Turks and Caicos Islands have been used since 1900.

12 Pence = 1 Shilling

Values for unused stamps are for examples with original gum as defined in the catalogue introduction. Very fine examples of Nos. 1-42 will have generally rough perforations that cut into the design on one or more sides due to the narrow spacing of the stamps on the plates and imperfect perforating methods. Stamps with perfs clear of the design on all four sides are extremely scarce and will command substantially higher prices.

Because of the printing and imperfect perforating methods, stamps are often found scissor separated. Prices will not be adversely affected on those stamps where the scissor cut does not remove the perforations.

Watermark

Wmk. 5 — Small Star

Queen Victoria — A1

Perf. 11½ to 13

1867 Unwmk. Engr.

1 A1 1p rose 67.50 67.50
2 A1 6p gray black 270.00 *270.00*
3 A1 1sh slate blue 105.00 67.50
Nos. 1-3 (3) 442.50 405.00

Perf. 11 to 13x14 to 15

1873-79 Wmk. 5

4 A1 1p lake 57.50 57.50
5 A1 1p dull red ('79) 62.50 67.50
a. Horiz. pair, imperf. btwn. *30,000.*
b. Perf. 11-12 *1,100.*
6 A1 1sh violet *5,750.* *2,250.*

Stamps offered as No. 6 are often examples from which the surcharge has been removed.

Stamps of 1867-79 Surcharged in Black

a

b

c

12 settings of the ½p.

1881 Unwmk. *Perf. 11 to 13*

7 (a) ½p on 6p gray blk 100.00 *175.00*
7A (b) ½p on 6p gray blk 100.00 *150.00*
8 (b) ½p on 1sh slate bl 140.00 *200.00*
a. Double surcharge 8,250.
8B (c) ½p on 1sh slate bl *11,000.*
c. Without fraction bar
d. Double surcharge 16,000.
e. #8a and #8Bd in pair 27,000.

d

e

Perf. 11 to 13x14 to 15

Wmk. 5

9 (a) ½p on 1p dull red 210.00 350.00
a. Double surcharge 6,500.
10 (b) ½p on 1p dull red 90.00 *150.00*
a. Double surcharge 8,250.
11 (c) ½p on 1p dull red 190.00 *250.00*
a. Double surcharge *6,500.*
12 (d) ½p on 1p dull red 315.00
a. Without fraction bar 1,150.
b. Double surcharge
13 (e) ½p on 1p dull red 675.00
14 (a) ½p on 1sh violet 300.00 450.00
a. Double surcharge 4,000.
15 (b) ½p on 1sh violet 155.00 *300.00*
a. Without fraction bar 675.00
b. Double surcharge 7,750.
16 (c) ½p on 1sh violet 105.00 *220.00*

f

g

h

9 settings of the 2½p.

Perf. 11 to 13

Unwmk.

17 (f) 2½p on 6p gray blk *16,000.*
18 (g) 2½p on 6p gray blk 425. *600.*
a. Horiz. pair, imperf. between *45,000.*
b. Double surcharge *18,500.*
19 (h) 2½p on 6p gray blk 250. *475.*
a. Double surcharge *17,500.*

i

j

Perf. 11 to 13x14 to 15

Wmk. 5

20 (i) 2½p on 1sh violet *4,250.*
21 (h) 2½p on 1sh violet 625.00 *975.00*
22 (j) 2½p on 1sh violet *13,500.*

k

l

m

n

Perf. 11 to 13

Unwmk.

24 (k) 2½p on 6p gray blk *9,500.*
25 (k) 2½p on 1sh slate bl *28,000.*
26 (l) 2½p on 1sh slate bl 1,500.
27 (m) 2½p on 1sh slate bl *3,750.*
a. Without fraction bar *15,000.*
28 (n) 2½p on 1sh slate bl *15,000.*

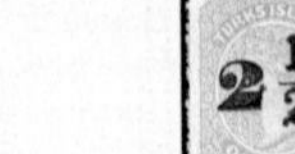

o

Perf. 11 to 13x14 to 15

Wmk. 5

29 (l) 2½p on 1p dull red 750.00
30 (o) 2½p on 1p dull red 1,550.
31 (l) 2½p on 1sh violet 875.00 1,000.
a. Double surcharge of "½" *5,000.*
32 (o) 2½p on 1sh violet 1,350.
b. Double surcharge of "½" *9,500.*

p

q

r

6 settings of the 4p.

Perf. 11 to 13

Unwmk.

33 (p) 4p on 6p gray black 120.00 175.00
34 (q) 4p on 6p gray black 440.00 *600.00*
35 (r) 4p on 6p gray black 800.00 *500.00*

Examples of No. 33 with top of "4" painted in are sometimes offered as No. 35.

Perf. 11 to 13x14 to 15

Wmk. 5

36 (r) 4p on 1p dull red 950.00 625.00
a. Inverted surcharge 3,250.
37 (p) 4p on 1p dull red 850.00 550.00
a. Inverted surcharge
38 (p) 4p on 1sh violet 500.00 *750.00*
39 (q) 4p on 1sh violet *2,750.*

Wmk. Crown and C C (1)

1881 Engr. *Perf. 14*

40 A1 1p brown red 87.50 105.00
a. Diagonal half used as ½p on cover
41 A1 6p olive brown 165.00 215.00
42 A1 1sh slate green 210.00 155.00
Nos. 40-42 (3) 462.50 475.00

A2

1881 Typo.

43 A2 4p ultramarine 170.00 67.50

1882-95 Engr. Wmk. 2

44 A1 1p orange brn ('83) 100.00 35.00
a. Half used as ½p on cover 5,000.
45 A1 1p car lake ('89) 9.00 7.00
46 A1 6p yellow brn ('89) 5.50 *8.00*
47 A1 1sh black brn ('87) 7.50 7.50
a. 1sh deep brown 7.50 5.50

Typo.

Die A

48 A2 ½p dull green ('85) 8.00 7.00
a. ½p blue green ('82) 30.00 32.50
49 A2 2½p red brown ('82) 50.00 20.00
50 A2 4p gray ('84) 42.50 5.00
a. Half used as 2p on cover 5,000.

Die B

51 A2 ½p gray green ('94) 7.00 4.50
52 A2 2½p ultra ('93) 7.50 5.00
53 A2 4p dk vio & bl ('95) 25.00 27.50

For descriptions of dies A and B see "Dies of British Colonial Stamps" in table of contents.

1887 Engr. *Perf. 12*

54 A1 1p carmine lake 47.50 10.00
a. Horiz. pair, imperf. btwn. 30,000.

No. 49 Surcharged in Black

1889

55 A2 1p on 2½p red brn 25.00 *22.50*
a. Double surcharge
b. Double surcharge, one inverted
c. "One" omitted 1,750.
d. Half used as ½p on cover 5,250.

No. 55c caused by the misplacement of the surcharge. Stamps also exist from the same sheet reading "Penny One."

No. 50 Surcharged in Black

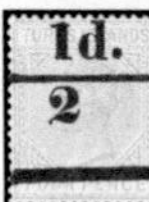

Two types of surcharge:
Type I — Upper bar continuous across sheet.
Type II — Upper bar breaks between stamps.

1893

56 A2 ½p on 4p gray (I) 210.00 160.00
a. Type II 3,750. 1,500.

This surcharge exists in five settings.

A3

1894 Typo.

57 A3 5p olive grn & carmine 12.50 *27.50*
a. Diag. half used as 2½p on cover 5,000.

TUVALU

tü-'vä-,ü

LOCATION — A group of islands in the Pacific Ocean northeast of Australia.
GOVT. — Independent state in the British Commonwealth
AREA — 9½ sq. mi.
POP. — 10,588 (1999 est.)
CAPITAL — Fongafale

Tuvalu, formerly Ellice Islands, consists of nine islands.

Australian dollar

Catalogue values for all unused stamps in this country are for Never Hinged items.

Watermark

Wmk. 380 — "POST OFFICE"

Gilbert and Ellice Islands Types of 1971 Overprinted in Violet Blue or Silver (35c)

No. 1

No. 12

Wmk. 373

1976, Jan. 1 Litho. *Perf. 14*

No.	Type	Description	Unused	Used
1	A18	1c	1.00	.50
2	A19	2c	1.25	.70
a.		Wmk. 314 sideways	200.00	25.00
b.		Wmk. 314 upright	1,400.	140.00
3	A19	3c Wmk. 314	2.00	1.00
a.		Wmk. 373	.65	.45
4	A19	4c	1.25	.70
5	A19	5c Wmk. 314	1.25	*1.00*
6	A18	6c	1.25	.70
7	A18	8c Wmk. 314	1.25	*1.00*
8	A18	10c Wmk. 314	1.25	*1.25*
9	A18	15c	2.00	.80
10	A19	20c	1.25	*1.00*
11	A19	25c Wmk. 314	8.00	2.75
a.		Wmk. 373	.70	*.60*
12	A19	35c	2.00	1.10
13	A18	50c	1.25	*1.00*
a.		Wmk. 314	47.50	22.50
14	A18	$1	1.25	*1.25*
a.		Wmk. 314	110.00	70.00
15	A18	$2	1.60	1.25
		Nos. 1-15 (15)	27.85	16.00

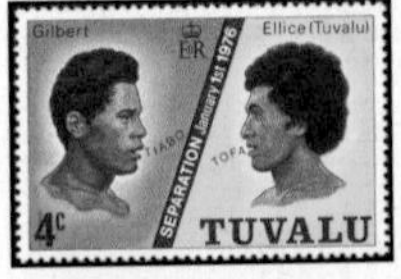

Men from Gilbert and Ellice — A1

Designs: 10c, Map of Gilbert and Ellice Islands, vert. 35c, Gilbert and Ellice canoes.

1976, Jan. 1 Wmk. 373

No.	Type	Description	Unused	Used
16	A1	4c multicolored	.50	.60
17	A1	10c multicolored	.65	.70
18	A1	35c multicolored	.90	1.00
		Nos. 16-18 (3)	2.05	2.30

Separation of the Gilbert and Ellice Islands.

50c Coin and Octopus — A2

New coinage: 10c, 10c-coin and red-dyed crab. 15c, 20c-coin and flyingfish. 35c, $1-coin and green turtle.

Wmk. 373

1976, Apr. 21 Litho. *Perf. 14*

No.	Type	Description	Unused	Used
19	A2	5c bister & multi	.30	.25
20	A2	10c ultra & multi	.40	.30
21	A2	15c blue & multi	.60	.40
22	A2	35c lt green & multi	1.10	.70
		Nos. 19-22 (4)	2.40	1.65

Map of Niulakita, Leathery Turtle — A3

2c, Map of Nukulaelae and sleeping mat. 4c, Map of Nui and talo vegetable. 5c, Map of Nanumanga and grass dancing skirt. 6c, Map of Nukufetau and coconut crab. 8c, Map of Funafuti and banana tree. 10c, Map of Tuvalu Islands. 15c, Map of Niutao and flyingfish. 20c, Map of Vaitupu and maneapa (house). 25c, Map of Nanumea and palu fish hook. 35c, Te Ano Game, horiz. 50c, Canoe pole fishing, horiz. $1, Reef fishing by flare, horiz. $2, House, horiz. $5, Colony Ship M.V. Nivanga, horiz.

1976 Wmk. 373 Litho. *Perf. 13½*

No.	Type	Description	Unused	Used
23-37	A3	Set of 15	30.00	8.50

Issue dates: $5, Sept. 1; others July 1. See #58-70. For overprints see #85-91.

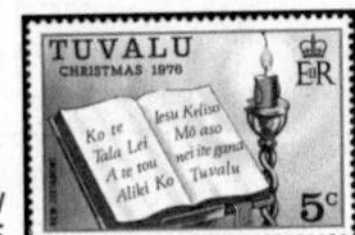

New Testament — A5

Designs: 20c, Lotolelei Church, Nanumea. 25c, Kelupi Church, Nui. 30c, Mataloa o Tuvalu Church, Vaitupu. 35c, Palataiso o Keliso Church, Nanumanga.

Perf. 14x14½

1976, Oct. 6 Litho. Wmk. 373

No.	Type	Description	Unused	Used
38-42	A5	Set of 5	4.50	2.75

Christmas 1976. Printed in sheets of 10 stamps and 2 labels.

Prince Philip Carried Ashore at Vaitupu — A6

Designs: 15c, Queen and Prince Philip on Buckingham Palace balcony. 50c, Queen Leaving Buckingham Palace for coronation.

1977, Feb. 9 Litho. *Perf. 13½x14*

No.	Type	Description	Unused	Used
43	A6	15c multicolored	.70	.60
44	A6	35c multicolored	.90	*1.00*
45	A6	50c multicolored	1.40	1.40
a.		Souv. sheet, #43-45, perf. 15	4.50	4.50
		Nos. 43-45 (3)	3.00	3.00

25th anniv. of the reign of Elizabeth II.

Health (Microscope) — A7

20c, Education (blackboard). 30c, Fruit growing (palm). 35c, Map of South Pacific Territory.

1977, May 4 Litho. *Perf. 13½x14*

No.	Type	Description	Unused	Used
46	A7	5c lilac & multi	.50	.30
47	A7	20c orange & multi	.50	.30
48	A7	30c yellow grn & multi	.50	.30
49	A7	35c lt blue & multi	.75	.45
		Nos. 46-49 (4)	2.25	1.35

South Pacific Commission, 30th anniv.

Swearing-in Ceremony and Scout Emblem — A8

Designs (Scout Emblem and): 20c, Scouts in outrigger canoe. 30c, Scouts under sun shelter. 35c, Lord Baden-Powell.

Perf. 13½x14

1977, Aug. 10 Litho. Wmk. 373

No.	Type	Description	Unused	Used
50	A8	5c multicolored	.30	.30
51	A8	20c multicolored	.30	.30
52	A8	30c multicolored	.50	.50
53	A8	35c multicolored	.50	.50
		Nos. 50-53 (4)	1.60	1.60

Scouting in Tuvalu (Ellice Islands), 50th anniv.

Hurricane Beach and Coral — A9

Designs: 20c, Boring apparatus on "Porpoise," vert. 30c, Map of islands showing line of dredgings to prove Darwin's theory, vert. 35c, Charles Darwin and "Beagle."

Perf. 13½

1977, Nov. 2 Unwmk. Litho.

No.	Type	Description	Unused	Used
54	A9	5c multicolored	.35	.35
55	A9	20c multicolored	.35	.35
56	A9	30c multicolored	.55	.45
57	A9	35c multicolored	.55	.45
		Nos. 54-57 (4)	1.80	1.60

1896-97 Royal Soc. of London Expeditions to explore coral reefs by dredging and boring.

Types of 1976

Designs: 30c, Fatele, local dance. 40c, Screw pine. Others as before.

1977-78 Unwmk. *Perf. 13½*

No.	Type	Description	Unused	Used
58	A3	1c multicolored	.30	.25
59	A3	2c multicolored	.30	.25
60	A3	4c multicolored	.30	.25
61	A3	5c multicolored	.30	.25
62	A3	6c multicolored	.30	.25
63	A3	8c multicolored	.30	.25
64	A3	10c multicolored	.30	.25
66	A3	20c multicolored	1.25	.85
67	A3	25c multicolored	.85	.30
68	A3	30c multi, horiz.	.35	.35
69	A3	40c multi, horiz.	.45	.50
70	A3	$5 multi, horiz.	3.50	3.50
		Nos. 58-70 (12)	8.50	7.25

Issued: #58, 61, 63-64, 67, 1977; others, 1978.

Pacific Pigeon — A10

Wild Birds of Tuvalu: 20c, Reef heron. 30c, Fairy tern. 40c, Lesser frigate bird.

Perf. 14x13½

1978, Jan. 25 Litho. Unwmk.

No.	Type	Description	Unused	Used
73	A10	8c lilac & multi	.80	.50
74	A10	20c ocher & multi	1.05	.70
75	A10	30c dull green & multi	1.30	.95
76	A10	40c brt green & multi	1.30	1.10
		Nos. 73-76 (4)	4.45	3.25

Lawedua A11

Ships: 20c, Tug Wallacia. 30c, Freighter Cenpac Rounder. 40c, Pacific Explorer.

1978, Apr. 5 Unwmk. *Perf. 13½x14*

No.	Type	Description	Unused	Used
77	A11	8c multicolored	.30	.25
78	A11	20c multicolored	.30	.30
79	A11	30c multicolored	.40	.35
80	A11	40c multicolored	.50	.50
		Nos. 77-80 (4)	1.50	1.40

Canterbury Cathedral A12

Designs: 30c, Salisbury Cathedral. 40c, Wells Cathedral. $1, Hereford Cathedral.

1978, June 2 Litho. *Perf. 13½x14*

No.	Type	Description	Unused	Used
81	A12	8c multicolored	.30	.25
82	A12	30c multicolored	.30	.25
83	A12	40c multicolored	.30	.25
84	A12	$1 multicolored	.30	.25
a.		Souv. sheet, #81-84, perf. 15	.60	.60
		Nos. 81-84 (4)	1.20	1.00

25th anniv. of coronation of Elizabeth II. #81-84 were also issued in bklt. panes of 2.

Types of 1976 Ovptd.

1978, Oct. 1 Litho. *Perf. 13½*

No.	Type	Description	Unused	Used
85	A3	8c multicolored	.30	.25
86	A3	10c multicolored	.30	.25
87	A3	15c multicolored	.30	.25
88	A3	20c multicolored	.30	.25
89	A3	30c multi, horiz.	.30	.25
90	A3	35c multi, horiz.	.30	.25
91	A3	40c multi, horiz.	.30	.25
		Nos. 85-91 (7)	2.10	1.75

Independence, Oct. 1, 1978. Overprint in 3 lines on vert. stamps, 1 line on horiz.

White Frangipani — A13

Wild Flowers: 20c, Zephyrantes rosea. 30c, Gardenia taitensis. 40c, Clerodendron inerme.

1978, Oct. 4 Unwmk. *Perf. 14*

No.	Type	Description	Unused	Used
92	A13	8c multicolored	.30	.25
93	A13	20c multicolored	.30	*.30*
94	A13	30c multicolored	.30	*.40*
95	A13	40c multicolored	.35	*.70*
		Nos. 92-95 (4)	1.25	1.65

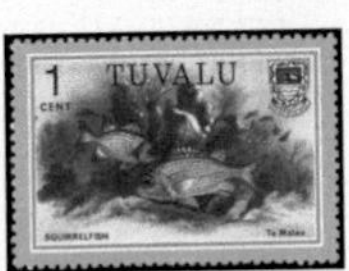

Squirrelfish A14

Fish: 2c, Yellow-banded goatfish. 4c, Imperial angelfish. 5c, Rainbow butterfly. 6c, Blue angelfish. 8c, Blue striped snapper. 10c, Orange clownfish. 15c, Chevroned coralfish. 20c, Fairy cod. 25c, Clown triggerfish. 30c, Long-nosed butterfly. 35c, Yellowfin tuna. 40c, Spotted eagle ray. 45c, Black-tipped rock cod. 50c, Hammerhead shark. 70c, Lionfish, vert. $1, White-barred triggerfish, vert. $2, Beaked coralfish, vert. $5, Tiger shark, vert.

1979, Jan. 24 Litho. *Perf. 14*

No.	Type	Description	Unused	Used
96	A14	1c multicolored	.30	.25
97	A14	2c multicolored	.30	.25
98	A14	4c multicolored	.30	.25
99	A14	5c multicolored	.30	.25
100	A14	6c multicolored	.30	.25
101	A14	8c multicolored	.30	.25
102	A14	10c multicolored	.30	.25
103	A14	15c multicolored	.30	.25
104	A14	20c multicolored	.30	.25
105	A14	25c multicolored	.30	.25
106	A14	30c multicolored	.30	.25
107	A14	35c multicolored	.30	.25
108	A14	40c multicolored	.30	.30
108A	A14	45c multicolored	.85	.60
109	A14	50c multicolored	.30	.25
110	A14	70c multicolored	.30	.30
111	A14	$1 multicolored	.35	.35

112 A14 $2 multicolored .85 .85
113 A14 $5 multicolored 2.00 2.00
Nos. 96-113 (19) 8.55 7.65

No. 108A issued June 16, 1981.
#101, 104, 106, 108 and #102, 105, 107, 108A were also issued in booklet panes of 4.
For surcharge & overprints see #150, O1-O19.

Capt. Cook — A15

Designs: 30c, Flag raising on new island. 40c, Observation of transit of Venus. $1, Death of Capt. Cook.

1979, Feb. 14 ***Perf. 14x14½***
114 A15 8c multicolored .30 .25
115 A15 30c multicolored .30 .25
116 A15 40c multicolored .30 .25
117 A15 $1 multicolored .30 .30
a. Strip of 4, #114-117 1.40 1.40

Bicentenary of death of Capt. James Cook (1728-1779). Nos. 114-117 printed se-tenant horizontally in sheets of 12 (4x3) with gutters between horizontal rows.

Grumman Goose over Nukulaelae A16

Grumman Goose over: 20c, Vaitupu. 30c, Nui. 40c, Funafuti.

1979, May 16 **Litho.** ***Perf. 14x13½***
118 A16 8c multicolored .30 .25
119 A16 20c multicolored .30 .25
120 A16 30c multicolored .30 *.30*
121 A16 40c multicolored .30 .30
Nos. 118-121 (4) 1.20 1.10

Inauguration of internal air service.

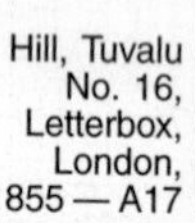
Hill, Tuvalu No. 16, Letterbox, London, 1855 — A17

Hill, Stamps of Tuvalu and: 40c, No. 17, Penny Black. $1, No. 18, mail coach.

1979, Aug. 20 **Litho.** ***Perf. 13½x14***
122 A17 30c multicolored .30 .25
123 A17 40c multicolored .30 .25
124 A17 $1 multicolored .35 .35
a. Souvenir sheet of 3, #122-124 1.00 1.00
Nos. 122-124 (3) .95 .85

Sir Rowland Hill (1795-1879), originator of penny postage.

Boy — A18

Designs: Children of Tuvalu.

1979, Oct. 20 **Litho.** ***Perf. 14***
125 A18 8c multicolored .30 .25
126 A18 20c multicolored .30 .25
127 A18 30c multicolored .30 .25
128 A18 40c multicolored .30 .25
Nos. 125-128 (4) 1.20 1.00

International Year of the Child.

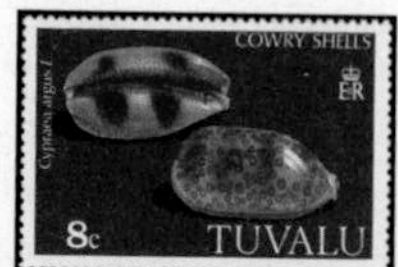
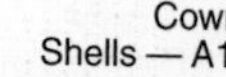
Cowry Shells — A19

1980, Feb. **Litho.** ***Perf. 14***
129 A19 8c Cypraea Argus .30 .25
130 A19 20c Cypraea scurra .30 .25
131 A19 30c Cypraea carneola .30 .30
132 A19 40c Cypraea aurantium .40 .40
Nos. 129-132 (4) 1.30 1.20

Philatelic Bureau, Funafuti, Tuvalu No. 28, Arms, London 1980 Emblem A20

Coat of Arms, London 1980 Emblem and: 20c, Gilbert and Ellice #41, Nukulaelae cancel, Tuvalu #24. 30c, US airmail cover. $1, Map of Tuvalu.

1980, Apr. 30 **Litho.** ***Perf. 13½x14***
133 A20 10c multicolored .30 .25
134 A20 20c multicolored .30 .25
135 A20 30c multicolored .30 .30
136 A20 $1 multicolored .55 .55
a. Souvenir sheet of 4, #133-136 1.75 1.75
Nos. 133-136 (4) 1.45 1.35

London 80 Intl. Stamp Exhib., May 6-14.

Queen Mother Elizabeth, 80th Birthday — A21

1980, Aug. 14 **Litho.** ***Perf. 14***
137 A21 50c multicolored .40 .40

Issued in sheets of 10 plus 2 labels.

Aethaloessa Calidalis — A22

20c, Parotis suralis. 30c, Dudua aprobola. 40c, Decadarchis simulans.

1980, Aug. 20 **Litho.** ***Perf. 14***
138 A22 8c shown .30 .25
139 A22 20c multicolored .30 .25
140 A22 30c multicolored .30 .30
141 A22 40c multicolored .30 .30
Nos. 138-141 (4) 1.20 1.10

Air Pacific Heron (First Regular Air Service to Tuvalu, 1964) — A23

Aviation Anniversaries: 20c, Hawker Siddeley 748 (air service to Tuvalu). 30c, Sunderland Flying Boat (War time service to Funafuti, 1945. 40c, Orville Wright and Flyer (Wright brothers' first flight, 1903).

1980, Nov. 5 **Litho.** ***Perf. 14***
142 A23 8c multicolored .30 .25
143 A23 20c multicolored .30 .25
144 A23 30c multicolored .30 .25
145 A23 40c multicolored .30 .30
Nos. 142-145 (4) 1.20 1.05

Hypolimnas Bolina Elliciana — A24

1981, Feb. 3 **Litho.** ***Perf. 14½***
146 A24 8c shown .30 .30
147 A24 20c Hypolimnas, diff. .30 .30
148 A24 30c Hypolimnas, diff. .35 .35
149 A24 40c Junonia vallida .55 .55
Nos. 146-149 (4) 1.50 1.50

No. 109 Surcharged

1981, Feb. 24 **Litho.** ***Perf. 14***
150 A14 45c on 50c multicolored .60 .60

Elizabeth, 1809 — A25

25c, Rebecca, 1819. 35c, Independence II, 1821. 40c, Basilisk, 1872. 45c, Royalist, 1890. 50c, Olivebank, 1920.

Wmk. 373

1981, May 13 **Litho.** ***Perf. 14***
151 A25 10c shown .30 .25
152 A25 25c multicolored .30 .25
153 A25 35c multicolored .30 .25
154 A25 40c multicolored .30 .30
155 A25 45c multicolored .35 .35
156 A25 50c multicolored .45 .45
Nos. 151-156 (6) 2.00 1.85

See Nos. 216-221, 353-356, 410-413.

Prince Charles, Lady Diana, Royal Yacht Charlotte A25a

Prince Charles and Lady Diana A25b

No. 157, Couple, Carolina. No. 158, Couple. No. 159, Victoria and Albert III. No. 161, Britannia.

Wmk. 380

1981, July 10 **Litho.** ***Perf. 14***
157 A25a 10c multicolored .30 .25
a. Blkt. pane of 4, perf. 12, unwmkd. .60
158 A25b 10c multicolored .30 .25
159 A25a 45c multicolored .30 .25
160 A25b 45c like #158 .30 .25
a. Blkt. pane of 2, perf. 12, unwmkd. 1.00
161 A25a $2 multicolored .50 .50
162 A25b $2 like #158 1.40 1.40
Nos. 157-162 (6) 3.10 2.90

Royal wedding. Issued in sheets of 7 (6 design A25a; 1 design A25b). Set of 3 $12.
For surcharges see Nos. B1-B2.

Souvenir Sheet

1981, Dec. **Litho.** ***Perf. 12***
163 A25b $1.50 Couple 1.00 1.00

Admission to UPU — A26

Wmk. Harrison's, London

1981, Nov. 19 **Engr.** ***Perf. 14½x14***
164 A26 70c dark blue .45 .45
165 A26 $1 dark red brown .65 .65
a. Souv. sheet of 2, #164-165, unwmkd. 1.40 1.40

Amatuku Maritime School — A27

1982, Feb. 17 **Litho.** ***Perf. 13½x14***
166 A27 10c Map .30 .25
167 A27 25c Motorboat .30 .25
168 A27 35c School, dock .30 .30
169 A27 45c Flag, ship .40 .40
Nos. 166-169 (4) 1.30 1.20

A27a

Wmk. 380

1982, May 19 **Litho.** ***Perf. 14***
170 A27a 10c Caroline of Brandenburg-Ansbach, 1714 .30 .25
171 A27a 45c Brandenburg-Ansbach arms .30 .25
172 A27a $1.50 Diana .50 .50
Nos. 170-172 (3) 1.10 1.00

21st birthday of Princess Diana, July 1.

Nos. 170-172 Overprinted "ROYAL BABY"

1982, July 14 **Litho.** ***Perf. 14***
173 A27a 10c multicolored .30 .30
174 A27a 45c multicolored .30 .30
175 A27a $1.50 multicolored .40 .40
Nos. 173-175 (3) 1.00 1.00

Birth of Prince William of Wales, June 21.

Scouting Year — A28

1982, Aug. 18
176 A28 10c Emblems .30 .25
177 A28 25c Campfire .30 .30
178 A28 35c Parade .35 .35
179 A28 45c Scout .40 .40
Nos. 176-179 (4) 1.35 1.30

Visit of Queen Elizabeth II and Prince Philip — A29

25c, Arms, Duke of Edinburgh's Personal Standard. 45c, Flags. 50c, Queen Elizabeth II, maps.

1982, Oct. 26 **Litho.** ***Perf. 14***
180 A29 25c multicolored .30 .25
181 A29 45c multicolored .30 .30
182 A29 50c multicolored .35 .35
a. Souvenir sheet of 3, #180-182 1.25 1.25
Nos. 180-182 (3) .95 .90

Handicrafts A30

1c, Fisherman's hat, lures, hooks. 2c, Cowrie shell handbags. 5c, Wedding & baby food baskets. 10c, Canoe model. 15c, Women's sun hats. 20c, Climbing rope. 25c, Pandanus baskets. 30c, Tray, coconut stands. 35c, Pandanus pillows, shell necklaces. 40c, Round baskets, fans. 45c, Reef sandals, fish trap. 50c, Rat trap, vert. 60c, Waterproof boxes, vert. $1, Pump drill, adze, vert. $2, Fisherman's hat, canoe bailers, vert. $5, Fishing rod, lures, scoop nets, vert.

1983-84 **Litho.** ***Perf. 14***
183 A30 1c multicolored .30 .25
184 A30 2c multicolored .30 .25
185 A30 5c multicolored .30 .25
186 A30 10c multicolored .30 .25
186A A30 15c multicolored 2.25 *2.50*
187 A30 20c multicolored .30 .25
188 A30 25c multicolored .30 .25
188A A30 30c multicolored 2.00 2.00

189 A30 35c multicolored .40 .30
190 A30 40c multicolored .30 *.45*
191 A30 45c multicolored .35 *.55*
192 A30 50c multicolored .40 .60
192A A30 60c multicolored 2.75 2.00
193 A30 $1 multicolored .40 *.60*
194 A30 $2 multicolored .60 *.75*
195 A30 $5 multicolored 1.00 *1.10*
Nos. 183-195 (16) 12.25 12.35

Issued: 15c, 1984; others, 3/14/83.

For surcharges & overprints see #207, 230, O20-O32.

Commonwealth Day — A31

Wmk. 373

1983, Mar. 14 Litho. *Perf. 14*
196 A31 20c Fishing industry .30 .25
197 A31 35c Traditional dancing .30 .25
198 A31 45c Satellite view .30 .25
199 A31 50c First container ship .30 .30
Nos. 196-199 (4) 1.20 1.05

Dragonflies A32

10c, Pantala flavescens. 35c, Anax guttatus. 40c, Tholymis tillarga. 50c, Diplacodes bipunctata.

1983, May 25 Wmk. 380
200 A32 10c multicolored .30 .25
201 A32 35c multicolored .50 .50
202 A32 40c multicolored .60 .60
203 A32 50c multicolored .65 .65
Nos. 200-203 (4) 2.05 2.00

Boys Brigade Centenary A33

1983, Aug. 10 Wmk. 373
204 A33 10c Running, emblem .30 .25
205 A33 35c Canoeing .30 .30
206 A33 $1 Officer, boys .75 .75
Nos. 204-206 (3) 1.35 1.30

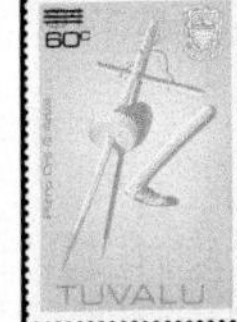

No. 193 Surcharged in Black

1983, Aug. 26 Wmk. 380
207 A30 60c on $1 multi 1.00 .60

First Manned Flight Bicentenary A34

25c, Montgolfier balloon, vert. 35c, McKinnon Turbo Goose. 45c, Beechcraft Super King Air 200. 50c, Double Eagle II Balloon, vert.

1983, Sept. 21 Wmk. 373
208 A34 25c multicolored .30 .30
209 A34 35c multicolored .40 .40
210 A34 45c multicolored .45 .45
211 A34 50c multicolored .55 .55
a. Souvenir sheet of 4, #208-211 1.75 1.75
Nos. 208-211 (4) 1.70 1.70

World Communications Year — A35

25c, Conch Shell Trumpet, vert. 35c, Radio Operator, vert. 45c, Teleprinter. 50c, Transmitting station.

1983, Nov. 18 Wmk. 380
212 A35 25c multicolored .30 .25
213 A35 35c multicolored .30 .30
214 A35 45c multicolored .35 .35
215 A35 50c multicolored .40 .40
Nos. 212-215 (4) 1.35 1.30

Ship Type of 1981

1984, Feb. 16 Wmk. 380
216 A25 10c Titus, 1897 .30 .25
217 A25 20c Malaita, 1905 .30 .25
218 A25 25c Aymeric, 1906 .30 .25
219 A25 35c Anshun, 1965 .35 .35
220 A25 45c Beaverbank, 1970 .40 .40
221 A25 50c Benjamin Bowring, 1981 .55 .55
Nos. 216-221 (6) 2.20 2.05

Leaders of the World
Large quantities of some Leaders of the World issues were sold at a fraction of face value when the printer was liquidated.

Historic Locomotives A36

1c, Class GS-4, US, 1941. 15c, AD-60, Australia, 1952. 40c, C38, Australia, 1943. 60c, Achilles England, 1892.

Se-tenant Pairs, #a.-b.
a. — Side and front views.
b. — Action scene.

Perf. 12½x13

1984, Feb. 29 Unwmk.
222 A36 1c multicolored .30 .25
223 A36 15c multicolored .30 .25
224 A36 40c multicolored .45 .45
225 A36 60c multicolored .65 .65
Nos. 222-225 (4) 1.70 1.60

See Nos. 235-246, 291-294, 320-323.

No. 191 Surcharged
Wmk. 380

1984, Feb. 1 Litho. *Perf. 14*
230 A30 30c on 45c multi .40 .40

For overprint see No. O25.

Beach Flowers — A38

25c, Ipomoea pes-caprae. 45c, Ipomoea macrantha. 50c, Triumfetta procumbens. 60c, Portulaca quadrifida.

1984, May 30
231 A38 25c multicolored .30 .25
232 A38 45c multicolored .40 .40
233 A38 50c multicolored .50 .50
234 A38 60c multicolored .65 .65
Nos. 231-234 (4) 1.85 1.80

Train Type of 1984

No. 235, Class 9700, Japan, 1897. No. 236, Casey Jones, US, 1896. No. 237, Class 231C/K, France, 1909. No. 238, Triplex, US, 1914. No. 239, Class 370, Gt. Britain, 1981. No. 240, Class 4F, Gt. Britain, 1924. No. 241, Class 640, Italy, 1907. No. 242, Tornado, Gt. Britain, 1888. No. 243, Broadlands, Gt. Britain, 1967. No. 244, Locomotion, Gt. Britain, 1825. No. 245, C57, Japan, 1937. No. 246, Class 4500, France, 1906.

Se-tenant Pairs, #a.-b.
a. — Side and front views.
b. — Action scene.

1984 Litho. *Perf. 12½x13*
235 A36 1c multicolored .30 .25
236 A36 10c multicolored .30 .25
237 A36 15c multicolored .30 .25
238 A36 15c multicolored .30 .25
239 A36 20c multicolored .30 .25
240 A36 25c multicolored .30 .25
241 A36 30c multicolored .30 .30
242 A36 40c multicolored .30 .30
243 A36 50c multicolored .35 .35
244 A36 60c multicolored .50 .50
245 A36 $1 multicolored .75 .75
246 A36 $1 multicolored .75 .75
Nos. 235-246 (12) 4.75 4.45

Issued: Nos. 235, 237, 241, 245, 10/4; others, 6/27.

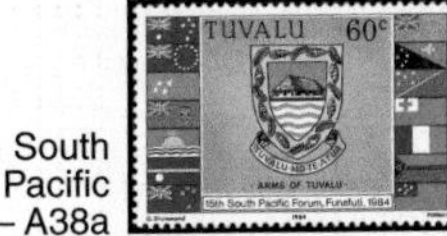

15th South Pacific Forum — A38a

1984, Aug. 21 Litho. *Perf. 14*
255 A38a 60c National flag .55 .55
256 A38a 60c Tuvalu crest .55 .55

Ausipex '84 — A38b

1984, Aug. 21 *Perf. 14*
257 A38b 60c Exhib. emblem .45 .45
258 A38b 60c Royal Exhibi. Building .45 .45

A. Shrewsbury Playing Cricket — A39

Cricket players in action or portrait.

Se-tenant Pairs #a.-b.

1984, Nov. 5 Litho. *Perf. 12½*
259 A39 5c shown .30 .25
260 A39 30c H. Verity .50 .50
261 A39 50c E.H. Hendren .50 .50
262 A39 60c J. Briggs .60 .60
Nos. 259-262 (4) 1.90 1.85

Drawings, Christmas 1984 — A40

1984, Nov. 14 Litho. *Perf. 14½x14*
267 A40 15c By Eli Faalata .30 .25
268 A40 40c By Toakai Niutao .30 .30
269 A40 50c By Falesa Teuila .40 .40
270 A40 60c By Piuani Talie .50 .50
Nos. 267-270 (4) 1.50 1.45

Classic Automobiles A41

Sketch listed first followed by angled view: 1c, Morris Minor, 1949. 15c, Studebaker Avanti, 1963. 50c, Chevrolet International Six, 1929. $1, Allard J2, 1950.

Se-tenant Pairs, #a.-b.
a. — Side and front views.
b. — Action scene.

1984, Dec. 7 Litho. *Perf. 12½x13*
271 A41 1c multicolored .30 .30
272 A41 15c multicolored .30 .30
273 A41 50c multicolored .60 .60
274 A41 $1 multicolored 1.25 1.25
Nos. 271-274 (4) 2.45 2.45

See Nos. 299-302, 332-339, 391-396, 414-425.

John J. Audubon A42

#279a, Common flicker. #279b, Say's phoebe. #280a, Townsend's warbler. #280b, Bohemian waxwing. #281a, Prothonotary warbler. #281b, Worm-eating warbler. #282a, Broad-winged hawk. #282b, Northern harrier.

1985, Feb. 12 Litho. *Perf. 12½*
279 A42 1c Pair, #a.-b. .30 .30
280 A42 25c Pair, #a.-b. .45 .45
281 A42 50c Pair, #a.-b. .90 .90
282 A42 70c Pair, #a.-b. 1.10 1.10
Nos. 279-282 (4) 2.75 2.75

Birds and Eggs — A43

15c, Black-naped tern. 40c, Black noddy. 50c, White-tailed tropicbird. 60c, Sooty tern.

1985, Feb. 27 *Perf. 14*
287 A43 15c multicolored .30 .25
288 A43 40c multicolored .60 .45
289 A43 50c multicolored .75 .50
290 A43 60c multicolored .90 .70
Nos. 287-290 (4) 2.55 1.90

Train Type of 1984

5c, Churchward, U.K. 10c, Class K.F., China. 30c, Class 99.77, East Germany. $1, Pearson, U.K.

Se-tenant Pairs, #a.-b.
a. — Side and front views.
b. — Action scene.

1985, Mar. 19 *Perf. 12½*
291 A36 5c multicolored .30 .25
292 A36 10c multicolored .30 .25
293 A36 30c multicolored .40 .40
294 A36 $1 multicolored 1.25 1.25
Nos. 291-294 (4) 2.25 2.15

Automobile Type of 1984

1c, Rickenbacker, 1923. 20c, Detroit-Electric, 1914. 50c, Packard Clipper, 1941. 70c, Audi Quattro, 1982.

Se-tenant Pairs, #a.-b.
a. — Side and front views.
b. — Action scene.

1985, Apr. 3
299 A41 1c multicolored .30 .30
300 A41 20c multicolored .30 .30
301 A41 50c multicolored .65 .65
302 A41 70c multicolored 1.00 1.00
Nos. 299-302 (4) 2.25 2.25

World War II Aircraft — A44

15c, Curtiss P-40N. 40c, Consolidated B-24D Liberator. 50c, Lockheed PV-1 Ventura. 60c, Douglas C-54 Skymaster.

1985, May 29 Litho. *Perf. 14*
307 A44 15c multicolored 1.00 .60
308 A44 40c multicolored 1.15 .85
309 A44 50c multicolored 1.15 1.30
310 A44 60c multicolored 1.15 1.30
a. Souvenir sheet of 4, #307-310 4.00 4.00
Nos. 307-310 (4) 4.45 4.05

Queen Mother, 85th Birthday A45

Designs: No. 311a, Facing right. No. 311b, Facing left. Nos. 312a, 317a, Facing right, diff. Nos. 312b, 317b, Facing front. Nos. 313a, 316a, Waving to crowd. Nos. 313b, 316b, Facing front, diff. No. 314a, Facing front. No.

314b, Facing left. No. 315a, As a young woman. No. 315b, As Queen Consort.

1985-86 Litho. *Perf. 12½*

311 A45 5c Pair, #a.-b. .30 .30
312 A45 30c Pair, #a.-b. .30 .30
313 A45 60c Pair, #a.-b. .50 .50
314 A45 $1 Pair, #a.-b. .80 .80
Nos. 311-314 (4) 1.90 1.90

Souvenir Sheets

315 A45 $1.20 #a.-b. 1.90 1.90
316 A45 $2 #a.-b. 4.50 4.50
317 A45 $3 #a.-b. 6.50 6.50

Issued: #316-317, 6/10/86; others, 7/4/85.

Train Type of 1984

10c, 1936 Green Arrow, U.K. 40c, 1982 G.M. (EMD) SD-50, US. 65c, 1932 DRG Flying Hamburger, Germany. $1, 1908 JNR Class 1070, Japan.

Se-tenant Pairs, #a.-b.
a. — Side and front views.
b. — Action scene.

1985, Sept. 18

320 A36 10c multicolored .30 .25
321 A36 40c multicolored .50 .50
322 A36 65c multicolored .65 .65
323 A36 $1 multicolored .70 .70
Nos. 320-323 (4) 2.15 2.10

Girl Guides, 75th Anniv. — A46

1985, Aug. 28 Litho. *Perf. 15*

328 A46 15c Playing guitar .30 .25
329 A46 40c Camping .50 .50
330 A46 50c Flag bearer .60 .60
331 A46 60c Guides' salute .70 .70
a. Souvenir sheet of 4, #328-331 2.00 2.00
Nos. 328-331 (4) 2.10 2.05

Car Type of 1984

5c, 1929 Cord L-29, US. 10c, 1932 Horch 670 V-12, Germany. 15c, 1901 Lanchester, UK. 35c, 1950 Citroen 2 CV, France. 40c, 1957 MGA, UK. 55c, 1962 Ferrari 250-GTO, Italy. $1, 1932 Ford V-8, US. $1.50, 1977 Aston Martin-Lagonda, UK.

a. — Side and front views.
b. — Action scene.

1985, Oct. 8 *Perf. 12½*

332-339 A41 Set of 8 pairs 4.00 4.00

Crabs — A47

15c, Stalk-eyed ghost. 40c, Red and white painted. 50c, Red-spotted. 60c, Red hermit.

1986, Jan. 7 *Perf. 15*

348 A47 15c multicolored .30 .30
349 A47 40c multicolored .60 .60
350 A47 50c multicolored .75 .75
351 A47 60c multicolored .90 .90
Nos. 348-351 (4) 2.55 2.55

Souvenir Sheet of 2

Fischer & Karpov, World Chess Champions; Rotary Intl., 80th Anniv. — A48

No. 352a, American and Soviet flags, chess board & knight. No. 352b, Rotary Intl. emblem.

1986, Mar. 19 Litho. *Perf. 13x12½*

352 A48 $3 #a.-b. 6.50 6.50

No. 352 exists with plain or decorated border.

Ship Type of 1981

15c, Messenger of Peace. 40c, John Wesley. 50c, Duff. 60c, Triton.

1986, Apr. 14 *Perf. 15*

353 A25 15c multicolored .30 .30
354 A25 40c multicolored .80 .80
355 A25 50c multicolored .90 .90
356 A25 60c multicolored 1.00 1.00
Nos. 353-356 (4) 3.00 3.00

Queen Elizabeth II, 60th Birthday A49

Various portraits.

1986, Apr. 21 *Perf. 12½*

357 A49 10c multicolored .30 .25
358 A49 90c multicolored .35 .35
359 A49 $1.50 multicolored .60 .60
360 A49 $3 multi, vert. 1.10 1.10
Nos. 357-360 (4) 2.35 2.30

Souvenir Sheet

361 A49 $4 multicolored 3.00 3.00

Peace Corps, 25th Anniv. — A50

1986, May 22 *Perf. 14*

362 A50 50c multicolored .80 .80

For overprint see No. 374.

AMERIPEX '86 — A51

1986, May 22 *Perf. 14x13½*

363 A51 60c multicolored .80 .80

A52

Players and teams: 1c, South Korea. 5c, France. 10c, W. Germany, 1974. 40c, Italy. 60c, W. Germany vs. Holland, 1974. $1, Canada. $2, Northern Ireland. $3, England.

1986, June 30 Litho. *Perf. 15*

364 A52 1c multi .30 .25
365 A52 5c multi .30 .25
366 A52 10c multi .30 .25
367 A52 40c multi .40 .40

Size: 60x40mm

Perf. 13x12½

368 A52 60c multi .50 .50
369 A52 $1 multi .80 .80
370 A52 $2 multi 1.75 1.75
371 A52 $3 multi 2.40 2.40
Nos. 364-371 (8) 6.75 6.60

Souvenir Sheets

372 A52 $1.50 like #369 1.75 1.75
373 A52 $2.50 like #370 3.00 3.00

1986 World Cup Soccer Championships. Nos. 366 and 368 picture emblem; others picture character trademark.

No. 362 Ovptd. with STAMPEX '86 Emblem

1986, Aug. 4 Litho. *Perf. 14*

374 A50 50c multicolored .70 .70

A53

Wedding of Prince Andrew and Sarah Ferguson A54

#381a, Andrew, vert. #381b, Couple, vert. #382a, Andrew. #382b, Princess Diana, Sarah.

Perf. 12½

1986, July 18 Litho. Unwmk.

381 A53 60c Pair, #a.-b. .75 .75
382 A53 $1 Pair, #a.-b. 1.25 1.25

Souvenir Sheet

Perf. 13x12½

383 A54 $6 Newlyweds 3.00 3.00

No. 382a pictures Westminster Abbey in LR. For overprints see Nos. 389-390.

Geckos — A55

1986, July 30 Litho. *Perf. 14*

384 A55 15c Mourning gecko .30 .30
385 A55 40c Oceanic stump-toed .90 .80
386 A55 50c Azure-tailed skink 1.20 1.05
387 A55 60c Moth skink 1.65 1.40
Nos. 384-387 (4) 4.05 3.55

Souvenir Sheet

South Pacific Forum, 15th Anniv. — A56

Flags and maps: a, Australia. b, Cook Islands. c, Micronesia. d, Fiji. e, Kiribati. f, Nauru. g, New Zealand. h, Niue. i, Papua New Guinea. j, Solomon Islands. k, Tonga. l, Tuvalu. m, Vanuatu. n, Western Samoa.

Wmk. 380

1986, Aug. 4 Litho. *Perf. 15*

388 Sheet of 14 + label 9.00 9.00
a.-n. A56 40c any single .60 .60

No. 388 has center label picturing Executive Committee headquarters, Suva, Fiji.

Nos. 381-382 Ovptd. "Congratulations to T.R.H. The Duke & Duchess of York" in Silver

1986 Unwmk. *Perf. 12½*

389 A53 60c Pair, #a.-b. 1.75 1.75
390 A53 $1 Pair, #a.-b. 2.75 2.75

Exist tete-beche.

Car Type of 1984

15c, 1953 Cooper, UK. 40c, 1964 Rover 2000, UK. 50c, 1930 Ruxton, US. 60c, 1950 Jowett Jupiter, UK. 90c, 1964 Cobra Daytona Coupe, US. $1.50, 1903 Packard Model F "Old Pacific," US.

Se-tenant Pairs, #a.-b.
a. — Side and front views.
b. — Action scene.

1986, Oct. Litho. *Perf. 12½*

391-396 A41 Set of 6 pairs 3.50 3.50

Marine Life — A57

1986, Nov. 5 Unwmk. *Perf. 14*

397 A57 15c Sea star .95 .95
398 A57 40c Pencil urchin 1.60 1.60
399 A57 50c Fragile coral 1.75 1.75
400 A57 60c Pink coral 2.00 2.00
Nos. 397-400 (4) 6.30 6.30

See Nos. 465-468, 524-527.

Souvenir Sheets

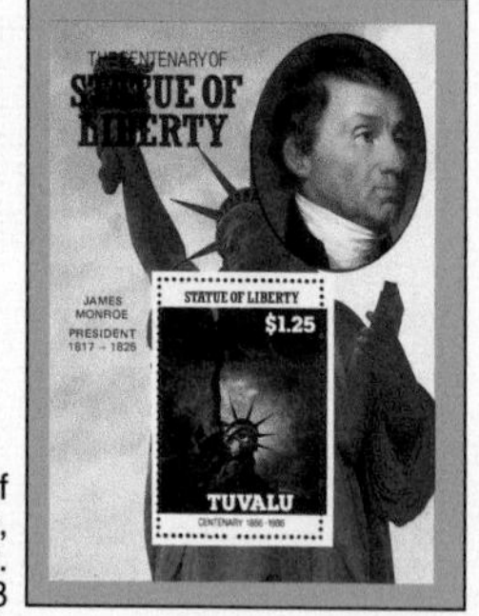

Statue of Liberty, Cent. A58

Various views of the statue.

1986, Nov. 24

401 A58 $1.25 multicolored .45 .45
402 A58 $1.50 multicolored .65 .65
403 A58 $1.80 multicolored .80 .80
404 A58 $2 multicolored .85 .85
405 A58 $2.25 multicolored 1.05 1.05
406 A58 $2.50 multicolored 1.10 1.10
407 A58 $3 multicolored 1.40 1.40
408 A58 $3.25 multicolored 1.45 1.45
409 A58 $3.50 multicolored 1.75 1.75
Nos. 401-409 (9) 9.50 9.50

A perforated set of sixteen 65c stamps commemorating the Statue of Liberty centennial in a different design were printed but never issued. The stamps were sold in the liquidation sale of the printer.

Ships Type of 1981

1987, Feb. 4 Unwmk. *Perf. 14*

410 A25 15c Southern Cross IV .70 .70
411 A25 40c John Williams VI 1.55 1.55
412 A25 50c John Williams IV 1.75 1.75
413 A25 60c M.S. Southern Cross 1.75 1.75
Nos. 410-413 (4) 5.75 5.75

Car Type of 1984

1c, 1938 Talbot-Lago, France. 2c, 1930 Dupont Model G, US. 5c, 1950 Riley RM, U.K. 10c, 1915 Chevrolet Baby Grand, US. 20c, 1968 Shelby Mustang GT 500 KR, US. 30c, 1952 Ferrari 212 Export Barchetta, Italy. 40c, 1912 Peerless Model 48-Six, US. 50c, 1954 Sunbeam Alpine, U.K. 60c, 1969 Matra-Ford MS80, France. 70c, 1934 Squire 1-Litre, U.K. 75c, 1931 Talbot 105, U.K. $1, 1928 Plymouth Model Q, US.

Se-tenant Pairs, #a.-b.
a. — Side and front views.
b. — Action scene.

Perf. 12½

1987, May 7 Litho. Unwmk.

414-425 A41 Set of 12 pairs, #a.-b. 6.50 6.50
425c Souv. sheet of 2 2.50 2.50

Ferns — A59

15c, Nephrolepis saligna. 40c, Asplenium nidus. 50c, Microsorum scolopendria. 60c, Pteris tripartita.
$1.50, Psilotum nudum.

1987, July 7 Wmk. 380 *Perf. 14*

438 A59 15c multicolored .30 .25
439 A59 40c multicolored .65 .65
440 A59 50c multicolored .80 .80
441 A59 60c multicolored .85 .85
Nos. 438-441 (4) 2.60 2.55

Souvenir Sheet

442 A59 $1.50 multicolored 2.50 2.50

A60

#443a, 444b, 445a, 456b, Flowers, all diff. #443b, 444a, 445b, 456a, Woman wearing fou, all diff.

1987, Aug. 12 Wmk. 380

443 A60 15c Pair, #a.-b. .35 .35
444 A60 40c Pair, #a.-b. .85 .85
445 A60 50c Pair, #a.-b. 1.00 1.00
446 A60 60c Pair, #a.-b. 1.35 1.35
Nos. 443-446 (4) 3.55 3.55

Crayfish and Coconut Crabs — A61

Wmk. 380

1987, Nov. 11 Litho. *Perf. 14*

451 A61 40c Coconut crabs .80 .60
452 A61 50c Painted crayfish 1.00 .75
453 A61 60c Ocean crayfish 1.20 .95
Nos. 451-453 (3) 3.00 2.30

Photograph of Queen Victoria, 1897, by Downey — A62

60c, Elizabeth and Philip on their wedding day, 1947. 80c, Elizabeth, Charles, Philip, c. 1950. $1, Elizabeth, Anne, 1950. $2, Elizabeth, 1970. $3, Elizabeth, children, 1950.

1987, Nov. 20 Unwmk. *Perf. 15*

454-458 A62 Set of 5 3.50 3.50

Souvenir Sheet

459 A62 $3 red org & blk 3.00 3.00

Accession of Queen Victoria to the throne of England, sesquicentennial; wedding of Queen Elizabeth II and Prince Philip, 40th anniv.

16th World Scout Jamboree, Australia, 1987-88 — A63

Jamboree and Australia bicentennial emblems plus: 40c, Aborigine, Ayer's Rock. 60c, Capt. Cook, by Dance, and HMS Endeavor. $1, Scout and Scout Park Arch. $1.50, Koala and kangaroo. $2.50, Lord and Lady Baden-Powell.

Perf. 13x12½

1987, Dec. 2 Litho. Unwmk.

460 A63 40c multicolored .35 .35
461 A63 60c multicolored .50 .50
462 A63 $1 multicolored .85 .85
463 A63 $1.50 multicolored 1.15 1.15
Nos. 460-463 (4) 2.85 2.85

Souvenir Sheet

464 A63 $2.50 multicolored 2.50 2.50

Marine Life Type of 1986

Unwmk.

1988, Feb. 29 Litho. *Perf. 15*

465 A57 15c Spanish dancer .55 .35
466 A57 40c Hard corals 1.30 .75
467 A57 50c Feather stars 1.60 .95
468 A57 60c Staghorn corals 1.90 1.10
Nos. 465-468 (4) 5.35 3.15

Birds — A64

5c, Jungle fowl. 10c, White tern. 15c, Brown noddy. 20c, Phoenix petrel. 25c, Pacific golden plover. 30c, Crested tern. 35c, Sooty tern. 40c, Bristle-thighed curlew. 45c, Eastern bar-tailed godwit. 50c, Reef heron. 55c, Greater frigatebird. 60c, Red-footed booby. 70c, Red-necked stint. $1, New Zealand long-tailed cuckoo. $2, Red-tailed tropicbird. $5, Banded rail.

1988, Mar. 2 *Perf. 15*

469 A64 5c multicolored .30 .25
470 A64 10c multicolored .30 .25
471 A64 15c multicolored .30 .25
472 A64 20c multicolored .30 .25
473 A64 25c multicolored .30 .25
474 A64 30c multicolored .30 .30
475 A64 35c multicolored .30 .30
476 A64 40c multicolored .30 .30
477 A64 45c multicolored .30 .30
478 A64 50c multicolored .30 .30
479 A64 55c multicolored .30 .30
480 A64 60c multicolored .35 .35
481 A64 70c multicolored .40 .40
482 A64 $1 multicolored .70 .70
483 A64 $2 multicolored 1.25 1.25
484 A64 $5 multicolored 3.10 3.10
Nos. 469-484 (16) 9.10 8.85

For overprints see Nos. 676-679, 796-799, O33-O48.

Intl. Red Cross and Red Crescent Organizations, 125th Annivs. — A65

15c, Jean-Henri Dunant. 40c, Junior Red Cross. 50c, Care for the handicapped. 60c, First aid training.
$1, Lecture.

Perf. 12½

1988, May 9 Litho. Unwmk.

485 A65 15c multicolored .30 .25
486 A65 40c multicolored .30 .25
487 A65 50c multicolored .30 .25
488 A65 60c multicolored .30 .30
Nos. 485-488 (4) 1.20 1.05

Souvenir Sheet

489 A65 $1.50 multicolored 2.25 2.25

A66

Voyages of Capt. Cook A67

Designs: 20c, HMS *Endeavour* (starboard side). 40c, *Endeavour* (stern). 50c, Landing, Tahiti, 1769, vert. 60c, Maori chief, vert. 80c, *Resolution* and native Hawaiian sail ship. $1, Cook, by Sir Nathaniel Dance-Holland (1735-1811), vert. $2.50, Antarctic icebergs surrounding the *Resolution.*

1988, June 15 Litho. *Perf. 12½*

490-495 A66 Set of 6 3.75 3.75

Souvenir Sheet

496 A67 $2.50 shown 7.50 7.50

Fungi — A68

40c, Ganoderma applanatum. 50c, Pseudoepicoccum cocos. 60c, Rigidoporus zonalis. 90c, Rigidoporus microporus.

1988, July 25 Litho. *Perf. 15*

497 A68 40c multicolored .55 .55
498 A68 50c multicolored .65 .65
499 A68 60c multicolored .75 .75
500 A68 90c multicolored 1.05 1.05
Nos. 497-500 (4) 3.00 3.00

See Nos. 520-523.

1988 Summer Olympics, Seoul — A69

Perf. 12½

1988, Aug. 19 Litho. Unwmk.

501 A69 10c Rifles, target .30 .30
502 A69 20c Judo .30 .30
503 A69 40c One-man kayak .60 .60
504 A69 60c Swimming .85 .85
505 A69 80c Yachting 1.10 1.10
506 A69 $1 Balance beam 1.60 1.60
Nos. 501-506 (6) 4.75 4.75

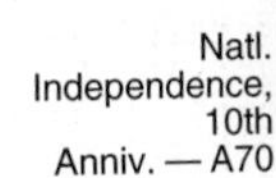

Natl. Independence, 10th Anniv. — A70

60c, Queen Elizabeth in boat. 90c, In sedan chair. $1.20, Seated at dais.

Wmk. 380

1988, Sept. 28 Litho. *Perf. 14*

507 A70 60c multi .60 .60
a. Souvenir sheet of 1 .70 .70
508 A70 90c multi .90 .90
a. Souvenir sheet of 1 1.05 1.05
509 A70 $1 shown 1.00 1.00
a. Souvenir sheet of 1 1.20 1.20
510 A70 $1.20 multi 1.25 1.25
a. Souvenir sheet of 1 1.45 1.45
Nos. 507-510 (4) 3.75 3.75

Nos. 507-508 and 510 vert.

Christmas A71

Unwmk.

1988, Dec. 5 Litho. *Perf. 14*

511 A71 15c Mary .30 .30
512 A71 40c Christ child .65 .65
513 A71 60c Joseph .90 .90
Nos. 511-513 (3) 1.85 1.85

Souvenir Sheet

514 A71 $1.50 Heraldic angel 2.00 2.00

Palm-frond or Pandanus-leaf Skirts — A72

1989, Mar. 31 Litho. *Perf. 14*

515 A72 40c multi .50 .50
516 A72 50c multi, diff. .65 .65
517 A72 60c multi, diff. .75 .75
518 A72 90c multi, diff. 1.10 1.10
Nos. 515-518 (4) 3.00 3.00

Souvenir Sheet

519 A72 $1.50 multi, vert. 3.50 3.50

Fungi Type of 1988

40c, Trametes muelleri. 50c, Pestalotiopsis palmarum. 60c, Trametes cingulata. 90c, Schizophyllum commune.

1989, May 24 Litho. *Perf. 14*

520 A68 40c multicolored .65 .65
521 A68 50c multicolored 1.45 1.45
522 A68 60c multicolored 1.80 1.80
523 A68 90c multicolored 2.60 2.60
Nos. 520-523 (4) 6.50 6.50

Marine Life Type of 1986

40c, Pennant coralfish. 50c, Anemone fish. 60c, Batfish. 90c, Threadfin coralfish.

1989, July 31 Litho. *Perf. 14*

524 A57 40c multicolored 1.05 1.05
525 A57 50c multicolored 1.35 1.35
526 A57 60c multicolored 1.60 1.60
527 A57 90c multicolored 2.80 2.80
a. Miniature sheet of 4, #524-527 7.50 7.50
Nos. 524-527 (4) 6.80 6.80

Souvenir Sheet

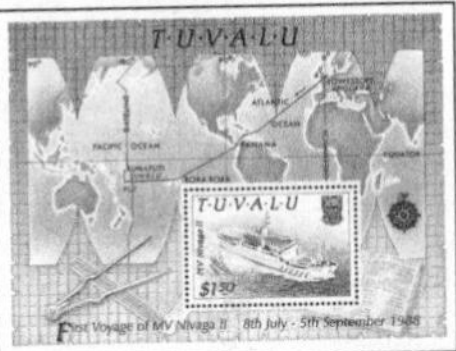

Maiden Voyage of M.V. *Nivaga II,* 1988 A73

1989, Oct. 9 Litho. *Perf. 14*

528 A73 $1.50 multicolored 4.75 4.75

Christmas — A74

Unwmk.

1989, Nov. 29 Litho. *Perf. 14*

529 A74 40c Conch shell .55 .55
530 A74 50c Flower bouquet .80 .80
531 A74 60c Germinated coconut .90 .90
532 A74 90c Shell jewelry 1.25 1.25
Nos. 529-532 (4) 3.50 3.50

Tropical Trees — A75

15c, Cocus nucifera. 30c, Rhizophora samoensis. 40c, Messerschmidia argentea. 50c, Pandanus tectorius. 60c, Hernandia nymphaeifolia. 90c, Pisonia grandis.

1990, Feb. 28 Litho. *Perf. 14½*

533 A75 15c multicolored .40 .40
534 A75 30c multicolored .70 .70
535 A75 40c multicolored .85 .85
536 A75 50c multicolored 1.05 1.05
537 A75 60c multicolored 1.30 1.30
538 A75 90c multicolored 2.25 2.25
Nos. 533-538 (6) 6.55 6.55

Penny Black, 150th Anniv. — A76

1990, May 3 Litho. *Perf. 14*

539 A76 15c multicolored .55 .55
540 A76 40c multicolored 1.45 1.45
541 A76 90c multicolored 3.50 3.50
Nos. 539-541 (3) 5.50 5.50

Souvenir Sheet

542 A76 $2 multicolored 5.00 5.00

Stamp World London '90.

World War II Ships — A77

Designs: 15c, Japanese merchant conversion, 1940. 30c, USS Unimak, seaplane tender, 1944. 40c, Amagari, Japanese Hubuki class, 1942. 50c, AO-24 USS Platte, Nov. 1, 1943. 60c, Japanese Shumushu Class (Type A) escort. 90c, CV-22 USS Independence.

1990

543-548 A77 Set of 6 10.00 10.00

Flowers — A78

1990, Sept. 21 Litho. *Perf. 14½*

549 A78 15c Erythrina fusca .30 .30
550 A78 30c Capparis cordifolia .40 .40
551 A78 40c Portulaca pilosa .55 .55
552 A78 50c Cordia subcordata .65 .65
553 A78 60c Scaevola taccada .80 .80
554 A78 90c Suriana maritima 1.20 1.20
Nos. 549-554 (6) 3.90 3.90

UN Development Program, 40th Anniv. — A79

40c, Surveyor. 60c, Communications station. $1.20, Fishing boat Te Tautai.

1990, Nov. 20 Litho. *Perf. 14*

555 A79 40c multicolored 1.40 1.40
556 A79 60c multicolored 1.90 1.90
557 A79 $1.20 multicolored 3.75 3.75
Nos. 555-557 (3) 7.05 7.05

Christmas — A80

1990, Nov. 20

558 A80 15c Mary and Joseph .30 .30
559 A80 40c Nativity .90 .90
560 A80 60c Shepherds 1.35 1.35
561 A80 90c Three Kings 1.95 1.95
Nos. 558-561 (4) 4.50 4.50

Seashells — A81

40c, Murex ramosus. 50c, Conus marmoreus. 60c, Trochus niloticus. $1.50, Cypraea mappa.

1991, Jan. 18 Litho. *Perf. 14*

562 A81 40c multicolored 1.00 1.00
563 A81 50c multicolored 1.35 1.35
564 A81 60c multicolored 1.45 1.45
565 A81 $1.50 multicolored 3.25 3.25
Nos. 562-565 (4) 7.05 7.05

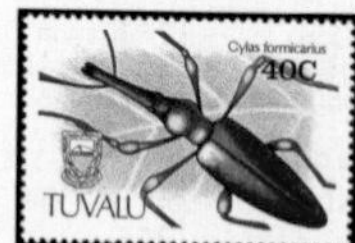

Insects — A82

40c, Cylas formicarius. 50c, Heliothis armiger. 60c, Spodoptera litura. $1.50, Agrius convolvuli.

1991, Mar. 22 Litho. *Perf. 14*

566 A82 40c multicolored 1.10 1.10
567 A82 50c multicolored 1.40 1.40
568 A82 60c multicolored 1.60 1.60
569 A82 $1.50 multicolored 3.90 3.90
Nos. 566-569 (4) 8.00 8.00

Endangered Marine Life — A83

40c, Green turtle. 50c, Humpback whale. 60c, Hawksbill turtle. $1.50, Sperm whale.

1991, May 31 Litho. *Perf. 14*

570 A83 40c multi .75 .75
571 A83 50c multi .90 .80
572 A83 60c multi 1.20 1.20
573 A83 $1.50 multi 2.90 2.90
Nos. 570-573 (4) 5.75 5.65

A84

1991, July 31 Litho. *Perf. 14*

574 A84 40c Soccer 1.00 1.00
575 A84 50c Volleyball 1.30 1.30
576 A84 60c Lawn tennis 1.60 1.60
577 A84 $1.50 Cricket 3.60 3.60
Nos. 574-577 (4) 7.50 7.50

9th South Pacific Games.

World War II Ships — A85

40c, USS Tennessee. 50c, IJN Haguro. 60c, HMS Achilles. $1.50, USS North Carolina.

1991, Oct. 15 Litho. *Perf. 14*

578 A85 40c multi 2.75 2.00
579 A85 50c multi 2.95 2.75
580 A85 60c multi 3.65 2.95
581 A85 $1.50 multi 7.75 7.75
Nos. 578-581 (4) 17.10 15.45

Christmas — A86

Various traditional dance costumes.

1991, Dec. 13

582 A86 40c multicolored 1.15 1.15
583 A86 50c multicolored 1.45 1.45
584 A86 60c multicolored 1.75 1.75
585 A86 $1.50 multicolored 4.40 4.40
Nos. 582-585 (4) 8.75 8.75

A87

Constellations.

1992, Jan. 29 Litho. *Perf. 14*

586 A87 40c Southern Fish 1.10 1.10
587 A87 50c Scorpio 1.40 1.40
588 A87 60c Sagittarius 1.75 1.75
589 A87 $1.50 Southern Cross 4.25 4.25
Nos. 586-589 (4) 8.50 8.50

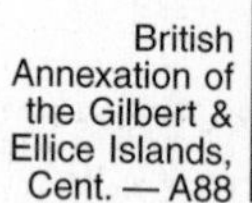

British Annexation of the Gilbert & Ellice Islands, Cent. — A88

40c, King George VI. 50c, King George V. 60c, King Edward VII. $1.50, Queen Victoria.

1992, Mar. 23 Litho. *Perf. 14*

590 A88 40c multi 1.00 1.00
591 A88 50c multi 1.25 1.25
592 A88 60c multi 1.60 1.60
593 A88 $1.50 multi 4.25 4.25
Nos. 590-593 (4) 8.10 8.10

Discovery of America, 500th Anniv. — A89

Columbus and: 40c, Queen Isabella & King Ferdinand of Spain. 50c, Polynesians. 60c, South American Indians. $1.50, North American Indians.

1992, May 22 Litho. *Perf. 14*

594 A89 40c black & dk blue .80 .80
595 A89 50c blk & dk plum .85 .85
596 A89 60c blk & dk grn 1.00 1.00
597 A89 $1.50 blk & dk pur 2.35 2.35
Nos. 594-597 (4) 5.00 5.00

World Columbian Stamp Expo '92, Chicago.

Fish — A90

Designs: 15c, Bluespot butterflyfish. 20c, Pink parrotfish. 25c, Stripe surgeonfish. 30c, Moon wrasse, 35c, Harlequin filefish. 40c, Bird wrasse. 45c, Black-finned pigfish. 50c, Blue-green chromis. 60c, Hump-headed Maori wrasse. 70c, Ornate coralfish, vert. 90c, Saddled butterflyfish, vert. $1, Vagabond butterflyfish, vert. $2, Longfin bannerfish, vert. $3, Moorish idol, vert.

1992, July 15

598-611 A90 Set of 14 11.00 11.00

For overprints & surcharge see #629-632, 716.

1992 Summer Olympics, Barcelona — A91

40c, Discus. 50c, Javelin. 60c, Shotput. $1.50, Track & field.
$2, Olympic stadium.

1992, July 27 Litho. *Perf. 14*

612 A91 40c multi .60 .60
613 A91 50c multi .75 .75
614 A91 60c multi 1.05 1.05
615 A91 $1.50 multi 2.60 2.60
Nos. 612-615 (4) 5.00 5.00

Souvenir Sheet

616 A91 $2 multi 3.75 3.75

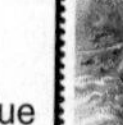

Blue Coral — A92

Various views of blue coral.

1992, Sept. 1

617 A92 10c multicolored .75 .75
618 A92 25c multicolored 1.65 1.65
619 A92 30c multicolored 1.65 1.65
620 A92 35c multicolored 1.95 1.95
Nos. 617-620 (4) 6.00 6.00

World Wildlife Fund.

Christmas — A93

Designs: 40c, Fishermen seeing angel. 50c, Fishermen sailing canoes toward island. 60c, Adoration of the fishermen. $1.50, Flowers, shell necklaces.

1992, Dec. 25 Litho. *Perf. 14*

621 A93 40c multicolored .70 .70
622 A93 50c multicolored .85 .85
623 A93 60c multicolored .95 .95
624 A93 $1.50 multicolored 2.50 2.50
Nos. 621-624 (4) 5.00 5.00

Wild Flowers — A94

40c, Calophyllum inophyllum. 50c, Hibiscus tiliaceus. 60c, Lantana camara. $1.50, Plumeria rubra.

1993, Feb. 2 Litho. *Perf. 14*

625 A94 40c multicolored .65 .65
626 A94 50c multicolored .80 .80
627 A94 60c multicolored .85 .85
628 A94 $1.50 multicolored 2.00 2.00
Nos. 625-628 (4) 4.30 4.30

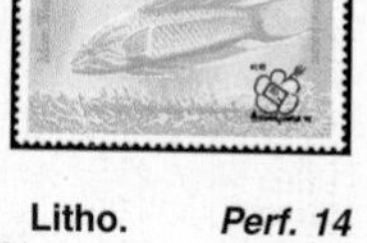

Nos. 601, 603, & 605-606 Ovptd.

1992, Sept. 1 Litho. *Perf. 14*

629 A90 30c on #601 .85 .85
630 A90 40c on #603 1.00 1.00
631 A90 50c on #605 1.50 1.50
632 A90 60c on #606 1.65 1.65
Nos. 629-632 (4) 5.00 5.00

World War II in the Pacific, 50th Anniv. — A95

40c, Japanese bombers. 50c, Anti-aircraft gun, vert. 60c, Using flame thrower. $1.50, Map of Funafuti Atoll, vert.

1993, Apr. 23 Litho. *Perf. 14*

633 A95 40c multicolored 1.20 1.20
634 A95 50c multicolored 1.45 1.45
635 A95 60c multicolored 1.70 1.70
636 A95 $1.50 multicolored 4.75 4.75
Nos. 633-636 (4) 9.10 9.10

Souvenir Sheet

Indopex '93 A96

1993, May 29 *Perf. 14x14½*
637 A96 $1.50 Cepora perimale 4.50 4.50

Marine Life — A97

1993, June 29 Litho. *Perf. 14*

638	A97	40c Giant clam	.55	.55
639	A97	50c Anemone crab	.70	.70
640	A97	60c Octopus	.90	.90
641	A97	$1.50 Green turtle	2.10	2.10
		Nos. 638-641 (4)	4.25	4.25

Coronation of Queen Elizabeth II, 40th Anniv. — A98

Queen: 40c, Riding in parade with Prince Phillip. 50c, Drinking coconut milk. 60c, Holding umbrella. $1.50, With natives. $2, Coronation ceremony.

1993, July 5

642	A98	40c multicolored	.60	.60
643	A98	50c multicolored	.75	.75
644	A98	60c multicolored	.95	.95
645	A98	$1.50 multicolored	2.30	2.30
		Nos. 642-645 (4)	4.60	4.60

Souvenir Sheet

646 A98 $2 multicolored 6.50 6.50

Souvenir Sheet

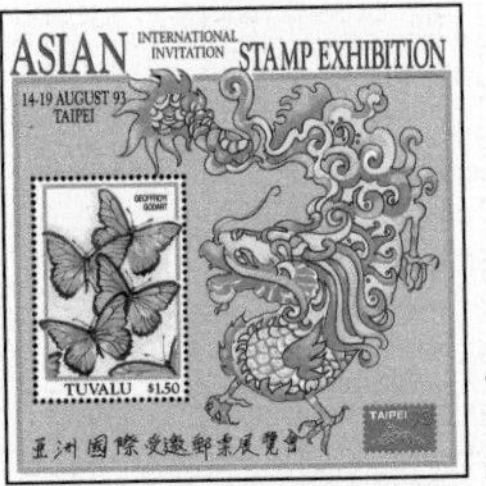

Taipei '93 A99

Litho. & Typo.

1993, Aug. 14 *Perf. 14½x14*
647 A99 $1.50 Geoffroyi godart 4.25 4.25

Souvenir Sheet

Bangkok '93 A100

$1.50, Paradisea staudinger.

1993, Oct. 1 Litho. *Perf. 14x14½*
648 A100 $1.50 multi 3.00 3.00

Greenhouse Effect — A101

Beach scene with: 40c, Sun at UR. 50c, Sun at UL. 60c, Crab on beach. $1.50, Sea gull in flight.

1993, Nov. 2 Litho. *Perf. 13½*

649	A101	40c multicolored	.45	.45
650	A101	50c multicolored	.60	.60
651	A101	60c multicolored	.80	.80
652	A101	$1.50 multicolored	1.90	1.90
a.		Souvenir sheet of 4, #649-652, perf. 14½x14	4.75	4.75
		Nos. 649-652 (4)	3.75	3.75

Christmas — A102

50c, Candle, flowers. 60c, Angel, flowers. $1.50, Palm tree, candles.

1993, Dec. 6 Litho. *Perf. 13½*

653	A102	40c shown	.50	.50
654	A102	50c multicolored	.60	.60
655	A102	60c multicolored	.75	.75
656	A102	$1.50 multicolored	1.75	1.75
		Nos. 653-656 (4)	3.60	3.60

Souvenir Sheet

Hong Kong '94 A103

1994, Feb. 18 *Perf. 14½x14*
657 A103 $2 Monarch 5.25 5.25

Scenic Views — A104

50c, Beach, trees, diff. 60c, Boats, ocean. $1.50, Boats, beach.

1994, Feb. 18 Litho. *Perf. 14*

658	A104	40c shown	.45	.45
659	A104	50c multi	.55	.55
660	A104	60c multi	.65	.65
661	A104	$1.50 multi	1.65	1.65
		Nos. 658-661 (4)	3.30	3.30

New Year 1994 (Year of the Dog) — A105

40c, Irish setter. 50c, Golden retriever. 60c, West Highland terrier. $1.50, German shepherd.

1994, Apr. 23 Litho. *Perf. 14*

662	A105	40c multicolored	.70	.70
663	A105	50c multicolored	.80	.80
664	A105	60c multicolored	1.00	1.00
665	A105	$1.50 multicolored	2.50	2.50
		Nos. 662-665 (4)	5.00	5.00

A106

1994, June 7

666	A106	40c Australia	.40	.40
667	A106	50c England	.55	.55
668	A106	60c Argentina	.60	.60
669	A106	$1.50 Germany	1.65	1.65
		Nos. 666-669 (4)	3.20	3.20

Souvenir Sheet

670 A106 $2 US 4.50 4.50

1994 World Cup Soccer Championships, US.

Seashells — A107

40c, Umbonium giganteum. 50c, Turbo petholatus. 60c, Planaxis savignyi. $1.50, Hydatina physis.

1994, Aug. 16 Litho. *Perf. 14*

671	A107	40c multicolored	.50	.50
672	A107	50c multicolored	.60	.60
673	A107	60c multicolored	.75	.75
674	A107	$1.50 multicolored	1.85	1.85
		Nos. 671-674 (4)	3.70	3.70

Souvenir Sheet

PHILAKOREA '94 — A108

1994, Aug. 16
675 A108 $1.50 Pekinese dog 3.50 3.50

Nos. 469-470, 476-477 Ovptd.

1994, Aug. 31 Litho. *Perf. 15*

676	A64	5c multicolored	.30	.30
677	A64	10c multicolored	.30	.30
678	A64	40c multicolored	.75	.75
679	A64	45c multicolored	.80	.80
		Nos. 676-679 (4)	2.15	2.15

First Manned Moon Landing, 25th Anniv. A109

a, 40c, Saturn V. b, 50c, Apollo 11. c, 60c, Neil Armstrong. d, $1.50, Splash-down.

1994, Oct. 31 *Perf. 14*
680 A109 Strip of 4, #a.-d. 4.00 4.00

Christmas A110

40c, Boys playing in water. 50c, Islanders, fish being gathered. 60c, People seated under canopy, food. $1.50, Traditional dancers.

1994, Dec. 15 Litho. *Perf. 14*

681	A110	40c multicolored	.50	.50
682	A110	50c multicolored	.55	.55
683	A110	60c multicolored	.65	.65
684	A110	$1.50 multicolored	1.80	1.80
		Nos. 681-684 (4)	3.50	3.50

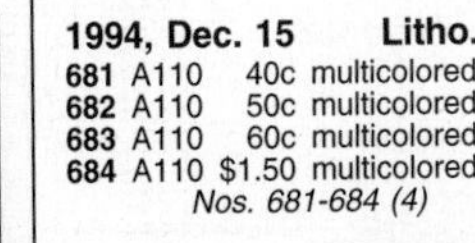

New Year 1995 (Year of the Boar) — A111

40c, One pig. 50c, Pig, piglet. 60c, Three pigs. $1.50, Sow nursing litter.

1995, Jan. 30 Litho. *Perf. 14*
685-688 A111 Set of 4 3.25 3.25

FAO, 50th Anniv. — A112

40c, Men with vegetables in wheelbarrow. 50c, Man with sack of vegetables. 60c, Girl cleaning vegetables. $1.50, Girl mixing food.

1995, Mar. 31 Litho. *Perf. 14*
689-692 A112 Set of 4 3.25 3.25

Visit South Pacific Year — A113

1995, May 26 Litho. *Perf. 14*

693	A113	40c shown	.45	.45
694	A113	50c Sailboat	.60	.60
695	A113	60c Hut	.70	.70
696	A113	$1.50 Home, beach	1.75	1.75
		Nos. 693-696 (4)	3.50	3.50

Pacific Coastal Orchids — A114

40c, Dendrobium comptonii. 50c, Dendrobium aff. involutum. 60c, Dendrobium rarum. $1.50, Grammatophyllum scriptum.

1995, July 28 Litho. *Perf. 14*
697-700 A114 Set of 4 4.00 4.00

Souvenir Sheet

Jakarta '95, Asian World Stamp Exhibition — A116

1995, Aug. 19 Litho. *Perf. 12*
702 A116 $1 Traditional dancer 2.50 2.50

For overprint see No. 715.

Souvenir Sheet

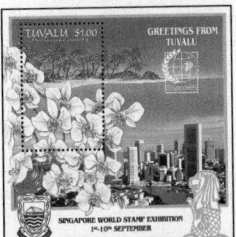

Singapore '95 World Stamp Exhibition — A117

$1, Phalaenopsis amabillis.

1995, Sept. 1
703 A117 $1 multicolored 2.25 2.25

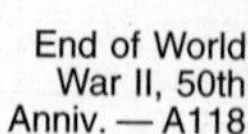

End of World War II, 50th Anniv. — A118

40c, Soldier with sub-machine gun, map of Japan, Tuvalu. 50c, Soldier holding rifle, landing exercise on beach. 60c, US Marine, offshore air and sea battle. $1.50, Soldier firing rifle, atomic mushroom cloud.

1995, Aug. 19 Litho. *Perf. 14*
704-707 A118 Set of 4 7.75 7.75

Souvenir Sheet

UN, 50th Anniv. A119

a, Rowing in outrigger canoes. b, UN New York headquarters.

1995, Oct. 24 *Perf. 14½*
708 A119 $1 Sheet of 2, #a.-b. 3.00 3.00

Christmas A120

Scores and verses to Christmas carols and: 40c, Map of island, "Silent Night." 50c, Boy carolers, "O Come All Ye Faithful." 60c, Girl carolers, "The First Noel." $1.50, Angel, "Hark the Herald Angels Sing."

1995, Dec. 15 Litho. *Perf. 14*
709-712 A120 Set of 4 3.25 3.25

Miniature Sheet

Independence, First Tuvalu Postage Stamps, 20th Anniv. — A121

a, 40c, #16. b, 60c, #17. c, $1, #18.

1996, Jan. 1 Litho. *Perf. 14*
713 A121 Sheet of 3, #a.-c. 4.25 4.25

Miniature Sheet

New Year 1996 (Year of the Rat) A122

Stylized rats: a, Looking right. b, Facing left, drinking from container.

1996, Feb. 23 Litho. *Perf. 14x14½*
714 A122 50c Sheet of 2, #a.-b. 2.00 2.00
c. Ovptd. in sheet margin 2.00 2.00
d. With added inscription in sheet margin 2.00 2.00

No. 714c is overprinted in sheet margin with exhibition emblem of Hongpex '96.

No. 714d is inscribed in sheet margin with two exhibition emblems of China '96. Issued: 5/18.

No. 702 Ovptd. in Gold

1996, Mar. 21 Litho. *Perf. 12*
715 A116 $1 multicolored 2.40 2.40

No. 604 Surcharged in Black, Red & Blue

1996, Oct. 21 Litho. *Perf. 14*
716 A90 $1 on 45c multi 2.10 2.10

1996 Summer Olympic Games, Atlanta — A123

1996, Sept. 11 Litho. *Perf. 14*
717 A123 40c Beach volleyball .50 .50
718 A123 50c Swimming .60 .60
719 A123 60c Weight lifting .75 .75
720 A123 $1.50 David Tua, boxer 1.90 1.90
Nos. 717-720 (4) 3.75 3.75

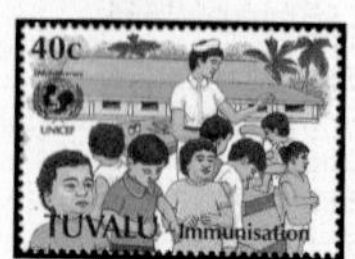

UNICEF, 50th Anniv. — A124

1996, Oct. 28
721 A124 40c Immunization .40 .40
722 A124 50c Education for life .50 .50
723 A124 60c Water tank project .60 .60
724 A124 $1.50 Hydroponic farm 1.70 1.70
Nos. 721-724 (4) 3.20 3.20

Christmas — A125

Designs: 40c, Magi following star. 50c, Shepherds seeing star. 60c, Adoration of the Magi. $1.50, Nativity scene.

1996, Nov. 25 *Perf. 14½*
725 A125 40c multicolored .55 .55
726 A125 50c multicolored .60 .60
727 A125 60c multicolored .75 .75
728 A125 $1.50 multicolored 1.85 1.85
Nos. 725-728 (4) 3.75 3.75

Fish — A126

25c, Bluetail mullet. 30c, Queen fish leatherskin. 40c, Paddletail. 45c, Long-nose emperor. 50c, Long-snouted unicornfish. 55c, Brigham's snapper. 60c, Red bass. 70c, Red jobfish. 90c, Leopard flounder. $1, Red snapper. $2, Longtail snapper. $3, Black trevally.

1997, Mar. 15 *Perf. 14*
729 A126 25c multicolored .30 .30
730 A126 30c multicolored .30 .30
731 A126 40c multicolored .40 .40
732 A126 45c multicolored .50 .50
Complete bklt., 4 ea #729-732 10.00
733 A126 50c multicolored .55 .55
734 A126 55c multicolored .55 .55
735 A126 60c multicolored .65 .65
736 A126 70c multicolored .70 .70
737 A126 90c multicolored .95 .95
738 A126 $1 multicolored 1.00 1.00
739 A126 $2 multicolored 1.95 1.95
a. Souv. sheet of 1, wmk. 373 3.00 3.00
740 A126 $3 multicolored 3.00 3.00
Nos. 729-740 (12) 10.85 10.85

No. 739a for return of Hong Kong to China, July 1, 1997.

Souvenir Sheet

New Year 1997 (Year of the Ox) A127

1997, June 20 Litho. *Perf. 14*
741 A127 $2 multicolored 3.00 3.00

Hong Kong '97.

Ducks and Drakes — A128

1997, May 29 Litho. *Perf. 14*
742 A128 40c White pekin .50 .50
743 A128 50c Muscovy .60 .60
744 A128 60c Pacific black .75 .75
745 A128 $1.50 Mandarin 1.85 1.85
Nos. 742-745 (4) 3.70 3.70

PACIFIC 97.

Domestic Cats — A129

40c, Korat king. 50c, Long-haired ginger kitten. 60c, Shaded cameo. $1.50, American Maine coon.

1997, June 20
746 A129 40c multicolored .50 .50
747 A129 50c multicolored .65 .65
748 A129 60c multicolored .75 .75
749 A129 $1.50 multicolored 1.85 1.85
Nos. 746-749 (4) 3.75 3.75

Queen Elizabeth II and Prince Philip, 50th Wedding Anniv. A130

Designs: No. 750, Queen, Prince standing in open vehicle. No. 751, Queen in yellow hat. No. 752, Queen holding umbrella. No. 753, Queen reading, Prince up close. No. 754, Three pictures of Queen. No. 755, Prince in top hat, Queen.

$2, Queen, Prince riding in open carriage, horiz.

Wmk. 373

1997, Oct. 1 Litho. *Perf. 14½*
750 40c multicolored .45 .45
751 40c multicolored .45 .45
a. A130 Pair, #750-751 .90 .90
752 50c multicolored .55 .55
753 50c multicolored .55 .55
a. A130 Pair, #752-753 1.10 1.10
754 60c multicolored .65 .65
755 60c multicolored .65 .65
a. A130 Pair, #754-755 1.30 1.30
Nos. 750-755 (6) 3.30 3.30

Souvenir Sheet

756 A130 $2 multicolored 2.50 2.50

No. 756 contains one 38x32mm stamp.

Traditional Activities A131

Christmas: 40c, Turtle hunting. 50c, Pole fishing. 60c, Canoe racing. $1.50, Traditional dance.

Perf. 13½x13

1997, Nov. 25 Litho. Wmk. 373
757 A131 40c multicolored .45 .45
758 A131 50c multicolored .55 .55
759 A131 60c multicolored .65 .65
760 A131 $1.50 multicolored 1.65 1.65
Nos. 757-760 (4) 3.30 3.30

Souvenir Sheet

New Year 1998 (Year of the Tiger) A132

1998, Feb. 2 Litho. *Perf. 13*
761 A132 $1.40 multicolored 1.75 1.75

Diana, Princess of Wales (1961-97)

Common Design Type

Designs: a, Wearing red evening dress. b, Wearing black evening dress. c, Wearing tiara. d, With collar up on coat.

Perf. 14½x14

1998, Mar. 31 Litho. Wmk. 373
762 CD355 80c Sheet of 4, #a.-d. 3.50 3.50

No. 762 sold for $3.20 + 20c, with surtax from international sales being donated to the Princess Diana Memorial Fund and surtax from national sales being donated to designated local charity.

Royal Air Force, 80th Anniv.

Common Design Type of 1993 Re-inscribed

Designs: 40c, Hawker Woodcock. 50c, Vickers Victoria. 60c, Bristol Brigand $1.50, De Haviland DHC 1 Chipmunk.

No. 767: a, Sopwith Pup. b, Armstrong Whitworth FK8. c, North American Harvard. d, Vultee Vengeance.

Wmk. 384

1998, Apr. 1 Litho. *Perf. 13½*
763 CD350 40c multicolored .50 .50
764 CD350 50c multicolored .60 .60
765 CD350 60c multicolored .75 .75
766 CD350 $1.50 multicolored 1.65 1.65
Nos. 763-766 (4) 3.50 3.50

Souvenir Sheet

767 CD350 $1 Sheet of 4, #a.-d. 4.25 4.25

Ships — A133

Designs: 40c, "Los Reyes," "Santiago," 1567. 50c, "Morning Star," missionary topsail schooner, 1867. 60c, "The Light," brigantine of Church of the Resurrection, 1870. $1.50, New Zealand missionary schooner, 1900.

Wmk. 373

1998, May 19 Litho. *Perf. 14*
768 A133 40c multicolored .45 .45
769 A133 50c multicolored .50 .50
770 A133 60c multicolored .65 .65
771 A133 $1.50 multicolored 1.40 1.40
Nos. 768-771 (4) 3.00 3.00

Dolphins and Porpoises A134

40c, Bottlenose dolphin. 50c, Dall's porpoise. 60c, Harbor porpoise. $1.50, Common dolphin.

Perf. 13½x13

1998, Aug. 21 **Litho.** **Wmk. 384**

772 A134 40c multicolored .45 .45
773 A134 50c multicolored .60 .60
774 A134 60c multicolored .70 .70
775 A134 $1.50 multicolored 1.80 1.80
Nos. 772-775 (4) 3.55 3.55

Greenpeace, Save Our Seas — A135

Marine life: 20c, Bleached platygyra daedalea, psammocora digitata. 30c, Bleached acropora robusta. 50c, Bleached acropora hyacinthus. $1, Bleached acropora danai, montastrea curta.

$1.50, Bleached seriatopora, bleached stylophora.

Wmk. 373

1998, Nov. 6 **Litho.** ***Perf. 14½***

776 A135 20c multicolored .30 .30
777 A135 30c multicolored .40 .40
778 A135 50c multicolored .70 .70
779 A135 $1 multicolored 1.15 1.15
Nos. 776-779 (4) 2.55 2.55

Souvenir Sheet

780 A135 $1.50 multicolored 2.00 2.00

Intl. Year of the Ocean (#780).

Christmas — A136

40c, Flight into Egypt. 50c, Angel speaking to shepherds. 60c, Nativity. $1.50, Adoration of the Magi.

1998, Nov. 20 ***Perf. 14½x14***

781 A136 40c multicolored .40 .40
782 A136 50c multicolored .50 .50
783 A136 60c multicolored .60 .60
784 A136 $1.50 multicolored 1.50 1.50
Nos. 781-784 (4) 3.00 3.00

Independence, 20th Anniv. — A137

Stamps on stamps, Prime Ministers: 40c, #722, Bikenibeu Paeniu. 60c, Kamuta Latasi. 90c, Tomasi Puapua. $1.50, Design like #166, Toaripi Lauti.

Wmk. 384

1998, Oct. 1 **Litho.** ***Perf. 14***

785 A137 40c multicolored .45 .45
786 A137 60c multicolored .70 .70
787 A137 90c multicolored .90 .90
788 A137 $1.50 multicolored 1.45 1.45
a. Souvenir sheet, #785-788 3.50 3.50
Nos. 785-788 (4) 3.50 3.50

Souvenir Sheet

New Year 1999 (Year of the Rabbit) A138

Perf. 14½x14

1999, Feb. 16 **Litho.** **Wmk. 373**

789 A138 $2 multicolored 2.75 2.75

Australia '99, World Stamp Expo — A139

Maritime history: 40c, Heemskerck, 1642. 50c, HMS Endeavour, 1769. 90c, PS Sophie Jane, 1831. $1.50, P&O SS Chusan, 1852. $2, HM Brig "Supply."

1999, Mar. 19 ***Perf. 14***

790 A139 40c multicolored .45 .45
791 A139 50c multicolored .50 .50
792 A139 90c multicolored 1.00 1.00
793 A139 $1.50 multicolored 1.55 1.55
Nos. 790-793 (4) 3.50 3.50

Souvenir Sheet

794 A139 $2 multicolored 2.25 2.25

Nos. 472, 475, 479, 482 Ovptd.

1999, June 11 **Litho.** ***Perf. 15***

796 A64 20c on #472 .30 .30
797 A64 35c on #475 .40 .40
798 A64 55c on #479 .70 .70
799 A64 $1 on #482 1.15 1.15
Nos. 796-799 (4) 2.55 2.55

50% of the sales of Nos. 796-799 will be donated to the Kosovo Relief Fund.

1st Manned Moon Landing, 30th Anniv.

Common Design Type

40c, Lift-off. 60c, Lunar module prepares to touchdown. 90c, Ascent stage approaches Command module. $1.50, Recovery.

$2, Looking at earth from moon.

Perf. 14x13¾

1999, July 20 **Litho.** **Wmk. 384**

800 CD357 40c multicolored .50 .50
801 CD357 60c multicolored .70 .70
802 CD357 90c multicolored 1.20 1.20
803 CD357 $1.50 multicolored 1.60 1.60
Nos. 800-803 (4) 4.00 4.00

Souvenir Sheet

Perf. 14

804 CD357 $2 multicolored 2.75 2.75

No. 804 contains one circular stamp 40mm in diameter.

Queen Mother's Century

Common Design Type

Queen Mother: 40c, With King George VI inspecting bomb damage. 60c, With daughters at Balmoral. 90c, With Princes Harry and William, 95th birthday. $1.50, As colonel-in-chief of Queen's Dragoon Guards.

$2, Age 6 photo, photo of Yuri Gagarin.

Wmk. 384

1999, Aug. 16 **Litho.** ***Perf. 13½***

805 CD358 40c multicolored .45 .45
806 CD358 60c multicolored .70 .70
807 CD358 90c multicolored 1.10 1.10
808 CD358 $1.50 multicolored 1.75 1.75
Nos. 805-808 (4) 4.00 4.00

Souvenir Sheet

809 CD358 $2 multicolored 3.00 3.00

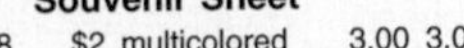

Flowers A141

No. 810: a, Fetai. b, Ateate. c, Portulacacae lueta. d, Tamoloc. e, Beach pea. f, Pomegranate (red letters).

No. 811: a, Cup of gold. b, Rock rose. c, Bower plant. d, Lavender star. e, Hybrid mandevilla. f, Pomegranate (white letters).

No. 812, Scrambled eggs, vert.

Perf. 13¾

1999, Nov. 22 **Litho.** **Unwmk.**

810 A141 90c Sheet of 6, #a.-f. 6.50 6.50
811 A141 90c Sheet of 6, #a.-f. 6.50 6.50

Souvenir Sheet

812 A141 $3 multi 5.50 5.50

A142

Millennium — A143

No. 813, Lady of peace with frame.

No. 814: a, Like No. 813, no frame. b, Olive branch. c, Dove. d. Lion. e, Lamb. f, War crowning peace.

No. 815: Sun on horizon, clock, computer keyboard.

Perf. 14½x14¼

1999, Dec. 31 **Litho.**

813 A142 90c multi 1.25 1.25
814 A142 90c Sheet of 6, #a.-f. 6.75 6.75

Souvenir Sheet

Perf. 14

815 A143 $2 multi 4.00 4.00

No. 813 printed in sheets of 6.

Worldwide Fund for Nature — A144

Sand tiger shark: a, 10c, Close-up of head. b, 30c, Facing left. c, 50c, Swimming above seaweed. d, 60c, Three sharks.

Perf. 13¼x13½

2000, Feb. 7 **Litho.** **Unwmk.**

816 A144 Strip of 4, #a.-d. 3.00 3.00
e. Souvenir sheet, 2 #816 6.50 6.50

Souvenir Sheet

Stamps Without WWF Emblem

817 A144 Sheet of 4, #a.-d 2.75 2.75

Marine Life and Birds A145

No. 818, each 90c: a, Common tern. b, White-tailed tropicbird. c, Red emperor snapper. d, Clown triggerfish. e, Longfin bannerfish. f, Harlequin tuskfish.

No. 819, each 90c: a, Wilson's storm petrel. b, Common dolphin. c, Spotted seahorse. d, Threeband demoiselle. e, Coral hind. f, Palette surgeonfish.

No. 820, each 90c: a, Great frigatebird. b, Brown booby. c, Dugong. d, Red knot. e, Common starfish. f, Hawksbill turtle.

No. 821, each 90c: a, Manta ray. b, White shark. c, Hammerhead shark. d, Tiger shark. e, Great barracuda. f, Leatherback turtle.

No. 822, each 90c: a, Whale shark. b, Six-spot grouper. c, Bluestreak cleaner wrasse. d, Lemon shark. e, Spotted trunkfish. f, Long-nosed butterflyfish.

No. 823, each 90c: a, Chevroned butterflyfish. b, Mandarinfish. c, Bicolor angelfish. d, Copperbanded butterflyfish. e, Clown anemonefish. f, Lemonpeel angelfish.

Each $3: No. 824, Picassofish. No. 825, Pygmy parrotfish. No. 826, Sailfish.

2000, Mar. 8 ***Perf. 14***

Sheets of 6, #a.-f.

818-823 A145 Set of 6 45.00 45.00

Souvenir Sheets

824-826 A145 Set of 3 17.50 17.50

Butterflies — A146

No. 827, each 90c: a, Birdwing. b, Tailed emperor. c, Orchid swallowtail. d, Union Jack. e, Long-tailed blue. f, Common Jezabel.

No. 828, each 90c: a, Caper white. b, Common Indian crow. c, Eastern flat. d, Cairns birdwing. e, Monarch. f, Meadow argus.

No. 829, each 90c, horiz.: a, Glasswing. b, Leftwing. c, Moth butterfly. d, Blue triangle. e, Beak. f, Plane.

Each $3: No. 830, Great egg-fly. No. 831, Palmfly, horiz.

2000, May 1 **Sheets of 6, #a.-f.**

827-829 A146 Set of 3 22.50 22.50

Souvenir Sheets

830-831 A146 Set of 2 10.00 10.00

Birds A147

#832, each 90c: a, Red-billed leiothrix. b, Gray shrike-thrush. c, Great frigatebird. d, Common kingfisher. e, Chestnut-breasted finch. f, White tern.

#833, each 90c: a, White-collared kingfisher. b, Scaled petrel. c, Superb blue wren. d, Osprey. e, Great cormorant. f, Peregrine falcon.

#834, each 90c: a, Rainbow lorikeet. b, White-throated tree creeper. c, White-tailed kingfisher. d, Golden whistler. e, Black-bellied plover. f, Beach thick-knee.

Each $3: #835, Morepork. #836, Broad-billed prion, horiz.

Illustration reduced.

2000, June 1 **Litho.** ***Perf. 14***

Sheets of 6, #a-f

832-834 A147 Set of 3 22.50 22.50

Souvenir Sheets

835-836 A147 Set of 2 7.50 7.50

Dogs and Cats A148

No. 837: a, Fox terrier. b, Collie. c, Boston terrier. d, Pembroke Welsh corgi. e, Pointer. f, Dalmatian.

No. 838, vert.: a, Dalmatian. b, Boston terrier. c, Fox terrier. d, Pointer. e, Pembroke Welsh corgi. f, Collie.

No. 839, vert. (denominations in orange): a, Ticked taboy oriental shorthair. b, Balinese. c, Somali. d, Chinchilla Persian. e, Tonkinese. f, Japanese bobtail.

No. 840, vert. (denominations in green): a, Lilac oriental shorthair. b, Balinese. c, Somali. d, Chinchilla Persian. e, Tonkinese. f, Japanese bobtail.
No. 841, Scottish terrier. No. 842, Oriental shorthair, vert.
Illustration reduced.

2000, July 3 Litho. *Perf. 14*
Sheets of 6, #a-f

837-840 A148 90c Set of 4 24.00 24.00

Souvenir Sheets

841-842 A148 $3 Set of 2 8.00 8.00

Birds and Animals A149

No. 843, horiz.: a, Brown noddy. b, Great frigatebird. c, Emperor angelfish. d, Common dolphin. e, Hermit crab. f, Threadfin butterflyfish.
No. 844, horiz.: a, Red-footed booby. b, Red-tailed tropicbird. c, Black-bellied plover. d, Common tern. e, Ruddy turnstone. f, Sanderling.
$3, Great frigatebird.

2000, Aug. 3 Sheets of 6, #a-f

843-844 A149 90c Set of 2 14.50 14.50

Souvenir Sheet

845 A149 $3 Great frigatebird 3.75 3.75

New Year 2000 and 2001 (Years of the Dragon and Snake) — A150

Designs: 40c, Dragon. 60c, Snake. 90c, Snake, diff. $1.50, Dragon, diff.

2001, Jan. 15 Litho. *Perf. 13½x13¼*

846-849 A150 Set of 4 6.00 6.00

Motofoua Secondary School Fire, 1st Anniv. — A151

Fire trucks: 60c, Anglo specialist rescue uUnit. 90c, Anglo 4800 water/foam tender. $1.50, Bronto 33-2T1 combined telescopic ladder/hydralulic platform. $2, Anglo 450 LRX water tender.
$3, Wormold "Arrestor" ARFFV.

2001, Mar. 9 Litho. *Perf. 13¼*

850-853 A151 Set of 4 7.50 7.50

Souvenir Sheet

854 A151 $3 multi 5.00 5.00

.tv Corporation A152

Palm fronds, satellite dish and: 40c, Woman. 60c, Dancers. 90c, Man. $1.50, Child.
$2, Map.

2001, May 30 Litho. *Perf. 14¼x14½*

855-858 A152 Set of 4 4.75 4.75

Souvenir Sheet

859 A152 $2 multi 4.00 4.00

Souvenir Sheet

Phila Nippon '01 A153

2001, Aug. 1 *Perf. 13*

860 A153 $3 multi 3.25 3.25

Nos. 806-808 Overprinted in Gold

No. 805 Surcharged in Gold

Wmk. 384

2001, Aug. 4 Litho. *Perf. 13½*

860A	CD358	60c multi	.75	.75
860B	CD358	90c multi	1.10	1.10
860C	CD358	$1.50 multi	1.75	1.75
860D	CD358	$2 on 40c multi	2.50	2.50
	Nos. 860A-860D (4)		6.10	6.10

No. 809 Surcharged in Gold

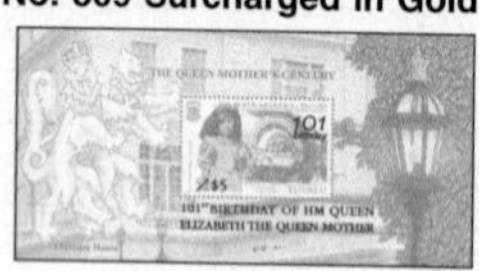

2001, Aug. 4 Wmk. 384 *Perf. 13½*
Souvenir Sheet

861 CD358 $5 on $2 multi 6.00 6.00

Fauna — A154

Designs: 25c, Mosquito. 30c, Giant African snail. 40c, Cockroach. 45c, Stick insect. 50c, Green stink bug. 55c, Dragonfly. 60c, Monarch caterpillar. 70c, Coconut beetle. 90c, Honeybee. $1, Monarch butterfly. $2, Common eggfly butterfly. $3, Painted lady butterfly.

Unwmk.

2001, Oct. 31 Litho. *Perf. 13*

862	A154	25c multi	.40	.40
863	A154	30c multi	.50	.50
864	A154	40c multi	.65	.65
865	A154	45c multi	.75	.75
866	A154	50c multi	.80	.80
867	A154	55c multi	.90	.90
868	A154	60c multi	1.00	1.00
869	A154	70c multi	1.10	1.10
870	A154	90c multi	1.50	1.50
871	A154	$1 multi	1.60	1.60
872	A154	$2 multi	3.25	3.25
873	A154	$3 multi	5.00	5.00
	Nos. 862-873 (12)		17.45	17.45

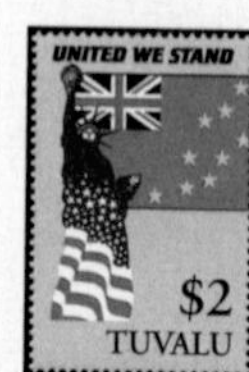

United We Stand — A155

Statue of Liberty and Tuvalu flag: No. 874, $2, Blue background. No. 875, $2, Yellow background.

2002, Jan. 10 *Perf. 14*

874-875 A155 Set of 2 5.00 5.00

Paintings Depicting Chapter Scenes From "The Tale of Genji" A156

No. 876, 40c — Chapter: a, 1. b, 2. c, 3. d, 4. e, 5. f, 6.
No. 877, 60c — Chapter: a, 8. b, 9. c, 10. d, 11. e, 12. f, 13.
No. 878, 90c — Chapter: a, 15. b, 16, c, 17. d, 18. e, 19, f, 20.
No. 879, $4 — Chapter 7. No. 880, $4, Chapter 14. No. 881, $4, Chapter 21.

2002, Apr. 24 Litho. *Perf. 14¼*
Sheets of 6, #a-f

876-878 A156 Set of 3 12.50 12.50

Imperf

879-881 A156 Set of 3 11.00 11.00

Nos. 876-878 each contain six 37x50mm stamps.

UN Special Session on Children and Convention on Rights of the Child — A157

Designs: 40c, Boy in wheelchair. 60c, Boy and girl sitting near fence. 90c, Nauti Primary School, Funafuti. $4, Mother and child.
No. 886: a, Taulosa Karl. b, Simalua Jacinta Enele.

2002, May 8 Litho. *Perf. 13¼x13½*

882-885 A157 Set of 4 4.25 4.25

Souvenir Sheet

886 A157 $1 Sheet of 2, #a-b 3.50 3.50

For surcharge, see No. 971A.

Reign of Queen Elizabeth II, 50th Anniv. A158

No. 887: a, Princes William and Harry. b, Queen in blue green suit. c, Queen and Prince Philip. d, Queen wearing red hat.
$4, Queen on horseback.

2002, June 17 *Perf. 14¼*

887 A158 $1.50 Sheet of 4, #a-d 7.75 7.75

Souvenir Sheet

888 A158 $4 multi 5.50 5.50

2002 World Cup Soccer Championships, Japan and Korea — A159

No. 889: a, Tom Finney. b, Poster from 1974 World Cup. c, Portuguese player and flag. d, Uruguayan player and flag. e, Suwon World Cup Stadium, Seoul (56x42mm).
$4, Johann Cruyff.

2002, July 15 *Perf. 14*

889 A159 90c Sheet of 5, #a-e 6.00 6.00

Souvenir Sheet

890 A159 $4 multi 5.25 5.25

Queen Mother Elizabeth (1900-2002) — A160

No. 891: a, 60c, Wearing tiara (lilac shading at UL) (26x29mm). b, 60c, Wearing tiara (lilac shading at UR) (26x29mm). c, 90c, In crowd, holding bouquet of flowers (lilac shading at UL) (28x23mm). d, 90c, Receiving flowers from children (lilac shading at UR) (28x23mm). e, 90c, With teddy bear (lilac shading at UL) (28x23mm). f, With man, woman and children (lilac shading at UR) (28x23mm). g, Color photograph (40x29mm).
No. 892, $2, lilac shading at UL: a, As child, with another young girl. b, As older woman.
No. 893, $2, lilac shading at UR: a, Smelling flower. b, Wearing brooch.

Perf. Compound x14¼ (60c), 13¼x10¾ (90c), 13¼x14¼ ($1.50)

2002, Aug. 12

891 A160 Sheet of 7, #a-g 6.50 6.50

Souvenir Sheets
Perf. 14¾

892-893 A160 Set of 2 7.75 7.75

20th World Scout Jamboree, Thailand — A161

No. 894 — Merit badges: a, Citizenship in the World. b, First Aid. c, Personal Fitness. d, Environmental Science.
$5, Lord Robert Baden-Powell.

2002, Oct. 2 *Perf. 14¼*
894 A161 $1.50 Sheet of 4, #a-d 6.50 6.50

Souvenir Sheet

895 A161 $5 multi 6.00 6.00

Intl. Year of Mountains — A162

No. 896, horiz.: a, Mt. Fitzroy, Chile. b, Mt. Foraker, US. c, Mt. Fuji, Japan. d, Mt. Malaku, Nepal and China.
$4, Mt. Godwin Austen, Kashmir.

2002, Oct. 2
896 A162 $1.50 Sheet of 4, #a-d 7.00 7.00

Souvenir Sheet

897 A162 $4 multi 7.00 7.00

Elvis Presley (1935-77) — A163

2002, Dec. 27 **Litho.** *Perf. 14¼*
898 A163 $1 multi 1.50 1.50

No. 898 was printed in sheets of 6. Value, $7.50.

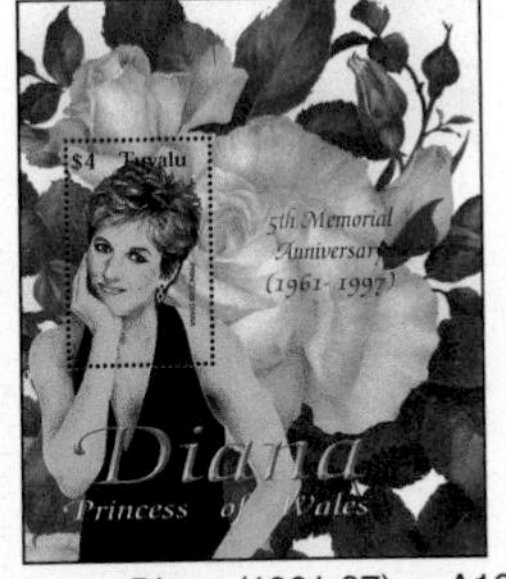

Princess Diana (1961-97) — A164

No. 899 — Diana wearing: a, Black dress, no necklace. b, Black dress, choker necklace. c, Blue dress. d, Blue green scarf. e, Pink blouse, hand at chin. f, Pink dress.
$4, Black dress, hand on chin.

2002, Dec. 27 *Perf. 14*
899 A164 $1 Sheet of 6, #a-f 7.50 7.50

Souvenir Sheet

900 A164 $4 multi 5.00 5.00

Year of the Horse (in 2002) — A165

Various horses: 40c, 60c, 90c, $2.
No. 905: a, Head of horse, seahorse. b, Heads of horse, three seahorses.

2003, Jan. 23 *Perf. 13¼*
901-904 A165 Set of 4 5.00 5.00

Souvenir Sheet

905 A165 $1.50 Sheet of 2, #a-b 4.50 4.50

New Year 2003 (Year of the Ram) — A166

No. 906: a, Green and black background. b, White background. c, Blue background.

2003, Feb. 1 *Perf. 14x13¾*
906 A166 75c Vert. strip of 3, #a-c 6.00 6.00

No. 906 printed in sheets containing two strips.

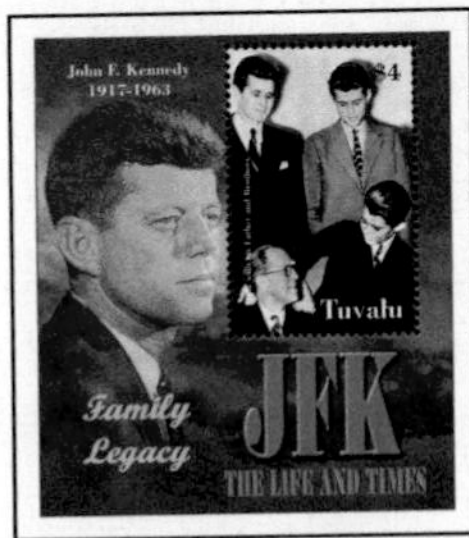

Pres. John F. Kennedy (1917-63) — A167

No. 907: a, In Solomon Islands, 1943. b, On PT 109, 1942. c, Receiving medal for gallantry, 1944. d, Campaigning for Senate, 1952.
$4, With father and brothers.

2003, Mar. 24 *Perf. 14*
907 A167 $1.75 Sheet of 4, #a-d 8.50 8.50

Souvenir Sheet

908 A167 $4 multi 4.75 4.75

Powered Flight, Cent. A168

No. 909, $1.75: a, Orville Wright in early plane, 1903. b, Wilbur Wright and King Alfonso XIII of Spain, 1909. c, Wilbur Wright's plane, 1908. d, Gabriel Voisin's plane piloted by Léon Delagrange, 1907.
No. 910, $1.75: a, Voisin's motor boat powered glider, 1905. b, Trajan Vuia's single winged plane, 1906. c, Santos-Dumont's biplane, 1906. d, Orville Wright circles parade ground, 1908.
No. 911, $4, Wright Brothers biplane in flight, 1908. No. 912, $4, Glenn Curtiss pilots June Bug, 1908.

2003, May 19 **Litho.** *Perf. 14*

Sheets of 4, #a-d

909-910 A168 Set of 2 16.50 16.50

Souvenir Sheets

911-912 A168 Set of 2 9.00 9.00

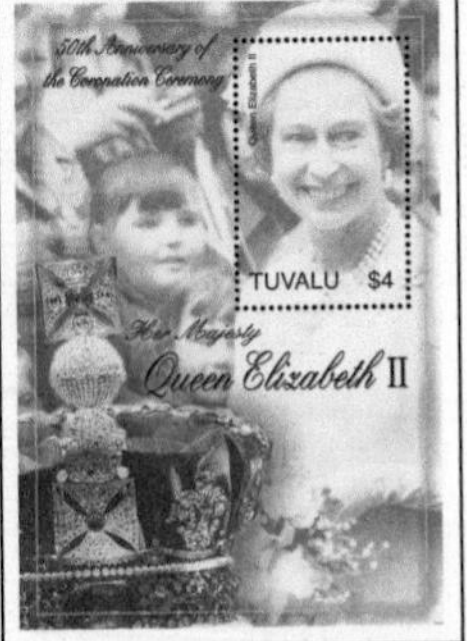

Coronation of Queen Elizabeth II, 50th Anniv. — A169

No. 913: a, Wearing gray dress. b, Wearing tiara. c, Wearing yellow hat.
$4, Wearing hat and pearl necklace.

2003, Aug. 11
913 A169 $2 Sheet of 3, #a-c 7.50 7.50

Souvenir Sheet

914 A169 $4 multi 5.00 5.00

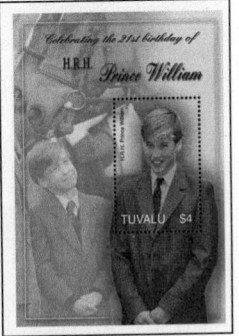

Prince William, 21st Birthday A170

No. 915: a, Wearing school cap. b, Wearing blue shirt. c, Wearing polo helmet.
$4, Wearing suit and tie.

2003, Aug. 11
915 A170 $1.50 Sheet of 3, #a-c 6.50 6.50

Souvenir Sheet

916 A170 $4 multi 5.75 5.75

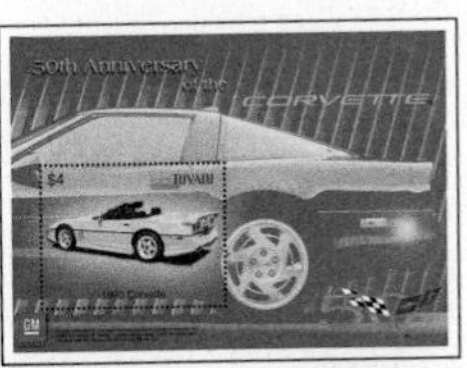

General Motors Automobiles — A171

No. 917, $1 — Corvettes: a, Yellow 1979. b, Red 1979. c, Silver 1979. d, 1980.
No. 918, $1.50 — Cadillacs: a, 1931 V-16 Sport Phaeton. b, 1959 Eldorado convertible. c, 1979 Seville Elegante. d, 1983 Seville Elegante.
No. 919, $4, 1990 Corvette. No. 920, $4, 1954 Cadillac Coupe de Ville.

2003, Sept. 8 *Perf. 13¾*

Sheets of 4, #a-d

917-918 A171 Set of 2 11.50 11.50

Souvenir Sheets

919-920 A171 Set of 2 8.75 8.75

Corvettes, 50th anniv.; Cadillacs, 100th anniv.

Tour de France Bicycle Race, Cent. A172

No. 921: a, Gastone Nencini, 1960. b, Jacques Anquetil, 1961. c, Anquetil, 1962. d, Anquetil, 1963.
$4, Jan Janssen, 1968.

2003, Oct. 6 *Perf. 13¾x13¼*
921 A172 $1 Sheet of 4, #a-d 6.50 6.50

Souvenir Sheet

922 A172 $4 multi 6.50 6.50

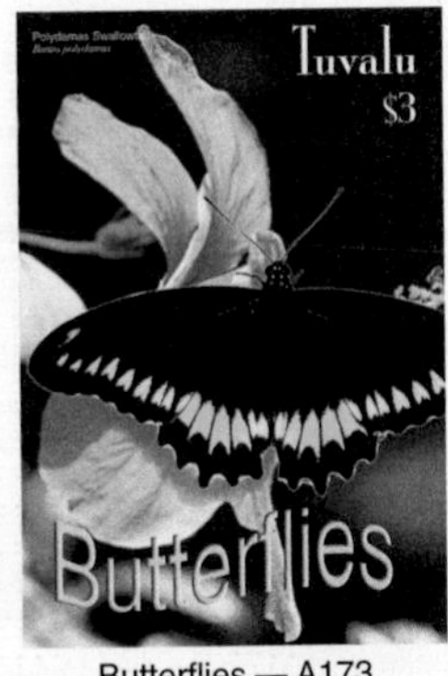

Butterflies — A173

No. 923, horiz.: a, Malachite. b, White M hairstreak. c, Giant swallowtail. d, Bahamian swallowtail.
$3, Polydamas swallowtail.

2003, Dec. 16 *Perf. 14*
923 A173 $1.25 Sheet of 4, #a-d 6.50 6.50

Imperf

924 A173 $3 multi 3.50 3.50

No. 923 contains four 42x28mm stamps.

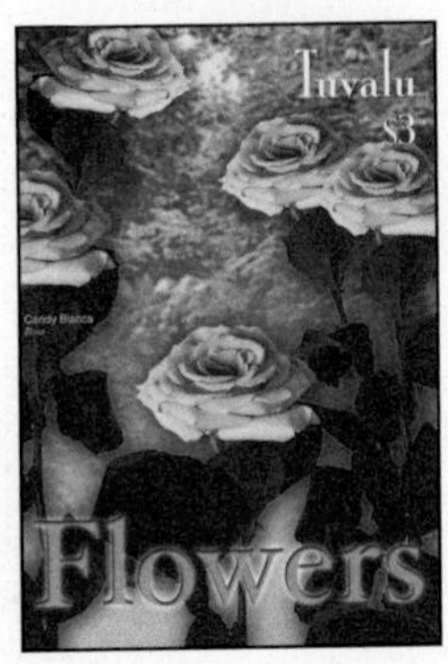

Flowers A174

No. 925: a, Rhododendron. b, Golden Artist tulip. c, Golden Splendor lily. d, Flamingo flower.
$3, Candy Bianca rose.

2003, Dec. 16 *Perf. 14*
925 A174 $1.25 Sheet of 4, #a-d 8.25 8.25

Imperf

926 A174 $3 multi 5.00 5.00

No. 925 contains four 28x42mm stamps.

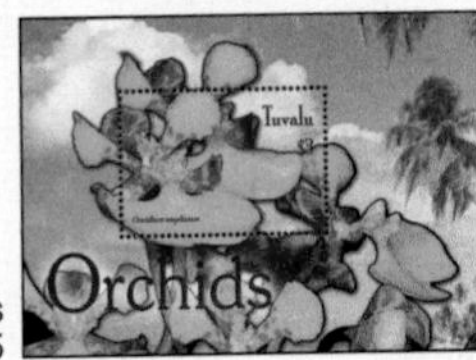

Orchids A175

No. 927, vert.: a, Dimerandra emarginata. b, Oncidium lanceanum. c, Isochilus linearis. d, Oeceoclades maculata.
$3, Oncidium ampliatum.

2003, Dec. 16 *Perf. 14*
927 A175 $1.25 Sheet of 4, #a-d 6.00 6.00

Souvenir Sheet

928 A175 $3 multi 3.75 3.75

Birds A176

No. 929: a, Blue-gray gnatcatcher. b, White-eyed vireo. c, Clapper rail. d, Sandhill crane.
$3, Grasshopper sparrow.

2003, Dec. 16
929 A176 $1.25 Sheet of 4, #a-d 6.25 6.25

Souvenir Sheet

930 A176 $3 multi 3.00 3.00

New Year 2004 (Year of the Monkey) — A177

Paintings by Chang Dai-chen: 75c, Monkey and Old Tree. $1.50, Two Monkeys.

2004, Jan. 4 ***Perf. 13½***
931 A177 75c multi 4.00 4.00

Souvenir Sheet

932 A177 $1.50 multi 4.50 4.50

No. 931 printed in sheets of 4.

Paintings by Norman Rockwell A178

No. 933, vert.: a, 100th Year of Baseball. b, The Locker Room (The Rookie). c, The Dug-out. d, Game Called Because of Rain.
$3, New Kids in the Neighborhood.

2004, Jan. 30 ***Perf. 14¼***
933 A178 $1.25 Sheet of 4, #a-d 7.50 7.50

Souvenir Sheet

934 A178 $3 multi 5.50 5.50

2004 AmeriStamp Expo, Norfolk, Va. (#933).

Paintings by Pablo Picasso (1881-1973) — A179

No. 935, vert.: a, Seated Woman. b, Woman in Armchair. c, Bust of Françoise. d, Head of a Woman.
$4, Françoise Gilot with Paloma and Claude.

2004, Mar. 1 Litho. ***Perf. 14¼***
935 A179 $1.50 Sheet of 4, #a-d 9.50 9.50

Imperf

936 A179 $4 multi 5.75 5.75

No. 935 contains four 37x50mm stamps.

Paintings by Paul Gauguin (1848-1903) A180

Designs: 50c, Les Seins aux Fleurs Rouges. 60c, Famille Tahitienne. No. 939, $1, Tahitiennes sur la Plage. $2, Jeune Fille à L'Eventail.
No. 941, $1: a, Nafea Faa Ipoipo. b, Le Cheval Blanc. c, Pape Moe. d, Contes Barbares.
$4, Femmes de Tahiti, horiz.

2004, Mar. 1 ***Perf. 14¼***
937-940 A180 Set of 4 7.00 7.00
941 A180 $1 Sheet of 4, #a-d 7.00 7.00

Imperf

Size: 93x73mm

942 A180 $4 multi 7.00 7.00

Paintings in the Hermitage, St. Petersburg, Russia — A181

Designs: 50c, Philadelphia and Elizabeth Wharton, by Anthony Van Dyck. 80c, A Glass of Lemonade, by Gerard Terborch. $1, A Mistress and Her Servant, by Pieter de Hooch. $1.20, Portrait of a Man and His Three Sons, by Bartholomaeus Bruyn the Elder.
$4, The Milkmaid's Family, by Louis le Nain, horiz.

2004, Mar. 1 ***Perf. 14¼***
943-946 A181 Set of 4 4.75 4.75

Imperf

Size: 80x68mm

947 A181 $4 multi 6.00 6.00

Fight Against HIV and AIDS — A182

Designs: 60c, Speaker at conference. 90c, Speaker and dais. $1.50, People standing in front of banner. $2, People seated at dais.
$3, Conference participants.

2004, May 17 ***Perf. 13x13½***
948-951 A182 Set of 4 7.00 7.00

Souvenir Sheet

952 A182 $3 multi 5.25 5.25

Souvenir Sheet

Inauguration of Republic of China President Chen Shui-bian — A183

No. 953: a, Pres. Chen Shui-bian. b, Saufatu Sopoanga, Prime Minister of Tuvalu.

2004, May 20 ***Perf. 13½x13¼***
953 A183 $2 Sheet of 2, #a-b 5.25 5.25

Souvenir Sheet

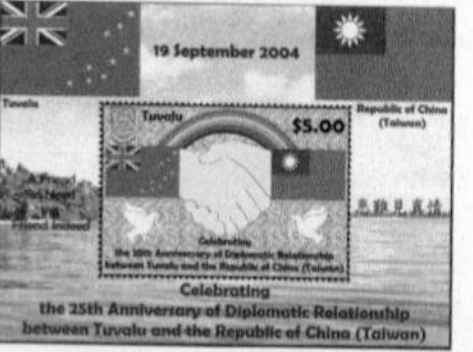

Diplomatic Relations Between Tuvalu and the Republic of China, 25th Anniv. A183a

2004, Sept. 19 Litho. ***Perf. 13¼x13***
953C A183a $5 multi 6.00 6.00

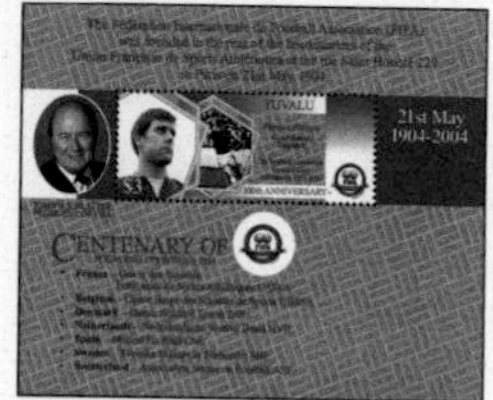

FIFA (Fédération Internationale de Football Association), Cent. — A184

No. 954: a, Sebastiano Rossi. b, Clarence Seedorf. c, Zico. d, Jack Charlton.
$3, Geoff Hurst.

Perf. 12¾x12½

2004, Nov. 29 **Litho.**
954 A184 $1 Sheet of 4, #a-d 6.00 6.00

Souvenir Sheet

955 A184 $3 multi 5.00 5.00

Miniature Sheet

World Peace A185

No. 956: a, Alfred Nobel. b, Doves. c, Nelson Mandela.

2005, Jan. 14 ***Perf. 12¾***
956 A185 $1.50 Sheet of 3, #a-c 6.50 6.50

Miniature Sheet

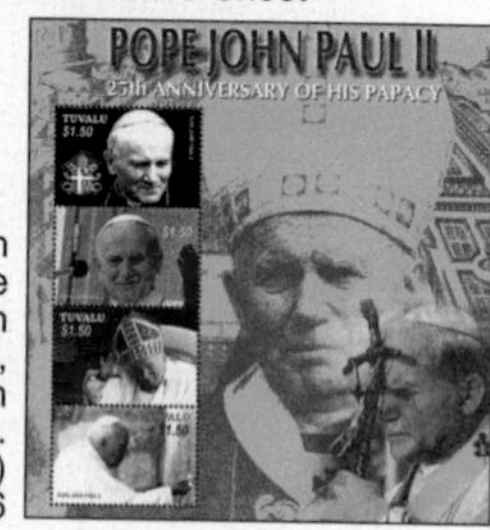

Election of Pope John Paul II, 25th Anniv. (in 2003) A186

No. 957: a, With papal arms. b, At microphone. c, Wearing miter. d, Placing prayer in Wailing Wall, Jerusalem.

2005, Jan. 14
957 A186 $1.50 Sheet of 4, #a-d 9.50 9.50

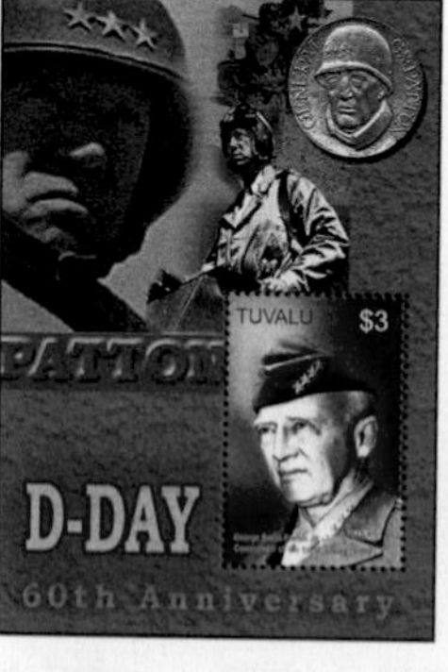

D-Day, 60th Anniv. (in 2004) A187

No. 958: a, Gen. George C. Marshall. b, Adm. Sir Ramsay Bertram Home. c, Gen. Walter Bedell Smith. d, Field Marshal Alan Francis Brooke.
$3, Gen. George S. Patton.

2005, Jan. 14
958 A187 $1.50 Sheet of 4, #a-d 10.00 10.00

Souvenir Sheet

959 A187 $3 multi 5.25 5.25

Dogs — A188

Designs: 20c, Rat terrier. 75c, Large Spanish hound. $1, Lundehund. $2, Beagle harrier.
$3, Old Danish pointer.

2005, Apr. 26 Litho. ***Perf. 13¾x13¼***
960-963 A188 Set of 4 6.50 6.50

Souvenir Sheet

964 A188 $3 multi 5.00 5.00

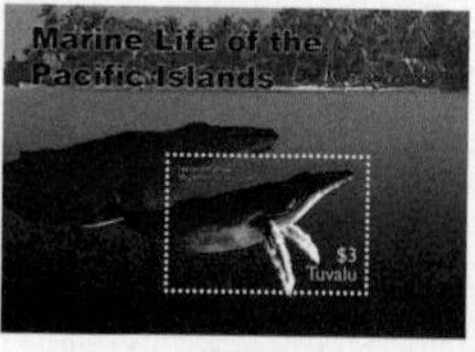

Marine Life A189

No. 965: a, Striped-face unicornfish. b, Great barracuda. c, Blue-ringed octopus. d, Giant clam.
$3, Humpback whale.

2005, Apr. 26 ***Perf. 13¼x13¾***
965 A189 $1 Sheet of 4, #a-d 7.00 7.00

Souvenir Sheet

966 A189 $3 multi 6.00 6.00

Medicinal Plants — A190

No. 967: a, Common toadflax. b, Pomegranate. c, Black horehound. d, Agnus castus
$3, Black henbane.

2005, Apr. 26 ***Perf. 13¾x13¼***
967 A190 $1 Sheet of 4, #a-d 6.75 6.75

Souvenir Sheet

968 A190 $3 multi 5.25 5.25

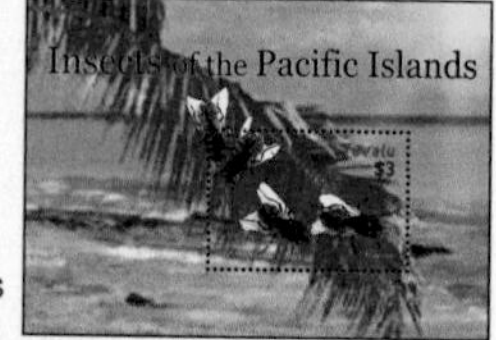

Insects A191

No. 969, vert.: a, Louse fly. b, Predacious dung beetle. c, Ladybug. d, Mosquito.
$3, House fly.

2005, Apr. 26 ***Perf. 13¾x13¼***
969 A191 $1 Sheet of 4, #a-d 6.75 6.75

Souvenir Sheet

Perf. 13¼x13¾

970 A191 $3 multi 5.25 5.25

Pope John Paul II (1920-2005) and Queen Elizabeth II — A192

2005, July 12 *Perf. 13½*
971 A192 $4 multi 6.50 6.50

No. 886 Surcharged

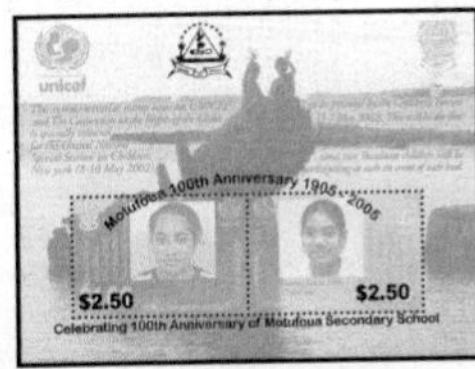

Methods and Perfs As Before

2005, July 17
971A A157 Sheet of 2 7.75 7.75
b. $2.50 on $1 #886a 3.75 3.75
c. $2.50 on $1 #886b 3.75 3.75

Battle of Trafalgar, Bicent. A193

No. 972: a, HMS Victory collides with French ship Redoubtable. b, Admiral Horatio Nelson. c, HMS Victory leads the British fleet. d, Nelson breaths his last breath.
$3, Admiral Cuthbert Collingwood.

2005, July 28 *Perf. 12*
972 A193 $1.50 Sheet of 4, #a-d 10.00 10.00

Souvenir Sheet

973 A193 $3 multi 5.25 5.25

World Cup Soccer Championships, 75th Anniv. — A194

No. 974: a, Thomas Berthold. b, Bobby Charlton. c, Klaus Augenthaler.
$3, Thomas Strunz.

2005, July 28 *Perf. 13¼*
974 A194 $2 Sheet of 3, #a-c 10.00 10.00

Souvenir Sheet

Perf. 12

975 A194 $3 multi 5.25 5.25

End of World War II, 60th Anniv. A195

No. 976, $2: a, Sir Winston Churchill. b, Gen. Charles de Gaulle. c, Newspaper report on death of Adolf Hitler.

No. 977, $2: a, Pres. Harry S. Truman. b, Newspaper report on end of war. c, Gen. Dwight D. Eisenhower.
No. 978, $3, Gen. George S. Patton. No. 979, $3, Brig. Gen. Paul W. Tibbets, Jr. and Enola Gay.

2005, Sept. 21 *Perf. 12¾*

Sheets of 3, #a-c

976-977 A195 Set of 2 20.00 20.00

Souvenir Sheets

978-979 A195 Set of 2 10.00 10.00

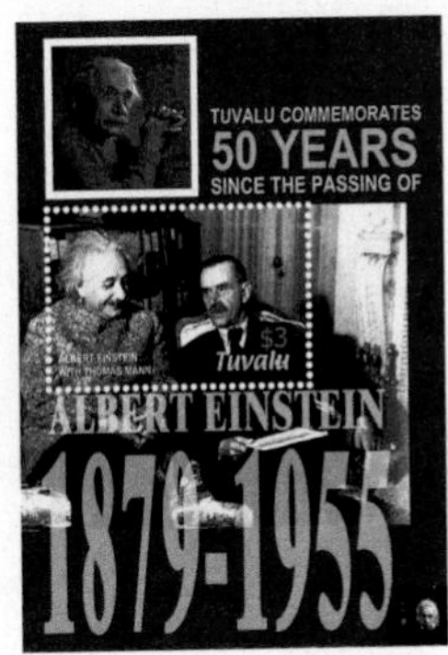

Albert Einstein (1879-1955), Physicist — A196

No. 981 — Einstein and: a, Hendrik Lorentz. b, Fritz Haber. c, David Ben-Gurion.
$3, Einstein with Thomas Mann.

2005, Sept. 21
980 A196 $2 Sheet of 3, #a-c 10.00 10.00

Souvenir Sheet

981 A196 $3 multi 5.00 5.00

Rotary International, Cent. — A197

No. 982: a, Child. b, Hand holding pills. c, Children.
$3, Paul P. Harris, founder.

2005, Nov. 28
982 A197 $2 Sheet of 3, #a-c 10.00 10.00

Souvenir Sheet

983 A197 $3 multi 5.00 5.00

Hans Christian Andersen (1805-75), Author — A198

No. 984: a, Andersen seated. b, Sculpture of Andersen. c, Head of Andersen.
$3, Statue of Andersen.

2005, Nov. 28
984 A198 $2 Sheet of 3, #a-c 10.00 10.00

Souvenir Sheet

985 A198 $3 multi 5.00 5.00

A199

Elvis Presley (1935-77) — A200

No. 987 — Presley and: a, Gable and top of column of house. b, Roofline of house. c, Bottom of column of house. d, Archway of house.

2006, Jan. 30 *Perf. 13½*
986 A199 $3 multi 4.50 4.50
987 A200 $3 Sheet of 4, #a-d 18.00 18.00

No. 986 printed in sheets of 4.

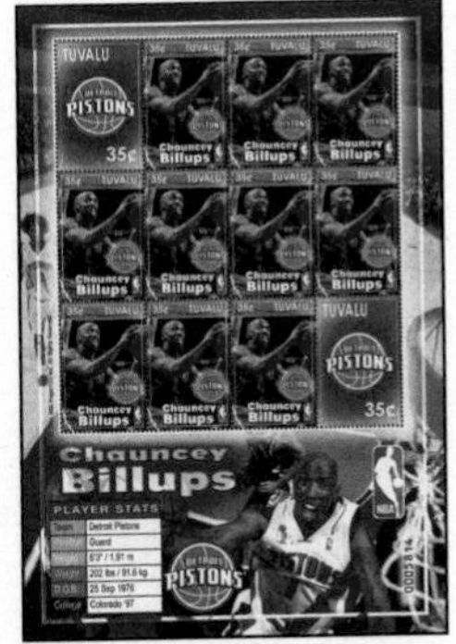

National Basketball Association Players and Team Emblems — A201

No. 988, 35c: a, Emblem of Detroit Pistons. b, Chauncey Billups.
No. 989, 35c: a, Emblem of New Jersey Nets. b, Rodney Buford.
No. 990, 35c: a, Emblem of Boston Celtics. b, Ricky Davis.
No. 991, 35c: a, Emblem of Miami Heat. b, Udonis Haslem
No. 992, 35c: a, Emblem of Indiana Pacers, horiz. b, Stephen Jackson.
No. 993, 35c: a, Emblem of Minnesota Timberwolves. b, Wally Szczerbiak.

2006, Jan. 30 *Perf. 13¼*

Sheets of 12, 2 #a, 10 #b

988-993 A201 Set of 6 45.00 45.00

Souvenir Sheet

2006 World Cup Soccer Championships, Germany — A202

No. 994 — Player and uniform for: a, 90c, Spain. b, $1, South Korea. c, $1.50, France. d, $2, United States.

2006, June 9 **Litho.** *Perf. 13¼*
994 A202 Sheet of 4, #a-d 8.25 8.25

Corals — A203

Designs: 10c, Montipora aequituberculata. 25c, Montipora capricornis. 30c, Montipora verrucosa. 40c, Acropora caroliniana. 50c, Acropora aculeus. 60c, Acropora anthocercis. 65c, Acropora granulosa. 80c, Acropora rosaria. 90c, Acropora cerealis. $1, Acropora yongei. $2, Acropora echinata. $5, Astreopora myriophthalma.

2006, Oct. 12 *Perf. 12¾*
995 A203 10c multi .30 .25
996 A203 25c multi .40 .40
997 A203 30c multi .45 .45
998 A203 40c multi .60 .60
999 A203 50c multi .75 .75
1000 A203 60c multi .90 .90
1001 A203 65c multi 1.00 1.00
1002 A203 80c multi 1.25 1.25
1003 A203 90c multi 1.40 1.40
1004 A203 $1 multi 1.50 1.50
1005 A203 $2 multi 3.00 3.00
1006 A203 $5 multi 7.50 7.50
Nos. 995-1006 (12) 19.05 19.00

Miniature Sheets

Pres. John F. Kennedy (1917-63) — A204

No. 1007, $1.30: a, On PT109, 1942. b, Receiving medal for gallantry, 1944. c, Portrait with brown background. d, In Ensign's uniform, 1941.
No. 1008, $1.30: a, Wearing bow tie. b, Wearing tan suit. c, With Eleanor Roosevelt. d, Portrait and U.S. Capitol.

2006, Sept. 21 **Litho.** *Perf. 13½*

Sheets of 4, #a-d

1007-1008 A204 Set of 2 15.50 15.50

Queen Elizabeth II, 80th Birthday A205

No. 1009: a, As child holding dog. b, Wearing crown and holding scepter. c, Wearing jacket. d, Wearing sash and tiara.
$3, Wearing crown.

2006, Sept. 21
1009 A205 $1.30 Sheet of 4, #a-d 7.75 7.75

Souvenir Sheet

1010 A205 $3 multi 4.50 4.50

Space Achievements — A206

No. 1011 — Space Shuttle Discovery's return to space: a, Nose of Shuttle, open cargo doors, text in white reading down. b, Tail of Shuttle, stars, Earth, text in red reading across. c, Tail and wings of Shuttle, open cargo doors, text in red reading down. d, Astronaut on robotic arm. e, Head-on view of Shuttle nose, text in red reading across. f, Robotic arm, text in red and white.
No. 1012 — International Space Station: a, Top of rocket boosters. b, Space Station, text in white reading across. c, Space Shuttle. d, Space Station, text in white reading up.
$3, Calipso Satellite.

2006
1011 A206 $1 Sheet of 6, #a-f 9.50 9.50

1012 A206 $1.30 Sheet of 4, #a-d 7.75 7.75

Souvenir Sheet

1013 A206 $3 multi 4.50 4.50

Issued: No. 1011, 12/21; Nos. 1012-1013, 9/21.

Miniature Sheet

Wolfgang Amadeus Mozart (1756-91), Composer — A207

No. 1014: a, Mozart gazing out window. b, Mozart family, 1780. c, Mozart, 1763. d, Art deco illustration of the young Mozart.

2006, Oct. 26

1014 A207 $1.30 Sheet of 4, #a-d 8.00 8.00

Rembrandt (1606-69), Painter — A208

Designs: 10c, Woman in Bed. 20c, The Flight into Egypt. 35c, The Suicide of Lucretia. 95c, Esther Preparing to Intercede with Ahasuerus. $1, Rembrandt's Mother. $2, Child with Dead Peacock.

$3, The Abduction of Ganymede.

2006, Nov. 9 ***Perf. 14¼***

1015-1020 A208 Set of 6 7.25 7.25

Imperf

Size: 76x106mm

1021 A208 $3 multi 4.75 4.75

Worldwide Fund for Nature (WWF) — A209

Various Pygmy killer whales.

2006, Nov. 9 ***Perf. 13½***

1022	Horiz. strip of 4	11.00	11.00
a.	A209 40c Four whales	.65	.65
b.	A209 60c Two whales	.95	.95
c.	A209 90c Four whales, diff.	1.40	1.40
d.	A209 $5 Two whales, diff.	8.00	8.00
e.	Miniature sheet, 2 each #1022a-1022d	22.00	22.00

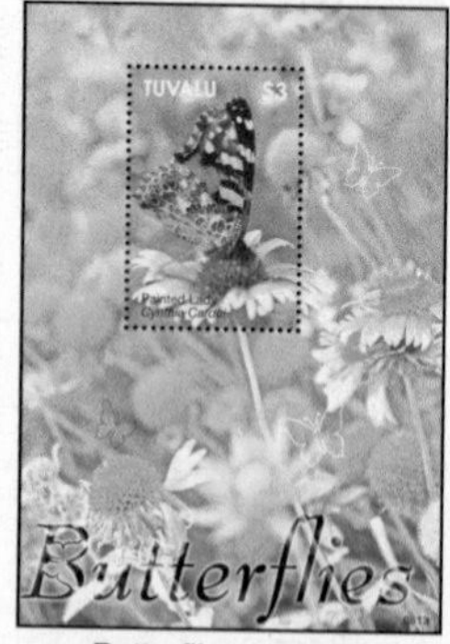

Butterflies — A210

No. 1023: a, Tailed jay. b, Ixias undatus. c, Hebomoia leucippe detanii. d, Rajah Brooke's birdwing.

$3, Painted lady.

2006, Nov. 23

1023 A210 $1 Sheet of 4, #a-d 6.00 6.00

Souvenir Sheet

1024 A210 $3 multi 4.00 4.00

Birds A211

No. 1025: a, Reed warbler. b, Indian pitta. c, Gurney's pitta. d, Northern shrike.

$3, Black-backed fairy wren.

2006, Nov. 23

1025 A211 $1 Sheet of 4, #a-d 7.00 7.00

Souvenir Sheet

1026 A211 $3 multi 5.00 5.00

Miniature Sheet

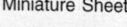

Wedding of Queen Elizabeth II and Prince Philip, 60th Anniv. A212

No. 1027: a, Photograph, denomination in pink. b, Drawing, denomination in white. c, Photograph, denomination in light green. d, Drawing, denomination in pink. e, Photograph, denomination in white. f, Drawing, denomination in light green.

2007, May 1 **Litho.** ***Perf. 13¼***

1027 A212 $1 Sheet of 6, #a-f 8.00 8.00

Princess Diana (1961-97) — A213

No. 1028: a, Wearing black and white hat, pink frame. b, Wearing beige dress, pink frame. c, Wearing pink hat, pink frame. d, Wearing pink hat, lilac frame. e, Wearing beige dress, no frame. f, Wearing black and white hat, lilac frame.

$3, Princess Diana in Tomb of King Seti I, Egypt.

2007, May 1

1028 A213 $1 Sheet of 6, #a-f 8.00 8.00

Souvenir Sheet

1029 A213 $3 multi 5.00 5.00

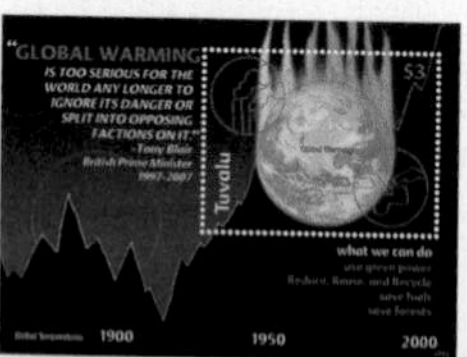

Global Warming A214

No. 1030, $1: a, Windmills. b, Smokestacks, graph of atmospheric carbon dioxide. c, Tree seedling. d, Robotic arm lifting logs, thermometer. e, Recycling emblem. f, Thermometer, graph of global temperatures.

No. 1031, $1 — Text: a, Cause: Deforestation. b, Effect: Melting ice cap. c, Cause: Industrialization. d, Effect: Warmer temperature. e, Cause: Traffic. f, Effect: Extreme weather.

No. 1032, $1 — Text: a, Effect: Habitats destroyed. b, Prevention: Use renewable energy. c, Effect: Coral reef bleaching. d, Prevention: Recycle. e, Effect: Erratic weather patterns. f, Prevention: Plant trees.

No. 1033, $3, Earth on fire, smokestacks, automobile getting fuel. No. 1034, $3, Windmills. No. 1035, $3, Plant in parched soil, vert.

2007, July 21 **Litho.**

Sheets of 6, #a-f

1030-1032 A214 Set of 3 32.50 32.50

Souvenir Sheets

1033-1035 A214 Set of 3 16.00 16.00

First Helicopter Flight, Cent. — A215

Designs: 20c, BO-105. 75c, NH 90, horiz. $1, S-65/RH-53D, horiz. $2, AH 64 Apache, horiz.

No. 1040, horiz.: a, BO-105, diff. b, S-65/RH-53D, diff. c, AH 64 Apache, diff. d, NH 90, diff.

$3, HUP Retriever, horiz.

2007, July 28 ***Perf. 13¼***

1036-1039 A215 Set of 4 5.50 5.50

1040 A215 $1.30 Sheet of 4, #a-d 7.00 7.00

Souvenir Sheet

1041 A215 $3 multi 4.75 4.75

Scouting, Cent. — A216

Scout: 20c, On bicycle. 75c, At campfire. $1, Playing cricket. $2, Shooting arrow.

$3, Dove, Scouting flag, vert.

2007, Aug. 15

1042-1045 A216 Set of 4 6.50 6.50

Souvenir Sheet

1046 A216 $3 multi 5.00 5.00

No. 1046 contains one 37x51mm stamp.

Paintings by Qi Baishi (1864-1957) — A217

No. 1047: a, A Good Wind for Thousands of Miles, top half. b, As "a," bottom half. c, The Yuxia and Lianhua Mountains, top half. d, As "c," bottom half. e, Autumn Landscape with Cormorants, top half. f, As "e," bottom half.

No. 1048: a, Grasshopper on a Branch. b, Fish and Catfish.

$3, Ink Landscape.

2007, Sept. 21

1047 A217 $1 Sheet of 6, #a-f 11.00 11.00

1048 A217 $2.50 Sheet of 2, #a-b 9.00 9.00

Souvenir Sheet

1049 A217 $3 multi 5.50 5.50

Princess Diana (1961-97) — A218

Litho. & Embossed

2007, Oct. 1 ***Serpentine Die Cut***

Without Gum

1050 A218 $9 gold & multi 14.00 14.00

Miniature Sheet

Elvis Presley (1935-77) — A219

No. 1051: a, Holding guitar. b, Wearing white shirt. c, Wearing suit and tie. d, Wearing Hawaiian shirt. e, Wearing blue shirt. f, Wearing Army uniform.

2007, Oct. 1 **Litho.** ***Perf. 13¼***

1051 A219 90c Sheet of 6, #a-f 8.00 8.00

Miniature Sheet

Pres. John F. Kennedy (1917-63) — A220

No. 1052 — Kennedy: a, Pointing, text at left. b, Pointing, text at right. c, Not pointing, text at left. d, Not pointing, text at right.

2007, Oct. 15 ***Perf. 12¾***

1052 A220 $1 Sheet of 4, #a-d 6.50 6.50

Miniature Sheet

Marilyn Monroe (1926-62), Actress — A221

No. 1053: a, Wearing white boa. b, Wearing black dress, denomination in white. c, Wearing black and white dress, denomination in purple. d, Wearing beige dress.

2007, Oct. 15

1053 A221 $1 Sheet of 4, #a-d 7.50 7.50

Miniature Sheet

Pope Benedict XVI A222

No. 1054: a, Photomosaic (Pope's ear). b, Photomosaic (Pope's neck and shoulder). c, Photomosaic (Pope's chest). d, Photograph of Pope.

2007, Nov. 11 *Perf. 12¼x12*
1054 A222 $1.30 Sheet of 4, #a-d 7.50 7.50

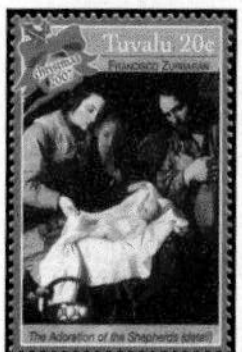

Christmas — A223

Paintings: 20c, The Adoration of the Shepherds, by Francisco Zurbaran. 75c, Madonna and Child with Angels, by Hans Memling. $1, The Nativity, by Maestro Esiguo. $2, The Nativity, by Philippe de Champaigne.

2007, Dec. 14 *Perf. 14*
1055-1058 A223 Set of 4 7.00 7.00

Miniature Sheet

2008 Summer Olympics, Beijing — A224

No. 1059: a, Baseball. b, Fencing. c, Field hockey. d, Gymnastics.

2008, Jan. 8 Litho. *Perf. 12¾*
1059 A224 60c Sheet of 4, #a-d 4.25 4.25

Miniature Sheet

New Year 2008 (Year of the Rat) A225

No. 1060 — Rat and Chinese character with yellow background color at: a, LR. b, LL. c, UR. d, UL.

2008, Feb. 28 *Perf. 12*
1060 A225 $1.30 Sheet of 4, #a-d 9.75 9.75

Taiwan Tourist Attractions — A226

No. 1061, horiz.: a, River and Red Suspension Bridge. b, Chinese New Year dragon. c, National Palace Museum. d, Taipei Main Railroad Station. e, Golden Waterfall, Jin Gua Shi. f, National Concert Hall, Taipei.
$2, Buddhist temple.

2008, Mar. 15 *Perf. 13¼*
1061 A226 50c Sheet of 6, #a-f 5.50 5.50

Souvenir Sheet

1062 A226 $2 multi 3.75 3.75

Flowers of the Holy Land A227

No. 1063: a, Crocuses. b, Aleppo adonis. c, Wild chamomile. d, Fig buttercup. e, Dwarf chicory. f, Queen mallow.
$2, Yellow crocus.

2008, May 14 *Perf. 11½x11¼*
1063 A227 50c Sheet of 6, #a-f 5.00 5.00

Souvenir Sheet

1064 A227 $2 multi 4.00 4.00

2008 World Stamp Championship, Israel.

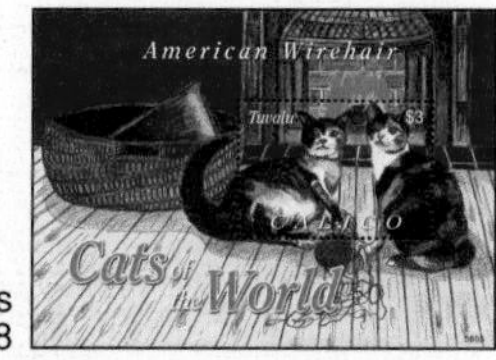

Cats A228

No. 1065: a, Siberian. b, California spangled. c, Siamese. d, Burmilla. e, European shorthair. f, Devon rex.
$3, American wirehair.

2008, May 31 *Perf. 13¼*
1065 A228 $1 Sheet of 6, #a-f 11.50 11.50

Souvenir Sheet

1066 A228 $3 multi 5.75 5.75

Miniature Sheet

Orchids A229

No. 1067: a, Vuylstekeara cambria. b, Dendrobium nobile (pink petals). c, Phalaenopsis nivacolor. d, Cattleya trianae. e, Dendrobium nobile (purple and green petals). f, Cymbidium alexanderi.

2008, June 15 *Perf. 11½x11¼*
1067 A229 $1 Sheet of 6, #a-f 11.50 11.50

A230

Elvis Presley (1935-77) — A231

No. 1068 — Presley: a, Without microphone. b, Holding microphone in right hand. c, Holding microphone in both hands.
No. 1069 — Presley: a, In white suit, yellow spirals at left and right. b, In leather jacket, yellow spirals at left and right. c, In white suit, yellow spirals at left. d, In white suit, yellow spirals at right. e, In leather jacket, yellow spirals at left. f, In white suit, no yellow spirals.

2008 *Perf. 11½x11¼*
1068 Horiz. strip of 3 5.75 5.75
a.-c. A230 $1 Any single 1.90 1.90

Perf. 13¼

1069 A231 $1 Sheet of 6, #a-f 9.50 9.50

Issued: No. 1068, 7/14; No. 1069, 9/11. No. 1068 was printed in sheets containing two of each stamp.

Miniature Sheet

Birds A232

No. 1070: a, Magnificent frigatebird. b, Townsend's warbler. c, Sooty tern. d, Common noddy. e, Masked booby. f, Red-tailed tropicbird.

2008, July 25 *Perf. 13¼*
1070 A232 $1 Sheet of 6, #a-f 11.50 11.50

Visit to Lourdes of Pope Benedict XVI — A233

2008, Aug. 31 Litho.
1071 A233 $1.30 multi 2.10 2.10

Printed in sheets of 4.

Miniature Sheets

A234

Space Exploration, 50th Anniv. (in 2007) — A235

No. 1072: a, Saturn V rocket carrying Apollo 11 on launch pad. b, Buzz Aldrin's footprint on Moon. c, Apollo 11 command module. d, Apollo 11 commander Neil A. Armstrong. e, Command module pilot Michael Collins. f, Lunar module pilot Edwin "Buzz" Aldrin.
No. 1073, $1.30 — Chandra X-ray Observatory with: a, Orange nebula at center. b, Stars in background. c, Red background. d, Blue green background.
No. 1074, $1.30 — Sputnik 1: a, Opened up. b, In orbit, satellite above denomination. c, R-7 Senyorka rocket. d, In orbit, with antenna running through denomination.
No. 1075, $1.30 — Cassini-Huygens probe: a, Cassini-Huygens in laboratory. b, Titan IV-B Centaur launch vehicle. c, Cassini-Huygens, Saturn. d, Cassini-Huygens, Saturn and Titan.
No. 1076, $1.30 — Galileo probe: a, Galileo in laboratory. b, Galileo, Europa, Jupiter and Io. c, Galileo probe (orange background). d, Jupiter, Io, Galileo and Ganymede.

2008, Sept. 11 *Perf. 13¼*
1072 A234 $1 Sheet of 6, #a-f 9.50 9.50

Sheets of 4, #a-d

1073-1076 A235 Set of 4 32.50 32.50

Miniature Sheet

Solo Aerial Circumnavigation of Wiley Post, 75th Anniv. — A236

No. 1077: a, Post wearing pressure suit. b, Post and airplane. c, The Winnie Mae. d, Post atop airplane. e, Post and wife, Mae. f, Harold Gatty, navigator.

2008, Oct. 23 *Perf. 13¼*
1077 A236 $1.30 Sheet of 6, #a-f 13.50 13.50

Miniature Sheet

Princess Diana (1961-97) — A237

No. 1078 — Princess Diana at: a, Left, denomination on lilac background. b, Right (Princess looking to left). c, Left, denomination on white background. d, Right (Princess looking to right).

2008, Nov. 25
1078 A237 $1.30 Sheet of 4, #a-d 9.25 9.25

Christmas — A238

Designs: 60c, Holly leaves and berries. 90c, Ornament. $1, Gift. $2.50, Candy cane.

2008, Nov. 25 *Perf. 14¼x14¾*
1079-1082 A238 Set of 4 6.50 6.50

Miniature Sheet

New Year 2009 (Year of the Ox) A239

No. 1083: a, 60c. b, 90c. d, $1.20. d, $2.50.

2009, Jan. 20 Litho. *Perf. 11½*
1083 A239 Sheet of 4, #a-d 7.00 7.00

Miniature Sheet

Inauguration of US President Barack Obama — A240

No. 1084: a, Pres. Abraham Lincoln. b, Emancipation Proclamation. c, Dr. Martin

Luther King, Jr. d, King at March on Washington. e, Pres. Barack Obama. f, Obama giving victory speech.

2009, Jan. 20
1084 A240 $1.30 Sheet of 6, #a-f, + 3 label 10.50 10.50

Miniature Sheet

Elvis Presley (1935-77) — A241

No. 1085 — Presley and: a, Red bird. b, Sun. c, Black bird. d, Flames. e, Sequin eagle. f, Peacock.

2009, Mar. 12
1085 A241 $1 Sheet of 6, #a-f 8.75 8.75

Miniature Sheet

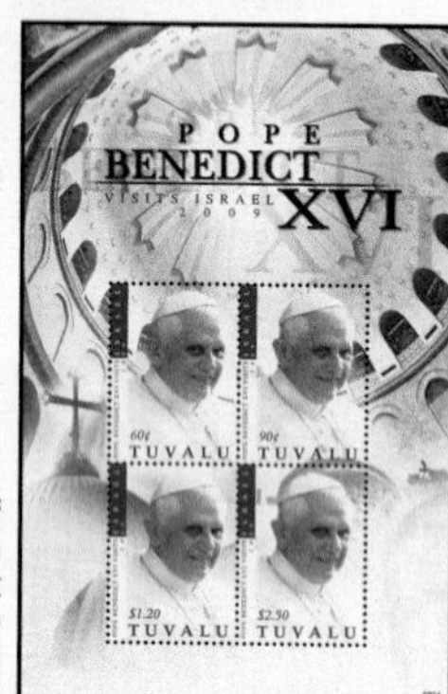

Visit of Pope Benedict XVI to Israel A242

No. 1086: a, 60c. b, 90c. c, $1.20. d, $2.50.

2009, Apr. 23
1086 A242 Sheet of 4, #a-d 7.50 7.50

Miniature Sheets

A243

Michael Jackson (1958-2009), Singer — A244

No. 1087 — Jackson and stage lighting above country name in: a, Blue. b, White. c, Orange. d, Red, with fireworks.

No. 1088 — Jacskon: a, Wearing jacket and hat, tie above "U." b, Holding microphone. c, Wearing sunglasses. d, Wearing jacket and hat, tie above "L."

2009, July 7 ***Perf. 13¼x13***
1087 A243 $1.30 Sheet of 4, #a-d 8.25 8.25

Perf. 13x13¼
1088 A244 $1.30 Sheet of 4, #a-d 8.25 8.25

Miniature Sheet

The Obama Family A245

No. 1089 — a, First Lady Michelle Obama. b, Pres. Barack Obama. c, Barack Obama and dog, Bo. d, Obama family with dog.

2009, July 13 ***Perf. 13½***
1089 A245 $1.30 Sheet of 4, #a-d 8.75 8.75

Miniature Sheet

The Three Stooges A246

No. 1090 — The Three Stooges in various scenes with country name in: a, Red brown. b, Blue. c, Yellow brown. d, Green.

2009, July 14 ***Perf. 11½***
1090 A246 $1.30 Sheet of 4, #a-d 8.75 8.75

Miniature Sheets

First Man on the Moon, 40th Anniv. A247

No. 1091: a, Golden olive branch left on Moon. b, Apollo 11 Command Module. c, Saturn V rocket. d, Astronaut Neil Armstrong. e, Congressional Space Medal of Honor. f, Apollo 11 Lunar Module.

No. 1092: a, Buzz Aldrin on Moon. b, Saturn V rocket taking off with Apollo 11. c, Apollo 11 Command Module. d, Apollo 11 crewmen awaiting pickup.

2009, July 20 ***Perf. 13½***
1091 A247 $1 Sheet of 6, #a-f 9.00 9.00
1092 A247 $1.30 Sheet of 4, #a-d 7.75 7.75

Miniature Sheet

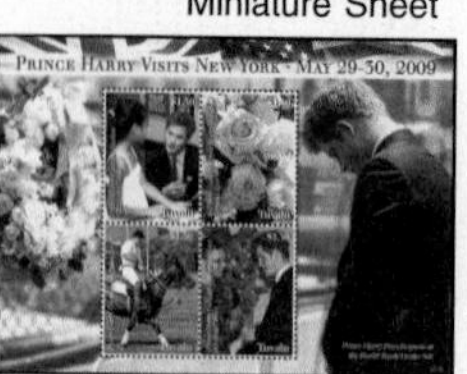

Visit of Prince Harry to New York A248

No. 1093: a, Prince Harry and woman at Harlem Children's Zoo. b, Wreath laid by Prince Harry at World Trade Center site. c, Prince Harry playing polo. d, Prince Harry and soldier at Veterans Affairs Medical Center.

2009, Aug. 25 ***Perf. 12x11½***
1093 A248 $1.30 Sheet of 4, #a-d 8.00 8.00

Souvenir Sheet

Diplomatic Relations Between Tuvalu and the Republic of China, 30th Anniv. — A249

2009, Sept. 19 ***Perf. 13½***
1094 A249 $5 multi 8.75 8.75

Christmas — A250

Designs: 60c, Stuffed reindeer, Santa Claus suit and hat with Tuvalu flag. 90c, Bells, Christmas ornament with Tuvalu flag. $1, Cloth Christmas decorations, Tuvalu arms. $2, Santa Claus on cake, bell with Tuvalu flag.

2009, Nov. 25 ***Perf. 13½x13***
1095-1098 A250 Set of 4 8.25 8.25

Miniature Sheet

Pres. John F. Kennedy (1917-63) — A251

No. 1099 — Pres. Kennedy: a, Seated at desk. b, With wife, Jacqueline. c, With son, John, Jr. d, At podium.

2009, Nov. 28 ***Perf. 12x11½***
1099 A251 $1.30 Sheet of 4, #a-d 9.50 9.50

Butterflies A252

Designs: 60c, Hyposcada kezia. 90c, Heteronympha mirifica. No. 1102, $1, Libythea geoffroy. $2.50, Protographium leosthenes.

No. 1104, $1: a, Horago selina. b, Ornithoptera victoriae. c, Polyura eudamippus. d, Catopsilia scylla. e, Graphium mendana. f, Melanitis amabilis.

2009, Nov. 28 ***Perf. 11½***
1100-1103 A252 Set of 4 8.50 8.50
1104 A252 $1 Sheet of 6, #a-f 10.00 10.00

Miniature Sheet

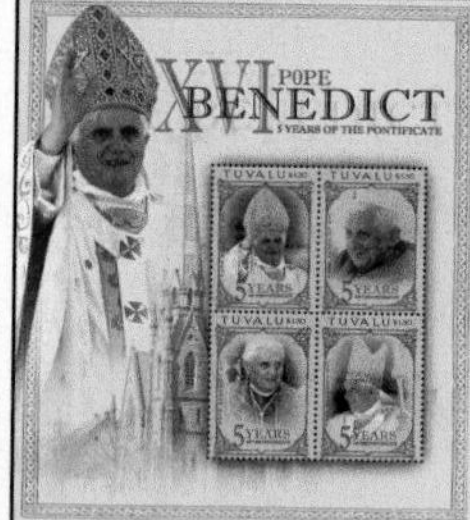

Reign of Pope Benedict XVI, 5th Anniv. — A252a

No. 1104G — Pope Benedict XVI: h, Waving. i, Wearing red vestments, facing left. j, Wearing red vestments, facing right. k, Holding crucifix.

2009, Dec. 10 ***Perf. 12x11½***
1104G A252a $1.30 Sheet of 4, #h-k 9.50 9.50

Miniature Sheet

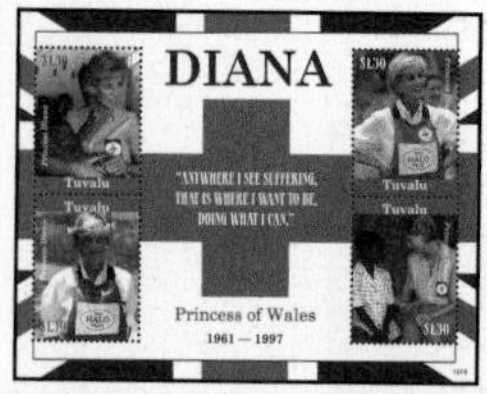

Princess Diana (1961-97) — A252b

No. 1104L: m, Holding infant. b, With arms on hips. c, Wearing face shield. d, Talking with child.

2009, Dec. 20
1104L A252b $1.30 Sheet of 4, #m-p 9.25 9.25

Miniature Sheet

Elvis Presley (1935-77) — A253

No. 1105 — Presley: a, With hands at bottom of guitar. b, With one hand over guitar strings. c, With hand over guitar strings and hand holding neck of guitar. d, Playing guitar and singing.

2010, Jan. 9 ***Perf. 13½***
1105 A253 $1.30 Sheet of 4, #a-d 9.25 9.25

Boy Scouts of America, Cent. A254

No. 1106, $1.30: a, Scout saluting. b, Scout planting tree.

No. 1107, $1.30: a, Scout with backpack and walking stick. b, Scout fishing.

2010, Feb. 1 **Pairs, #a-b** **Litho.**
1106-1107 A254 Set of 2 9.00 9.00

Nos. 1106-1107 were each printed in sheets containing two pairs.

Souvenir Sheet

Elvis Presley (1935-77) — A255

No. 1108: a, Presley facing left. b, Presley and guitar neck.

2010, Jan. 8 ***Imperf.***
Without Gum
1108 A255 $6 Sheet of 2, #a-b 21.50 21.50

Miniature Sheet

Earth Day, 40th Anniv. A256

No. 1109 — Various drawings by children: a, 50c. b, 60c, c, 90c, d, $1.50.

2010, Apr. 22 *Perf. 13¼*

1109 A256 Sheet of 4, #a-d 6.50 6.50

Miniature Sheets

Battle of Britain, 70th Anniv. A257

No. 1110, $1.30: a, Winston Churchill (black-and-white photograph). b, Coventry Cathedral in ruins. c, London in ruins (bicyclists at left). d, London in ruins (automobiles and trucks on street).

No. 1111, $1.30: a, Winston Churchill (color photograph). b, Messerschmitt BF 109E. c, Emblems of Luftwaffe and Royal Air Force. d, Supermarine Spitfire.

2010, Apr. 23 **Sheets of 4, #a-d**

1110-1111 A257 Set of 2 19.50 19.50

Palaces of the World A258

No. 1112, horiz.: a, Imperial Palace, Tokyo, Japan. b, Dolmabahçe Palace, Istanbul, Turkey. c, Winter Palace, St. Petersburg, Russia. d, Schönbrunn Palace, Vienna, Austria. e, Summer Palace, Beijing, China. f, Buckingham Palace, London, England.

$3, Palace of Versailles, Versailles, France.

2010, July 28 *Perf. 11½*

1112 A258 $1 Sheet of 6, #a-f 11.00 11.00

Souvenir Sheet

1113 A258 $3 multi 5.50 5.50

Souvenir Sheets

A259

A260

A261

Elvis Presley (1935-77) — A262

2010, July 28 *Perf. 14¼*

1114 A259 $3 multi 5.50 5.50
1115 A260 $3 multi 5.50 5.50
1116 A261 $3 multi 5.50 5.50
1117 A262 $3 multi 5.50 5.50
Nos. 1114-1117 (4) 22.00 22.00

Girl Guides, Cent. A263

No. 1118 — Drawings of Girl Guides in sepia and: a, Four Girl Guides in blue uniforms. b, Girl Guide wearing red neckerchief. c, Girl Guide with bongo drum. d, Two Girl Guides wearing red neckerchiefs.

$3, Centenary emblem, six Girl Guides, vert.

2010, Aug. 16 *Perf. 12½x12*

1118 A263 $1.30 Sheet of 4, #a-d 9.50 9.50

Souvenir Sheet

Perf. 11¼x11½

1119 A263 $3 multi 5.50 5.50

Miniature Sheets

A264

Pres. Abraham Lincoln (1809-65) — A265

No. 1120 — Lincoln with denomination in: a, Orange. b, Rose. c, Blue. d, Green.

No. 1121: Lincoln with country name in: a, Green. b, Purple. c, Dark red. d, Red brown.

2010, Aug. 21 *Perf. 13¼x13*

1120 A264 $1.30 Sheet of 4, #a-d 9.50 9.50

Perf. 12

1121 A265 $1.30 Sheet of 4, #a-d 9.50 9.50

Souvenir Sheets

Popes and their Coats of Arms A266

No. 1122, $4: a, Pope John Paul II. b, Arms of Pope John Paul II.

No. 1123, $4: a, Pope Benedict XVI. b, Arms of Pope Benedict XVI.

2010, Aug. 30 *Imperf.*

Sheets of 2, #a-b Without Gum

1122-1123 A266 Set of 2 30.00 30.00

Election of Pres. John F. Kennedy, 50th Anniv. A267

No. 1124, $1.30 — Gray frames and blue panels with Kennedy: a, Talking with Tobacco Association representative at Greenbrier Hotel, 1958. b, Signing Cuban quarantine proclamation, 1962. c, Campaigning, 1960. d, At televised debate, 1960.

No. 1125, $1.30 — Olive green frames and brown panels with Kennedy: a, With wife, Jacqueline, on sailboat. b, Reading newspaper on the Honey Fitz, 1963. c, With wife and children, 1962. d, With wife in limousine, 1961.

No. 1126, $1.30 — Bluish black frames and red panels: a, Kennedy with son, John, Jr. b, Crowd at Grand Rapids, Michigan campaign rally, 1960. c, Kennedy debating Richard M. Nixon, 1960. d, Kennedy at lectern at 1960 campaign rally.

2010, Sept. 12 *Perf. 12*

Sheets of 4, #a-d

1124-1126 A267 Set of 3 30.00 30.00

Frédèric Chopin (1810-49), Composer — A268

No. 1127: Various portraits of Chopin facing: a, Left. b, Right. c, Left, diff. d, Right diff.

No. 1128, $3, Chopin, black background.

No. 1129, $3, Chopin, brown background.

2010, Sept. 12

1127 A268 $1.30 Sheet of 4, #a-d 10.00 10.00

Souvenir Sheets

1128-1129 A268 Set of 2 12.00 12.00

Miniature Sheets

A269

Pope Benedict XVI A270

No. 1130 — Pope Benedict XVI and: a, "XVI" above building at right. b, "I" of "XVI" above building ar right. c, Crowd, window of Vatican City building at UL. d, Crowd, pillars of Vatican City building at UL.

No. 1131 — Pope Benedict XVI and: a, Part of building to left of face. b, No building to left or right of face. c, Purple area to left of face. d, Purple area to left of face with white spot near tip of ear.

2010, Sept. 21 *Perf. 12x12½*

1130 A269 $1.30 Sheet of 4, #a-d 7.50 7.50
1131 A270 $1.30 Sheet of 4, #a-d 7.50 7.50

Miniature Sheets

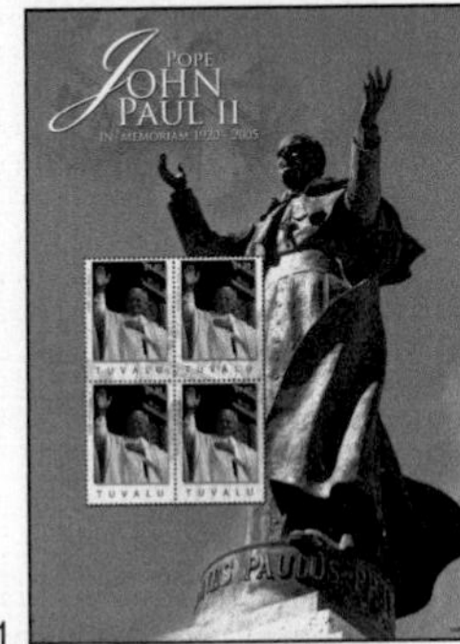

A271

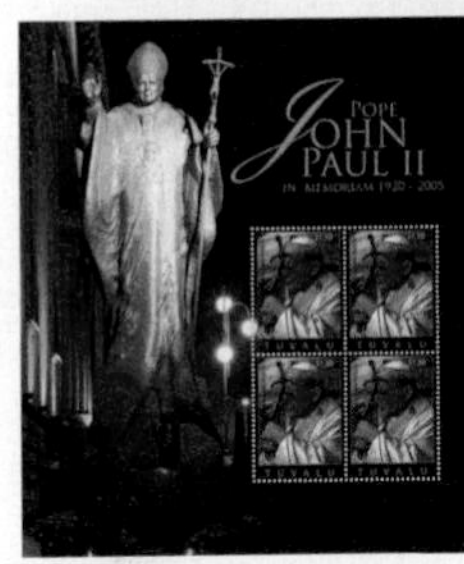

Pope John Paul II (1920-2005) — A272

No. 1132 — Pope John Paul II waving and: a, "T" of "Tuvalu" on pillar, lower part of first "U" in "Tuvalu" above arch. b, "T" of "Tuvalu" on arc, lower part of first "U" in "Tuvalu" above arc. c, Country name over area with darker gray area near "L" in "Tuvalu." d, Darker gray lines to left of first "U," below "V," to right of "A," and to left of second "U" in "Tuvalu."

No. 1133 — Pope John Paul II holding crucifix and: a, Light area in frame next to lower left corner of photo. b, Blackish brown frame.

2010, Oct. 7

1132 A271 $1.30 Sheet of 4, #a-d 10.50 10.50
1133 A272 $1.30 Sheet of 4, #1133a, 3 #1133b 10.50 10.50

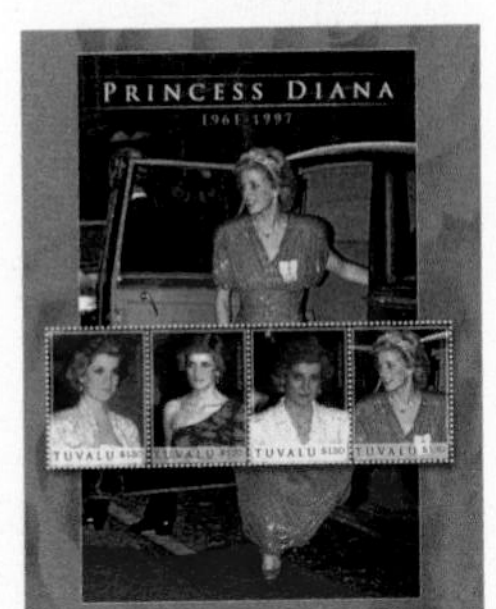

Princess Diana (1961-97) — A273

No. 1134 — Princess Diana wearing: a, White jacket and dress, tan background. b,

Red and black dress. c, White jacket, black background. d, Red and white tress, tiara.
No. 1135, $3, Strapless white dress. No. 1136, $3, Red and white hat.

2010, Oct. 28 ***Perf. 12***
1134 A273 $1.30 Sheet of 4, #a-d 10.50 10.50

Souvenir Sheets

1135-1136 A273 Set of 2 12.50 12.50

Miniature Sheets

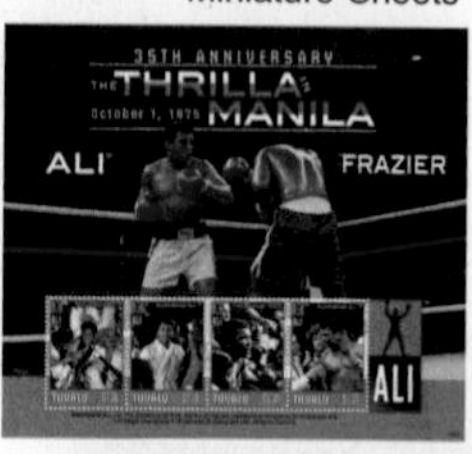

A274

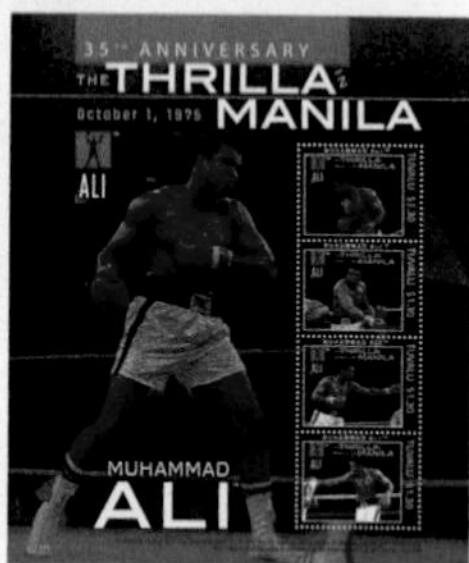

Fight Between Muhammad Ali and Joe Frazier, Manila, 35th Anniv. — A275

No. 1137: a, Ali wearing robe encircled by reporters with eight microphones. b, Ali wearing robe, standing. c, Ali, bare-chested, facing right, talking to reporters. d, Ali, bare-chested, looking left, talking to reporters.
No. 1138 — Ali in boxing ring: a, White rope at lower right. b, Frazier at lower left, white and red ropes at lower right. c, Ali with arm extended to right, white rope at bottom. d, Ali with arm extended to left, white and red ropes at bottom.

2010, Nov. 25 ***Perf. 11¼x11½***
1137 A274 $1.30 Sheet of 4, #a-d 9.00 9.00

Perf. 11½x11¼

1138 A275 $1.30 Sheet of 4, #a-d 9.00 9.00

Christmas — A276

Details of paintings: 60c, Pierre Bladelin Triptych, by Rogier van der Weyden. 90c, Annunciation, by Pietro Cavallini. $1, Altarpiece of the Virgin, by Jacques Daret. $2, Nativity, by Matthias Grunewald.

2010, Nov. 25 ***Perf. 12***
1139-1142 A276 Set of 4 9.00 9.00

Nos. 1139-1142 each were printed in sheets of 4.

2010 World Cup Soccer Championships, South Africa — A277

No. 1143, $1 — Scenes from June 16, 2010 Spain vs. Switzerland match (Spain in red shirts): a, Spanish player #15 and Swiss goalie. b, Spanish player #22 and Swiss player #17. c, Spanish player #8 and Swiss players #8 and #6. d, Spanish players #15 and #3 and Swiss player #16.
No. 1144, $1 — Scenes from June 21, 2010 Spain vs. Honduras match (Spain in red shirts): a, Spanish players #7 and #8. b, Spanish player #10 and Honduran player #11. c, Spanish player #8 and Honduran player #8. d, Spanish players #11 and #16 and Honduran players #11 and #12.
No. 1145, $1 — Scenes from June 25, 2010 Spain vs. Chile match (Spain in black shirts): a, Spanish players #7 and #10. b, Spanish player #9 and Chilean player #3. c, Spanish players #5, #14 and #16 and Chilean player #10. d, Spanish player #11 and Chilean player #7.
No. 1146, $1 — Scenes from June 29, 2010 Spain vs. Portugal match (Spain in red shirts): a, Spanish goalie leaping into arms of Spanish player #19. b, Spanish player #16 and Portuguese player #23. c, Spanish player #7. d, Spanish player falling and Portuguese player #23.
No. 1147, $1 — Scenes from July 3, 2010 Spain vs. Paraguay match (Spain in black shirts): a, Spanish players #8 and #10 and Paraguayan player #16. b, Spanish goalie (player #1). c, Spanish player #16 and Paraguayan player #3. d, Spanish player #15 and Paraguayan player #21.
No. 1148, $1 — Scenes from July 7, 2010 Spain vs. Germany match (Spain in red shirts): a, Spanish player #11 and German player #15 (with hand on Spanish player's back). b, Spanish player #8 and German player #7. c, Spanish player #6 and German player #6. d, Spanish player #11 and German player #15 (both players with arms extended).
No. 1149, $1 — Scenes from July 11, 2010 Spain vs. Netherlands match (Spain in black shirts): a, Spanish player #15 and Netherlands player #4. b, Spanish player #15 on knees and Netherlands player #10. c, Spanish player #7 and Netherlands player #4. d, Spanish player #10 and Netherlands player #9.
$3, Spanish team celebrating championship.

2010, July 11 **Sheets of 4, #a-d**
1143-1149 A277 Set of 7 52.50 52.50

Souvenir Sheet

1150 A277 $3 multi 5.50 5.50

Nos. 1143-1150 could not have been issued on the stated day of issue as Nos. 1149 and 1150 depict photographs taken that day.

Miniature Sheet

Expo 2010, Shanghai — A278

No. 1151 — Expo 2010 emblem and various views of Green Island: a, 60c. b, 90c. c, $1.50. d, $2.

2010, Aug. 25 ***Perf. 13¼***
1151 A278 Sheet of 4, #a-d 9.25 9.25

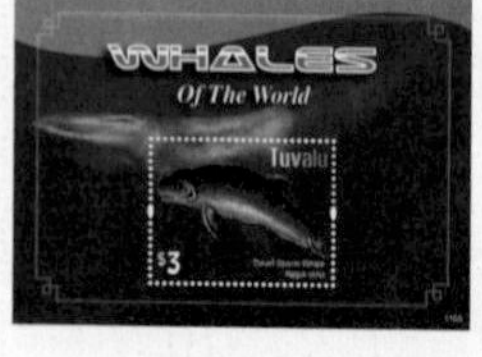

Whales A279

No. 1152: a, Orca. b, Short-finned pilot whale. c, Melon-headed whale. d, Pygmy killer whale. e, False killer whale. f, Sperm whale.
$3, Dwarf sperm whale.

2011, Jan. 30 ***Perf. 13 Syncopated***
1152 A279 $1 Sheet of 6, #a-f 11.75 11.75

Souvenir Sheet

1153 A279 $3 multi 5.75 5.75

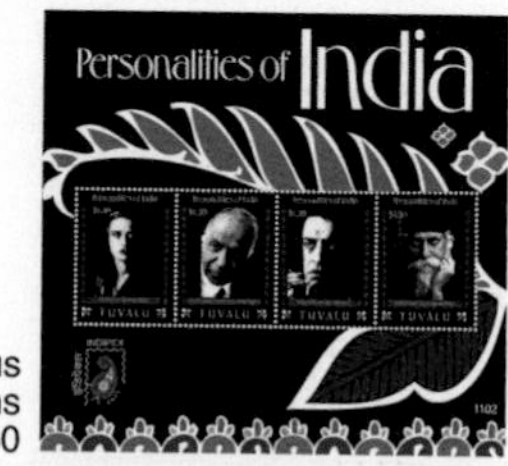

Famous Indians A280

No. 1154: a, Amrita Sher-Gil (1913-41), painter. b, Subrahmanyan Chandrasekhar (1910-95), astrophysicist. c, Satyajit Ray (1921-92), filmmaker. d, Rabindranath Tagore (1861-1941), writer.
$3, Mohandas K. Gandhi (1869-1948), nationalist leader.

2011, Feb. 12 ***Perf. 12¾x12½***
1154 A280 $1.30 Sheet of 4, #a-d 10.50 10.50

Souvenir Sheet

Perf. 13¼

1155 A280 $3 multi 6.25 6.25

Indipex 2011 Intl. Philatelic Exhibition, New Delhi. No. 1155 contains one 38x50mm stamp.

Miniature Sheets

A281

Elvis Presley (1935-77) — A282

No. 1156 — Presley: a, Standing, with arm extended. b, With both hands near microphone. c, Holding microphone with arm at side. d, With bent knees and arm extended.
No. 1157 — Presley: a, Standing in front of man on stage. b, With guitar, audience in background. c, Playing guitar. d, Holding microphone.

2011, Feb. 15 ***Perf. 13 Syncopated***
1156 A281 $1.30 Sheet of 4, #a-d 10.50 10.50

Perf. 12

1157 A282 $1.30 Sheet of 4, #a-d 10.50 10.50

Personalities of the U.S. Civil War — A283

No. 1158: a, Head of Pres. Abraham Lincoln. b, Lieutenant General Ulysses S. Grant. c, Major General George G. Meade. d, Lincoln, standing.
No. 1159, horiz.: a, Lincoln, no hands visible. b, Lincoln, with hand on chin.

2011, Feb. 28 ***Perf. 13 Syncopated***
1158 A283 $1.30 Sheet of 4, #a-d 10.50 10.50

Souvenir Sheet

Perf. 12

1159 A283 $3 Sheet of 2, #a-b 12.50 12.50

A284

Statue of Liberty, 125th Anniv. A285

No. 1160 — Statue of Liberty and: a, Gray backround, "86" at left b, Blue background, denomination at LL. c, Gray and purple background, denomination at UL. d, Gray background, "20" at right.
No. 1161: a, Side view of statue. b, Head of statue.

2011, Mar. 15 ***Perf. 13 Syncopated***
1160 A284 $1.30 Sheet of 4, #a-d 11.00 11.00

Souvenir Sheet

1161 A285 $1.50 Sheet of 2, #a-b 6.50 6.50

Beatification of Pope John Paul II — A286

Pope John Paul II: No. 1162, $1, Greeting crowd. No. 1163, $1, With mass attendants, reading. $3, Pope John Paul II in crowd, diff.

2011, Apr. 15 ***Perf. 13 Syncopated***
1162-1163 A286 Set of 2 4.25 4.25

Souvenir Sheet

Perf. 12

1164 A286 $3 multi 6.50 6.50

Nos. 1162 and 1163 were printed in a sheet of six containing three of each stamp.

Wedding of Prince William and Catherine Middleton — A287

No. 1165, $1.30: a, Couple, facing forward. b, Bride.
No. 1166, $1.30: a, Groom waving. b, Couple, looking at each other.
$3, Couple, kissing.

2011, Apr. 29 ***Perf. 12***

Pairs, #a-b

1165-1166 A287 Set of 2 11.50 11.50

Souvenir Sheet

Perf. 11¼x11½

1167 A287 $3 multi 6.50 6.50

Nos. 1165-1166 each were printed in sheets containing two pairs. No. 1167 contains one 30x79mm stamp. Nos. 1165-1167 could not have been issued on the stated day of issue because stamps have photographs taken that day, which was the day of the wedding.

Parrots A288

No. 1168: a, Western rosella. b, Australian ringneck. c, Budgerigar. d, Northern rosella. e, Red-capped parrot. f, Regent parrot.
$3, Red-winged parrot.

2011, June 6 ***Perf. 12***
1168 A288 $1 Sheet of 6, #a-f 13.00 13.00

Souvenir Sheet

1169 A288 $3 multi 6.50 6.50

Personalizable Stamp — A289

2011, June 15 ***Perf. 14¼x14¾***
1170 A289 20c multi .45 .45

A290

Meeting of U.S. Pres. Barack Obama and Australian Prime Minister Julia Gillard — A291

No. 1171: a, Prime Minister Gillard and Pres. Obama, no hands visible. b, Obama. c, Gillard and Obama shaking hands. d, Gillard.
No. 1172: a, Gillard. b, Obama.

2011, June 15 ***Perf. 11½x12***
1171 A290 $1.30 Sheet of 4, #a-d 11.50 11.50

Souvenir Sheet

1172 A291 $1.25 Sheet of 2, #a-b 5.50 5.50

First Man in Space, 50th Anniv. A292

No. 1173, $1.30, horiz.: a, Sergei Korolev (1907-66), spacecraft designer, and rocket. b, Yuri Gagarin, first man in space, with helmet. c, Erecting rocket from train. d, John Glenn, U.S. astronaut.
No. 1174, $1.30, horiz.: a, Vostok capsule. b, Vostok 1A rocket. c, Vostok Memorial. d, Virgil Grissom, U.S. astronaut.
No. 1175, $3, Gagarin wearing brown uniform. No. 1176, $3, Gagarin wearing white uniform and medal.

2011, June 27 ***Perf. 12½x12***

Sheets of 4, #a-d

1173-1174 A292 Set of 2 22.50 22.50

Souvenir Sheets

Perf. 11¼x11½

1175-1176 A292 Set of 2 13.00 13.00

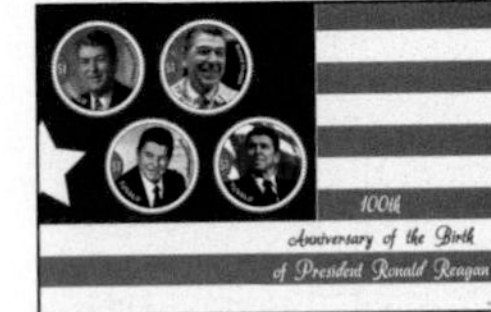

U.S. Pres. Ronald Reagan (1911-2004) — A293

No. 1177 — Pres. Reagan: a, Wearing red and blue striped tie, b, Wearing overcoat, striped shirt and polka dot tie. c, Wearing black suit. d, With American flag in background.
No. 1178 — Pres. Reagan: a, Wearing maroon patterned tie. b, Wearing striped tie, American flag in background.

2011, June 30 **Litho.** ***Perf.***
1177 A293 $1 Sheet of 4, #a-d 8.50 8.50

Souvenir Sheet

1178 A293 $3 Sheet of 2, #a-b 13.00 13.00

Miniature Sheets

U.S. Civil War, 150th Anniv. A294

No. 1179, $1.30 — Eagle, shield, Union and Confederate flags, General Robert E. Lee, Major General John Pope, and scenes from Second Battle of Bull Run, Aug. 28-30, 1862: a, Soldiers carrying Union flag at center. b, General Sigel's Corps at the battle site. c, Soldiers marching, green background. d, Battle scene, horses and building at right.
No. 1180, $1.30 — Eagle, shield, Union and Confederate flags, General Braxton Bragg, Major General William S. Rosecrans, and scenes from Battle of Stones River, Dec. 31, 1862-Jan. 2, 1863: a, Gen. Rosecrans rallies troops at Stones River. b, Union Army flees a Confederate onslaught. c, Confederates frontal attack on the Union. d, General Rosecrans tries to save his army.
No. 1181, $1.30 — Eagle, shield, Union and Confederate flags, General Robert E. Lee, General Ulysses S. Grant and scenes from the Battle of the Wilderness, May 5-7, 1864: a, Battle near Orange Court House Plank Road. b, The gloom at the outset in dense woods. c, Army of the Potomac charging the enemy. d, Carrying a wounded soldier to safety.

2011, July 4 ***Perf. 12½x12***

Sheets of 4, #a-d

1179-1181 A294 Set of 3 34.00 34.00

Miniature Sheets

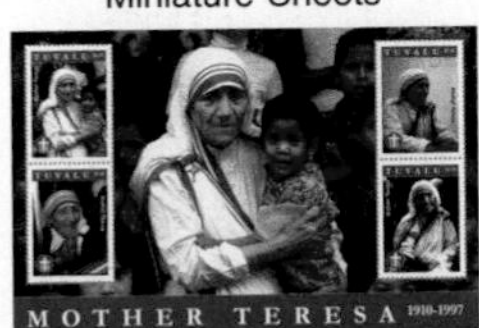

Mother Teresa (1910-97), Humanitarian — A295

No. 1182, $1.30 — Mother Teresa: a, Holding child, children in background. b, With wall inscribed "Peace" in background. c, With hands held together. d, Holding Nobel Peace Prize diploma and medal box.
No. 1183, $1.30 — Mother Teresa: a, Black-and-white photograph of head. b, With Pres. Ronald Reagan and wife, Nancy. c, Holding baby, door in background. d, Under umbrella.

Perf. 12x12½, 11¼ (#1183)

2011, July 5 **Sheets of 4, #a-d**
1182-1183 A295 Set of 2 22.50 22.50

Miniature Sheets

Woodblock Prints of Morning Glories — A296

Woodblock Prints of Mount Fuji, by Hiroshige — A297

No. 1184: a, Unopened buds on vine. b, Brownish purple flower with thin, spiked leaves, three Japanese characters at LL. c, Red flower on vine. d, Pink flowers on thin vine running horizontally. e, Pink flower on thick vine running vertically. f, Dark red and black flower on thin vine, one Japanese character at LL.
No. 1185: a, Mount Fuji above village. b, Mount Fuji with hill in foreground. c, Reflection of Mount Fuji in lake. d, Ocean wave and Mount Fuji.

2011, July 28 ***Perf. 13 Syncopated***
1184 A296 $1 Sheet of 6, #a-f 12.50 12.50

Perf. 12

1185 A297 $1.30 Sheet of 4, #a-d 11.00 11.00

PhilaNippon '11 Intl. Philatelic Exhibition, Yokohama.

Princess Diana (1961-97) — A298

No. 1186 — Princess Diana wearing: a, Tiara. b, Dark dress. c, Pearl necklace and hat with striped ribbon. d, Dress with ruffled collar.
$3, Princess Diana wearing pearl necklace and hat with black ribbon.

2011, Aug. 1 ***Perf. 12½x12***
1186 A298 $1.30 Sheet of 4, #a-d 11.00 11.00

Souvenir Sheet

Perf. 11½

1187 A298 $3 multi 6.25 6.25

Souvenir Sheets

War Horses A299

Carriage Horses A300

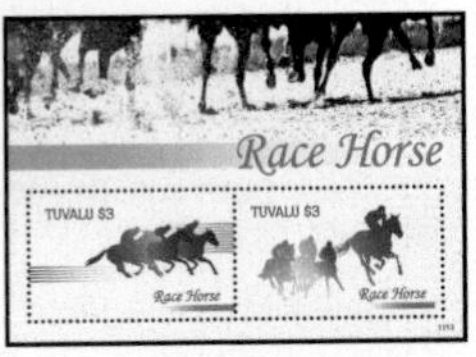

Race Horses A301

No. 1188: a, Denomination at LR. b, Denomination at LL.
No. 1189: a, White horse pulling man and woman in carriage. b, Silhouette of horse and carriage.
No. 1190: a, Three horses. b, Four horses.

2011, Aug. 31 **Litho.** ***Perf. 12***
1188 A299 $3 Sheet of 2, #a-b 12.50 12.50
1189 A300 $3 Sheet of 2, #a-b 12.50 12.50
1190 A301 $3 Sheet of 2, #a-b 12.50 12.50
Nos. 1188-1190 (3) 37.50 37.50

Miniature Sheet

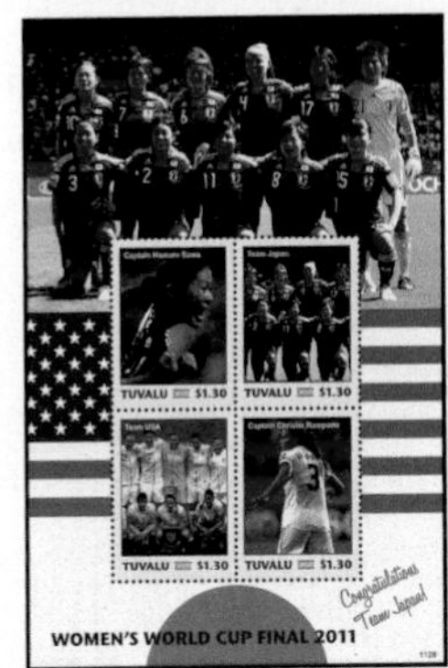

2011 Women's World Cup Soccer Championships, Germany — A302

No. 1191: a, Japanese team captain Homare Sawa. b, Japanese Team. c, U.S. team. d, U.S. team captain Christie Rampone.

2011, Sept. 21 ***Perf. 12x12½***
1191 A302 $1.30 Sheet of 4, #a-d 10.50 10.50

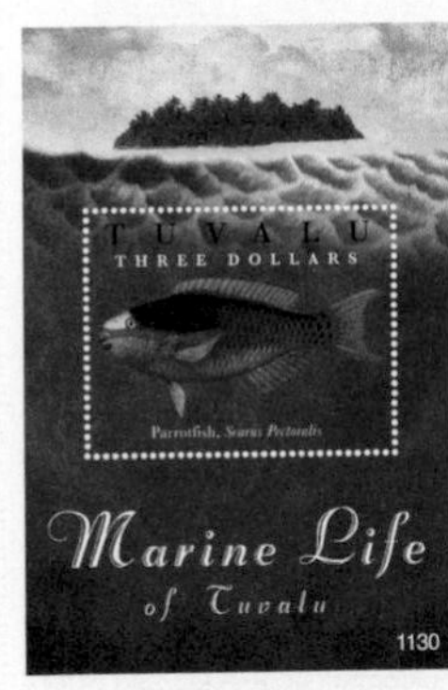

Marine Fauna A303

No. 1192: a, Christmas shearwater. b, Flying fish. c, Albacore tuna. d, Pantropical spotted dolphin. e, Pygmy killer whale.
$3, Parrotfish.

2012, Jan. 1 ***Perf. 13x13¼***
1192 A303 $1 Sheet of 5, #a-e 10.50 10.50

Souvenir Sheet

Perf. 13¼

1193 A303 $3 multi 6.25 6.25

No. 1192 contains five 40x30mm stamps.

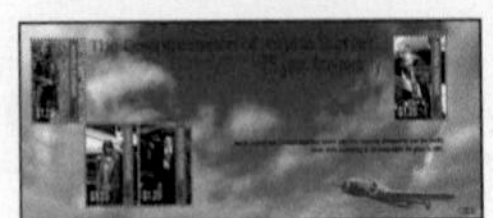

Disappearance of Amelia Earhart, 75th Anniv. — A304

No. 1194 — Earhart: a, Wearing leather pilot's helmet, brick wall in background. b, Without pilot's helmet, airplane fuselage in background. c, Wearing leather pilot's helmet, airplane propeller in background. d. Without pilot's helmet, airplane propeller in background.

$3.50, Earhart on side of airplane.

2012, Feb. 6 *Perf. 13*

1194 A304 $1.25 Sheet of 4, #a-d 11.00 11.00

Souvenir Sheet

1195 A304 $3.50 multi 7.75 7.75

Miniature Sheet

Sinking of the Titanic, Cent. A305

No. 1196: a, Smokestacks. b, Mast and aft deck. c, Flagpole and ship's stern.

$3.50, Flagpole and ship's stern, diff.

2012, Apr. 15 *Perf. 13 Syncopated*

1196 A305 $1.50 Sheet of 3, #a-c 9.25 9.25

Souvenir Sheet

1197 A305 $3.50 multi 7.25 7.25

Climate Change Awareness — A306

Inscriptions: No. 1198, $1, Plant a tree to help reduce greenhouse gases. No. 1199, $1, Turning off lights to save energy. No. 1200, $1, Distillation plants turn seas into clean drinking water. No. 1201, $1, Crops that are genetically enhanced to grow near salt water. No. 1202, $1, Mangrove trees encourage new land formation.

2012, May 1 *Perf. 14*

1198-1202 A306 Set of 5 10.50 10.50

Expo 2012, Yeosu, South Korea.

Souvenir Sheets

Elvis Presley (1935-77) — A307

Designs: No. 1203, $3.50, Red background, Presley on stage. No. 1204, $3.50, Red background, close-up of Presley. No. 1205, $3.50, Red background, two photographs of Presley. No. 1206, $3.50, Light blue background, black-and-white photograph of Presley. No. 1207, $3.50, Light blue background, color photograph of Presley.

2012, May 14 *Perf. 12¾*

1203-1207 A307 Set of 5 35.00 35.00

2012 Summer Olympics, London — A308

No. 1208 — British flag on simulated Olympic medals in: a, Bronze. b, Silver. c, Gold.

$1.50, Olympic rings, colored stripes, London landmarks, vert.

2012, May 30 *Perf.*

1208 A308 50c Sheet of 3, #a-c 3.00 3.00

Souvenir Sheet

Perf. 12¼x12

1209 A308 $1.50 multi 3.00 3.00

No. 1209 contains one 30x50mm stamp. Exists Imperf. Value, $25.

Souvenir Sheets

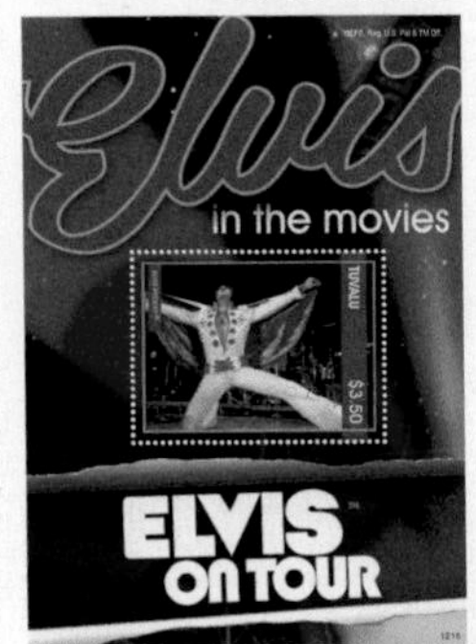

A309

A310

A311

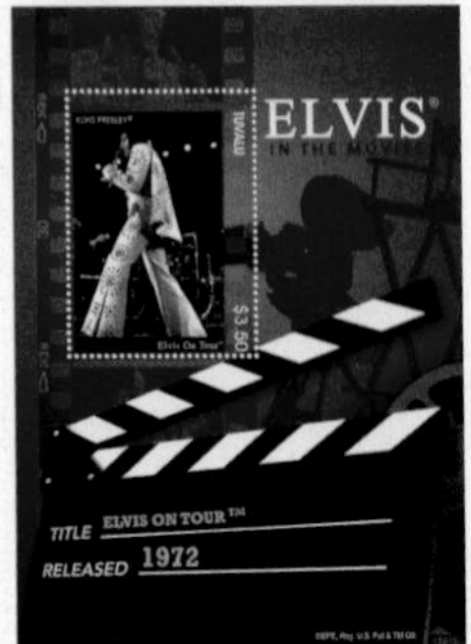

Elvis Presley (1935-77) — A312

2012, June 27 *Perf. 13¼*

1210 A309 $3.50 multi 6.75 6.75
1211 A310 $3.50 multi 6.75 6.75
1212 A311 $3.50 multi 6.75 6.75
1213 A312 $3.50 multi 6.75 6.75
Nos. 1210-1213 (4) 27.00 27.00

Fish — A313

Designs: 10c, Epibulus insidiator. 40c, Zanclus cornutus. 60c, Anampses cuvier. 90c, Rhinecanthus verrucosus. $1, Lactoria fornasini. $1.25, Enchelycore pardalis. $1.50, Diodon liturosus. $1.75, Anampses elegans. $2, Thalassoma trilobatum. $2.75, Pomacanthus imperator. $3.25, Pomacanthus semicirculatus. $5, Cheilinus fasciatus.

2012, July 15 *Perf. 13¾*

1214 A313 10c multi .25 .25
1215 A313 40c multi .85 .85
1216 A313 60c multi 1.25 1.25
1217 A313 90c multi 1.90 1.90
1218 A313 $1 multi 2.10 2.10
1219 A313 $1.25 multi 2.75 2.75
1220 A313 $1.50 multi 3.25 3.25
1221 A313 $1.75 multi 3.75 3.75
1222 A313 $2 multi 4.25 4.25
1223 A313 $2.75 multi 6.00 6.00
1224 A313 $3.25 multi 7.00 7.00
1225 A313 $5 multi 10.50 10.50
Nos. 1214-1225 (12) 43.85 43.85

Dogs — A314

No. 1226: a, Duck tolling retriever. b, Berger Picard. c, Chow chow. d, Great Dane. e, Labrador retriever.

2012, July 15 *Perf. 14*

1226 Sheet of 5 10.50 10.50
a.-e. A314 $1 Any single 2.10 2.10

Exists Imperf.

Miniature Sheet

Cats — A315

No. 1227: a, Siamese. b, Devon Rex. c, American wirehair. d, Cornish Rex. e, Burmese.

2012, Aug. 7

1227 A315 80c Sheet of 5, #a-e 8.50 8.50

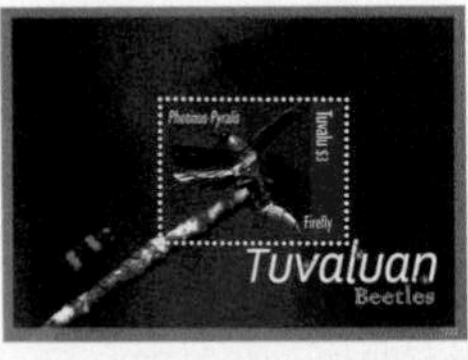

Beetles A316

No. 1228: a, Asian lady beetle. b, Blister beetle. c, Water beetle. d, Clytus arietis.

$3, Firefly.

2012, Sept. 5

1228 A316 $1.25 Sheet of 4, #a-d 10.50 10.50

Souvenir Sheet

Perf. 12

1229 A316 $3 multi 6.00 6.00

Paintings by Raphael A317

No. 1230: a, St. Margaret. b, Saint Michael Vanquishing Satan. c, Portrait of Elisabetta Gonzaga. d, The Holy Family.

$3, St. Margaret, diff.

2012, Sept. 5 *Perf. 12¾*

1230 A317 $1 Sheet of 4, #a-d 7.50 7.50

Souvenir Sheet

1231 A317 $3 multi 6.25 6.25

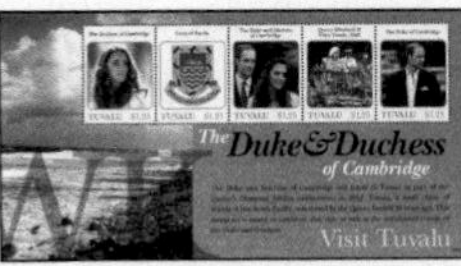

Visit of Duke and Duchess of Cambridge to Tuvalu — A318

No. 1232: a, Duchess of Cambridge. b, Crest of Tuvalu. c, Duke and Duchess of Cambridge. d, Queen Elizabeth II visiting Tuvalu, 1982. e, Duke of Cambridge.

$3.50, Duke and Duchess of Cambridge, horiz.

2012, Oct. 1 *Perf. 14*

1232 A318 $1.25 Sheet of 5, #a-e 13.00 13.00

Souvenir Sheet

Perf. 12

1233 A318 $3.50 multi 7.25 7.25

No. 1233 contains one 50x30mm stamp. No. 1232 exists imperf.

Reign of Queen Elizabeth II, 60th Anniv. A319

No. 1234 — Queen Elizabeth II and: a, Prince Philip on Great Wall of China, 1986. b, Park ranger with hat at Yosemite National Park, 1983. c, Emperor Haile Selassie at Tis-sisal Falls, Ethiopia, 1965. d, Prince Philip at Taj Mahal, 1961.

$3.50, Queen Elizabeth II and sailor in Tuvalu, 1982, vert.

2012, Dec. 31 *Perf. 13 Syncopated*

1234 A319 $1.25 Sheet of 4, #a-d 10.50 10.50

Souvenir Sheet

1235 A319 $3.50 multi 7.50 7.50

World Humanitarian Day — A320

No. 1236: a, Earth. b, Dove with olive branch. c, Peace symbol. d, Red cross.

$3.50, Heart.

2013, Mar. 21 *Perf. 13¾*

1236 A320 $1.20 Sheet of 4, #a-d 10.00 10.00

Souvenir Sheet

1237 A320 $3.50 multi 7.50 7.50

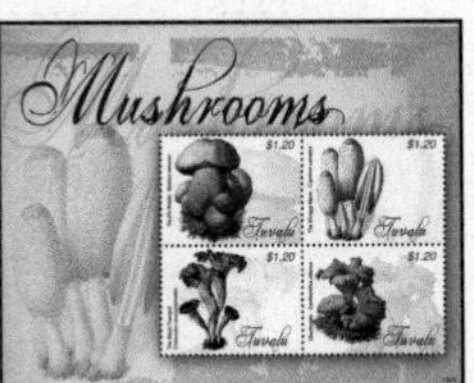

Mushrooms — A321

No. 1238: a, Devil's bolete. b, Shaggy mane. c, Black trumpet. d, Chanterelle.

$3.50, Entoloma clypeatum, vert.

2013, Apr. 29 *Perf. 12*

1238 A321 $1.20 Sheet of 4, #a-d 10.00 10.00

Souvenir Sheet

1239 A321 $3.50 multi 7.25 7.25

A322

Flowers A323

No. 1240: a, Medinilla magnifica. b, Alpinia purpurata. c, Nymphaea rubra. d, Crotalaria retusa.

No. 1241: a, Hibiscus rosa-sinensis. b, Gardenia taitensis. c, Hibiscus brackenridgei. d, Ranunculus lyallii.

No. 1242, Etlingera elatior. No. 1243, Tecomanthe speciosa, vert.

2013, Apr. 29 ***Perf. 14***

1240 A322 $1.20 Sheet of 4, #a-d 10.00 10.00

Perf. 12

1241 A323 $1.20 Sheet of 4, #a-d 10.00 10.00

Souvenir Sheet

1242 A322 $3.50 multi 8.25 8.25
1243 A323 $3.50 multi 8.25 8.25

A324

Election of Pope Francis A325

No. 1244: a, White smoke rising from chimney of Sistine Chapel. b, Pope Francis waving and holding crucifix. c, Pope Francis in window. d, Head of Pope Francis.

$8, Pope Francis waving.

2013, June 3 **Litho.** ***Perf. 14***

1244 A324 $1.20 Sheet of 4, #a-d 9.25 9.25

Souvenir Sheet Without Gum

Litho., Margin Embossed With Foil Application

Imperf

1245 A325 $8 multi 15.50 15.50

Miniature Sheet

Seashells — A326

No. 1246: a, Depressed cowry. b, Japanese wonder shell. c, Fluted giant clam. d, Chambered nautilus. e, Precious wentletrap.

Perf. 13 Syncopated

2013, June 3 **Litho.**

1246 A326 $1 Sheet of 5, #a-e 9.50 9.50

Tel Aviv 2013 International Stamp Exhibition.

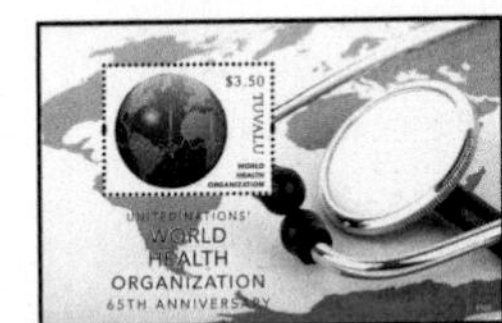

World Health Organization, 65th Anniv. — A327

No. 1247 — Globe and inscription: a, World Tuberculosis Day. b, World Immunization Week. c, World Health Day. d, World AIDS Day. e, World No Tobacco Day. f, World Blood Donor Day.

$3.50, Globe and inscription "World Health Organization."

2013, June 25

1247 A327 90c Sheet of 6, #a-f 10.00 10.00

Souvenir Sheet

1248 A327 $3.50 multi 6.50 6.50

Dolphins A328

No. 1249: a, Short-finned pilot whale. b, Risso's dolphin. c, Pacific white-sided dolphin. d, Northern right whale dolphin.

$3.50, Melon-headed whale.

2013, July 24 ***Perf. 12***

1249 A328 $1.25 Sheet of 4, #a-d 9.00 9.00

Souvenir Sheet

1250 A328 $3.50 multi 6.50 6.50

Miniature Sheets

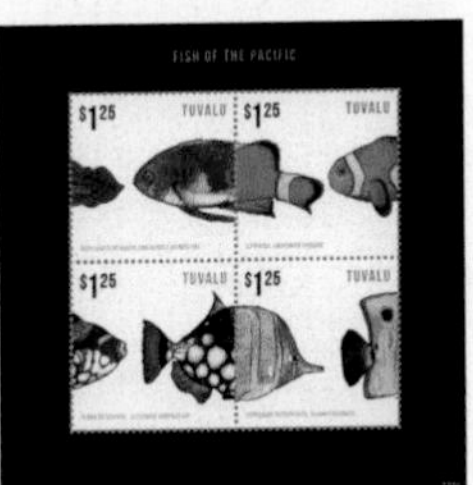

Fish A329

No. 1251, $1.25: a, Blue-head fairy wrasse. b, Clownfish. c, Clown triggerfish. d, Copperband butterflyfish.

No. 1252, $1.25: a, Scribbled angelfish. b, Flame angelfish. c, Harlequin tuskfish. d, Flameback angelfish.

2013, July 24 ***Perf. 13¾***

Sheets of 4, #a-d

1251-1252 A329 Set of 2 18.00 18.00

Temples of Thailand A330

No. 1253: a, Wat Pha Sorn Kaew. b, Wat Pho. c, Wat Phra Kaew. d, Wat Phra Singh.

$3.50, Wat Suthat.

2013, July 30 **Litho.**

1253 A330 $1.20 Sheet of 4, #a-d 7.50 7.50

Souvenir Sheet

1254 A330 $3.50 multi 5.50 5.50

Thailand 2013 World Stamp Exhibition, Bangkok.

Coronation of Queen Elizabeth II, 60th Anniv. — A331

No. 1255 — Queen Elizabeth II: a, Waving. b, Wearing tiara. c, Wearing white hat. d, Watching young Prince Charles at play.

$3.50, Queen Elizabeth II, diff.

2013, Oct. 7 **Litho.** ***Perf. 13¾***

1255 A331 $1.20 Sheet of 4, #a-d 8.50 8.50

Souvenir Sheet

1256 A331 $3.50 multi 6.00 6.00

Birth of Prince George of Cambridge — A332

No. 1257: a, Duke and Duchess of Cambridge, Prince George. b, Prince Charles, Princess Diana, Prince William. c, Princess Diana holding Prince William. d, Duchess of Cambridge holding Prince George.

$3.50, Duke and Duchess of Cambridge, Prince George, diff.

2013, Oct. 7 **Litho.** ***Perf. 14***

1257 A332 $1.20 Sheet of 4, #a-d 9.25 9.25

Souvenir Sheet

Perf. 12

1258 A332 $3.50 multi 6.25 6.25

Miniature Sheet

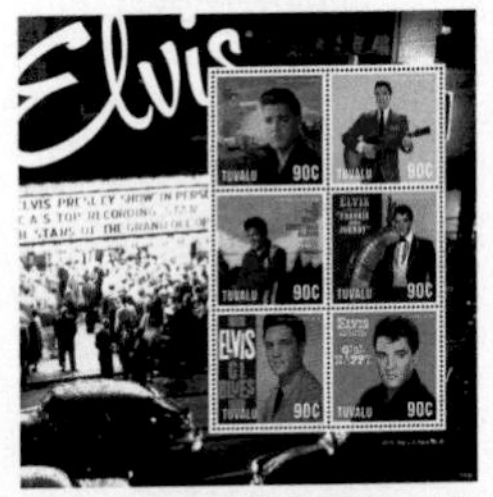

Elvis Presley (1935-77) — A333

No. 1259: a, Album cover for *Elvis' Christmas Album,* Presley to right of text. b, Presley playing guitar. c, Album cover for *Elvis' Christmas Album,* Presley to left of text. d, *Frankie and Johnny* album cover. e, *G.I. Blues* album cover. f, *Girl Happy* album cover.

2013, Dec. 2 **Litho.** ***Perf. 13¾***

1259 A333 90c Sheet of 6, #a-f 9.25 9.25

Orange Blossom Special — A334

2013, Dec. 9 **Litho.** ***Perf. 12½***

1260 A334 60c multi 1.10 1.10

Souvenir Sheet

Perf. 13½

1261 A334 $3.50 multi 6.25 6.25

No. 1260 was printed in sheets of 9. No. 1261 contains one 38x51mm stamp.

Meeting of Pres. Barack Obama and Queen Elizabeth II A335

No. 1262: a, Queen Elizabeth II. b, Pres. Barack Obama. c, Michelle Obama. d, Prince Philip.

No. 1263, horiz.: a, Pres. Obama. b, Michelle Obama.

$3.50, Queen Elizabeth II and Pres. Obama.

Perf. 12½, 13½ (#1263)

2013, Dec. 9 **Litho.**

1262 A335 $1.20 Sheet of 4, #a-d 8.75 8.75
1263 A335 $1.75 Sheet of 2, #a-b 6.25 6.25

Souvenir Sheet

1264 A335 $3.50 multi 6.25 6.25

No. 1263 contains two 51x38mm stamps.

A336

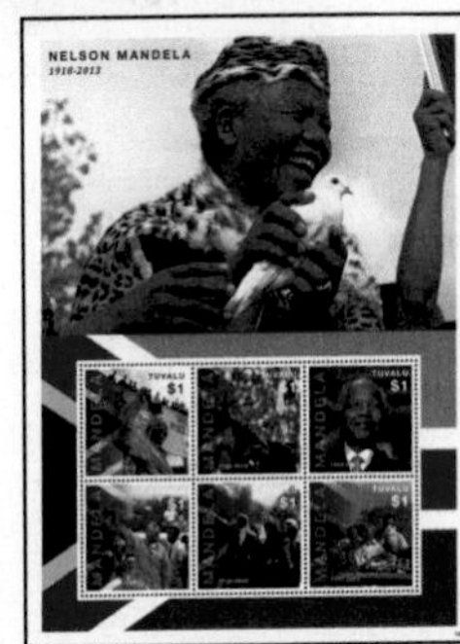

Nelson Mandela (1918-2013), President of South Africa — A337

No. 1266 — South African flag and Mandela: a, With fist raised, sign at right. b, With fist raised, standing at lectern. c, Wearing suit and tie. d, Standing in crowd with fist raised, man to Mandela's right. e, Waving at crowd, wife, Winnie, to Mandela's right. f, Holding on to railing.

2013, Dec. 15 **Litho.** ***Perf. 13¾***

1265 A336 $1 multi 1.90 1.90
1266 A337 $1 Sheet of 6, #a-f 11.00 11.00

No. 1265 was printed in sheets of 6.

Pope John Paul II (1920-2005) — A338

No. 1267 — Pope John Paul II with denomination in: a, Black. b, White.
$3.50, Pope John Paul II, horiz.

2013, Dec. 23 Litho. *Perf. 14*

1267 A338 $1.20 Horiz. pair, #a-b 4.25 4.25

Souvenir Sheet

1268 A338 $3.50 multi 6.25 6.25

No. 1267 was printed in sheets containing two pairs.

World War I, Cent. A339

No. 1269: a, Army Recruiting Office, Southwark, London, England, 1915. b, U.S. Sergeant Alvin C. York, 1919. c, Victory parade, London, 1919. d, French soldier at Battle of Verdun wearing gas mask, 1916. e, U.S. General John J. Pershing, 1918. f, Women working in ammunition factory, France, 1914.
$4, U.S. Army recruiting poster, vert.

2014, Mar. 5 Litho. *Perf. 13¾*

1269 A339 $1.20 Sheet of 6, #a-f 12.25 12.25

Souvenir Sheet

Perf. 12½

1270 A339 $4 multi 6.75 6.75

No. 1270 contains one 38x51mm stamp.

Characters From *Downton Abbey* Television Series — A340

No. 1271: a, Sir Richard Carlisle. b, Lady Mary Crawley. c, Matthew Crawley. d, Dr. Richard Clarkson.
$3.50, Matthew Crawley and Lady Mary Crawley, horiz.

2014, Mar. 5 Litho. *Perf. 14*

1271 A340 $1.20 Sheet of 4, #a-d 9.00 9.00

Souvenir Sheet

1272 A340 $3.50 multi 6.50 6.50

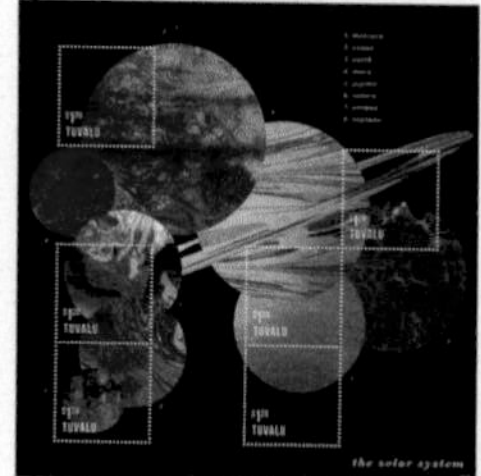

Solar System A341

No. 1273: a, Jupiter. b, Neptune, rings of Saturn. c, Earth and Venus. d, Saturn and Uranus. e, Venus and Mercury. f, Uranus.
$4.50, Sun.

2014, Mar. 24 Litho. *Perf. 13¾*

1273 A341 $1.20 Sheet of 6, #a-f 13.50 13.50

Souvenir Sheet

1274 A341 $4.50 multi 8.50 8.50

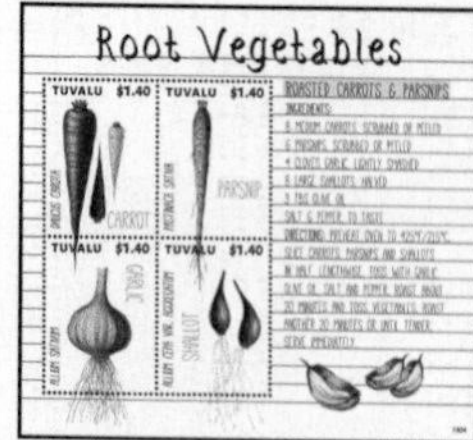

Vegetables — A342

No. 1275, $1.40: a, Carrots. b, Parsnip. c, Garlic. d, Shallots.
No. 1276, $1.40: a, Kohlrabi. b, Turnip. c, Sweet potato. d, Onion.
No. 1277, $2.25, horiz.: a, Radishes. b, Fennel.
No. 1278, $2.25, horiz.: a, Potato. b, Leek.

2014, Apr. 23 Litho. *Perf. 14*

Sheets of 4, #a-d

1275-1276 A342 Set of 2 21.00 21.00

Souvenir Sheets of 2, #a-b

1277-1278 A342 Set of 2 17.00 17.00

Giant Pacific Octopus A343

No. 1279: Various photographs of octopus, as shown.
$4.50, Octopus, vert.

2014, May 8 Litho. *Perf. 13¾*

1279 A343 50c Block of 4, #a-d 3.75 3.75

Souvenir Sheet

Perf. 12¾

1280 A343 $4.50 multi 8.50 8.50

No. 1280 contains one 38x51mm stamp.

Meeting of Queen Elizabeth II and Pope Francis — A344

Designs: No. 1281, Queen Elizabeth II and Pope Francis shaking hands, orange yellow frame.
No. 1282: a, Queen Elizabeth II, Prince Philip and Pope Francis shaking hands, tan frame. b, Queen Elizabeth II and Pope Francis, flowers in background, green frame. c, Queen Elizabeth II and Pope Francis seated, green frame. d, Queen Elizabeth II, Prince Philip, Pope Francis and other men, tan background.
$3.50, Queen Elizabeth II and Pope Francis, vert.

2014, July 21 Litho. *Perf. 14*

1281 A344 $1.20 multi 2.25 2.25
1282 A344 $1.20 Sheet of 4, #a-d 9.00 9.00

Souvenir Sheet

Perf. 12¾

1283 A344 $3.50 multi 6.50 6.50

No. 1281 was printed in sheets of 4. No. 1283 contains one 38x51mm stamp.

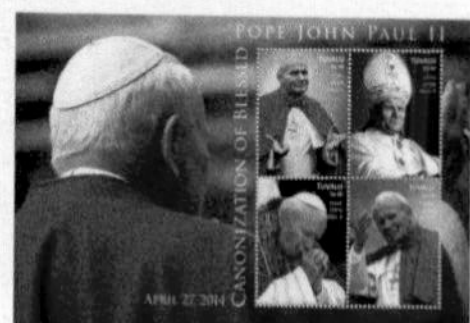

A345

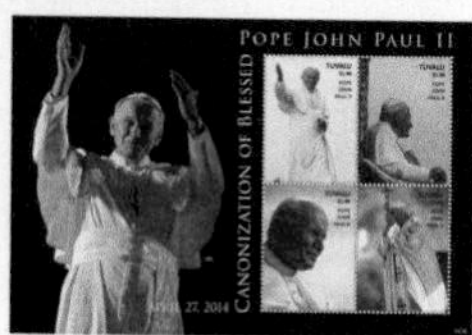

A346

A347

Canonization of Pope John Paul II — A348

Various photographs of Pope John Paul II, as shown.

2014, July 21 Litho. *Perf. 14*

1284 A345 $1.40 Sheet of 4, #a-d 10.50 10.50
1285 A346 $1.40 Sheet of 4, #a-d 10.50 10.50

Souvenir Sheets

1286 A347 $2.25 Sheet of 2, #a-b 8.50 8.50
1287 A348 $2.25 Sheet of 2, #a-b 8.50 8.50

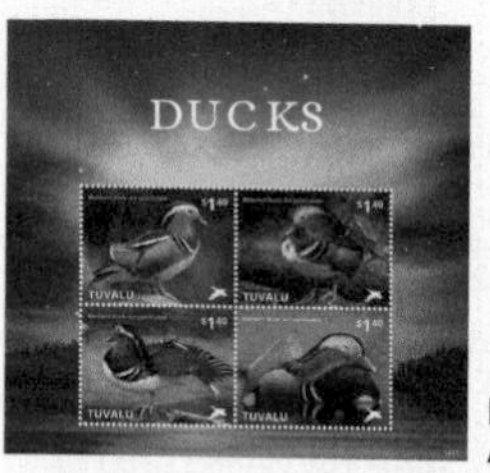

Ducks A349

No. 1288, $1.40: a, Mandarin duck facing right. b, Mandarin duck facing left. c, Mandarin duck with wing extended. d, Mandarin duck in water.
No. 1289, $1.40: a, Female wood duck. b, Mallard. c, Male wood duck. d, Mandarin duck facing left, diff.
No. 1290, $2.25: a, Wood duck, diff. b, Mandarin duck, diff.
No. 1291, $2.25, vert.: a, Mallard. b, Mandarin duck, diff.

2014, July 21 Litho. *Perf. 14*

Sheets of 4, #a-d

1288-1289 A349 Set of 2 21.00 21.00

Souvenir Sheets of 2, #a-b

1290-1291 A349 Set of 2 17.00 17.00

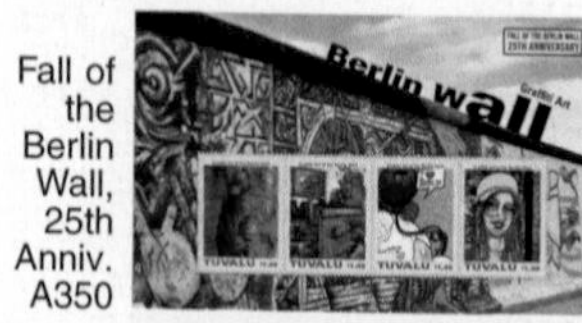

Fall of the Berlin Wall, 25th Anniv. A350

No. 1292 — Berlin Wall graffiti depicting: a, Red bear. b, Animal with boxing gloves, graffiti artist. c, Stylized flower and cartoon balloon. d, Woman wearing cap.
$5, "Change Your Life."

2014, Aug. 14 Litho. *Perf. 14*

1292 A350 $1.40 Sheet of 4, #a-d 10.50 10.50

Souvenir Sheet

Perf. 12¾

1293 A350 $5 multi 9.25 9.25

No. 1293 contains one 38x51mm stamp.

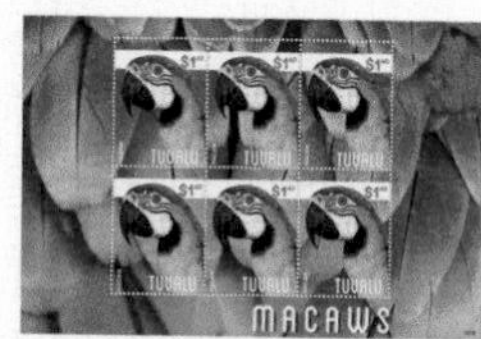

A351

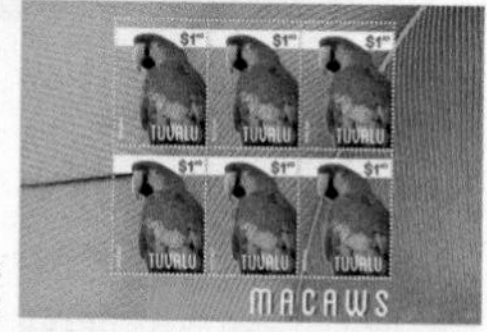

Macaws A352

Nos. 1294 and 1295: a-f, Macaw with different feather lines and colors in background, as shown.
No. 1296, horiz. — Macaw with denomination at: a, Right. b, Left.
$4.50, Macaw, diff.

2014, Aug. 14 Litho. *Perf. 14*

1294 A351 $1.40 Sheet of 6, #a-f 15.50 15.50
1295 A352 $1.40 Sheet of 6, #a-f 15.50 15.50

Souvenir Sheets

Perf. 12¾

1296 A352 $2.25 Sheet of 2, #a-b 8.50 8.50
1297 A352 $4.50 multi 8.50 8.50

No. 1296 contains two 51x38mm stamps. No. 1297 contains one 38x51mm stamp.

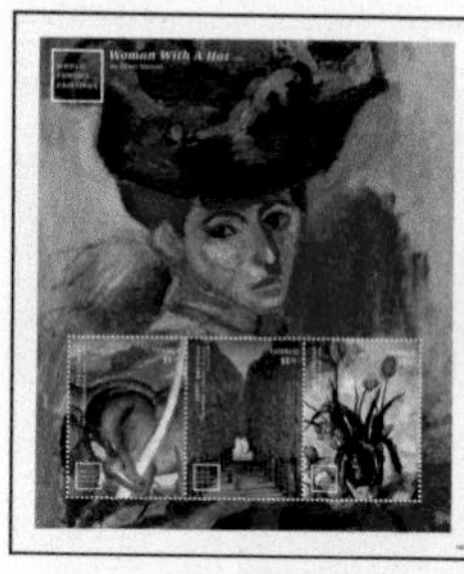

Paintings A353

No. 1298, $1.50: a, The Large Blue Horses, by Franz Marc. b, The Avenue in the Port at Saint-Cloud, by Henri Rousseau. c, Tulips in a Vase, by Paul Cézanne.
No. 1299, $1.50: a, Woman Reading, by Henri Matisse. b, Pyramid of Skulls, by Cézanne. c, Self-portrait with Pipe, by Vincent van Gogh.
No. 1300, $4.50, Nighthawks, by Edward Hopper. No. 1301, $4.50, Portrait of Père Tanguy, by van Gogh.

2014, Aug. 14 Litho. *Perf. 12¾*

Sheets of 3, #a-c

1298-1299 A353 Set of 2 18.00 18.00

Imperf

Size: 100x100mm

1300-1301 A353 Set of 2 18.00 18.00

Sharks A354

No. 1302, $1.40: a, Whale shark. b, Hammerhead shark. c, Caribbean reef shark. d, Great white shark.
No. 1303, $1.40: a, Whitetip shark. b, Gray reef shark. c, Leopard shark. d, Tiger shark.
No. 1304: a, Whale shark, diff. b, Gray reef shark, diff.
$4.50, Blacktip reef shark.

Perf. 14, 12¾ (#1303, 1305)

2014, Sept. 3 Litho.

Sheets of 4, #a-d

1302-1303 A354 Set of 2 22.50 22.50

Souvenir Sheets

1304 A354 $2.25 Sheet of 2, #a-b 9.00 9.00
1305 A354 $4.50 multi 9.00 9.00

No. 1303 contains four 51x38mm stamps. No. 1305 contains one 51x38mm stamp.

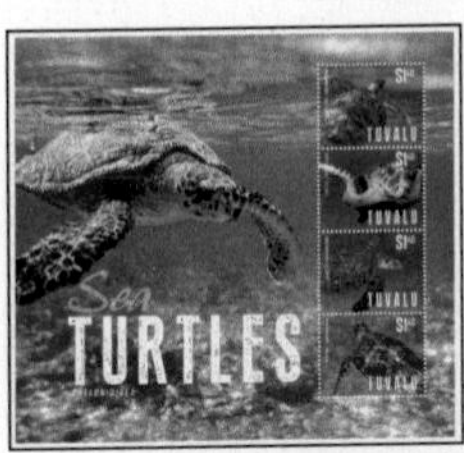

A355

A356

A357

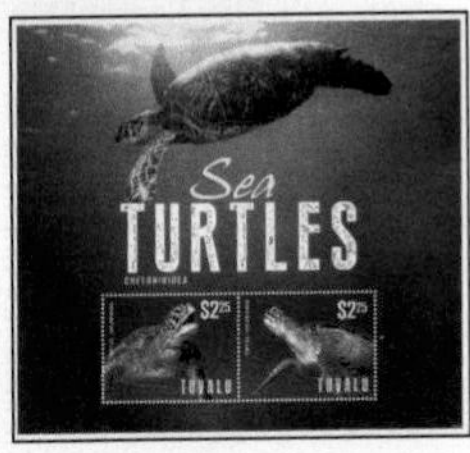

Sea Turtles A358

Various sea turtles, as shown.

2014, Sept. 3 Litho. *Perf. 12*

1306 A355 $1.40 Sheet of 4, #a-d 10.00 10.00
1307 A356 $1.40 Sheet of 4, #a-d 10.00 10.00

Souvenir Sheets

Perf. 12¾

1308 A357 $2.25 Sheet of 2, #a-b 8.00 8.00
1309 A358 $2.25 Sheet of 2, #a-b 8.00 8.00

Christmas — A359

Paintings by Peter Paul Rubens: $1.40, The Adoration of the Magi. $1.50, The Elevation of the Cross. $1.75, Adoration of the Shepherds. $2.25, The Holy Family.

2014, Nov. 24 Litho. *Perf. 13¼*

1310-1313 A359 Set of 4 12.00 12.00

Surfing A360

No. 1314, $1.40 — Various silhouettes of surfers with central background color of: a, Light blue green. b, Blue violet. c, Red. d, Bister.

No. 1315, $1.40, horiz. — Surfboards decorated with: a, Palm tree and sun. b, Flowers and wave. c, Vine and stripes. d, Waves.

No. 1316, $2.25 — Various silhouettes of surfers with central background color of: a, Light blue green (surfer's hands visible). b, Blue (surfer's hands not visible).

No. 1317, $2.25, horiz. — Surfboards decorated with: a, Waves, diff. b, Vine.

Perf. 13¾, 12 (#1315, 1317)

2014, Dec. 16 Litho.

Sheets of 4, #a-d

1314-1315 A360 Set of 2 18.50 18.50

Souvenir Sheets of 2, #a-b

1316-1317 A360 Set of 2 15.00 15.00

Nos. 1316 and 1317 each contain two 50x30mm stamps.

Inaugural Mass of Pope Benedict XVI A361

No. 1318 — Pope Benedict XVI: a, On steps. b, Wearing zucchetto, waving. c, Swinging censer. d, Wearing miter, waving.
$4.50, Pope Benedict XVI waving, diff.

2014, Dec. 31 Litho. *Perf. 14*

1318 A361 $1.40 Sheet of 4, #a-d 9.25 9.25

Souvenir Sheet

Perf. 12

1319 A361 $4.50 multi 7.25 7.25

No. 1319 contains one 30x50mm stamp.

Souvenir Sheet

St. John Paul II (1920-2005) — A362

2015, Feb. 2 Litho. *Perf. 14*

1320 A362 $3.50 multi 7.00 7.00

Corals A363

No. 1321: a, Bubble coral. b, Frogspawn coral. c, Mushroom coral. d, Brain coral.
$4.50, Coral on giant clam.

2015, Feb. 2 Litho. *Perf. 14*

1321 A363 $1.40 Sheet of 4, #a-d 12.25 12.25

Souvenir Sheet

Perf. 12

1322 A363 $4.50 multi 9.75 9.75

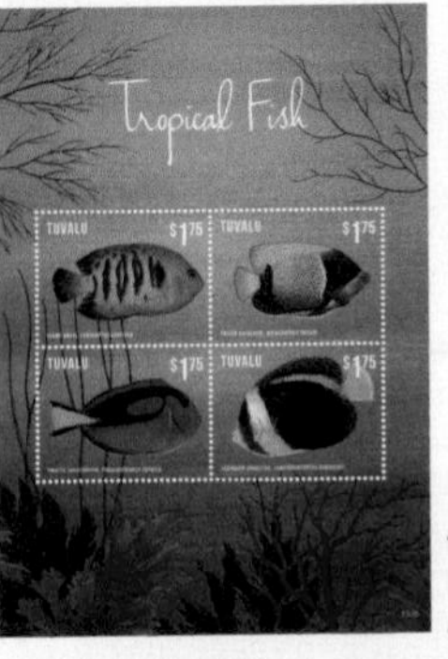

Tropical Fish A364

No. 1323, $1.75: a, Flame angelfish. b, Passer angelfish. c, Palette surgeonfish. d, Scribbled angelfish.

No. 1324, $1.75: a, Clown triggerfish. b, Powder blue surgeonfish. c, Clown anemonefish. d, Emperor angelfish.

No. 1325, $2.25: a, Southern orange-lined cardinalfish. b, Yellow tang.

No. 1326, $2.25: a, Coral grouper. b, Fire clownfish.

2015, Mar. 2 Litho. *Perf. 14*

Sheets of 4, #a-d

1323-1324 A364 Set of 2 22.00 22.00

Souvenir Sheets of 2, #a-b

Perf. 12¾

1325-1326 A364 Set of 2 14.00 14.00

Nos. 1325-1326 each contain two 51x38mm stamps.

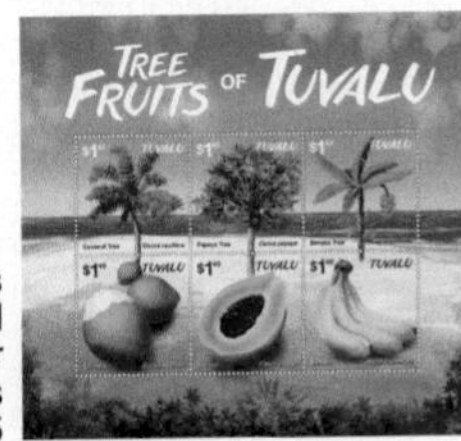

Trees and Their Fruits A365

No. 1327: a, Coconut tree. b, Papaya tree. c, Banana tree. d, Coconuts. e, Papaya. f, Bananas.

No. 1328: a, Pandanus tectorius tree. b, Pandanus tectorius fruit.

2015, Mar. 2 Litho. *Perf. 13¾*

1327 A365 $1.40 Sheet of 6, #a-f 13.50 13.50

Souvenir Sheet

1328 A365 $2.25 Sheet of 2, #a-b 7.00 7.00

Paintings of World War I Scenes A366

No. 1329, $1.40 — Details from *Gassed,* by John Singer Sargent: a, Soldiers with bandaged eyes, middle soldier carrying rifle on shoulder. b, Soldiers with bandaged eyes, all wearing helmets. c, Soldiers, man at left holding backpack of another soldier. d, Line of soldiers in distance.

No. 1330, $1.40 — Paintings by Alfred Théodore Joseph Bastien: a, *Cavalry and Tanks at Arras, 1918* (51x38mm). b, *Canadian Sentry, Moonlight, Neuville-Vitasse* (51x76mm). c, *Throwing Grenades* (51x38mm). d, *Canadian Cavalry Ready in a Wood* (51x38mm).

No. 1331, $4.50, *Street in Arras,* by Sargent. No. 1332, $4.50, *Canadian Gunners in the Mud,* by Bastien.

Perf. 13¾ (#1329), 12¾

2015, Mar. 2 Litho.

Sheets of 4, #a-d

1329-1330 A366 Set of 2 17.50 17.50

Souvenir Sheets

1331-1332 A366 Set of 2 14.00 14.00

Nos. 1331-1332 each contain one 51x38mm stamp.

Sites in London A367

No. 1333: a, Tower Bridge. b, London Eye. c, Westminster Abbey. d, Buckingham Palace. e, Saint Paul's Cathedral.
$4.50, Palace of Westminster.

2015, Apr. 13 Litho. *Perf. 14*

1333 A367 $1.40 Sheet of 5, #a-e 11.50 11.50

Souvenir Sheet

Perf. 12

1334 A367 $4.50 multi 7.25 7.25

2015 Europhilex Stamp Exhibition, London. No. 1334 contains one 80x30mm stamp.

Pope Francis Presiding Over Feb. 14, 2015 Consistory — A368

No. 1335: a, Pope Francis and Pope Benedict XVI. b, Pope Benedict XVI. c, Pope Francis blessing cardinal. d, Back of Pope Francis, Pope Benedict XVI.
$4.50, Pope Francis at pulpit.

2015, May 4 Litho. *Perf. 14*

1335 A368 $1.40 Sheet of 4, #a-d 9.00 9.00

Souvenir Sheet

1336 A368 $4.50 multi 7.25 7.25

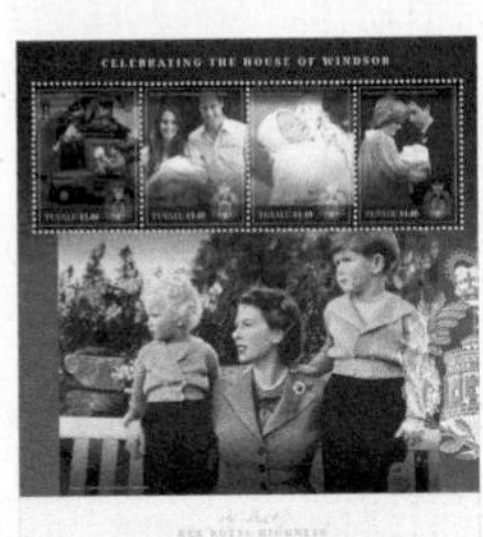

Birth of Princess Charlotte of Cambridge — A369

No. 1337: a, Princess Elizabeth and Prince Charles. b, Duke and Duchess of Cambridge with Prince George. c, Princess Charlotte of Cambridge. d, Prince Charles, Princess Diana holding Prince William.
$4.50, Duchess of Cambridge and Princess Charlotte.

2015, May 25 Litho. *Perf. 12*

1337 A369 $1.40 Sheet of 4, #a-d 8.75 8.75

Souvenir Sheet

1338 A369 $4.50 multi 7.00 7.00

Long-Reigning British Monarchs — A370

No. 1339: a, Queen Victoria. b, Queen Elizabeth II. c, King George III. d, King George V. e, King George VI. f, King George IV. g, King Edward VII. h, King William IV.
$4.50, Queen Elizabeth II, diff.

2015, May 25 Litho. *Perf. 12¾*

1339 A370 $1 Sheet of 8, #a-h 13.00 13.00

Souvenir Sheet

1340 A370 $4.50 multi 7.00 7.00

Italian World War II Aircraft A371

No. 1341: a, Reggiane Re. 2005 Sagittario. b, CANT Z.501 Gabbiano. c, Macchi C.200 Saetta. d, Savoia-Marchetti SM.81 Pipistrello.
$4.50, CANT Z.1007bis Alcione, vert.

2015, May 25 Litho. *Perf. 12*

1341 A371 $1.40 Sheet of 4, #a-d 10.00 10.00

Souvenir Sheet

1342 A371 $4.50 multi 7.50 7.50

No. 1342 contains one 30x40mm stamp.

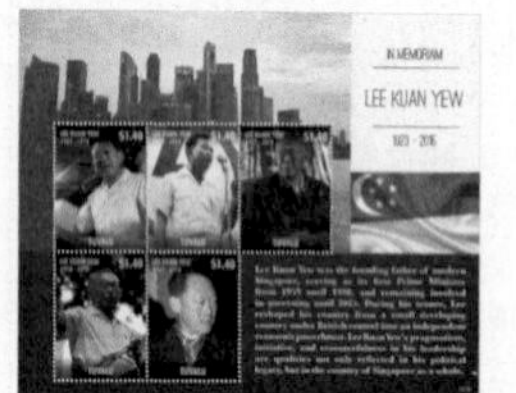

Lee Kuan Yew (1923-2015), Prime Minister of Singapore — A372

No. 1343 — Lee Kuan Yew: a, With microphone at left. b, In black-and-white photograph. c, Wearing blue and red robe. d, With microphone stand at LR. e, Waring black jacket.
$4.50, Lee Kuan Yew, diff.

2015, May 25 Litho. *Perf. 14*

1343 A372 $1.40 Sheet of 5, #a-e 9.25 9.25

Souvenir Sheet

Perf. 12¾

1344 A372 $4.50 multi 6.00 6.00

No. 1344 contains one 38x51mm stamp.

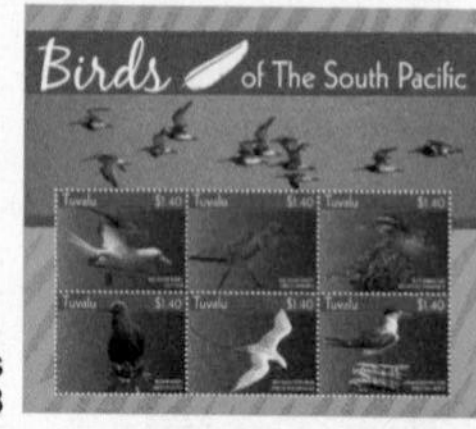

Birds A373

No. 1345: a, Red-footed booby. b, Bar-tailed godwit. c, Buff-banded rail. d, Brown noddy. e, Red-tailed tropicbird. f, Greater crested tern.
$4.50, Great frigatebird.

2015, May 25 Litho. *Perf. 12*

1345 A373 $1.40 Sheet of 6, #a-f 13.00 13.00

Souvenir Sheet

1346 A373 $4.50 multi 7.00 7.00

Sites in Singapore — A374

No. 1347: a, Chinese Garden. b, Cloud Forest, Gadens by the Bay. c, Pulau Ubin. d, Swan Lake. e, Da Bogong Temple, Kusu Island. f, Super Trees, Gardens by the Bay.
$4.50, Chinese Garden, diff.

2015, Aug. 3 Litho. *Perf. 12*

1347 A374 $1.40 Sheet of 6, #a-f 14.50 14.50

Souvenir Sheet

1348 A374 $4.50 multi 7.50 7.50

Singapore 2015 Intl. Stamp Exhibition.

Waterfalls — A375

No. 1349: a, Erawan Falls, Thailand. b, Rio Celeste Waterfall, Costa Rica. c, Krushuna's Waterfalls, Bulgaria. d, Kamienczyk Waterfall, Poland.
$4.50, Air Terjun Tiu Kelep Waterfall, Indonesia.

2015, Sept. 8 Litho. *Perf. 13½*

1349 A375 $1.40 Sheet of 4, #a-d 8.00 8.00

Souvenir Sheet

1350 A375 $4.50 multi 6.50 6.50

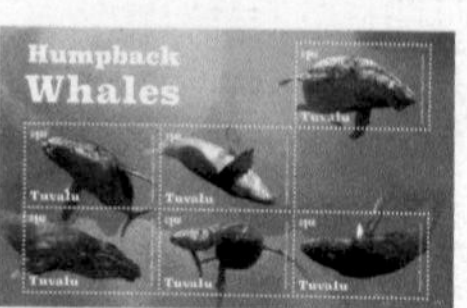

Humpback Whales — A376

No. 1351 — Various whales, as shown.
$4.50, Two Humpback whales, vert.

2015, Nov. 2 Litho. *Perf. 12*

1351 A376 $1.40 Sheet of 6, #a-f 12.00 12.00

Souvenir Sheet

1352 A376 $4.50 multi 6.50 6.50

Gold Medalists in 1896 Olympics — A377

No. 1353: a, William Welles Hoyt (1875-1954), pole vaulter, U.S. b, Launceston Elliot (1874-1930), weight lifter, Great Britain. c, Léon Flameng (1877-1917), cyclist, France. d, Sumner Paine (1868-1904), shooter, U.S.
$4.50, John Boland (1870-1958), tennis player, Great Britain.

2016, Jan. 18 Litho. *Perf. 14*

1353 A377 $1.40 Sheet of 4, #a-d 10.00 10.00

Souvenir Sheet

Perf. 12¾

1354 A377 $4.50 multi 8.00 8.00

No. 1354 contains one 38x51mm stamp.

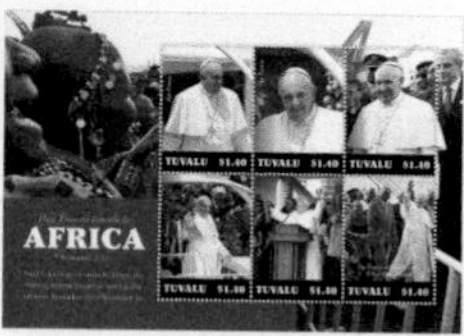

Pope Francis in Africa A378

No. 1355 — Pope Francis: a, With curved rail at UR. b, With curved rail and flowers at UR. c, Standing with military officers. d, Holding railing and waving. e, Behind pulpit, waving with both hands. f, Walking with Kenyan Pres. Uhuru Kenyatta and his wife.
$4.50, Pope Francis, diff.

2016, Jan. 28 Litho. *Perf. 14*

1355 A378 $1.40 Sheet of 6, #a-f 13.50 13.50

Souvenir Sheet

Perf.

1356 A378 $4.50 multi 7.50 7.50

No. 1356 contains one 33x43mm oval stamp.

Female Characters in *Star Trek* Television Shows — A379

No. 1357: a, Chief Medical Officer Beverly Crusher. b, Communications Officer Nyota Uhura. c, Captain Kathryn Janeway. d, Communications Officer Hoshi Sato. e, Deep Space 9 First Officer Kira Nerys. f, Science Officer Jadzia Dax.
$4.50, Former Borg Drone Seven of Nine.

2016, Jan. 28 Litho. *Perf. 12*

1357 A379 $1.40 Sheet of 6, #a-f 12.00 12.00

Souvenir Sheet

1358 A379 $4.50 multi 6.50 6.50

Souvenir Sheets

Elvis Presley (1935-77) — A380

Inscriptions: No. 1359, $4.50, Receives five gold records at once. No. 1360, $4.50, Shipping out for Germany.

2016, Jan. 28 Litho. *Perf. 12*

1359-1360 A380 Set of 2 14.00 14.00

Muhammad Ali (1942-2016), Boxer — A381

Various photographs of Ali.

2016, Jan. 28 Litho. *Perf. 12*

1361 A381 $1.40 Sheet of 4, #a-d 8.00 8.00

Souvenir Sheet

1362 A381 $4.50 multi 6.50 6.50

No. 1362 contains one 51x38mm stamp.

A382

A383

A384

Common Thresher Shark — A385

2016, Apr. 1 Litho. *Perf. 14*

1363	Strip of 4	9.75	9.75
a.	A382 $1.50 multi	2.40	2.40
b.	A383 $1.50 multi	2.40	2.40
c.	A384 $1.50 multi	2.40	2.40
d.	A385 $1.50 multi	2.40	2.40
e.	Souvenir sheet of 8, 2 each #1363a-1363d	19.50	19.50

Worldwide Fund for Nature (WWF).

New York City Landmarks — A386

No. 1364: a, Brooklyn Bridge. b, Grand Central Terminal. c, Gapstow Bridge, Central Park.
$7, New York City skyline.

2016, Apr. 29 Litho. *Perf. 12½*

1364 A386 $2.50 Sheet of 3, #a-c 10.75 10.75

Souvenir Sheet

Perf. 14

1365 A386 $7 multi 11.00 11.00

2016 World Stamp Show, New York. No. 1364 contains one 120x40mm stamp.

A387

Visit of U.S. President Barack Obama to Cuba — A388

No. 1366: a, Cuban Pres. Raúl Castro (40x30mm). b, Pres. Obama (40x30mm). c, Presidents Castro and Obama (40x30mm). d, Pres. Castro, Pres. Obama and wife, Michelle (40x30mm). e, Presidents Obama and Castro, flags of Cuba and U.S. (80x30mm).

No. 1367 — Pres. Obama: a, With microphone at left of tie. b, Waving, no fingers visible. c, With microphone at right of tie. d, Waving, fingers visible.

No. 1368, vert.: a, Pres. Obama. b, Pres. Castro.

2016, Sept. 23 Litho. *Perf. 14*
1366 A387 $2 Sheet of 5, #a-e 15.50 15.50

Perf. 13¾

1367 A388 $2 Sheet of 4, #a-d 12.50 12.50

Souvenir Sheet

Perf. 12

1368 A388 $3 Sheet of 2, #a-b 9.25 9.25

No. 1368 contains two 30x50mm stamps.

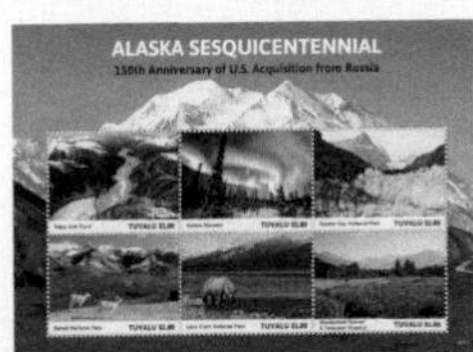

Purchase of Alaska by the U.S., 150th Anniv. (in 2017) — A389

No. 1369: a, Tracy Arm Fjord. b, Aurora Borealis. c, Glacier Bay National Park. d, Denali National Park. e, Lake Clark National Park. f, Mendenhall Glacier and fireweed meadow.

$5.50, Denali National Park, vert.

2016, Dec. 30 Litho. *Perf. 14*
1369 A389 $1.80 Sheet of 6, #a-f 15.50 15.50

Souvenir Sheet

Perf. 12½

1370 A389 $5.50 multi 8.00 8.00

No. 1370 contains one 38x51mm stamp.

Star Trek Television Series, 50th Anniv. — A390

No. 1371 — Scenes featuring Lieutenant Uhura from episodes: a, Plato's Stepchildren. b, Mirror, Mirror. c, The Trouble with Tribbles. d, The Conscience of the King.

$5.50, The Changeling, horiz.

2016, Dec. 30 Litho. *Perf. 14*
1371 A390 $2.50 Sheet of 4, #a-d 14.50 14.50

Souvenir Sheet

Perf. 12½

1372 A390 $5.50 multi 8.00 8.00

No. 1372 contains one 51x38mm stamp.

Miniature Sheets

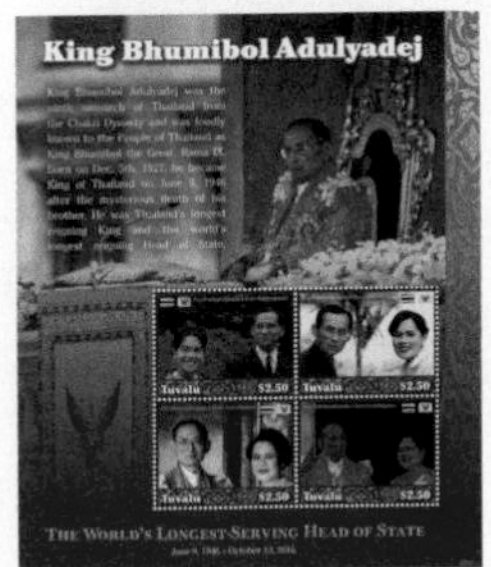

Thailand King Bhumibol Adulyadej (1927-2016) — A391

No. 1373 — Various photographs of King Bhumibol Adulyadej and Queen Sirikit, as shown.

No. 1374 — King Bhumibol Adulyadej with: a, Queen Elizabeth II (black-and white photograph). b, Queen Elizabeth II (color photograph). c, Pres. George W. Bush. d, Pres. Bill Clinton and wife, Hillary. e, Russian President Vladimir Putin. f, French President Jacques Chirac.

2017, Jan. 11 Litho. *Perf. 14*
1373 A391 $2.50 Sheet of 4, #a-d 15.00 15.00
1374 A391 $2.50 Sheet of 6, #a-f 23.00 23.00

Shimon Peres (1923-2016), President of Israel — A392

No. 1375: a, Pres. Barack Obama. b, Pres. Peres, U.S. flag in background. c, Peres and Senator Hillary Clinton. d, Peres, soldier in background. e, Obama, soldier in background. f, Benjamin Netanyahu, Prime Minister of Israel.

2017, Feb. 15 Litho. *Perf. 14*
1375 A392 $1.80 Sheet of 6, #a-f 16.50 16.50

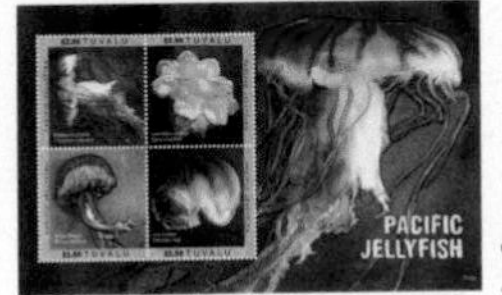

Jellyfish A393

No. 1376: a, Northern sea nettle. b, Lion's mane jellyfish. c, Mauve stinger. d, Jelly blubber.

No. 1377: a, White-spotted jellyfish. b, Sea wasp.

2017, Feb. 15 Litho. *Perf. 13¾*
1376 A393 $2.50 Sheet of 4, #a-d 17.50 17.50

Souvenir Sheet

1377 A393 $4.50 Sheet of 2, #a-b 15.75 15.75

Miniature Sheet

Environmental Protection — A394

No. 1378: a, Lightbulb. b, Two bottles. c, Recycling bin. d, Water faucet. e, Shopping bag. f, Recycling emblem.

Perf. 13¼x12½

2017, Feb. 28 Litho.
1378 A394 $1.80 Sheet of 6, #a-f 16.50 16.50

Miniature Sheets

A395

Pres. John F. Kennedy (1917-63) — A396

No. 1379 — Pres. Kennedy: a, With wife, Jacqueline, at their wedding. b, With wife, and daughter, Caroline (black-and-white photograph). c, With wife and daughter on lawn. d, With wife and daughter, cane chair in background.

No. 1380 — Pres. Kennedy: a, Taking oath of office. b, Sitting at desk, photographer in background. c, Standing behind microphone. d, Standing, photographer in background.

2017, Apr. 14 Litho. *Perf. 14*
1379 A395 $2.50 Sheet of 4, #a-d 15.00 15.00
1380 A396 $2.50 Sheet of 4, #a-d 15.00 15.00

Expo 2017, Astana, Kazakhstan — A397

No. 1381: a, Kazakhstan Pres. Nursultan Nazarbayev cutting ribbon (35x35mm). b, National emblem of Kazakhstan (35x35mm). c, Capsule laying ceremony (70x35mm). d, Emblem of Expo 2017 (35x35mm).

$5.50, Emblem of Expo 2017 and Bayterek Tower, vert.

2017, June 23 Litho. *Perf. 13¾*
1381 A397 $2.50 Sheet of 4, #a-d 15.50 15.50

Souvenir Sheet

Perf. 12½

1382 A397 $5.50 multi 8.50 8.50

No. 1382 contains one 38x51mm stamp.

Miniature Sheets

A398

Princess Diana (1961-97) — A399

No. 1383 — Princess Diana wearing: a, Black hat with brim. b, White hat with black ribbon. c. Light blue hat. d, Dark green brimless hat.

No. 1384 — Princess Diana wearing: a, Sailor's cap with crest. b, Black and white hat with wide brim. c, White hat. d, Red Cross uniform.

2017, June 26 Litho. *Perf. 14*
1383 A398 $2.50 Sheet of 4, #a-d 15.50 15.50
1384 A399 $2.50 Sheet of 4, #a-d 15.50 15.50

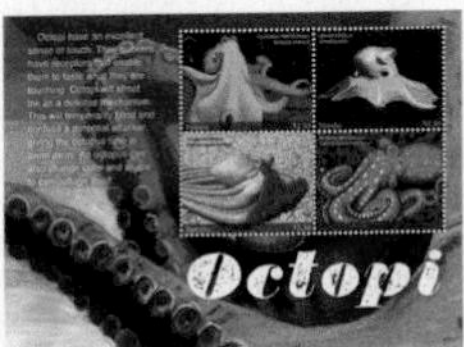

Octopi A400

No. 1385: a, Caribbean reef octopus. b, Dumbo octopus. c, Longarm octopus. d, White-spotted octopus.

No. 1386: a, Common octopus. b, Blanket octopus.

Perf. 12½x13¼

2017, Sept. 11 Litho.
1385 A400 $2.50 Sheet of 4, #a-d 14.00 14.00

Souvenir Sheet

1386 A400 $4 Sheet of 2, #a-b 11.00 11.00

A401

World War II, 75th Anniv. — A402

No. 1387: a, Allied troops in the South Pacific. b, Troops and native carriers on Kokoda Trail.

No. 1388: a, Allied troops in the South Pacific, diff, b, Troops and native carriers.

2017, Oct. 26 Litho. *Perf. 14*
1387 A401 $2.50 Pair, #a-b 8.50 8.50
1388 A402 $2.50 Pair, #a-b 8.50 8.50

Nos. 1387-1388 were each printed in sheets containing two pairs.

Hayabusa 2 Space Mission — A403

No. 1389: a, Hayabusa sample collector. b, Hayabusa 2 near 1999 JU3 asteroid, Minerva on asteroid. c, Hayabusa 2 near asteroid. d, Hayabusa 2 returning to Earth.

$5.50, Launch of Hayabusa 2, vert.

2017, Oct. 26 Litho. *Perf. 14*
1389 A403 $2.50 Sheet of 4, #a-d 15.50 15.50

Souvenir Sheet

Perf. 12

1390 A403 $5.50 multi 8.50 8.50

Saltwater Rays A404

No. 1391: a, Devil ray. b, Reef manta ray. c, Cownose ray. d, Spotted eagle ray. e, Blue-spotted stingray.

$5.50, Giant oceanic manta ray.

2017, Oct. 26 Litho. *Perf.*
1391 A404 $2 Sheet of 5, #a-e 15.50 15.50

Souvenir Sheet

Perf. 12½

1392 A404 $5.50 Sheet of 2, #a-b 9.25 9.25

No. 1392 contains one 51x38mm stamp.

Dolphins
A405

No. 1393: a, Three Bottlenose dolphins. b, Head of Bottlenose dolphin. c, Two Bottlenose dolphins. d, Bottlenose dolphin and Atlantic spotted dolphin.
No. 1394, vert.: a, Bottlenose dolphin. b, Bottlenose dolphin and Atlantic spotted dolphin.

2017, Dec. 4 Litho. *Perf. 14*
1393 A405 $2.50 Sheet of 4, #a-d 16.50 16.50

Souvenir Sheet
Perf. 12½
1394 A405 $4 Sheet of 2, #a-b 13.25 13.25

No. 1394 contains two 38x51mm stamps.

Butterflies — A406

No. 1395: a, Pearl-bordered fritillary. b, Small tortoiseshell. c, Old world swallowtail. d, American painted lady.
$5.50, Common blue butterfly.

2017, Dec. 4 Litho. *Perf. 13¾*
1395 A406 $2.50 Sheet of 4, #a-d 16.75 16.75

Souvenir Sheet
Perf.
1396 A406 $5.50 multi 9.25 9.25

No. 1396 contains one 38mm diameter stamp.

Underwater Caves — A407

No. 1397: a, Two divers in Chan Hol, Mexico. b, Orda Cave, Russia. c, South China Sea, Malaysia. d, One diver in Chan Hol.
No. 1398: a, Tux Kubaxa, Mexico. b, Cabo de Gata, Spain.

2017, Dec. 4 Litho. *Perf. 14*
1397 A407 $2.50 Sheet of 4, #a-d 16.00 16.00

Souvenir Sheet
Perf. 12½
1398 A407 $4 Sheet of 2, #a-b 12.50 12.50

No. 1398 contains two 51x38mm stamps.

A408

Tuvalu Beaches
A409

Various photographs of beaches, as shown.

2017, Dec. 26 Litho. *Perf. 14*
1399 A408 $2.50 Sheet of 4, #a-d 16.00 16.00

Souvenir Sheet
Perf. 12
1400 A409 $2.50 Sheet of 3, #a-c 12.00 12.00

Elvis Presley (1935-77) — A410

No. 1401 — Presley in movies: a, *Stay Away Joe*. b, *Harum Scarum*. c, *Roustabout*.

2017, Dec. 26 Litho. *Perf. 13¾*
1401 Horiz. strip of 3 8.50 8.50
a. A410 $1.50 multi 2.40 2.40
b. A410 $1.80 multi 2.75 2.75
c. A410 $2 multi 3.25 3.25

Printed in sheets containing 2 each Nos. 1401a-1401c.

Miniature Sheet

Wedding of Queen Elizabeth II and Prince Philip, 70th Anniv.
A411

No. 1402: a, Queen Elizabeth II wearing wedding dress. b, Wedding dress and tiara. c, Queen Elizabeth II and Prince Philip on wedding day. d, Engagement ring.

2017, Dec. 26 Litho. *Perf. 12*
1402 A411 $2.50 Sheet of 4, #a-d 16.00 16.00

Miniature Sheet

Visit to South Korea of Pres. Donald Trump
A412

No. 1403: a, U.S. First Lady Melania Trump. b, Pres. Trump. c, South Korean Pres. Moon Jae-in. c, South Korean First Lady Kim Jung-sook.

2018, Jan. 24 Litho. *Perf. 12*
1403 A412 $2.50 Sheet of 4, #a-d 16.00 16.00

A413

A414

Inauguration of Pres. Donald Trump — A415

No. 1404: a, Melania Trump and Karen Pence. b, Pres. Trump and Vice-President Mike Pence. c, Pres. Barack Obama and Vice-President Joe Biden. d, Michelle Obama and Jill Biden. e, Melania Trump. f, Pres. Trump. g, Pres. Obama. h, Michelle Obama.
No. 1405: a, $2, Ivanka Trump (30x40mm). b, $2, Jared Kushner (30x40mm). c, $3, Melania Trump (30x40mm). d, $4, Pres. Trump (30x40mm). e, $5, Pres. Trump speaking before Congress (60x40mm).
No. 1406: a, $3, Vice-President Pence and his wife, Karen. b, $4, Presidential Seal. c, $5, Pres. Trump and wife, Melania.

2018, Mar. 21 Litho. *Perf. 14*
1404 A413 $2 Sheet of 8, #a-h 26.00 26.00
1405 A414 Sheet of 5, #a-e 26.00 26.00

Souvenir Sheet
Perf. 12½
1406 A415 Sheet of 3, #a-c 19.50 19.50

Souvenir Sheet

Engagement of Prince Harry and Meghan Markle — A416

2018, Mar. 21 Litho. *Perf. 12½*
1407 A416 $5.50 multi 9.00 9.00

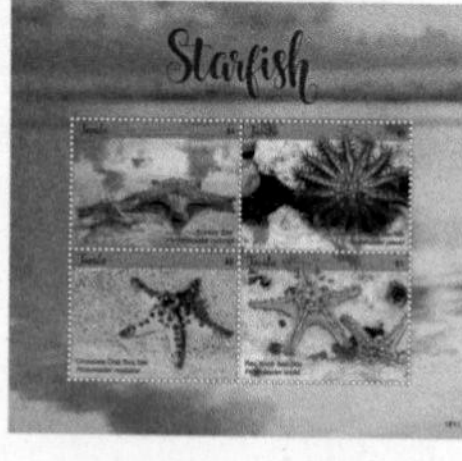

Starfish
A417

No. 1408: a, Knobby star. b, Crown-of-thorns starfish. c, Chocolate chip sea star. d, Red knob sea star.
No. 1409, vert.: a, $3, Red sea star. b, $5, Blue sea star.

2018, Mar. 21 Litho. *Perf. 14*
1408 A417 $2.50 Sheet of 4, #a-d 16.25 16.25

Souvenir Sheet
1409 A417 Sheet of 2, #a-b 13.00 13.00

Miniature Sheet

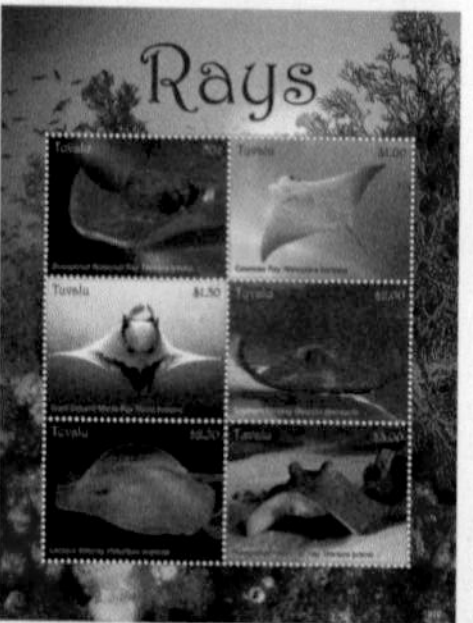

Rays
A418

No. 1410: a, 50c, Blue-spotted ribbontail ray swimming. b, $1, Cownose ray. c, $1.50, Giant oceanic manta ray. d, $2, Southern stingray. e, $2.50, Leopard whipray. f, $3, Blue-spotted ribbontail ray on ocean floor.

2018, Mar. 21 Litho. *Perf. 14*
1410 A418 Sheet of 6, #a-f 18.50 18.50

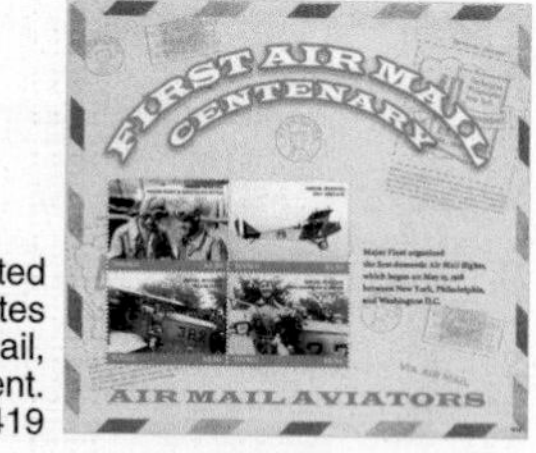

United States Air Mail, Cent.
A419

No. 1411: a, Major Reuben H. Fleet and Lieutenant George Boyle looking at map. b, DH-4 airplane. c, Major Fleet with arm on airplane. d, Pilot James Edgerton and his sister.
$5, United States #C1.

2018, Apr. 3 Litho. *Perf. 14*
1411 A419 $2.50 Sheet of 4, #a-d 17.00 17.00

Souvenir Sheet
Perf. 12½
1412 A419 $5 multi 7.50 7.50

No. 1412 contains one 51x38mm stamp.

Coronation of Queen Elizabeth II, 65th Anniv. — A420

No. 1413: a, $1, Queen Elizabeth II on throne with rod and scepter. b, $2, Procession. c, $3, Queen Elizabeth II and family. d, $4, Queen Elizabeth II on throne, diff.
$5, Queen Elizabeth II and Prince Philip, vert.

2018, May 30 Litho. *Perf. 14*
1413 A420 Sheet of 4, #a-d 16.25 16.25

Souvenir Sheet
1414 A420 $5 multi 7.50 7.50

Fruit
A421

No. 1415: a, $2, Papaya (incorrectly identified as "Pomegranate.") b, $2.50, Coconut. c, $3, Cavendish banana.
No. 1416: a, $3.50, Pomegranate. b, $4, Pink grapefruit.

2018, May 30 Litho. *Perf. 13¾*
1415 A421 Sheet of 3, #a-c 11.50 11.50

Souvenir Sheet
1416 A421 Sheet of 2, #a-b 11.50 11.50

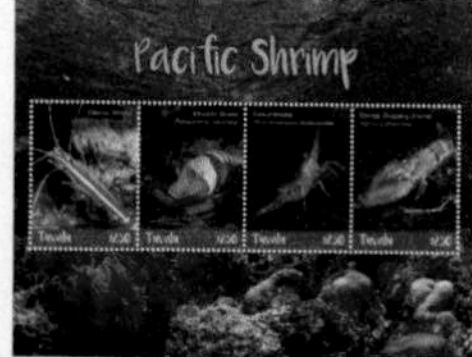

Shrimp
A422

No. 1417 — $2.50: a, Cleaner shrimp. b, Emperor shrimp. c, Camel shrimp. d, Orange snapping shrimp.
No. 1418 — $3.70: a, Peacock mantis shrimp. b, Modest snapping shrimp.

2018, May 30 Litho. *Perf. 14*
1417 A422 Sheet of 4, #a-d 16.50 16.50

Souvenir Sheet
Perf. 12½
1418 A422 Sheet of 2, #a-b 12.50 12.50

No. 1418 contains two 38x51mm stamps.

Coconut Crabs A423

No. 1419 — Various photographs of coconut crab: a, $1. b, $2. c, $3. d, $4.
No. 1420: a, $3, Crab on leaf. b, $4, Crab on ground.

2018, May 30 Litho. *Perf. 14*
1419 A423 Sheet of 4, #a-d 15.00 15.00

Souvenir Sheet
Perf. 12
1420 A423 Sheet of 2, #a-b 10.50 10.50

Orchids A424

No. 1421: a, $1, Encyclia cordigera. b, $2, Trichocentrum cavendishianum. c, $3, Sobralia macrantha. d, $4, Otoglossum coronarium.
No. 1422: a, $3, Guarianthe aurantiaca. b, $4, Guarianthe skinneri.

2018, May 30 Litho. *Perf. 14*
1421 A424 Sheet of 4, #a-d 16.50 16.50

Souvenir Sheet
Perf. 12½
1422 A424 Sheet of 2, #a-b 11.25 11.25

No. 1422 contains two 38x51mm stamps.

Miniature Sheet

Summit Meeting Between U.S. Pres. Donald Trump and North Korean Chairman Kim Jong Un, Singapore — A425

No. 1423: a, Kim and Trump standing in front of flags. b, Trump and Kim standing in front of building. c, Kim and Trump, sitting and shaking hands. d, Kim and Trump standing and shaking hands.

2018 Litho. *Perf. 14*
1423 A425 $2.50 Sheet of 4, a-d 15.00 15.00

No. 1423, which shows photographs taken at the summit, was stated to have been issued on June 12, which was the date of the summit.

Miniature Sheet

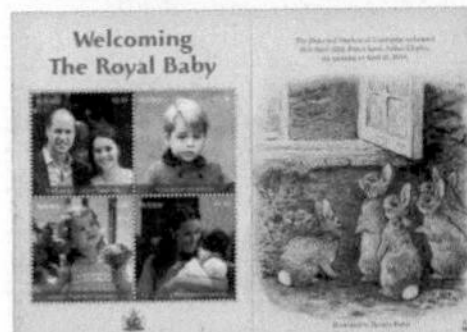

Birth of Prince Louis of Cambridge — A426

No. 1424: a, Duke and Duchess of Cambridge. b, Prince George of Cambridge. c, Princess Charlotte of Cambridge. d, Duchess of Cambridge holding Prince Louis.

2018, Sept. 8 Litho. *Perf. 13¾*
1424 A426 $2.50 Sheet of 4, #a-d 16.50 16.50

Wedding of Prince Harry and Meghan Markle A427

No. 1425: a, Bride and groom, Queen Elizabeth II and Princes Philip, Princes Charles and Duchess of Cornwall, Duke and Duchess of Cambridge with their children and Doria Ragland, mother of the bride. b, Queen Elizabeth II and Prince Philip. c, Bride and groom with bridesmaids and page boys. d, Bride and groom with Ragland.
$5, Bride and groom, vert.

2018, Sept. 8 Litho. *Perf. 12*
1425 A427 $3 Sheet of 4, #a-d 20.50 20.50

Souvenir Sheet
Perf. 12½
1426 A427 $5 multi 8.50 8.50

No. 1426 contains one 38x51mm stamp.

Miniature Sheet

Nebulae A428

No. 1427: a, $1, Eight-Burst Nebula (NGC 3132). b, $2, Bug Nebula (NGC 6302). c, $3, Open cluster in Rosette Nebula (NGC 2244). d, $4, Carina Nebula (NGC 3372).

2018, Dec. 5 Litho. *Perf.*
1427 A428 Sheet of 4, #a-d 14.00 14.00

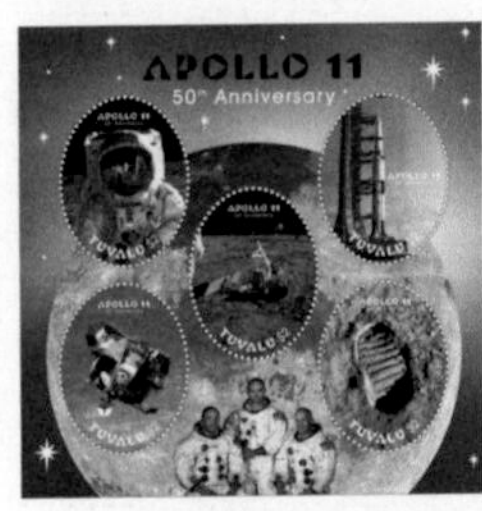

Flight of Apollo 11, 50th Anniv. (in 2019) A429

No. 1428: a, Astronaut on Moon. b, Launch of Apollo 11. c, Equipment and U.S. flag on lunar surface. d, Lunar Module leaving Moon. e, Footprint on lunar surface.
$5, Lunar Module and mission emblem, horiz.

2018, Dec. 5 Litho. *Perf.*
1428 A429 $2 Sheet of 5, #a-e 17.00 17.00

Souvenir Sheet
Perf. 12½
1429 A429 $5 multi 8.50 8.50

No. 1429 contains one 51x38mm stamp.

Tawny Nurse Shark A430

No. 1430: a, $1, Shark's head. b, $2, Shark, mouth not visible. c, $3, Two sharks. d, $4, Shark, mouth visible.
$5, Shark, horiz.

2018, Dec. 5 Litho. *Perf.*
1430 A430 Sheet of 4, #a-d 16.00 16.00

Souvenir Sheet
Perf. 14
1431 A430 $5 multi 8.00 8.00

No. 1431 contains one 80x30mm stamp.

Nudibranchs — A431

No. 1432: a, 50c, Variable neon slug. b, $1, Mediterranean violet aeolid. c, $1.50, Spanish shawl. d, $2, Magnificent sea slug. e, $2.50, Willan's chromodoris. f, $3, Hilton's aeolid.
$5, Crested aeolis.

2018, Dec. 5 Litho. *Perf. 14*
1432 A431 Sheet of 6, #a-f 17.00 17.00

Souvenir Sheet
1433 A431 $5 multi 8.25 8.25

Souvenir Sheet

Plumeria Rubra Flowers A432

No. 1434 — Various flowers: a, $2. b, $3. c, $4.

2019, Apr. 2 Litho. *Perf. 13¾*
1434 A432 Sheet of 3, #a-c 13.00 13.00

Striped Dolphins A433

No. 1435: a, $2, Two dolphins. b, $3, One dolphin. c, $4, Two dolphins, diff.
$7, One dolphin, vert.

2019, Apr. 10 Litho. *Perf. 12*
1435 A433 Sheet of 3, #a-c 14.50 14.50

Souvenir Sheet
1436 A433 $7 multi 14.50 14.50

Miniature Sheet

World War I, Cent. A434

No. 1437 — Various British and German troops greeting each other during Christmas truce: a, $1. b, $2. c, $3. d, $4.

2019, Apr. 15 Litho. *Perf. 12*
1437 A434 Sheet of 4, #a-d 16.00 16.00

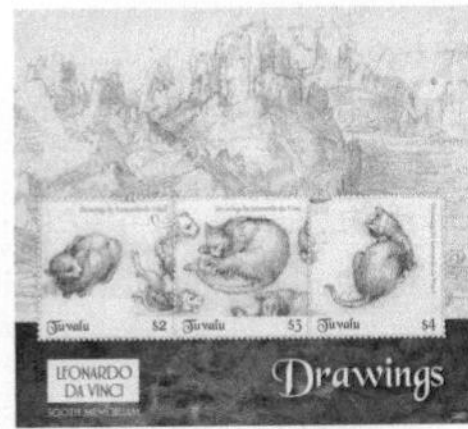

A435

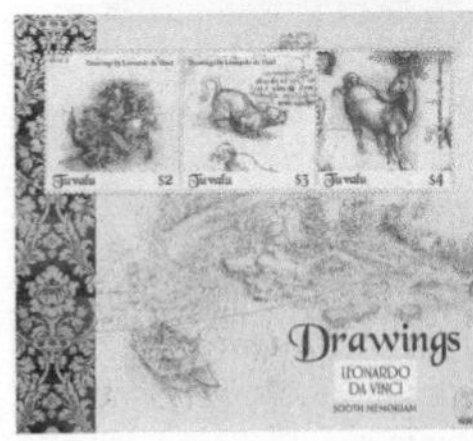

Drawings by Leonardo da Vinci (1452-1519) — A436

No. 1438 — Various cats: a, $2. b, $3. c, $4.
No. 1439: a, $2, Rider and horse. b, $3, Cat. c, $4, Horse, diff.
No. 1440, vert.: a, Animal seated in chair. b, Eagle on globe.

2019, Apr. 18 Litho. *Perf. 13¾*
1438 A435 Sheet of 3, #a-c 13.00 13.00
1439 A436 Sheet of 3, #a-c 13.00 13.00

Souvenir Sheet
Perf. 12
1440 A436 $4 Sheet of 2, 3a-b 11.50 11.50

No. 1440 contains two 30x50mm stamps.

Souvenir Sheets

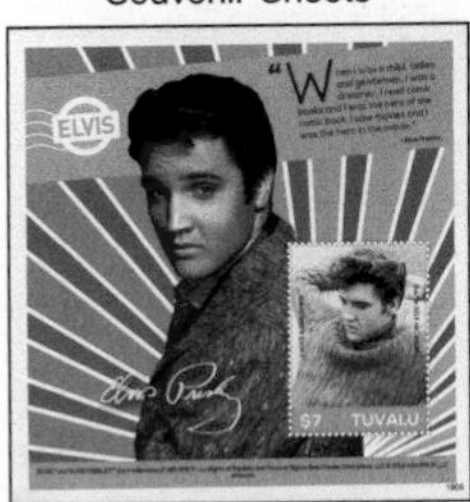

Elvis Presley (1935-77) — A437

Inscriptions: No. 1441, $7, I was a dreamer. No. 1442, $7, Elvis signs first movie contract. No. 1443, $7, Live concerts. No. 1444, $7, The loss of Elvis's mother, horiz.

2019, Apr. 23 Litho. *Perf. 14*
1441-1444 A437 Set of 4 40.00 40.00

A438

Day Octopi A439

Nos. 1445 and 1446 — Various photographs of octopi with denominations of: a, $2. b, $3. c, $4.
$7, Day octopus and fish.

2019, May 1 Litho. *Perf. 12*

1445 A438 Sheet of 3, #a-c 15.00 15.00
1446 A439 Sheet of 3, #a-c 15.00 15.00

Souvenir Sheet

Perf. 12½

1447 A439 $7 multi 11.50 11.50

No. 1447 contains one 38x51mm stamp.

Miniature Sheet

Birth of Archie Mountbatten-Windsor — A440

No. 1448: a, $1, Backs of Duke and Duchess of Sussex. b, $2, Duke and Duchess of Sussex with baby. c, $3, Duke and Duchess of Sussex with baby, diff. d, $4, Archie Mountbatten-Windsor.

2019, July 3 Litho. *Perf. 12*

1448 A440 Sheet of 4, #a-d 16.00 16.00

Hawksbill Sea Turtle A441

No. 1449 — Various images of Hawksbill sea turtle: a, $1. b, $2. c, $3. d, $4.
$7, Hawksbill sea turtle, diff.

2019, July 31 Litho. *Perf. 14*

1449 A441 Sheet of 4, #a-d 14.25 14.25

Souvenir Sheet

Perf. 12½

1450 A441 $7 multi 11.50 11.50

Singpex 2019 International Philatelic Exhibition, Singapore. No. 1450 contains one 51x38mm stamp.

Miniature Sheet

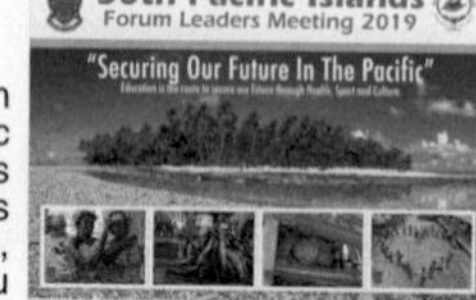

50th Pacific Islands Leaders Meeting, Tuvalu A442

No. 1451: a, Local dancers. b, Local fishing game. c, Local fruit. d, SDA Primary students.

2019, Aug. 12 Litho. *Perf. 13x13¼*

1451 A442 $2.50 Sheet of 4, #a-d 16.00 16.00

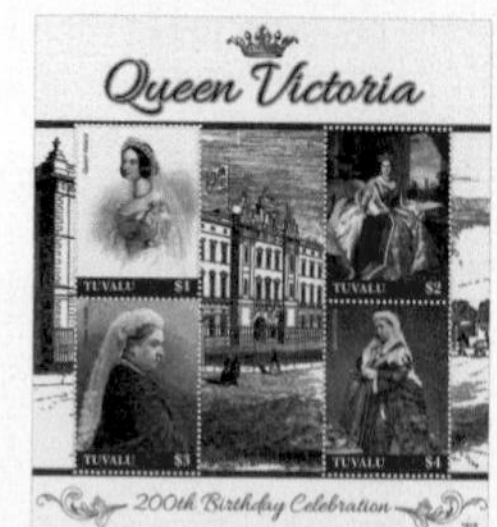

Queen Victoria (1819-1901) — A443

No. 1452 — Various images of Queen Victoria: a, $1. b, $2. c, $3. d, $4.
$7, Queen Victoria, diff.

2019, Sept. 9 Litho. *Perf. 14*

1452 A443 Sheet of 4, #a-d 16.00 16.00

Souvenir Sheet

Perf. 12

1453 A443 $7 multi 11.00 11.00

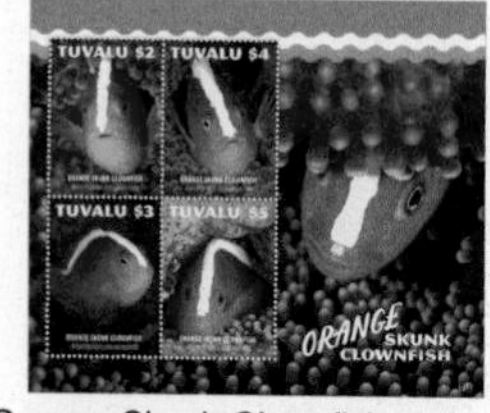

Orange Skunk Clownfish — A444

No. 1454 — Various images of Orange skunk clownfish: a, $2. b, $3. c, $4. d, $5.

2019, Sept. 9 Litho. *Perf. 14*

1454 A444 Sheet of 4, #a-d 22.00 22.00

Surgeonfish — A445

No. 1455: a, $1, Powder blue tang. b, $1, Achilles tang. c, $1.50, Striped surgeonfish. d, $1.50, Blue tang. e, $2, Bluespine unicornfish. f, $2, Blonde naso tang.

2019, Sept. 18 Litho. *Perf. 14*

1455 A445 Sheet of 6, #a-f 14.00 14.00

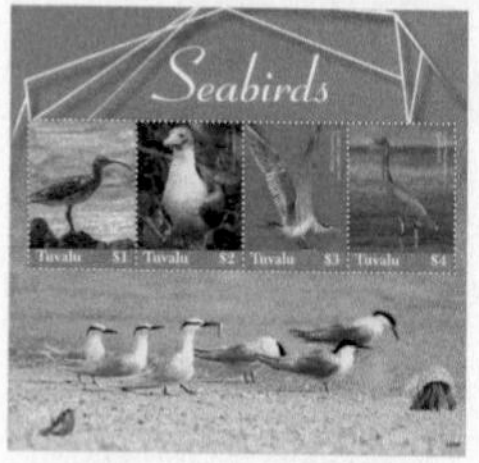

Seabirds A446

No. 1456: a, $1, Bristle-thighed curlew. b, $2, Red-footed booby. c, $3, Greater crested tern. d, $4, Pacific reef heron.
$7, Black-naped tern.

2019, Sept. 18 Litho. *Perf. 12*

1456 A446 Sheet of 4, #a-d 16.00 16.00

Souvenir Sheet

1457 A446 $7 multi 11.50 11.50

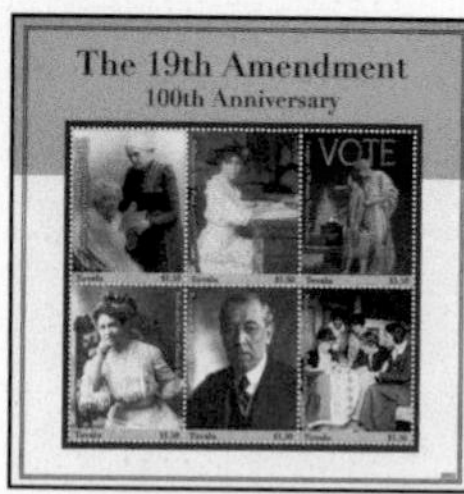

Passage of 19th Amendment to the United States Constitution, Cent. — A447

No. 1458: a, Elizabeth Cady Stanton (1815-1902), Susan B. Anthony (1820-1906), suffragists. b, Alice Paul (1885-1977), suffragist. c, League of Women Voters poster. d, Mary Church Terrell (1863-1954), suffragist. e, Pres. Woodrow Wilson (1856-1924). f, National Woman's Party leaders.
$7, Suffragists demonstrating in Chicago, 1916, horiz.

2020, June 17 Litho. *Perf. 14*

1458 A447 $1.50 Sheet of 6, #a-f 12.50 12.50

Souvenir Sheet

Perf. 12

1459 A447 $7 multi 9.75 9.75

Dorje Chang Buddha III, Religious Leader — A448

No. 1460 — Color of top panel: a, Blue green. b, Blue violet.

2020, Aug. 7 Litho. *Perf. 13¼x12½*

1460 A448 $1.50 Pair, #a-b 4.50 4.50

Printed in sheets of 6 containing 3 each of Nos. 1460a-1460b.

Miniature Sheet

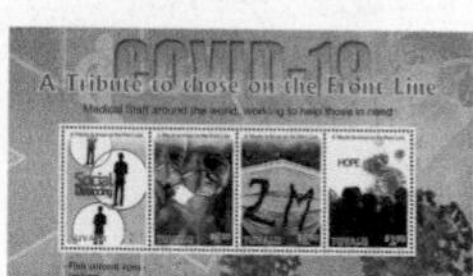

Campaign Against COVID-19 Pandemic — A449

No. 1461: a, Social distancing. b, Health care worker with protective face mask and magnifying glass. c, Protective face mask with "2M" inscription. d, Silhouettes of people, viruses and "hope."

2020, Aug. 11 Litho. *Perf. 14*

1461 A449 $2.50 Sheet of4, #a-d 15.00 15.00

Miniature Sheet

World War II Victory in Europe (V-E Day), 75th Anniv. A450

No. 1462: a, Wilhelm Keitel (1882-1946), German field marshal. b, Harry S Truman (1884-1972), 33rd President of the United States. c, Dwight D. Eisenhower (1890-1969), Supreme Commander of Allied Forces. d, Alfred Jodl (1890-1946), German general.

2020, Sept. 30 Litho. *Perf. 14*

1462 A450 $2.50 Sheet of 4, #a-d 14.50 14.50

A451

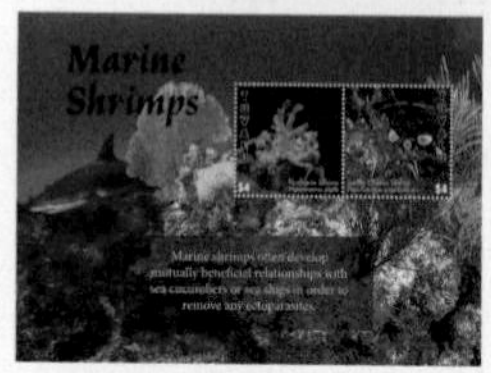

Shrimp A452

No. 1463: a, Mantis shrimp. b, Bumblebee shrimp. c, Peppermint shrimp. d, Marbled shrimp. e, Tiger pistol shrimp.
No. 1464: a, Harlequin shrimp. b, Spotted cleaner shrimp.

2020, Sept. 30 Litho. *Perf. 13¾*

1463 A451 $2 Sheet of 5, #a-e 14.50 14.50

Souvenir Sheet

1464 A452 $4 Sheet of 2, #a-b 11.50 11.50

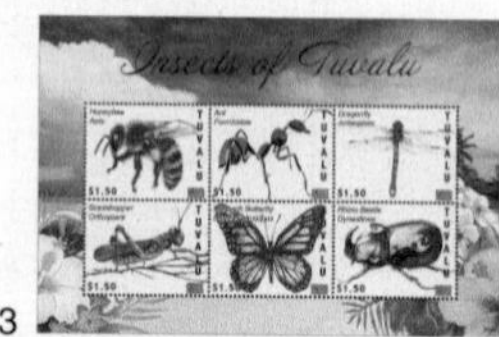

A453

Insects A454

No. 1465: a, Honeybee. b, Ant. c, Dragonfly. d, Grasshopper. e, Monarch butterfly. f, Rhino beetle.
$7, Cicada.

2020, Sept. 30 Litho. *Perf. 14*

1465 A453 $1.50 Sheet of 6, #a-f 13.00 13.00

Souvenir Sheet

Perf. 12

1466 A454 $7 multi 10.00 10.00

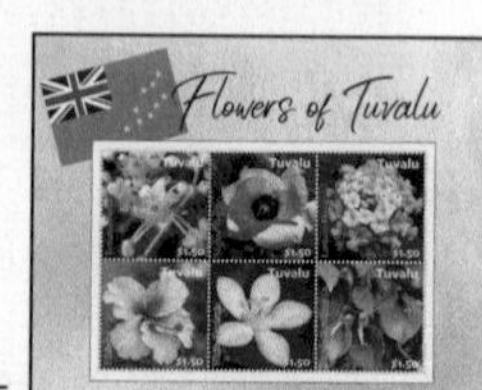

A455

Flowers A456

No. 1467: a, Tamanu flower. b, Mahoe flower. c, Lantana flower. d, Hibiscus. e, White gardenia. f, Purple coraltree.
$7, Plumeria.

2020, Sept. 30 Litho. *Perf. 13¾*

1467 A455 $1.50 Sheet of 6, #a-f 13.00 13.00

Souvenir Sheet

Perf. 12

1468 A456 $7 multi 10.00 10.00

Butterflies — A457

No. 1469: a, 50c, Great eggfly butterfly. b, $1, Green-spotted triangle butterfly. c, $1.50, Great eggfly butterfly, diff. d, $2, Green-spotted triangle butterfly, diff. e, $2.50, Great eggfly butterfly, diff. f, $3, Green-spotted triangle butterfly, diff.
$5.50, Chocolate argus butterfly.

2020, Nov. 2 Litho. *Perf. 14*

1469 A457 Sheet of 6, #a-f 15.00 15.00

Souvenir Sheet

Perf. 12

1470 A457 $5.50 multi 7.75 7.75

Miniature Sheet

Tanks of the Vietnam War A458

No. 1471: a, M60 Patton tank. b, M551 Sheridan tank. c, M113 Armored cavalry assault vehicle. d, M67 "Zippo" flame thrower tank.

2020, Nov. 2 Litho. *Perf. 12½*

1471 A458 $2.50 Sheet of 4, #a-d 14.00 14.00

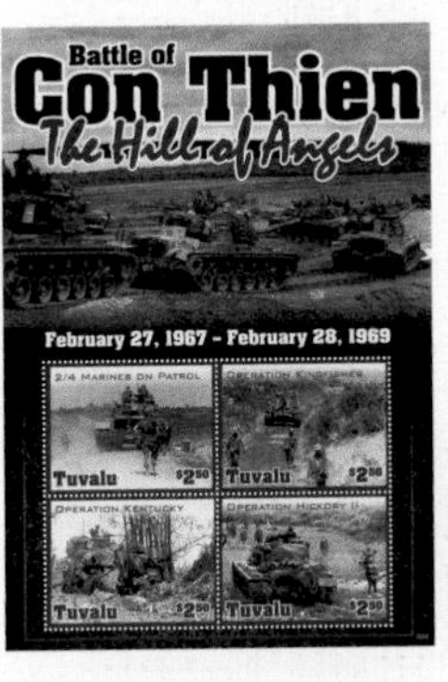

Vietnam War Battle of Con Thien A459

No. 1472: a, 2/4 Marines on patrol. b, Operation Kingfisher. c, Operation Kentucky. d, Operation Hickory II.
$5.50, Marines on search and destroy mission.

2020, Nov. 2 Litho. *Perf. 12½*

1472 A459 $2.50 Sheet of 4, #a-d 14.00 14.00

Souvenir Sheet

1473 A459 $5.50 multi 7.75 7.75

Paintings by Raphael (1483-1520) — A460

No. 1474 — Details of Saint John the Baptist Preaching, 1505: a, $1.75. b, $2.25. c, $2.75. d, $3.25.
$5.50, Detail of Saint John the Baptist Preaching, diff.

2020, Nov. 30 Litho. *Perf. 14*

1474 A460 Sheet of 4, #a-d 15.00 15.00

Souvenir Sheet

Perf. 12½

1475 A460 $5.50 multi 8.25 8.25

No. 1475 contains one 38x51mm stamp.

A461

Ludwig van Beethoven (1770-1827), Composer — A462

No. 1476 — Image of Beethoven: a, 1882 engraving. b, 1869 engraving. c, Portrait. d, 1900 engraving. e, Engraving by W. Holl.
$7, Seventeen-year-old Beethoven playing before Wolfgang Amadeus Mozart.

2020, Nov. 30 Litho. *Perf. 14*

1476 A461 $2 Sheet of 5, #a-e 15.00 15.00

Souvenir Sheet

Perf. 12½

1477 A462 $7 black 10.50 10.50

Mohandas K. Gandhi (1869-1948), Indian Nationalist Leader — A463

No. 1478 — Photograph of Gandhi from: a, 1942 (writing). b, 1890s (as law student). c, 1886 (with brother, Laxmidas). d, 1946 (with Jawaharlal Nehru). e, 1931 (wearing robe). f, 1931 (with textile workers).
$5.50, Gandhi spinning yarn, 1940s.

2020, Nov. 30 Litho. *Perf. 14*

1478 A463 $1.80 Sheet of 6, #a-f 16.00 16.00

Souvenir Sheet

Perf. 12½

1479 A463 $5.50 multi 8.25 8.25

No. 1479 contains one 38x51mm stamp.

A464

United Nations, 75th Anniv. A465

No. 1480: a, Flags and bushes outside of United Nations buildings, New York. b, United Nations General Assembly. c, United Nations flag. d, Flags outside of United Nations building.
$7.25, United Nations Building.

2020, Nov. 30 Litho. *Perf. 14*

1480 A464 $2.75 Sheet of 4, #a-d 16.50 16.50

Souvenir Sheet

Perf. 12½

1481 A465 $7.75 multi 11.50 11.50

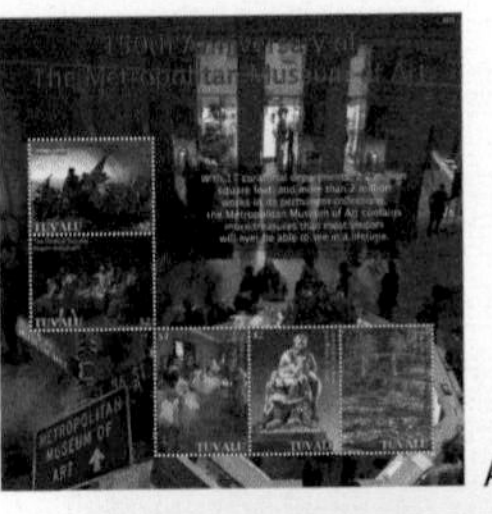

A466

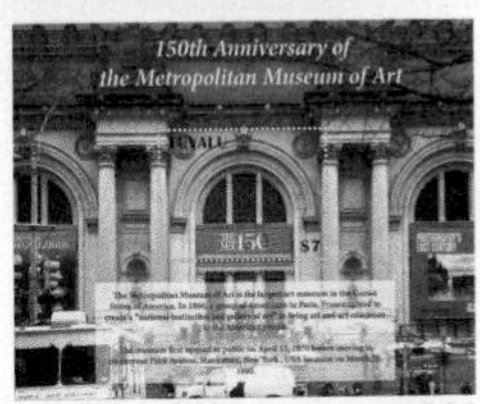

Metropolitan Museum of Art, New York City, 150th Anniv. — A467

No. 1482: a, Washington Crossing the Delaware, painting by Emanuel Leutze (1818-68). b, The Death of Socrates, painting by Jacques-Louis David (1748-1825). c, The Dance Class, painting by Edgar Degas (1834-1917), vert. d, Ugolino and His Sons, sculpture by Jean-Batiste Carpeaux (1827-75), vert. e, Bridge Over the Lily Pond, painting by Claude Monet (1840-1926), vert.
$7, Muesum entrance.

2020, Nov. 30 Litho. *Perf. 14*

1482 A466 $2 Sheet of 5, #a-e 15.00 15.00

Souvenir Sheet

Perf. 12½

1483 A467 $7 multi 10.50 10.50

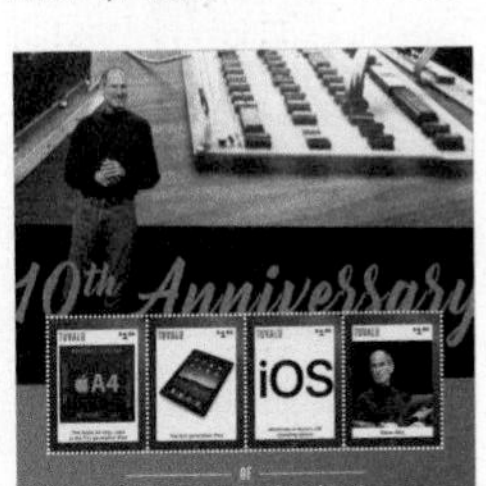

First Generation iPad, 10th Anniv. — A468

No. 1484: a, Apple A4 chip. b, First generation iPad. c, Wordmark of Apple's iOS operating system. d, Steve Jobs (1955-2011), chairman of Apple, holding iPad.
$5.50, Jobs holding iPad, diff.

2020, Nov. 30 Litho. *Perf. 14*

1484 A468 $1.80 Sheet of 4, #a-d 10.50 10.50

Souvenir Sheet

Perf. 12½

1485 A468 $5.50 multi 8.25 8.25

No. 1485 contains one 38x51mm stamp.

A469

Rabbits A470

No. 1486: a, White rabbit with gray ears. b, White rabbit. c, Gray rabbit in field. d, Rabbit and chick.
No. 1487: a, Rabbit facing left. b, Rabbit facing forward.

2020, Nov. 30 Litho. *Perf. 14*

1486 A469 $2.50 Sheet of 4, #a-d 15.00 15.00

Souvenir Sheet

1487 A470 $4 Sheet of 2, #a-b 12.00 12.00

Manta Rays A471

No. 1488: a, Mobula birostris and sea floor. b, Underside of Mobula alfredi. c, Underside of Mobula birostris. d, Mobula alfredi and sea floor. e, Side view of Mobula birostris.
No. 1489 — Mobula birostris with denomination in: a, Black. b, White.

2020, Nov. 30 Litho. *Perf. 13¾*

1488 A471 $2 Sheet of 5, #a-e 15.00 15.00

Souvenir Sheet

1489 A471 $4 Sheet of 2, #a-b 12.00 12.00

Jellyfish A472

No. 1490: a, Chrysaora hysoscella. b, Crossota. c, Aurelia aurita. d, Physalia physalis. e, Cubozoa.
No. 1491: a, Cyanea capillata. b, Rhizostoma pulmo.

2020, Nov. 30 Litho. *Perf. 13¾*

1490 A472 $2 Sheet of 5, #a-e 15.00 15.00

Souvenir Sheet

1491 A472 $4 Sheet of 2, #a-b 12.00 12.00

A473

Sea Turtles A474

No. 1492 — Drawings of sea turtles as seen from: a, Above. b, Side. c, Front. d, Below.
No. 1493 — Drawings of sea turtle: a, Facing left. b, Facing forward.

2020, Nov. 30 Litho. *Perf. 14*
1492 A473 $2.50 Sheet of 4, #a-d 15.00 15.00

Souvenir Sheet

1493 A474 $4 Sheet of 2, #a-b 12.00 12.00

Australian Landscapes — A475

No. 1494: a, Twelve Apostles. b, Whitsunday Islands. c, Nitmiluk National Park. d, Bunble Bungles. e, Pinnacles. f, Uluru.
$5.50, Great Barrier Reef.

2020, Dec. 7 Litho. *Perf. 14*
1494 A475 $1.80 Sheet of 6, #a-f 17.00 17.00

Souvenir Sheet
Perf. 12

1495 A475 $5.50 multi 8.50 8.50

No. 1495 contains one 50x30mm stamp.

A476

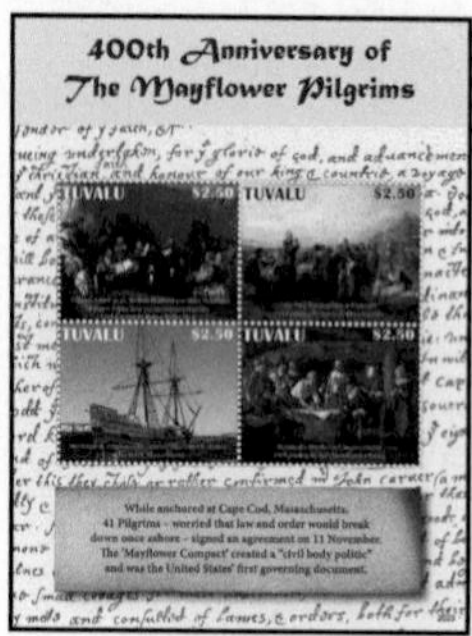

A478

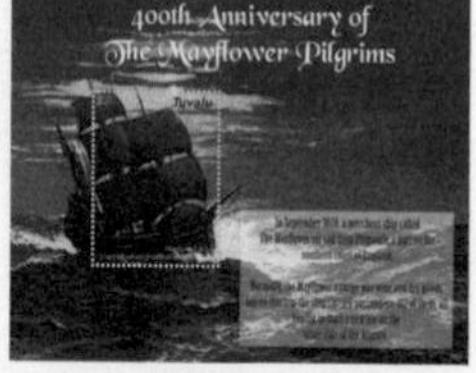

Arrival of Pilgrims in North America, 400th Anniv. A479

No. 1498: a, Embarkation of the Pilgrims, painting by Robert Walter Weir (1803-89). b, The First Thanksgiving at Plymouth, painting by Jennie A. Brownscombe (1850-1936). c, Mayflower II, replica of original Mayflower. d, The Signing of the Mayflower Compact, painting by Jean Leon Gerome Ferris (1863-1930).
$7, Mayflower at Sea, painting by A. S. Burbank (1855-1946).

Forbidden City, Beijing, 600th Anniv. — A477

No. 1496: a, Bronze statue of turtle. b, Bronze statue of crane. c, Imperial Guardian Lion. d, Copper and iron vat.
$7, Gate of Supreme Harmony.

2020, Dec. 20 Litho. *Perf. 14*
1496 A476 $2.50 Sheet of 4, #a-d 15.50 15.50

Souvenir Sheet

1497 A477 $7 multi 11.00 11.00

2020, Dec. 20 Litho. *Perf. 14*
1498 A478 $2.50 Sheet of 4, #a-d 15.50 15.50

Souvenir Sheet
Perf. 12½

1499 A479 $7 multi 11.00 11.00

A480

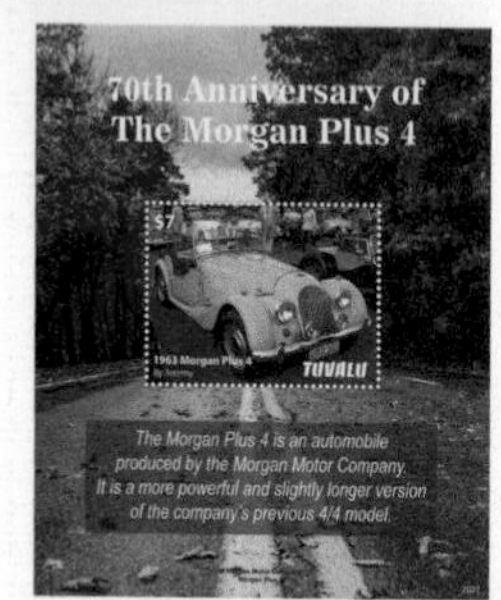

Morgan Plus 4 Automobiles, 70th Anniv. — A481

No. 1500 — Morgan Plus 4 from: a, 1995, painted green. b, 1999. c, 1993. d, 1995, painted blue.
$7, 1963 Morgan Plus 4.

2020, Dec. 20 Litho. *Perf. 14*
1500 A480 $2.50 Sheet of 4, #a-d 15.50 15.50

Souvenir Sheet
Perf. 12½

1501 A481 $7 multi 11.00 11.00

A482

Range Rovers, 50th Anniv. A483

No. 1502: a, 2014 Land Range Rover. b, 2017 Land Range Rover. c, 2016 Range Rover Sport. d, 2018 Land Range Rover Velar.
$7, 2012 Land Range Rover.

2020, Dec. 20 Litho. *Perf. 14*
1502 A482 $2.50 Sheet of 4, #a-d 15.50 15.50

Souvenir Sheet

1503 A483 $7 multi 11.00 11.00

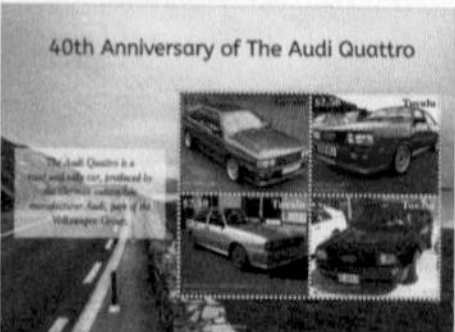

A484

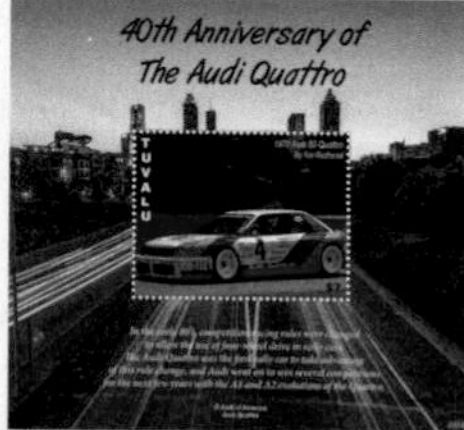

Audi Quattro Automobiles, 40th Anniv. — A485

No. 1504: a, 1987 Audi Quattro. b, 1988 Audi Quattro. c, 1980 Audi Quattro ARTZ Limousine. d, 1990s Audi Sport Quattro.
$7, 1970 Audi 90 Quattro.

2020, Dec. 20 Litho. *Perf. 14*
1504 A484 $2.50 Sheet of 4, #a-d 15.50 15.50

Souvenir Sheet
Perf. 12½

1505 A485 $7 multi 11.00 11.00

A486

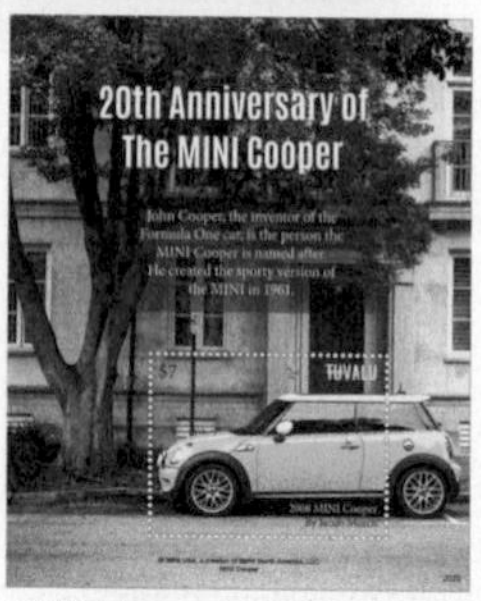

Mini Cooper Automobiles Manufactured by BMW, 20th Anniv. — A487

No. 1506: a, 2005 BMW Mini Cooper. b, 2019 BMW Mini Cooper. c, 2000 Rover Mini Cooper. d, 1965 Morris Mini Cooper.
$7, 2008 Mini Cooper.

2020, Dec. 20 Litho. *Perf. 14*
1506 A486 $2.50 Sheet of 4, #a-d 15.50 15.50

Souvenir Sheet
Perf. 12½

1507 A487 $7 multi 11.00 11.00

Miniature Sheet

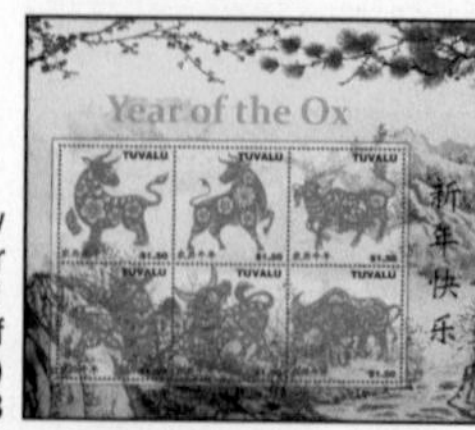

New Year 2021 (Year of the Ox) A488

No. 1508 — Ox with: a, Head at left, looking to right, three legs visible. b, Head at right, looking to left, four legs visible. c, Head at left, looking to left, one eye visible. d, Head at right, looking to left, three legs visible. e, Head at left, looking to right, grass and flower near hooves. f, Head at left, both eyes visible.

2021, Jan. 8 Litho. *Perf. 13¾*
1508 A488 $1.50 Sheet of 6 #a-f 14.00 14.00

Seahorses — A489

No. 1509: a, Tiger tail seahorse. b, Big-belly seahorse. c, Longsnout seahorse. d, Pacific seahorse.
$7, White's seahorse.

2021, Mar. 1 Litho. *Perf. 13¼x13½*
1509 A489 $2.50 Sheet of 4, #a-d 15.50 15.50

Souvenir Sheet

1510 A489 $7 multi 11.00 11.00

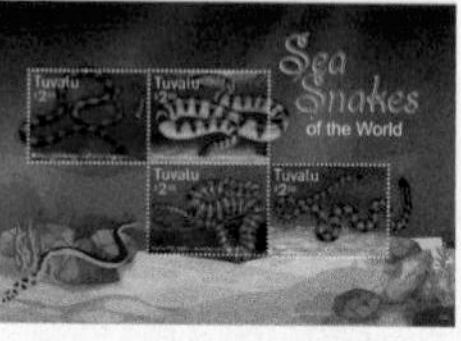

Sea Snakes A490

No. 1511: a, Blue-lipped sea krait. b, Hardwicke's sea snake. c, Marine file snake. d, Persian Gulf sea snake.
$7, Yellow-bellied sea snake.

2021, Mar. 1 Litho. *Perf. 13½x13¼*
1511 A490 $2.50 Sheet of 4, #a-d 15.50 15.50

Souvenir Sheet

1512 A490 $7 multi 11.00 11.00

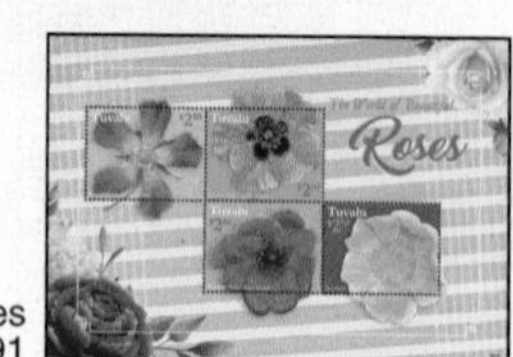

Roses A491

No. 1513: a, Rosa glauca. b, Rosa persica. c, Rosa moyesii. d, Rosa canina.
$7, Rosa gallica.

2021, Mar. 1 Litho. *Perf. 13½x13¼*
1513 A491 $2.50 Sheet of 4, #a-d 15.50 15.50

Souvenir Sheet

1514 A491 $7 multi 11.00 11.00

Joseph R. Biden, Jr. 46th President of the United States — A492

No. 1515 — Pres. Biden: a, Wearing blue and red striped tie. b, Holding microphone. c, Wearing face mask. d, Standing behind microphones. e, Without tie. f, Holding coffee cup.
$7, Biden waving.

Perf. 13¼x13½
2021, Mar. 15 Litho.
1515 A492 $1.46 Sheet of 6, #a-f 13.50 13.50

Souvenir Sheet
Perf. 14x14¼

1516 A492 $7 multi 11.00 11.00

No. 1516 contains one 38x51mm stamp.

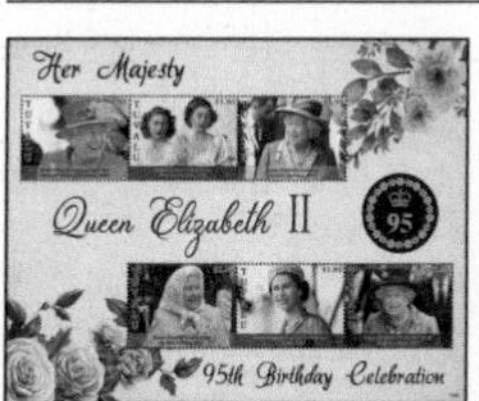
95th Birthday of Queen Elizabeth II
A493

No. 1517 — Queen Elizabeth II: a, At opening of Alexandra Gardens Bandstand, 2016. b, With her sister, Princess Margaret, 1946. c, In Frankfurt, Germany, 2015. d, At 90th birthday celebration, 2016. e, On royal visit to Jersey, 1957. f, Visiting Islington College, 2011.
$7, Queen Elizabeth II wearing blue jacket, 2011, vert.

Perf. 13½x13¼

2021, Mar. 15 Litho.

1517 A493 $1.95 Sheet of 6, #a-f 18.00 18.00

Souvenir Sheet

Perf. 14x14¼

1518 A493 $7 multi 11.00 11.00

No. 1518 contains one 38x51mm stamp.

Prince Philip (1921-2021) — A494

No. 1519 — Prince Philip: a, With Queen Elizabeth II. b, With soldiers. c, In coach with Queen Elizabeth II. d, Near lamps.
$7, Prince Philip seated with Queen Elizabeth II, vert.

2021 Litho. *Perf. 14*

1519 A494 $2.50 Sheet of 4, #a-d 15.50 15.50

Souvenir Sheet

1520 A494 $7 multi 11.00 11.00

Nos. 1519-1520 are claimed to have been issued on April 9, the day Prince Philip died.

Yellowstone National Park, 150th Anniv. (in 2022) — A495

No. 1521: a, Grand Canyon of the Yellowstone. b, Grand Prismatic Spring. c, Mammoth Hot Springs. d, Buffalos. e, Madison River. f, Sheepeater Cliffs.
$7, Old Faithful Geyser, vert.

2021, May 7 Litho. *Perf. 14*

1521 A495 $1.50 Sheet of 6, #a-f 14.00 14.00

Souvenir Sheet

Perf. 12

1522 A495 $7 multi 11.00 11.00

No. 1522 contains one 30x50mm stamp.

Birds
A496

No. 1523: a, Christmas shearwater. b, Bar-tailed godwit. c, Ruddy turnstone. d, Great frigatebird. e, Mallard. f, Pacific reef heron.
No. 1524, vert. — Red-footed booby with denomination at: a, UL. b, UR.

2021, May 17 Litho. *Perf. 14*

1523 A496 $1.50 Sheet of 6, #a-f 14.00 14.00

Souvenir Sheet

1524 A496 $4 Sheet of 2, #a-b 12.50 12.50

Grasshoppers — A497

No. 1525: a, $1, Grasshopper with head with white spots. b, $2, Grasshopper with brown head on leaf. c, $2, Grasshopper facing left. d, $3, Brown grasshopper with black spots facing left. e, $3, Green grasshopper with yellow eyes facing forward.
$7, Grasshopper on plant.

2021, May 17 Litho. *Perf. 14*

1525 A497 Sheet of 5, #a-e 17.00 17.00

Souvenir Sheet

Perf. 12½

1526 A497 $7 multi 11.00 11.00

No. 1526 contains one 51x38mm stamp.

Hibiscus Rosa-sinensis — A498

No. 1527 — Flower color a, $1, Red orange. b, $1, White. c, $1, Blue. d, $2, Pink. e, $2, Red violet. f, $2, Yellow.
$7, Two red flowers, horiz.

2021, May 17 Litho. *Perf. 13¾*

1527 A498 Sheet of 6, #a-f 14.00 14.00

Souvenir Sheet

Perf. 14

1528 A498 $7 multi 11.00 11.00

No. 1528 contains one 80x30mm stamp.

Dorje Chang Buddha III, Religious Leader — A499

2021, July 5 Litho. *Perf. 13¼*

1529 A499 $1.50 multi 2.25 2.25

Miniature Sheet

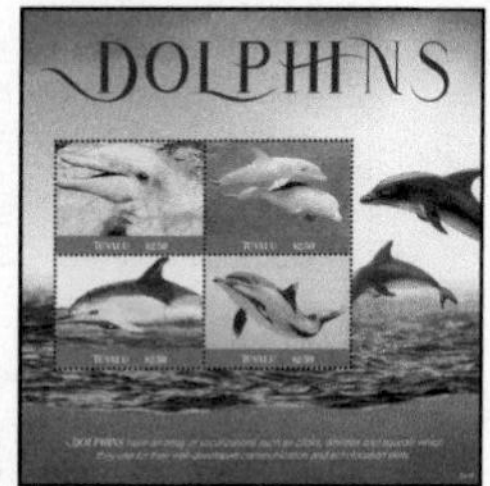
Dolphins
A500

No. 1530: a, Head of dolphin. b, Two dolphins. c, Dolphin above water's surface. d, Dolphin below water.

2021, July 5 Litho. *Perf. 14*

1530 A500 $2.50 Sheet of 4, #a-d 15.00 15.00

Miniature Sheet

Marine Life
A501

No. 1531: a, Pocillopora coral. b, Koi fish. c, Green sea turtle. d, Starfish.

2021, July 5 Litho. *Perf. 14*

1531 A501 $2.50 Sheet of 4, #a-d 15.00 15.00

Miniature Sheet

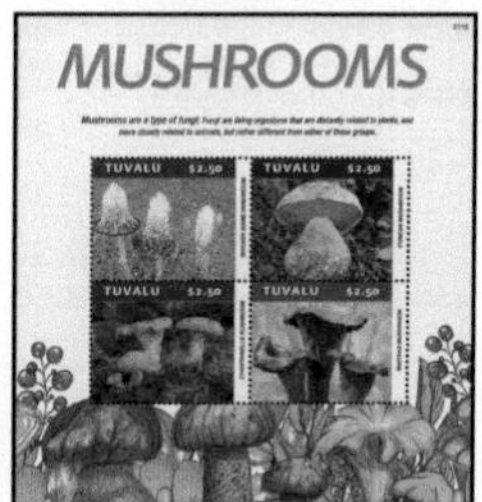
Mushrooms — A502

No. 1532: a, Shaggy mane mushrooms. b, Porcini mushroom c, Chantarelle mushrooms. d, Maitake mushrooms.

2021, July 5 Litho. *Perf. 14*

1532 A502 $2.50 Sheet of 4, #a-d 15.00 15.00

Miniature Sheet

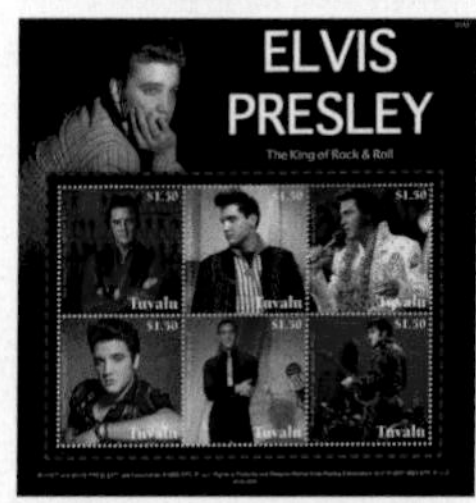
Elvis Presley (1935-77) — A503

No. 1533 — Presley: a, Wearing red shirt and black vest. b, Wearing striped shirt and jacket. c, Holding microphone. d, Wearing red, black and gray striped shirt. e, Wearing shirt and tie. f, Playing guitar.

2021, July 5 Litho. *Perf. 13¾*

1533 A503 $1.50 Sheet of 6, #a-f 13.50 13.50

10th Wedding Anniversary of Duke and Duchess of Cambridge — A504

No. 1534: a, Duke and Duchess of Cambridge, Eiffel Tower in background. b, Duchess of Cambridge with Queen Elizabeth II. c, Duke and Duchess of Cambridge with arms interlocked. d, Duke of Cambridge with Queen Elizabeth II.
No. 1535: a, Duchess of Cambridge. b, Duke of Cambridge.

2021, July 5 Litho. *Perf. 14*

1534 A504 $2.50 Sheet of 4, #a-d 15.00 15.00

Souvenir Sheet

1535 A504 $4 Sheet of 2, #a-b 12.00 12.00

3rd Wedding Anniversary of Duke and Duchess of Sussex — A505

No. 1536 — Duke and Duchess of Sussex: a, Duke at right, wearing blue jacket and tie. b, Duke at left, wearing white jacket. c, Duke at right, holding umbrella. d, Duke at left, wearing gray jacket and black tie.
$7, Duke and Duchess of Cambridge, horiz.

2021, July 5 Litho. *Perf. 13¾*

1536 A505 $2.50 Sheet of 4, #a-d 15.00 15.00

Souvenir Sheet

Perf. 12

1537 A505 $7 multi 10.50 10.50

No. 1537 contains one 50x30mm stamp.

Miniature Sheet

2020 Summer Olympics, Tokyo — A506

No. 1538: a, Gymnastics. b, Soccer. c, Tennis. d, Track and field.

2021, Aug. 2 Litho. *Perf. 13¾*

1538 A506 $2.50 Sheet of 4, #a-d 15.00 15.00

The 2020 Summer Olympics were postponed until 2021 because of the COVID-19 pandemic.

Souvenir Sheet

Ripple Cryptocurrency — A507

2021, Aug. 24 Litho. *Perf. 12½*
1539 A507 $30 multi 44.00 44.00

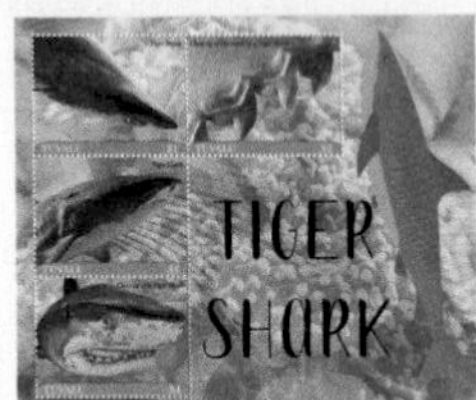

Tiger Sharks A508

No. 1540: a, $1, Side view of head of Tiger shark. b, $2, Teeth of Tiger shark. c, $3, Tiger shark, diff. d, $4, Head and mouth of Tiger shark.
$7, Tiger shark, diff.

2021, Oct. 11 Litho. *Perf. 14*
1540 A508 Sheet of 4, #a-d 15.00 15.00

Souvenir Sheet
Perf. 12½

1541 A508 $7 multi 10.50 10.50

No. 1541 contains one 51x38mm stamp.

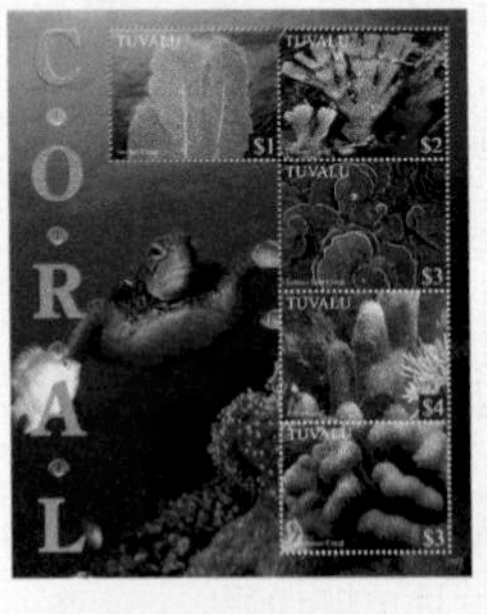

Corals A509

No. 1542: a, $1, Seafan coral. b, $2, Elkhorn coral. c, $3, Lettuce leaf coral. d, $3, Cauliflower coral. e, $4, Pillar coral.
$7, Staghorn coral.

2021, Oct. 11 Litho. *Perf. 14*
1542 A509 Sheet of 5, #a-e 19.50 19.50

Souvenir Sheet
Perf. 12½

1543 A509 $7 multi 10.50 10.50

No. 1543 contains one 51x38mm stamp.

Coconut Palm Trees A510

No. 1544: a, $1.50, Close-up of palm leaf. b, $2, Coconuts on palm tree. c, $2.50, Coconuts. d, $3, Top of palm tree without coconuts. e, $3.50, Coconuts on palm tree, diff.
$7, Coconut palm tree, diff.

2021, Oct. 11 Litho. *Perf. 14*
1544 A510 Sheet of 5, #a-e 19.00 19.00

Souvenir Sheet
Perf. 12½

1545 A510 $7 multi 10.50 10.50

No. 1545 contains one 51x38mm stamp.

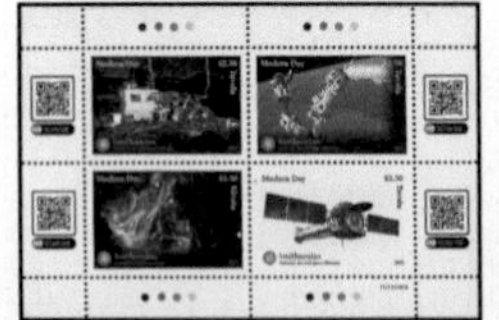

A511

A512

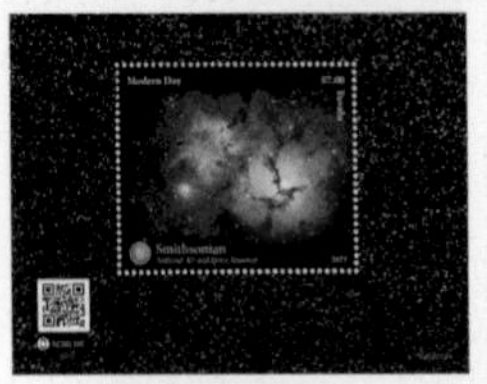

A513

Space Exploration — A514

No. 1546: a, Smithsonian Institution National Air and Space Museum display of Mars Rover. b, Astronaut and mechanical arm in space. c, Photograph of astronomical object from Hubble Space Telescope. d, Satellite.
No. 1547: a, International Space Station. b, Astronaut working in space. c, Photograph of astronomical object from Hubble Space Telescope, diff. d, Spacecraft with solar panels.
No. 1548, Photograph of astronomical object from Hubble Space Telescope, diff. No. 1549, International Space Station, diff.

2021, Oct. 1 Litho. *Perf. 13*
1546 A511 $2.50 Sheet of 4, #a-d 14.50 14.50
1547 A512 $3.50 Sheet of 4, #a-d 20.50 20.50

Souvenir Sheets
Perf. 13¼x13

1548 A513 $7 multi 10.50 10.50
1549 A514 $7 multi 10.50 10.50

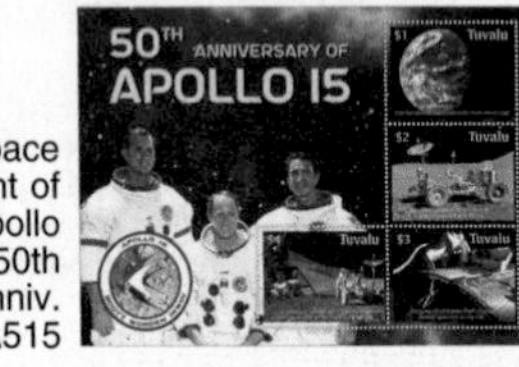

Space Flight of Apollo 15, 50th Anniv. A515

No. 1550: a, $1, Photograph of Earth taken from Apollo 15. b, $2, Apollo 15 Lunar Rover on Moon. c, $3, Astronaut Alfred Worden working outside of space capsule. d, $4, Lunar Module pilot James Irwin loading Lunar Rover on Moon.
$7, Commander David Scott doing geology work near Lunar Rover on Moon.

2021, Dec. 1 Litho. *Perf. 14*
1550 A515 Sheet of 4, #a-d 14.50 14.50

Souvenir Sheet
Perf. 12½

1551 A515 $7 multi 10.00 10.00

No. 1551 contains one 51x38mm stamp.

Miniature Sheet

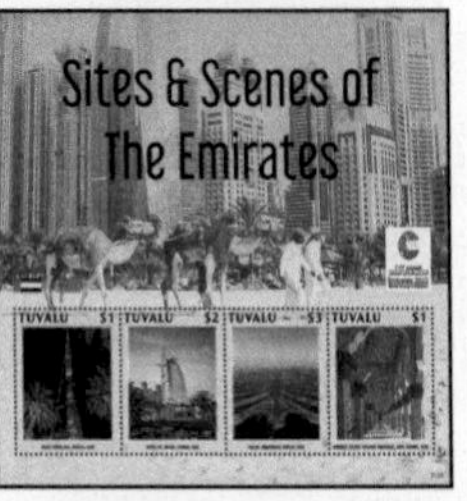

Tourist Attractions of the United Arab Emirates — A516

No. 1552: a, $1, Burj Khalifa, Dubai. b, $2, Burj Al Arab, Dubai. c, $3, Palm Jumeirah, Dubai. d, $4, Sheikh Zayed Grand Mosque, Abu Dhabi.

2022, Jan. 19 Litho. *Perf. 14*
1552 A516 Sheet of 4, #a-d 14.00 14.00

Emirates 2022 World Stamp Exhibition, Dubai.

Miniature Sheet

New Year 2022 (Year of the Tiger) A517

No. 1553 — Various tigers with denomination of : a, $1. b, $1.50. c, $2. d, $2.50. e, $3.

2022, Feb. 1 Litho. *Perf. 13¾*
1553 A517 Sheet of 5, #a-e 14.00 14.00

Reign of Queen Elizabeth II (1926-2022), 70th Anniv. — A518

No. 1554 — Queen Elizabeth II: a, Sitting behind microphone at Sandringham Estate. b, At Ascot Racecourse. c, Wearing crown at Buckingham Palace. d, At Liverpool Line Street Station. e, With dog at Balmoral Castle.
$7, Queen Elizabeth II wearing white scarf at Windsor.

2022, Feb. 6 Litho. *Perf. 14*
1554 A518 $1.70 Sheet of 5, #a-e 12.50 12.50

Souvenir Sheet
Perf. 12½

1555 A518 $6.70 multi 9.75 9.75

No. 1555 contains one 38x51mm stamp.

Miniature Sheet

Gold Medalists at 2022 Winter Olympics, Beijing — A519

No. 1556: a, Johann Strolz, Alpine skiing, flag of Austria. b, Therese Johaug, Biathlon, flag of Norway. c, Max Parrot, Snowboarding, flag of Canada. d, Eileen Gu, Snowboarding, flag of People's Republic of China.

Perf. 12½x13¼

2022, Mar. 25 Litho.
1556 A519 $2.50 Sheet of 4, #a-d 15.00 15.00

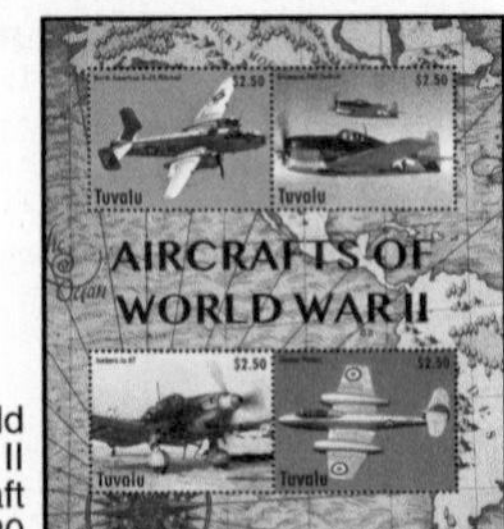

World War II Aircraft A520

No. 1557: a, North American B-25 Mitchell. b, Grumman F6F Hellcat. c, Junkers Ju 87. d, Gloster Meteor.
$7, Yakovlev Yak-3.

2022, Apr. 4 Litho. *Perf. 14*
1557 A520 $2.50 Sheet of 4, #a-d 14.00 14.00

Souvenir Sheet
Perf. 12

1558 A520 $7 multi 10.00 10.00

No. 1558 contains one 50x30mm stamp.

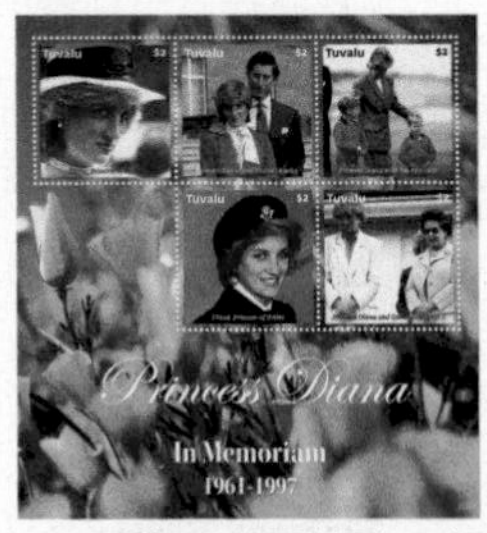

Princess Diana (1961-97) — A521

No. 1559 — Princess Diana: a, Wearing white hat with black band. b, With husband, Prince Charles. c, With her children, Princes William and Harry. d, Wearing British Red Cross uniform. e, With Queen Elizabeth II.
$7, Princess Diana wearing white hat, vert.

2022, Apr. 4 Litho. *Perf. 13¾*
1559 A521 $2 Sheet of 5, #a-e 14.00 14.00

Souvenir Sheet
Perf. 12½

1560 A521 $6.25 multi 8.75 8.75

No. 1560 contains one 38x51mm stamp.

Honey Bees A522

No. 1550 — Photographs of various bees with denomination of: a, $1. b, $2. c, $3. d, $4.
$7, Bee on flower.

2022, June 17 Litho. *Perf. 14*
1561 A522 Sheet of 4, #a-d 14.00 14.00

Souvenir Sheet
Perf. 12½

1562 A522 $7 multi 9.75 9.75

No. 1562 contains one 51x38mm stamp.

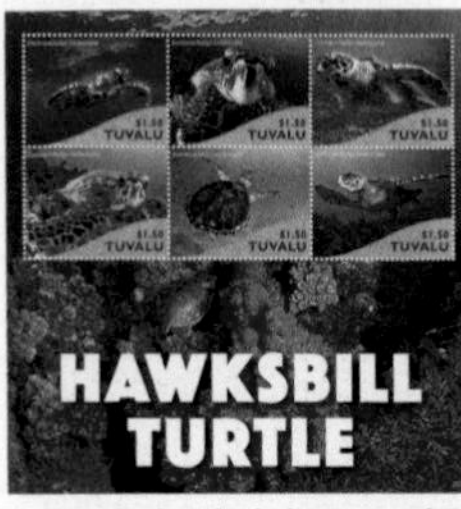

Eretmochelys Imbricata — A523

No. 1563 — Hawksbill turtle: a, Swimming to right in open water. b, Head. c, Swimming to left above sea floor, rear of turtle not visible. d, Swimming to right above sea floor. e, Swimming, top of shell visible. f, Swimming to left above sea floor, rear of turtle visible.
$7, Head of Hawksbill turtle, diff.

2022, June 17 Litho. *Perf. 14*
1563 A523 $1.50 Sheet of 6, #a-f 12.50 12.50

Souvenir Sheet
Perf. 12½

1564 A523 $7 multi 9.75 9.75

No. 1564 contains one 51x38mm stamp.

40th Birthday of Prince William
A524

No. 1565: a, $1, Prince William with his wife, Catherine. b, $2, Prince William with Queen Elizabeth II, 2016. c, $3, Prince William in Japan, 2015. d, $4, Prince William with wife and children, 2022.
$7, Prince William in Japan, 2015, vert.

2022, July 11 Litho. *Perf. 14*

1565	A524	Sheet of 4, #a-d	14.00	14.00

Souvenir Sheet

Perf. 12½

1566	A524	$7 multi	10.00	10.00

No. 1566 contains one 38x51mm stamp.

SEMI-POSTAL STAMPS

Nos. 159-160 Srchd. and Ovptd. "TONGA CYCLONE / RELIEF / 1982" in 1 or 3 Lines

Wmk. 380

1982, May 20 Litho. *Perf. 14*

B1	A25a	45c + 20c multi	.35	.35
B2	A25b	45c + 20c multi	.35	.35

POSTAGE DUE STAMPS

Arms of Tuvalu — D1

1981, May 13 Litho. *Perf. 14*

J1	D1	1c brt rose lil & blk	.30	.25
J2	D1	2c grnsh bl & blk	.30	.25
J3	D1	5c yellow brn & blk	.30	.25
J4	D1	10c blue grn & blk	.30	.25
J5	D1	20c chocolate & blk	.30	.25
J6	D1	30c orange & blk	.30	.25
J7	D1	40c ultra & blk	.30	.25
J8	D1	50c yellow grn & blk	.30	.30
J9	D1	$1 brt lilac & blk	.55	.55
		Nos. J1-J9 (9)	2.95	2.60

1982-83 *Perf. 14x15*

J1a	D1	1c bright rose lilac & black	.30	.25
J2a	D1	2c greenish blue & black	.30	.25
J3a	D1	5c yellow brown & black	.30	.25
J4a	D1	10c blue green & black	.30	.25
J5a	D1	20c chocolate & black	.30	.25
J6a	D1	30c orange & black	.35	.30
J7a	D1	40c ultra & black	.45	.35
J8a	D1	50c yellow green & black	.55	.45
J9a	D1	$1 bright lilac & black	.90	.65
		Nos. J1a-J9a (9)	3.75	3.00

Issued: 1c-20c, 11/25/82 (inscribed "1982"); 30c-$1, 5/25/83 (inscribed "1983").

OFFICIAL STAMPS

Nos. 96-113 Overprinted "OFFICIAL"

1981 Litho. Unwmk. *Perf. 14*

O1	A14	1c multicolored	.30	.25
O2	A14	2c multicolored	.30	.25
O3	A14	4c multicolored	.30	.25
O4	A14	5c multicolored	.30	.25
O5	A14	6c multicolored	.30	.25
O6	A14	8c multicolored	.30	.25
O7	A14	10c multicolored	.30	.25
O8	A14	15c multicolored	.30	.25
O9	A14	20c multicolored	.30	.25
O10	A14	25c multicolored	.30	.25
O11	A14	30c multicolored	.30	.30
O12	A14	35c multicolored	.30	.30
O13	A14	40c multicolored	.35	.35
O14	A14	45c multicolored	.40	.40
O15	A14	50c multicolored	.45	.45
O16	A14	70c multicolored	.55	.55
O17	A14	$1 multicolored	.70	.70
O18	A14	$2 multicolored	1.60	1.60
O19	A14	$5 multicolored	3.50	3.50
		Nos. O1-O19 (19)	11.15	10.65

No. 207 Surcharged and Overprinted

Wmk. 380

1983, Aug. Litho. *Perf. 14*

O20	A30	60c on $1 multi	.75	.75

Nos. 185-186A, 188, 230, 188A-195 Ovptd.

1984 Litho. Wmk. 380 *Perf. 14*

O21	A30	5c multicolored	.30	*.35*
O22	A30	10c multicolored	.30	*.35*
O23	A30	15c multicolored	.30	*.65*
O24	A30	25c multicolored	.30	*.55*
O25	A30	30c on 45c multi	.50	.65
O25A	A30	30c multicolored	.30	*.65*
O26	A30	35c multicolored	.40	*.70*
O27	A30	40c multicolored	.45	*.70*
O28	A30	45c multicolored	.50	*.70*
O29	A30	50c multicolored	.50	*.65*
O29A	A30	60c multicolored	.60	*.90*
O30	A30	$1 multicolored	.75	.90
O31	A30	$2 multicolored	1.20	1.00
O32	A30	$5 multicolored	2.85	2.25
		Nos. O21-O32 (14)	9.25	11.00

Issued: #O23, O29A, Apr. 30; others Feb. 1.

Nos. 469-484 Overprinted "OFFICIAL"

1989, Feb. 22 Litho. *Perf. 15*

O33	A64	5c multicolored	.30	.25
O34	A64	10c multicolored	.30	.25
O35	A64	15c multicolored	.30	.25
O36	A64	20c multicolored	.30	.25
O37	A64	25c multicolored	.30	.30
O38	A64	30c multicolored	.40	.40
O39	A64	35c multicolored	.45	.45
O40	A64	40c multicolored	.50	.50
O41	A64	45c multicolored	.60	.60
O42	A64	50c multicolored	.65	.65
O43	A64	55c multicolored	.70	.70
O44	A64	60c multicolored	.75	.75
O45	A64	70c multicolored	.90	.90
O46	A64	$1 multicolored	1.25	1.25
O47	A64	$2 multicolored	2.50	2.50
O48	A64	$5 multicolored	6.50	6.50
		Nos. O33-O48 (16)	16.70	16.50

For the following islands all are types of Tuvalu unless otherwise specified.
See note following Tuvalu No. 221.

Leaders of the World
Large quantities of some Leaders of the World sets, including unissued stamps, were sold at a fraction of face value when the printer was liquidated.

FUNAFUTI

Catalogue values for all unused stamps in this country are for Never Hinged items.

Locomotive Type of 1984

No. 1, 1919 Class C51, Japan. No. 2, 1935 F.C.C. Andes Class, Peru. No. 3, 1934 Kolhapur Class, UK. No. 4, 1941 V.R. Class H, Australia. No. 5, 1885 S.A.R. Class Y, Australia. No. 6, 1951 Class 4, UK. No. 7, 1928 Class U, UK. No. 8, 1923 Eryri Cog, UK. No. 9, 1927 Royal Scot Class, UK. No. 10, 1828 Lancashire Witch, UK. No. 11, 1906 NY, NH & H RR Class EP-1, US. No. 12, 1942 Springbok Class B1, UK. No. 13, 1827 Royal George, UK. No. 14, 1926 Northern Pacific Class A5, US. No. 15, 1900 Aberdare Class 2600, UK. No. 16, 1829 Sans Pareil, UK. No. 17, 1924 EST Class 241A, France. No. 18, 1911 Class 8K, UK. No. 19, 1913 Sir Gilbert Claughton, UK. No. 20, 1920 Sherlock Holmes, UK. No. 21, 1949 Class K1, UK. No. 22, 1925 Class P1, UK. No. 23, 1940 SNCF Class 232R, France. No. 24, 1904 B&O Class DD-1.

Se-tenant Pairs, #a.-b.
a. — Side and front views.
b. — Action scene.

Perf. 12½x13

1984-86 Litho. Unwmk.

1	A36	5c multicolored	.30	.25
2	A36	5c multicolored	.30	.25
3	A36	15c multicolored	.30	.25
4	A36	15c multicolored	.30	.25
5	A36	15c multicolored	.30	.25
6	A36	20c multicolored	.30	.25
7	A36	20c multicolored	.30	.25
8	A36	25c multicolored	.30	.25
9	A36	30c multicolored	.30	.30
10	A36	35c multicolored	.35	.35
11	A36	35c multicolored	.35	.35
12	A36	40c multicolored	.35	.35
13	A36	40c multicolored	.35	.35
14	A36	40c multicolored	.35	.35
15	A36	40c multicolored	.35	.35
16	A36	50c multicolored	.55	.55
17	A36	50c multicolored	.55	.55
18	A36	55c multicolored	.55	.55
19	A36	60c multicolored	.60	.60
20	A36	60c multicolored	.60	.60
21	A36	60c multicolored	.60	.60
22	A36	$1 multicolored	1.00	1.00
23	A36	$1 multicolored	1.00	1.00
24	A36	$1.50 multicolored	1.50	1.50
		Nos. 1-24 (24)	11.75	11.35

Issued: #3, 6, 9, 12, 16, 19, 4/16/84; 1, 4, 8, 10, 13, 18, 20, 22, 12/24/84; 2, 5, 11, 14, 17, 23, 4/29/85; 7, 15, 21, 24, 12/30/86.
1986 stamps not inscribed "Leaders of the World."

Automobile Type of 1984

No. 25, 1957 Triumph TR3A, UK. No. 26, 1932 Nash Special 8 Convertible, US. No. 27, 1937 Cord 812 Supercharged, US. No. 28, 1925 AC Six, UK. No. 29, 1924 Alfa Romeo P2, Italy. No. 30, 1935 Aston Martin Ulster, UK. No. 31, 1948 Morgan 4+4, UK. No. 32, 1906 Renault GP, France. No. 33, 1903 Cadillac Model A. No. 34, 1971 Porsche 917K, Germany. No. 35, 1913 Simplex 75HP, US. No. 36, 1939 Delahaye Type 165, France. No. 37, 1938 Opel Admiral, Germany. No. 38, 1936 Jaguar SS 100, UK. No. 39, 1965 Aston Martin DB5, UK. No. 40, 1977 Porsche 935.

Se-tenant Pairs, #a.-b.
a. — Side and front views.
b. — Action scene.

1984-87

25	A41	1c multicolored	.30	.25
26	A41	1c multicolored	.30	.25
27	A41	10c multicolored	.30	.25
28	A41	10c multicolored	.30	.25
29	A41	20c multicolored	.30	.25
30	A41	30c multicolored	.30	.30
31	A41	40c multicolored	.40	.40
32	A41	40c multicolored	.40	.40
33	A41	55c multicolored	.55	.55
34	A41	60c multicolored	.60	.60
35	A41	60c multicolored	.60	.60
36	A41	75c multicolored	.75	.75
37	A41	80c multicolored	.80	.80
38	A41	$1 multicolored	1.00	1.00
39	A41	$1 multicolored	1.00	1.00
40	A41	$1.50 multicolored	1.60	1.60
		Nos. 25-40 (16)	9.50	9.25

Issued: #25, 27, 31, 38, 9/13/84; 26, 30, 33, 34, 2/8/85; 28-29, 32, 35-37, 39-40, 8/27/87.
1987 stamps not inscribed "Leaders of the World."

Queen Mother Type of 1985

Hats: #45a, Blue feathered. #45b, White. #46a, 50a, Pink. #46b, 50b, Tiara. #47a, 51a, Blue. #47b, 51b, Blue with veil covering face. #48a, Blue. #48b, Tiara. #49a, Headband. #49b, Hat.

1985-86 *Perf. 13x12½*

45	A45	5c Pair, #a.-b.	.30	.30
46	A45	25c Pair, #a.-b.	.40	.40
47	A45	80c Pair, #a.-b.	1.20	1.20
48	A45	$1.05 Pair, #a.-b.	1.40	1.40
		Nos. 45-48 (4)	3.30	3.30

Souvenir Sheets of 2

49	A45	$1.05 #a.-b.	2.50	2.50
50	A45	$2 #a.-b.	2.75	2.75
51	A45	$3 #a.-b.	4.75	4.75

Issued: #45-49, 8/26; #50-51, 1/3/86.

Elizabeth II 60th Birthday Type

10c, Trooping the colors. 50c, Tiara. $1.50, As young woman, 1952. $3.50, Tiara, diff., vert.
$5, Scarf.

1986, Apr. 21 *Perf. 13x12½, 12½x13*

52	A49	10c multi	.30	.25
53	A49	50c multi	.35	.35
54	A49	$1.50 multi	1.10	1.10
55	A49	$3.50 multi	2.75	2.75
		Nos. 52-55 (4)	4.50	4.45

Souvenir Sheet

56	A49	$5 multi	4.00	4.00

Royal Wedding Type of 1986

#59a, Andrew holding rifle, vert. #59b, Sarah Ferguson, vert. #60a, Couple. #60b, Prince Philip and Andrew.

1986, July 23

59	A53	60c Pair, #a.-b.	1.25	1.25
60	A53	$1 Pair, #a.-b.	2.00	2.00

Souvenir Sheet

61	A56	$4 Newlyweds	4.75	4.75

Nos. 59-60 Ovptd. in Silver "Congratulations to T.R.H. The Duke & Duchess of York"

1986, July 23

62	A53	60c Pair, #a.-b.	2.00	2.00
63	A53	$1 Pair, #a.-b.	3.75	3.75

Royal Anniversaries
A1

1987 *Perf. 15*

66	A1	20c Queen Victoria	.30	.30
67	A1	50c George VI, Family	.65	.65
68	A1	75c Elizabeth	1.05	1.05
69	A1	$1.20 Elizabeth, Philip	1.75	1.75
70	A1	$1.75 Elizabeth, diff.	2.50	2.50
		Nos. 66-70 (5)	6.25	6.25

Souvenir Sheet

71	A1	$3 Elizabeth, Family	3.75	3.75

Elizabeth's 40th wedding anniv., Queen Victoria's accession to the throne, sesquicentennial.

Summer Olympics Type of 1988

1988, Aug. 19 *Perf. 13x12½*

72	A69	10c Hurdles	.30	.25
73	A69	20c High jump	.30	.25
74	A69	40c Running	.50	.50
75	A69	50c Discus	.60	.60
76	A69	80c Pole vault	1.00	1.00
77	A69	90c Javelin	1.10	1.10
		Nos. 72-77 (6)	3.80	3.70

NANUMAGA

Automobile Type of 1984

No. 1, 1903 De Dion-Bouton Single Cylinder. No. 2, 1955 Ford Thunderbird. No. 3, 1966 Lotus Elan, UK. No. 4, 1915 Stutz Bearcat. No. 5, 1915 Dodge 4-Cylinder Touring Car. No. 6, 1976 Jaguar XJ-S, UK. No. 7, 1928 Morgan Super Sports, UK. No. 8, 1906 Spyker, Holland. No. 9, 1957 Dual-Ghia, US. No. 10, 1966 Lamborghini P400 Miura Coupe, Italy. No. 11, 1947 Kaiser Traveler, US. No. 12, 1951 Lancia Aurelia, Italy. No. 13, 1963 Chevrolet Corvette Coupe. No. 14, 1949 Jaguar XK 120, UK. No. 15, 1930 Renault Reinastella, France. No. 16, 1938 Alvis Speed 25, UK. No. 17, 1956 Studebaker Golden Hawk. No. 18, 1909 Alco, US. No. 19, 1966 Shelby GT-350 Coupe, US. No. 20, 1968 Mercedes 300 SEL, Germany. No. 21, 1953 BRM V-16, UK. No. 22, 1910 Lozier Briarcliff, US.

Se-tenant Pairs, #a.-b.
a. — Side and front views.
b. — Action scene.

Perf. 12½x13

1984-87 Litho. Unwmk.

1	A41	5c multicolored	.30	.25
2	A41	5c multicolored	.30	.25
3	A41	5c multicolored	.30	.25
4	A41	10c multicolored	.30	.25
5	A41	10c multicolored	.30	.25
6	A41	10c multicolored	.30	.25
7	A41	10c multicolored	.30	.25
8	A41	15c multicolored	.30	.25
9	A41	20c multicolored	.30	.25
10	A41	25c multicolored	.35	.35
11	A41	25c multicolored	.35	.35
12	A41	25c multicolored	.35	.35
13	A41	30c multicolored	.40	.40
14	A41	40c multicolored	.55	.55
15	A41	40c multicolored	.55	.55

16 A41 50c multicolored .60 .60
17 A41 60c multicolored .80 .80
18 A41 75c multicolored 1.00 1.00
19 A41 $1 multicolored 1.50 1.50
20 A41 $1 multicolored 1.50 1.50
21 A41 $1 multicolored 1.50 1.50
22 A41 $1 multicolored 1.50 1.50
Nos. 1-22 (22) 13.65 13.20

Issued: #1, 4, 10, 14, 19, 6/11/84; #2, 5, 16, 20, 12/24/84; #6, 11, 18, 21, 7/23/85; #3, 7-9, 12, 15, 17, 22, 8/6/87.

1987 stamps not inscribed "Leaders of the World."

British Monarchs — A2

Se-tenant Pairs, #a.-b.

a. — Left stamp.

b. — Right stamp.

1984, Nov. 27 ***Perf. 13x12½***

23 A2 10c Richard I .30 .25
24 A2 20c Richard I, diff. .30 .25
25 A2 30c Third Crusade .35 .35
26 A2 40c Alfred the Great .45 .45
27 A2 50c Alfred, diff. .55 .55
28 A2 $1 Battle of Edington 1.10 1.10
Nos. 23-28 (6) 3.05 2.95

Locomotive Type of 1984

10c, 1906 NYC & HR Class S. 25c, 1884 T.R. Class B, Australia. 50c, 1902 Decapod, UK. 60c, 1846 Coppernob, UK.

Se-tenant Pairs, #a.-b.

a. — Side and front views.

b. — Action scene.

1985, Apr. 3 ***Perf. 12½x13***

29 A36 10c multicolored .30 .25
30 A36 25c multicolored .40 .40
31 A36 50c multicolored .75 .75
32 A36 60c multicolored .90 .90
Nos. 29-32 (4) 2.35 2.30

Flowers A3

#33a, Tecophilaea cyanocrocus. #33b, Lilium pardalinum. #34a, Canarina abyssinica. #34b, Vanda coerulea. #35a, Lathyrus maritimus. #35b, Narcissus tazetta. #36a, Bauera sessiflora. #36b, Thelymitra venosa.

1985, May 3 ***Perf. 13x12½***

33 A3 25c Pair, #a.-b. .30 .30
34 A3 30c Pair, #a.-b. .35 .35
35 A3 40c Pair, #a.-b. .55 .55
36 A3 50c Pair, #a.-b. .70 .70
Nos. 33-36 (4) 1.90 1.90

Queen Mother Type of 1985

Hats: #45a, White. #45b, Blue feathered. #46a, 50a, Violet blue wide-brimmed. #46b, 50b, Blue green wide-brimmed. #47a, 51a, Tiara. #47b, 51b, Light blue. #48a, Dark blue. #48b, Black.

#49a, As young girl. #49b, As young woman.

1985-86

45 A45 15c Pair, #a.-b. .30 .30
46 A45 55c Pair, #a.-b. 1.00 1.00
47 A45 65c Pair, #a.-b. 1.10 1.10
48 A45 90c Pair, #a.-b. 1.60 1.60
Nos. 45-48 (4) 4.00 4.00

Souvenir Sheets of 2

49 A45 $1.15 #a.-b. 1.75 1.75
50 A45 $2.10 #a.-b. 2.50 2.50
51 A45 $2.50 #a.-b. 3.00 3.00

Issued: #41-49, 9/5; 50-51, 1/3/86.

Elizabeth II 60th Birthday Type

1986, Apr. 21 ***Perf. 13x12½, 12½x13***

52 A49 5c White hat .30 .25
53 A49 $1 As young woman .35 .35
54 A49 $1.75 Tam .65 .65
55 A49 $2.50 Tiara, vert. .80 .80
Nos. 52-55 (4) 2.10 2.05

Souvenir Sheet

56 A49 $4 Portrait 3.00 3.00

World Cup Soccer Championships, Mexico — A4

Players and teams from participating countries.

Perf. 12½x13, 13x12½

1986, June 30

57 A4 1c Uruguay, vert. .30 .25
58 A4 5c Morocco, vert. .30 .25
59 A4 5c Hungary, vert. .30 .25
60 A4 10c Poland, vert. .30 .25
61 A4 20c Argentina, vert. .30 .25
62 A4 35c Bulgaria .30 .25
63 A4 50c Portugal, vert. .30 .25
64 A4 60c Belgium .30 .30
65 A4 75c France .30 .30
66 A4 $1 Canada, vert. .40 .40
67 A4 $2 Germany .60 .60
68 A4 $4 Scotland, vert. 1.25 1.25
Nos. 57-68 (12) 4.95 4.60

Royal Wedding Type of 1986

#71a, Prince Andrew, vert. #71b, Sarah Ferguson, vert. #72a, Prince Philip, Andrew. #72b, Prince Andrew.

1986, July 23

71 A53 60c Pair, #a.-b. 1.10 1.10
72 A53 $1 Pair, #a.-b. 1.90 1.90

Souvenir Sheet

73 A56 $4 Couple 4.00 4.00

Nos. 71-72 Ovptd. in Silver "Congratulations to T.R.H. The Duke & Duchess of York"

1986, Oct. 26

74 A53 60c Pair, #a.-b. 2.00 2.00
75 A53 $1 Pair, #a.-b. 3.75 3.75

Royal Anniversaries A5

15c, Queen Victoria. 35c, Princesses Margaret and Elizabeth. 60c, Elizabeth holding Princess Anne. $1.50, Elizabeth, Philip. $1.75, Elizabeth wearing tiara.

$3, Elizabeth.

1987, Oct. 15 ***Perf. 15***

78 A5 15c multicolored .30 .25
79 A5 35c multicolored .30 .30
80 A5 60c multicolored .40 .40
81 A62 $1.50 multicolored 1.05 1.05
82 A62 $1.75 multicolored 1.15 1.15
Nos. 78-82 (5) 3.20 3.15

Souvenir Sheet

83 A5 $3 multicolored 2.50 2.50

Elizabeth's 40th wedding anniv.; Victoria's accession to the throne, sesquicentennial.

NANUMEA

Locomotive Type of 1984

No. 1, 1940 Class E94, Germany. No. 2, 1946 Class 2251, UK. No. 3, 1941 Bantam Cock Class V4, UK. No. 4, 1902 Class C1, UK. No. 5, 1952 S.N.C.F. CC 7121, France. No. 6, 1903 La France Frenchmen Class, UK. No. 7, 1929 5700 Class, UK. No. 8, 1954 S.N.C.F. Class BB 1200, France. No. 9, 1881 Fairlight Class G, UK. No. 10, 1928 V.R. Class S, Australia.

Se-tenant Pairs, #a.-b.

a. — Side and front views.

b. — Action scene.

Perf. 12½x13

1984-85 **Litho.** **Unwmk.**

1 A36 1c multicolored .30 .25
2 A36 15c multicolored .30 .30
3 A36 20c multicolored .30 .30
4 A36 30c multicolored .30 .30
5 A36 35c multicolored .40 .40
6 A36 40c multicolored .45 .45
7 A36 50c multicolored .55 .55
8 A36 50c multicolored .55 .55
9 A36 60c multicolored .60 .60
10 A36 60c multicolored .60 .60
Nos. 1-10 (10) 4.35 4.30

Issued: Nos. 2-4, 6-7, 9, 4/30; others, 2/8/85.

Cricket Players Type of 1984

1c, J.A. Snow. 10c, C.J. Tavare. 40c, G.B. Stevenson. $1, P. Carrick.

Se-tenant Pairs, #a.-b.

1984, Oct. 9 ***Perf. 13x12½***

11 A39 1c multicolored .30 .30
12 A39 10c multicolored .30 .30
13 A39 40c multicolored .75 .75
14 A39 $1 multicolored 1.75 1.75
Nos. 11-14 (4) 3.10 3.10

Automobile Type of 1984

No. 15, 1965 Humber Supersnipe, UK. No. 16, 1934 Singer 9, UK. No. 17, 1948 Holden FX 2.1 Liter Sedan, Australia. No. 18, 1953 Buick Skylark. No. 19, 1951 Simca Aronde, France. No. 20, 1967 Toyota 2000 GT, Japan. No. 21, 1960 Elva Courier, UK. No. 22, 1952 Bentley Continental, UK. No. 23, 1938 Hispano-Suiza V12 Saoutchik Cabriolet, Spain/France. No. 24, 1913 Peugeot Bebe, France. No. 25, 1935 Bluebird V (LSR), UK. No. 26, 1978 Mazda RX7, Japan. No. 27, 1970 Lola T70, UK. No. 28, 1908 Locomobile, US.

Se-tenant Pairs, #a.-b.

a. — Side and front views.

b. — Action scene.

1985-86 ***Perf. 12½x13***

15 A41 5c multicolored .30 .25
16 A41 10c multicolored .30 .25
17 A41 15c multicolored .30 .25
18 A41 20c multicolored .30 .30
19 A41 20c multicolored .30 .30
20 A41 35c multicolored .45 .45
21 A41 40c multicolored .50 .50
22 A41 50c multicolored .60 .60
23 A41 50c multicolored .60 .60
24 A41 50c multicolored .60 .60
25 A41 60c multicolored .70 .70
26 A41 60c multicolored .70 .70
27 A41 75c multicolored .80 .80
28 A41 $2 multicolored 2.50 2.50
Nos. 15-28 (14) 8.95 8.80

Issued: Nos. 15, 21-22, 25, 1/14; Nos. 17-18, 23, 26, 2/22; Nos. 16, 19-20, 24, 27-28, 12/30/86.

Cats A6

#29a, American short-hair. #29b, Turkish Angora. #30a, Korat. #30b, American Maine Coon. #31a, Himalayan. #31b, Shaded Cameo. #32a, Long-haired ginger. #32b, Siamese Seal Point.

1985, May 28 ***Perf. 13x12½***

29 A6 5c Pair, #a.-b. .30 .25
30 A6 30c Pair, #a.-b. .45 .45
31 A6 50c Pair, #a.-b. .70 .70
32 A6 $1 Pair, #a.-b. 1.40 1.40
Nos. 29-32 (4) 2.85 2.80

Queen Mother Type of 1985

Hats: #41a, 47a, Light gray. #41b, 47b, Light blue. #42a, Lavender. #42b, Blue. #43a, Purple. #43b, Pink. #44a, 46a, Blue. #44b, 46b, Blue flowered. #45a, Feathered. #45b, Veiled.

1985-86

41 A45 5c Pair, #a.-b. .30 .25
42 A45 30c Pair, #a.-b. .30 .30
43 A45 75c Pair, #a.-b. .75 .75
44 A45 $1.05 Pair, #a.-b. .90 .90
Nos. 41-44 (4) 2.25 2.20

Souvenir Sheets of 2

45 A45 $1.20 #a.-b. 2.25 2.25
46 A45 $1 #a.-b. 1.00 1.00
47 A45 $4 #a.-b. 4.00 4.00

Issued: #41-45, 9/5; 46-47, 1/10/86.

Elizabeth II 60th Birthday Type

1986, Apr. 21 ***Perf. 13x12½, 12½x13***

48 A49 10c As teenager .30 .25
49 A49 80c As young woman .30 .30
50 A49 $1.75 Red hat .75 .75
51 A49 $3 Tiara, vert. 1.35 1.35
Nos. 48-51 (4) 2.70 2.65

Souvenir Sheet

52 A49 $4 Green print hat 3.00 3.00

1986 World Cup Soccer Championships, Mexico — A7

1c, Italy, 1934. 2c, Italy, 1938. 5c, Uruguay, 1950. 10c, Brazil, 1958. 25c, Argentina vs. Holland, 1978. 40c, Brazil vs. Czechoslovakia, 1962. 50c, Uruguay vs. Argentina, 1930. 75c, West Germany vs. Hungary, 1954. 90c, Brazil, 1970. $1, West Germany, 1974. $2.50, Italy vs. West Germany, 1982. $4, England, 1966.

1986, June 10 ***Perf. 13x12½***

53 A7 1c multicolored .30 .25
54 A7 2c multicolored .30 .25
55 A7 5c multicolored .30 .25
56 A7 10c multicolored .30 .25
57 A7 25c multicolored .30 .25
58 A7 40c multicolored .30 .25
59 A7 50c multicolored .30 .30
60 A7 75c multicolored .30 .30
61 A7 90c multicolored .30 .30
62 A7 $1 multicolored .35 .35
63 A7 $2.50 multicolored .80 .80
64 A7 $4 multicolored 1.20 1.20
Nos. 53-64 (12) 5.05 4.75

Royal Wedding Type of 1986

No. 65, Prince Andrew in jeep, vert. No. 66, Sarah Ferguson, vert. No. 67, Couple. No. 68, Prince Andrew, Princess Anne and parents.

No. 69, Newlyweds.

1986, July 23 ***Perf. 13x12½, 12½x13***

65 A53 60c multicolored .40 .40
66 A53 60c multicolored .40 .40
67 A53 $1 multicolored .65 .65
68 A53 $1 multicolored .65 .65
Nos. 65-68 (4) 2.10 2.10

Souvenir Sheet

69 A56 $4 multicolored 3.50 3.50

Nos. 65-68 Ovptd. in Silver "Congratulations to T.R.H. The Duke & Duchess of York"

#70a, Prince Andrew in jeep. #70b, Sarah Ferguson. #71a, Couple. #71b, Prince Andrew, Princess Anne and parents.

1986, Oct. 28

70 A53 60c Pair, #a.-b. 2.00 2.00
71 A53 $1 Pair, #a.-b. 3.75 3.75

Elizabeth 40th Wedding Anniv. Type

40c, Victoria. 60c, Elizabeth & Philip, wedding portrait. 80c, Elizabeth, Philip & Prince Charles. $1, Elizabeth, Princess Anne. $2, Elizabeth.

$3, Royal family, diff.

1987, Oct. 15 ***Perf. 15***

74 A62 40c multicolored .30 .30
75 A62 60c multicolored .40 .40
76 A62 80c multicolored .50 .50
77 A62 $1 multicolored .60 .60
78 A62 $2 multicolored 1.25 1.25
Nos. 74-78 (5) 3.05 3.05

Souvenir Sheet

79 A62 $3 multicolored 3.00 3.00

Queen Victoria's accession to the throne, 150th anniv.

NIUTAO

Automobile Type of 1984

No. 1, 1930 Bentley 4½ Liter Supercharged, UK. No. 2, 1935 Wolseley Hornet Special, UK.

No. 3, 1920 Crossley 25/30HP, UK. No. 4, 1976 Cadillac Eldorado 7-Liter V-8. No. 5, 1968 Austin Mini Cooper, UK. No. 6, 1958 BMW 507 Cabriolet, W. Germany. No. 7, 1963 Porsche 365C Cabriolet, W. Germany. No. 8, 1971 Tyrrell Ford 001, UK.

Se-tenant Pairs, #a.-b.

a. — Side and front views.

b. — Action scene.

Perf. 12½x13

1984-85 Litho. Unwmk.

1	A41	15c multicolored	.30	.25
2	A41	20c multicolored	.35	.35
3	A41	25c multicolored	.45	.45
4	A41	30c multicolored	.55	.55
5	A41	40c multicolored	.75	.75
6	A41	40c multicolored	.75	.75
7	A41	50c multicolored	.90	.90
8	A41	60c multicolored	1.05	1.05
		Nos. 1-8 (8)	5.10	5.05

Issued: Nos. 1, 4-5, 7, 4/16; Nos. 2-3, 6, 8, 5/2/85.

Locomotive Type of 1984

No. 9, 1830 Planet, UK. No. 10, 1863 Prince, UK. No. 11, 1943 Gordon Austerity Class, UK. No. 12, 1830 Northumbrian, UK. No. 13, 1879 Merddin Emrys, UK. No. 14, 1829 Agenoria, UK. No. 15, 1909 Atchison, Topeka & Santa Fe, 1301. No. 16, 1897 Class 6200, Japan. No. 17, 1938 F.M.S.R. Class O, Malaya. No. 18, 1880 1F, UK. No. 19, 1908 Class E550, Italy. No. 20, 1914 J.N.R. Class 6760, Japan.

Se-tenant Pairs, #a.-b.

a. — Side and front views.

b. — Action scene.

1984-85

9	A36	5c multicolored	.30	.25
10	A36	10c multicolored	.30	.25
11	A36	10c multicolored	.30	.25
12	A36	20c multicolored	.30	.30
13	A36	30c multicolored	.40	.40
14	A36	40c multicolored	.55	.55
15	A36	45c multicolored	.55	.55
16	A36	50c multicolored	.65	.65
17	A36	60c multicolored	.65	.65
18	A36	75c multicolored	.90	.90
19	A36	$1 multicolored	1.35	1.35
20	A36	$1.20 multicolored	1.60	1.60
		Nos. 9-20 (12)	7.85	7.70

Issue dates: Nos. 9-10, 12, 14, 16, 19, Sept. 17; Nos. 11, 13, 15, 18, 20, Aug. 21, 1985.

Cricket Players Type of 1984

1c, S.G. Hinks. 15c, C. Penn. 50c, T.M. Alderman. $1, K.B.S. Jarvis.

Se-tenant Pairs, #a.-b.

a. — Head.

b. — Action scene.

1985, Jan. 7 ***Perf. 13x12½***

21	A39	1c multicolored	.30	.25
22	A39	15c multicolored	.30	.30
23	A39	50c multicolored	1.00	1.00
24	A39	$1 multicolored	1.85	1.85
		Nos. 21-24 (4)	3.45	3.40

Audubon Bicentennial Type

#25a, Purple finch. #25b, White-throated sparrow. #26a, Anna's hummingbird. #26b, Smith's longspur. #27a, White-tailed kite. #27b, Harris' hawk. #28a, Northern oriole. #28b, Great crested flycatcher.

1985, Apr. 4

25	A42	5c Pair, #a.-b.	.30	.25
26	A42	15c Pair, #a.-b.	.30	.30
27	A42	25c Pair, #a.-b.	.50	.50
28	A42	$1 Pair, #a.-b.	2.05	2.05
		Nos. 25-28 (4)	3.15	3.10

Queen Mother Type of 1985

Hat: #37a, Light blue. #37b, Yellow. #38a, 43a, Black. #38b, 43b, Blue. #39a, Tiara. #39b, Pink. #40a, 42a, White. #40b, 42b, Blue. #41a, As young woman. #41b, Feathered.

1985-86

37	A45	15c Pair, #a.-b.	.30	.25
38	A45	35c Pair, #a.-b.	.75	.75
39	A45	70c Pair, #a.-b.	1.60	1.60
40	A45	95c Pair, #a.-b.	2.10	2.10
		Nos. 37-40 (4)	4.75	4.70

Souvenir Sheets

41	A45	$1.05 #a.-b.	1.05	1.05
42	A45	$1.50 #a.-b.	1.50	1.50
43	A45	$4 #a.-b.	3.75	3.75

Issued: #37-41, 9/4; #42-43, 1/10/86.

Elizabeth II 60th Birthday Type

1986, Apr. 21 ***Perf. 13x12½, 12½x13***

44	A49	5c White & gray hat	.30	.25
45	A49	60c Infant	.30	.30
46	A49	$1.50 Flowered white hat	.60	.60
47	A49	$3.50 Tiara, vert.	1.45	1.45
		Nos. 44-47 (4)	2.65	2.60

Souvenir Sheet

48	A49	$5 With tiara, diff.	3.90	3.90

For overprints see Nos. 58-62.

Royal Wedding Type

#51a, Couple, vert. #51b, Sarah Ferguson, vert. #52a, Prince Andrew. #52b, Sarah in evening gown.

1986, July 23 ***Perf. 12½x13, 13x12½***

51	A53	60c Pair, #a.-b.	.75	.75
52	A53	$1 Pair, #a.-b.	1.75	1.75

Souvenir Sheet

53	A56	$4 Newlyweds	3.25	3.25

Nos. 51-52 Ovptd. in Silver "Congratulations to T.R.H. The Duke & Duchess of York"

1986, Oct. 28

54	A53	60c Pair, #a.-b.	2.00	2.00
55	A53	$1 Pair, #a.-b.	3.75	3.75

Nos. 44-48 Ovptd. in Gold "40th WEDDING ANNIVERSARY OF H.M. QUEEN ELIZABETH II"

1987, Mar. ***Perf. 13x12½, 12½x13***

58	A49	5c multicolored	.30	.25
59	A49	60c multicolored	.45	.45
60	A49	$1.50 multicolored	1.15	1.15
61	A49	$3.50 multicolored	2.75	2.75
		Nos. 58-61 (4)	4.65	4.60

Souvenir Sheet

62	A49	$5 multicolored	3.50	3.50

NUI

Locomotives Type of 1984

No. 1, 1911 Class 8800, Japan. No. 2, 1932 Soviet Union Railways Class SU. No. 3, 1847 Jenny Lind Type, UK. No. 4, 1907 Victorian Government Railways Class A2, Australia. No. 5, same, 1950 Class R. No. 6, 1913 Class 9600, Japan. No. 7, 1934 LMS Stanier Tilbury Class 4P, UK. No. 8, 1924 Jinty Class 3, UK. No. 9, 1928 Boston & Albany Class D12. No. 10, 1847 Iron Duke Class, UK. No. 11, 1917 Wabash Railroad Class L. No. 12, 1943 South Australian Government Railways 520 Class. No. 13, 1885 Tennant Class 1463, UK. No. 14, 1947 No. 10000, UK. No. 15, 1848 Padarn Railway Fire Queen, UK. No. 16, 1935 Princess Margaret Rose Class 8P, UK. No. 17, 1932 Soviet Union Railways Class IS. No. 18, 1973 D.B. Class ET403, W. Germany. No. 19, 1916 E. Tenn. & W. N. Carolina R.R. No. 10. No. 20, 1973 D.B. Class 151, W. Germany. No. 21, 1909 Tasmanian Goverment Railways Class K Garratt. No. 22, 1927 B&O President Class. No. 23, 1832 Mohawk & Hudson Railroad Experiment. No. 24, 1934 Union Pacific Railroad, M-10000 Streamliner.

Se-tenant Pairs, #a.-b.

a. — Side and front views.

b. — Action scene.

1984-88 Litho. ***Perf. 12½x13***

1	A36	5c multicolored	.30	.25
2	A36	5c multicolored	.30	.25
3	A36	10c multicolored	.30	.25
4	A36	10c multicolored	.30	.25
5	A36	15c multicolored	.30	.25
6	A36	15c multicolored	.30	.25
7	A36	20c multicolored	.30	.25
8	A36	25c multicolored	.30	.30
9	A36	25c multicolored	.30	.30
10	A36	25c multicolored	.30	.30
11	A36	25c multicolored	.30	.30
12	A36	30c multicolored	.35	.35
13	A36	35c multicolored	.40	.40
14	A36	40c multicolored	.45	.45
15	A36	40c multicolored	.45	.45
16	A36	50c multicolored	.55	.55
17	A36	50c multicolored	.55	.55
18	A36	60c multicolored	.60	.60
19	A36	60c multicolored	.60	.60
20	A36	75c multicolored	.80	.80
21	A36	75c multicolored	.80	.80
22	A36	$1 multicolored	1.10	1.10
23	A36	$1 multicolored	1.10	1.10
24	A36	$1.25 multicolored	1.40	1.40
		Nos. 1-24 (24)	12.45	12.10

Issued: Nos. 5, 8, 12, 16, 3/19; Nos. 1, 6, 9, 22, 2/22/85; Nos. 3, 10, 13, 14, 18, 20, 23, 24, 8/7/87; Nos. 2, 4, 7, 11, 15, 17, 19, 21, 1/29/88.

1987 and 1988 stamps not inscribed "Leaders of the World."

British Monarchs Type of Nanumaga

1984, July 18 ***Perf. 13x12½***

Se-tenant Pairs, #a.-b.

25	A2	1c Queen Anne	.30	.25
26	A2	5c Henry V	.30	.25
27	A2	15c Henry V, diff.	.30	.25
28	A2	40c Queen Anne, diff.	.45	.45
29	A2	50c Queen Anne, diff.	.60	.60
30	A2	$1 Henry V, diff.	1.00	1.00
		Nos. 25-30 (6)	2.95	2.80

Automobile Type of 1984

No. 31, 1909 Buick. No. 32, 1966 Oldsmobile Toronado. No. 33, 1947 Railton Mobil Special, UK. No. 34, 1924 Opel Laubfrosch, Germany. No. 35, 1966 Jensen FF, UK. No. 36, 1963 Lotus-Climax GP MK 25, UK. No. 37, 1910 Delaunay Belleville, France. No. 38, 1956 Jensen 541, UK. No. 39, 1924 Hispano-Suiza H6 Boulogne, France. No. 40, 1972 Citroen-Maserati S.M. Coupe, France.

Se-tenant Pairs, #a.-b.

a. — Side and front views.

b. — Action scene.

1985 ***Perf. 12½x13***

31	A41	5c multicolored	.30	.25
32	A41	15c multicolored	.30	.30
33	A41	25c multicolored	.55	.55
34	A41	30c multicolored	.55	.55
35	A41	40c multicolored	.75	.75
36	A41	40c multicolored	.75	.75
37	A41	50c multicolored	1.05	1.05
38	A41	60c multicolored	1.15	1.15
39	A41	90c multicolored	1.70	1.70
40	A41	$1.10 multicolored	2.10	2.10
		Nos. 31-40 (10)	9.20	9.15

Issued: #33-35, 37, 4/2; #31-32, 36, 38-40, 10/9.

Cricket Players Type of 1984

1c, S.C. Goldsmith. 40c, S.N.V. Waterton. 60c, A. Sidebottom. 70c, A.A. Metcalfe.

Se-tenant Pairs, #a.-b.

1985, May 27 ***Perf. 13x12½***

41	A39	1c multicolored	.30	.25
42	A39	40c multicolored	.50	.50
43	A39	60c multicolored	.75	.75
44	A39	70c multicolored	1.00	1.00
		Nos. 41-44 (4)	2.55	2.50

Queen Mother Type of 1985

#49a, 54a, Purple. #49b, 54b, Tiara. #50a, Light blue. #50b, Lavender. #51a, Violet. #51b, White. #52a, 55a, Light blue. #52b, 55b, Tiara. #53a, White. #53b, Black.

1985-86

49	A45	5c Pair, #a.-b.	.30	.25
50	A45	50c Pair, #a.-b.	.90	.90
51	A45	75c Pair, #a.-b.	1.40	1.40
52	A45	85c Pair, #a.-b.	1.60	1.60
		Nos. 49-52 (4)	4.20	4.15

Souvenir Sheets of 2

53	A45	$1.15 #a.-b.	2.50	2.50
54	A45	$1.50 #a.-b.	2.00	2.00
55	A45	$3.50 #a.-b.	4.50	4.50

Issued: #49-53, 9/4; 54-55, 1/8/86.

Elizabeth II 60th Birthday Type

1986, Apr. 21 ***Perf. 13x12½, 12½x13***

56	A49	10c Feathered hat	.30	.25
57	A49	80c As young woman	.45	.45
58	A49	$1.75 Tiara	.85	.85
59	A49	$3 Tiara, diff., vert.	1.50	1.50
		Nos. 56-59 (4)	3.10	3.05

Souvenir Sheet

60	A49	$4 Portrait	3.25	3.25

Royal Wedding Type of 1986

#63a, Couple, vert. #63b, Prince Andrew, vert. #64a, Couple, Queen Elizabeth II. #64b, Andrew as young boy.

1986, July 23 ***Perf. 12½x13, 13x12½***

63	A53	60c Pair, #a.-b.	.85	.85
64	A53	$1 Pair, #a.-b.	1.15	1.15

Souvenir Sheet

65	A56	$4 Sarah in wedding dress	4.00	4.00

Nos. 63-64 Ovptd. in Silver "Congratulations to T.R.H. The Duke & Duchess of York"

1986, Oct. 28

66	A53	60c Pair, #a.-b.	1.90	1.90
67	A53	$1 Pair, #a.-b.	3.50	3.50

Elizabeth 40th Wedding Anniv. Type of Funafuti

1987, Oct. 15 ***Perf. 15***

70	A1	20c Queen Victoria	.30	.25
71	A1	50c George VI, Family	.35	.35
72	A1	75c Elizabeth	.50	.50
73	A1	$1.20 Elizabeth, Philip	.80	.80
74	A1	$1.75 Elizabeth, diff.	1.20	1.20
		Nos. 70-74 (5)	3.15	3.10

Souvenir Sheet

75	A1	$3 Elizabeth, Family	2.25	2.25

Queen Victoria's accession to the throne, sesquicentennial.

NUKUFETAU

Automobile Type of 1984

No. 1, 1904 Mercedes 28 PS, Germany. No. 2, 1966 Ford GT40 Mark II. No. 3, 1911 Vauxhall Prince Henry, UK. No. 4, 1956 Lincoln Continental Mark II. No. 5, 1950 Bristol 400, UK. No. 6, 1913 Morris Oxford "Bullnose," UK. No. 7, 1923 Austin Seven Tourer. No. 8, 1921 Bugatti Type 13 "Brescia," France. No. 9, 1967 Monteverdi, Switzerland. No. 10, 1925 Lancia Lambda, Italy. No. 11, 1938 Panhard Dynamic, France. No. 12, 1960 A.C. Ace, UK. No. 13, 1950 Land Rover Model 80, UK.

Se-tenant Pairs, #a.-b.

a. — Side and front views.

b. — Action scene.

Perf. 12½x13

1984-85 Litho. Unwmk.

1	A41	5c multicolored	.30	.25
2	A41	10c multicolored	.30	.25
3	A41	10c multicolored	.30	.25
4	A41	15c multicolored	.30	.25
5	A41	20c multicolored	.30	.30
6	A41	25c multicolored	.50	.50
7	A41	30c multicolored	.55	.55
8	A41	50c multicolored	1.00	1.00
9	A41	50c multicolored	1.00	1.00
10	A41	60c multicolored	1.00	1.00
11	A41	60c multicolored	1.00	1.00
12	A41	75c multicolored	1.15	1.15
13	A41	$1.50 multicolored	2.75	2.75
		Nos. 1-13 (13)	10.45	10.25

Issued; #2, 6-8, 10, 5/23; others, 6/26/85.

British Monarchs Type of Nanumaga

1984, Nov. 27 ***Perf. 13x12½***

Se-tenant Pairs, #a.-b.

14	A2	1c Mary II	.30	.30
15	A2	10c Mary II, diff.	.30	.30
16	A2	30c Mary II, diff.	.35	.35
17	A2	50c Henry IV	.60	.60
18	A2	60c Henry IV, diff.	.65	.65
19	A2	$1 Henry IV, diff.	1.05	1.05
		Nos. 14-19 (6)	3.25	3.25

Cricket Players Type of 1984

1985, Jan. 7

Se-tenant Pairs, #a.-b.

20	A39	1c D.G. Aslett	.30	.25
21	A39	10c N.R. Taylor	.30	.25
22	A39	55c S. Oldham	.60	.60
23	A39	$1 C.W.J. Athey	1.30	1.30
		Nos. 20-23 (4)	2.50	2.40

Locomotive Type of 1984

No. 24, 1900 Class XV, Germany. No. 25, 1859 ECR Class Y, UK. No. 26, 1923 Nord Super Pacific, France. No. 27, 1905 LNWR Experiment Class, UK. No. 28, 1941 SR Merchant Navy Class, UK. No. 29, 1830 S. Carolina Railroad Best Friend of Charleston. No. 30, 1941 SR No. 1, UK. No. 31, 1987 Class 89, UK. No. 32, 1923 Southern Pacific Railroad Class 4300, US. No. 33, 1956 New South Wales Government Railways Class 46. No. 34, 1953 D.B. Class V200, Germany. No. 35, 1936 Union Railroad Class S-7, US. No. 36, 1877 Phildelphia & Reading Railroad Camelback. No. 37, 1968 J.N.R. Class 381, Japan. No. 38, 1933 Rio Grande Southern Railroad Galloping Goose Railcar, US. No. 39, 1935 Chicago, Milwaukee, St. Paul & Pacific Class A.

Se-tenant Pairs, #a.-b.

a. — Side and front views.

b. — Action scene.

1985-88

24	A36	1c multicolored	.30	.25
25	A36	5c multicolored	.30	.25
26	A36	10c multicolored	.30	.25
27	A36	10c multicolored	.30	.25
28	A36	15c multicolored	.30	.30
29	A36	20c multicolored	.40	.40
30	A36	25c multicolored	.55	.55
31	A36	30c multicolored	.65	.65

32 A36 40c multicolored .85 .85
33 A36 50c multicolored 1.10 1.10
34 A36 60c multicolored 1.25 1.25
35 A36 60c multicolored 1.25 1.25
36 A36 60c multicolored 1.25 1.25
37 A36 70c multicolored 1.50 1.50
38 A36 $1 multicolored 2.25 2.25
a. Souvenir sheet of 2 2.50 2.50
39 A36 $1.50 multicolored 3.25 3.25
Nos. 24-39 (16) 15.80 15.60

Issued: Nos. 24, 26, 34, 37, 4/2/85; Nos. 29, 32, 35, 39, 3/20/86; Nos. 25, 27-28, 30-31, 33, 36, 38, 38a, 9/10/87.

1986 and 1987 stamps not inscribed "Leaders of the World."

Queen Mother Type of 1985

Hat: #44a, Wide-brimmed blue. #44b, Tiara. #45a, Tiara. #45b, Lavender. #46a, Blue. #46b, White stole. #47a, 50a, White. #47b, 50b, Blue. #48a, 49a, White. #48b, 49b, Wide-brimmed.

1985, Sept. 5 *Perf. 13x12½*
44 A45 10c Pair, #a.-b. .30 .25
45 A45 45c Pair, #a.-b. .80 .80
46 A45 65c Pair, #a.-b. 1.10 1.10
47 A45 $1 Pair, #a.-b. 1.75 1.75
Nos. 44-47 (4) 3.95 3.90

Souvenir Sheets of 2
48 A45 $1.10 #a.-b. 2.00 2.00
49 A45 $1.75 #a.-b. 2.25 2.25
50 A45 $3 #a.-b. 3.25 3.25

Elizabeth II 60th Birthday Type

1986, Apr. 21 *Perf. 13x12½, 12½x13*
51 A49 5c Scarf .30 .25
52 A49 40c Tiara .30 .25
53 A49 $2 Bareheaded .70 .70
54 A49 $4 Tiara, vert. 1.75 1.75
Nos. 51-54 (4) 3.05 2.95

Souvenir Sheet
55 A49 $5 Blue hat 3.00 3.00

For overprints see Nos. 65-69.

Royal Wedding Type of 1986

#58a, Couple, vert. #58b, Andrew, vert. #59a, Andrew, parents. #59b, Andrew.

1986, July 22
58 A53 60c Pair, #a.-b. 1.00 1.00
59 A53 $1 Pair, #a.-b. 1.50 1.50

Souvenir Sheet
60 A56 $4 Wedding ceremony 4.00 4.00

Nos. 58-59 Ovptd. in Silver "Congratulations to T.R.H. The Duke & Duchess of York"

1986, Oct. 28
61 A53 60c Pair, #a.-b. 2.00 2.00
62 A53 $1 Pair, #a.-b. 3.50 3.50

Nos. 51-55 Ovptd. in Gold "40th WEDDING ANNIVERSARY OF H.M. QUEEN ELIZABETH II"

1987, Oct. 15
65 A49 5c multicolored .30 .25
66 A49 40c multicolored .30 .30
67 A49 $2 multicolored 1.00 1.00
68 A49 $4 multicolored 1.95 1.95
Nos. 65-68 (4) 3.55 3.50

Souvenir Sheet
69 A49 $5 multicolored 3.25 3.25

NUKULAELAE

Locomotive Type of 1984

No. 1, 1891 Calbourne Class 02, UK. No. 2, 1912 K.P.E.V. Class T18, Germany. No. 3, 1942 SNCF Class 141P, France. No. 4, 1962 Class 47, UK. No. 5, 1941 Union Pacific Big Boy, US. No. 6, 1955 DRB 83-10, Germany. No. 7, 1940 S.N.C.F. 160-A-1, France. No. 8, 1901 Class AEG High Speed Railcar, Germany. No. 9, 1839 Albion Railroad Samson, Canada. No. 10, 1907 Saint Class, UK. No. 11, 1900 Nord De Glehn Atlantic, France. No. 12, 1851 Folkstone Class, UK. No. 13, 1914 J.N.R. Class 8620, Japan. No. 14, 1936 Class 8F, UK. No. 15, 1857 Shannon, UK. No. 16, 1948 Class A1, UK. No. 17, 1955 E.A.R. Class 59, Kenya. No. 18, 1897 V.R. Class Na, Australia. No. 19, 1859 Undine Class, UK. No. 20, 1935 Turbomotive, UK.

Se-tenant Pairs, #a.-b.
a. — Side and front views.
b. — Action scene.

Perf. 12½x13
1984-86 Litho. Unwmk.
1 A36 5c multicolored .30 .25
2 A36 5c multicolored .30 .25
3 A36 10c multicolored .30 .25
4 A36 10c multicolored .30 .25
5 A36 15c multicolored .30 .25
6 A36 15c multicolored .30 .25
7 A36 20c multicolored .30 .25
8 A36 25c multicolored .30 .25
9 A36 25c multicolored .30 .25
10 A36 40c multicolored .45 .45
11 A36 40c multicolored .45 .45
12 A36 40c multicolored .45 .45
13 A36 50c multicolored .55 .55
14 A36 50c multicolored .55 .55
15 A36 80c multicolored .95 .95
16 A36 $1 multicolored 1.20 1.20
17 A36 $1 multicolored 1.20 1.20
18 A36 $1 multicolored 1.20 1.20
19 A36 $1 multicolored 1.20 1.20
20 A36 $1.50 multicolored 1.75 1.75
Nos. 1-20 (20) 12.65 12.20

Issued: Nos. 1, 5, 10, 16, 5/23; Nos. 2, 7, 11, 17, 12/12; Nos. 3, 8, 13, 18, 3/24/85; Nos. 4, 6, 9, 12, 14, 15, 19-20, 7/11/86.

1986 stamps not inscribed "Leaders of the World."

Cricket Players Type of 1984

1984, Aug. 8 *Perf. 13x12½*
Se-tenant Pairs, #a.-b.
21 A39 5c D.B. Close .30 .25
22 A39 15c G. Boycott .30 .25
23 A39 30c D.L. Bairstow .45 .45
24 A39 $1 T.G. Evans 1.25 1.25
Nos. 21-24 (4) 2.30 2.20

Automobile Type of 1984

No. 25, 1924 Bugatti Type 35, France. No. 26, 1908 Sizaire-Naudin, France. No. 27, 1965 Sunbeam Tiger, UK. No. 28, 1907 Napier 60HP Touring Car, UK. No. 29, 1975 BMW 2002 TII, Germany. No. 30, 1910 Austro-Daimler Prince Henry, Austria. No. 31, 1927 La Salle, US. No. 32, 1901 Oldsmobile Curved Dash Buckboard. No. 33, 1955 Rover 90, UK. No. 34, 1948 Chrysler Town & Country.

Se-tenant Pairs, #a.-b.
a. — Side and front views.
b. — Action scene.

1985 *Perf. 12½x13*
25 A41 5c multicolored .30 .25
26 A41 10c multicolored .30 .25
27 A41 25c multicolored .40 .40
28 A41 35c multicolored .60 .60
29 A41 35c multicolored .60 .60
30 A41 50c multicolored .85 .85
31 A41 50c multicolored .85 .85
32 A41 70c multicolored 1.10 1.10
33 A41 75c multicolored 1.25 1.25
34 A41 $1 multicolored 1.45 1.45
Nos. 25-34 (10) 7.70 7.60

Issue dates: Nos. 25, 28, 30, 32, Feb. 8; Nos. 26-27, 29, 31, 33-34, July 23.

Dogs
A8

#35a, Hungarian vizsla. #35b, Bearded collie. #36a, Bernese mountain dog. #36b, Boxer. #37a, Labrador retriever. #37b, Shetland sheepdog. #38a, Welsh springer spaniel. #38b, Scottish terrier.

1985, Apr. 30
35 A8 5c Pair, #a.-b. .30 .25
36 A8 20c Pair, #a.-b. .35 .35
37 A8 50c Pair, #a.-b. .90 .90
38 A8 70c Pair, #a.-b. 1.25 1.25
Nos. 35-38 (4) 2.80 2.75

Queen Mother Type of 1985

Hat: #47a, Purple. #47b, Blue. #48a, 52a, Tiara. #48b, 52b, Lavender. #49a, 53a, Pink. #49b, 53b, Dark blue. #50a, Light purple. #50b, Light blue. #51a, As young girl. #51b, Lace.

1985-86
47 A45 5c Pair, #a.-b. .30 .25
48 A45 25c Pair, #a.-b. .45 .45
49 A45 85c Pair, #a.-b. 1.60 1.60
50 A45 $1 Pair, #a.-b. 2.00 2.00
Nos. 47-50 (4) 4.35 4.30

Souvenir Sheets of 2
51 A45 $1.20 #a.-b. 1.75 1.75
52 A45 $1.20 #a.-b. 1.50 1.50
53 A45 $3.50 #a.-b. 4.75 4.75

Issued: #46-51, 9/4; #52-53, 1/8/86.

Elizabeth II 60th Birthday Type

1986, Apr. 21 *Perf. 13x12½, 12½x13*
54 A49 10c White hat .30 .25
55 A49 $1 As young woman .55 .55
56 A49 $1.50 In orange dress .85 .85
57 A49 $3 Tiara, vert. 1.50 1.50
Nos. 54-57 (4) 3.20 3.15

Souvenir Sheet
58 A49 $4 In brown dress 3.00 3.00

Royal Wedding Type of 1986

#61a, Andrew, vert. #61b, Couple, vert. #62a, Sarah Ferguson and Princess Diana. #62b, Andrew.

1986, July 23 *Perf. 12½x13, 13x12½*
61 A53 60c Pair, #a.-b. 1.10 1.10
62 A53 $1 Pair, #a.-b. 1.75 1.75

Souvenir Sheet
63 A56 $4 Sarah in wedding dress 4.50 4.50

Nos. 61-62 Ovptd. in Silver "Congratulations to T.R.H. The Duke & Duchess of York"

1986, Oct. 28
64 A53 60c Pair, #a.-b. 2.00 2.00
65 A53 $1 Pair, #a.-b. 3.25 3.25

Queen Elizabeth II 40th Wedding Anniv. Type of Nanumaga

15c, Queen Victoria. 35c, Princesses Margaret and Elizabeth. 60c, Elizabeth holding Princess Anne. $1.50, Elizabeth, Philip. $1.75, Elizabeth wearing tiara.
$3, Elizabeth.

1987, Oct. 15 *Perf. 15*
68 A5 15c multicolored .30 .25
69 A5 35c multicolored .50 .50
70 A5 60c multicolored .75 .75
71 A5 $1.50 multicolored 2.10 2.10
72 A5 $1.75 multicolored 2.40 2.40
Nos. 68-72 (5) 6.05 6.00

Souvenir Sheet
73 A5 $3 multicolored 4.00 4.00

Queen Victoria's accession to the throne, sesquicentennial.

VAITUPU

Automobile Type of 1984

No. 1, 1961 Lotus Elite, UK. No. 2, 1950 MG TD Midget, UK. No. 3, 1932 Hillman Minx, UK. No. 4, 1905 White Model E Steam Car, US. No. 5, 1935 Auburn Supercharged 851, US. No. 6, 1981 Renault RE20, France. No. 7, 1928 Lea-Francis Hyper. No. 8, 1940 Packard Darrin. No. 9, 1938 Graham, US. No. 10, 1968 Chevrolet Camaro. No. 11, 1957 Renault Dauphine-Gordini, France. No. 12, 1930 Packard Eight. No. 13, 1926 Miller Special, US. No. 14, 1950 Healey Silverstone, UK. No. 15, 1970 De Tomaso Pantera, Italy. No. 16, 1927 Bentley 3-Liter, UK.

Se-tenant Pairs, #a.-b.
a. — Side and front views.
b. — Action scene.

Perf. 12½x13
1984-85 Litho. Unwmk.
1 A41 5c multicolored .30 .25
2 A41 15c multicolored .30 .25
3 A41 15c multicolored .30 .25
4 A41 15c multicolored .30 .25
5 A41 25c multicolored .30 .25
6 A41 25c multicolored .30 .25
7 A41 30c multicolored .30 .25
8 A41 30c multicolored .30 .25
9 A41 30c multicolored .30 .25
10 A41 40c multicolored .35 .35
11 A41 40c multicolored .35 .35
12 A41 50c multicolored .45 .45
13 A41 50c multicolored .45 .45
14 A41 60c multicolored .55 .55
15 A41 60c multicolored .55 .55
16 A41 $1 multicolored .90 .90
Nos. 1-16 (16) 6.30 5.85

Issued: Nos. 2, 5, 7, 12, Mar. 19; Nos. 1, 3, 6, 8, 10, 13-14, 16, Dec. 12; Nos. 4, 9, 11, 15, Apr. 4, 1985.

British Monarchs Type of Nanumaga

1984, July 18 *Perf. 13x12½*
Se-tenant Pairs, #a.-b.
17 A2 1c Richard III .30 .25
18 A2 5c Charles I .30 .25
19 A2 15c Charles I, diff. .30 .25
20 A2 40c Richard III, diff. .50 .50
21 A2 50c Richard III, diff. .60 .60
22 A2 $1 Charles I, diff. 1.15 1.15
Nos. 17-22 (6) 3.15 3.00

Locomotive Type of 1984

No. 23, 1929 D.R.G. V3201, Germany. No. 24, 1841 G.W.R. Leo Class, UK. No. 25, 1937 New York Central Railroad Class J3a. No. 26, 1949 Richmond, Fredericksburg & Potomac Railroad Class E8. No. 27, 1845 Columbine, UK. No. 28, 1954 BR Class 2MT, UK. No. 29, 1980 Amtrak Class AEM-7. No. 30, 1981 Via Rail LRC Class MPA-27a, Canada. No. 31, 1983 British Columbia Railway Class GF6C. No. 32, 1888 D&H Class B, India. No. 33, 1936 D.R. Class 45, Germany. No. 34, 1904 Northern Pacific Railway Class W, US. No. 35, 1855 W. & A. R.R. General, US. No. 36, 1938 Chicago & North Western Railway Class E-4. No. 37, 1911 J.N.R. Class 9020 Mallet, Japan. No. 38, 1977 Chicago Regional Transportation Authority Class F40.

Se-tenant Pairs, #a.-b.
a. — Side and front views.
b. — Action scene.

1985-87 *Perf. 12½x13*
23 A36 5c multicolored .30 .25
24 A36 10c multicolored .30 .25
25 A36 10c multicolored .30 .25
26 A36 15c multicolored .30 .30
27 A36 25c multicolored .55 .55
28 A36 25c multicolored .55 .55
29 A36 25c multicolored .55 .55
30 A36 35c multicolored .75 .75
31 A36 45c multicolored .95 .95
32 A36 50c multicolored 1.10 1.10
33 A36 60c multicolored 1.25 1.25
34 A36 65c multicolored 1.40 1.40
35 A36 80c multicolored 1.75 1.75
36 A36 85c multicolored 1.90 1.90
37 A36 $1 multicolored 2.25 2.25
38 A36 $1 multicolored 2.25 2.25
Nos. 23-38 (16) 16.45 16.30

Issued: Nos. 24, 27, 32-33, 3/7/85; Nos. 23, 28, 35, 37, 1/16/86; Nos. 25-26, 29-31, 34, 36, 38, 9/10/87.

1986 and 1987 stamps not inscribed "Leaders of the World."

A9

Butterfly illustrations by Roger V. Vigurs: #39a, Marpesia petreus. #39b, Pseudolycaena marsyas. #40a, Charaxes jasius. #40b, Junonia coenia. #41a, Palaeochrysophanus hippothoe. #41b, Sticopthalma camadeva. #42a, Phoebis avellaneda. #42b, Apatura iris.

1985, Mar. 12 *Perf. 13x12½*
39 A9 5c Pair, #a.-b. .30 .25
40 A9 15c Pair, #a.-b. .30 .30
41 A9 50c Pair, #a.-b. 1.00 1.00
42 A9 75c Pair, #a.-b. 1.60 1.60
Nos. 39-42 (4) 3.20 3.15

Queen Mother Type of 1985

Hat: #51a, 57a, Light blue. #51b, 57b, White. #52a, Tiara. #52b, Lavender. #53a, 56a, Violet. #53b, 56b, Green. #54a, Blue. #54b, Pink. #55a, Looking up. #55b, Looking forward.

1985-86
51 A45 15c Pair, #a.-b. .30 .25
52 A45 40c Pair, #a.-b. .75 .75
53 A45 65c Pair, #a.-b. 1.10 1.10
54 A45 95c Pair, #a.-b. 1.90 1.90
Nos. 51-54 (4) 4.05 4.00

Souvenir Sheets of 2
55 A45 $1.10 #a.-b. 2.10 2.10
56 A45 $2 #a.-b. 2.25 2.25
57 A45 $2.50 #a.-b. 3.00 3.00

Issued: #51-55, 8/28; 56-57, 1/8/86.

Elizabeth II 60th Birthday Type

1986, Apr. 21 ***Perf. 13x12½, 12½x13***

No.	Type	Description	Unused	Used
58	A49	5c Green hat	.30	.25
59	A49	60c As young woman	.30	.25
60	A49	$2 Flowered hat	.65	.65
61	A49	$3.50 Tiara, vert.	1.05	1.05
		Nos. 58-61 (4)	2.30	2.20

Souvenir Sheet

No.	Type	Description	Unused	Used
62	A49	$5 Straw hat	3.00	3.00

For overprints see Nos. 72-76.

Royal Wedding Type of 1986

#65a, Andrew, vert. #65b, Sarah Ferguson, vert. #66a, Charles, Andrew. #66b, Couple.

1986, July 18 ***Perf. 12½x13, 13x12½***

No.	Type	Description	Unused	Used
65	A53	60c Pair, #a.-b.	1.10	1.10
66	A53	$1 Pair, #a.-b.	1.75	1.75

Souvenir Sheet

No.	Type	Description	Unused	Used
67	A56	$4 Newlyweds	4.00	4.00

Nos. 65-66 Ovptd. in Silver "Congratulations to T.R.H. The Duke & Duchess of York"

1986, Oct. 28

No.	Type	Description	Unused	Used
68	A53	60c Pair, #a.-b.	2.00	2.00
69	A53	$1 Pair, #a.-b.	3.00	3.00

Nos. 58-62 Ovptd. in Gold "40th WEDDING ANNIVERSARY OF H.M. QUEEN ELIZABETH II"

1987, Oct. 15 ***Perf. 13x12½, 12½x13***

No.	Type	Description	Unused	Used
72	A49	5c multicolored	.30	.25
73	A49	60c multicolored	.40	.40
74	A49	$2 multicolored	1.40	1.40
75	A49	$3 multicolored	2.10	2.10
		Nos. 72-75 (4)	4.20	4.15

Souvenir Sheet

No.	Type	Description	Unused	Used
76	A49	$5 multicolored	4.00	4.00

UBANGI-SHARI

ü-'baŋ-gē 'shär-ē

(Ubangi-Shari-Chad)

LOCATION — In Western Africa, north of the equator
GOVT. — French Colony
AREA — 238,767 sq. mi.
POP. — 833,916
CAPITAL — Bangui

In 1910 French Congo was divided into the three colonies of Gabon, Middle Congo and Ubangi-Shari and officially named "French Equatorial Africa." Under that name in 1934 the group, with the territory of Chad included, became a single administrative unit. See Gabon.

100 Centimes = 1 Franc

Stamps of Middle Congo Ovptd. in Black

1915-22 **Unwmk.** ***Perf. 14x13½***

Chalky Paper

No.	Type	Description	Unused	Used
1	A1	1c ol gray & brn	.35	.70
a.		Double overprint	190.00	
b.		Imperf.	60.00	
2	A1	2c violet & brn	.35	.70
3	A1	4c blue & brn	.70	.70
4	A1	5c dk grn & bl	.70	1.00
5	A1	5c yel & bl ('22)	1.00	1.40
6	A1	10c carmine & bl	1.40	1.00
7	A1	10c dp grn & bl grn ('22)	1.00	1.40
8	A1	15c brn vio & rose	1.75	2.10
9	A1	20c brown & blue	3.50	4.25

No. 8 is on ordinary paper

Overprinted

No.	Type	Description	Unused	Used
10	A2	25c blue & grn	2.10	2.10
11	A2	25c bl grn & gray ('22)	1.40	1.40
12	A2	30c scarlet & grn	2.10	2.10
13	A2	30c dp rose & rose ('22)	1.00	1.40
14	A2	35c vio brn & bl	5.50	5.50
15	A2	40c dl grn & brn	5.50	7.00
16	A2	45c vio & red	5.50	7.00
17	A2	50c bl grn & red	7.00	7.00
18	A2	50c blue & grn ('22)	1.00	1.40
19	A2	75c brown & bl	14.00	14.00
20	A3	1fr dp grn & vio	14.00	14.00
21	A3	2fr vio & gray grn	14.00	17.50
22	A3	5fr blue & rose	42.50	42.50
		Nos. 1-22 (22)	126.35	136.15

For surcharges see Nos. B1-B2.

Middle Congo of 1907-22 Ovptd. in Black or Red

1922

No.	Type	Description	Unused	Used
23	A1	1c violet & grn	.70	1.00
a.		Overprint omitted	170.00	190.00
b.		Imperf.	40.00	
24	A1	2c grn & salmon	.70	1.00
25	A1	4c ol brn & brn	1.00	1.40
a.		Overprint omitted	200.00	225.00
26	A1	5c indigo & rose	1.00	1.40
27	A1	10c dp grn & gray grn	1.75	2.10
28	A1	15c lt red & dl bl	1.75	2.10
29	A1	20c choc & salmon	5.00	5.50

Overprinted

No.	Type	Description	Unused	Used
30	A2	25c vio & salmon	7.00	8.50
31	A2	30c rose & pale rose	2.75	3.50
32	A2	35c vio & grn	4.75	5.00
33	A2	40c ind & vio (R)	4.75	5.00
34	A2	45c choc & vio	4.75	5.00
35	A2	50c dk bl & pale bl	2.75	3.50
36	A2	60c on 75c vio, *pnksh*	3.50	4.25
37	A2	75c choc & sal	5.00	6.25
38	A3	1fr grn & dl bl (R)	10.50	11.00
a.		Overprint omitted	275.00	
39	A3	2fr grn & salmon	14.00	14.00
40	A3	5fr grn & ol brn	21.00	25.00
		Nos. 23-40 (18)	92.65	105.50

Nos. 23-29 with Additional Ovpt. in Black, Blue or Red

1924-33

No.	Type	Description	Unused	Used
41	A1	1c vio & grn (Bl)	.35	.50
a.		"OUBANGUI CHARI" omitted	140.00	140.00
42	A1	2c grn & sal (Bl)	.35	.55
a.		"OUBANGUI CHARI" omitted	140.00	140.00
b.		Double overprint	150.00	
43	A1	4c ol brn & brn (Bl)	.35	.55
a.		Double overprint (Bl + Bk)	175.00	
b.		"AEF" omitted	160.00	
44	A1	5c ind & rose	.35	.55
a.		"OUBANGUI CHARI" omitted	130.00	
45	A1	10c dp grn & gray grn	.70	.85
46	A1	10c red org & bl ('25)	.70	.70
47	A1	15c sal & dl bl	.80	.85
48	A1	15c sal & dl bl (Bl) ('26)	1.00	1.40
49	A1	20c choc & salmon (Bl)	1.25	1.40

On Nos. 41-49 the color in ( ) refers to the overprint "Afrique Equatoriale Francaise."

Overprinted

No.	Type	Description	Unused	Used
50	A2	25c vio & salmon (Bl)	.70	.70
a.		Imperf.		
51	A2	30c rose & pale rose (Bl)	.70	1.00
52	A2	30c choc & red ('25)	.70	1.00
a.		"OUBANGUI CHARI" omitted	140.00	
53	A2	30c dk grn & grn ('27)	1.40	1.75
54	A2	35c vio & grn (Bl)	.70	1.00
a.		"OUBANGUI CHARI" omitted	275.00	
55	A2	40c ind & vio (Bl)	.70	1.00
56	A2	45c choc & vio (Bl)	1.00	1.40
57	A2	50c dk bl & pale bl (R)	.70	.70
58	A2	50c gray & bl vio ('25) (R)	1.40	1.40
59	A2	60c on 75c dk vio, *pnksh* (R)	.70	.55
60	A2	65c org brn & bl ('28)	1.40	1.75
61	A2	75c choc & sal (Bl)	1.75	2.10
62	A2	75c dp bl & lt bl ('25) (R)	1.40	1.40
a.		"OUBANGUI CHARI" omitted	140.00	
63	A2	75c rose & dk brn ('28)	2.10	2.50
64	A2	90c brn red & pink ('30)	4.25	5.00
65	A3	1fr grn & ind (Bk + Bl) ('25)	.70	1.00
66	A3	1fr grn & ind (R + Bl)	1.40	2.10
67	A3	1.10fr bister & bl ('28)	3.50	3.50
68	A3	1.25fr mag & lt grn ('33)	10.50	10.50
69	A3	1.50fr ultra & bl ('30)	7.00	7.00
70	A3	1.75fr dk brn & dp buff ('33)	10.50	14.00
71	A3	2fr grn & red	1.40	2.10
a.		"OUBANGUI CHARI" omitted	1,250.	1,050.
b.		"OUBANGUI CHARI" double	1,200.	
72	A3	3fr red vio ('30)	5.00	5.50
73	A3	5fr grn & ol brn (Bl)	4.50	5.50
		Nos. 41-73 (33)	69.95	81.80

On Nos. 65, 66 the first overprint color refers to OUBANGUI CHARI.

For surcharges see Nos. 74-81.

Types of 1924 Issue Surcharged with New Values in Black or Red

1925-26

No.	Type	Description	Unused	Used
74	A3	65c on 1fr vio & ol	2.10	2.10
a.		"65" omitted	140.00	
75	A3	85c on 1fr vio & ol	2.10	2.10
a.		"AFRIQUE EQUATORIALE FRANCAISE" omitted	140.00	160.00
b.		Double surcharge	160.00	
76	A3	1.25fr on 1fr dk bl & ultra (R) ('26)	1.40	2.25
a.		"1f25" omitted	165.00	

Bars cover old denomination on No. 76.

Types of 1924 Issue Surcharged with New Values and Bars

1927

No.	Type	Description	Unused	Used
77	A2	90c on 75c brn red & rose red	2.10	2.75
78	A3	1.50fr on 1fr ultra & bl	2.10	2.75
79	A3	3fr on 5fr org brn & dl red	3.50	3.50
80	A3	10fr on 5fr ver & vio	17.50	19.00
81	A3	20fr on 5fr vio & gray	27.50	29.00
		Nos. 77-81 (5)	52.70	57.00

Common Design Types pictured following the introduction.

Colonial Exposition Issue

Common Design Types

1931 **Engr.** ***Perf. 12½***

Name of Country Typo. in Black

No.	Type	Description	Unused	Used
82	CD70	40c deep green	5.00	5.00
83	CD71	50c violet	5.00	5.00
84	CD72	90c red orange	5.50	5.50
a.		Imperf.	120.00	
85	CD73	1.50fr dull blue	5.50	5.50
		Nos. 82-85 (4)	21.00	21.00

SEMI-POSTAL STAMPS

Regular Issue of 1915 Surcharged

1916 **Unwmk.** ***Perf. 14x13½***

Chalky Paper

No.	Type	Description	Unused	Used
B1	A1	10c + 5c car & blue	2.75	3.25
a.		Inverted surch.		160.00
b.		Double surcharge		160.00
c.		Double surch., one invtd.	125.00	125.00
d.		Vertical surcharge	140.00	140.00
e.		No period under "C"	17.50	17.50

Regular Issue of 1915 Surcharged in Carmine

No.	Type	Description	Unused	Used
B2	A1	10c + 5c car & blue	1.75	2.10

POSTAGE DUE STAMPS

Postage Due Stamps of France Overprinted

1928 **Unwmk.** ***Perf. 14x13½***

No.	Type	Description	Unused	Used
J1	D2	5c light blue	1.40	2.10
J2	D2	10c gray brown	1.75	2.10
J3	D2	20c olive green	1.75	2.10
J4	D2	25c bright rose	1.75	2.10
J5	D2	30c light red	1.75	2.10
J6	D2	45c blue green	1.75	2.10
J7	D2	50c brown violet	2.50	3.50
J8	D2	60c yellow brown	2.75	3.50
J9	D2	1fr red brown	3.50	5.00
J10	D2	2fr orange red	7.00	7.00
J11	D2	3fr bright violet	7.00	7.00
		Nos. J1-J11 (11)	32.90	38.60

Landscape — D3

Emile Gentil — D4

1930 **Typo.**

No.	Type	Description	Unused	Used
J12	D3	5c dp bl & olive	.70	1.05
J13	D3	10c dk red & brn	1.05	1.40
J14	D3	20c green & brn	1.05	1.40
J15	D3	25c lt bl & brn	1.40	1.75
J16	D3	30c bis brn & Prus bl	2.50	2.75
J17	D3	45c Prus bl & ol	3.25	3.50
J18	D3	50c red vio & brn	5.25	6.00
J19	D3	60c gray lil & bl blk	5.50	5.50
J20	D4	1fr bis brn & bl blk	5.25	6.00
J21	D4	2fr violet & brown	5.50	7.00
J22	D4	3fr dp red & brn	7.00	8.50
		Nos. J12-J22 (11)	38.45	44.85

Stamps of Ubangi-Shari were replaced in 1936 by those of French Equatorial Africa.

UGANDA

ü-'gan-də

LOCATION — East Africa, at the Equator and separated from the Indian Ocean by Kenya and Tanzania
GOVT. — Independent state
AREA — 91,343 sq. mi.
POP. — 21,619,700 (1999 est.)
CAPITAL — Kampala

Stamps of 1898-1902 were replaced by those issued for Kenya, Tanganyika and Uganda. Uganda became independent October 9, 1962.

Cowries (50 = 4 Pence)
16 Annas = 1 Rupee (1896)
100 Cents = 1 Shilling (1962)

Catalogue values for unused stamps in this country are for Never Hinged items, beginning with Scott 79 in the regular postage section and Scott J1 in the postage due section.

Unused values for Nos. 2-68 are for stamps without gum. Very fine examples will be evenly cut and will show at least two full typewritten framelines.

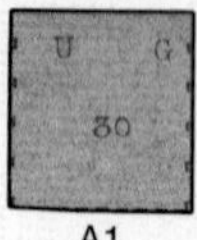

A1

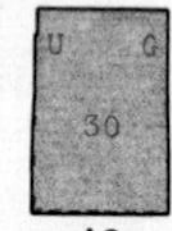

A2

Nos. 1-53 were produced with a typewriter by Rev. Ernest Millar of the Church Missionary Society. They were 20-26mm wide, with nine stamps in a horizontal row. Later two more were added to each row, and the stamps became narrower, 16-18mm.

Rev. Millar got a new typewriter in 1895, and the stamps he typed on it have a different appearance. A violet ribbon in the machine, inserted late in 1895, resulted in Nos. 35-53.

Nos. 1-53 are on thin, tough, white paper, laid horizontally with traces of a few vertical lines.

Forgeries of Nos. 1-53 are known.

Without Gum
Wide Letters
Typewritten on Thin Laid Paper
Stamps 20 to 26mm wide

1895 Unwmk. *Imperf.*

1 A1 10(c) black *5,750.* 3,000.
2 A1 20(c) black *9,600.* *2,350.*
a. "U A" instead of "U G" *7,750.*
3 A1 30(c) black *2,500.* *2,000.*
4 A1 40(c) black *7,750.* 2,850.
5 A1 50(c) black *1,800.* *1,400.*
a. "U A" instead of "U G" *8,750.*
6 A1 60(c) black *3,250.* 2,850.

Surcharged with New Value in Black, Pen-written

9 A1 10 on 30(c) black *85,000.*
10 A1 10 on 50(c) black *85,000.*
11 A1 15 on 10(c) black *60,000.*
12 A1 15 on 20(c) black *85,000.*
13 A1 15 on 40(c) black *72,500.*
14 A1 15 on 50(c) black *85,000.*
15 A1 25 on 50(c) black *85,000.*
16 A1 50 on 60(c) black *85,000.*

Stamps 16 to 18mm wide

17 A1 5(c) black 4,000. *1,650.*
18 A1 10(c) black *4,000.* *2,000.*
19 A1 15(c) black *2,500.* *1,900.*
a. Vertically laid paper *6,500.*
20 A1 20(c) black *4,000.* *1,900.*
a. Vertically laid paper *8,250.*
21 A1 25(c) black *2,250.* *2,000.*
22 A1 30(c) black *10,000.* *10,000.*
23 A1 40(c) black *9,500.* *9,500.*
24 A1 50(c) black *4,750.* *5,750.*
25 A1 60(c) black *10,000.* *11,000.*

Narrow Letters
Stamps 16 to 18mm wide

26 A2 5(c) black *2,000.*
27 A2 10(c) black *2,150.*
28 A2 15(c) black *2,150.*
29 A2 20(c) black *1,800.*
30 A2 25(c) black *2,150.*
31 A2 30(c) black *2,250.*
32 A2 40(c) black *2,000.*
33 A2 50(c) black *2,200.*
34 A2 60(c) black *3,200.*
35 A2 5(c) violet *900.* *825.*
36 A2 10(c) violet *825.* *825.*
37 A2 15(c) violet *1,300.* *750.*
38 A2 20(c) violet *600.* *375.*
a. "G A" instead of "U G"
b. Vertically laid paper 3,850.
39 A2 25(c) violet *2,300.* *2,000.*
40 A2 30(c) violet *2,850.* *1,400.*
41 A2 40(c) violet *2,850.* *1,900.*
42 A2 50(c) violet *2,500.* 1,900.
43 A2 100(c) violet *3,250.* 3,750.

As a favor to a philatelist, 35c and 45c denominations were made in black and violet. They were not intended for postal use and no rate called for those denominations.

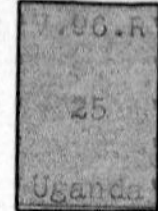

1896

44 A3 5(c) violet *950.* *1,250.*
45 A3 10(c) violet *1,050.* *825.*
46 A3 15(c) violet *950.* *950.*
47 A3 20(c) violet *500.* *275.*
48 A3 25(c) violet *875.* *1,150.*
49 A3 30(c) violet *950.* *1,050.*
50 A3 40(c) violet *1,150.* *1,150.*
51 A3 50(c) violet *950.* *1,000.*
52 A3 60(c) violet *2,000.* *2,500.*
53 A3 100(c) violet *1,900.* 2,500.

A4

Overprinted "L" in Black

1896 Typeset White Paper

54 A4 1a black (thin "1") 210. 190.
a. Small "O" in "POSTAGE" 1,550. 1,300.
55 A4 2a black 140. *140.*
a. Small "O" in "POSTAGE" 615. *750.*
56 A4 3a black 300. *375.*
a. Small "O" in "POSTAGE" 2,000. *2,250.*
57 A4 4a black 150. *180.*
a. Small "O" in "POSTAGE" 625.

Yellowish Paper

58 A4 8a black 225. *350.*
a. Small "O" in "POSTAGE" 1,675. *2,100.*
59 A4 1r black 425. *500.*
a. Small "O" in "POSTAGE" 2,250.
60 A4 5r black 29,500. 29,500.

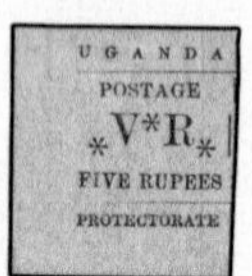

A4a

Without Overprint
White Paper

61 A4a 1a black (thin "1") 125.00 110.00
a. Small "O" in "POSTAGE" 700.00 675.00
62 A4a 1a black (thick "1") 26.00 *30.00*
a. Small "O" in "POSTAGE" 95.00 *110.00*
63 A4a 2a black 32.50 *40.00*
a. Small "O" in "POSTAGE" 110.00 *140.00*
64 A4a 3a black 32.50 *50.00*
a. Small "O" in "POSTAGE" 135.00 *200.00*
65 A4a 4a black 35.00 *37.50*
a. Small "O" in "POSTAGE" 125.00 *140.00*

Yellowish Paper

66 A4a 8a black 42.50 *50.00*
a. Small "O" in "POSTAGE" 155.00 *200.00*
67 A4a 1r black 95.00 *110.00*
a. Small "O" in "POSTAGE" 400.00 *475.00*
68 A4a 5r black 325.00 *400.00*
a. Small "O" in "POSTAGE" 1,000. *1,250.*

A5

Queen Victoria — A6

1898-1902 Engr. Wmk. 2 *Perf. 14*

69 A5 1a red 7.50 4.50
70 A5 1a car rose ('02) 2.50 2.00
71 A5 2a brown 12.00 *11.00*
72 A5 3a gray 22.50 *50.00*
73 A5 4a dark green 18.00 *12.50*
74 A5 8a olive gray 15.00 *32.50*

Wmk. 1

75 A6 1r ultra 60.00 *70.00*
76 A6 5r brown 95.00 *100.00*
Nos. 69-76 (8) 232.50 *282.50*

British East Africa No. 72 Overprinted in Black

1902 Wmk. 2

77 A8 ½a yellow green 3.75 2.75
a. Inverted overprint *2,200.*
b. Double overprint *2,800.*
c. Pair, one without overprint *5,500.*

British East Africa No. 76 Overprinted in Red

78 A8 2½a dark blue 6.00 4.00
a. Double overprint 650.00

Catalogue values for unused stamps in this section, from this point to the end of the section, are for Never Hinged items.

Ripon Falls and Speke Monument — A8

Wmk. 314

1962, July 28 Engr. *Perf. 14*

79 A8 30c vermilion & blk .45 .30
80 A8 50c violet & blk .45 .25
81 A8 1.30sh green & blk 1.50 .30
82 A8 2.50sh ultra & blk 3.00 2.00
Nos. 79-82 (4) 5.40 2.85

Cent. of the discovery of the source of the Nile by John Hanning Speke.

Independent State

Murchison Falls A9

Mulago Hospital, X-Ray Service A10

Designs: 10c, Tobacco growing. 15c, Coffee growing. 20c, Ankole cattle. 30c, Cotton growing. 50c, Mountains of the Moon. 1.30sh, Rubaga and Namirembe Cathedrals and Kibuli Mosque. 2sh, Makerere College and students. 5sh, Copper mining. 10sh, Cement factory. 20sh, Parliament.

Perf. 14½x14, 14x14½

1962, Oct. 9 Photo. Unwmk.

83 A9 5c Prus green .25 .25
84 A9 10c red brown .25 .25
85 A9 15c grn, blk & car .25 .25
86 A9 20c bister & pur .25 .25
87 A9 30c brt blue .25 .25
88 A9 50c bluish grn & blk .25 .25
89 A10 1sh bl grn, sep & red 1.00 .25
90 A10 1.30sh pur & ocher .30 .25
91 A10 2sh grnsh bl, blk & dk car .50 .80
92 A10 5sh dk grn & red 9.00 2.00
93 A10 10sh red brn & slate 4.75 4.50
94 A10 20sh blue & pale brn 5.50 *20.00*
Nos. 83-94 (12) 22.55 29.30

Uganda's independence, Oct. 9, 1962.

Crowned Crane — A11

1965, Feb. 20 Photo. *Perf. 14½*

95 A11 30c bl grn, blk, yel & red .25 .25
96 A11 1sh30c ultra, blk, yel & red .75 .40

Intl. Trade Fair at Lugogo Stadium, Kampala, Feb. 20-28.

Black Bee-eater A12

African Jacana A13

Arms of Uganda and Birds: 15c, Orange weaver. 20c, Narina trogon. 30c, Sacred ibis. 40c, Blue-breasted kingfisher. 50c, Whale-headed stork. 65c, Black-winged red bishop. 1sh, Ruwenzori turaco. 1.30sh, African fish eagle. 2.50sh, Great blue turaco. 5sh, Lilac-breasted roller. 10sh, Black-collared lovebird. 20sh, Crowned crane.

Perf. 14½x14, 14x14½

1965, Oct. 9 Photo. Unwmk.

Birds in Natural Colors

Size: 17x21mm, 21x17mm

97 A12 5c lt vio bl & blk .25 .25
98 A13 10c dull blue & red .25 .25
99 A12 15c dk brown & org .25 .25
100 A12 20c bister & brt grn .25 .25
101 A13 30c hen brn & blk 1.25 .25
102 A12 40c lt yel grn & red .90 1.50
103 A12 50c dp pur & gray .25 .25
104 A13 65c gray & brick red 2.75 3.25

Perf. 14½

Size: 41x25mm, 25x41mm

105 A13 1sh lt blue & blk .40 .25
106 A12 1.30sh yel & red brn 4.75 .30
107 A13 2.50sh brt yel grn & blk 3.25 .60
108 A12 5sh lil gray & vio bl 5.75 4.00
109 A13 10sh lt brown & blk 12.50 13.00
110 A13 20sh olive grn & blk 25.00 37.50
Nos. 97-110 (14) 57.80 61.90

Parliament Building — A14

13th Commonwealth Parliamentary Assoc. Conf.: 30c, Animal carvings from entrance hall of Uganda Parliament. 50c, Arms of Uganda. 2.50sh, Parliament Chamber.

1967, Oct. 26 Photo. *Perf. 14½*

111 A14 30c multicolored .25 .25
112 A14 50c multicolored .25 .25
113 A14 1.30sh multicolored .25 .25
114 A14 2.50sh multicolored .25 1.50
Nos. 111-114 (4) 1.00 2.25

Cordia Abyssinica A15

Black-galled Acacia A16

Flowers: 10c, Grewia similis. 15c, Cassia didymobotrya. 20c, Coleus barbatus. 30c, Ochna ovata. 40c, Ipomoea spathulata (morning glory). 50c, Spathodea nilotica (flame tree). 60c, Oncoba spinosa. 70c, Carissa edulis. 1.50sh, Clerodendrum myricoides (blue butterfly bush). 2.50sh, Acanthus arboreus. 5sh, Kigelia aethiopium (sausage tree). 10sh, Erythrina abyssinica (Uganda coral). 20sh, Monodora myristica.

Perf. 14½x14, 14

1969, Oct. 9 Photo. Unwmk.

115 A15 5c multicolored .25 .25
116 A15 10c multicolored .25 .25
117 A15 15c multicolored .25 .25
118 A15 20c multicolored .25 .25
119 A15 30c multicolored .25 .25
120 A15 40c gray & multi .25 .25
121 A15 50c tan & multi .25 .25
122 A15 60c multicolored .25 .25
123 A15 70c multicolored .25 .25

Perf. 14

124 A16 1sh multicolored .35 .25
125 A16 1.50sh multicolored .55 .25
126 A16 2.50sh multicolored .70 .25
127 A16 5sh multicolored 1.25 .25
128 A16 10sh multicolored 3.00 .55
129 A16 20sh tan & multi 7.75 1.25
Nos. 115-129 (15) 15.85 5.05

1971-73 On glazed Paper

115a A16 5c multi .40 .25
116a A16 10c multi .40 .25
118a A16 20c multi .40 .25
122a A16 60c multi 17.50 .40
123a A16 70c multi 1.00 .40
124a A16 1sh multi 1.00 .40
125a A16 1.50sh multi .50 .25
126a A16 2.50sh multi 1.25 .25
127a A16 5sh multi 1.75 .25
128a A16 10sh multi 3.50 .25
129a A16 20sh multi 12.00 .25
Nos. 115a-129a (11) 39.70 3.20

Values of Nos. 124-129 are for canceled-to-order stamps. Cancellations were printed on Nos. 128-129. Postally used examples sell for higher prices.

Nos. 125-126, 129 Surcharged

1975, Sept. 29 Photo. Perf. 14

130 A16 2sh on 1.50sh multi 1.05 1.75
131 A16 3sh on 2.50sh multi 20.50 37.50
132 A16 40sh on 20sh multi 8.25 15.00
Nos. 130-132 (3) 29.80 54.25

Millet — A17

Ugandan Crops: 20c, Sugar cane. 30c, Tobacco. 40c, Onions. 50c, Tomatoes. 70c, Tea. 80c, Bananas. 1sh, Corn. 2sh, Pineapple. 3sh, Coffee. 5sh, Oranges. 10sh, Peanuts. 20sh, Cotton. 40sh, Beans.

1975, Oct. 9 Photo. Perf. 14x14½
Size: 21x17mm
Multicolored, Name Panel as follows

133 A17 10c lt brown .25 .25
134 A17 20c blue .25 .25
135 A17 30c vermilion .25 .25
136 A17 40c lilac .25 .25
137 A17 50c olive .25 .25
138 A17 70c brt green .25 .25
139 A17 80c purple .25 .25

Perf. 14½
Size: 41x25mm

140 A17 1sh ocher .25 .25
141 A17 2sh slate .25 .25
142 A17 3sh blue .30 .40
143 A17 5sh yellow green .35 .55
144 A17 10sh brown red .70 1.10
145 A17 20sh rose lilac 1.50 2.25
146 A17 40sh orange 2.75 4.25
Nos. 133-146 (14) 7.85 10.80

See #195-198. For surcharge & overprints see #175, 203-206, 227-244, 253-257.

Communications Type of Tanzania 1976

Designs: 50c, Microwave tower. 1sh, Cordless switchboard and operators, horiz. 2sh, Telephones of 1880, 1930 and 1976. 3sh, Message switching center, horiz.

1976, Apr. 15 Litho. Perf. 14½

147 A6a 50c blue & multi .25 .25
148 A6a 1sh red & multi .25 .25
149 A6a 2sh yellow & multi .25 .25
150 A6a 3sh multicolored .25 .25
a. Souvenir sheet of 4 1.40 1.40
Nos. 147-150 (4) 1.00 1.00

Telecommunications development in East Africa. No. 150a contains 4 stamps similar to Nos. 147-150 with simulated perforations.

Olympics Type of Tanzania 1976

Designs: 50c, Akii Bua, Ugandan hurdler. 1sh, Filbert Bayi, Tanzanian runner. 2sh, Steve Muchoki, Kenyan boxer. 3sh, Olympic torch, flags of Kenya, Tanzania and Uganda.

1976, July 5 Litho. Perf. 14½

151 A6b 50c blue & multi .25 .25
152 A6b 1sh red & multi .25 .25
153 A6b 2sh yellow & multi .30 .30
154 A6b 3sh blue & multi .50 .40
a. Souv. sheet of 4, #151-154, perf. 13 5.50 5.00
Nos. 151-154 (4) 1.30 1.20

21st Olympic Games, Montreal, Canada, July 17-Aug. 1.

Railway Type of Tanzania 1976

Designs: 50c, Tanzania-Zambia Railway. 1sh, Nile Bridge, Uganda. 2sh, Nakuru Station, Kenya. 3sh, Class A locomotive, 1896.

1976, Oct. 4 Litho. Perf. 14

155 A6c 50c lilac & multi .25 .25
156 A6c 1sh emerald & multi .35 .25
157 A6c 2sh brt rose & multi .65 .45
158 A6c 3sh yellow & multi 1.00 .65
a. Souv. sheet, #155-158, perf 13 3.25 3.25
Nos. 155-158 (4) 2.25 1.60

Rail transport in East Africa.

Fish Type of Tanzania 1977

1977, Jan. 10 Litho. Perf. 14½

159 A6d 50c Nile perch .25 .25
160 A6d 1sh Tilapia .30 .25
161 A6d 3sh Sailfish .80 .60
162 A6d 5sh Black marlin 1.10 1.00
a. Souvenir sheet of 4, #159-162 5.50 5.50
Nos. 159-162 (4) 2.45 2.10

Festival Type of Tanzania 1977

Festival Emblem and: 50c, Masai tribesmen bleeding cow. 1sh, Dancers from Uganda. 2sh, Makonde sculpture, Tanzania. 3sh, Tribesmen skinning hippopotamus.

1977, Jan. 15 Perf. 13½x14

163 A6e 50c multicolored .25 .25
164 A6e 1sh multicolored .25 .25
165 A6e 2sh multicolored .40 .35
166 A6e 3sh multicolored .60 .60
a. Souvenir sheet of 4, #163-166 2.00 2.00
Nos. 163-166 (4) 1.50 1.45

2nd World Black and African Festival, Lagos, Nigeria, Jan. 15-Feb. 12.

Rally Type of Tanzania 1977

Safari Rally Emblem and: 50c, Automobile passing through village. 1sh, Winner at finish line. 2sh, Car passing through washout. 5sh, Car, elephants and Mt. Kenya.

1977, Apr. 5 Litho. Perf. 14

167 A6f 50c multicolored .25 .25
168 A6f 1sh multicolored .25 .25
169 A6f 2sh multicolored .35 .25
170 A6f 5sh multicolored .85 .75
a. Souvenir sheet of 4, #167-170 2.25 2.25
Nos. 167-170 (4) 1.70 1.50

25th Safari Rally, Apr. 7-11.

Church Type of Tanzania 1977

Designs: 50c, Rev. Canon Apolo Kivebulaya. 1sh, Uganda Cathedral. 2sh, Early grass-topped Cathedral. 5sh, Early tent congregation, Kigezi.

1977, June 30 Litho. Perf. 14

171 A6g 50c multicolored .25 .25
172 A6g 1sh multicolored .25 .25
173 A6g 2sh multicolored .25 .25
174 A6g 5sh multicolored .60 .60
a. Souvenir sheet of 4, #171-174 1.50 1.50
Nos. 171-174 (4) 1.35 1.35

Church of Uganda, centenary.

Type of 1975 Surcharged with New Value and 2 Bars

1977, Aug. 22 Photo. Perf. 14x14½

175 A17 80c on 60c bananas .40 .25

No. 175 was not issued without surcharge.

Wildlife Type of Tanzania 1977

Wildlife Fund Emblem and: 50c, Pancake tortoise. 1sh, Nile crocodile. 2sh, Hunter's hartebeest. 3sh, Red colobus monkey. 5sh, Dugong.

1977, Sept. 26 Litho. Perf. 14x13½

176 A6h 50c multicolored .25 .25
177 A6h 1sh multicolored .45 .40
178 A6h 2sh multicolored 2.00 1.00
179 A6h 3sh multicolored 2.75 1.40
180 A6h 5sh multicolored 2.75 2.50
a. Souvenir sheet of 4, #177-180 8.50 6.00
Nos. 176-180 (5) 8.20 5.55

Endangered species.

Soccer Type of Tanzania

Soccer Cup and: 50c, Soccer scene and Joe Kadenge. 1sh, Mohammed Chuma receiving trophy, and his portrait. 2sh, Shot on goal and Omari S. Kidevu. 5sh, Backfield defense and Polly Ouma.

1978, May 3 Litho. Perf. 14x13½

181 A8a 50c green & multi .25 .25
182 A8a 1sh lt brown & multi .25 .25
183 A8a 2sh lilac & multi .30 .30
184 A8a 5sh dk blue & multi .90 .90
a. Souvenir sheet of 4, #181-184 2.00 2.00
Nos. 181-184 (4) 1.70 1.70

World Soccer Cup Championships, Argentina, June 1-25.
See Nos. 203-206.

Crop Type of 1975

Designs as before.

1978, June Litho. Perf. 14½
Size: 41x25mm
Multicolored, Name Panel as follows

195 A17 5sh blue .25 .25
196 A17 10sh rose lilac .45 .45
197 A17 20sh brown .90 .90
198 A17 40sh deep orange 1.90 1.90
Nos. 195-198 (4) 3.50 3.50

For overprint see Nos. 241-244.

Shot Put — A18

1978, July 10 Litho. Perf. 14

199 A18 50c shown .25 .25
200 A18 1sh Broad jump .25 .25
201 A18 2sh Running .25 .25
202 A18 5sh Boxing .55 1.00
a. Souv. sheet, #199-202, perf 12 2.25 2.25
Nos. 199-202 (4) 1.30 1.75

Commonwealth Games, Edmonton, Canada, Aug. 3-12.
For overprints see Nos. 249-252.

Soccer Type of Tanzania 1978 Inscribed "WORLD CUP 1978"

Designs: 50c, Backfield defense and Polly Ouma. 2sh, Shot on goal and Omari S. Kidevu. 5sh, Soccer scene and Joe Kadenge. 10sh, Mohammed Chuma receiving trophy, and his portrait.

1978, Sept. 11 Perf. 14x13½

203 A8a 50c dk blue & multi .25 .25
204 A8a 2sh lilac & multi .30 .25
205 A8a 5sh green & multi .70 .90
206 A8a 10sh lt brown & multi 1.35 1.75
a. Souv. sheet of 4, #203-206, perf. 12 3.50 3.50
Nos. 203-206 (4) 2.60 3.15

World Cup Soccer Championship winners.
For overprint see Nos. 253-257.

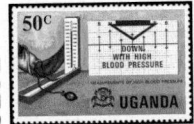

Blood Pressure Gauge and Chart — A19

1978, Sept. 25 Litho. Perf. 14

207 A19 50c shown .25 .25
208 A19 1sh Heart .25 .25
209 A19 2sh Retina .35 .30
210 A19 5sh Kidneys .80 1.10
a. Souvenir sheet of 4, #207-210 2.75 2.75
Nos. 207-210 (4) 1.65 1.90

World Health Day and Hypertension Month.

Cattle Unloaded from Plane — A20

Flyer 1 and: 1.50sh, "Islander" on runway, Kampala. 2.70sh, Coffee loaded on transport jet. 10sh, Concorde.

1978, Dec. 16

211 A20 1sh multicolored .25 .25
212 A20 1.50sh multicolored .25 .25
213 A20 2.70sh multicolored .45 .40
214 A20 10sh multicolored 1.90 1.40
a. Souvenir sheet of 4, #211-214 3.00 3.00
Nos. 211-214 (4) 2.85 2.30

75th anniversary of 1st powered flight.
For overprints see Nos. 258-261.

Elizabeth II Leaving Owen Falls Dam — A21

Designs: 1.50sh, Coronation regalia. 2.70sh, Coronation ceremony. 10sh, Royal family on balcony of Buckingham Palace.

1979, Mar. 1 Litho. Perf. 12½x12

215 A21 1sh multicolored .25 .25
216 A21 1.50sh multicolored .25 .25
217 A21 2.70sh multicolored .25 .25
218 A21 10sh multicolored .65 1.25
a. Souvenir sheet of 4, #215-218 2.00 2.00
Nos. 215-218 (4) 1.40 2.00

25th anniv. of coronation of Elizabeth II.
For overprints see Nos. 245-248.

Bishop Joseph Kiwanuka — A22

Designs: 1.50sh, Lubaga Cathedral. 2.70sh, Ugandan pilgrims and St. Peter's, Rome. 10sh, Friar Lourdel-Mapeera, missionary.

1979, Feb. 15 Perf. 14

219 A22 1sh multicolored .25 .25
220 A22 1.50sh multicolored .25 .25
221 A22 2.70sh multicolored .25 .25
222 A22 10sh multicolored .70 .90
a. Souvenir sheet of 4, #219-222 2.00 2.00
Nos. 219-222 (4) 1.45 1.65

Ugandan Catholic Church, centenary.
See No. 274. For overprints see Nos. 262-265.

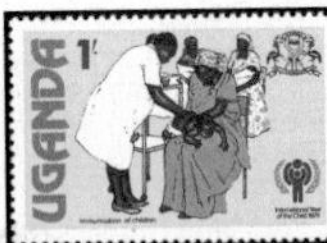

Child Receiving Vaccination — A23

IYC Emblem and: 1.50sh, Handicapped children playing. 2.70sh, Ugandan IYC emblem. 10sh, Teacher and pupils.

1979, July 16 Litho. Perf. 14

223 A23 1sh multicolored .25 .25
224 A23 1.50sh multicolored .25 .25
225 A23 2.70sh multicolored .25 .30
226 A23 10sh multicolored .50 .90
a. Souvenir sheet of 4, #223-226 1.75 1.75
Nos. 223-226 (4) 1.25 1.70

International Year of the Child.
For overprints see Nos. 266-269.

Nos. 133-146, 195-198, 215-218 Overprinted "UGANDA / LIBERATED / 1979"

1979, July 12 Photo. Perf. 14x14½
Size: 21x17mm

227 A17 10c multicolored .25 .25
228 A17 20c multicolored .25 .25
229 A17 30c multicolored .25 .25
230 A17 40c multicolored .25 .25
231 A17 50c multicolored .25 .25
232 A17 70c multicolored .25 .25
233 A17 80c multicolored .25 .25

Perf. 14½
Size: 41x25mm

234 A17 1sh multicolored .25 .25
235 A17 2sh multicolored .25 .25
236 A17 3sh multicolored .25 .25
237 A17 5sh multicolored .35 .30
238 A17 10sh multicolored .70 .60
239 A17 20sh multicolored 1.50 1.50
240 A17 40sh multicolored 3.00 3.00
Nos. 227-240 (14) 8.05 7.90

1979 Litho. Perf. 14½
Multicolored, name panel as follows

241 A17 5sh blue .45 .35
242 A17 10sh rose lilac .85 .70
243 A17 20sh brown 1.60 1.40
244 A17 40sh deep orange 3.25 2.75
Nos. 241-244 (4) 6.15 5.20

1979, July 12 Litho. Perf. 12½x12

245 A21 1sh multicolored .25 .25
246 A21 1.50sh multicolored .25 .25
247 A21 2.70sh multicolored .25 .25
248 A21 15sh on 10sh multi 1.40 1.10
a. Souvenir sheet of 4 2.50
Nos. 245-248 (4) 2.15 1.85

No. 248a contains Nos. 245-247 and a 15sh in design of No. 218. Issued Aug. 1.

Nos. 199-202, 203-206, 211-214, 219-222, 223-226 Overprinted "UGANDA LIBERATED 1979"

1979, Aug. 1 Litho. Perf. 14

249 A18 50c multicolored .25 .25
250 A18 1sh multicolored .25 .25
251 A18 2sh multicolored .25 .25
252 A18 5sh multicolored .40 .35

1979, Aug. 1 *Perf. 14x13½*

253 A8a 50c multi .25 .25
255 A8a 2sh multi (#204) .25 .25
256 A8a 5sh multi .40 .35
257 A8a 10sh multi .85 .70

Overprint exists on No. 183.

1979, Aug. 1 *Perf. 14*

258 A20 1sh multicolored .25 .25
259 A20 1.50sh multicolored .25 .25
260 A20 2.70sh multicolored .30 .25
261 A20 10sh multicolored 1.05 .85

1979, Aug. 1

262 A22 1sh multicolored .25 .25
263 A22 1.50sh multicolored .25 .25
264 A22 2.70sh multicolored .25 .25
265 A22 10sh multicolored .80 .70

1979, Aug. 16

266 A23 1sh multicolored .25 .25
267 A23 1.50sh multicolored .25 .25
268 A23 2.70sh multicolored .25 .25
269 A23 10sh multicolored .85 .80
a. Souvenir sheet of 4, #266-269 2.50 2.50
Nos. 249-269 (20) 7.90 7.25

ITU Emblem, Radio Waves — A24

1979, Sept. 11

270 A24 1sh lt gray & multi .25 .25
271 A24 1.50sh orange & multi .25 .25
272 A24 2.70sh yellow & multi .25 .25
273 A24 10sh blue & multi .35 .90
Nos. 270-273 (4) 1.10 1.65

50th anniv. of Intl. Radio Consultative Committee (CCIR) of the ITU.

No. 222a Redrawn and Inscribed FREEDOM OF WORSHIP DECLARED

Souvenir Sheet

1979, Sept. *Perf. 12*

274 Sheet of 4 2.00 2.00
a. A22 1sh No. 219 .25 .25
b. A22 1.50sh No. 220 .25 .25
c. A22 2.70sh No. 221 .25 .25
d. A22 10sh No. 222 1.25 1.25

In top panel of margin scrolls and coat of arms have been replaced by inscription.

A25

1979, Nov. 12 **Litho.** *Perf. 14*

275 A25 1sh #110 .25 .25
276 A25 1.50sh #112 .25 .25
277 A25 2.70sh #94 .25 .30
278 A25 10sh #69 .40 1.00
a. Souvenir sheet of 4, #275-278 1.25 1.25
Nos. 275-278 (4) 1.15 1.80

Sir Rowland Hill (1795-1879), originator of penny postage.
For overprints see Nos. 293-296.

Thomson's Gazelle — A26

Designs: 10c, Impalas. 20c, Large-spotted genet. 50c, Bush babies. 80c, Wild hunting dogs. 1sh, Lions. 1.50sh, Mountain gorillas. 2sh, Zebras. 2.70sh, Leopards. 3.50sh, Black rhinoceroses. 5sh, Defassa waterbucks. 10sh, African black buffaloes. 20sh, Hippopotami. 40sh, African elephants.

1979, Dec. 3 **Litho.** *Perf. 14*

No Date Imprint Below Design

Size: 21x17mm

279 A26 10c multicolored .25 .25
280 A26 20c multicolored .25 .25
281 A26 30c multicolored .25 .25
282 A26 50c multicolored .25 .25
283 A26 80c multicolored .25 .25

Size: 39x25mm

284 A26 1sh multicolored .25 .25
a. Imprint "1982" .45 .25
285 A26 1.50sh multicolored .25 .25
286 A26 2sh multicolored .25 .25
a. Imprint "1982" .60 .30
287 A26 2.70sh multicolored .25 .25
288 A26 3.50sh multicolored .30 .25
289 A26 5sh multicolored .45 .40
a. Imprint "1982" .60 .60
290 A26 10sh multicolored .85 .85
291 A26 20sh multicolored 1.15 1.15
292 A26 40sh multicolored 3.00 3.00
Nos. 279-292 (14) 8.00 7.90

Nos. 284, 286, 289 reissued inscribed 1982. See Nos. 400-406. For surcharges see Nos. 386-392.

Nos. 275-278a Overprinted: "LONDON 1980"

1980, May 6 **Litho.** *Perf. 14*

293 A25 1sh multicolored .25 .25
294 A25 1.50sh multicolored .25 .25
295 A25 2.70sh multicolored .30 .25
296 A25 10sh multicolored 1.10 1.10
a. Souvenir sheet of 4, #293-296 2.00 2.00
Nos. 293-296 (4) 1.90 1.85

London 80 Intl. Stamp Exhib., May 6-14.

Paul Harris Wheeling Rotary Cart — A27

1980, Aug. **Litho.** *Perf. 14*

297 A27 1sh Rotary emblem, vert. .25 .25
298 A27 20sh shown 1.60 1.60
a. Souvenir sheet of 2, #297-298 2.25 2.25

Rotary International, 75th anniversary.

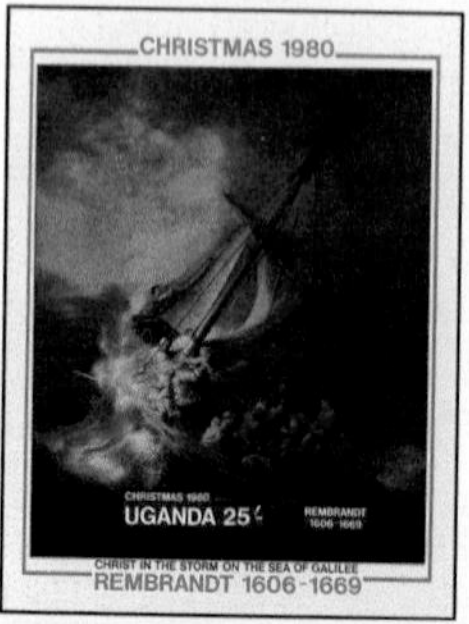

Soccer, Flags of Olympic Participants, Flame — A28

1980, Dec. 29 **Litho.** *Perf. 14*

299 A28 1sh shown .25 .25
300 A28 2sh Relay race .25 .25
301 A28 10sh Hurdles .25 .25
302 A28 20sh Boxing .75 .75
Nos. 299-302 (4) 1.50 1.50

Souvenir Sheet

303 Sheet of 4 2.00 2.00
a. A28 2.70sh like #299 .25 .25
b. A28 3sh like #300 .25 .25
c. A28 5sh like #301 .35 .30
d. A28 25sh like 302 1.60 1.40

22nd Summer Olympic Games, Moscow, July 19-Aug. 3.

Nos. 299-303 Overprinted with Sport, Winner and Country

1980, Dec. 29

304 A28 1sh multicolored .25 .25
305 A28 2sh multicolored .25 .25
306 A28 10sh multicolored .60 .60
307 A28 20sh multicolored 1.15 1.15
Nos. 304-307 (4) 2.25 2.25

Souvenir Sheet

308 Sheet of 4 2.25 2.25
a. A28 2.70sh like #304 .25 .25
b. A28 3sh like #305 .25 .25
c. A28 5sh like #306 .35 .30
d. A28 25sh like #307 1.60 1.40

Souvenir Sheet

Christ in the Storm on the Sea of Galilee, by Rembrandt — A29

1980, Dec. 31 *Imperf.*

309 A29 25sh multicolored 5.50 5.50

Christmas 1980.

Heinrich von Stephan and UPU Emblem — A30

2sh, UPU headquarters. 2.70sh, Mail plane, 1935. 10sh, Mail train, 1927.

1981, June 2 **Litho.** *Perf. 14*

310 A30 1sh shown .25 .25
311 A30 2sh multicolored .35 .25
312 A30 2.70sh multicolored .45 .35
313 A30 10sh multicolored 1.40 1.25
a. Souvenir sheet of 4, #310-313 3.75 3.75
Nos. 310-313 (4) 2.45 2.10

Von Stephan (1831-97), UPU founder.

Common Design Types pictured following the introduction.

Royal Wedding Issue

Common Design Type

10sh, Couple. 50sh, Tower of London. 200sh, Prince Charles.
250sh, Royal mews.

1981 **Litho.** *Perf. 14*

314 CD331a 10sh multi .25 .25
a. 10sh on 1sh .25 .25
315 CD331a 50sh multi .25 .25
a. 50sh on 5sh .25 .25
316 CD331a 200sh multi 1.35 1.25
a. 200sh on 20sh 1.75 1.25
Nos. 314-316 (3) 1.85 1.75
Nos. 314a-316a (3) 2.25 1.75

Souvenir Sheet

317 CD331 250sh multi 1.25 1.25
a. 250sh on 25sh, light orange 1.25 1.25

Royal wedding. Issue dates: surcharges, July 13; others, July 29. Nos. 314-316 also issued in sheets of 5 plus label, perf. 12, in changed colors.
For overprints see Nos. 342-345.

Sleeping Woman Before Green Shutters, by Picasso — A31

Picasso Birth Centenary: 20sh, Bullfight. 30sh, Nude Asleep on a Landscape. 200sh, Interior with a Girl Drawing. 250sh, Minotaur.

1981, Sept. 21 **Litho.** *Perf. 14*

318 A31 10sh multicolored .25 .25
319 A31 20sh multicolored .30 .25
320 A31 30sh multicolored .40 .30
321 A31 200sh multicolored 2.00 2.75

Size: 120x146mm

Imperf

322 A31 250sh multicolored 2.50 4.00
Nos. 318-322 (5) 5.45 7.55

Intl. Year of the Disabled — A32

1sh, Sign language. 10sh, Teacher in wheelchair. 50sh, Retarded children. 200sh, Blind man.

1981, Dec. *Perf. 15*

323 A32 1sh multicolored .25 .25
324 A32 10sh multicolored .25 .25
325 A32 50sh multicolored .60 .65
326 A32 200sh multicolored 1.50 2.00
a. Souvenir sheet of 4, #323-326 4.50 4.50
Nos. 323-326 (4) 2.60 3.15

1982 World Cup Soccer — A33

Designs: Various soccer players.

1982, Jan. 11 **Litho.** *Perf. 14*

327 A33 1sh multicolored .25 .25
328 A33 10sh multicolored .25 .25
329 A33 50sh multicolored .50 .75
330 A33 200sh multicolored 2.50 2.25
Nos. 327-330 (4) 3.50 3.50

Souvenir Sheet

331 A33 250sh World Cup 4.00 4.00

TB Bacillus Centenary — A34

1sh, Dr. Robert Koch. 10sh, Microscope. 50sh, Inoculation. 100sh, Bacteria under microscope.
150sh, Medical School.

1982, June 14 **Litho.**

332 A34 1sh multi .30 .30
333 A34 10sh multi .50 .35
334 A34 50sh multi 2.25 1.60
335 A34 100sh multi 4.50 3.25
Nos. 332-335 (4) 7.55 5.50

Souvenir Sheet

336 A34 150sh multi 6.00 3.50

Peaceful Uses of Outer Space — A35

5sh, Mpoma Satellite Earth Station. 10sh, Pioneer II. 50sh, Columbia space shuttle. 100sh, Voyager II, Saturn.
150sh, Columbia shuttle.

1982, May 17 **Litho.** *Perf. 15*

337 A35 5sh multicolored .30 .35
338 A35 10sh multicolored .30 .35
339 A35 50sh multicolored 1.45 1.40
340 A35 100sh multicolored 3.00 2.75
Nos. 337-340 (4) 5.05 4.85

Souvenir Sheet

341 A35 150sh multicolored 4.50 4.50

Nos. 314-317 Overprinted: "21st BIRTHDAY / HRH Princess of Wales / JULY 1 1982"

1982, July 7 *Perf. 14*

342 CD331 10sh multicolored .25 .25
343 CD331 50sh multicolored .25 .25
344 CD331 200sh multicolored 1.50 1.50
Nos. 342-344 (3) 2.00 2.00

Souvenir Sheet

345 CD331 250sh multicolored 3.00 2.50

Also issued in sheets of 5 + label in changed colors, perf. 12x12½.

20th Anniversary of Independence
A 150sh souvenir sheet showing the Coat of Arms was not issued.

Hornbill — A36

20sh, Superb starling. 50sh, Bateleur eagle. 100sh, Saddle-bill stork.
200sh, Laughing dove.

1982, July 12

346 A36 1sh shown .25 .25
347 A36 20sh multi .60 .60
348 A36 50sh multi 1.35 1.40
349 A36 100sh multi 3.00 2.90
Nos. 346-349 (4) 5.20 5.15

Souvenir Sheet

350 A36 200sh multi 11.50 10.00

Scouting Year — A37

5sh, Scouts. 20sh, Trophy presentation. 50sh, Helping disabled. 100sh, First aid instruction.
150sh, Baden-Powell.

1982, Aug. 23

351 A37 5sh multicolored .30 .30
352 A37 20sh multicolored .75 .60
353 A37 50sh multicolored 1.90 1.60
354 A37 100sh multicolored 3.75 3.25
Nos. 351-354 (4) 6.70 5.75

Souvenir Sheet

355 A37 150sh multicolored 4.50 4.00

For overprints see Nos. 376-380.

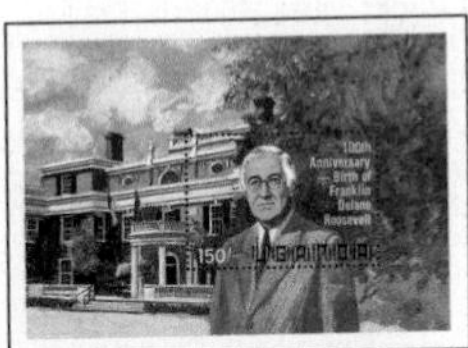

Franklin D. Roosevelt (1882-1945) — A38

Roosevelt and Washington: 50sh, 200sh, Inaugurations. No. 358, Mount Vernon. No. 359, Hyde Park.

1982, Sept. Litho.

356 A38 50sh multicolored .50 .50
357 A38 200sh multicolored 2.00 2.00

Souvenir Sheets

358 A38 150sh multicolored 1.50 1.50
359 A38 150sh multicolored 1.50 1.50

Italy's Victory in 1982 World Cup — A39

1982, Oct. Litho. *Perf. 14½*

359A A39 10sh Players .25 .25
359B A39 200sh Team 2.50 2.50

Souvenir Sheet

359C A39 250sh Globe 2.50 2.50

A39a

5sh, Dancers. 20sh, Traditional currency. 50sh, Village. 100sh, Drums.

1983, Mar. 14 Litho. *Perf. 14*

360 A39a 5sh multicolored .25 .25
361 A39a 20sh multicolored .25 .25
362 A39a 50sh multicolored .40 .40
363 A39a 100sh multicolored .60 .60
Nos. 360-363 (4) 1.50 1.50

Commonwealth Day.

St. George and the Dragon, by Raphael — A40

20sh, St. George and the Dragon, 1505. 50sh, Moses Parts the Red Sea. 200sh, Expulsion of Heliodorus.
250sh, Leo the Great and Attila, 1513.

1983, Apr.

364 A40 5sh multicolored .25 .25
365 A40 20sh multicolored .25 .25
366 A40 50sh multicolored .60 .60
367 A40 200sh multicolored 1.60 1.60
Nos. 364-367 (4) 2.70 2.70

Souvenir Sheet

368 A40 250sh multicolored 2.75 2.75

A41

7th Non-aligned Summit Conference A42

1983, Aug. 15 Litho. *Perf. 14½*

369 A41 5sh multicolored .25 .25
370 A42 200sh multicolored 1.50 1.50

African Elephants and World Wildlife Emblem — A43

5sh, Three adults with elephant bones. 10sh, Three adults walking. 30sh, Elephants standing in water hole. 70sh, Adults with calf.

1983, Aug. 22 *Perf. 15*

371 A43 5sh multicolored *.90 .90*
372 A43 10sh multicolored *1.45 1.45*
373 A43 30sh multicolored *3.50 3.50*
374 A43 70sh multicolored *9.00 9.00*
Nos. 371-374 (4) 14.85 14.85

Nos. 371-374 were reprinted in 1990, perf 14. Value $25.

Souvenir Sheet

375 A43 300sh Zebras, vert. *6.25 5.25*

No. 375 does not have the WWF emblem.
See Nos. 948-953.

Nos. 351-355 Ovptd. or Srchd. "BOYS BRIGADE CENTENARY 1883-1983"

1983, Sept. 19 Litho. *Perf. 14*

376 A37 5sh multicolored .25 .25
377 A37 20sh multicolored .25 .25
378 A37 50sh multicolored .40 .40
379 A37 400sh on 100sh multi 2.50 2.50
Nos. 376-379 (4) 3.40 3.40

Souvenir Sheet

380 A37 150sh multicolored 2.25 2.25

World Communications Year — A44

Designs: 20sh, Mpoma Satellite Earth Station. 50sh, Railroad, Computer Operator. 70sh, Filming Lions. 100sh, Pilots, Radio Communications. 300sh, Communications Satellite.

1983, Oct. 3 Litho. *Perf. 15*

381 A44 20sh multicolored .25 .25
382 A44 50sh multicolored .65 .65
383 A44 70sh multicolored .85 .85
384 A44 100sh multicolored 1.25 1.25
Nos. 381-384 (4) 3.00 3.00

Souvenir Sheet

385 A44 300sh multicolored 2.00 2.00

Nos. 279, 281-285, 289 Surcharged

1983, Nov. 7 Litho. *Perf. 14*

386 A26 100sh on 10c multi .70 .70
387 A26 135sh on 1sh multi .85 .85
388 A26 175sh on 30c multi 1.00 1.00
389 A26 200sh on 50c multi 1.40 1.40
390 A26 400sh on 80c multi 3.00 3.00
391 A26 700sh on 5sh multi 4.75 4.75
392 A26 1000sh on 1.50sh 6.50 6.50
Nos. 386-392 (7) 18.20 18.20

World Food Day — A45

1984, Jan. 12 Litho. *Perf. 14*

393 A45 10sh Plowing .50 .50
394 A45 300sh Banana crop 3.75 3.75

Christmas A46

10sh, Nativity. 50sh, Sheperds and Angel. 175sh, Flight into Egypt. 400sh, Angels Blowing Trumpets.
300sh, Three Kings.

1983, Dec. 12 Litho. *Perf. 14*

395 A46 10sh multicolored .25 .25
396 A46 50sh multicolored .30 .30
397 A46 175sh multicolored .70 .70
398 A46 400sh multicolored 1.75 1.75
Nos. 395-398 (4) 3.00 3.00

Souvenir Sheet

399 A46 300sh multicolored 2.25 2.25

Animal Type of 1979

1983, Dec. 19

400 A26 100sh like No. 284 .70 .70
401 A26 135sh like No. 285 .85 .85
402 A26 175sh like No. 286 1.00 1.00
403 A26 200sh like No. 287 1.40 1.40
404 A26 400sh like No. 288 3.00 3.00
405 A26 700sh like No. 292 4.75 4.75
406 A26 1000sh like No. 291 6.50 6.50
Nos. 400-406 (7) 18.20 18.20

1984 Summer Olympics — A48

1983 *Perf. 14½*

417 A48 5sh Ruth Kyalisiima .25 .25
418 A48 115sh Javelin .50 .50
419 A48 155sh Wrestling .65 .65
420 A48 175sh Rowing .85 .85
Nos. 417-420 (4) 2.25 2.25

Souvenir Sheet

421 A48 500sh Akii-Bua 2.00 2.00

For overprints see Nos. 458-462.

Intl. Civil Aviation Org., 40th Anniv. — A49

5sh, Passenger service. 115sh, Cargo service. 155sh, Police airwing. 175sh, Soroti Flying School plane.
250sh, Hot air balloon.

1984, Sept.

422 A49 5sh multi .45 .45
423 A49 115sh multi 1.75 1.75
424 A49 155sh multi 2.50 2.50
425 A49 175sh multi 3.50 3.50
Nos. 422-425 (4) 8.20 8.20

Souvenir Sheet

426 A49 250sh multi 3.50 3.50

Butterflies — A50

5sh, Silver-barred Charaxes. 115sh, Western Emperor Swallowtail. 155sh, African Giant Swallowtail. 175sh, Blue Salamis.
250sh, Veinted Yellow.

1984, Oct. Litho. *Perf. 14½*

427 A50 5sh multi .35 .35
428 A50 115sh multi 2.50 2.50
429 A50 155sh multi 3.50 3.50
430 A50 175sh multi 4.00 4.00
Nos. 427-430 (4) 10.35 10.35

Souvenir Sheet

431 A50 250sh multi 5.00 5.00

Freshwater Fish — A51

5sh, Nothobranchius taeniopygus. 10sh, Bagrus dogmac. 50sh, Polypterus senegalus. 100sh, Clarias. 135sh, Mormyrus kannume. 175sh, Synodontis victoriae. 205sh, Haplochromis brownae. 400sh, Lates niloticus. 700sh, Protopterus aethiopicus. 1000sh, Barbus radcliffii. 2500sh, Malapterus electricus.

1985 Litho. *Perf. 15*

432 A51 5sh multicolored .55 .55
433 A51 10sh multicolored .80 .55
434 A51 50sh multicolored 1.50 .45
435 A51 100sh multicolored 1.50 .45
436 A51 135sh multicolored 2.50 1.40
437 A51 175sh multicolored 2.50 2.40
438 A51 205sh multicolored 2.50 *2.75*
439 A51 400sh multicolored 2.50 *3.00*
440 A51 700sh multicolored 2.50 *3.50*
441 A51 1000sh multicolored 2.50 *3.50*
442 A51 2500sh multicolored 3.00 *4.75*
Nos. 432-442 (11) 22.35 23.30

Issued: #432-435, 437-441, 4/1; #436, 442, 6/10.
For overprints see Nos. 490-494.

Easter — A52

5sh, The Last Supper. 115sh, Jesus confronts doubting Thomas. 155sh, Crucifixion. 175sh, Pentecost.
250sh, Last prayer in garden.

1985, May 13 Litho. *Perf. 14*

443 A52 5sh multicolored .50 .50
444 A52 115sh multicolored 1.60 1.60
445 A52 155sh multicolored 1.75 *2.50*
446 A52 175sh multicolored 2.25 *3.25*
Nos. 443-446 (4) 6.10 7.85

Souvenir Sheet

447 A52 250sh multicolored 1.25 1.25

UN Child Survival Campaign A53

5sh, Mother breastfeeding. 115sh, Growth monitorization. 155sh, Immunization. 175sh, Oral rehydration therapy.
500sh, Expectant Mother, food.

1985, July 1

448 A53 5sh multi .35 .35
449 A53 115sh multi 1.90 1.90
450 A53 155sh multi 2.50 2.50
451 A53 175sh multi 3.00 3.00
Nos. 448-451 (4) 7.75 7.75

Souvenir Sheet

452 A53 500sh multi 5.25 5.25

Audubon Birth Bicent. — A54

115sh, Acrocephalus schoenobaenus. 155sh, Ardeola ibis. 175sh, Galerida gristata. 500sh, Aythya fuligula.
1000sh, Strix aluco.

1985, July

453 A54 115sh multi 1.90 1.75
454 A54 155sh multi 2.25 1.90
455 A54 175sh multi 1.90 2.25
456 A54 500sh multi 3.00 *4.75*
Nos. 453-456 (4) 9.05 10.65

Souvenir Sheet

457 A54 1000sh multi 11.00 11.00

See Nos. 469-473.

Nos. 417-421 Ovptd. or Srchd. with Winners Names, Medals and Countries in Gold

Gold medalists: 5sh, Benita Brown-Fitzgerald, US, 100-meter hurdles. 115sh, Arto Haerkoenen, Finland, javelin. 155sh, Atsuji Miyahara, Japan, 115-pound Greco-Roman wrestling. 100sh, West Germany, quadruple sculls. 1200sh, Edwin Moses, US, 400-meter hurdles.

1985, July *Perf. 15*
458 A48 5sh multicolored .25 .25
459 A48 115sh multicolored .35 .35
460 A48 155sh multicolored .50 .50
461 A48 1000sh on 175sh multi 3.00 3.00
Nos. 458-461 (4) 4.10 4.10

Souvenir Sheet

462 A48 1200sh on 500sh multi 3.50 3.50

UN Decade for Women — A56

5sh, Natl. Women's Day, Mar. 8. 115sh, Girl Guides 75th anniv., horiz. 155sh, Mother Theresa, 1979 Nobel Peace Prize laureate. 1000sh, Queen Mother. #467, Queen Mother inspecting troops. #468, like 115sh, horiz.

1985 **Litho.** *Perf. 14*
463 A56 5sh multicolored .25 .25
464 A56 115sh multicolored 1.75 1.60
465 A56 155sh multicolored 2.90 2.50
466 A56 1000sh multicolored 1.40 1.75
Nos. 463-466 (4) 6.30 6.10

Souvenir Sheets

467 A56 1500sh multicolored 3.00 3.00
468 A56 1500sh multicolored 4.50 4.50

Issued: #466-467, Aug. 21; others, Nov. 1.

Audubon Type of 1985

5sh, Rock ptarmigan. 155sh, Sage grouse. 175sh, Lesser yellowlegs. 500sh, Brown-headed cowbird.
1000sh, Whooping crane.

1985, Dec. 23 *Perf. 12½x12*
469 A54 5sh multi .50 .40
470 A54 155sh multi 2.00 2.00
471 A54 175sh multi 2.00 *2.50*
472 A54 500sh multi 3.50 *4.50*
Nos. 469-472 (4) 8.00 9.40

Souvenir Sheet

Perf. 14

473 A54 1000sh multi 9.50 9.50

UN, 40th Anniv. — A57

Designs: 10sh, Forest resources, vert. 180sh, UN Peace-keeping Force. 200sh, Emblem, UN Development Project. 250sh, Intl. Peace Year. 2000sh, Natl., UN flags, vert. 2500sh, Flags, UN Building, New York, vert.

1986, Feb. *Perf. 15*
474 A57 10sh multicolored .25 .25
475 A57 180sh multicolored .35 .35
476 A57 200sh multicolored .45 .45
477 A57 250sh multicolored .55 .55
478 A57 2000sh multicolored 4.25 4.25
Nos. 474-478 (5) 5.85 5.85

Souvenir Sheet

479 A57 2500sh multicolored 3.25 3.25

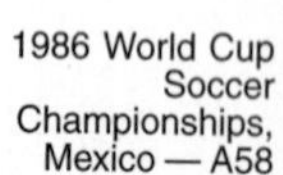

1986 World Cup Soccer Championships, Mexico — A58

Various soccer plays.

1986, Mar. *Perf. 14*
480 A58 10sh multicolored .30 .30
481 A58 180sh multicolored .90 .60
482 A58 250sh multicolored 1.00 .75
483 A58 2500sh multicolored 5.75 *6.50*
Nos. 480-483 (4) 7.95 8.15

Souvenir Sheet

484 A58 3000sh multicolored 5.50 5.50

No. 484 contains vert. stamp.
For overprints see Nos. 514-518.

A59

Halley's Comet A60

Designs: 50sh, Arecibo radio telescope, Puerto Rico, and Tycho Brahe (1546-1601), Danish astronomer. 100sh, Recovery of Astronaut John Glenn, US space capsule, Caribbean, 1962. 140sh, Adoration of the Magi, 1301, by Giotto (1276-1337). 2500sh, Sighting, 1835, Davy Crockett at The Alamo.

1986, Mar. **Litho.** *Perf. 14*
485 A59 50sh multicolored .30 .25
486 A59 100sh multicolored .40 .25
487 A59 140sh multicolored .60 .45
488 A59 2500sh multicolored 5.25 *6.25*
Nos. 485-488 (4) 6.55 7.20

Souvenir Sheet

489 A60 3000sh multicolored 7.50 7.50

For overprints see Nos. 519-523.

Nos. 437, 439-442 and 468 Ovptd. "NRA LIBERATION / 1986" in Silver or Black

1986, Apr. *Perf. 15*
490 A51 175sh multi 1.25 1.10
490A A51 400sh multi 2.50 2.50
491 A51 700sh multi 3.75 3.75
492 A51 1000sh multi (Bk) 4.00 4.00
493 A51 2500sh multi (Bk) 6.50 *7.75*
Nos. 490-493 (5) 18.00 19.10

Souvenir Sheet

Perf. 14

494 A56 1500sh multi (Bk) 6.25 4.75

No. 494 ovptd. in one line in margin. A 400sh also exists with silver overprint. All stamps exist with overprint colors transposed.

Queen Elizabeth II, 60th Birthday

Common Design Type

100sh, At London Zoo, c. 1938. 140sh, At the races, 1970. 2500sh, Sandringham, 1982. 3000sh, Engagement, 1947.

1986, Apr. 21 *Perf. 14*
495 CD339 100sh multi .25 .25
496 CD339 140sh multi .25 .25
497 CD339 2500sh multi 3.75 3.75
Nos. 495-497 (3) 4.25 4.25

Souvenir Sheet

498 CD339 3000sh multi 4.25 4.25

AMERIPEX '86 — A61

50sh, Niagara Falls. 100sh, Jefferson Memorial. 250sh, Liberty Bell. 1000sh, The Alamo. 2500sh, George Washington Bridge. 3000sh, Grand Canyon.

1986, May 22 *Perf. 15*
499 A61 50sh multicolored .30 .30
500 A61 100sh multicolored .30 .30
501 A61 250sh multicolored .50 .50
502 A61 1000sh multicolored 1.90 1.90
503 A61 2500sh multicolored 4.50 4.50
Nos. 499-503 (5) 7.50 7.50

Souvenir Sheet

504 A61 3000sh multicolored 3.75 3.75

Statue of Liberty, cent.

A62

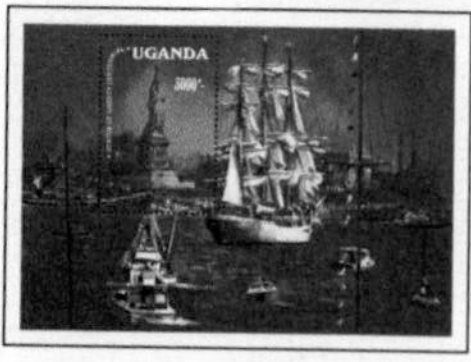

Statue of Liberty, Cent. A63

Tall ships, Operation Sail: 50sh, Gloria, Colombia, vert. 100sh, Mircea, Romania, vert. 140sh, Sagres II, Portugal. 2500sh, Gazela Primero, US.

1986, July *Perf. 14*
505 A62 50sh multicolored .75 .60
506 A62 100sh multicolored 1.00 .60
507 A62 140sh multicolored 1.75 1.25
508 A62 2500sh multicolored 7.75 *10.00*
Nos. 505-508 (4) 11.25 12.45

Souvenir Sheet

509 A63 3000sh multicolored 4.50 4.50

Royal Wedding Issue, 1986

Common Design Type

Designs: 50sh, Prince Andrew and Sarah Ferguson. 140sh, Andrew and Princess Anne. 2500sh, At formal affair. 3000sh, Couple diff.
Nos. 510-512 horiz.

1986, July 23
510 CD340 50sh multicolored .25 .25
511 CD340 140sh multicolored .25 .25
512 CD340 2500sh multicolored 3.75 *4.50*
Nos. 510-512 (3) 4.25 5.00

Souvenir Sheet

513 CD340 3000sh multicolored 5.00 5.00

Nos. 480-484 Ovptd. or Surcharged "WINNERS Argentina 3 W. Germany 2" in Gold in 2 or 3 Lines

1986, Sept. 15 **Litho.** *Perf. 14*
514 A58 50sh on 10sh multi .25 .25
515 A58 180sh multicolored .25 .25
516 A58 250sh multicolored .30 .30
517 A58 2500sh multicolored 3.25 *3.75*
Nos. 514-517 (4) 4.05 4.55

Souvenir Sheet

518 A58 3000sh multicolored 6.00 6.00

Nos. 485-489 Ovptd. with Halley's Comet Emblem

1986, Oct. 15 **Litho.** *Perf. 14*
519 A59 50sh multicolored .35 .35
520 A59 100sh multicolored .60 .40
521 A59 140sh multicolored .80 .70
522 A59 2500sh multicolored 6.75 *8.00*
Nos. 519-522 (4) 8.50 9.45

Souvenir Sheet

523 A60 3000sh multicolored 6.50 6.50

Christian Martyrs — A64

Designs: 50sh, St. Kizito. 150sh, St. Kizito educating Ganda converts. 200sh, Execution of Bishop James Hannington. 1000sh, Mwanga's execution of converts, cent. 1500sh, King Mwanga sentencing Christians to death.

1986, Oct. 15
524 A64 50sh multicolored .25 .25
525 A64 150sh multicolored .25 .25
526 A64 200sh multicolored .50 .50
527 A64 1000sh multicolored 2.00 *3.00*
Nos. 524-527 (4) 3.00 4.00

Souvenir Sheet

528 A64 1500sh multicolored 2.25 2.25

A65

Christmas — A66

Paintings by Albrecht Durer and Titian: 50sh, Madonna of the Cherries. 150sh, Madonna and Child, vert. 200sh, Assumption of the Virgin, vert. 2500sh, Praying Hands, vert. No. 533, Adoration of the Magi. No. 534, Presentation of the Virgin in the Temple.

1986, Nov. 26 **Litho.** *Perf. 14*
529 A65 50sh multicolored .25 .25
530 A65 150sh multicolored .55 .25
531 A65 200sh multicolored .75 .30
532 A65 2500sh multicolored 5.50 *7.00*
Nos. 529-532 (4) 7.05 7.80

Souvenir Sheets

533 A66 3000sh multicolored 5.00 5.00
534 A66 3000sh multicolored 5.00 5.00

Birds and Animals — A67

2sh, Red-billed firefinch. 5sh, African pygmy kingfisher. 10sh, Scarlet-chested sunbird. 25sh, White rhinoceros. 35sh, Lion. 45sh, Cheetahs. 50sh, Cordon bleu. 100sh, Giant eland. No. 543, Carmine bee-eaters. No. 544, Cattle egret, zebra.

1987 *Perf. 15*
535 A67 2sh multi .40 .35
536 A67 5sh multi .55 .35
537 A67 10sh multi .80 .35
538 A67 25sh multi 1.25 .95
539 A67 35sh multi 1.25 1.25
540 A67 45sh multi 1.50 *1.75*
541 A67 50sh multi 1.75 *2.10*
542 A67 100sh multi 2.75 *3.75*
Nos. 535-542 (8) 10.25 10.85

Souvenir Sheets

543 A67 150sh multi 4.50 4.50
544 A67 150sh multi 4.50 4.50

Issue dates: Nos. 535-537, 541, 543, Nov. 2; Nos. 538-540, 542-544, July 22.

Transportation Innovations A68

2sh, Eagle, 1987. 3sh, Bremen, 1928. 5sh, Winnie Mae, 1933. 10sh, Voyager, 1986. 15sh, Chanute biplane glider, 1896. 25sh, Norge, 1926. 35sh, Curtis biplane, USS Pennsylvania, 1911. 45sh, Freedom 7, 1961. 100sh, Concorde, 1976.

1987, Aug. 14
545 A68 2sh multicolored .30 .30
546 A68 3sh multicolored .30 .30
547 A68 5sh multicolored .35 .35
548 A68 10sh multicolored .50 .50
549 A68 15sh multicolored .80 .80
550 A68 25sh multicolored 1.10 1.10
551 A68 35sh multicolored 1.75 1.75
552 A68 45sh multicolored 2.00 2.00
553 A68 100sh multicolored 5.75 *6.75*
Nos. 545-553 (9) 12.85 13.85

1988 Summer Olympics, Seoul — A69

Flags and athletes.

1987, Oct. 5 *Perf. 14½x14*

554 A69 5sh Torch bearer .25 .25
555 A69 10sh Swimming .30 .30
556 A69 50sh Cycling 1.25 1.25
557 A69 100sh Gymnastic rings 2.50 2.50
Nos. 554-557 (4) 4.30 4.30

Souvenir Sheet

558 A69 150sh Boxing 4.00 *4.50*

A70

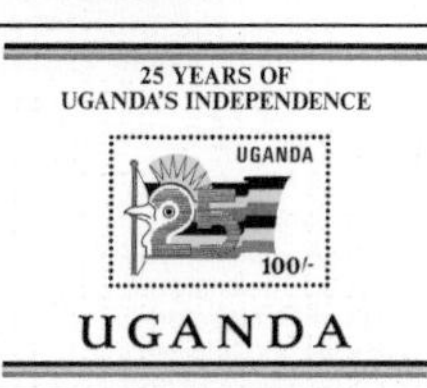

Natl. Independence, 25th Anniv. — A71

10sh, Mulago Hospital. 25sh, Independence Monument. 50sh, High Court.

1987, Oct. 8

559 A70 5sh shown .25 .25
560 A70 10sh multicolored .45 .45
561 A70 25sh multicolored .90 .90
562 A70 50sh multicolored 1.75 1.75
Nos. 559-562 (4) 3.35 3.35

Souvenir Sheet

563 A71 100sh shown 3.25 3.25

A72

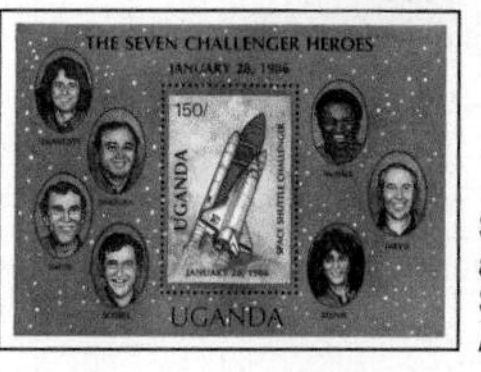

Science and Space A73

Designs: 5sh, Hippocrates, father of modern medicine, caduceus and surgeons. 25sh, Albert Einstein and Theory of Relativity equation. 35sh, Sir Isaac Newton and Optics Theory. 45sh, Karl Benz (1844-1929), German engineer, automobile pioneer, and the Velocipede, Mercedes-Benz sports coupe and manufacturers' emblems.

1987, Nov. 2 *Perf. 14½x14*

564 A72 5sh multicolored .60 .60
565 A72 25sh multicolored 2.50 2.50
566 A72 35sh multicolored 3.00 3.00
567 A72 45sh multicolored 3.75 3.75
Nos. 564-567 (4) 9.85 9.85

Souvenir Sheet

Perf. 14x14½

568 A73 150sh shown 5.75 5.75

Birds — A74

5sh, Golden-backed weaver. 10sh, Hoopoe. 15sh, Red-throated bee-eater. 25sh, Lilac-breasted roller. 35sh, Pygmy goose. 45sh, Scarlet-chested sunbird. 50sh, Crowned crane. 100sh, Long-tailed fiscal shrike.
No. 577, African barn owl, horiz. No. 578, African fish-eagle, horiz.

1987, Nov. 2 **Litho.** *Perf. 14*

569 A74 5sh multicolored .75 *.75*
570 A74 10sh multicolored 1.60 1.40
571 A74 15sh multicolored 1.75 1.40
572 A74 25sh multicolored 2.25 1.90
573 A74 35sh multicolored 2.50 2.10
574 A74 45sh multicolored 2.75 2.75
575 A74 50sh multicolored 2.75 2.75
576 A74 100sh multicolored 5.00 *5.00*
Nos. 569-576 (8) 19.35 18.05

Souvenir Sheets

577 A74 150sh multicolored 4.25 4.25
578 A74 150sh multicolored 4.25 4.25

14th World Boy Scout Jamboree, Australia, 1987-88 — A75

Activities: 5sh, Stamp collecting, Uganda Nos. 84 and 116. 25sh, Planting trees, Natl. flag. 35sh, Canoeing on Lake Victoria. 45sh, Hiking and camping. 150sh, Logo of 1987 jamboree and natl. Boy Scout organization emblem.

1987, Nov. 20

579 A75 5sh multicolored .30 .30
580 A75 25sh multicolored 1.10 1.10
581 A75 35sh multicolored 1.60 1.60
582 A75 45sh multicolored 1.90 1.90
Nos. 579-582 (4) 4.90 4.90

Souvenir Sheet

583 A75 150sh multicolored 4.75 4.75

Christmas A76

The life of Christ and the Virgin pictured on bas-reliefs, c. 1250, and a tapestry from France: 5sh, The Annunciation. 10sh, The Nativity. 50sh, Flight into Egypt. 100sh, The Adoration of the Magi. 150sh, The Mystic Wine Tapestry.

1987, Dec. 18

584 A76 5sh multicolored .25 .25
585 A76 10sh multicolored .25 .25
586 A76 50sh multicolored 1.40 *1.75*
587 A76 100sh multicolored 2.60 *3.00*
Nos. 584-587 (4) 4.50 5.25

Souvenir Sheet

588 A76 150sh multicolored 4.75 4.75

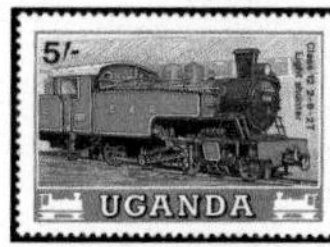

Locomotives A77

Designs: 5sh, Class 12 2-6-2T light shunter. 10sh, Class 92 1Co-Co1 diesel electric. 15sh, Class 2-8-2. 25sh, Class 2-6-2T light shunter. 35sh, Class 4-8-0. 45sh, Class 4-8-2. 50sh, Class 4-8-4+4-8-4 Garratt. 100sh, Class 87 1Co-Co1 diesel electric. No. 597, Class 59 4-8-2+2-8-4 Garratt. No. 598, Class 31 2-8-4.

1988, Jan. 18

589 A77 5sh multicolored .25 .25
590 A77 10sh multicolored .45 .45
591 A77 15sh multicolored .70 .65
592 A77 25sh multicolored 1.00 1.00
593 A77 35sh multicolored 1.60 1.25
594 A77 45sh multicolored 2.00 1.75
595 A77 50sh multicolored 2.10 1.90
596 A77 100sh multicolored 4.25 2.75
Nos. 589-596 (8) 12.35 10.00

Souvenir Sheets

597 A77 150sh multicolored 5.00 5.00
598 A77 150sh multicolored 5.00 5.00

Minerals — A78

1sh, Columbite-tantalite. 2sh, Galena. 5sh, Malachite. 10sh, Cassiterite. 35sh, Ferberite. 50sh, Emerald. 100sh, Monazite. 150sh, Microcline.

1988, Jan. 18

599 A78 1sh multicolored .25 .25
600 A78 2sh multicolored .25 .25
601 A78 5sh multicolored .25 .25
602 A78 10sh multicolored .35 .35
603 A78 35sh multicolored 1.50 1.50
604 A78 50sh multicolored 2.00 2.00
605 A78 100sh multicolored 3.50 3.50
606 A78 150sh multicolored 5.25 5.25
Nos. 599-606 (8) 13.35 13.35

1988 Summer Olympics, Seoul — A79

5sh, Hurdles. 25sh, High jump. 35sh, Javelin. 45sh, Long jump.
150sh, Medals, five-ring emblem.

1988, May 16 **Litho.** *Perf. 14*

607 A79 5sh multi .30 .30
608 A79 25sh multi .55 *.75*
609 A79 35sh multi .60 *.75*
610 A79 45sh multi .85 *1.00*
Nos. 607-610 (4) 2.30 2.80

Souvenir Sheet

611 A79 150sh multi 2.25 2.25

For overprints see Nos. 651-655.

Flowers — A80

5sh, Spathodea campanulata. 10sh, Gloriosa simplex. 20sh, Thevetica peruviana, vert. 25sh, Hibiscus schizopetalus. 35sh, Aframomum sceptrum. 45sh, Adenium obesum. 50sh, Kigelia africana, vert. 100sh, Clappertonia ficifolia.
No. 620, Costus spectabiis. No. 621, Canarina abyssinica, vert.

1988, July 28 **Litho.** *Perf. 15*

612 A80 5sh multicolored .60 .25
613 A80 10sh multicolored .60 .25
614 A80 20sh multicolored .80 .60
615 A80 25sh multicolored .80 .80
616 A80 35sh multicolored .80 *.85*
617 A80 45sh multicolored .80 *1.10*
618 A80 50sh multicolored 1.00 *1.40*
619 A80 100sh multicolored 1.50 *2.25*
Nos. 612-619 (8) 6.90 7.50

Souvenir Sheets

620 A80 150sh multicolored 3.50 3.50
621 A80 150sh multicolored 3.50 3.50

Intl. Red Cross, 125th Anniv. — A81

10sh, "AIDS". 40sh, Immunize children. 70sh, Relief distribution. 90sh, First aid.
150sh, Jean-Henri Dunant, vert.

1988, Oct. 28 **Litho.** *Perf. 14*

622 A81 10sh multicolored .30 .30
623 A81 40sh multicolored 1.00 1.00
624 A81 70sh multicolored 2.00 2.00
625 A81 90sh multicolored 2.50 2.50
Nos. 622-625 (4) 5.80 5.80

Souvenir Sheet

626 A81 150sh multicolored 3.00 3.00

Paintings by Titian — A82

Designs: 10sh, Portrait of a Lady, c. 1508. 20sh, Portrait of a Man, 1507. 40sh, Portrait of Isabella d'Este, c. 1534. 50sh, Portrait of Vincenzo Mosti, 1520. 70sh, Pope Paul III Farnese, c. 1545. 90sh, Violante, 1515. 100sh, Lavinia, Titian's Daughter, c. 1565. 250sh, Portrait of Dr. Parma, c. 1515. No. 635, The Speech of Alfonso D'Avalos, c. 1540. No. 636, Cain and Abel.

1988, Oct. 31 *Perf. 14*

627 A82 10sh multicolored .25 .25
628 A82 20sh multicolored .40 .40
629 A82 40sh multicolored .60 .60
630 A82 50sh multicolored .75 .75
631 A82 70sh multicolored .85 .85
632 A82 90sh multicolored .90 .90
633 A82 100sh multicolored 1.10 1.10
634 A82 250sh multicolored 2.10 2.10
Nos. 627-634 (8) 6.95 6.95

Souvenir Sheets

635 A82 350sh multicolored 3.50 3.50
636 A82 350sh multicolored 3.50 3.50

Game Preserves — A83

Designs: 10sh, Giraffes, Kidepo Valley Natl. Park. 25sh, Zebras, Lake Mburo Natl. Park. 100sh, African buffalo, Murchison Falls Natl. Park. 250sh, Pelicans, Queen Elizabeth Natl. Park. 350sh, Roan antelopes, Lake Mburo Natl. Park.

1988, Nov. 18 **Litho.** *Perf. 14*

637 A83 10sh multicolored .45 .25
638 A83 25sh multicolored 1.60 .65
639 A83 100sh multicolored 3.25 3.25
640 A83 250sh multicolored 9.00 9.00
Nos. 637-640 (4) 14.30 13.15

Souvenir Sheet

641 A83 350sh multicolored 4.25 4.25

WHO 40th Anniv., Alma Ata Declaration 10th Anniv. — A84

10sh, Primary health care. 25sh, Mental health. 45sh, Rural health care. 100sh, Dental care. 200sh, Postnatal care.
350sh, Conference Hall, Alma-Ata, USSR.

1988, Dec. 1

642 A84 10sh multicolored .25 .25
643 A84 25sh multicolored .45 .45
644 A84 45sh multicolored .75 .75
645 A84 100sh multicolored 1.60 1.60
646 A84 200sh multicolored 3.00 3.00
Nos. 642-646 (5) 6.05 6.05

Souvenir Sheet

647 A84 350sh multicolored 4.25 4.25

Miniature Sheet

Christmas, Mickey Mouse 60th Birthday — A85

Walt Disney characters: No. 648a, Santa Claus. b, Goofy. c, Mickey Mouse. d, Huey at conveyor belt. e, Dewey packing building blocks. f, Donald Duck. g, Chip-n-Dale. h, Louie at conveyor belt controls. No. 649, Preparing reindeer for Christmas eve flight. No. 650, Mickey loading sleigh with toys, horiz.

1988, Dec. 2 *Perf. 13½x14, 14x13½*

648 A85 Sheet of 8 10.00 10.00
a.-h. 50sh any single .80 .80

Souvenir Sheets

649 A85 350sh multicolored 5.25 5.25
650 A85 350sh multicolored 5.25 5.25

Nos. 607-611 Ovptd. or Surcharged to Honor Olympic Winners

5sh: "110 M HURDLES / R. KINGDOM / USA"
25sh: "HIGH JUMP / G. AVDEENKO / USSR"
35sh: "JAVELIN / T. KORJUS / FINLAND"
300sh: "LONG JUMP / C. LEWIS / USA"

1989, Jan. 30 **Litho.** *Perf. 14*

651 A79 5sh multicolored .25 .25
652 A79 25sh multicolored .30 .30
653 A79 35sh multicolored .35 .35
654 A79 300sh on 45sh multi 3.25 3.25
Nos. 651-654 (4) 4.15 4.15

Souvenir Sheet

655 A79 350sh on 150sh multi 5.00 5.00

1990 World Cup Soccer Championships, Italy — A86

Various action scenes.

1989, Apr. 24 Litho. Perf. 14

656 A86 10sh multi, vert. .45 .45
657 A86 25sh multicolored .70 .70
658 A86 75sh multicolored 1.60 1.60
659 A86 200sh multi, vert. 2.75 2.75
Nos. 656-659 (4) 5.50 5.50

Souvenir Sheet

660 A86 300sh multicolored 3.75 3.75

Mushrooms — A87

10sh, Suillus granulatus. 15sh, Omphalotus olearius. 45sh, Oudemansiella radicata. 50sh, Clitocybe nebularis. 60sh, Macrolepiota rhacodes. 75sh, Lepista nuda. 150sh, Suillus luteus. 200sh, Agaricus campestris.

No. 669, Schizophyllum commune. No. 670, Bolbitius vitellinus.

1989, Aug. 14 Litho. Perf. 14

661 A87 10sh multicolored .45 .45
662 A87 15sh multicolored .55 .55
663 A87 45sh multicolored 1.15 1.15
664 A87 50sh multicolored 1.15 1.15
665 A87 60sh multicolored 1.20 1.20
666 A87 75sh multicolored 1.40 1.40
667 A87 150sh multicolored 2.60 2.60
668 A87 200sh multicolored 2.75 2.75
Nos. 661-668 (8) 11.25 11.25

Souvenir Sheets

669 A87 350sh multicolored 6.00 6.00
670 A87 350sh multicolored 6.00 6.00

"The Thirty-six Views of Mt. Fuji" — A88

Prints by Hokusai (1760-1849): 10sh, Fuji and the Great Wave off Kanagawa. 15sh, Fuji from Lake Suwa. 20sh, Fuji from Kajikazawa. 60sh, Fuji from Shichirigahama. 90sh, Fuji from Ejiri in Sunshu. 120sh, Fuji Above Lightning. 200sh, Fuji from Lower Meguro in Edo. 250sh, Fuji from Edo. No. 679, The Red Fuji from the Foot. No. 680, Fuji from Umezawa.

1989, May 15 Litho. Perf. 14x13½

671 A88 10sh multicolored .35 .35
672 A88 15sh multicolored .35 .35
673 A88 20sh multicolored .35 .35
674 A88 60sh multicolored .90 .90
675 A88 90sh multicolored 1.40 1.40
676 A88 120sh multicolored 2.00 2.00
677 A88 200sh multicolored 2.75 2.75
678 A88 250sh multicolored 3.00 3.00
Nos. 671-678 (8) 11.10 11.10

Souvenir Sheets

679 A88 500sh multicolored 5.25 5.25
680 A88 500sh multicolored 5.25 5.25

Hirohito (1901-1989), Showa emperor, and Akihito, Heisei emperor of Japan.

PHILEXFRANCE '89 — A89

1989, July 7 Litho. Perf. 14

681 A89 20sh No. 1 .60 .60
682 A89 70sh No. 10 1.50 1.50
683 A89 100sh No. 48 1.75 1.75
684 A89 250sh No. 67 3.50 3.50
a. Souvenir sheet of 4, #681-684 10.00 10.00
Nos. 681-684 (4) 7.35 7.35

No. 684a sold for 500sh.

2nd All African Scout Jamboree, Aug. 3-15 — A90

1989, Aug. 3 Litho. Perf. 14

685 A90 10sh Fatal child ailments .35 .35
686 A90 70sh Raising poultry 1.50 1.50
687 A90 90sh Immunization 1.90 1.90
688 A90 100sh Brick-making 1.90 1.90
Nos. 685-688 (4) 5.65 5.65

Souvenir Sheet

689 A90 500sh Natl. emblem, vert. 5.25 5.25

Scouting, 75th anniv.
For surcharges see Nos. 1301-1304.

Miniature Sheet

Wildlife at Waterhole — A91

Designs: a, Saddle-billed stork. b, White pelican. c, Marabou stork. d, Egyptian vulture, giraffes. e, Bateleur eagle, antelope. f, African elephant. g, Giraffe. h, Goliath heron. i, Black rhinoceros, zebras. j, Zebras, oribi. k, African fish eagle. l, Hippopotamus. m, Black-backed jackal, white pelican. n, Cape buffalo. o, Olive baboon. p, Bohor reedbuck. q, Lesser flamingo, serval. r, Shoebill stork. s, Crowned crane. t, Impala. No. 691, Lion. No. 692, Long-crested eagle.

1989, Sept. 12 Perf. 14½x14

690 A91 Sheet of 20 22.00 22.00
a.-t. 30sh any single .60 .60

Souvenir Sheets

691 A91 500sh multicolored 5.25 5.25
692 A91 500sh multicolored 5.25 5.25

1st Moon Landing, 20th Anniv. — A92

Quotations and scenes from the Apollo 11 mission: 10sh, Launch vehicle, Moon. 20sh, Eagle lower stage on Moon. 30sh, Columbia. 50sh, Eagle landing. 70sh, Aldrin on Moon. 250sh, Armstrong on ladder. 300sh, Eagle ascending. 350sh, Aldrin, diff.

No. 701, Liftoff. No. 702, Parachute landing.

1989, Oct. 20 Litho. Perf. 14

693 A92 10sh multicolored .35 .35
694 A92 20sh multicolored .35 .35
695 A92 30sh multicolored .65 .65
696 A92 50sh multicolored .90 .90
697 A92 70sh multicolored 1.30 1.30
698 A92 250sh multicolored 4.50 4.50
699 A92 300sh multicolored 5.00 5.00
700 A92 350sh multicolored 6.00 6.00
Nos. 693-700 (8) 19.05 19.05

Souvenir Sheets

701 A92 500sh multicolored 5.00 5.00
702 A92 500sh multicolored 5.00 5.00

Nos. 693-697 and 699 horiz.

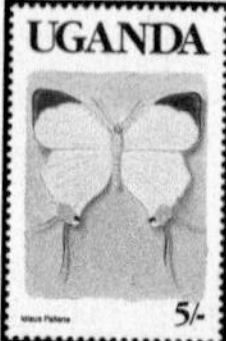
Butterflies — A93

5sh, Ioalus pallene. 10sh, Hewitsonia boisduvali. 20sh, Euxanthe wakefeildi. 30sh, Papilio echerioides. 40sh, Acraea semivitrea. 50sh, Colotis antevippe. 70sh, Acraea perenna. 90sh, Charaxes cynthia. 100sh, Euphaedra neophroa. 150sh, Cymothoe beckeri. 200sh, Vanessula milca. 400sh, Mimacraea marshalli. 500sh, Axiocerses amanga. 1000sh, Precis hierta.

1989, Nov. 13 "UGANDA" in Black

703 A93 5sh multicolored .65 .65
704 A93 10sh multicolored .70 .70
705 A93 20sh multicolored 1.10 1.10
706 A93 30sh multicolored 1.25 1.25
707 A93 40sh multicolored 1.40 1.40
708 A93 50sh multicolored 1.40 1.40
709 A93 70sh multicolored 1.75 1.75
710 A93 90sh multicolored 1.75 1.75
711 A93 100sh multicolored 1.75 1.75
712 A93 150sh multicolored 2.25 2.25
713 A93 200sh multicolored 2.25 2.25
714 A93 400sh multicolored 3.25 3.25
715 A93 500sh multicolored 3.50 3.50
716 A93 1000sh multicolored 4.50 4.50
Nos. 703-716 (14) 27.50 27.50

See Nos. 826-839 for "UGANDA" in blue.

Explorers of Africa — A94

Designs: 10sh, John Speke (1827-64), satellite view of Lake Victoria. 25sh, Sir Richard Burton (1821-90), satellite view of Lake Tanganyika. 40sh, Richard Lander (1804-34), bronze ritual figure of the Bakota tribe. 90sh, Rene Caillie (1799-1838), mosque. 125sh, Dorcas gazelle and Sir Samuel Baker (1821-93), discoverer of Lake Albert. 150sh, Phoenician galley and Necho II (d. 595 B.C.), king of Egypt credited by Herodotus with sending an expedition to circumnavigate Africa. 250sh, Vasco da Gama (c. 1460-1524), 1st European to sail around the Cape of Good Hope, and caravel. 300sh, Sir Henry Stanley (1841-1904), discoverer of Lake Edward, and Lady Alice . No. 725, Dr. David Livingstone (1813-73), discoverer of Victoria Falls, and steam launch Ma-Robert. No. 726, Mary Kingsley (1862-1900), ethnologist, and tail-spot climbing perch.

1989, Nov. 15 Litho. Perf. 14

717 A94 10sh multicolored .30 .30
718 A94 25sh multicolored .35 .35
719 A94 40sh multicolored .55 .55
720 A94 90sh multicolored 1.10 1.10
721 A94 125sh multicolored 1.60 1.60
722 A94 150sh multicolored 1.90 1.90
723 A94 250sh multicolored 3.25 3.25
724 A94 300sh multicolored 3.75 3.75
Nos. 717-724 (8) 12.80 12.80

Souvenir Sheets

725 A94 500sh multicolored 5.25 5.25
726 A94 500sh multicolored 5.25 5.25

Anniversaries and Events — A95

10sh, Bank emblem. 20sh, Satellite dishes, arrows. 75sh, Nehru. 90sh, Pan-American Dixie Clipper. 100sh, Locomotion, Stephenson. 150sh, Concorde cockpit. 250sh, Wapen von Hamburg, Leopoldus Primus. 300sh, Concorde cockpit, crew.

No. 735, Storming of the Bastille. No. 736, Emperor Frederick I Barbarossa, charter.

1989, Dec. 12

727 A95 10sh multicolored .30 .30
728 A95 20sh multicolored .30 .30
729 A95 75sh multicolored 2.40 2.40
730 A95 90sh multicolored 2.40 2.40
731 A95 100sh multicolored 2.40 2.40
732 A95 150sh multicolored 3.75 3.50
733 A95 250sh multicolored 3.75 3.50
734 A95 300sh multicolored 4.75 4.75
Nos. 727-734 (8) 20.05 19.55

Souvenir Sheets

735 A95 500sh multicolored 5.25 5.25
736 A95 500sh multicolored 5.25 5.25

African Development Bank 25th anniv. (10sh); World Telecommunications Day, May 17 (20sh); Birth cent. of Jawaharlal Nehru, 1st prime minister of independent India (75sh); 1st scheduled transatlantic airmail flight, 50th anniv. (90sh); 175th anniv. of the invention of the 1st steam locomotive by George Stephenson and opening of the Stockton & Darlington Railway in 1825 (100sh); 1st test flight of the Concorde, 20th anniv. (150sh, 300sh); Port of Hamburg, 800th anniv. (250sh, No. 736); and French revolution bicent. (No. 735).

Christmas — A96

Religious paintings by Fra Angelico: 10sh, Madonna and Child. 20sh, Adoration of the Magi. 40sh, Virgin and Child Enthroned with Saints. 75sh, The Annunciation. 100sh, St. Peter Martyr triptych center panel. 150sh, Virgin and Child Enthroned with Saints, diff. 250sh, Virgin and Child Enthroned. 350sh, Annalena Altarpiece. No. 745, Bosco ai Frati Altarpiece. No. 746, Madonna and Child with Twelve Angels.

1989, Dec. 18

737 A96 10sh multicolored .25 .25
738 A96 20sh multicolored .25 .25
739 A96 40sh multicolored .50 .50
740 A96 75sh multicolored .85 .85
741 A96 100sh multicolored 1.00 1.00
742 A96 150sh multicolored 1.40 1.40
743 A96 250sh multicolored 2.00 2.00
744 A96 350sh multicolored 2.25 2.25
Nos. 737-744 (8) 8.50 8.50

Souvenir Sheets

745 A96 500sh multicolored 3.00 3.00
746 A96 500sh multicolored 3.00 3.00

Orchids — A97

10sh, Aerangis kotschyana. 15sh, Angraecum infundibulare. 45sh, Cyrtorchis chailluana. 50sh, Aerangis rhodosticta. 100sh, Eulophia speciosa. 200sh, Calanthe sylvatica. 250sh, Vanilla imperialis. 350sh, Polystachya vulcanica.

No. 755, Ansellia africana. No. 756, Ancistrochilus rothschildianus.

1989, Dec. 18

747 A97 10sh multicolored .30 .30
748 A97 15sh multicolored .30 .30
749 A97 45sh multicolored .70 .70
750 A97 50sh multicolored .75 .75
751 A97 100sh multicolored 1.40 1.40
752 A97 200sh multicolored 3.00 3.00
753 A97 250sh multicolored 3.50 3.50
754 A97 350sh multicolored 5.00 5.00
Nos. 747-754 (8) 14.95 14.95

Souvenir Sheets

755 A97 500sh multicolored 6.75 6.75
756 A97 500sh multicolored 6.75 6.75

For overprints see Nos. 782-786A.

EXPO '90, Osaka — A98

Flowering trees — 10sh, Thevetia peruviana. 20sh, Acanthus eminens. 90sh, Gnidia glauca. 150sh, Oncoba spinosa. 175sh, Hibiscus rosa-sinensis. 400sh, Jacaranda mimosifolia. 500sh, Erythrina abyssinica. 700sh, Bauhinia purpurea.

No. 765, Delonix regia. No. 766, Cassia didymobatrya.

1990, Apr. 17 Litho. Perf. 14

757 A98 10sh multi .30 .30
758 A98 20sh multi .30 .30
759 A98 90sh multi .70 .70
760 A98 150sh multi 1.00 1.00
761 A98 175sh multi 1.10 1.10
762 A98 400sh multi 1.75 1.75
763 A98 500sh multi 2.00 2.00
764 A98 700sh multi 2.25 2.25
Nos. 757-764 (8) 9.40 9.40

Souvenir Sheets

765 A98 1000sh multi 5.50 5.50
766 A98 1000sh multi 5.50 5.50

World War II Milestones A99

Designs: 5sh, Allies penetrate west wall, Dec. 3, 1944. 10sh, VE Day, May 8, 1945. 20sh, US forces capture Okinawa, June 22, 1945. 75sh, DeGaulle named commander of all Free French forces, Apr. 4, 1944. 100sh, US troops invade Saipan, June 15, 1944. 150sh, Allied troops launch Operation Market Garden, Sept. 17, 1944. 200sh, Gen. MacArthur returns to Philippines, Oct. 20, 1944. 300sh, US victory at Coral Sea, May 8, 1942. 350sh, First battle of El Alamein, July 1, 1942. 500sh, Naval battle at Guadalcanal, Nov. 12, 1942. 1000sh, Battle of Britain.

1990, June 8 Litho. *Perf. 14*

767 A99 5sh multicolored .30 .30
768 A99 10sh multicolored .30 .30
769 A99 20sh multicolored .30 .30
770 A99 75sh multicolored .60 .60
771 A99 100sh multicolored .80 .80
772 A99 150sh multicolored 1.15 1.15
773 A99 200sh multicolored 1.40 1.40
774 A99 300sh multicolored 2.50 2.50
775 A99 350sh multicolored 3.00 3.00
776 A99 500sh multicolored 4.00 4.00
Nos. 767-776 (10) 14.35 14.35

Souvenir Sheet

777 A99 1000sh multicolored 6.50 6.50

Queen Mother, 90th Birthday A100

1990, July 5

778 250sh Hands clasped 1.00 1.00
779 250sh Facing left 1.00 1.00
780 250sh Holding dog 1.00 1.00
a. A100 Strip of 3, #778-780 4.25 4.25
Nos. 778-780 (3) 3.00 3.00

Souvenir Sheet

781 A100 1000sh like No. 778 4.00 4.00

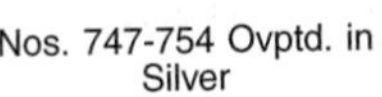

Nos. 747-754 Ovptd. in Silver

Nos. 755-756 Ovptd. in Silver in Sheet Margin

1990 Litho. *Perf. 14*

782 A97 10sh on No. 747 1.00 1.00
782A A97 15sh on No. 748 1.00 1.00
782B A97 45sh on No. 749 1.50 1.50
783 A97 50sh on No. 750 1.50 1.50
783A A97 100sh on No. 751 1.90 1.90
784 A97 200sh on No. 752 2.50 2.50
785 A97 250sh on No. 753 2.50 2.50
785A A97 350sh on No. 754 3.00 3.00
Nos. 782-785A (8) 14.90 14.90

Souvenir Sheet

786 A97 500sh on No. 755 5.00 5.00
786A A97 500sh on No. 756 5.00 5.00

Issue dates: 15sh, 45sh, 100sh, 350sh, No. 786A, Nov.; others, July 30.

Pan African Postal Union, 10th Anniv. — A101

Designs: 750sh, UN Conference on the least developed countries, Paris, Sept. 3-14.

1990, Aug. 3 Litho. *Perf. 14*

787 A101 80sh multicolored 1.25 1.25

Souvenir Sheet

788 A101 750sh multicolored 3.75 3.75

Great Britain No. O1 — A102

Designs: 50sh, Canada #12. 100sh, Baden #4b. 150sh, Switzerland #3L1. 200sh, US #C3a. 300sh, Western Australia #1. 500sh, Uganda #29. 600sh, Great Britain #2. No. 797, Uganda #29. No. 798, Sir Rowland Hill.

1990, Aug. 6 Litho. *Perf. 14*

789 A102 25sh multicolored .35 .35
790 A102 50sh multicolored .65 .65
791 A102 100sh multicolored 1.25 1.25
792 A102 150sh multicolored 1.50 1.50
793 A102 200sh multicolored 1.75 1.75
794 A102 300sh gray & black 2.25 2.25
795 A102 500sh multicolored 2.50 2.50
796 A102 600sh multicolored 2.50 2.50
Nos. 789-796 (8) 12.75 12.75

Souvenir Sheets

Size: 108x77mm

797 A102 1000sh multicolored 5.75 5.75

Size: 119x85mm

798 A102 1000sh scarlet & blk 5.75 5.75

Penny Black, 150th anniversary. Nos. 797-798, Stamp World London '90.

Birds — A103

10sh, African jacana. 15sh, Ground hornbill. 45sh, Kori bustard, vert. 50sh, Secretary bird. 100sh, Egyptian geese. 300sh, Goliath heron, vert. 500sh, Ostrich, vert. 650sh, Saddlebill stork, vert.

No. 807, Volturine guinea fowl, vert. No. 808, Lesser flamingo, vert.

1990, Sept. 3 Litho. *Perf. 14*

799 A103 10sh multicolored .90 .90
800 A103 15sh multicolored .90 .90
801 A103 45sh multicolored 1.10 1.10
802 A103 50sh multicolored 1.10 1.10
803 A103 100sh multicolored 1.75 1.75
804 A103 300sh multicolored 3.00 3.00
805 A103 500sh multicolored 4.00 4.00
806 A103 650sh multicolored 4.25 4.25
Nos. 799-806 (8) 17.00 17.00

Souvenir Sheets

807 A103 1000sh multicolored 5.75 5.75
808 A103 1000sh multicolored 5.75 5.75

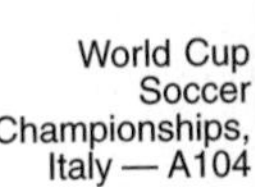

World Cup Soccer Championships, Italy — A104

Players from various national teams.

1990, Sept. 24

809 A104 50sh Cameroun .25 .25
810 A104 100sh Egypt .50 .50
811 A104 250sh Ireland 1.25 1.25
812 A104 600sh West Germany 3.25 3.25
Nos. 809-812 (4) 5.25 5.25

Souvenir Sheets

813 A104 1000sh Sweden 5.25 5.25
814 A104 1000sh Scotland 5.25 5.25

WHO, Promote Better Health A105

Walt Disney characters in scenes promoting improved health: 10sh, Mickey, Minnie Mouse having a good breakfast. 20sh, Huey, Dewey and Louie looking before crossing street. 50sh, Mickey, Donald Duck against smoking. 90sh, Mickey saving Donald from choking. 100sh, Mickey, Goofy using seat belts. 250sh, Mickey, Minnie avoiding drugs. 500sh, Donald, Daisy exercising. 600sh, Mickey showing bicycle safety. No. 823, Mickey, friends at doctor's office. No. 824, Mickey, friends walking.

1990, Oct. 19 Litho. *Perf. 13½x13*

815 A105 10sh multicolored .30 .30
816 A105 20sh multicolored .30 .30
817 A105 50sh multicolored .45 .45
818 A105 90sh multicolored .75 .75
819 A105 100sh multicolored .85 .85
820 A105 250sh multicolored 1.75 1.75
821 A105 500sh multicolored 4.00 4.00
822 A105 600sh multicolored 4.50 4.50
Nos. 815-822 (8) 12.90 12.90

Souvenir Sheets

823 A105 1000sh multicolored 6.00 6.00
824 A105 1000sh multicolored 6.00 6.00

Butterfly Type of 1989

3000sh, Euphaedra eusemoides. 4000sh, Acraea natalica. 5000sh, Euphaedra themis.

"Uganda" in Blue

1990-92 Litho. *Perf. 14*

826 A93 10sh like #704 .65 .65
827 A93 20sh like #705 .75 .75
a. Imprint "1991" .85 .75
828 A93 30sh like #706 .75 .75
829 A93 40sh like #707 .75 .75
830 A93 50sh like #708 1.00 1.00
831 A93 70sh like #709 1.00 1.00
832 A93 90sh like #710 1.10 1.10
833 A93 100sh like #711 1.10 1.10
a. Imprint "1991" 1.20 1.10
834 A93 150sh like #712 1.50 1.50
835 A93 200sh like #713 1.90 1.90
a. Imprint "1991" 1.90 1.90
836 A93 400sh like #714 2.25 2.25
837 A93 500sh like #715 2.25 2.25
838 A93 1000sh like #716 4.50 4.50
839 A93 2000sh like #716 11.00 11.00
a. Imprint "1991" 5.50 5.50
840 A93 3000sh multi 13.50 13.50
841 A93 4000sh multi 14.50 14.50
842 A93 5000sh multi 14.50 14.50
Nos. 826-842 (17) 73.00 73.00

Issue dates: 10sh, 20sh, 30sh, 40sh, 70sh, 90sh, 100sh, 150sh, 200sh, 2000sh, 11/90. 50sh, 400sh, 500sh, 1000sh, 11/4/91. 3000sh, 4000sh, 10/9/92.

Nos. 826-829, 831-835, 839-842 do not have a year date imprint below design. Nos. 830, 836-838 are inscribed "1991" below design.

Christmas — A106

Details from paintings by Rubens: 10sh, 500sh, The Baptism of Christ. 20sh, 150sh, 400sh, 600sh, St. Gregory the Great and Other Saints. 100sh, Saints Nereus, Domitilla and Achilleus. 300sh, Saint Augustine. No. 853, Victory of Eucharistic Truth Over Heresy, horiz. No. 854, Triumph of Faith, horiz.

1990, Dec. 17 Litho. *Perf. 14*

845 A106 10sh multicolored .25 .25
846 A106 20sh multicolored .25 .25
847 A106 100sh multicolored .80 .80
848 A106 150sh multicolored 1.10 1.10
849 A106 300sh multicolored 1.75 1.75
850 A106 400sh multicolored 1.90 1.90
851 A106 500sh multicolored 2.00 2.00
852 A106 600sh multicolored 2.25 2.25
Nos. 845-852 (8) 10.30 10.30

Souvenir Sheets

853 A106 1000sh multicolored 5.25 5.25
854 A106 1000sh multicolored 5.25 5.25

Natl. Census — A107

Design: 1000sh, Counting on fingers, houses, people.

1990, Dec. 28 Litho. *Perf. 14*

855 A107 20sh multicolored 1.00 1.00

Souvenir Sheet

856 A107 1000sh multicolored 5.00 5.00

Wetlands Fauna — A108

No. 857: a, Damselfly. b, Purple gallinule. c, Sitatunga. d, Purple heron. e, Bushpig. f, Vervet monkey. g, Long reed frog. h, Malachite kingfisher. i, Marsh mongoose. j, Painted reed frog. k, Jacana. l, Charaxes butterfly. m, Nile crocodile. n, Herald snake. o, Dragonfly. p, Lungfish.

No. 858, Nile monitor, horiz.

1991, Jan. 1 Litho. *Perf. 14*

857 A108 70sh Sheet of 16, #a.-p. 21.00 21.00

Souvenir Sheet

858 A108 1000sh multi 11.50 11.50

Fish — A109

Designs: 10sh, Haplochromis limax. 20sh, Notobranchius palmqvisti. 40sh, Distichodus affinis. 90sh, Haplochromis sauvagei. 100sh, Aphyosemion calliurum. 350sh, Haplochromis johnstoni. 600sh, Haplochromis dichrourus. 800sh, Hemichromis bimaculatus. No. 867, Haplochromis sp. No. 868, Aphyosemion striatum.

1991, Jan. 18 Litho. *Perf. 14*

859 A109 10sh multicolored .30 .30
860 A109 20sh multicolored .30 .30
861 A109 40sh multicolored .30 .30
862 A109 90sh multicolored .55 .55
863 A109 100sh multicolored .65 .65
864 A109 350sh multicolored 1.60 1.60
865 A109 600sh multicolored 3.25 3.25
866 A109 800sh multicolored 4.00 4.00
Nos. 859-866 (8) 10.95 10.95

Souvenir Sheets

867 A109 1000sh multicolored 6.50 6.50
868 A109 1000sh multicolored 6.50 6.50

1992 Summer Olympics, Barcelona — A110

20sh, Women's hurdles. 40sh, Long jump. 125sh, Table tennis. 250sh, Soccer. 500sh, 800-meter race.

No. 874 Women's 4x100-meter relay, horiz. No. 875, Opening ceremony, horiz.

1991, Feb. 25 Litho. *Perf. 14*

869 A110 20sh multicolored .25 .25
870 A110 40sh multicolored .25 .25
871 A110 125sh multicolored .80 .80
872 A110 250sh multicolored 1.75 1.75
873 A110 500sh multicolored 3.25 3.25
Nos. 869-873 (5) 6.30 6.30

Souvenir Sheets

874 A110 1200sh multicolored 5.00 5.00
875 A110 1200sh multicolored 5.00 5.00

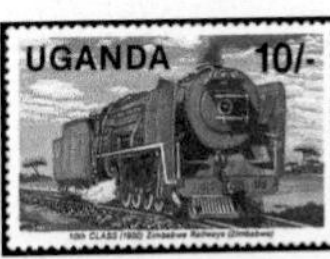

Trains — A111

Designs: 10sh, 10th Class, Zimbabwe. 20sh, 12th Class, Zimbabwe. 80sh, Tribal class, Tanzania and Zambia. 200sh, 4-6-0 Type, Egypt. 300sh, Mikado, Sudan. 400sh, Mountain class Garrat, Uganda. 500sh, Mallet Type, Uganda. 1000sh, 5 F 1 Electric locomotive, South Africa. No. 884, 4-8-2 Type, Egypt. No. 885, Atlantic type, Egypt. No. 886, 4-8-2 Type, Angola. No. 887, Mallet Compound Type, Natal.

1991, Apr. 2 Litho. *Perf. 14*

876 A111 10sh multicolored .30 .30
877 A111 20sh multicolored .30 .30
878 A111 80sh multicolored .45 .45
879 A111 200sh multicolored 1.30 1.30

880 A111 300sh multicolored 1.75 1.75
881 A111 400sh multicolored 2.40 2.40
882 A111 500sh multicolored 3.00 3.00
883 A111 1000sh multicolored 5.75 5.75
Nos. 876-883 (8) 15.25 15.25

Souvenir Sheets

884 A111 1200sh multicolored 4.50 4.50
885 A111 1200sh multicolored 4.50 4.50
886 A111 1200sh multicolored 4.50 4.50
887 A111 1200sh multicolored 4.50 4.50

Even though Nos. 886-887 have the same issue date as Nos. 876-885, their dollar value was lower when they were released.

Phila Nippon '91 — A112

Walt Disney characters in Japan: 10sh, Scrooge McDuck celebrating Ga-No-Iwai. 20sh, Mickey removes shoes before entering Minnie's home. 70sh, Cartman Goofy leading horse. 80sh, Daisy, Minnie exchange gifts. 300sh, Minnie kneels at entrance to home. 400sh, Mickey, Donald in volcanic sand bath. 500sh, Clarabelle Cow enjoys incense burning. 1000sh, Mickey, Minnie writing New Year cards. No. 896, Mickey, Donald and Goofy in public bath. No. 897, Mickey and friends playing Japanese music.

1991, May 29 Litho. *Perf. 14x13½*

888 A112 10sh multicolored .25 .25
889 A112 20sh multicolored .25 .25
890 A112 70sh multicolored .45 .45
891 A112 80sh multicolored .50 .50
892 A112 300sh multicolored 1.90 1.90
893 A112 400sh multicolored 2.40 2.40
894 A112 500sh multicolored 3.25 3.25
895 A112 1000sh multicolored 6.00 6.00
Nos. 888-895 (8) 15.00 15.00

Souvenir Sheets

896 A112 1200sh multicolored 7.50 7.50
897 A112 1200sh multicolored 7.50 7.50

17th World Scout Jamboree, Korea — A113

Designs: 20sh, Lord Baden-Powell. 80sh, Scouts collecting stamps. 100sh, Scout encampment, NY World's Fair, 1939. 150sh, Cover of 1st Scout Handbook. 300sh, Cooking over campfire. 400sh, Neil Armstrong, Edwin Aldrin, 1st scouts on moon. 500sh, Hands raised for Scout Pledge. 1000sh, Statue to Unknown Scout, Gilwell Park, England. No. 906, William D. Boyce, Lord Baden-Powell, Rev. L. Hadley. No. 907, 17th Jamboree Emblem.

1991, May 27 *Perf. 14*

898 A113 20sh multicolored .30 .30
899 A113 80sh multicolored .45 .45
900 A113 100sh multicolored .55 .55
901 A113 150sh grn & blk .80 .80
902 A113 300sh multicolored 1.50 1.50
903 A113 400sh multicolored 2.10 2.10
904 A113 500sh multicolored 2.50 2.50
905 A113 1000sh multicolored 4.75 4.75
Nos. 898-905 (8) 12.95 12.95

Souvenir Sheets

906 A113 1200sh multicolored 7.00 7.00
907 A113 1200sh cream & blk 7.00 7.00

For surcharge see No. 1305.

Paintings by Vincent Van Gogh A114

Paintings: 10sh, Snowy Landscape with Arles in the Background. 20sh, Peasant Woman Binding Sheaves, vert. 60sh, The Drinkers. 80sh, View of Auvers. 200sh, Mourning Man, vert. 400sh, Still Life: Vase with Roses. 800sh, The Raising of Lazarus. 1000sh, The Good Samaritan, vert. No. 916, First Steps. No. 917, Village Street and Steps in Auvers with Figures.

1991, June 26 Litho. *Perf. 13½*

908 A114 10sh multicolored .25 .25
909 A114 20sh multicolored .25 .25
910 A114 60sh multicolored .35 .35
911 A114 80sh multicolored .45 .45
912 A114 200sh multicolored 1.15 1.15
913 A114 400sh multicolored 2.25 2.25
914 A114 800sh multicolored 4.50 4.50
915 A114 1000sh multicolored 5.75 5.75
Nos. 908-915 (8) 14.95 14.95

Size: 102x76mm

Imperf

916 A114 1200sh multicolored 7.00 7.00
917 A114 1200sh multicolored 7.00 7.00

Royal Family Birthday, Anniversary
Common Design Type

No. 926, Elizabeth, Philip. No. 927, Sons, Diana, Charles.

1991, July 5 Litho. *Perf. 14*

918 CD347 20sh multi .25 .25
919 CD347 70sh multi .25 .25
920 CD347 90sh multi .40 .40
921 CD347 100sh multi .45 .45
922 CD347 200sh multi .80 .80
923 CD347 500sh multi 1.75 1.75
924 CD347 600sh multi 2.25 2.25
925 CD347 1000sh multi 3.50 3.50
Nos. 918-925 (8) 9.65 9.65

Souvenir Sheets

926 CD347 1200sh multi 4.00 4.00
927 CD347 1200sh multi 4.00 4.00

20sh, 100sh, 200sh, 1000sh, No. 927, Charles and Diana, 10th wedding anniversary. Others, Queen Elizabeth II, 65th birthday.

Charles de Gaulle, Birth Cent. — A115

Designs: 20sh, Portrait, vert. 70sh, Liberation of Paris, 1944, vert. 90sh, With King George VI, 1940, vert. 100sh, Reviewing Free French forces, 1940. 200sh, Making his appeal on BBC, 1940. 500sh, In Normandy, 1944. 600sh, At Albert Hall, 1940. 1000sh, Becoming President of France, 1959, vert. No. 936, Entering Paris, 1944, vert. No. 937, With Eisenhower, 1942.

1991, July 15 *Perf. 14*

928 A115 20sh multicolored .25 .25
929 A115 70sh multicolored .30 .30
930 A115 90sh multicolored .40 .40
931 A115 100sh multicolored .45 .45
932 A115 200sh multicolored .85 .85
933 A115 500sh multicolored 2.10 2.10
934 A115 600sh multicolored 2.50 2.50
935 A115 1000sh multicolored 4.25 4.25
Nos. 928-935 (8) 11.10 11.10

Souvenir Sheets

936 A115 1200sh multicolored 6.00 6.00
937 A115 1200sh multicolored 6.00 6.00

Mushrooms — A116

Designs: 20sh, Volvariella bingensis. 70sh, Agrocybe broadwayi. 90sh, Camarophyllus olidus. 140sh, Marasmius arborescens. 180sh, Marasmiellus subcinereus. 200sh, Agaricus campestris. 500sh, Chlorophyllum molybdites. 1000sh, Agaricus bingensis. No. 946, Leucocoprinus cepaestipes, horiz. No. 947, Laccaria lateritia, horiz.

1991, July 19 Litho. *Perf. 14*

938 A116 20sh multicolored .25 .25
939 A116 70sh multicolored .30 .30
940 A116 90sh multicolored .40 .40
941 A116 140sh multicolored .60 .60
942 A116 180sh multicolored .75 .75
943 A116 200sh multicolored .80 .80
944 A116 500sh multicolored 2.40 2.40
945 A116 1000sh multicolored 4.75 4.75
Nos. 938-945 (8) 10.25 10.25

Souvenir Sheets

946 A116 1200sh multicolored 4.50 4.50
947 A116 1200sh multicolored 4.50 4.50

World Wildlife Type of 1983

1991, Aug. 1

948 A43 100sh as No. 371 .80 .80
949 A43 140sh as No. 372 1.15 1.15
950 A43 200sh as No. 373 1.50 1.50
951 A43 600sh as No. 374 4.50 4.50
Nos. 948-951 (4) 7.95 7.95

Souvenir Sheets

Perf. 13x12½

952 A43 1200sh Giraffe 8.00 8.00
953 A43 1200sh Rhinoceros 8.00 8.00

World Wildlife Fund. Nos. 952-953 do not have the WWF emblem.

Flowers in Royal Botanical Gardens, Kew — A118

No. 954: a, Cypripedium calceolus. b, Rhododendron thomsonii. c, Ginkgo biloba. d, Magnolia campbellii. e, Wisteria sinensis. f, Clerodendrum ugandense. g, Eulophia horsfallii. h, Aerangis rhodosticta. i, Abelmoschus moschatus. j, Gloriosa superba. k, Carissa edulis. l, Ochna kirkii. m, Canarina abyssinica. n, Nymphaea caerulea. o, Ceropegia succulenta. p, Strelitzia reginae. q, Strongylodon macrobotrys. r, Victoria amazonica. s, Orchis militaris. t, Sophora microphylla.

No. 955 — Royal Botanic Gardens, Melbourne, Australia: a, Anigozanthos manglesii. b, Banksia grandis. c, Clianthus formosus. d, Gossypium sturtianum. e, Callistemon lanceolatus. f, Saintpaulia ionantha. g, Calodendrum capense. h, Aloe ferox. i, Bolusanthus speciosus. j, Lithops schwantesii k, Protea repens. l, Plumbago capensis. m, Clerodendrum thomsoniae. n, Thunbergia alata. o, Schotia latifolia. p, Epacris impressa. q, Acacia pycnantha. r, Telopea speciosissima. s, Wahlenbergia gloriosa. t, Eucalyptus globulus. No. 956, The Pagoda, Kew. No. 957, Temple of the Winds, Melbourne.

1991, Nov. 25 Litho. *Perf. 14½*

954 A118 100sh Sheet of 20, #a.-t. 12.00 12.00
955 A118 90sh Sheet of 20, #a.-t. 8.00 8.00

Souvenir Sheets

956 A118 1400sh multicolored 8.00 8.00
957 A118 1400sh multicolored 5.50 5.50

No. 956 contains one 30x38mm stamp.

While Nos. 955 and 957 have the same issue date as Nos. 954 and 956, their dollar value was lower when released.

Christmas — A120

Paintings by Piero Della Francesca: 20sh, Madonna with Child and Angels. 50sh, The Baptism of Christ. 80sh, Polyptych of Mercy. 100sh, The Madonna of Mercy. 200sh, The Legend of the True Cross: The Annunciation. 500sh, Pregnant Madonna. 1000sh, Polyptych of St. Anthony: The Annunciation. 1500sh, The Nativity. No. 968, The Brera Altarpiece. No. 969, Polyptych of St. Anthony.

1991, Dec. 18 Litho. *Perf. 12*

960 A120 20sh multicolored .25 .25
961 A120 50sh multicolored .25 .25
962 A120 80sh multicolored .35 .35
963 A120 100sh multicolored .45 .45
964 A120 200sh multicolored .85 .85
965 A120 500sh multicolored 2.10 2.10
966 A120 1000sh multicolored 4.25 4.25
967 A120 1500sh multicolored 6.50 6.50
Nos. 960-967 (8) 15.00 15.00

Souvenir Sheets

Perf. 14½

968 A120 1800sh multicolored 7.50 7.50
969 A120 1800sh multicolored 7.50 7.50

Boy Scouts — A121

Designs: 20sh, Boy Scout Monument, Silver Bay, NY and Ernest Thompson Seton, first chief scout. 50sh, Tree house and Daniel Beard, Boy Scout pioneer, vert. 1500sh, Boy Scout emblem.

1992, Jan. 6 Litho. *Perf. 14*

970 A121 20sh multicolored .90 .90
971 A121 50sh multicolored 1.25 1.25

Souvenir Sheet

972 A121 1500sh multicolored 6.50 6.50

YMCA-Boy Scouts partnership, Lord Robert Baden-Powell, 50th death anniv. in 1991 (#970) and 17th World Scout Jamboree, Korea (#971-972).

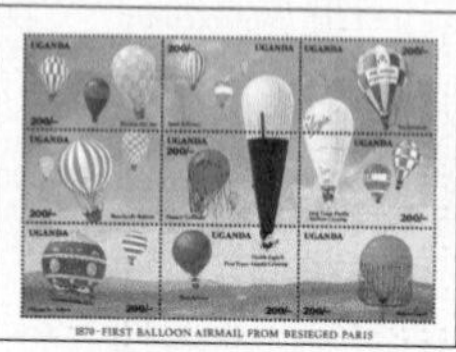

Balloons — A122

Balloons: a, Modern Hot Air. b, Sport. c, Pro Juventute. d, Blanchard's. e, Nadar's Le Geant. f, First trans-Pacific balloon crossing. g, Montgolfier's. h, Paris, Double Eagle II, used in first trans-Atlantic balloon crossing. i, Tethered.

1992, Jan. 6 Litho. *Perf. 14*

974 A122 200sh Sheet of 9, #a.-i. 9.50 9.50

Japanese Attack on Pearl Harbor, 50th Anniv. (in 1991) — A123

Designs: a, Japanese bombers attack USS Vestal. b, Japanese Zero fighter. c, Zeros over burning USS Arizona. d, Battleship Row, USS Nevada under way. e, Japanese Val dive bomber. f, US Dauntless dive bomber attacking Hiryu. g, Japanese planes over Midway Island. h, US Buffalo fighter plane. i, US Wildcat fighters over carrier. j, USS Yorktown and Hammann torpedoed by Japanese submarine.

1992, Jan. 6 *Perf. 14½x15*

975 A123 200sh Sheet of 10, #a.-j. 12.50 12.50

Battle of Midway, 50th anniv. (#975f-975j). Inscription for No. 975i incorrectly describes fighters as Hellcats.

Anniversaries and Events — A124

Designs: 400sh, Glider No. 8. 500sh, Man breaking pieces from Berlin Wall. 700sh, Portrait of Mozart and scene from "The Magic Flute." 1200sh, Electric locomotive.

1992, Jan. 6 Litho. *Perf. 14*

976 A124 400sh multicolored 1.60 1.60
977 A124 500sh multicolored 2.00 2.00
978 A124 700sh multicolored 6.50 6.50
Nos. 976-978 (3) 10.10 10.10

Souvenir Sheet

979 A124 1200sh multicolored 5.75 5.75

Otto Lillienthal, hang glider, cent. (in 1991) (#976). Brandenburg Gate, Bicent. (#977), Wolfgang Amadeus Mozart, death bicent. (#978), Trans-Siberian Railway, cent. (#979).

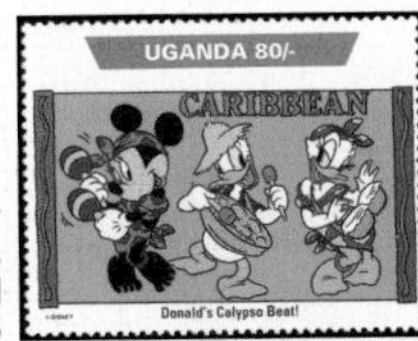

Walt Disney Characters on World Tour — A125

Designs: 20sh, Safari surprise in Africa. 50sh, Pluto's tail of India. 80sh, Donald's calypso beat in Caribbean. 200sh, Goofy pulling rickshaw in China. 500sh, Minnie, Mickey on camel in Egypt. 800sh, Wrestling, Japanese style. 1000sh, Goofy bullfighting in Spain. 1500sh, Mickey scoring in soccer game. No. 988, Daisy singing opera in Germany. No. 989, Mickey and Pluto as Cossack dancers in Moscow.

1992, Feb. *Perf. 13*

980	A125	20sh multi	.30	.30
981	A125	50sh multi	.30	.30
982	A125	80sh multi	.30	.30
983	A125	200sh multi	.70	.70
984	A125	500sh multi	1.75	1.75
985	A125	800sh multi	3.00	3.00
986	A125	1000sh multi	3.50	3.50
987	A125	1500sh multi	5.25	5.25
		Nos. 980-987 (8)	15.10	15.10

Souvenir Sheets

988	A125	2000sh multi, vert.	7.50	7.50
989	A125	2000sh multi, vert.	7.50	7.50

Queen Elizabeth II's Accession to the Throne, 40th Anniv.

Common Design Type

No. 994, Queen, waterfalls. No. 995, Queen, dam.

1992, Feb. 6 **Litho.** *Perf. 14*

990	CD348	100sh multi	.50	.50
991	CD348	200sh multi	.75	.75
992	CD348	500sh multi	2.00	2.00
993	CD348	1000sh multi	4.25	4.25
		Nos. 990-993 (4)	7.50	7.50

Souvenir Sheets

994	CD348	1800sh multi	6.00	6.00
995	CD348	1800sh multi	6.00	6.00

Dinosaurs A126

50sh, Kentrosaurus. 200sh, Iguanodon. 250sh, Hypsilophodon. 300sh, Brachiosaurus. 400sh, Peloneustes. 500sh, Pteranodon. 800sh, Tetra- lophodon. 1000sh, Megalosaurus.

1992, Apr. 8 **Litho.** *Perf. 14*

996	A126	50sh multi	.35	.35
997	A126	200sh multi	.65	.65
998	A126	250sh multi	1.25	1.25
999	A126	300sh multi	1.00	1.00
1000	A126	400sh multi	1.75	1.75
1001	A126	500sh multi	1.60	1.60
1002	A126	800sh multi	2.50	2.50
1003	A126	1000sh multi	4.50	4.50
		Nos. 996-1003 (8)	13.60	13.60

Souvenir Sheets

1004	A126	2000sh like #1003	6.50	6.50
1005	A126	2000sh like #998	6.50	6.50

Nos. 1004-1005 printed in continuous design.

While Nos. 997, 999, 1001-1002, 1005 have the same release date as Nos. 996, 998, 1000, 1003-1004, their value in relation to the dollar was lower when they were released.

Easter — A127

Paintings: 50sh, The Entry into Jerusalem (detail), by Giotto. 100sh, Pilate and the Watch from psalter of Robert de Lisle. 200sh, The Kiss of Judas (detail), by Giotto. 250sh, Christ Washing the Feet of the Disciples, illumination from Life of Christ. 300sh, Christ Seized in the Garden from Melissande Psalter. 500sh, Doubting Thomas, illumination from Life of Christ. 1000sh, The Marys at the Tomb (detail), artist unknown. 2000sh, The Ascension, from 14th century Florentine illuminated manuscript.

Limoge enamels: No. 1014, Agony at Gethsemane. No. 1015, The Piercing of Christ's Side.

1992 **Litho.** *Perf. 13½x14*

1006	A127	50sh multi	.25	.25
1007	A127	100sh multi	.30	.30
1008	A127	200sh multi	.70	.70
1009	A127	250sh multi	.75	.75
1010	A127	300sh multi	.90	.90
1011	A127	500sh multi	1.50	1.50
1012	A127	1000sh multi	3.00	3.00
1013	A127	2000sh multi	6.25	6.25
		Nos. 1006-1013 (8)	13.65	13.65

Souvenir Sheets

1014	A127	2500sh multi	7.00	7.00
1015	A127	2500sh multi	7.00	7.00

Musical Instruments — A128

1992, July 20 **Litho.** *Perf. 14*

1016	A128	50sh Adungu	.25	.25
1017	A128	100sh Endingidi	.30	.30
1018	A128	200sh Akogo	.65	.65
1019	A128	250sh Nanga	.75	.75
1020	A128	300sh Engoma	.90	.90
1021	A128	400sh Amakondere	1.25	1.25
1022	A128	500sh Akakyenkye	1.50	1.50
1023	A128	1000sh Ennanga	3.00	3.00
		Nos. 1016-1023 (8)	8.60	8.60

Discovery of America, 500th Anniv. — A129

Designs: 50sh, World map, 1486. 100sh, Map of Africa, 1508. 150sh, New World, 1500. 200sh, Nina, astrolabe. 600sh, Quadrant, Pinta. 800sh, Hour glass. 900sh, 15th century compass. 2000sh, World map, 1492. No. 1032, 1490 Map by Henricus Martellus, 1490. No. 1033, Sections of 1492 globe.

1992, July 24 **Litho.** *Perf. 14*

1024	A129	50sh multi	.25	.25
1025	A129	100sh multi	.25	.25
1026	A129	150sh multi	.25	.25
1027	A129	200sh multi	.70	.70
1028	A129	600sh multi	2.00	2.00
1029	A129	800sh multi	2.60	2.60
1030	A129	900sh multi	2.75	2.75
1031	A129	2000sh multi	2.25	2.25
		Nos. 1024-1031 (8)	11.05	11.05

Souvenir Sheets

1032	A129	2500sh multi, vert.	6.50	6.50
1033	A129	2500sh multi	4.50	4.50

World Columbian Stamp Expo '92, Chicago.

While Nos. 1024-1026, 1031 and 1033 have the same issue date as Nos. 1027-1030 and 1032, their value in relation to the dollar was lower when they were released.

Hummel Figurines — A130

No. 1034, Little Laundry Girl. No. 1035, Scrub Girl. No. 1036, Sweeper Girl. No. 1037, Little Mother. No. 1038, Little Mountaineer. No. 1039, Little Knitter. No. 1040, Little Cowboy. No. 1041, Little Astronomer.

No. 1042: a, Like #1034. b, Like #1035. c, Like #1036. d, Like #1037.

No. 1043: a, Like #1039. b, Like #1038. c, Like #1040. d, Like #1041.

1992, Aug. 28 **Litho.** *Perf. 14*

1034	A130	50sh multi	.25	.25
1035	A130	200sh multi	.65	.65
1036	A130	250sh multi	.70	.70
1037	A130	300sh multi	.90	.90
1038	A130	600sh multi	1.30	1.30
1039	A130	900sh multi	1.75	1.75
1040	A130	1000sh multi	2.25	2.25
1041	A130	1500sh multi	4.50	4.50
		Nos. 1034-1041 (8)	12.30	12.30

Souvenir Sheets

1042	A130	500sh Sheet of 4, #a.-d.	6.75	6.75
1043	A130	500sh Sheet of 4, #a.-d.	6.75	6.75

While Nos. 1034, 1038-1040, 1043 have the same release date as Nos. 1035-1037, 1041-1042, their value in relation to the dollar was lower when they were released.

1992 Summer Olympics, Barcelona — A131

50sh, Javelin. 100sh, High jump, horiz. 200sh, Pentathlon (Fencing). 250sh, Volleyball. 300sh, Women's platform diving. 500sh, Team cycling. 1000sh, Tennis. 2000sh, Boxing, horiz.

No. 1052, Baseball. No. 1053, Basketball.

1992 **Litho.** *Perf. 14*

1044	A131	50sh multi	.35	.35
1045	A131	100sh multi	.35	.35
1046	A131	200sh multi	.55	.55
1047	A131	250sh multi	.65	.65
1048	A131	300sh multi	.80	.80
1049	A131	500sh multi	1.30	1.30
1050	A131	1000sh multi	2.75	2.75
1051	A131	2000sh multi	5.25	5.25
		Nos. 1044-1051 (8)	12.00	12.00

Souvenir Sheets

1052	A131	2500sh multi	5.75	5.75
1053	A131	2500sh multi	5.75	5.75

Wild Animals — A132

50sh, Spotted hyena. 100sh, Impala. 200sh, Giant forest hog. 250sh, Pangolin. 300sh, Golden monkey. 800sh, Serval. 1000sh, Bush genet. 3000sh, Defassa waterbuck.

No. 1062, Mountain gorilla. No. 1063, Hippopotamus.

1992, Sept. 25 **Litho.** *Perf. 14*

1054	A132	50sh multi	.25	.25
1055	A132	100sh multi	.25	.25
1056	A132	200sh multi	.45	.45
1057	A132	250sh multi	.55	.55
1058	A132	300sh multi	.70	.70
1059	A132	800sh multi	1.75	1.75
1060	A132	1000sh multi	2.25	2.25
1061	A132	3000sh multi	6.75	6.75
		Nos. 1054-1061 (8)	12.95	12.95

Souvenir Sheets

1062	A132	2500sh multi	5.50	5.50
1063	A132	2500sh multi	5.50	5.50

Birds — A133

Designs: 20sh, Red necked falcon. 30sh, Yellow-billed hornbill. 50sh, Purple heron. 100sh, Regal sunbird. 150sh, White-brown robin chat. 200sh, Shining-blue kingfisher. 250sh, Great blue turaco. 300sh, Emerald cuckoo. 500sh, Abyssinian roller. 800sh, Crowned crane. 1000sh, Doherty's bush shrike. 2000sh, Splendid glossy starling. 3000sh, Little bee eater. 4000sh, Red-headed lovebird.

1992, Aug. **Litho.** *Perf. 15x14*

1064	A133	20sh multi	.35	.35
1065	A133	30sh multi	.35	.35
1066	A133	50sh multi	.35	.35
1067	A133	100sh multi	.35	.35
1068	A133	150sh multi	.40	.40
1069	A133	200sh multi	.55	.55
1070	A133	250sh multi	.70	.70
1071	A133	300sh multi	.75	.75
1072	A133	500sh multi	1.40	1.40
1073	A133	800sh multi	2.25	2.25
1074	A133	1000sh multi	2.75	2.75
1075	A133	2000sh multi	5.50	5.50
1076	A133	3000sh multi	8.50	8.50
1076A	A133	4000sh multi	11.00	11.00
		Nos. 1064-1076A (14)	35.20	35.20

Issued: 3000sh, Oct.; others, Aug.?

Walt Disney's Goofy, 60th Anniv. A134

Scenes from Disney animated films: 50sh, Hawaiian Holiday, 1937, vert. 100sh, The Nifty Nineties, 1941, vert. 200sh, Mickey's Fire Brigade, 1935, vert. 250sh, The Art of Skiing, 1941. 300sh, Mickey's Amateurs, 1937. 1000sh, Boat Builders, 1938. 1500sh, The Olympic Champ, 1942, vert. 2000sh, The Olympic Champ, 1942, vert. No. 1085, Goofy and Wilbur, 1939. No. 1086, Goofy's family tree, vert.

Perf. 13½x14, 14x13½

1992, Nov. 2 **Litho.**

1077	A134	50sh multi	.25	.25
1078	A134	100sh multi	.25	.25
1079	A134	200sh multi	.50	.50
1080	A134	250sh multi	.65	.65
1081	A134	300sh multi	.80	.80
1082	A134	1000sh multi	2.50	2.50
1083	A134	1500sh multi	4.00	4.00
1084	A134	2000sh multi	5.25	5.25
		Nos. 1077-1084 (8)	14.20	14.20

Souvenir Sheets

1085	A134	3000sh multi	7.50	7.50
1086	A134	3000sh multi	7.50	7.50

Souvenir Sheet

UN Headquarters, New York City — A135

1992, Oct. 28 **Litho.** *Perf. 14*

1087	A135	2500sh multi	7.50	7.50

Postage Stamp Mega Event '92, NYC.

Christmas — A136

Details or entire paintings by Zurbaran: 50sh, The Annunciation (angel at left). 200sh, The Annunciation (angel at right). 250sh, The Virgin of the Immaculate Conception. 300sh, The Virgin of the Immaculate Conception (detail). 800sh, 900sh, The Holy Family with Saints Anne, Joachim and John the Baptist (800sh, entire, 900sh, detail). 1000sh, Adoration of the Magi (entire). 2000sh, Adoration of the Magi. No. 1096, The Virgin of the Immaculate Conception (Virgin with arms outstretched). No. 1097, The Virgin of the Immaculate Conception (Virgin with arms folded).

1992, Nov. 16 **Litho.** *Perf. 13½x14*

1088	A136	50sh multi	.25	.25
1089	A136	200sh multi	.45	.45
1090	A136	250sh multi	.60	.60
1091	A136	300sh multi	.75	.75
1092	A136	800sh multi	2.00	2.00
1093	A136	900sh multi	2.25	2.25
1094	A136	1000sh multi	2.40	2.40
1095	A136	2000sh multi	4.75	4.75
		Nos. 1088-1095 (8)	13.45	13.45

Souvenir Sheets

1096	A136	2500sh multi	7.00	7.00
1097	A136	2500sh multi	7.00	7.00

World Health Organization A137

Anniversaries and Events — A138

Designs: 50sh, Improving household food security. 200sh, Continue to breastfeed. 250sh, At four months old, give breast milk and soft food. No. 1101, Drink water from a safe and protected source. No. 1102, Jupiter, Voyager 2. No. 1103, Mother holding baby. No. 1104, Impala. No. 1105, Zebra. No. 1106, Count Ferdinand von Zeppelin, zeppelin. 2000sh, Neptune, Voyager 2. 3000sh, Count Zeppelin, zeppelin, diff. No. 1109, Voyager 2, Jupiter, diff. No. 1110, Wart hog. No. 1111, Doctor examining child, Lions Intl. emblem. No. 1112, Count Zeppelin, balloon.

1992 Litho. *Perf. 14*

1098 A137 50sh multi .25 .25
1099 A137 200sh multi .40 .40
1100 A137 250sh multi .50 .50
1101 A137 300sh multi .60 .60
1102 A138 300sh multi 1.40 1.40
1103 A137 800sh multi 1.60 1.60
1104 A138 800sh multi 3.25 3.25
1105 A138 1000sh multi 3.75 3.75
1106 A138 1000sh multi 2.00 2.00
1107 A138 2000sh multi 9.75 9.75
1108 A138 3000sh multi 6.00 6.00
Nos. 1098-1108 (11) 29.50 29.50

Souvenir Sheets

1109 A138 2500sh multi 7.75 7.75
1110 A138 2500sh multi 7.75 7.75
1111 A138 2500sh multi 7.75 7.75
1112 A138 2500sh multi 7.75 7.75

WHO (#1098-1101, 1103). Intl. Space Year (#1102, 1107, 1109). Earth Summit, Rio de Janeiro (#1104-1105, 1110). Count Zeppelin, 75th anniv. of death (#1106, 1108, 1112). Lions Intl., 75th anniv. (#1111).

Issue dates: Nos. 1098-1103, 1106, 1109, 1112, Nov.; others, Dec.

1993 Visit of Pope John Paul II to Uganda — A139

A139a

Designs: 50sh, Cathedral in Kampala, site of Papal Mass, Kampala, hands releasing doves. 200sh, Site of Papal Mass, Pope. 250sh, Ugandan man, Pope. 300sh, Three Ugandan Catholic leaders, Pope. 800sh, Pope waving, Ugandan map and flag. 900sh, Ugandan woman, Pope wearing mitre. 1000sh, Pope, Ugandan flag, site of Papal Mass. 2000sh, Ugandan flag, Pope waving.

No. 1121, Pope at door of airplane, vert. No. 1122, Pope delivering message at podium, vert.

No. 1123, Pope John Paul II. No. 1124, Pope with hands raised.

1993, Feb. 1 Litho. *Perf. 14*

1113 A139 50sh multi .30 .30
1114 A139 200sh multi .50 .50
1115 A139 250sh multi .60 .60
1116 A139 300sh multi .70 .70
1117 A139 800sh multi 1.75 1.75
1118 A139 900sh multi 1.90 1.90
1119 A139 1000sh multi 2.25 2.25
1120 A139 2000sh multi 4.50 4.50
Nos. 1113-1120 (8) 12.50 12.50

Souvenir Sheets

1121 A139 3000sh multi 6.25 6.25
1122 A139 3000sh multi 6.25 6.25

Embossed

Perf. 12

1123 A139a 5000sh gold 22.50 22.50

Souvenir Sheet

Imperf

1124 A139a 5000sh gold 22.50 22.50

Miniature Sheet

Louvre Museum, Bicent. — A140

Details or entire paintings by Rembrandt: No. 1125a, Self-Portrait with an Easel. b, Birds of Paradise. c, The Beef Carcass. d, The Supper at Emmaus. e, Hendrickje Stoffels. f, Titus, Son of the Artist. g, The Holy Family (left). h, The Holy Family (right).

2500sh, Philosopher in Meditation, horiz.

1993, Apr. 5 Litho. *Perf. 12*

1125 A140 500sh Sheet of 8, #a.-h. + label 10.00 10.00

Souvenir Sheet

Perf. 14½

1126 A140 2500sh multi 6.50 6.50

Dogs — A141

50sh, Afghan hound. 100sh, Newfoundland. 200sh, Siberian huskies. 250sh, Briard. 300sh, Saluki. 800sh, Labrador retriever, vert. 1000sh, Greyhound. 1500sh, Pointer.

No. 1135, Cape hunting dog. No. 1136, Norwegian elkhound.

1993, May 28 Litho. *Perf. 14*

1127 A141 50sh multi .45 .45
1128 A141 100sh multi .45 .45
1129 A141 200sh multi .80 .80
1130 A141 250sh multi 1.00 1.00
1131 A141 300sh multi 1.40 1.40
1132 A141 800sh multi 3.50 3.50
1133 A141 1000sh multi 4.00 4.00
1134 A141 1500sh multi 6.50 6.50
Nos. 1127-1134 (8) 18.10 18.10

Souvenir Sheets

1135 A141 2500sh multi 11.00 11.00
1136 A141 2500sh multi 11.00 11.00

Miniature Sheet

Coronation of Queen Elizabeth II, 40th Anniv. — A142

No. 1137: a, 50sh, Official coronation photograph. b, 200sh, Orb, Rod of Equity & Mercy. c, 500sh, Queen during coronation ceremony. d, 1500sh, Queen Elizabeth II, Princess Margaret.

2500sh, The Crown, by Grace Wheatley, 1959.

1993, June 2 Litho. *Perf. 13½x14*

1137 A142 Sheet, 2 each #a.-d. 7.50 7.50

Souvenir Sheet

Perf. 14

1138 A142 2500sh multicolored 7.00 7.00

No. 1138 contains one 28x42mm stamp.

Miniature Sheet

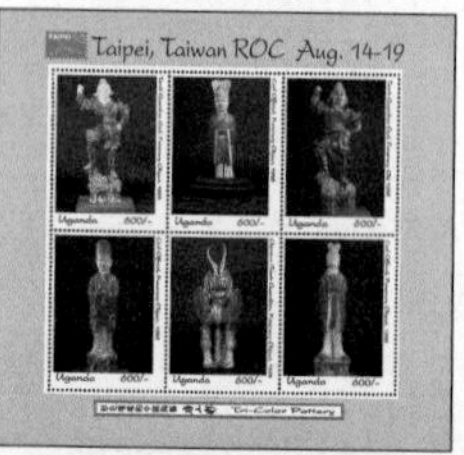

Taipei '93 — A143

Funerary objects: No. 1139a, Tomb guardian god. b, Civil official. c, Tomb guardian god, diff. d, Civil official, diff. e, Chimera. f, Civil official, diff.

2500sh, Statue of Sacred Mother, Ceremonial Hall, Taiyuan, Shanxi.

1993, Sept. 22 Litho. *Perf. 14x13½*

1139 A143 600sh Sheet of 6, #a.-f. 7.50 7.50

Souvenir Sheet

1140 A143 2500sh multicolored 7.00 7.00

With Bangkok '93 Emblem

Thai sculpture: No. 1141a, Standing Buddha, 13th-15th cent. b, Crowned Buddha, 13th cent. c, Thepanom, 15th cent. d, Crowned Buddha, 12th cent. e, Four-armed Avalokitesvara, 9th cent. f, Lop Buri standing Buddha, 13th cent.

2500sh, Buddha, interior of Wat Mahathat.

1993, Sept. 22

1141 A143 600sh Sheet of 6, #a.-f. 7.50 7.50

Souvenir Sheet

1142 A143 2500sh multicolored 7.00 7.00

With Indopex '93 Emblem

Japanese Wayang Puppets, Indonesia: No. 1143a, Bupati karma, Prince of Wangga. b, Rahwana. c, Sondjeng Sandjata. d, Raden Damar Wulan. e, Klitik figure. f, Hanaman.

2500sh, Candi Mendut in Kedu Plain, Java, Indonesia.

1993, Sept. 22 Litho. *Perf. 13½x14*

1143 A143 600sh Sheet of 6, #a.-f. 7.50 7.50

Souvenir Sheet

1144 A143 2500sh multicolored 7.00 7.00

A144

50sh, Gutierrez, Voeller. 200sh, Tomas Brolin. 250sh, Gary Lineker. 300sh, Munoz, Butragueno. 800sh, Carlos Valderrama. 900sh, Diego Maradona. 1000sh, Pedro Troglio. 2000sh, Enzo Scifo.

No. 1153, Brazil coaches. No. 1154, De Napoli, Skuhravy, horiz.

1993, Oct. 1 Litho. *Perf. 14*

1145 A144 50sh multi .35 .35
1146 A144 200sh multi .60 .60
1147 A144 250sh multi .75 .75
1148 A144 300sh multi .85 .85
1149 A144 800sh multi 2.40 2.40
1150 A144 900sh multi 2.55 2.55
1151 A144 1000sh multi 3.00 3.00
1152 A144 2000sh multi 6.00 6.00
Nos. 1145-1152 (8) 16.50 16.50

Souvenir Sheets

1153 A144 2500sh multi 7.25 7.25
1154 A144 2500sh multi 7.25 7.25

1994 World Cup Soccer Championships, US.

A145

Cathedrals of the World: 50sh, York Minster, England. 100sh, Notre Dame, Paris. 200sh, Little Metropolis, Athens. 250sh, St. Patrick's, New York. 300sh, Ulm, Germany. 800sh, St. Basil's, Moscow. 1000sh, Roskilde, Denmark. 2000sh, Seville, Spain. No. 1163, Namirembe, Uganda. No. 1163A, St. Peter's, Vatican City.

1993, Nov. 3 *Perf. 14*

1155 A145 50sh multi .35 .35
1156 A145 100sh multi .35 .35
1157 A145 200sh multi .65 .65
1158 A145 250sh multi .70 .70
1159 A145 300sh multi .95 .95
1160 A145 800sh multi 2.25 2.25
1161 A145 1000sh multi 3.00 3.00
1162 A145 2000sh multi 5.75 5.75
Nos. 1155-1162 (8) 14.00 14.00

Souvenir Sheets

1163 A145 2500sh multi 7.50 7.50
1163A A145 2500sh multi 7.50 7.50

Christmas — A146

Details or entire woodcut, The Virgin with Carthusian Monks, by Durer: 50sh, 200sh, 300sh, 2000sh.

Details or entire paintings by Raphael: 100sh, 800sh, Sacred Family. 250sh, The Virgin of the Rose. 1000sh, Holy Family (Virgin with Beardless Joseph).

No. 1172, 2500sh, The Virgin with Carthusian Monks, by Durer. No. 1173, 2500sh, Sacred Family, by Raphael.

1993, Nov. 19 Litho. *Perf. 13½x14*

1164-1171 A146 Set of 8 13.50 13.50

Souvenir Sheets

1172-1173 A146 Set of 2 15.00 15.00

Mickey Mouse, Friends with Dinosaurs A147

Disney characters depicted with: 50sh, Stegosaurus. 100sh, Pterandom. 200sh, Mamenchisaurus. 250sh, Rock painting. 300sh, Dino "sails." 500sh, Diplodocus. 800sh, Mamenshisaurus, diff. 1000sh, Triceratops.

No. 1182, 2500sh, Tyrannosaurus rex, Mickey. No. 1183, 2500sh, Minnie, Mickey, mamenchisaurus, diff.

1993, Dec. 22 Litho. *Perf. 14x13½*

1174-1181 A147 Set of 8 12.00 12.00

Souvenir Sheets

1182-1183 A147 Set of 2 12.00 12.00

Rinderpest Campaign — A148

1993, Dec. 29 *Perf. 14*

1184 A148 200sh multicolored 1.00 1.00

Picasso (1881-1973) — A149

Paintings: 100sh, Woman in Yellow, 1907. 250sh, Gertrude Stein, 1906. 2500sh, Woman by a Window, 1956.

1993, Dec. 29

1185-1186 A149 Set of 2 1.50 1.50

Souvenir Sheet

1187 A149 2500sh multicolored 7.50 7.50

Copernicus (1473-1543) A150

Telescopes: 500sh, Early. 1000sh, Modern. 2500sh, Copernicus.

1993, Dec. 29
1188-1189 A150 Set of 2 4.50 4.50

Souvenir Sheet

1190 A150 2500sh multicolored 7.50 7.50

Polska '93 — A151

Paintings: 800sh, Creation of the World, by S. I. Witkiewicz par J. Gloqowski, 1921. 1000sh, For the Right to Work, by Andrezej Strumillo, 1952. 2500sh, Temptation of St. Anthony I, by S. I. Witkiewicz (1908-21), horiz.

1993, Dec. 29
1191-1192 A151 Set of 2 5.75 5.75

Souvenir Sheet

1193 A151 2500sh multicolored 7.00 7.00

World Meteorological Day — A152

Designs: 50sh, Weather station, horiz. 200sh, Observatory at Meteorological Training School, Entebbe. 250sh, Satellite receiver at National Meteorological Center, horiz. 300sh, Reading temperatures, National Center, Entebbe, horiz. 400sh, Automatic weather station. 800sh, Destruction by hail storm, horiz. 2500sh, Barograph, horiz.

1993, Dec. 29
1194-1199 A152 Set of 6 10.50 10.50

Souvenir Sheet

1200 A152 2500sh multi 8.25 8.25

Fruits and Crops — A153

Designs: 50sh, Passiflora edulis. 100sh, Helianthus annus. 150sh, Musa sapientum. 200sh, Vanilla fragrans. 250sh, Ananas comosus. 300sh, Artocarpus heterophyllus. 500sh, Sorghum bicolor. 800sh, Zea mays.
No. 1209, 2000sh, Sesamum indicum. No. 1210, 2000sh, Coffea canephora.

1993, Dec. 29
1201-1208 A153 Set of 8 7.50 7.50

Souvenir Sheets

1209-1210 A153 Set of 2 10.00 10.00

Automotive Anniversaries A154

No. 1211: a, 1903 Model A Ford, Henry Ford. b, Model T Snowmobile at 1932 Winter Olympics, Jack Shea. c, Lee Iacocca, Ford Mustang at New York World's Fair. d, Jim Clark, Lotus-Ford winning 1965 Indianapolis 500 race.
No. 1212: a, 1994 Mercedes Benz S600 Coupe. b, 1955 Mercedes Benz W196 Grand Prix Champion car, Juan Manuel Fangio. c, 1938 Mercedes Benz W125 road speed record holder, Rudolph Caracciola. d, Carl Benz, 1893 Benz Viktoria.
No. 1213, Carl Benz, vert. No. 1214, Henry Ford, vert.

1994, Jan. 18 Litho. *Perf. 14*
1211 A154 700sh Strip of 4, #a.-d. 5.75 5.75
1212 A154 800sh Strip of 4, #a.-d. 6.75 6.75

Souvenir Sheets

1213 A154 2500sh multicolored 6.00 6.00
1214 A154 2500sh multicolored 6.00 6.00

First Ford motor, cent. (#1211, #1214). First Benz four-wheel car, cent. (#1212, #1213).

A155

Hong Kong '94 — A156

Stamps, religious shrines, Repulse Bay: No. 1215, Hong Kong #531. No. 1216, #1163.
Snuff boxes, Qing Dynasty: No. 1217a, Glass painted enamel with pavilion. b, Porcelain with floral design. c, Porcelain with quail design. d, Porcelain with openwork design. e, Agate with pair of dogs. f, Agate with man on donkey.

1994, Feb. 18 Litho. *Perf. 14*
1215 A155 500sh multicolored .90 .90
1216 A155 500sh multicolored .90 .90
a. Pair, #1215-1216 1.75 1.75

Miniature Sheet

1217 A156 200sh Sheet of 6, #a.-f. 3.75 3.75

Nos. 1215-1216 issued in sheets of 5 pairs. No. 1216a is continuous design.
New Year 1994 (Year of the Dog) (#1217e).

Miniature Sheet

1994 World Cup Soccer Championships, US — A157

Designs: No. 1218a, Georges Grun, Belgium. b, Oscar Ruggeri, Argentina. c, Frank Rijkaard, Holand. d, Magid "Tyson" Musisi, Uganda. e, Donald Keeman, Holland. f, Igor Shallmov, Russia.
No. 1219, 2500sh, RFK Stadium, Washington DC. No. 1220, 2500sh, Ruud Gullit, Holland.

1994, June 27 Litho. *Perf. 14*
1218 A157 500sh Sheet of 6, #a.-f. 10.50 10.50

Souvenir Sheets

1219-1220 A157 Set of 2 12.00 12.00

Heifer Project Intl., 50th Anniv. — A158

1994, June 29 Litho. *Perf. 14*
1221 A158 100sh multicolored 2.25 2.25

Moths — A159

Designs: 100sh, Lobobunaea goodii. 200sh, Bunaeopsis hersilia. 300sh, Rufoglanis rosea. 350sh, Acherontia atropos. 400sh, Euchloron megaera. 500sh, Epiphora rectifascia. 1000sh, Polyphychus coryndoni.
Lobobunaea goodii: No. 1230, 2500sh, Wings down. No. 1231, 2500sh, Wings extended.

1994, July 13
1222-1229 A159 Set of 8 8.75 8.75

Souvenir Sheets

1230-1231 A159 Set of 2 12.00 12.00

Native Crafts — A160

Designs: 100sh, Wood stool. 200sh, Wood & banana fiber chair. 250sh, Raffia & palm leaves basket. 300sh, Wool tapestry showing tree planting. 450sh, Wool tapestry showing hair grooming. 500sh, Wood sculpture, drummer. 800sh, Decorated gourds. 1000sh, Lady's bag made from bark cloth.
No. 1240, 2500sh, Raffia baskets. No. 1241, 2500sh, Papyrus hats.

1994, July 18
1232-1239 A160 Set of 8 8.25 8.25

Souvenir Sheets

1240-1241 A160 Set of 2 11.00 11.00

Cats — A161

Cat, historic landmark: 50sh, Turkish angora, Blue Mosque, Turkey, horiz. 100sh, Japanese bobtail, Mt. Fuji, Japan, horiz. 200sh, Norwegian forest cat, windmill, Holland, horiz. 300sh, Egyptian mau, pyramids, Egypt. 450sh, Rex, Stonehenge, England. 500sh, Chartreux, Eiffel Tower, France, horiz. 1000sh, Burmese, Shwe Dagon Pagoda, Burma. 1500sh, Maine coon, Pemaquid Point Lighthouse, Maine.
No. 1250, 2500sh, Russian blue, horiz. No. 1251, 2500sh, Manx, horiz.

1994, July 22
1242-1249 A161 Set of 8 14.00 14.00

Souvenir Sheets

1250-1251 A161 Set of 2 15.00 15.00

ILO, 75th Anniv. — A162

1994, July 29
1252 A162 350sh multicolored 1.25 1.25

PHILAKOREA '94 — A163

Designs: 100sh, Eight story Sari pagoda, Paekyangsa. 350sh, Ch'omsongdae (Natl. treasure). 1000sh, Pulguksa Temple exterior.
2500sh, Bronze mural, Pagoda Park, Seoul.

1994, Aug. 8
1253-1255 A163 Set of 3 2.75 2.75

Souvenir Sheet

1256 A163 2500sh multicolored 4.50 4.50

Intl. Year of the Family — A164

1994, Aug. 11
1257 A164 100sh multicolored 1.10 1.10

D-Day, 50th Anniv. — A165

Designs: 300sh, Mulberry Harbor pierhead moves into position. 1000sh, Mulberry Harbor floating bridge lands armor.
2500sh, Ships, Mulberry Harbor.

1994, Aug. 11
1258 A165 300sh multicolored .85 .85
1259 A165 1000sh multicolored 2.75 2.75

Souvenir Sheet

1260 A165 2500sh multicolored 6.00 6.00

A166

Intl. Olympic Committee, Cent. — A167

Designs: 350sh, John Akii-bua, Uganda, 100-meter hurdles, 1972. 900sh, Heike Herkel, Germany, high jump, 1992.
2500sh, Aleksei Urmanov, Russia, figure skating, 1994.

1994, Aug. 11
1261 A166 350sh multicolored .70 .70
1262 A166 900sh multicolored 1.75 1.75

Souvenir Sheet

1263 A167 2500sh multicolored 5.50 5.50

First Manned Moon Landing, 25th Anniv. A168

No. 1264 — Project Mercury astronauts: a, 50sh, Alan B. Shepard, Jr., Freedom 7. b, 100sh, M. Scott Carpenter, Aurora 7. c, 200sh, Virgil I. Grissom, Liberty Bell 7. d, 300sh, L. Gordon Cooper, Jr., Faith 7. e, 400sh, Walter M. Schirra, Jr., Sigma 7. f, 500sh, Donald K. Slayton, Apollo-Soyuz, 1975. g, 600sh, John H. Glenn, Jr., Friendship 7.
3000sh, Apollo 11 anniv. emblem.

1994, Aug. 11
1264 A168 Sheet of 7, #a.-g, + 2 labels 10.50 10.50

Souvenir Sheet

1265 A168 3000sh multi 10.50 10.50

A169

Disney's The Lion King A169a

No. 1266: a, Baby Simba. b, Mufasa, Simba, Sarabi. c, Young Simba, Nala. d, Timon. e, Rafiki. f, Pumbaa. g, Hyenas. h, Scar. i, Zazu.
No. 1267: a, Rafiki, Mufasa. b, Rafiki, Mufasa, Sarabi. c, Rafiki, Simba. d, Scar, Zazu. e, Rafiki seeing vision. f, Simba, Scar. g, Simba, Nala. h, Simba trying on mane. i, Simba, Nala, Zazu.
No. 1268: a, Scar plots evil plan. b, Mufasa rescues Simba. c, Destroying Mufasa. d, Simba escaping hyenas. e, Timon, Pumbaa, Simba. f, Simba, Timon, Pumbaa sing Hakuna Matata. g, Rafiki. h, Simba, Nala. i, Simba seeing reflection.

No. 1269, 2500sh, Simba, Timon. No. 1270, 2500sh, Characters of the Lion King, vert. No. 1271, 2500sh, Simba's colorful animal kingdom.
No. 1271A, Mufasa, Simba. No. 1271B, Mufasa, Simba on back, standing on rock.
Illustration A169a reduced.

Perf. 14x13½, 13½x14

1994, Sept. 30

1266 A169 100sh Sheet of 9, #a.-i. 2.75 2.75
1267 A169 200sh Sheet of 9, #a.-i. 5.75 5.75
1268 A169 250sh Sheet of 9, #a.-i. 7.50 7.50
Nos. 1266-1268 (3) 16.00 16.00

Souvenir Sheets

1269-1271 A169 Set of 3 17.50 17.50

Litho. & Embossed

Perf. 11½

1271A A169a 5000sh gold
1271B A169a 5000sh gold

Sierra Club, Cent. — A170

No. 1272, horiz.: a, 200sh, Cheetahs. b, 250sh, Cheetah kittens. c, 300sh, African wild dog. d, 500sh, African wild dog. e, 600sh, Grevy's zebra. f, 800sh, Chimpanzee. g, 1000sh, Grevy's zebra.
No. 1273: a, 100sh, Chimpanzee. b, 200sh, Chimpanzee. c, 250sh, African wild dog. d, 300sh, Cheetah. e-f, 500sh, 600sh, Gelada baboon. g, 800sh, Grevy's zebra. h, 1000sh, Gelada baboon.

1994, Nov. 9

1272 A170 Sheet of 7, #a.-g. + label 8.50 8.50
1273 A170 Sheet of 8, #a.-h. 8.75 8.75

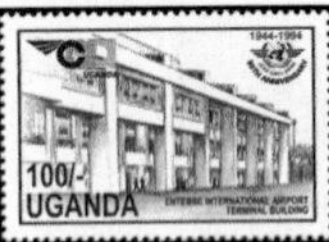

ICAO, 50th Anniv. — A171

Designs: 100sh, Entebbe Intl. Airport terminal building. 250sh, Entebbe control tower.

1994, Nov. 14 **Litho.** ***Perf. 14***

1274 A171 100sh multicolored .90 .90
1275 A171 250sh multicolored 1.60 1.60

Environmental Protection — A172

Designs: 100sh, Stop poaching. 250sh, Waste disposals. 350sh, Overfishing is a threat. 500sh, Deforestation.

1994, Nov. 15

1276-1279 A172 Set of 4 4.00 4.00

Christmas — A173

Paintings: 100sh, Adoration of the Christ Child, by Fillipino Lippi. 200sh, The Holy Family Rests on the Flight into Egypt, by Annibale Carracci. 300sh, Madonna with Christ Child ant St. John, by Piero di Cosimo. 350sh, The Conestabile Madonna, by Raphael. 450sh, Madonna and Child with Angels, after Antonio Rossellino. 500sh, Madonna and Child with St. John, by Raphael. 900sh, Madonna and Child, by Luca Signorelli. 1000sh, Madonna with the Child Jesus, St. John and an Angel, in style of Pier Francesco Fiorentino.
No. 1288, 2500sh, The Madonna of the Magnificat, by Sandro Botticelli. No. 1289, 2500sh, Adoration of the Magi, by Fra Angelico & Filippo Lippi.

1994, Dec. 5 **Litho.** ***Perf. 13½x14***

1280-1287 A173 Set of 8 10.00 10.00

Souvenir Sheets

1288-1289 A173 Set of 2 11.00 11.00

Tintoretto (1518-94) — A174

Details or entire paintings: 100sh, Self-portrait. 300sh, A Philosopher. 400sh, The Creation of the Animals, horiz. 450sh, The Feast of Belshazzar, horiz. 500sh, The Raising of the Brazen Serpent. 1000sh, Elijah Fed by the Angel.
No. 1296, 2000sh, Finding of Moses. No. 1297, 2000sh, Moses Striking Water from a Rock.

1995, Feb. 7 **Litho.** ***Perf. 13½***

1290-1295 A174 Set of 6 7.00 7.00

Souvenir Sheets

1296-1297 A174 Set of 2 10.50 10.50

Birds — A175

No. 1298: a, White-faced tree duck. b, European shoveler. c, Hartlaub's duck. d, Milky eagle-owl. e, Avocet. f, African fish eagle. g, Spectacled weaver. h, Black-headed gonolek. i, Great crested grebe. j, Red-knobbed coot. k, Woodland kingfisher. l, Pintail. m, Squacco heron. n, Purple gallinule. o, African darter. p, African jacana.
No. 1299, 2500sh, Fulvous tree duck. No. 1300, 2500sh, Pygmy goose.

1995, Apr. 24 **Litho.** ***Perf. 14***

1298 A175 200sh Sheet of 16, #a.-p. 14.00 14.00

Souvenir Sheets

1299-1300 A175 Set of 2 11.00 11.00

Nos. 685-688, 906 Surcharged

1995, June 1 **Litho.** ***Perf. 14***

1301 A90 100sh on #688 multi .25 .25
1302 A90 450sh on 70sh #686 1.25 1.25
1303 A90 800sh on 90sh #687 2.00 2.00
1304 A90 1500sh on 10sh #685 3.75 3.75
Nos. 1301-1304 (4) 7.25 7.25

Souvenir Sheet

1305 A113 2500sh on 1200sh multi 6.00 6.00

UN, 50th Anniv. — A176

Designs: 1000sh, Hands releasing butterflies, dragonfly, dove.
No. 1308, Infant's hand holding adult's finger.

1995, July 6 **Litho.** ***Perf. 14***

1306 A176 450sh shown 1.00 1.00
1307 A176 1000sh multicolored 2.25 2.25

Souvenir Sheet

1308 A176 2000sh multicolored 4.00 4.00

FAO, 50th Anniv. A177

No. 1309 — Corn huskers: a, 350sh, Young woman. b, 500sh, Old woman, girl. c, 1000sh, Woman with baby on back.
2000sh, Boy beside bore well for livestock, irrigation.

1995, July 6

1309 A177 Strip of 3, #a.-c. 2.75 2.75

Souvenir Sheet

1310 A177 2000sh multicolored 4.00 4.00

A178

End of World War II, 50th Anniv. — A179

No. 1311: a, Russian 152mm gun fires into center of Berlin. b, Soviets capture Moltke Bridge. c, Emperor William Memorial Church, now war memorial. d, Brandenburg Gate falls to Russian tanks. e, US B-17's continue to devastate industrial Germany. f, Soviet tanks enter Berlin. g, Hitler's chancellery lies in ruins. h, Reichstag burns.
Flags of countries each forming "VJ:" No. 1312a, Australia. b, Great Britain. c, New Zealand. d, US. e, China. f, Canada.
No. 1313, Waving Soviet flag from atop building in Berlin. No. 1314, US flag, combat soldier.

1995, July 6

1311 A178 500sh Sheet of 8, #a.-h. + label 11.00 11.00
1312 A179 600sh Sheet of 6, #a.-f. + label 8.75 8.75

Souvenir Sheets

1313 A178 2500sh multi 7.00 7.00
1314 A179 2500sh multi 7.50 7.50

No. 1313 contains one 56x42mm stamp.

Rotary Intl., 90th Anniv. — A180

Rotary emblem and: No. 1315, Paul Harris. No. 1316, Natl. flag.

1995, July 6 **Litho.** ***Perf. 14***

1315 A180 2000sh multicolored 4.00 4.00

Souvenir Sheet

1316 A180 2000sh multicolored 4.00 4.00

Queen Mother, 95th Anniv. — A181

No. 1317: a, Drawing. b, Waving. c, Formal portrait. d, Green blue outfit.
2500sh, Pale blue outfit.

1995, July 6 ***Perf. 13½x14***

1317 A181 500sh Block or strip of 4, #a.-d. 7.50 7.50

Souvenir Sheet

1318 A181 2500sh multicolored 7.25 7.25

No. 1317 was issued in sheets of 8 stamps.
Sheets of Nos. 1317-1318 exist with with black border and text "In Memoriam/1900-2002" in sheet margins.

Dinosaurs A182

Designs: 150sh, Velociraptor. 200sh, Psittacosaurus. 350sh, Dilophosaurus. 400sh, Kentrosaurus. 500sh, Stegosaurus. 1500sh, Pterodaustro.
No. 1325, vert: a, Archaeopteryx. b, Quetzalcoatlus. c, Pteranodon (b, d). d, Brachiosa (g, h). e, Tsintaosaur. f, Allosaur (g-h). g, Tyranosaur (f, i-k). h, Apatosaur (l). i, Giant dragonfly. j, Dimorphodon. k, Triceratops (l). l, Compsognathus.
No. 1326, 2000sh, Parasaurolophus. No. 1327, 2000sh, Shunosaurus.

1995, July 15 ***Perf. 14***

1319-1324 A182 Set of 6 9.00 9.00
1325 A182 300sh Sheet of 12, #a.-l. 11.00 11.00

Souvenir Sheets

1326-1327 A182 Set of 2 9.50 9.50

Reptiles — A183

50sh, Rough scaled bush viper. 100sh, Pygmy python. 150sh, Three horned chameleon. 200sh, African rock python. 350sh, Nile monitor. 400sh, Savannah monitor. 450sh, Bush viper. 500sh, Nile crocodile. 700sh, Bell's hinged tortoise. 900sh, Rhinoceros viper. 1000sh, Gaboon viper. 2000sh, Spitting cobra. 3000sh, Leopard tortoise. 4000sh, Puff adder. 5000sh, Common house gecko. 6000sh, Dwarf chameleon. 10,000sh, Boomslang.

1995 **Litho.** ***Perf. 14x15***

1328 A183 50sh multi .25 .25
1329 A183 100sh multi .25 .25
1330 A183 150sh multi .30 .30
1331 A183 200sh multi .40 .40
1332 A183 350sh multi .70 .70
1333 A183 400sh multi .85 .85
1334 A183 450sh multi .95 .95
1335 A183 500sh multi 1.00 1.00

Size: 38x24mm

Perf. 14

1336 A183 700sh multi 1.40 1.40
1337 A183 900sh multi 1.90 1.90
1338 A183 1000sh multi 2.00 2.00
1339 A183 2000sh multi 4.00 4.00
1340 A183 3000sh multi 6.25 6.25
1341 A183 4000sh multi 8.25 8.25
1341A A183 5000sh multi 10.00 10.00
1341B A183 6000sh multi 12.00 12.00
1341C A183 10,000sh multi 20.00 20.00
Nos. 1328-1341C (17) 70.50 70.50

Issued: 5000sh, 6000sh, 10,000sh, 11/20; others, 8/21.
Compare with Nos. 1550-1552.

Nsambya Church — A184

Designs: 450sh, Namilyango College. 500sh, Intl. Cooperative Alliance, cent. 1000sh, UN Volunteers, 25th anniv.

1995, Sept. 7 **Litho.** ***Perf. 14***

1342-1345 A184 Set of 4 4.00 4.00

Mill Hill Missionaries in Uganda, cent. (#1342-1343).

Scenic Landscapes & Waterfalls of Uganda — A185

Designs: No. 1346, 50sh, Bwindi Forest. No. 1347, 50sh, Sipi Falls, vert. No. 1348, 100sh, Karamoja. No. 1349, 100sh, Murchison Falls. No. 1350, 450sh, Sunset, Lake Mburo Natl. Park. No. 1351, 450sh, Bujagali Falls. No. 1352, 500sh, Sunset, Gulu District. No. 1353, 500sh, Two Falls, Murchison. No. 1354, 900sh, Kabale District. No. 1355, 900sh, Falls, Rwenzoris, vert. No. 1356, 1000sh, Rwenzori

Mountains. No. 1357, 1000sh, Falls, Rwenzoris, diff., vert.

1995, Sept. 14
1346-1357 A185 Set of 12 12.50 12.50

1996 Summer Olympics, Atlanta — A186

Athletes: 50sh, Peter Rono, runner. 350sh, Reiner Klimke, dressage. 450sh, German cycling team. 500sh, Grace Birungi, runner. 900sh, Francis Ogola, track. 1000sh, Nyakana Godfrey, welter-weight boxer.
No. 1364, 2500sh, Rolf Dannenberg, discus, vert. No. 1365, 2500sh, Sebastian Coe, runner.

1995, Sept. 21
1358-1363 A186 Set of 6 7.25 7.25
Souvenir Sheets
1364-1365 A186 Set of 2 9.50 9.50

Domestic Animals — A187

No. 1366: a, Peafowl (e). b, Pouter pigeon. c, Rock dove. d, Rouen duck. e, Guinea fowl. f, Donkey. g, Shetland pony. h, Palomino. i, Pigs. j, Border collie. k, Merino sheep. l. Milch goat. m, Black dutch rabbit. n, Lop rabbit. o, Somali cat (p). p, Asian cat.
No. 1367, 2500sh, Saddle bred horses. No. 1368, 2500sh, Oxen.

1995, Oct. 2
1366 A187 200sh Sheet of 16, #a.-p. 12.50 12.50
Souvenir Sheets
1367-1368 A187 Set of 2 12.00 12.00

Boy Scouts at Immunization Centers — A188

Designs: 150sh, Dressing children for weighing, vert. 350sh, Helping mothers carry children, vert. 450sh, Checking health cards. 800sh, Assisting in immunization. 1000sh, Weighing children, vert.

1995, Oct. 18 Litho. *Perf. 14*
1369-1373 A188 Set of 5 6.00 6.00

Establishment of Nobel Prize Fund, Cent. — A189

No. 1374, 300sh: a, Hideki Yukawa, physics, 1949. b, F.W. DeKlerk, peace, 1993. c, Nelson Mandela, peace, 1993. d, Odysseus Elytis, literature, 1979. e, Ferdinand Buisson, peace, 1927. f, Lev Landau, physics, 1962. g, Halldor Laxness, literature, 1955. h, Wole Soyinka, literature, 1986. i, Desmond Tutu, peace, 1984. j, Susumu Tonegawa, physiology or medicine, 1987. k, Louis de Broglie, physics, 1929. l, George Seferis, literature, 1963.
No. 1375, 300sh: a, Hermann Staudinger, chemistry, 1953. b, Fritz Haber, chemistry, 1918. c, Bert Sakmann, physiology or medicine, 1991. d, Adolf O.R. Windaus, chemistry, 1928. e, Wilhelm Wien, physics, 1911. f, Ernest Hemingway, literature, 1954. g, Richard M. Willstätter, chemistry, 1915. h, Stanley Cohen, physiology or medicine, 1986. i, J. Hans D. Jensen, physics, 1963. j, Otto H. Warburg, physiology or medicine, 1931. k, Heinrich O. Wieland, chemistry, 1927. l, Albrecht Kossel, physiology or medicine, 1910.
No. 1376, 2000sh, Werner Forssmann, physiology or medicine, 1956. No. 1377, 2000sh, Nelly Sachs, literature, 1966.

1995, Oct. 31 Sheets of 12, #a-l
1374-1375 A189 Set of 2 20.00 20.00
Souvenir Sheets
1376-1377 A189 Set of 2 10.50 10.50

Christmas — A190

Details or entire paintings of the Madonna and Child, by: 150sh, Hans Holbein the Younger. 350sh, Procaccini. 500sh, Pisanello. 1000sh, Crivelli. 1500sh, Le Nain.
No. 1383, 2500sh, The Holy Family, by Andrea Del Sarto. No. 1384, 2500sh, Madonna and Child, by Bellini.

1995, Nov. 30 Litho. *Perf. 13½x14*
1378-1382 A190 Set of 5 7.50 7.50
Souvenir Sheets
1383-1384 A190 Set of 2 11.00 11.00

Orchids — A191

Designs: 150sh, Ansellia africana. 450sh, Satyricum crassicaule. 500sh, Polystachya cultriformis. 800sh, Disa erubescens.
No. 1389: a, Aerangis iuteoalba. b, Satyrium sacculatum. c, Bolusiella maudiae. d, Habenaria attenuata. e, Cyrtorchis arcuata. f, Eulophia angolensis. g, Tridactyle bicaudata. h, Eulophia horsfallii. i, Diaphananthe fragrantissima.
No. 1390, 2500sh, Diaphananthe pulchella. No. 1391, 2500sh, Rangaeris amaniensis.

1995, Dec. 8 *Perf. 14*
1385-1388 A191 Set of 4 6.00 6.00
Miniature Sheet
1389 A191 350sh Sheet of 9, #a.-i. 12.50 12.50
Souvenir Sheets
1390-1391 A191 Set of 2 12.00 12.00

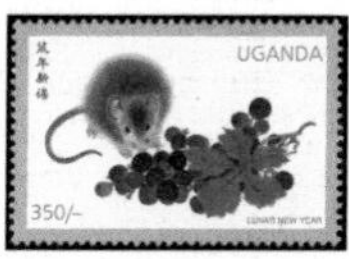
New Year 1996 (Year of the Rat) — A192

Rat eating: a, Purple grapes. b, Radishes. c, Corn. d, Squash.
2000sh, Green grapes.

1996, Jan. 29 Litho. *Perf. 14*
1392 A192 350sh Block of 4, #a.-d. 2.50 2.50
e. Miniature sheet, No. 1392 2.50 2.50
Souvenir Sheet
1393 A192 2000sh multicolored 3.00 3.00

No. 1392 issued in sheets of 16 stamps.

Miniature Sheet

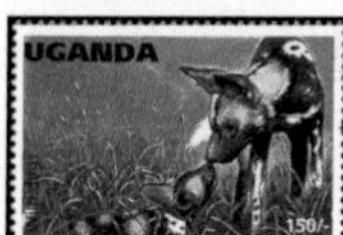
Wildlife — A193

No. 1394: a, 150sh, Wild dogs. b, 200sh, Fish eagle. c, 250sh, Hippopotamus. d, 350sh, Leopard. e, 400sh, Lion. f, 450sh, Lioness. g, 500sh, Meerkat. h, 550sh, Black rhinoceros.
No. 1395: a, 150sh, Gorilla. b, 200sh, Cheetah. c, 250sh, Elephant. d, 350sh, Thomson's gazelle. e, 400sh, Crowned crane. f, 450sh, Sattlebill. g, 500sh, Vulture. h, 550sh, Zebra.
No. 1396, 2000sh, Giraffe, vert. No. 1397, 2000sh, Gray heron.

1996, Mar. 27 Litho. *Perf. 14*
1394 A193 Sheet of 8, #a.-h. 6.25 6.25
1395 A193 Sheet of 8, #a.-h. 6.75 6.75
Souvenir Sheets
1396-1397 A193 Set of 2 9.00 9.00

Disney Characters on the Orient Express A194

Designs: 50sh, From London to Constantinople via Calais. 100sh, From Paris to Athens. 150sh, Ticket for the Pullman. 200sh, Pullman Corridor. 250sh, Dining car. 300sh, Staff beyond reproach. 600sh, Fun in the Pullman. 700sh, 1901 Unstoppable train enters the buffet in Frankfurt station. 800sh, 1929 passage detained five days by snowstorm. 900sh, Filming "Murder on the Orient Express."
No. 1408, 2500sh, Donald Duck in engine. No. 1409, 2500sh, Mickey, Goofy, Minnie waving from back of train.

1996, Apr. 15 *Perf. 14x13½*
1398-1407 A194 Set of 10 12.50 12.50
Souvenir Sheets
1408-1409 A194 Set of 2 13.00 13.00

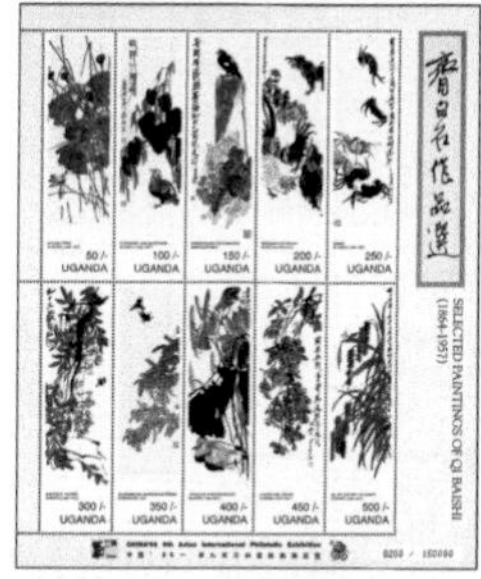
Paintings by Qi Baishi (1864-1957) — A195

No. 1410: a, 50sh, Autumn Pond. b, 100sh, Partridge and Smartweed. c, 150sh, Begonias and Mynah. d, 200sh, Chrysanthemums, Cocks and Hens. e, 250sh, Crabs. f, 300sh, Wisterias and Bee. g, 350sh, Smartweed and Ink-drawn Butterflies. h, 400sh, Lotus and Mandarin Ducks. i, 450sh, Lichees and Locust. j, 500sh, Millet and Preying Mantis.
No. 1411: a, Locust, flowers. b, Crustaceans.

1996, May 8 Litho. *Perf. 15x14*
1410 A195 Sheet of 10, #a.-j. 8.00 8.00
Souvenir Sheet
Perf. 14
1411 A195 800sh Sheet of 2, #a.-b. 7.50 7.50

No. 1411 contains two 48x34mm stamps. The captions on Nos. 1410c and 1410d are transposed.
CHINA '96, 9th Asian Intl. Philatelic Exhibition.
See Nos. 1475-1476.

Queen Elizabeth II, 70th Birthday A196

No. 1412: a, Portrait. b, As young woman, wearing crown jewels. c, Wearing red hat, coat.
2000sh, Portrait, diff.

1996, July 10 *Perf. 13½x14*
1412 A196 500sh Strip of 3, #a.-c. 3.25 3.25
Souvenir Sheet
1413 A196 2000sh multicolored 4.00 4.00

No. 1412 was issued in sheets of 9 stamps.

Jerusalem, 3000th Anniv. — A197

No. 1414: a, 300sh, Knesset Menorah. b, 500sh, Jerusalem Theater. c, 1000sh, Israel Museum.
2000sh, Grotto of the Nativity.

1996, July 10 *Perf. 14*
1414 A197 Sheet of 3, #a.-c. 3.75 3.75
Souvenir Sheet
1415 A197 2000sh multicolored 3.75 3.75

For overprint see Nos. 1556-1557.

Radio, Cent. — A198

Entertainers: 200sh, Ella Fitzgerald. 300sh, Bob Hope. 500sh, Nat "King" Cole. 800sh, Burns & Allen.
2000sh, Jimmy Durante.

1996, July 10 *Perf. 13½x14*
1416-1419 A198 Set of 4 3.75 3.75
Souvenir Sheet
1420 A198 2000sh multicolored 4.00 4.00

Mushrooms — A199

No. 1421: a, 150sh, Coprinus disseminatus. b, 300sh, Caprinus radians. c, 350sh, Hygrophorus coccineus. d, 400sh, Marasmius siccus. e, 450sh, Cortinarius collinitus. f, 500sh, Cortinarius cinnabarinus. g, 550sh, Coltricia cinnamomea. h, 1000sh, Mutinus elegans.
No. 1422, 2500sh, Inocybe soroia. No. 1423, 2500sh, Flammulina velutipes.

1996, June 24 *Perf. 14*
1421 A199 Sheet of 8, #a.-h. 6.50 6.50
Souvenir Sheets
1422-1423 A199 Set of 2 9.00 9.00

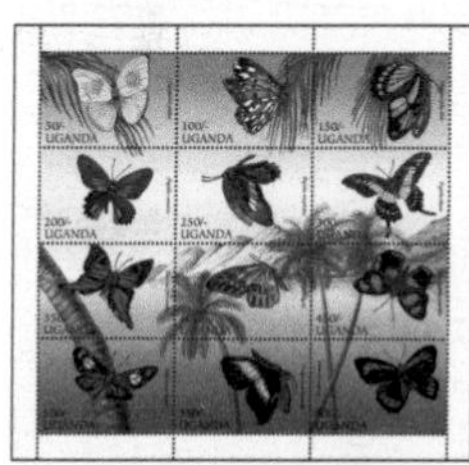
Butterflies — A200

No. 1424: a, 50sh, Catopsilia philea. b, 100sh, Dione vanillae. c, 150sh, Metemorpha dido. d, 200sh, Papilio sesotris. e, 250sh, Papilio neophilus. f, 300sh, Papilio thoas. g, 350sh, Dione periander. h, 400sh, Morpho cipris. i, 450sh, Catonephele numilia. j, 500sh, Heliconius doris. k, 550sh, Prepona antimache. l, 600sh, Eunica alcmena.
No. 1425, 2500sh, Caligo martia. No. 1426, 2500sh, Heliconius doris.

1996, June 26
1424 A200 Sheet of 12, #a.-l. 9.00 9.00
Souvenir Sheets
1425-1426 A200 Set of 2 10.00 10.00

UNICEF, 50th Anniv. — A201

Designs: 450sh, Two children. 500sh, Two children wearing hats. 550sh, Boy in classroom.
2000sh, Mother and child, vert.

1996, July 10 Litho. *Perf. 14*
1427-1429 A201 Set of 3 4.00 4.00

Souvenir Sheet

1430 A201 2000sh multicolored 4.00 4.00

UNESCO, 50th Anniv. A202

Natl. Parks: 450sh, Darien, Panama. 500sh, Los Glaciares, Argentina. 550sh, Tubbatha Reef Marine Park, Philippines.
2500sh, Rwenzori Mountains, Uganda.

1996, July 10
1431-1433 A202 Set of 3 4.75 4.75

Souvenir Sheet

1434 A202 2500sh multicolored 6.25 6.25

Trains A203

No. 1435: a, Loco Type B.B.B., Japan, 1968. b, Stephenson's "Rocket," 1829. c, "Austria," 1843. d, 19th cent. type. e, Loco Anglo-Indian, India, 1947. f, Type CoCo DB, Germany.
No. 1436: a, "Lady of Lynn," Great Western, England. b, Chinese type, 1930. c, Meyer-Ritson, Chile. d, Union Pacific "Centennial," US. e, "581" Japanese Natl. Railway, Japan, 1968. f, Co.Co. Series "120" DB, Germany.
No. 1437, 2500sh, Mallard, Great Britain. No. 1438, 2500sh, "99" Type 1-5-0, Germany.

1996, July 25
1435 A203 450sh Sheet of 6, #a.-f. 5.50 5.50
1436 A203 550sh Sheet of 6, #a.-f. 6.50 6.50

Souvenir Sheets

1437-1438 A203 Set of 2 10.00 10.00

Uganda Post Office, Cent. — A204

Designs: 150sh, Emblem. 450sh, Post bus service. 500sh, Modern mail transportation means. 550sh, "100," #48, #59.

1996, Aug. 30 Litho. *Perf. 14*
1439-1442 A204 Set of 4 6.00 6.00

Fruits — A205

Designs: 150sh, Mango, vert. 350sh, Orange, vert. 450sh, Paw paw, vert. 500sh, Avocado, vert. 550sh, Watermelon.

1996, Oct. 8 Litho. *Perf. 14*
1443-1447 A205 Set of 5 6.00 6.00

Christmas — A206

Details or entire paintings: 150sh, Annunciation, by Lorenzo Di Credi. 350sh, Madonna of the Loggia (detail), by Botticelli. 400sh, Virgin in Glory with Child and Angels, by Lorenzetti P. 450sh, Adoration of the Child, by Filippino Lippi. 500sh, Madonna of the Loggia, by Botticelli. 550sh, The Strength, by Bottticelli.

No. 1454, 2500sh, Holy Allegory, by Giovanni Bellini, horiz. No. 1455, 2500sh, The Virgin on the Throne with Child and Saints, by Ghirlandaio, horiz.

1996, Nov. 18 *Perf. 13½x14*
1448-1453 A206 Set of 6 5.75 5.75

Souvenir Sheets

Perf. 14x13½

1454-1455 A206 Set of 2 10.00 10.00

Sylvester Stallone in Movie, "Rocky III" — A207

1996, Nov. 21 Litho. *Perf. 14*
1456 A207 800sh Sheet of 3 5.50 5.50

1996 Summer Olympic Games, Atlanta — A208

Scenes from first Olympic Games in US, St. Louis, 1904: 350sh, Steamboat race, stadium. 450sh, Boxer George Finnegan. 500sh, Quadriga race (ancient games). 800sh, John Flanagan, hammer throw, vert.

1996, Dec. 8
1457-1460 A208 Set of 4 4.75 4.75

Traditional Attire — A209

Designs: 150sh, Western region, vert. 350sh, Karimo Jong women, vert. 450sh, Ganda. 500sh, Acholi.
No. 1465, vert. — Headdresses: a, Acholi. b, Alur. c, Bwola dance. d, Madi. e, Karimojong. f, Karimojong with feathers.

1997, Jan. 2
1461-1464 A209 Set of 4 4.00 4.00
1465 A209 300sh Sheet of 6, #a.-f. 5.00 5.00

New Year 1997 (Year of the Ox) — A210

Paintings of oxen: Nos. 1466a, 1467b, Walking left. Nos. 1466b, 1467b, Calf nursing. Nos. 1466c, 1467d, Calf lying down, adult. Nos. 1466d, 1467c, Adult lying down.
1500sh, Calf, vert.

1997, Jan. 24 Litho. *Perf. 14*
1466 A210 350sh Strip of 4, #a.-d. 4.25 4.25
1467 A210 350sh Sheet of 4, #a.-d. 4.25 4.25

Souvenir Sheet

1468 A210 1500sh multicolored 4.25 4.25

No. 1466 was issued in sheets of 4 vert. strips.

World Wildlife Fund — A211

No. 1469 — Rothschild's giraffe: a, Running. b, One bending neck across another's back. c, Head up close. d, Young giraffe, adult facing opposite directions.
2500sh, like #1469d, horiz.

1997, Feb. 12
1469 A211 300sh Strip of 4, #a.-d. 4.00 4.00

Souvenir Sheet

1470 A211 2500sh multicolored 6.50 6.50

No. 1469 was issued in sheets of 4 strips with each strip in a different order.
No. 1470 does not have the WWF emblem.

Souvenir Sheet

Mural from Tomb in Xian A212

1996, May 8 Litho. *Perf. 14*
1471 A212 500sh multicolored 3.00 3.00

China '96. No. 1471 was not available until March 1997.

Promulgation of the Constitution, Oct. 8, 1995 A213

Designs: 150sh, shown. 350sh, Scroll. 550sh, Closed book, vert.

1997, Feb. 25 *Perf. 14x13½*
1472-1474 A213 Set of 3 3.25 3.25

Paintings Type of 1996

No. 1475 — Paintings by Wu Changshuo (1844-1927): a, 50sh, Red Plum Blossom and Daffodil. b, 100sh, Peony. c, 150sh, Rosaceae. d, 200sh, Pomegranate. e, 250sh, Peach, Peony, and Plum Blossom. f, 300sh, Calyx canthus. g, 350sh, Chrysanthemum. h, 400sh, Calabash. i, 450sh, Chrysanthemum, diff. j, 500sh, Cypress tree.
No. 1476: a, 550sh, Litchi. b, 1000sh, Water lily.

1997, Mar. 5 *Perf. 14x15*
1475 A195 Sheet of 10, #a.-j. 6.50 6.50

Souvenir Sheet

Perf. 14

1476 A195 Sheet of 2, #a.-b. 3.50 3.50

Hong Kong '97. No. 1476 contains two 51x38mm stamps.

Summer Olympic Winners — A214

No. 1477: a, 150sh, Sohn Kee-chung, marathon, 1936. b, 200sh, Walter Davis, high jump, 1952. c, 250sh, Roland Matthes, swimming, 1968. d, 300sh, Akii Bua, 400m hurdles, 1972. e, 350sh, Wolfgang Nordwig, pole vault, 1972. f, 400sh, Wilma Rudolph, 4x100m relay, 1960. g, 450sh, Abebe Bikila, marathon, 1964. h, 500sh, Edwin Moses, 400m hurdles, 1984. i, 550sh, Randy Williams, long jump, 1972.
No. 1478: a, 150sh, Bob Hayes, 100m, 1964. b, 200sh, Rod Milburn, 110m hurdles, 1972. c, 250sh, Filbert Bayi, running, 1976. d, 300sh, H. Kipchoge Keino, steeple chase, 1972. e, 350sh, Ron Ray, running, 1976. f, 400sh, Joe Frazier, boxing, 1976. g, 450sh, Carl Lewis, 100m race, 1984. h, 500sh, Gisela Mauermayer, discus, 1936. i, 550sh, Dietmar Mogenburg, high jump, 1984.

1997, Mar. 3 Litho. *Perf. 14*

Sheets of 9, #a-i

1477-1478 A214 Set of 2 15.00 15.00

No. 1478h is inscribed shot put in error.

Disney's "Toy Story" A215

No. 1479, vert.: a, Woody. b, Buzz Lightyear. c, Bo Peep. d, Hamm. e, Slinky. f, Rex.
No. 1480: a, Woody on Andy's bed. b, "Get this wagon train a-movin." c, Bo Peep, blocks. d, Buzz Lightyear. e, Slinky, Rex. f, Woody hides. g, Buzz, Woody. h, Rex, Slinky, Buzz. i, Buzz, Woody on bed.
No. 1481: a, Woody telling Buzz he's sheriff. b, Green Army on alert. c, Woody, Buzz compete. d, Woody sights alien. e, Buzz ponders fate. f, "The Cla-a-a-a-a-a-w." g, Intergalactic emergency. h, Buzz, Woody argue at gas station. i, Buzz, Woody give chase.
No. 1482, 2000sh, Woody spots an intruder, vert. No. 1483, 2000sh, Andy's toys, vert. No. 1484, 2000sh, Buzz Lightyear in space, vert.

1997, Apr. 2 *Perf. 14x13½, 13½x14*
1479 A215 100sh Sheet of 6, #a.-f. 2.75 2.75
1480 A215 150sh Sheet of 9, #a.-i. 6.00 6.00
1481 A215 200sh Sheet of 9, #a.-i. 7.25 7.25

Souvenir Sheets

1482-1484 A215 Set of 3 21.00 21.00

Man in Space — A216

No. 1484A: b, Pioneer 10. c, Voyager 1. d, Viking Orbiter. e, Pioneer, Venus 1. f, Mariner 9. g, Galileo Entry Probe. h, Mariner 10. i, Voyager 2.
No. 1485: a, Sputnik 1. b, Apollo. c, Soyuz. d, Intelsat 1. e, Manned maneuvering unit. f, Skylab. g, Telstar 1. h, Hubble telescope.
No. 1486, Space shuttle Challenger. No. 1486A, Mars Viking Lander Robot.

1997, Apr. 16 Litho. *Perf. 14*
1484A A216 250sh Sheet of 8, #b.-i. 5.00 5.00
1485 A216 300sh Sheet of 8, #a.-h. 5.50 5.50

Souvenir Sheet

1486 A216 2000sh multicolored 4.75 4.75
1486A A216 2000sh multicolored 5.00 5.00

No. 1486 contains one 34x61mm stamp, No. 1486A one 61x35mm stamp.

Deng Xiaoping (1904-97), Chinese Leader A217

Designs: a, 500sh. b, 550sh. c, 1000sh.
2000sh, Portrait, diff.

1997, May 9
1487 A217 Sheet of 3, #a.-c. 5.50 5.50

Souvenir Sheet

1488 A217 2000sh multicolored 4.75 4.75

Environmental Protection — A218

No. 1489: a-d, Various water hyacinths.
No. 1490: a, Buffalo. b, Uganda kob. c, Guinea fowl. d, Malibu stork.
2500sh, Gorilla.

1997, May 14
1489 A218 500sh Sheet of 4, #a.-d. 3.75 3.75
1490 A218 550sh Sheet of 4, #a.-d. 4.25 4.25

Souvenir Sheet

1491 A218 2500sh multicolored 5.25 5.25

Queen Elizabeth II, Prince Philip, 50th Wedding Anniv. — A219

No. 1492: a, Queen. b, Royal arms. c, Queen in purple outfit, Prince. d, Prince, Queen in white hat. e, Buckingham Palace. f, Prince Philip.
2000sh, Queen in wedding dress.

1997, June 2 **Litho.** ***Perf. 14***
1492 A219 200sh Sheet of 6, #a.-f. 7.00 7.00

Souvenir Sheet

1493 A219 2000sh multicolored 4.75 4.75

Paul E. Harris (1868-1947), Founder of Rotary, Intl. — A220

Designs: 1000sh, Combating hunger, Harris. 2500sh, First Rotarians, Gustavus H. Loehr, Sylvester Schiele, Hiram E. Shorey, Paul E. Harris.

1997, June 2
1494 A220 1000sh multicolored 3.00 3.00

Souvenir Sheet

1495 A220 2500sh multicolored 4.50 4.50

Heinrich von Stephan (1831-97) A221

No. 1496 — Portrait of Von Stephan and: a, Chinese post boat. b, UPU emblem. c, Russian special post.
2500sh, Von Stephan, French postman on stilts.

1997, June 2
1496 A221 800sh Sheet of 3, #a.-c. 4.50 4.50

Souvenir Sheet

1497 A221 2500sh multicolored 4.50 4.50

PACIFIC 97.

Chernobyl Disaster, 10th Anniv. — A222

Designs: 500sh, UNESCO. 700sh, Chabad's Children of Chernobyl.

1997, May 21 **Litho.** ***Perf. 14x13½***
1498 A222 500sh multicolored 1.50 1.50
1499 A222 700sh multicolored 2.00 2.00

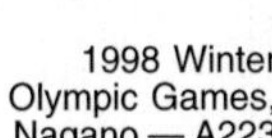

1998 Winter Olympic Games, Nagano — A223

Designs: 350sh, Men's slalom, vert. 450sh, Two-man bobsled, vert. 800sh, Women's slalom. 2000sh, Men's speed skating.
No. 1504: a, Ski jumping. b, Giant slalom. c, Cross-country skiing. d, Ice hockey. e, Man, pairs figure skating. f, Woman, pairs figure skating.
No. 1505, 2500sh, Downhill skiing. No. 1506, 2500sh, Women's figure skating.

1997, June 23 **Litho.** ***Perf. 14***
1500-1503 A223 Set of 4 7.25 7.25
1504 A223 500sh Sheet of 6, #a.-f. 6.25 6.25

Souvenir Sheets

1505-1506 A223 Set of 2 9.00 9.00

Makerere University, 75th Anniv. A224

Designs: 150sh, Main building, administration block. 450sh, East African School of Librarianship, vert. 500sh, Buyana stock farm. 550sh, Ceramic dish, School of Architectural and Fine Arts.

1997, July 31 ***Perf. 14x13½, 13½x14***
1507-1510 A224 Set of 4 3.50 3.50

Mahatma Gandhi (1869-1948) — A225

Various portraits.

1997, Oct. 5 **Litho.** ***Perf. 14***
1511 A225 600sh multicolored 2.50 2.50
1512 A225 700sh multicolored 2.75 2.75

Souvenir Sheet

1513 A225 1000sh multicolored 4.50 4.50

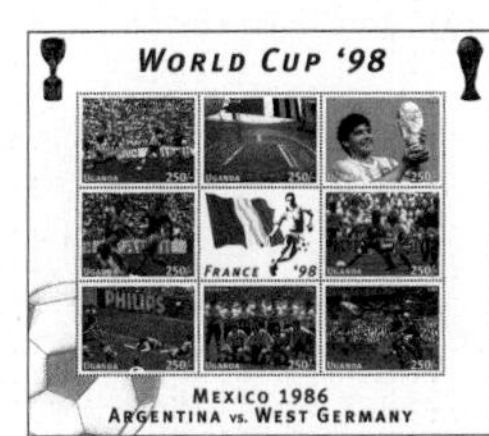

1998 World Cup Soccer Championships, France — A226

No. 1514, vert: a, 200sh, Fritz Walter, Germany. b, 300sh, Daniel Passarella, Argentina. c, 450sh, Dino Zoff, Italy. d, 500sh, Bobby Moore, England. e, 600sh, Diego Maradona, Argentina. f, 550sh, Franz Beckenbauer, West Germany.
No. 1515 — Argentina vs. West Germany, Mexico City, 1986: a, d, e, f, h, Action scenes. b, Azteca Stadium. c, Argentine player holding World Cup. g, Argentina team picture.
No. 1516 — Top tournament scorers: a, Paulo Rossi. b, Mario Kempes. c, Gerd Muller. d, Grzegorz Lato. e, Ademir. f, Eusebio Ferreica da Silva. g, Salvatore (Toto) Schillaci. h, Leonidas da Silva. i, Gary Lineker.
No. 1517, 2000sh, England, 1966. No. 1518, 2000sh, W. Germany, 1990.

1997, Oct. 3 **Litho.** ***Perf. 14***
1514 A226 Sheet of 6, #a.-f. 5.50 5.50
1515 A226 250sh Sheet of 8, #a.-h. 5.00 5.00
1516 A226 250sh Sheet of 9, #a.-i. + label 5.00 5.00

Souvenir Sheets

1517-1518 A226 Set of 2 8.50 8.50

Diana, Princess of Wales (1961-97) — A227

1997, Dec. 1
1519 A227 60sh multicolored 2.00 2.00

No. 1519 was issued in sheets of 6.

Christmas — A228

Sculpture, entire paintings or details: 200sh, Putto and Dolphin, by Andrea del Verrocchio. 300sh, The Fall of the Rebel Angels, by Pieter Bruegel the Elder. 400sh, The Immaculate Conception, by Murillo. 500sh, Music-making Angel, by Rosso Fiorentino. 600sh, Cupid and Psyche, by Adolphe-William Bouguereau. 700sh, Cupid and Psyche, by Antonio Canova.
No. 1526, 2500sh, Virgin, Angels from The Assumption of the Virgin, by El Greco. No. 1527, 2500sh, Angel from The Assumption of the Virgin, by El Greco.

1997, Dec. 1
1520-1525 A228 Set of 6 5.75 5.75

Souvenir Sheets

1526-1527 A228 Set of 2 8.50 8.50

New Year 1998 (Year of the Tiger) — A229

Various paintings of tigers: No. 1528: a, Looking backward. b, Jumping. c, Lying, looking forward. d, Lying, mouth open.
1500sh, On cliff.

1998, Jan. 16 **Litho.** ***Perf. 13½***
1528 A229 350sh Sheet of 4, #a.-d. 3.25 3.25

Souvenir Sheet

1529 A229 1500sh multicolored 3.00 3.00

Tourist Attractions A230

Designs: 300sh, Namugongo Martyrs Shrine, vert. 400sh, Kasubi Tombs. 500sh, Tourist boat, Kazinga Channel. 600sh, Elephant. 700sh, Bujagali Falls, Jinja.

1998, Feb. 6 **Litho.** ***Perf. 14***
1530-1534 A230 Set of 5 6.25 6.25

Mother Teresa (1910-97) A231

No. 1535: a-h, Various portraits. 2000sh, With Diana, Princess of Wales (1961-97).

1998, Feb. 9 **Litho.** ***Perf. 14***
1535 A231 300sh Sheet of 8, #a.-h. 7.00 7.00

Souvenir Sheet

1536 A231 2000sh multicolored 6.50 6.50

Nos. 1535a, 1535d-1535e, 1535h are each 22x36mm.

UNICEF in Uganda, 30th Anniv. — A232

Designs: 300sh, "Support for children with disabilities." 400sh, "Safeguard children against polio." 600sh, "Sanitation... responsibility for all." 700sh, "Children's right to basic education."

1998, Mar. 6 ***Perf. 13½x14***
1537-1540 A232 Set of 4 6.00 6.00

Dinosaurs — A233

Designs, horiz: 300sh, Pteranodon. 400sh, Diplodocus. 500sh, Lambeosaurus. 600sh, Centrosaurus. 700sh, Parasaurolophus.
No. 1546: a, Cetiosaurus. b, Brontosaurus. c, Brachiosaurus. d, Deinonychus. e, Dimetrodon. f, Megalosaurus.
No. 1547, 2500sh, Tyrannosaurus. No. 1548, 2500sh, Iguanodon.

1998, Mar. 24 **Litho.** ***Perf. 14***
1541-1545 A233 Set of 5 5.50 5.50
1546 A233 600sh Sheet of 6, #a.-f. 8.00 8.00

Souvenir Sheets

1547-1548 A233 Set of 2 12.00 12.00

Nos. 1547-1548 each contain one 43x57mm stamp.

Writers — A234

No. 1549: a, Rita Dove. b, Mari Evans. c, Sterling A. Brown. d, June Jordan. e, Stephen Henderson. f, Zora Neale Hurston.

1998, Apr. 6
1549 A234 300sh Sheet of 6, #a.-f. 4.25 4.25

Reptiles — A235

Designs: 300sh, Armadillo girdled lizard. 600sh, Spotted sandveld lizard. 700sh, Bell's ringed tortoise.

1998, Apr. 21 ***Perf. 13½***
1550 A235 300sh multicolored .75 .75
1551 A235 600sh multicolored 1.50 1.50
1552 A235 700sh multicolored 1.75 1.75
Nos. 1550-1552 (3) 4.00 4.00

Compare with Nos. 1328-1335.

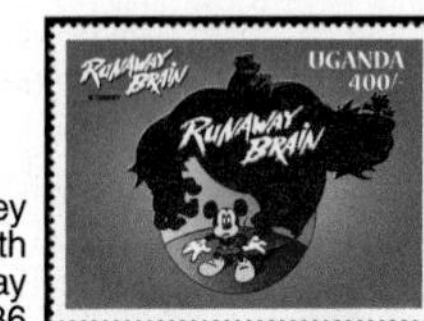

Mickey Mouse, 70th Birthday A236

No. 1553 — Scenes from cartoon, "Runaway Brain:" a, Mickey afraid of shadow. b, Mickey petting Pluto, newspaper. c, Mickey playing computer game, Pluto. d, Mickey, Minnie running. e, Mickey as target of experiment. f, Minnie being held captive by Pete on top of skyscraper. g, Mickey throwing lasso. h, Mickey surrounding Pete with rope. i, Mickey, Minnie holding onto rope above skyscrapers.
No. 1554, 3000sh, Mickey, Minnie embracing on top of skyscraper. No. 1555, 3000sh, Mickey, Minnie kissing on raft, vert.

1998, May 4 **Litho.** ***Perf. 14x13½***
1553 A236 400sh Sheet of 9, #a.-i. 9.75 9.75

Souvenir Sheets

1554-1555 A236 Set of 2 13.50 13.50

Nos. 1414-1415 Ovptd.

1998, May 13 Litho. *Perf. 14*

1556 A197 Sheet of 3, #a.-c. (#1414) 3.75 3.75

Souvenir Sheet

1557 A197 2000sh multi (#1415) 4.00 4.00

Sheet margins of Nos. 1556-1557 each contain additional overprint, "ISRAEL 98 — WORLD STAMP EXHIBITION/TEL-AVIV 13-21 MAY 1998."

Sailing Ships — A237

No. 1558, 1000sh: a, Fishing schooner. b, Chesapeake oyster boat. c, Java Sea schooner.

No. 1559, 1000sh: a, Santa Maria, 15th cent. galleon. b, Mayflower, 15th cent. galleon. c, Bark.

No. 1560, 3000sh, Boat with lateen sails. No. 1561, 3000sh, Thames River barge, vert.

1998, June 2 Litho. *Perf. 13x13½*

Sheets of 3, #a-c + Label

1558-1559 A237 Set of 2 12.00 12.00

Souvenir Sheets

1560-1561 A237 Set of 2 12.00 12.00

Nos. 1560-1561 are continuous designs.

Aircraft — A238

No. 1562: a, US F4F Wildcat. b, Japanese Zero. c, British Spitfire. d, British Harrier. e, S3A Viking. f, US Corsair.

No. 1563: a, Dornier Do-X transatlantic flyer, 1929. b, German Zucker mail rocket, 1930. c, X-15 Rocket Plane, 1955. d, Goddard's Rocket, 1930's. e, Wright brothers' flight, 1903. f, 160R Sikorsky helicopter, 1939.

No. 1564, 2500sh, P40 Tomahawk. No. 1565, 2500sh, SH346 Seabat.

1998, July 24 Litho. *Perf. 14*

1562 A238 500sh Sheet of 6, #a.-f. 7.00 7.00

1563 A238 600sh Sheet of 6, #a.-f. 8.25 8.25

Souvenir Sheets

1564-1565 A238 Set of 2 11.00 11.00

Flowers of the Mediterranean — A239

No. 1566, vert: a, Onosma. b, Rhododendron luteum. c, Paeonia mascula. d, Geranium macorrhizum. e, Cyclamen graecum. f, Lilium rhodopaedum. g, Narcissus pseudonarcissus. h, Paeonia rhodia. i, Aquilegia amaliae.

No. 1567: a, Paeonia peregrina. b, Muscari comutatum. c, Sternbergia. d, Dianthus. e, Verbascum. f, Aubrieta gracilis. g, Galanthus nivalis. h, Campanula incurva. i, Crocus sieberi.

No. 1568, 2000sh, Paeonia parnassica, vert. No. 1569, 2000sh, Pancratium maritimum, vert.

1998, Sept. 23 Litho. *Perf. 14*

1566 A239 300sh Sheet of 9, #a.-i. 5.00 5.00

1567 A239 600sh Sheet of 9, #a.-i. 9.00 9.00

Souvenir Sheets

1568-1569 A239 Set of 2 10.00 10.00

Christmas A240

Birds: 300sh, Bohemian waxwing. 400sh, House sparrow. 500sh, Black-capped chickadee. 600sh, Eurasian bullfinch. 700sh, Painted bunting. 1000sh, Northern cardinal.

No. 1576, 2500sh, Winter wren, vert. No. 1577, 2500sh, Red-winged blackbird, vert.

1998, Dec. 3 Litho. *Perf. 14*

1570-1575 A240 Set of 6 7.00 7.00

Souvenir Sheets

1576-1577 A240 Set of 2 11.00 11.00

Diana, Princess of Wales (1961-97) — A241

No. 1578: a, Inscription panel at left. b, Panel at right.

1998, Dec. 28 Litho. *Perf. 14½*

1578 A241 700sh Horiz. pair, #a-b 2.00 2.00

No. 1578 was issued in sheets of 3 pairs.

Picasso — A242

Paintings: 500sh, Woman Reading, 1935, vert. 600sh, Portrait of Dora Maar, 1937, vert. 700sh, Des Moiselles D'Avignon, 1907.

2500sh, Night Fishing at Antibes, 1939, vert.

1998, Dec. 28 *Perf. 14½x13, 13x14½*

1579-1581 A242 Set of 3 4.00 4.00

Souvenir Sheet

1582 A242 2500sh multicolored 4.75 4.75

Gandhi — A243

1998, Dec. 28 *Perf. 14*

1583 A243 600sh Portrait 5.50 5.50

Souvenir Sheet

1584 A243 2500sh Family portrait, horiz. 7.00 7.00

No. 1583 was issued in sheets of 4.

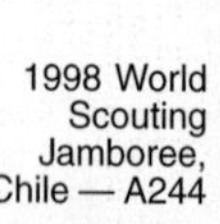

1998 World Scouting Jamboree, Chile — A244

No. 1585: a, Cub Scouts greet Pres. Eisenhower, Georgia, 1956. b, Uncle Dan Beard at 90th birthday party, 1990. c, Future Vice President Hubert Humphrey leads South Dakota troop, 1934.

2000sh, Young scout, tamed beaver, vert.

1998, Dec. 28

1585 A244 700sh Sheet of 3, #a.-c. 6.00 6.00

Souvenir Sheet

1586 A244 2000sh multicolored 4.00 4.00

New Year 1999 (Year of the Rabbit) — A245

No. 1587 — Rabbits: a, White. b, With carrot. c, Brown & white. e, Black & white.

1999, Jan. 4

1587 A245 350sh Sheet of 4, #a.-d. 4.00 4.00

Souvenir Sheet

1588 A245 1500sh Rabbit, diff. 4.00 4.00

Uganda Post Office — A246

1999, Jan. 18

1589 A246 300sh multicolored 1.75 1.75

Traditional Hairstyles — A247

Hairstyle, region: 300sh, Iru, Bairu. 500sh, Enshunju, Bahima. 550sh, Elemungole, Karamojong. 600sh, Longo, Langi. 700sh, Ekikuura, Bahima.

1999, Feb. 1

1590-1594 A247 Set of 5 6.25 6.25

Marine Life — A248

No. 1595: a, Wolffish. b, Equal sea star. c, Purple sea urchin. d, Mountain crab.

No. 1596: a, Blue marlin. b, Arctic tern. c, Common dolphin. d, Blacktip shark. e, Manta ray. f, Blackedge moray. g, Loggerhead turtle. h, Sailfin tang. i, Two-spotted octopus.

No. 1597, 2500sh, Sea nettle jellyfish. No. 1598, 2500sh, Decatopecten striatus.

1999, Mar. 15 Litho. *Perf. 14*

1595 A248 500sh Sheet of 4, #a.-d. 3.50 3.50

1596 A248 500sh Sheet of 9, #a.-i. 9.00 9.00

Souvenir Sheets

1597-1598 A248 each 9.50 9.50

Intl. Year of the Ocean.

Intl. Year of the Elderly — A249

Designs: 300sh, Income generating activity. 500sh, Learning from each other. 600sh, Leisure time for the aged. 700sh, Distributing food to the aged.

1999, July 19 Litho. *Perf. 13x13½*

1599-1602 A249 Set of 4 5.50 5.50

First Manned Moon Landing, 30th Anniv. — A250

No. 1603: a, Apollo 11 launch. b, Apollo 11 command and service modules. c, Edwin E. Aldrin, Jr. on lunar module ladder. d, Saturn V ready to launch. e, Lunar module descending. f, Aldrin on moon.

No. 1604: a, Freedom 7. b, Gemini 4. c, Apollo 11 command and service modules, diff. d, Vostok 1. e, Saturn V. f, Lunar module on moon.

No. 1605, 3000sh, Aldrin with scientific experiment. No. 1606, 3000sh, Command module re-entry.

1999, Nov. 24 Litho. *Perf. 13¾*

1603 A250 600sh Sheet of 6, #a.-f. 7.00 7.00

1604 A250 700sh Sheet of 6, #a.-f. 8.00 8.00

Souvenir Sheets

1605-1606 A250 Set of 2 14.00 14.00

Queen Mother (b. 1900) — A251

No. 1607: a, With stole. b, At wedding. c, With tiara (black and white photo). d, With tiara (color photo).

3000sh, Visiting Cambridge, 1961.

1999, Nov. 24 *Perf. 14*

1607 A251 1200sh Sheet of 4, #a.-d. 10.00 10.00

Souvenir Sheet

Perf. 13¾

1608 A251 3000sh multi 8.00 8.00

No. 1608 contains one 38x51mm stamp.

Hokusai Paintings — A252

No. 1609: a, Dragon Flying Over Mount Fuji (dragon). b, Famous Poses From the Kabuki Theater (one figure). c, Kitsune No Yomeiri. d, Dragon Flying Over Mount Fuji (Mount Fuji). e, Famous Poses From the Kabuki Theater (two figures). f, Girl Holding Cloth.

3000sh, Japanese Spaniel.

1999, Nov. 24 Litho. *Perf. 13¾*

1609 A252 700sh Sheet of 6, #a.-f. 8.00 8.00

Souvenir Sheet

1610 A252 3000sh multicolored 6.25 6.25

Birds — A253

Designs: 300sh, African penduline tit. 1000sh, Yellow-fronted tinkerbird. 1200sh, Zebra waxbill. 1800sh, Sooty anteater chat.

No. 1615: a, Gray-headed kingfisher. b, Green-headed sunbird. c, Speckled pigeon. d, Gray parrot. e, Barn owl. f, Gray crowned crane. g, Shoebill. h, Black heron.

No. 1616: a, Scarlet-chested sunbird. b, Lesser honeyguide. c, African palm swift. d, Swamp flycatcher. e, Lizard buzzard. f, Osprey. g, Cardinal woodpecker. h, Pearl-spotted owlet.

No. 1617: a, Fox's weaver. b, Chin-spot flycatcher. c, Blue swallow. d, Purple-breasted sunbird. e, Knob-billed duck. f, Red-collared widowbird. g, Ruwenzori turaco. h, African cuckoo hawk.

No. 1618, 3000sh, Four-banded sandgrouse. No. 1619, 3000sh, Paradise whydah.

1999, Dec. 6 *Perf. 14*

1611-1614 A253 Set of 4 9.75 9.75

1615 A253 500sh Sheet of 8, #a.-h. 9.00 9.00

1616 A253 600sh Sheet of 8, #a.-h. 10.50 10.50

1617 A253 700sh Sheet of 8, #a.-h. 12.50 12.50

Souvenir Sheets

1618-1619 A253 Set of 2 14.50 14.50

Primates — A254

Designs: 300sh, L'hoesti monkey. 400sh, Blue monkey. 500sh, Patas monkey. 600sh, Red-tailed monkey. 700sh, Black and white colobus. 1000sh, Mountain gorilla.
2500sh, Olive baboon.

1999, Nov. 19 Litho. *Perf. 13½x14*

1620-1625 A254 Set of 6 7.00 7.00

Souvenir Sheet

1626 A254 2500sh multicolored 5.50 5.50

Butterflies A255

Designs: 300sh, Epiphora bauhiniae, vert. 400sh, Phylloxiphia formosa. 500sh, Bunaea alcinoe, vert. 600sh, Euchloron megaera. 700sh, Argema mimosae, vert. 1800sh, Denephila nerii.
3000sh, Lobobunaea angasana.

Perf. 13½x13¼, 13¼x13½

2000, Jan. 19 Litho.

1627-1632 A255 Set of 6 9.25 9.25

Souvenir Sheet

1633 A255 3000sh multi 7.75 7.75

A256

UPU, 125th anniv. (in 1999): 600sh, Postman, two women, girl. 700sh, Woman, girl, mail box. 1200sh, Postman in horse-drawn wagon.

2000, Jan. 28 Litho. *Perf. 14*

1634-1636 A256 Set of 3 5.50 5.50

A257

No. 1637, 600sh — Orchids: a, Angraecum eichcerianum. b, Angraecum leonis. c, Arpophyllum giganteum. d, Bulbophyllum barbigerum. e, Angraecum ciryamae. f, Aerangis ellisii. g, Disa uniflora. h, Eulophia alta. i, Ancistrochilius stylosa.

No. 1638, 600sh: a, Eulophia paivenna. b, Ansellia gigantea. c, Anglaecopsis gracillima. d, Bonatea steudneri. e, Bulbophyllum falcatum. f, Aerangis citrata. g, Eulophiella elisabethae. h, Aerangis rhodosticta. i, Angraecum scottianum.

No. 1639, 700sh: a, Grammangis ellisii. b, Eulophia stenophylia. c, Oeoniella polystachys. d, Cymbidiella humblotti. e, Polystachya bella. f, Vanilla polycepis. g, Eulophileea roemplerana. h, Habenaria englerana. i, Ansellia frallana.

No. 1640, 700sh: a, Eulophia orthoplectra. b, Cirrhopetalum umbellatum. c, Eulophiella rolfei. d, Eulophia porphyroglossa. e, Eulopia petersii. f, Cyrtorchis arcuata. g, Eurychone rothschildiana. h, Eulophia quartiniana. i, Eulophia stenophylia (one flower).

No. 1641, 3000sh, Polystachya tayloriana, horiz. No. 1642, 3000sh, Ancistrochilus rothschildianus, horiz. No. 1643, 3000sh, Calanthe corymbosa, horiz. No. 1644, 3000sh, Cymbidiella rhodochila, horiz.

2000, Feb. 18 Sheets of 9, #a.-i.

1637-1638 A257 Set of 2 20.00 20.00
1639-1640 A257 Set of 2 25.00 25.00

Souvenir Sheets

1641-1644 A257 Set of 4 21.00 21.00

Butterflies — A258

Designs: 300sh, Short-tailed admiral. 400sh, Guineafowl. 1200sh, Club-tailed charaxes. 1800sh, Cymothoe egesta.

No. 1649: a, Charaxes anrticlea. b, Epitola posthumus. c, Beautiful monarch. d, Blue-banded nymph. e, Euxanthe crossleyi. f, African map. g, Western blue charaxes. h, Noble.

No. 1650: a, Green-veined charaxes. b, Ansorge's leaf butterfly. c, Crawshay's sapphire blue. d, Palla ussheri. e, Friar. f, Blood-red cymothoe. g, Mocker. h, Charaxes eupale.

No. 1651: a, Aeraea pseudolycia. b, Veined yellow. c, Buxton's hairstreak. d, Iolaus isomenias. e, Veined swallowtail. f, Figtree blue. g, Scarlet tip. h, Precis octavia.

No. 1652, 3000sh, African monarch. No. 1653, 3000sh, Kigezi swordtail.

2000, May 24 Litho. *Perf. 14*

1645-1648 A258 Set of 4 7.75 7.75
1649 A258 500sh Sheet of 8, #a-h 8.00 8.00
1650 A258 600sh Sheet of 8, #a-h 8.00 8.00
1651 A258 700sh Sheet of 8, #a-h 9.00 9.00

Souvenir Sheets

1652-1653 A258 Set of 2 11.00 11.00

The Stamp Show 2000, London (Nos. 1649-1653).

Popes A259

No. 1654: a, Agapetus II (946-55). b, Alexander II (1061-73). c, Anastasius IV (1153-54). d, Benedict VIII (1012-24). e, Benedict VII (974-83). f, Calixtus II (1119-24).

No. 1655, Celestine III (1191-98).

2000, June 28 *Perf. 13¾*

1654 A259 900sh Sheet of 6, #a-f 14.00 14.00

Souvenir Sheet

1655 A259 3000sh multi 7.00 7.00

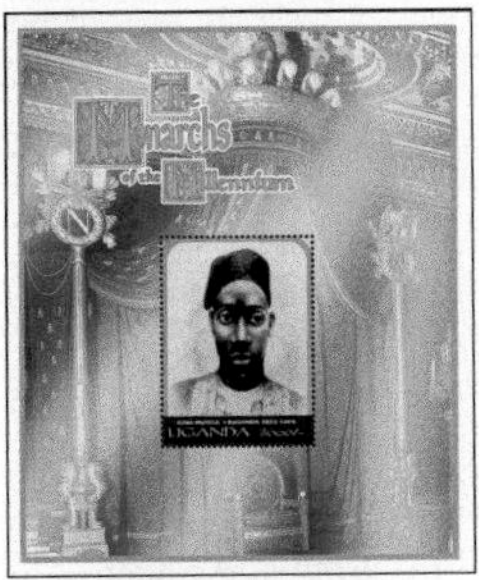

Monarchs — A260

No. 1655A: b, Philip II of France (1180-1223). c, Richard I of England (1189-99). d, William I of England (1066-87).

No. 1656: a, Boris III of Bulgaria (1918-43). b, Holy Roman Emperor Charles V (1519-58). c, Pedro II of Brazil (1831-89). d, Empress Elizabeth of Austria (1854-98). e, Francis Joseph of Austria (1848-1916). f, Frederick I of Bohemia (1619-20).

No. 1657, Mutesa I of Buganda (1191-98). No. 1657A, Cwa II Kabaleega.

2000, June 28 *Perf. 13¾*

1655A A260 900sh Sheet of 3, #b-d 5.00 5.00
1656 A260 900sh Sheet of 6, #a-f 9.00 9.00

Souvenir Sheets

1657 A260 3000sh multi 5.50 5.50
1657A A260 3000sh multi 5.50 5.50

Millennium — A261

No. 1658 — Highlights of 1850-1900: a, Opening of Japan. b, First safe elevator. c, Bessemer process of steel production. d, Florence Nightingale establishes nursing as a professsion. e, Louis Pasteur proposes germ theory of disease. f, First oil well drilled. g, Charles Darwin publishes *The Origin of Species*. h, Gregor Mendel discovers laws of heredity. i, Alfred Nobel invents dynamite, j, Suez Canal opens. k, Invention of the telephone. l, Invention of the electric light. m, World's time zones established. n, Invention of the electric motor. o, Motion pictures appear. p, US Civil War (57x37mm). q, Restoration of the Olympic Games.

Illustration reduced.

2000, June 28 *Perf. 12¾x12½*

1658 A261 300sh Sheet of 17, #a-q + label 15.00 15.00

Millennium A262

Designs: 300sh, Education for all. 600sh, Nile River. 700sh, Non-traditional exports. 1800sh, Tourism.

2000, July 24 *Perf. 14½*

1659-1662 A262 Set of 4 6.00 6.00

Common Market for Eastern and Southern Africa — A263

Designs: 500sh, Border checkpoint before and after COMESA treaty. 1400sh, Open border checkpoint.

2000, July 24

1663-1664 A263 Set of 2 2.50 2.50

Modern British Commonwealth, 50th Anniv. — A264

Designs: 600sh, Flags. 1200sh, Map.

2000, July 24

1665-1666 A264 Set of 2 2.25 2.25

Trains — A265

Designs: 300sh, Kenya Railways A 60 Class 4-8-2+2-8-4. 400sh, Mozambique Railways Baldwin 2-8-0. 600sh, Uganda Railways 73 Class German locomotive. 700sh, South Africa Railways Baby Garratt. 1200sh, Uganda Railways 82 Class French locomotive. 1400sh, East Africa Railway Beyer Garratt 4-8-2+2-8-4. 1800sh, Rhodesian Railways 2-8-2+2-8-2 Beyer Garratt. 2000sh, East African Railways Garratt.

No. 1675, 700sh: a, Uganda Railways 36 Class German locomotive. b, South African Railways Class 19D 4-8-2. c, Algeria Railways Garratt 4-8-2+2-8-4. d, Cameroon Railways French locomotive. e, South Africa railways electric freight locomotive. f, Rhodesia Railways 14A Class 2-8-2. g, British-built Egyptian railways locomotive. h, Uganda Railways 73 Class German locomotive, diff.

No. 1676, 700sh: a, 36 Class German locomotive (no counrtry specified). b, Rhodesian Railways 12th Class locomotive. c, Rhodesian Railways Garratt. d, 62 Class German locomotive. e, South Africa Railways Beyer Garratt. f, Sudan Railways locomotive. g, Nigerian Railways locomotive. h, 4-8-0 South Africa Railways.

No. 1677, 3500sh, East African Railways locomotive. No. 1678, 3500sh, Rhodesian Railways Alco 2-8-0. No. 1679, 3500sh, Egyptian State Railways 4-8-2.

2000, Aug. 14 *Perf. 14*

1667-1674 A265 Set of 8 14.00 14.00

Sheets of 8, #a-h

1675-1676 A265 Set of 2 18.00 18.00

Souvenir Sheets

1677-1679 A265 Set of 3 17.50 17.50

Nos. 1677-1679 each contain one 56x42mm stamp.

Christmas A266

Artwork by: 300sh, Drateru Fortunate Oliver, vert. 400sh, Brenda Tumwebaze. 500sh, Joseph Mukiibi, vert. 600sh, Paul Serunjogi. 700sh, Edward Maswere. 1200sh, Ndeba Harriet. 1800sh, Jude Kasagga, vert.

No. 1687, 3000sh, Nicole Kwiringira, vert. No. 1688, 3000sh, Michael Tinkamanyire, vert.

2000, Dec. 14 Litho. *Perf. 14*

1680-1686 A266 Set of 7 10.00 10.00

Souvenir Sheets

1687-1688 A266 Set of 2 12.50 12.50

New Year 2001 (Year of the Snake) A267

No. 1689: a, Snake with tongue out. b, Snake wrapped around person. c, Snake with open mouth. d, Snake hanging from branch.

2001, Jan. 5

1689 A267 600sh Sheet of 4, #a-d 5.00 5.00

Souvenir Sheet

1690 A267 2500sh shown 7.50 7.50

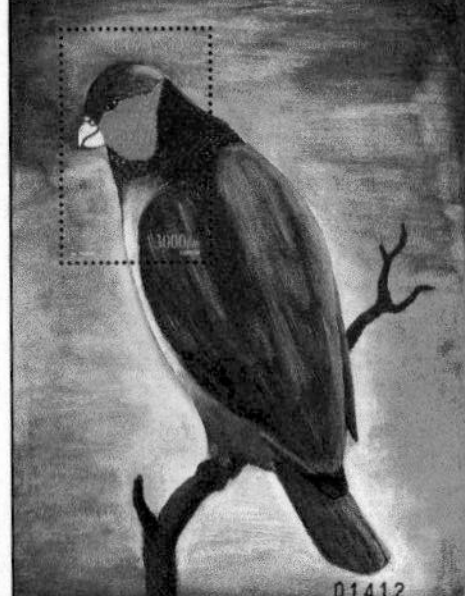

Wildlife A268

No. 1691: a, Bongo, horiz. b, Black rhinoceros, horiz. c, Leopard.

No. 1692, 3000sh, Parrot. No. 1693, 3000sh, Mountain gorillas, horiz.

Perf. 13¼x13¾, 13¾x13¼

2001, Feb. 5

1691 A268 600sh Strip of 3, #a-c 5.00 5.00

Souvenir Sheets

1692-1693 A268 Set of 2 12.50 12.50

No. 1691 was issued in sheets of 9 comprised of three strips of 3.

Holy Year 2000 — A269

Designs: 300sh, Holy Family. 700sh, Madonna and Child. 1200sh, Nativity, horiz.

2001, Apr. 4 Litho. *Perf. 13¼*

1694-1696 A269 Set of 3 4.50 4.50

East African School of Library and Information Science, Makerere University, Kampala — A270

Nairobi University, Kenya — A271

Universities and Flags on Map — A272

Design: 1200sh, Nkrumah Hall, University of Dar es Salaam, Tanzania.

2001, Apr. 23

1697 A270 300sh multi .40 .40
1698 A271 400sh multi .50 .50
1699 A270 1200sh multi 1.50 1.50
1700 A272 1800sh multi 2.25 2.25
Nos. 1697-1700 (4) 4.65 4.65

World Meteorological Organization, 50th Anniv. (in 2000) — A273

Designs: 300sh, Anemometer, vert. 2000sh, Tropical sun recorder.

2001, May 28

1701-1702 A273 Set of 2 5.00 5.00

UN High Commissioner for Refugees A274

Designs: 300sh, Ensure crop production. 600sh, Ensure community participation. 700sh, Ensure improved skills. 1800sh, Ensure improved health and water services.

2001, June 15

1703-1706 A274 Set of 4 6.50 6.50

Phila Nippon '01, Japan — A275

Designs: 600sh, Kikunojo Segawa I and Danjuro Ichikawa as Samurai, by Kiyonobu II. 700sh, Kamezo Tchimura as a Warrior, by Kiyohiro. 1000sh, Danjuro Ichikawa as Shirobei, by Kiyomitsu. 1200sh, Actor Sangoro Arashi, by Shunsho. 1400sh, Koshiro Matsumoto IV as Sukenari Juro, by Kiyonaga. 2000sh, Pheasant on Pine Branch, by Kiyomasu II.
3500sh, Tale of Ise, by Eishi.

2001, Aug. 1 Litho. *Perf. 14*

1707-1712 A275 Set of 6 10.00 10.00

Souvenir Sheet

1713 A275 3500sh multi 5.00 5.00

Cats and Dogs — A276

Designs: 400sh, Tabby British shorthair. 900sh, Turkish cat.
No. 1716, 600sh, horiz.: a, Blue and cream shorthair. b, Manx. c, Angora. d, Red and white British shorthair. e, Turkish cat, diff. f, Egyptian mau.
No. 1717, 1400sh, horiz.: a, Red tabby shorthair. b, Japanese bobtail. c, Siamese. d, Tabby Persian. e, Black and white Persian. f, Blue Russian.
No. 1718, 3500sh, Blue-eyed British shorthair. No. 1719, 3500sh, Calico American shorthair.

2001, Aug. 23

1714-1715 A276 Set of 2 2.00 2.00

Sheets of 6, #a-f

1716-1717 A276 Set of 2 19.00 19.00

Souvenir Sheets

1718-1719 A276 Set of 2 15.00 15.00

2001, Aug. 23

Designs: 1100sh, German shepherd. 1200sh, Irish setter.
No. 1722, 700sh, horiz.: a, Rottweiler. b, Flat-coated retriever. c, Samoyed. d, Poodle. e, Maltese. f, Irish terrier.
No. 1723, 1300sh, horiz: a, English sheepdog. b, German shepherd, diff. c, Great Dane. d, Boston terrier. e, Bull terrier. f, Australian terrier.
No. 1724, 3500sh, Bloodhound. No. 1725, 3500sh, Pointer, horiz.

1720-1721 A276 Set of 2 3.75 3.75

Sheets of 6, #a-f

1722-1723 A276 Set of 2 19.00 19.00

Souvenir Sheets

1724-1725 A276 Set of 2 15.00 15.00

APS Stampshow, Chicago (#1723).

Royal Navy Submarines, Cent. — A277

No. 1726, vert.: a, HMS Tribune. b, HMS Royal Oak. c, HMS Invincible. d, HMS Dreadnought. e, HMS Ark Royal. f, HMS Cardiff.

2001, Aug. 27

1726 A277 1000sh Sheet of 6, #a-f 12.50 12.50

Souvenir Sheet

1727 A277 3500sh HMS Triad 7.50 7.50

Queen Victoria (1819-1901) — A278

No. 1728: a, Wearing tiara. b, Wearing white head covering, looking right. c, Wearing black hat. d, Wearing red dress with blue sash. e, Wearing white head covering, looking left. f, With hand on chin.
3500sh, Wearing black, hat, diff.

2001, Aug. 27

1728 A278 1000sh Sheet of 6, #a-f 10.00 10.00

Souvenir Sheet

1729 A278 3500sh multi 6.00 6.00

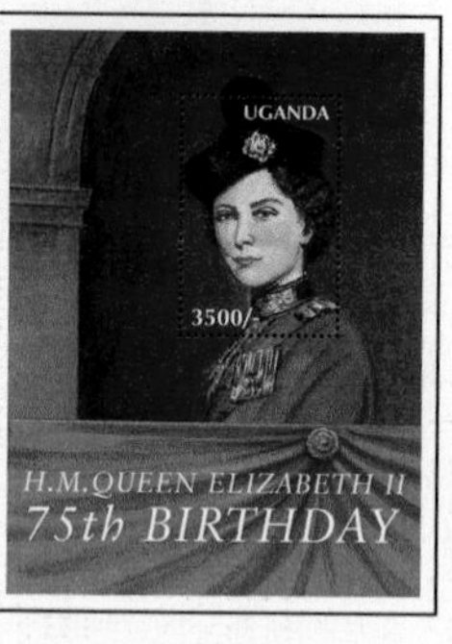

Queen Elizabeth II, 75th Birthday A279

No. 1730: a, In 1926. b, In 1931. c, In 1939. d, In 1955. e, In 1963. f, In 1999.
3500sh, Wearing cap.

2001, Aug. 27

1730 A279 1000sh Sheet of 6, #a-f 10.00 10.00

Souvenir Sheet

1731 A279 3500sh multi 6.00 6.00

Toulouse-Lautrec Paintings — A280

No. 1732: a, Woman Combing Her Hair. b, The Toilette. c, The English Girl at the Star in Le Havre.
3500sh, Ambassadeurs: Aristide Bruant.

2001, Aug. 27 Litho. *Perf. 13¾*

1732 A280 1500sh Sheet of 3, #a-c 7.50 7.50

Souvenir Sheet

1733 A280 3500sh multi 6.75 6.75

Monet Paintings A281

No. 1734, horiz.: a, Storm, Belle-Ile Coast. b, The Manneporte, Etretat. c, The Rocks at Pourville, Low Tide. d, The Wild Sea.
3500sh, Sunflowers.

2001, Aug. 27

1734 A281 1200sh Sheet of 4, #a-d 9.00 9.00

Souvenir Sheet

1735 A281 3500sh multi 6.75 6.75

Year of Dialogue Among Civilizations — A282

Perf. 13¾x13¼

2001, Nov. 16 Litho.

1736 A282 3000sh multi 7.50 7.50

Intl. Volunteers Year — A283

Designs: 300sh, Ebola outbreak. 700sh, Save life, donate blood. 2000sh, Collective effort for clean water.

2001, Nov. 16 *Perf. 13¼x13¾*

1737-1739 A283 Set of 3 5.00 5.00

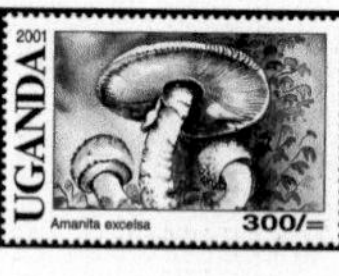

Mushrooms A284

Designs: 300sh, Amanita excelsa. 500sh, Coprinus cinereus. 600sh, Scleroderma aurantium. 700sh, Armillaria mellea. 1200sh, Leopiota procera. 2000sh, Flammulina velutipes.
3000sh, Amanita phalloides.

2001, Nov. 26 *Perf. 14½*

1740-1745 A284 Set of 6 8.00 8.00

Souvenir Sheets

1746 A284 3000sh multi 4.50 4.50
1746A A284 3000sh multi 4.50 4.50

Christmas — A285

Musical instruments: 400sh, Single skin long drum. 800sh, Animal horn trumpet, horiz. 1000sh, Bugisu clay drum. 1200sh, Musical bow. 1400sh, Pan pipes. 2000sh, Log xylophones, horiz.
No. 1753, 3500sh, Eight-stringed giant bow harp. No. 1754, Nativity scene, horiz.

2001 *Perf. 13¾x13¼, 13¼x13¾*

1747-1752 A285 Set of 6 12.50 12.50

Souvenir Sheets

1753-1754 A285 Set of 2 13.50 13.50

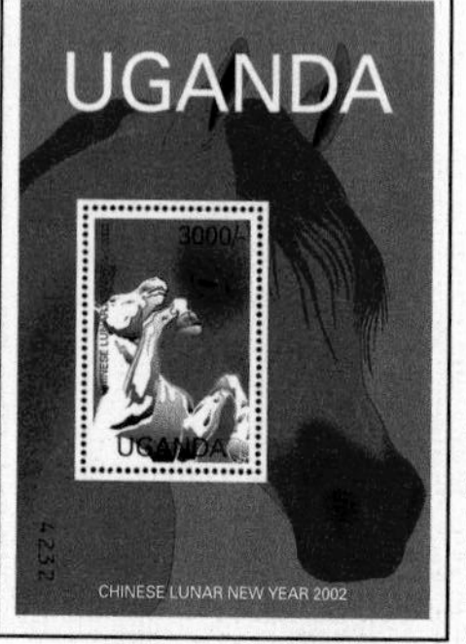

New Year 2002 (Year of the Horse) A286

No. 1755: a, White horse facing left. b, Dark brown and gray brown horse facing right with all feet on ground. c, Tan and brown horse facing right, with two feet raised.
3000r, Rearing horse.

2002, May 8 Litho. *Perf. 14x14¼*

1755 A286 1200sh Sheet of 3, #a-c 4.50 4.50

Souvenir Sheet

1756 A286 3000sh multi 3.75 3.75

Historic Sites of East Africa — A287

Designs: 400sh, Namugongo Shrine Church, Uganda. 800sh, Maruhubi Palace

Ruins, Zanzibar, Tanzania. 1200sh, Kings' Burial Grounds, Mparo, Uganda. 1400sh, Old Law Courts, Mombasa, Kenya, vert.

2002, May 8 *Perf. 14½*
1757-1760 A287 Set of 4 4.75 4.75

Reign of Queen Elizabeth II, 50th Anniv. A288

No. 1761: a, Wearing blue dress. b, Wearing blue and red hat. c, Without hat. d, Wearing blue hat.
3500sh, Wearing brown hat.

2002, June 17 *Perf. 14¼*
1761 A288 1500sh Sheet of 4, #a-d 7.50 7.50

Souvenir Sheet

1762 A288 3500sh multi 4.50 4.50

8th Intl. Interdisciplinary Congress on Women, Kampala — A289

Designs: 400sh, Women, building. 1200sh, Makerere University arms, vert.

Perf. 13¼x13¾, 13¾x13¼
2002, July 8
1763-1764 A289 Set of 2 2.00 2.00

United We Stand — A290

2002, July 15 *Perf. 13¾x13¼*
1765 A290 1500sh multi 1.90 1.90
Printed in sheets of 4.

Intl. Year of Mountains — A291

No. 1766: a, Tateyama, Japan. b, Mt. Nikko, Japan. c, Mt. Hodaka, Japan.
3500sh, Mt. Fuji, Japan.

2002, July 15 *Perf. 13¼x13¾*
1766 A291 2000sh Sheet of 3, #a-c 7.50 7.50

Souvenir Sheet

1767 A291 3500sh multi 4.50 4.50

2002 Winter Olympics, Salt Lake City — A292

Designs: No. 1768, 1200sh, Cross-country skiing. No. 1769, 1200sh, Ski jumping.

2002, July 15 *Perf. 13¾x13¼*
1768-1769 A292 Set of 2 3.00 3.00
1769a Souvenir sheet, #1768-1769 3.00 3.00

20th World Scout Jamboree, Thailand — A293

No. 1770: a, Scout in forest, 1930s. b, Scout saluting. c, Scouts hiking. d, Scout badge.
3500sh, Lord Robert Baden-Powell.

2002 *Perf. 13¼x13¾*
1770 A293 1400sh Sheet of 4, #a-d 7.00 7.00

Souvenir Sheet
Perf. 13¾x13¼

1771 A293 3500sh multi 4.50 4.50

Mammals, Insects, Flowers and Mushrooms — A294

Designs: 400sh, Ceratotherium simum. 800sh, Macrotermes subhyalinus. No. 1774, 1200sh, Gloriosa superba. 1400sh, Cyptotrama asprata.

No. 1776, 1000sh, horiz. — Insects: a, Nudaurelia cytherea. b, Locusta migratoria. c, Anacridium aegyptium. d, Sternotomis bohemanni. e, Papilio dardanus. f, Mantis polyspilota.

No. 1777, 1000sh, horiz. — Mushrooms: a, Termitomyces microcarpus. b, Agaricus trisulphuratus. c, Macrolepiota zeyheri. d, Lentinus stupeus. e, Lentinus sajor-caju. f, Lentinus velutinus.

No. 1778, 1200sh, horiz. — Flowers: a, Canarina eminii. b, Vigna unguiculata. c, Gardenia ternifolia. d, Canavalia rosea. e, Hibiscus calyphyllus. f, Nymphaea lotus.

No. 1779, 1200sh, horiz. — Mammals: a, Kobus kob. b, Alcelaphus buselaphus. c, Damaliiscus lunatus. d, Papio anubis. e, Panthera leo. f, Phacochoerus africanus.

No. 1780, 4000sh, Glossina austeni, horiz. No. 1781, 4000sh, Podoscypha parvula, horiz. No. 1782, 4000sh, Abutilon grandiflorum, horiz. No. 1783, 4000sh, Kobus ellipsiprymnus.

2002, Nov. 6 **Litho.** *Perf. 14*
1772-1775 A294 Set of 4 4.75 4.75

Sheets of 6, #a-f

1776-1779 A294 Set of 4 35.00 35.00

Souvenir Sheets

1780-1783 A294 Set of 4 20.00 20.00

A295

Pres. John F. Kennedy (1917-63) — A296

Various photos.

2002, Dec. 30
1784 A295 1200sh Sheet of 4, #a-d 6.00 6.00
1785 A296 1400sh Sheet of 4, #a-d 7.00 7.00

A297

Pres. Ronald Reagan A298

Various photos.

2002, Dec. 30
1786 A297 1200sh Sheet of 4, #a-d 6.00 6.00
1787 A298 1400sh Sheet of 4, #a-d 7.00 7.00

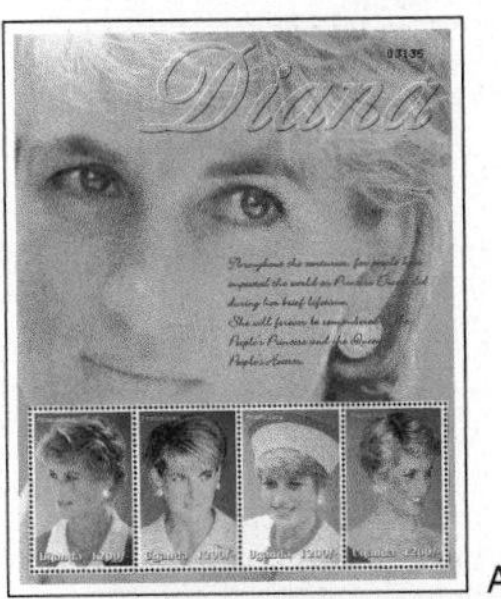

A299

Princess Diana (1961-97) — A300

2002, Dec. 30
1788 A299 1200sh Sheet of 4, #a-d 6.00 6.00
1789 A300 2000sh Sheet of 4, #a-d 10.00 10.00

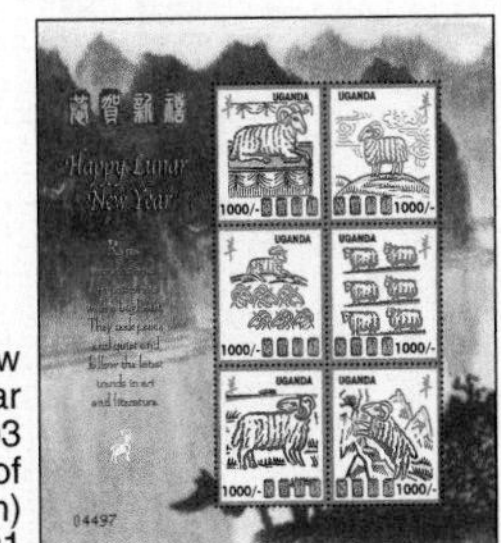

New Year 2003 (Year of the Ram) A301

No. 1790: a, Ram on stage. b, Ram on hill. c, Ram on hill, six ram's heads. d, Six rams. e, Ram in field. f, Ram on mountainside.

2003, Feb. 1 *Perf. 14¼x14*
1790 A301 1000sh Sheet of 6, #a-f 7.50 7.50

Japanese Art — A302

Designs: 400sh, Beauty Arranging Her Hair, by Eisen Keisai. 1000sh, Geishas, by Tsukimaro Kitagawa. 1200sh, Woman Behind a Screen, by Chikanobu Toyohara. 1400sh, Geishas, by Kitagawa, diff.

No. 1795: a, Scene in a Villa (basin in foreground), by Kinichika Toyohara. b, Scene in a Villa (screen at left), by Kunichika Toyohara. c, Visiting a Flower Garden (two people), by Kunisada Utagawa. d, Visiting a Flower Garden (one person), by Utagawa.

5000sh, Woman and Children, by Chikakazu.

2003, May 26 **Litho.** *Perf. 14¼*
1791-1794 A302 Set of 4 5.00 5.00
1795 A302 1200sh Sheet of 4, #a-d 6.00 6.00

Souvenir Sheet

1796 A302 5000sh multi 6.25 6.25

Rembrandt Paintings — A303

Designs: 400sh, Jacob Blessing the Sons of Joseph. 1000sh, A Young Woman in Profile With Fan. 1200sh, The Apostle Peter Kneeling. 1400sh, The Painter Hendrick Martensz Sorgh.

No. 1801: a, Portrait of Margaretha de Geer. b, Portrait of a White Haired Man. c, Portrait of Nicolaes Ruts. d, Portrait of Catrina Hooghsaet.

5000sh, Joseph Accused by Potiphar's Wife.

2003, May 26
1797-1800 A303 Set of 4 5.00 5.00
1801 A303 1400sh Sheet of 4, #a-d 7.00 7.00

Souvenir Sheet

1802 A303 5000sh multi 6.25 6.25

Paintings of Joan Miró — A304

Designs: 400sh, Group of Personages in the Forest. 800sh, Nocturne. 1200sh, The Smile of a Tear. 1400sh, Personage Before the Sun.

No. 1807, vert: a, Man's Head III. b, Catalan Peasant by Moonlight. c, Woman in the Night. d, Seated Woman.

No. 1808, 3500sh, Self-portrait II. No. 1809, 3500sh, Woman with Three Hairs, Birds and Constellations.

2003, May 26 *Perf. 14¼*
1803-1806 A304 Set of 4 4.75 4.75
1807 A304 1400sh Sheet of 4, #a-d 7.00 7.00

Imperf

Size: 103x82mm

1808-1809 A304 Set of 2 8.75 8.75

Buganda Princess Katrina-Sarah Ssangalyambogo, 2nd Birthday — A305

Princess and: 400sh, Bulange (government office building). 1200sh, Twekobe (palace), vert. 1400sh, Drummer, vert.

Perf. 13x13¼, 13¼x13

2003, June 16

1810-1812 A305 Set of 3 3.75 3.75

Coronation of Queen Elizabeth II, 50th Anniv. — A306

No. 1813: a, As toddler. b, As young woman, wearing flowered hat. c, Wearing robe and feathered hat.
3500sh, Wearing crown.

2003, July 15 ***Perf. 14***

1813 A306 2000sh Sheet of 3, #a-c 7.50 7.50

Souvenir Sheet

1814 A306 3500sh multi 4.50 4.50

Prince William, 21st Birthday A307

No. 1815: a, Wearing cap. b, Wearing blue striped shirt. c, Wearing white shirt.
5000sh, With hand on chin.

2003, July 15

1815 A307 2000sh Sheet of 3, #a-c 7.50 7.50

Souvenir Sheet

1816 A307 5000sh multi 6.25 6.25

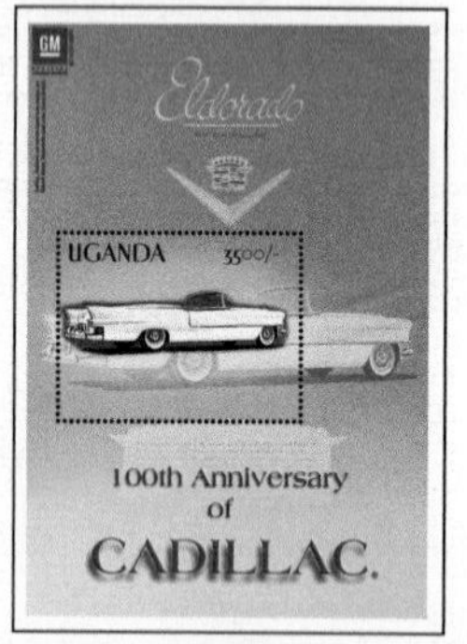

General Motors Automobiles — A308

No. 1817, 1200sh — Cadillacs: a, 1979 Seville Elegante. b, 1998 Eldorado Touring Coupe. c, 2002 Escalade. d, 1983 Seville Elegante.
No. 1818, 1400sh — Corvettes: a, 1970. b, 1972. c, 1982 Collector Edition. d, 1977.
No. 1819, 3500sh, Cadillac Eldorado convertible, 1950s. No. 1820, 3500sh, 1982 Collector Edition Corvette, diff.

2003, July 15 ***Perf. 14¼***

Sheets of 4, #a-d

1817-1818 A308 Set of 2 13.00 13.00

Souvenir Sheets

1819-1820 A308 Set of 2 8.75 8.75

Millennium Development Goals — A309

Designs: No. 1821, 400sh, Promote gender equity and empower women. No. 1822, 400sh, Improve maternal health. 600sh, Ensure environmental sustainability. 1000sh, Reduce child mortality. No. 1825, 1200sh, Eradicate extreme poverty and hunger. No. 1826, 1200sh, Combat HIV, AIDS, malaria and other diseases. 1400sh, Achieve universal primary education. 2000sh, Develop a global partnership for development.

2003, Oct. 24 ***Perf. 14½***

1821-1828 A309 Set of 8 10.50 10.50

Dances and Costumes — A310

Dances: 400sh, Entogoro. 800sh, Karimojong. 1400sh, Teso.
No. 1832 — Costumes: a, Kiga. b, Acholi. c, Karimojong. d, Ganda.

2003, Nov. 10 ***Perf. 14***

1829-1831 A310 Set of 3 3.25 3.25

1832 A310 1200sh Sheet of 4, #a-d 6.00 6.00

Christmas — A311

Dances: 300sh, Journey to Bethlehem. 400sh, Shepherds and angels. 1200sh, Nativity. 1400sh, Adoration of the Magi.
3000sh, Holy Family.

2003, Nov. 10

1833-1836 A311 Set of 4 4.25 4.25

Souvenir Sheet

1837 A311 3000sh multi 3.75 3.75

All-Africa Conference on Assuring Food and Nutrition Security in Africa by 2020, Kampala A312

Map of Africa, food basket, Intl. Food Policy Research Institute emblem and: 400sh, Boy. 1400sh, Boy, diff.

2004, Aug. 31 **Litho.** ***Perf. 14¼***

1838-1839 A312 Set of 2 2.25 2.25

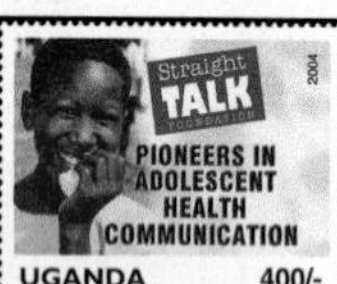

Straight Talk Foundation A313

Child and: 400sh, "Pioneers in Adolescent Health Communication." 1200sh, "Communication for Better Adolescent Health," vert.

2004, Sept. 22

1840-1841 A313 Set of 2 2.00 2.00

Campaign Against Child Labor — A314

Inscriptions: 400sh, "Stop Child Domestic Labor." 2000sh, "Keep the Community Informed."

2004, Sept. 22

1842-1843 A314 Set of 2 3.00 3.00

Rotary International, Cent. (in 2005) — A315

Rotary emblem and: 400sh, "Celebrate Rotary." 1200sh, "A Century of Service / A New Century of Success," vert.

2004, Sept. 22

1844-1845 A315 Set of 2 2.00 2.00

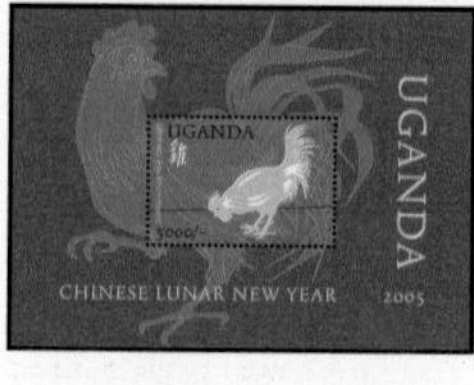

New Year 2005 (Year of the Rooster) A316

No. 1846 — Rooster shades: a, Blue. b, Orange. c, Purple. d, Red.
5000sh, Yellow.

2005, Apr. 4 **Litho.** ***Perf. 14***

1846 A316 1200sh Sheet of 4, #a-d 6.00 6.00

Souvenir Sheet

1847 A316 5000sh multi 6.25 6.25

Fight Against Tuberculosis, HIV and Leprosy — A317

WHO emblem and: No. 1848, 400sh, Ill man in blanket. No. 1849, 400sh, Doctor holding arm of ill man. No. 1850, 400sh, Mother and infant. No. 1851, 400sh, Infant in blanket. No. 1852, 400sh, Leper with artificial leg. No. 1853, 400sh, Leper wearing crucifix.

2005, May 31 ***Perf. 13x12¾***

1848-1853 A317 Set of 6 3.00 3.00

Flowering Plants — A318

Designs: 100sh, Clerodendrum sp. 400sh, Calliandra haematocephala. 600sh, Asteraceae compositae. 850sh, Angraecum sp. 900sh, Delonix regia. 1100sh, Bidens grantii. 1200sh, Musa sapientum. 1400sh, Begonia coccinea. 1600sh, Impatiens walleriana. 2000sh, Strelitzia reginae. 5000sh, Tecomaria capensis. 6000sh, Ixora hybrida. 10,000sh, Datura suaveolens. 20,000sh, Cucurbita pepo.

Perf. 12¾x13½

2005, June 22 **Litho.**

1854	A318	100sh	multi	.25	.25
1855	A318	400sh	multi	.45	.45
1856	A318	600sh	multi	.70	.70
1857	A318	850sh	multi	1.00	1.00
1858	A318	900sh	multi	1.10	1.10
1859	A318	1100sh	multi	1.25	1.25
1860	A318	1200sh	multi	1.40	1.40
1861	A318	1400sh	multi	1.60	1.60
1862	A318	1600sh	multi	1.90	1.90
1863	A318	2000sh	multi	2.40	2.40
1864	A318	5000sh	multi	5.75	5.75
1865	A318	6000sh	multi	7.00	7.00
1866	A318	10,000sh	multi	11.50	11.50
1867	A318	20,000sh	multi	23.00	23.00
	Nos. 1854-1867 (14)			59.30	59.30

Fish — A319

Designs: 400sh, Synodontis afrofischeri. 600sh, Protopterus aethiopicus. 1100sh, Clarias gariepinus. 1200sh, Rastrineobola agentea. 1600sh, Bagrus docmac. 2000sh, Schilbe mystus.
No. 1874: a, Mormyrus kannume. b, Barbus jacksonni. c, Bagrus docmac, diff. d, Labeo victorianus.

2005, Oct. 6 **Litho.** ***Perf. 13¼***

1868-1873 A319 Set of 6 8.75 8.75

Souvenir Sheet

1874 A319 1000sh Sheet of 4, #a-d 5.00 5.00

Western Union in Africa, 10th Anniv. — A320

Designs: 400sh, Map of Africa, olive branches. 1600sh, Globe. 2000sh, Globe and flags, vert.

2006, July 20 **Litho.** ***Perf. 14¼***

1875-1877 A320 Set of 3 5.00 5.00

Bank of Uganda, 40th Anniv. — A321

Designs: 400sh, Bank emblem. 600sh, Bank emblem, building, wildlife. 1600sh, Bank emblem, Tilapia nilotica. 2000sh, Bank emblem, mountain gorilla.

2006, Oct. 3 ***Perf. 13¼***

1878-1881 A321 Set of 4 5.75 5.75

Wetlands — A322

Designs: 400sh, Cattle and herdsman at water, Ramsar Convention emblem. 1600sh, People and birds near stream. 2000sh, Fishermen at Lake George.

2006 ***Perf. 13x13½***

1882-1884 A322 Set of 3 5.00 5.00

2007 Commonwealth Heads of Government Meeting, Kampala — A323

Flag of Uganda and: 400sh, Commonwealth Heads of Government Meeting emblem. 1600sh, Boniface Kiprop, runner. 2000sh, Dorcas Inzikuru, runner. 5000sh, Arms of Uganda, vert.

2007, Nov. 27 **Litho.** ***Perf. 13x13½***

1885-1888 A323 Set of 4 10.50 10.50

24th UPU Congress, Geneva — A324

People in native costumes: No. 1889, Karimojong man.
No. 1890: a, Omwenda women. b, Ebibaraho man. c, Kikoyi women. d, Kanzu men. e, Gomesi women.

2007, Dec. 7 **Litho.** ***Perf. 13¼x13***

1889 A324 1600sh multi 1.90 1.90

1890 A324 1600sh Horiz. strip of 5, #a-e 9.50 9.50

The UPU Congress was moved from Nairobi, Kenya, to Geneva because of political unrest.

Miniature Sheet

2008 Summer Olympics, Beijing — A325

No. 1891: a, Javelin. b, Running. c, Boxing. d, Swimming.

2008, June 18 ***Perf. 12***
1891 A325 1000sh Sheet of 4, #a-d 5.00 5.00

Worldwide Fund for Nature (WWF) — A326

No. 1892 — Spotted hyena: a, Running. b, With pack, devouring prey. c, Adult and juveniles. d, Two juveniles.

2008, June 18 ***Perf. 13¼***
1892 Strip of 4 5.00 5.00
a.-d. A326 1000sh Any single 1.25 1.25
e. Sheet of 8, 2 each #1892a-1892d 10.00 10.00

Reign of Aga Khan, 50th Anniv. (in 2007) — A327

Designs: No. 1893, 400sh, Diamond Trust Building. No. 1894, 400sh, Kampala Serena Hotel. No. 1895, 400sh, Jubilee Insurance Company Building.

No. 1896: a, School children (madrasa program). b, Ismaili Jamatkhana, Kampala. c, Aga Khan High School (educational services). d, Air Uganda airplane. e, Dam (Bujagali hydropower project).

2008, Sept. 30 **Litho.** ***Perf. 14½***
1893-1895 A327 Set of 3 1.50 1.50
1896 A327 1100sh Horiz. strip of 5, #a-e 6.50 6.50
f. Souvenir sheet of 1, #1896b — —

Peony — A328

2009, Apr. 10 **Litho.** ***Perf. 13¼***
1897 A328 1600sh multi 1.50 1.50

Printed in sheets of 8 + central label.

Miniature Sheet

China 2009 World Stamp Exhibition, Luoyang — A329

No. 1898 — Tourist attractions in China: a, Longmen Grottoes, Luoyang. b, Bridge over Pearl River, Guangzhou. c, Twin Temples on Fir Lake, Guilin. d, Yu Yuan Garden, Shanghai.

2009, Apr. 10 ***Perf. 12***
1898 A329 1000sh Sheet of 4, #a-d 3.75 3.75

Miniature Sheet

Pres. Abraham Lincoln (1809-65) — A330

No. 1899 — Photographs of Lincoln taken in: a, 1857 (wearing vest). b, 1864. c, 1863. d, 1857 (without vest).

2009, Apr. 10 ***Perf. 13¼***
1899 A330 2000sh Sheet of 4, #a-d 7.50 7.50

Miniature Sheet

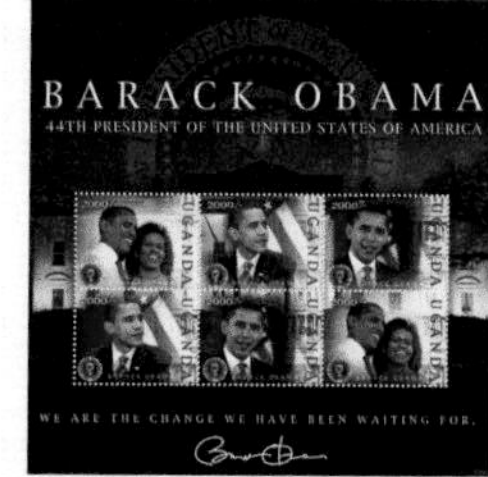

Inauguration of US Pres. Barack Obama — A331

No. 1900: a, Pres. Obama and wife, Michelle, balustrade over heads. b, Pres. Obama with blue striped tie, window at left. c, Pres. Obama with red and gold tie, balustrade above head. d, As "b," window above head. e, As "c," White House portico lamp above head. f, As "a," windows over heads.

2009, Apr. 10 ***Perf. 11½x11¼***
1900 A331 2000sh Sheet of 6, #a-f 11.00 11.00

Miniature Sheets

A332

Michael Jackson (1958-2009), Singer — A333

No. 1901: a, Wearing tan jacket, no microphone shown. b, Wearing blue and white shirt, no microphone shown. c, Wearing blue jacket, with microphone. d, Wearing tan jacket, with microphone.

No. 1902: a, Facing right, microphone at mouth. b, Holding microphone on stand. c, Behind microphone on stand. d, Facing left, microphone at mouth.

2009 ***Perf. 13¼x13***
1901 A332 2000sh Sheet of 4, #a-d 8.50 8.50
1902 A333 2000sh Sheet of 4, #a-d 8.50 8.50

The printer of Nos. 1901-1902 claims the stamps were issued June 25, the day Michael Jackson died. The editors doubt this claim.

Chinese Aviation, Cent. A334

No. 1903: a, Q-5. b, Q-5C. c, JH-7A. d, JH-7 on ground.
4000sh, JH-7 in flight.

2009, Nov. 12 ***Perf. 14¼***
1903 A334 2000sh Sheet of 4, #a-d 8.50 8.50

Souvenir Sheet

1904 A334 4000sh multi 4.25 4.25

Aeropex 2009, Beijing. No. 1903 contains four 42x33mm stamps.

Miniature Sheet

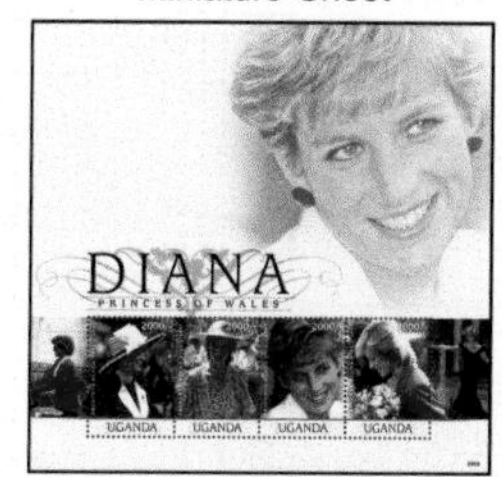

Princess Diana (1961-97) — A335

No. 1905 — Princess Diana: a, Wearing black and white hat. b, Wearing pink hat. c, Wearing white blouse. d, Holding flowers.

2010, Feb. 15 ***Perf. 11½***
1905 A335 2000sh Sheet of 4, #a-d 8.00 8.00

Miniature Sheet

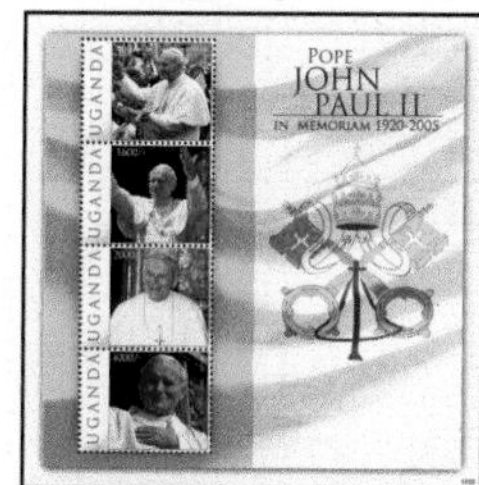

Pope John Paul II (1920-2005) — A336

No. 1906 — Pope John Paul II: a, 400sh, Greeting crowd. b, 1600sh, With arms raised. c, 2000sh, Standing in front of painting. d, 4000sh, With hand on chest.

2010, June 24
1906 A336 Sheet of 4, #a-d 7.25 7.25

Souvenir Sheet

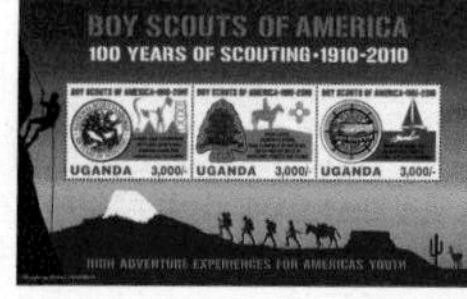

Boy Scouts of America, Cent. A337

No. 1907 — Emblem of: a, National Scout Jamboree. b, Philmont Scout Ranch, Cimarron, New Mexico. c, Florida High Adventure Sea Base.

2010, Oct. 14 ***Perf. 13½***
1907 A337 3000sh Sheet of 3, #a-c 8.00 8.00

Miniature Sheets

A338

Pope Benedict XVI A339

No. 1908 — Various photographs of Pope Benedict XVI with denomination at upper right: a, 400sh. b, 1600sh. c, 2000sh. d, 4000sh.

No. 1909 — Various photographs of Pope Benedict XVI with denomination at upper left: a, 400sh. b, 1600sh. c, 2000sh. d, 4000sh.

2011, Feb. 25 ***Perf. 12***
1908 A338 Sheet of 4, #a-d 6.75 6.75
1909 A339 Sheet of 4, #a-d 6.75 6.75

Miniature Sheets

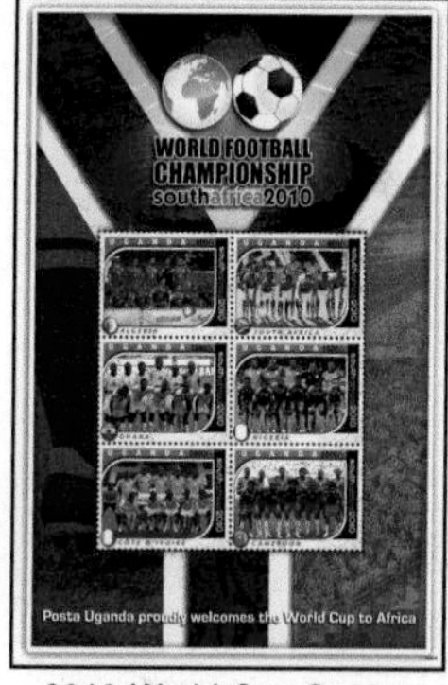

2010 World Cup Soccer Championships, South Africa — A340

No. 1910 — Team from: a, 400sh, Algeria. b, 400sh, South Africa. c, 1600sh, Ghana. d, 1600sh, Nigeria. e, 3000sh, Ivory Coast. f, 3000sh, Cameroun.

No. 1911 — Team from: a, 900sh, Italy. b, 900sh, Brazil. c, 1100sh, Japan. d, 1100sh, New Zealand. e, 4000sh, Australia. f, 4000sh, United States.

2011, Feb. 25 **Litho.** ***Perf. 12***
Sheets of 6, #a-f
1910-1911 A340 Set of 2 18.50 18.50

Disease Prevention — A341

Inscriptions: 400sh, Treat livestock against nagana. 900sh, Treat humans against sleeping sickness, horiz. 1600sh, War against tsetse flies in Uganda, horiz. 3000sh, Empower communities against trypanosomiasis, horiz.

2011, Jan. 18 ***Perf. 13x13½, 13½x13***
1912-1915 A341 Set of 4 5.25 5.25

Souvenir Sheet

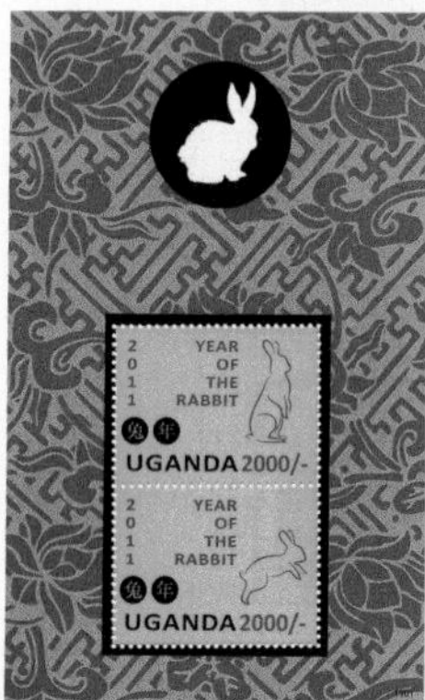

New Year 2011 (Year of the Rabbit) A342

No. 1916: a, Rabbit standing on hind legs. b, Rabbit leaping.

2011, Feb. 1 ***Perf. 12***

1916 A342 2000sh Sheet of 2, #a-b 3.50 3.50

Wedding of Prince William and Catherine Middleton — A343

No. 1917 — Stamps with blue panels: a, 600sh, Bride standing. b, 2500sh, Couple.
No. 1918 — Stamps with red panels: a, 600sh, Bride in coach. b, 2500sh, Couple waving.

2011, Apr. 29 ***Perf. 13¼x13***

Pairs, #a-b

1917-1918 A343 Set of 2 7.50 7.50

Nos. 1917-1918 each were printed in sheets containing two pairs. Nos. 1917-1918 could not have been issued on the stated day of issue, as the stamps show photographs of the wedding that day.

A344

A345

A346

A347

A348

A349

A350

A351

A352

A353

A354

A355

A356

A357

A358

A359

A360

A361

A362

Gorillas A363

2011, June 18 ***Perf. 14½***

1919 Block of 10 3.00 3.00
a. A344 400sh multi .30 .30
b. A345 400sh multi .30 .30
c. A346 400sh multi .30 .30
d. A347 400sh multi .30 .30
e. A348 400sh multi .30 .30
f. A349 400sh multi .30 .30
g. A350 400sh multi .30 .30
h. A351 400sh multi .30 .30
i. A352 400sh multi .30 .30
j. A352 400sh multi .30 .30
1920 Vert. strip of 5 4.00 4.00
a. A354 1000sh multi .80 .80
b. A355 1000sh multi .80 .80
c. A356 1000sh multi .80 .80
d. A357 1000sh multi .80 .80
e. A358 1000sh multi .80 .80
1921 Vert. strip of 5 6.25 6.25
a. A359 1600sh multi 1.25 1.25
b. A360 1600sh multi 1.25 1.25
c. A361 1600sh multi 1.25 1.25
d. A362 1600sh multi 1.25 1.25
e. A363 1600sh multi 1.25 1.25
Nos. 1919-1921 (3) 13.25 13.25

Pan-African Postal Union, 30th anniv. (in 2010).

AIDS Prevention — A364

Emblems and: 700sh, Philly Bongoley Lutaaya (1951-89), musician. 1500sh, Man and woman receiving information about AIDS at clinic, horiz. 1800sh, Medical workers in laboratory, horiz. 1900sh, People holding candles, horiz. 2700sh, AIDS ribbon within frame with simulated perforations and cancel. 3400sh, Family at home, horiz.

Perf. 13¼x13, 13x13¼

2012, Mar. 29 **Litho.**

1922-1927 A364 Set of 6 9.75 9.75

Discovery of human immunodeficiency virus, 30th anniv.

Wildlife A365

No. 1928 — Primates: a, 3400sh, De Brazza's monkey. b, 3400sh, Brown greater galago. c, 4100sh, Patas monkey. d, 4100sh, L'Hoest's monkey.
No. 1929 — Wildcats: a, 3400sh, Cheetah chasing Thomson's gazelle. b, 3400sh, Lions. c, 4100sh, Leopards. d, 4100sh, Caracals.
No. 1930 — Two African bush elephants: a, 3400sh, Elephant at right facing left. b, 3400sh, Elephant at right facing forward. c, 4100sh, Elephant at right facing left. d, 4100sh, Elephant at right facing forward.
No. 1931 — Owls: a, 3400sh, Pel's fishing owls. b, 3400sh, African wood owls. c, 4100sh, Spotted eagle-owls. d, 4100sh, Cape eagle-owls.
No. 1932 — Kingfishers: a, 3400sh, Pied kingfisher. b, 3400sh, Gray-headed kingfishers. c, 4100sh, Malachite kingfishers. d, 4100sh, Malachite kingfisher, Pied kingfisher.
No. 1933 — Birds of prey: a, 3400sh, Tawny eagle. b, 3400sh, Bateleurs. c, 4100sh, Osprey. d, 4100sh, Rüppell's vulture.
No. 1934 — Butterflies: a, 3400sh, Silver-barred charaxes. b, 3400sh, Green-banded swallowtail. c, 4100sh, Crossley's forest queen. d, 4100sh, Acraea swordtail.
No. 1935 — Fish: a, 3400sh, Haplochromis katonga. b, 3400sh, Haplochromis nyererei. c, 4100sh, Lates niloticus. d, 4100sh, Mormyrus macrocephalus.
No. 1936 — Reptiles: a, 3400sh, Graceful chameleon. b, 3400sh, Leopard tortoise. c, 4100sh, Gaboon viper. d, 4100sh, Nile crocodile.
No. 1937 — Endangered species: a, 3400sh, Beaudoin's snake eagles. b, 3400sh, African golden cats. c, 4100sh, Cheetahs. d, 4100sh, Checkered elephant shrews.
No. 1938, 8300sh, Blue monkeys. No. 1939, 8300sh, Leopards, diff. No. 1940, 8300sh, Two African bush elephants, diff. No. 1941, 8300sh, Verreaux's eagle-owl. No. 1942, 8300sh, Gray-headed kingfishers, diff. No. 1943, 8300sh, Western marsh harriers. No. 1944, 8300sh, Two Precis octavia. No. 1945, 8300sh, Haplochromis petronius. No. 1946, 8300sh, Gaboon viper, diff. No. 1947, 8300sh. Black-crowned crane.

2012, Mar. 30 **Litho.** ***Perf. 13¼***

Sheets of 4, #a-d

1928-1937 A365 Set of 10 120.00 120.00

Souvenir Sheets

1938-1947 A365 Set of 10 62.50 62.50

Miniature Sheets

A366

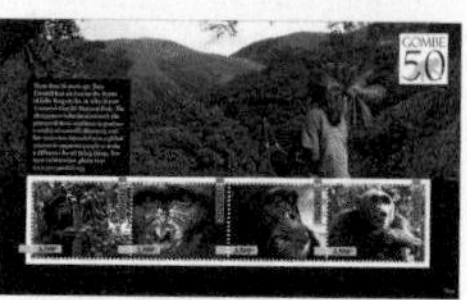

Chimpanzees — A367

Various photographs of chimpanzees, as shown.

2012, Apr. 11 **Litho.** ***Perf. 12***

1948 A366 3500sh Sheet of 4, #a-d 17.50 17.50
1949 A367 3500sh Sheet of 4, #a-d 17.50 17.50

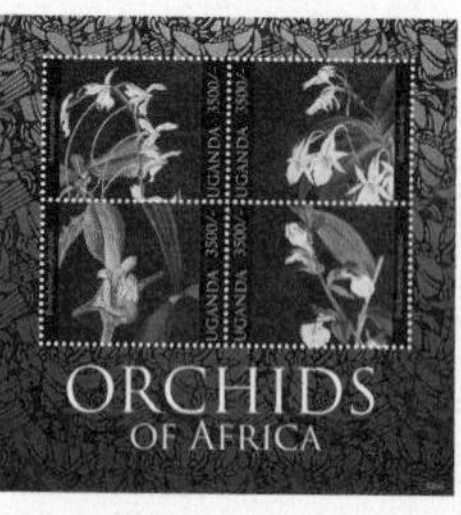

Orchids A368

No. 1950: a, Aerangis arachnopus. b, Angraecum leonis. c, Bulbophyllum calyptratum. d, Brachycorythis macrantha.
10,000sh, Bulbophyllum sandersonii, vert.

2012, Apr. 11 **Litho.** ***Perf. 12***

1950 A368 3500sh Sheet of 4, #a-d 11.50 11.50

Souvenir Sheet

Perf. 12½

1951 A368 10,000sh multi 8.25 8.25

No. 1951 contains one 38x51mm stamp.

Endangered Animals — A369

No. 1952: a, Addax. b, Cheetah. c, Western lowland gorilla. d, Mountain zebra. e, Dama gazelle.
10,000sh, Ostrich.

2012, Apr. 11 **Litho.** ***Perf. 14***

1952 A369 3000sh Sheet of 5, #a-e 12.50 12.50

Souvenir Sheet

Perf. 12½

1953 A369 10,000sh multi 8.25 8.25

No. 1953 contains one 51x38mm stamp.

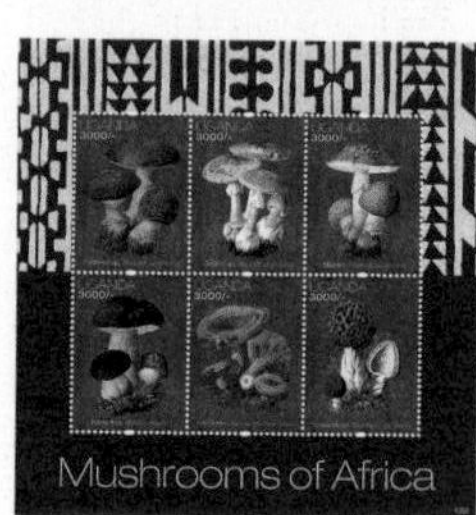

Mushrooms — A370

No. 1954: a, Panther cap. b, Death cap. c, Blusher. d, Penny bun. e, Saffron milk cap. f, Yellow morel.
No. 1955: a, Amethyst deceiver. b, Mica cap.

Perf. 13 Syncopated

2012, Apr. 11 **Litho.**

1954 A370 3000sh Sheet of 6, #a-f 15.00 15.00

Souvenir Sheet

1955 A370 5000sh Sheet of 2, #a-b 8.25 8.25

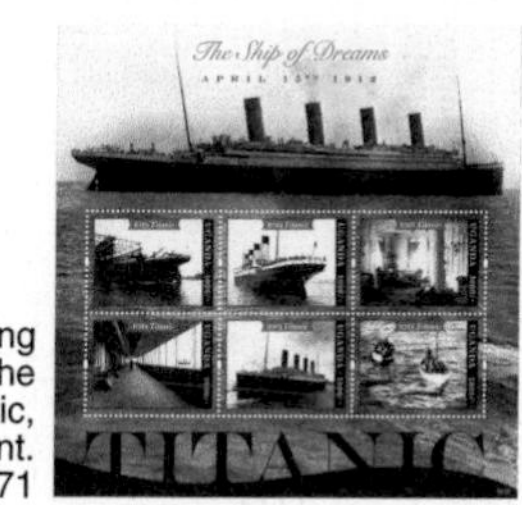

Sinking of the Titanic, Cent. A371

No. 1956: a, Titanic under construction. b, Stern of Titanic. c, Table and chairs. d, Deck. e, Bow of Titanic. f, Lifeboats.
10,000d, Titanic, diff.

Perf. 13 Syncopated

2012, Apr. 11 **Litho.**

1956 A371 3000sh Sheet of 6, #a-f 15.00 15.00

Souvenir Sheet

1957 A371 10,000sh multi 8.25 8.25

American Civil War, 150th Anniv. — A372

No. 1958 — Abraham Lincoln and detail from Battle of Chattanooga print published by Kurz and Allison: a, Red panel at top. b, White panel at top, no flag. c, Blue panel at top. d, White panel at top, flag visible.
10,000sh, Lincoln, Battle of Spotsylvania print by Kurz and Allison.

Perf. 13 Syncopated

2012, Apr. 11 **Litho.**

1958 A372 3500sh Sheet of 4, #a-d 11.50 11.50

Souvenir Sheet

1959 A372 10,000sh multi 8.25 8.25

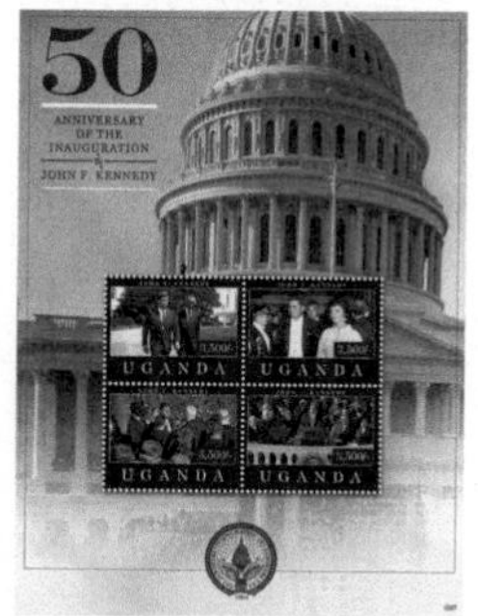

Inauguration of Pres. John F. Kennedy, 50th Anniv. (in 2011) — A373

No. 1960 Pres. Kennedy: a, With Vice President Lyndon B. Johnson. b, With wife, Jacqueline. c, Taking oath of office. d, Delivering inaugural speech.
10,000sh, Pres. Kennedy speaking, vert.

2012, Apr. 11 **Litho.** ***Perf. 12***

1960 A373 3500sh Sheet of 4, #a-d 11.50 11.50

Souvenir Sheet

1961 A373 10,000sh multi 8.25 8.25

Princess Diana (1961-97) — A374

No. 1962 — Princess Diana: a, Holding flowers. b, Wearing hat. c, Without hat.
10,000sh, Princess Diana wearing hat, diff.

Perf. 13 Syncopated

2012, Apr. 11 **Litho.**

1962 A374 3500sh Sheet of 3, #a-c 8.50 8.50

Souvenir Sheet

Perf. 12

1963 A374 10,000sh multi 8.25 8.25

No. 1963 contains one 30x50mm stamp.

Paintings by Peter Paul Rubens (1577-1640) — A375

No. 1964: a, 3400sh, The Deposition. b, 3400sh, The Martyrdom of St. Stephen. c, 4100sh, The Last Judgment. d, 4100sh, Christ and Mary Magdalene.
8300sh, Christ at Simon the Pharisee, horiz.

2012, July 26 **Litho.** ***Perf. 13¼***

1964 A375 Sheet of 4, #a-d 12.00 12.00

Souvenir Sheet

1965 A375 8300sh multi 6.75 6.75

Yuri Gagarin (1934-68), First Man in Space — A376

No. 1966: a, 3400sh, Gagarin, Vostok 1 in orbit. b, 3400sh, Gagarin, MiG-15. c, 4100sh, Monuments to Gagarin. d, 4100sh, Gagarin in helmet, launch of Vostok 1.
8300sh, Gagarin, launch of Vostok 1, diff.

2012, July 26 **Litho.** ***Perf. 13¼***

1966 A376 Sheet of 4, #a-d 12.00 12.00

Souvenir Sheet

1967 A376 8300sh multi 6.75 6.75

Chess Match Between Deep Blue Computer and Garry Kasparov, 15th Anniv. — A377

No. 1968: a, 3400sh, Kasparov standing at right, television screens at left. b, 3400sh, Kasparov and flags. c, 4100sh, Kasparov seated, computer display of chess board. d, 4100sh, Kasparov seated, television screens at left.
8300sh, Kasparov, chess board, arm of human and mechanical arm wrestling.

2012, July 26 **Litho.** ***Perf. 13¼***

1968 A377 Sheet of 4, #a-d 12.00 12.00

Souvenir Sheet

1969 A377 8300sh multi 6.75 6.75

Whitney Houston (1963-2012), Singer — A378

No. 1970 — Two images of Houston with larger image of Houston (without microphone) with: a, 3400sh, Hand on cheek. b, 3400sh, Eyes shut. c, 4100sh, Strapless gown. d, 4100sh, Dress with zipper, with hand touching side of head.
8300sh, Houston, diff.

2012, July 26 **Litho.** ***Perf. 13¼***

1970 A378 Sheet of 4, #a-d 12.00 12.00

Souvenir Sheet

1971 A378 8300sh multi 6.75 6.75

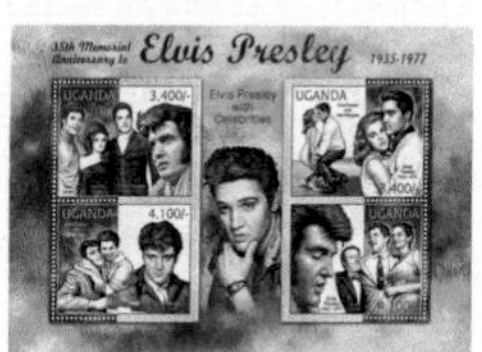

Elvis Presley (1935-77) — A379

No. 1972 — Presley with: a, 3400sh, Wife, Priscilla, and Tom Jones. b, 3400sh, Ann-Margret. c, 4100sh, Sophia Loren. d, 4100sh, Lou Costello and Jane Russell.
8300sh, Presley with Muhammad Ali.

2012, July 26 **Litho.** ***Perf. 13¼***

1972 A379 Sheet of 4, #a-d 12.00 12.00

Souvenir Sheet

1973 A379 8300sh multi 6.75 6.75

Elvis Presley (1935-77) — A380

No. 1974 — Presley with guitar, with frame color of: a, Dark blue green. b, Light blue green. c, Blue green.
10,000sh, Presley holding microphone.

2012, July 26 **Litho.** ***Perf. 12***

1974 A380 3500sh Sheet of 4, #1974a, 1974b, 2 #1974c 11.50 11.50

Souvenir Sheet

1975 A380 10,000sh multi 8.00 8.00

Olympic Rings and Stylized Torch — A381

Stadia for the 2012 Summer Olympics, London — A382

No. 1977: a, Olympic Stadium. b, Wembley Stadium. c, Old Trafford Stadium.

2012, Aug. 3 **Litho.** ***Perf. 13¼x13***

1976 A381 1500sh multi 1.25 1.25

Perf. 13¼

1977 Vert. strip of 3 2.60 2.60
a.-c. A382 1050sh Any single .85 .85

No. 1976 was issued in sheets of 8.

Independence, 50th Anniv. — A383

Designs: 700sh, 50th anniv. emblem. 1800sh, Independence Monument. 2700sh, Flag of Uganda.

2012, Oct. 9 **Litho.** ***Perf. 14***

1978-1980 A383 Set of 3 4.00 4.00

Transportation — A385

No. 1983 — Sailboats, with inscriptions: a, 3400sh, "2010 Extreme Sailing Series, skipper of The Wave, Muscat." b, 3400sh, "McDougall at PUMA Moth Worlds, 2010." c, 4100sh, "Tom Slingsby, ISAF World Sailor of the Year, 2010." d, 4100sh, "Bahrain Pindar Team, Langenargen, World Match Racing Tour 2009."
No. 1984 — Steam trains: a, 3400sh, Tornado 60163. b, 3400sh, Furness Railway No. 20. c, 4100sh, Terrier 32662. d, 4100sh, Brighton Works DS 377.
No. 1985 — High-speed trains: a, 3400sh, Transrapid TR-09, "2012" at LL. b, 3400sh,Transrapid TR-09, "2012" at UR. c, 4100sh, CR380A, black denomination at LL. d, 4100sh, CR380A, white denomination at UR.
No. 1986 — Airplanes: a, 3400sh, Airbus A380. b, 3400sh, Boeing 747-8. c, 4100sh, Aerospatiale BAC Concorde. d, 4100sh, Boeing 777-300.
No. 1987 — Airships: a, 3400sh, LZ-127. b, 3400sh, Hindenburg (LZ-129). c, 4100sh, USS Macon (ZRS-5). d, 4100sh, LZ-17 Sachsen.
No. 1988 — Formula 1 race cars and drivers: a, 3400sh, McLaren-Mercedes car, Lewis Hamilton. b, 3400sh, Lotus-Renault car, Kimi Räikkönen. c, 4100sh, Mercedes car, Michael Schumacher. d, 4100sh, Red Bull Racing-Renault car, Sebastian Vettel.
No. 1989 — Motorcycles: a, 3400sh, Kawasaki VERSYS 650. b, 3400sh, Ferrari V4 Superbike Concept. c, 4100sh, Honda V4 Concept. d, 4100sh, Yamaha YZF R1 1000.
No. 1990 — Unmotorized vehicles: a, 3400sh, Horse and cart. b, 3400sh, Paddleboat. c, 4100sh, Velomobile. d, 4100sh, Skateboard.
No. 1991 — Special transport vehicles: a, 3400sh, 1964 Ford F-600 Young fire truck. b, 3400sh, 1975 Plymouth Grand Fury and 1999 Ford Crown Victoria police cars, 1970 Harley-Davidson FLH police motorcycle. c, 4100sh, 1968 Citroen DS and 2008 Ford E450 Horton Type III ambulances. d, 4100sh, 2010 Ford F550 Gurkha MAPV police vehicle, 1970 Harley-Davidson FLH police motorcycle.
No. 1992 — Futuristic concept cars: a, 3400sh, Audi A9 concept car. b, 3400sh, Peugeot Touch concept car. c, 4100sh, Lotus Esquive concept car. d, 4100sh, Honda 3R-C concept car.
No. 1993, 8300sh, Extreme Sailing Series, Boston, 2011. No. 1994, 8300sh, Brighton Blue Bell steam train, clock. No. 1995, 8300sh, Bombardier Zefiro 380. No. 1996, 8300sh, Boeing 747-8, diff. No. 1997, 8300sh, Hindenburg (LZ-129), diff. No. 1998, 8300sh, Ferrari car, Fernando Alonso. No. 1999, 8300sh, Suzuki Biplane concept motorcycle. No. 2000, 8300sh, Hang glider. No. 2001, 8300sh, 1949 Mack L Model fire trucks. No. 2002, 8300sh, Lotus Hot Wheels concept car.

2012, Oct. 22 **Litho.** ***Perf. 13¼***

Sheets of 4, #a-d

1983-1992 A385 Set of 10 120.00 120.00

Souvenir Sheets

1993-2002 A385 Set of 10 65.00 65.00

Endangered Animals — A386

No. 2003 — Chimpanzees: a, 3400sh, Adult and juvenile. b, 3400sh, Adult. c, 4100sh, Adult, diff. d, 4100sh, Adult on tree branch.

No. 2004 — Gorillas: a, 3400sh, Two adult Gorilla gorilla facing right, denomination at top center. b, 3400sh, Gorilla gorilla and Gorilla beringei facing left, denomination at UL. c, 4100sh, Gorilla gorilla and Gorilla beringei. d, 4100sh, Two adult Gorilla beringei beringei and juvenile.

No. 2005 — Lions: a, 3400sh, Female on rock. b, 3400sh, Male and female, animal name at UR. c, 4100sh, Female stalking. d, 4100sh, Male.

No. 2006 — Lions: a, 3400sh, Head of male, female looking left, animal name at top center. b, 3400sh, Two males and one female. c, 4100sh, Female and cub. d, 4100sh, Female and head of cub.

No. 2007 — Cheetahs: a, 3400sh, Running left. b, 3400sh, Standing. c, 4100sh, Walking right. d, 4100sh, Resting.

No. 2008 — Elephants: a, 3400sh, Two animals, animal name above country name. b, 3400sh, Two animals, front animal facing left, animal name at UL. c, 4100sh, Four animals, animal name at UL. d, 4100sh, Two animals, animal name above country name.

No. 2009 — Elephants: a, 3400sh, One animal. b, 3400sh, Two animals walking side-by-side, animal name at UL. c, 4100sh, Adult and juvenile. d, 4100sh, One animal.

No. 2010 — Birds of prey: a, 3400sh, Neophron percnopterus in flight. b, 3400sh, Gyps rueppellii on branch. c, 4100sh, Gyps rueppellii facing right. d, 4100sh, Neophron percnopterus on rock.

No. 2011 — Secretary bird: a, 3400sh, Facing right, in flight. b, 3400sh, Facing left, in flight. c, 4100sh, Head of bird facing right and bird facing left. d, 4100sh, Two birds facing left.

No. 2012, 8300sh, Pan troglodytes (chimpanzee). No. 2013, 8300sh, Gorilla beringei, Gorilla beringei beringei (gorillas). No. 2014, 8300sh, Male and female Panthera leo (lions). No. 2015, 8300sh, Male Panthera leo (lion). No. 2016, 8300sh, Acinonyx jubatus (cheetah). No. 2017, 8300sh, One Loxodonta africana (elephant). No. 2018, 8300sh, Three Loxodonta africana (elephants). No. 2019, 8300sh, Gyps rueppelli (bird of prey), diff. No. 2020, 8300sh, Two Sagittarius serpentarius facing left (secretary birds).

2012, Nov. 8 Litho. *Perf. 13¼*

Sheets of 4, #a-d

2003-2011	A386	Set of 9	100.00	100.00

Souvenir Sheets

2012-2020	A386	Set of 9	55.00	55.00

Compare No. 2020 with No. 2022.

A387

A388

A389

Worldwide Fund for Nature (WWF) — A390

Secretary Bird — A391

2012, Nov. 8 Litho. *Perf. 13x13¼*

2021	Horiz. strip of 4	12.00	12.00
a.	A387 4100sh multi	3.00	3.00
b.	A388 4100sh multi	3.00	3.00
c.	A389 4100sh multi	3.00	3.00
d.	A390 4100sh multi	3.00	3.00
e.	Souvenir sheet of 4, #2021a-2021d	12.00	12.00
f.	Souvenir sheet of 8, 2 each #2021a-2021d	24.00	24.00

Souvenir Sheet

Perf. 12¾x13¼

2022	A391	8300sh multi	6.25	6.25

Compare No. 2022 with No. 2020.

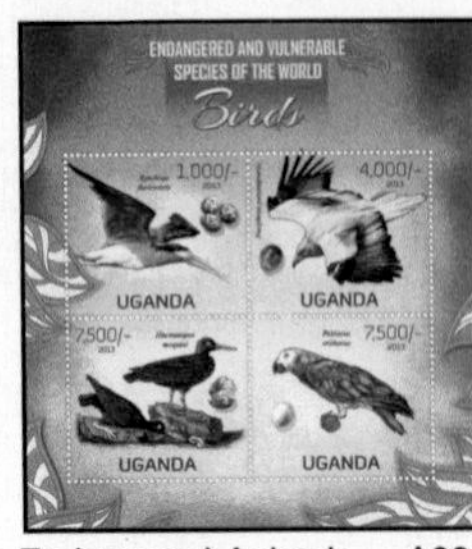

Endangered Animals — A392

No. 2023 — Birds and their eggs: a, 1000sh, Rynchops flavirostris. b, 4000sh, Neophron percnopterus. c, 7500sh, Haematopus moquini. d, 7500sh, Psittacus erithacus.

No. 2024 — Turtles: a, 1000sh, Aldabrachelys gigantea. b, 4000sh, Kinixys homeana. c, 7500sh, Testudo kleinmanni. d, 7500sh, Malacochersus tornieri.

No. 2025 — Dolphins: a, 1800sh, Orcaella brevirostris. b, 1800sh, Sousa chinensis. c, 7500sh, Lipotes vexillifer. d, 7500sh, Tursiops truncatus ponticus.

No. 2026 — Fish: a, 1800sh, Thunnus maccoyii. b, 1800sh, Schilbe mystus. c, 7500sh, Cheilinus undulatus. d, 7500sh, Oxynotus centrina.

No. 2027 — Butterflies: a, 1800sh, Apodemia mormo langei. b, 1800sh, Heraclides aristodemus ponceanus. c, 7500sh, Lycaeides melissa samuelis. d, 7500sh, Speyeria zerene behrensii.

No. 2028 — Reptiles: a, 1800sh, Osteolaemus tetraspis. b, 1800sh, Cordylus cataphractus. c, 7500sh, Crocodylus cataphractus. d, 7500sh, Acanthodactylus pardalis.

No. 2029, 4000sh — Hippopotami: a, Adult and juvenile Choeropsis liberiensis. b, Hippopotamus amphibius on land. c, Hippopotamus amphibius in water. d, Adult Choeropsis liberiensis with open mouth.

No. 2030, 4000sh — Wildcats: a, Prionailurus rubiginosus. b, Uncia uncia. c, Oreailurus jacobitus. d, Prionailurus viverrinus.

No. 2031, 4000sh — Lycaon pictus: a, Head of dog and two dogs standing. b, Dog and tree. c, Two dogs standing. d, Two dogs resting.

No. 2032, 4000sh — Predators: a, Gymnogyps californianus. b, Canis simensis. c, Alligator sinensis. d, Panthera pardus orientalis.

No. 2033, 7500sh, Struthio camelus and egg. No. 2034, 7500sh, Pyxis arachnoides. No. 2035, 7500sh, Platanista gangetica. No. 2036, 7500sh, Squatina squatina. No. 2037, 7500sh, Icaricia icarioides missionensis. No. 2038, 7500sh, Furcifer labordi. No. 2039, 7500sh, Hippopotamus amphibius on land, diff. No. 2040, 7500sh, Panthera tigris. No. 2041, 7500sh, Lycaon pictus, diff. No. 2042, 7500sh, Cuon alpinus.

2013, July 8 Litho. *Perf. 13¼*

Sheets of 4, #a-d

2023-2032	A392	Set of 10	140.00	140.00

Souvenir Sheets

2033-2042	A392	Set of 10	60.00	60.00

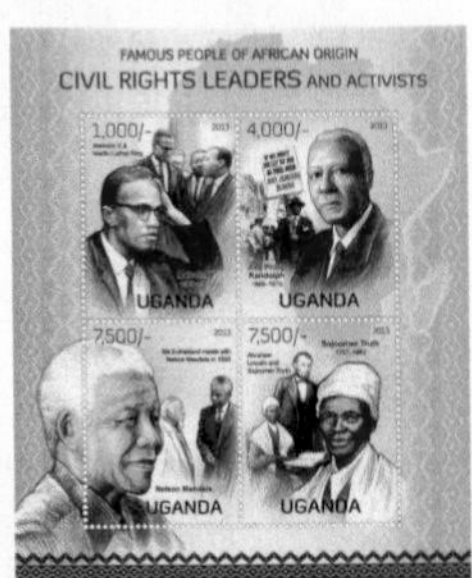

Famous People of African Heritage A393

No. 2043 — Civil rights leaders and activists: a, 1000sh, Malcolm X and Dr. Martin Luther King, Jr. b, 4000sh, Asa Philip Randolph. c, 7500sh, Nelson Mandela and Bill Sutherland. d, 7500sh, Sojourner Truth with Abraham Lincoln.

No. 2044 — Nobel laureates: a, 1000sh, Kofi Annan, 2001 Peace laureate. b, 4000sh, Desmond Tutu, 1984 Peace laureate. c, 7500sh, Wole Soyinka, 1986 Literature laureate, and short-eared owl. d, 7500sh, Wangari Maathai, 2004 Peace laureate.

No. 2045 — Olympic champions: a, 1000sh, Jesse Owens. b, 4000sh, Abebe Bikila. c, 7500sh, Maria Mutola. d, 7500sh, Derartu Tulu.

No. 2046 — Boxing champions: a, 1000sh, Joe Frazier and Muhammad Ali. b, 4000sh, Joe Louis. c, 7500sh, George Foreman and Shannon Briggs. d, 7500sh, Mike Tyson and Evander Holyfield.

No. 2047 — Tennis players: a, 1000sh, Serena Williams. b, 4000sh, Venus Williams. c, 7500sh, Venus Williams and trophy. d, 7500sh, Serena Williams and trophy.

No. 2048 — Baseball players: a, 1800sh, Willie Mays. b, 1800sh, Dan Bankhead. c, 7500sh, Satchel Paige. d, 7500sh, Larry Doby.

No. 2049 — Basketball players: a, 1800sh, Scottie Pippen and Michael Jordan. b, 1800sh, Earvin "Magic" Johnson. c, 7500sh, Charles Barkley. d, 7500sh, Karl Malone.

No. 2050 — Soccer players: a, 1800sh, Roger Milla. b, 1800sh, Nwankwo Kanu. c, 7500sh, Abedi Pele. d, 7500sh, Samuel Eto'o.

No. 2051— Entertainers: a, 1800sh, Morgan Freeman. b, 1800sh, Denzel Washington. c, 7500sh, Eddie Murphy. d, 7500sh, Oprah Winfrey with Pres. Barack Obama and wife, Michelle.

No. 2052 — Paintings of Henry Ossawa Tanner (1859-1937): a, 1800sh, The Annunciation. b, 1800sh, Mary. c, 7500sh, The Banjo Lesson. d, 7500sh, Spinning by Firelight.

No. 2053, 7500sh, Dr. Martin Luther King, Jr. No. 2054, 7500sh, Pres. Barack Obama. No. 2055, 7500sh, Stephen Kiprotich. No. 2056, 7500sh, Floyd Patterson and Muhammad Ali. No. 2057, 7500sh, Serena and Venus Williams. No. 2058, 7500sh, Jackie Robinson. No. 2059, 7500sh, Michael Jordan. No. 2060, 7500sh, Didier Drogba. No. 2061, 7500sh, Will Smith. No. 2062, 7500sh, Portrait of the Artist's Wife, by Tanner.

2013, July 8 Litho. *Perf. 13¼*

Sheets of 4, #a-d

2043-2052	A393	Set of 10	150.00	150.00

Souvenir Sheets

2053-2062	A393	Set of 10	60.00	60.00

Dogs A394

No. 2063, 3000sh: a, Coton de Tulear. b, Rhodesian ridgeback. c, Catahoula cur. d, Walker coonhound.

No. 2064, 3000sh: a, English mastiff. b, Basenji. c, Boerboel. d, Boxer.

No. 2065, 8800sh, Afghan hound, vert. No. 2066, 8800sh, German shepherd, vert.

2013, Sept. 7 Litho. *Perf. 13¾*

Sheets of 4, #a-d

2063-2064	A394	Set of 2	19.00	19.00

Souvenir Sheets

Perf. 12½

2065-2066	A394	Set of 2	14.00	14.00

Nos. 2065-2066 each contain one 38x51mm stamp.

Stephen Kiprotich, 2012 Olympic Gold Medalist in Marathon — A395

Kiprotich: 700sh, Running. 1900sh, Holding Ugandan flag approaching finish line. 2700sh, Holding Ugandan flag, horiz. 3400sh, On knees, horiz.

2013, Nov. 25 Litho. *Perf. 13*

2067-2070	A395	Set of 4	7.00	7.00

Stamps on Stamps A396

No. 2071, 2500sh — Stamps depicting cats: a, Azerbaijan #533. b, Czech Republic #3078. c, People's Republic of China #1853. d, France #3203.

No. 2072, 2500sh — Stamps depicting butterflies: a, Viet Nam #1310. b, Laos #692. c, Hungary #2314. d, Nicaragua #1570.

No. 2073, 2500sh — Stamps depicting owls: a, Hungary #C228. b, France #1338. c, Republic of China #4053. d, Zimbabwe #544.

No. 2074, 2500sh — Stamps depicting turtles: a, New Zealand #1698. b, Unauthorized Benin sticker. c, Tanzania #1128. d, Viet Nam #1968.

No. 2075, 2500sh — Stamps depicting dinosaurs: a, Tanzania #1220. b, Australia #1344. c, Marshall Islands #925i. d, New Zealand #1183.

No. 2076, 2500sh — Stamps depicting Worldwide Fund for Nature emblem: a, Central Africa #325. b, Algeria #875. c, Aruba #104. d, Indonesia #1383.

No. 2077, 2500sh — Stamps depicting orchids: a, Cuba #2328. b, Cambodia #1893. c, Virgin Islands #704. d, Liechtenstein #467.

No. 2078, 2500sh — Stamps depicting minerals: a, Azerbaijan #420. b, Togo #1857. c, Cambodia #1777. d, French Southern & Antarctic Territories #315.

No. 2079, 7500sh, Poland #1216 (cat). No. 2080, 7500sh, Cambodia #694 (butterfly). No. 2081, 7500sh, Cuba #2542 (prehistoric owl). No. 2082, 7500sh, Viet Nam #1969 (turtle). No. 2083, 7500sh, Mali #505 (dinosaur). No. 2084, 7500sh, Viet Nam #2281 (Worldwide Fund for Nature). No. 2085, 7500sh, Equatorial Guinea sticker (orchid). No. 2086, 7500sh, North Korea #3455 (minerals).

2013, Nov. 25 Litho. *Perf. 13¼*

Sheets of 4, #a-d

2071-2078	A396	Set of 8	65.00	65.00

Souvenir Sheets

2079-2086	A396	Set of 8	50.00	50.00

Miniature Sheet

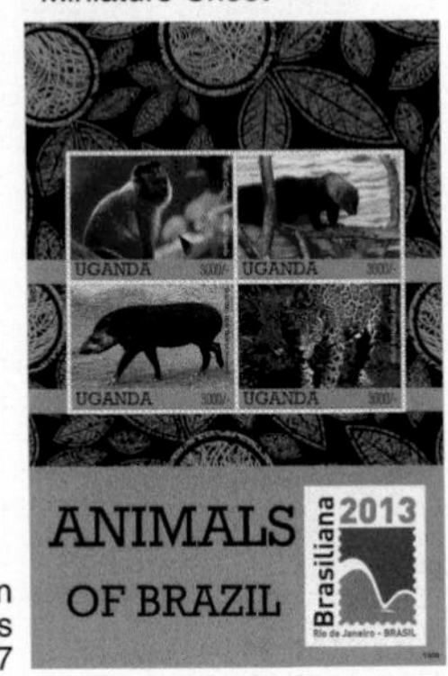

Brazilian Animals A397

No. 2087: a, Tufted capuchin monkey. b, Tayra eira barara. c, Brazilian tapir. d, Jaguar.

2013, Dec. 31 Litho. *Perf. 14*

2087	A397	3000sh Sheet of 4, #a-d	9.50	9.50

Brasiliana 2013 World Philatelic Exhibition, Rio de Janeiro.

Miniature Sheet

Mao Zedong (1893-1976), Chinese Communist Leader — A398

No. 2088 — Photographs of: a, Mao, 1938. b, Mao, 1948. c, Mao, 1954. d, Mao, 1961. e, Mao, undated. f, Great Wall of China.

2013, Dec. 31 Litho. *Perf. 14*
2088 A398 500sh Sheet of 6, #a-f 2.40 2.40

Birth of Prince George of Cambridge — A399

No. 2089: a, Duchess of Cambridge. b, Duke and Duchess of Cambridge, Prince George. c, Prince George. d, Duke of Cambridge.
8800sh, Duke and Duchess of Cambridge, Prince George, vert.

2013, Dec. 31 Litho. *Perf. 14*
2089 A399 3000sh Sheet of 4, #a-d 9.50 9.50

Souvenir Sheet
Perf. 12½
2090 A399 8800sh multi 7.00 7.00
No. 2090 contains one 38x51mm stamp.

Awarding of Nobel Peace Prize to Nelson Mandela, 20th Anniv. A400

No. 2091 — Color of image of Mandela at left: a, Olive brown. b, Red brown. c, Green. d, Blue.
8800sh, Mandela at awards ceremony.

2013, Dec. 31 Litho. *Perf. 14*
2091 A400 3000sh Sheet of 4, #a-d 9.50 9.50

Souvenir Sheet
2092 A400 8800sh multi 7.00 7.00

Miniature Sheets

A401

Nelson Mandela (1918-2013), President of South Africa — A402

No. 2093: a, Color photograph of Mandela waving. b, Color photograph of Mandela's face. c, Mandela behind microphones. d, Person holding newspaper with story on Mandela's release from prison.
No. 2094: a, Black-and-white photograph of Mandela waving. b, Color photograph of Mandela waving, diff. c, Black-and-white photograph of Mandela and other people. d, Mandela holding candle.

2013, Dec. 31 Litho. *Perf. 13¾*
2093 A401 4400sh Sheet of 4, #a-d 14.00 14.00
2094 A402 4400sh Sheet of 4, #a-d 14.00 14.00

Sikhs in Uganda, Cent. A403

Designs: 700sh, Khanda (Sikh symbol). 1100sh, Nishan Sahib (Sikh flag). 2700sh, Golden Temple, Amritsar, India. 3400sh, Sikh Temple, Kampala.

2014, Jan. 17 Litho. *Perf. 12¾*
2095-2098 A403 Set of 4 6.50 6.50

A404

A405

New Year 2014 (Year of the Horse) A406

No. 2101 — Horse and Chinese character for "horse" with background color of: a, Dull yellow green ("Year of the Horse" at LL). b, Orange. c, Pink. d, Red brown. e, Lilac. f, Dull green ("Year of the Horse" at UR).
8800sh, Horse, vert.

2014, Apr. 1 Litho. *Perf. 13¾*
2099 A404 1300sh multi 1.00 1.00
2100 A405 1300sh multi 1.00 1.00

Miniature Sheet
Perf. 14
2101 A406 2250sh Sheet of 6, #a-f 10.50 10.50

Souvenir Sheet
Perf. 12½
2102 A406 8800sh multi 7.00 7.00
No. 2102 contains one 38x51mm stamp.

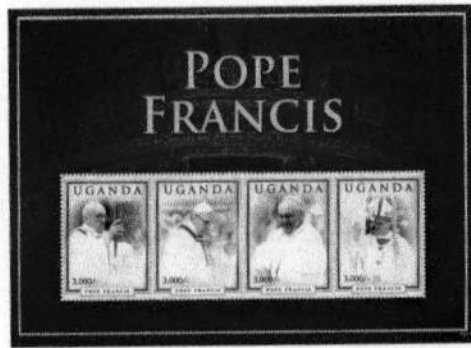

Pope Francis A407

No. 2103 — Pope Francis: a, Holding Bible. b, Looking down, facing right. c, Facing left, with hand lifted. d, Holding crucifix.
8800sh, Pope Francis, diff.

2014, Apr. 1 Litho. *Perf. 14*
2103 A407 3000sh Sheet of 4, #a-d 9.50 9.50

Souvenir Sheet
2104 A407 8800sh multi 7.00 7.00

African Animals A408

No. 2105: a, Debrazza's monkey. b, Aardvark. c, African wild dog. d, Okapi.
8800sh, Antelope.

2014, Apr. 1 Litho. *Perf. 14*
2105 A408 3000sh Sheet of 4, #a-d 9.50 9.50

Souvenir Sheet
Perf. 12
2106 A408 8800sh multi 7.00 7.00

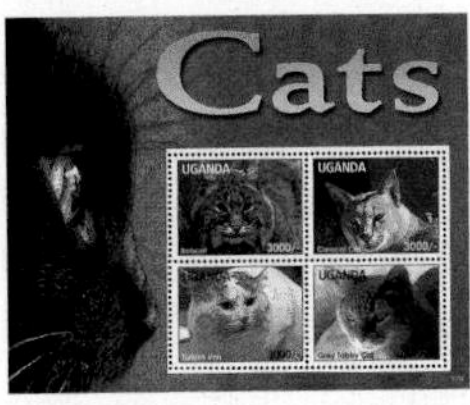

Cats A409

No. 2107: a, Bobcat. b, Caracal. c, Turkish Van. d, Gray tabby cat.
8800sh, Calico cat, vert.

2014, Apr. 1 Litho. *Perf. 12*
2107 A409 3000sh Sheet of 4, #a-d 9.50 9.50

Souvenir Sheet
Perf. 14
2108 A409 8800sh multi 7.00 7.00

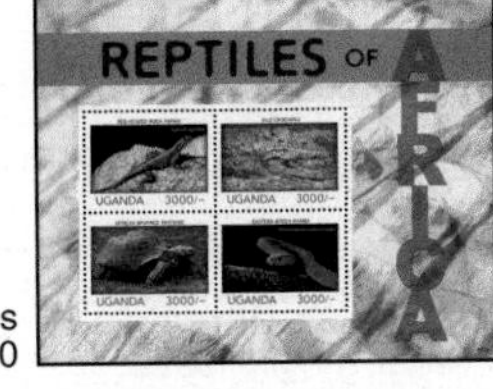

Reptiles A410

No. 2109: a, Red-headed rock agama. b, Nile crocodile. c, African spurred tortoise. d, Eastern green mamba.
8800sh, Cape cobra, vert.

2014, Apr. 1 Litho. *Perf. 12*
2109 A410 3000sh Sheet of 4, #a-d 9.50 9.50

Souvenir Sheet
2110 A410 8800sh multi 7.00 7.00

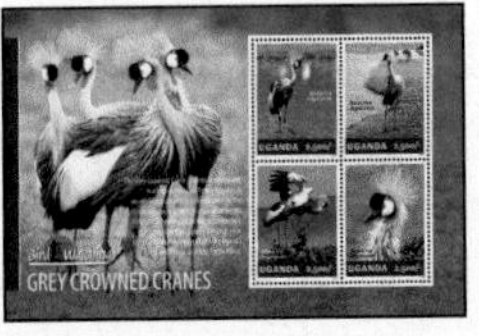

Bird Watching A411

No. 2111, 2500sh — Balearica regulorum: a, Crane near water, Latin name in white at right. b, Crane near water, Latin name in black at left. c, Crane in nest, Latin name in white at LL. d, Head of crane, Latin name in black at LL.
No. 2112, 2500sh — Flamingos: a, Phoenicopterus andinus. b, Phoenicopterus roseus. c, Phoenicopterus chilensis. d, Phoenicopterus ruber.
No. 2113, 2500sh — Falcons: a, Falco rupicoloides. b, Falco biarmicus. c, Falco peregrinus. d, Falco naumanni.
No. 2114, 2500sh — Parrots: a, Ara chloroptera. b, Probosciger aterrimus. c, Cacatua galerita. d, Ara ambiguus.
No. 2115, 2500sh — Water birds: a, Larus argentatus. b, Eudocimus ruber. c, Alcedo atthis. d, Ardea alba.
No. 2116, 2500sh — Vultures: a, Vultur gryphus. b, Gyps fulvus. c, Gyps coprotheres. d, Trigonoceps occipitalis.
No. 2117, 2500sh — Hornbills: a, Rhyticeros undulatus. b, Bucorvus leadbeateri. c, Tropicranus albocristatus. d, Tockus erythrorhynchus.
No. 2118, 2500sh — Eagles: a, Aquila chrysaetos. b, Terathopius ecaudatus. c, Haliaeetus leucocephalus. d, Harpia harpyja.
No. 2119, 2500sh — Hummingbirds: a, Colibri thalassinus. b, Hylocharis chrysura. c, Coeligena lutetiae. d, Colibri thalassinus in flight.
No. 2120, 2500sh — Bee-eaters: a, Two Merops philippinus. b, Merops apiaster. c, One Merops philippinus. d, Merops bullockoides.
No. 2121, 7500sh, Blaearica regulorum, diff. No. 2122, 7500sh, Phoenicopterus minor. No. 2123, 7500sh, Falco tinnunculus. No. 2124, 7500sh, Ara ararauna. No. 2125, 7500sh, Diomedea epomophora. No. 2126, 7500sh, Gypaetus barbatus. No. 2127, 7500sh, Tockus leucomelas. No. 2128, 7500sh, Haliaeetus albicilla. No. 2129, 7500sh, Archilochus alexandri. No. 2130, 7500sh, Merops viridis.

2014, Apr. 1 Litho. *Perf. 13¼*
Sheets of 4, #a-d
2111-2120 A411 Set of 10 80.00 80.00

Souvenir Sheets
2121-2130 A411 Set of 10 60.00 60.00
Nos. 2121-2130 each contain one 36x51mm stamp.

Domestic Animals A412

No. 2131, 2500sh — Apis mellifera: a, On yellow flower, Latin name in black. b, On white flower, Latin name in black. c, Flying below pink flower, Latin name in white. d, On red flower, latin name in white.
No. 2132, 2500sh — Betta splendens: a, One fish with yellow fins. b, One fish with red fins, facing forward, Latin name at UL. c, Two fish. d, One fish with red fins, facing backwards, Latin name at UR.
No. 2133, 2500sh — Carassius auratus auratus: a, Fish, aquarium gravel in foreground, Latin name at UL in one line. b, Fish, Latin name at UL in two lines. c, Fish and aquarium grass, Latin name at LL. d, Two fish, Latin name at UR.
No. 2134, 2500sh — Cats: a, Persian. b, Abyssinian. c, Bengal. d, Russian Blue.
No. 2135, 2500sh — Dogs: a, Papillon. b, Yorkshire terrier. c, Jack Russell terrier. d, Chihuahua.
No. 2136, 2500sh — Dogs: a, Elo. b, French bulldog. c, Beagle. d, Doberman pinscher.
No. 2137, 2500sh — Equus ferus caballus: a, White and brown horses running b, Adult and foal running. c, Gray horse. d, Two horses standing in field.
No. 2138, 2500sh — Canaries: a, Serinus mozambicus, Latin name in black. b, Serinus canaria. c, Serinus canaria domestica. d, Serinus mozambicus, Latin name in white.
No. 2139, 2500sh — Farm animals: a, Anser anser domesticus. b, Ovis aries. c, Oryctolagus cuniculus. d, Gallus gallus domesticus.
No. 2140, 2500sh — Capra aegagrus hircus: a, Goat, Latin name in black at UR on one line. b, Goats, Latin name at UR on three lines. c, Adult and juvenile goats, Latin name at UL on two lines. d, Goat, Latin name at LL.
No. 2141, 7500sh, Apis mellifera and honeycomb. No. 2142, 7500sh, Betta splendens, diff. No. 2143, 7500sh, Carassius auratus auratus, diff. No. 2144, 7500sh, Egyptian Mau cats. No. 2145, 7500sh, Bichon Frise. No. 2146, 7500sh, American cocker spaniel. No. 2147, 7500sh, Equus ferus caballus, diff. No. 2148, 7500sh, Serinus canaria, diff. No. 2149, 7500sh, Bos taurus. No. 2150, 7500sh, Capra aegagrus hircus, diff.

2014, Apr. 1 Litho. *Perf. 13¼*
Sheets of 4, #a-d
2131-2140 A412 Set of 10 80.00 80.00

Souvenir Sheets
2141-2150 A412 Set of 10 60.00 60.00
Nos. 2141-2150 each contain one 36x51mm stamp.

Hibiscus Flowers A413

No. 2151: a, Pink Hibiscus rosa-sinensis. b, Red Hibiscus rosa-sinensis. c, Hibiscus arnottianus. d, Hibiscus clayi. e, Hibiscus kokio. f, Hibiscus splendens.
10,000sh, Hibiscus mutabilis.

2014, Dec. 1 Litho. *Perf. 12½*

2151 A413 3200sh Sheet of 6, #a-f 14.00 14.00

Souvenir Sheet

2152 A413 10,000sh multi 7.25 7.25

Canoninzation of Ugandan Martyrs, 50th Anniv. (in 2014) — A414

Designs: 700sh, Uganda Martyrs with Bishop Leon Livinhac, 1885. 900sh, 2012 Uganda Martyrs' Day celebration. 1000sh, Uganda Martyrs' Basilica, Namugongo. 1800sh, 2010 Uganda Martyrs' Day celebration. 2000sh, St. Achilles Kiwanuka, vert. 2700sh, St. Kizito. 3200sh, Kasubi Nabulagala, 1881. 3400sh, Map of Uganda, Pope Francis, Ugandan Martyrs, Uganda Martyr's Basilica, flags of Vatican City and Uganda, vert.
No. 2161, 10,000sh, Relics of the Uganda Martyrs. No. 2162, 10,000sh, Uganda Martyrs' Shrine, Namugongo, 2014.

Perf. 13½x13, 13x13½

2015, Nov. 27 Litho.

2153-2160 A414 Set of 8 — —

Souvenir Sheets

2161-2162 A414 Set of 2 — —

Visit of Pope Francis to Uganda — A415

Designs: 500sh, Pope Francis, Martyrs' Museum, Namugongo. 700sh, Pope Francis waving. 1000sh, Pope Francis seated, no glasses, vert. 1100sh, Pope Francis wearing miter, vert. 1800sh, Pope Francis wearing zucchetto, no glasses, vert. 1900sh, Pope Francis wearing zucchetto, wearing glasses, vert. 2700sh, Pope Francis seated, wearing glasses. 3400sh, Pope Francis waving, wearing zucchetto, vert.
No. 2171, 10,000sh, Pope Francis, Munyonyo Martyrs' Shrine. No. 2172, 10,000sh, Pope Francis, Uganda Martyrs' Shrine, Namugongo.

Perf. 13½x13, 13x13½

2015, Nov. 27 Litho.

2163-2170 A415 Set of 8 — —

Souvenir Sheets

2171-2172 A415 Set of 2 — —

Primates — A416

Designs: 100sh, Bush baby. 500sh, Chimpanzees. 700sh, Black and white colobus. 800sh, Olive baboon. 900sh, De Brazza's monkey, vert. 1000sh, L'Hoest's monkey, vert. 1100sh, Baby mountain gorilla. 1800sh, Vervet monkey. 1900sh, Adult mountain gorilla. 2000sh, Blue monkey, vert. 2700sh, Olive baboons. 3000sh, Golden monkey. 3400sh, Chimpanzee, vert.

Perf. 13½x13, 13x13½

2017, May 5 Litho.

2173-2185 A416 Set of 13 — —

Inauguration of Isimba Hydropower Plant — A418

No. 2190 — Flags of Uganda and People's Republic of China and various aerial views of Isimba Hydropower Plant with denominations of: a, 3500sh. b, 4000sh. c, 7500sh. d, 15,000sh.
No. 2191, 20,000sh, Like No. 2190a. No. 2192, 20,000sh, Like No. 2190b. No. 2193, 20,000sh, Like No. 2190c. No. 2194, 20,000sh, Like No. 2190d.

2019, Mar. 21 Litho. *Perf. 13*

2190 A418 Sheet of 4, #a-d — —

Souvenir Sheets

2191-2194 A418 Set of 4 — —

SEMI-POSTAL STAMPS

Catalogue values for all unused stamps in this section are for never Hinged items.

PAPU (Pan African Postal Union), 18th Anniv. — SP1

No. B1, Mountain gorilla.

1998, Jan. 18 Litho. *Perf. 14*

B1 SP1 300sh +150sh multi 1.10 1.10

POSTAGE DUE STAMPS

Catalogue values for unused stamps in this section are for Never Hinged items.

Type of Kenya, 1967

Perf. 14x13½

1967, Jan. 3 Litho. Unwmk.

J1	D1	5c red	.25	*5.00*
J2	D1	10c green	.25	*6.00*
J3	D1	20c dark blue	.25	*6.00*
J4	D1	30c reddish brown	.40	*8.00*
J5	D1	40c red lilac	.60	*18.00*
J6	D1	1sh orange	1.75	*15.00*
		Nos. J1-J6 (6)	3.50	58.00

1970, Mar. 31 *Perf. 14x15*

J1a	D1	5c red	.25	*4.00*
J2a	D1	10c green	.25	*3.00*
J3a	D1	20c dark blue	.30	*4.00*
J4a	D1	30c reddish brown	.40	*5.00*
J5a	D1	40c red lilac	.60	*7.50*
		Nos. J1a-J5a (5)	1.80	23.50

1973 *Perf. 15*

J1b	D1	5c red	.25	*2.25*
J2b	D1	10c green	.25	*2.25*
J3b	D1	20c dark blue	.70	*6.00*
J4b	D1	30c reddish brown	.95	*9.00*
J5b	D1	40c red lilac	1.60	*13.50*
J6b	D1	1sh orange	4.00	*24.00*
		Nos. J1b-J6b (6)	7.75	57.00

Nos. J1-J6 Overprinted in Black "LIBERATED / 1979"

1979, Dec. Litho. *Perf. 14*

J7	D1	5c red	.25	*.70*
J8	D1	10c green	.25	*.70*
J9	D1	20c violet blue	.25	*.70*
J10	D1	30c reddish brown	.25	*1.00*
J11	D1	40c red lilac	.25	*1.00*
J12	D1	1sh orange	.60	*1.25*
		Nos. J7-J12 (6)	1.85	5.35

Wildlife — D2

1985, Mar. 11 Litho. *Perf. 15x14*

J13	D2	5sh Lion	.25	*.95*
J14	D2	10sh African buffalo	.25	*.95*
J15	D2	20sh Kob antelope	.60	*1.40*
J16	D2	40sh Elephant	1.25	*2.10*
J17	D2	50sh Zebra	1.25	*2.10*
J18	D2	100sh Rhinoceros	1.75	*3.50*
		Nos. J13-J18 (6)	5.35	11.00

UKRAINE

yü-'krān

LOCATION — In southeastern Europe, bordering on the Black Sea
GOVT. — Republic
AREA — 231,900 sq. mi.
POP. — 48,760,474 (2001)
CAPITAL — Kyiv

Following the collapse of the Russian Empire, a national assembly met at Kyiv and declared the Ukrainian National Republic on Jan. 22, 1918. During three years of civil war, the Ukrainian army, as well as Bolshevik, White Russian, Allied and Polish armies, fought back and forth across the country. By November, 1920, Ukraine was finally occupied by Soviet forces, and Soviet stamps were used from that time, until the recreation of the independent Ukraine on Aug. 24, 1991.

200 Shahiv = 100 Kopiyok (Kopecks) = 1 Karbovanets (Ruble)
100 Shahiv = 1 Hryvnia
100 Kopiyok = 1 Karbovanets (1992)
100 Kopiyok = 1 Hryvnia (1996)

Catalogue values for unused stamps in this country are for Never Hinged items, beginning with Scott 100 in the regular postage section, Scott B9 in the semi-postal section, and Scott F1 in the registration section.

Watermarks

Wmk. 116 — Crosses and Circles

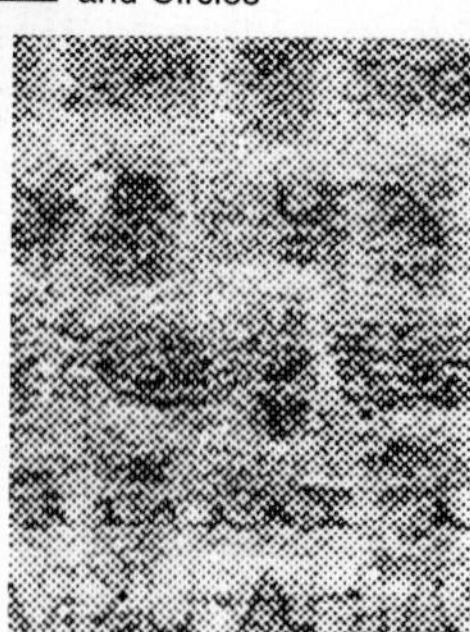
Wmk. 399

Republic's Trident Emblem A1

Ukrainian Peasant A2

Allegorical Ukraine A3

Trident A4

Inscription of Value — A5

1918, July Typo. *Imperf.*

Thin Paper

1	A1	10sh buff	.35	*1.10*
2	A2	20sh brown	.35	*1.10*
3	A3	30sh ultra	.35	*1.10*
a.		30sh blue	2.75	*6.50*
4	A4	40sh green	.35	*1.10*
5	A5	50sh red	.35	*1.10*
		Nos. 1-5 (5)	1.75	*5.50*

The stamps of this issue exist perforated or pin-perforated unofficially.
Forgeries of this set exist on a very thin, glossy paper.
These designs were earlier (April, 1918) utilized for money tokens, printed on thin cardboard, perforated 11½, and bearing an inscription on the reverse "Circulates on par with coins" in Ukrainian. These tokens exist favor canceled but were not postage stamps. Value uncanceled, $6 each.

Stamps of Russia Overprinted in Violet, Black, Blue, Red, Brown or Green

This trident-shaped emblem was taken from the arms of the Grand Prince Volodymyr and adopted as the device of the Ukrainian Republic.
In the early months of independence, Russian stamps were commonly used, but the influx of large quantities of stamps from Russia made it necessary to take measures to protect postal revenue. In August, 1918, local post offices were ordered to send their existing stocks of Russian stamps to regional centers, where they were overprinted with the trident arms. Unoverprinted Russian stamps were declared invalid after October 1, although they were often accepted for use.
This overprint was handstamped, typographed or lithographed. It was applied in various cities in the Ukraine and there are numerous types.

Nos. 6-47 represent the basic Russian stamps that received these overprints. Values are for the most common overprint variety.
For a detailed listing of these overprints, see the *Scott Classic Specialized Catalogue of Stamps and Covers 1840-1940.*

The basic Russian stamps to which Trident overprints were applied

A8

A9

A11

A12

A13

A14

A15

On Stamps of 1902-03

1918 Wmk. 168 *Perf. 13½*

6 A12 3½r black & gray *100.00 75.00*
7 A12 7r black & yellow *100.00 75.00*

On Stamps of 1909-18
Lozenges of Varnish on Face

Perf. 14, 14½x15

Unwmk.

8 A14 1k orange .25 *.35*
9 A14 2k green .25 *.35*
10 A14 3k red .25 *.35*
11 A15 4k carmine .25 *.35*
12 A14 5k claret .25 *.35*
13 A14 7k light blue .25 *.35*
14 A15 10k dark blue .25 *.35*
15 A11 14k blue & rose .25 *.35*
16 A11 15k red brn & bl .25 *.35*
17 A8 20k blue & car .25 *.35*
18 A11 25k grn & gray vio .40 *.50*
19 A11 35k red brn & grn .25 *.35*
20 A8 50k violet & grn .25 *.35*
21 A11 70k brown & org .25 *.35*

Perf. 13½

22 A9 1r lt brn, brn & org .55 *.75*
23 A12 3½r mar & lt grn 1.25 *2.50*
24 A13 5r dk bl, grn & pale bl 7.50 *11.00*
25 A12 7r dk grn & pink 9.00 *12.00*
26 A13 10r scar, yel & gray 13.00 *18.00*
Nos. 6-26 (21) 234.95 *199.30*

On Stamps of 1917
Perf. 14, 14½x15

27 A14 10k on 7k light blue .75 *1.00*
28 A11 20k on 14k bl & rose .75 *1.00*

On Stamps of 1917-18
Imperf

29 A14 1k orange .25 *.35*
30 A14 2k gray green .25 *.35*
31 A14 3k red .25 *.35*
32 A15 4k carmine .25 *.35*
33 A14 5k claret .90 *1.50*
34 A11 15k red brn & bl .25 *.35*
35 A8 20k bl & car .75 *1.50*
36 A11 25k grn & gray vio 60.00 —
37 A11 35k red brn & grn .25 *.35*
38 A8 50k violet & grn .30 *.35*
39 A11 70k brown & org .25 *.35*
40 A9 1r pale brn, brn & red org .25 *.60*
41 A12 3½r mar & lt grn 1.00 *2.50*
42 A13 5r dk bl, grn & pale bl 1.50 *3.00*
43 A12 7r dk grn & pink 2.50 *4.00*
44 A13 10r scar, yel & gray 70.00 *85.00*
Nos. 29-44 (16) 138.95 *100.90*

PF1

Russian Stamps AR1-AR3.

Wmk. 171 Litho.

Perf. 14, 14½x14¾

45 PF1 1k red, *buff* 5.00 *25.00*
46 PF1 5k green, *buff* 20.00 *120.00*
47 PF1 10k brown, *buff* 35.00 *350.00*
Nos. 45-47 (3) 60.00 *495.00*

Nos. 45-47 were used and accepted as postage stamps during stamp shortages.

The trident overprint was applied by favor to Russia Nos. 88-104, 110-111, the Romanov issue.

For surcharges see Russian Offices in the Turkish Empire Nos. 320-339.

A6

1919, Jan. Litho.

48 A6 20h red & green 10.00 *25.00*

Because of its high face value, No. 48 was used primarily on money transfer forms or parcel receipts. Used value is for a postally used example.

Nos. 1 and 5 Surcharged

1919, Feb. Unwmk. *Imperf.*

49 A1 35k on 10sh buff 9.00 *20.00*
50 A5 70k on 50sh red 70.00 *50.00*
a. Surcharge inverted 60.00

Nos. 49 and 50 were originally believed to have been created by the Soviets in the Ukraine in April, 1919, but more recent research seems to indicate that they were created by the White (Don) Army operating in eastern Ukraine at the request of the Ukrainian government. Correctly franked covers have been recorded from the February-June 1919 period.

Excellent forged surcharges exist.

Ukrainian Soviet Socialist Republic

During 1920/1921, hyperinflation of the ruble created a desperate need for stamps to pay ever-rising postal rates. Many Russian cities and districts surcharged existing stocks of Russian stamps in needed denominations for provisional use.

In June 1920 the national government of the Soviet Ukrainian Republic authorized the Kharkiv post office to create such surcharges for use in the Kharkiv region and in adjacent oblasts. Both unoverprinted Russian stamps and stamps bearing the regional trident overprints of Katerynoslav, Kharkiv and Kyiv were surcharged to raise their face value 100-fold. They were sold at 236 post offices in the Ukraine from June 1920 through Feb. 1921.

In Feb. 1922 three Russian postal savings stamps were surcharged for provisional use by the Kyiv post office, at the direction of the central government. As with the Kharkiv surcharges, these stamps were distributed over a wide area within the country.

KHARKIV ISSUE

Ukrainian and Russian Stamps Handstamp Surcharged

Ukrainian trident overprinted issues and unoverprinted Russian stamps revalued 100-fold by changing denominations from kopecks to rubles.

Two types of overprint: type I, Cyrillic RUB (not including periods) 9.5mmx6.5mm; type II, 8.5mmx6.5mm.

Number of basic Ukrainian or Russian stamp shown in parentheses.

On Katerynoslav Trident Ovpt. Issue of 1918

Type I Reading Upward

1920, June

51 A11 15k red brown & blue (#16a) 75.00 75.00

Kharkiv Trident Ovpt. Issue of 1918

52 A14 1k orange (#8b) 100.00 *60.00*
a. Surcharge reading downward 150.00 150.00
53 A14 2k green (#9b) 100.00 *65.00*
54 A14 3k red (#10b) 80.00 *40.00*
55 A11 15k red brn & blue (#16b) 40.00 35.00
56 A8 20k blue & car (#17b) 200.00 *175.00*
a. Surcharge reading downward 300.00 300.00
57 A11 20k on 14k blue & rose (#28b) 170.00 *190.00*

Imperf

58 A14 1k orange (#29b) 75.00 *75.00*
a. Surcharge reading downward 120.00 120.00
59 A14 2k green (#30b) 250.00 *250.00*
60 A14 3k red (#31b) 40.00 *40.00*

On Kyiv Trident Ovpt. Issue of 1918

No. 61

No. 63

On Kyiv II Overprint

61 A14 1k orange (#8f) 40.00 *40.00*

Imperf

62 A14 1k orange (#29f) 40.00 *50.00*
a. Surcharge reading downward — —

On Kyiv III Overprint

63 A14 3k red (#31g) 15.00 *20.00*

On Russian Arms Issue of 1909-18

No. 64

64 A14 1k orange (#73) 50.00 *50.00*
65 A14 2k green (#74) 10.00 *15.00*
a. Surcharge reading downward 15.00 20.00
66 A14 3k red (#75) 10.00 15.00
a. Surcharge reading downward 25.00 20.00
67 A15 4k red (#76) 325.00
68 A14 5k claret (#77) 7.00 6.00
a. Surcharge reading downward 20.00 20.00
69 A15 10k dk blue (#79) 15.00 15.00
a. Surcharge reading downward 90.00 *100.00*
70 A11 15k red brn & blue (#81) 7.00 6.00
a. Surcharge reading downward 10.00 10.00
71 A8 20k blue & car (#82) 10.00 *6.00*
a. Surcharge reading downward 15.00 12.00

Imperf

72 A14 1k orange (#119) 50.00 *36.00*
a. Surcharge reading downward 100.00 100.00
73 A14 2k green (#120) 45.00 *55.00*
74 A14 3k red (#121) 30.00 *36.00*
75 A14 5k claret (#123) 9.00 7.00
a. Surcharge reading downward 25.00 25.00
76 A11 15k red brn & blue (#125) 120.00 *130.00*
a. Surcharge reading downward — —

Type II Reading Upward

On Kharkiv Trident Ovpt. Issue of 1918

No. 79a

77 A14 3k red (#31b) 35.00 *40.00*

On Kyiv Trident Ovpt. Issue of 1918

78 A14 1k orange (#29f) 20.00 *25.00*

On Russian Arms Issue of 1919-18
Perf. 14x14½

79 A14 2k green (#74) 6.00 *7.00*
a. Surcharge reading downward 12.00 12.00
80 A14 5k claret (#77) 8.00 7.00
a. Surcharge reading downward 15.00 12.00
81 A15 10k dk blue (#79) 18.00 18.00
a. Surcharge reading downward 100.00 *115.00*
82 A11 15k red brn & blue (#81) 8.00 7.00
a. Surcharge reading downward 12.00 10.00
83 A8 20k blue & car (#82) 8.00 *7.00*

Imperf

84 A14 2k green (#120) 50.00 *60.00*

KYIV ISSUE

Russian Postal Savings Stamps Handstamp Surcharged

1922, Feb. Wmk. 171

85 7500 (r) on 5k, green, *buff* 50.00 50.00
a. Surcharge reading downward 60.00 55.00
86 8000 (r) on 5k, green, *buff* 150.00 90.00
a. Surcharge reading downward 180.00 150.00
87 15000 (r) on 10k, brown, *buff* 300.00 150.00
a. Surcharge reading downward 450.00 250.00

Nos. 85-87 are normally found on stamps watermarked with a vertical diamond pattern (Wmk. 171) but also exist on paper watermarked sideways, with both upward and downward-reading surcharges. These are rare and are worth approximately 8 times the values shown.

Nos. 1-5 surcharged in grivni (hryven) with the Polish eagle were sold as Polish occupation issues. They are of private origin.

Nos. 1-3 and 5 overprinted diagonally as above ("South Russia") are believed to be of private origin.

A lithographed set of 14 stamps (1h-200h) of these types, perf. 11½, was prepared in 1920, but never placed in use. Value, set $5.

All values exist imperf., some with inverted centers. Trial printings exist on various papers, including inverted, multiple, omitted and misaligned center vignettes. These are from the printer's waste.

This set handstamped "VILNA UKRAINA / 1921" and 6 values additionally overprinted "DOPLATA" are of private origin.

In 1923 the Ukrainian government-in-exile in Warsaw prepared an 11-value set, consisting of the 10h, 20h and 40h denominations of the unissued 1920 set surcharged and overprinted with the Cyrillic "UPP," supposedly intended as a Field Post issue for a planned invasion of the Ukraine. The invasion never occurred, and the stamps were never issued. Value $15.

For German stamps overprinted "Ukraine" see Russia Nos. N29-N48.

Catalogue values for unused stamps in this section, from this point to the end of the section, are for Never Hinged items.

Cossacks in Ukraine, 500th Anniv. — A20

Design: No. 101, Ukrainian emigrants to Canada.

1992, Mar. 1 Litho. *Perf. 12*

100	A20 15k multicolored		.45	.45
101	A20 15k multicolored		.45	.45

Ukrainian emigration to Canada, centennial (No. 101). Dated 1991.

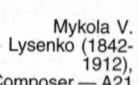

Mykola V. Lysenko (1842-1912), Composer — A21

1992, Mar. 22 *Perf. 13*

102 A21 100k multicolored .65 .65

Numerous trident overprints on Soviet stamps exist. Many of them are legitimate local issues and were in official use. Locally produced stamps also exist.

Ukrainian Girl — A22

1992 Litho. *Perf. 12x12½*

118	A22	50k bright blue	.25	.25
119	A22	70k bister	.25	.25
121	A22	1kb yellow green	.25	.25
122	A22	2kb purple	.25	.25
124	A22	5kb blue	.25	.25
126	A22	10kb red	.40	.40
128	A22	20kb green	1.60	1.60
130	A22	50kb brown	2.40	2.40
		Nos. 118-130 (8)	5.65	5.65

Issued: Nos. 124, 126, 128, 130, 5/16; 118-119, 121-122, 6/17.

Mykola I. Kostomarov (1817-1885), Writer — A23

1992, May 16 Photo. *Perf. 12x11½*

133 A23 20k olive green .65 .65

1992 Summer Olympics, Barcelona

A24 A25

1992, July 25 Litho. *Perf. 13*

134	A24 3kb yel green & multi	.40	.40
135	A25 4kb multicolored	.50	.50
136	A24 5kb buff & multi	.70	.70
	Nos. 134-136 (3)	1.60	1.60

World Forum of Ukrainians, Kyiv — A26

1992, Aug. 19 Litho. *Perf. 13*

137 A26 2kb multicolored .70 .70

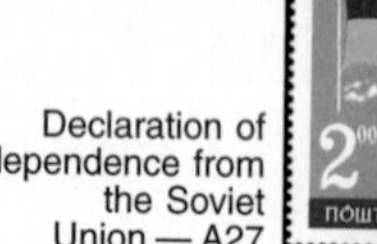

Declaration of Independence from the Soviet Union — A27

1992, Aug. 19 *Perf. 13½x13*

138 A27 2kb multicolored .70 .70

Souvenir Sheet

Union of Ukrainian Philatelists, 25th Anniv. — A28

1992, Aug. 19 *Perf. 12*

139 A28 2kb multicolored 1.10 1.10

Intl. Letter Writing Week — A29

1992, Oct. 4 *Perf. 13x13½*

140 A29 5kb multicolored .55 .55

World Congress of Ukrainian Lawyers, Kyiv — A30

1992, Oct. 18 Litho. *Perf. 13*

141 A30 15kb multicolored .90 .90

Ukrainian Diaspora in Austria — A31

Perf. 13½x14½

1992, Nov. 27 Litho.

142 A31 5kb multicolored .55 .55

Embroidery — A32

1992, Nov. 16 Litho. *Perf. 11½x12*

143 A32 50k black & orange .65 .65

Mohyla Academy, Kyiv, 360th Anniv. — A33

1992, Nov. 27 Litho. *Perf. 12x12½*

144 A33 1.50kb multicolored .70 .70

Souvenir Sheet

Ukrainian Medal Winners, 1992 Summer Olympics, Barcelona — A34

1992, Dec. 14 Litho. *Perf. 14*

145 A34 10kb multicolored 2.50 2.50

Coats of Arms — A35

1993, Feb. 15 Litho. *Perf. 14x13½*

148	A35 3kb Lviv	.65	.65
150	A35 5kb Kyiv	1.10	1.10

See No. 292.

Cardinal Joseph Slipyj (1892-1984) — A36

1993, Feb. 17 Litho. *Perf. 14x13½*

166 A36 15kb multicolored 1.25 1.25

1st Vienna-Cracow-Lviv-Kyiv Air Mail Flight, 75th Anniv. — A37

1993, Mar. 31 *Perf. 13½x14*

167	A37 35kb Biplane	.75	.75
168	A37 50kb Jet	1.00	1.00

Easter — A39

1993, Apr. 18 Litho. *Perf. 13½*

169 A39 15kb multicolored .95 .95

UN Declaration of Human Rights, 45th Anniv. — A40

Design: 5kb, Country Wedding in Lower Austria, by Ferdinand Georg Waldmuller.

Perf. 14½x13½

1993, June 11 Litho.

170 A40 5kb multicolored 1.60 1.60

A41 A41a

A41b A41c

A41d A41e

A41f A41g

A41h

Villagers at Work: 50kb, No. 177, Reaper with scythe. 100kb, No. 183, Ox carts. No. 173, 200kb, 500kb, Reapers with sickles. No. 174, Farmer with oxen. 150kb, 300kb, No. 181, Shepherd. No. 180, Bee keeper. No. 182, Fisherman. No. 185, Potter. (Illustrations A41a-A41h help identify the Cyrillic characters, not the designs.)

Perf. 12x12½, 14 (#174, 180, 182, 184)

1993-98 Litho.

171	A41	50kb green	.40	.40
172	A41	100kb blue	.40	.40
173	A41c	(100kb) brown	.50	.50
174	A41e	(100kb) magenta	.60	.60
175	A41	150kb red	.40	.40
176	A41	200kb orange	.50	.50
177	A41d	(250kb) green	.50	.50
178	A41	300kb violet	.50	.50
179	A41	500kb brown	.50	.50
180	A41f	(1800kb) org brn	.50	.50
181	A41a	(5000kb) red	1.50	1.50
182	A41g	(5300kb) blue	1.00	1.00
183	A41b	(10,000kb) blue	.80	.80
a.		Perf. 14	6.75	6.75
184	A41h	(17,000kb) red brn	1.75	1.75
		Nos. 171-184 (14)	9.85	9.85

Nos. 174, 181 issued for domestic letter rate; Nos. 177, 180 for letters within the Commonwealth of Independent States; Nos. 183-184 for mail abroad, surface and airmail. Actual amounts sold for varied with inflation. No. 183a sold for 30k on date of issue and was used for the domestic rate.

Issued: 50, 100, 150, 200, 300, 500kb, 12/18/93; No. 181, 183a, 5/28/94; No. 173, 177, 7/2/94; No. 174, 182, 10/15/94; No. 180, 184, 11/12/94; No. 183, 12/30/98.

Famine Deaths, 60th Anniv. — A42

1993, Sept. 12 Litho. *Perf. 12*

188 A42 75kb brown .70 .70

First Ukrainian Postage Stamp, 75th Anniv. — A43

1993, Oct. 9

189 A43 100kb blue & brown .70 .70

Stamp Day.

Liberation of Kyiv, 50th Anniv. — A44

1993, Nov. 6 Litho. *Perf. 12*

190 A44 75kb multicolored .70 .70

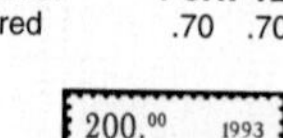

A45

1994, Jan. 15 Litho. *Perf. 12*

191 A45 200kb black & red 1.25 1.25

Agapit, Kyivan Rus physician, Middle Ages.

A46

Endangered species: No. 192, Erythronium dens, canis. No. 193, Cypripedium calceolus.

1994, Feb. 19 *Perf. 12x12½*

192 A46 200kb multicolored .60 .60
193 A46 200kb multicolored .60 .60

Independence Day — A47

1994, Sept. 3 **Litho.** *Imperf.*

194 A47 5000kb multicolored 1.50 1.50

No. 194 has simulated perforations.

Kyiv University — A47a

Litho. & Engr.

1994, Sept. 24 *Perf. 13x13½*

194A A47a 10,000kb multi .85 .85

Souvenir Sheet

Perf. 12½x13

194B A47a 25,000kb multi 2.25 2.25

No. 194B contains one 40x27mm stamp.

Liberation of Soviet Areas, 50th Anniv. — A48

Battle maps and: a, Katyusha rockets, liberation of Russia. b, Fighter planes, liberation of Ukraine. c, Combined offensive, liberation of Belarus.

1994, Oct. 8 **Litho.** *Perf. 12½x12*

195 A48 500kb Block of 3, #a.-c., + label 1.25 1.25

See Russia No. 6213, Belarus No. 78.

Excavation of Trypillia culture, Cent. — A49

1994, Dec. 17 **Litho.** *Perf. 12x12½*

196 A49 4000kb multicolored .45 .45

1st Books Printed in Ukrainian, 500th Anniv. — A50

1994, Dec. 17 *Perf. 13½*

197 A50 4000kb multicolored .45 .45

Sofiyivka Natural Park, Bicent. — A51

1994, Dec. 17 *Perf. 12½x12*

198 A51 5000kb multicolored .65 .65

Ilya Y. Repin (1844-1930), Painter — A52

1994, Dec. 17 *Perf. 12x12½*

199 A52 4000kb multicolored .45 .45

City of Uzhhorod, 1100th Anniv. — A53

1995, Jan. 28 **Litho.** *Perf. 12*

200 A53 5000kb multicolored .50 .50

Ivan Franko (1856-1916), Writer A54

Ivan Puliuj (1845-1918), Physicist A55

No. 203, Lesia Ukrainka (1871-1913), poet.

1995, Feb. 2 *Perf. 13½*

201 A54 3000kb multicolored .30 .30
202 A55 3000kb multicolored .40 .40
203 A54 3000kb multicolored .30 .30
Nos. 201-203 (3) 1.00 1.00

Falco Peregrinus — A56

1995, Apr. 15 **Litho.** *Perf. 12*

204 A56 5000kb shown .40 .40
205 A56 10,000kb Grus grus .80 .80

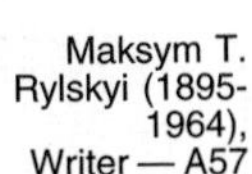

Maksym T. Rylskyi (1895-1964), Writer — A57

1995, Apr. 15 *Perf. 13½x14*

206 A57 50,000kb multicolored 1.25 1.25

End of World War II, 50th Anniv. — A58

1995, May 9 **Litho.** *Perf. 13½*

207 A58 100,000kb multicolored 1.75 1.75

Artek, Intl. Children's Camp — A59

1995, June 16 **Litho.** *Perf. 13½*

208 A59 5000kb multicolored .55 .55

Famous Writers — A60

Design: 1000kb, Ivan Kotliarevskyi (1769-1838), depiction of his poem, "Eneida." 3000kb, Taras Shevchenko (1814-61), his book, "Kobzar."

1995, July 8

209 A60 1000kb multicolored .40 .40
210 A60 3000kb multicolored .40 .40

Hetman Petro Konashevych-Sahaidachny — A61

1995, July 22 **Litho.** *Perf. 13½*

211 A61 30,000kb multicolored .85 .85

Arms of Luhansk — A62

1995 **Litho.** *Perf. 13½*

212 A62 10,000kb shown .40 .40
213 A62 10,000kb Chernihiv 1.00 1.00

Issued: No. 212, 9/15; No. 213, 10/22.

Hetman Bohdan Khmelnytsky (Khmelnytskyi; 1593?-1657) — A63

1995, Sept. 23 **Litho.** *Perf. 12½x12*

214 A63 40,000kb multi .90 .90

Hetman Ivan Mazepa (1640?-1709) A64

1995, Oct. 14 *Perf. 13½*

215 A64 30,000kb multi .85 .85

European Nature Protection Year — A65

1995, Oct. 14

216 A65 50,000kb multi 1.10 1.10

Intl. Children's Day — A66

1995, Oct. 22

217 A66 50,000kb multi 1.00 1.00

UN, 50th Anniv. — A67

1995, Oct. 24 *Perf. 12x12½*

218 A67 50,000kb multi 1.00 1.00

A68

1995, Dec. 9 *Perf. 13½*

219 A68 50,000kb multi 1.00 1.00

Ivan Karpenko-Karyi, playwright, actor.

Mikhailo Hrushevskyi, 1st Ukrainian President — A69

1995, Dec. 9

220 A69 50,000kb multi .90 .90

P. Safarik (1795-1861), Writer — A70

1995, Dec. 27

221 A70 30,000kb green 1.00 1.00

Trolleybus A71

Streetcar A72

City Bus — A73

1995, Dec. 27 **Litho.** *Perf. 14*

No Year Date

222 A71 (1000kb) blue violet .25 .25
a. Imprint "2003" 1.25 1.25
b. Imprint "2005" 1.25 1.25
c. Imprint "2006" 1.25 1.25
223 A72 (2000kb) green 2.75 2.75
224 A73 (3000kb) red 1.00 .80
a. Imprint "2006" .25 .25
Nos. 222-224 (3) 4.00 3.80

The postal rate that No. 223 paid was sharply increased greatly affecting the cost of the stamp at the post offices.

Imprinted values issued: No. 222a, 2003; No. 222b, 12/1/05; No. 222c, 2/3/06. No. 224a, 9/28/06.

Taras Shevchenko University Astronomical Observatory, Kyiv, 150th Anniv. — A74

a, 20,000 l, Early astronomical instruments. b, 30,000 l, Telescope. c, 50,000 l, Observatory, sun.

1996, Jan. 13 ***Perf. 12***
225 A74 Strip of 3, #a.-c. 1.75 1.75

Souvenir Sheet

1994 Winter Olympics, Lillehammer — A75

Medalists: a, 40,000kb, Valentina Tserbe, bronze, biathlon. b, 50,000kb, Oksana Bayul, gold, figure skating.

1996, Jan. 13
226 A75 Sheet of 2, #a.-b. 1.60 1.60

Ahatanhel Krymskyi (1871-1942), Writer — A76

1996, Jan. 15 ***Perf. 13½***
227 A76 20,000kb bister & brown .70 .70

Kharkiv Zoo, Cent. — A77

1996, Mar. 23 ***Perf. 12½x12***
228 A77 20,000kb multicolored .65 .65

Ivan S. Kozlovskyi (1900-93), Opera Singer — A78

1996, Mar. 23 ***Perf. 13½***
229 A78 20,000kb multicolored .65 .65

Motion Pictures, Cent. — A79

Oleksandr Dovzhenko, film maker, house.

1996, Mar. 23 ***Perf. 12½x12***
230 A79 4000kb multicolored .70 .70

No. 230 was issued se-tenant with two labels showing scenes from films.

Chernobyl Nuclear Disaster, 10th Anniv. — A80

1996, Apr. 26 Litho. ***Perf. 13½***
231 A80 20,000kb multicolored .65 .65

Symyrenko Family — A81

Vasyl Fedorovych (1835-1915), Volodymyr Levkovych (1891-1938), Levko Platonovych (1855-1920).

1996, May 25
232 A81 20,000kb multicolored .65 .65

Vasil Stefanyk (1871-1936), Writer — A82

1996, June 29
233 A82 20,000kb multicolored .65 .65

Mykola M. Myklukho-Maklai (1846-88), Explorer, Philologist — A83

Litho. & Engr.

1996, July 17 ***Perf. 13½***
234 A83 40,000kb multicolored 1.25 1.25

1996 Summer Olympic Games, Atlanta A84

Modern Olympic Games, Cent. A85

1996, July 19 Litho. ***Perf. 13½***
235 A84 20,000kb Wrestling .40 .40
236 A84 40,000kb Handball .80 .80
237 A85 40,000kb Greek athletes 1.10 1.10
Nos. 235-237 (3) 2.30 2.30

Souvenir Sheet
Perf. 12

238 A84 100,000kb Gymnast 1.75 1.75

Independence, 5th Anniv. — A86

1996, Aug. 24 ***Perf. 13½***
239 A86 20,000kb multicolored .70 .70

First Ukrainian Satellite, "Sich-1" — A87

1996, Aug. 31
240 A87 20,000kb multicolored .70 .70

Locomotives A88

Designs: 20,000kb, Steam, class OD. 40,000kb, Diesel class 2 TE-116.

1996, Aug. 31
241 A88 20,000kb multicolored .65 .65
242 A88 40,000kb multicolored 1.25 1.25
a. Pair, #241-242 2.25 2.25

Airplanes Designed by O.K. Antonov (1906-84) — A89

No. 243, Glider A-15, portrait of Antonov. No. 244, AN-2. No. 245, AN-124. No. 246, AN-225.

1996, Sept. 14
243 A89 20,000kb multicolored .55 .55
244 A89 20,000kb multicolored .55 .55
245 A89 40,000kb multicolored .55 .55
246 A89 40,000kb multicolored .55 .55
a. Block of 4, #243-246 2.25 2.25

Ivan Piddubnyi (1871-1949), Wrestler — A90

1996, Nov. 16
247 A90 40k multicolored .85 .85

First Ukrainian Antarctic Expedition — A91

1996, Nov. 23
248 A91 20k multicolored 1.50 1.50

A92

Flowers: 20k, Leontopodium alpinum. 40k, Narcissus anqustifolius.

1996, Nov. 23
249 A92 20k multicolored .55 .55
250 A92 40k multicolored .80 .80
a. Pair, #249-250 + label 1.50 1.50

A93

1996, Dec. 7 Litho. ***Perf. 13½***
251 A93 20k multicolored .60 .60

UNESCO, 50th anniv.

Viktor S. Kosenko, Composer, Birth Cent. — A94

1996, Dec. 21 Litho. ***Perf. 13½***
252 A94 20k multicolored .65 .65

St. Sophia's Cathedral, Kyiv — A95

Illinska (St. Elijah) Church, Subotiv — A96

St. George Church, Drohobych — A97

No. 256, Troitska Cathedral, Novomoskovsk.

1996, Dec. 25
253 A95 20k multicolored .40 .40
254 A96 20k multicolored .40 .40
255 A97 20k multicolored .40 .40
256 A97 20k multicolored .40 .40
a. Block of 4, #253-256 2.00 2.00

UNICEF, 50th Anniv. — A98

1996, Dec. 31
257 A98 20k multicolored .60 .60

Petro Mohyla (1596-1647), Metropolitan of Kyiv — A99

1996, Dec. 31
258 A99 20k multicolored .60 .60

Wild Animals — A100

1997, Mar. 22 Litho. ***Perf. 13½***
259 A100 20k Lynx lynx .90 .90
260 A100 20k Ursos arctos .90 .90
a. Pair, #259-260 + label 2.75 2.75

Cathedral of the Exaltation of the Holy Cross, Poltava, 17th Cent. — A101

Designs: No. 262, St. George's Cathedral, Lviv, 18th cent. No. 263, Protection Fortified Church, Sutkivtsi, 14-15th cent.

1997, Apr. 19 Litho. ***Perf. 13½***
261 A101 20k multicolored .90 .90
262 A101 20k multicolored .90 .90
263 A101 20k multicolored .90 .90
Nos. 261-263 (3) 2.70 2.70

Legendary Founders of Kyiv — A101a

Europa: a, Kyi (holding staff and shield) and Shchek (holding sword). b, Khoriv (holding sword, leaning on shield) and sister, Lybid.

1997, May 6 Litho. & Engr. *Perf. 13*
264 A101a 40k Sheet of 2, #a.-b. 9.00 9.00

4th Natl. Philatelic Exhibition, Cherkasy — A102

Design: Statue of Taras Shevchenko, stamps, exhibition hall.

1997, May 17 Litho. *Perf. 13½*
265 A102 10k multicolored .65 .65

Yurii V. Kondratiuk (1897-1942), Space Pioneer — A103

1997, June 21 *Perf. 12½x12*
266 A103 20k multicolored .90 .90

Constitution, 1st Anniv. — A104

1997, June 28 *Perf. 13½*
267 A104 20k multicolored .70 .70

Midsummer Festival of Ivan Kupalo — A104a

1997, July 5 Litho. *Perf. 13½*
268 A104a 20k multicolored .70 .70

Princess Olha A105

Sultana Roksoliana A106

1997, July 12 Litho. *Perf. 13½*
269 A105 40k multicolored 1.15 1.00
270 A106 40k multicolored 1.15 1.00

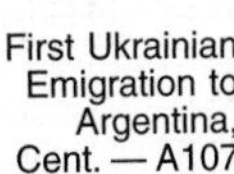

First Ukrainian Emigration to Argentina, Cent. — A107

Design: Monument to poet Taras Shevchenko, Buenos Aires.

1997, Aug. 16 Litho. *Perf. 13½*
271 A107 20k multicolored .75 .75

For Exceptional Service — A108

Order of Yaroslav the Wise A109

Medals for: No. 273, Military Service. 30k, Bravery. 40k, Order of Bohdan Khmelnytsky. No. 276, Honored Service.

No. 277: a, Medal hanging from chain. b, 8-point star.

Litho. & Engr.

1997, Aug. 20 *Perf. 13½*
272 A108 20k multicolored .45 .45
273 A108 20k multicolored .45 .45
274 A108 30k multicolored .70 .70
275 A108 40k multicolored .90 .90
276 A108 60k multicolored 1.25 1.25
a. Strip of 5, #272-276 5.00 5.00

Souvenir Sheet

Perf. 13

277 A109 60k Sheet of 2, #a.-b. 5.25 5.25

Nos. 277a-277b are each 35x50mm.

Hetman A110

No. 278, Dmytro "Baida" Vyshnevetskyj (?-1563), boats, archers. No. 279, Pylyp Orlyk (1672-1742), Stockholm harbor, crowd in Thessaloniki street.

1997, Sept. 13 Litho. *Perf. 12½x12*
278 A110 20k multicolored .95 .95
279 A110 20k multicolored .95 .95

See Nos. 357-358, 376-377, 412-413, 449-451, 510-511.

Solomiia Krushelnytska (Salomea Krusceniski, 1872-1952), Actress, Singer — A111

1997, Sept. 23 Litho. *Perf. 13½*
280 A111 20k multicolored .85 .85

Airplanes — A112

Designs: 20k, Antonov An-74 TK-200. 40k, Antonov An-38-100.

1997, Oct. 30
281 A112 20k multicolored .60 .60
282 A112 40k multicolored 1.40 1.40

Ships — A113

20k, Zavyietnyj, 1903. 40k, Serhii Korolev, 1970, Academician.

1997, Dec. 6 Litho. *Perf. 13½*
283 A113 20k multicolored .60 .60
284 A113 40k multicolored 1.40 1.40

A114

1997, Dec. 6 Litho. *Perf. 12x12½*
285 A114 40k multi + label 1.75 1.75

Participation of Ukrainian astronaut in US space shuttle mission.

Vasyl Krychevskyi (1872-1952), Painter and Architect. — A115

1997, Dec. 20 *Perf. 13½*
286 A115 10k multicolored .75 .75

Christmas — A116

1997, Dec. 20
287 A116 20k multicolored .85 .85

Traditional Handicrafts A117

Region: #288, Rooster, Dnipropetrovsk. #289, Vest, Chernivtsi. #290, Ram, Poltava. #291, Molded design, Ivano-Frankivsk.

1997, Dec. 20
288 A117 20k multicolored .75 .75
289 A117 20k multicolored .75 .75
290 A117 40k multicolored 1.25 1.25
291 A117 40k multicolored 1.25 1.25
Nos. 288-291 (4) 4.00 4.00

Perf. 11½

288a 20k .75 .75
289a 20k .75 .75
290a 40k 1.25 1.25
291a 40k 1.25 1.25
b. Sheet, 2 each #288a-291a 8.00 8.00

Nos. 288-291 have colored border. Nos. 288a-291a do not.

Arms Type of 1993

Arms of Transcarpathia (Zakarpattya).

1997, Dec. 30 Litho. *Perf. 13½*
292 A35 20k multicolored .90 .90

A118

Wildlife: a, 20k, Skylark. b, 40k, White-tailed eagle. c, 20k, Black stork. d, 40k, Long-eared hedgehog. e, 20k, Garden dormouse. f, 40k, Wild boar.

1997, Dec. 30 Litho. *Perf. 11½*
293 A118 Sheet of 6, #a.-f. 5.00 5.00

Hryhorii Skovoroda (1722-94), Philosopher — A119

Litho. & Engr.

1997, Dec. 27 *Perf. 13½*
294 A119 60k multicolored 1.10 1.10

Volodymyr Sosiura (1898-1965), Poet — A120

1998, Jan. 6 Litho. *Perf. 13½*
295 A120 20k multicolored 1.00 1.00

1998 Winter Olympic Games, Nagano — A121

1998, Feb. 14 Litho. *Perf. 13½*
296 A121 20k Figure skating .65 .65
297 A121 20k Biathlon .65 .65

Bilhorod Dnistrovskyi Fortress, 2500th Anniv. — A122

1998, Apr. 21 Litho. *Perf. 13½*
298 A122 20k multicolored .80 .80

UKRFILEKS 98 Natl. Philatelic Exhibition, Sevastopol — A123

Design: Frigate, "Hetman Sahaidachnyi."

1998, Apr. 28 Litho. *Perf. 13½*
299 A123 30k multi + label .85 .85

European Bank of Reconstruction and Development — A124

Obverse, reverse of Ukrainian coins: a, 1k, Gold, 11th cent. b, 1k, Silver, 11th cent. c, 60k, 500h St. Sophia Cathedral gold coin. d, 60k, 200h Taras Shevchenko gold coin. e, 30k, 1,000,000k Bohdan Khmelnytsky silver coin. f, 30k, 10h Petro Mohyla silver coin.

Litho. & Engr.

1998, May 8 *Perf. 13½*
300 A124 Sheet of 6, #a.-f. 10.00 10.00

Ivan Kupalo Natl. Festival — A125

1998, May 16 Litho. *Perf. 13½*
301 A125 40k multicolored 2.10 2.10

Europa.

Souvenir Sheet

Askania Nova Nature Preserve, Cent. — A126

a, 40k, Deer. b, 60k, Przewalski horses.

1998, May 16 Litho. *Perf. 11½*
302 A126 Sheet of 2, #a.-b. 3.25 3.25

Paintings from Lviv Picture Gallery — A127

Designs: No. 303, Portrait of Maria Theresa, by J.E. Liotard. No. 304, Man with a Cello, by Gerard von Honthorst. 40k, Madonna and Child, 17th cent. Lviv School.
1.20h, Madonna and Child and Two Saints, by 16th cent. Italian school.

1998, June 20 *Perf. 13½*
303 A127 20k multicolored .30 .30
304 A127 20k multicolored .30 .30
305 A127 40k multicolored .55 .55
a. Strip of 3, #303-305 1.40 1.40

Souvenir Sheet

306 A127 1.20h multicolored 2.25 2.25

Souvenir Sheet

Polytechnical Institute, Kyiv, Cent. — A128

1998, June 27 Litho. *Perf. 11½*
307 A128 1h multicolored 4.00 4.00

Askold & Dyr — A129

Litho. & Engr.

1998, July 4 *Perf. 13½*
308 A129 3h multi + label 3.25 3.25

Hetman Bohdan Khmelnytsky — A130

Designs: a, 30k, Battle scene, denomination LR. b, 2k, Portrait of Khmelnytsky. c, 30k, Battle scene, denomination LL. d, 40k, denomination LR. e, 60k, Battle scene. f, 40k, Battle scene, denomination LL.

1998, July 25 Litho. & Engr.
309 A130 Sheet of 6, #a.-f. 5.50 5.50

Ukrainian uprising, 350th anniv.

Town of Halych, 1100th Anniv. — A131

1998, Aug. 1 Litho.
310 A131 20k multicolored .70 .70

Queen Anna Yaroslavna (1024?-75) — A132

1998, Aug. 8
311 A132 40k multicolored .85 .85

Yurii Lysianskyi (1773-1837), Explorer — A133

1998, Aug. 13
312 A133 40k multicolored 1.10 1.10

Natalia Uzhvii (1898-1986), Stage Actress — A134

1998, Sept. 8 Litho. *Perf. 13½*
313 A134 40k multicolored 1.00 1.00

Polytechnical Institute, Kyiv, Cent. — A135

Designs: 10k, W.L. Kirpichov, first president. No. 315, E.O. Paton, bridge. No. 316, S.P. Timoschenko, mathematical formula. 30k, Igor I. Sikorsky, biplane. 40k, Sergei P. Korolev, rocket, satellite.

1998, Sept. 10 *Perf. 12½x12*
314 A135 10k multicolored .55 .55
315 A135 20k multicolored .55 .55
316 A135 20k multicolored .55 .55
317 A135 30k multicolored 1.00 1.00
318 A135 40k multicolored 1.00 1.00
a. Strip of 5, #314-318 4.25 4.25

World Post Day — A136

1998, Sept. 19 Litho. *Perf. 13½*
319 A136 10k multicolored .70 .70

Ukrainian Book, 1000th Anniv. — A137

1998, Sept.19
320 A137 20k multicolored .65 .65

Church Architecture A138

Designs: No. 321, Church of the Transfiguration, Chernihiv, 11th cent. No. 322, Church of the Holy Protection, Kharkiv, 17th cent.

1998, Sept. 21
321 A138 20k multicolored .70 .70
322 A138 20k multicolored .70 .70

World Wildlife Fund — A139

Branta ruficollis: a, f, 20k, Adults. b, g, 30k, Female on nest. c, h, 40k, Female with goslings. d, i, 60k, Adults, goslings.

1998, Oct. 10 Litho. *Perf. 13½*
323 A139 Block of 4, #a.-d. 4.00 4.00
e. Block of 4, perf. 11½, #f.-i. 4.75 4.75
j. Sheet of 2, #323e 9.50 9.50

Antonov Airplanes — A140

1998, Nov. 28 Litho. *Perf. 13½*
324 A140 20k Antonov 140 .60 .60
325 A140 40k Antonov 70 .80 .80

Hetman Type of 1997

Design: Petro Doroshenko (1627-98).

1998, Nov. 28 Litho. *Perf. 12½x12*
326 A141 20k multicolored .80 .80

Borys D. Hrinchenko (1863-1910), Writer — A142

1998, Dec. 4 Litho. *Perf. 13½*
327 A142 20k multicolored .85 .85

Christmas — A143

1998, Dec. 11
328 A143 30k multicolored 1.00 1.00

Ukrainians in Australia, 50th Anniv. — A144

1998, Dec. 20
329 A144 40k multicolored .85 .85

Illintsi Meteor Impact Area — A145

1998, Dec. 25
330 A145 40k multicolored 1.00 1.00

Universal Declaration of Human Rights, 50th Anniv. — A146

Paintings of various flowers by Kateryna Bilokur (1900-61): 30k, 1940. 50k, 1959.

1998, Dec. 25
331 A146 30k multicolored .60 .60
332 A146 50k multicolored .95 .95
a. Pair, #331-332 +label 1.60 1.60

Serhii Paradzhanov (1924-90), Film Director — A147

1999, Feb. 27 Litho. *Perf. 13½*
333 A147 40k multi + label 1.10 1.10

Volodymyr Ivasiuk (1949-79), Composer A148

1999, Mar. 4
334 A148 30k multicolored .60 .60

Scythian Gold — A149

1999, Mar. 20
335 A149 20k Clasp .30 .30
336 A149 40k Boar .50 .50
337 A149 50k Young elk .70 .70
338 A149 1h Necklace 1.10 1.10
a. Block of 4, #335-338 2.75 2.75

Spring Easter Dance — A150

1999, Apr. 7
339 A150 30k multicolored .50 .50

Europa A151

Synevyr Natl. Park: a, 50k, Wooden monuments on bank of Tereblyia River. b, 1h, Thymallus thymallus, river scene.

1999, Apr. 24
340 A151 Pair, #a.-b. 2.75 2.75

Panas Myrnyi (1849-1920), Writer — A152

1999, May 13
341 A152 40k multicolored .65 .65

Honoré de Balzac (1799-1850), Writer — A153

1999, May 20
342 A153 40k multicolored .65 .65

Council of Europe, 50th Anniv. — A154

1999, May 22
343 A154 40k multicolored .65 .65

Aleksandr Pushkin (1799-1837), Poet — A155

1999, June 6
344 A155 40k multi + label .65 .65

Sailboats A156

No. 345: a, Bark (Baidak), double sails, one man at tiller. b, Cossack (Chaika), single sail, rowers.

1999, June 26
345 A156 30k Pair, #a.-b. 1.10 1.10

Souvenir Sheet

Yaroslav the Wise A157

1999, July 2 Litho. *Perf. 11½*
346 A157 1.20h multicolored 2.00 2.00

Principality of Halytsko-Volynskyi, 800th Anniv. — A158

1999, July 27 *Perf. 13½*
347 A158 50k multicolored 1.00 .80

Natl. Museum of Art, Cent. — A159

Designs: a, 30k, Icon of St. George. b, 60, Girl in a Red Hat, by O.O. Murashko.

1999, July 27
348 A159 Pair, #a.-b. + label 1.50 1.00

Bee Keeping in Ukraine — A160

1999, Aug. 7
349 A160 30k Bee on flower 1.00 1.00

UPU, 125th Anniv. — A161

1999, Aug. 14 Litho. *Perf. 13½*
350 A161 30k multicolored .60 .60

Poltava, 1100th Anniv. — A162

1999, Aug. 14
351 A162 30k multicolored .70 .70

Presidential Medals — A163

Designs: 30k, Order of Princess Olga.
No. 353: a, Medal with trident. b, Medal with star.

1999, Aug. 17 Litho. & Engr.
352 A163 30k multicolored .65 .65

Souvenir Sheet of 2

353 A163 2.50h #a.-b. 6.00 6.00

No. 353 contains two 35x50mm stamps.

Polish-Ukrainian Cooperation in Nature Conservation — A164

a, Cervus elaphus. b, Felis silvestris.

1999, Sept. 22 Litho. *Perf. 13½*
354 A164 1.40h Pair, #a.-b. 3.00 2.00

See Poland Nos. 3477-3478.

National Bank — A165

1999, Sept. 28 Litho. & Engr.
355 A165 3h multicolored 2.75 2.40

Souvenir Sheet

356 A165 5h multicolored 5.00 5.00

Hetman Type of 1997

Designs: No. 357, Ivan Vyhovskyi (d. 1664), cavalry in water. No. 358, Pavlo Polubotok (1660-1724), ships in water.

1999 Litho. *Perf. 12¼x12*
357 A110 30k multi .65 .65
358 A110 30k multi .65 .65

Issued: No. 357, 11/20; No. 358, 12/22.

A166

Christmas A167

1999, Nov. 26 Wmk. 399 *Perf. 13½*
359 A166 30k multi .40 .40

Unwmk.

360 A167 60k multi .80 .80

Children's Art — A168

a, Spacecraft, alien creatures. b, Elephant in space. c, Rocket and space car on planet.

1999, Nov. 30 Unwmk. *Perf. 11½*
361 A168 10k Strip of 3, #a.-c. 2.00 2.00

Fauna — A169

Designs: a, 40k, Desmana moschata. b, 60k, Gyps fulvus. c, 40k, Lucanus cervus.

1999, Dec. 9 *Perf. 13½*
362 A169 Strip of 3, #a.-c. 1.75 1.75

Church of St. Andrew, Kyiv A170

1999, Dec. 12
363 A170 60k multi + label 1.25 1.25

Mushrooms — A171

Designs: a, 30k, Armillariella mellea. b, 30k, Paxillus atrotomentosus. c, 30k, Pleurotus ostratus. d, 40k, Cantharellus cibarius. e, 60k, Agaricus campester.

1999, Dec. 15 *Perf. 11½*
364 A171 Sheet of 5, #a.-e., + label 4.00 4.00

New Year 2000 A172

1999, Dec. 18 *Perf. 13½*
365 A172 50k multi + label 1.50 1.50

Motor Vehicles A173

a, Kraz-65032 truck. b, Tavriia Nova car.

1999, Dec. 18 Litho.
366 A173 30k Pair, #a.-b. 1.00 1.00

Works of Maria Prymachenko A174

Denomination colors: a, Green. b, Violet.

1999, Dec. 22
367 A174 30k Pair, #a.-b., + central label 1.00 1.00

Halshka Hulevychivna, Philanthropist — A175

1999, Dec. 25 *Perf. 13½*
368 A175 30k multi .60 .60

Zoogeographic Endowment Fund — A176

Animals from: a, 10k, Carpathian Reserve. b, 30k, Polissia Reserve. c, 40k, Kaniv Reserve. d, 60k, Trakhtemyriv Reserve. e, 1h, Askaniia-Nova Reserve (ram, birds). f, 1h, Kara-Dag Reserve (birds).

1999, Dec. 28 *Perf. 11½*
369 A176 Sheet of 6, #a.-f. 6.00 4.00

Christianity, 2000th Anniv. — A177

Designs: a, Mother of God mosaic, St. Sofia Cathedral, Kyiv, 11th cent. b, Christ Pantocrator fresco, Church of the Savior's Transfiguration, Polotsk, Belarus, 12th cent. c, Volodymyr Madonna, Tretiakov Gallery, Moscow, 12th cent.

2000, Jan. 5 **Litho.** *Perf. 11½*
370 A177 80k Sheet of 3, #a.-c. 5.00 4.25

Souvenir Sheet

Opera and Ballet Theaters A178

No. 371: a, National Academic, Kyiv. b, Odessa State, Odessa. c, Kharkov State Academic, Kharkov. d, Ivan Franko State Academic, Lviv.

2000, Jan. 29 **Litho.** *Perf. 11½*
371 A178 40k Sheet of 4, #a.-d. 5.50 5.50

Kyiv Bridges A179

No. 372: a, 10k, Moscow Bridge. b, 30k, Y. O. Paton Bridge. c, 40k, Pedestrian park bridge. d, 60k, Subway bridge.

2000, Jan. 29 *Perf. 12¼x12*
372 A179 Block of 4, #a.-d. 2.50 2.50

Souvenir Sheet

Peresopnytsia Gospel — A180

2000, Feb. 8 *Perf. 11½*
373 A180 1.50h multi 3.00 3.00

A181

2000, Feb. 11 *Perf. 13½*
374 A181 30k multi 1.60 .50

Oksana Petrusenko (1900-40), opera singer

Marusia Churai, 17th Cent. Singer — A182

2000, Feb. 18
375 A182 40k multi .90 .90

Hetman Type of 1997

Designs: No. 376, Danylo Apostol (1654-1734), church, burning castle. No. 377, Ivan Samoylovych (d. 1690), tent, winter scene.

2000 *Perf. 12¼x12*
376 A110 30k multi .90 .90
377 A110 30k multi .90 .90

Issued: No. 376, 2/22; No. 377, 3/3.

World Meteorological Organization, 50th Anniv. — A183

2000, Mar. 10 **Litho.** *Perf. 13½*
378 A183 30k multi 1.10 1.10

Europa Issue
Common Design Type

2000, Mar. 29 **Litho.** *Perf. 13½*
379 CD17 3h multi 4.50 3.00

Souvenir Sheets

Easter Eggs A184

No. 380: a, 30k, Egg with black and red star design, Podillia region. b, 30k, Flower egg, Chernihiv region. c, 30k, Egg with leaf design, Kyiv region. d, 30k, Egg with green, white and yellow geometric design, Odesa region. e, 70k, Egg with reindeer design, Hutsulschyna region. f, 70k, Egg with cross design, Volyn region.

2000, Apr. 28 *Perf. 11½*
380 A184 Sheet of 6, #a-f 4.25 4.25

Stamp Exhibitions — A185

No. 381: a, Woman in native costume, Austria #2. b, Man in native costume, Great Britain #1.

2000, May 20
381 A185 80k Sheet of 2, #a-b 3.75 3.75

WIPA 2000 Stamp Exhibition, Vienna; The Stamp Show 2000, London.

Donetsk Oblast A186

City of Kyiv A187

2000 *Perf. 12¼x12*
382 A186 30k multi .70 .70
383 A187 30k multi .70 .70

Regional and administrative areas. Issued: No. 382, 5/26; No. 383, 5/28.

6th Natl. Philatelic Exhibition, Donetsk A188

2000, May 28 **Litho.** *Perf. 12¼x12*
384 A188 30k multi .70 .70

City of Ostroh, 900th Anniv. — A189

2000, June 16 **Litho.** *Perf. 13½*
385 A189 30k multi .70 .70

2000 Summer Olympics, Sydney — A190

2000, June 26

386	A190 30k High jump	.50	.50
387	A190 30k Boxing	.50	.50
388	A190 70k Yachting	.85	.85
389	A190 1h Rhythmic gymnastics	1.50	1.50
	Nos. 386-389 (4)	3.35	3.35

Petro Prokopovych (1775-1850), Apiarist — A191

2000, July 12 **Litho.** *Perf. 13½*
390 A191 30k multi .80 .80

Shipbuilding — A192

2000, July 14

391	A192 Pair	1.90	1.90
a.	40k Ship St. Paul	.70	.70
b.	70k Ship St. Nicholas	1.10	1.10

Tetiana Pata (1884-1976), Artist — A193

No. 392: a, Leafy Plants with Flowers, 1950s. b, Viburnum Berries and Bird, 1957.

2000, July 21

392	A193 Horiz. pair, #a-b + central label	1.10	1.10
a.-b.	40k Any single	.50	.50

Dubno, 900th Anniv. — A194

2000, July 28
393 A194 30k multi .70 .70

Harvest Festival — A195

2000, Aug. 4
394 A195 30k multi .70 .70

Souvenir Sheet

Presidential Symbols — A196

Designs: a, Flag. b, Mace. c, Seal. d, Badge.

2000, Aug. 18 **Litho.** *Perf. 11½*
395 A196 60k Sheet of 4, #a-d 5.00 5.00

Regional and Administrative Areas

Volynska Oblast A197

Autonomous Republic of Crimea A198

2000 *Perf. 12¼x12*
396 A197 30k multi .70 .70
397 A198 30k multi .70 .70

Issued: No. 396, 8/23; No. 397, 10/20.

Kyiv Post Office, 225th Anniv. A199

2000, Sept. 3 *Perf. 11½*
398 A199 30k multi .70 .70

Endangered Amphibians — A200

No. 399: a, 30k, Triturus vulgaris. b, 70k, Salamandra salamandra.

2000, Sept. 8 *Perf. 13½*
399 A200 Pair, #a-b 1.75 1.75

Yurij Drohobych (1450-94), Writer — A201

2000, Sept. 12
400 A201 30k multi .70 .70

Souvenir Sheet

Carpathian National Park — A202

No. 401: a, Mt. Breskul, 1911 meters. b, Mt. Hoberla, 2061 meters.

2000, Sept. 15 *Perf. 11½*

401 A202 80k Sheet of 2, #a-b 5.00 5.00

Flowers A203

Designs: a, Marigolds. b, Chamomiles. c, Hollyhocks. d, Poppies. e, Periwinkles. f, Cornflowers. g, Morning glories. h, Martagon lilies. i, Peonies. j, Bluebells.

2000, Oct. 6

402 A203 30k Sheet of 10, #a-j 8.00 8.00

Children's Folk Tales — A204

Designs: a, "Ivasyk and Telesyk," (boy in boat, witch). b, "The Crooked Duck," (couple with duck). c, "The Cat and the Rooster."

2000, Nov. 3

403 30k Horiz. strip of 3 2.25 2.25
a.-c. A204 Any single .55 .55

New Year 2001 — A205

2000, Nov. 24

404 A205 30k multi .80 .80

St. Onufrius Church, Lviv A206

Church of Christ's Birth, Velyke A207

Design: 70k, Church of the Resurrection, Sumy.

2000, Dec. 8 *Perf. 13½*

405 A206 30k multi .60 .60
406 A207 30k multi .60 .60
407 A207 70k multi 1.20 1.20
Nos. 405-407 (3) 2.40 2.40

Souvenir Sheet

St. Vladimir (c. 956-1015), Kyivan Prince — A208

2000, Dec. 15 *Perf. 11½*

408 A208 2h multi 4.50 4.50

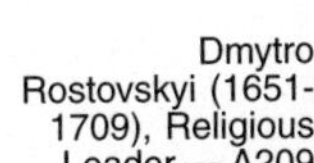

Dmytro Rostovskyi (1651-1709), Religious Leader — A209

2001, Jan. 16 **Litho.** *Perf. 13½*

409 A209 75k multi 1.25 1.25

Love — A210

2001, Jan. 26

410 A210 30k multi .70 .70

Souvenir Sheet

Prince Danylo Romanovych (1201-64) — A211

2001, Feb. 1 *Perf. 11½*

411 A211 3h multi 3.50 3.50

Hetman Type of 1997

Designs: 30k, Yuryi Khmelnytski (1641-85), as monk in Turkish prison, Kamianets-Podilskyi fortifications. 50k, Mykhailo Khanenko (1620-80), leading troops, relinquishing power.

2001, Feb. 20 *Perf. 12¼x12*

412-413 A110 Set of 2 1.00 1.00

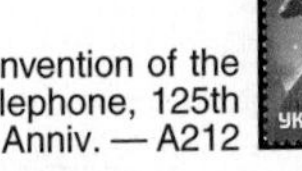

Invention of the Telephone, 125th Anniv. — A212

2001, Mar. 6 *Perf. 13½*

414 A212 70k multi 1.00 1.00

Children's Art — A213

Art by: 10k, Alyna Nochvaj. 30k, Olyia Pynych. 40k, Dasha Chemberzhi.

2001, Mar. 7 *Perf. 11½*

415-417 A213 Set of 3 1.10 1.10

Hollyhocks A214

Marigolds A215

Sunflower A216

Viburnum Opulus Berries A217

Wheat — A218

2001, Apr. 4 **Litho.** *Perf. 13¾*

418 A214 (10k) multi .25 .25
419 A215 (30k) multi .25 .25
420 A216 (71k) multi .50 .50
b. Imprint "2003" 3.00 3.00
c. Imprint "2004" 2.50 2.50
421 A217 (2.66h) multi 1.75 .85
b. Imprint "2003" 2.50 2.50
c. Imprint "2005" 2.00 2.00
d. Imprint "2006" 2.50 2.50
422 A218 (3.65h) multi 2.50 1.00
b. Imprint "2003" 3.75 3.75
c. Imprint "2004" 3.75 3.75
d. Imprint "2005" 2.50 2.50
e. Imprint "2006" 2.50 2.50
Nos. 418-422 (5) 5.25 2.85

2006, Oct. 9 *Perf. 11½*

Dated 2006

418a A214 (10k) multi 1.10 1.10
419a A215 (30k) multi 1.10 1.10
420a A216 (71k) multi 1.25 1.25
421a A217 (2.66h) multi 4.50 4.50
422a A218 (3.65h) multi 6.00 6.00
Nos. 418a-422a (5) 13.95 13.95

Nos. 418a-422a were issued only in No. F2b.

See Nos. 453-454, 466-468, 515, 572, 606-609.

Folktales A219

No. 423: a, The Fox and Wolf (fox on sleigh, fish). b, The Mitten (bear, fox, wolf, rabbit mouse, frog). c, Sirko the Dog (wolf with bottle, dog).

2001, Apr. 14 *Perf. 13½*

423 A219 30k Horiz. strip of 3, #a-c 1.40 1.40

Ships A220

No. 424: a, 20k, Twelve Apostles. b, 30k, Three Priests.

2001, Apr. 20

424 A220 Horiz. pair, #a-b 1.25 1.25

Europa A221

Fish, jellyfish, seaweed: a, 28x40mm. b, 56x40mm.

2001, Apr. 27

425 A221 1h Horiz. pair, #a-b 3.00 3.00

Holy Trinity — A222

2001, May 15

426 A222 30k multi .50 .50

Souvenir Sheet

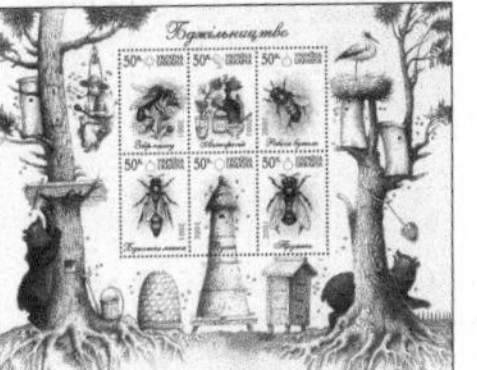

Apiculture — A223

No. 427: a, Bee on flower. b, Plant cutting, jar of honey, bowl of pollen, jars. c, Worker on honeycomb. d, Queen. e, Hive. f, Drone.

2001, May 22 *Perf. 11½*

427 A223 50k Sheet of 6, #a-f 6.50 6.50

Souvenir Sheet

Kyievo-Pecherska Monastery, 950th Anniv. — A224

2001, May 25

428 A224 1.50h multi 2.00 2.00

Visit of Pope John Paul II, June 23-27 — A225

2001, June 15 *Perf. 13½*

429 A225 3h multi 2.50 2.50

Regional and Administrative Areas

Zakarpatska Oblast A226

Kharkivska Oblast A227

Chernihivska Oblast A228

Kirovohradska Oblast — A229

2001 **Litho.** *Perf. 12¼x12*

430 A226 30k multi .60 .60
431 A227 30k multi .60 .60
432 A228 30k multi .60 .60
433 A229 30k multi .60 .60
Nos. 430-433 (4) 2.40 2.40

Issued: No. 430, 6/29; No. 431, 8/18; No. 432, 9/21; No. 433, 9/22.

Souvenir Sheet

Icons From Khanenko Art Museum — A230

No. 434: a, 20k, Virgin and Child, 28x40mm. b, 30k, St. John the Baptist, 28x40mm. c, Saints Serhyi and Bacchus, 56x40mm.

2001, July 12 **Litho.** *Perf. 11½*

434 A230 Sheet of 3, #a-c 1.25 1.25

Endangered Species — A231

No. 435: a, Milvus milvus. b, Scirtopoda telum.

2001, July 24 *Perf. 13*
435 A231 1h Vert. pair, #a-b 1.75 1.75

Dmytro Bortnianskyi (1751-1825), Composer — A232

2001, July 26
436 A232 20k multi .50 .50

Soccer — A233

2001, Aug. 10
437 A233 50k multi .70 .70

Souvenir Sheet

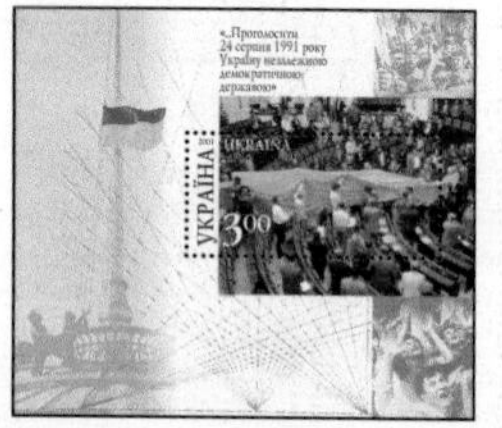

Independence, 10th Anniv. — A234

2001, Aug. 15 *Perf. 11½*
438 A234 3h multi 2.75 2.75

7th Natl. Philatelic Exhibition, Dnipropetrovsk — A235

2001, Oct. 7 Litho. *Perf. 12¼x12*
439 A235 30k multi .55 .55

Year of Dialogue Among Civilizations — A236

2001, Oct. 9 *Perf. 13*
440 A236 70k multi 2.00 2.00

Souvenir Sheet

Black Sea Marine Life A237

No. 441: a, 30k, Seahorses. b, 70k, Dolphins, birds.

2001, Oct. 19 *Perf. 11½*
441 A237 Sheet of 2, #a-b 2.40 2.40

Christmas A238

2001, Nov. 9 *Perf. 12¼x12*
442 A238 30k multi .65 .65

St. Nicholas — A239

2001, Nov. 16 *Perf. 13*
443 A239 30k multi .65 .65

Happy New Year — A240

2001, Nov. 23
444 A240 30k multi .65 .65

Poets A241

No. 445: a, Taras Shevchenko (1814-61), Ukrainian poet. b, Akakii Tsereteli (1840-1915), Georgian poet.

2001, Dec. 19
445 A241 40k Horiz. pair, #a-b .90 .90

See Georgia No. 276.

Regional Costumes

Kyivshchyna Region — A242

Chernihivshchyna Region — A243

Poltavshchyna Region — A244

No. 446: a, 20k, Two women. b, 50k, Man and woman.
No. 447: a, 20k, Musicians and girl. b, 50k, Bride and groom, boy.
No. 448: a, 20k, Priest and family. b, 50k, Two women.

2001, Dec. 20 *Perf. 13¼*
446 A242 Horiz. pair, #a-b .60 .60
447 A243 Horiz. pair, #a-b .60 .60
448 A244 Horiz. pair, #a-b .60 .60
c. Souvenir sheet, #446-448, perf. 11½ 2.00 2.00
Nos. 446-448 (3) 1.80 1.80

Hetman Type of 1997

Designs: No. 449, 40k, Pavlo Teteryia (d. 1670) holding scepter, people in town, horsemen and carriage heading for town. No. 450, 40k, Demyian Mnohohrishnyi, receiving scepter, boats in river. No. 451, 40k, Ivan Briukhovetskyi (d. 1668), battle scenes.

2002, Jan. 17 *Perf. 12¼x12*
449-451 A110 Set of 3 1.10 1.10

Scythian Military History A245

No. 452: a, Archer on horseback. b, Swordsman in battle. c, Commander on horseback, warrior. d, Female warrior.

2002, Jan. 29 *Perf. 13*
452 A245 40k Block of 4, #a-d 1.25 1.25

Flower Type of 2001 and

Periwinkle — A246

2002 Litho. *Perf. 13¾*
Year imprint
453 A246 5k multi, "2002" .50 .50
a. Perf. 11½, dated "2006" 1.50 1.50
b. As #453, dated "2004" .75 .75
c. As #453, dated "2005" .75 .75
d. As #453, dated "2006" .75 .75
454 A214 10k multi, "2002" .50 .50
a. Perf. 11½, dated "2006" 1.50 1.50
b. As #454, dated "2003" .75 .75
c. As #454, dated "2005" .75 .75
d. As #454, dated "2006" .75 .75

Issued: No. 453, 2/1; No. 453b, 7/19/04; No. 453c, 2005; No. 453d, 12/1/05. No. 454, 2/26; No. 454b, 2003; No. 454c, 2005; No. 454d, 12/1/05. Nos. 453a-454a, 10/9/06. Nos. 453a-454a were issued only in No. F2b.

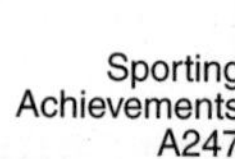

Sporting Achievements A247

Designs: No. 455, 40k, Zhanna Pintusevich-Block winning 100-meter dash at 2001 World Track and Field Championships. No. 456, 40k, Swimmer at 2000 Summer Olympics.

2002, Feb. 15 *Perf. 13*
455-456 A247 Set of 2 .80 .80

Regional and Administrative Areas

Kyivska Oblast A248

2002, Feb. 18 *Perf. 12¼x12*
457 A248 40k multi .50 .50

Shipbuilding — A249

No. 458: a, Frigate Sizopol and coast. b, Brigantine Perseus.

2002, Feb. 22 *Perf. 13½*
458 A249 40k Horiz. pair, #a-b .80 .80

Issuance of First Stamp After Independence, 10th Anniv. — A250

2002, Mar. 1
459 A250 40k No. 100 .80 .80

Leonid Hlibov (1827-93), Writer — A251

2002, Mar. 4 Litho. *Perf. 13¼*
460 A251 40k multi .50 .50

Ruslan Ponomariov, Winner of 16th World Chess Championships A252

2002, Mar. 29 *Perf. 13½*
461 A252 3.50h multi 2.00 2.00

Souvenir Sheet

Europa A253

No. 462: a, Lion. b, Tiger, horiz.

2002, Apr. 4 *Perf. 11½*
462 A253 1.75h Sheet of 2, #a-b 3.75 3.75

Palm Sunday — A254

2002, Apr. 19 *Perf. 13½*
463 A254 40k multi .45 .45

Worldwide Fund for Nature (WWF) — A255

Various views of Elaphe situla: a, 40k. b, 70k. c, 80k. d, 2.50h.

2002, May 25 *Perf. 13½*
464 A255 Block of 4, #a-d 2.50 2.50
e. Perf. 11½ 3.50 3.50

Souvenir Sheet

Opera and Ballet Theaters A256

No. 465: a, Donetsk (tree at center). b, Dnipropetrovsk (trees at side).

2002, May 31 ***Perf. 11½***
465 A256 1.25h Sheet of 2, #a-b 1.25 1.25

Flower Type of 2001 and

Blue Cornflower A257

Lilac A258

2002 **Litho.** ***Perf. 13¾***
Year Imprint

466 A215 30k multi, "2002" .50 .50
a. Perf. 11½, dated "2006" 1.75 1.75
b. As #466, dated "2003" .70 .70
c. As #466, dated "2004" .70 .70
d. As #466, dated "2005" .70 .70
e. As #466, dated "2006" .70 .70
467 A257 45k multi, "2002" .50 .50
a. Perf. 11½, dated "2006" 1.75 1.75
b. As #467, dated "2003" .70 .70
c. As #467, dated "2004" .70 .70
d. As #467, dated "2005" .70 .70
e. As #467, dated "2006" .70 .70
468 A258 (80k) multi, "2002" .80 .80
a. Perf. 11½, dated "2006" 2.50 2.50
b. As #468, dated "2003" 1.00 1.00
c. As #468, dated "2004" 1.00 1.00

Issued: Issued: No. 466, 6/1/02; No. 466b4/17/03; No. 466c, 1/22/04; No. 466d, 2/3/05; No. 466e, 12/1/05. No. 467, 9/19/02; No. 467b, 4/17/03; No. 467c, 2/6/04; No. 467d, 4/29/05; No. 467e, 3/3/06. No. 468, 7/5/02; No. 468b, 2003; No. 468c, 7/19/04.

Nos. 466a-468a issued 10/9/06. Nos. 466a-468a were issued only in No. F2b.

Regional and Administrative Areas

Luhanska Oblast A259

Chernivetska Oblast A260

Odeska Oblast A261

Cherkaska Oblast A262

Sumska Oblast A263

2002 ***Perf. 12¼x12***
469 A259 40k multi .50 .50
470 A260 40k multi .50 .50
471 A261 45k multi .50 .50
472 A262 45k multi .50 .50
473 A263 45k multi .50 .50
Nos. 469-473 (5) 2.50 2.50

Issued: No. 469, 6/2; No. 470, 6/27; No. 471, 9/20. No. 472, 10/9; No. 473, 10/21.

Endangered Species — A264

No. 474: a, Phalacrocorax aristotelis. b, Phocoena phocoena.

2002, June 14 **Litho.** ***Perf. 13***
474 A264 70k Pair, #a-b 1.50 1.50

Mykola Leontovich (1877-1921), Composer — A265

2002, June 21 ***Perf. 13½***
475 A265 40k multi .50 .50

Souvenir Sheet

Black Sea Nature Reserve A266

No. 476: a, Haematopus ostralegus (40x28mm). b, Larus genei (40x28mm). c, Iris pumila (22x26mm). d, Numenius arquata (26x22mm). e, Charadrius alexandrinus (26x22mm).

2002, July 13 ***Perf. 11½***
476 A266 50k Sheet of 5, #a-e 2.50 2.50

Folk Tales A267

No. 477: a, Fox and Pancake. b, Mr. Cat. c, Speckled Chicken.

2002, July 19 ***Perf. 14¼x14***
477 A267 40k Horiz. strip of 3, #a-c .70 .70

Art of Hanna Sobachko-Shostak A268

No. 478: a, Cage for Starlings, 1963 (peach background). b, Vase with Flowers, 1964 (red background). c, Chamomile Flowers, 1964 (yellow background).

2002, Aug. 9 ***Perf. 14x14¼***
478 Horiz. strip of 3 .90 .90
a.-c. A268 45k Any single .30 .30

Space Pioneers A269

Designs: 40k, Yurii V. Kondratiuk (1897-1942). 45k, Mykhailo Yianhel (1911-71). 50k, Mykola Kybalchych (1853-81). 70k, Serhii Korolov (1907-66).

2002, Aug. 23 ***Perf. 12¼x12***
479-482 A269 Set of 4 1.60 1.60

See Nos. 500-503.

Marine Life A270

No. 483: a, Phoca caspica. b, Huso huso ponticus.

2002, Sept. 6 ***Perf. 14x14¼***
483 A270 75k Horiz. pair, #a-b 1.25 1.25

See Kazakhstan No. 386.

Khotyn, 1000th Anniv. A271

2002, Sept. 21 ***Perf. 12¼x12***
484 A271 40k multi .50 .50

Odesaphil 2002 Stamp Exhibition, Odesa — A272

2002, Oct. 5 **Litho.** ***Perf. 14¼x14***
485 A272 45k multi .50 .50

Paintings of Kyiv by Taras Shevchenko (1814-61) A273

Designs: 45k, Askold's Tomb. 75k, Dnieper River Shoreline. 80k, St. Alexander's Church.

Perf. 13¾x14½
2002, Nov. 15 **Litho.**
486-488 A273 Set of 3 1.10 1.10

See Nos. 516-519, 548-551, 590-593.

Happy New Year — A274

2002, Nov. 22 ***Perf. 14x14¼***
489 A274 45k multi .65 .65

Regional Costumes

Vinychyna Region — A275

Cherkashchyna Region — A276

Ternopilska Region — A277

No. 490: a, Family, rainbow. b, Family, fruit tree.
No. 491: a, Four girls holding hands. b, Couple gathering crops.
No. 492: a, Priest blessing family. b, People with Easter baskets.

2002, Dec. 6 ***Perf. 13¼***
490 A275 45k Horiz. pair, #a-b .45 .45
491 A276 45k Horiz. pair, #a-b .45 .45
492 A277 45k Horiz. pair, #a-b .45 .45
c. Souvenir sheet, #490-492, perf. 11½ 4.25 4.25
Nos. 490-492 (3) 1.35 1.35

Folk Tales A278

No. 493: a, Koza-Dezera (cow on bridge). b, The Straw Bull. c, The Fox and Crane.

2003, Jan. 17 **Litho.** ***Perf. 14¼x14***
493 A278 45k Horiz. strip of 3, #a-c .75 .75

Speed Skating — A279

2003, Jan. 24 ***Perf. 14x14¼***
494 A279 65k multi .55 .55

Military History A280

No. 495: a, War with Goths, 4th cent. (soldier with spear and shield) b, Battles with Huns, 5th cent. (archer). c, Balkan campaigns, 6th cent. (soldier with hatchet). d, Battles with the Avars, 6th cent. (soldier with spears).

2003, Feb. 7
495 A280 45k Block of 4, #a-d 1.10 1.10

Shipbuilding — A281

No. 496: a, Steamship Grozny (denomination at left. b, Steamship Odessa (denomination at right).

2003, Feb. 14
496 A281 1h Horiz. pair, #a-b 1.40 1.40

Mikola Arkas (1853-1909), Composer — A282

2003, Feb. 21
497 A282 45k multi .45 .45

Souvenir Sheet

Javorivsky National Nature Park — A283

No. 498: a, 1h, Alcede atthis (32x44mm). b, 1h, Cypripedium calceolus (36x41mm). c, 1.50h, Eudia pavonia, horiz. (44x32mm)

2003, Mar. 3 ***Perf. 11½***
498 A283 Sheet of 3, #a-c 2.50 2.50

Europa A284

Poster by Oleksiy Shtanko: a, Virgin Mary with dove. b, Guardian angel.

2003, Mar. 21 ***Perf. 11½***
499 A284 1.75h Horiz. pair, #a-b 3.50 3.50
c. Booklet pane, 2 #499 + central label 12.50 —
Complete booklet, #499c 12.50

Space Pioneers Type of 2002

Designs: 45k, Olkeksandr Zasiadko (1779-1837). 65k, Kostyantin Konstantinov (1817-71). 70k, Valyntyn Hlushko (1908-89). 80k, Volodymyr Chelomei (1914-84).

2003, Apr. 11 Litho. ***Perf. 13¾x14½***
500-503 A269 Set of 4 1.60 1.60

Ukrainian Red Cross Society, 85th Anniv. A285

2003, Apr. 18
504 A285 45k multi .50 .50

Regional and Administrative Areas

Dnipropetrovska Oblast — A286

Lvivska Oblast A287

Khmelnytska Oblast — A288

Mykolayivska Oblast — A289

Zaporizhiya Oblast A290

2003
505 A286 45k multi .45 .45
506 A287 45k multi .45 .45
507 A288 45k multi .45 .45
508 A289 45k multi .45 .45
509 A290 45k multi .45 .45
Nos. 505-509 (5) 2.25 2.25

Issued: No. 505, 4/21; No. 506, 5/8; No. 507, 9/26; No. 508, 10/4; No. 509, 10/11.

Hetman Type of 1997

Designs: No. 510, 45k, Ivan Skoropadskiy (1646-1722) wearing robe, serfs in field, subjects bowing. No. 511, 45k, Kyrylo Rozumovskiy (1728-1803) holding scepter, attack of palace, palace ruins.

2003, May 22
510-511 A110 Set of 2 .75 .75

Souvenir Sheet

Volodymyr Monomakh (1053-1125), Grand Prince of Kyiv — A291

2003, May 28 ***Perf. 11½***
512 A291 3.50h multi 2.25 2.25

Owls A292

No. 513: a, Bubo bubo. b, Strix uralensis. c, Strix aluco. d, Strix nebulosa. e, Glaucidium passerinum. f, Aegolius funereus. g, Otus scops. h, Athene noctua. i, Tyto alba. j, Asio otus. k, Asio flammeus. l, Surnia ulula. Size of # 513e-513h: 25x27mm; others: 25x36mm.

2003, June 14
513 A292 45k Sheet of 12, #a-l 6.50 6.50

Oleksandr Myshuha (1853-1922), Opera Singer — A293

2003, June 20 ***Perf. 13¼***
514 A293 45k multi .50 .50

Sweet Pea — A294

2003, July 4 ***Perf. 13¾***

Year Imprint

515 A294 65k multi, "2003" 1.25 1.25
a. Perf. 11½, dated "2006" 2.50 2.50
b. As #515, dated "2004" 2.00 2.00
c. As #515, dated "2005" 1.25 1.25

Issued: No. 515b, 2/6/04; No. 515c, 2/1/05. No. 515a issued 10/9/06. No. 515a was issued only in No. F2b.

Paintings Type of 2002

Paintings of Kyiv: No. 516, 45k, Podil, by Mykhailo Sazhyn, 1840. No. 517, 45k, Kyiv-Pecherska Monastery, by Vasyl Timm, 1857. No. 518, 45k, Ruins of St. Irene Monastery, by Sazhyn, 1846. No. 519, 45k, View of Old City from Yaroslav Embankment, by Timm, 1854.

2003, July 18 ***Perf. 13¾x14½***
516-519 A273 Set of 4 1.50 1.50

Customs and Traditions A295

No. 520: a, Celebration of the Harvest (Church, flowers and insects). b, Ascension (Church, fruit).

2003, July 25 ***Perf. 14¼x14***
520 A295 45k Horiz. pair, #a-b .50 .50

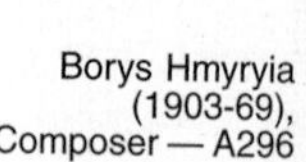

Borys Hmyryia (1903-69), Composer — A296

2003, Aug. 5 ***Perf. 14x14¼***
521 A296 45k multi .45 .45

Souvenir Sheet

Manyiavskyi Monastery — A297

No. 522: a, Denomination at LL. b, Denomination at LR.

2003, Aug. 15 ***Perf. 11x11½***
522 A297 1.25h Sheet of 2, #a-b 1.75 1.75

Yevpatoriya, 2500th Anniv. A298

2003, Aug. 29 ***Perf. 13¾x14½***
523 A298 45k multi .50 .50

Ancient Trade Routes A299

No. 524: a, Arrival of Scandinavian seamen in rowboat, coin of Danish King Svend Estridsen. b, Silver coin of Prince Volodymyr Sviatoslavovych, Slavic warship with sail.

2003, Sept. 17 ***Perf. 11½***
524 A299 80k Vert. pair, #a-b, + central label .90 .90
c. Booklet pane, #524 3.75 —
d. Booklet pane, #524a 2.50 —
e. Booklet pane, #524b 2.50 —
Complete booklet, #524c, 524d, 524e 9.00

Hryhoryi Kvitka-Osnovyianenko (1778-1843), Writer — A300

2003, Nov. 14 Litho. ***Perf. 14¼x14***
525 A300 45k multi .50 .50

Famine of 1932-33 A301

2003, Nov. 21 ***Perf. 13¾x14½***
526 A301 45k multi .50 .50

Christmas — A302

Litho. with Foil Application

2003, Nov. 25 ***Perf. 13¼x13½***
527 A302 45k multi 1.00 1.00

New Year's Greetings — A303

2003, Nov. 25 Litho. ***Perf. 13½***
528 A303 45k multi 1.00 1.00

Regional Costumes

Kharkiv Region A304

Sumy Region A305

Donetsk Region A306

No. 529: a, Women, religious icons. b, Family, lute.
No. 530: a, Woman, men. b, Group of women.
No. 531: a, Family, sled. b, Workers in field.

2003, Dec. 19 ***Perf. 13¼***
529 A304 45k Horiz. pair, #a-b .80 .80
530 A305 45k Horiz. pair, #a-b .80 .80
531 A306 45k Horiz. pair, #a-b .80 .80
c. Souvenir sheet, #529-531, perf. 11½ 3.50 3.50

Unification of Ukraine and Western Ukraine, 85th Anniv. A307

2004, Jan. 22 Litho. ***Perf. 13¾x14½***
532 A307 45k multi .40 .40

Stanislav Ludkevych (1879-1979), Composer — A308

2004, Jan. 24 ***Perf. 13¼***
533 A308 45k multi .40 .40

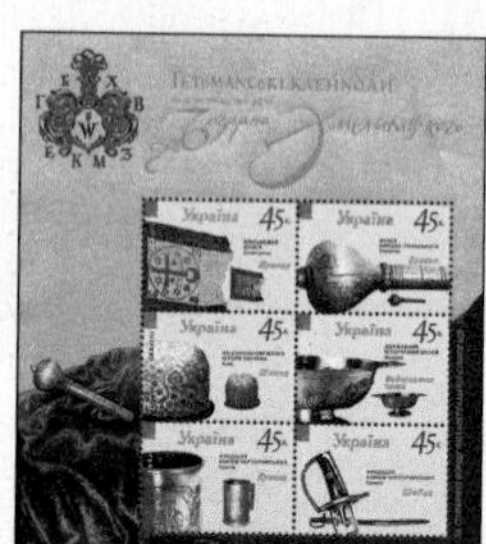

Possessions of Hetman Bohdan Khmelnytsky — A309

No. 534: a, Flag. b, Mace. c, Cap. d, Chalice decorated with leaves. e, Tankard. f, Sword.

Litho. With Foil Application

2004, Jan. 29 ***Perf. 11½***
534 A309 45k Sheet of 6, #a-f 2.00 2.00

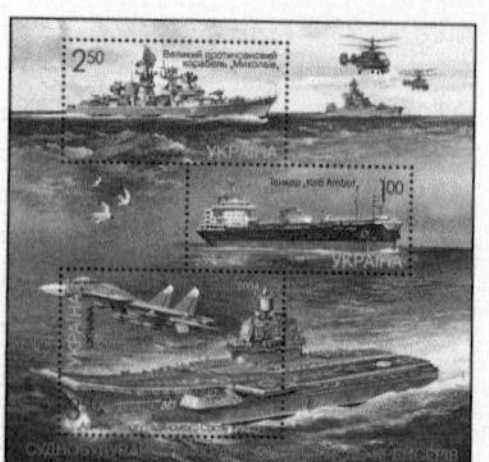

Shipbuilding — A310

No. 535: a, 1h, Oil tanker Kriti Amber (55x26mm). b, 2.50h, Anti-submarine ship Mikolayiv (55x29mm). c, 3.50h Aircraft carrier Admiral Kuznetzov (55x40mm).

2004, Feb. 21 **Litho.** ***Perf. 11½***
535 A310 Sheet of 3, #a-c 4.25 4.25

Regional and Administrative Areas

Ternopilska Oblast A311

2004, Mar. 3 ***Perf. 13¾x14½***
536 A311 45k multi .50 .50

Membership in UNESCO, 50th Anniv. — A312

2004, Mar. 19 ***Perf. 14¼x14***
537 A312 45k multi .50 .50

Butterflies — A313

No. 538: a, 45k, Endromis versicolora. b, 75k, Smerinthus ocellatus. c, 80k, Catocala fraxini. d, 2.60h, Apatura ilia. e, 3.50h, Papilio machaon.

2004, Mar. 26 ***Perf. 8***
538 A313 Sheet of 5, #a-e 4.75 6.00

Famous Ukrainians A314

Designs: No. 539, 45k, Serhyi Lyfar (1904-86), ballet dancer and choreographer. No. 540, 45k, Maria Zankovetska (1854-1934), actress. No. 541, 45k, Mykhaylo Maksymovych (1804-73), historian.

2004 **Litho.** ***Perf. 14x14¼***
539-541 A314 Set of 3 1.25 1.25

Issued: No. 539, 4/2, Nos. 540-541, 7/23.
See Nos. 574-575, 613-614, 641, 655-656, 750-751, 757-758.

Zenit-1 Rocket — A315

2004, Apr. 14
542 A315 45k multi .50 .50

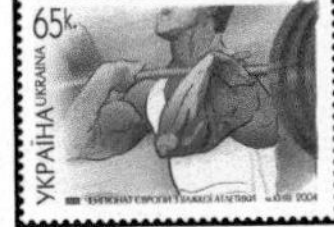

European Weight Lifting Championships, Kyiv — A316

2004, Apr. 20
543 A316 65k multi .50 .50

Miniature Sheet

Europa A317

No. 544: a, 45k, Lastivchyne Hnizdo (22x33mm). b, 75k, Carpathian Mountains (22x33mm). c, 2.61h, Khotyn Castle (29x33mm). d, 3.52h, Pecherska Lavra (39x28mm).

2004, Apr. 23 ***Perf. 11½***
544 A317 Sheet of 4, #a-d 6.25 6.25

UEFA (European Football Union), 50th Anniv. — A318

2004, May 17 ***Perf. 14¼x14***
545 A318 3.52h multi 1.75 1.75

FIFA (Fédération Internationale de Football Association), Cent. — A319

No. 546: a, 45k, Player #11. b, 75k, Player #6. c, 80k, Fan. d, 2.61h, Two women players.

2004, May 17 ***Perf. 13¼***
546 A319 Block of 4, #a-d 2.75 2.75

Symon Petlura (1879-1926), Political Leader — A320

2004, May 21
547 A320 45k multi .50 .50

Painting Type of 2002

Designs: No. 548, 45k, Kiev with St. Andrew's Church, by unknown artist, 1889. No. 549, 45k, Fountain Near the Golden Gate, by Petro Levchenko, 1910. No. 550, 45k, Spring in Kurenivka, by Abram Manevych, 1914-15. No. 551, 45k, St. Michael's Cathedral From the South, by Mykola Burachek, 1919.

2004, June 11 ***Perf. 13¾x14½***
548-551 A273 Set of 4 1.25 1.25

Folktales A321

No. 552: a, The Cat. b, Ivasyk Telesyk. c, The Fat Man.

2004, June 18 ***Perf. 14¼x14***
552 A321 45k Horiz. strip of 3, #a-c .90 .90

2004 Summer Olympics, Athens — A322

2004, June 26 ***Perf. 14x14¼***
553 A322 2.61h multi 1.40 1.40

Regional and Administrative Areas

Rovenska Oblast A323

Khersonska Oblast A324

Poltavska Oblast A325

2004 ***Perf. 13¾x14½***
554 A323 45k multi .50 .50
555 A324 45k multi .50 .50
556 A325 45k multi .50 .50

Issued: No. 554, 7/16; No. 555, 8/20; No. 556, 9/22.

Balaklava, 2500th Anniv. A327

Perf. 13¾x14½
2004, Aug. 14 **Litho.**
557 A327 45k multi .50 .50

Kharkiv, 350th Anniv. — A328

2004, Aug. 20 ***Perf. 14¼x14***
558 A328 45k multi .50 .50

Bridges A329

No. 559: a, Inhulskyi Bridge (open drawbridge). b, Darnytska Bridge (three arches above roadway). c, B. M. Preobrazhenskoho Bridge (arches below roadway). d, Southern Buh Bridge (swing bridge).

2004, Aug. 25 ***Perf. 13¾x14½***
559 A329 45k Block of 4, #a-d 1.25 1.25

No. 194B Surcharged

Litho. & Engr.
2004, Sept. 15 ***Perf. 12½x13***
560 A47a 2.61h on 25,000kb multi 1.50 1.50

Taras Shevchenko University, 170th anniv.

Kirovohrad, 250th Anniv. A330

Perf. 13¾x14¼
2004, Sept. 17 **Litho.**
561 A330 45k multi .50 .50

Military History A331

No. 562: a, Infantryman of Prince Oleg, 10th cent. b, National militia, 11th-12th cent. c, Archer on horseback, 12th cent. d, Cavalryman for Danylo Halyts, 13th cent.

2004, Oct. 15 ***Perf. 14x14¼***
562 A331 45k Block of 4, #a-d 1.40 1.40

Miniature Sheet

Birds of the Danube Nature Reserve A332

No. 563: a, 45k, Cygnus olor. b, 75k, Phalacrocorax pygmaeus. c, 80k, Egretta alba. d, 2.61h, Anser anser. e, 3.52h, Platalea leucordia.

2004, Oct. 26 ***Perf. 11½***
563 A332 Sheet of 5, #a-e 4.75 4.75

Khartron Control Systems in Space — A333

1516 Battle Between Cossacks and Tartars Using Fiery Projectiles A334

2004, Nov. 12 ***Perf. 14x14¼***
564 A333 45k multi .50 .50
565 A334 45k multi .50 .50

Christmas — A335

No. 566: a, Magi facing right ("2" in background). b, Magi facing left ("5" in background). c, Nativity ("0" in background).

Litho. With Foil Application

2004, Nov. 26 ***Perf. 13¼***
566 Horiz. strip of 4, #a-b, 2 #c 1.00 1.00
a.-c. A335 45k Any single, gold & multi .25 .25

Numbers in background of strip of 4 read "2005."

New Year's Greetings — A336

No. 567: a, Santa Claus, large trees at left ("2" in background). b, Santa Claus, large trees at right ("5" in background). c, Tree and gifts ("0" in background).

2004, Nov. 26

567 Horiz. strip of 4, #a-b, 2 #c 1.00 1.00
a.-c. A336 45k Any single, silver & multi .25 .25

Numbers in background of strip of 4 read "2005."

Ukrainian and Iranian Aircraft A337

No. 568: a, Antonov-140, Ukraine (denomination at left). b, Iran-140, Iran (denomination at right).

2004, Nov. 30 Litho. ***Perf. 11½***

568 Horiz. pair + central label 1.10 1.00
a.-b. A337 80k Either single .50 .50

See Iran No. 2907.

Regional Costumes

Lvivshchyna Region — A338

Ivano-Frankivshchyna Region — A339

Hutsulshchyna Region — A340

No. 569: a, Family, rooster. b, Family, pitcher.
No. 570: a, Musicians. b, Dancers at wedding.
No. 571: a, Men, child, lamb. b, Family, cradle.

2004, Dec. 10 ***Perf. 13¼***

569 A338 60k Horiz. pair, #a-b .70 .70
570 A339 60k Horiz. pair, #a-b .70 .70
571 A340 60k Horiz. pair, #a-b .70 .70
c. Miniature sheet, #569-571, perf. 11½ 2.10 2.10

Poppy — A341

2005, Jan. 14 Litho. ***Perf. 13¾***

Date Imprint

572 A341 1h multi, "2005" 1.10 1.10
a. Perf. 11½, dated "2006" 2.75 2.75
b. As #572, dated "2006" 1.10 1.10

No. 572b issued 5/23/06.
No. 572a issued 10/9/06. No. 572a was issued only in No. F2b.

November - December 2004 Protests Against Rigged Elections A342

2005, Jan. 23 ***Perf. 11½***

573 A342 45k multi .45 .45

Printed in sheets of 7 + label.

Famous Ukrainians Type of 2004

Design: No. 574, Pavlo Virskyi (1905-75), choreographer. No. 575, Volodymyr Vynnychenko (1880-1951), writer and statesman.

2005 Litho. ***Perf. 14x14¼***

574 A314 45k multi .45 .45
575 A314 45k multi .45 .45

Issued. No. 574, 2/4; No. 575, 7/15.

Miniature Sheet

Moths A343

No. 576: a, 45k, Acherontia atropos. b, 75k, Catocala sponsa. c, 80k, Staurophora celsia. d, 2.61h, Marumba quercus. e, 3.52h,Saturnia pyri.

2005, Feb. 11 ***Perf. 11½***

576 A343 Sheet of 5, #a-e 5.00 5.00

Regional and Administrative Areas

Vinnytska Oblast A344

Sevastopol City A345

Ivano-Frankivska Oblast — A346

Zhitomyrska Oblast A347

2005 ***Perf. 13¾x14½***

577 A344 45k multi .45 .45
578 A345 45k multi .45 .45
579 A346 45k multi .45 .45
580 A347 70k multi .55 .55
Nos. 577-580 (4) 1.90 1.90

Issued: No. 577, 2/23; No. 578, 6/11; No. 579, 7/16; 70k, 9/10.

Paintings by Ivan Aivazovskyi — A348

No. 581: a, Sea — Koktebel, 1853. b, Towers on the Rock Near the Bosporus, 1859.

2005, Mar. 4 Litho. ***Perf. 14x14¼***

581 A348 Horiz. pair, #a-b, + central label .90 .90
a.-b. 45k Either single .45 .45

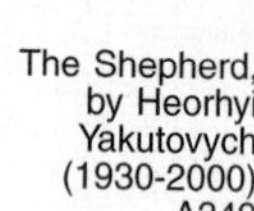

The Shepherd, by Heorhyi Yakutovych (1930-2000) A349

Litho. & Engr.

2005, Mar. 26 ***Perf. 11½***

582 A349 3.52h silver & gray blue 2.10 2.10

Cosmos-1 Satellite — A350

Zenit-2 Rocket — A351

Designs: No. 585, Dnepr rocket. No. 586, Cyclone-3 rocket.

2005, Apr. 12 Litho. ***Perf. 14x14¼***

583 A350 45k shown .40 .40
584 A351 45k shown .40 .40
585 A351 45k multi .40 .40
586 A351 45k multi .40 .40
Nos. 583-586 (4) 1.60 1.60

A352

End of World War II, 60th Anniv. A353

2005 ***Perf. 14x14¼***

587 A352 45k multi .55 .55

Souvenir Sheet

Perf. 11½

588 A353 80k multi .80 .80

Issued: 45k, 4/22; 80k, 5/7. No. 587 issued in sheets of 8 + central label.

Ninth Intl. Philatelic Exhibition, Kyiv A354

2005, May 17 ***Perf. 13¾x14½***

589 A354 45k multi .45 .45

Painting Type of 2002

Paintings of Kyiv: 45k, New Street, by Serhyi Shyshko, 1966. 75k, Park in Winter, by Shyshko, 1960. 80k, Sacred Sophia, by Yuryi Khymych, 1965. 1h, Khreshchatyk Boulevard, by Khymych, 1967, vert.

Perf. 13¾x14½, 14½x13¾

2005, May 18

590-593 A273 Set of 4 2.75 2.75

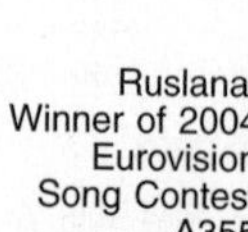

Ruslana, Winner of 2004 Eurovision Song Contest A355

Logo for 2005 Eurovision Song Contest — A356

2005, May 19 ***Perf. 11½***

594 A355 45k multi .45 .45
595 A356 2.50h multi 1.50 1.50

Europa A357

Nos. 596 and 597: a, 2.61h, Bowl of borscht, beets, onions, garlic, tomatoes, pepper, beans, lard, parsley and dill. b, 3.52h, Lidded tureen, cabbage, carrots, onion, garlic, pepper.

2005, May 20 ***Perf. 11½***

Stamp Size: 45x32mm

596 A357 Horiz. pair, #a-b 4.25 4.25

Booklet Stamps

Stamp Size: 40x27mm

Perf. 14x14¼

597 A357 Horiz. pair, #a-b 6.00 6.00
c. Booklet pane, 2 #597 12.00 —
Complete booklet, #597c 12.00

Complete booklet sold for 19.38h.

Development of the Cyrillic Alphabet — A358

Litho. & Embossed

2005, May 21 ***Perf. 14¼x14***

598 A358 45k multi .50 .50

Souvenir Sheet

Flora and Fauna in Karadazkyi Nature Reserve — A359

No. 599: a, 45k, Falco cherrug (33x40mm). b, 70k, Ascalaphus macaronius (29x35mm). c, 2.50h, Tursiops truncatus ponticus (33x33mm). d, 3.50h, Martes foina (49x33mm).

2005, July 28 Litho. ***Perf. 11½***

599 A359 Sheet of 4, #a-d 3.50 3.50

World Summit on the Information Society, Tunis — A360

2005, Aug. 12 ***Perf. 14x14¼***

600 A360 2.50h multi 1.40 1.40

Series Ov Locomotive A361

Series C Locomotive A362

Series Shch Locomotive A363

Series Ye Locomotive A364

2005, Aug. 31

601 A361 70k multi .55 .55
602 A362 70k multi .55 .55
603 A363 70k multi .55 .55
604 A364 70k multi .55 .55
Nos. 601-604 (4) 2.20 2.20

Nos. 601-604 were each printed in sheets of 11 + label.

Sumy, 350th Anniv. A365

2005, Sept. 2

605 A365 45k multi .45 .45

Nasturtium A366

Water Lily A367

Violets A368

Wild Rose A369

2005 Date imprint *Perf. 13¾*

606 A366 25k multi .65 .65
a. Perf. 11½, dated "2006" 1.10 1.10
b. As #606, dated "2006" 1.50 1.50
607 A367 70k multi 1.35 1.35
a. Perf. 11½, dated "2006" 1.50 1.50
b. As #607, dated "2006" 1.35 1.35
608 A368 (1.53h) multi 1.50 1.50
a. Perf. 11½, dated "2006" 4.00 4.00
b. As #608, dated "2006" 1.50 1.50
609 A369 (2.55h) multi 2.50 2.50
a. Perf. 11½, dated "2006" 5.00 5.00
b. As #609, dated "2006" 2.50 2.50
Nos. 606-609 (4) 6.00 6.00

Issued: No. 606, 9/8/05; No. 606b, 2/7/06. No. 607, 9/12/05; No. 607b, 2/7/06. No. 608, 12/16/05; No. 608b, 9/28/06. No. 609, 11/25/05; No. 609a, 6/5/06.

Nos. 606a-609a issued 10/9/06. Nos. 606a-609a were issued only in No. F2b.

Horses A370

No. 610: a, Novoolexandrivskyi heavy draft horse (brown horse facing left with four-line inscription). b, Orlov-Rostopchin (white horse). c, Ukrainian riding horse (brown horse facing left with three-line inscription). d, Thoroughbred (brown horse facing right).

2005, Sept. 15 *Perf. 11½*

610 A370 70k Block of 4, #a-d 1.60 1.60

"Safety - Green Light" — A371

"Give a Helping Hand" — A372

"No to Drugs" — A373

2005, Oct. 14 *Perf. 14x14¼*

611 Horiz. strip of 3 1.40 1.40
a. A371 70k multi .45 .45
b. A372 70k multi .45 .45
c. A373 70k multi .45 .45

Military History A374

No. 612: a, Commander Bobrok Volnyets at Battle of Kulikovo, 1380. b, Artillerymen and riflemen, 14th-15th cent. c, Knight Ivanko Sushyk at Grunwald, 1410. d, Prince Konstiantyn Ostrozkyi at Orsha, 1512.

2005, Oct. 22

612 A374 70k Block of 4, #a-d 1.60 1.60

Famous Ukrainians Type of 2004

Designs: No. 613, Dmytro Yiavornytskyi (1855-1940), historian. No. 614, Oleg Antonov (1906-84), aircraft designer.

2005-06 **Litho.**

613 A314 70k multi .50 .50
614 A314 70k multi .50 .50

Issued: No. 613, 11/7; No. 614, 2/7/06.

Christmas — A375

Litho. With Foil Application

2005, Nov. 11 *Perf. 13¼*

615 A375 70k multi .50 .50

New Year's Day — A376

2005, Nov. 11 **Litho.**

616 A376 70k multi .50 .50

St. Barbara's Church, Vienna, Austria A377

2005, Dec. 9 *Perf. 14¼x14*

617 A377 75k multi + label .65 .65

Lviv National Museum, Cent. A378

No. 618: a, Archangel Michael, by unknown artist (denomination at right). b, Dalmatynka, by Teofil Kopystynskyi (denomination at left).

2005, Dec. 13 **Litho.**

618 A378 70k Horiz. pair, #a-b, + central label 1.00 1.00

Regional Costumes

Zhytomyrshchyna Region — A379

Rivnenshchyna Region — A380

Volyn Region A381

No. 619: a, Family and dog, St. Basil's Day. b, Man and woman, St. Zosyma's Day.

No. 620: a, People with animals, St. George's Day. b, Men, women and musician, Sts. Peter and Paul's Day.

No. 621: a, People with buckets, Annunciation Day. b, Family and cat, St. Nicholas's Day.

2005, Dec. 20 *Perf. 13¼*

619 A379 70k Horiz. pair, #a-b .90 .90
620 A380 70k Horiz. pair, #a-b .90 .90
621 A381 70k Horiz. pair, #a-b .90 .90
c. Miniature sheet, #619-621, perf. 11½ 4.00 4.00

Europa Stamps, 50th Anniv. — A382

Designs: Nos. 622a, 623a, 1.30h, 50th anniversary emblem. Nos. 622a, 622b, 2.50h, CEPT emblem.

2006, Jan. 5 **Litho.** *Perf. 13¼*

With Names of Designers at Right of Stamps

622 A382 Vert. pair, #a-b 2.25 2.25

Souvenir Sheet

Without Names of Designers at Right of Stamps

Perf. 11½

623 A382 Sheet of 2, #a-b 2.25 2.25

Art by Hryhoryi Narbut (1886-1920) A383

Litho. & Engr.

2006, Mar. 10 *Perf. 11½*

624 A383 3.33h multi 2.10 2.10

Printed in sheets of 11 + label.

Miniature Sheet

Traditional Women's Headdresses — A384

No. 625: a, Drawing of woman wearing fur hat. b, Woman, facing left, wearing black hat with brown ribbon. c, Drawing of woman facing left, wearing undecorated head covering. d, Woman wearing large floral head covering. e, Woman wearing red kerchief. f, Woman wearing small floral head covering. g, Woman wearing white kerchief with red dots. h, Woman wearing brown kerchief with knot in front. i, Drawing of woman, facing right, wearing undecorated head covering. j, Woman wearing floral headcovering with thin black edge. k, Woman wearing kerchief with floral pattern. l, Woman wearing small floral head covering with ribbon.

2006, Mar. 30 **Litho.** *Perf. 11½*

625 A384 70k Sheet of 12, #a-l 5.50 5.50

Coronas-1 Satellite — A385

Designs: No. 627, Welding in space. No. 628, International observation of Halley's Comet.

2006, Apr. 12 *Perf. 14x14¼*

Color of Panel Denomination Panel

626 A385 85k gray .70 .70
627 A385 85k red brown .70 .70
628 A385 85k dull brown .70 .70
Nos. 626-628 (3) 2.10 2.10

Europa A386

Designs: Nos. 629a, 630a, 2.50h, Earth and Saturn. Nos. 629b, 630b, 3.50h, Earth and Jupiter.

2006, Apr. 28 *Perf. 11½*

Top Cyrillic Inscription in Black

629 A386 Horiz. pair, #a-b 4.25 4.25

Top Cyrillic Inscription in Red

630 A386 Booklet pane of 2, #a-b + 2 labels 8.00 8.00
Complete booklet, #630 8.00

Nos. 630a-630b are 52x26mm. No. 630 sold for 11.52h.

2006 World Cup Soccer Championships, Germany — A387

Designs: 2.50k, Ukrainian soccer players. 3.50k, Soccer ball.

2006, May 4

631-632 A387 Set of 2 4.50 4.50

Georgia, Ukraine, Azerbaijan and Moldova Summit, Kiev — A388

2006, May 23 *Perf. 14x14¼*

633 A388 70k multi .65 .65

Paintings of Kiev A389

Designs: No. 634, 70k, Zaborovskyi Gate, by Boris Tulin, 1987 (shown). No. 635, 70k, Olha Basystiuk Sings, by Tulin, 1987. No. 636, 70k, Kiev-Peherska Lavra, by Oleksandr Hubarev, 1990. No. 637, 70k, Andrew's Alley, by Hubarev, 1983.

2006, May 24 *Perf. 13¾x14¼*

634-637 A389 Set of 4 2.25 2.25

Souvenir Sheet

Lviv, 750th Anniv. A390

No. 638 — View of Lviv, 1618 and: a, 70k, Coat of arms (38x31mm). b, 2.50h, Coin (69x31mm).

2006, June 16 *Perf. 11½*

638 A390 Sheet of 2, #a-b 2.10 2.10

Miniature Sheet

Fauna of Shatskyi National Park A391

No. 639: a, Lanius excubitor (28x40mm). b, Lynx lynx (33x35mm). c, Anguilla anguilla

(41x29mm). d, Bufo calamita (28x29mm). e, Mustela erminea (45x29mm).

2006, July 14
639 A391 70k Sheet of 5, #a-e 3.00 3.00

Miniature Sheet

Cossack Leaders A392

No. 640: a, Ivan Bohun (denomination at UL). b, Ivan Honta (denomination at UR). c, Ivan Pidkova (denomination at LL). d, Ivan Sirko (denomination at LR).

Litho. & Engr. With Foil Application
2006, Aug. 18
640 A392 3.50h Sheet of 4, #a-d 8.50 8.50

Famous Ukrainians Type of 2004

Design: Ivan Franko (1856-1916), writer.

2006, Aug. 27 Litho. *Perf. 14x14¼*
641 A314 70k multi .65 .65

Series L Locomotive A393

Series SO Locomotive A394

Series YS Locomotive A395

Series FD Locomotive A396

2006, Sept. 15

642	A393 70k multi		.60	.60
643	A394 70k multi		.60	.60
644	A395 70k multi		.60	.60
645	A396 70k multi		.60	.60
	Nos. 642-645 (4)		2.40	2.40

Each stamp printed in sheets of 11 + label.

Tenth Natl. Philatelic Exhibition, Lviv A397

2006, Oct. 6 Litho. & Embossed
646 A397 70k multi .65 .65

Miltary History A398

No. 647: a, Cossack-siroma, 16th-17th cent. b, Naval campaigns of 16th-18th cents. c, Khmelnychna national liberation movement (soldiers aiming guns), 17th cent. d, Haidamachnya national liberation movement (soldier with sword), 17th cent.

2006, Nov. 3 Litho. *Perf. 14x14¼*
647 A398 70k Block of 4, #a-d 2.40 2.40

Horses in Sports A399

No. 648: a, Dressage. b, Horse racing. c, Harness racing. d, Show jumping.

2006, Nov. 17 *Perf. 11½*
648 A399 70k Block of 4, #a-d 2.60 2.60

Printed in sheets containing two each of Nos. 648a-648d.

St. Nicholas's Day — A400

No. 649: a, Children following angel. b, Angel and St. Nicholas.

Litho. With Foil Application
2006, Nov. 17 *Perf. 13¼*
649 A400 70k Horiz. pair, #a-b 1.00 1.00

Christmas — A401

2006, Nov. 24 *Perf. 14¼x14*
650 A401 70k multi .65 .65

Lviv, 750th Anniv. — A402

Litho. & Engr.
2006, Dec. 1 *Perf. 14x13¾*
651 A402 3.50h multi 2.75 2.75

Printed in sheets of 10 + 5 labels. See Austria No. 2075.

Regional Costumes

Zaporizhzha Region — A403

Khersonshchyna Region — A404

Odeshchyna Region — A405

No. 652: a, People with flags, candle, and swords, St. Michael's Day. b, People and horses, Assumption Day.

No. 653: a, Women and spinning wheel, St. Catherine's Day. b, Men and oxen, St. Elias's Day.

No. 654: a, People and pig, St. Barbara and St. Sava's Day. b, People and fish, St. Boris and St. Hlib's Day.

2006, Dec. 15 Litho. *Perf. 13¼*

652	A403 70k Horiz. pair, #a-b		.75	.75
653	A404 70k Horiz. pair, #a-b		.75	.75
654	A405 70k Horiz. pair, #a-b		.75	.75
c.	Miniature sheet, #652-654, perf. 11½		2.25	2.25

Famous Ukrainians Type of 2004

Designs: No. 655, 70k, Metropolitan Ivan Ohienko (1882-1972). No. 656, 70k, Igor Stravinsky (1882-1971), composer.

2007 Litho. *Perf. 14x14¼*
655-656 A314 Set of 2 1.25 1.25

Issued: No. 655, 1/12; No. 656, 6/8.

Conjoined Pots A406

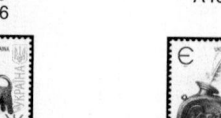

Candelabra A407

Clay Bull A408

Inkwell A409

Mug A410

Rag Doll A411

Folk decorative art: 3k, Horse figurine. 5k, Whistle. 10k, Jug. 50k, Spinning wheel. 60k, Demijohn. 70k, Circular water container. 85k, Ladle. 1h, Decorated cup with handle. 2h, Pitcher with handle.

2007 Litho. *Perf. 13¾*
Date Imprint

657	A406 1k multi, "2007"	.30	.30
a.	Imprint "2007-II"	.30	.30
658	A406 3k multi, "2007"	.30	.30
a.	Imprint "2007-II"	.30	.30
b.	Imprint "2008"	.50	.50
659	A406 5k multi, "2007"	.30	.30
a.	Imprint "2007-II"	.30	.30
b.	Imprint "2008"	.30	.30
c.	Imprint "2008-II"	.50	.50
d.	Imprint "2008-III"	.50	.50
e.	Imprint "2010"	.40	.40
f.	Imprint "2010-II"	1.75	1.75
g.	Imprint "2011"	1.75	1.75
660	A406 10k multi, "2007"	.30	.30
a.	Imprint "2007-II"	.30	.30
b.	Imprint "2008"	.50	.50
c.	Imprint "2008-II"	.50	.50
d.	Imprint "2008-III"	.50	.50
e.	Imprint "2008-IV"	.50	.50
f.	Imprint "2009"	.30	.30
g.	Imprint "2010"	.60	.60
h.	Imprint "2010-II"	.60	.60
i.	Imprint "2011"	.70	.70
j.	Imprint "2011-II"	.70	.70
661	A406 50k multi, "2007"	.40	.40
a.	Imprint "2007-II"	.40	.40
b.	Imprint "2008"	.50	.50
c.	Dated "2009"	.50	.50
d.	Imprint "2009-II"	.50	.50
e.	Imprint "2010"	.75	.75
f.	Imprint "2010-II"	.75	.75
g.	Imprint "2011"	.50	.50
h.	Imprint "2011-II"	.50	.50
i.	Imprint "2012"	.25	.25
662	A406 60k multi, "2007"	.50	.50
a.	Imprint "2008"	.50	.50
b.	Imprint "2008-II"	.75	.75
663	A406 70k multi, "2007"	.50	.50
a.	Imprint "2007-II"	.50	.50
b.	Imprint "2008"	.75	.75
c.	Imprint "2008-II"	.75	.75
d.	Imprint "2008-III"	.75	.75
664	A406 85k multi, "2007"	.75	.75
a.	Imprint "2007-II"	.75	.75
b.	Imprint "2008"	.90	.90
665	A406 1h multi, "2007"	.75	.75
a.	Imprint "2007-II"	.75	.75
b.	Imprint "2008"	.80	.80
c.	Imprint "2008-II"	.80	.80
d.	Imprint "2009"	.80	.80
e.	Imprint "2009-II"	.80	.80
f.	Imprint "2010"	.85	.85
g.	Imprint "2010-II"	.85	.85
h.	Imprint "2011"	.60	.60
i.	Imprint "2011-II"	.60	.60
666	A407 (1.52h) multi, "2007"	.80	.80
a.	Imprint "2007-II"	.80	.80
b.	Imprint "2008"	1.00	1.00
c.	Imprint "2010"	1.00	1.00
d.	Imprint "2011"	1.00	1.00
667	A406 2h multi, "2007"	1.40	1.40
a.	Imprint "2007-II"	1.40	1.40
b.	Imprint "2008"	1.40	1.40
c.	Imprint "2008-II"	2.00	2.00
d.	Dated "2009"	1.40	1.40
e.	Imprint "2009-II"	1.50	1.50
f.	Imprint "2010"	1.50	1.50
g.	Imprint "2010-II"	1.50	1.50
h.	Imprint "2010-III"	1.50	1.50
i.	Imprint "2011"	1.00	1.00
j.	Imprint "2011-II"	1.00	1.00
k.	Imprint "2011-III"	.60	.60
l.	Imprint "2012"	.60	.60
668	A408 (2.48h) multi, "2007"	1.25	1.25
a.	Imprint "2007-II"	1.25	1.25
b.	Imprint "2008"	1.25	1.25
669	A409 (3.33h) multi, "2007"	1.75	1.75
a.	Imprint "2007-II"	1.75	1.75
b.	Imprint "2008"	1.75	1.75
670	A410 (3.79h) multi, "2007"	2.00	2.00
a.	Imprint "2008"	2.00	2.00
b.	Imprint "2011"	2.00	2.00
671	A411 (10.10h) multi, "2007"	5.25	5.25
a.	Imprint "2007-II"	5.25	5.25
b.	Imprint "2008"	5.25	5.25
c.	Imprint "2011"	5.25	5.25
	Nos. 657-671 (15)	16.55	16.55

Issued: No. 657, 4/14/07, No. 657a, 12/07. No. 658, 4/14/07; No. 658a,9/6/07; No. 658b, 2008. No. 659, 3/16/07; No. 659a, 9/8/07; No. 659b, 2/08; No. 659c, 9/27/08; No. 659d, 10/27/08; No. 659e, 3/24/10; No. 659f, 8/13/10; No. 659g, 6/7/11. No. 660, 4/14/07; No. 660a, 11/16/07; No. 660b, 4/18/08; No. 660c, 5/30/08; No. 660d, 9/5/08; No. 660e, 2008; No. 660f, 9/7/09; No. 660g, 2/8/10; No. 660h, 8/13/10; Nos. 660i-660j, 6/7/11. No. 661, 1/26/07; No. 661a, 5/07; No. 661b, 8/22/08; No. 661c, 6/10/09; No. 661d, 9/7/09; No. 661e, 2/8/10; No. 661f, 8/13/10; Nos. 661g-661h, 6/7/11; No. 661i, 2012. No. 662, 1/26/07; No. 662a, 6/18/08; No. 662b, 8/22/08. No. 663, 1/26/07; No. 663a, 9/6/07; No. 663b, 4/11/08; No. 663c, 5/30/08; No. 663d, 7/28/08. No. 664, 1/26/07; No. 664a, 8/13/07; No. 664b, 8/22/08. No. 665, 4/6/07; No. 665a, 12/07; No. 665b, 7/26/08; No. 665c, 2008; Nos. 665d, 665e, 2009; No. 665f, 2/8/10; No. 665g, 8/13/10; Nos. 665h-665i, 6/7/11. No. 666, 4/6/07; No. 666a, 10/24/07; No. 666b, 10/21/08; No. 666c, 8/13/10; No. 666d, 6/7/11. No. 667, 3/16/07; No. 667a, 10/24/07; Nos. 667b, 667c, 9/27/08; No. 667d, 7/16/09; No. 667e, 9/7/09; No. 667f, 2/8/10; No. 667g, 3/24/10; No. 667h, 2010; Nos. 667i-667k, 6/7/11, No. 667l, 2012. No. 668, 4/6/07; No. 668a, 11/16/07; No. 668b, 10/17/08. No. 669, 4/14/07; No. 669a, 12/07; No. 669b, 11/08. No. 670, 3/16/07: No. 670a, 11/8/08; No. 670b, 6/7/11. NO. 671, 3/16/07; No. 671a, 11/16/07; No. 671b, 11/8/08; No. 671c, 6/7/11.

For surcharges, see Nos. 803-804.
See Nos. 720, 764, 817-820.

St. Michael's Cathedral, Adelaide, Australia — A412

2007, Feb. 9 *Perf. 13¼*
672 A412 3.35k multi + label 1.75 1.75

Souvenir Sheet

Taras Shevchenko (1814-61), Poet — A413

No. 673: a, 2.50h, Drawing of Shevchenko's house, poem (66x40mm). b, 3.35k, Shevchenko (36x40mm).

Litho. With Foil Application
2007, Feb. 23 *Perf. 11½*
673 A413 Sheet of 2, #a-b 3.25 3.25

Wedding Rings A414

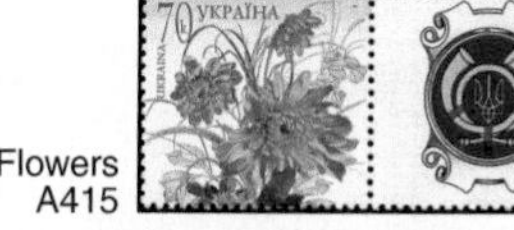

Flowers
A415

Pechersk Lavra Monastery, Kiev — A416

Oranta Monument — A417

2007, Mar. 1 Litho. *Perf. 11½*

674 A414 70k multi + label		2.00	2.00
675 A415 70k multi + label		2.00	2.00
676 A416 70k multi + label		2.00	2.00
677 A417 70k multi + label		2.00	2.00
	Nos. 674-677 (4)	8.00	8.00

Nos. 674-676 were printed in sheets of 22 stamps + 22 labels that could be personalized, and sold for 60.60h per sheet. No. 677 was printed in sheets of 18 stamps + 18 labels that could be personalized, and sold for 54.60h per sheet. Labels shown are generic.

Space Exploration
A418

Designs: No. 678, 70k, Leonid Kadeniuck, first Ukrainian cosmonaut. No. 679, 70k, Sea Launch rocket lifting off.

2007, Apr. 12 *Perf. 14x14¼*

678-679 A418 Set of 2 .80 .80

Europa
A419

Nos. 680 and 681: a, 2.50h, Scout emblem, neckerchief and "100." b, 3.35h, Scouts.

2007, Apr. 28 *Perf. 14x14¼*

Stamp Size: 40x28mm

680 A419 Horiz. pair, #a-b 3.50 3.50

Stamp Size: 45x33mm

Perf. 11½

681 A419 Booklet pane of 2, #a-b 7.50 —
Complete booklet, #681 7.50

Scouting, cent. No. 681 sold for 11.52h.

Paintings of Kiev
A420

Designs: No. 682, 70k, Sunny Day, Yaroslaviv Val, by Vitalii Petrovskyi, 1997. No. 683, 70k, Street of Recollections, by Tetiana Kuhai, 2004 (red panel), vert. No. 684, 70k, Kiev Walk, by Yulia Kuznietsova, 2004 (lilac panel), vert. No. 685, 70k, Snowing, by Maria Lashkevych, 2007.

Perf. 13¾x14½, 14½x13¾

2007, May 18

682-685 A420 Set of 4 2.25 2.25

Miniature Sheets

Dogs
A421

Cats
A422

No. 686: a, Pug. b, Irish setter. c, Alaskan malamute. d, Basset hound. e, Bull mastiff. f, American cocker spaniel.

No. 687: a, American shorthair. b, Sphynx. c, Scottish fold. d, Snowshoe. e, Russian blue. f, Somali.

2007, June 15 *Perf. 11½*

686 A421 70k Sheet of 6, #a-f 2.75 2.75
687 A422 70k Sheet of 6, #a-f 2.75 2.75

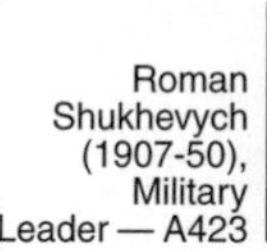

Roman Shukhevych (1907-50), Military Leader — A423

2007, June 29 *Perf. 14x14¼*

688 A423 70k multi .55 .55

TE1 Diesel Locomotive
A424

TE2 Diesel Locomotive
A425

TE3 Diesel Locomotive
A426

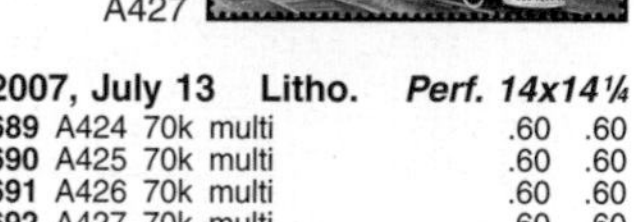

TE7 Diesel Locomotive
A427

2007, July 13 Litho. *Perf. 14x14¼*

689 A424 70k multi		.60	.60
690 A425 70k multi		.60	.60
691 A426 70k multi		.60	.60
692 A427 70k multi		.60	.60
	Nos. 689-692 (4)	2.40	2.40

Each stamp printed in sheets of 11 + label.

Miniature Sheet

Wedding Headdresses — A428

No. 693: a, Woman facing right wearing floral headdress with gray ribbon behind head. b, Woman facing left wearing gathered fabric headdress with broad red headband. c, Woman facing left wearing floral headdress with broad red ribbon at back. d, Woman facing right wearing ribboned floral headdress. e, Woman facing forward wearing tall red headdress with black and white spots. f, Woman wearing fabric headdress. g, Woman wearing headdress with wide floral ring above smaller floral rings. h, Man wearing hat and jacket with high collar. i, Woman facing left wearing tall floral headdress covering ear. j, Man wearing tall hat and collarless shirt with decorated front. k, Woman wearing headdress with one floral ring above broad red headband. l, Man wearing hat with chinstrap.

2007, Aug 23 Litho. *Perf. 11½*

693 A428 70k Sheet of 12, #a-l 5.75 5.75

Dnieper River Fish Preservation — A429

No. 694: a, Acipenser gueldenstaedtii. b, Zingel zingel.

2007, Sept. 6

694	Horiz. pair + central label	3.00	3.00
a.	A429 1.50h multi	1.25	1.25
b.	A429 2.50h multi	1.75	1.75

See Moldova No. 569.

Pereyaslav Khmelnytskyi, 1100th Anniv. — A430

2007, Sept. 16 *Perf. 14x14¼*

695 A430 70k multi .60 .60

Worldwide Fund for Nature (WWF) — A431

No. 696 — Pelecanus onocrotalus: a, 70k, In flight. b, 1.50h, In water. c, 2.50h, Two birds. d, 3.50h, One bird standing.

2007, Sept. 20 *Perf. 14x14¼*

696	A431 Block of 4, #a-d	4.25	4.25
e.	Miniature sheet, 4 each #696a-696d, perf. 11½, + 4 labels	17.00	17.00

Souvenir Sheet

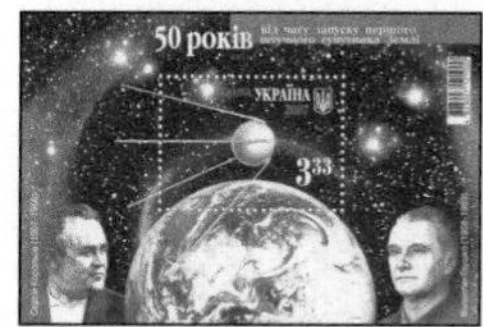

Launch of Sputnik 1, 50th Anniv. — A432

2007, Oct. 4 *Perf. 11½*

697 A432 3.33h multi 2.25 2.25

Miniature Sheets

A433

Peasant Houses
A434

No. 698 — House from: a, Podillya, with ox cart in front. b, Kiev, with couple, cat and pumpkins in front. c, Lemkivschyna, with horse and ducks in front. d, Hutsulschyna, with horse in front. e, Volyn, with wheat sheaves in front. f, Slobozhanschyna, with sunflowers at sides of house.

No. 699 — House from: a, Polissya, with basket weavers and horse in front. b, Khorolschyna, with children rolling hoop in front. c, Bukovyna, with couple in doorway. d, Boikivschyna, with dog and people carrying bundles of sticks in front. e, Poltava, people threshing grain in front. f, Lower Dnieper area, with man with fishing net in front.

2007, Oct. 24

698 A433 70k Sheet of 6, #a-f 2.75 2.75
699 A434 70k Sheet of 6, #a-f 2.75 2.75

Christmas and New Year's Day — A435

No. 700: a, Angels in sled. b, Angels with Christmas tree.

Litho. With Foil Application

2007, Nov. 16 *Perf. 13½*

700 A435 70k Horiz. pair, #a-b .80 .80

Christmas and New Year's Day — A436

2007, Nov. 23 *Perf. 11½*

701 A436 1h multi + label 2.75 2.75

Printed in sheets of 18 stamps + 18 labels that could be personalized.

2012 European Soccer Championships, Poland and Ukraine — A437

2007, Dec. 22

702 A437 3.33h multi 2.10 2.10

Regional Costumes

Khmelnytska Region — A438

Bukovyna Region — A439

Zakarpatyia Region — A440

No. 703: a, Potter and carolers, Christmas. b, People celebrating St. Simeon's Day, horses.

No. 704: a, Woman holding cross, man, woman, fruit basket, St. Ephrosinia's Day. b, Man holding violin, women and children, Ascension Day.

No. 705: a, Men and blacksmith holding mugs, Kuzma and Demyan Day. b, People near cross and candle, Easter.

2007, Dec. 22 Litho. *Perf. 13¼*

703 A438 70k Horiz. pair, #a-b .75 .75
704 A439 70k Horiz. pair, #a-b .75 .75
705 A440 70k Horiz. pair, #a-b .75 .75
c. Miniature sheet, #703-705, perf. 11½ 2.25 2.25

Aries A441

Taurus A442

Gemini A443

Cancer A444

Leo — A445

Virgo — A446

Libra A447

Scorpio A448

Sagittarius A449

Capricorn A450

Aquarius A451

Pisces A452

2008, Jan. 18 *Perf. 14¼x14*

706 A441 1h multi .80 .80
707 A442 1h multi .80 .80
708 A443 1h multi .80 .80
709 A444 1h multi .80 .80
710 A445 1h multi .80 .80
711 A446 1h multi .80 .80
712 A447 1h multi .80 .80
713 A448 1h multi .80 .80
714 A449 1h multi .80 .80
715 A450 1h multi .80 .80
716 A451 1h multi .80 .80
717 A452 1h multi .80 .80
Nos. 706-717 (12) 9.60 9.60

2008 Summer Olympics, Beijing — A453

No. 718: a, 1h, Archery. b, 1.30h, Fencing. c, 2.47h, Cycling. d, 3.33h, Rowing.

Litho. With Foil Application

2008, Jan. 26 *Perf. 11½*

718 A453 Block of 4, #a-d 4.25 4.25

Roses and Hearts A454

2008, Feb. 6 Litho. *Perf. 11½*

719 A454 1h multi + label 2.00 2.00

Printed in sheets of 22 stamps + 22 labels that could be personalized that sold for 69.90h. Label shown is generic.

Folk Decorative Art Type of 2007

Design: Carved pipe.

2008, Feb. 15 Litho. *Perf. 13¾*

720 A406 30k multi, "2008" .50 .50
a. Imprint "2008-II" .40 .40
b. Imprint "2009" .50 .50
c. Imprint "2009-II" .50 .50
d. Imprint "2010" .75 .75
e. Imprint "2010-II" .90 .90
f. Imprint "2011" .75 .75
g. Imprint "2012" .75 .75

Issued: No. 720a, 7/26/08; No. 720b, 7/16/09; No. 720c, 2009; No. 720d, 2/1/10; No. 720e, 8/13/10. No. 720f, 6/7/11. No. 720g, 2012.

Paintings by Taras Shevchenko (1814-61) — A455

Designs: 1h, Gypsy Fortune Teller. 1.52h, Kateryna. 2.47h, Self-portrait.

Litho. With Foil Application

2008, Feb. 23 *Perf. 11½*

721-723 A455 Set of 3 3.00 3.00

Europa A456

No. 724 — Letter writers with: a, 2.47h, Quill pen. b, 3.33h, Computer.

2008, Mar. 12 Litho. *Perf. 13¼*

724 A456 Horiz. pair, #a-b 3.75 3.75

A booklet containing two 37x30mm perf. 11½ stamps like Nos. 724a-724b sold for 12.84h.

Nicolay Gogol (1809-52), Writer — A457

No. 725: a, 1.52h, Gogol, gun, quill pen and inkwell, pipe. b, 2.47h, Taras Bulba on horseback.

2008, Mar. 21 *Perf. 14x14¼*

725 A457 Pair, #a-b 2.25 2.25

Easter — A458

Litho. With Foil Application

2008, Apr. 11 *Perf. 13¼*

726 A458 1h multi .75 .75

Miniature Sheet

18th and 19th Century Decorative Clocks — A459

No. 727: a, French mantle clock with clock as chariot wheel, 19th cent. (33x33mm). b, Russian mantle clock with nymphs, 19th cent. (33x33mm). c, French mantle clock with nude woman and nymphs on goats, 19th cent. (33x33mm). d, French clock by Charles Baltazar with blue green frame and nymph on top, 18th cent. (33x45mm). e, French clock with woman with shield on top, 18th cent. (33x45mm). f, German clock with woman trumpeter on top, 18th cent. (33x45mm). g, English clock with landscape above face, 18th cent. (33x45mm). h, Austrian clock with pillars at sides, 19th cent. (33x45mm). i, French mantle clock with birds at top, 19th cent. (33x45mm).

Litho. With Foil Application

2008, Apr. 18 *Perf. 11½*

727 A459 1h Sheet of 9, #a-i 5.25 5.25

Miniature Sheets

Dogs A460

Cats A461

No. 728: a, Smooth-haired dachshund. b, American bulldog. c, Rottweiler. d, Chow chow. e, Schnauzer. f, German shepherd.

No. 729: a, Persian. b, Selkirk Rex. c, Exotic shorthair. d, Burmese. e, Siamese. f, Kuril Island bobtail.

2008, May 16 Litho.

728 A460 1r Sheet of 6, #a-f 3.50 3.50
729 A461 1r Sheet of 6, #a-f 3.50 3.50

Miniature Sheet

Crimean Nature Reserve A462

No. 730: a, Aegypius monachus (31x38mm). b, Cranes and swans (36x31mm). c, Cervus elaphus (47x31mm). d, Silene jailensis and insect (31x31mm).

2008, June 18

730 A462 1h Sheet of 4, #a-d 2.60 2.60

Souvenir Sheets

Ukrainian Postage Stamps, 90th Anniv. A463

No. 731: a, 2.47h, Ukraine #1. b, 3.33h, Ukraine #2.

No. 732: a, 1h, Ukraine #4. b, 2.47h, Ukraine #5. c, 3.33j, Ukraine #3.

2008, July 4

731 A463 Sheet of 2, #a-b, + 2 labels 3.25 3.25
732 A463 Sheet of 3, #a-c, + label 3.75 3.75

Souvenir Sheet

Myhailivskyi Monastery, 900th Anniv. — A464

2008, July 11

733 A464 3.33h multi 2.00 2.00

TEP10 Diesel Locomotive A465

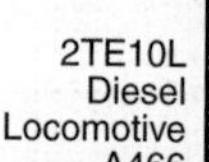

2TE10L Diesel Locomotive A466

M62 Diesel Locomotive A467

TE109 Diesel Locomotive A468

2008, Aug. 8 *Perf. 14x14¼*

734 A465 1h multi .60 .60
735 A466 1h multi .60 .60
736 A467 1h multi .60 .60
737 A468 1h multi .60 .60
Nos. 734-737 (4) 2.40 2.40

Each stamp printed in sheets of 11 + label.

Christmas Carols — A469

Songs of Spring — A470

Songs of the Cossacks A471

Songs of the Chumaks A472

2008, Sept. 5 ***Perf. 13½***

738 A469 1h multi		.60	.60
739 A470 1h multi		.60	.60
740 A471 1h multi		.60	.60
741 A472 1h multi		.60	.60
	Nos. 738-741 (4)	2.40	2.40

Ukrainian musical heritage.

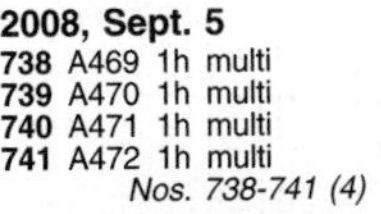
Jewelry A473

No. 742: a, 2.47h, Earring, 12th-13th cent. b, 3.33h, Pendant, 19th cent.

2008, Sept. 18 ***Perf. 11½***

742 A473 Horiz. pair, #a-b, + central label 3.50 3.50

See Azerbaijan No. 885.

Ukrainian and Swedish Military and Political Alliances of 17th and 18th Centuries — A474

Litho. With Foil Application

2008, Oct. 1

743 A474 1h multi .70 .70

A475

Ninth Natl. Philatelic Exhibition, Chernivtsi — A476

2008, Oct. 3 **Litho.** ***Perf. 14x14¼***

744 A475 1h multi .70 .70

Perf. 11½

745 A476 1h multi + label 4.25 4.25

No. 745 was printed in sheets of 10 stamps + 10 labels that could be personalized that sold for 88.38h. Label shown is generic.

Chernivtsi, 600th Anniv. — A477

2008, Oct. 4 ***Perf. 14x14¼***

746 A477 1h multi .70 .70

Sacking of Baturyn, 300th Anniv. — A478

2008, Oct. 24 ***Perf. 14¼x14***

747 A478 1h multi .70 .70

Christmas A479

New Year's Day A480

Litho. With Foil Application

2008, Nov. 21 ***Perf. 11½***

748 A479 1h multi .70 .70
749 A480 1h multi .70 .70

Famous Ukrainians Type of 2004

Designs: No. 750, 1h, Marko Vovchok (1833-1907), writer. No. 751, 1h, Vyachyslav Chornovil (1937-99), politician.

2008 **Litho.** ***Perf. 14x14¼***

750-751 A314 Set of 2 1.40 1.40

Issued: No. 750, 11/28; No. 751, 12/24.

Miniature Sheet

Headdresses — A481

No. 752: a, Woman facing right wearing brown and red headdress and red necklace. b, Woman facing forward wearing white headdress wrapping under chin. c, Woman facing left with headdress with blue-tipped tassels above eyes. d, Woman facing right wearing white headdress. e, Woman facing forward wearing brown, red and green headdress and red necklace. f, Woman facing forward wearing white, red and green headdress, denomination in white. g, Woman wearing headdress and laurel wreath. h, Woman wearing white, gray and red headdress. i, Woman facing left wearing white, red and green headdress with floral pattern over red striped forehead band. j, Man wearing brown hat. k, Woman facing forward wearing headdress with lace trim on forehead. l, Man wearing black and red hat.

2008, Dec. 10 ***Perf. 11½***

752 A481 1h Sheet of 12, #a-l 7.25 7.25

Regional Costumes

Crimea Region A482

Dnipropetrovshchyna Region — A483

Luhanshchyna Region — A484

No. 753: a, People with grapes, Feast of the Transfiguration. b, Baby being christened.

No. 754: a, Bride and groom receiving crowns. b, Three women at Harvest Festival.

No. 755: a, Musicians, Feast of Saints Cyril and Methodius. b, People and church on hill, Feast of the Miracle Worker.

2008, Dec. 25 **Litho.** ***Perf. 13¼***

753 A482 1h Horiz. pair, #a-b		.75	.75
754 A483 1h Horiz. pair, #a-b		.75	.75
755 A484 1h Horiz. pair, #a-b		.75	.75
c.	Miniature sheet, #753-755, perf. 11½	2.25	2.25
	Nos. 753-755 (3)	2.25	2.25

Stephan Bandera (1909-59), Nationalist Leader — A485

2009, Jan. 1

756 A485 1h multi .60 .60

Famous Ukrainians Type of 2004

Designs: 1h, Stepan Rudanskyi (1834-73), poet. 2.20h, Sholem Aleichem (1859-1916), writer.

2009 ***Perf. 14x14¼***

757-758 A314 Set of 2 1.40 1.40

Issued: No. 757, 1/17; No. 758, 2/18.

Souvenir Sheet

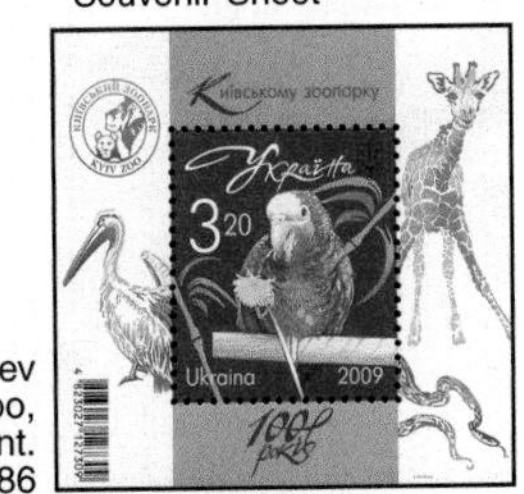
Kiev Zoo, Cent. A486

2009, Feb. 20 **Litho.** ***Perf. 11½***

759 A486 3.20h multi 2.00 2.00

Paintings by Taras Shevchenko — A487

Designs: No. 760, 1.50h, Portrait of I. I. Lyzohub, 1846-47. No. 761, 1.50h, Portrait of E. V. Keikuatova, 1847. No. 762, 1.50h, Village Family, 1843, horiz.

Litho. With Foil Application

2009, Mar. 9

760-762 A487 Set of 3 1.75 1.75

Nos. 760-762 each were printed in sheets of 11 + label.

Preservation of Polar Regions — A488

No. 763: a, Academician Vernadskiy Antarctic Station. b, Iceberg.

2009, Mar. 18

763 A488 3.30h Pair, #a-b 2.75 2.75

Printed in sheets containing 4 of each stamp and a central label.

Folk Art Type of 2007

Designs: Tile depicting Cossack on horse.

2009, Mar. 25 **Litho.** ***Perf. 13¾***

764 A406 1.50h multi		.60	.60
a.	Imprint "2009-II"	.75	.75
b.	Imprint "2010"	.75	.75
c.	Imprint "2010-II"	.75	.75
d.	Imprint "2011"	.75	.75
e.	Imprint "2011-II"	.75	.75
f.	Imprint "2011-III"	.75	.75
g.	Imprint "2009-III"	—	—

Issued: No. 764a, 7/16; Nos. 764b, 764c, 2010. Nos. 764d, 764e, 6/7/11. No. 764f, 6/7/11.

Souvenir Sheet

Nikolai Gogol (1809-52), Writer — A489

No. 765: a, 1.50h, Scene from "Night Before Christmas." b, 2.20h, Gogol.

Litho. With Foil Application

2009, Apr. 1 ***Perf. 11½***

765 A489 Sheet of 2, #a-b 2.00 2.00

Europa A490

No. 766: a, Telescope and star chart. b, Map of solar system, Galileo Galilei and his telescope.

2009, Apr. 17 **Litho.** ***Perf. 13¾x14¼***

Size: 52x25mm

766	Horiz. pair	5.00	5.00
a.	A490 3.75h multi	2.00	2.00
b.	A490 5.25h multi	3.00	3.00

Intl. Year of Astronomy. A booklet containing a pane with a pair of 57x28mm perf. 11½ stamps like Nos. 766a-766b sold for 18.42h. Value, $10.

Architecture in China and Ukraine — A491

No. 767: a, Stork Tower, Shanghai. b, Golden Gate, Kiev.

2009, Aug. 14 ***Perf. 11½***

767	Horiz. pair + central label	4.25	4.25
a.	A491 3.85h multi	1.75	1.75
b.	A491 5.40h multi	2.25	2.25

Miniature Sheet

Gorgany Game Reserve A492

No. 768: a, Tetrao urogallus (40x37mm). b, Pinus cembra (30x47mm). c, Arnica montana (40x40mm). d, Felis silvestris (57x30mm).

2009, Sept. 29

768 A492 1.50h Sheet of 4, #a-d 3.00 3.00

Electric Locomotive VL26 A493

Electric Locomotive VL41 A494

Diesel Locomotive 2TE116 A495

Diesel Locomotive 2TE121 A496

2009, Oct. 22 ***Perf. 13¾x14¼***

769 A493 1.50h multi 1.10 1.10
770 A494 1.50h multi 1.10 1.10
771 A495 1.50h multi 1.10 1.10
772 A496 1.50h multi 1.10 1.10
Nos. 769-772 (4) 4.40 4.40

Miniature Sheet

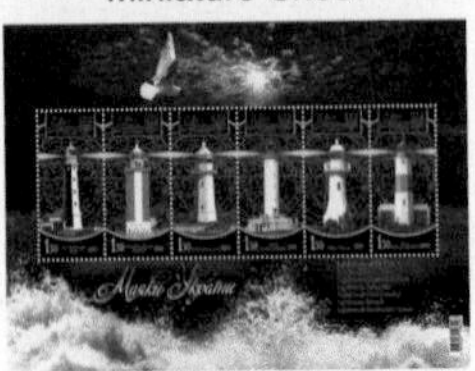

Lighthouses — A497

No. 773: a, Kyz-Aulskyi Lighthouse (blue top). b, Luparivskyi Front Lighthouse (base with vertical red and white stripes). c, Yaltinskyi Lighthouse (white, with hexagonal base). d, Vorontsovskyi Lighthouse (red top). e, Sarych Lighthouse (white, with circular base). f, Berdianskyi Lower Lighthouse (base with horizontal red and white stripes).

2009, Oct. 30 ***Perf. 11½***

773 A497 1.50h Sheet of 6, #a-f 4.75 4.75

Ukrainian Supreme Liberation Council, 65th Anniv. — A498

2009, Nov. 27 ***Perf. 14¼x14***

774 A498 1.50h multi .75 .75

A499 A500

A501 Songs — A502

2009, Nov. 27 ***Perf. 11½***

775 A499 1.50h multi .95 .95
776 A500 1.50h multi .95 .95
777 A501 2h multi 1.15 1.15
778 A502 2h multi 1.15 1.15
Nos. 775-778 (4) 4.20 4.20

Christmas — A503

New Year 2010 A504

Litho. With Foil Application

2009, Dec. 9 ***Perf. 11½***

779 A503 1.50h multi .65 .65

Perf. 13¾x14¼

780 A504 1.50h multi .65 .65

White Sukholimanskiy Grapes and Vineyard — A505

White Muscat Grapes, Sailboat and Vineyard A506

2009, Dec. 15 **Litho.** ***Perf. 11½***

781 A505 1.50h multi .65 .65
782 A506 1.50h multi .65 .65

Narodny Rukh (People's Movement) Party, 20th Anniv. — A507

2009, Dec. 19 ***Perf. 13¾***

783 A507 1.50h multi .65 .65

Miniature Sheet

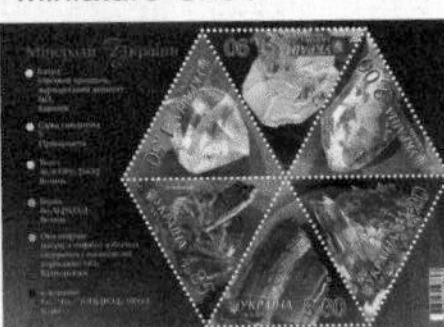

Minerals A508

No. 784: a, 1.50h, Quartz. b, 1.90h, Native sulphur. c, 2h, Topaz. d, 2.20h, Beryl. e, 3.30h, Tiger's eye. f, 4.85h, Kertschenite.

Litho. & Embossed

2009, Dec. 23 ***Perf. 11½***

784 A508 Sheet of 6, #a-h 7.75 7.75

2010 Winter Olympics, Vancouver — A509

No. 785: a, 1.50h, Cross-country skiing. b, 1.50h, Biathlon. c, 2h, Freestyle skiing. d, 2h, Luge.

Litho. With Foil Application

2010, Feb. 5 ***Perf. 11½***

785 A509 Horiz. strip of 4, #a-d 3.50 3.50

Souvenir Sheet

Taras Shevchenko (1814-61), Poet — A510

No. 786: a, 1.50h, Woman at butter churn, poem (66x40mm). b, 2h, Self-portrait (36x40mm).

2010, Mar. 9

786 A510 Sheet of 2, #a-b 1.75 1.75

Souvenir Sheet

Constitution of Pylyp Orlik, 300th Anniv. — A511

2010, Mar. 29 **Litho.**

787 A511 1.50h multi .85 .85

Victory in World War II, 65th Anniv. — A512

2010, Apr. 15 ***Perf. 13¼***

788 A512 1.50h multi .75 .75

Souvenir Sheets

Prepared But Unissued Postage Stamps of Ukrainian National Republic, 90th Anniv. A513

No. 789: a, 1.50h, Unissued 1h stamp. b, 1.50h, Unissued 10h stamp. c, 2h, Unissued 2h stamp. d, 2h, Unissued 15h stamp.

No. 790: a, 1.50h, Unissued 20h stamp. b, 1.50h, Unissued 40h stamp. c, 2h, Unissued 30h stamp. d, 2h, Unissued 50h stamp.

2010, Apr. 22 ***Perf. 11½***

Sheets of 4, #a-d, + Label

789-790 A513 Set of 2 6.50 6.50

Europa A514

Nos. 791 and 792 — Scenes from children's books: a, 2.20h, Mare's Head. b, 3.30h, Gold Shoe.

Litho. With Foil Application

2010, Apr. 30 ***Perf. 13¼***

791 A514 Horiz. pair, #a-b 2.50 2.50

Perf. 11½

792 A514 Booklet pane of 2, #a-b, + central label 5.00 —
Complete booklet, #792 5.00

Nos. 792a and 792b are 43x41mm. No. 792 sold for 10.50h.

Famous Ukrainians Type of 2004

Designs: 1h, Oleksandr Potebnia (1835-91), linguist. 1.50h, Mykola Pyrohov (1810-81), surgeon.

2010 **Litho.** ***Perf. 14x14¼***

793 A314 1h multi .55 .55
794 A314 1.50h multi .75 .75

Issued: No. 793, 9/10; No. 794, 6/2.

Wladimir and Vitali Klitschko, Boxers — A515

2010, June 8

795 A515 1.50h multi .85 .85

Flowers A516

Litho. With Foil Application

2010, Aug. 11 ***Perf. 13¼x13½***

796 A516 (1.50h) multi + label 3.75 3.75

No. 796 was printed in sheets of 10 stamps + 10 labels that could be personalized that sold for 105h. The label shown is generic.

DE1 Electric Locomotive A517

DC3 Electric Locomotive A518

TEM103 Diesel Locomotive A519

TEP150 Diesel Locomotive A520

2010, Sept. 4 **Litho.** ***Perf. 14x14¼***

797 A517 1h multi .45 .45
798 A518 1.50h multi .60 .60
799 A519 2h multi .85 .85
800 A520 2h multi .85 .85
Nos. 797-800 (4) 2.75 2.75

Nos. 797-800 each printed in sheets of 11 + label.

Sculptures by Johann Georg Pinsel — A521

No. 801: a, 1.50h, Mother of God. b, 2h, Angel.

2010, Sept. 8 ***Perf. 13¼***

801 A521 Horiz. pair, #a-b 1.25 1.25

Miniature Sheet

National Technical University Kharkhiv Polytechnical Institute, 125th Anniv. — A522

No. 802: a, 1.50h, O. M. Beketov (1862-1941), architect. b, 1.50h, P. P. Kopniaev (1867-1932), electrical engineer. c, 1.50h, O. M. Liapunov (1857-1918), mathematician. d, 1.50h, E. I. Orlov (1865-1944), chemical engineer. e, 1.50h, M. D. Pylchykov (1857-1908), physicist. f, 1.50h, V. M. Khrushchov (1882-1941), electrical engineer. g, 2h, V. L. Kyrpychov (1845-1913), mechanical engineer. h, 2h, M. M. Beketov (1827-1911), chemist. i, 2h, L. D. Landau (1908-68), theoretical physicist. j, 2m, P. M. Mukhachov (1861-1935), engineer. k, 2h, V. A. Stieklov (1863-1926), mathematician.

2010, Sept. 16 ***Perf. 11½***

802 A522 Sheet of 11, #a-k, + label 7.75 7.75

Nos. 657a, 658a, 658b Surcharged

Methods and Perfs As Before

2010, Oct. 6
803 A406 1.50h on 3k #658a 1.25 1.25
a. A406 1.50h on 3k #658b 1.25 1.25
804 A406 2h on 1k #657a 1.75 1.75

Miniature Sheet

Lighthouses — A523

No. 805: a, 1.50h, Tendrivskyi Lighthouse (with two horizontal black bands). b, 1.50h, Pavlovskyi Fort Lighthouse (hexagonal with brown vertical stripe). c, 1.50h, Khersoneskyi Lighthouse (round white lighthouse with ten windows). d, 2h, Sanzhiiskyi Lighthouse (hexagonal white lighthouse with two windows). e, 2h, Tarkhankutskyi Lighthouse (round white lighthouse with four windows). f, 2h, Illichivskyi Lighthouse (with horizontal red bands).

2010, Oct. 8 Litho. *Perf. 11½*
805 A523 Sheet of 6, #a-f 4.50 4.50

Leaders of Cossack Rebellions — A524

No. 806: a, 1.50h, Kryshtof Kosynskyi (1545-93). b, 2h, Bohdan Mykoshynskyi.

2010, Oct. 15 *Perf. 14x14¼*
806 A524 Block of 2, #a-b, + 2 labels 2.50 2.50

Military History A525

No. 807: a, 1.50h, Danubian Sich (country name in brown). b, 1.50h, Cossack regiments of 1812 (country name in blue). c, 2h, Defense of Sevastopol (country name in blue). d, 2h, Ataman Yakiv Kukharenko on horse (country name in brown).

2010, Oct. 29
807 A525 Block of 4, #a-d 2.75 2.75

Hetman Pavlo Polubotok (1660-1724) A526

Litho. With Foil Application

2010, Oct. 29
808 A526 1.50h multi .65 .65

Miniature Sheet

Kiev Metro, 50th Anniv. A527

No. 809: a, 1.50h, Dorohzhychi Station escalators. b, 1.50h, Train. c, 2h, Lukianivska Station exterior. d, 2h, Tunnel under construction.

2010, Nov. 3 Litho. *Perf. 11½*
809 A527 Sheet of 4, #a-d 2.75 2.75

Cabernet Sauvignon Grapes and Estate A528

2010, Dec. 17
810 A528 1.50h multi .65 .65

Miniature Sheet

Fauna of Sviati Hory National Park A529

No. 811: a, 1h, Zerynthia polyxena (38x30mm). b, 1.50h, Luscinia svecica (38x30mm). c, 1.50h, Lutra lutra (38x37mm). d,2h, Emys orbicularis (38x37mm).

2010, Dec. 28
811 A529 Sheet of 4, #a-d 2.50 2.50

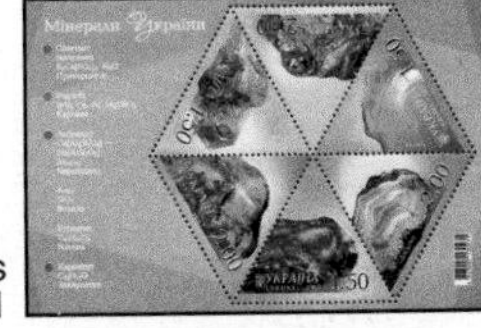

Signing of the Universal Declaration of Human Rights, 60th Anniv. — A530

2010, Dec. 31 *Perf. 14x14¼*
812 A530 1.50h multi .65 .65

Miniature Sheet

Minerals A531

No. 813: a, 1.50h, Syngenite (brown mineral). b, 1.50h, Amber. c, 1.50h, Labradorite (black and red mineral). d, 2h, Carpathite (black arnd brown mineral). e, 2h, Agate (mineral with rings). f, 2h, Rhodonite (red and gray mineral).

Litho. & Embossed

2010, Dec. 31 *Perf. 11½*
813 A531 Sheet of 6, #a-f 4.00 4.00

First Man in Space, 50th Anniv. A532

2011, Apr. 12 Litho. *Perf. 14x14¼*
814 A532 6h multi 2.25 2.25

Georgy Beregovoi (1921-95), Cosmonaut — A533

2011, Apr. 16 *Perf. 14¼x14*
815 A533 2.20h multi .75 .75

Kazashka Katya, Painting by Taras Shevchenko (1814-61) — A534

Litho. With Foil Application

2011, May 21 *Perf. 11½*
816 A534 1.50h multi .60 .60

Folk Decorative Art Type of 2007

Designs: 1.90h, Tobacco pouch. 2.20h, Powder flask. 6h, Bandura. 7h, Bowl with lid.

2011 Litho. *Perf. 13¾*
817 A406 1.90h multi .75 .75
a. Imprint "2011-II" .50 .50
818 A406 2.20h multi .85 .85
a. Imprint "2011-II" .55 .55
819 A406 6h multi 2.40 2.40
820 A406 7h multi 2.75 2.75
Nos. 817-820 (4) 6.75 6.75

Issued: Nos. 817-820, 6/7. Nos. 817a, 818a, 6/7.

Leaders of Cossack Rebellions — A535

No. 821: a, 1.50h, Hryhorii Loboda. b, 2h, Severyn Nalyvaiko.

2011, June 9 *Perf. 14x14¼*
821 A535 Block of 2, #a-b, + 2 labels 1.40 1.40

Ukrainian Constitution, 15th Anniv. — A536

Litho. & Embossed With Foil Application

2011, June 17 *Perf. 11½*
822 A536 6h multi 2.25 2.25

Miniature Sheet

Farmhouse and Animals — A537

No. 823: a, 1.50h, Cat. b, 1.50h, Birds. c, 1.50h, Pig. d, 2h, Cow. e, 2h, Dog.

2011, June 25 Litho.
823 A537 Sheet of 5, #a-e 3.25 3.25

Personalized Stamp — A538

Litho. With Foil Application

2011, June 25 *Perf. 11½*
824 A538 (1.50h) multi + label 2.75 2.75

No. 824 was printed in sheets of 18 + 18 labels that could be personalized. The label shown, depicting the national arms and posthorns, is the generic label image.
Compare with type A552.

Trains A539

Designs: 1.50h, Diesel train DPL1. 1.90h, Diesel train, DEP 02. 2.20h, Electric train EPL 2T. 6h, Electric train EPL 9T.

2011, July 5 Litho. *Perf. 14x14¼*
825-828 A539 Set of 4 4.25 4.25

First Flight of Dirigible "Kiev," Cent. A540

2011, Aug. 5
829 A540 2.20h multi .90 .90

Emigration of Ukrainians to Brazil, 120th Anniv. — A541

2011, Aug. 24 *Perf. 14¼x14*
830 A541 2.20h multi .90 .90

Independence, 20th Anniv. — A542

Litho. With Foil Application

2011, Aug. 24 *Perf. 14x14¼*
831 A542 2.20h multi .90 .90

"The Snow Queen" Fairy Tale A543

No. 832: a, 1.50h, Snow Queen in horse-drawn sleigh flying above town (43x26mm). b, 6h, Crow and girl (26x26mm).

2011, Sept. 1 Litho. *Perf. 11½*
832 A543 Horiz. pair, #a-b 2.75 2.75

12th Natl. Philatelic Exhibition, Odessa — A544

2011, Sept. 9 *Perf. 14x14¼*
833 A544 4.30h multi 1.75 1.75

Miniature Sheet

Prepared but Unissued Ukrainian National Republic Stamps, 90th Anniv. A545

No. 834: a, 1.50h, Unissued 5h stamp. b, 1.50h, Unissued 3h stamp. c, 2h, Unissued 60h stamp. d, 2h, Unissued 80h stamp. e, 6h, Unissued 100h stamp. f, 7h, Unissued 200h stamp.

2011, Sept. 12 *Perf. 11½*
834 A545 Sheet of 6, #a-f 7.75 7.75

Tetiana Markus (1921-43), Anti-Nazi Resistance Fighter
A546

2011, Sept. 21 *Perf. 14x14¼*
835 A546 1.50h multi .55 .55

Babi Yar Massacres, 70th Anniv. — A547

2011, Sept. 29 *Perf. 13¼*
836 A547 2.20h multi 1.25 1.25

Motion Picture *Natalka Poltavka,* 75th Anniv.
A548

No. 837: a, 1.50h, People. b, 6h, Woman.

Litho. With Foil Application

2011, Sept. 30 *Perf. 14x14¼*
837 A548 Horiz. pair, #a-b 2.75 2.75

Lvov National University, 350th Anniv.
A549

2011, Oct. 11 Litho. *Perf. 11½*
838 A549 1.50h multi .55 .55

Regional Communications Commonwealth, 20th Anniv. — A550

2011, Oct. 14
839 A550 1.90h multi .75 .75

Mykhailo Yanhel (1911-71), Missile Designer — A551

2011, Oct. 25 *Perf. 13¼*
840 A551 1.50h multi .80 .80

Personalized Stamp — A552

Litho. With Foil Application

2011, Nov. 1 *Perf. 11½*
841 A552 (1.80h) multi + label 2.75 2.75

No. 841 was printed in sheets of 12 + 12 labels that could be personalized. The label shown, depicting the national arms and posthorns, is the generic label image.

Compare with type A538.

St. Sophia's Cathedral, Kyiv, 1000th Anniv. — A553

No. 842: a, Painting above three arches. b, Round ceiling painting.

2011, Nov. 18
842 Horiz. pair + central label 3.00 3.00
a. A553 1.90h multi .75 .75
b. A553 6h multi 2.25 2.25

Miniature Sheet

Amphibians — A554

No. 843: a, 1.80h, Pelophylax esculentus. b, 1.80h, Hyla arborea. c, 2.20h, Pelophylax lessonae. d, 2.20h, Rana dalmantina. e, 4.30h, Pelophylax ridibundus.

2011, Nov. 22 Litho.
843 A554 Sheet of 5, #a-e 4.50 4.50

Miniature Sheet

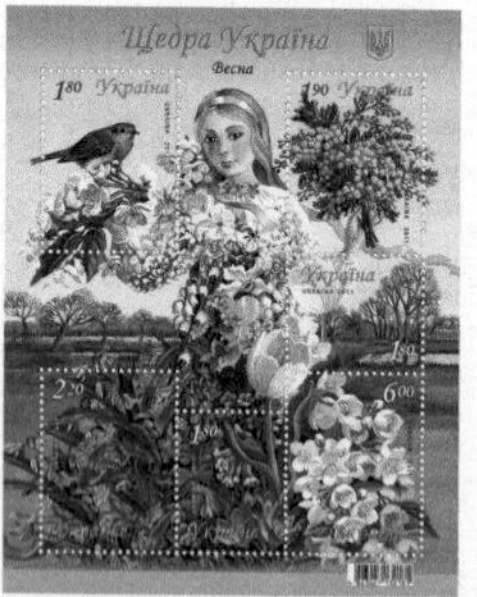

Spring
A555

No. 844: a, 1.80h, Bird on flower branch held by woman (30x40mm). b, 1.80h, Bare trees, white flowers and pond (30x21mm). c, 1.80h, Purple and yellow flowers (24x32mm). d. 1.90h, Cut flowers held by woman (30x40mm). e, 2.20h, Purple flowers (30x40mm). f, 6h, White flowers (30x40mm).

Litho. With Foil Application

2011, Nov. 25
844 A555 Sheet of 6, #a-f 5.50 5.50

Traminer Grapes and Vineyard
A556

Aligoté Grapes and Vineyard
A557

2011, Nov. 30 Litho.
845 A556 1.90h multi .70 .70
846 A557 4.30h multi 1.60 1.60

Campaign Against AIDS, 30th Anniv. — A558

2011, Dec. 1 *Perf. 13¼*
847 A558 1.80h multi .90 .90

Commonwealth of Independent States, 20th Anniv. — A559

2011, Dec. 8 *Perf. 13½*
848 A559 2.20h multi .90 .90

Miniature Sheet

Natural Wonders of Ukraine
A560

No. 849: a, Lake Svityaz (dark blue denomination). b, Lake Synevir (light blue denomination). c, Bug River rapids (red denomination). d, Hill near Dniester River (red denomination). e, Deer in Askania-Nova Nature Reserve (white denomination). f, Podilsky Tovtry Park (orange denomination). g, Marble Cave of the Crimea (white denomination).

2011, Dec. 19 *Perf. 11½*
849 A560 2.20h Sheet of 7, #a-g 6.00 6.00

Europa
A561

No. 850: a, 2.20h, Bird-shaped opening in forest canopy. b, 4.30h, Star in opening in snow-covered forest canopy.

2011, Dec. 20 *Perf. 13¼*
850 A561 Horiz. pair, #a-b 2.75 2.75

Intl. Year of Forests.

Christmas and New Year's Greetings — A562

No. 851: a, Grandfather Frost with bag of toys. b, People outside of church.

2011, Dec. 23 *Perf. 11½*
851 A562 1.80h Horiz. pair, #a-b 1.40 1.40

Miniature Sheet

Water Mills
A563

No. 852 — Various mills: a, 1.80h. b, 2.20h. c, 6.50h. d, 7.70h.

2011, Dec. 28
852 A563 Sheet of 4, #a-d 6.50 6.50

Tree Leaves and Fruit — A564

Designs: 5k, Sorbus aucuparia. 20k, Robinia pseudoacacia. 30k, Fraxinus excelsior. 40k, Juglans regia. 50k, Aesculus hippocastanum. 70k, Betula pendula. 2h, Quercus robur. 2.50h, Acer platanoides. 3h, Tilia cordata. 4h, Fagus sylvatica. 5h, Alnus incana. 8h, Ulmus laevis. 10h, Populus tremula.

2012-16 Litho. *Perf. 13¾*

853 A564 5k multi .30 .30
a. Imprint "2012-II" .30 .30
b. Imprint "2012-III" .30 .30
c. Imprint "2013" .30 .30
d. Imprint "2014" .30 .30
e. Imprint "2014-II" .30 .30
f. Imprint "2015" .30 .30
g. Imprint "2015-II" .30 .30
h. Imprint "2016" .30 .30
i. Imprint "2016-II" .30 .30
854 A564 20k multi .30 .30
a. Imprint "2012-II" .30 .30
b. Imprint "2012-III" .30 .30
c. Imprint "2013" .30 .30
d. Imprint "2014" .30 .30
e. Imprint "2015" .30 .30
f. Imprint "2015-II" .30 .30
g. Imprint "2016" .30 .30
h. Imprint "2016-II" .30 .30
855 A564 30k multi .30 .30
a. Imprint "2012-II" .30 .30
b. Imprint "2012-III" .30 .30
c. Imprint "2013" .30 .30
d. Imprint "2013-II" .30 .30
e. Imprint "2013-III" .30 .30
f. Imprint "2014" .30 .30
g. Imprint "2016" .30 .30
856 A564 40k multi .30 .30
a. Imprint "2012-II" .30 .30
b. Imprint "2012-III" .30 .30
c. Imprint "2013" .30 .30
d. Imprint "2014" .30 .30
e. Imprint "2015" .30 .30
f. Imprint "2015-II" .30 .30
g. Imprint "2016" .30 .30
857 A564 50k multi .30 .30
a. Imprint "2012-II" .30 .30
b. Imprint "2012-III" .30 .30
c. Imprint "2013" .30 .30
d. Imprint "2013-II" .30 .30
e. Imprint "2013-III" .30 .30
f. Imprint "2014" .30 .30
g. Imprint "2014-II" .30 .30
h. Imprint "2014-III" .30 .30
i. Imprint "2015" .30 .30
j. Imprint "2016" .30 .30
858 A564 70k multi .30 .30
a. Imprint "2012-II" .30 .30
b. Imprint "2013" .30 .30
c. Imprint "2014" .30 .30
d. Imprint "2016" .30 .30
859 A564 2h multi .90 .90
a. Imprint "2012-II" .90 .90
b. Imprint "2012-III" .90 .90
c. Imprint "2013" .90 .90
d. Imprint "2013-II" .90 .90
e. Imprint "2014" .85 .85
f. Imprint "2014-II" .85 .85
g. Imprint "2014-III" .85 .85
h. Imprint "2016" .50 .50
i. Imprint "2016-II" .50 .50
860 A564 2.50h multi 1.00 1.00
a. Imprint "2012-II" 1.00 1.00
b. Imprint "2012-III" 1.00 1.00
c. Imprint "2013" 1.00 1.00
d. Imprint "2013-II" 1.00 1.00
e. Imprint "2016" 1.00 1.00
861 A564 3h multi 1.25 1.25
a. Imprint "2012-II" 1.25 1.25
b. Imprint "2013" 1.25 1.25
c. Imprint "2014" 1.00 1.00
d. Imprint "2015" .70 .70
e. Imprint "2015-II" .70 .70
f. Imprint "2016" .70 .70
g. Imprint "2016-II" .70 .70
862 A564 4.80h multi 2.00 2.00
a. Imprint "2012-II" 2.00 2.00
b. Imprint "2012-III" 2.00 2.00
c. Imprint "2013" 2.00 2.00
d. Imprint "2013-II" 2.00 2.00
e. Imprint "2016" 2.00 2.00
863 A564 5h multi 2.00 2.00
a. Imprint "2013" 2.00 2.00
b. Imprint "2014" 2.00 2.00
c. Imprint "2014-II" 2.00 2.00
d. Imprint "2015" 1.25 1.25
e. Imprint "2016" 1.25 1.25
864 A564 8h multi 3.25 3.25
a. Imprint "2013" 3.25 3.25
b. Imprint "2014" 3.00 3.00
c. Imprint "2016" 3.00 3.00
865 A564 10h multi 4.00 4.00
a. Imprint "2015" 2.25 2.25
b. Imprint "2016" 2.25 2.25
c. Imprint "2016-II" 2.25 2.25
Nos. 853-865 (13) 16.20 16.20

Issued: 5k, 30k, 50k, 2h, 2/3; 20k, 40k, 70k, 2.50h, 1/14; 3h, 4.80h, 5h, 8h, 10h, 1/24. Nos. 853c, 857c, 1/11/13. Nos. 855g, 858d, 860e, 862e, 864c, 3/17/17.

See Nos. 882-883, 909, 942-943, 996, 1025-1026.

A565

A566

A567

Personalized Stamps — A568

2012, Feb. 20 Litho. *Perf. 11½*

Background Color

Cyrillic Country Name in Yellow

866 A565	(1.80h) violet blue + label	3.50	3.50
867 A566	(1.80h) blue + label	3.50	3.50

Cyrillic Country Name in Blue

868 A567	(1.80h) blue + label	3.50	3.50

Cyrillic Country Name in Pink

869 A568	(1.80h) blue + label	3.50	3.50
	Nos. 866-869 (4)	14.00	14.00

Nos. 866-869 were each printed in sheets of 14 + 14 labels that could be personalized. The labels shown, depicting a soccer ball and various stadiums used for the 2012 European Soccer Championships, are generic.

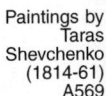

Paintings by Taras Shevchenko (1814-61) A569

Designs: 2h, Fortification at Raim, 1848. 2.50h, Moonlit Night on Kos-Aral, 1849 (49x28mm).

Litho. With Foil Application

2012, Mar. 9

870-871 A569	Set of 2	1.75	1.75

Souvenir Sheet

National Arms and Flag, 20th Anniv. — A570

No. 872: a, 2h, Arms. b, 3h, Flag.

2012, Mar. 23 *Perf. 11½*

872 A570	Sheet of 2, #a-b	1.90	1.90

Ivano-Frankivsk, 350th Anniv. — A571

2012, May 7 Litho. *Perf. 13¾x14¼*

873 A571	2h multi	.80	.80

Mykhailo Stelmakh (1912-83), Writer — A572

2012, May 24 *Perf. 13¼*

874 A572	2h multi	.80	.80

Printed in sheets of 11 + label.

A573

A574

A575

A576

A577

2012 UEFA European Soccer Championships, Poland and Ukraine — A578

No. 878 — Buildings in: a, Lviv (country name in purple). b, Kyiv (country name in yellow green). c, Kharkiv (country name in yellow). d, Donetsk (country name in red).

No. 879: a, Lviv Stadium (country name in purple). b, Olympic Stadium, Kyiv (country name in yellow green). c, Metalist Stadium, Kharkiv (country name in yellow). d, Donbass Stadium, Donetsk (country name in red).

No. 880: a, Emblem of 2012 tournament. b, Soccer ball, crowd.

2012 *Perf. 14x14¼*

875 A573	4.80h multi	1.60	1.60
876 A574	12h multi	4.00	4.00
877 A575	27.60h multi	10.00	10.00
878 A576	4.80h Block of 4, #a-d	6.50	6.50
879 A577	4.80h Block of 4, #a-d	6.50	6.50
	Nos. 875-879 (5)	30.90	30.90

Souvenir Sheet

Perf. 11½

880 A578	27.60h Sheet of 2, #a-b	20.00	20.00

Issued: No. 875, 6/1; No. 876, 6/8; No. 877, 6/8; Nos. 878-879, 5/28; No. 880, 6/11.

The souvenir sheet containing three 13.80h stamps was issued on June 25 and sold for 300h. The souvenir sheet containing one 62.55h stamp was issued on May 11 and sold for 360h.

Europa A579

No. 881: a, 4h, Musicians in costume. b, 5.60h, Mountain and direction post.

2012, June 13 *Perf. 14x14¼*

881 A579	Horiz. pair, #a-b	3.75	3.75
c.	Booklet pane of 2, #881a-881b, perf. 11½	8.75	—
	Complete booklet, #881c	8.75	

No. 881 was printed in sheets of 5 pairs + 2 labels. Complete booklet sold for 17.10h.

Tree Leaves and Fruit
A580 A581

Designs: (4.30h), Acer pseudoplatanus. (8.10h), Salix alba.

2012, July 25 *Perf. 13¾*

882 A580	(4.30h) multi	1.60	1.60
a.	Imprint "2016"	1.60	1.60
883 A581	(8.10h) multi	3.00	3.00
a.	Imprint "2016"	3.00	3.00

Issued: Nos. 882a, 883a, 3/17/17.

A582

A583

Railway Passenger Cars A584

2012, July 27 *Perf. 14x14¼*

884 A582	2h multi	.70	.70
885 A583	2h multi	.70	.70
886 A584	2h multi	.70	.70
	Nos. 884-886 (3)	2.25	2.25

Nos. 884-886 each were printed in sheets of 11 + label.

2012 Summer Olympics, London — A585

No. 887: a, 2h, Canoeing. b, 2h, High jump. c, 2.50h, Running. d, 5.30h, Shot put.

Litho. With Foil Application

2012, July 27 *Perf. 11½*

887 A585	Block of 4, #a-d	4.25	4.25

13th National Philatelic Exhibition, Odessa — A586

2012, Aug. 10 *Perf. 13¼*

888 A586	2h multi	.80	.80

Miniature Sheet

Ukrainian Soviet Socialist Republic Semi-Postal Stamps of 1923, 89th Anniv. — A587

No. 889: a, 2h, #B4. b, 2.50h, #B1. c, 4.30h, #B3. d, 4.80h, #B2.

2012, Aug. 13 Litho. *Perf. 11½*

889 A587	Sheet of 4, #a-d, + label	5.25	5.25

Pavel Popovich (1930-2009), Cosmonaut A588

2012, Aug. 15 *Perf. 14x14¼*

890 A588	2k multi	.75	.75

Miniature Sheet

Farm Animals A589

No. 891: a, 2h, Horse. b, 2h, Goat. c, 2h, Ducks. d, 2.50h, Chicken. e, 2.50h, Rabbit.

2012, Aug. 18 *Perf. 11½*

891 A589	Sheet of 5, #a-e	4.25	4.25

Personalized Stamp — A590

2012, Aug. 23

892 A590	(2h) multi + label	3.50	3.50

No. 892 was printed in sheets of 18 + 18 labels that could be personalized. The label shown, depicting the national arms and posthorns, is the generic label image.

Fairy Tale "Zaliznonosa Bosorkania" — A591

No. 893: a, 2h, Man, man with long nose, cat (43x26mm). b, 2.50h, Men on horse (26x26mm).

2012, Sept. 1 *Perf. 11½*

893 A591	Horiz. pair, #a-b	1.75	1.75

Miniature Sheet

Fruits and Flowers A592

No. 894: a, 2h, Cerasus vulgaris (30x45mm). b, 2h, Tagetes patula (30x50mm). c, 2.50h, Alcea rosea (30x50mm). d, 3.30h, Fragaria vesca (30x50mm).

Litho. With Foil Application

2012, Sept. 1

894 A592 Sheet of 4, #a-d 3.75 3.75

Ginsburg Apartment House, Kyiv, Cent. A593

2012, Sept. 14 Litho. ***Perf. 14x14¼***

895 A593 2h multi .80 .80

Sudak, 1800th Anniv. A594

2012, Sept. 20 ***Perf. 11½***

896 A594 2h multi .80 .80

Souvenir Sheet

Donetsk Region, 80th Anniv. A595

2012, Sept. 25

897 A595 2h multi .80 .80

Miniature Sheet

Nikita Botanical Gardens, 200th Anniv. A596

No. 898: a, 2h, Gazebo (38x31mm). b, 2h, Administration Building (45x31mm). c, 2.50h, Arbor and steps (50x33mm). d, 5.30h, Echinocereus (50x33mmm).

Litho. With Foil Application

2012, Oct. 4

898 A596 Sheet of 4, #a-d 4.50 4.50

Sun and Flowers, by Aliona Panasiuk, Winning Design in Children's Stamp Designing Contest — A597

2012, Oct. 9 Litho. ***Perf. 13¼***

899 A597 2h multi .80 .80

Chyhyryn, 500th Anniv. A598

2012, Oct. 14 ***Perf. 14x14¼***

900 A598 2h multi .80 .80

Battle of Blue Waters, 650th Anniv. A599

2012, Oct. 24

901 A599 2h multi .80 .80

Miniature Sheet

Windmills — A600

No. 902: a, 2h, Four-bladed windmill in winter. b, 2.50h, Six-bladed windmill. c, 3.30h, Six-bladed windmill, diff. d, 4.80h, Four-bladed windmill, diff.

2012, Nov. 9 ***Perf. 11½***

902 A600 Sheet of 4, #a-d 4.50 4.50

Andrii Malyshko (1912-70), Poet — A601

2012, Nov. 14 ***Perf. 13¼***

903 A601 2h multi .80 .80

No. 903 was printed in sheets of 11 + label.

Miniature Sheet

Seven Wonders of Ukraine A602

No. 904: a, Akkerman Fortress (name in light blue). b, Khotyn Fortress (name in light green). c, Vorontsov Palace (wall in front). d, Lutsk Castle (name in red). e, Mytropolychyi Palace (diamonds on roof). f, Kamianets-Podilskyi Fortress (with curving road). g, Kachanivka Palace (with cupola and pillars).

2012, Nov. 29 ***Perf. 11½***

904 A602 2.50h Sheet of 7, #a-g 6.75 6.75

Christmas and New Year's Day A603

No. 905: a, Tree, angel, bird, sleigh, candle, house. b, Decoration, grain, bowl and spoon, church and house.

Litho. With Foil Application

2012, Dec. 8

905 A603 2h Horiz. pair, #a-b 1.60 1.60

No. 905 was printed in sheets containing 6 pairs and 3 labels

Miniature Sheet

Frogs and Toads A604

No. 906: a, 2h, Bufo bufo. b, 2h, Bombina variegata. c, 4.30h, Bufo viridis. d, 5.40h, Pelobates fuscus. e, 5.40h, Rana temporaria.

2012, Dec. 17 Litho.

906 A604 Sheet of 5, #a-e 7.25 7.25

Traditional Women's Costume — A605

2012, Dec. 28 ***Perf. 13¼***

907 A605 2h multi .80 .80

Film, *Man with a Movie Camera,* by Dziga Vertov, 83rd Anniv. A606

No. 908: a, Lens and eye. b, Camera.

2012, Dec. 29

908 A606 2h Horiz. pair, #a-b 1.60 1.60

Morus Alba Leaf and Fruit — A607

2013, Jan. 11 ***Perf. 13¾***

909 A607 (4k) multi 1.75 1.75
a. Imprint "2013-II" 1.75 1.75
b. Imprint "2016" 1.75 1.75

Issued: No. 909b, 3/17/17.

Souvenir Sheet

Charter of Volodymyr II Monomakh, 900th Anniv. — A608

2013, Feb. 22 ***Perf. 11½***

910 A608 6.40h multi 2.50 2.50

Vladimir Vernadsky (1863-1945), Mineralogist — A609

2013, Feb. 28 ***Perf. 13¼***

911 A609 2h multi .80 .80

No. 911 was printed in sheets of 11 + label.

Honta and Zalizniak, by Mykola Storozhenko A610

Fate, by Oleksandr Ivakhnenko A611

Litho. With Foil Application

2013, Mar. 9 ***Perf. 11½***

912 A610 3.30h multi 1.25 1.25
913 A611 4.80h multi 1.75 1.75

Nos. 912-913 each were printed in sheets of 11 + label.

Semen Hulak-Artemovskyi (1813-73), Composer — A612

2013, Mar. 25 Litho. ***Perf. 14x14¼***

914 A612 2h multi .80 .80

12-791 Rail Car — A613

15-1547-03 Rail Tanker A614

19-7017-01 Rail Tanker A615

20-7032 Rail Car — A616

2013, Mar. 27

915 A613 2h multi .80 .80
916 A614 2h multi .80 .80
917 A615 2.50h multi .95 .95
918 A616 2.50h multi .95 .95
Nos. 915-918 (4) 3.50 3.50

Nos. 915-918 each were printed in sheets of 11 + label.

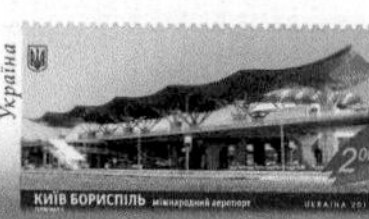

Boryspil International Airport, Kyiv — A617

2013, Apr. 2

919 A617 2h multi .80 .80

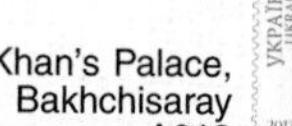

Khan's Palace, Bakhchisaray A618

Ayu-Dag Mountain — A619

Crimean Tourist Attractions — A620

No. 922: a, 2h, Valley of Ghosts, near Alushta (26x40mm). b, 2h, St. John's Cathedral, Kerch (37x26mm). c, 2.50h, Wine barrels and grapes, Masandra (37x26mm). d, 2.50h, Urn (26x40mm). e, 4.80h, Southern coast (56x26mm).

2013, Apr. 24 *Perf. 14x14¼*
920 A618 2h multi .80 .80
921 A619 2.50h multi .95 .95

Miniature Sheet

Perf. 11½

922 A620 Sheet of 5, #a-e 5.00 5.00

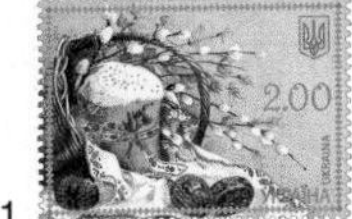

Easter — A621

2013, Apr. 30 *Perf. 14x14¼*
923 A621 2h multi .80 .80

Saints Cyril and Methodius — A622

2013, May 22 *Perf. 14¼x13¾*
924 A622 2.50h multi 1.25 1.25

Slavic writing, 1150th anniv.

Souvenir Sheet

Medals for First All-Russian Olympiad, Kyiv, Cent. — A623

2013, May 25 *Perf. 11½*
925 A623 4.80h multi 2.25 2.25

Europa A624

No. 926 — Postal vehicles: a, 4h, 1953 Moskvich 400. b, 5.60h, 2013 MAZ-5440 truck.

2013, May 29 *Perf. 14x14¼*
926 A624 Pair, #a-b 3.75 3.75
c. Booklet pane of 2, #926a-926b, perf. 11½ 7.50 —
Complete booklet, #926c 7.50

Complete booklet sold for 12.12h.

Children's Day — A625

No. 927: a, Rainbow, boy on one knee giving heart to girl in wheelchair. b, Children and balloons.

2013, May 31 *Perf. 13¼*
927 A625 2h Pair, #a-b 1.75 1.75

St. Volodymyr's Cathedral, Sevastopol A626

2013, June 27 Litho. *Perf. 14x14¼*
928 A626 3.30h multi 1.75 1.75

Souvenir Sheet

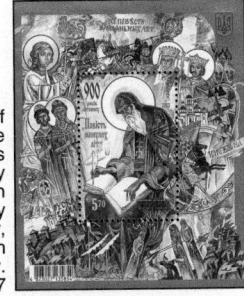

Tale of Bygone Years (History of Kievan Rus), by Nestor, 900th Anniv. A627

Litho. With Foil Application

2013, July 26 *Perf. 11½*
929 A627 5.70h multi 2.50 2.50

Souvenir Sheet

Christianization of Kievan Rus, 1025th Anniv. — A628

Litho., Margin Litho. With Foil Application

2013, July 28 *Perf. 11½*
930 A628 5.40h multi 2.40 2.40

See Belarus No. 870, Russia No. 7466.

Personalized Stamp — A629

2013, Aug. 19 Litho. *Perf. 11½*
931 A629 (2h) sil & blk + label 3.00 3.00

No. 931 was printed in sheets of 28 stamps + 28 labels that could be personalized. The label shown, deptincting the national arms and posthorns, is the generic label image.

Compare with type A727, A765, A866, A887.

Miniature Sheet

Breads A630

No. 932: a, 2h, Loaf of white bread. b, 2h, Kolache with hole in middle. c, 2.50h, Loaf of black bread. d, 2.50h, Three bubliks. e, 4.80h, Decorated korovai.

2013, Aug. 20 Litho. *Perf. 11½*
932 A630 Sheet of 5, #a-e, + 4 labels 6.50 6.50

Dnepropetrovsk Skyline — A631

2013, Aug. 23 Litho. *Perf. 14x14¼*
933 A631 2h multi .95 .95

Miniature Sheet

Dnepropetrovsk Oblast — A632

No. 934: a, 2h, Trinity Cathedral (35x26mm). b, 2h, Dnepropetrovsk skyline (35x26mm). c, 2.50h, Zenit-3SLB rocket (35x26mm). d, 3.30h, Painting of rooster and flowers from Petrekivka area (43x52mm).

2013, Aug. 23 Litho. *Perf. 11½*
934 A632 Sheet of 4, #a-d 4.50 4.50

Pumpkins, by Evdokim Voloshinov (1824-1913) A633

2013, Aug. 24 Litho. *Perf. 14x14¼*
935 A633 2h multi .95 .95

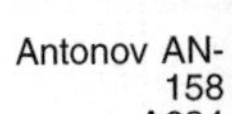

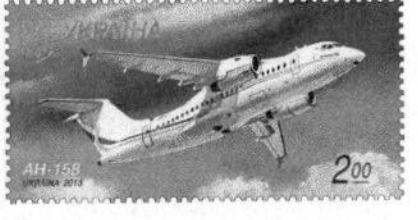

Antonov AN-158 A634

2013, Aug. 31 Litho. *Perf. 14x14¼*
936 A634 2h multi .95 .95

Water Tower, Vinnitsa — A635

2013, Sept. 5 Litho. *Perf. 14¼x14*
937 A635 2h multi .85 .85

Miniature Sheet

Vinnitsa Oblast A636

No. 938: a, 2h, Dniester River (26x36mm). b, 2h, Trinity Monastery, Brailov (26x36mm). c, 2.50h, Shcherbatov Palace, Nemyriv (45x23mm). d, 4.80h, Roshen Fountain, Vinnitsa (56x30mm).

2013, Sept. 9 Litho. *Perf. 11½*
938 A636 Sheet of 4, #a-d 4.00 4.00

Souvenir Sheet

Beheading of St. John the Baptist Monastery, Lyadova, 1000th Anniv. — A637

Litho. With Foil Application

2013, Sept. 15 *Perf. 11½*
939 A637 4.30h multi 1.75 1.75

Post Rider — A638

2013, Oct. 9 Litho. *Perf. 13½*
940 A638 2h multi .85 .85

Miniature Sheet

Autumn A639

No. 941: a, 2h, Sorbus aucuparia (30x45mm). b, 2h, Citrullus lanatus (30x50mm). c, 2.50h, Dahlia (30x50mm). d, 3.30h, Boletus edulis (30x50mm).

Litho. With Foil Application

2013, Oct. 14 *Perf. 11½*
941 A639 Sheet of 4, #a-d 3.75 3.75

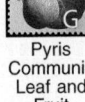

Hippophae Rhamnoides Leaf and Fruit A640

Pyris Communis Leaf and Fruit A641

2013 Litho. *Perf. 13¾*
942 A640 (5.60h) multi 1.75 1.75
a. Imprint "2016" 1.75 1.75
943 A641 (6.40h) multi 2.25 2.25
a. Imprint "2016" 2.25 2.25

Issued: No. 942, 11/5; No. 943, 10/22. Nos. 942a, 943a, 3/17/17.

Vera Kholodnaya (1893-1919), Film Actress — A642

2013, Oct. 31 Litho. *Perf. 14x14¼*
944 A642 2h multi .85 .85

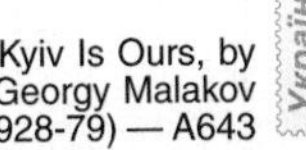

Kyiv Is Ours, by Georgy Malakov (1928-79) — A643

2013, Nov. 6 Litho. *Perf. 13¼*
945 A643 2h multi .85 .85

Liberation of Kyiv, 70th anniv.

Miniature Sheet

Winter on the Farm A644

No. 946: a, 2h, Squirrel in tree (32x24mm). b, 2h, Birds in tree (32x24mm). c, 2.50h, Children with Christmas decoration (32x48mm). d, 2.50h, Turkey (32x24mm).

2013, Nov. 22 Litho. *Perf. 11½*
946 A644 Sheet of 4, #a-d 3.50 3.50

Olha Kobylianska (1863-1942), Writer — A645

2013, Nov. 27 Litho. *Perf. 14x14¼*
947 A645 2h multi .85 .85

Christmas A646

Litho. With Foil Application

2013, Dec. 6 *Perf. 13½*
948 A646 2h multi .85 .85

Mykola Amosov (1913-2002), Surgeon — A647

2013, Dec. 6 Litho. *Perf. 13¼*
949 A647 2h multi .85 .85

Printed in sheets of 11 + label.

Miniature Sheet

Pectoral, 4th Cent. A648

No. 950 — Part of pectoral with denomination at: a, 4h, LL (33x29mm). b, 4h, LR (33x29mm). c, 5.60h, UL (40x29mm). d, 5.60h, LL (40x29mm).

Litho. & Embossed With Foil Application

2013, Dec. 12 *Perf. 11½*
950 A648 Sheet of 4, #a-d 8.50 8.50

Ports of Ukraine and Morocco A649

No. 951: a, 2h, Odessa, Ukraine. b, 3.30h, Tangiers, Morocco.

2013, Dec. 18 Litho. *Perf. 11½*
951 A649 Horiz. pair, #a-b 3.00 3.00

See Morocco No. 1182.

Churches in Ukraine and Romania — A650

No. 952: a, 2h, Church of the Savior, Berestovo, Ukraine. b, 3.30h, Church of the Sucevita Monastery, Romania.

Litho. With Foil Application

2013, Dec. 21 *Perf. 11½*
952 A650 Horiz pair, #a-b, + central label 3.00 3.00

See Romania Nos. 5509-5510.

Miniature Sheets

A651

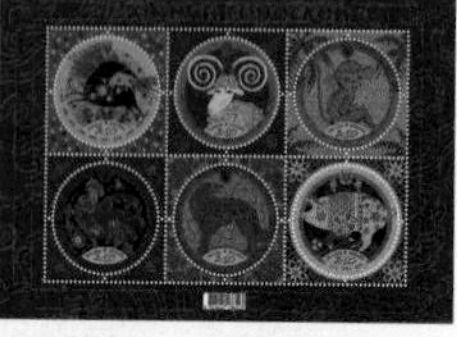

Chinese Zodiac Animals A652

No. 953: a, Rat. b, Ox. c, Tiger. d, Rabbit. e, Dragon. f, Snake.
No. 954: a, Horse. b, Goat. c, Monkey. d, Rooster. e, Dog. f, Pig.

Litho. With Foil Application

2013, Dec. 25 *Perf. 13½*
953 A651 2.50h Sheet of 6, #a-f 6.50 6.50
954 A652 2.50h Sheet of 6, #a-f 6.50 6.50

Bunch of Daisies, by Andrey Guk — A653

2014, Jan. 24 Litho. *Perf. 13¼*
955 A653 2h multi .60 .60

Leonid Kravchuk, First President of Ukraine, 80th Birthday — A654

2014, Jan. 31 Litho. *Perf. 14x14¼*
956 A654 2h multi .60 .60

Ukrainian Women's Biathlon Relay Team for 2014 Winter Olympics — A655

2014, Jan. 31 Litho. *Perf. 14x14¼*
957 A655 3.30h multi 1.90 1.90

No. 957 was printed in sheets of 16 + 4 labels.

On Apr. 15, No. 957 was overprinted in gold Cyrillic text to commemorate the victory of the biathlon team at the Winter Olympics. It was produced in limited quantities. Value, *$17.50.*

Miniature Sheet

Architecture in Kyiv of Wladislaw Horodecki (1863-1930) — A656

No. 958: a, 2h, Sculpture of lion from House of Chimeras (33x30mm). b, 2h, Sculpture of woman and frogs from House of Chimeras (33x30mm). c, 2h, Karaite Kenesa (33x30mm). d, 3.30h, National Art Museum (40x30mm). e, 4.80h, St. Nicholas Cathedral (33x60mm). f, 5.60h, House of Chimeras (40x30mm).

Litho. & Engr.

2014, Feb. 14 *Perf. 11½*
958 A656 Sheet of 10, #958a, 958b, 2 each #958c-958f 15.00 15.00

Icon Depicting Archangel Gabriel — A657

2014, Feb. 18 Litho. *Perf. 13½*
959 A657 4.80h multi 1.75 1.75

No. 959 was printed in sheets of 8 + central label.

Art School, Kirovohrad A658

2014, Feb. 27 Litho. *Perf. 14x14¼*
960 A658 2h multi .75 .75

Miniature Sheet

Kirovohrad Oblast — A659

No. 961: a, 2h, Ascension Cathedral (30x37mm). b, 2h, Scythian stele (30x37mm). c, 2.50h, Kropivnitsky Theater (35x26mm). d, 4.80h, Dancers (52x47mm).

2014, Feb. 27 Litho. *Perf. 11½*
961 A659 Sheet of 4, #a-d 3.25 3.25

Ukrposhta (Ukrainian Postal Service), 20th Anniv. — A660

Litho. & Embossed With Foil Application

2014, Mar. 25 *Perf. 14¼x14*
962 A660 2h multi .75 .75

Metropolitan Vasily Lipkivski (1864-1937) — A661

2014, May 8 Litho. *Perf. 13¼*
963 A661 2h multi .75 .75

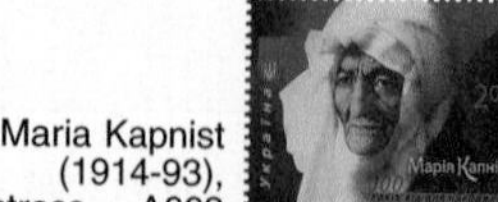

Maria Kapnist (1914-93), Actress — A662

2014, May 16 Litho. *Perf. 14x14¼*
964 A662 2h multi .75 .75

Children Playing and UNICEF Emblem — A663

2014, May 29 Litho. *Perf. 13½*
965 A663 2h multi .75 .75

Still Life with a Chocolate Mill, by Juan de Zurbarán — A664

2014, May 29 Litho. *Perf. 14x14¼*
966 A664 5.70h multi 1.75 1.75

No. 966 was printed in sheets of 8 + central label.

Sikorsky Ilya Muromets Airplane A665

2014, June 17 Litho. *Perf. 14x14¼*
967 A665 2h multi .75 .75

Europa — A666

Designs: 4.80h, Painting depicting Cossack Mamay playing kobza. 5.70h, Kobza.

2014, July 25 Litho. *Perf. 11½*
968 A666 4.80h multi 1.40 1.40
a. Booklet pane of 1 3.00 —
969 A666 5.70h multi 1.75 1.75
a. Booklet pane of 1 4.00 —
Complete booklet, #968a, 969a 7.00

Reply of the Zaporozhian Cossacks to Sultan Mehmed IV of the Ottoman Empire, by Ilya Y. Repin (1840-1930) A667

2014, July 29 Litho. *Perf. 11½*
970 A667 3.30h multi 1.10 1.10

No. 970 was printed in sheets of 8 + central label.

Cacti — A668

Designs: 2h, Gymnocalycium anisitsii. 2.50h, Opuntia microdasys. 3.30h, Pilosocereus palmeri. 4.80h, Graptopetalum bellum.

Perf. 13½x13¼

2014, Aug. 15 Litho.
971 A668 2h multi .85 .85
972 A668 2.50h multi 1.10 1.10

Perf. 14¼x14

Size: 25x52mm

973 A668 3.30h multi 1.35 1.35

Size: 28x40mm

974 A668 4.80h multi 2.10 2.10
Nos. 971-974 (4) 5.40 5.40

2013 Euromaidan Demonstrations A669

2014, Aug. 22 Litho. *Perf. 11½*
975 A669 2h multi .80 .80

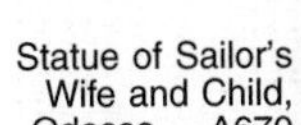

Statue of Sailor's Wife and Child, Odessa — A670

2014, Sept. 2 Litho. *Perf. 13½*
976 A670 2h multi .80 .80

Miniature Sheet

Odessa Oblast A671

No. 977: a, 2h, Akkerman Fortress (53x25mm). b, 2.50h, Port of Odessa (40x30mm). c, 2.50h, St. Nikolai Church, Vilkove (40x30mm). d, 5.70h, Ilyichevsk Lighthouse and ship (58x45mm).

2014, Sept. 2 Litho. *Perf. 11½*
977 A671 Sheet of 4, #a-d 4.75 4.75

Monument to Shipbuilders, Mykolaiv — A672

2014, Sept. 13 Litho. *Perf. 13½*
978 A672 2h multi .80 .80

Miniature Sheet

Mykolaiv Oblast A673

No. 979: a, 2h, Traffic circles and bridges (26x37mm). b, 2.50h, Kasperovskaya Cathedral of Our Lady, Mykolaiv (37x26mm). c, 2.50h, Buzky Gard National Park (37x26mm). d, 5.70h, Ship factory (51x52mm).

2014, Sept. 13 Litho. *Perf. 11½*
979 A673 Sheet of 4, #a-d 4.75 4.75

Portrait of V. L. Kochubey, by Taras Shevchenko (1814-61) A674

Gifts in Chigrin, 1644, Etching by Shevchenko A675

A676

No. 982: a, 3.30h, Portraits of Lusha Polusmak and Kobza player (56x35mm). b, 5.70h, Self-portrait of Shevchenko (36x35mm).

Litho. With Foil Application
2014, Sept. 26 *Perf. 11½*
980 A674 2h multi .80 .80
981 A675 2.50h multi 1.00 1.00

Souvenir Sheet
982 A676 Sheet of 2, #a-b 3.50 3.50

Nos. 980-981 were each printed in sheets of 11 + label.

A Lady in Black, by Boris Grigoriev (1886-1939) — A677

2014, Oct. 6 Litho. *Perf. 13½*
983 A677 2h multi .80 .80

No. 983 was printed in sheets of 8 + central label.

Pigeons — A678

Designs: No. 984, 2h, Kryukovsky pigeon (white bird). No. 985, 2h, Odessa Turman pigeon (brown and white bird). 2.50h, Kiev Tumbler pigeon. 3.30h, Micholaivsky Shield Tumbler pigeon.

2014, Oct. 10 Litho. *Perf. 14x14¼*
984-987 A678 Set of 4 3.25 3.25

World War II Liberation of Ukraine, 70th Anniv. — A679

Litho. With Foil Application
2014, Oct. 28 *Perf. 11½*
988 A679 2h multi .90 .90

Chernivtsi Post Office, 125th Anniv. — A680

Perf. 14x14¼ Syncopated
2014, Oct. 31 Litho.
989 A680 2h multi .80 .80

Self-Adhesive

Tereshchenko Family — A681

No. 990: a, 4.80h, Tereshchenko coat of arms. b, 5.70h, Artemi Tereshchenko (1794-1877), industrialist.

Litho. With Foil Application
2014, Nov. 14 *Perf. 11½*
990 A681 Sheet of 2, #a-b 3.00 3.00

Christmas and New Year's Day — A682

Litho. With Foil Application
2014, Nov. 14 *Perf. 14¼x14*
991 A682 2h multi .75 .75

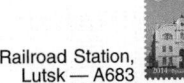

Railroad Station, Lutsk — A683

2014, Dec. 4 Litho. *Perf. 14¼x14*
992 A683 2h multi .65 .65

Miniature Sheet

Volyn Oblast A684

No. 993: a, Statue of Lesya Ukrainka, Lutsk (27x41mm). b, 2h, Lake, Okonsk (27x28mm). c, 2.50h, Angel (30x28mm). d, 4.20h, Monastery, Zimne (56x39mm).

2014, Dec. 4 Litho. *Perf. 11½*
993 A684 Sheet of 4, #a-d 3.25 3.25

Army Day — A685

Perf. 14x14¼ Syncopated
2014, Dec. 5 Litho.
994 A685 2h multi .65 .65

Miniature Sheet

Flora and Fauna in Winter A686

No. 995: a, 2h, Lepus timidus (30x56mm). b, 2h, Sciurus vulgaris (30x56mm). c, 3.30h, Parus major (37x40mm). d, 3.30h, Viburnum opulus (30x56mm).

Litho. With Foil Application
2014, Dec. 19 *Perf. 11½*
995 A686 Sheet of 4, #a-d 3.25 3.25

Tree Leaves and Fruit Type of 2012
Serpentine Die Cut 12¾x12¼
2014, Dec. 22 Litho.
Self-Adhesive
996 A564 2h Quercus robur .65 .65

Souvenir Sheet

Archaeological Artifacts — A687

No. 997 — Artifacts from: a, Trypillian culture, Ukraine (6th-3rd millennium B.C.). b, Mohenjo-Daro, Pakistan.

2014, Dec. 25 Litho. *Perf. 11½*
997 A687 4.80h Sheet of 2, #a-b 2.60 2.60

See Pakistan No. 1219.

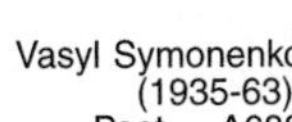

Vasyl Symonenko (1935-63), Poet — A688

2015, Jan. 8 Litho. *Perf. 14x14¼*
998 A688 2h multi .65 .65

Unity Day — A689

Litho. With Foil Application
Perf. 14¼x14 Syncopated
2015, Jan. 22
999 A689 2h multi .65 .65

Heroes Day — A690

2015, Feb. 20 Litho. *Perf. 13½*
1000 A690 2h multi .65 .65

Mykhailo Verbytsky (1815-70), Composer A691

2015, Mar. 4 Litho. *Perf. 13¾x14¼*
1001 A691 2h multi .65 .65

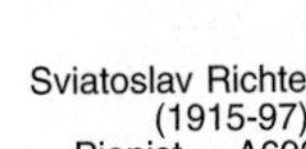

Sviatoslav Richter (1915-97), Pianist — A692

2015, Mar. 20 Litho. *Perf. 13¼*
1002 A692 2h multi .65 .65

Boris von Loutzky (1865-c. 1943), Automobile Manufacturer A693

2015, Apr. 10 Litho. *Perf. 14x14½*
1003 A693 2h multi .65 .65

Memorial Day — A694

2015, May 8 Litho. *Perf. 11½*
1004 A694 2h multi .65 .65

Crimean Tatars — A695

Designs: No. 1005, 3h, Tatar building (Ilk Qirim Hanlarinin Dürbesi). No. 1006, 3h, Coppersmith (Bakirci Usta). No. 1007, 3h, Haytarma dancers (Haytarma Oyuni). No.

1008, 3h, Tatar warrior on horseback (Qirimtatar Askeri).

2015, May 14 Litho. *Perf. 13½x13¼*
1005-1008 A695 Set of 4 3.00 3.00

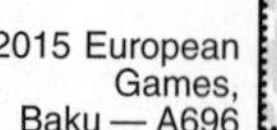

2015 European Games, Baku — A696

2015, June 5 Litho. *Perf. 14x14½*
1009 A696 4.40h multi .75 .75

Elie Metchnikoff (1845-1916), Zoologist and Bacteriologist A697

2015, July 21 Litho. *Perf. 13½*
1010 A697 4.80h multi .75 .75

Funicular, Kyiv — A698

KTV-55-2 Tram, Kyiv — A699

2015, July 24 Litho. *Perf. 14½x14*
1011 A698 2h multi .35 .35
1012 A699 2.40h multi .40 .40

Souvenir Sheet

Prince Vladimir the Great (c. 958-1015) — A700

Litho. With Foil Application
2015, July 28 *Perf. 11½*
1013 A700 12.90h multi 3.00 3.00

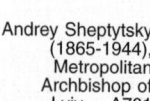

Andrey Sheptytsky (1865-1944), Metropolitan Archbishop of Lviv — A701

2015, July 29 Litho. *Perf. 13½*
1014 A701 2.40h multi .45 .45

Yuriy Fedkovych National University, Chernivtsi — A702

2015, Aug. 7 Litho. *Perf. 13½*
1015 A702 2.40h multi .45 .45

Miniature Sheet

Chernivtsi Oblast — A703

No. 1016: a, 2.40h, Cinderella Cave (30x28mm). b, 2.40h, Dormition Cathedral (26x40mm). c, 3h, Malanka Festival participants (37x28mm). d, 6h, Khotyn Fortress (56x39mm).

2015, Aug. 7 Litho. *Perf. 11½*
1016 A703 Sheet of 4, #a-d 2.25 2.25

Europa — A704

Designs: 4.80h, Cart. 5.40h, Girl on swing.

2015, Aug. 11 Litho. *Perf. 11½*
1017-1018 A704 Set of 2 1.75 1.75

A booklet containing a pane of two 31x44mm stamps like Nos. 1017-1018 sold for 22.50h.

A705

A706

A707

Cattle — A708

2015, Aug. 14 Litho. *Perf. 14x14½*
1019 A705 2.40h multi .40 .40
1020 A706 2.40h multi .40 .40
1021 A707 2.40h multi .40 .40
1022 A708 2.40h multi .40 .40
Nos. 1019-1022 (4) 1.60 1.60

Solomiya Krushelnytska Monument, Ternopil — A709

2015, Aug. 28 Litho. *Perf. 14x14½*
1023 A709 2.40h multi .45 .45

Miniature Sheet

Ternopil Oblast A710

No. 1024: a, 2.40h, Zalishchyky (40x23mm). b, 2.40h, Ternopil at night (40x23mm). c, 3h, Berezhany (23x37mm). d, 6h, Sculpture of angel, Assumption Cathedral, Buchach (58x40mm).

2015, Aug. 28 Litho. *Perf. 11½*
1024 A710 Sheet of 4, #a-d 2.25 2.25

Cornus Mas Leaf and Fruit A711

Euonymus Europaeus Leaf and Fruit A712

2015 Litho. *Perf. 13¾*
1025 A711 (2.40h) multi .45 .45
a. Imprint "2016" .45 .45
1026 A712 (5.40h) multi, imprint "2015" 1.10 1.10
a. Imprint "2016" 1.10 1.10
b. Imprint "2016-II" 1.10 1.10
c. Sheet of 20, #853h, 854g, 855g, 856g, 857j, 858d, 859h, 860e, 861f, 862e, 863e, 864c, 865b, 882a, 883a, 909b, 942a, 943a, 1025a, 1026a 25.00 25.00

Self-Adhesive
Serpentine Die Cut 12¼
1027 A712 (5.40h) multi 1.10 1.10

Issued: No. 1025, 9/15. Nos. 1026, 1027, 11/19/15. No. 1026c, 3/17/17.

Souvenir Sheet

National University of Kyiv-Mohyla Academy, 400th Anniv. — A713

Litho. With Foil Application
2015, Sept. 18 *Perf. 11½*
1028 A713 7.65h multi 1.40 1.40

Souvenir Sheet

Pochayiv Monastery, 775th Anniv. — A714

2015, Sept. 21 Litho. *Perf. 11½*
1029 A714 22.10h multi 5.00 5.00

St. Mary's Church, Boryspil — A715

2015, Sept. 30 Litho. *Perf. 14x14½*
1030 A715 2.40h multi .45 .45

Miniature Sheet

Kyiv Oblast A716

No. 1031: a, 2.40h, Horse riding, Kievan Rus Park, Kopachiv (35x26mm). b, 2.40h, Binoklevydna vessel, 5th millennium B.C. (35x26mm). c, 3h, Church of the Protective Veil, Parhomivka (35x26mm). d, 6h, Flowers on the Fence, painting by Kateryna Bilokur (35x33mm).

2015, Sept. 30 Litho. *Perf. 11½*
1031 A716 Sheet of 4, #a-d 3.00 3.00

Mosaic by Nicholas Roerich (1874-1947) A717

2015, Oct. 7 Litho. *Perf. 13½*
1032 A717 3h multi .55 .55

Roerich Pact, 80th anniv. Values are for stamps with surrounding selvage.

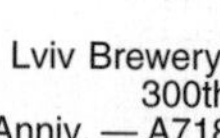

Lviv Brewery, 300th Anniv. — A718

2015, Oct. 8 Litho. *Perf. 13½*
1033 A718 2.40h multi .45 .45

No. 1033 was printed in sheets of 8 + 4 corner labels.

Postcrossing — A719

Serpentine Die Cut 12¼
2015, Oct. 9 Litho.
Self-Adhesive
1034 A719 (15.57h) multi 3.00 3.00

Anna and Mariya Muzychuk, Chess Champions A720

2015, Oct. 10 Litho. *Perf. 11½*
1035 A720 2.40h multi .45 .45

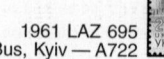

Ukrainian Defender's Day — A721

2015, Oct. 12 Litho. *Perf. 13½*
1036 A721 2.40h multi .45 .45

Values are for stamps with surrounding selvage.

1961 LAZ 695 Bus, Kyiv — A722

1963 Kyiv-4 Trolley Bus, Kyiv — A723

2015 Litho. *Perf. 14½x14*

1037 A722 2.40h multi .45 .45
1038 A723 2.40h multi .45 .45

Issued: No. 1037, 10/30; No. 1038, 11/6.

Souvenir Sheet

Princely Ostrogski Family — A724

No. 1039: a, 3.45h, Prince Konstanty Wasyl Ostrogski (1526-1608) (30x47mm). b, 5.25h, Princess Elizaveta Ostrogska (1539-82) (32x40mm). c, 7.65h, Hetman Konstanty Ostrogski (1460-1530) (30x54mm).

Litho. With Foil Application

2015, Nov. 3 *Perf. 11½*

1039 A724 Sheet of 3, #a-c 3.50 3.50

Orchids — A725

Designs: No. 1040, 2.40h, Ophrys taurica. No. 1041, 2.40h, Cephalanthera rubra. No. 1042, 2.40h, Epipactis palustris.

2015, Nov. 19 Litho. *Perf. 14¼x14*

1040-1042 A725 Set of 3 2.10 2.10

Nos. 1040-1042 were each printed in sheets of 8 + label.

Christmas and New Year's Day — A726

Litho. With Foil Application

2015, Dec. 2 *Perf. 13½*

1043 A726 2.40h multi .75 .75

Personalized Stamp — A727

2015, Dec. 10 Litho. *Perf. 11½*

1044 A727 (2.40h) multi + label 4.50 4.50

No. 1044 was printed in sheets of 9 stamps + 9 labels that could be personalized. The label shown, depicting the national arms and posthorn, is the generic label image.

Compare with type A629, A765, A866, A887.

St. Paraskevi Church, Kwiaton, Poland and St. George's Church, Drohobych, Ukraine
A728

2015, Dec. 18 Litho. *Perf. 11½*

1045 A728 5.40h multi 1.50 1.50

Wooden Churches of the Carpathian Region of Poland and Ukraine UNESCO World Heritage Site. See Poland No. 4208.

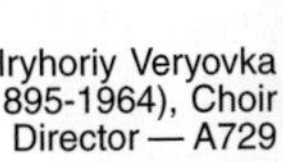

Hryhoriy Veryovka (1895-1964), Choir Director — A729

Perf. 14x14¼ Syncopated

2015, Dec. 25 Litho.

1046 A729 2.40h multi .70 .70

Gazebo, Khortytsia A730

2016, Jan. 15 Litho. *Perf. 14¼x14*

1047 A730 2.40h multi .70 .70

Miniature Sheet

Zaporizhia Oblast — A731

No. 1048: a, 2.40h, Buildings, Khortytsia National Reseve (37x28mm). b, 2.40h, Mi-8MSB helicopter (37x28mm). c, 3h, Sculpture of woman (26x45mm). d, 6h, Hydroelectric power station on Dnieper River (56x35mm).

2016, Jan. 15 Litho. *Perf. 11½*

1048 A731 Sheet of 4, #a-d 3.00 3.00

Uzhhorod Railway Station — A732

2016, Mar. 4 Litho. *Perf. 14¼x13¾*

1049 A732 2.40h multi .70 .70

Miniature Sheet

Zakarpattia Oblast — A733

No. 1050: a, 2.40h, Palanok Castle, Mukachevo (42x42mm). b, 2.40h, Shypit Waterfall (42x42mm). c, 3h, St. Nicholas Church, Svalyava (42x42mm). d, 6h, Ukrainian woman in traditional costume (62x62mm).

2016, Mar. 4 Litho. *Perf. 11½*

1050 A733 Sheet of 4, #a-d 3.00 3.00

Troop Carrier — A734

BM Tank — A735

Perf. 14 Syncopated

2016, Mar. 25 Litho.

1051 A734 2.40h multi .45 .45
1052 A735 2.40h multi .45 .45

Illustration by Anatoliy Bazylevich for Poem *Aeneid* — A736

2016, Apr. 15 Litho. *Perf. 13¼*

1053 A736 5.25h multi 1.00 1.00

Europa — A737

2016, Apr. 15 Litho. *Perf. 14x14¼*

1054 A737 (15.27h) multi 1.90 1.90

Think Green Issue.

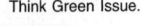

Chernobyl Nuclear Disaster, 30th Anniv. — A738

2016, Apr. 26 Litho. *Perf. 11½*

1055 A738 2.40h multi .45 .45

Tell Me the Truth, Painting by Ivan Marchuk — A739

2016, May 12 Litho. *Perf. 13½*

1056 A739 2.40h multi .45 .45

Mikhail Bulgakov (1891-1940), Writer A740

2016, May 13 Litho. *Perf. 14x14¼*

1057 A740 2.40h multi .45 .45

National Soccer Team A741

2016, May 22 Litho. *Perf. 14x14¼*

1058 A741 7.65h multi 1.40 1.40

Miniature Sheet

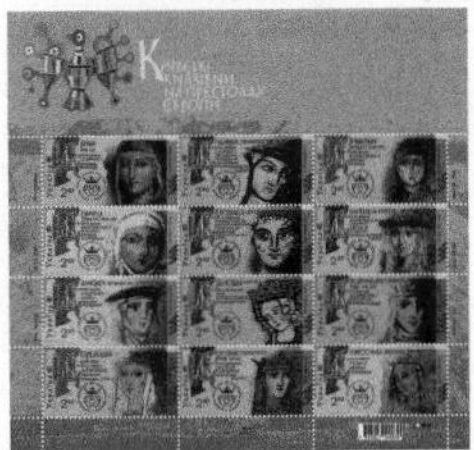

Kievan Princesses on European Thrones — A742

No. 1059 — Princess: a, Anne (1032-75), Queen consort of French King Henry I. b, Malmfred (c.1095-1137), Queen consort of Norwegian King Sigurd Iand Danish King Eric II. c, Wyszeslawa (1047-89), Queen of Poland. d, Euphemia (1096-1138), Queen consort of Hungarian King Coloman. e, Eupraxia (c. 1071-1100), Consort of Holy Roman Emperor Henry IV. f, Elisaveta (1025-76), Queen consort of Norwegian King Harald III. g, Anastasia (1074-1094), Queen consort of Hungarian King Andrew I. h, Zbyslava (1090-1114), Queen consort of Polish King Wladyslaw II. i, Dobroniga (c. 1012-87), Duchess consort of Polish Duke Casimir I. j, Predslava (c. 1090-1109), wife of Hungarian Prince Almos. k, Eupraxia-Dobrodjeja (1108-72), wife of Byzantine Co-emperor Alexios Komnenos. l, Euphrosyne (1130-93), Queen consort of Hungarian King Géza II.

2016, May 27 Litho. *Perf. 11½*

1059 A742 2.40h Sheet of 12, #a-l 7.25 7.25

Personalized Stamp — A743

2016, May 27 Litho. *Perf. 11½*

1060 A743 (2.40h) multi + label 1.00 1.00

No. 1044 was printed in sheets of 28 stamps + 28 labels that could be personalized. The label shown, depicting the national arms and posthorn, is the generic label image.

Ivan Mykolaichuk (1941-87), Movie Actor A744

2016, June 15 Litho. *Perf. 14x14¼*

1061 A744 2.40h multi .45 .45

Frigate Hetman Sahaydachniy A745

Perf. 14x14¼ Syncopated

2016, July 2 Litho.

1062 A745 5.40h multi 1.00 1.00

2016 Summer Olympics, Rio de Janeiro — A746

2016, July 23 Litho. *Perf. 11½*

1063 A746 4.40h multi .75 .75

Souvenir Sheet

Kolomyia, 775th Anniv. — A747

2016, Aug. 19 Litho. *Perf. 11½*

1064 A747 7.65h multi 1.40 1.40

Luhansk Railroad Station — A748

2016, Aug. 23 Litho. *Perf. 14¼x14*

1065 A748 2.40h multi .45 .45

Miniature Sheet

Luhansk Oblast A749

No. 1066: a, 2.40h, Luhansk University Institute of Culture and Arts (37x25mm). b, 2.40h, Paeonia tenuifolia (37x25mm). c, 3h, St. Alexander Nevsky Church, Seleznivka (37x25mm). d, 6h, Marmota bobak (37x37mm).

2016, Aug. 23 Litho. *Perf. 11½*
1066 A749 Sheet of 4, #a-d 3.00 3.00

Order of Freedom — A750

Litho. With Foil Application
2016, Aug. 24 *Perf. 13¼*
1067 A750 7.65h gold & multi 1.40 1.40

Jewish Culture — A751

Designs: 3h, Freilachs dancers. No. 1069, 4.40h, People at synagogue, Zhovka. No. 1070, 4.40h, Blowing of the shofar on Rosh Hashanah. 5.40h, Tailor.

2016, Aug. 27 Litho. *Perf. 13¼*
1068-1071 A751 Set of 4 3.75 3.75

Vegetables — A752

Designs: 2.40h, Solanum lycopersicum. 3h, Cucumis sativus. 4.40h, Solanum melongena. 5.40h, Capsicum annuum.

Die Cut Perf. 14
2016, Sept. 27 Litho.
Self-Adhesive
1072-1075 A752 Set of 4 3.25 3.25

Mykhailo Hrushevsky (1866-1934), Historian and Head of Ukrainian Central Council — A753

2016, Sept. 29 Litho. *Perf. 14¼x14*
1076 A753 2.40h multi .45 .45

No. 1076 was printed in sheets of 14 + central label.

Babi Yar Massacre, 75th Anniv. — A754

2016, Sept. 29 Litho. *Perf. 14¼x14*
1077 A754 2.40h multi .45 .45

Bohdan Stupka (1941-2012), Movie Actor — A755

2016, Oct. 5 Litho. *Perf. 14x14¼*
1078 A755 2.40h multi .45 .45

Fire Trucks A756

Designs: 2.40h, 1948 PMH-3. 3h, 1921 Magirus. 4.40h, 1916 Benz-Gaggenau.

2016, Oct. 12 Litho. *Perf. 14x14¼*
1079-1081 A756 Set of 3 1.75 1.75

Nos. 1079-1081 were each printed in sheets of 9 + label.

Miniature Sheet

Motocross Racers and Their Motorcycles — A757

No. 1082: a, Leonid Bratkovsky, M-72 motorcycle without number, 1956. b, Igor Grigoriev, CZ motorcycle No. 8, 1963. c, Vadim Horulko, Kovrovets motorcycle No. 233, 1965. d, Alexei Kibirin, CZ motorcycle without number, 1972. e, Leonid Shinkarenko, CZ motorcycle No. 15, 1967. f, Anatoly Ovchinnikov, CZ motorcycle No. 34, 1973. g, Vladimir Kavinov, KTM motorcycle No. 19, 1977. h, Boris Poganovsky, Evgeniy Nechiporenko, Dnepr motorcycle and sidecar, 1975. i, Evgeniy Rybalchenko, CZ motorcycle No. 18, 1975.

2016, Oct. 28 Litho. *Perf. 14x14¼*
1082 A757 3h Sheet of 9, #a-i 5.00 5.00

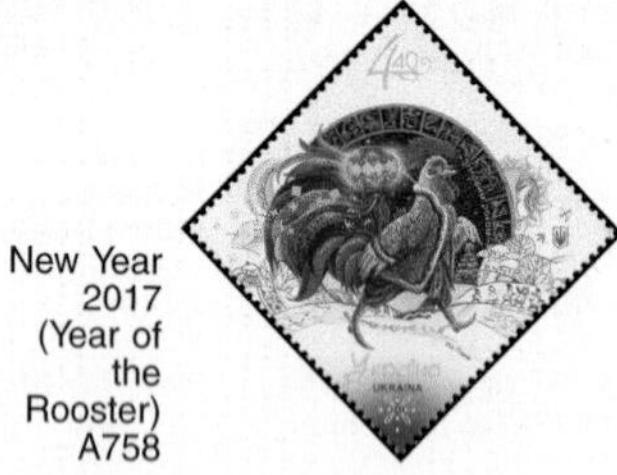

New Year 2017 (Year of the Rooster) A758

Litho. With Foil Application
2016, Nov. 11 *Perf. 13½*
1083 A758 4.40h gold & multi .75 .75

Personalized Stamp — A759

2016, Dec. 1 Litho. *Perf. 11½*
1084 A759 (2.40h) multi + label *2.75 2.75*

No. 1084 was printed in sheets of 9 stamps + 9 labels that could be personalized. The label shown, depicting the national arms and posthorn, is the generic label image.

Worldwide Fund for Nature (WWF) — A760

No. 1085 — Myotis bechsteinii: a, Hanging. b, Crawling (Latin name at top). c, Flying. d, Crawling (Latin name at left).

2016, Dec. 30 Litho. *Perf. 11½*
1085 A760 (16.25h) Block of 4, #a-d 7.50 7.50

Souvenir Sheet

Paleolithic Era — A761

No. 1086: a, Mammoth hunt. b, Shelter, food retrieval and fire starting

2017, Jan. 20 Litho. *Perf. 11½*
1086 A761 7.50h Sheet of 2, #a-b 2.75 2.75

After the Storm, by Arkhip Kuindzhi (c.1842-1910) A762

2017, Jan. 27 Litho. *Perf. 11½*
1087 A762 4.40h multi .85 .85

Flax, by Tetyana Yablonska (1917-2005) A763

2017, Feb. 24 Litho. *Perf. 13¼*
1088 A763 5.40h multi 1.00 1.00

No. 1088 was printed in sheets of 8 + label.

Ukrainian Revolution, Cent. A764

2017, Mar. 4 Litho. *Perf. 14x14¼*
1089 A764 3h multi .55 .55

Personalized Stamp — A765

2017, Mar. 6 Litho. *Perf. 11½*
1090 A765 (2.40h) sil & black + label 3.00 3.00
a. Dated "2018" 3.00 3.00

No. 1090 was printed in sheets of 8 stamps + 8 labels that could be personalized + a large central label. The label shown, depicting the national arms and posthorn, is the generic label image.

Compare with type A629, A727, A866, A887.

Jamala, Winner of 2016 Eurovision Song Contest — A766

2017, May 5 Litho. *Perf. 13¼*
1091 A766 4h multi .75 .75

Diplomatic Relations Between Ukraine and the United States, 25th Anniv. — A767

2017, May 8 Litho. *Perf. 14¼x14*
1092 A767 4.40h multi .85 .85

Souvenir Sheet

Holy Roman Empress Maria Theresa (1717-80) — A768

2017, May 13 Litho. *Perf. 11½*
1093 A768 (22h) multi 3.25 3.25

See Austria No. 2677, Croatia No. 1038, Hungary No. 4433, Slovenia No. 1219.

Souvenir Sheet

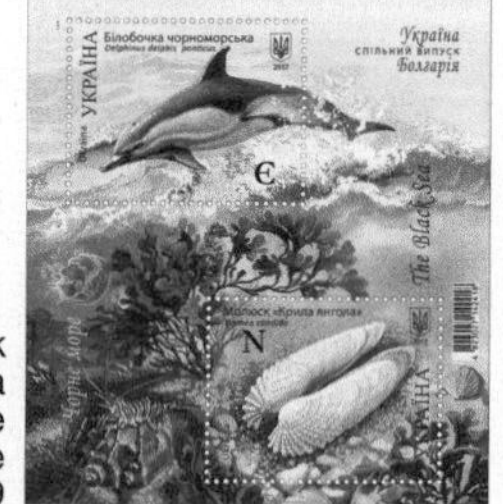

Black Sea Marine Life A769

No. 1094: a, (18h), Barnea candida. b, (22h), Delphinus delphis ponticus.

2017, May 22 Litho. *Perf. 11½*
1094 A769 Sheet of 2, #a-b 5.50 5.50

See Bulgaria No. 4808.

Miniature Sheet

Characters in Folk Tale *Nikita the Tanner* — A770

No. 1095: a, 2.40h, Dragon (49x26mm). b, 3h, Grandfather Danilo (26x26mm). c, 3h, Squirrel Belka Kamikaze (23x25mm). d, 5.40h, Nikita Kozumyaka on snail (42x51mm).

2017, June 1 Litho. *Perf. 11½*
1095 A770 Sheet of 4, #a-d 2.50 2.50

Europa A771

Designs: Nos. 1096a, 1097, Medzhybizh Castle. Nos. 1096b, 1098, Olesko Castle.

2017, June 9 Litho. *Perf. 14x14¼*
1096 Horiz. pair 1.40 1.40
a. A771 5h multi .65 .65
b. A771 5.80h multi .75 .75

Booklet Stamps
Perf. 11½

1097 A771 12.80h multi 3.50 3.50
a. Booklet pane of 1 3.50 3.50
1098 A771 12.80h multi 3.50 3.50
a. Booklet pane of 1 3.50 3.50
Complete booklet, #1097a, 1098a 7.00

Arms of Chop A772

Arms of Marinin A773

Arms of Yalta A774

Arms of Klesiv A775

Arms of Yenakiieve A776

Arms of Nizhyn A777

Arms of Shatsk A778

Arms of Parutyne A779

2017 Litho. *Perf. 13¾*
1099 A772 (40k) multi .25 .25
a. Dated "2017-II" .25 .25
b. Dated "2017-III" .25 .25
c. Dated "2018" .25 .25
d. Dated "2018-II" .25 .25
e. Dated "2019" .25 .25
1100 A773 (50k) multi .25 .25
a. Dated "2017-II" .25 .25
b. Dated "2017-III" .25 .25
c. Dated "2018" .25 .25
1101 A774 (4h) multi .55 .55
a. Dated "2017-II" .55 .55
b. Dated "2017-III" .50 .50
d. Dated "2018" .55 .55
e. Dated "2019" .75 .75
f. Dated "2019-II" .75 .75
1102 A775 (5h) multi .65 .65
a. Dated "2017-II" .65 .65
b. Dated "2017-III" .65 .65
c. Dated "2018" .60 .60
d. Dated "2018-II" .65 .65
e. Dated "2019" 1.25 1.25
f. Dated "2019-II" 1.25 1.25
1103 A776 (5.20h) multi .70 .70
a. Dated "2017-II" .70 .70
b. Dated "2018" .70 .70
1104 A777 (8h) multi 1.10 1.10
a. Dated "2017-II" 1.10 1.10
b. Dated "2017-III" 1.10 1.10
c. Dated "2018" 1.00 1.00
d. Dated "2018-II" 1.10 1.10
e. Dated "2019" 1.50 1.50
f. Dated "2019-II" 1.50 1.50
1105 A778 (10h) multi 1.40 1.40
a. Dated "2017-II" 1.40 1.40
b. Dated "2018" 1.25 1.25
c. Dated "2018-II" 1.40 1.40
d. Dated "2019" 1.75 1.75
1106 A779 (53.10h) multi 7.25 7.25
a. Dated "2018" 7.25 7.25
b. Dated "2019" 5.75 5.75
Nos. 1099-1106 (8) 12.15 12.15

Issued: Nos. 1099, 1100, 6/13; No. 1101, 6/10; Nos. 1102-1105, 6/20; No. 1106, 9/28.

One Way, by Roman Minin — A780

2017, July 2 Litho. *Perf. 13¼*
1107 A780 4h multi .55 .55

Roald Hoffmann, 1981 Nobel Laureate in Chemistry — A781

2017, July 18 Litho. *Perf. 13¼*
1108 A781 5h gold & multi .65 .65

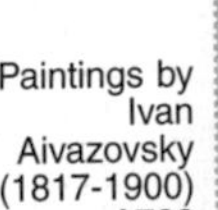

Paintings by Ivan Aivazovsky (1817-1900) A782

Designs: 3h, Yalta, 1864. 8.80h, Evening in the Crimea, 1848.

2017, July 29 Litho. *Perf. 14*
1109 A782 3h multi .45 .45

Souvenir Sheet
Perf. 11½

1110 A782 8.80h multi 1.25 1.25

No. 1109 was printed in sheets of 8 + label.

Military Transportation A783

Designs: 3h, BTR-4 armored transport. 5.40h, AN-178 airplane.

Perf. 14x14¼ Syncopated

2017, Aug. 11 Litho.
1111-1112 A783 Set of 2 1.25 1.25

Medicinal Plants — A784

Designs: No. 1113, 4h, Chelidonium majus. No. 1114, 4h, Tilia cordata. 5h, Symphytum officinale. 5.80h, Cichorium intybus.

2017, Aug. 18 Litho. *Perf. 14¼x14*
1113-1116 A784 Set of 4 2.60 2.60

Ukrainian Fashion Week — A785

2017, Sept. 3 Litho. *Perf. 13¼*
1117 A785 8h multi 1.10 1.10

No. 1117 was printed in sheets of 8 + central label.

ECr1 Tarpan Train — A786

2017, Sept. 22 Litho. *Perf. 14¼x14*
1118 A786 4h multi .55 .55

Miniature Sheet

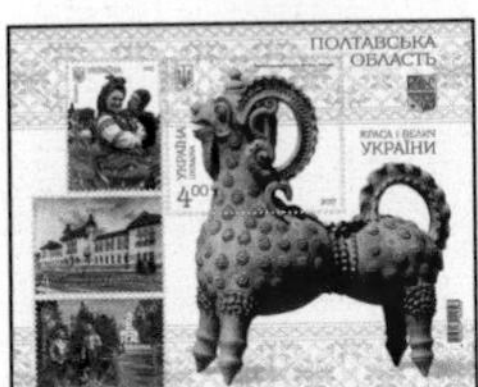

Poltava Oblast A787

No. 1119: a, Costumed participants at Sorochynska Fair (28x38mm). b, Goat sculpture (52x45mm). c, Vasyl Krychevsky Ethnographic Museum, Poltava (38x28mm). d, Statues and buildings at Mirgorod Resort (38x28mm).

2017, Sept. 22 Litho. *Perf. 11½*
1119 A787 4h Sheet of 4, #a-d 2.25 2.25

Khmelnitsky City Hall and Sculpture — A788

2017, Sept. 23 Litho. *Perf. 13¼*
1120 A788 4h multi .55 .55

Miniature Sheet

Khmelnitsky Oblast — A789

No. 1121: a, Intercession Church (37x28mm). b, Cave of Atlantis (37x28mm). c, Riverside cliffs near Subich (37x28mm). d, Kamyanets-Podilsky Fortress (70x70mm diamond).

Perf. 11½, 8¼ (#1121d)

2017, Sept. 23 Litho.
1121 A789 4h Sheet of 4, #a-d 2.25 2.25

International Year of Sustainable Tourism for Development — A790

2017, Sept. 29 Litho. *Perf. 14¼x14*
1122 A790 3h multi .40 .40

No. 1122 was printed in sheets of 8 + central label.

Dancers A791

Farrier A792

Gypsy Van — A793

Fortune Teller — A794

2017, Sept. 30 Litho. *Perf. 13¼*
1123 A791 4h multi .55 .55
1124 A792 4h multi .55 .55
1125 A793 5h multi .70 .70
1126 A794 5h multi .70 .70
Nos. 1123-1126 (4) 2.50 2.50

Roma culture in Ukraine.

Artemy Vedel (c. 1767-1808), Composer — A795

2017, Oct. 5 Litho. *Perf. 13¼*
1127 A795 4h multi .55 .55

Premiere of Film *Storozhova Zastava* — A796

2017, Oct. 10 Litho. *Perf. 11½*
1128 A796 4h multi .55 .55

No. 1128 was printed in sheets of 8 + central label.

Miniature Sheet

Cossack Seals A797

No. 1129 — Seal of: a, Zaporozhian Army, 1763. b, Hetman Bohdan Khmelnytsky, 17th cent. c, Kodak Palanka, 18th cent. d, Petro Doroshenko, 1656-59. e, Zaporozhian sergeant, 17th-18th cent. f, Semen Rakovich, 1672-91.

2017, Oct. 14 Litho. *Perf. 11½*
1129 A797 5h Sheet of 6, #a-f 4.25 4.25

Fire Fighting A798

Designs: No. 1130, 4h, KrAZ-63221 fire truck. No. 1131, 4h, GPM-54 fire tank. No. 1132, 5h, An-32P fire plane. No. 1133, 5h, PK-10/130 (UMS 1000) fire boat.

2017, Oct. 17 Litho. *Perf. 13¾x14¼*
1130-1133 A798 Set of 4 2.50 2.50

Nos. 1130-1133 were each printed in sheets of 9 + label.

Ukrainian National Republic, Cent. A799

2017, Nov. 7 Litho. *Perf. 14x14¼*
1134 A799 4h gold & multi .55 .55

Sharpening of Saws, by Oleksandr Bohomazov (1880-1930) A800

2017, Nov. 10 Litho. *Perf. 13½*
1135 A800 4h multi .55 .55

Christmas — A801

Litho. With Foil Application

2017, Nov. 30 ***Perf. 13½***
1136 A801 4h sil & multi .55 .55

Apostles Peter and Paul Beryl Crystal — A802

2017, Dec. 19 Litho. ***Perf. 14x14¼***
1137 A802 4h multi .55 .55

Miniature Sheet

Zhytomyr Oblast A803

No. 1138: a, Doll (35x44mm). b, St. Barbara's Church, Berdychiv (26x37mm). c, Chatsky Head rock formation (26x37mm). d, Radomysl Castle and statue of angel (26x37mm).

2017, Dec. 19 Litho. ***Perf. 11½***
1138 A803 4h Sheet of 4, #a-d 2.25 2.25

Uman A804

Sheshory A805

Taki Odesa A806

Luhansk Steppe A807

Serpentine Die Cut 11¾

2017, Dec. 22 Litho.

Self-Adhesive

1139 A804 4h multi		.55	.55
1140 A805 4h multi		.55	.55
1141 A806 4h multi		.55	.55
1142 A807 4h multi		.55	.55
	Nos. 1139-1142 (4)	2.20	2.20

Nos. 1139-1142 were each printed in sheets of 8 + label.

Miniature Sheet

State Seals A808

No. 1143: a, Seal of Ukrainian Central Rada and Mykhailo Hrushevsky (1866-1934), President of Central Rada. b, Seal of Ukrainian People's Republic and Volodymyr Vynnychenko (1880-1951), Prime Minister. c, Seal of the State Secretariat and Pavlo Skoropadskyi (1873-1945). d, Seal of the Directorate of Ukraine and Symon Petliura (1879-1926), Chairman of Directorate.

Litho. & Embossed

2018, Jan. 22 ***Perf. 11½***
1143 A808 9h Sheet of 4, #a-d 4.75 4.75

Oleksandr Shalimov (1918-2006), Surgeon — A809

2018, Jan. 23 Litho. ***Perf. 14x14¼***
1144 A809 5h multi .65 .65

2018 Winter Olympics, PyeongChang, South Korea — A810

2018, Jan. 23 Litho. ***Perf. 13½***
1145 A810 9h multi 1.25 1.25

Values are for stamps with surrounding selvage.

Arms of Lokachi — A811

2018, Mar. 16 Litho. ***Perf. 13¾***

1146 A811 (4h) multi	.55	.55
a. Dated "2018-II"	.55	.55
b. Dated "2019"	.70	.70
c. Dated "2019-II"	.70	.70

A812

Characters From Animated Film *The Stolen Princess: Ruslan and Ludmila* A813

Serpentine Die Cut 11¾

2018, Mar. 30 Litho.

Self-Adhesive

1147 A812 5h multi	.70	.70
1148 A813 5h multi	.70	.70

Souvenir Sheet

Trypillian Neolithic Culture A814

No. 1149: a, 9h, Agriculture. b, 15h, Melting of metal ore.

2018, Apr. 24 Litho. ***Perf. 11½***
1149 A814 Sheet of 2, #a-b 3.25 3.25

Raising of Ukrainian Flag on Black Sea Ships, Cent. — A815

2018, Apr. 27 Litho. ***Perf. 14¼x14***
1150 A815 5h multi .70 .70

Suprematist Composition 1, by Kazimir Malevich (1879-1935) — A816

2018, Apr. 28 Litho. ***Perf. 13¼***
1151 A816 5h sil & multi .70 .70

No. 1151 was printed in sheets of 8 + label.

2018 UEFA Champions League Final, Kyiv — A817

2018, May 20 Litho. ***Perf. 14¼x14***
1152 A817 9h multi 1.25 1.25

The Girl on a Background of a Persian Carpet, by Mykhailo Vrubel (1856-1910) — A818

2018, June 19 Litho. ***Perf. 11½***
1153 A818 5h multi .70 .70

See No. 1164.

Four Evangelists Bridge, Mukachevo A819

Plebanivka Viaduct — A820

2018, June 27 Litho. ***Perf. 14¼x14***

1154 A819 (26.24h) multi	3.00	3.00
1155 A820 (39.36h) multi	4.50	4.50

Booklet Panes of 1
Stamp Size:45x30mm
Perf. 11½

1156 A819 (26.24h) multi	5.25	—
1157 A820 (39.36h) multi	7.75	—
Complete booklet, #1156, 1157	13.00	

Europa. Nos. 1154-1155 were each printed in sheets of 9 + 3 labels. Complete booklet sold for 111h.

Miniature Sheet

Insects A821

No. 1158: a, Mantis religiosa. b, Lyristes plebejus. c, Sympetrum flaveolum. d, Calopteryx virgo. e, Decticus verrucivorus. f, Apatura ilia. g, Bombus hortorum.

Litho. With Foil Application

2018, July 3 ***Perf. 11½***
1158 A821 7.50h Sheet of 7, #a-g 6.50 6.50

Flowers — A822

Designs: No. 1159, 5h, Rosa canina. No. 1160, 5h, Pulmonaria obscura. No. 1161, 5h, Hypericum maculatum. No. 1162, 5h, Valeriana officinalis.

2018, July 13 Litho. ***Perf. 13¼***
1159-1162 A822 Set of 4 2.75 2.75

Nos. 1159-1162 were each printed in sheets of 9 + 3 labels.

Selman A. Waksman (1888-1973), 1952 Nobel Laureate in Physiology or Medicine — A823

2018, July 22 Litho. ***Perf. 13¼***
1163 A823 7.50h multi 1.00 1.00

Souvenir Sheet

Paintings by Mykhailo Vrubel (1856-1910) — A824

No. 1164: a, 5h, Self-portrait (33x47mm). b, 7.50h, Angel with Censer and Candle (25x47mm). c, 7.50h, Like No. 1153 (30x47mm).

Litho. With Foil Application

2018, July 27 ***Perf. 11½***
1164 A824 Sheet of 3, #a-c 2.75 2.75

Paintings — A825

Designs: 5h, Bride, by Olesya Hudyma. 7h, Kiss, by Vsevolod Maksymovych (1894-1914). 9h, Mother and Child, by Vera Barinova-Kuleba.

Litho. With Foil Application

2018, Aug. 14 ***Perf. 13½***
1165-1167 A825 Set of 3 3.00 3.00

Nos. 1165-1167 were each printed in sheets of 8 + label.

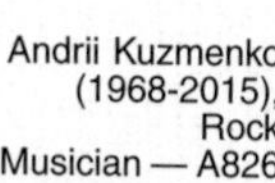

Andrii Kuzmenko (1968-2015), Rock Musician — A826

2018, Aug. 17 Litho. ***Perf. 14***
1168 A826 9h multi 1.25 1.25

Dormition Cathedral, Kharkiv — A827

2018, Aug. 23 Litho. ***Perf. 13¼***
1169 A827 5h multi .70 .70

Miniature Sheet

Kharkiv Oblast A828

No. 1170: a, Polovtsian statues (26x37mm). b, Our Savior Orthodox Church, Volodymyrivka (37x26mm). c, Fireworks over Freedom Square, Kharkiv (35x45mm). d, Sharivka Palace, Sharivka (37x26mm).

2018, Aug. 23 Litho. *Perf. 11½*
1170 A828 5h Sheet of 4, #a-d 2.75 2.75

Personalized Stamp — A829

2018, Sept. 10 Litho. *Perf. 11½*
1171 A829 (8h) multi + label 2.75 2.75

No. 1171 was printed in sheets of 6 stamps + 6 labels that could be personalized. The label shown, depicting the national arms and posthorn, is the generic label image.

Souvenir Sheets

Stamps of Ukraine and Western Ukraine A830

Coats of Arms A831

Peasants From 1918 100-Hryvnia Note — A832

No. 1172: a, Ukraine #4. b, Western Ukraine #3.

No. 1173: a, Arms of Ukrainian People's Republic (denomination at UR). b, Arms of Ukrainian State (denomination at UL).

No. 1174: Peasant with: a, Sickle and sheaf of grain. b, Hammer.

2018 Litho. *Perf. 11½*

1172 A830 15h Sheet of 2, #a-b		4.00	4.00
1173 A831 15h Sheet of 2, #a-b		4.00	4.00
1174 A832 15h Sheet of 2, #a-b		4.00	4.00
Nos. 1172-1174 (3)		12.00	12.00

Issued: No. 1172, 10/9; No. 1173, 10/10; No. 1174, 10/11. Ukrfilexpo 2018, Kyiv. A booklet containing imperforate examples of Nos. 1172-1174 was printed in limited quantities and sold for 255h.

Soldiers — A833

Designs: No. 1175, 7h, Soldier wearing helmet. No. 1176, 7h, Soldier aiming rifle.

2018, Oct. 12 Litho. *Perf. 11½*
1175-1176 A833 Set of 2 1.90 1.90

Innovations — A834

Designs: 7h, First electric tram (picture of horse on tracks with electric motors). 10.50h, Piezomotor. 13h, Corneal transplantation.

2018, Nov. 2 Litho. *Perf. 13¼*
1177-1179 A834 Set of 3 4.00 4.00

Miniature Sheet

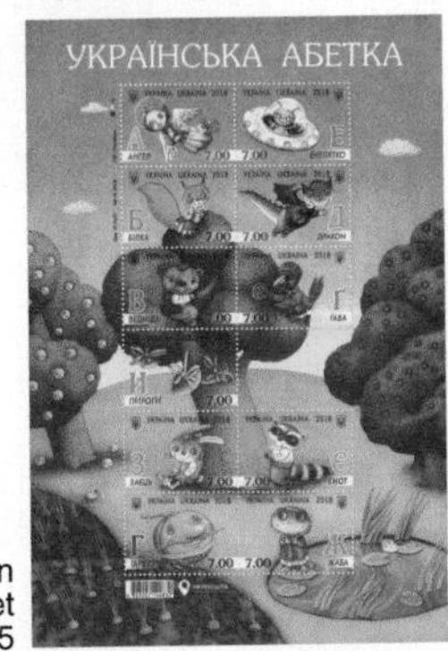

Ukrainian Alphabet A835

No. 1180 — Cyrillic letter of Ukrainian alphabet, Ukrainian word and picture of: a, Angel. b, Alien in spaceship. c, Squirrel. d, Dragon. e, Bear. f, Crow. g, Pierogies wrapped in ribbons hanging from tree. h, Hare. i, Raccoon. j, Pumpkin. k, Toad.

2018, Nov. 9 Litho. *Perf. 11½*
1180 A835 7h Sheet of 11, #a-k 9.00 9.00

Chicken Kiev — A836

2018, Nov. 12 Litho. *Perf. 11½*
1181 A836 7h multi .95 .95

No. 1181 was printed in sheets of 8 + 3 labels.

100th Birthday of Borys Paton, Chairman of National Academy of Sciences — A837

2018, Nov. 28 Litho. *Perf. 13¼*
1182 A837 7h multi .95 .95

Miniature Sheet

Flora and Fauna of Carpathian Biosphere Reserve — A838

No. 1183: a, Lucanus cervus (30x33mm). b, Fagus sylvatica (30x33mm). c, Coccothraustes coccothraustes (37x30mm). d, Rhododendron myrtifolia (30x45mm). e, Narcissus angustifolius (30x45mm). f, Ursus arctos (37x33mm).

2018, Nov. 30 Litho. *Perf. 11½*
1183 A838 7h Sheet of 6, #a-f 5.50 5.50

2018 Ukrainian Winter Paralympics Athletes — A839

2018, Dec. 3 Litho. *Perf. 14x14¼*
1184 A839 (8h) multi .95 .95

No. 1184 was printed in sheets of 9 + label.

St. Catherine's Church, Chernihiv — A840

2018, Dec. 7 Litho. *Perf. 13¼*
1185 A840 7h multi .95 .95

Miniature Sheet

Chernihiv Oblast — A841

No. 1186: a, Hetman's Capital, Baturyn (30x31mm). b, Aerial view of Desna River (38x47mm). c, Chernihiv Train Station (37x26mm). d, Kachanivka Palace (30x31mm).

2018, Dec. 7 Litho. *Perf. 11½*
1186 A841 7h Sheet of 4, #a-d 3.75 3.75

New Year 2019 (Year of the Pig) — A842

Litho. With Foil Application

2018, Dec. 14 *Perf. 11½*
1187 A842 (8h) gold & multi .95 .95

Embroidery From Vinnytsia A843

Embroidery From Lviv A844

Embroidery From Kyiv A845

Embroidery From Poltava A846

2018, Dec. 14 Litho. *Perf. 11½*

1188 A843	7h multi	.95	.95
1189 A844	7h multi	.95	.95
1190 A845	(27.74h) multi	4.00	4.00
1191 A846	(27.74h) multi	4.00	4.00
Nos. 1188-1191 (4)		9.90	9.90

Nos. 1188-1191 were each printed in sheets of 8 + central label.

St. Nicholas — A847

2018, Dec. 19 Litho. *Perf. 14¼x14*
1192 A847 (8h) multi .95 .95

Icon of Virgin Mary and Crucified Jesus, Okhtyrka — A848

2018, Dec. 24 Litho. *Perf. 13¼*
1193 A848 7h multi .95 .95

Miniature Sheet

Sumy Oblast A849

No. 1194: a, Owl in Desna-Starogutsky National Nature Park. b, Holy Resurrection Cathedral, Sumy. c, Round Courtyard, Trostyanets. d, Oleksandr Dovzhenko Hlukhiv National Pedagogical University, Hlukhiv.

2018, Dec. 24 Litho. *Perf. 11½*
1194 A849 7h Sheet of 4, #a-d 3.75 3.75

Souvenir Sheet

Church Bells A850

No. 1195: a, Mazepa Bell, St. Sophia's Cathedral, Kyiv, 1705. b, Bell, Cathedral of the Nativity, Chisinau, Moldova, 1838.

Litho. & Embossed

2018, Dec. 26 *Perf. 11½*
1195 A850 (27.39h) Sheet of 2, #a-b, + central label 7.50 7.50

See Moldova No. 1011.

Unification of Ukraine and Western Ukraine, Cent. — A851

2019, Jan. 22 Litho. *Perf. 14x14¼*
1196 A851 8h silver & multi .85 .85

Souvenir Sheet

Cimmerian Warriors — A852

2019, Feb. 27 Litho. *Perf. 11½*

1197 A852 30h multi 3.25 3.25

"Love is to Quench His Thirst" A853

"Love is to Give Her Flowers" A854

"Love is to Dedicate a Song to Her" A855

"Love is to Make Him Pierogis" A856

Serpentine Die Cut 12

2019, Mar. 6 Litho.

Self-Adhesive

1198 Block or horiz. strip of 4 3.50
- *a.* A853 8h multi .85 .85
- *b.* A854 8h multi .85 .85
- *c.* A855 8h multi .85 .85
- *d.* A856 8h multi .85 .85

Council of Europe, 70th Anniv. — A857

European Court of Human Rights, 60th Anniv. A858

2019, Mar. 15 Litho. *Perf. 13¼*

1199 A857 8h multi .85 .85

Perf. 14x14¼

1200 A858 8h multi .85 .85

Alexander Vertinsky (1889-1957), Singer — A859

2019, Mar. 21 Litho. *Perf. 11½*

1201 A859 8h multi .85 .85

Greek Women and Child A860

Men Dancing A861

Easter Preparations A862

Church of St. John the Precursor, Kerch A863

2019, Mar. 22 Litho. *Perf. 13¼*

1202 A860 8h multi .85 .85
1203 A861 8h multi .85 .85
1204 A862 8h multi .85 .85
1205 A863 8h multi .85 .85
Nos. 1202-1205 (4) 3.40 3.40

Greek culture in Ukraine.

Life Triptych, by Fedir Krychevsky (1879-1947) — A864

No. 1206 — Triptych section: a, Love (28x58mm, panel at left). b, Family (43x58mm). c, Return (28x58mm, panel at right).

2019, Apr. 12 Litho. *Perf. 11½*

1206 A864 8h Horiz. strip of 3, #a-c 2.50 2.50

Valeriy Lobanovskyi (1939-2002), Soccer Coach — A865

2019, Apr. 18 Litho. *Perf. 14x14¼*

1207 A865 8h multi .75 .75

Personalized Stamp — A866

2019, Apr. 19 Litho. *Perf. 11½*

1208 A866 (8h) gold & black + label 1.50 1.50

No. 1208 was printed in sheets of 28 stamps + 28 labels that could be personalized. The label shown, depicting the Ukrposhta emblem is the generic label image.

Compare with type A629, A727, A765, A887.

Miniature Sheet

Cyrillic Alphabet A867

No. 1209: a, Rooster, Cyrillic letter for "P." b, Magpie, Cyrillic letter for "S." c, Fox, Cyrillic letter for "L." d, Turkey, Cyrillic letter for "I." e, Cat, Cyrillic letter for "K." f, Mouse, Cyrillic letter for "M." g, Rhinoceros, Cyrillic letter for "N." h, Deer, Cyrillic letter for "O." i, Hedgehog, Cyrillic letter for "Ji." j, Fish, Cyrillic letter for "J." k, Crawfish, Cyrillic letter for "R."

2019, Apr. 26 Litho. *Perf. 11½*

1209 A867 8h Sheet of 11, #a-k 9.00 9.00

Kyiv Cake — A868

2019, May 17 Litho. *Perf. 11½*

1210 A868 10h multi .90 .90

No. 1210 was printed in sheets of 8 + 3 labels.

Ciconia Ciconia — A869

Luscinia Luscinia — A870

2019, May 22 Litho. *Perf. 11½*

Stamps With Gray Frames

1211 A869 (26.90h) multi 3.00 3.00
1212 A870 (26.90h) multi 3.00 3.00

Europa. Stamps similar to Nos. 1211-1212, but lacking gray frames, were printed in a booklet containing panes of 1 of each stamp. The booklet sold for 108h.

Monument to Saint Volodymyr (c.958-1015), Kyiv — A871

2019, May 25 Litho. *Perf. 14x14¼*

1213 A871 8h multi .85 .85

Miniature Sheet

City of Kyiv A872

No. 1214: a, St. Andrew's Church (23x37mm). b, Monument to Bohdan Khmelnytsky (37x28mm). c, Kyiv skyline (37x35mm). d, Horodecki House (37x28mm). e, Church and buildings on Andriyivskyy Descent (23x37mm).

2019, May 25 Litho. *Perf. 11½*

1214 A872 8h Sheet of 5, #a-e 4.25 4.25

Member of Black Cossacks Cavalry Regiment A873

Member of Ukrainian Galician Army A874

2019, June 9 Litho. *Perf. 11½*

1215 A873 8h multi .85 .85
1216 A874 8h multi .85 .85

Soldiers of the 1917-21 Ukrainian War of Independence.

Map of Ukraine A875

2019, June 27 Litho. *Die Cut*

Self-Adhesive

1217 A875 (8h) multi .85 .85

Mine and Tailings Near Makiivka A876

2019, July 5 Litho. *Perf. 14x14¼*

1218 A876 8h multi .85 .85

Miniature Sheet

Donetsk Oblast A877

No. 1219: a, Sviatohirsk Assumption Monastery, Sviatohirsk (47x35mm). b, Belosaraiskiy Lighthouse (37x26mm). c, Stone Tombs Reserve, Nazarivka (37x26mm). d, Mine tailings and field of sunflowers, Kurahivka. (47x35mm).

2019, July 5 Litho. *Perf. 11½*

1219 A877 8h Sheet of 4, #a-d 3.25 3.25

Souvenir Sheet

Odessa Film Studio, Cent. A878

No. 1220: a, Entrance gate. b, First Pavilion.

2019, July 19 Litho. *Perf. 11½*

1220 A878 15h Sheet of 2, #a-b 3.25 3.25

Miniature Sheet

Flora and Fauna of Mezynskyi National Nature Park — A879

No. 1221: a, Cuculus canorus. b, Canis lupus. c, Capreolus capreolus. d, Nymphoides peltatum. e, Callimorpha dominula.

2019, July 27 Litho. *Perf. 11½*

1221 A879 8h Sheet of 5, #a-e 4.25 4.25

Panteleimon Kulish (1819-97), Writer — A880

2019, Aug. 2 Litho. *Perf. 14¼x14*
1222 A880 8h multi .85 .85

St. Sophia Cathedral, Rome — A881

2019, Aug. 20 Litho. *Perf. 14x14¼*
1223 A881 10h multi 1.00 1.00

No. 1223 was printed in sheets of 9 + label.

A882

A883

A884

Embroidery Designs — A885

2019, Aug. 23 Litho. *Perf. 11½*

1224	A882	8h multi	.80	.80
1225	A883	8h multi	.80	.80
1226	A884	15h multi	1.40	1.40
1227	A885	15h multi	1.40	1.40
		Nos. 1224-1227 (4)	4.40	4.40

Nos. 1224-1227 were each printed in sheets of 8 + central label.

Vyshhorod Mother of God Icon — A886

2019, Aug. 28 Litho. *Perf. 11½*
1228 A886 10h multi .90 .90

Personalized Stamp — A887

2019, Sept. 10 Litho. *Perf. 11½*
1229 A887 (8h) multi + label 2.25 2.25

No. 1229 was printed in sheets of 9 stamps + 9 labels that could be personalized. The label shown, depicting the Ukrposhta emblem, is the generic label image.
Compare with type A629, A727, A765, A866.

Reign of Grand Prince of Kyiv, Yaroslav the Wise (c. 978-1054), 1000th Anniv. — A888

2019, Sept. 20 Litho. *Perf. 14¼x14*
1230 A888 10h gold & multi .90 .90

No. 1230 was printed in sheets of 8 + 2 labels.

Universal Postal Union, 145th Anniv. — A889

2019, Oct. 8 Litho. *Perf. 13¼*
1231 A889 (27h) multi 2.00 2.00

Filming of Movie *The Rising Hawk* (Zakhar Berkut) in Ukraine — A890

2019, Oct. 9 Litho. *Perf. 13¼*
1232 A890 8h gold & multi .85 .85

No. 1232 was printed in sheets of 8 + central label.

Souvenir Sheet

The Galagan Family A891

No. 1233: a, Coat of arms of the Galagan Family. b, Pavlo Galagan (1853-69) and Galagan College, vert. c, Hryhorii Galagan (1819-88), founder of Galagan College, vert.

2019, Oct. 10 Litho. *Perf. 11½*
1233 A891 10h Sheet of 3, #a-c 2.75 2.75

Mosaic Depicting Archangel Michael, Kyiv — A892

2019, Nov. 6 Litho. *Perf. 13½*
1234 A892 8h gold & multi .85 .85

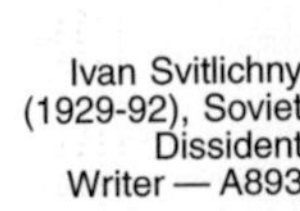

Ivan Svitlichny (1929-92), Soviet Dissident Writer — A893

2019, Nov. 22 Litho. *Perf. 14x14¼*
1235 A893 8h multi .85 .85

Miniature Sheet

Endangered Fish — A894

No. 1236: a, Gymnocephalus acerinus (40x28mm). b, Acipenser ruthenus (40x28mm). c, Carassius carassius (49x28mm). d, Romanogobio uranoscopus (49x28mm). e, Barbus waleckii (49x28mm). f, Lota lota (49x28mm). g, Rhynchocypris percnurus (40x28mm). h, Zingel streber (40x28mm).

2019, Dec. 17 Litho. *Perf. 11½*
1236 A894 8h Sheet of 8, #a-h 6.50 6.50

Christmas — A895

No. 1237: a, St. Nicholas, angels and houses (33x30mm). b, Santa Claus over house's chimney, snowman, people around Christmas tree (33x30mm). c, Carolers with bells on staff, masked caroler, cat (33x30mm). d, Church, houses, carolers, cat and snowmen (33x50mm). e, Priest, people, snowman and dog near christening hole in ice (33x30mm).

Litho. With Foil Application

2019, Dec, 18 *Perf. 11½*
1237 A895 (8h) Block of 5, #a-e, + label 3.50 3.50

Before the Rain, Lviv, by Maksym Kisilvo — A896

2019, Dec. 19 Litho. *Perf. 14¼x14*
1238 A896 (8h) multi .85 .85

Miniature Sheet

Lviv Oblast A897

No. 1239: a, Dominican Church, Lviv, painting by Viktor Zhmak (51x51mm). b, Svirz Castle (33x28mm). c, St. Nicholas Church, Lviv (33x28mm). d, Kamianskyi Waterfall (33x28mm).

2019, Dec. 19 Litho. *Perf. 11½*
1239 A897 8h Sheet of 4, #a-d 3.25 3.25

Ludwig van Beethoven (1770-1827), Composer A898

2020, Jan. 14 Litho. *Perf. 14x14¼*
1240 A898 17h multi 1.75 1.75

Soldier and Damaged Donetsk Airport Control Tower — A899

2020, Jan. 22 Litho. *Perf. 14¼x14*
1241 A899 (8h) multi 1.00 1.00

2014 Battles of Donetsk Airport.

Penguin — A900

2020, Jan. 28 Litho. *Perf. 13½*
1242 A900 (8h) multi 1.00 1.00

Discovery of Antarctica, 200th anniv. Values are for stamps with surrounding selvage.

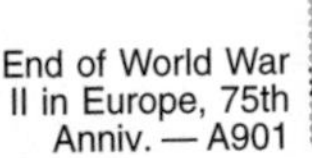

End of World War II in Europe, 75th Anniv. — A901

Litho. & Embossed

2020, May 8 *Perf. 14¼x14*
1243 A901 9h multi .95 .95

Masked Medical Worker and Soldier — A902

2020, May 29 Litho. *Perf. 13¼*
1244 A902 (9h) multi 1.00 1.00

Campaign against COVID-19 pandemic.

Arms of Staryi Merchyk A903

Arms of Burshtyn A904

Arms of Kryvche A905

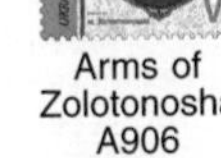

Arms of Zolotonosha A906

Arms of Fontanka A907

Arms of Tetiiv A908

2020 Litho. *Perf. 13¾*

1245	A903	(50k) multi	.25	.25
1246	A904	(3h) multi	.30	.30
1247	A905	(8h) multi	.80	.80
1248	A906	(9h) multi	.80	.80
1249	A907	(13.50h) multi	1.40	1.40
1250	A908	(17h) multi	1.75	1.75
		Nos. 1245-1250 (6)	5.30	5.30

Issued: Nos. 1245-1246, 6/3; Nos. 1247, 1249, 9/15; Nos. 1248, 1250, 9/24.

Ivan Franko National Drama Theater, Cent. A909

2020, June 19 Litho. *Perf. 11½*
1251 A909 9h multi 1.00 1.00

No. 1251 was printed in sheets of 8 + 4 labels.

Fedir Feketa (1789-1839), Postman
A910

2020, June 25 Litho. *Perf. 11½*
1252 A910 (26.70h) multi 3.00 3.00

Ancient Postal Routes. Europa.
A booklet containing a pane of one 51x35mm stamp having the same franking value as No. 1252 sold fo 62h.

Philadelphus
A911

Lavandula
A912

Serpentine Die Cut
2020, July 15 Litho.
Booklet Stamps
Self-Adhesive

1253 A911 13.50h multi 1.40 1.40
a. Booklet pane fo 8 11.50
1254 A912 13.50h multi 1.40 1.40
a. Booklet pane fo 8 11.50

Nos. 1253-1254 are impregnated with the scent of the flower they depict.

A913

Sofia Karaffa-Korbut (1924-96) and Her Illustrations of Characters From *The Forest Song,* Play by Lesia Ukrainka (1871-1913) — A914

2020, July 25 Litho. *Perf. 11½*
1255 A913 9h gold & multi .65 .65
1256 A914 9h sil & multi .65 .65

Order of the Iron Cross — A915

Litho. With Foil Application
2020, Aug. 18 *Perf. 13¼*
1257 A915 11h gold & multi 1.10 1.10

Queue for Bread, by Ivan Botko (1914-90)
A916

Perf. 14¼x13¾
2020, Aug. 20 Litho.
1258 A916 9h multi .90 .90

Miniature Sheet

Kherson Oblast
A917

No. 1259: a, Dzharylhach Island (37x28mm). b, Polovets (Cuman) statue of woman, Askania-Nova (37x28mm). c, Oleksii Shovkunenko Art Museum, Kherson (37x28mm). d, Cervus nippon (49x44mm).

2020, Aug. 20 Litho. *Perf. 11½*
1259 A917 9h Sheet of 4, #a-d 3.75 3.75

Schönborn Castle, Chynadiyovo
A918

Germans Celebrating Christmas
A919

Polka Dancers
A920

German Farmers
A921

2020, Aug. 28 Litho. *Perf. 13¼*
1260 A918 9h multi .90 .90
1261 A919 9h multi .90 .90
1262 A920 9h multi .90 .90
1263 A921 9h multi .90 .90
Nos. 1260-1263 (4) 3.60 3.60

German culture in Ukraine.

Souvenir Sheet

Scythian Battles
A922

No. 1264: a, 9h, Scythian battle with Macedonians, 339 B.C. b, 27h, Scythian battle with army of Zopyrion, 331 B.C.

Litho. With Foil Application
2020, Sept. 11 *Perf. 11½*
1264 A922 Sheet of 2, #a-b 3.75 3.75

Ukrphilex 2020 Philatelic Exhibition, Kharkiv. A booklet containing No. 1264 was produced in limited quantities and sold for 150h.

Miniature Sheet

Cyrillic Alphabet
A923

No. 1265: a, Snow-covered cottage, Cyrillic letter for "Kh." b, Moon, Cyrillic soft sign. c, Soup in cauldron over fire, Cyrillic letter for "Yu." d, Goat, Cyrillic letter for "Ts." e, Calf, Cyrillic letter for "T." f, Boots, Cyrillic letter for "Ch." g, Man smiling, Cyrillic letter for "Oo." h, Pike (fish), Cyrillic letter for "Shch." i, Top of snow-covered tree, Cyrillic letter for "Ya." j, Paint can, Cyrillic letter for "F." k, Bottom of tree with pine cones, Cyrillic letter for "Sh."

2020, Sept. 12 Litho. *Perf. 11½*
1265 A923 9h Sheet of 11, #a-k 7.00 7.00

Miniature Sheet

Lighthouses — A924

No. 1266: a, Yevpatorliskyi Lighthouse (lighthouse with red and white stripes). b, Byrluchyi Lighthouse (white octagonal lighthouse). c, Illinskyi Lightouse (white lighthouse with semi-circular windows). d, Stanislav-Adzhyholskyi Rear Lighthouse (circular red steel bar lighthouse). e, Mehanomskyi Lighthouse (white octagonal lighthouse surrounded by fence). f, Zmiinyi Lighthouse (lighthouse with trident symbol).

2020, Sept. 15 Litho. *Perf. 11½*
1266 A924 9h Sheet of 6, #a-f 5.50 5.50

Miniature Sheet

Endangered Birds — A925

No. 1267: a, Circus pygargus. b, Falco naumanni, vert. c, Aquila chrysaetos, vert. d, Pandion haliaetus. e, Hieraaetus pennatus, vert. f, Aquila pomarina. g, Circus macrourus. h, Buteo rufinus, vert.
Horiz. stamps are 47x32mm; vert. stamps are 33x45mm.

2020, Oct. 7 Litho. *Perf. 11½*
1267 A925 9h Sheet of 8, #a-h 7.25 7.25

BTR4-MB1 Armored Personnel Carrier — A926

BM-21UM Berest Rocket Launcher — A927

Perf. 14x14¼ Syncopated
2020, Oct. 9 Litho.
1268 A926 9h multi .90 .90
1269 A927 9h multi .90 .90

Cossack of 1st Bohdan Khmelnytskyi Ukrainian Regiment
A928

Cossack of Sich Riflemen Detachment
A929

Cossack of 1st Ukrainian Syniozhupanna Division — A930

2020, Oct. 13 Litho. *Perf. 11½*
1270 A928 9h multi .90 .90
1271 A929 9h multi .90 .90
1272 A930 9h multi .90 .90
Nos. 1270-1272 (3) 2.70 2.70

Uniforms of paramilitary factions in the 1917-21 Ukrainian Revolution.

Kyrylo Osmak (1890-1960), President of Supreme Ukrainian Liberation Council — A931

2020, Oct. 30 Litho. *Perf. 14¼x14*
1273 A931 9h multi .90 .90

Marko Kropyvnytskyi (1840-1910), Playwright and Song Writer — A932

2020, Nov. 12 Litho. *Perf. 11½*
1274 A932 9h multi .90 .90

No. 1274 was printed in sheets of 7 + 3 labels.

Mykhailo Starytskyi (1840-1904), Writer — A933

2020, Nov. 12 Litho. *Perf. 13¼*
1275 A933 (9h) multi .90 .90

No. 1275 was printed in sheets of 8 + central label.

Mykola Rudenko (1920-2004), Writer and Human Rights Activist — A934

Mykhailo Gorin (1930-2013), Human Rights Activist — A935

Svyatoslav Karavansky (1920-2016), Linguist and Soviet Political Prisoner — A936

2020, Nov. 20 Litho. *Perf. 14x4¼*

1276 Strip of 3 2.70 2.70
a. A934 (9h) multi .90 .90
b. A935 (9h) multi .90 .90
c. A936 (9h) multi .90 .90

Animated Movie *Mavka, The Forest Song* A937

Serpentine Die Cut 11¾

2020, Nov. 30 Litho.

Self-Adhesive

1277 A937 (9h) multi .90 .90

Railroad Viaduct, Vorokhta A938

2020, Dec. 4 Litho. *Perf. 14x14¼*

1278 A938 (9h) multi .90 .90

Miniature Sheet

Ivano-Frankivsk Oblast — A939

No. 1279: a, Bowl crafted by Olexa Bakhmatiuk (1820-82) (63x44mm). b, Church of the Nativity of the Virgin, Vorokhta (37x28mm). c, Hutsul bride and groom on horseback (37x28mm). d, Dovbush Rocks (37x28mm).

2020, Dec. 4 Litho. *Perf. 11½*

1279 A939 9h Sheet of 4, #a-d 3.75 3.75

Ukrainian Woman and Jewelry A940

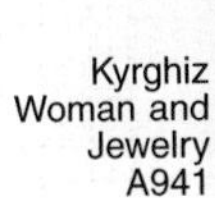

Kyrghiz Woman and Jewelry A941

Litho. & Embossed

2020, Dec. 8 *Perf. 11½*

1280 Horiz. pair 2.80 2.80
a. A940 (13.50h) multi 1.40 1.40
b. A941 (13.50h) multi 1.40 1.40

See Kyrgyz Express Post No. 136.

Blue Bull, by Maria Prymachenko (1908-97) — A942

Litho. With Foil Application

2020, Dec. 10 *Perf. 11½*

1281 A942 (9h) gold & multi .90 .90

Characters From Animated Cartoon Series *Cossacks* A943

Serpentine Die Cut 11¾

2020, Dec. 18 Litho.

Self-Adhesive

1282 A943 (9h) multi .90 .90

Miniature Sheet

Regional Costumes — A944

No. 1283: a, Mykolayiv Oblast men and child. b, Mykolayiv Oblast man, woman and child. c, Kirovohrad Oblast man, women and child celebrating Christmas. d, Kirovohrad Oblast man and woman with horse and cat on Palm Sunday. e, Kyiv Region woman, child and man with dove. f, Kyiv Region women assisting bathing woman.

2020, Dec. 24 Litho. *Perf. 11½*

1283 A944 11h Sheet of 6, #a-f 6.50 6.50

Personalized Stamp — A945

2020, Dec. 24 Litho. *Perf. 11½*

1284 A945 (9h) multi + label 1.90 1.90

No. 1284 was printed in sheets of 9 stamps + 9 labels that could be personalized. The label shown, depicting the Ukrposhta emblem, is the generic label image.

Stained-Glass Windows of Lviv — A946

No. 1285 — Stained-glass window depicting: a, V (9h), Flowers, from 7 Soborna Square (40x31mm). b, V (9h), Curves and loops, from Dominican Church (40x31mm). c, V (9h), Two angels, from Church of the Heart of Jesus (40x31mm). d, V (9h), Archangel, from Armenian Cathedral (40x31mm). e, M (13.50h), Jesus praying, from Church of St. Anthony (40x46mm). f, M (13.50h), Mary wearing crown, from Church of the Assumption (40x46mm). g, F (17h), Mary with halo of stars, from Latin Cathedral (39x53mm).

Litho. With Holographic Foil

2020, Dec. 30 *Perf. 11½*

1285 A946 Sheet of 7, #a-g 5.75 5.75

Order of Heroes of the Heavenly Hundred — A947

2021, Feb. 19 Litho. *Perf. 11½*

1286 A947 (11h) multi 1.10 1.10

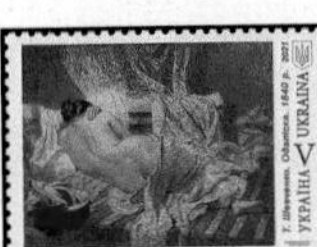

Odalisque, by Taras Shevchenko (1814-61) A948

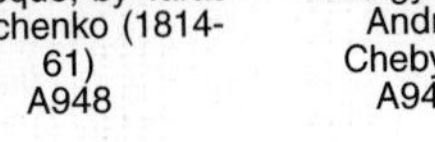

Energy II, by Andriy Chebykin A949

2021, Mar. 5 Litho. *Perf. 11½*

1287 A948 (9h) multi .65 .65

Perf. 13¼

1288 A949 (9h) multi .65 .65

Miniature Sheet

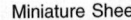

Ukrainian Armed Forces A950

No. 1289 — Emblem and member of: a, Missile and Artillery Forces, wearing dress uniform and beret. b, Mechanized Infantry, wearing helmet and goggles. c, Presidential Regiment, saluting. d, Air Defense Forces, with walkie-talkie. e, Mountain Infantry, near mountain. f, Army Aviation Brigade, wearing dress uniform and cap. g, Member of Tank Brigade, in front of tank. h, Female soldier in dress uniform.

2021, Mar. 14 Litho. *Perf. 13¼*

1289 A950 (9h) Sheet of 8, #a-h 5.25 5.25

Chernobyl Nuclear Disaster, 35th Anniv. A951

2021, Apr. 26 Litho. *Perf. 14x14¼*

1290 A951 (9h) multi .65 .65

Shirt Embroidery From Dnipropetrovsk Region A952

Shirt Embroidery From Rivne Region A953

Shirt Embroidery From Ternopil Region A954

Shirt Embroidery From Luhansk Region A955

2021, May 21 Litho. *Perf. 11½*

1291 A952 (9h) multi .65 .65
1292 A953 (9h) multi .65 .65
1293 A954 (17h) multi 1.25 1.25
1294 A955 (17h) multi 1.25 1.25
Nos. 1291-1294 (4) 3.80 3.80

Nos. 1291-1294 were each printed in sheets of 8 + central label.

Deforestation A956

Wolf and Tree Stump A957

2021, June 9 Litho. *Perf. 14¼*

1295 A956 (27h) multi 2.00 2.00
1296 A957 (27h) multi 2.00 2.00

Europa. A booklet containing a pane of two perf. 11½ 30x42mm stamps like Nos. 1295-1296 sold for 108.30h.

2020 European Soccer Championships A958

2021, June 11 Litho. *Perf. 13¼*

1297 A958 (17h) multi 1.25 1.25

The 2020 European Soccer Championships were postponed until 2021 because of the COVID-19 pandemic.

Miniature Sheet

Sevastopol — A959

No. 1298: a, Balaklava Bay (40x28mm). b, Buildings and monument near Sevastopol Quay (40x28mm). c, Saint Vladimir Cathedral and Ruins of the 1935 Basilica (40x28mm). d, Monument to Sunken Ships (35x56mm).

2021, June 14 Litho. *Perf. 11½*

1298 A959 11h Sheet of 4, #a-d 3.25 3.25

Sevastopol, on the Crimean Peninsula, was annexed by Russia in 2014.

Lesia Ukrainka (1871-1913), Writer — A960

2021, July 9 Litho. *Perf. 11½*

1299 A960 27h sil & multi 2.00 2.00

2020 Summer Olympics, Tokyo — A961

2021, July 11 Litho. *Perf. 13½*

1300 A961 (17h) sil & multi 1.30 1.30

The 2020 Summer Olympics were postponed until 2021 because of the COVID-19 pandemic.

Arms of Bolhrad A962

Arms of Bohodukhiv A963

Arms of Komarno A964

Arms of Bakhmut A965

Arms of Koropets A966

Arms of Kremenchuk A967

2021-22 Litho. *Perf. 13¾*

1301	A962	(50k)	multi	.30	.25
1302	A963	(50k)	multi	.30	.25
1303	A964	(5.25h)	multi	.40	.40
1304	A965	(8h)	multi	.60	.60
1305	A966	(13.50h)	multi	1.00	1.00
1306	A967	(17h)	multi	1.30	1.30
	Nos. 1301-1306 (6)			3.90	3.80

Issued: Nos. 1301, 1305, 7/16; No. 1302, 1/21/22; No. 1303, 12/1; Nos. 1304, 1306, 9/29.

Miniature Sheet

Birds A970

No. 1309: a, Tetrastes bonasia, b, Tetrao urogallus. c, Phasianus colchicus. d, Coturnix coturnix, e, Lagopus lagopus. f, Perdix perdix. g, Lyrurus tetrix. h, Alectoris chukar.

2021, Aug. 6 Litho. *Perf. 11½*
1309 A970 9h Sheet of 8, #a-h 5.50 5.50

Shmuel Yosef Agnon (1888-1970), 1966 Nobel Laureate in Literature — A971

2021, Aug. 17 Litho. *Perf. 13¼*
1310 A971 (40h) multi 3.00 3.00

See Israel No. 2293.

Independence Monument, Kyiv — A972

Litho. With Foil Application
2021, Aug. 17 *Perf. 11½*
1311 A972 (9h) gold & multi .70 .70

Souvenir Sheet
Perf. 11½ on 3 Sides
1312 A972 33h gold & multi 2.50 2.50

No. 1312 contains one 40x70mm stamp.

Souvenir Sheet

Battle of Chocim, by Józef Brandt (1841-1915) — A973

2021, Sept. 2 Litho. *Perf. 11½*
1313 A973 (40h) multi 3.00 3.00

Battle of Chocim, 400th anniv. See Lithuania No. 1190, Poland No. 4567.

Souvenir Sheet

Paintings by Eugen Zotow (1881-1953) — A974

No. 1314: a, View of Vaduz Castle (47x32mm). b, Self-portrait, (32x32mm).

2021, Sept. 6 Litho. *Perf. 11½*
1314 A974 (27h) Sheet of 2, #a-b 4.25 4.25

See Liechtenstein No. 1844.

Astronomical Observatory of Ivan Franko National University of Lviv — A976

2021, Sept. 14 Litho. *Perf. 11½*
1316 A976 (9h) multi .70 .70

Cherkasy Dam and Kremenchug Reservoir — A977

Perf. 13¾x14¼
2021, Sept. 18 Litho.
1317 A977 (9h) multi .70 .70

Miniature Sheet

Cherkasy Oblast — A978

No. 1318: a, Monument to Taras Shevchenko, Kaniv (38x52mm). b, Holy Ascension Church and windmills, Vodianyky (40x26mm). c, Sofiivka Arboretum, Uman (40x26mm). d, Wedding Palace, Cherkasy, at night (40x26mm).

2021, Sept. 18 Litho. *Perf. 11½*
1318 A978 11h Sheet of 4, #a-d 3.50 3.50

Mykolayiv Astronomical Observatory, 200th Anniv. — A979

2021, Sept. 28 Litho. *Perf. 11½*
1319 A979 (9h) multi .70 .70

Miniature Sheet

Horodecki House (House With Chimaeras), Kyiv — A980

No. 1320: a, 11h, Architectural ornamentation depicting elephant and buck (31x31mm). b, 11h, Architectural ornamentation depicting rhinoceros and elephant (31x31mm). c, 16h, Architectural ornamentation of battle between eagle and panther (31x31mm). d, 16h, Wladyslaw Horodecki (1863-1930), building's architect (31x31mm). e, 33h, Horodecki House (94x47mm).

Litho. (11h, 33h), Litho. With Foil Application (16h)
2021, Oct. 4 *Perf. 11½*
1320 A980 Sheet of 5, #a-e, + 2 labels 6.75 6.75

Second Winter Campaign of the Ukrainian National Army, Cent. — A981

2021, Oct. 13 Litho. *Perf. 14¼x14*
1321 A981 (10.50h) multi .80 .80

Hydrofoil Voshod A982

2021, Oct. 22 Litho. *Perf. 14x14¼*
1322 A982 (10.50h) multi .80 .80

1921 Zaporozhets Tractor A983

2021, Oct. 22 Litho. *Perf. 14x14¼*
1323 A983 (10.50h) multi .80 .80

Machine Gunner, Third Iron Rifle Divison A984

Commander, First Auto Panzer Division A985

Ukrainian Sich Rifleman — A986

2021, Oct. 29 Litho. *Perf. 14¼x14*

1324	A984	(10.50h)	multi	.80	.80
1325	A985	(10.50h)	multi	.80	.80
1326	A986	(10.50h)	multi	.80	.80
	Nos. 1324-1326 (3)			2.40	2.40

Military uniforms of the 1917-21 Ukrainian Revolution.

Minesweeper Cherkasy — A987

2021, Nov. 19 Litho. *Perf. 14x14¼*
1327 A987 (10.50h) multi .80 .80

Order of Danylo Halytskyi — A988

Litho. With Foil Application
2021, Dec. 6 *Perf. 13½*
1328 A988 (13h) gold & multi .95 .95

Christmas A989

Litho. With Foil Application
2021, Dec. 7 *Perf. 13½*
1329 A989 (10.50h) gold & multi .80 .80

Amber — A990

2021, Dec. 15 Litho. *Perf. 14¼x14*
1330 A990 (10.50h) multi .80 .80

Miniature Sheet

Rivne Oblast A991

No. 1331: a, Dubno Castle. b, Tarakaniv Fort and dirt path. c, Railroad tracks running through Love Tunnel near Kievan. d, Museum entrance, Peresopnytsia.

2021, Dec. 15 Litho. *Perf. 11½*
1331 A991 (10.50h) Sheet of 4, #a-d 3.25 3.25

Yevhen Chykalenko (1861-1929), Publisher and Philanthropist A992

2021, Dec. 21 Litho. *Perf. 14*
1332 A992 (10.50h) multi .80 .80

Trident — A993

2022, Jan. 21 Litho. *Perf. 13¼*
1333 A993 (12h) black & yellow .85 .85

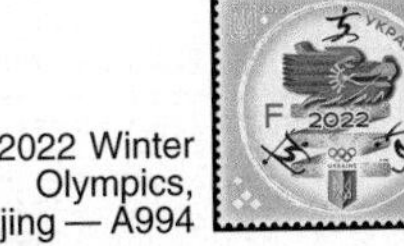

2022 Winter Olympics, Beijing — A994

2022, Jan. 23 Litho. *Perf. 13¼*
1334 A994 (23h) multi 1.60 1.60

A998

Winning Art in Defiance to Russian Invasion of Ukraine Stamp Design Contest — A999

2022, Apr. 12 Litho. *Perf. 14¼x14*
1338 A998 (23h) multi — —

Perf. 13¼

1339 A999 (44h) multi — —

A1000

Winning Art in Defiance to Russian Invasion of Ukraine Stamp Design Contest With Date
A1001

2022, May 23 Litho. *Perf. 14½x14*
1340 A1000 (23h) multi + label — —

Perf. 14x14¼

1341 A1001 (44h) multi + label — —

Children's Art — A1002

2022, June 28 Litho. *Perf. 13¼*
1342 A1002 (12h) multi — —

A1004

Tractor With Ukrainian Flag Towing Damaged Russian Tank — A1005

2022, July 28 Litho. *Perf. 13½x13¾*
1344 A1004 (18h) multi — —

Perf. 13¼

1345 A1005 (55h) multi — —
a. Tete-beche pair — —

Oct. 8, 2022 Explosion on the Crimean Bridge — A1011

2022, Nov. 4 Litho. *Perf. 14¼x14*
1351 A1011 (18h) multi — —

No. 1351 was printed in sheets of 7 + 2 labels.

SEMI-POSTAL STAMPS

Ukrainian Soviet Socialist Republic

"Famine"
SP1

Taras H. Shevchenko
SP2

"Death" Stalking Peasant
SP3

"Ukraine" Distributing Food
SP4

Perf. 14½x13½, 13½x14½

1923, June Litho. Unwmk.

B1	SP1	10k + 10k gray bl & blk	1.00	*5.50*
B2	SP2	20k + 20k vio brn & org brn	1.00	*5.50*
B3	SP3	90k + 30k db & blk, *straw*	1.00	*6.75*
B4	SP4	150k + 50k red brn & blk	1.00	*9.50*
		Nos. B1-B4 (4)	4.00	*27.25*

Imperf., Pairs

B1a	SP1	10k + 10k	50.00	*120.00*
B2a	SP2	20k + 20k	50.00	*120.00*
B3a	SP3	90k + 30k	50.00	*120.00*
B4a	SP4	150k + 50k	50.00	*120.00*

The values of these stamps are in karbovanets, which by 1923 converted to rubles at 100 to 1.

Wmk. 116
Same Colors

B5	SP1	10k + 10k	*40.00*	*70.00*
B6	SP2	20k + 20k	*40.00*	*70.00*
a.		Imperf., pair	2,500.	
B7	SP3	90k + 30k	*40.00*	*70.00*
B8	SP4	150k + 50k	*40.00*	*70.00*
		Nos. B5-B8 (4)	*160.00*	*280.00*

Catalogue values for unused stamps in this section, from this point to the end of the section, are for Never Hinged items.

Charity and Health Fund — SP5

1994, Jan. 15 Litho. *Perf. 12*
B9 SP5 150kb +20kb multi 1.10 .80

Third Natl. Philatelic Exhibition, Lviv — SP6

1995, Sept. 23 Litho. *Perf. 13½*
B10 SP6 50,000kb +5000kb multi 1.20 1.20

Souvenir Sheet

Zymnenska Icon of Madonna and Child — SP7

1999, Sept. 4 Litho. *Perf. 11½*
B11 SP7 1.20h +10k multicolored 3.75 3.75

Intl. Year of the Elderly.

Miniature Sheet

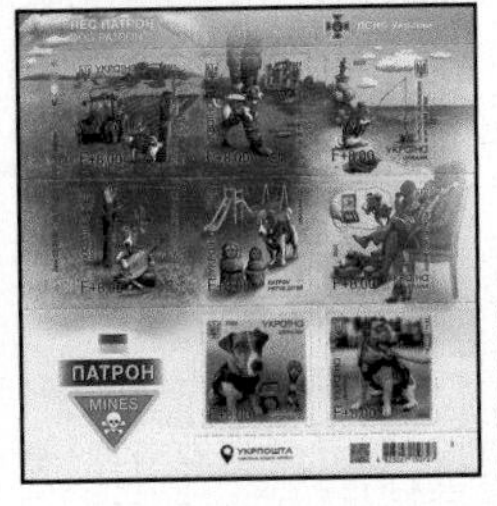

Rescue Dog Named Patron
SP8

No. B12 — Patron: a, Unrinating on unexploded Russian bomb. b, Wearing mask and cape. c, Fishing for mines. d, Playing balalaika. e, Growling at Russian nesting dolls hiding hand grenade. f, Dreaming of receiving a medal. g, With medal and trophy. h, On leash.

Die Cut Perf. 14

2022, Sept. 1 Litho.

Self-Adhesive

B12 SP8 (23h) +8h Sheet of 8, #a-h — —

Surtax for support of animal shelters and purchase of mine detection equipment.

Miniature Sheet

Tribute to Ukrainian Military
SP9

No. B13: a, Airborne Assault Force members wearing red berets, rooster on balcony. b, Sailor, ship and lighthouse. c, Ground Force members carrying baby. d, Territorial Defense Force members and refugees. e, Special Operations Force member with special equipment on helmet. f, Air Force pilot and airplanes.

2022, Oct. 14 Litho. *Perf. 13¾x14¼*
B13 SP9 (12h) +8h Sheet of 6, #a-f — —

REGISTRATION STAMPS

Catalogue values for unused stamps in this section are for Never Hinged items.

Trident — R1

2001, Apr. 1 Litho. *Perf. 13¾*

F1	R1	(10.84h) multi	8.00	7.25
a.		Imprint "2003"	9.00	7.25
b.		Perf. 11½, dated "2006"	7.25	7.25

Issued: No. F1a, 1/28/03; No. F1b, 10/9/06. No. F1b was issued only in No. F2c.

Trident With Frame — R2

2005-06 Litho. *Perf. 13¾*

F2	R2	(10.10h) multi	7.00	7.00
a.		Imprint "2006"	7.00	7.00
b.		Perf. 11½, dated "2006"	7.00	7.00
c.		Sheet of 18, #418a-422a, 453a-454a, 466a-468a, 515a, 572a, 606a-609a, F1b, F2b	25.00	25.00

Issued: No. F2, 10/28/05; No. F2a, 2/7/06; No. F2b, 10/9/06. No. F2b was issued only in No. F2c. No. F2c sold for 35.41h and exists imperf.

MILITARY STAMPS

COURIER FIELD POST ISSUE

Nos. 1-5, 48 Surcharged

Кур'єрсько-
польова
Пошта.
10 Гривень

1920, Aug. 26

M1	A1	10h on 10sh buff	20.00	—
a.		Inverted surcharge	80.00	
M2	A2	10h on 20sh brown	40.00	—
M3	A3	10h on 30sh ultramarine	50.00	—
M4	A4	10h on 40sh green	55.00	—
a.		Inverted surcharge	215.00	
M5	A5	10h on 50sh red	50.00	—
M6	A1	20h on 10sh buff	55.00	—
M7	A2	20h on 20sh brown	15.00	—
a.		Inverted surcharge	60.00	
M8	A3	20h on 30sh ultramarine	40.00	—
a.		Inverted surcharge	160.00	
M9	A4	20h on 40sh green	40.00	—
M10	A5	20h on 50sh red	40.00	—
a.		Inverted surcharge	160.00	
M11	A1	40h on 10sh buff	200.00	—
M12	A2	40h on 20sh brown	100.00	—
M13	A3	40h on 30sh ultramarine	400.00	—
M14	A4	40h on 40sh green	200.00	—
M15	A5	40h on 50sh red	400.00	—
M16	A6	40h on 20hr red & green	—	—

Nos. M1-M16 were prepared to facilitate communications between the Ukrainian government-in-exile at Tarnow, Poland, and its military units in the field.

Only two examples of No. M16 are known, one unused and one used on cover.

Forged surcharges and cancellations exist.

UMM AL QIWAIN

'um-al-kī-'wīn

LOCATION — Oman Peninsula, Arabia, on Arabian Gulf
GOVT. — Sheikdom under British protection
AREA — 300 sq. mi.
POP. — 5,700

Umm al Qiwain is one of six Persian Gulf sheikdoms to join the United Arab Emirates which proclaimed independence Dec. 2, 1971. See United Arab Emirates.

100 Naye Paise = 1 Rupee
100 Dirham = 1 Riyal (1967)

Catalogue values for all unused stamps in this country are for Never Hinged items.

Sheik Ahmed bin Rashid al Mulla and Gazelles — A1

Photogravure and Lithographed

1964, June 29 Unwmk. *Perf. 14*

Size: 35x22mm

1	A1	1np shown	.25	.25
2	A1	2np Snake	.25	.25
3	A1	3np Hyena	.25	.25
4	A1	4np Conspicuous trig-gerfish	.25	.25
5	A1	5np Fish	.25	.25
6	A1	10np Silver angelfish	.30	.25
7	A1	15np Palace	.30	.25
8	A1	20np Umm al Qiwain	.30	.25
9	A1	30np Tower	.35	.30

Size: 42x26mm

10	A1	40np as 1np	.35	.30
11	A1	50np as 2np	.45	.35
12	A1	70np as 3np	.75	.40
13	A1	1r as 4np	1.00	.50
14	A1	1.50r as 4np	1.25	.65
15	A1	2r as 10np	1.75	.90

Size: 52x33mm

16	A1	3r as 15np	3.00	2.00
17	A1	5r as 20np	5.25	3.25
18	A1	10r as 30np	9.00	6.00
		Nos. 1-18 (18)	25.30	16.65

National Stadium, Tokyo, and Discobolus A2

Designs: 1r, 2r, National Stadium, Tokyo. 1.50r, Indoor swimming arena. 3r, Komazawa Gymnasium. 4r, Stadium entrance.

1964, Nov. 25 Photo. *Perf. 14*

19	A2	50np multi	.30	.25
20	A2	1r multi	.50	.25
21	A2	1.50r multi	.65	.25
22	A2	2r multi	1.00	.25
23	A2	3r multi	1.25	.45
24	A2	4r multi	2.50	.85
25	A2	5r multi	3.25	1.00
		Nos. 19-25 (7)	9.45	3.30

18th Olympic Games, Tokyo, Oct. 10-25, 1964. Perf. and imperf. souvenir sheets contain 4 stamps similar to #22-25 in changed colors. Size: 145x115mm.

A3

Designs: 10np, Pres. Kennedy's funeral cortege leaving White House. 15np, Mrs. Kennedy with children, and Robert Kennedy following coffin. 50np, Horse-drawn caisson. 1r, Presidents Truman and Eisenhower, and Margaret Truman Daniels. 2r, Pres. Charles de Gaulle, Emperor Haile Selassie, Chancellor Ludwig Erhart, Sir Alec Douglas-Home and King Frederick IX. 3r, Kennedy family on steps of St. Matthew's Cathedral. 5r, Honor guard at tomb. 7.50r, Portrait of Pres. John F. Kennedy.

Perf. 14½

1965, Jan. 20 Unwmk. Photo.

Black Design with Gold Inscriptions

Size: 29x44mm

26	A3	10np pale blue	.25	.25
27	A3	15np pale yellow	.25	.25
28	A3	50np pale green	.30	.25
29	A3	1r pale pink	.60	.35
30	A3	2r pale green	1.00	.45

Size: 33x51mm

31	A3	3r pale gray	1.75	.65
32	A3	5r pale blue	3.00	.90
33	A3	7.50r pale yellow	4.00	1.50
		Nos. 26-33 (8)	11.15	4.60

Pres. John F. Kennedy. A souvenir sheet contains 2 stamps similar to Nos. 32-33 with pale green (5r) and pale salmon (7.50r) backgrounds, size: 29x44mm. Size of sheet: 114x70mm.

A4

Designs: 10d, Astronaut on Moon. 20d, Landing module approaching moon. 30d, Apollo XII on launching pad. 50d, Commanders Charles Conrad, Jr., Alan L. Bean, Richard F. Gordon, Jr., earth and moon, horiz. 75d, Earth and Apollo XII, horiz. 1r, Sheik Ahmed, rocket and lunar landing module, horiz.

1969, Nov. 19 Litho. *Perf. 14½*

34	A4	10d multi	.25
35	A4	20d multi	.35
36	A4	30d multi	.45
37	A4	50d emerald & multi	.55
38	A4	75d purple & multi	1.00
39	A4	1r dk bl & multi	1.75
		Nos. 34-39 (6)	4.35

US Apollo XII moon landing mission, 11/14-24/69.

Two imperf. souvenir sheets of 3 exist, containing stamps similar to Nos. 34-36 and Nos. 37-39.

A5

1970, May 29 Litho. *Perf. 14*

40	A5	10d James A. Lovell	.25
41	A5	30d Fred W. Haise, Jr.	.40
42	A5	50d John L. Swigert, Jr.	.90
a.		Souv. sheet of 3, #40-42	2.00
		Nos. 40-42 (3)	1.55

Safe return of the crew of Apollo 13.

A6

Designs: 5d, 1.25r, EXPO '70 Emblem. 10d, 20d, Japanese Pavilion.

1970, Aug. 14 Litho. *Perf. 13½x14*

43	A6	5d yellow & multi	.25
44	A6	10d blue & multi	.35
45	A6	20d red & multi	.45
48	A6	1.25r red & multi	.90
		Nos. 43-48 (4)	1.95

EXPO '70 Intl. Exhib., Osaka, Japan, Mar. 15-Sept. 13, 1970.

A 40d and 1r, showing the Emperor and Empress of Japan, and a souvenir sheet containing these and Nos. 43-45, 48 were prepared, but not issued.

A7

Uniforms: 10d, Private, North Lancashire Regiment. 20d, Royal Navy seaman. 30d, Officer, North Lancashire (Loyal) Regiment. 50d, Private, York and Lancaster Regiment. 75d, Royal Navy officer. 1r, Officer, York and Lancaster Regiment.

1970, Oct. 12 Litho. *Perf. 14½x14*

49	A7	10d multi	.25
50	A7	20d multi	.35
51	A7	30d multi	.55
a.		Souv. sheet of 3, #49-51	2.75
52	A7	50d buff & multi	.90
53	A7	75d multi	1.25
54	A7	1r buff & multi	1.75
a.		Souv. sheet of 3, #52-54	4.00
		Nos. 49-54 (6)	5.05

British landings on the Trucial Coast, 150th anniv.

Stamps of Umm al Qiwain were replaced in 1972 by those of United Arab Emirates.

AIR POST STAMPS

Type of Regular Issue, 1964

Photogravure and Lithographed

1965 Unwmk. *Perf. 14*

Size: 42x26mm

C1	A1	15np as #1	.25	.25
C2	A1	25np as #2	.25	.25
C3	A1	35np as #3	.25	.25
C4	A1	50np as #4	.60	.25
C5	A1	75np as #5	1.10	.30
C6	A1	1r as #6	1.40	.40

Size: 52x33mm

C7	A1	2r as #7	2.25	.55
C8	A1	3r as #8	3.25	.75
C9	A1	5r as #9	4.50	1.25
		Nos. C1-C9 (9)	13.85	4.25

Issued: #C7-C9, Nov. 6; others, Oct. 18.

AIR POST OFFICIAL STAMPS

Type of Regular Issue, 1964

Size: 42x26mm

Photogravure and Lithographed

1965, Dec. 22 Unwmk. *Perf. 14*

CO1	A1	75np as #6	1.00	.30

Size: 52x33mm

CO2	A1	2r as #7	2.50	.75
CO3	A1	3r as #8	3.75	1.00
CO4	A1	5r as #9	5.00	1.50
		Nos. CO1-CO4 (4)	12.25	3.55

OFFICIAL STAMPS

Type of Regular Issue, 1964

Size: 42x26mm

Photogravure and Lithographed

1965, Dec. 22 Unwmk. *Perf. 14*

O1	A1	25np as #1	.35	.25
O2	A1	40np as #2	.45	.25
O3	A1	50np as #3	.75	.25
O4	A1	75np as #4	1.00	.30
O5	A1	1r as #5	1.25	.35
		Nos. O1-O5 (5)	3.80	1.40

UNITED ARAB EMIRATES

yu-,nī-təd 'ar-əb i-'mi,ə,r-əts

(Trucial States)

LOCATION — Arabia, on Arabian Gulf
GOVT. — Federation of sheikdoms
AREA — 32,300 sq. mi.
POP. — 2,377,453 (1995)
CAPITAL — Abu Dhabi

The UAE was formed Dec. 2, 1971, by the union of Abu Dhabi, Ajman, Dubai, Fujeira, Sharjah and Umm al Qiwain. Ras al Khaima joined in Feb. 1972.

1,000 Fils = 1 Dinar
100 Fils = 1 Dirham (1973)

Catalogue values for all unused stamps in this country are for Never Hinged items.

Abu Dhabi Nos. 56-67 Overprinted

1972, Aug. Litho. Unwmk. *Perf. 14*

1	A10	5f multicolored	3.25	3.25
2	A10	10f multicolored	3.25	3.25
3	A10	25f multicolored	5.00	5.00
4	A10	35f multicolored	6.50	6.50
5	A10	50f multicolored	11.00	11.00
6	A10	60f multicolored	12.00	12.00
7	A10	70f multicolored	16.00	16.00
8	A10	90f multicolored	20.00	20.00
9	A11	125f multicolored	65.00	65.00
10	A11	150f multicolored	90.00	90.00
11	A11	500f multicolored	210.00	210.00
12	A11	1d multicolored	400.00	400.00
		Nos. 1-12 (12)	842.00	842.00

The overprint differs.

Nos. 1-12 were used in Abu Dhabi. Nos. 2-3 were placed on sale later in Dubai & Sharjah.

Map and Flag of UAE — A1

Almagta Bridge, Abu Dhabi — A2

Designs: 10f, Like 5f. 15f, 35f, Coat of arms of UAE (eagle). 75f, Khor Fakkan, Sharjah. 1d, Steel Clock Tower, Dubai. 1.25d, Buthnah Fort, Fujeira. 2d, Alfalaj Fort, Umm al Qiwain. 3d, Khor Khwair, Ras al Khaima. 5d, Palace of Sheik Rashid bin Humaid al Nuaimi, Ajman. 10d, Sheik Zayed bin Sultan al Nahayan, Abu Dhabi.

1973, Jan. 1 Unwmk. *Perf. 14½*

Size: 41x25mm

13	A1	5f multicolored	.25	.25
14	A1	10f multicolored	.25	.25
15	A1	15f blue & multi	.40	.25
16	A1	35f olive & multi	.60	.25

Perf. 14x15

Size: 45x29½mm

17	A2	65f multicolored	.85	.85
18	A2	75f multicolored	1.20	1.25
19	A2	1d multicolored	1.35	1.25
20	A2	1.25d multicolored	3.00	2.00
21	A2	2d multicolored	33.00	12.50
22	A2	3d multicolored	6.75	6.75
23	A2	5d multicolored	7.50	7.50
24	A2	10d multicolored	17.00	16.00
		Nos. 13-24 (12)	72.15	49.10

For surcharge see No. 68.

Festival Emblem — A3

1973, Mar. 27 Litho. *Perf. 13½x14*

25	A3	10f shown	7.00	.35
26	A3	1.25d Trophy	16.00	9.00

National Youth Festival, Mar. 27.

Pedestrian Crossing in Dubai — A4

35f, Traffic light school crossing sign, vert. 1.25d, Traffic policemen with car & radio, vert.

1973, Apr. 1 ***Perf. 13½x14, 14x13½***

27	A4	35f green & multi	4.00	1.75
28	A4	75f blue & multi	7.50	3.50
29	A4	1.25d violet & multi	13.00	6.00
		Nos. 27-29 (3)	24.50	11.25

Traffic Week, Apr. 1-7.

Human Rights Flame and People — A5

1973, Dec. 10 **Litho.** ***Perf. 14½x14***

30	A5	35f blue, blk & org	1.15	1.20
31	A5	65f red, blk & org	4.00	2.50
32	A5	1.25d olive, blk & org	7.50	5.00
		Nos. 30-32 (3)	12.65	8.70

25th anniversary of the Universal Declaration of Human Rights.

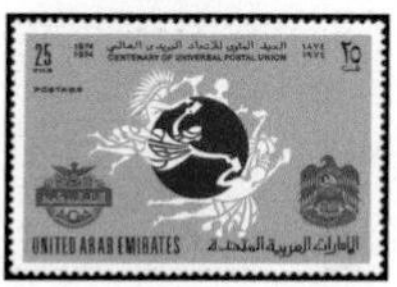

UPU and Arab Postal Union Emblems A6

1974, Aug. 5 **Litho.** ***Perf. 14x14½***

33	A6	25f multicolored	1.60	.80
34	A6	60f emerald & multi	2.60	1.40
35	A6	1.25d lt brown & multi	5.25	3.50
		Nos. 33-35 (3)	9.45	5.70

Centenary of Universal Postal Union.

Health Care — A7

Education A8

Designs: 65f, Construction. 1.25d, UAE flag, UN and Arab League emblems.

1974, Dec. 2 **Litho.** ***Perf. 13½***

36	A7	10f multicolored	.90	.35
37	A8	35f multicolored	2.40	.80
38	A8	65f blue & brown	2.60	1.25
39	A8	1.25d multicolored	5.50	2.60
		Nos. 36-39 (4)	11.40	5.00

Third National Day.

Arab Man and Woman Holding Candle over Book — A9

Man and Woman Reading Book — A10

1974, Dec. 27 ***Perf. 14x14½, 14½x14***

40	A9	35f deep ultra & multi	2.25	.50
41	A10	65f orange brn & multi	2.50	1.00
42	A10	1.25d gray & multi	5.50	2.00
		Nos. 40-42 (3)	10.25	3.50

World Literacy Day.

Oil Degassing Station A11

50f, Off-shore drilling platform. 100f, Underwater storage tank. 125f, Oil production platform.

1975, Mar. 10 **Litho.** ***Perf. 13x13½***

43	A11	25f multicolored	1.20	.45
44	A11	50f multicolored	2.60	.80
45	A11	100f multicolored	6.50	2.00
46	A11	125f multicolored	9.00	2.40
a.		Souvenir sheet of 4, #43-46	32.00	24.00
		Nos. 43-46 (4)	19.30	5.65

9th Arab Petroleum Conference.

Three stamps to commemorate the 2nd Gulf Long Distance Swimming Championship were prepared in June, 1975, but not issued. Value $500.

Jabal Ali Earth Station A12

Jabal Ali Earth Station: 35f, 65f, Communications satellite over globe.

1975, Nov. 8 **Litho.** ***Perf. 13***

47	A12	15f multicolored	1.00	.30
48	A12	35f multicolored	2.40	.55
49	A12	65f multicolored	4.00	.90
50	A12	2d multicolored	9.00	3.25
		Nos. 47-50 (4)	16.40	5.00

Various Scenes A13

Sheik Hamad, Fujeira Ruler A14

Supreme Council Members (Sheikdom rulers): 60f, Sheik Rashid bin Humaid al Naimi, Ajman. 80f, Sheik Ahmed bin Rashid al Mulla, Umm al Qiwain. 90f, Sheik Sultan bin Mohammed al Qasimi, Sharjah. 1d, Sheik Saqr bin Mohammed al Qasimi, Ras al Khaima. 140f, Sheik Rashid bin Said al Maktum, Dubai. 5d, Sheik Zayed bin Sultan al Nahayan, Abu Dhabi.

1975, Dec. 2 **Litho.** ***Perf. 14***

51	A13	10f multicolored	.70	.25
52	A14	35f multicolored	1.75	.90
53	A14	60f multicolored	2.60	1.75
54	A14	80f multicolored	3.75	2.75
55	A14	90f multicolored	4.25	3.00
56	A14	1d multicolored	4.50	3.50
57	A14	140f multicolored	6.25	4.50
58	A14	5d multicolored	26.00	18.00
		Nos. 51-58 (8)	49.80	34.65

Fourth National Day.

Students and Lamp of Learning — A15

Arab Literacy Day: 15f, Lamp of learning.

1976, Feb. 8 **Litho.** ***Perf. 14***

59	A15	15f orange & multi	.60	.30
60	A15	50f ultra & multi	2.00	.80
61	A15	3d multicolored	9.75	6.25
		Nos. 59-61 (3)	12.35	7.35

Children Crossing Street — A16

Traffic Week: 15f, Traffic lights and signals, vert. 80f, Road and traffic lights.

Perf. 14½x14, 14x14½

1976, Apr. 1 **Litho.**

62	A16	15f brt blue & multi	2.00	1.00
63	A16	80f blue & multi	7.50	3.75
64	A16	140f ocher & multi	14.50	8.00
		Nos. 62-64 (3)	24.00	12.75

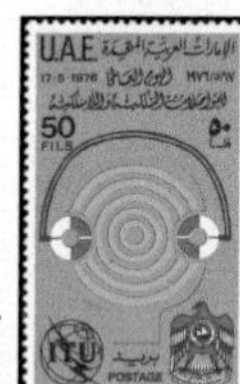

Waves and Ear Phones, ITU Emblem, Coat of Arms — A17

1976, May 17 **Litho.** ***Perf. 14***

65	A17	50f gray grn & multi	1.50	.55
66	A17	80f pink & multi	3.00	1.00
67	A17	2d tan & multi	6.50	2.60
		Nos. 65-67 (3)	11.00	4.15

International Telecommunications Day.

No. 18 Surcharged

1976 **Litho.** ***Perf. 14x15***

68	A2	50f on 75f multi	*42.50*	*17.00*

Coat of Arms — A18

1976, Aug. 15 **Litho.** ***Perf. 11½***

69	A18	5f dull rose	.30	*.25*
70	A18	10f golden brown	.30	*.25*
71	A18	15f orange	.40	.35
72	A18	35f dull red brn	.60	.25
73	A18	50f bright lilac	.80	.40
74	A18	60f bister	1.00	.50
75	A18	80f yellow green	1.20	.60
76	A18	90f ultra	1.60	.65
77	A18	1d blue	1.75	.65
78	A18	140f olive green	3.00	1.20
79	A18	150f rose violet	4.25	1.60
80	A18	2d slate	4.50	1.75
81	A18	5d blue green	10.50	5.00
82	A18	10d lilac rose	19.50	11.50
		Nos. 69-82 (14)	49.70	24.95

See Nos. 91-104.

Sheik Zayed — A19

1976, Dec. 12 **Litho.** ***Perf. 13***

83	A19	15f rose & multi	5.00	.50
84	A19	140f blue & multi	9.75	4.00

5th National Day.

Symbolic Falcon and Globe — A20

1976, Dec. 15 ***Perf. 14x13½***

85	A20	80f yellow & multi	5.00	1.20
86	A20	2d red & multi	9.00	5.00

International Falconry Congress, Abu Dhabi, Dec. 1976.

A21

1976, Dec. 30 **Litho.** ***Perf. 13***

87	A21	50f multicolored	4.00	1.20
88	A21	80f multicolored	8.00	2.40

Mohammed Ali Jinnah (1876-1948), 1st Governor General of Pakistan.

A22

APU emblem, members' flags.

1977, Apr. 12 **Litho.** ***Perf. 13½x14***

89	A22	50f multicolored	5.00	1.20
90	A22	80f multicolored	7.25	3.00

Arab Postal Union, 25th anniversary.

Arms Type of 1976

1977, July 25 **Litho.** ***Perf. 11½***

91	A18	5f dull rose & blk	.40	.35
92	A18	10f gldn brn & blk	.40	.35
93	A18	15f dull org & blk	.55	.45
94	A18	35f lt brown & blk	1.40	.50
95	A18	50f brt lilac & blk	1.60	.55
96	A18	60f bister & blk	1.75	.60
97	A18	80f yel grn & blk	1.75	.60
98	A18	90f ultra & blk	2.75	.95
99	A18	1d blue & blk	4.00	1.40
100	A18	140f ol grn & blk	6.00	1.90
101	A18	150f rose vio & blk	6.50	2.25
102	A18	2d slate & blk	10.00	3.25
103	A18	5d bl grn & blk	22.50	8.25
104	A18	10d lil rose & blk	37.50	24.50
		Nos. 91-104 (14)	97.10	45.90

Man Reading Book, UAE Arms, UN Emblem — A23

1977, Sept. 8 **Litho.** ***Perf. 14x13½***

105	A23	50f green, brn & gold	3.00	.65
106	A23	3d blue & multi	10.00	4.50

International Literacy Day.

A set of three stamps for the 6th Natl. Day was withdrawn from sale on the day of issue, Dec. 2, 1977. Value, $850.

Post Horn and Sails — A24

1979, Apr. 14 Photo. *Perf. 12x11½*

107 A24 50f multicolored 1.00 .80
108 A24 5d multicolored 7.00 5.00

Gulf Postal Organization, 2nd Conf., Dubai.

Arab Achievements A25

1980, Mar. 22 Litho. *Perf. 14x14½*

109 A25 50f multicolored .60 .40
110 A25 140f multicolored 1.75 1.00
111 A25 3d multicolored 3.75 2.25
Nos. 109-111 (3) 6.10 3.65

9th National Day — A26

1980, Dec. 2 Litho. *Perf. 13½*

112 A26 15f multicolored .50 .30
113 A26 50f multicolored 1.60 .80
114 A26 80f multicolored 2.00 1.20
115 A26 150f multicolored 3.00 1.75
Nos. 112-115 (4) 7.10 4.05

Souvenir Sheet

Perf. 13½x14

116 A26 3d multicolored 12.00 12.00

Family on Graph — A27

1980, Dec. 15

117 A27 15f shown .65 .30
118 A27 80f Symbols 2.25 1.00
119 A27 90f like #118 3.00 1.75
120 A27 2d like #117 6.00 4.00
Nos. 117-120 (4) 11.90 7.05

1980 population census.

Hegira (Pilgrimage Year) — A28

1980, Dec. 18 *Perf. 14x13½*

121 A28 15f multicolored .40 .25
122 A28 80f multicolored 1.60 1.00
123 A28 90f multicolored 2.25 1.20
124 A28 140f multicolored 3.50 2.00
Nos. 121-124 (4) 7.75 4.45

Souvenir Sheet

125 A28 2d multicolored 9.25 9.25

No. 125 contains one 36x57mm stamp.

OPEC Emblem A29

1980, Dec. 21 *Perf. 14*

126 A29 50f Men holding OPEC emblem, vert. 1.00 .40
127 A29 80f like #126 1.60 1.00
128 A29 90f shown 1.75 1.20
129 A29 140f like #128 3.25 1.75
Nos. 126-129 (4) 7.60 4.35

Souvenir Sheet

130 A29 3d like #128 14.50 14.50

Traffic Week — A30

15f, 80f, Crossing guard, students, traffic light. 50f, 5d, Crossing guard, traffic light and signs.

1981, Mar. 26 Litho. *Perf. 14½*

131 A30 15f multicolored .55 .25
132 A30 50f multicolored 1.00 .60
133 A30 80f multicolored 2.00 1.20
134 A30 5d multicolored 9.00 6.00
Nos. 131-134 (4) 12.55 8.05

Size of Nos. 131 and 133: 25½x35mm.

10th Natl. Day — A31

1981, Dec. 2 Litho. *Perf. 15x14*

135 A31 25f Cogwheel .60 .35
136 A31 150f Soldiers 4.00 2.00
137 A31 2d UN emblem 5.25 2.40
Nos. 135-137 (3) 9.85 4.75

Intl. Year of the Disabled — A32

Perf. 14½x14, 14x14½

1981, Dec. 26 Litho.

138 A32 25f Couple .60 .30
139 A32 45f Man in wheel-chair, vert. 1.20 .90
140 A32 150f like #139 4.00 2.00
141 A32 2d like #138 6.00 2.60
Nos. 138-141 (4) 11.80 5.80

Natl. Arms — A33

1982-86

142 A33 5f multicolored .25 .25
143 A33 10f multicolored .25 .25
144 A33 15f multicolored .25 .25
145 A33 25f multicolored .25 .25
145A A33 35f multicolored .25 .25
146 A33 50f lt. blue & multi .35 .35
146A A33 50f dark blue & multi 2.40 1.20
147 A33 75f multicolored .50 .50
148 A33 100f multicolored .75 .75
149 A33 110f multicolored .80 .80
150 A33 125f multicolored 1.20 1.15
151 A33 150f multicolored 1.40 1.00
151A A33 175f multicolored 1.60 1.00

Size: 23x27mm

Perf. 13

152 A33 2d multicolored 1.75 1.30
152A A33 250f multicolored 1.90 1.15
153 A33 3d multicolored 3.00 1.55
154 A33 5d multicolored 5.00 2.60
155 A33 10d multicolored 10.50 6.75
156 A33 20d multicolored 20.00 11.00
157 A33 50d multicolored 40.00 20.00
Nos. 142-157 (20) 92.40 52.35

Issued: 35f, 175f, 250f, 12/15/84; 50d, 2/6/86; others, 3/7/82.

6th Arab Gulf Soccer Championships — A34

1982, Apr. 4 Litho. *Perf. 14*

167 A34 25f Emblem, flags 1.00 .50
168 A34 75f Eagle, soccer ball, stadium, vert. 2.60 1.90
169 A34 125f Players, vert. 3.50 2.40
170 A34 3d like 75f, vert. 7.50 6.25
Nos. 167-170 (4) 14.60 11.05

2nd Disarmament Meeting — A35

1982, Oct. 24 Litho. *Perf. 13x13½*

171 A35 25f multicolored .55 .25
172 A35 75f multicolored 1.60 1.75
173 A35 125f multicolored 3.00 1.90
174 A35 150f multicolored 3.25 2.40
Nos. 171-174 (4) 8.40 6.30

11th Natl. Day — A36

Designs: 25f, 150f, Skyscraper, communications tower, natl. crest, castle turret, open book, flag. 75f, 125f, Sun, bird, vert.

1982, Dec. 2 Litho. *Perf. 14½*

175 A36 25f multicolored .50 .35
176 A36 75f multicolored 1.90 1.30
177 A36 125f multicolored 2.60 1.75
178 A36 150f multicolored 3.00 2.25
Nos. 175-178 (4) 8.00 5.65

A37

1983, Dec. 20 Litho. *Perf. 14x14½*

179 A37 25f multicolored .65 .25
180 A37 150f multicolored 3.00 1.30
181 A37 2d multicolored 4.00 2.40
182 A37 3d multicolored 5.75 3.00
Nos. 179-182 (4) 13.40 6.95

World Communications Year.

A38

Arab Literacy Day: 25f, 75f, Oil lamp, open Koran. 35f, 3d, Scribe.

1983, Jan. 8 Litho. *Perf. 14½*

183 A38 25f multicolored *32.50 60.00*
184 A38 35f multicolored 1.25 .65
185 A38 75f multicolored *32.50 55.00*
186 A38 3d multicolored 8.00 4.00

Nos. 183 and 185 withdrawn from sale on day of issue because of an error in Koranic inscription.

INTELSAT, 20th Anniv. — A39

1984, Nov. 24 Litho. *Perf. 14½*

187 A39 2d multicolored 4.50 4.00
188 A39 2.50d multicolored 6.50 5.75

13th Natl. Day — A40

Flag, portrait of an Emir and building or view from each capital.

1984, Dec. 2 *Perf. 14½x13½*

189 A40 1d Building, pavilion 2.00 1.25
190 A40 1d Fortress, cannon 2.00 1.25
191 A40 1d Port, boats 2.00 1.25
192 A40 1d Fortress 2.00 1.25
193 A40 1d Oil refinery 2.00 1.25
194 A40 1d Building, garden 2.00 1.25
195 A40 1d Oil well, palace 2.00 1.25
Nos. 189-195 (7) 14.00 8.75

Tidy Week — A41

1985, Mar. 15 *Perf. 12½*

196 A41 5d multicolored 9.25 8.00

A42

1985, Sept. 10 *Perf. 13½x14½*

197 A42 2d multicolored 5.75 3.75
198 A42 250f multicolored 8.00 5.25

World Junior Chess Championships, Sharjah, Sept. 10-27.

14th Natl. Day — A43

1985, Dec. 2 *Perf. 14x13½*

199 A43 50f multicolored .60 .45
200 A43 3d multicolored 5.75 3.75

Population Census — A44

1985, Dec. 16

201 A44 50f multicolored .90 .45
202 A44 1d multicolored 2.40 1.15
203 A44 3d multicolored 6.25 3.00
Nos. 201-203 (3) 9.55 4.60

Intl. Youth Year — A45

50f, Silhouettes, sapling, vert. 175f, Globe, open book. 2d, Youth carrying world, vert.

1985, Dec. 23 *Perf. 14½*

204 A45 50f multicolored .80 .55
205 A45 175f multicolored 2.40 1.30
206 A45 2d multicolored 3.00 1.75
Nos. 204-206 (3) 6.20 3.60

Women and Family Day — A46

1986, Mar. 21 *Perf. 13½*

207 A46 1d multicolored 1.20 .80
208 A46 3d multicolored 3.75 2.60

General Postal Authority, 1st Anniv. — A47

Designs: 50f, 250f, Posthorn, map, natl. flag, globe. 1d, 2d, Emblem, globe, vert.

1986, Apr. 1

209 A47 50f multicolored .50 .40
210 A47 1d multicolored 1.00 .65
211 A47 2d multicolored 2.60 1.75
212 A47 250f multicolored 3.00 2.25
Nos. 209-212 (4) 7.10 5.05

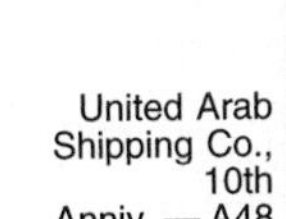

United Arab Shipping Co., 10th Anniv. — A48

1986, Aug. 20 *Perf. 13x13½*

213 A48 2d shown 3.75 2.25
214 A48 3d Ship's bow, vert. 4.50 3.00

A49

1986, Sept. 1 *Perf. 13½x13*

215 A49 250f multicolored 3.50 1.35
216 A49 3d multicolored 4.25 1.55

Emirates Telecommunications Corp., Ltd., 10th anniv.

Hawk — A50

1986, Sept. 9 Photo. *Perf. 15x14*

Booklet Stamps

Background Color

217 A50 50f pale green .75 .75
218 A50 75f pink 1.25 1.25
219 A50 125f gray 2.00 2.00
a. Bklt. pane, 75f, 125f, 2 50f 8.00 8.00
Complete booklet, #219a 13.00
Nos. 217-219 (3) 4.00 4.00

Emirates Airlines, 1st Anniv. — A51

1986, Oct. 25 *Perf. 13½*

220 A51 50f Jet, camel 1.40 1.00
221 A51 175f Jet 4.50 3.50

State Crests, GCC Emblem — A52

1986, Nov. 2 *Perf. 13*

222 A52 50f shown .65 .50
222A A52 175f like no. 223 2.25 1.75
223 A52 3d Tree, emblem 3.75 3.50
Nos. 222-223 (3) 6.65 5.75

Gulf Cooperation Council supreme council 7th session, Abu Dhabi, Nov. 1986. No. 222A incorrectly inscribed "1.75f."

15th Natl. Day — A53

1986, Dec. 2 Litho. *Perf. 13½*

224 A53 50f shown .90 .45
225 A53 1d like 50f 2.00 1.30
226 A53 175f Flag, emblem 3.75 2.25
227 A53 2d like 175f 3.75 2.60
Nos. 224-227 (4) 10.40 6.60

27th Chess Olympiad, Dubai A54

1986, Nov. 14 *Perf. 12½*

228 A54 50f Skyscraper, vert. 1.15 .65
229 A54 2d shown 4.50 3.75
230 A54 250f Tapestry, diff. 5.75 4.50
a. Souv. sheet, #228-230, perf 13 18.00 18.00
Nos. 228-230 (3) 11.40 8.90

No. 230a exists imperf. Value, $35.

Arab Police Day — A55

1986, Dec. 18 *Perf. 13½*

231 A55 50f multicolored 1.40 .80
232 A55 1d multicolored 2.40 2.00

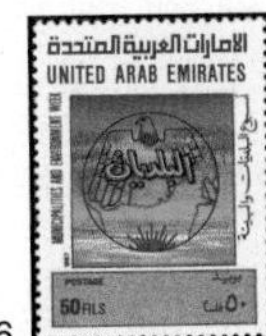

A56

1987, Mar. 15

233 A56 50f multicolored 1.40 .80
234 A56 1d multicolored 2.40 2.00

Municipalities and Environment Week.

A57

1987, Apr. 10

235 A57 200f multicolored 3.00 3.00
236 A57 250f multicolored 3.25 3.25

UAE Flight Information Region, 1st anniv.

Conservation — A58

50f, Water. 2d, Solar energy, oil well.

1987, May 25

237 A58 50f multicolored .80 .80
238 A58 2d multicolored 7.00 7.00

A59

1987, June 23

239 A59 1d multicolored 1.40 1.40
240 A59 3d multicolored 3.75 3.75

United Arab Emirates University, 10th anniv.

1st Shipment of Crude Oil from Abu Dhabi, 25th Anniv. A60

1987, July 4 *Perf. 13*

241 A60 50f Oil rig .65 .65
242 A60 1d Drilling well, vert. 1.55 1.55
243 A60 175f Crew, drill 2.40 2.40
244 A60 2d Oil tanker 2.60 2.60
Nos. 241-244 (4) 7.20 7.20

Arab Palm Tree and Date Day — A61

1987, Sept. 15 Litho. *Perf. 14x15*

245 A61 50f shown .75 .75
246 A61 1d Tree, fruit, diff. 1.30 1.30

A62

1987, Nov. 21 Litho. *Perf. 13x13½*

247 A62 2d multicolored 2.40 2.40
248 A62 250f multicolored 3.00 3.00

Intl. Year of Shelter for the Homeless.

A63

1987, Dec. 15 *Perf. 13½*

249 A63 1d multicolored 1.60 1.60
250 A63 2d multicolored 3.75 3.75

Salim Bin Ali Al-Owais (b. 1887), poet.

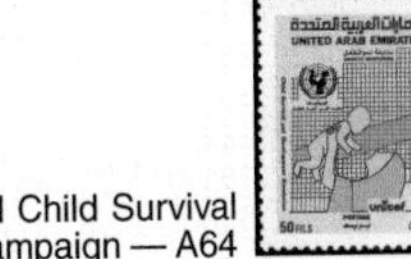

UN Child Survival Campaign — A64

50f, Growth monitoring. 1d, Immunization. 175f, Oral rehydration therapy. 2d, Breast feeding, horiz.

1987, Oct. 25 Litho. *Perf. 13*

251 A64 50f multicolored .50 .40
252 A64 1d multicolored 1.00 .80
253 A64 175f multicolored 1.60 1.40
254 A64 2d multicolored 1.75 1.55
Nos. 251-254 (4) 4.85 4.15

Abu Dhabi Intl. Airport, 6th Anniv. — A65

1988, Jan. 2

255 A65 50f Control tower .70 .70
256 A65 50f Terminal interior .70 .70
257 A65 100f Aircraft over airport 1.60 1.60
258 A65 100f Aircraft at gates 1.60 1.60
Nos. 255-258 (4) 4.60 4.60

Natl. Arts Festival — A66

1988, Mar. 21 Litho. *Perf. 13½*

259 A66 50f multicolored 1.00 1.00
260 A66 250f multicolored 3.00 3.00

Youth Cultural Festival — A67

Winning children's drawings of a design contest sponsored by the Ministry of Education and the Sharjah Cultural and Information Department.

Perf. 13x13½, 13½x13 (262)

1988, May 25 Litho.

261 A67 50f Net fisherman .60 .40
262 A67 1d Woman, vert. 1.15 1.00
263 A67 1.75d Youth as flower 1.75 1.60
264 A67 2d Recreation 2.25 2.00
Nos. 261-264 (4) 5.75 5.00

Palestinian Uprising — A68

1988, June 28 Litho. *Perf. 13½*

265 A68 2d multicolored 2.25 1.75
266 A68 250f multicolored 3.00 2.25

A69

Banks — A70

1988, July 16 Litho. *Perf. 13½*

267 A69 50f multicolored 2.00 2.00
268 A70 50f multicolored 2.00 2.00

Abu Dhabi Natl. Bank, Ltd., 20th anniv. (No. 267); Natl. Bank of Dubai, Ltd., 25th anniv. (No. 268).

Port Rashid, Dubai, 16th Anniv. — A71

1988, Aug. 31 Litho. *Perf. 13½*

269	A71	50f Ground transportation	.50	.50
270	A71	1d Piers	1.00	1.00
271	A71	175f Ship at dock	2.00	2.00
272	A71	2d Ship, unloading cranes	2.25	2.25
		Nos. 269-272 (4)	5.75	5.75

1988 Summer Olympics, Seoul — A72

1988, Sept. 17 *Perf. 15x14½*

273	2d Swimming	2.60	2.60
274	250f Cycling	3.25	3.25
a.	A72 Pair, #273-274	6.00	6.00

Ras Al Khaima Natl. Museum, 1st Anniv. — A74

1988, Nov. 19 Litho. *Perf. 14*

275	A74	50f Vase, vert.	.60	.45
276	A74	3d Gold crown	2.60	1.75

18th Arab Scout Conference, Nov. 29-Dec. 3, Abu Dhabi — A75

1988, Nov. 29 *Perf. 12½*

277	A75	1d multicolored	1.00	1.00

10th Arbor Day — A76

Perf. 13½x13, 13x13½

1989, Mar. 6 Litho.

278	A76	50f Ghaf, vert.	.50	.50
279	A76	100f Palm	1.00	1.00
280	A76	250f Dahlia blossom	2.25	2.25
		Nos. 278-280 (3)	3.75	3.75

Sharjah Intl. Airport, 10th Anniv. — A77

1989, Apr. 21 Litho. *Perf. 13½*

281	A77	50f multicolored	.75	.75
282	A77	100f multicolored	1.75	1.75

Postal Service, 80th Anniv. — A78

1989, Aug. 19 Litho. *Perf. 13x13½*

283	A78	50f Seaplane	.80	.80
284	A78	3d Ship	5.25	5.25

Al-Ittihad Newspaper, 20th Anniv. — A79

1989, Oct. 20 Litho. *Perf. 13½*

285	A79	50f shown	.60	.60
286	A79	1d Al Ittihad Press	1.00	1.00

Gulf Investment Corporation, 5th Anniv. — A80

1989, Nov. 25

287	A80	50f multicolored	.60	.60
288	A80	2d multicolored	2.60	2.60

Child on Crutches, Hands — A81

Designs: 2d, Crouched youth, cracked earth, bread in hand, horiz.

1989, Dec. 5 *Perf. 15x14, 14x15*

289	A81	2d multicolored	2.25	2.25
290	A81	250f shown	2.60	2.60

Intl. Volunteer's Day, Red Crescent Soc.

Bank Building — A82

50f, Emblem, architecture.

1989, Dec. 20 *Perf. 13½*

291	A82	50f multicolored	.60	.60
292	A82	1d shown	1.00	1.00

Commercial Bank of Dubai, Ltd., 20th Anniv.

Astrolabe, Manuscript Page and Ship of Bin Majid, 15th Cent. Navigator and Writer — A83

1989, Dec. 25 *Perf. 13x13½, 13½x13*

293	A83	1d shown	1.00	1.00
294	A83	3d Ship, page, vert.	3.50	3.50

Heritage revival.

3rd Al Ain Festival — A84

1990, Jan. 17 *Perf. 13½*

295	A84	50f multicolored	.60	.60
296	A84	1d multicolored	1.55	1.55

Falcon — A85

1990, Feb. 17 Litho. *Perf. 11½*

Granite Paper

297	A85	5f multicolored	.25	.25
298	A85	20f multicolored	.25	.25
299	A85	25f multicolored	.25	.25
301	A85	50f multicolored	.40	.35
302	A85	100f multicolored	1.75	1.00
303	A85	150f multicolored	3.00	1.40
304	A85	175f multicolored	3.25	1.60

Size: 21x26mm

Perf. 11½x12

306	A85	2d multicolored	4.50	2.40
307	A85	250f multicolored	5.00	2.60
309	A85	3d multicolored	6.25	3.00
310	A85	5d multicolored	9.00	5.25
311	A85	10d multicolored	18.00	10.50
312	A85	20d multicolored	30.00	18.00
313	A85	50d multicolored	80.00	50.00
		Nos. 297-313 (14)	161.90	96.85

See also Nos. 726A-726G.

Children's Cultural Festival — A86

1990, Mar. 10 Litho. *Perf. 13½*

316	A86	50f multicolored	.50	.50
317	A86	250f multicolored	2.00	2.00

Red Crescent Society — A87

1990, Aug. 5 Litho. *Perf. 14x15*

318	A87	175f shown	1.55	1.55
319	A87	2d Starving child	2.00	2.00

Dubai Chamber of Commerce and Industry, 25th Anniv. — A88

1990, July 1 *Perf. 13*

320	A88	50f multicolored	.60	.60
321	A88	1d multicolored	1.20	1.20

World Cup Soccer Championships, Italy — A89

UAE emblem, character trademark and: 1d, Leaning Tower of Pisa, desert, vert. 2d, Soccer ball, vert. 250f, Circle of flags. 3d, Map, vert.

1990, June 8 *Perf. 13½*

322	A89	50f multicolored	.60	.60
323	A89	1d multicolored	1.20	1.20
324	A89	2d multicolored	2.40	2.40
325	A89	250f multicolored	3.25	3.25
		Nos. 322-325 (4)	7.45	7.45

Souvenir Sheet

Perf. 12½

326	A89	3d multicolored	5.75	5.75

A90

1990, Sept. 22 Litho. *Perf. 13½*

327	A90	50f shown	.60	.60
328	A90	1d Emblem, 30 years	1.75	1.75
329	A90	175f Emblem, drop of oil	3.00	3.00
		Nos. 327-329 (3)	5.35	5.35

Organization of Petroleum Exporting Countries (OPEC), 30th anniv.

A91

Flowers: No. 330, Argyrolobeum roseum. No. 331, Lamranthus roseus. No. 332, Centavrea pseudo sinaica. No. 333, Calotropis procera. No. 334, Nerium oleander. No. 335, Catharanthus roseus. No. 336, Hibiscus rosa sinensis. No. 337, Bougainvillea glabra.

1990, Aug. 25 *Perf. 14x14½*

330	A91	50f multicolored	.75	.75
331	A91	50f multicolored	.75	.75
332	A91	50f multicolored	.75	.75
333	A91	50f multicolored	.75	.75
a.		Souvenir sheet of 4, #330-333	3.75	3.75
334	A91	50f multicolored	.75	.75
335	A91	50f multicolored	.75	.75
336	A91	50f multicolored	3.25	3.25
337	A91	50f multicolored	3.25	3.25
a.		Souvenir sheet of 4, #334-337	14.00	14.00
		Nos. 330-337 (8)	11.00	11.00

Environmental Pollution — A92

1990, Oct. 8 Litho. *Perf. 13*

338	A92	50f Water pollution	.40	.40
339	A92	3d Air pollution	2.60	2.60

Central Bank, 10th Anniv. — A93

1990, Dec. 2 *Perf. 13½*

340	A93	50f shown	.40	.40
341	A93	175f Bank building, horiz.	2.60	2.60

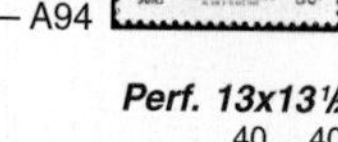

Intl. Conference on High Salinity Tolerant Plants — A94

1990, Dec. 8 *Perf. 13x13½*

342	A94	50f Tree	.40	.40
343	A94	250f Water, trees	2.25	2.25

Grand Mosque, Abu Dhabi — A95

2d, Al Jumeirah Mosque, Dubai, vert.

Perf. 13½x13, 13x13½

1990, Nov. 26

344	A95	1d multicolored	.90	.90
345	A95	2d multicolored	3.75	3.75

Abu Dhabi Intl. Fair — A96

1991, Jan. 16 Litho. *Perf. 13x13½*

346	A96	50f multicolored	.80	.80
347	A96	2d multicolored	2.00	2.00

A97

1991, May 17 Litho. *Perf. 14x13½*

348	A97	2d multicolored	2.40	2.40
349	A97	3d multicolored	3.75	3.75

World Telecommunications Day.

A98

1991, June 18 *Perf. 13½*
350 A98 1d Sheikh Saqr Mosque 1.20 1.20
351 A98 2d King Faisal Mosque 2.60 2.60

Children's Paintings — A99

Designs: 50f, Celebration. 1d, Women waving flags. 175f, Women playing blind-man's buff. 250f, Women dancing for men.

1991, July 15 Litho. *Perf. 14x13½*
352 A99 50f multicolored .50 .40
353 A99 1d multicolored 1.15 .80
354 A99 175f multicolored 2.00 1.75
355 A99 250f multicolored 2.40 2.00
Nos. 352-355 (4) 6.05 4.95

Fish — A100

1991, Aug. 5 Litho. *Perf. 13½x14*
356 A100 50f Yellow marked butterflyfish .50 .50
357 A100 50f Golden trevally .50 .50
358 A100 50f Two banded porgy .50 .50
359 A100 50f Red snapper .50 .50
360 A100 1d Three banded grunt 1.00 1.00
361 A100 1d Rabbit fish 1.00 1.00
362 A100 1d Black bream 1.00 1.00
363 A100 1d Greasy grouper 1.00 1.00
a. Min. sheet of 8, #356-363 7.00 7.00
Nos. 356-363 (8) 6.00 6.00

A101

Intl. Aerospace Exhibition, Dubai: 175f, Jet fighter over Dubai Intl. Airport. 2d, Fighter silhouette over airport.

1991, Nov. 3 Litho. *Perf. 13½*
364 A101 175f multicolored 1.75 1.75
365 A101 2d multicolored 2.00 2.00

A102

Sheikh Rashid Bin Said Al Maktum (1912-90), Ruler of Dubai and: 50f, Airport, vert. 175f, City skyline, vert. 2d, Waterfront, satellite dish.

1991, Oct. 7 *Perf. 13*
366 A102 50f multicolored .40 .40
367 A102 1d multicolored .90 .90
368 A102 175f multicolored 1.60 1.60
369 A102 2d multicolored 1.75 1.75
Nos. 366-369 (4) 4.65 4.65

Civil Defense Day — A103

1991, Oct. 8 Litho. *Perf. 13½*
370 A103 50f multicolored .60 .60
371 A103 1d multicolored 1.40 1.40

A104

A105

A106

20th Natl. Day — A107

#374, Emir at left, fortress, cannon. #377, Fortress on rocky outcropping. #378, Emir at right, fortress, cannon. 3d, Sheikh Said bin Sultan al Nahayan, Defense Forces.

1991, Dec. 2 Litho. *Perf. 13*
372 A104 75f multicolored 1.00 1.00
373 A105 75f multicolored 1.00 1.00
374 A105 75f multicolored 1.00 1.00
375 A106 75f multicolored 1.00 1.00
376 A107 75f multicolored 1.00 1.00
377 A107 75f multicolored 1.00 1.00
378 A107 75f multicolored 1.00 1.00

Imperf

Size: 70x90mm

378A A107 3d multicolored 8.00 8.00
Nos. 372-378A (8) 15.00 15.00

On Nos. 372-378 portions of the design were applied by a thermographic process producing a shiny, raised effect.

A108

1991, Nov. 16 *Perf. 13½*
379 A108 50f lt green & multi .40 .40
380 A108 3d orange & multi 3.25 3.25

Gulf Cooperaton Council, 10th anniv.

A109

1992, Jan. 15 Litho. *Perf. 13½*
381 A109 175f pink & multi 2.20 2.20
382 A109 250f lt blue & multi 2.50 2.50

Abu Dhabi National Oil Co., 20th anniv.

Al-Jahli Castle Al-Ain — A110

1992, Apr. 20 Litho. *Perf. 13½*
383 A110 2d multicolored 1.75 1.75
384 A110 250f multicolored *47.50 47.50*

Expo '92, Seville.

No. 384 was withdrawn because of poor rendition of Arabic word for "postage."

A111

Mosques: 50f, Sheikh Rashid bin Humaid al Nuaimi, Ajman. 1d, Sheikh Ahmed Bin Rashid Al Mualla, Umm Al Quwain.

1992, Mar. 26 *Perf. 14x13½*
385 A111 50f multicolored .80 .80
386 A111 1d multicolored 1.60 1.60

See Nos. 417-418.

Week of the Deaf Child — A112

1992, Apr. 20 *Perf. 13½x13*
387 A112 1d shown 1.40 1.40
388 A112 3d Ear with hearing aid 3.25 3.25

Zayed Seaport, 20th Anniv. A113

1992, June 28 Litho. *Perf. 13½*
389 A113 50f Aerial view .45 .45
390 A113 1d Cargo transport 1.10 1.10
391 A113 175f Ship docked 2.10 2.10
392 A113 2d Map 2.40 2.40
Nos. 389-392 (4) 6.05 6.05

1992 Summer Olympics, Barcelona — A114

1992, July 25 Litho. *Perf. 14x13½*
393 A114 50f Yachting .50 .50
394 A114 1d Running .95 .95
395 A114 175f Swimming 1.90 1.90
396 A114 250f Cycling 2.10 2.10
Nos. 393-396 (4) 5.45 5.45

Souvenir Sheet

396A A114 3d Equestrian 4.75 4.75

Children's Paintings — A115

1992, Aug. 15 *Perf. 13½x14*
397 A115 50f Playing soccer .50 .50
398 A115 1d Playing in field 1.00 1.00
399 A115 2d Playground 2.25 2.25
400 A115 250f Children among trees 3.00 3.00
Nos. 397-400 (4) 6.75 6.75

Intl. Bank of United Arab Emirates, 15th Anniv. — A116

Design: 175f, Bank emblem.

Litho. & Embossed

1992, Sept. 9 *Perf. 11*
401 A116 50f gold & multi .75 .75

Size: 35x41mm

Perf. 11½

402 A116 175f lake, gold & vio 2.25 2.25

Traditional Musical Instruments A116a

No. 402A, Tambourah, vert. No. 402B, Oud, vert. No. 402C, Rababah, vert. No. 402D, Mizmar, shindo. No. 402E, Tabel, hibban. No. 402F, Marwas, duff.

1992, Oct. 17 Litho. *Perf. 13½*
402A A116a 50f multicolored .50 .50
402B A116a 50f multicolored .50 .50
402C A116a 50f multicolored 1.00 1.00
g. Sheet, #402A-402C, perf. 12¾ 3.00 3.00
402D A116a 1d multicolored 2.00 2.00
402E A116a 1d multicolored 2.00 2.00
402F A116a 1d multicolored 2.00 2.00
h. Sheet, #402D-402F, perf. 12¾ 6.00 6.00
Nos. 402A-402F (6) 8.00 8.00

Camels — A117

Designs: 50f, Race. 1d, Used for transportation, vert. 175f, Harnessed for obtaining water from well. 2d, Roaming free, vert.

1992, Dec. 23 Litho. *Perf. 13½*
403 A117 50f multicolored .50 .30
404 A117 1d multicolored 1.25 .70
405 A117 175f multicolored 2.50 1.25
406 A117 2d multicolored 2.75 1.50
Nos. 403-406 (4) 7.00 3.75

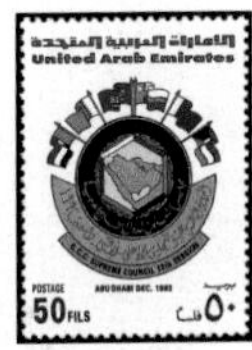
A118

1992, Dec. 21
407 A118 50f multicolored 1.00 1.00
408 A118 2d yellow & multi 4.50 4.50

Gulf Cooperation Council, 13th session.

A119

1993, Jan. 28 Litho. *Perf. 13½*
409 A119 2d shown 2.00 2.00
410 A119 250f Building, fishing boat 3.50 3.50

Dubai Creek Golf and Yacht Club.

Tourism — A120

1993, Jan. 16
411 A120 50f Golf, horiz. .60 .60
412 A120 1d Fishing 1.20 1.20
413 A120 2d Boating, horiz. 2.40 2.40
414 A120 250f Motor vehicle touring, horiz. 3.00 3.00
Nos. 411-414 (4) 7.20 7.20

Natl. Youth Festival — A121

1993, Mar. 27 Litho. *Perf. 14x13½*

415 A121 50f violet & multi .90 .90
416 A121 3d red brown & multi 3.75 3.75

Mosque Type of 1992

50f, Thabit bin Khalid Mosque, Fujeira. 1d, Sharq al Morabbah Mosque, Al Ain.

1993, Feb. 16 *Perf. 13½*

417 A111 50f multicolored 1.00 1.00
418 A111 1d multicolored 2.00 2.00

Shells — A122

25f, Conus textile. 50f, Pinctada radiata. 100f, Murex scolopax. 150f, Natica pulicaris. 175f, Lambis truncata sebae. 200f, Cardita bicolor. 250f, Cypraea grayana. 300f, Cymatium trilineatum.

1993, Apr. 3 Litho. *Perf. 13*

419 A122 25f multicolored .35 .35
420 A122 50f multicolored .50 .50
421 A122 100f multicolored 1.00 1.00
422 A122 150f multicolored 1.50 1.50
423 A122 175f multicolored 2.25 2.25
424 A122 200f multicolored 2.50 2.50
425 A122 250f multicolored 3.00 3.00
426 A122 300f multicolored 4.00 4.00
Nos. 419-426 (8) 15.10 15.10

Campaign Against Drugs — A123

Design: 1d, Skull, drugs, vert.

1993, Aug. 21 Litho. *Perf. 13½*

427 A123 50f multicolored 1.60 1.60
428 A123 1d multicolored 2.25 2.25

A124

Natl. Bank of Abu Dhabi, 25th Anniv.: 50f, Abu Dhabi skyline, bank emblem. 1d, Bank emblem. 175f, Bank building, emblem. 2d, Skyline, emblem, diff.

Litho. & Typo.

1993, Sept. 15 *Perf. 11½*

429 A124 50f silver & multi .45 .45
430 A124 1d silver & multi .90 .90
431 A124 175f silver & multi 2.00 2.00
432 A124 2d silver & multi 2.25 2.25
Nos. 429-432 (4) 5.60 5.60

A125

Dubai Ports Authority: 50f, Aerial view of port. 1d, Loading cargo. 2d, Aerial view, diff. 250f, Globe.

1993, Nov. 10 Litho. *Perf. 13½*

433 A125 50f purple & multi .50 .50
434 A125 1d green & multi 1.20 1.20
435 A125 2d orange & multi 2.40 2.40
436 A125 250f pink & multi 3.00 3.00
Nos. 433-436 (4) 7.10 7.10

Natl. Day — A126

Children's paintings: 50f, Soldiers saluting flag. 1d, Two women sitting, one standing, flag, vert. 175f, Flag, boat. 2d, Flags atop castle tower.

1993, Dec. 2 Litho. *Perf. 13½*

437 A126 50f multicolored .50 .50
438 A126 1d multicolored 1.20 1.20
439 A126 175f multicolored 2.25 2.25
440 A126 2d multicolored 2.40 2.40
Nos. 437-440 (4) 6.35 6.35

Archaeological Discoveries A127

Designs: 50f, Tomb. 1d, Rectangular artifact. 175f, Animal-shaped artifact. 250f, Bowl.

1993, Dec. 15 *Perf. 14x13½*

441 A127 50f multicolored .50 .50
442 A127 1d multicolored 1.15 1.15
443 A127 175f multicolored 2.00 2.00
444 A127 250f multicolored 2.60 2.60
Nos. 441-444 (4) 6.25 6.25

10th Childrens' Festival, Sharjah — A128

Children's paintings: 50f, Children with balloons, flags. 1d, Children playing, three trees. 175f, Child with picture, girls with balloons. 2d, House, children playing outdoors.

1994, Mar. 19 Litho. *Perf. 13x13½*

445 A128 50f green & multi .50 .50
446 A128 1d blue & multi 1.25 1.25
447 A128 175f red violet & multi 2.10 2.10
448 A128 2d carmine & multi 2.25 2.50
Nos. 445-448 (4) 6.10 6.35

Arabian Horses — A129

50f, Brown horse on hind feet, vert. 1d, White horse. 175f, Head of brown horse, vert. 250f, Head of white and brown horse.

1994, Jan. 25 *Perf. 13x13½, 13½x13*

449 A129 50f multicolored .50 .50
450 A129 1d multicolored 1.20 1.20
451 A129 175f multicolored 2.00 2.00
452 A129 250f multicolored 2.60 2.60
Nos. 449-452 (4) 6.30 6.30

10th Conference of Arab Towns, Dubai — A130

Perf. 13x13½, 13½x13

1994, May 15 Litho.

453 A130 50f Map, city, vert. .50 .40
454 A130 1d shown 2.00 1.75

Pilgrimage to Mecca — A131

1994, Apr. 29 Litho. *Perf. 13x13½*

455 A131 50f shown .75 .75
456 A131 2d Holy Ka'aba 2.75 2.75

Intl. Year of the Family — A132

Intl. Olympic Committee, Cent. — A133

Arab Housing Day — A134

Writers Assoc., 10th Anniv. — A135

1994, June 15 *Perf. 13x13½*

457 A132 1d multicolored 1.40 1.40
458 A133 1d multicolored 1.40 1.40

Perf. 13½x13

459 A134 1d multicolored 1.40 1.40
460 A135 1d multicolored 1.40 1.40
Nos. 457-460 (4) 5.60 5.60

Archaeological Finds, Al Qusais, Dubai — A136

Designs: 50f, Lidded pitcher, vert. 1d, Pointed-handle pitcher. 175f, Pitcher, arm-shaped handle. 250f, Short round vase.

1994, Aug. 16 Litho. *Perf. 13½*

461 A136 50f multicolored .55 .55
462 A136 1d multicolored 1.30 1.30
463 A136 175f multicolored 2.20 2.20
464 A136 250f multicolored 3.00 3.00
Nos. 461-464 (4) 7.05 7.05

Environmental Protection A137

Designs: 50f, Arabian leopard. 1d, Gordon's wildcat. 2d, Caracal. 250f, Sand cat.

1994, Oct. 10 Litho. *Perf. 13½*

465 A137 50f multicolored .50 .50
466 A137 1d multicolored 1.25 1.25
467 A137 2d multicolored 3.25 3.25
468 A137 250f multicolored 3.75 3.75
Nos. 465-468 (4) 8.75 8.75

12th Arab Gulf Soccer Championships, Abu Dhabi — A138

1994, Nov. 3 Litho. *Perf. 13½*

469 A138 50f Ball, emblem, vert. .55 .55
470 A138 3d Soccer players 3.75 3.75

Birds — A139

50f, Merops orientalis. 175f, Halcyon chloris. 2d, Dromas ardeola. 250f, Coracias benghalensis. 3d, Phoenicopterus ruber.

1994, Dec. 12

471 A139 50f multicolored .50 .50
472 A139 175f multicolored 2.60 2.60
473 A139 2d multicolored 3.00 3.00
474 A139 250f multicolored 4.50 4.50
Nos. 471-474 (4) 10.60 10.60

Souvenir Sheet

475 A139 3d multi, vert. 6.50 6.50

Archaeological Finds, Mulaiha, Sharjah — A140

Designs: 50f, Front of carved horse, vert. 175f, Ancient coin, vert. 2d, Inscription on metal, vert. 250f, Inscription on stone.

1995, Jan. 25 Litho. *Perf. 13½*

476 A140 50f multicolored .45 .45
477 A140 175f multicolored 1.75 1.75
478 A140 2d multicolored 2.40 2.40
479 A140 250f multicolored 2.60 2.60
Nos. 476-479 (4) 7.20 7.20

Natl. Dances — A141

1995, Feb. 14

480 A141 50f Al-Naashat .50 .50
481 A141 175f Al-Ayaalah 1.75 1.75
482 A141 2d Al-Shahhoh 2.00 2.00
Nos. 480-482 (3) 4.25 4.25

A142

1995, Mar. 19 Litho. *Perf. 13½*

483 A142 50f Helicopters .40 .40
484 A142 1d Emblem 1.10 1.10
485 A142 175f Warships, horiz. 2.25 2.25
486 A142 2d Artillery, horiz. 2.50 2.50
Nos. 483-486 (4) 6.25 6.25

Intl. Defense Exhibition & Conf., Abu Dhabi.

A143

1d, Arab League emblem. 2d, FAO emblem. 250f, UN emblem.

1995, Mar. 22

487 A143 1d multicolored 1.00 1.00
488 A143 2d multicolored 2.25 2.25
489 A143 250f multicolored 3.00 3.00
Nos. 487-489 (3) 6.25 6.25

50th Anniv. of Arab League, FAO & UN.

General Post Office Authority, 10th Anniv. — A144

1995, Apr. 1

490 A144 50f multicolored .60 .60

First Gulf Cooperation Council Philatelic Exhibition, Abu Dhabi — A145

1995, Apr. 11 Litho. *Perf. 13½*
491 A145 50f multicolored .60 .60

Traditional Games, Ajman Museum — A146

50f, Boy with hoop, stick. 175f, Girl on swing. 2d, Boy, girl playing stick game within marked boundary. 250f, Two girls playing game with stones.

1995, Aug. 28 Litho. *Perf. 13½x13*
492 A146 50f multicolored .40 .40
493 A146 175f multicolored 1.55 1.55
494 A146 2d multicolored 1.75 1.75
495 A146 250f multicolored 2.00 2.00
Nos. 492-495 (4) 5.70 5.70

A147

Birds: 50f, Falco naumanni. 175f, Phalacrocorax nigrogularis. 2d, Cursorius cursor. 250f, Upupa epops.

1995, Sept. 25
496 A147 50f multicolored .65 .65
497 A147 175f multicolored 2.25 2.25
498 A147 2d multicolored 2.75 2.75
499 A147 250f multicolored 3.25 3.25
Nos. 496-499 (4) 8.90 8.90

See Nos. 528-532.

A148

Natl. Census: 50f, Stylized family, building. 250f, Mosque, skyscrapers, stylized family.

1995, Nov. 20
500 A148 50f multicolored 1.00 1.00
501 A148 250f multicolored 4.00 4.00

National Day — A149

Children's paintings: 50f, People wearing feathered headdresses, palm trees, building. 175f, Girls with flags, balloons, flowers. 2d, Trees, family in front of house holding balloons, flags. 250f, Groups of children along street watching parade of cars.

1995, Dec. 2 *Perf. 13x13½*
502 A149 50f multicolored .45 .45
503 A149 175f multicolored 1.25 1.25
504 A149 2d multicolored 1.40 1.40
505 A149 250f multicolored 1.75 1.75
Nos. 502-505 (4) 4.85 4.85

Environmental Protection A150

50f, Dugong dugon. 2d, Delphinus delphis. 3d, Megaptera novaeangliae.

1996, Jan. 25 Litho. *Perf. 13x13½*
506 A150 50f multicolored .60 .60
507 A150 2d multicolored 2.60 2.60
508 A150 3d multicolored 3.75 3.75
a. Souvenir sheet, #506-508 6.25 6.25
Nos. 506-508 (3) 6.95 6.95

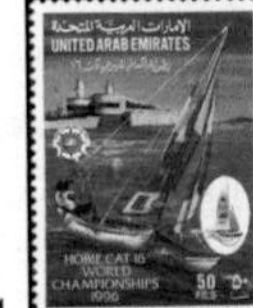

A151

1996, Feb. 27 *Perf. 13½*
509 A151 50f shown 1.00 1.00
510 A151 3d Building, beach 4.00 4.00

Hobie Cat 16 World Sailing Championships.

A152

Archaelogical Finds, Fujeira Museum: 50f, Two-handled pitcher. 175f, Kettle. 250f, Bracelet. 3d, Metal ornament, horiz.

1996, Apr. 15
511 A152 50f multicolored .50 .50
512 A152 175f multicolored 1.50 1.50
513 A152 250f multicolored 2.50 2.50
514 A152 3d multicolored 3.50 3.50
Nos. 511-514 (4) 8.00 8.00

1996 Summer Olympic Games, Atlanta — A153

Perf. 13½x14, 14x 13½
1996, July 19 Litho.
515 A153 50f Shooting .50 .50
516 A153 1d Cycling, vert. 1.50 1.50
517 A153 250f Running, vert. 2.50 2.50
518 A153 350f Swimming 3.50 3.50
Nos. 515-518 (4) 8.00 8.00

Women's Union, 21st Anniv. — A154

Perf. 14x13½, 13½x14
1996, Aug. 15
519 A154 50f Emblem, vert. .75 .75
520 A154 3d shown 3.50 3.50

A155

1996, Sept. 15 *Perf. 14x13½*
521 A155 1d shown .75 .75
522 A155 250f Soccer player 2.10 2.10

11th Asian Soccer Cup Championship.

A156

UN Campaign Against Illegal Use of Drugs: 50f, World with snake around it. 3d, Half of man's face, half of skull, hypodermic needle, pills.

1996, Oct. 15 *Perf. 13½*
523 A156 50f multicolored .75 .75
524 A156 3d multicolored 3.00 3.00

Sheikh Saeed Al-Maktoum House, Cent. — A157

Designs: 250f Sheikh Saeed, close-up view of house. 350f, Overall view of house.

1996, Nov. 12 Litho. *Perf. 13x13½*
525 A157 50f multicolored .50 .50
526 A157 250f multicolored 1.75 1.75
527 A157 350f multicolored 2.50 2.50
Nos. 525-527 (3) 4.75 4.75

Bird Type of 1995

Designs: 50f, Pterocles exustus. 150f, Otus brucei. 250f, Hypocolus ampelinus. 3d, Irania gutturalis. 350f, Falco concolor.

1996, Nov. 18 *Perf. 14x13½*
528 A147 50f multicolored .50 .50
529 A147 150f multicolored 1.75 1.75
530 A147 250f multicolored 2.75 2.75
531 A147 3d multicolored 3.25 3.25
532 A147 350f multicolored 3.75 3.75
Nos. 528-532 (5) 12.00 12.00

Children's Paintings — A158

50f, Face. 1d, Boats. 250f, Flowers. 350f, Woman in long dress, palm tree, tent.

Perf. 14x13½, 13½x14
1996, Nov. 19
533 A158 50f multi, vert. .35 .35
534 A158 1d multi .80 .80
535 A158 250f multi, vert. 2.25 2.25
536 A158 350f multi, vert. 2.75 2.75
Nos. 533-536 (4) 6.15 6.15

Sheik Zayed bin Sultan al Nahayan, Accession to the Throne of Abu Dhabi, 30th Anniv. — A158a

A159

Sheik and: 50f, 250f, Flowers. 1d, 350f, Date palm.

1996, Dec. 2 Photo. *Perf. 12*
537 A158a 50f red & multi .45 .45
538 A158a 1d olive & multi .75 .75
539 A158a 250f purple & multi 1.75 1.75
540 A158a 350f gray & multi 2.40 2.40
Nos. 537-540 (4) 5.35 5.35

Photo. & Embossed
Imperf
Size: 90x70mm

541 A159 5d On horseback, gazelles 7.50 7.50

Anniversaries — A160

Photo. & Embossed
1996, Dec. 2 *Perf. 12*
542 A160 50f red violet & multi .75 .75
543 A160 1d silver & multi 1.75 1.75

Sheik Zayed bin Sultan al Nahayan's accession to the throne of Abu Dhabi, 30th anniv., Creation of United Arab Emirates, 25th anniv.

Natl. Day, 25th Anniv. — A161

50f, 150f, Seven rulers of United Arab Emirates. 1d, 3d, Heraldic eagle, national flag. 5d, Score of Natl. Anthem.

1996, Dec. 2 Granite Paper
544 A161 50f green & multi .70 .70
545 A161 1d multicolored 1.25 1.25
546 A161 150f tan & multi 1.60 1.60
547 A161 3d multicolored 3.25 3.25
Nos. 544-547 (4) 6.80 6.80

Photo. & Embossed
Imperf
Size: 70x90mm

547A A161 5d multicolored 4.50 4.50

Butterflies — A162

1997, Jan. 28 Litho. *Perf. 14x13½*
548 A162 50f Agrodiaetus loewii .60 .60
549 A162 1d Papilio machaon 1.25 1.25
550 A162 150f Orithya 1.90 1.90
551 A162 250f Chrysippus 3.25 3.25
Nos. 548-551 (4) 7.00 7.00

Dubai Shopping Festival — A163

Perf. 13¼x13¾, 13¾x13¼
1997, Feb. 22 Litho.
552 A163 50f shown 1.00 1.00
553 A163 250f Shopping bag, vert. 3.50 3.50

Intl. Defense Exhibition & Conference — A164

50f, Helicopter airlifting jeep. 1d, Emblem. 250f, Artillery, emblem. 350f, Ships, emblem.

1997, Mar. 16 Litho. *Perf. 13½*
554 A164 50f multicolored .50 .50
555 A164 1d multicolored .85 .85
556 A164 250f multicolored 2.25 2.25
557 A164 350f multicolored 3.00 3.00
Nos. 554-557 (4) 6.60 6.60

Emirates Bank Group, 20th Anniv. — A165

Perf. 13¾x13¼
1997, Mar. 23 Litho.
568 A165 50f multi .75 .75
569 A165 1d buff & multi 2.00 2.00
a. Souv. sheet, #568-569, imperf. 5.00 5.00

No. 569a sold for 5d.

Technical Education and National Development Conference — A166

1997, Apr. 6 ***Perf. 13¾x13¼***
570 A166 50f shown .75 .75
571 A166 250f Emblem 2.75 2.75

Sharjah Heritage — A167

Designs: 50f, Coins. 3d, Museum.

1997, June 17 **Litho.** ***Perf. 13½***
572 A167 50f multicolored .75 .75
573 A167 3d multicolored 3.25 3.25

Emirates Philatelic Association — A168

Perf. 13¾x13¼, 13¼x13¾
1997, June 24 **Litho.**
574 A168 50f shown .75 .75
575 A168 250f Stamps, horiz. 3.00 3.00

Children's Paintings — A169

50f, Cats. 1d, Children playing. 250f, Children, moon, vert. 3d, Abstract.

1997, Sept. 15 **Litho.** ***Perf. 13½***
576 A169 50f multicolored .55 .55
577 A169 1d multicolored .95 .95
578 A169 250f multicolored 2.25 2.25
579 A169 3d multicolored 3.00 3.00
Nos. 576-579 (4) 6.75 6.75

Reunion, by Sheikha Hassan Maktoum al Maktoum — A170

Mindscape, by Sarah Majid al Futtaim A170a

Blue Musings, by Maha Abdulla Al Mazroui — A170b

The Pause, by Khulood Mattar Rashid A170c

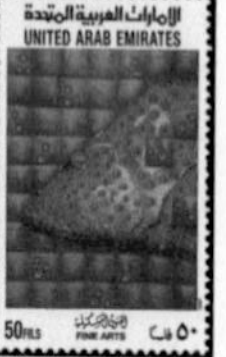

The Seas I, by Sheikha Sawsan Abdulaziz Al Qasimi — A170d

Still Life, by Sheikha Bodour Sultan Al Qasimi A170e

The Opening, by Tina Ahmed and Others — 170f

1997, Oct. 25 **Litho.** ***Perf. 13¾***
580 A170 50f multi 1.25 1.25
581 A170a 50f multi 1.25 1.25
582 A170b 50f multi 1.25 1.25
583 A170c 50f multi 1.25 1.25
584 A170d 50f multi 1.25 1.25
585 A170e 50f multi 1.25 1.25
Nos. 580-585 (6) 7.50 7.50

Imperf
586 A170f 5d multi 6.50 6.50

Intl. Aerospace Exhibition, Dubai — A171

Perf. 13½x13¾
1997, Nov. 16 **Litho.**
587 A171 250f Jet fighter 2.25 2.25
588 A171 3d VTOL airplane 2.75 2.75

26th National Day — A172

Sheikh Zayed bin Sultan al Nahayan and: 50f, Gardens. 1d, Trees and mountains. 150f, Water, trees and mountains. 250f, Roadway.

1997, Dec. 2 **Litho.** ***Perf. 13½x13¾***
589 A172 50f multi .45 .45
590 A172 1d multi .75 .75
591 A172 150f multi 1.20 1.20
592 A172 250f multi 1.75 1.75
Nos. 589-592 (4) 4.15 4.15

3rd Afro-Arab Trade Fair — A173

Perf. 13x13¼, 13¼x13
1997, Dec. 6 **Litho.**
593 A173 150f Emblem, vert. 1.25 1.25
594 A173 350f Handshake 2.75 2.75

Arthropods — A174

50f, Blepharopsis mendica. 150f, Galeodes sp. 250f, Crocothemis arythraea. 350f, Xylocopa aestuans.

1998, Feb. 25 **Litho.** ***Perf. 13¼***
595 A174 50f multicolored .45 .45
596 A174 150f multicolored 1.20 1.20
597 A174 250f multicolored 2.00 2.00
598 A174 350f multicolored 2.60 2.60
Nos. 595-598 (4) 6.25 6.25

ISAF World Sailing Championship A175

Various sailboats.

Perf. 13¼x13, 13x13¼
1998, Mar. 2 **Litho.**
599 A175 50f multi, vert. .40 .40
600 A175 1d multi 1.00 1.00
601 A175 250f multi 1.75 1.75
602 A175 3d multi, vert. 2.40 2.40
Nos. 599-602 (4) 5.55 5.55

A176

Triple Intl. Defense Exhibition & Conf., Abu Dhabi: 50f, Combat soldiers in protective gear, horiz. 1d, Emblem over world map, skyline of Abu Dhabi. 150f, Electronic gear. 350f, Missile battery, electronic warfare components.

1998, Mar. 15 **Litho.** ***Perf. 13½***
603 A176 50f multicolored .45 .45
604 A176 1d multicolored 1.25 1.25
605 A176 150f multicolored 2.10 2.10
606 A176 350f multicolored 3.00 3.00
Nos. 603-606 (4) 6.80 6.80

A177

1998, Apr. 20 **Litho.** ***Perf. 13½***
607 A177 50f shown .40 .40
608 A177 3d Emblem, monument 3.00 3.00

Sharjah, 1998 Arab cultural capital.

World Environment Day — A178

1998, May 17 **Litho.** ***Perf. 13½***
609 A178 1d Landscape, oryx 1.50 1.50
610 A178 350f multicolored 2.75 2.75

Henna — A179

Various designs painted on hands.

1998, Sept. 9 **Litho.** ***Perf. 13½***
611 A179 50f multicolored .60 .60
612 A179 1d multicolored .90 .90
613 A179 150f multicolored 1.40 1.40
614 A179 2d multicolored 1.75 1.75
615 A179 250f multicolored 2.25 2.25
616 A179 3d multicolored 2.75 2.75
Nos. 611-616 (6) 9.65 9.65

Art — A180

50f, Fish. 250f, Mosque, palm trees, vert. 350f, Door, jar.

1998, Oct. 20 **Litho.** ***Perf. 13½***
617 A180 50f multicolored .50 .50
618 A180 1d shown .95 .95
619 A180 250f multicolored 2.25 2.25
620 A180 350f multicolored 3.25 3.25
Nos. 617-620 (4) 6.95 6.95

27th National Day — A181

1998, Dec. 2 **Litho.** ***Perf. 13x13¼***
621 A181 50f Mountain road .45 .45
622 A181 350f Boat, city skyline 4.25 4.25

Flowers — A182

Designs: 25f, Indigofera arabica. 50f, Centaureum pulchellum. 75f, Lavandula citriodora. 1d, Taverniera glabra. 150f, Convolvulus deserti. 2d, Capparis spinosa. 250f, Rumex vesicrius. 3d, Anagallis arvensis. 350f, Tribulus arabicus. 5d, Reichardia tinitana.

1998, Dec. 8 **Litho.** ***Perf. 13¼x13¾***
623 A182 25f multicolored .25 .25
624 A182 50f multicolored .45 .45
625 A182 75f multicolored .60 .60
626 A182 1d multicolored .80 .80
627 A182 150f multicolored 1.25 1.25
628 A182 2d multicolored 1.60 1.60
629 A182 250f multicolored 2.10 2.10
630 A182 3d multicolored 2.50 2.50
631 A182 350f multicolored 2.75 2.75
632 A182 5d multicolored 4.00 4.00
Nos. 623-632 (10) 16.30 16.30

Arthropods — A183

50f, Anthia duodecimguttata. 150f, Daphnis nerii. 250f, Acorypha glaucopsis. 350f, Androctonus crassicauda.

1999, Mar. 15 **Litho.** ***Perf. 13½x14***
633 A183 50f multicolored .50 .50
634 A183 150f multicolored 1.15 1.15
635 A183 250f multicolored 2.25 2.25
636 A183 350f multicolored 3.50 3.50
Nos. 633-636 (4) 7.40 7.40

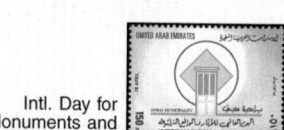

Intl. Day for Monuments and Sites — A184

1999, Apr. 18 **Litho.** ***Perf. 13x13½***
637 A184 150f shown 1.50 1.50
638 A184 250f Fort 2.75 2.75

UPU, 125th Anniv. — A185

1999 **Litho.** ***Perf. 13½x13***
639 A185 50f shown 1.00 1.00
640 A185 350f Emblem, "125" 2.75 2.75

Imperf
Size: 90x70mm
641 A185 5d Hemispheres 5.25 5.25

Environmental Protection A186

Marine life: 50f, Lamprometra klunzingeri. 150f, Pelagia noctiluca. 250f, Hexabranchus sanguineus. 3d, Siphonochalina siphonella.

1999, Nov. 3 Litho. ***Perf. 13½x14***

642 A186 50f multi	.50	.50
643 A186 150f multi	1.60	1.60
644 A186 250f multi	2.60	2.60
645 A186 3d multi	3.00	3.00
Nos. 642-645 (4)	7.70	7.70

Handicrafts — A187

Designs: 50f, Lacemaking. 1d, Embroidery. 250f, Woman with wickerwork. 350f, Finished wickerwork.

1999, Nov. 8 ***Perf. 14x13½***

646 A187 50f multi	.50	.50
647 A187 1d multi	1.15	1.15
648 A187 250f multi	3.00	3.00
649 A187 350f multi	4.50	4.50
Nos. 646-649 (4)	9.15	9.15

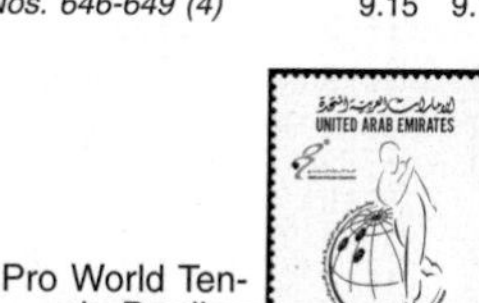

14th Pro World Ten-pin Bowling Championships A188

Designs: 50f, Emblem. 250f, Bowler, pins, Abu Dhabi skyline.

1999, Nov. 16 Litho. ***Perf. 14x13½***
650-651 A188 Set of 2 2.60 2.60

Children's Art — A189

Art by: 50f, Nooran Khaleefa. 1d, Khawla Al Hawal. 150f, Khawla Salem. 250f, Fatimah Ibrahim.

1999, Dec. 15 ***Perf. 13x13½***
652-655 A189 Set of 4 4.75 4.75

Millennium — A190

Falcon and "2000" in: 50f, Gray and silver. 250f, Blue and gold.

1999, Dec. 22 ***Perf. 13½x13***
656-657 A190 Set of 2 2.25 2.25

Dubai Ports and Customs, Cent. — A191

50f, Old building. 3d, Modern building.

2000, Jan. 26 ***Perf. 13x13½***
658-659 A191 Set of 2 5.00 5.00

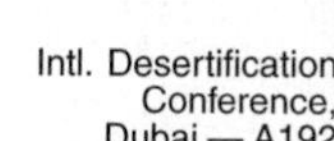

Intl. Desertification Conference, Dubai — A192

2000, Feb. 12 ***Perf. 13½x13***
660 A192 250f multi 3.00 3.00

Environmental Protection A193

Designs: 50f, Palm trees, Al Gheel. 250f, Aggah Beach.

2000, Feb. 29 Litho. ***Perf. 13x13½***

661 A193 50f multi	.50	.50
662 A193 250f multi	2.50	2.50

2000 Summer Olympics, Sydney — A194

Emblem and: 50f, Swimmer. 2d, Runner. 350f, Shooter.

2000, Sept. 16 Litho. ***Perf. 13x13½***
663-665 A194 Set of 3 4.75 4.75

Dubai Intl. Holy Koran Award — A195

50f, Medal on ribbon of flags. 250f, Sheikh Zayed bin Sultan al Nahayan and UAE flag.

2000, Sept. 23 ***Perf. 13½x13***
666-667 A195 Set of 2 3.50 3.50

World Meteorological Organization, 50th Anniv. — A196

Designs: 50f, Barometer and modern map. 250f, Gauge's pointer and old map.

2000
668-669 A196 Set of 2 3.50 3.50

Expansion of Dubai Intl. Airport — A197

Denominations: 50f, 350f.

2000, Nov. 4 Litho. ***Perf. 13x13½***
670-671 A197 Set of 2 5.75 5.75

Development and Environment — A198

Designs: 50f, Smile. 250f, Flower. 3d, Heart as leaf. 350f, Heart as globe.

2001, Mar. 20 Litho. ***Perf. 13¼x13***
672-675 A198 Set of 4 8.75 8.75

Dubai Millennium, Winner of 2000 Dubai World Cup — A199

Designs: 3d, Horse's head. 350f, Horse at track.

2001, Mar. 24 ***Perf. 13x13¼***
676-677 A199 Set of 2 7.50 7.50

Sultan Bin Ali Al Owais (1925-2000), Poet — A200

Designs: 50f, Calligraphy. 1d, Portrait.

2001, Apr. 30 ***Perf. 13¼x13***
678-679 A200 Set of 2 3.00 3.00

Arab Bank for Investment and Foreign Trade, 25th Anniv. — A201

Designs: 50f, Emblem. 1d, Emblem, diff.

2001, July 7 Litho. ***Perf. 13¼x13***
680-681 A201 Set of 2 2.25 2.25

7th GCC Postage Stamp Exhibition, Dubai — A202

2001, July 10
682 A202 50f multi 1.40 1.40

Traditional Boats — A203

Designs: 50f, Shahoof. 250f, Bagarah. 3d, Sam'aa. 350f, Jalboot.

2001, Aug. 25 ***Perf. 14x13¼***
683-686 A203 Set of 4 10.00 10.00

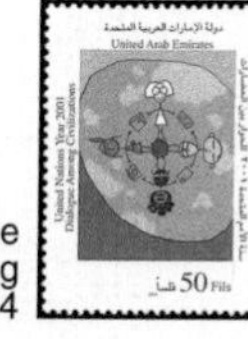

Year of Dialogue Among Civilizations — A204

Designs: 50f, Emblem. 250f, Branch with multicolored leaves.

2001, Oct. 9 ***Perf. 13¼x13***
687-688 A204 Set of 2 3.75 3.75

Emirates Post — A205

Falcons and inscription: 50f, Changing. 250f, Growing. 3d, Achieving.

2001, Sept. 15 ***Perf. 13x13¼***
689-691 A205 Set of 3 7.50 7.50

Children's Art — A206

Designs: 1d, Mosque. 250f, Boatbuilding. 3d, Man pouring coffee, vert. 350f, Falconry.

Perf. 14x13¼, 13¼x14
2001, Nov. 12 Litho.
692-695 A206 Set of 4 10.50 10.50

Unification of Armed Forces, 25th Anniv. — A207

2001, Dec. 30 ***Perf. 13¼x13***
696 A207 1d multi 2.25 2.25

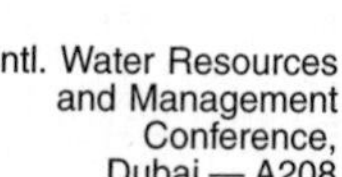
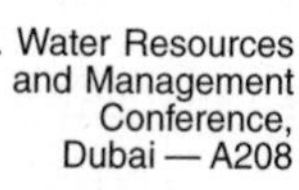

Intl. Water Resources and Management Conference, Dubai — A208

2002, Feb. 2
697 A208 50f multi 1.60 1.60

UAE University, 25th Anniv. — A209

Background colors: 50f, Blue. 1d, Red.

2002, Mar. 25 ***Perf. 13¼x14***
698-699 A209 Set of 2 2.75 2.75

Arabian Saluki — A210

Various salukis: 50f, 150f, 250f, 3d.

2002, Apr. 29 Litho. ***Perf. 13½x13¼***
700-703 A210 Set of 4 11.00 11.00

Emirates Post, 1st Anniv. — A211

"1" and: 50f, Ring of text. 3d, Emblem.

2002, May 29 ***Perf. 13¼x13***
704 A211 50f blue 1.60 1.60

Souvenir Sheet

Perf. 14¼

705 A211 3d multi 9.25 9.25

No. 705 contains one 45x35mm stamp.

Rashid Bin Salim Al-Suwaidi Al-Khadhar (1905-80), Poet — A212

Designs: 50f, Text. 250f, Portrait.

2002, July 17 Litho. ***Perf. 13½x13¼***
706-707 A212 Set of 2 5.25 5.25

Children's Creativity — A213

Designs: 50f, Antelope and boat, by Amna al-Bloushi. 1d, Children, by Fahd al-Habsi. 2d, Earth holding flower, by Hana Mohammed. 250f, Fish, by Hatem al-Dhaheri. 3d, Child holding Earth, by Abdulla Ridha. 350f, Stick figures, by Yousef al-Sind. 5d, Emblem of Latifa Bint Mohammed Award for Childhood Creativity (29x39mm).

Perf. 13x13¼, 13¼x13 (5d)

2002, Oct. 9
708-714 A213 Set of 7 17.50 17.50

Sheikh Hamdan Bin Rashid Al-Maktoum Award for Medical Sciences — A214

Designs: 50f, Award, emblem, sand dunes. 250f, Caduceus, map.

2002, Oct. 21 ***Perf. 13x13¼***
715-716 A214 Set of 2 4.75 4.75

31st National Day — A215

Landmarks in the Emirates: Nos. 717, 724a, 50f, Ajman. Nos. 718, 724b, 50f, Sharjah. Nos. 719, 724c, 50f, Dubai. Nos. 720, 724d, 50f, Abu Dhabi. Nos. 721, 724e, 50f, Ras al Khaima. Nos. 722, 724f, Fujeira. Nos. 723, 724g, Umm al Qiwain.

2002, Dec. 2 Litho. ***Perf. 13¼x14***
717-723 A215 Set of 7 7.50 7.50

Souvenir Sheet
Litho. & Embossed
Imperf

724 Sheet of 7 12.50 12.50
a.-g. A215 50f Any single 1.50 1.50

No. 724 sold for 5d.

Thuraya Satellite Communications A216

Denominations: 25f, 250f.

2002 Litho. ***Perf. 14***
725-726 A216 Set of 2 2.75 2.75

Issued: 25f, 1/27; 250f, 1/6.

Falcon Type of 1990

2003-04 Litho. ***Perf. 11½***
Granite Paper

726A A85 125f multi 2.25 .90

Size: 21x26mm
Perf. 11½x11¾

726B A85 225f multi 2.75 1.50
726C A85 275f multi 3.50 2.00
726D A85 325f multi 4.25 2.75
726E A85 375f multi 4.50 1.90
726F A85 4d multi 4.75 2.25
726G A85 6d multi 7.25 3.00
Nos. 726A-726G (7) 29.25 14.30

Issued: 125f, 2/23; 225f, 11/24/04; 275f, 325f, 375f, 4/13; 4d, 6d, 9/16.

Items in Al Ain National Museum — A217

Designs: 50f, Jar from Hili tombs. 275f, Pottery from Umm an-Nar tombs. 4d, Bronze axe. 6d, Soapstone vessel.

2003, Feb. 25 ***Perf. 14x13½***
727-730 A217 Set of 4 11.50 11.50

National Bank of Dubai, 40th Anniv. A218

Panel color: 50f, Blue. 4d, Orange. 6d, Red.

2003, Apr. 15 Litho. ***Perf. 14x13¼***
731-733 A218 Set of 3 8.75 8.75

Miniature Sheet

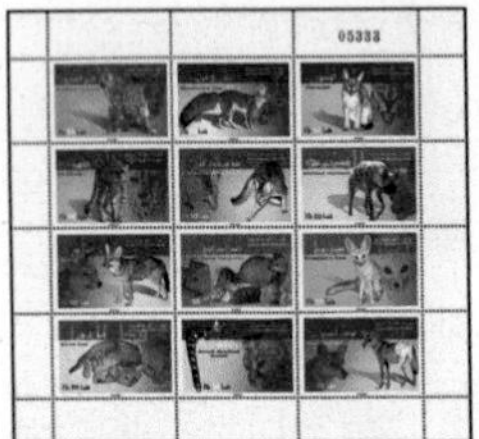
Wildlife A218a

No. 733A: b, Arabian leopard. c, Blanford's fox. d, Caracal. e, Cheetah. f, Gordon's wild cat. g, Striped hyena. h, Jackal. i, White-tailed mongoose. j, Ruppell's fox. k, Sand cat. l, Small spotted genet. m, Arabian wolf.

2003, June 10 Litho. ***Perf. 14½***
733A A218a 50f Sheet of 12, #b-m 9.00 9.00

Coins — A219

Designs: 50f, Dirham of Caliph Al Walid bin Abdul Malik. 125f, Arab Sasanian Dirham of Caliph Abdul Malik Bin Marwan. 275f, Dinar of Al Mustansir Billah Al Fatimi. 375f, Dinar of Caliph Abdul Malik bin Marwan.

5d, Dirham of Caliph Muhammed Al Ameen to mark election of Mousa Al Natiq Bilhaq.

2003, July 20 Litho. ***Perf. 13¼x13¾***
734-737 A219 Set of 4 7.50 7.50

Size: 106x73mm
Imperf

738 A219 5d multi 20.00 20.00

Sheikh Zayed bin Sultan al Nahayan, 37th Anniv. of Accession as Ruler of Abu Dhabi — A220

Sheikh Zayed and: 50f, Camel and sand dune. 175f, Modern buildings.

2003, Aug. 6 Litho. ***Perf. 13***
739-740 A220 Set of 2 2.75 2.75

World Youth Soccer Championships, United Arab Emirates — A221

2003, Sept. 7 ***Perf. 13x13¼***
741 A221 375f multi 3.75 3.75

World Bank Boards of Governors Annual Meetings, Dubai — A222

Emblem and: 50f, Emirates Tower. 175f, Falcon. 275f, Mosque domes, horiz. 375f, Dhow. 5d, English and Arabic text.

Perf. 13¼x13, 13x13¼

2003, Sept. 23 Litho.
742-745 A222 Set of 4 8.50 8.50

Imperf
Size: 118x74mm

746 A222 5d multi 15.00 15.00

Peace — A223

Dove and: 50f, Zakharafs. 225f, Door and wind tower. 275f, Columns. 325f, Water taxi.

2003, Oct. 1 ***Perf. 13x13¼***
747-750 A223 Set of 4 9.50 9.50

Traditional Housing — A224

Designs: 50f, Palm frond house. 175f, Mud house. 275f, Stone house. 325f, Tent.

2003, Oct. 20 ***Perf. 13½x14***
751-754 A224 Set of 4 9.00 9.00

Falcons — A225

Designs: 50f, Peregrine falcon. 125f, Hybrid gyr-peregrine falcon. 275f, Gyrfalcon. 375f, Saker falcon.

2003, Nov. 17 ***Perf. 13¼x14***
755-758 A225 Set of 4 9.00 9.00

Poetry of Saeed Bin Ateej Al Hamli (1875-1919) A226

Poetry: 125f, Four short lines. 175f, Four long lines.

2003, Dec. 29 ***Perf. 13x13¼***
759-760 A226 Set of 2 3.25 3.25

Mohammed Bin Saeed Bin Ghubash (1899-1969), Religious Scholar — A227

Designs: 50f, Portrait. 175f, Books.

2004, Apr. 5 Litho. ***Perf. 13¼x14***
761-762 A227 Set of 2 3.00 3.00

Fourth Family Meeting — A228

Color of hands: 375f, Orange. 4d, Purple.

2004, Apr. 19
763-764 A228 Set of 2 7.00 7.00

FIFA (Fédération Internationale de Football Association), Cent. — A229

2004, May 21 Litho. ***Perf. 13x13¼***
765 A229 375f multi 2.75 2.75

Handicrafts by Special Needs Persons — A230

Designs: 50f, Handcrafted vase. 125f, Painting. 275f, Framed branch. 5d, Pottery artwork.

2004, June 29 ***Perf. 13¼x13***
766-769 A230 Set of 4 8.50 8.50

2004 Summer Olympics, Athens — A231

Olympic rings and: 50f, Track athlete. 125f, Rifle shooter. 275f, Swimmer. 375f, 2004 Athens Olympics emblem, torch bearer.

2004, Aug. 13 Litho. ***Perf. 13x13¼***
770-773 A231 Set of 4 8.25 8.25

Endangered or Extinct Persian Gulf Marine Life — A232

Designs: 50f, Black finless porpoise. 175f, Serranidae. 275f, Whale shark. 375f, Dugongidae.

2004, Sept. 26 ***Perf. 14***
774-777 A232 Set of 4 8.00 8.00
777a Booklet pane, 2 each #774-777 9.50 —
Complete booklet, #777a 9.50

Operation Emirates Solidarity for Mine Clearance in South Lebanon — A233

Flags and: 275f, Person clearing mines. 375f, Map, people clearing mines, horiz.

2004, Oct. 25 ***Perf. 13x12¾, 12¾x13***
778-779 A233 Set of 2 5.75 5.75

Sheik Dr. Sultan bin Mohammed al-Qassimi, Ruler of Sharjah — A234

Color of denomination: 50f, Orange brown. 125f, Green. 275f, Red brown. 4d, Blue.

2004, Nov. 30 ***Perf. 13½x14***
780-783 A234 Set of 4 7.25 7.25

Traditional Women's Clothing — A235

Designs: 50f, Drawers. 125f, Robe. 175f, Gown. 225f, Jalabia. 275f, Scarf. 375f, Yashmak.

2004, Dec. 29 **Litho.** ***Perf. 14***
784-789 A235 Set of 6 8.00 8.00
789a Booklet pane, #784-789 8.00 8.00
Complete booklet, #789a 8.00

Dubai Aluminum, 25th Anniv. — A236

Designs: 50f, Smelting complex. 275f, Smelting complex, sheikhs (brown background). 375f, Like 275f, blue background.

2005, Jan. 8 ***Perf. 13***
790-792 A236 Set of 3 5.00 5.00

10th Dubai Shopping Festival — A237

Designs: 50f, Emblem. 125f, Emblem, diff. 275f, Emblem and "10," green background. 375f, Emblem and "10," red background.

2005, Jan. 12 ***Perf. 13¼x13***
793-796 A237 Set of 4 7.00 7.00

2nd Intl. Gathering of Scouting and Belonging, Sharjah — A238

Designs: 50f, Emblem. 375f, Scouts and truck.

2005, Apr. 1 **Litho.** ***Perf. 13¼x14***
797-798 A238 Set of 2 4.75 4.75

Shaikha Fatima Bint Mubarak, Women's Rights Activist — A239

2005, Apr. 10 ***Perf. 14½***
799 A239 50f multi 3.00 3.00

Al Majedi Bin Dhaher, 17th Century Poet — A240

Poetry and: 50f, Sand. 175f, Bricks.

2005, May 30 **Litho.** ***Perf. 14½***
800-801 A240 Set of 2 2.00 2.00

Reptiles — A241

Designs: 50f, Agama. 125f, Desert monitor. 225f, Sand lizard. 275f, Dune sand gecko. 375f, Spiny-tailed lizard. 5d, Sand skink.

2005, Aug. 2 ***Perf. 13¾***
802-807 A241 Set of 6 14.50 14.50
807a Booklet pane, #802-807 15.00 —
Complete booklet, #807a 15.00

Accession of Sheik Khalifa Bin Zayed Al Nahyan, 1st Anniv. A242

Sheik Khalifa: 50f, With a child. 175f, With another sheik. 275f, With another sheik, diff. 375f, Kissing sheik.

2005, Nov. 3 **Litho.** ***Perf. 14x13¼***
808-811 A242 Set of 4 8.00 8.00
811a Sheet of 4, #808-811 10.00 10.00

No. 811a sold for 10d.

2005 Census — A243

Emblem at: 50f, Bottom. 375f, Left, horiz.

Perf. 13¼x13, 13x13¼
2005, Nov. 10
812-813 A243 Set of 2 3.25 3.25

Desert Plants — A244

Designs: 50f, Leptadenia pyrotechnica. 125f, Lycium shawii. 225f, Calotropis procera. 275f, Prosopis cineraria. 325f, Zizyphus spina-christi. 375f, Acacia tortilis.

2005, Nov. 27 **Litho.** ***Perf. 13½***
814-819 A244 Set of 6 12.50 12.50
819a Booklet pane, #814-819 13.00 —
Complete booklet, #819a 13.00

34th National Day — A245

Children's art: 50f, Flower in Arabic script, by Shaimaa Mohammed Al Halabi. 125f, Ring of children, by Muaz Jamal Ahmed Hassan, horiz. 275f, Hands, by Pithani Srinidhi. 375f, Doves, flag and plants, by Lina Abu Baker Mukhtar, horiz.

2005, Dec. 2 ***Perf. 14¼***
820-823 A245 Set of 4 7.00 7.00

Pearl Diving Tools — A246

Designs: 50f, F'ttam (nose clip). 125f, Al Khabet (finger protectors). 175f, Al Dayeen (basket). 275f, Sea rock (diver's weight). 375f, Diver's outfit.

2005, Dec. 21 ***Perf. 14***
824-828 A246 Set of 5 *11.00 11.00*

A souvenir sheet containing Nos. 824-828 with pearl halves affixed to each stamp sold for 100d. Value, $77.50.

Gulf Cooperation Council Day for Autistic Children — A247

2006, Apr. 4 **Litho.** ***Perf. 13***
829 A247 4d multi *3.00 3.00*

Souvenir Sheet

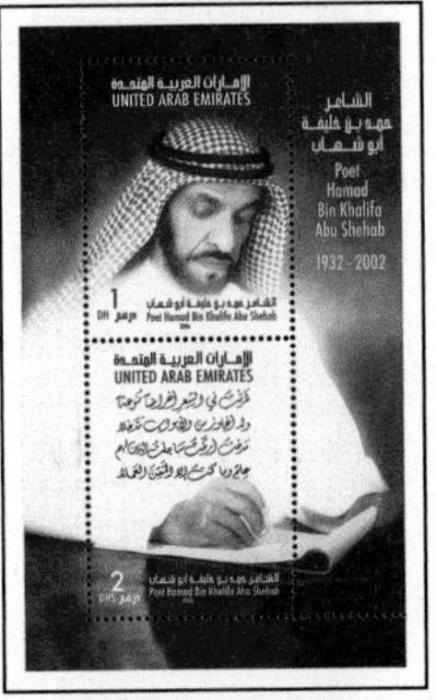

Hamad Bin Khalifa Abu Shehab (1932-2002), Poet — A248

No. 830: a, 1d, Head. b, 2d, Hands, poetry in Arabic text.

2006, Apr. 26 ***Perf. 14¼***
830 A248 Sheet of 2, #a-b 4.00 4.00

A249

Gulf Cooperation Council, 25th Anniv. — A250

Litho. with Foil Application
2006, May 25 ***Perf. 14***
831 A249 1d multi 3.50 3.50

Imperf
Size: 165x105mm
832 A250 5d multi 13.00 13.00

See Bahrain Nos. 628-629, Kuwait Nos. 1646-1647, Oman Nos. 477-478, Qatar Nos. 1007-1008, and Saudi Arabia No. 1378.

Dubai Police, 50th Anniv. — A251

2006, June 1 ***Perf. 13¼x13***
833 A251 1d multi 2.00 2.00

19th Asian Stamp Exhibition, Dubai — A252

Designs: 1d, shown. 4d, Four towers.

Litho. With Foil Application
2006, June 24 ***Perf. 13¾***
834-835 A252 Set of 2 4.00 4.00

Dubai Intl. Holy Koran Award, 10th Anniv. — A253

2006, July 24 **Litho.** ***Perf. 14x13½***
836 A253 1d multi 1.00 1.00

Al Raha Beach Developments — A254

Designs: 1d, Khor Al Raha. 2d, Al Lissaily. 350f, Al Wateed (40x40mm). 4d, Al Bandar (40x40mm).

2006, Sept. 18 **Litho.** ***Perf. 13***
837-840 A254 Set of 4 8.00 8.00

UPU Strategy Conference, Dubai — A255

Designs: 1d, Green arrows. 4d, Blue and green arrows.

Litho. & Embossed
2006, Sept. 27 ***Perf. 14x13½***
841-842 A255 Set of 2 6.00 6.00

12th Gulf Cooperation Council Postage Stamp Exhibition — A256

2006, Nov. 13 **Litho.** ***Perf. 13¼x13***
843 A256 1d multi 1.10 1.10

35th National Day — A257

2006, Dec. 1
844 A257 1d multi 1.75 1.75

A souvenir sheet containing one stamp sold for 10d.

Sheikh Mohammed bin Rashid al Maktoum, Prime Minister A258

Sheikh Mohammed: 1d, Wearing kaffiyeh. 4d, Wearing polo helmet (44x53mm).

Litho. With 3-Dimensional Plastic Affixed

2006, Dec. 2 ***Serpentine Die Cut 9***

Self-Adhesive

845-846 A258 Set of 2 4.25 4.25

Gazelles — A259

Designs: 1d, Tahr. 2d, Sand gazelle. 3d, Mountain gazelle. 350f, Arabian oryx.

2006, Nov. 29 **Litho.** ***Perf. 14***

847-850 A259 Set of 4 8.75 8.75
850a Souvenir sheet, #847-850 8.75 8.75

Intl. Volunteers Day — A260

Man giving items to: 2d, Two children. 4d, Three children.

2006, Dec. 5 ***Perf. 13x13¼***

851-852 A260 Set of 2 5.00 5.00

Women's Jewelry — A261

Designs: 1d, Mariya um alnairat. 150f, Mortasha. 2d, Shaghab bu shouk. 3d, Shahid ring. 350f, Bushuq. 4d, Tassah.

2006, Dec. 31 ***Perf. 13x13¼***

853-858 A261 Set of 6 10.00 10.00
858a Booklet pane, #853-858 13.00 —
Complete booklet, #858a 15.00

Falcon — A262

2007, Jan. 31 ***Perf. 13¼x13***

Background Color

859	A262	1d buff	.75	.75
860	A262	150f gray	1.20	1.20
861	A262	2d lilac	1.50	1.50
862	A262	3d yellow	2.25	2.25
863	A262	350f yel green	2.60	2.60
864	A262	4d pink	3.25	3.25
865	A262	5d blue vio	3.75	3.75
		Nos. 859-865 (7)	15.30	15.30

Booklet Stamps

Self-Adhesive

Serpentine Die Cut 12½

Background Color

865A	A262	1d buff	.75	.75
865B	A262	150f gray	1.20	1.20
865C	A262	2d lilac	1.50	1.50
865D	A262	3d yellow	2.25	2.25
865E	A262	350f yel green	2.60	2.60
865F	A262	4d pink	3.25	3.25
865G	A262	5d blue vio	3.75	3.75
h.		Booklet pane, #865A-865G	17.50	—
		Complete booklet, #865Gh	17.50	
		Nos. 865A-865G (7)	15.30	15.30

See Nos. 937, 959-965, 1043A, 1043D, 1081-1085.

Dubai Tennis Championships A263

Background colors: 1d, Orange. 3d, Red violet.

2007, Feb. 19 ***Perf. 14***

866-867 A263 Set of 2 3.25 3.25

18th Arabian Gulf Soccer Cup Championships, Abu Dhabi — A264

Arabian Gulf Cup with frame in: 1d, Red. 3d, Green.

2007, May 9 **Litho.** ***Perf. 14x13¾***

868-869 A264 Set of 2 3.25 3.25
869a Souvenir sheet, #868-869 9.50 9.50

No. 869a sold for 10d.

Etisalat (Telecommunications Company), 30th Anniv. — A265

Denomination color: 1d, Blue. 3d, Orange red. 350f, Purple. 4d, Red.

2007, May 17 ***Perf. 13x13¼***

870-873 A265 Set of 4 9.50 9.50

Each stamp has a die cut opening.

Souvenir Sheet

World Blood Donor Day — A266

No. 874 — World Blood Donor Day emblem and: a, 1d, Heart. b, 3d, Blood drop.

2007, June 14 ***Perf. 13***

874 A266 Sheet of 2, #a-b 3.75 3.75

Sheikh Ahmed Mohamed Hasher Al Maktoum, UAE's First Olympic Gold Medalist — A267

2007, July 17 ***Perf. 14x13½***

875 A267 3d multi 3.50 3.50

A268

Emirates Bank, 30th Anniv. — A269

Perf. 14x13¾ (A268), 14 (A269)

2007, Aug. 28

876	A268	1d blue & multi	1.10	1.10
877	A269	150f blue & multi	1.60	1.60
878	A268	3d brn & multi	3.50	3.50
879	A269	350f brn & multi	3.75	3.75
a.		Souvenir sheet, #876-879	10.50	10.50
		Nos. 876-879 (4)	9.95	9.95

No. 879a sold for 15d.

Emirates Banks Association, 25th Anniv. A270

2007, Oct. 4 ***Perf. 13¾***

880 A270 1d red & bis brn 2.00 2.00

Abu Dhabi Islamic Bank, 10th Anniv. — A271

Differing backgrounds with denominations of: 1d, 150f, 2d, 3d.

2007, Nov. 8 **Litho.** ***Perf. 14¼***

881-884 A271 Set of 4 10.00 10.00
884a Souvenir sheet, #881-884 10.00 10.00

Abu Dhabi Police, 50th Anniv. — A272

Litho. With Foil Application

2007, Nov. 14 ***Perf. 13¼x14***

885 A272 1d multi 1.00 1.00

Children's Art — A273

Designs: Nos. 886, 892, Woman and two men in prayer. Nos. 887, 893, Woman presenting gift to another woman, vert. Nos. 888, 894, Children facing mosque. Nos. 889, 895, Hands holding child giving item to woman, vert. Nos. 890, 896, Child helping man across street. Nos. 891, 897, Child helping handicapped person, vert.

2007, Nov. 29 **Litho.** ***Perf. 14***

886	A273	1d multi	.90	.90
887	A273	150f multi	1.35	1.35
888	A273	2d multi	1.75	1.75
889	A273	3d multi	2.75	2.75
890	A273	350f multi	3.00	3.00
891	A273	4d multi	3.50	3.50
		Nos. 886-891 (6)	13.25	13.25

Booklet Stamps

Self-Adhesive

Die Cut Perf. 11¼x12, 12x11¼

892	A273	1d multi	1.25	1.25
893	A273	150f multi	1.90	1.90
894	A273	2d multi	2.50	2.50
895	A273	3d multi	4.00	4.00
896	A273	350f multi	4.50	4.50
897	A273	4d multi	5.25	5.25
a.		Complete booklet, #892-897	19.50	19.50
		Nos. 892-897 (6)	19.40	19.40

Complete booklet is stapled in center with one stamp per page and with the center leaf of the booklet having stamps on both sides.

Souvenir Sheet

Sheikh Mohammed Al Khazraji (1919-2006), Chief Justice — A274

No. 898: a, 1d, Facing right. b, 3d, Facing forward.

2007, Dec. 9 ***Perf. 13½x13¾***

898 A274 Sheet of 2, #a-b 4.00 4.00

Al Abbas Group, 40th Anniv. — A275

Denominations: 1d, 150f, 2d, 3d.

2007, Dec. 16 ***Perf. 14¼***

899-902 A275 Set of 4 7.50 7.50

Al Rostamani Group, 50th Anniv. — A276

Background colors: 1d, Gray. 150f, Prussian blue.

2007, Dec. 23 ***Perf. 13x13¼***

903-904 A276 Set of 2 7.00 7.00

Union Properties, 20th Anniv. — A277

Designs: 1d, Emblem. 150f, F1 Theme Park, Dubai, horiz. 2d, Uptown. 3d, Green community, horiz.

Perf. 13¼x13½, 13½x13¼

2007, Dec. 27

905-908 A277 Set of 4 6.00 6.00
908a Souvenir sheet, #905-908 10.00 10.00

No. 908a sold for 15d.

Federal National Council, 36th Anniv. — A278

2008, Feb. 12 ***Perf. 13¼***

909 A278 1d multi 1.40 1.40

National Bank of Abu Dhabi, 40th Anniv. — A279

"40" and: 1d, Yellow panel at top. 150f, Yellow panel at top. 225d, White panel at top. 4d, White panel at top.

2008, Feb. 13 ***Perf. 13***

910-913 A279 Set of 4 11.00 11.00
913a Souvenir sheet, #910-913 15.00 15.00

No. 913a sold for 15d.

Municipality and Planning Department of Ajman — A280

Emblems of: 1d, Municipality and Planning Department. 150f, Ajman Urban Planning Conference. 2d, E-services. 4d, Geographic Information Systems.

2008, Mar. 24 Litho. ***Perf. 13¼***

914-917 A280 Set of 4 11.00 11.00
917a Souvenir sheet, #914-917, perf. 13¼x14¼ 15.00 15.00

No. 917a sold for 15d.

Souvenir Sheet

Hamdan Bin Rashid Al Maktoum Award for Distinguished Academic Performance — A281

No. 918: a, 1d, Emblem and "10." b, 2d, Rashid Al Maktoum, emblem.

2008, Apr. 1 ***Perf. 13¼***

918 A281 Sheet of 2, #a-b 5.00 5.00

Traditional Souqs A282

Marketplaces: 1d, Spice Souq, Dubai. 150f, Al Arsa Souq, Sharjah. 2d, Gold Souq, Dubai. 3d, Old Souq, Abu Dhabi.

Litho. & Embossed

2008, Apr. 20 ***Perf. 13½x13¼***

919-922 A282 Set of 4 6.75 6.75

Drydocks World, 25th Anniv. — A283

Designs: 1d, Shown. 4d, Emblem, dhow, horiz.

Perf. 13¼x13, 13x13¼

2008, June 4 **Litho.**

923-924 A283 Set of 2 7.00 7.00

Sharjah Intl. Airport, 75th Anniv. A284

2008, July 7 ***Perf. 13½***

925 A284 1d multi 1.00 1.00

2008 Summer Olympics, Beijing — A285

Emblem of Beijing Olympics, emblems of five sports and: 1d, Yellow orange background. 4d, Olympic torch, vert. 475f Olympic torch, diff., vert. 550f, Red violet background.
10d, Olympic torch, vignettes of Nos. 926-929.

2008, Aug. 4 ***Perf. 14x13¼, 13¼x14***

926-929 A285 Set of 4 8.50 8.50

Size: 120x120mm

Imperf

930 A285 10d multi 7.00 7.00

Gulf News, 30th Anniv. A286

Background color: 1d, Blue. 150f, Maroon. 225f, Orange.

2008, Sept. 30 ***Perf. 13½x13¼***

Granite Paper

931-933 A286 Set of 3 4.00 4.00

A souvenir sheet containing Nos. 931-933 sold for 15d.

Souvenir Sheet

Arab Postal Day A287

No. 934 — Emblem and: a, 1d, World map, pigeon. b, 225f, Camel caravan.

Litho. & Silkscreened With Foil Application

2008, Oct. 10

934 A287 Sheet of 2, #a-b 4.00 4.00

Miniature Sheets

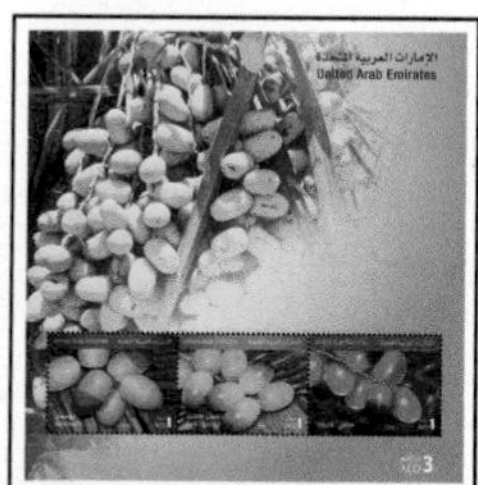

Date Varieties A288

No. 935: a, Abuman. b, Jash Hamad. c, Msalli.
No. 936, vert.: a, Farth. b, Mirzaban. c, Abukibal. d, Salani.

2008, Oct. 22 Litho. ***Perf. 13x13¼***

935 A288 1d Sheet of 3, #a-c 6.00 6.00

Perf. 13¼x13

936 A288 1d Sheet of 4, #a-d 7.00 7.00

Falcon Type of 2007 Inscribed "Priority"

Litho. & Embossed

2008, Dec. 2 ***Perf. 13¼x14***

Background Color

937 A262 2d vermilion 2.25 2.25

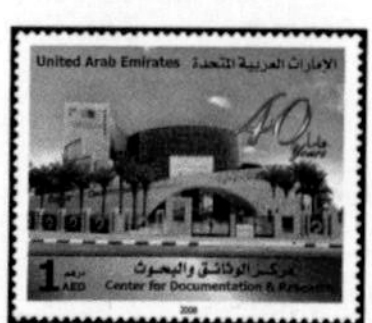

Center for Documentaion and Research, 40th Anniv. — A289

Designs: 1d, Building. 4d, Sheikhs and crowd of people. 10d, Sheikhs, vert.

2008, Dec. 2 Litho. ***Perf. 14¼***

939 A289 1d multi .85 .85

940 A289 4d multi 3.25 3.25

Miniature Sheet

Litho With 3-Dimensional Plastic Affixed

Self-Adhesive

Serpentine Die Cut 9

941 A289 10d multi 10.00 10.00

Eid Al Adha — A290

Designs: 1d, Al Eidiya. 3d, Eid prayers.

Litho. With Foil Application

2008, Dec. 6 ***Perf. 13¾***

942-943 A290 Set of 2 4.00 4.00
943a Souvenir sheet, #942-943 110.00 110.00

No. 943a sold for 6d.

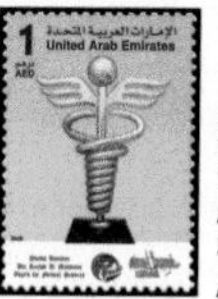

Sheikh Hamdan Bin Rashid Al Maktoum Award for Medical Science, 10th Anniv. — A291

Designs: 1d, Award. 2d, Special Recognition Award. 3d, Sheikh Hamdan Bin Rashid Al Maktoum, award. 4d, 10th anniversary emblem.

2008, Dec. 15 Litho. ***Perf. 13¼***

944-947 A291 Set of 4 9.50 9.50
947a Souvenir sheet, #944-947 80.00 80.00

No. 947a sold for 15d.

Dubai Duty Free, 25th Anniv. A292

Designs: 1d, 25th anniversary emblem in gray. 2d, 25th anniversary emblem in red. 3d, Dubai Duty Free shop. 4d, Shop, diff.

2008, Dec. 20 Litho. ***Perf. 13¼x13***

948-951 A292 Set of 4 8.75 8.75
951a Souvenir sheet, #948-951 80.00 80.00

Universal Declaration of Human Rights, 60th Anniv. — A293

Color of top panel: 1d, Red brown. 4d, Orange and yellow.

Perf. 13¾x13½

2008, Dec. 31 **Litho.**

952-953 A293 Set of 2 5.00 5.00
953a Souvenir sheet, #952-953 70.00 70.00

No. 953a sold for 6d.

Second Arab Stamp Exhibition, Dubai — A294

Serpentine Die Cut 12½

2009, Mar. 5 Litho. & Embossed

Self-Adhesive

Printed on Clear Plastic Film

954 A294 1d multi 1.00 1.00

No. 954 has white backing paper.

Emirates Center for Strategic Studies and Research (ECSSR), 15th Anniv. — A295

Designs: 1d, Books published by ECSSR. 150f, UAE Federation Library. 2d, Media monitoring room. 4d, ECSSR Building.

2009, Mar. 26 Litho. ***Perf. 13¼***

Granite Paper

955-958 A295 Set of 4 7.00 7.00
958a Souvenir sheet, #955-958 40.00 40.00

No. 958a sold for 10d.

Falcon Type of 2007 Redrawn

2009, Apr. 2 Litho. ***Perf. 13¼x13***

Background Color

959	A262	25f black	.25	.25
960	A262	1d dark buff	.55	.55
961	A262	150f brownish gray	.80	.80
962	A262	2d gray lilac	1.10	1.10
963	A262	10d orange	5.50	5.50
964	A262	20d lt greenish blue	11.00	11.00
965	A262	50d dark green	27.50	27.50
		Nos. 959-965 (7)	46.70	46.70

Nos. 959-965 are dated 2009 and lack the buff curved line to the left of the Arabic country name found on Nos. 859-865. Denominations for Nos. 960 and 962 use "AED" rather than the "Dh." or "Dhs." used on Nos. 859 and 861.

Rashid Bin Tannaf (1910-99), Poet — A296

Rashid Bin Tannaf: 1d, Wearing kaffiyeh. 4d, Without kaffiyeh.

2009, Apr. 30 ***Perf. 13¼***

Granite Paper

966-967 A296 Set of 2 3.50 3.50

A souvenir sheet containing Nos. 966-967 sold for 15d.

Discovery of Umm An Nar Culture, 50th Anniv. — A297

Umm An Nar tomb with background color of: 1d, Red brown. 150f, Brown. 4d, Olive green.

2009, June 28 ***Perf. 13x13¼***

968-970 A297 Set of 3 5.00 5.00

Jerusalem, Capital of Arab Culture — A298

2009, Aug. 3 ***Perf. 13¼x13***

971 A298 2d multi 2.25 2.25

Postal Services in the Emirates, Cent. A299

Covers bearing: 1d, Pakistan Nos. 1, 2, 5 and 12. 150f, Trucial States No. 4, Oman Nos. 21 and 52. 4f, United Arab Emirates No. 3, Dubai Nos. 80 and 83, and Sharjah stamp. 5d,

Withdrawn United Arab Emirates National Day stamp of 1977.
10d, Various India stamps.

2009, Aug. 19 *Perf. 13¼*
Granite Paper
972-975 A299 Set of 4 9.00 9.00
Souvenir Sheet
976 A299 10d multi 27.00 27.00

38th National Day — A300

2009, Dec. 2 *Perf. 13*
977 A300 1d multi .90 .90

FIFA 2009 Club World Cup Soccer Championships, Abu Dhabi — A301

Designs: 1d, Shown. 10d, Similar to 1d, with United Arab Emirates flag at right.

2009, Dec. 19 *Perf. 13¾*
978 A301 1d multi 1.25 1.25
Souvenir Sheet
Perf. 13
979 A301 10d multi 35.00 35.00
No. 979 contains one 40x40mm stamp.

Securities and Commodities Authority, 10th Anniv. — A302

Emblem and: 1d, Numerals and squares. 2d, Text on computer screen, graphs. 3d, Emirates Securities Market trading board. 5d, Falcon and numerals.

2010, Feb. 1 *Perf. 13*
Granite Paper
980-983 A302 Set of 4 9.50 9.50
A souvenir sheet containing No. 983 sold for 15d.

Emirates Aluminum, 3rd Anniv. — A303

Designs: 1d, Emblem. 2d, Hand holding frame with picture of smelting complex. 3d, Falcon, horse. 5d, United Arab Emirates flag.

2010, Feb. 24 *Perf. 13x14¼*
984-987 A303 Set of 4 6.50 6.50
987a Souvenir sheet, #984-987, perf. 14¼ 10.00 10.00
No. 987a sold for 15d.

United Arab Emirates Pavilion, Expo 2010, Shanghai — A304

Pavilion: 1d, In daylight. 550f, At dusk.

Litho. With Foil Application
2010, May 13 *Perf. 13¼x13*
988-989 A304 Set of 2 4.75 4.75

Diplomatic Relations Between United Arab Emirates and Republic of Korea, 30th Anniv. — A305

No. 990: a, 1d, Flag of United Arab Emirates and air-conditioning tower. b, 550f, Flag of South Korea and Mt. Amisan Chimney, Gyeongbokgung Palace.

2010, June 17 **Litho.** *Perf. 13x13¼*
990 A305 Horiz. pair, #a-b 4.25 4.25
See South Korea No. 2337.

Jebel Ali Free Zone, 25th Anniv. — A306

Designs: 1d, Zone in 1986. 2d, Zone in 1997. 3d, Zone in 2009. 4d, 25th anniversary emblem.

2010, June 30 *Perf. 13¼x13½*
991-994 A306 Set of 4 8.50 8.50
994a Sheet of 4, #991-994, perf. 14¼x13½ 22.00 22.00
No. 994a sold for 15d.

Souvenir Sheet

2010 Youth Olympics, Singapore — A307

2010, Aug. 19 *Perf. 13¾*
995 A307 475f multi 2.75 2.75

Sheikh Zayed Grand Mosque — A308

Designs: 1d, Mosque. 5d, Mosque, horiz. 25d, Mosque, diff., horiz.

Perf. 13½x13¼, 13¼x13½
2010, Aug. 29 **Litho.**
996-997 A308 Set of 2 5.50 5.50
Litho. & Embossed With Foil Application
Imperf
Size:145x110mm
998 A308 25d gold & multi 18.50 18.50

Old Schools A309

Designs: 1d, Al Nehyania School, Abu Dhabi. 150f, Al Ahmadiya School, Dubai. 4d, Al Eslah School, Sharjah.

Perf. 13½x13¾
2010, Sept. 19 **Litho.**
999-1001 A309 Set of 3 3.75 3.75
A souvenir sheet containing Nos. 999-1001 sold for 15d.

Organization of the Petroleum Exporting Countries, 50th Anniv. — A310

2010, Sept. 27 *Perf. 13*
1002 A310 1d multi .75 .75

World Post Day — A311

Designs: 1d, Dove holding envelope. 550f, Universal Postal Union emblem.

2010, Oct. 9 *Perf. 13¼x13*
1003-1004 A311 Set of 2 5.00 5.00

Miniature Sheet

Sea Birds A312

No. 1005: a, 1d, Black-headed gull. b, 150f, Crab plover. c, 2d, Gray heron ardea. d, 3d, Sooty gull. e, 450f, Socotra cormorant. f, 550f, Caspian gull.

2010, Nov. 4 **Litho.** *Perf. 13*
Granite Paper
1005 A312 Sheet of 6, #a-f, + label 12.50 12.50

DP World Marine Terminal Operators A313

DP World emblem and various port scenes: 1d, 2d, 3d, 4d.

2010, Nov. 9 *Perf. 14¼x13¾*
Granite Paper
1006-1009 A313 Set of 4 7.50 7.50
1009a Sheet of 4, #1006-1009 10.00 10.00
No. 1009a sold for 15d.

Yas Marina Racing Circuit, Abu Dhabi A314

Designs: 1d, Race car on track. 550f, Grandstands.

2010, Nov. 14 *Perf. 13¼x13*
1010-1011 A314 Set of 2 5.00 5.00

Watani (National Identity) — A315

Designs: 1d, Four stylized fingerprints. 150f, Map of United Arab Emirates composed of fingerprints, vert.

2010, Dec. 2 *Perf. 13x13½, 13½x13*
1012-1013 A315 Set of 2 2.40 2.40

39th National Day A316

Nos. 1014 and 1015 — Winning designs in children's stamp design contest: a, Four automobiles, people waving flags and signs. b, Children with flags around grills. c, Flag of United Arab Emirates, tower. d, Four people, flags, towers. e, Children with balloons. f, Flag and "December 2."

2010, Dec. 2 *Perf. 13*
1014 A316 1d Sheet of 6, #a-f 6.00 6.00
Stamp Size: 35x26mm
Self-Adhesive
Serpentine Die Cut 12¾
1015 A316 1d Booklet pane of 12, 2 each #a-f 12.00 12.00

Ghaf Tree — A317

2011, Mar. 31 *Perf. 13¼*
1016 A317 1d green 1.00 1.00
A souvenir sheet containing No. 1016 and a 4d stamp with a ghaf tree seed and a plastic netting affixed to it sold for 40d.

17th Gulf Cooperation Council Postage Stamp Exhibition, Abu Dhabi — A318

2011, Apr. 4 *Perf. 13*
1017 A318 150f multi 2.00 2.00

Miniature Sheet

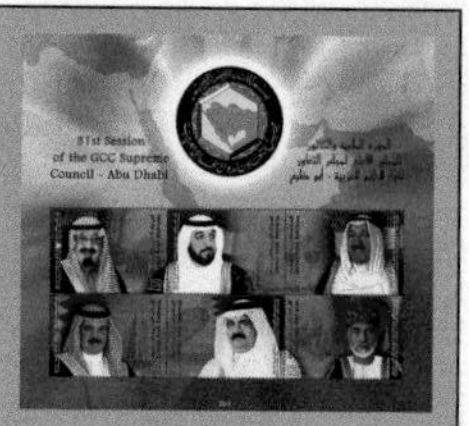

31st Session of the Gulf Cooperation Council Supreme Council, Abu Dhabi — A319

No. 1018 — Various buildings and: a, King Abdullah, flag of Saudi Arabia. b, Sheikh Khalifa, flag of United Arab Emirates. c, Sheikh Sabah, flag of Kuwait. d, King Hamad, flag of Bahrain. e, Sheikh Hamad, flag of Qatar. f, Sultan Qaboos, flag of Oman.

2011, Apr. 5 *Perf. 13½x13¾*
1018 A319 150f Sheet of 6, #a-f 6.50 6.50

Fifth Gulf Federation for Cancer Control Conference, Sharjah — A320

2011, May 31 Litho. *Perf. 14x13½*
Granite Paper

1019 A320 1d multi 1.10 1.10

Emblem of Sheikha Fatima Bint Mubarak — A321

Litho. With Foil Application

2011, July 24 *Perf. 13*

1020 A321 1d multi 2.00 2.00

Al Bidyah Mosque, Fujeira — A322

Designs: 1d, Archway. 150f, Mosque exterior.
15d, Mosque exerior, wall carving.

2011, Aug. 27 Litho. *Perf. 14x14¼*

1021 A322 1d multi 1.00 1.00
1022 A322 150f multi 1.50 1.50

Litho. & Embossed
Imperf
Size: 130x80mm

1023 A322 15d multi 8.25 8.25

No. 1023 contains one 40x40mm perforated label.

Fauna of Bu Tinah Island — A323

Designs: No. 1024, 1d, Dugong (35x35mm). No. 1025, 1d, One fish (35x35mm). No. 1026, 1d, Three fish (35x35mm). No. 1027, 1d, Crab (35x35mm). No. 1028, 1d, Bird (35x35mm). No. 1029, 1d, Coral (35x35mm). No. 1030, 1d, Coral (48x30mm). No. 1031, 1d, Dolphin (48x30mm). No. 1032, 1d, Flamingos (48x30mm). No. 1033, 1d, Sea turtle (48x30mm).
15d, Sea turtle, dugong, dolphins, coral, crab, birds.

Perf. 13¼, 13¼x13½ (#1030-1033)

2011, Nov. 30 Litho.

1024-1033 A323 Set of 10 18.00 18.00

Size: 120x70mm
Imperf

1034 A323 15d multi 20.00 20.00

40th National Day — A324

2011, Dec. 2 *Perf. 13½x13¾*
Granite Paper

1035 A324 1d multi 1.00 1.00

Winter Plants A325

Designs: No. 1036, 1d, Bladder dock. No. 1037, 1d, Cart-track plant. No. 1038, 1d, Arta. No. 1039, 1d, Hawa. No. 1040, 150f, Rohida tree. No. 1041, 150f, Puncturevine.

2011, Dec. 26 *Perf. 14x13*

1036-1041 A325 Set of 6 7.00 7.00

Camels A326

Designs: 1d, Four camels. 4d, One camel.

2011, Dec. 29 *Perf. 13¾*

1042-1043 A326 Set of 2 3.75 3.75

A souvenir sheet containing one each of Nos. 1042-1043 sold for 15d.

Falcon Type of 2007 Redrawn With Area Inside Falcon Shaded

2011 Litho. *Perf. 13¼x13*
Background Color Dated "2011"

1043A	A262	1d yel ochre	.75	.75
1043B	A262	2d lilac	—	—
1043C	A262	3d yellow		—
1043D	A262	5d dull ultra	3.75	3.75

Denominations on Nos. 1043A-1043D use "AED" instead of "Dh." or "Dhs."

Sultan Bin Ali Al Owais Cultural Foundation, 25th Anniv. — A327

Designs: 1d, Sultan and "25." 15d, Sultan and "25," diff.

Perf. 13¾x13½

2012, Mar. 14 Litho.

1044 A327 1d multi 1.00 1.00

Litho. With Foil Application
Size: 100x120mm
Imperf

1045 A327 15d multi + label 8.25 8.25

22nd Al Gaffal 60-Foot Traditional Dhow Sailing Race — A328

No. 1046: a, 1d, View of dhow from air. b, 5d, View of dhow from surface of water.
15d, Various dhows.

2012, May 26 Litho. *Perf. 13¼x13½*

1046 A328 Horiz. pair, #a-b 3.75 3.75

Size: 185x85mm
Imperf

1047 A328 15d multi + 5 labels 8.25 8.25

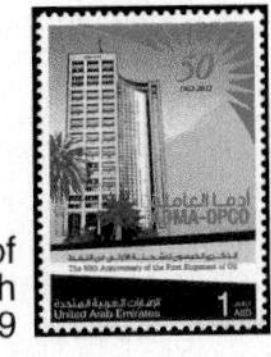

First Shipment of Crude Oil, 50th Anniv. — A329

Designs: 1d, Abu Dhabi Marine Operating Company Building. 150f, Offshore oil rig and birds. 3d, Oil platforms and dolphins, horiz. 4d, Oil tanker and tanks, horiz.
15d, Emblem of Abu Dhabi Marine Operating Company, vignettes of Nos. 1048-1051.

Litho. With Foil Application
Perf. 13¼x13½, 13½x13¼

2012, July 4

1048-1051 A329 Set of 4 7.00 7.00

Size: 120x95mm
Imperf

1052 A329 15d multi + 5 labels 8.25 8.25

Liwa Date Festival — A330

Designs: 1d, Bowl of dates, palm frond. 5d, Dates, palm frond.
15d, Dates, trees, rug, horiz.

2012, July 17 *Perf. 14*

1053-1054 A330 Set of 2 4.50 4.50

Size: 120x80mm
Imperf

1055 A330 15d multi 9.50 9.50

Arab Post Day — A331

Perf. 13½x13¼

2012, Aug. 15 Litho.

1056 A331 225f multi 1.75 1.75

World Energy Forum 2012, Dubai — A332

Emblems of World Energy Forum and Supreme Council of Energy and: 1d, "E=WEF." 2d, Building in Dubai. 3d, Solar energy collector. 4d, Sheikhs Khalifa Bin Zayed Al Nahyan and Mohammed bin Rashid al Maktoum.

2012, Oct. 22 *Perf. 14*

1057-1060 A332 Set of 4 6.00 6.00
1060a Souvenir sheet of 4, #1057-1060 8.25 8.25

No. 1060a sold for 15d.

Snakes — A333

No. 1061: a, Arabian horned viper. b, Carpet viper. c, Arabian rearfang. d, Sochurek's saw-scaled viper. e, Sand boa.
25d, Snakes depicted on Nos. 1061a-1061e.

2012, Nov. 1 *Perf. 14x13½*

1061		Vert. strip of 5	11.50	11.50
a.	A333	1d multi	.75	.75
b.	A333	150f multi	1.15	1.15
c.	A333	3d multi	2.25	2.25
d.	A333	4d multi	3.00	3.00
e.	A333	550f multi	4.00	4.00

Size: 130x100mm
Imperf

1062 A333 25d multi + 5 perf. 14x13½ labels 14.00 14.00

A334

41st National Day A335

Ruler and scene from: No. 1064, 4d, Abu Dhabi. No. 1065, 4d, Ajman. No. 1066, 4d, Dubai. No. 1067, 4d, Fujeira. No. 1068, 4d, Ras al Khaima. No. 1069, 4d, Sharjah. No. 1070, 4d, Umm al Qiwain.

Litho. & Embossed With Foil Application

2012, Nov. 29 *Perf. 14¼*

1063 A334 1d multi .55 .55

Imperf

1064-1070 A335 Set of 7 15.50 15.50

Al Ahmadiya School, Dubai, Cent. — A336

No. 1071: a, School room, sheikh and student. b, School building.
6d, Sheikh, various pictures of school.

2012, Dec. 12 Litho. *Perf. 13¼*

1071		Horiz. pair	1.40	1.40
a.	A336	1d multi	.55	.55
b.	A336	150f multi	.85	.85

Size: 144x94mm
Litho. With Foil Application
Imperf

1072 A336 6d multi 3.75 3.75

United Arab Emirates Soccer Team, Champions of 21st Gulf Cup Tournament — A337

Designs: 2d, Team. 6d, Gulf Cup, vert.

2013, Feb. 10 Litho. *Perf. 13¼*

1073 A337 2d multi 1.10 1.10

Souvenir Sheet
Perf. 13¼x12¾

1074 A337 6d multi 3.25 3.25

No. 1074 contains one 30x50mm stamp.

Mother's Day — A338

Litho. With Foil Application

2013, Mar. 21 *Perf. 13*

1075 A338 3d red vio & gold 1.75 1.75

Postal Services in Abu Dhabi, 50th Anniv. A339

50th anniv. emblem and: 1d, Abu Dhabi #26, 80 on covers. 150f, Abu Dhabi #62 on cover, block of Abu Dhabi #10. 3d, Abu Dhabi #42 on cover, block of Abu Dhabi #14. 4d, Abu Dhabi #39, 46 on cover, Abu Dhabi #80, pair of Abu Dhabi #18.

10d, Photographs of various post offices in Abu Dhabi from 1963, 1968, 1975 and 1993, various stamps.

2013, Mar. 30 Litho. *Perf. 14xx13¼*
1076-1079 A339 Set of 4 5.25 5.25

Imperf

Size: 100x100mm

1080 A339 10d multi 5.50 5.50

No. 1080 contains four labels showing the various post offices.

Falcon Type of 2007 Redrawn With Area Inside Falcon Shaded

2013, Apr. 7 *Perf. 14*

Dated "2013"
Background Color

1081	A262	1d yellowish buff	.55	.55
1082	A262	150f grayish sepia	.80	.80
1083	A262	3d dull yellow	1.75	1.75
1084	A262	5d violet blue	2.75	2.75
1085	A262	6d white	3.25	3.25
		Nos. 1081-1085 (5)	9.10	9.10

Denominations on Nos. 1081, 1083-1084 use "AED" instead of "Dh." or "Dhs." used on Nos. 859, 862 and 865. Background colors and color of shading within falcon differ on Nos. 860, 961 and 1082.

Yahsat, Communications Satellite of United Arab Emirates — A340

2013, May 13 *Perf. 14*
1086 A340 4d multi 2.25 2.25

Fazza Heritage Championships A341

Designs: 1d, Diver in free diving competition. 150f, Yola (traditional dance) competition.

2013, July 28 Litho. *Perf. 13½*
1087-1088 A341 Set of 2 1.40 1.40

Oryxes A342

Designs: 1d, Oryxes standing and on ground. 150f, Oryxes battling. 3d, Four oryxes running.

15d, Oryxes.

2013, Aug. 26 Litho. *Perf. 13*
1089-1091 A342 Set of 3 3.00 3.00

Size: 180x100mm

Imperf

1092 A342 15d multi + 3 labels 8.25 8.25

Abu Dhabi International Triathlon A343

2013, Oct. 31 Litho. *Perf. 12¾x13¼*
1093 A343 3d multi 1.75 1.75

Qasr al-Hosn, Oldest Stone Building in Abu Dhabi A344

Designs: 1d, Aerial view, desert in background. 150f, Man in doorway (40x30mm). 2d, Gate. 3d, Aerial view, skyscrapers in background (40x30mm).

8d, Colorized aerial view denoting additions to building.

Perf. 12¾x13¼, 14 (150f, 3d)
Litho. With Foil Application

2013, Nov. 25
1094-1097 A344 Set of 4 4.25 4.25

Size: 131x81mm

Imperf

1098 A344 8d multi 4.50 4.50

10th Dubai International Film Festival — A345

No. 1099 — Horse's head and: a, Top of "1" in "10." b, Top of "0" in "10." c, Bottom of "1" in "10." d, Bottom of "0" in "10."

Litho. With Foil Application

2013, Dec. 3 *Perf. 13¼x13¾*
1099 A345 3d Block of 4, #a-d 6.50 6.50

Emirates National Bank of Dubai, 50th Anniv. — A346

Designs: 1d, Orange and white arcs from bank's emblem. 2d, Bank's emblem and 50th anniv. ribbon. 3d, 50th anniv. ribbon. 4d, Arabic text in circle.

2013, Dec. 18 Litho. *Perf. 13*
1100-1103 A346 Set of 4 5.50 5.50
1103a Souvenir sheet of 4, #1100-1103 5.50 5.50

Coffee Tools — A347

Designs: 1d, Al Tawa and Al Mehmas (roasting pan and mixer). 150f, Al Menhaz and Al Rashad (mortar and pestle). 3d, Al Dallah (coffee pot). 4d, Al Fenjan (coffee cup).

10d, Man roasting coffee beans, labels without denominations, similar to Nos.1104-1107.

2013, Dec. 24 Litho. *Perf. 13x13¼*
1104-1107 A347 Set of 4 5.25 5.25

Souvenir Sheet

Imperf

1108 A347 10d multi + 4 labels 5.50 5.50

Parts of the design of No. 1108 have a scratch-and-sniff sandalwood scent.

Jumeirah Islamic Archaeological Site — A348

Designs: 1d, Walls and pillars. 150f, Walls.

2013, Dec. 30 Litho. *Perf. 14x14¼*
1109-1110 A348 Set of 2 1.40 1.40

Emirates Center for Strategic Studies and Research, 20th Anniv. — A349

Building, stylized globe emblem and background color of: 1d, Gray. 150f, Purple. 2d, Green. 4d, Brown.

10d, Stylized globe emblem and labels without denominations similar to Nos. 1111-1114.

2014, Jan. 2 Litho. *Perf. 13*
1111-1114 A349 Set of 4 4.75 4.75

Souvenir Sheet

Imperf

1115 A349 10d multi + 4 labels 5.50 5.50

Souvenir Sheet

Crown Prince Hamdan, Sixth Anniv. of Accession — A350

Litho. With Foil Application

2014, Feb. 1 *Perf. 14½*
1116 A350 3d multi 1.75 1.75

Sharjah, 2014 Islamic Cultural Capital — A351

2014, Apr. 15 Litho. *Perf. 14*
1117 A351 3d multi 1.75 1.75

Miniature Sheet

Union Supreme Court, 40th Anniv. A352

No. 1118 — Anniversary emblem and background color of: a, Red. b, Green. c, White. d, Blue.

2014, May 8 Litho. *Perf. 13¼x13½*
1118 A352 1d Sheet of 9, 3 #1118a, 2 each #1118b-1118d 5.00 5.00

Zayed Humanitarian Day — A353

2014, July 17 Litho. *Perf. 14¼*
1119 A353 1d multi .55 .55

Expo 2020, Dubai A354

No. 1120: a, Denomination at left. b, Denomination at right.

10d, Emblem and perforated labels without denominations similar to Nos. 1120a-1120b.

2014, Sept. 30 Litho. *Perf. 13x13½*
1120 A354 3d Horiz. pair, #a-b 3.25 3.25

Size: 160x90mm

Imperf

1121 A354 10d multi + 2 labels 5.50 5.50

Flag Day — A355

Litho. With Foil Application

2014, Nov. 3 *Perf. 14*
1122 A355 3d multi 1.75 1.75

43rd National Day — A356

Litho. & Embossed

2014, Dec. 2 *Perf. 14¼*
1123 A356 1d multi .55 .55

History of Civil Aviation in Dubai A357

Designs: 1d, Airplane, Sheikh Sa'id bin Maktum, 1937 agreement to build airport. 3d, Airport, Sheikh Rashid, text of 1966 decree creating Department of Civil Aviation. 5d, Sheikh Mohammed, airplanes and airport.

2014, Dec. 7 Litho. *Perf. 13¼*
1124-1126 A357 Set of 3 5.00 5.00

Miniature Sheets

First United Arab Emirates Currency A358

No. 1127 — Obverse and reverse of 1973 coins: a, 1-dirham coin depicting pitcher. b, 50-fils coin depicting oil derricks. c, 25-fils coin depicting gazelle. d, 10-fils coin depicting dhow. e, 5-fils coin depicting fish. f, 1-fils coin depicting date palms.

No. 1128 — Fronts and backs of banknotes: a, 1973 1-dirham note. b, 1973 50-dirham note. c, 1973 5-dirham note. d, 1973 100-dirham note. e, 1973 10-dirham note. f, 1976 1000-dirham note.

Litho. & Embossed

2014, Dec. 25 *Serpentine Die Cut*

Self-Adhesive

1127	A358 Sheet of 6	4.25	
a.-c.	1d Any single	.55	.55
d.-f.	150f Any single	.85	.85

Litho. & Embossed With Foil Application

Serpentine Die Cut 13

1128	A358 Sheet of 6	10.50	
a.-b.	2d Either single	1.10	1.10
c.-d.	3d Either single	1.75	1.75
e.-f.	4d Either single	2.25	2.25

History of Civil Aviation in Abu Dhabi A359

Abu Dhabi Intl. Airport: 1d, Control tower and airplane in flight. 150f, Interior of terminal.

2014, Dec. 31 Litho. *Perf. 13¼*
1129-1130 A359 Set of 2 1.40 1.40

Sharjah, Arab Tourism Capital — A360

2015, Mar. 3 Litho. *Perf. 14¼*
1131 A360 3d multi 1.75 1.75

A souvenir sheet containing one perf. 13¼x13½ example of No. 1131 sold for 10d.

Oil Production Anniversaries A361

2015, Apr. 2 Litho. *Perf. 13¼x13½*
1132 A361 3d multi 1.75 1.75

First crude oil shipment, 50th anniv.; concession agreement, 75th anniv.

Women's Museum — A362

No. 1133 — Various photographs of women with bottom inscription of: a, Women's contribution to economic activity in the 70's. b, Women's education in UAE in the 70's. c, 1st batch of female students, 1953-1954. d, Al Riwah folklore dance. e, The 1st women museum in the Arab world - Dubai.

Litho. With Foil Application

2015, June 17 *Perf. 14¼*
1133 Horiz. strip of 5 8.75 8.75
a.-e. A362 3d Any single 1.75 1.75

Strategic Projects A363

No. 1134: a, Masdar City. b, Etihad Rail. c, Khalifa Port. d, Shams I Solar Power Plant.

2015, July 30 Litho. *Perf. 14¼*
1134 A363 1d Block of 4, #a-d 2.25 2.25

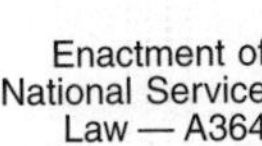

Enactment of National Service Law — A364

2015, Sept. 17 Litho. *Perf. 13x13½*
1135 A364 1d multi .55 .55

Stylized Blind Man — A365

2015, Oct. 15 Litho. *Perf. 13x13½*
1136 A365 3d black 1.75 1.75

International White Cane Day. No. 1136 was printed in sheets of 2.

Diplomatic Relations Between United Arab Emirates and Kazakhstan — A366

No. 1137: a, Sheikh Khalifa, flag of United Arab Emirates. b, Pres. Nursultan Nazarbayev, flag of Kazakhstan.

2015, Oct. 28 Litho. *Perf. 14*
1137 A366 3d Horiz. pair, #a-b 3.25 3.25

See Kazakhstan No. 758.

QR Code — A367

2015, Nov. 22 Litho. *Perf. 14¼*
1138 A367 3d multi 1.75 1.75

Commemoration Day — A368

Designs: 3d, Soldiers and flag. 10d, Soldiers, woman carrying flag, airplanes, skyline and people, horiz.

Litho. With Foil Application

2015, Nov. 30 *Perf. 14*
1139 A368 3d multi 1.75 1.75

Size: 142x92mm

Imperf

1140 A368 10d multi + label 5.50 5.50

44th National Day — A369

Litho. With Foil Application

2015, Dec. 2 *Perf. 14*
1141 A369 1d multi .55 .55

Automobile and Touring Club of the United Arab Emirates, 50th Anniv. — A370

Designs: 1d, Club headquarters. 3d, 50th anniversary emblem.
15d, Car, motorcycle and rider, club headquarters, 50th anniversary emblem.

2015, Dec. 12 Litho. *Perf. 14*
1142-1143 A370 Set of 2 2.25 2.25

Souvenir Sheet

Litho. With Foil Application

Imperf

1144 A370 15d multi + 2 labels 8.25 8.25

Dubai Chamber of Commerce, 50th Anniv. — A371

Various depictions of Dubai Chamber of Commerce Building.

Litho. With Foil Application

2015, Dec. 31 *Perf. 13¼x13*
1145 Horiz. strip of 4 5.50 5.50
a. A371 1d multi .55 .55
b. A371 2d multi 1.10 1.10
c. A371 3d multi 1.60 1.60
d. A371 4d multi 2.25 2.25

Souvenir Sheet

Imperf

1146 A371 10d multi + 4 labels 5.50 5.50

Burj Khalifa, 6th Anniv. — A372

2016, Jan. 24 Litho. *Perf. 14¼*
1147 A372 3d multi 3.00 3.00

Khalifa International Award for Date Palm and Agricultural Innovation A373

Perf. 12¾x13¼

2016, Mar. 15 Litho.
1148 A373 3d multi 1.75 1.75

Dubai Tour Bicycle Race — A374

Designs: Nos. 1149a, 1151, 1d, Cyclists racing past buildings. Nos. 1149b, 1150, 1d, Boy waving at cyclists.

2016, June 8 Litho. *Perf. 13x13½*
1149 A374 1d Vert. pair, #a-b 1.10 1.10

Booklet Stamps

Self-Adhesive

Serpentine Die Cut 8¾x9

1150 A374 1d multi .55 .55
1151 A374 1d multi .55 .55
a. Booklet pane of 8, 4 each #1150-1151 4.50

Arab Postal Day A375

No. 1152 — Letters circling globe, with background color of: a, 1d, Blue. b, 2d, Green.

Litho. & Silk-Screened

2016, Aug. 21 *Perf. 12¾x13½*
1152 A375 Horiz. pair, #a-b 1.75 1.75

Al Jahili Fort, Venue of 2016 Aga Khan Award for Architecture Ceremonies — A376

Litho. With Foil Application

2016, Nov. 6 *Perf. 14*
1153 A376 3d gold & multi 1.75 1.75

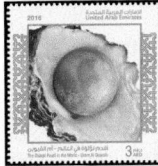

Pearl of the U.A.E., World's Oldest Natural Pearl — A377

Designs: 3d, Pearl in oyster. 10d, Pearl in oyster, horiz.

Litho. & Silk-Screened

2016, Nov. 15 *Perf. 14*
1154 A377 3d gold & multi 1.75 1.75

Size: 140x90mm

Imperf

1155 A377 10d multi + label 5.50 5.50

45th National Day — A378

Litho. With Foil Application

2016, Dec. 2 *Perf. 14*
1156 A378 1d gold & multi .55 .55

A379

Etihad Museum, Dubai — A380

2016, Dec. 2 Litho. *Perf. 13¼x13½*
1157 A379 3d multi 1.75 1.75

Foil Application on Clear Plastic

Self-Adhesive

Serpentine Die Cut 11

1158 A380 3d gold 1.75 1.75

Government of Abu Dhabi, 50th Anniv. — A381

Perf. 13½x13¼

2016, Dec. 20 Litho.
1159 A381 3d brown ochre 1.75 1.75

National Program for Happiness and Positivity — A382

No. 1160: a, Flag of United Arab Emirates. b, Sun. c, Three stick-figure people. d, Water. e, Rain cloud. f, Flower g, Happy face. h, Palm tree.
15d, Program emblem, flag, sun, stick-figure people, water, rain cloud, flower, happy face, and palm tree.

Perf. 13, 13x13x14x13 (#1160e-1160h)

2017, Mar. 20 **Litho.**

1160 A382 2d Sheet of 8, #a-h 20.00 20.00

Souvenir Sheet

Imperf

1161 A382 15d multi + label 8.25 8.25

Hope Probe Mars Mission of United Arab Emirates Space Agency — A383

2017, Aug. 16 **Litho.** *Perf. 14¼*

1162 A383 3d multi 1.75 1.75

A384

Year of Giving — A385

Serpentine Die Cut12½x12¼

2017, Sept. 5 **Litho.**

Self-Adhesive

1163 A384 3d multi 1.75 1.75

Serpentine Die Cut 10¾x9½

1164 A385 3d multi 1.75 1.75

Nos. 1164-1165 were printed together on sheets containing 3 of each stamp.

Intl. Year of Sustainable Tourism for Development A386

Designs: No. 1165, 3d, Burj Khalifa, Dubai. No. 1166, 3d, Al Noor Island, Sharjah. No. 1167, 3d, Fujairah Fort, Fujairah. No. 1168, 3d, Ajman Museum, Ajman. No. 1169, 3d, Al Shohadaa (Martyrs' Memorial), Umm al Qiwain. No. 1170, 3d, Emirates Palace, Abu Dhabi. No. 1171, 3d, Al Jazirah al Hamra ruins, Ras al Khaima.

2017, Nov. 14 **Litho.** *Perf. 14*

1165-1171 A386 Set of 7 11.50 11.50

Abu Dhabi Police, 60th Anniv. A387

No. 1172: a, Police emblem with eagle. b, 60th anniversary emblem.

15d, Police emblem and non-denominated labels similar to Nos. 1172a-1172b.

Litho. With Foil Application

2017, Nov. 21 *Perf. 13*

1172 A387 3d Horiz. pair, #a-b 3.25 3.25

Size: 141x91mm

Imperf

1173 A387 15d multi + 2 labels 8.25 8.25

Sheikh Zayed Heritage Festival — A388

2017, Dec. 1 **Litho.** *Perf. 13*

1174 A388 3d multi 1.75 1.75

46th National Day — A389

Litho. & Embossed

2017, Dec. 2 *Perf. 14*

1175 A389 3d multi 1.75 1.75

Dubai Police Emblem A390

No. 1176 — Colors: a, Green and mint green. b, Green and myrtle green.

2018, Jan. 14 **Litho.** *Perf. 13*

1176 A390 3d Horiz. pair, #a-b 3.25 3.25

A souvenir sheet containing No. 1176b sold for 15d.

Abu Dhabi Tour Bicycle Race — A391

Litho. With Foil Application

2018, Feb. 21 *Perf. 13*

1177 A391 3d multi 1.75 1.75

A392

Diplomatic Relations Between United Arab Emirates and People's Republic of China, 34th Anniv. — A393

No. 1178 — Flags of People's Republic of China and United Arab Emirates and text: a, "Celebrating 34 Years of Diplomatic Relations." b, "President Xi Jinping state visit to UAE."

No. 1179: a, People's Republic of China President Xi Jinping. b, Sheikh Khalifa.

2018, July 19 **Litho.** *Perf. 14*

1178 A392 2d Horiz. pair, #a-b 3.25 3.25

1179 A393 2d Horiz. pair, #a-b 3.25 3.25

Tawazun Economic Council, 25th Anniv. (in 2017) — A394

No. 1180: a, Emblem for Tawazun Economic Council. b, "25 years."

Litho. (#1180a), Litho. & Embossed With Foil Application (#1180b).

2018, Aug. 27 *Perf. 13*

1180 A394 3d Horiz. pair, #a-b 3.25 3.25

International Telecommunication Union Plenipotentiaries Conference, Dubai — A395

2018, Oct. 29 **Litho.** *Perf. 13*

1181 A395 3d multi 1.75 1.75

Arab Reading Challenge — A396

No. 1182 — Star medal and: a, Prime Minister Mohammed bin Rashid Al Maktoum. b, Books and lock.

Litho. & Embossed

2018, Oct. 30 *Perf. 13x13¼*

1182 A396 3d Pair, #a-b 3.25 3.25

47th National Day — A397

2018, Dec. 2 **Litho.** *Perf. 13¼x13*

1183 A397 3d multi 1.75 1.75

Sheikh Zayed bin Sultan Al Nahyan (1918-2004), First President of United Arab Emirates — A398

Designs: 3d, Sheikh Zayed. 100d, Sheikh Zayed at Founder's Memorial, Abu Dhabi.

2018, Dec. 26 **Litho.** *Perf. 13x13¼*

1184 A398 3d multi 1.75 1.75

Size: 178x128mm

Imperf

1185 A398 100d multi 55.00 55.00

2019 Asian Cup Soccer Tournament, United Arab Emirates — A399

2019, Jan. 7 **Litho.** *Perf. 14½*

1186 A399 3d multi 1.75 1.75

Grand Imam of Al-Azhar Ahmad-Al Tayyeb and Pope Francis — A400

2019, Feb. 4 **Litho.** *Perf. 14*

1187 A400 3d multi 1.75 1.75

Human Fraternity Meeting, Abu Dhabi.

Emirates Center for Strategic Studies and Research, 25th Anniv. — A401

2019, Feb. 10 **Litho.** *Perf. 13½*

1188 A401 3d multi 1.75 1.75

Organization of Islamic Cooperation, 50th Anniv. — A402

2019, Mar. 1 **Litho.** *Perf. 14*

1189 A402 3d multi 1.75 1.75

Sharjah, 2019 World Book Capital A403

No. 1190 — Stamp color: a, Dull violet blue. b, Blue green.

2019, Apr. 23 **Litho.** *Perf. 14*

1190 A403 3d Pair, #a-d 3.25 3.25

No. 1190 was printed in sheets containing four pairs.

Souvenir Sheet

Sharjah, 2019 World Book Capital — A403a

2019, Apr. 23 **Litho.** *Imperf.*

1191 A403a 15d multi + 2 labels 8.25 8.25

A404

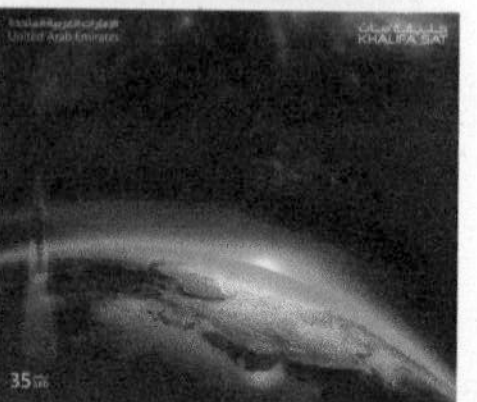

Launch of KhalifaSat — A405

No. 1192: a, Rocket launch (22x77mm). b, Palm Jumeirah artificial archipelago (30x30mm). c, KhalifaSat (43x51mm).

35d, Rocket launch and orbiting satellite.

Perf. 13¾x14 (#1192a), 13¼ (#1192b), 14x14¼ (#1192c)

2019, July 7 **Litho.**

1192 A404 3d Sheet of 3, #a-c 5.00 5.00

Litho. With Lenticular Lens Affixed

Size: 125x105mm

Without Gum

Imperf

1193 A405 35d multi 19.00 19.00

Mohandas K. Gandhi (1869-1948), Indian Nationalist Leader — A406

No. 1194: a, Photograph of Gandhi. b, 150th anniversary emblem.

2019, Aug. 24 Litho. *Perf. 14x14½*
1194 A406 3d Pair, #a-b 3.25 3.25

Express Mail Service, 20th Anniv. — A407

2019, Sept. 10 Litho. *Perf. 13x13¼*
1195 A407 3d multi 1.75 1.75

Miniature Sheet

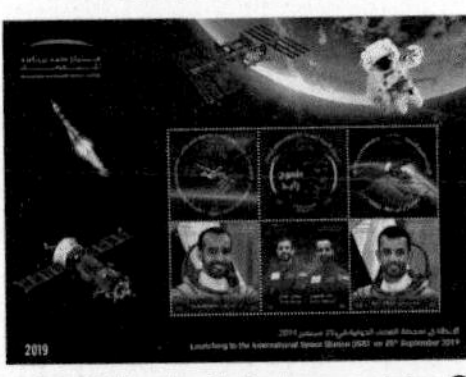

Launch of Emirati Astronaut to Serve on International Space Station — A408

No. 1196: a, International Space Station. b, Drawing of Sheikh as a constellation. c, Soyuz spacecraft. d, Astronaut Hazzaa Al Mansoori. e, Al Mansoori and Backup Astronaut Sultan Al Neyadi. f, Al-Neyadi.

2019, Sept. 25 Litho. *Perf. 13*
1196 A408 3d Sheet of 6, #a-f 9.75 9.75

Miniature Sheet

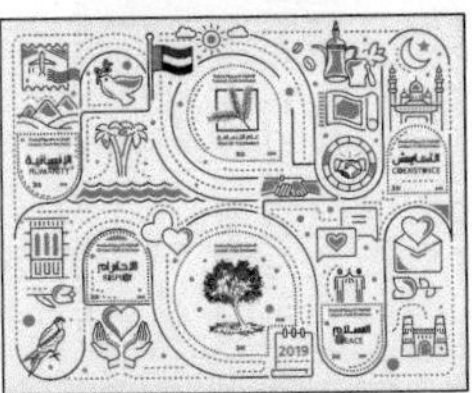

Year of Tolerance — A409

No. 1197: a, "Humanity" (35x35mm). b, Year of Tolerance emblem (52x52mm). c, "Coexistence" (34x38mm). d, "Respect" (34x38mm). e, Tree (68x68mm). f, "Peace" (34x36mm).

Litho. & Embossed With Foil Application

2019, Nov. 14 *Perf. 10½*
1197 A409 3d Sheet of 6, #a-f 10.00 10.00

Flag of Palestinian Authority, Doves and Dome of the Rock, Jerusalem A410

2019, Nov. 17 Litho. *Perf. 13¼*
1198 A410 3d multi 1.75 1.75

Jerusalem, capital of Palestinian Authority.

2019 Sharjah Stamp Exhibition — A411

No. 1199: a, 2d, Emirates Philatelic Association emblem. b, 3d, Exhibition emblem.

2019, Nov. 19 Litho. *Perf. 14*
1199 A411 Pair, #a-b 2.75 2.75

48th National Day A412

No. 1200: a, United Arab Emirates flag. b, Sheikhs and United Arab Emirates flag.

2019, Dec. 2 Litho. *Perf. 13¼*
1200 A412 3d Horiz. pair, #a-b 3.25 3.25

Abu Dhabi Chamber Of Commerce and Industry, 50th Anniv. — A413

Litho. With Foil Application

2019, Dec. 16 *Perf. 14¼*
1201 A413 3d multi 1.75 1.75

Opening of Sharjah Mosque — A414

Litho. & Embossed With Foil Application

2019, Dec. 19 *Perf. 14*
1202 A414 3d multi 1.75 1.75

Miniature Sheet

Emirates Post, 110th Anniv. A415

No. 1203: a, Motor scooter and "Courier Services" (36x25mm). b, Sealed parcel and "Parcel Services" (36x25mm). c, Envelopes, postal card, clock, tree and mailbox (56x32mm). d, Airmail envelope and "Registered Mail Services" (36x25mm). e, Emirates Post emblem (66x41mm). f, Mailbox and "Post Box Services" (36x25mm). g, EMS emblem and "Express Mail Services" (36x25mm). h, Mail van and drone (48x28mm). i, Mail truck and "Delivering happiness" (72x30mm).

Die Cut Perf. 13, 13¼x13 (#1203c, 1203i)

2019, Dec. 30 Litho.

Self-Adhesive

1203 A415 3d Sheet of 9, #a-i 15.00 15.00

New "Wheelchair" Symbol — A416

No. 1204 — Denomination color: a, White. b, Ultra.

2020, Feb. 20 Litho. *Perf. 13¼x13*
1204 A416 3d Pair, #a-d 3.25 3.25

No. 1204 was printed in sheets containing four pairs.

Souvenir Sheet

Tribute to Workers During the COVID-19 Pandemic — A417

2020, May 10 Litho. *Imperf.*
1205 A417 19d multi + label 10.50 10.50

Perforated label within No. 1205 lacks country name or denomination.

Arab League, 75th Anniv. — A418

Litho. & Embossed With Foil Application

2020, June 9 *Perf. 14¼*
1206 A418 3d gold & multi 1.75 1.75

No. 1206 was printed in sheets of 4.

A419

A420

A421

Dubai Buildings — A422

2020, June 28 Litho. *Perf. 13¼*

1207	Sheet of 4	7.00	7.00
a.	A419 3d multi	1.75	1.75
b.	A420 3d multi	1.75	1.75
c.	A421 3d multi	1.75	1.75
d.	A422 3d multi	1.75	1.75

Dubai, 2020 capital of Arab media.

International Year of Plant Health — A423

2020, Aug. 20 Litho. *Perf. 13¼*
1208 A423 3d multi 1.75 1.75

Miniature Sheet

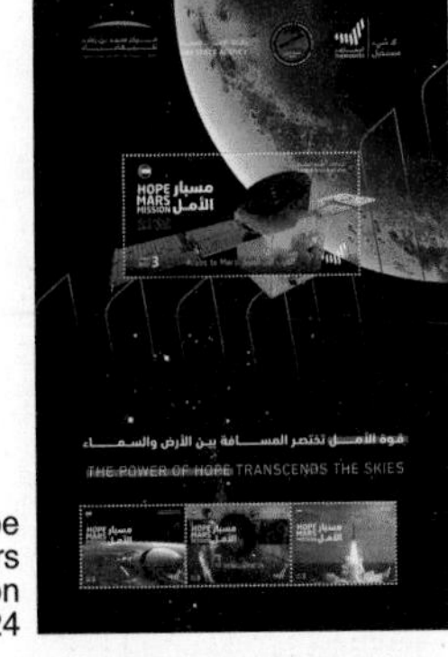

Hope Mars Mission A424

No. 1209: a, Probe and Mars (90x45mm). b, Rocket over Earth (40x30mm). c, Technicians and probe (40x30mm). d, Rocket launch (40x30mm).

Perf. 13¼ (#1209a), 13x13¼ (others)

2020, Oct. 20 Litho.
1209 A424 3d Sheet of 4, #a-d 7.00 7.00

A425

A426

A427

A428

Wahat Al Karama (Oasis of Dignity) War Memorial, Abu Dhabi — A429

2020, Oct. 25 Litho. *Perf. 13¾x14*

1210	Horiz. strip of 4	7.00	7.00
a.	A425 3d multi	1.75	1.75
b.	A426 3d multi	1.75	1.75
c.	A427 3d multi	1.75	1.75
d.	A428 3d multi	1.75	1.75

Imperf

1211 A429 15d multi + label 8.25 8.25

Souvenir Sheet

Barakah Nuclear Power Plant A430

2020, Oct. 25 Litho. *Perf. 14¼*
1212 A430 3d multi 1.75 1.75

Miniature Sheet

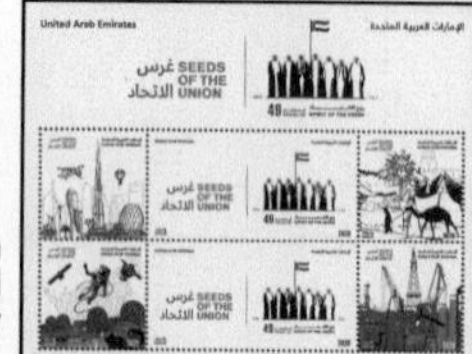

49th National Day A431

No. 1213: a, Airplane, balloon, wind generators, Burj Khalifa, Dubai (30x30mm). b, Palm tree, man leading camel, Al Jahili Fort (30x30mm). c, Astronaut and satellites (30x30mm). d, Cranes, oil tanker, derricks and pump (30x30mm). e, Sheikhs and flag of United Arab Emirates (60x30mm).

2020, Dec. 2 Litho. *Perf. 13¼*

1213 A431 3d Sheet of 6, #1213a-1213d, 2 #1213e 10.00 10.00

Miniature Sheet

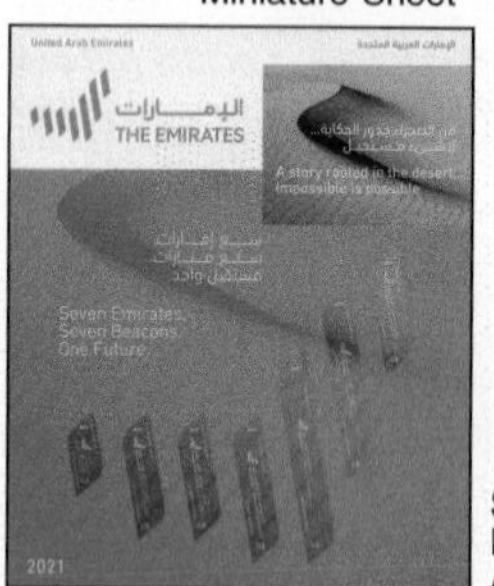

Sand Dunes A432

No. 1214 — Inscription "Impossible is Possible" and sand dune, with tip-to-tip measurement of: a, 31mm. b, 46mm, with bottom dark striation above denomination. c, 46mm, with botton dark striation below denomination. d, 54mm. e, 77mm. f, 68mm. g, 46mm, with denomination only on dark striation on stamp.

2021, Apr. 11 Litho. *Die Cut*

Self-Adhesive

1214 A432 Sheet of 7 12.50
a.-g. 3d Any single 1.75 1.75

Khor Fakkan Amphitheater A433

Litho. & Embossed

2021, July 7 *Perf. 13¾*

1215 A433 3d multi 1.75 1.75

Size: 150x120mm

Imperf

1216 A433 20d Amphitheater, diff. 11.00 11.00

Souvenir Sheet

Birds A434

No. 1217: a, Houbara bustard. b, Stone curlew.

2021, Sept. 5 Litho. *Perf. 14*

1217 A434 3d Sheet of 2, #a-b 3.25 3.25

Buildings at Expo 2020, Dubai — A435

No. 1218: a, United Arab Emirates Pavilion. b, Mission Possible — Opportunity Pavilion. c, Al Wasl Plaza. d, Alif — Mobility Pavilion. e, Terra-sustainability Pavilion.

Litho. & Embossed

2021, Oct. 1 *Perf. 13¾*

1218 Sheet of 5 8.75 8.75
a.-e. A435 3d Any single 1.75 1.75

Expo 2020 was postponed until 2021 because of the COVID-19 pandemic.

National Anniversaries of United Arab Emirates and Kazakhstan — A437

No. 1220: a, Flags of United Arab Emirates and Kazakhstan. b, Emblems commemorating the 50th anniv. of the formation of the United Arab Emirates and the 30th anniv. of the independence of Kazakhstan.

Litho. (#1220a), Litho. & Embossed (#1220b)

2021, Oct. 10 *Perf. 13½*

1220 A437 3d Vert. pair, #a-b 3.25 3.25

Printed in sheets containing two vertical pairs. See Kazakhstan No.

Souvenir Sheet

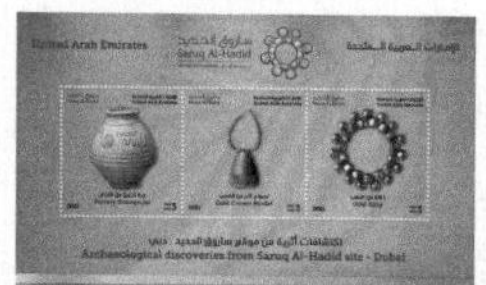

Discoveries From Saruq Al-Hadid Archaeological Site — A438

No. 1221: a, Pottery storage jar. b, Gold crown model. c, Gold ring.

Litho. & Embossed

2021, Nov. 4 *Perf. 14x13¼*

1221 A438 3d Sheet of 3, #a-b 5.00 5.00

Mohammed Bin Rashid Al Maktoum Creative Sports Award — A439

2021, Nov. 23 Litho. *Perf. 13½*

1222 A439 3d multi 1.75 1.75

Emblem of 50th National Day A440

Emirs and Crown Princes of the Seven Emirates A441

Emirs and Crown Princes of the Seven Emirates A442

Sheikh Humaid bin Rashid Al Nuaimi, Ruler of Ajman A443

Sheikh Mohamed bin Zayed Al Nahyan, Ruler of Abu Dhabi — A444

Sheikh Mohammed bin Rashid Al Maktoum, Ruler of Dubai — A445

Sheikh Mohammed bin Rashid Al Maktoum, Ruler of Sharjah — A446

Sheikh Hamad bin Mohammed Al Sharqi, Ruler of Fujeira — A447

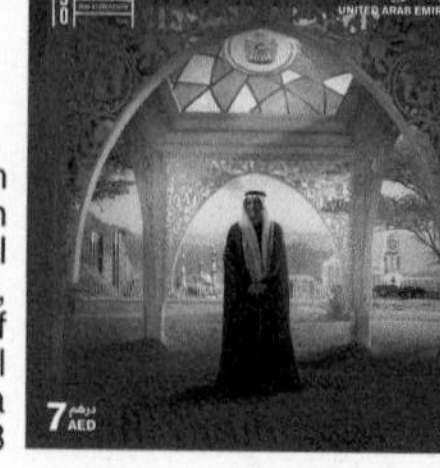

Sheikh Saud bin Saqr Al Qasimi, Ruler of Ras al Khaima A448

Sheikh Saud bin Rashid Al Mualla, Ruler of Umm al Qiwain A449

2021, Dec. 2 Litho. *Perf. 14¾x14¼*

1223 Pair 1.10 1.10
a. A440 1d multi .55 .55
b. A441 1d multi .55 .55

Imperf

1224 A442 7d multi 4.00 4.00
1225 A443 7d multi 4.00 4.00
1226 A444 7d multi 4.00 4.00
1227 A445 7d multi 4.00 4.00
1228 A446 7d multi 4.00 4.00
1229 A447 7d multi 4.00 4.00
1230 A448 7d multi 4.00 4.00
1231 A449 7d multi 4.00 4.00
Nos. 1224-1231 (8) 32.00 32.00

50th National Day. Four self-adhesive stamps, each affixed to a credit card-size piece of plastic were created in limited quantities. Three of these items sold for 250d, and the fourth sold for 2021d.

Souvenir Sheet

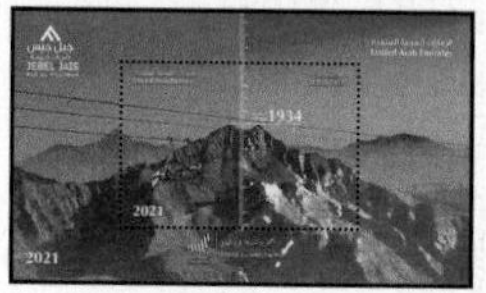

Ministry of the Interior, 50th Anniv. A450

No. 1232: a, Emblem of the Ministry of the Interior. b, 50th anniversary emblem.

2021, Dec. 21 Litho. *Perf. 13¼*

1232 A450 3d Sheet of 2, #a-b 3.25 3.25

Souvenir Sheet

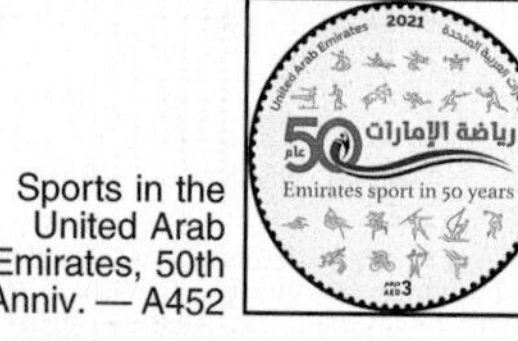

Jebel Jais and Person Riding Zip Line A451

2021, Dec. 22 Litho. *Perf. 13¼x13*

1233 A451 3d multi 1.75 1.75

Sports in the United Arab Emirates, 50th Anniv. — A452

2021, Dec. 27 Litho. *Perf.*

1234 A452 3d multi 1.75 1.75

No. 1234 was printed in sheets of 3.

Qasr Al Watan (Presidential Palace), Abu Dhabi — A453

2021, Dec. 31 Litho. *Perf. 13½*

1235 A453 3d multi 1.75 1.75

No. 1235 was printed in sheets of 3.

2022 World Stamp Exhibition, Dubai — A454

2022, Jan. 19 Litho. *Perf. 13¼x13*

1236 A454 3d multi 1.75 1.75

Souvenir Sheet

National Anniversaries of United Arab Emirates and India — A455

No. 1237: a, Flag of United Arab Emirates and 50th anniversary emblem. b, Flag of India and 75th anniversary emblem.

Litho. & Embossed

2022, Feb. 18 *Perf. 13¼x14*

1237 A455 3d Sheet of 2, #a-b 3.25 3.25

Formation of the United Arab Emirates, 50th anniv. (in 2021), independence of India, 75th anniv. See India No.

Map of United Arab Emirates and Emblem for Khalifa International Prize for Date Palm and Agricultural Innovation A456

2022, Mar. 14 Litho. *Perf. 13x13¼*

1238 A456 3d multi 1.75 1.75

Arab League Summit, Algiers — A457

Litho. & Embossed

2022, Nov. 1 *Perf.*

1239 A457 3d multi 1.75 1.75

No. 1239 was printed in sheets of 2.

Miniature Sheet

Hamdan Bin Mohammed Bin Rashid Al Maktoum International Photography Award, 10th Anniv. — A458

No. 1240: a, Photographer, light green background. b, Photographer, grayish blue background. c, 10th anniversary emblem. d, Photographer, light brown background.

Litho With Foil Application (#1240c), Litho. (others)

2022, Nov. 16 *Perf. 14*

1240 A458 3d Sheet of 4, #a-d 6.50 6.50

Gulf Cooperation Council, 40th Anniv. — A472

2022, Dec. 12 Litho. *Perf. 13½*

1247 A472 3d multi 1.75 1.75

A474

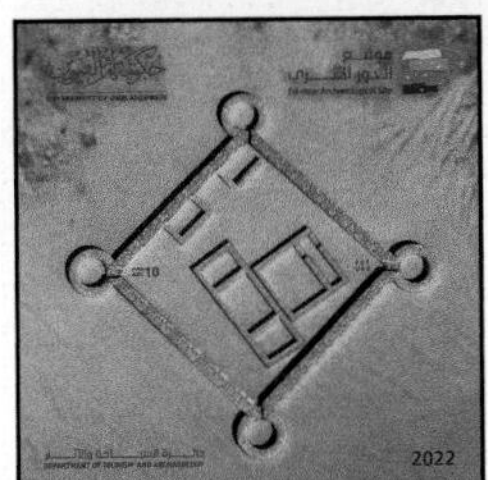

Ed-Dour Archaeological Site — A475

No. 1249: a, Building ruins. b, Curved wall of Ed-Dour fort. c, Four stone structures. 10d, Aerial view of fort.

Litho., Sheet Margin Litho. & Embossed

2022, Dec. 12 *Perf. 13x13¼*

1249 A474 3d Sheet of 3, #a-c 5.00 5.00

Litho. & Embossed

Imperf

1250 A475 10d multi 5.50 5.50

Souvenir Sheet

Diplomatic Relations Between United Arab Emirates and Egypt, 50th Anniv. — A476

2023, Jan. 19 Litho. *Perf. 14*

1251 A476 3d multi 1.75 1.75

Souvenir Sheet

62nd National Day of Kuwait A478

No. 1253: a, Flags of United Arab Emirates and Kuwait. b, Falcon head from emblem of United Arab Emirates and emblem of Kuwait.

2023, Feb. 25 Litho. *Perf. 13*

1253 A478 3d Sheet of 2, #a-b 3.25 3.25

Souvenir Sheet

World Padel Tour A479

No. 1254 — Padel racket with: a, Red handle. b, Blue handle.

2023, Feb. 26 Litho. *Die Cut*

Self-Adhesive

1254 A479 3d Sheet of 2, #a-b 3.25 3.25

UPPER SENEGAL & NIGER

'ə-pər ˌse-nə-gäl and 'nī-jər

LOCATION — In Northwest Africa, north of French Guinea and Ivory Coast
GOVT. — A former French Colony
AREA — 617,600 sq. mi.
POP. — 2,474,142
CAPITAL — Bamako

In 1921 the name of this colony was changed to French Sudan and postage stamps so inscribed were placed in use.

100 Centimes = 1 Franc

Gen. Louis Faidherbe A1

Oil Palms A2

Dr. N. Eugène Ballay — A3

Perf. 14x13½

1906-07 Unwmk. Typo.

Name of Colony in Red or Blue

1	A1	1c slate	1.40	1.75
2	A1	2c brown	1.75	2.10
b.		Imperf., pair	120.00	
3	A1	4c brn, *gray bl*	2.50	2.50
4	A1	5c green	5.50	2.75
b.		Imperf., pair	600.00	
5	A1	10c car (B)	6.25	2.75
b.		Imperf., pair	150.00	
6	A1	15c vio ('07)	4.25	*5.00*
7	A2	20c black & red, *azure*	5.50	5.50
a.		Imperf., pair	150.00	
8	A2	25c bl, *pnksh*	17.50	4.25
9	A2	30c vio brn, *pnksh*	7.00	5.50
10	A2	35c blk, *yellow*	5.50	5.00
11	A2	40c car, *az* (B)	9.00	9.00
12	A2	45c brn, *grnsh*	10.50	*11.00*
13	A2	50c dp vio	10.50	*11.00*
14	A2	75c bl, *org*	10.50	*12.00*
15	A3	1fr blk, *azure*	25.00	*27.50*
16	A3	2fr bl, *pink*	45.00	*52.50*
17	A3	5fr car, *straw* (B)	95.00	*105.00*
		Nos. 1-17 (17)	262.65	265.10

Camel with Rider — A4

1914-17 *Perf. 13½x14*

18	A4	1c brn vio & vio	.35	*.45*
19	A4	2c gray & brn vio	.35	*.45*
20	A4	4c black & blue	.35	*.45*
21	A4	5c yel grn & bl grn	1.05	.50
b.		Booklet pane of 4	—	
c.		Complete booklet	2,000.	
22	A4	10c red org & rose	2.50	2.10
23	A4	15c choc & org ('17)	2.10	1.05
b.		Booklet pane of 4	80.00	
c.		Complete booklet	1,400.	
24	A4	20c brn vio & blk	2.10	2.10
25	A4	25c ultra & bl	2.10	1.40
b.		Booklet pane of 4	100.00	
26	A4	30c ol brn & brn	2.10	*2.10*
27	A4	35c car rose & vio	3.50	2.50
28	A4	40c gray & car rose	2.10	1.40
29	A4	45c bl & ol brn	2.10	2.10
30	A4	50c black & green	2.75	*2.75*
31	A4	75c org & ol brn	2.75	*2.75*
32	A4	1fr brown & brn vio	2.75	*3.50*
33	A4	2fr green & blue	3.50	*3.50*
34	A4	5fr violet & black	12.50	*14.00*
		Nos. 18-34 (17)	44.95	43.10

See Burkina Faso for types of this issue that escaped overprinting.

For surcharges see No. B1, French Sudan Nos. 21-49, Niger Nos. 1-28.

SEMI-POSTAL STAMP

Regular Issue of 1914 Surcharged in Red

1915 Unwmk. *Perf. 13½x14*

B1 A4 10c + 5c red orange & rose 2.10 2.10

POSTAGE DUE STAMPS

Natives — D1

1906 Unwmk. Typo. *Perf. 14x13½*

J1	D1	5c green, *greenish*	3.50	3.50
J2	D1	10c red brown	7.00	7.00
J3	D1	15c dark blue	10.50	10.50
J4	D1	20c black, *yellow*	14.00	7.00
J5	D1	50c violet	27.50	*27.50*
J6	D1	60c black, *buff*	21.00	*21.00*
J7	D1	1fr black, *pinkish*	35.00	*37.50*
		Nos. J1-J7 (7)	118.50	114.00

D2

1914

J8	D2	5c green	1.10	*1.40*
a.		Imperf., pair	90.00	
J9	D2	10c rose	1.60	*1.75*
J10	D2	15c gray	1.60	*1.75*
J11	D2	20c brown	1.60	*1.75*
J12	D2	30c blue	2.40	*2.60*
J13	D2	50c black	2.00	*2.25*
J14	D2	60c orange	7.25	*7.75*
J15	D2	1fr violet	7.25	*7.75*
a.		Imperf., pair	130.00	90.00
		Nos. J8-J15 (8)	24.80	27.00

Stamps of Upper Senegal and Niger were superceded in 1921 by those of French Sudan.

UPPER SILESIA

ˈə-pər sīˈlē-zhˌē-ˌə

LOCATION — Formerly in eastern Germany and prior to World War I a part of Germany.

A plebiscite held under the terms of the Treaty of Versailles failed to determine the status of the country, the voting resulting about equally in favor of Germany and Poland. Accordingly, the League of Nations divided the territory between Germany and Poland.

100 Pfennig = 1 Mark
100 Fennigi = 1 Marka

Plebiscite Issues

A1

Perf. 14x13½

1920, Feb. 20 Typo. Unwmk.

1	A1	2½pf slate	.40	*.80*
2	A1	3pf brown	.40	*.85*
3	A1	5pf green	.30	*.80*
4	A1	10pf dull red	.40	*.90*
5	A1	15pf violet	.25	*.80*
6	A1	20pf blue	.25	*.80*
a.		Imperf., pair	275.00	—
7	A1	50pf violet brn	4.75	*8.00*
8	A1	1m claret	5.00	*12.00*
9	A1	5m orange	5.00	*12.00*
		Nos. 1-9 (9)	16.75	*36.95*
		Set, never hinged	55.00	

Black Surcharge

I II III IV

10	A1	5pf on 15pf vio (I)	*100.00*	*400.00*
		Never hinged	*375.00*	
a.		Type II	100.00	*400.00*
b.		Type III	100.00	*400.00*
c.		Type IV	100.00	*400.00*
11	A1	5pf on 20pf blue (I)	1.10	*3.25*
		Never hinged	3.00	
a.		Type II	1.25	*3.75*
b.		Type III	1.60	*4.00*
c.		Type IV	2.00	*5.00*

Red Surcharge

I II III IV

12	A1	10pf on 20pf bl (I)	1.10	*3.25*
		Never hinged	3.00	
a.		Type II	1.10	*3.25*
b.		Type III	1.10	*3.25*
c.		Type IV	1.10	*3.25*
d.		Imperf.	60.00	*240.00*

Black Surcharge

Type I Type II Type III Type IV Type V

13	A1	50pf on 5m org (I), shiny ovpt.	30.00	*52.50*
		Never hinged	200.00	
a.		Type II	32.50	*55.00*
b.		Type III	35.00	*87.50*
c.		Type IV	35.00	*87.50*
d.		Type V	42.50	*120.00*
e.		Type I, matte ovpt.	37.50	*87.50*

Nos. 10-13 are found with many varieties including surcharges inverted, double and double inverted.

Dove with Olive Branch Flying over Silesian Terrain — A2

A3

1920, Mar. 26 Typo. *Perf. 13½x14*

15	A2	2½pf gray	.55	*.80*
16	A2	3pf red brown	.55	*.80*
17	A2	5pf green	.55	*.80*
18	A2	10pf dull red	.55	*.80*
19	A2	15pf violet	.55	*.80*
20	A2	20pf blue	.80	*2.00*
21	A2	25pf dark brown	.55	*.80*
22	A2	30pf orange	.55	*.80*
23	A2	40pf olive green	.55	*2.00*

Perf. 14x13½

24	A3	50pf gray	1.00	*.80*
25	A3	60pf blue	.55	*1.60*
26	A3	75pf deep green	1.60	*2.00*
27	A3	80pf red brown	1.60	*1.10*
28	A3	1m claret	1.60	.80
29	A3	2m dark brown	1.40	.80
30	A3	3m violet	1.40	.80
31	A3	5m orange	4.00	*4.50*
		Nos. 15-31 (17)	18.35	22.00
		Set, never hinged	67.50	

Nos. 18-28 Overprinted in Black or Red

1921, Mar. 20

32	A2	10pf dull red	4.00	*10.00*
33	A2	15pf violet	4.00	*10.00*
34	A2	20pf blue	5.50	*14.00*
35	A2	25pf dk brn (R)	12.00	*32.50*
36	A2	30pf orange	10.00	*20.00*
37	A2	40pf olive grn (R)	11.00	*20.00*

Overprinted

38	A3	50pf gray (R)	11.00	*27.50*
39	A3	60pf blue	12.00	*22.50*
40	A3	75pf deep green	12.00	*27.50*
a.		75pf blue green	*1,650.*	*1,850.*
41	A3	80pf red brown	20.00	*35.00*
42	A3	1m claret	24.00	*65.00*
		Nos. 32-42 (11)	125.50	*284.00*
		Set, never hinged	700.00	

Inverted or double overprints exist on Nos. 32-33, 35-40. Counterfeit overprints exist.

Type of 1920 and Surcharged

1922, Mar.

45	A3	4m on 60pf ol grn	.80	*2.00*
46	A3	10m on 75pf red	1.25	*2.75*
47	A3	20m on 80pf orange	6.50	*16.00*
		Nos. 45-47 (3)	8.55	*20.75*
		Set, never hinged	32.00	

Stamps of the above design were a private issue not recognized by the Inter-Allied Commission of Government. Value, set of 7, $65 unused, $225 never hinged, $225 used.

OFFICIAL STAMPS

German Stamps of 1905-20 Handstamped in Blue

1920, Feb. Wmk. 125 *Perf. 14, 14½*

On Stamps of 1906-19

O1	A22	2pf gray	1.10	*1.25*
O3	A22	2½pf gray	.55	*.65*
O4	A16	3pf brown	.55	*.65*
O5	A16	5pf green	.55	*.65*
O6	A22	7½pf orange	.55	*.65*
O7	A16	10pf car rose	.55	*.65*
O8	A22	15pf dk violet	.55	*.65*
O9	A16	20pf blue violet	.55	*.65*
O10	A16	25pf org & blk, *yel*	8.00	*6.50*
O11	A16	30pf org & blk, *buff*	.55	*.65*
O12	A22	35pf red brown	.55	*.65*
O13	A16	40pf lake & blk	.55	*.65*
O14	A16	50pf vio & blk, *buff*	.55	*.65*
O15	A16	60pf magenta	.55	*.65*
O16	A16	75pf green & blk	.55	*.65*
O17	A16	80pf lake & blk, *rose*	6.50	*8.00*
O18	A17	1m car rose	1.10	*1.25*
O19	A21	2m gray blue	5.25	*6.50*

On National Assembly Stamps of 1919-20

O25	A23	10pf car rose	.90	*1.10*
O26	A24	15pf choc & bl	1.60	*2.00*
O27	A25	25pf green & red	3.25	*4.00*
O28	A25	30pf red vio & red	2.50	*3.00*

On Semi-Postal Stamps of 1919

O30	A16	10pf + 5pf carmine	6.50	*8.00*
O31	A22	15pf + 5pf dk vio	6.50	*8.00*
		Nos. O1-O31 (24)	50.35	*58.05*

Red Handstamp

O5a	A16	5pf	10.00	*14.00*
O8a	A22	15pf	6.50	*10.00*
O9a	A16	20pf	6.50	*10.00*
O13a	A16	40pf	20.00	*30.00*
O16a	A16	75pf	20.00	*30.00*
O26a	A24	15pf	1.10	*1.25*
		Nos. O5a-O26a (6)	64.10	*95.25*

Values of Nos. O1-O31 are for reprints made with a second type of handstamp differing in minor details from the original (example: period after "S" is round instead of the earlier triangular form). Originals are scarce. Counterfeits exist.

Germany No. 65C with this handstamp is considered bogus by experts.

Local Official Stamps of Germany, 1920, Overprinted

1920, Apr. *Perf. 14*

O32	LO2	5pf bl green	.30	*1.50*
O33	LO3	10pf rose	.30	*1.50*
O34	LO4	15pf violet brn	.30	*1.50*
O35	LO5	20pf deep ultra	.30	*1.50*
O36	LO6	30pf orange, *buff*	.30	*1.50*
O37	LO7	50pf violet, *buff*	.80	*3.00*
O38	LO8	1m red, *buff*	6.50	*15.00*
		Nos. O32-O38 (7)	8.80	*25.50*

Same Overprint on Official Stamps of Germany, 1920-21

1920-21

O39	O1	5pf green	1.00	*8.00*
O40	O2	10pf carmine	.25	*1.50*
O41	O3	15pf violet brn	.25	*1.50*
O42	O4	20pf deep ultra	.25	*1.50*
O43	O5	30pf orange, *buff*	.25	*1.50*
O44	O6	40pf carmine rose	.25	*1.50*
O45	O7	50pf violet, *buff*	.25	*1.50*
O46	O8	60pf red brown	.25	*1.50*
O47	O9	1m red, *buff*	.25	*1.50*
O48	O10	1.25m dk blue, *yel*	.25	*1.50*
O49	O11	2m dark blue	7.25	*12.00*
O50	O12	5m brown, *yel*	.25	*1.50*

1922, Feb. Wmk. 126

O51	O11	2m dark blue	.25	*1.00*
		Nos. O39-O51 (13)	11.00	*36.00*

This overprint is found both horizontal, reading upright or inverted, and vertical, reading up or down. These variations generally command no premium over the values above.

The overprint also exists on most values double and double, one inverted, in the above formats, as well as at a 45 degree angle, upreading and downreading, either upright or inverted. These varieties generally sell for 25-100 percent over the value of normal examples.

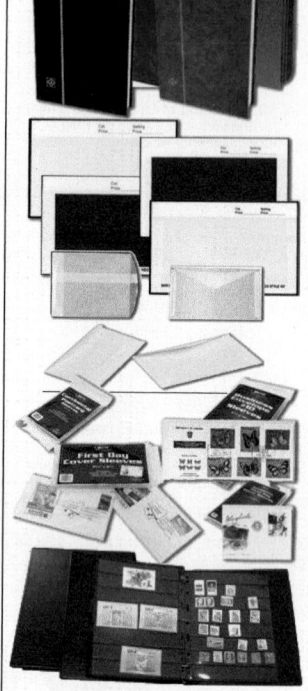

URUGUAY

'yur-ə-,gwā

LOCATION — South America, between Brazil and Argentina and bordering on the Atlantic Ocean
GOVT. — Republic
AREA — 68,037 sq. mi.
POP. — 3,137,668 (1996)
CAPITAL — Montevideo

120 Centavos = 1 Real
8 Reales = 1 Peso
100 Centesimos = 1 Peso (1859)
1000 Milesimos = 1 Peso (1898)

Watermarks

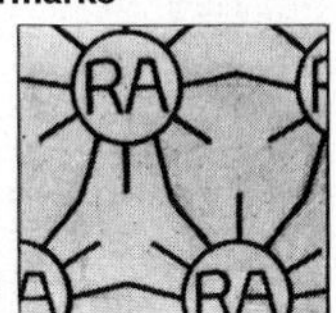

Wmk. 90 — Large Sun and RA

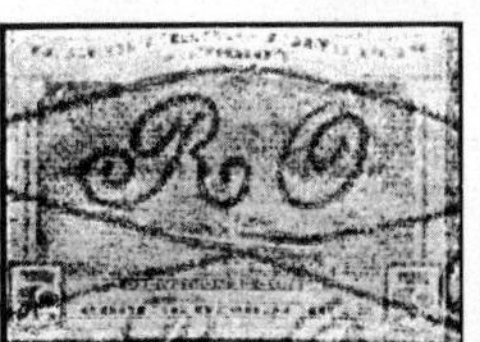

Wmk. 187 — R O in Diamond

Wmk. 188 — REPUBLICA O. DEL URUGUAY

Wmk. 189 — Caduceus

Wmk. 227 — Greek Border and REPUBLICA O. DEL URUGUAY in Alternate Curved Lines

Wmk. 327 — Coat of Arms

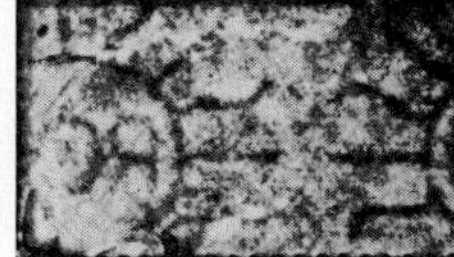

Wmk. 332 — Large Sun and R O U

Catalogue values for unused stamps in this country are for Never Hinged items, beginning with Scott 534 in the regular postage section, Scott B5 in the semi-postal section, Scott C113 in the airpost section, Scott CB1 in the airpost semi-postal section, Scott E9 in the special delivery section, and Scott Q64 in the parcel post section.

CARRIER ISSUES

Issued by Atanasio Lapido, Administrator-General of Posts

A1 A1a
"El Sol de Mayo"

Unwmk.

1856, Oct. 1 Litho. *Imperf.*

1 A1 60c blue 450. 450.
2 A1 80c green 500. 500.
3 A1 1r vermilion 400. 400.

1857, Oct. 1

3B A1a 60c blue *2,750.* —

Nos. 1-3B were spaced very closely on the stone. Very fine examples will have clear margins on three sides and touching or slightly cut into the frames on the fourth (consult the grading illustrations in the catalogue introduction). All genuinely used examples are pen canceled. Certification by a recognized authority is recommended.

Stamps with tiny faults, such as small thin spots, sell for about 75% of the values of sound examples.

See Nos. 410-413, 771A.

A2

1858, Mar.

4 A2 120c blue 575. *725.*
c. Tête bêche pair —
5 A2 180c green 150. *225.*
c. Thick paper 550.
d. Tête bêche pair —
6 A2 240c dull ver 150. *1,300.*
c. 180c in stone of 240c —
d. Thick paper (dull ver) — —
e. 240c setenant with a vacant space *5,000.*
Nos. 4-6 (3) 875.00 *2,250.*

Nos. 4-6e have been extensively forged. Certification by a recognized authority is recommended.

GOVERNMENT ISSUES

A3

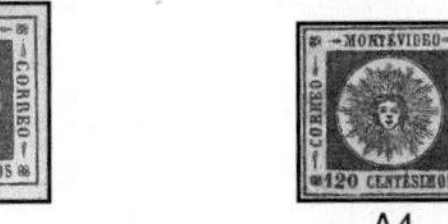

A4

1859, June 26 Thin Numerals

7 A3 60c lilac 55.00 35.00
a. 60c gray lilac 50.00 35.00
8 A3 80c orange 450.00 75.00
a. 80c yellow 350.00 60.00
9 A3 100c brown lake 100.00 70.00
a. 100c brown rose 150.00 100.00
10 A3 120c blue 55.00 30.00
a. 120c slate blue 75.00 30.00
11 A3 180c green 22.00 *26.00*
12 A3 240c vermilion 90.00 90.00
Nos. 7-12 (6) 772.00 *326.00*

1860 Thick Numerals

13 A4 60c dull lilac 25.00 12.00
a. 60c gray lilac 40.00 15.00
b. 60c brown lilac 35.00 18.00
c. 60c red lilac 120.00 60.00
d. As "a," fine impression (1st printing) 150.00 55.00
14 A4 80c yellow 50.00 25.00
a. 80c orange 120.00 26.00
15 A4 100c rose 100.00 55.00
a. 100c carmine 110.00 55.00
16 A4 120c blue 45.00 25.00
17 A4 180c yellow grn 425.00 375.00
a. 180c deep green 425.00 *450.00*
Nos. 13-17 (5) 645.00 *492.00*

No. 13 was first printed (1860) in sheets of 192 (16x12) containing 24 types. The impressions are very clear; paper is whitish and of better quality than that of the later printings. In the 1861-62 printings, the layout contains 12 types and the subjects are spaced farther apart.

Coat of Arms — A5

1864, Apr. 13

18 A5 6c rose 18.00 12.00
a. 6c carmine 40.00 30.00
b. 6c red 40.00 30.00
c. 6c brick red 120.00 60.00
20 A5 6c salmon 500.00 *500.00*
21 A5 8c green 25.00 25.00
a. Tête bêche pair 850.00
22 A5 10c yellow 32.50 25.00
a. 10c ocher 35.00 25.00
23 A5 12c blue 15.00 12.00
a. 12c dark blue 27.50 18.00
b. 12c slate blue 30.00 20.00

No. 20, which is on thicker paper, was never placed in use.

Stamps of 1864 Surcharged in Black

1866, Jan. 1

24 A5 5c on 12c blue 30.00 *50.00*
a. 5c on 12c slate blue 33.00 *67.50*
b. Inverted surcharge 165.00
c. Double surcharge 165.00
d. Pair, one without surcharge
e. Triple surcharge 60.00
25 A5 10c on 8c brt grn 30.00 *50.00*
a. 10c on 8c dl grn 30.00 *55.00*
b. Tête bêche pair 325.00
c. Double surcharge 165.00
26 A5 15c on 10c ocher 35.00 *90.00*
a. 15c on 10c yellow 40.00 *100.00*
b. Inverted surcharge 165.00
c. Double surcharge 165.00
27 A5 20c on 6c rose 40.00 *80.00*
a. 20c on 6c rose red 42.50 *82.50*
b. Inverted surcharge 165.00
c. Double surcharge 165.00
d. Pair, one without surcharge
28 A5 20c on 6c brick red *400.00*
a. Double surcharge 550.00
Nos. 24-27 (4) 135.00 *270.00*

Many counterfeits exist.

No. 28 was not issued.

Coat of Arms and Numeral of Value — A7

A8

A8a

A8b

A8c

Type I

Type II

ONE CENTESIMO:

Type I — The wavy lines behind "CENTESIMO" are clear and distinct. Stamps 4mm apart.

Type II — The wavy lines are rough and blurred. Stamps 3mm apart.

1866, Jan. 10 *Imperf.*

29 A7 1c black (type II) 5.00 *7.50*
a. 1c black (type I) 5.00 *7.50*
30 A8 5c blue 6.00 4.00
a. 5c dull blue 5.00 2.50
b. 5c ultramarine 32.50 10.00
c. Numeral with white flag 25.00 12.00
d. "ENTECIMOS" 25.00 12.00
e. "CENTECIMO" 25.00 12.00
f. "CENTECIMOS" with small "S" 25.00 12.00
g. Pelure paper 125.00 125.00
h. Thick paper
i. "MONTCVIDEO" 25.00 12.00
31 A8a 10c yellow green 20.00 7.00
a. 10c blue green 20.00 7.00
b. "I" of "CENTECIMOS" omitted 30.00 14.00
c. "CENIECIMOS" 27.50 14.00
d. "CENTRCIMOS" 30.00 14.00
32 A8b 15c orange yel 30.00 15.00
a. 15c yellow 30.00 15.00
33 A8c 20c rose 35.00 15.00
a. 20c lilac rose 35.00 15.00
b. Thick paper 50.00 17.50
Nos. 29-33 (5) 96.00 48.50

See Nos. 34-38. For overprint see No. O11.

Engraved plates were prepared for Nos. 30 to 33 but were not put in use. The stamps were printed from lithographic transfers from the plate. In 1915 a few reprints of the 15c were made from the engraved plate by a California philatelic society, each sheet being numbered and signed by officers of the society; then the plate was defaced.

1866-67 *Perf. 8½ to 13½*

34 A7 1c black 6.50 20.00
35 A8 5c blue 5.00 2.50
a. 5c dark blue 5.00 1.00
b. Numeral with white flag 27.50 12.00
c. "ENTECIMOS" 27.50 12.00
d. "CENTECIMO" 27.50 12.00
e. "CENTECIMOS" with small "S" 20.00 8.00
f. Pelure paper 10.00 20.00
36 A8a 10c green 12.00 4.00
a. 10c yellow green 14.00 4.00
b. "CENIECIMOS" 35.00 14.00
c. "I" of "CENTECIMOS" omitted 35.00 14.00
d. "CENTRCIMOS" 35.00 14.00
e. Pelure paper 100.00 20.00
37 A8b 15c orange yel 21.00 6.00
a. 15c yellow 21.00 6.00
b. Thin paper 25.00 10.00
38 A8c 20c rose 25.00 10.00
a. 20c brown rose 25.00 10.00
b. Thin paper 30.00 15.00
c. Thick paper 30.00 15.00
Nos. 34-38 (5) 69.50 42.50

A9

A10

A11

A12

1877-79 Engr. *Rouletted 8*

39 A9 1c red brown 1.00 .50
40 A10 5c green 1.25 .50
a. Thick paper 5.00 2.50
41 A11 10c vermilion 2.40 .80
42 A11 20c bister 4.50 1.25
43 A11 50c black 16.00 3.50
43A A12 1p blue ('79) 62.50 22.50
Nos. 39-43A (6) 87.65 29.05

The first printing of the 1p had the coat of arms smaller with quarterings reversed. These "error" stamps were not issued, and all were ordered burned. One example is known to have been in a celebrated Uruguayan collection and a few others exist.

See No. 44. For overprints and surcharges see Nos. 52-53, O1-O8, O10, O19.

1880, Nov. 10 Litho. *Rouletted 6*

44 A9 1c brown .50 .60
a. Imperf., pair 10.00
b. Rouletted 12½ 2.50 2.50
c. With white label 35.00

Joaquin Suárez — A13

1881, Aug. 25 *Perf. 12½*

45 A13 7c blue 2.50 2.50
a. Imperf., pair 10.00 10.00

For overprint see No. O9.

A14

Devices from Coat of Arms — A14a

1882, May 15

46 A14 1c bluish green 1.50 1.50
a. 1c yellow green 6.50 3.25
b. Imperf., pair 13.00
47 A14a 2c rose 1.25 1.00
a. Imperf., pair 15.00

These stamps bear numbers from 1 to 100 according to their position on the sheet.

Counterfeits of Nos. 46 and 47 are plentiful.

See Nos. 1132-1133. For overprints see Nos. 54, O12-O13, O20.

Coat of Arms
A15 A16

Gen. Máximo Santos
A17

General José Artigas
A18

Perf. 12, 12x12½, 12x13, 13x12

1883, Mar. 1

48	A15	1c green	1.40	1.00
49	A16	2c red	2.40	1.40
50	A17	5c blue	3.00	1.75
51	A18	10c brown	5.25	2.60
		Nos. 48-51 (4)	12.05	6.75

Imperf., Pairs

48a	A15	1c	7.00
49a	A16	2c	7.00
50a	A17	5c	7.00
51a	A18	10c	20.00

For overprints see Nos. O14-O18.

No. 40 Overprinted in Black

1883, Sept. 24 ***Rouletted 8***

52	A10 5c green	1.10	.75
a.	Double overprint	18.00	18.00
b.	Overprint reading down	6.00	6.00
c.	"Provisorio" omitted	7.00	7.00
d.	"1883" omitted	5.00	5.00

No. 52 with overprint in red is a color essay.

No. 41 Surcharged in Black

1884, Jan. 15

53	A11 1c on 10c ver	.50	.50
a.	Small figure "1"	4.25	4.25
b.	Inverted surcharge	4.25	4.25
c.	Double surcharge	9.75	5.00

No. 47 Overprinted in Black

Perf. 12½

54	A14a 2c rose	.75	.75
a.	Double overprint	20.00	
b.	Imperf., pair	50.00	

A22

A23

No. 56 has smaller numerals and the sun around the face is rounder.

Thick Paper

1884, Jan. 25 **Litho.** **Unwmk.**

55	A22 5c lt ultra	2.50	1.20
a.	Imperf., pair	7.50	4.50

Thin Paper

Perf. 12½, 13 and Compound

56	A23 5c blue	1.50	.75
a.	Imperf., pair	14.00	

For overprints see Nos. O21-O22.

A24

A24a

A24b

Artigas
A25

Santos
A26

A27

A28

1884-88 **Engr.** ***Rouletted 8***

57	A24	1c gray	1.00	.70
58	A24	1c olive	.90	.50
59	A24	1c green	.80	.50
60	A24a	2c vermilion	15.00	8.00
60A	A24a	2c rose ('88)	.50	.30
61	A24b	5c deep blue	1.00	.40
62	A24b	5c violet ('86)	.60	.30
63	A24b	5c lt bl ('88)	.60	.30
64	A25	7c dk brown	2.50	1.00
65	A25	7c org ('88)	2.40	.90
66	A26	10c olive brn	2.75	.90
67	A27	20c red violet	6.75	2.50
68	A27	20c bis brn ('88)	6.75	2.50
69	A28	25c gray violet	4.50	1.70
70	A28	25c ver ('88)	3.50	1.10
		Nos. 57-70 (15)	49.55	21.60

Some examples of No. 61 reacted with Potassium ferrocyanide, and the humidity during printing to stain the paper an uneven bluish color that can be seen under the gum.

For overprints see Nos. 73, 98-99, O23-O34, O36-O39, O61.

A29

1887, Oct. 17 **Litho.** ***Rouletted 9***

71	A29 10c lilac	3.00	1.50
a.	10c gray lilac	3.00	1.50

For overprint see No. O40.

A30

1888, Jan. 1 **Engr.** ***Rouletted 8***

72	A30 10c violet	.60	.30

For overprint see No. O35.

No. 62 Overprinted in Black

1889, Oct. 14

73	A24b 5c violet	.40	.40
a.	Inverted overprint	8.00	8.00
b.	Inverted "A" for "V" in "Provisorio"	4.00	4.00

No. 73 with overprint in red is a color essay.

Coat of Arms
A32

Numeral of Value
A33

A34

A35

A36

A37

Justice
A38

Mercury
A39

A40

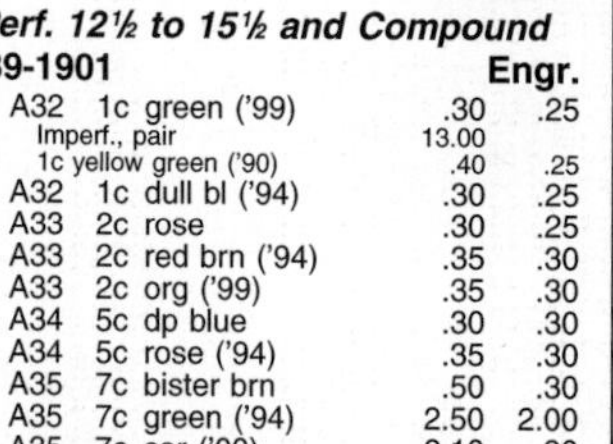

Perf. 12½ to 15½ and Compound

1889-1901 **Engr.**

74	A32	1c green ('99)	.30	.25
a.		Imperf., pair	13.00	
b.		1c yellow green ('90)	.40	.25
75	A32	1c dull bl ('94)	.30	.25
76	A33	2c rose	.30	.25
77	A33	2c red brn ('94)	.35	.30
78	A33	2c org ('99)	.35	.30
79	A34	5c dp blue	.30	.30
80	A34	5c rose ('94)	.35	.30
81	A35	7c bister brn	.50	.30
82	A35	7c green ('94)	2.50	2.00
83	A35	7c car ('00)	2.10	.90
84	A36	10c blue grn	4.60	.40
a.		Printed on both sides	50.00	
85	A36	10c org ('94)	4.90	1.00
86	A37	20c orange	5.50	.60
87	A37	20c brown ('94)	6.75	2.00
88	A37	20c lt blue ('00)	4.50	.50
a.		20c greenish blue	5.50	.50
89	A38	25c red brown	5.50	1.50
90	A38	25c ver ('94)	6.50	3.50
91	A38	25c bis brn ('01)	5.50	.50
92	A39	50c lt blue	8.00	4.50
93	A39	50c lilac ('94)	12.50	6.25
94	A39	50c car ('01)	8.25	1.25
95	A40	1p lilac	17.00	5.00
96	A40	1p lt blue ('94)	27.50	7.50
97	A40	1p dp grn ('01)	20.00	2.50
a.		Imperf., pair	90.00	
		Nos. 74-97 (24)	144.35	42.15

For surcharges and overprints see Nos. 100-101, 142, 180, 185, C1-C3, O41-O60, O89-O91, O108-O109.

Nos. 59 and 62 Overprinted in Red

a

b

1891-92 ***Rouletted 8***

98	A24 (a) 1c green ('92)	.40	.40
a.	Inverted overprint	7.25	7.25
b.	Double overprint	9.50	9.50
c.	Double ovpt., one invtd.	3.00	2.50
d.	"PREVISORIO"	4.00	4.00
99	A24b (b) 5c violet	.30	.30
a.	"1391"	4.00	2.75
b.	Double overprint	5.00	3.50
c.	Inverted overprint	5.00	3.50
d.	Double ovpt., one invtd.	6.00	3.75

Nos. 86 and 81 Surcharged in Black or Red

c

d

Perf. 12½ to 15½ and Compound

1892

100	A37 (c) 1c on 20c org (Bk)	.40	.40
a.	Inverted surcharge	6.00	6.00
101	A35 (d) 5c on 7c bis brn (R)	.40	.40
a.	Inverted surcharge	1.00	1.00
b.	Double surcharge, one invtd.	3.00	3.00
c.	Double surcharge	3.00	3.00
d.	Vertical surcharge	12.00	
e.	"PREVISORIO"	3.00	3.00
f.	"Cinco" omitted	5.50	

No. 101 with surcharge in green is a color essay.

Several surcharge errors of date and misspelling of "Centésimos" exist. Value $15.

A45

A46

Arms
A47

Peace
A48

1892 **Engr.**

102	A45	1c green	.60	.25
103	A46	2c rose	.60	.25
104	A47	5c blue	5.00	2.40
105	A48	10c orange	12.00	5.00
		Nos. 102-105 (4)	18.20	7.90

Issued: 1c, 2c, 3/9; 5c, 4/19; 10c, 12/15.

Liberty
A49

Arms
A50

1894, June 2

106	A49 2p carmine	27.50	17.00
107	A50 3p dull violet	27.50	17.00

Gaucho
A51

Solis Theater
A52

Locomotive
A53

Bull's Head
A54

Ceres
A55

Sailing Ship
A56

Liberty
A57

Mercury
A58

Coat of Arms
A59

Montevideo Fortress
A60

Cathedral in Montevideo — A61

Perf. 12 to 15½ and Compound

1895-99

108 A51 1c bister .50 .30
109 A51 1c slate bl ('97) .50 .30
a. Printed on both sides 20.00
110 A52 2c blue 1.00 .30
111 A52 2c claret ('97) 1.00 .30
112 A53 5c red 1.00 .30
113 A53 5c green ('97) 1.00 .30
a. Imperf., pair 20.00
114 A53 5c grnsh bl ('99) 1.00 .40
115 A54 7c deep green 7.75 2.50
116 A54 7c orange ('97) 3.50 1.25
117 A55 10c brown 2.60 .50
118 A56 20c green & blk 8.00 .85
119 A56 20c cl & blk ('97) 5.00 .60
120 A57 25c red brn & blk 6.50 1.50
a. Center inverted 2,000.
121 A57 25c pink & bl ('97) 3.50 .60
122 A58 50c blue & blk 8.00 3.50
123 A58 50c grn & brn ('97) 5.00 1.25
124 A59 1p org brn & blk 15.00 4.00
125 A59 1p yel brn & bl ('97) 9.50 3.50
126 A60 2p violet & grn 36.50 22.50
127 A60 2p bis & car ('97) 9.50 2.00
128 A61 3p carmine & blue 32.50 20.00
129 A61 3p lil & car ('97) 12.50 2.50
Nos. 108-129 (22) 171.35 69.25

All values of this issue exist imperforate but they were not issued in that form.

For overprints and surcharges see Nos. 138-140, 143, 145, 147, O62-O78.

President Joaquin Suárez
A62 A63

Statue of President Suárez — A64

Perf. 12½ to 15 and Compound

1896, July 18

130 A62 1c brown vio & blk .25 .25
131 A63 5c pale bl & blk .25 .25
132 A64 10c lake & blk 1.00 .40
Nos. 130-132 (3) 1.50 .90

Dedication of Pres. Suárez statue.

For overprints and surcharge see Nos. 133-135, 144, 146, 152, O79-O81.

Same Overprinted in Red

e

f

1897, Mar. 1

133 A62 (e) 1c brn vio & blk .40 .40
a. Inverted overprint 6.00 6.00
134 A63 (e) 5c pale blue & blk .50 .40
a. Inverted overprint 10.00 6.00
135 A64 (f) 10c lake & blk 1.00 .60
a. Inverted overprint 10.00 9.00
b. Double overprint 10.00 10.00
Nos. 133-135 (3) 1.90 1.40

"Electricity" — A68

1897-99 **Engr.**

136 A68 10c red 6.50 .40
137 A68 10c red lilac ('99) 3.00 .50

For overprints see Nos. 141, O82-O83.

Regular Issues Overprinted in Red or Blue

1897, Sept. 26

138 A51 1c slate bl (R) 1.00 .65
a. Inverted overprint 4.75 4.75
139 A52 2c claret (Bl) 1.50 1.25
a. Inverted overprint 4.75 4.75
140 A53 5c green (Bl) 2.10 1.75
a. Inverted overprint 7.75 7.75
b. Double overprint
141 A68 10c red (Bl) 3.50 2.40
a. Inverted overprint 17.00 17.00
Nos. 138-141 (4) 8.10 6.05

Commemorating the Restoration of Peace at the end of the Civil War.

Issue for use only on the days of the National Fête, Sept. 26-28, 1897.

Regular Issues Surcharged in Black, Blue or Red

1898, July 25

142 A32 ½c on 1c bl (Bk) .40 .40
a. Inverted surcharge 3.00 3.00
143 A51 ½c on 1c bis (Bl) .40 .40
a. Inverted surcharge 3.00
b. Double surcharge 3.00
144 A62 ½c on 1c brn vio & blk (R) .40 .40
145 A52 ½c on 2c blue (Bk) .40 .40
146 A63 ½c on 5c pale bl & blk (R) .40 .40
a. Double surcharge 7.50
147 A54 ½c on 7c dp grn (R) .40 .40
Nos. 142-147 (6) 2.40 2.40

The 2c red brown of 1894 (#77) was also surcharged like #142-147 but was not issued. Value $12.

Liberty — A69

1898-99 **Litho.** ***Perf. 11, 11½***

148 A69 5m rose .30 .25
149 A69 5m purple ('99) .30 .25

Statue of Artigas — A70

1899-1900 **Engr.** ***Perf. 12½, 14, 15***

150 A70 5m blue .30 .25
151 A70 5m orange ('00) .30 .25

No. 135 With Additional Surcharge in Black

1900, Dec. 1

152 A64 5c on 10c lake & blk .50 .30
a. Black bar covering "1897" omitted 18.00

Cattle
A72

Girl's Head
A73

Shepherdess — A74

Perf. 13½ to 16 and Compound

1900-10 **Engr.**

153 A72 1c yellow green .40 .30
154 A73 5c dull blue .80 .30
155 A73 5c slate grn ('10) .80 .30
156 A74 10c gray violet 1.00 .30
Nos. 153-156 (4) 3.00 1.20

For surcharges and overprints see Nos. 179, 184, O84, O86, O88, O106-O107.

Eros and Cornucopia
A75

Basket of Fruit
A76

1901, Feb. 11

157 A75 2c vermilion .30 .30
158 A76 7c brown orange 2.00 .40

For surcharges and overprints see Nos. 197-198, O85, O87, O105.

General Artigas
A78

Cattle
A79

Eros
A80

Cow
A81

Shepherdess
A82

Numeral
A83

Justice — A84

1904-05 **Litho.** ***Perf. 11½***

160 A78 5m orange .50 .30
a. 5m yellow .50 .30
161 A79 1c green .60 .30
a. Imperf., pair 4.25
162 A80 2c dp orange .50 .30
a. 2c orange red 2.00 .30
b. Imperf., pair 3.75
163 A81 5c blue 1.00 .30
a. Imperf., pair 4.25
164 A82 10c dk violet ('05) .60 .30
165 A83 20c gray grn ('05) 3.00 .55
166 A84 25c olive bis ('05) 4.00 .85
Nos. 160-166 (7) 10.20 2.90

Design of No. 163 measures 17x23mm. See No. 170.

For overprints see Nos. 167-169, O92-O98, O101-O103.

Nos. 160-166 were printed with a papermarkers sheet watermark "Clyde First Quality" that appears on some stamps.

Overprinted Diagonally in Carmine or Black

1904, Oct. 15

167 A79 1c green (C) .55 .40
168 A80 2c deep orange (Bk) .85 .40
169 A81 5c dark blue (C) 1.60 .60
Nos. 167-169 (3) 3.00 1.40

End of the Civil War of 1904. In the first overprinting, "Paz 1904" appears at a 50-degree angle; in the second, at a 63-degree angle.

A85

Size: 19¼x25½mm

1906, Feb. 23 **Litho.** **Unwmk.**

170 A85 5c dark blue 1.10 .25
a. Imperf., pair 6.00

See No. 163.

A86

1906-07

171 A86 5c deep blue .30 .30
172 A86 7c orange brn ('07) .70 .50
173 A86 50c rose 5.00 1.25
Nos. 171-173 (3) 6.00 2.05

Cruiser "Montevideo"
A87

1908, Aug. 23 **Typo.** ***Rouletted 13***

174 A87 1c car & dk grn 2.00 1.50
175 A87 2c green & dk grn 2.00 1.50
176 A87 5c org & dk grn 2.00 1.50
Nos. 174-176 (3) 6.00 4.50

Center Inverted

174a A87 1c 300.00 300.00
175a A87 2c 300.00 300.00
176a A87 5c 300.00 300.00
Nos. 174a-176a (3) 900.00 900.00

Imperf., Pairs

174b A87 1c 30.00
175b A87 2c 30.00
176b A87 5c 30.00

Independence of Uruguay, declared Aug. 25, 1825. Counterfeits exist.

For surcharges and overprints see Nos. 186, O99-O100, O104, O110.

View of the Port of Montevideo
A88

Wmk. 187

1909, Aug. 24 **Engr.** ***Perf. 11½***

177 A88 2c lt brown & blk 1.25 1.20
178 A88 5c rose red & blk 1.25 1.20

Issued to commemorate the opening of the Port of Montevideo, Aug. 25, 1909.

Nos. 156, 91 Surcharged

Perf. 14 to 16

1909, Sept. 13 **Unwmk.**

179 A74 8c on 10c dull vio .75 .25
a. "Contesimos" 4.00 2.00
180 A38 23c on 25c bis brn 1.75 .60

Centaur — A89

Wmk. 187

1910, May 22 **Engr.** ***Perf. 11½***

182 A89 2c carmine red .60 .40
183 A89 5c deep blue .60 .40

Cent. of Liberation Day, May 25, 1810.

The 2c in deep blue and 5c in carmine red were prepared for collectors.

Stamps of 1900-06 Surcharged

g

h

Perf. 14 to 16, 11½

1910, Oct. 6 Unwmk.

Black Surcharge

184 A72 (g) 5m on 1c yel grn .25 .25
a. Inverted surcharge 4.50 3.75

Dark Blue Surcharge

185 A39 (h) 5c on 50c dull red .40 .25
a. Inverted surcharge 5.00 5.00

Blue Surcharge

186 A86 (i) 5c on 50c rose .80 .45
a. Double surcharge 20.00
b. Inverted surcharge 10.00 8.75
Nos. 184-186 (3) 1.45 .95

Artigas A90

"Commercial Progress" A91

1910, Nov. 21 Engr. *Perf. 14, 15*

187 A90 5m dk violet .25 .25
188 A90 1c dp green .25 .25
189 A90 2c orange red .25 .25
190 A90 5c dk blue .25 .25
191 A90 8c gray blk .40 .25
192 A90 20c brown 4.00 .25
193 A91 23c dp ultra 6.00 .40
194 A91 50c orange 9.00 1.25
195 A91 1p scarlet 15.00 1.25
Nos. 187-195 (9) 35.40 4.40

See Nos. 199-210. For overprints see Nos. 211-213, O118-O124.

Symbolical of the Posts — A92

1911, Jan. 6 Wmk. 187 *Perf. 11½*

196 A92 5c rose car & blk .80 .60

1st South American Postal Cong., at Montevideo, Jan. 1911.

No. 158 Surcharged in Red or Dark Blue

Perf. 14 to 16

1911, May 17 Unwmk.

197 A76 2c on 7c brn org (R) .40 .40
198 A76 5c on 7c brn org (Bl) .40 .25
a. Inverted surcharge 8.50 8.50

Centenary of the battle of Las Piedras, won by the forces under Gen. Jose Gervasio Artigas, May 8, 1811.

Types of 1910

FOUR AND FIVE CENTESIMOS:
Type I — Large numerals about 3mm high.
Type II — Small numerals about 2¼mm high.

1912-15 Typo. *Perf. 11½*

199 A90 5m violet .25 .25
a. 5m purple .50 .25
200 A90 5m magenta .25 .25
a. 5m dull rose .50 .25
201 A90 1c green ('13) .25 .25
202 A90 2c brown org .25 .25
203 A90 2c rose red ('13) .25 .25
a. 2c deep red ('14) .50 .25
204 A90 4c org (I) ('14) .25 .25
a. 4c orange (II) ('15) .50 .25
b. 4c yellow (II) ('13) .50 .25
205 A90 5c dull bl (I) .40 .25
a. 5c blue (II) .50 .25
206 A90 8c ultra ('13) .50 .25
207 A90 20c brown ('13) 4.50 .25
a. 20c chocolate 4.50 .25
208 A91 23c dk blue ('15) 10.00 .60
209 A91 50c orange ('14) 10.00 1.50
210 A91 1p vermilion ('15) 30.00 1.25
Nos. 199-210 (12) 56.90 5.60

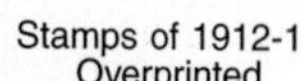

Stamps of 1912-15 Overprinted

1913, Apr. 4

211 A90 2c brown orange .85 .50
a. Inverted overprint 5.00 4.50
212 A90 4c yellow .85 .50
213 A90 5c blue .85 .50
Nos. 211-213 (3) 2.55 1.50

Cent. of the Buenos Aires Cong. of 1813.

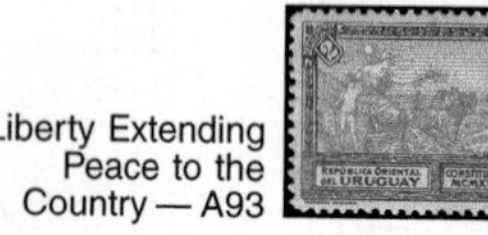

Liberty Extending Peace to the Country — A93

1918, Jan. 3 Litho.

214 A93 2c green & red .85 .50
215 A93 5c buff & blue .85 .50

Promulgation of the Constitution.

Statue of Liberty, New York Harbor — A94

Perf. 14, 15, 13½

1919, July 15 Engr.

217 A94 2c carmine & brn 1.00 .25
218 A94 4c orange & brn 1.00 .25
a. Roulette 1,600. 1,300.
219 A94 5c blue & brn 1.25 .40
220 A94 8c org brn & ind 1.25 .40
221 A94 20c ol bis & blk 3.50 .80
222 A94 23c green & blk 7.00 1.25
Nos. 217-222 (6) 15.00 3.35

Peace at end of World War I.
Perf 13½ used only on 2c, 20c, 23c.

Harbor of Montevideo — A95

1919-20 Litho. *Perf. 11½*

225 A95 5m violet & blk .25 .25
226 A95 1c green & blk .25 .25
227 A95 2c red & blk .25 .25
228 A95 4c orange & blk .35 .25
229 A95 5c ultra & slate .45 .25
230 A95 8c gray bl & lt brn .60 .25
231 A95 20c brown & blk 1.75 .35
232 A95 23c green & brn 3.25 .65
233 A95 50c brown & blue 5.75 2.00
234 A95 1p dull red & bl 11.50 3.00
Nos. 225-234 (10) 24.40 7.50

For overprints see Nos. O125-O131.

José Enrique Rodó — A96

1920, Feb. 28 Engr. *Perf. 14, 15*

235 A96 2c car & blk .55 .40
236 A96 4c org & bl .65 .50
237 A96 5c bl & brn .75 .55
Nos. 235-237 (3) 1.95 1.45

Issued to honor José Enrique Rodó, author. For surcharges see Nos. P2-P4.

Mercury — A97

1921-22 Litho. *Perf. 11½*

238 A97 5m lilac .25 .25
239 A97 5m gray blk ('22) .25 .25
240 A97 1c lt grn .25 .25
241 A97 1c vio ('22) .25 .25
242 A97 2c fawn .50 .25
243 A97 2c red ('22) .50 .25
244 A97 3c bl grn ('22) .70 .25
245 A97 4c orange .50 .25
246 A97 5c ultra .60 .25
247 A97 5c choc ('22) .70 .25
248 A97 12c ultra ('22) 2.75 .60
249 A97 36c ol grn ('22) 9.00 2.75
Nos. 238-249 (12) 16.25 5.85

See Nos. 254-260. For overprint and surcharge see Nos. E1, P1.

Dámaso A. Larrañaga (1771-1848), Bishop, Writer, Scientist and Physician — A98

1921, Dec. 10 Unwmk.

250 A98 5c slate 5.00 1.00

Mercury Type of 1921-22

1922-23 Wmk. 188

254 A97 5m gray blk .25 .25
255 A97 1c violet ('23) .25 .25
a. 1c red violet .25 .25
256 A97 2c pale red .25 .25
257 A97 2c deep rose ('23) .30 .25
259 A97 5c yel brn ('23) .65 .25
260 A97 8c salmon pink ('23) 1.00 .90
Nos. 254-260 (6) 2.70 2.15

Equestrian Statue of Artigas — A99

Unwmk.

1923, Feb. 26 Engr. *Perf. 14*

264 A99 2c car & sepia .40 .25
265 A99 5c vio & sepia .40 .25
266 A99 12c blue & sepia .40 .25
Nos. 264-266 (3) 1.20 .75

Southern Lapwing — A100

Perf. 12½, 11½x12½

1923, June 25 Litho. Wmk. 189

Size: 18x22½mm

267 A100 5m gray .25 .25
268 A100 1c org yel .25 .25
269 A100 2c lt vio .25 .25
270 A100 3c gray grn .30 .25
271 A100 5c lt bl .30 .25
272 A100 8c rose red .55 .50
273 A100 12c dp bl .55 .50
274 A100 20c brn org 1.40 .50
275 A100 36c emerald 7.00 7.00
276 A100 50c orange 10.00 10.00
277 A100 1p brt rose 32.50 20.00
278 A100 2p lt grn 42.50 20.00
Nos. 267-278 (12) 95.85 59.75

See #285-298, 309-314, 317-323, 334-339. For surcharges and overprints see Nos. 345-348, O132-O148, P5-P7.

Battle Monument — A101

1923, Oct. 12 Wmk. 188 *Perf. 11½*

279 A101 2c dp grn .55 .40
280 A101 5c scarlet .55 .40
281 A101 12c dk bl .55 .40
Nos. 279-281 (3) 1.65 1.20

Unveiling of the Sarandi Battle Monument by José Luis Zorrilla, Oct. 12, 1923.

"Victory of Samothrace" A102

Unwmk.

1924, July 29 Typo. *Perf. 11*

282 A102 2c rose 20.00 10.00
283 A102 5c mauve 20.00 10.00
284 A102 12c brt bl 20.00 10.00
Nos. 282-284 (3) 60.00 30.00

Olympic Games. Sheets of 20 (5x4).
Five hundred sets of these stamps were printed on yellow paper for presentation purposes. They were not on sale at post offices. Value for set, $1,500.

Lapwing Type of 1923

First Redrawing

Imprint: "A. BARREIRO Y RAMOS"

1924, July 26 Litho. *Perf. 12½, 11½*

Size: 17¼x21½mm

285 A100 5m gray blk .25 .25
286 A100 1c fawn .25 .25
287 A100 2c rose lil .30 .25
288 A100 3c gray grn .25 .25
289 A100 5c chalky blue .25 .25
290 A100 8c pink .50 .25
291 A100 10c turq blue .40 .25
292 A100 12c slate blue .50 .25
293 A100 15c lt vio .50 .25
294 A100 20c brown .75 .30
295 A100 36c salmon 12.00 8.00
296 A100 50c greenish gray 17.50 12.00
297 A100 1p buff 50.00 22.50
298 A100 2p dl vio 67.50 22.50
Nos. 285-298 (14) 150.95 67.55

Landing of the 33 "Immortals" Led by Juan Antonio Lavalleja A103

Perf. 11, 11½

1925, Apr. 19 Wmk. 188

300 A103 2c salmon pink & blk 1.40 .80
301 A103 5c lilac & blk 1.40 .80
302 A103 12c blue & blk 1.40 .80
Nos. 300-302 (3) 4.20 2.40

Cent. of the landing of the 33 Founders of the Uruguayan Republic.

Legislative Palace — A104

Perf. 11½

1925, Aug. 24 Unwmk. Engr.

303 A104 5c vio & blk 1.25 .80
304 A104 12c bl & blk 1.25 .80

Dedication of the Legislative Palace.

General Fructuoso Rivera — A105

Wmk. 188

1925, Sept. 24 Litho. *Perf. 11*

305 A105 5c light red .50 .40

Centenary of Battle of Rincón. See No. C9.

Battle of Sarandí — A106

1925, Oct. 12 *Perf. 11½*

306 A106 2c bl grn 1.25 1.00
307 A106 5c dl vio 1.25 1.00
308 A106 12c dp bl 1.25 1.00
Nos. 306-308 (3) 3.75 3.00

Centenary of the Battle of Sarandi.

Lapwing Type of 1923
Second Redrawing
Imprint: "Imprenta Nacional"

1925-26 ***Perf. 11, 11½, 10½***
Size: 17½x21¾mm

No.	Type	Description	Unused	Used
309	A100	5m gray blk	.45	.25
310	A100	1c dl vio	.55	.25
311	A100	2c brt rose	.70	.25
312	A100	3c gray grn	.55	.40
313	A100	5c dl bl ('26)	.90	.25
314	A100	12c slate blue	8.00	.40
		Nos. 309-314 (6)	11.15	1.80

The design differs in many small details from that of the 1923-24 issues. These stamps may be readily identified by the imprint and perforation.

Lapwing Type of 1923
Third Redrawing
Imprint: "Imp. Nacional" at center

1926-27 ***Perf. 11, 11½, 10½***
Size: 17½x21¾mm

No.	Type	Description	Unused	Used
317	A100	5m gray	.30	.25
318	A100	1c lt vio ('27)	1.60	.55
319	A100	2c red	1.10	.40
320	A100	3c gray grn	1.60	.65
321	A100	5c lt bl	.50	.25
322	A100	8c pink ('27)	2.25	.80
323	A100	36c rose buff	12.00	4.00
		Nos. 317-323 (7)	19.35	6.90

These stamps may be distinguished from preceding stamps of the same design by the imprint.

Philatelic Exhibition Issue

Post Office at Montevideo — A107

Unwmk.
1927, May 25 **Engr.** ***Imperf.***

No.	Type	Description	Unused	Used
330	A107	2c green	4.75	3.50
a.		Sheet of 4	20.00	20.00
331	A107	5c dull red	4.75	3.50
a.		Sheet of 4	20.00	20.00
332	A107	8c dark blue	4.75	3.50
a.		Sheet of 4	20.00	20.00
		Nos. 330-332 (3)	14.25	10.50

Printed in sheets of 4 and sold at the Montevideo Exhibition. Lithographed counterfeits exist.

Lapwing Type of 1923
Fourth Redrawing
Imprint: "Imp. Nacional" at right
Perf. 11, 11½

1927, May 6 **Litho.** **Wmk. 188**
Size: 17¾x21¾mm

No.	Type	Description	Unused	Used
334	A100	1c gray vio	.40	.25
335	A100	2c vermilion	.40	.25
336	A100	3c gray grn	.80	.35
337	A100	5c blue	.40	.25
338	A100	8c rose	3.00	.80
339	A100	20c gray brn	4.00	1.60
		Nos. 334-339 (6)	9.00	3.50

The design has been slightly retouched in various places. The imprint is in italic capitals and is placed below the right numeral of value.

No. 292 Surcharged in Red

1928, Jan. 13 **Unwmk.** ***Perf. 11½***

No.	Type	Description	Unused	Used
345	A100	2c on 12c slate blue	2.00	2.00
346	A100	5c on 12c slate blue	2.00	2.00
347	A100	10c on 12c slate blue	2.00	2.00
348	A100	15c on 12c slate blue	2.00	2.00
		Nos. 345-348 (4)	8.00	8.00

Issued to celebrate the inauguration of the railroad between San Carlos and Rocha.

General Rivera — A108

1928, Apr. 19 **Engr.** ***Perf. 12***

No.	Type	Description	Unused	Used
349	A108	5c car rose	.50	.35

Centenary of the Battle of Las Misiones.

Artigas (7 dots in panels below portrait.) — A109

Imprint: "Waterlow & Sons. Ltd., Londres"

Perf. 11, 12½, 13x13½, 12½x13, 13x12½

1928-43 **Size: 16x19½mm**

No.	Type	Description	Unused	Used
350	A109	5m black	.25	.25
350A	A109	5m org ('43)	.25	.25
351	A109	1c dk vio	.25	.25
352	A109	1c brn vio ('34)	.25	.25
352A	A109	1c vio bl ('43)	.25	.25
353	A109	2c dp grn	.25	.25
353A	A109	2c brn red ('43)	.25	.25
354	A109	3c bister	.25	.25
355	A109	3c dp grn ('32)	.25	.25
355A	A109	3c brt grn ('43)	.25	.25
356	A109	5c red	.25	.25
357	A109	5c ol grn ('33)	.25	.25
357A	A109	5c dl pur ('43)	.25	.25
358	A109	7c car ('32)	.25	.25
359	A109	8c dk bl	.25	.25
360	A109	8c brn ('33)	.25	.25
361	A109	10c orange	.25	.25
362	A109	10c red org ('32)	.60	.40
363	A109	12c dp bl ('32)	.40	.25
364	A109	15c dl bl	.40	.25
365	A109	17c dk vio ('32)	.80	.25
366	A109	20c ol brn	.65	.25
367	A109	20c red brn ('33)	1.25	.50
368	A109	24c car rose	.90	.35
369	A109	24c yel ('33)	.80	.40
370	A109	36c ol grn ('33)	1.40	.50
371	A109	50c gray	2.40	1.25
372	A109	50c blk ('33)	3.50	1.60
373	A109	50c blk brn ('33)	3.00	1.25
374	A109	1p yel grn	7.00	4.00
		Nos. 350-374 (30)	27.35	15.50

1929-33 ***Perf. 12½***
Size: 22 to 22½x28½ to 29½mm

No.	Type	Description	Unused	Used
375	A109	1p ol brn ('33)	6.00	4.00
376	A109	2p dk grn	17.00	9.00
377	A109	2p dl red ('32)	20.00	16.00
378	A109	3p dk bl	25.00	17.00
379	A109	3p blk ('32)	23.00	20.00
380	A109	4p violet	28.00	17.00
381	A109	4p dk ol grn ('32)	30.00	20.00
382	A109	5p car brn	32.50	23.00
383	A109	5p red org ('32)	30.00	23.00
384	A109	10p lake ('33)	92.50	70.00
385	A109	10p dp ultra ('33)	92.50	70.00
		Nos. 375-385 (11)	396.50	289.00

See Nos. 420-423, 462. See type A135.

Equestrian Statue of Artigas — A110

1928, May 1

No.	Type	Description	Unused	Used
386	A110	2p Prus bl & choc	16.00	7.75
387	A110	3p dp rose & blk	23.00	12.00

Symbolical of Soccer Victory — A111

1928, July 29

No.	Type	Description	Unused	Used
388	A111	2c brn vio	16.00	9.25
389	A111	5c dp red	16.00	9.25
390	A111	8c ultra	16.00	9.25
		Nos. 388-390 (3)	48.00	27.75

Uruguayan soccer victories in the Olympic Games of 1924 and 1928. Printed in sheets of 20, in panes of 10 (5x2).

Gen. Eugenio Garzón — A112

1928, Aug. 25 ***Imperf.***

No.	Type	Description	Unused	Used
391	A112	2c red	1.40	1.40
a.		Sheet of 4	6.50	6.50
392	A112	5c yel grn	1.40	1.40
a.		Sheet of 4	6.50	6.50
393	A112	8c dp bl	1.40	1.40
a.		Sheet of 4	6.50	6.50
		Nos. 391-393 (3)	4.20	4.20

Dedication of monument to Garzon. Issued in sheets of 4. Lithographed counterfeits exist.

Black River Bridge — A113

Gauchos Breaking a Horse — A114

Peace A115

Montevideo A116

Liberty and Flag of Uruguay A117

Liberty with Torch and Caduceus A118

Statue of Artigas A124

Artigas Dictating Instructions for 1813 Congress A119

Seascape A120

Montevideo Harbor, 1830 A121

Liberty and Coat of Arms — A122

Montevideo Harbor, 1930 — A123

1930, June 16 ***Perf. 12½, 12***

No.	Type	Description	Unused	Used
394	A113	5m gray blk	.25	.25
395	A114	1c dk brn	.25	.25
396	A115	2c brn rose	.25	.25
397	A116	3c yel grn	.25	.25
398	A117	5c dk bl	.25	.25
399	A118	8c dl red	.35	.25
400	A119	10c dk vio	.50	.35
401	A120	15c bl grn	.65	.50
402	A121	20c indigo	.80	.65
403	A122	24c red brn	1.10	.80
404	A123	50c org red	3.00	2.00
405	A124	1p black	6.00	3.00
406	A124	2p bl vio	14.00	8.50
407	A124	3p dk red	20.00	14.00
408	A124	4p red org	23.00	19.00
409	A124	5p lilac	35.00	22.50
		Nos. 394-409 (16)	105.65	72.80

Cent. of natl. independence and the promulgation of the constitution.

Type of 1856 Issue
Values in Centesimos
Wmk. 227

1931, Apr. 11 **Litho.** ***Imperf.***

No.	Type	Description	Unused	Used
410	A1	2c gray blue	3.00	2.00
a.		Sheet of 4	15.00	15.00
411	A1	8c dull red	3.00	2.00
a.		Sheet of 4	15.00	15.00

No.	Type	Description	Unused	Used
412	A1	15c blue black	3.00	2.00
a.		Sheet of 4	15.00	15.00

Wmk. 188

No.	Type	Description	Unused	Used
413	A1	5c light green	3.00	2.00
a.		Sheet of 4	15.00	15.00
		Nos. 410-413 (4)	12.00	8.00

Sold only at the Philatelic Exhibition, Montevideo, Apr. 11-15, 1931. Issued in sheets of 4.

Juan Zorrilla de San Martin, Uruguayan Poet — A125

1932, June 6 **Unwmk.** ***Perf. 12½***

No.	Type	Description	Unused	Used
414	A125	1½c brown violet	.25	.25
415	A125	3c green	.25	.25
416	A125	7c dk blue	.25	.25
417	A125	12c lt blue	.40	.25
418	A125	1p chocolate	20.00	13.00
		Nos. 414-418 (5)	21.15	14.00

Semi-Postal Stamp No. B2 Surcharged

1932, Nov. 1 ***Perf. 12***

No.	Type	Description	Unused	Used
419	SP1	1½c on 2c + 2c dp grn	1.00	.35

Artigas Type of 1928
Imprint: "Imprenta Nacional" at center

1932-35 **Litho.** ***Perf. 11, 12½***
Size: 15¾x19¼mm

No.	Type	Description	Unused	Used
420	A109	5m lt brown ('35)	.25	.25
421	A109	1c pale violet ('35)	.25	.25
422	A109	15m black	.25	.25
423	A109	5c bluish grn ('35)	.50	.25
		Nos. 420-423 (4)	1.25	1.00

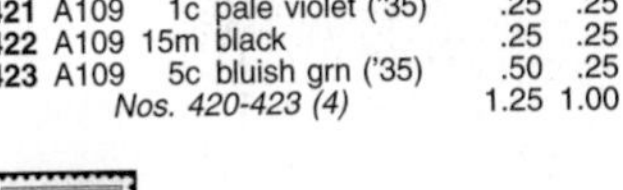

Gen. J. A. Lavalleja — A126

1933, July 12 **Engr.** ***Perf. 12½***

No.	Type	Description	Unused	Used
429	A126	15m brown lake	.25	.25

Flag of the Race and Globe — A127

Perf. 11, 11½, 11x11½

1933, Aug. 3 **Litho.**

No.	Type	Description	Unused	Used
430	A127	3c blue green	.60	.25
431	A127	5c rose	.60	.25
432	A127	7c lt blue	.60	.25
433	A127	8c dull red	1.15	.55
434	A127	12c deep blue	.75	.25
435	A127	17c violet	2.00	.80
436	A127	20c red brown	4.00	1.60
437	A127	24c yellow	4.00	1.75
438	A127	36c orange	5.75	2.40
439	A127	50c olive gray	6.25	3.00
440	A127	1p bister	15.00	6.25
		Nos. 430-440 (11)	40.70	17.35

Raising of the "Flag of the Race" and of the 441st anniv. of the sailing of Columbus from Palos, Spain, on his first voyage to America.

Sower — A128

Perf. 11½, 12¾ (#443)

1933, Aug. 28 **Unwmk.**

No.	Type	Description	Unused	Used
441	A128	3c blue green	.65	.25
442	A128	5c dull violet	1.00	.25
443	A128	7c lt blue	1.00	.25
444	A128	8c deep red	2.10	.50
445	A128	12c ultra	5.25	1.00
		Nos. 441-445 (5)	10.00	2.25

3rd Constituent National Assembly.

Juan Zorrilla de San Martin — A129

1933, Nov. 9 **Engr.** ***Perf. 12½***

446	A129	7c slate	.25	.25

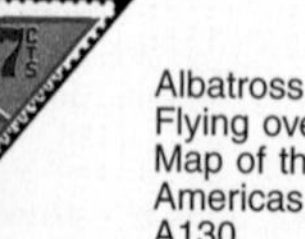

Albatross Flying over Map of the Americas A130

1933, Dec. 3 **Typo.** ***Perf. 11½***

447	A130	3c green, blk & brn	2.75	2.00
448	A130	7c turq bl, brn & blk	1.60	.80
449	A130	12c dk bl, gray & ver	2.40	1.60
450	A130	17c ver, gray & vio	5.00	2.75
451	A130	20c yellow, bl & grn	6.00	3.50
452	A130	36c red, blk & yel	7.75	5.50
		Nos. 447-452 (6)	25.50	16.15

7th Pan-American Conf., Montevideo. Issued in sheets of 6. Value $200. For overprints see Nos. C61-C62.

General Rivera — A131

1934, Feb. **Engr.** ***Perf. 12½***

453	A131	3c green	.25	.25

Stars Representing the Three Constitutions A132

1934, Mar. 23 **Typo.**

454	A132	3c yellow grn & grn	.60	.40
455	A132	7c org red & red	.60	.40
456	A132	12c ultra & blue	2.00	.80

Perf. 11½

457	A132	17c brown & rose	2.50	1.25
458	A132	20c yellow & gray	3.50	1.60
459	A132	36c dk vio & bl grn	3.50	1.60
460	A132	50c black & blue	7.00	3.25
461	A132	1p dk car & vio	16.00	6.75
		Nos. 454-461 (8)	35.70	16.05

First Year of Third Republic.

Artigas Type of 1928

Imprint: "Barreiro & Ramos S. A."

1934, Nov. 28 **Litho.**

462	A109	50c brown black	6.00	2.50

"Uruguay" and "Brazil" Holding Scales of Justice — A133

1935, May 30 **Unwmk.** ***Perf. 11***

463	A133	5m brown	.80	.40
464	A133	15m black	.40	.25
465	A133	3c green	.40	.25
466	A133	7c orange	.40	.25
467	A133	12c ultra	.80	.60
468	A133	50c brown	4.00	2.50
		Nos. 463-468 (6)	6.80	4.25

Visit of President Vargas of Brazil.

Florencio Sánchez — A134

1935, Nov. 7

469	A134	3c green	.25	.25
470	A134	7c brown	.25	.25
471	A134	12c blue	.55	.35
		Nos. 469-471 (3)	1.05	.85

Florencio Sanchez (1875-1910), author.

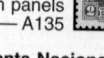

Artigas (6 dots in panels below portrait) — A135

Imprint: "Imprenta Nacional" measuring 7.5 mm at center

1936-44 ***Perf. 11, 12½***

474	A135	5m org brn ('37)	.25	.25
475	A135	5m lt brown ('39)	.25	.25
476	A135	1c lt violet ('37)	.25	.25
477	A135	2c brown ('37)	.25	.25
478	A135	2c green ('39)	.25	.25
479	A135	5c brt blue ('37)	.25	.25
480	A135	5c bluish grn ('39)	.40	.25
481	A135	12c dull blue ('38)	.40	.25
482	A135	20c fawn	1.40	.35
a.		Imprint 9mm, perf. 11	*40.00*	*10.00*
482A	A135	20c rose ('44)	1.00	.40
483	A135	50c brown black	3.00	.80
a.		Imprint 9mm, perf. 11	*250.00*	*50.00*

Size: 21½x28½mm

483A	A135	1p brown	8.50	3.00
483B	A135	2p blue	14.00	12.00
483C	A135	3p gray black	20.00	16.00
		Nos. 474-483C (14)	50.20	34.55

See Nos. 488, and 576. See type A109.

Power Dam on Rio Negro — A136

1937-38

484	A136	1c dull violet	.25	.25
485	A136	10c blue	.50	.25
486	A136	15c rose	1.25	.65
487	A136	1p choc ('38)	6.25	2.50
		Nos. 484-487 (4)	8.25	3.65

Imprint: "Imprenta Nacional" at right

1938

488	A135	1c bright violet	.40	.25

International Law Congress, 1889 — A137

1939, July 16 **Litho.** ***Perf. 12½***

489	A137	1c brown orange	.25	.25
490	A137	2c dull green	.25	.25
491	A137	5c rose ver	.25	.25
492	A137	12c dull blue	.65	.40
493	A137	50c lt violet	2.60	1.50
		Nos. 489-493 (5)	4.00	2.65

50th anniversary of the Montevideo Congress of International Law.

Artigas — A138

1939-43 **Litho.** **Unwmk.**

Size: 15¾x19mm

494	A138	5m dl brn org ('40)	.25	.25
495	A138	1c blue	.25	.25
496	A138	2c lt violet	.25	.25
497	A138	5c violet brn	.25	.25
498	A138	8c rose red	.25	.25
499	A138	10c green	.50	.25
500	A138	15c dull blue	1.25	.60

Size: 24x29½mm

501	A138	1p dull brn ('41)	2.50	1.00
502	A138	2p dl rose vio ('40)	7.00	3.00
503	A138	4p orange ('43)	9.25	4.00
504	A138	5p ver ('41)	14.00	6.00
		Nos. 494-504 (11)	35.75	16.10

See No. 578.

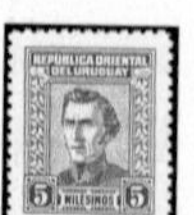

Artigas —A138a

Redrawn: Horizontal lines in portrait background

1940-44 **Size: 17x21mm**

505	A138a	5m brn org ('41)	.25	.25
506	A138a	1c lt blue	.25	.25
507	A138a	2c lt violet ('41)	.25	.25
508	A138a	5c violet brn	.25	.25
509	A138a	8c sal pink ('44)	.25	.25
510	A138a	10c green ('41)	.40	.25
511	A138a	50c olive bis ('42)	6.25	1.75
511A	A138a	50c yel grn ('44)	4.75	1.75
		Nos. 505-511A (8)	12.65	5.00

See Nos. 568-575, 577, 601, 632, 660-661. For surcharges see Nos. 523, 726.

Juan Manuel Blanes, Artist — A139

1941, Aug. 11 **Engr.** ***Perf. 12½***

512	A139	5m ocher	.25	.25
513	A139	1c henna brown	.25	.25
514	A139	2c green	.25	.25
515	A139	5c rose carmine	.60	.25
516	A139	12c deep blue	1.25	.60
517	A139	50c dark violet	4.75	3.25
		Nos. 512-517 (6)	7.35	4.85

Francisco Acuna de Figueroa — A140

1942, Mar. 18 **Unwmk.**

518	A140	1c henna brown	.25	.25
519	A140	2c deep green	.25	.25
520	A140	5c rose carmine	.25	.25
521	A140	12c deep blue	1.00	.40
522	A140	50c dark violet	3.25	2.50
		Nos. 518-522 (5)	5.00	3.65

Issued in honor of Francisco Acuna de Figueroa, author of the National anthem.

No. 506 Surcharged in Red

1943, Jan. 27

523	A138a	5m on 1c lt bl	.25	.25

Coat of Arms — A141

1943, Mar. 12 **Litho.**

524	A141	1c on 2c dl vio brn (R)	.25	.25
525	A141	2c on 2c dl vio brn (V)	.25	.25
a.		Inverted surcharge	20.00	20.00

Nos. 524-525 are unissued stamps surcharged. See Nos. 546-555, Q67, Q69, Q74-Q76.

Clio — A142

1943, Aug. 24

526	A142	5m lt violet	.25	.25
527	A142	1c lt ultra	.25	.25
528	A142	2c brt rose	.50	.25
529	A142	5c buff	.50	.25
		Nos. 526-529 (4)	1.50	1.00

100th anniversary of the Historic and Geographic Institute of Uruguay.

Swiss Colony Monument — A143

Overprinted and Surcharged in Various Colors

1944, May 18 ***Perf. 11, 12½***

530	A143	1c on 3c dull grn (R)	.25	.25
531	A143	5c on 7c brn red (B)	.25	.25
532	A143	10c on 12c dk bl (Br)	.65	.25
		Nos. 530-532 (3)	1.15	.75

Founding of the Swiss Colony, 50th anniv. Nos. 530-532 are unissued stamps surcharged.

YMCA Seal — A144

1944, Sept. 8 ***Perf. 12½***

533	A144	5c blue	.25	.25

100th anniv. of the YMCA.

Catalogue values for unused stamps in this section, from this point to the end of the section, are for Never Hinged items.

"La Educación del Pueblo" A145

José Pedro Varela A146

A147

Monument — A148

Perf. 11½

1945, June 13 **Litho.** **Unwmk.**

534	A145	5m brt green	.55	.25
535	A146	1c dp brown	.55	.25

Perf. 12½

536	A147	2c rose red	.55	.25
537	A148	5c blue	.55	.25
a.		Perf. 11½	.55	.25
		Nos. 534-537 (4)	2.20	1.00

José Pedro Varela, author, birth cent.

Santiago Vazquez A149

Silvestre Blanco A150

Eduardo Acevedo A151

Bruno Mauricio de Zabala A152

José Pedro Varela A153

José Ellauri A154

Gen. Luis de Larrobla — A155

Engraved (5m, 5c, 10c); Lithographed

1945-47 ***Perf. 10½, 11, 11½, 12½***
538 A149 5m purple ('46) .30 .25
539 A150 1c yel brn ('46) .30 .25
540 A151 2c brown vio .30 .25
541 A152 3c grn & dp grn ('47) .30 .25
542 A153 5c brt carmine .30 .25
543 A154 10c ultra .50 .25
544 A155 20c dp grn & choc ('47) 1.50 .50
Nos. 538-544 (7) 3.50 2.00

No. C86A Surcharged in Blue

1946, Jan. 9 ***Perf. 12½***
545 AP7 20c on 68c pale vio brn 1.50 .60

Inauguration of the Black River Power Dam. See No. C120.

Type A141 Overprinted

1946-51 Unwmk. Litho. ***Perf. 12½***
546 A141 5m orange ('49) .60 .25
a. Inverted overprint
547 A141 2c dl vio brn ('47) .60 .25
548 A141 3c green .60 .25
549 A141 5c ultra ('51) .60 .25
550 A141 10c orange brn .60 .25
551 A141 20c dk green 1.00 .25
552 A141 50c brown 5.50 1.00
553 A141 3p lilac rose 20.00 5.00
Nos. 546-553 (8) 29.50 7.50

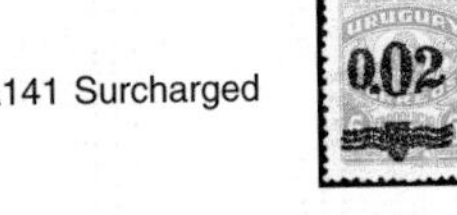
Type A141 Surcharged

1947-48
554 A141 2c on 5c ultra ('48) .55 .25
555 A141 3c on 5c ultra .55 .25

Statue of Ariel A158

Bust of José Enrique Rodó A159

Bas-relief A160

Bas-relief A161

Perf. 12½
1948, Jan. 30 Unwmk. Engr.
Center in Orange Brown
556 A158 1c grnsh gray .30 .25
557 A159 2c purple .30 .25
558 A160 3c green .30 .25
559 A161 5c red violet .30 .25
560 A160 10c dp orange .50 .25
561 A161 12c ultra .55 .25
562 A158 20c rose violet 1.10 .25
563 A159 50c dp carmine 3.50 .90
Nos. 556-563 (8) 6.85 2.65

Dedication of the Rodó monument.

View of the Port, Paysandú A162

Arms of Paysandú A163

1948, Oct. 9 **Litho.**
564 A162 3c blue green .30 .25
565 A163 7c ultra .85 .25

Exposition of Industry and Agriculture, Paysandú, October-November 1948.

Santa Lucia River Highway Bridge — A164

1948, Dec. 10
566 A164 10c dark blue 1.10 .25
567 A164 50c green 2.90 1.00

Redrawn Artigas Types of 1940, 1936, 1939

1948-51 Litho. ***Perf. 12½***
568 A138a 5m gray ('49) .30 .25
569 A138a 1c rose vio ('50) .30 .25
570 A138a 2c orange .30 .25
571 A138a 2c choc ('50) .30 .25
572 A138a 3c blue green .30 .25
572A A138a 7c violet blue .30 .25
573 A138a 8c rose car ('49) .30 .25
574 A138a 10c orange brn ('51) .30 .25
575 A138a 12c blue ('51) .30 .25
576 A135 20c violet 1.00 .25
577 A138a 20c rose pink ('51) 2.25 .25

Size: 18x21¾mm
578 A138 1p lilac rose ('51) 6.00 .25
Nos. 568-578 (12) 11.95 3.00

Nos. 571-572A also exist perf. 11.

Plowing — A165

Mounted Cattle Herder — A166

1949, Apr. 29 Unwmk. ***Perf. 12½***
579 A165 3c blue grn .30 .25
580 A166 7c blue .85 .25

4th Regional American Conf. of Labor, 1949.

Cannon, Rural and Urban Views — A167

1950, Oct. 11 **Litho.**
581 A167 1c lilac rose .30 .25
582 A167 3c green .35 .25
583 A167 7c deep blue 1.00 .25
Nos. 581-583 (3) 1.65 .75

200th anniv. of the founding of Cordón, a district of Montevideo.

Symbolical of Soccer Matches — A168

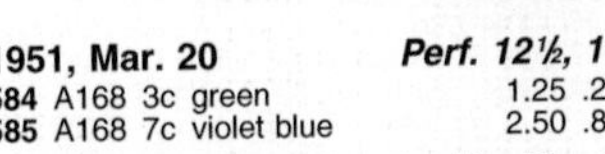

1951, Mar. 20 ***Perf. 12½, 11***
584 A168 3c green 1.25 .25
585 A168 7c violet blue 2.50 .80

4th World Soccer Championship, Rio de Janeiro.

Gen. José Artigas A169

Flight of the People A170

1c, 2c, 5c, Various equestrian portraits of Artigas. 7c, Dictating instructions. 8c, In congress. 10c, Artigas' flag. 14c, At the citadel. 20c, Arms of Artigas. 50c, In Paraguay. 1p, Bust.

Engraved and Photogravure
1952, Jan. 7 Unwmk. ***Perf. 13½***
586 A169 5m slate .30 .25
587 A169 1c bl & blk .30 .25
588 A169 2c pur & red brn .30 .25
589 A170 3c aqua & dk brn .30 .25
590 A169 5c red org & blk .30 .25
591 A170 7c ol & blk .40 .25
592 A170 8c car & blk .55 .25
593 A170 10c choc, brt ultra & crim .55 .25
594 A169 14c dp bl .55 .25
595 A169 20c org yel, dp ultra & car 1.20 .25
596 A169 50c org brn & blk 2.40 .40
597 A169 1p bl gray & cit 4.50 1.25
Nos. 586-597 (12) 11.65 4.15

Centenary (in 1950) of the death of Gen. José Artigas.

Plane and Stagecoach — A171

1952, Oct. 9 Photo. ***Perf. 13½x13***
598 A171 3c bl grn .35 .25
599 A171 7c blk brn .35 .25
600 A171 12c ultra .95 .25
Nos. 598-600 (3) 1.65 .75

75th anniv. (in 1949) of the UPU.

Redrawn Artigas Type of 1940-44
1953, Feb. 23 Litho. ***Perf. 11***
Size: 24x29½mm
601 A138a 2p fawn 20.00 8.50

Franklin D. Roosevelt — A172

1953, Apr. 9 Engr. ***Perf. 13½***
602 A172 3c green .30 .25
603 A172 7c ultra .35 .25
604 A172 12c blk brn 1.00 .25
Nos. 602-604 (3) 1.65 .75

5th Postal Cong. of the Americas & Spain.

Ceibo, Natl. Flower A173

Horse Breaking A174

Legislature Building A175

"Island of Seals" (Southern Sea Lions) A176

Designs: 2c, 10c, 5p, Ombu tree. 3c, 50c, Passion Flower. 7c, 3p, Montevideo fortress. 12c, 2p, Outer gate, Montevideo.

Perf. 13x13½, 13½x13, 12½x13, 13x12½
Photo. (5m, 3c, 20c, 50c); Engr.
1954, Jan. 14 **Unwmk.**
605 A173 5m multi .30 .25
606 A174 1c car & blk .30 .25
607 A174 2c brn & grn .30 .25
608 A173 3c multi .30 .25
609 A175 5c pur & red brn .30 .25
610 A173 7c brn & grn .30 .25
611 A176 8c car & ultra .55 .25
612 A174 10c org & grn .45 .25
613 A175 12c dp ultra & dk brn .30 .25
614 A174 14c rose lil & blk .30 .25
615 A173 20c grn, brn, gray & car 1.00 .25
616 A173 50c car & multi 2.50 .25
617 A175 1p car & red brn 3.00 1.00
618 A175 2p car & blk brn 5.00 1.60
619 A173 3p lil & grn 6.00 2.00
620 A176 4p dp brn & dp ultra 17.50 5.00
621 A174 5p vio bl & grn 13.00 4.00
Nos. 605-621 (17) 51.40 16.60

For surcharges see Nos. 637-639, 750, C299.

Fair Entrance — A177

1956, Jan. 19 Litho. ***Perf. 11***
622 A177 3c pale olive green .30 .25
623 A177 7c blue .30 .25
Nos. 622-623,C166-C168 (5) 4.05 1.60

First Exposition of National Products.

José Batlle y Ordonez, Birth Centenary — A178

Design: 7c, Full length portrait.

Perf. 13½
1956, Dec. 15 Wmk. 90 Photo.
624 A178 3c rose red .30 .25
625 A178 7c sepia .30 .25
Nos. 624-625,C169-C172 (6) 3.95 1.90

No. 624 Surcharged

No. 625 Surcharged

1957-58
626 A178 5c on 3c ('58) .55 .25
627 A178 10c on 7c .55 .25
a. Surcharge inverted 25.00 25.00

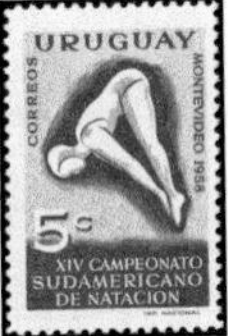
Diver — A179

Design: 10c, Swimmer at start, horiz.

Perf. 10½, 11½
1958, Feb. 15 Litho. Unwmk.
628 A179 5c brt bl grn .40 .25
629 A179 10c brt bl .85 .25

14th South American swimming meet, Montevideo.

Eduardo Acevedo — A180

1958, Mar. 19 ***Perf. 11½, 10½***

630 A180 5c lt ol grn & blk .55 .25
631 A180 10c ultra & blk .55 .25

Eduardo Acevedo (1856-1948), lawyer, legislator, minister of foreign affairs, birth cent.

Redrawn Artigas Type of 1940-44

1958, Sept. 25 **Litho.** ***Perf. 11***

632 A138a 5m blue .55 .25

Baygorria Hydroelectric Works — A181

1958, Oct. 30 **Unwmk.** ***Perf. 11***

633 A181 5c yel grn & blk .30 .25
634 A181 10c brn org & blk .30 .25
635 A181 1p bl gray & blk 1.50 .25
636 A181 2p rose & blk 3.00 .55
Nos. 633-636 (4) 5.10 1.30

Nos. 608, 610 and 605 Surcharged

Photogravure and Engraved

1958-59 ***Perf. 13x13½***

637 A173 5c on 3c multi ('59) .55 .25
638 A173 10c on 7c brn & grn .55 .25
639 A173 20c on 5m multi .55 .25
Nos. 637-639 (3) 1.65 .75

Gabriela Mistral — A182

Wmk. 327

1959, July 6 **Litho.** ***Perf. 11½***

640 A182 5c green .45 .25
641 A182 10c dark blue .55 .25
642 A182 20c red .70 .25
Nos. 640-642 (3) 1.70 .75

Gabriela Mistral, Chilean poet and educator.

Carlos Vaz Ferreira — A183

1959, Sept. 3 ***Perf. 11***

643 A183 5c blk & lt bl .45 .25
644 A183 10c blk & ocher .45 .25
645 A183 20c blk & ver .45 .25
646 A183 50c blk & vio .60 .25
647 A183 1p blk & grn .95 .25
Nos. 643-647 (5) 2.90 1.25

Ferreira (1872-1958), educator and author.

A184

Wmk. 332

1960, May 16 **Litho.** ***Perf. 12***

648 A184 3c red lil & blk .30 .25
649 A184 5c dp vio & blk .30 .25
650 A184 10c brt bl & blk .30 .25
651 A184 20c chocolate & blk .35 .25
652 A184 1p gray & blk .55 .25
653 A184 2p org & blk 1.30 .25
654 A184 3p olive grn & blk 2.10 .40
655 A184 4p yel brn & blk 2.50 .75
656 A184 5p brt red & blk 3.25 .75
Nos. 648-656 (9) 10.95 3.40

Dr. Martin C. Martinez (1859-1940), statesman.

A185

1960, June 6 **Wmk. 332** ***Perf. 12***

657 A185 10c Uprooted oak emblem .45 .25

Issued to publicize World Refugee Year, July 1, 1959-June 30, 1960. See No. C207.

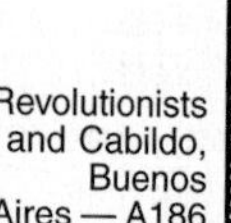

Revolutionists and Cabildo, Buenos Aires — A186

1960, Nov. 4 **Litho.** ***Perf. 12***

658 A186 5c bl & blk .45 .25
659 A186 10c bl & ocher .45 .25
Nos. 658-659,C208-C210 (5) 2.65 1.25

150th anniv. of the May Revolution of 1810.

Redrawn Artigas Type of 1940-44

1960-61 **Wmk. 332** ***Perf. 11***

660 A138a 2c gray .55 .25
661 A138a 50c brn ('61) .55 .25

Gen. Manuel Oribe (1796?-1857), Revolutionary Leader, Pres. of Uruguay (1835-38) — A187

1961, Mar. 4 **Litho.** ***Perf. 12***

671 A187 10c brt bl & blk .45 .25
672 A187 20c bis & blk .60 .25
673 A187 40c grn & blk .60 .25
Nos. 671-673 (3) 1.65 .75

Cavalry Charge — A188

1961, June 12 **Wmk. 332** ***Perf. 12***

674 A188 20c bl & blk .45 .25
675 A188 40c emer & blk .70 .25

150th anniversary of the revolution.

Welfare, Justice and Education — A189

1961, Aug. 14 **Wmk. 322** ***Perf. 12***

676 A189 2c bister & lilac .50 .25
677 A189 5c bister & orange .50 .25
678 A189 10c bister & scarlet .50 .25
679 A189 20c bister & yel grn .50 .25
680 A189 50c bister & light vio .50 .25
681 A189 1p bister & blue .50 .25
682 A189 2p bister & citron 1.40 .25
683 A189 3p bister & gray 2.00 .65
684 A189 4p bister & light bl 3.00 .80
685 A189 5p bister & chocolate 3.40 1.25
Nos. 676-685 (10) 12.80 4.45

Inter-American Economic and Social Conference of the Organization of American States, Punta del Este, August, 1961. See Nos. C233-C244.

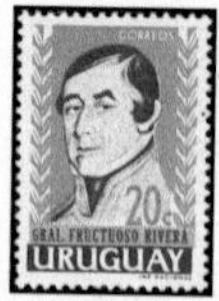

Gen. José Fructuoso Rivera — A190

Wmk. 332

1962, May 29 **Litho.** ***Perf. 12***

686 A190 10c brt red & blk .55 .25
687 A190 20c bis & blk .55 .25
688 A190 40c grn & blk .55 .25
Nos. 686-688 (3) 1.65 .75

Issued to honor Gen. José Fructuoso Rivera (1790-1854), first President of Uruguay.

Spade, Grain, Swiss "Scarf" and Hat — A191

1962, Aug. 1 **Wmk. 332** ***Perf. 12***

689 A191 10c bl, blk & car .50 .25
690 A191 20c lt grn, blk & car .50 .25
Nos. 689-690,C245-C246 (4) 2.30 1.10

Swiss Settlement in Uruguay, cent.

Bernardo Prudencio Berro — A192

1962, Oct. 22 **Litho.** ***Perf. 12***

691 A192 10c grnsh bl & blk .55 .25
692 A192 20c yel brn & blk .55 .25

Pres. Bernardo P. Berro (1803-1868).

Damaso Larrañaga A193

1963, Jan. 24 **Wmk. 332** ***Perf. 12***

693 A193 20c lt bl grn & dk brn .55 .25
694 A193 40c tan & dk brn .55 .25

Damaso Antonio Larranaga (1771-1848), teacher, writer and founder of National Library.

Rufous-bellied Thrush — A194

Birds: 50c, Rufous ovenbird. 1p, Chalk-browed mockingbird. 2p, Rufous-collared sparrow.

1963, Apr. 1 **Wmk. 332** ***Perf. 12***

695 A194 2c rose, brn & blk .30 .25
696 A194 50c lt brn & blk .75 .25
697 A194 1p tan, brn & blk 2.00 .25
698 A194 2p lt brn, blk & gray 3.75 .60
Nos. 695-698 (4) 6.80 1.35

Thin frame on No. 696, no frame on No. 698.

UPAE Emblem — A195

1963, May 31 **Litho.**

699 A195 20c ultra & blk .45 .25
Nos. 699,C252-C253 (3) 1.90 .75

50th anniv. of the founding of the Postal Union of the Americas and Spain, UPAE. For surcharge see No. C321.

Wheat Emblem — A196

1963, July 8 **Wmk. 332** ***Perf. 12***

700 A196 10c grn & yel .45 .25
701 A196 20c brn & yel .45 .25
Nos. 700-701,C254-C255 (4) 2.25 1.25

FAO "Freedom from Hunger" campaign.

Anchors — A197

1963, Aug. 16

702 A197 10c org & vio .40 .25
703 A197 20c dk red & gray .50 .25
Nos. 702-703,C256-C257 (4) 2.50 1.20

Voyage around the world by the Uruguayan sailing vessel "Alferez Campora," 1960-63.

Large Intestine, Congress Emblem — A198

1963, Dec. 9 **Litho.**

704 A198 10c lt grn, blk & dk car .50 .25
705 A198 20c org, yel, blk & dk car .60 .25

1st Uruguayan Proctology Cong., Montevideo, Dec. 9-15.

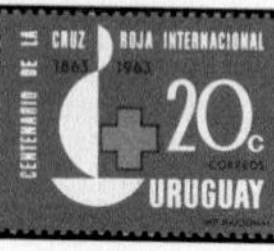

Red Cross Centenary Emblem — A199

Imprint: "Imp. Nacional"

1964, June 5 **Wmk. 332** ***Perf. 12***

706 A199 20c blue & red .50 .25
707 A199 40c gray & red .60 .25

Centenary of International Red Cross.

No. 706 exists with imprint missing. Value $4.

Luis Alberto de Herrera — A200

1964, July 22 **Litho.** **Unwmk.**

708 A200 20c dl grn, bl & blk .45 .25
709 A200 40c lt bl, bl & blk .45 .25
710 A200 80c yel org, bl & blk .45 .25
711 A200 1p lt vio, bl & blk .60 .25
712 A200 2p gray, bl & blk .90 .50
Nos. 708-712 (5) 2.85 1.50

Herrera (1873-1959), leader of Herrerista party and member of National Government Council.

Nile Gods Uniting Upper and Lower Egypt (Abu Simbel) — A201

1964, Oct. 30 Wmk. 332 *Perf. 12*
713 A201 20c multi .35 .25
Nos. 713,C266-C267 (3) 2.20 1.00

UNESCO world campaign to save historic monuments in Nubia. See No. C267a.

Pres. John F. Kennedy — A202

1965, Mar. 5 Wmk. 327 *Perf. 11½*
714 A202 20c gold, emer & blk .45 .25
a. Gold omitted
715 A202 40c gold, redsh brn & blk .50 .25
a. Gold omitted
Nos. 714-715,C269-C270 (4) 2.35 1.30

Tete Beche Pair of 1864, No. 21a — A203

1965, Mar. 19 Wmk. 332 *Perf. 12*
716 A203 40c black & green .55 .25

1st Rio de la Plata Stamp Show, sponsored jointly by the Argentine and Uruguayan philatelic associations, Montevideo, Mar. 19-28. See No. C271. For overprint see No. 736.

Benito Nardone — A204

40c, Benito Nardone before microphone.

1965, Mar. 25 Litho.
717 A204 20c blk & emer .55 .25
718 A204 40c blk & emer, vert. .60 .25

1st anniversary of the death of Benito Nardone, president of the Council of Government.

Artigas Quotation A205

40c, Artigas bust, quotation. 80c, José Artigas.

Perf. 12x11½
1965, May 17 Litho. Wmk. 327
719 A205 20c bl, yel & red .40 .25
720 A205 40c vio bl, cit & blk .40 .25
721 A205 80c brn, yel, red & bl .60 .25
Nos. 719-721,C273-C275 (6) 3.75 1.75

José Artigas (1764-1850), leader of the independence revolt against Spain.

Soccer — A206

Designs: 40c, Basketball. 80c, Bicycling. 1p, Woman swimmer.

1965, Aug. 3 Litho. Wmk. 327
722 A206 20c grn, org & blk .30 .25
723 A206 40c hn brn, cit & blk .30 .25
724 A206 80c gray, red & blk .30 .25
725 A206 1p bl, yel grn & blk .30 .25
Nos. 722-725,C276-C281 (10) 5.60 3.45

18th Olympic Games, Tokyo, 10/10-25/64.

No. 572A Surcharged in Red

1965 Unwmk. *Perf. 12½*
726 A138a 10c on 7c vio bl .55 .25

No. B5 Srchd.

1966, Jan. 25 Wmk. 327 *Perf. 11½*
727 SP2 4c on 5c + 10c grn & org .55 .25

Association of Uruguayan Architects, 50th anniv.

Winston Churchill — A207

Wmk. 332
1966, Apr. 29 Litho. *Perf. 12*
728 A207 40c car, dp ultra & brn .55 .25

Sir Winston Spencer Churchill, statesman and World War II leader. See No. C284.

Arms of Rio de Janeiro and Sugar Loaf Mountain — A208

1966, June 9 Litho. Wmk. 332
729 A208 40c emer & brn .55 .25

400th anniversary of the founding of Rio de Janeiro. See No. C285.

Army Engineer — A209

1966, June 17 Litho.
730 A209 20c blk, red, vio bl & yel .55 .25

50th anniversary of the Army Engineers Corps.

Daniel Fernandez Crespo — A210

Portraits: No. 732, Washington Beltran. No. 733, Luis Batlle Berres.

1966, Sept. 16 Wmk. 332 *Perf. 12*
731 A210 20c lt bl & blk .55 .25
732 A210 20c lt bl & dk brn .55 .25
733 A210 20c brick red & blk .55 .25
Nos. 731-733 (3) 1.65 .75

Issued to honor political leaders.

Old Printing Press — A211

1966, Oct. 14 Photo. *Perf. 12*
734 A211 20c tan, grnsh gray & dk brn .55 .25

50th anniversary of State Printing Office.

Fireman — A212

1966, Oct. 21 Litho.
735 A212 20c red & blk .75 .25

Issued to publicize fire prevention. Printed with alternating red and black labels inscribed: "Prevengase del fuego! Del pueblo y para el pueblo." Value, pair with tab $1.

No. 716 Overprinted in Red

1966, Nov. 4
736 A203 40c blk & grn .55 .25

2nd Rio de la Plata Stamp Show, Buenos Aires, Apr. 1966, and cent. of Uruguay's 1st surcharged issue. See No. C298.

General Leandro Gomez — A213

#738, Gen. Juan Antonio Lavalleja. #739, Aparicio Saravia, revolutionary, on horseback.

Wmk. 332
1966, Nov. 24 Litho. *Perf. 12*
737 A213 20c slate, blk & dp bl .55 .25
738 A213 20c red, blk & bl .55 .25
739 A213 20c blue & blk, horiz. .55 .25
Nos. 737-739 (3) 1.65 .75

Montevideo Planetarium A214

1967, Jan. 13 Wmk. 332 *Perf. 12*
740 A214 40c pink & blk .55 .25

10th anniv. of the Montevideo Municipal Planetarium. See No. C301.

Sunflower, Cow and Emblem — A215

1967, Jan. 13 Litho.
741 A215 40c dk brn & yel .55 .25

Young Farmers' Movement, 20th anniv.

Church of San Carlos — A216

1967, Apr. 17 Wmk. 332 *Perf. 12*
742 A216 40c lt bl, blk & dk red .65 .25

Bicentenary of San Carlos.

Eduardo Acevedo — A217

1967, Apr. 17
743 A217 20c grn & brn .50 .25
744 A217 40c org & grn .60 .25

Issued to honor Eduardo Acevedo, lawyer, legislator and Minister of Foreign Affairs.

Arms of Carmelo — A218

1967, Aug. 11 Litho. *Perf. 12*
745 A218 40c lt & dk bl & ocher .55 .25

Founding of Carmelo, 150th anniv.

José Enrique Rodó — A219

2p, Portrait of Rodó and sculpture, horiz.

1967, Oct. 6 Wmk. 332 *Perf. 12*
746 A219 1p gray, brn & blk .55 .25
747 A219 2p rose claret, blk & tan .55 .25

50th anniversary of the death of José Enrique Rodó, author.

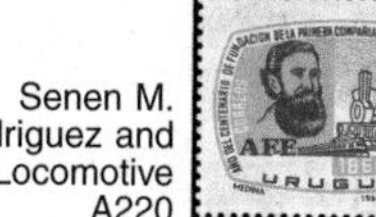

Senen M. Rodriguez and Locomotive A220

1967, Oct. 26 Litho. *Perf. 12*
748 A220 2p ocher & dk brn .65 .25

Centenary of the founding of the first national railroad company.

Child and Map of Americas — A221

1967, Nov. 10 Wmk. 332 *Perf. 12*
749 A221 1p vio & red .55 .25

Inter-American Children's Institute, 40th anniv.

No. 610 Surcharged in Red

Perf. 13x13½
1967, Nov. 10 Engr. Unwmk.
750 A173 1p on 7c brn & grn .55 .25

Cocoi Heron — A222

Birds: 1p, Great horned owl. 3p, Brown-headed gull, horiz. No. 754, White-faced tree duck, horiz. No. 754A, Black-tailed stilts. 5p, Wattled jacanas, horiz. 10p, Snowy egret, horiz.

1968-70 Wmk. 332 Litho. *Perf. 12*
751 A222 1p dl yel & brn 2.10 .40
752 A222 2p bl grn & blk 2.10 .40
753 A222 3p org, gray & blk ('69) 1.60 .35

754 A222 4p brn, tan & blk 3.50 .60
754A A222 4p ver & blk ('70) 1.60 .35
755 A222 5p lt red brn, blk & yel 4.00 .60
756 A222 10p lil & blk 7.25 .80
Nos. 751-756 (7) 22.15 3.50

Concord Bridge, Presidents of Uruguay, Brazil — A223

1968, Apr. 3
757 A223 6p brown .55 .25

Opening of Concord Bridge across the Uruguay River by Presidents Jorge Pacheco Areco of Uruguay and Arthur Costa e Silva of Brazil.

Soccer Player and Trophy — A224

1968, May 29 **Litho.**
758 A224 1p blk & yel .55 .25

Victory of the Penarol Athletic Club in the Intercontinental Soccer Championships of 1966.

St. John Bosco, Symbols of Education and Industry — A225

1968, July 31 **Wmk. 332** ***Perf. 12***
759 A225 2p brn & blk .55 .25

75th anniv. of the Don Bosco Workshops of the Salesian Brothers.

Sailors' Monument, Montevideo A226

Designs: 6p, Lighthouse and buoy, vert. 12p, Gunboat "Suarez" (1860).

1968, Nov. 12 **Litho.** ***Perf. 12***
760 A226 2p gray ol & blk .45 .25
761 A226 6p lt grn & blk .45 .25
762 A226 12p brt bl & blk .45 .25
Nos. 760-762,C340-C343 (7) 4.05 1.75

Sesquicentennial of National Navy.
For surcharge see No. Q101.

Oscar D. Gestido — A227

1968, Dec. 6 **Wmk. 332** ***Perf. 12***
763 A227 6p brn, dp car & bl .55 .25

First anniversary of the death of President Oscar D. Gestido.

Gearwheel, Grain and Two Heads — A228

1969, Mar. 17 **Litho.** ***Perf. 12***
764 A228 2p blk & ver .55 .25

25th anniversary of Labor University.

Bicyclists — A229

1969, Mar. 21 **Wmk. 332**
765 A229 6p dk bl, org & emer .50 .25

1968 World Bicycle Championships. See No. C347.

Gymnasts and Club Emblem — A230

1969, May 8 **Wmk. 332** ***Perf. 12***
766 A230 6p blk & ver .55 .25

75th anniversary of L'Avenir Athletic Club.

Baltasar Brum (1883-1933) — A231

Former presidents: No. 768, Tomas Berreta (1875-1947).

1969 **Litho.** ***Perf. 12***
767 A231 6p rose red & blk .55 .25
768 A231 6p car rose & blk .55 .25

Fair Emblem A232

1969, Aug. 15 **Wmk. 332** ***Perf. 12***
769 A232 2p multi .55 .25

Issued to publicize the 2nd Industrial World's Fair, Montevideo, 1970.

Diesel Locomotive — A233

Design: No. 771, Old steam locomotive and modern railroad cars.

1969, Sept. 19 **Litho.** **Wmk. 332**
770 6p car, blk & ultra .60 .25
771 6p car, blk & ultra .60 .25
e. A233 Pair, #770-771 1.30 1.30

Centenary of Uruguayan railroads. No. 771e has continuous design and label between pairs.
For surcharges see Nos. Q102-Q103.

Souvenir Sheet

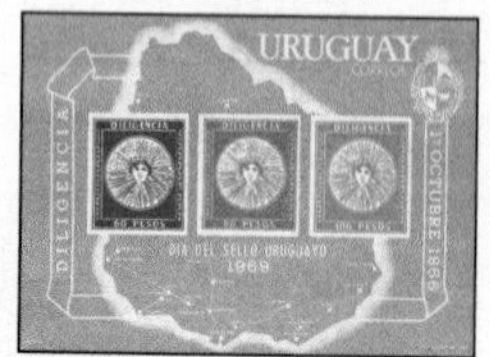

Diligencia Issue, 1856 — A233a

1969, Oct. 1 ***Imperf.***
771A A233a Sheet of 3 8.25 8.00
b. 60p blue 2.00 2.00
c. 80p green 2.60 2.60
d. 100p red 3.00 3.00

Stamp Day 1969. No. 771A contains stamps similar to No. 1-3, with denominations in pesos.

No. 771A was re-issued Apr. 15, 1972, with black overprint for 15th anniv. of 1st Lufthansa flight from Uruguay to Germany and the Munich Olympic Games. Value $30.

"Combat" and Sculptor Belloni A234

1969, Oct. 22 **Wmk. 332** ***Perf. 12***
772 A234 6p olive, slate grn & blk .65 .25

José L. Belloni (1882-), sculptor.

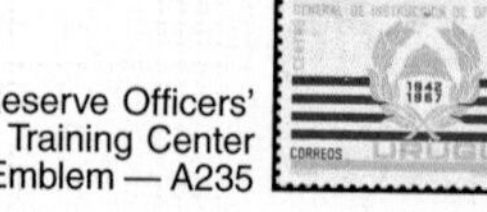

Reserve Officers' Training Center Emblem — A235

Design: 2p, Training Center emblem, and officer in uniform and as civilian.

1969, Nov. 5 **Litho.**
773 A235 1p yel & dk bl .55 .25
774 A235 2p dk brn & lt bl .55 .25

Reserve Officers' Training Center, 25th anniv.

Map of Americas and Sun — A236

1970, Apr. 20 **Wmk. 332** ***Perf. 12***
775 A236 10p dp bl & gold .65 .25

11th meeting of the governors of the Inter-American Development Bank, Punta del Este.

Stylized Pine — A237

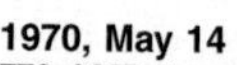

1970, May 14
776 A237 2p red, blk & brt grn .60 .25

2nd National Forestry and Wood Exhibition.

Artigas' Ancestral Home in Sauce — A238

1970, June 18 **Wmk. 332** ***Perf. 12***
777 A238 15p ver, ultra & blk .65 .25

Map of Uruguay, Sun and Sea — A239

1970, July 8 **Litho.**
778 A239 5p greenish blue .60 .25

Issued for tourist publicity.

EXPO '70 Emblem, Mt. Fuji and Uruguay Coat of Arms — A240

EXPO '70 Intl. Exhibition, Osaka, Japan, 3/15-9/13: No. 780, Geisha. No. 781, Sun Tower. No. 782, Youth pole.

1970, Aug. 5 **Wmk. 332** ***Perf. 12***
779 A240 25p grn, slate bl & yel .65 .30
780 A240 25p org, slate bl & grn .65 .30
781 A240 25p yel, slate bl & pur .65 .30
782 A240 25p pur, slate bl & org .65 .30
a. Block of 4, #779-782 2.90 2.90

Cobbled Street in Colonia del Sacramento — A241

1970, Oct. 21 **Litho.** ***Perf. 12***
783 A241 5p blk & multi .60 .25

290th anniv. of the founding of Colonia del Sacramento, the 1st European settlement in Uruguay.

Mother and Son by Edmundo Prati in Salto — A242

1970, Nov. 4 **Litho.**
784 A242 10p grn & blk .70 .30

Issued to honor mothers.

URUEXPO Emblem — A243

1970, Dec. 9 **Wmk. 332** ***Perf. 12***
785 A243 15p bl, brn org & vio .65 .40

URUEXPO '70, National Philatelic Exposition, Montevideo, Sept. 26-Oct. 4.

Children Holding Hands, and UNESCO Emblem A244

Children's Drawings: No. 786, Two girls holding hands, vert. No. 788, Boy sitting at school desk, vert. No. 789, Astronaut and monster.

1970, Dec. 29 **Litho.** ***Perf. 12½***
786 A244 10p multi .60 .35
787 A244 10p multi .60 .35
788 A244 10p dp car & multi .60 .35
789 A244 10p bl & multi .60 .35
a. Block of 4, #786-789 + 2 labels 2.60 2.60

International Education Year.

Alfonso Espinola (1845-1905), Physician, Professor and Philanthropist — A245

1971, Jan. 13 **Wmk. 332** ***Perf. 12***
790 A245 5p dp org & blk .60 .25

Exposition Poster — A246

1971 **Litho.** ***Perf. 12***
791 A246 15p multi .60 .25

Uruguay Philatelic Exposition, 1971, Montevideo, March 26-Apr. 19.

5c Coin of 1840, Obverse — A247

Design: #793, 1st coin of Uruguay, reverse.

1971, Apr. 16 Wmk. 332 *Perf. 12*
792 A247 25p bl, brn & blk .85 .60
793 A247 25p bl, brn & blk .85 .50
a. Pair, #792-793 2.00 2.00

Numismatists' Day.

Domingo Arena, Lawyer and Journalist — A248

1971, May 3 Wmk. 332 *Perf. 12*
794 A248 5p dk car .55 .25

National Anthem — A249

1971, May 19 Litho.
795 A249 15p bl, blk & yel .65 .40

José F. Arias, Physician — A250

1971, May 25 Wmk. 332 *Perf. 12*
796 A250 5p sepia .70 .25

Eduardo Fabini, Bar from "Campo" — A251

1971, June 2 Litho.
797 A251 5p dk car rose & blk .85 .30

Eduardo Fabini (1882-1950), composer, and 40th anniversary of first radio concert.

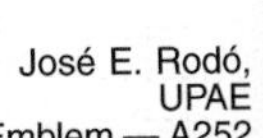

José E. Rodó, UPAE Emblem — A252

1971, July 15 Wmk. 332 *Perf. 12*
798 A252 15p ultra & blk .90 .40

José Enrique Rodó (1871-1917), writer, first Uruguayan delegate to Congress of the Postal Union of the Americas and Spain.

Water Cart and Faucet — A253

1971, July 17
799 A253 5p ultra & multi .60 .25

Centenary of Montevideo's drinking water system.

Sheep and Cloth — A254

Design: 15p, Sheep, cloth and bale of wool.

1971, Aug. 7
800 A254 5p grn & gray .50 .25
801 A254 15p dk bl, grnsh bl & gray .60 .25

Wool Promotion.

José Maria Elorza and Merilin Sheep — A255

1971, Aug. 10
802 A255 5p lt bl, grn & blk .55 .25

José Maria Elorza, developer of the Merilin sheep.

Criollo Horse — A256

1971, Aug. 11
803 A256 5p blk, gray bl & org 1.00 .25

Bull and Ram — A257

1971, Aug. 13
804 A257 20p red, grn, blk & gold .70 .35

Centenary of Rural Association of Uruguay; 19th International Cattle Breeding Exposition, and 66th National Cattle Championships at Prado, Aug. 1971.

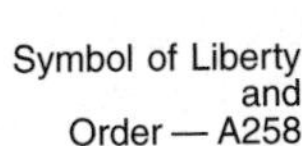

Symbol of Liberty and Order — A258

20p, Policemen, flag of Uruguay and emblem.

1971
805 A258 10p gray, blk & bl .55 .25
806 A258 20p dk bl, blk, lt bl & gold .60 .25

To honor policemen killed on duty. Issue dates: 10p, Sept. 9; 20p, Nov. 4.

10p Banknote of 1896 A259

Design: No. 808, Reverse of 10p note.

1971, Sept. 23
807 A259 25p dl grn, gold & blk .75 .50
808 A259 25p dl grn, gold & blk .75 .50
a. Pair, #807-808 + label 1.75 1.75

75th anniversary of Bank of the Republic.

Farmer and Arms of Durazno — A260

1971, Oct. 11
809 A260 20p gold, bl & blk .75 .25

Sesquicentennial of the founding of Durazno.

Emblem and Laurel A261

1971, Oct. 20
810 A261 10p vio bl, gold & red .75 .25

Winners of Liberator's Cup, American Soccer Champions, 1971.
For surcharge see No. 825.

Voter Casting Ballot — A262

Design: 20p, Citizens voting, horiz.

1971, Nov. 22 Wmk. 332 *Perf. 12*
811 A262 10p bl & blk .55 .25
812 A262 20p bl & blk .55 .25

Universal, secret and obligatory franchise.

Map of Uruguay on Globe — A263

1971, Dec. 23
813 A263 20p lt bl & vio brn .75 .25

7th Littoral Expo., Paysandu, 3/26-4/11.

Juan Lindolfo Cuestas — A264

No. 815, Julio Herrera y Obes. No. 816, Claudio Williman. No. 817, José Serrato. No. 818, Andres Martinez Truebá.

1971, Dec. 27
814 A264 10p shown .50 .25
815 A264 10p multicolored .50 .25
816 A264 10p multicolored .50 .25
817 A264 10p multicolored .50 .25
818 A264 10p multicolored .50 .25
a. Horiz. strip of 5, #814-818 2.75 2.75

Presidents of Uruguay.

Souvenir Sheet

Uruguay No. 4, Cathedral of Montevideo and Plaza de la Constitucion — A265

1972, Jan. 17 *Imperf.*
819 A265 120p brn, bl & dp rose 1.50 1.00

Stamp Day 1971 (release date delayed). See Nos. 834-835, 863.

Bartolomé Hidalgo — A266

1972, Feb. 28 *Perf. 12*
820 A266 5p lt brn, blk & red .80 .25

Bartolomé Hidalgo (1788-1822), Uruguayan-Argentine poet.

Missa Solemnis, by Beethoven — A267

1972, Apr. 20 Litho. Wmk. 332
822 A267 20p lil, emer & blk .65 .25

12th Choir Festival of Eastern Uruguay.

Dove and Wounded Bird — A268

1972, May 9
823 A268 10p ver & multi .65 .25

To honor Dionision Disz (age 9), who died saving his sister.

Columbus Arch, Colon — A269

1972, June 21
824 A269 20p red, bl & blk .65 .25

Centenary of Colon, now suburb of Montevideo.

No. 810 Surcharged in Silver

(Surcharge 69mm wide)

1972, June 30
825 A261 50p on 10p multi .75 .25

Winners of the 1971 Intl. Soccer Cup.

Tree Planting — A270

1972, Aug. 5 Wmk. 332 *Perf. 12*
826 A270 20p grn & blk .60 .25

Afforestation program.

"Collective Housing" — A271

1972, Sept. 30 Litho.
827 A271 10p dp bl & multi .60 .25

Publicity for collective housing plan.

Amethyst — A272

Uruguayan Gem Stones: 9p, Agate. 15p, Chalcedony.

1972, Oct. 7

828	A272	5p gray & multi	.70	.25
829	A272	9p gray bl & multi	.70	.25
830	A272	15p gray grn & multi	1.10	.25
		Nos. 828-830 (3)	2.50	.75

Uniform of 1830 — A273

Design: 20p, Lancer.

1972, Nov. 21 **Litho.**

831	A273	10p multi	.40	.25
832	A273	20p rose red & multi	.80	.25

Red Cross and Map of Uruguay — A274

1972, Dec. 11 **Wmk. 332** ***Perf. 12***

833	A274	30p multi	.65	.25

75th anniv. of the Uruguayan Red Cross.

Stamp Day Type of 1972

Souvenir Sheets

Designs: 200p, Coat of arms type of 1864 similar to Nos. 18, 20-21, but 60p, 60p and 80p. 220p, Similar to Nos. 22-23, but 100p and 120p.

1972, Dec. 20 ***Imperf.***

834	A265	200p multi	1.50	.60
835	A265	220p multi	2.00	.75

Stamp Day 1972. 1st printed cancellations, 200th anniv., #834; Decree establishing regular postal service, cent., #835.

Scales of Justice, Olive Branch — A275

1972, Dec. 27 **Wmk. 332** ***Perf. 12***

836	A275	10p gold, dk & lt bl	.55	.25

Civil Rights Law for Women, 25th anniv.

Gen. José Artigas — A276

1972-74 **Wmk. 332** **Litho.** ***Perf. 12***

837	A276	5p yel ('74)	.35	.25
838	A276	10p dk bis ('74)	.35	.25
839	A276	15p emer ('74)	.35	.25
840	A276	20p lilac ('73)	.35	.25
841	A276	30p lt bl ('73)	.35	.25
842	A276	40p dp org ('73)	.35	.25
843	A276	50p ver ('73)	.35	.25
844	A276	75p ap grn ('73)	.35	.25
845	A276	100p emerald	.35	.25
846	A276	150p choc ('73)	.35	.25
847	A276	200p dk bl ('73)	.65	.30
848	A276	250p pur ('73)	.75	.35
849	A276	500p gray ('73)	1.90	.60
849A	A276	1000p blue ('73)	3.75	1.25
		Nos. 837-849A (14)	10.55	5.00

For surcharges see Nos. 929-932.

Hand Holding Cup; Grain, Map of Americas — A277

1973, Jan. 9

850	A277	30p rose red, yel & blk	.55	.25

Intl. Institute for Agricultural Research, 39th anniv.

Elbio Fernandez and José P. Varela — A278

1973, Jan. 16

851	A278	10p dl grn, gold & blk	.55	.25

Society of Friends of Public Education, cent.

Map of Americas, "1972" and Columbus — A279

1973, Jan. 30

852	A279	50p purple	.55	.25

Tourist Year of the Americas 1972.

Carlos Maria Ramirez, Scales and Books — A280

No. 854, Justino Jimenez de Arechaga. No. 855, Juan Andres Ramirez. No. 856, Justino E. Jimenez de Arechaga.

1973, Feb. 15

853	A280	10p shown	.50	.25
854	A280	10p multicolored	.50	.25
855	A280	10p multicolored	.50	.25
856	A280	10p multicolored	.50	.25
a.		Horiz. strip, #853-856 + label	2.25	2.25

Professorship of Constitutional Rights, cent.

Provincial Map of Uruguay — A281

1973, Feb. 27 **Litho.** ***Perf. 12½x12***

857	A281	20p bl & multi	.65	.25

See No. 1167.

Francisco de los Santos — A282

1973, May 16 **Wmk. 332** ***Perf. 12***

858	A282	20p grn & blk	.60	.25

Soldiers' Day and Battle of Piedras. Santos was a courier who went through enemy lines.

No. C319 Surcharged in Black

Souvenir Sheet

1973, May 9 **Litho.** ***Imperf.***

859	AP57	100p on 5p multi	1.50	1.00

Founding of Cordoba in Argentina, 400th anniv.

Friar, Indians, Church — A283

1973, July 25 ***Perf. 12***

860	A283	20p lt ultra, pur & blk	.55	.25

Villa Santo Domingo Soriano, first Spanish settlement in Uruguay.

Symbolic Fish — A284

1973, Aug. 15

861	A284	100p bl & multi	.75	.25

First station of Oceanographic and Fishery Service, Montevideo.

A285

Sun over flower in Italian colors.

1973, Sept.

862	A285	100p multi	.55	.25

Italian Chamber of Commerce of Uruguay.

Stamp Day Type of 1972

Souvenir Sheet

Design: 240p, Thin numeral sun type of 1859 and street scene.

Wmk. 332

1973, Oct. 1 **Litho.** ***Imperf.***

863	A265	240p grn, org & blk	1.75	1.50

Stamp Day 1973.

Herrera — A286

1973, Nov. 12 ***Perf. 12***

866	A286	50p gray, brn & dk brn	.55	.25

Centenary of the birth of Luis Alberto de Herrera.

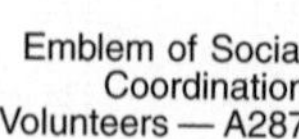

Emblem of Social Coordination Volunteers — A287

Wmk. 352

1973, Nov. 19 **Litho.** ***Perf. 12***

867	A287	50p bl & multi	.60	.25

Festival of Nations, Montevideo.

Arm with Arteries and Heart — A288

1973, Nov. 22

868	A288	50p blk, red & pink	.55	.25

3rd Cong. of the Pan-American Federation of Blood Donors, Montevideo, Nov. 23-25.

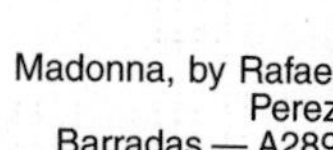

Madonna, by Rafael Perez Barradas — A289

1973, Dec. 10 **Litho.** **Wmk. 332**

869	A289	50p grn, gray & yel grn	.65	.25

Christmas 1973.

Nicolaus Copernicus — A290

1973, Dec. 26 **Litho.**

870	A290	50p grn & multi	.70	.25

500th anniversary of the birth of Nicolaus Copernicus (1473-1543), Polish astronomer.

Praying Hands and Andes — A291

75p, Statue of Christ on mountain, and flower.

1973, Dec. 26 **Litho.**

871	A291	50p blk, lt grn & ultra	.50	.25
872	A291	75p bl, blk & org	.60	.25

Survival and rescue of victims of airplane crash.

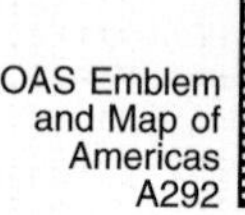

OAS Emblem and Map of Americas A292

1974, Jan. 14 **Wmk. 332** ***Perf. 12***

873	A292	250p gray & multi	1.10	.40

25th anniversary of the Organization of American States (OAS).

Scout Emblems and Flame — A293

1974, Jan. 21

874	A293	250p multi	1.10	.40

1st Intl. Boy Scout Games, Montevideo, 1974.

Hector Suppici Sedes and Car — A294

1974, Jan. 28 ***Perf. 12***

875	A294	50p sep, grn & blk	.95	.25

70th anniversary of the birth of Hector Suppici Sedes (1903-1948), automobile racer.

Three Gauchos — A295

1974, Mar. 20 Litho. Wmk. 332

876 A295 50p multi .85 .25

Centenary of the publication of "Los Tres Gauchos Orientales" by Antonio D. Lussich.

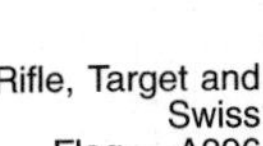

Rifle, Target and Swiss Flag — A296

1974, Apr. 2

877 A296 100p multi .70 .25

Centenary of the Swiss Rifle Association.

Map of Uruguay and Compass Rose — A297

1974, Apr. 23 Litho.

878 A297 50p multi .65 .25

Military Geographical Service.

Montevideo Stadium Tower — A298

Design: 75p, Soccer player, Games' emblem, horiz. 1000p, similar to 75p.

1974, May 7 Wmk. 332 *Perf. 12*

879 A298 50p multi .35 .25
880 A298 75p multi .35 .25
881 A298 1000p multi 23.00 9.50

World Cup Soccer Championship, Munich, June 13-July 7.

No. 881 had limited distribution. A souvenir sheet of one No. 881 was not valid for postage. Value, $50.

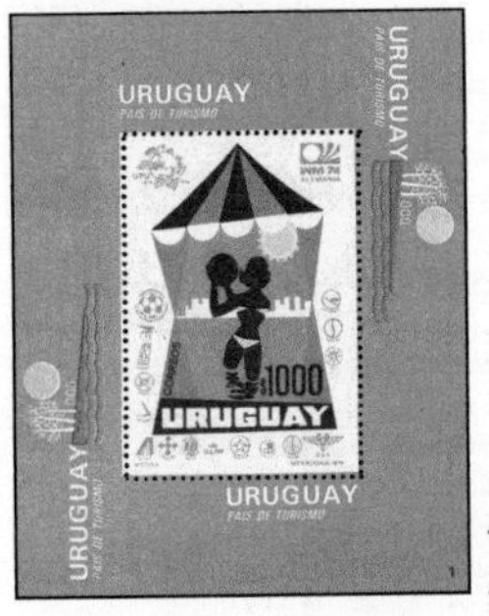

Tourism A299

Wmk. 332

1974, June 6 Litho. *Perf. 12*

882 A299 1000p multicolored 36.00 35.00

No. 882 had limited distribution.

Old and New School and Founders A300

1974, May 21

883 A300 75p black & bister .65 .25

Centenary of the Osimani-Llerena Technical School at Salto, founded by Gervasio Osimani and Miguel Llerena.

Gardel and Score — A301

Wmk. 332

1974, June 24 Litho. *Perf. 12*

884 A301 100p multi .75 .25

Carlos Gardel (1887-1935), singer and motion picture actor. See No. 1173.

Volleyball and Net — A302

1974, July 11 Wmk. 332 *Perf. 12*

885 A302 200p lil, yel & blk .75 .25

First anniversary of Women's Volleyball championships, Montevideo, 1973.

"Protect your Heart" — A303

1974, July 24 Litho.

886 A303 75p ol grn, yel & red .70 .25

Heart Foundation publicity.

Portrait and Statue — A304

1974, Aug. 5

887 A304 75p dk & lt bl .65 .25

Centenary (in 1973) of the founding of San José de Mayo by Eusebio Vidal.

A305

Artigas statue, Buenos Aires, flags of Uruguay and Argentina.

1974, Aug. 13 *Perf. 12½*

888 A305 75p multicolored .70 .25

Unveiling of Artigas monument, Buenos Aires.

A306

1974, Sept. 24 Wmk. 332 *Perf. 12*

889 A306 100p Radio tower and waves .65 .25

50th anniv. of Broadcasting in Uruguay.

URUEXPO 74 Emblem — A307

URUEXPO Emblem and Old Map of Montevideo Bay — A308

1974

890 A307 100p blk, dk bl & red .40 .25
891 A308 300p sepia, red & grn .95 .60

URUEXPO 74 Philatelic Exhibition, 10th anniversary of Philatelic Circle of Uruguay (100p) and 250th anniversary of fortification of Montevideo.

Issue dates: 100p, Oct. 1; 300p, Oct. 19.

Letters and UPU Emblem — A309

UPU Cent.: 200p, UPU emblem, letter, and globe.

1974, Oct. 9

892 A309 100p lt bl & multi .30 .25
893 A309 200p lil, blk & gold .40 .25
Nos. 892-893,C395-C396 (4) 3.50 2.50

A 1000p souvenir sheet was not valid for postage. Value $45.

Artigas Statue and Map of Lavalleja — A310

1974, Oct. 17 *Perf. 12*

894 A310 100p ultra & multi .70 .25

Unveiling of Artigas statue in Minas, Lavalleja.

Ship in Dry Dock, Arsenal's Emblem — A312

1974, Nov. 15 Litho. Wmk. 332

896 A312 200p multi .70 .30

Centenary of Naval Arsenal, Montevideo.

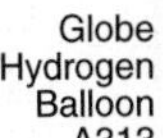

Globe Hydrogen Balloon A313

No. 898, Farman biplane. No. 899, Castaibert monoplane. No. 900, Bleriot monoplane. No. 901, Military and civilian pilots' emblems. No. 902, Nieuport biplane. No. 903, Breguet-Bidon fighter. No. 904, Caproni bomber.

1974, Nov. 20

897 A313 100p shown .75 .35
898 A313 100p multicolored .75 .35
899 A313 100p multicolored .75 .35
900 A313 100p multicolored .75 .35
a. Strip of 4, #897-900 3.25 3.25
901 A313 150p multicolored .75 .35
902 A313 150p multicolored .75 .35
903 A313 150p multicolored .75 .35
904 A313 150p multicolored .75 .35
a. Strip of 4, #901-904 3.25 3.25
Nos. 897-904 (8) 6.00 2.80

Aviation pioneers.

Sugar Loaf Mountain and Summit Cross A314

1974, Nov. 30

905 A314 150p multicolored .70 .25

Cent. of the founding of Sugar Loaf City.

Adoration of the Kings — A315

1974 *Perf. 12*

906 A315 100p shown .50 .25
907 A315 150p Three Kings .50 .25
Nos. 906-907,C400 (3) 1.70 .75

Christmas 1974. See No. C401. Issue dates: 100p, Dec. 17; 150p, Dec. 19.

Nike, Fireworks, Rowers and Club Emblem — A316

1975, Jan. 27 Litho. Wmk. 332

908 A316 150p gray & multi .45 .25

Centenary of Montevideo Rowing Club.

Treaty Signing, by José Zorilla de San Martin A317

1975, Feb. 12 *Perf. 12*

909 A317 100p multi .95 .25

Commercial Treaty between Great Britain and Uruguay, 1817.

Rose — A318

1975, Mar. 18 Litho. Wmk. 332
910 A318 150p multicolored 1.00 .40

Bicentenary of city of Rosario.

"The Oath of the 33," by Juan M. Blanes A319

1975, Apr. 16 ***Perf. 12***
911 A319 150p gold & multi .70 .25

Sesquicentennial of liberation movement.

Ship, Columbus and Ancient Map — A320

1975, Oct. 9 Litho. Wmk. 332
912 A320 1p gray & multi 1.60 .80

Hispanic Stamp Day.

Leonardo Olivera and Santa Teresa Fort — A321

Artigas as Young and Old Man — A322

1975 Litho. Wmk. 332 ***Perf. 12***
913 A321 10c org & multi .50 .25
914 A322 50c vio bl & multi 1.00 .40

Sesquicentennial of the capture of Fort Santa Teresa (10c) and of Uruguay's declaration of independence (50c).
Issue dates: 10c, Oct. 20; 50c, Oct. 17.

Battle of Rincon, by Diogenes Hequet — A323

No. 916, Artigas' Home, Ibiray, Paraguay. 25c, Battle of Sarandi, by J. Manuel Blanes.

1975 Litho.
915 A323 15c gold & blk .50 .25
916 A323 15c gold & multi .50 .25
917 A323 25c gold & multi .85 .30
Nos. 915-917 (3) 1.85 .80

Uruguayan independence. Nos. 915 and 917, 150th anniversary of Battles of Rincon and Sarandi. No. 916, 50th anniversary of school at Artigas mansion.
Issued: #915, 10/23; #916, 11/18; #917, 11/28.

"En Familia," by Sanchez — A324

Florencio Sanchez — A325

Plays by Sanchez: #919, Barranca Abajo. #920, M'Hijo el Doctor. #921, Canillita.

1975, Oct. 31 Wmk. 332 ***Perf. 12***
918 A324 20c gray, red & blk .55 .25
919 A324 20c bl, grn & blk .55 .25
920 A324 20c red, bl & blk .55 .25
921 A324 20c grn, gray & blk .55 .25
922 A325 20c multi .55 .25
a. Block of 5 stamps + 4 labels 4.00 4.00

Florencio Sanchez (1875-1910), dramatist, birth centenary. Nos. 918-922 printed se-tenant in sheets of 30 stamps and 20 labels.

Maria Eugenia Vaz Ferreira — A326

Design: No. 924, Julio Herrera y Reissig.

1975
923 A326 15c yel, blk & brn .60 .25
924 A326 15c org, blk & maroon .60 .25

Maria Eugenia Vaz Ferreira (1875-1924), poetess, and Julio Herrera y Reissig (1875-1910), poet, birth anniversaries.
Issue dates: #923, Dec. 9; #924, Dec. 29.

A327

Virgin and Child — A328

Fireworks A329

1975
925 A327 20c bl & multi .65 .40
926 A328 30c blk & multi 1.25 .60
927 A329 60c multi 1.60 .75
Nos. 925-927 (3) 3.50 1.75

Christmas 1975.
Issued: 20c, 12/16; 30c, 12/15; 60c, 12/11.

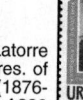

Col. Lorenzo Latorre (1840-1916), Pres. of Uruguay (1876-80) — A330

1975, Dec. 30 ***Perf. 12***
928 A330 15c multicolored .60 .25

Nos. 840, 842-843, 849A Surcharged

1975
929 A276 10c on 20p lilac .40 .25
930 A276 15c on 40p orange .40 .25
931 A276 50c on 50p ver .70 .45
932 A276 1p on 1000p blue 1.20 .95
Nos. 929-932 (4) 2.70 1.90

There are two surcharge types for Nos. 929 and 930. Values are the same.

Ariel, Stars, Book and Youths — A331

1976, Jan. 12 Litho. Wmk. 332
933 A331 15c grn & multi .60 .25

75th anniversary of publication of "Ariel," by Jose Enrique Rodo (1872-1917), writer.

Water Sports — A332

1976, Mar. 12 Litho. Wmk. 332
934 A332 30c multicolored .70 .25

23rd South American Swimming, Diving and Water Polo Championships.

Telephone — A333

1976, Apr. 9 ***Perf. 12***
935 A333 83c multicolored .85 .30

Centenary of first telephone call by Alexander Graham Bell, Mar. 10, 1876.

"Plus Ultra" and Columbus' Ships — A334

Wmk. 332
1976, May 10 Litho. ***Perf. 12***
936 A334 63c gray & multi .75 .30

Flight of Dornier "Plus Ultra" from Spain to South America, 50th anniversary.

A335

Dornier "Wal" and Boeing 727, hourglass.

1976, May 24
937 A335 83c gray & multi .75 .30

Lufthansa German Airline, 50th anniv.

A336

Designs: 10c, Olympics. 15c, Telephone, cent. 25c, UPU, cent., UN #2. 50c, World Cup Soccer Championships, Argentina, 1978.

1976, June 3 ***Perf. 11½***
938 A336 10c shown *2.00 1.00*
939 A336 15c multicolored *2.00 1.00*
940 A336 25c multicolored *2.00 1.00*
941 A336 50c multicolored *2.00 1.00*
Nos. 938-941 (4) 8.00 4.00

Nos. 938-941 had limited distribution.
A souvenir sheet containing one each, Nos. 938-941, was not valid for postage. Value $45.

Louis Braille — A340

1976, June 7
942 A340 60c blk & brn 1.25 .40

Sesquicentennial of the invention of the Braille system of writing for the blind by Louis Braille (1809-1852).

Signing of US Declaration of Independence A341

1976, June 21
943 A341 1.50p multicolored 2.75 2.00

American Bicentennial.

The Candombe, by P. Figari — A342

Wmk. 332
1976, July 29 Litho. ***Perf. 12***
944 A342 30c ultra & multi .70 .25

Abolition of slavery, sesquicentennial.

Gen. Fructuoso Rivera Statue — A343

1976, Aug. 2
945 A343 5p on 10p multi 4.25 2.00

No. 945 was not issued without surcharge.

General Accounting Office — A344

Wmk. 332
1976, Aug. 24 Litho. ***Perf. 12***
946 A344 30c bl, blk & brn .60 .25

National General Accounting Office, sesquicentennial.

Old Pump, Emblem and Flame — A345

1976, Sept. 6

947 A345 20c red & blk 1.10 .25

First official fire fighting service, centenary.

Southern Lapwing A346

Mburucuya Flower A347

Spearhead A348

Figurine A349

La Yerra, by J. M. Blanes A350

The Gaucho, by Blanes A351

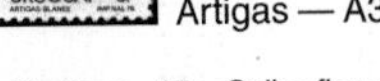

Artigas — A352

Designs: 15c, Ceibo flower.

1976-79 Litho. Wmk. 332 *Perf. 12*

948	A346	1c	violet	.30	.25
949	A347	5c	lt grn	.30	.25
950	A347	15c	car rose	.30	.25
951	A348	20c	gray	.30	.25
952	A349	30c	gray blue	.30	.25
953	A352	45c	brt bl ('79)	.30	.25
954	A350	50c	grnsh bl ('77)	.30	.25
955	A351	1p	dk brn ('77)	.70	.25
956	A352	1p	brt yel ('79)	.30	.25
957	A352	1.75p	bl grn ('79)	.55	.35
958	A352	1.95p	gray ('79)	.55	.35
959	A352	2p	dl grn ('77)	1.50	.45
960	A352	2p	lil rose ('79)	.60	.40
961	A352	2.65p	vio ('79)	.70	.45
962	A352	5p	dk bl	4.75	2.25
963	A352	10p	brn ('77)	9.00	2.25
			Nos. 948-963 (16)	20.75	8.75

"Diligencia" Uruguay No. 1 — A353

Wmk. 332

1976, Sept. 26 Litho. *Perf. 12*

964 A353 30c bister, red & blue .70 .25

Philatelic Club of Uruguay, 50th anniv.

Games' Emblem — A354

1976, Oct. 26 Litho. *Perf. 12*

965 A354 83c gray & multi 1.25 .50

5th World University Soccer Championships.

World Cup Soccer Championships, Argentina A355

Anniversaries and Events: 30c, 1976 Summer Olympics, Montreal. 50c, Viking spacecraft. 80c, Nobel prizes, 75th anniv.

1976, Nov. 12 *Perf. 12*

966	A355	10c	multicolored	2.00	1.25
967	A355	30c	multicolored	2.00	1.25
968	A355	50c	multicolored	2.00	1.25
969	A355	80c	multicolored	2.00	1.25
			Nos. 966-969 (4)	8.00	5.00

Nos. 966-969 had limited distribution. See Nos. C424-C425.

Eye and Spectrum A356

1976, Nov. 24

970 A356 20c blk & multi .75 .25

Foresight prevents blindness.

Map of Montevideo, 1748 — A357

45c, Montevideo Harbor, 1842. 70c, First settlers, 1726. 80c, Coin with Montevideo arms, vert. 1.15p, Montevideo's first coat of arms, vert.

Wmk. 332

1976, Dec. 30 Litho. *Perf. 12*

971	A357	30c	multi	.35	.25
972	A357	45c	multi	.35	.25
973	A357	70c	multi	.60	.30
974	A357	80c	multi	1.00	.40
975	A357	1.15p	multi	1.50	.55
			Nos. 971-975 (5)	3.80	1.75

Founding of Montevideo, 250th anniversary.

Symbolic of Flight — A358

1977, May 7 Litho. *Perf. 12*

976 A358 80c multicolored 1.00 .50

50th anniversary of Varig airlines.

Artigas Mausoleum A359

1977, June 17 Litho. *Perf. 12*

977 A359 45c multicolored .75 .30

A360

1977, July 5 Wmk. 332

978 A360 45c Map of Uruguay, arch .70 .30

Centenary of Salesian Brothers' educational system in Uruguay.

A361

Anniversaries and events: 20c, Werner Heisenberg, Nobel Prize for Physics. 30c, World Cup Soccer Championships, Uruguay Nos. 282, 390. 50c, Lindbergh's trans-Atlantic flight, 50th anniv. 1p, Rubens 400th birth anniv.

1977, July 21

979	A361	20c	shown	1.25	.90
980	A361	30c	multicolored	1.25	.90
981	A361	50c	multicolored	1.25	.90
982	A361	1p	multicolored	1.25	.90
a.			Strip, 2 ea #979-982 + 2 labels	10.00	8.00
			Nos. 979-982 (4)	5.00	3.60

Nos. 979-982 had limited distribution.

A souvenir sheet containing Nos. 979-982, imperf., was not valid for postage. It sold for 8p. Value, $35. See Nos. C426-C427.

Children — A362

1977, Aug. 10 Litho. *Perf. 12*

983 A362 45c multi .75 .30

Interamerican Children's Inst., 50th anniv.

"El Sol de Mayo" — A363

1977, Oct. 1 Litho. *Perf. 12*

984 A363 45c multi .75 .50

Stamp Day 1977.

Windmills — A364

1977, Sept. 29 Wmk. 332

985 A364 70c yel, car & blk .75 .30

Spanish Heritage Day.

Souvenir Sheet

View of Sans (Barcelona), by Barradas — A365

1977, Oct. 7 Litho. *Perf. 12*

986 A365 Sheet of 2 5.50 5.00

a.-b. 5p, single stamp 2.25 2.25

ESPAMER '77 Philatelic Exhibition, Barcelona, Oct. 7-13.

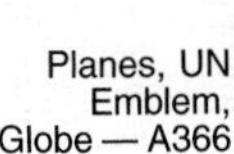

Planes, UN Emblem, Globe — A366

1977, Oct. 17

987 A366 45c multi .70 .25

30th anniv. of Civil Aviation Organization.

Holy Family — A367

Santa Claus A368

1977, Dec. 1 Wmk. 332

988 A367 45c multi .55 .25

989 A368 70c blk, yel & red .55 .25

Christmas 1977.

Map of Rio Negro Province — A369

1977, Dec. 16

990 A369 45c multi .65 .25

Rio Negro Dam; development of agriculture, livestock and beekeeping. See Nos. 1021-1033.

Mail Collection — A370

No. 992, Mail truck. No. 993, Post office counter. No. 994, Postal boxes. No. 995, Mail sorting. No. 996, Pigeonhole sorting. No. 997, Route sorting (seated carriers). No. 998, Home delivery. No. 999, Special delivery (motorcyclists). No. 1000, Airport counter.

1977, Dec. 21

991	A370	50c	shown	.60	.25
992	A370	50c	multicolored	.60	.25
993	A370	50c	multicolored	.60	.25
994	A370	50c	multicolored	.60	.25
995	A370	50c	multicolored	.60	.25
996	A370	50c	multicolored	.60	.25
997	A370	50c	multicolored	.60	.25
998	A370	50c	multicolored	.60	.25
999	A370	50c	multicolored	.60	.25
1000	A370	50c	multicolored	.60	.25
a.			Strip of 10, #991-1000	10.00	7.50

Uruguayan postal service, 150th anniv.

Edison's Phonograph, 1877 — A371

1977, Dec. 30

1001 A371 50c vio brn & yel .65 .25

Centenary of invention of the phonograph.

"R", Rainbow and Emblem — A372

1977, Dec. 30 **Wmk. 332**

1002 A372 50c multi .65 .25

World Rheumatism Year.

Emblem and Diploma — A373

1978, Mar. 27 **Litho.** ***Perf. 12***

1003 A373 50c multi .65 .25

50th anniversary of Military College.

Erhard Schon by Albrecht Durer (1471-1528) A374

Painting: 50c, Self-Portrait by Peter Paul Rubens (1577-1640).

1978, June 13 ***Perf. 12½***

1004 A374 25c blk & brn *1.40 1.25*
1005 A374 50c brn & blk *2.50 2.25*

Nos. 1004-1005 had limited distribution. See Nos. C430-C432.

Map and Arms of Artigas Department A375

Wmk. 332

1978, June 16 **Litho.** ***Perf. 12***

1006 A375 45c multi .70 .25

Souvenir Sheet

Anniversaries — A376

Designs: 2p, Papilio thoas. No. 1007b, "100." No. 1007c, Argentina '78 emblem and globes. 5p, Model T Ford.

Wmk. 332

1978, Aug. 24 **Litho.** ***Perf. 12***

1007 A376 Sheet of 4 31.00 25.00
a. 2p multi 4.00 3.25
b. 4p multi 8.00 6.50
c. 4p multi 8.00 6.50
d. 5p multi 10.00 8.50

75th anniv. of 1st powered flight; URUEXPO '78 Phil. Exhib.; Parva Domus social club, cent.; 11th World Cup Soccer Championship, Argentina, June 1-25; Ford motor cars, 75th anniv.

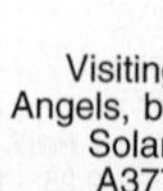

Visiting Angels, by Solari A377

Designs (Details from No. 1008b): No. 1008a, Second angel. No. 1008c, Third angel.

1978, Sept. 13 **Unwmk.**

1008 Strip of 3 2.50 2.00
a. A377 1.50p, 19x30mm .50 .40
b. A377 1.50p, 38x30mm .50 .40
c. A377 1.50p, 19x30mm .50 .40

Solari, Uruguayan painter.

Bernardo O'Higgins A378

#1010, José de San Martin and monument.

1978 **Wmk. 332**

1009 A378 1p multi .55 .25
1010 A378 1p multi .55 .25

Benardo O'Higgins (1778-1842 and José de San Martin (1778-1850), South American liberators.

Issued: #1009, Sept. 13; #1010, Oct. 10.

Telephone Dials — A379

1978, Sept. 25

1011 A379 50c multi .65 .25

Automation of telephone service.

Symbolic Stamps A380

Iberian Tile Pattern A381

1978, Oct. 31

1012 A380 50c multi .55 .25
1013 A381 1p multi .55 .25

Stamp Day (50c) and Spanish heritage (1p).

Boeing 727 — A382

1978, Nov. 27

1014 A382 50c multi .85 .25

Inauguration of Boeing 727 flights by PLUNA Uruguayan airlines, Nov. 1978.

Angel Blowing Horn — A383

1978, Dec. 7

1015 A383 50c multi .50 .25
1016 A383 1p multi .75 .25

Christmas 1978.

Flag Flying on Plaza of the Nation — A384

1978, Dec. 15 ***Perf. 12½***

1017 A384 1p multicolored .65 .25

A385

Wmk. 332

1978, Dec. 27 **Litho.** ***Perf. 12***

1018 A385 1p blk, red & yel .55 .25

Horacio Quiroga (1868-1928), short story writer.

Arch, Olympic Rings, Lake Placid and Moscow Emblems A386

7p, Olympic Rings, Lake Placid '80 emblem.

1979, Apr. 28 **Litho.** ***Perf. 12***

1019 A386 5p multi 2.50 1.20
1020 A386 7p multi 3.25 1.20

81st Session of Olympic Organizing Committee, Apr. 3-8 (5p), and 13th Winter Olympic Games, Lake Placid, NY, Feb. 12-24.

Souvenir Sheets

1021 Sheet of 4 *36.00 35.00*
a. A386 3p similar to #1019
b. A386 5p Olympic rings
c. A386 7p Rider looking back
d. A386 10p Rider facing forward

1022 Sheet of 4 *36.00 35.00*
a. A386 3p similar to #1020
b. A386 5p Uruguay '79
c. A386 7p World Chess Olympics '78
d. A386 10p Sir Rowland Hill, Great Britain stamp

No. 1022d shows Great Britain No. 836, but with 11p denomination. No. 1021c-1021d have continuous design.

Nos. 1021-1022 had limited distribution. Except for No. 1022d, singles were sold for postal use in 1980. Nos. 1021-1022 exist imperf. Same values.

Map and Arms of Paysandu A387

Map and Arms of Maldonado A388

1979-81

1023 A387 45c shown .60 .40
1024 A387 45c Salto .60 .40
1025 A388 45c shown .60 .40
1026 A387 45c Cerro Largo .60 .40
1027 A387 50c Treinta y Tres .60 .40
1028 A387 50c Durazno ('80) .60 .40
1029 A388 2p Rocha ('81) .60 .40
1030 A388 2p Flores .60 .40
Nos. 1023-1030 (8) 4.80 3.20

See No. 990.

Sapper with Pickax, 1837 — A389

Army Day: No. 1039, Artillery man with cannon, 1830.

1979, May 18 **Litho.** ***Perf. 12***

1038 A389 5p multi 1.75 1.00
1039 A389 5p multi 1.75 1.00

Madonna and Child by Durer — A390

Anniversaries and events: 80c, World Cup Soccer Championships, Spain. 1.30p, Sir Rowland Hill, Greece No. 117.

1979, June 18 ***Perf. 12***

1040 A390 70c brn & gray 8.75 4.75
1041 A390 80c multicolored 6.75 4.00
1042 A390 1.30p multicolored 6.75 4.00
Nos. 1040-1042 (3) 22.25 12.75

Nos. 1040-1042 had limited distribution. Issued in sheets of 24 containing 6 blocks of 4 with margin around. See #C437-C438.

Salto Dam — A391

1979, June 19

1043 A391 2p multi 1.00 .30

Crandon Institute Emblem, Grain — A392

1979, July 19

1044 A392 1p vio bl & bl .55 .25

Crandon Institute (private Methodist school), centenary.

IYC Emblem, Smiling Kites A393

Cinderella A394

1979

1045 A393 2p multi .75 .25
1046 A394 2p multi .75 .25

International Year of the Child. Issue dates: No. 1045, July 23; No. 1046, Aug. 29.

Uruguay Coat of Arms 150th Anniversary — A395

1979, Sept. 6

1047 A395 8p multi 3.00 1.40

Virgin and Child — A396

Wmk. 332

1979, Nov. 19 **Litho.** ***Perf. 12***

1048 A396 10p multi 2.50 1.60

Christmas 1979; Intl. Year of the Child.

Symbols, by Torres-Garcia — A397

1979, Nov. 12
1049 A397 10p yel & blk 3.25 1.60

Joaquín Torres-Garcia (1874-1948), painter.

UPU and Brazilian Postal Emblems A398

1979, Oct. 11
1050 A398 5p multi 1.50 .80

18th UPU Congress, Rio, Sept.-Oct.

Dish Antenna and Sun — A400

Perf. 12x11½
1979, Nov. 26 Litho. Wmk. 332
1052 A400 10p multi 3.25 1.25

Telecom '79, 3rd World Telecommunications Exhibition, Geneva, Sept. 20-26.

Spanish Heritage Day — A401

1979, Dec. 3 ***Perf. 12***
1053 A401 10p multi 2.25 1.50

Silver Coin Centenary A402

Designs: Obverse and reverse of coins in denominations matching stamps.

1979, Dec. 26

1054	A402	10c multi	.45	.25
1055	A402	20c multi	.45	.25
1056	A402	50c multi	.45	.25
1057	A402	1p multi	.85	.25
		Nos. 1054-1057 (4)	2.20	1.00

Souvenir Sheet

A403

1980, Jan. 10

1058	A403 Sheet of 4		4.50	3.50
a.	1p Police emblem		.40	.30
b.	2p Security Agent		.65	.50
c.	3p Policeman, 1843		.95	.75
d.	4p Cadet, 1979		1.25	1.00

Police force sesquicentennial.

Light Bulb, Thomas Edison A404

1980, Jan. 18
1059 A404 2p multi .90 .25

Centenary of electric light (1979).

Bass and Singer — A405

1980, Jan. 30

1060	Sheet of 4	4.50	3.00
a.	A405 2p Radio waves	.95	.65
b.	A405 2p shown	.95	.65
c.	A405 2p Ballerina	.95	.65
d.	A405 2p Television waves	.95	.65

Performing Arts Society, 50th anniversary.

Stamp Day — A406

1980, Feb.
1061 A406 1p multi .70 .25

La Leyenda Patria — A407

1980, Feb. 26
1062 A407 1p multi .75 .25

Printers' Association, 50th Anniversary — A408

1980, Feb.
1063 A408 1p multi .60 .25

Lufthansa Cargo Container Service Inauguration A409

1980, Apr. 12 Unwmk. ***Perf. 12½***
1064 A409 2p multi .85 .25

Conf. Emblem, Banners — A410

1980, Apr. 28 Wmk. 332 ***Perf. 12***
1065 A410 2p multi .75 .25

8th World Hereford Conf., Punta del Este and Livestock Exhib., Prado/Montivideo.

Man, Woman and Birds — A411

1980 Litho. ***Perf. 12***
1066 A411 1p multi .85 .25

International Year of the Child (1979).

Latin-American Lions, 9th Forum — A412

1980, May 6 Wmk. 332 ***Perf. 12***
1067 A412 1p multi .85 .25

Souvenir Sheet

Army Day, May 18 — A413

1980, May 16

1068	A413 Sheet of 4	6.00	5.00
a.	2p Rifleman, 1814	1.25	1.00
b.	2p Cavalry officer, 1830	1.25	1.00
c.	2p Private Liberty Dragoons, 1826	1.25	1.00
d.	2p, Artigas Militia officer, 1815	1.25	1.00

Arms of Colonia A414

Colonia, 1680 A415

1980, June 17 Litho. ***Perf. 12***
1069 A414 50c multi 1.75 .25

Souvenir Sheet

1070	Sheet of 4	4.00	3.00
a.	A415 1p shown	.85	.65
b.	A415 1p 1680, diff.	.85	.65
c.	A415 1p 1980	.85	.65
d.	A415 1p 1980, diff.	.85	.65

Colonia, 300th anniversary.

Rotary Emblem on Globe — A416

1980, July 8
1071 A416 5p multi 1.75 .90

Rotary International, 75th anniversary.

Hand Putting Out Cigarette — A417

1980, Sept. 8 **Photo.**
1072 A417 1p multi .85 .25

World Health Day and anti-smoking campaign.

Artigas — A418

Wmk. 332
1980-85 Litho. ***Perf. 12½***

1073	A418	10c blue ('81)	.70	.25
1074	A418	20c orange	.50	.25
1075	A418	50c red	.50	.25
1076	A418	60c yellow	.50	.25
1077	A418	1p gray	1.00	.25
1078	A418	2p brown	1.00	.25
1079	A418	3p brt grn	1.75	.40
1080	A418	4p brt bl ('82)	2.25	.50
1081	A418	5p green ('82)	1.25	.25
1082	A418	6p brt org ('85)	.50	.25
1083	A418	7p lil rose ('82)	5.50	.80
1084	A418	10p blue ('82)	2.25	.40
1085	A418	12p blk ('85)	1.10	.25
1086	A418	15.50p emer ('85)	1.40	.35
1087	A418	20p dk vio ('82)	5.00	.80
1088	A418	30p lt brn ('82)	7.00	.80
1089	A418	50p gray bl ('82)	16.75	1.90
		Nos. 1073-1089 (17)	48.95	8.20

Christmas 1980 — A419

1980, Dec. 15 Litho. ***Perf. 12***
1090 A419 2p multi .85 .25

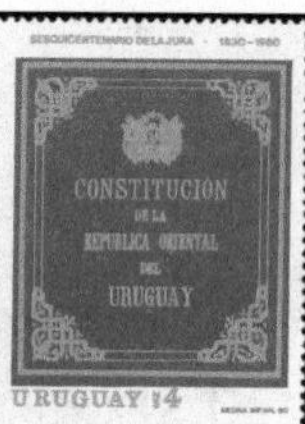

Constitution Title Page — A420

1980, Dec. 23 ***Perf. 12½***
1091 A420 4p brt bl & gold 1.25 .55

Sesquicentennial of Constitution.

A421

No. 1092, Montevideo Stadium. No. 1093, Soccer gold cup. No. 1094, Flags.

1980, Dec. 30 ***Perf. 12***
1092 A421 5p multicolored 2.25 1.00

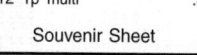

1093	A421	5p multicolored	2.25	1.00

Size: 25x79mm

1094	A421	10p multicolored	2.25	1.00
a.		Souv. sheet of 3, #1092-1094	13.00	13.00
		Nos. 1092-1094 (3)	6.75	3.00

Soccer Gold Cup Championship, Montevideo.

No. 1094 exists imperf. Value, $21.

A422

1981, Jan. 27
1095 A422 2p multi .85 .25

Spanish Heritage Day.

UPU Membership Centenary A423

1981, Feb. 6
1096 A423 2p multi .85 .25

Alexander von Humboldt (1769-1859), German Explorer and Scientist — A424

1981, Feb. 19
1097 A424 2p multi 1.25 .25

Intl. Education Congress and Fair, Montevideo (1980) — A425

1981, Mar. 31
1098 A425 2p multi .85 .25

Hand Holding Gold Cup — A426

1981, Apr. 8

1099	A426	2p multi	.95	.25
1100	A426	5p multi	1.50	.50

1980 victory in Gold Cup Soccer Championship.

Eighth Notes on Map of Americas — A427

1981, Apr. 28
1101 A427 2p multi .85 .25

Inter-American Institute of Musicology, 40th anniv.

World Tourism Conference, Manila, Sept. 27, 1980 — A428

Wmk. 332

1981, June 1 Litho. *Perf. 12*
1102 A428 2p multi .85 .25

Inauguration of PLUNA Flights to Madrid — A429

1981, May 12

1103	A429	2p multi	.50	.25
1104	A429	5p multi	1.10	.45
1105	A429	10p multi	2.40	.95
		Nos. 1103-1105 (3)	4.00	1.65

Army Day — A430

No. 1106, Cavalry soldier, 1843. No. 1107, Infantryman, 1843.

Wmk. 332

1981, May 18 Litho. *Perf. 12*

1106	A430	2p multicolored	.85	.25
1107	A430	2p multicolored	.85	.25

Natl. Atomic Energy Commission, 25th Anniv. — A431

1981, July 20
1108 A431 2p multi .85 .25

Europe-South American Soccer Cup — A432

1981, Aug. 4
1109 A432 2p multi 1.10 .25

Stone Tablets, Salto Grande Excavation A433

1981, Sept. 10
1110 A433 2p multi 1.00 .25

10th Lavalleja Week — A434

1981, Oct. 3
1111 A434 4p multi 1.60 .45

Intl. Year of the Disabled — A435

Wmk. 332

1981, Oct. 26 Litho. *Perf. 12*
1112 A435 2p multi .85 .25

UN Environmental Law Meeting Montevideo, Oct. 28-Nov. 6 — A436

1981, Oct. 28
1113 A436 5p multi 1.60 .45

A437

1981, Oct. 13
1114 A437 2p multi .85 .25

50th anniv. of ANCAP (Natl. Administration of Combustible Fuels, Alcohol and Cement).

Souvenir Sheets

Uruguay 81 Intl. Philatelic Exhibition — A438

No. 1114A: b, Copa de Oro trophy. c, Soccer player kicking ball.

No. 1115: a, Chess pieces. b, Prince Charles and Lady Diana, flags of Uruguay and Great Britain.

Wmk. 332

1981, Nov. 23 Litho. *Perf. 12*

1114A	A438	5p Sheet of 2, #b-c	*37.00*	*35.00*
1115	A438	5p Sheet of 2, #a-b	*27.50*	*27.50*

1982 World Cup Soccer Championships, Spain (No. 1114Ac), World Chess Championships, Atlanta (No. 1115a); Wedding of Prince Charles and Lady Diana (No. 1115b). Nos. 1114A-1115 exist imperf., which were not valid for postage. Value, $57.

Topographical Society Sesequicentennial A439

1981, Dec. 5 *Perf. 12*
1116 A439 2p multi 1.00 .25

See No. 1407.

Bank of Uruguay, 85th Anniv. A440

1981, Dec. 17 *Perf. 12½*
1117 A440 2p multi .85 .25

Palmar Dam — A441

1981, Dec. 22 *Perf. 12*
1118 A441 2p multi 1.00 .25

Christmas 1981 — A442

1981, Dec. 23
1119 A442 2p multi .85 .25

Pres. Joaquin Suarez Bicentenary — A443

1982, Mar. 15
1120 A443 5p multi 1.50 .50

Artillery Captain, 1872, Army Day — A444

Wmk. 332

1982, May 18 Litho. *Perf. 12*

1121	A444	3p shown	1.25	.25
1122	A444	3p Florida Battalion, 1865	1.25	.25

See Nos. 1136-1137.

Cent. (1981) of Pinocchio, by Carlo Collodi — A445

1982, June 17
1123 A445 2p multi .95 .25

2nd UN Conference on Peaceful Uses of Outer Space, Vienna, Aug. 9-21 — A446

1982, June 3
1124 A446 3p multi 1.50 .70

World Food Day — A447

1982
1125 A447 2p multi .90 .25

25th Anniv. of Lufthansa's Uruguay-Germany Flight — A448

3p, Lockheed L-1049-G Super Constellation. 7p, Boeing 747.

1982, Apr. 14 Unwmk. *Perf. 12½*

1126	A448	3p multicolored	1.25	.40
1127	A448	7p multicolored	3.00	.80

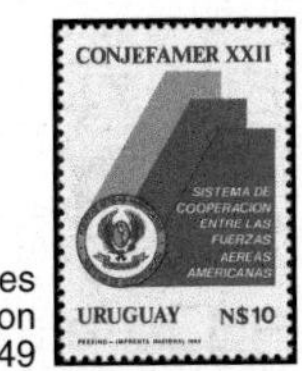

American Air Forces Cooperation System — A449

1982, Apr. 14 Wmk. 332 ***Perf. 12***
1128 A449 10p Emblem 3.25 .80

Juan Zorilla de San Martin (1855-1931), Painter — A450

1982, Aug. 18 ***Perf. 12½***
1129 A450 3p Self-portrait 1.20 .40

165th Anniv. of Natl. Navy — A451

1982, Nov. 15 ***Perf. 12***
1130 A451 3p Navy vessel Capitan Miranda 1.25 .40

Natl. Literacy Campaign — A452

1982, Nov. 30
1131 A452 3p multi .75 .25

Stamp Day — A453

1982, Dec. 23 ***Perf. 12½***
1132 A453 3p like #46 .65 .25
1133 A453 3p like #47 .65 .25
a. Pair, #1132-1133 1.90 1.90

These stamps bear numbers from 1 to 100 according to their position on the sheet.

Christmas 1982 — A454

1983, Jan. 4 ***Perf. 12***
1134 A454 3p multi 1.00 .25

Eduardo Fabini (1882-1950), Composer A455

1983, May 10
1135 A455 3p gold & brn .90 .25

Army Day Type of 1982

Designs: No. 1136, Military College cadet, 1885. No. 1137, 2nd Cavalry Regiment officer, 1885.

1983, May 18
1136 A444 3p multi .95 .25
1137 A444 3p multi .95 .25

Visit of King Juan Carlos and Queen Sofia of Spain, May — A456

1983, May 20 **Unwmk.**
1138 A456 3p Santa Maria, globe .90 .40
1139 A456 7p Profiles, flags 2.10 .80

Size of No. 1138: 29x39mm.

Brasiliana '83 Emblem A457

80th Anniv. of First Automobile in Uruguay A458

Opening of UPAE Building, Montevideo A459

Jose Cuneo (1887-1977), Painter A460

1982 World Cup — A461

Graf Zeppelin Flight Over Montevideo, 50th Anniv. (1984) — A462

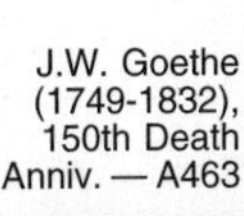

J.W. Goethe (1749-1832), 150th Death Anniv. — A463

First Space Shuttle Flight — A464

1983 Litho. Wmk. 332 ***Perf. 12***
1140 A457 3p multi 1.25 1.00
1141 A458 3p multi 1.25 1.00
1142 A459 3p multi 1.25 1.00
1143 A460 3p multi 1.25 1.00
a. Souvenir sheet of 4 7.50 7.50
1144 A461 7p multi 1.75 1.50
1145 A462 7p multi 1.75 1.50
1146 A463 7p multi 1.75 1.50
1147 A464 7p multi 1.75 1.50
a. Souvenir sheet of 4 12.50 12.50
Nos. 1140-1147 (8) 12.00 10.00

No. 1143a contains stamps similar to Nos. 1140-1143. No. 1147a stamps similar to Nos. 1144-1147. Nos. 1143a and 1147a for URUEXPO '83 and World Communications Year.

Issued: #1142, 6/8; #1143, 1146, 9/29; #1143a, 1147a, 6/9; #1140, 7/22; #1144, 12/13; #1146, 9/20; #1145, 12/8.

Bicentenary of City of Minas — A465

Wmk. 332
1983, Oct. 17 Litho. ***Perf. 12***
1148 A465 3p Founder 1.00 .25

World Communications Year — A466

1983, Nov. 30
1149 A466 3p multi .85 .25

Garibaldi Death Centenary — A467

1983, Dec. 5
1150 A467 7p multi 1.50 .40

Christmas 1983 — A468

Lithographed and Embossed (Braille)

1983, Dec. 21 ***Perf. 12½***
1151 A468 4.50p multi 1.00 .25

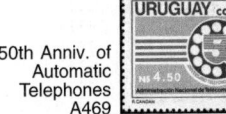

50th Anniv. of Automatic Telephones A469

1983, Dec. 27 ***Perf. 12***
1152 A469 4.50p multi .95 .25

Simon Bolivar, Battle Scene — A470

Wmk. 332
1984, Mar. 28 Litho. ***Perf. 12***
1153 A470 4.50p brn & gldn brn 1.50 .40

Gen. Leandro Gomez — A471

1984, Jan. 2
1154 A471 4.50p multi .85 .25

American Women's Day — A472

1984, Feb. 18
1155 A472 4.50p Flags, emblem .85 .25

Reunion Emblem — A473

1984, Mar. 23
1156 A473 10p multi 1.50 .45

Intl. Development Bank Governors, 25th annual reunion, Punta del Este.

50th Anniv. of Radio Club of Uruguay (1983) — A474

1984, Apr. 11
1157 A474 7p multi 1.25 .30

A475

1984, Feb. 7 Litho. ***Perf. 12***
1158 A475 4.50p multi .85 .25

Intl. Maritime Org., 25th anniv.

A476

1984, May 2 Litho. ***Perf. 12***
1159 A476 4.50p multi .90 .25

1930 World Soccer Championships, Montevideo.

Department of San Jose de Mayo, 200th Anniv. — A477

1984, May 9 Litho. ***Perf. 12***
1160 A477 4.50p multi .85 .25

Tourism, 50th Anniv. — A478

1984, May 15 Litho. ***Perf. 12***
1161 A478 4.50p multi .85 .25

Military Uniforms — A479

No. 1162, Artillery Regiment, 1895. No. 1163, Cazadores, 2nd battalion.

1984, June 19 Litho. ***Perf. 12***
1162 A479 4.50p multicolored .90 .25
1163 A479 4.50p multicolored .90 .25

Artigas on the Plains — A480

1984, July 2 Litho. ***Perf. 12***
1164 A480 4.50p bl & blk .75 .30
1165 A480 8.50p bl & redsh brn 1.50 .40

A. Penarol Soccer Club — A481

1984, Aug. 21 Litho. ***Perf. 12***
1166 A481 4.50p Championship trophy .85 .25

Provincial Map Type of 1973

1984, Sept. 21 Litho. ***Perf. 12***
1167 A281 4.50p multi .85 .25

Childrens Council, 50th Anniv. — A482

1984, Oct. 11 Litho. ***Perf. 12***
1168 A482 4.50p multi .75 .25

Christmas — A483

1984 Litho. ***Perf. 12***
1169 A483 6p multi 1.00 .30

A484

1985, Feb. 13 Litho. ***Perf. 12***
1170 A484 4.50p multi .85 .25

1st Jr. World Jai Alai Championships.

Don Bruno Mauricio de Zabala, 300th Birth Anniv. — A485

1985, Apr. 16 Litho. ***Perf. 12***
1171 A485 4.50p multi .85 .25

Intl. Olympic Committee, 90th Anniv. — A486

Design: Olympic rings, Los Angeles and Sarajevo 1984 Games emblems.

1985, May 22 ***Perf. 12½***
1172 A486 12p multi 1.25 .50

Carlos Gardel, (1890-1935), Entertainer — A487

1985, June 21 ***Perf. 12***
1173 A487 6p lt gray, red brn & bl .85 .25

Catholic Circle of Workers, Cent. — A488

Wmk. 332

1985, June 21 Litho. ***Perf. 12***
1174 A488 6p Cross, clasped hands .55 .25

Icarus, by Hans Erni — A489

1985, July Photo. Wmk. 332
1175 A489 4.50p multi .85 .25

Intl. Civil Aviation Org., 40th anniv.

American Air Forces Cooperation System, 25th Anniv. — A490

1985, July
1176 A490 12p Emblem, flags .85 .25

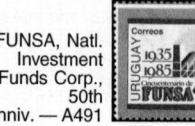

FUNSA, Natl. Investment Funds Corp., 50th Anniv. — A491

1985, July 31 Litho. Wmk. 332
1177 A491 6p multi .85 .25

Intl. Youth Year — A492

1985, Aug. 28
1178 A492 12p mar & blk .65 .25

Installation of Democratic Government A493

1985, Aug. 30
1179 A493 20p brt pur, yel ocher & dk grnsh bl 1.10 .40

Intl. Book Fair — A494

1985
1180 A494 20p multi 1.00 .35

Military School, Cent. — A495

1985, Nov. 29 Litho. ***Perf. 12***
1181 A495 10p multi .65 .25

Department of Flores, Cent. — A496

1985, Dec. 9
1182 A496 6p Map, arms .65 .25

Christmas 1985 — A497

1985, Dec. 23
1183 A497 10p multi .80 .30
1184 A497 22p multi 1.10 .30

Day of Hispanic Solidarity — A498

1985, Dec. 27
1185 A498 12p Isabel Monument .85 .25

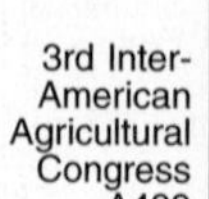

3rd Inter-American Agricultural Congress A499

Wmk. 332

1986, Jan. 7 Photo. ***Perf. 12***
1186 A499 12p blk, dl yel & red .75 .25

UPU Day — A500

1986, Jan. 14 Litho. ***Perf. 12***
1187 A500 15.50p multi .85 .25

1985 Census — A501

1986, Jan. 21
1188 A501 10p multi .65 .25

Conaprole, 50th Anniv. — A502

1986, Jan. 25
1189 A502 10p gold, brt ultra & bl .75 .25

UN, 40th Anniv. — A503

Wmk. 332

1986, Feb. 26 Litho. ***Perf. 12***
1190 A503 20p multi .85 .25

Brokers and Auctioneers Assoc., 50th Anniv. — A504

1986, Mar. 19
1191 A504 10p multi .65 .25

Gen. Manuel Ceferino Oribe (1792-1857), President — A505

Portraits: Nos. 1196, 1200, 2p, 7p, 15p, 20p, Oribe. Nos. 1195, 1209, 1211, 3p, Lavalleja. Nos. 1199, 1208, 1210, 30p, 100p, 200p, Artigas. No. 1198, 17p, 22p, 26p, 45p, 75p, Rivera.

1986-89 ***Perf. 12½***

1192	A505	1p	dl grn	.35	.25
1193	A505	2p	scarlet	.35	.25
1194	A505	3p	ultra	.35	.25
1195	A505	5p	dark blue	.35	.25
1196	A505	5p	violet blue	.35	.25
1197	A505	7p	tan	.35	.25
1198	A505	10p	lilac rose	.35	.25
1199	A505	10p	brt green	.35	.25
1200	A505	10p	bluish grn	.35	.25
1201	A505	15p	dull blue	.35	.25
1202	A505	17p	deep blue	.40	.25
1203	A505	20p	light brown	.35	.25
1204	A505	22p	violet	.35	.25
1205	A505	26p	olive blk	.50	.25
1206	A505	30p	pale org	.50	.25
1207	A505	45p	dark red	.50	.25
1208	A505	50p	dp bis	.90	.60
1209	A505	50p	bright pink	.35	.25
1210	A505	60p	dark gray	1.40	.60
1211	A505	60p	orange	.35	.25
1211A	A505	75p	red orange	.55	.25
1211B	A505	100p	dl red brn	2.10	.80
1211C	A505	200p	brt yel grn	3.25	1.25
	Nos. 1192-1211C (23)			15.00	8.00

The 22p is airmail.

Issued: 1p, 7p, 4/18; #1195, 30p, 6/16; #1198, 22p, 9/24; #1208, 8/5; 100p, 7/2; 2p, 6/16/87; 3p, #1210, 8/14/87; #1199, 17p, 8/4/87; 26p, 9/2/87; 15p, 9/9/88; 45p, 12/20/88; 200p, 10/19/88; #1211A, 5/19/89; #1211, 7/27/89; #1196, 1203, 8/15/89; #1209, 12/12/89; #1200, 1989.

See Nos. 1321-1329.

Italian Chamber of Commerce in Uruguay — A506

1986, May 5 *Perf. 12*
1212 A506 20p multi .85 .25

A507

1986, May 28 **Photo.** *Perf. 12*
1213 A507 20p multi .95 .30

1986 World Cup Soccer Championships, Mexico.

A508

Wmk. 332
1986, May 19 **Litho.** *Perf. 12*
1214 A508 10p multi .85 .30

Genocide of the Armenian people, 71st anniv.

A509

1986, June 16
1215 A509 10p multi .70 .25

El Dia Newspaper, cent.

Garcia, Peruvian Flag — A510

1986, July 14
1216 A510 20p multi .65 .25

State visit of Pres. Alan Garcia of Peru.

Simon Bolivar, Gen. Sucre, Map — A511

1986, July 24
1217 A511 20p multi .90 .25

State visit of Pres. Jaime Lusinchi of Venezuela.

State Visit of Pres. Jose Sarney of Brazil — A512

1986, July 31
1218 A512 20p multi .85 .25

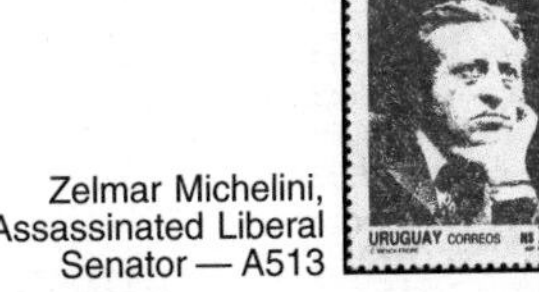

Zelmar Michelini, Assassinated Liberal Senator — A513

1986, Aug. 21
1219 A513 10p vio bl & rose lake .70 .25

B'nai B'rith of Uruguay, 50th Anniv. — A514

1986, Sept. 10
1220 A514 10p red, gold & red brn .95 .30

General Agreement on Tariffs & Trade (GATT) Committee Meeting, Punta del Este — A515

1986, Sept. 15
1221 A515 10p multi .75 .25

Scheduled Flights between Uruguay and Spain, 40th Anniv. — A516

1986, Sept. 22
1222 A516 20p multi .85 .30

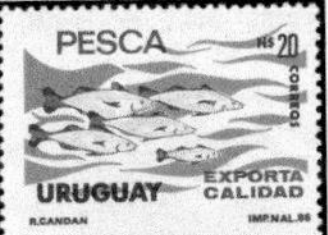

Fish Exports — A517

1986, Oct. 1
1223 A517 20p multi .85 .30

Wool Exports — A518

1986, Oct. 15
1224 A518 20p multi .85 .30

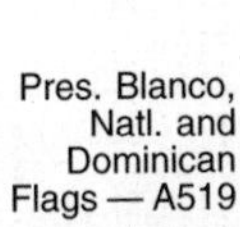

Pres. Blanco, Natl. and Dominican Flags — A519

1986, Oct. 29
1225 A519 20p multi .85 .25

State visit of Pres. Salvador Jorge Blanco of the Dominican Republic.

State Visit of Pres. Sandro Pertini of Italy — A520

1986, Oct. 31
1226 A520 20p grn & buff .85 .25

State Visit of Pres. Raul Alfonsin of Argentina — A521

1986, Nov. 10
1227 A521 20p multi .85 .25

Exists imperf. Value, $20.

Hispanic Solidarity Day — A522

Design: Felipe and Santiago, the patron saints of Montevideo, and cathedral.

Wmk. 332
1987, Jan. 12 **Litho.** *Perf. 12*
1228 A522 10p rose lake & blk .85 .30

JUVENTUS, 50th Anniv. (in 1986) — A523

1987, Jan. 28
1229 A523 10p brt yel, blk & ultra .70 .25

Juventus, a Catholic sports, culture and leisure organization.

Hector Gutierrez Ruiz (1934-1976), Politician
A524

Intl. Symposium on Science and Technology
A525

1987, Feb. 23
1230 A524 10p brn & deep mag .65 .25
1231 A525 20p multi .90 .25

Ruiz represented Uruguay at an earlier science and technology symposium.

Visit of Pope John Paul II to La Plata Region — A526

1987, Mar. 31
1232 A526 50p blk & deep org 1.25 .50

Dr. Jose F. Arias (1885-1985), Founder of the University of Crafts — A527

1987, Apr. 28
1233 A527 10p multi .70 .25

Jewish Community in Uruguay, 70th Anniv. — A528

1987, July 8
1234 A528 10p blk, org & brt bl .85 .30

Pluna Airlines, 50th Anniv. (in 1986) — A529

1987, Sept. 16
1235 A529 10p Dragon Fly .45 .25
1236 A529 20p Douglas DC-3 .60 .25
1237 A529 25p Vickers Viscount .90 .25
1238 A529 30p Boeing 707 1.00 .25
Nos. 1235-1238 (4) 2.95 1.00

Artigas Antarctic Station — A530

1987, Sept. 28
1239 A530 20p multi 1.25 .50

Uruguay Mortgage Bank, 75th Anniv. — A531

1987, Oct. 14
1240 A531 26p multi .85 .25

Exports — A532

1987, Oct. 28
1241 A532 51p Beef 1.00 .40
1242 A532 51p Milk products 1.00 .40

Christmas 1987 — A533

1987, Dec. 21
1243 A533 17p Nativity, vert. .60 .25
1244 A533 66p shown 1.20 .50

State Visit of Jose Napoleon Duarte, President of El Salvador — A534

1988, Jan. 12
1245 A534 20p brt olive grn & Prus blue .85 .25

VARIG Airlines, 60th Anniv. (in 1987) — A535

1988, Feb. 9

1246 A535 66p blk, blue & brt yel 1.25 1.00

Post Office Stamp Foundation — A536

Wmk. 332

1988, Feb. 9 Litho. *Perf. 12*

1247 A536 30p on 10+5p brt blue, blk & yel 1.40 .30

No. 1247 not issued without surcharge.

Intl. Peace Year — A537

1988, Feb. 11

1248 A537 10p multi .65 .25

Euskal Erria, 75th Anniv. (in 1987) — A538

1988, Mar. 9

1249 A538 66p multi 1.10 .40

Basque-Uruguayan diplomatic relations.

Air Force, 75th Anniv. — A539

1988, Mar. 11

1250 A539 17p multi .65 .25

Interamerican Children's Institute, 60th Anniv. — A540

Wmk. 332

1988, Mar. 28 Litho. *Perf. 12*

1251 A540 30p apple grn, blk & grn .75 .25

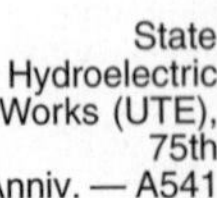

State Hydroelectric Works (UTE), 75th Anniv. — A541

Designs: No. 1253, Baygorria Dam. No. 1254, Gabriel Terra Dam. No. 1255, Constitucion Dam. No. 1256, Dams on map.

1988, Apr. 20

1252 A541 17p multi .35 .25
1253 A541 17p multi .35 .25
1254 A541 51p multi 1.00 .30
1255 A541 51p multi 1.00 .30
1256 A541 66p multi 1.40 .45
Nos. 1252-1256 (5) 4.10 1.55

Dated 1987.

Postal Union of America and Spain (UPAE), 75th Anniv. (in 1987) — A542

1988, May 10

1257 A542 66p multi 1.10 .45

Israel, 40th Anniv. — A543

1988, May 17

1258 A543 66p lt ultra & blk 1.40 .35

Postal Messenger of Peace A544

1988, May 24

1259 A544 66p multi 1.10 .35

Portrait, *La Cumparsita* Tango — A545

1988, June 7

1260 A545 17p Parade, horiz. .55 .25
1261 A545 51p Score 1.80 .55

Gerardo H. Matos Rodrigues, composer.

Firemen, Cent. — A546

17p, Pablo Banales, founder. 26p, Fireman, 1900. 34p, Emblem, horiz. 51p, Merry Weather fire engine, 1907, horiz. 66p, Fire pump, 1888, horiz. 100p, Ladder truck, 1921.

1988, June 21

1262 A546 17p multi .50 .25
1263 A546 26p multi .55 .25
1264 A546 34p multi .75 .30
1265 A546 51p multi 1.10 .45
1266 A546 66p multi 1.75 .65

Size: 44x24½mm

1267 A546 100p multi 2.75 1.10
Nos. 1262-1267 (6) 7.40 3.00

Capitan Miranda Trans-world Voyage, Cent. A547

1988, July 28

1268 A547 30p multi .65 .25

Exports — A548

1988

1269 A548 30p Citrus fruit .40 .25
1270 A548 45p Rice .85 .25
1271 A548 55p Footwear 1.00 .25
1272 A548 55p Leather and furs 1.00 .35
Nos. 1269-1272 (4) 3.25 1.10

Issued: 30p, #1272, 9/14; 45p, #1271, 8/23.

Natl. Museum of Natural History, 150th Anniv. — A549

30p, Usnea densirostra fossil. 90p, Toxodon platensis bone, Quaternary period.

1988, Sept. 20

1273 A549 30p blk, yel & red brn .60 .25
1274 A549 90p blk, ultra & beige 1.40 .65
a. Pair, #1273-1274 3.00 2.50

Battle of Carpinteria, 150th Anniv. (in 1986) A550

1988, Nov. 23

1275 A550 30p multi .65 .25

Horiz. row contains two stamps, label, then two more stamps.

Christmas — A551

1988, Dec. 21

1276 A551 115p multi 1.40 1.00

A552

Paintings: a, Manolita Pina, 1920, by J. Torres Garcia. b, 78 Squares and Rectangles, by J.P. Costigliolo. c, Print publicizing an exhibition of works by Pedrero Figari, 1945. d, Self-portrait, 1947, by J. Torres Garcia.

1988, Dec. 27

1277 Block or strip of 4 + label 5.50 4.50
a.-d. A552 115p any single 1.00 .65

No. 1277 can be collected as a vert. or horiz. strip of 4, or block of 4, with label.

Spanish Heritage Day — A553

1989, Jan. 9

1278 A553 90p multi 1.00 .40
1279 A553 115p multi 1.50 .50

Armenian Organization Hnchakian, Cent. — A554

Wmk. 332

1989, June 7 Litho. *Perf. 12*

1280 A554 210p red, yel & blue 2.00 .70

Joint issue between Ukraine and Kyrgyzstan. See Kyrgyz Express Post No. 136.

French Revolution, Bicentennial A555

No. 1281, Plumb line, frame. No. 1282, Liberty tree. No. 1283, Eye in sunburst. No. 1284, Liberty.

1989, July 3

1281 A555 50p multi .45 .25
1282 A555 50p multi .45 .25
1283 A555 210p multi 1.80 .45
1284 A555 210p multi 1.80 .45
Nos. 1281-1284 (4) 4.50 1.40

Use Postal Codes A556

50p, Montevideo Dept. map. 210p, National map, vert.

1989, July 25

1285 A556 50p multi .60 .25
1286 A556 210p multi 1.60 .45

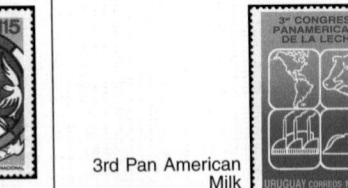

3rd Pan American Milk Congress — A557

1989, Aug. 24

1287 A557 170p sky blue & ultra 1.40 .45

A558

Wmk. 332

1989, Aug. 29 Photo. *Perf. 12*

1288 A558 170p multicolored 1.40 .30

Joaquin Jose da Silva Xavier.

A559

1989, Aug. 31

1289 A559 210p blk, red & bl 1.60 .35

Inter-Parliamentary Union Conf., London.

FAO Emblem, Map, Citrus Slice — A560

1989, Sept. 11

1290 A560 180p multicolored 1.40 .35

8th Conf., Intergovernmental Group on Citrus Fruits.

UN Decade for the Disabled A561

1989, Oct. 4

1291 A561 50p shown .60 .25
1292 A561 210p Disabled people 1.40 .45

America Issue — A562

Nacurutu artifact and UPAE emblem.

1989, Oct. 11 ***Perf. 12½***

1293 A562 60p multicolored 1.10 .40
1294 A562 180p multicolored 3.90 1.10

City of Pando, Bicentennial A563

1989, Dec. 27 Litho. *Perf. 12*

1295 A563 60p multicolored .65 .25

Christmas — A564

70p, Virgin of Trienta y Tres. 210p, Barradas, horiz.

1989, Dec. 19

1296 A564 70p multi .60 .25
1297 A564 210p multi 1.75 .45

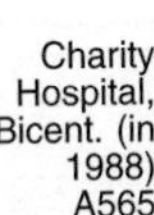

Charity Hospital, Bicent. (in 1988) A565

1990, Jan. 23 Wmk. 332

1298 A565 60p multicolored .95 .70

Provincial Arms and Maps — A566

1990

1299 A566 70p Soriano .60 .40
1300 A566 70p Florida, vert. .70 .45
1301 A566 90p Canelones .75 .50
1302 A566 90p Lavalleja, vert. .75 .50
1303 A566 90p San Jose, vert. .75 .50
1304 A566 90p Rivera .75 .50
Nos. 1299-1304 (6) 4.30 2.85

Dated 1989.

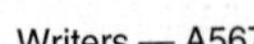

Writers — A567

Designs: a, Luisa Luisi (1883-1940). b, Javier de Viana (1872-1926). c, Delmira Agustini (1886-1914). d, J. Zorrilla de San Martin (1855-1931). e, Alfonsina Storni (1892-1938). f, Julio Casal (1889-1954). g, Juana de Ibarbourou (1895-1979). h, Carlos Roxlo (1861-1926).

1990, Mar. 20

1320 Block of 8 + 2 labels 8.00 6.00
a.-b. A567 60p any single .45 .45
c.-d. A567 75p any single .60 .60
e.-f. A567 170p any single 1.25 1.25
g.-h. A567 210p any single 1.60 1.60

Printed in sheets of 4 blocks of 4 separated by vert. and horiz. rows of 5 labels. Position of denomination varies to form border around each block.

Dated 1989.

Portraits Type of 1986

25p, 30p, Lavalleja. 60p, 90p, Rivera. 100p, 150p, 300p, 500p, 1000p, Artigas.

1990 Litho. Wmk. 332 *Perf. 12½*

1321 A505 25p orange .35 .25
1322 A505 30p ultra .35 .25
1323 A505 60p purple .35 .25
1324 A505 90p org red .70 .30
1325 A505 100p brown 1.75 .35
1326 A505 150p dk blue green 1.00 .50
1327 A505 300p blue 1.75 1.00
1328 A505 500p orange red 3.00 1.10
1329 A505 1000p red 6.00 3.00
Nos. 1321-1329 (9) 15.25 7.00

Issued: 30p, 60p, 7/17; 90p, 3/24; 150p, 6/22; 300p, 7/5; 500p, 3/22; 1000p, 7/24.

A568

1990, Apr. 3 ***Perf. 12***

1346 A568 70p multicolored .65 .40

City of Mercedes, bicent. Dated 1989.

A569

1990, Apr. 24

1347 A569 210p multicolored 1.50 1.25

Intl. Agricultural Development Fund, 10th anniv. Dated 1989.

Traffic Safety — A570

Designs: a, Bus, car. b, Don't drink and drive. c, Cross on the green light. d, Obey traffic signs.

1990, May 28

1348 A570 70p Block of 4, #a.-d. 2.50 1.50

General Artigas — A571

1990, June 18

1349 A571 60p red & blue .70 .45

A572

1990, June 26

1350 A572 70p multicolored .65 .40

Intl. Mothers' Day. Dated 1989.

A573

Treaty of Montevideo, 1889: a, Gonzalo Ramirez. b, Ildefonso Garcia. c, Flags at left. d, Flags at right.

1990, July 10

1351 A573 60p Block of 4, #a.-d. 2.60 1.75

Nos. 1351c-1351d printed in continuous design. Dated 1989.

Microphone, Tower — A574

b, Newspaper boy. c, Television camera. d, Books.

1990, Sept. 26

1352 A574 70p Block of 4, #a.-d. 3.00 2.00

Carlos Federico Saez (1878-1901) A575

Portraits: b, Pedro Blanes Viale (1879-1926). c, Edmundo Prati (1889-1970). d, Jose L. Zorrilla de San Martin (1891-1975).

1990, Dec. 26

1353 Block of 4 5.00 4.00
a.-b. A575 90p any single .50 .50
c.-d. A575 210p any single 1.10 1.10

Prevent Forest Fires — A576

Wmk. 332

1990, Oct. 26 Litho. *Perf. 12*

1354 A576 70np multicolored 2.25 2.00

America Issue A577

Designs: 120p, Odocoileus bezoarticus. 360p, Peltophorum dubium, vert.

1990, Nov. 6

1355 A577 120p multi 1.25 1.00
1356 A577 360p multi 3.75 3.50

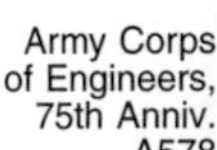

Army Corps of Engineers, 75th Anniv. A578

1991, Jan. 21

1357 A578 170p multicolored 1.25 1.00

The Nativity by Brother Juan B. Maino — A579

1990, Dec. 24

1358 A579 170p bister & multi 1.25 1.00
1359 A579 830p silver & multi 5.00 4.75

Organization of American States, Cent. (in 1989) — A580

Wmk. 332

1991, Mar. 21 Litho. *Perf. 12*

1360 A580 830p bl, blk & yel 4.75 4.50

Prevention of AIDS A581

1991, Mar. 8

1361 A581 170p bl & multi 1.25 1.00
1362 A581 830p grn & multi 5.00 4.75

Carnival A582

1991, Feb. 19

1363 A582 170p multicolored 1.25 1.00

Education A583

Expanding youth's horizons: a, Stone ax, megalithic monument. b, Wheel, pyramids. c, Printing press, solar system. d, Satellite, diagram.

Wmk. 332

1991, Apr. 23 Litho. *Perf. 12*

1364 Block of 4 3.50 3.50
a.-b. A583 120p any single .40 .40
c.-d. A583 330p any single 1.25 1.25

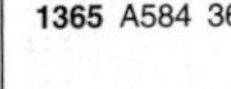

Natl. Cancer Day — A584

1991, June 17

1365 A584 360p red & black 1.40 1.10

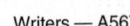

A585

Exports of Uruguay — A586

Perf. 12½x13, 13x12½

1991 Litho. Wmk. 332

1366 A585 120p Textiles .50 .40
1367 A586 120p Clothing .65 .35
1368 A585 400p Semiprecious stones, granite 2.90 1.40
Nos. 1366-1368 (3) 4.05 2.15

Issued: #1366, 400p, 4/23; #1367, 6/26.

7th Pan American Maccabiah Games — A587

1991, July 4 Perf. 12½x13
1369 A587 1490p multicolored 4.75 *6.00*

Dornier Wal, Route Map — A588

1991, July 5 Perf. 12
1370 A588 1510p multicolored 4.75 4.50

Espamer '91.

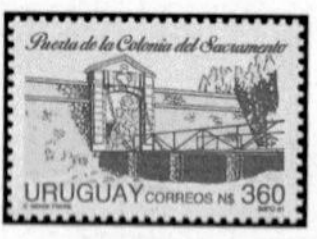

Entrance to Sacramento Colony — A589

Railroads and Trains: 540p, 825p, First locomotive, 1869. 600p, like 360p. 800p, Entrance to Sacramento Colony. 1510p, 2500p, Horse-drawn streetcar.

Wmk. 332

1991-2002 Litho. Perf. 12

1378 A589 360p brn & yel 1.10 .60
1378A A589 540p dk bl & gray 1.60 .95
1379 A589 600p brn, yel & blk 1.10 .85
1379A A589 800p ol grn & dk ol grn 1.10 .95
1379B A589 825p bl, gray & blk 1.60 1.25
1380 A589 1510p ol bis & emer 4.75 3.00
1382 A589 2500p ol bis, emer & blk 4.00 3.00
Nos. 1378-1382 (7) 15.25 10.60

Issued: 360p, 540p, 1510p, July 19; 825p, Feb. 11, 1992; 2500p, May 29, 2002; 600p, June 18, 1992; 800p, Feb. 9, 1993.

For surcharges, see Nos. 2011B, 2057-2059.

Sagrada Family College, Cent. — A590

College of the Immaculate Heart of Mary, Cent. — A591

Wmk. 332

1991, June 26 Litho. Perf. 12
1383 A590 360p multicolored 1.00 .90
1384 A591 1370p multicolored 4.00 3.75

Constitutional Oath — A592

1991, July 17
1385 A592 360p multicolored 1.10 .90

Swiss Confederation, 700th Anniv. — A593

1991, Aug. 1 Perf. 13x12½
1386 A593 1510p multicolored 5.50 5.25

Souvenir Sheet
Perf. 12

1387 A593 3000p multicolored 11.00 11.00

Photography, 150th Anniv. — A594

Perf. 12½x13
1991, Sept. 12 Litho. Wmk. 332
1388 A594 1370p multi 3.75 3.50

Actors Society of Uruguay, 50th Anniv. — A595

1991, Aug. 24 Perf. 12
1389 A595 450p blk & red 1.50 1.25

CREA (Agriculture Association), 25th Anniv. — A596

1991, Sept. 14 Perf. 12½x13
1390 A596 450p multicolored 1.50 1.25

Whitbread Around the World Race — A597

1991, Aug. 20 Perf. 13x12½
1391 A597 1510p multicolored 4.25 4.00

Amerigo Vespucci (1454-1512) A598

America Issue: 450p, First landing at River Plate, 1602, vert.

1991, Oct. 11 Perf. 12
1392 A598 450p yel & brn 1.50 1.25
1393 A598 1740p ol & brn 4.25 3.50

Automobiles A599

Designs: 350p, Gladiator, 1902. 1370p, E.M.F., 1909. 1490p, Renault, 1912. 1510p, Clement-Bayard, 1903, vert.

1991, Oct. 18 Perf. 12½x13, 13x12½
1394 A599 360p multicolored 1.00 .90
1395 A599 1370p multicolored 3.75 3.50
1396 A599 1490p multicolored 3.75 3.50
1397 A599 1510p multicolored 3.75 3.50
Nos. 1394-1397 (4) 12.25 11.40

Team Nacional Montevideo, Winners of Toyota and Europe-South America Soccer Cups — A600

Wmk. 332

1991, Nov. 8 Litho. Perf. 12
1398 A600 450p shown 1.50 1.25
1399 A600 450p Emblem, trophy, vert. 1.50 1.25

Margarita Xirgu (1888-1969), Actress A601

1991, Oct. 4
1400 A601 360p yel & brn 1.25 1.00

INTERPOL, 60th Congress — A602

1991, Oct. 30
1401 A602 1740p multicolored 3.75 3.50

Maria Auxiliadora Institute, Cent. A603

1991, Nov. 11
1402 A603 450p multicolored 1.50 1.25

Technological Laboratory, 25th Anniv. A604

1991, Nov. 11
1403 A604 1570p dk bl & lt bl 3.25 3.00

The Table by Zoma Baitler A605

1991, Oct. 18
1404 A605 360p multicolored 1.50 1.25

World Food Day — A606

1991,Oct. 16 Perf. 12½x13
1405 A606 1740p multicolored 4.25 4.00

Ships A607

Designs: a, Steam yacht, Gen. Rivera. b, Coast Guard cutter, Salto. c, Cruiser, Uruguay. d, Tanker, Pte. Oribe.

Wmk. 332

1991, Oct. 4 Litho. Perf. 12
1406 Block of 4 11.00 10.00
a.-b. A607 450p any single 1.25 1.25
c.-d. A607 1570p any single 3.50 3.50

Topographical Society Type of 1981

1991, Dec. 3 Perf. 12½
1407 A439 550p multi 1.25 1.00

Topographical Society, 160th anniv.

World AIDS Day — A608

1991, Dec. 1
1408 A608 550p bl, blk & brt yel 1.00 1.00
1409 A608 2040p lt grn, blk & lil 4.00 3.50

Export Industries A609

Wmk. 332

1991, Mar. 20 Litho. Perf. 12½
1410 A609 120p multicolored .65 .40

Christmas — A610

1991, Dec. 24 Perf. 12
1411 A610 550p Angel 1.25 1.10
1412 A610 2040p Adoration of the Angels 3.50 3.25

Muscians A611

Designs: a, Juan de Dios Filiberto. b, Pintin Castellanos. c, Francisco Canaro. d, Anibal Troilo.

Wmk. 332

1992, Jan. 20 Photo. *Perf. 12*
1413 A611 450p Block of 4, #a-d 4.00 3.50

Patricio Aylwin, Pres. of Chile — A612

Perf. 11½x12

1992, Mar. 23 Litho. Unwmk.
1415 A612 550p multicolored 1.10 .85

Penarol, Winners of Liberator's Cup in Club Soccer — A612a

Perf. 13x12½

1992, May 29 Litho. Wmk. 332
1415A A612a 600p yel & blk 1.50 1.25

Souvenir Sheet

Perf. 12

1415B A612a 3000p yel & blk 5.25 5.00

La Paz City, 120th Anniv. — A612b

1992, May 25 *Perf. 13x12½*
1415C A612b 550p multicolored 1.10 .85

World No-Smoking Day — A613

Wmk. 332

1992, May 31 Litho. *Perf. 12*
1416 A613 2500p multicolored 4.00 3.75

United Nations World Health Day — A614

Wmk. 332

1992, July 28 Litho. *Perf. 13*
1417 A614 2500p bl, lt bl & red 4.00 3.75

Mercosur — A615

1992, Aug. 5 Photo. *Perf. 12*
1418 A615 2500p multicolored 4.00 3.75

Olymphilex '92, Barcelona A616

Wmk. 332

1992, Aug. 8 Photo. *Perf. 12*
1419 A616 2900p multicolored 4.75 4.50

Discovery of America, 500th Anniv. — A617

Perf. 11½x12, 12x11½

1992, Oct. 10 Litho. Unwmk.
1420 A617 700p Ship, masts, vert. 1.50 1.25
1421 A617 2900p Globe, ship 4.25 4.00

Jose Pedro Varela Natl. Teachers College, 50th Anniv. — A618

1992, Oct. 22 *Perf. 12x11½*
1422 A618 700p multicolored 1.10 .90

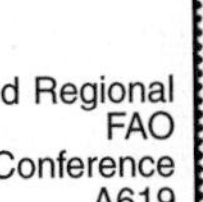

22nd Regional FAO Conference A619

Designs: 2500p, Emblems. 2900p, Emblems, children with food basket.

1992, Sept. 28
1423 A619 2500p multicolored 3.25 3.00
1424 A619 2900p multicolored 4.00 3.75

Intl. Conf. on Nutrition, Rome, Italy (#1424).

Cesar Vallejo (1892-1938), Poet — A620

1992, Sept. 30
1425 A620 2500p brn & dk brn 3.50 3.25

A621

1992, Oct. 26 *Perf. 11½x12*
1426 A621 700p gray, red & blk 1.10 .90

Assoc. of Wholesalers and Retailers, cent.

A622

Perf. 11½x12

1992, Oct. 10 Litho. Unwmk.
1427 A622 700p black, blue & grn 1.25 1.00

Monument to Columbus, cent.

A623

Ruins and lighthouse, Colonia del Sacramento.

1992, Oct. 10
1428 A623 700p multicolored 1.50 1.25

Discovery of America, 500th anniv.

A624

1992, Oct. 19
1429 A624 700p red lil, rose lil & blk 1.50 1.25

Columbus Philanthropic Society, cent.

A625

1992, Oct. 19
1430 A625 2900p multicolored 4.00 3.75

Judaism in the Americas, 500th anniv.

A626

1992, Oct. 30
1431 A626 2900p multicolored 4.00 3.75

Lebanon Society of Uruguay, 50th anniv.

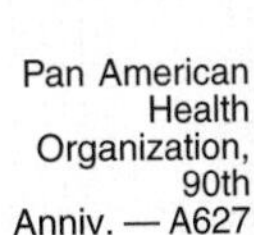

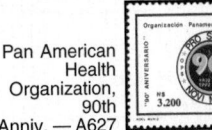

Pan American Health Organization, 90th Anniv. — A627

Perf. 12x11½

1992, Dec. 15 Litho. Unwmk.
1432 A627 3200p blk, bl & yel 4.00 3.75

22nd Lions Club Forum for Latin America and the Caribbean A628

1992, Dec. 2
1433 A628 2700p multicolored 3.25 3.25

Christmas — A629

1992, Dec. 1 *Perf. 11½x12*
1434 A629 800p Nativity scene 1.25 1.00
1435 A629 3200p Star in sky 3.75 3.50

General Manuel Oribe, Birth Bicent. — A630

Designs: No. 1436, Oribe, Oriental College. No. 1437, Oribe in military dress uniform, vert.

Perf. 12x11½, 11½x12

1992, Dec. 8 Litho. Unwmk.
1436 A630 800p multicolored 1.25 1.00
1437 A630 800p multicolored 1.25 1.00

Logosofia, 60th Anniv. — A631

1992, Dec. 29 *Perf. 12x11½*
1438 A631 800p blue & yellow 1.25 1.00

Immigrants' Day — A632

1992, Dec. 4 *Perf. 11½x12*
1439 A632 800p black & green 1.25 1.00

ANDEBU, 70th Anniv. — A633

Caritas of Uruguay, 30th Anniv. — A634

1992, Dec. 22 Photo. *Perf. 12x11½*
1440 A633 2700p Satellite 3.25 3.00
1441 A634 3200p Map, huts by water 4.00 3.75

A635

1992, Dec. 18 *Perf. 11½x12*
1442 A635 800p brown & yellow 1.25 1.00

Jose H. Molaguero S. A., 50th anniv.

A636

Perf. 11½x12

1993, Mar. 1 Litho. Unwmk.
1443 A636 80c multicolored 1.10 .90

Wilson Ferreira Aldunate.

Economic Science and Accountancy College, Cent. — A637

Perf. 12x11½

1993, Apr. 15 Photo. Unwmk.
1444 A637 1p multicolored 1.40 1.10

Souvenir Sheet

Polska '93, Intl. Philatelic Exhibition — A638

a, Lech Walesa. b, Pope John Paul II.

1993, May 3 ***Perf. 11½x12***
1445 A638 2p Sheet of 2, #a.-b. 24.00 24.00

A639

A639a

A639b

A639c

A639d

A639e

A639f

A639g

A639h

Design A639g shows the Postal Administration Tower.

ONE PESO (Letter Box — A639):
Type I — "Bugon vecinal 1879" 21½mm, letter box 23½mm high.
Type II — "Bugon vecinal 1879" 22mm, letter box 22½mm high.
Type III — "Bugon vecinal 1879" 19½mm, letter box 21mm high.
There are other differences among the three types.

Perf. 12½, 12 (#1449, 1465)

1993-99 Litho. Wmk. 332
1446 A639 50c gray ol & yel .35 .25
1447 A639 1p lt brn & yel (I) .55 .45
a. Type II .90 .60
b. Type III, unwatermarked .60 .35
c. Type III, photo., unwmkd. .65 .35
1448 A639a 1p org yel & bl 1.10 .90
1449 A639b 1p org & bl .75 .65
1450 A639c (1.20p) blue .90 .70
1451 A639c (1.40p) green .95 .75
1452 A639d 1.40p yel & bl .95 .75
1453 A639c (1.60p) red 1.50 1.20
1454 A639 1.80p bl & yel 1.25 1.40
1455 A639c (1.80p) brown 1.50 1.20
1456 A639c (2p) gray 1.50 1.20
1457 A639c (2.30p) lilac 1.90 1.60
1458 A639 2.60p bl, yel & grn 1.90 1.60
1459 A639e (2.60p) grn & yel 1.90 1.60

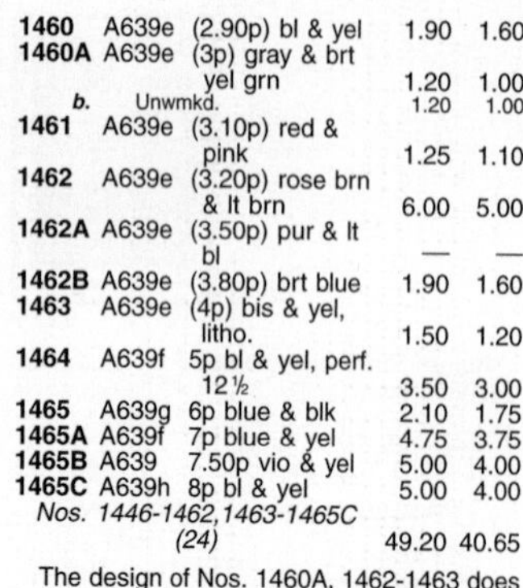

1460 A639e (2.90p) bl & yel 1.90 1.60
1460A A639e (3p) gray & brt yel grn 1.20 1.00
b. Unwmkd. 1.20 1.00
1461 A639e (3.10p) red & pink 1.25 1.10
1462 A639e (3.20p) rose brn & lt brn 6.00 5.00
1462A A639e (3.50p) pur & lt bl — —
1462B A639e (3.80p) brt blue 1.90 1.60
1463 A639e (4p) bis & yel, litho. 1.50 1.20
1464 A639f 5p bl & yel, perf. 12½ 3.50 3.00
1465 A639g 6p blue & blk 2.10 1.75
1465A A639f 7p blue & yel 4.75 3.75
1465B A639 7.50p vio & yel 5.00 4.00
1465C A639h 8p bl & yel 5.00 4.00
Nos. 1446-1462,1463-1465C (24) 49.20 40.65

The design of Nos. 1460A, 1462-1463 does not include "PORTE MINIMO." There are minor design differences between #1464 and 1465A.

Issued: #1448, 4/15/93; #1450, 8/2/93; #1451, 12/1/93; #1452, 1/4/94; #1453, 4/4/94; #1455, 8/1/94; #1454 8/9/94; #1449, 10/3/94; 1456, 12/1/94. #1457, 4/1/95; #1458, (2.60p), 8/10/95; 50c, #1447, 8/27/96; #1460, (3.10p), (3.50p), 4/1/96; 7.50p, 5/21/96; 5p, 1997; (3.80p), 5/9/97; #1463, 8/1/97; 6p, 8/13/97; (3.50p), 7/28/98; (3p), 2/1/99. #1460Ab, 1999.

For surcharges, see Nos. 2056, 2106, 2186, 2269

Interior Fire Service, 50th Anniv. — A640

Perf. 11½x12

1993, May 28 Litho. Unwmk.
1466 A640 1p multicolored 1.25 1.00

15th Congress of UPAEP — A641

1993, June 21
1467 A641 3.50p multicolored 4.00 3.75

Uruguayan Navy, 175th Anniv. — A642

Sailing ship, Pedro Campbell, first admiral.

Perf. 12x11½

1993, June 28 Litho. Wmk. 332
1468 A642 1p multicolored 1.50 1.25

Intl. University Society, 25th Anniv. — A643

1993, July 2
1469 A643 1p multicolored 1.40 1.10

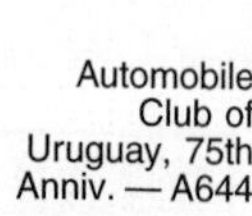

Automobile Club of Uruguay, 75th Anniv. — A644

1993, July 19 Photo. Unwmk.
1470 A644 3.50p 1910 Hupmobile 4.00 3.75

Uruguay Battalion in UN Peacekeeping Force, Cambodia A645

Perf. 12x11½

1993, Aug. 6 Litho. Unwmk.
1471 A645 1p multicolored 1.50 1.25

Souvenir Sheet

Brasiliana '93 — A646

World Cup Soccer Champions: a, Uruguay, 1930, 1950. b, Brazil, 1958, 1962, 1970.

1993, July 28 ***Perf. 11½x12***
1472 A646 2.50p Sheet of 2, #a.-b. 9.50 9.00

State Television Channel 5, 30th Anniv. — A647

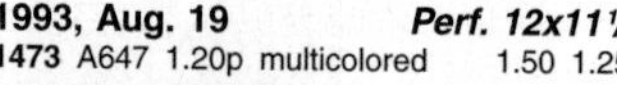

1993, Aug. 19 ***Perf. 12x11½***
1473 A647 1.20p multicolored 1.50 1.25

ANDA, 60th Anniv. — A648

Perf. 12½

1993, Sept. 24 Litho. Unwmk.
1474 A648 1.20p multicolored 1.50 1.25

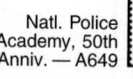

Natl. Police Academy, 50th Anniv. — A649

1993, Sept. 24
1475 A649 1.20p multicolored 1.60 1.40

Newspaper Diario El Pais, 75th Anniv. — A650

Perf. 12½

1993, Sept. 30 Litho. Unwmk.
1476 A650 1.20p multicolored 1.60 1.40

Latin American Conference on Rural Electrification A651

1993, Oct. 11
1477 A651 3.50p multicolored 4.00 3.75

B'nai B'rith, 150th Anniv. — A652

1993, Oct. 13
1478 A652 3.70p multicolored 4.00 3.75

A653

Fauna — A654

1993 Photo. Wmk. 332 ***Perf. 12½***
1482 A653 20c Seriema bird .65 .35
1484 A653 30c Dragon bird 1.10 .50
1486 A653 50c Anteaters, horiz. 2.40 .75
1492 A654 1.20p Giant armadillo 2.90 2.40
Nos. 1482-1492 (4) 7.05 4.00

Issued: 1.20p, 8/3/93; 20c, 30c, 50c, 10/22/93.

For surcharges, see Nos. 2011A, 2055, 2150, 2185.

America Issue — A655

1.20p, Caiman latirostris. 3.50p, Athene cunicularia, vert.

Perf. 12½

1993, Oct. 6 Litho. Unwmk.
1504 A655 1.20p multicolored 1.50 1.50
1505 A655 3.50p multicolored 5.00 4.25

Souvenir Sheet

Whitbread Trans-Global Yacht Race — A656

1993, Oct. 22 ***Perf. 11½x12***
1506 A656 5p multicolored 5.25 5.00

Beatification of Mother Francisca Rubatto — A657

1993, Oct. 29 Wmk. 332 ***Perf. 12***
1507 A657 1.20p multicolored 1.50 1.25

Intl. Year of Indigenous People — A658

Perf. 13x12½

1993, Oct. 29 Unwmk.
1508 A658 3.50p multicolored 3.50 3.25

Rotary Club of Montevideo, 75th Anniv. — A658a

Perf. 12½

1993, Nov. 10 Litho. Unwmk.

1508A A658a 3.50p dk bl & bis 3.75 3.50

Rhea Americana — A659

1993, Dec. 20 Litho. *Perf. 12*

1509 A659 20c shown .90 .75
1510 A659 20c With chicks .90 .75
1511 A659 50c Head 2.10 1.75
1512 A659 50c Two walking 2.10 1.75
Nos. 1509-1512 (4) 6.00 5.00

World Wildlife Fund.

Children's Rights Day — A660

1994, Jan. 4 *Perf. 12½*

1513 A660 1.40p multicolored 1.60 1.40

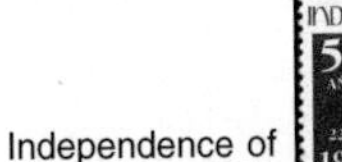

Independence of Lebanon, 50th Anniv. — A661

1993, Nov. 22

1514 A661 3.70p multicolored 3.50 3.25

Eduardo Victor Haedo — A662

1993, Nov. 24

1515 A662 1.20p multicolored 1.40 1.20

Christmas — A663

1993, Dec. 7

1516 A663 1.40p shown 1.40 1.25
1517 A663 4p Nativity, diff. 4.00 3.75

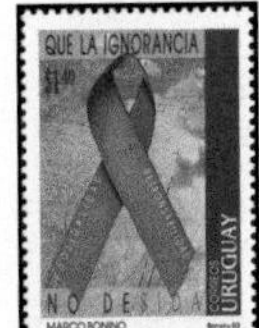

Intl. AIDS Day — A664

1993, Dec. 1

1518 A664 1.40p multicolored 2.25 2.00

Souvenir Sheets

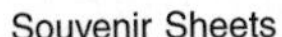

Anniversaries & Events — A665

Designs: No. 1519a, Switzerland #3L1, 1913 Swiss private air mail stamp. b, Germany #C39, Uruguay #C426c. c, Uruguay #C372, US #C76. d, Uruguay #C282a, US #C104.
No. 1520a, Switzerland Types A1, A2. b, Switzerland #B541.

1993, Nov. 18

1519 A665 1p #a.-d. 12.50 12.50
1520 A665 2.50p #a.-b. 12.50 12.50

Swiss postage stamps, 150th anniv. (#1519a, 1520). Dr. Hugo Eckener, 125th anniv. of birth (#1519b). First man on moon, 25th anniv. (#1519c). 1994 World Cup Soccer Championships, US (#1519d).
Nos. 1519-1520 exist imperf. Value $30.

17th Inter-American Naval Conference A666

1994, Mar. 21 Litho. *Perf. 12½*

1521 A666 3.70p multicolored 3.50 3.25

A667

1994, Mar. 11 *Perf. 12½*

1522 A667 4p multicolored 4.00 3.75

5th World Sports Congress, Punta del Este.

A668

Unwmk.

1994, Apr. 4 Litho. *Perf. 12*

1523 A668 3.90p multicolored 3.50 3.25

Latin America Youth Organization, 7th conference.

A669

1994, Apr. 18

1524 A669 4.30p multicolored 4.00 3.75

4th World Congress on Merino Wool.

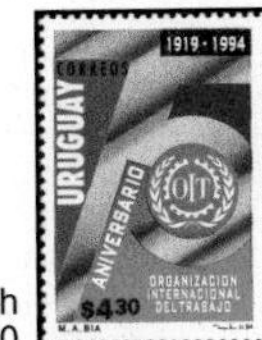

ILO, 75th Anniv. — A670

1994, Apr. 28 *Perf. 12½*

1525 A670 4.30p multicolored 3.75 3.50

Miniature Sheet

1994 Winter Olympic Medal Winners — A671

Designs: a, Katja Seizinger. b, Markus Wasmeier. c, Vreni Schneider. d, Gustav Weder.

1994, May 6 *Perf. 12*

1526 A671 1.25p Sheet of 4, #a.-d. 10.00 10.00

No. 1526 exists demonitized and imperf on paper with watermark 322. This item was sold with No. 1526 and has a matching serial number. Same value.

Miniature Sheet

1994 World Cup Soccer Championships, US — A672

a, Soccer ball, flags of Uruguay, Brazil. b, Ball, flags of Italy, Argentina. c, Ball, flags of Germany, Great Britain. d, Olympic Rings.

1994, May 16

1527 A672 1.25p Sheet of 4, #a.-d. 10.00 10.00

Uruguay, Olympic soccer gold medalists, 1924-1928 (#1527d).
See note after No. 1526.

Clemente Estable (1894-1976), Biologist — A673

1994, May 23 Litho. *Perf. 12½*

1528 A673 1.60p olive & black 1.60 1.40

Electoral Court, 70th Anniv. — A674

1994, June 7

1529 A674 1.60p multicolored 1.60 1.40

Natl. Commission to Prevent Tapeworms A675

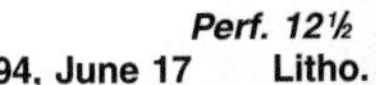

Perf. 12½

1994, June 17 Litho. Unwmk.

1530 A675 1.60p multicolored 3.25 2.00

Souvenir Sheet

Cesareo L. Berisso, First Aviator to Land at Natl. Airport, Carrasco A676

1994, June 21 *Perf. 12*

1531 A676 5p multicolored 4.25 4.00

Intl. Cooperatives, 150th Anniv. — A677

1994, July 1 *Perf. 12½*

1532 A677 4.30p multicolored 3.75 3.50

Commission on Integration of Regional Electricity, 30th Anniv. — A678

1994, July 8

1533 A678 1.60p multicolored 1.50 1.25

Abate Pierre — A679

Perf. 12½

1994, Aug. 5 Litho. Unwmk.

1534 A679 4.80p multicolored 4.00 3.75

Intl. Year of the Family — A680

1994, July 28

1535 A680 4.80p multicolored 4.00 3.75

The Man of Lugano, by Goffredo Sommavilla (1850-1944) A681

Perf. 12½

1994, Aug. 15 Litho. Unwmk.

1536 A681 4.80p multicolored 4.00 3.75

First Manned Moon Landing, 25th Annvi. — A682

1994, July 20

1537 A682 3p multicolored 3.25 3.00

Intl. Olympic Committee, Cent. — A683

1994, Aug. 23
1538 A683 4.80p multicolored 4.00 3.75

Elbio Fernandez School, 125th Anniv. — A684

Perf. 12½
1994, Aug. 29 Litho. Unwmk.
1539 A684 1.80p multicolored 1.60 1.40

A685

1994, Sept. 10 ***Perf. 12***
1540 A685 1.80p black & blue 1.60 1.35

Gral. Aparicio Saravia, 90th Death Anniv.

A686

1994, Sept. 30 ***Perf. 12½***
1541 A686 4.80p multicolored 3.75 *3.75*

6th Latin American Urban Congress.

General Assoc. of Uruguayan Authors, 65th Anniv. — A687

Perf. 12½
1994, Sept. 26 Litho. Unwmk.
1542 A687 1.80p multicolored 1.60 1.25

America Issue — A688

1994, Oct. 10
1543 A688 1.80p Stagecoach 1.75 1.50
1544 A688 4.80p Paddle steamer 4.75 4.50

A689

Perf. 12½
1994, Oct. 28 Litho. Unwmk.
1545 A689 2p multicolored 1.75 1.50

Assoc. of Directors of Marketing, 50th anniv.

A690

1994, Nov. 25
1546 A690 2p multicolored 2.00 1.75

YMCA in Uruguay, 85th anniv.

Lottery, 55th Anniv. — A691

1994, Nov. 21
1547 A691 2p multicolored 2.00 1.75

First Intl. Seminar to Promote Roads in Uruguay, Punta del Este — A692

1994, Oct. 14
1548 A692 2p multicolored 1.75 1.50

Uruguayan Press Assoc., 50th Anniv. — A693

1994, Oct. 24
1549 A693 2p multicolored 2.00 1.75

Miniature Sheet

Natl. Mint, 150th Anniv. — A694

Portions of old coin press and: a, Mint building. b, 1844 Copper coin. c, 1844 Silver coin. d, Montevideo silver peso.

1994, Oct. 17 ***Perf. 12***
1550 A694 1.50p Sheet of 4, #a.-d. 9.25 8.00

No. 1550 exists demonitized and imperf. on paper with watermark 332. This item was sold with No. 1550 and has matching serial numbers. Same value.

Miniature Sheet

Natl. Navy — A695

Ships: a, ROU Uruguay, ROU Artigas. b, ROU Fortuna. c, ROU Uruguay. d, ROU Cte. Pedro Campbell.

1994, Nov. 15
1551 A695 1.50p Sheet of 4, #a.-d. 8.00 7.00

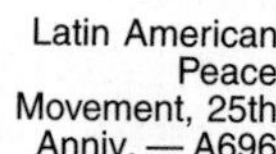

Latin American Peace Movement, 25th Anniv. — A696

1994, Nov. 15 ***Perf. 12½***
1552 A696 4.30p multicolored 3.25 3.25

4th Conference of the Latin American and Caribbean Organization of High Fiscal Entities, Montevideo A697

1994, Dec. 5
1553 A697 5.50p multicolored 4.25 4.00

Christmas — A698

1994, Dec. 2
1554 A698 2p shown 1.25 1.25
1555 A698 5.50p Star, tree, house 4.50 4.00

Uruguayan Red Cross & Red Crescent Societies, 75th Anniv. — A699

Perf. 12½
1994, Dec. 20 Litho. Unwmk.
1556 A699 5p multicolored 3.75 3.50

City Post Office — A700

1995-97 Litho. Wmk. 332 ***Perf. 12***
1557 A700 20c yellow green .55 .50
1565 A700 10p brown 7.25 6.75
1566 A700 10p dark brown 4.00 3.75

Unwmk.
1566A A700 10p clar & blk 4.00 3.75
Nos. 1557-1566A (4) 15.80 14.75

Issued: 20c, 1/11/95; 10p, 5/21/96; #1566, 1566A, 1997.
Denomination has no decimal places on Nos. 1566-1566A.

Naval Aviation, 70th Anniv. — A704

Perf. 12½
1995, Feb. 7 Litho. Unwmk.
1567 A704 2p multicolored 1.75 1.50

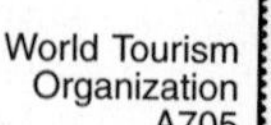
World Tourism Organization A705

Designs: No. 1568, Ranch house, sheep herders. No. 1569, Water recreation park. No. 1570, Native wildlife. No. 1571, Beach resort.

1995, Feb. 13
1568 A705 5p multicolored 3.50 3.50
1569 A705 5p multicolored 3.50 3.50
1570 A705 5p multicolored 3.50 3.50
1571 A705 5p multicolored 3.50 3.50
Nos. 1568-1571 (4) 14.00 14.00

17th World Conference of Lifeguard Services — A706

1995, Feb. 15
1572 A706 5p multicolored 3.50 3.50

Rotary Intl., 90th Anniv. — A707

1995, Feb. 22
1573 A707 5p multicolored 3.50 3.50

ICAO, 50th Anniv. — A708

1995, Mar. 14
1574 A708 5p multicolored 3.50 3.25

Pietro Mascagni (1863-1945), Composer A709

Perf. 12½
1995, Mar. 30 Litho. Unwmk.
1575 A709 5p multicolored 3.75 3.50

Miniature Sheet

Butterflies — A710

Designs: a, Phoebis neocypris. b, Diogas erippus. c, Euryades duponcheli. d, Automeris coresus.

1995, June 15 Litho. ***Perf. 12½***
1576 A710 5p Sheet of 4, #a.-d. 13.00 12.50

Wild Dog — A711

1995, May 17 Litho. ***Perf. 12½***
1577 A711 2.30p multicolored 2.25 2.00

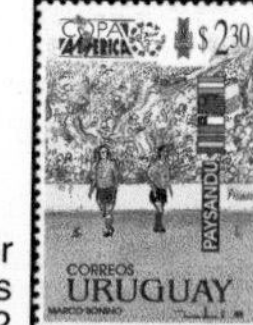
America Cup Soccer Championships A712

Game scenes, flags of participating countries, match sites: a, Paysandu. b, Rivera. c, Ball (no site). d, Montevideo. e, Maldonado.

1995, July 4

1578 A712 2.30p Strip of 5, #a.-e. 8.25 7.00

No. 1578 is a continuous design.

FAO, 50th Anniv. — A713

1995, July 7

1579 A713 5.50p multicolored 3.50 3.25

UN Peace-Keeping Missions — A714

1995, July 14 Litho. *Perf. 12½*

1580 A714 2.30p multicolored 2.00 1.75

Visit of Italy's Pres. Oscar Luigi Scalfaro — A715

1995, July 21

1581 A715 5.50p multicolored 3.50 3.50

A716

1995, July 24

1582 A716 5p multicolored 3.25 3.25

Rotary Intl., 90th anniv.

A717

1995, Sept. 22

1583 A717 2.60p multicolored 1.90 1.60

Jose Pedro Varela, 150th birth anniv.

Miniature Sheet

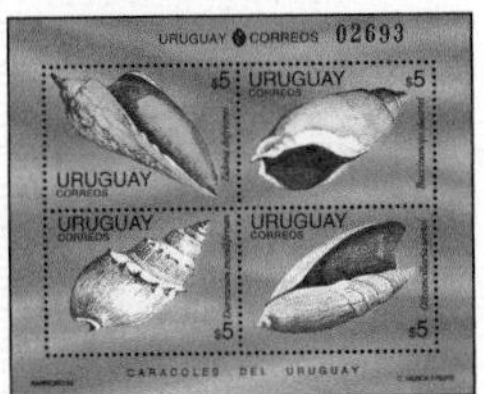

Shells — A718

a, Zidona dufresnei. b, Boccinanops duartei. c, Dorsanum moniliferum. d, Olivancillaria uretai.

1995, Aug. 4

1584 A718 5p Sheet of 4, #a.-d. 21.00 20.00

America Issue — A719

Designs: 3p, Dicksonia sellowiana, vert. 6p, Chrysocyon brachyurus.

Unwmk.

1995, Oct. 10 Litho. *Perf. 12*

1585 A719 3p multicolored 2.00 1.75

1586 A719 6p multicolored 4.00 3.75

Carlos Gardel, Musician — A720

1995, Sept. 4 *Perf. 12½*

1587 A720 5.50p blue & black 3.50 3.25

Flowers — A721

Designs: a, Notocactus roseinflorus. b, Verbena chamaedryfolia. c, Bauhinia candicans. d, Tillandsia aeranthos. e, Eichhornia crassipes.

1995, Sept. 12

1588 A721 3p Strip of 5, #a.-e. 11.00 10.00

Miniature Sheet

Uruguay's Artigas Antarctic Scientific Research Base, 10th Anniv. — A722

Designs: a, 2.50p, Albatross. b, 4p, Fairchild FAU572. c, 4p, ROU Vanguard. d, 2.50p, PTS/M Amphibian transporter.

1995, Oct. 13

1589 A722 Sheet of 4, #a.-d. 12.00 12.00

Uruguayan Antarctic Institute, 20th anniv.

No. 1589 exists demonitized and imperf. on paper with watermark 332. This item was sold with No. 1589 and has matching serial numbers. Same value.

Holocaust Memorial — A723

1995, Sept. 27 Litho. *Perf. 13x12½*

1590 A723 6p multicolored 6.25 6.00

UN, 50th Anniv. — A724

1995, Oct. 24 Litho. *Perf. 12*

1591 A724 6p multicolored 3.75 3.50

Early Locomotives A725

No. 1592, Beyer & Peacock, 1876. No. 1593, Criollo, 1895. No. 1594, Beyer & Peacock, 1910.

1995, Nov. 7

1592 A725 3p multicolored 2.25 2.00

1593 A725 3p multicolored 2.25 2.00

1594 A725 3p multicolored 2.25 2.00

Nos. 1592-1594 (3) 6.75 6.00

Uruguayan Navy, 178th Anniv. — A726

No. 1595, Sailing ship, Artiguista. No. 1596, ROU Pte. Rivera. No. 1597, ROU Montevideo.

1995, Nov. 15 *Perf. 12½*

1595 A726 3p multicolored 2.25 2.00

1596 A726 3p multicolored 2.25 2.00

1597 A726 3p multicolored 2.25 2.00

Nos. 1595-1597 (3) 6.75 6.00

Motion Pictures, Cent. — A727

1995, Dec. 13

1598 A727 6p Lumiere Brothers 4.25 4.00

A728

Christmas — A729

1995, Dec. 15

1599 A728 2.90p multicolored 1.75 1.50

1600 A729 6.50p multicolored 4.00 3.75

Modern Olympic Games, Cent. — A730

Designs: a, Equestrian event, Atlanta 1996. b, Ski jumper, Nagano 1988. c, Torch bearer, Sydney 2000. d, Skier, Salt Lake City 2002.

1996, Jan. 30 Litho. *Perf. 12½*

1601 A730 2.50p Sheet of 4, #a.-d. 10.50 9.50

Latin America Philatelic Exposition.

No. 1601 exists demonitized and imperf. on paper with watermark 332. This item was sold with No. 1601 and has matching serial numbers. Same value.

Carnival Personalities — A732

1996, Feb. 16 Litho. *Perf. 12½*

1603 A732 2.90p Rosa Luna 2.25 2.00

1604 A732 2.90p Pepino 2.25 2.00

1605 A732 2.90p Santiago Luz 2.25 2.00

Nos. 1603-1605 (3) 6.75 6.00

Golf in Uruguay — A733

Designs: a, Cantegril Country Club. b, Cerro Golf Club. c, Fay Crocker. d, Lago Golf Club. e, Golf Club of Uruguay.

1996, Feb. 27

1606 A733 2.90p Strip of 5, #a.-e. 13.00 12.00

No. 1606 was issued in sheets of 25 stamps.

Famous People, Events — A734

Designs: a, Statue, Cardinal Barbieri (1892-1979). b, Yitzhak Rabin (1922-95), Nobel Peace Prize. c, Soccer players, First World Cup Soccer Championship, Grand Park Central, July 13, 1930. d, Robert Stolz (1880-1975), composer.

1996, Mar. 8

1607 A734 2.50p Sheet of 4, #a.-d. 8.00 7.00

Philatelic Academy of Uruguay. The Stamp of Today, SODRE TV Chanel 5, 10th anniv.

Montevideo, Capital of Latin American Culture — A735

1996, Mar. 5

1608 A735 2.90p Solis Theater, 1837 2.00 1.75

a. Booklet pane of 3 *7.00*

Complete booklet, #1608a *7.50*

General Census — A736

1996, Apr. 29

1609 A736 3.20p multicolored 2.00 1.75

1998 World Cup Soccer Championships, France — A737

a, Player in early uniform, Olympic champions, 1924-28, world cup champions, 1930-50, older trophy. b, Trophy, player. d, Two children playing, UNICEF emblem, soccer emblems. e, Olympic rings, two players, eliminations for Atlanta '96.

1996, Apr. 10

1610 A737 2.50p Sheet of 4, #a.-d. 8.75 8.50

Latin America Philatelic Exposition.

No. 1610 exists demonitized and imperf. on paper with watermark 332. This item was sold with No. 1610 and has matching serial numbers. Same value.

Bones from Indian Burial Grounds — A738

1996, Apr. 18
1611 A738 3.20p multicolored 2.00 1.75

Alfredo Zitarrosa (1936-89), Guitarist — A739

1996, Mar. 15 ***Perf. 12***
1612 A739 3p multicolored 2.25 2.00

Prehistoric Animals — A740

Designs: a, Glyptodon claripes. b, Macrauchenia patachonica. c, Toxodon platensis. d, Glossotherium robostum. e, Titanosaurus.

1996, Apr. 18 ***Perf. 12½***
1613 A740 3.20p Strip of 5, #a.-e. 11.25 10.00

No. 1613 was issued in sheets of 25 stamps.

Taking Care of Planet Earth, Everyone's Responsibility, by Soraya Campanella
A741

Unwmk.
1996, June 5 **Litho.** ***Perf. 12***
1614 A741 3.20p multicolored 2.00 1.75

Souvenir Sheet

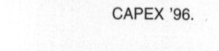

Calidris Canutus A742

1996, May 28 ***Perf. 12½***
1615 A742 12p multicolored 11.25 11.00

CAPEX '96.

Early Methods of Transportation — A743

Designs: a, 1912 Dion-Buton omnibus. b, 1928 Ford Model A. c, 1940 Raleigh bicycle. d, 1926 Magirus firetruck. e, 1917 Hotchkiss ambulance.

1996, May 21
1616 A743 3.20p Strip of 5, #a.-e. 11.25 10.00

No. 1616 was issued in sheets of 25 stamps.

Sailing Ships — A744

Designs: a, Our Lady of Encina, 1726. b, San Francisco. c, Ships of E. Moreau. d, Bold Lady. e, Our Lady of the Light.

1996, June 17 **Litho.** ***Perf. 12½***
1617 A744 3.20p Strip of 5, #a.-e. 9.75 8.50

No. 1617 was issued in sheets of 25 stamps.

Landscape in Las Flores, by Carmelo de Arzadun — A745

1996, July 15 **Litho.** ***Perf. 12½***
1618 A745 3.50p multicolored 2.00 1.75

Jewish Community in Uruguay, 80th Anniv. — A746

1996, July 29
1619 A746 7.50p multicolored 4.25 4.00

A747

Scientists from Uruguay — A748

No. 1620, Enrique Legrand (1861-1939). No. 1621, Victor Bertullo (1919-79). No. 1622, Tomas Beno Hirschfeld (1939-86). No. 1623, Miguel C. Rubino (1886-1945).

1996, July 30
1620 A747 3.50p multicolored 2.10 1.90
1621 A747 3.50p multicolored 2.10 1.90
1622 A748 3.50p multicolored 2.10 1.90
1623 A748 3.50p multicolored 2.10 1.90
Nos. 1620-1623 (4) 8.40 7.60

Bank of Uruguay, Cent. A749

1996, Sept. 9 ***Perf. 12***
1624 A749 3.50p 10p note 2.25 2.00
a. Booklet pane, #1624 3.00
1625 A749 3.50p 500p note 2.25 2.00
a. Booklet pane, #1625 3.00
Complete bklt., #1624a, 1625a 6.00

Souvenir Sheet

Otto Lilienthal (1848-1896) — A750

1996, Aug. 30
1626 A750 12p multicolored 6.75 6.50

AEROFILA '96.

Scientists A751

No. 1627, Albert Einstein. No. 1628, Aristotle. No. 1629, Isaac Newton.

1996, Sept. 3 ***Perf. 12½***
1627 A751 7.50p multicolored 4.25 4.00
1628 A751 7.50p multicolored 4.25 4.00
1629 A751 7.50p multicolored 4.25 4.00
Nos. 1627-1629 (3) 12.75 12.00

National Heritage — A752

Designs: No. 1630, Map of Gorriti Island showing locations of Spanish forts, 18th cent. No. 1631, Narbona Church, 18th cent.

Perf. 13x12½
1996, Sept. 12 **Litho.** **Unwmk.**
1630 A752 3.50p multicolored 1.95 1.75
1631 A752 3.50p multicolored 1.95 1.75

Rural Assoc., 125th Anniv. — A753

1996, Sept. 20 ***Perf. 12½x13***
1632 A753 3.50p multicolored 2.00 1.75

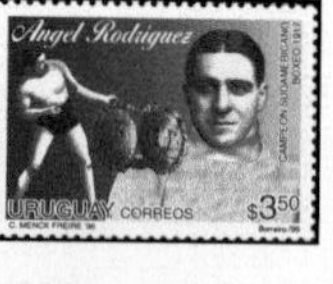

Marine Life — A754

a, Carchardon carcharias. b, Alopias vulpinus. c, Notorynchus cepedianus. d, Squatina dumerili.

1996, Sept. 23
1633 A754 3.50p Sheet of 4, #a.-d. 9.00 8.00

Istanbul '96.

Sports Champions from Uruguay — A755

Designs: a, Angel Rodriguez, boxing, 1917. b, Leandro Noli, cycling, 1939. c, Eduardo G. Risso, rowing, 1948. d, Estrella Puente, javelin, 1949. e, Oscar Moglia, basketball, 1956.

1996, Oct. 1
1634 A755 3.50p Strip of 5, #a.-e. 10.75 9.50

Traditional Costumes — A756

America issue: 3.50p, Gaucho. 7.50p, Woman of the campana.

1996, Oct. 11 ***Perf. 13x12½***
1635 A756 3.50p multicolored 1.50 1.75
1636 A756 7.50p multicolored 4.75 4.00

3rd Space Conference of the Americas A757

1996, Nov. 4 **Wmk. 332** ***Perf. 12***
1637 A757 3.50p multicolored 2.40 2.10

Comic Strips, Cent. — A758

"Peloduro," by Julio E. Suarez.

1996, Nov. 7
1638 A758 4p multicolored 2.60 2.40

Health Institute, Cent. — A759

1996, Nov. 20
1639 A759 4p multicolored 2.10 1.90

Church of the 7th Day Adventists in Uruguay, Cent. — A760

Wmk. 332
1996, Nov. 26 **Litho.** ***Perf. 12½***
1640 A760 3.50p multicolored 2.00 1.75

Felix de Azara (1746-1811), Naturalist A761

1996, Nov. 20 ***Perf. 12***
1641 A761 4p multicolored 2.25 2.00

Fish — A762

Designs: No. 1642, Cynolebia nigripinnis. No. 1643, Cynolebia viarius.

Unwmk.
1997, Feb. 24 **Litho.** ***Die Cut***
Self-Adhesive
1642 A762 4p multicolored 2.25 2.00
1643 A762 4p multicolored 2.25 2.00

Popular Festivals — A763

#1644, Natl. Folklore Festival, Durazno. #1645, Traditional Gaucho Festival, Tacuarembo.

1997 **Wmk. 332** ***Perf. 12½***
1644 A763 4p multi 2.50 2.25
1645 A763 4p multi, vert. 2.50 2.25

Issued: #1644, 1/30; #1645, 3/10.
See Nos. 1653-1656.

Mushrooms A764

Designs: a, Tricholoma nudum. b, Agaricus xanthodermus. c, Russula sardonia. d, Microsporum canis. e, Polyporus versicolor.

1997, Feb. 7
1646 A764 4p Strip of 5, #a.-e 13.00 12.00

No. 1646 was issued in sheets of 25 stamps.

Ports — A765

No. 1647, Colonia. No. 1648, Punta del Este. No. 1649, Santiago Vázquez. No. 1650, Buceo.

1997, Feb. 28 Litho. *Die Cut*
Self-Adhesive

1647 A765 4p multicolored 2.25 2.00
1648 A765 4p multicolored 2.25 2.00
1649 A765 4p multicolored 2.25 2.00
1650 A765 4p multicolored 2.25 2.00
Nos. 1647-1650 (4) 9.00 8.00

Artigas' Lancers, Bicent. — A766

1997, Mar. 10 Wmk. 332 *Perf. 12½*
1651 A766 4p multicolored 2.25 2.00

Military Academy, 50th Anniv. — A767

1997, Mar. 13
1652 A767 4p multicolored 2.25 2.00

Popular Festivals Type of 1997

Coat of arms and: No. 1653, Performers under outdoor pavilion, Beer Week. No. 1654, Ruben Lena, bridge, river, Olimar River Festival, vert. No. 1655, Guitar, man on horse, Festival de Minas Y Abril. No. 1656, Family around person on horseback, Roosevelt Park.

1997 Litho.
1653 A763 5p multicolored 2.75 2.75
1654 A763 5p multicolored 2.75 2.75
1655 A763 5p multicolored 2.75 2.75

Die Cut
Unwmk.
Self-Adhesive

1656 A763 5p multicolored 2.75 2.75
Nos. 1653-1656 (4) 11.00 11.00

Lions Intl. (#1656). Issued: #1653, 3/23; #1654, 3/24; #1655, 4/26; #1656, 3/21.

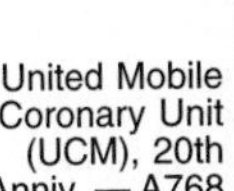

United Mobile Coronary Unit (UCM), 20th Anniv. — A768

1997, Apr. 4 Unwmk. *Die Cut*
Self-Adhesive
1657 A768 5p multicolored 2.75 2.50

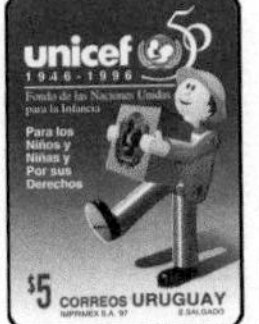

UNICEF, 50th Anniv. — A769

1997, Apr. 8 *Die Cut*
Self-Adhesive
1658 A769 5p multicolored 2.75 2.50

Lighthouses — A770

Various birds and: a, Anchorena Tower, 1920. b, Farallón Lighthouse, 1870. c, José Ignacio Lighthouse, 1877. d, Santa Maria Lighthouse, 1874. e, Vigía Tower, 18th cent.

1997, Apr. 22 *Die Cut*
Self-Adhesive
1659 A770 5p Strip of 5, #a.-e. 16.00 15.00

Prehistoric Animals — A771

Designs: a, Devincenzia gallinali. b, Smilodon populator. c, Mesosaurus tenuidens. d, Doedicurus clavicaudatus. e, Artigasia magna.

1997, May 5 *Die Cut*
Self-Adhesive
1660 A771 5p Strip of 5, #a.-e. 16.00 15.00

A772

Ecclesiastical Provinces A772a

No. 1661, Church, diocese of Salto. No. 1662, Church, diocese of Melo. No. 1663, Bishop Jacinto Vera, 1st bishop of Montevideo. No. 1664, Msgr. Mariano Soler, 1st archbishop of Montevideo.

Wmk. 332
1997, May 9 Litho. *Perf. 12½*
1661 A772 5p multicolored 2.75 2.50
1662 A772 5p multicolored 2.75 2.50
1663 A772a 5p multicolored 2.75 2.50
1664 A772a 5p multicolored 2.75 2.50
Nos. 1661-1664 (4) 11.00 10.00

Youth Stamp Collecting A773

Designs: a, 2p, Boy, "Philately?" b, 2p, Boy thinking of stamps. c, 2p, Girl with soccer ball, boy. d, 1p, Boy looking at stamps in album. e, 1p, Boy with tongs and magnifying glass.

1997, May 25 Unwmk.
1665 A773 Strip of 5, #a.-e. 5.25 4.00

PACIFIC 97 — A774

1997, May 29 *Perf. 12*
1666 A774 10p Rynchops niger 5.25 5.00

Maccio Theater of San Jose, 85th Anniv. — A775

1997, June 5 Wmk. 332 *Perf. 12½*
1667 A775 5p multicolored 2.75 2.50

Inter-American Institute of Children, 70th Anniv. — A776

1997, June 9 Unwmk.
1668 A776 5p multicolored 2.75 2.50

Colony of Sacramento A777

1997, July 4
1669 A777 5p multicolored 2.75 2.50

Punta del Este, 90th Anniv. — A778

1997, July 1
1670 A778 5p multicolored 2.75 2.50

Uruguayan Comics — A779

Scenes from comics by: No. 1671, Julio E. Suarez (Peloduro). No. 1672, Geoffrey Foladori.

Perf. 12½
1997, June 30 Litho. Unwmk.
1671 A779 5p multicolored 2.25 2.00
1672 A779 5p multicolored 2.25 2.00

Zionism, Cent. — A780

Design: Theodor Herzl (1860-1904), founder of Zionist movement.

1997, July 17
1673 A780 5p multicolored 3.25 3.00

Children's Painting A781

Geranoaetus Melanoleucus A782

1997, July 21 Litho. *Die Cut*
Self-Adhesive
1674 A781 15p multicolored *10.50 10.00*
a. Dated "1999" *10.50 10.00*
1675 A782 25p multicolored *16.00 16.00*
a. Type II ('04) *10.00 10.00*
b. Dated "1998" *16.00 16.00*
c. Dated "1999" *16.00 16.00*
d. Dated "2005" *10.00 10.00*

Type I stamps have printer's name at right, designer's name at left, and have an eagle's head that is rounder, with its edge making a sharper angle with the right margin than on type II. Type II stamps have the printer's name at left and the designer's name at right.

See Nos. 1840, 1850, 1853, 1855.

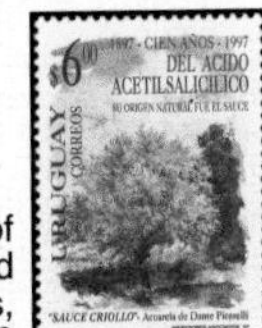

Isolation of Acetylsalicylic Acid from Willow Trees, Cent. — A783

1997, Aug. 12 Litho. *Perf. 12½*
1676 A783 6p multicolored 2.25 2.00
a. Booklet pane of 2 6.50
Complete booklet, #1676a 6.75

Department of Salto — A784

1997, Aug. 26
1677 A784 6p multicolored 2.25 2.00

Felix Mendelssohn (1809-47) A785

No. 1679, Johannes Brahms (1833-97).

1997, Sept. 1
1678 A785 6p multicolored 2.00 1.75
1679 A785 6p multicolored 2.00 1.75
a. Pair, #1678-1679 4.75 4.25

Natural History Museum of Montevideo, 160th Anniv. — A786

Designs: a, Lucas Kraguevich, paleontologist. b, Jose Arechavaleta, botanist. c, Garibaldi J. Devincenzi, zoologist. d, Antonio Taddei, archaelogist.

1997, Sept. 3
1680 A786 6p Strip of 4, #a.-d. 8.50 7.50

Mercosur (Common Market of Latin America) — A787

1997, Sept. 26 *Perf. 12*
1681 A787 11p multicolored 4.00 3.75

See Argentina, No. 1975; Bolivia No. 1019; Brazil, No. 2646; Paraguay, No. 2564.

Souvenir Sheet

Passiflora Coerulea — A788

1997, Sept. 26 *Perf. 12½*
1682 A788 15p multicolored 5.25 5.00

1st Philatelic Exhibition of Mercosur countries.

Heinrich von Stephan (1831-97) — A789

1997, Oct. 9
1683 A789 11p multicolored 4.00 3.75

Souvenir Sheet

Spanish-Uruguayan Monument — A790

1997, Oct. 9
1684 A790 15p Monument 5.25 5.00

Philatelic Exhibition, Spain 1997.

America Issue — A791

Designs: 6p, Woman carrying mail. 11p, Man delivering letters.

1997, Oct. 10
1685 A791 6p multicolored 2.00 1.75
1686 A791 11p multicolored 3.75 3.50

Artigas Scientific Base, Antarctica A792

1997, Oct. 15 ***Perf. 12***
1687 A792 6p Pygoscelis papua 2.25 2.00

Painting, by Domingo Laporte (1855-1928) A793

1997, Oct. 21 ***Perf. 12½***
1688 A793 6p multicolored 2.25 2.00

Galicia House, 80th Anniv. — A794

1997, Oct. 24
1689 A794 6p multicolored 2.25 2.00

3rd Intl. Congress of Aeronautical and Space History, Montevideo A795

Perf. 12½
1997, Oct. 27 Litho. Unwmk.
1690 A795 6p Arme 2 Biplane 2.25 2.00

1st Biennial Interparliamentary Exhibition of MERCOSUR Paintings, Montevideo — A796

1997, Oct. 28
1691 A796 11p multicolored 3.75 3.50

Souvenir Sheet

Pope John Paul II, Holy Year 2000 A797

1997, Nov. 7
1692 A797 10p multicolored 8.25 8.00

Third Intl. Assembly Punta del Este, and of arrival of first Polish colonists at River Plate, cent.

Uruguayan Navy, 180th Anniv. — A798

1997, Nov. 14
1693 A798 6p multicolored 2.25 2.00

Shanghai '97 Intl. Stamp and Coin Exhibition — A799

No. 1694: a, 3.50p, Front and back of 1 peso coin. b, 3.50p, Chinese flag, Hong Kong harbor, flower, junk. c, 4p, Michael Schumacher, Formula 1 driving champion, Ferrari. d, 4p, Sojourner on Mars, Pathfinder Mission.

No. 1695: a, 3.50p, Martina Hingis, 1997 Wimbledon Ladies' champion. b, 3.50p, Jan Ullrich, 1997 Tour de France winner. c, 4p, Soccer players, 1998 World Cup Soccer Championship, France. d, 4p, Ski jumper, 1998 Winter Olympic Games, Nagano.

1997, Nov. 19
1694 A799 Sheet of 4, #a.-d. 6.25 6.00
1695 A799 Sheet of 4, #a.-d. 6.25 6.00

Christmas — A800

1997, Nov. 20
1696 A800 6p Magi 2.00 2.00
1697 A800 11p Madonna & Child 4.00 3.75

Uruguayan Sportsmen A801

Designs: a, Adesio Lombardo, Olympic bronze medalist, basketball, Helsinki, 1952. b, Guillermo Douglas, Olympic bronze medalist, single sculls, Rome, 1932. c, Obdulio Varela, soccer player on 1950 World Cup championship team. d, Atilio Francois, silver medalist, 1947 World Cycling Championships, Paris. e, Juan López Testa, South American 100 meters champion, 1947.

1997, Nov. 26
1698 A801 6p Strip of 5, #a.-e. 11.25 10.00

Mevifil '97, 1st Intl. Exhibition of Philatelic Audio-Visual and Computer Systems A802

1997, Dec. 1 ***Perf. 12***
1699 A802 11p multicolored 3.75 3.50

INDEPEX '97 — A803

Early vehicles, inventors: a, 1st Land Rover, 1947. b, Henry Ford (1863-1947), Model A. c, Robert Bosch (1861-1942), inventor of automotive components. d, Rudolf Diesel (1858-1913), patented first diesel engine, 1897.

1997, Dec. 8 ***Perf. 12½***
1700 A803 6p Strip of 4, #a.-d. 9.00 8.00

Naval Academy of Uruguay, 90th Anniv. — A804

1997, Dec. 12
1701 A804 6p multicolored 2.25 2.00

Supreme Court of Uruguay, 90th Anniv. — A805

1997, Dec. 12
1702 A805 6p multicolored 2.25 2.00

Uruguayan Post Office, 170th Anniv. — A806

1997, Dec. 19
1703 A806 6p multicolored 2.25 2.00

MEVIR (Movement for Eradication of Unsanitary Rural Housing), 90th Anniv. — A807

Design: Homes, Dr. A. Gallinal, logo.

1997, Dec. 26
1704 A807 6p multicolored 2.25 2.00

Construction Projects — A808

a, Preparation. b, Planning. c, Execution.

1997, Dec. 29 ***Perf. 12***
1705 A808 6p Strip of 3, #a.-c. 6.75 6.00
d. Booklet pane, #1705 7.75 7.25
Complete booklet, #1705d 8.00 7.25

Souvenir Sheet

1897 Revolution, Cent. — A809

Design: Gen. Antonio "Chiquito" Saravia and Col. Diego Lamas.

1997, Dec. 30 ***Perf. 12½***
1706 A809 15p multicolored 5.00 4.50

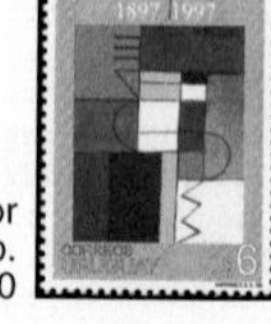

Painting by Héctor Ragni (b. 1898) — A810

1998, Feb. 6
1707 A810 6p multicolored 2.25 2.00

Naval Station, Montevideo A811

1998, Feb. 13
1708 A811 6p multicolored 2.25 2.00

Native Trees — A812

a, Butia capitata. b, Grove of butia capitata. c, Grove of phytolacca dioica. d, Phytolacca dioica.

1998, Mar. 20 ***Perf. 12***
1709 A812 6p Block of 4, #a.-d. 8.00 7.50

Museum of Humor — A813

Cartoons: No. 1710, by Oscar Abín. No. 1711, by Emilio Cortinas.

1998, Mar. 13 ***Perf. 12½***
1710 A813 6p multicolored 2.00 1.75
1711 A813 6p multicolored 2.00 1.75
a. Pair, #1710-1711 4.50 4.00

Wilson Ferreira Aldunate (1919-88) — A814

1998, Mar. 17 *Perf. 12*
1712 A814 6p multicolored 2.25 2.00

Fossilized Animals — A815

Designs: a, Testudinites sellowi. b, Proborhyaena gigantea. c, Propachyrucos schiaffinos. d, Stegomastodon platensis.

1998, Mar. 26
1713 A815 6p Block of 4, #a.-d. 8.50 8.00

Israel '98, State of Israel, 50th Anniv. — A816

1998, Mar. 31 *Perf. 12*
1714 A816 12p multicolored 4.00 3.75

Birds A820

a, Plyborus plancus. b, Cygnus melancoryphus. c, Platalea ajaja. d, Theristicus caudatus.

1998, Apr. 30
1718 A820 6p Block of 4, #a.-d. 9.50 9.00

Organization of American States, 50th Anniv. — A821

1998, Apr. 14 Litho. *Perf. 12¾x12½*
1719 A821 12p multi 4.90 4.50

61st World Congress of Sports Journalism — A822

1998, Apr. 21 Litho. *Perf. 12*
1720 A822 6p multicolored 2.60 2.40

Land Settlement Institute, 50th Anniv. — A823

1998, Apr. 22 Litho. *Perf. 12¾x12½*
1721 A823 6p multi 2.60 2.40

Souvenir Sheet

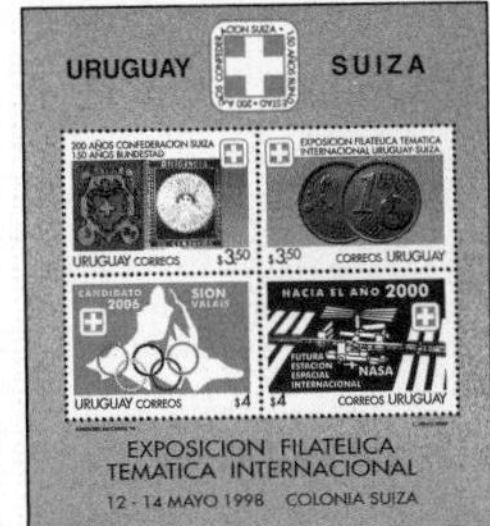

Intl. Topical Philatelic Exhibition, Nueva Helvecia — A824

Cross and: a, 3.50p, Switzerland #5, Uruguay #1. b, 3.50p, Obverse and reverse of Euro coin. c, 4p, Olympic rings and mountain. d, 4p, Space station.

1998, May 12 *Perf. 12½x12¾*
1722 A824 Sheet of 4, #a.-d. 8.50 8.00

Swiss Republic, bicent.

Souvenir Sheet

Whales — A825

a, 3.50p, Balaeneoptera physalus (b). b, 3.50p, Balaeneoptera acutorostrata. c, 4p, Megaptera novaeangliae (d). d, 4p, Eubalaena australis (c).

1998, May 15 Litho. *Perf. 12½*
1723 A825 Sheet of 4, #a.-d. 8.00 7.50

Ambiente '98, Maia, Portugal; Intl. Year of the Ocean; Expo '98, Lisbon.

1983 Labor Day Democracy Demonstrations A826

Perf. 12¼x12¾
1998, May 27 Litho. Wmk. 332
1724 A826 6p brn & blk 2.60 2.40

See Nos. 1740, 1775.

Street Cars — A827

Historic Montevideo trams: a, English "La Comercial," 1906. b, German Transatlantica Co., 1907. c, Transatlantica, 1908. d, Transatlantica double decker, 1916.

1998, May 29 Litho. *Perf. 12*
1725 A827 6p Block of 4, #a.-d. 8.00 7.50

Juvalux '98 — A828

Wildcats: a, Felis colocola. b, Felis pardalis. c, Felis wiedil. d, Panthera onca.

Unwmk.
1998, June 18 Litho. *Perf. 12*
1726 A828 6p Block of 4, #a.-d. 9.00 8.50

Ships — A829

a, "Sirus." b, Gunboat "18 de Julio." c, Transport, "Maldonado." d, "Instituto de Pesca No. 1."

1998, June 25 Litho. *Perf. 12*
1727 A829 6p Block of 4, #a.-d. 8.00 7.50

Jesuit Mission Church, Calera de las Huérfanas A830

Perf. 12½x12¾
1998, July 24 Litho. Unwmk.
1728 A830 12p multi 5.00 4.75

Monument to the Peace of 1872, San José de Mayo, 125th Anniv. — A831

1998, July 31 *Perf. 12¾x12½*
1729 A831 6p multi 2.25 2.00

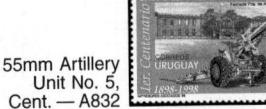

155mm Artillery Unit No. 5, Cent. — A832

1998, Aug. 7 *Perf. 12½x12¾*
1730 A832 6p multi 2.60 2.00

Butterflies A833

1998, Aug. 14 Litho. *Perf. 12*
1731 A833 6p Eacles imperialis 2.75 2.50
1732 A833 6p Protoparce luceti-us 2.75 2.50
a. Pair, #1731-1732 6.50 6.00

First Monument to José Artigas, San José de Mayo, Cent. — A834

Perf. 12¾x12½
1998, Aug. 24 Litho.
1733 A834 6p multi 2.60 2.40

A835

1998, Aug. 28
1734 A835 6p multi 2.60 2.40

Dr. Mauricio López Lombo (1918-93), zoo founder.

A836

1998, Aug. 31
1735 A836 6p multi 2.60 2.40

Falleri-Balzo Music Conservatory, Montevideo, cent.

José Fernández Vergara (1810-1906), Founder of Pueblo Vergara — A837

1998, Sept. 8
1736 A837 6p multi 2.60 2.40

Souvenir Sheet

El Pais Newspaper, 80th Anniv. — A838

1998, Sept. 14 *Perf. 12½x12¾*
1737 A838 12p multi 5.00 4.75

Collective Medical Assistance Institute, 145th Anniv. — A839

1998, Sept. 24 *Perf. 12¾x12½*
1738 A839 6p multi 2.60 2.40

Postal Link Between Montevideo and Corunna, Spain, 230th Anniv. — A840

1998, Sept. 24
1739 A840 12p multi 4.75 4.50

Espamer '98, Buenos Aires.

Labor Day Type

6p, March of the Social and Cultural Assoc. of Public School Students, 9/25/83.

Perf. 12½x12¾

1998, Sept. 25 **Wmk. 332**
1740 A826 6p brn & blk 2.60 2.40

Iberoamericana '98 Philatelic Exhibition, Maia, Portugal — A841

Airplanes: a, Junkers J52. b, Spad VII. c, Ansaldo SVA-10. d, Neybar.

Unwmk.

1998, Oct. 2 **Litho.** ***Perf. 12***
1741 A841 6p Block of 4, #a.-d. 9.75 8.75

Death of Chilean Pres. Salvador Allende, 25th Anniv. — A842

Perf. 12¼x12¾

1998, Oct. 2 **Litho.** **Unwmk.**
1742 A842 12p multi 4.25 3.75

50th Anniv. of Enrique Rodríguez Fabregat (1885-1976) as UN Commissioner for Palestine — A843

1998, Oct. 5 ***Perf. 12¾x12½***
1743 A843 6p multi 2.60 2.40

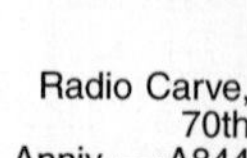

Radio Carve, 70th Anniv. — A844

1998, Oct. 7 **Litho.** ***Perf. 12½x12¾***
1744 A844 6p multi 2.60 2.40

World Post Day — A845

1998, Oct. 9 **Litho.** ***Perf. 12½x12¾***
1745 A845 12p multi 4.75 4.50

Ilsapex '98, Johannesburg.

America Issue A846

Famous women: 6p, Julia Guarino (1897-1985), first woman architect in South America. 12p, Dr. Paulina Luisi (1875-1950).

1998, Oct. 9 **Litho.** ***Perf. 12***
1746 A846 6p multi 2.75 2.00
1747 A846 12p multi 5.50 4.00

Assoc. of Inland Pharmacies, 50th Anniv. — A847

1998, Oct. 10 ***Perf. 12½x12¾***
1748 A847 6p multi 2.60 2.40

Postal Services — A847a

Serpentine Die Cut 11¼

1998, Oct. 15 **Litho.** **Unwmk.**

Self-Adhesive

1748A A847a 25p multi 7.75 7.50
b. Dated "1999" 7.75 7.50

Classic Vehicles — A848

Designs: a, 1950 Lancia fire engine. b, 1946 Maserati San Remo. c, 1954 Alfa Romeo trolley bus. d, 1936 Fiat Topolino.

1998, Oct. 23 **Litho.** ***Perf. 12***
1749 A848 6p Block of 4, #a.-d. 9.50 8.50

Italia'98.

Artists — A849

Designs: No. 1750, Sculpture, "Motherhood," and self-portrait of Nerses Ounanian (1920-57). No. 1751, Illustrations from book "Piquín y Chispita," by Serafin J. Garcia (1905-85), vert. No. 1752, Musical score by Héctor M. Artola (1903-82), vert.

Perf. 12½x12¾, 12¾x12½

1998, Oct. 27 **Litho.**
1750 A849 6p multi 2.60 2.40
1751 A849 6p multi 2.60 2.40
1752 A849 6p multi 2.60 2.40
Nos. 1750-1752 (3) 7.80 7.20

Juvenalia '98 — A850

1998, Oct. 30 **Litho.** ***Perf. 12¾x12½***
1753 A850 6p multi 2.60 2.40

Souvenir Sheet

Uruguay-Germany Philatelic Exhibition, Montevideo — A851

Designs: a, 3.50p, Zeppelin cover, Zeppelin NT. b, 3.50p, Germany #1592, Germany Berlin #9N584, German Democratic Republic #2791, mail box. c, 4p, Brandenburg Gate, Volkswagen Beetle, Konrad Adenauer. d, 4p, Airplane, German mark note and coin.

1998, Nov. 6 **Litho.** ***Perf. 12½x12¾***
1754 A851 Sheet of 4, #a.-d. 8.50 7.50

IBRA '99, 150th anniv. of German stamps (#1754a, 1754b), 50th anniv. of Federal Republic of Germany (#1754c), 50th anniv. of German mark (#1754d).

16th Congress of Expenditure Control Boards — A852

1998, Nov. 9
1755 A852 12p blue & silver 4.75 4.50

Uruguayan Chamber of Industries, Cent. — A853

1998, Nov. 9
1756 A853 6p multi 2.60 2.40

Flowers — A854

1p, Oxalis pudica. 4p, Oxalis pudica (white). 5p, Oxalis pudica (purple). 6p, Eugenia uniflora. 7p, Eugenia uniflora. 9p, Eugenia uniflora. 10p, Aechmea recurvata. 14p, Acca sellowiana. 50p, Acca sellowiana.

Serpentine Die Cut 11¼

1998-99 **Self-Adhesive** **Litho.**
1757 A854 1p "98" date .70 .30
a. "99" in inscription .65 .30
b. "2000" in inscription .65 .30
c. "2001" in inscription .65 .30
d. "2002" in inscription .65 .30
1760 A854 4p multi 1.60 1.00
1761 A854 5p multi 1.40 .80
1762 A854 6p multi 3.00 1.75
1763 A854 7p multi 3.00 1.75
1765 A854 9p multi 9.25 5.50
1766 A854 10p "98" date 3.25 2.75
a. "99" in inscription 3.00 2.75
b. "2002" in inscription 3.00 2.75
1770 A854 14p multi 6.50 3.75
1771 A854 50p multi 16.00 9.50
Nos. 1757-1771 (9) 44.70 27.10

Issued: 7p, 2/4/99; 4p, 12/23/99; 14p, 8/6/99; 1p, 6p, 10p, 50p, 1998. 9p, 1999. 5p, 2/19/02.

Reprints issued: #1757a, 12/7/99; #1757b, 12/15/00; #1757c, 2/24/01; #1757d, 5/22/02. #1766a, 12/7/99; #1766b, 2/8/02.

Christmas A855

Designs: 6p, The Virgin's Descent to Reward St. Ildefons' Writings (detail), by El Greco. 12p, St. Peter's Tears (detail), by Bartolomé Esteban Murillo.

1998, Nov. 23 **Litho.** ***Perf. 12***
1772 A855 6p multi 2.50 2.40
1773 A855 12p multi 6.00 5.50

Paso Del Molina Neighborhood of Montevideo, 250th Anniv. — A856

1998, Nov. 26 ***Perf. 12½x12¾***
1774 A856 6p multi 2.60 2.40

Labor Day Type

6p, Proclamation at the Obelisk, 11/27/83.

Perf. 12¼x12¾

1998, Nov. 27 **Litho.** **Wmk. 332**
1775 A826 6p brn & blk 2.60 2.40

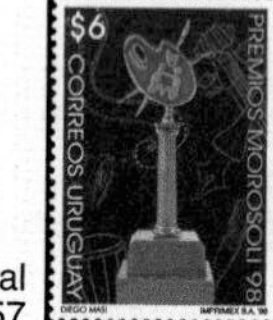

Morosoli Cultural Awards — A857

Perf. 12¾x12½

1998, Nov. 27 **Litho.** **Unwmk.**
1776 A857 6p multi 2.60 2.40

Universal Declaration of Human Rights, 50th Anniv. — A858

1998, Dec. 10 ***Perf. 12½x12¾***
1777 A858 6p multi 2.60 2.40

Uruguayan Olympic Committee, 75th Anniv. A859

1998, Dec. 15 ***Perf. 12***
1778 A859 6p multi 2.60 2.40

Uruguayan Sportsmen — A860

Designs: a, Juan Lopez (1907-83), soccer coach. b, Hector Scarone (1899-1967), soccer player. c, Leandro Gomez Harley (1902-79), basketball player, hurdler. d, Liberto Corney (1905-55), boxer.

1998, Dec. 15 ***Perf. 12¾x12½***
1779 A860 6p Block of 4, #a.-d. 9.50 9.00

Famous Uruguayans A861

Designs: No. 1780: Dr. Roberto Caldeyro Barcia (1921-96), physiologist. No. 1781, Dr. José Verocay (1876-1923), pathologist. No. 1782, Dr. José L. Duomarco (1905-85), medical researcher.

Perf. 12¼x12¾

1998, Dec. 18 **Litho.** **Unwmk.**
1780 A861 6p multi 2.60 2.40
1781 A861 6p multi 2.60 2.40
1782 A861 6p multi 2.60 2.40
Nos. 1780-1782 (3) 7.80 7.20

Emile Zola's "J'accuse" Letter, Cent. (in 1998) — A862

1999, Jan. 4 Litho. ***Perf. 12½x12¾***
1783 A862 14p multicolored 6.00 5.50

Las Cañas Resort, Fray Bentos — A863

1999, Feb. 26
1784 A863 7p multicolored 2.50 2.25

Rio de la Plata Boundary Treaty, 25th Anniv. — A864

1999, Mar. 15
1785 A864 7p multicolored 2.90 2.60

Famous Uruguayans A865

Designs: No. 1786, Joaquin Torres Garcia (1874-1949), painter. No. 1787, Luis Ernesto Aroztegui (1930-94), textile artist. No. 1788, Juan José Morosoli (1899-1957), writer.

1999, Mar. 26
1786 A865 7p multicolored 3.75 3.25
1787 A865 7p multicolored 3.75 3.25
1788 A865 7p multicolored 3.75 3.25
Nos. 1786-1788 (3) 11.25 9.75

Birds and Flowering Trees — A866

a, Psidium cattleianum, Pipraeidea melanonota. b, Tabebuia ipe, Chlorostilbon aureoventris. c, Duranta repens, Tangara preciosa. d, Citharexylum montevidense, Tachuris rubigastra.

1999, Apr. 14 Litho. ***Perf. 12¼x12¾***
1789 A866 7p Block of 4, #a.-d. 8.75 7.75

Carriages A867

Designs: a, Break de chasse. b, Mylord. c, Coupé trois quarts. d, Break de champ.

1999, Apr. 29 Litho. ***Perf. 12½x12¾***
1790 A867 7p Block of 4, #a.-d. 11.50 10.00

National Soccer Team, Cent. A868

Designs: a, B. Céspedes, M. Nebel, C. Céspedes, team's first field. b, H. Castro, P. Cea, A. Ciocca, team flag. c, R. Porta, A García, S. Gambetta, team headquarters.

1999, May 5 Litho. ***Perf. 12***
1791 A868 7p Strip of 3, #a.-c. 7.75 7.00
Complete booklet, #1791 8.00

Children's Millennium Stamp Design Contest Winners — A869

Designs: a, By Stefani Andrea Furtado. b, By Pilar Trujillo. c, By Lucia Lavie. d, By Cecilia Chopitea.

1999, May 6 Litho. ***Perf. 12½x12¾***
1792 A869 7p Block of 4, #a.-d. 11.00 10.00

Jorge Chebataroff (1909-84), Geographer, Botanist — A870

1999, May 14
1793 A870 7p multicolored 2.90 2.60

Formation of Infantry Brigade No. 1, 60th Anniv. — A871

Paintings: No. 1794, Infantry Battalion No. 2 at Battle of Montecaseros, 1852. No. 1795, Infantry Brigade No. 1 at Battle of Estero Bellaco, 1866. No. 1796, Infantry Battalion No. 1 at Battle of Boquerón, 1866.

1999, May 18
1794 A871 7p multicolored 2.75 2.50
1795 A871 7p multicolored 2.75 2.50
1796 A871 7p multicolored 2.75 2.50
Nos. 1794-1796 (3) 8.25 7.50

Villa de la Restauracion, 150th Anniv. — A872

1999, May 24 ***Perf. 12¾x12½***
1797 A872 7p multicolored 2.90 2.50

Souvenir Sheet

Barcelona, Spain Soccer Team, Cent. — A873

1999, May 28 Litho. ***Perf. 12½x12¾***
1798 A873 15p multi 4.50 4.25

1st Festival of Film Critics, Montevideo — A874

1999, June 2 ***Perf. 12¾x12¼***
Booklet Stamp
1799 A874 7p multi 2.50 2.25
a. Booklet pane, 2 #1799 5.50
Complete booklet, #1799a 6.50

Philex France 99 — A875

Horses: a, Arabian. b, Quarter horse. c, Thoroughbred. d, Shetland pony.

Perf. 12½x12¾
1999, June 10 Litho.
1800 A875 7p Block of 4, #a.-d. 9.00 7.75

Publication "Marcha," 60th Anniv. — A876

Perf. 12¼x12¾
1999, June 23 Litho.
1801 A876 7p multi 2.90 2.60

Permanent Home for "Espacio Ciencia" Science Exhibits — A877

1999, July 2 ***Perf. 12¾x12¼***
1802 A877 7p multi 2.90 2.60

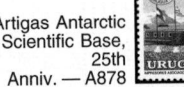

Artigas Antarctic Scientific Base, 25th Anniv. — A878

1999, July 12 ***Perf. 12¼x12¾***
1803 A878 7p multi 2.75 2.50

Republic of Uruguay University, 150th Anniv. — A879

1999, July 19
1804 A879 7p yel & blk 2.90 2.60

UNESCO Regional Office, 50th Anniv. — A880

1999, July 20 ***Perf. 12¾x12¼***
1805 A880 7p multi 2.90 2.60

The Last Charruas A881

a, One seated, one standing. b, Two seated.

1999, July 22 Litho. ***Perf. 12¾x12½***
1806 A881 7p Pair, #a.-b. 5.50 5.00

Souvenir Sheet

Millennium — A882

a, 3.50p, Apollo space program. b, 3.50p, Soccer players, 2000 Olympic Games, Sydney. c, 4p, Centenary of Zeppelins. d, 4p, #C60.

1999, July 30 Litho. ***Perf. 12½x12¾***
1807 A882 Sheet of 4, #a.-d. 11.00 10.00

UPU, 125th anniv., Bangkok 2000, Espana 2000, WIPA 2000, Hanover World's Fair.

El Galpón Theater, Montevideo, 50th Anniv. — A883

1999, Aug. 3 ***Perf. 12¾x12¼***
1808 A883 7p multi 2.90 2.60

China 1999 World Philatelic Exhibition — A884

Sea planes: a, Piper J-3. b, Short Sunderland.

1999, Aug. 18 ***Perf. 12¼x12¾***
1809 A884 7p Pair, #a.-b. 4.50 4.00

Dogs — A885

Designs: a, Cocker spaniel. b, German shepherd. c, Dalmatian. d, Basset hound.

Perf. 12¾x12½
1999, Aug. 24 Litho.
1810 A885 7p Block of 4, #a.-d. 10.50 9.50

Insects & Flowers — A886

a, Halictidae, Oxalis sp. b, Apanteles sp., Epidendrum paniculosum. c, Metabolosia univita, Baccharis trimera. d, Compositae, Cantarido.

Perf. 12½x12¾
1999, Sept. 10 Litho.
1811 A886 7p Block of 4, #a.-d. 8.75 7.75

A887

Uruguayan Artists: No. 1812, Orlando Aldama (1904-87), writer. No. 1813, Julio Martínez Oyanguren (1901-73), guitarist.

Perf. 12¾x12½
1999, Sept. 13 Litho.
1812 A887 7p multi 3.00 2.75
1813 A887 7p multi 3.00 2.75

A888

Perf. 12¾x12¼

1999, Sept. 18 **Litho.**

1814 A888 7p multi 2.75 2.50

Cultural heritage of Mercosur countries.

First Uruguayan Participation in Olympics, Paris, 1924 — A889

Designs: a, Poster, medal. b, Medal, medal-winning soccer team.

1999, Sept. 30 ***Perf. 12¼x12¾***

1815 A889 7p Pair, #a.-b. 6.00 5.50

Intl. Year of Older Persons — A890

1999, Oct. 1 **Litho.** ***Perf. 12¼x12¾***

1816 A890 7p multi 2.90 2.50

Philatelic Witches Sabbath, by Mariano Barbasán A891

1999, Oct. 1 ***Perf. 12***

1817 A891 7p multi 2.90 2.50

Stamp Day.

America Issue, A New Millennium Without Arms — A892

7p, Arms in trash can. 14p, Earth, satellites.

1999, Oct. 6 ***Perf. 13¾x12¼***

1818 A892 7p multi 3.25 3.00

1819 A892 14p multi 5.00 4.75

Inter-American Development Bank, 40th Anniv. — A893

1999, Oct. 6 ***Perf. 12¼x12¾***

1820 A893 7p multi 2.90 2.00

Winner of Older Person's Stamp Design Contest — A894

1999, Oct. 8

1821 A894 7p multi 2.90 2.00

El Ceibo Society, 50th Anniv. — A895

1999, Oct. 8

1822 A895 7p multi 2.90 2.00

Third Intl. Conference of Ministers for Sports, Punta del Este — A896

1999, Oct. 13 ***Perf. 12***

1823 A896 7p multi 2.90 2.00

Souvenir Sheets

Official Service of Broadcasting, Television and Entertainment — A897

No. 1824: a, 4p, Television cameraman. b, 4p, Building. c, 3p, Radio studio. d, 3p, Film cameraman.

No. 1825: a, 4p, Symphony orchestra. b, 4p, Chamber music group. c, 3p, Chorus. d, 3p, Ballet dancers.

1999, Oct. 22 ***Perf. 12¼x12¾***

1824 A897 Sheet of 4, #a.-d. 6.50 5.50

1825 A897 Sheet of 4, #a.-d. 6.50 5.50

Uruguayan Standards Institute, 60th Anniv. — A898

1999, Nov. 3

1826 A898 7p multi 2.90 2.00

A899

1999, Nov. 3 ***Perf. 12¾x12¼***

1827 A899 7p multi 2.90 2.00

Vice-President Hugo Batalla (1926-98).

A900

Cover of 4/29/29 Mundo Uruguayo magazine.

1999, Nov.12

1828 A900 7p multi 2.90 2.00

Exhibition of art and design from the 1920s, Blanes Museum, Montevideo.

Millennium — A901

No. 1829 — Various buildings and: a, "1999." b, "2000."

1999, Nov. 23 **Litho.** ***Perf. 12***

1829 A901 3.50p Pair, #a.-b. 3.00 2.00

Celmar Poumé (1924-83), Cartoonist — A902

1999, Nov. 26 ***Perf. 12¾x12¼***

1830 A902 7p multi 2.90 2.00

Christmas A903

9p, Tree with ornaments. 18p, Carolers.

Perf. 12¼x12¾, 12¾x12¼

1999, Dec. 3

1831 A903 9p multi 3.50 3.25

1832 A903 18p multi, vert. 6.50 6.25

Tannat Wines, 20th Anniv. — A904

1999, Dec. 9 ***Perf. 12***

1833 A904 9p shown 3.50 3.00

1834 A904 9p Wine drinker 3.50 3.00

New Maldonado Department Governmental Building — A905

1999, Dec. 11 ***Perf. 12¼x12¾***

1835 A905 9p multi 3.50 3.00

Types of 1997 and

Crow's Gorge Nature Reserve A907

Chilean Lapwing A908

Design: 2p, Penitente Waterfall, vert. 5p, Chilean Lapwing (*Vanellus chilensis*). 10p, Crow's Gorge Nature Reserve. No. 1841, Gruta del Palacio, vert. 100p, Sierra de los Caracoles.

Serpentine Die Cut 11¼, Die Cut (#1836A, 1840, 1850, 1853)

2000-06	**Self-Adhesive**		**Litho.**
1836 A907	2p multi, "2001"	.45	.45
b.	Dated "2002"	.30	.30
1836A A908	5p multi	.55	.55
1837 A907	10p multi	1.00	1.00
1838 A907	11p multi	2.50	2.40
1840 A781	20p multi, "2000"	5.25	5.00
a.	Dated "2001"	5.25	5.00
1841 A907	20p multi, "2001"	5.75	5.50
a.	Dated "2006"	5.75	5.50
1850 A782	32p multi	9.00	8.50
1853 A782	80p multi	22.00	21.00
1854 A907	100p multi	17.00	16.50
1855 A782	100p multi	9.50	9.00
1855A A782	100p multi	9.50	9.00
	Nos. 1836-1855A (11)	82.50	78.90

Issued: 32p, 1/20. No. 1840, 80p, 12/12. 11p, 3/16/01. No. 1841, 4/26/01. 2p, 8/1/01. No. 1854, 2/13/02. No. 1855, 10/5/04. 5p, 12/1/06; 10p, 10/18/06; No. 1855A, 9/26/06.

No. 1855 has straight numerals in denomination. No. 1855A has slanted numerals.

50th Anniv of Artistic Career of Carlos Páez Vilaró A916

2000, Jan. 15 **Litho.** ***Perf. 12***

1856 A916 9p multi 3.50 3.40

Orchids A917

No. 1857: a, 5p, Laelia purpurata. b, 4p, Cattleya corcovado. c, 4p, Cattleya sp. "hybrid." d, 5p, Laelia tenebrosa.

2000, Mar. 3

1857 A917 Block of 4, #a.-d. 8.00 7.00

Lighthouses A918

No. 1858: a, 5p, Isla de Flores, 1828. b, 4p, Punta del Este, 1860. c, 4p, Cabo Polonio, 1881. d, 5p, Punta Brava, 1876.

2000, Mar. 14

1858 A918 Block of 4, #a.-d. 8.50 7.50

Carlos Quijano (1900-84), Economics Journalist A919

2000, Mar. 30 ***Perf. 12¼x12¾***

1859 A919 9p multi 3.75 3.50

The Gold Rush, Starring Charlie Chaplin, 75th Anniv. — A920

2000, Apr. 7 **Litho.** ***Perf. 12¼x12¾***

1860 A920 18p multi 7.25 6.75

Lubrapex 2000 Stamp Show, Brazil.

El Cordón Neighborhood of Montevideo, 250th Anniv. — A921

2000, Apr. 10 **Litho.** ***Perf. 12¼x12¾***

1861 A921 9p multi 3.75 3.50

Mural "Espina de la Cruz," by Children of Mercedes A922

a, 5p, Branches. b, 4p, Two red flowers.

2000, Apr. 26 *Perf. 12¼x12*
1862 A922 Pair, #a-b 4.00 3.50

Francisco García y Santos (1856-1921), Government Official — A923

2000, May 2 *Perf. 12¾x12¼*
1863 A923 9p multi 3.75 3.50

Uruguayan Notaries Assoc., 125th Anniv. — A924

2000, May 9 Litho. *Perf. 12¾x12¼*
1864 A924 9p multi 3.75 3.50

Intl. Museum Day — A925

2000, May 18 Litho. *Perf. 12¾x12¼*
1865 A925 9p multi 3.75 3.50

Stampin' the Future Children's Stamp Design Contest Winners — A926

Artwork by: a, 5p, Helena Perez. b, 4p, Maria Pia Pereyra. c, 4p, Virginia Regueiro. d, 5p, Blanca E. Lima.

2000, June 2 Litho. *Perf. 12*
1866 A926 Block of 4, #a-d 8.00 7.00

Club Soriano, 90th Anniv. — A927

2000, June 9 Litho. *Perf. 12¼x12¾*
1867 A927 9p multi 3.75 3.50

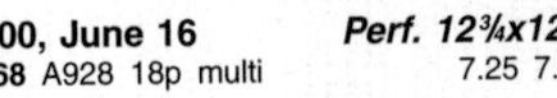

Antonio Rupenian, Founder of Radio Armenia — A928

2000, June 16 *Perf. 12¾x12¼*
1868 A928 18p multi 7.25 7.00

"1900 Generation" Writers, Cent. — A929

Perf. 12¾x12¼

2000, June 22 Litho.
1869 A929 9p multi 3.75 3.50

Cacti A930

No. 1870: a, 5p, Notocactus ottonis. b, 4p, Echinopsis multiplex.

2000, July 4 *Perf. 12¼*
1870 A930 Horiz. pair, #a-b 4.50 3.75

Uruguayan Soccer Association, Cent. — A931

No. 1871: a, 5p, Players marching. b, 4p, Team photo. c, 4p, Stadium, World Cup. d, 5p, Players in action, World Cup.

2000, July 14 Litho. *Perf. 12¼x12*
1871 A931 Block of 4, #a-d 10.50 9.50

Opera Anniversaries — A932

No. 1872: a, 9p, Scene from Carmen, composer Georges Bizet. b, 9p, Scene from Tosca, composer Giacomo Puccini.

2000, July 20
1872 A932 Pair, #a-b 7.00 6.25

Carmen, 125th anniv.; Tosca, cent.

Latin American Integration Association, 20th Anniv. — A933

2000, Aug. 11 *Perf. 12¾x12¼*
1873 A933 18p multi 7.50 7.25

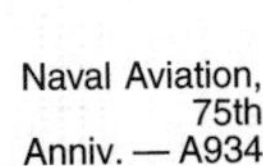

Naval Aviation, 75th Anniv. — A934

2000, Aug. 18 *Perf. 12¼x12¾*
1874 A934 9p multi 3.75 3.50

ORT, 120th Anniv. — A935

2000, Aug. 28
1875 A935 9p multi 4.00 3.50

Luis de la Robla (1780-1844), First Postmaster General — A936

2000, Aug. 28 *Perf. 12¾x12¼*
1876 A936 9p multi 4.00 3.50

Gonzalo Rodriguez (1971-99), Race Car Driver — A937

a, 9p, Rodriguez, dark blue car. b, 9p, Rodriguez holding trophy, light blue car.

2000, Sept. 11 *Perf. 12x12¼*
1877 A937 Pair, #a-b 8.00 7.50

Gen. José Artigas (1764-1850) A938

2000, Sept. 22 Litho. *Perf. 12¼*
1878 A938 9p multi + label 4.25 3.75

España 2000 Intl. Philatelic Exhibition — A939

Birds: a, 5p, Donacospiza albifrons. b, 4p, Geositta cunicularia. c, 4p, Phacellodomus striaticollis. d, 5p, Cacicus chrysopterus.

2000, Sept. 27 *Perf. 12*
1879 A939 Block of 4, #a-d 8.25 7.25

Soka Gakkai International, 25th Anniv. — A940

2000, Oct. 2 *Perf. 12¼x12¾*
1880 A940 18p multi 7.75 7.25

America Issue, Fight Against AIDS A941

No. 1881: a, 9p, Tic-tac-toe game with condoms and crosses. b, 18p, Syringe and red ribbon.

2000, Oct. 10 *Perf. 12¼*
1881 A941 Horiz. pair, #a-b 10.00 9.50

Mercosur Cultural Heritage Day — A942

2000, Oct. 14 *Perf. 12¾x12¼*
1882 A942 18p multi 7.75 7.25

Dragon, by Luis Mazzey (1895-1983) A943

2000, Oct. 19 *Perf. 12¼x12¾*
1883 A943 9p multi 3.75 3.25

Fire Fighters — A944

Designs: No. 1884, 9p, At car crash. No. 1885, 9p, Searching for victims, vert.

Perf. 12¼x12¾, 12¾x12¼

2000, Oct. 26
1884-1885 A944 Set of 2 8.50 8.00

Prof. Julio Ricaldoni (1906-93), Structural Engineer — A945

2000, Nov. 13 *Perf. 12¼x12¾*
1886 A945 9p multi 3.25 3.00

29th Conference on Structural Engineering, Punta del Este.

Training Ship "Capitan Miranda," 70th Anniv. — A946

2000, Nov. 15
1887 A946 9p multi 5.50 5.00

Holy Roman Emperor Charles V (1500-58) A947

2000, Nov. 22 **Litho.**
1888 A947 22p multi 8.25 8.00

Christmas A948

Designs: 11p, Fireworks. 22p, Holy Family.

2000, Dec. 1
1889-1890 A948 Set of 2 19.50 18.50

Sarandi del Yi, 125th Anniv. — A949

2000, Dec. 14 *Perf. 12¾x12¼*
1891 A949 11p multi 6.75 6.25

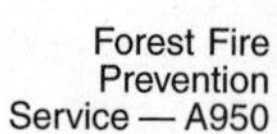

Forest Fire Prevention Service — A950

2001, Feb. 9 Litho. ***Perf. 12½x12¾***
1892 A950 11p multi 6.75 6.25

Amphibians and Reptiles A951

No. 1893: a, Phyllomedusa iheringii. b, Acanthochelys spixii. c, Phrynops hilarii. d, Scinax sqalirostris.

2001, Feb. 15 ***Perf. 12***
1893 A951 11p Block of 4, #a-d 22.50 21.50

Paysandú Rowing Club, Cent. — A952

2001, Feb. 28 ***Perf. 12½x12¾***
1894 A952 11p multi 6.50 6.25

17th Congress of Latin American Confederation of Congress Organizers — A953

2001, Mar. 2 ***Perf. 12¾x12½***
1895 A953 11p multi 6.50 6.25

City of Belén, Bicent. — A954

2001, Mar. 14
1896 A954 11p multi 6.50 6.00

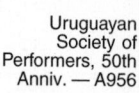

David, by Michelangelo, 500th Anniv. — A955

2001, Mar. 22
1897 A955 22p multi 12.50 12.00

Uruguayan Society of Performers, 50th Anniv. — A956

2001, Mar. 26 ***Perf. 12½x12¾***
1898 A956 11p multi 6.50 6.00

Casal Catalá, 75th Anniv. — A957

2001, Apr. 20 ***Perf. 12¾x12½***
1899 A957 11p multi 6.50 6.00

Universidad Mayor de la República Engineering Faculty, 85th Anniv. — A958

2001, Apr. 30
1900 A958 11p blue 6.75 6.25

Rodolfo V. Tálice (1899-1999), Biologist — A959

2001, May 2 ***Perf. 12½x12¾***
1901 A959 11p multi 6.50 6.00

Montevideo Lions Club, 50th Anniv. — A960

2001, May 14 ***Perf. 12¾x12½***
1902 A960 11p multi 6.50 6.25

Invention of the Telephone, 125th Anniv. — A961

2001, May 22 ***Perf. 12½x12¾***
1903 A961 22p multi 12.50 12.50

Snakes A962

No. 1904: a, Philodryas olfersii. b, Bothrops alternatus.

2001, May 28 ***Perf. 12***
1904 A962 11p Horiz. pair, #a-b 14.50 13.50

Juan Manuel Blanes (1830-1901), Painter — A963

2001, June 8 Litho. ***Perf. 12½x12¾***
1905 A963 11p multi 6.75 6.25

Start of Pediatrics Teaching by Dr. Luis Morquio, Cent. — A964

2001, June 15 ***Perf. 12¾x12½***
1906 A964 11p multi 7.00 6.75

The Ring of the Nibelung, by Richard Wagner A965

No. 1907: a, The Rhinegold (El Oro del Rin). b, The Valkyrie (La Walquiria). c, Siegfried (Sigfrido). d, The Twilight of the Gods (El Ocaso de los Dioses).

2001, June 29 ***Perf. 12***
1907 A965 11p Block of 4, #a-d 28.00 27.00

Intl. Organization for Migration, 50th Anniv. — A966

2001, July 5 ***Perf. 12¾x12½***
1908 A966 22p blue & black 13.50 13.50

Thomas Alva Edison (1847-1931) — A967

2001, July 12
1909 A967 22p multi 6.25 6.00

Laying of Foundation Stone for Montevideo Port, Cent. — A968

2001, July 18 ***Perf. 12½x12¾***
1910 A968 11p multi 6.75 6.25

Fowl A969

No. 1911: a, New Hampshire. b, Orpington-Buff. c, Araucanas. d, Leghorn-Light brown.

2001, July 30 ***Perf. 12***
1911 A969 11p Block of 4, #a-d 17.00 16.00

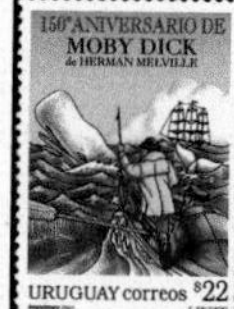

Moby Dick, by Herman Melville, 150th Anniv. — A970

2001, Aug. 2 ***Perf. 12¾x12½***
1912 A970 22p multi 13.00 12.50

Bernardo González Pecotche (1901-63), Founder of Logosophy — A971

2001, Aug. 7 ***Perf. 12***
1913 A971 11p multi 6.75 6.25

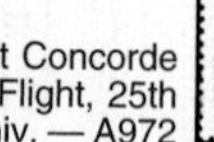

First Concorde Flight, 25th Anniv. — A972

2001, Aug. 10 ***Perf. 12½x12¾***
1914 A972 22p multi 13.00 12.50

Rose Varieties A973

No. 1915: a, Louis Philippe. b, Souvenir de Mme. Léonie Viennot. c, Kronenbourg. d, Lady Hillingdon.

2001, Aug. 16 ***Perf. 12***
1915 A973 11p Block of 4, #a-d 26.00 25.00

Apiculture — A974

No. 1916: a, Apiculturists. b, Bee on flower.

2001, Sept. 12
1916 A974 12p Horiz. pair, #a-b 15.00 14.00

Town of Dolores, Bicent. — A975

2001, Sept. 21 ***Perf. 12¾x12½***
1917 A975 12p multi 5.25 5.00

Uruguay Philatelic Club, 75th Anniv. — A976

Sun and inscription: No. 1918, 12p, "75 Años." No. 1919, 12p, "1er Presidente / Dr. Miguel A. Paez Formoso."

2001, Sept. 26 ***Perf. 12½x12¾***
1918-1919 A976 Set of 2 14.50 14.00

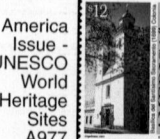

America Issue - UNESCO World Heritage Sites A977

Buildings from Historic Quarter of Colonia del Sacramento: a, 12p, Basilica del Santisimo. b, 24p, San Benito de Palermo Chapel.

2001, Sept. 28 ***Perf. 12***
1920 A977 Horiz. pair, #a-b 19.50 19.00

Carlos Amoretti, 50th Anniv. as Artist — A978

2001, Oct. 2 ***Perf. 12½x12¾***
1921 A978 12p multi 7.25 7.00

Town of Sauce, 150th Anniv. — A979

2001, Oct. 12 ***Perf. 12¾x12½***
1922 A979 12p multi 8.75 8.50

Uruguay - Japan Diplomatic Relations, 80th Anniv. — A980

Perf. 12¼x12¾
2001, Sept. 24 **Litho.**
1923 A980 24p multi 13.00 12.50

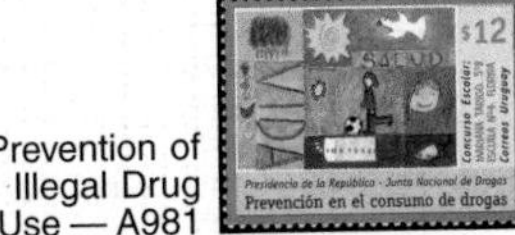

Prevention of Illegal Drug Use — A981

2001, Oct. 16
1924 A981 12p multi 9.00 8.50

Year of Dialogue Among Civilizations — A982

2001, Oct. 23 ***Perf. 12¾x12¼***
1925 A982 24p multi 10.00 10.00

Honorary Committee for Fighting Cancer — A983

2001, Oct. 29
1926 A983 12p multi 9.00 8.50

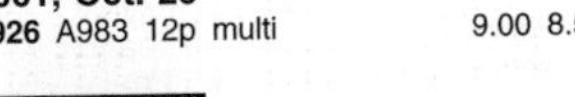

Ultimas Noticias Newspaper, 20th Anniv. — A984

2001, Oct. 31
1927 A984 12p multi 8.75 8.50

Sauce Basketball Club, 50th Anniv. — A985

2001, Nov. 9 ***Perf. 12¼x12¾***
1928 A985 12p multi 8.75 8.50

Blood Donor's Day — A986

2001, Nov. 12 ***Perf. 12¾x12¼***
1929 A986 12p multi 8.75 8.50

Juan Zorrilla de San Martín (1855-1931), Writer — A987

2001, Nov. 13 ***Perf. 12¼x12¾***
1930 A987 12p multi 8.75 8.50

Uruguayan Navy's Hydrographic Ship "Oyarvide" A988

2001, Nov. 14
1931 A988 12p multi 9.00 8.50

Uruguayan Visit of Rotary Intl. President Richard King and Wife Cherie — A989

2001, Nov. 20 ***Perf. 12¾x12¼***
1932 A989 24p multi 10.00 10.00

Peñarol Athletic Club, 110th Anniv. A990

2001, Nov. 22 ***Perf. 12***
1933 A990 12p multi 8.75 8.50

Julio Sosa (1926-64), Tango Singer — A991

2001, Nov. 26 ***Perf. 12¾x12¼***
1934 A991 12p multi 9.00 8.50

José Nasazzi (1901-68), Soccer Player — A992

2001, Nov. 29
1935 A992 12p multi 9.00 8.50

Christmas — A993

Paintings of Adoration of the Shepherds, by: 12p, José Ribera. 24p, Anton Raphael Mengs.

2001, Dec. 6
1936-1937 A993 Set of 2 16.00 15.00

Church of San Carlos, Bicent. — A994

2001, Dec. 7
1938 A994 12p multi 9.00 8.75

National Museum of Visual Arts, 90th Anniv. A995

2001, Dec. 12 ***Perf. 12***
1939 A995 12p multi 9.00 8.75

State Insurance Bank, 90th Anniv. — A996

2001, Dec. 20 ***Perf. 12¾x12¼***
1940 A996 12p multi 9.00 8.75

Guettarda Uruguensis A997

2001, Dec. 21 ***Perf. 12¼x12¾***
1941 A997 24p multi 15.00 15.00

St. Josemaría Escrivá de Balaguer (1902-75) — A998

Balaguer and quotes: a, "El trabajo es. . ." b, "Quieres de verdad. . ." c, "La santidad. . ." d, "Que busques. . ."

2002, Jan. 9 ***Perf. 12***
1942 A998 12p Block of 4, #a-d 17.50 16.50

Uruguayan Association of Directors of Carnivals and Folk Festivals, 50th Anniv. — A999

Feet of: a, Ringmaster. b, Clown. c, Acrobat.

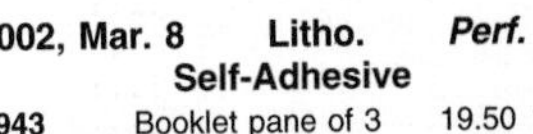

2002, Mar. 8 **Litho.** ***Perf. 12½***
Self-Adhesive

1943		Booklet pane of 3	19.50	17.50
a.-b.	A999	6p Either single	4.50	4.00
c.	A999	12p black	8.50	8.00
		Booklet, #1943	20.00	20.00

Christianity in Armenia, 1700th Anniv. — A1000

2002, Apr. 23 ***Perf. 12***
1944 A1000 12p multi 7.50 7.00

New Year 2003 (Year of the Horse) — A1001

2002, May 14 ***Perf. 12¾x12¼***
1945 A1001 24p multi 9.25 9.00

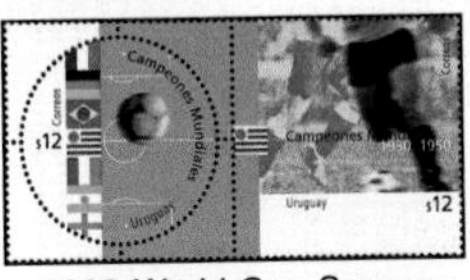

2002 World Cup Soccer Championships, Japan and Korea — A1002

No. 1946: a, Flags, soccer ball, and field (38mm diameter). b, Soccer players, years of Uruguayan championships.

2002, May 21 ***Perf. 12¾***
1946 A1002 12p Horiz. pair, #a-b 12.50 12.00

See Argentina No. 2184, Brazil No. 2840, France No. 2891, Germany No. 2163 and Italy No. 2526.

Book Day — A1003

2002, May 24 ***Perf. 12¾x12¼***
1947 A1003 12p multi 7.25 7.00

Inter-American Children's Institute, 75th Anniv. — A1004

2002, June 10 ***Perf. 12¼x12¾***
1948 A1004 12p multi 7.25 7.00

Department of Tacuarembó, 165th Anniv. — A1005

2002, June 14
1949 A1005 12p multi 7.00 6.75

Cerro de Montevideo Lighthouse, Bicent. — A1006

Designs: 12p, Old lighthouse. 24p, New lighthouse, vert.

Perf. 12¼x12¾, 12¾x12¼

2002, June 24

1950-1951 A1006 Set of 2 12.50 12.00

Villa Constitución, 150th Anniv. — A1007

2002, July 11 *Perf. 12¼x12¾*

1952 A1007 12p multi 5.90 5.50

"We Are United" — A1008

2002, July 17

1953 A1008 6p multi 3.75 3.50

Printed in sheets of 3 + label. Value $12.

Natural Uruguay — A1009

2002, July 22 **Litho.**

1954 A1009 24p blue & orange 10.50 10.00

Montevideo Botanical Gardens, Cent. — A1010

No. 1955: a, Botanical Gardens building, Erythrina cristigalli. b, Rhodophiala bifida. c, Prof. Atilio Lombardo and Tillandsia arequitae. d, Heteropterys dumetorum.

2002, July 31 *Perf. 12*

1955 Horiz. strip of 4 22.00 20.00

a.-d. A1010 12p Any single 5.00 5.00

Montevideo Wanderers Soccer Team, Cent. — A1011

2002, Aug. 1 *Perf. 12¾x12¼*

1956 A1011 12p black 5.50 5.00

Sportsmen A1012

Designs: No. 1957, 12p, Lorenzo Fernández, soccer player. No. 1958, 12p, Josè Leandro Andrade, soccer player. No. 1959, 12p, Alvaro Gestido, soccer player. No. 1960, 12p, César L. Gallardo, fencer. No. 1961, 12p, Pedro Petrone, soccer player.

2002, Aug. 16 *Perf. 12¼x12¾*

1957-1961 A1012 Set of 5 18.00 17.00

Elvis Presley (1935-77) — A1013

2002, Aug. 19 *Perf. 12¾x12¼*

1962 A1013 24p multi 8.25 8.00

Agustín Bisio (1894-1952), Poet — A1014

2002, Aug. 30 *Perf. 12¾x12¼*

Self-Adhesive

1963 A1014 12p multi 5.50 5.00

City of Artigas, 150th Anniv. — A1015

2002, Sept. 12 *Perf. 12¾x12¼*

Self-Adhesive

1964 A1015 12p multi 4.90 4.50

Uruguayan Cooperative Society of Bus Services, 65th Anniv. — A1016

2002, Sept. 16 *Perf. 12¼x12¾*

1965 A1016 12p multi 5.25 5.00

Psychoanalysis, Cent. — A1017

2002, Sept. 20 *Perf. 12*

1966 A1017 12p multi 4.90 4.50

24th Latin American Psychoanalysis Congress, Montevideo.

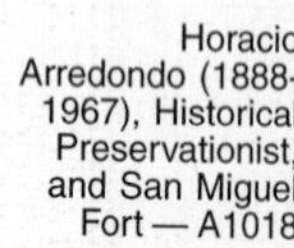

Horacio Arredondo (1888-1967), Historical Preservationist, and San Miguel Fort — A1018

2002, Sept. 20 *Perf. 12¼x12¾*

1967 A1018 12p multi 4.50 4.00

Paso del Rey Barracks Natl. Historic Monument A1019

2002, Sept. 23 *Perf. 12*

1968 A1019 12p multi 5.00 4.75

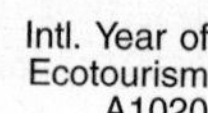
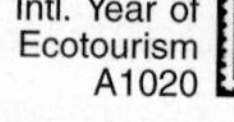

Intl. Year of Ecotourism A1020

2002, Sept. 24 **Litho.**

1969 A1020 12p multi 5.00 4.75

Uruguayan Postal Services, 175th Anniv. — A1021

Designs: No. 1970, Postal Services headquarters, Montevideo. No. 1971, Letter box.

2002, Oct. 9 *Perf. 12¾x12¼*

1970 A1021 12p multi 4.50 4.25

Souvenir Sheet

Imperf

1971 A1021 12p multi 4.50 4.25

First Equestrian Statue of Brig. Gen. Juan Antonio Lavalleja, Cent. — A1022

2002, Oct. 11 *Perf. 12¾x12¼*

1972 A1022 12p multi 4.50 4.25

America Issue — Youth, Education and Literacy — A1023

"ANALFABETISMO" in: 12p, Word search puzzle. 24p, Bowl of alphabet soup.

2002, Oct. 16 *Perf. 12¼x12¾*

1973-1974 A1023 Set of 2 12.50 12.00

Christmas — A1024

2002, Nov. 4 *Perf. 12¾x12¼*

1975 A1024 12p multi 5.50 5.00

Association of Uruguayan Pharmacies, 65th Anniv. — A1025

2002, Nov. 8 **Litho.**

1976 A1025 12p multi 5.00 4.75

Tannat Wine — A1026

2002, Nov. 13

1977 A1026 12p multi 5.00 4.75

Uruguayan Navy, 185th Anniv. — A1027

2002, Nov. 13 *Perf. 13½*

1978 A1027 12p multi 3.00 2.75

National Organ and Tissue Bank, 25th Anniv. — A1028

2002, Nov. 15

1979 A1028 12p multi 4.50 4.25

Taxis in Uruguay, Cent. — A1029

2002, Nov. 25 *Perf. 12¼x12¾*

1980 A1029 12p multi 4.25 4.00

Brig. Gen. Manuel Oribe (1792-1857) — A1030

2002, Nov. 28 *Perf. 12¾x12¼*

1981 A1030 12p multi 4.25 4.00

George Harrison (1943-2001), Rock Musician — A1031

2002, Nov. 29 *Perf. 13½*

1982 A1031 24p multi 8.25 8.00

Pan-American Health Organization, Cent. — A1032

2002, Dec. 2

1983 A1032 12p multi 4.25 4.00

Uruguayan Participation in U.N. Peace Keeping Missions, 50th Anniv. — A1033

2002, Dec. 6 *Perf. 12¼x12¾*

1984 A1033 12p multi 4.25 4.00

Alfredo Testoni (1919-2000), Artist — A1034

2002, Dec. 9 *Perf. 13½*

1985 A1034 12p multi 4.00 3.75

Mercosur A1035

Designs: 12p, Ship and coastline. 24p, Beach.

2002, Dec. 12
1986-1987 A1035 Set of 2 12.00 11.50

Battle of Ituzaingó, 175th Anniv. — A1036

2002, Dec. 17 **Litho.**
1988 A1036 12p multi 4.25 4.00

Battle of Juncal, 175th Anniv. — A1037

2002, Dec. 17
1989 A1037 12p multi 4.25 4.00

Town of Juanicó, 130th Anniv. — A1038

2002, Dec. 23 ***Perf. 12¼x12¾***
1990 A1038 12p multi 4.00 3.50

Uruguay on World Map — A1039

2003, Jan. 17 **Litho.** ***Perf. 12¼x12¾***
1991 A1039 12p multi 3.00 2.75

Busqueda Weekly, 30th Anniv. — A1040

2003, Jan. 29
1992 A1040 12p multi 3.00 2.75

Water Goddess Iemanja — A1041

2003, Jan. 29 ***Perf. 12¾x12¼***
1993 A1041 12p multi 2.75 2.50

Uruguay - People's Republic of China Diplomatic Relations, 15th Anniv. A1042

2003, Jan. 31 ***Perf. 12***
1994 A1042 12p multi 4.00 3.75

New Year 2003 (Year of the Ram) — A1043

2003, Feb. 7 ***Perf. 12¾x12¼***
1995 A1043 5p multi 1.10 .90

Explorers — A1044

Explorers and maps of their voyages: a, Christopher Columbus, 4th voyage, 1502. b, Juan Díaz de Solís, 1516. c, Sebastian Cabot, 1526-30. d, Hernando Arias de Saavedra, 1597-1618.

2003, Feb. 14 ***Perf. 12***
1996 Horiz. strip of 4 9.25 8.25
a.-d. A1044 12p Any single 1.75 1.75

Communications Services Regulatory Union, 2nd Anniv. — A1045

2003, Feb. 21 ***Perf. 12¼x12¾***
1997 A1045 12p multi 2.40 2.00

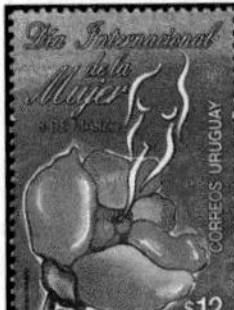

Intl. Women's Day — A1046

2003, Mar. 7 ***Perf. 12¾x12¼***
1998 A1046 12p multi 2.60 2.25

City of Treinta y Tres, 150th Anniv. — A1047

2003, Mar. 10 ***Perf. 12¼x12¾***
1999 A1047 12p multi 2.60 2.25

Butterflies A1048

No. 2000: a, Heliconius erato. b, Junonia evarete. c, Dryadula phaetusa. d, Parides perrhebus.

2003, Mar. 18 ***Perf. 12***
2000 A1048 12p Block of 4, #a-d 10.00 9.00

First Presidency of José Batlle y Ordóñez, Cent. — A1049

No. 2001 — Batlle y Ordóñez: a, Wearing overcoat. b, Wearing presidential sash. c, With head on hand. d, Wearing white jacket.

2003, Mar. 25 ***Perf. 12***
2001 Horiz. strip of 4 10.00 9.00
a.-d. A1049 12p Any single 2.00 2.00

Rural Women's Crafts — A1050

No. 2002: a, Basket weaving. b, Knitting. c, Pottery making. d, Food canning. e, Jewelry making.

2003, Mar. 23 **Litho.** ***Perf. 12***
2002 Horiz. strip of 5 12.00 11.00
a.-e. A1050 12p Any single 2.00 2.00

Farruco's Chapel — A1051

2003, Apr. 4 **Litho.** ***Perf. 12¾x12¼***
2003 A1051 12p multi 2.60 2.25

Natural Foods — A1052

2003, Apr. 9 ***Perf. 12¼x12¾***
2004 A1052 12p multi 2.60 2.25

Cerros Azules Caiman Farm — A1053

Serpentine Die Cut 11¼
2003, Apr. 10
Self-Adhesive
2005 A1053 12p multi 2.60 2.25

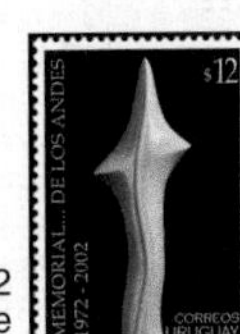

Memorial to 1972 Airplane Crash in the Andes — A1054

2003, Apr. 22 ***Perf. 12¾x12¼***
2006 A1054 12p multi 2.40 2.10

Military Center — A1055

2003, May 21
2007 A1055 12p multi 2.40 2.10

May 18, 1811 Military Museum, 150th Anniv. — A1056

2003, May 26 ***Perf. 12***
2008 A1056 12p multi 2.25 1.90

Casa de Ximénes and Las Bóvedas, Montevideo Historical District A1057

2003, May 30 ***Perf. 12¼***
2009 A1057 14p multi 2.60 2.25

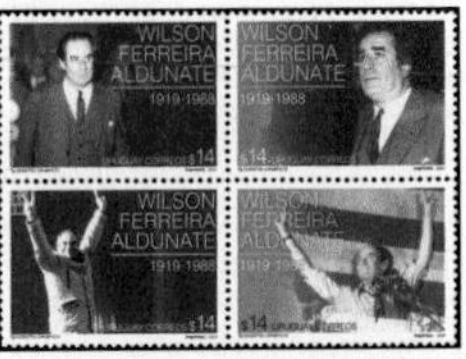

Wilson Ferreira Aldunate (1919-88), Politician — A1058

No. 2010: a, Brown background. b, Green background. c, Dark violet background, text at right. d, Light violet background, text at left.

2003, June 16 **Litho.** ***Perf. 12***
2010 A1058 14p Block of 4, #a-d 8.00 7.00

Olympic Soccer Gold Medal, 75th Anniv. — A1059

2003, June 18
2011 A1059 14p multi 3.00 2.75

Nos. 1382, 1492 Overprinted in Gold

Methods, Perfs and Watermarks as Before

2003, June 18
2011A A654 (14p) on 1.20p #1492 1.75 1.50
Complete booklet of 10 17.50
2011B A589 (36p) on 2500p #1382 4.75 4.50
Complete booklet of 10 47.50

Compare No. 2011A with No. 2055.

Richard Anderson College, 70th Anniv. — A1060

2003, July 15
2012 A1060 14p multi 3.00 2.75

Santa Isabel del Paso de los Toros, Cent. A1061

2003, July 17
2013 A1061 14p multi 3.00 2.75

National Association of Affiliates, 70th Anniv. — A1062

2003, July 24
2014 A1062 14p multi 3.00 2.75

Jesús María College, Carrasco, 50th Anniv. — A1063

2003, Aug. 4
2015 A1063 14p multi 3.00 2.75

Philatelic Academy of Uruguay, 25th Anniv. — A1064

2003, Aug. 5
2016 A1064 14p multi 3.00 2.75

Palacio Heber — A1065

2003, Aug. 14
2017 A1065 14p multi 3.00 2.75

Parva Domus Magna Quies, 125th Anniv. — A1066

2003, Aug. 15
2018 A1066 14p multi 2.90 2.50

Security Dept. Commission of Interior Ministry, 4th Anniv. — A1067

2003, Aug. 18
2019 A1067 14p multi 2.90 2.50

First International Victory of Uruguayan Soccer Team, Cent. — A1068

2003, Sept. 12 ***Perf. 12½x12¾***
2020 A1068 14p multi 2.90 2.50

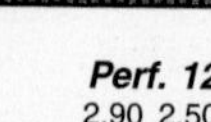

Lauro Ayestarán (1913-66), Musicologist A1069

2003, Sept. 19 ***Perf. 12***
2021 A1069 14p multi 2.90 2.50

Asociacion Española Primera de Socorros Mutuos Hospital, 150th Anniv. — A1070

2003, Sept. 19 ***Perf. 12½x12¾***
2022 A1070 14p multi 2.90 2.50

Dr. Manuel Quintela Clinical Hospital, 50th Anniv. — A1071

2003, Sept. 23 ***Perf. 12***
2023 A1071 14p multi 2.90 2.50

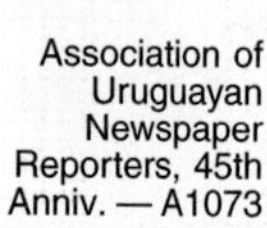

Society of Friends of Public Education, 135th Anniv. — A1072

2003, Sept. 24
2024 A1072 14p multi 2.90 2.50

Association of Uruguayan Newspaper Reporters, 45th Anniv. — A1073

2003, Sept. 29 ***Perf. 12½x12¾***
2025 A1073 14p multi 2.90 2.50

Pres. Fructuoso Rivera (c. 1788-1854) — A1074

2003, Oct. 1 ***Perf. 12***
2026 A1074 14p multi 2.90 2.50

Naval Club, 75th Anniv. — A1075

2003, Oct. 1 ***Perf. 12½x12¾***
2027 A1075 14p multi 2.90 2.50

Malos Pensamientos Radio Program A1076

2003, Oct. 3
2028 A1076 14p multi 2.90 2.50

Successes in Intl. Events by Milton Wynants, Cyclist — A1077

2003, Oct. 7 ***Perf. 12¾x12½***
2029 A1077 14p multi 2.90 2.50

Ente Nazionale Assistenza Sociale in Uruguay, 50th Anniv. — A1078

2003, Oct. 9 ***Perf. 12½x12¾***
2030 A1078 14p multi 2.90 2.50

City of Cardona, Cent. — A1079

2003, Oct. 10 ***Perf. 12***
2031 A1079 14p multi 2.90 2.50

Construction League of Uruguay, 84th Anniv. — A1080

2003, Oct. 14 ***Perf. 12¾x12½***
2032 A1080 14p multi 2.90 2.50

María Tsakos Foundation, 25th Anniv. — A1081

2003, Oct. 15
2033 A1081 14p multi 2.90 2.50

America Issue — Flora and Fauna — A1082

Designs: 14p, Prosopis affinis. 36p, Agouti paca paca.

2003, Oct. 22 ***Perf. 12½x12¾***
2034-2035 A1082 Set of 2 9.75 9.00

Independence of Lebanon, 60th Anniv. — A1083

2003, Oct. 24
2036 A1083 14p olive grn & red 2.90 2.50

Souvenir Sheet

Masons in Uruguay, 147th Anniv. A1084

2003, Oct. 29 ***Perf. 12¾x12½***
2037 A1084 14p multi 2.90 2.50

Cacho Bochinche Television Show, 30th Anniv. — A1085

2003, Oct. 29 ***Perf. 12½x12¾***
2038 A1085 14p multi 2.90 2.50

Morenada, 50th Anniv. — A1086

2003, Oct. 29
2039 A1086 14p multi 2.90 2.50

Brig. Gen. Juan A. Lavalleja (c. 1786-1853) — A1087

2003, Oct. 30 ***Perf. 12***
2040 A1087 14p multi 2.90 2.50

Souvenir Sheet

Election of Pope John Paul II, 25th Anniv. A1088

No. 1089 — Uruguayan flag and: a, Pope John Paul II, Vatican arms. b, Polish eagle, map of Latin America.

2003, Oct. 31
2041 A1088 12p Sheet of 2, #a-b 5.50 5.00

Union of Latin American Polish Societies and Organizations, 10th anniv. (No. 2041b).

Souvenir Sheet

2006 World Cup Soccer Championships, Germany — A1089

No. 2042 — World Cup trophy and: a, Uruguayan flag, J. A. Schiaffino. b, German flag, Fritz Walter.

2003, Oct. 31
2042 A1089 12p Sheet of 2, #a-b 5.25 4.50

Christmas — A1090

2003, Nov. 7 ***Perf. 12¾x12½***
2043 A1090 14p multi 2.60 2.25

A1091

2003, Nov. 10 ***Perf. 12½x12¾***
2044 A1091 14p multi 2.50 2.00

Italian Chamber of Commerce of Uruguay, 120th Anniv.

Visit of Manuel Fraga Iribarne, President of Spanish Autonomous Community of Galicia — A1092

2003, Nov. 10
2045 A1092 14p multi 2.50 2.00

San Gregorio de Polanco, 150th Anniv. — A1093

2003, Nov. 14
2046 A1093 14p multi 2.50 2.00

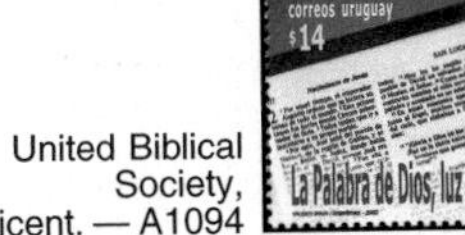
United Biblical Society, Bicent. — A1094

2003, Nov. 24
2047 A1094 14p multi 2.50 2.00

R.O.U. Paysandu A1095

2003, Nov. 25 ***Perf. 12***
2048 A1095 14p multi 2.50 2.00

University Culture Foundation, 35th Anniv. — A1096

2003, Nov. 28
2049 A1096 14p multi 2.50 2.00

Uruguayan Air Force, 50th Anniv. — A1097

2003, Dec. 4
2050 A1097 14p multi 2.50 2.00

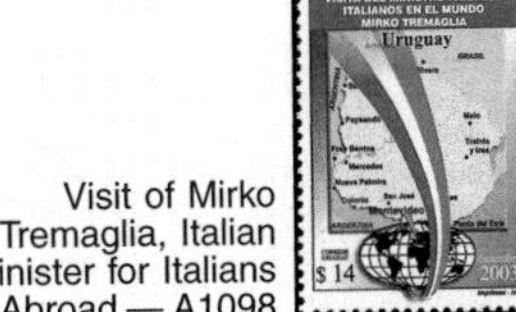
Visit of Mirko Tremaglia, Italian Minister for Italians Abroad — A1098

2003, Dec. 15
2051 A1098 14p multi 2.50 2.00

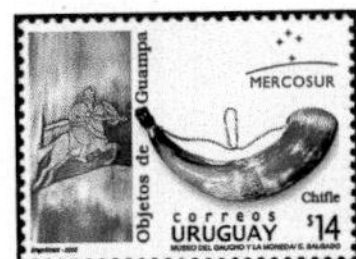
Mercosur A1099

Designs: 14p, Horn. 36p, Silver stirrup.

2003, Dec. 16
2052-2053 A1099 Set of 2 8.50 8.00

Powered Flight, Cent. — A1100

2003, Dec. 19
2054 A1100 14p multi 2.50 2.25

Nos. 1378, 1382, 1458 and 1492 Surcharged in Black or Blue Violet

j

k

Methods and Perfs. as Before

2004 **Wmk. 332**

2055	A654(j)	1p on 1.20p #1492	.45	.40
2056	A639(j)	2p on 2.60p #1458 (BV)	.45	.40
2057	A589(k)	5p on 2500p #1382	.90	.50
2058	A589(k)	10p on 360p #1378	1.75	1.20
2059	A589(k)	50p on 825p #1379B	6.75	6.00
		Nos. 2055-2059 (5)	10.30	8.50

Issued: Nos. 2055-2056, 1/19; Nos. 2057-2058, 2/16; No. 2059, 3/23. Obliterator on Nos. 2055 and 2056 covers the centesimos portion of the denomination.

Compare No. 2055 with No. 2011A.

Birds A1101

No. 2060: a, Puffinus gravis. b, Macronectes halli. c, Daption capense. d, Diamedea melanophrys.

Unwmk.

2004, Jan. 22 **Litho.** ***Perf. 12***
2060 A1101 14p Block of 4, #a-d 9.25 8.25

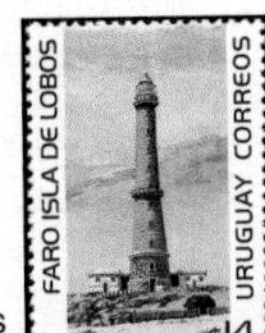
Isla de Lobos Lighthouse — A1102

No. 2061: a, Isla de Flores Lighthouse. b, Farallon Lighthouse. c, La Panela Lighthouse. d, Banco Ingles Floating Lighthouse.

2004, Feb. 10 **Litho.** ***Perf. 12***
2061 A1102 10p Block of 4, #a-d 6.50 5.50
2062 A1102 14p shown 2.25 2.00

Abitab, 10th Anniv. — A1103

Unwmk.

2004, Feb. 12 **Litho.** ***Perf. 12***
2063 A1103 14p multi 2.50 2.10

National Naval Prefecture, 175th Anniv. — A1104

2004, Feb. 20 **Litho.** ***Perf. 12***
2064 A1104 14p multi 2.50 2.25

Maté Containers — A1105

No. 2065: a, Maté de Cáliz. b, Maté de Plata Colonial. c, Maté de Calabaza.

2004, Mar. 4
2065 A1105 5p Strip of 3, #a-c 3.00 2.25

33 Orientales Mechanized Infantry Battalion No. 10, Cent. — A1106

2004, Mar. 12
2066 A1106 14p multi 2.50 2.25

Intl. Water Day — A1107

2004, Mar. 25
2067 A1107 14p multi 2.50 2.25

Regional Energy Integration Commission, 40th Anniv. — A1108

2004, Mar. 25
2068 A1108 14p multi 2.50 2.25

Grenadier Guards, 80th Anniv. — A1109

2004, Apr. 1
2069 A1109 14p multi 2.50 2.25

Expansion of La Teja Refinery A1110

2004, Apr. 2
2070 A1110 14p multi 2.50 2.25

Florida Infantry Batallion No. 1, 175th Anniv. — A1111

2004, Apr. 16
2071 A1111 14p multi 2.50 2.25

Tribute to Servicemen A1112

2004, May 26
2072 A1112 14p multi 2.50 2.25

Medicinal Plants — A1113

No. 2073: a, Malva sylvestris. b, Achyrocline satureiodes, c, Baccharis trimera. d, Mentha x piperita.

2004, June 3
2073 A1113 Strip of 4 18.00 17.00
a.-d. 36p Any single 4.00 4.00

Map and Arms of Montevideo Department A1114

2004, June 17
2074 A1114 14p multi 2.50 2.25
a. Booklet pane of 2 5.00 —
Complete booklet, #2074a 5.00

No. 2074a sold for 35p.

Carlos Gardel (1890-1935), Singer — A1115

2004, June 24 **Litho.** ***Perf. 12***
2075 A1115 14p multi 2.50 2.25

Campaign Against Illegal Drugs — A1116

2004, June 25 **Litho.** ***Perf. 12***
2076 A1116 14p multi 2.50 2.25

Renán Rodríguez, Politician A1117

2004, Aug. 10
2077 A1117 14p multi 2.50 2.25

Maimonides (1135-1204), Philosopher
A1118

2004, Aug. 12
2078 A1118 16p multi 2.50 2.25

Galician Center, Montevideo, 125th Anniv.
A1119

2004, Aug. 30
2079 A1119 16p multi 2.50 2.25

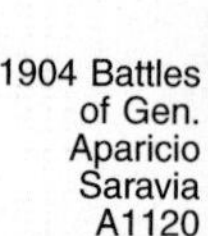

1904 Battles of Gen. Aparicio Saravia
A1120

No. 2080 — Battle of: a, Illescas. b, Fray-Marcos. c, Paso del Parque. d, Masoller.

2004, Sept. 8
2080 Block of 4 5.50 4.50
a.-d. A1120 10p Any single 1.10 1.10

Highway Patrol, 50th Anniv. — A1121

2004, Sept. 15 ***Perf. 12½x12¾***
2081 A1121 16p multi 2.50 2.25

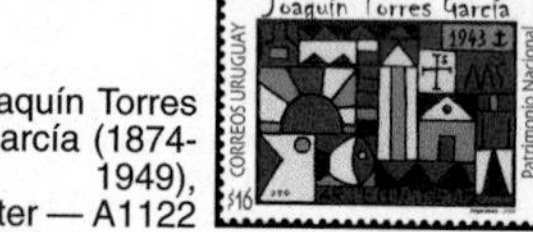

Joaquín Torres García (1874-1949), Painter — A1122

2004, Sept. 19
2082 A1122 16p multi 2.50 2.25

Magisterial Cooperative, 75th Anniv. — A1123

2004, Sept. 22
2083 A1123 16p multi 2.50 2.25

Army Administrative Corps, Cent. — A1124

2004, Sept. 22
2084 A1124 16p multi 2.50 2.25

FIFA (Fédération Internationale de Football Association), Cent. — A1125

2004, Oct. 5 ***Perf. 12***
2085 A1125 37p multi 5.00 4.75

Uruguay - Republic of Korea Diplomatic Relations, 40th Anniv. A1126

2004, Oct. 7
2086 A1126 16p multi 2.50 2.25

Montevideo Cathedral, Bicent. — A1127

2004, Oct. 19 **Litho.** ***Perf. 12***
2087 A1127 16p multi 2.50 2.25

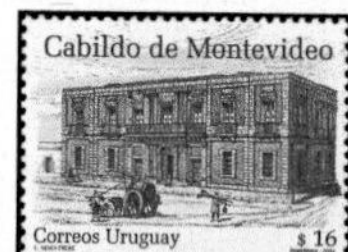

Montevideo Council Building A1128

2004, Oct. 22 **Litho.** ***Perf. 12***
2088 A1128 16p multi 2.50 2.25

Tomás Toribio House — A1129

2004, Oct. 22
2089 A1129 16p multi 2.50 2.25

America Issue - Environmental Protection A1130

Dirty and clean: 16p, Water. 37p, Birds.

2004, Oct. 26
2090-2091 A1130 Set of 2 8.00 7.25

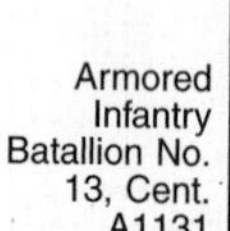

Armored Infantry Batallion No. 13, Cent. A1131

2004, Nov. 16
2092 A1131 16p multi 2.50 2.25

Corner Store, 18th Cent. — A1132

2004, Nov. 22
2093 A1132 16p multi 2.50 2.25

PriceWaterhouseCoopers in Uruguay, 85th Anniv. — A1133

2004, Dec. 7
2094 A1133 16p multi 2.50 2.25

Review of Court Clerks, Cent. — A1134

2004, Dec. 8
2095 A1134 16p multi 2.50 2.25

Christmas — A1135

2004, Dec. 14
2096 A1135 16p multi 2.50 2.25

Water Conservation A1136

2004, Dec. 21
2097 A1136 37p multi 5.50 5.00

Souvenir Sheet

Punta del Este A1137

2004, Dec. 27
2098 A1137 16p multi 3.75 3.50

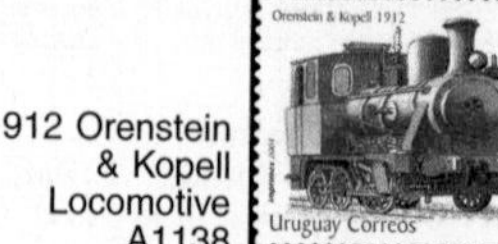

1912 Orenstein & Kopell Locomotive A1138

Serpentine Die Cut 11¼
2004, Dec. 28 **Self-Adhesive**
2099 A1138 30p multi 5.25 5.00

Rotary International, Cent. — A1139

2005, Feb. 23 **Litho.** ***Perf. 12***
2100 A1139 37p multi 8.00 7.50

Bridges A1140

No. 2101: a, Chuy del Tacuarí Bridge. b, Barra Bridge, Maldonado. c, Mauá Bridge Yaguarón River. d, Castells Bridge, Víboras.

2005, Mar. 18
2101 A1140 16p Block of 4, #a-d 12.00 10.00

Ninth Meeting of Latin American Energy Regulators A1141

2005, Apr. 5
2102 A1141 16p multi 2.75 2.50

"Liberating Dragoons" Ninth Mechanized Cavalry Regiment, Cent. A1142

2005, Apr. 11
2103 A1142 16p multi 2.75 2.50

Armenian Genocide, 90th Anniv. — A1143

2005, Apr. 25
2104 A1143 16p multi 2.50 2.25

Fingerprint Analysis in Uruguay, Cent. A1144

2005, Apr. 26
2105 A1144 16p multi 2.75 2.50

No. 1446 Surcharged

Wmk. 332
2005, May 27 **Litho.** ***Perf. 12½***
2106 A639 2p on 50c #1446 .75 .50

Fountains — A1145

Designs: No. 2107, 10p, Constitution Plaza Fountain. No. 2108, 10p, Botanical Garden Fountain. No. 2109, 10p, Athlete's Fountain, Rodó Park. 37p, Cordier Fountain, Prado, horiz.

2005, June 8 **Litho.** ***Perf. 12***
2107-2110 A1145 Set of 4 11.00 10.00

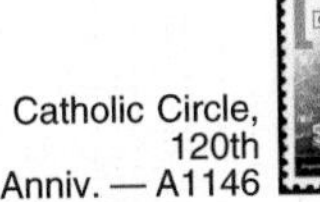

Catholic Circle, 120th Anniv. — A1146

2005, June 9
2111 A1146 16p multi 2.90 2.50

SOS Children's Villages, 45th Anniv. — A1147

2005, June 23
2112 A1147 16p multi 2.90 2.50

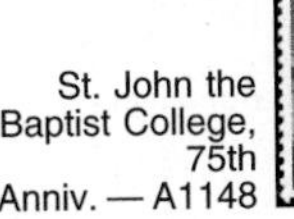

St. John the Baptist College, 75th Anniv. — A1148

2005, June 24
2113 A1148 16p multi 2.90 2.50

Souvenir Sheet

Death of Pope John Paul II and Election of Pope Benedict XVI A1149

No. 2114: a, Cross and statue of Pope John Paul II, Montevideo. b, Pope Benedict XVI.

Perf. 12x11¾
2005, July 15 Litho. Unwmk.
2114 A1149 10p Sheet of 2, #a-b 6.50 6.00

Medical Association Assistance Center, 70th Anniv. — A1150

2005 ***Perf. 12***
2115 A1150 16p multi 2.75 2.50

Inscribed "Correos Uruguay" at Right

Perf. 12¾x12½
2116 A1150 16p multi 2.75 2.50

Issued: No. 2115, 7/19; No. 2116, 8/4.

Seminary College, 125th Anniv. — A1151

Designs: No. 2117, 16p, St. Ignatius of Loyola, college building. No. 2118, 16p, College building.

2005, July 29 ***Perf. 12***
2117-2118 A1151 Set of 2 5.00 4.50

General Liber Seregni (1916-2004) — A1152

No. 2119 — Inscriptions: a, Vocacion. b, Comienzo. c, Liberacion. d, Reconocimiento.

2005
2119 A1152 16p Block of 4, #a-d 13.50 10.00
e. Booklet pane, #2119 12.50 —
Complete booklet, #2119e 13.00

Issued: No. 2119, 8/1; No. 2119e, 10/11.

Pope John Paul II (1920-2005) A1153

2005, Aug. 11 ***Perf. 13½x13¾***
2120 A1153 37p multi 5.75 5.50

Europa Stamps, 50th Anniv. — A1154

Designs: 16p, Landscape, by C. De Arzadun, Spain #1263. 37p, The Emus, by De Arzadun, Spain, #1126, vert.

Perf. 13¾x13½, 13½x13¾
2005, Aug. 11 Litho.
2121-2122 A1154 Set of 2 8.50 8.00

Urutem 2005 Philatelic Exhibition — A1155

2005, Aug. 15 Litho. ***Perf. 12***
2123 A1155 16p multi 2.75 2.50

Legislative Palace, 80th Anniv. — A1156

2005, Aug. 24 Litho. ***Perf. 12***
2124 A1156 16p multi 2.75 2.50

Estadio Centenario, 75th Anniv. A1157

Children's art: No. 2125, $16, Stadium, by Jonatan Belón. No. 2126, 16p, "75" made with flag and soccer field, by Sofia Arca.

2005, Aug. 30
2125-2126 A1157 Set of 2 5.25 4.75

Carlos Solé, Soccer Broadcaster A1158

2005, Sept. 20
2127 A1158 16p multi 2.90 2.60

World Cup Soccer Championships, 75th Anniv. — A1159

Designs: No. 2128, 16p, Parade of athletes. No. 2129, 16p, Handshake before match. No. 2130, 16p, Awarding of World Cup. 37p, Flags of Germany and Uruguay, emblem of 2006 World Cup Soccer Championships, Germany.

2005, Oct. 3
2128-2131 A1159 Set of 4 13.00 12.00

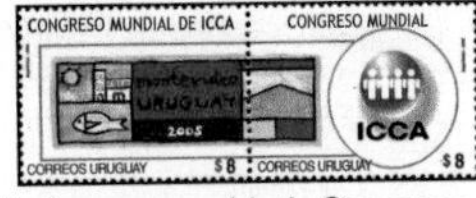

44th Congress of Intl. Congress and Convention Association, Montevideo — A1160

No. 2132: a, Fish sun and buildings. b, Association emblem.

2005, Nov. 4 Litho. ***Perf. 12***
2132 A1160 8p Horiz. pair, #a-b 2.75 2.50

Uruguay River Fish A1161

No. 2133: a, Rhamdia sapo. b, Odontesthes bonariensis. c, Hoplias malabaricus. d, Pygocentrus nattereri.

2005, Nov. 22
2133 A1161 16p Block of 4, #a-d 10.00 9.00

El Escolar Magazine, 50th Anniv. — A1162

2005, Nov. 23
2134 A1162 16p multi 3.25 3.00

Customhouse Brokers Association, 70th Anniv. — A1163

2005, Nov. 25
2135 A1163 16p multi 2.75 2.50

Detail From Mural, *Oficios,* by Julio Alpuy A1164

2005, Dec. 1
2136 A1164 16p multi 2.75 2.50

Writers — A1165

Designs: 16p, Juan Zorilla de San Martin (1855-1931). 37p, Constancio C. Vigil (1876-1954).

2005, Dec. 9
2137-2138 A1165 Set of 2 8.50 8.00

Commercial and Industrial Center of Salto, Cent. A1166

2005, Dec. 12
2139 A1166 16p multi 2.75 2.50

Central Español Soccer Team, Cent. — A1167

2005, Dec. 12
2140 A1167 16p multi 2.75 2.50

Christmas A1168

2005, Dec. 12
2141 A1168 16p multi 2.75 2.50

Montevideo Atheneum, 137th Anniv. — A1169

2005, Dec. 14 Litho.
2142 A1169 16p multi 2.75 2.50

1924 Paris Olympics, 80th Anniv. (in 2004) — A1170

Designs: No. 2143, 16p, Andrés Mazali, soccer gold medalist. No. 2144, 16p, Juan Pedro Cea, soccer gold medalist. No. 2145, 16p, Alfredo Ghierra, soccer gold medalist. 37p, Urn showing soccer players, vert.

2005, Dec. 20 ***Perf. 12***
2143-2146 A1170 Set of 4 13.00 12.00

America Issue, Fight Against Poverty — A1171

Designs: 16p, Children, teacher and school. 37p, Men with shovel.

2005, Dec. 22
2147-2148 A1171 Set of 2 8.00 7.50

Capitán Miranda, 75th Anniv. A1172

No. 2149: a, Capitán Miranda in 1930. b, Capitán Miranda in 2005. c, Capt. Francisco P. Miranda (1869-1925). d, Crests of ships Capitán Miranda, Cádiz, and Montevideo.

2005, Dec. 28
2149 A1172 16p Block of 4, #a-d 10.00 9.00

No. 1492 Surcharged in Brown

2005? Photo. Wmk. 332 ***Perf. 12½***
2150 A654 1p on 1.20p #1492 .85 .60

Obliterator on No. 2150 covers the "20" of original denomination. Compare with Nos. 2055 and 2011A.

Maldonado, 250th Anniv. A1173

Designs: No. 2151, 16p, San Fernando Cathedral. No. 2152, 16p, Dragoon Quarters.

2006, Feb. 22 Litho. ***Perf. 12***
2151-2152 A1173 Set of 2 5.50 5.00

Alfredo Zitarrosa (1936-89), Singer — A1174

Zitarrosa and: No. 2153, 16p, Guitar, violin. No. 2154, 16p, Guitar, violin, vert.

2006, Mar. 10
2153-2154 A1174 Set of 2 5.00 4.50

Solís Theater, 150th Anniv. A1175

2006, Mar. 28
2155 A1175 16p multi 2.75 2.50

Diario Español Newspaper, Cent. — A1176

2006, May 15
2156 A1176 16p multi 2.75 2.50

Public Enterprise Day — A1177

2006, May 19
2157 A1177 16p black 2.75 2.50

Assassinated Politicians A1178

Designs: No. 2158, 16p, Héctor Gutiérrez Ruiz (1934-76). No. 2159, 16p, Zelmar Michelini (1924-76). No. 2160, 16p, Michelini and Gutiérrez Ruiz.

2006, June 1
2158-2160 A1178 Set of 3 7.75 7.00

SODRE Symphonic Orchestra, 75th Anniv. A1179

2006, June 20
2161 A1179 16p black 2.50 2.25

Masons in Uruguay, 150th Anniv. — A1180

2006, Aug. 15
2162 A1180 16p multi 2.75 2.50

Horse Breeds A1181

No. 2163: a, Appaloosa. b, Percheron. c, Belgian Heavy Draft. d, Criollo.

2006, Aug. 18
2163 A1181 16p Block of 4, #a-d 10.50 9.50

First Uruguayan Postage Stamps, 150th Anniv. A1182

2006, Sept. 29
2164 A1182 16p multi 2.75 2.50

Eladio Dieste (1917-2000), Architect A1183

2006, Oct. 3
2165 A1183 16p multi 2.75 2.50

Syndical Unification Congress, 40th Anniv. — A1184

No. 2166: a, Marchers with banner. b, Marchers with flag.

2006, Oct. 3
2166 A1184 16p Horiz. pair, #a-b 5.50 5.00

Diplomatic Relations Between Uruguay and the Sovereign Military Order of Malta, 40th Anniv. — A1185

2006, Oct. 4
2167 A1185 16p multi 2.75 2.50

Paysandú, 250th Anniv. — A1186

2006, Oct. 12
2168 A1186 16p multi 2.75 2.50

Dr. Washington Beltrán (1914-2003), Politician — A1187

2006, Oct. 25
2169 A1187 16p multi 2.75 2.50

16th Ibero-American Summit, Montevideo A1188

2006, Nov. 1 Litho. ***Perf. 12***
2170 A1188 37p multi 5.25 5.00

Salto, 250th Anniv. — A1189

2006, Nov. 7 Litho. ***Perf. 12***
2171 A1189 16p multi 2.75 2.50

Channel 10, 50th Anniv. A1190

2006, Nov. 8 Litho. ***Perf. 12***
2172 A1190 16p multi 2.75 2.50

America Issue, Energy Conservation — A1191

No. 2173: a, 16p, Screw-in fluorescent light bulbs. b, 37p, Solar panels.

2006, Nov. 17 Litho. ***Perf. 12***
2173 A1191 Horiz. pair, #a-b 8.00 7.50

Sports — A1192

Designs: No. 2174, 16p, Indoor soccer. No. 2175, 16p, Handball. No. 2176, 16p, Rugby. No. 2177, 16p, Tennis.

2006, Nov. 30
2174-2177 A1192 Set of 4 11.00 10.00

Christmas — A1193

2006, Dec. 7
2178 A1193 37p multi 5.25 5.00

Musical Instruments A1194

Designs: 15p, Guitar. 37p, Drum, horiz.

2006, Dec. 11
2179-2180 A1194 Set of 2 8.00 7.50

Ocean Liners and Ports A1195

No. 2181: a, Queen Mary 2, Montevideo. b, Costa Fortuna, Montevideo. c, Zuiderman, Montevideo. d, Star Princess, Punta del Este.

2006, Dec. 18
2181 A1195 37p Block of 4, #a-d 24.00 22.50

Uruguayan Lottery, 150th Anniv. A1196

2006, Dec. 22 Litho. ***Perf. 12***
2182 A1196 15p multi 2.75 2.50

Optimist Class Yacht World Championships — A1197

2006, Dec. 28 Litho. ***Perf. 12***
2183 A1197 37p multi 5.75 5.50

Uruguay Post Emblem A1198

Serpentine Die Cut 11¼
2006, Dec. 29 Litho.
Self-Adhesive
2184 A1198 15p multi 2.75 2.40

No. 1492 Surcharged in Golden Brown

No. 1454 Surcharged in Black and Silver

Methods, Perfs, and Watermarks As Before

2007, Jan. 24

2185 A654 1p on 1.20p #1492 .85 .60
2186 A639 2p on 1.80p #1454 .85 .60

Compare No. 2185 with Nos. 2011A, 2055 and 2150.

Punta del Este, Cent. A1199

Unwmk.

2007, Jan. 26 Litho. *Perf. 12*
2187 A1199 37p multi 5.25 5.00

José Nasazzi Children's Soccer Cup — A1200

2007, Feb. 5 Litho. *Perf. 12*
2188 A1200 15p multi 2.25 2.00

Julia Arévalo (1898-1985), Politician A1201

2007, Mar. 8 Litho. *Perf. 12*
2189 A1201 15p multi 2.25 2.25

Souvenir Sheet

Ministry of Transportation and Public Works, Cent. — A1202

No. 2190: a, 5p, Highway construction crew. b, 10p, Airplanes at airport. c, 15p, Bridge.

2007, Mar. 12 Litho. *Perf. 12¼*
2190 A1202 Sheet of 3, #a-c 5.25 4.50

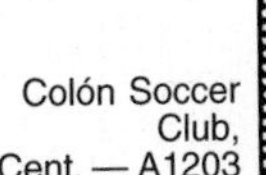

Colón Soccer Club, Cent. — A1203

2007, Mar. 12 Litho. *Perf. 12*
2191 A1203 15p multi 2.50 2.25

Campaign Against Dengue Fever — A1204

Serpentine Die Cut 11¼

2007, Mar. 28 Self-Adhesive
2192 A1204 15p multi 2.50 2.25

National Cadastre, Cent. — A1205

2007, Apr. 12 *Perf. 12*
2193 A1205 15p multi 2.50 2.25

Regional Art Meeting — A1206

2007, June 8
2194 A1206 15p multi 2.50 2.25

Shells A1207

No. 2195: a, 5p, Aequipecten tehuelchus. b, 5p, Trophon pelseneeri. c, 10p, Americominella duartei. d, 10p, Conus clenchi.

2007, June 26
2195 A1207 Block of 4, #a-d 5.00 4.00

Giuseppe Garibaldi (1807-82), Italian Leader — A1208

Designs: 15p, Ship, Garibaldi on horseback. 37p, Garibaldi, ship.

2007, July 4
2196-2197 A1208 Set of 2 7.00 7.00
2197a Horiz. pair, #2196-2197 7.50 7.00

See Brazil Nos. 3021-3022.

Guichón, Cent. — A1209

2007, July 13
2198 A1209 15p multi 2.50 2.25

Souvenir Sheet

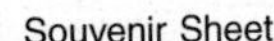

La Estrella del Sur Publication, Bicent. — A1210

2007, July 19 *Perf. 12½x12¾*
2199 A1210 15p multi 2.75 2.50

Agronomy Faculties, Cent. — A1211

2007, July 30
2200 A1211 15p multi 2.25 2.00

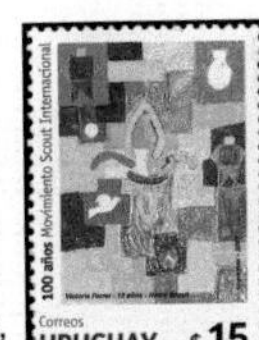

Scouting, Cent. — A1212

Children's drawings: No. 2201, 15p, Scout emblem, by Victoria Ferrer. No. 2202, 15p, Scouts at Flag Ceremony, by Paula Barrios.

No. 2203, horiz.: a, Knot, Lord Robert Baden-Powell and Duke of Connaught. b, Knot, International Scout emblem patch.

2007, Aug. 9 *Perf. 12*
2201-2202 A1212 Set of 2 4.50 4.00

Souvenir Sheet

2203 A1212 25p Sheet of 2, #a-b 7.50 7.00

Three Musicians in Primary Colors, by José Gurvich (1927-74) A1213

2007, Aug. 17
2204 A1213 15p multi 2.25 2.00

Diplomatic Relations Between Uruguay and Guatemala, Cent. — A1214

No. 2205: a, 15p, Santa Catarina Arch, Antigua, Guatemala. b, 37p, City gate, Colonia del Sacramento, Uruguay.

2007, Sept. 3 Litho. *Perf. 12½x12¾*
2205 A1214 Horiz. pair, #a-b 7.50 7.00

See Guatemala No. 583.

German College and High School, Montevideo, 150th Anniv. — A1215

No. 2206: a, Anniversary emblem. b, Children's drawing of girl and colors of flags of Germany and Uruguay.

2007, Sept. 5 *Perf. 12*
2206 Horiz. pair + central label 4.50 4.00
a.-b. A1215 15p Either single 1.75 1.75

Occupations A1216

Designs: 1p, Peanut vendor. 7p, Knife grinder, vert. 10p, Organ grinder, vert. 25p, Barber, vert. 50p, Druggist, vert.

Serpentine Die Cut 11¼

2007, Oct. 6 Self-Adhesive

2207 A1216 1p multi	.30	.30
2208 A1216 7p multi	1.15	1.15
2209 A1216 10p multi	1.15	1.15
2210 A1216 25p multi	3.50	3.50
2211 A1216 50p multi	7.00	7.00
Nos. 2207-2211 (5)	13.10	13.10

See Nos. 2253, 2282, 2290, 2292-2295, B13.

Marine Mammal Conservation A1217

2007, Oct. 12 *Die Cut*

Self-Adhesive

2212 A1217 37p multi 5.25 5.00

Butterflies — A1218

No. 2213: a, 5p, Eurybia lycisca. b, 10p, Catagramma excelsior pastazza. c, 15p, Agrias claudina. d, 20p, Marpesia marcella.

2007, Oct. 26 *Perf. 12½x12¾*
2213 A1218 Block of 4, #a-d 9.00 8.00

Torrijos - Carter Panama Canal Treaties, 30th Anniv. — A1219

2007, Nov. 5 *Perf. 12*
2214 A1219 37p multi 5.25 5.00

America Issue, Education For All — A1220

Designs: 15p, Rectangles. 37p, Squares and rectangles.

2007, Nov. 22
2215-2216 A1220 Set of 2 7.50 7.00

Naval School, Cent. A1221

2007, Dec. 5 *Perf. 12x11¾*
2217 A1221 12p multi 2.00 1.75

Diplomatic Relations Between Uruguay and Russia, 150th Anniv. — A1223

No. 2218: a, 12p, Sacred Heart of Jesus Sanctuary, Uruguay. b, 37p, St. Basil's Cathedral, Russia.

2007, Dec. 21 Litho. *Perf. 12*
2218 A1223 Horiz. pair, #a-b + central label 6.50 6.00

Christmas — A1224

2007, Dec. 21
2219 A1224 12p multi 2.00 1.75

Architecture — A1225

Designs: 12p, House, by Julio Vilamajó. 37p, Joaquín Torres García Building, by Carlos Ott.

2007, Dec. 28
2220-2221 A1225 Set of 2 7.50 7.00

Nelly Goitiño (1924-2007), Actress and Director — A1226

2008, Mar. 24 Litho. *Perf. 12*
2222 A1226 12p multi 2.00 1.75

Natl. Association of Milk Producers, 75th Anniv. — A1227

2008, Apr. 23 Litho. *Perf. 12*
2223 A1227 12p multi 2.25 2.00

Israel, 60th Anniv. — A1228

2008, May 8
2224 A1228 37p multi + label 5.50 5.00

Diplomatic Relations Between Uruguay and the People's Republic of China, 20th Anniv. A1229

Designs: No. 2225, 12p, Terracotta warriors, China. No. 2226, 12p, The Three Chiripás, painting by J. M. Blaines.

2008, May 19 Litho. *Perf. 12*
2225-2226 A1229 Set of 2 4.10 3.50

Dr. Juan J. Crottogini (1908-96), Gynecologist — A1230

2008, May 27 Litho. *Perf. 12*
2227 A1230 12p multi 2.25 2.00

Souvenir Sheet

Uruguayan Artisans Association, 25th Anniv. — A1231

2008, May 29 *Perf. 12½x12¾*
2228 A1231 12p multi 2.25 2.00

Discount Bank, 50th Anniv. A1232

2008, June 4 *Perf. 12*
Self-Adhesive
2229 A1232 12p multi 2.25 2.00

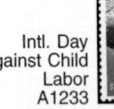

Intl. Day Against Child Labor A1233

2008, June 12
2230 A1233 12p multi 2.25 2.00

Birds — A1234

Designs: 12p, Piranga flava. 37p, Cyanocorax chrysops, vert.

2008, June 20
2231-2232 A1234 Set of 2 7.50 7.00

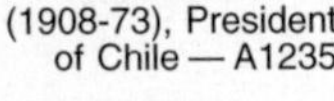

Salvador Allende (1908-73), President of Chile — A1235

2008, June 26
2233 A1235 37p multi 5.75 5.50

Francisco Gómez House, 120th Anniv. as Montevideo Government Building — A1236

2008, July 11 *Perf. 12*
2234 A1236 12p multi 2.25 2.00

Hospital Centenaries A1237

Designs: No. 2235, 12p, Dr. Raul Amorin Cal Hospital, Florida. No. 2236, 12p, Central Hospital of the Armed Forces. No. 2237, 12p, Pereira Rossell Hospital Center.

2008, July 15
2235-2237 A1237 Set of 3 6.25 5.50

2008 Summer Olympics, Beijing — A1238

No. 2238: a, 2p, Pole vault. b, 5p, Cycling. c, 10p, Swimming. d, 20p, Kayaking.

2008, July 22
2238 A1238 Block of 4, #a-d 6.00 5.00

Intl. Swimming Federation (FINA), Cent. — A1239

2008, July 22
2239 A1239 37p multi 5.25 5.00

Club Español, Montevideo, 130th Anniv. — A1240

2008, Aug. 28 Litho. *Perf. 12*
2240 A1240 12p multi 2.25 2.00

Carlos Vaz Ferreira (1872-1958), Philosopher A1241

2008, Sept. 25 Litho. *Perf. 12*
2241 A1241 12p multi 2.25 2.00

Latin American and Caribbean Coalition A1242

2008, Sept. 25
2242 Horiz. strip of 3 6.25 5.50
a. A1242 10p Three people 1.40 1.40
b. A1242 12p Three people, diff. 1.75 1.75
c. A1242 15p Four people 2.00 2.00

Souvenir Sheet

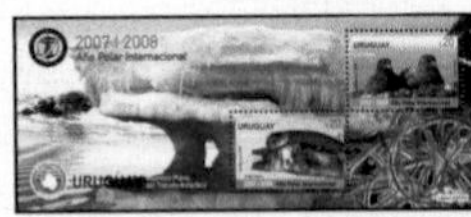

Intl. Polar Year A1243

No. 1243: a, Skuas. b, Arctocephalus gazella.

2008, Oct. 7
2243 A1243 20p Sheet of 2, #a-b 6.50 6.00

America Issue, National Festivals — A1244

Designs: 12p, Guitarist, dancers. 37p, Dancer, costumed drummers.

Perf. 12¾x12½, 12 (37p)
2008, Oct. 24
2244-2245 A1244 Set of 2 7.50 7.00

Dr. Roberto De Bellis (1938-2007), Hematologist A1245

2008, Oct. 29 *Perf. 12*
2246 A1245 12p multi 2.00 1.75

José "Pepe" Sasía, Soccer Player — A1246

2008, Nov. 20 Litho. *Perf. 12*
2247 A1246 12p multi 2.25 2.00

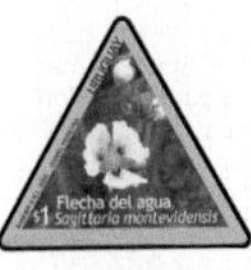

Flowers — A1247

Designs: 1p, Sagittaria montevidensis. 2p, Lantana camara. 10p, Calliandra parvifolia. 17p, Erythrina crista-galli. 25p, Prunus subcoriacea.

2008-09 **Litho.** ***Die Cut***

Self-Adhesive

2248 A1247	1p multi		.35	.30
2249 A1247	2p multi		.35	.30
2250 A1247	10p multi		1.60	1.40
a.	Dated "2009"		1.60	1.40
2251 A1247	17p multi		2.60	2.25
2252 A1247	25p multi		4.00	3.50
	Nos. 2248-2252 (5)		8.90	7.75

Issued: 1p, 2p, 3/12/09; 10p, 25p, 11/28; 17p, 12/18.
No. 2250a, 5/15/09.
See Nos. 2265-2266, 2287.

Occupations Type of 2007

2008, Dec. 7 ***Die Cut***

Self-Adhesive

2253 A1216 8p Pasta makers 1.50 1.25

Ministry of Foreign Affairs, 180th Anniv. A1248

2008, Dec. 10 **Litho.** ***Perf. 12***

2254 A1248 37p multi 5.75 5.50

Christmas A1249

2008, Dec. 24

2255 A1249 12p multi 2.25 2.00

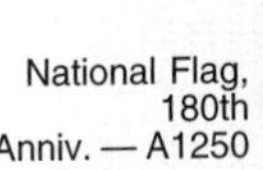

National Flag, 180th Anniv. — A1250

2008, Dec. 29

2256 A1250 37p multi 5.75 5.50

Pres. Baltasar Brum (1883-1933) A1251

2009, Mar. 4 ***Perf. 12½x12¾***

2257 A1251 12p multi 2.00 1.75

Delmira Agustini (1886-1914), Poet — A1252

2009, Mar. 26

2258 A1252 12p multi 2.00 1.75

Miguelete, Cent. — A1253

2009, Mar. 27 ***Perf. 12¾x12½***

2259 A1253 12p multi 2.00 1.75

Fray Bentos, 150th Anniv. A1254

2009, Apr. 15 **Litho.** ***Perf. 12***

2260 A1254 12p multi 2.00 1.75

City of Florida, 200th Anniv. — A1255

2009, Apr. 24 ***Perf. 12¾x12½***

2261 A1255 12p multi 2.00 1.75

Carnival Costume Designed by Juan Mascheroni — A1256

2009, May 28 ***Die Cut***

Self-Adhesive

2262 A1256 37p multi 5.75 5.50

Souvenir Sheet

Intl. Year of Astronomy — A1257

No. 2263: a, 10p, Intl. Year of Astronomy emblem. b, 12p, Galileo Galilei at Inquisition. c, 25p, Head of Galileo.

2009, June 4 ***Perf. 12***

2263 A1257 Sheet of 3, #a-c 7.25 6.50

Juan Carlos Onetti (1909-94), Writer — A1258

2009, July 1 ***Perf. 12½x12¾***

2264 A1258 12p multi 2.00 1.75

Flowers Type of 2008-09

Designs: 30p, Tessaria absinthioides. 50p, Eichhornia crassipes.

2009, July 14 ***Die Cut***

Self-Adhesive

2265 A1247 30p multi 4.50 4.25
2266 A1247 50p multi 7.50 7.00

Souvenir Sheet

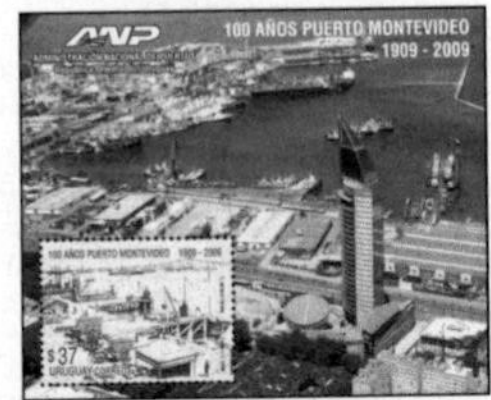

Port of Montevideo, Cent. — A1259

2009, July 21 ***Perf. 12***

2267 A1259 37p multi 5.75 5.50

Charles Darwin (1809-82), Naturalist — A1260

No. 2268: a, 12p, Head of Darwin, evolution of humans. b, 37p, HMS Beagle.

2009, Aug. 31

2268 A1260 Horiz. pair, #a-b 7.50 7.00

No. 1454 Surcharged

Method, Perf. and Watermark As Before

2009, Sept. 10

2269 A639 1p on 1.80p #2269 .65 .40

Obliterator covers the centisimos portion of the denomination.

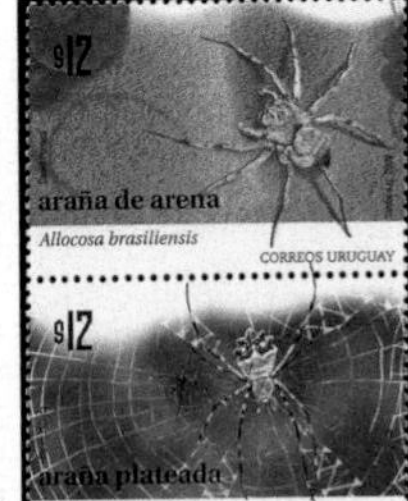

Spiders A1261

No. 2270: a, Allocosa brasiliensis. b, Argiope argentata.

2009, Sept. 24 **Litho.** ***Perf. 12***

2270 A1261 12p Vert. pair, #a-b 4.00 3.50

Acipenser Gueldenstaedtii and Caviar — A1262

Unwmk.

2009, Sept. 30 **Litho.** ***Perf. 12***

2271 A1262 37p multi 6.00 5.50

Intl. Labor Organization, 90th Anniv. — A1263

2009, Oct. 7

2272 A1263 37p multi 5.75 5.50

Butterflies and Birds — A1264

No. 2273: a, Hamadryas amphione. b, Anartia amathea. c, Tachuris rubrigasta. d, Colaptes melanochloros.

2009, Oct. 13

2273 A1264 12p Block of 4, #a-d 7.25 6.00

America Issue, Traditional Games — A1265

Designs: 12p, Hand holding stone for Taba. 37p, Taba Game, painting by Juan Manuel Blanes.

2009, Oct. 23 ***Perf. 12½x12¾***

2274-2275 A1265 Set of 2 7.00 6.25

Government House Museum, 10th Anniv. — A1266

2009, Nov. 6 ***Perf. 12***

2276 A1266 12p multi + label 2.25 2.00

Christmas — A1267

2009, Nov. 17 ***Perf. 12¾x12½***

2277 A1267 12p multi 1.90 1.60

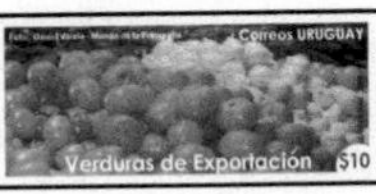

Exports A1268

Designs: 10p, Vegetables. 25p, Fruits.

2009, Nov. 19 ***Die Cut***

Self-Adhesive

2278 A1268 10p multi 1.40 1.25
2279 A1268 25p multi 3.75 3.25

Inter-American Development Bank, 50th Anniv. — A1269

2009, Nov. 24 ***Perf. 12¾x12½***

2280 A1269 37p multi 5.25 4.75

Christian Youth Association (YMCA) in Uruguay, Cent. — A1270

2009, Nov. 25

2281 A1270 12p multi 1.90 1.60

Occupations Type of 2007

2009, Nov. 27 ***Die Cut***

Self-Adhesive

2282 A1216 8p Grocer, vert. 1.50 1.25

Chauffeur's Protection Center, Montevideo, Cent. — A1271

2009, Dec. 3 ***Perf. 12½x12¾***

2283 A1271 12p multi 2.25 2.00

Souvenir Sheet

Battle of the River Plate, 70th Anniv. A1272

No. 2284: a, 10p, HMS Ajax. b, 12p, HMSNZ Achilles. c, 15p, HMS Exeter.

2009, Dec. 16 ***Perf. 12***
2284 A1272 Sheet of 3, #a-c 6.25 5.50

Official Service of Broadcasting, Television and Entertainment, 80th Anniv. — A1273

2009, Dec. 18 ***Perf. 12¾x12½***
2285 A1273 37p multi 5.75 5.50

Alba Roballo (1908-96), Politician A1274

2010, Mar. 8 Litho. ***Perf. 12***
2286 A1274 12p multi 2.00 1.75

Flowers Type of 2008-09

2010, Apr. 12 ***Die Cut***
Self-Adhesive
2287 A1247 12p Erithrina crista-galli 2.25 2.00

Historic Hotels — A1275

Designs: No. 2288, 12p, Gran Hotel Concordia, Salto. No. 2289, 12p, Hotel Colón, Piriápolis.

2010, May 26 ***Perf. 12¾x12½***
2288-2289 A1275 Set of 2 4.10 3.50

Occupations Type of 2007

Designs: 5p, Street vendor with basket, vert. 7p, Candy vendor, vert. 10p, Shoemaker, vert. 17p, Cuarteador (man on horseback), vert. 25p, Fish vendor, vert. 30p, Ice cream vendor with pushcart.

2010 Litho. ***Die Cut***
Self-Adhesive

2290	A1216	5p multi	.80	.75
2291	A1216	7p multi	1.10	1.00
2292	A1216	10p multi	1.60	1.50
2293	A1216	17p multi	2.75	2.50
2294	A1216	25p multi	4.00	3.75
2295	A1216	30p multi	5.00	4.50
		Nos. 2290-2295 (6)	15.25	14.00

Issued: 5p, 10p, 5/27; 17p, 30p, 8/10; 25p, 8/19; 7p, 10/20.

First Russians in Uruguay, 150th Anniv. — A1276

Perf. 12¾x12½
2010, June 11 **Litho.**
2296 A1276 37p multi 5.75 5.50

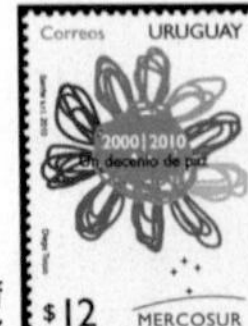
Decade of Peace — A1277

2010, June 30
2297 A1277 12p multi 2.00 1.75

Souvenir Sheet

Frédéric Chopin (1810-49), Composer — A1278

No. 2298: a, 12p, Chopin. b, 37p, Piano.

2010, July 21 ***Perf. 12***
2298 A1278 Sheet of 2, #a-b 7.50 7.00

Diplomatic Relations Between Uruguay and Romania, 75th Anniv. — A1279

2010, July 23 ***Perf. 12¾x12½***
2299 A1279 37p multi 5.75 5.25

Asturian Center, Montevideo, Cent. — A1280

2010, Aug. 28
2300 A1280 37p multi 5.75 5.50

Sporting Club Uruguay, Cent. — A1281

2010, Sept. 1 Litho. ***Perf. 12***
2301 A1281 12p multi 2.00 1.75

Diplomatic Relations Between Uruguay and Greece, 135th Anniv. A1282

2010, Sept. 8 Litho. ***Perf. 12***
2302 A1282 37p multi 5.75 5.25

Florencio Sánchez (1875-1910), Playwright A1283

2010, Sept. 17 ***Perf. 12¼x12¾***
2303 A1283 12p multi 2.00 1.75

Restoration of Democracy in Uruguay, 25th Anniv. — A1284

Perf. 12¾x12½
2010, Sept. 21 **Litho.**
2304 A1284 12p multi 2.00 1.75

Mario Benedetti (1920-2009), Writer — A1285

No. 2305 — Benedetti at: a, Right. b, Left.

2010, Sept. 25 ***Perf. 12½x12¾***
2305 A1285 12p Horiz. pair, #a-b 5.00 4.00
c. Booklet pane of 2, #2305a-2305b 5.00 —
Complete booklet, #2305c 5.00

No. 2305c sold for 30p.

Flowers and Birds A1286

No. 2306: a, Bauhinia forficata var. pruinosa. b, Furnarius rufus. c, Guira guira. d, Passiflora coerulea.

2010, Sept. 30
2306 A1286 12p Block of 4, #a-d 8.00 7.00

Uruguay as Antarctic Treaty Consultative Member, 25th Anniv. — A1287

2010, Oct. 8 Litho. ***Perf. 12½x12¾***
2307 A1287 37p multi 5.75 5.50

Christmas — A1288

2010, Oct. 29 ***Perf. 12¾x12½***
2308 A1288 12p multi 2.00 1.60

America Issue A1289

No. 2309 — Flag of Uruguay and: a, 12p, National anthem. b, 37p, National coat of arms.

2010, Nov. 8
2309 A1289 Horiz. pair, #a-b 7.50 7.00

Blue Uniform of Uruguay Soccer Team, Cent. — A1290

No. 2310: a, Team of 1910. b, Team of 2010, emblem of 2010 World Cup Soccer Tournament, South Africa (84x30mm).

2010, Nov. 15 ***Perf. 12½x12¾***
2310 Horiz. pair 4.25 3.75
a.-b. A1290 12p Either single 2.00 1.75

Cruise Ships and Their Ports of Call A1291

No. 2311: a, MSC Lirica, Punta del Este. b, Veendam, Montevideo. c, Silver Whisper, Punta del Este and Casapueblo. d, Splendour of the Seas, Punta del Este and Isla de Lobos.

2010, Nov. 19 ***Perf. 12***
2311 A1291 37p Block of 4, #a-d 22.50 21.00

Souvenir Sheet

First Airplane Flights in Uruguay, Cent. A1292

No. 2312 — Airplane and: a, Armand Prevost, pilot of Dec. 7, 1910 flight. b, Bartolomeo Cattaneo, pilot of Dec. 16, 1910 flight.

2010, Nov. 30 ***Perf. 12¾x12½***
2312 A1292 37p Sheet of 2, #a-b, + central label 11.00 10.50

El Telégrafo Newspaper, Paysandu, Cent. — A1293

2010, Dec. 9 ***Perf. 12¾x12½***
2313 A1293 12p multi 2.00 1.75

Socialist Party of Uruguay, Cent. — A1294

2010, Dec. 10 ***Perf. 12½x12¾***
2314 A1294 12p multi 2.00 1.75

Paintings by Eduardo Vernazza (1910-91) — A1295

Paintings by Carmelo Arden Quin (1913-2010) — A1296

No. 2315: a, "Gato con Botas," - Ballet Ruso. b, Personaje Femenino - Opera China (Dan).

No. 2316: a, Couronnes I. b, Dualité - Periode Indienne.

2010, Dec. 22 ***Perf. 12¾x12½***
2315 A1295 12p Horiz. pair, #a-b 4.00 3.50

Perf. 12½x12¾
2316 A1296 12p Horiz. pair, #a-b 4.00 3.50

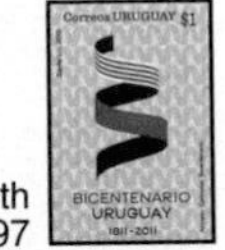
Independence, 200th Anniv. — A1297

2011, Jan. 3 Self-Adhesive ***Die Cut***
2317 A1297 1p multi .55 .30

Artisan Crafts — A1298

Designs: 2p, Baskets, thistles and cattails. No. 2319, Handbag, wool (lana). No. 2320, Iron toy car (hierro). 12p, Wooden sheep, wood. 20p, Silver container. 22p, Bamboo sculpture, bamboo. 37p, Ceramic pot. 44p, Wire sculpture. 200p, Leather basket, cow.

2011 Self-Adhesive *Die Cut*

2318 A1298 2p multi .40 .40
2319 A1298 10p multi 1.50 1.50
2320 A1298 10p multi 1.50 1.50
2321 A1298 12p multi 1.75 1.75
2322 A1298 20p multi 3.00 3.00
2323 A1298 22p multi 3.25 3.25
2324 A1298 37p multi 5.50 5.50

Size: 27x19mm

2325 A1298 44p multi 6.50 6.50

Size: 42x30mm

2326 A1298 200p multi 32.50 30.00
Nos. 2318-2326 (9) 55.90 53.40

Issed: 2p, 1/31; No. 2319, 37p, 3/23; No. 2320, 22p, 12/15; 12p, 20p, 4/12; 44p, 5/13; 200p, 5/6.

25th Gaucho Culture Festival, Tacuarembó A1299

No. 2327: a, Cauldron, meat on grill. b, Bola, gaucho on horse. c, Spurs, gaucho on horse.

2011, Feb. 3 ***Perf. 12***
2327 Horiz. strip of 3 5.75 5.00
a.-c. A1299 12p Any single 1.75 1.60

Uruguayan Independence, bicent.

Rabindranath Tagore (1861-1941), Poet — A1300

2011, Feb. 16 ***Perf. 12¾x12½***
2328 A1300 37p multi 5.00 4.75

Indipex 2011 Intl. Philatelic Exhibition, New Delhi.

Battle of Las Piedras, by Juan Luis and Juan Manuel Blanes A1301

2011, Feb. 25
2329 A1301 12p multi 2.00 1.75

Uruguayan Army, Uruguayan Independence, bicent.

Cry of Asencio, Bicent. A1302

No. 2330: a, 12p, Hand on sword, hand on knife, spears. b, 37p, Bearded man with spear, horse, hand on knife.

2011, Feb. 28
2330 A1302 Horiz. pair, #a-b 7.50 7.00

Uruguayan Independence, bicent.

Gen. Leandro Gómez (1811-65) — A1303

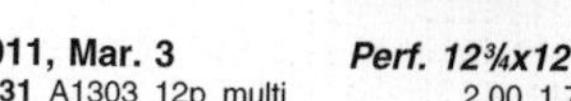

2011, Mar. 3 ***Perf. 12¾x12½***
2331 A1303 12p multi 2.00 1.75

Souvenir Sheet

Las Llamadas, by Carlos Páez Vilaró — A1304

2011, Mar. 4 ***Litho.***
2332 A1304 37p multi 5.25 5.00

Famous Women A1305

Designs: No. 2333, 12p, Petrona Rosende (1787-1862), writer. No. 2334, 12p, Josefa Oribe (1789-1835), independence supporter.

2011, Mar. 8 ***Perf. 12***
2333-2334 A1305 Set of 2 3.75 3.00

Uruguayan Independence, bicent.

Uruguay No. 196 — A1306

2011, Mar. 23 ***Perf. 12¾x12½***
2335 A1306 37p multi 5.25 5.00

Postal Union of the Americas, Spain and Portugal (UPAEP), cent.

Planeta Building, Atlántida A1307

2011, Apr. 8 ***Perf. 12½x12¾***
2336 A1307 12p multi 2.00 1.75

Atlántida, cent.

Mother's Day — A1308

2011, May 11 ***Die Cut***
Self-Adhesive
2337 A1308 12p multi 2.00 1.75

Monte Carlo TV Channel 4, 50th Anniv. — A1309

2011, May 11 ***Perf. 12½x12¾***
2338 A1309 12p multi 2.00 1.75

Battle of Las Piedras, Bicent. A1310

2011, May 12 ***Perf. 12***
2339 A1310 12p multi 2.00 1.75

Uruguayan Independence, bicent.

2011 Copa América Soccer Tournament, Argentina — A1311

2011, June 15 ***Perf. 12¾x12½***
2340 A1311 37p multi 5.25 5.00

Aitona, by Ignacio Iturria — A1312

2011, June 29 ***Perf. 12½x12¾***
2341 A1312 12p multi 2.00 1.75

Basque Center, Montevideo, cent.

Campaign Against Human Immunodeficiency Virus, 30th Anniv. — A1313

2011, June 30 ***Perf. 12¾x12½***
2342 A1313 12p multi 2.00 1.75

Natl. Physical Education Commission, Cent. — A1314

2011, July 20 ***Perf. 12½x12¾***
2343 A1314 12p multi 2.00 1.75

Uruguay, Champions of 2011 Copa América Soccer Tournament A1315

No. 2344: a, Cristian Rodriguez. b, Alvaro Pereira. c, Abel Hernández. d, Luis Suárez. e, Nicolás Lodeiro. f, Sebastián Abreu. g, Diego Pérez. h, Fernando Muslera. i, Diego Forlán. j, Team manager Washington Tabárez. k, Edinson Cavani. l, Sebastián Eguren. m, Martín Cáceres. n, Diego Godín. o, Egidio Arévalo. p, Alvaro González. q, Maximiliano Pereira. r, Juan Castillo. s, Diego Lugano. t, Walter Gargano. u, Mauricio Victorino. v, Andrés Scotti. w, Martín Silva. x, Sebastián Coates.

2011, Aug. 11 ***Perf. 12***
2344 Sheet of 24 26.00 20.00
a.-x. A1315 6p Any single .85 .75

Intl. Year of Forests A1316

2011, Sept. 21 ***Litho.***
2345 A1316 12p multi 2.00 1.75

America Issue, Mailboxes — A1317

Designs: 12p, Cylindrical mailbox, Avenida 18 de Julio, Montevideo. 37p, Rectangular mailbox, Plaza Independecia, Montevideo.

2011, Sept. 30 ***Perf. 12¾x12½***
2346-2347 A1317 Set of 2 7.50 7.00

Diplomatic Relations Between Japan and Uruguay, 90th Anniv. — A1318

2011, Oct. 5 ***Perf. 12***
2348 A1318 37p multi + label 5.25 5.00

La Redota (Exodus of Gen. José Artigas and Supporters), Bicent. — A1319

2011, Oct. 13
2349 A1319 12p multi 2.00 1.75

Uruguayan Independece, bicent.

Souvenir Sheet

China Zorrilla, Actress A1320

2011, Oct. 18 ***Perf. 12½x12¾***
2350 A1320 37p multi 5.25 5.00

Whale Watching A1321

No. 2351 — Eubalaena australis: a, 12p, Tail above surface near boat. b, 12p, Tail below water. c, 37p, At water's surface near land. d, 37p, Diving underwater.

2011, Nov. 16 ***Litho.***
2351 A1321 Block of 4, #a-d 15.00 14.00

Isla de Flores National Park A1322

2011, Nov. 16 ***Perf. 12***
2352 A1322 12p multi 2.00 1.75

Cruise Ships A1323

No. 2353: a, Seabourn Sojourn near José Batlle y Ordonez Power Plant. b, Asuka II near Joaquín Torres García Telecommunications Tower. c, Costa Victoria in Port of Montevideo. d, AIDAcara near Cerro de Montevideo.

2011, Nov. 22
2353 A1323 37p Block of 4, #a-d 20.00 19.00

PLUNA Airlines, 75th Anniv. A1324

2011, Nov. 22
2354 A1324 12p multi 2.00 1.75

Tango Musicians A1325

No. 2355: a, César Zagnoli (1911-2002). b, Juan D'Arienzo (1900-76). c, Donato Racciatti (1918-2000).

Perf. 12½x12¾
2011, Nov. 30 **Litho.**
2355 Horiz. strip of 3 5.75 5.00
a.-c. A1325 12p Any single 1.60 1.60

Christmas A1326

2011, Dec. 7 ***Perf. 12***
2356 A1326 12p multi 2.00 1.75

Souvenir Sheet

Intl. Year of Chemistry — A1327

2011, Dec. 9 ***Perf. 12½x12¾***
2357 A1327 37p multi 5.25 5.00

Diplomatic Relations Between Uruguay and the Czech Republic and Slovakia, 90th Anniv. A1328

2011, Dec. 13 ***Perf. 12***
2358 A1328 37p multi 5.25 5.00

Paintings A1329

Designs: No. 2359, Formas, by María Freire. No. 2360, Composición 17 de Julio - 1968, by Freire, vert.
No. 2361, vert.: a, Crepúsculo, by Vicente Martín. b, Dama con Mandolina, by Martín.

2011, Dec. 19 ***Perf. 12½x12¾***
2359 A1329 12p multi 1.75 1.60

Perf. 12¾x12½
2360 A1329 12p multi 1.75 1.60
2361 Horiz. pair 3.75 3.25
a.-b. A1329 12p Either single 1.75 1.60
Nos. 2359-2361 (3) 7.25 6.45

Intl. Year of People of African Descent — A1330

Paintings by Mary Porto Casas: 12p, La Lancera. 37p, Mandela, horiz.

2011, Dec. 27 ***Perf. 12***
2362-2363 A1330 Set of 2 7.00 6.50

State Insurance Bank, Cent. A1331

2011, Dec. 27
2364 A1331 12p multi 2.00 1.75

Independence, 200th Anniv. — A1332

No. 2365: a, Indigenous man with headband holding stick. b, Man of African descent with hat and gun.

2011, Dec. 28 **Litho.**
2365 A1332 12p Horiz. pair, #a-b 4.00 3.50

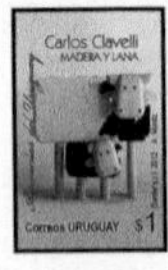

Items Made by Artisans — A1333

No. 2366: a, Cows made of wood and wool, by Carlos Clavelli. b, Woolen garment, by Siv Göransson. c, Leather container and lid, by Albertina Morelli. d, Silver pendant, bu Nilda Echenique. e, Wire ball, by Gustavo Genta.

2012, Jan. 31 ***Die Cut***
Self-Adhesive
2366 Horiz. strip of 5 2.75 1.25
a.-e. A1333 1p Any single .50 .25

Written and Sign Language Letters and Their Corresponding International Signal Flags — A1334

Letter: 5p, A. 10p, M. 12p, O. 20p, S. 50p, G. 60p, I.

2012 **Self-Adhesive** ***Die Cut***
2367 A1334 5p multi .85 .65
2368 A1334 10p multi 1.60 1.25
2369 A1334 12p multi 1.90 1.45
2370 A1334 20p multi 3.00 2.40
2371 A1334 50p multi 8.25 6.25

Size: 27x19mm
2372 A1334 60p multi 10.00 7.50
Nos. 2367-2372 (6) 15.90 15.90

Issued: 5p, 2/9; 10p, 2/28; 12p, 50p, 60p, 4/11; 20p, 5/16.

Intl. Women's Day — A1335

2012, Mar. 7 ***Perf. 12½x12¾***
2373 A1335 12p multi 2.00 1.75

Palacio Gandós, Montevideo — A1336

2012, Mar. 15 ***Perf. 12¾x12½***
2374 A1336 37p multi 5.25 5.00

Annual Board of Governors Meeting of the Inter-American Development Bank and Inter-American Investment Corporation, Montevideo.

Enrique V. Iglesias, Ex-President of Inter-American Development Bank — A1337

2012, Mar. 20 **Litho.**
2375 A1337 37p multi 5.00 4.75

2012 Summer Olympics, London — A1338

No. 2376: a, Soccer, ArcelorMittal Orbit. b, Cycling, St. Paul's Cathedral. c, Yachting, Tower Bridge. d, Hurdler, Big Ben and Parliament.

2012, Mar. 30 ***Perf. 12***
2376 A1338 15p Block of 4, #a-d 9.00 8.00

Diplomatic Relations Between Uruguay and Ukraine, 20th Anniv. A1339

2012, Apr. 25
2377 A1339 37p multi 5.75 5.50

Nueva Helvecia Colony, 150th Anniv. — A1340

2012, Apr. 25 ***Perf. 12½x12¾***
2378 A1340 12p multi 2.10 1.90

Euskal Erria Basque Fellowship Center, Montevideo, Cent. — A1341

2012, May 25
2379 A1341 37p multi 5.25 5.00

World Blood Donation Day — A1342

2012, June 14 ***Die Cut***
Self-Adhesive
2380 A1342 12p multi 2.25 2.00

Intl. Year of Cooperatives A1343

2012, July 6 ***Perf. 12½x12¾***
2381 A1343 12p multi 2.25 2.00

Uruguay Mortgage Bank, 120th Anniv. — A1344

Perf. 12¾x12½
2012, Aug. 10 **Litho.**
2382 A1344 12p multi 2.25 2.00

Fauna A1345

No. 2383: a, Paroaria coronata, Pyrocephalus rubinus. b, Charadrius modestus, Caiman latirostris. c, Pontoporia blainvilleii. d, Xylocopa augusti, Rhinella schneideri.

Perf. 12½x12¾
2012, Aug. 31 **Litho.**
2383 A1345 12p Block of 4, #a-d 7.00 6.00

Intl. Democracy Day — A1346

2012, Sept. 13 ***Perf. 12¾x12½***
2384 A1346 37p multi 5.75 5.50

Anibal Barrios Pintos (1918-2011), Writer, and Sculpture of Aboriginal People — A1347

2012, Sept. 27 ***Perf. 12½x12¾***
2385 A1347 12p multi 2.00 1.75

America Issue — A1348

Legend of: No. 2386, 12p, The Ceibo Flower. No. 2387, 12p, The Black Shepherd.

2012, Sept. 28 *Perf. 12¾x12½*
2386-2387 A1348 Set of 2 3.75 3.25

Crops Grown for Alternative Energy Sources A1349

Designs: No. 2388, 12p, Saccharum officinarum. No. 2389, 12p, Helianthus annuus.

2012, Oct. 5 *Perf. 12½x12¾*
2388-2389 A1349 Set of 2 3.75 3.25

Souvenir Sheet

25th Universal Postal Union Congress, Doha, Qatar — A1350

2012, Oct. 6 *Perf. 12¾x12½*
2390 A1350 37p multi 5.75 5.50

National Directorate of Mining and Geology, Cent. — A1351

2012, Oct. 22 **Litho.**
2391 A1351 12p multi 2.25 2.00

Tourist Attractions and Cruise Ships — A1352

No. 2392 — Attraction and ship: a, Colonia del Sacramento Lighthouse, National Geographic Explorer. b, Yacht Club Uruguay, Puerto del Buceo, Celebrity Infinity. c, Santa Teresa Fortress, Grand Celebration. d, Argentino Hotel, Piriápolis, MSC Magnifica.

2012, Oct. 22 *Perf. 12*
2392 Horiz. strip of 4 21.00 20.00
a.-d. A1352 37p Any single 5.00 5.00

National Road Safety Union — A1353

Designs: 5p, Stop sign. 10p, Martini glasses. 15p, Passenger with hands over seat belt. 20p, Triangular warning sign with helmeted head of person. 45p, Speed limit sign. 50p, Blue ribbon. 70p. National Road Safety Union emblem. 100p, Road Safety Decade inscription on diamond warning sign.

2012, Oct. 24 ***Die Cut***
Self-Adhesive

2393 A1353 5p multi 1.00 1.00
2394 A1353 10p multi 2.00 2.00
2395 A1353 15p multi 2.50 2.25
2396 A1353 20p multi 3.50 3.00
2397 A1353 45p multi 8.00 6.50
a. Vert. strip of 5, 2 #2396, 3 #2397 35.00
2398 A1353 50p multi 10.50 7.50
a. Vert strip of 5, #2393, 2395, 2396, 2 #2398 30.00
2399 A1353 70p multi 12.50 10.00
2400 A1353 100p multi 19.00 15.00
a. Vert. strip of 5, #2393, 2394, 2395, 2399, 2400 40.00
Nos. 2393-2400 (8) 59.00 47.25

National Fire Fighting Directorate, 125th Anniv. — A1354

No. 2401 — Fire fighting emblem, fire fighter in protective clothing and: a, Building fire. b, Forest fire. c, Bronto Skylift F68HLA. d, Refinery fire.

2012, Oct. 26 *Perf. 12½x12¾*
2401 A1354 12p Block of 4, #a-d 8.00 7.00

Virginia Brindis de Salas (1908-58), Poet — A1355

2012, Oct. 31 *Perf. 12¾x12½*
2402 A1355 12p multi 2.25 2.00

Paintings — A1356

Designs: No. 2403, 12p, Recreo, by Petrona Viera. No. 2404, 12p, Construcción, by Augusto Torres.

2012, Oct. 31 **Litho.**
2403-2404 A1356 Set of 2 4.50 4.00

National Administration of Electrical Transmission and Usage, Cent. — A1357

No. 2405: a, Rincón de Baygorria Dam, linemen working on wires. b, High tension wire tower, engineer with chart. c, Wind generators. d, Palace of Light, José Battle y Ordoñez Center, worker with hard hat.

2012, Oct. 31 *Perf. 12½x12¾*
2405 A1357 12p Horiz. strip of 4, #a-d, + 4 labels 8.00 7.00

Tango Music — A1358

No. 2406: a, Double bass used in tango music. b, Francisco Canaro (1888-1964), tango orchestra leader. c, Edgardo Pedroza (1926-2000), tango orchestra leader.

2012, Nov. 23
2406 Horiz. strip of 3 16.50 16.00
a. A1358 15p multi 2.25 2.25
b.-c. A1358 45p Either single 6.50 6.50

Christmas — A1359

2012, Nov. 23 *Perf. 12¾x12½*
2407 A1359 15p multi 2.50 2.25

Club Neptuno, Cent. — A1360

2012, Dec. 3 **Litho.**
2408 A1360 15p multi 2.25 2.25

Etchepare Colony for Psychiatric Care, Cent. — A1361

2012, Dec. 4 *Perf. 12*
2409 A1361 15p multi 2.25 2.25

Independent Party, 10th Anniv. — A1362

2012, Dec. 17 *Perf. 12½x12¾*
2410 A1362 15p multi 2.25 2.25

Souvenir Sheet

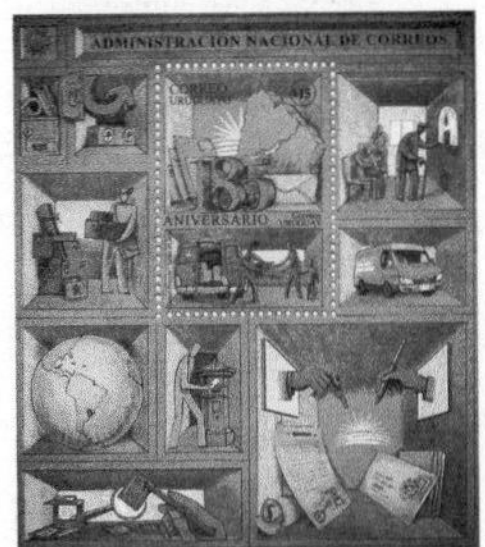

National Postal Administration, 185th Anniv. — A1363

2012, Dec. 21 *Perf. 12¾x12½*
2411 A1363 15p multi 2.50 2.25

Rural Workers — A1364

Designs: 1p, Farmer tending to field (agricultor). 5p, Fence builders (alambrador), 10p, Workers tending sheep (esquillador). 15p, Beekeeper and hives (apicultor). 25p, Fruit harvester (recolectora). 30p, Cattle driver (arriero). 45p, Worker processing fish (pesca). 50p, Woman milking cow (tambera). 60p, Woman moving logs (leñadora).

2013 **Litho.** ***Die Cut***
Self-Adhesive

2412 A1364 1p multi .30 .30
2413 A1364 5p multi .85 .80
2414 A1364 10p multi 1.60 1.50
2415 A1364 15p multi 2.40 2.25
2416 A1364 25p multi 4.00 3.75
2417 A1364 30p multi 4.75 4.50
2418 A1364 45p multi 7.00 6.75
2419 A1364 50p multi 7.75 7.50
2420 A1364 60p multi 9.50 9.00
Nos. 2412-2420 (8) 37.30 35.55

Passage of Law No. 18,441 limiting hours of rural workers.

Issued: 1p, 10p, 2/22; 5p, 7/9; 15p, 60p, 5/17; 25p, 4/18; 30p, 50p, 3/8; 45p, 4/30.

Carnival Costume Designed by Juan Mascheroni — A1365

Perf. 12¾x12½
2013, Feb. 28 **Litho.**
2421 A1365 15p multi 2.50 2.25

Souvenir Sheet

Military Aviation in Uruguay, Cent. A1366

2013, Mar. 16 *Perf. 12*
2422 A1366 15p multi 3.00 2.75

Harald Edelstam (1913-89), Swedish Diplomat — A1367

2013, Mar. 17 *Perf. 12¾x12½*
2423 A1367 45p multi 7.25 7.00

Edelstam rescued Cuban diplomats, Chilean activists and Uruguayan refugees from persecution during the 1973 Chilean coup.

Defensor Sporting Club, Cent. — A1368

2013, Mar. 20 *Perf. 12½x12¾*
2424 A1368 15p multi 2.50 2.25

No. 2424 was printed in sheets of 8 + central label.

Famous Women — A1369

No. 2425: a, María "Tota" Quinteros (1918-2001) holding sign showing kidnapped daughter, Elena (1945-76). b, Jorgelina Martínez (1926-2009), labor leader. c, María Viñas Sendic (1943-2003), labor leader.

2013, Mar. 21 *Perf. 12¾x12½*
2425 Strip of 3 7.25 6.50
a.-c. A1369 15p Any single 2.25 2.00

Nibya Mariño, Pianist — A1370

2013, Mar. 22 *Perf. 12½x12¾*
2426 A1370 15p multi 2.50 2.25

No. 2426 was printed in sheets of 8 + central label.

Patient Safety Day — A1371

2013, Apr. 11 ***Perf. 12¾x12½***
2427 A1371 15p multi 1.90 2.25

Instructions of the Year XIII, Bicent. — A1372

2013, May 3 ***Perf. 12***
2428 A1372 15p multi 2.50 2.25

Souvenir Sheet

Red Cross Coach, 1897 A1373

2013, May 30 **Litho.**
2429 A1373 15p multi 2.50 2.25

Paintings A1374

No. 2430: a, Zíngaras, by Rafael Barradas (1890-1929). b, Bodegón (Still Life), by Augusto Torres (1913-92).

Perf. 12½x12¾
2013, June 11 **Litho.**
2430 A1374 15p Horiz. pair, #a-b 5.00 4.50

World Day of Autism Awareness — A1375

2013, June 12 ***Perf. 12¾x12½***
2431 A1375 15p multi 2.25 2.25

City of San Carlos II, by Daniel Arteta — A1376

2013, July 8 ***Perf. 12½x12¾***
2432 A1376 15p multi 2.50 2.25

San Carlos, 250th Anniv.

Amanda Rorra (1924-2005), Afro-Uruguayan Activist — A1377

2013, July 25 **Litho.** ***Perf. 12¾x12½***
2433 A1377 15p multi 2.50 2.25

Intl. Year of Quinoa — A1378

2013, July 26 **Litho.** ***Perf. 12½x12¾***
2434 A1378 45p multi 6.75 6.50

Calabrian Association of Uruguay, 50th Anniv. — A1379

2013, Aug. 2 **Litho.** ***Perf. 12½x12¾***
2435 A1379 45p multi 6.75 6.50

No. 2435 was printed in sheets of 8 + central label.

Tabernacle, Sculpture by Octavio Podestá A1380

Perf. 12½x12¾
2013, Aug. 22 **Litho.**
2436 A1380 15p multi 2.50 2.25

Insects A1381

No. 2437: a, Borellia bruneri. b, Diloboderus abderus. c, Sulcophanaeus menelas. d, Apis mellifera.

Perf. 12½x12¾
2013, Aug. 30 **Litho.**
2437 A1381 15p Block of 4, #a-d, + 2 labels 10.50 9.50

International Day of Democracy — A1382

Perf. 12¾x12½
2013, Sept. 15 **Litho.**
2438 A1382 45p multi 6.25 6.00

Care Centers for Children and Families, 25th Anniv. — A1383

Perf. 12¾x12½
2013, Sept. 16 **Litho.**
2439 A1383 15p multi 2.50 2.25

Andrés Aguiar (d. 1849), Soldier for Giuseppe Garibaldi in First Italian War of Independence A1384

Perf. 12¾x12½
2013, Sept. 21 **Litho.**
2440 A1384 45p multi 7.25 7.00

Susana Dalmás (1948-2012), Politician — A1385

Perf. 12¾x12½
2013, Sept. 26 **Litho.**
2441 A1385 15p multi 2.50 2.25

Tango Heritage A1386

No. 2442: a, Bandoneon. b, Musician playing violin and Romeo Gavioli (1913-57), singer. c, Microphone and Carlos Roldán (1913-73), singer.

Perf. 12½x12¾
2013, Sept. 26 **Litho.**
2442 Horiz. strip of 3 25.00 24.00
a.-c. A1386 45p Any single 8.00 8.00

Association of Chemists and Pharmacists of Uruguay, 125th Anniv. — A1387

Perf. 12¾x12½
2013, Sept. 27 **Litho.**
2443 A1387 15p multi 2.50 2.25

Montevideo, 2013 Ibero-American Cultural Capital — A1388

No. 2444: a, Eduardo Galeano, writer. b, Daniel Viglietti, musician. c, Ruben Rada, musician. d, Sara Nieto, ballerina.

2013, Oct. 2 **Litho.** ***Perf. 12¾x12½***
2444 Horiz. strip of 4 10.50 9.50
a.-d. A1388 15p Any single 2.25 2.25
e. Booklet pane of 4, #2444a-2444d 10.50 —
Complete booklet, #2444e 10.50

The Annunciation of Sarah, Painting by José Gurvich — A1389

2013, Oct. 29 **Litho.** ***Perf. 12½x12¾***
2445 A1389 45p multi 5.75 5.50

Diplomatic relations between Uruguay and Israel, 65th anniv. See Israel No. 1989.

SODRE Juvenile Orchestra — A1390

No. 2446: a, Child's legs, French horn. b, Violin and bow.

2013, Nov. 4 **Litho.** ***Perf. 12¾x12½***
2446 A1390 15p Horiz. pair, #a-b 5.00 4.50

Internet and Integrated Systems — A1391

2013, Nov. 7 **Litho.** ***Perf. 12¾x12½***
2447 A1391 45p multi 5.75 5.50

Exports A1392

No. 2448: a, 15p, Wine grapes. b, 15p, Sides of beef. c, 45p, Wine bottle and barrels. d, 45p, Dish of beef and vegetables.

2013, Nov. 8 **Litho.** ***Perf. 12½x12¾***
2448 A1392 Block of 4, #a-d 21.00 20.00

Souvenir Sheet

Brasiliana 2013 Intl. Philatelic Exhibition, Rio de Janeiro — A1393

No. 2449 — Brasiliana 2013 emblem and illustrations from song lyrics by Vinicius de Moraes (1913-80): a, 15p, Young man and woman (25x35mm). b, 45p, Woman with head covering (42x31mm).

Perf. 12, 12½x12¾ (45p)
2013, Nov. 20 **Litho.**
2449 A1393 Sheet of 2, #a-b 10.00 9.50

Christmas A1394

Perf. 12½x12¾
2013, Nov. 22 **Litho.**
2450 A1394 15p multi 2.50 2.25

Wildlife A1395

No. 2451: a, Calidris canutus rufa. b, Chelonia mydas.

2013, Dec. 4 **Litho.** ***Perf. 12¾x12½***
2451 A1395 15p Horiz. pair, #a-b 5.50 5.00

Printed in sheets containing 4 pairs and 5 labels.

High-Speed Ferry Francisco A1396

2013, Dec. 5 **Litho.** ***Perf. 12***
2452 A1396 45p multi 5.75 5.50

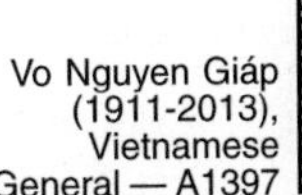

Vo Nguyen Giáp (1911-2013), Vietnamese General — A1397

Perf. 12¾x12½

2013, Dec. 10 **Litho.**

2453 A1397 45p multi 5.75 5.50

Diplomatic relations between Uruguay and Viet Nam, 20th anniv.

Rampla Juniors Soccer Team, Cent. — A1398

Perf. 12½x12¾

2013, Dec. 11 **Litho.**

2454 A1398 15p multi 2.50 2.25

Return to Uruguay of Children of Exiles, 30th Anniv. — A1399

2013, Dec. 17 **Litho.** ***Die Cut***

Self-Adhesive

2455 A1399 20p multi 3.50 3.25

Campaign Against Discrimination A1400

Perf. 12¾x12½

2013, Dec. 19 **Litho.**

2456 A1400 45p multi 5.75 5.50

America issue.

New Year 2014 (Year of the Horse) — A1401

2014, Jan. 31 **Litho.** ***Perf. 12¾x12½***

2457 A1401 15p multi 2.50 2.25

Carnaval Costume — A1402

Perf. 12¾x12½

2014, Feb. 25 **Litho.**

2458 A1402 15p multi 2.50 2.25

Hugo Chávez (1954-2013), President of Venezuela — A1403

No. 2459 — Chávez: a, 15p, Waving. b, 45p, Holding map of South America.

2014, Mar. 5 **Litho.** ***Perf. 12½x12¾***

2459 A1403 Horiz. pair, #a-b 8.00 7.50

Florida Infantry Batallion No. 1, 185th Anniv. — A1404

2014, Mar. 6 **Litho.** ***Perf. 12½x12¾***

2460 A1404 15p multi 2.25 2.00

Luisa Cuesta, Leader in Mothers and Relatives of Disappeared Uruguayans Movement A1405

2014, Mar. 7 **Litho.** ***Perf. 12½x12¾***

2461 A1405 15p multi 2.00 1.75

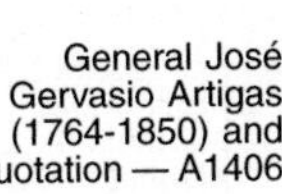

General José Gervasio Artigas (1764-1850) and Quotation — A1406

Artigas and quotation starting with: 1p, "Sean los orientales. . ." 10p, "Que los Más infelices. . ." 15p, "La libertad de América. . ." 30p, "La causa. . ." 50p, "Nada podemos esperar. . ." 100p, "Todas las provincias. . ."

2014 **Litho.** ***Die Cut***

Self-Adhesive

2462	A1406	1p multi	.30	.30
2463	A1406	10p multi	1.50	1.50
2464	A1406	15p multi	2.25	2.25
2465	A1406	30p multi	2.60	2.60
2466	A1406	50p multi	7.50	7.50
2467	A1406	100p multi	15.00	15.00
	Nos. 2462-2467 (6)		29.15	29.15

Issued: 1p, 6/12; 10p, 6/2; 15p, 11/19; 30p, 50p, 3/7; 100p, 4/7. See No. B14.

Uruguayan Transparency Law — A1407

2014, Apr. 10 **Litho.** ***Perf. 12¾x12½***

2468 A1407 15p multi 2.25 2.00

South American Athletic Institution, Cent. — A1408

2014, Apr. 22 **Litho.** ***Perf. 12¾x12½***

2469 A1408 15p multi 2.25 2.00

No. 2469 printed in sheets of 8 + central label.

Section 20 of the Communist Party of Uruguay National Historical Monument A1409

2014, Apr. 23 **Litho.** ***Perf. 12½x12¾***

2470 A1409 15p multi 2.25 2.00

University Sports League, Cent. — A1410

2014, May 5 **Litho.** ***Perf. 12½x12¾***

2471 A1410 15p multi 2.25 2.00

No. 2471 was printed in sheets of 8 + central label.

Uruguay Society of Architects, Cent. — A1411

2014, May 22 **Litho.** ***Perf. 12¾x12½***

2472 A1411 15p multi 2.25 2.00

Souvenir Sheet

Alcides Ghiggia, Soccer Player A1412

No. 2473 — Uruguayan flag and: a, Ghiggia playing soccer. b, Ghiggia in 2014.

2014, May 28 **Litho.** ***Perf. 12¾x12½***

2473 A1412 15p Sheet of 2, #a-b 5.00 4.50

Souvenir Sheet

Battle of Buceo, 200th Anniv. A1413

2014, June 4 **Litho.** ***Perf. 12½x12¾***

2474 A1413 45p multi 5.75 5.50

Mafalda, Comic Strip by Quino, 50th Anniv. A1414

No. 2475 — Mafalda and: a, 15p, Globe wrapped in bandage. b, 45p, Globe with banners.

2014, June 17 **Litho.** ***Perf. 12***

2475 A1414 Pair, #a-b 8.00 7.50

No. 2475 was printed in sheets containing three pairs.

Paintings A1415

No. 2476: a, El Pozo, by Ernesto Laroche (1879-1940). b, Portrait of María de Castro de Figari, by Pedro Blanes Viale (1879-1926).

2014, July 15 **Litho.** ***Perf. 12¾x12½***

2476 A1415 15p Horiz. pair, #a-b 4.50 4.00

Tranqueras, Cent. — A1416

2014, July 22 **Litho.** ***Perf. 12½x12¾***

2477 A1416 15p multi 2.25 2.00

Famous People — A1417

Designs: No. 2478, 15p, Federico García Vigil, conductor. No. 2479, 15p, Cristina Morán, actress.

Perf. 12¾x12½

2014, Aug. 13 **Litho.**

2478-2479 A1417 Set of 2 4.50 4.00

Second Intl. Decade of the World's Indigenous Peoples — A1418

2014, Sept. 2 **Litho.** ***Perf. 12¾x12½***

2480 A1418 45p multi 5.75 5.50

Miniature Sheet

A1419

No. 2481: a, 15p, La Estanzuela Experimental Station, cent. (scientist and building). b, 15p, Int'l. Day of Biodiversity (zebra and flamingo). c, 15p, World Environment Day (butterfly on flower). d, 45p, Intl. Year of Family Farming.

Perf. 12½x12¾

2014, Sept. 16 **Litho.**

2481 A1419 Sheet of 4, #a-d 13.00 12.00

People Doing Community Service — A1420

Perf. 12½x12¾

2014, Sept. 22 **Litho.**

2482 A1420 15p multi 2.25 2.00

Pinnipeds — A1421

No. 2483 — Emblem of Chile Philatelic Society and: a, Arctocephalus australis. b, Otaria flavescens.

Perf. 12½x12¾

2014, Sept. 29 **Litho.**

2483 A1421 15p Pair, #a-b 4.00 3.50

Diplomatic Relations Between Uruguay and South Korea, 50th Anniv. — A1422

No. 2484 — Dancers and drummers from: a, 15p, Uruguay. b, 45p, South Korea.

2014, Oct. 7 Litho. *Perf. 12½x12¾*
2484 A1422 Horiz. pair, #a-b 7.75 7.00

See South Korea Nos. 2433-2434.

Visit of Charles de Gaulle to Uruguay, 50th Anniv. — A1423

Uruguayan and French flags, de Gaulle and: 15p, Buildings. 45p, Ship.

2014, Oct. 9 Litho. *Perf. 12¾x12½*
2485-2486 A1423 Set of 2 8.00 7.50

Nos. 2485-2486 were printed in sheets of 8 containing 4 of each stamp.

Souvenir Sheet

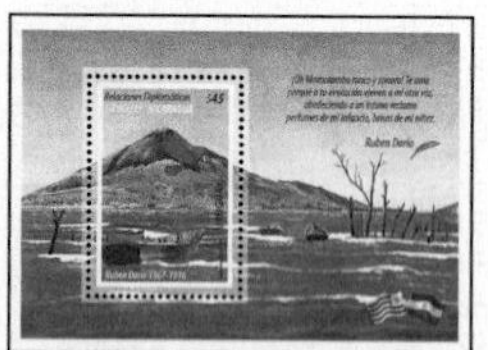

Diplomatic Relations Between Uruguay and Nicaragua — A1424

2014, Oct. 10 Litho. *Perf. 12¾x12½*
2487 A1424 45p multi 5.75 5.50

Souvenir Sheet

Anniversaries of Parliamentary Organizations — A1425

No. 2488: a, 15p, Interparliamentary Union, 125th anniv. b, 45p, Latin American Parliament, 50th anniv.

2014, Oct. 15 Litho. *Perf. 12¾x12½*
2488 A1425 Sheet of 2, #a-b 8.00 7.50

General José Gervasio Artigas (1764-1850) and Quotation — A1426

Artigas and quotation starting with: C, "Sólo aspiro. . ." S, "Mi autoridad. . ."

2014, Nov. 1 Litho. *Die Cut*
Self-Adhesive

2489 A1426 C multi 2.75 2.50
2490 A1426 S multi 7.75 7.50
a. Dated "2015" 5.25 5.00
b. Dated "2016" 4.50 4.25
c. Dated "2018" 4.00 3.75

On day of issue, No. 2489 sold for 15p and No. 2490 sold for 60p.

Issued: No. 2490a, 11/23/15; No. 2490c, 12/20/18.

Fauna — A1427

Designs: No. 2491, 15p, Melanophryniscus sanmartini. No. 2492, 15p, Desmodus rotundus.

2014, Nov. 5 Litho. *Perf. 12¾x12½*
2491-2492 A1427 Set of 2 4.00 3.50

Nos. 2491-2492 were printed in sheets of 8 containing 4 of each stamp.

Christmas — A1428

Perf. 12¾x12½

2014, Nov. 12 Litho.
2493 A1428 15p multi 2.25 2.00

Silvio B. Previale Intl. Accordion Festival, Salto — A1429

Perf. 12¾x12½

2014, Nov. 14 Litho.
2494 A1429 15p multi 2.25 2.00

Diplomatic Relations Between Uruguay and Surinam, 35th Anniv. — A1430

2014, Dec. 9 Litho. *Perf. 12¾x12½*
2495 A1430 50p multi 6.75 6.50

Campaign Against Discrimination Towards Indigenous People — A1431

2014, Dec. 9 Litho. *Perf. 12*
2496 A1431 50p multi 6.75 6.50

Ana Josefa Barbera, 19th Cent. Philanthropist A1432

Perf. 12¾x12½

2014, Dec. 12 Litho.
2497 A1432 15p multi 2.25 2.00

Closure of Auschwitz Concentration Camp, 70th Anniv. — A1433

No. 2498: a, 15p, Ana Benkel de Vinocur (1926-2006), author and survivor of Auschwitz. b, 50p, Tracks leadting to Auschwitz gate, barbed wire.

2015, Jan. 28 Litho. *Perf. 12½x12¾*
2498 A1433 Pair, #a-b 10.50 10.00

Battle of Paysandú, 150th Anniv. — A1434

No. 2499: a, 15p, Paysandú Basilica. b, 50p, Corvette Parnahyba.

2015, Feb. 6 Litho. *Perf. 12¾x12½*
2499 A1434 Horiz. pair, #a-b 9.00 8.50

URUJAM 2015 Intl. Scout Jamboree, Las Cañas — A1435

2015, Feb. 6 Litho. *Perf. 12½x12¾*
2500 A1435 50p multi 8.25 8.00

Liverpool Soccer Team of Uruguay, Cent. — A1436

Perf. 12¾x12½

2015, Feb. 10 Litho.
2501 A1436 15p multi 2.25 2.00

Carnaval A1437

Perf. 12½x12¾

2015, Feb. 11 Litho.
2502 A1437 15p multi 2.25 2.00

New Year 2015 (Year of the Goat) — A1438

Perf. 12¾x12½

2015, Feb. 19 Litho.
2503 A1438 15p multi 2.25 2.00

Prof. Belela Herrera, Vice Chancellor of Uruguay A1439

2015, Mar. 6 Litho. *Perf. 12½x12¾*
2504 A1439 15p multi 2.25 2.00

Sport Federation Centenaries — A1440

No. 2505 — Centenary of: a, Uruguayan Volleyball Federation. b, Uruguayan Basketball Federation.

Perf. 12½x12¾

2015, Mar. 18 Litho.
2505 A1440 15p Horiz. pair, #a-b 4.25 3.75

Souvenir Sheet

Armenian Genocide, Cent. — A1441

2015, Apr. 7 Litho. *Perf. 12¾x12½*
2506 A1441 50p multi 6.25 6.00

Elevation of Montevideo Archbishop Daniel Sturla to Cardinal — A1442

2015, Apr. 21 Litho. *Perf. 12¾x12½*
2507 A1442 50p multi 7.25 7.00
a. Souvenir sheet of 1 7.25 7.00

No. 2507 was printed in sheets of 5.

General José Gervasio Artigas (1764-1850) — A1443

Serpentine Die Cut 9x9¾

2015 Self-Adhesive Litho.

2508 A1443 3p purple & multi .35 .25
2509 A1443 5p red org & multi .50 .35
2510 A1443 10p cerise & multi 1.00 .70
2511 A1443 15p blue & multi 1.60 1.10
2512 A1443 20p org red & multi 2.10 1.50
2513 A1443 30p grn & multi 3.25 2.25
Nos. 2508-2513 (6) 8.80 6.15

Issued: 3p, 5/5; 5p, 7/10; 10p, 9/4; 15p, 8/20; 20p, 5/20; 30p, 5/8.

Miniature Sheet

Wetlands Fauna A1444

No. 2514: a, Amblyramphus holosericus. b, Rynchops niger intercedens. c, Phoenicopterus chilensis. d, Egretta thula. e, Theristicus caerulescens. f, Hydrochoerus hydrochaeris. g, Xanthopsar flavus. h, Philodryas aestiva. i, Neohelice granulatus. j, Melanophryniscus montevidensis.

2015, June 5 Litho. *Perf. 12½x12¾*
2514 A1444 15p Sheet of 10, #a-j, + 3 labels 16.00 11.00

12th Meeting of the Conference of the Parties to the Ramsar Convention on Wetlands, Punta del Este.

José Luis Massera (1915-2002), Mathematician A1445

2015, June 8 Litho. *Perf. 12½x12¾*
2515 A1445 15p multi 1.60 1.10

Miniature Sheet

International Telecommunication Union, 150th Anniv. — A1446

No. 2516: a, AntelSat, first Uruguayan satellite and ITU 150th anniv. emblem. b, AntelSat el primer satélite uruguayo.

Perf. 12½x12¾
2015, June 18 Litho.
2516 A1446 Sheet of 8, #2516b, 7 #2516a, + central label 15.75 11.50
a. 15p multi 1.40 1.10
b. 50p multi 4.75 3.75

Technological Laboratory of Uruguay, 50th Anniv. — A1447

2015, July 8 Litho. *Perf. 12½x12¾*
2517 A1447 15p multi 1.60 1.10

Souvenir Sheet

Diplomatic Relations Between Uruguay and Egypt, 83rd Anniv. — A1448

No. 2518: a, 15p, Sistrum. b, 50p, Funerary mask of Eso-Eris mummy.

2015, July 23 Litho. *Perf. 12¾x12½*
2518 A1448 Sheet of 2, #a-b 6.25 4.75

Grand Orient of Uruguay, 25th Anniv. — A1449

Perf. 12½x12¾
2015, Aug. 17 Litho.
2519 A1449 15p multi 1.60 1.10

Paintings A1450

No. 2520: a, The Red Shawl, by Carlos Federico Sáez (1878-1901). b, Eros and Psyche, by Anhelo Hernández (1922-2010).

Perf. 12¾x12½
2015, Aug. 27 Litho.
2520 A1450 15p Horiz. pair, #a-b 3.25 2.10

St. John Bosco (1815-88) A1451

2015, Sept. 8 Litho. *Perf. 12½x12¾*
2521 A1451 15p multi 1.60 1.10

Democracy in Uruguay, 30th Anniv. — A1452

Perf. 12½x12¾
2015, Sept. 14 Litho.
2522 A1452 15p multi 1.60 1.10

Galán y Rocha Hospital, Paysandú, Cent. — A1453

Perf. 12½x12¾
2015, Sept. 24 Litho.
2523 A1453 15p multi 1.60 1.10

Miniature Sheet

Owls A1454

No. 2524: a, Aegolius harrisii. b, Bubo virginianus. c, Athene cunicularia. d, Megascops choliba. e, Tyto alba. f, Asio flammeus. g, Glaucidium brasilianum. h, Asio clamator.

Perf. 12½x12¾
2015, Sept. 30 Litho.
2524 A1454 15p Sheet of 8, #a-h 12.00 8.25

Carrasco International Airport, Montevideo — A1455

2015, Oct. 2 Litho. *Perf. 12*
2525 A1455 15p multi 1.60 1.10

Provisional Regulations of the Eastern Provice to Promote the Campaign and Security of its Landowners A1456

2015, Oct. 9 Litho. *Perf. 12*
2526 A1456 15p multi 1.60 1.10

No. 2526 was printed in sheets of 10 + central label.

United Nations, 70th Anniv. A1457

No. 2527 — Uruguayan United Nations Peacekeeper with child in: a, 15p, Congo. b, 50p, Haiti.

2015, Oct. 20 Litho. *Perf. 12*
2527 A1457 Horiz. pair, #a-b 6.75 4.50

Famous People — A1458

Designs: No. 2528, 15p, Prof. Daniel Vidart, anthropologist. No. 2529, 15p, Ida Holz, computer engineer.

2015, Oct. 21 Litho. *Perf. 12¾x12½*
2528-2529 A1458 Set of 2 3.25 2.10

Dropping of Atomic Bombs on Hiroshima and Nagasaki, 70th Anniv. — A1459

No. 2530: a, Peace Statue, Nagasaki. b, Atomic Bomb Dome, Hiroshima.

2015, Oct. 23 Litho. *Perf. 12*
2530 A1459 50p Pair, #a-b 9.25 6.75

Energy Balance in Uruguay, 50th Anniv. — A1460

No. 2531: a, Water splash, wind generator, refinery, emblem of Ministry of Industry, Energy and Mining, b, Solar panels, sunflower, bar graph.

2015, Nov. 11 Litho. *Perf. 12*
2531 A1460 20p Vert. pair, #a-b 4.00 2.75

Eight Hour Work Day Law, Cent. A1461

2015, Nov. 17 Litho. *Perf. 12*
2532 A1461 20p multi 2.00 1.40

Maria del Pilar, Afro-Uruguayan Woman Freed in 1815 — A1462

2015, Dec. 3 Litho. *Perf. 12*
2533 A1462 20p multi 2.00 1.40

International Year of Soils — A1463

2015, Dec. 3 Litho. *Perf. 12*
2534 A1463 60p multi 5.50 4.00

Cruise Ships and Tourist Sites A1464

No. 2535: a, MS Zaandam, Calle de los Suspiros, Colonia del Sacramento. b, MSC Splendida, Estadio Centenario, Montevideo. c, Costa Favolosa, Cabo Polonio Lighthouse. d, Norwegian Sun, Port of Punta del Este.

2015, Dec. 4 Litho. *Perf. 12*
2535 A1464 20p Block of 4, #a-d 8.00 5.50

Campaign Against Human Trafficking A1465

2015, Dec. 7 Litho. *Perf. 12*
2536 A1465 60p multi 5.50 4.00

America Issue.

Tourist Sites in Salto — A1466

Designs: No. 2537, 20p, Hot Springs of Arapey. No. 2538, 20p, Nuestra Señora del Carmen Church, Campanario.

Perf. 12¾x12½
2015, Dec. 14 Litho.
2537-2538 A1466 Set of 2 4.00 2.75

Nos. 2537-2538 were printed in sheets of 8 containing four of each stamp + central label.

Christmas A1467

2015, Dec. 15 Litho. *Perf. 12*
2539 A1467 20p multi 2.00 1.40

Souvenir Sheet

Tango Music Personalities — A1468

No. 2540: a, Horacio Ferrer (1933-2014), composer. b, Astor Piazzolla (1921-92), bandoneon player.

Perf. 12½x12¾

2015, Dec. 22 **Litho.**
2540 A1468 60p Sheet of 2, #a-b 11.00 8.00

Souvenir Sheet

International Year of Light — A1469

Perf. 12½x12¾

2015, Dec. 23 **Litho.**
2541 A1469 60p multi 5.50 4.00

New Year 2016 (Year of the Monkey) — A1470

2016, Jan. 28 **Litho.** ***Perf. 12¾x12½***
2542 A1470 20p multi 2.00 1.40

Poster for 1915-16 Summer Festival and Carnival — A1471

2016, Feb. 19 **Litho.** ***Perf. 12***
2543 A1471 20p multi 2.00 1.25

No. 2543 was printed in sheets of 5 + label.

Souvenir Sheet

Tacuarembo Gaucho Festival, 30th Anniv. — A1472

2016, Mar. 4 **Litho.** ***Perf. 12¾x12½***
2544 A1472 20p multi 2.00 1.25

Intl. Women's Day A1473

No. 2545: a, Enriqueta Compte y Riqué (1866-1949), founder of first South American kindergarten. b, Female rider in Lancers of Aparicio. c, State Commitment to End Gender-based Violence.

2016, Mar. 8 **Litho.** ***Perf. 12¾x12½***
2545 A1473 20p Strip of 3, #a-c 6.00 3.75

Police Women — A1474

2016, Mar. 11 **Litho.** ***Perf. 12***
2546 A1474 20p multi 2.00 1.25

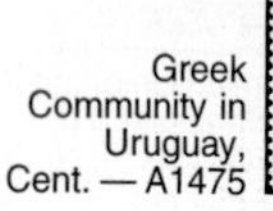

Greek Community in Uruguay, Cent. — A1475

Perf. 12½x12¾

2016, Mar. 16 **Litho.**
2547 A1475 20p multi 2.00 1.25

Souvenir Sheet

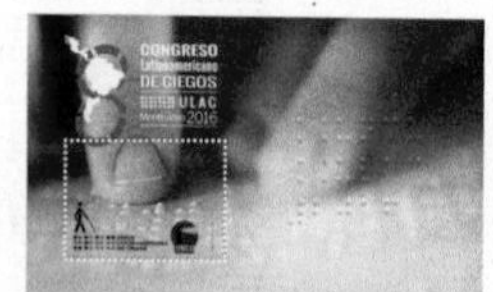

Eighth Latin American Congress for the Blind, Montevideo — A1476

Litho., Sheet Margin Litho. & Embossed

2016, Apr. 20 ***Perf. 12½x12¾***
2548 A1476 20p multi 2.00 1.25

Treaty of Asunción, 25th Anniv. — A1477

2016, Apr. 25 **Litho.** ***Perf. 12***
2549 A1477 60p multi 5.50 4.00

No. 2549 was printed in sheets of 24 + label.

Souvenir Sheet

William Shakespeare (1564-1616), Writer — A1478

2016, Apr. 28 **Litho.** ***Perf. 12¾x12½***
2550 A1478 60p multi 5.50 4.00

International Year of Pulses — A1479

2016, May 20 **Litho.** ***Perf. 12¾x12½***
2551 A1479 60p multi 5.50 4.00

Dámaso Antonio Larrañaga (1771-1848), Founder of National Library — A1480

2016, May 26 **Litho.** ***Perf. 12½x12¾***
2552 A1480 20p multi 2.00 1.40

National Library, 200th anniv. No. 2552 was printed in sheets of 8 + central label.

General José Gervasio Artigas (1764-1850) — A1481

Serpentine Die Cut 9¾x9

2016 **Self-Adhesive** **Litho.**

Portrait Color

2553	A1481	20p green	2.00	1.40
a.		Dated "2017"	2.50	1.50
b.		Dated "2018"	1.40	1.40
2554	A1481	30p blue	2.75	2.00
a.		Dated "2019"	2.75	1.90
2555	A1481	50p red	4.00	3.25
a.		Dated "2017"	6.00	3.50
b.		Dated "2018"	3.50	3.50
c.		Dated "2019"	4.75	3.25
2556	A1481	60p yellow	5.50	4.00
2557	A1481	200p purple	18.00	13.00
a.		Dated "2019"	11.00	11.00
		Nos. 2553-2557 (5)	32.25	23.65

Issued: 20p, 50p, 5/30; 30p, 60p, 6/6; 200p, 6/14; No. 2553a, 1/27/17; No. 2555a, 3/24/17; Nos. 2553b, 2555a, 3/23/18; No. 2554a, 1/10/19; No. 2555a, 2/25/19; No. 2557a, 12/16/19. See Nos. 2586-2588, 2622-2624, 2649-2650.

Souvenir Sheet

Naval Oceanographic, Hydrographic and Meteorological Service, Cent. — A1482

2016, May 31 **Litho.** ***Perf. 12½x12¾***
2558 A1482 20p multi 2.00 1.40

Souvenir Sheet

Uruguayan Mission to Rescue Ernest Shackleton Expedition on Elephant Island, Cent. — A1483

No. 2559: a, Lieutenant Ruperto Elichiribehety (1888-1929), rescue mission leader, and crew. b, Mirounga leonina. c, Fishing boat Instituto No. 1.

Perf. 12½x12¾

2016, June 10 **Litho.**
2559 A1483 20p Sheet of 3, #a-c 6.00 4.00

Symphony Orchestra of Official Service of Broadcasting, Television and Entertainment, 85th Anniv. — A1484

2016, June 20 **Litho.** ***Perf. 12***
2560 A1484 20p multi 2.00 1.40

Copa América Soccer Championships, Cent. — A1485

No. 2561: a, Héctor Rivadavia Gómez (1880-1931), director of South American Soccer Federation. b, Players from 1916 Uruguay championship team.

2016, June 24 **Litho.** ***Perf. 12***
2561 A1485 20p Pair, #a-b 4.00 2.75

Diplomatic Relations Between Uruguay and Germany, Cent. — A1486

No. 2562 — Flags of Uruguay and Germany and: a, Uruguayan Legislative Palace. b, German Reichstag.

2016, July 14 **Litho.** ***Perf. 12½x12¾***

2562		Horiz. pair + central label	11.00	5.50
a.	A1486	20p multi	2.75	1.40
b.	A1486	60p multi	8.00	4.00

Printed in sheets containing 3 each Nos. 2562a-2562b and 3 labels.

University of the Republic Engineering Faculty, Cent. — A1487

2016, July 20 **Litho.** ***Perf. 12***
2563 A1487 20p multi 2.00 1.40

National Ports Administration, Cent. — A1488

2016, July 21 **Litho.** ***Perf. 12½x12¾***
2564 A1488 20p multi 2.00 1.40

No. 2564 was printed in sheets of 8 + central label.

National Party, 180th Anniv. — A1489

Perf. 12½x12¾

2016, Aug. 10 **Litho.**
2565 A1489 20p multi 2.00 1.40

2016 Summer Olympics, Rio de Janeiro — A1490

No. 2566: a, Tennis. b, Rowing. c, Marathon. d, Equestrian.

2016, Aug. 12 **Litho.** ***Perf. 12***
2566 A1490 20p Block or vert. strip of 4, #a-d 8.00 5.75

El Cuello Azul II, Painting by Gladys Afamado — A1491

2016, Aug. 31 **Litho.** ***Perf. 12***
2567 A1491 20p multi 2.00 1.40

Trees and Blossoms — A1492

No. 2568: a, Jacaranda mimosifolia. b, Handroanthus impetiginosus. c, Erythrina crista-galli. d, Peltophorum dubium.

2016, Sept. 21 Litho. ***Perf. 12***
2568 A1492 20p Block or horiz. strip of 4, #a-d 8.50 5.75

Printed in sheets of 8 (2 each Nos. 2568a-2568d), + 4 labels.

Miniature Sheet

Stained-Glass Windows From José Pedro Varela, Pedagogical Museum — A1493

No. 2569: a, Fisica (Physics). b, Pedagogia (Pedagogy). c, Historia (History). d, Higiene (Hygiene). e, Astronomia (Astronomy). f, Quimica (Chemistry).

2016, Sept. 22 Litho. ***Perf. 12***
2569 A1493 20p Sheet of 6, #a-f 12.50 8.50

Heritage Day — Public Education.

Souvenir Sheet

Garcilaso de la Vega (1539-1616), Historian — A1494

Perf. 12¾x12½
2016, Sept. 28 Litho.
2570 A1494 60p multi 5.75 4.25

Butterflies A1495

No. 2571: a, Junonia genovesa hilaris. b, Mechanitis lysimnia lysimnia. c, Choricea licursis.

2016, Oct. 7 Litho. ***Perf. 12½x12¾***
2571 Strip of 3 6.25 4.25
a.-c. A1495 20p Any single 1.75 1.40

Printed in sheets of 9 (3 each #2571a-2571c) + 3 labels.

Souvenir Sheet

Miguel de Cervantes (1547-1616), Writer — A1496

2016, Oct. 12 Litho. ***Perf. 12¾x12½***
2572 A1496 60p multi 5.75 4.25

Banco Republica, 120th Anniv. — A1497

2016, Oct. 21 Litho. ***Perf. 12½x12¾***
2573 A1497 20p multi 2.10 1.40

No. 2573 was printed in sheets of 6 + central label.

Río Negro Department Tourism A1498

Designs: No. 2574, 20p, Cerdocyon thous. No. 2575, 20p, Machinery in Anglo Meat Packing Plant UNESCO World Heritage Site.

Perf. 12½x12¾
2016, Nov. 16 Litho.
2574-2575 A1498 Set of 2 4.25 2.75

Nos. 2474-2475 were printed together in sheets containing four of each stamp.

Christmas — A1499

2016, Nov. 28 Litho. ***Perf. 12***
2576 A1499 20p multi 2.10 1.40

Tourism A1500

No. 2577 — Cruise ships and tourist attractions: a, Crystal Serenity and Phleocryptes melanops. b, Crown Princess and canoe on lake. c, Fram and blind man with guide dog. d, Prinsendam and Palacio Salvo, Montevideo.

2016, Dec. 1 Litho. ***Perf. 12***
2577 A1500 20p Block or horiz. strip of 4, #a-d 8.50 5.50

Antonio Sayago (d. 1902), Afro-Uruguayan Musician A1501

2016, Dec. 2 Litho. ***Perf. 12½x12¾***
2578 A1501 20p multi 2.10 1.40

Líber Seregni (1916-2004), Military Officer and Politician — A1502

No. 2579: a, Color photograph of Seregni. b, Drawing of Seregni holding loudspeaker. c, Sepia photograph of Seregni.

Perf. 12¾x12½
2016, Dec. 12 Litho.
2579 Booklet pane of 3 6.25 —
a.-c. A1502 20p Any single 1.75 1.60
Complete booklet, #2579 6.25

Complete booklet sold for 70p.

Steam Plant, Aguas Corrientes, Coat of Arms of Canelones Deparatment and Map of Uruguay A1503

Church, Villa Soriano, Coat of Arms of Soriano Deparatment and Map of Uruguay A1504

San Carlos Bull Ring, Colonia del Sacramento, Coat of Arms of Colonia Deparatment and Map of Uruguay A1505

2016 Litho. ***Perf. 12½x12¾***
2580 A1503 20p multi 2.10 1.40
2581 A1504 20p multi 2.10 1.40
2582 A1505 20p multi 2.10 1.40
Nos. 2580-2582 (3) 6.30 4.20

Issued: No. 2580, 12/13; Nos. 2581-2582, 12/15.

Olga Delgrossi, Tango Singer — A1506

Perf. 12½x12¾
2016, Dec. 15 Litho.
2583 A1506 20p multi 2.10 1.40

Ida Vitale, Poet — A1507

Perf. 12¾x12½
2016, Dec. 23 Litho.
2584 A1507 20p multi 2.10 1.40

New Year 2017 (Year of the Rooster) A1508

2017, Jan. 22 Litho. ***Perf. 12½x12¾***
2585 A1508 20p multi 2.10 1.50

Artigas Type of 2016
Serpentine Die Cut 9¾x9
2017 Self-Adhesive Litho.
Dated "2017"
Portrait Color

2586 A1481 3p blue .45 .25
a. Dated "2019" .30 .25
2587 A1481 5p orange .60 .35
a. Dated "2018" .35 .35
b. Dated "2021" .30 .30
2588 A1481 10p magenta 1.20 .70
a. Dated "2018" .70 .70
b. Dated "2019" 1.25 .65
c. Dated "2021" .45 .45
Nos. 2586-2588 (3) 2.25 1.30

Issued: 3p, 5p, 2/2; 10p, 2/14; No. 2586a, 12/4/19; No. 2587a, 12/3/18; No. 2588a, 4/5/18; No. 2588b, 1/10/19; Nos. 2587b, 2588c, 11/5/21.

Souvenir Sheet

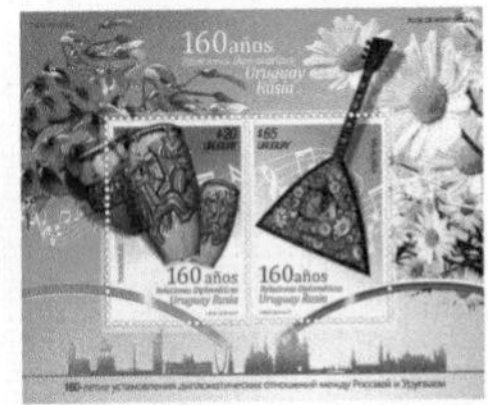

Diplomatic Relations Between Uruguay and Russia, 160th Anniv. — A1509

No. 2589 — Decorated musical insturments: a, Drums, Uruguay. b, Balalaika, Russia.

Perf. 12¾x12½
2017, Feb. 16 Litho.
2589 A1509 Sheet of 2 6.25 6.25
a. 20p multi 1.50 1.50
b. 65p multi 4.75 4.75

Candombe, Painting by Carlos Páez Vilaró — A1510

Perf. 12½x12¾
2017, Feb. 24 Litho.
2590 A1510 20p multi 2.10 1.50

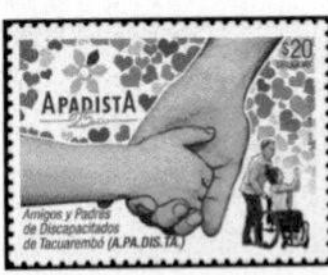

Friends and Parents of the Disabled of Tacuarembó (APADISTA), 25th Anniv. — A1511

2017, Mar. 8 Litho. ***Perf. 12***
2591 A1511 20p multi 2.10 1.40

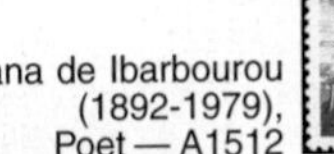

Juana de Ibarbourou (1892-1979), Poet — A1512

2017, Mar. 8 Litho. ***Perf. 12¾x12½***
2592 A1512 20p multi 2.10 1.40

No. 2592 was printed in sheets of 8 + central label.

Souvenir Sheet

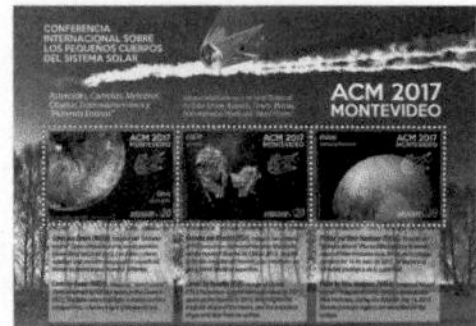

Asteroids, Comets and Meteors International Conference, Montevideo — A1513

No. 2593: a, Dwarf planet Ceres. b, Comet CG67P. c, Pluto.

2017, Apr. 9 Litho. ***Perf. 12½x12¾***
2593 A1513 20p Sheet of 3, #a-c 6.25 4.25

Club Atlético Progreso Soccer Team, Cent. — A1514

2017, Apr. 27 Litho. ***Perf. 12½x12¾***
2594 A1514 20p multi 2.10 1.40

No. 2594 was printed in sheets of 8 + central label.

Lions Clubs International, Cent. — A1515

2017, Apr. 28 Litho. ***Perf. 12½x12¾***
2595 A1515 65p multi 6.25 4.75

José Enrique Rodó (1871-1917), Writer — A1516

2017, May 3 Litho. ***Perf. 12½x12¾***
2596 A1516 20p multi 2.10 1.40

No. 2596 was printed in sheets of 8 + central label.

Premiere of La Cumparsita, Tango Song by Geraldo Matos Rodríguez, Cent. — A1517

2017, May 8 Litho. ***Perf. 12¾x12½***
2597 A1517 65p multi 6.25 4.75
a. Souvenir sheet of 1 6.25 4.75

Commission for the Eradication of Unhealthy Rural Housing (MEVIR), 50th Anniv. — A1518

2017, May 17 Litho. ***Perf. 12½x12¾***
2598 A1518 20p multi 2.10 1.40

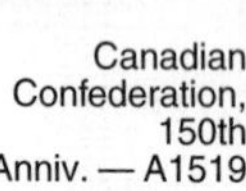

Canadian Confederation, 150th Anniv. — A1519

No. 2599: a, Moraine Lake, Alberta. b, Inukshuk.

Perf. 12½x12¾
2017, June 27 Litho.
2599 Horiz. pair + central label 8.25 6.25
a. A1519 20p multi 1.90 1.40
b. A1519 65p multi 6.25 4.75

Souvenir Sheet

Central Bank of Uruguay, 50th Anniv. A1520

No. 2600 — 2017 Central Bank of Uruguay 2000-peso coin: a, 20p, Obverse. b, 65p, Reverse.

Litho. & Embossed
2017, July 7 ***Perf. 12¾x12½***
2600 A1520 Sheet of 2, #a-b 8.50 6.25

Arrival in Uruguay of Mother Francisca Rubatto (1844-1904), Founder of Capuchin Sisters of Mother Rubatto, 125th Anniv. — A1521

2017, Aug. 8 Litho. ***Perf. 12½x12¾***
2601 A1521 20p multi 2.10 1.40

Diplomatic Relations Between Uruguay and Belarus, 25th Anniv. — A1522

No. 2602: a, 20p, Solís Theater, Montevideo. b, 65p, Bolshoi Theater of Belarus, Minsk.

2017, Sept. 7 Litho. ***Perf. 12¾x12½***
2602 A1522 Horiz. pair, #a-b, + central label 8.50 6.00

See Belarus No. 1070.

Banco de Previsión Social (Social Security Institute), 50th Anniv. — A1523

Perf. 12½x12¾
2017, Sept. 16 Litho.
2603 A1523 20p multi 2.10 1.40

2017 World Chess Youth Championships, Montevideo — A1524

Perf. 12¾x12½
2017, Sept. 25 Litho.
2604 A1524 65p multi 6.25 4.50

Cooperation and Friendship Between Uruguay and the United States, 150th Anniv. — A1525

2017, Oct. 2 Litho. ***Perf. 12½x12¾***
2605 A1525 65p multi 6.25 4.50

1910 Beyer Peacock Class N3 2-6-0 Locomotive No. 120 — A1526

2017, Oct. 10 Litho. ***Perf. 12½x12¾***
2606 A1526 65p multi 6.25 4.50

Obdulio J. Varela (1917-96), Captain of 1950 World Cup Champion Uruguayan Soccer Team — A1527

2017, Oct. 27 Litho. ***Perf. 12¾x12½***
2607 A1527 20p multi 2.10 1.40

First Year of Uruguay as Associate Observer in Community of Portuguese Language Countries — A1528

2017, Oct. 31 Litho. ***Perf. 12¾x12½***
2608 A1528 65p multi 6.25 4.50

Souvenir Sheet

Uruguayan Navy, 200th Anniv. — A1529

No. 2609: a, MBB Bo105 helicopter. b, Schooner Capitán Miranda. c, Frigate Uruguay.

Perf. 12½x12¾
2017, Nov. 13 Litho.
2609 A1529 20p Sheet of 3, #a-c 6.25 4.25

Universal Declaration of Democracy, 20th Anniv. — A1530

Perf. 12¾x12½
2017, Nov. 15 Litho.
2610 A1530 65p multi 6.25 4.50

Christmas — A1531

Perf. 12¾x12½
2017, Nov. 29 Litho.
2611 A1531 20p multi 2.10 1.40

Gregorio, the Town Crier — A1532

2017, Dec. 4 Litho. ***Perf. 12¾x12½***
2612 A1532 20p multi 2.10 1.40

Forma II, by Guillermo Fernández (1928-2007) — A1533

2017, Dec. 8 Litho. ***Perf. 12¾x12½***
2613 A1533 20p multi 2.10 1.40

Egg of Pachycymbiola Brasiliana on La Paloma Beach, Rocha — A1534

Perf. 12½x12¾
2017, Dec. 14 Litho.
2614 A1534 65p multi 6.25 4.50

Colonia Department Tourism — A1535

No. 2615: a, Heterothalamus alienus in Davyt Blancarena Park. b, Sailboat and parasailers near Costa del Immigrante.

Perf. 12¾x12½
2017, Dec. 18 Litho.
2615 A1535 20p Horiz. pair, #a-b 4.25 2.75

Uruguayan Postal Service, 190th Anniv. — A1536

No. 2616: a, Francisco de los Santos, last messenger of José Gervasio Artigas. b, Uruguay Post van.

Perf. 12½x12¾
2017, Dec. 21 Litho.
2616 A1536 20p Horiz. pair, #a-b 4.25 2.75

Souvenir Sheet

Diplomatic Relations Between Uruguay and People's Republic of China, 30th Anniv. — A1537

No. 2617 — Flags of Uruguay and People's Republic of China and: a, 20p, Tamandua tetradactyla (lesser anteater), Handroanthus impetiginosus. b, 65p, Ailuropoda melanoleuca (giant panda), Bambusa vulgaris.

2018, Jan. 23 Litho. ***Perf. 12½x12¾***
2617 A1537 Sheet of 2, #a-b 7.75 6.00

New Year 2018 (Year of the Dog) — A1538

Perf. 12¾x12½
2018, Feb. 10 Litho.
2618 A1538 65p multi 5.75 4.75

Carnival Costume — A1539

Perf. 12¾x12½

2018, Feb. 16 **Litho.**
2619 A1539 20p multi 2.00 1.40

Gen. Victor Licandro (1918-2011) — A1540

Perf. 12¾x12½

2018, Feb. 26 **Litho.**
2620 A1540 20p multi 2.00 1.40

International Women's Day — A1541

No. 2621: a, Rural woman, farm field. b, Afro-American woman, building.

2018, Mar. 8 **Litho.** ***Perf. 12½x12¾***
2621 A1541 20p Horiz. pair, #a-b 4.00 3.00

Artigas Type of 2016

Serpentine Die Cut 9¾x9

2018 **Self-Adhesive** **Litho.**

Dated "2018"

Portrait Color

2622 A1481 1p gray grn .30 .25
a. Dated "2021" .30 .30
2623 A1481 80p sepia 8.00 5.75
a. Dated "2019" 4.75 4.25
2624 A1481 100p red lilac 8.50 7.00
a. Dated "2019" 8.25 5.50
Nos. 2622-2624 (3) 16.80 13.00

Issued: 1p, 3/19; 80p, 4/4; 100p, 4/5; No. 2623a, 12/12/19; No. 2624a, 12/16/19; No. 2622a, 12/2/21.

Miniature Sheet

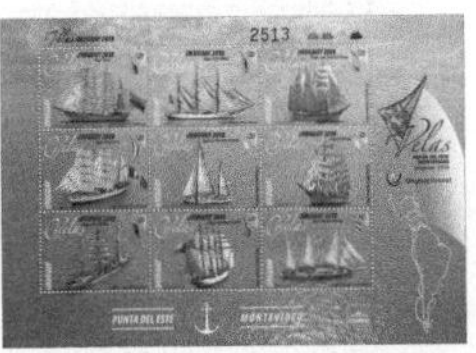

Tall Ships A1542

No. 2625 — Ship and flag of: a, 20p, Gloria, Colombia. b, 20p, Cisne Branco, Brazil. c, 20p, Juan Sebastián Elcano, Spain. d, 20p, Cuauhtémoc, Mexico. e, 20p, Dr. Bernardo Houssay, Argentina. f, 20p, Libertad, Argentina. g, 20p, Simón Bolívar, Venezuela. h, 20p, Esmerelda, Chile. i, 65p, Capitán Miranda, Uruguay.

2018, Apr. 13 **Litho.** ***Perf. 12½x12¾***
2625 A1542 Sheet of 9, #a-i 22.00 16.00

Oscar W. Tabárez, Soccer Player and Manager A1543

2018, May 4 **Litho.** ***Perf. 12½x12¾***
2626 A1543 20p multi 2.00 1.40

Dr. Martin Luther King (1929-68), Civil Rights Leader — A1544

2018, June 7 **Litho.** ***Perf. 12¾x12½***
2627 A1544 65p multi 5.75 4.25

No. 2627 was printed in sheets of 8 + central label.

Bid by Uruguay, Argentina and Paraguay to Host 2030 World Cup Soccer Championships A1545

Perf. 12½x12¾

2018, June 14 **Litho.**
2628 A1545 20p multi 2.00 1.40

No. 2628 was printed in sheets of 5 + 4 labels.

Automobile Club of Uruguay, Cent. — A1546

No. 2629: a, 1904 Clement Bayard. b, 1948 Fordson truck. c, 1900 Delin. d, 1925 Ford Model T.

2018, July 12 **Litho.** ***Perf. 12½x12¾***
2629 A1546 20p Block of 4, #a-d 8.00 5.25

Cry of Asencio of the Blandengues de Artigas Cavalry Regiment, Cent. — A1547

2018, July 20 **Litho.** ***Perf. 12½x12¾***
2630 A1547 20p multi 2.00 1.40

150th Liver Transplant Performed in Uruguay — A1548

2018, July 23 **Litho.** ***Perf. 12¾x12½***
2631 A1548 20p multi 2.00 1.40

Student Martyrs Day, 50th Anniv. — A1549

Perf. 12½x12¾

2018, Aug. 14 **Litho.**
2632 A1549 20p multi 2.00 1.25

Heriberto P. Coates (1866-1940), Founder of Rotary Club of Montevideo, and Hotel Pyramides A1550

Perf. 12½x12¾

2018, Aug. 17 **Litho.**
2633 A1550 20p multi 2.00 1.25

Rotary Club of Montevideo, cent.

Items in Uruguayan Museums — A1551

No. 2634: a, 20p, Colonial era vessel, from Antonio Taddei Museum, Canalones. b, 65p, Homage to Gardel, mural by the Gregorio Workshop, from San Gregorio de Polanco Open Air Museum of Art, Tacuarembó.

Perf. 12¾x12½

2018, Aug. 28 **Litho.**
2634 A1551 Horiz. pair, #a-b 7.75 5.25

San Fructuoso Cathedral, Tacuarembó, Cent. — A1552

2018, Aug. 30 **Litho.** ***Perf. 12***
2635 A1552 20p multi 1.90 1.25

Olimpia Athletic Club, Cent. — A1553

Perf. 12¾x12½

2018, Sept. 10 **Litho.**
2636 A1553 20p multi 1.90 1.25

No. 2636 was printed in sheets of 8 + central label.

Abel Carlevaro Casal (1916-2001), Guitar Teacher and Composer A1554

Perf. 12½x12¾

2018, Sept. 18 **Litho.**
2637 A1554 20p multi 1.90 1.25

No. 2637 was printed in sheets of 8 + central label.

Universal Declaration of Human Rights, 70th Anniv. — A1555

Perf. 12¾x12½

2018, Sept. 28 **Litho.**
2638 A1555 65p multi 5.50 4.00

Birds A1556

No. 2639: a, Cathartes aura. b, Ramphastos toco.

2018, Oct. 9 **Litho.** ***Perf. 12¾x12½***
2639 A1556 20p Horiz. pair, #a-b 3.75 2.50

Tourism in Treinta y Tres. No. 2639 was printed in sheets of 4 pairs + central label.

Souvenir Sheet

Untitled Painting by Gabriel Vuljevas A1557

2018, Oct. 11 **Litho.** ***Perf. 12½***
2640 A1557 65p multi 5.50 4.00

Independence of Lithuania, cent.

Vichadero, Cent. — A1558

2018, Oct. 19 **Litho.** ***Perf. 12½x12¾***
2641 A1558 20p multi 1.90 1.25

Ana Gasquen, Slave Ordered to be Freed by Gen. José Artigas in 1818 — A1559

2018, Oct. 24 **Litho.** ***Perf. 12¾x12½***
2642 A1559 20p multi 1.90 1.25

Souvenir Sheet

National Institute of Colonization, 70th Anniv. — A1560

No. 2643: a, Man and woman in farm field. b, Farm worker, tractor, farm house, corn stalks.

2018, Oct. 31 **Litho.** ***Perf. 12½***
2643 A1560 20p Sheet of 2, #a-b 3.75 2.50

Colorín Colorado, by Luis Alberto Solari (1918-93) A1561

2018, Nov. 5 **Litho.** ***Perf. 12½x12¾***
2644 A1561 22p multi 2.00 1.40

Miniature Sheet

Ducks A1562

No. 2645: a, Anas bahamensis. b, Anas georgica. c, Netta peposaca. d, Anas sibilatrix.

2018, Nov. 7 **Litho.** ***Perf. 12½x12¾***
2645 A1562 22p Sheet of 4, #a-d 8.25 5.50

Mariano Mores (1918-2016), Tango Composer and Pianist — A1563

2018, Nov. 9 Litho. ***Perf. 12½x12¾***
2646 A1563 65p multi 5.50 4.00

Javier de Viana (1868-1926), Writer — A1564

Perf. 12¾x12½
2018, Nov. 21 **Litho.**
2647 A1564 22p multi 2.00 1.40

International Year of Corals — A1565

Perf. 12½x12¾
2018, Nov. 23 **Litho.**
2648 A1565 65p multi 5.50 4.00

Artigas Type of 2016
Serpentine Die Cut 9¾x9
2018-19 **Litho.**
Self-Adhesive
Portrait Color

2649	A1481	2p pink	.30	.25
a.		Dated "2021"	.30	.30
2650	A1481	22p lilac	1.75	1.40
2651	A1481	65p yellow green	4.75	4.00
2652	A1481	70p bistre	4.50	3.75
		Nos. 2649-2652 (4)	11.30	9.40

Issued: 2p, 1/10/19; 22p, 12/3; 65p, 2/26/19. 70p, 12/12/19; No. 2649a, 12/2/21.

Christmas — A1566

Perf. 12¾x12½
2018, Dec. 12 **Litho.**
2653 A1566 22p multi 2.00 1.40

America Issue A1567

No. 2654 — Domesticated animals: a, 22p, Lamb. b, 65p, Dog.

Perf. 12½x12¾
2018, Dec. 19 **Litho.**
2654 A1567 Horiz. pair, #a-b 7.50 5.50

End of World War I, Cent. — A1568

Perf. 12¾x12½
2018, Dec. 21 **Litho.**
2655 A1568 65p multi 5.50 4.00

Souvenir Sheet

Uruguayan Diplomatic Recognition of the Palestinian Authority — A1569

2018, Dec. 31 **Litho.** ***Perf. 12***
2656 A1569 65p multi 5.50 4.00

New Year 2019 (Year of the Pig) — A1570

2019, Jan. 24 Litho. ***Perf. 12¾x12½***
2657 A1570 65p multi 5.00 4.00

Wilson Ferreira Aldunate (1919-88), Politician — A1571

2019, Feb. 4 Litho. ***Perf. 12¾x12½***
2658 A1571 22p multi 1.90 1.40

Carnival A1572

No. 2659: a, Fermina "Martha" Gularte (1919-2002), dancer. b, Carlos María "Pirulo" Albín (1919-95), dancer. c, Juan Angel "El Cacique" Silva (1919-2003), drummer.

Perf. 12¾x12½
2019, Feb. 20 **Litho.**
2659 A1572 22p Horiz. strip of 3, #a-c 5.75 4.00
d. Booklet pane of 3, #2659a-2659c 6.00 —
Complete booklet, #2659d 6.75

Complete booklet sold for 80p.

Rigoberta Menchú Tum, 1992 Nobel Peace Laureate — A1573

2019, Mar. 8 Litho. ***Perf. 12¾x12½***
2660 A1573 65p multi 5.00 4.00

No. 2660 was printed in sheets of 8 + central label.

Angela Davis, Professor and Political Activist — A1574

Perf. 12¾x12½
2019, Mar. 21 **Litho.**
2661 A1574 65p multi 5.00 4.00

No. 2661 was printed in sheets of 8 + central label.

Julio César Benítez (1940-68) and Victoriano Santos Iriarte (1902-68), Soccer Players — A1575

Perf. 12½x12¾
2019, Mar. 27 **Litho.**
2662 A1575 22p multi 1.90 1.40

Racing Club de Montevideo soccer team, cent. No. 2662 was printed in sheets of 8 + central label.

Uruguay Chamber of Construction, Cent. A1576

2019, Mar. 29 **Litho.** ***Perf. 12***
2663 A1576 22p multi 1.90 1.40

Paysandú Tourism — A1577

No. 2664: a, Nasua nasua. b, Leopardus braccatus.

2019, Apr. 5 Litho. ***Perf. 12¾x12½***
2664 A1577 22p Horiz. pair, #a-b 3.25 2.60

Pascual Harriague (1819-94), Viticulturist — A1578

2019, Apr. 8 Litho. ***Perf. 12¾x12½***
2665 A1578 22p multi 1.90 1.25

International Labor Organization, Cent. A1579

2019, Apr. 25 **Litho.** ***Perf. 12***
2666 A1579 65p multi 5.00 3.75

Adolfo Aguirre González (1919-99), Professor and Founder of Left Liberation Front — A1580

2019, Apr. 25 Litho. ***Perf. 12¾x12½***
2667 A1580 22p multi 1.90 1.25

No. 2667 was printed in sheets of 8 + central label.

International Celiac Disease Day — A1581

2019, May 8 Litho. ***Perf. 12½x12¾***
2668 A1581 22p multi 1.90 1.25

Santiago Chalar (1938-94), Physician and Guitarist A1582

2019, May 14 Litho. ***Perf. 12½x12¾***
2669 A1582 22p multi 1.90 1.25

No. 2669 was printed in sheets of 8 + central label.

National Soccer Team, 120th Anniv. — A1583

2019, May 14 Litho. ***Perf. 12½x12¾***
2670 A1583 22p multi 1.90 1.25

No. 2670 was printed in sheets of 8 + central label.

Souvenir Sheet

Leonardo da Vinci (1452-1519), Painter — A1584

2019, May 15 Litho. ***Perf. 12½x12¼***
2671 A1584 65p multi 5.00 3.75

Souvenir Sheet

Amado Nervo (1870-1919), Writer and Diplomat — A1585

2019, May 31 Litho. ***Perf. 12½x12¼***
2672 A1585 65p multi 5.00 3.75

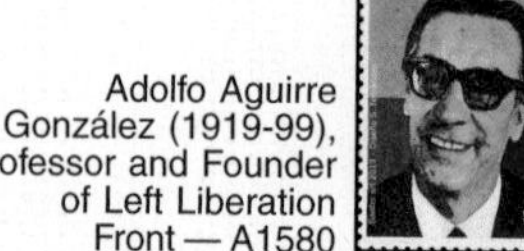

Caretta Caretta and Plastic Bag — A1586

2019, June 5 Litho. ***Perf. 12½x12¾***
2673 A1586 65p multi 5.00 3.75

Julio "Kanela" Sosa, (1933-2019), Dancer and Choreographer A1587

Perf. 12¾x12½
2019, June 14 **Litho.**
2674 A1587 22p multi 1.90 1.25

The Kiss, by Pablo Picasso (1881-1973) — A1588

Perf. 12¾x12½
2019, June 21 **Litho.**
2675 A1588 65p multi 5.00 3.75

Souvenir Sheet

Walt Whitman (1819-92), Poet — A1589

Perf. 12½x12¼

2019, June 28 **Litho.**
2676 A1589 65p multi 5.00 3.75

Bicycle Path System — A1590

2019, July 4 **Litho.** *Perf. 12½x12¾*
2677 A1590 22p multi 1.90 1.40

Souvenir Sheet

Diplomatic Relations Between Uruguay and Israel, 70th Anniv. — A1591

No. 2678: a, Mazama gouazoubira. b, Capra nubiana.

2019, July 15 **Litho.** *Perf. 12½x12¾*
2678 A1591 Sheet of 2 10.75 5.25
a. 22p multi 2.50 1.25
b. 65p multi 8.00 4.00

Joaquín "Ansina" Lenzina (1760-1860), Assistant to José Gervasio Artigas — A1592

2019, July 22 **Litho.** *Perf. 12¾x12½*
2679 A1592 22p multi 1.90 1.40

First Man on the Moon, 50th Anniv. A1593

2019, July 23 **Litho.** *Perf. 12¾x12½*
2680 A1593 65p multi 5.00 3.75

The design, when viewed through red and blue glasses, becomes three-dimensional.

Teapot Designed by Marianne Brandt, 1924 — A1594

2019, Aug. 6 **Litho.** *Perf. 12¾x12½*
2681 A1594 65p multi 5.00 3.50

Bauhaus Art School, cent.

United Nations Population Fund, 50th Anniv. — A1595

Perf. 12½x12¾

2019, Aug. 14 **Litho.**
2682 A1595 65p multi 5.00 3.50

Souvenir Sheet

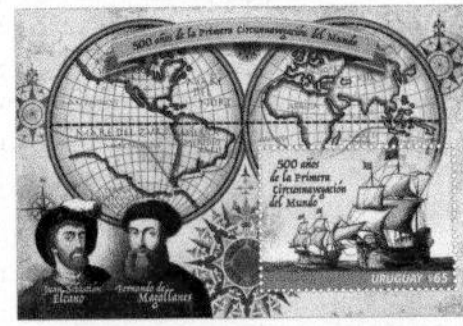

Circumnavigation by Ferdinand Magellan's Expedition, 500th Anniv. — A1596

2019, Sept. 3 **Litho.** *Perf. 12½x12¾*
2683 A1596 65p multi 5.00 3.50

Uruguay National Team for 2019 Rugby World Cup, Japan A1597

2019, Sept. 9 **Litho.** *Perf. 12*
2684 A1597 22p multi 1.90 1.25

No. 2684 was printed in sheets of 5 + label.

Martha Montaner (1955-2016), Senator — A1598

Perf. 12¾x12½

2019, Sept. 16 **Litho.**
2685 A1598 22p multi 1.90 1.25

Amalia de la Vega (1919-2000), Singer — A1599

Perf. 12¾x12½

2019, Sept. 26 **Litho.**
2686 A1599 22p multi 1.90 1.25

No. 2686 was printed in sheets of 8 + central label.

National Emergency System, 10th Anniv. — A1600

2019, Oct. 4 **Litho.** *Perf. 12¾x12½*
2687 A1600 22p multi 1.90 1.25

America Issue A1601

No. 2688 — Traditional foods: a, Asado (beef roast). b, Postre "Chajá" (sponge cake with meringue and fruit).

2019, Oct. 9 **Litho.** *Perf. 12½x12¾*
2688 A1601 Horiz. pair 2.00 4.75
a. 22p multi 1.75 1.25
b. 65p multi 5.00 3.50

World Diabetes Day — A1602

2019, Oct. 25 **Litho.** *Perf. 12½x12¾*
2689 A1602 22p multi 1.90 1.25

Souvenir Sheet

Italian Military Aviation Mission to South America, Cent. A1603

No. 2690: a, Ansaldo A-1 Balilla. b, Caproni Ca.3, Macchi M.7.

2019, Nov. 1 **Litho.** *Perf. 12½x12¾*
2690 A1603 70p Sheet of 2, #a-b 10.75 7.50

Rectangles and Squares MMDLXIX, by José Pedro Costigliolo (1902-85) — A1604

2019, Nov. 6 **Litho.** *Perf. 12¾x12½*
2691 A1604 25p multi 2.10 1.40

25th San Felipe and Santiago 10,000 Meter Race A1605

2019, Nov. 7 **Litho.** *Perf. 12*
2692 A1605 25p multi 2.10 1.40

Ministry of Transportation and Public Works Projects in Montevideo — A1606

No. 2693: a, Adela Reta National Auditorium. b, Executive Tower.

Perf. 12½x12¾

2019, Nov. 11 **Litho.**
2693 A1606 25p Horiz. pair, #a-b 4.25 2.75

Gustavo Nocetti (1959-2002), Tango Singer — A1607

Perf. 12¾x12½

2019, Nov. 19 **Litho.**
2694 A1607 25p multi 2.10 1.40

No. 2694 was printed in sheets of 8 + central label.

International Year of Indigenous Languages — A1608

Perf. 12¾x12½

2019, Nov. 21 **Litho.**
2695 A1608 25p multi 2.10 1.40

No. 2695 was printed in sheets of 8 + central label.

Plants, Birds and Insects A1609

No. 2696: a, Hylocharis chrysura, Myrrhinium var. octandrum. b, Marpesia petreus petreus, Tillandsia aeranthos. c, Xilocopa frontalis, Luehea divaricata. d, Harmonia axyridis, Hypericum connatum.

Perf. 12½x12¾

2019, Nov. 25 **Litho.**
2696 A1609 25p Block or horiz. strip of 4, #a-d 8.50 5.25

Printed in sheets containing two blocks + 4 labels.

Souvenir Sheet

Mohandas K. Gandhi (1869-1948), Indian Nationalist Leader — A1610

No. 2697: a, Gandhi with walking stick. b, Head of Gandhi.

Perf. 12¾x12½

2019, Nov. 27 **Litho.**
2697 A1610 70p Sheet of 2, #a-b, + central label 10.75 7.50

Souvenir Sheet

UNESCO, 70th Anniv. — A1611

2019, Dec. 2 **Litho.** *Perf. 12*
2698 A1611 70p multi 5.50 3.75

Adela Pellegrino, Historian — A1612

2019, Dec. 5 **Litho.** *Perf. 12¾x12½*
2699 A1612 25p multi 2.10 1.40

Christmas — A1613

2019, Dec. 9 Litho. *Perf. 12¾x12½*
2700 A1613 25p multi 2.10 1.40

Campaign to Combat Gender-Based Violence — A1613a

2019, Dec. 12 Litho. *Die Cut*
Self-Adhesive
2700A A1613a S multi 1.90 1.25

No. 2700A sold for 22p on day of issue.

Souvenir Sheet

Prado Museum, Madrid, 200th Anniv. A1614

Perf. 12¾x12½
2019, Dec. 17 Litho.
2701 A1614 70p multi 5.00 3.75

New Year 2020 (Year of the Rat) — A1615

2020, Jan. 20 Litho. *Perf. 12¾x12½*
2702 A1615 70p multi 4.75 3.75

Carnival Costume Designed by Rosario Viñoly — A1616

Perf. 12¾x12½
2020, Feb. 13 Litho.
2703 A1616 25p multi 1.90 1.30

Piriápolis Tourism A1617

No. 2704: a, Piriá's Castle, home of city founder, Francisco Piriá. b, Beach and chaise lounges with wheels.

Perf. 12¾x12½
2020, Feb. 21 Litho.
2704 A1617 25p Horiz. pair, #a-b 3.50 2.60

Souvenir Sheet

First Photograph in Uruguay, 180th Anniv. — A1618

2020, Feb. 27 Litho. *Perf. 12*
2705 A1618 25p multi 1.90 1.30

Idea Vilariño (1920-2009), Writer — A1619

Perf. 12¾x12½
2020, Mar. 10 Litho.
2706 A1619 25p multi 1.90 1.25

No. 2706 was printed in sheets of 8 + central label.

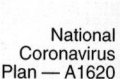

National Coronavirus Plan — A1620

2020, May 13 Litho. *Perf. 12½x12¾*
2707 A1620 25p multi 1.90 1.25

Women's Fashion A1621

No. 2708: a, 25p, Florencia Alba wearing clothes designed by Gonzalo guigou. b, 70p, Sharif Dogliotti wearing clothes designed by Gustavo García.

2020, May 13 Litho. *Perf. 12¾x12½*
2708 A1621 Horiz. pair, #a-b 6.75 4.50

Jacinto Ventura de Molina (1766-1841), Writer — A1622

2020, July 31 Litho. *Perf. 12¾x12½*
2709 A1622 25p multi 1.90 1.25

María Auxiliadora Delgado (1937-2019), First Lady of Uruguay — A1623

2020, July 31 Litho. *Perf. 12¾x12½*
2710 A1623 25p multi 1.90 1.25

No. 2710 was printed in sheets of 8 + central label.

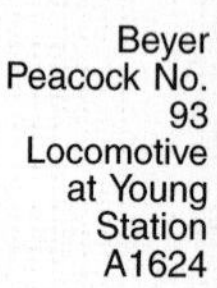

Beyer Peacock No. 93 Locomotive at Young Station A1624

2020, Aug. 17 Litho. *Perf. 12*
2711 A1624 25p multi 1.90 1.25

Town of Young, cent.

Latin American Integration Association, 40th Anniv. — A1625

Perf. 12¾x12½
2020, Aug. 28 Litho.
2712 A1625 70p multi 4.75 3.25

Architecture in Montevideo — A1626

No. 2713: a, 25p, Jackson Chapel, Church of the Holy Family, designed by Victor Rabú. b, 70p, Lapido Building, designed by Juan María Aubriot and Ricardo Valabrega.

2020, Sept. 3 Litho. *Perf. 12¾x12½*
2713 A1626 Horiz. pair, #a-b 6.75 4.50

America issue.

Tsakos Group, 50th Anniv. A1627

María Tsakos Foundation Headquarters A1628

Perf. 12½x12¾
2020, Sept. 21 Litho.
2714 A1627 70p multi 5.00 3.50

Perf. 12¾x12½
2715 A1628 70p multi 5.00 3.50

Nos. 2714 and 2715 were each printed in sheets of 2 + central label.

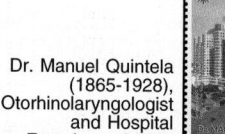

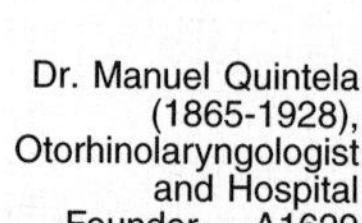
Dr. Manuel Quintela (1865-1928), Otorhinolaryngologist and Hospital Founder — A1629

Perf. 12¾x12½
2020, Sept. 25 Litho.
2716 A1629 25p multi 1.90 1.25

Miniature Sheet

World Tourism Day A1630

No. 2717 — Inscriptions: a, Safari minero (Mining safari). b, Valle Edén-Ecotoruism (Edén Valley-Ecotourism). c, Area Protegida Valle del Lunarejo (Lunarejo Valley Protected Area). d, Area Protegida Paso Centurion (Centurion Pass Protected Area). e, Canotaje / Pesca Artesenal (Rafting / Artisanal Fishing). f, Enotourism Ruta del Vino (Oenotourism Wine Route). g, Quesos y Lacteos (Cheese and Dairy Products). h, Tirolesa, Rapel, Mountain Bike (Ziplining, Rappelling, Mountain Biking). i, Area Protegida Cerro Verde (Cerro Verde Protected Area). j, Aceite de Oliva (Olive Oil).

Perf. 12½x12¾
2020, Sept. 30 Litho.
2717 A1630 25p Sheet of 10, #a-j 19.00 12.00

Souvenir Sheet

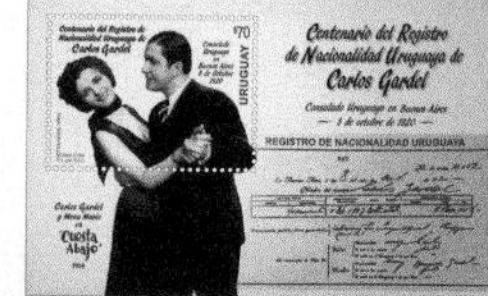
Application for Uruguayan Citizenship by Carlos Gardel (1890-1935), Tango Singer, Cent. — A1631

2020, Oct. 8 Litho. *Perf. 12½x12¾*
2718 A1631 70p multi 4.75 3.25

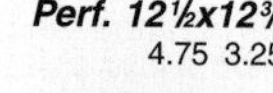

Mariano Arana, Architect and Mayor of Montevideo A1632

Francisco "Panchito" Nolé, Musician A1633

Margarita Kemayd, Swimmer — A1634

2020, Oct. 9 Litho. *Perf. 12¾x12½*
2719 Strip of 3 5.75 3.75
a. A1632 25p multi 1.90 1.25
b. A1633 25p multi 1.90 1.25
c. A1634 25p multi 1.90 1.25

Human Rights for Migrants A1635

2020, Oct. 9 Litho. *Perf. 12½x12¾*
2720 A1635 25p multi 1.90 1.25

Souvenir Sheet

Florence Nightingale (1820-1910), Nurse — A1636

2020, Oct. 22 Litho. *Perf. 12¾x12½*
2721 A1636 70p multi 4.75 3.25

Souvenir Sheet

Diplomatic Relations Between Uruguay and Poland, Cent. — A1637

No. 2722 — Storks: a, 25p, Ciconia maguari. b, 70p, Ciconia ciconia.

2020, Oct. 23 Litho. *Perf. 12¾x12½*
2722 A1637 Sheet of 2, #a-b 6.75 4.50

Miniature Sheet

Ludwig van Beethoven (1770-1827), Composer — A1638

No. 2723: a, Flautist. b, Cellist. c, Violinist. d, Horn players.

2020, Oct. 27 Litho. *Perf. 12¼x12¾*
2723 A1638 70p Sheet of 4, #a-d 13.00 13.00

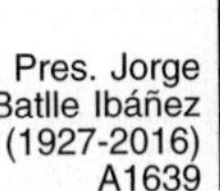

Pres. Jorge Batlle Ibáñez (1927-2016) A1639

2020, Oct. 29 Litho. *Perf. 12½x12¾*
2724 A1639 25p multi 1.25 1.25

Minas de Corrales, Cent. — A1640

2020, Nov. 9 Litho. *Perf. 12¾x12½*
2725 A1640 27p multi 1.30 1.30

Souvenir Sheet

Uruguayan Society of Surgery, Cent. — A1641

No. 2726: a, 27p, Surgeons and surgical instruments. b, 75p, Surgeons operating on patient.

Perf. 12¾x12¼
2020, Nov. 11 Litho.
2726 A1641 Sheet of 2, #a-b 5.00 5.00

Souvenir Sheet

The Songs of Maldoror, Poetic Novel by Isidore Ducasse (Comte de Lautréamont) (1846-70) — A1642

Perf. 12¾x12¼
2020, Nov. 24 Litho.
2727 A1642 75p multi 3.50 3.50

José María Iparraguirre (1820-81), Poet and Musician — A1643

No. 2728: a, Iparraguirre. b. Iparraguirre playing guitar.

2020, Dec. 3 Litho. *Perf. 12*
2728 Pair + 2 labels 4.75 4.75
a. A1643 27p multi 1.25 1.25
b. A1643 75p multi 3.50 3.50

Souvenir Sheet

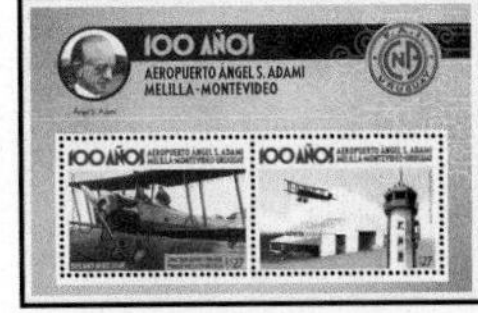

Angel S. Adami Airport, Montevideo, Cent. — A1644

No. 2729: a, Avro 504K biplane. b, Biplane, hangar and control tower.

2020, Dec. 7 Litho. *Perf. 12¼x12¾*
2729 A1644 27p Sheet of 2, #a-b 2.60 2.60

Flowers and Pollinators — A1645

No. 2730: a, Cucurbita manima, Xilocopa augusti. b, Sesbania punicea, Augochlora amphitrite.

2020, Dec. 8 Litho. *Perf. 12¼x12¾*
2730 A1645 27p Pair, #a-b 2.60 2.60

Printed in sheets containing 3 each Nos. 2730a-2730b + 2 labels.

Miniature Sheet

M'Bopicuá Biopark, 20th Anniv. — A1646

No. 2731: a, Porphyrio martinica. b, Gubernatrix cristata. c, Leopardus wiedii. d, Pecari tojacu.

2020, Dec. 9 Litho. *Perf. 12¼x12¾*
2731 A1646 27p Sheet of 4, #a-d 5.25 5.25

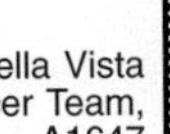

Bella Vista Soccer Team, Cent. — A1647

Perf. 12¼x12¾
2020, Dec. 10 Litho.
2732 A1647 27p multi 1.25 1.25

No. 2732 was printed in sheets of 8 + central label.

Miniature Sheet

Christmas — A1648

No. 2733 — Stained-glass windows of Jackson Chapel, Montevideo, depicting: a, Annunciation. b, Nativity. c, Adoration of the Magi. d, Young Jesus preaching in the temple. e, Flight into Egypt.

2020, Dec. 16 Litho. *Perf. 12*
2733 A1648 27p Sheet of 5, #a-e, + label 6.50 6.50

Miniature Sheet

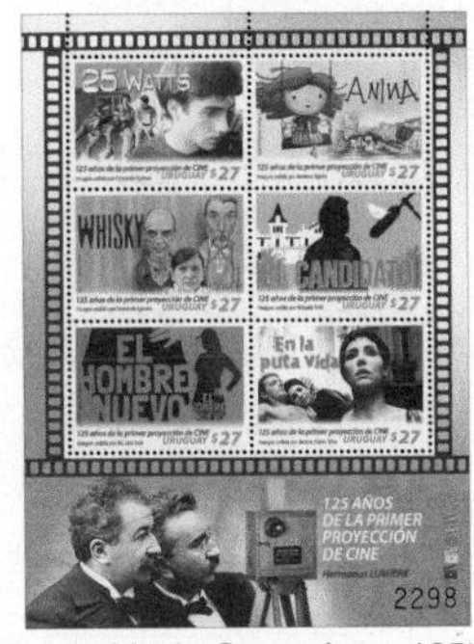

Public Movie Screenings, 125th Anniv. — A1649

No. 2734 — Uruguayan-produced movies: a, 25 Watts, 2001. b, Anina, 2013. c, Whisky, 2004. d, El Candidato (The Candidate), 2016. e, El Hombre Nuevo (The New Man), 2015. f, En la Puta Vida (In this Tricky Life), 2001.

Perf. 12¼x12¾
2020, Dec. 18 Litho.
2734 A1649 27p Sheet of 6, #a-f 7.75 7.75

New Year 2021 (Year of the Ox) — A1650

2021, Feb. 1 Litho. *Perf. 12¾x12¼*
2735 A1650 75p multi 3.50 3.50

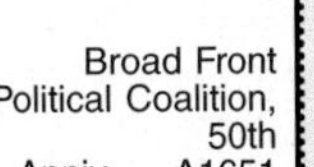

Broad Front Political Coalition, 50th Anniv. — A1651

2021, Feb. 4 Litho. *Perf. 12¼x12¾*
2736 A1651 27p multi 1.25 1.25

Susana Sienra (1920-2016), Wife of Exiled Political Leader Wilson Ferreria Aldunate A1652

2021, Mar. 8 Litho. *Perf. 12¼x12¾*
2737 A1652 27p multi 1.25 1.25

María Espínola Espínola (1878-1963), Educator — A1653

Perf. 12¾x12¼
2021, Mar. 18 Litho.
2738 A1653 27p multi 1.25 1.25

No. 2738 was printed in sheets of 8 + central label.

Uruguay Fencing Federation, Cent. — A1654

No. 2739: a, Fencers in wheelchairs. b, Fencers. c, Fencer and Nicolas Revello.

2021, May 27 Litho. *Perf. 12¼x12¾*
2739 A1654 Strip of 3 6.00 6.00
a.-b. 27p Either single 1.25 1.25
c. 75p multi 3.50 3.50

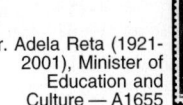

Dr. Adela Reta (1921-2001), Minister of Education and Culture — A1655

2021, July 9 Litho. *Perf. 12¾x12½*
2740 A1655 27p multi 1.25 1.25

2020 Summer Olympics, Tokyo A1656

2021, July 14 Litho. *Perf. 12*
2741 A1656 75p multi 3.50 3.50

The 2020 Summer Olympics were postponed until 2021 because of the COVID-19 pandemic.

Diplomatic Relations Between Uruguay and Japan, Cent. — A1657

2021, July 27 Litho. *Perf. 12½x12¾*
2742 A1657 75p multi 3.50 3.50

Beneficial Insects — A1658

Design: Trifolium pratense and Bombus bellicosus.

2021, July 29 Litho. *Perf. 12½x12¾*
2743 A1658 27p multi 1.25 1.25

Souvenir Sheet

Albino Camelus Dromidarius — A1659

Perf. 12¾x12½
2021, Aug. 11 Litho.
2744 A1659 27p multi 1.30 1.30

Talice Reserve and Ecopark, 30th anniv.

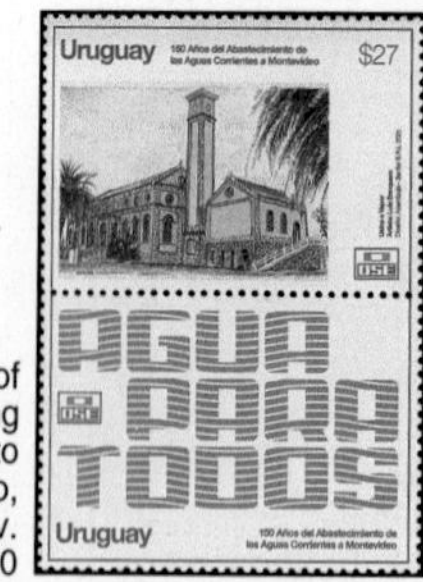

Delivery of Drinking Water to Montevideo, 150th Anniv. A1660

2021, Aug. 17 **Litho.** ***Perf. 12***
2745 A1660 27p multi + label 1.30 1.30

Portrait of a Tall Man, Painting by Manuel Espínola Gómez (1921-2003) — A1661

Perf. 12¾x12½

2021, Aug. 19 **Litho.**
2746 A1661 27p multi 1.30 1.30

Souvenir Sheet

ROU 24 Pedro Campbell — A1662

Perf. 12½x12¾

2021, Aug. 30 **Litho.**
2747 A1662 75p multi 3.50 3.50

First Uruguayan Antarctic naval mission, 30th anniv.

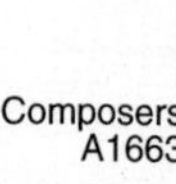

Composers A1663

No. 2748: a, Ramón Rodríguez (1886-1957). b, César Cortinas (1890-1918). c, Luis Sambucetti (1860-1926).

2021, Sept. 1 **Litho.** ***Perf. 12½x12¾***
2748 Strip of 3 4.00 4.00
a.-c. A1663 27p Any single 1.30 1.30

Printed in sheets of 9 containing 3 strips.

José Enrique Rodó (1871-1917), Writer — A1664

Perf. 12¾x12½

2021, Sept. 23 **Litho.**
2749 A1664 27p multi 1.25 1.25

Peñarol Athletic Club, 130th Anniv. A1665

2021, Sept. 28 **Litho.** ***Perf. 12***
2750 A1665 27p multi 1.25 1.25

Dr. Roberto Caldeyro-Barcia (1921-96), Perinatologist A1666

Perf. 12½x12¾

2021, Sept. 29 **Litho.**
2751 A1666 27p multi 1.25 1.25

Rural Association of Uruguay, 150th Anniv. — A1667

2021, Oct. 3 **Litho.** ***Perf. 12½x12¾***
2752 A1667 27p multi 1.25 1.25

No. 2752 was printed in sheets of 8 + central label.

Mercosur, 30th Anniv. — A1668

2021, Oct. 18 **Litho.** ***Perf. 12½x12¾***
2753 A1668 75p multi 3.50 3.50

Xacobeo Holy Year A1669

No. 2754: a, Way of St. James route marker in Montevideo (sister city of Santiago de Compostela, Spain) and sailboat. b, Pilgrims and Santiago de Compostela Cathedral.

2021, Oct. 18 **Litho.** ***Perf. 12***
2754 A1669 Horiz. pair 4.75 4.75
a. 27p multi 1.25 1.25
b. 75p multi 3.50 3.50

Carlos Julio Pereyra (1922-2020), Politician A1670

"I Say Yes to Youth in Parliament" A1671

2021, Oct. 19 **Litho.** ***Perf. 12½x12¾***
2755 A1670 27p multi 1.25 1.25
2756 A1671 75p multi 3.50 3.50

Democracy Day.

Bank of the Oriental Republic of Uruguay, 125th Anniv. — A1672

2021, Oct. 22 **Litho.** ***Perf. 12½x12¾***
2757 A1672 27p multi 1.25 1.25

No. 2757 was printed in sheets of 3 + 3 labels.

Souvenir Sheet

Trucks of General Celestino Bové Combat Engineers Batallion — A1673

2021, Oct. 27 **Litho.** ***Perf. 12¾x12½***
2758 A1673 27p multi 1.25 1.25

General Celestino Bové Combat Engineers Batallion No. 4, cent.

Durazno, 200th Anniv. A1674

No. 2759: a, Bicentennial emblem, building and flags of Uruguay. b, Bicentennial emblem.

2021, Oct. 29 **Litho.** ***Perf. 12¾x12½***
2759 A1674 27p Horiz. pair, #a-b 2.50 2.50

Printed in sheets containing four pairs + central label.

America Issue A1675

No. 2760: a, Tourists partaking in outdoor activities. b, Tourists traveling during COVID-19 pandemic.

Perf. 12½x12¾

2021, Nov. 10 **Litho.**
2760 A1675 Horiz. pair 5.00 5.00
a. 30p multi 1.40 1.40
b. 75p multi 3.50 3.50

Souvenir Sheet

Diplomatic Relations Between Uruguay and Czech Republic and Slovakia, Cent. — A1676

No. 1676: a, Prague Castle, Czech Republic. b, Bratislava Castle, Slovakia.

2021, Nov. 17 **Litho.** ***Perf. 12***
2761 A1676 75p Sheet of 2, #a-b 6.75 6.75

Souvenir Sheet

Canticle of Hell A1677

Perf. 12½x12¾

2021, Nov. 24 **Litho.**
2762 A1677 75p multi 3.50 3.50

Dante Alighieri (c. 1265-1321), writer.

Anita Garibaldi (1821-49), Italian Revolutionary A1678

Perf. 12½x12¾

2021, Nov. 25 **Litho.**
2763 A1678 75p multi 3.50 3.50

See Brazil No. 3466.

Generation of '45 Writers — A1679

No. 2764: a, Emir Rodríguez Monegal (1921-85). b, Amanda Berenguer (1921-2010). c, José Pedro Díaz (1921-2006).

Perf. 12½x12¾

2021, Nov. 30 **Litho.**
2764 Strip of 3 4.25 4.25
a.-c. A1679 30p Any single 1.40 1.40

Souvenir Sheet

Naval School Building, Cent. A1680

2021, Dec. 9 **Litho.** ***Perf. 12½x12¾***
2765 A1680 30p multi 1.40 1.40

Crabs — A1681

No. 1681: a, Callinectes sapidus. b, Leptuca uruguayensis.

Perf. 12½x12¾

2021, Dec. 17 **Litho.**
2766 A1681 30p Vert. pair, #a-b, + bottom label 2.75 2.75

Printed in sheets containing four each Nos. 2766a-2766b + 4 labels.

Christmas — A1682

Perf. 12¾x12½

2021, Dec. 17 **Litho.**
2767 A1682 30p multi 1.40 1.40

New Year 2022 (Year of the Tiger) — A1683

2022, Jan. 27 Litho. *Perf. 12¾x12½*
2768 A1683 75p multi 3.50 3.50

General Artigas Military High School, 75th Anniv. — A1684

Perf. 12¾x12½
2022, Mar. 15 Litho.
2769 A1684 30p multi 1.50 1.50

Oriental Ladies Philanthropic Society — A1685

Perf. 12¾x12½
2022, Mar. 23 Litho.
2770 A1685 30p multi 1.50 1.50

Artigas Department Tourism — A1686

No. 2771: a, Samba dancer. b, Geode.

2022, Apr. 8 Litho. *Perf. 12¾x12½*
2771 A1686 30p Horiz. pair, #a-b 3.00 3.00

Printed in sheets containing four pairs + central label.

Juanicó, 150th Anniv. — A1687

2022, May 13 Litho. *Perf. 12½x12¾*
2772 A1687 30p multi 1.50 1.50

Association of Hotels and Restaurants of Uruguay, Cent. — A1688

2022, May 19 Litho. *Perf. 12¾x12½*
2773 A1688 30p multi 1.50 1.50

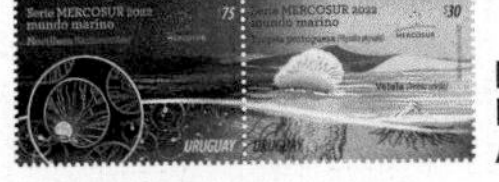

Marine Life A1689

No. 2774: a, Physalia physalis, Velella velella. b, Noctiluca scintillans.

2022, June 1 Litho. *Perf. 12½x12¾*
2774 A1689 Horiz. pair 5.25 5.25
a. 30p multi 1.50 1.50
b. 75p multi 3.75 3.75

Pres. Tabaré Vázquez (1940-2020), and Children A1690

Perf. 12½x12¾
2022, June 20 Litho.
2775 A1690 30p multi 1.60 1.60

International Day of Parliamentarism A1691

Perf. 12½x12¾
2022, June 30 Litho.
2776 A1691 75p multi 4.00 4.00

Interparliamentary Union, 133rd anniv.

Souvenir Sheet

Flagging of Navy Ships Purchased From Germany, 30th Anniv. — A1692

Perf. 12½x12¾
2022, Aug. 19 Litho.
2777 A1692 30p multi 1.50 1.50

Climb Up the Hill, Painting by Aldo Peralta (1933-78) A1693

Perf. 12½x12¾
2022, Aug. 31 Litho.
2778 A1693 30p multi 1.50 1.50

Historical and Cultural Institute and Museum of Fine Arts of San José, 75th anniv.

Amílcar Vasconcellos (1915-99), Minister of Economy and Finance A1694

Perf. 12½x12¾
2022, Sept. 15 Litho.
2779 A1694 30p multi 1.50 1.50

Democracy Day.

Concepción "China" Zorrilla (1922-2015), Actress and Director — A1695

Perf. 12¾x12½
2022, Sept. 20 Litho.
2780 A1695 30p multi 1.50 1.50

Souvenir Sheet

Crash of Uruguayan Air Force Flight 571 in the Andes, 50th Anniv. — A1696

2022, Oct. 7 Litho. *Perf. 12¾x12½*
2781 A1696 45p multi 2.25 2.25

National Administration of Power Plants and Electrical Transmissions, 110th Anniv. — A1697

2022, Oct. 21 Litho. *Perf. 12¾x12½*
2782 A1697 30p multi 1.50 1.50

Souvenir Sheet

Misiones Armored Cavalry Regiment No. 5, 125th Anniv. — A1698

Perf. 12½x12¾
2022, Nov. 16 Litho.
2783 A1698 32p multi 1.60 1.60

Pasteur Hospital, Montevideo, Cent. — A1699

Perf. 12¾x12½
2022, Nov. 22 Litho.
2784 A1699 84p multi 4.25 4.25

Dancers — A1700

Perf. 12¾x12½
2022, Nov. 28 Litho.
2785 A1700 84p multi 4.25 4.25

America issue.

Souvenir Sheet

Charrúa Combat Engineers Battalion No. 3, Cent. — A1701

Perf. 12¾x12½
2022, Nov. 29 Litho.
2786 A1701 32p multi 1.60 1.60

Christmas — A1702

Perf. 12¾x12½
2022, Dec. 19 Litho.
2787 A1702 32p multi 1.60 1.60

Punta del Diablo Tourism A1703

No. 2788: a, Fishing boat. b, Punta Palmar Lighthouse.

Perf. 12½x12¾
2022, Dec. 21 Litho.
2788 A1703 32p Pair, #a-b 1.60 1.60

Printed in sheets containing 3 each of Nos. 2788a-2788b.

New Year 2023 (Year of the Rabbit) — A1704

2023, Jan. 19 Litho. *Perf. 12¾x12½*
2789 A1704 84p multi 4.50 4.50

Rural Woman With Basket of Farm Crops — A1705

Perf. 12¾x12½
2023, Mar. 29 Litho.
2790 A1705 32p multi 1.75 1.75

Biodiversity — A1706

No. 2791: a, Collage of animals and marine life created by school children. b, Bird from collage. c, Fish from collage. d, Mammal from collage.

Perf. 12½x12¾
2023, Mar. 30 Litho.
2791 A1706 32p Block or strip of 4, #a-d 6.75 6.75

SEMI-POSTAL STAMPS

Indigent Old Man — SP1

Unwmk.

1930, Nov. 13 Engr. *Perf. 12*

B1 SP1 1c + 1c dark violet .30 .30
B2 SP1 2c + 2c deep green .30 .30
B3 SP1 5c + 5c red .45 .45
B4 SP1 8c + 8c gray violet .45 .45
Nos. B1-B4 (4) 1.50 1.50

The surtax on these stamps was for a fund to assist the aged.

For surcharge see No. 419.

Catalogue values for unused stamps in this section, from this point to the end of the section, are for Never Hinged items.

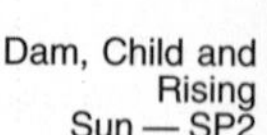

Dam, Child and Rising Sun — SP2

Wmk. 327

1959, Sept. 29 Litho. *Perf. 11½*

B5 SP2 5c + 10c green & org .30 .25
B6 SP2 10c + 10c dk bl & org .30 .25
B7 SP2 1p + 10c purple & org .80 .50
Nos. B5-B7, CB1-CB2 (5) 2.20 1.80

National recovery. For surcharges see Nos. 727, Q100.

Souvenir Sheet

Taipei '96, Intl. Philatelic Exhibition — SP3

Unwmk.

1996, Oct. 21 Litho. *Perf. 12*

B8 SP3 7p +3p multi 8.25 8.00

Gen. Artigas Central Railway Station, Montevideo, Cent. — SP4

a, Baldwin, 1889. b, Hudswell Clarke, 1895. c, Luis Andreoni, engineer & architect. d, Hawthorn Leslie, 1914. e, General Electric, 1954.

Perf. 12½

1997, July 15 Litho. Unwmk.

B9 SP4 4p +1p, Strip of 5, #a.-e. 13.00 12.00

Diana, Princess of Wales (1961-97) — SP5

Designs: No. B10, In protective clothing. No. B11, In blue blouse. No. B12, In white.

1998, Jan. 15 Litho. *Perf. 12½*

B10 SP5 2p +1p multi 2.75 2.50
B11 SP5 2p +1p multi 2.75 2.50

Souvenir Sheet

Perf. 12

B12 SP5 12p +3p multi 15.00 15.00

No. B12 contains one 35x50mm stamp.

Occupations Type of 2008

Serpentine Die Cut 11¼

2007, Nov. 18 Litho.

Self-Adhesive

B13 A1216 5p +2p Baker 1.10 .90

General José Gervasio Artigas (1764-1850) and Quotation — SP6

2014, Apr. 28 Litho. *Die Cut*

Self-Adhesive

B14 SP6 15p+2p multi 2.90 2.50

AIR POST STAMPS

No. 91 Overprinted in Dark Blue, Red or Green

1921-22 Unwmk. *Perf. 14*

C1 A38 25c bister brn (Bl) 18.00 15.00
a. Black overprint 800.00 800.00
C2 A38 25c bister brn (R) 7.00 7.00
a. Inverted overprint 100.00 100.00
C3 A38 25c bister brn (G) ('22) 7.00 7.00
Nos. C1-C3 (3) 32.00 29.00

This overprint, on No. C3, also exists in light yellow green. Value, $85 unused and used.

No. C1a was not issued. Some authorities consider it an overprint color trial.

AP2

Wmk. 188

1924, Jan. 2 Litho. *Perf. 11½*

C4 AP2 6c dark blue 2.50 2.00
C5 AP2 10c scarlet 3.50 3.00
C6 AP2 20c deep green 5.00 5.00
Nos. C4-C6 (3) 11.00 10.00

Heron — AP3

1925, Aug. 24 *Perf. 12½*

Inscribed "MONTEVIDEO"

C7 AP3 14c blue & blk 35.00 25.00

Inscribed "FLORIDA"

C8 AP3 14c blue & blk 35.00 17.50

These stamps were used only on Aug. 25, 1925, the cent. of the Assembly of Florida, on letters intended to be carried by airplane between Montevideo and Florida, a town 60 miles north. The stamps were not delivered to the public but were affixed to the letters and canceled by post office clerks. Later uncanceled stamps came on the market.

One authority believes Nos. C7-C8 served as registration stamps on these two attempted special flights.

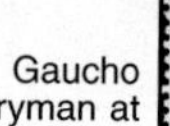

Gaucho Cavalryman at Rincón — AP4

1925, Sept. 24 *Perf. 11*

C9 AP4 45c blue green 17.50

Centenary of Battle of Rincon. Used only on Sept. 24. No. C9 was affixed and canceled by post office clerks.

Albatross — AP5

1926, Mar. 3 Wmk. 188 *Imperf.*

C10 AP5 6c dark blue 2.00 2.00
C11 AP5 10c vermilion 2.50 2.50
C12 AP5 20c blue green 3.00 3.00
C13 AP5 25c violet 3.50 3.50
Nos. C10-C13 (4) 11.00 11.00

Excellent counterfeits exist.

1928, June 25 *Perf. 11*

C14 AP5 10c green 3.00 2.00
C15 AP5 20c orange 5.00 3.00
C16 AP5 30c indigo 5.00 3.00
C17 AP5 38c green 8.50 6.00
C18 AP5 40c yellow 8.50 6.00
C19 AP5 50c violet 10.00 7.50
C20 AP5 76c orange 20.00 17.50
C21 AP5 1p red 20.00 15.00
C22 AP5 1.14p indigo 45.00 35.00
C23 AP5 1.52p yellow 75.00 60.00
C24 AP5 1.90p violet 95.00 75.00
C25 AP5 3.80p red 225.00 170.00
Nos. C14-C25 (12) 520.00 400.00

Counterfeits of No. C25 exist.

1929, Aug. 23 Unwmk.

C26 AP5 4c olive brown 3.00 3.00

The design was redrawn for Nos. C14-C26. The numerals are narrower, "CENTS" is 1mm high instead of 2½mm and imprint letters touch the bottom frame line.

Pegasus — AP6

1929-43 Engr. *Perf. 12½*

Size: 34x23mm

C27 AP6 1c red lilac ('30) .40 .40
C28 AP6 1c dk blue ('32) .40 .40
C29 AP6 2c yellow ('30) .40 .40
C30 AP6 2c olive grn ('32) .40 .40
C31 AP6 4c Prus blue ('30) .70 .70
C32 AP6 4c car rose ('32) .70 .70
C33 AP6 6c dull vio ('30) .70 .70
C34 AP6 6c red brown ('32) .70 .70
C35 AP6 8c red orange 3.00 2.50
C36 AP6 8c gray ('30) 4.00 3.00
C36A AP6 8c brt green ('43) 2.50 2.00
C37 AP6 16c indigo 2.00 1.50
C38 AP6 16c rose ('30) 3.25 3.00
C39 AP6 24c claret 3.00 2.50
C40 AP6 24c brt violet ('30) 4.25 3.50
C41 AP6 30c bister 3.00 2.75
C42 AP6 30c dk green ('30) 2.00 1.50
C43 AP6 40c dk brown 5.50 5.00
C44 AP6 40c yel org ('30) 6.00 5.00
C45 AP6 60c blue green 5.00 3.25
C46 AP6 60c emerald ('30) 8.50 7.00
C47 AP6 60c dp orange ('31) 3.00 2.00
C48 AP6 80c dk ultra 8.00 7.00
C49 AP6 80c green ('30) 15.00 12.00
C50 AP6 90c light blue 8.00 6.00
C51 AP6 90c dk olive grn ('30) 15.00 12.00
C52 AP6 1p car rose ('30) 10.00 7.50
C53 AP6 1.20p olive grn 22.00 20.00
C54 AP6 1.20p dp car ('30) 30.00 26.00
C55 AP6 1.50p red brown 25.00 20.00
C56 AP6 1.50p blk brn ('30) 20.00 15.00
C57 AP6 3p deep red 40.00 35.00
C58 AP6 3p ultra ('30) 30.00 25.00
C59 AP6 4.50p black 75.00 55.00
C60 AP6 4.50p redsh pur ('30) 45.00 35.00
C60A AP6 10p dp ultra ('43) 17.00 12.00
Nos. C27-C60A (36) 419.40 336.40

See Nos. C63-C82. For surcharges see Nos. C106-C112, C114.

Nos. 450, 452 Overprinted in Red

1934, Jan. 1 *Perf. 11½*

C61 A130 17c ver, gray & vio 20.00 15.00
a. Sheet of 6 140.00
b. Gray omitted 150.00
c. Double overrprint 150.00
C62 A130 36c red, blk & yel 20.00 15.00
a. Sheet of 6 140.00

7th Pan-American Conference, Montevideo.

Pegasus Type of 1929

1935 Engr. *Perf. 12½*

Size: 31½x21mm

C63 AP6 15c dull yellow 2.50 2.00
C64 AP6 22c brick red 1.50 1.40
C65 AP6 30c brown violet 2.50 2.00
C66 AP6 37c gray lilac 1.40 1.00
C67 AP6 40c rose lake 2.00 1.40
C68 AP6 47c rose 4.00 3.50
C69 AP6 50c Prus blue 1.40 .80
C70 AP6 52c dp ultra 4.00 3.50
C71 AP6 57c grnsh blue 2.00 1.75
C72 AP6 62c olive green 1.75 .80
C73 AP6 87c gray green 5.00 4.00
C74 AP6 1p olive 3.50 2.25
C75 AP6 1.12p org brown 3.50 2.25
C76 AP6 1.20p bister brn 15.00 12.00
C77 AP6 1.27p red brown 15.00 13.00
C78 AP6 1.62p rose 10.00 9.00
C79 AP6 2p brown rose 17.00 14.00
C80 AP6 2.12p dk slate grn 17.00 14.00
C81 AP6 3p dull blue 15.00 13.00
C82 AP6 5p orange 60.00 60.00
Nos. C63-C82 (20) 184.05 161.65

Counterfeits exist.

For surcharges, see Nos. C106-C112.

Power Dam on Rio Negro — AP7

Imprint: "Imp. Nacional" at center

1937-41 Litho.

C83 AP7 20c lt green ('38) 5.50 4.00
C84 AP7 35c red brown 8.00 6.50
C85 AP7 62c blue grn ('38) .80 .30
C86 AP7 68c yel org ('38) 2.00 1.50
C86A AP7 68c pale vio brn ('41) 1.75 .70
C87 AP7 75c violet 7.50 5.00
C88 AP7 1p dp pink ('38) 2.50 1.75
C89 AP7 1.38p rose ('38) 25.00 20.00
C90 AP7 3p dk blue ('40) 17.00 12.00
Nos. C83-C90 (9) 70.05 51.75

Imprint at left

C91 AP7 8c pale green ('39) 2.50 .75
C92 AP7 20c lt green ('38) 7.50 1.25

For surcharge and overprint see Nos. 545, C120.

Plane over Sculptured Oxcart — AP8

1939-44 *Perf. 12½*

C93 AP8 20c slate .50 .40
C94 AP8 20c lt violet ('43) .80 .80
C95 AP8 20c blue ('44) .60 .40
C96 AP8 35c red 1.00 .80

C97 AP8 50c brown org 1.00 .30
C98 AP8 75c deep pink 1.10 .25
C99 AP8 1p dp blue ('40) 3.25 .60
C100 AP8 1.38p brt vio 5.50 2.25
C101 AP8 1.38p yel org ('44) 5.00 4.00
C102 AP8 2p blue 8.00 1.40
a. Perf. 11 7.00 1.10
C103 AP8 5p rose lilac 10.00 2.25
C104 AP8 5p blue grn ('44) 15.00 7.00
C105 AP8 10p rose ('40) 100.00 65.00
Nos. C93-C105 (13) 151.75 85.45

Counterfeits exist. These differ in design detail and are perfed other than 12½.

For surcharges see Nos. C116-C119.

Nos. C68, C71, C75, C73, C77-C78, C80 Surcharged in Red or Black

1944, Nov. 22

C106 AP6 40c on 47c 1.00 1.00
C107 AP6 40c on 57c (R) 1.00 1.00
C108 AP6 74c on 1.12p 1.00 1.00
C109 AP6 79c on 87c 2.00 2.00
C110 AP6 79c on 1.27p 3.00 3.00
C111 AP6 1.20p on 1.62p 2.00 2.00
C112 AP6 1.43p on 2.12p (R) 2.00 2.00
Nos. C106-C112 (7) 12.00 12.00

Catalogue values for unused stamps in this section, from this point to the end of the section, are for Never Hinged items.

Legislature Building — AP9

Unwmk.

1945, May 11 Engr. *Perf. 11*

C113 AP9 2p ultra 5.25 2.00

Type of 1929, Srchd. in Violet

1945, Aug. 14 *Perf. 12½*

C114 AP6 44c on 75c brown 2.00 .50
a. Double overprint 45.00

Allied Nations' victory in Europe.

"La Eolo" — AP10

1945, Oct. 31 *Perf. 11*

C115 AP10 8c green 4.25 1.00

Nos. C97 and C101 Srchd. in Violet, Black or Blue

1945-46 *Perf. 12½*

C116 AP8 14c on 50c (V) ('46) 1.75 .50
a. Inverted surcharge 85.00
C117 AP8 23c on 1.38p 1.75 .50
a. Inverted surcharge 175.00
C118 AP8 23c on 50c 1.75 .50
a. Inverted surcharge 175.00
C119 AP8 1p on 1.38p (Bl) 1.75 .50
a. Inverted surcharge 175.00
Nos. C116-C119 (4) 7.00 2.00

Victory of the Allied Nations in WWII.

No. C85 Overprinted in Black

1946, Jan. 9

C120 AP7 62c blue green 2.25 1.00

Issued to commemorate the inauguration of the Black River Power Dam.

AP11

1946-49 Black Overprint Litho.

C121 AP11 8c car rose .40 .25
a. Inverted overprint
C122 AP11 50c brown .85 .25
a. Double overprint 25.00
C123 AP11 1p lt bl 1.60 .40
C124 AP11 2p ol ('49) 4.25 2.00
C125 AP11 3p lil rose 7.50 3.00
C126 AP11 5p rose car 12.50 6.00
Nos. C121-C126 (6) 27.10 11.90

Four-Motored Plane — AP12

National Airport — AP13

1947-49 *Perf. 11½, 12½*

C129 AP12 3c org brn ('49) .25 .25
C130 AP12 8c car rose ('49) .45 .25
C131 AP12 14c ultra .75 .30
C132 AP12 23c emerald .60 .25
C133 AP13 1p car & brn ('49) 1.75 .40
C134 AP13 3p ultra & brn ('49) 4.50 1.60
C135 AP13 5p grn & brn ('49) 10.00 4.00
C136 AP13 10p lil rose & brn 16.00 6.00
Nos. C129-C136 (8) 34.30 13.05

Counterfeits exist, perf 11¼. Design size of genuine stamps is 34½x24mm, while forgeries are 33½x23½mm.

See Nos. C145-C164. For surcharges see Nos. C206, Q94.

AP14

Black Overprint

1948, June 9 *Perf. 12½*

C137 AP14 12c blue .35 .25
C138 AP14 24c Prus grn .75 .25
C139 AP14 36c slate blue .85 .35
Nos. C137-C139 (3) 1.95 .85

School of Architecture, University of Uruguay — AP15

Designs: 27c, Medical School. 31c, Engineering School. 36c, University.

1949, Dec. 7

C141 AP15 15c carmine .40 .25
C142 AP15 27c chocolate .40 .25
C143 AP15 31c dp ultra .80 .25
C144 AP15 36c dull green 1.10 .35
Nos. C141-C144 (4) 2.70 1.10

Founding of the University of Uruguay, cent.

Plane Type of 1947-49

1952-59 Unwmk. *Perf. 11, 12½*

C145 AP12 10c blk ('54) .30 .25
C146 AP12 10c lt red ('58) .30 .25
a. Imperf., pair 30.00
C147 AP12 15c org brn .45 .25
a. Vert. pair, imperf btwn. 42.50
C148 AP12 20c lil rose ('54) .55 .25
C149 AP12 21c purple .60 .25
C150 AP12 27c yel grn ('57) .60 .25
C151 AP12 31c chocolate .75 .25
C152 AP12 36c ultra .60 .25
C153 AP12 36c blk ('58) .60 .25
C154 AP12 50c lt bl ('57) 1.10 .50
C155 AP12 50c bl blk ('58) .75 .25
C156 AP12 62c dl sl bl ('53) 1.40 .50
C157 AP12 65c rose ('53) 1.40 .50
C158 AP12 84c org ('59) 1.75 .70
C159 AP12 1.08p vio brn 2.60 .80
C160 AP12 2p Prus bl 3.75 1.40
C161 AP12 3p red org 5.50 1.75
C162 AP12 5p dk gray grn 10.50 4.00
C163 AP12 5p gray ('57) 5.50 2.50
C164 AP12 10p dp grn ('55) 26.00 12.50
Nos. C145-C164 (20) 65.00 27.65

Planes and Show Emblem — AP16

Unwmk.

1956, Jan. 5 Litho. *Perf. 11*

C166 AP16 20c ultra .85 .40
C167 AP16 31c olive grn 1.00 .30
C168 AP16 36c car rose 1.60 .40
Nos. C166-C168 (3) 3.45 1.10

First Exposition of National Products.

Type of Regular Issue and

José Batlle y Ordonez AP17

Designs: 10c, Full-face portrait without hand. 36c, Portrait facing right.

Perf. 13½

1956, Dec. 15 Wmk. 90 Photo.

C169 A178 10c magenta .65 .25
C170 A178 20c grnsh blk .65 .25
C171 AP17 31c brown .80 .40
C172 A178 36c bl grn 1.25 .50
Nos. C169-C172 (4) 3.35 1.40

Stamp of 1856 and Stagecoach AP18

1956, Dec. 15 Litho.

C173 AP18 20c grn, bl & pale yel .90 .30
C174 AP18 31c brn, bl & lt bl 1.00 .40
C175 AP18 36c dp claret & bl 1.75 .55
Nos. C173-C175 (3) 3.65 1.25

1st postage stamps of Uruguay, cent.

Organization of American States, 10th Anniv. — AP19

Perf. 11, 11½ (No. C177)

1958, June 19 Unwmk.

C176 AP19 23c blue & blk .60 .25
C177 AP19 34c green & blk .80 .25
C178 AP19 44c cerise & blk .95 .40
Nos. C176-C178 (3) 2.35 .90

Universal Declaration of Human Rights, 10th Anniv. — AP20

1958, Dec. 10 *Perf. 11*

C179 AP20 23c blk & blue .50 .25
C180 AP20 34c blk & yel grn .90 .25
C181 AP20 44c blk & org red 1.10 .45
Nos. C179-C181 (3) 2.50 .95

"Flight" from Monument to Fallen Aviators — AP21

1959 Litho. *Perf. 11*

Size: 22x37½mm

C182 AP21 3c bis brn & blk .45 .25
C183 AP21 8c brt lil & blk .45 .25
C184 AP21 38c black .45 .25
C185 AP21 50c citron & blk .45 .25
C186 AP21 60c vio & blk .55 .25
C187 AP21 90c ol grn & blk .60 .25
C188 AP21 1p blue & blk .70 .25
C189 AP21 2p ocher & blk 2.25 .55
C190 AP21 3p grn & blk 3.00 .95
C191 AP21 5p vio brn & blk 4.50 1.50
C192 AP21 10p dp rose car & blk 13.00 4.25
Nos. C182-C192 (11) 26.40 9.00

See Nos. C211-C222. For surcharge see No. Q97.

Alberto Santos-Dumont AP22

1959, Feb. 13 Wmk. 327 *Perf. 11½*

C193 AP22 31c multi .70 .25
C194 AP22 36c multi .70 .25

Airplane flight of Alberto Santos-Dumont, Brazilian aeronaut, in 1906 in France.

Girl and Waves — AP23

Designs: 38c, 60c, 1.05p, Compass and map of Punta del Este.

1959, Mar. 6 *Perf. 11½*

C195 AP23 10c ocher & lt bl .40 .25
C196 AP23 38c grn & bis .40 .25
C197 AP23 60c lilac & bister .60 .25
C198 AP23 90c red org & grn .80 .25
C199 AP23 1.05p blue & bister 1.25 .55
Nos. C195-C199 (5) 3.45 1.55

50th anniv. of Punta del Este, seaside resort.

Torch, YMCA Emblem and Chrismon AP24

Wmk. 327

1959, Dec. 22 Litho. *Perf. 11½*

C200 AP24 38c emer, blk & gray .55 .25
C201 AP24 50c bl, blk & gray .55 .25
C202 AP24 60c red, blk & gray 1.00 .50
Nos. C200-C202 (3) 2.10 1.00

50th anniv. of the YMCA in Uruguay.

José Artigas and George Washington — AP25

1960, Mar. 2 *Perf. 11½x12*

C203 AP25 38c red & blk .50 .25
C204 AP25 50c brt bl & blk .50 .25
C205 AP25 60c dp grn & blk .85 .25
Nos. C203-C205 (3) 1.85 .75

Pres. Eisenhower's visit to Uruguay, Feb. 1960.

No. C204 exists imperforate, but was not regularly issued in this form.

No. C150 Surcharged

1960, Apr. 8 Unwmk. *Perf. 11*
C206 AP12 20c on 27c yel grn .75 .25
a. Perf. 12½ .75 .25

Refugees and WRY Emblem — AP26

Size: 24x35mm

1960, June 6 Wmk. 332
C207 AP26 60c brt lil rose & blk .60 .25

World Refugee Year, 7/1/59-6/30/60.

Type of Regular Issue, 1960

Wmk. 332

1960, Nov. 4 Litho. *Perf. 12*
C208 A186 38c bl & ol grn .45 .25
C209 A186 50c bl & ver .45 .25
C210 A186 60c bl & pur .85 .25
Nos. C208-C210 (3) 1.75 .75

Type of 1959 Redrawn with Silhouette of Airplane Added

1960-61 Litho. *Perf. 12*
C211 AP21 3c blk & pale vio .35 .25
C212 AP21 20c blk & crimson .35 .25
C213 AP21 38c blk & pale bl .35 .25
C214 AP21 50c blk & buff .35 .25
C215 AP21 60c blk & dp grn .45 .25
C216 AP21 90c blk & rose .50 .25
C217 AP21 1p blk & gray .70 .25
C218 AP21 2p blk & yel grn 1.00 .25
C219 AP21 3p blk & red lil 1.25 .25
C220 AP21 5p blk & org ver 1.90 .50
C221 AP21 10p blk & yel 4.00 1.60
C222 AP21 20p blk & dk bl ('61) 8.75 3.25
Nos. C211-C222 (12) 19.95 7.60

Pres. Gronchi and Flag Colors — AP27

1961, Apr. 17 Wmk. 332 *Perf. 12*
C223 AP27 90c multi .50 .25
C224 AP27 1.20p multi .75 .25
C225 AP27 1.40p multi .75 .40
Nos. C223-C225 (3) 2.00 .90

Visit of President Giovanni Gronchi of Italy to Uruguay, April, 1961.

Carrasco National Airport — AP28

1961, May 16 Wmk. 332 *Perf. 12*

Building in Gray

C226 AP28 1p lt vio .35 .25
C227 AP28 2p ol gray .75 .25
C228 AP28 3p orange 1.40 .40
C229 AP28 4p purple 1.60 .50
C230 AP28 5p aqua 2.25 .70
C231 AP28 10p lt ultra 4.50 1.25
C232 AP28 20p maroon 6.50 2.50
Nos. C226-C232 (7) 17.35 5.85

Type of Regular "CIES" Issue, 1961

1961, Aug. 3 Litho. Wmk. 332
C233 A189 20c blk & org .40 .25
C234 A189 45c blk & grn .40 .25
C235 A189 50c blk & gray .40 .25
C236 A189 90c blk & plum .40 .25
C237 A189 1p blk & dp rose .45 .25
C238 A189 1.40p blk & lt vio .60 .25
C239 A189 2p blk & bister .65 .25
C240 A189 3p blk & lt bl 1.10 .30
C241 A189 4p blk & yellow 1.60 .55
C242 A189 5p blk & blue 1.60 .85
C243 A189 10p blk & yel grn 3.50 1.50
C244 A189 20p blk & dp pink 7.00 2.75
Nos. C233-C244 (12) 18.10 7.70

Swiss Flag, Plow, Wheat Sheaf — AP29

1962, Aug. 1 Wmk. 332 *Perf. 12*
C245 AP29 90c car, org & blk .50 .25
C246 AP29 1.40p car, bl & blk .80 .35

Cent. of the Swiss Settlement in Uruguay.

Red-crested Cardinal — AP30

Birds: 45c, White-capped tanager, horiz. 90c, Vermilion flycatcher. 1.20p, Great kiskadee, horiz. 1.40p, Fork-tailed flycatcher.

1962, Dec. 5 Litho. *Perf. 12*
C247 AP30 20c gray, blk & red .30 .25
C248 AP30 45c multi .60 .25
C249 AP30 90c crim rose, blk & lt brn 1.50 .25
C250 AP30 1.20p lt bl, blk & yel 1.90 .25
C251 AP30 1.40p blue & sepia 2.40 .30
Nos. C247-C251 (5) 6.70 1.30

No frame on #C248, thin frame on #C251. See #C258-C263. For surcharge see #C320.

Type of Regular UPAE Issue, 1963

1963, May 31 Wmk. 332 *Perf. 12*
C252 A195 45c bluish grn & blk .55 .25
C253 A195 90c magenta & blk .90 .25

Freedom from Hunger Type of Regular Issue

1963, July 9 Wmk. 332 *Perf. 12*
C254 A196 90c red & yel .45 .25
C255 A196 1.40p violet & yel .90 .50

"Alferez Campora" — AP31

1963, Aug. 16 Litho.
C256 AP31 90c dk grn & org .50 .25
C257 AP31 1.40p ultra & yel 1.10 .45

Voyage around the world by the Uruguayan sailing vessel "Alferez Campora," 1960-63.

Bird Type of 1962

Birds: 1p, Glossy cowbird (tordo). 2p, Yellow cardinal. 3p, Hooded siskin. 5p, Sayaca tanager. 10p, Blue and yellow tanager. 20p, Scarlet-headed marsh-bird. All horizontal.

1963, Nov. 15 Wmk. 332 *Perf. 12*
C258 AP30 1p vio bl, blk & brn org .65 .25
C259 AP30 2p lt brn, blk & yel 1.60 .30
C260 AP30 3p yel, brn & blk 2.10 .50
C261 AP30 5p emer, bl grn & blk 3.50 .70
C262 AP30 10p multi 7.50 1.25
C263 AP30 20p gray, org & blk 16.50 7.75
Nos. C258-C263 (6) 31.85 10.75

Frame on Nos. C260-C263.

Pres. Charles de Gaulle — AP32

2.40p, Flags of France and Uruguay.

1964, Oct. 9 Litho. *Perf. 12*
C264 AP32 1.50p multi .55 .25
C265 AP32 2.40p multi 1.25 .35

Charles de Gaulle, Pres. of France, Oct. 1964.

Submerged Statue of Ramses II — AP33

Design: 2p, Head of Ramses II.

1964, Oct. 30 Litho. Wmk. 332
C266 AP33 1.30p multi .35 .25
C267 AP33 2p bis, red brn & brt bl 1.50 .50
a. Souv. sheet of 3, #713, C266-C267, imperf. 3.00 3.00

UNESCO world campaign to save historic monuments in Nubia.

National Flag — AP34

1965, Feb. 18 Wmk. 332 *Perf. 12*
C268 AP34 50p gray, dk bl & yel 8.75 4.00

Kennedy Type of Regular Issue

1965, Mar. 5 Wmk. 327 *Perf. 11½*
C269 A202 1.50p gold, lil & blk .45 .25
C270 A202 2.40p gold, brt bl & blk .95 .55

Issue of 1864, No. 23 — AP35

6c, 8c, 10c denominations of 1864 issue.

Wmk. 332

1965, Mar. 19 Litho. *Perf. 12*
C271 Sheet of 10 5.50 4.50

"URUGUAY" at bottom

a. AP35 1p blue & black .40 .35
b. AP35 1p brick red & black .40 .35
c. AP35 1p green & black .40 .35
d. AP35 1p ocher & black .40 .35
e. AP35 1p carmine & black .40 .35

"URUGUAY" at top

f. AP35 1p blue & black .40 .35
g. AP35 1p brick red & black .40 .35
h. AP35 1p green & black .40 .35
i. AP35 1p ocher & black .40 .35
j. AP35 1p carmine & black .40 .35

1st Rio de la Plata Stamp Show, sponsored jointly by the Argentine and Uruguayan philatelic associations, Montevideo, Mar. 19-28. No. C271 contains two horizontal rows of stamps and two rows of labels; Nos. C271a-C271e are in first row, Nos. C271f-C271j in second row. Adjacent labels in top and bottom rows.

For overprint see No. C298.

National Arms — AP36

1965, Apr. 30 Wmk. 332 *Perf. 12*
C272 AP36 20p multi 2.25 1.10

Type of Regular Issue and

Artigas Monument — AP37

Designs: 1.50p, Artigas and wagontrain. 2.40p, Artigas quotation.

Perf. 11½x12, 12x11½

1965, May 17 Litho. Wmk. 327
C273 AP37 1p multi .45 .25
C274 A205 1.50p multi .65 .25
C275 A205 2.40p multi 1.25 .50
Nos. C273-C275 (3) 2.35 1.00

José Artigas (1764-1850), leader of the independence revolt against Spain.

Olympic Games Type of Regular Issue

Designs: 1p, Boxing. 1.50p, Running. 2p, Fencing. 2.40p, Sculling. 3p, Pistol shooting. 20p, Olympic rings.

1965, Aug. 3 Litho. *Perf. 12x11½*
C276 A206 1p red, gray & blk .30 .25
C277 A206 1.50p emer, bl & blk .30 .25
C278 A206 2p dk car, bl & blk .50 .25
C279 A206 2.40p lt ultra, org & blk .70 .35
C280 A206 3p lil, yel & blk 1.00 .50
C281 A206 20p dk vio bl, pink & lt bl 1.60 .85
Nos. C276-C281 (6) 4.40 2.45

Souvenir Sheet

Designs: 5p, Stamp of 1924, No. 284. 10p, Stamp of 1928, No. 389.

C282 Sheet of 2 3.00 2.50
a. 5p buff, blue & black 1.10 .95
b. 10p blue, black & rose red 1.60 1.40

18th Olympic Games, Tokyo, 10/10-25/64.

ITU Emblem and Satellite — AP38

1966, Jan. 25 Wmk. 332 *Perf. 12*
C283 AP38 1p bl, bluish blk & ver .75 .25

Cent. of the ITU (in 1965).

Winston Churchill — AP39

1966, Apr. 29 Wmk. 332 *Perf. 12*
C284 AP39 2p car, brn & gold .65 .25

Rio de Janeiro Type of Regular Issue

1966, June 9 Wmk. 332 *Perf. 12*
C285 A208 80c dp org & brn .65 .25

International Cooperation Year Emblem — AP40

1966, June 9 Litho.
C286 AP40 1p bluish grn & blk .65 .25

UN International Cooperation Year.

President Zalman Shazar of Israel — AP41

1966, June 21 Wmk. 327
C287 AP41 7p multi 1.00 .30

Visit of Pres. Zalman Shazar of Israel.

Crested Screamer — AP42

1966, July 7 Wmk. 327 *Perf. 12*
C288 AP42 100p bl, blk, red & gray 8.75 2.25

Jules Rimet Cup, Soccer Ball and Globe — AP43

1966, July 11 **Litho.**
C289 AP43 10p dk pur, org & lil 1.00 .30

World Cup Soccer Championship, Wembley, England, July 11-30.

Bulls — AP44

1966 **Wmk. 327, 332 (10p)**

C290	AP44	4p Hereford	.30	.25
C291	AP44	6p Holstein	.30	.25
C292	AP44	10p Shorthorn	.65	.25
C293	AP44	15p Aberdeen Angus	1.10	.35
C294	AP44	20p Norman	2.25	.55
C295	AP44	30p Jersey	3.00	.85
C296	AP44	50p Charolais	4.50	1.50
		Nos. C290-C296 (7)	12.10	4.00

Issued to publicize Uruguayan cattle. Issued: 4p, 50p, 8/13; 6p, 30p, 8/29; 10p, 15p, 20p, 9/26.

Boiso Lanza, Early Plane and Space Capsule — AP45

1966, Oct. 14 **Litho.** ***Perf. 12***
C297 AP45 25p ultra, blk & lt bl 1.10 .50

Issued to honor Capt. Juan Manuel Boiso Lanza, pioneer of military aviation.

No. C271 Overprinted in Black

1966, Nov. 4 **Wmk. 332**
C298 Sheet of 10 7.00 4.50

"URUGUAY" at bottom
a.-e. AP35 1p each .50 .35

"URUGUAY" at top
f.-j. AP35 1p each .35 .35

2nd Rio de la Plata Stamp Show, Buenos Aires, Apr. 1966, sponsored by the Argentine and Uruguayan philatelic associations, and for the cent. of Uruguay's 1st surcharged issue. The addition of black numerals makes the designs resemble the surcharged issue of 1866, Nos. 24-28.

Labels in top row are overprinted "SEGUNDA MUESTRA 1966," in bottom row "SEGUNDAS JORNADAS 1966" and "CENTENARIO DEL SELLO / ESCUDITO RESELLADO" in both rows. One label each in top and bottom rows is overprinted "BUENOS AIRES / ABRIL 1966."

No. 613 Surcharged in Dark Blue

Perf. 12½x13
1966, Dec. 17 **Engr.** **Unwmk.**
C299 A175 1p on 12c .75 .25

Philatelic Club of Uruguay, 40th anniv.

Dante Alighieri — AP46

Wmk. 332
1966, Dec. 27 **Litho.** ***Perf. 12***
C300 AP46 50c sepia & bister .80 .25

Dante Alighieri (1265-1321), Italian poet.

Planetarium Projector — AP47

1967, Jan. 13 **Wmk. 332** ***Perf. 12***
C301 AP47 5p dl bl & blk .85 .30

Montevideo Municipal Planetarium, 10th anniv.

Archbishop Makarios and Map of Cyprus — AP48

1967, Feb. 14 **Wmk. 332** ***Perf. 12***
C302 AP48 6.60p rose lil & blk .75 .25

Visit of Archbishop Makarios, president of Cyprus, Oct. 21, 1966.

Dr. Albert Schweitzer Holding Fawn — AP49

1967, Mar. 31 **Litho.** **Wmk. 332**
C303 AP49 6p grn, blk, brn & sal 1.00 .80

Albert Schweitzer (1875-1965), medical missionary.

Corriedale Ram — AP50

Various Rams: 4p, Ideal. 5p, Romney Marsh. 10p, Australian Merino.

1967, Apr. 5

C304	AP50	3p red org, blk & gray	1.60	.25
C305	AP50	4p emer, blk & gray	1.60	.25
C306	AP50	5p ultra, blk & gray	1.60	.25
C307	AP50	10p yel, blk & gray	1.60	.50
		Nos. C304-C307 (4)	6.40	1.25

Uruguayan sheep raising.

Flag of Uruguay and Map of the Americas AP51

1967, Apr. 8
C308 AP51 10p dk gray, bl & gold .75 .25

Meeting of American Presidents, Punta del Este, Apr. 10-12.

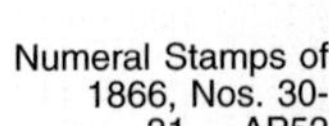

Numeral Stamps of 1866, Nos. 30-31 — AP52

Design: 6p, Nos. 32-33; diff. frame.

Wmk. 332
1967, May 10 **Litho.** ***Perf. 12***

C309	AP52	3p bl, yel grn & blk	.60	.25
a.		Souvenir sheet of 4	2.00	1.50
C310	AP52	6p bis, dp rose & blk	.90	.30
a.		Souvenir sheet of 4	3.00	2.50

Cent. of the 1866 numeral issue. Nos. C309a-C310a each contain 4 stamps similar to Nos. C309 and C310 respectively (the arrangement of colors differs in the souvenir sheets).

Ansina, Portrait by Medardo Latorre — AP53

1967, May 17
C311 AP53 2p gray, dk bl & red .65 .25

Issued to honor Ansina, servant of Gen. José Artigas.

Plane Landing — AP54

1967, May 30
C312 AP54 10p red, bl, blk & yel .80 .25

30th anniv. (in 1966) of PLUNA Airline.

Shooting for Basket AP55

Basketball Game AP56

Basketball Players in Action: No. C314, Driving (ball shoulder high). No. C315, About to pass (ball head high). No. C316, Ready to pass (ball held straight in front). No. C317, Dribbling with right hand.

1967, June 9

C313	AP55	5p multi	.50	.25
C314	AP55	5p multi	.50	.25
C315	AP55	5p multi	.50	.25
C316	AP55	5p multi	.50	.25
C317	AP55	5p multi	.50	.25
a.		Strip of 5, Nos. C313-C317	2.85	1.60

Souvenir Sheet
C318 AP56 10p org, brt grn & blk 2.00 1.75

5th World Basketball Championships, Montevideo, May 1967.
For overprint see No. C349.

José Artigas, Manuel Belgrano, Flags of Uruguay and Argentina — AP57

Wmk. 332
1967, June 19 **Litho.** ***Imperf.***
C319 AP57 5p bl, grn & yel 1.50 1.25

3rd Rio de la Plata Stamp Show, Montevideo, Uruguay, June 18-25.
For surcharge see No. 859.

Nos. C248 and C252 Surcharged in Gold

1967, June 22 ***Perf. 12***
C320 AP30 5.90p on 45c multi .70 .25
C321 A195 5.90p on 45c multi .70 .25

Don Quixote and Sancho Panza, Painted by Denry Torres AP58

1967, July 10
C322 AP58 8p bister brn & brn .85 .25

Issued in honor of Miguel de Cervantes Saavedra (1547-1616), Spanish novelist.
For surcharge see No. C356.

Stone Axe — AP59

Designs: 15p, Headbreaker stones. 20p, Spearhead. 50p, Birdstone. 75p, Clay pot. 100p, Ornitholite (ritual sculpture), Balizas, horiz. 150p, Lasso weights (boleadores). 200p, Two spearheads.

1967-68 **Wmk. 332** ***Perf. 12***

C323	AP59	15p gray & blk	.45	.25
C324	AP59	20p gray & blk	.45	.25
C325	AP59	30p gray & blk	1.00	.25
C326	AP59	50p gray & blk	1.25	.25
C327	AP59	75p brn & blk	2.25	.35
C328	AP59	100p gray & blk	3.00	.70
C329	AP59	150p gray & blk ('68)	3.75	.70
C330	AP59	200p gray & blk ('68)	6.00	1.50
		Nos. C323-C330 (8)	18.15	4.25

Railroad Crossing — AP60

1967, Dec. 4
C331 AP60 4p blk, yel & red 1.00 .25

10th Pan-American Highway Congress, Montevideo.

Lions Emblem and Map of South America — AP61

1967, Dec. 29
C332 AP61 5p pur, yel & emer .95 .25

50th anniversary of Lions International.

Boy Scout — AP62

1968, Jan. 24 **Litho.**
C333 AP62 9p sepia & brick red 1.00 .30

Issued in memory of Robert Baden-Powell, founder of the Boy Scout organization.

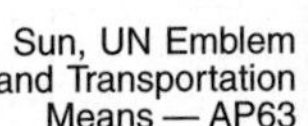

Sun, UN Emblem and Transportation Means — AP63

1968, Feb. 29 **Wmk. 332** ***Perf. 12***
C334 AP63 10p gray, yel, lt & dk bl .75 .25

Issued for International Tourist Year.

Octopus — AP64

Marine Fauna: 20p, Silversides. 25p, Characin. 30p, Catfish, vert. 50p, Squid, vert.

1968 Wmk. 332 *Perf. 12*

C335	AP64	15p lt grn, bl & blk	.90	.25
C336	AP64	20p brn, grn & bl	.90	.25
C337	AP64	25p multi	1.25	.25
C338	AP64	30p bl, grn & blk	1.50	.50
C339	AP64	50p dp org, grn & dk bl	2.40	.65
		Nos. C335-C339 (5)	6.95	1.90

Issued: 30p, 50p, 10/10; 15p, 20p, 25p, 11/5.

Navy Type of Regular Issue

Designs: 4p, Naval Air Force. 6p, Naval arms. 10p, Signal flags, vert. 20p, Corsair (chartered by General Artigas).

1968, Nov. 12 Litho.

C340	A226	4p bl, blk & red	.45	.25
C341	A226	6p multi	.45	.25
C342	A226	10p lt ultra, red & yel	.50	.25
C343	A226	20p ultra & blk	1.30	.25
		Nos. C340-C343 (4)	2.70	1.00

Rowing — AP65

1969, Feb. 11 Wmk. 332 *Perf. 12*

C344	AP65	30p shown	.65	.25
C345	AP65	50p Running	1.00	.35
C346	AP65	100p Soccer	1.75	.55
		Nos. C344-C346 (3)	3.40	1.15

19th Olympic Games, Mexico City, 10/12-27/68.

Bicycling Type of Regular Issue

Designs: 20p, Bicyclist and globe, vert.

1969, Mar. 21 Wmk. 332 *Perf. 12*

C347 A229 20p bl, pur & yel .80 .25

"EFIMEX 68" and Globe — AP66

1969, Apr. 10 Wmk. 332 *Perf. 12*

C348 AP66 20p dk grn, red & bl .85 .25

EFIMEX '68, International Philatelic Exhibition, Mexico City, Nov. 1-9, 1968.

No. C318 Ovptd. with Names of Participating Countries, Emblem, Bars, etc. and "CAMPEONATO MUNDIAL DE VOLEIBOL"

1969, Apr. 25

Souvenir Sheet

C349 AP56 10p org, brt grn & blk 1.40 1.10

Issued to commemorate the World Volleyball Championships, Montevideo, Apr. 1969.

Book, Quill and Emblem — AP67

1969, Sept. 16 Litho. *Perf. 12*

C350 AP67 30p grn, org & blk 1.00 .25

10th Congress of Latin American Notaries.

Automobile Club Emblem — AP68

1969, Oct. 7 Wmk. 332 *Perf. 12*

C351 AP68 10p ultra & red .75 .25

50th anniv. (in 1968) of the Uruguayan Automobile Club.

ILO Emblem — AP69

1969, Oct. 29 Litho. *Perf. 12*

C352 AP69 30p dk bl grn & blk .85 .25

50th anniv. of the ILO.

Exhibition Emblem — AP70

1969, Nov. 15 Wmk. 332 *Perf. 12*

C353 AP70 20p ultra, yel & grn .85 .25

ABUEXPO 69 Philatelic Exhibition, San Pablo, Brazil, Nov. 15-23.

Rotary Emblem and Hemispheres AP71

1969, Dec. 6 *Perf. 12*

C354 AP71 20p ultra, bl & bis 1.00 .30

South American Regional Rotary Conference and the 50th anniv. of the Montevideo Rotary Club.

Dr. Luis Morquio — AP72

1969, Dec. 22 Litho. Wmk. 332

C355 AP72 20p org red & brn .75 .25

Centenary of the birth of Dr. Luis Morquio, pediatrician.

No. C322 Surcharged "FELIZ AÑO 1970 / 6.00 / PESOS"

1969, Dec. 24

C356 AP58 6p on 8p bis brn & brn .75 .25

Issued for New Year 1970.

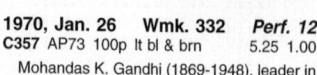

Mahatma Gandhi and UNESCO Emblem — AP73

1970, Jan. 26 Wmk. 332 *Perf. 12*

C357 AP73 100p lt bl & brn 5.25 1.00

Mohandas K. Gandhi (1869-1948), leader in India's fight for independence.

Evaristo C. Ciganda — AP74

1970, Mar. 10 Litho.

C358 AP74 6p brt grn & brn .75 .25

Ciganda, author of the 1st law for teachers' pensions, birth cent.

Giuseppe Garibaldi — AP75

1970, Apr. 7 Unwmk. *Perf. 12*

C359 AP75 20p rose car & pink .95 .25

Centenary of Garibaldi's command of foreign legionnaires in the Uruguayan Civil War.

Fur Seal — AP76

Designs: 20p, Rhea, vert. 30p, Common tegu (lizard). 50p, Capybara. 100p, Mulita armadillo. 150p, Puma. 200p, Nutria.

1970-71 Wmk. 332 *Perf. 12*

C361	AP76	20p pur, emer & blk	1.00	.25
C362	AP76	30p emer, yel & blk	1.10	.30
C363	AP76	50p dl yel & brn	2.10	.50
C365	AP76	100p org, sep & blk	3.00	.75
C366	AP76	150p emer & brn	2.10	.85
C367	AP76	200p brt rose, brn & blk ('71)	5.50	2.25
C368	AP76	250p gray, bl & blk	7.50	2.25
		Nos. C361-C368 (7)	22.30	7.15

Soccer and Mexican Flag — AP77

1970, June 2 Litho. *Perf. 12*

C369 AP77 50p multi 1.10 .50

9th World Soccer Championships for the Jules Rimet Cup, Mexico City, 5/30-6/21.

"U N" and Laurel — AP78

1970, June 26 Wmk. 332 *Perf. 12*

C370 AP78 32p dk bl & gold .85 .25

25th anniversary of the United Nations.

Eisenhower and US Flag — AP79

1970, July 14 Litho.

C371 AP79 30p gray, vio bl & red .85 .25

Issued in memory of Gen. Dwight David Eisenhower, 34th Pres. of US (1890-1969).

Neil A. Armstrong Stepping onto Moon AP80

1970, July 21

C372 AP80 200p multi 4.25 1.50

1st anniv. of man's 1st landing on the moon.

Flag of the "Immortals" AP81

1970, Aug. 24 Wmk. 332 *Perf. 12*

C373 AP81 500p bl, blk & red 6.25 6.00

The 145th anniversary of the arrival of the 33 "Immortals," the patriots, who started the revolution for independence.

Congress Emblem with Map of South America — AP82

1970, Sept. 16 Unwmk. *Perf. 12*

C374 AP82 30p bl, dk bl & yel .85 .25

Issued to publicize the 5th Pan-American Congress of Rheumatology, Punta del Este.

Souvenir Sheet

Types of First Air Post Issue AP83

1970, Oct. 1 Wmk. 332 *Perf. 12½*

C375	AP83	Sheet of 3	3.75	3.00
a.		25p brown (Bl)	1.10	.90
b.		25p brown (R)	1.10	.90
c.		25p brown (G)	1.10	.90

Stamp Day. #C375 contains 3 stamps similar to #C1-C3, but with denominations in pesos.

Flags of ALALC Countries — AP84

1970, Nov. 23 Litho. *Perf. 12*

C376 AP84 22p multi .85 .25

For the Latin-American Association for Free Trade (Asociación Latinoamericana de Libre Comercio).

Yellow Fever, by J. M. Blanes — AP85

1971, June 8 Wmk. 332 *Perf. 12*

C377 AP85 50p blk, dk red brn & yel 1.00 .35

Juan Manuel Blanes (1830-1901), painter.

Racial Equality, UN Emblem — AP86

1971, June 28 **Litho.**
C378 AP86 27p blk, pink & bis .85 .25

Intl. Year Against Racial Discrimination.

Congress Emblem with Maps of Americas AP87

1971, July 6 **Wmk. 332** ***Perf. 12***
C379 AP87 58p dl grn, blk & org .95 .40

12th Pan-American Congress of Gastroenterology, Punta del Este, Dec. 5-10, 1971.

Committee Emblem — AP88

1971, Nov. 29
C380 AP88 30p bl, blk & yel .85 .25

Inter-governmental Committee for European Migration.

Llama and Mountains — AP89

1971, Dec. 30
C381 AP89 37p multi 1.10 .40

EXFILIMA '71, Third Inter-American Philatelic Exposition, Lima, Peru, Nov. 6-14.

Munich Olympic Games Emblem — AP90

Designs (Munich '72 Emblem and): 100p, Torchbearer. 500p, Discobolus.

1972, Feb. 1 ***Perf. 11½x12***
C382 AP90 50p blk, red & org .40 .25
C383 AP90 100p multi .75 .40
C384 AP90 500p multi 4.00 2.00
Nos. C382-C384 (3) 5.15 2.65

20th Olympic Games, Munich, 8/26-9/11.

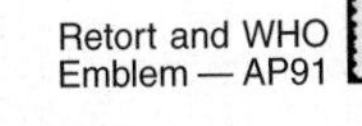

Retort and WHO Emblem — AP91

1972, Feb. 22 ***Perf. 12***
C385 AP91 27p multi .65 .25

50th anniversary of the discovery of insulin by Frederick G. Banting and Charles H. Best.

Ship with Flags Forming Sails — AP92

1972, Mar. 6 **Wmk. 332**
C386 AP92 37p multi .85 .25

Stamp Day of the Americas.

1924 and 1928 Gold Medals, Soccer AP93

Design: 300p, Olympic flag, Motion and Munich emblems, vert.

1972, June 12 **Litho.** ***Perf. 12***
C387 AP93 100p bl & multi .90 .75
C388 AP93 300p multi 2.60 2.25

20th Olympic Games, Munich, 8/26-9/11.

Cross — AP94

1972, Aug. 10
C389 AP94 37p vio & gold .70 .25

Dan A. Mitrione (1920-70), slain US official.

Interlocking Squares and UN Emblem — AP95

1972, Aug. 16
C390 AP95 30p gray & multi .70 .25

3rd UN Conf. on Trade and Development (UNCTAD III), Santiago, Chile, Apr.-May 1972.

Brazil's "Bull's-eye," 1843 — AP96

Wmk. 332

1972, Aug. 26 **Litho.** ***Perf. 12***
C391 AP96 50p grn, yel & bl .70 .25

4th Inter-American Philatelic Exhibition, EXFILBRA, Rio de Janeiro, Aug. 26-Sept. 2.

Map of South America, Compass Rose — AP97

1972, Sept. 28
C392 AP97 37p multi .70 .25

Uruguay's support for extending territorial sovereignty 200 miles into the sea.

Adoration of the Kings and Shepherds, by Rafael Perez Barradas — AP98

1972, Oct. 12
C393 AP98 20p lemon & multi + label .80 .25

Christmas 1972 and first biennial exhibition of Uruguayan painting, 1970.

WPY Emblem — AP99

Wmk. 332

1974, Aug. 20 **Litho.** ***Perf. 12***
C394 AP99 500p gray & red 1.25 .60

World Population Year 1974.

Soccer, Olympics and UPU Emblems — AP100

AP100a

Anniversaries and events: Nos. C396 and C397 are same design as No. C395.

No. C398a, 17th UPU Congress, Lausanne. No. C398b, World Soccer Federation, 1st South American president. No. C398c, 1976 Summer and Winter Olympics, Innsbruck and Montreal.

1974, Aug. 30
C395 AP100 200p grn & multi 1.40 1.00
C396 AP100 300p org & multi 1.40 1.00
C397 AP100 500p lt. bl & multi 12.50 9.00

Souvenir Sheet

With Blue Frame

C398 AP100a Sheet of 3 72.50 50.00
a.-c. 500p any single 15.00 11.00

Centenary of Universal Postal Union.
Nos. C397-C398 had limited distribution.

Mexico No. O1 and Mexican Coat of Arms — AP101

Wmk. 332

1974, Oct. 15 **Litho.** ***Perf. 12***
C399 AP101 200p multi .85 .25

EXFILMEX '74 5th Inter-American Philatelic Exhibition, Mexico City, Oct. 26-Nov. 3.

Christmas Type of 1974

240p, Kings following star. 2500p, Virgin & Child.

1974
C400 A315 240p multi .70 .25

Miniature Sheet

C401 A315 2500p multi 4.75 4.50

Issued: 240p. Dec. 27; 2500p, Dec. 31.

Spain No. 1, Colors of Spain and Uruguay AP102

1975, Mar. 4
C402 AP102 400p multi .85 .25

Espana 75, International Philatelic Exhibition, Madrid, Apr. 4-13.

Souvenir Sheet

Nos. C253, 893 and C402 AP103

Wmk. 332

1975, Apr. 4 **Litho.** ***Perf. 12***
C403 AP103 Sheet of 3 5.75 5.00
a. 1000p No. C253 1.75 1.50
b. 1000p No. 893 1.75 1.50
c. 1000p No. C402 1.75 1.50

Espana 75 Intl. Phil. Exhib., Madrid, Apr. 4-13.

1976 Summer & Winter Olympics, Innsbruck & Montreal — AP104

1975, May 16 ***Perf. 12***
C404 AP104 400p shown 1.40 .60
C405 AP104 600p Flags, Olympic rings 2.25 .95

Souvenir Sheets

C406 Sheet of 2 44.00 40.00
a. AP104 500p Montreal emblem 11.00 11.00
b. AP104 1000p Innsbruck emblem 24.00 24.00
C407 Sheet of 2 42.50 40.00
a. AP104 500p Emblems, horiz. 11.00 11.00
b. AP104 1000p Flags, horiz. 24.00 24.00

Nos. C404-C407 had limited distribution.

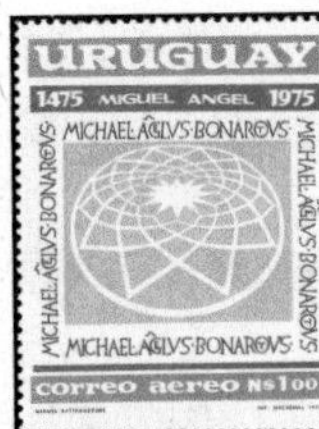

Floor Design for Capitol, Rome — AP105

1975, Aug. 15
C408 AP105 1p multi 1.50 1.25

500th birth anniversary of Michelangelo Buonarroti (1475-1564), Italian sculptor, painter and architect.

Apollo-Soyuz Space Mission, USA & Uruguay Independence — AP106

Anniversaries and events: 15c, Apollo-Soyuz spacecraft. 20c, Apollo-Soyuz spacecraft. 25c, Artigas monument, vert. 30c, George Washington, Pres. Artigas. No. C412, Early Aircraft, vert. No. C413a, Apollo spacecraft, astronauts. No. C413b, US and Uruguayan Declarations of Independence. No.

C413c, Modern aircraft. No. C413d, UN Secretaries General. No. C414c, Boiso Lanza, aviation pioneer. 1p, Flags of UN and Uruguay.

1975, Sept. 29

C409	AP106 10c multicolored	1.75	1.50
C410	AP106 15c multicolored	2.50	2.10
C411	AP106 25c multicolored	3.25	2.60
C412	AP106 50c multicolored	4.25	3.50
	Nos. C409-C412 (4)	11.75	9.70

Souvenir Sheets

C413	Sheet of 4	47.00	45.00
a.-d.	AP106 40c any single	10.00	10.00
C414	Sheet of 4	47.00	45.00
a.	AP106 20c multicolored	2.50	2.50
b.	AP106 30c multicolored	6.25	6.25
c.	AP106 50c multicolored	10.00	10.00
d.	AP106 1p multicolored	21.00	21.00

Nos. C409-C414 had limited distribution.

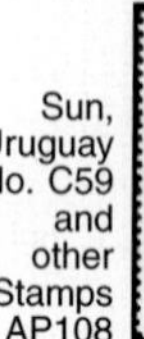

Sun, Uruguay No. C59 and other Stamps AP108

Wmk. 332

1975, Oct. 13 Litho. *Perf. 12*

C415	AP108 1p blk, gray & yel	3.25	1.25

Uruguayan Stamp Day.

Montreal Olympic Emblem and Argentina '78 AP109

Flags of US and Uruguay AP110

UPU and UPAE Emblems — AP111

Wmk. 332

1975, Oct. 14 Litho. *Perf. 11½*

C416	AP109 1p multi	2.25	.80
C417	AP110 1p multi	2.25	.80
C418	AP111 1p multi	2.25	.80
a.	Souvenir sheet of 3, #C418b-C418d	32.00	20.00
b.	AP109 2p multi	10.50	6.50
c.	AP110 2p multi	10.50	6.50
d.	AP111 2p multi	10.50	6.50
	Nos. C416-C418 (3)	6.75	2.40

EXFILMO '75 and ESPAMER '75 Stamp Exhibitions, Montevideo, Oct. 10-19.

Ocelot — AP112

Design: No. C420, Oncidium bifolium.

1976, Jan. Litho. *Perf. 12*

C419	AP112 50c vio bl & multi	1.50	.50
C420	AP112 50c emer & multi	1.50	.50

Souvenir Sheets

Olympics, Soccer, Telecommunications and UPU — AP113

1976, June 3 *Perf. 11½*

C422	AP113 Sheet of 3	57.50	55.00
a.	30c Soccer player	5.50	5.50
b.	70c Alexander Graham Bell	13.00	13.00
c.	1p UPU emblem, UN #5	19.00	19.00
C423	Sheet of 3	57.00	55.00
a.	AP113 40c Discus thrower	6.00	6.00
b.	AP113 60c Telephone, cent.	8.50	8.50
c.	AP113 2p UPU emblem, UN #11	24.00	24.00

Nos. C422-C423 had limited distribution.

Anniversaries and Events Type of 1976

Souvenir Sheets

20c, Frederick Passy, Henri Dunant. 35c, Nobel prize, 75th anniv. 40c, Viking spacecraft. 60c, 1976 Summer Olympics, Montreal. 75c, US space missions. 90c, 1976 Summer Olympics, diff.

World Cup Soccer Championships, Argentina: 1p, Uruguay, 1930 champions. 1.50p, Uruguay, 1950 champions.

1976, Nov. 12 *Perf. 12*

C424	Sheet of 4	47.00	45.00
a.	A355 20c multicolored	2.50	2.50
b.	A355 40c multicolored	4.75	4.75
c.	A355 60c multicolored	6.50	6.50
d.	A355 1.50p multicolored	.16.00	16.00
C425	Sheet of 4	47.00	45.00
a.	A355 35c multicolored	5.00	5.00
b.	A355 75c multicolored	7.00	7.00
c.	A355 90c multicolored	8.00	8.00
d.	A355 1p multicolored	10.00	10.00

Nos. C424-C425 had limited distribution.

Nobel Prize Type of 1977

Souvenir Sheets

Anniversaries and events: 10c, World Cup Soccer Championships. 40c, Victor Hess, Nobel Prize in Physics. 60c, Max Plank, Nobel Prize in Physics. 80c, Graf Zeppelin, Concorde. 90c, Virgin and Child by Rubens. 1.20p, World Cup Soccer Championships, diff. 1.50p, Eduardo Bonilla, Count von Zeppelin. 2p, The Nativity by Rubens.

1977, July 21

C426	Sheet of 4	42.00	40.00
a.	A361 10c multicolored	1.00	1.00
b.	A361 60c multicolored	4.25	4.25
c.	A361 80c multicolored	6.00	6.00
d.	A361 2p multicolored	14.50	14.50
C427	Sheet of 4	42.00	40.00
a.	A361 40c multicolored	2.60	2.60
b.	A361 90c multicolored	6.50	6.50
c.	A361 1.20p multicolored	7.75	7.75
d.	A361 1.50p multicolored	11.50	11.50

Nos. C426-C427 had limited distribution.

Uruguay Natl. Postal System, 150th Anniv. — AP114

1977, July 27

C428	AP114 8p multicolored	10.00	10.00

Souvenir Sheet

C429	AP114 10p multicolored	17.50	17.00

No. C428, imperf., was not valid for postage. Souvenir sheets sold in the package with No. C429 were not valid for postage.

For overprint see No. C435.

Paintings Type of 1978

Paintings: 1p, St. George Slaying Dragon by Durer. 1.25p, Duke of Lerma by Rubens. No. 432a, Madonna and Child by Durer. No. 432b, Holy Family by Rubens. No. 432c, Flight from Egypt by Francisco de Goya (1746-1828).

1978, June 13 *Perf. 12½*

C430	A374 1p brn & blk	4.50	4.00
C431	A374 1.25p blk & brn	4.50	4.50

Souvenir Sheet

C432	Sheet of 3	25.00	25.00
a.-c.	A374 1p any single	6.00	6.00

Nos. C430-C432 had limited distribution.

Souvenir Sheet

ICAO, 30th Anniv. and 1st Powered Flight, 75th Anniv. AP115

Designs: a, Concorde, Dornier DO-x. b, Graf Zeppelin, Wright Brothers' Flyer. c, Space shuttle and De Pinedo's plane.

1978, June 13

C433	AP115 Sheet of 3	37.00	35.00
a.-c.	1p any single	10.00	10.00

No. C433 had limited distribution.

Souvenir Sheet

World Cup Soccer Championships, Argentina — AP116

1978, June 13 *Perf. 12*

C434	AP116 Sheet of 3	57.00	55.00
a.	50c multicolored	4.00	4.00
b.	1.50p multicolored	10.00	10.00
c.	2p multicolored	16.00	16.00

No. C434 had limited distribution.

No. C428 Overprinted in Black

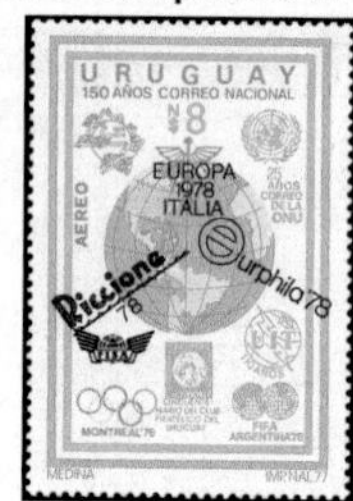

1978, Aug. 28

C435	AP114 8p multicolored	7.75	3.50

No. C435 had limited distribution.

Madonna and Child Type of 1979

Various Madonna and Child etchings by Albrecht Dürer with Intl. Year of the Child emblem at: a, UL. b, UR.

Wmk. 332

1979, June 18 Litho. *Perf. 12½*

C436	A390 1.50p Sheet of 2, #a-b	27.50	26.00

No. C436 had limited distribution.

Boiso Lanza, Wright Brothers AP117

75th anniv. of powered flight.

1979, June 18 *Perf. 12½*

C437	AP117 1.80p multicolored	4.00	1.90

No. C437 had limited distribution.

Issued in sheet of 24 containing 6 blocks of 4r with margin around. See Nos. 1040-1042.

Souvenir Sheet

1982 World Cup Soccer Championships, Spain — AP118

1979, June 18 *Perf. 12*

C438	AP118 Sheet of 3	42.00	40.00
a.	50c Jules Rimet cup	2.50	2.50
b.	2.50p Uruguay flag	10.00	10.00
c.	3p Espana '82	14.00	14.00

No. C438 had limited distribution.

Souvenir Sheet

Rowland Hill Cent. AP119

1979, June 18

C439	AP119 Sheet of 2	42.00	40.00
a.	2p Uruguay #1, C1	16.00	16.00
b.	2p Great Britain #1, 836	16.00	16.00

No. C439 had limited distribution.

AIR POST SEMI-POSTAL STAMPS

Catalogue values for unused stamps in this section are for Never Hinged items.

Type of Semi-Postal Stamps, 1959

Wmk. 327

1959, Dec. 29 Litho. *Perf. 11½*

CB1	SP2 38c + 10c brown & org	.30	.30
CB2	SP2 60c + 10c gray grn & org	.50	.50

Issued for national recovery.

SPECIAL DELIVERY STAMPS

No. 242 Overprinted

1921, Aug. Unwmk. *Perf. 11½*

E1	A97 2c fawn	.70	.25
a.	Double overprint	4.25	

Caduceus — SD1

Imprint: "IMP. NACIONAL."

1922, Dec. 2 Litho. Wmk. 188

Size: 21x27mm

E2	SD1 2c light red	.50	.25

1924, Oct. 1

E3	SD1 2c pale ultra	.50	.25

1928 Unwmk. *Perf. 11*

E4	SD1 2c light blue	.50	.25

Imprint: "IMPRA. NACIONAL."

1928-36 Wmk. 188

Size: 16½x19½mm.

E5	SD1 2c black, *green*	.30	.25

Unwmk.

E6 SD1 2c blue green ('29) .30 .25

Perf. 11½, 12½

E7 SD1 2c blue ('36) .30 .25
Nos. E5-E7 (3) .90 .75

1944, Oct. 23 *Perf. 12½*

E8 SD1 2c salmon pink .25 .25

Catalogue values for unused stamps in this section, from this point to the end of the section, are for Never Hinged items.

1947, Nov. 19

E9 SD1 2c red brown .30 .25

No. E9 Surcharged in Black

1957, Oct. 30

E10 SD1 5c on 2c red brown .30 .25

LATE FEE STAMPS

Galleon and Modern Steamship — LF1

Wmk. Crossed Keys in Sheet

1936, May 18 Litho. *Perf. 11*

I1 LF1 3c green .55 .55
I2 LF1 5c violet .95 .95
I3 LF1 6c blue green 1.10 1.10
I4 LF1 7c brown 1.30 1.30
I5 LF1 8c carmine 1.50 1.50
I6 LF1 12c deep blue 2.25 2.25
Nos. I1-I6 (6) 7.65 7.65

POSTAGE DUE STAMPS

D1

1902 Unwmk. Engr. *Perf. 14 to 15*

Size: 21¼x18½mm

J1 D1 1c blue green .75 .30
J2 D1 2c carmine .75 .30
J3 D1 4c gray violet .80 .30
J4 D1 10c dark blue 1.75 .70
J5 D1 20c ocher 2.50 1.25
Nos. J1-J5 (5) 6.55 2.85

Surcharged in Red

1904

J6 D1 1c on 10c dk bl 1.25 1.25
a. Inverted surcharge 12.00 12.00

1913-15 Litho. *Perf. 11½*

Size: 22½x20mm

J7 D1 1c lt grn .75 .30
J8 D1 2c rose red .75 .30
J9 D1 4c dl vio 1.00 .30
J10 D1 6c dp brn 1.00 .50

Size: 21¼x19mm

J11 D1 10c dl bl 1.50 .60
Nos. J7-J11 (5) 5.00 2.00

Imprint: "Imprenta Nacional"

1922 **Size: 20x17mm**

J12 D1 1c bl grn .50 .30
J13 D1 2c red .50 .30
J14 D1 3c red brn .70 .50
J15 D1 4c brn vio .50 .30
J16 D1 5c blue .80 .50
J17 D1 10c gray grn 1.00 .60
Nos. J12-J17 (6) 4.00 2.50

1926-27 Wmk. 188 *Perf. 11*

Size: 20x17mm

J18 D1 1c bl grn ('27) .50 .25
J19 D1 3c red brn ('27) .50 .25
J20 D1 5c slate blue .50 .25
J21 D1 6c light brown .50 .50
Nos. J18-J21 (4) 2.00 1.25

1929 Unwmk. *Perf. 10½, 11*

J22 D1 1c blue green .25 .25
J23 D1 10c gray green .50 .25

Figure of Value Redrawn (Flat on sides)

1932 **Wmk. 188**

J24 D1 6c yel brn .50 .25

Imprint: "Casa A. Barreiro Ramos S. A."

1935 Unwmk. Litho. *Perf. 12½*

Size: 20x17mm

J25 D1 4c violet .50 .25
J26 D1 5c rose .50 .25

Type of 1935

Imprint: "Imprenta Nacional" at right

1938

J27 D1 1c blue green .25 .25
J28 D1 2c red brown .25 .25
J29 D1 3c deep pink .25 .25
J30 D1 4c light violet .25 .25
J31 D1 5c blue .25 .25
J32 D1 8c rose .25 .25
Nos. J27-J32 (6) 1.50 1.50

OFFICIAL STAMPS

Regular Issues Handstamped in Black, Red or Blue

Many double and inverted impressions exist of the handstamped overprints on Nos. O1-O83. Prices are the same as for normal stamps or slightly more.

On Stamps of 1877-79

1880-82 Unwmk. *Rouletted 8*

O1 A9 1c red brown 4.00 3.50
O2 A10 5c green 3.00 2.50
O3 A11 20c bister 3.25 3.25
O4 A11 50c black 22.00 22.00
O5 A12 1p blue 22.00 22.00
Nos. O1-O5 (5) 54.25 53.25

On No. 44

Rouletted 6

O6 A9 1c brown ('81) 6.00 6.00

On Nos. 43-43A

Rouletted 8

O7 A11 50c black (R) 17.00 16.00
O8 A12 1p blue (R) 22.50 20.00

On Nos. 45, 41, 37a

Perf. 12½

O9 A13 7c blue (R) ('81) 4.25 3.25

Rouletted 8

O10 A11 10c ver (Bl) 2.00 2.00

Perf. 13½

O11 A8b 15c yellow (Bl) 5.00 4.50

1883 On Nos. 46-47 *Perf. 12½*

O12 A14 1c green 6.50 6.50
O13 A14a 2c rose 9.50 9.50

On Nos. 50-51

Perf. 12½, 12x12½, 13

O14 A17 5c blue (R) 4.00 4.00
a. Imperf., pair 4.50
O15 A18 10c brown (Bl) 6.50 6.50
a. Imperf., pair 6.00

No. 48 Handstamped

1884 *Perf. 12½*

O16 A15 1c green 35.00 32.50

Overprinted as No. O1 in Black On Nos. 48-49

1884 *Perf. 12, 12x12½, 13*

O17 A15 1c green 35.00 32.50
O18 A16 2c red 12.00 9.50

On Nos. 53-56

Rouletted 8

O19 A11 1c on 10c ver 2.00 1.60
a. Small "1" (No. 53a) 5.00

Perf. 12½

O20 A14a 2c rose 6.50 6.50
O21 A22 5c ultra 6.50 6.50
O22 A23 5c blue 5.00 2.00
Nos. O17-O22 (6) 67.00 58.60

On Stamps of 1884-88

1884-89 *Rouletted 8*

O23 A24 1c gray 12.00 5.50
O24 A24 1c green ('88) 2.50 1.60
O25 A24 1c olive grn 3.25 1.75
O26 A24a 2c vermilion 1.00 .60
O27 A24a 2c rose ('88) 2.25 1.25
O28 A24b 5c slate blue 2.25 1.25
O29 A24b 5c slate bl, *bl* 6.50 5.00
O30 A24b 5c violet ('88) 6.50 5.00
O31 A24b 5c lt blue ('89) 6.50 5.00
O32 A25 7c dk brown 3.25 1.60
O33 A25 7c orange ('89) 3.25 2.25
O34 A26 10c olive brn 2.00 .90
O35 A30 10c violet ('89) 16.00 9.50
O36 A27 20c red violet 3.00 1.60
O37 A27 20c bister brn ('89) 16.00 7.00
O38 A28 25c gray violet 3.50 2.50
O39 A28 25c vermilion ('89) 16.00 7.00
Nos. O23-O39 (17) 105.75 59.30

The OFICIAL handstamp, type "a," was also applied to No. 73, the 5c violet with "Provisorio" overprint, but it was not regularly issued.

1887 On No. 71 *Rouletted 9*

O40 A29 10c lilac 5.00

No. O40 was not regularly issued.

On Stamps of 1889-1899

Perf. 12½ to 15 and Compound

1890-1900

O41 A32 1c green .80 .25
O43 A32 1c blue ('95) 2.00 2.00
O44 A33 2c rose .80 .25
O45 A33 2c red brn ('95) 2.50 2.50
O46 A33 2c orange ('00) .80 .80
O47 A34 5c deep blue 1.50 1.50
O48 A34 5c rose ('95) 2.00 2.00
O49 A35 7c bister brown 1.25 .80
O50 A35 7c green ('95) 25.00
O51 A36 10c blue green 1.25 .80
O52 A36 10c orange ('95) 25.00 25.00
O53 A37 20c orange 1.25 .80
O54 A37 20c brown ('95) 25.00
O55 A38 25c red brown 1.25 .80
O56 A38 25c ver ('95) 55.00
O57 A39 50c lt blue 4.50 4.50
O58 A39 50c lilac ('95) 5.50 5.50
O59 A40 1p lilac 7.00 5.00
O60 A40 1p lt blue ('95) 40.00 22.50

Nos. O50, O52, O54, O56 and O60 were not regularly issued.

1891 On No. 99 *Rouletted 8*

O61 A24b 5c violet 1.50 1.25
a. "1391" 9.00

On Stamps of 1895-99

Perf. 12½ to 15 and Compound

1895-1900

O62 A51 1c bister .60 .60
O63 A51 1c slate blue ('97) 1.25 .55
O64 A52 2c blue .25 .25
O65 A52 2c claret ('97) 1.25 .55
O66 A53 5c red .80 .55
O67 A53 5c green ('97) 1.25 .55
O68 A53 5c grnsh blue ('00) .95 .75
O69 A54 7c deep green .50 .50
O70 A55 10c brown .50 .50
O71 A56 20c green & blk .80 .80
O72 A56 20c claret & blk ('97) 4.50 2.25
O73 A57 25c red brn & blk .80 .80
O74 A57 25c pink & bl ('97) 4.50 2.25
O75 A58 50c blue & blk .95 .95
O76 A58 50c grn & brn ('97) 5.75 2.75
O77 A59 1p org brn & blk 4.75 4.75
O78 A59 1p yel brn & bl ('97) 9.25 5.75
a. Inverted overprint
Nos. O62-O78 (17) 38.65 25.10

1897, Sept. On Nos. 133-135

O79 A62 1c brown vio & blk 1.25 1.00
O80 A63 5c pale bl & blk 1.75 1.00
O81 A64 10c lake & blk 1.75 1.10
Nos. O79-O81 (3) 4.75 3.10

Perf. 12½ to 15 and Compound

1897-1900 On Nos. 136-137

O82 A68 10c red 4.00 1.50
O83 A68 10c red lilac ('00) 2.00 1.25

Regular Issue of 1900-01 Overprinted

1901 *Perf. 14 to 16*

O84 A72 1c yellow green .55 .25
O85 A75 2c vermilion .70 .25
O86 A73 5c dull blue .70 .25
O87 A76 7c brown orange .95 .50
O88 A74 10c gray violet 1.00 .55
O89 A37 20c lt blue 8.50 4.00
O90 A38 25c bister brown 1.60 .80
O91 A40 1p deep green 11.00 6.00
a. Inverted overprint 15.00 8.00
Nos. O84-O91 (8) 25.00 12.60

Most of the used official stamps of 1901-1928 have been punched with holes of various shapes, in addition to the postal cancellations.

Regular Issue of 1904-05 Overprinted

1905 *Perf. 11½*

O92 A79 1c green .50 .25
O93 A80 2c orange red .50 .25
O94 A81 5c deep blue .50 .25
O95 A82 10c dark violet 1.00 .40
O96 A83 20c gray green 3.25 1.00
a. Inverted overprint
O97 A84 25c olive bister 2.25 .80
Nos. O92-O97 (6) 8.00 2.95

Regular Issues of 1904-07 Overprinted

1907, Mar.

O98 A79 1c green .25 .25
O99 A86 5c deep blue .25 .25
O100 A86 7c orange brown .25 .25
O101 A82 10c dark violet .25 .25
O102 A83 20c gray green .40 .35
a. Inverted overprint 4.00
O103 A84 25c olive bister .50 .40
O104 A86 50c rose .95 .70
Nos. O98-O104 (7) 2.85 2.45

Regular Issues of 1900-10 Overprinted

1910, July 15 *Perf. 14½ to 16*

O105 A75 2c vermilion 8.75 4.00
O106 A73 5c slate green 5.25 3.00
O107 A74 10c gray violet 2.75 1.25
O108 A37 20c grnsh blue 2.75 1.25
O109 A38 25c bister brown 4.50 2.40

Perf. 11½

O110 A86 50c rose 6.00 2.50
a. Inverted overprint 20.00 15.00
Nos. O105-O110 (6) 30.00 14.40

Peace—O1

1911, Feb. 18 **Litho.**

O111 O1 2c red brown .40 .25
O112 O1 5c dark blue .40 .40
O113 O1 8c slate .40 *.65*
O114 O1 20c gray brown .55 *.95*
O115 O1 23c claret .80 *.95*
O116 O1 50c orange 1.60 1.25
O117 O1 1p red 4.00 1.50
Nos. O111-O117 (7) 8.15 5.95

Regular Issue of 1912-15 Overprinted

1915, Sept. 16

O118 A90 2c carmine .55 .40
O119 A90 5c dark blue .55 .40
O120 A90 8c ultra .55 .40
O121 A90 20c dark brown 1.25 .50

O122 A91 23c dark blue 4.00 3.50
O123 A91 50c orange 6.00 3.50
O124 A91 1p vermilion 8.00 4.00
Nos. O118-O124 (7) 20.90 12.70

Regular Issue of 1919 Overprinted

1919, Dec. 25
O125 A95 2c red & black 1.00 .50
a. Inverted overprint 3.50
O126 A95 5c ultra & blk 1.10 .55
O127 A95 8c gray bl & lt brn 1.10 .55
a. Inverted overprint 3.50
O128 A95 20c brown & blk 2.40 1.00
O129 A95 23c green & brn 2.40 1.00
O130 A95 50c brown & bl 5.00 2.50
O131 A95 1p dull red & bl 12.00 5.00
a. Double overprint 15.00
Nos. O125-O131 (7) 25.00 11.10

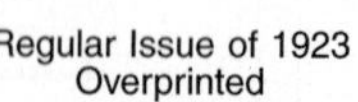

Regular Issue of 1923 Overprinted

1924 Wmk. 189 *Perf. 12½*
O132 A100 2c violet .25 .25
O133 A100 5c light blue .25 .25
O134 A100 12c deep blue .30 .25
O135 A100 20c buff .40 .25
O136 A100 36c blue green 1.75 1.25
O137 A100 50c orange 3.50 2.50
O138 A100 1p pink 6.25 5.00
O139 A100 2p lt green 12.00 10.00
Nos. O132-O139 (8) 24.70 19.75

Same Overprint on Regular Issue of 1924

1926-27 Unwmk. *Imperf.*
O140 A100 2c rose lilac .50 .25
O141 A100 5c pale blue .80 .25
O142 A100 8c pink ('27) 1.00 .25
O143 A100 12c slate blue 1.20 .25
O144 A100 20c brown 2.50 .50
O145 A100 36c dull rose 4.00 1.00
Nos. O140-O145 (6) 10.00 2.50

Regular Issue of 1924 Overprinted

1928 *Perf. 12½*
O146 A100 2c rose lilac 1.50 .95
O147 A100 8c pink 1.50 .50
O148 A100 10c turq blue 2.00 .50
Nos. O146-O148 (3) 5.00 1.95

Since 1928, instead of official stamps, Uruguay has used envelopes with "S. O." printed on them, and stamps of many issues which are punched with various designs such as star or crescent.

NEWSPAPER STAMPS

No. 245 Surcharged

1922, June 1 Unwmk. *Perf. 11½*
P1 A97 3c on 4c orange .40 .40
a. Inverted surcharge 9.50 9.50
b. Double surcharge 2.50 2.50

Nos. 235-237 Surcharged

1924, June 1 *Perf. 14½*
P2 A96 3c on 2c car & blk .40 .40
P3 A96 6c on 4c red org & bl .40 .40
P4 A96 9c on 5c bl & brn .40 .40
Nos. P2-P4 (3) 1.20 1.20

Nos. 288, 291, 293 Overprinted or Surcharged in Red

1926 *Imperf.*
P5 A100 3c gray green .80 .25
a. Double overprint 1.00 1.00
P6 A100 9c on 10c turq bl .95 .40
a. Double surcharge 1.00 1.00
P7 A100 15c light violet 1.25 .50
Nos. P5-P7 (3) 3.00 1.15

PARCEL POST STAMPS

Mercury — PP1

Imprint: "IMPRENTA NACIONAL"
Inscribed "Exterior"
Size: 20x29½mm
Perf. 11½

1922, Jan. 15 Litho. Unwmk.
Q1 PP1 5c grn, *straw* .25 .25
Q2 PP1 10c grn, *bl gray* .40 .25
Q3 PP1 20c grn, *rose* 2.10 .55
Q4 PP1 30c grn, *blue grn* 2.10 .25
Q5 PP1 50c grn, *gray grn* 3.50 .50
Q6 PP1 1p grn, *org* 5.25 1.75
Nos. Q1-Q6 (6) 13.60 3.55

Inscribed "Interior"
Q7 PP1 5c grn, *straw* .25 .25
Q8 PP1 10c grn, *bl gray* .25 .25
Q9 PP1 20c grn, *rose* 1.00 .25
Q10 PP1 30c grn, *bl grn* 1.40 .25
Q11 PP1 50c grn, *blue* 2.25 .35
Q12 PP1 1p grn, *org* 6.00 1.25
Nos. Q7-Q12 (6) 11.15 2.60

Imprint: "IMP. NACIONAL"
Inscribed "Exterior"

1926, Jan. 20 *Perf. 11½*
Q13 PP1 20c grn, *rose* 1.75 .50

Inscribed "Interior"
Perf. 11
Q14 PP1 5c grn, *yellow* .40 .25
Q15 PP1 10c grn, *bl gray* .50 .25
Q16 PP1 20c grn, *rose* 1.00 .25
Q17 PP1 30c grn, *bl grn* 1.75 .40
Nos. Q13-Q17 (5) 5.40 1.65

Inscribed "Exterior"

1926 *Perf. 11½*
Q18 PP1 5c blk, *straw* .40 .25
Q19 PP1 10c blk, *bl gray* .65 .25
Q20 PP1 20c blk, *rose* 1.75 .25

Inscribed "Interior"
Q21 PP1 5c blk, *straw* .40 .25
Q22 PP1 10c blk, *bl gray* .50 .25
Q23 PP1 20c blk, *rose* 1.00 .25
Q24 PP1 30c blk, *bl grn* 1.75 .40
Nos. Q18-Q24 (7) 6.45 1.90

PP2

Perf. 11, 11½

1927, Feb. 22 Wmk. 188
Q25 PP2 1c dp bl .25 .25
Q26 PP2 2c lt grn .25 .25
Q27 PP2 4c violet .25 .25
Q28 PP2 5c red .25 .25
Q29 PP2 10c dk brn .40 .25
Q30 PP2 20c orange .65 .40
Nos. Q25-Q30 (6) 2.05 1.65

See Nos. Q35-Q38, Q51-Q54.

PP3

Size: 15x20mm

1928, Nov. 20 *Perf. 11*
Q31 PP3 5c blk, *straw* .25 .25
Q32 PP3 10c blk, *gray blue* .25 .25
Q33 PP3 20c blk, *rose* .50 .25
Q34 PP3 30c blk, *green* .80 .25
Nos. Q31-Q34 (4) 1.80 1.00

Type of 1927 Issue

1929-30 Unwmk. *Perf. 11, 12½*
Q35 PP2 1c violet .25 .25
Q36 PP2 1c ultra ('30) .25 .25
Q37 PP2 2c bl grn ('30) .25 .25
Q38 PP2 5c red ('30) .25 .25
Nos. Q35-Q38 (4) 1.00 1.00

Nos. Q35-Q38, and possibly later issues, occasionally show parts of a papermaker's watermark.

PP4

1929, July 27 Wmk. 188 *Perf. 11*
Q39 PP4 10c orange .50 .50
Q40 PP4 15c slate blue .50 .50
Q41 PP4 20c ol brn .50 .50
Q42 PP4 25c rose red 1.00 .50
Q43 PP4 50c dark gray 2.00 1.00
Q44 PP4 75c violet 8.00 6.00
Q45 PP4 1p gray green 7.50 3.00
Nos. Q39-Q45 (7) 20.00 12.00

For overprints see Nos. Q57-Q63.

Ship and Train — PP5

1938-39 Unwmk. *Perf. 12½*
Q46 PP5 10c scarlet .40 .25
Q47 PP5 20c dk bl .60 .25
Q48 PP5 30c lt vio ('39) .95 .25
Q49 PP5 50c green 1.75 .25
Q50 PP5 1p brn org 2.50 1.10
Nos. Q46-Q50 (5) 6.20 2.10

See Nos. Q70-Q73, Q80, Q88-Q90, Q92-Q93, Q95.

Type of 1927 Redrawn

1942-55? Litho. *Perf. 12½*
Q51 PP2 1c vio ('55)
Q52 PP2 2c bl grn .25 .25
Q54 PP2 5c lt red ('44) .25 .25

The vertical and horizontal lines of the design have been strengthened, the "2" redrawn, etc. No. Q51 has oval "O" in CENTESIMO, 2¼mm from frame line at right; No. Q35 has round "O" 1¾mm from frame line.

Numeral of Value — PP6

1943, Apr. 28 Engr.
Q55 PP6 1c dk car rose .25 .25
Q56 PP6 2c grnsh blk .25 .25

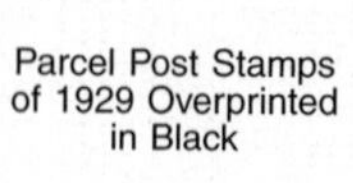

Parcel Post Stamps of 1929 Overprinted in Black

1943, Dec. 15 Wmk. 188 *Perf. 11*
Q57 PP4 10c orange 1.00 .50
Q58 PP4 15c slate blue 1.00 .50
Q59 PP4 20c olive brn 1.00 .50
Q60 PP4 25c rose red 1.50 1.00
Q61 PP4 50c dk gray 2.50 2.00
Q62 PP4 75c violet 5.00 4.00
Q63 PP4 1p gray grn 8.00 4.50
Nos. Q57-Q63 (7) 20.00 13.00

Catalogue values for unused stamps in this section, from this point to the end of the section, are for Never Hinged items.

Bank of the Republic PP7

University PP8

Perf. 12½

1945, Sept. 5 Litho. Unwmk.
Q64 PP7 1c green .55 .25
Q65 PP8 2c brt vio .55 .25

See Nos. Q77-Q79, Q84.

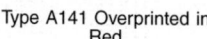

Custom House — PP9

1946, Dec. 11 *Perf. 11½*
Q66 PP9 5c yel brn & bl .55 .25

Type A141 Overprinted in Red

1946, Dec. 27 *Perf. 12½*
Q67 A141 1p light blue 1.20 .25

See Nos. Q69, Q76.

Mail Coach — PP11

1946, Dec. 23
Q68 PP11 5p red & ol brn 20.00 5.00

Type A141 Overprinted in Black

1947
Q69 A141 2c dull violet brn .55 .25

See Nos. Q74-Q76.

Type of 1938

1947-52 Unwmk. *Perf. 12½*
Size: 16x19.5mm (5c, 30c)
Q70 PP5 5c brown org ('52) .40 .25
Size: 17x20.5mm
Q71 PP5 10c violet .40 .25
Q72 PP5 20c vermilion .70 .25
Q73 PP5 30c blue 1.40 .25
Nos. Q70-Q73 (4) 2.90 1.00

Type of 1947

1948-49 Black Overprint
Q74 A141 1c rose lilac ('49) .40 .25
Q75 A141 5c ultra .40 .25
Q76 A141 5p rose carmine 7.00 1.75
Nos. Q74-Q76 (3) 7.80 2.25

Types of 1945

1950
Q77 PP8 1c vermilion .55 .25
Q78 PP7 2c chalky blue .55 .25

1952 *Perf. 11*
Q79 PP7 10c blue green .55 .25

Type of 1938-39

1954 *Perf. 12½*
Q80 PP5 20c carmine .55 .25

Custom House — PP13

1p, State Railroad Administration Building.

1955 Unwmk. Litho. *Perf. 12½*

Q81 PP13 5c brown	.35	.25
Q82 PP13 1p light ultra	2.50	1.60

See Nos. Q83, Q85-Q86, Q96. For surcharge see No. Q87.

Types of 1945 and 1955

Design: 20c, Solis Theater.

1956-57 *Perf. 11*

Q83 PP13 5c gray ('57)	.60	.25
Q84 PP7 10c lt olive grn	.50	.25
Q85 PP13 20c yellow	.50	.25
Q86 PP13 20c lt red brn ('57)	.50	.25
Nos. Q83-Q86 (4)	2.10	1.00

No. Q83 Surcharged with New Value in Red

1957

Q87 PP13 30c on 5c gray	.55	.25

Type of 1938-39

1957-60 Wmk. 327 *Perf. 11*

Q88 PP5 20c lt blue ('59)	.45	.25

Unwmk.

Q89 PP5 30c red lilac	.45	.25

Perf. 12½

Q90 PP5 1p dk blue ('60)	.85	.50
Nos. Q88-Q90 (3)	1.75	1.00

Nos. Q88 and Q93 are in slightly larger format-17¼x21mm instead of 16x19½mm.

National Printing Works — PP14

1960, Mar. 23 Wmk. 327 *Perf. 11*

Q91 PP14 30c yellow green	.55	.25

Type of 1938-39

1962-63 Wmk. 332 *Perf. 11*

Q92 PP5 50c slate green	.40	.25

Perf. 10½

Q93 PP5 1p blue grn ('63)	.85	.50

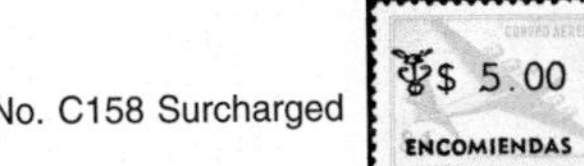

No. C158 Surcharged

1965 Unwmk. *Perf. 11*

Q94 AP12 5p on 84c orange	.60	.25

For use on regular and air post parcels.

Types of 1938-55

1p, State Railroad Administration Building.

1966 Litho. *Perf. 10½*

Q95 PP5 10c blue green	.55	.25

Wmk. 327

Q96 PP13 1p brown	.55	.25

No. C184 Surcharged in Red

1966 Unwmk. *Perf. 11*

Q97 AP21 1p on 38c black	.55	.25

Plane and Bus — PP15

Design: 20p, Plane facing left and bus; "Encomiendas" on top.

Wmk. 332

1969, July 8 Litho. *Perf. 12*

Q98 PP15 10p blk, crim & bl grn	.45	.25
Q99 PP15 20p bl, blk & yel	.70	.25

No. B7 Surcharged

1971, Feb. 3 Wmk. 327 *Perf. 11½*

Q100 SP2 60c on 1p + 10c	1.50	.60

No. 761 Surcharged in Red

1971, Nov. 12 Wmk. 332 *Perf. 12*

Q101 A226 60c on 6p lt grn & blk	.70	.25

Nos. 770-771 Surcharged

1972, Nov. 6 Litho. *Perf. 12*

Q102 A233 1p on 6p multi (#770)	1.75	.55
Q103 A233 1p on 6p multi (#771)	1.75	.55
a. Pair, #Q102-Q103	3.50	1.10

See note after No. 771.

Parcels and Arrows — PP16

Old Mail Truck — PP17

Designs: Early means of mail transport.

1974 Wmk. 332 Litho. *Perf. 12*

Q104 PP16 75p shown	.40	.25
Q105 PP17 100p shown	.60	.30
Q106 PP17 150p Steam engine	1.40	.95
Q107 PP17 300p Side-wheeler	1.40	.75
Q108 PP17 500p Plane	2.00	1.00
Nos. Q104-Q108 (5)	5.80	3.25

Issue dates: 75p, Feb. 13; others, Mar. 6.

UZBEKISTAN

ˌuz-ˌbe-ki-ˈstan

LOCATION — Central Asia, bounded by Kazakhstan, Turkmenistan, Tajikistan, Afghanistan and Kyrgyzstan
GOVT. — Independent republic, member of the Commonwealth of Independent States
AREA — 172,741 sq. mi.
POP. — 25,155,064 (2001 est.)
CAPITAL — Tashkent (Toshkent)

With the breakup of the Soviet Union on Dec. 26, 1991, Uzbekistan and ten former Soviet republics established the Commonwealth of Independent States.

100 Kopecks = 1 Ruble
100 Tiyin = 1 Sum

Catalogue values for all unused stamps in this country are for Never Hinged items.

Princess Nodira (1792-1842) — A1

Perf. 11½x12

1992, May 7 Unwmk. Photo.

1 A1 20k multicolored	.45	.45

For surcharge, see No. 749.

Melitaea Acreina — A2

1992, Aug. 31 Litho. *Perf. 12*

2 A2 1r multicolored	.40	.40

For surcharge, see No. 752.

Independence from Soviet Union, 1st Anniv. — A3

1992, Sept. 25 Photo. *Perf. 12*

3 A3 1r multicolored	.40	.40

Khiva Mosque, 19th Cent. — A4

1992, Oct. 20 *Perf. 11½*

4 A4 50k multicolored	.40	.40

For surcharge, see No. 750.

Samarkand A5

1992, Oct. 28 Litho. *Perf. 13x13½*

5 A5 10r multicolored	.60	.60

Winner of 1992 Aga Khan Award for Architecture. For surcharge, see No. 753.

Samovar, 19th Cent. — A6

1992, Nov. 20 *Perf. 12x11½*

6 A6 50k multicolored	.40	.40

For surcharge, see No. 751.

Fauna — A7

Designs: 1r, Teratoscincus scincus. No. 8, Naja oxiana. No. 9, Ondatra zibethica, vert. 3r, Pandion haliaetus, vert. 5r, Remiz pendulinus, vert. 10r, Dryomys nitedula, vert. 15r, Varanus griseus. 20r, Cervus elaphus baktrianus.

1993, Mar. 12 Litho. *Perf. 12*

7 A7 1r multicolored	.25	.25
8 A7 2r multicolored	.25	.25
9 A7 2r multicolored	.25	.25
10 A7 3r multicolored	.25	.25
11 A7 5r multicolored	.25	.25
12 A7 10r multicolored	.25	.25
13 A7 15r multicolored	.50	.50
Nos. 7-13 (7)	2.00	2.00

Souvenir Sheet

14 A7 20r multicolored	1.00	1.00

For surcharges, see Nos. 769-776.

Russia Nos. 4596-4600, 5838, 5841-5843, 5984 Surcharged in Vio Bl, Brt Bl, Bl, Red, Blk and Grn

a

Methods and perfs as before

1993

15	A2765 2r on 1k (#5838, BB)	.60	.60
16	A2138 8r on 4k (#4599, Bl)	.55	.55
17	A2138 15r on 2k (#4597)	4.50	4.50
18	A2765 15r on 2k (#5984)	4.50	4.50
19	A2765 15r on 3k (#5839, R)	4.50	4.50
20	A2765 15r on 4k (#4599, V)	4.50	4.50
21	A2765 15r on 4k (#5840, R)	4.50	4.50
22	A2765 15r on 5k (#5841)	4.50	4.50
23	A2139 15r on 6k (#4600, R)	4.50	4.50
24	A2765 15r on 7k (#5985a, R)	4.50	4.50
25	A2765 15r on 10k (#5842)	4.50	4.50
26	A2765 15r on 15k (#5843, R)	4.50	4.50
27	A2138 20r on 4k (#4599, Bk)	.75	.75
28	A2139 30r on 3k (#4598, G)	.75	.75
28A	A2138 100r on 1k (#4596, R)	.90	.90
29	A2138 500r on 1k (#4596, Bl)	5.25	5.25
	Nos. 15-29 (16)	53.80	53.80

No. 18 exists imperf.

Flag and Coat of Arms — A8

Perf. 12x12½, 11½x12 (#33)

1993, June 10 Litho.

30 A8 8r multicolored	.30	.30
31 A8 15r multicolored	.35	.35
33 A8 50r multicolored	.85	.85
34 A8 100r multicolored	2.00	2.00
Nos. 30-34 (4)	3.50	3.50

No. 33 is 19x26½mm.

Flowers — A9

No. 38, Dianthus uzbekistanicus. No. 39, Colchicum kesselringii. No. 40, Crocus alatavicus. No. 41, Salvia bucharica. No. 42, Tulipa kaufmanniana. No. 43, Tulipa greigii. No. 44, Tulip.

1993, Sept. 10 *Perf. 12*

38 A9 20r multicolored	.25	.25
39 A9 20r multicolored	.25	.25
40 A9 25r multicolored	.25	.25
41 A9 25r multicolored	.25	.25
42 A9 30r multicolored	.30	.30
43 A9 30r multicolored	.30	.30
Nos. 38-43 (6)	1.60	1.60

Souvenir Sheet

44 A9 50r multicolored	1.00	1.00

For surcharges, see Nos. 777-783.

Coat of Arms — A10

1994-95 Litho. *Perf. 12*
Denomination Expressed as "1.00"

45 A10 1s green 1.75 1.75

Perf. 11½x12

46 A10 75s claret .40 .40

Issued: 1s, 3/20/95; 75s, 7/2. See Nos. 151A-154, 167-171, 228-237, 405-415.

1995 Litho. *Perf. 14*
Denominations Expressed With "CYM"

46A A10 1s green — —
47 A10 2s green 2.00 2.00

Size: 20x33mm

48 A10 3s carmine 2.00 2.00
49 A10 6s carmine 3.00 3.00
49A A10 15s blue 3.00 3.00

Denomination Shown with Decimal

50 A10 3s carmine .50 .50
51 A10 6s blue 1.75 1.75
Nos. 45-51 (8) 14.40 14.40

Issued: 15s, 12/26; 2s, 3s, 6s, 4/18.
See Nos. 151A-154, 167-171, 228-237, 405-415.

Arms Type of 1994-95

1997, Dec. 30 Litho. *Perf. 14*
Size: 14x22mm

51A A10 6s green 22.50 22.50

No. 51A is dated 1997.

Statue of Tamerlane, Tashkent — A10a

1994, Sept. 1 Litho. *Perf. 12½x12*

52 A10a 20t multicolored .45 .45

For surcharge, see No. 761.

Bakhouddin, 675th Anniv. — A11

1994, Aug. 1 *Perf. 12½x12*

55 A11 100s multi + label .50 .50

Souvenir Sheet

President's Cup Intl. Tennis Tournament, Tashkent — A12

1994, June 3 *Perf. 12x12½*

56 A12 500s multicolored 1.25 1.25

Ulugh Beg (1394-1449), Astronomer — A13

30t, Portals of Samarkand. 35t, Portals of Bukhara. 40t, Globe, astrolabe. 45t, Statue. 60t, Portrait.

1994, Sept. 15 Litho. *Perf. 12x12½*

57 A13 30t multi + label .30 .30
58 A13 35t multi + label .30 .30
59 A13 40t multi + label .30 .30
60 A13 45t multil .70 .70
Nos. 57-60 (4) 1.60 1.60

Souvenir Sheet

61 A13 60t multicolored .75 .75

For surcharges, see Nos. 762-766.

Russia Nos. 4596, 5113, 5839, 5840, 5843, 5984 Surcharged in Red Violet or Red

b

Methods and perfs as before

1995, Jan.

61A A2138(a) 2s on 1k (#4596, R) *1.50 1.50*
61B A2765(a) 2s on 3k (#5839, R) *1.50 1.50*
61C A2765(b) 200s on 2k (#5984) *1.50 1.50*
61D A2765(b) 200s on 4k (#5840) *1.50 1.50*
61E A2436(b) 200s on 5k (#5113) *1.50 1.50*
61F A2765(b) 200s on 15k (#5843) *1.50 1.50*
Nos. 61A-61F (6) *9.00 9.00*

No. 61C exists imperf. Value *$7.50.*

Souvenir Sheet

End of World War II, 50th Anniv. A14

1995, May 8 Litho. *Perf. 12*

62 A14 20s multicolored 3.00 3.00

Souvenir Sheet

UPU A15

1995, Sept. 21

63 A15 20s multicolored 2.50 2.50

Capra Falconeri — A16

1995, Aug. 15 *Perf. 12½*

64 A16 6s shown .95 .55
65 A16 10s Three on mountain 1.60 .85
66 A16 10s Up close 1.60 .85
67 A16 15s Lying down 2.50 1.40
Nos. 64-67 (4) 6.65 3.65

World Wildlife Fund.

Intl. Tennis Tournament, Tashkent '95 — A17

1995, Aug. 25 *Perf. 14*

68 A17 10s multicolored 2.25 2.25

Silk Road Architecture — A19

Designs: 6s, Mosque, 15th cent. No. 71, Blue-domed mosque, ruins, 15th cent. No. 72, Mosque with 4 minarets, 19th cent. No. 73, Cylindrical-style mosque, 19th cent. 20s, Map of mosque sites, camel, mosque.

1995, Aug. 28 Litho. *Perf. 12x12½*

70 A19 6s multicolored 1.25 1.25
71 A19 10s multicolored 2.50 2.50
72 A19 10s multicolored 2.50 2.50
73 A19 15s multicolored 3.75 3.75
Nos. 70-73 (4) 10.00 10.00

Souvenir Sheet

74 A19 20s multicolored 6.00 6.00

Folktales A20

6s, Man wrestling with creature, woman spilling bowls. No. 76, Man looking at stork, nest of eggs. No. 77, Women watching man cut into watermelon full of gold coins. No. 78, Creature carrying woman. 15s, Man holding beads, parrot.

1995, Aug. 24

75 A20 6s multi + label 2.40 2.40
76 A20 10s multicolored 3.25 3.25
77 A20 10s multicolored 3.25 3.25
78 A20 10s multicolored 3.25 3.25
79 A20 15s multicolored 5.00 5.00
Nos. 75-79 (5) 17.15 17.15

Moths — A21

6s, Karanasa abramovi. No. 81, Colias romanovi. No. 82, Parnassius delphius. No. 83, Neohipparchia fatua. No. 84, Chasara staudingeri. No. 85, Colias wiskotti. 15s, Parnassius tianschanicus.
20s, Colias christophi.

1995, Oct. 10 *Perf. 12½x12*

80 A21 6s multicolored 1.40 1.40
81 A21 10s multicolored 2.25 2.25
82 A21 10s multicolored 2.25 2.25
83 A21 10s multicolored 2.25 2.25
84 A21 10s multicolored 2.25 2.25
85 A21 10s multicolored 2.25 2.25
86 A21 15s multicolored 3.00 3.00
Nos. 80-86 (7) 15.65 15.65

Souvenir Sheet

87 A21 20s multicolored 3.75 3.75

Aircraft — A22

1995, Oct. 10

88 A22 6s JIN-2 1.25 1.25
89 A22 10s IL-76 2.00 2.00
90 A22 10s KA-22 2.00 2.00
91 A22 10s AN-8 2.00 2.00
92 A22 10s AN-22 2.00 2.00
93 A22 10s AN-12 2.00 2.00
94 A22 15s IL-114 3.00 3.00
Nos. 88-94 (7) 14.25 14.25

Souvenir Sheet

95 A22 20s like No. 94 4.25 4.25

Wildlife from Tashkent Zoo — A23

Designs: 6s, Camelus ferus. No. 97, Aegypius monachus. No. 98, Ursus arctos isabellinus. No. 99, Zebra. No. 100, Macaca mulatta. No. 101, Pelecanus crispus. 15s, Loxodonta africana.
20s, Capra falconeri.

1995, Nov. 30 *Perf. 12x12½*

96 A23 6s multicolored 1.10 1.10
97 A23 10s multicolored 1.75 1.75
98 A23 10s multicolored 1.75 1.75
99 A23 10s multicolored 1.75 1.75
100 A23 10s multicolored 1.75 1.75
101 A23 10s multicolored 1.75 1.75
102 A23 15s multicolored 2.50 2.50
Nos. 96-102 (7) 12.35 12.35

Souvenir Sheet

103 A23 20s multicolored 3.25 3.25

Wild Animals — A24

Designs: 10s, Ovis ammon bocharensis. No. 105, Ovis ammon severtzov. No. 106, Cervus elaphus bactrianus. No. 107, Capra sibirica. No. 108, Ovis ammon karelini. No. 109, Ovis ammon cycloceros. 20s, Saiga tatarica.
25s, Gazella subgutturosa.

1996, Feb. 16 *Perf. 12½x12*

104 A24 10s multicolored 1.25 1.25
105 A24 15s multicolored 1.90 1.90
106 A24 15s multicolored 1.90 1.90
107 A24 15s multicolored 1.90 1.90
108 A24 15s multicolored 1.90 1.90
109 A24 15s multicolored 1.90 1.90
110 A24 20s multicolored 2.75 2.75
Nos. 104-110 (7) 13.50 13.50

Souvenir Sheet

111 A24 25s multicolored 3.50 3.50

Painting — A25

1995, Oct. Litho. *Perf. 12x12½*

112 A25 15s multicolored 2.75 2.75

Souvenir Sheet

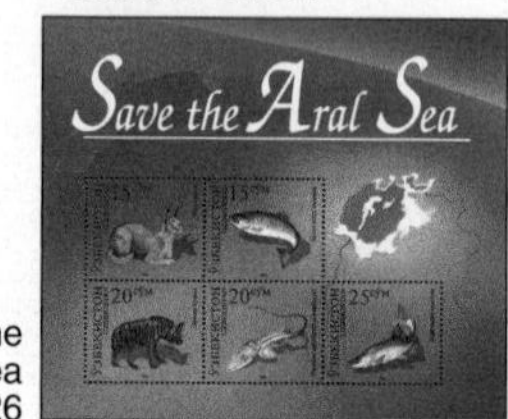

Save the Aral Sea A26

a, 15s, Felis caracal. b, 15s, Salmo trutta aralensis. c, 20s, Hyaena hyaena. d, 20t, Pseudoscaphirynchus kaufmanni. e, 25t, Aspiolucius esocinus.

1996, May 15 *Perf. 14*

113 A26 Sheet of 5, #a.-e. 5.00 5.00

See Kazakhstan No. 145, Kyrgyzstan No. 107, Tadjikistan No. 91, Turkmenistan No. 52.

1996 Summer Olympic Games, Atlanta — A27

1996, June 23 Litho. *Perf. 12½x12*

114 A27 6s Soccer .60 .60
115 A27 10s Equestrian event 1.25 1.25
116 A27 15s Boxing 1.75 1.75
117 A27 20s Cycling 2.50 2.50
Nos. 114-117 (4) 6.10 6.10

Souvenir Sheet

Tamerlane (1336-1405) — A28

1996, Aug. 31 Litho. *Perf. 14*

118	A28	20s multicolored	3.50	3.50
a.		Inscribed "1336-1404," perf 12x12½	*5.00*	*5.00*

Issued: No. 118a, 8/9/96.

Souvenir Sheet

Independence Day — A29

1996, Aug. 27 Litho. *Perf. 12x12½*

119	A29	20s multicolored	2.50	2.50

Tashkent Tennis Cup Championship — A30

1996, Sept. 2 Litho. *Perf. 14*

121	A30	12s green	11.00	11.00

A31

1996, Sept. 18 *Perf. 14*

122	A31	15s Faijzulla Khodjaev	6.50	6.50

A32

1996, Oct. 14 Litho. *Perf. 14*

123	A32	15s black & buff	6.50	6.50

Abdurauf Fitrat (1886-1996).

Futuristic Space Travel — A33

9s, Shuttle-type vehicle. No. 126, Vehicle in front of sun. No. 127, Sun's rays, vehicle traveling left. No. 128, Large vehicle, sun in distance. No. 129, Saucer-shaped vehicle landing on planet. 25s, Two men in cockpit. 30s, Two different space vehicles.

1997, Mar. 17

124	A33	9s multi, vert.	.90	.90
125	A33	15s shown	1.35	1.35
126	A33	15s multi	1.35	1.35
127	A33	15s multi	1.35	1.35
128	A33	15s multi, vert.	1.35	1.35
129	A33	15s multi, vert.	1.35	1.35
130	A33	25s multi, vert.	2.00	2.00
		Nos. 124-130 (7)	9.65	9.65

Souvenir Sheet

131	A33	30s multi, vert.	5.00	5.00

Fairy Tales — A34

No. 132, Genie. No. 133, Bird. No. 134, Child holding mirror in front of couple. No. 135, Ape. No. 136, Face of creature, horse. No. 137, Large bird attacking deer. 30s, Two people kneeling before throne.
35s, Man on horse.

1997, Apr. 18

132	A34	15s multicolored	1.10	1.10
133	A34	15s multicolored	1.10	1.10
134	A34	20s multicolored	1.40	1.40
135	A34	20s multicolored	1.40	1.40
136	A34	25s multicolored	1.60	1.60
137	A34	25s multicolored	1.60	1.60
138	A34	30s multicolored	2.25	2.25
		Nos. 132-138 (7)	10.45	10.45

Souvenir Sheet

139	A34	35s multicolored	6.50	6.50

Abdulhamid Sulaymon, Birth Cent. — A35

1997, June 20

140	A35	6s lilac, black & gray	*4.75*	*4.75*

Pantera Pardus Tullianus — A36

Designs: No. 142, Yawning. No. 143, Stretching. 25s, Walking on fallen tree.
30s, With mouth open.

1997, May 28

141	A36	9s multicolored	.95	.95
142	A36	15s multicolored	1.75	1.75
143	A36	15s multicolored	1.75	1.75
144	A36	25s multicolored	3.25	3.25
		Nos. 141-144 (4)	7.70	7.70

Souvenir Sheet

145	A36	30s multicolored	3.75	3.75

No. 145 contains one 30x40mm stamp.

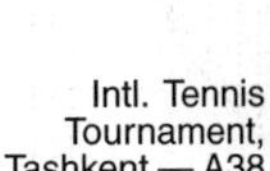

Sites on Silk Road — A37

In Bukhara: No. 146, Ancient citadel. No. 147, Tomb of Ismail Samani, vert.
In Khiva: No. 148, Minaret, vert. No. 149, Fortress wall with open door.
No. 150, Mosque, Bukhara. No. 151, Minaret, Khiva, diff., vert.

1997 Litho. *Perf. 14*

146	A37	15s multicolored	2.50	2.50
147	A37	15s multicolored	2.50	2.50
148	A37	15s multicolored	2.50	2.50
149	A37	15s multicolored	2.50	2.50
		Nos. 146-149 (4)	10.00	10.00

Souvenir Sheets

150	A37	30s multicolored	3.00	3.00
151	A37	30s multicolored	3.00	3.00

Issued: Nos. 146-147, 150, 10/7; Nos. 148-149, 151, 10/8.

Arms Type of 1994 Redrawn

1998 Litho. *Perf. 14*

Size: 14x22mm

151A	A10	2s green	.40	.40
152	A10	3s carmine, "1998"	1.25	1.25
a.		Dated "1999"	.50	.50
153	A10	6s green, "1998"	3.00	3.00
a.		Dated "1999"	.70	.70
153A	A10	12s green	2.75	2.75
153B	A10	15s red	1.75	1.75
154	A10	45s blue	4.25	4.25
		Nos. 151A-154 (6)	13.40	13.40

Nos. 152-154 have country name "O'ZBEKISTON" at top and "POCHTA 1998" at bottom.
Issued: 6s, 2/25; 12s, 15s, 45s, 3/25; 2s, 4/16; 3s, 4/17.

Intl. Tennis Tournament, Tashkent — A38

Emblem and: No. 155, President's Cup. No. 156, Tennis player. No. 157, Camel.

1997 Litho. *Perf. 14*

155	A38	6s blue & grn	*4.00*	*4.00*
156	A38	6s blue & grn	*4.00*	*4.00*
157	A38	6s blue & grn	*4.00*	*4.00*
		Nos. 155-157 (3)	*12.00*	*12.00*

Automobiles — A39

a, 9s, Tico. b, 12s, Damas. c, 15s, Nexia.

1997, Sept. 19 Litho. *Perf. 14*

158	A39	Block of 3, #a.-c. + label	6.00	6.00

Tennis Tournament — A40

1998, Aug. 17 Litho. *Perf. 14*

159	A40	15s multicolored	1.25	1.25

Sharq Taronlalari Intl. Music Festival — A41

1998, July 15

160	A41	15s multicolored	1.00	1.00

Berdekh Monument — A42

1998, Aug. 17

161	A42	15s blue & brown	1.00	1.00

Kamal ud-Din Behzad, Painter — A43

1998, Aug. 17

162	A43	15s multicolored	1.40	1.40

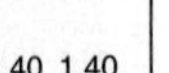

Imam al-Buhkari — A44

1998, June 26

163	A44	15s multicolored	1.00	1.00

Ahmad al-Farghani, Astronomer — A45

1998, June 26

164	A45	15s multicolored	1.50	1.50

Folktales A46

Designs: a, 8s, Woman holding baby. b, 10s, "Alpomish" over rainbow. c, 15s, Three men seated before fire. d, 15s, Man talking to man with sword. e, 18s, Man riding horse. f, 18s, Knight with longbow, squire with arrow. g, 20s, Swordmaker at work. h, 20s, Man fighting lion. i, 25s, Man, woman walking arm in arm.

1998, Nov. 27 Litho. *Perf. 14*

165	A46	Sheet of 9, #a.-i.	7.50	7.50

No. 165 is a continuous design.

Arms Type of 1994 Redrawn

1999-2001 Litho. *Perf. 14*

Size: 14x23mm

167	A10	5s blue green, "2000"	*2.00*	*2.00*
a.		Dated "2004"	2.25	2.25
b.		Dated "2005"	2.25	2.25
168	A10	6s green	*1.00*	*1.00*
168A	A10	10s dk green	*.50*	*.50*
d.		10s blue grn, dated "2004"	*1.50*	*1.50*
168B	A10	15s lt blue	*.85*	*.85*
168C	A10	17s dk blue	*.90*	*.90*
169	A10	30s blue	*1.00*	*1.00*
170	A10	40s rose, "2000"	*1.50*	*1.50*
b.		Dated "2001"	*1.25*	*1.25*
170A	A10	45s rose	*2.75*	*2.75*
c.		45s carmine, dated "2001"	*3.00*	*3.00*
171	A10	60s rose car	*2.75*	*2.75*
		Nos. 167-171 (9)	*13.25*	*13.25*

Issued: 6s, 3/22/99. 15s, 17s, 30s, 45s, 12/5/00. 5s, 60s, 1/17/01; No. 168A, 40s, 2/5/01. No. 168Ad, 6/15/04.
Nos. 167-171 have country name "O'ZBEKISTON" at top and "POCHTA" and year at bottom. Stamps issued in 2001 are inscribed "2000."
No. 168 is inscribed "6 so'm." No. 153 is inscribed "6-00."

Trains — A47

Locomotives: No. 172, OV steam, 1897-1917. No. 173, EA steam, 1931-35. 28s, FD steam, 1931-41. 36s, SO steam, 1934-52. No. 176, VL-22 electric. No. 177, KCh. 69s, TEP-6.

1999, May 11 Litho. *Perf. 14*

172	A47	18s multicolored	*.70*	*.70*
173	A47	18s multicolored	*.70*	*.70*
174	A47	28s multicolored	*1.00*	*1.00*
175	A47	36s multicolored	*1.10*	*1.10*
176	A47	56s multicolored	*2.00*	*2.00*
177	A47	56s multicolored	*2.00*	*2.00*
178	A47	69s multicolored	*2.25*	*2.25*
		Nos. 172-178 (7)	*9.75*	*9.75*

A48

Designs: 18s, Horse rearing.
No. 180, horiz.: a, 36s, Robed rider on horse. b, 28s, White horse. c, 69s, Jockey on race horse.
75s, Black horse, horiz.

1999, May 25

179 A48 18s multicolored *1.75 1.75*
180 A48 Vert. strip of 3, #a.-c. *4.00 4.00*

Souvenir Sheet

181 A48 75s multicolored *3.25 3.25*

No. 180 printed in sheets of 8 stamps containing 2 strips and one each of Nos. 180a and 180c.

A49

No. 182 — Story of Badal Qorachi: a, 18s, Woman, deer. b, 18s, Two archers on horses. c, 28s, Archer on horse. d, 36s, White giant. e, 56s, Black giant. f, 56s, Troll, cat, bones. g, 69s, Man, woman.
75s, Woman on sofa, demon, horiz.

1999, June 8

182 A49 Sheet of 7, #a.-g. + label *7.50 7.50*

Souvenir Sheet

183 A49 75s multicolored *3.25 3.25*

A50

Reptiles: No. 184, Trapelus sanguinolentus.
No. 185, horiz.: a, 18s, Eremias arguta. b, 18s, Vipera ursinii. c, 28s, Phrynocephalus mystaceus. d, 36s, Agkistrodon halys. e, 56s, Eumeces schneideri. f, 69s, Vipera lebetina.
75s, Two lizards, horiz.

1999, June 22

184 A50 56s multicolored *1.25 1.25*
185 A50 Sheet of 6, #a.-f. *6.25 6.25*

Souvenir Sheet

186 A50 75s multicolored *3.75 3.75*

A51

1999, July 7

187 A51 45s light green & black *1.60 1.60*

UPU, 125th anniv.

A52

1999, July 21

188 A52 30s green & claret *1.25 1.25*

Muhammadrizo Erniyozbek ogli-Ogahiy, poet.

A53

Birds of Prey: No. 189, Circaetus qallicus. No. 190, Falco tinnunculus. No. 191, Aquila chrysaetos. No. 192, Gyps fulvus. 36s, Falco cherrug. 56s, Gypaetus barbatus. 60s, Pandion haliaetus.
75s, Bird, hatchlings.

1999, Oct. 22 Litho. *Perf. 14x13¾*

189 A53 15s multi *.70 .70*
190 A53 15s multi *.70 .70*
191 A53 18s multi *.90 .90*
192 A53 18s multi *.90 .90*
193 A53 36s multi *1.25 1.25*
194 A53 56s multi *1.75 1.75*
195 A53 60s multi *2.00 2.00*
Nos. 189-195 (7) 8.20 8.20

Souvenir Sheet

196 A53 75s multi *4.00 4.00*

A54

Soccer.

1999, Nov. 8

197 A54 15s Two players *.65 .65*
198 A54 18s Two players, diff. *.65 .65*
199 A54 28s Two players, diff. *.85 .85*
200 A54 28s Player, goalie *.85 .85*
201 A54 36s Player, goalie, diff. *1.50 1.50*
202 A54 56s Two players, diff. *1.75 1.75*
203 A54 69s Two players, diff. *2.25 2.25*
Nos. 197-203 (7) 8.50 8.50

Souvenir Sheet

Perf. 13¾x14

204 A54 75s Two players, horiz. *4.00 4.00*

A55

Prehistoric Animals: a, 28s, Meqaneura. b, 28s, Mesosaurus. c, 36s, Rhamphorhynchus. d, 36s, Styracosaurus albertensis. e, 56s, Trachodon annectens. f, 56s, Tarbosaurus bataar. g, 69s, Arsinoitherium. h, 75s, Phororhacos.

1999, Dec. 13 Litho. *Perf. 14x13¾*

205 A55 Sheet of 8, #a.-h. *12.00 12.00*

Uzbek National Circus — A56

28s, Woman and lion. No. 207, 36s, Acrobat with bow and arrow. No. 208, 36s, Acrobat. No. 209, 56s, Clown on horse. No. 210, 56s, Two riders on horse. 69s, Wire walker.
100s, Woman, camels, llamas, horiz.

2000. Jan. 4 *Perf. 14*

206 A56 28s multi *.95 .95*
207 A56 36s multi *.95 .95*
208 A56 36s multi *.95 .95*
209 A56 56s multi *1.90 1.90*
210 A56 56s multi *1.90 1.90*
211 A56 69s multi *2.25 2.25*
Nos. 206-211 (6) 8.90 8.90

Souvenir Sheet

212 A56 100s multi *3.25 3.25*

Horses A57

Designs: 69s, Horses pulling carriage.
No. 214: a, 36s, Horse in dressage competition. b, 36s, Horse jumping fences. c, 56s, Horses in race. d, 56s, Horse jumping steeplechase fence. e, 75s, Horse with sulky. f, 75s, Race winner.

2000, Feb. 1

213 A57 69s multi *2.00 2.00*
214 A57 Sheet of 6, #a.-f. *10.00 10.00*

Ajiniyoz Qo'siboy, Poet — A58

2000, Mar. 31 Litho. *Perf. 14*

215 A58 28s multi *1.25 1.25*

Famous Islamic Scholars A59

Designs: No. 216, 60s, Burhan al-Din al-Marghinani. No. 217, 60s, Imam Abu Mansur al-Maturidi, horiz.

2000, Oct. 24 Stamp + label

216-217 A59 Set of 2 *3.25 3.25*

UN High Commissioner for Refugees, 50th Anniv. — A60

2000, Dec. 11

218 A60 125s multi + label *2.25 2.25*

Bats — A61

Designs: 15s, Tadarida teniotis. 30s, Otonycteris hemprichi. 45s, Nyctalus lasiopterus, vert. 50s, Myotis frater, vert. 60s, Rhinolophus hipposideros, vert. 90s, Barbastella leucomelas, vert. 125s, Nyctalus noctula, vert.
160s, Unidentified bat, vert.

2001, Feb. 23 *Perf. 13¾x14, 14x13¾*

219-225 A61 Set of 7 *6.00 6.00*

Souvenir Sheet

226 A61 160s multi *2.75 2.75*

Dated 2000.

Native Costumes — A62

2001, Feb. 26 *Perf. 14x13¾*

227 Horiz. strip of 5 + label *7.00 7.00*
a. A62 45s multi *.60 .60*
b. A62 50s multi, diff. *.70 .70*
c. A62 60s multi, diff. *.80 .80*
d. A62 90s multi, diff. *1.15 1.15*
e. A62 125s multi, diff. *1.75 1.75*

Dated 2000.

Arms Type of 1994 Redrawn

2001-05 Litho. *Perf. 14*

Size: 14x23mm

228 A10 15s emerald *.70 .70*
229 A10 17s dull green *.70 .70*
230 A10 20s dull green *.70 .70*
231 A10 25s bright blue *.70 .70*
232 A10 30s sky blue *.70 .70*
232A A10 30s blue green *.90 .90*
b. Dated "2004" *.90 .90*
c. pale blue grn, dated "2005" *.90 .90*
233 A10 33s gray blue *.90 .90*
234 A10 45s red *1.25 1.25*
235 A10 50s rose *1.40 1.40*
236 A10 60s rose pink *1.75 1.75*
237 A10 100s rose, "2001" *2.50 2.50*
a. red, Dated "2003" *1.50 1.50*
Nos. 228-237 (11) 12.20 12.20

Issued: 15s, 17s, 25s, 33s, 50s, 60s, 100s, 4/3; 20s, 30s, 4/11; 45s, 6/22. No. 232A, 5/26/03; No. 232Aa, 6/15/04; No. 232Ab, 3/25/05. No. 237a, 5/26/03.

Ali Shir Nava'i (1441-1501), Poet — A63

2001, Apr. 11

238 Horiz. strip of 5 + label *8.25 8.25*
a. A63 60s Hayrat ul-abror *1.00 1.00*
b. A63 70s Farhod va Shirin *1.00 1.00*
c. A63 85s Layli va Majnun *1.25 1.25*
d. A63 90s Sab'ai sayyora *1.25 1.25*
e. A63 125s Saddi Iskandariy *1.75 1.75*

World Environment Day — A64

2001, June 20

239 A64 100s multi *2.10 2.10*

Avesto, 2700th Anniv. — A65

2001, June 20

240 A65 160s multi *2.50 2.50*

Souvenir Sheet

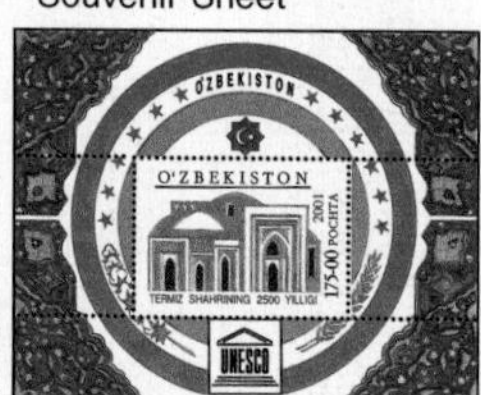

Termiz, 2500th Anniv. A66

2001, June 20

241 A66 175s multi *3.75 3.75*

Souvenir Sheet

Independence, 10th Anniv. — A67

2001, June 20

242 A67 175s multi *3.50 3.50*

Souvenir Sheet

Regional Communications Cooperation — A68

2001, June 20

243 A68 175s multi *3.25 3.25*

10th Anniv. of Independence Issue

Vertical Label

Horizontal Label

Tourist Hotel A69

Monuments A70

Inauguration of Pres. Islam Karimov — A71

Pres. Karimov at United Nations — A72

Pres. Karimov at Istanbul Summit — A73

Hirmon — A74

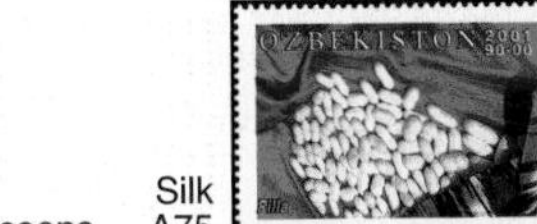

Silk Cocoons — A75

Fergana Refinery — A76

Power Station — A77

Daewoo Auto Factory — A78

Securities Exchange — A79

Kamchik Tunnel — A80

Pres. Karimov and US Pres. Clinton — A81

Pres. Karimov and Russian Pres. Vladimir Putin — A82

Pres. Karimov and Japanese Emperor Akihito — A83

Pres. Karimov and Chinese Pres. Jiang Zemin — A84

Pres. Karimov and German Chancellor Gerhard Schröder — A85

Pres. Karimov and French Pres. Jacques Chirac — A86

Pres. Karimov and British Prime Minister John Major — A87

Pres. Karimov and Iranian Pres. Ali Mohammad Khatami — A88

Pres. Karimov and Egyptian Pres. Hosni Mubarak — A89

Pres. Karimov and Italian Pres. Carlos Ciampi — A90

Pres. Karimov and Indian Pres. Kocheril Narayanan A91

Pres. Karimov and Pope John Paul II — A92

Textile Workers A93

Shurtan Gas Complex A94

Muborak Refinery A95

Oil Pipeline A96

Solar Collector — A97

Soldiers with Flag — A98

Missiles — A99

Soldiers Training — A100

Kurash Sports Complex — A101

New Year's Celebration A102

Mother and Child — A103

Wedding — A104

Bukhara Refinery A105

Nuclear Power Plant A106

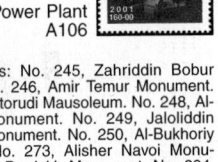

A70 Designs: No. 245, Zahriddin Bobur Monument. No. 246, Amir Temur Monument. No. 247, Al-Motorudi Mausoleum. No. 248, Al-Marginoniy Monument. No. 249, Jaloliddin Manguberdi Monument. No. 250, Al-Bukhoriy Mausoleum. No. 273, Alisher Navoi Monument. No 274, Berdakh Monument. No. 284, Alpomish Monument. No. 288, Al-Fargoni Monument.

2001 Litho. ***Perf. 14x13¾, 13¾x14***

Stamp + Label with Same Orientation

No.	Type	Value	Color	Unused	Used
244	A69	60s	multi	.50	.50
245	A70	60s	multi	.50	.50
246	A70	70s	multi	.50	.50
247	A70	75s	multi	.50	.50
248	A70	75s	multi	.50	.50
249	A70	85s	multi	.70	.70
250	A70	90s	multi	.70	.70
251	A71	90s	multi	.70	.70
252	A72	90s	multi	.70	.70
253	A73	90s	multi	.70	.70
254	A74	90s	multi	.70	.70
255	A75	90s	multi	.70	.70
256	A76	90s	multi	.70	.70
257	A77	90s	multi	.70	.70
258	A78	90s	multi	.70	.70
259	A79	90s	multi	.70	.70
260	A80	90s	multi	.70	.70
261	A81	95s	multi	.80	.80
262	A82	95s	multi	.80	.80
263	A83	95s	multi	.80	.80
264	A84	95s	multi	.80	.80
265	A85	95s	multi	.80	.80
266	A86	95s	multi	.80	.80
267	A87	95s	multi	.80	.80
268	A88	95s	multi	.80	.80
269	A89	95s	multi	.80	.80
270	A90	95s	multi	.80	.80
271	A91	95s	multi	.80	.80
272	A92	95s	multi	.80	.80
273	A70	115s	multi	1.00	1.00
274	A70	115s	multi	1.00	1.00
275	A93	115s	multi	1.00	1.00
276	A94	115s	multi	1.00	1.00
277	A95	115s	multi	1.00	1.00
278	A96	115s	multi	1.00	1.00
279	A97	115s	multi	1.00	1.00
280	A98	115s	multi	1.00	1.00
281	A99	115s	multi	1.00	1.00
282	A100	115s	multi	1.00	1.00
283	A101	115s	multi	1.00	1.00
284	A70	125s	multi	1.00	1.00
285	A102	125s	multi	1.00	1.00
286	A103	125s	multi	1.00	1.00
287	A104	125s	multi	1.00	1.00
288	A70	160s	multi	1.25	1.25
289	A105	160s	multi	1.25	1.25
290	A106	160s	multi	1.25	1.25
	Nos. 244-290 (47)			*39.25*	*39.25*

Nos. 244-290 were each printed in sheets of 2 stamps and 2 labels.

See No. 363.

Uzbekistan Arms — A107

Uzbekistan Flag — A108

Motor Vehicles A109

Central Bank Building A110

Bank Association Building A111

Tashkent Khokimiyat Building A112

Central Trade Center Building — A113

Shurtan Gas Complex — A114

Shurtan Gas Complex — A115

Couple with Baby — A116

Children A117

Farm Equipment A118

Airplanes A119

Constitution A120

Majlis Hall — A121

Gold Ingots and Coins — A122

Muruntay Gold Mine — A123

Independence Day Celebrations A124

Independence Day Celebrations A125

A109 Designs: No. 292a, Nexia. No. 292b, Damas. No. 293a, Tico. No. 293b, Matiz.

A118 Designs: No. 298a, Case 2022 cotton picker. No. 298b, SHR-100 tractor.

A119 Designs: No. 299a, IL-76 MF cargo plane. No. 299b, IL-114-100 passenger plane.

291	Pair with central label	*1.50*	*1.50*
a.	A107 90s multi	*.75*	*.75*
b.	A108 90s multi	*.75*	*.75*
292	Pair with central label	*1.50*	*1.50*
a.-b	A109 90s Any single	*.75*	*.75*
293	Pair with central label	*1.50*	*1.50*
a.-b.	A109 90s multi	*.75*	*.75*
294	Pair with central label	*1.50*	*1.50*
a.	A110 90s multi	*.75*	*.75*
b.	A111 90s multi	*.75*	*.75*
295	Pair with central label	*1.50*	*1.50*
a.	A112 90s multi	*.75*	*.75*
b.	A113 90s multi	*.75*	*.75*
296	Pair with central label	*2.25*	*2.25*
a.	A114 115s multi	*1.10*	*1.10*
b.	A115 115s multi	*1.10*	*1.10*
297	Pair with central label	*2.25*	*2.25*
a.	A116 125s multi	*1.10*	*1.10*
b.	A117 125s multi	*1.10*	*1.10*
298	Pair with central label	*2.50*	*2.50*
a.-b.	A118 160s Any single	*1.25*	*1.25*
299	Pair with central label	*1.75*	*1.75*
a.	A119 90s multi	*.75*	*.75*
b.	A119 115s multi	*.95*	*.95*
300	Pair with central label	*1.50*	*1.50*
a.	A120 115s multi	*.90*	*.90*
b.	A121 60s multi	*.50*	*.50*
301	Pair with central label	*1.75*	*1.75*
a.	A122 115s multi	*.90*	*.90*
b.	A123 90s multi	*.60*	*.60*
302	Pair with central label	*1.75*	*1.75*
a.	A124 125s multi	*.95*	*.95*
b.	A125 90s multi	*.70*	*.70*
	Nos. 291-302 (12)	*21.25*	*21.25*

Nos. 291-302 printed in sheets of four stamps and two labels (two pairs).

See Nos. 361-362, 364-366, 371.

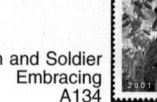

Theater — A126

Theater — A127

Theater A128

Medals A129

Combine — A130

Combine — A131

Pres. Karimov and Farmers — A132

Soldier Taking Oath Before Flag — A133

Man and Soldier Embracing A134

Frontier Guards and Dog A135

Athletes A136

Soldiers in Formation A137

Diver Training — A138

Decontamination Training — A139

Modern Architecture — A140

Armed Forces A141

Archaeology — A142

High School A143

Uzbekistan on World Map — A144

A129 Designs: No. 304a, Dostelik. No. 304b, I Darajali "Shon-Sharaf." No. 304c, II Darajali "Shon-Sharaf." No. 305a, I Darajali Sog'lom Avlod Uchun. No. 305b, II Darajali Sog'lom Avlod Uchun. No. 305c, Mehnat Shuhrati. No. 306a, Jaloliddin Manguberdi. No. 306b, Buyuk Xizmatlari Uchun. No. 306c, El-Yurt Hurmati. No. 307a, Oltin Yildiz. No. 307b, Mustaqillik. No. 307c, Amir Temur.

A136 Designs: No. 310a, Muhammadqodir Abdullayev. No. 310b, Lina Cheryazova. No. 310c, Artur Grigoryan. No. 312a, 160s, Armen Bagdasarov. No. 312b, 160s, Rustam Qosimjonov. No. 312c, 115s, Otabek Kosimov. No. 312d, 115s, Iroda To'laganova. No. 312e, 100s, Dilshod Muxtorov. No. 312e, 115s, Oksana Chusovitina.

No. 313: a, Temuriylar Tarixi Muzeyi (Amir Temur Museum). b, Oqsaroy. c, Oliy Majlis. d, Motamsaro Ona (Monument to Grieving Mother). e, Shahidlar Xotirasi (Respect Monument). f, Interkontinental mehmonxonasi (Intercontinental Hotel). g, Milliy Bank (National Bank). h, Yunusobod Sport Majmuasi (Yunusobod Sport Complex).

No. 314: a, 60s, Infantrymen, tank. b, 70s, Airplane and crew. c, 80s, Helicopter and crew. d, 90s, Soldier directing tank with flags. e, 90s, Minesweeper. f, 115s, Soldiers in classroom. g, 160s, Tanks. h, 60s, Artillery.

No. 315: a, 75s, Pot. b, 75s, Artifact with arch. c, 75s, Artifact with hole at top and side. d, 80s, Broken pot. e, 80s, Anthropomorphic figure with arms. f, 80s, Buddha. g, 80s, Costumed figure. h, 80s, Disk. i, 80s, Anthropomorphic figure missing arm. j, 80s, Box. k, 80s, Face.

303	Strip of 3 + label	*1.90*	*1.90*
a.	A126 90s multi	*.60*	*.60*
b.	A127 90s multi	*.60*	*.60*
c.	A128 90s multi	*.60*	*.60*
304	Strip of 3 + label	*3.25*	*3.25*
a.-c.	A129 160s Any single	*1.00*	*1.00*
305	Strip of 3 + label	*3.25*	*3.25*
a.-c.	A129 160s Any single	*1.00*	*1.00*
306	Strip of 3 + label	*3.25*	*3.25*
a.-c.	A129 160s Any single	*1.00*	*1.00*
307	Strip of 3 + label	*3.25*	*3.25*
a.-c.	A129 160s Any single	*1.00*	*1.00*

308	Strip of 3 + label	3.25	3.25
a.	A130 160s multi	1.00	1.00
b.	A131 160s multi	1.00	1.00
c.	A132 160s multi	1.00	1.00
309	Strip of 3 + label	2.25	2.25
a.	A133 60s multi	.45	.45
b.	A134 80s multi	.60	.60
c.	A135 90s multi	.70	.70
310	Strip of 3 + label	3.00	3.00
a.	A136 160s multi	1.25	1.25
b.-c.	A136 115s Any single	.85	.85
311	Block of 3 + label	2.25	2.25
a.	A137 115s multi	.80	.80
b.	A138 80s multi	.60	.60
c.	A139 70s multi	.50	.50
	Nos. 303-311 (9)	*25.65*	*25.65*

Sheets

312	A136 Sheet of 6, #a-f, + 3 labels	6.50	6.50
313	A140 115s Sheet of 8, #a-h, + label	8.50	8.50
314	A141 Sheet of 8, #a-h, + label	6.50	6.50
315	A142 Sheet of 11, #a-k, + label	7.50	7.50

Souvenir Sheets

316	A143 160s multi	2.50	2.50
317	A144 175s multi	2.75	2.75

Labels have same orientation as stamps and are at left side of strips on Nos. 303-310, and at UR on No. 311. No. 312 contains three different labels.

See No. 370.

Commonwealth of Independent States, 10th Anniv. — A145

2001, Nov. 8 ***Perf. 13¾x14***

318 A145 60s multi 1.40 1.40

Artwork of Oral Tansiqboyev — A146

No. 319: a, 100s, Mening Qo'shig'im (My Song). b, 125s, Angren-Qo'qon Tog'yo'li (Angren-Kokand Mountain Road).

2001, Nov. 8

319 A146 Pair, #a-b, with central label 4.00 4.00

Flowers — A147

Designs: 45s, Zygophyllum bucharicum. 50s, Viola hissarica. 60s, Bergenia hissarica. 70s, Eremurus hilariae. 85s, Salvia korolkowii. 90s, Lamyropappus schakaptaricus. 145s, Punica granatum.

175s, Undescribed flowers.

2002, May 10 Litho. ***Perf. 14x13¾***

320-326 A147 Set of 7 7.00 7.00

Souvenir Sheet

327 A147 175s multi 3.50 3.50

Hominids A148

No. 328: a, 40s, Dryopithecus maior. b, 45s, Homo erectus modjokertensis. c, 50s, Pithecanthropus erectus. d, 60s, Australopithecus afarensis. e, 70s, Zinjanthropus boisei. f, 85s, Homo sapiens neanderthalensis. g, 90s, Sinanthropus pekinensis. h, 125s, Protanthropus heidelbergensis. i, 160s, Homo sapiens fossilis.

2002, May 10 ***Perf. 13¾x14***

328 A148 Sheet of 9, #a-i, + 3 labels 8.50 8.50

Protection of Ozone Layer — A149

2002, June 7 Litho. ***Perf. 13¾x14***

329 A149 40s multi 1.40 1.40

Souvenir Sheet

City of Shahrisabz, 2700th Anniv. — A150

2002, June 14 ***Perf. 14***

330 A150 30s multi 1.25 1.25

Uzbek Sports — A151

Designs: 45s, Chavgon. 50s, Poyga. 60s, Kamondan otish. 70s, Qiz quvmoq. 85s, Ro'molcha olish. 90s, Kurash. 145s, Uloq.

175s, Ro'molcha olish, diff.

2002, July 26 ***Perf. 13¾x14***

331-337 A151 Set of 7 6.25 6.25

Souvenir Sheet

338 A151 175s multi 2.75 2.75

Ancient Coins A152

No. 339: a, 30s, Silver tetradrachm of Eucratides I c. 171-135 BC, obverse. b, 45s, As "a," reverse. c, 60s, Silver coin of Buxoro, obverse. d, 90s, As "c," reverse. e, 125s, Silver miri of Tamerlane, 1370-1405, obverse. f, 160s, As "e," reverse.

2002, Aug. 1

339 A152 Block of 6, #a-f 6.50 6.50

See Nos. 367-369.

City of Nukus, 70th Anniv. — A153

2002, Oct. 2

340 A153 100s multi 1.60 1.60

Iris Varieties — A154

Designs: 15s, Qoraqum. 30s, Solnechniy zaychik. 45s, Simfoniya. 50s, Chimyon. 60s, Ikar. 90s, Babye leto. 125s, Toshkent.

160s, Askiya.

2002, Oct. 2 ***Perf. 14x13¾***

341-347 A154 Set of 7 7.00 7.00

Souvenir Sheet

348 A154 160s multi 2.50 2.50

Uzbekistan postal officials have declared the following items as "illegal":

Sheets of eight stamps depicting Trains (4 different sheets with denominations of 56s, 75s, 95s and 125s);

Sheets of six stamps with various denominations depicting Birds (2 different), Animals, Year of the Snake, Chiroptera, Lizards, Chess;

Sheets of one label and five stamps with various denominations depicting Perissodactyla;

Souvenir sheets of one depicting Trains (8 different 36s sheets, 4 different 56s sheets, 2 different 75s sheets).

G'afur G'ulom (1903-66), Poet — A155

2003, May 4 Litho. ***Perf. 13¾x14***

349 A155 1000s brown 5.75 5.75

European Bank Annual Meeting Issue

Vertical Label

Horizontal Label

National Bank, Tashkent A156

Kaltaminor Minaret, Khiva A157

Aloqabank, Tashkent — A158

Pres Karimov and European Bank for Reconstruction and Development Pres. Jean Lemierre — A159

Islamkhodja Minaret, Khiva — A160

East Gates, Khiva A161

Samanid Museum, Bukhara A162

Ark, Bukhara A163

Women's Traditional Dress A164

Women's Traditional Dress A165

Women's Traditional Dress A166

Women's Traditional Dress A167

Women's Traditional Dress A168

A157 Designs: 630s, Gumbazi Sayyidon Mausoleum, Shahrisabz. 920s, Go'ri Amir Mausoleum, Samarqand. 970s, Chorminor Madrasasi, Bukhara. 1330s, Registon, Samarqand, horiz.

2003, May 4 ***Perf. 14x13¾, 13¾x14***

Stamp + Label with Same Orientation

350	A156 520s multi	6.25	6.25
351	A157 520s multi	6.25	6.25
352	A157 630s multi	7.25	7.25
353	A157 920s multi	11.00	11.00
354	A157 970s multi	12.00	12.00
355	A158 970s multi	12.00	12.00
356	A157 1330s multi	15.00	15.00
357	A159 1330s multi	15.00	15.00
358	Horiz. pair with central label	14.00	14.00
a.	A160 580s multi	6.25	6.25
b.	A161 520s multi	6.25	6.25
359	Horiz. pair with central label	21.00	21.00
a.	A162 1170s multi	12.50	12.50
b.	A163 630s multi	7.00	7.00
360	Horiz. strip of 5 with flanking label	27.50	27.50
a.	A164 240s multi	2.75	2.75
b.	A165 320s multi	4.00	4.00
c.	A166 520s multi	6.25	6.25
d.	A167 580s multi	6.25	6.25
e.	A168 630s multi	7.25	7.25

Types of 2001-02

Stamp + Label with Same Orientation

361	A110 520s multi	6.25	6.25
362	A111 580s multi	6.25	6.25
363	Horiz. pair with central label	14.00	14.00
a.	A74 170s multi	2.00	2.00
b.	A93 920s multi	11.00	11.00
364	Horiz. pair with central label	9.75	9.75
a.	A107 240s multi	2.75	2.75
b.	A108 520s multi	6.25	6.25
365	Horiz. pair with central label	10.00	10.00
a.	A114 630s multi	7.25	7.25
b.	A115 240s multi	2.75	2.75
366	Horiz. pair with central label	10.00	10.00
a.	A122 520s multi	6.25	6.25
b.	A123 320s multi	4.00	4.00

367 Horiz. pair with flanking label 14.00 14.00
a. A152 520s Like #339a 6.25 6.25
b. A152 520s Like #339b 6.25 6.25

368 Horiz. pair with flanking label 14.00 14.00
a. A152 580s Like #339c 6.25 6.25
b. A152 580s Like #339d 6.25 6.25

369 Horiz. pair with flanking label 15.00 15.00
a. A152 630s Like #339e 7.25 7.25
b. A152 630s Like #339f 7.25 7.25

370 A140 Sheet of 8 + central label 60.00 60.00
a. 520s Like #313a 6.25 6.25
b. 970s Like #313b 12.00 12.00
c. 580s Like #313c 6.25 6.25
d. 630s Like #313d 7.25 7.25
e. 320s Like #313e 4.00 4.00
f. 630s Like #313f 7.25 7.25
g. 920s Toshkent shahar hokimiyati (mayor's house) 11.00 11.00
h. 240s Like #313h 2.75 2.75

Type of 2001 Redrawn

371 Horiz. pair with central label 19.00 19.00
a. A109 630s Like #292a 7.25 7.25
b. A109 970s Like #293b 12.00 12.00
Nos. 350-371 (22) 325.50 325.50

Famous Men — A169

Designs: 125s, Komil Yormatov, film director. 500s, Jo'raxon Sultonov, singer.

2003, July 8 ***Perf. 13¾x14***
372-373 A169 Set of 2 5.00 5.00

Birds — A170

Designs: No. 374, 100s, Ciconia ciconia asiatica. No. 375, 100s, Ciconia nigra. No. 376, 125s, Platalea leucorodia. No. 377, 125s, Phoenicopterus ruber.

2003, Sept. 17 ***Perf. 14x13¾***
374-377 A170 Set of 4 5.50 5.50

Caps — A171

Designs: No. 378, 100s, Kula-tung. No. 379, 100s, Erkaklar do'ppisi. No. 380, 100s, Bayram do'ppisi. No. 381, 125s, Ayollar do'ppisi. No. 382, 125s, Ayollar taxya-do'ppisi. No. 383, 155s, Erkaklar do'ppisi, diff. No. 384, 155s, Bolalar bayram do'ppisi.

2003, Oct. 7
378-384 A171 Set of 7 11.00 11.00

Paintings A172

No. 385: a, Tong. Onalik, by R. Ahmedov. b, Baxt, by S. Ayitbayev.

2003, Nov. 19
385 A172 970s Horiz. pair, #a-b 12.00 12.00

See Kazakhstan No. 434.

Abuxoliq G'ijduvoniy, Bukhara, 900th Anniv. — A173

2003, Nov. 28 ***Perf. 13¾x14***
386 A173 125s multi + label 1.60 1.60

Souvenir Sheet

2004 Summer Olympics, Athens — A174

2004, June 15 Litho. ***Perf. 14x13¾***
387 A174 205s multi 3.00 3.00

Ma'murjon Uzoqov (1904-63), Singer A175

Abdulla Qodiriy (1894-1938), Writer A176

2004, Oct. 11 ***Perf. 14***
388 A175 100s lt blue & blk 1.50 1.50
389 A176 125s lt blue & blk 1.75 1.75

Grapes — A177

Designs: 60s, Kaltak. No. 391, 100s, Oq husayni. No. 392, 100s, Kattaqo'rg'on. No. 393, 125s, Echkemar. No. 394, 125s, Qizil Xurmoni. 155s, Qora Andijon. 210s, Parkent.

2004, Oct. 11 ***Perf. 14x13¾***
390-396 A177 Set of 7 12.00 12.00

Jewelry of 19th and 20th Centuries — A178

Inscriptions: 60s, Tumor, Samarqand. No. 398, 100s, Tumor, Toshkent. No. 399, 100s, Qi'ltiqtumor, Qo'qon. No. 400, 125s, Tumor, Buxoro. No. 401, 125s, Bo'yintumor, Toshkent. 155s, Qo'ltiqtumor, Buxoro. 210s, Tumor, Buxoro, diff.

2004, Oct. 18
397-403 A178 Set of 7 12.00 12.00

Kitab State Geological Reserve, 25th Anniv. — A179

2004, Dec. 1
404 A179 100s multi + label 2.00 2.00

Arms Type of 1994 Redrawn

2004-06 Litho. ***Perf. 14***
Size: 14x23mm

405 A10 35s blue green .25 .25
406 A10 60s green .35 .35
a. blue green, dated "2005" .35 .35
407 A10 65s blue green .40 .40
408 A10 125s chalky blue .60 .60
409 A10 200s red .85 .85
410 A10 250s blue 1.10 1.10
411 A10 290s red 1.25 1.25
412 A10 350s blue 1.50 1.50
413 A10 430s red 1.75 1.75
414 A10 2500s red 10.00 10.00
415 A10 3700s blue 14.00 14.00
Nos. 405-415 (11) 32.05 32.05

Issued: No. 406, 6/15; Nos. 406a, 408, 4/15/05; others, 1/5/06. Nos. 405, 407, 409-415 are dated "2005," though issued in 2006.

Oybek (1905-68), Writer — A180

2005, Apr. 25 Litho. ***Perf. 14x13¾***
416 A180 125s multi 1.60 1.60

Miniature Sheet

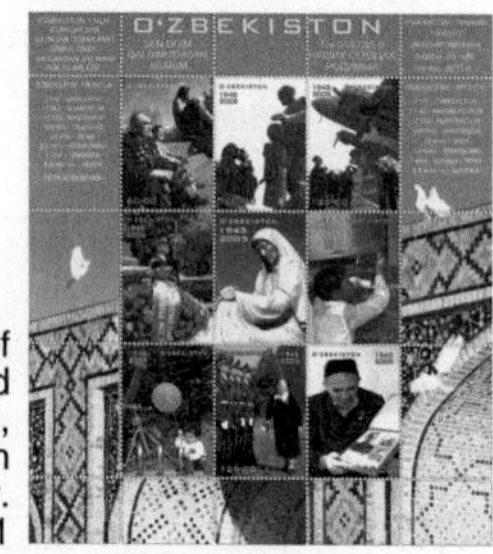
End of World War II, 60th Anniv. A181

No. 417: a, 60s, Veterans at war memorial. b, 60s, Child with balloon at memorial. c, 100s, Sculptures. d, 100s, Child looking at memorial. e, 125s, Veterans looking at airplane sculpture. f, 125s, Woman passing soldiers. g, 155s, Soldier and floral display. h, 155s, Man looking at scrapbook.

2005, May 6
417 A181 Sheet of 8, #a-h, + central label 8.50 8.50

Tashkent University of Information Technologies, 50th Anniv. — A182

2005, May 25 ***Perf. 13¾x14***
418 A182 125s multi + label 1.90 1.90

Qarshi, 2700th Anniv. — A183

2005, Aug. 1
419 A183 125s multi 1.25 1.25

Doves — A184

No. 420: a, 85s, Qopqon-chinni. b, 85s, Ruyan. c, 100s, Novvoti. d, 100s, Oq kaptar. e, 125s, Juk. f, 125s, Chelkar. g, 155s, Udi. h, 155s, Gulsor.
210s, Buxoro kaptari.

2005, Sept. 15
420 A184 Sheet of 8, #a-h 6.75 6.75

Souvenir Sheet

421 A184 210s multi 2.75 2.75

Miniature Sheet

Toreutic Art A185

No. 422: a, 60s, Teapot with ribbed ornamentation. b, 60s, Teapot with round ornamentation. c, 100s, Teapot, diff. d, 125s, Teapot, diff. 155s, Teapot-samovar. 340s, Teapot with square lid.

2005, Oct. 25
422 A185 Sheet of 6, #a-f 7.50 7.50

Ma'mun Academy, 1000th Anniv. — A186

2005, Dec. 15 ***Perf. 13¾x14***
423 A186 430s multi 3.00 3.00

Paintings A187

Designs: No. 424, 200s, Ko'i, by V. I. Yenin. No. 425, 200s, Osuda Kun, by B. Boboyev, vert. No. 426, 250s, Samarqand, Navro'z, by G. Abdurahmanov, vert. No. 427, 250s, Qo'qondagi Choyxona, by J. Umarbekov, vert. No. 428, 300s, Oqtosh, by R. Ahmedov, vert. No. 429, 300s, Yoz, by Y. P. Melnikov, vert. 350s, Kuz, by N. Qo'ziboyev, vert.

2006, Jan. 3 ***Perf. 13¾x14, 14x13¾***
424-430 A187 Set of 7 10.50 10.50

Dated 2005.

Rustam Qosimjonov, Intl. Chess Federation World Champion A188

2006, Jan. 5 ***Perf. 13¾x14***
431 A188 200s multi 1.75 1.75

Dated 2005.

Medalists at 2004 Summer Olympics, Athens — A189

Designs: No. 432, 200s, Artur Taymazov, 120kg freestyle wrestling gold medalist. No. 433, 200s, Aleksandr Doxturushvili, 74kg Greco-Roman wrestling gold medalist. 250s, Magomed Ibragimov, 96kg freestyle wrestling silver medalist. 350s, O'tkir Haydarov and Bahodir Sultonov, 81kg and 54kg boxing bronze medalists, horiz.

2006, Jan. 5 ***Perf. 14x13¾, 13¾x14***
432-435 A189 Set of 4 *6.50 6.50*

Dated 2005.

2006 Winter Olympics, Turin — A190

Designs: 1540s, Skiing. 2155s, Figure skating.

2006, May 19 Litho. ***Perf. 14x13¾***
436-437 A190 Set of 2 14.00 14.00

Musical Instruments — A191

Designs: 200s, Tanbur and Qashqar rubobi. 250s, Surnay and Tor. 290s, Surnay and Doira. 350s, Nay and Dutor. 410s, G'ijjak. 430s, Nog'om. 580s, Tanbur and Chang.

2006, May 19
438-444 A191 Set of 7 10.00 10.00

Dogs — A192

Designs: 350s, Labrador retriever. 540s, Cocker spaniel. 600s, German shepherd. 780s, Asian sheepdog.
1150s, Collie and German shepherd.

2006, May 19 ***Perf. 13¾x14***
445-448 A192 Set of 4 9.00 9.00

Souvenir Sheet

449 A192 1150s multi 4.00 4.00

Souvenir Sheet

2006 World Cup Soccer Championships, Germany — A193

2006, May 19 ***Perf. 14x13¾***
450 A193 720s multi 3.50 3.50

Fish A194

No. 451: a, 45s, Salmo trutta aralensis. b, 90s, Acipenser nudiventris. c, 250s, Pseudoscaphirhynchus kaufmanni. d, 300s, Barbus brachcephalus.
1010s, Aspiolucius esocinus.

2006, July 10 ***Perf. 13¾x14***
451 A194 Sheet of 4, #a-d 3.50 3.50

Souvenir Sheet

452 A194 1010s multi 4.25 4.25

Bell Tower, Tashkent A195

Alisher Navoiy Theater A196

2006, Aug. 10 ***Perf. 14x13¾***
453 A195 55s green .55 .55

Perf. 13¾x14

454 A196 90s emerald .75 .75

See Nos. 543, 545, 548, 597, 599. Compare with Type A249.

Butterflies A197

Designs: 45s, Papilio alexanor. 90s, Parnassius mnemosyne. 200s, Parnassius apollonius. 250s, Parnassius maximinus. 300s, Parnassius honrathi. No. 460, 350s, Hypermnestra helios. No. 461, 350s, Parnassius charltonius.
1010s, Parnassius actius.

2006, Aug. 10 ***Perf. 13¾x14***
455-461 A197 Set of 7 6.75 6.75

Souvenir Sheet

462 A197 1010s multi 5.00 5.00

15th Anniv. of Independence Issue

Horizontal Label

Vertical Label

Pres. Islam Karimov and Indian Prime Minister Manmohan Singh A198

School and Children, Kokand A199

House of Children's Creativity A200

Senate Chamber A201

Emblem of 2005 Intl. Cotton Fair, Tashkent, and Cotton Boll — A202

Pres. Karimov and People's Republic of China Chairman Hu Jintao A203

Pres. Karimov and Latvian Pres. Vaire Vike-Fraiberg — A204

Qungirot Soda Factory A205

Leaders at Shanghai Cooperation Organization Summit, Tashkent — A206

Cement Factory — A207

Railroad Construction A208

Pres. Karimov and Graduates of Vaseda University A209

Monument of Independence and Humanism — A210

Mine A211

Bronze Smelter A212

Festival A213

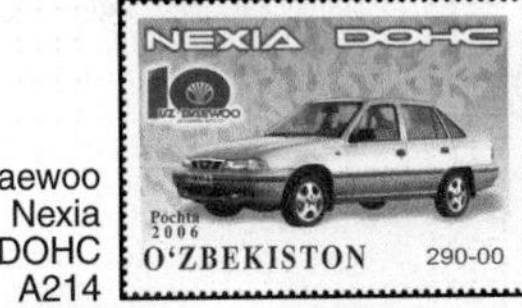

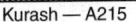

Daewoo Nexia DOHC A214

Kurash — A215

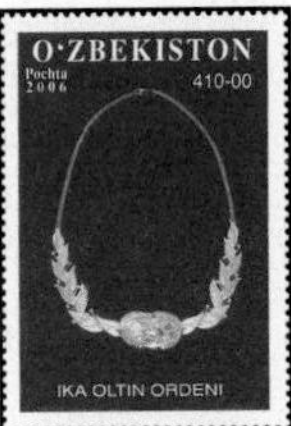

Intl. Kurash Association Medal — A216

Pres. Karimov and Cotton Pickers A217

Pres. Karimov and Cotton Pickers A218

Pres. Karimov and Farmers A219

Roads A220

Textiles A221

Military A222

Sports A223

A198 Designs — Pres. Karimov and: No. 466, Malaysian King Tuanku Syed Sirajuddin. No. 470, Writer Said Akhmad. No. 474, Slovenian Pres. Janez Drnovsek. No. 477, Russian Pres. Vladimir Putin. No. 480, South Korean Pres. Roh Moo-hyun. No. 483, Uzbek labor leader.

A200 Designs: No. 469, Humanism Arch. No. 478, Medical School, Margilan. No. 484, Tashkent Railway Station. No. 486, Senate Building.

A206 Design: No. 482, Leaders at Euro-Asian Economic Union meeting.

A207 Design: No. 481, Angren Coal Mine.

A213 Design: No. 489b, 90s, Festival, diff.

A214 Design: No. 490b, 200s, Daewoo Damas II.

A215 Designs: No. 491b, 90s, Kurash, diff. No. 491c, 100s, Kurash, diff.

A216 Designs: No. 492b, 580s, FILA Wrestling medal. No. 492c, 720s, National Olympic Committee medal.

No. 494: a, 90s, Winding mountain road. b, 180s, Road construction. c, 55s, Highway.

No. 495: a, 410s, Workers and textile mill machinery. b, 580s, Women holding skeins of thread. c, 250s, Textile mill machinery.

No. 496: a, 410s, Soldiers in joint Uzbekistan-Russia anti-terrorism exercises, flags. b, 100s, Graduation of cadets. c, 250s, Soldiers at desks.

No. 497: a, 580s, Pres. Karimov and student athletes. b, 45s Stadium. c, 55s, Swimming meet. d, 90s, Athletes with medals. e, 200s, Karate. f, 250s, Soccer. g, 100s, Synchronized swimming. h, 290s, Equestrian event.

Perf. 13¾x14, 14x13¾

2006, Aug. 25

Stamp + Label With Same Orientation

463 A198 45s multi .55 .55
464 A199 45s multi .55 .55
465 A200 45s multi .55 .55
466 A198 55s multi .55 .55
467 A201 90s multi .55 .55
468 A202 90s multi .55 .55
469 A200 95s multi .55 .55
470 A198 100s multi .55 .55
471 A203 200s multi .90 .90
472 A204 200s multi .90 .90
473 A205 200s multi .90 .90
474 A198 250s multi 1.15 1.15
475 A206 250s multi 1.15 1.15
476 A207 250s multi 1.15 1.15
477 A198 290s multi 1.35 1.35
478 A200 290s multi 1.35 1.35
479 A208 290s multi 1.35 1.35
480 A198 350s multi 1.35 1.35
481 A207 350s multi 1.35 1.35
482 A206 410s multi 1.75 1.75
483 A198 430s multi 1.90 1.90
484 A200 430s multi 1.90 1.90
485 A209 580s multi 2.75 2.75
486 A200 720s multi 3.50 3.50
487 A210 1010s multi 4.75 4.75
Nos. 463-487 (25) 33.85 33.85

Pairs

488 Horiz. pair with central label 1.10 1.10
a. A211 45s multi .55 .55
b. A212 55s multi .55 .55
489 Horiz. pair with central label 1.10 1.10
a. A213 55s multi .55 .55
b. A213 90s multi .55 .55
490 Horiz. pair with central label 2.25 2.25
a. A214 290s multi 1.35 1.35
b. A214 200s multi .90 .90
Nos. 488-490 (3) 4.45 4.45

Strips

491 Strip of 3 + label 3.00 3.00
a. A215 430s multi 1.90 1.90
b. A215 90s multi .55 .55
c. A215 100s multi .55 .55
492 Strip of 3 + label 8.00 8.00
a. A216 410s multi 1.75 1.75
b. A216 580s multi 2.75 2.75
c. A216 720s multi 3.50 3.50
493 Strip of 3 + label 2.75 2.75
a. A217 200s multi .90 .90
b. A218 250s multi 1.15 1.15
c. A219 90s multi .55 .55
Nos. 491-493 (3) 13.75 13.75

Sheets

494 A220 Sheet of 3, #a-c, + label 1.45 1.45
495 A221 Sheet of 3, #a-c, + label 5.50 5.50
496 A222 Sheet of 3, #a-c, + label 3.50 3.50
497 A223 Sheet of 8, #a-h, + label 7.50 7.50
Nos. 494-497 (4) 17.95 17.95

Nos. 463-475, 477-480, 482-486 were printed in sheets of 2 stamps and 2 labels. Nos. 476, 481 and 487 were printed in sheets of 5 stamps and 5 labels. Nos. 488-490 were printed in sheets of 4 stamps and 2 labels (2 pairs).

National Flag, 15th Anniv. A224

2006, Nov. 1 ***Perf. 13¾x14***
498 A224 600s multi + label 2.50 2.50

Miniature Sheet

Intl. Year of Deserts and Desertification — A225

No. 499: a, 45s, Oxyura leucocephala. b, 250s, Haliaeetus albicilla. c, 350s, Phalcrocorax pygmaeus. d, 350s, Marmaronetta angustirostris.

2006, Nov. 1
499 A225 Sheet of 4, #a-d 4.75 4.75

Roses — A226

Designs: 45s, Rosa divina. 90s, Rosa maracandica. 250s, Rosa persica. 350s, Rosa vassilczencoi.
600s, Rosa divina, diff.

2006, Nov. 1 ***Perf. 14x13¾***
500-503 A226 Set of 4 3.75 3.75

Souvenir Sheet

504 A226 600s multi 2.00 2.00

Souvenir Sheet

Year of Charity and Medical Workers A227

2006, Nov. 17 ***Perf. 13¾x14***
505 A227 720s multi 2.75 2.75

Souvenir Sheet

Regional Communications Commonwealth, 15th Anniv. — A228

2006, Nov. 17
506 A228 1010s multi 4.50 4.50

2006 Asian Games, Doha, Qatar — A229

Designs: 90s, High jump. 250s, Tennis. No. 509, 350s, Basketball. No. 510, 350s, Soccer.

2006, Dec. 27 Litho. ***Perf. 13¾x14***
507-510 A229 Set of 4 *4.25 4.25*

Diplomatic Relations Between Uzbekistan and People's Republic of China, 15th Anniv. — A230

2006, Dec. 29
511 A230 200s multi *1.25 1.25*

Admission to the United Nations, 15th Anniv. — A231

2007, Mar. 1
512 A231 410s multi *1.75 1.75*

Souvenir Sheet

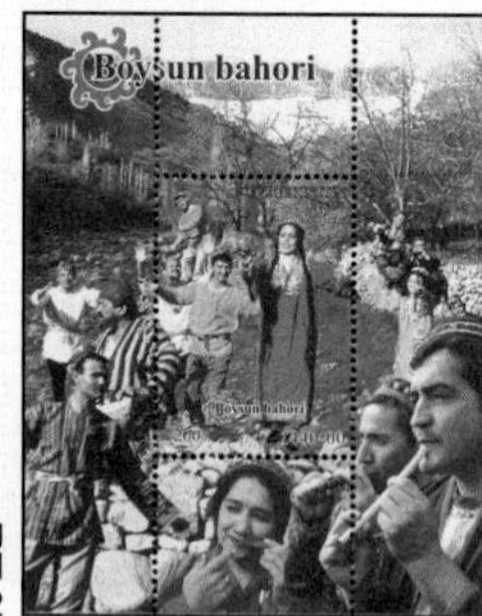
Spring Festival A232

2007, Mar. 1 ***Perf. 14x13¾***
513 A232 1440s multi *5.75 5.75*

2007 Winter Asian Games, Changchun, People's Republic of China — A233

Designs: 250s, Figure skating. 350s, Skiing.

2007, Mar. 1
514-515 A233 Set of 2 *2.75 2.75*

Abdulla Qahhor (1907-68), Writer — A234

No. 516: a, 350s, Scene from "Shohi So'zana." b, 420s, Qahhor.

2007, May 31 ***Perf. 13¾x14***
516 A234 Horiz. pair, #a-b *3.00 3.00*

Souvenir Sheets

A235

A236

A237

Architecture — A238

No. 517: a, 200s, Norbo'tabiy Madrasasi (madrassa). b, 410s, Daxmai Shohon Maqbarasi (mausoleum). c, 430s, Xudoyorxon Saroyi (palace).

No. 518: a, 250s, Modarixon Madrasasi (madrassa). b, 420s, Mir Arab Madrasasi (madrassa). c, 430s, Chor Bakr Me'moriy Majmuasi (mausoleum).

No. 519: a, 90s, Qo'shdarvoza (city gate). b, 250s, Muhammad Rahimxon Madrasasi (madrassa). c, 1010s, Pahlavon Mahmud Maqbarasi (mausoleum).

No. 520: a, 300s, Yunusxon Maqbarasi (mausoleum). b, 350s, Baroqxon Madrasasi (madrassa). c, 750s, Abulqosim Madrasasi (madrassa).

2007, May 31 ***Perf. 13¾x14, 14x13¾***
517 A235 Sheet of 3, #a-c, + label *4.00 4.00*
518 A236 Sheet of 3, #a-c, + label *4.00 4.00*
519 A237 Sheet of 3, #a-c, + label *5.00 5.00*
520 A238 Sheet of 3, #a-c, + label *5.00 5.00*
Nos. 517-520 (4) *18.00 18.00*

Margilan, 2000th Anniv. — A239

2007, June 30 *Perf. 14x13¾*
521 A239 350s multi *1.40 1.40*

Quddus Muhammadiy (1907-99), Poet — A240

2007, July 30 *Perf. 13¾x14*
522 A240 410s light blue & blk *1.60 1.60*

Berries — A241

Designs: 100s, Fragaria. 250s, Ribes nigrum. 580s, Rubus idaeus. 720s, Grossularia reclinata.

2007, July 30 **Litho.**
523-526 A241 Set of 4 *6.50 6.50*

Jewelry — A242

Designs: 300s, Yarim tirnoq. 350s, Ko'krak do'zi, horiz. 670s, Shovkala, horiz. 720s, Bodomoy.

2007, July 30 *Perf. 14x13¾, 13¾x14*
527-530 A242 Set of 4 *7.75 7.75*

Miniature Sheets

Samarqand, 2750th Anniv. — A243

No. 531: a, 45s, Registon Maydoni, Ulug'bel Madrasasi. b, 55s, Registon Maydoni, Sherdor Madrasasi. c, 100s, Registon Maydoni, Tillakori Madrasasi. d, 180s, Amir Temur Maqbarasi, Umumiy Ko'rinishi. e, 200s, Bibixonim Masjidi. f, 250s, Ruhobod Maqbarasi. g, 490s, Registon Maydoni, Umumiy Ko'rinishi. h, 720s, Shohisinda Majmuasi, Qo'shgumbazli Maqbara.

No. 532, vert.: a, 90s, Imom al-Moturidiy Maqbarasi. b, 100s, Imom Buxoriy Maqbarasi. c, 180s, Amir Temur Maqbarasi Kirish Peshtoqi. d, 200s, Amir Temur Haykali (statue). e, 410s, Bibixonim Maqbarasi. f, 680s, Shohizinda Majmuasi. g, 700s, Bibixonim Masjidi Kirish Peshtoqi. h, 1150s, Shohizinda Majmuasi, Tuman Oqo Maqbarasi.

2007, July 30 *Perf. 13¾x14*
531 A243 Sheet of 8, #a-h, + central label *7.50 7.50*

Perf. 14x13¾
532 A243 Sheet of 8, #a-h, + central label *12.50 12.50*

Acinonyx Jubatus — A244

Designs: 90s, Leaping. 490s, Resting. 680s, Walking. 780s, Standing. 1440s, Adult with juvenile, vert.

2007, Oct. 3 *Perf. 13¾x14*
533-536 A244 Set of 4 *7.25 7.25*

Souvenir Sheet
Perf. 14x13¾
537 A244 1440s multi *5.25 5.25*

Souvenir Sheet

Tashkent Subway, 30th Anniv. A245

No. 538: a, 540s, Train and system map. b, 780s, Subway emblem and station entrance.

2007, Nov. 20 *Perf. 14x13¾*
538 A245 Sheet of 2, #a-b *5.00 5.00*

Constitution, 15th Anniv. — A246

2007, Dec. 5 **Litho.**
539 A246 600s multi *2.25 2.25*

Miniature Sheet

Zahiruddin Muhammad Babur (1483-1530), Founder of Mughal Dynasty — A247

No. 540 — Inscriptions: a, 200s, Boburning toj kiyib Farg'ona taxtiga chiqishi (Coronation). b, 250s, Boburning Samarqandliklar tomonidan tantana bilan kutib olinishi (Samarqand people welcome Babur). c, 350s, Bobur Hirotda Sulton Huseyn xonadonida (Babur at Sultan Hussein's house). d, 350s, Bengaliya elchisi Bobur qabulida (Babur receives Bengal ambassador). e, 350s, Babur. f, 410s, Qobul qal'asining qamaldan ozod etilishi (Babur freeing Kabul fortress). g, 490s, Bobur Dehli atrofidagi maqbaralami ziyorat qilmoqda (Babur views Delhi mausoleum). h, 540s, Qobul atrofidagi Xo'ja Seyoron chashmasi (Xo'ja Seyoron Spring near Kabul). i, 680s, Bobur Mon Sing va Bikramojit saroylarini tomosha qilmoqda (Babur views Man Singh and Bikramajit Palaces).

2008, Feb. 13
540 A247 Sheet of 9, #a-i *12.50 12.50*

National Academic Drama Theater A248

Alisher Navoiy Theater A249

2008, Feb. 28 *Perf. 13¾x14*
541 A248 45s blue *.55 .55*
542 A249 90s dark green *.55 .55*

No. 542 has thicker lettering than No. 454.

Architecture Types of 2006-08

2008 Litho. *Perf. 13¾x14, 14x13¾*

543	A195	30s green	.35	.35
544	A249	75s dark green	.35	.35
545	A195	85s dark green	.40	.40
546	A248	100s red	.40	.40
547	A249	150s dark green	.55	.55
548	A195	160s green	.60	.60
549	A248	200s red	.75	.75
550	A249	250s blue	.90	.90
551	A249	310s dark green	1.10	1.10
552	A248	350s blue	1.25	1.25
		Nos. 543-552 (10)	*6.65*	*6.65*

Issued: 75s, 85s, 150s, 310s, 350s, 4/1; 30s, 7/15; 100s, 11/25; 160s, 200s, 250s, 4/1. See Nos. 598, 600-601.

Yahyo Gulomov (1908-77), Archaeologist — A250

2008, June 25 Litho. *Perf. 13¾x14*
553 A250 150s multi *.70 .70*

2008 Summer Olympics, Beijing — A251

Designs: 150s, Judo. 200s, Boxing. 250s, Running. 310s, Rhythmic gymnastics, vert.

Perf. 13¾x14, 14x13¾
2008, June 25
554-557 A251 Set of 4 *5.50 5.50*

Flowers — A252

Designs: 150s, Cousinia butkovii. 200s, Cousinia dshisakensis. 250s, Cousinia adenophora. 310s, Cousinia angreni.

2008, June 25 *Perf. 14x13¾*
558-561 A252 Set of 4 *3.00 3.00*

Intl. Swimming Federation (FINA), Cent. — A253

No. 562: a, 310s, Water polo. b, 450s, Synchronized swimming.

No. 563: a, 620s, Diving. b, 750s, Freestyle swimming.

2008, July 24 *Perf. 14x13¾*
Horiz. Pairs, #a-b, + Central Label
562-563 A253 Set of 2 *8.00 8.00*

Souvenir Sheet

Navoi, 50th Anniv. A254

No. 564: a, 930s, Farkhad monument, Culture Palace. b, 1250s, Gold bars.

2008, Oct. 22 *Perf. 13¾x14*
564 A254 Sheet of 2, #a-b, + 2 labels *7.75 7.75*

Writers — A255

Designs: 620s, Maqsud Shayxzoda (1908-67). 750s, Mirzakalon Ismoiliy (1908-86).

2008, Nov. 5
565-566 A255 Set of 2 *4.50 4.50*

Men's Traditional Costumes — A256

2008, Dec. 31 *Perf. 14x13¾*
567 Horiz. strip of 4 + label *9.50 9.50*
a. A256 310s Joma *1.00 1.00*
b. A256 350s Yaktak *1.10 1.10*
c. A256 750s Erkalar liboslari *2.50 2.50*
d. A256 1250s Joma, diff. *4.50 4.50*

Louis Braille (1809-52), Educator of the Blind — A257

2009, Feb. 2 Litho. *Perf. 13¾x14*
568 A257 620s multi *2.00 2.00*

Intl. Year of Astronomy — A258

No. 569: a, 350s, Observatory of Sultan Ulugh Beg, Samarkand. b, 750s, Statue of Ulugh Beg.

2009, Mar. 22 *Perf. 14x13¾*
569 A258 Horiz. pair, #a-b, + central label *3.75 3.75*

Birds — A259

2009, Apr. 8 *Perf. 13¾x14*
570 Horiz. strip of 4 *7.00 7.00*
a. A259 310s Rufibrenta ruticollis *1.05 1.05*
b. A259 350s Cygnus cygnus *1.15 1.15*
c. A259 620s Aythya nyroca *2.00 2.00*
d. A259 750s Anser erythropus *2.60 2.60*

A260

A261

A262

A263

A264

Children's Art — A265

2009, June 1 ***Perf. 13¾x14***

571 A260 200s multi .60 .60
572 A261 200s multi .60 .60
573 A262 200s multi .60 .60

Perf. 14x13¾

574 A263 200s multi .60 .60
575 A264 200s multi .60 .60
576 A265 200s multi .60 .60
Nos. 571-576 (6) 3.60 3.60

2010 Youth Olympic Games, Singapore — A266

Designs: 450s, Basketball. 750s, Soccer, horiz.

2009, July 1 ***Perf. 14x13¾, 13¾x14***

577-578 A266 Set of 2 3.75 3.75

Miniature Sheet

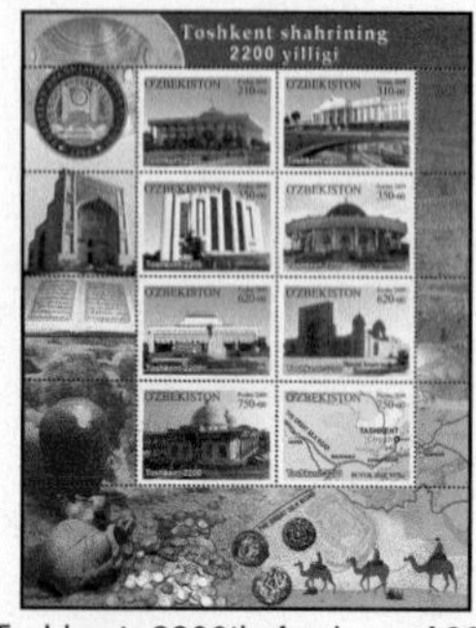
Tashkent, 2200th Anniv. — A267

No. 579: a, 310s, Majlis Building (Oliy Majlis binosi). b, 310s, Senate Building (Senat binosi). c, 350s, Intl. Business Center (Xalqaro biznes markazi). d, 350s, Temurids History Museum (Temuriylar tarixi davlat muzeyi). e, 620s, Turkistan Palace (Turkiston saroyi). f, 620s, Madrassa (Hazrat Imom majmuasi Baroqxon madrasasi). g, 750s, Museum of Victims of Oppression. h, 750s, Map of Great Silk Road.

2009, Aug. 17 ***Perf. 13¾x14***

579 A267 Sheet of 8, #a-h 12.00 12.00

Cities Along the Great Silk Road — A268

Designs: 350s, Khiva. 750s, Madrassa, Tashkent.
1250s, Samarkand Gate, Bukhara.

2009, Oct. 9 ***Perf. 14x13¾***

580-581 A268 Set of 2 3.00 3.00

Souvenir Sheet

582 A268 1250s multi 3.50 3.50

Theater Types of 2009

2009, Dec. 1 **Litho.** ***Perf. 13¾x14***

583 A249 450s red 1.40 1.40
584 A248 600s blue 1.60 1.60

Circus Performers — A269

Designs: 450s, Two women on horse. 600s, Three women on two horses. 1200s, Three women on horse.

2009, Dec. 28 ***Perf. 14x13¾***

585-587 A269 Set of 3 6.50 6.50

Carpet Designs — A270

No. 588: a, Samarqand, 19th cent. b, Andijon, 20th cent.
No. 589: a, Bukhara, 19th cent. b, Tashkent, 20th cent.

2009, Dec. 28 ***Perf. 13¾x14***

588 Horiz. pair + central label 4.50 4.50
a. A270 450s multi 1.25 1.25
b. A270 1200s multi 3.25 3.25
589 Horiz. pair + central label 4.50 4.50
a. A270 600s multi 1.25 1.25
b. A270 1000s multi 3.25 3.25

Endangered Flora — A271

Designs: 450s, Fritillaria eduardii. 1200s, Iridodictyum winklerii.

2010, Jan. 26 ***Perf. 14x13¾***

590-591 A271 Set of 2 4.75 4.75

Tashkent Zoo Animals — A272

Designs: 450s, Macaca sinica. 800s, Macaca fascicularis. 1000s, Mandrillus sphinx. 1650s, Lemur catta, horiz.

2010, Feb. 12 ***Perf. 14x13¾***

592-594 A272 Set of 3 5.50 5.50

Souvenir Sheet

Perf. 13¾x14

595 A272 1650s multi 4.50 4.50

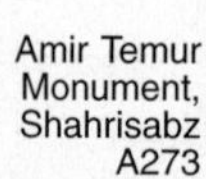

Amir Temur Monument, Shahrisabz A273

Qarshi Railroad Station — A274

2010, Mar. 29 ***Perf. 13¾x14***

596 Horiz. pair + central label 5.25 5.25
a. A273 800s multi 2.00 2.00
b. A274 1200s multi 3.25 3.25

Sites in Kashkadarya Vilayet.

Architecture Types of 2006-08

2010, Apr. 1 ***Perf. 14x13¾, 13¾x14***

597 A195 25s green .40 .40
598 A248 100s green .40 .40
599 A195 110s green .40 .40
600 A248 125s green .40 .40
601 A248 200s green .40 .40
Nos. 597-601 (5) 2.00 2.00

Endangered Birds — A275

Designs: 400s, Chettusia gregaria. 800s, Myiophonus caeruleus. 1000s, Tichodroma muraria. 1200s, Grus leucogeranus.
1900s, Cygnus olor.

2010, Apr. 15 ***Perf. 14x13¾***

602-605 A275 Set of 4 6.25 6.25

Souvenir Sheet

606 A275 1900s multi 4.75 4.75

No. 606 contains one 37x52mm stamp.

43rd Annual Meeting of the Asian Development Bank Board of Governors Issue

Horizontal Label

Vertical Label

Combine A276

Irrigation Canal — A277

Bukhara Oil Refinery — A278

Fergana Oil Refinery — A279

Tractor Trailer — A280

Train — A281

Poytaxt Business Center — A282

Uzbekistan Forum — A283

Sitorai Mohi Xosa Palace, Bukhara — A284

Hazrati Imam Complex, Tashkent A285

Majlis — A286

Conservatory Building — A287

Arch — A288

Tashkent Business Center — A289

Senate Building — A290

White Palace — A291

Highway Cloverleaf A292

Highway and Bridge — A293

Two Highways A294

Bridge Over Highway — A295

Seamstresses A296

Pottery Shop — A297

Water Polo — A298

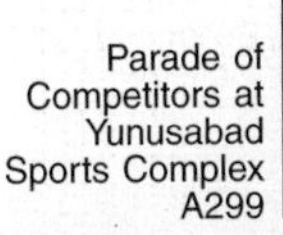

Parade of Competitors at Yunusabad Sports Complex A299

Construction Vehicles — A300

Railway Bridge — A301

Daewoo Automobile Plant — A302

Tashkent Tractor Factory — A303

Students in Laboratory A304

Children in Computer Class — A305

Flag of Uzbekistan A306

Coat of Arms A307

Bank Association Building A308

Central Bank Building A309

Man and Woman in Traditional Clothes A310

Man , Woman and Child in Traditional Clothes A311

Infant and Nurse A312

Surgeons in Operating Room — A313

2010, Apr. 15 *Perf. 13¾x14*

607 Horiz. pair + central label *5.50 5.50*
a. A276 800s multi *2.50 2.50*
b. A277 1000s multi *3.00 3.00*
608 Horiz. pair + central label *5.50 5.50*
a. A278 800s multi *2.50 2.50*
b. A279 1000s multi *3.00 3.00*
609 Horiz. pair + central label *6.25 6.25*
a. A280 800s multi *2.50 2.50*
b. A281 1200s multi *3.75 3.75*
610 Horiz. pair + central label *6.25 6.25*
a. A282 800s multi *2.50 2.50*
b. A283 1200s multi *3.75 3.75*
611 Horiz. pair + central label *6.25 6.25*
a. A284 800s multi *2.50 2.50*
b. A285 1200s multi *3.75 3.75*
612 Horiz. pair + central label *6.25 6.25*
a. A286 800s multi *2.50 2.50*
b. A287 1200s multi *3.75 3.75*
613 Horiz. pair + central label *6.25 6.25*
a. A288 800s multi *2.50 2.50*
b. A289 1200s multi *3.75 3.75*
614 Horiz. pair + central label *6.25 6.25*
a. A290 800s multi *2.50 2.50*
b. A291 1200s multi *3.75 3.75*
615 Horiz. pair + central label *6.25 6.25*
a. A292 900s multi *2.50 2.50*
b. A293 1100s multi *3.75 3.75*
616 Horiz. pair + central label *6.25 6.25*
a. A294 900s multi *2.50 2.50*
b. A295 1100s multi *3.75 3.75*
617 Horiz. pair + central label *6.50 6.50*
a. A296 900s multi *2.75 2.75*
b. A297 1200s multi *3.75 3.75*
618 Horiz. pair + central label *6.50 6.50*
a. A298 900s multi *2.75 2.75*
b. A299 1200s multi *3.75 3.75*
619 Horiz. pair + central label *6.75 6.75*
a. A300 1000s multi *3.00 3.00*
b. A301 1200s multi *3.75 3.75*
620 Horiz. pair + central label *6.75 6.75*
a. A302 1000s multi *3.00 3.00*
b. A303 1200s multi *3.75 3.75*
621 Horiz. pair + central label *6.75 6.75*
a. A304 1000s multi *3.00 3.00*
b. A305 1200s multi *3.75 3.75*
622 Horiz. pair + central label *6.75 6.75*
a. A306 1000s multi *3.00 3.00*
b. A307 1200s multi *3.75 3.75*

Perf. 14x13¾

623 Horiz. pair + central label *6.25 6.25*
a. A308 800s multi *2.50 2.50*
b. A309 1200s multi *3.75 3.75*
624 Horiz. pair + central label *6.50 6.50*
a. A310 900s multi *2.75 2.75*
b. A311 1200s multi *3.75 3.75*
625 Horiz. pair + central label *6.50 6.50*
a. A312 900s multi *2.75 2.75*
b. A313 1200s multi *3.75 3.75*
Nos. 607-625 (19) *120.25 120.25*

Miniature Sheet

Victory in World War II, 65th Anniv. A314

No. 626: a, 400s, Young people giving flowers to veterans. b, 800s, Ceremony at Grieving Mother Monument. c, 1000s, Soldier, women and children. d, 1200s, Celebratory ceremony with soldiers.

2010, May 9 *Perf. 13¾x14*
626 A314 Sheet of 4, #a-d *8.00 8.00*

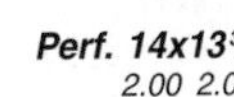

2010 Youth Olympics, Singapore — A315

2010, July 12 *Perf. 14x13¾*
627 A315 800s multi *2.00 2.00*

Uzbekistan-China Gas Pipeline — A316

2010, July 15 **Litho.**
628 A316 250s multi *.85 .85*

Miniature Sheet

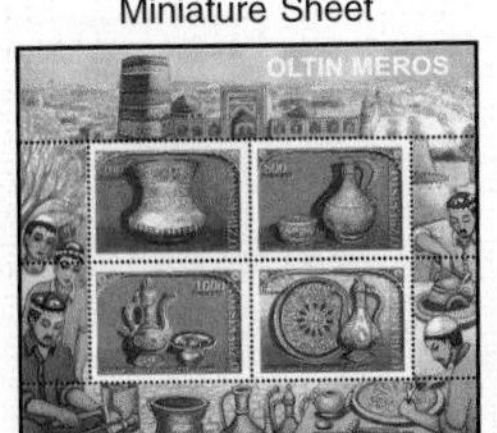

19th Century Copperware — A317

No. 629: a, 400s, Bucket, Central Asia. b, 800s, Bowl and pitcher, Khiva. c, 1000s, Pitcher and warming plate, Kokand. d, 1200s, Tray and pitcher, Khiva and Bukhara.

2010, Aug. 25 *Perf. 13¾x14*
629 A317 Sheet of 4, #a-d *8.00 8.00*

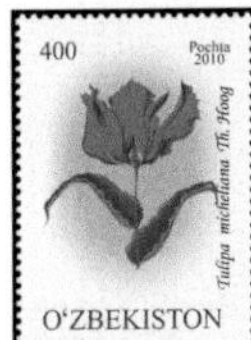

Tulips — A318

Designs: 400s, Tulipa micheliana. 800s, Tulipa dasystemon. No. 632, 1000s, Tulipa lehmaniana. No. 633, 1200s, Tulipa bifloriformis.

No. 634: a, 1000s, Three Tulipa dasystemon. b, 1900s, One Tulipa dasystemon, rock.

2010, Sept. 27 *Perf. 14x13¾*
630-633 A318 Set of 4 *6.25 6.25*

Souvenir Sheet

634 A318 Sheet of 2, #a-b *5.75 5.75*

Fish — A319

Designs: 800s, Pterois volitans. No. 636, 1000s, Trichogaster leeri. 1200s, Carassius auratus.

No. 638: a, 1000s, Pterophyllum scalare. b, 1900s, Trichogaster leeri, diff.

2010, Oct. 9 *Perf. 13¾x14*
635-637 A319 Set of 3 *6.00 6.00*

Souvenir Sheet

638 A319 Sheet of 2, #a-b *6.00 6.00*

16th Asian Games, Guangzhou, China — A320

2010, Oct. 25 **Litho.**
639 A320 800s multi *2.00 2.00*

Protection of Polar Regions and Glaciers — A321

2010, Oct. 25 *Perf. 14x13¾*
640 A321 900s multi *2.75 2.75*

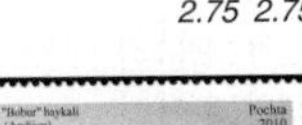

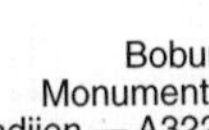

Bobur Monument, Andijon — A322

Olympic Sports College, Andijon — A323

2010, Dec. 30 *Perf. 13¾x14*
641 Horiz. pair + central label *5.25 5.25*
a. A322 900s multi *2.25 2.25*
b. A323 1200s multi *3.00 3.00*

Sites in Andijon Vilayet.

Soyib Xo'jayev (1910-82), Actor — A324

2010, Dec. 30 *Perf. 14x13¾*

642	A324 900s multi	2.25	2.25

Seventh Asian Winter Games, Astana and Almaty — A325

Designs: 800s, Figure skater. 900s, Freestyle skier.

2011, Jan. 5

643-644	A325 Set of 2	4.00	4.00

Flowers — A326

Designs: 800s, Lagochilus vevedenskyi. 900s, Echinops babtagensis. No. 647, 1000s, Saxifraga hirculus. 1200s, Nathaliella alaica.

No. 649: a, 1000s, Eremus korolkovii, plant 21mm tall. b, 1900s, Eremus korolkovii, plant 37mm tall.

2011, Mar. 31

645-648	A326 Set of 4	6.75	6.75

Souvenir Sheet

649	A326 Sheet of 2, #a-b	5.25	5.25

Miniature Sheet

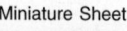

Carved Wood Items A327

No. 650: a, 800s, Table, 1983. b, 900s, Round covered box, 1984. c, 1000s, Lavh, 1990. d, 1200s, Decorative pumpkin, 1985.

2011, Apr. 12 *Perf. 13¾x14*

650	A327 Sheet of 4, #a-d	7.50	7.50

A328

A329

A330

Children's Art — A331

2011, June 1

651	A328 500s multi	.85	.85
652	A329 500s multi	.85	.85
653	A330 500s multi	.85	.85
654	A331 500s multi	.85	.85
	Nos. 651-654 (4)	3.40	3.40

Independence, 20th Anniv. Issue

Vertical Label

Horizontal Label

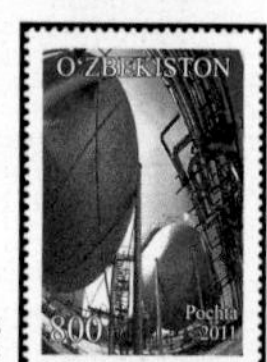

Navoiyazot Gas Tanks — A332

Maxam-Chirchiq Fertilizer Plant — A333

Wedding Hall, Termez — A334

Archaeological Museum, Termez — A335

Plaza, Urgench — A336

Al-Xorazmi Monument, Urgench — A337

Theater, Bukhara — A338

Monument, Bukhara — A339

Jokorgi Kenes Building, Nukus — A340

Berdaq Museum, Nukus — A341

Sports Complex, Namangan A342

Aloqabank Building, Namangan A343

Daewoo Automotive Plant — A344

Captiva, Epica and Spark Automobiles, Car Dealership A345

Highway Cloverleaf A346

Highway Overpass A347

Regional Pre-natal Center, Gulistan — A348

Denausky Medical Association Hospital — A349

Independence Day Celebrations A350

Ballet Dancers — A351

High Jumper Svetlana Radzivil — A352

Judoka Rishat Sabirov and Opponent A353

Zarafshansky Gold Mining Complex A354

Bekabadsky Metallurgical Complex A355

Wedding Hall, Samarkand A356

Concert Hall, Samarkand A357

Academic Lyceum, State University, Karshi — A358

Fergana Branch of Tashkent University of Information Technology A359

Youth Center, Andijan — A360

College of Light Industry, Andijan — A361

Worker at Control Center of MTS-Uzbekistan Company A362

Uztelecom Control Center — A363

Textile Factory, Bukhara — A364

Gulistansky Textile Factory — A365

Talimarzhdansky Power Plant — A366

Sogdiana Substation A367

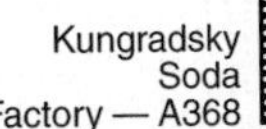

Kungradsky Soda Factory — A368

Shurtangas Oil Pumps — A369

Mountains in Winter — A370

Mountains in Spring — A371

Gissar National Park — A372

Gissar National Park — A373

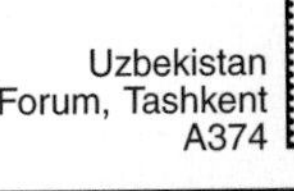
Uzbekistan Forum, Tashkent A374

Educational Center, Tashkent A375

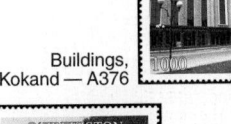

Buildings, Kokand — A376

Park Gazebos, Kokand — A377

Isuzu Automotive Factory, Samarqand A378

Isuzu Truck — A379

Bodomzor Subway Station — A380

Train on Tashguzar-Baysun-Kumkurgan Bridge — A381

Eski Machit Dancers — A382

Musicians With Karnays — A383

National Library and Monument to Amir Temur (Tamerlane) A384

Perf. 14x13¾ (#655, 666), 13¾x14

2011, Aug. 29 **Litho.**

655 Horiz. pair + central label 3.50 3.50
a. A332 800s multi 1.40 1.40
b. A333 1200s multi 2.10 2.10
656 Horiz. pair + central label 3.50 3.50
a. A334 800s multi 1.40 1.40
b. A335 1200s multi 2.10 2.10
657 Horiz. pair + central label 3.50 3.50
a. A336 800s multi 1.40 1.40
b. A337 1200s multi 2.10 2.10
658 Horiz. pair + central label 3.50 3.50
a. A338 800s multi 1.40 1.40
b. A339 1200s multi 2.10 2.10
659 Horiz. pair + central label 3.50 3.50
a. A340 800s multi 1.40 1.40
b. A341 1200s multi 2.10 2.10
660 Horiz. pair + central label 3.50 3.50
a. A342 800s multi 1.40 1.40
b. A343 1200s multi 2.10 2.10
661 Horiz. pair + central label 3.50 3.50
a. A344 800s multi 1.40 1.40
b. A345 1200s multi 2.10 2.10
662 Horiz. pair + central label 3.50 3.50
a. A346 800s multi 1.40 1.40
b. A347 1200s multi 2.10 2.10
663 Horiz. pair + central label 3.50 3.50
a. A348 800s multi 1.40 1.40
b. A349 1200s multi 2.10 2.10
664 Horiz. pair + central label 3.50 3.50
a. A350 800s multi 1.40 1.40
b. A351 1200s multi 2.10 2.10
665 Horiz. pair + central label 3.50 3.50
a. A352 800s multi 1.40 1.40
b. A353 1200s multi 2.10 2.10
666 Horiz. pair + central label 3.75 3.75
a. A354 900s multi 1.60 1.60
b. A355 1200s multi 2.10 2.10
667 Horiz. pair + central label 3.75 3.75
a. A356 900s multi 1.60 1.60
b. A357 1200s multi 2.10 2.10
668 Horiz. pair + central label 3.75 3.75
a. A358 900s multi 1.60 1.60
b. A359 1200s multi 2.10 2.10
669 Horiz. pair + central label 3.75 3.75
a. A360 900s multi 1.60 1.60
b. A361 1200s multi 2.10 2.10
670 Horiz. pair + central label 3.75 3.75
a. A362 900s multi 1.60 1.60
b. A363 1200s multi 2.10 2.10
671 Horiz. pair + central label 3.75 3.75
a. A364 900s multi 1.60 1.60
b. A365 1200s multi 2.10 2.10
672 Horiz. pair + central label 3.75 3.75
a. A366 900s multi 1.60 1.60
b. A367 1200s multi 2.10 2.10
673 Horiz. pair + central label 3.75 3.75
a. A368 900s multi 1.60 1.60
b. A369 1200s multi 2.10 2.10
674 Horiz. pair + central label 3.75 3.75
a. A370 900s multi 1.60 1.60
b. A371 1200s multi 2.10 2.10
675 Horiz. pair + central label 3.75 3.75
a. A372 900s multi 1.60 1.60
b. A373 1200s multi 2.10 2.10
676 Horiz. pair + central label 4.00 4.00
a. A374 1000s multi 1.90 1.90
b. A375 1200s multi 2.10 2.10
677 Horiz. pair + central label 4.00 4.00
a. A376 1000s multi 1.90 1.90
b. A377 1200s multi 2.10 2.10
678 Horiz. pair + central label 4.00 4.00
a. A378 1000s multi 1.90 1.90
b. A379 1200s multi 2.10 2.10
679 Horiz. pair + central label 4.00 4.00
a. A380 1000s multi 1.90 1.90
b. A381 1200s multi 2.10 2.10
680 Horiz. pair + central label 4.00 4.00
a. A382 1000s multi 1.90 1.90
b. A383 1200s multi 2.10 2.10

Litho. & Embossed With Foil Application

Perf. 14

681 A384 15,000s multi 26.00 26.00
Nos. 655-681 (27) *122.00 122.00*

Souvenir Sheet

Regional Communications Commonwealth, 20th Anniv. — A385

2011, Nov. 1 **Litho.** ***Perf. 14x13¾***
682 A385 2000s multi 3.25 3.25

Campaign Against AIDS, 30th Anniv. — A386

2011, Dec. 16
683 A386 900s multi 2.25 2.25

Miniature Sheet

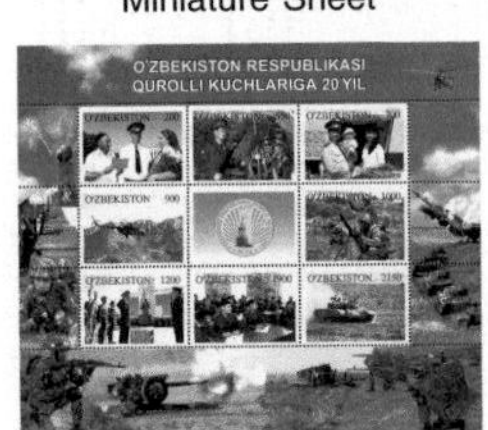
Uzbekistan Armed Forces, 20th Anniv. — A387

No. 684: a, 200s, Soldier with parents. b, 550s, Soldier reading proclamation, honor guard with flag. c, 700s, Soldier with wife and child. d, 900s, Helicopter. e, 1000s, Soldiers in camouflage. f, 1200s, Soldiers taking oath. g, 1900s, Military academy classroom. h, 2150s, Tank.

2012, Jan. 3 ***Perf. 13¾x14***
684 A387 Sheet of 8, #a-h, + central label 18.00 18.00

Monuments — A388

Monuments commemorating: 100s, 450s, 600s, Amir Temur (Tamerlane, 1336-1405), conqueror. 150s, 170s, Berdaq (1827-1900), poet. 250s, 300s, Muhammad Al-Khorezmi (c. 780-c.850), mathematician, horiz.

2012 ***Perf. 14x13¾, 13¾x14***
685 A388 100s green .25 .25
686 A388 150s green .30 .30
687 A388 170s green .35 .35
688 A388 250s green .55 .55
689 A388 300s green .60 .60
690 A388 450s green .95 .95
691 A388 600s green 1.25 1.25
Nos. 685-691 (7) *4.25 4.25*

Issued: 100s, 5/5; others, 4/5. See Nos. 711-713, 723-725, 736, 754-755, 799.

Paintings — A389

Designs: 800s, Onalik O'ylari, by Rakhim Ahmedov. 900s, Lagan O'yini, by Dzhavlon Umarbekov. 1000s, Bog'da, by Shorasul Shoahmedov. 1200s, Chavgon O'yini, by Shoahmedov.

2012, June 5 ***Perf. 14x13¾***
692-695 A389 Set of 4 7.50 7.50

Flowers — A390

Designs: 800s, Hedysarum angrenicum. 900s, Cousinia glabriseta. No. 698, 1000s, Oxytropis pseudoleptophysa. 1200s, Phlomoides tschimganica.

No. 700: a, 1000s, Scorzonera bungei. b, 1900s, Spirostegia bucharica.

2012, June 5
696-699 A390 Set of 4 6.25 6.25

Souvenir Sheet

700 A390 Sheet of 2, #a-b 5.00 5.00

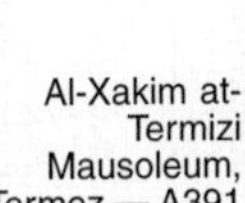

Al-Xakim at-Termizi Mausoleum, Termez — A391

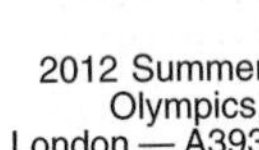
Riders in Game of Ulok-kupkari A392

2012, June 20 ***Perf. 13¾x14***
701 Horiz. pair + central label 4.00 4.00
a. A391 900s multi 1.75 1.75
b. A392 1200s multi 2.25 2.25

2012 Summer Olympics, London — A393

2012, July 27
702 A393 800s multi 1.75 1.75

Endangered Animals — A394

Designs: 400s, Mellivora capensis indica. 800s, Falco pelegrinoides. No. 705, 1000s, Hemiechinus hypomelas. 1200s, Lutra lutra seistanicus.

No. 707, Lynx lynx isabellina.

2012, Aug. 27 ***Perf. 14x13¾***
703-706 A394 Set of 4 6.25 6.25

Souvenir Sheet

707 A394 1000s multi 1.75 1.75

Miniature Sheet

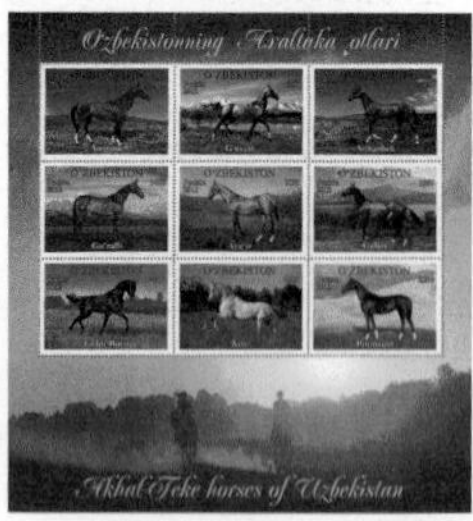

Akhal-Teke Horses — A395

No. 708: a, 950s, Amirana. b, 950s, G'ayrat. c, 950s, Asmanbek. d, 1050s, Go'zalli. e, 1050s, Ayg'ir. f, 1050s, Gallas. g, 2200s, Geldi Botir. h, 2200s, Xon. i, 2200s, Potmagul.

2012, Sept. 25 ***Perf. 14***
708 A395 Sheet of 9, #a-i *20.00 20.00*

Miniature Sheet

Soccer in Uzbekistan, Cent — A396

No. 709 — Various soccer players: a, 600s. b, 650s, c, 950s. d, 1050s. e, 1150s. f, 1300s. g, 2200s. h, 2500s.

2012, Sept. 25 ***Perf. 13¾x14***
709 A396 Sheet of 8, #a-h, + central label *15.00 15.00*

2012 Summer Olympics, London — A397

2012, Oct. 25 **Litho.**
710 A397 900s multi *1.75 1.75*

Monuments Type of 2012

Monument commemorating: 50s, 200s, Berdaq. 350s, Muhammad Al-Khorezmi, horiz.

2012, Nov. 9 ***Perf. 14x13¾, 13¾x14***
711 A388 50s green *.30 .30*
712 A388 200s green *.50 .50*
713 A388 350s green *.85 .85*
Nos. 711-713 (3) .85 .85

Tashkent Zoo Animals — A398

Designs: 400s, Threskiornis aethiopicus. 800s, Dolichotis patagonum. 1000s, Struthio camelus.
1200s, Elephas maximus.

2012, Dec. 28 ***Perf. 14x13¾***
714-716 A398 Set of 3 *4.25 4.25*

Souvenir Sheet

717 A398 1200s multi *2.25 2.25*

Flora and Fauna of Chatkal National Biosphere Reserve — A399

Designs: No. 718, 800s, Trichius fasciatus. No. 719, 900s, Juno tubergeniana. No. 720, 1000s, Bubo bubo. No. 721, 1200s, Ursus arctos isabellinus.
No. 722, vert: a, 1000s, Marmota menzbieri. b, 1900s, Marmota menzbieri, diff.

2012, Dec. 28 ***Perf. 13¾x14***
718-721 A399 Set of 4 *5.50 5.50*

Souvenir Sheet

Perf. 14x13¾

722 A399 Sheet of 2, #a-b *4.50 4.50*

Monuments Type of 2012

Monuments commemorating: 110s, Amir Temur (Tamerlane, 1336-1405), conqueror. 400s, 1500s, Muhammad Al-Khorezmi (c. 780-c. 850), mathematician, horiz.

Perf. 14x13¾, 13¾x14

2013, June 5 **Litho.**
723 A388 110s green *.25 .25*
724 A388 400s green *.60 .60*
725 A388 1500s green *2.25 2.25*
Nos. 723-725 (3) 3.10 3.10

Architecture of the Great Silk Road — A400

Designs: 1400s, Buildings, Bukhara. 1500s, Kutlug-Murad-inak Madrassa, Khiva.
3200s, Ota Darvoza, Khiva, and map of Great Silk Road.

2013, June 5 **Litho.** ***Perf. 14***
726-727 A400 Set of 2 4.50 4.50

Souvenir Sheet

728 A400 3200s multi 5.00 5.00

Flora — A401

Designs: 1400s, Cousinia platystegia. 1500s, Diospyros lotus.

2013, June 17 **Litho.** ***Perf. 14***
729-730 A401 Set of 2 4.75 4.75

Sports — A402

Designs: No. 731, 1500s, Judo. No. 732, 1500s, Fencing.

2013, June 17 **Litho.** ***Perf. 14***
731-732 A402 Set of 2 5.00 5.00

2013 Summer Universiade, Kazan, Russia (No. 731); 2013 Asian Youth Games, Nanjing, People's Republic of China (No. 732).

Miniature Sheet

Jewelry A403

No. 733: a, 1400s, Earrings from Bukhara, 19th cent. b, 1400s, Bracelet from Samarkand, 19th cent. c, 1500s, Round cincture from Fergana, 20th cent. d, 1500s, Heart-shaped pendant from Bukhara, 19th cent.

2013, Sept. 25 **Litho.** ***Perf. 14***
733 A403 Sheet of 4, #a-d *10.00 10.00*

2014 Winter Olympics, Sochi, Russia — A404

2014, Jan. 31 **Litho.** ***Perf. 14x13¾***
734 A404 1200s multi 2.50 2.50

Yonboshqal'a Fortress — A405

Gas Complex — A406

2014, Jan. 31 **Litho.** ***Perf. 13¾x14***
735 Horiz. pair + central label 5.50 5.50
a. A405 1500s multi 2.50 2.50
b. A406 2000s multi 3.00 3.00

Sites in Karakalpakstan Region.

Monuments Type of 2012

Design: 1000s, Muhammad Al-Khorezmi (c. 780-c. 850), mathematician, horiz.

2014, Apr. 10 **Litho.** ***Perf. 13¾x14***
736 A388 1000s green *1.50 1.50*

Flowers — A407

Designs: 1300s, Delphinium knorringianum. 1500s, Corydalis severzowii.
3200s, Juno magnifica.

2014, Apr. 10 **Litho.** ***Perf. 14***
737-738 A407 Set of 2 *3.50 3.50*

Souvenir Sheet

739 A407 3200s multi *4.00 4.00*

A408

A409

Children's Art — A410

Perf. 13¾x14, 14x13¾

2014, May 30 **Litho.**
740 A408 1200s multi *1.25 1.25*
741 A409 1200s multi *1.25 1.25*
742 A410 1200s multi *1.25 1.25*
Nos. 740-742 (3) 3.75 3.75

Fauna — A411

Designs: 1000s, Chlamydotis undulata. 1300s, Tetrax tetrax.
3200s, Saiga tatarica.

2014, May 30 **Litho.** ***Perf. 14***
743-744 A411 Set of 2 3.00 3.00

Souvenir Sheet

745 A411 3200s multi 3.75 3.75

17th Asian Games, Incheon, South Korea — A412

2014, July 30 **Litho.** ***Perf. 13¾x14***
746 A412 1200s multi 1.90 1.90

Paintings — A413

Designs: 1500s, Ilhom Parisi, by Shorasul Shoahmedov. 2100s, Teatr, by Muzaffar Polatov.

2014, Oct. 16 **Litho.** ***Perf. 14x13¾***
747-748 A413 Set of 2 4.75 4.75

Nos. 1-2, 4-6 Surcharged

Methods and Perfs. As Before

2014, Nov. 3
749 A1 300s on 20k #1 .55 .55
750 A4 300s on 50k #4 .55 .55
751 A6 300s on 50k #6 .55 .55
752 A2 500s on 1r #2 .85 .85
753 A5 1900s on 10r #5 3.25 3.25
Nos. 749-753 (5) 5.75 5.75

Monuments Type of 2012

Monument commemorating: 290s, Berdaq. 500s, Amir Temur (Tamerlane).

2014, Nov. 6 **Litho.** ***Perf. 14x13¾***
754 A388 290s green .60 .60
755 A388 500s green 1.00 1.00

Bobur Park, Namangan A414

Mosque, Namangan A415

2015, Jan. 22 **Litho.** ***Perf. 13¼x14***
756 Horiz. pair + central label 2.50 2.50
a. A414 1000s multi 1.10 1.10
b. A415 1200s multi 1.40 1.40

Tashkent Zoo Animals — A416

Designs: 1000s, Phasianus colchicus. 1200s, Anthropoides virgo, Balearica pavonina. 2100s, Hystrix indica.
2500s, Canis lupus, vert.

2015, Jan. 22 **Litho.** ***Perf. 13¾x14***
757-759 A416 Set of 3 4.75 4.75

Souvenir Sheet

Perf. 14x13¾

760 A416 2500s multi 2.75 2.75

No. 52 Surcharged

Methods and Perfs. As Before

2015, Apr. 15

761 A10a 300s on 20t #52 .65 .65

Nos. 57-61 Surcharged

Nos. 762-765 surcharged in black. No. 766 surcharged in blue.

Methods and Perfs. As Before

2015, Apr. 15

762 A13 1000s on 30t + label #57 .85 .85
763 A13 1000s on 35t + label #58 .85 .85
764 A13 1000s on 40t + label #59 .85 .85
765 A13 1900s on 45t #60 1.60 1.60
Nos. 762-765 (4) 4.15 4.15

Souvenir Sheet

766 A13 1900s on 60t #61 4.00 4.00

A417

Victory in World War II, 70th Anniv. — A418

2015, Apr. 15 Litho. *Perf. 14*

767 Horiz. pair + central label 3.25 3.25
a. A417 1000s multi 1.50 1.50
b. A418 1200s multi 1.75 1.75

Miniature Sheet

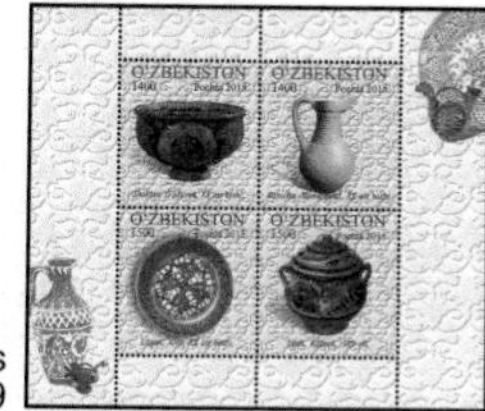
Ceramics A419

No. 768: a, 1400s, Bowl. b, 1400s, Pitcher. c, 1500s, Plate. d, 1500s, Bowl with lid.

2015, Apr. 15 Litho. *Perf. 14*

768 A419 Sheet of 4, #a-d 5.50 5.50

Nos. 7-14 Surcharged

Nos. 769-775 surcharged in black. No. 776 surcharged in dark blue.
Large Surcharged Numeral: Nos. 769, 774, 776.
Small Surcharged Numeral: Nos. 770-773, 775.

Methods and Perfs. As Before

2015, June 15

769 A7 200s on 2r #8 .30 .30
770 A7 200s on 3r #10 .30 .30
771 A7 500s on 1r #7 .60 .60
772 A7 500s on 2r #9 .60 .60
773 A7 500s on 5r #11 .60 .60
774 A7 500s on 10r #12 .60 .60
775 A7 500s on 15r #13 .60 .60
Nos. 769-775 (7) 3.60 3.60

Souvenir Sheet

776 A7 3900s on 20r #14 4.50 4.50

Nos. 38-44 Surcharged

Nos. 777-782 surcharged in black. No. 783 surcharged in blue.

Methods and Perfs. As Before

2015, June 16

777 A9 400s on 20r #38 .50 .50
778 A9 400s on 20r #39 .50 .50
779 A9 400s on 25r #41 .50 .50
780 A9 400s on 30r #43 .50 .50
781 A9 600s on 25r #40 .65 .65
782 A9 600s on 30r #42 .65 .65
Nos. 777-782 (6) 3.30 3.30

Souvenir Sheet

783 A9 1000s on 50r #44 1.40 1.40

Sports — A420

Designs: 1200s, Gymnastics. 1500s, Pole vault.

2015, Aug. 20 Litho. *Perf. 14*

784-785 A420 Set of 2 3.00 3.00

Flowers — A421

Designs: 1300s, Amygdalus. 1500s, Dipsacus laciniatus.
3200s, Thermopsis alterniflora.

2015, Aug. 20 Litho. *Perf. 14*

786-787 A421 Set of 2 3.50 3.50

Souvenir Sheet

788 A421 3200s multi 2.75 2.75

Fruit — A422

Designs: 1500s, Cydonia oblonga. 1800s, Punica granatum.

2015, Oct. 9 Litho. *Perf. 13*

789-790 A422 Set of 2 *3.75 3.75*

Values are for stamps with surrounding selvage.

Zomin Sanitarium A423

Aydar Lake — A424

2015, Dec. 14 Litho. *Perf. 13¾x14*

791 Horiz. pair + central label *2.50 2.50*
a. A423 1500s multi *1.25 1.25*
b. A424 1500s multi *1.25 1.25*

Sites in Jizzakh Region.

Souvenir Sheet

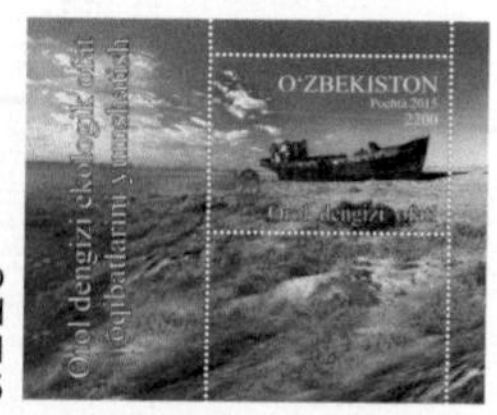
Ship Hulk and Camel A425

2016, Jan. 5 Litho. *Perf. 14*

792 A425 2200s multi *2.00 2.00*

Shrinkage of the Aral Sea.

Souvenir Sheet

International Telecommunication Union, 150th Anniv. — A426

2016, Jan. 22 Litho. *Perf. 14*

793 A426 2500s multi *2.10 2.10*

Fauna — A427

Designs: 1000s, Cetonia aurata. 1200s, Mustela eversmanni.1500s, Salmo trutta oxianus. 1800s, Upupa epops.
2500s, Merops apiaster.

2016, Jan. 22 Litho. *Perf. 14*

794-797 A427 Set of 4 *4.00 4.00*

Souvenir Sheet

798 A427 2500s multi *2.00 2.00*

Monuments Type of 2012

Design: 700s, Monument to Berdaq (1827-1900), poet.

2016, May 23 Litho. *Perf. 14x13¾*

799 A388 700s green .75 .75

2016 Summer Olympics, Rio de Janeiro — A428

Designs: 1900s, Weight lifting. 2100s, Long jump, vert.

Perf. 13¾x14, 14x13¾

2016, May 23 Litho.

800-801 A428 Set of 2 3.00 3.00

Silk Road Landmarks A429

Designs: 1500s, Ayoz Fortress. 1700s, Ko'k-Gumbaz (Blue Dome) mosque, Karshi.
3200s, Ark Fortress, Bukhara.

2016, May 23 Litho. *Perf. 13¾x14*

802-803 A429 Set of 2 2.50 2.50

Souvenir Sheet

804 A429 3200s multi 2.50 2.50

Flowers — A430

Designs: 1300s, Capparis spinosa. 1500s, Datúra métel.
2500s, Paeonia tenuifolia.

2016, May 23 Litho. *Perf. 14*

805-806 A430 Set of 2 2.10 2.10

Souvenir Sheet

807 A430 2500s multi 1.90 1.90

Fauna — A431

Designs: 1500s, Latrodectus tredecimguttatus. 1900s, Testudo horsfieldii.
2100s, Coracias garrulus.

2016, May 23 Litho. *Perf. 14*

808-809 A431 Set of 2 2.50 2.50

Souvenir Sheet

810 A431 2100s multi 1.75 1.75

Miniature Sheet

Independence, 25th Anniv. — A432

No. 811: a, 1200s, Bunyodkor Stadium, Tashkent. b, 1200s, Minor Mosque, Tashkent. c, 1500s, Ustyurt Gas and Chemical Complex. d, 1500s, Chevrolet automobile dealership. e, 2100s, Afrosiyob high-speed train. f, 2100s, Graduates. g, 2500s, Soldiers. h, 2500s, Mother and child.

2016, Aug. 31 Litho. *Perf. 13¾x14*

811 A432 Sheet of 8, #a-h, + central label 11.50 11.50

Animals at Tashkent Zoo — A433

Designs: 1700s, Neofelis nebulosa. 1900s, Haliaeetus albicilla. 2100s, Ramphastos vitellinus.
2500s, Eos bornea.

2016, Dec. 30 Litho. *Perf. 14*

812-814 A433 Set of 3 4.75 4.75

Souvenir Sheet

815 A433 2500s multi 1.90 1.90

Miniature Sheet

Traditional Costumes — A434

No. 816: a, 1900, Groom, 19th cent. b, 2100s, Bridesmaid, 20th cent. c, 2500s, Costume for boy's circumcision, 19th cent. d, 2500s, Woman, 1930-1940s.

2016, Dec. 30 Litho. *Perf. 14x13¾*
816 A434 Sheet of 4, #a-d 7.00 7.00

Syr Darya River — A435

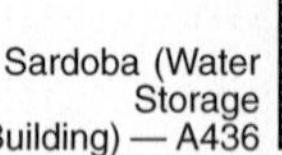

Sardoba (Water Storage Building) — A436

2017, Feb. 28 Litho. *Perf. 13¾x14*
817 Horiz. pair + central label 2.25 2.25
a. A435 1300s multi 1.00 1.00
b. A436 1500s multi 1.25 1.25

Birds — A437

Designs: 100s, Grus grus. 200s, Coturnix coturnix. 250s, Ciconia ciconia. 300s, 600s, Columba livia. 350s, 700s, Luscinia luscinia. 400s, Pica pica, horiz. 500s, Cygnus olor, horiz.

Perf. 14x13¾, 13¾x14

2017, Mar. 30 Litho.

818	A437	100s magenta	.25	.25
819	A437	200s blue	.25	.25
820	A437	250s blue	.25	.25
821	A437	300s blue	.25	.25
822	A437	350s blue	.25	.25
823	A437	400s magenta	.30	.30
824	A437	500s magenta	.40	.40
825	A437	600s magenta	.45	.45
826	A437	700s magenta	.55	.55
		Nos. 818-826 (9)	2.95	2.95

See Nos. 834-838, 845-856, 879-881, 926-927.

Theater A438

No. 827: a, Scene from "Sadoqat." b, Alisher Navoi State Academic Bolshoi Theater, Tashkent. c, Scene from "To'maris."

2017, May 12 Litho. *Perf. 13¾x14*
827 Horiz. strip of 3 3.25 3.25
a. A438 1000s multi .65 .65
b. A438 1800s multi 1.10 1.10
c. A438 2200s multi 1.50 1.50

Flowers — A439

Designs: 1300s, Hibiscus hybridus. 1900s, Crocus sativus.
2400s, Eremurus lactiflorus.

2017, May 12 Litho. *Perf. 14*
828-829 A439 Set of 2 2.10 2.10

Souvenir Sheet

830 A439 2400s multi 1.60 1.60

Fruit — A440

Designs: 1300s, Ficus carica. 1600s, Prunus persica.

2017, June 9 Litho. *Perf. 13*
831-832 A440 Set of 2 1.75 1.75

Values are for stamps with surrounding selvage.

Gold Medalists at 2016 Summer Olympics — A441

No. 833: a, 1800s, Ruslan Nurudinov, weight lifting. b, 1900s, Xasanboy Do'smatov, boxing.

2017, June 9 Litho. *Perf. 14x13¾*
833 A441 Horiz. pair, #a-b, + central label 2.25 2.25

Birds Type of 2017

Designs: 50s, Columba livia. 150s, Cygnus olor, horiz. 450s, Ciconia ciconia. 550s, Pica pica, horiz. 900s. Luscinia luscinia.

Perf. 14x13¾, 13¾x14

2017, July 21 Litho.

834	A437	50s emerald	.25	.25
835	A437	150s emerald	.25	.25
836	A437	450s emerald	.45	.45
837	A437	550s emerald	.55	.55
838	A437	900s emerald	.85	.85
		Nos. 834-838 (5)	2.35	2.35

Souvenir Sheets

Fountain on Khadra Square, Tashkent A443

Yunus Rajabov Metro Station, Tashkent A444

2017, Oct. 5 Litho. *Perf. 14x13¾*
840 A443 2700s multi 1.60 1.60
841 A444 4000s multi 2.40 2.40

Souvenir Sheet

Uzbekistan Constitution, 25th Anniv. — A445

2017, Dec. 4 Litho. *Perf. 14x13¾*
842 A445 4000s multi 2.25 2.25

Uzbek Cuisine — A446

Designs: 1800s, Palov. 1900s, Somsa.

2018, Jan. 16 Litho. *Perf. 14*
843-844 A446 Set of 2 2.10 2.10

A booklet issued on Jan. 30, 2018 commemorating Pres. Islam Karimov containing a pane of 14 stamps and 32 pairs of stamps with central labels was printed in limited quantities.

Birds Type of 2017

Designs: 650s, Columba livia. 800s, 2500s, Luscinia luscinia. 1000s, 1300s, 1800s, Cygnus olor, horiz. 2600s, Grus grus. 2800s, 4550s, Ciconia ciconia. 3500s, Coturnix coturnix. 7800s, 15,800s, Pica pica, horiz.

2018 Litho. *Perf. 14x13¾, 13¾x14*

845	A437	650s brt mag	.35	.35
846	A437	800s blue green	.45	.45
847	A437	1000s blue green	.55	.55
848	A437	1300s blue	.75	.75
849	A437	1800s magenta	1.00	.00
850	A437	2500s brt mag	1.40	1.40
851	A437	2600s blue	1.50	1.50
852	A437	2800s brt mag	1.60	1.60
853	A437	3500s blue green	2.00	2.00
854	A437	4550s blue	2.60	2.60
855	A437	7800s brt mag	4.50	4.50
856	A437	15,800s blue	9.00	9.00
		Nos. 845-856 (12)	25.70	24.70

Issue date: Nos. 845, 848, 3/28; Nos. 846, 851, 854-855, 4/10; Nos. 847, 850, 852-853, 856, 2/22; No. 849, 8/17.

Uzbekistan's Membership in UNESCO, 25th Anniv. — A447

2018, July 9 Litho. *Perf. 13¾x14*
857 A447 5800s multi 3.25 3.25

Zangiota Mosque, Tashkent A448

Lake Urungach A449

2018, July 9 Litho. *Perf. 13¾x14*
858 Horiz. pair + central label 3.00 3.00
a. A448 2700s multi 1.40 1.40
b. A449 2800s multi 1.60 1.60

Attractions of the Tashkent Region.

18th Asian Games, Jakarta — A450

Designs: 2700s, Kurash wrestling. 2800s, Soccer.

2018, Aug. 6 Litho. *Perf. 13¾x14*
859-860 A450 Set of 2 3.00 3.00

Miniature Sheet

Flora and Fauna of Zomin Nature Reserve A451

No. 861: a, 900s. Corvus corax. b, 1000s, Sus scrofa. c, 1800s, Juniperus. d, 2700s, Vulpes vulpes. e, 2800s, Eremurus. f, 3200s, Alectoris chukar. g, 3400s, Ziziphora. h, 3700s, Noctuidae.

2018, Aug. 6 Litho. *Perf. 13*
861 A451 Sheet of 8, #a-h 11.00 11.00

Miniature Sheet

Railroad Stations A452

No. 862 — Station at: a, 900s, Samarkand. b, 900s, Jizzakh. c, 1100s, Qarshi. d, 1100s, Andijan. e, 1800s, Bukhara. f, 1800s, Urgench. g, 3700s, South Tashkent. h, 3700s, Nukus. i, 6500s, Tashkent.

2018, Aug. 17 Litho. *Perf. 13¾x14*
862 A452 Sheet of 9, #a-i 25.00 25.00

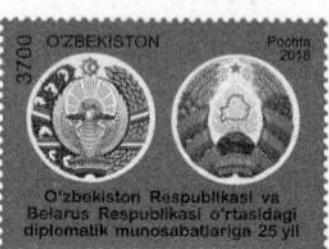

Diplomatic Relations Between Uzbekistan and Belarus, 25th Anniv. — A453

2018, Nov. 23 Litho. *Perf. 13¾x14*
863 A453 3700s multi 2.10 2.10

See Belarus No. 1121.

Fauna A454

Designs: 900s, Coccinella septempunctata. 1100s, Phrynocephalus interscapularis. 2700s, Carpodacus erythrinus, vert. 2800s, Rhombomys opimus.
3400s, Sciurus vulgaris, vert.

Perf. 13¾x14, 14x13¾

2018, Nov. 23 Litho.
864-867 A454 Set of 4 4.25 4.25

Souvenir Sheet

868 A454 3400s multi 1.90 1.90

Paintings by Pavel Benkov (1879-1949) A455

Designs: 1100s, Girl with a Dutar. 2800s, Artists in Shahizinde.
3200s, Lyabi hauz Water Carriers.

2018, Dec. 20 Litho. *Perf. 13¾x14*
869-870 A455 Set of 2 2.40 2.40

Souvenir Sheet

871 A455 3200s multi 1.10 1.10

Miniature Sheet

Flowers A456

No. 872: a, 900s, Adonis vernalis. b, 1000s, Viola tricolor. c, 2700s, Iris hippolyti. d, 2800s, Tagetes.

2019, Jan. 24 Litho. *Perf. 14x13¾*
872 A456 Sheet of 4, #a-d 4.25 4.25

Mausoleum of Abduhalik Gijduvani (1103-79) — A457

Mausoleum of Bahauddin Naqshbandi (1318-89) — A458

2019, Feb. 1 Litho. *Perf. 13¾x14*
873 A457 4000s multi + label 2.25 2.25
874 A458 4200s multi + label 2.25 2.25

Scenes From Uzbek Films A459

Scene from: 3200s, Tahir and Zuhra, 1945. 3500s, You Are Not an Orphan, 1963. 6200s, The Adventures of Nasreddin, 1947.

2019, Feb. 1 Litho. *Perf. 13¾x14*
875-876 A459 Set of 2 3.75 3.75

Souvenir Sheet

877 A459 6200s multi 3.25 3.25

Souvenir Sheet

Alisher Navoi Metro Station, Tashkent A460

2019, Feb. 1 Litho. *Perf. 13¾x14*
878 A460 4200s multi 2.25 2.25

Birds Type of 2017

Design: 1510s, Luscinia luscinia.

2019 Litho. *Perf. 14x13½*
879 A437 1510s blue .80 .80

Issued: 1510s, 2/1.

Birds Type of 2017

Designs: 1600s, Coturnix coturnix. 3200s, Pica pica, horiz.

2020 Litho. *Perf. 14x13¾, 13¾x14*
880 A437 1600s magenta .80 .80
881 A437 3200s blue grn 1.75 1.75

Issued, 1600s, 3200s, 2/5/20.

Deggaroni Mosque, Karmana — A461

Monument to Alisher Navoi (1441-1501), Poet, Navoiy — A462

2019, June 7 Litho. *Perf. 13½x14*
882 Horiz. pair, #a-b, + central label 4.00 4.00
a. A461 3600s multi 2.00 2.00
b. A462 3600s multi 2.00 2.00

Navoiy Region attractions.

2019 Asian Soccer Cup Tournament, United Arab Emirates — A463

2019 World Track and Field Championships, Doha, Qatar — A464

2019, June 7 Litho. *Perf. 14*
883 A463 3600s multi 2.00 2.00
884 A464 3600s multi 2.00 2.00

Miniature Sheet

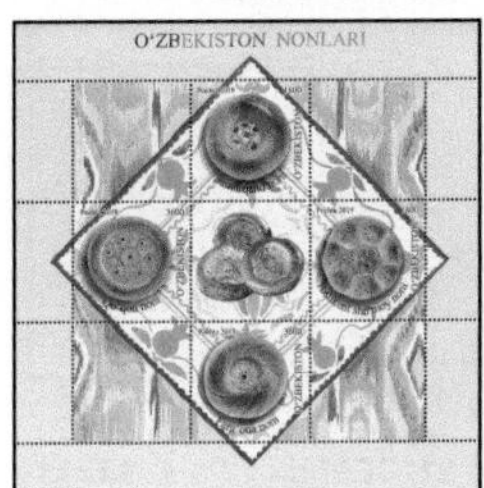

Breads A465

No. 885: a, 1800s, Samarqand noni. b, 1800s, Toshkent shirmoy noni. c, 3600s, Qo'qon noni. d, 3600s, Farg'ona noni.

2019, June 7 Litho. *Perf. 13*
885 A465 Sheet of 4, #a-d, + 5 labels 5.75 5.75

Tashkent Zoo Animals A466

Designs: 3600s, Python molurus bivittatus. No. 887, 3700s, Aix galericulata. No. 888, 3700s, Equus caballus. 6500s, Panthera tigris altaicus. 7200s, Giraffa camelopardalis giraffa, vert.

2019, June 21 Litho. *Perf. 13¾x14*
886-889 A466 Set of 4 8.50 8.50

Souvenir Sheet

Perf. 14x13¾

890 A466 7200s multi 3.50 3.50

Souvenir Sheet

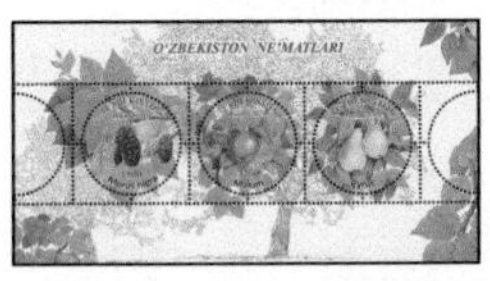

Fruit A467

No. 891: a, 1800s, Morus nigra (blackberries). b, 3200s, Malus (apples). c, 3600s, Pyrus (pears).

2019, July 11 Litho. *Perf. 13*
891 A467 Sheet of 3, #a-c 4.50 4.50

Miniature Sheet

Minerals A468

No. 892 — Inscriptions: a, 1800s, Flyuorit-calsit brekchiyasi. b, 3700s, Marmar Oniks. c, 6500s, Tasmali Feruza qora slanesda. d, 10,700s, Feruza.

2019, July 11 Litho. *Perf. 13*
892 A468 Sheet of 4, #a-d 11.50 11.50

Animals A469

Designs: No. 893, 3200s, Aquila chrysaetos. No. 894, 3200s, Equus hemionus, vert. 3700s, Phoenicopterus roseus, vert. 6500s, Panthera uncia.

Perf. 13¾x14, 14x13¾

2019, Aug. 27 Litho.
893-896 A469 Set of 4 8.25 8.25

Great Silk Road — A470

Camel caravan stops along Great Silk Road: 3600s, 3700s. 6500s, Camel caravan, diff.

2019, Aug. 23 Litho. *Perf. 14*
897-898 A470 Set of 2 3.50 3.50

Souvenir Sheet

899 A470 6500s multi 3.25 3.25

Miniature Sheets

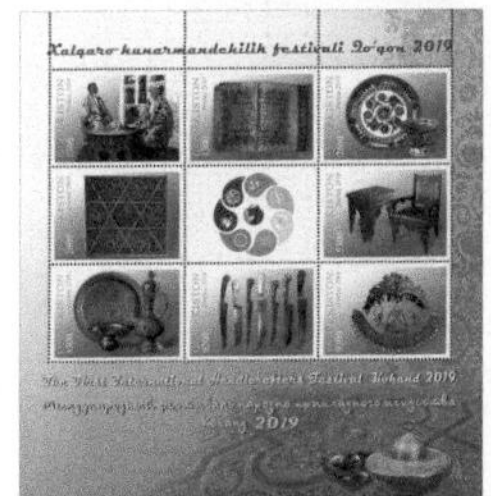

A471

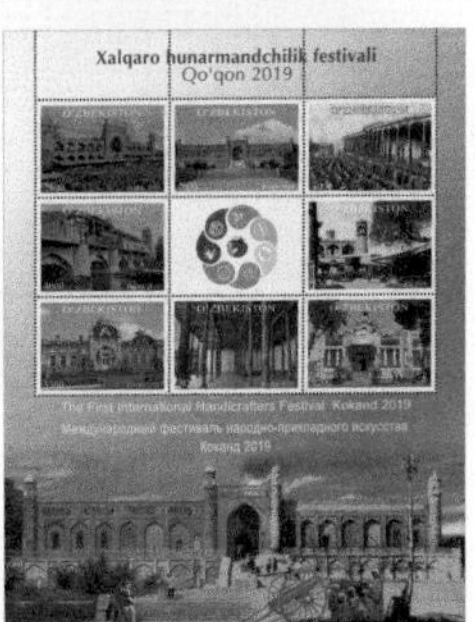

First International Handicrafters Festival, Kokand — A472

No. 900: a, 1300s, Two men at table. b, 1300s, Book. c, 2600s, Plate and bowl. d, 2600s, Decorated square. e, 5300s, Chair and small table. f, 5300s, Plate, bowl and pitcher. g, 9200s, Knives. h, 9200s, Jewelry.

No. 901: a, 2600s, Mosque with crowd of people. b, 2600s, Two people at mosque. c, 4000s, Mosque with crowd of people, diff. d, 4000s, Waterway under mosque. e, 5300s, Mosque and horse-drawn cart. f, 5300s, Building with fence. g, 9200s, Pillars supporting roof. h, 9200s, Building, diff.

2019, Sept. 5 Litho. *Perf. 13¾x14*
900 A471 Sheet of 8, #a-h, + central label 30.00 30.00
901 A472 Sheet of 8, #a-h, + central label 35.00 35.00

Souvenir Sheet

Mohandas K. Gandhi (1869-1948), Indian Nationalist Leader — A473

2019, Oct. 2 Litho. *Perf. 13¾x14*
902 A473 6200s multi 3.00 3.00

Souvenir Sheet

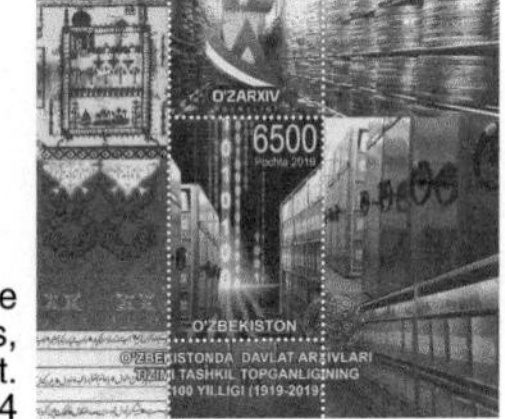

State Archives, Cent. A474

2019, Oct. 21 Litho. *Perf. 14*
903 A474 6500s multi 3.25 3.25

Scenes from Folk Tale, *Zumrad and Kimmat* — A475

Various scenes.

2019, Oct. 23 Litho. *Perf. 14*
904 Horiz. strip of 5 + flanking label 14.50 14.50
a. A475 1800s multi .90 .90
b. A475 3600s multi 1.75 1.75
c. A475 6500s multi 3.25 3.25
d. A475 7200s multi 3.50 3.50
e. A475 10,700s multi 5.00 5.00

Miniature Sheet

Mushrooms — A476

No. 905: a, 3200s, Morchella esculenta. b, 3400s, Pleurotus ostreatus. c, 3500s, Pleurotus eryngii. d, 5800s, Lepista saeva.

2019, Dec. 10 Litho. *Perf. 13¾x14*
905 A476 Sheet of 4, #a-d 7.75 7.75

Miniature Sheet

Flora and Fauna of Kyzylkum State Resereve — A477

No. 906: a, 3200s, Gazella subgutturosa. b, 3400s, Haloxylon persicum. c, 3500s, Alhagi pseudalhagi. d, 5800s, Canis aureus. e, 6200s, Trapelus sanguinolentus. f, 10,400s, Pterocles orientalis.

2019, Dec. 10 Litho. *Perf. 13¾x14*
906 A477 Sheet of 6, #a-f 16.00 16.00

Souvenir Sheet

Tumaris of Saki
A478

2019, Dec. 20 Litho. *Perf. 13¾x14*
907 A478 9200s multi 4.50 4.50

Souvenir Sheet

Uzbek State Puppet Theater, 80th Anniv.
A479

2020, Jan. 15 Litho. *Perf. 13¾x14*
908 A479 15,800s multi 7.75 7.75

Souvenir Sheet

Muqimiy State Musical Theater, 80th Anniv.
A480

2020, Jan. 25 Litho. *Perf. 14*
909 A480 15,800s multi 7.75 7.75

Dated 2019.

Shaykhontohur Mosque, Tashkent — A481

Tashkent City Convention Center and Hilton Hotel
A482

2020, Feb. 27 Litho. *Perf. 14*
910 Horiz. pair, #a-b, + central label 7.00 7.00
a. A481 5300s multi 2.50 2.50
b. A482 9200s multi 4.50 4.50

Dated 2019.

Souvenir Sheet

Novruz Holiday
A483

2020, Mar. 20 Litho. *Perf. 14*
911 A483 11,200s multi 5.50 5.50

Minerals — A484

No. 912: a, Feruza (turquoise). b, Ametist (amethyst). c, Lazurit (lazurite).

2020, Mar. 30 Litho. *Perf. 13*
912 Horiz. strip of 3, #a-c, + flanking label 5.50 5.50
a. A484 1900s multi .95 .95
b. A484 3100s multi 1.50 1.50
c. A484 6400s multi 3.00 3.00

Souvenir Sheet

End of World War II, 75th Anniv.
A485

2020, May 8 Litho. *Perf. 14*
913 A485 7300s multi 3.75 3.75

Souvenir Sheet

Alisher Navoi National Library, 150th Anniv.
A486

2020, May 26 Litho. *Perf. 14*
914 A486 15,800s multi 9.00 9.00

Miniature Sheet

Winning Art in Children's Stamp Design Contest — A487

No. 915: a, 3200s, Winter, by Ulugbekov Fozilbek. b, 3400s, Spring, by Yamoldinova Renata. c, 5300s, Autumn, by Bakhtiyorova Gulsanam. d, 7300s, Summer, by Makhmudzhanova Nilufar.

2020, July 17 Litho. *Perf. 14*
915 A487 Sheet of 4, #a-d 12.50 12.50

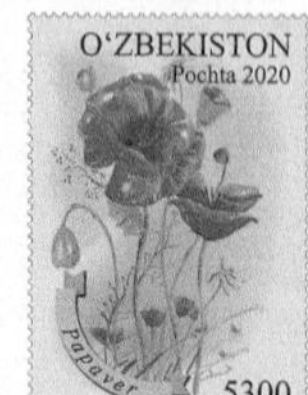

Poppies — A488

2020, July 17 Litho. *Perf. 14x13¾*
916 A488 5300s multi 2.60 2.60

No. 916 was printed in sheets of 3 + label.

Olympic Reserve Sports College, Fergana — A489

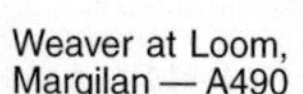

Weaver at Loom, Margilan — A490

2020, Oct. 7 Litho. *Perf. 13¾x14*
917 Horiz. pair + central label 3.25 3.25
a. A489 3200s multi 1.50 1.50
b. A490 3500s multi 1.75 1.75

Bukhara, 2020 Cultural Capital of the Islamic World
A491

2020, Nov. 27 Litho. *Perf. 13¾x14*
918 A491 7300s multi + label 3.00 3.00

United Nations, 75th Anniv. — A492

2020, Dec. 21 Litho. *Perf. 14x13¾*
919 A492 7300s multi 3.00 3.00

Abu Reyhan al-Biruni (973-c. 1050), Persian Scholar and Writer
A493

2020, Dec. 30 Litho. *Perf. 14*
920 A493 9200s multi 3.75 3.75

Souvenir Sheet

Fountain in Alisher Navoi Park, Navoi
A494

2020, Dec. 30 Litho. *Perf. 14*
921 A494 6500s multi 2.75 2.75

Uzbek Cuisine — A495

Designs: 6200s, Manti. 9200s, Lag'mon.

2021, Jan. 12 Litho. *Perf. 14*
922-923 A495 Set of 2 6.25 6.25

Souvenir Sheet

Rock Band Yalla, 50th Anniv. (in 2020)
A496

2021, Jan. 15 Litho. *Perf. 13¾*
924 A496 8800s multi 3.50 3.50

Souvenir Sheet

Alisher Navoi (1441-1501), Poet — A497

2021, Feb. 9 Litho. *Perf. 13¾*
925 A497 13,600s multi 5.50 5.50

Birds Type of 2017

Designs: 1900s, Grus grus. 3800s, Ciconia ciconia.

2021 Litho. *Perf. 14x13¾*
926 A437 1900s magenta .95 .95
927 A437 3800s blue 1.90 1.90

Issued: 1900s, 4/1; 3800s, 3/20.

Miniature Sheet

Flowers
A498

No. 928: a, 3800s, Pyracantha coccinea. b, 5900s, Primula fedtschenkoi. c, 7600s, Fritillaria karelinii. d, 11,500s, Hydrangea macrophylla.

2021, June 28 Litho. *Perf. 14*
928 A498 Sheet of 4, #a-d 14.00 14.00

Souvenir Sheet

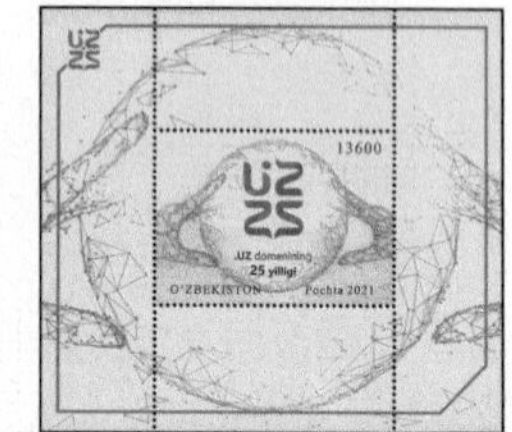

Use of ".uz" as Uzbekistan's Internet Domain, 25th Anniv. — A499

2021, June 29 Litho. *Perf. 14*
929 A499 13,600s multi 6.75 6.75

Souvenir Sheet

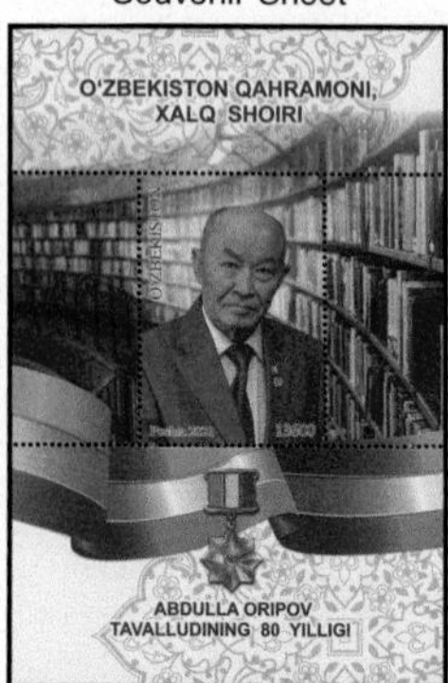

Abdulla Oripov (1941-2016), Poet — A500

2021, June 29 Litho. *Perf. 14*
930 A500 13,600s multi 6.75 6.75

Medal for Faithful Service A501

Medal for Courage A502

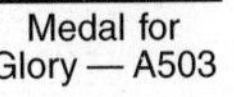

Medal for Glory — A503

Creator of the Future Medal — A504

2021, Sept. 15 Litho. *Perf. 14*

931	Horiz. strip of 4 + central label	14.00	14.00
a.	A501 3800s multi	1.90	1.90
b.	A502 5900s multi	3.00	3.00
c.	A503 7600s multi	3.75	3.75
d.	A504 10,000s multi	5.00	5.00

Souvenir Sheet

Regional Communications Commonwealth, 30th Anniv. — A505

2021, Oct. 20 Litho. *Perf. 14*

932 A505 9500s multi 4.75 4.75

Souvenir Sheets

A506

A507

A508

A509

A510

A511

A512

A513

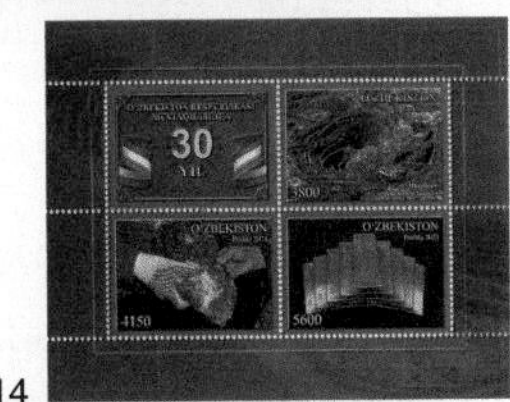

A514

A515

A516

A517

A518

A519

A520

A521

Independence, 30th Anniv. — A522

No. 933: a, 3800s, Flower Garden Park, Tashkent. b, 4150s, Sculpture garden. c, 5600s, Greenhouse.

No. 934: a, 3800s, Women cooking at large cauldron. b, 4150s, Singers and musicians. c, 5600s, Textiles.

No. 935: a, 3800s, Tashkent metallurgical factory. b, 4150s, Rolls of metal on pallets. c, 5600s, Roll of metal on machine.

No. 936: a, 3800s, Chevrolet Equinox. b, 4150s, Chevrolet Tracker. c, 5600s, Chevrolet Malibu.

No. 937: a, 3800s, Hazrat Imam Mosque complex b, 4150s, Bibi-Khanym Mosque, Samarkand. c, 5600s, Kalta Minor and Muhammad Amin Khan Madrasa, Khiva.

No. 938: a, 3800s, TZST CE 220 cotton harvester. b, 4150s, Machinery. c, 5600s, Worker monitoring machine gauges.

No. 939: a, 3800s, Children's National Medical Center, Tashkent. b, 4150s, Medical equipment. c, 5600s, Magnetic resonance imaging machine.

No. 940: a, 3800s, Muhammad Al-Xorazmiy School, Tashkent. b, 4150s, Students at desks. c, 5600s, Computer room.

No. 941: a, 3800s, Murontov Gold Mine, Navoiy. b, 4150s, Miners handling ore. c, 5600s, Gold bars.

No. 942: a, 3800s, Registon Plaza Hotel, Samarkand. b, 4150s, Hotel lobby as seen from upper floor. c, 5600s, Hotel lobby as seen from lobby floor.

No. 943: a, 3800s, Metro train to Sergeli District, Tashkent. b, 4150s, Metro train in station. c, 5600s, Metro train in station, diff.

No. 944: a, 3800s, Soldiers with guns. b, 4150s, Armored troop transports. c, 5600s, Military airplane.

No. 945: a, 3800s, Humo Arena, Tashkent. b, 4150s, Ice hockey players and referee. c, 5600s, Figure skaters.

No. 946: a, 3800s, Monument in New Uzbekistan Park, Tashkent. b, 4150s, Statues of men. c, 5600s, Statues of men and horses.

No. 947: a, 3800s, Female gold embroiderers. b, 4150s, Clothing with gold embroidery. c, 5600s, Gold decorated containers.

No. 948: a, 3800s, Carved wood items. b, 4150s, Plates. c, 5600s, Tables.

No. 949: a, 3800s, Zither. b, 4150s, Tanbur. c, 5600s, Drums.

2021, Oct. 20 Litho. *Perf. 14*

933	A506	Sheet of 3, #a-c, + label	4.25	4.25
934	A507	Sheet of 3, #a-c, + label	4.25	4.25
935	A508	Sheet of 3, #a-c, + label	4.25	4.25
936	A509	Sheet of 3, #a-c, + label	4.25	4.25
937	A510	Sheet of 3, #a-c, + label	4.25	4.25
938	A511	Sheet of 3, #a-c, + label	4.25	4.25
939	A512	Sheet of 3, #a-c, + label	4.25	4.25
940	A513	Sheet of 3, #a-c, + label	4.25	4.25
941	A514	Sheet of 3, #a-c, + label	4.25	4.25
942	A515	Sheet of 3, #a-c, + label	4.25	4.25
943	A516	Sheet of 3, #a-c, + label	4.25	4.25
944	A517	Sheet of 3, #a-c, + label	4.25	4.25
945	A518	Sheet of 3, #a-c, + label	4.25	4.25
946	A519	Sheet of 3, #a-c, + label	4.25	4.25
947	A520	Sheet of 3, #a-c, + label	4.25	4.25
948	A521	Sheet of 3, #a-c, + label	4.25	4.25
949	A522	Sheet of 3, #a-c, + label	4.25	4.25
		Nos. 933-949 (17)	72.25	72.25

Mausoleum of Khoja Abdi-Darun, Samarkand A523

Mausoleum of Pres. Islam Karimov, Samarkand A524

2021, Oct. 26 Litho. *Perf. 14*

950	Horiz. pair + central label	5.00	5.00
a.	A523 3800s multi	2.00	3.00
b.	A524 5900s multi	3.00	3.00

Cats A525

No. 951: a, 5900s, Bengal cat. b, 7600s, Persian cat.

2021, Oct. 26 Litho. *Perf. 14*

951 A525 Pair, #a-b 6.75 6.75

Miniature Sheet

Hydroelectric Power Plants — A526

No. 952: a, 4150s, Oxangaron Gesi Building. b, 4150s, Tuyabogiz Gesi Building. c, 4150s, Qamchiq Gesi Building. d, 5600s, Katta Farg'ona Kanali Ges-1 Building. e, 5600s, Uzbekgidroenergo Headquarters. f, 5600s, Topolon Reservoir. g, 9500s, Zarchob-1 Gesi Building. h, 9500s, Topolong Ges-34 Building. i, 9500s, Qodiriya Gesi Building.

2021, Nov. 22 Litho. *Perf. 14*

952 A526 Sheet of 9, #a-i 24.00 24.00

VANUATU

ˌvan-ˌwä-ˈtü

LOCATION — Island group in south Pacific Ocean northeast of New Caledonia
GOVT. — Republic
AREA — 5,700 sq. mi.
POP. — 189,036 (1999 est.)
CAPITAL — Port Vila

The Anglo-French condominium of New Hebrides (Vol. 5) became the independent state of Vanuatu July 30, 1980.

Hebrides franc Vatu (1981)

Catalogue values for all unused stamps in this country are for Never Hinged items.

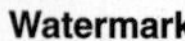

Watermark

Wmk. 387 — Squares and Rectangles

Erromango Is. and Kaori Tree — A44

Designs: 10fr, Archipelago and man making copra. 15fr, Espiritu Santo Island and cattle. 20fr, Efate Island and Post Office, Vila. 25fr, Malakula Island and headdresses. 30fr, Aoba and Maewo Islands and pig tusks. 35fr, Pentecost Island and land diving. 40fr, Tanna Island and Prophet John Frum's Red Cross. 50fr, Shepherd Island and canoe with sail. 70fr, Banks Island and dancers. 100fr, Ambrym Island and carvings. 200fr, Aneityum Island and decorated baskets. 500fr, Torres Islands and fishing with bow and arrow.

Wmk. 373

1980, July 30 Litho. ***Perf. 14***

280 A44 5fr multicolored .25 .25
281 A44 10fr multicolored .25 .25
282 A44 15fr multicolored .25 .30
283 A44 20fr multicolored .30 .40
284 A44 25fr multicolored .40 .45
285 A44 30fr multicolored .50 .60
286 A44 35fr multicolored .55 .65
287 A44 40fr multicolored .55 .75
288 A44 50fr multicolored .60 .90
289 A44 70fr multicolored 1.10 1.25
290 A44 100fr multicolored 1.10 1.00
291 A44 200fr multicolored 1.25 1.75
292 A44 500fr multicolored 2.25 *3.75*
Nos. 280-292 (13) 9.35 12.30

Inscribed in French

Unwmk.

280a A44 5fr multicolored .35 .25
281a A44 10fr multicolored .50 .25
282a A44 15fr multicolored .55 .45
283a A44 20fr multicolored .60 .50
284a A44 25fr multicolored .70 .55
285a A44 30fr multicolored .70 .65
286a A44 35fr multicolored .75 .80
287a A44 40fr multicolored 1.10 .90
288a A44 50fr multicolored 1.20 1.10
289a A44 70fr multicolored 1.75 1.50
290a A44 100fr multicolored 1.75 1.60
291a A44 200fr multicolored 2.00 2.75
292a A44 500fr multicolored 4.75 5.25
Nos. 280a-292a (13) 16.70 16.55

Rotary Emblem — A52

1980, Sept. 16 Wmk. 373

293 A52 10fr Emblem, horiz. .25 .25
294 A52 40fr shown .50 .50

Inscribed in French

Unwmk.

293a A52 10fr multicolored .25 .25
294a A52 40fr multicolored .70 .70

75th anniv. of Rotary Intl. and 8th anniv. of Port Vila Rotary Club (40fr).

Kiwanis Emblem — A53

1980, Sept. 16 Wmk. 373

295 A53 10fr shown .25 .25
296 A53 40fr Emblem, horiz. .75 .75

Inscribed in French

Unwmk.

295a A53 10fr multicolored .25 .25
296a A53 40fr multicolored 1.00 1.00

New Zealand District Kiwanis Convention, Port Vila, Sept. 16-18.

Christmas — A54

Paintings: 10fr, Virgin and Child, by Michael Pacher. 15fr, Virgin and Child, by Hans Memling. 30fr, Rest on the Flight to Egypt, by Adriaen van der Werff.

1980, Nov. 12 Wmk. 373

297 A54 10fr multicolored .25 .25
298 A54 15fr multicolored .25 .25
299 A54 30fr multicolored .40 .40
Nos. 297-299 (3) .90 .90

Erythrura Trichroa — A55

20fr, Chalcophaps indica. 30fr, Pachycephala pectoralis. 40fr, Ptilinopus tannensis.

1981, Feb. 18

300 A55 10fr shown .50 .30
301 A55 20fr multicolored .75 .65
302 A55 30fr multicolored 1.20 1.00
303 A55 40fr multicolored 1.60 1.25
Nos. 300-303 (4) 4.05 3.20

Duke of Edinburgh's 60th Birthday — A56

1981, June 10 ***Perf. 14x14½***

304 A56 15v Tribesman, portrait .25 .25
305 A56 25v Portrait .25 .25
306 A56 35v Family .25 .25
307 A56 45v shown .25 .25
Nos. 304-307 (4) 1.00 1.00

Common Design Types

pictured following the introduction.

Royal Wedding Issue

Common Design Type

1981, July 29

308 CD331 15v Bouquet .25 .25
309 CD331 45v Charles .35 .35
310 CD331 75v Couple .55 .55
Nos. 308-310 (3) 1.15 1.15

First Anniv. of Independence A57

1981, July 19

311 A57 15v Map, flag, vert. .25 .25
312 A57 25v Emblem .25 .25
313 A57 45v Anthem .40 .40
314 A57 75v Arms, vert. .55 .55
Nos. 311-314 (4) 1.45 1.45

Christmas A58

Children's drawings: 15v, Three kings. 25v, Girl holding lamb, vert. 35v, Butterfly-angel. 45v, Gift bearer, vert.

Wmk. 373

1981, Nov. 11 Litho. ***Perf. 14***

315 A58 15v multicolored .25 .25
316 A58 25v multicolored .25 .25
317 A58 35v multicolored .40 .40
318 A58 45v multicolored .60 .60
a. Souvenir sheet, #315-318 2.25 2.25
Nos. 315-318 (4) 1.50 1.50

Broadbills — A59

20v, Rainbow lorries. 25v, Buff-bellied flycatchers. 45v, Fantails.

1982, Feb. 8 ***Perf. 14½x14***

319 A59 15v shown .60 .60
320 A59 20v multicolored .80 .80
321 A59 25v multicolored 1.00 1.00
322 A59 45v multicolored 1.75 1.75
Nos. 319-322 (4) 4.15 4.15

Orchids — A60

1v, Flickengeria comata. 2v, Calanthe triplicata. 10v, Dendrobium sladei. 15v, Dendrobium mohlianum. 20v, Dendrobium macrophyllum. 25v, Dendrobium purpureum. 30v, Robiquetia mimus. 35v, Dendrobium mooreanum. 45v, Spathoglottis plicata. 50v, Dendrobium seemannii. 75v, Dendrobium conanthum. 100v, Dendrobium macranthum. 200v, Coelogyne lamellata. 500v, Bulbophyllum longiscapum.

Perf. 14x13½, 13½x14

1982, June 15

323 A60 1v multicolored .25 .70
324 A60 2v multicolored .25 .75
325 A60 10v multicolored .30 .40
326 A60 15v multicolored .40 .35
327 A60 20v multicolored .50 .40
328 A60 25v multicolored .75 .70
329 A60 30v multicolored .90 1.10
330 A60 35v multicolored 1.00 1.25
331 A60 45v multicolored 1.20 1.40
332 A60 50v multicolored 1.40 1.75
333 A60 75v multicolored 2.25 2.75
334 A60 100v multicolored 2.60 2.75
335 A60 200v multicolored 3.25 4.25
336 A60 500v multicolored 6.25 9.25
Nos. 323-336 (14) 21.30 27.80

Nos. 330-333 horiz.
For surcharges see Nos. 383, 512, 551-554, 586-589A, B1.

Scouting Year — A61

Wmk. 373

1982, Sept. 1 Litho. ***Perf. 14***

337 A61 15v Around campfire .35 .35
338 A61 20v First aid .35 .35
339 A61 25v Signal tower .45 .45
340 A61 45v Building raft 1.00 1.00
341 A61 75v Scout sign 1.40 1.40
Nos. 337-341 (5) 3.55 3.55

Christmas A62

Details from Nativity painting. 35v, 45v horiz.

1982, Nov. 16

342 A62 15v multicolored .35 .35
343 A62 25v multicolored .55 .55
344 A62 35v multicolored .80 .80
345 A62 45v multicolored 1.00 1.00
a. Souvenir sheet of 4, #342-345 3.00 3.00
Nos. 342-345 (4) 2.70 2.70

Hypolimnas Octocula — A63

1983, Jan. 17 ***Perf. 14½***

346 Pair 1.75 1.60
a. A63 15v shown .75 .75
b. A63 15v Euploea sylvester .75 .75
347 Pair 2.00 2.00
a. A63 20v Polyura sacco .90 .90
b. A63 20v Papilio canopus .90 .90
348 Pair 2.75 2.40
a. A63 25v Parantica pumila 1.25 1.20
b. A63 25v Luthrodes cleotas 1.25 1.20
Nos. 346-348 (3) 6.50 6.00

A64

1983, Mar. 14 ***Perf. 13½x14***

349 A64 15v Pres. Sokomanu .25 .25
350 A64 20v Fisherman .25 .25
351 A64 25v Herdsman, cattle .30 .30
352 A64 75v Flags, map .65 .65
Nos. 349-352 (4) 1.45 1.45

Commonwealth Day. 20v, 75v inscribed in French.

Economic Zone — A65

a, Thunnus albacares. b, Map. c, Matthew Isld. d, Hunter Isld. e, Epinephelus morrhua, etelis carbunculus. f, Katsuwonus pelamis.

Perf. 14x13½

1983, May 23 Litho. Wmk. 373

353 Sheet of 6 4.25 4.25
a.-f. A65 25v multicolored .65 .65

Manned Flight Bicentenary A66

Balloons or Airships: 15v, Montgolfiere, 1783. 20v, J.A.C. Charles 1st hydrogen balloon, 1783. 25v, Blanchard & Jeffries 1st English Channel crossing, 1785. 35v, H. Giffard's 1st mechanically powered airship, 1852.

40v, Renard and Krebs' airship, 1884. 45v, Graf Zeppelin's 1st transworld flight, 1929.

1983, Aug. 4 Litho. *Perf. 14*

354	A66	15v multi, vert.	.30	.30
355	A66	20v multi, vert.	.35	.35
356	A66	25v multi, vert.	.45	.45
357	A66	35v multi	.60	.60
358	A66	40v multi	.75	.75
359	A66	45v multi	.85	.85
		Nos. 354-359 (6)	3.30	3.30

For overprint see No. 372.

World Communications Year — A67

15v, Mail transport, Bauerfield Airport. 20v, Switchboard operator. 25v, Telex operator. 45v, Satellite earth station.

1983, Oct. 10 Litho. Wmk. 373

360	A67	15v multicolored	.25	.25
361	A67	20v multicolored	.40	.40
362	A67	25v multicolored	.55	.55
363	A67	45v multicolored	.95	.95
a.		Souv. sheet of 4, #360-363 + 3 labels	5.25	5.25
		Nos. 360-363 (4)	2.15	2.15

No. 363a issued for WCY and 75th anniv. of New Hebrides stamps.

Local Fungi — A68

15v, Cymatoderma elegans, vert. 25v, Lignosus rhinoceros, vert. 35v, Stereum ostrea. 45v, Ganoderma boninenze, vert.

1984, Jan. 9 Litho. *Perf. 14*

364	A68	15v multicolored	.80	.80
365	A68	25v multicolored	.90	.90
366	A68	35v multicolored	1.50	1.50
367	A68	45v multicolored	1.75	1.75
		Nos. 364-367 (4)	4.95	4.95

Lloyd's List Issue

Common Design Type

1984, Apr. 30 Litho. *Perf. 14½x14*

368	CD335	15v Port Vila	.25	.25
369	CD335	20v Induna	.35	.35
370	CD335	25v Air Vanuatu jet	.50	.50
371	CD335	45v Brahman Express	.75	.75
		Nos. 368-371 (4)	1.85	1.85

No. 359 Overprinted "UPU CONGRESS / HAMBURG"

1984, June 11 Wmk. 373 *Perf. 14*

372	A66	45v multicolored	.85	.85

Cattle — A69

1984, July 3 Litho. *Perf. 14*

373	A69	15v Charolais	.25	.25
374	A69	25v Charolais-Afrikaner	.40	.40
375	A69	45v Friesian	.70	.70
376	A69	75v Charolais-Brahman	1.30	1.30
		Nos. 373-376 (4)	2.65	2.65

Ausipex '84 A70

Ships.

1984, Sept. 7

377	A70	25v Makambo	.60	.50
378	A70	45v Rockton	1.10	1.00
379	A70	100v Waroonga	2.10	*4.00*
a.		Souvenir sheet of 3, #377-379	5.00	*5.25*
		Nos. 377-379 (3)	3.80	5.50

Christmas A71

25v, Father Christmas, child in hospital. 45v, Nativity. 75v, Father Christmas, children.

1984, Nov. 19 Litho. Wmk. 373

380	A71	25v multicolored	.50	.30
381	A71	45v multicolored	.90	.75
382	A71	75v multicolored	1.50	1.50
		Nos. 380-382 (3)	2.90	2.55

No. 323 Surcharged

1985, Jan. 22 Litho. *Perf. 14x13½*

383	A60	5v on 1v multi	1.25	1.00

Ceremonial Dance Costumes — A71a

1985, Jan. 22 *Perf. 14*

384	A71a	20v Ambrym Island	.35	.35
385	A71a	25v Pentecost Island	.50	.50
386	A71a	45v Women's Grade Ceremony, S.W. Malakula	.80	.80
387	A71a	75v Same, men's	1.25	1.25
		Nos. 384-387 (4)	2.90	2.90

Audubon Birth Bicent. — A72

Peregrine falcons.

Wmk. 373

1985, Mar. 26 Litho. *Perf. 14*

388	A72	20v multicolored	1.00	1.00
389	A72	35v multicolored	1.20	1.20
390	A72	45v multicolored	1.40	1.40
391	A72	100v multicolored	2.40	2.40
		Nos. 388-391 (4)	6.00	6.00

Queen Mother 85th Birthday

Common Design Type

Perf. 14½x14

1985, June 7 Wmk. 384

392	CD336	5v Wedding photo	.25	.25
393	CD336	20v 80th birthday celebration	.45	.45
394	CD336	35v At Ancona, Italy	.60	.60
395	CD336	55v Holding Prince Henry	.95	.95
		Nos. 392-395 (4)	2.25	2.25

Souvenir Sheet

396	CD336	100v At Covent Garden Opera	3.00	3.00

EXPO '85, Tsukuba — A73

35v, Mala naval patrol boat. 45v, Japanese fishing fleet, Port Vila. 55v, Mobile Force Band. 100v, Prime Minister Walter H. Lini.

1985, July 26 Wmk. 373 *Perf. 14*

397	A73	35v multicolored	.65	.40
398	A73	45v multicolored	.80	.60
399	A73	55v multicolored	.90	.70
400	A73	100v multicolored	1.00	*1.60*
a.		Souvenir sheet of 4, #397-400	4.00	4.00
		Nos. 397-400 (4)	3.35	3.30

Natl. independence, 5th anniv.

Intl. Youth Year — A74

Children's drawings.

1985, Sept. 16 Wmk. 373 *Perf. 14*

401	A74	20v Alain Lagaliu	.55	.55
402	A74	30v Peter Obed	.65	.65
403	A74	50v Mary Estelle	1.00	1.00
404	A74	100v Abel M rani	1.75	1.75
		Nos. 401-404 (4)	3.95	3.95

Natl. and UN Flags, Map — A75

1985, Sept. 24 Litho. *Perf. 14*

405	A75	45v multicolored	1.50	1.25

Admission of Vanuatu to UN, 4th anniv.

Sea Slugs — A76

20v, Chromodoris elisa bethina. 35v, Halgerda aurantiomaculata. 55v, Chromodoris kuniei. 100v, Notodoris minor.

1985, Nov. 11 Wmk. 373 *Perf. 14½*

406	A76	20v multicolored	.35	.35
407	A76	35v multicolored	.70	.70
408	A76	55v multicolored	.95	.95
409	A76	100v multicolored	1.75	1.75
		Nos. 406-409 (4)	3.75	3.75

Nos. 407-408 horiz. See Nos. 497-500.

Scuba Diving — A77

1986, Jan. 22 Wmk. 384 *Perf. 14*

410	A77	30v shown	.80	.50
411	A77	35v Volcanic eruption	.90	.60
412	A77	55v Land diving	.90	.80
413	A77	100v Wind surfing	1.25	*2.00*
		Nos. 410-413 (4)	3.85	3.90

See No. 479.

Queen Elizabeth II 60th Birthday

Common Design Type

Designs: 20v, With Prince Charles and Princess Anne, 1951. 35v, At christening of Prince William, the Music Room, Buckhingham Palace, 1982. 45v, State visit, 1985. 55v, State visit to Mexico, 1974. 100v, Visiting Crown Agents' offices, 1983.

1986, Apr. 21 Litho. *Perf. 14x14½*

414	CD337	20v scar, blk & sil	.25	.25
415	CD337	35v ultra & multi	.45	.45
416	CD337	45v green & multi	.50	.50
417	CD337	55v violet & multi	.65	.65
418	CD337	100v multicolored	1.25	1.25
		Nos. 414-418 (5)	3.10	3.10

For overprints & surcharges see #465-469, B2-B6.

AMERIPEX '86 — A78

45v, SS President Coolidge. 55v, As troop ship, 1942. 135v, Site of sinking, 1942.

1986, May 19 Wmk. 373 *Perf. 14*

419	A78	45v multicolored	1.40	.70
420	A78	55v multicolored	1.60	.90
421	A78	135v multicolored	2.75	2.25
a.		Souvenir sheet of 3, #419-421	6.25	6.25
		Nos. 419-421 (3)	5.75	3.85

Halley's Comet — A79

30v, Comet, deity statue. 45v, Family sighting comet. 55v, Comet over SW Pacific. 100v, Edmond Halley, manuscript.

1986, June 23 Wmk. 384 *Perf. 14½*

422	A79	30v multicolored	1.20	1.20
423	A79	45v multicolored	1.25	1.25
424	A79	55v multicolored	1.60	1.60
425	A79	100v multicolored	2.10	2.10
		Nos. 422-425 (4)	6.15	6.15

Coral — A80

1986, Oct. 27 Wmk. 373 *Perf. 14*

426	A80	20v Daisy	.70	.70
427	A80	45v Organ pipe	1.50	1.50
428	A80	55v Sea fan	1.75	1.75
429	A80	135v Soft	4.50	4.50
		Nos. 426-429 (4)	8.45	8.45

Intl. Peace Year — A81

30v, Children of the world. 45v, Child praying. 55v, UN building, negotiators. 135v, Peoples working in harmony.

1986, Nov. 3 Litho. *Perf. 14*

430	A81	30v multi	.65	.65
431	A81	45v multi	1.00	1.00
432	A81	55v multi	1.25	1.25
433	A81	135v multi	3.00	3.00
		Nos. 430-433 (4)	5.90	5.90

Automotives A82

20v, Datsun 240Z, 1969. 45v, Model A Ford, 1927. 55v, Unic, 1924-25. 135v, Citroen DS19, 1975.

1987, Jan. 22

434	A82	20v multi	.35	.35
435	A82	45v multi	.65	.65
436	A82	55v multi	.80	.80
437	A82	135v multi	1.90	1.90
		Nos. 434-437 (4)	3.70	3.70

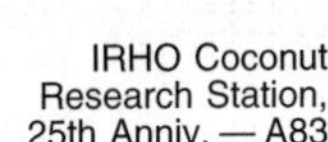

IRHO Coconut Research Station, 25th Anniv. — A83

35v, Nursery. 45v, Cocos nucifera tree. 100v, Cocos nucifera fruit. 135v, Station.

1987, May 13 *Perf. 14½x14*

438	A83	35v multicolored	.55	.55
439	A83	45v multicolored	.85	.85
440	A83	100v multicolored	1.25	1.25
441	A83	135v multicolored	1.75	1.75
		Nos. 438-441 (4)	4.40	4.40

Fish — A84

1v, Cirrhitichthys aprinus. 5v, Zanclus cornutus. 10v, Canthigaster cinctus. 15v, Amphiprion rubrocinctus. 20v, Acanthurus lineatus. 30v, Thalassoma hardwicki. 35v,

Anthias tuka. 40v, Adioryx microstomus. 45v, Balistoides conspicillum. 50v, Xyrichtys taeniouris. 55v, Hemitaurich-thys polyepis. 65v, Pterois volitans. 100v, Paracirrhites forsteri. 300v, Balistapus undulatus. 500v, Chaetodon ephippium.

Perf. 14x14½

1987, July 15 Wmk. 384

442 A84 1v multicolored .25 .25
443 A84 5v multicolored .25 .25
444 A84 10v multicolored .25 .25
445 A84 15v multicolored .30 .30
446 A84 20v multicolored .40 .40
447 A84 30v multicolored .55 .55
448 A84 35v multicolored .60 .60
449 A84 40v multicolored .65 .65
450 A84 45v multicolored .85 .85
451 A84 50v multicolored .90 .90
452 A84 55v multicolored 1.00 1.00
453 A84 65v multicolored 1.10 1.10
454 A84 100v multicolored 2.10 2.10
455 A84 300v multicolored 5.50 5.50
456 A84 500v multicolored 7.75 7.75
Nos. 442-456 (15) 22.45 22.45

Insects — A85

45v, Xylotrupes gideon. 55v, Phyllodes imperialis. 65v, Cyphogaster. 100v, Othreis fullonia.

1987, Sept. 22 Wmk. 373 *Perf. 14*

457 A85 45v multicolored .90 .90
458 A85 55v multicolored 1.00 1.00
459 A85 65v multicolored 1.40 1.40
460 A85 100v multicolored 2.00 2.00
Nos. 457-460 (4) 5.30 5.30

Christmas Carols — A86

1987, Nov. 10 *Perf. 13½x14*

461 A86 20v Away in a Manger .40 .40
462 A86 45v Once in Royal David's City .85 .85
463 A86 55v While Shepherds Watched Their Flocks 1.00 1.00
464 A86 65v We Three Kings of Orient Are 1.25 1.25
Nos. 461-464 (4) 3.50 3.50

Nos. 414-418 Ovptd. in Silver "40TH WEDDING ANNIVERSARY"

Perf. 14x14½

1987, Dec. 9 Litho. Wmk. 384

465 CD337 20v scar, blk & sil .45 .45
466 CD337 35v ultra & multi .60 .60
467 CD337 45v green & multi .75 .75
468 CD337 55v violet & multi .80 .80
469 CD337 100v multicolored 1.50 1.50
Nos. 465-469 (5) 4.10 4.10

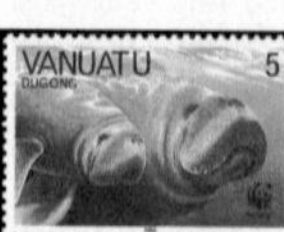

World Wildlife Fund — A87

Dugongs.

1988, Feb. 29 *Perf. 13x13½*

470 A87 5v Mother, calf .90 .40
471 A87 10v Adult 1.40 .40
472 A87 20v Two adults 1.90 1.10
473 A87 45v Herd 3.25 2.75
Nos. 470-473 (4) 7.45 4.65

Australia Bicentennial — A88

Burns Philp emblem, bicent. emblem and steamships.

1988, May 18 Wmk. 373 *Perf. 12*

474 A88 20v S.S. Tambo .35 .35
475 A88 45v S.S. Induna .75 .75
476 A88 55v S.S. Morinda .90 .90
477 A88 65v S.S. Marsina 1.00 1.00
Nos. 474-477 (4) 3.00 3.00

Capt. James Cook (1728-1779), Explorer — A89

Perf. 14 on 2 or 3 Sides

1988, July 29 Wmk. 384

478 A89 45v black & red .75 .75

SYDPEX '88. No. 478 printed in panes of 10 plus 5 center labels picturing a map of Vanuatu, HMS Resolution, exhibition emblem, HMS Endeavour or a map of Australia.

Tourism Type of 1986
Souvenir Sheet
Wmk. 373

1988, Aug. 24 Litho. *Perf. 14*

479 Sheet of 2 4.25 4.25
a. A77 55v like No. 412 1.10 1.10
b. A77 100v like No. 413 2.25 2.25

EXPO '88. Nos. 479a-479b are dated 1988 and "Vanuatu" is inscribed in violet blue.

1988 Summer Olympics, Seoul — A90

1988, Sept. 19 *Perf. 13½x14*

480 A90 20v Boxing .25 .25
481 A90 45v Track events .70 .70
482 A90 55v Signing Olympic agreement .85 .85
483 A90 65v Soccer 1.00 1.00
Nos. 480-483 (4) 2.80 2.80

Souvenir Sheet

484 A90 150v Tennis 3.50 3.50

Intl. Tennis Federation, 75th anniv. (150v).

Lloyds of London, 300th Anniv.
Common Design Type

Designs: 20v, Lloyds new building, 1988. 55v, Cargo ship Shirrabank, horiz. 65v, Adela, horiz. 145v, Excursion steamer General Slocum on fire in New York Harbor, 1904.

1988, Oct. 25 Wmk. 384 *Perf. 14*

485 CD341 20v multicolored .35 .35
486 CD341 55v multicolored 1.00 1.00
487 CD341 65v multicolored 1.00 1.00
488 CD341 145v multicolored 2.50 2.50
Nos. 485-488 (4) 4.85 4.85

FAO — A91

Perf. 14½x14, 14x14½

1988, Nov. 14

489 A91 45v Tending crops .80 .80
490 A91 55v Fishing, vert. .90 .90
491 A91 65v Animal husbandry, vert. .90 .90
492 A91 120v Produce market 1.10 1.10
Nos. 489-492 (4) 3.70 3.70

Christmas — A92

Carols: 20v, Silent Night, Holy Night. 45v, Angels From the Realms of Glory. 65v, O Come All Ye Faithful. 155v, In That Poor Stable How Charming Jesus Lies.

1988, Dec. 1 Litho. *Perf. 14½x14*

493 A92 20v multicolored .35 .35
494 A92 45v multicolored .55 .55
495 A92 65v multicolored .65 .65
496 A92 155v multicolored 1.60 1.60
Nos. 493-496 (4) 3.15 3.15

Marine Life Type of 1985

Shrimp.

1989, Feb. 1 *Perf. 14*

497 A76 20v Periclimenes brevicarpalis .30 .30
498 A76 45v Lysmata grabhami .75 .75
499 A76 65v Rhynchocinetes 1.00 1.00
500 A76 150v Stenopus hispidus 1.90 1.90
Nos. 497-500 (4) 3.95 3.95

Economic & Social Commission for Asia and the Pacific (ESCAP) — A93

20v, Consolidated Catalina. 45v, Douglas DC-3. 55v, Embraer EMB110 Bandeirante. 200v, Boeing 737-300.

Perf. 12x12½

1989, Apr. 5 Litho. Wmk. 373

501 A93 20v multicolored .75 .75
502 A93 45v multicolored 1.05 1.05
503 A93 55v multicolored 1.20 1.20
504 A93 200v multicolored 3.75 3.75
Nos. 501-504 (4) 6.75 6.75

Inauguration of the Sydney-Noumea-Espiritu Santo Service, 1948 (20v).

PHILEXFRANCE '89 — A94

Exhibition emblem and: No. 505a, Porte de Versailles Hall Number 1. No. 505b, Eiffel Tower. No. 506, Revolt of French Troops, Nancy, 1790.

1989, July 5 Wmk. 373 *Perf. 12*

505 A94 Pair 4.00 4.00
a.-b. 100v any single 1.75 1.75

Souvenir Sheet
Perf. 14
Wmk. 384

506 A94 100v multicolored 2.00 2.00

French revolution, bicent.

Moon Landing, 20th Anniv.
Common Design Type

Apollo 17: 45v, Command module in space. 55v, Harrison Schmitt, Gene Cerman and Ron Evans. 65v, Mission emblem. 120v, Liftoff. 100v, Recovery of Apollo 11 crew after spashdown.

1989, July 20 Wmk. 384 *Perf. 14*
Size of Nos. 508-509: 29x29mm

507 CD342 45v multicolored 1.15 1.15
508 CD342 55v multicolored 1.15 1.15
509 CD342 65v multicolored 1.30 1.30
510 CD342 120v multicolored 2.25 2.25
Nos. 507-510 (4) 5.85 5.85

Souvenir Sheet

511 CD342 100v multicolored 2.75 2.75

No. 324 Surcharged

Perf. 14x13½

1989, Oct. 18 Litho. Wmk. 373

512 A60 100v on 2v multi 4.75 4.75

STAMPSHOW '89, Melbourne.

World Stamp Expo '89 — A95

Perf. 14x13½

1989, Nov. 6 Litho. Wmk. 384

513 A95 65v New Hebrides #256 3.75 3.75

Souvenir Sheet

514 Sheet of 2 9.50 9.50
a. A95 65v New Hebrides #254 3.00 3.00
b. A95 100v The White House (detail) 5.00 5.00

Flora — A96

45v, Alocasia macrorrhiza. 55v, Acacia spirorbis. 65v, Metrosideros collina. 145v, Hoya australis.

Perf. 12½x12

1990, Jan. 5 Wmk. 373

515 A96 45v multicolored .70 .70
516 A96 55v multicolored .85 .85
517 A96 65v multicolored 1.00 1.00
518 A96 145v multicolored 2.25 2.25
Nos. 515-518 (4) 4.80 4.80

A97

Stamp World London '90 Exhibition emblem and simulated stamps or stamps on stamps: 45v, Kava (simulated stamps). 65v, Luganville P.O. exterior, interior (simulated stamps). 100v, Propeller plane, 19th cent. packet (simulated stamps). 150v, New Hebrides #187-188, first day cancellation. 200v, Great Britain #1, Vanuatu #281.

1990, Apr. 30 *Perf. 13x13½*

519 A97 45v multicolored .70 .70
520 A97 65v multicolored 1.10 1.10
521 A97 100v multicolored 1.50 1.50
522 A97 200v multicolored 3.00 3.00
Nos. 519-522 (4) 6.30 6.30

Souvenir Sheet

523 A97 150v multicolored 5.00 5.00

Penny Black, 150th anniv. No. 523 margin pictures first day cancel and cachet.

Independence, 10th Anniv. — A98

25v, Natl. Council of Women Emblem. 50v, Pres. Frederick Kalomuana Timakata. 55v, Preamble to Constitution. 65v, Vanuaaku Pati flag. 80v, Reserve Bank. 150v, Prime Minister Walter H. Lini.

1990, July 30 *Perf. 14*

524 A98 25v multicolored .35 .35
525 A98 50v multicolored .80 .80
526 A98 55v multicolored .90 .90
527 A98 65v multicolored 1.00 1.00
528 A98 80v multicolored 1.25 1.25
Nos. 524-528 (5) 4.30 4.30

Souvenir Sheet

529 A98 150v multi 5.75 5.75

Miniature Sheet

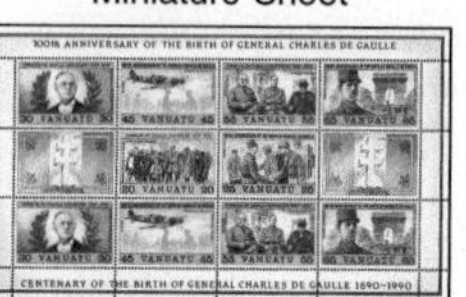

Charles De Gaulle (1890-1970) — A99

Wmk. 373

1990, Nov. 22 Litho. *Perf. 14*

530 A99 Sheet, 2 ea #530c-530f + 2 labels 20.00 20.00
a. 20v At Bayeux, after D-day landing 4.00 4.00
b. 25v Alsace, 1945 4.00 4.00
c. 30v Portrait 1.60 1.60
d. 45v Spitfire, Biggin Hill, 1942 1.75 1.75
e. 55v Casablanca, 1943 1.90 1.90
f. 65v Day of Glory, Paris, 1944 2.00 2.00

Christmas — A100

1990, Dec. 5 *Perf. 13*

531 Strip of 5 4.25 4.25
a. A100 25v Angel facing right .50 .50
b. A100 50v Shepherds .75 .75
c. A100 65v Nativity .80 .80
d. A100 70v The Three Kings .85 .85
e. A100 80v Angel facing left .85 .85

Butterflies — A101

25v, Parthenos sylvia. 55v, Euploea leucostictos. 80v, Lampides boeticus. 150v, Danaus plexippus.

Perf. 14x14½

1991, Jan. 9 **Wmk. 384**

532 A101 25v multicolored .45 .45
533 A101 55v multicolored .90 .90
534 A101 80v multicolored 1.40 1.40
535 A101 150v multicolored 2.50 2.50
Nos. 532-535 (4) 5.25 5.25

Art Festival — A102

Wmk. 373

1991, May 2 **Litho.** *Perf. 13½*

536 A102 25v Dance .30 .30
537 A102 65v Weaving .80 .80
538 A102 80v Carving 1.00 1.00
539 A102 150v Music 1.90 1.90
Nos. 536-539 (4) 4.00 4.00

Elizabeth & Philip, Birthdays
Common Design Types
Wmk. 384

1991, June 17 **Litho.** *Perf. 14½*

540 CD345 65v multicolored 1.00 1.00
541 CD346 70v multicolored 1.10 1.10
a. Pair, #540-541 + label 2.50 2.50

Phila Nippon '91 — A103

Birds: 50v, White-collared kingfisher. 55v, Green palm lorikeet. 80v, Scarlet robin. 100v, Pacific swallow. 150v, Reef heron.

Wmk. 373

1991, Nov. 15 **Litho.** *Perf. 14½*

542 A103 50v multicolored .70 .70
543 A103 55v multicolored .70 .70
544 A103 80v multicolored 1.00 1.00
545 A103 100v multicolored 1.20 1.20
Nos. 542-545 (4) 3.60 3.60

Souvenir Sheet

546 A103 150v multicolored 2.50 2.50

Fight Against AIDS — A104

Designs: 25v, Multiple partners, unsafe sex can spread AIDS. 65v, AIDS victim and care giver. 80v, AIDS kills, shark. 150v, Children's playground.

1991, Nov. 29 **Wmk. 384** *Perf. 14*

547 A104 25v multicolored .55 .55
548 A104 65v multicolored 1.00 1.00
549 A104 80v multicolored 1.25 1.25
550 A104 150v multicolored 2.25 2.25
Nos. 547-550 (4) 5.05 5.05

Nos. 324-326 & 329 Surcharged

Perf. 14x13½

1991, June 12 **Litho.** **Wmk. 373**

551 A60 20v on 2v #324 .55 .55
552 A60 60v on 10v #325 1.50 1.50
553 A60 70v on 15v #326 1.90 1.90
554 A60 80v on 30v #329 2.00 2.00
Nos. 551-554 (4) 5.95 5.95

Queen Elizabeth II's Accession to the Throne, 40th Anniv.
Common Design Type

1992, Feb. 6 **Wmk. 384** *Perf. 14*

555 CD349 20v multicolored .30 .30
556 CD349 25v multicolored .35 .35
557 CD349 60v multicolored .75 .75
558 CD349 65v multicolored .85 .85

Wmk. 373

559 CD349 70v multicolored .85 .85
Nos. 555-559 (5) 3.10 3.10

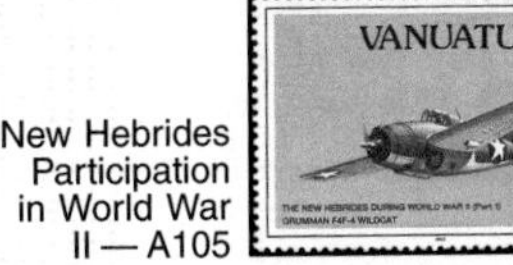
New Hebrides Participation in World War II — A105

Designs: 50v, Grumman F4F-4 Wildcat. 55v, Douglas SBD-3 Dauntless. 65v, Consolidated PBY-5A Catalina. 80v, USS Hornet. 200v, Vought-Sikorsky OS2U-3.

Perf. 13½x14

1992, May 22 **Litho.** **Wmk. 373**

560 A105 50v multicolored 2.25 2.25
561 A105 55v multicolored 2.25 2.25
562 A105 65v multicolored 2.50 2.50
563 A105 80v multicolored 3.50 3.50
Nos. 560-563 (4) 10.50 10.50

Souvenir Sheet

564 A105 200v multicolored 10.50 10.50

World Columbian Stamp Expo, Chicago (No. 564).
See Nos. 590-594, 664-667.

Vanuatu's Membership in the World Meteorological Organization, 10th Anniv. — A106

Designs: 25v, Meteorological station, Port Vila. 60v, Cyclone near Vanuatu seen by Japanese satellite GMS 4. 80v, Weather chart showing cyclone. 105v, Cyclone warning broadcast by radio.

1992, June 20 *Perf. 14*

565 A106 25v multicolored .35 .35
566 A106 60v multicolored .85 .85
567 A106 80v multicolored 1.10 1.10
568 A106 105v multicolored 1.20 1.20
Nos. 565-568 (4) 3.50 3.50

1992 Melanesian Cup — A107

1992, July 20 *Perf. 13½x14*

569 A107 20v Soccer team, trophy .40 .40
570 A107 65v Soccer players 1.00 1.00
571 A107 70v Men's track 1.25 1.25
572 A107 80v Women's track 1.25 1.25
Nos. 569-572 (4) 3.90 3.90

1992 Summer Olympics, Barcelona (#571-572).
For surcharges see Nos. 621-622.

World Food Day — A108

Designs: 20v, "Breast is best." 70v, Central Hospital, Port Vila. 80v, "Give your children a healthy future." 150v, Nutritious food.

1992, Oct. 16 **Wmk. 384** *Perf. 14*

573 A108 20v green & brown .35 .35
574 A108 70v brown & green .85 .85
575 A108 80v green & brown 1.00 1.00
576 A108 150v brown & green 1.90 1.90
Nos. 573-576 (4) 4.10 4.10

Turtles — A109

55v, Leatherback turtle. 65v, Loggerhead turtle. 70v, Hawksbill turtle. 80v, Green turtle. 200v, Green turtle hatchlings.

1992, Dec. 15 *Perf. 14x14½*

577 A109 55v multicolored 1.15 1.15
578 A109 65v multicolored 1.25 1.25
579 A109 70v multicolored 1.75 1.75
580 A109 80v multicolored 2.25 2.25
Nos. 577-580 (4) 6.40 6.40

Souvenir Sheet

581 A109 200v multicolored 5.25 5.25

Hibiscus — A110

Designs: 25v, Light pink hibiscus rosa-sinensis. 55v, Hibiscus tiliaceus. 80v, Red hibiscus rosa-sinensis. 150v, Dark pink hibiscus rosa-sinensis.

Wmk. 384

1993, Mar. 3 **Litho.** *Perf. 14*

582 A110 25v multicolored .40 .40
583 A110 55v multicolored .85 .85
584 A110 80v multicolored 1.05 1.05
585 A110 150v multicolored 2.00 2.00
Nos. 582-585 (4) 4.30 4.30

Nos. 331, 333-335 Surcharged

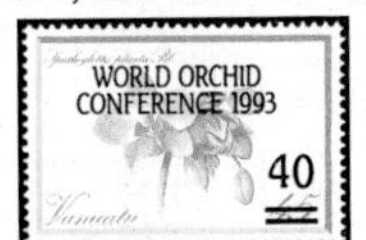

Perf. 13½x14, 14x13½

1993, Apr. 21 **Litho.** **Wmk. 373**

586 A60 40v on 45v #331 .85 .85
587 A60 55v on 75v #333 1.10 1.10
588 A60 65v on 100v #334 1.40 1.40
589 A60 150v on 200v #335 3.00 3.00
Nos. 586-589 (4) 6.35 6.35

Size and location of surcharge varies.

No. 326 Surcharged

1993, June 1

589A A60 20v on 35v #326 6.75 6.75

World War II Type of 1992

20v, Grumman F6F-3 Hellcat. 55v, Lockheed P-38F Lightning. 65v, GrummanTBF-1 Avenger. 80v, USS Essex. 200v, Douglas C-47 Dakota.

1993, June 30 *Perf. 13½*

590 A105 20v multicolored .90 .90
591 A105 55v multicolored 2.50 2.50
592 A105 65v multicolored 3.00 3.00
593 A105 80v multicolored 3.75 3.75
Nos. 590-593 (4) 10.15 10.15

Souvenir Sheet

594 A105 200v multicolored 9.75 9.75

Island Scenes — A111

Designs: 5v, Iririki Island, Port Vila. 10v, Iririki Island, yachts. 15v, Court House, Port Vila. 20v, Two girls, Pentecost Island. 25v, Women dancers, Tanna Island. 30v, Market, Port Vila. 45v, Man with canoe, Erakor Island, vert. 50v, Coconut trees, Champagne Beach. 55v, Coconut trees, North Efate Islands. 60v, Fish (Banks Group). 70v, Sea fan, Tongoa Island, vert. 75v, Espiritu Santo Island. 80v, Sailboat at sunset, Port Vila Bay, vert. 100v, Mele Waterfall, vert. 300v, Yasur Volcano, Tanna Island, vert. 500v, Erakor Island.

1993, July 7 *Perf. 14x14½, 14½x14*

595 A111 5v multicolored .25 .25
596 A111 10v multicolored .25 .25
597 A111 15v multicolored .30 .30
598 A111 20v multicolored .40 .40
599 A111 25v multicolored .45 .45
600 A111 30v multicolored .55 .50
601 A111 45v multicolored .80 .80
602 A111 50v multicolored .90 .90
603 A111 55v multicolored 1.00 1.00
604 A111 60v multicolored 1.10 1.10
605 A111 70v multicolored 1.25 1.25
606 A111 75v multicolored 1.40 1.40
a. Souvenir sheet, #596, 603, 604, 606 ('94) 4.75 4.75
607 A111 80v multicolored 1.40 1.40
608 A111 100v multicolored 1.75 1.75
609 A111 300v multicolored 5.25 5.25
610 A111 500v multicolored 8.75 8.75
Nos. 595-610 (16) 25.80 25.75

No. 606a, Philakorea '94 International Stamp Exhibition.
For surcharges see Nos. 619-620, 742-745A, 745D.

Shells — A112

55v, Trochus niloticus. 65v, Lioconcha castrensis. 80v, Turbo petholatus. 150v, Pleuroploca trapezium.

Wmk. 373

1993, Sept. 15 **Litho.** *Perf. 14½*

611 A112 55v multi 1.40 1.40
612 A112 65v multi 1.75 1.75
613 A112 80v multi 2.00 2.00
614 A112 150v multi 4.00 4.00
Nos. 611-614 (4) 9.15 9.15

See Nos. 632-635, 654-657.

Louvre Museum, Bicent. — A113

Paintings by De La Tour: 25v, St. Joseph the Carpenter. 55v, The Newborn. 80v, Adoration of the Shepherds (detail). 150v, Adoration of the Shepherds (entire).

Wmk. 373

1993, Nov. 10 **Litho.** *Perf. 14*

615 A113 25v multicolored .40 .40
616 A113 55v multicolored .85 .85
617 A113 80v multicolored 1.25 1.25
618 A113 150v multicolored 2.50 2.50
Nos. 615-618 (4) 5.00 5.00

Nos. 570, 572, 598, 600 Surcharged

1993, Dec. 6 Litho. Wmk. 373
Perfs. as Before

No.	Type	Description	Unused	Used
619	A111	15v on 20v #598	.30	.30
620	A111	25v on 30v #600	.40	.40
621	A107	55v on 65v #570	1.00	1.00
622	A107	70v on 80v #572	1.25	1.25
		Nos. 619-622 (4)	2.95	2.95

Service Organizations — A114

Hong Kong '94: 25v, Kiwanis Intl., Charity Races, vert. 60v, Lions Intl. Twin Otter on mercy mission. 75v, Rotary Intl. fighting malaria, vert. 150v, Red Cross blood donar service. 200v, Emblems of service organizations.

Perf. 14x15, 15x14
1994, Feb. 18 Litho. Wmk. 373

No.	Type	Description	Unused	Used
623	A114	25v multicolored	.40	.40
624	A114	60v multicolored	1.10	1.10
625	A114	75v multicolored	1.25	1.25
626	A114	150v multicolored	2.50	2.50
		Nos. 623-626 (4)	5.25	5.25

Souvenir Sheet

No.	Type	Description	Unused	Used
627	A114	200v multicolored	3.50	3.50

Intl. Year of the Family — A115

1994, Mar. 2 ***Perf. 14***

No.	Type	Description	Unused	Used
628	A115	25v vio & rose brn	.35	.35
629	A115	60v ver & dk grn	.85	.85
630	A115	90v green & sepia	1.20	1.20
631	A115	150v brn & vio bl	2.10	2.10
		Nos. 628-631 (4)	4.50	4.50

Shell Type of 1993

60v, Cyprea argus. 70v, Conus marmoreus. 85v, Lambis chiragra. 155v, Chicoreus brunneus.

1994, May 31 Litho. ***Perf. 12***

No.	Type	Description	Unused	Used
632	A112	60v multicolored	1.25	1.25
633	A112	70v multicolored	1.25	1.25
634	A112	85v multicolored	1.90	1.90
635	A112	155v multicolored	3.25	3.25
		Nos. 632-635 (4)	7.65	7.65

Tourism — A116

Designs: a, 25v, Slit gong (drum), traditional hut. b, 75v, Volcano, boats. c, 90v, Sailboats, airplane, green palm lorikeet. d, 200v, Helicopter, woman with tray of fruit.

1994, July 27 Litho. ***Perf. 13½***

No.	Type	Description	Unused	Used
636	A116	Strip of 4, #a.-d.	8.00	8.00

Anemonefish A117

1994, Aug. 16 Litho. ***Perf. 12***

No.	Type	Description	Unused	Used
637	A117	55v Pink	2.10	2.10
638	A117	70v Clark's	2.75	2.75
639	A117	80v Red & black	2.90	2.90
640	A117	140v Orange-fin	5.25	5.25
a.		Souvenir sheet of 1	3.50	3.50
		Nos. 637-640 (4)	13.00	13.00

Philakorea '94 (#640a).

ICAO, 50th Anniv. — A118

Designs: 25v, 1950 Qantas Catalina. 60v, 1956 Tai Douglas DC3. 75v, 1966 New Hebrides Airways Drover. 90v, 1994 Air Vanuatu Boeing 737.

1994, Dec. 7

No.	Type	Description	Unused	Used
641	A118	25v multicolored	.60	.60
642	A118	60v multicolored	1.60	1.60
643	A118	75v multicolored	1.90	1.90
644	A118	90v multicolored	2.50	2.50
		Nos. 641-644 (4)	6.60	6.60

Hibiscus — A119

1995, Feb. 1 Litho. ***Perf. 12***

No.	Type	Description	Unused	Used
645	A119	25v The Path	.40	.40
646	A119	60v Old Frankie	1.05	1.05
647	A119	90v Fijian white	1.50	1.50
648	A119	200v Surf rider	3.50	3.50
		Nos. 645-648 (4)	6.45	6.45

Lizards — A120

Designs: 25v, Emoia nigromarginata. 55v, Nactus multicarinatus. 70v, Lepidodactylus. 80v, Emoia caerulocauda. 140v, Emoia sanfordi.

1995, Apr. 12

No.	Type	Description	Unused	Used
649	A120	25v multicolored	.45	.45
650	A120	55v multicolored	1.10	1.10
651	A120	70v multicolored	1.35	1.35
652	A120	80v multicolored	1.45	1.45
653	A120	140v multicolored	2.75	2.75
		Nos. 649-653 (5)	7.10	7.10

Shell Type of 1993

25v, Epitonium scalare. 55v, Strombus latissimus. 90v, Conus bullatus. 200v, Pterynotus pinnatus.

1995, June 1

No.	Type	Description	Unused	Used
654	A112	25v multicolored	.55	.55
655	A112	55v multicolored	1.10	1.10
656	A112	90v multicolored	1.75	1.75
657	A112	200v multicolored	4.25	4.25
		Nos. 654-657 (4)	7.65	7.65

Anniversaries A121

Designs: 25v, Girls wearing traditional head pieces. 55v, Stylized picture of natives dancing, vert. 60v, Children, doves, natl. flag, UN flag, vert. 75v, Embroidered tapestry of native, vert. 90v, Troops parading. 140v, Group in traditional ceremony.

Perf. 14x13½, 13½x14
1995, July 28 Litho.

No.	Type	Description	Unused	Used
658	A121	25v multicolored	.45	.45
659	A121	55v multicolored	.85	.85
660	A121	60v multicolored	.85	.85
661	A121	75v multicolored	1.30	1.30
662	A121	90v multicolored	1.40	1.40
663	A121	140v multicolored	2.25	2.25
a.		Souvenir sheet of 1	4.25	4.25
		Nos. 658-663 (6)	7.10	7.10

UN, 50th anniv. (#660). Singapore 95 (#663a). Others, independence, 15th anniv.

World War II Type of 1992

60v, SB2C Helldiver. 70v, Spitfire Mk VIII. 75v, F4U-1A Corsair. 80v, PV1 Ventura. 140v, Japanese surrender, USS Missouri.

1995, Sept. 1 Litho. ***Perf. 12½***

No.	Type	Description	Unused	Used
664	A105	60v multicolored	2.75	2.75
665	A105	70v multicolored	3.00	3.00
666	A105	75v multicolored	3.00	3.00
667	A105	80v multicolored	3.50	3.50
		Nos. 664-667 (4)	12.25	12.25

Souvenir Sheet
Perf. 13½

No.	Type	Description	Unused	Used
667A	A105	140v multicolored	9.00	9.00

No. 667A for Singapore 95.

Artifacts — A122

Ambae money mat and: a, 25v, Rambaramp mortuary effigy, Malakula. b, 60v, Wusi pot, Espiritu Santo. c, 75v, Slit gong, Efate Island. d, 90v, Tapa cloth, Erromango Island.
Nos. 668e, 668f, like No. 668d.

1995, Nov. 22 Litho. ***Perf. 13½x13***

No.	Type	Description	Unused	Used
668	A122	Strip of 4, #a.-d.	5.50	5.50
e.		90v Perf. 14	1.50	1.50
f.		Souvenir sheet, #668e	2.75	2.75

No. 668f, 9th Asian Intl. Philatelic Exhibition, Beijing.
Issued: Nos. 668e, 668f, Dec. 1995.
See No. 720.

Fishing — A123

1996, Feb. 1 Litho. ***Perf. 14***

No.	Type	Description	Unused	Used
669	A123	55v Cast net	1.00	1.00
670	A123	75v Reef	1.25	1.25
671	A123	80v Deep water, vert.	1.25	1.25
672	A123	140v Game, vert.	2.50	2.50
		Nos. 669-672 (4)	6.00	6.00

Flying Bats — A124

No. 673, Notopteris macdonaldi, facing left. No. 674, Pteropus anetianus, green leaves on tree, vert. No. 675, Pteropus anetianus, diff., vert. No. 676, Notopteris macdonaldi, diff.
No. 677, vert: a, 90v, Pteropus tonganus. b, 140v, Pteropus tonganus, diff.

1996, Apr. 3 Litho. ***Perf. 14***

No.	Type	Description	Unused	Used
673	A124	25v multicolored	.70	.55
674	A124	25v multicolored	.70	.55
675	A124	25v multicolored	.70	.55
676	A124	25v multicolored	.70	.55
		Nos. 673-676 (4)	2.80	2.20

Souvenir Sheet

No.	Type	Description	Unused	Used
677	A124	Sheet of 2, #a.-b.	5.25	5.25

World Wildlife Fund (Nos. 673-676). 9th Asian Intl. Philatelic Exhibition (No. 677).

UNICEF, 50th Anniv. — A125

Unwmk.
1996, June 5 Litho. ***Perf. 14***

No.	Type	Description	Unused	Used
678	A125	55v Immunizations	1.10	1.10
679	A125	60v Breast feeding	1.40	1.40

Radio, Cent. — A126

60v, Airplane, radio signal. 75v, Radio Vanuatu. 80v, Guglielmo Marconi. 90v, Ship, radio signal.

1996, June 5 ***Perf. 14½***

No.	Type	Description	Unused	Used
680	A126	60v multicolored	1.00	1.00
681	A126	75v multicolored	1.20	1.20
682	A126	80v multicolored	1.25	1.25
683	A126	90v multicolored	1.50	1.50
a.		Block of 4, #680-683	6.50	6.50

Modern Olympic Games, Cent. — A127

Designs: 25v, Marie Kapalu, Tawai Keiruan, Baptiste Firiam, Tava Kalo, 1996 athletes from Vanuatu. 70v, 1996 Athletes in training. 75v, 1950's Athletes. 200v, 1896 Athletes.

1996, July 17 Litho. ***Perf. 14***

No.	Type	Description	Unused	Used
684	A127	25v multicolored	.45	.45
685	A127	70v multicolored	1.25	1.25
686	A127	75v multicolored	1.25	1.25
687	A127	200v multicolored	3.75	3.75
		Nos. 684-687 (4)	6.70	6.70

Christmas — A128

Children of various races holding candles in front of churches: a, 25v, Presbyterian, Roman Catholic. b, 60v, Church of Christ. c, 75v, 7th Day Adventist, Apostolic. d, 90v, Anglican.

1996, Sept. 11 Litho. ***Perf. 14***

No.	Type	Description	Unused	Used
688	A128	Strip of 4, #a.-d.	4.50	4.50

No. 688 is a continuous design.

Hibiscus — A129

1996, Nov. 13 Litho. ***Perf. 13½***

No.	Type	Description	Unused	Used
689	A129	25v Lady Cilento	.50	.50
690	A129	60v Kinchen's Yellow	1.25	1.25
691	A129	90v D.J. O'Brien	1.75	1.75
692	A129	200v Cuban Variety	3.75	3.75
a.		Sheet of 2, #689, #692	6.00	6.00
		Nos. 689-692 (4)	7.25	7.25

Hong Kong '97. No. 692a issued 2/12/97.

Diving — A130

Designs: 70v, Coral Garden. 75v, Lady of the President Coolidge. 90v, "Boris," Queensland grouper. 140v, Wreck of the President Coolidge.

1997, Jan. 15 Litho. ***Perf. 14½x14***

No.	Type	Description	Unused	Used
693	A130	70v multicolored	1.25	1.25
694	A130	75v multicolored	1.25	1.25
695	A130	90v multicolored	1.50	1.50
696	A130	140v multicolored	2.50	2.50
a.		Souvenir sheet, #694, 696	6.00	6.00
b.		Souvenir sheet, #693-696	10.00	10.00
		Nos. 693-696 (4)	6.50	6.50

Pacific '97 (#696a).

Birds — A131

25v, Sharp-tailed sandpiper. 55v, Crested tern. 60v, Little pied cormorant. 75v, Brown booby. 80v, Reef heron. 90v, Red-tailed tropic bird.

1997, June 4 Litho. *Perf. 13½x14*

No.	Type	Value	Description	Unused	Used
697	A131	25v	multi	.55	.55
698	A131	55v	multi	1.10	1.10
699	A131	60v	multi	1.20	1.20
700	A131	75v	multi	1.40	1.40
701	A131	80v	multi, vert.	1.40	1.40
702	A131	90v	multi, vert.	1.75	1.75
			Nos. 697-702 (6)	7.40	7.40

Air Vanuatu, 10th Anniv. — A132

Designs: 25v, Pilot at controls. 60v, Airplane being serviced, cargo loaded. 90v, Serving drinks to passengers. 200v, Passengers leaving plane upon arrival at Vanuatu.

1997, Apr. 2 *Perf. 14½x14*

No.	Type	Value	Description	Unused	Used
703	A132	25v	multicolored	.45	.45
704	A132	60v	multicolored	1.10	1.10
705	A132	90v	multicolored	1.75	1.75
706	A132	200v	multicolored	3.75	3.75
			Nos. 703-706 (4)	7.05	7.05

No. 704 is 81x31mm.

Thomas A. Edison (1847-1931) — A133

Designs: 60v, Light bulb, Edison. 70v, Hydro dam, Santo. 200v, Port Vila by dusk.

1997, Aug. 27 Litho. *Perf. 12*

No.	Type	Value	Description	Unused	Used
707		60v	multicolored	1.00	1.00
708		70v	multicolored	1.25	1.25
709		200v	multicolored	3.50	3.50
a.	A133		Block of 3, #707-709 + label	7.25	7.25

No. 709 is 80x30mm.

Fish — A134

Designs: 25v, Yellow-faced angelfish. 55v, Flame angelfish. 60v, Lemonpeel angelfish. 70v, Emperor angelfish. 140v, Multi-barred angelfish.

1997, Nov. 12 Litho. *Perf. 14x13½*

No.	Type	Value	Description	Unused	Used
710	A134	25v	multicolored	.45	.45
711	A134	55v	multicolored	1.00	1.00
712	A134	60v	multicolored	1.20	1.20
713	A134	70v	multicolored	1.25	1.25
714	A134	140v	multicolored	2.50	2.50
			Nos. 710-714 (5)	6.40	6.40

Architecture in Vanuatu — A135

Designs: 30v, Fale-Espiritu Santo. 65v, Natl. Cultural Center. 80v, University of the South Pacific. 200v, Chief's Nakamal.

1998, Feb. 11 Litho. *Perf. 14½x14*

No.	Type	Value	Description	Unused	Used
715	A135	30v	multicolored	.45	.45
716	A135	65v	multicolored	1.00	1.00
717	A135	80v	multicolored	1.20	1.20
718	A135	200v	multicolored	3.00	3.00
			Nos. 715-718 (4)	5.65	5.65

Diana, Princess of Wales (1961-97)
Common Design Type

Various portraits: a, 75v. b, 85v. c, 145v.

1998, Mar. 31 Litho. *Perf. 14½x14*

No.	Type	Value	Description	Unused	Used
718A	CD355	95v	multicolored	1.50	1.50

Sheet of 4

No.	Type	Description	Unused	Used
719	CD355	#a.-c., 718A	6.50	6.50

No. 719 sold for 400v + 50v, with surtax from international sales being donated to The Diana, Princess of Wales Memorial Fund and surtax from national sales being donated to designated local charity.

Artifacts Type of 1995

Tribal masks: a, 30v, South West Malakula. b, 65v, North Ambrym. c, 75v, Gana Island Banks. d, 85v, Uripiv Island, Malakula. e, 95v, Vao Island, Malakula, and Central South Pentecost.

1998, June 3 Litho. *Perf. 14½*

No.	Type	Description	Unused	Used
720	A122	Strip of 5, #a.-e.	7.25	7.25

Butterflies A136

30v, Danaus plexippus. 60v, Hypolimnas bolina. 65v, Eurema hecabe. 75v, Nymphalidae. 95v, Precis villida. 205v, Tirumala hamata.

1998, July 23 Litho. *Die Cut*
Self-Adhesive

No.	Type	Value	Description	Unused	Used
721	A136	30v	multicolored	.55	.55
722	A136	60v	multicolored	1.10	1.10
723	A136	65v	multicolored	1.25	1.25
724	A136	75v	multicolored	1.60	1.60
725	A136	95v	multicolored	1.90	1.90
726	A136	205v	multicolored	3.25	3.25
a.			Souvenir sheet of 1	5.00	5.00
			Nos. 721-726 (6)	9.65	9.65

Singpex '98 (#726a).

Volcanoes A137

30v, Yasur, Tanna. 60v, Marum & Benbow, Ambrym. 75v, Gaua. 80v, Lopevi. 145v, Ambae.

1998, Oct. 23 Litho. *Perf. 15x14*

No.	Type	Value	Description	Unused	Used
728	A137	30v	multicolored	.45	.45
729	A137	60v	multicolored	.90	.90
730	A137	75v	multicolored	1.20	1.20
731	A137	80v	multicolored	1.20	1.20
732	A137	145v	multicolored	2.25	2.25
			Nos. 728-732 (5)	6.00	6.00

Early Explorers A138

Explorer, ship: 34v, Pedro Fernandez de Quiros, San Pedro y Paulo, 1606. 73v, Louis-Antoine de Bougainville, Boudeuse, 1768. 84v, Capt. James Cook, HMS Resolution, 1774. 90v, Jean-Fancois de Galaup de la Perousse, Astrolabe, 1788. 96v, Jules Sebastien-Cesar Dumont d'Urville, Astrolabe, "1788."

1999, Feb. 17 Litho. *Perf. 14*

No.	Type	Value	Description	Unused	Used
733	A138	34v	multicolored	.50	.50
734	A138	73v	multicolored	1.60	1.60
735	A138	84v	multicolored	1.90	1.90
a.			Souv. sheet, #733-735	3.75	3.75
736	A138	90v	multicolored	1.90	1.90
737	A138	96v	multicolored	2.00	2.00
a.			Souv. sheet, #734, 736-737	5.50	5.50
			Nos. 733-737 (5)	7.90	7.90

No. 735a was released for Australia '99 World Stamp Expo on 3/19/99; No. 737a for PhilexFrance 99.

Birds — A139

34v, Vanuatu kingfisher. 67v, Shining cuckoo. 73v, Peregrine falcon. 107v, Rainbow lorikeet.

1999, May 12 Litho. *Perf. 14*

No.	Type	Value	Description	Unused	Used
738	A139	34v	multicolored	.75	.75
739	A139	67v	multicolored	1.25	1.25
			Booklet, 5 #739	7.00	
740	A139	73v	multicolored	1.50	1.50
741	A139	107v	multicolored	2.25	2.25
a.			Sheet of 1	4.75	4.75
b.			Sheet of 1 with China 1999 emblem in margin	5.75	5.75
			Nos. 738-741 (4)	5.75	5.75

Issued: #741b, 8/18.

Nos. 601, 603-605, 607, 608 Surcharged

Perf. 14½x14, 14x14½

1998-2000 Litho.

No.	Type	Value	Description	Unused	Used
742	A111	1v	on 100v #608	.25	.25
742A	A111	2v	on 45v #601	.25	.25
743	A111	2v	on 55v #603	.25	.25
744	A111	3v	on 60v #604	.25	.25
744A	A111	3v	on 75v #606	.25	.25
745	A111	4v	on 45v #601	.25	.25
745A	A111	5v	on 70v #605		
745B	A111	34v	on 20v #598	.50	.50
745C	A111	67v	on 300v #609	1.00	1.00
745D	A111	73v	on 80v #607	—	
			Nos. 742-745D (10)	3.00	3.00

Issued: No. 742, No. 742A, 743, 744, 745, 745A, 12/18/98; No. 744A, 4/27/99; Nos. 745B, 745C, 745D, 2/17/00.

Ceremonial Dancers — A140

1v, Banks Islands. 2v, Small Nambas, Laman-Malakula. 3v, Small Nambas, Malakula. 5v, Smol Bag Theatre. 107v, South West Bay, Malakula. 200v, Big Nambas, Malakula. 500v, Pentacost.

1999, July 14 *Perf. 14*

No.	Type	Value	Description	Unused	Used
746	A140	1v	multicolored	.25	.25
747	A140	2v	multicolored	.25	.25
748	A140	3v	multicolored	.25	.25
749	A140	5v	multicolored	.25	.25
750	A140	107v	multicolored	1.60	1.60
751	A140	200v	multicolored	3.25	3.25
752	A140	500v	multicolored	7.75	7.75
			Nos. 746-752 (7)	13.60	13.60

See Nos. 788-791.

Poisonous Fish — A141

Designs: 34v, Pterois antennata. 84v, Pterois antennata, diff. 90v, Pterois volitans. 96v, Pterois volitans, diff.

1999, Oct. 13 Litho. *Perf. 14¼*

No.	Type	Value	Description	Unused	Used
753	A141	34v	multi	.70	.70
754	A141	84v	multi	1.75	1.75
755	A141	90v	multi	2.00	2.00
756	A141	96v	multi	2.25	2.25
			Nos. 753-756 (4)	6.70	6.70

Millennium — A142

Designs: a, 34v, Fish. b, 68v, Girl, land diver, vert. c, 84v, Fetish, vert. d, 90v, Bird, flowers. e, 96v, Man with conch shell.

1999, Dec. 1 *Perf. 14½*

No.	Type	Description	Unused	Used
757	A142	Sheet of 5, #a.-e.	6.50	6.50

Souvenir Sheet

Queen Mother, 100th Birthday A143

a, 107v, As child. b, 100v, As old woman.

Litho. with Foil Application

2000, May 22 *Perf. 13¼*

No.	Type	Description	Unused	Used
758	A143	Sheet of 2, #a-b	5.00	5.00

The Stamp Show 2000, London.

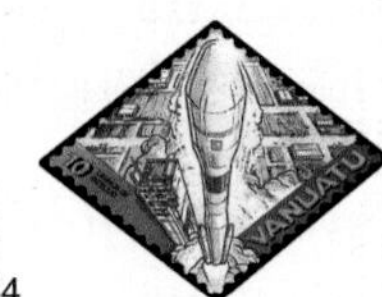

Intelsat — A144

Designs: 10v, Launch vehicle. 34v, Port Vila ground station. 100v, Intelsat 802 over Vaunatu. 225v, Intelsat and Tam Tam drum.

Litho. with Foil Application

2000, June 21 *Die Cut Perf. 10*
Self-Adhesive

No.	Type	Description	Unused	Used
759-762	A144	Set of 4	7.00	7.00
762a		Souvenir sheet, #760, 762	5.25	5.25

World Stamp Expo 2000, Anaheim (#762a).

Independence, 20th Anniv., UN Peace Year — A145

Artwork: 34v, Abstract painting by Sero Kuautonga. 67v, Tapa cloth by Moses Pita. 73v, Tapestry by Juliet Pita. 84v, Natora wood carving by Emmanuel Watt. 90v, Watercolor by Joseph John.

2000, July 29 Litho. *Perf. 13¾x13¼*

No.	Type	Description	Unused	Used
763-767	A145	Set of 5	8.00	8.00
		Booklet, 5 #764	6.50	

2000 Summer Olympics, Sydney — A146

Designs: 56v, Runner. 67v, Weight lifter. 90v, High jumper. 96v, Boxer.

2000, Sept. 15 *Perf. 13¼x13*

No.	Type	Description	Unused	Used
768-771	A146	Set of 4	5.50	5.50
		Booklet, 5 #769	6.00	

Dolphins — A147

34v, Common. 73v, Spotted. 84v, Spinner. 107v, Bottlenose.

2000, Nov. 30 Litho. *Perf. 12½*
772-775 A147 Set of 4 6.50 6.50
775a Souvenir sheet, #774-775 5.50 5.50

Hong Kong 2001 Stamp Exhibition (#775a).

Birds — A148

Designs: 35v, Cardinal honeyeater. 60v, Vanuatu white-eye. 90v, Santo Mountain starling. 100v, Royal parrotfinch. 110v, Vanuatu Mountain honeyeater.

2001, Feb. 1 Litho. *Perf. 14*
776-780 A148 Set of 5 10.50 10.50
780a Horiz. strip, #776-780 10.50 10.50

Exports — A149

Designs: 35v, Vanilla. 75v, Cacao. 90v, Coffee. 110v, Copra.

2001, Apr. 11 *Perf. 13¼x13*
781-784 A149 Set of 4 6.00 6.00

Whales — A150

Designs: 60v, Sperm. 80v, Humpback, vert. 90v, Blue.

Perf. 14½x14¾, 14¾x14½
2001, July 18 Litho.
785-787 A150 Set of 3 6.00 6.00
787a Souvenir sheet, #785-787, perf. 14½ 6.25 6.25

See New Caledonia No. 874.

Ceremonial Dancers Type of 1999

Designs: 35v, Snake dance, Banks Islands, horiz. 100v, Toka Dance, Tanna, horiz. 300v, Rom Dance, Ambryn, horiz. 1000v, Brasive Dance, Futuna, horiz.

2001, Sept. 12 Litho. *Perf. 13x13¼*
788 A140 35v multi .75 .75
789 A140 100v multi 2.10 2.10
790 A140 300v multi 6.25 6.25

Litho. With Foil Application
791 A140 1000v multi 20.00 20.00
Nos. 788-791 (4) 29.10 29.10

Sand Drawings — A151

Various sand drawings and: a, Four people on beach. b, Man standing in canoe in water. c, Man sitting on canoe, man rowing canoe. d, Canoe, shelter.

Perf. 12¾x13½
2001, Nov. 28 Litho.
792 A151 60v multi 1.00 1.00
792A A151 90v multi 1.50 1.50
792B A151 110v multi 1.90 1.90
792C A151 135v multi 2.40 2.40
d. Horiz. strip of 4 + central label 9.00 9.00

Intl. Year of Ecotourism — A152

Designs: Nos. 793, 798a, 35v, Mount Yasur, Pentecost Island land diver, dancers. Nos. 794, 798b, 60v Dancers, man making kava. Nos. 795, 798c, 75v, Siri Falls, flowers, birds, vert. Nos. 796, 798d, 110v, Kayakers, scuba diver, vert. Nos. 797, 798e, 135v, Beach bungalows, tourists.

2002, Jan. 30 Litho. *Perf. 14*
Stamps + Label
793-797 A152 Set of 5 8.75 8.75

Souvenir Sheet
Without Labels
Perf. 14½x14¾
798 A152 Sheet of 5, #a-e 8.75 8.75

Nos. 793, 794, and 797 are 38x26mm and Nos. 795-796 are 26x38mm, while Nos. 798a, 798b, and 798e are 37x25mm and Nos. 798c-798d are 25x37mm.

Horses — A153

Designs: 35v, Working horses. 60v, Cattle roundup. 75v, Horse racing. 80v, Tourism and horses. 200v, Wild Tanna horse.

2002, Mar. 27 *Perf. 14¾x14*
799-803 A153 Set of 5 8.25 8.25
803a Souvenir sheet of 1 4.25 4.25
803b Souvenir sheet of 1 with Philakorea 2002 emblem 4.25 4.25

Issued: No. 803b, 7/31/02.

Soccer — A154

Designs: 35v, Children's soccer. 80v, Under 17 soccer. 110v, Women's soccer. 135v, International soccer.

2002, May 31 Litho. *Perf. 13¾*
804-807 A154 Set of 4 7.00 7.00

Value is for stamps with surrounding selvage.

Reforestation A155

No. 808: a, Girl with seedling of Artocarpus atilis. b, Boy and man planting seedling of Endospermum medullosum. c, Canoe carver with Gyrocarpus americanus log. d, Mother and child with Dracontomelon vitiense fruit.

Serpentine Die Cut
2002, July 31 Litho.
Self-Adhesive
808 Horiz. strip of 4 6.75
a. A155 35v multi .80 .80
b. A155 60v multi 1.40 1.40
c. A155 90v multi 1.90 1.90
d. A155 110v multi 2.50 2.50

Dugongs — A156

Designs: 35v, Pair nuzzling. 75v, Pair swimming. 80v, One swimming. 135v, One on ocean floor.

2002, Sept. 25 Litho. *Perf. 13¾*
812-815 A156 Set of 4 6.25 6.25
815a Souvenir sheet, #814-815 7.00 7.00

Orchids A157

Designs: 35v, Dendrobium gouldii. 60v, Dendrobium polysema. 90v, Dendrobium spectabile. 110v, Flickingeria comata.

2002, Nov. 27 Litho. *Perf. 13¼*
816-819 A157 Set of 4 6.25 6.25

Year of Cattle — A158

Cattle Breeds: 35v, Limousin. 80v, Charolais. 110v, Simmental. 135v, Red Brahman.

2003, Jan. 29 *Perf. 13*
820-823 A158 Set of 4 7.50 7.50

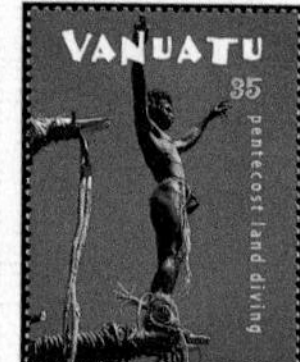

Pentecost Island Land Divers — A159

Designs: 35v, Diver on platform. 80v, Diver in air. 110v, Dancers, platform. 200v, Diver and platform (35x90mm).

2003, Mar. 26 *Perf. 13¾x13¼*
824-827 A159 Set of 4 9.50 9.50
827a Souvenir sheet of 1 5.25 5.25

Snorkeling — A160

Various people snorkeling: 35v, 80v, 90v, 110v, 135v. 80v and 90v are vert.

2003, May 28 Litho. *Perf. 13¾*
828-832 A160 Set of 5 7.50 7.50
832a Souvenir sheet, #828-832, perf. 13¼ 8.25 8.25

Natanggura Palm — A161

Half of palm nut and: 35v, Man planting palm tree, carved dolphins. 80v, Man weaving thatch for roof, carved turtle. 90v, Carver, carved lizard. 135v, Carvers, carved fish.

2003, July 23 *Perf. 13¾x13¼*
833-836 A161 Set of 4 5.75 5.75

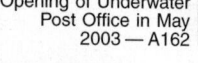

Opening of Underwater Post Office in May 2003 — A162

2003, Sept. 24 *Perf. 13¾*
837 A162 90v multi 2.25 2.25

Sea Horses — A163

Designs: 60v, Hippocampus kuda. 90v, Hippocampus histrix. 200v, Hippocampus bargibanti.

2003, Sept. 24
838-840 A163 Set of 3 6.00 6.00
840a Souvenir sheet of 1 4.50 4.50

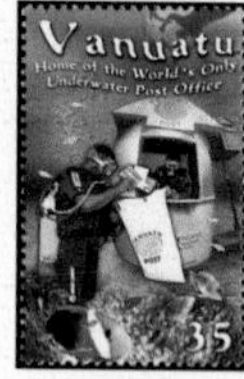

Moths — A164

Designs: 35v, Daphnis hypothous. 90v, Hippotion celerio. 110v, Euchromia creusa. 135v, Eudocima salaminia.

2003, Nov. 26 *Perf. 13½*
841-844 A164 Set of 4 6.50 6.50

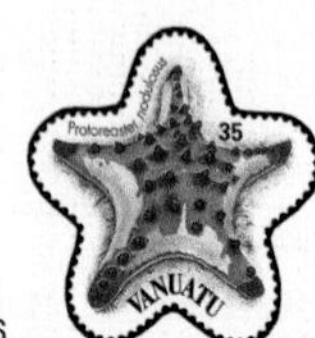

Activities at Underwater Post Office — A165

Designs: 35v, Workers placing mail in bag. 80v, Swimmer placing mail in mail box. 110v, Swimmer at counter. 220v, Clerk at counter, swimmer near mail box.

2004, Jan. 30 *Perf. 13¾x13½*
845-848 A165 Set of 4 8.25 8.25
848a Souvenir sheet of 1 4.50 4.50

2004 Hong Kong Stamp Expo (#848a).

Starfish — A166

Designs: 35v, Protoreaster nodulosus. 60v, Linckia laevigata. 90v, Fromia monilis. 250v, Echinaster callosus.

Serpentine Die Cut
2004, Apr. 28 Litho.
Self-Adhesive
849-852 A166 Set of 4 8.25 8.25

Red-tailed Tropicbird — A167

Designs: 35v, Adult and juvenile. 50v, Adult and chick, vert. 75v, Adult flying above juvenile, vert. 135v, Adult in flight. 200v, Adult pair.

2004, July 14 Litho. *Perf. 13¾*
853-857 A167 Set of 5 10.50 10.50
857a Souvenir sheet, #853-857, perf. 13½ 11.50 11.50

Musket Cove to Port Vila Yacht Race, 25th Anniv. A168

Various yachts: 35v, 80v, 90v, 200v. 80v and 200v are vert.

2004, Sept. 18 *Perf. 14¼*

858-861	A168	Set of 4	10.00 10.00
861a		Souvenir sheet of 1	5.25 5.25

Joint issue between Vanuatu and Fiji. See Fiji Nos. 1024-1027

Miniature Sheet

Marine Life A169

No. 862: a, Red and black anemonefish. b, Longfin bannerfish. c, Goldman's sweetlips. d, Green turtle. e, Clark's anemonefish. f, Harlequin sweetlips. g, Yellowtail coris. h, Emperor angelfish. i, Hairy red hermit crab, leaf oyster. j, Spotfin lionfish. k, Yellow-lipped sea krait. l, Clam.

Serpentine Die Cut 13¼

2004, Nov. 24 **Litho.**

Self-Adhesive

862 A169 35v Sheet of 12, #a-l 11.00 11.00

Christmas A170

Serpentine Die Cut 13

2004, Nov. 24 **Self-Adhesive**

863 A170 80v multi 2.25 2.25

Sunsets — A171

Designs: 60v, Sailboat. 80v, Man with raised arm, vert. 90v, Sailboats, vert. 135v, Man blowing conch shell.

2005, Jan. 19 ***Perf. 14x14½, 14½x14***

864-867 A171 Set of 4 9.25 9.25

Miniature Sheet

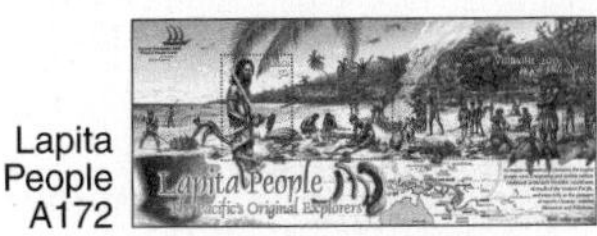

Lapita People A172

No. 868: a, 50v, Man holding tool, vert. b, 70v, People cleaning fish. c, 110v, People tending fire and carrying animal to fire. d, 200v, Women making baskets, mother and child, vert.

2005, Mar. 2 ***Perf. 13¼***

868 A172 Sheet of 4, #a-d 11.50 11.50

Pacific Explorer 2005 World Stamp Expo, Sydney.

Volcano Post — A173

Mail box on Mount Yasur and: 35v, Five tourists. 80v, Native woman. 100v, Three postal workers. 250v, Postal worker removing mail.

2005, May 31 **Litho.** ***Perf. 14x14¼***

869-872	A173	Set of 4	10.00 10.00
872a		Souvenir sheet of 1	5.75 5.75

Souvenir Sheet

Independence, 25th Anniv. — A174

No. 873: a, 35v, Vanuatu natives celebrating. b, 50v, Soldiers raising Vanuatu flag, 1980. c, 400v, Children and statue of family.

2005, July 30 **Litho.** ***Perf. 13***

873 A174 Sheet of 3, #a-c 12.50 12.50

Miniature Sheet

Corals A175

No. 874: a, Lace coral. b, Star coral. c, Sun coral (Tubastraea sp.). d, Plate coral. e, Brown anthelia. f, Bubble coral. g, Flowerpot coral. h, Cup coral. i, Daisy coral. j, Sun coral (Tubastraea diaphana). k, Mushroom-feather coral. l, Sun coral (Tubastraea micrantha).

Serpentine Die Cut 13½x13¼

2005, Sept. 7 **Litho.**

Self-Adhesive

874 A175 35v Sheet of 12, #a-l 11.00 11.00

Landscapes — A176

Designs: 80v, Horse and rider on beach. 90v, Palm trees. 110v, Waterfall. 135v, Harbor.

2005, Nov. 16 **Litho.** ***Perf. 14¼x14***

875-878 A176 Set of 4 11.00 11.00

Miniature Sheet

Reef Shells A177

No. 879: a, Crocus clam. b, Pearl oyster. c, Gold-ringer cowrie. d, Cock-a-comb oyster. e, Tiger cowrie. f, Textile cone. g, Marlinspike. h, Vibex bonnet. i, Erosa cowrie. j, Scorpion conch. k, Honey cowrie. l, Umbilical ovula.

Serpentine Die Cut 13½

2006, Feb. 8 **Self-Adhesive**

879 A177 35v Sheet of 12, #a-l 11.00 11.00

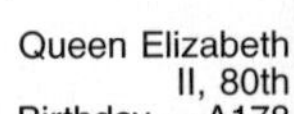

Queen Elizabeth II, 80th Birthday — A178

Queen: 50v, As young woman in Army uniform. 100v, Without hat. No. 882, 110v, With blue hat. No. 883, 200v, With yellow hat.

No. 884: a, 110v, Like 100v. b, 200v, Like No. 882.

2006, Apr. 21 **Litho.** ***Perf. 14***

With White Frames

880-883 A178 Set of 4 8.00 8.00

Souvenir Sheet

Without White Frames

884 A178 Sheet of 2, #a-b 5.75 5.75

Souvenir Sheet

Arrival in Vanuatu of Pedro Fernandez de Quiros, 400th Anniv. — A179

2006, May 10 ***Perf. 13¼***

885 A179 350v multi 7.50 7.50

2006 World Cup Soccer Championships, Germany — A180

Various soccer players, 2006 World Cup emblem on soccer jersey: 35v, 80v, 110v, 135v.

2006, June 9 **Litho.** ***Die Cut***

Self-Adhesive

886-889	A180	Set of 4	7.00 7.00
889a		Souvenir sheet, #886-889	7.00 7.00

Flowers — A181

Designs: 5v, Passiflora foetida. 10v, Hibiscus rosa-sinensis. 20v, Cereus undatus. 40v, Strelitzia reginae. 50v, Spathodea campanulata. 70v, Delonix regia. 90v, Hibiscus hilaceus. 100v, Nymphaea sp. 150v, Plumeria obtusa. 500v, Allamanda cathartica. 1000v, Thunbergia grandiflora.

Serpentine Die Cut 11¾

2006, July 1 **Self-Adhesive**

890	A181	5v multi	.25	.25
891	A181	10v multi	.25	.25
892	A181	20v multi	.35	.35
893	A181	40v multi	.65	.65
894	A181	50v multi	.80	.80
895	A181	70v multi	1.10	1.10
896	A181	100v multi	1.60	1.60
897	A181	150v multi	2.50	2.50
898	A181	500v multi	8.00	8.00
899	A181	1000v multi	16.50	16.50

Inscribed "International Post" at Left

900	A181	5v multi	.25	.25
901	A181	10v multi	.25	.25
902	A181	20v multi	.35	.35
903	A181	50v multi	.80	.80
904	A181	90v multi	1.40	1.40
905	A181	100v multi	1.60	1.60
906	A181	500v multi	8.00	8.00
907	A181	1000v multi	16.50	16.50
		Nos. 890-907 (18)	61.15	61.15

Miniature Sheet

Worldwide Fund for Nature (WWF) — A182

No. 908: a, 70v, Giant grouper and coral. b, 90v, Giant grouper and smaller fish. c, 100v, Juvenile giant groupers. d, 150v, Giant grouper, smaller fish, diff.

2006, Oct. 4 **Litho.** ***Perf. 13¼***

908 A182 Sheet, 2 each #a-d 15.00 15.00

Shipwreck of the SS President Coolidge A183

Designs: 90v, Diver, corals. 100v, Divers, fish. 130v, Shipwreck, fish. 150v, Ship sinking, sailors leaving ship (85x30mm).

No. 913: a, 90v, Like #909. b, 100v, Like #910. c, 130v, Like #911. d, 150v, Like #912.

2006, Nov. 29 **Litho.** ***Perf. 13¼***

Stamps Inscribed "International Post"

909-912 A183 Set of 4 9.00 9.00

Souvenir Sheet

Stamps Without "International Post"

913 A183 Sheet of 4, #a-d 9.00 9.00

Reef Heron — A184

Reef heron: 10v, With wings extended. 20v, Standing on land, vert. 50v, With fish in bill, vert. 70v, Head. 250v, Chicks.

2007, Feb. 9 **Litho.** ***Perf. 14½***

914-918	A184	Set of 5	8.00 8.00
918a		Souvenir sheet, #914-918	8.00 8.00

Diving at Million Dollar Point — A185

Designs: Nos. 919, 923a, 90v, Divers near submerged jeep. Nos. 920, 923b, 100v, Divers near submerged truck, vert. (42x60mm). Nos. 921, 923c, 130v, Diver, diff. Nos. 922, 923d, 150v, Diver, lionfish.

2007, Apr. 18 ***Perf. 13¼***

Stamps Inscribed "International Post"

919-922 A185 Set of 4 9.00 9.00

Souvenir Sheet

Stamps Without "International Post"

923 A185 Sheet of 4, #a-d 9.00 9.00

Fruit — A186

Designs: 30v, Bananas. 40v, Watermelon. 70v, Limes. 100v, Papayas. 250v, Coconuts.

2007, June 27 ***Serpentine Die Cut***

Self-Adhesive

924-928 A186 Set of 5 9.50 9.50

James A. Michener (1907-97), Writer — A187

Michener: 40v, With pen. 90v, At typewriter. 130v, With island natives. 350v, Holding book.

2007, Aug. 22 ***Perf. 14½***

929-932 A187 Set of 4 11.50 11.50

Banded Iguana — A188

Designs: 50v, Two iguanas, two flowers. 70v, Iguana on branch. 100v, Iguana. 250v, Iguana on flower bud.

Serpentine Die Cut 15

2007, Nov. 7 **Litho.**

Self-Adhesive

933-936 A188 Set of 4 9.25 9.25
936a Souvenir sheet, #935-936 7.75 7.75

Air Vanuatu, 20th Anniv. A189

Designs: 40v, Three airplanes at airport. 90v, Boeing 737-800. 130v, Boeing 737-300. 180v, Twin Otter. 250v, ATR 42.

2007-08 ***Serpentine Die Cut 15***

937 A189	40v multi	.75	.75
938 A189	90v multi	1.75	1.75
939 A189	130v multi	2.50	2.50
940 A189	180v multi	3.50	3.50
941 A189	250v multi	4.75	4.75
	Nos. 937-941 (5)	13.25	13.25

First flight of Boeing 737-800 (#938). Issued: 40v, 130v, 180v, 250v, 11/23; 90v, 1/17/08.

Coconut Crabs — A190

Crab on: 60v, Beach. 500v, Tree, vert.

Perf. 13½x13¼, 13¼x13½

2008, Feb. 20 **Litho.**

942-943 A190 Set of 2 13.00 13.00
943a Souvenir sheet, #942-943 13.00 13.00

Miniature Sheet

2008 Summer Olympics, Beijing — A191

No. 944: a, 10v, Archery. b, 40v, Athletics. c, 60v, Table tennis. d, 90v, Weight lifting.

2008, June 18 **Litho.** ***Perf. 12***

944 A191 Sheet of 4, #a-d 4.25 4.25

Underwater Post Office — A192

Designs: 40v, Underwater postal workers carrying sacks of mail, fish with postcard. 80v, Postal worker, fish with letters. 100v, Postal workers in raft, fish with mail. 200v, Underwater post office, fish and marine life with letters.

2008, July 30 **Litho.** ***Die Cut***

Self-Adhesive

945-948 A192 Set of 4 8.50 8.50

Tourism A193

Scenes and website addresses of: No. 949, 90v, Vanuatu Tourism. No. 950, 90v, Breakas Beach Resort. No. 951, 90v, Iririki Island Resort and Spa. No. 952, 90v, Le Lagon Resort. No. 953, 90v, The Melanesian Hotel. No. 954, 90v, Le Meridien Resort Spa and Casino. No. 955, 90v, Sebel Hotel.

2008, Aug. 27 ***Perf. 15x14¾***

949-955 A193 Set of 7 13.00 13.00

Miniature Sheet

Nudibranchs — A194

No. 956: a, Risbecia tryoni. b, Phyllidia coelestis. c, Flabellina rubrolineata. d, Chromodoris lochi. e, Chromodoris elisabethina. f, Jorunna funebris. g, Glossodoris rufomarginata. h, Phyllidia ocellata. i, Chromodoris geometrica. j, Phyllidia madangensis. k, Hexabranchus sanguineus. l, Glossodoris atromarginata.

Serpentine Die Cut 13¼

2008, Oct. 8 **Self-Adhesive**

956 A194 40v Sheet of 12, #a-l 8.50 8.50

Birds — A195

Designs: 45v, Eastern reef heron. 100v, Great crested tern. 130v, White-tailed tropicbird. 250v, Fairy tern.

2008, Nov. 26 **Litho.** ***Perf. 14½x15***

957-960 A195 Set of 4 9.00 9.00
960a Souvenir sheet of 1 #960 5.00 5.00

Romance in Vanuatu — A196

Couples in Vanuatu, website addresses for: No. 961, 90v, Bride and groom wearing flowers (Events Vanuatu). No. 962, 90v, Bride and groom with wine glasses (Events Vanuatu). No. 963, 90v, Man and woman sitting on beach (Air Vanuatu). No. 964, 90v, Man and woman sitting on chaise lounges (Breakas Beach Resort). No. 965, 90v, Man and woman at table (White Grass Ocean Resort).

2009, Jan. 28 **Litho.** ***Die Cut***

Self-Adhesive

961-965 A196 Set of 5 7.00 7.00

Mystery (Inyeug) Island — A197

Designs: Nos. 966, 970a, 90v, Boat dock. Nos. 967, 970b, 100v, Snorkelers and boat, horiz. Nos. 968, 970c, 130v, Sailboat and trees, horiz. Nos. 969, 970d, 200v, Man and woman on outrigger canoe on beach.

2009, Mar. 28 **Litho.** ***Perf. 14***

Stamps Inscribed "International Post"

966-969 A197 Set of 4 8.25 8.25

Souvenir Sheet

Stamps Without "International Post"

970 A197 Sheet of 4, #a-d 8.25 8.25

Peonies — A198

2009, Apr. 10 **Litho.** ***Perf. 13¼***

971 A198 100v multi 1.75 1.75

Printed in sheets of 8.

Plumeria Flowers A199

Various plumeria flowers: 90v, 100v, 130v, 150v.

2009, May 14 ***Perf. 14½x14***

972-975 A199 Set of 4 8.00 8.00

Souvenir Sheet

Hong Kong 2009 Intl. Stamp Exhibition — A200

2009, May 14 ***Perf. 13½***

976 A200 Sheet of 2, Pitcairn Islands #685a, Vanuatu #976a 8.50 8.50
a. 150v Two pandas 4.25 4.25

Joint issue between Vanuatu and Pitcairn Islands.

No. 976 sold for 310v and New Zealand $5, and is identical to Pitcairn Islands No. 685.

Souvenir Sheet

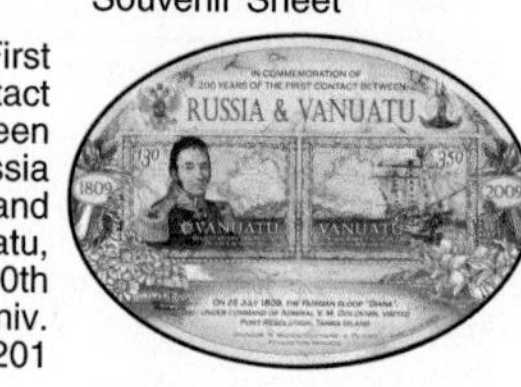

First Contact Between Russia and Vanuatu, 200th Anniv. A201

No. 977 — Map and: a, 130v, Russian Admiral V. M. Golovnin. b, 350v, Russian ship, "Diana."

2009, July 28 ***Perf. 13¼***

977 A201 Sheet of 2, #a-b 8.50 8.50

Charles Darwin (1809-82), Naturalist — A202

No. 978 — Darwin, birds and: a, Tortoises. b, Iguanas.

2009, Sept. 2 ***Perf. 13¼x13½***

978 A202 200v Horiz. pair, #a-b, + central label 7.50 7.50

Worldwide Fund for Nature (WWF) — A203

No. 979 — Beach thick-knee: a, Adult on nest, bird in flight. b, Adult and chick on ground, two birds in flight. c, Two adults at water's edge, bird in flight. d, Adult on beach, bird in flight.

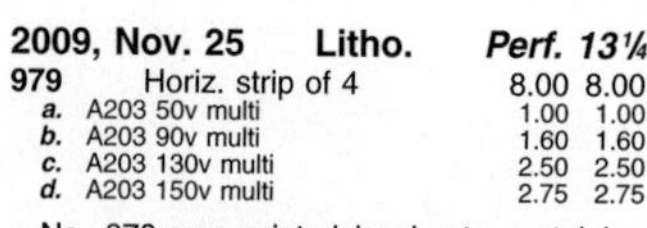

2009, Nov. 25 **Litho.** ***Perf. 13¼***

979	Horiz. strip of 4	8.00	8.00
a.	A203 50v multi	1.00	1.00
b.	A203 90v multi	1.60	1.60
c.	A203 130v multi	2.50	2.50
d.	A203 150v multi	2.75	2.75

No. 979 was printed in sheets containing two strips.

Souvenir Sheet

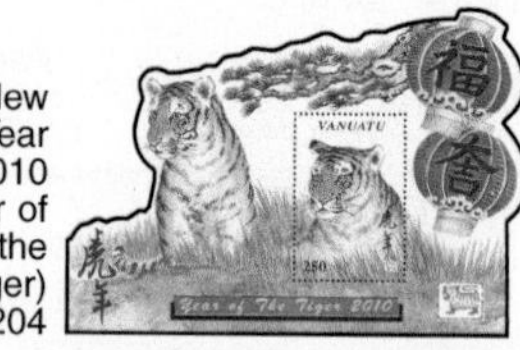

New Year 2010 (Year of the Tiger) A204

2010, Feb. 14 ***Perf. 13¼***

980 A204 250v multi 5.00 5.00

Miniature Sheet

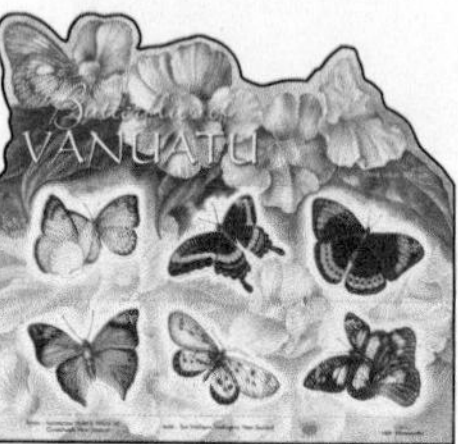

Butterflies — A205

No. 981: a, Calopsilia pomona. b, Papilio godeffroyi. c, Hypolimnas octocula. d, Doleschallia bisaltide. e, Acraea andromacha. f, Danaus affinis.

2010, Apr. 14 ***Die Cut***

Self-Adhesive

981 A205 100v Sheet of 6, #a-f 11.00 11.00

Tourism — A206

Designs: 40v, Dugong off Epi Island. 140v, Snake Dance, Banks Island, horiz. 160v, Iririki Resort, Efate Island. 190v, Mt. Yasur Volcano, Tanna Island, horiz.

Perf. 13¼x13¾, 13¾x13¼

2010, Apr. 30

982 A206 40v multi .75 .75
a. Perf. 14 .75 .75

Inscribed "International Post" at Left

983 A206	140v multi	2.75	2.75
984 A206	160v multi	3.00	3.00
985 A206	190v multi	3.50	3.50
	Nos. 982-985 (4)	10.00	10.00

Miniature Sheet

Perf. 14

986	Sheet of 4, #982a, 986a-986c	10.50	10.50
a.	A206 140v Like #983, without "International Post" at left	2.75	2.75
b.	A206 160v Like #984, without "International Post" at left	2.90	2.90
c.	A206 190v Like #985, without "International Post" at left	3.75	3.75

Expo 2010, Shanghai (#986).

Cats — A207

Color of cat: 10v, White. 100v, Black and white. 160v, Brown and white. 190v, Gray and white.

2010, July 14 ***Perf. 14½x14***

987-990 A207 Set of 4 8.50 8.50

Souvenir Sheet

2010 Youth Olympics, Singapore — A208

2010, Aug. 14 *Perf. 13¼*
991 A208 500v multi 8.50 8.50

"Smile With Us" — A209

Designs: No. 992, 20v, Man, statues in background. No. 993, 20v, Two women. No. 994, 20v, Three children. No. 995, 20v, Fish. No. 996, 20v, Dugong. No. 997, 100v, Woman. No. 998, 100v, Divers at Underwater Post Office. No. 999, 100v, Island. No. 1000, 100v, Dolphin. No. 1001, 100v, Airplane.

2010, Dec. 15 *Perf. 13½*
992-1001 A209 Set of 10 11.00 11.00
996a Horiz. strip of 5, #992-996 1.75 1.75
1001a Horiz. strip of 5, #997-1001 9.00 9.00

Turtles — A210

No. 1002: a, Green turtles, "International Post" at left. b, Green turtles, "International Post" at right. c, Hawksbill turtle, "International Post" at left. d, Hawksbill turtles, "International Post" at right.

2011, Jan. 26 *Perf. 13½x13¼*
1002 Horiz. strip of 4 + central label 7.75 7.75
a.-d. A210 100v Any single 1.75 1.75

Tanna Coffee — A211

Designs: No. 1003, 100v, Short black. No. 1004, 100v, Long black. 140v, Latte. 160v, Cappuccino.

2011, Mar. 23 *Perf. 14½x14*
1003-1006 A211 Set of 4 9.75 9.75

Worldwide Fund for Nature (WWF) — A212

No. 1007 — Massena's lorikeet: a, Bird facing left. b, Bird on branch. c, Two birds on branch. d, Bird on palm frond.

2011, May 25 **Litho.** *Perf. 14*
1007 Horiz. strip of 4 8.50 8.50
a. A212 40v multi .80 .80
b. A212 60v multi 1.25 1.25
c. A212 140v multi 2.90 2.90
d. A212 160v multi 3.25 3.25
e. Sheet of 8, 2 each #1007a-1007d 17.50 17.50

Green and Golden Bell Frog — A213

Designs: 45v, Frog on branch. 70v, Frog in flower. 140v, Three frogs in flower. 200v, Frog on cut branch.

2011, July 27 *Perf. 14¼*
1008-1011 A213 Set of 4 9.00 9.00
1011a Souvenir sheet of 2, #1010-1011 7.00 7.00

Beaches A214

Designs: No. 1012, 100v, Airplane on beach of Eratap Island, birds. No. 1013, 100v, Trees near Champagne Beach, Espiritu Santo Island, turtles. 140v, Woman on beach at Havannah Harbor, Efate Island, shells. 160v, Beach on Pele Island, fish.

2011, Sept. 28 *Perf. 14x14½*
1012-1015 A214 Set of 4 10.00 10.00

A gritty substance has been applied to the beach portions of the stamp designs.

Flowers — A215

Designs: No. 1016, 100v, Heliconia psittacorum. No. 1017, 100v, Heliconia rostrata. 140v, Strelitzia reginae. 180v, Heliconia caribaea variety.

2011, Dec. 7 *Perf. 14½x14*
1016-1019 A215 Set of 4 10.50 10.50

Dragonflies — A216

Designs: 40v, Yellow-striped flutterer. 90v, Globe skimmer. 140v, Fiery skimmer. 250v, Painted grasshawk.

2012, Feb. 22 *Perf. 14¼*
1020-1023 A216 Set of 4 11.00 11.00
1023a Souvenir sheet of 2, #1021, 1023 7.00 7.00

Diplomatic Relations Between Vanuatu and People's Republic of Chin, 30th Anniv. A217

2012, Mar. 26 *Perf. 12*
1024 A217 90v multi 1.75 1.75

Birds — A218

Designs: 10v, Southern shrikebill. 20v, Silvereyes. 40v, Red-bellied fruuit doves. 50v, Pacific imperial pigeon. 70v, Long-tailed trillers. 90v, Vanuatu scrubfowl. 100v, Streaked fantails. 140v, Dark brown honeyeater. 160v, Vanuatu petrels. 400v, Ruddy turnstones. 500v, Purple swamphens. 1000v, Striated mangove heron. 40v and 70v lack blue triangle and airplane.

2012, May 2 **Litho.** *Perf. 14¼*
1025 A218 10v multi .25 .25
1026 A218 20v multi .40 .40
1027 A218 40v multi .80 .80
1028 A218 50v multi 1.00 1.00
1029 A218 70v multi 1.40 1.40
1030 A218 90v multi 1.75 1.75
1031 A218 100v multi 2.00 2.00
1032 A218 140v multi 3.00 3.00
1033 A218 160v multi 3.25 3.25
1034 A218 400v multi 8.00 8.00
1035 A218 500v multi 10.00 10.00
1036 A218 1000v multi 20.00 20.00
a. Souvenir sheet of 12, #1025-1036 52.50 52.50
Nos. 1025-1036 (12) 51.85 51.85

Reign Of Queen Elizabeth II, 60th Anniv. — A219

No. 1037 — Queen Elizabeth II: a, 250v, On horse. b, 300v, Waving.

2012, June 1 *Perf. 13¼x13½*
1037 Horiz. pair + central label 11.00 11.00
a. A219 250v multi 5.00 5.00
b. A219 300v multi 6.00 6.00

Kiwanis Charity Race Day — A220

Kiwanis emblem and various race horses: 35v, 50v, 150v, 250v.

Perf. 14x14¼
2012, July 12 **Litho.** **Unwmk.**
1038-1041 A220 Set of 4 10.50 10.50

Nov. 14, 2012 Partial Solar Eclipse — A221

People in boats and diagram of position of Sun and Moon at various times during eclipse: 40v, 60v, 160v, 180v.

Perf. 14x14¼
2012, Oct. 31 **Litho.** **Unwmk.**
1042-1045 A221 Set of 4 9.75 9.75

Vanuatu Red Cross Society, 30th Anniv. — A222

Vanuatu Red Cross Society emblem, anniversary emblem and: 60v, Workers removing boxes from small boat. 100v, Hand under water running from faucet.

Perf. 14x14¼
2012, Dec. 5 **Litho.** **Wmk. 387**
1046-1047 A222 Set of 2 3.50 3.50

Greetings — A223

Designs: 80v, Children and flowers. 100v, Snorkeler, fish, coral reef. 140v, Volcano. 160v, Aerial view of islands, butterflies.

Wmk. 387
2012, Dec. 5 **Litho.** *Perf. 14½*
1048-1051 A223 Set of 4 10.50 10.50

Sam's Animal Welfare Association A224

Various dogs and people: 40v, 60v, 160v, 200v.

Perf. 14x14¼
2013, Feb. 27 **Litho.** **Wmk. 387**
1052-1055 A224 Set of 4 10.00 10.00
1055a Souvenir sheet of 2, #1054-1055 8.00 8.00

Worldwide Fund for Nature (WWF) — A225

Various depictions of orange spot filefish.

Wmk. 387
2013, Mar. 28 **Litho.** *Perf. 14*
1056 Horiz. strip of 4 9.00 9.00
a. A225 30v multi .65 .65
b. A225 70v multi 1.60 1.60
c. A225 100v multi 2.25 2.25
d. A2225 200v multi 4.50 4.50

Printed in sheets of 8 containing 2 each #1056a-1056d.

Waterfalls — A226

Designs: 40v, Siri Falls, Gaua. 100v, Big Wota Falls, Northern Maewo. 140v, Saser Twin Falls, Vanua Lava. 160v, Mele Cascades, Efate.

Perf. 14¼x14
2013, June 26 **Litho.** **Wmk. 387**
1057-1060 A226 Set of 4 9.25 9.25

Birth of Prince George of Cambridge A227

Designs: 40v, Duke of Cambridge holding Prince George. 60v, Duchess of Cambridge holding Prince George. 100v, Duke and Duchess of Cambridge, Prince George. 250v, Prince George.

Perf. 13¾x13¼
2013, Sept. 18 **Litho.** **Unwmk.**
1061-1064 A227 Set of 4 9.50 9.50

Christmas A228

Santa Claus: 40v, In hammock. 100v, Snorkeling near underwater post office, vert. 160v, In sleigh above island, vert. 250v, Looking at card in Vanuatu post office lobby.

Perf. 13½
2013, Nov. 6 **Litho.** **Unwmk.**
1065-1068 A228 Set of 4 12.00 12.00

Souvenir Sheet

Underwater Post Office, 10th Anniv. — A229

Unwmk.
2013, Dec. 11 **Litho.** *Perf. 14*
1069 A229 350v multi 7.50 7.50

Submarine Cable Between Fiji and Vanuatu — A230

No. 1070: a, Workers, ship and cable with floats. b, Divers examining cable. c, Electronic cables plugged into machine.

Litho. With Foil Application

2014, Jan. 15 ***Perf. 14½x14***

1070 Horiz. strip of 6 + central label, #1070a-1070c, Fiji #1304a-1304c 14.50 14.50
a. A230 40v multi .65 .65
b. A230 130v multi 2.10 2.10
c. A230 190v multi 3.25 3.25

No. 1070 sold for 750v in Vanuatu and $13.30 in Fiji. See Fiji No. 1304.

Wan Smolbag International Theater Festival, 25th Anniv. — A231

Art for: 10v, *9 Long 1 Step Wan* music compact disc. 40v, Film *Vanua-tai. . .of Land and Sea.* 120v, Television show *Love Patrol.* 300v, Film *Las Kad.*

2014, May 7 **Litho.** ***Perf. 14x14¼***
1071-1074 A231 Set of 4 10.00 10.00

Cocktail Glasses and Flowers — A232

Flower and cocktail glass containing: 70v, Fire. 100v, Underwater post office. 180v, Woman drinking at beach. 250v, Sailboat at sea.

2014, July 23 **Litho.** ***Die Cut***
Self-Adhesive
1075-1078 A232 Set of 4 13.00 13.00

Extreme Sports A233

Designs: 50v, Kiteboarding. 120v, People riding off-road buggies, vert. 160v, Parasailing, vert. 190v, Jet boating.

2014, Oct. 29 **Litho.** ***Perf. 14½***
1079-1082 A233 Set of 4 10.50 10.50

Nelson Mandela (1918-2013), President of South Africa — A234

Flags of South Africa and Vanuatu, various pictures of Mandela and quotes starting with: 40v, "Action without vision. . ." 120v, "Education is the most powerful weapon. . ." 150v, "Sport has the power to inspire. . ." 200v, "Forgiveness liberates the soul. . ."

2014, Dec. 5 **Litho.** ***Perf. 14x14¼***
1083-1086 A234 Set of 4 10.50 10.50

Items Made in Vanuatu — A235

Designs: 20v, Items made by ACTIV Association. 80v, Venui Vanilla. 150v, Health and beauty products by The Summit. 300v, Jewelry by Vanuatu Bijouterie.

2015, Mar. 11 **Litho.** ***Perf. 14½x14***
1087-1090 A235 Set of 4 10.50 10.50

Restaurants A236

Designs: No. 1091, 120v, Eratap. No. 1092, 120v, Francesca's. No. 1093, 120v, The Havannah. No. 1094, 120v, L'Houstalet.

2015, Oct. 28 **Litho.** ***Perf. 14x14½***
1091-1094 A236 Set of 4 8.75 8.75

2016 Summer Olympics, Rio de Janeiro — A237

Designs: 40v, Table tennis, taekwondo. 90v, Rowing, beach volleyball. 150v, Boxing, rowing. 200v, Rowing, judo.

2016, May 11 **Litho.** ***Perf. 14x14¼***
1095-1098 A237 Set of 4 9.25 9.25

Swimming Holes — A238

Designs: 10v, Matevulu Blue Hole, Santo Island. 100v, Riri Blue Hole, Santo Island. 180v, Nanda Blue Hole, Santo Island. 250v, Blue Lagoon, Efate Island.

2017, July 19 **Litho.** ***Perf. 14***
1099-1102 A238 Set of 4 10.50 10.50

Miniature Sheet

2017 Pacific Mini Games, Port Vila A239

No. 1103: a, 20v, Boxing. b, 20v, Beach volleyball. c, 30v, Women's netball. d, 30v, 3-on-3 basketball. e, 30v, Tennis. f, 40v, Soccer. g, 40v, Table tennis. h, 60v, Archery. i, 80v, Golf. j, 80v, Weight lifting. k, 90v, Judo. l, 130v, Shot put. m, 150v, Rugby sevens. n, 180v, Karate.

2017, Nov. 25 **Litho.** ***Perf. 14¼x14***
1103 A239 Sheet of 14, #a-n 18.00 18.00

New Year 2018 (Year of the Dog) — A240

Designs: 180v, Two dogs. 350v, One dog.

2018, Feb. 1 **Litho.** ***Perf. 13¼***
1104-1105 A240 Set of 2 10.00 10.00
1105a Souvenir sheet of 2, #1104-1105 10.00 10.00

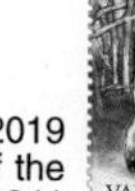

New Year 2019 (Year of the Pig) — A241

Designs: 180v, Pig and piglets. 350v, Stylized pig and piglets, diff.

2018, Dec. 10 **Litho.** ***Perf. 13¼***
1106-1107 A241 Set of 2 9.25 9.25

Campaign Against Plastic Pollution — A242

Designs: 60v, Children showing plastic trash collected on beach. 180v, Diver photographing marine life. 250v, Woman giving plastic bottle to child. 350v, Children swimming underwater, marine life.

2019, Oct. 9 **Litho.** ***Perf. 14***
1108-1111 A242 Set of 4 14.50 14.50

Birds — A243

Designs: 90v, Swamp harrier. 150v, Brahminy kite. 180v, Brown goshawk. 300v, Peregrine falcon.

2019, Dec. 11 **Litho.** ***Perf. 14x14¼***
1112-1115 A243 Set of 4 12.50 12.50

Souvenir Sheet

New Year 2020 (Year of the Rat) A244

No. 1116: a, 180v, Rat. b, 350v, Chinese character for "rat."

2020, Jan. 25 **Litho.** ***Perf. 13¼x13½***
1116 A244 Sheet of 2, #a-b 9.00 9.00

Red Panda — A245

Various depictions of Red pandas: 60v, 80v, 90v, 100v.
400v, Red panda in tree.

2021, May 25 **Litho.** ***Perf. 13***
1117-1120 A245 Set of 4 6.25 6.25

Souvenir Sheet

Perf. 13¼x13

1121 A245 400v multi 7.50 7.50

No. 1121 contains one 48x40mm stamp.

Miniature Sheets

A246

Satellites A247

Various unnamed satellites, as shown.

2021, May 25 **Litho.** ***Perf. 13¼***
1122 A246 100v Sheet of 6, #a-f 11.00 11.00
1123 A247 150v Sheet of 6, #a-f 17.00 17.00

Miniature Sheets

A248

Items From Smithsonian Institution — A249

No. 1124: a, Skull of dinosaur. b, Giant panda. c, Butterfly on flower. d, Peacock. e, Rock crystal. f, Fish.

No. 1125: a, Bell X-1 "Glamorous Glennis" jet. b, Bwa butterfly mask. c, Bella Coola Raven mask. d, Edison light bulb. e, Draisine. f, Hope Diamond.

2021, May 25 Litho. *Perf. 13*

1124	A248	180v	Sheet of 6, #a-f	20.00	20.00
1125	A249	190v	Sheet of 6, #a-f	21.00	21.00

SEMI-POSTAL STAMPS

No. 324 Surcharged

Nos. 414-418 Surcharged

Wmk. 373 (No. B1), 384
Perf. 14x13½, 14x14½

1987, May 12 Litho.

B1	A60	20v +10v on 2v	1.00	1.00
B2	CD337	20v +10v	1.00	1.00
B3	CD337	35v +15v	1.75	1.75
B4	CD337	45v +20v	1.90	1.90
B5	CD337	55v +25v	3.75	3.75
B6	CD337	100v +50v	4.00	4.00
		Nos. B1-B6 (6)	13.40	13.40

Old value of #B1 obliterated by 2 horizontal bars. Surcharge indicated by text "Surcharge +10."

VATICAN CITY

'va-ti-kən 'si-tē

LOCATION — Western Italy, directly outside the western boundary of Rome

GOVT. — Independent state subject to certain political restrictions under a treaty with Italy

AREA — 108.7 acres

POP. — 870 (1999 est.)

100 Centesimi = 1 Lira

100 Cents = 1 Euro (2002)

Catalogue values for unused stamps in this country are for Never Hinged items, beginning with Scott 68 in the regular postage section, Scott C1 in the airpost section, Scott E3 in the special delivery section, and Scott J7 in the postage due section.

Certificates for often forged or never hinged high value items are advised.

Watermarks

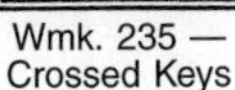

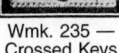

Wmk. 235 — Crossed Keys

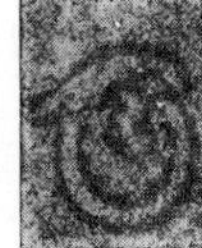

Wmk. 277 — Winged Wheel

Papal Arms — A1

Pope Pius XI — A2

Unwmk.

1929, Aug. 1 Engr. *Perf. 14*

Surface-Colored Paper

1	A1	5c dk brn & pink	.25	.25
2	A1	10c dk grn & lt grn	.25	.35
3	A1	20c violet & lilac	.75	.65
4	A1	25c dk bl & lt bl	.95	.75
5	A1	30c indigo & yellow	1.10	.85
6	A1	50c ind & sal buff	1.60	.90
7	A1	75c brn car & gray	2.25	1.50

Photo.

White Paper

8	A2	80c carmine rose	1.60	.50
9	A2	1.25 l dark blue	2.60	1.10
10	A2	2 l olive brown	5.25	2.25
11	A2	2.50 l red orange	4.50	3.75
12	A2	5 l dk green	5.25	*12.00*
13	A2	10 l olive blk	11.00	*17.00*
		Nos. 1-13,E1-E2 (15)	74.85	*75.35*
		Set, never hinged	265.00	

The stamps of Type A1 have, in this and subsequent issues, the words "POSTE VATICANE" in rows of colorless letters in the background.

For surcharges and overprints see Nos. 14, 35-40, 61-67, J1-J6, Q1-Q13.

No. 5 Surcharged in Red

1931, Oct. 1

14	A1	25c on 30c ind & yel	3.00	2.25
		Never hinged	10.00	

Arms of Pope Pius XI A5

Vatican Palace and Obelisk A6

Vatican Gardens A7

Pope Pius XI A8

St. Peter's Basilica — A9

1933, May 31 Engr. Wmk. 235

19	A5	5c copper red	.25	.25
a.		Imperf., pair	600.00	*825.00*
20	A6	10c dk brn & blk	.25	.25
21	A6	12½c dp grn & blk	.25	.25
22	A6	20c orange & blk	.25	.25
a.		Vertical pair imperf. between and at bottom	750.00	
23	A6	25c dk olive & blk	.25	.25
a.		Imperf., pair	425.00	*600.00*
24	A7	30c blk & dk brn	.25	.25
25	A7	50c vio & dk brn	.25	.25
26	A7	75c brn red & dk brn	.25	.25
27	A7	80c rose & dk brn	.25	.25
28	A8	1 l violet & blk	7.50	7.50
29	A8	1.25 l dk bl & blk	22.50	13.50
30	A8	2 l dk brn & blk	52.50	37.50
31	A8	2.75 l dk vio & blk	67.50	*90.00*
32	A9	5 l blk brn & dk grn	.25	.25
33	A9	10 l dk bl & dk grn	.25	.30
34	A9	20 l blk & dp grn	.40	*.50*
		Nos. 19-34,E3-E4 (18)	153.85	152.70
		Set, never hinged	375.00	

Nos. 8-13 Surcharged in Black

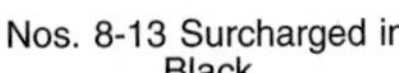

No. 36 No. 36a

1934, June 16 Unwmk.

35	A2	40c on 80c	40.00	18.00
36	A2	1.30 l on 1.25 l	180.00	90.00
a.		Small figures "30" in "1.30"	*22,500.*	*16,000.*
		Never hinged	*28,000.*	
37	A2	2.05 l on 2 l	240.00	30.00
a.		No comma btwn. 2 & 0	*1,500.*	*1,000.*
		Never hinged	*3,000.*	
38	A2	2.55 l on 2.50 l	150.00	250.00
a.		No comma btwn. 2 & 5	*800.00*	*900.00*
		Never hinged	*1,600.*	
b.		Narrow spacing ('37)	*225.00*	*250.00*
39	A2	3.05 l on 5 l	500.00	450.00
40	A2	3.70 l on 10 l	450.00	550.00
		Nos. 35-40 (6)	1,560.	1,388.
		Set, never hinged	2,900.	

A second printing of Nos. 36-40 was made in 1937. The 2.55 l and 3.05 l of the first printing and 1.30 l of the second printing sell for more. For more detailed listings, see Scott *Classic Specialized Catalogue of Stamps and Covers 1840-1940.*

Tribonian Presenting Pandects to Justinian I A10

Pope Gregory IX Promulgating Decretals A11

1935, Feb. 1 Photo.

41	A10	5c red orange	4.50	4.50
42	A10	10c purple	4.50	4.50
43	A10	25c green	22.50	22.50
44	A11	75c rose red	50.00	42.50
45	A11	80c dark brown	45.00	37.50
46	A11	1.25 l dark blue	50.00	42.50
		Nos. 41-46 (6)	176.50	154.00
		Set, never hinged	850.00	

Intl. Juridical Congress, Rome, 1934.

Doves and Bell A12

Allegory of Church and Bible A13

St. John Bosco A14

St. Francis de Sales A15

1936, June 22

47	A12	5c blue green	1.50	1.50
48	A13	10c black	1.50	1.50
49	A14	25c yellow green	37.50	15.00
50	A12	50c rose violet	1.50	1.50
51	A13	75c rose red	47.50	*40.00*
52	A14	80c orange brn	5.00	*6.00*
53	A15	1.25 l dark blue	5.00	*6.00*
54	A15	5 l dark brown	3.00	*7.50*
		Nos. 47-54 (8)	102.50	79.00
		Set, never hinged	360.00	

World Exposition of the Catholic Press, 1936.

Crypt of St. Cecilia in Catacombs of St. Calixtus — A16

Basilica of Sts. Nereus and Achilleus in Catacombs of St. Domitilla — A17

1938, Oct. 12 ***Perf. 14***

55	A16	5c bister brown	.50	.50
56	A16	10c deep orange	.50	.50
57	A16	25c deep green	.60	.60
58	A17	75c deep rose	10.00	10.00
59	A17	80c violet	25.00	25.00
60	A17	1.25 l blue	30.00	30.00
		Nos. 55-60 (6)	66.60	66.60
		Set, never hinged	200.00	

Intl. Christian Archaeological Congress, Rome, 1938.

Interregnum Issue

Nos. 1-7 Overprinted in Black

1939, Feb. 20 ***Perf. 14***

61	A1	5c dk brn & pink	26.00	7.50
62	A1	10c dk grn & lt grn	1.00	.25
63	A1	20c violet & lilac	1.00	.25
64	A1	25c dk bl & lt bl	3.25	*5.00*
65	A1	30c indigo & yellow	1.00	.25
a.		Pair, one without ovpt.	*4,000.*	
66	A1	50c indigo & sal buff	1.00	.25
67	A1	75c brn car & gray	1.00	.25
		Nos. 61-67 (7)	34.25	13.75
		Set, never hinged	135.00	

Catalogue values for unused stamps in this section, from this point to the end of the section, are for Never Hinged items.

Coronation of Pope Pius XII — A18

1939, June 2 **Photo.**

68	A18	25c green	3.00	.40
69	A18	75c rose red	.70	.70
70	A18	80c violet	8.50	4.00
71	A18	1.25 l deep blue	.70	.70
		Nos. 68-71 (4)	12.90	5.80

Coronation of Pope Pius XII, Mar. 12, 1939.

Arms of Pope Pius XII — A19

Pope Pius XII
A20 A21

Wmk. 235

1940, Mar. 12 **Engr.** ***Perf. 14***

72	A19	5c dark carmine	.45	.25
a.		Imperf, pair	*1,000.*	
73	A20	1 l purple & blk	.45	.25
74	A21	1.25 l slate bl & blk	.45	.25
a.		Imperf., pair	*1,000.*	*1,500.*
75	A20	2 l dk brn & blk	2.00	2.00
76	A21	2.75 l dk rose vio & blk	2.50	2.50
		Nos. 72-76 (5)	5.85	5.25

See Nos. 91-98. For surcharges see Nos. 102-109.

A22

Picture of Jesus inscribed "I have Compassion on the Multitude."

1942, Sept. 1 **Photo.** **Unwmk.**

77	A22	25c dk blue green	.25	.25
78	A22	80c chestnut brown	.25	.25
79	A22	1.25 l deep blue	.25	.25
		Nos. 77-79 (3)	.75	.75

See Nos. 84-86, 99-101.

A23

Consecration of Archbishop Pacelli by Pope Benedict XV.

1942, Jan. 16

80	A23	25c myr grn & gray grn	.25	.25
81	A23	80c dk brn & yel grn	.25	.25
82	A23	1.25 l sapphire & vio bl	.25	.25
83	A23	5 l vio blk & gray blk	.35	.50
		Nos. 80-83 (4)	1.10	1.25

25th anniv. of the consecration of Msgr. Eugenio Pacelli (later Pope Pius XII) as Archbishop of Sardes.

Type of 1942
Inscribed MCMXLIII

1944, Jan. 31

84	A22	25c dk blue green	.25	.25
85	A22	80c chestnut brown	.25	.25
86	A22	1.25 l deep blue	.25	.25
		Nos. 84-86 (3)	.75	.75

Raphael Sanzio — A24

Designs: 80c, Antonio da Sangallo. 1.25 l, Carlo Maratti. 10 l, Antonio Canova.

1944, Nov. 21 **Wmk. 235** **Photo.**

87	A24	25c olive & green	.35	.25
88	A24	80c cl & rose vio	.60	.50
a.		Dbl. impression of center	*3,000.*	
89	A24	1.25 l bl vio & dp bl	.80	.40
a.		Imperf., pair	*1,900.*	*2,400.*
90	A24	10 l bister & ol brn	2.00	2.00
		Nos. 87-90 (4)	3.75	3.15

400th anniv. of the Pontifical Academy of the Virtuosi of the Pantheon.

Types of 1940

1945, Mar. 5 **Engr.** **Unwmk.**

91	A19	5c gray	.25	.25
a.		Imperf., pair	400.00	
92	A19	30c brown	.25	.25
a.		Imperf., pair	625.00	
93	A19	50c dark green	.25	.25
94	A21	1 l brown & blk	.25	.25
95	A21	1.50 l rose car & blk	.25	.25
a.		Imperf., pair	625.00	
96	A21	2.50 l dp ultra & blk	.25	.25
a.		Imperf, pair	625.00	
97	A20	5 l rose vio & blk	.30	*.25*
98	A20	20 l gray grn & blk	.40	*.40*
		Nos. 91-98,E5-E6 (10)	3.45	3.65

Nos. 91-96 exist in pairs imperf. between, some vertical, some horizontal. Value, each pair $500.

Type of 1942
Inscribed MCMXLIV
Wmk. 277

1945, Sept. 12 **Photo.** ***Perf. 14***

99	A22	1 l dk blue green	.25	.25
100	A22	3 l dk carmine	.25	.25
a.		Jesus image omitted	225.00	225.00
101	A22	5 l deep ultra	.25	.25
a.		Jesus image omitted	225.00	225.00
		Nos. 99-101 (3)	.75	.75

Nos. 99-101 exist in pairs imperf. between, both horizontal and vertical. Value, each pair $140.

Pairs imperf. horizontally exist of 3 lire (value $150) and 5 lire (value $200).

Nos. 91 to 98 Surcharged with New Values and Bars in Black or Blue

Two types of 25c on 30c:
I — Surcharge 16mm wide.
II — Surcharge 19mm wide.

Two types of 1 l on 50c:
I — Surcharge bars 5mm wide.
II — Bars 4mm wide.

1946, Jan. 9 **Unwmk.** ***Perf. 14***

102	A19	20c on 5c	.25	.25
a.		Inverted surcharge	1,200.	—
103	A19	25c on 30c (I)	.25	.25
a.		Type II	.40	.25
b.		Inverted surcharge (II)	1,200.	—
104	A19	1 l on 50c (I)	.25	.25
a.		Type II	20.00	6.00
105	A21	1.50 l on 1 l (Bl)	.25	.25
a.		Double surcharge	500.00	
106	A21	3 l on 1.50 l	.25	.25
107	A21	5 l on 2.50 l	.50	.30
a.		Double surcharge	500.00	
108	A20	10 l on 5 l	1.75	.60
109	A20	30 l on 20 l	4.25	2.00
		Nos. 102-109,E7-E8 (10)	18.75	9.65

Nos. 102, 105-109 exist in horizontal pairs, imperf. between. Value, each pair $150.

Vertical pairs imperf. between exist of Nos. 102, 106-107 (value, each $150) and of No. 104a (value $250).

Nos. 102-108 exist in pairs, one without surcharge. Value, Nos. 102-105, each pair $600.; Nos. 106-108, each pair $900.

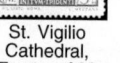

St. Vigilio Cathedral, Trent — A28

St. Angela Merici — A29

Designs: 50c, St. Anthony Zaccaria. 75c, St. Ignatius of Loyola. 1 l, St. Cajetan Thiene. 1.50 l, St. John Fisher. 2 l, Christoforo Cardinal Madruzzi. 2.50 l, Reginald Cardinal Pole. 3 l, Marello Cardinal Cervini. 4 l, Giovanni Cardinal del Monte. 5 l, Emperor Charles V. 10 l, Pope Paul III.

Perf. 14, 14x13½

1946, Feb. 21 **Photo.** **Unwmk.**

Centers in Dark Brown

110	A28	5c olive bister	.25	.25
111	A29	25c purple	.25	.25
112	A29	50c brown orange	.25	.25
113	A29	75c black	.25	.25
114	A29	1 l dk violet	.25	.25
115	A29	1.50 l red orange	.25	.25
116	A29	2 l yellow green	.25	.25
117	A29	2.50 l deep blue	.25	.25
118	A29	3 l brt carmine	.25	.25
119	A29	4 l ocher	.25	.25
120	A29	5 l brt ultra	.25	.25
121	A29	10 l dp rose car	.25	.25
a.		Imperf., pair	1,900.	
		Nos. 110-121,E9-E10 (14)	3.50	3.50

Council of Trent (1545-63), 400th anniv.

Vertical pairs imperf. between exist of Nos. 110-111, 113-119, 121 (value, each pair $500).

Horizontal pairs imperf. between exist of Nos. 113 and 117 (value $600 each) and No. 121 (value $675).

Horizontal pairs, imperf. vertically, exist of Nos. 119 (value $250) and No. 121 (value $275).

Vertical pairs, imperf. horizontally, exist of Nos. 110-114, 116-118 (value $75 each pair) and No. 121 (value $120).

Basilica of St. Agnes — A40

Basilica of the Holy Cross in Jerusalem — A41

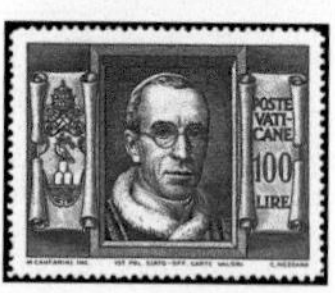

Pope Pius XII — A42

Basilicas: 3 l, St. Clement, 5 l, St. Prassede. 8 l, St. Mary in Cosmedin. 16 l, St. Sebastian. 25 l, St. Lawrence. 35 l, St. Paul. 40 l, St. Mary Major.

Perf. 14, 14x13½

1949, Mar. 7 **Photo.** **Wmk. 235**

122	A40	1 l dark brown	.25	.25
123	A40	3 l violet	.25	.25
124	A40	5 l deep orange	.25	.25
a.		Perf. 14x13½	18.50	7.50
125	A40	8 l dp blue grn	.25	.25

Perf. 14, 13½x14

126	A41	13 l dull green	4.00	4.00
127	A41	16 l dk olive brn	.35	.30
a.		Perf. 14	.50	.30
128	A41	25 l car rose	7.50	1.00
129	A41	35 l red violet	45.00	15.00
a.		Perf. 13½x14	47.50	15.00
130	A41	40 l blue	.35	.30
a.		Perf. 13½x14	.40	.30

Engr.
Perf. 14

131	A42	100 l sepia	4.50	4.50
		Nos. 122-131,E11-E12 (12)	137.70	65.60

All values come in two perfs except the 100 l.

Nos. 127, 128 exist imperf horizontally, Nos. 125-126 exist imperf vertically. Value in pairs $200 each pair.

Nos. 130-131 exist imperf. Value, No. 131 pair, $3,750.

For surcharge, see No. 154,

Jesus Giving St. Peter the Keys to Heaven A43

Cathedrals of St. Peter, St. Paul, St. John Lateran and St. Mary Major A44

Pope Boniface VIII Proclaiming Holy Year in 1300 — A45

Pope Pius XII in Ceremony of Opening the Holy Door — A46

Wmk. 277

1949, Dec 21 **Photo.** ***Perf. 14***

132	A43	5 l red brn & brn	.25	.25
133	A44	6 l ind & yel brn	.25	.25
134	A45	8 l ultra & dk grn	.85	.55
135	A46	10 l green & slate	.25	.25
136	A43	20 l dk grn & red brn	1.40	.30
137	A44	25 l sepia & dp blue	.75	.25
138	A45	30 l grnsh blk & rose lil	2.50	1.10
139	A46	60 l blk brn & brn rose	1.40	1.10
		Nos. 132-139 (8)	7.65	4.05

Holy Year, 1950.

Palatine Guard and Statue of St. Peter — A47

1950, Sept. 12

140	A47	25 l sepia	7.50	4.50
141	A47	35 l dark green	3.50	4.50
142	A47	55 l red brown	2.00	*4.50*
		Nos. 140-142 (3)	13.00	13.50

Centenary of the Palatine Guard.

Pope Pius XII Making Proclamation A48

Crowd at St. Peter's Basilica A49

1951, May 8 **Unwmk.**

143	A48	25 l chocolate	11.00	1.00
144	A49	55 l bright blue	4.75	14.50

Proclamation of the Roman Catholic dogma of the Assumption of the Virgin Mary, Nov. 1, 1950.

A50

Pope Pius X — A51

Perf. 14x13½

1951, June 3 Photo. Wmk. 235

Background of Medallion in Gold

145	A50	6 l purple	.25	.25
146	A50	10 l Prus green	.25	.25
147	A51	60 l blue	7.00	7.00
148	A51	115 l brown	22.50	22.50
		Nos. 145-148 (4)	30.00	30.00

Council of Chalcedon — A52

Pope Leo I Remonstrating with Attila the Hun — A53

1951, Oct. 31 Engr. *Perf. 14x13½*

149	A52	5 l dk gray green	.50	.40
a.		Pair, imperf. horiz.	*1,400.*	
150	A53	25 l red brown	3.50	3.00
a.		Horiz. pair, imperf. btwn.	*4,000.*	*4,000.*
151	A52	35 l carmine rose	8.00	6.00
152	A53	60 l deep blue	25.00	17.50
153	A52	100 l dark brown	47.50	37.50
		Nos. 149-153 (5)	84.50	64.40

Council of Chalcedon, 1500th anniv.

No. 126 Surcharged with New Value and Bars in Carmine

1952, Mar. 15 ***Perf. 14***

154	A41	12 l on 13 l dull grn	2.00	1.35
a.		Perf. 13½x14	2.00	1.00
b.		Pair, one without surcharge	1,250.	1,250.
c.		Surcharge inverted	*5,000.*	
d.		As "a," surcharge double	2,000.	

Roman States Stamp and Stagecoach A54

1952, June 9 Engr. *Perf. 13*

155	A54	50 l sep & dp bl, *cr*	5.00	5.00
a.		Souvenir sheet	160.00	160.00

1st stamp of the Papal States, cent.

#155a contains 4 stamps similar to #155, with papal insignia and inscription in purple. Singles from the souvenir sheet differ slightly from #155. The colors are closer to black and blue, and the cream tone of the paper is visible on the back.

No. 155a exists imperforate.

St. Maria Goretti — A55

Perf. 13½x14

1953, Feb. 12 Photo. Wmk. 235

156	A55	15 l dp brown & vio	4.75	2.50
157	A55	35 l dp rose & brn	3.50	2.50

Martyrdom of St. Maria Goretti, 50th anniv.

St. Peter — A56

Designs: 5 l, Pius XII and Roman sepulcher. 10 l, St. Peter and Tomb of the Apostle. 12 l, Sylvester I and Constantine Basilica. 20 l, Julius II and Bramante's plans. 25 l, Paul III and the Apse. 35 l, Sixtus V and dome. 45 l, Paul V and facade. 60 l, Urban VIII and the canopy. 65 l, Alexander VII and colonnade. 100 l, Pius VI and the sacristy.

Perf. 13½x13, 14

1953, Apr. 23 Engr.

158	A56	3 l dk red brn & blk	.25	.25
159	A56	5 l slate & blk	.25	.25
160	A56	10 l dk green & blk	.25	.25
161	A56	12 l chestnut & blk	.25	.25
162	A56	20 l violet & blk	.25	.25
163	A56	25 l dk brown & blk	.25	.25
164	A56	35 l dk carmine & blk	.25	.25
165	A56	45 l olive brn & blk	.25	.25
166	A56	60 l dk blue & blk	.25	.25
167	A56	65 l car rose & blk	.25	.25
168	A56	100 l rose vio & blk	.25	.25
		Nos. 158-168,E13-E14 (13)	3.35	3.25

Nos. 158, 163, 165, and 166 exist imperf. Value $900 each pair.

St. Clare of Assisi — A57

Unwmk.

1953, Aug. 12 Photo. *Perf. 13*

169	A57	25 l aqua, yel brn & vio brn	2.00	2.00
170	A57	35 l brn red, yel brn & vio brn	20.00	15.00

Death of St. Clare of Assisi, 700th anniv.

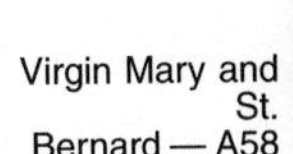
Virgin Mary and St. Bernard — A58

1953, Nov. 10

171	A58	20 l ol grn & dk vio brn	.75	.75
172	A58	60 l brt bl & ol grn	7.50	5.50

Death of St. Bernard of Clairvaux, 800th anniv.

Peter Lombard Medal — A59

1953, Dec. 29

173	A59	100 l lil rose, bl, dk grn & yel	37.50	27.50

Peter Lombard, Bishop of Paris 1159.

Pope Pius XI and Vatican City — A60

1954, Feb. 12 Wmk. 235

174	A60	25 l bl, red brn & cr	1.25	1.00
175	A60	60 l yel brn & dp bl	3.50	3.00

Signing of the Lateran Pacts, 25th anniv.

Pope Pius IX — A61

Portraits: (At left) - 6 l, 20 l, Pope Pius IX. (At right) — 4 l, 12 l, 35 l, Pope Pius XII.

1954, May 26 Engr. *Perf. 13*

176	A61	3 l violet	.25	.25
177	A61	4 l carmine	.25	.25
178	A61	6 l plum	.25	.25
179	A61	12 l blue green	1.00	.25
180	A61	20 l red brown	.90	.85
181	A61	35 l ultra	2.00	2.00
		Nos. 176-181 (6)	4.65	3.85

Marian Year; centenary of the dogma of the Immaculate Conception.

St. Pius X — A62

1954, May 29 Photo.

Colors (except background): Yellow and Plum

182	A62	10 l dark brown	.30	.25
183	A62	25 l violet	2.75	1.50
184	A62	35 l dk slate gray	4.75	3.25
		Nos. 182-184 (3)	7.80	5.00

Canonization of Pope Pius X, May 20, 1954.

#182-184 exist imperf. Value, each pair $800.

Basilica of St. Francis of Assisi — A63

1954, Oct. 1 Photo. *Perf. 14*

185	A63	20 l dk vio gray & cr	2.00	1.60
186	A63	35 l dk brown & cream	1.50	1.50

Consecration of the Basilica of St. Francis of Assisi, 200th anniv.

St. Augustine — A64

1954, Nov. 13

187	A64	35 l blue green	1.25	.90
188	A64	50 l redsh brown	1.90	1.75

1600th birth anniv. of St. Augustine.

Madonna of the Gate of Dawn, Vilnius — A65

1954, Dec. 7

189	A65	20 l pink & multi	1.60	1.15
190	A65	35 l blue & multi	10.00	8.50
191	A65	60 l multicolored	15.00	13.25
		Nos. 189-191 (3)	26.60	22.90

Issued to mark the end of the Marian Year.

St. Boniface and Fulda Abbey — A66

1955, Apr. 28 Engr. *Perf. 13*

192	A66	10 l grnsh gray	.25	.25
193	A66	35 l violet	.60	.60
a.		Imperf., pair	550.00	
194	A66	60 l brt blue green	.75	.70
		Nos. 192-194 (3)	1.60	1.55

1200th death anniv. of St. Boniface.

No. 193 also exists imperf horizontally (value $325) and vertically (value $250).

Pope Sixtus II and St. Lawrence — A67

Wmk. 235

1955, June 27 Photo. *Perf. 14*

195	A67	50 l carmine	4.25	2.00
196	A67	100 l deep blue	2.75	2.00

Fra Angelico (1387-1455), painter. Design is from a Fra Angelico fresco.

No. 196 exists imperf. Value, pair $400.

Pope Nicholas V — A68

1955, Nov. 28

197	A68	20 l grnsh bl & ol brn	.30	.25
198	A68	35 l rose car & ol brn	.40	.30
199	A68	60 l yel grn & ol brn	.75	.40
		Nos. 197-199 (3)	1.45	.95

Death of Pope Nicholas V, 500th anniv.

St. Bartholomew and Church of Grottaferrata — A69

1955, Dec. 29

200	A69	10 l brown & gray	.25	.25
201	A69	25 l car rose & gray	.50	.30
202	A69	100 l dk green & gray	2.00	1.50
		Nos. 200-202 (3)	2.75	2.05

900th death anniv. of St. Bartholomew, abbot of Grottaferrata.

Capt. Gaspar Roust — A70

6 l, 50 l, Guardsman. 10 l, 60 l, Two drummers.

1956, Apr. 27 Engr. *Perf. 13*

No.	Type	Value	Color	Unused	Used
203	A70	4 l	dk carmine rose	.25	.25
204	A70	6 l	deep orange	.25	.25
205	A70	10 l	deep ultra	.25	.25
206	A70	35 l	brown	.55	.55
207	A70	50 l	violet	.75	.60
208	A70	60 l	blue green	.85	.65
			Nos. 203-208 (6)	2.90	2.55

450th anniv. of the Swiss Papal Guard.

St. Rita of Cascia — A71

1956, May 19 Photo. *Perf. 14*

No.	Type	Value	Color	Unused	Used
209	A71	10 l	gray green	.25	.25
210	A71	25 l	olive brown	.55	.55
211	A71	35 l	ultra	.35	.35
			Nos. 209-211 (3)	1.15	1.15

500th death anniv. of St. Rita of Cascia.

Pope Paul III Confirming Society of Jesus — A72

1956, July 31 Engr. *Perf. 13*

No.	Type	Value	Color	Unused	Used
212	A72	35 l	dk red brown	.50	.50
213	A72	60 l	blue gray	.95	.95

400th death anniv. of St. Ignatius of Loyola, founder of the Society of Jesus.

St. John of Capistrano — A73

1956, Oct. 30 *Perf. 14*

No.	Type	Value	Color	Unused	Used
214	A73	25 l	slate blk & grn	2.00	2.00
215	A73	35 l	dk brn car & brn	.75	.75

5th cent. of the death of St. John of Capistrano, leader in the war against the Turks.

Black Madonna of Czestochowa — A74

1956, Dec. 20

No.	Type	Value	Color	Unused	Used
216	A74	35 l	dk blue & blk	.25	.25
217	A74	60 l	green & ultra	.45	.45
218	A74	100 l	brn & dk car rose	.90	.80
			Nos. 216-218 (3)	1.60	1.50

300th anniv. of the proclamation of the Madonna of Czestochowa as "Queen of Poland."

St. Domenico Savio — A75

6 l, 60 l, Sts. Domenico Savio and John Bosco.

1957, Mar. 21 Wmk. 235 *Perf. 13½*

No.	Type	Value	Color	Unused	Used
219	A75	4 l	red brown	.25	.25
220	A75	6 l	brt carmine	.25	.25
221	A75	25 l	green	.25	.25
222	A75	60 l	ultra	1.20	.95
			Nos. 219-222 (4)	1.95	1.70

Death cent. of St. Domenico Savio.

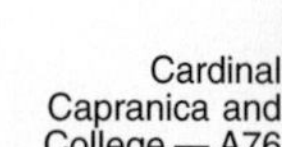

Cardinal Capranica and College — A76

Design: 10 l, 100 l, Pope Pius XII.

1957, June 27 Engr. *Perf. 13*

No.	Type	Value	Color	Unused	Used
223	A76	5 l	dk carmine rose	.25	.25
224	A76	10 l	pale brown	.25	.25
225	A76	35 l	grnsh black	.25	.25
226	A76	100 l	ultra	.50	.50
			Nos. 223-226 (4)	1.25	1.25

500th anniv. of Capranica College, oldest seminary in the world.

Pontifical Academy of Science — A77

1957, Oct. 9 Photo. *Perf. 14*

No.	Type	Value	Color	Unused	Used
227	A77	35 l	dk blue & green	.65	.65
228	A77	60 l	brown & ultra	.65	.65

Pontifical Academy of Science, 20th anniv.

Mariazell — A78

High Altar — A79

1957, Nov. 14 Engr. *Perf. 13½*

No.	Type	Value	Color	Unused	Used
229	A78	5 l	green	.25	.25
230	A79	15 l	slate	.25	.25
231	A78	60 l	ultra	.70	.25
232	A79	100 l	violet	.90	.85
			Nos. 229-232 (4)	2.10	1.60

Mariazell shrine, Austria, 800th anniv.

Apparition of the Virgin Mary — A80

Designs: 10 l, 35 l, Sick man and basilica. 15 l, 100 l, St. Bernadette.

Perf. 13x14

1958, Feb. 21 Wmk. 235

No.	Type	Value	Color	Unused	Used
233	A80	5 l	dark blue	.25	.25
234	A80	10 l	blue green	.25	.25
235	A80	15 l	reddish brown	.25	.25
236	A80	25 l	rose carmine	.25	.25
237	A80	35 l	gray brown	.25	.25
238	A80	100 l	violet	.25	.25
			Nos. 233-238 (6)	1.50	1.50

Centenary of apparition of the Virgin Mary at Lourdes and the establishment of the shrine.

Pope Pius XII — A81

60 l, 100 l, Vatican pavilion at Brussels fair.

1958, June 19 Engr. *Perf. 13*

No.	Type	Value	Color	Unused	Used
239	A81	35 l	claret	.30	.25

Perf. 13x14

No.	Type	Value	Color	Unused	Used
240	A81	60 l	fawn	.55	.55
241	A81	100 l	violet	1.75	1.25
242	A81	300 l	ultra	1.40	1.10
a.			Souvenir sheet of 4, #239-242	20.00	20.00
			Nos. 239-242 (4)	4.00	3.15

Universal and Intl. Exposition, Brussels.

Statue of Pope Clement XIII by Canova — A82

Statues: 10 l, Clement XIV. 35 l, Pius VI. 100 l, Pius VII.

1958, July 2 *Perf. 14*

No.	Type	Value	Color	Unused	Used
243	A82	5 l	brown	.25	.25
244	A82	10 l	carmine rose	.25	.25
245	A82	35 l	blue gray	.25	.25
246	A82	100 l	dark blue	.85	.85
			Nos. 243-246 (4)	1.60	1.60

Antonio Canova (1757-1822), sculptor.

Interregnum Issue

St. Peter's Keys and Papal Chamberlain's Insignia — A83

Wmk. 235

1958, Oct. 21 Photo. *Perf. 14*

No.	Type	Value	Color	Unused	Used
247	A83	15 l	brn blk, *yel*	1.40	1.40
248	A83	25 l	brown black	.25	.25
249	A83	60 l	brn blk, *pale vio*	.25	.25
			Nos. 247-249 (3)	1.90	1.90

Pope John XXIII — A84

Design: 35 l, 100 l, Coat of Arms.

1959, Apr. 2 Photo. *Perf. 14*

No.	Type	Value	Color	Unused	Used
250	A84	25 l	car rose, bl & buff	.25	.25
251	A84	35 l	multicolored	.25	.25
252	A84	60 l	rose car, bl & ocher	.25	.25
253	A84	100 l	multicolored	.25	.25
			Nos. 250-253 (4)	1.00	1.00

Coronation of Pope John XXIII, 11/4/58.

Pope Pius XI — A85

1959, May 25 Wmk. 235 *Perf. 14*

No.	Type	Value	Color	Unused	Used
254	A85	30 l	brown	.25	.25
255	A85	100 l	violet blue	.25	.25

Lateran Pacts, 30th anniversary.

St. Lawrence — A86

Portraits of Saints: 25 l, Pope Sixtus II. 50 l, Agapitus. 60 l, Filicissimus. 100 l, Cyprianus. 300 l, Fructuosus.

1959, May 25

No.	Type	Value	Color	Unused	Used
256	A86	15 l	red, brn & yel	.25	.25
257	A86	25 l	lilac, brn & yel	.25	.25
258	A86	50 l	Prus bl, blk & yel	.25	.25
259	A86	60 l	ol grn, brn & bis	.25	.25
260	A86	100 l	maroon, brn & yel	.25	.25
261	A86	300 l	bis brn & dk brn	.50	.35
			Nos. 256-261 (6)	1.75	1.60

Martyrs of Emperor Valerian's persecutions.

Radio Tower and Archangel Gabriel — A87

1959, Oct. 27 Photo. *Perf. 14*

No.	Type	Value	Color	Unused	Used
262	A87	25 l	rose, org yel & dk brn	.25	.25
263	A87	60 l	multicolored	.25	.25

2nd anniv. of the papal radio station, St. Maria di Galeria.

St. Casimir, Tower of Gedimines and Cathedral, Vilnius — A88

1959, Dec. 14 Engr. Wmk. 235

No.	Type	Value	Color	Unused	Used
264	A88	50 l	brown	.25	.25
265	A88	100 l	dull green	.25	.25

500th anniv. (in 1958) of the birth of St. Casimir, patron saint of Lithuania.

Nativity by Raphael — A89

1959, Dec. 14 Engr. *Perf. 13½*

No.	Type	Value	Color	Unused	Used
266	A89	15 l	dark gray	.25	.25
267	A89	25 l	magenta	.25	.25
268	A89	60 l	bright ultra	.25	.25
			Nos. 266-268 (3)	.75	.75

St. Antoninus — A90

25 l, 110 l, St. Antoninus preaching.

Perf. 13x14

1960, Feb. 29 Wmk. 235

No.	Type	Value	Color	Unused	Used
269	A90	15 l	ultra	.25	.25
270	A90	25 l	turquoise	.25	.25
271	A90	60 l	brown	.30	.30
272	A90	110 l	rose claret	.60	.60
			Nos. 269-272 (4)	1.40	1.40

5th cent. of death of St. Antoninus, bishop of Florence.

Transept of Lateran Basilica — A91

1960, Feb. 29 Photo. *Perf. 14*

No.	Type	Value	Color	Unused	Used
273	A91	15 l	brown	.25	.25
274	A91	60 l	black	.25	.25

Roman Diocesan Synod, February, 1960.

Flight into Egypt by Fra Angelico — A92

Designs: 10 l, 100 l, St. Peter Giving Alms to the Poor, by Masaccio. 25 l, 300 l, Madonna of Mercy, by Piero della Francesca.

1960, Apr. 7 Wmk. 235 *Perf. 14*

No.	Type	Value	Color	Unused	Used
275	A92	5 l	green	.25	.25
276	A92	10 l	gray brown	.25	.25
277	A92	25 l	deep carmine	.25	.25
278	A92	60 l	lilac	.35	.35

279 A92 100 l ultra 1.40 1.40
280 A92 300 l Prus green 1.00 1.00
Nos. 275-280 (6) 3.50 3.50

World Refugee Year, 7/1/59-6/30/60.

Cardinal Sarto's Departure from Venice — A93

35 l, Pope John XXIII praying at coffin of Pope Pius X. 60 l, Body of Pope Pius X returning to Venice.

1960, Apr. 11 Engr. *Perf. 13½*

281 A93 15 l brown .25 .25
282 A93 35 l rose carmine .75 .75
283 A93 60 l Prus green 1.75 1.75
Nos. 281-283 (3) 2.75 2.75

Return of the body of Pope Pius X to Venice.

Feeding the Hungry — A94

"Acts of Mercy," by Della Robbia: 10 l, Giving drink to the thirsty. 15 l, Clothing the naked. 20 l, Sheltering the homeless. 30 l, Visiting the sick. 35 l, Visiting prisoners. 40 l, Burying the dead. 70 l, Pope John XXIII.

1960, Nov. 8 Photo. *Perf. 14*
Centers in Brown

284 A94 5 l red brown .25 .25
285 A94 10 l green .25 .25
286 A94 15 l slate .25 .25
287 A94 20 l rose carmine .25 .25
288 A94 30 l violet blue .25 .25
289 A94 35 l violet brown .25 .25
290 A94 40 l red orange .25 .25
291 A94 70 l ocher .25 .25
Nos. 284-291,E15-E16 (10) 2.50 2.50

Holy Family by Gerard van Honthorst — A95

1960, Dec. 6 Wmk. 235 *Perf. 14*

292 A95 10 l slate grn & slate blk .25 .25
293 A95 15 l sepia & ol blk .25 .25
294 A95 70 l grnsh bl & dp bl .25 .25
Nos. 292-294 (3) .75 .75

St. Vincent de Paul — A96

Designs: 70 l, St. Louisa de Marillac. 100 l, St. Louisa and St. Vincent.

1960, Dec. 6

295 A96 40 l dull violet .25 .25
296 A96 70 l dark gray .30 .30
297 A96 100 l dk red brown .60 .40
Nos. 295-297 (3) 1.15 .95

Death of St. Vincent de Paul, 300th anniv.

St. Meinrad — A97

Designs: 40 l, Statue of Our Lady of Einsiedeln. 100 l, Einsiedeln monastery, horiz.

1961, Feb. 28 *Perf. 14*

298 A97 30 l dark gray .50 .40
299 A97 40 l lt violet .90 .75
300 A97 100 l brown 1.75 1.50
Nos. 298-300 (3) 3.15 2.65

Death of St. Meinrad, 1,100th anniv.; Einsiedeln Abbey, Switzerland.

Pope Leo the Great Defying Attila — A98

Wmk. 235
1961, Apr. 6 Photo. *Perf. 14*

301 A98 15 l rose brown .25 .25
302 A98 70 l Prus green .60 .60
303 A98 300 l brown black 1.75 1.75
Nos. 301-303 (3) 2.60 2.60

Death of Pope Leo the Great (St. Leo Magnus), 1,500th anniv. The design is from a marble bas-relief in St. Peter's Basilica.

St. Paul Arriving in Rome, 61 A.D. — A99

10 l, 30 l, Map showing St. Paul's journey to Rome. 20 l, 200 l, First Basilica of St. Paul, Rome.

1961, June 13 Wmk. 235 *Perf. 14*

304 A99 10 l Prus green .25 .25
305 A99 15 l dl red brn & gray .25 .25
306 A99 20 l red org & gray .25 .25
307 A99 30 l blue .25 .25
308 A99 75 l org brn & gray .30 .30
309 A99 200 l blue & gray 1.40 1.00
Nos. 304-309 (6) 2.70 2.30

Arrival of St. Paul in Rome, 1,900th anniv.

1861 and 1961 Mastheads A100

70 l, Editorial offices. 250 l, Rotary press.

1961, July 4

310 A100 40 l red brn & blk .25 .25
311 A100 70 l blue & blk .60 .60
312 A100 250 l yellow & blk 2.00 2.00
Nos. 310-312 (3) 2.85 2.85

Centenary of L'Osservatore Romano, Vatican's newspaper.

St. Patrick's Purgatory, Lough Derg — A101

10 l, 40 l, St. Patrick, marble sculpture.

Wmk. 235
1961, Oct. 6 Photo. *Perf. 14*

313 A101 10 l buff & slate grn .25 .25
314 A101 15 l blue & sepia .25 .25
315 A101 40 l yellow & bl grn .25 .25
316 A101 150 l Prus bl & red brn .45 .30
Nos. 313-316 (4) 1.20 1.05

Death of St. Patrick, 1,500th anniv.

Arms of Roncalli Family — A102

Designs: 25 l, Church at Sotto il Monte. 30 l, Santa Maria in Monte Santo, Rome. 40 l, Church of San Carlo al Corso, Rome (erroneously inscribed with name of Basilica of Sts. Ambrosius and Charles, Milan). 70 l, Altar, St. Peter's, Rome. 115 l, Pope John XXIII.

1961, Nov. 25

317 A102 10 l gray & red brn .25 .25
318 A102 25 l ol bis & sl grn .25 .25
319 A102 30 l vio bl & pale pur .25 .25
320 A102 40 l lilac & dk blue .25 .25
321 A102 70 l gray grn & org brn .25 .25
322 A102 115 l choc & slate .25 .25
Nos. 317-322 (6) 1.50 1.50

80th birthday of Pope John XXIII.

"The Adoration" by Lucas Chen — A103

1961, Nov. 25 Center Multicolored

323 A103 15 l bluish green .25 .25
324 A103 40 l gray .25 .25
325 A103 70 l pale lilac .25 .25
Nos. 323-325 (3) .75 .75

Christmas.

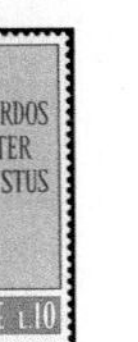

Draining of Pontine Marshes Medal by Pope Sixtus V, 1588 — A104

40 l, 300 l, Map of Pontine Marshes showing 18th cent. drainage under Pope Pius VI.

1962, Apr. 6 Wmk. 235 *Perf. 14*

326 A104 15 l dark violet .25 .25
327 A104 40 l rose carmine .25 .25
328 A104 70 l brown .25 .25
329 A104 300 l dull green .40 .40
Nos. 326-329 (4) 1.15 1.15

WHO drive to eradicate malaria.

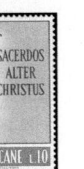

"The Good Shepherd" A105

Wheatfield (Luke 10:2) A106

1962, June 2 Photo.

330 A105 10 l lilac & black .25 .25
331 A106 15 l blue & ocher .25 .25
332 A105 70 l lt green & blk .25 .30
333 A106 115 l fawn & ocher 1.40 1.00
334 A105 200 l brown & black 1.60 1.25
Nos. 330-334 (5) 3.75 3.05

Issued to honor the priesthood and to stress its importance as a vocation.

"The Good Shepherd" is a fourth-century statue in the Lateran Museum, Rome.

St. Catherine of Siena — A107

1962, June 12

335 A107 15 l brown .25 .25
336 A107 60 l brt violet .30 .25
337 A107 100 l blue .45 .40
Nos. 335-337 (3) 1.00 .90

Canonization of St. Catherine of Siena, 500th anniv. The portrait is from a fresco by Il Sodoma, Church of St. Dominic, Siena.

Paulina M. Jaricot — A108

1962, July 5 Portrait Multicolored

338 A108 10 l pale violet .25 .25
339 A108 50 l dull green .25 .25
340 A108 150 l gray .45 .40
Nos. 338-340 (3) .95 .90

Paulina M. Jaricot (1799-1862), founder of the Society for the Propagation of the Faith.

Sts. Peter and Paul — A109

Design: 40 l, 100 l, "The Invincible Cross," relief from sarcophagus.

Wmk. 235
1962, Sept. 25 Photo. *Perf. 14*

341 A109 20 l lilac & brown .25 .25
342 A109 40 l lt brown & blk .25 .25
343 A109 70 l bluish grn & brn .25 .25
344 A109 100 l sal pink & blk .25 .25
Nos. 341-344 (4) 1.00 1.00

6th Congress of Christian Archeology, Ravenna, Sept. 23-28.

"Faith" by Raphael — A110

Designs: 10 l, "Hope." 15 l, "Charity." 25 l, Arms of Pope John XXIII and emblems of the Four Evangelists. 30 l, Ecumenical Congress meeting in St. Peter's. 40 l, Pope John XXIII on throne. 60 l, Statue of St. Peter. 115 l, The Holy Ghost as a dove (symbolic design).

Photo.; Center Engr. on 30 l
1962, Oct. 30

345 A110 5 l brt blue & blk .25 .25
346 A110 10 l green & blk .25 .25
347 A110 15 l ver & sepia .25 .25
348 A110 25 l ver & slate .25 .25
349 A110 30 l lilac & blk .25 .25
350 A110 40 l dk carmine & blk .25 .25
351 A110 60 l dk grn & dp org .25 .25
352 A110 115 l crimson .25 .25
Nos. 345-352 (8) 2.00 2.00

Vatican II, the 21st Ecumenical Council of the Roman Catholic Church, which opened Oct. 11, 1962. Nos. 345-347 show "the Three Theological Virtues" by Raphael.

Nativity Scene — A111

Set in India, following a design by Marcus Toano.

1962, Dec. 4 Center Multicolored

353 A111 10 l gray .25 .25
354 A111 15 l brown .25 .25
355 A111 90 l dull green .75 .25
Nos. 353-355 (3) 1.25 .75

Miracle of the Loaves and Fishes by Murillo — A112

Design: 40 l, 200 l, "The Miraculous Catch of Fishes" by Raphael.

Wmk. 235

1963, Mar. 21 Photo. *Perf. 14*

356 A112 15 l brn & dk brn .25 .25
357 A112 40 l rose red & blk .25 .25
358 A112 100 l blue & dk brn .25 .25
359 A112 200 l bl grn & blk .25 .25
Nos. 356-359 (4) 1.00 1.00

FAO "Freedom from Hunger" campaign.

Pope John XXIII — A113

1963, May 8

360 A113 15 l red brown .25 .25
361 A113 160 l black .25 .25

Awarding of the Balzan Peace Prize to Pope John XXIII.

Interregnum Issue

Keys of St. Peter and Papal Chamberlain's Insignia — A114

1963, June 15 Wmk. 235 *Perf. 14*

362 A114 10 l dk brown .25 .25
363 A114 40 l dk brown, *yel* .25 .25
364 A114 100 l dk brown, *vio* .25 .25
Nos. 362-364 (3) .75 .75

Pope Paul VI — A115

Design: 40 l, 200 l, Arms of Pope Paul VI.

1963, Oct. 16 Engr. *Perf. 13x14*

365 A115 15 l black .25 .25
366 A115 40 l carmine .25 .25
367 A115 115 l redsh brown .25 .25
368 A115 200 l slate blue .25 .25
Nos. 365-368 (4) 1.00 1.00

Coronation of Pope Paul VI, June 30, 1963.

St. Cyril — A116

Designs: 70 l, Map of Hungary, Moravia and Poland, 16th century. 150 l, St. Methodius.

Wmk. 235

1963, Nov. 22 Photo. *Perf. 14*

369 A116 30 l violet black .25 .25
370 A116 70 l brown .25 .25
371 A116 150 l rose claret .25 .25
Nos. 369-371 (3) .75 .75

1100th anniv. of the beginning of missionary work among the Slavs by Sts. Cyril and Methodius. The pictures of the saints are from 16th century frescoes in St. Clement's Basilica, Rome.

African Nativity Scene — A117

1963, Nov. 22

372 A117 10 l brn & pale brn .25 .25
373 A117 40 l ultra & brown .25 .25
374 A117 100 l gray olive & brn .25 .25
Nos. 372-374 (3) .75 .75

The design is after a sculpture by the Burundi artist Andreas Bukuru.

Church of the Holy Sepulcher, Jerusalem — A118

15 l, Pope Paul VI. 25 l, Nativity Church, Bethlehem. 160 l, Well of the Virgin Mary, Nazareth.

1964, Jan. 4 Wmk. 235 *Perf. 14*

375 A118 15 l black .25 .25
376 A118 25 l rose brown .25 .25
377 A118 70 l brown .25 .25
378 A118 160 l ultra .25 .25
Nos. 375-378 (4) 1.00 1.00

Visit of Pope Paul VI to the Holy Land, Jan. 4-6.

St. Peter from Coptic Church at Wadi-es-Sebua, Sudan — A119

Design: 20 l, 200 l, Trajan's Kiosk, Philae.

1964, Mar. 10 Photo.

379 A119 10 l ultra & red brn .25 .25
380 A119 20 l multicolored .25 .25
381 A119 70 l gray & red brn .25 .25
382 A119 200 l gray & multi .25 .25
Nos. 379-382 (4) 1.00 1.00

UNESCO world campaign to save historic monuments in Nubia.

Pietà by Michelangelo — A120

Designs: 15 l, 100 l, Pope Paul VI. 250 l, Head of Mary from Pietà.

1964, Apr. 22 Wmk. 235 *Perf. 14*

383 A120 15 l violet blue .25 .25
384 A120 50 l dark brown .25 .25
385 A120 100 l slate blue .25 .25
386 A120 250 l chestnut .25 .25
Nos. 383-386 (4) 1.00 1.00

New York World's Fair, 1964-65.

Isaiah by Michelangelo — A121

10 l, Michelangelo, after Jacopino del Conte. 25 l, Isaiah. 30 l, Delphie Sibyl. 40 l, Jeremiah. 150 l, Joel.

1964, June 16 Engr. *Perf. 13½x14*

387 A121 10 l multicolored .25 .25
388 A121 25 l multicolored .25 .25
389 A121 30 l multicolored .25 .25
390 A121 40 l multicolored .25 .25
391 A121 150 l multicolored .25 .25
Nos. 387-391 (5) 1.25 1.25

Michelangelo Buonarroti (1475-1564). Designs are from the Sistine Chapel.

The Good Samaritan A122

Perf. 14x13½

1964, Sept. 22 Engr. Wmk. 235

392 A122 10 l red brown & red .25 .25
393 A122 30 l dark blue & red .25 .25
394 A122 300 l gray & red .25 .25
Nos. 392-394 (3) .75 .75

Cent. (in 1963) of the founding of the Intl. Red Cross.

Nos. 392 and 394 exist with the red cross omitted.

Birthplace of Cardinal Nicolaus Cusanus — A123

Design: 200 l, Cardinal's sepulcher, Church of San Pietro in Vincoli, Rome.

1964, Nov. 16 Wmk. 235

395 A123 40 l dull blue grn .25 .25
396 A123 200 l rose red .25 .25

German cardinal Nicolaus Cusanus (Nicolaus Krebs of Kues) (1401-1464).

Japanese Nativity Scene by Kimiko Koseki — A124

1964, Nov. 16 Photo. *Perf. 14*

397 A124 10 l multicolored .25 .25
a. Yellow omitted
398 A124 15 l black & multi .25 .25
399 A124 135 l bister & multi .25 .25
Nos. 397-399 (3) .75 .75

Pope Paul VI and Map of India and Southeast Asia — A125

Designs: 15 l, Pope Paul VI at prayer. 25 l, Eucharistic Congress altar, Bombay, horiz. 60 l, Gateway of India, Bombay, horiz.

1964, Dec. 2

400 A125 15 l dull violet .25 .25
401 A125 25 l green .25 .25
402 A125 60 l brown .25 .25
403 A125 200 l dull violet .25 .25
Nos. 400-403 (4) 1.00 1.00

Trip of Pope Paul VI to India, Dec. 2-5, 1964.

Uganda Martyrs — A126

Various groups of Martyrs of Uganda.

Perf. 13½x14

1965, Mar. 16 Engr. Wmk. 235

404 A126 15 l Prus green .25 .25
405 A126 20 l brown .25 .25
406 A126 30 l ultra .25 .25
407 A126 75 l black .25 .25
408 A126 100 l rose red .25 .25
409 A126 160 l violet .25 .25
Nos. 404-409 (6) 1.50 1.50

Canonization of 22 African martyrs, 10/18/64.

Dante by Raphael — A127

Designs: 40 l, Dante and the 3 beasts at entrance to the Inferno. 70 l, Dante and Virgil at entrance to Purgatory. 200 l, Dante and Beatrice in Paradise. (40 l, 70 l, 200 l, by Botticelli.)

Photogravure and Engraved

1965, May 18 *Perf. 13½x14*

410 A127 10 l bis brn & dk brn .25 .25
411 A127 40 l rose & dk brn .25 .25
412 A127 70 l lt grn & dk brn .25 .25
413 A127 200 l pale bl & dk brn .25 .25
Nos. 410-413 (4) 1.00 1.00

Birth of Dante Alighieri, 700th anniv.

St. Benedict by Perugino — A128

Design: 300 l, View of Monte Cassino.

1965, July 2 Photo. *Perf. 14*

414 A128 40 l brown .25 .25
415 A128 300 l dark green .25 .25

Conferring of the title Patron Saint of Europe upon St. Benedict by Pope Paul VI; restoring of the Abbey of Monte Cassino.

Pope Paul VI Addressing UN Assembly — A129

30 l, 150 l, UN Headquarters and olive branch.

1965, Oct. 4 Wmk. 235 *Perf. 14*

416 A129 20 l brown .25 .25
417 A129 30 l sapphire .25 .25
418 A129 150 l olive green .25 .25
419 A129 300 l rose violet .25 .25
Nos. 416-419 (4) 1.00 1.00

Visit of Pope Paul VI to the UN, NYC, Oct. 4.

Peruvian Nativity Scene — A130

1965, Nov. 25 Engr. *Perf. 13½x14*

420 A130 20 l rose claret .25 .25
421 A130 40 l red brown .25 .25
422 A130 200 l gray green .25 .25
Nos. 420-422 (3) .75 .75

Cartographer — A131

Designs: 5 l, Pope Paul VI. 10 l, Organist. 20 l, Painter. 30 l, Sculptor. 40 l, Bricklayer. 55 l, Carpenter. 75 l, Plowing farmer. 90 l, Blacksmith. 130 l, Scholar.

1966, Mar. 8 Photo. *Perf. 14*

423 A131 5 l sepia .25 .25
424 A131 10 l violet .25 .25
425 A131 15 l brown .25 .25
426 A131 20 l gray green .25 .25
427 A131 30 l brown red .25 .25
428 A131 40 l Prus green .25 .25
429 A131 55 l dark blue .25 .25
430 A131 75 l dk rose brown .25 .25
431 A131 90 l carmine rose .25 .25
432 A131 130 l black .25 .25
Nos. 423-432,E17-E18 (12) 3.00 3.00

The Pope's portrait is from a bas-relief by Enrico Manfrini; the arts and crafts designs are bas-reliefs by Mario Rudelli from the chair in the Pope's private chapel.

King Mieszko I and Queen Dabrowka — A132

Designs: 25 l, St. Adalbert (Wojciech) and Cathedrals of Wroclaw and Gniezno. 40 l, St. Stanislas, Skalka Church, Wawel Cathedral and Castle, Cracow. 50 l, Queen Jadwiga (Hedwig), Holy Gate with Our Lady of Mercy, Vilnius, and Jagellon University Library, Cracow. 150 l, Black Madonna of Czestochowa, cloister and church of Bright Mountain, Czestochowa, and St. John's Cathedral, Warsaw. 220 l, Pope Paul VI blessing students and farmers.

Perf. 14x13½

1966, May 3 Engr. Wmk. 235

433 A132	15 l	black	.25	.25
434 A132	25 l	violet	.25	.25
435 A132	40 l	brick red	.25	.25
436 A132	50 l	claret	.25	.25
437 A132	150 l	slate blue	.25	.25
438 A132	220 l	brown	.25	.25
		Nos. 433-438 (6)	1.50	1.50

Millenium of Christianization of Poland.

Pope John XXIII Opening Vatican II Council — A133

Designs: 15 l, Ancient Bible on ornate display stand. 55 l, Bishops celebrating Mass. 90 l, Pope Paul VI greeting Patriarch Athenagoras I. 100 l, Gold ring given to participating bishops. 130 l, Pope Paul VI carried in front of St. Peter's.

1966, Oct. 11 Photo. *Perf. 14*

439 A133	10 l	red & black	.25	.25
440 A133	15 l	brown & green	.25	.25
441 A133	55 l	blk & brt rose	.25	.25
442 A133	90 l	slate grn & blk	.25	.25
443 A133	100 l	green & ocher	.25	.25
444 A133	130 l	orange brn & brn	.25	.25
		Nos. 439-444 (6)	1.50	1.50

Conclusion of Vatican II, the 21st Ecumenical Council of the Roman Catholic Church, Dec. 8, 1965.

Nativity, Sculpture by Scorzelli — A134

1966, Nov. 24 Wmk. 235 *Perf. 14*

445 A134	20 l	plum	.25	.25
446 A134	55 l	slate green	.25	.25
447 A134	225 l	yellow brown	.25	.25
		Nos. 445-447 (3)	.75	.75

St. Peter, Fresco, Catacombs, Rome — A135

Designs: 20 l, St. Paul, fresco from Catacombs, Rome. 55 l, Sts. Peter and Paul, glass painting, Vatican Library. 90 l, Baldachin by Bernini, St. Peter's, Rome. 220 l, Interior of St. Paul's, Rome.

Perf. 13½x14

1967, June 15 Photo. Unwmk.

448 A135	15 l	multi	.25	.25
449 A135	20 l	multi	.25	.25
450 A135	55 l	multi	.25	.25
451 A135	90 l	multi	.25	.25
452 A135	220 l	multi	.25	.25
		Nos. 448-452 (5)	1.25	1.25

Martyrdom of the Apostles Peter and Paul, 1,900th anniv.

Cross, People and Globe — A136

1967, Oct. 13 Wmk. 235 *Perf. 14*

453 A136	40 l	carmine rose	.25	.25
454 A136	130 l	brt blue	.25	.25

3rd Congress of Catholic Laymen, Rome, Oct. 11-18.

Sculpture of Shepherd Children of Fatima — A137

Designs: 50 l, Basilica at Fatima. 200 l, Pope Paul VI praying before statue of Virgin of Fatima.

1967, Oct. 13 *Perf. 13½x14*

455 A137	30 l	multi	.25	.25
456 A137	50 l	multi	.25	.25
457 A137	200 l	multi	.25	.25
		Nos. 455-457 (3)	.75	.75

Apparition of the Virgin Mary to 3 shepherd children at Fatima, 50th anniv.

Christmas Issue

Nativity, 9th Century Painting on Wood — A138

1967, Nov. 28 Photo. Unwmk.

458 A138	25 l	purple & multi	.25	.25
459 A138	55 l	gray & multi	.25	.25
460 A138	180 l	green & multi	.25	.25
		Nos. 458-460 (3)	.75	.75

Pope Paul VI — A139

Designs: 55 l, Monstrance from fresco by Raphael. 220 l, Map of South America.

1968, Aug. 22 Wmk. 235 *Perf. 14*

461 A139	25 l	blk & dk red brn	.25	.25
462 A139	55 l	blk, gray & ocher	.25	.25
463 A139	220 l	blk, lt bl & sep	.25	.25
		Nos. 461-463 (3)	.75	.75

Visit of Pope Paul VI to the 39th Eucharistic Congress in Bogotá, Colombia, Aug. 22-25.

Holy Infant of Prague — A140

Engraved and Photogravure

1968, Nov. 28 *Perf. 13½x14*

464 A140	20 l	plum & pink	.25	.25
465 A140	50 l	vio & pale vio	.25	.25
466 A140	250 l	dk bl & lt bluish gray	.25	.25
		Nos. 464-466 (3)	.75	.75

The Resurrection, by Fra Angelico de Fiesole — A141

Easter Issue

Perf. 13½x14

1969, Mar. 6 Engr. Wmk. 235

467 A141	20 l	dk carmine & buff	.25	.25
468 A141	90 l	green & buff	.25	.25
469 A141	180 l	ultra & buff	.25	.25
		Nos. 467-469 (3)	.75	.75

Common Design Types pictured following the introduction.

Europa Issue

Common Design Type

Perf. 13½x14

1969, Apr. 28 Photo. Wmk. 235

Size: 36½x27mm

470 CD12	50 l	gray & lt brn	.25	.25
471 CD12	90 l	vermilion & lt brn	.25	.25
472 CD12	130 l	olive & lt brn	.25	.25
		Nos. 470-472 (3)	.75	.75

Pope Paul VI with African Children — A142

Designs: 55 l, Pope Paul VI and African bishops. 250 l, Map of Africa with Kampala, olive branch and compass rose.

Perf. 13½x14

1969, July 31 Photo. Wmk. 235

473 A142	25 l	bister & brown	.25	.25
474 A142	55 l	dk red & brown	.25	.25
475 A142	250 l	multicolored	.25	.25
		Nos. 473-475 (3)	.75	.75

Visit of Pope Paul VI to Uganda, 7/31-8/2.

Pope Pius IX — A143

Designs: 50 l, Chrismon, emblem of St. Peter's Circle. 220 l, Pope Paul VI.

Perf. 13½x14

1969, Nov. 18 Engr. Wmk. 235

476 A143	30 l	red brown	.25	.25
477 A143	50 l	dark gray	.25	.25
478 A143	220 l	deep plum	.25	.25
		Nos. 476-478 (3)	.75	.75

Centenary of St. Peter's Circle, a lay society dedicated to prayer, action and sacrifice.

Mt. Fuji and EXPO '70 Emblem — A144

EXPO '70 Emblem and: 25 l, EXPO '70 emblem. 40 l, Osaka Castle. 55 l, Japanese Virgin and Child, by Domoto in Osaka Cathedral. 90 l, Christian Pavilion.

1970, Mar. 16 Photo. Unwmk.

479 A144	25 l	gold, red & blk	.25	.25
480 A144	40 l	red & multi	.25	.25
481 A144	55 l	brown & multi	.25	.25
482 A144	90 l	gold & multi	.25	.25
483 A144	110 l	blue & multi	.25	.25
		Nos. 479-483 (5)	1.25	1.25

EXPO '70 Intl. Exhibition, Osaka, Japan, Mar. 15-Sept. 13.

Centenary Medal, Jesus Giving St. Peter the Keys — A145

Designs: 50 l, Coat of arms of Pope Pius IX. 180 l, Vatican I Council meeting in St. Peter's, obverse of centenary medal.

Engr. & Photo.; Photo. (50 l)

1970, Apr. 29 *Perf. 13x14*

484 A145	20 l	orange & brown	.25	.25
485 A145	50 l	multicolored	.25	.25
486 A145	180 l	ver & brn	.25	.25
		Nos. 484-486 (3)	.75	.75

Centenary of the Vatican I Council.

Christ, by Simone Martini — A146

25 l, Christ with Crown of Thorns, by Rogier van der Weyden. 50 l, Christ, by Albrecht Dürer. 90 l, Christ, by El Greco. 180 l, Pope Paul VI.

1970, May 29 Photo. *Perf. 14x13*

487 A146	15 l	gold & multi	.25	.25
488 A146	25 l	gold & multi	.25	.25
489 A146	50 l	gold & multi	.25	.25
490 A146	90 l	gold & multi	.25	.25
491 A146	180 l	gold & multi	.25	.25
		Nos. 487-491 (5)	1.25	1.25

Ordination of Pope Paul VI, 50th anniv.

Adam, by Michelangelo; UN Emblem — A147

UN Emblem and: 90 l, Eve, by Michelangelo. 220 l, Olive branch.

1970, Oct. 8 Photo. *Perf. 13x14*

492 A147	20 l	multi	.25	.25
493 A147	90 l	multi	.25	.25
494 A147	220 l	multi	.25	.25
		Nos. 492-494 (3)	.75	.75

25th anniversary of the United Nations.

Pope Paul VI — A148

Designs: 55 l, Holy Child of Cebu, Philippines. 100 l, Madonna and Child, by Georg Hamori, Darwin Cathedral, Australia. 130 l, Cathedral of Manila. 220 l, Cathedral of Sydney.

1970, Nov. 26 Photo. Unwmk.

495 A148	25 l	multi	.25	.25
496 A148	55 l	multi	.25	.25
497 A148	100 l	multi	.25	.25
498 A148	130 l	multi	.25	.25
499 A148	220 l	multi	.25	.25
		Nos. 495-499 (5)	1.25	1.25

Visit of Pope Paul VI to the Far East, Oceania and Australia, Nov. 26-Dec. 5.

Angel Holding Lectern — A149

Sculptures by Corrado Ruffini: 40 l, 130 l, Crucified Christ surrounded by doves. 50 l, like 20 l.

1971, Feb. 2 *Perf. 13x14*

500 A149	20 l	multicolored	.25	.25
501 A149	40 l	dp orange & multi	.25	.25
502 A149	50 l	purple & multi	.25	.25
503 A149	130 l	multicolored	.25	.25
		Nos. 500-503 (4)	1.00	1.00

Intl. year against racial discrimination.

Madonna and Child by Francesco Ghissi — A150

Paintings: Madonna and Child, 40 l, by Sassetta (Stefano di Giovanni); 55 l, Carlo Crivelli; 90 l, by Carlo Maratta. 180 l, Holy Family, by Ghisberto Ceracchini.

1971, Mar. 26 Photo. *Perf. 14*

504 A150 25 l gray & multi .25 .25
505 A150 40 l gray & multi .25 .25
506 A150 55 l gray & multi .25 .25
507 A150 90 l gray & multi .25 .25
508 A150 180 l gray & multi .25 .25
Nos. 504-508 (5) 1.25 1.25

St. Dominic, Sienese School — A151

Portraits of St. Dominic: 55 l, by Fra Angelico. 90 l, by Titian. 180 l, by El Greco.

1971, May 25 Unwmk. *Perf. 13x14*

509 A151 25 l multi .25 .25
510 A151 55 l multi .25 .25
511 A151 90 l multi .25 .25
512 A151 180 l multi .25 .25
Nos. 509-512 (4) 1.00 1.00

St. Dominic de Guzman (1170-1221), founder of the Dominican Order.

St. Stephen, from Chasuble, 1031 — A152

180 l, Madonna as Patroness of Hungary, 1511.

1971, Nov. 25

513 A152 50 l multi .25 .25
514 A152 180 l black & yellow .25 .25

Millenium of the birth of St. Stephen (975?-1038), king of Hungary.

Bramante — A153

Designs: 25 l, Bramante's design for dome of St. Peter's. 130 l, Design for spiral staircase.

1972, Feb. 22 Engr. *Perf. 13½x14*

515 A153 25 l dull yellow & blk .25 .25
516 A153 90 l dull yellow & blk .25 .25
517 A153 130 l dull yellow & blk .25 .25
Nos. 515-517 (3) .75 .75

Bramante (real name Donato d'Agnolo; 1444-1514), architect.

St. Mark in Storm, 12th Century Mosaic A154

Map of Venice, 1581 A155

Design: 180 l, St. Mark's Basilica, Painting by Emilio Vangelli.

Unwmk.

1972, June 6 Photo. *Perf. 14*

518 A154 25 l lt brown & multi .25 .25
519 A155 Block of 4 1.00 1.00
a.-d. 50 l, UL, UR, LL, LR, each .25 .25
520 A154 180 l lt blue & multi 1.10 1.10
a. Souvenir sheet, #518-520 2.50 2.50
Nos. 518-520 (3) 2.35 2.35

UNESCO campaign to save Venice.
NO. 520a exists imperforate.

Gospel of St. Matthew, 13th Century, French — A156

Illuminated Initials from: 50 l, St. Luke's Gospel, Biblia dell'Aracoeli 13th century, French. 90 l, Second Epistle of St. John, 14th century, Bologna. 100 l, Apocalypse of St. John, 14th century, Bologna. 130 l, Book of Romans, 14th century, Central Italy.

1972, Oct. 11 *Perf. 14x13½*

521 A156 30 l multi .25 .25
522 A156 50 l multi .25 .25
523 A156 90 l multi .25 .25
524 A156 100 l multi .25 .25
525 A156 130 l multi .25 .25
Nos. 521-525 (5) 1.25 1.25

Intl. Book Year. Illustrations are from illuminated medieval manuscripts.

Luigi Orione — A157

Design: 180 l, Lorenzo Perosi and music from "Hallelujah."

1972, Nov. 28 Photo. *Perf. 14x13½*

526 A157 50 l rose, lilac & blk .25 .25
527 A157 180 l orange, grn & blk .25 .25

Secular priests Luigi Orione (1872-1940), founder of CARITAS, Catholic welfare organization; and Lorenzo Perosi (1872-1956), composer.

Cardinal Bessarion — A158

40 l, Reading Bull of Union between the Greek and Latin Churches, 1439, from bronze door of St. Peter's. 130 l, Coat of arms from tomb, Basilica of Holy Apostles, Rome.

Perf. 13x14

1972, Nov. 28 Wmk. 235 Engr.

528 A158 40 l dull green .25 .25
529 A158 90 l carmine .25 .25
530 A158 130 l black .25 .25
Nos. 528-530 (3) .75 .75

Johannes Cardinal Bessarion (1403?-1472), Latin Patriarch of Constantinople, who worked for union of the Greek and Latin Churches. Portrait by Cosimo Rosselli in Sistine Chapel.

Eucharistic Congress Emblem — A159

Designs: 75 l, Head of Mary (Pietá), by Michelangelo. 300 l, Melbourne Cathedral.

1973, Feb. 27 Photo. Unwmk.

531 A159 25 l violet & multi .25 .25
532 A159 75 l olive & multi .25 .25
533 A159 300 l multicolored .30 .30
Nos. 531-533 (3) .80 .80

40th Intl. Eucharistic Congress, Melbourne, Australia, Feb. 18-25.

St. Teresa — A160

Designs: 25 l, St. Teresa's birthplace, Alençon. 220 l, Lisieux Basilica.

1973, May 23 Engr. & Photo.

534 A160 25 l black & pink .25 .25
535 A160 55 l black & yellow .25 .25
536 A160 220 l black & lt blue .25 .25
Nos. 534-536 (3) .75 .75

St. Teresa of Lisieux and of the Infant Jesus (1873-1897), Carmelite nun.

Copernicus — A161

Designs: 20 l, 100 l, View of Torun.

1973, June 19 Engr. *Perf. 14*

537 A161 20 l dull green .25 .25
538 A161 50 l brown .25 .25
539 A161 100 l lilac .25 .25
540 A161 130 l dark blue .25 .25
Nos. 537-540 (4) 1.00 1.00

Nicolaus Copernicus (1473-1543), Polish astronomer.

St. Wenceslas A162

90 l, Arms of Prague Diocese. 150 l, Spire of Prague Cathedral. 220 l, St. Adalbert.

1973, Sept. 25 Photo. *Perf. 14*

541 A162 20 l shown .25 .25
542 A162 90 l multicolored .25 .25
543 A162 150 l multicolored .25 .25
544 A162 220 l multicolored .25 .25
Nos. 541-544 (4) 1.00 1.00

Millenium of Prague Latin Episcopal See.

St. Nerses Shnorali — A163

25 l, Church of St. Hripsime. 90 l, Armenian khatchkar, a stele with cross and inscription.

Engr. & Litho.

1973, Nov. 27 *Perf. 13x14*

545 A163 25 l tan & dk brown .25 .25
546 A163 90 l lt violet & blk .25 .25
547 A163 180 l lt green & sepia .25 .25
Nos. 545-547 (3) .75 .75

Armenian Patriarch St. Nerses Shnorali (1102-1173).

Noah's Ark, Rainbow and Dove (Mosaic) A164

Design: 90 l, Lamb drinking from stream, and Tablets of the Law (mosaic).

1974, Apr. 23 Litho. *Perf. 13x14*

548 A164 50 l gold & multi .25 .25
549 A164 90 l gold & multi .25 .25

Centenary of the Universal Postal Union.

"And There was Light" — A165

Designs: 25 l, Noah's Ark, horiz. 50 l, The Annunciation. 90 l, Nativity (African). 180 l, Hands holding grain (Spanish inscription: The Lord feeds his people), horiz. Designs chosen through worldwide youth competition in connection with 1972 Intl. Book Year.

Perf. 13x14, 14x13

1974, Apr. 23 Photo.

550 A165 15 l brown & multi .25 .25
551 A165 25 l yellow & multi .25 .25
552 A165 50 l blue & multi .25 .25
553 A165 90 l green & multi .25 .25
554 A165 180 l rose & multi .25 .25
Nos. 550-554 (5) 1.25 1.25

"The Bible: the Book of Books."

St. Thomas Aquinas Teaching — A166

Designs: 50 l, Students (left panel). 220 l, Students (right panel). Designs from a painting in the Convent of St. Mark in Florence, by an artist from the School of Fra Angelico.

Sizes: 50 l, 220 l, 20x36mm, 90 l, 26x36mm

Engr. & Litho.

1974, June 18 Unwmk. *Perf. 13x14*

555 A166 50 l dk brown & gold .25 .25
556 A166 90 l dk brown & gold .25 .25
557 A166 220 l dk brown & gold .25 .25
a. Strip of 3, #555-557 .90 .90

St. Thomas Aquinas (1225-1274), scholastic philosopher.

St. Bonaventure — A167

Woodcuts: 40 l, Civita Bagnoregio. 90 l, Tree of Life (13th century).

1974, Sept. 26 Photo. *Perf. 13x14*

558 A167 40 l gold & multi .25 .25
559 A167 90 l gold & multi .25 .25
560 A167 220 l gold & multi .75 .25
Nos. 558-560 (3) 1.25 .75

St. Bonaventure (Giovanni di Fidanza; 1221-1274), scholastic philosopher.

Christ, St. Peter's Basilica
A168

Pope Paul VI Giving his Blessing
A169

Holy Year 1975: 10 l, Christus Victor, Sts. Peter and Paul. 30 l, Christ. 40 l, Cross surmounted by dove. 50 l, Christ enthroned. 55 l, St. Peter. 90 l, St. Paul. 100 l, St. Peter. 130 l, St. Paul. 220 l, Arms of Pope Paul VI. Designs of 10 l, 25 l, are from St. Peter's; 30 l, 40 l, from St. John Lateran; 50 l, 55 l, 90 l, from St. Mary Major; 100 l, 130 l, from St. Paul outside the Walls.

1974, Dec. 19 Photo. *Perf. 13x14*

561 A168 10 l multi .25 .25
562 A168 25 l multi .25 .25
563 A168 30 l multi .25 .25
564 A168 40 l multi .25 .25
565 A168 50 l multi .25 .25
566 A168 55 l multi .25 .25
567 A168 90 l multi .25 .25
568 A168 100 l multi .25 .25
569 A168 130 l multi .25 .25
570 A169 220 l multi .25 .25
571 A169 250 l multi .25 .25
Nos. 561-571 (11) 2.75 2.75

Pentecost, by El Greco — A170

1975, May 22 Engr. *Perf. 13x14*

572 A170 300 l car rose & org .60 .60

Fountain, St. Peter's Square
A171

Fountains of Rome: 40 l, Piazza St. Martha, Apse of St. Peter's. 50 l, Borgia Tower and St. Peter's. 90 l, Belvedere Courtyard. 100 l, Academy of Sciences. 200 l, Galleon.

Litho. & Engr.

1975, May 22 *Perf. 14*

573 A171 20 l buff & blk .25 .25
574 A171 40 l pale violet & blk .25 .25
575 A171 50 l salmon & blk .25 .25
576 A171 90 l pale citron & blk .25 .25
577 A171 100 l pale green & blk .25 .25
578 A171 200 l pale blue & blk .25 .25
Nos. 573-578 (6) 1.50 1.50

European Architectural Heritage Year.

Miracle of Loaves and Fishes, Gilt Glass — A172

Designs: 150 l, Painting of Christ, from Comodilla Catacomb. 200 l, Raising of Lazarus. All works from 4th century.

Perf. 14x13½

1975, Sept. 25 Photo. Unwmk.

579 A172 30 l multi .25 .25
580 A172 150 l brown & multi .25 .25
581 A172 200 l green & multi .25 .75
Nos. 579-581 (3) .75 1.25

9th Intl. Congress of Christian Archaeology.

Investiture of First Librarian Bartolomeo Sacchi by Pope Sixtus IV — A173

Designs: 100 l, Pope Sixtus IV and books in old wooden press, from Latin Vatican Codex 2044, vert. 250 l, Pope Sixtus IV visiting Library, fresco in Hospital of the Holy Spirit. Design of 70 l is from fresco by Melozzo di Forli in Vatican Gallery.

Perf. 14x13½, 13½x14

1975, Sept. 25 Litho. & Engr.

582 A173 70 l gray & lilac .25 .25
583 A173 100 l lt yellow & grn .25 .25
584 A173 250 l gray & red .25 .25
Nos. 582-584 (3) .75 .75

Founding of the Vatican Apostolic Library, 500th anniv.

Mt. Argentario Monastery
A174

St. Paul of the Cross, by Giovanni Della Porta
A175

Design: 300 l, Basilica of Sts. John and Paul and burial chapel of Saint.

1975, Nov. 27 Photo. *Perf. 14x13½*

585 A174 50 l multi .25 .25
586 A175 150 l multi .25 .25
587 A174 300 l multi .30 .30
Nos. 585-587 (3) .80 .80

Bicentenary of death of St. Paul of the Cross, founder of the Passionist religious order in 1737.

Praying Women, by Fra Angelico — A176

International Women's Year: 200 l, Seated women, by Fra Angelico.

1975, Nov. 27 *Perf. 13½x14*

588 A176 100 l multi .25 .25
589 A176 200 l multi .25 .25

Virgin and Child in Glory, by Titian — A177

Design: 300 l, The Six Saints, by Titian. Designs from "The Madonna in Glory with the Child Jesus and Six Saints."

1976, May 13 Engr. *Perf. 14x13½*

590 A177 100 l rose magenta .25 .25
591 A177 300 l rose magenta .30 .30
a. Pair, #590-591 .75 .75

Titian (1477-1576), painter.

A178

Designs: 150 l, Eucharist, wheat and globe. 200 l, Hands Holding Eucharist. 400 l, Hungry mankind reaching for the Eucharist.

1976, July 2 Photo. *Perf. 13½x14*

592 A178 150 l gold, red & bl .25 .25
593 A178 200 l gold & blue .25 .30
594 A178 400 l gold, grn & brn .30 .80
Nos. 592-594 (3) .80 1.35

41st Intl. Eucharistic Congress, Philadelphia, PA, Aug. 1-8.

A179

Details from Transfiguration by Raphael: 30 l, Moses Holding Tablets. 40 l, Transfigured Christ. 50 l, Prophet Elijah with book. 100 l, Apostles John and Peter. 150 l, Group of women. 200 l, Landscape.

1976, Sept. 30 Photo. *Perf. 13½x14*

595 A179 30 l ocher & multi .25 .25
596 A179 40 l red & multi .25 .25
597 A179 50 l violet & multi .25 .25
598 A179 100 l multicolored .25 .25
599 A179 150 l green & multi .25 .25
600 A179 200 l ocher & multi .25 .25
Nos. 595-600 (6) 1.50 1.50

St. John's Tower — A180

Roman Views: 100 l, Fountain of the Sacrament. 120 l, Fountain at entrance to the gardens. 180 l, Basilica, Cupola of St. Peter's and Sacristy. 250 l, Borgia Tower and Sistine Chapel. 300 l, Apostolic Palace and Courtyard of St. Damasius.

Litho. & Engr.

1976, Nov. 23 *Perf. 14*

601 A180 50 l gray & black .25 .25
602 A180 100 l salmon & dk brn .25 .25
603 A180 120 l citron & dk grn .25 .25
604 A180 180 l pale gray & blk .25 .25
605 A180 250 l yellow & brn .25 .25
606 A180 300 l pale lilac & mag .25 .25
Nos. 601-606 (6) 1.50 1.50

The Lord's Creatures
A181

70 l, Brother Sun. 100 l, Sister Moon and Stars. 130 l, Sister Water. 170 l, Praise in infirmities and tribulations. 200 l, Praise for bodily death. Designs are illustrations by Duilio Cambellotti for "The Canticle of Brother Sun," by St. Francis.

1977, Mar. 10 Photo. *Perf. 14x13½*

607 A181 50 l multi .25 .25
608 A181 70 l multi .25 .25
609 A181 100 l multi .25 .25
610 A181 130 l multi .25 .25
611 A181 170 l multi .25 .25
612 A181 200 l multi .25 .25
Nos. 607-612 (6) 1.50 1.50

St. Francis of Assisi, 750th death anniv.

Sts. Peter and Paul — A182

Design: 350 l, Pope Gregory XI and St. Catherine of Siena. Designs are after fresco by Giorgio Vasari.

1977, May 20 Engr. *Perf. 14*

613 170 l black .30 .25
614 350 l black .45 .45
a. A182 Pair, #613-614 .85 .85

Return of Pope Gregory XI from Avignon, 600th anniv.

Dormition of the Virgin — A183

Design: 400 l, Virgin Mary in Heaven. Both designs after miniatures in Latin manuscripts, Vatican Library.

1977, July 5 Photo. *Perf. 13½x14*

615 A183 200 l multi .25 .25
616 A183 400 l multi .40 .40

Feast of the Assumption.

The Nile Deity, Roman Sculpture
A184

Sculptures: 120 l, Head of Pericles. 130 l, Roman Couple Joining Hands. 150 l, Apollo Belvedere, head. 170 l, Laocoon, head. 350 l, Apollo Belvedere, torso.

1977, Sept. 29 *Perf. 14x13½*

617 A184 50 l multi .25 .25
618 A184 120 l multi .25 .25
619 A184 130 l multi .25 .25
620 A184 150 l multi .25 .25
621 A184 170 l multi .25 .25
622 A184 350 l multi .25 .25
Nos. 617-622 (6) 1.50 1.50

Classical sculptures in Vatican Museums.

Creation of Man and Woman
A185

Designs: 70 l, Three youths in the furnace. 100 l, Adoration of the Kings. 130 l, Raising of Lazarus. 200 l, The Good Shepherd. 400 l, Chrismon, Cross, sleeping soldiers (Resurrection). Designs are bas-reliefs from Christian sarcophagi, 250-350 A.D., found in Roman excavations.

1977, Dec. 9 Photo. *Perf. 14x13½*

623 A185 50 l multi .25 .25
624 A185 70 l multi .25 .25
625 A185 100 l multi .25 .25
626 A185 130 l multi .25 .25
627 A185 200 l multi .25 .25
628 A185 400 l multi .25 .25
Nos. 623-628 (6) 1.50 1.50

Madonna with the Parrot and Rubens Self-portrait — A186

1977, Dec. 9 *Perf. 13½x14*

629 A186 350 l multi .50 .50

Peter Paul Rubens (1577-1640).

Pope Paul VI, by Lino Bianchi Barriviera — A187

Design: 350 l, Christ's Face, by Pericle Fazzini and arms of Pope Paul VI.

1978, Mar. 9 Photo. *Perf. 14*

630 A187 350 l multi .40 .40
631 A187 400 l multi .45 .45

80th birthday of Pope Paul VI.

Pope Pius IX (1792-1878) — A188

Designs: 130 l, Arms of Pope Pius IX. 170 l, Seal of Pius IX, used to sign definition of Dogma of Immaculate Conception.

Litho. & Engr.

1978, May 9 *Perf. 13x14*

632 A188 130 l multi .25 .25
633 A188 170 l multi .25 .25
634 A188 200 l multi .25 .25
Nos. 632-634 (3) .75 .75

Interregnum Issues

Keys of St. Peter and Papal Chamberlain's Insignia — A189

1978, Aug. 23 **Photo.** *Perf. 14*

635 A189 120 l purple & lt green .25 .25
636 A189 150 l purple & salmon .25 .25
637 A189 250 l purple & yellow .25 .25
Nos. 635-637 (3) .75 .75

Keys of St. Peter and Papal Chamberlain's Insignia — A190

1978, Oct. 12 **Photo.** *Perf. 14*

638 A190 120 l black & multi .25 .25
639 A190 200 l black & multi .25 .25
640 A190 250 l black & multi .25 .25
Nos. 638-640 (3) .75 .75

Pope John Paul I, Pope from Aug. 26 to Sept. 28, 1978 — A191

Pope John Paul I: 70 l, Sitting on his throne. 250 l, Walking in Vatican garden. 350 l, Giving blessing, horiz.

1978, Dec. 11 *Perf. 13x14, 14x13*

641 A191 70 l multi .25 .25
642 A191 120 l multi .25 .25
643 A191 250 l multi .25 .25
644 A191 350 l multi .25 .25
Nos. 641-644 (4) 1.00 1.00

Arms of Pope John Paul II — A192

Designs: 250 l, Pope John Paul II raising hand in blessing. 400 l, Jesus giving keys to St. Peter.

Litho. & Engr.

1979, Mar. 22 *Perf. 14x13*

645 A192 170 l black & multi .25 .25
646 A192 250 l black & multi .30 .30
647 A192 400 l black & multi .45 .45
Nos. 645-647 (3) 1.00 1.00

Inauguration of pontificate of Pope John Paul II.

Martyrdom of St. Stanislas — A193

Designs: 150 l, St. Stanislas appearing to the people. 250 l, Gold reliquary, 1504, containing saint's head. 500 l, View of Cracow Cathedral.

1979, May 18 **Photo.** *Perf. 14*

648 A193 120 l multi .25 .25
649 A193 150 l multi .25 .25
650 A193 250 l multi .30 .30
651 A193 500 l multi .50 .50
Nos. 648-651 (4) 1.30 1.30

900th anniversary of martyrdom of St. Stanislas (1030-1079), patron saint of Poland.

St. Basil the Great Instructing Monk — A194

St. Basil the Great, 16th cent. of death: 520 l, St. Basil the Great visiting the sick.

Engr. & Photo.

1979, June 25 *Perf. 13½x14*

652 A194 150 l multi .25 .25
653 A194 520 l multi .55 .55

Father Secchi, Solar Protuberance, Spectrum and Meteorograph — A195

Father Angelo Secchi (1818-1878), astronomer, solar protuberance, spectrum and: 220 l, Spectroscope. 300 l, Telescope.

Litho. & Engr.

1979, June 25 *Perf. 14x13½*

654 A195 180 l multi .25 .25
655 A195 220 l multi .25 .25
656 A195 300 l multi .30 .30
Nos. 654-656 (3) .80 .80

Vatican City — A196

Papal Arms and Portraits: 70 l, Pius XI. 120 l, Pius XII. 150 l, John XXIII. 170 l, Paul VI. 250 l, John Paul I. 450 l, John Paul II.

1979, Oct. 11 **Photo.** *Perf. 14x13½*

657 A196 50 l multi .25 .25
658 A196 70 l multi .25 .25
659 A196 120 l multi .25 .25
660 A196 150 l multi .25 .25
661 A196 170 l multi .25 .25
662 A196 250 l multi .25 .25
663 A196 450 l multi .40 .40
Nos. 657-663 (7) 1.90 1.90

Vatican City State, 50th anniversary.

Infant, by Andrea Della Robbia, IYC Emblem — A197

IYC Emblem and Della Robbia Bas Reliefs, Hospital of the Innocents, Florence.

Engr. & Photo.

1979, Nov. 27 *Perf. 13½x14*

664 A197 50 l multi .25 .25
665 A197 120 l multi .25 .25
666 A197 200 l multi .25 .25
667 A197 350 l multi .30 .30
Nos. 664-667 (4) 1.05 1.05

International Year of the Child.

Abbot Desiderius Giving Codex to St. Benedict A198

Illuminated Letters and Illustrations, Codices, Vatican Apostolic Library: 100 l, St. Benedict writing the Rule. 150 l, Page from the Rule. 220 l, Death of St. Benedict. 450 l, Montecassino (after painting by Paul Bril).

1980, Mar. 21 **Photo.** *Perf. 14x13½*

668 A198 80 l multi .25 .25
669 A198 100 l multi .25 .25
670 A198 150 l multi .25 .25
671 A198 220 l multi .25 .25
672 A198 450 l multi .40 .40
Nos. 668-672 (5) 1.40 1.40

St. Benedict of Nursia (patron saint of Europe), 1500th birth anniversary.

Bernini, Medallion Showing Baldacchino in St. Peter's — A199

Gian Lorenzo Bernini (1598-1680), Architect (Self-portrait and Medallion): 170 l, St. Peter's Square with third wing (never built). 250 l, Bronze chair, Doctors of the Church. 350 l, Apostolic Palace stairway.

1980, Oct. 16 **Litho.** *Perf. 14x13½*

673 A199 80 l multicolored .25 .25
674 A199 170 l multicolored .25 .25
675 A199 250 l multicolored .30 .30
676 A199 350 l multicolored .40 .40
Nos. 673-676 (4) 1.20 1.20

St. Albertus Magnus on Mission of Peace — A200

1980, Nov. 18 **Litho.** *Perf. 13½x14*

677 A200 300 l shown .35 .35
678 A200 400 l As bishop .50 .50

St. Albertus Magnus, 700th death anniv.

Communion of the Saints — A201

1980, Nov. 18 *Perf. 14x13½*

679 A201 250 l shown .30 .30
680 A201 500 l Christ and saints .50 .50

Feast of All Saints.

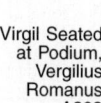

Guglielmo Marconi and Pope Pius XI, Vatican Radio Emblem, Vatican Arms — A202

Designs: 150 l, Microphone, Bible text. 200 l, St. Maria di Galeria Radio Center antenna, Archangel Gabriel statue. 600 l, Pope John Paul II.

1981, Feb. 12 **Photo.** *Perf. 14x13½*

681 A202 100 l shown .25 .25
682 A202 150 l multicolored .25 .25
683 A202 200 l multicolored .25 .25
684 A202 600 l multicolored .50 .50
Nos. 681-684 (4) 1.25 1.25

Vatican Radio, 50th anniversary.

Virgil Seated at Podium, Vergilius Romanus A203

1981, Apr. 23 **Litho.** *Perf. 14*

685 A203 350 l multicolored .40 .40
686 A203 600 l multicolored .60 .60
Set, with labels 1.75 1.75

2000th birth anniversary of Virgil.
Issued in sheets of 16 stamps plus 9 labels. Value $15.

Congress Emblem — A204

Congress Emblem and: 150 l, Virgin appearing to St. Bernadette. 200 l, Pilgrims going to Lourdes. 500 l, Bishop and pilgrims.

1981, June 22 **Photo.**

687 A204 80 l multicolored .25 .25
688 A204 150 l multicolored .25 .25
689 A204 200 l multicolored .25 .25
690 A204 500 l multicolored .50 .50
Nos. 687-690 (4) 1.25 1.25

42nd Intl. Eucharistic Congress, Lourdes, France, July 16-23.

Intl. Year of the Disabled — A205

1981, Sept. 29 **Photo.** *Perf. 14x13½*

691 A205 600 l multicolored .65 .65

Jan van Ruusbroec, Flemish Mystic, 500th Birth Anniv. — A206

Litho. & Engr.

1981, Sept. 29 *Perf. 13½x14*

692 A206 200 l shown .25 .25
693 A206 300 l Portrait .30 .30

1980 Journeys of Pope John Paul II — A207

50 l, Papal arms. 100 l, Map of Africa. 120 l, Crucifix. 150 l, Baptism. 200 l, African bishop. 250 l, Visiting sick. 300 l, Notre Dame, France. 400 l, UNESCO speech. 600 l, Christ of the Andes, Brazil. 700 l, Cologne Cathedral, Germany. 900 l, John Paul II.

1981, Dec. 3 **Photo.** *Perf. 13½x14½*

694 A207 50 l multicolored .25 .25
695 A207 100 l multicolored .25 .25
696 A207 120 l multicolored .25 .25
697 A207 150 l multicolored .25 .25
698 A207 200 l multicolored .25 .25
699 A207 250 l multicolored .30 .30
700 A207 300 l multicolored .30 .30
701 A207 400 l multicolored .35 .35
702 A207 600 l multicolored .50 .50
703 A207 700 l multicolored .65 .65
704 A207 900 l multicolored .95 .95
a. Complete booklet, 8 each #694, 695, 698, 699 ('82) 27.50
Nos. 694-704 (11) 4.30 4.30

700th Death Anniv. of St. Agnes of Prague — A208

Designs: 700 l, Handing order to Grand Master of the Crosiers of the Red Star. 900 l, Receiving letter from St. Clare.

1982, Feb. 16 Photo. *Perf. 13½x14*

705 A208 700 l multicolored .75 .75
706 A208 900 l multicolored 1.10 1.10

Pueri Cantores — A209

Luca Della Robbia (1400-1482), Sculptor: No. 708, Pueri Cantores, diff. No. 709, Virgin in Prayer (44x36mm).

Photo. & Engr.

1982, May 21 *Perf. 14*

707 A209 1000 l multicolored .80 .80
708 A209 1000 l multicolored .80 .80
709 A209 1000 l multicolored .80 .80
a. Strip of 3, #707-709 3.50 3.50

St. Teresa of Avila (1515-1582) — A210

Sketches of St. Teresa by Riccardo Tommasi-Ferroni.

1982, Sept. 23 Photo.

710 A210 200 l multicolored .25 .25
711 A210 600 l multicolored .75 .75
712 A210 1000 l multicolored 1.10 1.10
Nos. 710-712 (3) 2.10 2.10

Christmas — A211

Nativity Bas-Reliefs: 300 l, Wit Stwosz, Church of the Virgin Mary, Cracow. 450 l, Enrico Manfrini.

Photo. & Engr.

1982, Nov. 23 *Perf. 14*

713 A211 300 l multicolored .40 .40
714 A211 450 l multicolored .55 .55

400th Anniv. of Gregorian Calendar — A212

Sculpture Details, Tomb of Pope Gregory XIII, St. Peter's Basilica: 200 l, Surveying the globe. 300 l, Receiving Edict of Reform. 700 l, Presenting edict.

1982, Nov. 23 Engr. *Perf. 13½x14*

715 A212 200 l multicolored .25 .25
716 A212 300 l multicolored .35 .35
717 A212 700 l multicolored .80 .80
a. Souvenir sheet of 3, #715-717 2.25 2.25
Nos. 715-717 (3) 1.40 1.40

Souvenir Sheets

The Papacy and Art, US 1983 Exhibition — A213

1983, Mar. 10 Litho. *Perf. 13½x14*

718 A213 Sheet of 6 3.25 3.25
a. 100 l Greek Vase .30 .25
b. 200 l Italian vase .30 .25
c. 250 l Female terra-cotta bust .40 .35
d. 300 l Marcus Aurelius bust .40 .35
e. 350 l Bird fresco .50 .40
f. 400 l Pope Clement VIII vestment .50 .40

1983, June 14 Litho. *Perf. 13½x14*

719 A213 Sheet of 6 3.00 3.00
a. 100 l Horse's head, Etruscan terra cotta .35 .30
b. 200 l Horseman, Greek fragment .35 .30
c. 300 l Male head, Etruscan .45 .40
d. 400 l Apollo Belvedere head .45 .40
e. 500 l Moses, Roman fresco .55 .45
f. 1000 l Madonna and Child, by Bernardo Daddi .60 .45

1983, Nov. 10 Litho. *Perf. 13½x14*

720 A213 Sheet of 6 3.50 3.50
a. 150 l Greek cup, Oedipus and the Sphinx .40 .35
b. 200 l Etruscan bronze statue of a child .40 .35
c. 350 l Emperor Augustus marble statue .50 .45
d. 400 l Good Shepherd marble statue .50 .45
e. 500 l St. Nicholas Saving a ship by G. da Fabriano .60 .50
f. 1200 l The Holy face by G. Rouault .75 .60

Vatican Collection: The Papacy and Art - US 1983 exhibition, New York, Chicago, San Francisco.

Extraordinary Holy Year, 1983-84 (1950th Anniv. of Redemption) — A214

Sketches by Giovanni Hajnal.

1983, Mar. 10 Photo. & Engr.

721 A214 300 l Crucifixion .30 .30
722 A214 350 l Christ the Redeemer .35 .35
723 A214 400 l Pope .40 .40
724 A214 2000 l Holy Spirit 2.00 2.00
Nos. 721-724 (4) 3.05 3.05

Theology, by Raphael (1483-1517) — A215

Allegories, Room of the Segnatura.

1983, June 14

725 A215 50 l shown .25 .25
726 A215 400 l Poetry .35 .35
727 A215 500 l Justice .50 .50
728 A215 1200 l Philosphy 1.40 1.40
Nos. 725-728 (4) 2.50 2.50

Gregor Johann Mendel (1822-1884), Biologist — A216

Phases of pea plant hybridization.

Photo. & Engr.

1984, Feb. 28 *Perf. 14x13½*

729 A216 450 l multicolored .45 .45
730 A216 1500 l multicolored 1.75 1.75

St. Casimir of Lithuania (1458-1484) — A217

1984, Feb. 28 *Perf. 14*

731 A217 550 l multicolored .60 .60
732 A217 1200 l multicolored 1.25 1.25

Pontifical Academy of Sciences A218

1984, June 18 Litho. & Engr.

733 A218 150 l shown .25 .25
734 A218 450 l Secret Archives .50 .50
735 A218 550 l Apostolic Library .75 .75
736 A218 1500 l Observatory 1.75 1.75
Nos. 733-736 (4) 3.25 3.25

Papal Journeys A218a

1984-85 Photo. *Perf. 13½x14½*

737 A218a 50 l Pakistan .25 .25
738 A218a 100 l Philippines .25 .25
739 A218a 150 l Guam .25 .25
740 A218a 250 l Japan .25 .25
741 A218a 300 l Alaska .25 .25
742 A218a 400 l Africa .35 .35
743 A218a 450 l Portugal .40 .40
a. Bklt. pane, 4 ea #738, 741-743 + 4 labels ('85) 10.00
Complete booklet, #743a 10.00
744 A218a 550 l Grt. Britain .80 .80
745 A218a 1000 l Argentina 1.25 1.25
746 A218a 1500 l Switzerland 2.50 2.50
747 A218a 2500 l San Marino 4.00 4.00
748 A218a 4000 l Spain 6.00 6.00
Nos. 737-748 (12) 16.55 16.55

Issued: Nos. 737-748, 10/2/84; No. 743a, 3/14/85.

St. Damasus I (b. 304) — A219

St. Damasus I and: 200 l, Sepulchre of Sts. Marcellinus and Peter. 500 l, Epigraph of St. Januarius. 2000 l, Basilica, Church of the Martyrs Simplicius, Faustinus and Beatrice.

1984, Nov. 27 Photo. *Perf. 14x13½*

749 A219 200 l multicolored .35 .35
750 A219 500 l multicolored .70 .70
751 A219 2000 l multicolored 2.25 2.25
Nos. 749-751 (3) 3.30 3.30

St. Methodius (d. 885) — A220

St. Methodius and: 500 l, Madonna and Christ. 600 l, St. Cyril, carrying the body of St. Clement I. 1700 l, Sts. Benedict and Cyril, patrons of Europe.

Photo. & Engr.

1985, May 7 *Perf. 13½x14*

752 A220 500 l multicolored .50 .50
753 A220 600 l multicolored .70 .70
754 A220 1700 l multicolored 2.25 2.25
Nos. 752-754 (3) 3.45 3.45

St. Thomas More (1477-1535) A221

St. Thomas More (from a portrait by Hans Holbein) and: 250 l, map of British Isles. 400 l, Frontispiece of Utopia. 2000 l, Frontispiece of Domenico Regi's biography of More.

Litho. & Engr.

1985, May 7 *Perf. 14x13½*

755 A221 250 l multicolored .40 .40
756 A221 400 l multicolored .50 .50
757 A221 2000 l multicolored 2.60 2.60
Nos. 755-757 (3) 3.50 3.50

St. Gregory VII (c. 1020-85) — A222

Designs: 150 l, Eagle from Byzantine door, St. Paul's Basilica, Rome. 450 l, St. Gregory blessing. 2500 l, Sarcophagus.

Perf. 13½x14, 14x13½

1985, June 18 Photo.

758 A222 150 l multi, vert. .25 .25
759 A222 450 l multi, vert. .60 .45
760 A222 2500 l multicolored 2.75 2.50
Nos. 758-760 (3) 3.60 3.20

43rd Intl. Eucharistic Congress — A223

Emblem, host, cross and: 100 l, Outline map of Africa. 400 l, Altar and Assembly of Bishops. 600 l, African chalice. 2300 l, African Christian family.

Photo. & Engr.

1985, June 18 *Perf. 13½x14*

761 A223 100 l multicolored .25 .25
762 A223 400 l multicolored .45 .40
763 A223 600 l multicolored .55 .55
764 A223 2300 l multicolored 2.60 2.60
Nos. 761-764 (4) 3.85 3.80

Concordat Agreement Ratification A224

1985, Oct. 15 Photo. *Perf. 14x13½*

765 A224 400 l Papal arms, map of Italy .60 .60

Coaches — A225

1985, Oct. 15 Litho. & Engr.

766 A225 450 l dp lil rose & int bl .45 .45
767 A225 1500 l brt bl & dp lil rose 1.50 1.50
a. Souvenir sheet of 2, #766-767, perf. 13½x12½ 3.00 3.00

Italia '85.

Intl. Peace Year 1986 — A226

Biblical and gospel texts: 50 l, Isaiah 2:4. 350 l, Isaiah 52:7. 450 l, Matthew 5:9. 650 l,

Luke 2:14. 2000 l, Message for World Peace, speech of Pope John Paul II, Jan. 1, 1986.

1986, Apr. 14 Photo. ***Perf. 14***

768 A226 50 l multicolored .25 .25
769 A226 350 l multicolored .35 .35
770 A226 450 l multicolored .60 .60
771 A226 650 l multicolored .80 .80
772 A226 2000 l multicolored 2.25 2.25
Nos. 768-772 (5) 4.25 4.25

Vatican City A227

1986, Apr. 14 ***Perf. 13½x14***

773 A227 Block of 6 5.00 5.00
a.-f. 550 l, any single .70 .70

UNESCO World Heritage Campaign. No. 773 has continuous design.

Patron Saints of the Sick — A228

Designs: No. 774, St. Camillus de Lellis rescuing invalid during Tiber flood, by Pierre Subleyras (1699-1749). No. 775, St. John of God with invalids, by Gomez Moreno (1834-1918). 2000 l, Pope John Paul II visiting the sick.

Litho. & Engr.

1986, June 12 ***Perf. 13½x14***

774 A228 700 l multicolored .80 .80
775 A228 700 l multicolored .80 .80
776 A228 2000 l multicolored 2.50 2.50
Nos. 774-776 (3) 4.10 4.10

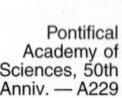

Pontifical Academy of Sciences, 50th Anniv. — A229

School of Athens (details), by Raphael: 1500 l, Scribes. 2500 l, Students learning math.

Litho. & Engr.

1986, Oct. 2 ***Perf. 14x13½***

777 A229 1500 l multicolored 1.75 1.75
778 A229 2500 l multicolored 3.00 3.00

Conversion of St. Augustine (354-430) in 387 — A230

Religious art: 300 l, St. Augustine reading St. Paul's Epistles, fresco by Benozzo Gozzoli (1420-1498), Church of St. Augustine, San Gimignano. 400 l, Baptism of St. Augustine, painting by Bartolomeo di Gentile (1470-1534), Vatican Art Gallery. 500 l, Ecstasy of St. Augustine, fresco by Benozzo Gozzoli, Church of St. Augustine. 2200 l, St. Augustine, detail of Disputa del Sacramento, fresco by Raphael (1483-1520), Room of the Segnatura, Apostolic Palace.

1987, Apr. 7 Photo. ***Perf. 13½x14***

779 A230 300 l multicolored .40 .40
780 A230 400 l multicolored .55 .55
781 A230 500 l multicolored .65 .65
782 A230 2200 l multicolored 3.00 3.00
Nos. 779-782 (4) 4.60 4.60

A231

Seals: 700 l, Church of Riga, 1234-1269. 2400 l, Marian Basilica of the Assumption, Aglona, 1780.

1987, June 2 Photo. ***Perf. 13½x14***

783 A231 700 l multicolored 1.25 1.25
784 A231 2400 l multicolored 3.25 3.25

Christianization of Latvia, 800th anniv.

Christianization Anniversaries — A232

Designs: 200 l, Christ, statue in the Lithuanian Chapel, Vatican Crypt. 700 l, Two Angels and Our Lady Holding the Body of Christ, by a Lithuanian artist. 3000 l, Lithuanian shrine.

1987, June 2 ***Perf. 13½x14***

785 A232 200 l multicolored .30 .30
786 A232 700 l multicolored 1.00 1.00
787 A232 3000 l multicolored 3.25 3.25
Nos. 785-787 (3) 4.55 4.55

Christianization of Lithuania, 600th anniv.

OLYMPHILEX '87, Rome, Aug. 29-Sept. 9 — A233

Details of mosaic from the Baths of Caracalla: 400 l, Judge. 500 l, Athlete. 600 l, Athlete, diff. 2000 l, Athlete, diff.

Litho. & Engr.

1987, Aug. 29 ***Perf. 14***

788 A233 400 l multicolored .40 .40
789 A233 500 l multicolored .50 .50
790 A233 600 l multicolored .60 .60
791 A233 2000 l multicolored 3.00 3.00
Nos. 788-791 (4) 4.50 4.50

Souvenir Sheet

792 Sheet of 4 + 4 labels 4.00 4.00
a. A233 400 l like No. 788 .40 .30
b. A233 500 l like No. 789 .50 .40
c. A233 600 l like No. 780 .60 .50
d. A233 2000 l 2.75 2.25

Stamps from souvenir sheet have a Greek border in blue surrounding vignettes (pictured). Nos. 788-791 have single line border in blue. No. 792 has 4 labels picturing the papal arms, a goblet, a crown and the exhibition emblem.

Inauguration of the Philatelic and Numismatic Museum — A235

Designs: 400 l, Philatelic department, Vatican City, No. 1. 3500 l, Numismatic department, 1000-lire coin of 1986.

1987, Sept. 29 Photo. ***Perf. 14x13½***

793 A235 400 l multicolored .50 .50
794 A235 3500 l multicolored 4.00 4.00

Journeys of Pope John Paul II, 1985-86 — A236

Designs: 50 l, Venezuela, Peru, Ecuador and Trinidad & Tobago, 1985. 250 l, The Netherlands, Luxembourg, Belgium, 1985. 400 l, Togo, Ivory Coast, Cameroun, Central Africa, Zaire, Kenya and Morocco, 1985. 500 l, Liechtenstein, 1986. 600 l, India, 1986. 700 l, Colombia, St. Lucia, 1986. 2500 l, France, 1986. 4000 l, Bangladesh, Singapore, Fiji, New Zealand, Australia and Seychelles, 1986.

1987, Oct. 27 Photo. ***Perf. 14x13½***

795 A236 50 l multicolored .25 .25
796 A236 250 l multicolored .50 .30
797 A236 400 l multicolored .60 .40
798 A236 500 l multicolored .80 .50
799 A236 600 l multicolored 1.00 .80
800 A236 700 l multicolored 1.50 1.00
801 A236 2500 l multicolored 5.50 4.25
802 A236 4000 l multicolored 8.50 7.00
Nos. 795-802 (8) 18.65 14.50

A237

Transfer of St. Nicholas Relics from Myra to Bari, 900th anniv.: 500 l, Arrival of relics at Bari. 700 l, Act of charity, three improverished women. 3000 l, Miraculous rescue of ship.

1987, Dec. 3 ***Perf. 13½x14***

803 A237 500 l multicolored 1.00 1.00
804 A237 700 l multicolored 1.50 1.25
805 A237 3000 l multicolored 10.00 8.00
Nos. 803-805 (3) 12.50 10.25

St. Nicholas of Bari (c. 270-352), bishop of Myra. Legend of Santa Claus originated because of his charitable works. Printed in sheets of 8 + 16 se-tenant labels picturing Santa Claus. Value, $60.

A238

Children and: 500 l, Sister of the Institute of the Daughters of Mary Help of Christians. 1000 l, St. John Bosco. 2000 l, Salesian lay brother. Printed in a continuous design.

1988, Apr. 19 **Photo.**

806 Strip of 3 4.00 4.00
a. A238 500 l multicolored .45 .40
b. A238 1000 l multicolored .75 .50
c. A238 2000 l multicolored 1.50 1.25

St. John Bosco (1815-1888), educator.

A239

50 l, Annunciation. 300 l, Nativity. 500 l, Pentecost. 750 l, Assumption. 1000 l, Mother of the Church. 2400 l, Refuge of Sinners.

1988, June 16 Photo. ***Perf. 13½x14***

807 A239 50 l multicolored .25 .25
808 A239 300 l multicolored .30 .25
809 A239 500 l multicolored .50 .40
810 A239 750 l multicolored .90 .60
811 A239 1000 l multicolored 1.25 .80
812 A239 2400 l multicolored 2.75 1.75
Nos. 807-812 (6) 5.95 4.05

Marian Year, 1987-88.

A240

Baptism of the Rus' of Kiev, Millennium: 450 l, "Prince St. Vladimir the Great," from a 15th cent. icon. 650 l, Cathedral of St. Sophia, Kiev. 2500 l, "Mother of God in Prayer," from a mosaic at the cathedral.

1988, June 16

813 A240 450 l multicolored .60 .45
814 A240 650 l multicolored .85 .65
815 A240 2500 l multicolored 3.00 2.25
Nos. 813-815 (3) 4.45 3.35

Paintings by Paolo Veronese (1528-1588) A241

Designs: 550 l, Marriage of Cana (Madonna and Christ) the Louvre, Paris. 650 l, Self-portrait of the Artist, Villa Barbaro of Maser, Treviso. 3000 l, Marriage of Cana (woman and two men).

Perf. 13½x14, 14x13½

1988, Sept. 29 Photo. & Engr.

816 A241 550 l multi, vert. .75 .45
817 A241 650 l multicolored .85 .55
818 A241 3000 l multi, vert. 4.00 2.50
Nos. 816-818 (3) 5.60 3.50

Christmas — A242

Luke 2:14 and: 50 l, Angel facing LR. 400 l, Angel facing UR. 500 l, Angel facing LL. 550 l, Shepherds. 850 l, Nativity. 1500 l, Magi.

1988, Dec. 12 Photo. ***Perf. 13½x14***

819 A242 50 l multicolored .25 .25
820 A242 400 l multicolored .40 .30
821 A242 500 l multicolored .55 .35
822 A242 550 l multicolored .65 .40
823 A242 850 l multicolored .90 .60
824 A242 1500 l multicolored 1.40 1.00
Nos. 819-824 (6) 4.15 2.90

Souvenir Sheet

825 Sheet of 6 4.00 4.00
a. A242 50 l gold & multi .25 .25
b. A242 400 l gold & multi .40 .30
c. A242 500 l gold & multi .50 .35
d. A242 550 l gold & multi .70 .40
e. A242 850 l gold & multi 1.00 .60
f. A242 1500 l gold & multi 1.50 1.00

No. 825 has continuous design.

Feast of the Visitation, 600th Anniv. — A243

Illuminations: 550 l, The Annunciation. 750 l, The Visitation (Virgin and St. Elizabeth). 2500 l, Mary, Elizabeth and infants.

1989, May 5 Photo. ***Perf. 13½x14***

826 A243 550 l multicolored .70 .40
827 A243 750 l multicolored .80 .55
828 A243 2500 l multicolored 2.60 1.90
Nos. 826-828 (3) 4.10 2.85

Souvenir Sheet

Gregorian Egyptian Museum, 150th Anniv. — A244

Designs: 400 l, Apis. 650 l, Isis and Apis dicephalous bust. 750 l, Statue of the physician Ugiahorresne. 2400 l, Pharaoh Mentuhotep.

Litho. & Engr.

1989, May 5 ***Perf. 14x13½***

829 A244 Sheet of 4 4.00 4.00
a. 400 l multicolored .30 .25
b. 650 l multicolored .40 .25
c. 750 l multicolored .55 .45
d. 2400 l multicolored 1.50 1.25

A245

Birds from engravings by Eleazar Albin in *Histoire Naturelle des Oiseaux,* 1750 — 100 l, Parrot. 150 l, Green woodpecker. 200 l, Crested and common wrens. 350 l, Kingfisher. 500 l, Red grosbeak of Virginia. 700 l, Bullfinch. 1500 l, Lapwing plover. 3000 l, French teal.

1989, June 13 Photo. *Perf. 12*
Granite Paper

830	A245	100 l	multicolored	.25	.25
831	A245	150 l	multicolored	.25	.25
832	A245	200 l	multicolored	.25	.25
833	A245	350 l	multicolored	.45	.25
834	A245	500 l	multicolored	.65	.30
835	A245	700 l	multicolored	.90	.45
836	A245	1500 l	multicolored	2.00	1.00
837	A245	3000 l	multicolored	4.00	2.00
			Nos. 830-837 (8)	8.75	4.75

A246

Symbols of the Eucharist.

Photo. & Engr.
1989, Sept. 29 *Perf. 13½x14*

838	A246	550 l	shown	.70	.40
839	A246	850 l	multi, diff.	1.00	.65
840	A246	1000 l	multi, diff.	1.25	.75
841	A246	2500 l	multi, diff.	3.25	1.90
			Nos. 838-841 (4)	6.20	3.70

44th Intl. Eucharistic Cong., Seoul, Oct. 5-8.

Ecclesiastical Hierarchy in the US, Bicent. — A247

Designs: 450 l, Basilica of the Assumption of the Blessed Virgin Mary, Baltimore. 1350 l, John Carroll (1735-1815), 1st bishop of Baltimore and the US. 2400 l, Cathedral of Mary Our Queen, Baltimore.

1989, Nov. 9 Photo. *Perf. 12*

842	A247	450 l	multicolored	.60	.40
843	A247	1350 l	multicolored	1.75	1.25
844	A247	2400 l	multicolored	3.25	2.00
			Nos. 842-844 (3)	5.60	3.65

Papal Journeys 1988 — A248

Papal arms, Pope John Paul II and maps: 50 l, Uruguay, Bolivia, Peru and Paraguay, May 7-19. 550 l, Austria, June 23-27. 800 l, Zimbabwe, Botswana, Lesotho, Swaziland and Mozambique, Sept. 10-19. 1000 l, France, Oct. 8-11. 4000 l, Pastoral visits in Italy, 1978-1988.

1989, Nov. 9 *Perf. 14x13½*

845	A248	50 l	multicolored	.25	.25
846	A248	550 l	multicolored	.80	.50
847	A248	800 l	multicolored	1.10	.70
848	A248	1000 l	multicolored	1.50	.90
849	A248	4000 l	multicolored	5.75	3.50
			Nos. 845-849 (5)	9.40	5.85

St. Angela Merici (c. 1474-1540) — A249

Designs: 700 l, The vision of the mystical stair, Prophecy of the Ursulines. 800 l, Evangelical counsel. 2800 l, Ursulines mission continued.

1990, Apr. 5 Photo. *Perf. 13½x14*

850	A249	700 l	multicolored	1.10	.80
851	A249	800 l	multicolored	1.25	.95
852	A249	2800 l	multicolored	4.25	3.25
			Nos. 850-852 (3)	6.60	5.00

Caritas Intl., 40th Anniv. — A250

Designs: 450 l, Abraham. 650 l, Three visitors. 800 l, Abraham and Sarah. 2000 l, Three visitors at Abraham's table.

1990, June 5 Photo. *Perf. 12x11½*
Granite Paper

853	A250	450 l	multicolored	.75	.45
854	A250	650 l	multicolored	1.25	.70
855	A250	800 l	multicolored	1.50	.85
856	A250	2000 l	multicolored	3.00	2.00
			Nos. 853-856 (4)	6.50	4.00

Souvenir Sheet

857	Sheet of 4	7.00	7.00
a.	A250 450 l like #853	.70	.60
b.	A250 650 l like #854	1.10	.90
c.	A250 800 l like #855	1.25	1.00
d.	A250 2000 l like #856	3.25	2.25

Nos. 853-856 have a single line border in gold. Nos. 857a-857d have no border line.

No. 857 with "Pro Terremotati 1997" overprinted in sheet margin exists in limited quantities, sold for 8000 l to assist earthquake victims in Umbria and Marche, but was not officially issued by Vatican postal authorities. It was sold in a folder depicting St. Francis of Assissi. Value $30.

A251

300 l, Ordination of St. Willibrord. 700 l, Stay in Antwerp. 3000 l, Leaving belongings, death.

1990, June 5 *Perf. 13½x14*

858	A251	300 l	multicolored	.50	.30
859	A251	700 l	multicolored	1.00	.70
860	A251	3000 l	multicolored	4.00	3.25
			Nos. 858-860 (3)	5.50	4.25

1300th anniv. of ministry of St. Willibrord.

A252

Diocese of Beijing-Nanking, 300th Anniv.: 500 l, Lake Beijing. 750 l, Church of the Immaculate Conception, Beijing, 1650. 1500 l, Lake Beijing, diff. 2000 l, Church of the Redeemer, Beijing, 1703.

1990, Oct. 2

861	A252	500 l	multicolored	.65	.45
862	A252	750 l	multicolored	1.00	.70
863	A252	1500 l	multicolored	2.10	1.40
864	A252	2000 l	multicolored	2.60	1.90
			Nos. 861-864 (4)	6.35	4.45

Christmas A253

Details from painting by Sebastiano Mainardi.

1990, Nov. 27 Photo. *Perf. 13*

865	A253	50 l	Choir of Angels	.25	.25
866	A253	200 l	St. Joseph	.30	.30
867	A253	650 l	Holy Child	1.10	1.10
868	A253	750 l	Madonna	1.25	1.25
869	A253	2500 l	Nativity scene, vert.	4.00	4.00
			Nos. 865-869 (5)	6.90	6.90

Paintings of the Sistine Chapel — A254

Different details from lunettes: 50 l, 100 l, Eleazar. 150 l, 250 l, Jacob. 350 l, 400 l, Josiah. 500 l, 650 l, Asa. 800 l, 1000 l, Zerubbabel. 2000 l, 3000 l, Azor.

1991, Apr. 9 Photo. *Perf. 11½*
Granite Paper

870	A254	50 l	multicolored	.25	.25
871	A254	100 l	multicolored	.25	.25
a.			Booklet pane of 6	.75	
872	A254	150 l	multicolored	.25	.25
a.			Booklet pane of 6	1.25	
873	A254	250 l	multicolored	.30	.30
874	A254	350 l	multicolored	.40	.40
875	A254	400 l	multicolored	.50	.50
876	A254	500 l	multicolored	.65	.65
877	A254	650 l	multicolored	.85	.85
a.			Booklet pane of 6	5.50	
			Complete booklet, #871a, 872a, 877a	8.00	
878	A254	800 l	multicolored	.90	.90
879	A254	1000 l	multicolored	1.25	1.25
880	A254	2000 l	multicolored	2.50	2.50
881	A254	3000 l	multicolored	3.75	3.75
			Nos. 870-881 (12)	11.85	11.85

Encyclical Rerum Novarum, Cent. — A255

Arms of Pope Leo XIII and: 600 l, Title page of Encyclical. 750 l, Allegory of Church's interest in workers, employers. 3500 l, Pope Leo XIII (1878-1903).

1991, May 23 Engr. *Perf. 14x13½*

882	A255	600 l	blue & dk grn	.90	.85
883	A255	750 l	sage grn & rose car	1.10	1.00
884	A255	3500 l	brt pur & dk bl	5.00	4.50
			Nos. 882-884 (3)	7.00	6.35

Vatican Observatory, Cent. — A256

Designs: 750 l, Astrograph for making photographic sky map, 1891. 1000 l, Zeiss Double Astrograph, Lake Castelgandolfo, 1935, horiz. 3000 l, New telescope, Vatican Observatory, Mt. Graham, Arizona, 1991.

Perf. 11½x12, 12x11½
1991, Oct. 1 Photo.
Granite Paper

885	A256	750 l	multicolored	1.00	1.00
886	A256	1000 l	multicolored	1.50	1.50
887	A256	3000 l	multicolored	4.25	4.25
			Nos. 885-887 (3)	6.75	6.75

Canonization of St. Bridget, 600th Anniv. — A257

Designs: 1500 l, Receiving Madonna's revelations. 2000 l, Receiving Christ's revelations.

1991, Oct. 1 *Perf. 12½x13*

888	A257	1500 l	multicolored	2.50	2.25
889	A257	2000 l	multicolored	3.50	3.25

Journeys of Pope John Paul II, 1990 — A258

Pope John Paul II and: 200 l, Cathedral of Immaculate Conception, Ouagadougou, Burkina Faso. 550 l, St. Vitus' Cathedral, Prague. 750 l, Our Lady of Guadaloupe's Basilica, Mexico. 1500 l, Ta' Pinu Sanctuary, Gozo. 3500 l, Cathedral of Christ the King, Gitega, Burundi.

Litho. & Engr.
1991, Nov. 11 *Perf. 13½x14*

890	A258	200 l	green & multi	.25	.25
891	A258	550 l	org brn & multi	.75	.75
892	A258	750 l	claret & multi	1.00	1.00
893	A258	1500 l	dk brn & multi	2.00	2.00
894	A258	3500 l	grn bl & multi	5.25	5.25
			Nos. 890-894 (5)	9.25	9.25

West Africa, Jan. 25-Feb. 1 (200 l); Czechoslovakia, Apr. 21-22 (550 l); Mexico, Curacao, May 6-14 (750 l); Malta, May 25-27 (1500 l); Tanzania, Burundi, Rwanda, Ivory Coast, Sept. 1-10 (3500 l).

A259

Special Assembly for Europe of Synod of Bishops: 300 l, Colonnade of St. Peter's Basilica. 500 l, St. Peter's Basilica and Square. 4000 l, Colonnade of St. Peter's Basilica, Apostolic Palace.

1991, Nov. 11 Engr. *Perf. 12½x13*

895	300 l	olive & blk	.50	.50
896	500 l	olive & blk	.90	.90
897	4000 l	olive & blk	6.00	6.00
a.		A259 Strip of 3, #895-897	6.50	6.50

No. 897a has continous design.

A260

Discovery and Evangelization of America, 500th Anniv.: 500 l, Christopher Columbus. 600 l, Saint Peter Claver. 850 l, La Virgen de los Reyes Catolicos. 1000 l, Bishop Bartolome de las Casas. 2000 l, Father Junipero Serra.

Charts: 1500 l, New World. 2500 l, Old World.

1992, Mar. 24 Photo. *Perf. 11½x12*
Granite Paper

898	A260	500 l	multicolored	.65	.65
899	A260	600 l	multicolored	.75	.75
900	A260	850 l	multicolored	1.00	1.00
901	A260	1000 l	multicolored	1.25	1.25
902	A260	2000 l	multicolored	2.50	2.50
			Nos. 898-902 (5)	6.15	6.15

Souvenir Sheet
Perf. 12

903	A260	Sheet of 2	7.00	7.00
a.		1500 l multicolored	2.25	2.25
b.		2500 l multicolored	3.75	3.75

Piero Della Francesca (d. 1492), Painter — A261

Frescoes: 300 l, 750 l (detail), Our Lady of Childbirth. 1000 l, 3000 l (detail), Resurrection.

1992, May 15 Photo. *Perf. 13½x14*

904	A261	300 l	multicolored	.40	.40
905	A261	750 l	multicolored	1.10	1.10
906	A261	1000 l	multicolored	1.40	1.40
907	A261	3000 l	multicolored	4.25	4.25
			Nos. 904-907 (4)	7.15	7.15

St. Giuseppe Benedetto Cottolengo (1786-1842) — A262

St. Giuseppe Benedetto Cottolengo: 650 l, Comforting the sick. 850 l, With Little House of Divine Providence.

1992, May 15 *Perf. 11½x12*
Granite Paper

908 A262 650 l multicolored 1.00 1.00
909 A262 850 l multicolored 1.40 1.40

A263

Plants of the New World: a, Frumentum indicum. b, Solanum pomiferum. c, Opuntia. d, Cacaos, cacavifera. e, Solanum tuberosum, capsicum, mordens. f, Ananas sagitae folio.

1992, Sept. 15 Photo. *Perf. 11½x12*
Granite Paper

910 Block of 6 7.50 7.50
a.-f. A263 850 l any single 1.10 1.10

A264

1992, Oct. 12 *Perf. 12½x13*
911 A264 700 l multicolored 1.25 1.10

4th General Conference of the Latin American Episcopacy.

Christmas — A265

Mosaics from Basilica of St. Maria Maggiore, Rome: 600 l, The Annunciation. 700 l, Nativity. 1000 l, Adoration of the Magi. 1500 l, Presentation to the Temple.

1992, Nov. 24 Photo. *Perf. 11½*
Granite Paper

912 A265 600 l multicolored 1.00 1.00
913 A265 700 l multicolored 1.15 1.15
914 A265 1000 l multicolored 1.35 1.35
915 A265 1500 l multicolored 2.75 2.75
Nos. 912-915 (4) 6.25 6.25

St. Francis Healing Man from Ilerda, by Giotto di Bondone (1266-1337) — A266

1993, Jan. 9 Litho. *Perf. 13½x14*
916 A266 1000 l multi + label 2.10 1.75

Prayer Meeting for Peace in Europe, Assisi.

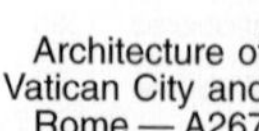

Architecture of Vatican City and Rome — A267

Buildings: 200 l, St. Peter's Basilica, Vatican City. 300 l, St. John Lateran Basilica, Rome. 350 l, St. Mary Major's Basilica, Rome. 500 l, St. Paul's Basilica, Rome. 600 l, Apostolic Palace, Vatican. 700 l, Lateran Apostolic Palace, Rome. 850 l, Papal Palace, Castel Gandolfo. 1000 l, Chancery Palace, Rome. 2000 l, Palace of the Propagation of the Faith, Rome. 3000 l, St. Calixtus Palace, Rome.

1993, Mar. 23 Photo. *Perf. 12x11½*
Granite Paper

917 A267 200 l multicolored .25 .25
a. Booklet pane of 4 1.10
918 A267 300 l multicolored .40 .40
a. Booklet pane of 4 1.60
919 A267 350 l multicolored .50 .50
a. Booklet pane of 4 2.00
920 A267 500 l multicolored .65 .65
a. Booklet pane of 4 2.75
Complete booklet, #917a, 918a, 919a, 920a 7.50
921 A267 600 l multicolored .80 .80
922 A267 700 l multicolored .95 .95
923 A267 850 l multicolored 1.00 1.00
924 A267 1000 l multicolored 1.25 1.25
925 A267 2000 l multicolored 2.60 2.60
926 A267 3000 l multicolored 3.75 3.75
Nos. 917-926 (10) 12.15 12.15

A268

Congress emblem, Vatican arms and: 500 l, Cross, grape vines. 700 l, Cross, hands breaking bread. 1500 l, Hands lifting chalice. 2500 l, Wheat, banner.

1993, May 22 Litho. *Perf. 14x13½*
927 A268 500 l multicolored .60 .60
928 A268 700 l multicolored .90 .90
929 A268 1500 l multicolored 1.90 1.90
930 A268 2500 l multicolored 3.00 3.00
Nos. 927-930 (4) 6.40 6.40

45th Intl. Eucharistic Congress, Seville.

A269

Traditio Legis Sarcophagus, St. Peter's Basilica: a, 200 l, Sacrifice of Isaac. b, 750 l, Apostle Peter receiving law from Jesus, Apostle Paul. c, 3000 l, Christ watching servant pouring water on Pilate's hands.

1993, May 22 Engr. *Perf. 13½x14*
931 A269 Triptych, #a.-c. 5.25 5.25

Ascension Day, May 20.

Contemporary Art — A270

Europa: 750 l, Crucifixion, by Felice Casorati (1886-1963). 850 l, Rouen Cathedral, by Maurice Utrillo (1883-1955).

1993, Sept. 29 Photo. *Perf. 13*
932 A270 750 l multicolored .95 .95
933 A270 850 l multicolored 1.00 1.00

Death of St. John of Nepomuk, 600th Anniv. — A271

2000 l, Buildings in Prague, Charles Bridge.

1993, Sept. 29 Litho. *Perf. 13½x14*
934 A271 1000 l multicolored 1.40 1.25
935 A271 2000 l multicolored 2.75 2.50

Travels of Pope John Paul II — A272

Visits to: 600 l, Senegal, Gambia, Guinea. 1000 l, Angola, St. Thomas and Prince. 5000 l, Dominican Republic.

1993, Nov. 23 Photo. *Perf. 12x11½*
Granite Paper

936 A272 600 l multicolored .75 .75
937 A272 1000 l multicolored 1.50 1.50
938 A272 5000 l multicolored 7.00 7.00
Nos. 936-938 (3) 9.25 9.25

Hans Holbein the Younger (1497?-1543), Painter — A273

Details or entire paintings: 700 l, 1000 l, Madonna of Solothurn. 1500 l, Self-portrait.

Litho. & Engr.

1993, Nov. 23 *Perf. 13½x14*
939 A273 700 l multicolored .90 .90
940 A273 1000 l multicolored 1.50 1.50
941 A273 1500 l multicolored 2.25 2.25
Nos. 939-941 (3) 4.65 4.65

Synod of Bishops, Special Assembly for Africa — A274

Designs: 850 l, Stylized crosier, dome with cross, vert. 1000 l, Crucifix, dome of St. Peter's Basilica, crosiers, African landscape.

Perf. 12½x13, 13x12½

1994, Apr. 8 **Photo.**
942 A274 850 l multicolored 1.25 1.25
943 A274 1000 l multicolored 1.50 1.50

The Restored Sistine Chapel A275

Frescoes, by Michelangelo: Creation of the Sun and Moon: No. 944, Sun. No. 945, God pointing toward moon. Creation of Man: No. 946, Adam. No. 947, God. Original Sin: No. 948, Adam, Eve taking apple from serpent. No. 949, Adam, Eve forced from Garden of Eden. The Flood: No. 950, People on dry ground. No. 951, People on stone outcropping.

4000 l, Detail of Last Judgment, Christ and the Virgin.

1994, Apr. 8 Photo. *Perf. 11½*
944 350 l multicolored .40 .40
945 350 l multicolored .40 .40
a. A275 Pair, #944-945 1.00 1.00
946 500 l multicolored .60 .60
947 500 l multicolored .60 .60
a. A275 Pair, #946-947 1.50 1.50
948 1000 l multicolored 1.50 1.50
949 1000 l multicolored 1.50 1.50
a. A275 Pair, #948-949 2.50 2.50
950 2000 l multicolored 4.00 4.00
951 2000 l multicolored 3.00 3.00
a. A275 Pair, 950-951 8.00 8.00
Nos. 944-951 (8) 12.00 12.00

Souvenir Sheet
Perf. 12

952 A275 4000 l multicolored 6.25 6.25

No. 952 contains one 36x54mm stamp.

European Inventions, Discoveries A276

Europa: 750 l, Progess from wheel to atom traced by white thread. 850 l, Galileo in center of solar system, scientific instruments.

1994, May 31 Litho. *Perf. 13x13½*
953 A276 750 l multicolored .95 .95
954 A276 850 l multicolored 1.10 1.10

Intl. Year of the Family — A277

Stained glass: 400 l, God creating man and woman. 750 l, Family under names of four Evangelists. 1000 l, Parents teaching son. 2000 l, Young man comforting elderly couple.

1994, May 31 Photo. *Perf. 13x14*
955 A277 400 l multicolored .50 .50
956 A277 750 l multicolored .95 .95
957 A277 1000 l multicolored 1.40 1.40
958 A277 2000 l multicolored 2.50 2.50
Nos. 955-958 (4) 5.35 5.35

Giovanni da Montecorvino (1247-1328), Missionary — A278

1994, Sept. 27 Litho. *Perf. 14*
959 A278 1000 l multicolored 1.75 1.75

Evangelization of China, 700th anniv.

13th Intl. Convention of Christian Archaeology, Split, Croatia — A279

Mosaics from Euphrasian Basilica, Parentium, Croatia, 6th Cent.: 700 l, Bishop Euphrasius, Archdeacon Claudius, Claudius' son. 1500 l, Madonna and Child, two angels. 3000 l, Christ, Apostles Peter & Paul.

1994, Sept. 27 *Perf. 13x14*
960 A279 700 l multicolored .90 .90
961 A279 1500 l multicolored 1.90 1.90
962 A279 3000 l multicolored 4.00 4.00
Nos. 960-962 (3) 6.80 6.80

Travels of Pope John Paul II — A280

Designs: 600 l, Benin, Uganda, Sudan. 700 l, Albania. 1000 l, Spain. 2000 l, Jamaica, Mexico, US. 3000 l, Lithuania, Latvia, Estonia.

1994, Nov. 18 Engr. *Perf. 13*
963 A280 600 l multicolored .85 .85
964 A280 700 l multicolored 1.00 1.00
965 A280 1000 l multicolored 1.40 1.40
966 A280 2000 l multicolored 2.75 2.75
967 A280 3000 l multicolored 4.25 4.25
Nos. 963-967 (5) 10.25 10.25

Christmas A281

The Nativity, by Il Tintoretto: 700 l, The Holy Family. No. 969, The Holy Family, two women. No. 970, Adoration of the shepherds.

1994, Nov. 18 Photo. *Perf. 11½*
Granite Paper

968 A281 700 l multicolored 1.00 1.00

Size: 45x27mm

969 A281 1000 l multicolored 1.50 1.50
970 A281 1000 l multicolored 1.50 1.50
a. Pair, #969-970 3.50 3.50
Nos. 968-970 (3) 4.00 4.00

Peace and Freedom — A282

1995, Mar. 25 Photo. *Perf. 14x13*

971 A282 750 l shown .90 .90
972 A282 850 l Hands clasp, dove 1.00 1.00

Europa.

Shrine of Loreto, 700th Anniv. — A283

Details of artworks from vaults of Sacristy: 600 l, St. Mark's, Angel with chalice, by Melozzo da Forli. 700 l, St. Mark's, Angel with lamb, by da Forli. 1500 l, 2500 l, St. John's, Music making angels, by Luca Signorelli.
No. 977, Marble carving showing Holy House of Loreto.

1995, Mar. 25 *Perf. 11½*

973 A283 600 l multicolored .75 .75
974 A283 700 l multicolored .85 .85
975 A283 1500 l multicolored 2.00 2.00
976 A283 2500 l multicolored 4.00 4.00
Nos. 973-976 (4) 7.60 7.60

Souvenir Sheet

977 A283 3000 l multicolored 3.75 3.75

No. 977 contains one 36x36mm stamp.

Radio, Cent. — A284

Designs: 850 l, Guglielmo Marconi, transmitting equipment. 1000 l, Archangel Gabriel, Pope John Paul II, Marconi broadcasting station, Vatican City.

1995, June 8 Photo. *Perf. 14*

978 A284 850 l multicolored 1.25 1.25
979 A284 1000 l multicolored 1.75 1.75

See Germany No. 1990, Ireland Nos. 973-974, Italy Nos. 2038-2039, San Marino Nos. 1336-1337.

A285

European Nature Conservation Year (Scenes in Vatican Gardens & Castel Gandolfo: 200 l, Fountain of the Triton, arches of rhyncospernum jasminoides. 300 l, Avenue of roses, Palazzo Barberini. 400 l, Statue of Apollo Citaredo. 550 l, Ruins of Domitian's Villa, Avenue of roses. 750 l, Acer negundo, Viale dell'Osservatorio. 1500 l, Belvedere garden. 2000 l, Fountain of the Eagle, Quercus ilex. 3000 l, Avenue of cypresses, equestrian statue.

1995, June 8 *Perf. 12*

Granite Paper

980 A285 200 l multicolored .25 .25
981 A285 300 l multicolored .35 .35
a. Booklet pane of 3 1.00
982 A285 400 l multicolored .50 .50
a. Booklet pane of 3 1.50
983 A285 550 l multicolored .70 .70
a. Booklet pane of 3 2.25
984 A285 750 l multicolored .90 .90
a. Booklet pane of 3 2.75
Complete booklet, #981a, 982a, 983a, 984a 7.50
985 A285 1500 l multicolored 1.90 1.90
986 A285 2000 l multicolored 2.50 2.50
987 A285 3000 l multicolored 3.75 3.75
Nos. 980-987 (8) 10.85 10.85

A286

Paintings of peace, by Paolo Guiotto: 550 l, Small hearts flying from large heart. 750 l, Stylized faces. 850 l, Doves in flight. 1250 l, Lymph reaching to smallest branches. 2000 l, Explosion of colors, people.

1995, Oct. 3 Photo. *Perf. 13½x13*

988 A286 550 l multicolored .65 .65
989 A286 750 l multicolored .85 .85
990 A286 850 l multicolored 1.00 1.00
991 A286 1250 l multicolored 1.40 1.40
992 A286 2000 l multicolored 2.25 2.25
Nos. 988-992 (5) 6.15 6.15

UN, 50th anniv.

A287

St. Anthony of Padua (1195-1231): 750 l, St. John of God (1495-1550). 3000 l, St. Philip Neri (1515-95).

Litho. & Engr.

1995, Oct. 3 *Perf. 13½x14*

993 A287 500 l green & brown .65 .65
994 A287 750 l violet & green .95 .95
995 A287 3000 l magenta & black 3.75 3.75
Nos. 993-995 (3) 5.35 5.35

A288

Scenes depicting life of Jesus Christ from illuminated manuscripts: 400 l, The Annunciation. 850 l, Nativity. 1250 l, Flight into Egypt. 2000 l, Jesus among the teachers.

1995, Nov. 20 Photo. *Perf. 12x11½*

Granite Paper

996 A288 400 l multicolored .50 .50
997 A288 850 l multicolored 1.10 1.10
998 A288 1250 l multicolored 1.60 1.60
999 A288 2000 l multicolored 2.50 2.50
Nos. 996-999 (4) 5.70 5.70

Towards the Holy Year 2000.

Travels of Pope John Paul II — A289

Designs: 1000 l, Giving greeting in Croatia, statue of Blessed Lady, Zagreb Cathedral. 2000 l, In Italy, lighthouse in Genoa, Orvieto Cathedral, Valley of Temples in Agrigento.

1995, Nov. 20 Litho. *Perf. 14½x14*

1000 A289 1000 l multicolored 1.50 1.50
1001 A289 2000 l multicolored 3.00 3.00

Religious Anniversaries — A290

Designs: 1250 l, Angel holding crosses, Union of Brest-Litovsk, 400th anniv. 2000 l, Cross with branches, Latin episcopal mitre, Byzantine mitre, Union of Uzhorod, 350th anniv.

1996, Mar. 16 Photo. *Perf. 13½x14*

1002 A290 1250 l multicolored 1.60 1.60
1003 A290 2000 l multicolored 2.50 2.50

A291

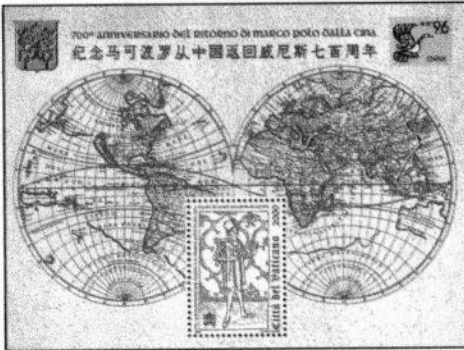
Marco Polo's Return from China, 700th Anniv. A292

Designs from miniatures, Bodleian Library, Oxford: 350 l, Marco Polo delivering Pope Gregory X's letter to Great Khan. 850 l, Great Khan dispensing alms to poor in Cambaluc. 1250 l, Marco Polo receiving golden book from Great Khan. 2500 l, Marco Polo in Persia listening to story of three Kings who go to Bethlehem to adore Jesus.
2000 l, Stylized portrait of Marco Polo drawn from first printed edition of "Il Milione."

1996, Mar. 15 *Perf. 11½*

Granite Paper

1004 A291 350 l multicolored .45 .45
1005 A291 850 l multicolored 1.10 1.10
1006 A291 1250 l multicolored 1.60 1.60
1007 A291 2500 l multicolored 3.25 3.25
Nos. 1004-1007 (4) 6.40 6.40

Souvenir Sheet

Perf. 12x11½

1008 A292 2000 l black 2.50 2.50

A293

Famous Women: 750 l, Gianna Baretta Molla (1922-62), physician. 850 l, Sister Edith Stein (1891-1942).

1996, May 7 Engr. *Perf. 13x14*

1009 A293 750 l blue 1.25 1.25
1010 A293 850 l brown 1.50 1.50

A294

Modern Olympic Games, Cent.: a, Statue of athlete. b, Athlete's torso. c, Hand. d, Statue of athlete reaching upward. e, Hercules.

1996, May 7 Photo. *Perf. 13*

1011 Strip of 5 10.00 10.00
a.-e. A294 1250 l any single 1.40 1.40

Ordination of Pope John Paul II, 50th Anniv. — A295

Designs: 500 l, Wawel Cathedral, Krakow. 750 l, Pope John Paul II giving blessing. 1250 l, Basilica of St. John Lateran, Rome.

1996, Oct. 12 Litho. *Perf. 14*

1012 A295 500 l multicolored .65 .65
1013 A295 750 l multicolored 1.00 1.00
1014 A295 1250 l multicolored 2.00 2.00
Nos. 1012-1014 (3) 3.65 3.65

Life of Jesus Christ from Illuminated Manuscripts — A296

Designs: 550 l, Baptism of Jesus at River Jordan. 850 l, Temptation in the desert. 1500 l, Cure of the leper. 2500 l, Jesus the teacher.

1996, Oct. 12 Photo. *Perf. 12x11½*

1015 A296 550 l multicolored .75 .75
1016 A296 850 l multicolored 1.50 1.25
1017 A296 1500 l multicolored 3.00 2.50
1018 A296 2500 l multicolored 5.00 3.50
Nos. 1015-1018 (4) 10.25 8.00

Christmas A297

Nativity, by Murillo (1618-82).

1996, Nov. 20 Litho. *Perf. 13½*

1019 A297 750 l multicolored 2.00 1.50

St. Celestine V (1215-96) — A298

No. 1021, St. Alfonso Maria De'Liguori (1696-1787).

1996, Nov. 20 *Perf. 13½x14*

1020 A298 1250 l multicolored 1.60 1.60
1021 A298 1250 l multicolored 1.60 1.60

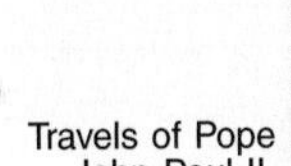

Travels of Pope John Paul II, 1995 — A299

Designs: 250 l, Jan. 11-21, Philippines, Papua New Guinea, Australia, Sri Lanka. 500 l, May 20-22, Czech Republic, Poland. 750 l, June 3-4, Belgium. 1000 l, June 30-July 3, Slovakia. 2000 l, Sept. 14-20, Cameroun, South Africa, Kenya. 5000 l, Oct. 4-9, UN headquarters, NY, US.

1996, Nov. 20 *Perf. 14x13½*

1022 A299 250 l blue & multi .35 .35
1023 A299 500 l blue green & multi .65 .65
1024 A299 750 l green & multi 1.00 1.00
1025 A299 1000 l brown & multi 1.25 1.25
1026 A299 2000 l gray & multi 2.50 2.50
1027 A299 5000 l pink & multi 6.75 6.75
Nos. 1022-1027 (6) 12.50 12.50

Papal Carriages and Automobiles A300

Designs: 50 l, Touring carriage. 100 l, Graham Paige. 300 l, Festive traveling carriage. 500 l, Citroen Lictoria VI. 750 l, Grand touring carriage. 850 l, Mercedes Benz. 1000 l, Festive half carriage. 1250 l, Mercedes Benz 300SEL. 2000 l, Touring carriage, diff. 4000 l, Fiat "Pope mobile."

1997, Mar. 20 Photo. *Perf. 12*

Granite Paper

1028 A300 50 l multicolored .25 .25
1029 A300 100 l multicolored .25 .25
a. Booklet pane of 4 .90
1030 A300 300 l multicolored .35 .35
a. Booklet pane of 4 1.50
1031 A300 500 l multicolored .60 .60
a. Booklet pane of 4 2.75
1032 A300 750 l multicolored .90 .90
a. Booklet pane of 4 4.00
Complete booklet, #1029a, 1030a, 1031a, 1032a 9.50

No.	Type	Value	Description	Unused	Used
1033	A300	850 l	multicolored	1.00	1.00
1034	A300	1000 l	multicolored	1.25	1.25
1035	A300	1250 l	multicolored	1.75	1.75
1036	A300	2000 l	multicolored	2.50	2.50
1037	A300	4000 l	multicolored	5.00	5.00
			Nos. 1028-1037 (10)	13.85	13.85

A301

Swiss Guard: 750 l, Guard in traditional attire. 850 l, Guard in armor with sword in front of iron gate.

1997, Mar. 20 Litho. *Perf. 13½*

No.	Type	Value	Description	Unused	Used
1038	A301	750 l	multicolored	.90	.90
1039	A301	850 l	multicolored	1.00	1.00
a.			Strip of 2 + 2 labels	1.90	1.90

Europa.

A302

1997, Apr. 23 Engr. *Perf. 14*

No.	Type	Value	Description	Unused	Used
1040	A302	850 l	deep violet	1.60	1.60

St. Adalbert (956-997). See Germany No. 1964, Poland No. 3337, Czech Republic No. 3012, Hungary No. 3569.

A303

"Looking at the Classics," Museum Exhibition — A304

Pictures from texts of Latin and Greek classics: 500 l, Aristotle observing and describing various species from man to insect, from his "De Historia Animalium." 750 l, Bacchus riding dragon, from "Metamorphoses" by Ovid. 1250 l, General haranguing his soldiers, from "Iliad" by Homer. 2000 l, Hannibal leaving Canne, two horsemen, foot soldier, from "Ab Urbe Condita" by Titus Livius.

Masks from "Comedies," by Terence: No. 1045: a, Man, woman. b, Two women. c, Two men.

1997, Apr. 23 Photo. *Perf. 14*

No.	Type	Value	Description	Unused	Used
1041	A303	500 l	multicolored	.60	.60
1042	A303	750 l	multicolored	.90	.90
1043	A303	1250 l	multicolored	1.50	1.50
1044	A303	2000 l	multicolored	2.40	2.40
			Nos. 1041-1044 (4)	5.40	5.40

Perf. 13½

No.	Type	Value	Description	Unused	Used
1045	A304	1000 l	Sheet of 3, #a.-c.	4.00	4.00

A305

46th Intl. Eucharistic Congress, Wroclaw, Poland: 650 l, Elements of the Eucharist, chalice, consecrated Host, arms of Wroclaw. 1000 l, The Last Supper, fish, Congress emblem. 1250 l, Wroclaw Cathedral, sheaf of wheat, holy spirit descending on church. 2500 l, "IHS" symbol of Christ on cross, doves, world with two hands on it.

1997, May 27 Photo. *Perf. 13*

No.	Type	Value	Description	Unused	Used
1046	A305	650 l	multicolored	.75	.70
1047	A305	1000 l	multicolored	1.25	1.10
1048	A305	1250 l	multicolored	1.50	1.40
1049	A305	2500 l	multicolored	3.25	2.75
			Nos. 1046-1049 (4)	6.75	5.95

A306

1997, Sept. 15 Litho. *Perf. 13x14*

No.	Type	Value	Description	Unused	Used
1050	A306	900 l	multicolored	.90	.70

Pope Paul VI (1897-1978).

No. 1050 was printed se-tenant with 4 labels. Value $2.00

St. Ambrose (d. 397) — A307

1997, Sept. 15 Photo. *Perf. 13x14*

No.	Type	Value	Description	Unused	Used
1051	A307	800 l	multicolored	1.50	1.25

Towards the Holy Year 2000 — A308

Illustrations of Christ's miracles: 400 l, Healing of paralyzed man. 800 l, Calming of the tempest. 1300 l, Multiplication of bread and fish. 3600 l, Peter's confession and conferment of primacy.

1997, Sept. 15 *Perf. 12*

Granite Paper

No.	Type	Value	Description	Unused	Used
1052	A308	400 l	multicolored	.60	.50
1053	A308	800 l	multicolored	1.25	1.00
1054	A308	1300 l	multicolored	2.50	2.00
1055	A308	3600 l	multicolored	7.00	6.00
			Nos. 1052-1055 (4)	11.35	9.50

1996 Travels of Pope John Paul II — A309

Designs: 400 l, Central & South America, Feb. 5-12. 900 l, Tunisia, Apr. 14. 1000 l, Slovenia , May 17-19. 1300 l, Germany, June 21-23. 2000 l, Hungary, Sept. 6-7. 4000 l, France, Sept. 19-22.

1997, Nov. 11 Litho. *Perf. 14x13½*

No.	Type	Value	Description	Unused	Used
1056	A309	400 l	multicolored	.50	.50
1057	A309	900 l	multicolored	1.00	1.00
1058	A309	1000 l	multicolored	1.50	1.50
1059	A309	1300 l	multicolored	2.00	2.00
1060	A309	2000 l	multicolored	3.00	3.00
1061	A309	4000 l	multicolored	6.00	6.00
			Nos. 1056-1061 (6)	14.00	14.00

Christmas A310

Detail from "The Nativity," by Benozzo Gozzoli (1420-97).

1997, Nov. 11 Photo. *Perf. 14*

No.	Type	Value	Description	Unused	Used
1062	A310	800 l	multicolored	1.60	1.40

Feasts of Sts. Peter and Paul, June 29th — A311

1998, Mar. 24 Photo. *Perf. 13*

No.	Type	Value	Description	Unused	Used
1063	A311	800 l	St. Peter	.95	.95
1064	A311	900 l	St. Paul	1.10	1.10

Europa.

The Popes of the Holy Years 1300-1525 — A312

Designs: 200 l, Boniface VIII, 1300. 400 l, Clement VI, 1350. 500 l, Boniface IX, 1390, 1400. 700 l, Martin V, 1423. 800 l, Nicholas V, 1450. 900 l, Sixtus IV, 1475. 1300 l, Alexander VI, 1500. 3000 l, Clement VII, 1525.

1998, Mar. 24 Litho. *Perf. 14*

No.	Type	Value	Description	Unused	Used
1065	A312	200 l	multicolored	.30	.30
1066	A312	400 l	multicolored	.50	.50
1067	A312	500 l	multicolored	.65	.65
1068	A312	700 l	multicolored	.85	.85
1069	A312	800 l	multicolored	1.00	1.00
1070	A312	900 l	multicolored	1.25	1.25
1071	A312	1300 l	multicolored	1.75	1.75
1072	A312	3000 l	multicolored	3.75	3.75
			Nos. 1065-1072 (8)	10.05	10.05

Nos. 1065-1072 were each printed se-tenant with a label picturing the respective papal arms.

See Nos. 1095-1102, 1141-1150.

Face on Shroud — A313

2500 l, Cathedral of Turin.

Litho. & Engr.

1998, May 19 *Perf. 13½x14*

No.	Type	Value	Description	Unused	Used
1073	A313	900 l	multicolored	1.00	1.00
1074	A313	2500 l	multicolored	3.00	3.00

Exposition of the Shroud of Turin.

A314

Frescoes of Angels, by Melozzo da Forli (1438-94), Basilica of Sts. Apostles, Rome: Angels playing various musical instruments.

1998, May 19 Photo. *Perf. 12*

Granite Paper

No.	Type	Value	Description	Unused	Used
1075	A314	450 l	multicolored	.65	.65
1076	A314	650 l	multicolored	.80	.80
1077	A314	800 l	multicolored	1.00	1.00
1078	A314	1000 l	multicolored	1.25	1.25
1079	A314	1300 l	multicolored	2.00	2.00
1080	A314	2000 l	multicolored	2.75	2.75
			Nos. 1075-1080 (6)	8.45	8.45

Towards Holy Year 2000 — A315

Episodes from the Life of Christ: 500 l, Triumphal entry into Jerusalem. 800 l, Washing of the feet. 1300 l, The Last Supper. 3000 l, Crucifixion.

1998, May 19 *Perf. 12*

Granite Paper

No.	Type	Value	Description	Unused	Used
1081	A315	500 l	multicolored	.60	.60
1082	A315	800 l	multicolored	.90	.90
1083	A315	1300 l	multicolored	1.75	1.75
1084	A315	3000 l	multicolored	3.50	3.50
			Nos. 1081-1084 (4)	6.75	6.75

Italia '98 — A316

1998, Oct. 23 Photo. *Perf. 14*

No.	Type	Value	Description	Unused	Used
1085	A316	800 l	Pope John Paul II	2.50	2.50

See Italy No. 2259 and San Marino No. 1430.

The Good Shepherd — A317

1998, Oct. 25 *Perf. 12 Vert.*

Granite Paper

Booklet Stamp

No.	Type	Value	Description	Unused	Used
1086	A317	900 l	multicolored	1.30	1.30
a.			Booklet pane of 5	6.50	
			Complete booklet, #1086a	6.50	

Italia '98.

Christian Sculptures — A318

Designs: a, 600 l, Peter's denial. b, 900 l, Praying woman. c, 1000 l, Christ and the Cyrenean. 2000 l, Christ with the Cross and Two Apostles.

Granite Paper

1998, Oct. 25 *Perf. 12*

No.	Type	Value	Description	Unused	Used
1087	A318		Sheet of 4, #a.-d.	6.50	6.50

Italia '98. Margin is embossed.

Christmas — A319

1998, Dec. 1 Litho. *Perf. 14x13½*

No.	Type	Value	Description	Unused	Used
1088	A319	800 l	multicolored	1.25	1.25

See Croatia No. 381.

1997 Travels of Pope John Paul II — A320

Designs: 300 l, Sarajevo, 4/12-13/97. 600 l, Prague, 4/25-27/97. 800 l, Beirut, 5/10-11/97. 900 l, Poland, 5/21-6/10/97. 1300 l, Paris, 8/21-24/97. 5000 l, Rio de Janeiro, 10/2-6/97.

1998, Dec. 1 *Perf. 12½*

No.	Type	Value	Description	Unused	Used
1089	A320	300 l	brown	.40	.40
1090	A320	600 l	green	.75	.75
1091	A320	800 l	brown	1.25	1.25
1092	A320	900 l	violet blue	1.50	1.50
1093	A320	1300 l	org brn	1.75	1.75
1094	A320	5000 l	org brn	6.50	6.50
			Nos. 1089-1094 (6)	12.15	12.15

Popes of the Holy Years Type of 1998

Popes: 300 l, Julius III, 1550. 600 l, Gregory XIII, 1575. 800 l, Clement VIII, 1600. 900 l, Urban VIII, 1625. 1000 l, Innocent X, 1650. 1300 l, Clement X, 1675. 1500 l, Innocent XII, 1700. 2000 l, Benedict XIII, 1725.

1999, Mar. 23 Litho. *Perf. 14*

1095 A312 300 l multicolored .55 .55
1096 A312 600 l multicolored 1.00 1.00
1097 A312 800 l multicolored 1.75 1.75
1098 A312 900 l multicolored 2.00 2.00
1099 A312 1000 l multicolored 2.25 2.25
1100 A312 1300 l multicolored 2.50 2.50
1101 A312 1500 l multicolored 3.00 3.00
1102 A312 2000 l multicolored 4.00 4.00
Nos. 1095-1102 (8) 17.05 17.05

Nos. 1095-1102 were each printed se-tenant with a label picturing the respective papal arms.

Flowers from Vatican Gardens and Papal Villa, Castelgandolfo A321

Europa: 800 l, John Paul II Rose. 900 l, Water lilies.

1999, Mar. 23 Litho. *Perf. 12½x13*

1103 A321 800 l multicolored 1.00 1.00
1104 A321 900 l multicolored 1.25 1.25
a. Pair, #1103-1104 + label 3.75 3.75

Padre Pio de Pietrelcina (1887-1968) A322

No. 1106: a, 1st church, San Giovanni Rotondo. b, New church, San Giovanni Rotondo. c, Like No. 1105.

1999, Apr. 27 Litho. *Perf. 14x13*

1105 A322 800 l multicolored 1.25 1.25

Souvenir Sheet

Perf. 13x13½

1106 A322 Sheet of 3 2.10 2.10
a. 300 l multi, vert. .35 .35
b. 600 l multi, vert. .70 .70
c. 900 l multi 1.00 1.00

Nos. 1106a-1106b are 30x40mm, No. 1106c is 60x40mm.

No. 1106 exists imperforate.

A323

Holy Places in Palestine A324

Nos. 1107-1111: 19th cent. watercolors, Pontifical Lateran University Library.

Map of Holy Land from "Geographia Blaviana," 17th cent — #1112: a, Mediterranean Sea, denomination, LL. b, Mediterranean Sea, denomination LR. c, Red Sea, Holy Land. d, Inscription identifying map.

1999, May 25 Photo. *Perf. 11½*

Granite Paper

1107 A323 200 l Bethlehem .25 .25
1108 A323 500 l Nazareth .55 .55
1109 A323 800 l Lake of Tiberias .85 .85
1110 A323 900 l Jerusalem 1.25 1.25
1111 A323 1300 l Mount Tabor 1.60 1.60
Nos. 1107-1111 (5) 4.50 4.50

Perf. 12x11¾

1112 A324 1000 l Sheet of 4, #a.-d. *11.00 11.00*

Towards Holy Year 2000 — A325

Events from life of Christ: 400 l, Deposition from the Cross. 700 l, Resurrection. 1300 l, Pentecost. 3000 l, Last Judgement.

1999, May 25 *Perf. 12x11¾*

Granite Paper

1113 A325 400 l multicolored .55 .55
1114 A325 700 l multicolored .90 .90
1115 A325 1300 l multicolored 1.75 1.75
1116 A325 3000 l multicolored 4.00 4.00
Nos. 1113-1116 (4) 7.20 7.20

Kosovo 1999 A326

1999, May 25 *Perf. 12¼*

Granite Paper

1117 A326 3600 l black 4.00 4.00

Proceeds from sale of stamp benefits victims of the fighting in Kosovo.

1998 Travels of Pope John Paul II — A327

600 l, Cuba, June 21-26. 800 l, Nigeria, Mar. 21-23. 900 l, Austria, June 19-21. 1300 l, Croatia, Oct. 2-4. 2000 l, Italy, Oct. 20.

1999, Oct. 12 Litho. *Perf. 14x13½*

1118 A327 600 l multicolored .85 .85
1119 A327 800 l multicolored .95 .95
1120 A327 900 l multicolored 1.05 1.05
1121 A327 1300 l multicolored 1.75 1.75
1122 A327 2000 l multicolored 2.50 2.50
Nos. 1118-1122 (5) 7.10 7.10

Council of Europe, 50th Anniv. — A328

1999, Oct. 12 Photo. *Perf. 11¾*

Granite Paper

1123 A328 1200 l multicolored 1.50 1.50

Christmas — A329

The Birth of Christ, by Giovanni di Pietro: 500 l, Joseph (detail). 800 l, Christ (detail). 900 l, Mary (detail). 1200 l, Entire painting.

Perf. 13¼x12½

1999, Nov. 24 Litho.

1124 A329 500 l multi .75 .75
1125 A329 800 l multi 1.25 1.25
1126 A329 900 l multi 1.50 1.50
1127 A329 1200 l multi 1.75 1.75
Nos. 1124-1127 (4) 5.25 5.25

Opening of the Holy Door for Holy Year 2000 — A330

Various panels of Holy Door. Stamps on No. 1136 lack white border.

1999, Nov. 24 Photo. *Perf. 11¾x12*

Granite Paper

1128 A330 200 l multi .30 .30
1129 A330 300 l multi .35 .35
1130 A330 400 l multi .45 .45
1131 A330 500 l multi .60 .60
1132 A330 600 l multi .70 .70
1133 A330 800 l multi .90 .90
1134 A330 1000 l multi 1.50 1.50
1135 A330 1200 l multi 2.25 2.25
Nos. 1128-1135 (8) 7.05 7.05

Souvenir Sheet

1136 Sheet of 8, #a.-h. 10.00 10.00
a. A330 200 l Like #1128 .30 .30
b. A330 300 l Like #1129 .40 .40
c. A330 400 l Like #1130 .50 .50
d. A330 500 l Like #1131 .60 .60
e. A330 600 l Like #1132 .70 .70
f. A330 800 l Like #1133 1.00 1.00
g. A330 1000 l Like #1134 1.25 1.25
h. A330 1200 l Like #1135 1.50 1.50

Holy Year 2000 — A331

Designs: 800 l, St. Peter's Basilica. 1000 l, Basilica of St. John Lateran. 1200 l, Basilica of St. Mary Major. 2000 l, Basilica of St. Paul.

2000, Feb. 4 Photo. *Perf. 11¾*

Granite Paper

1137 A331 800 l multi 1.00 .80
1138 A331 1000 l multi 1.40 1.25
1139 A331 1200 l multi 1.75 1.40
1140 A331 2000 l multi 2.50 2.25
Nos. 1137-1140 (4) 6.65 5.70

Popes of the Holy Year Type of 1998

Designs: 300 l, Benedict XIV, 1750. 400 l, Pius VI, 1775. 500 l, Leo XII, 1825. 600 l, Pius IX, 1875. 700 l, Leo XIII, 1900. 800 l, Pius XI, 1925. 1200 l, Pius XII, 1950. 1500 l, Paul VI, 1975. No. 1149, John Paul II with miter, 2000.

No. 1150, John Paul II with hand on chin, 2000.

2000, Feb. 4 Litho. *Perf. 13¾*

1141 A312 300 l multi + label .50 .50
1142 A312 400 l multi + label .75 .75
1143 A312 500 l multi + label 1.00 1.00
1144 A312 600 l multi + label 1.25 1.25
1145 A312 700 l multi + label 1.50 1.50
1146 A312 800 l multi + label 1.75 1.75
1147 A312 1200 l multi + label 2.25 2.25
1148 A312 1500 l multi + label 2.50 2.50
1149 A312 2000 l multi + label 5.50 5.50
Nos. 1141-1149 (9) 17.00 17.00

Souvenir Sheet

1150 A312 2000 l multi 2.00 2.00

No. 1150 contains one label.

Christianity in Iceland, 1000th Anniv. — A332

2000, Feb. 4 *Perf. 13¼x13¾*

1151 A332 1500 l multi 2.10 2.10

See Iceland Nos. 900-901.

Europa, 2000

Common Design Type

2000, May 9 Litho. *Perf. 13¼x13*

1152 CD17 1200 l multi 1.75 1.75

Printed in sheets of 10, with left and right side selvage of Priority Mail etiquettes.

Pope John Paul II, 80th Birthday — A333

800 l, Pope. 1200 l, Black Madonna of Jasna Gora. 2000 l, Pope's silver cross.

2000, May 9 Engr. *Perf. 13x12¾*

1153 A333 800 l purple 1.00 1.00
1154 A333 1200 l dark blue 1.75 1.50
1155 A333 2000 l green 3.00 2.50
Nos. 1153-1155 (3) 5.75 5.00

See Poland Nos. 3520-3522.

Restored Sistine Chapel Frescoes A334

Designs: 500 l, The Calling of St. Peter and St. Andrew, by Domenico Ghirlandaio. 1000 l, The Trials of Moses, by Sandro Botticelli. 1500 l, The Donation of the Keys, by Pietro Perugino. 3000 l, The Worship of the Golden Calf, by Cosimo Rosselli.

Perf. 11½x11¾

2000, May 9 Photo. Blue Frame

Granite Paper

1156 A334 500 l multi .80 .75
1157 A334 1000 l multi 1.25 1.25
1158 A334 1500 l multi 1.90 2.00
1159 A334 3000 l multi 4.00 3.50
Nos. 1156-1159 (4) 7.95 7.50

See Nos. 1172-1175, 1215-1218.

20th World Youth Day — A335

Various photos of Pope John Paul II and youth.

Perf. 13¾x13¼

2000, June 19 Litho.

Color of Cross

1160 A335 800 l red 1.00 1.00
1161 A335 1000 l green 1.25 1.10
1162 A335 1200 l violet 1.50 1.25
1163 A335 1500 l orange 2.25 1.75

Booklet Stamp

Self-Adhesive

Serpentine Die Cut 12

1164 A335 1000 l green 1.25 1.25
a. Booklet of 4 + 4 labels 6.00
Nos. 1160-1164 (5) 7.25 6.35

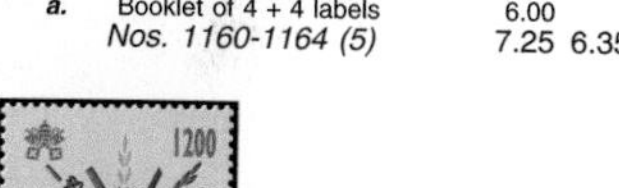

47th Intl. Eucharistic Congress — A336

2000, June 19 *Perf. 13x12½*

1165 A336 1200 l multi 1.50 1.50

Beatification of Pope John XXIII — A337

2000, Sept. 1 Photo. *Perf. 13¼x14*

1166 A337 1200 l multi 1.60 1.60

1999 Travels of Pope John Paul II — A338

#1167: a, Mexico, 1/22-28. b, Romania, 5/7-9. c, Poland, 6/17. d, Slovenia, 9/19. e, India and Georgia, 11/5-9.

2000, Sept. 1 ***Perf. 11¾***
Granite Paper

1167 Horiz. strip of 5 7.00 7.00
a.-e. A338 1000 l Any single 1.00 1.00

Christmas — A339

Frescoes in Basilica of St. Francis, Assisi, by Giotto: 800 l, Nativity. 1200 l, Infant Jesus. 1500 l, Mary. 2000 l, Joseph.

2000, Nov. 7 Photo. ***Perf. 11¾x11½***
Granite Paper

1168-1171 A339 Set of 4 9.00 7.00

Sistine Chapel Restoration Type of 2000

Paintings: 800 l, The Baptism of Christ, by Pietro Perugino. 1200 l, The Passage of the Red Sea, by Biagio d'Antonio. 1500 l, The Punishment of Korah and the Stoning of Moses and Aaron, by Sandro Botticelli. 4000 l, The Sermon on the Mount, by Cosimo Rosselli.

Perf. 11½x11¾
2001, Feb. 15 **Photo.**
Granite Paper
Red Frame

1172-1175 A334 Set of 4 9.75 8.00

Christian Conversion of Armenia, 1700th Anniv. — A340

Scenes from illuminated code of 1569: 1200 l, St. Gregory prepares to give King Tiridates human features. 1500 l, St. Gregory makes Agatangel write history of Armenians. 2000 l, St. Gregory and King Tiridates meet Emperor Constantine and Pope Sylvester I.

2001, Feb. 15 ***Perf. 11¾***
Granite Paper

1176-1178 A340 Set of 3 6.00 6.00

Year of Dialogue Among Civilizations — A341

2001, May 22 Litho. ***Perf. 14¼x14***
1179 A341 1500 l multi 1.75 1.75

Europa — A342

Designs: 800 l, Hands holding water above earth. 1200 l, Hand catching water.

2001, May 22 ***Perf. 13½x13¼***
1180-1181 A342 Set of 2 2.50 2.50

Giuseppe Verdi (1813-1901), Composer — A343

Verdi and: 800 l, Score from Nabucco. 1500 l, Costumes from Aida. 2000 l, Scenery from Othello.

2001, May 22 ***Perf. 13¼x14¼***
1182-1184 A343 Set of 3 5.50 5.50

2000 Travels of Pope John Paul II — A344

Designs: 500 l, Mount Sinai, Feb. 26. 800 l, Mount Nebo, Mar. 20. 1200 l, The Last Supper, Mar. 23. 1500 l, Holy Sepulchre, Mar. 26. 5000 l, Fatima, May 12.
3000 l, Western Wall.

2001, Sept. 25 Litho. ***Perf. 13¼***
1185-1189 A344 Set of 5 12.00 12.00

Souvenir Sheet
Perf. 13¼x14

1190 A344 3000 l multi 4.00 4.00

No. 1190 contains one 35x26mm stamp.

Remission of Debts of Poor Countries — A345

Various panels by Carlo di Camerino: 200 l, 400 l, 800 l, 1000 l, 1500 l.

2001, Sept. 25 Photo. ***Perf. 13***
1191-1195 A345 Set of 5 5.25 5.25

Giuseppe Toniolo Institute for Higher Studies, 80th Anniv. — A346

Litho. & Embossed
2001, Nov. 22 ***Perf. 12¾***
1196 A346 1200 l red & blue 1.75 1.75

Etruscan Museum Gold Objects A347

Designs: 800 l, Parade fibula. 1200 l, Earrings. 1500 l, Vulci fibula. 2000 l, Head of Medusa.

2001, Nov. 22 Photo. ***Perf. 13½***
1197-1200 A347 Set of 4 8.00 8.00

Christmas — A348

Artwork by Egino G. Weinert: 800 l, The Annunciation. 1200 l, The Nativity. 1500 l, Adoration of the Magi.

2001, Nov. 22 Litho. ***Perf. 13x13¼***
1201-1203 A348 Set of 3 4.75 3.75
1202a Booklet pane of 4 + 4 etiquettes 7.00
Booklet, #1202a 7.00

100 Cents = 1 Euro (€)

Depictions of Virgin Mary in Vatican Basilica — A349

Designs: 8c, Our Lady of Women in Labor. 15c, Our Lady with People Praying. 23c, Our Lady at the Tomb of Pius XII. 31c, Our Lady of the Fever. 41c, Our Lady of the Slap. 52c, Mary Immaculate. 62c, Our Lady Help of Christians. 77c, Virgin of the Deesis. €1.03, L'Addolorata. €1.55, Presentation of Mary at the Temple.

2002, Mar. 12 Litho. ***Perf. 13¼x13***
1204 A349 8c multi .30 .30
1205 A349 15c multi .40 .40
1206 A349 23c multi .60 .50
1207 A349 31c multi .65 .60
1208 A349 41c multi 1.00 .80
1209 A349 52c multi 1.25 1.10
1210 A349 62c multi 1.60 1.25
1211 A349 77c multi 2.00 1.75
1212 A349 €1.03 multi 2.75 2.50
1213 A349 €1.55 multi 4.50 4.00
Nos. 1204-1213 (10) 15.05 13.20

Pontifical Ecclesiastical Academy, 300th Anniv. — A350

No. 1214: a, Pope Clement XI. b, Academy building (46x33mm). c, Pope John Paul II.

2002, Mar. 12 Engr. ***Perf. 13¼x13***
1214 A350 Horiz. strip of 3 6.00 6.00
a.-c. 77c Any single 1.80 1.80

Sistine Chapel Restoration Type of 2000

Designs: 26c, The Temptation of Christ, by Sandro Botticelli. 41c, The Last Supper, by Cosimo Rosselli. 77c, Moses' Journey in Egypt, by Pietro Perugino. €1.55, The Last Days of Moses, by Luca Signorelli.

Perf. 11½x11¾
2002, June 13 **Photo.**
Granite Paper

1215-1218 A334 Set of 4 7.75 7.75

Europa A351

Christ and the Circus, by Aldo Carpi: 41c, Entire painting. 62c, Detail.

2002, June 13 ***Perf. 13¼***
1219-1220 A351 Set of 2 2.75 2.75

Roman States Postage Stamps, 150th Anniv. A352

Designs: 41c, Regina Viarum, Roman States #11. 52c, Cassian Way, Roman States #25. €1.03, Vatican walls, Vatican City #2.
€1.55, St. Peter's Basilica.

2002, June 13 ***Perf. 13x13¼***
1221-1223 A352 Set of 3 5.00 5.00

Souvenir Sheet
Perf.

1224 A352 €1.55 multi 4.00 4.00

No. 1224 contains one 31mm diameter stamp.

St. Leo IX (1002-54), Pope — A353

Designs: 41c, Portrait. 62c, In procession, receiving papal miter. €1.29, Reading from scroll, as prisoner of Normans.

2002, Sept. 26 Litho. ***Perf. 13x13¼***
1225-1227 A353 Set of 3 6.00 6.00

Cimabue (1240-1302), Artist — A354

Designs: 26c, Crucifix. 62c, Jesus Christ. 77c, Virgin Mary. €1.03, St. John.

2002, Sept. 26 Photo. ***Perf. 13¼x14***
1228-1231 A354 Set of 4 7.00 7.00

Nativity, by Pseudo Ambrogio di Baldese A355

2002, Nov. 21 Photo. ***Perf. 13***
1232 A355 41c multi 2.00 2.00

See New Zealand No. 1834.

2001 Travels of Pope John Paul II — A356

Designs: 41c, Greece, Syria and Malta, May 4-9. 62c, Ukraine, June 23-27. €1.55, Armenia and Kazakhstan, Sept. 22-27.

2002, Nov. 21 Litho. ***Perf. 13x13¼***
1233-1235 A356 Set of 3 6.50 6.50
1234a Booklet pane, 4 #1234 + 4 etiquettes 6.50
Booklet, #1234a 6.50

A357

Pontificate of John Paul II, 25th Anniv. — A358

No. 1236: a, Election as Pope, 1978. b, In Poland, 1979. c, In France, 1980. d, Assassination attempt, 1981. e, At Fatima, Portugal, 1982. f, Extraordinary Holy Year, 1983. g, At Quirinale Palace, Rome, 1984. h, World Youth Day, 1985. i, At synagogue, Rome, 1986. j, Pentecost vigil, 1987. k, At European Parliament, Strasbourg, France, 1988. l, Meeting with Mikhail Gorbachev, 1989. m, At Guinea-Bissau leper colony, 1990. n, At European Bishops' Synod, 1991. o, Publication of Catechism of the Catholic Church, 1992. p, Praying for the Balkans in Assisi, 1993. q, At Sistine Chapel, 1994. r, At UN Headquarters for 50th anniv. celebrations, 1995. s, In Germany, 1996. t, In Sarajevo, Bosnia & Herzegovina, 1997. u, In Cuba, 1998. v, Opening Holy Doors, 1999. w, World Youth Day, 2000. x, Closing Holy Doors, 2001. y, Addressing Italian Parliament, 2002.

2003, Mar. 20 Litho. ***Perf. 13x13¼***
1236 A357 Sheet of 25 27.50 27.50
a.-y. 41c Any single 1.00 .95

Etched on Silver Foil
Die Cut Perf. 12½x13
Self-Adhesive

1237 A358 €2.58 Pope John Paul II 9.00 9.00

Cancels can be easily removed from No. 1237.
See Poland Nos. 3668-3669.

Martyrdom of St. George, 1700th Anniv. — A359

2003, May 6 Litho. & Engr. ***Perf. 13***
1238 A359 62c multi 1.90 1.90

Europa — A360

Poster art for: 41c, 1975 Holy Year. 62c, Exhibition of Slav codices, incunabula and rare books at Sistine Hall, 1985.

2003, May 6 Litho. *Perf. 13¼x13*
1239-1240 A360 Set of 2 2.40 2.40

Masterpieces by Beato Angelico in Niccolina Chapel — A361

Designs: 41c, Diaconal Consecration of St. Lawrence. 62c, St. Stephen Preaching. 77c, Trial of St. Lawrence. €1.03, Stoning of St. Stephen.

2003, May 6 Photo. *Perf. 13¼*
1241-1244 A361 Set of 4 7.00 7.00

Beatification of Mother Teresa of Calcutta — A362

Perf. 13½x13¼
2003, Sept. 23 Litho.
1245 A362 41c multi + label 1.25 1.25

Printed in sheets of 5 + 5 different labels. Value $7.00

19th Century Artists — A363

Designs: 41c, Blessed Are the Pure at Heart, by Paul Gauguin. 62c, The Pietà, by Vincent van Gogh.

Perf. 13¼x13½
2003, Sept. 23 Photo.
1246 A363 41c multi 1.10 1.00
1247 A363 62c multi 1.75 1.50
a. Booklet pane of 4 + 4 etiquettes 7.00 —
Complete booklet, #1247a 7.00

Animals in Vatican Basilica Art — A364

Designs: 21c, Dragon. 31c, Camel. 77c, Horse. €1.03, Leopard.

2003, Sept. 23
1248-1251 A364 Set of 4 6.00 5.50

Canonization of Josemaría Escrivá de Balaguer, Oct. 6, 2003 — A365

2003, Nov. 18 Litho. *Perf. 14x13¼*
1252 A365 41c multi 1.10 1.10

2002 Travels of Pope John Paul II — A366

Designs: 62c, Bulgaria and Azerbaijan, May 22-26. 77c, Canada, Guatemala and Mexico, July 23-Aug. 2. €2.07, Poland, Aug. 16-19.

2003, Nov. 18 *Perf. 13x13¼*
1253-1255 A366 Set of 3 9.00 9.00

Christmas — A367

2003, Nov. 18
Stamp With White Border
1256 A367 41c multi 1.60 1.60
Souvenir Sheet
Stamp Without White Border
1257 A367 41c multi 1.75 1.75

Death of Pope Paul VI, 25th anniv. (#1257).

St. Pius V (1504-72) — A368

Altarpiece by Grazio Cossoli in Chapel of the Rosary, Santa Croce di Bosco Marengo: 4c, Detail depicting St. Pius V and flag. €2, Entire altarpiece.

Litho. & Silk Screened
2004, Mar. 18 *Perf. 13¼x13*
1258-1259 A368 Set of 2 5.50 5.50

2003 Travels of Pope John Paul II — A369

Designs: 60c, Spain, May 3-4. 62c, Bosnia & Herzegovina, June 22. 80c, Croatia, June 5-9. €1.40, Slovakia, Sept. 11-14.

2004, Mar. 18 Litho.
1260-1263 A369 Set of 4 11.50 11.50

Papal Visits to Poland A370

No. 1264, 45c: a, Pope with hand on chin. b, Pope praying. c, Pope carrying crucifix. d, Pope with crucifix against head.

No. 1265, 62c: a, Pope holding crucifix, diff. b, Pope with arm raised. c, Pope, wearing white, seated. d, Pope, wearing red cape, seated.

Litho. (Labels Litho. & Embossed)
2004, Mar. 18
Sheets of 4, #a-d, + 8 Labels
1264-1265 A370 Set of 2 13.00 13.00

See Poland Nos. 3724-3725.

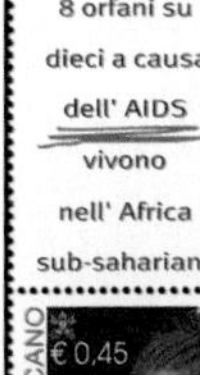

Children AIDS Victims — A371

2004, June 3 Photo. *Perf. 13¼x13*
1266 A371 45c multi + label 1.25 1.25

Printed in sheets of 6 + 6 stamp-sized labels (with different text) and 1 large central label. Value, $6.

Europa A372

Paintings of: 45c, Men on horses. 62c, People in garden.

2004, June 3 Litho. *Perf. 12¾x13¼*
1267-1268 A372 Set of 2 2.60 2.60

Flags and One-Euro Coins — A373

2004, June 3 Litho. *Perf. 13½*
1269 A373 4c Austria .25 .25
1270 A373 8c Belgium .25 .25
1271 A373 15c Finland .35 .35
1272 A373 25c France .60 .60
1273 A373 30c Germany .70 .70
1274 A373 40c Greece .95 .95
1275 A373 45c Vatican City 1.10 1.10
1276 A373 60c Ireland 1.40 1.40
1277 A373 62c Italy 1.50 1.50
1278 A373 70c Luxembourg 1.75 1.75
1279 A373 80c Monaco 1.90 1.90
1280 A373 €1 Netherlands 2.40 2.40
1281 A373 €1.40 Portugal 3.50 3.50
1282 A373 €2 San Marino 4.75 4.75
1283 A373 €2.80 Spain 6.75 6.75
Nos. 1269-1283 (15) 28.15 28.15

48th Intl. Eucharistic Congress — A374

Designs: 45c, Hands breaking bread over chalice. 65c, Hand raising eucharist.

2004, Sept. 16 Litho. *Perf. 13x13¼*
1284-1285 A374 Set of 2 3.00 3.00

Contemporary Religious Art in Vatican Museum Collection A375

Designs: 45c, Still Life with Bottles, by Giorgio Morandi. 60c, The Fall of an Angel, by Marino Marini. 80c, Landscape with Houses, by Ezio Pastorio. 85c, Tuscan Countryside, by Giulio Cesare Vinzio.

2004, Sept. 16 Photo. *Perf. 14x13¼*
1286 A375 45c multi 1.10 1.10
1287 A375 60c multi 1.50 1.50
a. Perf. 13½x13¼ 1.75 1.75
b. Booklet pane of 4 #1287a + 4 etiquettes 7.00 —
Complete booklet, #1287b 7.00
1288 A375 80c multi 2.25 2.25
1289 A375 85c multi 2.50 2.50
Nos. 1286-1289 (4) 7.35 7.35

Petrarch (1304-74), Poet — A376

2004, Nov. 18 Photo. *Perf. 13¼x13*
1290 A376 60c multi 1.60 1.60

Christmas A377

2004, Nov. 18 Litho. *Perf. 13¼*
1291 A377 80c multi 2.25 2.25

Interregnum Issue

Arms of St. Peter and Papal Chamberlain's Insignia — A378

Inscription colors: 60c, Blue. 62c, Red. 80c, Green.

2005, Apr. 12 Litho. *Perf. 13½x13*
1292-1294 A378 Set of 3 6.00 6.00

Pope Benedict XVI — A379

Pope Benedict XVI wearing: 45c, Stole. 62c, White vestments. 80c, Miter.

2005, June 2 Litho. *Perf. 13¼x13*
1295-1297 A379 Set of 3 5.25 5.25

Coronation of Pope Benedict XVI, Apr. 19, 2005.

20th World Youth Day — A380

2005, June 2
1298 A380 62c multi 1.50 1.50

See Germany No. 2343.

Europa — A381

Ceramic plates depicting fish painted by Pablo Picasso with background colors of: 62c, Orange. 80c, Blue.

2005, June 2 *Perf. 12½*
1299-1300 A381 Set of 2 4.00 4.00

Ratification of Modifications to Italy-Vatican Concordat, 20th Anniv. — A382

Arms of Vatican City and Italy and: 45c, Pen. €2.80, Map.

2005, June 9 Photo. *Perf. 13¼*
1301-1302 A382 Set of 2 8.00 8.00

See Italy Nos. 2677-2678.

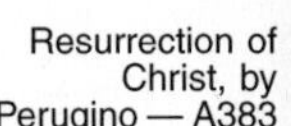

Resurrection of Christ, by Perugino — A383

Various painting details: 60c, 62c, 80c, €1. €2.80, Jesus Christ.

2005, June 9 ***Perf. 14x13¼***
1303-1306 A383 Set of 4 7.50 7.50

Souvenir Sheet
Perf. 13¼x13¾

1307 A383 €2.80 multi 7.25 7.25

No. 1307 contains one 29x60mm stamp.

Dinner at Emmaus, by Primo Conti — A384

2005, Nov. 10 **Litho.** ***Perf. 13x13¼***
1308 A384 62c multi 1.50 1.50

Eleventh General Assembly of the Synod of Bishops.

2004 Journeys of Pope John Paul II — A385

Designs: 45c, Bern, Switzerland, June 5-6. 80c, Lourdes, France, Aug. 14-15. €2, Loreto, Italy, Sept. 5.

2005, Nov. 10
1309-1311 A385 Set of 3 8.00 8.00

The Annunciation, by Raphael — A386

Designs: Nos. 1312, 1314a, Drawing of Angel, Painting of Virgin Mary. Nos. 1313, 1314b, Painting of Angel, drawing of Virgin Mary.

Litho. & Engr.
2005, Nov. 10 ***Perf. 13x13¼***
1312 A386 62c multi 1.60 1.60
1313 A386 €1 multi 2.75 2.75

Souvenir Sheet

1314 A386 €1.40 Sheet of 2, #a-b 7.00 7.00

See France No. 3153.

Swiss Papal Guards, 500th Anniv. — A387

Designs: 62c, Guard and drummers. 80c, Guards and St. Peter's Basilica.

2005, Nov. 22 **Litho.** ***Perf. 14x14¼***
1315-1316 A387 Set of 2 3.50 3.50

Nos. 1315-1316 each issued in sheets of 6. See Switzerland Nos. 1224-1225.

Christmas — A388

Details from Adoration of the Shepherds, by François Le Moyne: 45c, Shepherds and sheep. 62c, Angel. 80c, Madonna and Child.

2005, Nov. 22 ***Perf. 13¼x13***
1317-1319 A388 Set of 3 4.75 4.75
1319a Booklet pane of 4 #1319 8.00 —
Complete booklet, #1319a 8.00

Europa — A389

Designs: 62c, Praying hands, church, mosque and synagogue. 80c, Handshake, classroom.

2006, Mar. 16 **Litho.** ***Perf. 13x13¼***
1320-1321 A389 Set of 2 3.50 3.50

Jesuits — A390

Designs: 45c, Blessed Peter Faber (1506-46). 60c, St. Ignatius of Loyola (1491-1556). €2, St. Francis Xavier (1506-52).

2006, Mar. 16
1322-1324 A390 Set of 3 7.50 7.50

Andrea Mantegna (c. 1430-1506), Painter — A391

Designs: 60c, Madonna and Child. 85c, Saints Gregory and John the Baptist. €1, Saints Peter and Paul.

No. 1328 — San Zeno Polyptych: a, Country name at right. b, Country name at left.

2006, Mar. 16 **Photo.** ***Perf. 12¾***
1325-1327 A391 Set of 3 6.00 6.00

Souvenir Sheet
Perf. 13¼x13

1328 A391 €1.40 Sheet of 2, #a-b 7.00 7.00

No. 1328 contains two 21x37mm stamps.

Wolfgang Amadeus Mozart (1756-91), Composer A392

Litho. & Engr.
2006, June 22 ***Perf. 14x14¼***
1329 A392 80c multi 2.00 2.00

Issued in sheets of 6. Value, $15.

2005 Travels of Pope Benedict XVI — A393

Designs: 62c, National Eucharistic Congress, Bari, Italy, May 21-29. €1.40, World Youth Day, Cologne, Germany, Aug. 16-21.

2006, June 22 **Litho.** ***Perf. 13¼x13***
1330-1331 A393 Set of 2 4.00 4.00

St. Peter's Basilica, 500th Anniv. A394

No. 1332, 45c — 1506 medallion depicting: a, Allegory of architecture (denomination at LL). b, Architect Donato Bramante (denomination at UR).

No. 1333, 60c — 1506 medallion depicting: a, Pope Julius II (denomination at LL). b, Bramante's plan for St. Peter's Basilica (denomination at UR).

Litho. & Embossed
2006, June 22 ***Perf. 14***
Horiz. Pairs, #a-b
1332-1333 A394 Set of 2 6.00 6.00

Intl. Year of Deserts and Desertification — A395

Designs: 62c, Flowers, child on parched earth. €1, Trees, child and cattle.

2006, Oct. 12 **Litho.** ***Perf. 13½x13¼***
1334-1335 A395 Set of 2 4.25 4.25

Diplomatic Relations Between Vatican City and Singapore, 25th Anniv. — A396

Designs: 85c, Merlion and St. Peter's Basilica. €2, Flags of Singapore and Vatican City.

2006, Oct. 12 ***Perf. 13½x13***
1336-1337 A396 Set of 2 7.50 7.50

See Singapore Nos. 1232-1233.

Vatican Musum, 500th Anniv. — A397

Heads from Laocoon sculpture: 60c, Son of Laocoon. 65c, Laocoon. €1.40, Son of Laocoon, diff.

€2.80, Laocoon, horiz.

Litho. & Embossed
2006, Oct. 12 ***Perf. 13x13¼***
1338-1340 A397 Set of 3 7.00 7.00

Souvenir Sheet
Perf. 13 Horiz.

1341 A397 €2.80 multi 7.00 7.00

No. 1341 contains one 80x30mm stamp.

Christmas — A398

Stained glass from Pope's private chapel: 60c, Shepherds. 65c, Holy Family. 85c, Magi and Star of Bethlehem.

2006, Oct. 12 **Litho.** ***Perf. 13¼x13***
1342-1344 A398 Set of 3 5.50 5.50
1343a Booklet pane of 4 #1343 7.00 —
Complete booklet, #1343a 7.00

St. Francis of Paola (1416-1507) A399

Details from sculpture: 60c, Head of St. Francis. €1, Angel.

2007, Mar. 16 **Litho.** ***Perf. 13x13¼***
1345-1346 A399 Set of 2 4.25 4.25

Pope Benedict XVI, 80th Birthday A400

Pope Benedict XVI: 60c, Wearing zucchetto. 65c, Without head covering. 85c, Wearing miter.

2007, Mar. 16 ***Perf. 13¼x13***
Stamp + Label
1347-1349 A400 Set of 3 5.00 5.00

Issued in sheets of 4+4 labels. Value, set of 3, $17.50.

Europa — A401

Designs: 60c, Scouts reading map, Scout holding chick. 65c, Scouts around campfire.

2007, June 12 ***Perf. 13x13¼***
1350-1351 A401 Set of 2 3.50 3.50

Scouting, cent.

Christian Museum, 250th Anniv. — A402

Designs: 85c, Gilded glass depicting Saints Peter and Paul, silver vase. €2, Bronze lamp with monogram of Christ, silver bottle.

2007, June 12
1352-1353 A402 Set of 2 7.50 7.50

Carlo Goldoni (1707-93), Playwright A403

Goldoni and: 60c, Bridge, man, harlequin. 85c, Church, man, woman.

€2.80, Goldoni holding book.

2007, June 12 ***Perf. 13x13¼***
1354-1355 A403 Set of 2 3.75 3.75

Souvenir Sheet
Perf. 13

1356 A403 €2.80 multi 7.50 7.50

No. 1356 contains one 45x33mm stamp and was sold with side portions of the sheet folded to produce an effect like a theater curtain.

New Philatelic and Numismatic Museum — A404

No. 1357: a, Vatican City #37, 576, 1013, 1296. b, Four Vatican City coins.

Litho. & Embossed

2007, Sept. 20 ***Perf. 14***
1357 A404 60c Horiz. pair, #a-b 3.25 3.25

Treaty of Rome, 50th Anniv. — A405

Stars and: 15c, Atomium, Brussels. 30c, Eiffel Tower, Paris. 60c, Brandenburg Gate, Berlin. 65c, Plaza, Rome. €1, Castle, Luxembourg. €4, Buildings and bridges, Amsterdam. €2.80, Mother and child.

2007, Sept. 20 Litho. ***Perf. 13x13¼***
1358-1363 A405 Set of 6 18.00 18.00

Souvenir Sheet

Perf. 13x13¼ on 2 Sides
1364 A405 €2.80 multi 8.00 8.00

No. 1364 contains one 40x37mm stamp.

St. Elizabeth of Hungary (1207-31) — A406

2007, Nov. 20 ***Perf. 13¾***
1365 A406 65c multi 1.60 1.60

2006 Travels of Pope Benedict XVI — A407

Travels: 60c, Poland, May 25-28. 65c, Valencia, Spain, July 8-9. 85c, Germany, Sept. 9-14. €1.40, Turkey, Nov. 28-Dec. 1.

2007, Nov. 20 ***Perf. 13¼x13***
1366-1369 A407 Set of 4 9.75 9.75

Booklet Stamp
Self-Adhesive

1370 A407 85c Like #1368 2.50 2.50
a. Booklet pane of 4 10.00

Christmas — A408

Vatican arms and nave paintings in St. Andrew's Church, Luqa, Malta, by Giuseppe Calì: 60c, Madonna and Child. 65c, Holy Family with Women and Young Girl. 85c, Infant Jesus and Young Girl.

2007, Nov. 20
1371-1373 A408 Set of 3 5.50 5.50

See Malta Nos. 1319-1321.

Europa — A409

Designs: 60c, Envelope with cachet and cancels. 85c, Handwritten letter, Pope Benedict XVI.

2008, Mar. 6 Litho. ***Perf. 13¾***
1374-1375 A409 Set of 2 3.50 3.50

Sistine Chapel Paintings by Michelangelo, 500th Anniv. — A410

Designs: 5c, Libyan. 10c, Eritrean. 25c, Delphic Sibyl. 60c, Sibyl Cumana. 65c, Daniel. 85c, Jonah. €2, Ezekiel. €5, Zaccharias.

2008, Mar. 6 ***Perf. 13x13¼***
1376 A410 5c multi .25 .25
1377 A410 10c multi .30 .30
1378 A410 25c multi .75 .75
1379 A410 60c multi 1.75 1.75
1380 A410 65c multi 1.90 1.90
1381 A410 85c multi 2.40 2.40
1382 A410 €2 multi 5.50 5.50
1383 A410 €5 multi 14.00 14.00
Nos. 1376-1383 (8) 26.85 26.85

23rd World Youth Day — A411

2008, May 15 Litho. ***Perf. 13¾***
1384 A411 €1 multi 2.75 2.75

Visit of Pope Benedict XVI to United Nations — A412

2008, May 15
1385 A412 €1.40 multi 3.75 3.75

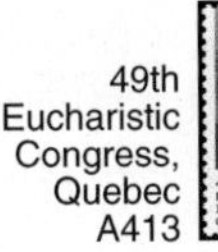

49th Eucharistic Congress, Quebec A413

Designs: 60c, Wedding at Cana, Washing of the Feet, Last Supper. 85c, Crucifixion, Resurrection, Disciples of Emmaus.

2008, May 15 ***Perf. 13¾x13¼***
1386-1387 A413 Set of 2 4.25 4.25

Apparition of the Virgin Mary at Lourdes, 150th Anniv. — A414

Designs: 65c, Pilgrims at Lourdes. 85c, Virgin Mary, Lourdes.

2008, May 15 Litho. ***Perf. 13x13¼***
1388-1389 A414 Set of 2 *9.50 9.50*

Nos. 1388-1389 each were printed in sheets of 4. Value, *$40.*

2007 Travels of Pope Benedict XVI — A415

Travels: 65c, Brazil, May 9-14. 85c, Austria, Sept. 7-9.

Litho. & Engr.

2008, Sept. 17 ***Perf. 12¾***
1390-1391 A415 Set of 2 4.50 4.50

Pauline Year — A416

Designs: 60c, Conversion of St. Paul. 65c, St. Paul preaching. 85c, St. Paul imprisoned.

2008, Sept. 17 Litho. ***Perf. 13¼x13***
1392-1394 A416 Set of 3 5.00 5.00

Issued in sheets of 4. Value, set, $20.

Postal Convention Between Vatican City and Sovereign Military Order of Malta — A417

2008, Nov. 13 Litho. ***Perf. 13¾***
1395 A417 €2.50 multi + label 7.00 7.00

Andrea Palladio (1508-80), Architect — A418

Designs: 65c, San Giorgio Maggiore Church, Venice. 85c, Villa Rotonda, Vicenza, Italy.
€2.80, Palladio.

2008, Nov. 13 ***Perf. 13¼x14***
1396-1397 A418 Set of 2 3.75 3.75

Souvenir Sheet

1398 A418 €2.80 multi 7.00 7.00

Christmas A419

Designs: 60c, Adoration of the Magi, by Raphael. 65c, Nativity, by Albrecht Dürer.

2008, Nov. 13 Litho. ***Perf. 13x13¼***
1399-1400 A419 Set of 2 3.00 3.00

Booklet Stamp
Self-Adhesive

Serpentine Die Cut 12½
1401 A419 60c multi 1.60 1.60
a. Booklet pane of 4 6.50

See Germany Nos. B1008-B1009.

Gibraltar Shrine to Our Lady of Europe, 700th Anniv. — A420

2009, Feb. 10 Litho. ***Perf. 14x14¾***
1402 A420 85c multi 2.25 2.25

Printed in sheets of 4. See Gibraltar No. 1182.

A421

Vatican City State, 80th Anniv. A422

Popes: No. 1403, 65c, Pius XI. No. 1404, 65c, Pius XII. No. 1405, 65c, John XXIII. No. 1406, 65c, Paul VI. No. 1407, 65c, John Paul I. No. 1408, 65c, John Paul II. No. 1409, Benedict XVI.
€2.80, Vatican City map.

2009, Feb. 10 ***Perf. 13½x14***
1403-1409 A421 Set of 7 11.50 11.50

Souvenir Sheet

1410 A422 €2.80 gray & blk 8.00 8.00

Europa — A423

Paintings from Astronomical Observations series by Donato Creti: 60c, The Sun. 65c, Saturn.

2009, May 20 Litho. ***Perf. 14¼***
1411-1412 A423 Set of 2 3.25 3.25

Intl. Year of Astronomy.

St. Frances of Rome (1384-1440) A424

Designs: 85c, St. Frances healing a poor man with an injured arm. €1, Miracle of the grapes.

2009, May 20 ***Perf. 13¼***
1413-1414 A424 Set of 2 4.75 4.75

World Book and Copyright Day — A425

Pontifical Biblical Institute, Cent. — A426

75th Intl. Federationo of Library Associations and Institutions General Conference, Milan — A427

2009, May 20 ***Perf. 14x14¾***
1415 A425 60c multi 1.75 1.75
1416 A426 85c multi 2.40 2.40
1417 A427 €1.40 multi 4.00 4.00
Nos. 1415-1417 (3) 8.15 8.15

Guglielmo Cardinal Massaja (1809-89), Missionary in Africa — A428

2009, Sept. 23 Litho. *Perf. 13¾*
1418 A428 60c brown 1.75 1.75

2008 Travels of Pope Benedict XVI — A429

Travels: 65c, France, Sept. 12-15. 85c, United States, Apr. 15-21. €1, Australia, July 12-21.

2009, Sept. 23
1419-1421 A429 Set of 3 7.00 7.00

A430

A431

The Disputation of the Holy Sacrament, by Raphael, 500th Anniv. — A432

Designs: Nos. 1422-1424, Various painting details. €3.30, Entire painting.

2009, Sept. 23 *Perf. 14*
1422 A430 65c multi 1.90 1.90
1423 A431 65c multi 1.90 1.90
1424 A432 65c multi 1.90 1.90
Nos. 1422-1424 (3) 5.70 5.70

Souvenir Sheet
Perf. 13¾

1425 A432 €3.30 multi 9.00 9.00

No. 1425 contains one 35x50mm stamp.

Italian Language Day — A433

2009, Oct. 21 Photo. *Perf. 13¼x13*
1426 A433 60c multi + label 1.60 1.60

Printed in sheets of 5 + 5 labels. Value, $10. See Italy No. 2966; San Marino No. 1801.

Composers A434

Designs: 65c, George Frideric Handel (1685-1759). 85c, Joseph Haydn (1732-1809). €5, Felix Mendelssohn Bartholdy (1809-47).

2009, Oct. 24 Litho. *Perf. 14¾x14*
1427-1429 A434 Set of 3 19.50 19.50

Convocation of Second Vatican Council, 50th Anniv. — A435

Litho. & Embossed

2009, Nov. 4 *Perf. 14*
1430 A435 60c multi 1.60 1.60

Louis Braille (1809-52), Educator of the Blind — A436

2009, Nov. 4 *Perf. 14¾x14*
1431 A436 65c multi 1.75 1.75

Christmas — A437

Madonna and Child Enthroned with Two Angels and Saints Joachim and Anne, by Francesco Melanzio: 60c, Detail. 65c, Entire painting.

2009, Nov. 4 Litho. *Perf. 12½*
1432 A437 60c multi 1.90 1.90
1433 A437 65c multi 2.00 2.00
a. Booklet pane of 4 8.00 8.00
Complete booklet, #1433a 8.00

Easter — A438

Litho. & Engr.

2010, Mar. 5 *Perf. 13x12¾*
1434 A438 65c multi 1.60 1.60

Sandro Botticelli (1445-1510), Painter — A439

Details of Sistine Chapel paintings: 60c, Women from *The Temptation of Christ.* 85c, Woman holding walking stick from *The Life of Moses.* €1.45, Woman carrying basket on head from *The Life of Moses.*

2010, Mar. 5 Litho. *Perf. 13¾x13½*
1435-1437 A439 Set of 3 8.25 8.25

The Deposition, by Caravaggio (1573-1610) — A440

2010, June 22 Litho. *Perf. 13¼x14*
1438 A440 65c multi 1.75 1.75

Europa — A441

Illustrations from *The Bible Narrated for Children*: 60c, Adam and Eve in the Garden of Eden. 65c, Jesus and children.

2010, June 22 *Perf. 13*
1439-1440 A441 Set of 2 3.25 3.25

Nos. 1439-1440 were printed in sheets of 6.

Sacerdotal Year — A442

Designs: €1.40, St. John Vianney (1786-1859) and priests. €1.50, The Good Shepherd, sheep and wolf.

2010, June 22 *Perf. 13¾x13½*
1441-1442 A442 Set of 2 8.25 8.25

Father Matteo Ricci (1552-1610), Missionary to China — A443

Designs: 5c, Ricci and Xu Guangqi, Chinese court official. €3.30, Ricci.

2010, June 22 *Perf. 14¾x14*
1443-1444 A443 Set of 2 9.50 9.50

Pope Leo XIII (1810-1903) — A444

2010, Sept. 20 Litho. *Perf. 14¾x14*
1445 A444 65c multi 1.90 1.90

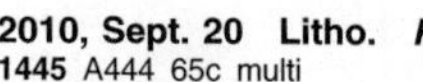

A445

Composers — A445a

Designs: 65c, Frédéric Chopin (1810-49). €1, Robert Schumann (1810-56). €4.40, Chopin and Schumann, horiz. (65x16mm).

2010, Sept. 20 *Perf. 13x12¾*
1446 A445 65c multi 2.00 2.00
1447 A445 €1 multi 3.00 3.00

Perf. 12¾ at Top

1448 A445a €4.40 multi + label 12.50 12.50
Nos. 1446-1448 (3) 17.50 17.50

A446

Reopening of the Vatican Library — A446a

Designs: 65c, Crucified Christ. 85c, Sts. Cosmas and Damian. €3.90, Medallion depicting Pope Sixtus V, vert.

2010, Sept. 20 *Perf. 14x13½*
1449 A446 65c multi 2.00 2.00
1450 A446 85c multi 2.50 2.50

Imperf

1451 A446a €3.90 multi 14.00 14.00
Nos. 1449-1451 (3) 18.50 18.50

No. 1451 is printed as a miniature book made up of two pieces of paper of different sizes. Both pieces of paper are printed on both sides, and are glued together. The cover of the book is the longer of the two pieces of paper, and is folded into three parts. The stamp, the front cover of the book, is the middle part of this piece of paper. The gum, applied to the left of the stamp, becomes the book's back cover when the longer piece of paper is folded. The title page of *De Nuptiis Philologiae et Mercurii* is to the right of the stamp, and is the book's first page. Text and illustrations are on the reverse of this picture and the stamp, and another picture depicting text and the seal of the Vatican Library is printed on the back of the gum. The second piece of paper, folded in half to constitute four pages of the book, has text and illustrations, and is glued to the back of longer sheet where the fold between the stamp and the photo is found. Values are for the complete item.

Approval of the Franciscan Rule, 800th Anniv. — A447

2010, Nov. 15 Litho. *Perf. 12¾*
1452 A447 65c multi 2.00 2.00

Writers — A448

Scenes from works by: 60c, Anton Chekhov (1860-1904). 65c, Leo Tolstoy (1828-1910).

2010, Nov. 15 *Perf. 14¼x14¾*
1453-1454 A448 Set of 2 3.75 3.75

2009 Travels of Pope Benedict XVI — A449

Travels: 10c, Cameroun and Angola, Mar. 17-23. 65c, Holy Land, May 8-15. 85c, Czech Republic, Sept. 26-28.

2010, Nov. 15 *Perf. 13x13¼*
1455-1457 A449 Set of 3 4.75 4.75

See Israel No. 1837.

Christmas — A450

Paintings: 60c, The Birth of Jesus, by Gheorghe Tattarascu. 65c, The Nativity and Adoration of the Shepherds, by the School of Murillo.

2010, Nov. 15 ***Perf. 13¼***
1458 A450 60c multi 1.75 1.75
1459 A450 65c multi 1.90 1.90

Booklet Stamps
Self-Adhesive
Serpentine Die Cut 12½

1460 A450 60c multi 1.75 1.75
a. Booklet pane of 4 7.00
1461 A450 65c multi 1.90 1.90
a. Booklet pane of 4 7.75

See Romania Nos. 5218-5219.

Easter A451

2011, Mar. 21 ***Perf. 12¾***
1462 A451 75c multi 2.25 2.25

Father Eusebio Kino (1645-1711), Missionary in Mexico — A452

2011, Mar. 21 ***Perf. 14¼x14¾***
1463 A452 €1.60 maroon & black 4.75 4.75

A453

Unification of Italy, 150th Anniv. — A454

Designs: No. 1464, 60c, Milan Cathedral and Lombardy-Venetia #6. No. 1465, 60c, Modena Cathedral and Modena #3. No. 1466, 60c, Uffizi Gallery, Palazzo Vecchio, Florence and Tuscany #4. No. 1467, 60c, San Carlo Square, Turin and Sardinia #1. No. 1468, 60c, Mt. Vesuvius and Naples, Two Sicilies #3, 13. No. 1469, 60c, Baptistry, Parma and Parma #4.

€1.50, Piazza del Popolo, Rome.

2011, Mar. 21 ***Perf. 12½***
1464-1469 A453 Set of 6 11.00 11.00

Souvenir Sheet

1470 A454 €1.50 multi 5.00 5.00

See Italy No. 3046.

Beatification of Pope John Paul II — A455

2011, Apr. 12 ***Perf. 13***
1471 A455 75c multi 2.50 2.50

Printed in sheets of 6. See Poland No. 4009.

World Youth Day, Madrid — A456

2011, June 21 ***Perf. 14x13½***
1472 A456 75c multi 2.10 2.10

See Spain No. 3797.

Europa A457

Detail from The Journey of Moses into Egypt, by Perugino: a, 60c, "Europa" at UL. b, 75c, "Europa" at UR.

2011, June 21 ***Perf. 13¾***
1473 A457 Horiz. pair, #a-b 4.00 4.00

Intl. Year of Forests.

Ordination of Pope Benedict XVI, 60th Anniv. A458

Designs: No. 1474, 75c, Shell, photograph from ordination as priest, June 29, 1951. No. 1475, 75c, Bear, photograph from installation as bishop, May 28, 1977. No. 1476, 75c, St. Corbinnian, photograph from installation as cardinal, June 27, 1977. No. 1477, 75c, Papal arms, photograph from installation as pope, Apr. 19, 2005.

2011, June 21 ***Perf. 13½x13¾***
1474-1477 A458 Set of 4 9.00 9.00

Miniature Sheet

L'Osservatore Romano (Official Vatican Newspaper), 150th Anniv. — A459

No. 1478 — Front pages of newspaper announcing election of Pope: a, Leo XIII. b, Pius X. c, Benedict XV. d, Pius XI. e, Pius XII. f, John XXIII. g, Paul VI. h, John Paul I. i, John Paul II. j, Benedict XVI.

2011, June 21 ***Perf. 14x14¾***
1478 A459 60c Sheet fo 10, #a-j 18.50 18.50

Mater et Magistra, Encyclical by Pope John XXIII, 50th Anniv. — A460

2011, Sept. 2 ***Perf. 13¾***
1479 A460 60c multi 1.75 1.75

Room of Heliodorus Frescoes by Raphael, 500th Anniv. A461

Details from The Expulsion of Heliodorus from the Temple. 75c, Left side of fresco. €1.60, Right side of fresco.

2011, Sept. 2 ***Perf. 14¼***
1480-1481 A461 Set of 2 7.00 7.00

Rudjer Boskovic (1711-87), Astronomer, and Dome of St. Peter's Basilica A462

2011, Sept. 13
1482 A462 €3.30 multi 10.00 10.00

See Croatia No. 810.

Composers — A463

Designs: 75c, Franz Liszt (1811-86). €1.60, Gustav Mahler (1860-1911).

2011, Nov. 18 **Litho.** ***Perf. 14x14¾***
1483-1484 A463 Set of 2 6.50 6.50

2010 Travels of Pope Benedict XVI — A464

Travels: 60c, Malta, Apr. 17-18. 75c, Portugal, May 11-14. €1.40, Cyprus, June 4-6. €1.60, United Kingdom, Sept. 16-19. €2, Spain, Nov. 6-7.

2011, Nov. 18 ***Perf. 13¼***
1485-1489 A464 Set of 5 18.00 18.00

Christmas — A465

Designs: 60c, Madonna and Child, Saints Benedict and Francis. 75c, Infant Jesus and animals.

2011, Nov. 18 ***Perf. 13¼***
1490 A465 60c multi 1.75 1.75
1491 A465 75c multi 2.00 2.00

Booklet Stamp
Self-Adhesive
Serpentine Die Cut 12½x12¼

1492 A465 75c multi 2.00 2.00
a. Booklet pane of 4 8.00

Easter — A466

2012, Mar. 1 ***Perf. 14¼x14¾***
1493 A466 75c multi 2.00 2.00

Father Christopher Clavius (1538-1612), Mathematician and Astronomer — A467

2012, Mar. 1 ***Perf. 14¼***
1494 A467 €1.60 black & red 4.50 4.50

Madonna of Foligno, by Raphael — A468

Sistine Madonna, by Raphael — A469

2012, Mar. 1 ***Perf. 13¼***
1495 A468 60c multi 1.75 1.75
1496 A469 75c multi 2.25 2.25

Souvenir Sheets

1497 A468 €1.40 multi 4.00 4.00
1498 A469 €2.40 multi 7.00 7.00

See Germany No. 2666.

St. Joan of Arc (c. 1412-31) — A470

Litho. & Engr.

2012, May 11 ***Perf. 13***
1499 A470 75c multi 2.00 2.00

See France No. 4220.

Seventh World Meeting of Families, Milan — A471

2012, May 11 **Litho.** ***Perf. 13¼x14***
1500 A471 €1.50 multi 4.00 4.00

Europa — A472

Designs: No. 1501, 75c, Dome of St. Peter's Basilica. No. 1502, 75c, Dove in stained-glass window, St. Peter's Basilica.

2012, May 11
1501-1502 A472 Set of 2 4.00 4.00

50th Intl. Eucharistic Congress, Dublin — A473

Designs: 75c, Celtic cross from the Rock of Cashel, Tipperary, Ireland. €1, Ardagh Chalice.

2012, May 11 ***Perf. 14¾x14***
1503-1504 A473 Set of 2 4.75 4.75

Pope John Paul I (1912-78) — A474

2012, Sept. 13 ***Perf. 14x13¾***
1505 A474 75c multi 2.00 2.00

No. 1505 was printed in sheets of 6.

Vatican Secret Archives, 400th Anniv. A475

No. 1506: a, Pope Benedict XVI. b, Sealed document. c, Pope Paul V.

2012, Sept. 13 *Perf. 13¾x13½*
1506 A475 75c Horiz. strip of 3, #a-c 6.00 6.00

No. 1506 was printed in sheets containing four strips.

Souvenir Sheet

Battle of the Milvian Bridge, 1700th Anniv. A476

2012, Sept. 13 *Perf. 14x13½*
1507 A476 €4.40 multi 11.50 11.50

See Italy No. 3136.

2011 Travels of Pope Benedict XVI — A477

Travels: 60c, Croatia, June 4-5. 75c, San Marino, June 19. €1.40, Spain, Aug. 18-21. €1.60, Germany, Sept. 22-25. €2, Benin, Nov. 18-20.

2012, Nov. 6 *Perf. 13½*
1508-1512 A477 Set of 5 17.50 17.50

Christmas — A478

Stained-glass windows by János Hajnal depicting: 60c, Annunciation. 75c, Holy Family and shepherd.

2012, Nov. 6 *Perf. 13¾*
1513-1514 A478 Set of 2 3.50 3.50
1514a Booklet pane of 8, 4 each #1513-1514 14.00 —
Complete booklet, #1514a 14.00

Souvenir Sheet

Restoration of the Colonnade of St. Peter's Square — A479

No. 1515 — Papal arms of: a, Alexander VII. b, Benedict XVI.

Litho. With Foil Application

2012, Nov. 20 *Perf. 13¾*
1515 A479 €10 Sheet of 2, #a-b *57.50 57.50*

Inscription in sheet margin "Officium Philatelicum et Nomismaticum" could be personalized.

Sculpture of Risen Christ, by Pericle Fazzini — A480

Perf. 13¼x13½

2013, Feb. 28 **Litho.**
1516 A480 85c multi 2.25 2.25

Easter.

Year of Faith A481

No. 1517 — Details from Faith, by Raphael: a, Putto, denomination at LL (20x38mm). b, Putto, denomination at LR (20x38mm). c, Faith with chalice and host (30x38mm).

2013, Feb. 28 *Perf. 13½x13¾*
1517 A481 Horiz. strip of 3 6.00 6.00
a.-b. 60c Either single 1.60 1.60
c. €1 multi 2.60 2.60

Souvenir Sheet

Mass of Bolsena, by Raphael A482

2013, Feb. 28 *Perf. 13½x13¾*
1518 A482 €4.80 multi 12.50 12.50

Miracle of Bolsena, 750th anniv.

Interregnum Issue

Angel and Sede Vacante Arms — A483

Background colors: 70c, Blue green. 85c, Blue. €2, Gray. €2.50, Yellow.

2013, Mar. 1 *Perf. 13¼x13*
1519-1522 A483 Set of 4 16.00 16.00

Pope Francis — A484

Various photographs of Pope Francis: 70c, 85c, €2, €2.50.

2013, May 2 *Perf. 13¼x14*
1523-1526 A484 Set of 4 16.00 16.00

See Argentina No. 2682, Italy No. 3179.

Giuseppe Gioachino Belli (1791-1863), Poet — A485

2013, May 2 *Perf. 14x14¾*
1527 A485 €1 multi 2.60 2.60

World Youth Day — A486

2013, May 2 *Perf. 13¼x13*
1528 A486 €1.90 multi 5.00 5.00

Europa — A487

Vatican City postal van and: 70c, St. Peter's Basilica. 85c, Globe.

2013, May 2
1529-1530 A487 Set of 2 4.00 4.00

Pope John XXIII (1881-1963) — A488

2013, June 12 *Perf. 14x13½*
1531 A488 85c multi 2.25 2.25

No. 1531 was printed in sheets of 9.

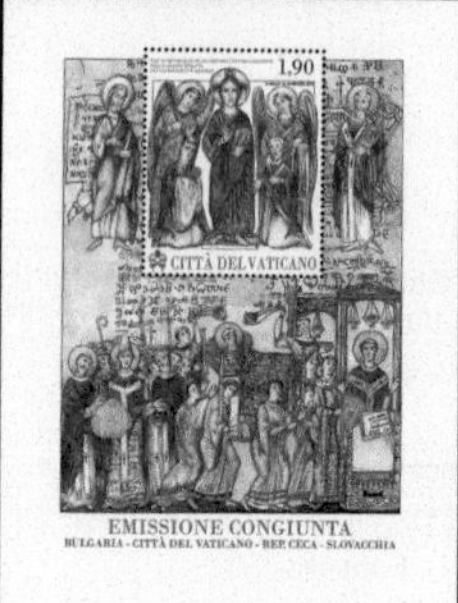

Edict of Milan, 1700th Anniv. — A489

Frescoes from the Oratory of St. Sylvester, Rome, depicting Pope Sylvester I and Emperor Constantine: 70c, 85c, €2.50.
€1.90, Pope Sylvester I showing icon depicting Sts. Peter and Paul to Emperor Constantine.

2013, June 12 *Perf. 13x13¼*
1532-1534 A489 Set of 3 11.00 11.00

Souvenir Sheet

1535 A489 €1.90 multi 5.25 5.25

See Italy No. 3178.

Souvenir Sheet

Mission of Sts. Cyril and Methodius to Slavic Lands, 1150th Anniv. — A490

Litho. & Engr.

2013, June 12 *Perf. 11¾*
1536 A490 €1.90 multi 5.25 5.25

See Bulgaria No. 4647, Czech Republic No. 3573, Slovakia No. 666.

Composers — A491

Designs: 70c, Giuseppe Verdi (1813-1901). 85c, Richard Wagner (1813-83).

2013, Aug. 30 **Litho.** *Perf. 14x14¾*
1537-1538 A491 Set of 2 4.25 4.25

Popes of the Renaissance — A492

Designs: 70c, Pope Julius II (1443-1513). €2, Pope Leo X (1475-1521).

2013, Aug. 30 *Perf. 13¾x13½*
1539-1540 A492 Set of 2 7.25 7.25

Raoul Follereau (1903-77), Journalist, and Lepers — A493

2013, Nov. 7 **Litho.** *Perf. 13¾*
1541 A493 €2 multi 5.50 5.50

World Leprosy Day.

2012 Travels of Pope Benedict XVI — A494

Travels: 70c, Mexico and Cuba, Mar. 23-29. 85c, Lebanon, Sept. 14-16.

2013, Nov. 7 **Litho.** *Perf. 14x13¾*
1542 A494 70c multi 1.90 1.90
1543 A494 85c multi 2.40 2.40
a. Booklet pane of 4, 2 each #1542-1543 8.75 —
Complete booklet, #1543a 8.75

Santa Maria di Nardò Cathedral, Lecce, Italy, 600th Anniv. — A495

Cathedral frescoes depicting: 5c, St. Augustine. 10c, Our Lady of Health. 15c, Madonna del Giglio. 25c, St. Nicholas of Myra. 45c, Christ Pantocrator.

2013, Nov. 7 **Litho.** *Perf. 13x13¼*
1544-1548 A495 Set of 5 2.75 2.75

Christmas — A496

Paintings by Pinturicchio: 70c, Nativity. 85c, Adoration of the Magi.

2013, Nov. 7 **Litho.** *Perf. 13¼x13¾*
1549-1550 A496 Set of 2 4.25 4.25

Nos. 1549-1550 each were printed in sheets of 8 + central label. See Finland (Aland Islands) Nos. 349-350.

27th Intl. Book Fair, Turin — A497

2014, Mar. 21 **Litho.** *Perf. 13*
1551 A497 70c multi 2.00 2.00

Easter — A498

2014, Mar. 21 Litho. *Perf. 13¾*
1552 A498 85c multi 2.40 2.40

Start of Second Year of Reign of Pope Francis — A499

Various photographs of Pope Francis with denomination in: 70c, Red. 85c, Blue. €2, Green. €2.50, Bister.

2014, Mar. 21 Litho. *Perf. 13½x13*
1553-1556 A499 Set of 4 17.00 17.00

See Philippines No. 3519.

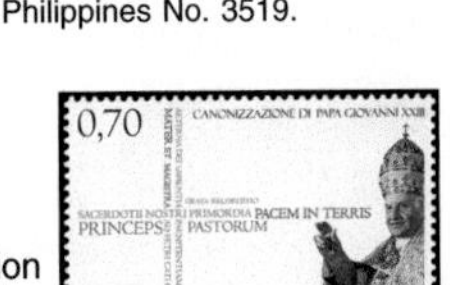

Canonization of Pope John XXIII — A500

2014, Mar. 21 Litho. *Perf. 13¼*
1557 A500 70c multi 2.00 2.00

See Italy No. 3228

Souvenir Sheet

Canonization of Popes John Paul II and John XXIII — A501

No. 1558: a, Pope John Paul II. b, Pope John XXIII.

Perf. 11½x11¼ Syncopated
2014, Mar. 21 Litho.
1558 A501 €1 Sheet of 2, #a-b 5.50 5.50

See Poland No. 4112.

A502

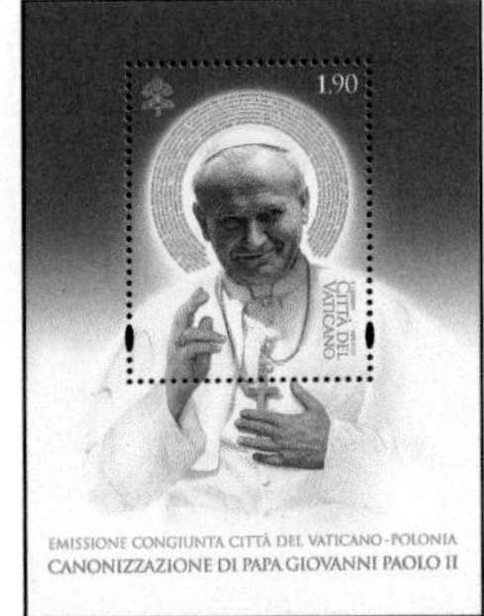

Canonization of Pope John Paul II — A503

Perf. 11½x11¾ Syncopated
2014, Mar. 21 Litho.
1559 A502 85c multi 2.40 2.40

Souvenir Sheets

Perf. 11¼x11½ Syncopated
1560 A503 €1.90 multi 5.25 5.25

Engr.
1561 A503 €2.50 bister 7.00 7.00

See Poland Nos. 4113-4115.

Charlie Chaplin (1889-1977), Film Actor — A504

2014, May 20 Litho. *Perf. 13½*
1562 A504 70c multi 1.90 1.90

Face of Christ, by El Greco (1541-1614) — A505

2014, May 20 Litho. *Perf. 14¾x14*
1563 A505 85c multi 2.40 2.40

Europa — A506

Pipe organ from: 70c, Basilica of St. John Lateran. 85c, St. Peter's Basilica.

2014, May 20 Litho. *Perf. 13¾*
1564-1565 A506 Set of 2 4.25 4.25

Emperor Charlemagne (742-814) — A507

Charlemagne: 85c, On horse. €1.90, With orb and scepter.

2014, May 20 Litho. *Perf. 13¾*
1566-1567 A507 Set of 2 7.50 7.50

Souvenir Sheet

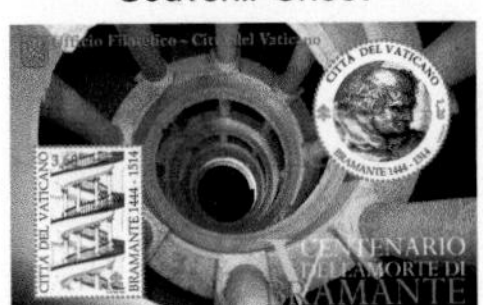

Donato Bramante (1444-1514), Architect — A508

No. 1568: a, €1.20, Bramante (38mm diameter). b, €3.60, Bramante Staircase, Octagonal Courtyard of the Belvedere (30x40mm).

Perf. (#1568a), Perf. 14¼ (#1568b)
2014, May 20 Litho.
1568 A508 Sheet of 2, #a-b 13.00 13.00

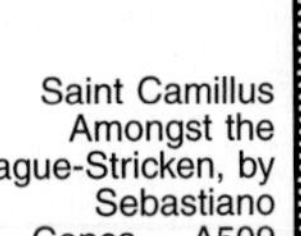

Saint Camillus Amongst the Plague-Stricken, by Sebastiano Conca — A509

2014, Aug. 28 Litho. *Perf. 13¼*
1569 A509 70c multi 1.90 1.90

St. Camillus de Lellis (1550-1614), founder of the Order of the Ministers of the Sick.

Richard Strauss (1864-1949), Composer — A510

2014, Aug. 28 Litho. *Perf. 13¾*
1570 A510 70c multi 1.90 1.90

Beatification of Pope Paul VI (1897-1978) — A511

2014, Aug. 28 Litho. *Perf. 13¼x13*
1571 A511 70c multi 1.90 1.90

No. 1571 was issued in sheets of 4.

Statue of St. Pius X (1835-1914), by Pier Enrico Astorri — A512

2014, Aug. 28 Litho. *Perf. 13*
1572 A512 €2 multi 5.25 5.25

Synod of Ayutthaya, 350th Anniv. — A513

2014, Aug. 28 Litho. *Perf. 13¾*
1573 A513 €2 multi 5.25 5.25

See Thailand No. 2822.

Fall of the Berlin Wall, 25th Anniv. — A514

Designs: 85c, Old woman holding chisel against wall. €3.60, Rainbow.

2014, Aug. 28 Litho. *Perf. 14¼*
1574 A514 85c multi 2.25 2.25

Souvenir Sheet
1575 A514 €3.60 multi 9.50 9.50

William Shakespeare (1564-1616), Writer — A515

2014, Nov. 21 Litho. *Perf. 13¾*
1576 A515 85c multi 2.10 2.10

Pauline Chapel Paintings by Michelangelo (1475-1564) — A516

Designs: 70c, Crucifixion of Saint Peter. 85c, Conversion of Saint Paul.

Perf. 11½x11¾
2014, Nov. 21 Litho.
1577-1578 A516 Set of 2 4.00 4.00

2013 Travels of Pope Francis — A517

Travels: 70c, Rio de Janeiro, Brazil, July 22-29. 85c, Lampedusa, Cagliari and Assisi, Italy, July 8, vert.

2014, Nov. 21 Litho. *Perf. 13¾*
1579 A517 70c multi 1.75 1.75
1580 A517 85c multi 2.10 2.10
a. Booklet pane of 4 8.50 —
Complete booklet, #1580a 8.50

Nativity, by Raúl Soldi (1905-94) — A518

2014, Nov. 21 Litho. *Perf. 13½*
1581 A518 85c multi 2.10 2.10

Christmas. See Argentina No. 2754.

Easter — A519

2015, Feb. 15 Litho. *Perf. 13¾*
1582 A519 80c multi 1.75 1.75

Public Display of the Shroud of Turin — A520

2015, Feb. 19 Litho. *Perf. 13¾*
1583 A520 95c multi 2.10 2.10

International Year of Light — A521

2015, Feb. 19 Litho. *Perf. 13¼*
1584 A521 €2.15 multi 4.75 4.75

Pope Francis — A522

Various photographs of Pope Francis: 80c, 95c, €2.30, €3.

2015, Feb. 19 Litho. *Perf. 14x14¾*
1585-1588 A522 Set of 4 18.50 18.50

St. John Bosco (1815-88) — A523

2015, May 19 Litho. *Perf. 12½*
1589 A523 80c multi 1.75 1.75

See Italy No. 3304.

International Telecommunication Union, 150th Anniv. — A524

2015, May 19 Litho. *Perf. 13½*
1590 A524 €2.15 multi 4.75 4.75

Europa — A525

Toys: 80c, Teddy bear, train, toy soldiers in Papal gendarmes uniforms. 95c, Toy soldiers in Swiss Guards uniforms, blocks, marble.

2015, May 19 Litho. *Perf. 13¾x13½*
1591-1592 A525 Set of 2 4.00 4.00

Souvenir Sheet

Events of 1945, 70th Anniv. A526

No. 1593: a, End of World War II. b, Founding of the United Nations.

2015, May 19 Litho. *Perf. 13¼*
1593 A526 €2 Sheet of 2, #a-b 9.00 9.00

Eighth World Meeting of Families, Philadelphia A527

2015, Sept. 2 Litho. *Perf. 13¾*
1594 A527 €2.30 multi 5.25 5.25

Armenian Religious Figures — A528

No. 1595: a, St. Gregory of Narek (951-1003). b, Blessed Ignatius Maloyan (1869-1915).

2015, Sept. 2 Litho. *Perf. 13¾*
1595 A528 €1 Horiz. pair, #a-b 4.50 4.50

Cent. of proclamation of St. Gregory of Narek as Doctor of the Church and martyrdom of Maloyan. No. 1595 printed in sheets containing two pairs.

Synod of Bishops, 50th Anniv. — A529

Designs: 80c, Pope Paul VI and bishops. 95c, Pope Francis and family.

2015, Sept. 2 Litho. *Perf. 13x13¼*
1596-1597 A529 Set of 2 4.00 4.00

14th General Assembly of the Synod of Bishops (No. 1597).

2014 Travels of Pope Francis — A530

Travels: No. 1598, 95c, Tirana, Albania, Sept. 21. No. 1599, 95c, Strasbourg, France, Nov. 25. No. 1600, 95c, Istanbul, Turkey, Nov. 28-30. €2.30, Seoul, South Korea, Aug. 13-18.

€3, Jerusalem, Israel, May 24-26.

2015, Sept. 2 Litho. *Perf. 14¾x14*
1598-1601 A530 Set of 4 12.00 12.00

Souvenir Sheet

Perf. 13¼

1602 A530 €3 multi 6.75 6.75

No. 1602 contains one 52x40mm stamp. See Israel No. 2075.

St. Colombanus of Bobbio (c. 543-615) — A531

2015, Nov. 19 Litho. *Perf. 14x14¾*
1603 A531 95c multi 2.00 2.00

Pope Innocent XII (1615-1700) — A532

2015, Nov. 19 Litho. *Perf. 13¾*
1604 A532 95c multi 2.00 2.00

St. Philip Neri (1515-95) and St. Teresa of Avila (1515-82) A533

Perf. 13¼x13½

2015, Nov. 19 Litho.
1605 A533 €2.30 multi 5.00 5.00

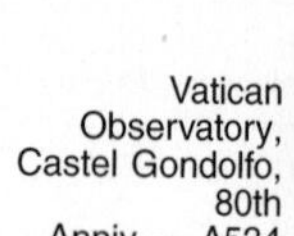
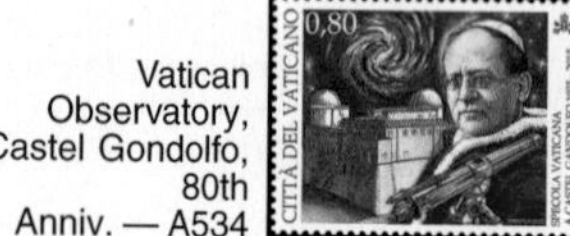

Vatican Observatory, Castel Gondolfo, 80th Anniv. — A534

Designs: 80c, Pope Pius XI (1857-1939), Papal Palace, Castel Gondolfo, Schmidt telescope. 95c, Pope Francis, Moon, refractor telescope.

2015, Nov. 19 Litho. *Perf. 13¾*
1606-1607 A534 Set of 2 3.75 3.75

Holy Year of Mercy — A535

Designs: 80c, Pope Francis, Holy Door, cross. 95c, Immaculate Conception.

2015, Nov. 19 Litho. *Perf. 13¼x13*
1608-1609 A535 Set of 2 3.75 3.75

Christmas — A536

Illustration of Nativity from Codices Urbinates Latini 239: 80c, Entire scene. 95c, Detail.

Perf. 11¼x11½ Syncopated

2015, Nov. 19 Litho.
1610-1611 A536 Set of 2 3.75 3.75
1611a Booklet pane of 4 #1611 8.00 —
Complete booklet, #1611a 8.00

Easter A537

No. 1612 — Stained-glass windows from Church of St. Angela Mercini, Milan: a, 95c, Crucifixion. b, €1, Resurrection.

2016, Feb. 1 Litho. *Perf. 14x14¾*
1612 A537 Pair, #a-b 4.25 4.25

Printed in sheets containing two pairs.

51st International Eucharistic Congress, Cebu City, Philippines — A538

Designs: 95c, Holy Child of Cebu. €1, Cebu Cathedral, Philippines.

2016, Feb. 1 Litho. *Perf. 13¾*
1613-1614 A538 Set of 2 4.25 4.25

Jubilee of Mercy — A539

Designs: 95c, People distributing bread on seashore. €1, People at well.

2016, Feb. 1 Litho. *Perf. 13¼x13*
1615-1616 A539 Set of 2 4.25 4.25

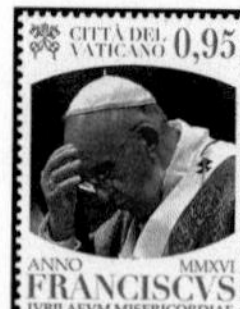

Pope Francis — A540

Variouis photographs of Pope Francis with denomination color of: 95c, Green. €1, Blue. €2.30, Orange. €3, Red.

2016, Feb. 1 Litho. *Perf. 13¼x13*
1617-1620 A540 Set of 4 16.00 16.00
1620a Souvenir sheet of 4, #1617-1620 16.00 16.00

Europa — A541

2016, May 10 Litho. *Perf. 13¾*
1621 A541 95c multi 2.25 2.25

Think Green Issue.

Vatican Gendarmerie, 200th Anniv. — A542

Designs: 95c, Papal gendarme in ceremonial uniform. €1, Gendarme in current uniform.

2016, May 10 Litho. *Perf. 14x14¾*
1622-1623 A542 Set of 2 4.50 4.50

Jubilee of Mercy — A543

Designs: 95c, Clothing the naked. €1, Sheltering the homeless.

2016, May 10 Litho. *Perf. 14¾x14*
1624-1625 A543 Set of 2 4.50 4.50

World Youth Day, Cracow, Poland — A544

Designs: €1, Pope Francis and youths. €4.50, Pope Francis.

Perf. 11¼x11½

2016, May 10 Photo.
1626 A544 €1 multi 2.40 2.40

Souvenir Sheet

Photo. & Engr.

Perf. 11¼x11

1627 A544 €4.50 multi 10.50 10.50

No. 1627 contains one 54x41mm stamp. See Poland Nos. 4223-4224.

Canonization of St. Teresa of Calcutta (Mother Teresa) — A545

2016, Sept. 2 Litho. *Perf. 13¾*
1628 A545 95c multi 2.10 2.10

Pope Innocent III (1160-1216) A546

2016, Sept. 13 Litho. *Perf. 13x13¼*
1629 A546 95c multi 2.10 2.10

St. Maximilian Kolbe (1894-1941) — A547

2016, Sept. 13 Litho. *Perf. 13¼x13*
1630 A547 €1 multi 2.25 2.25

Election of Virgin Mary as Patroness of Luxembourg, 350th Anniv. — A548

2016, Sept. 13 Engr. *Perf. 13x13¼*
1631 A548 €1 multi 2.25 2.25

See Luxembourg No. 1441.

Jubilee of Mercy — A549

Designs: 95c, Visiting the imprisoned. €1, Visting the sick.

2016, Sept. 13 Litho. *Perf. 13x13¼*
1632-1633 A549 Set of 2 4.50 4.50

Souvenir Sheet

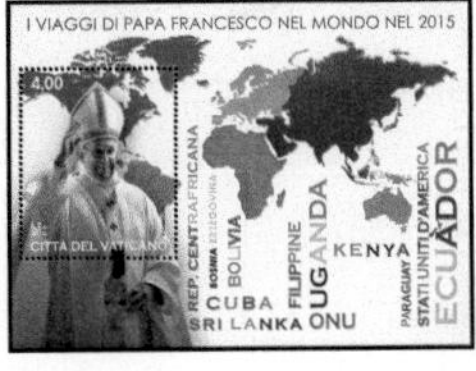
2015 Travels of Pope Francis A550

2016, Sept. 13 Litho. *Perf. 13x13¼*
1634 A550 €4 multi 9.00 9.00

St. Dominic (1170-1221), Founder of the Dominican Order — A551

2016, Nov. 17 Litho. *Perf. 13¼x13*
1635 A551 95c multi 2.10 2.10

Dominican Order, 800th anniv.

Pope Francis, 80th Birthday — A552

2016, Nov. 17 Litho. *Perf. 13x13¼*
1636 A552 €1 multi 2.25 2.25

No. 1636 was printed in sheets of 4.

Jubilee of Mercy — A553

Designs: 95c, Symbols of burial of the dead. €1, Jesus Christ and Holy Door.

2016, Nov. 17 Litho. *Perf. 14¾x14*
1637-1638 A553 Set of 2 4.25 4.25

Christmas — A554

Nativity ceramic by Giovanni della Robbia. 95c, Holy Family with St. Francis and St. Anthony of Padua. €1, Infant Jesus.

2016, Nov. 17 Litho. *Perf. 13¾x14*
1639 A554 95c multi 2.10 2.10
1640 A554 €1 multi 2.25 2.25
a. Booklet pane of 4 9.00 —
Complete booklet, #1640a 9.00

Lithuanian Grand Duke Vytautas and Bishop Motiejus A555

2017, Feb. 10 Litho. *Perf. 13¾*
1641 A555 €1 sil & multi 2.10 2.10

Diocese of Samogitia, Lithuania, 600th anniv. See Lithuania No. 1100.
No. 1641 was printed in sheets of 4. Value, $10.

Pope Alexander VII (1599-1667), His Coat of Arms and St. Peter's Square — A556

Francesco Borromini (1599-1667), Architect, and Church of Sant'Ivo alla Sapienza — A557

2017, Feb. 10 Litho. *Perf. 13¾*
1642 A556 95c multi 2.00 2.00
1643 A557 €1 multi 2.10 2.10

Pope Francis — A558

Various photographs of Pope Francis: 95c, €1, €2.30, €3.

2017, Feb. 10 Litho. *Perf. 13¼*
1644-1647 A558 Set of 4 15.50 15.50

Risen Christ From Flemish Tapestry by Pieter van Aelst — A559

Perf. 14¼x14½
2017, Feb. 10 Litho.
Stamp With White Frame
1648 A559 €1 multi 2.10 2.10

Souvenir Sheet
Stamp Without White Frame
Perf. 13x13¼
1649 A559 €4.50 multi 9.50 9.50

Easter. No. 1649 contains one 40x60mm stamp.

Pope Emeritus Benedict XVI, 90th Birthday — A560

2017, May 4 Litho. *Perf. 13½x13*
1650 A560 95c multi 2.10 2.10

No. 1650 was printed in sheets of 4.

Cardinal Domenico Bartolucci (1917-2013), Director of Sistine Chapel Choir — A561

2017, May 4 Litho. *Perf. 13x13¼*
1651 A561 95c multi 2.10 2.10

Apparition of the Virgin Mary at Fatima, Portugal, Cent. — A562

2017, May 4 Litho. *Perf. 13¼x13*
1652 A562 €2.55 multi 5.75 5.75

Martyrdom of Saints Peter and Paul, 1950th Anniv. — A563

Designs: 95c, St. Peter, rooster and keys. €1, St. Paul, book and sword.

2017, May 4 Litho. *Perf. 13¾*
1653-1654 A563 Set of 2 4.25 4.25

Europa — A564

Designs: 95c, Castel Gandolfo and Vatican Observatory. €1, Palace of Belvedere, Vatican City.

2017, May 4 Litho. *Perf. 13x13¼*
1655-1656 A564 Set of 2 4.25 4.25

St. Frances Xavier Cabrini (1850-1917), Founder of the Missionary Sisters of the Sacred Heart of Jesus — A565

2017, Sept. 7 Litho. *Perf. 14¼*
1657 A565 95c multi 2.25 2.25

Father Lorenzo Milani (1923-67), Educator of Poor in Italy — A566

2017, Sept. 7 Litho. *Perf. 13¼x13*
1658 A566 95c multi 2.25 2.25

Lay People, Children and St. Marcellino Champagnat (1789-1840) Founder of Marist Brothers — A567

2017, Sept. 7 Litho. *Perf. 13¼x13*
1659 A567 €1 multi 2.40 2.40

Marist Brothers, 200th anniv.

Publication of "Populorum Progressio" Encyclical by Pope Paul VI, 50th Anniv. A568

2017, Sept. 7 Litho. *Perf. 14*
1660 A568 €1 multi 2.40 2.40

No. 1660 was printed in sheets of 4.

Souvenir Sheet

Congregation for Oriental Churches, Cent. — A569

2017, Sept. 7 Litho. *Perf. 12 at Top*
1661 A569 €2.55 multi 6.00 6.00

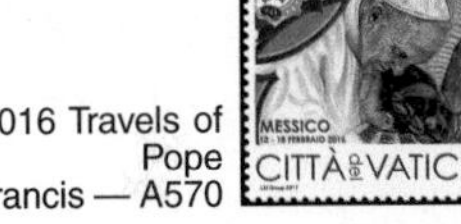
2016 Travels of Pope Francis — A570

Travels: No. 1662, 95c, Mexico, Feb. 12-18. No. 1663, 95c, Lesbos, Greece, Apr. 16. No. 1664, 95c, Armenia, June 24-26. No. 1665, 95c, Poland, July 27-31. No. 1666, 95c, Georgia and Azerbaijan, Sept. 30-Oct. 2. No. 1667, 95c, Sweden, Oct. 31-Nov. 1.

2017, Nov. 23 Litho. *Perf. 13x13¼*
1662-1667 A570 Set of 6 13.50 13.50

Protestant Reformation, 500th Anniv. — A571

2017, Nov. 23 Litho. *Perf. 13x13¼*
1668 A571 €1 gold & multi 2.40 2.40

St. Francis de Sales (1567-1622) — A572

2017, Nov. 23 Litho. *Perf. 13¼x13*
1669 A572 €2.55 multi 6.25 6.25

Christmas — A573

Designs: 95c, Annunciation. €1, Madonna and Child.

2017, Nov. 23 Litho. *Perf. 13¼x13*
1670 A573 95c multi 2.25 2.25
a. Booklet pane of 4 + 4 labels 9.00 —
Complete booklet, #1670a 9.00
1671 A573 €1 multi 2.40 2.40

Joint Issue between Vatican City and Monaco.
See Monaco Nos. 2908-2909.

Easter — A574

2018, Feb. 6 Litho. *Perf. 13¾*
1672 A574 95c multi 2.40 2.40

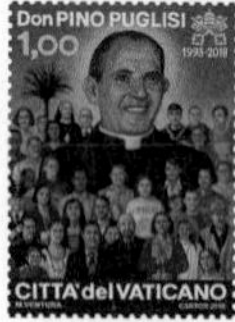
Blessed Giuseppe Puglisi (1937-1993), Palermo Priest Killed by Mafia — A575

2018, Feb. 6 Litho. *Perf. 13¼x13*
1673 A575 €1 multi 2.50 2.50

No. 1673 was printed in sheets of 6. Value, $15.

Pope Francis — A576

2017 photographs of Pope Francis: 95c, Celebrating Palm Sunday. €1, Holding pastoral staff. €2.30, Wearing miter on pastoral visit. €3, Holding candle.

2018, Feb. 6 Litho. *Perf. 13¼*
1674-1677 A576 Set of 4 18.00 18.00
1677a Souvenir sheet of 4, #1674-1677 18.00 18.00

The Adoration of the Magi (Detail), by Domenico Ghirlandaio — A577

2018, May 3 Litho. *Perf. 13¼*
1678 A577 95c multi 2.25 2.25

Centesimus Annus Pro Pontifice Foundation, 25th anniv.

Dome of Santa Maria del Fiore Cathedral, Florence, 600th Anniv. — A578

2018, May 3 Litho. *Perf. 13x13¼*
1679 A578 €1 multi 2.40 2.40

No. 1679 was printed in sheets of 4.

Bridges — A579

Designs: 95c, St. Peter and Ponte Sant'Angelo, Rome. €1, St. John Nepomuk and Charles Bridge, Prague.

2018, May 3 Litho. *Perf. 13¾*
1680-1681 A579 Set of 2 4.75 4.75

Europa.

Vatican Museum Statues — A580

Designs: 10c, Belvedere Apollo. 15c, Augustus of Prima Porto. 30c, Charity With Four Putti, by Gian Lorenzo Bernini. 95c, Perseus Triumphant, by Antonio Canova.

2018, May 3 Litho. *Perf. 13¼x13*
1682-1685 A580 Set of 4 3.75 3.75

European Year of Cultural Heritage.

Souvenir Sheet

Old Church Slavonic Liturgical Language, 1150th Anniv. — A581

2018, May 3 Litho. & Engr. *Perf. 13*
1686 A581 €5.95 multi 14.50 14.50

See Slovakia No. 791.

St. Pio of Pietrelcina (1887-1968) A582

2018, Sept. 6 Litho. *Perf. 14x13¼*
1687 A582 €1.10 multi 2.60 2.60

No. 1687 was printed in sheets of 4.

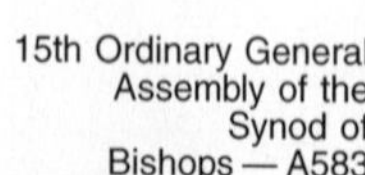

15th Ordinary General Assembly of the Synod of Bishops — A583

2018, Sept. 6 Litho. *Perf. 13¾*
1688 A583 €1.15 multi 2.75 2.75

Popes — A584

Designs: €1.10, Pope Paul VI (1897-1978). €1.15, Pope John Paul I (1912-78).

2018, Sept. 6 Litho. *Perf. 13¾*
1689-1690 A584 Set of 2 5.25 5.25

Canonization of Pope Paul VI.

Scientists — A585

Designs: €1.10, Father Angelo Secchi (1818-78), astronomer. €1.15, Maria Gaetana Agnesi (1718-99), mathematician.

2018, Sept. 6 Litho. *Perf. 13¼x13*
1691-1692 A585 Set of 2 5.25 5.25

Our Lady of Good Health Viewed From the Grand Canal, by Canaletto (1697-1768) — A586

Mary with the Child Venerated by St. Mark and St. Luke, by Tintoretto (1518-94) — A587

2018, Sept. 6 Litho. *Perf. 13¾x13¼*
1693 A586 €1.10 multi 2.60 2.60

Souvenir Sheet
Perf. 14x13½ on 3 Sides
1694 A587 €2.60 multi 6.00 6.00

Gioachino Rossini (1792-1868), Composer — A588

2018, Nov. 9 Litho. *Perf. 13¼x13*
1695 A588 €2.40 multi 5.50 5.50

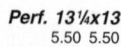

Universal Declaration of Human Rights, 70th Anniv. — A589

No. 1696: a, €1.10, Peace dove. b, €1.15, Man and woman.

2018, Nov. 9 Litho. *Perf. 13¼x13*
1696 A589 Pair, #a-b 5.25 5.25

Popes — A590

Designs: €1.10, St. Adeodatus I (570-618). €1.15, St. Zosimus (d. 418).

2018, Nov. 9 Litho. *Perf. 13x13¼*
1697-1698 A590 Set of 2 5.25 5.25

Souvenir Sheet

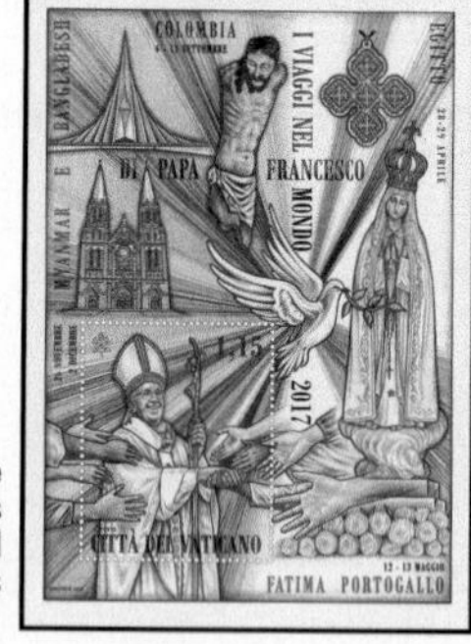
Pope Francis and Hands A591

2018, Nov. 9 Litho. *Perf. 14x13¼*
1699 A591 €1.15 multi 2.60 2.60

2017 travels of Pope Francis.

Christmas — A592

Designs: €1.10, Virgin Mary and angel. €1.15, Madonna and Child.

2018, Nov. 9 Litho. *Perf. 14x13¾*
1700-1701 A592 Set of 2 5.25 5.25
1701a Booklet pane of 4, 2 each #1700-1701 10.50 —
Complete booklet, #1701a 10.50

Pope Francis — A593

Color of vestments: €1.10, White. €1.15, Purple. €2.40, Red. €3, Green.

2019, Feb. 11 Litho. *Perf. 13¾*
1702-1705 A593 Set of 4 17.50 17.50

Easter — A594

2019, Feb. 11 Litho. *Perf. 13¼*
1706 A594 €1.10 multi 2.50 2.50

World Youth Day, Panama — A595

2019, Feb. 11 Litho. *Perf. 13x13¼*
1707 A595 €2.60 multi 6.00 6.00

Souvenir Sheet

Italo-Albanese Eparchy of Lungro, Cent. — A596

2019, Feb. 11 Litho. *Perf.*
1708 A596 €2.40 multi 5.50 5.50

Lateran Treaty, 90th Anniv. A597

No. 1709: a, Pope Pius XI (1857-1939). b. Pope Francis.

2019, Feb. 11 Litho. *Perf. 13¼x14*
1709 A597 Pair, #a-b 5.25 5.25
a. €1.10 multi 2.50 2.50
b. €1.15 multi 2.60 2.60

No. 1709 was printed in sheets containing two pairs.

Conciliation Hall, Lateran Palace, Site of Signing of the Lateran Treaty — A598

Serpentine Die Cut 11
2019, Feb. 11 Litho.
Self-Adhesive
1710 A598 €1.10 gold & multi 2.50 2.50

See Italy No. 3556.

A self-adhesive embroidered €8.40 stamp depicting the Papal Arms and commemorating the 90th anniversary of the Lateran Pacts and formation of the Vatican City State was offered only in a folder containing an unused example and a used example on cover. The folder sold for €28.

Bambino Gesù Pediatric Hospital, Rome, 150th Anniv. — A599

2019, Mar. 19 Litho. *Perf. 13¼x13*
1711 A599 €1.10 multi 2.50 2.50

See Italy No. 3563.

Giuseppe Diana (1958-94), Priest Murdered by the Camorra — A600

2019, Mar. 19 Litho. *Perf. 13¼x13*
1712 A600 €1.10 multi 2.50 2.50

Printed in sheets of 6.

Europa — A601

Designs: €1.10, Mallard duck. €1.15, Pigeon.

Perf. 13¾x13½
2019, Mar. 19 Litho.
1713-1714 A601 Set of 2 5.00 5.00

Marshal Józef Pilsudski (1867-1935) and Pope Benedict XV (1854-1922) A602

Perf. 11x11½ Syncopated
2019, Mar. 29 Litho.
1715 A602 €1.15 multi 2.60 2.60

Diplomatic relations between Vatican City and Poland, cent. See Poland No. 4408.

St. Jerome, by Leonardo da Vinci (1452-1519) — A603

2019, Apr. 29 Litho. *Perf. 13¼x13*
1716 A603 €1.15 multi 2.60 2.60

No. 1716 was printed in sheets of 4.

Souvenir Sheet

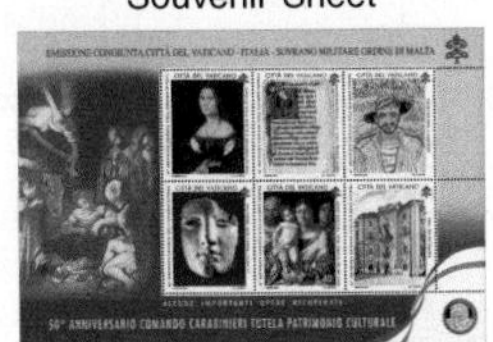

The Holy Family, by Andrea Mantegna (c. 1431-1506) — A604

2019, Apr. 29 Litho. *Perf. 13¼*
1717 A604 €5.40 multi + 5 labels 12.50 12.50

Carabinieri Unit for Protection of Cultural Heritage, 50th anniv.

Joint Issue between Vatican City and Italy. See Italy No. 3568.

St. Jean-Baptise de La Salle (1651-1719), Founder of the Institute of the Brothers of the Christian Schools, and Students — A605

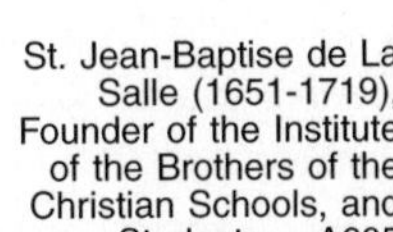

2019, May 31 Litho. *Perf. 13¼x14*
1718 A605 €1.15 multi 2.60 2.60

Souvenir Sheet

Conclusion of Restoration Work on the Sistine Chapel, 25th Anniv. — A606

No. 1719: a, 25c, St. John the Baptist wearing cape and codpiece, St. Andrew, and onlookers. b, 25c, St. Peter holding keys, St. Paul, and onlookers. c, €1.10, Jesus and Virgin Mary.

2019, May 31 Litho. *Perf. 13¼x13½*
1719 A606 Sheet of 3, #a-c 3.75 3.75

Souvenir Sheet

Visit of Pope Francis to Romania A607

2019, May 31 Litho. *Perf. 14¼*
1720 A607 €2.40 multi 5.50 5.50

See Romania No. 6277.

2018 Travels of Pope Francis — A608

Travels: €1.10, Chile and Peru, Jan. 15-22. €1.15, Geneva, Switzerland, June 21. €2.40, Ireland, Aug. 25-26. €3, Lithuania, Lavia and Estonia, Sept. 22-25.

2019, Sept. 10 Litho. *Perf. 13¾*
1721-1724 A608 Set of 4 17.00 17.00

Souvenir Sheet

Church of St. Peter, Capernaum, Israel — A609

2019, Sept. 10 Litho. *Perf.*
1725 A609 €1.15 multi 2.50 2.50

Diplomatic relations between Vatican City and Israel, 25th anniv. See Israel No. 2231.

Circolo San Pietro, 150th Anniv. — A610

2019, Nov. 4 Litho. *Perf. 13¼*
1726 A610 €1.10 multi 2.50 2.50

No. 1726 was printed in sheets of 6.

Rembrandt van Rijn (1606-69), Painter — A611

2019, Nov. 4 Litho. *Perf. 13¼x13½*
1727 A611 €1.15 multi 2.60 2.60

No. 1727 was printed in sheets of 6.

Ordination of Pope Francis, 50th Anniv. — A612

Pope Francis: €1.10, As young priest. €1.15, Wearing white cassock and pellegrina.

2019, Nov. 4 Litho. *Perf. 13*
1728-1729 A612 Set of 2 5.25 5.25

Christmas A613

Mosaic of: €1.10, Annunciation. €1.15, Nativity.

2019, Nov. 4 Litho. *Perf. 14x13½*
1730-1731 A613 Set of 2 5.25 5.25
1731a Booklet pane of 4, 2 each #1730-1731 10.50 —
Complete booklet, #1731a 10.50

The Sacrifice of Isaac, by Giambattista Tiepolo (1696-1770) — A614

2020, Feb. 14 Litho. *Perf. 13½x14*
1732 A614 €1.10 multi 2.50 2.50

No. 1732 was printed in sheets of 4.

Street Art Depicting Ascension of Jesus, Rome — A615

2020, Feb. 14 Litho. *Perf. 13½x13*
1733 A615 €1.15 multi 2.60 2.60

Easter.

St. Nicholas of Bari (270-343) — A616

2020, Feb. 14 Litho. *Perf. 13*
1734 A616 €1.15 multi 2.60 2.60

Pontificate of Pope Francis, 5th Anniv. — A617

Pope Francis with: €1.10, Lamb. €1.15, Dove. €2.40, Dog. €3, Cat.

2020, Feb. 14 Litho. *Perf. 13¼x13*
1735-1738 A617 Set of 4 17.00 17.00

Souvenir Sheet

Earth Day, 50th Anniv. A618

No. 1739: a, Flower bud, dandelion seeds, G clef and musical notes. b, Sailboat, dandelion seeds and musical notes, vert.

Perf. 13½x14, 14x13½
2020, Feb. 14 Litho.
1739 A618 Sheet of 2 3.25 3.25
a. 30c multi .70 .70
b. €1.10 multi 2.50 2.50

Pope Francis and Catholicos Karekin II Watering Tree — A619

2020, June 23 Litho. *Perf. 13¾*

1740 A619 €1.15 multi 2.60 2.60

International Year of Plant Health.

St. Teresa of Jesus of Los Andes (1900-20) — A620

2020, June 23 Litho. *Perf. 13¾*

1741 A620 €2.40 multi 5.50 5.50

Europa — A621

Maps of Roman postal routes depicting: €1.10, Cardo Massimo and Decumano Massimo, Turin. €1.15, Appian Way, Terracina.

Litho. With Foil Application

2020, June 23 *Perf. 13x13¼*

1742-1743 A621 Set of 2 5.00 5.00

Souvenir Sheet

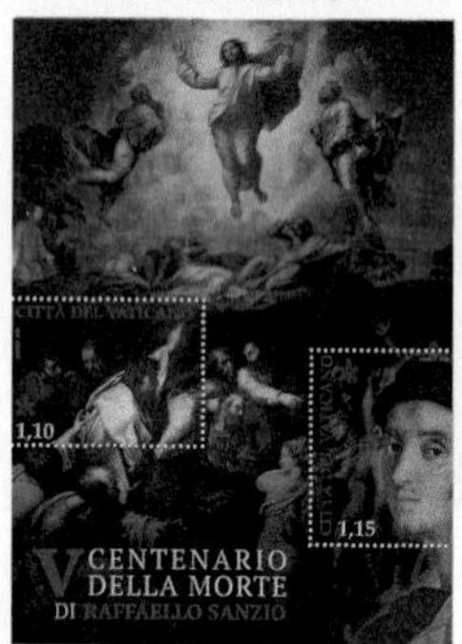

Paintings by Raphael (1483-1520) — A622

No. 1744: a, The Transfiguration. b, Self-portrait, vert.

Perf. 13x13¼ on 3 Sides (#1744a), 13¼x13 on 3 Sides (#1744b)

2020, June 23 Litho.

1744 A622 Sheet of 2 5.00 5.00
a. €1.10 multi 2.40 2.40
b. €1.15 multi 2.60 2.60

Declaration of St. Ephrem the Syrian (c. 306-73) as Doctor of the Church, Cent. — A623

2020, Sept. 10 Litho. *Perf. 13¾*

1745 A623 €1.15 multi 2.75 2.75

Pope Francis, Basilica of Our Lady of Peace, Yamoussoukro, Ivory Coast, and Ivory Coast Pres. Alassane Ouattara — A624

2020, Sept. 10 Litho. *Perf. 13¾*

1746 A624 €2.40 multi 5.75 5.75

Diplomatic relations between Vatican City and Ivory Coast, 50th anniv. See Ivory Coast No.

Souvenir Sheet

Apostleship of the Sea, Cent. — A625

No. 1747: a, Sailors on boat on stormy sea. b, Virgin Mary and infant Jesus, vert.

Perf. 14x13¼ (#1747a), 13¼x14 (#1747b)

2020, Sept. 10 Litho.

1747 A625 Sheet of 2 5.50 5.50
a. €1.10 multi 2.60 2.60
b. €1.15 multi 2.75 2.75

Vatican Public Security Inspectorate, 75th Anniv. — A626

Serpentine Die Cut 11

2020, Sept. 28 Photo.

Self-Adhesive

1748 A626 €1.10 multi 2.60 2.60

See Italy No. 3673.

St. John Paul II (1920-2005) A627

2020, Oct. 16 Litho. *Perf. 14¼x14*

1749 A627 €1.15 multi + label 2.75 2.75

No. 1749 was printed in sheets of 6 + 6 labels. See Poland No. 4510.

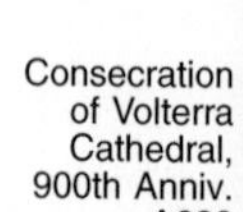

Consecration of Volterra Cathedral, 900th Anniv. A628

Serpentine Die Cut 9¼x8

2020, Nov. 10 Engr.

Self-Adhesive

1750 A628 €1.10 black 2.75 2.75

See Italy No. 3695.

Basilica of Aquileia — A629

2020, Nov. 10 Photo. *Perf. 13*

1751 A629 €1.10 multi 2.75 2.75

See Italy No. 3696

Ludwig van Beethoven (1770-1827), Composer A630

2020, Nov. 10 Litho. *Perf. 13x13¼*

1752 A630 €1.15 multi 2.75 2.75

Souvenir Sheet

Arms of Pope Francis A631

2020, Nov. 10 Litho. *Perf. 13x13¼*

1753 A631 €3 multi + 7 labels 7.25 7.25

2019 travels of Pope Francis. Labels show the destinations of Pope Francis in 2020.

Souvenir Sheet

Diplomatic Relations Between Vatican City and the European Union and Council of Europe, 50th Anniv. — A632

No. 1754: a, Council of Europe emblem. b, Flags of Vatican City and the European Union.

2020, Nov. 10 Litho. *Perf. 13¼x13*

1754 A632 Sheet of 2 5.50 5.50
a.-b. €1.15 Either single 2.75 2.75

A633

A634

Christmas — A635

Designs: €1.10, St. Peter's Basilica and Pope Francis holding the Lantern of Light from Bethlehem. €1.15, Star of Bethlehem from Basilica of the Nativity, Bethlehem, Christkindl Shrine, Steyer, Austria, and infant Jesus.

2020, Nov. 10 Litho. *Perf. 13¼x14*

1755 A633 €1.10 multi 2.60 2.60
1756 A634 €1.15 multi 2.75 2.75
a. Booklet pane of 4, 2 each #1755-1756 11.00 —
Complete booklet, #1756a 11.00

Souvenir Sheet

1757 A635 Sheet of 2 5.50 5.50
a. €1.10 multi 2.60 2.60
b. €1.15 multi 2.75 2.75

See Austria No. 2908.

Canons Regular of the Immaculate Conception, 150th Anniv. — A636

2021, Feb. 22 Litho. *Perf. 13½*

1758 A636 €1.10 multi 2.75 2.75

Easter — A637

2021, Feb. 22 Litho. *Perf. 13¼*

1759 A637 €1.15 multi 2.75 2.75

Meetings of Pope Francis and Other Religious Leaders — A638

Pope Francis meeting with: €1.10, Chief Rabbi of Rome Riccardo Shemuel Di Segni, 2016. €1.15, Grand Imam of Al-Azhar Ahmad al-Tayyib, 2017. €2.40, Supreme Buddhist Patriarch of Thailand Somdet Phra Ariyavongsagatanana IX, 2019. €3, Hindu leader Ndu-Kurukkal SivaSri T. Mahadeva, 2015.

2021, Feb. 22 Litho. *Perf. 13x13¼*

1760-1763 A638 Set of 4 18.50 18.50

Souvenir Sheet

Year of St. Joseph A639

Litho., Sheet Margin Litho. With Foil Application

2021, Feb. 22 *Perf. 14x13¾*

1764 A639 €3 multi 7.25 7.25

Souvenir Sheet

Vatican Media Outlets A640

No. 1765: a, Vatican Radio, 90th anniv. b, L'Osservatore Romano newspaper, 160th anniv.

2021, Feb. 22 Litho. ***Perf. 13x13¼***
1765 A640 Sheet of 2 8.50 8.50
a. €1.15 multi 2.75 2.75
b. €2.40 multi 5.75 5.75

Conversion of St. Ignatius of Loyola, 500th Anniv. — A641

2021, May 25 Litho. ***Perf. 13¾***
1766 A641 €1.15 multi 3.00 3.00

Saints Peter and Paul Association, 50th Anniv. — A642

2021, May 25 Litho. ***Perf. 13x13¼***
1767 A642 €1.15 multi 3.00 3.00

Endangered Birds — A643

Designs: €1.10, Falco tinnunculus. €1.15, Troglodytes troglodytes.

2021, May 25 Litho. ***Perf. 13¼x13***
1768-1769 A643 Set of 2 5.50 5.50
Europa.

Pope Sixtus V (1521-90) — A644

Designs: €2, Coat of arms of Pope Sixtus V. €2.50, Portrait of Pope Sixtus V, by Pietro Facchetti (1539-1613).

2021, May 25 Litho. ***Perf. 13¼x13***
1770-1771 A644 Set of 2 11.00 11.00

Souvenir Sheet

Walk of St. Anthony of Padua, 800th Anniv. A645

Perf. 13¾x13½ on 3 Sides
2021, May 25 Litho.
1772 A645 €2.40 multi 6.00 6.00

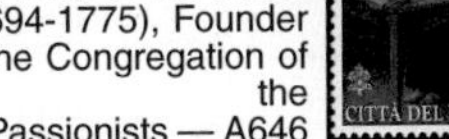

St. Paul of the Cross (1694-1775), Founder of the Congregation of the Passionists — A646

2021, Sept. 8 Litho. ***Perf. 13¼x13***
1773 A646 €1.10 multi 2.60 2.60

Congregation of the Passionists, 300th anniv.

Catholic University of the Sacred Heart, Cent. — A647

2021, Sept. 8 Litho. ***Perf. 13¼x13***
1774 A647 €1.10 multi 2.60 2.60

Saint Peter Examining Faith of Dante Alighieri — A648

2021, Sept. 8 Litho. ***Perf. 14***
1775 A648 €1.15 multi 2.75 2.75

Alighieri (c. 1265-1321), writer. No. 1775 was printed in sheets of 4.

Souvenir Sheet

Martyrdom of Saint Matthew, by Caravaggio (1571-1610) — A649

2021, Sept. 8 Litho. ***Perf. 14x13¾***
1776 A649 €5.40 multi 12.50 12.50

52nd International Eucharistic Congress, Budapest — A650

Congress emblem and: €1.10, Parliament Building, Budapest. €1.15, Map of Hungary, vert.

Perf. 13x13¼, 13¼x13
2021, Sept. 8 Litho.
1777-1778 A650 Set of 2 5.25 5.25

Abbey of Prémontré, France, 900th Anniv. — A651

2021, Nov. 9 Litho. ***Perf. 13¼***
1779 A651 €1.15 multi 2.60 2.60

5th World Day of the Poor — A652

No. 1780 — Pope Francis: a, At lunch table with guests. b, Preparing Eucharist during Mass.

2021, Nov. 9 Litho. ***Perf. 13¾***
1780 A652 Vert. pair 5.25 5.25
a. €1.10 multi 2.50 2.50
b. €1.15 multi 2.60 2.60

Emblem of Italian Bishops Conference and Map of the Mediterranean Area — A653

2021, Nov. 9 Litho. ***Perf. 13x13¼***
1781 A653 €2.40 multi 5.50 5.50

Feb. 23, 2020, visit by Pope Francis with Mediterranean area bishops in Bari, Italy.

Souvenir Sheet

Our Lady of the Southern Cross, Southern Cross Constellation, and Map of Australia — A654

2021, Nov. 9 Litho. ***Perf. 14¾***
1782 A654 €3 multi 6.75 6.75

Preparation for Jubilee 2025.

Christmas A655

Designs: €1.10, Magi following Star of Bethlehem. €1.15, Holy Family.

2021, Nov. 9 Litho. ***Perf. 13¾x14***
1783-1784 A655 Set of 2 5.25 5.25
1784a Booklet pane of 4, 2 each #1783-1784 10.50 —
Complete booklet, #1784a 10.50

Martyrdom of St. Marcian, 1900th Anniv. — A656

2022, Feb. 22 Litho. ***Perf. 13¾x14***
1785 A656 €1.10 multi 2.50 2.50

Easter — A657

Perf. 13¾x13½
2022, Feb. 22 Litho.
1786 A657 €1.15 multi 2.60 2.60

Election of Pope Adrian VI (1459-1523), 500th Anniv. — A658

2022, Feb. 22 Litho. ***Perf. 12***
1787 A658 €2 multi 4.50 4.50

Giovanni Battista de Rossi (1822-94), Archaeologist, and Excavated Hypogeum A659

2022, Feb. 22 Litho. ***Perf. 14x13¾***
1788 A659 €2.50 multi 5.75 5.75

Year of the Family — A660

Pope Francis: €1.10, At 2014 group wedding at St. Peter's Basilica. €1.15, Baptizing child. €2.40, Embracing child. €3, Embracing elderly woman.

2022, Feb. 22 Litho. ***Perf. 12***
1789-1792 A660 Set of 4 17.00 17.00

Souvenir Sheet

Pope Francis A661

Perf. 12 on 2 Sides
2022, Mar. 10 Litho.
1793 A661 €3 multi 6.75 6.75

Prayers of Pope Francis for COVID-19 pandemic, 2nd anniv.

St. Luigi Orione (1872-1940) A662

2022, May 16 Litho. ***Perf. 13x13¼***
1794 A662 €2.40 multi 5.00 5.00

No. 1794 was printed in sheets of 4. See Argentina No. 2959, Italy No. 3837.

Europa — A663

Detail of Sistine Rooms of the Vatican Museum painting depicting the transporting of the Egyptian obelisk to St. Peter's Square: 10c, Workers and horses. 30c, Obelisk on sled.

€1.15, Scaffolding for obelisk.

2022, May 16 Litho. ***Perf. 13¼x13***
1795-1796 A663 Set of 2 .85 .85

Souvenir Sheet

1797 A663 €1.15 multi 2.40 2.40

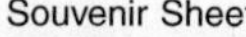

Souvenir Sheet

Tenth World Meeting of Families A664

2022, May 16 Litho. ***Perf. 13x13¼***
1798 A664 €1.15 multi 2.40 2.40

Souvenir Sheet

Our Lady of China, and Map of Asia A665

2022, May 16 Litho. ***Perf. 14¾***
1799 A665 €3 multi 6.25 6.25

Preparation for Jubilee 2025.

Santa Maria Pediatric Dispensary, Cent. — A666

2022, Sept. 1 Litho. ***Perf. 12***
1800 A666 €1.20 multi 2.40 2.40

Popes Francis and Pius XII (1876-1958), Institute for Religious Works — A667

2022, Sept. 1 Litho. ***Perf. 13¾***
1801 A667 €1.20 multi 2.40 2.40

Institute for Religious Works (Vatican Bank), 80th anniv.

Beatification of Pope John Paul I (1912-78) — A668

2022, Sept. 1 Litho. ***Perf. 13¾***
1802 A668 €1.25 multi 2.50 2.50

Concordat Between Vatican City and Latvia, Cent. — A669

2022, Sept. 1 Litho. ***Perf. 13¼x13½***
1803 A669 €1.25 multi 2.50 2.50

Joint issue between Vatican City and Latvia. See Latvia No. 1112.

Sun and Seed A670

2022, Sept. 1 Embroidered ***Imperf.***
Self-Adhesive
1804 A670 €7 multi 14.00 14.00

Decade for Ecosystem Restoration.

Palace of Spain as Spanish Embassy to the Vatican, 400th Anniv. — A671

2022, Nov. 16 Litho. ***Perf. 12***
1805 A671 €1.20 multi 2.50 2.50

Piacenza Cathedral, 900th Anniv. — A672

2022, Nov. 16 Litho. ***Perf. 13¼x13***
1806 A672 €1.20 multi 2.50 2.50

Father Paolo Manna (1872-1952), Missionary A673

2022, Nov. 16 Litho. ***Perf. 13x13¼***
1807 A673 €1.20 multi 2.50 2.50

Proclamation of St. Isidore of Seville (c. 560-636) as a Doctor of the Church, 300th Anniv. — A674

2022, Nov. 16 Litho. ***Perf. 13¼x13***
1808 A674 €1.25 multi 2.60 2.60

Diplomatic Relations Between Vatican City and Belarus, 30th Anniv. — A675

2022, Nov. 16 Litho. ***Perf. 13x13¼***
1809 A675 €1.25 multi 2.60 2.60

See Belarus No.

Resumption of Diplomatic Relations Between Vatican City and Mexico, 30th Anniv. — A676

2022, Nov. 16 Litho. ***Perf. 13¼x13***
1810 A676 €2.40 multi 5.00 5.00

See Mexico No. 3280.

Souvenir Sheet

2021 Travels of Pope Francis A677

2022, Nov. 16 Litho. ***Perf. 12½***
1811 A677 €1.25 multi 2.60 2.60

A678

Christmas — A679

Perf. 13¾x13½
2022, Nov. 16 Litho.
1812 A678 €1.20 multi 2.50 2.50
1813 A679 €1.25 multi 2.60 2.60

Pope Benedict XVI (1927-2022) A680

2023, Jan. 31 Litho. ***Perf. 12***
1814 A680 €1.25 multi 2.75 2.75

Easter — A681

2023, Feb. 27 Litho. ***Perf. 12***
1815 A681 €1.25 multi 2.75 2.75

Pontificate of Pope Francis, 10th Anniv. — A682

Designs: €1.20, Celebration of first Mass by Francis as Pope, 2013. €1.25, Pope Francis kissing Book of the Gospels, 2016. €2.40, Pope Francis hearing a confession. €3.10, First pastoral visit of Pope Francis to Lampedusa, Italy, 2013.

2023, Feb. 27 Litho. ***Perf. 13¼x13***
1816-1819 A682 Set of 4 17.00 17.00

Souvenir Sheet

Astronomer Copernicus, or Conversations with God, Painting by Jan Matejko (1838-93) — A683

2023, Feb. 27 Litho. ***Perf. 12***
1820 A683 €1.25 multi 2.75 2.75

Nicolaus Copernicus (1473-1543), astronomer. See Poland No. 4655.

Souvenir Sheet

Our Lady of Africa, and Map of Africa A684

2023, Feb. 27 Litho. ***Perf. 14¾***
1821 A684 €3.10 multi 6.75 6.75

Preparation for Jubilee 2025.

SEMI-POSTAL STAMPS

Holy Year Issue

Cross and Orb
SP1 SP2

1933 Unwmk. Engr. *Perf. 13x13½*

B1 SP1 25c + 10c green 4.75 *4.75*
B2 SP1 75c + 15c scarlet 8.25 *16.50*
B3 SP2 80c + 20c red brown 30.00 22.50
B4 SP2 1.25 l + 25c ultra 9.00 *17.00*
Nos. B1-B4 (4) 52.00 *60.75*
Set, never hinged 190.00

Catalogue values for unused stamps in this section, from this point to the end of the section, are for Never Hinged items.

Shrine of Our Lady of Mentorella, Italy, 1500th Anniv. — SP3

2010, Mar. 5 Litho. *Perf. 14¼x14¾*

B5 SP3 65c +20c multi 2.25 2.25

Printed in sheets of 6. Surtax for Haitian earthquake relief. Value, $12.50.

AIR POST STAMPS

Catalogue values for unused stamps in this section are for Never Hinged items.

Statue of St. Peter AP1

Dove of Peace over Vatican AP2

Elijah's Ascent into Heaven AP3

Our Lady of Loreto and Angels Moving the Holy House AP4

Wmk. 235

1938, June 22 Engr. *Perf. 14*

C1 AP1 25c brown .25 .25
C2 AP2 50c green .25 .25
C3 AP3 75c lake .25 .30
C4 AP4 80c dark blue .25 .45
C5 AP1 1 l violet .50 .50
C6 AP2 2 l ultra .75 .80
C7 AP3 5 l slate blk 2.50 2.50
C8 AP4 10 l dk brown vio 2.50 2.50
Nos. C1-C8 (8) 7.25 7.55

Dove of Peace Above St. Peter's Basilica AP5

House of Our Lady of Loreto AP6

Birds Circling Cross — AP7

1947, Nov. 10 Photo.

C9 AP5 1 l rose red .25 .25
C10 AP6 4 l dark brown .25 .25
C11 AP5 5 l brt ultra .25 .25
C12 AP7 15 l brt purple 1.00 2.10
C13 AP6 25 l dk blue green 2.75 2.75
C14 AP7 50 l dk gray 4.50 5.25
C15 AP7 100 l red orange 17.50 9.00
Nos. C9-C15 (7) 26.50 19.85

Nos. C13-C15 exist imperf. Value, each pair $1,000.

No. C15 exists in a horizontal pair, imperf between. Value, $500.

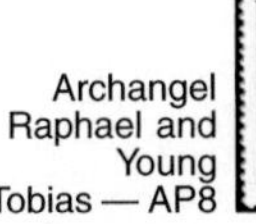

Archangel Raphael and Young Tobias — AP8

1948, Dec. 28 Engr. *Perf. 14*

C16 AP8 250 l sepia 52.50 10.00
C17 AP8 500 l ultra 550.00 375.00
Set, hinged 375.00

No. C16 exists imperforate.

Angels and Globe — AP9

1949, Dec. 3

C18 AP9 300 l ultra 30.00 12.50
C19 AP9 1000 l green 150.00 82.50
Set, hinged 95.00

Nos. C18-C19 exist imperforate.

UPU, 75th anniversary.

Franciscus Gratianus — AP10

1951, Dec. 20 *Perf. 14x13*

C20 AP10 300 l deep plum 325.00 220.00
C21 AP10 500 l deep blue 40.00 20.00
Set, hinged 200.00

Publication of unified canon laws, 800th anniv.

Dome of St. Peter's Basilica — AP11

1953, Aug. 10 *Perf. 13*

C22 AP11 500 l chocolate 35.00 9.00
C23 AP11 1000 l deep ultra 105.00 20.00
Set, hinged 47.50

See Nos. C33-C34.

Archangel Gabriel by Melozzo da Forli — AP12

Archangel Gabriel: 10 l, 35 l, 100 l, Annunciation by Pietro Cavallini. 15 l, 50 l, 300 l, Annunciation by Leonardo da Vinci.

1956, Feb. 12 Wmk. 235

C24 AP12 5 l gray black .25 .25
C25 AP12 10 l blue green .25 .25
C26 AP12 15 l deep orange .25 .25
C27 AP12 25 l dk car rose .25 .25
C28 AP12 35 l carmine .25 .25
C29 AP12 50 l olive brown .25 .25
C30 AP12 60 l ultra 2.75 2.25
C31 AP12 100 l orange brown .25 .25
C32 AP12 300 l deep violet .75 .75
Nos. C24-C32 (9) 5.25 4.75

Type of 1953

1958 *Perf. 13½*

C33 AP11 500 l grn & bl grn 7.50 4.00
a. Perf. 14 *4,000. 1,200.*
C34 AP11 1000 l dp mag .75 .75
a. Perf. 14 .75 .75

Nos. C33-C34 exist without watermark.

Obelisk of St. John Lateran — AP13

Obelisks, Rome: 10 l, 60 l, St. Mary Major. 15 l, 100 l, St. Peter. 25 l, 200 l, Piazza del Popolo. 35 l, 500 l, Trinita dei Monti.

1959, Oct. 27 Engr. *Perf. 13½x14*

C35 AP13 5 l dull violet .25 .25
C36 AP13 10 l blue green .25 .25
C37 AP13 15 l dk brown .25 .25
C38 AP13 25 l slate grn .25 .25
C39 AP13 35 l ultra .25 .25
C40 AP13 50 l yellow grn .25 .25
C41 AP13 60 l rose carmine .25 .25
C42 AP13 100 l bluish black .25 .25
C43 AP13 200 l brown .25 .25
C44 AP13 500 l orange brn .25 .25
Nos. C35-C44 (10) 2.50 2.50

Archangel Gabriel by Filippo Valle — AP14

1962, Mar. 13 Wmk. 235

C45 AP14 1000 l brown 1.25 .75
C46 AP14 1500 l dark blue 1.75 1.25

Jet over St. Peter's Cathedral — AP15

Designs: 40 l, 200 l, Radio tower and statue of Archangel Gabriel (like A87). 90 l, 500 l, Aerial view of St. Peter's Square and Vatican City.

1967, Mar. 7 Photo. *Perf. 14*

C47 AP15 20 l brt violet .25 .25
C48 AP15 40 l black & pink .25 .25
C49 AP15 90 l sl bl & dk gray .25 .25
C50 AP15 100 l black & salmon .25 .25
C51 AP15 200 l vio blk & gray .25 .25
C52 AP15 500 l dk brn & lt brn .25 .25
Nos. C47-C52 (6) 1.50 1.50

Archangel Gabriel by Fra Angelico — AP16

1968, Mar. 12 Engr. *Perf. 13½x14*

C53 AP16 1000 l dk car rose, *cr* 1.00 .75
C54 AP16 1500 l black, *cr* 1.75 1.50

St. Matthew, by Fra Angelico — AP17

The Evangelists, by Fra Angelico from Niccolina Chapel: 300 l, St. Mark. 500 l, St. Luke. 1000 l, St. John.

Engr. & Photo.
Perf. 14x13½

1971, Sept. 30 Unwmk.

C55 AP17 200 l blk & pale grn .25 .25
C56 AP17 300 l black & bister .25 .25
C57 AP17 500 l black & salmon .85 .60
C58 AP17 1000 l black & pale lil 1.00 .75
Nos. C55-C58 (4) 2.35 1.85

AP18

Seraph, mosaic from St. Mark's Basilica, Venice.

Litho. & Engr.

1974, Feb. 21 *Perf. 13x14*

C59 AP18 2500 l multicolored 2.50 2.00

AP19

Last Judgment, by Michelangelo: 500 l, Angel with Trumpet. 1000 l, Ascending figures. 2500 l, Angels with trumpets.

Litho. & Engr.

1976, Feb. 19 *Perf. 13x14*

C60 AP19 500 l sal, bl & brn 1.25 1.10
C61 AP19 1000 l sal, bl & brn 1.40 1.10
C62 AP19 2500 l sal, bl & brn 1.90 1.50
Nos. C60-C62 (3) 4.55 3.70

Radio Waves, Antenna, Papal Arms — AP20

1978, July 11 Engr. *Perf. 14x13*

C63 AP20 1000 l multicolored 1.00 .70
C64 AP20 2000 l multicolored 2.00 1.40
C65 AP20 3000 l multicolored 3.00 1.90
Nos. C63-C65 (3) 6.00 4.00

10th World Telecommunications Day.

Pope John Paul II Shaking Hands, Arms of Dominican Republic — AP21

Litho. & Engr.

1980, June 24 *Perf. 14x13½*

C66 AP21 200 l shown .25 .25
C67 AP21 300 l Mexico .30 .30
C68 AP21 500 l Poland .60 .60
C69 AP21 1000 l Ireland 1.10 1.10
C70 AP21 1500 l US 1.75 1.75
C71 AP21 2000 l UN 2.00 2.00
C72 AP21 3000 l with Dimitrios I, Turkey 3.50 3.50
Nos. C66-C72 (7) 9.50 9.50

Issued: 3000 l, Sept. 18; others June 24.

World Communications Year — AP22

Designs: 2000 l, Moses Explaining The Law to the People by Luca Signorelli. 5000 l, Paul Preaching in Athens, Tapestry of Raphael design.

1983, Nov. 10 *Perf. 14*

C73 AP22 2000 l multicolored 2.75 2.50
C74 AP22 5000 l multicolored 5.50 5.00

Journeys of Pope John Paul II, 1983-84 — AP23

Designs: 350 l, Central America, the Caribbean, 1983. 450 l, Warsaw Cathedral, Our Lady of Czestochowa, Poland, 1983. 700 l, Statue of Our Lady, Lourdes, France, 1983. 1000 l, Mariazell Sanctuary, St. Stephen's Cathedral, Austria, 1983. 1500 l, Asia, the Pacific, 1984. 2000 l, Einsiedeln Basilica, St. Nicholas of Flue, Switzerland, 1984. 2500 l, Quebec's Notre Dame Cathedral, five crosses of the Jesuit martyrs, Canada, 1984. 5000 l, Saragossa, Spain, Dominican Republic and Puerto Rico, 1984.

1986, Nov. 20 Photo. *Perf. 14x13½*

C75	AP23	350 l multicolored	.50	.50
C76	AP23	450 l multicolored	.65	.65
C77	AP23	700 l multicolored	1.00	1.00
C78	AP23	1000 l multicolored	1.50	1.50
C79	AP23	1500 l multicolored	2.25	2.25
C80	AP23	2000 l multicolored	3.25	3.25
C81	AP23	2500 l multicolored	4.00	4.00
C82	AP23	5000 l multicolored	8.00	8.00
		Nos. C75-C82 (8)	21.15	21.15

Papal Journeys Type of 1986

Designs: 450 l, Horseman, shepherdess, St. Peter's Basilica, Cathedral of Santiago in Chile, and the Sanctuary of Our Lady of Lujan, Argentina. 650 l, Youths and the Cathedral of Speyer, Federal Republic of Germany. 1000 l, St. Peter's Basilica, Altar of Gdansk, flowers and thorns. 2500 l, Crowd and American skyscrapers. 5000 l, Tepee at Fort Simpson, Canada, and American Indians.

1988, Oct. 27 Photo. *Perf. 14x13½*

C83	AP23	450 l multicolored	.65	.65
C84	AP23	650 l multicolored	.95	.95
C85	AP23	1000 l multicolored	1.50	1.50
C86	AP23	2500 l multicolored	3.50	3.50
C87	AP23	5000 l multicolored	7.25	7.25
		Nos. C83-C87 (5)	13.85	13.85

Uruguay, Chile and Argentina, Mar. 30-Apr. 14, 1987 (450 l); Federal Republic of Germany, Apr. 30-May 4, 1987 (650 l); Poland, June 8-14, 1987 (1000 l); US, Sept. 10-19, 1987 (2500 l); and Canada, Sept. 20, 1987 (5000 l).

Journeys of Pope John Paul II, 1989 — AP24

500 l, Africa. 1000 l, Scandinavia. 3000 l, Santiago de Compostela, Spain. 5000 l, Asia.

1990, Nov. 27 Photo. *Perf. 12*
Granite Paper

C88	AP24	500 l multicolored	.80	.80
C89	AP24	1000 l multicolored	1.60	1.60
C90	AP24	3000 l multicolored	5.00	5.00
C91	AP24	5000 l multicolored	8.00	8.00
		Nos. C88-C91 (4)	15.40	15.40

Madagascar, Reunion, Zambia and Malawi, Apr. 28-May 6 (500 l); Norway, Iceland, Finland, Denmark and Sweden, June 1-10 (1000 l); Korea, Indonesia and Mauritius, Oct. 6-16 (5000 l).

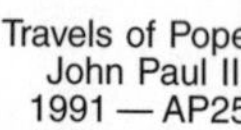

Travels of Pope John Paul II, 1991 — AP25

1992, Nov. 24 Photo. *Perf. 14*

C92	AP25	500 l multicolored	.65	.65
C93	AP25	1000 l multicolored	1.40	1.40
C94	AP25	4000 l multicolored	5.25	5.25
C95	AP25	6000 l multicolored	8.00	8.00
		Nos. C92-C95 (4)	15.30	15.30

Portugal, May 10-13 (500 l); Poland, June 1-9 (1000 l); Poland, Hungary, Aug. 13-20 (4000 l); Brazil, Oct. 12-21 (6000 l).

SPECIAL DELIVERY STAMPS

Pius XI — SD1

Unwmk.
1929, Aug. 1 Photo. *Perf. 14*

E1	SD1	2 l carmine rose	20.50	15.00
E2	SD1	2.50 l dark blue	17.00	18.50

For overprints see Nos. Q14-Q15.

Catalogue values for unused stamps in this section, from this point to the end of the section, are for Never Hinged items.

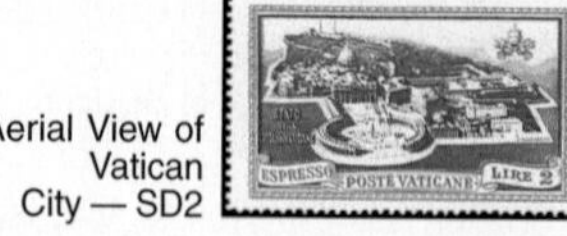
Aerial View of Vatican City — SD2

1933, May 31 Wmk. 235 Engr.

E3	SD2	2 l rose red & brn	.35	.35
E4	SD2	2.50 l dp blue & brn	.35	*.55*

1945, Mar. 2 Unwmk.

E5	SD2	3.50 l dk car & ultra	.50	.50
E6	SD2	5 l ultra & green	.75	*1.00*

Nos. E5 and E6 Srchd. with New Values and Bars in Black

1945, Dec. 29

E7	SD2	6 l on 3.50 l dk car & ultra	5.50	2.75
E8	SD2	12 l on 5 l ultra & grn	5.50	2.75

Vertical pairs imperf. between exist of No. E7 (value $150) and No. E8 (value $200).
Nos. E7-E8 exist in pairs, one without surcharge. Value, each pair, $1,250. Nos. E7-E8 exist in vertical pairs, imperforate between. Value, each pair, $1,250.

Bishop Matteo Giberti — SD3

Design: 12 l, Gaspar Cardinal Contarini.

1946, Feb. 21 Photo.
Centers in Dark Brown

E9	SD3	6 l dark green	.25	.25
E10	SD3	12 l copper brown	.25	.25

See note after No. 121.
No. E9 exists in horizontal pair, imperf between. Value, $1,250.
No. E10 exist imperf (value, pair, $1,900.) and part perf. (value, pair $150).
No. E10 exists in vertical pairs, imperf horizontally (value, each pair, $120).
Nos. E9-E10 exist in horizontal pairs, imperf vertically (value, each pair, $140).

St. Peter's Basilica — SD5

Design: 80 l, Basilica of St. John.

1949, Mar. 7 Wmk. 235 *Perf. 14*

E11	SD5	40 l slate gray	15.00	4.50
a.		Perf. 13½x14	32.50	8.00
E12	SD5	80 l chestnut brown	60.00	35.00
a.		Perf. 13½x14	55.00	32.50

No. E11 exists in vertical pairs, imperf horizontally. Value, $250.

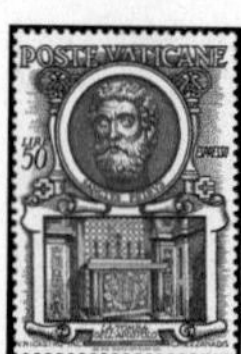
St. Peter and His Tomb — SD6

85 l, Pius XII and Roman sepulcher.

Perf. 13½x13, 14
1953, Apr. 23 Engr.

E13	SD6	50 l blue grn & dk brn	.25	.25
E14	SD6	85 l dp orange & dk brn	.35	.25

Arms of Pope John XXIII — SD7

1960 Photo. *Perf. 14*

E15	SD7	75 l red & brown	.25	.25
E16	SD7	100 l dk blue & brown	.25	.25

Pope Paul VI by Enrico Manfrini — SD8

Design: 150 l, Papal arms.

1966, Mar. 8 Wmk. 235 *Perf. 14*

E17	SD8	150 l black brown	.25	.25
E18	SD8	180 l brown	.25	.25

POSTAGE DUE STAMPS

Nos. 1-3 Overprinted in Black and Brown

1931, Oct. 1 Unwmk. *Perf. 14*

J1	A1	5c dk brown & pink	.35	*.75*
a.		Double frame	5,000.	
J2	A1	10c dk grn & lt grn	.35	*.75*
a.		Frame omitted	*5,250.*	
J3	A1	20c violet & lilac	1.90	2.25

No. 5 Surcharged

J4	A1	40c on 30c indigo & yel	2.25	*6.00*

Nos. 10-11 Surcharged

J5	A2	60c on 2 l olive brn	40.00	30.00
J6	A2	1.10 l on 2.50 l red org	11.00	*22.50*
		Nos. J1-J6 (6)	55.85	*62.25*
		Set, never hinged	190.00	

In addition to the surcharges, #J4-J6 are overprinted with ornamental frame as on #J1-J3.
No. J5 is valued in the grade of fine.

Catalogue values for unused stamps in this section, from this point to the end of the section, are for Never Hinged items.

Papal Arms — D1

Unwmk.
1945, Aug. 16 Typo. *Perf. 14*

J7	D1	5c black & yellow	.25	.25
J8	D1	20c black & lilac	.25	.25
J9	D1	80c black & salmon	.25	.25
J10	D1	1 l black & green	.25	.25
J11	D1	2 l black & blue	.25	.25
J12	D1	5 l black & gray	.25	.25
a.		Imperf., pair	150.00	150.00
		Nos. J7-J12 (6)	1.50	1.50

A second type of Nos. J7-J12 exists, in which the colored lines of the background are thicker. Value, $50.
The 20c and 5 lire exist in horizontal pairs imperf. vertically. Value, each $100.
The 20c, 80c, and 1l exists in horizontal pairs imperf. between. Value, each, $500.
The 1l exists in vertical pairs, imperf horizontally. Value, $175.

Papal Arms — D2

Perf. 13½x13
1954, Apr. 30 Wmk. 235 Engr.

J13	D2	4 l black & rose	.25	.25
J14	D2	6 l black & green	.30	.30
J15	D2	10 l black & yellow	.25	.25
J16	D2	20 l black & blue	.55	.55
J17	D2	50 l black & ol brn	.25	.25
J18	D2	70 l black & red brn	.25	.25
		Nos. J13-J18 (6)	1.85	1.85

No. J13 exists in vertical pairs, imperf horizontally. Value, $175.

Papal Arms — D3

Photo. & Engr.
1968, May 28 Wmk. 235 *Perf. 14*

J19	D3	10 l black, *grysh bl*	.25	.25
J20	D3	20 l black, *pale bl*	.25	.25
J21	D3	50 l black, *pale lil rose*	.25	.25
J22	D3	60 l black, *gray*	.25	.25
J23	D3	100 l black, *dull yel*	.25	.25
J24	D3	180 l black, *bluish lil*	.25	.25
		Nos. J19-J24 (6)	1.50	1.50

PARCEL POST STAMPS

Nos. 1-7 Overprinted

1931, Oct. 1 Unwmk. *Perf. 14*

Q1	A1	5c dk brown & pink	.25	.55
Q2	A1	10c dk grn & lt grn	.25	.55
Q3	A1	20c violet & lilac	7.50	2.60
Q4	A1	25c dk bl & lt bl	11.00	5.50
Q5	A1	30c indigo & yel	7.50	5.50
Q6	A1	50c indigo & sal buff	7.50	5.50
Q7	A1	75c brn car & gray	1.50	5.50
a.		Inverted overprint	1,000.	

Nos. 8-13 Overprinted

Q8	A2	80c carmine rose	1.10	5.50
Q9	A2	1.25 l dark blue	1.50	5.50
Q10	A2	2 l olive brown	1.10	5.50
a.		Inverted overprint	1,000.	*1,350.*
Q11	A2	2.50 l red orange	1.90	5.50
a.		Double overprint	1,000.	
b.		Inverted overprint	1,800.	
Q12	A2	5 l dark green	1.90	5.50
Q13	A2	10 l olive black	1.50	5.50
a.		Double overprint	1,275.	

Nos. E1-E2 Overprinted Vertically

Q14	SD1	2 l carmine rose	1.50	5.50
Q15	SD1	2.50 l dark blue	1.50	5.50
a.		Inverted overprint	1,000.	
		Nos. Q1-Q15 (15)	47.50	69.70
		Set, never hinged	160.00	

VENEZUELA

ˌve-nə-ˈzwā-lə

LOCATION — Northern coast of South America, bordering on the Caribbean Sea
GOVT. — Republic
AREA — 352,143 sq. mi.
POP. — 23,203,466 (1999 est.)
CAPITAL — Caracas

100 Centavos = 8 Reales = 1 Peso
100 Centesimos = 1 Venezolano (1879)
100 Centimos = 1 Bolivar (1880)

Watermark

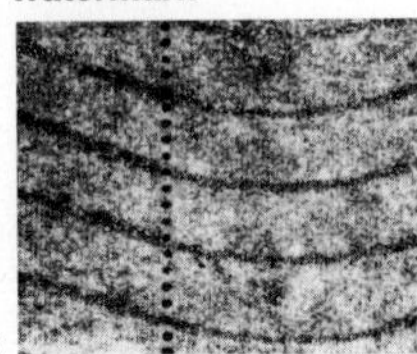
Wmk. 346

Catalogue values for unused stamps in this country are for Never Hinged items, beginning with Scott 743 in the regular postage section, Scott B2 in the semi-postal section, Scott C709 in the airpost section, and Scott E1 in the special delivery section.

Coat of Arms — A1

Fine Impression
No Dividing Line Between Stamps
Unwmk.

1859, Jan. 1 **Litho.** ***Imperf.***

1 A1 ½r yellow 60.00 12.00
a. ½r orange 60.00 12.00
b. Greenish paper *225.00*
2 A1 1r blue 450.00 15.00
a. Half used as ½r on cover *7,500.*
3 A1 2r red 42.50 15.00
a. 2r dull rose red 55.00 17.00
b. Half used as 1r on cover *1,250.*
c. Greenish paper 250.00 140.00
Nos. 1-3 (3) 552.50 42.00

Coarse Impression

1859-62 **Thick Paper**

4 A1 ½r orange ('61) 12.00 4.00
a. ½r yellow ('59) 500.00 30.00
b. ½r olive yellow 750.00 35.00
c. Bluish paper 575.00
d. ½r dull rose (error) 250,000. 350,000.
5 A1 1r blue ('62) 20.00 12.50
a. 1r pale blue 35.00 15.00
b. 1r dark blue 35.00 15.00
c. Half used as ½r on cover *7,500.*
d. Bluish paper 200.00
6 A1 2r red ('62) 45.00 80.00
a. 2r dull rose 55.00 80.00
b. Tête bêche pair *10,000.*
c. Half used as 1r on cover *400.00*
d. Bluish paper *225.00*
Nos. 4-6 (3) 77.00 96.50

In the fine impression, the background lines of the shield are more sharply drawn. In the coarse impression, the shading lines at each end of the scroll inscribed "LIBERTAD" are usually very heavy. Stamps of the coarse impression are closer together, and there is usually a dividing line between them.

Nos. 1-3 exist on thick paper and on bluish paper. Nos. 1-6 exist on pelure paper.

The greenish paper varieties (Nos. 1b and 3c) and the bluish paper varieties were not regularly issued.

Arms — A2

1862 **Litho.**

7 A2 ¼c green 20.00 *200.00*
8 A2 ½c dull lilac 20.00 *240.00*
a. ½c violet 40.00 210.00
9 A2 1c gray brown 42.50 *400.00*
Nos. 7-9 (3) 82.50 *840.00*

Counterfeits are plentiful. Forged cancellations abound on Nos. 7-17.

Eagle — A3

1863-64

10 A3 ½c pale red ('64) 55.00 *400.00*
a. ½c red 60.00 *400.00*
11 A3 1c slate ('64) 62.50 *160.00*
12 A3 ½r orange 7.75 3.50
13 A3 1r blue 17.00 8.50
a. 1r pale blue 30.00 13.00
b. Half used as ½r on cover *750.00*
14 A3 2r green 23.00 20.00
a. 2r deep yellow green 30.00 20.00
b. Quarter used as ½r on cover *7,500.*
c. Half used as 1r on cover *2,000.*

Counterfeits exist.

1865 **Redrawn**

15 A3 ½r orange 4.00 2.50

The redrawn stamp has a broad "N" in "FEDERACION." "MEDIO REAL" and "FEDERACION" are in thin letters. There are 52 instead of 49 pearls in the circle.

No. 15 in yellow is a postal forgery.

A4

1865-70

16 A4 ½c yel grn ('67) 275.00 *300.00*
17 A4 1c bl grn ('67) 275.00 *250.00*
18 A4 ½r brn vio (thin paper) 9.50 2.00
19 A4 ½r lil rose ('70) 9.50 3.25
a. ½r brownish rose 9.50 3.00
b. Tête bêche pair 200.00 *600.00*
20 A4 1r vermilion 45.00 15.00
a. Half used as ½r on cover *500.00*
21 A4 2r yellow 160.00 77.50
a. Half used as 1r on cover *3,000.*
Nos. 16-21 (6) 774.00 *647.75*

This issue is known unofficially rouletted.

Postal forgeries exist of the ½r.

One quarter of #21 used as ½r is a postal forgery.

For overprints see Nos. 37-48.

Overprinted in Very Small Upright Letters "Bolivar Sucre Miranda — Decreto de 27 de Abril de 1870", or "Decreto de 27 de Junio 1870" in Slanting Letters

Simón Bolívar — A5

(The "Junio" overprint is continuously repeated, in four lines arranged in two pairs, with the second line of each pair inverted.)

Un	1	Siete	7
Dos	2	Nueve	9
Tres	3	Quince	15
Cuatro	4	Veinte	20
Cinco	5	Cincuenta	50

1871-76 **Litho.**

22 A5 1c yellow 1.50 .40
a. 1c orange 2.10 .45
b. 1c brown orange ('76) 2.10 .40
c. 1c pale buff ('76) 2.10 .45
d. Laid paper 1.00 .75
23 A5 2c yellow 2.00 .45
a. 2c orange 4.00 .45
b. 2c brown orange 3.50 .75
c. 2c pale buff ('76) 3.50 .45
d. Laid paper 3.50 .55
e. Frame inverted *4,000.* *3,000.*
24 A5 3c yellow 3.00 .75
a. 3c orange 3.00 1.40
b. 3c pale buff ('76) 5.50 1.75
25 A5 4c yellow 4.00 .75
a. 4c orange 4.50 1.25
b. 4c brown orange ('76) 4.50 1.25
c. 4c buff ('76) 4.50 1.25
26 A5 5c yellow 4.00 .75
a. 5c orange 4.00 .90
b. 5c pale buff ('76) 4.00 .90
c. Laid paper 7.50 .90
27 A5 1r rose 4.00 2.00
a. 1r pale red 4.00 2.00
b. Laid paper 6.00 2.50
c. Half used as ½r on cover *1,500.*
28 A5 2r rose 4.50 2.00
a. 2r pale red 4.50 2.00
b. Laid paper 12.00 2.50
29 A5 3r rose 6.00 2.00
a. 3r pale red 6.00 2.00
30 A5 5r rose 5.75 1.00
a. 5r pale red 5.75 1.00
31 A5 7r rose 22.50 4.00
a. 7r pale red 22.50 4.00
32 A5 9r green 22.50 4.25
a. 9r olive green 22.50 6.00
33 A5 15r green 55.00 8.50
a. 15r gray green ('76) 55.00 8.50
b. Frame inverted *8,000.* *6,500.*
34 A5 20r green 77.50 20.00
a. Laid paper 110.00 35.00
35 A5 30r green 375.00 110.00
a. 30r gray green ('76) 600.00 160.00
b. Double overprint
36 A5 50r green 1,200. 300.00
a. 50r gray green ('76) 400.00
Nos. 22-34 (13) 212.25 46.85
Nos. 22-35 (14) 587.25 156.85

These stamps were made available for postage and revenue by official decree, and were the only stamps sold for postage in Venezuela from Mar., 1871 to Aug., 1873.

Due to lack of canceling handstamps, the majority of stamps were canceled with pen marks. Fiscal cancellations were also made with the pen. The values quoted are for pen-canceled stamps.

Different settings were used for the different overprints. Stamps with the upright letters were issued in 1871. Those with the slanting letters in one double line were issued in 1872-73. Those with the slanting overprint in two double lines were issued starting in 1874 from several different settings, those of 1877-78 showing much coarser impressions of the design than the earlier issues. The 7r and 9r are not known with this overprint. Stamps on laid paper (1875) are from a separate setting.

Stamps and Types of 1866-67 Overprinted in Two Lines of Very Small Letters Repeated Continuously

Overprinted "Estampillas de Correo — Contrasena"

1873, July 1

37 A4 ½r pale rose 70.00 13.00
a. ½r rose 70.00 13.00
b. Inverted overprint 175.00 75.00
c. Tête bêche pair *3,000.* *2,000.*
38 A4 1r vermilion 85.00 25.00
a. Inverted overprint — —
b. Half used as ½r on cover *5,500.*
39 A4 2r yellow 300.00 125.00
a. Inverted overprint — —
b. Half used as 1r on cover *12,000.*
Nos. 37-39 (3) 455.00 163.00

Overprinted "Contrasena — Estampillas de Correo"

1873, Nov.

40 A4 1c gray lilac 30.00 32.50
a. Inverted overprint 6.50 *17.00*
41 A4 2c green 125.00 90.00
a. Inverted overprint 40.00 50.00
b. As "a," half used as 1c on cover *7,500.*
42 A4 ½r rose 72.50 13.00
a. Inverted overprint 30.00 4.00
b. ½r pink 60.00 11.00
43 A4 1r vermilion 85.00 23.00
a. Inverted overprint 35.00 9.00
b. Half used as ½r on cover *300.00*
44 A4 2r yellow 325.00 160.00
a. Inverted overprint 110.00 50.00
b. Half used as 1r on cover *10,000.*
Nos. 40-44 (5) 637.50 318.50

Overprinted "Contrasena — Estampilla de Correos"

1875

45 A4 ½r rose 85.00 10.00
a. Inverted overprint 125.00 25.00
b. Double overprint 160.00 90.00
46 A4 1r vermilion 160.00 15.00
a. Inverted overprint 200.00 80.00
b. Tête bêche pair *3,500.* *3,000.*
c. Half used as ½r on cover *3,500.*

Overprinted "Estampillas de correo — Contrasena"

1876-77

47 A4 ½r rose 77.50 9.25
a. ½r pink 65.00 7.50
b. Inverted overprint 65.00 7.50
c. Both lines of overprint read "Contrasena" 75.00 17.50
d. Both lines of overprint read "Estampillas de correo" 75.00 17.50
e. Double overprint 125.00 35.00
48 A4 1r vermilion ('77) 92.50 23.00
a. Inverted overprint 85.00 24.00
b. Tête bêche pair *2,250.* *2,500.*
c. Half used as ½r on cover —

On Nos. 47 and 48 "correo" has a small "c" instead of a capital. Nos. 45 and 46 have the overprint in slightly larger letters than the other stamps of the 1873-76 issues.

Overprinted "Decreto de 27 Junio 1870" Twice, One Line Inverted

Simón Bolívar
A6 A7

1879 ***Imperf.***

49 A6 1c yellow 4.00 1.00
a. 1c orange 5.00 1.50
b. 1c olive yellow 5.50 1.75
50 A6 5c yellow 3.50 .50
a. 5c orange 2.50 .75
b. Double overprint 20.00 10.00
51 A6 10c blue 5.00 .50
52 A6 30c blue 7.75 1.00
53 A6 50c blue 7.75 1.00
54 A6 90c blue 40.00 12.00
55 A7 1v rose red 77.50 18.00
56 A7 3v rose red 130.00 55.00
57 A7 5v rose red 225.00 77.50
Nos. 49-57 (9) 500.50 166.50

In 1879 and the early part of 1880 there were no regular postage stamps in Venezuela and the stamps inscribed "Escuelas" were permitted to serve for postal as well as revenue purposes. Postally canceled stamps are extremely scarce. Values quoted are for stamps with cancellations of banks or business houses or with pen cancellations. Stamps with pen marks removed are sometimes offered as unused stamps, or may have fraudulent postal cancellations added.

Nos. 49-57 exist without overprint. These are proofs.

A8

A9

1880 ***Perf. 11***

58 A8 5c yellow 1.50 .50
a. 5c orange 1.50 .50
b. Printed on both sides 150.00 85.00
59 A8 10c yellow 2.50 .60
a. 10c orange 2.50 .60
60 A8 25c yellow 2.50 .60
a. 25c orange 2.75 .70
b. Printed on both sides 110.00 52.50
c. Impression of 5c on back *175.00* 90.00
61 A8 50c yellow 4.75 .80
a. 50c orange 5.25 .85
b. Half used as 25c on cover —
c. Printed on both sides 150.00 90.00
d. Impression of 25c on back 150.00 90.00
62 A9 1b pale blue 12.00 1.40
63 A9 2b pale blue 17.00 1.75
64 A9 5b pale blue 40.00 5.75
a. Half used as 2½b on cover —
65 A9 10b rose red 200.00 70.00
66 A9 20b rose red 1,200. 200.00
67 A9 25b rose red *5,000.* 500.00
Nos. 58-65 (8) 280.25 81.40

See note on used values below No. 57.

Bolívar — A10

1880 **Litho.** ***Perf. 11***

Thick or Thin Paper

68 A10 5c blue 15.00 7.25
a. Printed on both sides 225.00 140.00
69 A10 10c rose 20.00 12.00
a. 10c carmine 20.00 12.00
b. Double impression 90.00 75.00
c. Horiz. pair, imperf. btwn. 75.00 75.00
70 A10 10c scarlet 20.00 12.00
a. Horiz. pair, imperf. btwn. 75.00 75.00
71 A10 25c yellow 15.00 7.25
b. Thick paper 20.00 10.00
72 A10 50c brown 92.50 40.00
a. 50c deep brown 92.50 40.00
b. Printed on both sides 225.00 140.00
c. Half used as 25c on cover *5,000.*

73	A10 1b green	140.00	50.00
a.	Horiz. pair, imperf. btwn.	300.00	300.00
	Nos. 68-73 (6)	302.50	128.50

Nos. 68 to 73 were used for the payment of postage on letters to be sent abroad and the Escuelas stamps were then restricted to internal use.

Counterfeits of this issue exist in a great variety of shades as well as in wrong colors. They are on thick and thin paper, white or toned, and imperf. or perforated 11, 12 and compound. They are also found tête bêche. Counterfeits of Nos. 68 to 72 inclusive often have a diagonal line across the "S" of "CENTS" and a short line from the bottom of that letter to the frame below it. Originals of No. 73 show parts of a frame around "BOLIVAR."

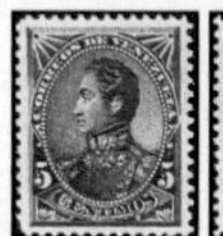

Simón Bolívar
A11 A12

A13

A14

A15

1882, Aug. 1 Engr. *Perf. 12*

74	A11 5c blue	.70	.35
75	A12 10c red brown	.70	.35
76	A13 25c yellow brown	1.10	.40
a.	Printed on both sides	50.00	27.50
77	A14 50c green	2.40	.70
a.	Half used as 25c on cover		500.00
78	A15 1b violet	4.50	1.75
	Nos. 74-78 (5)	9.40	3.55

Nos. 75-78 exist imperf. Value, set $32.50.

See Nos. 88, 92-95. For surcharges and overprints see Nos. 100-103, 108-112.

A16

A17

A18

A19

A20

A21

A22

A23

1882-88

79	A16 5c blue green	.25	.25
80	A17 10c brown	.25	.25
81	A18 25c orange	.25	.25
82	A19 50c blue	.25	.25
83	A20 1b vermilion	.25	.25
84	A21 3b dull vio ('88)	.25	.25
85	A22 10b dark brn ('88)	1.25	.80
86	A23 20b plum ('88)	1.50	.95
	Nos. 79-86 (8)	4.25	3.25

By official decree, dated Apr. 14, 1882, stamps of types A11 to A15 were to be used for foreign postage and those of types A16 to A23 for inland correspondence and fiscal use.

Issue date: Nos. 79-83, Aug. 1.

See Nos. 87, 89-91, 96-99. For surcharges and overprints see Nos. 104-107, 114-122.

1887-88 Litho. *Perf. 11*

87	A16 5c gray green	.45	.30
88	A13 25c yellow brown	55.00	22.50
89	A18 25c orange	.70	.45
90	A20 1b orange red ('88)	4.75	.90
	Nos. 87-90 (4)	60.90	24.15

Perf. 14

91	A16 5c gray green	95.00	40.00

Stamps of type A16, perf. 11 and 14, are from a new die with "ESCUELAS" in smaller letters. Stamps of the 1887-88 issue, perf. 12, and a 50c dark blue, perf. 11 or 12, are believed by experts to be from printer's waste.

Counterfeits of No. 91 have been made by perforating printers waste of No. 96.

Rouletted 8

92	A11 5c blue	40.00	17.00
93	A13 25c yel brown	15.00	10.00
94	A14 50c green	15.00	10.00
95	A15 1b purple	30.00	20.00
	Nos. 92-95 (4)	100.00	57.00

1887-88

96	A16 5c green	.25	.25
97	A18 25c orange	.25	.25
98	A19 50c dark blue	1.25	1.10
99	A21 3b purple ('88)	3.50	3.50
	Nos. 96-99 (4)	5.25	5.10

The so-called imperforate varieties of Nos. 92 to 99, and the pin perforated 50c dark blue, type A19, are believed to be from printer's waste.

Stamps of 1882-88 Handstamp Surcharged in Violet

1892 *Perf. 12*

100	A11 25c on 5c blue	*40.00*	*40.00*
101	A12 25c on 10c red brn	*16.00*	*16.00*
102	A13 1b on 25c yel brn	*16.00*	*16.00*
103	A14 1b on 50c green	*20.00*	*20.00*
	Nos. 100-103 (4)	*92.00*	*92.00*

See note after No. 107.

1892

104	A16 25c on 5c bl grn	*10.00*	*6.00*
105	A17 25c on 10c brown	*10.00*	*6.00*
106	A18 1b on 25c orange	*15.00*	*12.00*
107	A19 1b on 50c blue	*23.00*	*12.00*
	Nos. 104-107 (4)	*58.00*	*36.00*

Counterfeits of this surcharge abound.

Stamps of 1882-88 Overprinted in Red or Black

1893

108	A11 5c blue (R)	.55	.25
a.	Inverted overprint	3.25	3.25
b.	Double overprint	16.00	16.00
109	A12 10c red brn (Bk)	.90	.90
a.	Inverted overprint	4.00	4.00
b.	Double overprint	16.00	16.00
110	A13 25c yel brn (R)	.80	.50
a.	Inverted overprint	5.25	5.25
b.	Double overprint	16.00	16.00
c.	25c yel brn (Bk)	500.00	500.00
111	A14 50c green (R)	1.25	.80
a.	Inverted overprint	5.25	5.25
b.	Double overprint	27.50	27.50
112	A15 1b pur (R)	3.25	1.20
a.	Inverted overprint	10.00	10.00
	Nos. 108-112 (5)	6.75	3.65

1893

114	A16 5c bl grn (R)	.25	.25
a.	Inverted overprint	3.25	3.25
b.	Double overprint	5.25	5.25
115	A17 10c brn (R)	.25	.25
a.	Inverted overprint	3.25	3.25
116	A18 25c org (R)	.25	.25
a.	Inverted overprint	3.25	3.25
117	A18 25c org (Bk)	5.75	2.75
a.	Inverted overprint	8.25	5.00
118	A19 50c blue (R)	.25	.25
a.	Inverted overprint	3.25	3.25
119	A20 1b ver (Bk)	.60	.40
a.	Inverted overprint	4.00	4.00
120	A21 3b dl vio (R)	.90	.40
a.	Double overprint	8.25	8.25
121	A22 10b dk brn (R)	3.50	2.25
a.	Double overprint	10.00	10.00
b.	Inverted overprint	20.00	20.00
122	A23 20b plum (Bk)	3.00	3.00
a.	Double overprint	10.00	20.00
b.	Inverted overprint		
	Nos. 114-122 (9)	14.75	9.80

Counterfeits exist.

Simón Bolívar — A24

1893 Engr.

123	A24 5c red brn	.90	.25
124	A24 10c blue	3.25	1.25
125	A24 25c magenta	15.00	.50
126	A24 50c brn vio	4.25	.55
127	A24 1b green	5.75	1.25
	Nos. 123-127 (5)	29.15	3.80

Many shades exist in this issue, but their values do not vary.

Simón Bolívar — A25

1893

128	A25 5c gray	.25	.25
129	A25 10c green	.25	.25
130	A25 25c blue	.25	.25
131	A25 50c orange	.25	.25
132	A25 1b red vio	.25	.25
133	A25 3b red	.55	.25
134	A25 10b dl vio	.90	.80
135	A25 20b red brn	4.25	2.75
	Nos. 128-135 (8)	6.95	5.05

By decree of Nov. 28, 1892, the stamps inscribed "Correos" were to be used for external postage and those inscribed "Instruccion" were for internal postage and revenue purposes.

For surcharge see No. 230.

Until July 1, 1895, revenue stamps inscribed "Escuelas" or "Instruccion," fiscal stamps for the collection of taxes for primary schools, were used as both revenue stamps and as postage stamps. After that date, they were no longer to be used for postal purposes, but their use was permitted when supplies of regular postage stamps were temporarily exhausted. See Nos. AR1-AR86.

Landing of Columbus — A26

1893 *Perf. 12*

136	A26 25c magenta	20.00	.60

4th cent. of the discovery of the mainland of South America, also participation of Venezuela in the Intl. Exhib. at Chicago in 1893.

Map of Venezuela — A27

1896 Litho.

137	A27 5c yel grn	3.00	2.75
a.	5c apple green	3.00	2.75
138	A27 10c blue	4.00	5.50
139	A27 25c yellow	4.00	5.50
a.	25c orange	4.00	5.50
b.	Tête bêche pair	125.00	125.00
140	A27 50c rose red	55.00	25.00
a.	50c red	52.50	52.50
b.	Tête bêche pair	375.00	375.00
141	A27 1b violet	40.00	27.50
	Nos. 137-141 (5)	106.00	66.25

Gen. Francisco Antonio Gabriel de Miranda (1752-1816).

These stamps were in use from July 4 to Nov. 4, 1896. Later usage is known.

There are many forgeries of this issue. They include faked errors, imperforate stamps and many tête bêche. The paper of the originals is thin, white and semi-transparent. The gum is shiny and crackled. The paper of the reprints is often thick and opaque. The gum is usually dull, smooth, thin and only slightly adhesive.

Bolívar — A28

1899-1901 Engr.

142	A28 5c dk grn	1.00	.25
143	A28 10c red	1.25	.40
144	A28 25c blue	1.50	.55
145	A28 50c gray blk	2.00	1.00
146	A28 50c org ('01)	1.75	.50
147	A28 1b yel grn	32.50	15.00
149	A28 2b orange	400.00	225.00
	Nos. 142-147,149 (7)	440.00	242.70

For overprints, see Nos. 150-163.

Stamps of 1899 Overprinted in Black

1900

150	A28 5c dk grn	1.25	.40
a.	Inverted overprint	4.75	4.75
151	A28 10c red	1.25	.40
a.	Inverted overprint	6.50	6.50
b.	Double overprint	10.50	10.50
152	A28 25c blue	7.75	1.25
a.	Inverted overprint	13.00	13.00
153	A28 50c gray blk	4.00	.55
a.	Inverted overprint	12.00	12.00
154	A28 1b yel grn	1.75	.80
a.	Double overprint	13.00	13.00
b.	Inverted overprint	12.00	12.00
155	A28 2b orange	2.75	2.25
a.	Inverted overprint	35.00	35.00
b.	Double overprint	32.50	32.50
	Nos. 150-155 (6)	18.75	5.65

Initials are those of R. T. Mendoza.

Counterfeit overprints exist, especially of inverted and doubled varieties.

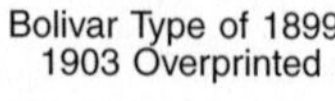

Bolivar Type of 1899-1903 Overprinted

1900

156	A28 5c dk grn	750.00	750.00
157	A28 10c red	750.00	750.00
158	A28 25c blue	600.00	600.00
159	A28 50c yel orange	23.00	1.60
160	A28 1b slate	1.25	1.00
a.	Without overprint	7,000.	—
	Nos. 156-160 (5)	2,124.	2,103.

Nos. 156-158 Overprinted

1900, Aug. 14

161	A28 5c green	8.00	.55
162	A28 10c red	7.00	1.00
163	A28 25c blue	8.00	1.00
	Nos. 161-163 (3)	23.00	2.55

Inverted Overprint

161a	A28 5c	9.25	9.25
162a	A28 10c	9.25	9.25
163a	A28 25c	12.00	12.00
	Nos. 161a-163a (3)	30.50	30.50

Overprint exists on each value without "Castro" or without "1900."

Type of 1893 Surcharged

1904, Jan. *Perf. 12*

230	A25 5c on 50c green	.80	.60
a.	"Vele"	23.00	23.00
b.	Surcharge reading up	1.00	.50
c.	Double surcharge	18.00	18.00

Gen. José de Sucre — A35

1904-09 Engr.
231 A35 5c bl grn .50 .25
232 A35 10c carmine .55 .25
233 A35 15c violet .90 .40
234 A35 25c dp ultra 6.50 .40
235 A35 50c plum 1.00 .50
236 A35 1b plum 1.10 .50
Nos. 231-236 (6) 10.55 2.30

Issue date: 15c, Dec. 1909. Others, July 1, 1904.

Pres. Cipriano Castro — A37

1905, July 5 Litho. *Perf. 11½*
245 A37 5c vermilion 3.25 3.25
a. 5c carmine 5.00 5.00
246 A37 10c dark blue 5.50 4.25
247 A37 25c yellow 2.00 1.50
Nos. 245-247 (3) 10.75 9.00

National Congress. Issued for interior postage only. Valid only for 90 days.
Various part-perforate varieties of Nos. 245-247 exist. Value, $15-$30.

Liberty — A38

1910, Apr. 19 Engr. *Perf. 12*
249 A38 25c dark blue 13.00 .70

Centenary of national independence.

Francisco de Miranda A39

Rafael Urdaneta A40

Bolívar — A41

1911 Litho. *Perf. 11½x12*
250 A39 5c dp grn .50 .25
251 A39 10c carmine .50 .25
252 A40 15c gray 5.75 .40
253 A40 25c dp bl 3.25 .60
a. Imperf., pair 40.00 50.00
254 A41 50c purple 3.50 .40
255 A41 1b yellow 3.50 1.50
Nos. 250-255 (6) 17.00 3.40

The 50c with center in blue was never issued although examples were postmarked by favor.
The centers of Nos. 250-255 were separately printed and often vary in shade from the rest of the design. In a second printing of the 5c and 10c, the entire design was printed at one time.

1913 Redrawn
255A A40 15c gray 3.50 2.25
255B A40 25c deep blue 2.00 .65
255C A41 50c purple 2.00 .65
Nos. 255A-255C (3) 7.50 3.55

The redrawn stamps have two berries instead of one at top of the left spray; a berry has been added over the "C" and "S" of "Centimos"; and the lowest leaf at the right is cut by the corner square.

Simón Bolívar — A42

1914, July Engr. *Perf. 13½, 14, 15*
256 A42 5c yel grn 37.50 .55
257 A42 10c scarlet 35.00 .50
258 A42 25c dark blue 5.75 .25
Nos. 256-258 (3) 78.25 1.30

Simón Bolívar — A43

Different frames.

Printed by the American Bank Note Co.

1915-23 *Perf. 12*
259 A43 5c green 4.25 .25
260 A43 10c vermilion 10.00 .60
261 A43 10c claret ('22) 10.00 .90
262 A43 15c dull ol grn 9.25 .60
263 A43 25c ultra 6.50 .25
a. 25c blue 13.00 .60
264 A43 40c dull green 23.00 11.50
265 A43 50c dp violet 6.50 .80
266 A43 50c ultra ('23) 17.00 4.75
267 A43 75c lt blue 57.50 23.00
a. 75c greenish blue 57.50 23.00
268 A43 1b dark gray 35.00 5.25
Nos. 259-268 (10) 179.00 47.90

See Nos. 269-285. For surcharges see Nos. 307, 309-310.

Type of 1915-23 Issue Re-engraved Printed by Waterlow & Sons, Ltd.

1924-39 *Perf. 12½*
269 A43 5c orange brn .55 .25
a. 5c yellow brown .55 .25
b. Horiz. pair, imperf. between 25.00 40.00
270 A43 5c green ('39) 12.50 1.00
271 A43 7½c yel grn ('39) 1.25 .40
272 A43 10c dk green .25 .25
273 A43 10c dk car ('39) 4.00 .25
274 A43 15c olive grn 2.25 .50
275 A43 15c brown ('27) .30 .25
276 A43 25c ultra 2.25 .25
277 A43 25c red ('28) .25 .25
a. Horiz. pair, imperf. btwn. 50.00 85.00
278 A43 40c dp blue ('25) .55 .25
279 A43 40c slate bl ('39) 8.00 1.25
280 A43 50c dk blue .55 .25
281 A43 50c dk pur ('39) 8.00 .85
282 A43 1b black .55 .25
283 A43 3b yel org ('25) 1.75 .95
284 A43 3b red org ('39) 13.00 4.25
285 A43 5b dull vio ('25) 19.00 8.50
Nos. 269-285 (17) 75.00 19.95

Perf. 14
269c A43 5c 7.00 2.00
272a A43 10c 7.00 2.00
274a A43 15c 8.25 2.75
276a A43 25c 12.00 4.75
280a A43 50c 35.00 14.00
282a A43 1b 42.50 27.00
Nos. 269c-282a (6) 111.75 52.50

The re-engraved stamps may readily be distinguished from the 1915 issue by the perforation and sometimes by the colors. The designs differ in many minor details which are too minute for illustration or description.

Bolívar and Sucre — A44

Perf. 11½x12, 12
1924, Dec. 1 Litho.
286 A44 25c grayish blue 2.75 .55

Redrawn
286A A44 25c ultra 3.50 .85

Centenary of the Battle of Ayacucho.
The redrawn stamp has a whiter effect with less shading in the faces. Bolivar's ear is clearly visible and the outline of his aquiline nose is broken.

A45

A46

Revenue Stamps Surcharged in Black or Red

1926 *Perf. 12, 12½*
287 A45 5c on 1b ol grn .65 .40
a. Double surcharge 8.00 8.00
b. Pair, one without surcharge 12.00 12.00
c. Inverted surcharge 8.00 8.00
288 A46 25c on 5c dk brn (R) .65 .40
a. Inverted surcharge 8.00 8.00
b. Double surcharge 8.00 8.00

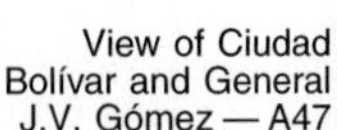

View of Ciudad Bolívar and General J.V. Gómez — A47

1928, July 21 Litho. *Perf. 12*
289 A47 10c deep green 1.00 .65
a. Imperf., pair 40.00

25th anniversary of the Battle of Ciudad Bolívar and the foundation of peace in Venezuela.

Simón Bolívar — A48

1930, Dec. 9
290 A48 5c yellow 1.00 .40
291 A48 10c dark blue 1.00 .40
292 A48 25c rose red 1.00 .40
Nos. 290-292 (3) 3.00 1.20

Imperf., Pairs
290a A48 5c 5.25 5.25
291a A48 10c 6.50 6.50
292a A48 25c 10.50 10.50

Death centenary of Simón Bolívar (1783-1830), South American liberator.
Nos. 290-292 exist part-perforate, including pairs imperf. between, imperf. horiz., imperf. vert. Value range, $6-12.

Simón Bolívar — A49

Various Frames
Bluish Winchester Security Paper

1932-38 Engr. *Perf. 12½*
293 A49 5c violet .50 .25
294 A49 7½c dk green ('37) 1.10 .40
295 A49 10c green .65 .25
296 A49 15c yellow 1.50 .25
297 A49 22½c dp car ('38) 3.50 .50
298 A49 25c red 1.25 .25
299 A49 37½c ultra ('36) 4.50 2.00
300 A49 40c indigo 4.50 .25
301 A49 50c olive grn 4.50 .40
302 A49 1b lt blue 6.00 .70
303 A49 3b brown 47.50 13.00
304 A49 5b yellow brn 65.00 17.50
Nos. 293-304 (12) 140.50 35.75

For surcharges see Nos. 308, 318-319, C223.

Arms of Bolívar — A50

1933, July 24 Litho. *Perf. 11*
306 A50 25c brown red 3.00 2.40
a. Imperf., pair 32.50 32.50

150th anniv. of the birth of Simón Bolívar. Valid only to Aug. 21.

Stamps of 1924-32 Surcharged in Black — (Blocks of Surcharge in Color of stamps)

1933
307 A43 7½c on 10c grn .50 .25
a. Double surcharge 2.50 2.50
b. Inverted surcharge 4.25 4.25
308 A49 22½c on 25c (#298) 2.00 .85
309 A43 22½c on 25c (#277) 1.50 1.50
a. Double surcharge 10.00 10.00
310 A43 37½c on 40c dp bl 2.00 .95
a. Double surcharge 11.50 11.50
b. Inverted surcharge 10.00 10.00
Nos. 307-310 (4) 6.00 3.55

Nurse and Child A51

River Scene A52

Gathering Cacao Pods A53

Cattle Raising A54

Plowing — A55

Perf. 11, 11½ or Compound
1937, July 1 Litho.
311 A51 5c deep violet .85 .35
312 A52 10c dk slate grn .85 .25
313 A53 15c yellow brn 1.50 .55
314 A51 25c cerise 1.50 .35
315 A54 50c yellow grn 10.00 4.25
316 A55 3b red orange 19.00 7.75
317 A51 5b lt brown 36.00 15.00
Nos. 311-317 (7) 69.70 28.50

Nos. 311-317 exist imperforate. Value for set $75. Nos. 311-315 exist in pairs, imperf. between; value range, $20-$30.
For overprints and surcharges see Nos. 321-324, 345, 376-377, 380-384.

No. 300 Surcharged in Black

1937, July *Perf. 12½*
318 A49 25c on 40c indigo 7.75 .95
a. Double surcharge 16.00 16.00
b. Inverted surcharge 13.00 13.00
c. Triple surcharge 32.50 32.50

No. 300 Surcharged

319 A49 25c on 40c indigo 440.00 350.00
a. Double surcharge

A56

1937, Oct. 28 Litho. *Perf. 10½*
320 A56 25c blue 1.25 .45

Acquisition of the Port of La Guaira by the Government from the British Corporation, June 3, 1937. Exists imperf. See Nos. C64-C65.
A redrawn printing of No. 320, with top inscription beginning "Nacionalización . . ." was prepared but not issued. Value, $40.
For surcharge see No. 385.

Stamps of 1937 Overprinted in Black

1937, Dec. 17 ***Perf. 11, 11½***

321	A51	5c deep violet	5.75	3.25
322	A52	10c dk slate grn	1.75	.75
a.		Inverted overprint	13.00	13.00
323	A51	25c cerise	1.50	.55
a.		Inverted overprint	16.00	16.00
324	A55	3b red orange	375.00	225.00
		Nos. 321-324 (4)	384.00	229.55

Part-perforate pairs exist of Nos. 321-322 and 324. Value range, $12.50 to $125.
See Nos. C66-C78.

Gathering Coffee Beans A57

Simón Bolívar A58

Post Office, Caracas — A59

1938 **Engr.** ***Perf. 12***

325	A57	5c green	.50	.25
326	A57	5c deep green	.50	.25
327	A58	10c car rose	.90	.25
328	A58	10c dp rose	.90	.25
329	A59	15c dk violet	1.75	.25
330	A59	15c olive grn	1.10	.25
331	A58	25c lt blue	.50	.25
332	A58	25c dk blue	.50	.25
333	A58	37½c dk blue	11.00	4.00
334	A58	37½c lt blue	3.50	.85
335	A59	40c sepia	26.00	7.75
336	A59	40c black	22.50	7.75
337	A57	50c olive grn	36.00	7.75
338	A57	50c dull violet	11.00	.85
339	A58	1b dp brown	15.00	5.50
340	A58	1b black brown	22.50	1.50
341	A57	3b orange	120.00	50.00
342	A59	5b black	19.00	7.75
		Nos. 325-342 (18)	293.15	95.70

See Nos. 400, 412.

Teresa Carreño — A60

1938, June 12 ***Perf. 11½x12***

343	A60	25c blue	5.75	.60

Teresa Carreno, Venezuelan pianist, whose remains were repatriated Feb. 14, 1938.
For surcharge see No. 386.

Bolívar Statue — A61

1938, July 24 ***Perf. 12***

344	A61	25c dark blue	6.50	.60

"The Day of the Worker."
For surcharge see No. 387.

Type of 1937 Surcharged in Black

1938 **Litho.** ***Perf. 11, 11½***

345	A51	40c on 5b lt brn	8.50	4.50
a.		Inverted surcharge	21.00	21.00

Gen. José I. Paz Castillo, Postmaster of Venezuela, 1859 — A62

1939, Apr. 19 **Engr.** ***Perf. 12½***

348	A62	10c carmine	2.50	.70

80th anniv. of the first Venezuelan stamp.

View of Ojeda — A63

1939, June 24 **Photo.**

349	A63	25c dull blue	9.25	.75

Founding of city of Ojeda.

Cristóbal Mendoza — A64

1939, Oct. 14 **Engr.** ***Perf. 13***

350	A64	5c green	.40	.25
351	A64	10c dk car rose	.40	.25
352	A64	15c dull lilac	1.00	.25
353	A64	25c brt ultra	.80	.25
354	A64	37½c dark blue	15.00	6.25
355	A64	50c lt olive grn	16.00	4.00
356	A64	1b dark brown	6.50	3.50
		Nos. 350-356 (7)	40.10	14.75

Mendoza (1772-1839), postmaster general.

Diego Urbaneja — A65

1940-43 ***Perf. 12***

357	A65	5c Prus green	.55	.25
357A	A65	7½c dk bl grn ('43)	.80	.30
358	A65	15c olive	.95	.30
359	A65	37½c deep blue	1.50	.70
360	A65	40c violet blue	1.10	.35
361	A65	50c violet	6.50	1.75
362	A65	1b dk violet brn	3.50	.90
363	A65	3b scarlet	9.50	3.75
		Nos. 357-363 (8)	24.40	8.30

See Nos. 399, 408, 410-411. For surcharges see Nos. 396, C226.

Battle of Carabobo, 1821 — A67

1940, June 13

365	A67	25c blue	6.75	.80

Birth of General JoséAntonio Páez, 150th anniv.

"Crossing the Andes" by Tito Salas — A68

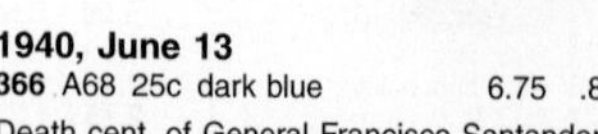

1940, June 13

366	A68	25c dark blue	6.75	.80

Death cent. of General Francisco Santander.

Monument and Urn containing Ashes of Simón Bolívar A69

Bed where Simón Bolívar was Born A70

Designs: 15c, "Christening of Bolivar" by Tito Salas. 20c, Bolivar's birthplace, Caracas. 25c, "Bolivar on Horseback" by Salas. 30c, Patio of Bolivar House, Caracas. 37½c, Patio of Bolivar's Birthplace. 50c, "Rebellion of 1812" by Salas.

1940-41

367	A69	5c turq green	.25	.25
368	A70	10c rose pink	.25	.25
369	A69	15c olive	.60	.25
370	A70	20c blue ('41)	1.00	.25
371	A69	25c lt blue	.60	.25
372	A70	30c plum ('41)	1.50	.25
373	A70	37½c dk blue	3.00	1.00
374	A70	50c purple	2.00	.50
		Nos. 367-374 (8)	9.20	3.00

110th anniv. of the death of Simón Bolívar.
See Nos. 397, 398, 403, 405-407, 409. For surcharges see Nos. 375, 401-402, C224, C237-C238.

No. 371 Surcharged In Black

1941

375	A69	20c on 25c lt blue	.60	.25
a.		Inverted surcharge	10.00	10.00

Nos. 311-312 Overprinted in Black

1941 ***Perf. 11½***

376	A51	5c deep violet	2.00	.50
a.		Double overprint	10.00	8.25
b.		Vert. pair, imperf. btwn.	14.00	14.00
c.		Inverted overprint	20.00	16.00
377	A52	10c dk slate grn	1.00	.30
a.		Double overprint	13.00	13.00

Symbols of Industry — A77

1942, Dec. 17 **Litho.** ***Perf. 12***

378	A77	10c scarlet	1.10	.25
a.		Imperf., pair	22.50	22.50

Grand Industrial Exposition, Caracas.

Caracas Cathedral — A78

1943 **Engr.**

379	A78	10c rose carmine	.75	.25

See No. 404.

Stamps of 1937 Overprinted in Black

1943 ***Perf. 11, 11½***

380	A51	5c deep violet	16.00	9.50
381	A52	10c dk slate grn	6.00	4.00
382	A54	50c yellow green	8.00	4.50
383	A55	3b red orange	45.00	22.00
		Nos. 380-383 (4)	75.00	40.00

Issued for sale to philatelists & sold only in sets.

Stamps of 1937-38 Surcharged in Black

1943 ***Perf. 11½, 10½, 12***

384	A51	20c on 25c cerise	30.00	30.00
385	A56	20c on 25c blue	77.50	77.50
386	A60	20c on 25c dk blue	15.00	15.00
387	A61	20c on 25c dk blue	15.00	15.00
a.		Inverted surcharge	42.50	42.50
		Nos. 384-387 (4)	137.50	137.50

Issued for sale to philatelists & sold only in sets.

Souvenir Sheet

A79

1944, Aug. 22 **Litho.** ***Perf. 12***

Flags in Red, Yellow, Blue & Black

388	A79	Sheet of 4	35.00	35.00
a.		5c Prussian green	3.00	.80
b.		10c rose	4.50	.80
c.		20c ultramarine	4.50	1.75
d.		1b rose lake	6.00	2.25

80th anniv. of Intl. Red Cross and 37th anniv. of Venezuela's joining.
No. 388 exists imperf. Value $60.

Antonio José de Sucre — A80

1945, Mar. 3 **Engr.** **Unwmk.**

389	A80	5c orange yellow	2.10	1.10
390	A80	10c dark blue	3.25	1.75
391	A80	20c rose pink	4.25	1.75
		Nos. 389-391,C206-C215 (13)	33.75	22.50

Birth of Antonio de Sucre, 150th anniv.

Andrés Bello A81

Gen. Rafael Urdaneta A82

1946, Aug. 24

392	A81	20c deep blue	.65	.35
393	A82	20c deep blue	.65	.35
		Nos. 392-393,C216-C217 (4)	3.50	1.20

80th anniversary of the death of Andrés Bello (1780?-1865), educator and writer, and the centenary of the death of Gen. Rafael Urdaneta.

Allegory of the Republic — A83

1946, Oct. 18 Litho. *Perf. 11½*
394 A83 20c light blue .80 .35
Nos. 394,C218-C221 (5) 5.60 3.95

Anniversary of Revolution of October, 1945. Exists imperf.

Anti-tuberculosis Institute, Maracaibo — A84

1947, Jan. 12
395 A84 20c ultra & yellow .80 .35
Nos. 395,C228-C231 (5) 6.90 5.15

12th Pan-American Health Conf., Caracas, Jan. 1947. Exists imperf. and part perf.

No. 362 Surcharged in Green

396 A65 15c on 1b dk vio brn .70 .30
a. Inverted surcharge 6.00 5.00
Nos. 396,C223-C227 (6) 30.50 24.00

Types of 1938-40

1947 Engr.
397 A69 5c green .25 .25
398 A70 30c black 1.00 .50
399 A65 40c red violet .95 .25
400 A59 5b deep orange 40.00 18.00
Nos. 397-400 (4) 42.20 19.00

In 1947 a decree authorized the use of 5c and 10c revenue stamps of the above type for franking correspondence. Other denominations were also used unofficially.

For surcharges see Nos. 876-883.

Nos. 398 and 373 Surcharged in Red

1947 Unwmk. *Perf. 12*
401 A70 5c on 30c black .40 .25
a. Inverted surcharge 5.00 5.00
402 A70 5c on 37½c dk bl .45 .25
a. Inverted surcharge 5.00 5.00

Types of 1938-43

1947-48
403 A69 5c brt ultra .25 .25
404 A78 10c red .25 .25
405 A69 15c rose car .50 .25
406 A69 25c violet .40 .25
407 A70 30c dk vio brn ('48) .50 .25
408 A65 40c orange ('48) .50 .25
409 A70 50c olive green .95 .25
410 A65 1b deep blue 1.75 .25
411 A65 3b gray 3.50 .90
412 A59 5b chocolate 13.00 5.00
Nos. 403-412 (10) 21.60 7.90

M. S. Republica de Venezuela — A85

Imprint: "American Bank Note Company"

1948-50 Engr. *Perf. 12*
413 A85 5c blue .25 .25
414 A85 7½c red org ('49) .70 .40
a. Booklet pane of 20
415 A85 10c car rose .55 .25
a. Booklet pane of 10
416 A85 15c gray ('50) .55 .25
417 A85 20c sepia .40 .25
418 A85 25c violet ('49) .55 .25
419 A85 30c orange ('50) 3.75 2.25
420 A85 37½c brown ('49) 1.75 1.40
421 A85 40c olive ('50) 2.50 1.75
422 A85 50c red violet ('49) .70 .25
423 A85 1b gray green 1.75 .55
Nos. 413-423 (11) 13.45 7.85

Grand Colombian Merchant Fleet. See Nos. 632-634, C256-C271, C554-C556. For surcharges see Nos. 450-451.

Santos Michelena — A86

1949, Apr. 25 *Perf. 12½*
424 A86 5c ultra .25 .25
425 A86 10c carmine .40 .25
426 A86 20c sepia 1.60 .60
427 A86 1b green 5.75 3.00
Nos. 424-427,C272-C277 (10) 16.50 9.70

Centenary of the death of Santos Michelena, Finance Minister, and the 110th anniversary of the Postal Convention of Bogota.

Christopher Columbus — A87

1949-50 Engr.
428 A87 5c deep ultra .45 .25
429 A87 10c carmine 1.50 .50
430 A87 20c dark brown 1.75 .60
431 A87 1b green 4.75 2.10
Nos. 428-431,C278-C283 (10) 18.45 8.65

450th anniversary (in 1948) of Columbus' discovery of the American mainland.

Issued: 5c, 10c, 1949; 20c, 1b, Jan. 1950.

Arms of Venezuela — A88

1948
432 A88 5c blue 1.40 .70
433 A88 10c red 1.75 .80

The 20c and 1b, type A88, and six similar air post stamps were prepared but not issued. Value, set of 8, about $125.

Gen. Francisco de Miranda — A89

1950, Mar. 28 Unwmk. *Perf. 12*
434 A89 5c blue .25 .25
435 A89 10c green .40 .25
436 A89 20c sepia .85 .35
437 A89 1b rose carmine 4.00 1.75
Nos. 434-437 (4) 5.50 2.60

Bicentenary of birth of General Francisco de Miranda.

Map and Population Chart — A90

1950, Sept. 1
438 A90 5c blue .25 .25
439 A90 10c gray .25 .25
440 A90 15c sepia .25 .25
441 A90 25c green .45 .25
442 A90 30c red .55 .25
443 A90 50c violet 1.10 .45
444 A90 1b red brown 2.75 1.40
Nos. 438-444,C302-C310 (16) 11.50 7.50

8th National Census of the Americas.

Alonso de Ojeda — A91

1950, Dec. 18 Photo. *Perf. 11½*
445 A91 5c deep blue .25 .25
446 A91 10c deep red .30 .25
447 A91 15c slate gray .35 .25
448 A91 20c ultra 1.40 .55
449 A91 1b blue green 5.50 2.75
Nos. 445-449 (5) 7.80 4.05
Nos. 445-449,C316-C321 (11) 15.75 8.10

450th anniversary (in 1949) of the discovery of the Gulf of Maracaibo.

Nos. 414 and 420 Surcharged in Black

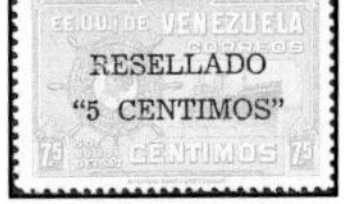

1951 Unwmk. *Perf. 12*
450 A85 5c on 7½c red org .35 .25
451 A85 10c on 37½c brn .35 .25
a. Inverted surcharge 16.00 16.00

Telegraph Stamps Surcharged in Black or Red

Grayish Security Paper

1951, June Engr.
452 5c on 5c brown .25 .25
453 10c on 10c green .25 .25
454 20c on 1b blk (R) .50 .25
455 25c on 25c carmine .65 .25
456 30c on 2b ol grn (R) .90 .70
Nos. 452-456 (5) 2.55 1.70

The 5c and 10c surcharges include quotation marks on each line and values are expressed "Bs. 0.05" etc.

Bolivar Statue, New York — A92

1951, July 13 *Perf. 12*
457 A92 5c green .25 .25
458 A92 10c car rose .40 .25
459 A92 20c ultra .40 .25
460 A92 30c slate gray .50 .25
461 A92 40c deep green .70 .25
462 A92 50c red brown 1.50 .50
463 A92 1b gray black 4.75 2.50
Nos. 457-463 (7) 8.50 4.25
Nos. 457-463,C322-C329 (15) 21.00 9.85

Relocation of the equestrian statue of Simon Bolivar in NYC, Apr. 19, 1951.

Arms of Carabobo and "Industry" — A93

1951 Unwmk. Photo. *Perf. 11½*
464 A93 5c green .25 .25
465 A93 10c red .25 .25
466 A93 15c brown 1.40 .25
467 A93 20c ultra 2.00 .25
468 A93 25c orange brn 2.25 .25
469 A93 30c blue 5.00 2.00
470 A93 35c purple 19.00 16.00
Nos. 464-470 (7) 30.15 19.25

Issue dates: 5c, 10c, Oct. 8; others, Oct. 29.

Arms of Zulia and "Industry"

471 A93 5c green .25 .25
472 A93 10c red .95 .25
473 A93 15c brown 2.10 .95
474 A93 20c ultra 2.75 1.25
475 A93 50c brown org 16.00 12.00
476 A93 1b dp gray grn 5.50 2.10
477 A93 5b rose violet 12.00 8.00
Nos. 471-477 (7) 39.55 24.80

Issued: 5c, 10c, Sept. 8; others, Sept. 20.

Arms of Anzoategui and Globe

478 A93 5c green .25 .25
479 A93 10c red .25 .25
480 A93 15c brown 2.25 1.00
481 A93 20c ultra 3.75 .25
482 A93 40c red orange 7.75 3.75
483 A93 45c rose violet 22.50 1.25
484 A93 3b blue gray 8.75 4.25
Nos. 478-484 (7) 45.50 11.00

Issue date: Nov. 9.

Arms of Caracas and Buildings

485 A93 5c green 1.25 .25
486 A93 10c red 1.75 .25
487 A93 15c brown 4.25 1.00
488 A93 20c ultra 8.50 1.00
489 A93 25c orange brn 11.50 2.25
490 A93 30c blue 11.00 2.50
491 A93 35c purple 110.00 62.50
Nos. 485-491 (7) 148.25 69.75

Issued: 5c, 10c, June 20; others, Aug. 6.

Arms of Tachira and Agricultural Products

492 A93 5c green .25 .25
493 A93 10c red .95 .25
494 A93 15c brown 1.75 .60
495 A93 20c ultra 4.25 1.10
496 A93 50c brown org 260.00 3.25
497 A93 1b dp gray grn 4.25 1.50
498 A93 5b dull purple 10.50 6.00
Nos. 492-498 (7) 281.95 12.95

Issue date: Aug. 9.

Arms of Venezuela and Statue of Simon Bolivar

499 A93 5c green 1.00 .25
500 A93 10c red .85 .25
501 A93 15c brown 7.50 1.50
502 A93 20c ultra 7.50 1.00
503 A93 25c orange brn 12.50 2.75
504 A93 30c blue 12.50 2.75
505 A93 35c purple 65.00 50.00
Nos. 499-505 (7) 106.85 58.50

Issue date: Aug. 6.

Arms of Miranda and Agricultural Products

1952
506 A93 5c green .25 .25
507 A93 10c red .25 .25
508 A93 15c brown 1.75 .25
509 A93 20c ultra 1.90 .25
510 A93 25c orange brn 2.50 1.10
511 A93 30c blue 4.25 1.90
512 A93 35c purple 26.00 18.00
Nos. 506-512 (7) 36.90 22.00

Arms of Aragua and Stylized Farm

513 A93 5c green .25 .25
514 A93 10c red .25 .25
515 A93 15c brown 1.90 .25
516 A93 20c ultra 1.90 .25
517 A93 25c orange brn 4.25 1.10
518 A93 30c blue 4.25 1.90
519 A93 35c purple 22.50 17.50
Nos. 513-519 (7) 35.30 21.50

Issue date: 20c, 30c, Mar. 24.

Arms of Lara, Agricultural Products and Rope

520 A93 5c green .25 .25
521 A93 10c red .25 .25
522 A93 15c brown 1.00 .25
523 A93 20c ultra 2.40 .25
524 A93 25c orange brn 2.75 1.75
525 A93 30c blue 5.25 1.40
526 A93 35c purple 21.00 13.00
Nos. 520-526 (7) 32.90 17.15

Issue date: 20c, 30c, Mar. 24.

Arms of Bolivar and Stylized Design

527 A93 5c green .25 .25
528 A93 10c red .25 .25
529 A93 15c brown .95 .25
530 A93 20c ultra 2.10 .25
531 A93 40c red orange 8.00 2.75
532 A93 45c rose violet 20.00 14.00
533 A93 3b blue gray 9.50 6.25
Nos. 527-533 (7) 41.05 24.00

Issue date: 20c, Mar. 24.

Arms of Sucre, Palms and Seascape

534 A93 5c green .25 .25
535 A93 10c red .25 .25
536 A93 15c brown 2.40 .25
537 A93 20c ultra 2.40 .25
538 A93 40c red orange 8.00 2.10
539 A93 45c rose violet 27.50 17.50
540 A93 3b blue gray 7.00 4.75
Nos. 534-540 (7) 47.80 25.35

Arms of Trujillo Surrounded by Stylized Tree

541 A93 5c green .25 .25
542 A93 10c red .25 .25
543 A93 15c brown 2.50 .25

544 A93 20c ultra 2.50 .60
545 A93 50c brown orange 15.00 7.25
546 A93 1b dp gray green 3.50 1.25
547 A93 5b dull purple 9.00 4.50
Nos. 541-547 (7) 33.00 14.35

Map of Delta Amacuro and Ship

1953-54

548 A93 5c green .25 .25
549 A93 10c red .25 .25
550 A93 15c brown .90 .25
551 A93 20c ultra 1.50 .25
552 A93 40c red orange 4.75 3.00
553 A93 45c rose violet 22.50 13.50
554 A93 3b blue gray 6.00 4.50
Nos. 548-554 (7) 36.15 22.00

Arms of Falcon and Stylized Oil Refinery

555 A93 5c green .25 .25
556 A93 10c red .25 .25
557 A93 15c brown 1.40 .25
558 A93 20c ultra 1.40 .25
559 A93 50c brown orange 7.25 3.50
560 A93 1b dp gray grn 4.50 2.75
561 A93 5b dull purple 13.50 7.25
Nos. 555-561 (7) 28.55 14.50

Issue date: 20c, Feb. 13.

Arms of Guarico and Factory

562 A93 5c green .25 .25
563 A93 10c red .25 .25
564 A93 15c brown 1.10 .25
565 A93 20c ultra 1.25 .25
566 A93 40c red orange 6.50 4.00
567 A93 45c rose violet 16.00 7.75
568 A93 3b blue gray 6.50 3.50
Nos. 562-568 (7) 31.85 16.25

Issue date: 20c, Feb. 13.

Arms of Merida and Church

569 A93 5c green .25 .25
570 A93 10c red .25 .25
571 A93 15c brown .85 .25
572 A93 20c ultra 2.10 .25
573 A93 50c brown orange 9.00 4.00
574 A93 1b dp gray green 2.50 1.75
575 A93 5b dull purple 9.00 5.25
Nos. 569-575 (7) 23.95 12.00

Issue date: 20c, Feb. 2.

Arms of Monagas and Horses

576 A93 5c green .25 .25
577 A93 10c red .25 .25
578 A93 15c brown 1.10 .25
579 A93 20c ultra 1.60 .90
580 A93 40c red orange 7.50 2.75
581 A93 45c rose violet 22.50 13.50
582 A93 3b blue gray 9.25 7.50
Nos. 576-582 (7) 42.45 25.40

Arms of Portuguesa and Forest

583 A93 5c green .25 .25
584 A93 10c red .25 .25
585 A93 15c brown .65 .25
586 A93 20c ultra 1.40 .25
587 A93 50c brown org 7.25 4.75
588 A93 1b dp gray grn 1.90 .80
589 A93 5b dull purple 8.00 5.25
Nos. 583-589 (7) 19.70 11.80

Issue date: 5c, 10c, Feb. 2.

Map of Amazonas and Orchid

590 A93 5c green 1.40 .25
591 A93 10c red 1.40 .25
592 A93 15c brown 3.00 .25
593 A93 20c ultra 8.50 .85
594 A93 40c red orange 10.00 3.00
595 A93 45c rose violet 16.00 7.75
596 A93 3b blue gray 24.00 8.50
Nos. 590-596 (7) 64.30 20.85

Issue date: Jan. 1954.

Arms of Apure, Horse and Bird

597 A93 5c green .25 .25
598 A93 10c red .25 .25
599 A93 15c brown 1.60 .25
600 A93 20c ultra 8.50 .25
601 A93 50c brown org 11.00 8.50
602 A93 1b dp gray grn 3.50 3.00
603 A93 5b dull purple 21.00 12.00
Nos. 597-603 (7) 46.10 24.50

Issue date: Jan. 1954.

Arms of Barinas, Cow and Horse

604 A93 5c green .25 .25
605 A93 10c red .25 .25
606 A93 15c brown .55 .25
607 A93 20c ultra 3.75 .55
608 A93 50c brown org 4.50 2.75
609 A93 1b dp gray grn 1.10 .55
610 A93 5b dull purple 10.00 5.00
Nos. 604-610 (7) 20.40 9.60

Issue date: Jan. 1954.

Arms of Cojedes and Cattle

611 A93 5c green .25 .25
612 A93 10c red .25 .25
613 A93 15c brown .25 .25
614 A93 20c ultra .25 .25
615 A93 25c orange brown 4.00 1.10
616 A93 30c blue 6.25 1.75
617 A93 35c purple 7.75 6.25
Nos. 611-617 (7) 19.00 10.10

Issue date: Dec, 17, 1953.

Arms of Nueva Esparta and Fish

618 A93 5c green .25 .25
619 A93 10c red .25 .25
620 A93 15c brown 1.40 .25
621 A93 20c ultra 1.60 .25
622 A93 40c red orange 7.25 2.75
623 A93 45c rose vio 17.50 10.00
624 A93 3b blue gray 8.00 5.50
Nos. 618-624 (7) 36.25 19.25

Issue date: Jan. 1954.

Arms of Yaracuy and Tropical Foliage

625 A93 5c green 1.50 .25
626 A93 10c red .25 .25
627 A93 15c brown 1.10 .25
628 A93 20c ultra 1.75 .25
629 A93 25c orange brn 2.50 1.10
630 A93 30c blue 2.75 .95
631 A93 35c purple 6.50 4.25
Nos. 625-631 (7) 16.35 7.30
Nos. 464-631 (168) 1,264. 514.15

Issue date: Jan. 1954.
See Nos. C338-C553.

Ship Type of 1948-50, Redrawn
Coil Stamps
Imprint: "Courvoisier S.A."

1952 Unwmk. Photo. *Perf. 11½x12*

632 A85 5c green 1.50 .25
633 A85 10c car rose 2.50 .25
634 A85 15c gray 9.00 .25
Nos. 632-634,C554-C556 (6) 22.50 1.50

Juan de Villegas and Cross of Father Yepez — A94

1952, Sept. 14 *Perf. 11½*

635 A94 5c green .25 .25
636 A94 10c red 1.25 .25
637 A94 20c dk gray bl 1.90 .60
638 A94 40c dp org 9.00 3.50
639 A94 50c brown 4.75 2.00
640 A94 1b violet 9.00 2.40
Nos. 635-640 (6) 26.15 9.00
Nos. 635-640,C557-C564 (14) 38.05 14.15

Founding of the city of Barquisimeto by Juan de Villegas, 400th anniv.

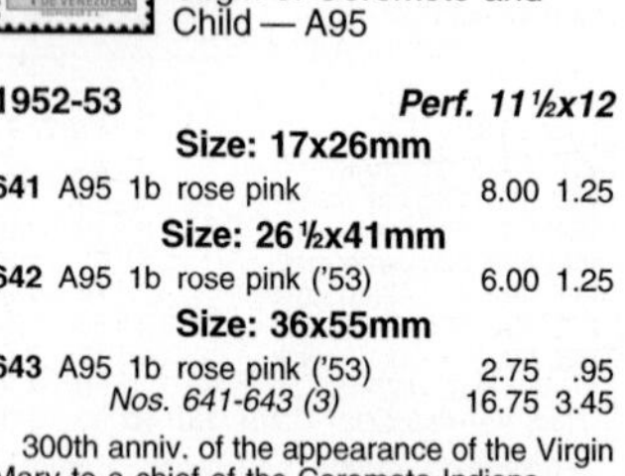

Virgin of Coromoto and Child — A95

1952-53 *Perf. 11½x12*

Size: 17x26mm

641 A95 1b rose pink 8.00 1.25

Size: 26½x41mm

642 A95 1b rose pink ('53) 6.00 1.25

Size: 36x55mm

643 A95 1b rose pink ('53) 2.75 .95
Nos. 641-643 (3) 16.75 3.45

300th anniv. of the appearance of the Virgin Mary to a chief of the Coromoto Indians.
Issue date: No. 641, Oct. 6.

Telegraph Stamps Surcharged in Black or Red

1952, Nov. 24 Engr. *Perf. 12*

Grayish Security Paper

644 5c on 25c car .35 .25
645 10c on 1b blk (R) .35 .25

Surcharged

1952, Dec.

646 20c on 25c car .35 .25
647 30c on 2b ol grn 2.10 1.40
648 40c on 1b blk (R) .85 .45
649 50c on 3b red org 2.75 1.60
Nos. 646-649 (4) 6.05 3.70

Post Office, Caracas — A96

Perf. 13x12½

1953-54 Unwmk. Photo.

650 A96 5c green .25 .25
a. Bklt. pane of 10
651 A96 7½c brt green .35 .25
652 A96 10c rose carmine .25 .25
a. Bklt. pane of 10
653 A96 15c gray .40 .25
654 A96 20c ultra .25 .25
655 A96 25c magenta .40 .25
656 A96 30c blue 1.90 .25
657 A96 35c brt red vio .85 .25
658 A96 40c orange 1.25 .40
659 A96 45c violet 1.90 .65
660 A96 50c red orange 1.25 .40
Nos. 650-660 (11) 9.05 3.45

Issued: 20c, 30c, 45c, 3/11; 7½c, 25c, 50c, 6/53; 5c, 10c, 2/54; 15c, 1954.
See Nos. C565-C575, C587-C589.

A96a

Type of 1953-54 Inscribed "Republica de Venezuela"

1955

661 A96a 5c green .25 .25
662 A96a 10c rose car .25 .25
663 A96a 15c gray .25 .25
664 A96a 20c ultra .25 .25
665 A96a 30c blue .65 .40
666 A96a 35c brt red vio .65 .25
667 A96a 40c orange 1.00 .25
668 A96a 45c violet 1.25 .50
Nos. 661-668 (8) 4.55 2.40
Nos. 661-668,C597-C606 (18) 10.80 7.05

Arms of Valencia and Industrial Scene — A97

1955, Mar. 26 Engr. *Perf. 12*

669 A97 5c brt grn .25 .25
670 A97 20c ultra .40 .25
671 A97 25c reddish brn .65 .25
672 A97 50c vermilion 1.00 .25
Nos. 669-672,C590-C596 (11) 4.50 2.75

Founding of Valencia del Rey, 400th anniv.

Coat of Arms — A98

1955, Dec. 9 Unwmk. *Perf. 11½*

673 A98 5c green 1.10 .25
674 A98 20c ultra 3.75 .25
675 A98 25c rose car 3.00 .25
676 A98 50c orange 3.75 .25
Nos. 673-676,C607-C612 (10) 18.65 3.50

1st Postal Convention, Caracas, 2/9-15/54.

Book and Map of the Americas — A99

1956 Photo. *Perf. 11½*

Granite Paper

677 A99 5c lt grn & bluish grn .25 .25
678 A99 10c lil rose & rose vio .25 .25
679 A99 20c ultra & dk bl .25 .25
680 A99 25c gray & lil gray .55 .25
681 A99 30c lt bl & bl .55 .25
682 A99 40c bis brn & brn .65 .25
683 A99 50c ver & red brn 1.40 .65
684 A99 1b lt pur & vio 2.25 1.10
Nos. 677-684 (8) 6.15 3.25
Nos. 677-684,C629-C635 (15) 10.85 5.55

Book Festival of the Americas, 11/15-30/56.

Simon Bolivar — A100

Engraved, Center Embossed

1957-58 Unwmk. *Perf. 13½*

685 A100 5c brt bl grn .25 .25
686 A100 10c red .25 .25
687 A100 20c lt slate bl .40 .25
688 A100 25c rose lake .40 .25
689 A100 30c vio blue .50 .25
690 A100 40c red orange .75 .25
691 A100 50c orange yel 1.10 .55
Nos. 685-691 (7) 3.65 2.05
Nos. 685-691,C636-C642 (14) 7.45 4.00

150th anniv. of the Oath of Monte Sacro and the 125th anniv. of the death of Simon Bolivar (1783-1830).
Issued: 10c, 50c, 1958; others, 11/15/57.

Hotel Tamanaco, Caracas — A101

1957-58 Engr. *Perf. 13*

692 A101 5c green .25 .25
693 A101 10c carmine .25 .25
694 A101 15c black .25 .25
695 A101 20c dark blue .30 .25
696 A101 25c dp claret .30 .25
697 A101 30c dp ultra .50 .25
698 A101 35c purple .30 .25
699 A101 40c orange .40 .25
700 A101 45c rose violet .50 .25
701 A101 50c yellow .70 .25
702 A101 1b dk slate grn 1.10 .45
Nos. 692-702 (11) 4.85 2.95
Nos. 692-702,C643-C657 (26) 14.35 8.60

Issued: 5c, 10c, Oct. 10, 1957; others, 1958.
For surcharge see No. 878.

Main Post Office, Caracas — A102

1958, May 14 Litho. *Perf. 14*

703 A102 5c emerald .25 .25
704 A102 10c rose red .25 .25
705 A102 15c gray .25 .25
706 A102 20c lt bl .25 .25
707 A102 35c red lilac .25 .25
708 A102 45c brt vio 1.25 .85
709 A102 50c yellow .30 .25
710 A102 1b lt ol grn .75 .40
Nos. 703-710 (8) 3.55 2.75
Nos. 703-710,C658-C670 (21) 15.15 11.75

See Nos. 748-750, C658-C670, C786-C792.
For surcharges see Nos. 865, C807, C856-C861.

Main Post Office, Caracas — A103

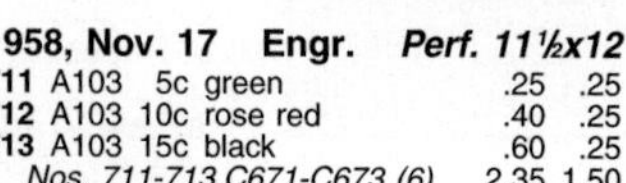

1958, Nov. 17 Engr. *Perf. 11½x12*

711 A103 5c green .25 .25
712 A103 10c rose red .40 .25
713 A103 15c black .60 .25
Nos. 711-713,C671-C673 (6) 2.35 1.50

Arms of Merida — A104

1958, Oct. 9 Photo. *Perf. 14x13½*

714 A104 5c green .25 .25
715 A104 10c bright red .25 .25
716 A104 15c greenish gray .25 .25

717 A104 20c blue .25 .25
718 A104 25c magenta .45 .25
719 A104 30c violet .25 .25
720 A104 35c light purple .30 .25
721 A104 40c orange .65 .25
722 A104 45c deep rose lilac .35 .25
723 A104 50c bright yellow .55 .25
724 A104 1b gray green 1.60 .55
Nos. 714-724 (11) 5.15 3.05
Nos. 714-724,C674-C689 (27) 14.00 9.90

400th anniversary of the founding of the city of Merida. For surcharge see No. 873.

Arms of Trujillo, Bolivar Monument and Trujillo Hotel — A105

1959, Nov. 17 Unwmk. *Perf. 14*

725 A105 5c emerald .25 .25
726 A105 10c rose .25 .25
727 A105 15c gray .25 .25
728 A105 20c blue .25 .25
729 A105 25c brt pink .35 .25
730 A105 30c lt ultra .50 .25
731 A105 35c lt pur .50 .25
732 A105 45c rose lilac .65 .35
733 A105 50c yellow .65 .25
734 A105 1b lt ol grn 1.60 .85
Nos. 725-734 (10) 5.25 3.20
Nos. 725-734,C690-C700 (21) 10.80 7.45

Founding of the city of Trujillo, 400th anniv.

Stadium — A106

1959 Mar. 10 Litho. *Perf. 13½*

735 A106 5c brt grn .35 .25
736 A106 10c rose pink .35 .25
737 A106 20c blue .60 .25
738 A106 30c dk bl .70 .25
739 A106 50c red lilac 1.10 .25
Nos. 735-739 (5) 3.10 1.25
Nos. 735-739,C701-C705 (10) 5.50 3.00

8th Central American and Caribbean Games, Caracas, Nov. 29-Dec. 14, 1958.
#735-739 exist imperf. Value, pair $25.

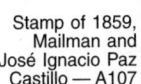

Stamp of 1859, Mailman and José Ignacio Paz Castillo — A107

Stamp of 1859 and: 50c, Mailman on horseback and Jacinto Gutierrez. 1b, Plane, train and Miguel Herrera.

1959, Sept. 15 Engr. *Perf. 13½x14*

740 A107 25c org yel .50 .25
741 A107 50c blue .50 .25
742 A107 1b rose red 1.25 .45
Nos. 740-742,C706-C708 (6) 3.90 1.90

Centenary of Venezuelan postage stamps.

Catalogue values for unused stamps in this section, from this point to the end of the section, are for Never Hinged items.

Alexander von Humboldt — A108

1960, Feb. 9 Unwmk. *Perf. 13½*

743 A108 5c grn & yel grn .55 .25
744 A108 30c vio bl & vio 1.60 .35
745 A108 40c org & brn org 2.10 .55
Nos. 743-745,C709-C711 (6) 8.95 2.15

Centenary of the death of Alexander von Humboldt, German naturalist and geographer.

Post Office Type of 1958

1960, July Litho. *Perf. 14*

748 A102 25c yellow .45 .35
749 A102 30c light blue .45 .35
750 A102 40c fawn .95 .35
Nos. 748-750 (3) 1.85 1.05

Newspaper, 1808, and View of Caracas, 1958 — A109

1960, June 6 Litho. *Perf. 14*

751 A109 10c rose & blk .65 .25
752 A109 20c lt blue & blk 1.10 .25
753 A109 35c lilac & blk 1.60 1.00
Nos. 751-753,C712-C714 (6) 10.60 3.75

150th anniv. (in 1958) of the 1st Venezuelan newspaper, Gazeta de Caracas.

Agustin Codazzi — A110

1960, June 15 Engr. Unwmk.

754 A110 5c brt green .30 .25
755 A110 15c gray 1.40 .25
756 A110 20c blue 1.10 .25
757 A110 45c purple 1.40 .50
Nos. 754-757,C715-C720 (10) 13.80 3.70

Centenary (in 1959) of the death of Agustin Codazzi, geographer.
For surcharges see Nos. 869, C884.

National Pantheon — A111

Pantheon in Bister

1960, May 9 Litho.

758 A111 5c emerald .30 .25
759 A111 20c brt blue .65 .25
760 A111 25c light olive 1.20 .25
761 A111 30c dull blue 1.40 .30
762 A111 40c fawn 2.00 .55
763 A111 45c lilac 1.90 .55
Nos. 758-763 (6) 7.45 2.15
Nos. 758-763,C721-C734 (20) 30.85 9.65

For surcharges see Nos. C894-C895.

Andres Eloy Blanco, Poet (1896-1955) — A112

1960, May 21 Unwmk. *Perf. 14*

Portrait in Black

764 A112 5c emerald .35 .25
765 A112 30c dull blue .50 .25
766 A112 50c yellow 1.10 .30
Nos. 764-766,C735-C737 (6) 6.85 1.85

For surcharge see No. C874.

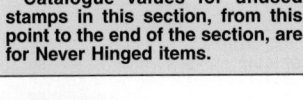

Independence Meeting of April 19, 1810, Led by Miranda — A113

1960, Aug. 19 Litho. *Perf. 13½*

Center Multicolored

767 A113 5c brt green .75 .25
768 A113 20c blue 1.60 .35
769 A113 30c violet blue 2.00 .45
Nos. 767-769,C738-C740 (6) 9.60 2.85

150th anniversary of Venezuela's Independence.
See Nos. 812-814, C804-C806. For surcharge see No. C893.

Drilling for Oil — A114

1960, Aug. 26 Engr. *Perf. 14*

770 A114 5c grn & slate grn 3.25 .95
771 A114 10c dk car & brn .35 .35
772 A114 15c gray & dull pur 1.50 .45
Nos. 770-772,C741-C743 (6) 10.60 3.20

Issued to publicize Venezuela's oil industry.

Luisa Cáceres de Arismendi — A115

Unwmk.

1960, Oct. 21 Litho. *Perf. 14*

Center Multicolored

773 A115 20c light blue 1.60 .40
774 A115 25c citron 1.10 .40
775 A115 30c dull blue 1.60 .55
Nos. 773-775,C744-C746 (6) 11.20 3.20

Death of Luisa Càceres de Arismendi, 94th anniv.

José Antonio Anzoategui — A116

1960, Oct. 29 Engr.

776 A116 5c emerald & gray ol .45 .25
777 A116 15c ol gray & dl vio .65 .25
778 A116 20c blue & gray vio .95 .25
Nos. 776-778,C747-C749 (6) 6.40 1.80

140th anniversary (in 1959) of the death of General José Antonio Anzoategui.

Antonio José de Sucre — A117

Unwmk.

1960, Nov. 18 Litho. *Perf. 14*

Center Multicolored

779 A117 10c deep rose .55 .25
780 A117 15c gray brown .60 .25
781 A117 20c blue 1.00 .40
Nos. 779-781,C750-C752 (6) 7.40 2.60

130th anniversary of the death of General Antonio José de Sucre.

Bolivar Peak, Merida — A118

Designs: 15c, Caroni Falls, Bolivar. 35c, Guacharo caves, Monagas.

1960, Mar. 22 *Perf. 14*

782 A118 5c emerald & grn 1.10 1.00
783 A118 15c gray & dk gray 3.50 3.25
784 A118 35c rose lil & lil 3.00 2.75
Nos. 782-784,C753-C755 (6) 16.60 15.25

Buildings and People — A119

1961 Litho. Unwmk.

Building in Orange

785 A119 5c emerald .30 .25
786 A119 10c carmine .30 .25
787 A119 15c gray .30 .25
788 A119 20c blue .30 .25
789 A119 25c lt red brown .30 .25
790 A119 30c dull blue .30 .25
791 A119 35c red lilac .75 .25
792 A119 40c fawn 1.10 .25
793 A119 45c brt violet 1.40 .30
794 A119 50c yellow 1.10 .25
Nos. 785-794 (10) 6.15 2.55

1960 national census. See #C756-C770. For surcharge see No. 866.

Rafael Maria Baralt — A120

1961, Mar. 11 Engr. *Perf. 14*

795 A120 5c grn & slate grn .30 .25
796 A120 15c gray & dull red brn .65 .25
797 A120 35c red lilac & lt vio 1.00 .25
Nos. 795-797,C771-C773 (6) 5.85 2.15

Rafael Maria Baralt, statesman, death cent. See Nos. C771-C773.

Yellow-headed Parrot — A121

1961, Sept. 6 Litho. *Perf. 14½*

798 A121 30c shown 1.40 .50
799 A121 40c Snowy egret 2.10 .50
800 A121 50c Scarlet ibis 3.50 .90
Nos. 798-800,C776-C778 (6) 10.90 4.25

Juan J. Aguerrevere A122

1961, Oct. 21 Unwmk. *Perf. 14*

801 A122 25c dark blue .60 .25
a. Souvenir sheet, imperf. 2.75 2.50

Centenary of the founding of the Engineering Society of Venezuela, Oct. 28, 1861.
No. 801a sold for 1b.
No. 801a exists with "Valor: Bs 1,00" omitted at lower left corner. Value, $7.

Battle of Carabobo, 1821 A123

1961, Dec. 1 *Perf. 14*

Center Multicolored

802 A123 5c emerald & blk .30 .25
803 A123 40c brown & blk .75 .25
Nos. 802-803,C779-C784 (8) 16.75 5.00

140th anniversary of Battle of Carabobo.

Oncidium Papilio Lindl. — A124

Orchids: 10c, Caularthron bilamellatum. 20c, Stanhopea Wardii Lodd. 25c, Catasetum pileatum. 30c, Masdevallia tovarensis. 35c, Epidendrum Stamfordianum Batem, horiz. 50c, Epidendrum atropurpureum Willd. 3b, Oncidium falcipetalum Lindl.

Perf. 14x13½, 13½x14

1962, May 30 Litho. Unwmk.

Orchids in Natural Colors

804 A124 5c black & orange .30 .25
805 A124 10c blk & brt grnsh bl .30 .25
806 A124 20c black & yel grn .65 .25
807 A124 25c black & lt blue .90 .25
808 A124 30c black & olive 1.00 .25
809 A124 35c black & yellow 1.10 .30
810 A124 50c black & gray 1.20 .35
811 A124 3b black & vio 7.50 2.75
Nos. 804-811 (8) 12.95 4.65
Nos. 804-811,C794-C803 (18) 33.60 13.90

For surcharges see Nos. 872, C885-C887.

Independence Type of 1960

Signing Declaration of Independence.

1962, June 11 *Perf. 13½*

Center Multicolored

812 A113 5c emerald .30 .25
813 A113 20c blue .65 .25
814 A113 25c yellow .95 .30
a. Souv. sheet, #812-814, imperf 3.75 3.25
Nos. 812-814,C804-C806 (6) 7.55 2.70

150th anniv. of the Venezuelan Declaration of Independence, July 5, 1811.

No. 814a sold for 1.50b.

Shot Put — A125

1962, Nov. 30 Litho. *Perf. 13x14*

815 A125 5c shown .40 .25
816 A125 10c Soccer .40 .25
817 A125 25c Swimming .55 .25
a. Souv. sheet, #815-817, imperf 4.00 3.50
Nos. 815-817,C808-C810 (6) 5.55 2.40

1st Natl. Games, Caracas, 1961. The stamps are arranged so that two pale colored edges of each stamp join to make a border around blocks of four.

No. 817a sold for 1.40b.

For surcharge see No. C899.

Vermilion Cardinal — A126

Birds: 10c, Great kiskadee. 20c, Glossy black thrush. 25c, Collared trogons. 30c, Swallow tanager. 40c, Long-tailed sylph. 3b, Black-necked stilt.

1962, Dec. 14 *Perf. 14x13½*

Birds in Natural Colors, Black Inscription

818 A126 5c brt yellow grn .30 .25
819 A126 10c violet blue .30 .25
820 A126 20c lilac rose .60 .25
821 A126 25c dull brown .70 .25
822 A126 30c lemon .90 .25
823 A126 40c lilac 1.10 .30
824 A126 3b fawn 8.00 3.00
Nos. 818-824 (7) 11.90 4.55
Nos. 818-824,C811-C818 (15) 29.60 14.35

For surcharges see Nos. 868, C880-C882.

Malaria Eradication Emblem, Mosquito and Map — A127

Lithographed and Embossed

Perf. 13½x14

1962, Dec. 20 Wmk. 346

825 A127 50c brown & black 1.00 .30

WHO drive to eradicate malaria. See Nos. C819-C819a.

White-tailed Deer — A128

Designs: 10c, Collared peccary. 35c, Collared titi (monkey). 50c, Giant Brazilian otter. 1b, Puma. 3b, Capybara.

Perf. 13½x14

1963, Mar. 13 Litho. Unwmk.

Multicolored Center; Black Inscriptions

826 A128 5c green .30 .25
827 A128 10c orange .30 .25
828 A128 35c red lilac .30 .25
829 A128 50c blue .65 .25
830 A128 1b rose brown 3.25 1.40
831 A128 3b yellow 7.50 3.50
Nos. 826-831 (6) 12.30 5.90
Nos. 826-831,C820-C825 (12) 26.60 12.50

For surcharges see #870-871, C888-C889.

Fisherman and Map of Venezuela — A129

1963, Mar. 21

832 A129 25c sal & dp ultra .30 .25
Nos. 832,C826-C827 (3) 2.55 1.30

FAO "Freedom from Hunger" campaign.

Cathedral of Bocono — A130

1963, May 30 Wmk. 346

833 A130 50c brn, red & turq grn, *buff* .90 .25

400th anniversary of the founding of Bocono. See No. C828.

St. Peter's Basilica, Rome — A131

1963, June 11 *Perf. 14x13½*

834 A131 35c dk bl, brn & buff .60 .25
835 A131 45c dk grn, red brn & buff .65 .25
Nos. 834-835,C829-C830 (4) 4.45 1.35

Vatican II, the 21st Ecumenical Council of the Roman Catholic Church.

National Flag — A132

1963, July 29 Unwmk. *Perf. 14*

836 A132 30c gray, red, yel & bl 1.25 .25

Centenary of Venezuela's flag and coat of arms. See No. C831.

Lake Maracaibo Bridge — A133

Perf. 13½x14

1963, Aug. 24 Wmk. 346

837 A133 30c blue & brown .55 .25
838 A133 35c bluish grn & brn .60 .25
839 A133 80c blue grn & brn 1.40 .45
Nos. 837-839,C832-C834 (6) 7.65 2.55

Opening of bridge over Lake Maracaibo. For surcharge see No. 875.

Map, Soldier and Emblem — A134

1963, Sept. 10 Unwmk.

840 A134 50c red, bl & grn, *buff* .90 .25

25th anniversary of the armed forces. See No. C835. For surcharge see No. C862.

Dag Hammarskjold and World Map — A135

Perf. 14x13½

1963, Sept. 25 Unwmk.

841 A135 25c dk bl, bl grn & ocher .35 .25
842 A135 55c grn, grnsh bl & ocher 1.40 .40
Nos. 841-842,C836-C837 (4) 5.35 1.85

"1st" anniv. of the death of Dag Hammarskjold, Secretary General of the UN, 1953-61.

See #C837a. For surcharges see #867, C875-C876.

Dr. Luis Razetti — A136

1963, Oct. 10 Litho.

843 A136 35c blue, ocher & brn .75 .25
844 A136 45c mag, ocher & brn 1.20 .25
Nos. 843-844,C838-C839 (4) 5.55 2.40

Dr. Luis Razetti, physician, birth cent.

Dr. Francisco A. Risquez — A137

Design: 20c, Dr. Carlos J. Bello.

1963, Dec. 31 *Perf. 11½x12*

845 A137 15c multicolored .65 .25
846 A137 20c multicolored .95 .25
Nos. 845-846,C840-C841 (4) 3.60 1.50

Cent. of the Intl. Red Cross.

Oil Field Workers — A138

10c, Oil refinery. 15c Crane & building construction. 30c, Cactus, train & truck. 40c, Tractor.

1964, Feb. 5 Litho. *Perf. 14x13½*

847 A138 5c multi .30 .25
848 A138 10c multi .30 .25
849 A138 15c multi .50 .25
850 A138 30c multi .85 .25
851 A138 40c multi .90 .25
Nos. 847-851 (5) 2.85 1.25
Nos. 847-851,C842-C846 (10) 4.85 2.65

Department of Industrial Development, cent.

Pedro Gual — A139

1964, Mar. 20 Unwmk. *Perf. 14*

852 A139 40c lt olive green .75 .25
853 A139 50c lt red brown 1.00 .30
Nos. 852-853,C847-C848 (4) 4.50 1.40

Pedro Gual (1784-1862), statesman.

Carlos Arvelo — A140

1964, Apr. 17 Engr. *Perf. 14x13½*

854 A140 1b dull bl & gray 1.75 .55

Centenary of the death of Dr. Carlos Arvelo (1784-1862), chief physician of Bolivar's revolutionary army, director of Caracas Hospital, rector of Central University and professor of pathology.

For surcharge see No. 874.

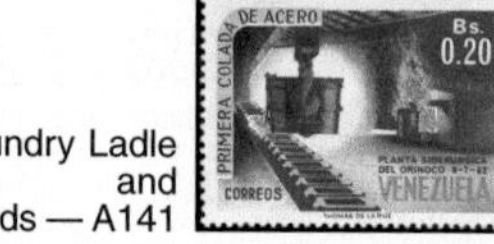

Foundry Ladle and Molds — A141

1964, May 22 *Perf. 14x13½*

855 A141 20c multicolored .50 .25
856 A141 50c multicolored .95 .25
Nos. 855-856,C849-C850 (4) 5.20 1.60

Orinoco Steel Mills.

Romulo Gallegos, Novelist, 80th Birthday — A142

Unwmk.

1964, Aug. 3 Litho. *Perf. 12*

857 A142 5c dk & lt green .30 .25
858 A142 10c bl & pale bl .30 .25
859 A142 15c dk & lt red lil .60 .25
Nos. 857-859,C852-C854 (6) 4.45 1.65

Angel Falls, Bolivar State — A143

Tourist Publicity: 10c, Tropical landscape, Sucre State. 15c, San Juan Peaks, Guarico. 30c, Net fishermen, Anzoategui. 40c, Mountaineer, Merida.

1964, Oct. 22 *Perf. 13½x14*

860 A143 5c multi .30 .25
861 A143 10c multi .30 .25
862 A143 15c multi .30 .25
863 A143 30c multi .85 .25
864 A143 40c multi 1.50 .25
Nos. 860-864 (5) 3.25 1.25

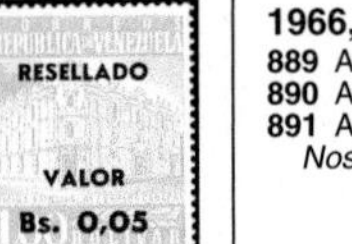

Issues of 1958-64 Surcharged in Black, Dark Blue or Lilac

1965

No.	Type	Description	Unused	Used
865	A102	5c on 1b (#710)	.90	.25
866	A119	10c on 45c (#793)	.30	.25
867	A135	15c on 55c (#842)	.30	.25
868	A126	20c on 3b (#824)	.30	.25
869	A110	25c on 45c (#757) (DB)	.30	.25
870	A128	25c on 1b (#830)	.65	.25
871	A128	25c on 3b (#831)	.70	.25
872	A124	25c on 3b (#811) (L)	.35	.25
873	A104	30c on 1b (#724)	.65	.25
874	A140	40c on 1b (#854)	1.50	.25
875	A133	60c on 80c (#839)	2.00	.40
		Nos. 865-875 (11)	7.95	2.90

Lines of surcharge arranged variously; old denomination obliterated with bars on Nos. 867, 870-872. See Nos. C856-C899.

Revenue Stamps of 1947 Surcharged in Red or Black

Imprint: "American Bank Note Co."; No. 882: (Imprint: "Bundesdruckerei Berlin")

1965 Engr. *Perf. 12, 13½ (No. 882)*

No.	Type	Description	Unused	Used
876	R1	5c on 5c emerald	.45	.25
877	R1	5c on 20c red brn	.45	.25
878	R1	10c on 10c brn ol	.45	.25
879	R1	15c on 40c grn	.45	.25
880	R1	20c on 3b dk bl (R)	.75	.25
881	R1	25c on 5b vio bl (R)	1.40	.35
882	R1	25c on 5b vio bl (R)	.75	.25
883	R1	60c on 3b dk bl (R)	1.75	.35
		Nos. 876-883 (8)	6.45	2.20

Type R1 is illustrated above No. 401.

John F. Kennedy and Alliance for Progress Emblem — A144

1965, Aug. 20 Photo. *Perf. 12x11½*

No.	Type	Description	Unused	Used
884	A144	20c gray	.65	.25
885	A144	40c bright lilac	1.00	.25
		Nos. 884-885,C900-C901 (4)	4.65	1.40

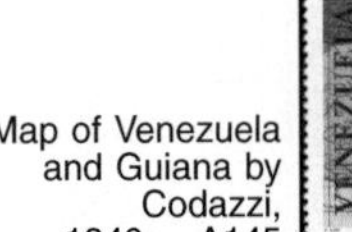

Map of Venezuela and Guiana by Codazzi, 1840 — A145

Maps of Venezuela and Guiana: 15c, by Juan M. Restrepo, 1827, horiz. 40c, by L. de Surville, 1778.

1965, Nov. 5 Litho. *Perf. 13½*

No.	Type	Description	Unused	Used
886	A145	5c multi	.30	.25
887	A145	15c multi	.60	.25
888	A145	40c multi	1.00	.25
a.		Souv. sheet, #886-888, imperf	6.50	8.00
		Nos. 886-888,C905-C907 (6)	5.05	1.65

Issued to publicize Venezuela's claim to part of British Guiana.

No. 888a sold for 85c.

Protesilaus Leucones — A146

Various Butterflies in Natural Colors Black Inscriptions

1966, Jan. 25 Litho. *Perf. 13½x14*

No.	Type	Description	Unused	Used
889	A146	20c lt olive grn	1.40	.25
890	A146	30c lt yellow grn	2.75	.25
891	A146	50c yellow	4.00	.30
		Nos. 889-891,C915-C917 (6)	16.05	2.30

Ship and Map of Atlantic Ocean — A147

1966, Mar. 10 Litho. *Perf. 13½x14*

No.	Type	Description	Unused	Used
892	A147	60c brown, bl & blk	2.50	.70

Bicentenary of the first maritime mail.

"El Carite" Dance A148

Various Folk Dances

Perf. 14x13½

1966, Apr. 5 Litho. Unwmk.

No.	Type	Description	Unused	Used
893	A148	5c gray & multi	.30	.25
894	A148	10c orange & multi	.30	.25
895	A148	15c lemon & multi	.50	.25
896	A148	20c lilac & multi	.60	.25
897	A148	25c brt pink & multi	.75	.35
898	A148	35c yel grn & multi	1.00	.40
		Nos. 893-898,C919-C924 (12)	14.10	4.70

Type of Air Post Stamps and

Arturo Michelena, Self-portrait A149

Paintings: 1b, Penthesileia, battle scene. 1.05b, The Red Cloak.

Perf. 12½x12, 12x12½

1966, May 12 Litho. Unwmk.

No.	Type	Description	Unused	Used
899	A149	95c sepia & buff	1.10	.65
900	AP74	1b multi	1.30	.65
901	AP74	1.05b multi	1.75	.65
		Nos. 899-901,C927-C929 (6)	8.60	4.20

Arturo Michelena (1863-1898), painter. Miniature sheets of 12 exist.

Construction Worker and Map of Americas — A150

Designs: 20c, as 10c. 30c, 65c, Labor monument. 35c, Machinery worker and map of Venezuela. 50c, Automobile assembly line.

1966, July 6 Litho. *Perf. 14x13½*

No.	Type	Description	Unused	Used
902	A150	10c yellow & blk	.35	.25
903	A150	20c lt grnsh bl & blk	.45	.25
904	A150	30c lt blue & vio	.45	.25
905	A150	35c lemon & olive	.65	.25
906	A150	50c brt rose & claret	1.00	.30
907	A150	65c salmon pink & brn	1.20	.35
		Nos. 902-907 (6)	4.10	1.65

2nd Conference of Ministers of Labor of the Organization of American States.

Velvet Cichlid — A151

Designs: 25c, Perch cichlid. 45c, Piranha.

1966, Aug. 31 Litho. *Perf. 13½x14*

No.	Type	Description	Unused	Used
908	A151	15c multicolored	.35	.25
909	A151	25c multicolored	.50	.25
910	A151	45c multicolored	1.25	.35
		Nos. 908-910,C933-C935 (6)	8.10	2.35

Nativity — A152

1966, Dec. 9 Litho. *Perf. 13½x14*

No.	Type	Description	Unused	Used
911	A152	65c violet & blk	1.25	.40

Christmas 1966.

Satellite, Radar, Globe, Plane and Ship — A153

1966, Dec. 28 *Perf. 13½x14*

No.	Type	Description	Unused	Used
912	A153	45c multi	1.00	.30

Ministry of Communications, 30th anniv.

Rubén Dario — A154

1967 Litho.

No.	Type	Description	Unused	Used
913	A154	70c gray bl & dk bl	1.50	.65

Rubén Dario (pen name of Felix Rubén García Sarmiento, 1867-1916), Nicaraguan poet, newspaper correspondent and diplomat.

Old Building and Arms, University of Zulia — A155

Perf. 13½x14

1967, Apr. 21 Litho. Unwmk.

No.	Type	Description	Unused	Used
914	A155	80c gold, blk & car	1.50	.65

University of Zulia founding, 75th anniv.

Front Page and Printing Press — A156

1968, June 27 Photo. *Perf. 14x13½*

No.	Type	Description	Unused	Used
915	A156	1.50b emer, blk & brn	2.00	.80

Newspaper Correo del Orinoco, 150th anniv.

Boll Weevil A157

Insect Pests: 20c, Corn borer, vert. 90c, Tobacco caterpillar.

Perf. 14x13½, 13½x14

1968, Aug. 30 Litho.

No.	Type	Description	Unused	Used
916	A157	20c multicolored	.60	.25
917	A157	75c olive & multi	1.75	.25
918	A157	90c multicolored	2.60	.35
		Nos. 916-918,C989-C991 (6)	8.60	1.60

Guayana Substation — A158

Designs: 45c, Guaira River Dam, horiz. 50c, Macagua Dam and power plant, horiz. 80c, Guri River Dam and power plant.

1968, Nov. 8 Litho.

No.	Type	Description	Unused	Used
919	A158	15c fawn & multi	.30	.25
920	A158	45c dl yel & multi	.90	.25
921	A158	50c bl grn & multi	1.20	.35
922	A158	80c blue & multi	1.90	.75
		Nos. 919-922 (4)	4.30	1.60

Electrification program.

House and Piggy Bank — A159

1968, Dec. 6 Litho. *Perf. 13½x14*

No.	Type	Description	Unused	Used
923	A159	45c blue & multi	1.00	.35

National Savings System.

Nursery and Child Planting Tree — A160

Designs: 15c, Child planting tree (vert.; this design used as emblem on entire issue). 30c, Waterfall, vert. 45c, Logging. 55c, Fields and village, vert. 75c, Palambra (fish).

Perf. 14x13½, 13½x14

1968, Dec. 19 Litho.

No.	Type	Description	Unused	Used
924	A160	15c multicolored	.50	.25
925	A160	20c multicolored	.50	.25
926	A160	30c multicolored	.55	.25
927	A160	45c multicolored	.75	.25
928	A160	55c multicolored	1.75	.35
929	A160	75c multicolored	1.20	.25
		Nos. 924-929 (6)	5.25	1.60
		Nos. 924-929,C1000-C1005 (12)	12.70	4.30

Issued to publicize nature conservation.

Colorada Beach, Sucre — A161

Designs: 45c, Church of St. Francis of Yare, Miranda. 90c, Stilt houses, Zulia.

1969, Jan. 24 *Perf. 13½x14*

No.	Type	Description	Unused	Used
930	A161	15c multicolored	.35	.25
931	A161	45c multicolored	1.10	.25
932	A161	90c multicolored	1.60	.75
		Nos. 930-932,C1006-C1008 (6)	4.85	2.00

Tourist publicity. For souvenir sheet see No. C1007a.

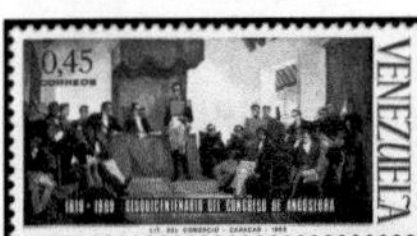

Bolivar Addressing Congress of Angostura A162

1969, Feb. 15 Litho. *Perf. 11*

No.	Type	Description	Unused	Used
933	A162	45c multicolored	1.10	.35

Sesquicentennial of the Congress of Angostura (Ciudad Bolivar).

Martin Luther King, Jr. — A163

1969, Apr. 1 Litho. ***Perf. 13½***

934 A163 1b bl, red & dk brn 1.40 .30

Rev. Dr. Martin Luther King, Jr. (1929-1968), American civil rights leader and recipient of the Nobel Peace Prize, 1964.

Tabebuia — A164

Trees: 65c, Erythrina poeppigiana. 90c, Platymiscium.

1969, May 30 Litho. ***Perf. 13½x14***

935 A164 50c multicolored .95 .25
936 A164 65c gray & multi 1.25 .25
937 A164 90c pink & multi 1.90 .40
Nos. 935-937,C1009-C1011 (6) 6.80 1.65

Issued to publicize nature conservation.

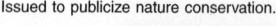

Still Life with Pheasant, by Rojas — A165

Paintings by Cristobal Rojas (1858-1890): 25c, On the Balcony, vert. 45c, The Christening. 50c, The Empty Place (family). 60c, The Tavern. 1b, Man's Arm, vert.

Perf. 14x13½, 13½x14

1969, June 27 Litho. Unwmk.

Size: 32x42mm, 42x32mm

938 A165 25c gold & multi .30 .25
939 A165 35c gold & multi .70 .25
940 A165 45c gold & multi 1.10 .30
941 A165 50c gold & multi 1.25 .35
942 A165 60c gold & multi 1.75 .45

Perf. 11

Size: 26x53mm

943 A165 1b gold & multi 2.40 .70
Nos. 938-943 (6) 7.50 2.30

ILO Emblem — A166

1969, July 28 ***Perf. 13½***

944 A166 2.50b claret & blk 2.75 1.50

50th anniv. of the ILO.

Charter and Coat of Arms — A167

Industrial Complex — A168

1969, Aug. 26 Litho. ***Perf. 13½***

945 A167 45c ultra & multi 1.00 .30
946 A168 1b multicolored 1.60 .40

Industrial development.

House with Arcade, Carora — A169

Designs: 25c, Ruins of Pastora Church. 55c, Chapel of the Cross. 65c, House of Culture.

1969, Sept. 8 ***Perf. 13x14½***

947 A169 20c multicolored .35 .25
948 A169 25c multicolored .55 .25
949 A169 55c multicolored 1.25 .30
950 A169 65c multicolored 1.60 .45
Nos. 947-950 (4) 3.75 1.25

400th anniversary of city of Carora.

Simon Bolivar in Madrid — A170

Designs: 10c, Bolivar's wedding, Madrid, 1802, horiz. 35c, Bolivar monument. Madrid.

Perf. 13½x14, 14x13½

1969, Oct. 28 Litho.

951 A170 10c multicolored .40 .25
952 A170 15c brn red & blk .70 .25
953 A170 35c multicolored .95 .25
a. Souvenir sheet of 2 3.00 2.50
Nos. 951-953 (3) 2.05 .75

Bolivar's sojourn in Spain. No. 953a contains 2 imperf. stamps similar to Nos. 952-953 with simulated perforation. Sold for 75c.

"Birds in the Woods" A171

Design: 45c, "Children in Summer Camp." Both designs are after children's paintings.

1969, Dec. 12 Litho. ***Perf. 12½***

954 A171 5c emerald & multi .35 .25
955 A171 45c red & multi 1.30 .40

Issued for Children's Day.

Map of Great Colombia — A172

1969, Dec. 16 Litho. ***Perf. 11½***

956 A172 45c multicolored .95 .25

150th anniversary of the founding of the State of Great Colombia.

St. Anthony's, Clarines — A173

Churches: 30c, Church of the Conception, Caroni. 40c, St. Michael's, Burbusay. 45c, St. Anthony's, Maturin. 75c, St. Nicholas, Moruy. 1b, Coro Cathedral.

1970, Jan. 15 ***Perf. 14***

957 A173 10c pink & multi .30 .25
958 A173 30c emerald & multi .40 .25
959 A173 40c yellow & multi .85 .25
960 A173 45c gray bl & multi 1.20 .30
a. Souvenir sheet of 1, imperf. 2.25 2.00
961 A173 75c yellow & multi 1.60 .45
962 A173 1b orange & multi 2.00 .55
Nos. 957-962 (6) 6.35 2.05

Colonial architecture.

No. 960a sold for 75c.

A174

Design: Seven Hills of Valera.

1970, Feb. 13 Litho. ***Perf. 13x14½***

963 A174 95c multicolored 1.50 .40

Sesquicentennial of the city of Valera.

A175

Flowers: 20c, Monochaetum Humboldtianum. 25c, Symbolanthus vasculosis. 45c, Cavedishia splendens. 1b, Befaria glauca.

1970, July 29 Litho. ***Perf. 14x13½***

964 A175 20c multicolored .60 .25
965 A175 25c multicolored 1.00 .25
966 A175 45c multicolored 1.40 .40
967 A175 1b multicolored 2.00 .55
Nos. 964-967,C1049-C1052 (8) 10.50 2.75

Battle of Boyaca, by Martin Tovar y Tovar — A176

1970, Aug. 7 ***Perf. 13½x14***

968 A176 30c multicolored .75 .25

150th anniversary of Battle of Boyaca.

Our Lady of Belén de San Mateo — A177

Designs: 35c, Pastoral Cross of Archbishop Silvestre Guevera y Lira, 1867. 40c, Our Lady of Valle. 90c, Virgin of Chiquinquira. 1b, Our Lady of Socorro de Valencia.

1970, Sept. 1 ***Perf. 14x13½***

969 A177 35c gray & multi .75 .25
970 A177 40c gray & multi .85 .25
971 A177 60c gray & multi 1.25 .40
a. Souvenir sheet of 1, imperf. 2.00 1.75
972 A177 90c gray & multi 1.50 .55
973 A177 1b gray & multi 2.00 .65
Nos. 969-973 (5) 6.35 2.10

The designs are from sculptures and paintings in various Venezuelan churches.

No. 971a sold for 75c.

Venezuela No. 22 and EXFILCA Emblem A178

Designs: 20c, EXFILCA emblem and flags of participating nations, vert. 70c, Venezuela No. C13 and EXFILCA emblem, vert.

1970, Nov. 28 Litho. ***Perf. 11***

974 A178 20c yellow & multi .55 .25
975 A178 25c dk blue & multi .65 .25
976 A178 70c brown & multi 1.25 .40
a. Souvenir sheet of 1, imperf. 2.00 1.75
Nos. 974-976 (3) 2.45 .90

EXFILCA 70, 2nd Interamerican Philatelic Exhibition, Caracas, Nov. 27-Dec. 6. No. 976a is a hexagon with each side 50mm long. Sold for 85c.

Guardian Angel, by Juan Pedro Lopez — A179

1970, Dec. 1 Litho. ***Perf. 14½x13½***

977 A179 45c dull yellow & multi .95 .30

Christmas 1970.

Jet and 1920 Plane — A180

1970, Dec. 10 ***Perf. 13x14***

978 A180 5c blue & multi .65 .25

Venezuelan Air Force, 50th anniversary.

Question Mark Full of Citizens — A181

1971, Apr. 30 Litho. ***Perf. 14x13½***

Light Green, Red & Black

979 Block of 4 5.00 2.25
a. A181 30c frame L & T 1.00 .70
b. A181 30c frame T & R 1.00 .70
c. A181 30c frame L & B 1.00 .70
d. A181 30c frame B & R 1.00 .70

National Census, 1971. Sheet of 20 contains 5 No. 979 and 5 blocks of 4 labels. See No. C1054.

Battle of Carabobo — A182

1971, June 21 ***Perf. 13½x14***

980 A182 2b blue & multi 2.40 1.25

Sesquicentennial of Battle of Carabobo.

Map of Federal District A183

Designs: State maps from — 15c, Monagas. 20c, Nueva Esparta. 25c, Portuguesa, vert. 45c, Sucre. 55c, Tachira, vert. 65c, Trujillo. 75c, Yaracuy. 85c, Zulia, vert. 90c, Amazonas, vert. 1b, Federal Dependencies.

1971 Litho. ***Perf. 13½x14, 14x13½***

981 A183 5c multi .55 .25
982 A183 15c multi .55 .25
983 A183 20c multi .55 .25
984 A183 25c multi .55 .25
985 A183 45c multi .60 .25
986 A183 55c multi .75 .25
987 A183 65c multi .85 .25
988 A183 75c multi 1.00 .30
989 A183 85c multi 1.25 .30
990 A183 90c multi 2.00 .30
991 A183 1b multi 2.10 .55
Nos. 981-991 (11) 10.75 3.20
Nos. 981-991,C1035-C1048 (25) 23.40 7.65

Issued: 5c, 7/15; 15c, 20c, 8/16; 25c, 45c, 9/15; 55c, 65c, 10/15; 75c, 85c, 11/15; 90c, 1b, 12/15.

Madonna and Child — A184

Design: #993, Madonna & Jesus in manger.

1971, Dec. 1 *Perf. 11*

992 A184 25c multicolored .80 .25
993 A184 25c multicolored .80 .25
a. Pair, #992-993 1.90 .60

Christmas 1971. Printed checkerwise.

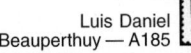

Luis Daniel Beauperthuy — A185

1971, Dec. 10 *Perf. 14x13½*

994 A185 1b vio bl & multi 1.50 .60

Dr. Luis Daniel Beauperthuy, scientist.

Globe in Heart Shape — A186

1972, Apr. 7 Litho. *Perf. 14x13½*

995 A186 1b red, ultra & blk 1.25 .60

"Your heart is your health," World Health Day 1972.

Flags of Americas and Arms of Venezuela — A187

Designs: 4b, Venezuelan flag. 5b, National anthem. 10b, Araguaney, national tree. 15b, Map, North and South America. All show flags of American nations in background.

1972, May 16 Litho. *Perf. 14x13½*

996 A187 3b multicolored 4.00 1.00
997 A187 4b multicolored 4.50 1.75
998 A187 5b multicolored 5.00 2.25
999 A187 10b multicolored 9.25 3.00
1000 A187 15b multicolored 13.50 4.25
Nos. 996-1000 (5) 36.25 12.25

"Venezuela in America."

Parque Central Complex — A188

#1002, Front view ("Parque Central" on top). #1003, Side view ("Parque Central" at right).

1972, July 25 *Perf. 11½*

1001 A188 30c yellow & multi .30 .25
1002 A188 30c blue & multi .30 .25
1003 A188 30c red & multi .30 .25
a. Strip of 3, #1001-1003 2.15 2.15

Completion of "Parque Central" middle-income housing project, Caracas.

Mahatma Gandhi A189

1972, Oct. 2 Litho. *Perf. 13½x14*

1004 A189 60c multicolored 1.50 .40

103rd birthday of Mohandas K. Gandhi (1869-1948), leader in India's fight for independence, advocate of non-violence.

Children Playing Music A190

Christmas: #1006, Children roller skating.

1972, Dec. 5 Litho. *Perf. 13½x14*

1005 30c multicolored .40 .25
1006 30c multicolored .40 .25
a. A190 Pair, #1005-1006 1.50 1.50

Indigo Snake — A191

Snake: 15c, South American chicken snake. 25c, Venezuelan lance-head. 30c, Coral snake. 60c, Casabel rattlesnake. 1b, Boa constrictor.

1972, Dec. 15 Litho. *Perf. 13½x14*

1007 A191 10c black & multi .60 .35
1008 A191 15c black & multi .60 .35
1009 A191 25c black & multi .85 .35
1010 A191 30c black & multi 1.00 .35
1011 A191 60c black & multi 1.90 .40
1012 A191 1b black & multi 2.75 .60
Nos. 1007-1012 (6) 7.70 2.40

Copernicus — A192

Designs: 5c, Model of solarcentric system. 15c, Copernicus' book "De Revolutionibus."

1973, Feb. 19 Litho. *Perf. 13½x14*

1013 5c multicolored .30 .25
1014 10c multicolored .50 .25
1015 15c multicolored .75 .25
a. A192 Strip of 3, #1013-1015 2.25 .90

Sun — A193

Designs: Planetary system — No. 1017, Earth. No. 1018, Mars. No. 1019, Saturn. No. 1020, Asteroids. No. 1021, Neptune. No. 1022, Venus. No. 1023, Jupiter. No. 1024, Uranus. No. 1025, Pluto. No. 1026, Moon. No. 1027, Mercury. No. 1028, Orbits and Saturn. No. 1029, Sun, Mercury, Venus, Earth. No. 1030, Jupiter, Uranus, Neptune, Pluto.

Size: 26½x29mm

1973 Litho. *Perf. 13½*

1016 A193 5c multi .40 .25
1017 A193 5c multi .40 .25
1018 A193 20c multi .85 .25
1019 A193 20c multi .65 .25
1020 A193 30c multi .70 .25
1021 A193 40c multi .85 .25
1022 A193 50c multi 1.25 .40
1023 A193 60c multi 1.50 .45
1024 A193 75c multi 1.75 .55
1025 A193 90c multi 2.25 .80
1026 A193 90c multi 3.25 .80
1027 A193 1b multi 3.50 .95

Size: 27x55mm

Perf. 12

1028 A193 10c multi .40 .25
1029 A193 15c multi .60 .25
1030 A193 15c multi .70 .25
a. Strip of 3, #1028-1030 1.75 1.75
Nos. 1016-1030 (15) 19.05 6.20

10th anniversary of Humboldt Planetarium. No. 1030a has continuous design showing solar system.

Issue dates: Nos. 1016, 1018, 1021, 1023-1025, Mar. 15; others Mar. 30.

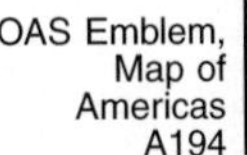

OAS Emblem, Map of Americas A194

1973, Apr. 30 Litho. *Perf. 13½x14*

1031 A194 60c multicolored .90 .30

Organization of American States, 25th anniv.

José Antonio Paez A195

Street of the Lancers, Puerto Cabello A196

Designs: 10c, Paez in uniform. 30c, Paez and horse, from old print. 2b, Paez at Battle of Centauro, horiz. 10c, 2b are after contemporary paintings.

1973 *Perf. 14x13½, 13½x14*

1032 A195 10c gold & multi .30 .25
1033 A195 30c red, blk & gold .45 .25
1034 A195 50c bl, vio bl & dk brn .75 .35
1035 A196 1b multicolored 1.60 .60
1036 A195 2b gold & multi 2.60 1.25
Nos. 1032-1036 (5) 5.70 2.70

Gen. José Antonio Paez (1790-1873), leader in War of Independence, President of Venezuela. The 1b for the sesquicentenary of the fall of Puerto Cabello.

Issue dates: Nos. 1033-1034, May 6; Nos. 1032, 1036, June 13; No. 1035, Nov. 8.

José P. Padilla, Mariano Montilla, Manuel Manrique A197

1b, Naval battle. 2b, Line-up for naval battle.

1973, July 27 Litho. *Perf. 12½*

1037 A197 50c multicolored .40 .25
1038 A197 1b multicolored 1.25 .45
1039 A197 2b multicolored 2.50 1.00
Nos. 1037-1039 (3) 4.15 1.70

150th anniv. of the Battle of Maracaibo.

Bishop Ramos de Lora — A198

1973, Aug. 1 Photo. *Perf. 14x13½*

1040 A198 75c gold & dk brn .85 .25

Sesquicentennial of the birth of Ramos de Lora (1722-1790), first Bishop of Merida de Maracaibo and founder of the Colegio Seminario, the forerunner of the University of the Andes.

Plane, Ship, Margarita Island — A199

1973, Sept. 8 Litho. *Perf. 14x13½*

1041 A199 5c multicolored .75 .25

Establishment of Margarita Island as a free port.

Map of Golden Road and Waterfall A200

Designs (Road Map and): 10c, Scarlet macaw. 20c, Church ruins. 50c, 60c, Indian mountain sanctuary. 90c, Colonial church. 1b, Flags of Venezuela and Brazil.

1973, Oct. 1 Litho. *Perf. 13*

1042 A200 5c black & multi .30 .25
1043 A200 10c black & multi .30 .25
1044 A200 20c black & multi 1.00 .25
1045 A200 50c black & multi 1.10 .35
1046 A200 60c black & multi 1.10 .35
1047 A200 90c black & multi 1.60 .40
1048 A200 1b black & multi 2.10 .55
Nos. 1042-1048 (7) 7.50 2.40

Completion of the Golden Road from Santa Elena de Uairen, Brazil, to El Dorado, Venezuela.

Issued: 50c, 60c, Oct. 30; others Oct. 1.

Gen. Paez Dam and Power Station — A201

1973, Oct. 14 *Perf. 14x13½*

1049 A201 30c multicolored .75 .25

Opening of the Gen. José Antonio Paez Dam and Power Station.

Child on Slide A202

Designs: No. 1051, Fairytale animals. No. 1052, Children's book. No. 1053, Children disembarking from plane for vacation.

1973, Dec. 4 Litho. *Perf. 12*

1050 A202 10c multicolored .65 .25
1051 A202 10c multicolored .65 .25
1052 A202 10c multicolored .65 .25
1053 A202 10c multicolored .65 .25
Nos. 1050-1053 (4) 2.60 1.00

Children's Foundation Festival.

King Following Star A203

Christmas: No. 1055, Two Kings.

1973, Dec. 5 Litho. *Perf. 14x13½*

1054 30c multicolored .75 .25
1055 30c multicolored .75 .25
a. A203 Pair, #1054-1055 1.90 1.90

Regional Map of Venezuela — A204

1973, Dec. 13 *Perf. 13½x14*

1056 A204 25c multicolored 1.00 .25

Introduction of regionalization.

Handicraft — A205

Designs: 35c, Industrial park. 45c, Cog wheels and chimney.

1973, Dec. 18 *Perf. 14x13½*

1057 A205 15c blue & multi .40 .25
1058 A205 35c multicolored .50 .25
1059 A205 45c yellow & multi .90 .25
Nos. 1057-1059 (3) 1.80 .75

Progress in Venezuela and jobs for the handicapped.

Map of Carupano and Revelers A206

1974, Feb. 22 *Perf. 13½x14*

1060 A206 5c multicolored .85 .25

10th anniversary of Carupano Carnival.

Congress Emblem — A207

1974, May 20 **Litho.** *Perf. 13½*

1061 A207 50c multicolored .85 .25

9th Venezuelan Engineering Congress, Maracaibo, May 19-25.

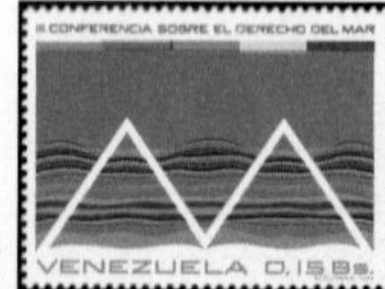

Waves and "M" — A208

Designs: Under-water photographs of deep-sea fish and marine life.

1974, June 20 **Litho.** *Perf. 12½*

1062 A208 15c multicolored .65 .25
1063 A208 35c multicolored .90 .25
1064 A208 75c multicolored 1.25 .30
1065 A208 80c multicolored 1.25 .40
Nos. 1062-1065 (4) 4.05 1.20

3rd UN Conference on the Law of the Sea, Caracas, June 20-Aug. 29.

Pupil and New School A209

"Pay your Taxes" Campaign: 10c, 15c, 20c, like 5c. 25c, 30c, 35c, 40c, Suburban housing development. 45c, 50c, 55c, 60c, Highway and overpass. 65c, 70c, 75c, 80c, Playing field (sport). 85c, 90c, 95c, 1b, Operating room. All designs include Venezuelan coat of arms, coins and banknotes.

1974 *Perf. 13½*

1066 A209 5c blue & multi .35 .25
1067 A209 10c ultra & multi .35 .25
1068 A209 15c violet & multi .35 .25
1069 A209 20c lilac & multi .35 .25
1070 A209 25c multicolored .35 .25
1071 A209 30c multicolored .90 .25
1072 A209 35c multicolored .35 .25
1073 A209 40c olive & multi .60 .25
1074 A209 45c multicolored .60 .25
1075 A209 50c green & multi .60 .25
1076 A209 55c multicolored 1.10 .40
1077 A209 60c multicolored .90 .30
1078 A209 65c bister & multi 2.00 .60
1079 A209 70c multicolored .95 .25
1080 A209 75c multicolored 1.40 .30
1081 A209 80c brown & multi 1.40 .30
1082 A209 85c ver & multi 1.40 .30
1083 A209 90c multicolored 1.40 .50
1084 A209 95c multicolored 2.40 1.10
1085 A209 1b multicolored 1.40 .45
Nos. 1066-1085 (20) 19.15 7.00

Bolivar at Battle of Junin — A210

1974, Aug. 6 **Litho.** *Perf. 13½x14*

1086 A210 2b multicolored 2.25 1.00

Sesquicentennial of the Battle of Junin.

Globe and UPU Emblem A211

Postrider, Ship, Steamer and Jet — A211a

1974, Oct. 9 *Perf. 12*

1087 A211 45c dk blue & multi .70 .35
1088 A211a 50c black & multi .80 .35

Centenary of Universal Postal Union.

Rufino Blanco-Fombona A212

Portraits of Blanco-Fombona and his books.

1974, Oct. 16 **Litho.** *Perf. 12½*

1089 A212 10c gray & multi .40 .30
1090 A212 30c yellow & multi .40 .30
1091 A212 45c multicolored .70 .30
1092 A212 90c buff & multi 1.10 .50
Nos. 1089-1092 (4) 2.60 1.40

Centenary of the birth of Rufino Blanco-Fombona (1874-1944), writer.

Children — A213

1974, Nov. 29 **Litho.** *Perf. 13½*

1093 A213 70c blue & multi .85 .35

Children's Foundation Festival.

General Sucre — A214

Globe with South American Map and Flags — A215

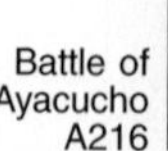

Battle of Ayacucho A216

1b, Map of South America with battles marked.

1974, Dec. 9 *Perf. 14x13½, 13½x14*

1094 A214 30c multicolored .30 .25
1095 A215 50c multicolored .50 .35
1096 A215 1b multicolored 1.10 .40
1097 A216 2b multicolored 2.25 .85
Nos. 1094-1097 (4) 4.15 1.85

Sesquicentennial of the Battle of Ayacucho.

Adoration of the Shepherds, by J. B. Mayno — A217

1974, Dec. 16 **Photo.** *Perf. 14x13½*

1098 30c Shepherd .50 .30
1099 30c Madonna & Child .50 .30
a. A217 Pair, #1098-1099 1.50 1.50

Christmas 1974.

Road Building, 1905 and El Ciempies Overpass, 1972 — A219

Designs: 20c, 1b, Jesus Muñoz Tebar, first Minister of Public Works. 25c, Bridges on Caracas-La Guaira Road, 1912 and 1953. 40c, View of Caracas, 1874 and 1974. 70c, Tucacas Railroad Station, 1911, and projected terminal, 1974. 80c, Anatomical Institute, Caracas, 1911, and Social Security Hospital, 1969. 85c, Quininari River Bridge, 1804, and Orinoco River Bridge, 1967.

1974, Dec. 18 **Litho.** *Perf. 12½*

1100 A219 5c ultra & multi .30 .30
1101 A219 20c ocher & blk .35 .30
1102 A219 25c blue & multi .45 .30
1103 A219 40c yellow & multi .45 .30
1104 A219 70c green & multi 2.10 .40
1105 A219 80c multicolored 1.75 .45
1106 A219 85c orange & multi 2.10 .45
1107 A219 1b red & black 2.40 .80
Nos. 1100-1107 (8) 9.90 3.30

Centenary of the Ministry of Public Works.

Women and IWY Emblem — A220

1975, Oct. 8 **Litho.** *Perf. 13½x14*

1108 A220 90c multicolored .85 .35

International Women's Year.

Scout Emblem and Tents — A221

1975, Nov. 11 **Litho.** *Perf. 13½x14*

1109 A221 20c multicolored .40 .30
1110 A221 80c multicolored .95 .40

14th World Boy Scout Jamboree, Lille-hammer, Norway, July 29-Aug. 7.

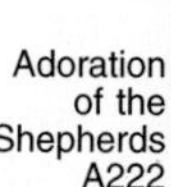

Adoration of the Shepherds A222

1975, Dec. 5 **Litho.** *Perf. 13½x14*

1111 30c multicolored .55 .40
1112 30c multicolored .55 .40
a. A222 Pair, #1111-1112 1.90 1.90

Christmas 1975.

Bolivar's Tomb — A224

Design: 1.05b, National Pantheon.

1976, Feb. 2 **Engr.** *Perf. 14x13½*

1113 A224 30c blue gray & ultra .40 .30
1114 A224 1.05b sepia & car 1.10 .40

Centenary of National Pantheon.

Bolivia Flag Colors — A225

1976, Mar. 22 **Litho.** *Perf. 13½*

1115 A225 60c multicolored .90 .35

Sesquicentennial of Bolivia's independence.

Aerial Map Survey — A226

1976, Apr. 8 *Perf. 13½x12½*

1116 A226 1b black & vio bl 1.25 .35

Natl. Cartographic Institute, 40th anniv.

Gen. Ribas' Signature — A227

José Felix Ribas — A228

1976, Apr. 26 Photo. *Perf. 12½x13*
1117 A227 40c red & green .60 .30

Perf. 13½
1118 A228 55c multicolored .90 .40

Gen. José Felix Ribas (1775-1815), independence hero, birth bicentenary.

Musicians of the Chacao School, by Armandio Barrios A229

Lamas's Colophon — A230

1976, May 13 Litho. *Perf. 13½*
1119 A229 75c multicolored 2.25 .80

Photo. *Perf. 12½x13*
1120 A230 1.25b buff, red & gray .95 .35

José Angel Lamas (1775-1814), composer, birth bicentenary.

Bolivar, by José Maria Espinoza — A231

1976 Engr. *Perf. 12*
Size: 18x22½mm
1121 A231 5c green .30 .25
1122 A231 10c lilac rose .30 .25
1123 A231 15c brown .30 .25
1124 A231 20c black .30 .25
1125 A231 25c yellow .30 .25
1126 A231 30c violet bl .30 .25
1127 A231 45c dk purple .30 .25
1128 A231 50c orange .30 .25
1129 A231 65c blue .40 .25
1130 A231 1b vermilion .50 .35

Size: 26x32mm
Perf. 12x11½
1131 A231 2b gray 1.00 .35
1132 A231 3b violet blue 1.60 .55
1133 A231 4b yellow 2.00 .75
1134 A231 5b orange 2.40 1.00
1135 A231 10b dull purple 5.50 2.00
1136 A231 15b blue 8.25 2.75
1137 A231 20b vermilion 10.50 3.75
Nos. 1121-1137 (17) 34.55 13.75

Issued: 5c-1b, May 17; 2b-20b, July 15.

Coil Stamps

1978, May 22 *Perf. 13½ Horiz.*
Size: 18x22½mm
1138 A231 5c green .45 .35
1139 A231 10c lilac rose .45 .35
1140 A231 15c brown .45 .35
1141 A231 20c black .45 .35
1142 A231 25c yellow .45 .35
1143 A231 30c violet blue .50 .35
1144 A231 45c dk purple .65 .35
1144A A231 50c orange .90 .35
1144B A231 65c blue 1.10 .35
1144C A231 1b vermilion 1.90 .35
Nos. 1138-1144C (10) 7.30 3.50

Black control number on back of every fifth stamp.

See Nos. 1305-1307, 1362-1366, 1401-1409, 1482, 1484, 1487, 1490. Compare with designs A405-A406.

Maze — A232

Central University — A233

Faculty Emblems — A234

1976, June 1 Litho. *Perf. 12½x13*
1145 A232 30c multicolored .40 .25
1146 A233 50c yel, org & blk .55 .25
1147 A234 90c black & yellow 1.10 .45
Nos. 1145-1147 (3) 2.05 .95

Central University of Venezuela, 250th anniv.

"Unity" — A235

Designs: 45c, 1.25b, similar to 15c.

1976, June 29 Litho. *Perf. 12½*
1148 A235 15c multicolored .40 .25
1149 A235 45c multicolored .55 .25
1150 A235 1.25b multicolored 1.10 .45
Nos. 1148-1150 (3) 2.05 .95

Amphictyonic Cong. of Panama, Sesqui.

Washington, US Bicent. Emblem — A236

US Bicentennial Emblem and: No. 1152, Jefferson. No. 1153, Lincoln. No. 1154, F. D. Roosevelt. No. 1155, J. F. Kennedy.

1976, July 4 Engr. *Perf. 14*
1151 A236 1b red brn & blk .95 .35
1152 A236 1b green & blk .95 .35
1153 A236 1b purple & blk .95 .35
1154 A236 1b blue & blk .95 .35
1155 A236 1b olive & blk .95 .35
Nos. 1151-1155 (5) 4.75 1.75

American Bicentennial.

Valve — A237

Computer drawings of valves & pipelines.

1976, Nov. 8 Photo. *Perf. 12½x14*
1156 A237 10c multicolored .40 .35
1157 A237 30c multicolored .40 .35
1158 A237 35c multicolored .50 .35
1159 A237 40c multicolored .50 .35
1160 A237 55c multicolored .65 .35
1161 A237 90c multicolored 1.10 .35
Nos. 1156-1161 (6) 3.55 2.10

Nationalization of the oil industry.

Nativity, by Barbaro Rivas — A238

1976, Dec. 1 Litho. *Perf. 13x14*
1162 A238 30c multicolored .85 .60

Christmas 1976.

Ornament — A239

Lithographed and Embossed

1976, Dec. 15 *Perf. 14x13½*
1163 A239 60c yellow & black .85 .35

Declaration of Bogota (economic agreements of Andean countries), 10th anniv.

Coat of Arms of Barinas A240

1977, May 25 Photo. *Perf. 12½x13*
1164 A240 50c multicolored .85 .25

400th anniv. of the founding of Barinas.

Crucified Christ, Patron Saint of La Grita — A241

1977, Aug. 6 Litho. *Perf. 13*
1165 A241 30c multicolored .75 .25

Founding of La Grita, 400th anniv. (in 1976).

Symbolic City — A242

1977, Aug. 26 Litho. *Perf. 13½*
1166 A242 1b multicolored .90 .30

450th anniversary of the founding of Coro.

Communications Symbols — A243

1977, Sept. 30 Litho. *Perf. 13½x14*
1167 A243 85c multicolored .90 .25

9th Interamerican Postal and Telecommunications Staff Congress, Caracas, Sept. 26-30.

Cable Connecting with TV, Telephone and Circuit Box — A244

1977, Oct. 12 Litho. *Perf. 14*
1168 A244 95c multicolored 1.20 .25

Inauguration of Columbus underwater cable linking Venezuela and the Canary Islands.

"Venezuela" — A245

Designs: "Venezuela" horizontal on 50c, 1.05b; reading up on 80c, 1.25b; reading down on 1.50b.

1977, Nov. 26 Photo. *Perf. 13½x13*
1169 A245 30c brt grn & blk .35 .25
1170 A245 50c dp org & blk .50 .25
1171 A245 80c bl gray & blk .80 .25
1172 A245 1.05b red & blk 1.10 .25
1173 A245 1.25b yel & blk 1.25 .25
1174 A245 1.50b dk gray brn & blk 1.50 .35
Nos. 1169-1174 (6) 5.50 1.60

Iron industry nationalization, 1st anniv.

Juan Pablo Duarte — A246

1977, Dec. 8 Engr. *Perf. 11x13*
1175 A246 75c black & magenta .80 .25

Duarte (1813-76), leader in liberation struggle.

Nativity, Colonial Sculpture — A247

1977, Dec. 15 Litho. *Perf. 13*
1176 A247 30c green & multi .65 .25

Christmas 1977.

OPEC Emblem — A248

1977, Dec. 20
1177 A248 1.05b brt & lt bl & blk 1.10 .25

50th Conference of Oil Producing and Exporting Countries, Caracas.

Bicyclist — A249

Design: 5c, Two bicyclists.

1978, Jan. 16 Litho. *Perf. 13½x13*
1178 A249 5c multi .35 .25
1179 A249 1.25b multi 1.40 .25

World Bicycling Championships, San Cristobal, Tachira, Aug. 22-Sept. 4.

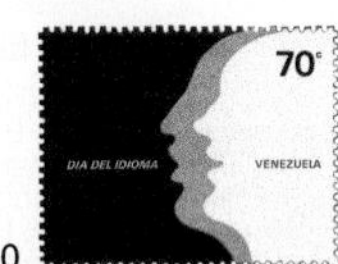

Profiles — A250

1978, Apr. 21 Litho. *Perf. 13½x14*
1180 A250 70c blk, gray & lil .90 .25

Language Day.
Issued in tete-beche pairs. Value $1.25.

Magnetic Computer Tape and Satellite — A251

1978, May 17 Litho. *Perf. 14*
1184 A251 75c violet blue 1.00 .25

10th World Telecommunications Day.

"1777-1977" A252

Goya's Carlos III as Computer Print A253

1978, June 23 Litho. *Perf. 12*
1185 A252 30c multicolored .35 .25
1186 A253 1b multicolored .95 .25

200th anniversary of Venezuelan unification.

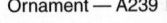

Bolivar Bicentenary

Juan Vicente Bolivar y Ponte, Father of Simon Bolivar
A254

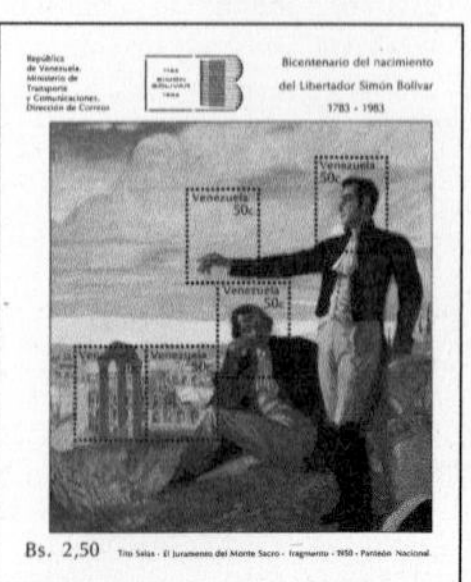

The Oath on Monte Sacro, Rome, by Tito Salas
A255

Designs: 30c, Bolivar as infant in nursemaid's arms (detail from design of No. 1189). No. 1189, Baptism of the Liberator, by Tito Salas, 1929.

1978, July 24 Engr. *Perf. 12½*
1187 A254 30c emerald & blk .35 .25
1188 A254 1b multicolored .95 .25

Souvenir Sheet
Litho.
Perf. 14

1189 A255 Sheet of 5 41.00 40.00
a. 50c, single stamp 1.50 1.50

1978, Dec. 17 Engr. *Perf. 12½*

Designs: 30c, Bolivar at 25. 1b, Simon Rodriguez. No. 1192, shown. (Bolivar's tutor).

1190 A254 30c multicolored .35 .25
1191 A254 1b rose red & blk .85 .25

Souvenir Sheet
Litho.
Perf. 14

1192 A255 Sheet of 5 25.00 24.00
a. 50c, single stamp 1.10 1.10

Size of souvenir sheet stamps: 20x24mm. Size of #1189: 154x130mm; #1192: 130x155mm.

1979, July 24 Engr. *Perf. 12½*

Designs: 30c, Alexander Sabes Petion, president of Haiti. 1b, Bolivar's signature.
No. 1195: a, Partial map of Jamaica, horiz. b, Partial map of Jamaica, vert. c, Bolivar, 1816. d, Luis Brion. e, Petion.

1193 A254 30c org, vio & blk .45 .25
1194 A254 1b red org & blk .80 .25

Souvenir Sheet
Litho.
Perf. 14

1195 A255 Sheet of 5 5.25 3.25
a.-e. 50c, any single .45 .35

Size of souvenir sheet stamps: 26x20, 20x26mm.

1979, Dec. 17 Engr. *Perf. 12½*

Designs: 30c, Bolivar. 1b, Slave. No. 1198, Freeing of the Slaves, by Tito Salas. (30c, 1b, details from design of No. 1198.)

1196 A254 30c multicolored .55 .25
1197 A254 1b multicolored .65 .25

Souvenir Sheet
Litho.
Perf. 14

1198 A255 Sheet of 5 7.75 5.50
a. 50c, single stamp 1.25 1.10

Simon Bolivar, birth centenary. Size of souvenir sheet stamps: 22x28mm.
See Nos. 1228-1230, 1264-1266, 1276-1284, 1294-1296, 1317-1322.

"T" and "CTV" — A256

Designs: Different arrangement of letters "T" and "CTV" for "Confederacion de Trabajeros Venezolanos."

1978, Sept. 27 Photo. *Perf. 13x13½*
1199 Strip of 5 2.00 2.00
a.-e. A256 30c, single stamp .40 .25
1200 Strip of 5 4.00 4.00
a.-e. A256 95c, single stamp .50 .25

Workers' Day.

Symbolic Design — A257

1978, Oct. 3 Litho. *Perf. 14*
1201 A257 50c dark brown 1.00 .35

Rafael Rangel, physician and scientist, birth centenary.

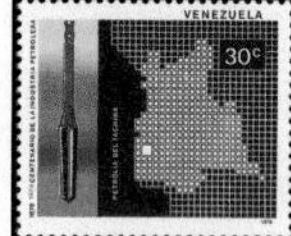

Drill Head, Tachira Oil Field Map — A258

"P" as Pipeline — A259

1978, Nov. 2 Litho. *Perf. 13½*
1202 A258 30c multicolored .35 .30
1203 A259 1.05b multicolored 1.40 .40

Centenary of oil industry.

Star — A260

1978, Dec. 6 Litho. *Perf. 14*
1204 A260 30c multicolored .85 .35

Christmas 1978.

"P T" — A261

1979, Feb. 8 Litho. *Perf. 12½*
1205 A261 75c black & red .65 .35

Creation of Postal and Telegraph Institute.

"Dam Holding Back Water" — A262

1979, Feb. 15 Photo. *Perf. 13½*
1206 A262 2b silver, gray & blk 1.10 .45

Guri Dam, 10th anniversary.

San Martin, by E. J. Maury
A263

60c, San Martin, by Mercedes. 70c, Monument, Guayaquil. 75c, San Martin's signature.

1979, Feb. 25 *Perf. 12½x13*
1207 A263 40c blue, blk & yel .45 .30
1208 A263 60c blue, blk & yel .55 .30
1209 A263 70c blue, blk & yel .70 .30
1210 A263 75c blue, blk & yel .70 .30
Nos. 1207-1210 (4) 2.40 1.20

José de San Martin (1778-1850), South American liberator.

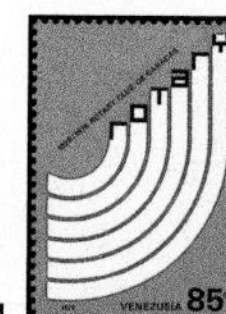

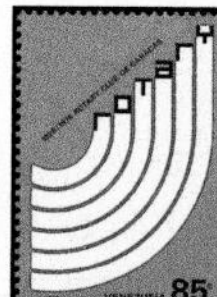

"Rotary" — A264

1979, Aug. 7 Litho. *Perf. 14x13½*
1211 A264 85c gold & blk .95 .35

Rotary Club of Caracas, 50th anniversary.

Our Lady of Coromoto Appearing to Children — A265

Engraved and Lithographed
1979, Aug. 23 *Perf. 13*
1212 A265 55c black & dp org .90 .35

Canonization of Our Lady of Coromoto, 25th anniv.

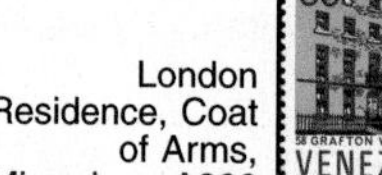

London Residence, Coat of Arms, Miranda — A266

1979, Oct. 23 Litho. *Perf. 14½x14*
1213 A266 50c multicolored .75 .35

Francisco de Miranda (1750-1816), Venezuelan independence fighter.

O'Leary, Maps of South America and United Kingdom — A267

1979, Nov. 6
1214 A267 30c multicolored .75 .35

Daniel O'Leary (1801-1854), general, writer.

A268

IYC Emblem and: 79c, Boy holding nest. 80c, Boys in water, bridge.

1979, Nov. 20 Litho. *Perf. 14½x14*
1215 A268 70c lt blue & blk .35 .25
1216 A268 80c multicolored .85 .25

International Year of the Child.

A269

1979, Dec. 1 Litho. *Perf. 13*
1217 A269 30c multicolored .75 .35

Christmas 1979.

Caudron Bomber, EXFILVE Emblem
A270

EXFILVE Emblem and: No. 1219, Stearman biplane. No. 1220, UH-1H helicopter. No. 1221, CF-5 jet fighter.

1979, Dec. 15 *Perf. 11x11½*
1218 A270 75c multicolored 1.00 .35
1219 A270 75c multicolored 1.00 .35
1220 A270 75c multicolored 1.00 .35
1221 A270 75c multicolored 1.00 .35
a. Block of 4, #1218-1221 4.25 3.50

Venezuelan Air Force, 59th anniv.; EXFILVE 79, 3rd Natl. Philatelic Exhibition, Dec. 7-17.

IPOSTEL Emblem, World Map — A271

1979, Dec. 27 *Perf. 11½*
1222 A271 75c multicolored .75 .35

Postal and Telegraph Institute, introduction of new logo.

Queen Victoria, Hill — A272

1980, Feb. 13 Litho. *Perf. 12½*
1223 A272 55c multicolored .75 .35

Sir Rowland Hill (1795-1879), originator of penny postage.

Dr. Augusto Pi Suner, Physiologist, Birth Centenary
A273

1980, Mar. 14 Litho. *Perf. 11½*
1224 A273 80c multicolored .75 .35

Spanish Seed Leaf — A274

Lithographed and Engraved
1980, Mar. 27 *Perf. 13*
1225 A274 50c multicolored .85 .35

Pedro Loefling (1729-56), Swedish botanist.

Juan Lovera (1778-1841), Artist — A275

1980, May 25 Litho. *Perf. 13½*
1226 A275 60c blue & dp org .50 .35
1227 A275 75c violet & org .70 .35

Bolivar Types of 1978

30c, Signing of document. 1b, House of Congress. #1230, Angostura Congress, by Tito Salas.

1980, July 24 Engr. *Perf. 12½*
1228 A254 30c multicolored .45 .25
1229 A254 1b multicolored .80 .25

Souvenir Sheet
Litho.
Perf. 14

1230 A255 Sheet of 5 5.25 5.25
a. 50c, single stamp .40 .40

Simon Bolivar (1783-1830), revolutionary. Size of souvenir sheet stamps: 25x20mm, 20x25mm.

Dancing Girls, by Armando Reveron — A276

1980, Aug. 17 Litho. *Perf. 13*
1231 A276 50c shown .40 .30

Size: 25x40mm

1232 A276 65c Portrait 1.00 .40

Armando Reveron (1889-1955), artist.

Bernardo O'Higgins — A277

Lithographed and Engraved

1980, Aug. 22 *Perf. 13x14*
1233 A277 85c multicolored 1.00 .35

Bernardo O'Higgins (1776-1842), Chilean soldier and statesman.

School Ship Simon Bolivar — A278

Frigate Mariscal Sucre — A279

Designs: No. 1236, Submarine Picua. No. 1237, Naval Academy.

Perf. 11½ (#1234), 11x11½

1980, Sept. 13 Litho.
1234 A278 1.50b shown 1.50 1.25
1235 A279 1.50b shown 1.50 1.25
1236 A279 1.50b multi 1.50 1.25
1237 A279 1.50b multi 1.50 1.25
Nos. 1234-1237 (4) 6.00 5.00

On No. 1236 "Picuda" is misspelled on stamp.

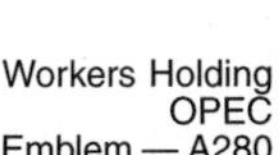

Workers Holding OPEC Emblem — A280

20th Anniv. of OPEC (Organization of Petroleum Exporting Countries): #1239, Emblem.

1980, Sept. 14 Litho. *Perf. 12x11½*
1238 A280 1.50b multicolored 1.00 .75
1239 A280 1.50b multicolored 1.00 .75

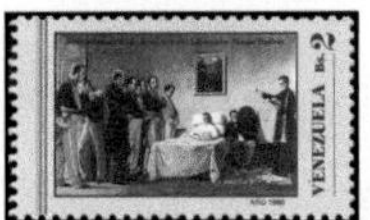

Death of Simon Bolivar — A281

1980, Dec. 17 Litho. *Perf. 11x11½*
1240 A281 2b multicolored 1.90 1.60

Simon Bolivar, 150th anniversary of death.

A282

Lithographed and Engraved

1980, Dec. 17 *Perf. 13x12½*
1241 A282 2b multicolored 1.10 .90

Gen. José Antonio Sucre, 150th anniv. of death.

Nativity, by Rubens — A283

1980, Dec. 19 Litho. *Perf. 14x13½*
1242 A283 1b multi 1.00 .60

Christmas 1980.

Helen Keller's Initials (Written and Braille) A284

Lithographed and Embossed

1981, Feb. 12 *Perf. 12½*
1243 A284 1.50b multicolored 1.10 .90

Helen Keller (1880-1968), blind and deaf writer and lecturer.

John Baptiste de la Salle — A285

1981, May 15 Litho. *Perf. 11½x11*
1244 A285 1.25b multicolored .80 .55

Christian Brothers' 300th anniv.

San Felipe City, 250th Anniv. — A286

1981, May 1 *Perf. 11½*
1245 A286 3b multicolored 1.40 1.10

Municipal Theater of Caracas Centenary A287

1981, June 28 Litho. *Perf. 12*
1246 A287 1.25b multicolored 2.25 2.00

A288

1981, Sept. 15 Litho. *Perf. 11½*
1247 A288 2b multicolored .85 .60

UPU membership centenary.

A289

1981, Oct. 14 Litho.
1248 A289 1b multicolored 1.00 .50

11th natl. population and housing census.

A290

1981, Dec. 3 Litho. *Perf. 11½*
1249 A290 95c multicolored .75 .50

9th Bolivar Games, Barquismeto.

Transportation A291

Designs: 1b, 19th Cent. Bicycle. 1.05b, Locomotive, 1926. 1.25b, Buick, 1937. 1.50b, Coach.

1981, Dec. 5 Photo. *Perf. 13x14*
1250 A291 1b multi .70 .60
1251 A291 1.05b multi 1.10 .65
1252 A291 1.25b multi 1.25 .90
1253 A291 1.50b multi 1.60 1.10
Nos. 1250-1253 (4) 4.65 3.25

See Nos. 1289-1292, 1308-1311.

Christmas 1981 — A292

1981, Dec. 21 Litho. *Perf. 11½*
1254 A292 1b multicolored .75 .50

50th Anniv. of Natural Science Society — A293

Designs: 1b, Mt. Autana. 1.50b, Sarisarinama. 2b, Guacharo Cave.

1982, Jan. 21 *Perf. 11½*
1255 A293 1b multi .80 .40
1256 A293 1.50b multi 1.25 .75
1257 A293 2b multi 1.60 .90
Nos. 1255-1257 (3) 3.65 2.05

20th Anniv. of Constitution A294

1982, Jan. 28 Photo. *Perf. 13x13½*
1258 A294 1.85b gold & blk 1.10 .90

A295

1982, Feb. 19 Litho. *Perf. 13½*
1259 A295 3b multicolored 1.60 1.40

20th anniv. of agricultural reform.

A296

1982, Mar. 12 Litho. *Perf. 13½*
1260 A296 1b blue & dk blue 1.00 .75

Jules Verne (1828-1905), science fiction writer.

Natl. Anthem Centenary (1981) — A297

1982, Mar. 26 *Perf. 11½*
1261 A297 1b multicolored .90 .65

1300th Anniv. of Bulgaria — A298

1982, June 2 Litho. *Perf. 13½*
1262 A298 65c multicolored .85 .60

6th Natl. 5-Year Plan, 1981-85 — A299

1982, June 11
1263 A299 2b multicolored .75 .50

Bolivar Types of 1978

30c, Juan José Rondon. 1b, José Antonio Anzoategui.

1982, July 24 Engr. *Perf. 12½*
1264 A254 30c multicolored .75 .50
1265 A254 1b multicolored .75 .50

Souvenir Sheet

Litho. *Perf. 14*
1266 A255 Sheet of 5 5.75 5.75
a.-e. 50c, any single .35 .35

Single stamps of No. 1266 show details from Battle of Boyaca, by Martin Tovar y Tovar. Size of souvenir sheet stamps: 19x26mm, 26x19mm.

Cecilio Acosta (1818-1881), Writer — A299a

1982, Aug. 13 Litho. *Perf. 11½*
1266F A299a 3b multicolored .90 .65

Aloe — A300

2.55b, Tortoise. 2.75b, Tara amarilla tree. 3b, Guacharo bird.

1982, Oct. 14 Photo. *Perf. 13*
1267 A300 1.05b multi .85 .75
1268 A300 2.55b multi 2.10 1.60
1269 A300 2.75b multi 2.25 1.75
1270 A300 3b multi 2.75 2.50
Nos. 1267-1270 (4) 7.95 6.60

Andres Bello (1781-1865), Statesman and Reformer — A301

1982, Nov. 20 Litho. *Perf. 12*

1271 A301 1.05b multicolored .60 .45
1272 A301 2.55b multicolored 1.25 1.00
1273 A301 2.75b multicolored 1.25 1.00
1274 A301 3b multicolored 1.60 1.25
Nos. 1271-1274 (4) 4.70 3.70

Christmas 1982 — A302

Design: Holy Family creche figures by Francisco J. Cardozo, 18th cent.

Photogravure and Engraved

1982, Dec. 7 *Perf. 13½*

1275 A302 1b multicolored .95 .40

Bolivar Types of 1978

No. 1276, Victory Monument, Carabobo. No. 1277, Monument to the Meeting plaque. No. 1278, Antonio de Sucre. No. 1279, Jose Antonio Paez. No. 1280, Sword hilt, 1824. No. 1281, Guayaquil Monument.

1982-83 Engr. *Perf. 12½*

1276 A254 30c multicolored .50 .35
1277 A254 30c multicolored .50 .35
1278 A254 30c multicolored .50 .35
1279 A254 1b multicolored .70 .35
1280 A254 1b multicolored .70 .35
1281 A254 1b multicolored .70 .35
Nos. 1276-1281 (6) 3.60 2.10

Souvenir Sheets

Litho.

Perf. 14

1282 A255 Sheet of 5 6.25 6.25
a.-e. 50c, any single .40 .40
1283 A255 Sheet of 5 6.25 6.25
a.-e. 50c, any single .40 .40
1284 A255 Sheet of 5 6.25 6.25
a.-e. 50c, any single .40 .40

No. 1282: Battle of Carabobo by Martin Tovar y Tovar; No. 1283, Monument to the Meeting; No. 1284, Battle of Ayacucho, by Martin Tovar y Tovar.

Issue dates: Nos. 1276-1277, 1279, 1281-1283, Dec. 17; others, Apr. 18, 1983.

Gen. Jose Francisco Bermudez A303

Antonio Nicolas Briceno, Liberation Hero A304

Perf. 13x13½, 15x14

1982, Dec. 23 Litho.

1285 A303 3b multicolored 1.90 1.60
1286 A304 3b multicolored 1.90 1.60

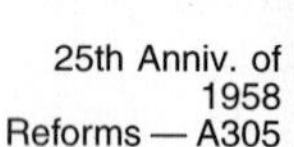

25th Anniv. of 1958 Reforms — A305

1983, Jan. 23 *Perf. 10½x10*

1287 A305 3b multicolored 1.40 1.00

A306

1983, Mar. 20 Photo. *Perf. 13½x13*

1288 A306 4b olive & red 1.00 .45

25th anniv. of Judicial Police Technical Dept.

Transportation Type of 1981

Designs: 75c, Lincoln, 1923. 80c, Locomotive, 1889. 85c, Willys truck, 1927. 95c, Cleveland motorcycle, 1920.

Perf. 13½x14½

1983, Mar. 28 Photo.

1289 A291 75c multi 1.30 1.00
1290 A291 80c multi 1.30 1.00
1291 A291 85c multi 1.60 1.00
1292 A291 95c multi 1.60 1.00
Nos. 1289-1292 (4) 5.80 4.00

A307

1983, May 17 Photo. *Perf. 13x12½*

1293 A307 2.85b multicolored 1.00 .75

World Communications Year.

Bolivar Types of 1978

Designs: 30c; Flags of Colombia, Peru, Chile, Venezuela, and Buenos Aires. 1b; Equestrian Statue of Bolivar.

Photo. & Engr. (#1294), Engr. (#1295)

1983, July 25 *Perf. 12½*

1294 A254 30c multicolored .55 .40
1295 A254 1b multicolored .80 .40

Souvenir Sheet

Litho.

Perf. 14

1296 A255 Sheet of 5 6.25 5.00
a.-e. 50c, any single .40 .40

Single stamps of No. 1296 show details of "The Liberator on the Silver Mountain of Potosi" Size of souvenir sheet stamps, 20x25mm.

A308

9th Pan-American Games — A309

Designs: No. 1298, Swimming. No. 1299, Cycling. No. 1300, Fencing. No. 1301, Runners. No. 1302, Weightlifting.

No. 1303: a, Baseball. b, Cycle wheel. c, Boxing glove. d, Soccer ball. e, Target.

Lithographed and Engraved

1983, Aug. 25 *Perf. 13*

1297 A308 2b multi .70 .35
1298 A308 2b multi .70 .35
1299 A308 2.70b multi .85 .60
1300 A308 2.70b multi .85 .60
1301 A308 2.85b multi 1.00 .75
1302 A308 2.85b multi 1.00 .75
Nos. 1297-1302 (6) 5.10 3.40

Souvenir Sheet

1303 Sheet of 5 17.50 16.00
a.-e. A309 1b, any single 3.50 3.00

No. 1303 for Copan '83. Size: 167x121mm.

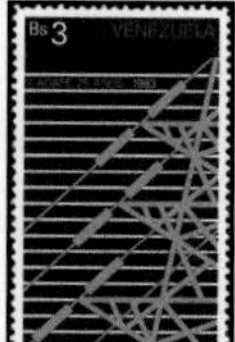

25th Anniv. of Cadafe (State Electricity Authority) — A310

1983, Oct. 27 Litho. *Perf. 14*

1304 A310 3b multicolored 1.60 1.40

Redrawn Bolivar Type of 1976

1983, Sept. 29 Engr. *Perf. 12*

Size: 26x32mm

1305 A231 25b blue green 11.50 10.00
1306 A231 30b brown 13.50 11.00
1307 A231 50b brt rose lilac 20.00 16.00
Nos. 1305-1307 (3) 45.00 37.00

Transportation Type of 1981

Various views of Caracas Metro.

1983, Dec. Photo. *Perf. 13½x14½*

1308 A291 55c multicolored .90 .75
1309 A291 75c multicolored .90 .75
1310 A291 95c multicolored .90 .75
1311 A291 2b multicolored 2.00 1.50
Nos. 1308-1311 (4) 4.70 3.75

Nativity — A311

1983, Dec. 1 Litho. *Perf. 13x14*

1312 A311 1b multi .75 .50

Christmas 1983.

A312

2.25p, Pitching tent. 2.55b, Planting tree. 2.75b, Mountain climbing. 3b, Camp site.

Lithographed and Engraved

1983, Dec. 14 *Perf. 12½x13*

1313 A312 2.25p multi .85 .70
1314 A312 2.55b multi .85 .70
1315 A312 2.75b multi 1.00 .70
1316 A312 3b multi 1.00 .70
Nos. 1313-1316 (4) 3.70 2.80

Scouting Year (1982).

Bolivar Types of 1978

Designs: No. 1317, Title page of "Opere de Raimondo Montecuccoli" (most valuable book in Caracas University Library). No. 1318, Pedro Gual, Congress of Panama delegate, 1826. No. 1319, Jose Maria Vargas (b. 1786), University of Caracas pres. No. 1320, José Faustino Sanchez Carrion, Congress of Panama delegate, 1826.

1984 Engr. *Perf. 12½*

1317 A254 30c multicolored .60 .35
1318 A254 30c multicolored .60 .35
1319 A254 1b multicolored .60 .35
1320 A254 1b multicolored .60 .35
Nos. 1317-1320 (4) 2.40 1.40

Souvenir Sheets

Litho.

Perf. 14

1321 A255 Sheet of 5 6.25 5.00
a.-e. 50c, any single .40 .40
1322 A255 Sheet of 5 6.25 5.00
a.-e. 50c, any single .40 .40

Single stamps of No. 1321 show details of Arts, Science and Education, fresco by Hector Poleo; 1322, Map of South America, 1829. Size of souvenir sheet stamps: 20x30mm; 27x20mm.

Issued: #1317, 1319, 1321, 1/19; others, 1/20.

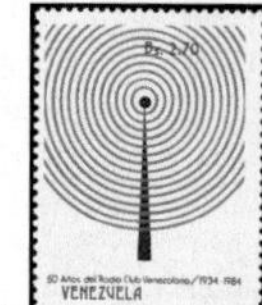

Radio Waves — A313

1984, Jan. 30 Litho. *Perf. 14x13*

1323 A313 2.70b multicolored .90 .65

Radio Club of Venezuela, 50th anniv.

Intelligentsia for Peace — A314

1984, Jan. 31

1324 A314 1b Doves .70 .50
1325 A314 2.70b Profile 1.40 .90
1326 A314 2.85b Flower, head 1.40 .90
Nos. 1324-1326 (3) 3.50 2.30

President Romulo Gallegos (1884-1969) A315

Gallegos: No. 1327, Portrait as a young man in formal dress. No. 1328, Portrait, 1948.

1984-85 Litho. *Perf. 11½*

1327 A315 1.70b royal bl, dl bl, beige & blk .90 .65
1328 A315 1.70b ocher, org brn & buff .90 .65

Issued: #1327, 10/12/84; #1328, 1/18/85.

See Nos. 1335-1336.

Pan-American Union of Engineering Associations, 18th Convention — A316

1984, Oct. 28

1329 A316 2.55b pale buff, dk bl .90 .65

Christmas 1984 — A317

1984, Dec. 3

1330 A317 1b multicolored .75 .50

Pope John Paul II, Statue of the Virgin of Caracas — A318

1985, Jan. 26 Litho. *Perf. 12*

1331 A318 1b multicolored 2.00 1.75

Papal visit, 1985.

Pascua City Bicent. — A319

1985, Feb. 10

1332 A319 1.50b multicolored .85 .60

Dr. Mario Briceno-Iragorry (b. 1897), Historian — A320

1985, Oct. Litho. *Perf. 12*

1333 A320 1.25b silver & ver .80 .50

Natl. St. Vincent de Paul Soc., Cent. — A321

1985, July

1334 A321 1b dk ol bis, ver & buff .85 .60

Gallegos Memorial Type of 1984-85

Designs: Gallegos, diff.

1985, Aug. 8

1335 A315 1.70b gray grn, dk gray grn & dl gray grn .90 .65

1336 A315 1.70b grn, sage grn & dl grn .90 .65

Dated 1984.

Latin American Economic System, 10th Anniv. — A322

1985, Aug. 15

1337 A322 4b black & red 2.25 2.00

Miniature Sheet

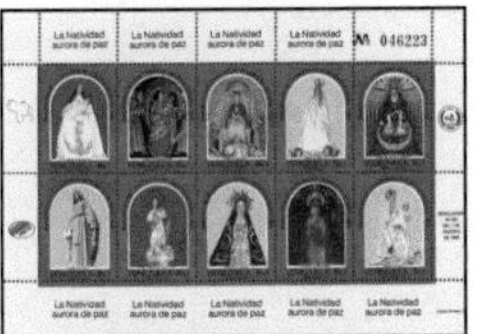

Virgin Mary, Birth Bimillennium — A323

Statues: a, Virgin of the Divine Shepherd. b, Chiquinquira Madonna. c, Coromoto Madonna. d, Valley Madonna. e, Virgin of Perpetual Succor. f, Virgin of Peace. g, Immaculate Conception Virgin. h, Soledad Madonna. i, Virgin of Consolation. j, Nieves Madonna.

1985, Sept. 9

1338 A323 Sheet of 10 9.50 7.00
a.-j. 1b, any single .50 .35

OPEC, 25th Anniv. — A324

1985, Sept. 13

1339 A324 6b multicolored 2.25 1.75

Opening of the Museum of Contemporary Art, Caracas — A325

1985, Oct. 24 *Perf. 13½*

1340 A325 3b multicolored 1.40 .90

Dated 1983.

UN, 40th Anniv. — A326

1985, Nov. 15 *Perf. 12*

1341 A326 10b brt blue & ver 2.50 2.25

Intl. Youth Year — A327

1985, Nov. 26

1342 A327 1.50b multicolored .85 .60

Christmas 1985 — A328

Nativity: a, Sheperds. b, Holy Family, Magi. Se-tenant in a continuous design.

1985, Dec. 2

1343 A328 Pair 2.25 1.75
a.-b. 2b, any single 1.00 .35

Dr. Luis Maria Drago (b. 1859), Politician — A329

1985, Dec. 20 *Perf. 13½*

1344 A329 2.70b tan, ver & sepia 1.25 .70

Dated 1984.

Miniature Sheet

Natl. Oil Industry, 10th Anniv. — A330

Designs: a, Industry emblem. b, Isla Oil Refinery. c, Bariven oil terminal. d, Pequiven refinery. e, Corpoven drilling rig. f, Maraven offshore rig. g, Intevep labs. h, Meneven refinery. i, Lagoven refinery. j, Emblem, early drilling rig.

1985, Dec. 13 *Perf. 12*

1345 A330 Sheet of 10 14.50 12.00
a.-b. 1b multi .35 .30
c.-d. 2b multi .65 .35
e.-f. 3b multi 1.20 .50
g.-h. 4b multi 1.50 .60
i.-j. 5b multi 1.75 .60

Simon Bolivar Memorial Coins — A331

1985, Dec. 18

1346 A331 2b multicolored .70 .50
1347 A331 2.70b multicolored 1.00 .65
1348 A331 3b multicolored 1.10 .75
Nos. 1346-1348 (3) 2.80 1.90

Dated 1984.

Guayana Development Corp., 25th Anniv. — A332

2b, Guayana City. 3b, Orinoco Steel Mill. 5b, Raul Leoni-Guri Hydro-electric Dam.

1985, Dec. 27

1349 A332 2b multicolored .65 .55
1350 A332 3b multicolored 1.10 .75
1351 A332 5b multicolored 1.80 1.40
Nos. 1349-1351 (3) 3.55 2.70

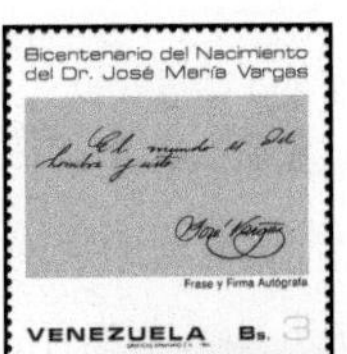

A333

Dr. Jose Vargas (1786-1854) — A334

Designs: No. 1352a, Handwriting and signature. b, Portrait, 1874, by Martin Tovar y Tovar. c, Statue, Palace of the Academies. d, Flags, EXFILBO '86 emblem. e, Vargas do Caracas Hospital. f, Frontispiece of lectures manual, 1842. g, Portrait, 1986, by Alirio Palacios. h, Gesneria vargasii. i, Bolivar-Vargas commemorative medal, 1955, 6th Natl. Medical Sciences Cong. j, Portrait, anonymous, 19th cent.

No. 1353a, Portrait, facing front. b, Portrait, facing left, Nos. 1352a, 1352d, 1352e, 1352h and 1352i have horizontal vignettes.

Miniature Sheet

1986, Mar. 10 Litho. *Perf. 12*

1352 Sheet of 10 11.00 11.00
a.-j. A333 3b, any single .90 .40

Souvenir Sheet

Imperf

1353 A334 Sheet of 2 14.00 13.50
a.-b. 15b, any single 6.00 1.00

EXFILBO '86, Mar. 10-17, Caracas, 1st Bolivarian exhibition.

Youths Painting School Wall — A335

1986, May 12 *Perf. 12*

1354 A335 3b shown .90 .75
1355 A335 5b Repairing desk 1.60 1.25

Founding and maintenance of educational institutions.

Francisco Miranda's Work for American Liberation, Bicent. (1981) — A336

Lithographed and Engraved

1986, Apr. 18 *Perf. 13*

1356 A336 1.05b multicolored .75 .50

Dated 1983.

INDULAC, 45th Anniv. — A337

2.55b, Milk trucks, vert. 2.70b, Map, vert. 3.70b, Milk processing plant.

1986, June 27 Litho. *Perf. 12*

1357 A337 2.55b multicolored .80 .65
1358 A337 2.70b multicolored .80 .65
1359 A337 3.70b multicolored 1.10 .65
Nos. 1357-1359 (3) 2.70 1.95

Industria Lactea (INDULAC), Venezuelan milk processing company.

Miniature Sheet

Viasa Venezuelan Airlines, 25th Anniv. — A338

a, Commemorative coin. b, Douglas DC-8 ascending. c, DC-8 taxiing. d, Boeing 747 in flight. e, DC-10 tails. f, Map of hemispheres. g, DC-10 taking off. h, Rear of DC-10 & DC8 on runway. i, DC-9 over mountains. j, Crew in cockpit.

1986, Aug. 11 Litho. *Perf. 12*

1360 A338 Sheet of 10 11.50 9.00
a.-e. 3b, any single .70 .40
f.-j. 3.25b, any single .90 .40

Miniature Sheet

Romulo Betancourt (1908-1981), President — A339

a, i, Portrait with natl. flag. b, j, Seated in armchair, smoking pipe. c, h, Wearing hat, text. d, f, Wearing sash of office. e, g, Reading.

1986, Sept. 28

1361 A339 Sheet of 10 12.50 10.00
a.-e. 2.70b, any single .60 .35
f.-j. 3b, any single .75 .35

Redrawn Bolivar Type of 1976

1986, Sept. 29 Litho. *Perf. 12½*

1362 A231 25c red .75 .35
1363 A231 50c blue .75 .35
1364 A231 75c pink .75 .35
1365 A231 1b orange .75 .35
1366 A231 2b brt yellow grn .90 .35
Nos. 1362-1366 (5) 3.90 1.75

Nos. 1362-1366 inscribed Armitano.
For surcharges see Nos. 1453-1464.

Re-opening of Zulia University, 40th Anniv. — A340

1986, Sept. 29

1367 A340 2.70b shown .65 .50
1368 A340 2.70b Library entrance .65 .50
a. Pair, #1367-1368 1.50 1.00

11th Congress of Architects, Engineers and Affiliated Professionals — A341

1986, Oct. 3

1369 1.40b multicolored .90 .65
1370 1.55b multicolored .90 .65
a. A341 Pair, #1369-1370 2.00 1.50

Fauna and Flora — A342

70c, Priodontes maximus. 85c, Espeletia angustifolia. 2.70b, Crocodylus intermedius. 3b, Brownea grandiceps.

1986, Sept. 12 Photo. *Perf. 13½*

1371 A342 70c multicolored .90 .70
1372 A342 85c multicolored .90 .70
1373 A342 2.70b multicolored .90 .70
1374 A342 3b multicolored 1.10 .80
Nos. 1371-1374 (4) 3.80 2.90

Miniature Sheet

State Visit of Pope John Paul II — A343

1986, Oct. 22 *Perf. 12*

1375 A343 Sheet of 10 10.00 7.50
a. 1b Pope, mountains .35 .30
b. 2b Bridge .50 .30
c. 3b Kissing the ground .65 .30
d. 3b Statue of Our Lady .65 .30
e. 4b Crosier, buildings 1.00 .30
f. 5.25b Waterfall 1.25 .40

#1375 contains 2 each #1375a-1375b, 1375e-1375f and one each #1375c-1375d.

Miniature Sheet

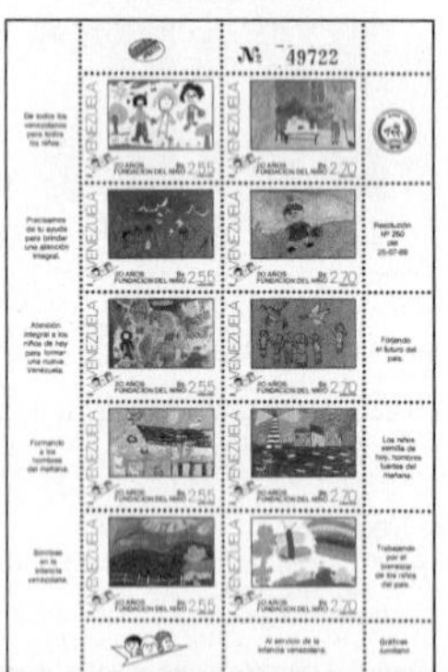

Children's Foundation, 20th Anniv. — A344

Children's drawings: a, Three children. b, Hearts, children, birds. c, Child, animals. d, Animals, house. e, Landscape. f, Child, flowers on table. g, Child holding ball. h, Children, birds. i, Lighthouse, port. j, Butterfly in flight.

1986, Nov. 10

1376 A344 Sheet of 10 8.00 5.50
a.-e. 2.55b, any single .55 .30
f.-j. 2.70b, any single .55 .30

Christmas — A345

Creche figures carved by Eliecer Alvarez.

1986, Nov. 10

1377 2b shown .60 .35
1378 2b Virgin and child .60 .35
a. A345 Pair, #1377-1378 1.40 .90

City Police, 25th Anniv. — A346

Emblem and: a, Emergency medical aid, helicopter. b, Security at sporting event. c, Bar code. d, Cadets in front of police academy. e, Motorcycle police.

1986, Dec. 10

1379 Strip of 5 5.25 4.00
a.-e. A346 2.70b, any single .65 .30

Folk Art — A347

Lithographed and Engraved

1987, Jan. 31 *Perf. 13*

1380 A347 2b Musical instrument .90 .65
1381 A347 2b Fabric .90 .65
1382 A347 3b Ceramic pot 1.20 .65
1383 A347 3b Basket work 1.20 .65
Nos. 1380-1383 (4) 4.20 2.60

Dated 1983. Nos. 1380, 1382 show Pre-Hispanic art.

A348

Lithographed and Engraved

1987, Feb. 27 *Perf. 14x14½*

1384 A348 2.55b multicolored 1.90 .50

Discovery of the Tubercle Bacillus by Robert Koch, Cent. (in 1982). Dated 1983.

Miniature Sheet

Easter 1987 — A349

Paintings and sculpture: a, Arrival of Jesus in Jerusalem. b, Christ at the Column. c, Jesus of Nazareth. d, The Descent. e, The Solitude. f, The Last Supper. g, Christ Suffering. h, The Crucifixion. i, Christ Entombed. j, The Resurrection.

1987, Apr. 2 Litho. *Perf. 12*

1385 A349 Sheet of 10 20.00 17.50
a.-e. 2b, any single 1.10 .30
f.-j. 2.25b, any single 1.25 .30

World Neurochemistry Congress — A350

3b, Bolivar and Bello, outdoor sculpture by Marisol Escobar. 4.25b, Retinal neurons.

1987, May 8 Litho. *Perf. 12*

1386 A350 3b multicolored .55 .30
1387 A350 4.25b multicolored .75 .30
a. Pair, #1386-1387 3.50 3.00

Miniature Sheet

Tourism — A351

Hotels: a, f, Barquisimeto Hilton. b, g, Lake Hotel Intercontinental, Maracaibo. c, h, Macuto Sheraton, Caraballeda. d, i, Melia Caribe, Caraballeda. e, j, Melia, Puerto la Cruz.

1987, May 29 Litho. *Perf. 12*

1388 A351 Sheet of 10 17.50 15.00
a.-e. 6b, any single 1.00 .35
f.-j. 6.50b, any single, diff. 1.00 .35

Natl. Institute of Canalization, 35th Anniv. — A352

2b, Map of Amazon territory waterways. 4.25b, Apure and Bolivar states waterways.

1987, June 25 Litho. *Perf. 12*

1389 A352 2b multicolored .35 .30
1390 A352 4.25b multicolored .65 .35
g. Pair, #1389-1390 1.75 1.25

Vicente Emilio Sojo (1887-1974), Composer A352a

2b, Academy of Fine Arts, Caracas. 4b, Sojos directing choir. 5b, Hymn to Bolivar score. 6b, Sojo, score on blackboard. 7b, Portrait, signature.

1987, July 1 Litho. *Perf. 12*

1390A Strip of 5 39.00 37.50
b. A352a 2b tan & sepia 1.25 1.25
c. A352a 4b tan & sepia 2.00 1.40
d. A352a 5b tan & sepia 2.00 1.40
e. A352a 6b tan & sepia 3.25 2.00
f. A352a 7b tan & sepia 4.00 2.00

Printed in sheets of 10 containing two strips of five, black control number (UR).

Simon Bolivar University, 20th Anniv. — A353

Designs: a, Bolivar statue by Roca Rey, 1973. b, Outdoor sculpture of solar panels by Alejandro Otero, 1972. c, Rectory, 1716. d, Laser. e, Owl, sculpture, 1973.

1987, July 9 Litho. *Perf. 12*

1391 Strip of 5 16.00 15.00
a. A353 2b multicolored .50 .30
b. A353 3b multicolored .75 .30
c. A353 4b multicolored 1.00 .30
d. A353 5b multicolored 1.25 .60
e. A353 6b multicolored 1.50 .60

Miniature Sheet

Ministry of Transportation and Communication — A354

Designs: a, Automobiles. b, Ship. c, Train, Cathedral. d, Letters, telegraph key. e, Communication towers. f, Highway. g, Airplane. h, Locomotive, rail caution signs. i, Satellite dish. j, Satellite in orbit.

1987, July 16

1392 A354 Sheet of 10 11.50 9.00
a.-e. 2b any single .35 .30
f.-j. 2.25b any single .35 .30

Nos. 1392a and 1392f, 1392b and 1392g, 1392c and 1392h, 1392d and 1392i, 1392e and 1392j have continuous designs.

Miniature Sheet

Venezuela Navigation Company, 70th Anniv. — A355

Designs: a, Corporate headquarters. b, Fork lift. c, Ship's Superstructure. d, Engine room. e, The Zulia. f, The Guarico. g, Ship's officer on the bridge. h, Bow of supertanker. i, Loading dock. j, Map of sea routes.

1987, July 31 Litho. *Perf. 12*

1393 A355 Sheet of 10 8.75 6.25
a.-b. 2b, any single .35 .30
c.-d. 3b, any single .35 .30
e.-f. 4b, any single .40 .30
g.-h. 5b, any single .50 .30
i.-j. 6b, any single .55 .30

Nos. 1393a, 1393c, 1393e, 1393g and 1393i in vertical strip; No. 1393b, 1393d, 1393f, 1393h and 1393j in vertical strip.

Miniature Sheet

Natl. Guard, 50th Anniv. — A356

a, f, Air-sea rescue. b, g, Traffic control. c, h, Environment and nature protection. d, i, Border control. e, j, Industrial security.

1987, Aug. 6

1394 A356 Sheet of 10 42.50 40.00
a.-e. 2b, any single .80 .30
f.-j. 4b, any single 1.50 .50

Discovery of America, 500th Anniv. (in 1992) — A357

20th cent. paintings (details): 2b, Departure from Port of Palos, by Jacobo Borges. 7b, Discovery of America, by Tito Salas. 11.50b, El Padre de las Casas, Protector of the Indians, by Salas. 12b, Trading in Venezuela at the Time of the Conquest, by Salas. 12.50b, Defeat of Guaicaipuro, by Borges.

1987, Oct. Litho. *Perf. 12*

1395 Strip of 5 12.00 11.00
a. A357 2b multi .35 .30
b. A357 7b multi .65 .35
c. A357 11.50b multi 1.00 .45
d. A357 12b multi 1.10 .55
e. A357 12.50b multi 1.25 .55

Christmas 1987 — A358

Paintings and sculpture representing the Spanish Colonial School, 18th cent.: 2b, *The Annunciation*, by Juan Pedro Lopez (1724-1787). 3b, *Nativity*, by Jose Francisco Rodriguez (1767-1818). 5.50b, *Adoration of the Magi*, anonymous. 6b, *Flight into Egypt*, by Lopez.

1987, Nov. 17 Litho. *Perf. 12*

1396 Block of 4 7.75 6.75
a. A358 2b multi .35 .30
b. A358 3b multi .35 .30
c. A358 5.50b multi .55 .35
d. A358 6b multi .65 .35

Miniature Sheet

Sidor Mills, 25th Anniv. — A359

Natl. steel production: a-d, Exterior view of steel plant (in a continuous design). e, Tower bearing the SIDOR emblem. f, Furnaces and molten steel flowing down gutters. g, Pooring steel rods. h, Slab mill. i, Steel rod production, diff. j, Anniv. emblem.

1987, Nov. 23

1397 A359 Sheet of 10 13.50 11.00
a. 2b multi .35 .30
b. 6b multi .85 .45
c. 7b multi 1.00 .55
d. 11.50b multi 1.60 .85
e. 12b black 1.90 .90
f. 2b multi .35 .30
g. 6b multi .85 .45
h. 7b multi 1.00 .55
i. 11.50b multi 1.60 .85
j. 12b multi 1.90 .90

Meeting of 8 Latin American Presidents, 1st Anniv. — A360

1987, Nov. 26

1398 A360 6b multicolored 1.00 .80

Pequiven Petrochemical Co., 10th Anniv. — A361

1987, Dec. 1

1399 Strip of 5 9.00 7.75
a. A361 2b Plastics .35 .30
b. A361 6b Refined oil products .70 .35
c. A361 7b Fertilizers .80 .35
d. A361 11.50b Installations 1.20 .65
e. A361 12b Expansion 1.40 .70

St. John Bosco (1815-88) A362

Portrait of Bosco and: 2b, Map, children. 3b, National Church, Caracas. 4b, Vocational training (printer's apprentice). 5b, Church of Mary Auxiliadora. 6b, Missionary school (nun teaching children).

1987, Dec. 8

1400 Strip of 5 5.25 4.00
a. A362 2b multicolored .35 .30
b. A362 3b multicolored .40 .35
c. A362 4b multicolored .50 .35
d. A362 5b multicolored .55 .35
e. A362 6b multicolored .70 .40

Redrawn Bolivar Type of 1976

1987, Dec. 31 Litho. *Perf. 12½*

1401	A231	3b emerald grn	.35	.25
1402	A231	4b gray	.55	.25
1403	A231	5b vermilion	.70	.25
1404	A231	10b dk ol bis	1.60	.50
1405	A231	15b rose claret	2.75	.90
1406	A231	20b bright blue	3.25	1.10
1407	A231	25b olive bister	4.50	1.75
1408	A231	30b dark violet	5.25	1.90
1409	A231	50b carmine	8.50	3.00
		Nos. 1401-1409 (9)	27.45	9.90

Nos. 1401-1409 inscribed Armitano.

29th Assembly of Inter-American Development Bank Governors A363

1988, Mar. 18 Litho. *Perf. 12*

1410 A363 11.50b multi 1.75 .80

Miniature Sheet

Republic Bank, 30th Anniv. — A364

Bank functions and finance projects: a, Personal banking at branch. b, Capital for labor. c, Industrial projects. d, Financing technology. e, Exports and imports. f, Financing agriculture. g, Fishery credits. h, Dairy farming development. i, Construction projects. j, Tourism trade development.

1988, Apr. 11

1411 A364 Sheet of 10 12.50 10.00
a.-e. 2b any single .40 .30
f.-j. 6b any single .60 .30

No. 1411 contains two strips of five.

Anti-Polio Campaign Day of Victory, May 25 — A365

Design: Polio victims pictured on bronze relief, Rotary and campaign emblems.

1988, May 20 Litho. *Perf. 12*

1412 A365 11.50b multi 1.60 1.40

Carlos Eduardo Frias (1906-1986), Founder of the Natl. Publicity Industry — A366

1988, May 27 Litho. *Perf. 12*

1414 A366 Pair 4.50 3.00
a. 4b multi .40 .30
b. 10b multi .85 .50

Publicity Industry, 50th anniv.

Venalum Natl. Aluminum Corp., 10th Anniv. — A367

Designs: 2b, Factory interior. 6b, Electric smelter. 7b, Aluminum pipes. 11.50b, Aluminum blocks moved by crane. 12b, Soccer team, aluminum equipment on playing field.

1988, June 10

1415 Strip of 5 11.50 7.50
a. A367 2b multi .60 .55
b. A367 6b multi 1.20 .55
c. A367 7b multi 1.40 .55
d. A367 11.50b multi 2.25 1.50
e. A367 12b multi 2.25 1.50

Nature Conservation A368

Birds: 2b, Carduelis cucullata. 6b, Eudocimus ruber. 11.50b, Harpia harpyja. 12b, Phoenicopterus ruber ruber. 12.50b, Pauxi pauxi.

1988, June 17 Litho. *Perf. 12*

1416 Strip of 5 10.00 7.50
a. A368 2b multi .35 .30
b. A368 6b multi .80 .35
c. A368 11.50b multi 1.50 .65
d. A368 12b multi 1.60 .65
e. A368 12.50b multi 1.60 .65

Army Day — A369

Military uniforms: a, Simon Bolivar in dress uniform, 1828. b, Gen.-in-Chief Jose Antonio Paez in dress uniform, 1821. c, Liberation Army division gen., 1810. d, Brig. gen., 1820. e, Artillery corpsman, 1836. f, Alferez Regiment parade uniform, 1988. g, Division Gen. No. 1 dress uniform, 1988. h, Line Infantry Regiment, 1820. i, Promenade Infantry, 1820. j, Light Cavalry, 1820.

1988, June 20

1417 Sheet of 10 17.50 15.00
a., f. A369 2b multi .35 .30
b., g. A369 6b multi .90 .35
c., h. A369 7b multi 1.10 .35
d., i. A369 11.50b multi 1.75 .60
e., j. A369 12b multi 1.90 .60

Scabbard, Sword and Signature — A370

Paintings by Tito Salas: 4.75b, *The General's Wedding.* 6b, Portrait. 7b, *Battle of Valencia.* 12b, *Retreat from San Carlos.*

1988, July 1 Litho. *Perf. 12*

1418 Strip of 5 10.00 7.50
a. A370 2b shown .45 .35
b. A370 4.75b multi .85 .35
c. A370 6b multi 1.00 .35
d. A370 7b multi 1.50 .40
e. A370 12b multi 3.25 .55

General Rafael Urdaneta (b. 1788).

General Santiago Marino (b. 1788), by Martin Tovar y Tovar — A371

1988, July

1419 A371 4.75b multi 1.10 .65

1988 Summer Olympics, Seoul — A372

1988, Aug. 2

1420 A372 12b multi 2.00 1.75

Electric Industry, Cent. — A373

Buildings, 1888: 2b, 1st Office. 4.75b, Jaime Carrillo and electrical plant. 10b, Bolivar Plaza. 11.50b, Baralt Theater. 12.50b, Central Thermoelectric Plant, Ramon Lagoon, 1988.

1988, Oct. 25 Litho. *Perf. 12*

1421 Strip of 5 7.75 6.50
a. A373 2b multi .35 .30
b. A373 4.75b multi .50 .35

c. A373 10b multi 1.00 .45
d. A373 11.50b multi 1.10 .55
e. A373 12.50b multi 1.25 .65

Christmas — A374

Designs: 4b, Nativity (left side), by Tito Salas, 1936. 6b, Christ child, anonymous, 17th cent. 15b, Nativity (right side).

1988, Dec. 9

1422	4b multi	.65	.35
1423	6b multi	1.20	.50
1424	15b multi	3.00	1.50
a.	A374 Strip, #1423, 2 ea #1422, 1424	8.25	7.00

Miniature Sheet

Marian Year — A375

Icons: a, Our Lady of Copacabana, Bolivia. b, Our Lady of Chiquinquira, Colombia. c, Our Lady of Coromoto, Venezuela. d, Our Lady of the Clouds, Ecuador. e, Our Lady of Antigua, Panama. f, Our Lady of the Evangelization, Peru. g, Our Lady of Lujan, Argentina. h, Our Lady of Altagracia, Dominican Republic. i, Our Lady of Aparecida, Brazil. j, Our Lady of Guadalupe, Mexico.

1988, Aug. 15 Litho. *Perf. 12*

1425	A375 Sheet of 10	15.00	12.50
a.-e.	4.75b any single	.60	.35
f.-j.	6b any single	.70	.45

Juan Manuel Cagigal Observatory, Cent. — A376

Designs: 2b, Bardou refracting telescope. 4.75b, Universal theodolite AUZ-27. 6b, Bust of Cagigal. 11.50b, Boulton cupola and night sky over Caracas in September. 12b, Satellite photographing Hurricane Allen.

1989, Sept. 5

1426	Strip of 5	8.00	6.75
a.	A376 2b multicolored	.35	.30
b.	A376 4.75b multicolored	.50	.40
c.	A376 6b multicolored	.70	.45
d.	A376 11.50b multicolored	1.20	.60
e.	A376 12b multicolored	1.40	.75

Comptroller-General's Office, 50th Anniv. — A377

1988, Oct. 14 Litho. *Perf. 12*

1427	A377 10b multi	1.40	1.10

Portrait of Founder Juan Pablo Rojas Paul, by Cristobal Rojas, 1890 — A378

6b, Commemorative medal.

1989, Oct. 21 Litho. *Perf. 12*

1428	A378 6b multi	.75	.50
1429	A378 6.50b shown	.75	.50
a.	Pair, #1428-1429	2.00	1.50

Natl. History Academy, cent.

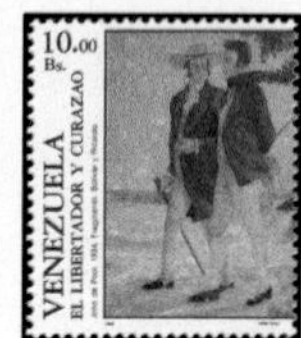

Portrait of Ricardo — A379

Paintings: No. 1430, Simon Bolivar and Dr. Mordechay Ricardo. No. 1430A, The Octagon. Nos. 1430-1430A printed in continuous design completing the painting *The Liberator in Curacao,* by John de Pool.

1989, Jan. 27 Litho. *Perf. 12*

1430	A379 10b multi	.85	.50
1430A	A379 10b multi	.85	.50
1430B	A379 11.50b shown	1.25	.65
c.	Strip of 5, #1430B, 2 ea #1430-1430A	10.50	9.25

Convention with Holy See, 25th Anniv. — A380

Designs: a, Raul Leoni, constitutional president, 1964-69. b, Cardinal Quintero, archbishop of Caracas, 1960-80. c, Arms of Cardinal Lebrun, archbishop of Caracas since 1980. d, Arms of Luciano Storero, titular archbishop of Tigimma. e, Pope Paul VI.

1989, May 4 Litho. *Perf. 12*

1431	Strip of 5	6.25	5.00
a.-b.	A380 4b any single	.50	.35
c.-d.	A380 12b any single	1.25	1.00
e.	A380 16b any single	1.75	1.25

Bank of Venezuela, Cent. — A381

Designs: a, *Cocoa Harvest,* by Tito Salas, 1946. b, *Teaching a Boy How to Grow Coffee,* by Salas, 1946. c, Bank headquarters, Caracas. d, Archive of the Liberator, Caracas. e, Aforestation campaign (seedling). f, Aforestation campaign (five youths planting seedlings). g, 50-Bolivar bank note (left side). h, 50-Bolivar bank note (right side). i, 500-Bolivar bank note (left side). j, 500-Bolivar bank note (right side).

1989, Aug. 1

1432	A381 Sheet of 10	15.00	12.50
a.-f.	4b any single	.40	.35
g.-j.	8b any single	1.00	.60

Nos. 1432g-1432h and 1432i-1432j printed in continuous designs.

America Issue — A382

UPAE emblem and pre-Columbian votive bisque artifacts: 6b, Vessel. 24b, Statue of a man.

1989

1433	A382 6b multicolored	.80	.25
1434	A382 24b multicolored	3.50	1.75
a.	Pair, #1433-1434	6.50	6.00

Miniature Sheet

Christmas — A383

Denomination at top: a, Shepherds, sheep. c, Angel appears to 3 shepherds. e, Holy Family. g, Two witnesses. i, Adoration of the kings.
Denomination at bottom: b, like a. d, like c. f, like e. h, like g. j, like i.

1989 Litho. *Perf. 12*

1435	Sheet of 10	14.00	11.50
a.-b.	A383 5b any single	.50	.35
c.-f.	A383 6b any single	.55	.35
g.-h.	A383 12b any single	1.25	.55
i.-j.	A383 15b any single	1.40	.75

Miniature Sheets

Bank of Venezuela Foundation, 20th Anniv. — A384

Tree and arms: No. 1436: a, Tabebuia chrysantha, national. b, Ceiba pentandra, Federal District. c, Myrospermum frutescens, Anzoategui. d, Pithecellobium saman, Aragua. e, Cedrela odorata, Barinas. f, Diptenyx punctata, Bolivar. g, Licania pyrofolia, Apure. h, Sterculia apetala, Carabobo.

No. 1437: a, Tabebuia rosea, Cojedes. b, Prosopis juliflora, Falcon. c, Copernicia tectorum, Guarico. d, Erythrina poeppigiana, Merida. e, Brawnea leucantha, Miranda. f, Mauritia flexuosa, Monagas. g, Malpighia glabra, Lara. h, Guaicum officinale, Nueva Esparta.

No. 1438: a, Swietenia macrophylla, Portuguesa. b, Platymiscium diadelphum, Sucre. c, Prumnopitys montana de Laub, Tachira. d, Roystonea venezuelana, Yaracuy. e, Cocos nucifera, Zulia. f, Hevea benthamiana, Federal Territory of Amazonas. g, Erythrina fusca, Trujillo. h, Rhizophora mangle, Territory of the Amacuro Delta.

1990, June 27 Litho. *Perf. 12*

1436	A384 Sheet of 8 + 2 labels	25.00	22.50
a.-f.	10b any single	.65	.35
g.	40b multicolored	2.50	1.25
h.	50b multicolored	3.25	1.60
1437	A384 Sheet of 8 + 2 labels	25.00	22.50
a.-f.	10b any single	.65	.35
g.	40b multicolored	2.50	1.25
h.	50b multicolored	3.25	1.60
1438	A384 Sheet of 8 + 2 labels	25.00	22.50
a.-f.	10b any single	.65	.35
g.	40b multicolored	2.50	1.25
h.	50b multicolored	3.25	1.60

Central Bank of Venezuela, 50th Anniv. — A385

Designs: a, Santa Capilla Headquarters, 1943. b, Headquarters, 1967. c, Left half of 500b Bank Note, 1940. d, Right half of 500b Bank Note, 1940. e, Sun of Peru decoration, 1825. f, Medals Ayacucho, 1824, Boyaca, 1820 and Liberators of Quito, 1822. g, Swords of Peru, 1825. h, Cross pendant, Bucaramanga, 1830. i, Medallion of George Washington, 1826. j, Portrait of Gen. O'Leary.

1990, Oct. 15

1439	Sheet of 10	17.50	15.00
a.-f.	A385 10b any single	.70	.40
g.-h.	A385 15b any single	1.00	.50
i.	A385 40b multicolored	2.75	1.40
j.	A385 50b multicolored	3.50	1.75

University of Zulia, Cent. — A386

Designs: a, Dr. Francisco Ochoa, founder. b, Dr. Jesus E. Lossada, President, 1946-47. c, Soil conservation. d, Developing alternative automotive fuels. e, Organ transplants.

1990, Sept. 18 Litho. *Perf. 12*

1440	Strip of 5	9.25	8.00
a.-b.	A386 10b any single	.50	.30
c.-d.	A386 15b any single	.75	.35
e.	A386 20b multicolored	1.10	.55

Christmas — A387

Paintings: a, St. Joseph and Child by Juan Pedro Lopez. b, The Nativity by Lopez. c, The Return from Egypt by Matheo Moreno. d, The Holy Family by unknown artist. e, The Nativity (oval painting) by Lopez.

1990, Nov. 25

1441	Strip of 5	8.75	7.50
a.-c.	A387 10b any single	.50	.30
d.-e.	A387 20b any single	1.10	.55

OPEC, 30th Anniv. — A388

a, Globe. b, Square emblem. c, Circular emblem. d, Diamond emblem. e, Flags.

1990, Dec. 21 Litho. *Perf. 12*

1442	Strip of 5	9.25	8.00
a.-b.	A388 10b any single	.70	.40
c.	A388 20b multicolored	1.50	.75
d.	A388 30b multicolored	2.10	1.00
e.	A388 40b multicolored	2.75	1.50

America Issue — A389

1990, Dec. 12 Litho. *Perf. 12*

1443	A389 10b Lake dwelling	1.50	.65
1444	A389 40b Coastline	4.00	2.25
a.	Pair, #1443-1444	6.50	6.00

Exfilve '90, Caracas — A389a

Designs: 40b, Bank of Venezuela 1000b note. 50b, Bank of Caracas 100b note.

1990, Nov. 16 Litho. *Imperf.*

1444B	A389a 40b multicolored	3.75	3.50
1444C	A389a 50b multicolored	4.75	4.50

No. 1444B, Bank of Venezuela, cent. No. 1444C, Bank of Caracas, cent.

St. Ignatius of Loyola (1491-1556) — A390

Designs: a, Jesuit quarters, Caracas. b, Death mask. c, Statue by Francisco de Vergara, 18th century. d, Statue of Our Lady of Montserrat, 11th century.

1991, Apr. 12 Litho. *Perf. 12*

1445	Strip of 4 + label	13.50	12.50
a.-b.	A390 12b any single	.55	.30
c.	A390 40b multicolored	2.00	.90
d.	A390 50b multicolored	2.25	1.10

Venezuelan-American Cultural Center, 50th Anniv. — A391

Designs: a, Elisa Elvira Zuloaga (1900-1980), painter & engraver. b, Gloria Stolk (1912-1979), writer. c, Caroline Lloyd (1924-1980), composer. d, Jules Waldman (1912-1990), publisher. e, William Coles (1908-1978), attorney.

1991, July 4 Litho. *Perf. 12*

1446	Strip of 5	13.50	12.50
a.-c.	A391 12b any single	.55	.30
d.	A391 40b multicolored	2.00	1.00
e.	A391 50b multicolored	2.25	1.10

Miniature Sheet

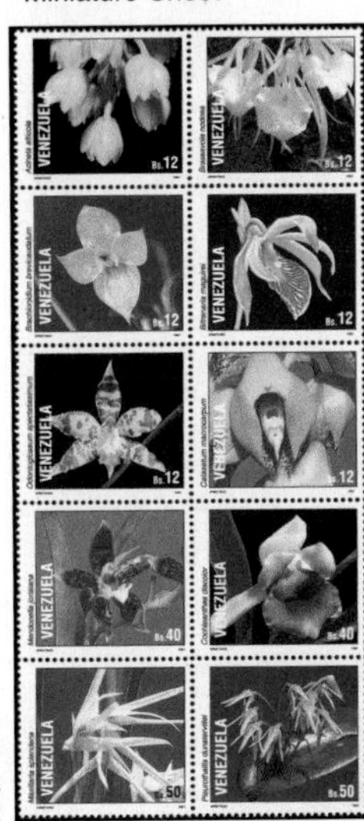

Orchids A392

Designs: No. 1447a, 12b, Acineta alticola. b, 12b, Brassavola nodosa. c, 12b, Brachionidium brevicaudatum. d, 12b, Bifrenaria maguirei. e, 12b, Odontoglossum spectatissimum. f, 12b, Catasetum macrocarpum. g, 40b, Mendocella jorisiana. h, 40b, Cochleanthes discolor. i, 50b, Maxillaria splendens. j, 50b, Pleurothallis dunstervillei. No. 1448, Cattleya violacea.

1991, Aug. 22 Litho. *Perf. 12*

1447 A392 Sheet of 10, #a.-j. 20.00 18.00

Souvenir Sheet

1448 A392 50b multicolored 18.00 18.00

No. 1448 contains one 42x37mm stamp.

Nos. 1447-1448 exist imperf. Values: No. 1447 $55; No. 1448 $25.

See Nos. 1499-1500, 1508-1509.

Democratic Action Party, 50th Anniv. — A393

Designs: a, People voting. b, Agricultural reform. c, Students and teachers. d, Nationalization of the petroleum industry.

1991, Sept. 13 Litho. *Perf. 12*

1449 A393 12b Block of 4, #a.-d. 5.25 4.25

America Issue — A394

Designs: 12b, Terepaima Chief. 40b, Paramaconi Chief.

1991, Oct. 24

1450	A394 12b multi	.75	.30
1451	A394 40b multi	2.50	1.50
a.	Pair, #1450-1451	5.00	4.50

Nos. 1450-1451 also exist imperf.

Children's Foundation, 25th Anniv. — A395

Children's drawings: a, 12b, Children in house. b, 12b, Playground. c, 12b, Carnival. d, 12b, Woman and girl walking by pond. e, 12b, Boy in hospital. f, 12b, Five children around tree. g, 40b, Two girls in colorful room. h, 40b, Classroom. i, 50b, Three children. j, 50b, Four children dancing.

1991, Oct. 31 Litho. *Perf. 12*

1452 A395 Sheet of 10, #a.-j. 19.50 17.00

Nos. 1362-1364 Surcharged

1991 Litho. *Perf. 12½*

1453	A231	5b on 25c red	.35	.30
1454	A231	5b on 75c pink	.35	.30
1455	A231	10b on 25c red	.65	.35
1456	A231	10b on 75c pink	.65	.35
1457	A231	12b on 50c blue	.85	.50
1458	A231	12b on 75c pink	.85	.50
1459	A231	20b on 50c blue	1.30	.70
1460	A231	20b on 75c pink	1.30	.70
1461	A231	40b on 50c blue	2.50	1.40
1462	A231	40b on 75c pink	2.50	1.40
1463	A231	50b on 50c blue	3.25	1.75
1464	A231	50b on 75c pink	3.25	1.75
		Nos. 1453-1464 (12)	17.80	10.00

Christmas A396

Children's art work: a, 10b, Wise men. b, 12b, Holy Family. c, 20b, Statues of Holy Family. d, 25b, Shepherds. e, 30b, Holy Family, cow, donkey.

1991, Nov. 14 Litho. *Perf. 12*

1465 A396 Strip of 5, #a.-e. 8.00 6.75

Souvenir Sheet

Exfilve '91, Caracas A397

1991, Nov. 29 Litho. *Perf. 12*

1466 A397 50b No. 136 3.75 3.50

Exists imperf. Value, $7.50.

Discovery of America, 500th Anniv. (in 1992) — A398

a, 12b, Coat of arms of Columbus. b, 12b, Santa Maria. c, 12b, Map by Juan de la Cosa. d, 40b, Sighting land. e, 50b, Columbus with Queen Isabella and King Ferdinand II.

1991, Dec. 12 Litho. *Perf. 12*

1468 A398 Strip of 5, #a.-e. 7.50 6.25

1992, Mar. 15

Designs: No. 1469a, 12b, Emblem for discovery of America Commission. b, 12b, Venezuelan pavillion, Expo '92. c, 12b, 15th century map of Spain. d, 12b, Portrait of Columbus, by Susy Dembo. e, 12b, Encounter, by Ivan Jose Rojas. f, 12b, 0x500 America, by Annella Armas. g, 40b, Imago-Mundi, by Alessandro Grechi. h, 40b, Long Journey, by Gloria Fiallo. i, 50b, Playa Dorado, by Carlos Riera. j, 50b, Irminaoro, by Erasmo Sanches Cedeno. No. 1470, Untitled work, by Muaricio Sanchez.

1469 A398 Sheet of 10, #a.-j. 20.00 18.00

1470 A398 50b multicolored 4.75 4.50

Expo '92, Seville. No. 1470 contains one 38x42mm stamp.

Protection of Nature — A399

Turtles: No. 1471a, Geochelone carbonaria, facing left. b, Geochelone carbonaria, facing right. c, Podocnemis expansa, facing left. d, Podocnemis expansa, swimming.

1992, June 12 Litho. *Perf. 12*

1471 A399 12b Block of 4, #a.-d. 11.00 11.00

World Wildlife Fund.

No. 1471 also exists imperf.

Miniature Sheet

Beatification of Josemaria Escriva — A400

Designs: a, 18b, Teaching in Venezuela, 1975. b, 18b, Celebrating mass. c, 18b, Parents, Jose Escriva and Dolores Albas. d, 18b, Text with autograph. e, 18b, Kissing feet of Madonna. f, 18b, Commemorative medallion. g, 60b, With Pope Paul VI. h, 60b, At desk, writing. i, 75b, Portrait. j, 75b, Portrait in St. Peter's Square, 1992.

1992, Oct. 2 Litho. *Perf. 12*

1472 A400 Sheet of 10, #a.-j. 20.00 18.00

Electrification of Southern Regions — A401

Designs: a, 12b, Roof of native hut. b, 12b, Transmission lines and towers. c, 12b, Horses running through pond. d, 40b, Workmen under tower. e, 50b, Baskets, crafts.

1992, July 15 Litho. *Perf. 12*

1473 A401 Strip of 5, #a.-e. 7.25 6.00

Miniature Sheet

Artwork, by Mateo Manaure — A402

Color of background: a, 12b, Red. b, 12b, Red violet. c, 12b, Gray. d, 12b, Violet brown. e, 40b, Brown. f, 40b, Blue. g, 50b, Blue violet. h, 50b, Black.

1993, July 23

1474 A402 Sheet of 8, #a.-h. + 2 labels 11.00 8.50

Bank of Maracaibo, 110th anniv.

Discovery of America, 500th Anniv. — A403

Paintings: a, 18b, The Third Trip, by Elio Caldera. b, 60b, Descontextura, by Juan Pablo Nascimiento.

1992, Nov. 20 Litho. *Perf. 12*

1476 A403 Pair, #a.-b. 4.50 4.00

Christmas — A404

Artwork by Lucio Rivas: a, 18b, Adoration of the Shepherds. b, 75b, Adoration of the Magi. 100b, Flight into Egypt.

1992, Dec. 3 Litho. *Perf. 12*

1477 A404 Pair, #a.-b. 4.00 3.50

Souvenir Sheet

1478 A404 100b multicolored 4.25 4.00

No. 1478 contains one 42x38mm stamp.

A405 A406

A407

Designs: 1b, 2b, Simon Bolivar. 5b, Natl. Pantheon. 10b, Victory Monument, Carabobo. 20b, Jose Antonio Paez. 25b, Luisa Caceres de Arismendi. 35b, Ezequiel Zamora. 40b, Cristobal Mendoza. No. 1490, Central University. No. 1491, Jose Felix Ribas. No. 1494, Manuel Piar. 200b, Simon Bolivar.

1993-94 Litho. *Perf. 12½*

Size: 18x22mm

1479	A405	1b silver	.40	.35
1480	A405	2b greenish blue	.40	.35
1482	A406	5b red	.40	.35
1484	A406	10b violet	.40	.35
1487	A407	20b olive green	.90	.60
1488	A407	25b red brown	.65	.50
1488A	A407	35b brt yel grn	1.50	.90
1489	A407	40b lt blue	1.10	.90
1490	A406	50b orange	2.40	1.10
1491	A407	50b lilac rose	1.50	1.25
1493	A407	100b brown	4.75	3.50
1494	A407	100b dark blue	3.00	2.40
1496	A407	200b brown	6.00	5.00
		Nos. 1479-1496 (13)	23.40	17.55

Nos. 1479-1493 inscribed Armitano.

See Nos. 1548-1562.

Orchid Type of 1991

Miniature Sheet

Designs: a, 20b, Cattleya percivaliana. b, 20b, Anguloa ruckeri. c, 20b, Chondrorhyncha flaveola. d, 20b, Stenia pallida. e, 20b, Zygosepalum lindeniae. f, 20b, Maxillaria triloris. g, 80b, Stanhopea wardii. h, 80b, Oncidium papilio. i, 100b, Oncidium hastilabium. j, 100b, Sobralia cattleya. 150b, Polycycnis muscifera.

1993, Apr. 1 Litho. *Perf. 12*

1499 A392 Sheet of 10, #a.-j. 20.00 18.00

Souvenir Sheet

1500 A392 150b multicolored 7.75 7.50

Miniature Sheet

Settlement of Tovar Colony, 150th Anniv. — A408

Designs: a, 24b, Woman. b, 24b, Children. c, 24b, Catholic Church, 1862. d, 24b, Statue of St. Martin of Tours, 1843. e, 24b, Fruits and vegetables. f, 24b, School, 1916. g, 80b, Home of founder, Augustin Codazzi, 1845. h, 80b, House of colony director, Alexander Benitz, 1845. i, 100b, Breidenbach Mill, 1860. j, 100b, Parade.

1993, Apr. 12 Litho. *Perf. 12*

1501 A408 Sheet of 10, #a.-j. 20.00 18.00

Miniature Sheet

19th Pan-American Railways Conference — A409

Designs: a, 24b, Tucacas steam locomotive. b, 24b, Halcon steam locomotive on Las Mostazas Bridge, 1894. c, 24b, Maracaibo locomotive. d, 24b, Tender, rail cars, Palo Grande Station. e, 24b, Fiat diesel locomotive, 1957. f, 24b, GP-9-L diesel locomotive, 1957. g, 80b, GP-15-L diesel locomotive, 1982. h, 80b, Metro subway train, Caracas. i, 100b, Electric locomotive. j, 100b, Passenger cars of electric train.

1993, May 25 Litho. *Perf. 12*

1502 A409 Sheet of 10, #a.-j. 25.00 22.50

Nos. 1502c-1502d, 1502i-1502j are continuous designs.

A410

World Day to Stop Smoking: a, 24b, Shown. b, 80b, "No smoking" emblem.

1993, May 27 Litho. *Perf. 12½x12*

1503 A410 Pair, #a.-b. 4.50 4.00

A411

America Issue: a, 24b, Amazona barbadensis. b, 80b, Ara macao.

1993, Oct. 7 Litho. *Perf. 12*

1504 A411 Pair, #a.-b. 7.25 6.75

Miniature Sheets

Native Indians — A412

Designs: No. 1505a, 1b, Two Yanomami children with painted bodies, spear. b, 1b, Yanomami woman preparing food. c, 40b, Two Panare children performing in Katyayinto ceremony. d, 40b, Panare man with nose flute. e, 40b, Taurepan man in canoe. f, 40b, Taurepan girl weaving. g, 40b, Piaroa woman with infant. h, 40b, Piaroa dancers wearing war masks. i, 100b, Hoti man blowing flute. j, 100b, Hoti woman carrying baby, basket over back.

150b, Child blowing traditional whistle.

1993, Nov. 25 Litho. *Perf. 12*

1505 A412 Sheet of 10, #a.-j. 14.50 12.00

Souvenir Sheet

1506 A412 150b multicolored 4.50 4.50

Christmas — A413

Nativity scene: a, f, 24b, Joseph. b, g, 24b, Madonna and Child. c, h, 24b, Shepherd boy, wise man holding gift, lambs. d, i, 80b, Wise man with hands folded, boy. e, j, 100b, Wise man presenting gift, boy with hands folded.

1993, Nov. 30

1507 A413 Sheet of 10, #a.-j. 17.50 15.00

Nos. 1507f-1507j are black, magenta & buff.

Orchid Type of 1991

Miniature Sheet

Designs: a, 35b, Chrysocycnis schlimii. b, 35b, Galeandra minax. c, 35b, Oncidium falcipetalum. d, 35b, Oncidium lanceanum. e, 40b, Sobralia violacea linden. f, 40b, Sobralia infundibuligera. g, 80b, Mendoncella burkei. h, 80b, Phragmipedium caudatum. i, 100b, Phragmipedium kaieteurum. j, 200b, Stanhopea grandiflora.

150b, Epidendrum elongatum.

1994, May 19 Litho. *Perf. 12*

1508 A392 Sheet of 10, #a.-j. 20.00 18.00

Souvenir Sheet

1509 A392 150b multicolored 4.00 3.75

No. 1509 contains one 42x37mm stamp.

Miniature Sheet of 10

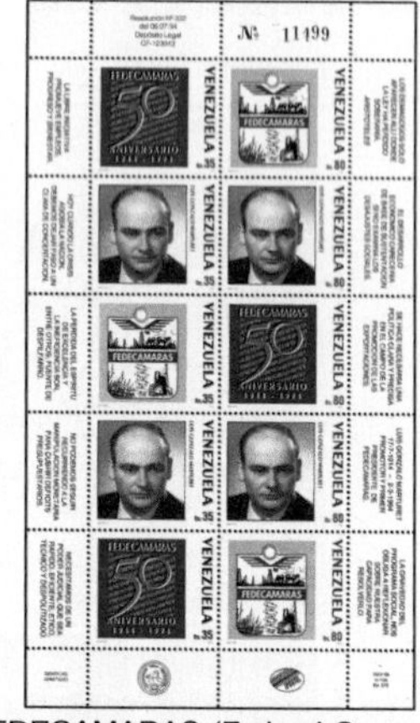

FEDECAMARAS (Federal Council of Production & Commerce Associations), 50th Anniv. — A414

a, 35b; f, 80b, Anniversary emblem. b, 35b; e, 80b, Luis Gonzalo Marturet (1914-64), 1st president. c, 35b; d, 80b, FEDECAMARAS emblem.

1994, July 17 Litho. *Perf. 12*

1510 A414 #c, f, 2 ea #a-b, d-e 16.00 13.50

Judicial Service — A415

1994, Sept. 13 Litho. *Perf. 12*

1511 A415 100b multicolored 2.00 1.75

Miniature Sheet

Christmas — A416

Paintings: a, 35b, g, 80b, The Nativity, by follower of Jose Lorenzo de Alvarado. b, 35b, h, 80b, Birth of Christ, 19th cent. c, 35b, i, 80b, The Nativity, diff., by follower of Jose Lorenzo de Alvarado. d, 35b, j, 80b, Adoration of the Magi, 17th cent.. e, 35b, f, 80b, Birth of Christ, by School of Tocuyo.

1994, Dec. 1

1512 A416 Sheet of 10, #a.-j. 16.00 13.50

Miniature Sheet

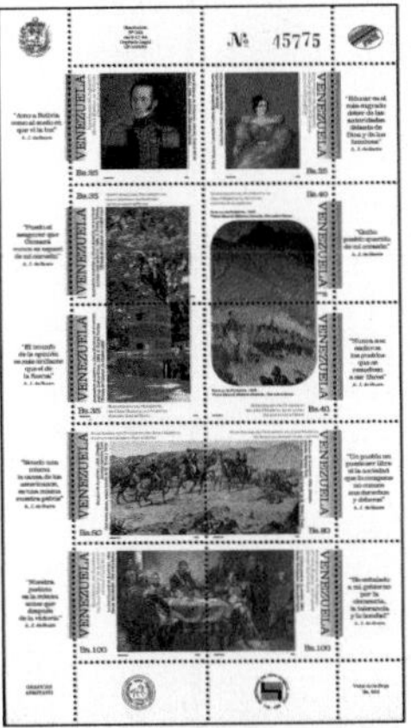

Antonio Jose de Sucre (1795-1830) — A417

Designs: No. 1513a, 25b, Portrait. b, 25b, Dona Mariana Carcelen Y Larrea Marquesa de Solanda. c, 35b, Top of equestrian monument. d, 35b, Bottom of monument. e, 40b, Painting of Battle of Pichincha, mountains at top. f, 40b, Painting of Battle of Pichincha, battle scent. g, 80b, Painting of Battle of Ayacucho, soldiers on horseback. h, 80b, Painting of Battle of Ayacucho, dead soldiers. i, 100b, Painting of Surrender at Ayachucho, general signing document. j, 100b, Painting of Surrender at Ayachucho, seated general at right.
150b, Portion of mural, Carabobo, by Pedro Centeno Vallenilla.

1995, Feb. 2
1513 A417 Sheet of 10, #a.-j. 16.00 13.50

Souvenir Sheet

1514 A417 150b multicolored 3.00 3.50

Postal Transportation — A418

a, 35b, Post office van. b, 80b, Airplane.

1995, Mar. 22 Litho. *Perf. 12*
1515 A418 Pair, #a.-b. 2.50 2.50

No. 1515 issued in sheets of 10 stamps.

Miniature Sheet

St. Jean-Baptiste de La Salle (1651-1719), Educator — A419

Denomination LR: a, 100b, Portrait. b, 35b, Students with microscope, academic education. c, 35b, Soccer players, sports education. d, 35b, Scouts at camp, citizenship education. e, 80b, La Salle College, Caracas.
Denomination LL: f, like #1516e. g, like #1516d. h, like #1516b. i, like #1516c. j, like #1516a.

1995, May 15
1516 A419 Sheet of 10, #a.-j. 13.50 11.00

Miniature Sheet

Founding of Salesian Order, Cent. — A420

Designs: a, 35b, St. John Bosco (1815-88), priest with child. b, 35b, Lonely child, Madonna and Child. c, 35b, Man running machine tool. d, 35b, Young men working with electronic instruments. e, 35b, Baseball game. f, 35b, Basketball game. g, 80b, People working in fields. h, 80b, Man looking at chili peppers. i, 100b, Young tribal natives receiving religious training. j, 100b, Tribal native.

1995, Apr. 26
1517 A420 Sheet of 10, #a.-j. 13.50 11.00

Miniature Sheet

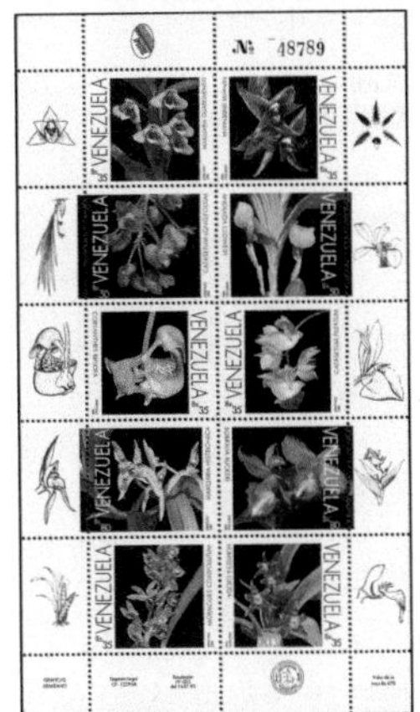

Orchids — A421

Designs: a, 35b, Maxillaria guareimensis. b, 35b, Paphinia lindeniana. c, 50b, Catasetum longifolium. d, 50b, Anguloa clowesii. e, 35b, Coryanthes biflora. f, 35b, Catasetum pileatum. g, 80b, Maxillaria histrionica. h, 80b, Sobralia ruckeri. i, 35b, Mormodes convolutum. j, 35b, Huntleya lucida.
150b, Catasetum barbatum.

1995, May 31 Litho. *Perf. 12*
1518 A421 Sheet of 10, #a.-j. 14.50 12.00

Souvenir Sheet

1519 A421 150b multicolored 3.75 3.50

No. 1519 contains one 42x36mm stamp.
See #1534-1535, 1563-1564, 1587-1588.

CAF (Andes Development Corporation), 25th Anniv. — A422

1995, June 7
1520 A422 80b multicolored 1.90 1.60

Miniature Sheet

Beatification of Mother Maria of San Jose — A423

Designs: a, 35b, In formal habit. b, 35b, Pope John Paul II. c, 35b, As young woman distributing Bibles. d, 35b, Doing embroidary work. e, 35b, Statue of Madonna, altar. f, 35b, Kneeling in devotions. g, 80b, Walking with Sisters in hospital. h, 80b, With patient in hospital. i, 100b, Working with children. j, 100b, Helping person seated along road.

1995, July 2
1521 A423 Sheet of 10, #a.-j. 13.50 11.00

Nos. 1521a-1521b, 1521c-1521d, 1521e-1521f, 1521g-1521h, 1521i-1521j are each continuous designs.

UN, 50th Anniv. A424

Designs: a, People from different countries unfurling UN flag. b, Emblem on UN flag.

1995, June 26
1522 A424 50b Pair, #a.-b. 3.75 3.25

Gen. José Gregorio Monagas (1795-1858), President, Liberator of the Slaves — A425

a, Portrait. b, Slave family with opened chains.

1995, July 26 Litho. *Perf. 12*
1523 A425 50b Pair, #a.-b. 2.90 2.40

Slave Rebellion, Bicent. — A426

Jose Leonardo Chirino and: a, Liberty leading the people (after Delacroix). b, Revolutionaries with weapons.

1995, Aug. 16
1524 A426 50b Pair, #a.-b. 3.00 2.50

Venezuelan Red Cross, Cent. — A427

Designs: a, 100b, Red Cross flag. b, 80b, Carlos J. Bello Hospital. c, 35b, Surgery scene. d, 35b, Rescue workers carrying victim. e, 35b, Care givers with child.

1995, Aug. 30
1525 A427 Strip of 5, #a.-e. 7.25 6.00

America Issue — A428

Environmental protection: a, 35b, Trees, lake. b, 80b, Flowers, hillside.

1995, Sept. 13 Litho. *Perf. 12*
1526 A428 Pair, #a.-b. 4.00 3.50

No. 1526 was issued in sheets of 10 stamps.
No. 1526 exists in two types: the heavy border at top is above "America" only: the heavy line extends over the denomination. Values the same.

Miniature Sheet

Native Aboriginals — A429

No. 1527: a, 25b, Kuana man seated on post. b, 25b, Kuana woman using stones to do laundry. c, 35b, Guahibo people, one playing flute. d, 35b, Guahibo shaman with child. e, 50b, Uruak man with tree branch. f, 50b, Uruak woman cooking. g, 80b, Warao woman spinning twine. h, 80b, Warao man, woman in boat. i, 100b, Bari men with bows, arrows. j, 100b, Bari man rubbing sticks to make fire.
150b, Young boy with bird.

1995, Oct. 18
1527 A429 Sheet of 10, #a.-j. 18.50 16.00

Souvenir Sheet

1528 A429 150b multicolored 5.25 5.00

See Nos. 1541-1542.

Miniature Sheet

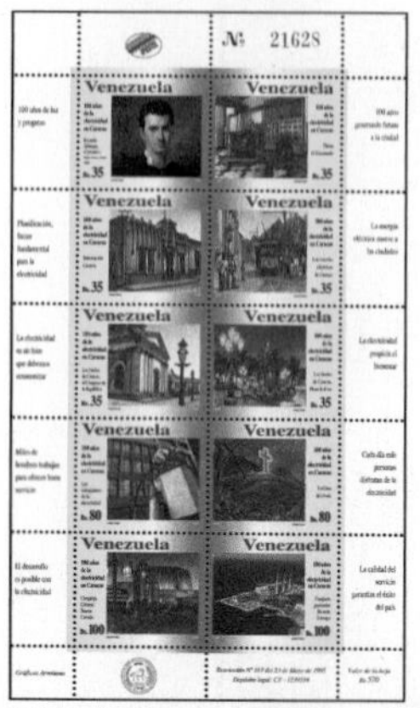

Electricity in Caracas, Cent. — A430

Designs: a, 35b, Ricardo Zuloaga, early pioneer. b, 35b, Early electric plant. c, 35b, Substation. d, 35b, 1908 Electric trams. e, 35b, Electric lampposts mandated by Congress, 1908. f, 35b, Lampposts, Bolivar Plaza. g, 80b, Electrical repairman. h, 80b, Lighted cross, Avila. i, 100b, Teresa Carreño Cultural Complex. j, 100b, Ricardo Zuloaga main generator plant.

1995, Nov. 6
1529 A430 Sheet of 10, #a.-j. 13.50 11.00

Miniature Sheet

Christmas — A431

Designs: a, 35b, The Annunciation. b, 35b, Being turned away at the inn. c, 100b, Birth of Christ in the stable. d, 35b, Angel appearing to shepherds. e, 35b, Three Magi. f, 40b, Christmas pageant. g, 40b, Children skating. h, 100b, Christmas presents. i, 40b, Women preparing food for holidays. j, 40b, Children, mother preparing food for holidays.

1995, Nov. 15
1530 A431 Sheet of 10, #a.-j. 12.50 10.00

Nos. 1530f-1530g, and 1530i-1530j are each continuous designs.

Miniature Sheet

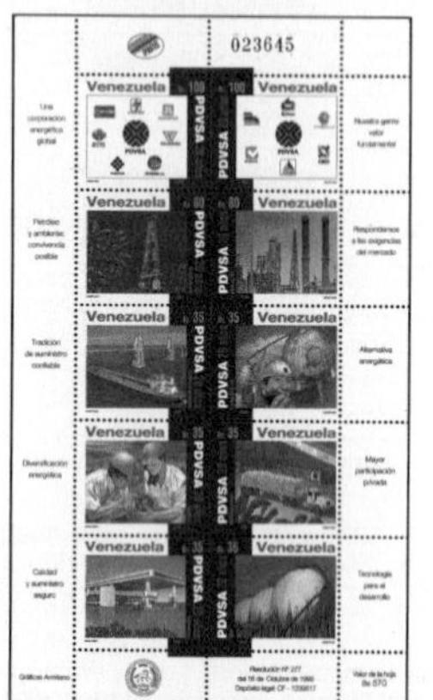

Petroleum Industries of South America (PDVSA), 20th Anniv. — A432

a, 35b, PDVSA emblem, 7 petroleum company emblems. b, PDVSA emblem, 6 petroleum company emblems. c, 80b, Oil derrick. d, 80b, Refinery. e, 35b, Oil tanker crossing under bridge. f, 35b, Worker, orimulsion tanks. g, 35b, Two people examining carbon. h, 35b, Semi truck hauling petrochemicals. i, 35b, Filling station. j, 35b, Gas storage tanks.

1995, Dec. 13 Litho. *Perf. 12*
1531 A432 Sheet of 10, #a.-j. 13.50 11.00

Miniature Sheet

Town of El Tocuyo, 450th Anniv. — A433

Designs: a, 35b, City arms. b, 35b, Workers in sugar cane field. c, Church of Our Lady of Immaculate Conception. d, Statue of Madonna inside church. e, 35b, Ruins of Temple of Santa Domingo. f. 35b, House of Culture. g, 80b, Cactus, vegetation. h, 80b, Cactus up close. i, 100b, Dancers with swords. j, 100b, Man playing guitar.

1995, Dec. 5
1532 A433 Sheet of 10, #a.-j. 13.50 11.00

Miniature Sheet

Vist of Pope John Paul II — A434

Statues of various saints, Pope and: a, 25b, Children. b, 25b, Man, woman. c, 40b, Man, woman, baby. d, 40b, Elderly man. e, 50b, Woman, boy. f, 50b, Sick person. g, 60b, Man in prison. h, 60b, Working man. i, 100b, People of various career fields. j, 100b, Priests, nuns.
200b, Pope John Paul II holding crucifix.

1996, Jan. 26
1533 A434 Sheet of 10, #a.-j. 14.50 12.00

Souvenir Sheet

1533K A434 200b multicolored 10.50 10.00

Orchid Type of 1995

Designs: a, Epidendrum fimbriatum. b, Myoxanthus reymondii. c, Catasetum pileatum. d, Ponthieva maculata. e, Maxillaria triloris. f, Scaphosepalum breve. g, Cleistes rosea. h, Maxillaria sophronitis. i, Catasetum discolor. j, Oncidium ampliatum.
200b, Odontoglossum naevium.

1996, May 31 Litho. *Perf. 12*
1534 A421 60b Sheet of 10, #a.-j. 13.50 11.00

Souvenir Sheet

1535 A421 200b multicolored 6.75 6.50

1996 Summer Olympic Games, Atlanta — A435

Designs: a, Emblem of Olympic Committee. b, Swimmer. c, Boxer. d, Cyclist. e, Medal winners.

1996, June 28 Litho. *Perf. 12*
1536 A435 130b Strip of 5, #a.-e. 10.25 9.00

No. 1536 was issued in a sheet of 10 stamps.

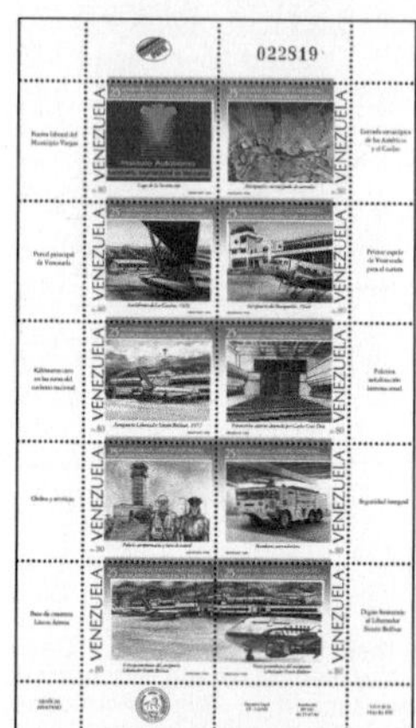

Maiquetia Intl. Airport, 25th Anniv. — A436

Designs: a, Symbol of automation. b, Map of airport flight routes. c, La Guaira Airdrome, 1929. d, Maiqueitia Airport, 1944. e, Simon Bolivar Airport, 1972. f, Interior view of terminal. g, Airport police, control tower. h, Airport firetruck. i, Airplane at terminal, Simon Bolivar Airport. j, Airplane on taxiway, Simon Bolivar Airport.

1996, Aug. 4
1537 A436 80b Sheet of 10, #a-j 15.00 12.50

America Issue — A437

Traditional costumes: a, 60b, Women's. b, 130b, Men's.

1996, Sept. 10
1538 A437 Pair, #a.-b. 4.25 3.75

No. 1538 was issued in sheets of 10 stamps.

Mario Briceño-Iragorry (1897-1958) A438

Portraits: a, As young man, Trujillo, 1913. b, At University of Mérida, 1919. c, As politician, 1944. d, As writer, 1947. e, As older man, Caracas, 1952.

1996, Sept. 24
1539 A438 80b Strip of 5, #a.-e. 7.75 6.50

No. 1539 was issued in sheets of 10 stamps.

Caracas Rotary Club, 70th Anniv. — A439

1996, Oct. 3
1540 A439 50b multicolored 1.10 .85

No. 1540 was issued in sheets of 10.

Native Aboriginal Type of 1995

Designs: a, 80b, Yukpa boy working in garden. b, 80b, Paraujanos girl carrying fruit. c, 80b, Kinaroes man, woman bundling cattails. d, 80b, Motilon man with bananas. e, 80b, Chaque mother carrying infant on back. f, 100b, Guajiros man, young woman fixing hair. g, 100b, Mucuchi man carrying pack on back. h, 100b, Mape man with bow and arrow. i, 100b, Macoa working with grain, painted faces. j, 100b, Yaruros man weaving.
200b, Woman breastfeeding infant.

1996, Oct. 11
1541 A429 Sheet of 10, #a.-j. 16.00 13.50

Souvenir Sheet

1542 A429 200b multicolored 3.50 3.25

Souvenir Sheet

Taipei '96, Intl. Philatelic Exhibition — A440

1996, Oct. 21 Litho. *Perf. 12*
1543 A440 200b Ara chloroptera *7.75 7.50*

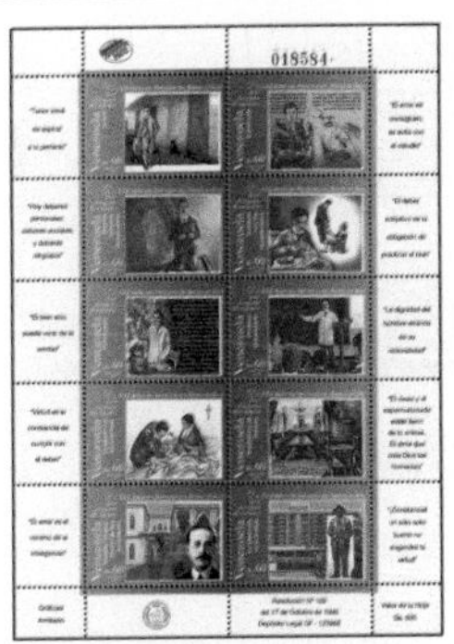

José Gregorio Hernández (1864-1908), Physician — A441

a, As young boy. b, As student, anatomy drawing. c, Praying, Madonna statue. d, Thinking of the needy. e, In research study. f, As professor of university. g, Comforting sick patient. h, Empty chair at academy. i, Vargas Hospital, statue, portrait of Hernández. j, Hospital named after Hernández, statue.
200b, Portrait of Hernández.

1996, Oct. 26 Litho. *Perf. 12*

1544 A441 60b Sheet of 10, #a.-j. 9.50 7.00

Souvenir Sheet

1545 A441 200b multicolored 3.00 2.75

No. 1545 contains one 42x36mm stamp.

Christmas — A442

Designs: a, 60b, Child setting up Nativity scene. b, 60b, Three men with guitars, woman. c, 60b, Rooster, people making music. d, 60b, People with painted faces dancing, singing. e, 60b, Men, woman playing drums, instruments. f, 80b, Exchanging gifts of food. g, 80b, Family at table, looking at gift of food. h, 80b, Child in hammock, presents. i, 80b, Parading replica of infant Jesus. j, 80b, Kissing feet of Christ Child.

1996, Nov. 7

1546 A442 Sheet of 10, #a.-j. 9.00 6.50

Andrés Eloy Blanco (1896-1955), Politician, Writer — A443

Designs: a, As adolescent. b, As Caracas city official, government building. c, With family. d, With democratic founders. e, As politician, building. f, As President of Constituent Assembly, building. g, As "Poet of Pueblo." h, Lincoln Memorial, as Chancellor of the Republic. i, Author of writings on Spain, sailing ship. j, Map of Spain, sailing ships, conquistador on horseback.

1997, Feb. 17 Litho. *Perf. 12*

1547 A443 100b Sheet of 10, #a.-j. 11.50 9.00

Simon Bolivar (1783-1830) — A444

1997, Mar. 7 Litho. *Perf. 13½x13*

1548	A444	15b	olive	.30	.25
1549	A444	20b	brown org	.30	.25
1550	A444	40b	dark brown	.40	.40
1551	A444	50b	rose claret	.65	.60
1552	A444	70b	deep violet	.90	.85
1553	A444	90b	deep blue	1.30	1.25
1554	A444	200b	dp grn bl	2.40	2.25
1555	A444	300b	dp bl grn	3.25	3.00
1556	A444	400b	gray	4.75	4.50
1557	A444	500b	pale sepia	5.50	5.25
1558	A444	600b	pale brown	6.00	5.75
1559	A444	800b	pale vio brn	7.75	7.25
1560	A444	900b	slate blue	8.00	7.50
1561	A444	1000b	dk org brn	8.50	8.00
1562	A444	2000b	olive bister	15.50	15.00
	Nos. 1548-1562 (15)			65.50	62.10

Orchid Type of 1995

Designs: a, Phragmipedium lindleyanum. b, Zygosepalum labiosum. c, Acacallis cyanea. d, Maxillaria camaridii. e, Scuticaria steelei. f, Aspasia variegata. g, Comparettia falcata. h, Scapyglottis stellata. i, Maxillaria ruffescens. j, Vanilla pompona.
250b, Rodriguezia lanceolata.

1997, May 30 *Perf. 12*

1563 A421 165b Sheet of 10, #a.-j. 17.50 15.00

Souvenir Sheet

1564 A421 250b multicolored 3.75 3.50

No. 1564 contains one 42x37mm stamp.

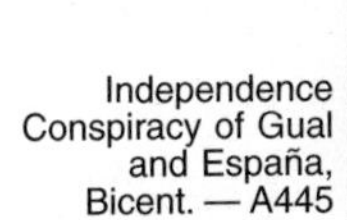

Independence Conspiracy of Gual and España, Bicent. — A445

#1565, José María España, proclamation for independence being read. #1566, España under arrest. #1567, Manuel Gual, soldiers. #1568, Gual fleeing through door, sailing ship, standing on Trinidad. #1569, Revolutionary flag, sailing ship.

1997, July 16

1565	A445	165b	multicolored	1.50	1.50
1566	A445	165b	multicolored	1.50	1.50
a.			Pair, #1565-1566	3.00	3.00
1567	A445	165b	multicolored	1.50	1.50
a.			Pair, #1566-1567	3.00	3.00
1568	A445	165b	multicolored	1.50	1.50
a.			Pair, #1567-1568	3.00	3.00
1569	A445	165b	multicolored	1.50	1.50
a.			Pair, #1565, 1569	3.00	3.00
b.			Pair, #1568-1569	3.00	3.00

Printed in sheet of 10 containing one each #1566a, 1567a, 1568a, 1569a-1569b. Value $18.50.

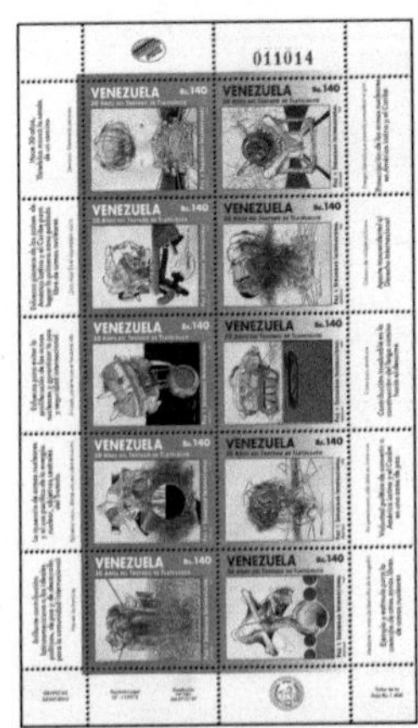

Treaty of Tlatelolco Banning Use of Nuclear Weapons in Latin America, 30th Anniv. — A446

Various stylized designs representing devastation resulting from use of nuclear weapons: a.-e., White inscriptions. f.-j., Black inscriptions.

1997, July 31

1570 A446 140b Sheet of 10, #a.-j. 17.50 15.00

Stories for Children — A447

"The Rabbit and the Tiger:" a, Rabbit, tiger carrying satchel. b, Watching rat figure digging. c, Watching turtle on his back. d, Rabbit. e. Rat in net, rabbit. f, Tiger, house, rat. g, Bird, rat, rabbit, bee, beehive. h, Rabbit, turtle. i, Tiger with stick over shoulder. j, Tiger with mouth open, bees.
250b, Rabbit, tiger.

1997, Aug. 7

1571 A447 55b Sheet of 10, #a.-j. 10.50 8.00

Souvenir Sheet

1572 A447 250b multicolored 3.50 3.25

No. 1572 contains one 42x37mm stamp.
The reverse of Nos. 1571a-1571j are each inscribed with parts of the childrens' story.

Unexpected Adventures of a Postman — A448

America Issue: 110b, Giving letter to woman with dog. 280b, With motor scooter in rain.

1997, Aug. 29 Litho. *Perf. 12*

1573	A448	110b	multicolored	2.00	2.00
1574	A448	280b	multicolored	3.50	3.50
a.			Pair, #1573-1574	7.75	7.25

No. 1574a was issued in sheets of 10 stamps.

Villa of Anauco Villa, Bicent. — A449

Designs: a, Inscription. b, Main entrance. c, Entrance corridor. d, Interior patio. e, Exterior corridor leading to kitchen. f, Kitchen. g, Stairs leading to balcony. h, Coach house. i, Stable. j, Outside stable, water trough.

1997, Sept. 23

1575 A449 110b Sheet of 10, #a.-j. 13.50 11.00

Independence in India, 50th Anniv. — A450

Designs: a, 165b, Jawaharlal Nehru. b, 200b, Sardar Patel, flag. c, 165b, Congressional building. d, 200b, Gandhi. e, 165b, Purification at the Ganges. f, 200b, Rabindranath Tagore. g, 165b, Motion picture industry. h, 200b, Traditional music. i, 165b, Insat-1B meteorological satellite. j, 200b, Use of modern technology.
250b, Minarets of Taj Majal.

1997, Oct. 2

1576 A450 Sheet of 10, #a.-j. 22.50 20.00

Souvenir Sheet

1577 A450 250b multicolored 3.50 3.25

Heinrich von Stephan (1831-97) — A451

a, 110b, Portrait. b, 280b, UPU emblem.

1997, Oct. 9 Litho. *Perf. 12*

1578 A451 Pair, #a.-b. 4.25 3.75

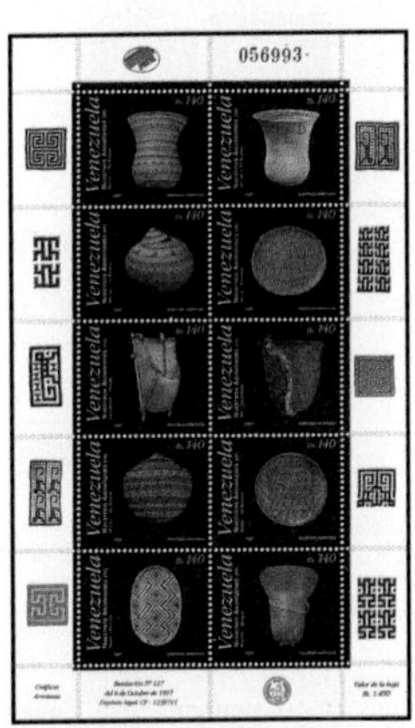

Wicker-work — A452

No. 1579: a, Red basket, Ye'Kuana. b, With handles, Ye'Kuana. c, Round, Ye'Kuana. d, Tray, Panare. e, Backpack, Pemon. f, With carrying strap, Yanomami. g, Round (dk brown), diff., Ye'Kuana. h, Tray, Ye'Kuana. i, Oval tray, Panare. j, Wide mouth, Warao.
250b, Square box with lid, Ye'Kuana.

1997, Oct. 24 *Perf. 12*

1579 A452 140b Sheet of 10, #a.-j. 17.50 15.00

Souvenir Sheet

1580 A452 250b multicolored 4.25 4.00

No. 1580 contains one 42x37mm stamp.

Christmas — A453

a, Annunciation. b, Mary, St. Elizabeth. c, No room at the inn. d, Nativity. e, Annunciation to shepherds. f, Adoration of the shepherds. g, Magi following star. h, Adoration of the Magi. i, Presentation of Christ child in temple. j, Flight into Egypt.

1997, Oct. 31
1581 A453 110b Sheet of 10, #a.-j. 13.50 11.00

7th Summit of Latin American Chiefs of State and Government, Isla de Margarita — A454

a, 165b, j, 200b, Social justice. b, 165b, i, 200b, Free elections. c, 165b, h, 200b, Summit emblem. d, 165b, g, 200b, Truthful information. e, 165b, f, 200b, Human rights.

1997, Nov. 5
1582 A454 Sheet of 10, #a.-j. 20.50 18.00

Diocese of Zulia, Cent. — A455

Churches: a, Convent. b, Church of St. Ann. c, Reliquary, Chiquinquira. d, Basilica of Chiquinquira and St. John of God. e, Church, Aranza. f, Cathedral, Maracaibo. g, Cathedral, Machiques. h, Archbishop's seal. i, Cathedral, Cabimas. j, Cathedral of the Virgin, San Carlos.

1997, Dec. 16
1583 A455 110b Sheet of 10, #a.-j. 12.50 10.00

Democracy in Venezuela, 40th Anniv. — A456

Designs: a, Commemorative emblem. b, Popular decision. c, Public education. d, Social development. e, Freedom of expression. f, Capital, constitution. g, Popular culture. h, Civil rights. i, Environmental protection. j, Social and civic participation.

1998, Feb. 19 Litho. *Perf. 12*
1584 A456 110b Sheet of 10, #a.-j. 14.50 12.00

Discovery of Margarita Island, 500th Anniv. — A457

Map of Margarita Islands and: a, 200b, Angel Rock. b, 265b, Christopher Columbus, ship. c, 200b, Simon Bolivar. d, 200b, Pearl diver. e, 265b, Statue of the Virgin del Valle, church. f, 100b, Mending fish net, fishermen in boats. g, 200b, Gen. Santiago Marino. h, 100b, Petronila Mata, cannon. i, 200b, Gen. Juan Bautista Arismendi. j, 100b, Parrot.
250b, Women weeping at the Lagoon of Martyrs, horiz.

1998, Mar. 26 Litho. *Perf. 12*
1585 A457 Sheet of 10, #a.-j. 19.50 17.00

Souvenir Sheet

1586 A457 250b multicolored 3.50 3.25

No. 1586 contains one 42x37mm stamp.

Orchid Type of 1995

a, Oncidium orthostates. b, Epidendrum praetervisum. c, Odontoglossum schilleranum. d, Bletia lansbergii. e, Caularthron bicornutum. f, Darwiniera bergoldii. g, Houlletia tigrina. h, Pleurothallis acuminata. i, Elleanthus lupulinus. j, Epidendrum ferrugineum.
250b, Pleurothallis immersa.

1998, May 29
1587 A421 185b Sheet of 10, #a.-j. 20.50 18.00

Souvenir Sheet

1588 A421 250b multicolored 3.50 3.25

No. 1588 contains one 42x37mm stamp.

Henri Pittier Natl. Park, 60th Anniv. — A458

Fauna: a, 140b, Crax pauxi. b, 150b, Spizaetus ornatus. c, 200b, Touit collaris. d, 200b, Trogon collaris. e, 350b, Cyanocorax yncas. f, 140b, Tersina viridis. g, 150b, Phyllomedusa trinitatis. h, 200b, Morpho peleides. i, 200b, Acrocinus longimanus. j, 350b, Dynastes hercules.

1998, July 17
1589 A453 Sheet of 10, #a.-j. 22.50 20.00

Comptroller General of the Republic, 60th Anniv. — A459

Designs: a, 140b, Gumersindo Torres Millet, founding Comptroller. b, 140b, Luis Antonio Pietri Yépez, first Comptroller of the democracy. c, 140b, View of capitol dome. d, 140b, Colors of flag (service to society). e, 200b, Simon Bolivar, coins. f, 200b, Various numbers on green background. g, 350b, Newspaper headlines (inform the public). h, 350b, Statue of justice (uphold law). i, 350b, Text of duties of the Comptroller General. j, 350b, Emblem, the 6th Assembly of the Latin American and Caribbean States Comptrollers.

1998, July 29
1590 A459 Sheet of 10, #a.-j. 22.50 20.00

Organization of the American States (OAS), 50th Anniv. — A460

a, 140b, Logo of the anniversary. b, 140b, OAS emblem. c, 350b, Flags forming double helix, US flag at center left. d, 150b, Deactivating land mine. e, 150b, Defending human rights. f, 200b, Simon Bolivar. g, 200b, Scroll, quill pen, inkwell. h, 350b, Flags forming double helix, Venezuelan flag at center right. i, 200b, Road sign with map of Americas. j, 200b, Mountain climbers.

1998, July 30
1591 A460 Sheet of 10, #a.-j. 20.00 17.50

Expo '98, Lisbon — A461

Designs: a, 140b, Bird, turtle, crab. b, 140b, Fishermen throwing net from boat. c, 150b, Seashells, turtle. d, 150b, Fish. e, 200b, Marine life, denomination, UR. f, 200b, Marine life, denomination LR. g, 200b, Man riding through river on horse. h, 200b, Cattle in river, monkey. i, 350b, Two sea birds. j, 350b, Monkey, waterfall, flower.

1998, July 31
1592 A461 Sheet of 10, #a.-j. 22.50 20.00

18th Central American and Caribbean Games, Maracaibo A462

Figures: a, 150b, Running. b, 200b, Playing basketball. c, 150b, Bowling. d, 200b, Boxing. e, 150b, Cycling. f, 200b, Fencing. g, 150b, Performing gymnastics. h, 200b, Weight lifting. i, 150b, Swimming. j, 200b, Playing tennis.

1998, Aug. 4
1593 A462 Sheet of 10, #a.-j. 17.50 15.00

Discovery of Venezuela, 500th Anniv. — A463

Designs: a, 350b, Christopher Columbus. b, 200b, Juan de la Cosa (1460?-1510), map. c, 200b, Huts built on stilts in water. d, 150b, Women of three different races. e, 140b, 13th cent. artifact. f, 350b, Alonso de Ojeda (1465-1515), map. g, 200b, Detail of map of Jodocus Hondius. h, 200b, Modern city. i, 150b, Various people of modern Venezuela. j, 140b, Statues of Catholic king and queen.

1998, Aug. 10
1594 A463 Sheet of 10, #a.-j. 20.50 18.00

A464

1998, Aug. 12
1595 A464 400b multicolored 3.75 3.50

Columbus' landing in Venezuela and exploration of Amerigo Vespucci, 500th anniv.
Joint issue between Venezuela and Italy. See Italy No. 2252.

Treaty of Amazon Cooperation, 20th Anniv. — A465

Designs: a, Casiquiare River, denomination LR. b, Casiquiare River, denomination LL. c, Bactris gasipaes. d, Neblinaria celiae. e, Paracheidon axelrodi. f, Dendrobates leucomelas. g, Nocthocrax urumatum. h, Speothos venaticus. i, Cocuy mountain. j. Neblina Mountains.

1998, Aug. 20
1596 A465 200b Sheet of 10, #a.-j. 20.50 18.00

Children's Story — A466

Cockroach Martinez and Perez Rat: a, Cockroach. b, Burro. c, Parrot. d, Insects with camera, pad. e, Cat. f, Cockroach, pig. g, Goat. h, Cockroach, rat. i, Rat. j, Cockroach, bird.
350b, Cockroach.

1998, Aug. 21 Litho. *Perf. 12*
1597 A466 130b Sheet of 10, #a.-j. 12.50 10.00

Souvenir Sheet

1598 A466 350b multicolored 4.25 4.00

State of Israel, 50th Anniv. — A467

a, 350b, Menorah. b, 350b, Moses, Ten Commandments. c, 200b, Theodore Herzl. d, 200b, King David. e, 140b, Blowing of Shofar. f, 350b, Torah. g, 350b, Praying at Wailing Wall. h, 200b, David Ben Gurion. i, 200b, Knesset. j, 140b, Book Museum.

1998, Sept. 15
1599 A467 Sheet of 10, #a.-j. 22.50 20.00

Souvenir Sheet

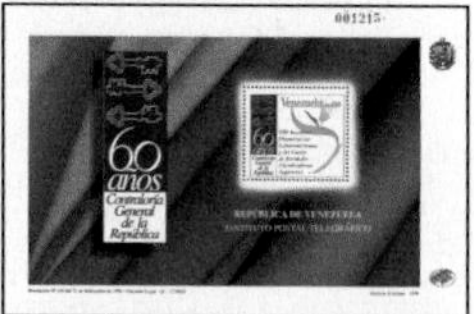
Comptroller General, 60th Anniv. — A468

1998, Sept.
1600 A468 480b multicolored 4.75 4.50

UPU, 125th Anniv. — A469

a, 100b, Customer at window, clerks at left. b, 100b, Scanning bar code, woman at right. c, 100b, Electronic mail. d, 100b, Hybrid mail. e, 100b, Business mail. f, 300b, Like "a," clerks at right. g, 300b, Like "b," woman at left. h, 300b, Like "c," large monitor at right. i, 300b, Like "d," woman at right. j, 300b, Like "e," building with stacks at left.

1998, Sept. 29
1601 A469 Sheet of 10, #a.-j. 12.50 10.00

Legendary Caciques — A470

a, Caruao. b, Manaure. c, Guacamayo. d, Tapiaracay. e, Mamacuri. f, Maniacuare. g, Mara. h, Chacao. i, Tamanaco. j, Tiuna.
500b, Indian.

1998, Oct. 9
1602 A470 420b Sheet of 10, #a.-j. 25.00 22.50

Souvenir Sheet

1603 A470 500b multicolored 4.25 4.00

Evangelism in Venezuela, 500th Anniv. — A471

No. 1604: a, 100b, Fr. Francisco de Córdoba, Fr. Juan Garcés. b, 100b, Fr. Matías Ruíz Blanco. c, 100b, Fr. Vincente de Requejada. d, 100b, Fr. José Gumilla. e, 100b, Fr. Antonio Gonzáles de Acuña. f, 300b, Fr. Pedro de Córdoba. g, 300b, Fr. Francisco de Pamplona. h, 300b, Fr. Bartolomé Díaz. i, 300b, Fr. Filipe Salvador Gilij. j, 300b, Don Mariano Martí.
350b, Emblem of Papal Nuncio.

1998, Oct. 24 Litho. *Perf. 12*
1604 A471 Sheet of 10, #a.-j. 16.00 13.50

Souvenir Sheet

1605 A471 350b multicolored 3.75 3.50

No. 1605 contains one 42x37mm stamp.

Special Olympics, 30th Anniv. — A472

180b: a, Carrying torch. b, Giving hug. c, Soccer players. d, Girl holding small flag. e, Girl performing gymnastics.
420b: f, Swimmer. g, Coach walking with athletes. h, Hitting volleyball. i, Particpants cheering. j, Coach instructing girl in softball.

1998, Oct. 30 Litho. *Perf. 12*
1606 A472 Sheet of 10, #a.-j. 17.50 15.00

Christmas — A473

Children standing in front of windows — 180b: a, Girl holding sparkler. b, Boy holding artist's brush, ornament. c, Girl with kite. d, Boy with pinwheel. e, Girls playing musical instruments.
420b: f, Boy on wagon. g, Girl with yo-yo, doll. h, Boy with bell. i, Girl with spool and thread. j, Boy on skateboard.

1998, Nov. 4
1607 A473 Sheet of 10, #a.-j. 17.50 15.00

America Issue A474

Famous women: a, 180b, Teresa de la Parra (1889-1936), writer. b, 420b, Teresa Carreño (1853-1917), pianist.

1998, Nov. 23
1608 A474 Pair, #a.-b. 4.25 3.75

William H. Phelps (1875-1965), Ornithologist A475

Portrait of Phelps and — 200b: a, Cephalopterus ornatus. b, Topaza pella. c, Grallaria excelsa phelpsi. d, Chrysolampis mosquitus. e, Tangara xanthogastra phelpsi.
300b: f, Radio transmitter. g, Mt. Phelps. h, Baseball and glove. i, Phelps Library. j, Cash register.

1998, Dec. 4
1609 A475 Sheet of 10, #a.-j. 18.50 16.00

Msgr. Jesús Manuel Jáuregui Moreno (1848-1905) — A476

Designs: a, Portrait as younger man. b, Christ on the cross. c, Our Mother of Angels Church. d, Madonna and Child. e, Portrait as older man.

1999, Jan. 30 Litho. *Perf. 12*
1610 A476 500b Strip of 5, #a.-e. 14.50 12.00

Holy Sacrament for the Consecration of the Republic of Venezuela, Cent. — A477

No. 1612: a, Man, elderly woman. b, Priest. c, Ostensorium (top). d, Boy with basketball, girl. e, Man, woman holding baby. f, Lady doctor. g, Woman. h, Ostensorium (base). i, Soldier. j, Native man holding spear.
500b, Hands of priest holding the Host.

1999, June 16 Litho. *Perf. 12*
1611 A477 250b Sheet of 10, #a.-j. 23.00 20.00

Souvenir Sheet

1612 A477 500b multicolored 2.50 2.25

No. 1612 contains one 42x37mm stamp.

Souvenir Sheet

Andino Parliament, 20th Anniv. — A478

1999 Litho. *Perf. 12*
1613 A478 500b multi 5.25 5.00

Christmas — A479

a, 500b, Betrothal of Joseph, Mary. b, 500b, Annunciation. c, 500b, Elizabeth, Mary. d, 500b, The search for lodging in Bethlehem. e, 500b, Birth of Jesus. f, 300b, Vision of the shepherds. g, 300b, Magi following star. h, 300b, Adoration of the Magi. i, 300b, Flight into Egypt. j, 300b, Slaughter of the innocents.

1999, Nov. 5 *Perf. 12x12¼*
1614 A479 Sheet of 10, #a.-j. 49.00 46.00

Souvenir Sheet

Expo 2000, Hanover A480

2000, July 8 Litho. *Perf. 12*
1615 A480 650b multi 6.25 6.00

2nd Summit of Heads of State and Government of OPEC Countries — A481

No. 1616 — Sites in Venezuela: a, 300b, Angel Falls. b, 300b, Llanos, Cojedes. c, 300b, Quebrada Jaspe. d, 300b, Morichal Largo. e, 300b, Auyantepuy, Carrao River. f, 400b, Lake Maracaibo. g, 400b, Humboldt Peak. h, 400b, Mochima. i, 400b, Morichal Largo River. j, 400b, Auyantepuy, from Uruyen.

No. 1617, 550b: a, Saudi Arabia. b, Algeria. c, United Arab Emirates. d, Indonesia. e, Iraq. f, Iran. g, Kuwait. h, Libya. i, Nigeria. j, Qatar.

2000, Sept. 26 Litho. *Perf. 12*
Sheets of 10, #a-j
1616-1617 A481 Set of 2 180.00 175.00

Christmas — A482

No. 1618: a, 300b, Angel and "Gloria." b, 300b, Angel and "a." c, 650b, Angel and "Dios." d, 300b, Angel and "en los." e, 300b, Angel and "Cielos." f, 300b, Shepherd and lamb. g, 550b, Joseph. h, 650b, Jesus. i, 550b, Mary. j, 300b, Woman with water jar.

2000, Nov. 29
1618 A482 Sheet of 10, #a-j 43.00 30.00

America Issue, A New Millennium Without Arms — A483

No. 1619: a, 300b, Finger in gun barrel. b, 650b, Man in heaven.

2000, Dec. 14
1619 A483 Vert. pair, #a-b 7.00 6.50

Educational Building and Endowment Foundation, 25th Anniv. — A484

No. 1620 — School buildings in: a, Caracas. b, Vargas State. c, Portuguesa State. d, Mérida State. e, Yaracuy State.

2001, May 9 Litho. *Perf. 12*
1620 Horiz. strip of 5 16.50 9.50
a.-c. A484 300b Any single 1.60 1.60
d.-e. A484 400b Any single 2.10 2.10

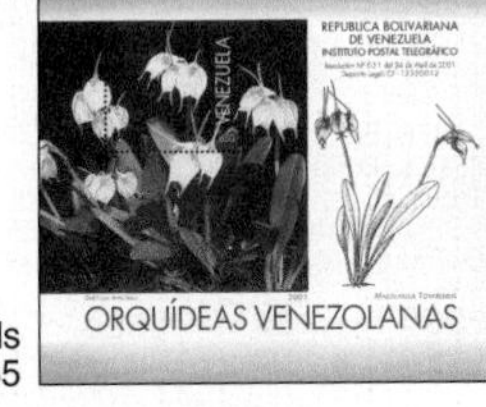

Orchids A485

No. 1621: a, 200b, Galeottia jorisiana. b, 200b, Lycaste longipetala. c, 300b, Coryanthes albertinae. d, 300b, Hexisea bidentata. e, 400b, Lycaste macrophylla. f, 400b, Masdevallia maculata. g, 550b, Ada aurantiaca. h, 550f, Kefersteinia graminea. i, 550b, Sobralia liliastrum. j, 550b, Gongora maculata.
650b, Masdevallia tovarensis.

2001, May 25
1621 A485 Sheet of 10, #a-j 32.50 30.00

Souvenir Sheet

1622 A485 650b multi 7.25 7.00

Blessed Josemaría Escrivá de Balaguer (1902-75), Founder of Opus Dei — A486

No. 1623: a, 300b, Portrait. b, 300b, Bell of Nuestra Senora de los Angeles Church. c, 300b, Figure of Infant Jesus. d, 300b, Escrivá with men. e, 550b, Escrivá with women. f, 550f, Escrivá receiving doctorate, 1972. g, 550b, Escrivá with children, 1975. h, 300b, Commemorative plaque, Caracas Cathedral. i, 550b, Color portrait. j, 300b, Beatification ceremony, St. Peter's Square, Vatican City.

2001, June 8
1623 A486 Sheet of 10, #a-j 35.00 32.50

Battle of Carabobo, 180th Anniv. — A487

No. 1624: a, Thomas I. Ferriar. b, Bolívar in Buenavista, by Martín Tovar y Tovar. c, Quote by Simón Bolívar. d, Commemorative column. e, Pedro Camejo. f, José Antonio Páez, by Tovar y Tovar. g, Santiago Mariño, by Tovar y Tovar. h, Simón Bolívar, by M. Eberstein. i, Manuel Cedeño, by Tito Salas. j, Ambrosio Plaza, by Salas.

2001, June 22
1624 A487 Sheet of 10 49.00 32.50
a.-e. 400b Any single 2.00 2.00
f.-j. 600b Any single 2.50 2.50

Christmas — A488

Holy Family and angel with: a, 200b, Clarinet. b, 200b, Guitar. c, 220b, Lute. d, 220b, Trumpet. e, 280b, Violin. f, 280b, Harp. g, 400b, Bagpipes. h, 400b, Pan pipes. i, 500b, Drum. j, 500b, Stringed instrument.

2001, Nov. 30 Litho. *Perf. 12*

1625 A488 Sheet of 10, #a-j 32.50 24.00

Navigational Signaling, 160th Anniv. — A489

Navigational aids: a, Margarita Aqueduct buoy. b, BNFA buoy. c, Punta Brava lighthouse. d, Punta Macolla lighthouse. e, Los Roques lighthouse. f, Isla Redonda lighthouse. g, Punta Faragoza lighthouse. h, Punta Ballena lighthouse. i, Punta Tigre lighthouse. j, Recalada de Güiria lighthouse.

2002, May 10 Litho. *Perf. 12*

1626 Sheet of 10 28.00 25.00
a.-b. A489 300b Either single 1.00 1.00
c.-f. A489 450b Any single 1.40 1.40
g.-j. A489 500b Any single 1.50 1.50

Symbolic Incorporation of Guacaipuro into National Pantheon A490

No. 1627: a, Tiaora and Caycape, sisters of Guacaipuro. b, Guacaipuro defeats Pedro de Miranda. c, Guacaipuro defeated by Juan Rodriguez Suárez. d, Killing in the gold mines. e, Death of Juan Rodriguez Suárez. f, Guacaipuro's escape from cabin fire. g, Death of Guacaipuro. h, Urquía, companion of Guacairpuro. i, Baruta, first son of Guacaipuro. j, Guacaipuro, Cacique of the Teques and Caracas people.

2002, Oct. 29 Litho. *Perf. 12*

1627 Sheet of 10 16.50 14.00
a. A490 200b multi .60 .60
b-g. A490 300b any single .75 .75
h. A490 350b multi .90 .90
i. A490 400b multi 1.00 1.00
j. A490 500b multi 1.25 1.25

Mission Robinson — A491

No. 1628: a, Toddler. b, Boy reading. c, Simón Bolívar and torch. d, Simón "Robinson" Rodriguez, Bolívar's teacher. e, Rodriguez and Eiffel Tower. f, Bolívar and flag. g, Bolívar and Rodriguez reading. h, Bolívar standing and Rodriguez seated. i, Rodriguez, men and women reading. j, Indians reading.

2003, Sept. 19 Litho. *Perf. 12x12¼*

1628 A491 Sheet of 10 12.50 8.50
a.-d. 300b Any single .60 .60
e.-f. 400b Either single 1.25 1.25
g.-j. 500b Any single 1.50 1.50

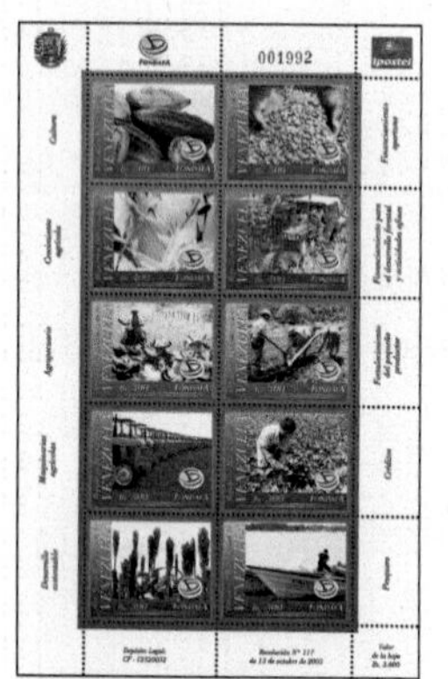

Agricultural, Fishery and Forestry Fund (FONDAFA) — A492

No. 1629: a, Cattle drive. b, Farmer plowing field. c, Row of tractors. d, Farmer tending crops. e, Corn in field. f, Boats. g, Ear of corn. h, Farmer in tractor in field. i, Cacao pods. j, Cacao beans.

2003, Nov. 7 *Perf. 12*

1629 A492 Sheet of 10 17.50 15.00
a.-f. 300b Any single 1.00 1.00
g.-h. 400b Either single 1.25 1.25
i.-j. 500b Either single 1.50 1.50

National Urban Development Fund (FONDUR), 28th Anniv. — A493

No. 1630: a, Barinas. b, Portuguesa. c, Carabobo. d, Miranda. e, Sucre. f, Trujillo. g, Táchira. h, Vargas. i, FONDUR emblem. j, Lara.

2003, Dec. 16 Litho. *Perf. 14¼*

1630 A493 Sheet of 10 11.50 9.00
a.-f. 300b Any single .90 .60
g.-h. 400b Either single 1.10 .90
i.-j. 500b Either single 1.40 1.10

Natl. Urban Transportation Fund (FONTUR), 12th Anniv. — A494

No. 1631: a, Av. Uruguay, Lara. b, Carretera del Páramo, Merida. c, Av. Cumanan-Cumanacoa, Sucre. d, Carratera Santa Lucia, Barinas. e, Francissco Fajardo Expressway, Caracas. f, Students. g, Paraiso Tunnel, Caracas. h, VIVEX Module. i, Row of buses. j, Av. Cruz Paredes, Barinas.

2003, Dec. 18 Litho. *Perf. 14¼*

1631 A494 Sheet of 10 11.50 9.00
a.-c. 300b Any single .75 .60
d.-f. 400b Any single 1.00 .75
g-j. 500b Any single 1.25 1.00

Natl. Telecommunications Commission (CONATEL) — A495

No. 1632: a, Three Amazonian children, two dogs and hammock. b, Caracas and mountain. c, Amazonian children with spears. d, Snow-covered Bolivar Peak. e, Amazonian child in canoe aiming arrow. f, Medina Beach. g, Amazonian children aiming arrows skyward. h, Angel Falls. i, Amazonian children making baskets. j, Coro Dunes.

2003, Dec. 23 Litho. *Perf. 12*

1632 A495 Sheet of 10 17.50 15.00
a.-d. 300b Any single 1.25 .95
e.-f. 400b Either single 1.60 1.25
g.-h. 500b Either single 2.00 1.60
i.-j. 600b Either single 2.50 2.00

Foundation for the Development of Community and Municipal Reconstruction (FUNDACOMUN), 42nd Anniv. — A496

No. 1633: a, Miranda. b, Trujillo. c, Mérida. d, Falcón. e, Vargas. f, Esparta. g, Caracas, denomination at left. h, Caracas, denomination at right. i, Barinas. j, Lara.

2004, Mar. 10 Litho. *Perf. 12*

1633 A496 Sheet of 10 13.50 11.00
a.-c. 300b Any single .90 .70
d.-f. 400b Any single 1.20 .95
g.-j. 500b Any single 1.40 1.10

Barrio Adentro Mission A497

No. 1634: a, Houses on hillside, people in doorway. b, Woman, house, ladder, people in alley. c, Woman, mother and child. d, Family, children. e, Boys playing baseball, boat. f, People near fence, man with cap. g, Man, sand dunes. h, Man with guitar, cows. i, Mountain, woman, cross and statue. j, Indians, river.

2004, Mar. 24 *Perf. 12*

1634 A497 Sheet of 10 19.50 17.00
a.-b. 300b Either single .55 .50
c.-f. 500b Any single .85 .70
g. 750b multi 1.40 1.20
h.-i. 1500b Either single 2.60 2.25
j. 1700b multi 2.75 2.40

Souvenir Sheet

Design: 1000b, Man pushing wheelbarrow, horiz.

1634K A497 1000b multi 5.25 5.00

No. 1634K contains one 41x36mm stamp.

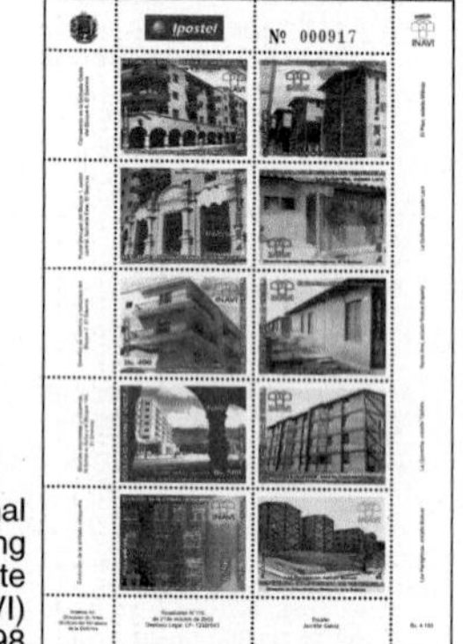

National Housing Institute (INAVI) A498

No. 1635: a, Apartment block 6, El Silencio. b, El Pilar. c, Central section of apartment block 1, El Silencio. d, La Quiboreña. e, Apartment block 7, El Silencio. f, Santa Ana. g, Apartment block 144, El Silencio. h, La Quiracha. i, Architectural drawings of Caracas buildings. j, Los Peregrinos.

2004, May 28 Litho. *Perf. 12*

1635 A498 Sheet of 10 12.50 10.00
a.-c. 300b Any single .75 .60
d.-f. 400b Any single 1.10 .90
g.-j. 500b Any single 1.30 1.00

National Aquatic Areas and Islands Institute (INEA) A499

No. 1636: a, INEA emblem. b, INEA emblem and headquarters. c, Marine firefighters, boats. d, Firetruck, marine firefighter moving drum. e, Sunken tugboat Gran Roque. f, Underwater view of Gran Roque. g, Tugboats. h, Large ships at port. i, Starfish, religious statue. j, Boats and birds.

2004, June 15

1636 A499 Sheet of 10 18.50 16.00
a.-b. 300b Either single .55 .50
c.-f. 500b Any single .95 .85
g. 600b multi 1.20 1.10

h. 1000b multi 1.90 1.70
i. 1500b multi 2.90 2.50
j. 1700b multi 3.25 2.90

A500

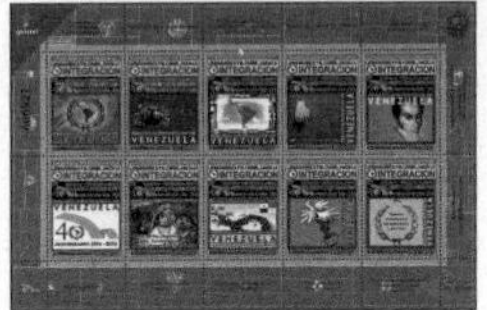

Latin American Parliament, 40th Anniv. — A501

No. 1637: a, Latin American Parliament emblem, 40th anniversary emblem. b, 40th anniversary emblem. c, Latin American Parliament flag and 40th anniversary emblem. d, Flags of member nations. e, Flags and Andrés Townsend Ezcurra. f, Flags and Luis Beltrán Prieto Figueroa. g, Flags and Nelson Carneiro. h, Plenary meeting room, Venezuela. i, Assembly hall, Sao Paolo. j, Latin American Parliament Building, Sao Paolo.

No. 1638: a, Latin American Parliament emblem. b, 40th Anniversary emblem. c, Mérida Session emblem. d, Charter of Social Rights. e, Flags and map of Latin America. f, Flag and map of Panama. g, Táchira Session emblem. h, Bird with ball and chain (social debt). i, Simón Bolivar. j, Constitutional Hypothesis.

2004, July 12

1637 A500 Sheet of 10 17.50 15.00
a.-c. 300b Any single .65 .55
d.-e. 450b Either single 1.00 .90
f.-g. 500b Either single 1.10 .95
h.-i. 1500b Either single 3.00 2.75
j. 1700b multi 3.25 2.90
1638 A501 Sheet of 10 17.50 15.00
a.-c. 300b Any single .65 .55
d.-e. 450b Either single 1.00 .90
f.-g. 500b Either single 1.10 .95
h.-i. 1500b Either single 3.00 2.75
j. 1700b multi 3.25 2.90

CVG Edelca, 40th Anniv. A502

No. 1639: a, Macagua Hydroelectric Station and Dam,, Ciudad Guayana. b, Electric transmission towers and lines. c, Electrical power equipment. d, Room, Guri. e, Native people. f, Guri Hydroelectric Station and Dam. g, Streetlights near Macagua Hydroelectric Station and Dam. h, Solar tower, by Alejandro Otero. i, Dam, Ecomuseum, Caroní. j, Gran Sabana.

No. 1640, Guri Hydroelectric Station and Dam.

2004, July 29

1639 A502 Sheet of 10 14.50 12.00
a.-b. 300b Either single .65 .55
c. 400b multi 1.00 .85
d.-g. 500b Any single 1.10 .95
h. 600b multi 1.25 1.10
i. 1000b multi 2.00 1.75
j. 1500b multi 3.00 2.75

Souvenir Sheet

1640 A502 1000b multi 6.25 6.00

No. 1640 contains one 41x36mm stamp.

United Nations Population Fund — A503

No. 1641 — Inscriptions: a, Los y las adolescentes . . . b, El comporttmiento . . . c, Las niñas tienen . . . d, Los seres humanos . . . e, Promovamos el empoderamiento . . . f, Los derechjos reproductivos . . . g, Por una maternidad sin riesgo. h, El derecho al desarrollo . . . i, Eliminemos la violencia . . . j, El condón protege vidas.

2004, Sept. 15

1641 A503 Sheet of 10 21.00 19.00
a.-d. 500b Any single 1.75 1.20
e.-j. 1000b Any single 2.40 2.10

National Parks Institute (INPARQUES) — A504

No. 1642 — Parks and: a, Food. b, Education. c, Recreation. d, Water. e, Landscapes. f, Biodiversity. g, Conservation. h, Electricity. i, Tourism. j, Ethnic people.

2004, Oct. 11 Litho. *Perf. 14¼x14½*

1642 A504 Sheet of 10 20.00 20.00
a.-b. 300b Either single .90 .90
c. 400b multi 1.40 1.40
d.-g. 500b Any single 1.60 1.60
h. 600b multi 1.75 1.75
i. 1000b multi 3.25 3.25
j. 1500b multi 4.50 4.50

National Tax and Customs Administration (SENIAT) — A505

No. 1643 — Inscriptions: a, Aporte a la educación, cultura y deporte (children). b, Aporte a la salud. c, Dile no al contrabando. d, Con tus tributos . . . e, Aporte a la educación, cultura y deporte (baseball players). f, Construcción de futuras . . . g, Aporte a la vialidad. h, Bienvenidos a un país . . . i, Aporte a la educación, cultura y deporte (building and palm tree). j, Aporte a la educación, cultura y deporte (modern building and sculpture).

2004, Oct. 15 Litho. *Perf. 12*

1643 A505 Sheet of 10 22.50 20.00
a.-d. 500b Any single 1.50 1.40
e.-j. 1000b Any single 2.40 2.10

A506

Banco Federal A507

No. 1644: a, Cerro El Avila, Caracas, 1945. b, Nuevo Circo, Caracas, 1970. c, Plaza Venezuela, Caracas, 1943. d, Sculpture by Francisco Narváez, Caracas, 1940. e, Baralt Theater, Maracaibo, 1883. f, Los Próceres, Caracas, 1956. g, El Paraíso Horse Track, Caracas, 1908. h, Bullfighter Luis Sánchez Olivares, Caracas, 1950. i, Funicular, Mérida, 1954. j, Angel Falls, Bolivar State, 1937. k, Banco Federal emblem, gold star. l, Banco Federal Building (sepia). m, Lake Bridge, Maracaibo, 1962. n, Virgin of Coromoto (sepia). o, El Silencio, Caracas, 1945.

No. 1645: a, San Fernando de Apure Church. b, Caracas Cathedral. c, Coro Cathedral. d, Santa Inés de Cumaná Cathedral. e, Our Lady of Chiquinquirá Basilica. f, Our Lady of Coromoto Basilica. g, St. Rose of Lima Church, Ortíz. h, Mérida Cathedral. i, Our Lady of the Assumption Cathedral. j, San Cristóbal Cathedral. k, Banco Federal emblem, silver star. l, Banco Federal Building (full color). m, Barquisimeto Cathedral. n, Virgin of Coromoto (full color). o, Valencia Cathedral.

2005, Jan. 20 Litho. *Perf. 14¼x14½*

1644 A506 Sheet of 15 26.00 25.00
a.-e. 300b Any single .75 .75
f.-h. 400b Any single 1.00 1.00
i.-j. 600b Either single 1.50 1.50
k.-l. 750b Either single 2.10 2.10
m.-n. 1000b Either single 2.75 2.75
o. 1700b multi 4.00 4.00
1645 A507 Sheet of 15 26.00 25.00
a.-e. 300b Any single .75 .75
f.-h. 400b Any single 1.00 1.00
i.-j. 600b Either single 1.50 1.50
k.-l. 750b Either single 2.10 2.10
m.-n. 1000b Either single 2.75 2.75
o. 1700b multi 4.00 4.00

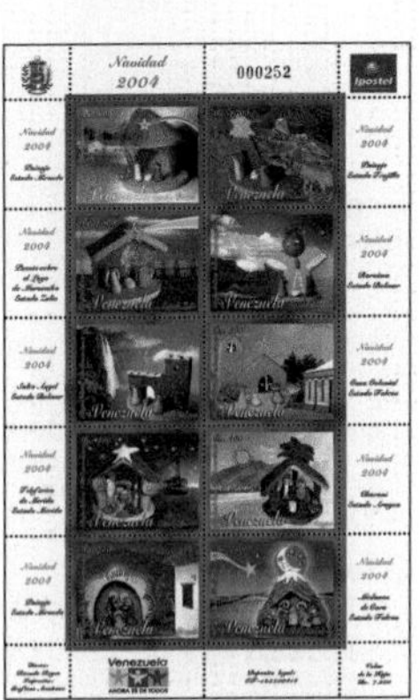

Christmas — A508

No. 1646 — Creche figures from various states: a, Bolívar. b, Falcón. c, Mérida. d, Aragua. e, Miranda. f, Miranda, diff. g, Falcón, diff. h, Zulia. i, Bolívar, diff. j, Trujillo.

2004, Dec. 23 *Perf. 12*

1646 A508 Sheet of 10 18.00 16.00
a.-b. 300b Either single .70 .65
c.-d. 400b Either single .85 .80
e. 600b multi 1.25 1.10
f.-g. 750b Either single 1.75 1.60
h.-i. 1000b Either single 2.25 2.10
j. 1700b multi 3.25 3.00

Souvenir Sheet

Incan and Modern Mail Deliverers — A509

2004 *Perf. 12*

1647 A509 1000b multi 4.75 4.50

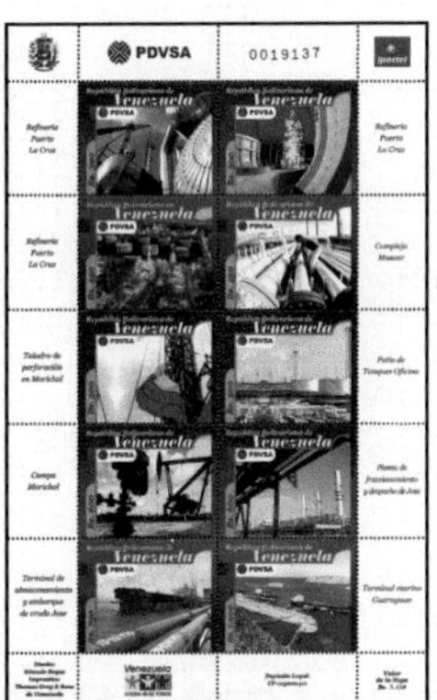

Petróleos de Venezuela, S. A. — A510

No. 1648: a, Crane above turbines, Puerto La Cruz Refinery. b, Night view of tower Puerto La Cruz Refinery. c, Aerial view of Puerto La Cruz refinery. d, Man inspecting pipes. e, Crane and Venezuelan flag. f, Storage tanks. g, Oil wells. h, Refinery towers. i, Oil tanker and pipes. j, Tankers at Guaraguao Marine Terminal.

2004, Nov. 24 Litho. *Perf. 14¼*

1648 A510 Sheet of 10 16.40 14.00
a.-b. 300b Either single .80 .70
c.-d. 450b Either single 1.00 .90
e.-f. 500b Either single 1.20 1.00
g.-h. 600b Either single 1.60 1.40
i. 750b multi 1.90 1.60
j. 1000b multi 2.50 2.25

Mountains A511

Designs: No. 1649, Bolivar Peak, Venezuela. No. 1650, Mt. Damavand, Iran.

2004 Litho. *Perf. 13*

1649 A511 1700b multi 3.00 3.00
1650 A511 1700b multi 3.00 3.00
a. Horiz. pair, #1649-1650 7.00 6.50

No. 1650 has "Republica Bolivariana de Venezuela" overprinted in black over vignette. No. 1650 exists without overprint. Nos. 1649 and 1650 without overprint were prepared for issue in 2004 but No. 1649 and 1650 with overprint were not placed on sale until 2006.

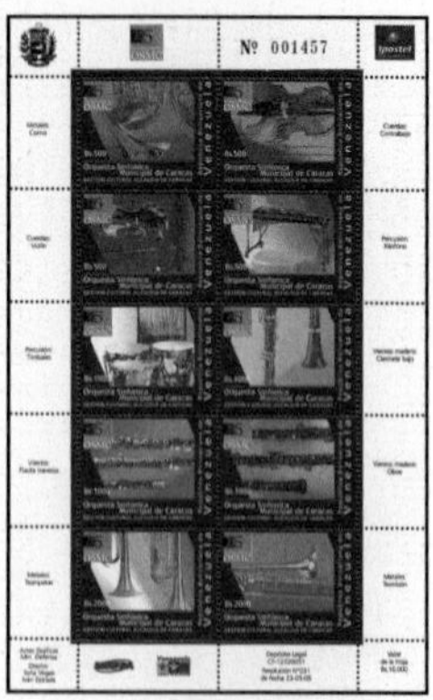

Caracas Municipal Symphony Orchestra, 25th Anniv. — A512

No. 1651: a, French horns. b, Bass (in blue) and bow. c, Violin and bow. d, Marimba. e, Timpani. f, Clarinets. g, Flutes. h, Oboes. i, Trumpets. j, Trombone.

2005 ***Perf. 12***

1651	A512	Sheet of 10	23.00	20.00
a.-d.		500b Any single	.95	.80
e.-h.		1000b Any single	2.10	1.75
i.-j.		2000b Either single	4.00	3.25

16th World Youth and Student Festival A513

No. 1652: a, Festival emblems from 1947-59. b, Festival emblems from 1962-2005. c, Festival emblem and joined arms. d, Festival emblem and text of Simón Bolívar's Vow of Monte Sacro. e, Festival emblem and Bolívar with outstretched arm, signature of Bolívar. f, Festival emblem and broken chain. g, Festival emblem, Bolívar. h, Festival emblem, dove. i, Festival emblem, dove, globe and hands. j, Festival emblem and hands.

1000b, Festival emblem and Bolívar with outstretched arm, horiz.

2005, Aug. 5 **Litho.** ***Perf. 12***

1652	A513	Sheet of 10	14.50	12.00
a.-d.		300b Any single	.85	.70
e.-i.		500b Any single	1.25	1.00
j.		1500b multi	3.75	3.00

Souvenir Sheet

Perf. 12x11¾

1653	A513	1000b multi	4.25	4.00

No. 1653 contains one 41x36mm stamp.

IPOSTEL — A514

No. 1654: a, IPOSTEL emblem, flag, Caracas Post Office. b, Postal vans. c, IPOSTEL emblem on envelope, Caracas Post Office. d, Postal motorcycles. e, Carmelitas Post Office. f, Airplane, postal bicycles. g, Falcón Post Office. h, Mail carriers. i, Zulia Post Office. j, Postal workers in San Martín.

No. 1655: a, Man, IPOSTEL emblem, letters. b, Postal worker, mail sacks. c, Mail on conveyor belt. d, Mail carriers with parcels. e, Postal workers sorting mail. f, Postal workers at Ribas Mission. g, Mail sacks. h, Doctor, medical equipment at Barrio Adentro Mission. i, Postal worker and postal machinery. j, Forklift and Mercal emblem.

2005, Oct. 10 ***Perf. 12***

1654	A514	Sheet of 10	26.00	23.00
a.-b.		300b Either single	.85	.75
c.-d.		400b Either single	1.00	.90
e.-f.		600b Either single	1.40	1.25
g.-i.		1700b Any single	4.00	3.50
j.		2000b multi	5.00	4.25
1655	A514	Sheet of 10	26.00	23.00
a.-b.		300b Either single	.85	.75
c.-d.		400b Either single	1.00	.90
e.-f.		600b Either single	1.40	1.25
g.-i.		1700b Any single	4.00	3.50
j.		2000b multi	5.00	4.25

Central Bank of Venezuela, 65th Anniv. — A515

No. 1656: a, Bank emblem. b, Caracas branch. c, Maracaibo branch. d, Venezuela Mint. e, Children's economic educational program. f, Numismatic Museum. g, Plaza Juan Pedro López. h, Gold bars. i, Bank notes and printing plates. j, Coins.

2005, Oct. 20 ***Perf. 12½x13½***

1656	A515	Sheet of 10	20.00	18.00
a.-b.		300b Either single	.65	.60
c.-d.		400b Either single	.80	.70
e.-f.		600b Either single	1.10	1.00
g.-h.		1500b Either single	2.75	2.50
i.-j.		1700b Either single	3.00	2.90

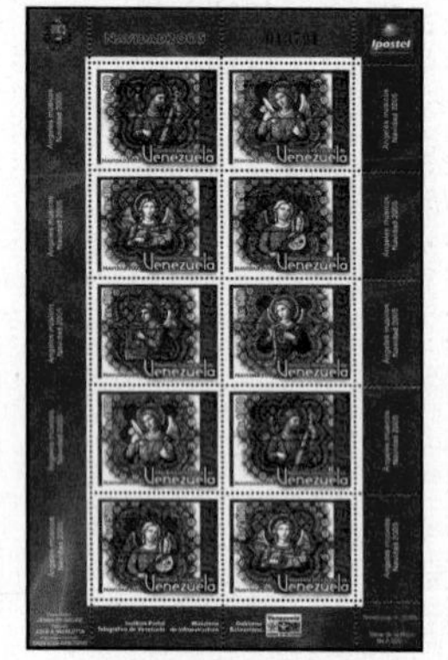

Christmas — A516

No. 1657 — Angel with: a, h, Long-necked stringed instrument with bow. b, j, Lute. c, Harp. d, g, Maracas. e, i, Stringed instrument with bow. f, Horn.

2005, Dec. 1 ***Perf. 12***

1657	A516	Sheet of 10	23.00	20.00
a.-c.		400b Any single	1.00	.80
d.-f.		600b Any single	1.50	1.25
g.-h.		1000b Either single	2.40	2.10
i.		1500b multi	3.25	2.90
j.		2000b multi	4.70	4.25

National Guard A517

No. 1658: a, Villa Zoila. b, Troops and building with ornate roof. c, Troops and automobiles. d, Troops saluting. e, Helicopter. f, Troops in inflatable raft. g, Three guardsmen at industrial site. h, Two guardsmen inspecting boxes. i, Guardsman with drug-sniffing dog. j, Guardsman, children.

2006, Feb. 23

1658	A517	Sheet of 10	26.00	24.00
a.-d.		300b Any single	.85	.80
e.-f.		400b Either single	1.00	.95
g.-h.		1500b Either single	3.75	3.50
i.-j.		2000b Either single	5.00	4.75

Banco Guayana, 50th Anniv. — A518

No. 1659 — Shimaraña people: a, People with painted faces. b, Archer and man with spear. c, Canoes on water. d, Women near dock. e, Man in canoe, woman's face. f, Children. g, Bow fishermen. h, Men, child, waterfall. i, Child. j, Women, dancer and river.

2006, Mar. 16

1659	A518	Sheet of 10	32.50	30.00
a.-b.		300b Either single	.90	.85
c.-f.		500b Any single	1.40	1.25
g.-h.		1700b Either single	4.75	4.25
i.-j.		2000b Either single	5.50	5.00

National Tax and Customs Administration (SENIAT) — A519

No. 1660 — Customs buildings in: a, Valencia. b, Puerto Cabello. c, Paraguachón. d, Santa Elena de Uairén. e, Maiquetia (in day). f, Maiquetia (at night). g, Ureña. h, Táchira. i, Barcelona. j, La Guaira.

2006, Mar. 22

1660	A519	Sheet of 10	20.00	18.00
a.-b.		400b Either single	.70	.60
c.-d.		500b Either single	.90	.75
e.-f.		700b Either single	1.20	1.00
g.-h.		1000b Either single	1.40	1.40
i.-j.		2000b Either single	3.50	3.00

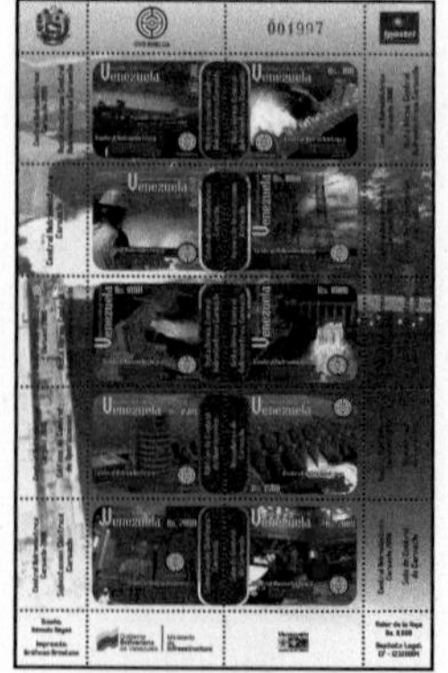

Carauchi Hydroelectric Dam Project — A520

No. 1661: a, Dam at night. b, Aerial view of dam. c, Worker at dam. d, Power lines. e, Aerial view of dam, water flowing to right. f, Aerial view of dam, water flowing straight ahead, descriptive text at left. g, Control tower. h, Spillway. i, Electrical substation. j, Control room.

No. 1662 — Rescued animals: a, Iguana iguana. b, Caluromys philander. c, Paleosuchus palpebrosus. d, Geochelone carbonaria. e, Cebus olivaceus. f, Choloepus didactylus. g, Tupinambis teguixin. h, Lora bejuca. i, Coendou prehensilis. j, Tamandua tetradactyla.

No. 1663, Aerial view of dam, water flowing straight ahead, descriptive text at top.

2006, Apr. 6

1661	A520	Sheet of 10	26.00	23.00
a.-b.		300b Either single	.75	.70
c.-f.		1000b Any single	2.10	1.80
g.-h.		1500b Either single	3.00	2.60
i.-j.		2000b Either single	4.50	4.00
1662	A520	Sheet of 10	26.00	23.00
a.-b.		300b Either single	.75	.70
c.-f.		1000b Any single	2.10	1.80
g.-h.		1500b Either single	3.00	2.60
i.-j.		2000b Either single	4.50	4.00

Souvenir Sheet

1663	A520	1000b multi	6.75	6.50

No. 1663 contains one 42x37mm stamp.

141st Extraordinary Meeting of OPEC — A521

No. 1664 — Petroleum facilities, meeting emblem and: a, "OPEP". b, Flag of United Arab Emirates flag. c, Flag of Libya. d, Flag of Iraq. e, Flag of Saudi Arabia. f, Flag of Indonesia. g, Flag of Nigeria. h, Flag of Algeria. i, Flag of Iran. j, Flag of Qatar. k, Flag of Venezuela. l, Flag of Kuwait.

2006, June 1

1664	A521	Sheet of 12	22.50	20.00
a.-b.		300b Either single	.65	.60
c.-h.		500b Any single	.80	.75
i.-j.		1500b Either single	2.50	2.25
k.-l.		2000b Either single	3.25	3.00

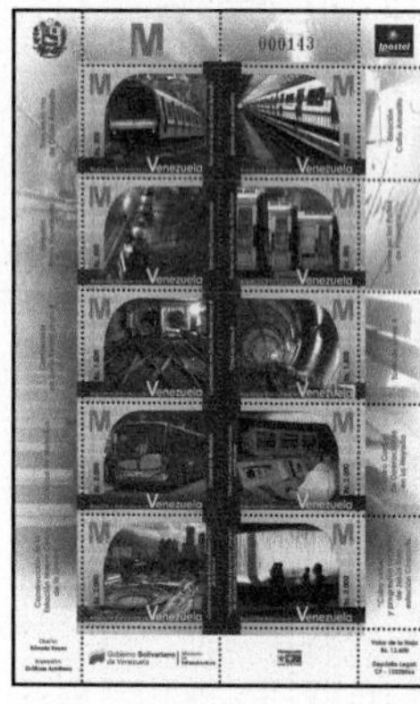

Caracas Mass Transit A522

No. 1665: a, Train on Yellow line. b, Yellow line station. c, Plaza Venezuela Station. d, Three trains. e, Train switches. f, Line 4 Tunnel. g, Metro bus. h, Control room. i, Construction of Line 4 Nuevo Circo Station. j, Art by Jesús Soto, Chacaíto Station.

2006, July 2

1665	A522	Sheet of 10	27.50	25.00
a.-b.		300b Either single	.65	.60
c.-d.		500b Either single	1.00	.90
e.-f.		1500b Either single	2.75	2.50
g.-j.		2000b Any single	3.60	3.25

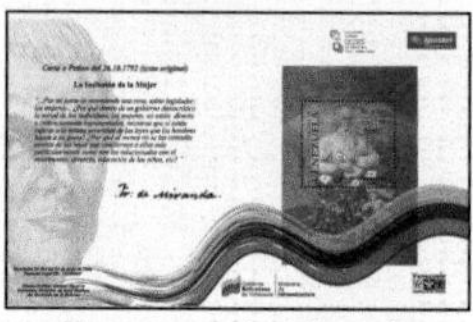

Francisco de Miranda University — A523

No. 1666, vert.: a, Miranda on horse. b, Miranda facing left. c, Nose, mouth and hand of Miranda. d, Statue of Miranda, Venezuelan flag. e, Miranda holding flag. f, Miranda at Venezuelan independence ceremonies. g, Miranda. h, Statues of Miranda. i, Miranda facing right. j, Miranda writing letter, ship.

No. 1667, Like #1666j.

2006, July 28

1666	A523	Sheet of 10	40.00	37.50
a.-d.		300b Any single	1.40	1.25
e.-f.		500b Either single	2.10	1.90
g.-h.		1500b Either single	5.75	5.25

i.-j.	2000b Either single	7.50	6.75

Souvenir Sheet

1667	A523 1500b multi	4.25	4.00

No. 1666 contains ten 35x45mm stamps.

Children's Art — A524

No. 1668: a, Flag of Liberty, by Elimar Sanchez. b, Miranda (Miranda and broken chain), by Gabriel Solano. c, Miranda and Catalina, by Elikarina Sánchez. d, Musical Aspects of Miranda (G clef), by Josmelys Díaz. e, Miranda Playing, by Nasser Sultan. f, Miranda and His Dreams, by Cynthia Urbina. g, Flag of Miranda, by Janem Sultan. h, Miranda Thinking, by Luis Miguel Martínez. i, Miranda and His Family, by Vianny Gonella. j, Diary of Miranda, by José A. Martínez.

2006

1668	A524 Sheet of 10	23.00	21.00
a.-d.	300b Any single	.80	.70
e.-f.	500b Either single	1.00	.95
g.-h.	1500b Either single	3.00	2.90
i.-j.	2000b Either single	4.25	3.90

Souvenir Sheet

CVG EDELCA, 43rd Anniv. — A525

2006

1669	A525 3500b multi	8.00	7.50

Central University, Caracas — A526

No. 1670: a, Exterior of Engineering Library. b, Interior of Engineering Library. c, Electrical Engineering Building. d, School of Engineering, Metallurgy and Material Sciences, Sculpture by Harry Abend. e, School of Civil Engineering. f, School of Chemical Engineering, Petroleum and Geology, Mines and Geophysics. g, Mural by Alejandro Otero at School of Engineering. h, Machinery at Institute of Materials and Structural Models. i, Fluid Mechanics Institute. j, Aulas Auditorium.

2006

1670	A526 Sheet of 10	49.00	47.00
a.-d.	400b Any single	.90	.85
e.-f.	600b Either single	1.40	1.25
g.-h.	3000b Either single	6.75	6.25
i.-j.	5000b Either single	10.50	9.75

Modern Art A527

No. 1671: a, Esfera Japón. b, Biface Naranja. c, Repetición y Progresión. d, Repetición Optica No. 2. e, Composición Dinámica. f, Muro Optico. g, Pardelas Interferentes. h, Espiral. i, Ambivalencia Dicembre. j, Estructura Cinética.
1500b, Espiral, diff.

2006

1671	A527 Sheet of 10	22.50	20.00
a.-b.	300b Either single	.95	.85
c.-f.	500b Any single	1.25	1.10
g.-j.	1000b Any single	2.75	2.50

Souvenir Sheet

1672	A527 1500b multi	4.50	4.25

No. 1671 contains ten 45x35mm stamps.

Transportation — A528

No. 1673: a, Airplane in flight. b, Simón Bolívar Intl. Airport, Maiquetía. c, Highway, Ayacucho. d, Highway, Barquisimeto. e, José Antonio Páez Highway. f, Caracas — La Guaira Viaduct. g, Line 3, Caracas Metro. h, Line 4, Caracas Metro. i, Maracaibo Metro. j, Teques Metro. k, Valencia Metro. l, Caracas — Tuy Medio tram.

2006

1673	A528 Sheet of 12	40.00	37.50
a.-g.	300b Any single	.90	.80
h.-j.	2000b Any single	4.75	4.50
k.-l.	3000b Either single	6.50	6.00

A529

Christmas — A530

No. 1674: a, Musicians. b, Toy. c, Top. d, Holiday table setting. e, Food. f, Letter to Baby Jesus. g, Illuminated cross. h, Yo-yo. i, Yo-yo, top and toy. j, Envelope with Holy Family.

No. 1675: a, Nativity. b, Food. c, Letter to Baby Jesus. d, IPOSTEL emblem with Holy Family.

2006

1674	A529 Sheet of 10	26.00	23.00
a.-b.	300b Either single	.80	.70
c.-d.	450b Either single	1.10	1.00
e.-f.	550b Either single	1.40	1.20
g.-h.	1000b Either single	2.50	2.25
i.	2000b multi	4.50	4.00
j.	3000b multi	6.75	6.00
1675	A530 Sheet of 4	9.25	8.25
a.-b.	300b Either single	.60	.55
c.	1000b multi	1.75	1.60
d.	2000b multi	3.50	3.25

Miniature Sheets

A531

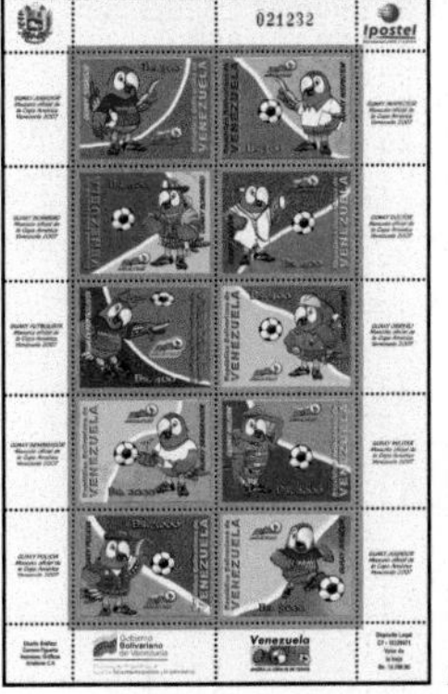

A532

2007 Copa America Soccer Tournament, Venezuela — A533

No. 1676: a, Mascot Guaky and soccer ball. b, City University Olympic Stadium, Caracas. c, José E. Pachencho Stadium, Maracaibo. d, Metropolitan Stadium, Lara. e, Agustín Tovar "La Carolina" Stadium, Barinas. f, General J. A. Anzoátegui Stadium, Puerto La Cruz. g, Cachamay Total Entertainment Center, Ciudad Guayana. h, Metropolitan Stadium, Mérida. i, Monumental Stadium, Maturin. j, Multisport Stadium, Pueblo Nuevo San Cristóbal.

No. 1677 — Mascots: a, Guaky Jugador. b, Guaky Inspector. c, Guaky Bombero. d, Guaky Doctor. e, Guaky Futbolista. f, Guaky Obrero. g, Guaky Sembrador. h, Guaky Militar. i, Guaky Policia. j, Guaky Jugador, diff.

No. 1678 — Mascot Guaky and emblem of soccer governing body of: a, Venezuela. b, Brazil. c, Argentina. d, Mexico. e, Colombia. f, Chile. g, Peru. h, Uruguay. i, Ecuador. j, Bolivia. k, Paraguay. l, United States.

2007, June 18 Litho. ***Perf. 12***

1676	A531 Sheet of 10	27.50	25.00
a.-b.	300b Either single	.55	.50
c.-f.	400b Any single	.70	.65
g.-h.	2000b Either single	3.25	3.00
i.	3000b multi	4.50	4.00
j.	5000b multi	7.75	7.00
1677	A532 Sheet of 10	27.50	25.00
a.-b.	300b Either single	.55	.50
c.-f.	400b Any single	.70	.65
g.-h.	2000b Either single	3.25	3.00
i.	3000b multi	4.50	4.00
j.	5000b multi	7.75	7.00
1678	A533 Sheet of 12	27.50	25.00
a.-d.	300b Any single	.55	.50
e.-h.	400b Any single	.70	.65
i.-j.	2000b Either single	2.75	2.50
k.	3000b multi	4.50	4.00
l.	5000b multi	7.25	6.50
	Nos. 1676-1678 (3)	82.50	75.00

Intelligence and Prevention Service (DISIP), 38th Anniv. — A534

No. 1679 — DISIP emblem and: a, El Helicoide (Headquarters Building), denomination in red, "Venezuela" in dark blue. b, Model of El Helicoide, denomination in dark blue, "Venezuela" in orange. c, Model of El Helicoide, denomination in yellow. d, El Helicoide being built, denomination in red, "Venezuela" in green. e, Cupola of El Helicoide, denomination in orange. f, Auditorium of El Helicoide, denomination in light blue, "Venezuela" in red. g, El Helicoide, denomination in green. h, El Helicoide, denomination in red. i, Garden outside El Helicoide. j, Plaza Bolívar.
3500b, El Helicoide, denomination in yellow.

2007, June 21

1679	A534 Sheet of 10	36.00	34.00
a.-f.	300b Any single	.70	.65
g.-h.	2000b Either single	4.20	4.00
i.	3000b multi	5.50	5.00
j.	5000b multi	9.50	9.00

Souvenir Sheet

1680	A534 3500b multi	7.25	7.00

No. 1680 contains one 42x37mm stamp.

Miniature Sheet

Simón Bolívar Center, Caracas A535

No. 1681: a, Muses de los Niños. b, Juan Pablo II buildings. c, Torres del Silencio. d, Palacio de Justicia. e, Parque Central building. f, Museo de Arte Contemporaneo de Caracas. g, Avenida Bolívar. h, Paseo Vargas. i, Teresa Carreño Theater. j, Cristobal Rojas.

2007, July 19

1681	A535 Sheet of 10	32.50	30.00
a.-d.	300b Any single	.65	.60
e.-f.	450b Either single	.90	.80
g.-h.	2000b Either single	4.50	4.00
i.	3000b multi	6.00	5.50
j.	5000b multi	11.00	10.00

Miniature Sheet

Christmas — A536

No. 1682 — Art: a, Resplendent God, by Hugo Rivero. b, Creole Christmas, by Vidalia González. c, Christmas Door, by Soccoro Peraza. d, Christmas, wood carvings by Orlando Campos. e, Christmas, wood carving by Tomás Flores. f, Christmas Wish, by Alberto Allup. g, St. Joseph, Virgin and Child, by Baldomero Higuera. h, Christmas, by Edgar Vegas. i, Holy Family, by Margarita Pérez de Lamanna. j, Merry Christmas, by Ana Teresa Pesce.

2007, Dec. 10

1682 A536 Sheet of 10 23.00 21.00
a.-d. 500b Any single 1.20 1.10
e.-h. 1000b Any single 2.50 2.40
i.-j. 1500b Either single 3.50 3.25

Miniature Sheet

Venezuelan Institute for Scientific Investigations (IVIC) — A537

No. 1683 — IVIC emblem and: a, Quimbiotec Blood Products Plant. b, Beatriz Roche Children's Band. c, Academic medal. d, Cubagua gargoyle. e, Advance Studies Center graduates. f, Bolívar and Bello Plaza. g, Molecular model. h, Investigative laboratory. i, Marcel Roche Library. j, Samuel Robinson Apartments.

No. 1684 — Artwork by: a, Linda Morales. b, Alberto Allup. c, Freddy Simoza. d, Orlando Campos.

2007, Dec. 14

1683 A537 Sheet of 10 28.00 25.00
a.-d. 500b Any single 1.20 1.00
e.-h. 1000b Any single 2.50 2.25
i.-j. 2000b Either single 5.00 4.50

Souvenir Sheet

1684 A537 500b Sheet of 4, #a-d 5.25 4.25

Miniature Sheet

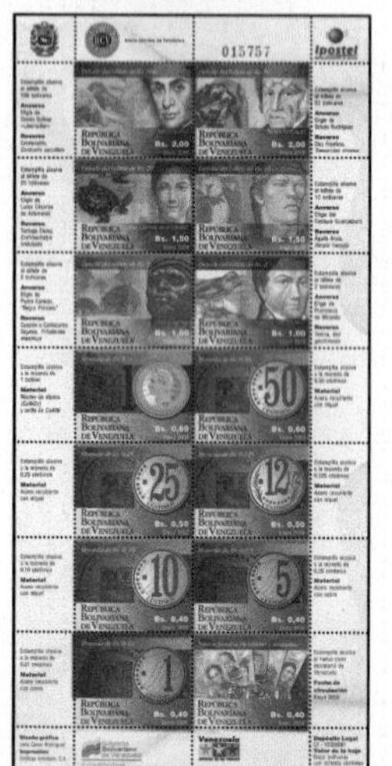

Coins and Banknotes of Revalued Currency — A538

No. 1685: a, Coins and banknotes. b, 1 centimo coin. c, 5 centimo coin. d, 10 centimo coin. e, 12½ centimo coin. f, 25 centimo coin. g, 50 centimo coin. h, 1 bolivar coin. i, Francisco de Miranda and Inia geoffrensis from 2 bolivar banknote. j, Pedro Camejo and Priodontes maximus from 5 bolivar banknote. k, Guaicaipuro and Harpia harpyja from 10 bolivar banknote. l, Luisa Cáceres de Arismendi and Eretmochelys imbricata from 20 bolivar banknote. m, Simón Rodríguez and Tremarctos ornatus from 50 bolivar banknote. n, Simon Bolivar and Carduelis cucullata from 100 bolivar banknote.

2008, May 7 Litho. *Perf. 12*

1685 A538 Sheet of 14 23.00 20.00
a.-d. 40c Any single .75 .65
e.-f. 50c Either single .85 .75
g.-h. 60c Either single 1.00 .90
i.-j. 1b Either single 1.75 1.50
k.-l. 1.50b Either single 2.50 2.25
m.-n. 2b Either single 3.50 3.25

Miniature Sheet

2008 Summer Olympics, Beijing — A539

No. 1686: a, Swimming. b, Weight lifting. c, Women's wrestling. d, Fencing.

2008, June 20 *Perf. 12*

1686 A539 1b Sheet of 4, #a-d 15.00 14.00

Miniature Sheet

Sites in Caracas A540

No. 1687: a, Palacio de las Academias. b, Sabana Grande Boulevard. c, Plaza El Venezolano. d, Abra Solar. e, Carmelitas Post Office. f, Plaza O'Leary. g, City Hall (Palacio Municipal). h, Reflecting pool (Paseo Monumental Los Próceres). i, Casona Anauco Arriba. j, Plaza Bolívar.

3b, Reflecting pool (Paseo Monumental Los Próceres).

2008, Oct. 9 Litho. *Perf. 12*

1687 A540 Sheet of 10 32.00 29.00
a.-b. 30c Either single .50 .45
c.-d. 40c Either single .65 .60
e.-f. 60c Either single .90 .85
g.-h. 1.50b Either single 2.10 1.90
i. 5b multi 7.25 6.50
j. 10b multi 14.00 13.00

Souvenir Sheet

1688 A540 3b multi 4.50 4.25

Miniature Sheet

Portraits of Simon Bolivar A541

No. 1689 — Portraits by: a, José M. Espinosa. b, Pierre Colf. c, Tito Salas. d, José Gil de Castro. e, Angel Zeballos. f, Gil de Castro, diff. g, Salas, diff. h, Juan Lovera. i, Unknown artist. j, Salas, diff. k, Salas, diff. l, Daniel Hernández.

2008 Litho. *Perf. 12*

1689 A541 Sheet of 12 32.00 29.00
a.-d. 30c Any single .50 .45
e.-g. 50c Any single .75 .65
h.-j. 1.50b Any single 2.10 1.10
k. 3b multi 4.50 3.75
l. 10b multi 14.00 12.00

Miniature Sheet

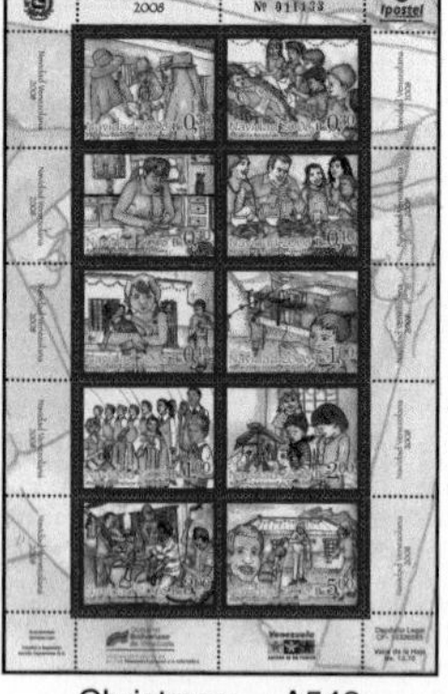

Christmas — A542

No. 1690: a, Four people wearing hats, baby. b, Children giving letters to baby Jesus. c, Woman in kitchen. d, Family eating holiday meal. e, Boy and girl with toys. f, Boys flying kite. g, Choir and musicians. h, Three children at small creche. i, Musicians. j, Children playing, house decorated with Christmas lights.

2008, Dec. 1 Litho. *Perf. 12*

1690 A542 Sheet of 10 20.00 18.00
a.-c. 30c Any single .45 .40
d.-e. 40c Either single .55 .50
f.-g. 1b Either single 1.40 1.20
h. 2b multi 2.60 2.40
i. 3b multi 3.75 3.25
j. 5b multi 6.25 5.50

Miniature Sheet

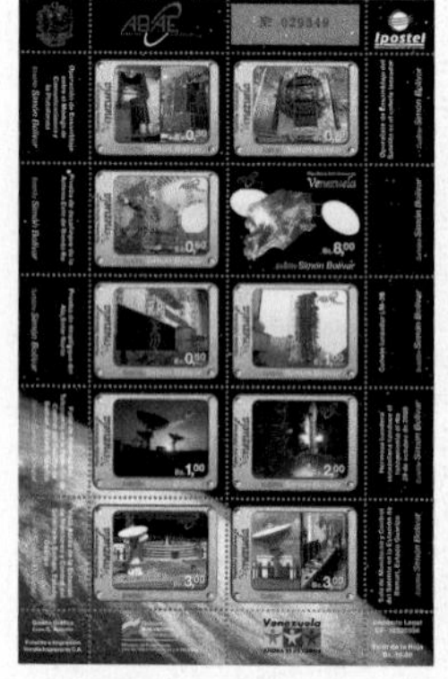

Simón Bolívar Satellite A543

No. 1691: a, Parts of satellite. b, Arm of satellite folded up. c, Satellite on scaffolds. d, Scaffolds and sign. e, Launch pad. f, Satellite dishes. g, Lift-off. h, Satellite dishes and control building. i, Satellite dish and control room. j, Satellite in space.

2009, Jan. 8

1691 A543 Sheet of 10 28.00 25.00
a.-b. 30c Either single .45 .40
c.-d. 60c Either single .70 .65
e.-f. 1b Either single 1.20 1.10
g. 2b multi 2.25 2.10
h.-i. 3b Either single 3.25 3.00
j. 8b multi 9.25 8.50

Miniature Sheet

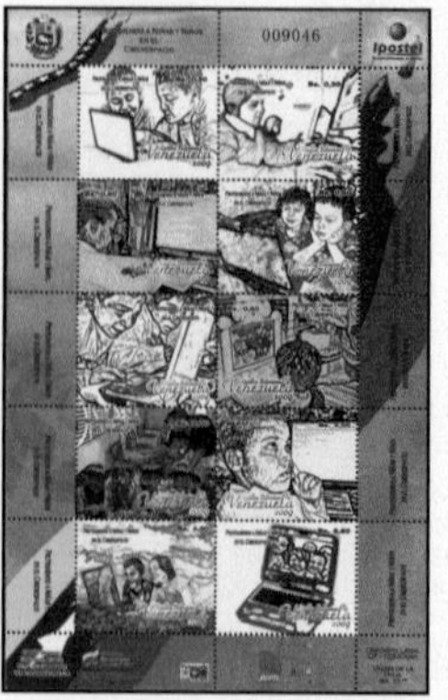

Protection of Children on the Internet — A544

No. 1692: a, Two boys at laptop computer. b, Two children at desktop computers. c, Man at computer. d, Two children at laptop computer, diff. (children at right). e, Two boys at laptop computer, diff. (Children at left). f, Child at computer with adult watching. g, Group of children in computer classroom. h, Boy with finger at ear near computer. i, Man and woman in field with computer. j, Laptop computer showing children on screen.

2009, May 15

1692 A544 Sheet of 10 25.00 22.50
a.-b. 30c Either single .45 .40
c.-f. 50c Any single .65 .55
g.-h. 2b Either single 2.60 2.25
i. 4b multi 5.00 4.50
j. 6.50b multi 8.75 7.75

Francisco de Miranda (1750-1816), Revolutionist in Venezuela and France — A545

2009, Oct. 15

1693 A545 1.50b multi 2.25 2.00
a. Souvenir sheet of 1, imperf. 3.50 3.25

See France No. 3729.

Miniature Sheets

Venezuelan Declaration of Independence, 200th Anniv. (in 2011) — A546

A547

Signers of the Venezuelan Declaration of Independence — A548

No. 1694: a, Part 7 of Declaration of Independence. b, Part 8. c, Part 9. d, Part 4. e, Part 5. f, Part 6. g, Part 2. h, Part 3. i, Part 1. j, Signatures. k, Signatures, diff. l, Simon Bolivar and map of North and South America.

No. 1695: a, Francisco de Miranda. b, Francisco Hernández. c, Salvador Delgado. d, Juan José de Maya. e, Juan Antonio Díaz Argote. f, Felipe Fermín Paul. g, Manuel Vicente Maya. h, Juan Toro. i, Francisco Policarpo Ortiz. j, Gabriel Pérez de Pagola. k, José Maria Ramírez. l, Fernando Toro.

No. 1696: a, Gabriel de Ponte. b, Lino de Clemente. c, Ramón Ignacio Méndez. d, Francisco Javier Ustáriz. e, Isidoro Antonio López Méndez. f, El Marqués del Toro. g, Juan Antonío Rodriguez Domínguez. h, José de Sata y Busy. i, José Vicente de Unda. j, Antonio Nicolás Briceño.

2009 Litho. *Perf. 12*

1694 A546 Sheet of 12 35.00 32.50
a.-c. 30c Any single .50 .45
d.-f. 50c Any single .75 .65
g.-h. 1b Either single 1.60 1.50
i.-j. 2b Either single 3.00 2.75
k. 3.50b multi 5.00 4.75
l. 9.50b multi 14.50 13.50
1695 A547 Sheet of 12 35.00 32.50
a.-c. 30c Any single .50 .45
d.-f. 50c Any single .75 .65
g.-h. 1b Either single 1.60 1.50
i.-j. 2b Either single 3.00 2.75
k. 3.50b multi 5.00 4.75
l. 9.50b multi 14.50 13.50
1696 A548 Sheet of 10 35.00 32.50
a. 30c multi .50 .45
b.-c. 50c Either single .75 .65
d.-f. 1b Any single 1.60 1.50
g.-h. 2b Either single 3.00 2.75
i. 3.50b multi 5.00 4.75
j. 9.50b multi 14.50 13.50
Nos. 1694-1696 (3) 105.00 97.50

Miniature Sheets

History of the Venezuelan Flag — A549

No. 1697 — Flag from: a, 1797. b, 1800. c, 1806 (Sun and Moon). d, 1806 (yellow, blue and red stripes). e, 1810. f, 1811. g, 1817 (7 stars). h, 1817 (8 stars). i, 1819. j, 1821 (arms in upper left corner).

No. 1698 — Flag from: a, 1821. b, 1830. c, 1836. d, 1859 (7 stars). e, 1859 (20 stars). f, 1863. g, 1905. h, 1930. i, 1954. j, 2006.

2009 Litho. *Perf. 12*

1697 A549 Sheet of 10 24.00 21.00
a.-b. 40c Either single .70 .60
c. 50c multi .80 .70
d. 60c multi .95 .85
e.-f. 1b Either single 1.75 1.50
g.-h. 2b Either single 3.25 2.90
i.-j. 3b Either single 4.50 4.00
1698 A549 Sheet of 10 24.00 21.00
a.-b. 40c Either single .70 .60
c. 50c multi .80 .70
d. 60c multi .95 .85
e.-f. 1b Either single 1.75 1.50
g.-h. 2b Either single 3.25 2.90
i.-j. 3b Either single 4.50 4.00

Miniature Sheets

History of the Venezuelan Coat of Arms — A550

No. 1699 — Arms from: a, 1591. b, 1811 (sun and banner). c, 1811 (dated 19 Abril de 1810). d, 1811 (dated 1811). e, 1812 (with 7 stars). f, 1812 (eagle with shield). g, 1819. h, 1821 (with eagle). i, 1821 (fasces and cornucopias). j, 1822.

No. 1700 — Arms from: a, 1830. b, 1834. c, 1836. d, 1856. e, 1863. f, 1871. g, 1905. h, 1930. i, 1954. j, 2006.

2009 Litho. *Perf. 12*

1699 A550 Sheet of 10 23.00 21.00
a.-b. 40c Either single .65 .60
c. 50c multi .75 .70
d. 60c multi .90 .85
e.-f. 1b Either single 1.60 1.50
g.-h. 2b Either single 3.00 2.90
i.-j. 3b Either single 5.75 5.50
1700 A550 Sheet of 10 23.00 21.00
a.-b. 40c Either single .65 .60
c. 50c multi .75 .70
d. 60c multi .90 .85
e.-f. 1b Either single 1.60 1.50
g.-h. 2b Either single 3.00 2.90
i.-j. 3b Either single 5.75 5.50

Miniature Sheet

Ayacucho Library, 35th Anniv. — A551

No. 1701 — Map color: a, Bister. b, Dark green. c, Dark blue. d, Lilac. e, Gray brown. f, Light blue. g, Yellow. h, Apple green. i, Brownish lilac. j, Gray.

2009 Litho. *Perf. 12*

1701 A551 Sheet of 10 34.00 31.00
a.-d. 30c Any single .55 .50
e.-f. 2b Either single 3.25 2.90
g.-h. 3.50b Either single 5.25 5.00
i.-j. 4b Either single 6.00 5.50

Miniature Sheet

Christmas — A552

No. 1702 — Religious art by: a, Lidoska Pirela. b, Miguel MarSán. c, Thays Arteaga. d, Gustavo Martínez. e, Orlando Campos. f, Daniel Sanseviero. g, Hugo Rivero. h, Edgar Vegas. i, Liliana Benítez. j, Alberto Allup.

2009

1702 A552 Sheet of 10 32.50 30.00
a.-d. 30c Any single .55 .50
e.-g. 50c Any single .85 .80
h. 3.10b multi 5.50 5.00
i. 4.20b multi 7.75 7.00
j. 6.50b multi 11.00 10.00

Miniature Sheets

A553

Signers of the Venezuelan Declaration of Independence — A554

No. 1703: a, Juan Germán Roscio. b, Fernando Peñalver. c, Martín Tovar Ponte. d, Ignacio Fernández. e, José Angel Alamo. f, Luis Ignacio Mendoza. g, Nicolás de Castro. h, Ignacio Ramón Briceño. i, Francisco Javier Yánes. j, Gabriel de Alcalá.

No. 1704: a, Mariano de la Cova. b, Juan Bermúdez. c, Francisco Isnardi. d, Manuel Plácido Maneiro. e, Juan Pablo Pacheco. f, José Luis Cabrera. g, Manuel Palacio. h, Juan Nepomuceno Quintana. i, Luis José de Cazorla. j, Francisco Javier de Mayz.

2009 *Perf. 12*

1703 A553 Sheet of 10 35.00 32.00
a.-b. 30c Either single .50 .45
c. 50c multi .75 .65
d.-f. 1b Any single 1.40 1.25
g.-h. 2b Either single 2.90 2.50
i. 3.50b multi 5.25 4.50
j. 9.50b multi 14.50 12.50
1704 A554 Sheet of 10 35.00 32.00
a.-b. 30c Either single .50 .45
c.-d. 50c Either single .75 .65
e.-f. 1b Either single 1.40 1.25
g.-h. 2b Either single 2.90 2.50
i. 3.50b multi 5.25 4.50
j. 9.50b multi 14.50 12.50

Miniature Sheet

Bolivarian Militia — A555

No. 1705 — General Command Building: a, Domed and crenellated tower. b, Columns and balcony. c, Flag above main entrance. d, Round crenellated tower in foreground. e, Round crenellated tower in background. f, Rectangular tower. g, Columns and Plaza of Honor. h, Militia members, round crenellated tower in background. i, Building. j, Building and flag.

2010, Apr. 21

1705 A555 Sheet of 10 44.00 41.00
a.-c. 1b Any single 1.25 1.10
d.-f. 2b Any single 2.50 2.25
g.-h. 4.50b Either single 5.00 4.75
i. 6b multi 7.00 6.25
j. 10.50b multi 13.50 12.50

Miniature Sheet

Prominent Figures of the First Republic of Venezuela — A556

No. 1706: a, Juan Germán Roscio (1763-1821). b, José Félix Ribas (1775-1815). c, Francisco Espejo (1758-1814). d, Isidoro López Méndez (1751-1814). e, Lino de Clemente (1767-1834). f, José Félix Sosa (1773-1814). g, Martín Tovar Ponte (1772-1843). h, Francisco Javier Ustáriz (1772-1814). i, Francisco Salias (1785-1834). j, José Cortés de Madariaga (1766-1826).

2010, Apr. 28

1706 A556 Sheet of 10 45.00 42.50
a.-b. 1b Either single 1.25 1.20
c.-f. 2.50b Any single 3.25 3.00
g.-i. 4b Any single 4.75 4.50
j. 12b multi 14.50 14.00

Manuela Sáenz (c. 1797-1856), Mistress of Simón Bolívar — A557

2010, May 24

1707 A557 2.50b multi 3.25 3.00

See Ecuadoe No. 2007.

Miniature Sheet

Scenes From Independence Day Military Parade — A558

No. 1708: a, National flag (Bandera Nacional). b, Athletes on float (Atletas). c, Women from cultural group wearing yellow and green dresses (Agrupaciones Culturales). d, People from cultural group wearing masks, red and white costumes (Agrupaciones Culturales). e, Women from cultural group wearing headdresses and white blouses (Agrupaciones Culturales). f, Indigenous people (Etnias Indígenas). g, People carrying flags (Estandartes FANB). h, Two uniformed men and white horse (Réplica de la Espada del Libertador). i, Soldiers from Venezuela Military Academy marching (Academia Militar de Venezuela). j, Sailors from Naval School (Escuela Naval). k, Students from Military Aviation School (Escuela de Aviación Militar). l, Students from National Guard Officer's Training School (EFOFAC). m, Students from Military Technical School (Escuela Técnical Militar). n, Male members of Bolivarian Militia wearing red pants (Milicia Bolivariana). o, Female members of Bolivarian Militia wearing white boots (Milicia Bolivariana). p, Rural militia (Milicia Campesina). q, AMX-30 tank. r, C-90 Escorpión tank. s, Dragón 300 armored fighting vehicle. t, E-11 Urutu armored personnel carrier. u, Oto Melara armored personnel carrier. v, Sultán tank. w, AMX-13 tank. x, Tank of Mechanized Infantry with banner (Infanteria Mecanizada del Ejército). y, Members of Brazil delegation. z, Members of Cuba delegation. aa, Members of Bolivia delegation. ab, Members of Nicaragua delegation. ac, Members of Argentina delegation. ad, Members of Ecuador delegation. ae, Members of Belarus delegation. af, Members of Dominican Republic delegation. ag, Members of Parachute battalion (Batallón de Paracaidistas). ah, Members of Caribbean Batallion (Batallón de Caribes). ai, Members of Forest Batallion (Batallón de Selva). aj, Special Forces wearing jungle camouflage with hoods (Fuerzas Especiales). ak, Special Forces members, man with black ski cap at right (Fuerzas Especiales). al, Special Forces members with open mouths and camouflage painted faces, white gun straps (Fuerzas Especiales). am, Special Forces members wearing red berets (Fuerzas Especiales). an, Special Forces members with fully-painted faces, black gun straps (Fuerzas Especiales). ao, Sukhoi 30MK2 jet. ap, F-16 jet. aq, K-8 jet. ar, MI-26T Panare helicopter. as, MI-35M Caribe helicopter. at, MI-17V5 Pemón helicopter. au, Sikorsky AS-61D helicopter. av, Mounted sqadron (Escuadrón de Caballería).

2010, Aug. 9

1708 A558 Sheet of 48 67.50 55.00
a.-x. 30c Any single .95 .75
y.-av. 1b Any single 1.75 1.40

Organization of Petroleum Exporting Countries (OPEC), 50th Anniv. — A559

No. 1709 — Paintings: a, Sembradores, by Ender Cepeda. b, Y Por Fin Nos Tocó Un Chorrito de Petróleo, by Soccorro Salinas. c, Cartografía Soberana, by Saúl Huerta. d, Serie Atardecer en Campos Petroleros, by Ernesto León. e, Como Caída del Cielo, by Rosa Contreras. f, Marea, by Morella Jurado. g, Julio, by Omar Carreño. h, Del Reventón al Barril Dorado, by Gabriel Bracho. i, Petróleo Nuestro de Cada Día, by Manuel Quintana Castillo. j, El Pozo y Las Ocho Estrellas, by Paúl Del Río.

12p, 50th anniversary emblem, horiz.

2010, Sept. 14

1709 A559 Sheet of 10 45.00 42.50
a.-c. 30c Any single .65 .60
d.-e. 50c Either single .65 .60
f.-g. 3b Either single 3.25 3.00
h. 8b multi 8.50 8.00
i.-j. 10b Either single 10.50 10.00

Souvenir Sheet

1710 A559 12b multi 14.75 14.50

No. 1710 contains one 42x37mm stamp.

Miniature Sheet

Central Bank of Venezuela Art Collection, 70th Anniv. — A560

No. 1711 — Paintings: a, Venezuela, by Armando Reverón. b, Formas en Equilibio N-1, by Angel Hurtado. c, Bananeros, by Camille Pissarro. d, La Pareja, by Armando Barrias. e, Left half of El Avila Visto Desde el Country Club (trees at left), by Manuel Cabré. f, Right half of El Avila Visto Desde el Country Club (trees at right), by Cabré.

2010, Nov. 24

1711 A560 Sheet of 6 35.00 34.00
a.-b. 30c Either single .45 .45
c. 5b multi 4.00 4.00
d. 8b multi 6.50 6.50
e.-f. 12.50b Either single 10.50 10.50

Miniature Sheet

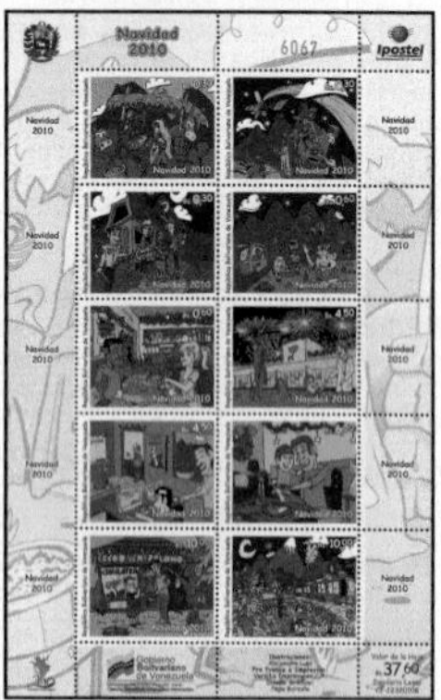

Christmas — A561

No. 1712: a, Nativity. b, Satellite over the three Magi. c, Musicians. d, Cable car, buildings on mountainside, children playing. e, Woman and man at market. f, Fireworks over building. g, Teacher and children in school room, boy working at computer. h, Father and son opening Christmas gift. i, Father and son outside of candy store. j, Child on blanket in plaza, people, bus.

2010, Dec. 7

1712	A561	Sheet of 10	35.00	32.50
a.-c.		30c Any single	.50	.45
d.-e.		60c Either single	.60	.55
f.-g.		4.50b Either single	3.75	3.50
h.		6.50b multi	5.40	5.00
i.-j.		10b Either single	8.25	7.75

Miniature Sheet

Venezuelan Antarctic Program — A562

No. 1713: a, Members of first expedition, 2008. b, Scientists taking measurements. c, Members of third expedition, 2010. d, Line of expedition members in snowstorm. e, Iceberg adrift. f, Antarctic base buildings, iceberg. g, Members of second expedition, 2009. h, Giant petrel. i, Penguins and ship, Barrientos Island. j, Whale at surface.

2010, Dec. 21 ***Perf. 12¼x12***

1713	A562	Sheet of 10	37.50	35.00
a.-b.		30c Either single	.55	.50
c.-d.		40c Either single	.55	.50
e.-f.		60c Either single	.80	.75
g.		6.50b multi	5.25	5.00
h.-i.		8.50b Either single	6.75	6.25
j.		13.50b multi	10.50	9.75

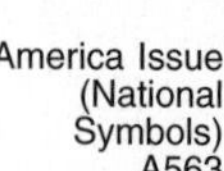

America Issue (National Symbols) A563

2011, Feb. 21 ***Perf. 14¼***

1714 A563 2b multi 2.00 1.75

Miniature Sheet

Army Day A564

No. 1715 — Uniform of: a, Batallón Bravos de Apure. b, Guardia de Honor del Libertador. c, Soldado Llanero. d, Batallón de Rifles. e, Batallón Tiradores de la Guardia. f, Cazadores Britanicos. g, Dragones de la Guardia. h, Husares de Páez. i, General de División Patriota. j, Campaña del Libertador.

2011, June 27 ***Perf. 12***

1715	A564	Sheet of 10	26.00	24.00
a.-b.		30c Either single	.30	.30
c.-e.		40c Any single	.30	.30
f.-g.		1.50b Either single	1.00	.90
h.		6.50b multi	4.25	4.00
i.		10b multi	6.50	6.00
j.		15.60b multi	9.75	9.00

Reunion of the Patriotic Society, by Tito Salas A565

The Pantheon of Heroes, by Arturo Michelena — A566

No. 1716: a, Woman in black dress at right (left fifth of painting). b, Three men seated on bench at right, man at lectern in foreground (fourth fifth of painting). c, Bearded man standing at right (right fifth of painting). d, Woman with white dress in foreground at table (second fifth of painting). e, As "a." f, As "b." g, Three men seated on bench at left, lectern in foreground (middle fifth of painting). h, As "d." i, As "b." j, As "g."

2011, June 27 ***Perf. 12***

1716	A565	Sheet of 10	32.50	30.00
a.-c.		30c Any single	.30	.30
d.-e.		60c Either single	.45	.40
f.		1.50b multi	.95	.90
g.-h.		8.50b Either single	5.40	5.00
i.-j.		12.50b Either single	7.50	7.00

Souvenir Sheet

1717 A566 18b multi 11.25 11.00

Miniature Sheet

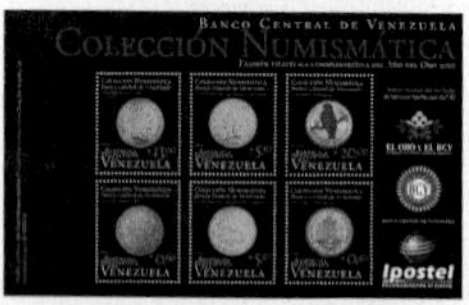

Central Bank of Venezuela Gold Coin Collection — A567

No. 1718: a, Reverse of 1975 Venezuela 1000b coin depicting arms. b, Reverse of 1886 Venezuela 100b coin depicting arms. c, Obverse of 1851 United States $20 coin depicting Liberty. d, Reverse of 1851 United States $20 coin depicting Great Seal. e, Obverse of 1886 Venezuela 100b coin depicting Simón Bolívar. f, Obverse of 1975 1000b coin depicting bird.

2011, Oct. 25

1718	A567	Sheet of 6	31.50	30.00
a.		40c multi	.35	.35
b.		60c multi	.40	.40
c.-d.		5.50b Either single	2.75	2.75
e.		13b multi	7.50	7.50
f.		20b multi	11.00	11.00

Stained Glass Windows at Supreme Justice Tribunal, by Alirio Rodríguez — A568

No. 1719 — Detail from window numbered: a, 1/10. b, 6/10. c, 2/10. d, 7/10. e, 3/10. f, 8/10. g, 4/10. h, 9/10. i, 5/10. j, 10/10. 25b, Detail from different window.

2011, Dec. 14

1719	A568	Sheet of 10	32.50	30.00
a.-b.		30c Either single	.35	.35
c.-d.		40c Either single	.35	.35
e.-f.		1.50b Either single	1.10	1.00
g.-h.		6.50b Either single	4.25	4.00
i.		12b multi	9.75	9.00
j.		15.60b multi	13.00	12.00

Souvenir Sheet

1720 A568 25b multi 18.00 17.50

Souvenir Sheet

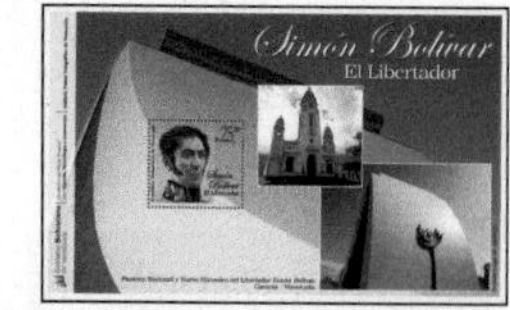

Simón Bolívar (1783-1830) — A569

2012, Sept. 27

1721 A569 25b multi 18.00 17.50

New Bolívar Mausoleum, Caracas.

Miniature Sheet

Luis Zambrano (1901-90), Inventor — A570

No. 1722 — Zambrano: a, Facing forward, wearing hat. b, Facing left, without hat. c, Fancing forward, without hat. d, Facing right, without hat. e, Working on machine with two men. f, Standing in front of machine. g, Touching wheel. h, Putting rod in machine. i, Wearing cap. j, Standing next to machine.

2012

1722	A570	Sheet of 10	27.50	25.00
a.-b.		30c Either single	.40	.35
c.-d.		40c Either single	.40	.35
e.-f.		1.50b Either single	1.10	1.00
g.		4b multi	3.25	3.00
h.-i.		6.50b Either single	5.50	5.00
j.		12.50b multi	11.00	10.00

Miniature Sheet

Pres. Hugo Chávez (1954-2013) — A571

No. 1723 — Pres. Chávez: a, Touching crucifix. b, Wearing beret and uniform, saluting. c, Hugging Venezuelan flag. d, Visiting school children. e, Hugging elderly woman. f, Holding flagpole. g, Shaking hands with person in crowd. h, Pointing finger. i, Wearing beret and uniform. j, Holding microphone.

20b, Wearing sash and necklace, vert.

2013, Apr. 9

1723	A571	Sheet of 10	17.50	15.00
a.-d.		30c Any single	.40	.35
e.		40c multi	.40	.35
f.-g.		1.50b Either single	.70	.60
h.		4.20b multi	1.90	1.60
i.		11.70b multi	5.00	4.25
j.		14b multi	5.75	5.00

Souvenir Sheet

1724 A571 20b multi 8.25 8.00

No. 1724 contains one 37x42mm stamp.

Miniature Sheet

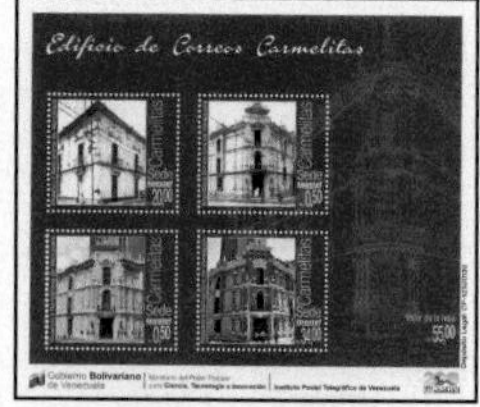

Correos Carmelitas Building, Caracas — A572

No. 1725: a, 50c, Black-and-white photograph. b, 50c, Color photograph of builing painted yellow. c, 20b, Black-and-white photograph of different corner of building. d, 34b, Color photograph of building painted red.

2014, Jan. 28 **Litho.** ***Perf. 12***

1725	A572	Sheet of 4	19.00	18.00
a.-b.		50c Either single	.25	.25
c.		20b multi	6.50	6.50
d.		34b multi	11.00	11.00

America Issue A573

No. 1726 — Pres. Hugo Chávez (1954-2013): a, Waving. b, Holding map of South America.

2014, Mar. 5 **Litho.** ***Perf. 12***

1726	A573	Pair	5.25	4.75
a.		1b multi	.30	.25
b.		12.50b multi	5.00	4.75

Works of the Revolution A574

No. 1727: a, Estadio Monumental de Maturín (soccer stadium). b, Tractor in field. c, Latin American Infantile Cardiological Hospital. d, Metrocable cable car. e, Bridge over Orinoco River. f, Buildings, Ciudad Caribia. g, Miranda Satellite. h, Children with computers (Canaima Education Project).

2014, Dec. 18 **Litho.** ***Perf. 12***

1727	Horiz. strip of 8	*59.00*	*57.00*
a.	A574 30c multi	*.25*	*.25*
b.	A574 40c multi	*.25*	*.25*
c.	A574 50c multi	*.25*	*.25*
d.	A574 3.50b multi	*1.10*	*1.10*
e.	A574 15.60b multi	*5.00*	*5.00*
f.	A574 25b multi	*8.00*	*8.00*
g.	A574 31.50b multi	*10.00*	*10.00*
h.	A574 100b multi	*32.00*	*32.00*

Miniature Sheet

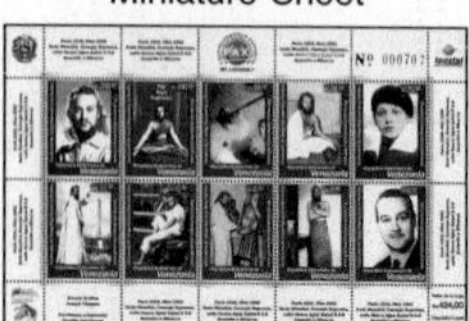

Serge Raynaud de la Ferrière (1916-62), Founder of Universal Great Brotherhood — A575

Various photograhphs of Ferrière: a, 30c. b, 40c. c, 50c. d, 80c. e, 12.50b. f, 25b. g, 34.50b. h, 50b. i, 100b. j, 200b.

2015, May 12 **Litho.** ***Perf. 12***

1728 A575 Sheet of 10, #a-j 17.50 15.00

Miniature Sheet

Pedro Camejo (1790-1821), Soldier in War of Independence Known as "Negro Primero" — A576

No. 1729 — Bust or statue of Camejo and various works or art or buildings: a, 30c. b, 50c. c, 4b. d, 9b. e, 15b. f, 38b. g, 45b. h, 80b. i, 100b. j, 200b.

2015, June 29 Litho. *Perf. 12*
1729 A576 Sheet of 10, #a-j 19.50 17.00

Miniature Sheet

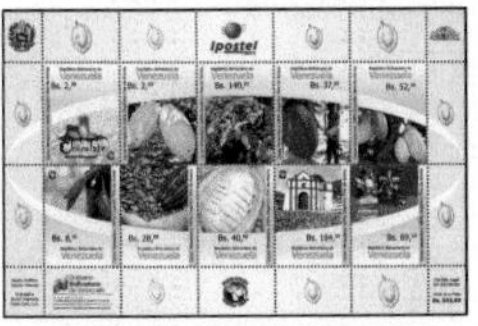

Cacao Farming and Processing — A577

No. 1730: a, 2b, Emblem of Chocolate Expoferia Internacional. b, 2b. Yellow cacao pods. c, 8b, Cacao buds and growing pods. d, 28b, Brown cacao pod and cocoa beans in sack. e, 37b, Farmer harvesting cacao pod. f, 40b, Opened cacao pod. g, 52b, Yellow and Green cacao pods on tree. h, 69b, Venezuelan flag, wrapped chocolate candy bars. i, 140b, Cacao flowers. j, 184b, Drying of cocoa beans and building.

2015, Oct. 1 Litho. *Perf. 12*
1730 A577 Sheet of 10, #a-j 16.00 13.50

Campaign to End Violence Against Women — A578

2015, Nov. 25 Litho. *Perf. 12*
1731 A578 338b multi 5.25 5.00

See Dominican Republic No. 1583, Ecuador No. 2173, Guatemala No. 717, El Salvador No.

Flora and Fauna A579

No. 1732 — Inscription: a, 50c, Sabana de Barinas. b, 10b, Reforestación del Parque Nacional Macarao. c, 46b, Arbol flamboyant (Delonix regia). d, 71b, Corocora colorada (Eudocimus ruber). e, 94b, Caimán del Orinoco (Cocodylus intermedius). f, 110b, Cangrejo Ermitaño (Coenobita clypeatus). g, 250b, Arbol araguaney (Handroanthus chrysanthus). h, 458b, Tortuga arrau (Podocnemis expansa).

2016, Oct. 13 Litho. *Perf. 12*
1732 A579 Block of 8, #a-h *11.00 9.00*

Christmas — A580

No. 1733 — Art by: a, 10b, Darianna Castillo. b, 20b, Romna Medina. c, 50b, Katherin Chacón. d, 70b, Dervis Nuñez. e, 90b, Pedro Crespo (Pan de Jamon, grapes, ensalada de gallina). f, 100b, Crespo (roast ham, hallacas). g, 300b, Enriqueta Aguiar. h, 500b, Mirelis Rojas.

2016, Dec. 1 Litho. *Perf. 12*
1733 A580 Block of 8, #a-h 12.00 10.00

Miniature Sheet

Biotechnology Organizations, 10th Anniv. — A581

No. 1734: a, 10b, Crop irrigation. b, 20b, Field and trees. c, 40b, Emblem of Comprehensive Dairy Development Program (PIDEL). d, 50b, Emblem of National Foundation for Development of Biotechnology (NADBIO) e, 100b, Emblem of Environment Ecology Education Program (PROECO). f, 150b, NADBIO and words. g, 160b, Two cows. h, 220b, Calf. i, 320b, Technician at microscope. j, 500b, Cattle at feed trough.

2017, Mar. 27 Litho. *Perf. 12*
1734 A581 Sheet of 10, #a-j 10.50 8.00

Ezequiel Zamora (1817-60), Soldier — A582

2017, May 19 Litho. *Perf. 12*
1735 A582 500b multi 2.75 2.50

POSTAL FISCAL STAMPS

Nos. 128-135 Overprinted

1900 *Perf. 12*

AR1	A25	5c gray	.25	.25
a.		Overprint inverted	8.00	8.00
AR2	A25	10c deep green	.25	.25
a.		Overprint inverted	8.00	8.00
AR3	A25	25c blue	.25	.25
a.		Overprint inverted	8.00	8.00
AR4	A25	50c orange	.25	.25
a.		Overprint inverted	8.00	8.00
AR5	A25	1b red violet	.30	.25
a.		Overprint inverted	8.00	8.00
AR6	A25	3b red orange	.50	.25
a.		Overprint inverted	8.00	8.00
AR7	A25	10b dull violet	1.25	.75
AR8	A25	20b red brown	7.50	7.50
		Nos. AR1-AR8 (8)	10.55	9.75

Type of 1893 Postage Stamps in Changed Colors Overprinted

1900 *Perf. 12*

AR9	A25	5c orange	.25	.25
AR10	A25	10c deep blue	.25	.25
AR11	A25	25c plum	.25	.25
AR12	A25	50c bright green	1.00	.25
AR13	A25	1b gray black	10.00	1.75
AR14	A25	3b red brown	2.00	1.00
AR15	A25	10b vermilion	12.00	3.50
AR16	A25	20b deep violet	20.00	5.00
		Nos. AR9-AR16 (8)	45.75	12.25

Type of 1893 Postage Stamps in Changed Colors Overprinted

1901

AR17	A25	1b gray black	.75	.50

Type of 1893 in Changed Colors

1901

AR18	A25	5c orange	.25	.25
AR19	A25	10c vermilion	.25	.25
AR20	A25	10c blue	.25	.25
AR21	A25	25c Prussian blue	.25	.25
AR22	A25	50c yellow green	.25	.25
AR23	A25	1b gray black	10.00	2.50
AR24	A25	3b red brown	.25	.25
AR25	A25	10b vermilion	.50	.45
AR26	A25	20b deep violet	1.00	.65
		Nos. AR18-AR26 (9)	13.00	5.10

Simón Bolivar — PF1

1904, July Engr. *Perf. 12*

AR27	PF1	5c green	.25	.25
AR28	PF1	10c gray	.25	.25
AR29	PF1	25c vermilion	.25	.25
AR30	PF1	50c yel org	.25	.25
AR31	PF1	1b claret	3.00	.40
AR32	PF1	3b blue	.50	.25
AR33	PF1	10b bluish gray	.75	.50
AR34	PF1	20b deep carmine	1.75	.50
		Nos. AR27-AR34 (8)	7.00	2.65

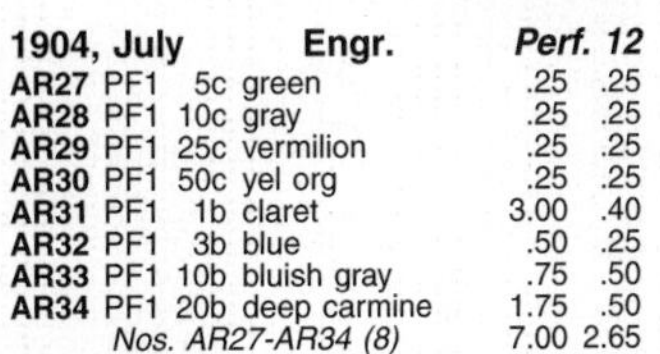

National Figures — PF2

5c, José Vargas (1786-1854), Independence leader and provisional president. 10c, De Avila. 25c, Miguel José Sanz, revolutionary jurist and educator. 50c, Antonio Guzman Blanco (1829-99), jurist, president. 1b, Andres Bello. 2b, Martin S. Sanabria (1831-1904), educator, cabinet minister. 3b, José Antonio Paez (1790-1873), revolutionary leader. 10b, Antonio José de Sucre known as the "Gran Mariscal de Ayacucho." 20b, Simón Bolivar, military and political leader.

1911 Litho. *Perf. 11½x12*

AR35	PF2	5c blue	.25	.25
AR36	PF2	10c pale yel & org	.25	.25
AR37	PF2	25c gray	.25	.25
AR38	PF2	50c scarlet	.25	.25
AR39	PF2	1b green	.25	.25
AR40	PF2	2b brown	.90	.50
AR41	PF2	3b blue violet	.90	.50
AR42	PF2	10b lilac	1.75	.75
AR43	PF2	20b blue	1.75	1.10
		Nos. AR35-AR43 (9)	6.55	4.10

Simón Bolivar — PF3

1914 Engr. *Perf. 14*

AR44	PF3	5c lilac	.25	.25
AR45	PF3	10c olive green	.25	.25
AR46	PF3	25c red brown	1.00	.25
AR47	PF3	50c rose carmine	1.50	.25
AR48	PF3	1b violet brown	1.50	.50
AR49	PF3	2b bister	3.25	1.50
AR50	PF3	3b gray blue	3.25	.50
AR51	PF3	10b orange brown	10.00	3.25
AR52	PF3	20b gray black	6.50	2.25
		Nos. AR44-AR52 (9)	27.50	9.00

PF4

PF5

Antonio José de Sucre — PF6

1915 *Perf. 12*

AR53	PF4	5c brown	.25	.25
AR54	PF5	10c blue	.25	.25
AR55	PF5	25c carmine	3.25	.25
AR56	PF5	50c red brown	.25	.25
AR57	PF4	1b green	.40	.25
AR58	PF4	2b gray brown	2.25	.25
AR59	PF6	3b violet	.25	.25
AR60	PF6	10b gray black	20.00	2.25
AR61	PF6	20b orange	.25	.25
		Nos. AR53-AR61 (9)	27.15	4.25

Type of 1915 in Changed Colors and

PF7

Antonio José de Sucre — PF8

1922

AR62	PF5	10c green	.40	.25
AR63	PF7	20c light blue	.40	.25
AR64	PF4	1b olive brown	.40	.25
AR65	PF4	2b carmine	.40	.25
AR66	PF6	10b yellow	.40	.25
AR67	PF8	50b claret	.40	.25
		Nos. AR62-AR67 (6)	2.40	1.50

Inscribed "EEUU VENEZUELA" — PF9

Pale Blue Security Imprint "EEUU VENEZUELA" on Face of Paper

1947 Engr. *Perf. 12*

AR68	PF9	5c green	.25	.25
AR69	PF9	10c yellow brown	.25	.25
AR70	PF9	20c red brown	.25	.25
AR71	PF9	40c green	.45	.25
AR72	PF9	50c light blue	.45	.25
AR73	PF9	1b violet	.45	.25
AR74	PF9	2b blue	.60	.45
AR75	PF9	3b blue	.60	.45
AR76	PF9	10b orange	4.50	2.50
		Nos. AR68-AR76 (9)	7.80	4.90

Nos. AR67-AR71, AR75 and AR76 overprinted, see Nos. 876-883.

Inscribed "REPUBLICA DE VENEZUELA" — PF10

Pale Blue Security Imprint "REPUBLICA DE VENEZUELA" on Face of Paper

1956

No.	Type	Value / Color	Unused	Used
AR77	PF10	5c green	.25	.25
AR78	PF10	10c yellow brown	.25	.25
AR79	PF10	20c red brown	.25	.25
AR80	PF10	40c green	.25	.25
AR81	PF10	50c blue	.45	.25
AR82	PF10	1b violet	.60	.40
AR83	PF10	2b deep violet	1.00	.85
AR84	PF10	3b dark blue	1.40	.85
AR85	PF10	5b ultramarine	2.50	1.75
AR86	PF10	10b orange	4.50	2.50
		Nos. AR77-AR86 (10)	11.45	7.60

SEMI-POSTAL STAMPS

A 5c green stamp of the Cruzada Venezolana Sanitaria Social portraying Simon Bolivar was overprinted "EE. UU. DE VENEZUELA CORREOS" in 1937.

It is stated that 50,000 stamps without control numbers on back were sold by post offices and 147,700 with control numbers on back were offered for sale by the Society at eight times face value.

Bolívar Funeral Carriage — SP1

Unwmk.

1942, Dec. 17 Engr. *Perf. 12*

No.	Type	Value / Color	Unused	Used
B1	SP1	20c + 5c blue	6.00	.65

Cent. of the arrival of Simón Bolivar's remains in Caracas. The surtax was used to erect a monument to his memory. See Nos. CB1-CB2.

Catalogue values for unused stamps in this section, from this point to the end of the section, are for Never Hinged items.

Red Cross Nurse — SP2

1975, Dec. 15 Litho. *Perf. 14*

No.	Type	Value / Color	Unused	Used
B2	SP2	30c + 15c multi	.40	.25
B3	SP2	50c + 25c multi	.60	.40

Surtax for Venezuelan Red Cross.

Carmen América Fernandez de Leoni SP3

Children in Home SP4

1976, June 7 Litho. *Perf. 13½*

No.	Type	Value / Color	Unused	Used
B4	SP3	30c + 15c multi	.30	.25
B5	SP4	50c + 25c multi	.50	.35

Surtax was for the Children's Foundation, founded by Carmen América Fernandez de Leoni in 1966.

Patient — SP5

1976, Dec. 8 Litho. *Perf. 14*

No.	Type	Value / Color	Unused	Used
B6	SP5	10c + 5c multi	.25	.25
B7	SP5	30c + 10c multi	.25	.25

Surtax was for Anti-tuberculosis Society.

AIR POST STAMPS

Air post stamps of 1930-42 perforated "GN" (Gobierno Nacional) were for official use.

Airplane and Map of Venezuela — AP1

1930 Unwmk. Litho. *Perf. 12*

No.	Type	Value / Color	Unused	Used
C1	AP1	5c bister brn	.25	.25
C2	AP1	10c yellow	.25	.25
a.		10c salmon	32.50	32.50
C3	AP1	15c gray	.25	.25
C4	AP1	25c lilac	.25	.25
C5	AP1	40c olive grn	.25	.25
a.		40c slate blue	45.00	
b.		40c slate green	45.00	
C6	AP1	75c dp red	.30	.25
C7	AP1	1b indigo	.45	.25
C8	AP1	1.20b blue grn	.70	.35
C9	AP1	1.70b dk blue	.90	.45
C10	AP1	1.90b blue grn	.90	.50
C11	AP1	2.10b dk blue	1.75	.65
C12	AP1	2.30b vermilion	1.75	.50
C13	AP1	2.50b dk blue	1.75	.50
C14	AP1	3.70b blue grn	1.75	1.10
C15	AP1	10b dull vio	5.25	2.40
C16	AP1	20b gray grn	8.00	4.50
		Nos. C1-C16 (16)	24.75	12.70

Issued: 10b, 6/8; 20b, 6/16; others, 4/5.

Nos. C1-C16 exist imperforate or partly perforated. Value, imperf set $200.

See Nos. C119-C126.

Airplane and Map of Venezuela — AP2

Bluish Winchester Security Paper

1932, July 12 Engr. *Perf. 12½*

No.	Type	Value / Color	Unused	Used
C17	AP2	5c brown	.45	.25
C18	AP2	10c org yel	.45	.25
C19	AP2	15c gray lilac	.45	.25
C20	AP2	25c violet	.45	.25
C21	AP2	40c ol grn	.85	.25
C22	AP2	70c rose	.60	.25
C23	AP2	75c red org	1.10	.25
C24	AP2	1b dk bl	1.20	.25
C25	AP2	1.20b green	2.60	.85
C26	AP2	1.70b red brn	5.25	.55
C27	AP2	1.80b ultra	2.60	.35
C28	AP2	1.90b green	6.50	3.50
C29	AP2	1.95b blue	7.25	2.75
C30	AP2	2b blk brn	4.50	2.25
C31	AP2	2.10b blue	10.50	6.00
C32	AP2	2.30b red	4.50	2.40
C33	AP2	2.50b dk bl	6.50	1.40
C34	AP2	3b dk vio	6.50	.85
C35	AP2	3.70b emerald	8.75	6.00
C36	AP2	4b red org	6.50	1.40
C37	AP2	5b black	7.25	2.40
C38	AP2	8b dk car	14.50	4.75
C39	AP2	10b dk vio	28.00	8.00
C40	AP2	20b grnsh slate	65.00	20.00
		Nos. C17-C40 (24)	192.25	65.45

Pairs imperf. between exist of the 1b (value $150); the 25c and 4b (value $300 each).

Air Post Stamps of 1932 Surcharged in Black

1937, June 4

No.	Type	Value / Color	Unused	Used
C41	AP2	5c on 1.70b red brn	11.00	7.00
C42	AP2	10c on 3.70b emer	11.00	7.00
C43	AP2	15c on 4b red org	5.00	3.50
C44	AP2	25c on 5b blk	5.00	3.50
C45	AP2	1b on 8b dk car	4.00	3.50
C46	AP2	2b on 2.10b bl	30.00	23.00
		Nos. C41-C46 (6)	66.00	47.50

Various varieties of surcharge exist, including double and triple impressions. No. C43 exists in pair imperf. between; value $30 unused, $50 used.

Allegory of Flight — AP3

Allegory of Flight — AP4

National Pantheon at Caracas AP5

Airplane AP6

Perf. 11, 11½ and Compound

1937, July 1 Litho.

No.	Type	Value / Color	Unused	Used
C47	AP3	5c brn org	.30	.40
C48	AP4	10c org red	.25	.25
C49	AP5	15c gray blk	.60	.40
C50	AP6	25c dk vio	.60	.40
C51	AP4	40c yel grn	1.10	.55
C52	AP3	70c red	1.10	.40
C53	AP5	75c bister	2.50	1.30
C54	AP3	1b dk gray	1.50	.55
C55	AP4	1.20b pck grn	6.50	4.25
C56	AP3	1.80b dk ultra	3.25	2.00
C57	AP5	1.95b lt ultra	10.00	7.75
C58	AP6	2b chocolate	4.25	2.75
C59	AP6	2.50b gray bl	11.50	11.50
C60	AP4	3b lt vio	6.50	4.50
C61	AP6	3.70b rose red	11.50	15.00
C62	AP5	10b red vio	25.00	15.00
C63	AP3	20b gray	30.00	23.00
		Nos. C47-C63 (17)	116.45	90.00

All values exist imperf, and all except the 3.70b part-perf.

Counterfeits exist.

For overprints & surcharges see Nos. C66-C78, C114-C118, C164-C167, C169-C172, C174-C180.

AP7

1937, Oct. 28 *Perf. 11*

No.	Type	Value / Color	Unused	Used
C64	AP7	70c emerald	1.40	.55
C65	AP7	1.80b ultra	2.25	1.00

Acquisition of the Port of La Guaira by the Government from the British Corporation, June 3, 1937. Nos. C64-C65 exist imperf. Value, set $275.

A redrawn printing of Nos. C64-C65, with lower inscription beginning "Nacionalización..." was prepared but not issued. Value, $40 each.

For overprints see Nos. C168, C173.

Air Post Stamps of 1937 Overprinted in Black

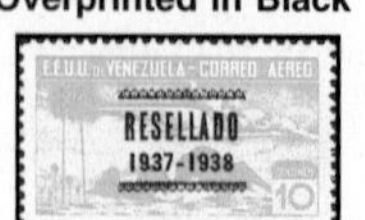

1937, Dec. 17 *Perf. 11, 11½*

No.	Type	Value / Color	Unused	Used
C66	AP4	10c org red	1.00	.70
a.		Inverted overprint	15.00	12.00
C67	AP6	25c dk vio	2.00	1.00
C68	AP4	40c yel grn	2.00	1.40
C69	AP3	70c red	1.50	1.00
a.		Inverted overprint	15.00	14.00
b.		Double overprint	20.00	16.00
C70	AP3	1b dk gray	2.00	1.40
a.		Inverted overprint	16.00	13.00
b.		Double overprint	13.00	
C71	AP4	1.20b pck grn	30.00	20.00
a.		Inverted overprint	77.50	
C72	AP3	1.80b dk ultra	5.75	2.40
C73	AP5	1.95b lt ultra	7.75	4.25
a.		Inverted overprint	60.00	40.00
C74	AP6	2b chocolate	50.00	23.00
a.		Inverted overprint	100.00	90.00
b.		Double overprint	82.50	82.50
C75	AP6	2.50b gray bl	50.00	19.00
a.		Double overprint	70.00	
b.		Inverted overprint	100.00	82.50
C76	AP4	3b lt vio	30.00	12.00
C77	AP5	10b red vio	72.50	40.00
C78	AP3	20b gray	77.50	47.50
a.		Double overprint	150.00	150.00
		Nos. C66-C78 (13)	332.00	173.65

Counterfeit overprints exist on #C77-C78.

View of La Guaira — AP8

National Pantheon — AP9

Oil Wells — AP10

1938-39 Engr. *Perf. 12*

No.	Type	Value / Color	Unused	Used
C79	AP8	5c green	1.25	.50
C80	AP8	5c dk grn	.35	.25
C81	AP9	10c car rose	1.80	.80
C82	AP9	10c scarlet	.35	.25
C83	AP8	12½c dull vio	.75	.55
C84	AP10	15c slate vio	3.75	1.25
C85	AP10	15c dk bl	1.10	.25
C86	AP8	25c dk bl	3.75	1.25
C87	AP8	25c bis brn	.35	.25
C88	AP10	30c vio ('39)	2.50	.25
C89	AP9	40c dk vio	4.50	1.25
C90	AP9	40c redsh brn	3.25	.25
C91	AP8	45c Prus grn ('39)	1.30	.25
C92	AP9	50c blue ('39)	1.60	.25
C93	AP10	70c car rose	1.10	.25
C94	AP8	75c bis brn	7.75	2.00
C95	AP8	75c ol bis	1.75	.25
C96	AP10	90c red org ('39)	1.30	.25
C97	AP9	1b ol & bis	9.00	2.75
C98	AP9	1b dk vio	1.60	.25
C99	AP10	1.20b orange	25.00	5.75
C100	AP10	1.20b green	2.50	.55
C101	AP8	1.80b ultra	2.50	.55
C102	AP9	1.90b black	7.00	2.75
C103	AP10	1.95b lt bl	5.50	2.50
C104	AP8	2b ol gray	57.50	15.00
C105	AP8	2b car rose	2.25	.70
C106	AP9	2.50b red brn	57.50	20.00
C107	AP9	2.50b orange	13.00	2.75
C108	AP10	3b bl grn	25.00	4.75
C109	AP10	3b ol gray	7.00	2.00
C110	AP8	3.70b gray blk	10.00	5.50
C111	AP10	5b red brn ('39)	10.00	2.00
C112	AP9	10b vio brn	25.00	2.40
C113	AP10	20b red org	75.00	25.00
		Nos. C79-C113 (35)	373.85	105.55

See Nos. C227a, C235-C236, C254-C255.

For surcharge see No. C227.

Nos. C51, C56, C58-C59, C61 Surcharged

1938, Apr. 15 *Perf. 11, 11½*

No.	Type	Value / Color	Unused	Used
C114	AP3	5c on 1.80b	.85	.60
a.		Inverted surcharge	12.50	7.50
C115	AP6	10c on 2.50b	3.00	1.40
a.		Inverted surcharge	10.00	7.50
C116	AP6	15c on 2b	1.40	1.10
C117	AP4	25c on 40c	1.75	1.40
C118	AP6	40c on 3.70b	3.50	3.25
		Nos. C114-C118 (5)	10.50	7.75

Plane & Map Type of 1930
White Paper; No Imprint

1938-39 Engr. *Perf. 12½*
C119 AP1 5c dk grn ('39) .30 .25
C120 AP1 10c org yel ('39) .55 .25
C121 AP1 12½c rose vio ('39) 1.10 .85
C122 AP1 15c dp bl .95 .25
C123 AP1 25c brown 1.10 .25
C124 AP1 40c olive ('39) 2.75 .40
C125 AP1 70c rose car ('39) 20.00 7.75
C126 AP1 1b dk bl ('39) 7.75 3.00
Nos. C119-C126 (8) 34.50 13.00

Monument to Sucre — AP11

Monuments at Carabobo
AP12 AP13

1938, Dec. 23 *Perf. 13½*
C127 AP11 20c brn blk .80 .30
C128 AP12 30c purple 1.20 .30
C129 AP13 45c dk bl 1.75 .25
C130 AP11 50c lt ultra 1.50 .25
C131 AP13 70c dk car 26.00 7.50
C132 AP12 90c red org 2.50 .75
C133 AP13 1.35b gray blk 3.00 1.00
C134 AP11 1.40b slate gray 12.00 2.75
C135 AP12 2.25b green 6.00 2.00
Nos. C127-C135 (9) 54.75 15.10

For surcharge see No. C198.

Simón Bolívar and Carabobo Monument AP14

1940, Mar. 30 *Perf. 12*
C136 AP14 15c blue .75 .25
C137 AP14 20c olive bis .75 .25
C138 AP14 25c red brn 2.75 .40
C139 AP14 40c blk brn 2.25 .25
C140 AP14 1b red lilac 5.00 .55
C141 AP14 2b rose car 11.00 1.40
Nos. C136-C141 (6) 22.50 3.10

"The Founding of Grand Colombia" AP15

1940, June 13
C142 AP15 15c copper brown 1.25 .45

Founding of the Pan American Union, 50th anniv.

Statue of Simón Bolívar, Caracas — AP16

1940-44
C143 AP16 5c dk grn ('42) .25 .25
C144 AP16 10c scar ('42) .25 .25
C145 AP16 12½c dull purple .75 .30
C146 AP16 15c blue ('43) .50 .25
C147 AP16 20c bis brn ('44) .50 .25
C148 AP16 25c bis brn ('42) .50 .25
C149 AP16 30c dp vio ('43) .50 .25
C150 AP16 40c blk brn ('43) .65 .25
C151 AP16 45c turq grn ('43) .65 .25
C152 AP16 50c blue ('44) .65 .25
C153 AP16 70c rose pink 2.00 .30
C154 AP16 75c ol bis ('43) 7.75 1.60
C155 AP16 90c red org ('43) 1.25 .30
C156 AP16 1b dp red lil ('42) .65 .25
C157 AP16 1.20b dp yel grn ('43) 2.50 .75
C158 AP16 1.35b gray blk ('42) 10.50 3.50
C159 AP16 2b rose pink ('43) 2.00 .25
C160 AP16 3b ol blk ('43) 3.25 .75
C161 AP16 4b black 2.50 .75
C162 AP16 5b red brn ('44) 20.00 8.00
Nos. C143-C162 (20) 57.60 19.00

See Nos. C232-C234, C239-C253. For surcharges see Nos. C225, C873.

Nos. C48, C50-C65 Overprinted

Perf. 11, 11½ & Compound
1943, Dec. 21
C164 AP4 10c orange red 2.00 .90
C165 AP6 25c dk violet 2.00 .90
C166 AP4 40c yellow grn 2.00 .90
C167 AP3 70c red 2.00 .90
C168 AP7 70c emerald 2.00 .90
C169 AP5 75c bister 2.00 .90
C170 AP3 1b dk gray 2.00 .90
C171 AP4 1.20b peacock grn 5.00 1.60
C172 AP3 1.80b dk ultra 5.00 1.60
C173 AP7 1.80b dk ultra 5.00 2.50
C174 AP5 1.95b lt ultra 6.00 3.25
C175 AP6 2b chocolate 6.00 3.25
C176 AP6 2.50b gray blue 5.00 3.25
C177 AP4 3b lt violet 6.00 3.25
C178 AP6 3.70b rose red 52.50 45.00
C179 AP5 10b red violet 12.00 10.00
C180 AP3 20b gray 27.50 20.00
Nos. C164-C180 (17) 144.00 100.00
Set, never hinged 275.00

Issued for sale to philatelists. Nos. C164-C169 were sold only in sets.
Nearly all are known with invtd. ovpt.

Flags of Venezuela and the Red Cross — AP17

Flags in red, yellow, blue and black

1944, Aug. 22 Litho. *Perf. 12*
C181 AP17 5c gray green .25 .25
C182 AP17 10c magenta .25 .25
C183 AP17 20c brt blue .25 .25
C184 AP17 30c violet bl .40 .25
C185 AP17 40c chocolate .55 .25
C186 AP17 45c apple green 1.75 .45
C187 AP17 90c orange 1.60 .45
C188 AP17 1b gray black 2.40 .45
Nos. C181-C188 (8) 7.45 2.60
Set, never hinged 12.00

80th anniv. of the Intl. Red Cross and 37th anniv. of Venezuela's joining the organization. Nos. C181-C188 exist imperf. and part perf. Value, imperf set $30.

Baseball Players — AP18

"AEREO" in dark carmine

1944, Oct. 12
C189 AP18 5c dull vio brn .30 .25
C190 AP18 10c gray green .50 .25
C191 AP18 20c ultra .50 .25
C192 AP18 30c dull rose 1.00 .40
C193 AP18 45c rose violet 2.00 .70
C194 AP18 90c red orange 3.50 1.40
C195 AP18 1b dark gray 4.00 1.40
C196 AP18 1.20b yellow grn 9.25 7.25
C197 AP18 1.80b ocher 12.00 9.25
Nos. C189-C197 (9) 33.05 21.15
Set, never hinged 55.00

7th World Amateur Baseball Championship Games, Caracas.
Nos. C189-C197 exist imperf, and all but 1b exist part perf. Value, imperf set $75.
Various errors of "AEREO" overprint exist.

No. C134 Surcharged in Black

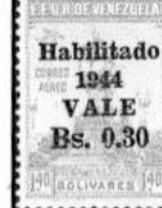

1944, Nov. 17 *Perf. 13½*
C198 AP11 30c on 1.40b .50 .50
a. Double surcharge 35.00 35.00
b. Inverted surcharge 13.50 13.50

Charles Howarth — AP19

1944, Dec. 21 Unwmk. *Perf. 12*
C199 AP19 5c black .25 .25
C200 AP19 10c purple .25 .25
C201 AP19 20c sepia .30 .25
C202 AP19 30c dull green .40 .25
C203 AP19 1.20b bister 2.00 1.90
C204 AP19 1.80b deep ultra 3.50 2.40
C205 AP19 3.70b rose 4.50 4.00
Nos. C199-C205 (7) 11.20 9.30
Set, never hinged 18.00

Cent. of founding of 1st cooperative shop in Rochdale, England, by Charles Howarth.
Nos. C199-C205 exist imperf. and part perf.

Antonio José de Sucre — AP20

1945, Mar. 3 Engr.
C206 AP20 5c orange .25 .25
C207 AP20 10c violet .25 .25
C208 AP20 20c grnsh blk .25 .25
C209 AP20 30c brt green .25 .25
C210 AP20 40c olive 1.10 1.10
C211 AP20 45c black brn 1.60 1.10
C212 AP20 90c redsh brn 2.10 1.10
C213 AP20 1b dp red lil 2.10 1.10
C214 AP20 1.20b black 6.25 5.25
C215 AP20 2b yellow 10.00 7.25
Nos. C206-C215 (10) 24.15 17.90
Set, never hinged 40.00

150th birth anniv. of Antonio Jose de Sucre, Grand Marshal of Ayacucho.

Type of 1946

1946, Aug. 24 *Perf. 12*
C216 A81 30c Bello 1.10 .25
C217 A82 30c Urdaneta 1.10 .25
Set, never hinged 2.75

Allegory of Republic — AP23

Perf. 11½
1946, Oct. 18 Litho. Unwmk.
C218 AP23 15c dp violet bl .40 .25
C219 AP23 20c bister brn .40 .25
C220 AP23 30c dp violet .50 .35
C221 AP23 1b brt rose 3.50 2.75
Nos. C218-C221 (4) 4.80 3.60
Set, never hinged 8.00

Anniversary of the Revolution of October, 1945. Exist imperf. and part perf.

Nos. 297, 371, C152 and 362 Surcharged in Black

1947, Jan. *Perf. 12*
C223 A49 10c on 22½c dp car .25 .25
a. Inverted surcharge 7.00 5.00
C224 A69 15c on 25c lt bl .40 .25
C225 AP16 20c on 50c blue .40 .25
a. Inverted surcharge 9.00 7.00
C226 A65 70c on 1b dk vio brn .75 .45
a. Inverted surcharge 9.00 5.00

Type of 1938 Surcharged in Black

C227 AP10 20b on 20b org red 28.00 22.50
a. Surcharge omitted 92.50 40.00
Nos. C223-C227 (5) 29.80 23.70
Set, never hinged 40.00

"J. R. G." are the initials of "Junta Revolucionaria de Gobierno."
Also exist: 20c on #C143, 10c on #371.

Anti-tuberculosis Institute, Maracaibo — AP24

1947, Jan. 12 Litho.
Venezuela Shown on Map in Yellow
C228 AP24 15c dark blue .45 .35
C229 AP24 20c dark brown .45 .35
C230 AP24 30c violet .45 .35
C231 AP24 1b carmine 4.75 3.75
Nos. C228-C231 (4) 6.10 4.80
Set, never hinged 16.00

12th Pan-American Health Conf., Caracas, Jan. 1947.
Nos. C228-C231 exist imperf., part perf. and with yellow omitted.

Types of 1938-40

1947, Mar. 17 Engr.
C232 AP16 75c orange 7.50 4.50
C233 AP16 1b brt ultra .70 .25
C234 AP16 3b red brown 17.50 8.00
C235 AP10 5b scarlet 15.00 5.00
C236 AP9 10b violet 20.00 7.50
Nos. C232-C236 (5) 60.70 25.25
Set, never hinged 85.00

On Nos. C235 and C236 the numerals of value are in color on a white table.

No. 370 Surcharged in Black

1947, June 20
C237 A70 5c on 20c blue .40 .25
C238 A70 10c on 20c blue .40 .25
a. Inverted surcharge 5.00 5.00
Set, never hinged 1.00

Types of 1938-44

1947-48 Engr.
C239 AP16 5c orange .25 .25
C240 AP16 10c dk green .25 .25
C241 AP16 12½ bister brn .45 .45
C242 AP16 15c gray .25 .25
C243 AP16 20c violet .25 .25
C244 AP16 25c dull green .25 .25
C245 AP16 30c brt ultra .45 .25
C246 AP16 40c green ('48) .25 .25
C247 AP16 45c vermilion .45 .25
C248 AP16 50c red violet .25 .25
C249 AP16 70c dk car 1.00 .45
C250 AP16 75c purple ('48) .65 .25
C251 AP16 90c black 1.00 .30
C252 AP16 1.20b red brn ('48) 1.25 .50
C253 AP16 3b dp blue 1.75 .50
C254 AP10 5b olive grn 9.25 5.00
C255 AP9 10b yellow 8.25 4.75
Nos. C239-C255 (17) 26.25 14.45
Set, never hinged 60.00

On Nos. C254 and C255 the numerals of value are in color on a white tablet.
Issue dates: 5c, 10c, Oct. 8. 15c, Dec. 2, 40c, 75c, 1.20b, May 10, 1948. Others, Oct. 27, 1947.

M. S. Republica de Venezuela — AP25

Imprint: "American Bank Note Company"

1948-50 Unwmk. *Perf. 12*

C256 AP25 5c red brown .25 .25
C257 AP25 10c deep green .25 .25
C258 AP25 15c brown .25 .25
C259 AP25 20c violet brn .35 .25
C260 AP25 25c brown black .35 .25
C261 AP25 30c olive green .35 .25
C262 AP25 45c blue green .65 .35
C263 AP25 50c gray black 1.00 .55
C264 AP25 70c orange 1.75 .55
C265 AP25 75c brt ultra 3.00 .75
C266 AP25 90c car lake 1.75 1.75
C267 AP25 1b purple 2.40 1.10
C268 AP25 2b gray 2.50 1.75
C269 AP25 3b emerald 9.75 5.50
C270 AP25 4b deep blue 4.50 5.50
C271 AP25 5b orange red 18.00 8.25
Nos. C256-C271 (16) 47.10 27.55
Set, never hinged 70.00

Issued to honor the Grand-Colombian Merchant Fleet. See Nos. C554-C556.

Issued: 5c, 10c, 15c, 25c, 30c, 1b, 7/9/48; 45c, 75c, 5b, 5/11/50; others, 3/9/49.

For surcharges see Nos. C863-C864.

Santos Michelena — AP26

1949, Apr. 25

C272 AP26 5c orange brn .25 .25
C273 AP26 10c gray .25 .25
C274 AP26 15c red orange .50 .50
C275 AP26 25c dull green 1.00 .80
C276 AP26 30c plum 1.00 .80
C277 AP26 1b violet 5.50 3.00
Nos. C272-C277 (6) 8.50 5.60
Set, never hinged 12.00

See note after No. 427.

Christopher Columbus AP27

1948-49 Unwmk. *Perf. 12½*

C278 AP27 5c brown ('49) .30 .25
C279 AP27 10c gray .30 .30
C280 AP27 15c orange ('49) .65 .30
C281 AP27 25c green ('49) 1.25 .65
C282 AP27 30c red vio ('49) 1.50 .95
C283 AP27 1b violet ('49) 6.00 2.75
Nos. C278-C283 (6) 10.00 5.20
Set, never hinged 16.00

See note after No. 431.

AP28

Symbols of global air mail.

1950 *Perf. 12*

C284 AP28 5c red brown .25 .25
C285 AP28 10c dk green .25 .25
C286 AP28 15c olive brn .25 .25
C287 AP28 25c olive gray .40 .30
C288 AP28 30c olive grn .55 .30
C289 AP28 50c black .40 .25
C290 AP28 60c brt ultra 1.10 .60
C291 AP28 90c carmine 1.40 .75
C292 AP28 1b purple 1.90 .50
Nos. C284-C292 (9) 6.50 3.45
Set, never hinged 10.50

75th anniv. of the UPU.

Issue dates: 5c, Jan. 28. Others, Feb. 19.

AP29

Araguaney, Venezuelan national tree.

Foliage in Yellow

1950, Aug. 25 Photo. *Perf. 11½*

C293 AP29 5c orange brn .30 .25
C294 AP29 10c blue grn .30 .25
C295 AP29 15c deep plum .65 .25
C296 AP29 25c dk gray grn 4.00 1.30
C297 AP29 30c red orange 5.00 1.60
C298 AP29 50c dark gray 2.50 .35
C299 AP29 60c deep blue 3.90 .80
C300 AP29 90c red 6.25 1.60
C301 AP29 1b rose violet 9.50 2.00
Nos. C293-C301 (9) 32.40 8.40
Set, never hinged 160.00

Issued to publicize Forest Week, 1950.

Census Type of 1950

1950, Sept. 1 Engr. *Perf. 12*

C302 A90 5c olive gray .25 .25
C303 A90 10c green .25 .25
C304 A90 15c olive green .25 .25
C305 A90 25c gray .45 .45
C306 A90 30c orange .65 .30
C307 A90 50c lt brown .45 .25
C308 A90 60c ultra .45 .25
C309 A90 90c rose carmine 1.40 .65
C310 A90 1b violet 1.75 1.75
Nos. C302-C310 (9) 5.90 4.40
Set, never hinged 9.50

Signing Act of Independence AP31

1950, Nov. 17

C311 AP31 5c vermilion .65 .25
C312 AP31 10c red brown .65 .25
C313 AP31 15c violet .90 .25
C314 AP31 30c brt blue 1.10 .40
C315 AP31 1b green 5.25 2.40
Nos. C311-C315 (5) 8.55 3.55
Set, never hinged 10.00

200th anniversary of the birth of Gen. Francisco de Miranda.

Alonso de Ojeda Type of 1950

1950, Dec. 18 Photo. *Perf. 11½*

C316 A91 5c orange brn .25 .25
C317 A91 10c cerise .30 .25
C318 A91 15c black brn .55 .25
C319 A91 25c violet .60 .30
C320 A91 30c orange 1.25 .50
C321 A91 1b emerald 5.00 2.50
Nos. C316-C321 (6) 7.95 4.05
Set, never hinged 12.00

Bolivar Statue Type of 1951

1951, July 13 Engr. *Perf. 12*

C322 A92 5c purple .80 .25
C323 A92 10c dull green .90 .25
C324 A92 20c olive gray .90 .25
C325 A92 25c olive green 1.00 .25
C326 A92 30c vermilion 1.20 .55
C327 A92 40c lt brown 1.20 .55
C328 A92 50c gray 2.75 1.00
C329 A92 70c orange 3.75 2.50
Nos. C322-C329 (8) 12.50 5.60
Set, never hinged 20.00

Queen Isabella I — AP34

1951, Oct. 12 Photo. *Perf. 11½*

C330 AP34 5c dk green & buff 2.25 .25
C331 AP34 10c dk red & cream 2.25 .25
C332 AP34 20c dp blue & gray 3.75 .25
C333 AP34 30c dk blue & gray 3.75 .25
a. Souv. sheet of 4, #C330-C333 22.50 *24.00*
Never hinged 33.00
Nos. C330-C333 (4) 12.00 1.00
Set, never hinged 14.00

500th anniv. of the birth of Queen Isabella I of Spain.

Bicycle Racecourse AP35

1951, Dec. 18 Engr. *Perf. 12*

C334 AP35 5c green 2.25 .25
C335 AP35 10c rose carmine 2.25 .25
C336 AP35 20c redsh brown 2.75 .70
C337 AP35 30c blue 3.50 1.00
a. Souv. sheet, #C334-C337 32.50 *35.00*
Never hinged 48.50
Nos. C334-C337 (4) 10.75 2.20
Set, never hinged 16.50

3rd Bolivarian Games, Caracas, Dec. 1951.

Arms of Carabobo and "Industry" — AP36

1951 Photo. *Perf. 11½*

C338 AP36 5c blue green 2.50 1.10
C339 AP36 7½c gray green 3.25 1.90
C340 AP36 10c car rose 2.50 1.10
C341 AP36 15c dark brown 3.25 1.10
C342 AP36 20c gray blue 3.50 1.10
C343 AP36 30c deep blue 9.50 1.60
C344 AP36 45c magenta 4.75 1.60
C345 AP36 60c olive brown 9.00 3.50
C346 AP36 90c rose brown 20.00 11.00
Nos. C338-C346 (9) 58.25 24.00

Issue date: Oct. 29.

Arms of Zulia and "Industry"

C347 AP36 5c blue green 1.25 .60
C348 AP36 10c car rose 1.25 .60
C349 AP36 15c dark brown 1.90 .60
C350 AP36 30c deep blue 12.50 4.00
C351 AP36 60c olive brown 7.50 1.25
C352 AP36 1.20b brown car 25.00 16.00
C353 AP36 3b blue gray 8.75 2.40
C354 AP36 5b purple brn 12.50 6.25
C355 AP36 10b violet 20.00 12.50
Nos. C347-C355 (9) 90.65 44.20

Issued: 5b, 9/8; 5c, 3b, 10b, 10/8; others, 10/29.

Arms of Anzoategui

C356 AP36 5c blue green 1.50 .85
C357 AP36 10c car rose 1.50 .85
C358 AP36 15c dk brown 2.00 .85
C359 AP36 25c sepia 2.40 .85
C360 AP36 30c deep blue 6.25 3.50
C361 AP36 50c henna brn 6.25 1.75
C362 AP36 60c olive brn 9.00 1.10
C363 AP36 1b purple 11.00 3.50
C364 AP36 2b violet gray 19.00 7.75
Nos. C356-C364 (9) 58.90 21.00

Issue date: Nov. 9.

Arms of Caracas and Buildings

C365 AP36 5c blue green 2.75 1.10
C366 AP36 7½c gray green 8.00 3.50
C367 AP36 10c car rose 1.90 1.10
C368 AP36 15c dk brown 19.00 2.50
C369 AP36 20c gray blue 12.50 2.50
C370 AP36 30c deep blue 21.00 4.75
C371 AP36 45c magenta 12.50 2.75
C372 AP36 60c olive brn 42.50 5.75
C373 AP36 90c rose brn 25.00 20.00
Nos. C365-C373 (9) 145.15 43.95

Issue date: Aug. 6.

Arms of Tachira and Agricultural Products

C374 AP36 5c blue green .90 .90
C375 AP36 10c car rose .90 .90
C376 AP36 15c dk brown 2.50 .90
C377 AP36 30c deep blue 32.50 3.75
C378 AP36 60c olive brn 26.00 3.75
C379 AP36 1.20b brown car 26.00 18.00
C380 AP36 3b blue gray 8.50 3.75
C381 AP36 5b purple brn 15.00 7.75
C382 AP36 10b violet 20.00 15.00
Nos. C374-C382 (9) 132.30 54.70

Issue date: Aug. 9.

Arms of Venezuela and Bolivar Statue

C383 AP36 5c blue green 1.75 .90
C384 AP36 7½c gray grn 4.50 2.75
C385 AP36 10c car rose 13.50 .90
C386 AP36 15c dk brown 10.00 2.75
C387 AP36 20c gray blue 13.50 2.25
C388 AP36 30c deep blue 24.50 4.75
C389 AP36 45c magenta 11.00 2.00
C390 AP36 60c olive brn 50.00 10.00
C391 AP36 90c rose brn 32.50 22.50
Nos. C383-C391 (9) 161.25 48.80

Issue date: Aug. 6.

Arms of Miranda and Agricultural Products

1952

C392 AP36 5c bl grn 1.00 .70
C393 AP36 7½c gray grn 1.75 1.00
C394 AP36 10c car rose 1.00 .70
C395 AP36 15c dk brn 2.10 .70
C396 AP36 20c gray blue 3.00 .85
C397 AP36 30c deep blue 6.00 1.40
C398 AP36 45c magenta 5.50 .70
C399 AP36 60c olive brn 10.50 1.90
C400 AP36 90c rose brn 45.00 27.50
Nos. C392-C400 (9) 75.85 35.45

Issue date: 7½c, 15c, 20c, 30c, Mar. 24.

Arms of Aragua and Stylized Farm

C401 AP36 5c blue green 2.50 .90
C402 AP36 7½c gray grn 2.25 1.25
C403 AP36 10c car rose 1.25 .90
C404 AP36 15c dk brown 7.75 1.10
C405 AP36 20c gray blue 3.75 1.10
C406 AP36 30c deep blue 11.00 1.25
C407 AP36 45c magenta 8.50 1.10
C408 AP36 60c olive brn 18.00 1.75
C409 AP36 90c rose brn 67.50 35.00
Nos. C401-C409 (9) 122.50 44.35

Issue date: 7½c, 15c, 20c, 30c, Mar. 24.

Arms of Lara, Agricultural Products and Rope

C410 AP36 5c blue green 2.25 .80
C411 AP36 7½c gray grn 2.00 1.10
C412 AP36 10c car rose 1.10 .80
C413 AP36 15c dk brown 3.50 .80
C414 AP36 20c gray blue 5.50 .80
C415 AP36 30c deep blue 11.00 1.60
C416 AP36 45c magenta 5.50 1.40
C417 AP36 60c olive brn 11.00 2.50
C418 AP36 90c rose brn 60.00 40.00
Nos. C410-C418 (9) 101.85 49.80

Issue date: 7½c, 15c, 20c, Mar. 24.

Arms of Bolivar and Stylized Design

C419 AP36 5c blue green 11.50 1.25
C420 AP36 10c car rose 1.00 .70
C421 AP36 15c dark brown 1.75 .70
C422 AP36 25c sepia 1.40 .70
C423 AP36 30c deep blue 8.00 3.25
C424 AP36 50c henna brn 5.40 1.40
C425 AP36 60c olive brn 9.00 1.75
C426 AP36 1b purple 8.00 1.40
C427 AP36 2b violet gray 18.00 6.25
Nos. C419-C427 (9) 64.05 17.40

Issue date: 15c, 30c, Mar. 24.

Arms of Sucre, Palms and Seascape

C428 AP36 5c blue green 1.00 .65
C429 AP36 10c car rose .65 .65
C430 AP36 15c dk brown 1.40 .65
C431 AP36 25c sepia 27.50 .65
C432 AP36 30c deep blue 9.25 2.75
C433 AP36 50c henna brn 4.25 1.00
C434 AP36 60c olive brn 5.25 2.10
C435 AP36 1b purple 6.75 1.60
C436 AP36 2b violet gray 15.00 7.50
Nos. C428-C436 (9) 71.05 17.55

Issue date: 15c, 30c, Mar. 24.

Arms of Trujillo Surrounded by Stylized Tree

C437 AP36 5c blue green 11.00 .70
C438 AP36 10c car rose .80 .40
C439 AP36 15c dk brown 3.00 .40
C440 AP36 30c deep blue 13.50 2.25
C441 AP36 60c olive brn 9.75 2.10
C442 AP36 1.20b rose red 8.75 5.00
C443 AP36 3b blue gray 4.25 3.10
C444 AP36 5b purple brn 9.25 3.50
C445 AP36 10b violet 16.00 8.25
Nos. C437-C445 (9) 76.30 25.70

Issue date: 5c, 30c, Mar. 24.

Map of Delta Amacuro and Ship

1953-54

C446 AP36 5c bl grn 1.25 .85
C447 AP36 10c car rose .85 .85
C448 AP36 15c dk brn 1.90 .96
C449 AP36 25c sepia 2.75 1.25
C450 AP36 30c dp bl 11.00 3.25
C451 AP36 50c hn brn 5.50 1.25
C452 AP36 60c ol brn 8.25 2.50
C453 AP36 1b purple 10.50 3.50
C454 AP36 2b vio gray 17.50 13.00
Nos. C446-C454 (9) 59.50 27.41

Issue date: 15c, 30c, Feb. 13.

Arms of Falcon and Stylized Oil Refinery

C455 AP36 5c bl grn 1.00 .50
C456 AP36 10c car rose .50 .50
C457 AP36 15c dk brn 1.00 .50
C458 AP36 30c dp bl 8.25 2.25
C459 AP36 60c ol brn 6.25 1.75
C460 AP36 1.20b rose red 7.75 7.25
C461 AP36 3b bl gray 8.25 4.50
C462 AP36 5b pur brn 13.50 9.25
C463 AP36 10b violet 13.50 10.50
Nos. C455-C463 (9) 60.00 37.00

Issue date: 10c, 15c, 30c, Feb. 13.

Arms of Guarico and Factory

C464 AP36 5c blue grn 1.10 .80
C465 AP36 10c car rose .80 .80
C466 AP36 15c dk brn 1.75 .80
C467 AP36 25c sepia 2.50 1.10
C468 AP36 30c dp bl 11.00 4.25
C469 AP36 50c hn brn 5.50 1.75
C470 AP36 60c ol brn 6.25 2.50
C471 AP36 1b purple 11.00 2.50
C472 AP36 2b vio gray 16.00 8.25
Nos. C464-C472 (9) 55.90 22.75

Issue date: 15c, 30c, Feb. 13.

Arms of Merida and Church

C473 AP36 5c bl grn .95 .80
C474 AP36 10c car rose .80 .80
C475 AP36 15c dk brn 1.50 .80
C476 AP36 30c dp bl 14.00 3.25
C477 AP36 60c ol brn 7.00 1.90
C478 AP36 1.20b rose red 12.00 7.00
C479 AP36 3b bl gray 7.00 3.25
C480 AP36 5b pur brn 13.50 7.00
C481 AP36 10b violet 19.00 12.00
Nos. C473-C481 (9) 75.75 36.80

Issue date: 10c, Feb. 2.

Arms of Monagas and Horses

C482 AP36 5c bl grn 1.10 .85
C483 AP36 10c car rose .85 .85
C484 AP36 15c dk brn 1.75 .85
C485 AP36 25c sepia 1.25 .85
C486 AP36 30c dp bl 16.00 4.25
C487 AP36 50c hn brn 6.50 2.10
C488 AP36 60c ol brn 7.50 2.10
C489 AP36 1b purple 11.00 2.75
C490 AP36 2b vio gray 15.00 7.50
Nos. C482-C490 (9) 60.95 22.10

Issue date: 10c, Feb. 2.

Arms of Portuguesa and Forest

C491 AP36 5c bl grn 4.00 1.25
C492 AP36 10c car rose .95 .95
C493 AP36 15c dk brn 2.40 .95
C494 AP36 30c dp bl 12.00 5.50
C495 AP36 60c ol brn 8.75 2.25
C496 AP36 1.20b rose red 20.00 12.00
C497 AP36 3b bl gray 7.00 4.00
C498 AP36 5b pur brn 12.50 7.00
C499 AP36 10b violet 18.00 15.00
Nos. C491-C499 (9) 85.60 48.90

Issue date: 5c, 10c, 30c, Feb. 2.

Map of Amazonas and Orchid

C500 AP36 5c bl grn 9.25 2.10
C501 AP36 10c car rose 2.10 2.10
C502 AP36 15c dk brn 9.25 2.10
C503 AP36 25c sepia 19.00 2.10
C504 AP36 30c dp bl 47.50 4.75
C505 AP36 50c hn brn 37.50 8.25
C506 AP36 60c ol brn 47.50 8.25
C507 AP36 1b purple 190.00 27.50
C508 AP36 2b vio gray 75.00 32.50
Nos. C500-C508 (9) 437.10 89.65

Issue date: Jan. 1954

Arms of Apure, Horse and Bird

C509 AP36 5c bl grn 1.60 .80
C510 AP36 10c car rose .80 .80
C511 AP36 15c dk brn 1.60 .80
C512 AP36 30c dp bl 6.25 2.75
C513 AP36 60c ol brn 5.75 1.40
C514 AP36 1.20b brn car 9.75 7.00
C515 AP36 3b bl gray 5.75 3.00
C516 AP36 5b pur brn 11.50 5.50
C517 AP36 10b violet 16.00 11.50
Nos. C509-C517 (9) 59.00 33.55

Issue date: Jan. 1954.

Arms of Barinas, Cow and Horse

C518 AP36 5c bl grn .50 .50
C519 AP36 10c car rose .50 .50
C520 AP36 15c dk brn 1.90 .50
C521 AP36 30c dp blue 6.50 2.50
C522 AP36 60c ol brn 6.50 1.25
C523 AP36 1.20b brn car 9.00 4.75
C524 AP36 3b bl gray 5.75 3.50
C525 AP36 5b pur brn 9.75 3.25
C526 AP36 10b violet 14.00 10.00
Nos. C518-C526 (9) 54.40 26.75

Issue date: Jan. 1954.

Arms of Cojedes and Cattle

C527 AP36 5c bl grn 7.75 1.10
C528 AP36 7½c gray grn 2.00 1.10
C529 AP36 10c car rose .60 .60
C530 AP36 15c dk brn .60 .60
C531 AP36 20c gray bl 1.50 .60
C532 AP36 30c dp blue 10.50 1.50
C533 AP36 45c mag 3.75 .90
C534 AP36 60c ol brn 7.75 1.25
C535 AP36 90c rose brn 9.25 5.25
Nos. C527-C535 (9) 43.70 12.90

Issue date: Dec.

Arms of Nueva Esparta and Fish

C536 AP36 5c bl grn 1.25 .65
C537 AP36 10c car rose .65 .65
C538 AP36 15c dk brn 2.10 .65
C539 AP36 25c sepia 3.50 .85
C540 AP36 30c dp bl 7.50 1.60
C541 AP36 50c hn brn 7.50 1.60
C542 AP36 60c ol brn 7.50 1.00
C543 AP36 1b purple 11.00 2.50
C544 AP36 2b vio gray 15.00 7.50
Nos. C536-C544 (9) 56.00 17.00

Issue date: Jan. 1954.

Arms of Yaracuy and Tropical Foliage

C545 AP36 5c bl grn 2.00 .75
C546 AP36 7½c gray grn 24.50 22.50
C547 AP36 10c car rose 1.10 .75
C548 AP36 15c dk brn 2.25 .75
C549 AP36 20c gray bl 3.75 .75
C550 AP36 30c dp bl 7.50 1.90
C551 AP36 45c mag 5.25 1.10
C552 AP36 60c ol brn 5.25 1.90
C553 AP36 90c rose brn 14.00 9.50
Nos. C545-C553 (9) 65.60 39.90
Nos. C338-C553 (216) 2,272. 841.61

Issue date: Jan. 1954.

Ship Type of 1948-50 Redrawn

Coil Stamps

Imprint: "Courvoisier S.A."

1952 **Unwmk.** ***Perf. 12x11½***
C554 AP25 5c rose brn 2.00 .25
C555 AP25 10c org red 3.25 .25
C556 AP25 15c ol brn 4.25 .25
Nos. C554-C556 (3) 9.50 .75

Barquisimeto Type of 1952

1952, Sept. 14 **Photo.** ***Perf. 11½***
C557 A94 5c blue green .25 .25
C558 A94 10c car rose .25 .25
C559 A94 20c dk blue .40 .25
C560 A94 25c black brn .60 .25
C561 A94 30c ultra .75 .25
C562 A94 40c brown org 3.50 1.50
C563 A94 50c dk ol grn 1.40 .40
C564 A94 1b purple 4.75 2.00
Nos. C557-C564 (8) 11.90 5.15

Caracas Post Office Type of 1953-54

1953, Mar. 11 ***Perf. 12½***
C565 A96 7½c yellow grn .25 .25
C566 A96 15c dp plum .25 .25
C567 A96 20c slate .25 .25
C568 A96 25c sepia .50 .25
C569 A96 40c plum .50 .25
C570 A96 45c rose vio .50 .25
C571 A96 50c red orange .75 .25
C572 A96 70c dk sl grn 1.50 .75
C573 A96 75c dp ultra 5.25 1.10
C574 A96 90c brown org 1.25 .60
C575 A96 1b violet blue 1.25 .60
Nos. C565-C575 (11) 12.25 4.80

See Nos. C587-C589, C597-C606.

Simon Rodriguez — AP39

1954, Feb. 28 ***Perf. 11½***
C576 AP39 5c blue green 3.75 .25
C577 AP39 10c car rose 3.75 .25
C578 AP39 20c gray blue 3.75 .25
C579 AP39 45c magenta 3.75 1.50
C580 AP39 65c gray green 8.75 6.00
Nos. C576-C580 (5) 23.75 8.25
Set, never hinged 35.00

Centenary of the death of Simon Rodriguez, scholar and tutor of Bolivar.

Quotation from Bolivar's Manifesto of 1824 — AP40

1954, Mar. 1 **Unwmk.**
C581 AP40 15c blk & brn buff 3.50 .25
C582 AP40 25c dk red brn & gray 3.50 .25
C583 AP40 40c dk red brn & red org 3.50 .25
C584 AP40 65c black & blue 3.50 1.00
C585 AP40 80c dk red brn & rose 3.50 .65
C586 AP40 1b pur & rose lil 8.50 .50
Nos. C581-C586 (6) 26.00 2.90
Set, never hinged 40.00

10th Inter-American Conf., Caracas, Mar. 1954.

P.O. Type of 1953

1954, Feb. **Photo.** ***Perf. 12½***
C587 A96 5c orange .40 .25
C588 A96 30c red brown 2.40 1.25
C589 A96 60c bright red 2.40 2.00
Nos. C587-C589 (3) 5.20 3.50
Set, never hinged 7.80

Valencia Arms Type of 1955

1955, Mar. 26 **Engr.** ***Perf. 12***
C590 A97 5c blue green .25 .25
C591 A97 10c rose pink .25 .25
C592 A97 20c ultra .25 .25
C593 A97 25c gray .25 .25
C594 A97 40c violet .35 .25
C595 A97 50c vermilion .35 .25
C596 A97 60c olive green .50 .25
Nos. C590-C596 (7) 2.20 1.75
Set, never hinged 5.00

P.O. Type of 1953 Inscribed: "Republica de Venezuela"

1955 **Photo.** ***Perf. 12½***
C597 A96a 5c orange .25 .25
C598 A96a 10c olive brn .25 .25
C599 A96a 15c deep plum .25 .25
C600 A96a 20c slate .25 .25
C601 A96a 30c red brn .25 .25
C602 A96a 40c plum .75 .40
C603 A96a 45c rose violet .75 .60
C604 A96a 70c dk slate grn 1.75 1.25
C605 A96a 75c deep ultra 1.00 .75
C606 A96a 90c brown org .75 .40
Nos. C597-C606 (10) 6.25 4.65
Set, never hinged 9.50

Caracas Arms Type of 1955

1955, Dec. 9 **Unwmk.** ***Perf. 11½***
C607 A98 5c yellow org .60 .25
C608 A98 15c claret brn .60 .25
C609 A98 25c violet blk .60 .25
C610 A98 40c red 1.75 .25
C611 A98 50c red orange 1.75 .25
C612 A98 60c car rose 1.75 1.25
Nos. C607-C612 (6) 7.05 2.50
Set, never hinged 16.00

University Hospital, Caracas — AP43

5c, 10c, 15c, 70c, O'Leary School, Barinas. 25c, 30c, 80c, University Hospital, Caracas. 40c, 45c, 50c, 1b, Caracas-La Guaira Highway. 60c, 65c, 75c, 2b, Towers of Simon Bolivar Center.

1956-57 **Unwmk.** ***Perf. 11½***
C613 AP43 5c orange 1.50 .25
C614 AP43 10c sepia 1.50 .25
C615 AP43 15c claret brown 1.50 .25
C616 AP43 20c dark blue 1.50 .25
C617 AP43 25c gray black 1.50 .25
C618 AP43 30c henna brown 2.25 .25
C619 AP43 40c bright crimson 2.25 .30
C620 AP43 45c brown violet 2.25 .30
C621 AP43 50c deep orange 2.25 .30
C622 AP43 60c olive green 2.25 .30
C623 AP43 65c bright blue 3.75 .30
C624 AP43 70c blue green 3.75 .30
C625 AP43 75c ultra 3.75 .45
C626 AP43 80c carmine rose 3.75 .25
C627 AP43 1b plum 3.75 .30
C628 AP43 2b dark car rose 3.75 .95
Nos. C613-C628 (16) 41.25 5.25
Set, never hinged 63.00

Issued: 20c, 40c, 45c, 50c, 1b, 11/5/56; others, 1957.

Book and Flags of American Nations — AP44

1956-57 **Granite Paper**
C629 AP44 5c orange & brn .55 .25
C630 AP44 10c brn & pale brn .55 .25
C631 AP44 20c blue & sapphire .55 .25
C632 AP44 25c gray vio & gray .55 .25
C633 AP44 40c rose red & pale pur .55 .25
C634 AP44 45c vio brn & gray brn .55 .25
C635 AP44 60c olive & gray ol 1.40 .80
Nos. C629-C635 (7) 4.70 2.30
Set, never hinged 7.40

Book Festival of the Americas, 11/15-30/56.
Issued: 5c, 40c, 11/15; others, 2/7/57.

Bolivar Type of 1957-58

Engraved; Center Embossed

1957-58 **Unwmk.** ***Perf. 13½***
C636 A100 5c orange .35 .25
C637 A100 10c olive gray .35 .25
C638 A100 20c blue .50 .25
C639 A100 25c gray black .55 .25
C640 A100 40c rose red .50 .25
C641 A100 45c rose lilac .55 .25
C642 A100 65c yellow brn 1.00 .45
Nos. C636-C642 (7) 3.80 1.95
Set, never hinged 5.75

Issued: 45c, 1958; others, Nov. 15, 1957.

Tamanaco Hotel Type of 1957-58

1957-58 **Engr.** ***Perf. 13***
C643 A101 5c dull yellow .35 .25
C644 A101 10c brown .35 .25
C645 A101 15c chocolate .35 .25
C646 A101 20c gray blue .35 .25
C647 A101 25c sepia .35 .25
C648 A101 30c violet bl .35 .25
C649 A101 40c car rose .35 .25
C650 A101 45c claret .35 .25
C651 A101 50c red org .35 .25
C652 A101 60c yellow grn .35 .25
C653 A101 65c orange brn 1.60 .90
C654 A101 70c slate .90 .45
C655 A101 75c grnsh blue .95 .55
C656 A101 1b dk claret .95 .55
C657 A101 2b dk gray 1.60 .70
Nos. C643-C657 (15) 9.50 5.65
Set, never hinged 15.00

Issue dates: 5c, 10c, Oct. 10; others, 1958.
For surcharge see No. C878.

Post Office Type of 1958

1958, May 14 **Litho.** ***Perf. 14***
C658 A102 5c dp yellow .30 .25
C659 A102 10c brown .30 .25
C660 A102 15c red brn .30 .25
C661 A102 20c lt blue .30 .25
C662 A102 25c lt gray .30 .25
C663 A102 30c lt ultra .30 .25
C664 A102 40c brt yel grn .30 .25
C665 A102 50c red orange .30 .25
C666 A102 60c rose pink .30 .25
C667 A102 65c red .30 .25
C668 A102 90c violet .50 .25
C669 A102 1b lilac .60 .25
C670 A102 1.20b bister brn 7.50 6.00
Nos. C658-C670 (13) 11.60 9.00
Set, never hinged 19.00

See Nos. C786-C792. For surcharges see Nos. C856-C861.

Post Office Type of 1958

Coil Stamps

1958 **Engr.** ***Perf. 11½x12***
C671 A103 5c deep yellow .35 .25
C672 A103 10c brown .35 .25
C673 A103 15c dark brown .40 .25
Nos. C671-C673 (3) 1.10 .75
Set, never hinged 1.25

Merida Type of 1958

1958, Oct. 9 **Photo.** ***Perf. 13½***
C674 A104 5c orange yellow .30 .25
C675 A104 10c gray brown .30 .25
C676 A104 15c dull red brn .30 .25
C677 A104 20c chalky blue .30 .25

C678 A104 25c brown gray .30 .25
C679 A104 30c violet bl .30 .25
C680 A104 40c rose car .30 .25
C681 A104 45c brt lilac .30 .25
C682 A104 50c red orange .45 .25
C683 A104 60c lt olive grn .35 .25
C684 A104 65c hennna brn 1.10 .75
C685 A104 70c gray black .65 .50
C686 A104 75c brt grnsh bl 1.30 1.20
C687 A104 80c brt vio bl .80 .55
C688 A104 90c blue green .80 .60
C689 A104 1b lilac 1.00 .75
Nos. C674-C689 (16) 8.85 6.85
Set, never hinged 13.50

Trujillo Type of 1959

1958, Nov. 17 Photo. *Perf. 14*
C690 A105 5c orange yel .25 .25
C691 A105 10c lt brown .25 .25
C692 A105 15c redsh brown .25 .25
C693 A105 20c lt blue .25 .25
C694 A105 25c pale gray .25 .25
C695 A105 30c lt vio blue .25 .25
C696 A105 40c brt yel grn .35 .25
C697 A105 50c red orange .35 .25
C698 A105 60c lilac rose .50 .35
C699 A105 65c vermilion 1.60 1.25
C700 A105 1b lilac 1.25 .65
Nos. C690-C700 (11) 5.55 4.25
Set, never hinged 9.00

Emblem — AP45

1959, Mar. 10 Litho. *Perf. 13½*
C701 AP45 5c yellow .30 .25
C702 AP45 10c red brown .30 .25
C703 AP45 15c orange .30 .25
C704 AP45 30c gray .60 .45
C705 AP45 50c green .90 .55
Nos. C701-C705 (5) 2.40 1.75
Set, never hinged 3.75

8th Central American and Caribbean Games, Caracas, Nov. 29-Dec. 14, 1958.
Exist imperf. Value, pair $25.

Stamp Centenary Type of 1959

Stamp of 1859 and: 25c, Mailman and José Ignacio Paz Castillo. 50c, Mailman on horseback and Jacinto Gutierrez. 1b, Plane, train and Miguel Herrera.

1959, Sept. 15 Engr. *Perf. 13½*
C706 A107 25c orange yel .30 .25
C707 A107 50c blue .45 .25
C708 A107 1b rose red .90 .45
Nos. C706-C708 (3) 1.65 .95
Set, never hinged 6.00

Catalogue values for unused stamps in this section, from this point to the end of the section, are for Never Hinged items.

Alexander von Humboldt Type of 1960

1960, Feb. 9 Unwmk.
C709 A108 5c ocher & brn .55 .25
C710 A108 20c brt bl & turq bl 1.75 .25
C711 A108 40c ol & ol grn 2.40 .50
Nos. C709-C711 (3) 4.70 1.00

Newspaper Type of 1960

1960, June 11 Litho. *Perf. 14*
C712 A109 5c yellow & blk 3.25 1.10
C713 A109 15c lt red brn & blk 1.60 .40
C714 A109 65c salmon & blk 2.40 .75
Nos. C712-C714 (3) 7.25 2.25

Agustin Codazzi Type of 1960

1960, June 15 Engr.
C715 A110 5c yel org & brn .30 .25
C716 A110 10c brn & dk brn .50 .25
C717 A110 25c gray & blk .70 .25
C718 A110 30c vio bl & sl 1.60 .25
C719 A110 50c org brn & brn 2.50 .50
C720 A110 70c gray ol & ol gray 4.00 .95
Nos. C715-C720 (6) 9.60 2.45

For surcharge see No. C884.

National Pantheon Type of 1960

1960, May 9 Litho.
Pantheon in Bister
C721 A111 5c dp bister .25 .25
C722 A111 10c red brown .25 .25
C723 A111 15c fawn .40 .25
C724 A111 20c lt blue .55 .25
C725 A111 25c gray 3.25 .40
C726 A111 30c lt vio bl 3.25 .65
C727 A111 40c brt yel grn .55 .25
C728 A111 45c lt violet .85 .25
C729 A111 60c deep pink 1.20 .45
C730 A111 65c salmon 1.20 .45
C731 A111 70c gray 1.75 .65
C732 A111 75c chalky blue 4.75 1.20
C733 A111 80c lt ultra 2.40 .95
C734 A111 1.20b bister brn 2.75 1.25
Nos. C721-C734 (14) 23.40 7.50

For surcharges see Nos. C894-C895.

Andres Eloy Blanco Type of 1960

1960, May 21 *Perf. 14*
Portrait in Black
C735 A112 20c blue .65 .25
C736 A112 75c grnsh blue 2.25 .40
C737 A112 90c brt violet 2.00 .40
Nos. C735-C737 (3) 4.90 1.05

For surcharge see No. C874.

Independence Type of 1960

1960, Aug. 19 Litho. *Perf. 13½*
Center Multicolored
C738 A113 50c orange .95 .40
C739 A113 75c brt grnsh blue 2.40 .65
C740 A113 90c purple 1.90 .75
Nos. C738-C740 (3) 5.25 1.80

Oil Refinery — AP46

Unwmk.
1960, Aug. 26 Engr. *Perf. 14*
C741 AP46 30c dk bl & sl bl 1.60 .40
C742 AP46 40c yel grn & ol 1.90 .45
C743 AP46 50c org & red brn 2.00 .60
Nos. C741-C743 (3) 5.50 1.45

Issued to publicize Venezuela's oil industry.

Luisa Cáceres de Arismendi Type of 1960

1960, Oct. 21 Litho. *Perf. 14*
Center Multicolored
C744 A115 5c bister 1.40 .40
C745 A115 10c redsh brown 2.00 .65
C746 A115 60c rose carmine 3.50 .80
Nos. C744-C746 (3) 6.90 1.85

José Antonio Anzoategui Type of 1960

1960, Oct. 29 Engr.
C747 A116 25c gray & brown 1.00 .25
C748 A116 40c yel grn & ol gray 1.60 .35
C749 A116 45c rose cl & dl pur 1.75 .45
Nos. C747-C749 (3) 4.35 1.05

Antonio José de Sucre Type of 1960

Unwmk.
1960, Nov. 18 Litho. *Perf. 14*
Center Multicolored
C750 A117 25c gray 1.25 .40
C751 A117 30c violet blue 1.75 .55
C752 A117 50c brown orange 2.25 .75
Nos. C750-C752 (3) 5.25 1.70

Type of Regular Issue, 1960

Designs: 30c, Bolivar Peak. 50c, Caroni Falls. 65c, Guacharo caves.

1960, Mar. 22 *Perf. 14*
C753 A118 30c vio bl & blk bl 3.00 2.75
C754 A118 50c brn org & brn 3.00 2.75
C755 A118 65c red org & red brn 3.00 2.75
Nos. C753-C755 (3) 9.00 8.25

Cow's Head, Grain, Man and Child — AP47

1961, Feb. 6 Litho. Unwmk.
Cow and Inscription in Black
C756 AP47 5c yellow .25 .25
C757 AP47 10c brown .25 .25
C758 AP47 15c redsh brn .25 .25
C759 AP47 20c dull blue .25 .25
C760 AP47 25c gray .25 .25
C761 AP47 30c violet bl .25 .25
C762 AP47 40c yellow grn .45 .25
C763 AP47 45c lilac .45 .25
C764 AP47 50c orange .45 .25
C765 AP47 60c cerise .65 .25
C766 AP47 65c red orange .80 .40
C767 AP47 70c gray 1.20 .55
C768 AP47 75c brt grnsh bl 1.00 .45
C769 AP47 80c brt violet 1.20 .40
C770 AP47 90c violet 1.60 .80
Nos. C756-C770 (15) 9.30 5.10

9th general census & 3rd agricultural census.
Issued: 5-15c, 30c, 60-65c, 75-80c, 2/6; others, 4/6.
For surcharges see Nos. C865-C866.

Rafael Maria Baralt Type of 1961

1961, Mar. 11 Engr. *Perf. 14*
C771 A120 25c gray & sepia 1.10 .40
C772 A120 30c dk blue & vio 1.20 .45
C773 A120 40c yel grn & ol grn 1.60 .55
Nos. C771-C773 (3) 3.90 1.40

Arms of San Cristobal — AP48

1961, Apr. 10 Litho.
Arms in Original Colors
C774 AP48 5c orange & blk .30 .25
C775 AP48 55c yel grn & blk .90 .30

400th anniversary of San Cristobal.
For surcharge see No. C879.

Bird Type of 1961

Birds: 5c, Troupial. 10c, Golden cock of the rock. 15c, Tropical mockingbird.

1961, Sept. 6 Unwmk. *Perf. 14½*
C776 A121 5c multicolored 1.90 1.10
C777 A121 10c multicolored .90 .60
C778 A121 15c multicolored 1.10 .65
Nos. C776-C778 (3) 3.90 2.35

Charge, Battle of Carabobo AP49

1961, Dec. 1 Litho. *Perf. 14*
Center Multicolored
C779 AP49 50c black & ultra .80 .25
C780 AP49 1.05b black & org 1.90 .50
C781 AP49 1.50b blk & lil rose 2.25 .50
C782 AP49 1.90b black & lilac 2.75 1.00
C783 AP49 2b black & gray 3.50 1.00
C784 AP49 3b black & grnsh bl 4.50 1.25
Nos. C779-C784 (6) 15.70 4.50

140th anniversary of Battle of Carabobo.
For surcharges see Nos. C867-C870.

Arms of Cardinal Quintero — AP50

1962, Mar. 1 Unwmk.
C785 AP50 5c lilac rose .50 .25
a. Souv. sheet of 1, imperf. 4.00 3.50

1st Venezuelan Cardinal, José Humberto Quintero.
No. C785a, issued Mar. 23, sold for 1b.

Post Office Type of 1958

1962, Apr. 12 Litho. *Perf. 13½x14*
C786 A102 35c citron .30 .25
C787 A102 55c gray olive .50 .25
C788 A102 70c bluish green .80 .30
C789 A102 75c brown orange 1.00 .25
C790 A102 80c fawn 1.00 .35
C791 A102 85c deep rose 1.50 .50
C792 A102 95c lilac rose 1.00 .45
Nos. C786-C792 (7) 6.10 2.35

For surcharges see Nos. C856-C861.

Archbishop Rafael Arias Blanco — AP51

1962, May 10 *Perf. 10½*
C793 AP51 75c red lilac .90 .30

4th anniversary (in 1961) of the anti-communist pastoral letter of the Archbishop of Caracas, Rafael Arias Blanco.

Orchid Type of 1962

Orchids: 5c, Oncidium volvox. 20c, Cycnoches chlorochilon. 25c, Cattleya Gaskelliana. 30c, Epidendrum difforme, horiz. 40c, Catasetum callosum Lindl, horiz. 50c, Oncidium bicolor Lindl. 1b, Brassavola nodosa Lindl, horiz. 1.05b, Epidendrum lividum Lindl. 1.50b, Schomburgkia undulata Lindl. 2b, Oncidium zebrinum.

Perf. 14x13½, 13½x14
1962, May 30 Litho. Unwmk.
Orchids in Natural Colors
C794 A124 5c blk & lt grn .30 .25
C795 A124 20c black .30 .25
C796 A124 25c black & fawn .65 .25
C797 A124 30c black & pink .60 .25
C798 A124 40c black & yel .65 .25
C799 A124 50c black & lil 1.00 .40
C800 A124 1b blk & pale rose 1.40 .60
C801 A124 1.05b blk & dp org 5.25 2.00
C802 A124 1.50b blk & pale vio 5.00 2.25
C803 A124 2b blk & org brn 5.50 2.75
Nos. C794-C803 (10) 20.65 9.25

For surcharges see Nos. C885-C887.

Independence Type of 1960

Signing Declaration of Independence.

1962, June 11 *Perf. 13½*
Center Multicolored
C804 A113 55c olive .80 .25
C805 A113 1.05b brt rose 2.60 .85
C806 A113 1.50b purple 2.25 .80
a. Souv. sheet of 3, #C804-C806, imperf. 6.00 5.00
Nos. C804-C806 (3) 5.65 1.90

No. C806a, issued Oct. 13, sold for 4.10b.
A buff cardboard folder exists with impressions of Nos. 812-814, C804-C806. Perforation is simulated. Sold for 5.60b. Value $11.
For surcharge see No. C893.

No. 710 Srchd. in Rose Carmine "BICENTENARIO DE UPATA 1762-1962 RESELLADO AEREO VALOR Bs. 2,00"

1962, July 7 *Perf. 13½x14*
C807 A102 2b on 1b lt ol grn 2.50 1.20

Upata, a village in the state of Bolivar, 200th anniv.

National Games Type of 1962

Perf. 13x14
1962, Nov. 30 Unwmk. Litho.
C808 A125 40c Bicycling .70 .30
C809 A125 75c Baseball .75 .40
C810 A125 85c Woman athlete 2.75 .95
a. Souv. sheet of 3, #C808-C810 imperf. 5.50 4.50
Nos. C808-C810 (3) 4.20 1.65

See note after No. 817.
No. C810a sold for 3b.
For surcharge see No. C899.

Bird Type of 1962

Birds: 5c, American kestrel. 20c, Black-bellied tree duck, horiz. 25c, Amazon kingfisher. 30c, Rufous-tailed chachalaca. 50c, Black-and-yellow troupial. 55c, White-naped nightjar. 2.30b, Red-crowned woodpecker. 2.50b, Black-moustached quail-dove.

1962, Dec. 14 *Perf. 14x13½, 13½x14*
Birds in Natural Colors; Black Inscription
C811 A126 5c car rose .25 .25
C812 A126 20c brt blue .60 .25
C813 A126 25c lt gray .70 .25
C814 A126 30c lt olive .80 .30
C815 A126 50c violet 1.25 .45
C816 A126 55c dp orange 2.10 .80
C817 A126 2.30b dl red brn 6.00 3.50
C818 A126 2.50b orange yel 6.00 4.00
Nos. C811-C818 (8) 17.70 9.80

For surcharges see Nos. C880-C882.

Malaria Eradication Emblem, Mosquito and Map — AP52

Lithographed and Embossed
Perf. 13½x14

1962, Dec. 20 **Wmk. 346**
C819 AP52 30c green & blk 1.00 .35
a. Souv. sheet of 2, #825, C819, imperf. 4.25 4.00

WHO drive to eradicate malaria. No. C819a sold for 2b.

Animal Type of Regular Issue

5c, Spectacle bear, vert. 40c, Paca. 50c, Three-toed sloths. 55c, Great anteater. 1.50b, South American tapirs. 2b, Jaguar.

Multicolored Center; Black Inscriptions
Perf. 14x13½, 13½x14

1963, Mar. 13 **Litho.** **Unwmk.**
C820 A128 5c yellow .25 .25
C821 A128 40c brt green .80 .25
C822 A128 50c lt violet 1.10 .40
C823 A128 55c brown olive 1.40 .45
C824 A128 1.50b gray 4.00 2.00
C825 A128 2b ultra 6.75 3.25
Nos. C820-C825 (6) 14.30 6.60

For surcharges see Nos. C888-C889.

Freedom from Hunger Type of 1963

40c, Map, shepherd. 75c, Map, farmer.

1963, Mar. 21
C826 A129 40c lt yel grn & dl red 1.00 .40
C827 A129 75c yellow & brown 1.25 .65

Arms of Bocono — AP53

1963, May 30 **Wmk. 346**
C828 AP53 1b multicolored 2.40 .65

400th anniversary of the founding of Bocono. For surcharge see No. C892.

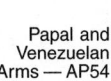

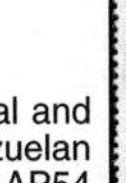

Papal and Venezuelan Arms — AP54

1963, June 11 ***Perf. 14x13½***
Arms Multicolored
C829 AP54 80c light green 1.60 .35
C830 AP54 90c gray 1.60 .50

Vatican II, the 21st Ecumenical Council of the Roman Catholic Church.
For surcharges see Nos. C871-C872.

Arms of Venezuela — AP55

1963, July 29 **Unwmk.** ***Perf. 14***
C831 AP55 70c gray, red, yel & bl 1.50 .50

Cent. of Venezuela's flag and coat of arms.
For surcharge see No. C883.

Lake Maracaibo Bridge — AP56

Wmk. 346
1963, Aug. 24 **Litho.** ***Perf. 14***
C832 AP56 90c grn, brn & ocher 1.75 .50
C833 AP56 95c blue, brn & och 1.75 .60
C834 AP56 1b ultra, brn & och 1.60 .50
Nos. C832-C834 (3) 5.10 1.60

Opening of bridge over Lake Maracaibo.
For surcharges see Nos. C897-C898.

Armed Forces Type of 1963

1963, Sept. 10 **Unwmk.**
C835 A134 1b red & bl, *buff* 2.40 1.00

For surcharge see No. C862.

Hammarskjold Type of 1963

1963, Sept. 25 **Unwmk.** ***Perf. 14***
C836 A135 80c dk bl, lt ultra & ocher 1.50 .50
C837 A135 90c dk bl, bl & ocher 2.10 .70
a. Souv. sheet of 4, #841-842, C836-C837, imperf. 5.25 5.25

No. C837a sold for 3b.
For surcharges see Nos. C875-C876.

Dr. Luis Razetti, Physician, Birth Cent. — AP57

1963, Oct. 10 **Engr.**
C838 AP57 95c dk blue & mag 1.80 .90
C839 AP57 1.05b dk brn & grn 1.80 1.00

For surcharges see Nos. C890-C891.

Red Cross Type of 1963

Designs: 40c, Sir Vincent K. Barrington. 75c, Red Cross nurse and child.

1963, Dec. 31 **Litho.** ***Perf. 11½x12***
C840 A137 40c multicolored .75 .40
C841 A137 75c multicolored 1.25 .60

Development Type of 1964

Designs: 5c, Loading cargo. 10c, Tractor and corn. 15c, Oil field workers. 20c, Oil refinery. 50c, Crane and building construction.

1964, Feb. 5 **Unwmk.** ***Perf. 14x13½***
C842 A138 5c multicolored .30 .25
C843 A138 10c multicolored .30 .25
C844 A138 15c multicolored .30 .25
C845 A138 20c multicolored .30 .25
C846 A138 50c multicolored .80 .40
Nos. C842-C846 (5) 2.00 1.40

Cent. of the Dept. of Industrial Development and to publicize the Natl. Industrial Expo.

Pedro Gual Type of 1964

1964, Mar. 20 ***Perf. 14x13½***
C847 A139 75c dull blue green 1.00 .40
C848 A139 1b bright pink 1.75 .45

Blast Furnace and Map of Venezuela — AP58

1964, May 22 **Litho.** ***Perf. 13½x14***
C849 AP58 80c multi 1.50 .45
C850 AP58 1b multi 2.25 .65

Issued to publicize the Orinoco steel mills.

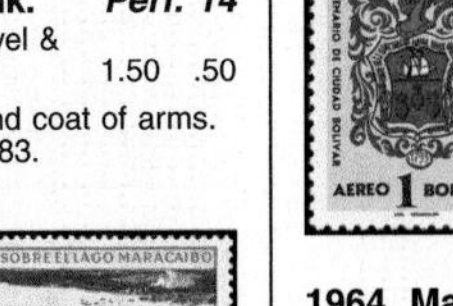
Arms of Ciudad Bolivar — AP59

1964, May 22 ***Perf. 10½***
C851 AP59 1b multi 1.75 1.00

Bicentenary of Ciudad Bolivar.

AP60

1964, Aug. 3 **Unwmk.** ***Perf. 11½***
C852 AP60 30c bister brn & yel .65 .25
C853 AP60 40c plum & pink 1.10 .25
C854 AP60 50c brn & tan 1.50 .40
Nos. C852-C854 (3) 3.25 .90

80th birthday of novelist Romulo Gallegos.

AP61

1964, Nov. 11 **Litho.** ***Perf. 14x13½***
C855 AP61 1b orange & dk vio 1.50 .65

Eleanor Roosevelt and 15th anniv. (in 1963) of the Universal Declaration of Human Rights.
For surcharge see No. C896.

Issues of 1947-64 Srchd. in Black, Dark Blue, Red, Carmine or Lilac with New Value and "RESELLADO / VALOR"

1965
C856 A102 5c on 55c (#C787) .65 .25
C857 A102 5c on 70c (#C788) .65 .25
C858 A102 5c on 80c (#C790) .65 .25
C859 A102 5c on 85c (#C791) .65 .25
C860 A102 5c on 90c (#C668) .65 .25
C861 A102 5c on 95c (#C792) .65 .25
C862 A134 5c on 1b (#C835) .85 .25
C863 AP25 10c on 3b (#C269) (C) .65 .25
C864 AP25 10c on 4b (#C270) (C) 1.10 .25
C865 AP47 10c on 70c (#C767) (C) .70 .25
C866 AP47 10c on 90c (#C770) (C) .65 .25
C867 AP49 10c on 1.05b (#C780) .90 .25
C868 AP49 10c on 1.90b (#C782) .65 .25
C869 AP49 10c on 2b (#C783) .70 .25
C870 AP49 10c on 3b (#C784) .70 .25
C871 AP54 10c on 80c (#C829) .65 .25
C872 AP54 10c on 90c (#C830) .65 .25
C873 AP16 15c on 3b (#C253) .70 .25
C874 A112 15c on 90c (#C737) .65 .25
C875 A135 15c on 80c (#C836) .65 .25
C876 A135 15c on 90c (#C837) .65 .25
C877 AP59 15c on 1b (#C851) .70 .25
C878 A101 20c on 2b (#C657) (R) .85 .25
C879 AP48 20c on 55c (#C775) (DB) .70 .25
C880 A126 20c on 55c (#C816) .90 .25
a. 25c on 55c (#C816)
C881 A126 20c on 2.30b (#C817) .70 .25
C882 A126 20c on 2.50b (#C818) .90 .25
C883 AP55 20c on 70c (#C831) .90 .25
C884 A110 25c on 70c (#C720) (DB) 1.00 .25
C885 A124 25c on 1.05b (#C801) (L) .70 .25
C886 A124 25c on 1.50b (#C802) (L) .70 .25
C887 A124 25c on 2b (#C803) (L) .90 .25
C888 A128 25c on 1.50b (#C824) .90 .25
C889 A128 25c on 2b (#C825) .90 .25
C890 AP57 25c on 95c (#C838) .85 .25
C891 AP57 25c on 1.05b (#C839) .90 .25
C892 AP53 30c on 1b (#C828) 1.10 .25
C893 A113 40c on 1.05b (#C805) (DB) .90 .25
C894 A111 50c on 65c (#C730) (DB) .65 .25
C895 A111 50c on 1.20b (#C734) (DB) 1.10 .25
C896 AP61 50c on 1b (#C855) .70 .25

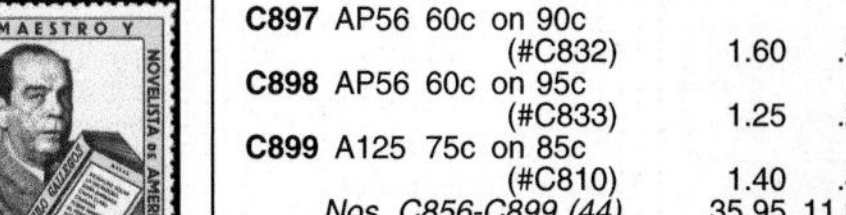
C897 AP56 60c on 90c (#C832) 1.60 .40
C898 AP56 60c on 95c (#C833) 1.25 .25
C899 A125 75c on 85c (#C810) 1.40 .40
Nos. C856-C899 (44) 35.95 11.30

Lines of surcharge arranged variously on Nos. C856-C899. Old denominations obliterated with bars on Nos. C862, C871-C873, C875-C877, C883, C885-C887, C889, C892, C896-C898. Vertical surcharge on Nos. C865-C866, C871-C872, C874, C878, C896.

Kennedy Type of 1965

1965, Aug. 20 **Photo.** ***Perf. 12x11½***
C900 A144 60c lt grnsh bl 1.40 .40
C901 A144 80c red brn 1.60 .50

Medical Federation Emblem — AP62

1965, Aug. 24 **Litho.** ***Perf. 13½x14***
C902 AP62 65c red org & blk 1.75 .75

20th anniversary of the founding of the Medical Federation of Venezuela.

Unisphere and Venezuela Pavilion — AP63

1965, Aug. 31 ***Perf. 14x13½***
C903 AP63 1b multi 1.35 .35

New York World's Fair, 1964-65.

Andrés Bello (1780?-1865), Educator and Writer — AP64

Perf. 14x13½
1965, Oct. 15 **Litho.** **Unwmk.**
C904 AP64 80c dk brn & org 1.60 .75

Map Type of 1965

Maps of Venezuela and Guiana: 25c, Map of Venezuela and Guiana by J. Cruz Cano, 1775. 40c, Map stamp of 1896 (No. 140). 75c, Map by the Ministry of the Exterior, 1965 (all horiz.).

1965, Nov. 5 ***Perf. 13½***
C905 A145 25c multi .65 .25
C906 A145 40c multi 1.10 .25
C907 A145 75c multi 1.40 .40
a. Souv. sheet of 3, #C905-C907, imperf. 16.00 14.00
Nos. C905-C907 (3) 3.15 .90

#C907a, issued June 7, 1966, sold for 1.65b.

ITU Emblem and Telegraph Poles — AP65

1965, Nov. 19 **Litho.** ***Perf. 13½x14***
C908 AP65 75c blk & ol grn 1.10 .40

Cent. of the ITU.

Simon Bolivar and Quotation — AP66

1965, Dec. 9 ***Perf. 14x13½***
C909 AP66 75c lt bl & dk brn 1.10 .40

Sesquicentennial of Bolivar's Jamaica letter, Sept. 6, 1815.

Children Riding Magic Carpet and Three Kings on Camels — AP67

1965, Dec. 16 ***Perf. 13½x14***

C910 AP67 70c yel & vio bl 1.60 .75

Children's Festival, 1965 (Christmas).

Fermin Toro — AP68

1965, Dec. 22 ***Perf. 14x13½***

C911 AP68 1b blk & org 1.25 .55

Death centenary of Fermin Toro (1808-1865), statesman and writer.

Winston Churchill AP69

1965, Dec. 29 ***Perf. 14½x13***

C912 AP69 1b lilac & blk 1.60 .55

Sir Winston Spencer Churchill (1874-1965), statesman and World War II leader.

ICY Emblem, Arms of Venezuela and UN Emblem — AP70

1965, Dec. 30 ***Perf. 13½x14***

C913 AP70 85c gold & vio blk 1.60 .55

International Cooperation Year, 1965.

OAS Emblem and Map of America — AP71

1965, Dec. 31 ***Perf. 14x13½***

C914 AP71 50c bl, blk & gold 1.35 .45

Organization of American States, 75th anniv.

Butterfly Type of 1966

1966, Jan. 25 Litho. ***Perf. 13½x14***

Various Butterflies in Natural Colors; Black Inscriptions

C915 A146 65c lilac 1.90 .40
C916 A146 85c blue 2.75 .50
C917 A146 1b salmon pink 3.25 .60
Nos. C915-C917 (3) 7.90 1.50

Farms of 1936 and 1966 — AP72

1966, Mar. 1 ***Perf. 14x13½***

C918 AP72 55c blk, yel & emer 1.25 .40

30th anniversary of the Ministry for Agriculture and Husbandry.

Dance Type of 1966

Various folk dances.

1966, Apr. 5 Litho. ***Perf. 14***

C919 A148 40c bl & multi 1.25 .35
C920 A148 50c multi 1.25 .40
C921 A148 60c vio & multi 1.00 .25
C922 A148 70c multi 2.00 .50
C923 A148 80c red & multi 2.40 .65
C924 A148 90c ocher & multi 2.75 .80
Nos. C919-C924 (6) 10.65 2.95

Title Page "Popule Meus" — AP73

1966, Apr. 15 ***Perf. 13½x14***

C925 AP73 55c yel grn, blk & bis .90 .45
C926 AP73 95c dp mag, blk & bis 1.10 .60

150th anniv. (in 1964) of the death of José Angel Lamas, composer of natl. anthem.

Circus Scene, by Michelena AP74

Paintings by Michelena: 1b, Miranda in La Carraca. 1.05b, Charlotte Corday.

Perf. 12x12½

1966, May 12 Litho. Unwmk.

C927 AP74 95c multi 1.20 .75
C928 AP74 1b multi 1.50 .75
C929 AP74 1.05b multi 1.75 .75
Nos. C927-C929 (3) 4.45 2.25

Cent. of the birth of Arturo Michelena (1863-1898), painter. Miniature sheets of 12 exist.

See Nos. 900-901.

Abraham Lincoln — AP75

1966, May 31 ***Perf. 13½x14***

C930 AP75 1b gray & blk 1.35 .75

Dr. José Gregorio Hernandez AP76

1966, July 29 Litho. ***Perf. 14x13½***

C931 AP76 1b brt bl & vio bl 1.75 .65

Centenary (in 1964) of the birth of Dr. José Gregorio Hernandez, physician.

Dr. Manuel Dagnino and Hospital — AP77

1966, Aug. 16 Litho. ***Perf. 13½x14***

C932 AP77 1b sl grn & yel grn 1.60 .55

Founding of Chiquinquira Hospital, cent.

Fish Type of 1966

Fish: 75c, Pearl headstander, vert. 90c, Swordtail characine. 1b, Ramirez's dwarf cichlid.

Perf. 14x13½, 13½x14

1966, Aug. 31

C933 A151 75c multi 2.00 .50
C934 A151 90c grn & multi 2.00 .50
C935 A151 1b multi 2.00 .50
Nos. C933-C935 (3) 6.00 1.50

Rafael Arevalo Gonzalez — AP78

1966, Sept. 13 Litho. ***Perf. 13½x14***

C936 AP78 75c yel bis & blk 1.50 .55

Centenary of the birth of Rafael Arevalo Gonzalez, journalist.

Simon Bolivar, 1816 — AP79

Bolivar Portraits: 25c, 30c, 35c, by José Gil de Castro, 1825. 40c, 50c, 60c, Anonymous painter, 1825. 80c, 1.20b, 4b, Anonymous painter, c. 1829.

Imprint: "Bundesdruckerei Berlin 1966"

1966 Multicolored Center

C937 AP79 5c lem & blk .30 .25
C938 AP79 10c lt ol grn & blk .30 .25
C939 AP79 20c grn & blk .30 .25
C940 AP79 25c salmon & blk .30 .25
C941 AP79 30c pink & blk .30 .25
C942 AP79 35c dl rose & blk .35 .25
C943 AP79 40c bis brn & blk .30 .25
C944 AP79 50c org brn & blk .50 .25
C945 AP79 60c brn red & blk .50 .25
C946 AP79 80c brt bl & blk .95 .35
C947 AP79 1.20b dl bl & blk 1.50 .65
C948 AP79 4b vio bl & blk 5.00 2.75
Nos. C937-C948 (12) 10.60 6.00

Issued to honor Simon Bolivar.

Issue dates: Nos. C937-C939, Aug. 15; Nos. C940-C942, Sept. 29; others, Oct. 14.

See Nos. C961-C972.

"Justice" — AP80

1966, Nov. 3 Litho. ***Perf. 14x13½***

C949 AP80 50c pale lil & red lil 1.10 .40

50th anniversary of the Academy of Political and Social Sciences.

Angostura Bridge, Orinoco River — AP81

1967, Jan. 6 Litho. ***Perf. 13½x14***

C950 AP81 40c multi .60 .25

Issued to commemorate the opening of the Angostura Bridge over the Orinoco River.

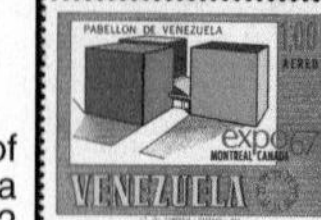
Pavilion of Venezuela AP82

1967, Apr. 28 Litho. ***Perf. 11x13½***

C951 AP82 1b multi 1.35 .40

EXPO '67, International Exhibition, Montreal, Apr. 28-Oct. 27, 1967.

Statue of Chief Guaicaipuro — AP83

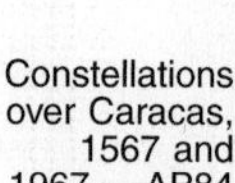

Constellations over Caracas, 1567 and 1967 — AP84

Designs: 45c, Captain Francisco Fajardo. 55c, Diego de Losada, the Founder. 65c, Arms of Caracas. 90c, Map of Caracas, 1578. 1b, Market on Plaza Mayor, 1800.

1967 Litho. ***Perf. 14x13½, 13½x14***

C952 AP83 15c multi .30 .25
C953 AP83 45c gold, car & brn .50 .25
C954 AP83 55c multi .50 .25
C955 AP84 60c blk, ultra & sil .65 .25
C956 AP83 65c multi .90 .30
C957 AP84 90c multi .35 .35
C958 AP84 1b multi 1.10 .40
Nos. C952-C958 (7) 4.30 2.05

400th anniv. of the founding of Caracas (1st issue). See Nos. C977-C982 (2nd issue).

Two souvenir sheets each contain single stamps similar to Nos. C952-C953, but with simulated perforation. Sold for 1b each. Size: 80x119mm. Value $45 each.

Issued: 55c, 65c, July 28; others, July 12.

Gen. Francisco Esteban Gomez — AP85

1967, July 31 Litho. ***Perf. 14x13½***

C959 AP85 90c multi 1.35 .60

150th anniversary, Battle of Matasiete.

Juan Vicente González — AP86

1967, Oct. 18 Litho. ***Perf. 14x13½***

C960 AP86 80c ocher & blk 1.35 .40

Centenary of the death (in 1866) of Juan Vicente González, journalist.

Bolivar Type of 1966

Imprint: "Druck Bruder Rosenbaum. Wien"

1967-68 Litho. ***Perf. 13½x14***

Multicolored Center

C961 AP79 5c lemon & blk .25 .25
C962 AP79 10c lemon & blk .25 .25
C963 AP79 20c grn & blk .35 .25
C964 AP79 25c salmon & blk .30 .25
C965 AP79 30c pink & blk .35 .25
C966 AP79 35c dl rose & blk .35 .25
C967 AP79 40c bis brn & blk .65 .25
C968 AP79 50c org brn & blk 5.00 .35
C969 AP79 60c brn red & blk 2.25 .90
C970 AP79 80c brt bl & blk 1.30 .50
C971 AP79 1.20b dl bl & blk 1.90 .35
C972 AP79 4b vio bl & blk 5.00 1.90
Nos. C961-C972 (12) 17.95 5.75

Issue dates: 20c, 30c, 50c, Nov. 24; 5c, 25c, 40c, Feb. 5, 1968; others, Aug, 28, 1967.

Child with Pinwheel — AP87

1967, Dec. 15 Litho. ***Perf. 14x13½***

C973 AP87 45c multi .65 .25
C974 AP87 75c multi .90 .30
C975 AP87 90c multi 1.20 .35
Nos. C973-C975 (3) 2.75 .90

Children's Festival.

Madonna with the Rosebush, by Stephan Lochner — AP88

1967, Dec. 19

C976 AP88 1b multi 1.75 .70

Christmas 1967.

Palace of the Academies, Caracas AP89

Views of Caracas: 50c, St. Theresa's Church, vert. 70c, Federal Legislature. 75c, University City. 85c, El Pulpo highways crossing. 2b, Avenida Libertador.

1967, Dec. 28 ***Perf. 13½x14, 14x13½***

C977 AP89 10c multi .30 .25
C978 AP89 50c lil & multi .40 .25
C979 AP89 70c multi .70 .25
C980 AP89 75c multi .80 .25
C981 AP89 85c multi .90 .30
C982 AP89 2b multi 2.50 .85
Nos. C977-C982 (6) 5.60 2.15

400th anniv. of Caracas (2nd issue).

Dr. José Manuel Nuñez Ponte (1870-1965), Educator — AP90

1968, Mar. 8 **Litho.** ***Perf. 14***

C983 AP90 65c multi .85 .35

De Miranda and Printing Press — AP91

Designs (Miranda Portraits and): 35c, Parliament, London. 45c, Arc de Triomphe, Paris. 70c, Portrait, vert. 80c, Portrait bust and Venezuelan flags, vert.

Perf. 13½x14, 14x13½

1968, June 20 **Litho.**

C984 AP91 20c yel brn, grn & brn .40 .25
C985 AP91 35c multi .60 .25
C986 AP91 45c lt bl & multi 1.10 .40
C987 AP91 70c multi 1.40 .35
C988 AP91 80c multi 1.60 .55
Nos. C984-C988 (5) 5.10 1.80

General Francisco de Miranda (1750?-1816), revolutionist, dictator of Venezuela.

Insect Type of 1968

Insect Pests: 5c, Red leaf-cutting ant, vert. 15c, Sugar cane beetle, vert. 20c, Leaf beetle.

Perf. 14x13½, 13½x14

1968, Aug. 30 **Litho.**

C989 A157 5c multi .65 .25
C990 A157 15c multi 1.25 .25
C991 A157 20c gray & multi 1.75 .25
Nos. C989-C991 (3) 3.65 .75

Three Keys — AP92

1968, Oct. 17 **Litho.** ***Perf. 14x13½***

C992 AP92 95c yel, vio & dk grn 1.50 .50

Natl. Comptroller's Office, 30th anniv.

Fencing AP93

Designs: 5c, Pistol shooting, vert. 15c, Running. 75c, Boxing. 5b, Sailing, vert.

Perf. 14x13½, 13½x14

1968, Nov. 6 **Litho.** **Unwmk.**

C993 AP93 5c vio, bl & blk .50 .30
C994 AP93 15c multi .60 .30
C995 AP93 30c yel grn, dk grn & blk .80 .30
C996 AP93 75c multi 1.50 .40
C997 AP93 5b multi 5.50 1.90
Nos. C993-C997 (5) 8.90 3.20

19th Olympic Games, Mexico City, 10/12-27.

Holy Family, by Francisco José de Lerma — AP94

1968, Dec. 4 **Litho.** ***Perf. 14x13½***

C998 AP94 40c multi .85 .25

Christmas 1968.

Dancing Children and Stars — AP95

1968, Dec. 13 **Litho.** ***Perf. 14x13½***

C999 AP95 80c vio & org 1.25 .50

Issued for the 5th Children's Festival.

Conservation Type of 1968

Designs: 15c, Marbled wood-quail, vert. 20c, Water birds, vert. 30c, Woodcarvings and tools, vert. 90c, Brown trout. 95c, Valley and road. 1b, Red-eyed vireo feeding young bronzed cowbird.

Perf. 13½x14, 14x13½

1968, Dec. 19 **Litho.**

C1000 A160 15c multi .50 .35
C1001 A160 20c multi .50 .35
C1002 A160 30c multi .60 .35
C1003 A160 90c multi 1.60 .45
C1004 A160 95c multi 2.50 .65
C1005 A160 1b multi 1.75 .55
Nos. C1000-C1005 (6) 7.45 2.70

Tourist Type of 1969

Designs: 15c, Giant cactus and desert, Falcon. 30c, Hotel Humboldt, Federal District. 40c, Cable car and mountain peaks, Merida.

1969, Jan. 24 ***Perf. 13½x14***

C1006 A161 15c multi .45 .25
C1007 A161 30c multi .50 .25
a. Souv. sheet of 2, #931, C1007, imperf. 2.40 2.10
C1008 A161 40c multi .85 .25
Nos. C1006-C1008 (3) 1.80 .75

Tree Type of 1969

Trees: 5c, Cassia grandis. 20c, Triplaris caracasana. 25c, Samanea saman.

1969, May 30 **Litho.** ***Perf. 13½x14***

C1009 A164 5c lt grn & multi .65 .25
C1010 A164 20c org & multi .95 .25
C1011 A164 25c lt vio & multi 1.10 .25
Nos. C1009-C1011 (3) 2.70 .75

Alexander von Humboldt, by Joseph Stieler — AP96

1969, Sept. 12 **Photo.** ***Perf. 14***

C1012 AP96 50c multi .90 .40

Alexander von Humboldt (1769-1859), naturalist and explorer.

Map of Maracaibo, 1562 — AP97

20c, Ambrosio Alfinger, Alfonso Pacheco, Pedro Maldonado, horiz. 40c, Maracaibo coat of arms. 70c, University Hospital. 75c, Monument to the Indian Mara. 1b, Baralt Square, horiz.

Perf. 13½x13, 13x13½

1969, Sept. 30 **Litho.**

C1013 AP97 20c lil & multi .40 .25
C1014 AP97 25c org & multi .50 .25
C1015 AP97 40c multi .55 .25
C1016 AP97 70c grn & multi 1.25 .35
C1017 AP97 75c brn & multi 1.50 .40
C1018 AP97 1b multi 1.75 .50
Nos. C1013-C1018 (6) 5.95 2.00

400th anniversary of Maracaibo.

Astronauts Neil A. Armstrong, Edwin E. Aldrin, Jr., Michael Collins and Moonscape AP98

1969, Nov. 18 **Litho.** ***Perf. 12½***

C1019 AP98 90c multi 1.75 .65
a. Souv. sheet of 1, imperf. 3.50 3.25

See note after US No. C76.

Virgin with the Rosary, 17th Century — AP99

Christmas: 80c, Holy Family, Caracas, 18th Cent.

1969, Dec. 1 **Litho.** ***Perf. 12½***

C1020 AP99 75c gold & multi 1.10 .35
C1021 AP99 80c gold & multi 1.50 .45
a. Pair, #C1020-C1021 2.60 2.40

Simon Bolivar, 1819, by M. N. Bate — AP100

Bolivar Portraits: 45c, 55c, like 15c. 65c, 70c, 75c Drawing by Francois Roulin, 1828. 85c, 90c, 95c, Charcoal drawing by José Maria Espinoza, 1828. 1b, 1.50b, 2b, Drawing by Espinoza, 1830.

1970, Mar. 16 **Litho.** ***Perf. 14x13½***

C1022 AP100 15c multi .30 .25
C1023 AP100 45c bl & multi .50 .25
C1024 AP100 55c org & multi .65 .25
C1025 AP100 65c multi .65 .30
C1026 AP100 70c bl & multi .75 .40
C1027 AP100 75c org & multi 1.00 .40
C1028 AP100 85c multi 1.20 .40
C1029 AP100 90c bl & multi 1.20 .45
C1030 AP100 95c org & multi 1.40 .50
C1031 AP100 1b multi 1.40 .50
C1032 AP100 1.50b bl & multi 1.50 .55
C1033 AP100 2b multi 3.25 1.75
Nos. C1022-C1033 (12) 13.80 6.00

Issued to honor Simon Bolivar (1783-1830), liberator and father of his country.

General Antonio Guzmán Blanco and Dr. Martin J. Sanabria AP101

1970, June 26 **Litho.** ***Perf. 13***

C1034 AP101 75c brt grn & multi .90 .30

Free obligatory elementary education, cent.

Map of Venezuela with Claim to Part of Guyana AP102

State map and arms. 55c, 90c, vert.

Perf. 13½x14, 14x13½

1970-71 **Litho.**

C1035 AP102 5c shown .40 .25
C1036 AP102 15c Apure .40 .25
C1037 AP102 20c Aragua .45 .25
C1038 AP102 20c Anzoategui .50 .25
C1039 AP102 25c Barinas .50 .25
C1040 AP102 25c Bolivar .50 .25
C1041 AP102 45c Carabobo .75 .25
C1042 AP102 55c Cojedes .80 .25
C1043 AP102 65c Falcon .85 .25
C1044 AP102 75c Guárico 1.00 .25
C1045 AP102 85c Lara 1.25 .30
C1046 AP102 90c Mérida 1.25 .30
C1047 AP102 1b Miranda 1.25 .40
C1048 AP102 2b Delta Amacuro Territory 2.75 .95
Nos. C1035-C1048 (14) 12.65 4.45

Issued: 5c, 7/15; 15c, #C1037, 1/18; #C1038-C1039, 2/15/71; #C1040, 45c, 3/15/71; 55c, 65c, 4/15; 75c, 85c, 5/15/71; 90c, 1b, 6/15/71; 2b, 7/15/71.

Flower Type of 1970

Flowers: 20c, Epidendrum secundum. 25c, Oyedaea verbesinoides. 45c, Heliconia villosa. 1b, Macleania nitida.

1970, July 29 **Litho.** ***Perf. 14x13½***

C1049 A175 20c multi .60 .25
C1050 A175 25c multi .75 .25
C1051 A175 45c multi 1.90 .35
C1052 A175 1b multi 2.25 .45
Nos. C1049-C1052 (4) 5.50 1.30

Caracciolo Parra Olmedo — AP104

1970, Nov. 16 **Photo.** ***Perf. 12½***

C1053 AP104 20c bl & multi .40 .25

Sesquicentennial of birth of Caracciolo Parra Olmedo (1819-1900), professor of law, rector of University of Merida.

Census Chart AP105

1971, Apr. 30 **Litho.** ***Perf. 13½x14***

C1054 Block of 4 6.50 2.50
a. AP105 70c, frame L & T 1.00 .55
b. AP105 70c, frame T & R 1.00 .55
c. AP105 70c, frame L & B 1.00 .55
d. AP105 70c, frame B & R 1.00 .55

See note after No. 979.

Cattleya Gaskelliana AP106

Orchids: 20c, Cattleya percivaliana, vert. 75c, Cattleya mossiae, vert. 90c, Cattleya violacea. 1b, Cattleya lawrenciana.

Perf. 14x13½, 13½x14

1971, Aug. 25

C1055 AP106 20c blk & multi .55 .25
C1056 AP106 25c blk & multi .80 .25
C1057 AP106 75c blk & multi 1.50 .50
C1058 AP106 90c blk & multi 2.10 .80
C1059 AP106 1b blk & multi 2.25 .90
Nos. C1055-C1059 (5) 7.20 2.70

40th anniversary of Venezuelan Society of Natural History. Issued in sheets of 5 stamps and one label with Society emblem in blue. Value $37.50.

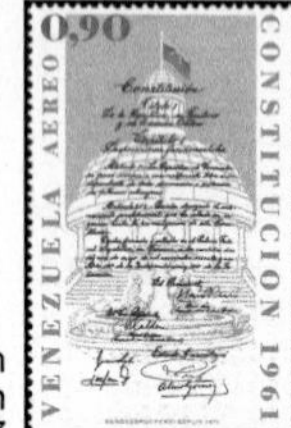

Draft of Constitution Superimposed on Capitol — AP107

1971, Dec. 29 Litho. *Perf. 13½*

C1060 AP107 90c multi .90 .40

Anniversary of 1961 Constitution.

AIR POST SEMI-POSTAL STAMPS

King Vulture — SPAP1

Unwmk.

1942, Dec. 17 Engr. *Perf. 12*

CB1 SPAP1 15c + 10c org brn 2.25 .60
CB2 SPAP1 30c + 5c violet 2.25 .75
Set, never hinged 7.50

See note after No. B1.

SPECIAL DELIVERY STAMPS

Catalogue values for unused stamps in this section are for Never Hinged items.

SD1

Perf. 12½

1949, Mar. 9 Unwmk. Engr.

E1 SD1 30c red .70 .30

SD2

Wmk. 116

1961, Apr. 7 Litho. *Perf. 13½*

E2 SD2 30c orange .65 .25

REGISTRATION STAMPS

Bolívar — R1

1899, May Unwmk. Engr. *Perf. 12*

F1 R1 25c yellow brown 4.50 2.50

No. F1 Overprinted

1900

F2 R1 25c yellow brown 2.25 1.50
a. Inverted overprint 32.50 32.50
b. Double overprint 40.00 40.00

Counterfeit overprints exist, especially of the varieties.

OFFICIAL STAMPS

For General Use

Coat of Arms — O1

Lithographed, Center Engraved

1898, May 1 Unwmk. *Perf. 12*

O1 O1 5c bl grn & blk .80 .55
O2 O1 10c rose & blk .95 .85
O3 O1 25c bl & blk 1.50 1.40
O4 O1 50c yel & blk 2.50 2.25
O5 O1 1b vio & blk 2.75 2.50
Nos. O1-O5 (5) 8.50 7.55

Nos. O4 and O5 Handstamp Surcharged in Magenta or Violet

1899, Nov.

O6 O1 5c on 50c yel & blk 4.75 4.50
O7 O1 5c on 1b vio & blk 20.00 18.00
O8 O1 25c on 50c yel & blk 20.00 18.00
O9 O1 25c on 1b vio & blk 12.00 11.00
Nos. O6-O9 (4) 56.75 51.50

Inverted Surcharge

O6a O1 5c on 50c 15.00 15.00
O7a O1 5c on 1b 40.00 40.00
O8a O1 25c on 50c 32.50 32.50
O9a O1 25c on 1b 32.50 32.50
Nos. O6a-O9a (4) 120.00 120.00

Nos. O6-O9 exist with double surcharge. Value each $18.50-$37.50.

Many of the magenta overprints have become violet. There are intermediate shades.

Counterfeit overprints exist.

Coat of Arms — O3

1900 Litho., Center Engr.

O14 O3 5c bl grn & blk .40 .40
O15 O3 10c rose & blk .55 .55
O16 O3 25c bl & blk .55 .55
O17 O3 50c yel & blk .55 .55
O18 O3 1b dl vio & blk .65 .65
Nos. O14-O18 (5) 2.70 2.70

O4

Imprint: "American Bank Note Co., N.Y."

1904, July Engr.

O19 O4 5c emerald & blk .25 .25
O20 O4 10c rose & blk .65 .65
O21 O4 25c blue & blk .65 .65
O22 O4 50c red brn & blk 4.25 4.25
a. 50c claret & black 4.25 4.25
O23 O4 1b red brn & blk 2.00 2.00
a. 1b claret & black 2.00 2.00
Nos. O19-O23 (5) 7.80 7.80

No Stars Above Shield — O5

1912 Lithographed in Caracas

O24 O5 5c grn & blk .55 .30
O25 O5 10c car & blk .55 .30
O26 O5 25c dk bl & blk .55 .30
O27 O5 50c pur & blk .55 .40
a. Center double 19.00
O28 O5 1b yel & blk 1.30 .80
Nos. O24-O28 (5) 3.50 2.10

PERFORATED OFFICIAL STAMPS

From 1925 through 1943, Venezuelan Official stamps consisted of regular and air post stamps punched with the initials "GN" (Gobierno Nacional). The perforated initials can appear either upright, inverted, or sideways, reading up or down on any given stamp and can be right-reading or left-reading, creating eight possible varieties.

Values for these varieties are the same.

No. OA1

1915-23 On Nos. 250//268

OA1 A43 5c green 4.25 .50
OA2 A43 10c vermilion 25.00 1.00
OA3 A43 10c claret ('22) 4.25 .60
OA4 A43 15c dull ol grn 9.25 .60
OA5 A43 25c ultramarine 25.00 1.00
OA6 A43 50c dp violet 9.25 .80
OA7 A43 50c ultra ('23) 25.00 4.75
OA8 A43 1b dark gray 25.00 4.75
Nos. OA1-OA8 (8) 127.00 14.00

1924-28 On Nos. 267//285

OA9 A43 5c orange brn .30 .25
OA10 A43 10c dk green .30 .25
OA11 A43 15c olive green 3.00 1.50
OA12 A43 15c brown ('27) .40 .25
OA13 A43 25c ultramarine 1.75 .25
OA14 A43 25c red ('28) .25 .25
OA15 A43 40c dp blue ('25) .80 .25
OA16 A43 50c dk blue .80 .25
OA17 A43 1b black .80 .25
OA18 A43 3b yel org ('25) 2.75 1.50
OA19 A43 5b dull vio ('25) 6.25 3.00
Nos. OA9-OA19 (11) 17.40 8.00

On Nos. 269c-282a

OA9a A43 5c orange brn 2.00 .40
OA10a A43 10c dk green 2.00 .40
OA11a A43 15c olive grn 1.50 .40
OA13a A43 25c ultramarine 1.75 .75
OA16a A43 50c dk blue 3.00 1.50
OA17a A43 1b black 12.50 6.00
Nos. OA9a-OA17a (6) 22.75 9.45

On No. 286

1924

OA18A A44 25c grayish blue 3.50 1.50

1926 On Nos. 287-288

OA19A A45 5c on 1b olive grn 1.25 1.25
OA20 A46 25c on 5c dk brown 1.75 1.75

On Nos. 289

1928

OA21 A47 10c deep grn 3.00 3.00

On Nos. 290-292

1930

OA22 A48 5c yellow 1.20 .85
OA23 A48 10c dark blue 1.25 .85
OA24 A48 25c rose red 2.00 1.00

On Nos. 293-304

1932-38

OA25 A49 5c violet .25 .25
OA26 A49 7½c dk green ('37) .30 .25
OA27 A49 10c green .25 .25
OA28 A49 15c yellow .50 .50
OA29 A49 22½c dp car ('38) .90 1.50
OA30 A49 25c red .50 .50
OA31 A49 37½c ultra ('36) 3.00 4.00
OA32 A49 40c indigo 2.00 .60
OA33 A49 50c olive grn 2.50 1.10
OA34 A49 1b lt blue 3.00 3.00
OA35 A49 3b brown 7.00 9.00
OA36 A49 5b yellow grn 20.00 10.00
Nos. OA25-OA36 (12) 40.20 30.95

On No. 306

1933

OA37 A50 25c brown red 2.00 .75

On Nos. 307-310

1933

OA38 A43 7½c on 10c grn 3.00 1.00
OA39 A43 22½c on 25c (#298) 2.00 .60
OA40 A43 22½c on 25c (#277) 2.00 .60
OA41 A43 37½c on 40c dp bl 2.25 .75
Nos. OA38-OA41 (4) 9.25 2.95

No. OA42

No. OA43

No. OA44

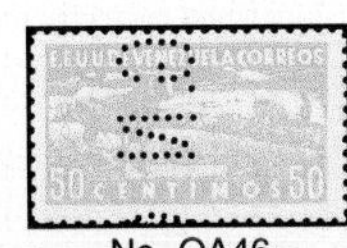

No. OA46

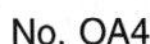

No. OA47

1937 **On Nos. 311-317**

No.	Design	Description	Unused	Used
OA42	A51	5c deep violet	1.25	1.00
OA43	A52	10c dk slate green	1.00	.80
OA44	A53	15c yellow brn	2.00	1.20
OA45	A51	25c cerise	1.25	1.25
OA46	A54	50c yellow grn	12.00	1.50
OA47	A55	3b red orange	21.00	10.00
OA48	A51	5b lt brown	60.00	20.00
		Nos. OA42-OA48 (7)	98.50	35.75

On No. 318

1937

No.	Design	Description	Unused	Used
OA49	A49	25c on 40c indigo	7.75	3.50

On No. 320

No.	Design	Description	Unused	Used
OA50	A56	25c blue	.90	.60

On Nos. 321-324

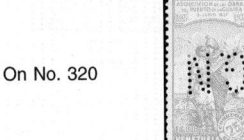

No.	Design	Description	Unused	Used
OA51	A51	5c deep violet	7.50	.40
OA52	A52	10c dk slate grn	2.75	1.20
OA53	A51	25c cerise	1.75	.60
OA54	A55	3b red orange	300.00	125.00
		Nos. OA51-OA54 (4)	312.00	127.20

No. OA55

No. OA57

No. OA59

1938 **On Nos. 325-342**

No.	Design	Description	Unused	Used
OA55	A57	5c green	.30	.25
OA56	A57	5c deep green	.30	.25
OA57	A58	10c car rose	.30	.25
OA58	A58	10c deep rose	.45	.45
OA59	A59	15c dk violet	.45	.25
OA60	A59	15c olive grn	.60	.25
OA61	A58	25c lt blue	.60	.50
OA62	A58	25c dark blue	.75	.50
OA63	A58	37½c dark blue	4.50	2.00
OA64	A58	37½c lt blue	.90	.60
OA65	A59	40c sepia	1.25	1.00
OA66	A59	40c black	5.00	2.50
OA67	A57	50c olive grn	5.50	2.50
OA68	A57	50c dull violet	2.50	1.25
OA69	A58	1b dp brown	4.25	1.50
OA70	A58	1b black brown	3.00	1.50
OA71	A57	3b orange	9.00	4.00
OA72	A59	5b black	8.00	3.00
		Nos. OA55-OA72 (18)	47.65	22.55

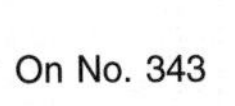

On No. 343

1938

No.	Design	Description	Unused	Used
OA73	A60	25c blue	4.75	2.00

On No. 344

1938

No.	Design	Description	Unused	Used
OA74	A61	25c dark blue	4.25	2.00

On No. 345

1938

No.	Design	Description	Unused	Used
OA75	A51	40c on 5b lt brn	5.00	3.00

On No. 348

1939

No.	Design	Description	Unused	Used
OA76	A62	10c carmine	2.10	.75

On No. 349

1939

No.	Design	Description	Unused	Used
OA77	A63	25c dull blue	6.00	3.00

On Nos. 350-356

1939

No.	Design	Description	Unused	Used
OA78	A64	5c green	.75	.25
OA79	A64	10c dk car rose	.75	.25
OA80	A64	15c dull lilac	1.50	.75
OA81	A64	25c brt ultra	2.50	.75
OA82	A64	37½c dark blue	15.00	6.25
OA83	A64	50c lt olive grn	15.00	6.25
OA84	A64	1b dark brown	10.00	7.50
		Nos. OA78-OA84 (7)	45.50	22.00

On Nos. 357-363

1940-43

No.	Design	Description	Unused	Used
OA85	A65	5c Prussian grn	.50	.25
OA86	A65	7½c dk bl grn ('43)	1.50	1.50
OA87	A65	15c olive	.80	.50
OA88	A65	37½c deep blue	3.00	2.00
OA89	A65	40c violet blue	1.75	1.00
OA90	A65	50c violet	3.50	1.75
OA91	A65	1b dk violet brn	3.50	1.00
OA92	A65	3b scarlet	9.50	3.50
		Nos. OA85-OA92 (8)	24.05	11.50

On No. 365

1940

No.	Design	Description	Unused	Used
OA93	A67	25c blue	4.75	1.25

On No. 366

1940

No.	Design	Description	Unused	Used
OA94	A68	25c dark blue	4.75	1.50

1940-41 **On Nos. 367-374**

No.	Design	Description	Unused	Used
OA95	A69	5c turq green	.60	.25
OA96	A70	10c rose pink	.90	.25
OA97	A69	15c olive	.60	.25
OA98	A70	20c blue ('41)	.60	.25
OA99	A69	25c lt blue	.90	.25
OA100	A70	30c plum ('41)	5.00	.25
OA101	A70	37½c dark blue	6.00	2.00
OA102	A70	50c purple	3.00	1.25
		Nos. OA95-OA102 (8)	17.60	4.75

On No. 375

1941

No.	Design	Description	Unused	Used
OA103	A69	20c on 25c lt blue	2.40	1.00

On Nos. 376-377

1941

No.	Design	Description	Unused	Used
OA104	A51	5c deep violet	3.00	1.50
OA105	A52	10c dk slate grn	3.00	1.50

On No. 378

1942

No.	Design	Description	Unused	Used
OA106	A77	10c scarlet	1.25	.50

Semi-Postal Stamp

On No. B1

1942

No.	Design	Description	Unused	Used
OAB1	SP1	20c + 5c blue	7.25	2.00

Air Post Stamps

On Nos. C1-C16

1930

No.	Design	Description	Unused	Used
OAC1	AP1	5c bister brn	.30	.25
OAC2	AP1	10c yellow	.30	.25
OAC3	AP1	15c gray	.30	.25
OAC4	AP1	25c lilac	.30	.25
OAC5	AP1	40c olive grn	.30	.25
OAC6	AP1	75c dp red	.30	.25
OAC7	AP1	1b indigo	.30	.25
OAC8	AP1	1.20b blue grn	.60	.35
OAC9	AP1	1.70b dk blue	.60	.60
OAC10	AP1	1.90b blue grn	.60	.60
OAC11	AP1	2.10b dk blue	.60	.60
OAC12	AP1	2.30b vermilion	.60	.60
OAC13	AP1	2.50b dk blue	.60	.60
OAC14	AP1	3.70b blue grn	3.00	3.00
OAC15	AP1	10b dull vio	8.00	8.00
OAC16	AP1	20b gray grn	12.00	12.00
		Nos. OAC1-OAC16 (16)	28.70	28.10

On Nos. C17-C40

1932

No.	Design	Description	Unused	Used
OAC17	AP2	5c brown	.30	.25
OAC18	AP2	10c org yel	.30	.25
OAC19	AP2	15c gray lilac	.30	.25
OAC20	AP2	25c violet	.40	.25
OAC21	AP2	40c ol grn	.40	.25
OAC22	AP2	70c rose	.40	.25
OAC23	AP2	75c red org	.60	.30
OAC24	AP2	1b dk blue	1.10	.30
OAC25	AP2	1.20b green	1.50	.60
OAC26	AP2	1.70b red brn	1.60	.40
OAC27	AP2	1.80b ultra	4.00	.40
OAC28	AP2	1.90b green	3.00	1.25
OAC29	AP2	1.95b blue	2.75	2.00
OAC30	AP2	2b blk brn	2.75	1.00
OAC31	AP2	2.10b blue	4.75	2.00
OAC32	AP2	2.30b red	2.75	1.50
OAC33	AP2	2.50b dk blue	2.75	1.50
OAC34	AP2	3b dk violet	3.00	1.25
OAC35	AP2	3.70b emerald	5.00	2.50
OAC36	AP2	4b red org	5.50	1.40
OAC37	AP2	5b black	3.75	1.25
OAC38	AP2	8b dk carmine	9.00	3.00
OAC39	AP2	10b dk violet	12.00	5.00
OAC40	AP2	20b grnsh slate	40.00	15.00
		Nos. OAC17-OAC40 (24)	107.90	42.15

On Nos. C41-C46

1937

No.	Design	Description	Unused	Used
OAC41	AP2	5c on 1.70b red brn	25.00	15.00
OAC42	AP2	10c on 3.70b emer	13.00	9.50
OAC43	AP2	15c on 4b red org	9.00	7.00
OAC44	AP2	25c on 5b black	9.00	7.00
OAC45	AP2	1b on 8b dk car	9.00	7.00
OAC46	AP2	2b on 2.10b bl	65.00	40.00
		Nos. OAC41-OAC46 (6)	130.00	85.50

No. OAC47

No. OAC48

No. OAC49

No. OAC50

1937 **On Nos. C47-C63**

No.	Design	Description	Unused	Used
OAC47	AP3	5c brn org	.50	.30
OAC48	AP4	10c org red	.60	.30
OAC49	AP5	15c gray blk	.60	.30
OAC50	AP6	25c dk violet	.60	.30
OAC51	AP4	40c yel grn	.90	.50
OAC52	AP5	70c red	.60	.50
OAC53	AP5	75c bister	2.50	1.50
OAC54	AP3	1b dk gray	.60	.25
OAC55	AP4	1.20b peacock grn	2.40	1.25
OAC56	AP3	1.80b dk ultra	1.75	1.25

No.	Design	Description	Unused	Used
OAC57	AP5	1.95b lt ultra	2.50	2.50
OAC58	AP6	2b chocolate	3.00	2.00
OAC59	AP6	2.50b gray bl	15.00	7.50
OAC60	AP4	3b lt violet	12.50	10.00
OAC61	AP6	3.70b rose red	9.00	9.00
OAC62	AP5	10b red violet	12.50	10.00
OAC63	AP5	20b gray	20.00	10.00
		Nos. OAC47-OAC63 (17)	85.55	57.45

On Nos. C64-C65

1937

No.	Design	Description	Unused	Used
OAC64	AP7	70c emerald	1.75	1.50
OAC65	AP7	1.80b ultra	2.40	2.40

On Nos. C66-C78

1937

No.	Design	Description	Unused	Used
OAC66	AP4	10c org red	2.00	1.50
OAC67	AP6	25c dk vio	3.00	2.50
OAC68	AP4	40c yel grn	3.25	2.75
OAC69	AP3	70c red	2.50	2.50
OAC70	AP3	1b dk gray	4.00	2.75
OAC71	AP4	1.20b pck grn	30.00	20.00
OAC72	AP3	1.80b dk ultra	7.50	2.40
OAC73	AP5	1.95b lt ultra	12.00	10.00
OAC74	AP6	2b chocolate	80.00	30.00
OAC75	AP6	2.50b gray bl	80.00	25.00
OAC76	AP4	3b lt vio	100.00	30.00
OAC77	AP5	10b red vio	200.00	90.00
OAC78	AP3	20b gray	325.00	150.00
		Nos. OAC66-OAC78 (13)	849.25	369.40

No. OAC80

No. OAC82

No. OAC84

1938-39 On Nos. C79-C113

No.	Design	Description	Unused	Used
OAC79	AP8	5c green	.75	.50
OAC80	AP8	5c dk grn	.75	.50
OAC81	AP9	10c car rose	.75	.60
OAC82	AP9	10c scarlet	.75	.25
OAC83	AP8	12½c dull vio	.75	.30
OAC84	AP10	15c slate vio	.75	.30
OAC85	AP10	15c dk blue	2.00	2.00
OAC86	AP8	25c dk blue	.75	.30
OAC87	AP8	25c bis brn	.75	.35
OAC88	AP10	30c vio ('39)	.75	.30
OAC89	AP9	40c dk violet	.75	.30
OAC90	AP9	40c redsh brn	2.10	1.50
OAC91	AP8	45c Prus grn ('39)	.75	.30
OAC92	AP9	50c blue ('39)	.75	.30
OAC93	AP10	70c car rose	.75	.40
OAC94	AP8	75c bis brn	1.50	1.25
OAC95	AP8	75c ol bis	1.25	.50
OAC96	AP10	90c red org ('39)	1.50	.70
OAC97	AP9	1b ol & bis	2.40	.70
OAC98	AP9	1b dk vio	1.50	.70
OAC99	AP10	1.20b orange	7.50	3.00
OAC100	AP10	1.20b green	1.50	.80
OAC101	AP8	1.80b ultra	1.50	.80
OAC102	AP9	1.90b black	2.40	1.50
OAC103	AP10	1.95b lt blue	3.00	1.50
OAC104	AP8	2b ol gray	20.00	4.50
OAC105	AP8	2b car rose	2.40	1.50
OAC106	AP9	2.50b red brn	20.00	6.50
OAC107	AP9	2.50b orange	3.00	1.50
OAC108	AP10	3b bl grn	30.00	6.00
OAC109	AP10	3b ol gray	4.00	2.50
OAC110	AP8	3.70b gray blk	10.00	4.00
OAC111	AP10	5b red brn ('39)	9.00	5.00
OAC112	AP9	10b vio brn	21.00	8.00
OAC113	AP10	20b red org	90.00	45.00
		Nos. OAC79-OAC113 (35)	247.30	104.15

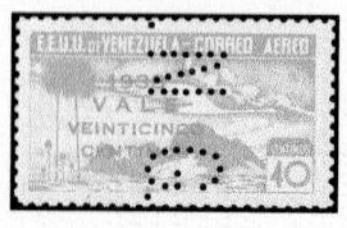

On Nos. C114-C118

1938

No.	Design	Description	Unused	Used
OAC114	AP3	5c on 1.80b	2.50	2.50
OAC115	AP6	10c on 2.50b	3.50	2.50
OAC116	AP6	15c on 2b	2.50	2.50
OAC117	AP4	25c on 40c	3.00	3.00
OAC118	AP6	40c on 3.70b	3.50	3.50
		Nos. OAC114-OAC118 (5)	15.00	14.00

1938-39 On Nos. C119-C126

No.	Design	Description	Unused	Used
OAC119	AP1	5c dk grn ('39)	.90	.30
OAC120	AP1	10c org yel ('39)	.90	.50
OAC121	AP1	12½c rose vio ('39)	.60	.30
OAC122	AP1	15c dp blue	.60	.30
OAC123	AP1	25c brown	.60	.30
OAC124	AP1	40c olive ('39)	3.50	1.00
OAC125	AP1	70c rose car ('39)	20.00	10.00
OAC126	AP1	1b rose car ('39)	7.75	3.50
		Nos. OAC119-OAC126 (8)	34.85	16.20

No. OAC127

No. OAC128

No. OAC129

1938 On Nos. C127-C135

No.	Design	Description	Unused	Used
OAC127	AP11	20c brn blk	.40	.30
OAC128	AP12	30c purple	2.50	2.00
OAC129	AP13	45c dk bl	.60	.50
OAC130	AP11	50c lt ultra	1.50	.30
OAC131	AP13	70c dk car	30.00	10.00
OAC132	AP12	90c red org	1.25	.50
OAC133	AP13	1.35b gray blk	2.10	.60
OAC134	AP11	1.40b slate gray	10.00	3.50
OAC135	AP12	2.25b green	6.00	2.50
		Nos. OAC127-OAC135 (9)	54.35	20.20

On Nos. C136-C141

1940

No.	Design	Description	Unused	Used
OAC136	AP14	15c blue	2.00	.60
OAC137	AP14	20c olive bis	2.00	.30
OAC138	AP14	25c red brn	3.50	.30
OAC139	AP14	40c blk brn	2.50	.30
OAC140	AP14	1b red lilac	5.00	1.75
OAC141	AP14	2b rose carmine	9.00	2.50
		Nos. OAC136-OAC141 (6)	24.00	5.75

On No. C142

1940

No.	Design	Description	Unused	Used
OAC142	AP15	15c copper brn	1.25	.50

On Nos. C143//C161

1940-43

No.	Design	Description	Unused	Used
OAC143	AP16	5c dk grn ('42)	.50	.25
OAC144	AP16	10c scarlet ('42)	.50	.25
OAC145	AP16	12½c dull pur	2.00	1.50
OAC146	AP16	15c blue ('43)	3.00	.60
OAC147	AP16	25c bis brn ('42)	2.00	.60
OAC148	AP16	40c blk brn ('43)	2.00	.60
OAC149	AP16	70c rose pink	1.75	.60
OAC150	AP16	75c ol bis ('43)	5.00	.60
OAC151	AP16	1b dp red lil ('42)	4.50	2.25
OAC152	AP16	1.35b gray blk ('42)	7.50	3.50
OAC153	AP16	3b ol blk ('43)	12.00	6.00
OAC154	AP16	4b black	13.00	6.00
		Nos. OAC143-OAC154 (12)	53.75	22.75

Air Post Semi-Official Stamps

On Nos. CB1-CB2

1942

No.	Design	Description	Unused	Used
OACB1	SPAP1	15c + 10c org brn	3.00	1.50
OACB2	SPAP1	30c + 5c violet	3.00	1.50

LOCAL STAMPS FOR THE PORT OF CARUPANO

In 1902 Great Britain, Germany and Italy, seeking compensation for revolutionary damages, established a blockade of La Guaira and seized the custom house. Carúpano, a port near Trinidad, was isolated and issued the following provisionals. A treaty effected May 7, 1903, referred the dispute to the Hague Tribunal.

A1

A2

1902 Typeset *Imperf.*

No.	Design	Description	Unused	Used
1	A1	5c purple, *orange*	27.00	
2	A2	10c black, *orange*	40.00	40.00
a.		Tête bêche pair	82.50	
3	A1	25c purple, *green*	32.50	32.50
4	A1	50c green, *yellow*	85.00	
5	A1	1b blue, *rose*	120.00	120.00
		Nos. 1-5 (5)	304.50	

A3

1902

No.	Design	Description	Unused	Used
6	A3	1b black, *yellow*	200.00	200.00
a.		Tête bêche pair		

A4

1903 Handstamped

No.	Design	Description	Unused	Used
7	A4	5c carmine, *yellow*	45.00	45.00
8	A4	10c green, *yellow*	92.50	92.50
9	A4	25c green, *orange*	45.00	45.00
10	A4	50c blue, *rose*	45.00	45.00
11	A4	1b violet, *gray*	45.00	45.00
12	A4	2b carmine, *green*	45.00	45.00
13	A4	5b violet, *blue*	45.00	45.00
		Nos. 7-13 (7)	362.50	362.50

Dangerous counterfeits exist of Nos. 1-13.

LOCAL STAMPS FOR THE STATE OF GUAYANA

Revolutionary Steamship "Banrigh" — A1

Control Mark

Control Mark on Block of 4

1903 Typo. *Perf. 12*

No.	Design	Description	Unused	Used
1	A1	5c black, *gray*	19.00	19.00
2	A1	10c black, *orange*	47.50	47.50
3	A1	25c black, *pink*	19.00	19.00
4	A1	50c black, *blue*	30.00	30.00
5	A1	1b black, *straw*	25.00	25.00
		Nos. 1-5 (5)	140.50	140.50

Nos. 1-5 can be found with or without the illustrated control mark which covers four stamps.

Counterfeits include the 10c and 50c in red and are from different settings from the originals. They are on papers differing in colors from the originals. All 5c on granite paper are bogus.

Coat of Arms — A2

1903

No.	Design	Description	Unused	Used
11	A2	5c black, *pink*	40.00	40.00
12	A2	10c black, *orange*	50.00	
13	A2	25c black, *gray blue*	40.00	40.00
a.		25c black, *blue*	40.00	
14	A2	50c black, *straw*	40.00	
15	A2	1b black, *gray*	30.00	30.00
		Nos. 11-15 (5)	200.00	

Postally used examples are very scarce, as are examples having 9 ornaments in horizontal borders. Nos. 11-15 pen canceled sell for same values as unused.

See note on controls after No. 5.

Counterfeits exist of Nos. 11-15. Stamps with 10 ornaments in horizontal borders are counterfeits.

Nos. 1-5, 11-15 were issued by a group of revolutionists and had a limited local use. The dates on the stamps commemorate the declaration of Venezuelan independence and a compact with Spain against Joseph Bonaparte.

VIET NAM

vē-'et-'näm

LOCATION — In eastern Indo-China
GOVT. — Kingdom
AREA — 123,949 sq. mi.
POP. — 77,311,210 (1999 est.)
CAPITAL — Hanoi

Viet Nam, which included the former French territories of Tonkin, Annam and Cochin China, became an Associated State of the French Union in 1949. The Communist Viet Minh obtained control of Northern Viet Nam in 1954, and the republic of South Viet Nam was established in October, 1955.

100 Cents (Xu) = 1 Piaster (Dong)

Catalogue values for unused stamps in this country are for Never Hinged items, beginning with Scott 27 in the regular postage section, Scott B2 in the semi-postal section, Scott C1 in the air-post section, Scott J1 in the postage due section, and Scott M1 in the military section.

Bongour Falls, Dalat A1

Emperor Bao-Dai A2

Designs: 20c, 2pi, 10pi, Imperial palace, Hué. 30c, 15pi, Lake, Hanoi. 50c, 1pi, Temple, Saigon.

Perf. 13x13½, 13½x13
Unwmk.

1951, June 6-Oct. 23 Photo.

1	A1	10c olive green	.25	.25
2	A1	20c deep plum	.50	.25
3	A1	30c blue	.50	.40
4	A1	50c red	1.00	.25
5	A1	60c brown	.50	.25
6	A1	1pi chestnut brn	.50	.25
7	A2	1.20pi yellow brn	3.50	2.00
8	A1	2pi purple	1.00	.25
9	A2	3pi dull blue	3.50	.25
10	A1	5pi green	2.75	.30
11	A1	10pi crimson	6.50	.35
12	A1	15pi red brown	22.50	2.50
13	A2	30pi blue green	50.00	3.00
		Nos. 1-13 (13)	93.00	10.30
		Set, never hinged	175.00	

Souvenir booklets exist comprising five gummed sheets of 1 containing Nos. 1, 2, 6, 9, 12, together with commemorative inscriptions. Value, $125.

Empress Nam-Phuong — A3

1952, Aug. 15 *Perf. 12½*

14	A3	30c dk pur, yel & brn	.60	.35
15	A3	50c blue, yel & brn	.80	.45
16	A3	1.50pi ol grn, yel & brn	1.75	.30
		Nos. 14-16 (3)	3.15	1.10
		Set, never hinged	6.00	

For surcharge see No. B1.

Globe and Lightning Bolt — A4

1952, Aug. 24 Engr. *Perf. 13*

17	A4	1pi greenish blue	2.00	1.25
		Never hinged	6.00	

Viet Nam's admission to the ITU, 1st anniv.

Coastal Scene and UPU Emblem — A5

1952, Sept. 12

18	A5	5pi red brown	1.75	1.50
		Never hinged	3.50	

Viet Nam's admission to the UPU, 1st anniv.

Bao-Dai and Pagoda of Literature, Hanoi — A6

1952, Nov. 10 *Perf. 12*

19	A6	1.50pi rose violet	1.75	1.25
		Never hinged	3.50	

39th birthday of Emperor Bao-Dai.

Crown Prince Bao-Long in Annamite Costume — A7

70c, 80c, 100pi, Prince in Annamite costume. 90c, 20pi, 50pi, Prince in Western uniform.

1954, June 15 *Perf. 13*

20	A7	40c aqua	.25	.40
21	A7	70c claret	.25	.40
22	A7	80c black brown	.25	*.40*
23	A7	90c dark green	.40	*1.25*
24	A7	20pi rose pink	1.25	*2.25*
25	A7	50pi violet	4.00	*7.00*
26	A7	100pi blue violet	6.00	*17.50*
		Nos. 20-26 (7)	12.40	*29.20*
		Set, never hinged, brown gum	25.00	
		Set, never hinged, white gum	40.00	

REPUBLIC OF VIET NAM

(South Viet Nam)

(Viet Nam Cong Hoa)

GOVT. — Republic
AREA — 66,280 sq. mi.
POP. — 19,600,000 (est. 1973)
CAPITAL — Saigon

Catalogue values for unused stamps in this section, from this point to the end of the section, are for Never Hinged items. Because of the tropical conditions, never hinged stamps must also be free of wrinkles, toning, and any other disturbance.

Mythological Turtle — A8

Unwmk.

1955, July 20 Engr. *Perf. 13*

27	A8	30c claret	1.25	.50
28	A8	50c dark green	3.75	1.75
29	A8	1.50pi bright blue	3.00	1.25
		Nos. 27-29 (3)	8.00	3.50

Refugees on Raft — A9

1955, Oct. 11

30	A9	70c crimson rose	1.00	1.00
31	A9	80c brown violet	3.00	3.00
32	A9	10pi indigo	5.50	5.50
33	A9	20pi vio, red brn & org	16.00	16.00
34	A9	35pi dk bl, blk brn & yel	25.00	25.00
35	A9	100pi dk grn, brn vio & org	65.00	65.00
		Nos. 30-35 (6)	115.50	115.50

1st anniv. of the flight of the North Vietnamese.

No. 34 is inscribed "Chiên-Dich-Huynh-Dê" (Operation Brotherhood) below design. See No. 54.

Post Office, Saigon — A10

1956, Jan. 10 *Perf. 12*

36	A10	60c bluish green	1.25	1.00
37	A10	90c violet	2.25	1.25
38	A10	3pi red brown	4.50	2.50
		Nos. 36-38 (3)	8.00	4.75

5th anniv. of independent postal service.
For overprints see Nos. 51-53.

Pres. Ngo Dinh Diem — A11

1956 Engr. *Perf. 13x13½*

39	A11	20c orange ver	.40	.25
40	A11	30c rose lilac	.75	.40
41	A11	50c brt carmine	.40	.40
42	A11	1pi violet	.75	.40
43	A11	1.50pi violet	1.10	.50
44	A11	3pi black brown	1.90	.60
45	A11	4pi dark blue	2.60	.70
46	A11	5pi red brown	3.00	.75
47	A11	10pi blue	3.75	1.25
48	A11	20pi gray black	7.50	2.25
49	A11	35pi green	18.00	4.00
50	A11	100pi brown	37.50	19.00
		Nos. 39-50 (12)	77.65	30.50

Nos. 36-38 Overprinted

1956, Aug. 6 *Perf. 12*

51	A10	60c bluish green	1.20	.60
52	A10	90c violet	2.00	.60
53	A10	3pi red brown	2.60	.90
		Nos. 51-53 (3)	5.80	2.10

The overprint reads: "Government Post Office Building."

No. 34 Overprinted

1956, Aug. 6

54	A9	35pi dk bl, blk brn & yel	9.00	6.00

Bamboo — A12

1956, Oct. 26 Litho. *Perf. 13x13½*

55	A12	50c scarlet	1.10	1.10
56	A12	1.50pi rose violet	1.10	1.10
57	A12	2pi brt green	1.50	1.50
58	A12	4pi deep blue	3.00	3.00
		Nos. 55-58 (4)	6.70	6.70

1st anniv. of the Republic.

Children — A13

1956, Nov. 7 Engr. *Perf. 13½x14*

59	A13	1pi lilac rose	.60	.40
60	A13	2pi blue green	.85	.40
61	A13	6pi purple	1.25	.40
62	A13	35pi violet blue	8.50	2.75
		Nos. 59-62 (4)	11.20	3.95

"Operation Brotherhood."

Hunters on Elephants — A14

Design: 90c, 2pi, 3pi, Mountain dwelling.

1957, July 7 Photo. *Perf. 13*

63	A14	20c yellow grn & pur	.75	.45
64	A14	30c bister & dp mag	.80	.55
65	A14	90c yel grn & dk brn	1.00	.65
66	A14	2pi green & ultra	1.75	.70
67	A14	3pi blue vio & brn	2.25	.80
		Nos. 63-67 (5)	6.55	3.15

Loading Cargo — A15

1957, Oct. 21 *Perf. 13½x13*

68	A15	20c rose violet	.25	.25
69	A15	40c lt olive grn	.30	.25
70	A15	50c lt carmine rose	.40	.40
71	A15	2pi ultra	1.10	.45
72	A15	3pi brt green	1.40	.55
		Nos. 68-72 (5)	3.45	1.90

9th Colombo Plan Conference, Saigon.

Torch, Map and Constitution — A16

1957, Oct. 26 Litho. *Perf. 13x13½*

73	A16	50c black, green & sal	.25	.25
74	A16	80c black, brt bl & mag	.30	.25
75	A16	1pi black, bl grn & brt car	.40	.40
76	A16	4pi blk, ol grn & fawn	.75	.45
77	A16	5pi blk, grnsh bl & cit	.75	.55
78	A16	10pi black, ultra & rose	1.50	.75
		Nos. 73-78 (6)	3.95	2.65

Republic of South Viet Nam, 2nd anniv.

Farmers, Tractor and Village — A17

1958, July 7 Engr. *Perf. 13½*

79	A17	50c yellow green	.35	.25
80	A17	1pi deep violet	.40	.25
81	A17	2pi ultra	.85	.45
82	A17	10pi brick red	2.25	.75
		Nos. 79-82 (4)	3.85	1.70

4th anniv. of the government of Ngo Dinh Diem.

Girl and Lantern — A18

1958, Sept. 27

No.	Type	Description	Unused	Used
83	A18	30c yellow	.30	.25
84	A18	50c dk carmine rose	.40	.25
85	A18	2pi dp carmine	.60	.40
86	A18	3pi blue green	1.00	.45
87	A18	4pi lt olive green	1.25	.50
		Nos. 83-87 (5)	3.55	1.85

Children's Festival.

A19

1958, Oct. 26 ***Perf. 13½***

No.	Type	Description	Unused	Used
88	A19	1pi dull red brown	.40	.25
89	A19	2pi bluish green	.75	.25
90	A19	4pi rose carmine	1.00	.45
91	A19	5pi rose lilac	1.50	.75
		Nos. 88-91 (4)	3.65	1.70

Issued for United Nations Day.

> Most South Viet Nam stamps from 1958 onward exist imperforate in issued and trial colors, and also in small presentation sheets in issued colors.

UNESCO Building, Paris — A20

1958, Nov. 3 ***Perf. 12½x13***

No.	Type	Description	Unused	Used
92	A20	50c ultra	.35	.25
93	A20	2pi bright red	.65	.25
94	A20	3pi lilac rose	.75	.40
95	A20	6pi violet	1.00	.60
		Nos. 92-95 (4)	2.75	1.50

UNESCO Headquarters in Paris opening, 11/3.

Torch and UN Emblem — A21

1958, Dec. 10 **Engr.** ***Perf. 13½***

No.	Type	Description	Unused	Used
96	A21	50c dark blue	.35	.25
97	A21	1pi brown carmine	.55	.25
98	A21	2pi yellow green	.80	.40
99	A21	6pi rose violet	1.25	.60
		Nos. 96-99 (4)	2.95	1.50

Signing of the Universal Declaration of Human Rights, 10th anniv.

Cathedral of Hué — A22

Thien Mu Pagoda, Hué — A23

National Museum — A24

50c, 2pi, Palace of Independence, Saigon.

1958-59 ***Perf. 13½***

No.	Type	Description	Unused	Used
100	A22	10c dk blue gray	.25	.40
101	A23	30c green ('59)	.40	.75
102	A24	40c dk green ('59)	.70	.65
103	A24	50c green ('59)	.80	.80
104	A24	2pi grnsh blue ('59)	2.00	1.75
105	A23	4pi dull purple ('59)	2.50	2.00
106	A24	5pi dk carmine ('59)	2.75	2.00
107	A22	6pi orange brown	3.25	2.00
		Nos. 100-107 (8)	12.65	10.35

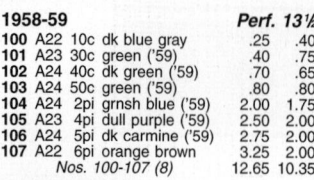

Trung Sisters on Elephants — A25

1959, Mar. 14 **Photo.** ***Perf. 13***

No.	Type	Description	Unused	Used
108	A25	50c multicolored	1.50	.75
109	A25	2pi ocher, grn & bl	2.25	1.20
110	A25	3pi emerald, vio & bis	2.75	1.50
111	A25	6pi multicolored	5.50	2.25
		Nos. 108-111 (4)	12.00	5.70

Sisters Trung Trac and Trung Nhi who resisted a Chinese invasion in 40-44 A.D.

Symbols of Agrarian Reforms — A26

1959, July 7 **Engr.** ***Perf. 13***

No.	Type	Description	Unused	Used
112	A26	70c lilac rose	.35	.25
113	A26	2pi dk grn & Prus bl	.50	.25
114	A26	3pi olive	.90	.35
115	A26	6pi dark red & red	1.75	1.10
		Nos. 112-115 (4)	3.50	1.95

5th anniv. of Ngo Dinh Diem's presidency.

Diesel Engine and Map of North and South Viet Nam — A27

1959, Aug. 7

No.	Type	Description	Unused	Used
116	A27	1pi lt violet & grn	.75	.75
117	A27	2pi gray & green	1.40	1.10
118	A27	3pi grnsh bl & grn	2.10	1.50
119	A27	4pi maroon & grn	3.00	2.25
		Nos. 116-119 (4)	7.25	5.60

Re-opening of the Saigon-Dongha Railroad.

Volunteer Road Workers — A28

1959, Oct. 26

No.	Type	Description	Unused	Used
120	A28	1pi org brn, ultra & grn	.70	.30
121	A28	2pi violet, org & grn	1.10	.45
122	A28	4pi dk bl, bl & bis	2.10	.50
123	A28	5pi bister, brn & ocher	2.60	.85
		Nos. 120-123 (4)	6.50	2.10

4th anniv. of the constitution, stressing communal development.

Boy Scout — A29

1959, Dec. **Engr.** ***Perf. 13***

No.	Type	Description	Unused	Used
124	A29	3pi brt yellow grn	.60	.25
125	A29	4pi deep lilac rose	1.25	.30
126	A29	8pi dk brn & lil rose	2.10	.65
127	A29	20pi Prus bl & bl grn	3.75	1.10
		Nos. 124-127 (4)	7.70	2.30

National Boy Scout Jamboree.

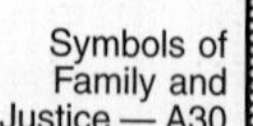

Symbols of Family and Justice — A30

1960

No.	Type	Description	Unused	Used
128	A30	20c emerald	.80	.80
129	A30	30c brt grnsh blue	.85	.85
130	A30	2pi orange & maroon	1.60	1.60
131	A30	6pi car & rose vio	1.75	1.75
		Nos. 128-131 (4)	5.00	5.00

Issued to commemorate the family code.

Refugee Family and WRY Emblem — A31

1960, Apr. 7 **Engr.** ***Perf. 13***

No.	Type	Description	Unused	Used
132	A31	50c brt lilac rose	.45	.25
133	A31	3pi brt green	.55	.30
134	A31	4pi scarlet	.65	.40
135	A31	5pi dp violet blue	.80	.60
		Nos. 132-135 (4)	2.45	1.55

World Refugee Year, 7/1/59-6/30/60.

Henri Dunant — A32

1960, May 8 **Cross in Carmine**

No.	Type	Description	Unused	Used
136	A32	1pi dark blue	.45	.30
137	A32	3pi green	1.40	.35
138	A32	4pi crimson rose	1.90	.50
139	A32	6pi dp lilac rose	2.25	.65
		Nos. 136-139 (4)	6.00	1.80

Centenary (in 1959) of the Red Cross idea.

Model Farm — A33

1960, July 7 ***Perf. 13***

No.	Type	Description	Unused	Used
140	A33	50c ultra	.50	.25
141	A33	1pi dark green	.60	.30
142	A33	3pi orange	1.00	.35
143	A33	7pi bright pink	1.60	.65
		Nos. 140-143 (4)	3.70	1.55

Establishment of communal rice farming.

Girl With Basket of Rice and Rice Plant — A34

1960, Nov. 21

No.	Type	Description	Unused	Used
144	A34	2pi emerald & green	.80	.40
145	A34	4pi blue & ultra	1.20	.60

Conf. of the UN FAO, Saigon, Nov. 1960.

Map and Flag of Viet Nam — A35

1960, Oct. 26 **Engr.** ***Perf. 13***

No.	Type	Description	Unused	Used
146	A35	50c grnsh bl, car & yel	.45	.25
147	A35	1pi ultra, car & yel	.55	.30
148	A35	3pi purple, car & yel	.95	.40
149	A35	7pi yel grn, car & yel	1.60	.60
		Nos. 146-149 (4)	3.55	1.55

Fifth anniversary of the Republic.

Agricultural Development Center, Tractor and Plow — A36

1961, Jan. 3 ***Perf. 13***

No.	Type	Description	Unused	Used
150	A36	50c red brown	.40	.25
151	A36	70c rose lilac	.55	.30
152	A36	80c rose red	.65	.40
153	A36	10pi bright pink	4.00	1.00
		Nos. 150-153 (4)	5.60	1.95

Plant and Child — A37

1961, Mar. 23 ***Perf. 13***

No.	Type	Description	Unused	Used
154	A37	70c light blue	.45	.25
155	A37	80c ultra	.60	.30
156	A37	4pi olive bister	.70	.45
157	A37	7pi grnsh bl & yel grn	1.25	.70
		Nos. 154-157 (4)	3.00	1.70

Child protection.

Pres. Ngo Dinh Diem — A38

1961, Apr. 29 ***Perf. 13***

No.	Type	Description	Unused	Used
158	A38	50c brt ultra	.80	.50
159	A38	1pi red	1.40	.90
160	A38	2pi lilac rose	1.50	1.10
161	A38	4pi brt violet	2.40	1.75
		Nos. 158-161 (4)	6.10	4.25

Second term of Pres. Ngo Dinh Diem.

Boy, Girl and Flaming Torch — A39

1961, July 7 **Engr.** ***Perf. 13***

No.	Type	Description	Unused	Used
162	A39	50c red	.35	.25
163	A39	70c bright pink	.35	.30
164	A39	80c ver & maroon	.45	.40
165	A39	8pi dp claret & mag	1.40	.75
		Nos. 162-165 (4)	2.55	1.70

Issued for Youth Day.

Saigon-Bien Hoa Highway Bridge — A40

1961, July 28

No.	Type	Description	Unused	Used
166	A40	50c yellow green	.45	.25
167	A40	1pi orange brown	.65	.30
168	A40	2pi dark blue	.75	.40
169	A40	5pi brt red lilac	1.75	.45
		Nos. 166-169 (4)	3.60	1.40

Opening of Saigon-Bien Hoa Highway.

Alexandre de Rhodes — A41

1961, Sept. 5

No.	Type	Description	Unused	Used
170	A41	50c rose carmine	.30	.25
171	A41	1pi claret	.40	.30
172	A41	3pi bister brown	.45	.40
173	A41	6pi emerald	1.25	.65
		Nos. 170-173 (4)	2.40	1.60

Alexandre de Rhodes (1591-1660), Jesuit missionary who introduced Roman characters to express the Viet Nam language.

Young Man with Torch, Sage, Pagoda — A42

1961, Oct. 26 ***Perf. 13***

No.	Type	Description	Unused	Used
174	A42	50c orange ver	.40	.25
175	A42	1pi brt green	.55	.30
176	A42	3pi rose red	.80	.40
177	A42	8pi rose lilac & brn	1.90	.75
		Nos. 174-177 (4)	3.65	1.70

Moral Rearmament of Youth Movement.

Temple Dedicated to Confucius — A43

1961, Nov. 4 **Engr.**

178	A43	1pi brt green	.50	.25
179	A43	2pi rose red	.75	.30
180	A43	5pi olive	1.90	.50
		Nos. 178-180 (3)	3.15	1.05

15th anniversary of UNESCO.

Earth Scraper Preparing Ground for Model Village — A44

1961, Dec. 11 ***Perf. 13***

181	A44	50c dark green	.80	.25
182	A44	1pi Prus bl & car lake	.90	.30
183	A44	2pi olive grn & brn	1.20	.40
184	A44	10pi Prus blue	4.25	.65
		Nos. 181-184 (4)	7.15	1.60

Agrarian reform program.

Man Fighting Mosquito and Emblem — A45

1962, Apr. 7 ***Perf. 13***

185	A45	50c brt lilac rose	.45	.25
186	A45	1pi orange	.45	.30
187	A45	2pi emerald	.60	.40
188	A45	6pi ultra	1.50	.65
		Nos. 185-188 (4)	3.00	1.60

WHO drive to eradicate malaria.

Postal Check Center, Saigon — A46

1962, May 15 **Engr.** ***Perf. 13***

189	A46	70c dull green	.30	.25
190	A46	80c chocolate	.35	.30
191	A46	4pi lilac rose	.85	.35
192	A46	7pi rose red	2.00	.55
		Nos. 189-192 (4)	3.50	1.45

Inauguration of postal checking service.

Madonna of Vang — A47

1962, July 7

193	A47	50c violet & rose red	.40	.25
194	A47	1pi red brn & indigo	.60	.30
195	A47	2pi brown & rose car	1.00	.40
196	A47	8pi green & dk blue	2.50	.65
		Nos. 193-196 (4)	4.50	1.60

Catholic shrine of the Madonna of Vang.

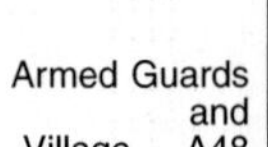

Armed Guards and Village — A48

1962, Oct. 26

197	A48	50c bright red	.35	.25
198	A48	1pi yellow green	.65	.30
199	A48	1.50pi lilac rose	1.00	.40
200	A48	7pi ultra	2.25	.65
		Nos. 197-200 (4)	4.25	1.60

"Strategic village" defense system.

Gougah Waterfall, Dalat — A49

1963, Jan. 3

201	A49	60c orange red	1.25	.30
202	A49	1pi bluish black	1.75	.45

62nd birthday of Pres. Ngo Dinh Diem; Spring Festival.

Trung Sisters' Monument and Vietnamese Women — A50

1963, Mar. 1 **Engr.**

203	A50	50c green	.25	.25
204	A50	1pi dk carmine rose	.40	.30
205	A50	3pi lilac rose	.60	.45
206	A50	8pi violet blue	1.25	.60
		Nos. 203-206 (4)	2.50	1.60

Issued for Women's Day.

Farm Woman with Grain — A51

1963, Mar. 21 ***Perf. 13***

207	A51	50c red	.40	.25
208	A51	1pi dk car rose	.45	.30
209	A51	3pi lilac rose	.65	.45
210	A51	5pi violet	1.00	.65
		Nos. 207-210 (4)	2.50	1.65

FAO "Freedom from Hunger" campaign.

Common Defense Emblem — A52

1963, July 7 **Engr.** ***Perf. 13***

211	A52	30c bister	.50	.25
212	A52	50c lilac rose	.70	.25
213	A52	3pi brt green	.95	.30
214	A52	8pi red	1.50	.65
		Nos. 211-214 (4)	3.65	1.45

Common defense effort. The inscription says: "Personalism-Common Progress."

Emblem — A53

1963, Oct. 26 ***Perf. 13***

215	A53	50c rose red	.35	.25
216	A53	1pi emerald	.50	.30
217	A53	4pi purple	1.00	.40
218	A53	5pi orange	1.75	.60
		Nos. 215-218 (4)	3.60	1.55

The fighting soldiers of the Republic.

Centenary Emblem and Map — A54

1963, Nov. 17 **Engr.**

Cross in Deep Carmine

219	A54	50c Prus blue	.35	.25
220	A54	1pi deep carmine	.70	.30
221	A54	3pi orange yellow	1.60	.40
222	A54	6pi brown	2.25	.65
		Nos. 219-222 (4)	4.90	1.60

Centenary of International Red Cross.

Constitution and Scales — A55

1963, Dec. 10 ***Perf. 13***

223	A55	70c orange	.30	.25
224	A55	1pi brt rose	.45	.30
225	A55	3pi green	.65	.40
226	A55	8pi ocher	1.25	.60
		Nos. 223-226 (4)	2.65	1.55

15th anniv. of the Universal Declaration of Human Rights.

Danhim Hydroelectric Station — A56

1964, Jan. 15 **Engr.**

227	A56	40c rose red	.30	.25
228	A56	1pi bister brown	.45	.30
229	A56	3pi violet blue	.75	.40
230	A56	8pi olive green	1.50	.60
		Nos. 227-230 (4)	3.00	1.55

Inauguration of the Danhim Hydroelectric Station.

Atomic Reactor — A57

1964, Feb. 3 ***Perf. 13***

231	A57	80c olive	.45	.25
232	A57	1.50pi brown orange	.70	.30
233	A57	3pi chocolate	.95	.45
234	A57	7pi brt blue	.90	.75
		Nos. 231-234 (4)	3.00	1.75

Peaceful uses of atomic energy.

Compass Rose, Barograph and UN Emblem — A58

1964, Mar. 23 **Engr.**

235	A58	50c bister	.25	.25
236	A58	1pi vermilion	.25	.25
237	A58	1.50pi rose claret	.50	.40
238	A58	10pi emerald	1.50	.70
		Nos. 235-238 (4)	2.50	1.60

4th World Meteorological Day, Mar. 23.

South Vietnamese Gesturing to North Vietnamese; Map — A59

1964, July 20 ***Perf. 13***

239	A59	30c dk grn, ultra & mar	.95	.25
240	A59	50c dk car rose, yel & blk	1.10	.30
241	A59	1.50pi dk bl, dp org & blk	1.50	.65
		Nos. 239-241 (3)	3.55	1.20

10th anniv. of the Day of National Grief, July 20, 1954, when the nation was divided into South and North Viet Nam.

Hatien Beach — A60

1964, Sept. 7 **Engr.** ***Perf. 13½***

242	A60	20c bright ultra	.35	.25
243	A60	3pi emerald	1.50	.40

Revolutionists and "Nov. 1" — A61

Designs: 80c, Soldier breaking chain. 3pi, Broken chain and date: "1-11 1963," vert.

1964, Nov. 1 **Engr.** ***Perf. 13***

244	A61	50c red lilac & indigo	.40	.25
245	A61	80c violet & red brn	.50	.30
246	A61	3pi dk blue & red	1.10	.70
		Nos. 244-246 (3)	2.00	1.25

Anniv. of November 1963 revolution.

Temple, Saigon — A62

Designs: 1pi, Royal tombs, Hué. 1.50pi, Fishermen and sailboats at Phan-Thiet beach. 3pi, Temple, Gia-Dhin.

1964-66 **Size: 35½x26mm** ***Perf. 13***

247	A62	50c fawn, grn & dl vio	.45	.25
248	A62	1pi olive bis & ind	.70	.30
249	A62	1.50pi ol gray & dk sl grn	.85	.40
250	A62	3pi vio, dk sl grn & cl	1.60	.65
		Nos. 247-250 (4)	3.60	1.60

Coil Stamp

Size: 23x17mm

250A	A62	1pi ol bis & ind ('66)	6.00	3.50

Issue date: Nos. 247-250, Dec. 2, 1964.

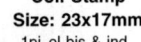

Hung Vuong and Au Co with their Children — A63

1965, Apr. **Engr.** ***Perf. 13***

251	A63	3pi car lake & org red	2.50	.45
252	A63	100pi brown vio & vio	12.00	3.50

Mythological founders of Viet Nam, c. 2000 B.C.

ITU Emblem, Insulator and TV Mast — A64

1965, May 17 **Engr.**

253	A64	1pi olive, dp car & bister	.50	.30
254	A64	3pi henna brn, car & lil	1.50	.45

ITU, centenary.

Buddhist Wheel of Life and Flames — A65

1.50pi, Wheel, lotus blossom and world map, horiz. 3pi, Wheel and Buddhist flag.

Inscribed: "Phat-Giao" (Buddhism)

1965, May 15 ***Perf. 13***

255 A65 50c dark carmine .90 .25
256 A65 1.50pi dk blue & ocher 1.20 .30
257 A65 3pi org brn & dk brn 1.50 .45
Nos. 255-257 (3) 3.60 1.00

Anniversary of Buddha's birth.

ICY Emblem and Women of Various Races — A66

1965, June 26

258 A66 50c bluish blk & bis .50 .25
259 A66 1pi dk brn & brn .75 .30
260 A66 1.50pi dark red & gray 1.25 .45
Nos. 258-260 (3) 2.50 1.00

International Cooperation Year.

Ixora — A67

Flowers: 80c, Orchid. 1pi, Chrysanthemum. 1.50pi, Lotus, horiz. 3pi, Plum blossoms.

1965, Sept. 10 **Engr.** ***Perf. 13***

261 A67 70c grn, slate grn & red .35 .25
262 A67 80c dk brn, lil & sl grn .50 .30
263 A67 1pi dk blue & yellow .65 .40
264 A67 1.50pi sl grn, dl grn & gray .85 .45
265 A67 3pi slate grn & org 1.60 .75
Nos. 261-265 (5) 3.95 2.15

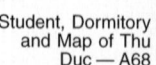

Student, Dormitory and Map of Thu Duc — A68

1965, Oct. 15 ***Perf. 13***

266 A68 50c dark brown .25 .25
267 A68 1pi bright green .40 .25
268 A68 3pi crimson .60 .30
269 A68 7pi dark blue violet 1.25 .55
Nos. 266-269 (4) 2.50 1.35

Issued to publicize higher education.

Farm Boy and Girl, Pig and 4-T Emblem — A69

4pi, Farm boy with chicken, village and 4-T flag.

1965, Nov. 25 **Engr.** ***Perf. 13***

270 A69 3pi emerald & dk red 1.20 .25
271 A69 4pi dull violet & plum 1.75 .30

10th anniv. of the 4-T Clubs and the National Congress of Young Farmers.

Basketball — A70

Designs: 1pi, Javelin. 1.50pi, Hand holding torch, athletic couple. 10pi, Pole vault.

1965, Dec. 14 **Engr.** ***Perf. 13***

272 A70 50c dk car & brn org .45 .25
273 A70 1pi brn org & red brn .65 .30
274 A70 1.50pi brt green 1.00 .40
275 A70 10pi red lil & brn org 2.40 .75
Nos. 272-275 (4) 4.50 1.70

Radio Tower — A71

Radio tower, telephone dial, map of Viet Nam.

1966, Apr. 24 **Engr.** ***Perf. 13***

276 A71 3pi brt blue & brn .50 .25
277 A71 4pi purple, red & blk .65 .30

Saigon microwave station.

Loading Hook and Globe — A72

1966, June 22 **Engr.** ***Perf. 13***

278 A72 3pi gray & dk car rose .35 .25
279 A72 4pi olive & dk purple .45 .30
280 A72 6pi brt grn & dk blue .80 .40
Nos. 278-280 (3) 1.60 .95

Appreciation of the help given by the free world.

Hands Reaching for Persecuted Refugees — A73

1966, July 20

281 A73 3pi brn, vio brn & olive .40 .25
282 A73 7pi claret, vio brn & dk pur 1.00 .30

Refugees from communist oppression.

Paper Soldiers, Votive Offering — A74

Designs: 1.50pi, Man and woman making offerings. 3pi, Floating candles in paper boats. 5pi, Woman burning paper offerings.

1966, Aug. 30 **Engr.** ***Perf. 13***

283 A74 50c red, blk & bis brn .65 .25
284 A74 1.50pi brown, emer & grn 1.00 .30
285 A74 3pi rose red & lake 1.40 .40
286 A74 5pi org brn, bis & dk brn 2.00 .65
Nos. 283-286 (4) 5.05 1.60

Wandering Souls Festival.

Oriental Two-string Violin — A75

Vietnamese Instruments: 3pi, Woman playing 16-string guitar. 4pi, Musicians playing two-string guitars. 7pi, Woman and boy playing flutes.

1966 **Engr.** ***Perf. 13***

Size: 35½x26mm

287 A75 1pi brown red & brn .75 .25
288 A75 3pi rose lilac & pur 1.10 .30
289 A75 4pi rose brown & brn 1.50 .40
290 A75 7pi dp blue & vio bl 2.25 .65
Nos. 287-290 (4) 5.60 1.60

Coil Stamp

Size: 23x17mm

290A A75 3pi rose lil & pur 8.00 3.00
b. Booklet pane of 5 *45.00*
Complete booklet, 2 #290Ab *185.00*

Nos. 287-290 were issued Sept. 28.

Complete booklet contains two vertical strips of 5 with selvage at either end. These strips were also sold loose without booklet cover.

WHO Building, Geneva, and Flag — A76

Designs: 50c, WHO Building and emblem, horiz. 8pi, WHO flag and building.

1966, Oct. 12

291 A76 50c purple & carmine .45 .25
292 A76 1.50pi red brn, vio bl & blk .65 .30
293 A76 8pi grnsh bl, vio bl & brn 1.40 .80
Nos. 291-293 (3) 2.50 1.35

Opening of WHO Headquarters, Geneva.

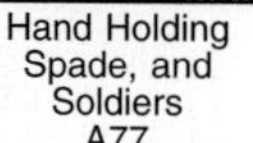
Hand Holding Spade, and Soldiers A77

Soldier and Workers A78

Designs: 1.50pi, Flag, workers. 4pi, Soldier and cavalryman.

1966, Nov. 1 **Engr.** ***Perf. 13***

294 A77 80c dull brn & red brn .35 .25
295 A77 1.50pi car rose, yel & brn .65 .30
296 A78 3pi brown & slate grn 1.25 .40
297 A78 4pi lilac, black & brn 1.75 .65
Nos. 294-297 (4) 4.00 1.60

3rd anniv. of the revolution against the government of Pres. Ngo Dinh Diem.

Symbolic Tree and UNESCO Emblem — A79

Designs: 3pi, Globe and olive branches. 7pi, Symbolic temple, horiz.

1966, Dec. 15 **Engr.** ***Perf. 13***

298 A79 1pi pink, brn & dk car .75 .25
299 A79 3pi dp bl, grn & brn org 1.00 .30
300 A79 7pi grnsh bl, dk bl & red 1.75 .65
Nos. 298-300 (3) 3.50 1.20

20th anniv. of UNESCO.

Bitter Melon — A80

1967, Jan. 12 **Engr.** ***Perf. 13***

301 A80 50c Cashew, vert. 1.25 .25
302 A80 1.50pi shown 1.60 .30
303 A80 3pi Sweetsop 2.00 .40
304 A80 20pi Areca nuts 5.00 .65
Nos. 301-304 (4) 9.85 1.60

Phan-Boi-Chau A81

Designs: 20pi, Phan-Chau-Trinh portrait and addressing crowd.

1967, Mar. 24 **Engr.** ***Perf. 13***

305 A81 1pi mar, red brn & dk brn .90 .25
306 A81 20pi vio, slate grn & blk 2.10 .80

Issued to honor Vietnamese patriots.

Woman Carrying Produce — A82

Labor Day: 1pi, Market scene. 3pi, Two-wheeled horse cart. 8pi, Farm scene with water buffalo.

1967, May 1 **Engr.** ***Perf. 13***

307 A82 50c vio bl, dk bl & ultra .25 .25
308 A82 1pi sl grn & dull pur .30 .30
309 A82 3pi dk carmine .50 .35
310 A82 8pi brt car rose & pur .95 .60
Nos. 307-310 (4) 2.00 1.50

Potter, Vases and Lamp — A83

Weavers and Potters — A84

Designs: 1.50pi, Vase and basket. 35d, Bag and lacquerware.

1967, July 22 **Engr.** ***Perf. 13***

311 A83 50c red brn, grn & ultra .25 .25
312 A83 1.50pi grnsh bl, car & blk .50 .30
313 A84 3pi red, vio & org brn 1.00 .40
314 A83 35pi bis brn, blk & dk red 3.25 1.40
Nos. 311-314 (4) 5.00 2.35

Issued to publicize Vietnamese handicrafts.

Wedding Procession A85

1967, Sept. 18 **Engr.** ***Perf. 13***

315 A85 3pi rose cl, dk vio & red 1.50 .45

Symbols of Stage, Music and Art — A86

Litho. & Engr.

1967, Oct. 27 ***Perf. 13***

316 A86 10pi bl gray, blk & red 1.50 .55

Issued to publicize the Cultural Institute.

"Freedom and Justice" — A87

Balloting — A88

"Establishment of Democracy" — A89

1967, Nov. 1 **Photo.**

317 A87 4pi mag, brn & ocher .80 .25
318 A88 5pi brown, yel & blk 1.25 .30
319 A89 30pi dl lil, indigo & red 2.50 .65
Nos. 317-319 (3) 4.55 1.20

National Day; general elections.

Pagoda and Lions Emblem — A90

1967, Dec. 5 Photo. *Perf. 13½x13*

320	A90	3pi multicolored	1.75	1.00

50th anniversary of Lions International.

Teacher with Pupils and Globe A91

1967, Dec. 10 *Perf. 13x13½*

321	A91	3pi tan, blk, yel & car	2.00	.65

International Literacy Day, Sept. 8, 1967.

Tractor and Village — A92

Rural Construction Program: 9pi, Bulldozer and home building. 10pi, Wheelbarrow, tractor and new building. 20pi, Vietnamese and Americans working together.

1968, Jan. 26 Photo. *Perf. 13½*

322	A92	1pi multicolored	.25	.25
323	A92	9pi lt blue & multi	1.00	.25
324	A92	10pi multicolored	1.25	.30
325	A92	20pi yel, red lil & blk	1.75	.65
		Nos. 322-325 (4)	4.25	1.45

WHO Emblem A93

1968, Apr. 7 Photo. *Perf. 13½*

326	A93	10pi gray grn, blk & yel	2.00	1.00

WHO, 20th anniversary.

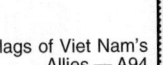

Flags of Viet Nam's Allies — A94

Designs: 1.50pi, Flags surrounding SEATO emblem. 3pi, Flags, handclasp, globe and map of Viet Nam. 50pi, Flags and handclasp.

1968, June 22 Photo. *Perf. 13½*

327	A94	1pi multicolored	.55	.25
328	A94	1.50pi multicolored	1.10	.30
329	A94	3pi multicolored	2.00	.40
330	A94	50pi multicolored	6.50	.95
		Nos. 327-330 (4)	10.15	1.90

Issued to honor Viet Nam's allies.

Three-wheeled Truck and Tractor — A95

Private Property Ownership: 80c, Farmer, city man and symbols of property. 2pi, Three-wheeled cart, taxi and farmers. 30pi, Taxi, three-wheeled cart and tractor in field.

Inscribed: "HUU-SAN-HOA CONG-NHAN VA NONG-DAN"

1968, Nov. 1 Photo. *Perf. 13½*

331	A95	80c multicolored	.25	.25
332	A95	2pi steel blue & multi	.30	.30
333	A95	10pi orange brn & multi	.95	.45
334	A95	30pi gray blue & multi	2.75	1.25
		Nos. 331-334 (4)	4.25	2.25

Human Rights Flame A96

Men of Various Races A97

1968, Dec. 10 Photo. *Perf. 13½*

335	A96	10pi multicolored	.70	.30
336	A97	16pi purple & multi	1.40	.40

International Human Rights Year.

UNICEF Emblem, Mother and Child — A98

6pi, Children flying kite with UNICEF emblem.

1968, Dec. 11

337	A98	6pi multicolored	1.25	.50
338	A98	16pi multicolored	2.25	.80

Workers and Train — A99

1.50pi, 3pi, Crane, train, map of Viet Nam.

1968, Dec. 15

339	A99	1.50pi multicolored	.70	.25
340	A99	3pi org, vio bl & grn	1.00	.30
341	A99	9pi multicolored	1.50	.40
342	A99	20pi multicolored	2.40	.65
		Nos. 339-342 (4)	5.60	1.60

Reopening of Trans-Viet Nam Railroad.

Farm Woman — A100

Vietnamese Women: 1pi, Merchant. 3pi, Nurses, horiz. 20pi, Three ladies.

1969, Mar. 23 Engr. *Perf. 13*

343	A100	50c vio bl, lil & ocher	.30	.25
344	A100	1pi grn, bis & dk brn	.50	.30
345	A100	3pi brown, blk & bl	.70	.40
346	A100	20pi lilac & multi	1.50	.60
		Nos. 343-346 (4)	3.00	1.55

Soldiers and Civilians — A101

Family Welcoming Soldier — A102

1969, June 1 Photo. *Perf. 13*

347	A101	2pi multicolored	.45	.25
348	A102	50pi multicolored	2.25	.60

Pacification campaign.

Man Reading Constitution, Scales of Justice — A103

Voters, Torch and Scales — A104

1969, June 9

349	A103	1pi yel org, yel & blk	.25	.25
350	A104	20pi multicolored	3.00	.50

Constitutional democracy. Phrase on both stamps: "Democratic and Governed by Law."

Mobile Post Office — A105

Mobile Post Office: 3pi, Window service. 4pi, Child with letter. 20pi, Crowd at window and postmark: "15, 12, 67."

1969, July 10

351	A105	1pi multicolored	.25	.25
352	A105	3pi multicolored	.60	.30
353	A105	4pi multicolored	.75	.45
354	A105	20pi ocher & multi	1.50	.75
		Nos. 351-354 (4)	3.10	1.75

Installation of the first mobile post office in Viet Nam.

Mnong-gar Woman — A106

1pi, Djarai woman. 50pi, Bahnar man.

1969, Aug. 29 Photo. *Perf. 13*

355	A106	1pi brt pink & multi	1.00	.40
356	A106	6pi sky blue & multi	1.75	.65
357	A106	50pi gray & multi	7.25	.95
		Nos. 355-357 (3)	10.00	2.00

Ethnic minorities in Viet Nam.

Civilians Becoming Soldiers — A107

General Mobilization: 3pi, Bayonet training. 5pi, Guard duty. 10pi, Farewell.

Inscribed: "TONG BONG VIEN"

1969, Sept. 20

358	A107	1.50pi orange & multi	.55	.25
359	A107	3pi purple & multi	1.10	.30
360	A107	5pi blk, red & ocher	1.75	.40
361	A107	10pi pink & multi	2.25	.65
		Nos. 358-361 (4)	5.65	1.60

ILO Emblem and Globe — A108

1969, Oct. 29 Photo. *Perf. 13*

362	A108	6pi blue grn, blk & gray	.75	.30
363	A108	20pi red, blk & gray	1.25	.45

ILO, 50th anniversary.

Pegu House Sparrow A109

Birds: 6pi, Moluccan munia. 7pi, Great hornbill. 30pi, Old world tree sparrow.

1970, Jan. 15 Photo. *Perf. 12½x14*

364	A109	2pi blue & multi	*1.00*	*.35*
365	A109	6pi orange & multi	*3.00*	*.70*
366	A109	7pi org brn & multi	*4.00*	*.70*
367	A109	30pi blue & multi	*14.00*	*2.10*
		Nos. 364-367 (4)	*22.00*	*3.85*

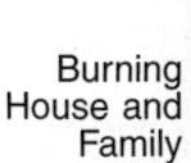

Burning House and Family A110

Design: 20pi, Family fleeing burning house and physician examining child.

1970, Jan. 31 Photo. *Perf. 13*

368	A110	10pi multicolored	1.25	.25
369	A110	20pi multicolored	2.00	.30

Mau Than disaster, 1968.

Vietnamese Costumes A111

Traditional Costumes: 1pi, Man, woman and priest, vert. 2pi, Seated woman with fan. 100pi, Man and woman.

Inscribed: "Y-PHUC CO TRUYEN"

1970, Mar. 13 Photo. *Perf. 13*

370	A111	1pi lt brown & multi	.35	.25
371	A111	2pi pink & multi	.45	.30
372	A111	3pi ultra & multi	.55	.40
373	A111	100pi multicolored	5.50	1.50
		Nos. 370-373 (4)	6.85	2.45

Issued for the Trung Sisters' Festival.

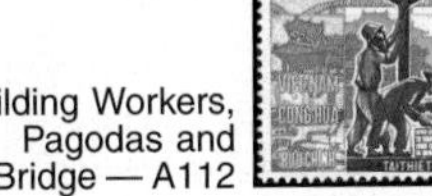

Building Workers, Pagodas and Bridge — A112

Rebuilding of Hué: 20pi, Concrete mixers and scaffolds.

1970, June 10 Litho. & Engr.

374	A112	6pi multicolored	.60	.30
375	A112	20pi rose lil, brn & bis	1.40	.45

Plower in Rice Field — A113

1970, Aug. 29 *Perf. 13*

376	A113	6pi multicolored	1.50	.45

"Land to the Tiller" agricultural reform program.

New Building and Scaffold — A114

Construction Work — A115

1970, Sept. 15 Engr. *Perf. 13*

377	A114	8pi pale ol & brn org	.75	.30
378	A115	16pi brn, indigo & yel	1.50	.45

Reconstruction after 1968 Tet Offensive.

Productivity Year Emblem — A116

1970, Oct. 3

379	A116	10pi multicolored	1.25	.45

Asian Productivity Year.

Nguyen-Dinh-Chieu A117

1970, Nov. 16 Engr. *Perf. 13½*

380 A117 6pi dull vio, red & brn .65 .30
381 A117 10pi grn, red & dk brn 1.10 .45

Nguyen-Dinh-Chieu (1822-1888), poet.

Education Year Emblem — A118

Litho. & Engr.

1970, Nov. 30 *Perf. 13*

382 A118 10pi pale brn, yel & blk 1.50 .65

International Education Year.

Parliament Building — A119

Design: 6pi, Senate Building.

1970, Dec.

383 A119 6pi lt bl, cit & dk brn .50 .30
384 A119 10pi multicolored 1.00 .45

6pi issued Dec. 8 for the 6th Cong.; 10pi issued Dec. 9 for the 9th General Assembly of the Asian Interparliamentary Union.

Dancers — A120

Designs: Various Vietnamese dancers and musicians. 6pi and 7pi horizontal.

1971, Jan. 12

385 A120 2pi ultra & multi .65 .30
386 A120 6pi pale green & multi 1.60 .35
387 A120 7pi pink & multi 1.90 .45
388 A120 10pi brown org & multi 2.25 .50
Nos. 385-388 (4) 6.40 1.60

For surcharge see No. 500.

Farmers and Law — A121

Agrarian Reform Law: 3pi, Tractor and law, dated 26.3.1970. 16pi, Farmers, people rejoicing and law book.

1971, Mar. 26 Engr. *Perf. 13*

389 A121 2pi vio bl, dk brn & dl org .35 .25
a. Dated "1970" 30.00
390 A121 3pi pale grn, brn & dk bl .55 .30
391 A121 16pi multicolored 2.50 .45
Nos. 389-391 (3) 3.40 1.00

No. 389 is dated "1971."

For surcharge see No. 482.

Courier on Horseback — A122

Design: 6pi, Mounted courier with flag.

Engr. & Photo.

1971, June 6 *Perf. 13*

392 A122 2pi violet & multi .30 .30
393 A122 6pi tan & multi 1.75 .45

Postal history.

Military and Naval Operations on Vietnamese Coast — A123

1971, June 19

394 A123 3pi multi + label 1.00 .45
395 A123 40pi multi + label 5.00 1.00

Armed Forces Day.

Deer — A124

1971, Aug. 20 Engr.

396 A124 9pi shown 1.25 .35
397 A124 30pi Tiger 3.75 .90

Rice Harvest — A125

30pi, Threshing and winnowing rice and rice plants. 40pi, Bundling and carrying rice.

Litho. & Engr.

1971, Sept. 28 *Perf. 13*

398 A125 1pi multicolored .40 .30
399 A125 30pi sal pink, dk pur & blk 2.10 .75
400 A125 40pi sepia, yel & grn 2.50 .80
Nos. 398-400 (3) 5.00 1.85

For surcharge see No. 496.

Inauguration of UPU Building, Bern — A126

1971, Nov. 9 Engr. *Perf. 13*

401 A126 20pi green & multi 1.75 .50

Fish — A127

Various Fish; 2pi vertical.

1971, Nov. 16 Photo. & Engr.

402 A127 2pi multicolored 1.10 .30
403 A127 10pi violet & multi 2.25 .45
404 A127 100pi lilac & multi 17.00 2.00
Nos. 402-404 (3) 20.35 2.75

Mailman and Woman on Water Buffalo — A128

Rural Mail: 10pi, Bird carrying letter. 20pi, Mailman with bicycle delivering mail to villagers.

Inscribed: "PHAT TRIEN BUU-CHINH NONG THON"

1971, Dec. 20 Engr. *Perf. 13*

405 A128 5pi multicolored .65 .30
406 A128 10pi multicolored 1.10 .45
407 A128 20pi multicolored 1.75 .60
Nos. 405-407 (3) 3.50 1.35

Trawler Fishermen, and Fish — A129

Publicity for Fishing Industry: 7pi, Net fishing from boat. 50d, Trawler with seine.

1972, Jan. 2 Engr. *Perf. 13*

408 A129 4pi pink, blk & blue .40 .25
409 A129 7pi lt blue, blk & red .65 .30
410 A129 50pi multicolored 3.50 1.60
Nos. 408-410 (3) 4.55 2.15

King Quang Trung (1752-1792) — A130

1972, Jan. 28 *Perf. 13½*

411 A130 6pi red & multi 1.00 .35
a. Booklet pane of 10 *90.00*
412 A130 20pi black & multi 3.00 1.20

No. 411a is imperf. horizontally.

Road Workers — A131

1972, Feb. 4

413 A131 3pi multicolored .50 .30
414 A131 8pi multicolored 1.00 .45

Community development.

Rice Farming — A132

1972, Mar. 26 Engr. *Perf. 13½*

415 A132 1pi shown .25 .25
416 A132 10pi Wheat farming 2.00 .30

Farmers' Day.

Plane over Dalat — A133

1972, Apr. 18 Engr. & Photo.

417 A133 10pi shown 2.00 .50
418 A133 10pi over Ha-tien 2.00 .50
419 A133 10pi over Hue 2.00 .50
420 A133 10pi over Saigon 2.00 .50
a. Block of 4, #417-420 *10.00* 7.50
421 A133 25pi like No. 417 4.50 .75
422 A133 25pi like No. 418 4.50 .75
423 A133 25pi like No. 419 4.50 .75
424 A133 25pi like No. 420 4.50 .75
a. Block of 4, #421-424 *20.00* 12.50
Nos. 417-424 (8) 26.00 5.00

20 years Air Viet Nam.

Scholar — A134

20pi, Teacher, pupils. 50pi, Scholar, scroll.

1972, May 5 Engr. & Litho.

425 A134 5pi multicolored .40 .30

Engr.

426 A134 20pi lt green & multi 1.75 .50
427 A134 50pi pink & multi 4.75 .90
Nos. 425-427 (3) 6.90 1.70

Ancient letter writing art.

Armed Farmer — A135

6pi, Civilian rifleman & Self-defense Forces emblem, horiz. 20pi, Man, woman training with rifles.

Engr. & Litho.

1972, June 15 *Perf. 13*

428 A135 2pi brt rose & multi 1.10 .35
429 A135 6pi multicolored 1.50 .50
430 A135 20pi lt violet & multi 2.40 .60
Nos. 428-430 (3) 5.00 1.45

Civilian Self-defense Forces.

Hands Holding Safe — A136

1972, July 10

431 A136 10pi lt blue & multi 1.25 .30
432 A136 25pi lt green & multi 2.25 .45

Treasury Bonds campaign.

Frontier Guard — A137

Designs: 10pi, 3 guards and horse, horiz. 40pi, Marching guards, horiz.

Engr. & Litho.

1972, Aug. 14 *Perf. 13*

433 A137 10pi olive & multi 1.00 .30
434 A137 30pi buff & multi 1.50 .50
435 A137 40pi lt blue & multi 2.50 .70
Nos. 433-435 (3) 5.00 1.50

Historic frontier guards.

Soldier Helping Wounded Man — A138

Designs: 16pi, Soldier on crutches and flowers. 100pi, Veterans' memorial, map and flag.

1972, Sept. 1

436 A138 9pi olive & multi 1.25 .35
437 A138 16pi yellow & multi 1.75 .45
438 A138 100pi lt blue & multi 6.00 1.40
Nos. 436-438 (3) 9.00 2.20

For surcharge see No. 483.

Tank, Memorial, Flag and Map A139

Soldiers and Map of Viet Nam A140

1972, Nov. 25 Litho. *Perf. 13*

439 A139 5pi multicolored 6.50 .30
440 A140 10pi ultra & multi 9.50 .45

Victory at Binh-Long.

Book Year Emblem and Globe — A141

Designs: 4pi, Emblem, books circling globe. 5pi, Emblem, books and globe.

1972, Nov. 30

441 A141 2pi dp carmine & multi .50 .25
442 A141 4pi blue & multi 1.10 .30
443 A141 5pi yellow bister & multi 1.40 .45
Nos. 441-443 (3) 3.00 1.00

International Book Year.

Liberated Vietnamese Family — A142

1973, Feb. 18 Litho. ***Perf. 13***

444 A142 10pi yellow & multi 2.00 1.20

To celebrate the 200,000th returnee.

Soldiers Raising Vietnamese Flag — A143

Design: 10pi, Victorious soldiers and map of demilitarized zone, horiz.

1973, Feb. 24 Litho. ***Perf. 13***

445 A143 3pi lilac & multi .80 .75
446 A143 10pi yellow grn & multi 2.00 1.50

Victory at Quang Tri.

Satellite, Storm over Viet Nam — A144

1973, Mar. 23 Litho. ***Perf. 12½x12***

447 A144 1pi lt blue & multi 1.25 .60

World Meteorological Day.
For surcharge see No. 497.

Farmers with Tractor, Symbol of Law — A145

Farmer Plowing with Water Buffalos — A146

Pres. Thieu Holding Agrarian Reform Law — A147

1973, Mar. 26 Litho. ***Perf. 12½x12***

448 A145 2pi lt green & multi 3.00 .60
449 A146 5pi orange & multi 3.00 .60

Perf. 11

450 A147 10pi blue & multi *115.00 30.00*
Nos. 448-450 (3) 121.00 31.20

3rd anniv. of the agrarian reform law; 5-year plan for rural development.
Value for No. 450 is for stamp with first day cancel. Commercially used examples are worth substantially more.
See No. 475.

INTERPOL Emblem and Side View of Headquarters A148

1pi, INTERPOL emblem and Headquarters. 2pi, INTERPOL emblem.

1973, Apr. 8 Litho. ***Perf. 12½x12***

451 A148 1pi olive & multi .45 .25
452 A148 2pi yellow & multi .75 .30
453 A148 25pi ocher, lilac & brn 3.25 .45
Nos. 451-453 (3) 4.45 1.00

Intl. Criminal Police Org., 50th anniv.
For surcharge see No. 498.

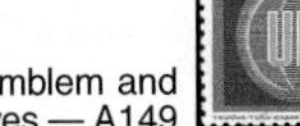

ITU Emblem and Waves — A149

2pi, Globe and waves. 3pi, ITU emblem.

1973, May 17

454 A149 1pi dull blue & multi .40 .25
455 A149 2pi brt blue & multi .65 .30
456 A149 3pi orange & multi 1.10 .45
Nos. 454-456 (3) 2.15 1.00

World Telecommunications Day.
For surcharge see No. 499.

Globe, Hand Holding House A150

Men Building Pylon A151

Design: 10pi, Fish in net, symbols of agriculture, industry and transportation.

1973, Nov. 6 Litho. ***Perf. 12x12½***

457 A150 8pi gray & multi .90 .25
458 A150 10pi vio bl, blk & gray 1.40 .30
459 A151 15pi blk, org & lil rose 1.75 .45
Nos. 457-459 (3) 4.05 1.00

National development.
For surcharge see No. 514.

Water Buffalos — A152

1973, Dec. 20 Litho. ***Perf. 12½x12***

460 A152 5pi shown 2.50 .50
461 A152 10pi Water buffalo 3.50 .75

Human Rights Flame, Three Races — A153

Design: 100pi, Human Rights flame, scales and people, vert.

1973, Dec. 29 ***Perf. 12½x12, 12x12½***

462 A153 15pi ultra & multi .50 .25
463 A153 100pi green & multi 2.75 .50

25th anniv. of Universal Declaration of Human Rights.

"25" and WHO Emblem — A154

Design: 15pi, WHO emblem, diff.

1973, Dec. 31 ***Perf. 12½x12***

464 A154 8pi orange, bl & brn .80 .30
465 A154 15pi lt brn, bl & brt pink 1.20 .45

25th anniversary of WHO.
For surcharge see No. 515.

Sampan Ferry — A155

Design: 10pi, Sampan ferry (different).

1974, Jan. 13 Litho. ***Perf. 14x13½***

466 A155 5pi lt blue & multi 1.25 .30
467 A155 10pi yellow grn & multi 2.00 .70

Sampan ferry women.

Soldiers of 7 Nations A156

American War Memorial A157

Map of South Viet Nam and Allied Flags — A158

Design: No. 469, Soldiers and flags of South Viet Nam, Korea, US, Australia New Zealand, Thailand and Philippines. Same flags shown on 8pi and 60pi.

1974, Jan. 28 ***Perf. 12½x12, 12x12½***

468 A156 8pi multicolored .55 .25
469 A156 15pi lt brown & multi 1.25 .30
470 A157 15pi multicolored 1.25 .30
471 A158 60pi multicolored 3.50 .60
Nos. 468-471 (4) 6.55 1.45

In honor of South Viet Nam's allies.
For surcharge see No. 516.

Trung Sisters on Elephants Fighting Chinese — A159

1974, Feb. 27 Litho. ***Perf. 12½x12***

472 A159 8pi green, citron & blk 1.00 .25
473 A159 15pi dp orange & multi 1.50 .30
474 A159 80pi ultra, pink & blk 3.50 .45
Nos. 472-474 (3) 6.00 1.00

Trung Trac and Trung Nhi, queens of Viet Nam, 39-43 A.D. Day of Vietnamese Women.

Pres. Thieu Type of 1973 and

Farmers Going to Work A160

Woman Farmer Holding Rice A161

1974, Mar. 26 Litho. ***Perf. 14***

475 A147 10pi blue & multi 1.50 .30

Perf. 12½x12, 12x12½

476 A160 20pi yellow & multi 1.50 .45
477 A161 70pi blue & multi 12.00 1.50
Nos. 475-477 (3) 15.00 2.25

Agriculture Day. Size of No. 475 is 31x50mm, No. 450 is 34x54mm and printed on thick paper. No. 475 has been extensively redrawn and first line of inscription in bottom panel changed to "26 THANG BA."
Value for No. 477 is for stamp with first day cancel. Commercially used examples are worth substantially more.

Hung Vuong with Bamboo Tallies — A162

Flag Inscribed: Hung Vuong, Founder of Kingdom — A163

1974, Apr. 2 ***Perf. 14x13½***

478 A162 20pi yellow & multi 1.50 .30
479 A163 100pi olive & multi 4.50 .45

Hung Vuong, founder of Vietnamese nation and of Hông-Bang Dynasty (2879-258 B.C.).

National Library — A164

New National Library Building: 15pi, Library, right facade and Phoenix.

1974, Apr. 14

480 A164 10pi orange, brn & blk .80 .75
481 A164 15pi multicolored 1.20 .90

Nos. 391 and 437 Srchd. with New Value and Two Bars in Red

1974 ***Perf. 13***

482 A121 25pi on 16pi multi 10.00 2.75
483 A138 25pi on 16pi multi 5.00 2.25

Memorial Tower, Saigon A165

Globe, Crane Lifting Crate A167

Crane with Flags, Globe and Map of Viet Nam — A166

Perf. 12x12½, 12½x12

1974, June 22 Litho.

484 A165 10pi blue & multi .55 .35
485 A166 20pi multicolored 1.25 .45
486 A167 60pi yellow & multi 3.25 .60
Nos. 484-486 (3) 5.05 1.40

International Aid Day.

Sun and Views of Saigon, Dalat Hué — A168

Cau-Bong Bridge, Nha Trang — A169

Thien-Mu Pagoda, Hué — A170

1974, July 12 ***Perf. 14x13½, 13½x14***

487 A168 5pi blue & multi 1.10 .30
488 A169 10pi blue & multi 1.10 .60
489 A170 15pi yellow & multi 1.90 1.00
Nos. 487-489 (3) 4.10 1.90

Tourist publicity.

Rhynchostylis Gigantea — A171

Orchids: 20pi, Cypripedium caliosum, vert. 200pi, Dendrobium nobile.

1974, Aug. 18

490 A171 10pi blue & multi .30 .40
491 A171 20pi yellow & multi .35 .45
492 A171 200pi bister & multi 6.00 1.25
Nos. 490-492 (3) 6.65 2.10

Hands Passing Letter, UPU Emblem A172

UPU Emblem and Woman A173

UPU Cent.: 30pi, World map, bird, UPU emblem.

Perf. 12½x12, 12x12½

1974, Oct. 9 **Litho.**

493	A172	20pi ultra & multi	.35	.30
494	A172	30pi orange & multi	.85	.45
495	A173	300pi gray & multi	2.75	1.25
		Nos. 493-495 (3)	3.95	2.00

Nos. 398, 447, 451, 454, 387 Srchd. with New Value and Two Bars in Red

1974-75

496	A125	25pi on 1pi multi	*13.50*	5.00
497	A144	25pi on 1pi multi	*13.50*	5.00
498	A148	25pi on 1pi multi	*13.50*	5.00
499	A149	25pi on 1pi multi	*19.00*	9.00
500	A120	25pi on 7pi multi	*16.00*	5.00
		Nos. 496-500 (5)	*75.50*	29.00

Issued: #496, 498, 1/1/75; others, 11/18/74.

Hien Lam Pavilion, Hué — A174

Throne, Imperial Palace, Hué — A175

Water Pavilion, Hué — A176

1975, Jan. 5 **Litho.** *Perf. 14x13½*

501	A174	25pi multicolored	1.40	1.40
502	A175	30pi multicolored	1.75	1.75
503	A176	60pi multicolored	2.10	2.10
		Nos. 501-503 (3)	5.25	5.25

Historic sites.

Symbol of Youth, Children Holding Flower A177

Family and Emblem A178

1975, Jan. 14 *Perf. 11½*

504	A177	20pi blue & multi	2.50	.35

Perf. 12½x12

505	A178	70pi yellow & multi	2.50	.35

Intl. Conf. on Children & Natl. Development.

Unicorn Dance A179

Boy Lighting Firecracker A180

Bringing New Year Gifts and Wishes — A181

Perf. 14x13½, 13½x14

1975, Jan. 26 **Litho.**

506	A179	20pi multicolored	2.50	.35
507	A180	30pi blue & multi	3.00	.50
508	A181	100pi bister & multi	7.00	1.00
		Nos. 506-508 (3)	12.50	1.85

Lunar New Year, Tet.

A182

A183

A184

Designs: 25pi, Military chief from play "San Hau." 40pi, Scene from "Tam Ha Nam Duong." 100pi, Warrior Luu-Kim-Dinn.

1975, Feb. 23

509	A182	25pi rose & multi	1.25	.45
510	A183	40pi lt green & multi	2.10	*.45*
511	A184	100pi violet & multi	7.50	.75
		Nos. 509-511 (3)	10.85	1.65

National theater.

Produce, Map of Viet Nam, Ship — A185

Irrigation Project — A186

1975, Mar. 26 **Litho.** *Perf. 12½x12*

512	A185	10pi multicolored	1.75	.75
513	A186	50pi multicolored	4.50	1.20

Agriculture Day; 5th anniv. of Agrarian Reform Law.

Nos. 457, 464, 468 Srchd. with New Value and Two Bars in Red

1975

514	A150	10pi on 8pi multi	34.00	10.00
515	A154	10pi on 8pi multi	21.00	6.00
516	A156	25pi on 8pi multi	10.00	4.00
		Nos. 514-516 (3)	65.00	20.00

In the 1980's a number of South Viet Nam stamps appeared on the market. These apparently had been printed before the collapse of the Republic but saw no postal use. These include, but are not limited to, sets of two for western electric and for rural electric, one each for history, library, New Year and cows, a set of three for transportation and a set of four for economic development.

SEMI-POSTAL STAMPS

Type of 1952 Surcharged in Carmine

Perf. 12x12½

1952, Nov. 10 **Unwmk.**

B1	A3	1.50pi + 50c bl, yel & brn	3.50	2.75
		Never hinged	7.50	

The surtax was for the Red Cross.

Catalogue values for unused stamps in this section, from this point to the end of the section, are for Never Hinged items. Because of the tropical conditions, never hinged stamps must also be free of wrinkles, toning, and any other disturbance.

Sabers and Flag — SP1

1952, Dec. 21 **Engr.** *Perf. 13*

B2	SP1	3.30pi + 1.70pi dp claret	2.25	2.00

The surtax was for the Wounded Soldiers' Aid Organization.

X-ray Camera and Patient — SP2

1960, Aug. 1 *Perf. 13*

B3	SP2	3pi + 50c bl grn & red	.90	.75

The surtax was for the Anti-Tuberculosis Foundation.

AIR POST STAMPS

Catalogue values for unused stamps in this section, from this point to the end of the section, are for Never Hinged items. Because of the tropical conditions, never hinged stamps must also be free of wrinkles, toning, and any other disturbance.

AP1

AP2

Perf. 13½x12½

1952-53 **Unwmk.** **Photo.**

C1	AP1	3.30pi dk brn red & pale yel grn	1.00	.50
C2	AP1	4pi brown & yellow	1.25	.35
C3	AP1	5.10pi dk vio bl & sal pink	1.25	.75
C4	AP2	6.30pi yellow & car	1.50	.85
		Nos. C1-C4 (4)	5.00	2.45

Issued: #C2, 11/24/53; others, 3/8/52.

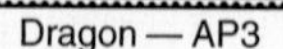
Dragon — AP3

Fish — AP4

1952, Sept. 3 **Engr.** *Perf. 13*

C5	AP3	40c red	1.40	.35
C6	AP3	70c green	2.40	.50
C7	AP3	80c ultra	2.40	.50
C8	AP3	90c brown	2.40	.50
C9	AP4	3.70pi deep magenta	5.25	.75
		Nos. C5-C9 (5)	13.85	2.60

Nos. C5-C9 exist imperforate in a souvenir booklet. Value, $175.

South Viet Nam

Phoenix AP5

1955, Sept. 7

C10	AP5	4pi violet & lil rose	2.50	1.75

Crane Carrying Letter — AP6

1960, Dec. 20. *Perf. 13*

C11	AP6	1pi olive	.75	.45
C12	AP6	4pi green & dk blue	1.75	.60
C13	AP6	5pi ocher & purple	2.00	.75
C14	AP6	10pi deep magenta	3.50	1.20
		Nos. C11-C14 (4)	8.00	3.00

POSTAGE DUE STAMPS

Catalogue values for unused stamps in this section, from this point to the end of the section, are for Never Hinged items. Because of the tropical conditions, never hinged stamps must also be free of wrinkles, toning, and any other disturbance.

Temple Lion — D1

Perf. 13x13½

1952, June 16 **Typo.** **Unwmk.**

J1	D1	10c red & green	.70	.60
J2	D1	20c green & yellow	1.00	.80
J3	D1	30c purple & orange	1.25	1.00
J4	D1	40c dk grn & sal rose	1.60	1.25
J5	D1	50c dp carmine & gray	2.10	1.75
J6	D1	1pi blue & silver	3.25	3.00
		Nos. J1-J6 (6)	9.90	8.40

South Viet Nam

Dragon — D2

1955-56

J7	D2	2pi red vio & org	.40	.30
J8	D2	3pi violet & grnsh bl	.55	.40
J9	D2	5pi violet & yellow	.60	.45
J10	D2	10pi dk green & car	.90	.65
J11	D2	20pi red & brt grn ('56)	2.00	1.50
J12	D2	30pi brt grn & yel ('56)	3.00	2.25
J13	D2	50pi dk red brn & yel ('56)	6.00	4.50
J14	D2	100pi pur & yel ('56)	12.00	9.00
		Nos. J7-J14 (8)	25.45	19.05

Nos. J11-J14 inscribed "BUU-CHINH" instead of "TIMBRE-TAXE."

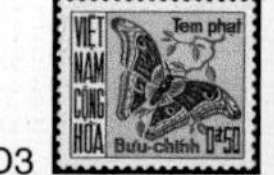
Atlas Moth — D3

Design: 3pi, 5pi, 10pi, Three butterflies.

1968, Aug. 20 Photo. ***Perf. 13½x13***

J15	D3	50c multicolored	*2.25*	.90
J16	D3	1pi multicolored	*2.75*	1.00
J17	D3	2pi multicolored	*5.00*	2.00
J18	D3	3pi multicolored	*6.75*	3.00
J19	D3	5pi multicolored	*12.00*	4.75
J20	D3	10pi multicolored	*18.00*	6.75
		Nos. J15-J20 (6)	*46.75*	18.40

Nos. J15-J18 Srchd. with New Value and Two Bars in Red

1974, Oct. 1

J21	D3	5pi on 3pi multi	2.00	1.50
J22	D3	10pi on 50c multi	2.00	1.50
J23	D3	40pi on 1pi multi	2.00	1.50
J24	D3	60pi on 2pi multi	2.00	1.50
		Nos. J21-J24 (4)	8.00	6.00

MILITARY STAMPS

Catalogue values for unused stamps in this section, from this point to the end of the section, are for Never Hinged items. Because of the tropical conditions, never hinged stamps must also be free of wrinkles, toning, and any other disturbance.

Soldier Guarding Village — M1

Rouletted 7½

1961, June Unwmk. Litho.

M1	M1	och, brn, dk grn & blk	*9.00*	*1.50*

1961, Sept. Typo.

M2	M1	org yel, dk grn & brn	*4.00*	*1.50*

Bottom inscription on No. M1 is black, brown on No. M2.

Battle and Refugees — M2

1969, Feb. 22 Litho. ***Imperf.***

M3	M2	red & green	*70.00*	*80.00*
a.		Booklet pane of 10	*700.00*	

VIET CONG

Local Communists (Viet Cong) formed the National Front for the Liberation of South Vietnam (NLF) on Dec. 20, 1960. During 1960-68, the NLF occupied large areas of the country and, in 1969, established a Provisional Revolutionary Government (PRG) to administer areas under its control. Despite major setbacks following its nationwide Tet Offensive in early 1968, the NLF continued its resistance and, following the North Vietnamese invasion in 1975 and collapse of the South Vietnamese government, the PRG took control of the country pending unification with the North in 1976.

100 Xu = 1 Dong

Catalogue values for all unused stamps in this country are for Never Hinged items.

3rd Anniversary of the National Liberation Front — A1

1963, Oct. 5 Litho. ***Perf. 11***

1	A1	20xu multi (English inscr.)	6.50	6.50
2	A1	20xu multi (French inscr.)	6.50	6.50
3	A1	20xu multi (Spanish inscr.)	6.50	6.50
		Nos. 1-3 (3)	19.50	19.50

Occupation of Village — A2

Design: No. 5, Firing on American helicopter.

1963, Oct. 5

4	A2	10xu multi	10.00	10.00
5	A2	10xu multi	10.00	10.00

Third anniversary of the revolution of the National Front for the Liberation of South Viet-nam (NLF).

Anti-government Demonstration — A3

Designs: 20xu, Harvesting rice with stacked rifles nearby. 30xu, Sinking of the *USS Card.*

1964, 20 Dec.

6	A3	10xu multi	5.00	5.00
7	A3	20xu multi	5.00	5.00
8	A3	30xu blkish grn & pl blue	5.00	5.00
a.		Strip of 3, #6-8	15.00	15.00
		Nos. 6-8 (3)	15.00	15.00

Fourth anniversary of the NLF.

U.S. Planes on Fire — A4

Nguyen Van Troi (1940-1964), Revolutionary Martyr — A4a

1965, Oct. 15

9	A4	10xu multi	6.00	6.00
10	A4a	20xu multi	6.00	6.00
		Nos. 9-11 (3)	18.00	18.00

Fifth anniversary of the NLF.

Viet Cong Flags, Maps and Globe — A4b

1965, Dec. 20

11	A4b	40xu multi	6.00	6.00

Viet Cong Soldiers Atop U.S. Tank — A5

Designs: No. 13, Guerrillas, flag, burning U.S. tank and armor, horiz. 30xu, Demonstrators with flag and banners.

1967, Dec. 20

12	A5	20xu multi	6.00	6.00
13	A5	20xu multi	6.00	6.00
14	A5	30xu multi	6.00	6.00
		Nos. 12-14 (3)	18.00	18.00

Seventh anniversary of the NLF.

"Guerrilla" — A6

Designs: 20xu, "Jungle Patrol," horiz. 30xu, "Women Soldiers." 40xu, "Towards the Future," horiz.

1968 ***Perf. 12***

15	A6	10xu multi	5.00	5.00
16	A6	20xu multi	5.00	5.00
17	A6	30xu multi	5.00	5.00
18	A6	40xu multi	5.00	5.00
		Nos. 15-19 (4)	20.00	20.00

Series of patriotic paintings, *The Struggle for Freedom.*

A7

A7a — 21

Designs: No. 19, Voting. No. 20, Bazooka crew and flaming U.S. planes. No. 21, Marchers with Viet Cong flag (English inscr.). No. 22, Marchers with Viet Cong flag (French inscr.).

1968, Dec. 20 ***Perf. 11***

19	A7	20xu multi	5.00	5.00
20	A7	20xu multi	5.00	5.00
21	A7a	30xu multi	5.00	5.00
22	A7a	30xu multi	5.00	5.00
		Nos. 19-22 (4)	20.00	20.00

Eighth anniversary of the NLF.

Lenin and Viet Cong Flag — A8

1970, Apr. 22

23	A8	20xu multi	4.50	4.50
24	A8	30xu multi	4.50	4.50
25	A8	50xu multi	5.50	5.50
26	A8	2d multi	6.50	6.50
		Nos. 23-26 (4)	21.00	21.00

Centenary of Lenin's birth.

Ho Chi Minh Watering Peach Tree — A9

1970, May 19

27	A9	20xu multi	4.50	4.50
28	A9	30xu multi	4.50	4.50
29	A9	50xu multi	5.50	5.50
30	A9	2d multi	6.50	6.50
		Nos. 27-30 (4)	21.00	21.00

80th birthday of Ho Chi Minh. Nos. 27-30 exist imperf.

Stylized Viet Cong Flag, Shattered Helmet — A10

1970, Dec. 20

31	A10	20xu multi	.75	.75
32	A10	30xu multi	1.50	1.50
33	A10	50xu multi	2.25	2.25
34	A10	3d multi	8.00	8.00
		Nos. 31-34 (4)	12.50	12.50

Tenth anniversary of the NLF. Nos. 31-34 exist imperf. Value, $25.

Viet Cong Home Guard A11

Designs: 30xu, Capturing U.S. tank. 50xu, Soldiers guarding farmers. 1d, Ambush.

1971, Feb. 15

35	A11	20xu multi	4.50	4.50
36	A11	30xu multi	4.50	4.50
37	A11	50xu multi	5.50	5.50
38	A11	1d multi	6.50	6.50
		Nos. 35-38 (4)	21.00	21.00

Tenth anniversary of the People's Liberation Armed Forces.

Life in Liberated Viet Nam — A12

Designs: 20xu, Children and teacher in classroom. 30xu, Women sewing Viet Cong flag. 40xu, Building village defenses. 50xu, Clinic. 1d, Harvesting.

1971, June 6

39	A12	20xu multi	0.75	0.75
40	A12	30xu multi	1.50	1.50
41	A12	40xu multi	2.50	2.50
42	A12	50xu multi	3.00	3.00
43	A12	1d multi	5.00	5.00
		Nos. 39-43 (5)	12.75	12.75

Second anniversary of the Provisional Government.

Harvesting Rice — A13

Designs: No. 45, Marchers with Viet Cong flag and banner. No. 46, School children, flag. No. 47, Women Home Guards. No. 48, Demonstrators, conference delegate. No. 49, Soldiers, tanks attacking.

1974, June 6

44	A13	10xu multi	2.00	2.00
45	A13	10xu multi	2.00	2.00
46	A13	10xu multi	2.00	2.00
47	A13	10xu multi	2.00	2.00
48	A13	10xu multi	2.00	2.00
a.		Strip of 5, #44-48	10.00	10.00
49	A13	10xu multi	2.00	2.00
		Nos. 44-49 (6)	12.00	12.00

Fifth anniversary of the Provisional Government. Nos. 44-49 exist imperf.

Soldiers with Ho Chi Minh — A14

1975, Feb. 28

50	A14	10xu multi	1.50	1.50
51	A14	20xu multi	2.00	2.00

For design A14 in smaller format, see Nos. 56-59.

Ho Chi Minh Watering Peach Tree — A15

Inscribed "Mien Nam Viet Nam"

1975

52	A15	5d multi	.40	.40
53	A15	10d multi	.75	.75
54	A15	30d multi, magenta frame	4.00	4.00
55	A15	30d multi, olive frame	4.00	4.00
		Nos. 52-55 (4)	9.15	9.15

85th Birthday of Ho Chi Minh, first issue. Issued: 10d, 5/7; 5d, 5/8; No. 54, 5/19; No. 55, 7/16.

Nos. 52-55 exist imperf.

See Nos. 60-61.

Type of 1975, Reduced Size (35.5x26mm)

1975-76

56	A14	15d green & black	0.75	0.75
57	A14	30d org red & black	1.75	1.75
58	A14	60d royal blue & black	2.50	2.50
59	A14	300d yellow & black	7.50	7.50
		Nos. 56-59 (4)	12.50	12.50

15th anniversary of the NLF. Issued: 30d, 9/2/75; 300d, 12/18/75; 15d, 60d, 1/15/76.

Ho Chi Minh — A16

1975, Oct. 6

60	A16	30d multi	1.25	1.25
61	A16	60d multi	2.25	2.25

85th Birthday of Ho Chi Minh, second issue.

PROVISIONAL SURCHARGES

Beginning in 1973, postmasters were authorized to surcharge their stocks with new values in the local currency to meet the postal rates of the Saigon government. With the fall of the South in 1975, stamps of the Provisional Revolutionary Government replaced South Vietnamese issues in the newly conquered territories. A wide variety of these local surcharges exist and all are scarce. Forgeries and fakes abound.

Fruits — A17

Designs: 20d, Cocos nucifera. 30d, Garcinia mangostana. 60d, Mangifera indica.

1976, Mar.

62	A17	20d multi	2.50	2.50
63	A17	30d multi	4.00	4.00
64	A17	60d multi	8.50	8.50
		Nos. 62-64 (3)	15.00	15.00

Nos. 62-64 exist imperf.

Types of North Vietnam Nos. 816-818

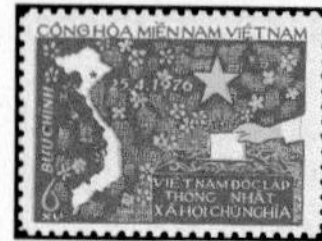

Inscribed "CONG HOA MIEN NAM VIET NAM"

Designs: No. 65, Map, hand placing ballot in ballot box. Nos. 66-67, Map, voters.

1976, Apr.

65	A279	6xu car red & br yellow	0.75	.25
66	A279a	6xu ultra & red	0.75	.25
67	A279a	12xu bright emerald & red	2.00	.75
		Nos. 65-67 (3)	3.50	1.25

First elections to United National Assembly. Issued: Nos. 65, 67, 4/15; No. 66, 4/25.

Nos. 65-67 exist imperf.

Flag — A18

1976, May 1

68	A18	30d multi	2.00	2.00

First anniversary of victory.

Type of North Vietnam Nos. 819-820

Inscribed "CONG HOA MIEN NAM VIET NAM."

Design: No. 70, "Doc Lap Thong Nhat Chu Nghia Xa Hoi."

1976, June 24

69	A280	6xu pur brn & multi	.75	.30
70	A280	12xu lt blue & multi	1.50	.50

First session of the Unified National Assembly.

VIET NAM, DEMOCRATIC REPUBLIC

(North Viet Nam)

LOCATION — In eastern Indo-China
GOVT. — Republic
AREA — 61,293 sq. mi.
POP. — 18,800,000 (1968 est.)
CAPITAL — Hanoi

Beginning in 1946, the Communist Viet Minh fought the French in a guerrilla war that ended with the French defeat at Dien Bien Phu in 1954. In an agreement signed in Geneva on July 21, 1954, Viet Nam was partitioned at the 17th parallel. The government in Hanoi controlled the north, and engaged in another protracted military campaign against American and South Vietnamese forces that led to the official reunification of the country under Communist control on July 2, 1976.

100 cents = 1 Dong
100 Xu = 1 Dong (1959)

All stamps are without gum unless otherwise indicated. Values for stamps with gum are for Never Hinged items.

Watermark

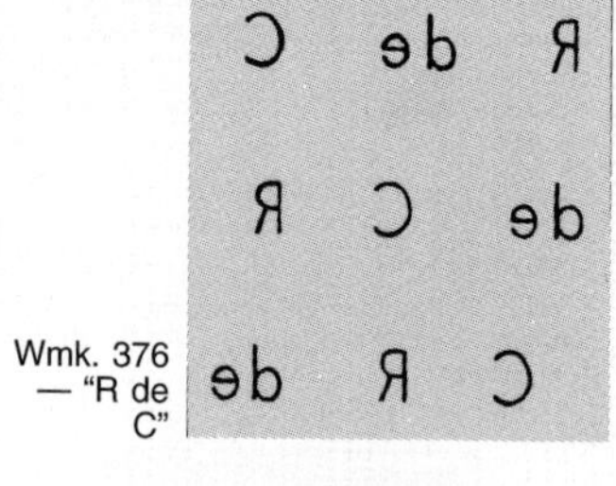

Wmk. 376 — "R de C"

VIET MINH ISSUES

Stamps and Types of Indo-China Overprinted or Surcharged

No. 236 Overprinted

Printing Methods and Perfs as Before

1945-46 Without Gum

1L1	A41	1pi yel grn (Yersin)	7.50	19.00

Nos. 238-239 (Rhodes) Ovptd.

1L2	A43	15c dk vio brn, perf. 11½	3.00	4.00
a.		Perf. 12	3.00	4.00
b.		Perf. 11½, green overprint	10.00	10.00
1L3	A43	30c org brn, perf. 11½	3.00	3.00
a.		Perf. 13½	6.00	6.00
b.		Perf. 12	30.00	—

No. 242 Overprinted

1L4	A44	50c dl red (Athlete)	20.00	25.00

No. 241 Ovptd.

1L5	A44	10c dk vio brn & yel (Athlete)	8.00	10.00

Nos. 218-222 (Petain) Overprinted

1L6	A32	3c olive brn, perf. 11½	3.00	3.00
a.		Perf. 12x14	10.00	
b.		Perf. 14	30.00	
1L7	A32	6c rose red	3.00	3.00
1L8	A32	10c dull grn (R)	5.00	5.00
1L9	A32	40c dk bl (R)	5.00	10.00
1L10	A32	40c slate bl (R)	10.00	20.00
		Nos. 1L6-1L10 (5)	26.00	41.00

Nos. 245-246 and Type (Pavie) Overprinted

1L11	A46	4c org yel	3.00	3.00
1L12	A46	10c dl grn	5.00	6.00
1L13	A46	20c dark red	3.00	3.00
		Nos. 1L11-1L13 (3)	11.00	12.00

No. 165A Overprinted

1L14	A22	25c dk bl (Planting Rice, R), top line 18 mm wide	80.00	90.00
a.		Top line 20 mm wide	67.50	9.00

Nos. 1L14-1L14a issued with gum.

No. 232 (Courbet) Overprinted

1L15	A39	3c lt brn	2.00	2.00
1L16	A39	6c car rose	2.00	2.00

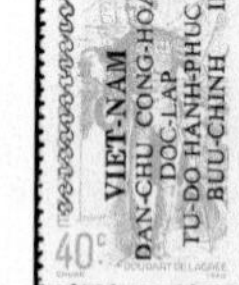

No. 261 (Lagree) Overprinted Vertically

1L17	A52	40c brt bl	5.00	15.00

Nos. 253-255 (Doumer) Overprinted

1L18	A50	2c red vio	2.00	2.00
1L19	A50	4c org brn	2.00	2.00
1L20	A50	10c dull grn	3.00	3.00
a.		"HANH-PHUC" inverted	22.00	—
		Nos. 1L18-1L20 (3)	7.00	7.00

No. 217 (Petain) Overprinted

Nos. 256-258 (Charner) Overprinted

1L21	A32	1c olive brn	2.00	2.00
1L22	A51	10c green	3.00	3.00
1L23	A51	20c red	5.00	15.00
1L24	A51	1pi pale yel grn	10.00	25.00
		Nos. 1L21-1L24 (4)	20.00	45.00

No. 230 and Type (Genouilly) Overprinted

1L25	A37	5c dull brown	2.00	2.00
1L26	A37	6c carmine rose	3.50	3.50

No. 210-212 (Sihanouk) Surcharged

1L27 A28 5d on 1c red org (Bl) 45.00 45.00
1L28 A28 10d on 6c violet (R) 50.00 50.00
1L29 A28 15d on 25c dp ultra (R) 50.00 50.00
Nos. 1L27-1L29 (3) 145.00 145.00

Nos. 225-226 (Sihanouk) Surcharged

No. 1L30

No. 1L31

1L30 A34 50xu on 1c reddish brn 4.00 —
1L31 A35 2d on 6c car rose 30.00 —

Nos. 213-214 (Elephant) Surcharged

1L32 A29 2d on 3c red brn (G) 45.00 45.00
1L33 A29 4d on 6c crim (G) 45.00 45.00

Nos. 247-248 (Pasquier) Surcharged Vertically

1L34 A47 1d on 5c brn vio 3.00 4.00
1L35 A47 2d on 10c dl grn 4.00 5.00

No. B30 (Cathedral) Surcharged

1L36 SP7 5d on 15c+60c brn pur 40.00 40.00

Nos. 259-260 (Lagree) Surcharged Vertically

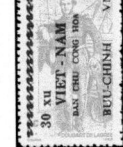

1L37 A52 30xu on 1c dl gray brn (R) 3.00 —
1L38 A52 3d on 15c dl rose vio 6.00 —

Nos. 243-244 (La Grandiere) Surcharged

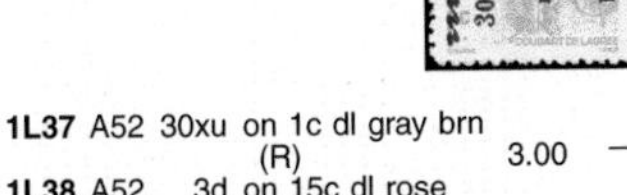

1L39 A45 1d on 5c dk brn (Bl) 8.00 8.00
1L40 A45 4d on 1c dull brn 4.00 6.00

Type of 1943 (Garnier) Srchd.

1L41 A42 30xu on 15c dp plum (R) 2.00 3.00

No. 237 (Garnier) Surcharged with New Value, "VIET-NAM DAN CHU CONG HOA BUU-CHINH," Wavy & Straight Line Obliterators

1L42 A42 5d on 1c dull ol bis 6.00 —

Nos. 249-252 (De Lanessan, Van Vollenhoven) Surcharged

No. 1L43

No. 1L44

No. 1L45

No. 1L46

1L43 A49 50xu on 1c ol brn 5.00 6.00
1L44 A48 60xu on 1c ol brn 5.00 5.00
1L45 A48 1.60d on 10c green 3.00 4.00
1L46 A49 3d on 15c dp red-dish pur (Bl) 4.00 6.00
Nos. 1L43-1L46 (4) 17.00 21.00

Nos. B30-B31 (Cathedral) Surcharged

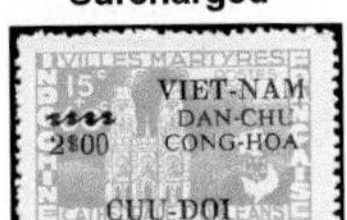

1L47 SP7 2d on 15c+60c pur brn 25.00 —
1L48 SP7 3d on 40c+1.10pi blue 25.00 —

No. 234 (Yersin) Surcharged

1L49 A41 +2d on 6c car rose 5.00 —

No. 233 (Behaine) Surcharged

1L50 A40 +3d on 20c dull red 9.00 9.00

No. 215 (Saigon Fair) Surcharged

1L51 A30 +4d on 6c car rose 5.00 6.00

No. 229 (Natl. Revolution) Surcharged

1L52 A36 +4d on 6c car rose 10.00 —

Nos. 213-214 Surcharged

1L53 A29 +5d on 3c reddish brown 8.00 10.00
1L54 A29 +10d on 6c crimson 8.00 12.00

Nos. 216, 224 Surcharged

1L55 A31 30xu +3d on 6c (Nam-Phuong) 2.00 3.00

Perf. 13½

1L56 A33 30xu +3d on 6c (Bao-Dai) 2.50 3.00
a. Perf. 12 30.00

Ho Chi Minh — VM1

1946 Litho. Unwmk. *Perf. 11½*
Without Gum

1L57 VM1 1h green 1.00 1.00
1L58 VM1 3h brt rose red 1.00 1.00
1L59 VM1 9h yellow bister 1.00 1.00

With Added Inscription

1L60 VM1 4h +6h Prus blue 2.50 5.00
1L61 VM1 6h +9h dp pur 2.50 5.00
Nos. 1L57-1L61 (5) 8.00 13.00

Ho Chi Minh — VM2

1948 Typo. *Perf. 7 Rough*
Thin, Rough, Brown Paper

1L62 VM2 2d brown, *buff* 20.00 160.00
1L63 VM2 5d red, *buff* 20.00 160.00

For surcharge and overprints see Nos. 50, O6-O7.

DEMOCRATIC REPUBLIC OF VIET NAM

From 1945-2002, all stamps are without gum unless otherwise indicated. Values for stamps with gum are for Never Hinged items.

Many North Vietnamese stamps are roughly perforated, especially issues before 1958.

Ho Chi Minh, Map of Vietnam — A1

1951-55 Unwmk. Litho. *Imperf.*

1 A1 100d brown 27.50 *20.00*
a. Perf. 11¼ ('55) 27.50 *20.00*
2 A1 100d green 27.50 *20.00*
a. Perf. 11¼ ('55) 27.50 *20.00*

Perf. 11¼

3 A1 200d red 20.00 *20.00*
a. Imperf. ('55) 20.00 *20.00*
Nos. 1-3 (3) 75.00 60.00

Nos. 1-3 printed on thin semi-transparent paper.

Nos. 1-3 used values are for cto. Postally used examples are worth about 5 times these values.

Counterfeits exist.

For surcharges, see Nos. 9-14, 36-38, and note before No. J1.

Blacksmith — A2

1953-55 *Perf. 11¼*

4 A2 100d violet 6.00 3.00
5 A2 500d brown 9.00 *8.00*

Issued: 100d, 6/53. 500d, 2/55.

Georgi Malenkov, Ho Chi Minh, Mao Tse-tung and Flags — A3

1954-55 *Perf. 11¼*

6 A3 50d brown & red, *brnish* 25.00 *25.00*
7 A3 100d red 25.00 *25.00*
8 A3 100d yellow & red, *brnish* 30.00 *30.00*
Nos. 6-8 (3) 80.00 *80.00*

Issued: 50d, 10/54; #7, 1/54; #8, 4/55.

No. 7 printed on thin, white paper.

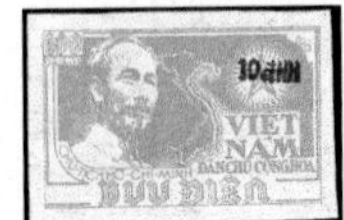

Nos. 1-3 Surcharged in Red or Blue

1954, Oct. *Imperf.*

9 A1 10d on 100d brown 22.50 *32.50*
10 A1 10d on 100d green 22.50 *32.50*

Perf. 11

11 A1 20d on 200d red (Bl) 22.50 *42.50*
Nos. 9-11 (3) 67.50 *107.50*

Nos. 1-3 Surcharged in Black, Red or Blue

1954, Oct. *Imperf.*

12 A1 10d on 100d brown (Bk, R or Bl) 26.00 *35.00*
13 A1 10d on 100d green (Bk, R or Bl) 26.00 *35.00*

Perf. 11

14 A1 20d on 200d red (Bk or Bl) 60.00 *75.00*
Nos. 12-14 (3) 112.00 *145.00*

Nos. 9-14 exist with counterfeit surcharges, counterfeit surcharges on counterfeit stamps, and with fantasy surcharges.

Victory at Dien Bien Phu — A4

1954-56 *Perf. 11¼*

17 A4 10d red brn & yel brn 25.00 *25.00*
a. Imperf 110.00 *110.00*
18 A4 50d red & org yel 20.00 *7.50*
a. Imperf 25.00 *15.00*
19 A4 150d brown & blue 20.00 *10.00*
a. Imperf 25.00 *15.00*
Nos. 17-19 (3) 65.00 *42.50*

Issued: Imperfs, 10/54; others, 1956. See #O5.

Used values for Nos. 17-19 are for postally used examples. The 10d exists cto, perf or imperf. Value about 1/10 those shown above.

Liberation of Hanoi — A5

1955, Jan. 1 *Perf. 11½*

20 A5 10d lt blue & bl 6.50 6.50
21 A5 50d dk grn & grn 8.00 8.00
22 A5 150d rose & brn red 10.00 12.00
Nos. 20-22 (3) 24.50 26.50

Nos. 20-22 used values are for postally used examples. Cto stamps are worth about $1 each.

Land Reform — A6

1955-56 *Perf. 11¼*

23 A6 5d lt green 18.00 4.75
24 A6 10d gray 18.00 4.75
25 A6 20d orange 18.00 6.00
26 A6 50d rose 18.00 6.00
27 A6 100d lt brown 37.50 6.00
Nos. 23-27 (5) 109.50 27.50

Issued: 100d, 12/55; 20d, 50d, 2/56; others, 6/56. See Nos. O8-O9.

Return of Government to Hanoi — A7

1956, Mar. 1 *Perf. 11¼*

28 A7 1000d violet 47.50 12.00
29 A7 1500d dk blue 65.00 12.00
30 A7 2000d turquoise 65.00 12.00
31 A7 3000d blue green 80.00 12.00
Nos. 28-31 (4) 257.50 48.00

Counterfeits exist, often imperf and offered as proofs.

Re-opening of Hanoi-China Railroad — A8

1956, Mar. 1

32 A8 100d dark blue 20.00 6.00
33 A8 200d blue green 20.00 6.00
34 A8 300d violet 40.00 6.00
35 A8 500d lilac brown 47.50 *6.00*
Nos. 32-35 (4) 127.50 24.00

Counterfeits exist, often imperf and offered as proofs.

Nos. 1-3 Surcharged

1954, Oct. *Imperf.*

36 A1 10d on 100d brown 25.00 *40.00*
37 A1 10d on 100d green 25.00 —

Perf. 11

38 A1 20d on 200d red 15.00 *15.00*
Nos. 36-38 (3) 65.00 *55.00*

Nos. 36-38 exist with counterfeit surcharges, counterfeit surcharges on counterfeit stamps, and with fantasy surcharges.

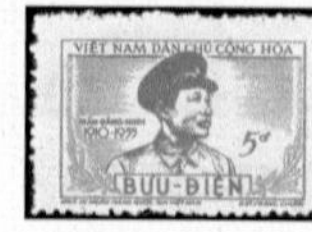

Tran Dang Ninh (1910-55), Guerrilla Leader — A9

1956, July **Litho.** *Perf. 11¼*

39 A9 5d bl grn & pale grn 4.50 *2.00*
40 A9 10d lilac & rose 4.50 *2.00*
41 A9 20d gr brn & dk gray 5.50 *3.00*
42 A9 100d dk blue pale bl 6.50 *3.50*
Nos. 39-42 (4) 21.00 *10.50*

Nos. 39-42 used values are for postally used. CTO value, set $2.50.

Mac Thi Buoi (1927-51), Guerrilla Leader — A10

1956, Nov. 3 *Perf. 11½*

43 A10 1000d rose & lilac rose 47.50 15.00
44 A10 2000d brown & bister 90.00 24.00
45 A10 4000d bl grn & green 190.00 35.00
46 A10 5000d ultra & lt blue 240.00 *60.00*
Nos. 43-46 (4) 567.50 *134.00*

Nos. 43-46 used values are for postally used. Cto value, set $40.

Counterfeits exist, often imperf and offered as proofs.

Bai Thuong Dam — A11

1956-58 *Perf. 11¼*

47 A11 100d vio bl & lil brn 10.00 *6.50*
a. Perf 13 11.00 *9.50*
48 A11 200d lilac & gr grn 11.00 *6.50*
a. Perf 13 12.50 *11.00*
49 A11 300d rose & lil brn 16.00 *12.00*
a. Perf 13 12.50 *11.00*
Nos. 47-49 (3) 37.00 25.00

Nos. 47-49 used values are for postally used. CTO values: Nos. 47-49, set $4; Nos. 47a-49a, set $5.50.

Issued: #47-49, 12/15/56; #47a-49a, 1958.

No. 1L63 Surcharged

1956, Dec. **Typo.** *Perf. 7 Rough*

50 VM2 50d on 5d org red, *brnish* 75.00 *50.00*
a. 50d on 5d dp red, *brnish* 90.00 100.00

Reprints and counterfeits exist.

Nam Dinh Textile Mill — A13

1957, Mar. **Litho.** *Perf. 12½*

51-53 A13 100d, 200d, 300d, set of 3 25.00 2.50
51a Perf. 11½ 6.00 6.00
51b Imperf 12.00 12.00
51c Perf. 11½x12½ 6.50 6.50
51d Imperf x perf 11½ 12.00 12.00

Nos. 51-53 used values are for cto. Postally used value, set $25.

Ho Chi Minh — A14

1957 *Perf. 12½*

54-57 A14 20d, 60d, 100d, 300d, set of 4 20.00 2.00

Nos. 54-57 used values are for cto. Postally used value, set $8.

Issued: 20d, 60d, 12/13; others, 5/19.

Fourth World Trade Union Congress, Leipzig — A15

1957, Aug. 1 *Perf. 12½*

58 A15 300d red violet 8.00 .75

No. 58 used value is for cto. Postally used value $5.50.

See Nos. O17-O20.

Democratic Republic, 12th Anniv. — A16

1957, Sept. 2 *Perf. 13*

59-60 A16 20d, 100d set of 2 *14.00* 2.00

Nos. 59-60 used values are for cto. Postally used value, set $5.50.

Presidents Voroshilov, Ho Chi Minh — A17

1957, Nov. 7 *Perf. 12½*

61-63 A17 100d, 500d, set of 1000d 3 45.00 30.00

Russian revolution, 40th anniv.

Used values from No. 64 on are for cto stamps. Postally used examples are worth substantially more.

Anti-illiteracy Campaign — A18

1958, Jan. 6 *Perf. 12½*

64-66 A18 50d, 150d, 1000d, set of 3 30.00 2.00

A19

1958, Mar. 8

67-68 A19 150d, 500d, set of 2 30.00 2.50

Physical education.

May Day — A20

1958, May 1

69-70 A20 50d, 150d, set of 2 10.00 1.10

Fourth Intl. Congress of Democratic Women, Vienna — A21

1958, May **Typo.**

71 A21 150d blue 8.00 .75

A22 A22a

A22: #72, 150d, #75, 2000d, Basket, lace & cup, vert.

A22a: #73, 150d, #74, 1000d, Potter.

1958 **Litho.**

72-75 A22, A22a Set of 4 25.00 2.00

Arts & Crafts Fair, Hanoi.

Issued: Nos. 72, 75, 6/26; others, 8/19.

Building the Reunification Railway — A23

1958, July 20

76-77 A23 50d, 150d, set of 2 8.00 .75

August Revolution, 13th Anniv. — A24

1958, Aug. 19

78-79 A24 150d, 500d, set of 2 7.00 1.10

Resistance Movement in South Viet Nam, 13th Anniv. — A25

1958, Sept. 23

80-81 A25 50d, 150d, set of 2 10.00 .75

A26

1958, Oct.

82 A26 150d grnsh blue & blk 3.00 .40

Tran Hung Dao (1253-1300).

A27

Hanoi Engineering Plant.

1958, Nov. 7 **Engr.** *Perf. 11½*

83 A27 150d brown 3.00 .40

Mutual Aid Teams — A28

1958, Nov. 7
84-85 A28 150d, 500d, set of 2 12.00 2.75

Ngoc Son Temple (Temple of Jade) — A29

1958, Dec. 1 Photo. *Perf. 12*
86-87 A29 150d, 2000d, set of 2 30.00 3.00

Rattanware Cooperative — A30

1958, Dec. 31
88 A30 150d greenish blue 2.75 .65

Ha Long Bay — A31

1959, Feb. 8
89-90 A31 150d, 350d, set of 2 7.00 2.00

Cam Pha Coal Mines — A32

1959, Mar. 3 Engr. *Perf. 11½*
91 A32 150d blue 8.50 .40

Trung Sisters — A33

1959, Mar. 14 Litho. *Perf. 11*
92-93 A33 5xu, 8xu, set of 2 8.00 1.10

World Peace Movement, 10th Anniv. — A34

1959, Apr. 15
94 A34 12xu purple, *rose* 2.50 .50

Xuan Quang Dam — A35

1959, May 1
95-96 A35 6xu, 12xu, set of 2 8.00 .70

Phu Loi Massacre — A36

1959, May 15
97-98 A36 12xu, 20xu, set of 2 5.50 .70

Hien Luong Bridge — A37

1959, July 20
99 A37 12xu black & carmine 3.00 .65

Me Tri Radio Station — A38

1959, Aug. 10
100-101 A38 3xu, 12xu, set of 2 4.50 1.00

Shooting — A39

Swimming — A39a

Wrestling — A39b

1959, Sept. 2

102	A39	1xu lt blue & dk blue	1.25	.35
103	A39a	6xu multicolored	2.00	.35
104	A39b	12xu brown rose	3.75	.35
		Nos. 102-104 (3)	7.00	1.05

People's Republic of China, 10th Anniv. — A40

1959, Oct. 1
105 A40 12xu multicolored 5.00 .70

Fruits — A41

Designs: 3xu, Coconuts. 12xu, Bananas. 30xu, Pineapple.

1959, Nov. 20
106-108 A41 Set of 3 9.00 1.00

People's Army, 15th Anniv. — A42

1959, Dec. 22
109 A42 12xu multicolored 3.00 .35

A43

1960, Jan. 6
110-111 A43 2xu, 12xu, set of 2 4.50 .70

Vietnamese Workers' Party, 30th Anniv.

A44

Ethnic costumes: 2xu, Ede. 10xu, Meo. No. 114, 12xu, Tay. No. 115, 12xu, Thai.

1960, Jan. 6
112-115 A44 Set of 4 8.50 2.00

Census — A45

Designs: 1xu, People. 12xu, Transmitting tower, dam, buildings, workers.

1960, Feb. 20
116-117 A45 Set of 2 3.50 1.00

No. 117 is 37x26mm.

Intl. Women's Day, 50th Anniv. — A46

1960, Mar. 8
118 A46 12xu multicolored 2.00 .70

A47

1960, Apr. 5
119-120 A47 4xu, 12xu, set of 2 60.00 20.00

Hung Vuong Temple.

A48

1960, Apr. 22
121-122 A48 5xu, 12xu, set of 2 6.00 1.00
121a Souv. sheet of 1, olive brown & blue, imperf. 70.00 65.00

Lenin. No. 121a exists on brownish paper.

Election of National Assembly Delegates — A49

1960, May 3 *Perf. 11*
123 A49 12xu multicolored, *rose* 1.50 .45

A50

1960, May 8
124-125 A50 8xu, 12xu, set of 2 5.00 .65

Viet Nam Red Cross.

A51

Ho Chi Minh, 70th Birthday: Nos. 128, 130, Ho with children.

1960, May 19

126	A51	4xu green & purple	2.25	.35
127	A51	12xu pink & brown	3.50	.35
128	A51	12xu multicolored	3.50	.35
		Nos. 126-128 (3)	9.25	1.05

Souvenir Sheets

Imperf

129	A51	10xu yel bis & brn, *rose*	12.00	—
130	A51	10xu multicolored	11.00	—

No. 128 is 25x39mm.

New Constitution — A52

1960, July 7
131 A52 12xu lemon & gray 2.50 1.00

National Day, 15th Anniv. — A53

1960, Sept. 2
132-133 A53 4xu, 12xu, set of 2 6.00 .65

Development A54

Designs: No. 134, Classroom. No. 135, Plowing. No. 136, Factory.

1960, Sept. 2
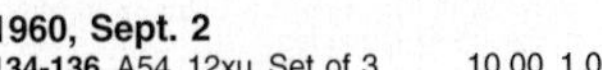
134-136 A54 12xu Set of 3 10.00 1.00

3rd Vietnamese Communist Party Congress — A55

1960, Sept. 4
137-138 A55 1xu, 12xu, set of 2 6.00 .65

World Federation of Trade Unions, 15th Anniv. — A56

1960, Oct. 3
139 A56 12xu black & vermilion 5.00 .35

Hanoi, 950th Anniv. — A57

1960, Oct. 10 Litho. *Perf. 11*

140-141 A57 8xu, 12xu, set of 2 7.00 .65

141a Souv. sheet of 1, imperf. 15.00 12.00

No. 141a exists on brownish paper.

15 Years' Achievements Exhibition — A58

1960, Oct. 20

142-143 A58 2xu, 12xu, set of 2 3.50 .65

World Federation of Democratic Youth, 15th Anniv. — A59

1960, Nov. 10

144 A59 12xu multicolored 3.00 .35

Trade Unions, 2nd Natl. Congress — A60

1961, Feb. 10

145 A60 12xu multicolored, *rose* 2.00 .35

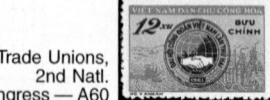

Vietnamese Women's Union, 3rd Natl. Congress — A61

1961, Mar. 8 Tinted Paper

146-147 A61 6xu, 12xu, set of 2 5.00 1.25

Animals — A62

Designs: 12xu, Rusa unicolor. 20xu, Helarctos malynus. 50xu, Elephas maximus. 1d, Hylobates leucogenys.

1961, Mar. 8

148-151 A62 Set of 4 25.00 3.50

Imperf., #148-151 60.00 60.00

Ly Tu Trong — A63

1961, Mar. 18

152-153 A63 2xu, 12xu, set of 2 3.00 .75

Youth Labor Union, 3rd Congress.

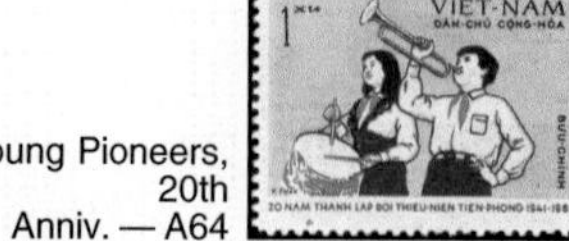

Young Pioneers, 20th Anniv. — A64

1961, May 2

154-155 A64 1xu, 12xu, set of 2 4.00 .75

Intl. Red Cross — A65

1961, May 8

156-157 A65 6xu, 12xu, set of 2 6.50 .70

Intl. Children's Day — A66

1961, June 1 *Perf. 11*

158-159 A66 4xu, 12xu, set of 2 5.50 .70

Yuri Gagarin's Space Flight — A67

1961, June 15

160-161 A67 6xu, 12xu, set of 2 21.00 2.00

Imperf., #160-161 27.00 —

Hanoi, Hue and Saigon — A68

1961, July 20

162-163 A68 12xu, 3d, set of 2 11.00 1.00

A69

1961, July 20

164-165 A69 12xu, 2d, set of 2 9.00 1.00

Imperf., #164-165 — —

Reunification campaign.

A70

1961, Aug. 21

166-167 A70 2xu, 12xu, set of 2 5.50 .70

Geological exploration.

Savings Campaign — A71

1961, Aug. 21

168-169 A71 3xu, 12xu, set of 2 5.00 .70

Ancient Towers — A72

Designs: 6xu, Thien Mu, Hue. 10xu, Pen Brush, Bac Ninh. No. 172, 12xu, Binh Son, Vinh Phuc. No. 173, 12xu, Cham, Phan Rang.

1961, Sept. 12

170-173 A72 Set of 4 9.00 3.75

Imperf., #170-173 25.00 12.00

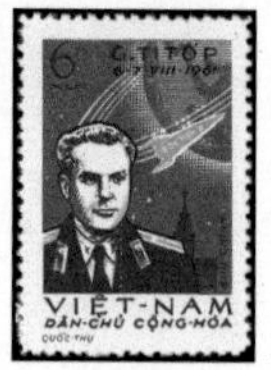

A73

6xu, 12xu, Gherman Titov's Space Flight.

1961, Oct. 17

174-175 A73 Set of 2 7.00 .80

Imperf., #174-175 11.00 10.00

A74

1961, Oct. 17

176 A74 12xu vermilion & black 3.00 .40

22nd Communist Party Congress, Moscow.

Port of Haiphong A75

1961, Nov. 7

177-178 A75 5xu, 12xu, set of 2 9.00 .80

A76

Musicians: No. 179, 12xu, Flutist. No. 180, 12xu, Cymbalist. 30xu, Dancer with fan. 50xu, Guitarist.

1961, Nov. 18 *Perf. 13½*

179-182 A76 Set of 4 14.00 2.00

Imperf., #179-182 18.00 20.00

182a Souvenir sheet, #179-182 55.00 50.00

Stamps on No. 182a are se-tenant and perfed on outside edges of the strip of 4.

5th World Trade Union Congress, Moscow — A77

1961, Dec. 4 *Perf. 11*

183 A77 12xu dp red lil & gray 2.00 .45

Natl. Resistance, 15th Anniv. — A78

1961, Dec. 4

184-185 A78 4xu, 12xu, set of 2 2.00 .65

Tet Holiday — A79

Designs: 6xu, Sow, piglets. 12xu, Poultry.

1962, Jan. 16 Litho.

186-187 A79 Set of 2 9.00 1.50

Tet Tree-Planting Festival — A80

1962, Jan. 16

188-189 A80 12xu, 40xu, set of 2 5.00 .80

Crops — A81

Designs: 2xu, Camellia sinensis. 6xu, Illicium verum. No. 192, 12xu, Coffea arabica. No. 193, 12xu, Ricinus communis. 30xu, Rhus succedanea.

1962, Mar. 1

190-194 A81 Set of 5 18.00 2.50

Folk Dances — A82

Designs: No. 195, 12xu, Rong Chieng. No. 196, 12xu, Bamboo. 30xu, Hat. 50xu, Parasol.

1962, Mar. 20 Photo. *Perf. 11½x12*

195-198 A82 Set of 4 20.00 2.25

Imperf., #195-198 22.00 20.00

Souvenir Sheet

199 A82 30xu like #195 18.00 16.00

First Five Year Plan — A83

Designs: 1xu, Kim Lien Apartments, Hanoi. 3xu, State farm. 8xu, Natl. Institute of Hydraulics.

1962, Apr. 10 Litho. *Perf. 11*

200-202 A83 Set of 3 3.50 1.25

A84

Flowers: No. 203, 12xu, Hibiscus rosa sinensis. No. 204, 12xu, Plumeria acutifolia. 20xu, Chrysanthemum indicum. 30xu, Nelumbium nuciferum. 50xu, Ipomoea pulchella.

Perf. 12½x11½

1962, Apr. 10 Photo.

203-207 A84 Set of 5 21.00 3.00

Imperf., #203-207 30.00 25.00

206a Souvenir sheet of 1 13.00 12.00

A85

1962, May 4 **Litho.** ***Perf. 11***
208 A85 12xu multicolored 3.00 .50

3rd Natl. Heroes of Labor Congress.

Harrow — A86

Dai Lai Lake — A87

1962, May 25
209-210 A86-A87 6xu, 12xu set of 2 4.00 .80

Visit by Gherman Titov — A88

Titov: 12xu, Waving at children. 20xu, Receiving medal from Ho Chi Minh. 30xu, Wearing space suit.

1962, June 12
211-213 A88 Set of 3 7.00 1.50
Imperf., #211-213 12.00 12.00

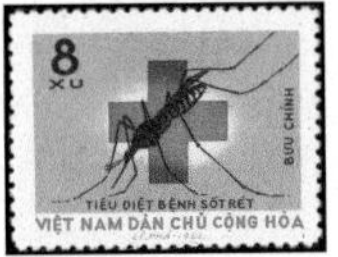
Anti-Malaria Campaign — A89

1962, July 9
214-216 A89 8xu, 12xu, 20xu, set of 3 7.50 1.50

War for Reunification — A90

1962, July 20
217 A90 12xu multicolored 2.50 .40

Ba Be Lake — A91

Design: No. 219, Ban Gioc Falls, vert.

1962, Aug. 14
218-219 A91 12xu Set of 2 4.00 .90

A stamp picturing a weight lifter exists, but was not released. Values: mint $120; used $130.

King Quang Trung (1752-92) — A92

1962, Sept. 16
220-221 A92 3xu, 12xu, set of 2 3.50 .70

Nguyen Trai (1380-1442) — A93

1962, Sept. 19
222-223 A93 3xu, 12xu, set of 2 3.50 .70

Food Crops — A94

Designs: 1xu, Peanuts. 4xu, Beans. 6xu, Sweet potatoes. 12xu, Corn. 30xu, Cassava.

1962, Oct. 10
224-228 A94 Set of 5 9.00 4.75
Imperf., #224-228

Animal Husbandry — A95

Designs: 2xu, Feeding poultry. No. 230, 12xu, Feeding pigs. No. 231, 12xu, Cattle grazing. No. 232, 12xu, Tending water buffalo.

1962, Nov. 28
229-232 A95 Set of 4 7.00 1.75

A stamp commemorating the 45th anniversary of the Russian Revolution exists, but was not issued. Value $200.

First Five Year Plan — A96

#233, Evening classes. #234, Clearing land.

1962, Dec. 28
233-234 A96 12xu Set of 2 5.00 .70

Flights of Vostok 3 and 4 — A97

12xu, Pavel Popovich, Vostok 4. 20xu, Andrian Nikolayev, Vostok 3. 30xu, Rockets lifting-off, vert.

1962, Dec. 28 ***Perf. 11***
235-237 A97 Set of 3 6.00 1.25
Imperf., #235-237 10.00 12.00

Guerrilla — A98

1963, Jan. 15
238-239 A98 5xu, 12xu, set of 2 3.50 .70

Hoang Hoa Tham (1846-1913) — A99

1963, Feb. 10
240-241 A99 6xu, 12xu, set of 2 3.00 .90

A100

First Five Year Plan — A100a

Designs: No. 242, Fertilizing rice paddy. No. 243, Lam Thao superphosphate plant.

1963, Feb. 25
242-243 A100-A100a 12xu Set of 2 3.50 .75

Karl Marx — A101

1963, Mar. 14
244-245 A101 3xu, 12xu, set of 2 3.00 .65

Nos. 244-245 are printed on greenish and rose toned paper respectively.

Fidel Castro, Vietnamese Soldiers — A102

1963, Apr. 17
246 A102 12xu multicolored 2.75 .50

May Day — A103

1963, May 8
247 A103 12xu multicolored 2.75 .45

A104

Intl. Red Cross, Cent. — A105

Design: No. 249, Child, syringe.

1963, May 8
248 A104 12xu grn, blk & red 1.50 .35
249 A104 12xu grn, red & blk 1.50 .35
250 A105 20xu multicolored 2.50 .35
Nos. 248-250 (3) 5.50 1.05

Mars 1 Spacecraft A106

6xu, 12xu (#252), Mars 1 approaching Mars. 12xu (#253), 20xu, Mars 1 entering orbit, vert.

1963, May 21
251-254 A106 Set of 4 7.50 1.50
Imperf., #251-254 17.00 15.00

Fishing Industry — A107

Designs: No. 255, Trawler, offshore fish. No. 256, Freshwater fish.

1963, July 3
255-256 A107 12xu Set of 2 9.00 .75

Ho Chi Minh, Nguyen Van Hien — A108

1963, July 20
257 A108 12xu multicolored 2.00 .35

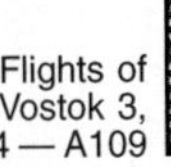
Flights of Vostok 3, 4 — A109

Designs: 12xu, Rockets in orbit. 20xu, Nikolayev. 30xu, Popovich.

1963, Aug. 11
258-260 A109 Set of 3 7.00 1.10
Imperf., #258-260 13.00 12.00

First Five Year Plan for Chemical Industry — A110

Designs: 3xu, Viet Tri Insecticide Factory. 12xu, Viet Tri Chemical Factory.

1963, Aug. 11
261-262 A110 Set of 2 3.25 .60

Fish — A111

Designs: No. 263, 12xu, Cyprinus carpio. No. 264, 12xu, Myloharyngodon piceus. No. 265, 12xu, Hypophthalmichthys molitrix. 20xu, Ophiocephalus caqua. 30xu, Tilapia mossambica.

1963, Sept. 10
263-267 A111 Set of 5 15.00 3.00
Imperf., #263-267 20.00 20.00
a. Souvenir Sheet Of 1, #266 60.00

A112

Birds: #268, 12xu, Francolinus stephenson. #269, 12xu, Acridotheres cristatellus. #270, 12xu, Halcyon smyrneusis. 20xu, Diardigallus diardi, horiz. 30xu, Egretta. 40xu, Psittacula alexandri.

Perf. 11½x12, 12x11½

1963, Oct. 15 **Photo.**
268-273 A112 Set of 6 35.00 3.50
Imperf., #268-273 50.00 45.00

Souvenir Sheet

274 A112 50xu Sheet of 1, like #272 80.00 80.00

A113

1963, Oct. 20 **Litho.** ***Perf. 11***
275 A113 12xu multicolored 1.75 .35

World Federation of Trade Unions Congress for Viet Nam.

GANEFO Games — A114

#276, 12xu, Swimming. #277, 12xu, Volleyball, vert. #278, 12xu, Soccer, vert. 30xu, High jump.

1963, Nov. 10
276-279 A114 Set of 4 4.50 1.50
Imperf., #276-279 7.00 6.00

A115

Flowers: 6xu, Rauwolfia verticillata. No. 281, 12xu, Sophora japonica. No. 282, 12xu, Fibraurea tinctoria. No. 283, 12xu, Chenopodium ambrosioides. 20xu, Momordica cochinchinensis.

1963, Dec. 3
280-284 A115 Set of 5 7.00 2.00
Imperf., #280-284 10.00 10.00

A116

1963, Dec. 20
285 A116 12xu multicolored 2.00 .35

World Day for Viet Nam.

A117

First Five-Year Plan — A118

6xu, Molten cast iron. #287, 12xu, Thai Nguyen Steel & Iron Works. #288, 12xu, Power lines.

1964, Jan. 25 **Litho.**
286-288 A117-A118 Set of 3 4.50 1.40

Intl. Quiet Sun Year — A119

1964, Jan. 25
289-290 A119 12xu, 50xu, set of 2 5.00 .80
Imperf., #289-290 20.00 17.50

Flights of Vostok 5 and 6 — A120

#291, 12xu, Rockets in orbit. #292, 12xu, Valery Bykovsky. 30xu, Valentina Tereshkova.

1964, Mar. 25
291-293 A120 Set of 3 6.00 1.00
Imperf., #291-293 12.00 12.00

A stamp commemorating the anniversary of the founding of the People's Democratic Republic of Korea was printed but not issued.

A121

Flowers: No. 294, 12xu, Persica vulgaris. No. 295, 12xu, Hibiscus mutabilis. No. 296, 12xu, Passiflora hispida. No. 297, 12xu, Saraca dives. 20xu, Michelia champaca. 30xu, Camellia amplexicaulis.

1964, Apr. 10 ***Perf. 11½x12***
294-299 A121 Set of 6 13.00 2.00
Imperf., #294-299 15.00 15.00

A122

Costumes: 6xu, Peasant, 19th cent. No. 301, 12xu, Woman wearing large hat, 19th cent. No. 302, 12xu, Woman carrying hat.

1964, Apr. 27 ***Perf. 11***
300-302 A122 Set of 3 5.00 1.00

Battle of Dien Bien Phu, 10th Anniv. — A123

Designs: 3xu, Artillery. 6xu, Machine gun emplacement. Nos. 305, 307c, Bomb disposal. Nos. 306, 307d, Farmer on tractor.

1964, May 7
303 A123 3xu red & black .80 .35
304 A123 6xu blue & black 1.20 .35
305 A123 12xu yel org & blk 2.00 .35
306 A123 12xu red lilac & black 2.00 .35
Nos. 303-306 (4) 7.50 1.60
Imperf., #303-306 12.00 12.00

Souvenir Sheet

Imperf

307 Sheet of 4 15.00 15.00
a. A123 3xu orange & black
b. A123 6xu yellow green & black
c. A123 12xu red, black & orange
d. A123 12xu blue & black

Ham Rong Bridge A124

1964, May 17
308 A124 12xu multicolored 2.50 .35

Wild Animals A125

Designs: No. 309, 12xu, Panthera tigris, vert. No. 310, 12xu, Pseudaxis axis, vert. No. 311, 12xu, Tapirus indicus. 20xu, Bubalus bubalis. 30xu, Rhinoceros bicornis. 40xu, Bibos banteng.

1964, June 2 ***Perf. 10½***
309-314 A125 Set of 6 15.00 2.25
Imperf., #309-314 21.00 25.00

Geneva Agreement on Viet Nam, 10th Anniv. — A126

Intl. Labor Federation Committee United with People of South Viet Nam — A127

1964, July 20 ***Perf. 11***
315-316 A126-A127 12xu Set of 2 2.50 .70

Nam Bac Ninh Pumping Station — A128

1964, Aug. 25
317 A128 12xu blue gray & black 1.50 .35

Liberation of Hanoi, 10th Anniv. — A129

6xu, People cheering soldiers in truck. 12xu, Construction, hammerhead crane.

1964, Oct. 10
318-319 A129 Set of 2 3.50 .70

Natl. Defense Games A130

Designs: 5xu, Rowing. No. 321, 12xu, Parachuting, vert. No. 322, 12xu, Gliders, vert. No. 323, 12xu, Shooting.

1964, Oct. 18
320-323 A130 Set of 4 6.50 2.25

Fruits — A131

Designs: No. 324, 12xu, Mangifera indica. No. 325, 12xu, Guarcinia mangostana. No. 326, 12xu, Nephelium litchi. 20xu, Anona squamosa. 50xu, Citrus medica.

1964, Oct. 31 **Photo.** ***Perf. 11½x12***
324-328 A131 Set of 5 11.00 2.00
Imperf., #324-328 15.00 12.00

World Solidarity Conference A132

Designs: a, Ba Dinh Hall. b, Vietnamese soldier shaking hands with foreign people. c, Fist, planes, submarine.

1964, Nov. 25 **Litho.** ***Perf. 11***
329 A132 12xu Strip of 3, #a.-c. 5.50 3.00

People's Army, 20th Anniv. — A133

Designs: No. 330, Soldiers, flag. No. 331a, Coast guards. No. 331b, Mounted border guards, vert.

1964, Dec. 22
330 A133 12xu multicolored 1.75 .35
331 A133 12xu Pair, #a.-b. 3.25 2.50
Nos. 330-331 (2) 5.00 2.85

Cuban Revolution, 6th Anniv. — A134

Designs: a, Vietnamese, Cuban flags. b, Cuban revolutionaries.

1965, Jan. 1
332 A134 12xu Pair, #a.-b. 4.00 .75

Economic & Cultural Development of Mountain Region — A135

Designs: 2xu, 3xu, Women pollinating corn. 12xu, Girls walking to school.

1965, Feb. 28
333-335 A135 Set of 3 3.00 1.00
Imperf., #333-335

A136

Vietnamese Worker's Party, 35th Anniv. — A137

Politicians: No. 336a, Le Hong Phong. b, Tran Phu. c, Hoang Van Thu. d, Ngo Gia Tu. e, Nguyen Van Cu.
No. 337a, Party flag. b, Worker, soldier.

1965, Feb. 3 **Litho.** ***Perf. 11***
336 A136 6xu Strip of 5, #a.-e. 15.00 15.00
337 A137 12xu Pair, #a.-b. 15.00 15.00
Nos. 336-337 (2) 30.00 30.00

Issued: No. 336, 2/3; No. 337, 1/30.

Transportation Ministers Conference, Hanoi — A138

12xu, 30xu, Nguyen Van Troi, locomotive.

1965, Mar. 23
338-339 A138 Set of 2 7.00 .70
Imperf., #338-339

Vignette on No. 339 is mirror image of No. 338.

Flight of Voskhod 1 — A139

20xu, Cosmonauts Komarov, Feoktistov, Yegorov, rocket, globe. 1d, Cosmonauts, rocket.

1965, Mar. 30
340-341 A139 Set of 2 8.00 .70
Imperf., #340-341 11.00 10.00

Lenin, 95th Birth Anniv. — A140

1965, Apr. 22 **Litho.**
342-343 A140 8xu, 12xu, set of 2 3.50 .70

A141

1965, May 19
344-345 A141 6xu, 12xu, set of 2 2.50 .70

Ho Chi Minh, 75th birthday.

A142

1965, May 19
346 A142 12xu multicolored 2.00 .35

Afro-Asian Conference, 10th anniv.

Trade Union Conference, Hanoi — A143

Designs: No. 347, Workers solidarity. No. 348, Soldiers, vert. No. 349, Naval battle.

1965, June 2
347-349 A143 12xu Set of 3 4.00 1.10

Wild Animals A144

Designs: No. 350, 12xu, Martes flavigula. No. 351, 12xu, Chrotogale owstoni. No. 352, 12xu, Manis pentadactyla. No. 353, 12xu, Presbytis delacouri, vert. 20xu, Petaurista lylei, vert. 50xu, Nycticebus pygmaeus, vert.

1965, June 24 **Photo.** ***Perf. 12***
350-355 A144 Set of 6 17.00 2.25
Imperf., #350-355 25.00 25.00

A145

1965, July 1 ***Perf. 11½x11***
356 A145 12xu multicolored 3.25 .35

6th Socialist Postal Ministers Conference.

A146

Nguyen Van Troi (1940-64). Denominations: 12xu, 50xu, 4d.

1965, July 20 **Litho.** ***Perf. 11***
357-359 A146 Set of 3 9.00 2.40

A147

Insects — A148

Designs: No. 360, 12xu, Tessaratoma papillosa. No. 361, 12xu, Rhynchocoris humeralis. No. 362, 12xu, Poeciliocoris latus.

No. 363, 12xu, Tosena melanoptera. 20xu, Cicada. 30xu, Fulgora candelaria.

1965, July 24 **Photo.**
360-362 A147 Set of 3 4.00 1.00
363-365 A148 Set of 3 10.00 1.00
Nos. 360-365 (6) 12.00 2.50
Imperf., #360-365 18.00 18.00

August Revolution, 20th Anniv. — A149

1965, Aug. 19 **Litho.**
366-367 A149 6xu, 12xu, set of 2 2.50 .70

Crustaceans A150

Designs: No. 368, 12xu, Penaeus indicus. No. 369, 12xu, Scylla serrata. No. 370, 12xu, Metapenaeus joyneri. No. 371, 12xu, Neptunus. 20xu, Palinurus japonicus. 50xu, Uca marionis.

1965, Aug. 19
368-373 A150 Set of 6 18.00 2.00
Imperf., #368-373 20.00 22.50

500th US Warplane Shot Down — A151

1965, Aug. 30
374 A151 12xu gray green & lilac 7.00 4.00

A152

Completion of 1st Five-Year Plan — A153

#375, Foundry worker. #376, Electricity, irrigation. #377, Public health, education. #378, Students, children playing. #379, Factory worker. #380, Agricultural workers.

1965
375-377 A152 12xu Set of 3 3.00 1.25
378-380 A153 12xu Set of 3 3.00 1.25
Imperf., #375-380

Issued: #375-377, 9/2; #378-380, 12/25.

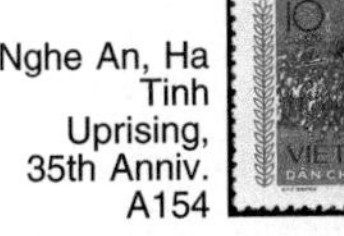
Nghe An, Ha Tinh Uprising, 35th Anniv. A154

1965, Sept. 12
381-382 A154 10xu, 12xu, set of 2 2.50 .80
Imperf., #381-382

Friendship Between Viet Nam, People's Republic of China, 16th Anniv. — A155

Designs: No. 383, Youth holding flags, Friendship Gate. No. 384, Children waving flags, walking through Gate, vert.

1965, Oct. 1
383-384 A155 12xu Set of 2 11.00 1.75

Flight of Voskhod 2 A156

#385, 12xu, Konstantin Tsiolkovsky, Sputnik I. #386, 12xu, Voskhod 2, A. Leonov, P. Belyayev. #387, 50xu, Yuri Gagarin. #388, 50xu, Leonov walking in space.

1965, Oct. 5
385-388 A156 Set of 4 7.50 3.25
Imperf., #385-388

A157

Norman R. Morrison, US anti-war demonstration.

1965, Nov. 22
389 A157 12xu black & red 2.50 .35

A158

Nguyen Du (1765-1820), poet: No. 390, 12xu, Birthplace. No. 391, 12xu, Museum. 20xu, Volume of poems entitled Kieu. 1d, Scene from Kieu.

1965, Nov. 25
390-393 A158 Set of 4 5.50 1.50

A159

Designs: No. 394, 12xu, Ho Chi Minh. No. 395, 12xu, Karl Marx. No. 396, 12xu, Lenin. 50xu, Frederich Engels.

Litho. & Engr. (#394), Litho.

1965, Nov. 28 ***Perf. 11½***
394-397 A159 Set of 4 5.50 1.50

Nos. 395-397 have white border.

Butterflies — A160

#398, 12xu, Cethosia cyane. #399, 12xu, Zelides sarpedon. #400, 12xu, Cethosia. #401, 12xu, Apatura ambica. 20xu, Papilio paris. 30xu, Tros aristolochiae.

1965, Nov. 18 **Litho.** ***Perf. 11***
398-403 A160 Set of 6 20.00 2.25
Imperf., #398-403 55.00 55.00

South Viet Nam Natl. Liberation Front, 5th Anniv. A161

1965, Dec. 20
404 A161 12xu lilac 2.50 .35
Imperf.

1st General Elections, 20th Anniv. — A162

1966, Jan. 6
405 A162 12xu black & red 2.50 .35

A163

Orchids: No. 406, 12xu, Vanda teres. No. 407, 12xu, Dendrobium meschatum. No. 408, 12xu, Dendrobium nobile. No. 409, 12xu, Dendrobium crystallinum. 20xu, Vandopsis gigantea. 30xu, Dendrobium.

1966, Jan. 10 ***Perf. 12***
406-411 A163 Set of 6 12.00 2.50
Imperf., #406-411 22.00 20.00

A164

1966, Jan. 18 ***Perf. 11***

412 A164 12xu multicolored 2.50 .35

Imperf.

New Year 1966 (Year of the Horse).

Reptiles — A165

#413, 12xu, Physignathus cocincinus. #414, 12xu, Gekko gecko. #415, 12xu, Trionyx sinensis. #416, 12xu, Testudo elongata. 20xu, Varanus salvator. 40xu, Eretmochelys imbricata.

1966, Feb. 25 ***Perf. 12x11½***

413-418 A165 Set of 6 12.00 2.25

Imperf., #413-418 20.00 20.00

Natl. Sports — A166

Designs: No. 419, Archery. No. 420, Wrestling. No. 421, Spear fighting.

1966, Mar. 25 ***Perf. 11***

419-421 A166 12xu Set of 3 4.50 1.10

6xu, 12xu, 1d stamps for running, swimming and shooting were printed but not issued.

Youth Labor Union, 35th Anniv. — A167

1966, Mar. 26

422 A167 12xu multicolored 1.75 .50

1000th US Warplane Shot Down — A168

1966, Apr. 29

423 A168 12xu multicolored 6.00 4.00

May Day — A169

1966, May 1

424 A169 6xu multicolored 1.75 .35

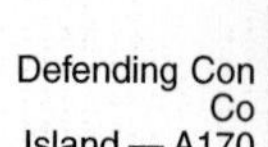

Defending Con Co Island — A170

1966, June 1

425 A170 12xu multicolored 2.50 .35

A171

1966, June 1

426 A171 12xu red & black 1.75 .35

Young Pioneers, 25th anniv.

A172

Designs: 3xu, View of Yenan. 12xu, Ho Chi Minh, Mao Tse-Tung.

1966, July 1

427-428 A172 Set of 2 4.00 .70

Imperf., #427-428

Chinese Communist Party, 45th anniv.

A173

Luna 9: 12xu, Flight path to moon. 50xu, In lunar orbit.

1966, Aug. 5

429-430 A173 Set of 2 7.00 1.25

Imperf., #429-430 9.00 10.00

A174

1966, Oct. 14

431 A174 12xu multicolored 10.00 3.00

With Additional Inscription: "NGAY 14.10.1966"

431A A174 12xu multicolored 15.00 3.75

Imperf., #431-431A

1500th US warplane shot down.

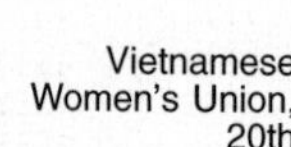

Victory in Dry Season Campaign A175

Designs: 1xu, 12xu (No. 433), Woman guerrilla carrying guns. 12xu (No. 434), Soldier escorting prisoners of war.

1966, Oct. 15

432-434 A175 Set of 3 5.00 1.25

Imperf., #432-434

See also No. 618A.

Vietnamese Women's Union, 20th Anniv. — A176

1966, Oct. 20

435 A176 12xu orange & black 2.00 .35

Imperf.

Birds — A177

Designs: No. 436, 12xu, Pitta moluccensis. No. 437, 12xu, Psarisomus dolhousiae. Nos. 438, 12xu, Alcedo atthis, vert. No. 439, 12xu, Oriolus chinensis, vert. 20xu, Upupa epops, vert. 30xu, Oriolus traillii.

1966, Oct. 31 ***Perf. 12x12½, 12½x12***

436-441 A177 Set of 6 10.00 2.50

Imperf., #436-441 25.00 25.00

GANEFO Asian Games — A178

Designs: No. 442, Soccer. No. 443, Shooting. No. 444, Swimming. No. 445, Running.

1966, Nov. 25 ***Perf. 11***

442-445 Set of 4 6.00 1.25

Imperf., #442-445 10.00 10.00

443a A178 12xu Pair, #442-443 3.50

445a A178 30xu Pair, #444-445 4.50

Nos. 443a-445a (2) 8.00

Ho Chi Minh's Appeal for Natl. Resistance, 20th Anniv. — A179

Designs: No. 446, Flags, workers. No. 447, Soldiers, workers, ships.

1967, Jan. 30

446-447 A179 12xu Set of 2 2.00 .80

See Nos. 501-504.

Rice Harvest A180

1967, Jan. 30

448 A180 12xu multicolored 1.50 .35

Bamboo — A181

No. 449, 12xu, Bambusa arundinaceu. No. 450, 12xu, Arundinaria rolleana. No. 451, 12xu, Arundinaria racemosa. No. 452, 12xu, Bambusa bingami. 30xu, Bambusa nutans. 50xu, Dendrocalamus patellaris.

1967, Feb. 2 ***Perf. 12x11½***

449-454 A181 Set of 6 8.00 2.25

Imperf., #449-454 12.00 10.00

Wild Animals A182

Designs: No. 455, 12xu, Cuon rutilans. No. 456, 12xu, Arctictis binturong. No. 457, 12xu, Arctonyx collaris. 20xu, Viverra zibetha. 40xu, Macaca speciosa. 50xu, Neofelis nebulosa.

1967, Mar. 26 **Litho.** ***Perf. 12***

455-460 A182 Set of 6 10.00 2.25

Imperf., #455-460 13.00 12.00

2000th US Aircraft Shot Down — A183

1967, June 5 ***Perf. 11***

461-462 A183 6xu, 12xu, set of 2 10.00 3.00

Fish — A184

#463, 12xu, Saurida filamentosa. #464, 12xu, Scomberomorus niphonius. #465, 12xu, Haplogenys mucronatus. 20xu, Lethrinus haematopterus. 30xu, Formio niger. 50xu, Lutianus erythropterus.

1967, July 25 ***Perf. 12***

463-468 A184 Set of 6 10.00 2.25

Imperf., #463-468 13.00 13.00

A185

Launch of 1st Chinese ballistic missile: 12xu, Missile, flag, agricultural scene. 30xu, Missile, Gate of Heavenly Peace.

1967, July 25 ***Perf. 11***

469-470 A185 Set of 2 8.00 2.50

Imperf., #469-470

A186

Russian October Revolution, 50th anniv.: 6xu, Lenin, revolutionary soldiers. No. 472a, 12xu, Lenin, armed mob. No. 472b, 12xu, Lenin, Marx, Vietnamese soldiers. 20xu, Cruiser Aurora.

1967, Oct. 15

471-473 A186 Set of 4 4.00 1.25

No. 472 is printed se-tenant.

2500th US Warplane Shot Down — A187

Design: No. 475, Plane in flames, vert.

1967, Nov. 6
474-475 A187 12xu Set of 2 9.00 3.50

Nos. 474-475 exist imperf. Value, set $40.

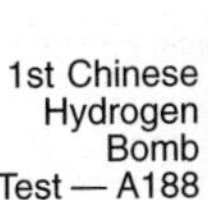

1st Chinese Hydrogen Bomb Test — A188

Designs: 12xu, Atomic symbol, Gate of Heavenly Peace. 20xu, Chinese lantern, atomic symbol, dove.

1967, Nov. 20
476-477 A188 Set of 2 6.50 1.50
Imperf., #476-477 32.00 30.00

No. 477 is 30x35mm.

A189

#478, 12xu, Rifle fire from trenches. #479, 12xu, Militia with captured US pilot. #480, 12xu, Factory anti-aircraft unit. #481, 12xu, Naval anti- aircraft unit. 20xu, Aerial dog-fight. 30xu, Heavy anti-aircraft battery.

1967, Dec. 19 ***Perf. 12***
478-483 A189 Set of 6 5.50 2.25

Chickens A190

Designs: No. 484, 12xu, White spotted cock, hen. No. 485, 12xu, Black hens. No. 486, 12xu, Bantam cock, hen. No. 487, 12xu, Bantam cock. 20xu, Fighting cocks. 30xu, Exotic hen. 40xu, Hen, chicks from Ho region. 50xu, Dong Cao's cock, hen.

1968, Feb. 29
484-491 A190 Set of 8 10.00 2.75
Imperf., #484-491 17.00 15.00

Victories of 1966-67 A191

No. 492: a, Soldier attacking US tank. b, Gunner firing on US ships. c, Burning stockade. d, Soldier firing mortar.

No. 493: a, Attacking US artillery. b, Escorting US prisoners. c, Interrogating refugees. d, Civilian demonstration.

1968, Mar. 5 ***Perf. 11***
492-493 A191 12xu Blocks of 4, set of 2 6.00 6.00
Imperf., #492-493

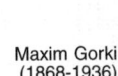

Maxim Gorki (1868-1936) A192

1968, Mar. 5
494 A192 12xu brown & black 1.50 .35
Imperf.

Roses — A193

Designs: No. 495, 12xu, Pale red. No. 496, 12xu, Orange. No. 497, 12xu, Pink. 20xu, Yellow, 30xu, Dark red. 40xu, Lilac.

1968, Apr. 25 Photo. ***Perf. 11½x12***
495-500 A193 Set of 6 10.00 2.25
Imperf., #495-500 15.00 15.00

Ho Chi Minh's Appeal for Resistance Type

Values and colors: No. 501, 6xu, greenish blue and yellow. No. 502, 12xu, vermilion. No. 503, 12xu, bright blue. No. 504, 12xu, brownish lilac.

1968, Apr. 25 Litho. ***Perf. 11***
Size: 25x17mm
501-504 A179 6xu, 12xu Set of 4 6.00 .75
Imperf., #501-504

Ho Chi Minh, Flag — A195

1968, May 19
505 A195 12xu brown & red 2.50 .40
Imperf.

Karl Marx — A196

1968, May 19
506 A196 12xu olive grn & blk 1.50 .35

3000th US Warplane Shot Down — A197

#507: a, 12xu, Anti-aircraft machine gunners. b, 12xu, Women firing anti-aircraft gun. #508: a, 40xu, Vietnamese plane shooting down US plane. b, 40xu, Anti-aircraft missile.

1968, June 25
507-508 A197 Set of 2 pairs 14.00 4.50
Imperf., #507-508

Handicrafts — A198

6xu, Rattan products. #510, 12xu, Ceramics. #511, 12xu, Bamboo products. 20xu, Ivory carving. 30xu, Lacquerware. 40xu, Silverware.

1968, July 5 ***Perf. 12***
509-514 A198 Set of 6 6.00 2.00
Imperf., #509-514 15.00 12.50

Martial Arts — A199

Designs: No. 515, 12xu, Saber fencing. No. 516, 12xu, Stick fighting. No. 517, 12xu, Dagger fighting. 30xu, Unarmed combat. 40xu, Chinese war sword fighting. 50xu, Duel with swords, shields.

1968, Oct. 25
515-520 A199 Set of 6 9.00 2.25
Imperf., #515-520 15.00 15.00

Architecture A200

Designs: No. 521, 12xu, Khue Van tower, vert. No. 522, 12xu, Bell tower, Keo pagoda, vert. 20xu, Covered bridge, Thay pagoda. 30xu, One-pillar pagoda, Hanoi, vert. 40xu, Gateway, Ninh Phuc pagoda. 50xu, Tay Phuong pagoda.

1968, Nov. 15
521-526 A200 Set of 6 5.50 2.50
Imperf., #521-526 10.00 10.00

Foreign Solidarity with Viet Nam — A201

#527, 12xu, Latin American guerrilla, vert. #528, 12xu, Cuban, Vietnamese militia. 20xu, Asian, African, Latin American soldiers, vert.

1968, Dec. 15 Wmk. 376 ***Perf. 12½***
With Gum
527-529 A201 Set of 3 4.00 2.25

Scenes of War — A202

Artworks: No. 530, 12xu, Defending the mines. No. 531, 12xu, Plowman with rifle, vert. 30xu, Repairing railway track. 40xu, Wreckage of US aircraft.

1968, Dec. 15 Wmk. 376 ***Perf. 12½***
With Gum
530-533 A202 Set of 4 4.00 2.50

Victories in South Viet Nam — A203

#534, 12xu, Tay Nguyen throwing grenade. #535, 12xu, Gun crews, Tri Thien. #536, 12xu, Nam Ngai shooting down US aircraft. 40xu, Insurgents, Tay Ninh, destroyed US armor. 50xu, Guerrillas preparing bamboo spike booby traps.

1969, Feb. 16 Unwmk. ***Perf. 11½***
534-538 A203 Set of 5 5.50 1.75

Timber Industry A204

Designs: 6xu, Loading timber trucks. No. 540, 12xu, Log raft running rapids. No. 541, 12xu, Launch towing log raft. No. 542, 12xu, Elephant hauling timber. No. 543, 12xu, Forest protection. 20xu, Water buffalo hauling log. 30xu, Hauling logs by overhead cable.

1969, Apr. 10
539-545 A204 Set of 7 8.00 2.50
Imperf., #539-545 15.00 15.00

Scenes of War — A205

Designs: No. 546, 12xu, Young guerrilla. No. 547, 12xu, Scout on patrol. 20xu, Female guerrilla, vert. 30xu, Halt at way station. 40xu, After a skirmish. 50xu, Liberated hamlet.

Perf. 12½x11½, 11½x12½
1969, June 20
546-551 A205 Set of 6 7.50 2.25
Imperf., #546-551 15.00 15.00

Tet Offensive Battles — A206

Designs: 8xu, 12xu (No. 553), Ben Tre. No. 554, 12xu, Mortar crew, Khe Sanh, vert. No. 555, 12xu, Two soldiers, flag, Hue, vert. No. 556, 12xu, Soldier running toward US Embassy, Saigon, vert.

1969, Sept. 20 ***Perf. 11***
552-556 A206 Set of 5 3.00 2.25
Imperf., #552-556

Liberation of Hanoi, 15th Anniv. — A207

#557, Soldier with flamethrower. #558, Children constructing toy buildings.

1969, Oct. 10
557-558 A207 12xu Set of 2 3.50 .65
Imperf., #557-558

A208

1969, Nov. 20
559 A208 12xu brn, blk & red 2.50 .35
Imperf.

Bertrand Russell Intl. War Crimes Tribunal, Stockholm and Roskilde.

A209

Fruits: No. 560, 12xu, Papaya. No. 561, 12xu, Grapefruit. 20xu, Tangerines. 30xu, Oranges. 40xu, Lychee nuts. 50xu, Persimmons.

1969, Nov. 20 ***Perf. 12***
560-565 A209 Set of 6 5.00 2.00
Imperf., #560-565 8.00 8.00

Viet Nam Labor Party, 40th Anniv. A210

Designs: No. 566, Nguyen Ai Quoc. No. 567, Ho Chi Minh. No. 568, Le Hong Phong. No. 569, Tran Phu. No. 570, Nguyen Van Cu.

1970, Feb. 3 *Perf. 11*
566-570 A210 12xu Set of 5 4.50 2.75
Imperf., #566-570

Nos. 568-570 are 40x25mm. Nos. 566-567 issued in vert. or horiz. se-tenant pairs. Nos. 568-570 issued in horizontal strips of 3.

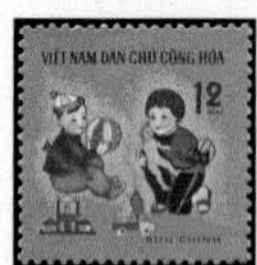
Children's Activities — A211

Designs: No. 571, 12xu, Playing with toys. No. 572, 12xu, Three boys at kindergarten. No. 573, 20xu, Tending a garden. No. 574, 20xu, Tending water buffaloes. 30xu, Feeding chickens. 40xu, Piano, violin duet. 50xu, Flying model airplane. 60xu, Walking to school.

1970, Mar. 8 *Perf. 12*
571-578 A211 Set of 8 6.00 2.75

For overprints see Nos. 2181-2188.

Lenin, Birth Centenary A212

Designs: 12xu, Making speech. 1d, Portrait.

1970, Apr. 22 *Perf. 11*
579-580 A212 Set of 2 4.00 .65
Imperf., #579-580

Shells — A213

No. 581, 12xu, Oc con lon. No. 582, 12xu, Oc xa cu. 20xu, Oc tien. 1d, Oc tu va.

1970, Apr. 26 *Perf. 12½x12*
581-584 A213 Set of 4 6.00 1.25
Imperf., #581-584 11.50 10.00

Ho Chi Minh — A214

12xu (#585, 588c, 588g), In 1930 (full face, no beard). 12xu (#586, 588b, 588f), In 1945 (facing right, beard). 2d, 6xu, (#587, 588a, 588e), In 1969 (full face, beard).

1970, May 19 *Perf. 11*
585-587 A214 Set of 3 4.50 1.10
Imperf., #585-587

Souvenir Sheets of 3

Imperf

588 Types of #585-587, #a.-c., orange background 8.00 7.00
588D Types of #585-587, #e.-g., pale lilac background 8.00 7.00

Stamps in souvenir sheets have white backgrounds. The 6xu stamp is larger than the 2d stamp. Nos. 588a and 588e, 588c and 588g are different colors.

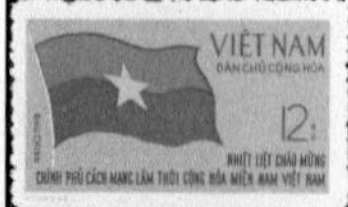
Vietcong Flag — A215

1970, June 6
589 A215 12xu multicolored 2.00 .35

Formation of Revolutionary Provisional Government of South Viet Nam, 1st anniv.

Fruits and Vegetables — A216

#590, 12xu, Watermelon. #591, 12xu, Pumpkin. 20xu, Cucumber. 50xu, Zucchini. 1d, Melon.

1970, July 15 *Perf. 12*
590-594 A216 Set of 5 5.00 1.75
Imperf., #590-594 12.00 12.00

Consumer Industries A217

#595, Coal miners, truck. #596, Power linesman, vert. #597, Textile worker, soldier, vert. #598, Stoker, power plant, vert.

Perf. 12x11½, 11½x12

1970, Aug. 25 **Litho. & Engr.**
595-598 A217 12xu Set of 4 3.50 1.25

Agriculture — A218

1970, Aug. 25 **Litho.** *Perf. 11*
599 A218 12xu multicolored 2.00 .35

Democratic Republic of Viet Nam, 25th Anniv. — A219

Famous people: #600, 12xu, Vo Thi Sau facing firing squad. #601, 12xu, Nguyen Van Troi, captors. #602, 12xu, Phan Din Giot attacking pillbox. #603, 12xu, Ho Chi Minh. 20xu, Nguyen Viet Xuan, troops in battle. 1d, Nguyen Van Be attacking tank with mine.

1970-71
600-605 A219 Set of 6 4.50 3.50
Imperf., #600-605

No. 603 is 41x28mm.
Issued 9/2-71: Nos. 600, 603, 604; 3/71: Nos. 601, 602, 605.

Indo-Chinese People's Summit Conf. — A220

1970, Oct. 25
606 A220 12xu multicolored 2.00 .35
Imperf.

Bananas — A221

Designs: No. 607, 12xu, Tay. No. 608, 12xu, Tieu. 50xu, Ngu. 1d, Mat.

1970, Oct. 25 *Perf. 12*
607-610 A221 Set of 4 6.50 1.25
Imperf., #607-610 12.00 12.00

Friedrich Engels — A222

1970, Nov. 28 *Perf. 11*
611-612 A222 12xu, 1d set of 2 3.00 .70

Snakes — A223

Designs: 12xu, Akistrodon ciatus. 20xu, Calliophis macclellandii. 50xu, Bungarus faciatus. 1d, Trimeresurus gramineus.

1970, Nov. 30 **Photo.** *Perf. 12x11½*
613-616 A223 Set of 4 5.50 .70
Imperf., #613-616 18.00 18.00

Natl. Liberation Front of South Viet Nam, 10th Anniv. — A224

Design: 6xu, Mother and child, flag, vert.

1970, Dec. 20 **Litho.** *Perf. 11*
617-618 A224 Set of 2 2.00 .70
Imperf., #617-618

Victory Type of 1966

1971, Mar.?
618A A175 2xu black & orange 2.00 .35

Launching of 1st Chinese Satellite, 1st Anniv. — A225

1971, Apr. 10
619-620 A225 12xu, 50xu Set of 2 5.50 .70
Imperf., #619-620

Ho Chi Minh — A226

Denominations: 1xu, 3xu, 10xu, 12xu.

1971, May 19
621-624 A226 Set of 4 2.50 1.25
Imperf., #621-624
624a Souvenir sheet of 1, imperf. 6.00 5.00

No. 624a contains one 52x52mm stamp.

Tay Son Uprising, Bicent. A227

1971, May 25
625-626 A227 6xu, 12xu, set of 2 2.50 .70
Imperf., #625-626

Marx, Music for The Internationale A228

1971, June 20 *Perf. 12½*
627 A228 12xu org, blk & red 2.50 .35
Imperf.

Paris Commune, cent.

Hai Thuong Lan Ong, Physician, 250th Birth Anniv. — A229

1971, July 1
628-629 A229 12xu, 50xu Set of 2 3.00 .70
Imperf., #628-629

Statues from Tay Phuong Pagoda — A230

Designs: No. 630, 12xu, Vasumitri. No. 631, 12xu, Kapimala. No. 632, 12xu, Dhikaca. No. 633, 12xu, Sangkayasheta. 30xu, Bouddha Nandi. 40xu, Rahulata. 50xu, Sangha Nandi. 1d, Cakyamuni.

1971, July 30 **Photo.** *Perf. 12*
630-637 A230 Set of 8 12.00 2.75
Imperf., #630-637 24.00 24.00

Ho Chi Minh Working Youth Union, 40th Anniv. — A231

1971, Sept. 7 **Litho.** *Perf. 11*
638 A231 12xu multicolored 1.50 .35
Imperf.

Flight of Luna 16 — A232

Luna 16: No. 639a, 12xu, Return from Moon. No. 639b, 12xu, Flight to Moon. 1d, On Moon.

1971, Sept. 17
639-640 A232 Set of 3 3.50 1.10
Imperf., #639-640 18.00 18.00

No. 639 is se-tenant.

Flight of Luna 17 — A233

Designs: No. 641, 12xu, Landing on Moon, vert. No. 642 12xu, On Moon. 1d, Lunakhod 1 crossing lunar crevasse.

1971, Oct. 15
641-643 A233 Set of 3 4.50 1.10
Imperf., #641-643 16.00 16.00

Five Tigers — A234

Folk paintings: No. 644, 12xu, White tiger. No. 645, 12xu, Red tiger. No. 646, 12xu, Yellow tiger. 40xu, Green tiger. 50xu, Black tiger. 1d, Five tigers.

1971, Nov. 25 ***Perf. 12***
644-649 A234 Set of 6 9.00 2.00
Imperf., #644-649 16.00 16.00

Size: 90x119mm

Imperf

650 A234 1d multicolored 14.00 12.00

Chinese Communist Party, 50th Anniv. — A235

1971, Dec. 1 ***Perf. 11***
651 A235 12xu multicolored 1.50 .35

Mongolian People's Republic, 50th Anniv. — A236

1971, Dec. 25
652 A236 12xu multicolored 1.50 .35

Folk Engravings from Dong Ho — A237

#653a, 12xu, Traditional wrestling. #653b, 12xu, Drum procession. #654a, 12xu, Gathering coconuts, vert. #654b, 12xu, Jealousy, vert. 40xu, Wedding of mice. 50xu, Frog school.

1972, Jan. 30
653-656 A237 Set of 6 9.00 4.25
Imperf., #653-656 10.00 10.00

No. 653 is tete-beche.
The 30xu in design of #654a is a proof.

3rd Natl. Trade Unions Congress — A238

Designs: 1xu, Workers facing right. 12xu, Workers facing left.

1972, May 1
657-658 A238 Set of 2 2.00 .70
Imperf., #657-658 10.00 10.00

Natl. Resistance, 25th Anniv. — A239

Designs: No. 659, Munitions worker. No. 660, Soldier in battle. No. 661, Woman in paddy field. No. 662, Text of Ho Chi Minh's appeal.

1972, May 5
659-662 A239 12xu Set of 4 3.00 1.25
Imperf., #659-662 20.00 20.00

Ho Chi Minh's Birthplace A240

Design: No. 664, Home in Hanoi.

1972, May 19
663-664 A240 12xu Set of 2 2.50 .70
Imperf., #663-664 5.00 5.00

A241

1972, June 20
665-666 A241 12xu Set of 2 5.00 2.00
Imperf., #665-666

3500th US warplane shot down.
Added inscription on No. 666 reads "NGAY 20.4.1972."

A242

Georgi Dimitrov (1882-1949), Bulgarian politician: No. 668, Dimitrov at Leipzig Court, 1933.

1972, Aug. 15
667-668 A242 12xu Set of 2 2.00 .70
Imperf., #667-668 5.00 5.00

Birds — A243

Designs: No. 669, 12xu, Lobivanellus indicus. No. 670, 12xu, Anas falcata. 30xu, Bubulcus ibis. 40xu, Gallicrex cinerea. 50xu, Prophyria porphyrio. 1d, Leptoptilos dubius.

1972, Oct. 12 ***Perf. 12***
669-674 A243 Set of 6 9.00 2.00
Imperf., #669-674 20.00 20.00

A244

4000th US warplane shot down: No. 676, Gunner holding rocket.

1972, Oct. 17 ***Perf. 11***
675-676 A244 12xu Set of 2 7.00 1.25
Imperf., #675-676 9.00

A245

Tay Nguyen folk dances: #677, 12xu, Drum. #678, 12xu, Umbrella. #679, 12xu, Shield. 20xu, Horse. 30xu, Ca Dong. 40xu, Rice pounding. 50xu, Khaen. 1d, Cham rong.

1972, Dec. 20 ***Perf. 12***
677-684 A245 Set of 8 8.00 2.50
Imperf., #677-684 10.00 10.00

Flight of Soyuz 11 — A246

Designs: 12xu, Soyuz 11 docking with Salyut laboratory. 1d, Soyuz 11 cosmonauts.

1972, Dec. 30 ***Perf. 11***
685-686 A246 Set of 2 3.00 .70
Imperf., #685-686 16.00 16.00

Wild Animals A247

Designs: 12xu, Cuon alpinus. 30xu, Panthera pardus. 50xu, Felis bengalensis. 1d, Lutra lutra.

1973, Feb. 15 ***Perf. 12½***
687-690 A247 Set of 4 6.50 1.50
Imperf., #687-690 22.00 22.00

Copernicus — A248

Copernicus and: No. 691a, 12xu, Armillary sphere. No. 691b, 12xu, Sun. 30xu, Signature, vert.

1973, Feb. 19 ***Perf. 11***
691-692 A248 Set of 3 3.50 1.75
Imperf., #691-692

Engravings on Ngoc Lu Bronze Drums A249

Designs: No. 693, Drummers (Nha Danh Trong). No. 694, Pounding rice (Nha Gia Gao). No. 695, Dancers (Mua). No. 696, War canoe (Thuyen). No. 697, Birds (Chim, Thu).

1973, Apr. 12
693-697 A249 12xu Set of 5 4.00 1.75
Imperf., #693-697

Wild Animals — A250

Designs: 12xu, Tragulus javanicus. 30xu, Capricornis sumatraensis. 50xu, Sus scrofa. 1d, Moschus moschiferus.

1973, May 25 ***Perf. 12x12½***
698-701 A250 Set of 4 4.50 1.25
Imperf., 698-701 12.00 12.00

Birds — A251

#702, 12xu, Pycnonotus jocosus. #703, 12xu, Megalurus palustris. 20xu, Capsychus saularis. 40xu, Rhipidura albicollis. 50xu, Parus major. 1d, Zosterops japonica.

1973, July 15 ***Perf. 12***
702-707 A251 Set of 6 6.00 2.10
Imperf., 702-707 15.00 15.00

Disabled Soldiers
A252 A252a

1973, July 27 ***Perf. 11***
708-709 A252, A252a 12xu Set of 2 *2.50 .80*
Imperf., #708-709

Nos. 708-709 were issued for the use of disabled soldiers.

Three Readiness Youth Movement A253

Designs: No. 710, Road building. No. 711, Open-air class. No. 712, On the march.

1973, Sept. 2
710-712 A253 12xu Set of 3 2.50 1.10
Imperf., #710-712

Democratic People's Republic of Korea, 25th Anniv. — A254

1973, Sept. 9
713 A254 12xu multicolored 1.50 .35
Imperf.

4181st US Warplane Shot Down — A255

Designs: No. 714, 12xu, US B-52 hit by air attack. No. 715, 12xu, US B-52, fighter crashing over Haiphong Harbor. No. 716, 12xu, Anti-aircraft battery. 1d, Aircraft wreckage caught in fishing net.

1973, Oct. 10
714-717 A255 Set of 4 8.00 1.75
Imperf., #714-717

Flowers — A256

6xu, 12xu (#719), Chrysanthemum (Cuc). #720, 12xu, Rose. #721, 12xu, Dahlia. #722, 12xu, Chrysanthemum (Bach mi). #723, 12xu, Chrysanthemum (Dai doa).

1974, Jan. 15
718-723 A256 Set of 6 35.00
Imperf., #718-723 75.00

Nos. 718-723 may not have been officially released.

Elephants — A257

#724, 12xu, Hauling logs. #725, 12xu, War elephant. 40xu, Setting logs in place. 50xu, Circus elephant. 1d, Carrying war supplies.

1974, Feb. 10 ***Perf. 11½***
724-728 A257 Set of 5 7.00 1.75
Imperf., #724-728 12.00 12.00

Victory at Dien Bien Phu, 20th Anniv. A258

Designs: a, Dien Bien Phu soldier's badge. b, Soldier waving victory flag.

1974, May 7 ***Perf. 11***

729 A258 12xu Pair, #a.-b. 2.50 .70
Imperf. 5.00 5.00

Three Responsibilities Women's Movement — A259

Designs: a, Armed worker, peasant. b, Female textile worker.

1974, June 1

730 A259 12xu Pair, #a.-b. 2.50 1.10
Imperf.

A260

Chrysanthemums: No. 731, 12xu, Brown. No. 732, 12xu, Yellow (Vang). 20xu, Ngoc Khong Tuoc. 30xu, White. 40xu, Kim. 50xu, Hong mi. 60xu, Gam. 1d, Lilac.

1974, June 20 ***Perf. 12x12½***

731-738 A260 Set of 8 6.50 4.00
Imperf., #731-738 11.00 11.00

A261

Industrial plants: No. 739, 12xu, Corchorus capsularis. No. 740, 12xu, Cyperus tojet jormis. 30xu, Morus alba.

1974, Aug. 15 ***Perf. 11***

739-741 A261 Set of 3 5.00 1.10
Imperf., #739-741 10.00 10.00

Liberation of Hanoi, 20th Anniv. — A262

Designs: a, Woman laying bricks. b, Soldier holding child waving flag.

1974, Oct. 10

742 A262 12xu Pair, #a.-b. 2.50 .70

Solidarity with Chilean Revolution — A263

Designs: No. 743, Pres. Salvador Allende, flag. No. 744, Pablo Neruda, poet.

1974, Oct. 15

743-744 A263 12xu Set of 2 2.50 .70
Imperf., #743-744 5.00 5.00

Marine Life — A264

Designs: No. 745, 12xu, Rhizostoma. No. 746, 12xu, Loligo. 30xu, Haleotis. 40xu, Pteria martensii. 50xu, Sepia officinalis. 1d, Palinurus japonicus.

1974, Oct. 25 ***Perf. 12½***

745-750 A264 Set of 6 7.00 2.10
Imperf., #745-750 12.00 12.00

People's Republic of Albania, 30th Anniv. A265

Designs: a, Natl. arms. b, Albanian, Vietnamese flags, women.

1974, Nov. 29 ***Perf. 11***

752 A265 12xu Pair, #a.-b. 2.00 .70
Imperf.

Paris Agreement on Vietnam, 2nd Anniv. A266

Designs: No. 753, Intl. Conference on Viet Nam in session, 5-line inscription. No. 754, Signing of Paris Agreement, 4-line inscription.

1975, Jan. 27

753-754 A266 12xu Set of 2 2.50 .70
Imperf.

Medicinal Plants — A267

Designs: No. 755, 12xu, Costus speciosus. No. 756, 12xu, Curcuma zedoaria. No. 757, 12xu, Rosa laevigata. 30xu, Erythrina indica. 40xu, Lilium brownii. 50xu, Hibiscus sagittifolius. 60xu, Papaver somniferum. 1d, Belamcanda chinensis.

1975, Feb. 8 ***Perf. 11½x12***

755-762 A267 Set of 8 7.50 2.75
Imperf., #755-762 12.50 12.50

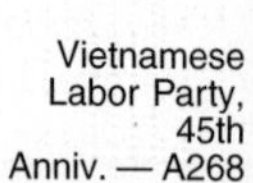

Vietnamese Labor Party, 45th Anniv. — A268

Designs: No. 763, 12xu, Tran Phu. No. 764, 12xu, Le Hong Phong. No. 765, 12xu, Nguyen Van Cu. No. 766, 12xu, Ngo Gia Tu. 60xu, Ho Chi Minh in 1924, vert.

1975, Feb. 3 ***Perf. 11***

763-767 A268 Set of 5 7.00 1.25
Imperf., #763-767 10.00 10.00

A269

Fruit: No. 768, 12xu, Achras sapota. No. 769, 12xu, Persica vulgaris. 20xu, Eugenia jambos. 30xu, Chrysophyllum cainito. 40xu, Lucuma mamosa. 50xu, Prunica granitum. 60xu, Durio ziberthinus. 1d, Prunus salicina.

1975, Apr. 25 ***Perf. 12x12½***

768-775 A269 Set of 8 7.00 2.50
Imperf., 768-775 12.00 12.00

A270

No. 776, 12xu. No. 777, 60xu.

1975, May 19 ***Perf. 11***

776-777 A270 Set of 2 3.50 1.10
Imperf., #776-777 10.00 10.00

Ho Chi Minh, 85th birthday.

People's Republic of Poland, 30th Anniv. — A271

1975, July 5

778-781 A271 1xu, 2xu, 3xu, 12xu, set of 4 3.00 .80
Imperf., #778-781

Flags — A272

Natl. Arms — A273

Flag of North Viet Nam and: No. 782, Draped flag. No. 783, Flag with star & cresent. No. 784, DDR flag and handshake.

1975

782-785 A272-A273 12xu Set of 4 6.00 .80
Imperf., #782-784

People's Republic of China, 25th anniv. (#782), Republic of Algeria, 20th anniv. (#783), German Democratic Republic, 25th anniv. (#784), liberation of Hungary, 30th anniv. (#785).

Issued: No. 782, 7/5. Nos. 783-785, 8/15.

Independence, 30th Anniv. — A274

#786, Flag. #787, Natl. arms. #788-789, Ho Chi Minh proclaiming independence.

1975, Sept. 2

786-788 A274 12xu Set of 3 3.00 1.10

Souvenir Sheet

Imperf

789 A274 20xu multi 20.00 15.00

No. 789 contains one 45x30mm stamp.

Reptiles — A275

#790, 12xu, Dermochelys coriacea. #791, 12xu, Physignathus cocincinus. 20xu, Hydrophis brookii. 30xu, Platysternum megacephalum. 40xu, Leiolepis belliana. 50xu, Python molurus. 60xu, Naja hannah. 1d, Draco maculatus.

1975, Nov. 25 ***Perf. 12***

790-797 A275 Set of 8 7.50 2.50
Imperf., #790-797 18.00 18.00

Butterflies A276

#798, 12xu, Pathysa antiphates. #799, 12xu, Danaus plexippus. 20xu, Cynautocera papilionaria. 30xu, Maenas salaminia. 40xu, Papilio machaon. 50xu, Ixias pyrene. 60xu, Eusemia vetula. 1d, Eriboea.

1976, Jan. 6

798-805 A276 Set of 8 8.00 2.50
Imperf., #798-805 22.50 22.50

No. 799 misspelled "Danais."

Lan Hoang Thao Orchid — A277

1976, Jan. 25 ***Perf. 11***

806-807 A277 6xu, 12xu, set of 2 4.00 1.25

See Nos. 854-855.

Wild Animals — A278

#808, 12xu, Callosciurus erythraeus. #809, 12xu, Paguma larvata. 20xu, Macaca mulatta. 30xu, Hystrix hodgsoni. 40xu, Nyctereutes procyonoides. 50xu, Selenarctos thibetanus. 60xu, Panthera pardus. 1d, Cynocephalus variegatus.

1976, Mar. 20 ***Perf. 12***

808-815 A278 Set of 8 6.50 2.25
Imperf., #808-815 13.00 13.00

A279

A279a

No. 816, Map, hand placing ballot in ballot box. Nos. 817, 818, Map, voters.

1976, Apr. 10 ***Perf. 11***

816 A279 6xu rose red & yel .75 .35
817 A279a 6xu brown & red .75 .35
818 A279a 12xu lt blue & red 2.00 .40
Imperf., #816-818
Nos. 816-818 (3) 3.50 1.10

1st Elections to Unified Natl. Assembly. Size of Nos. 817-818 is 35x22mm.

Identical stamps inscribed "Mien Nam Viet Nam" are National Front issues. Same values.

Unified Natl. Assembly, 1st Session — A280

Design: 12xu, Inscribed "Doc Lap Thong Nhat Chu Nghia Xa Hoi."

1976, June 24

819-820 A280 6xu, 12xu, set of 2 2.00 .70

Identical stamps inscribed "Mien Nam Viet Nam" are National Front issues. Same values.

A281

1976, June 24 ***Perf. 12x12½***
821 A281 12xu multicolored 1.50 .35

Reunification of Viet Nam.

A282

Orchids: No. 822, 12xu, Habenaria rhodocheila. No. 823, 12xu, Dendrobium devonianum. 20xu, Dendrobium tortile. 30xu, Doritis pulcherrima. 40xu, Dendrobium farmeri. 50xu, Dendrobium aggregatum. 60xu, Eria pannea. 1d, Paphiopedilum concolor.

1976, June 24 ***Perf. 12***
822-829 A282 Set of 8 8.00 1.50
Imperf., #822-829 13.00 13.00

DEMOCRATIC REPUBLIC OF VIET NAM (After Unification)

AREA — 128,000 sq. mi.
POP. — 77,311,210 (1999 est.)
CAPITAL — Hanoi

Vietnamese Red Cross, 30th Anniv. — A283

1976, July 27 ***Perf. 11***
830 A283 12xu multicolored 2.50 .35
Imperf.

Fish A284

#831, 12xu, Lutjanus sebae. #832, 12xu, Dampieria melanotaenia. 20xu, Therapon theraps. 30xu, Amphiprion bifasciatus. 40xu, Abudefduf sexfasciatus. 50xu, Heniochus acuminatus. 60xu, Amphiprion macrostoma. 1d, Symphorus spilurus.

1976, Aug. 15 ***Perf. 12***
831-838 A284 Set of 8 5.50 2.50
Imperf., #831-838 9.00 9.00

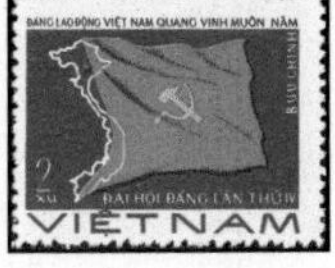

Viet Nam Worker's Party, 4th Natl. Congress — A285

1976, Nov. 12 ***Perf. 11***
839-844 A285 2, 3, 5, 10, 12, 20xu, set of 6 3.00 2.25

Viet Nam Communist Party, 4th Natl. Congress — A286

Designs: a, Agriculture, industry. b, Ho Chi Minh, worker, farmer, soldier, scientist.

Design size: 24.5mmx35mm

1976, Dec. 10
845 A286 12xu Pair, #a.-b. 2.50 .70
Imperf.

See Nos. 951-954.

Unification of Viet Nam — A287

1976, Dec. 14
846-847 A287 6xu, 12xu, set of 2 2.00 .70
Imperf., #846-847 4.50

General Offensive, 1975 — A288

Designs: 2xu, 50xu, Liberation of Buon Me Thuot. 3xu, 1d, Tanks liberating Da Nang. 6xu, 2d, Tank, soldiers liberating Presidential palace, Saigon.

1976, Dec. 14
848-853 A288 Set of 6 4.00 2.25

Lan Hoang Thao Orchid Type of 1976 Inscribed "VIET NAM" and "1976"

1976, Dec. **Litho.** ***Perf. 11***
854-855 A277 6xu, 12xu Set of 2 *45.00 25.00*

Dragonflies A289

#856, 12xu, Ho. #857, 12xu, Bao. 20xu, Canh dom. 30xu, Nuong. 40xu, Suoi. 50xu, Canh vang. 60xu, Canh khoang. 1d, Canh den.

1977, Jan. 25 ***Perf. 12***
856-863 A289 Set of 8 6.50 1.00
Imperf., #856-863 16.00 16.00

A290

Rare Birds: 12xu (#864), 60xu, Buceros bicornis. 12xu (#865), Ptilolaemus tickelli. 20xu, Berenicornis comatus. 30xu, Aceros undulatus. 40xu, Anthracoceros malabaricus. 50xu, Anthracoceros malayanus. 1d, Aceros nipalensis.

1977, Apr. 15
864-871 A290 Set of 8 6.50 1.75
Imperf., #864-871 9.00 9.00

A291

Bronze drum and: 4xu, Thang Long Tower. 5xu, Map. 12xu, Lotus blossom. 50xu, Flag.

1977, Apr. 25 ***Perf. 11***
872-875 A291 Set of 4 4.00 1.75
Imperf., #872-875

Natl. Assembly general elections, 1st anniv.

Beetles — A292

#876, 12xu, Black-spotted (Dom den). #877, 12xu, Yellow-spotted (Lang vang). 20xu, Veined (Van gach). 30xu, Green (Nhung xanh). 40xu, Green-spotted (Hoa xanh). 50xu, Black (Van den). 60xu, Leopard skin (Da bao). 1d, Nine-spotted (Chin cham).

1977, June 15 ***Perf. 12½x12***
876-883 A292 Set of 8 6.50 1.50
Imperf., #876-883 12.00 12.00

Wildflowers — A293

Designs: No. 884, 12xu, Thevetia peruviana. No. 885, 12xu, Broussonetia papvrifera. 20xu, Aleurites montana. 30xu, Cerbera manghes. 40xu, Cassia multijuga. 50xu, Cassia nodosa. 60xu, Hibiscus schizopetalus. 1d, Lagerstroemia speciosa.

1977, Aug. 19 ***Perf. 12x12½***
884-891 A293 Set of 8 4.50 1.50
Imperf., #884-891 10.00 10.00

A294

Dahlias: 6xu (#892), 12xu (#894), Pink. 6xu (#893), 12xu (#895), Orange.

1977, Sept. 10 ***Perf. 11***
892-895 A294 Set of 4 3.50 .60

See Nos. 921-924.

A295

Children drawing map of unified Viet Nam. Denominations: 4xu, 5xu, 10xu, 12xu, 30xu each have different colored border.

1977, Sept. 10
896-900 A295 Set of 5 4.50 1.50

Goldfish A296

Designs: No. 901, 12xu, Dong nai. No. 902, 12xu, Velvet (Hoa nhung). 20xu, Blue Chinese (Tau xanh). 30xu, Dragon-eyed (Mat bong). 40xu, Cam trang. 50xu, Five-colored (Ngu sac). 60xu, Dong nai. 1d, Thap cam.

1977, Oct. 20 ***Perf. 12***
901-908 A296 Set of 8 7.00 1.25
Imperf., #901-908 12.00 12.00

A297

Russian October Revolution, 60th anniv.: 12xu (No. 909, olive background), 12xu (No. 910, blue background), Ho Chi Minh, Lenin banner. 50xu, Mother holding child with flag. 1d, Workers, farmers, Moscow Kremlin, cruiser Aurora.

1977, Nov. 7
909-912 A297 Set of 4 3.00 1.25

A298

Songbirds: 12xu, Gracula religiosa. No. 914, 20xu, Garrulax canorus. No. 915, 20xu, Streptopelia chinensis. 30xu, Linius schach. 40xu, Garrulax formosus. 50xu, Garrulax chinensis. 60xu, Acridotheres cristatellus. 1d, Garrulax yersini.

1978, Jan. 25
913-920 A298 Set of 8 5.50 1.75
Imperf., #913-920 12.00 12.00

Cultivated Flower Type of 1977

5xu, 10xu, Sunflower. 6xu, 12xu, Pansy.

1978, Mar. 20 ***Perf. 11***
921-924 A294 Set of 4 4.00 .60

Intl. Children's Day (June 1977) — A299

1978, Mar. 20
925 A299 12xu multicolored 1.50 .35

Sports — A300

#926, 12xu, Discus. #927, 12xu, Long jump. 20xu, Hurdles. 30xu, Hammer throw. 40xu, Shot put. 50xu, Javelin. 60xu, Running. 1d, High jump.

1978, Apr. 10 ***Perf. 11½***
926-933 A300 Set of 8 4.00 1.25
Imperf., #926-933 10.00 10.00

A301

4th Viet Nam Trade Union Cong.: #934, Trade Union emblem. #935, Ho Chi Minh, workers.

1978, May 1 ***Perf. 11***
934-935 A301 10xu Set of 2 2.00 .70

A302

10xu, Ho Chi Minh conducting orchestra. 12xu, Ho Chi Minh's mausoleum, horiz.

1978, May 15
936-937 A302 Set of 2 2.00 .70

No. 937 is 39x23mm.

Young Pioneers' Cultural Palace, Hanoi — A303

1978, May 29
938 A303 10xu multicolored 1.50 .35

Intl. Children's Day.

Sculptures from Tay Phuong Pagoda — A304

Designs: No. 939, 12xu, Sanakavasa. No. 940, 12xu, Parsva. No. 941, 12xu, Punyasas. No. 942, 20xu, Kumarata. No. 943, 20xu, Nagarjuna. 30xu, Yayata. 40xu, Cadiep. 50xu, Ananda. 60xu, Buddhamitra. 1d, Asvagmosa.

1978, July 1 ***Perf. 12***
939-948 A304 Set of 10 8.00 1.50
Imperf., #939-948 20.00 20.00

Cuban Revolution, 25th Anniv. — A305

1978, July 20 ***Perf. 11***
949-950 A305 6xu, 12xu Set of 2 2.00 .70

Types of 1976

6xu (No. 951), 12xu (No. 953), like #845a. 6xu (No. 952), 12xu (No. 954), like #845b.

Design size: 18.5mmx23mm

1978, Aug. 15
951-954 A286 Set of 4 3.50 1.75

Space Exploration, 20th Anniv. A306

#955, 12xu, Sputnik. #956, 12xu, Venera 1. 30xu, Spacecraft docking. 40xu, Molniya 1. 60xu, Soyuz. 2d, Cosmonauts Gubarev, Grechko.

1978, Aug. 28 ***Perf. 12½x12***
955-960 A306 Set of 6 4.50 1.50
Imperf., #955-960 10.00 10.00

World Telecommunications Day — A307

Designs: a, Printed circuit. b, ITU emblem.

1978, Sept. 25 ***Perf. 11***
962 A307 12xu Pair, #a.-b. 2.00 .70
Imperf. 18.00 18.00

20th Congress of Socialist Postal Ministers A308

1978, Sept. 25
963 A308 12xu multicolored 1.50 .35

Chrysanthemums A309

No. 964, 12xu, Tim. No. 965, 12xu, Kim tien. 20xu, Hong. 30xu, Van tho. 40xu, Vang. 50xu, Thuy tim. 60xu, Vang mo. 1d, Nau do.

1978, Oct. 1 ***Perf. 12***
964-971 A309 Set of 8 5.00 1.25
Imperf., #964-971 12.00 12.00

Dinosaurs — A310

Designs: No. 972, 12xu, Plesiosaurus. No. 973, 12xu, Brontosaurus. 20xu, Iguanodon. 30xu, Tyrannosaurus rex. 40xu, Stegosaurus. 50xu, Mosasaurus. 60xu, Triceratops. 1d, Pteranodon.

1979, Jan. 1 **Litho.** ***Perf. 11½***
972-979 A310 Set of 8 9.00 1.25
Imperf., #972-979 17.00 17.00

No. 977 misspelled "Mozasaurus."

A311

1979, Jan. 1 ***Perf. 11***
980 A311 12xu multicolored 1.50 .35
Imperf. 5.00 5.00

Socialist Republic of Cuba, 20th anniv.

A312

Quang Trung's victory over the Chinese, 190th Anniv.: #981, Battle plan. #982, Quang Trung.

1979, Feb. 1
981-982 A312 12xu Set of 2 2.00 .70
a. Perf 12, #981-982 20.00

Albert Einstein, Physicist — A313

Designs: No. 983, 12xu, Einstein. No. 984, 60xu, Equation, sun, planets.

1979, Mar. 14
983-984 A313 12xu, 60xu, set of 2 6.00 .50

Domestic Animals A314

10xu, Ram. 12xu, Ox. 20xu, Ewe, lamb. 30xu, White water buffalo, vert. 40xu, Cow. 50xu, Goat. 60xu, Water buffalo, calf. 1d, Young goat, vert.

1979, Mar. 20 ***Perf. 12***
985-992 A314 Set of 8 5.50 1.25
Imperf., #985-992 9.00 9.00

Five Year Plan (1976-80) — A315

#993, 998, Map, emblem. #994, 999, Factory worker. #995, 1000, Peasant woman, tractor. #996, 1001, Soldier. #997, 1002, Man, atom, compass.

1979 ***Perf. 11***
993-997 A315 6xu Set of 5 5.00 1.50
998-1002 A315 12xu Set of 5 5.00 3.50
1000a Perf. 12
Nos. 993-1002 (2) 10.00 5.00

Issued: Nos. 993-997, 5/1. Nos. 998-1002, 6/1. Nos. 993, 996-1002 on toned paper.

Philaserdica '79, Intl. Stamp Exhibition, Sofia, Bulgaria — A316

1979, May 27 ***Perf. 12***
1003-1004 12xu, 30xu Set of 2 2.00 .70

Intl. Year of the Child — A317

12xu, Ho Chi Minh, children. 20xu, Nurse, mother, child. 50xu, Children with glider, painting supplies. 1d, Girls of different races.

1979, June 1 ***Perf. 11***
1005-1008 A317 Set of 4 3.50 1.25

Ornamental Birds A318

#1009, 12xu, Lophura diardi. #1010, 12xu, Tragopan temminckii. 20xu, Phasianus colchicus. 30xu, Lophura edwardsi. 40xu, Lophura nycthemera, vert. 50xu, Polyplectron germaini, vert. 60xu, Rheinhardia ocellata, vert. 1d, Pavo muticus, vert.

1979, June 16 ***Perf. 12***
1009-1016 A318 Set of 8 6.50 1.75
Imperf., #1009-1016 12.00 12.00

Orchids A319

Designs: No. 1017, 12xu, Dendrobium heterocacpum. No. 1018, 12xu, Cymbidium hybridum. 20xu, Rhynchostylis gigantea. 30xu, Dendrobium mobile. 40xu, Aerides falcatum. 50xu, Paphiopedilum callosum. 60xu, Vanda teres. 1d, Dendrobium phalaenopsis.

1979, Aug. 10 ***Perf. 12***
1017-1024 A319 Set of 8 6.50 1.75
Imperf., #1017-1024 12.00 12.00

Cats — A320

Designs: No. 1025, 12xu, Meo tam the. No. 1026, 12xu, Meo muop, vert. 20xu, Meo khoang, vert. 30xu, Meo dom van. 40xu, Meo muop dom, vert. 50xu, Meo vang, vert. 60xu, Meo xiem. 1d, Meo van am.

1979, Nov. 10
1025-1032 A320 Set of 8 6.00 2.75
Imperf., #1025-1032 13.00 13.00

Vietnamese People's Army, 25th Anniv. — A321

a, People greeting soldiers. b, Frontier guards.

1979, Dec. 22 ***Perf. 11***
1033 A321 12xu Pair, #a.-b. 5.00 .75

Roses — A322

Designs: 1xu, 12xu (No. 1036), Red, pink roses. 2xu, 12xu (No. 1037), Single pink rose.

1980, Jan. 1
1034-1037 A322 Set of 4 4.50 1.25

See Nos. 1084-1085.

Aquatic Flowers — A323

#1038, 12xu, Nelumbium nuciferum. #1039, 12xu, Nymphala stellata. 20xu, Ipomola reptans. 30xu, Nymphoides indicum. 40xu, Jussiala repens. 50xu, Eichhornia crassipes. 60xu, Monochoria voginalis. 1d, Nelumbo nucifera.

1980, Jan. 15 ***Perf. 12½***
1038-1045 A323 Set of 8 5.50 1.25
Imperf., #1038-1045 9.00 9.00

Vietnamese Communist Party, 50th Anniv. A324

Designs: No. 1046a, Ho Chi Minh proclaiming independence, 1945. No. 1046b, Peasants with banner, improvised weapons. No. 1047a, Map, soldiers, tanks storming palace. No. 1047b, Soldiers waving flag at Dien Bien Phu. 2d, Ho Chi Minh, soldiers and workers.

1980, Feb. 3 ***Perf. 11***
1046 A324 12xu Pair, #a.-b. 1.00 .65
1047 A324 20xu Pair, #a.-b. 1.00 .65
1048 A324 2d multicolored 2.00 .35
Nos. 1046-1048 (3) 4.00 1.65

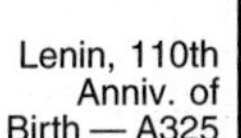

Lenin, 110th Anniv. of Birth — A325

1980, Apr. 22 ***Perf. 12***
1049-1051 A325 6xu, 12xu, 1d, set of 3 3.00 1.75

1980 Summer Olympics, Moscow — A326

#1052, 12xu, Hurdles. #1053, 12xu, Running. 20xu, Team handball. 30xu, Soccer. 40xu, Wrestling. 50xu, Gymnastics, horiz. 60xu, Swimming, horiz. 1d, Sailing, horiz.

1980, May 1 ***Perf. 12x12½, 12½x12***
1052-1059 A326 Set of 8 5.50 1.25
Imperf., #1052-1059 10.00 10.00

A327

Ho Chi Minh, 90th anniv. of birth: 12xu, In 1924. 40xu, As president.

1980, May 19 ***Perf. 11***
1060-1061 A327 Set of 2 2.00 1.00

A328

1980, June 15
1062 A328 5xu multicolored 1.00 .35

Intl. Children's Day.

Intercosmos '80, Soviet-Vietnamese Space Mission — A329

Designs: No. 1063, 12xu, Cosmonauts. No. 1064, 12xu, Soyuz 37 atop booster. 20xu, Soyuz 37. 40xu, Soyuz docking with Salyut space station. 1d, Soyuz firing retro-rockets. 2d, Parachute landing. 3d, Cosmonauts, Soyuz-Salyut station.

1980, July 24 ***Perf. 12x12½***
1063-1068 A329 Set of 6 6.50 1.00
Imperf., #1063-1068 10.00 10.00

Souvenir Sheet

1069 A329 3d multicolored 7.00 7.00
Imperf. 9.00 9.00

Saltwater Fish — A330

Designs: No. 1070, 12xu, Rhincodon typus. No. 1071, 12xu, Galeocerdo cuvier. 20xu, Orectolobus japonicus. 30xu, Heterodontus zebra. 40xu, Dasyatis uarnak. 50xu, Pristis microdon. 60xu, Sphyrna lewini. 1d, Myliobatis tobijei.

1980, Aug. 1 ***Perf. 12***
1070-1077 A330 Set of 8 6.00 1.75
Imperf., #1070-1077 14.00 14.00

A331

Post and Telecommunications Office, 35th Anniv.: 12xu, Ho Chi Minh reading newspaper. 20xu, Ho Chi Minh talking on telephone. 50xu, Kim Dong carrying bird in cage. 1d, Dish antenna.

1980, Aug. 15 **Litho.** ***Perf. 12½***
1078-1081 A331 Set of 4 3.00 1.25

A332

Natl. Telecommunications Day: No. 1082, Telephone switchboard operator. No. 1083, Train, map.

1980, Aug. 25 ***Perf. 11, 12 (#1083)***
1082-1083 A332 12xu Set of 2 2.50 .70

Rose Type of 1980

No. 1084, Pink. No. 1085, Red and pink.

1980, Aug. 25 ***Perf. 11***

Size: 20x24mm

1084-1085 A322 12xu Set of 2 4.50 .40

For surcharge see Nos. 1384A-1385.

Republic of Vietnam, 35th Anniv. — A333

Designs: No. 1086, 12xu, Ho Chi Minh. No. 1087, 12xu, Natl. arms. 40xu, Pac Bo Cave. 1d, Source of Lenin River, horiz.

1980, Sept. 2 ***Perf. 12½***
1086-1089 A333 Set of 4 3.50 1.25

A334

Natl. emblems: 6xu, Arms. No. 1091, 12xu, Flag, horiz. No. 1092, 12xu, Anthem.

1980, Sept. 20 ***Perf. 12***
1090-1092 A334 Set of 3 4.50 1.25

A335

Nguyen Trai, 600th birth anniv.: 12xu, Nguyen Trai. 50xu, Books, horiz. 1d, Ho Chi Minh reading commemorative stele, Con Son.

1980, Oct. 6 ***Perf. 11***
1093-1095 A335 Set of 3 4.50 1.25

For surcharge see No. 1386.

A336

Natl. Women's Union, 50th Anniv.: #1096, Ho Chi Minh, women. #1097, Group of 4 women.

1980, Oct. 20
1096-1097 A336 12xu Set of 2 1.75 .70

A337

Flowers: No. 1098, 12xu, Ipomoea pulchella. No. 1099, 12xu, Biguoniaceae venusta. 20xu, Petunia hybrida. 30xu, Trapaeolum majus. 40xu, Thunbergia grandiflora. 50xu, Anlamanda cathartica. 60xu, Campsis radicans. 1d, Bougainivillaea spectabilis.

1980, Nov. 20 ***Perf. 12½***
1098-1105 A337 Set of 8 5.75 1.25
Imperf., #1098-1105 10.00 10.00

Ornamental Fish — A338

Designs: No. 1106, 12xu, Betta splendens. No. 1107, 12xu, Symphysodon aequifasciata. 20xu, Poecilobrycon eques. 30xu, Gyrinocheilus aymonieri. 40xu, Barbus tetrazona. 50xu, Pterophyllum eimekei. 60xu, Xiphophorus helleri. 1d, Trichopterus sumatranus.

1981, Jan. 15 ***Perf. 12***
1106-1113 A338 Set of 8 5.75 3.00
Imperf., #1106-1113 10.00 9.00

26th Soviet Communist Party Congress — A339

20xu, Rocket, book. 50xu, Young people, flag.

1981, Feb. 23 ***Perf. 11***
1114-1115 A339 Set of 2 3.00 .70

Animals from Cuc Phuona Natl. Forest A340

#1116, 12xu, Hylobates concolor. #1117, 12xu, Macaca speciosa. 20xu, Selenarctos thibetanus. 30xu, Cuon alpinus. 40xu, Sus scrofa. 50xu, Cervus unicolor. 60xu, Panthera pardus. 1d, Panthera tigris.

1981, Apr. 10 ***Perf. 12½x12***
1116-1123 A340 Set of 8 7.50 1.50
Imperf., #1116-1123 13.00 13.00

Doves — A341

#1124, 12xu, Treron sieboldi. #1125, 12xu, Ducula aenea, vert. 20xu, Streptopelia tranquebarica, vert. 30xu, Macropygia unchall, vert. 40xu, Ducula badia, vert. 50xu, Treron apicauda. 60xu, Chalcophaps indica. 1d, Seimun treron seimundi.

1981, June 5 ***Perf. 12***
1124-1131 A341 Set of 8 6.00 3.00
Imperf., #1124-1131 10.00 9.00

Nectar-sucking Birds — A342

Designs: No. 1132, 20xu, Aethopyga siparaja. No. 1133, 20xu, Anthreptes singalensis. 30xu, Aethopyga saturata. 40xu, Aethopyga gouldiae. No. 1136, 50xu, Nectarinia chalcostetha. No. 1137, 50xu, Nectarinia hypogrammica. 60xu, Nectarinia sperata. 1d, Aethopyga nipalensis.

1981, Aug. 5 ***Perf. 12½x12***
1132-1139 A342 Set of 8 4.50 1.75
Imperf., #1132-1139 10.00 10.00

A343

1981, Aug. 5 ***Perf. 11***
1140 A343 12xu Lotus flower 3.50 .35

A343a

Design: Factory militiawoman.

1981, Aug. 5
1140A A343a 12xu yel & multi 20.00 .75

See Nos. M30-M31.

A344

Fruit: No. 1141, 20xu, Elaeagnus latifolia. No. 1142, 20xu, Fortunella japonica. 30xu, Nephelium lappaceum. 40xu, Averrhoa bilimbi. No. 1145, 50xu, Ziziphus mauritiana. No. 1146, 50xu, Fragaria vesca. 60xu, Bouea oppositifolia. 1d, Syzygium aqueum.

1981, Oct. 12 ***Perf. 12***
1141-1148 A344 Set of 8 5.25 1.25
Imperf., #1141-1148 10.00

A345

Planting trees: No. 1149, Ho Chi Minh. No. 1150, Three people.

1981, Nov. 15 ***Perf. 11***
1149-1150 A345 30xu Set of 2 1.75 .50

Tree planting festival.

Bulgaria, 1300th Anniv. — A346

1982, May 7 ***Perf. 11***
1151-1153 A346 30xu, 50xu, 2d, set of 3 5.00 1.10

Wild Animals A347

Designs: No. 1154, 30xu, Orangutan. No. 1155, 30xu, Bison bonasus. No. 1156, 40xu, Kangaroo. No. 1157, 40xu, Hippopotamus. No. 1158, 50xu, Rhinoceros sondaicus. No. 1159, 50xu, Giraffe. 60xu, Zebra. 1d, Lion.

1981, Dec. 9 ***Perf. 12½x12***
1154-1161 A347 Set of 8 4.50 1.50
Imperf., #1154-1161 9.00 9.00

A348

World Food Day: 30xu, 50xu, Woman holding sheaf of rice. 2d, FAO emblem, horiz.

1982, Jan. 26 ***Perf. 11***
1162-1164 A348 Set of 3 3.00 1.10

A349

1982, Feb. 19
1165-1166 A349 50xu, 5d, Set of 2 4.50 1.75

10th World Trade Unions Congress, Havana, Cuba.

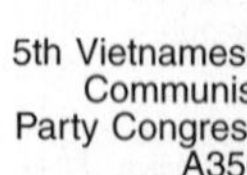

5th Vietnamese Communist Party Congress A350

Designs: No. 1167, 30xu, Ho Chi Minh. No. 1168, 30xu, Hammer, sickle. No. 1169, 30xu, Worker, dam. 50xu, Women harvesting rice. 1d, Ho Chi Minh.

1982
1167-1170 A350 Set of 4 4.00 1.50

Imperf

Size: 99x61 mm

1171 A350 1d multicolored 55.00 55.00

Issued: Nos. 1167-1168, 1171, 2/15; Nos. 1169-1170, 3/27.

Bees & Wasps — A351

Designs: No. 1172, 20xu, Ong bove. No. 1173, 20xu, Ong van xanh. 30xu, To vo nau. 40xu, Ong vang. No. 1176, 50xu, Ong dau nau. No. 1177, 50xu, To vo xanh. 60xu, Ong bau. 1d, Ong mat.

1982, Feb. 20 ***Perf. 12***
1172-1179 A351 Set of 8 4.50 1.50
Imperf., #1172-1179 10.00 10.00

Soccer — A352

#1180, 30xu, 3 players. #1181, 30xu, 2 players. #1182, 40xu, Striped background. #1183, 40xu, grass background. #1184, 50xu, Vertically striped background. #1185, 50xu, Horizonally striped background. 60xu, 1d, Various soccer scenes.

1982, Apr. 15
1180-1187 A352 Set of 8 4.50 1.25
Imperf., #1180-1187 10.00 10.00

For overprints see Nos. 2142-2149.

A353

Vietnamese Red Cross, 35th Anniv.: 1d, Red Cross emblem.

1982, May 15 ***Perf. 11***
1188-1189 A353 Set of 2 2.00 .70

A354

5th Natl. Women's Congress: No. 1190, Congress emblem, three women with arms raised. No. 1191, Congress emblem, faces of three women.

1982, May 19 ***Perf. 12***
1190-1191 A354 12xu Set of 2 2.00 .75

A355

Birds of Prey: No. 1192, 30xu, Microhierax melanoleucos. No. 1193, 30xu, Falco tinnunculus. 40xu, Aviceda leuphotes. No. 1195, 50xu, Icthyophaga nana. No. 1196, 50xu, Milvus korschun. 60xu, Neohierax harmandi, horiz. No. 1198, 1d, Elanus caeruleus, horiz. No. 1199, 1d, Circaetus gallicus.

1982, June 10
1192-1199 A355 Set of 8 7.50 1.75
Imperf., #1192-1199 12.00 12.00

A356

1982, May 16 ***Perf. 11***
1200-1201 A356 30xu, 3d, set of 2 4.50 2.00
Imperf., #1200-1201 45.00

Georgi Dimitrov (1882-1949), Bulgarian Communist leader.

Dahlias — A357

Designs (last word or two of Vietnamese inscription): No. 1202, 30xu, Da cam. No. 1203, 30xu, Do. 40xu, Canh se. No. 1205, 50xu, Do nhung. No. 1206, 50xu, Vang. 60xu, Do tuoi. No. 1208, 1d, Bien. No. 1209, 1d, Trang. Various flowers.

1982, July 15 ***Perf. 12x12½***
1202-1209 A357 Set of 8 6.50 2.25
Imperf., #1202-1209 12.00 12.00

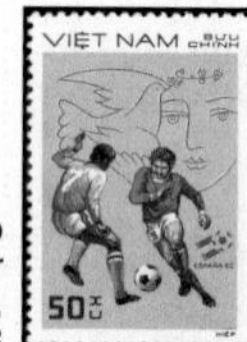
1982 World Cup Soccer Championships, Spain — A358

#1210, 50xu, Ball at bottom right. #1211, 50xu, Ball at right in air. #1212, 50xu, Ball at bottom center. #1213, 1d, 1 player. #1214, 1d, 3 players. 2d, 2 players.

1982, July 25 ***Perf. 12x12½***
1210-1215 A358 Set of 6 7.50 2.25
Imperf., #1210-1215 10.00 10.00

A359

1982, Apr. 22 ***Perf. 11***
1216 A359 30xu Natl. defense 1.50 .70

See No. M32.

A360

1982, Aug. 15
1217 A360 30xu multicolored 1.50 .35

Cuban victory at Giron (Bay of Pigs), 20th anniv.

World Environment Day — A361

#1219, Ho Chi Minh, children planting tree.

1982, Aug. 15
1218-1219 A361 30xu Set of 2 2.50 .70
Imperf., #1218-1219 35.00

A362

1982, Sept. 20
1220 A362 30xu multicolored 1.50 .35

Rabindranath Tagore (1861-1941), poet.

A363

Insects: No. 1221, 30xu, Catacanthus incarnatus. No. 1222, 30xu, Sycanus falleni. 40xu, Nezara viridula. No. 1224, 50xu, Lohita grandis. No. 1225, 50xu, Helcomeria spinosa. 60xu, Chrysocoris stollii. No. 1227, 1d, Pterygamia srayi. No. 1228, 1d, Tiarodes ostentans.

1982, Sept. 25 ***Perf. 12x12½***
1221-1228 A363 Set of 8 6.00 1.75
Imperf., #1221-1228 11.00 11.00

Russian Revolution, 65th Anniv. — A364

Design: No. 1230, Lenin, workers.

1982, Nov. 7 ***Perf. 11***
1229-1230 A364 30xu Set of 2 1.50 .70

9th South East Asian Games, New Delhi, India — A365

#1231, 30xu, Table tennis. #1232, 30xu, Swimming. 1d, Wrestling. 2d, Shooting.

1982, Nov. 19
1231-1234 A365 Set of 4 5.00 1.50

Fish — A366

Designs: No. 1235, 30xu, Samaris cristatus. No. 1236, 30xu, Tephrinectes sinensis. No. 1237, 40xu, Psettodes erumei. No. 1238, 40xu, Zebrias zebra. No. 1239, 50xu, Cynoglossus puncticeps. No. 1240, 50xu, Pardachirus pavoninus. 60xu, Brachirus orientalis. 1d, Psettina iijimae.

1982, Dec. 15 ***Perf. 12***
1235-1242 A366 Set of 8 5.50 1.50
Imperf., #1235-1242 13.00 13.00

Socialist Ideals — A367

#1243, 30xu, Agriculture. #1244, 30xu, Industry. 1d, Natl. defense. 2d, Health & education.

1982, Dec. 25 ***Perf. 11***
1243-1246 A367 Set of 4 5.00 1.50

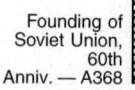

Founding of Soviet Union, 60th Anniv. — A368

1982, Dec. 30
1247 A368 30xu multicolored 2.00 .40
Imperf., #1247 35.00

Sampans — A369

Designs: 30xu, Docked. 50xu, With striped sails. 1d, Sampans on Red River. 3d, With white sails. 5d, With patched sail. 10d, Fast sampan, horiz.

1983, Jan. 10 ***Perf. 12½***

1248-1253 A369 Set of 6 7.00 2.00
Imperf., #1248-1253 12.00 12.00

Locomotives A370

30xu, Class 231-300. 50xu, Class 230-000. 1d, Class 140-601. 2d, Class 241-000. 3d, Class 141-500. 5d, Class 150-000. 8d, Class 40-300.

1983, Feb. 20 ***Perf. 13***

1254-1260 A370 Set of 7 7.00 2.50
Imperf., #1254-1260 15.00 15.00

1st Manned Balloon Flight, Bicent. — A371

Balloons: 30xu, Montgolfier. 50xu, Yellow. 1d, CA-11. 2d, Hot-air. 3d, Over harbor. 5d, Le Geant. 8d, Ascending. 10d, Montgolfier, diff.

1983, Mar. 25 **Litho.** ***Perf. 12½***

1261-1267 A371 Set of 7 7.50 2.00
Imperf., #1261-1267 15.00 15.00

Souvenir Sheet

Perf. 13

1268 A371 10d Sheet of 1 5.00 1.50

No. 1268 contains one 32x40mm stamp.

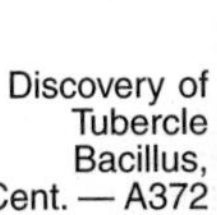

Discovery of Tubercle Bacillus, Cent. — A372

1983, Mar. 25 ***Perf. 11***

1269 A372 5d multicolored 2.75 .75

Laos-Cambodia-Viet Nam Summit — A373

1983, Mar. 25

1270-1271 A373 50xu, 5d Set of 2 2.50 .75
Imperf., #1270-1271 35.00

Cosmonauts A374

Designs: 30xu, Gubarev, Remek. No. 1273, 50xu, Klimuk, Hermaszewski. No. 1274, 50xu, Bykovsky, Jahn. No. 1275, 1d, Rukavishnikov, Ivanov. No. 1276, 1d, Farcas, Kubasov. No. 1277, 2d, Mendez, Romanenko. No. 1278, 2d, Gorbatko, Tuan. 5d, Dzhanibekov, Gurragcha. 8d, Popov, Prunariu. No. 1281, Gagarin.

1983, Apr. 1 ***Perf. 12½x12***

1272-1280 A374 Set of 9 8.50 2.00
Imperf., #1272-1280 14.00 14.00

Souvenir Sheet

1281 A374 10d multicolored 7.00 1.50

No. 1281 contains one 36x28mm stamp.

Reptiles — A375

Designs: No. 1282, 30xu, Teratolepis fasciata. No. 1283, 30xu, Chamaeleo jacksoni. No. 1284, 50xu, Uromastyx acanthinurus. No. 1285, 80xu, Heloderma suspectum. 1d, Cameleo menle. 2d, Amphibolurus barbatus. 5d, Chlamydosaurus kingi. 10d, Phrynosoma coronatum.

1983, Apr. 5 ***Perf.***

1282-1289 A375 Set of 8 7.00 3.00
Imperf., #1282-1289 13.00 13.00

Raphael (1483-1520), Painter — A375a

Designs: 30xu, Virgin Mother Seated on Chair. 50xu, Granduca, the Virgin Mother. 1d, Sistine Madonna. 2d, Marriage of Maria. 3d, The Gardener. 5d, Woman with Veil. 8d, 10d, Self-Portrait.

1983, Apr. 30 ***Perf. 12½***

1289A-1289G A375a Set of 7 7.00 2.00
Imperf., #1289A-1289G 15.00 15.00

Souvenir Sheet

Perf. 13

1289H A375a 10d multicolored 6.00 1.50

Chess Pieces — A376

Designs: 30xu, Vietnamese pawns. 50xu, Indian elephant. 1d, Scottish knight, bishop. 2d, Indian elephant, diff. 3d, Knight. 5d, Sailing ship. 8d, Jester, elephant. 10d, Modern pawns.

1983, May 9 ***Perf. 13***

1290-1296 A376 Set of 7 6.50 2.00
Imperf., #1290-1296 17.00 17.00

Souvenir Sheet

1297 A376 10d multicolored 7.00 1.50

No. 1297 contains one 28x36mm stamp.

Souvenir Sheet

TEMBAL '83 World Stamp Exhibition, Basel — A377

1983, May 21 ***Perf. 13***

1298 A377 10d multicolored 5.00 1.50

1984 Summer Olympics, Los Angeles — A378

Designs: 30xu, Long jump. 50xu, Running. 1d, Javelin. 2d, High jump, horiz. 3d, Hurdles, horiz. 5d, Shot put. 8d, Pole vault. 10d, Discus.

1983, June 13 **Litho.** ***Perf. 13***

1299-1305 A378 Set of 7 10.00 2.00
Imperf., #1299-1305 20.00 20.00

Souvenir Sheet

1306 A378 10d Sheet of 1 15.00 1.50

No. 1306 contains one 32x40mm stamp.

The issuance of this set has been questioned.

Souvenir Sheet

Brasiliana '83, Rio de Janeiro — A379

1983, July 20 ***Perf. 13***

1307 A379 10d Rhamphastos toco 10.00 2.50

Butterflies — A380

Designs: No. 1308, 30xu, Leptocircus meges. No. 1309, 30xu, Terias hecabe. No. 1310, 40xu, Zetides agamemnon. No. 1311, 40xu, Nyctalemon patroclus. No. 1312, 50xu, Papilio chaon. No. 1313, 50xu, Precis almana. 60xu, Thauria lathyi. 1d, Kallima inachus.

1983, July 30 **Litho.** ***Perf. 12***

1308-1315 A380 Set of 8 7.50 3.00
Imperf., #1308-1315 13.00 13.00

Souvenir Sheet

Bangkok '83 A381

1983, Aug. 4 ***Perf. 13***

1316 A381 10d multicolored 10.00 1.50

Karl Marx (1818-1883) — A382

No. 1317, 50xu. No. 1318, 10d,

1983, Oct. 10 ***Perf. 11***

1317-1318 A382 Set of 2 4.50 1.25
Imperf., #1317-1318 45.00

Phu Dong Sports Festival A383

1983, Oct. 10

1319-1320 A383 30xu, 1d, Set of 2 2.50 .70

World Food Day — A384

Design: 50xu, Infant, fish. 4d, Family.

1983, Oct. 10 ***Perf. 12½***

1321-1322 A384 Set of 2 2.00 .70
Imperf., #1321-1322 7.00

Mushrooms — A385

#1323, 50xu, Flammulina velutipes. #1324, 50xu, Pleurotus ostreatus. #1325, 50xu, Cantharellus cibarius. #1326, 50xu, Coprinus atramentarius. 1d, Volvariella volvacea. 2d, Agaricus silvaticus. 5d, Morchella esculenta. 10d, Amanita caesarea.

1983, Oct. 10 ***Perf. 12x12½***

1323-1330 A385 Set of 8 10.00 3.00
Imperf., #1323-1330 14.50

For overprints see Nos. 2150-2157.

World Communications Year — A386

50xu, Letter carrier. 2d, Mail sorting room. 8d, Switchboard operators. #1334, 10d, Radio operator, antenna. #1335, 10d, Telephone, letter, dish antenna, ship.

1983, Sept. 30 ***Perf. 12½***

1331-1334 A386 Set of 4 5.00 1.50

Souvenir Sheet

Perf. 13

1335 A386 10d Sheet of 1 2.75 1.50

5th Natl. Trade Unions Congress A387

50xu, Woman with flowers, Vietnam-Soviet Union Friendship Cultural Building. 2d, 30d, Welder.

1983, Nov. 16 ***Perf. 11***

1336-1338 A387 Set of 3 7.00 1.50

Water Birds — A388

Designs: No. 1339, 50xu, Ciconia nigra. No. 1340, 50xu, Ardea cinerea. No. 1341, 50xu, Ardea purpurea. No. 1342, 50xu, Ibis leucocephalus. 1d, Grus grus. 2d, Platalea minor. 5d, Nycticorax nycticorax. 10d, Anastomus oscitans.

1983, Nov. 20 ***Perf. 12x12½***
1339-1346 A388 Set of 8 8.50 3.00
Imperf., #1339-1346 16.00 16.00

No. 1343 inscribed "Grus grue."

World Peace Conference, Prague — A389

Designs: 50xu, Shown. 3d, 5d, 20d, Hands, globe, dove.

1983, Dec. 19 ***Perf. 11***
1347-1350 A389 Set of 4 8.50 2.00
Imperf., #1347-1350 70.00

1984 Winter Olympics, Sarajevo, Yugoslavia A390

#1351, 50xu, Cross-country skiing, vert. #1352, 50xu, Biathlon, vert. 1d, Speed skating, vert. 2d, Bobsled, vert. 3d, Hockey. 5d, Ski jumping. 6d, Slalom skiing. 10d, Pairs figure skating.

1984, Jan. 30 ***Perf. 12½***
1351-1357 A390 Set of 7 5.50 2.00
Imperf., #1351-1357 12.00 12.00

Souvenir Sheet

1358 A390 10d multicolored 4.50 1.50

No. 1358 contains one 40x32mm stamp.

Soviet Union-Vietnamese Projects, 1978-83 — A391

Designs: 20xu (No. 1359), 4d, Hoa Binh Hydro-electric project. 20xu (No. 1360), Vietnamese-Soviet Cultural Palace. 50xu, Thang Long Bridge.

1984, Jan. 31 **With Gum** ***Perf. 11***
1359-1362 A391 Set of 4 55.00

Endangered Animals A392

Designs: No. 1363, 50xu, Felis marmorata. No. 1364, 50xu, Panthera tigris. No. 1365, 50xu, Panthera pardus. No. 1366, 1d, Hylobates lar. No. 1367, 1d, Nycticebus coucang. No. 1368, 2d, Elephas indidus. No. 1369, 2d, Bos gaurus.

1984, Feb. 26 ***Perf. 12½x12***
1363-1369 A392 Set of 7 4.50 1.00
Imperf., #1363-1369 14.00 14.00

A393

Wildflowers: No. 1370, 50xu, Banhinia variegata. No. 1371, 50xu, Caesalpinia pulcherrima. 1d, Cassia fistula. 2d, Delonix regia. 3d, Artagotrys uncinatus. 5d, Corchorus olitorius. 8d, Banhinia grandiflora.

1984, Mar. 15 ***Perf. 12x12½***
1370-1376 A393 Set of 7 7.00 2.50
Imperf., #1370-1376 12.00 12.00

Souvenir Sheet

1377 A393 10d Delonix regia 4.50 1.50

Location of inscriptions differs on Nos. 1373, 1377.

A394

Orchids: No. 1378, 50xu, Cymbidium. No. 1379, 50xu, Brasse cattleya. 1d, Cattleya Dianx. 2d, Cymbidium, diff. 3d, Cymbidium hybridum. 5d, Phoenix winged orchids. 8d, Yellow Queen orchids.

1984, Mar. 28 ***Perf. 13***
1378-1384 A394 Set of 7 8.50 2.00
Imperf., #1378-1384 17.00 17.00

Nos. 1084-1085, 1093 Surcharged

a

b

1984, Apr. 25 ***Perfs. as before***
1384A A322(a) 50xu on 12xu #1084 *10.00* 6.00
1385 A322(a) 50xu on 12xu #1085 *10.00* 6.00
1386 A335(b) 50xu on 12xu #1093 *10.00* 4.00

Souvenir Sheet

Espana '84, Madrid A395

1984, Apr. 27 ***Perf. 12½***
1387 A395 10d Ciconia ciconia 5.00 2.50

Victory at Dien Bien Phu, 30th Anniv. — A396

No. 1388, 50xu; No. 1395, 10d, Ho Chi Minh, generals, battle map. #1389, 50xu, Troops, truck. No. 1390, 1d, Civilians carrying provisions. No. 1391, 2d, Men-hauling artillery. No. 1392, 3d, Anti-aircraft battery. No. 1393, 5d, Troops attacking enemy base. No. 1394, 8d, Troops waving flag.

1984, May 7 ***Perf. 12½***
1388-1394 A396 Set of 7 5.50 2.00

Souvenir Sheet

1395 A396 10d multicolored 4.50 1.50

Souvenir Sheet

UPU Congress, Hamburg '84 — A397

1984, June 19 ***Perf. 13***
1396 A397 10d Junkers JU-52 3M 5.00 1.50

Fish — A398

Designs: No. 1397, 30xu, Cypselurus spilopterus. No. 1398, 30xu, Ostracion cornutus. 50xu, Diodon hystrix. 80xu, Chelmon rostratus. 1d, Antennarius tridens. 2d, Pterois russelli. 5d, Mola mola. 10d, Minous monodactylus.

1984, June 25 **Litho.** ***Perf. 12***
1397-1404 A398 Set of 8 6.50 3.00
Imperf., #1397-1404 11.00 11.00

Ornamental Fish — A399

Designs: No. 1405, 50xu, Trichogaster trichopterus. No. 1406, 50xu, Brachydanio rerio. 1d, Macropodus opercularis. 2d, Gymnocorymbus ternetzi. 3d, Hyphessobrycon serpae. 5d, Labeo bicolor. 8d, Batta splendens.

1984, June 29 ***Perf. 12½***
1405-1411 A399 Set of 7 5.50 3.00
Imperf., #1405-1411 11.00 11.00

Vietnamese Trade Union Movement, 55th Anniv. — A400

Designs: No. 1412a, 50xu, House at 15 Hang Non St., Hanoi, vert. No. 1412b, 50xu, Nguyen Duc Canh, vert. 1d, Striking workers. 2d, Ho Chi Minh visiting factory. 3d, Hanoi Mechanical Engineering plant. 5d, Intl. trade union movement.

1984, July 20 ***Perf. 11***
1412-1416 A400 Set of 6 4.50 2.25
Imperf., #1412-1416 100.00

Souvenir Sheet

Imperf

1417 A400 2d like #1414 10.50 11.00

No. 1412 printed se-tenant. No. 1417 contains one 45x38mm stamp.

Rock Formations, Ha Long Bay — A401

#1418, 50xu, Hang-Bo Nau. #1419, 50xu, Nui Yen Ngua. #1420, 50xu, Hon Dua. #1421, 50xu, Hang Con Gai. #1422, 1d, Hon Coc. #1423, 1d, Hon Ga Choi. 2d, Hon Dinh Huong. 3d, Hon Su Tu. 5d, Hon Am. 8d, Nui Bai Tho.

1984, July 30 ***Perf. 12½x12***
1418-1427 A401 Set of 10 6.50 2.50
Imperf., #1418-1427 13.00 13.00

Dinosaurs A402

#1428, 50xu, Styracosaurus. #1429, 50xu, Diplodocus. #1430, 1d, Corythosaurus. #1431, 1d, Rhamphyorhynchus. 2d, Seymouria. 3d, Allosaurus. 5d, Dimetrodon. 8d, Brachiosaurus.

1984, Aug. 30
1428-1435 A402 Set of 8 12.00 3.00
Imperf., #1428-1435 15.00 15.00

Viet Nam-Laos-Cambodia Friendship — A403

1984, Aug. 30 ***Perf. 11***
1436-1437 A403 50xu, 10d, set of 2 5.50 .80
Imperf., #1436-1437 35.00

Souvenir Sheet

Ausipex '84, Melbourne, Australia — A404

1984, Sept. 20 ***Perf. 13***
1438 A404 10d Koala 11.00 1.50

Viet Nam-Cambodia Friendship Agreement, 5th Anniv. — A405

50xu, 3d, People, pagoda, statue. 50d, Dancers.

1984, Sept. 30 ***Perf. 11***
1439-1441 A405 Set of 3 11.00 4.00
Imperf., #1439-1441 50.00

Liberation of Hanoi, 30th Anniv. — A406

Designs: 50xu, Thang Long Bridge. 1d, Khue Van Gateway. 2d, Ho Chi Minh mausoleum.

1984, Oct. 5
1442-1444 A406 Set of 3 3.75 1.25
Imperf., #1442-1444 50.00

Vintage Automobiles A407

#1445, 50xu, Vis-a-Vis, vert. #1446, 50xu, Duc. 1d, Tonneau. 2d, Double phaeton. 3d, Landaulet. 5d, Torpedo. 6d, Coupe de Ville.

1984, Oct. 30 ***Perf. 12½x13, 13x12½***
1445-1451 A407 Set of 7 4.50 2.50
Imperf., #1445-1451 11.00 11.00

Lenin (1870-1924)
A408

Paintings of Lenin: 50xu, At his desk. 1d, Standing with revolutionaries. 3d, Speaking at factory. 5d, Meeting with farmers.

1984, Nov. 15 ***Perf. 12x12½***
1452-1455 A408 Set of 4 3.00 1.50
Imperf., #1452-1455 8.00 8.00

UNICEF
A409

Paintings: 30xu, Woman, soldiers. 50xu, Mother, children. 1d, Miner, family. 3d, Young girl, vert. 5d, Children playing on ground. 10d, Women, child, vert.

1984, Dec. 7 ***Perf. 12***
1456-1461 A409 Set of 6 5.00 2.75
Imperf., #1456-1461 10.00 10.00

A410

50xu, 30d. Frontier Forces, 25th anniv.

1984, Dec. 15 ***Perf. 11***
1462-1463 A410 Set of 2 11.00 1.90
Imperf., #1462-1463

See No. M39.

A411

Flora and Fauna: 20xu, Bubalus bubalis. 30xu, Felis marmorata. No. 1466, 50xu, Hibiscus rosa-sinensis. No. 1467, 50xu, Ailurus fulgens. No. 1468, 50xu, Rosa centifolia. No. 1469, 50xu, Betta splendens. No. 1470, 1d, Chrysanthemum sinense. No. 1471, 1d, Nymphaea ampla. No. 1472, 1d, Pelecanus onocrotalus. No. 1473, 1d, Panthera tigris. No. 1474, 2d, Nycticebus coucang. No. 1475, 2d, Macaca fascicularis. No. 1476, 2d, Dalia coccinea. 5d, Gekko gecko. 10d, Rhytidoceros bicornis.

1984, Dec. ***Perf. 12½x12***
1464-1478 A411 Set of 15 11.00 4.00
Imperf., #1464-1478 15.00

No. 1466 inscribed "Hybiscus." No. 1470 inscribed "Chrysanthemun."

A412

1985 ***Perf. 11***
1479-1480 A412 3d, 5d, set of 2 2.50 .80
Imperf., #1479-1480 30.00

New Year 1985 (Year of the Buffalo). Issued: 3d, 1/21; 5d, 4/30.

A413

1985, Apr. 26 ***Perf. 11***
1481 A413 2d Ho Chi Minh 1.00 .40
Imperf. 18.00

Vietnamese Communist Party, 55th anniv.

Military Victory in South Viet Nam, 10th Anniv. — A414

Designs: 1d, Soldiers advancing forward. 2d, 10d, Ho Chi Minh, tank, soldiers. 4d, Construction worker. 5d, Map, women.

1985, Apr. 30 ***Perf. 12½***
1482-1485 A414 Set of 4 4.00 1.50

Souvenir Sheet

Perf. 13

1486 A414 10d multicolored 3.50 1.75
Imperf. 10.00

Cactus — A415

Designs: No. 1487, 50xu, Echinocereus knippelianus. No. 1488, 50xu, Lemaireocereus thurberi. 1d, Notocactus haselbergii. 2d, Parodia chrysacanthion. 3d, Pelecyphora pseudopectinata. 5d, Rebutia frebrighii. 8d, Lobivia aurea.

1985, Mar. 30 ***Perf. 11½***
1487-1493 A415 Set of 7 6.50 2.50
Imperf., #1487-1493 15.00 15.00

Vietnamese People's Army, 40th Anniv. — A416

Designs: No. 1494, 50xu, Ho Chi Minh. No. 1495, 50xu, Taking oath on flag. 1d, Anti-aircraft missile. 2d, Soldiers, civilians working together. 3d, Tank entering grounds of presidential palace, Saigon. 5d, Soldier demonstrating use of rifle. 8d, Officers, soldiers, map. 10d, Four soldiers representing branches of military.

1984, Dec. 22 ***Perf. 12½***
1494-1500 A416 Set of 7 5.00 3.00

Souvenir Sheet

1501 A416 10d multi 3.50 1.50

End of World War II, 40th Anniv. — A417

Designs: 1d, 10d, Victory Monument. 2d, Vietnamese soldier. 4d, Dove, falling American eagle. 5d, Child, doves.

1985, June 5 ***Perf. 12x12½***
1502-1505 A417 Set of 4 4.00 1.50
Imperf., #1502-1505 15.00 15.00

Souvenir Sheet

1506 A417 10d multicolored 3.00 1.50

Liberation of Haiphong, 30th Anniv. — A418

Designs: 2d, Long Chau Lighthouse. 5d, An Duong Bridge, horiz.
10d, To Hieu (1912-44), vert.

1985, May 13 ***Perf. 11***
1507-1508 A418 Set of 2 2.00 .80
Imperf., #1507-1508 35.00

Souvenir Sheet

Imperf

1509 A418 10d multicolored 3.00 1.50

Ho Chi Minh, 95th Birth Anniv. A419

Ho Chi Minh: 1d, At battlefield. 2d, Reading. 4d, 10d, Portrait, vert. 5d, Writing.

1985, July 6 ***Perf. 12½***
1510-1513 A419 Set of 4 3.50 2.00

Souvenir Sheet

Perf. 13

1514 A419 10d multicolored 4.50 1.40

No. 1514 contains one 30x36mm stamp.

Motorcycles, Cent. — A420

Designs: No. 1515, 1d, 1895, Germany. No. 1516, 1d, 1898 tricycle, France. No. 1517, 2d, 1913 Harley-Davidson, US. No. 1518, 2d, 1918 Cleveland, US. 3d, 1935 Simplex, US. 4d, 1984 Minarelli, Italy. 6d, 1984 Honda, Japan. 10d, 1984 Honda racing bike.

1985, June 28 ***Perf. 13***
1515-1521 A420 Set of 7 5.00 2.75
Imperf., #1515-1521 14.00 14.00

Souvenir Sheet

1522 A420 10d multicolored 5.00 1.40

No. 1522 contains one 32x40mm stamp.

Argentina '85, Buenos Aires — A421

Wild animals: No. 1523, 1d, Aptenodytes pennati, vert. No. 1524, 1d, Dolichotis patagonum, vert. No. 1525, 2d, Panthera onca. No. 1526, 2d, Hydrochoerys capibara. 3d, Peterocnemia pennata, vert. 4d, Priodontes giganteus. 6d, Voltur gryphus. 10d, Lama glama, horiz.

1985, July 5 ***Perf. 12½***
1523-1529 A421 Set of 7 8.50 2.50
Imperf., #1523-1529 18.00 18.00

Souvenir Sheet

With Gum

Perf. 13

1530 A421 10d multicolored 11.00 1.50
Imperf., #1530 25.00

No. 1530 contains one 40x32mm stamp.

12th World Youth and Students Festival, Moscow — A422

No. 1531, 2d, Youth carrying flags, globe. No. 1532, 2d, Workers, power transmission lines. 4d, Lighthouse, coastal defense. 5d, Intl. festival.

1985, June 20 ***Perf. 12½***
1531-1534 A422 Set of 4 4.50 1.50
Imperf., #1531-1534 17.00 17.00

Souvenir Sheet

With Gum

Perf. 13

1535 A422 10d like #1531 5.50 1.25

Marine Life — A423

#1536, 3d, Nadoa tuberculata. #1537, 3d, Luidia maculata. #1538, 3d, Stichopus chloronotus. #1539, 3d, Holothuria monacaria. #1540, 4d, Astropyga radiata. #1541, 4d, Astropecten scoparius. #1542, 4d, Linckia laevigata.

1985, July 30 ***Perf. 12***
1536-1542 A423 Set of 7 7.50 2.75
Imperf., #1536-1542 19.00 19.00

Socialist Republic of Viet Nam, 40th Anniv. — A424

Designs: 2d, Construction. 3d, Hands shaking, doves. 5d, Flag, military forces. No. 1567, 10d, Flag, Ho Chi Minh.

1985, Aug. 28 ***Perf. 12½***
1543-1546 A424 Set of 4 4.00 1.90
Imperf., #1543-1546 20.00 20.00

Souvenir Sheet

Perf. 13

1547 A424 10d like #1543 4.00 3.00

No. 1547 contains one 32x40mm stamp.

Vietnamese Police Force, 40th Anniv. — A425

1985, Aug. 30 ***Perf. 11***
1548 A425 10d multicolored 4.00 .40
Imperf. 18.00

See No. M41.

1st Natl. Sports Festival — A426

Designs: 5d, Gymnastics. 10d, Gymnastics, running, swimming.

1985, Aug. 30
1549-1550 A426 Set of 2 4.00 .80
Imperf., #1549-1550 35.00

German Railways, 150th Anniv. A427

Various locomotives: #1551, 1d, Facing left. #1552, 1d, Facing right. #1553, 2d, Facing left. #1554, 2d, Facing right. 3d, 4d, 6d.

1985, Sept. 13 ***Perf. 12½***
1551-1557 A427 Set of 7 5.50 2.50
Imperf., #1551-1557 10.00 10.00

Souvenir Sheet

With Gum

Perf. 13

1558 A427 10d multicolored 3.75 1.50

No. 1558 contains one 32x40mm stamp.

Vietnamese Geological Survey, 30th Anniv. — A428

#1559, Drilling rigs. #1560, Aerial survey.

1985, Oct. 5 ***Perf. 11***

1559-1560 A428 1d Set of 2 2.50 .80

Italia '85 — A429

Vintage Italian cars: No. 1561, 1d, 1922 Alfa Romeo. No. 1562, 1d, 1932 Bianchi Berlina. No. 1563, 2d, 1928 Isotta Fraschini. No. 1564, 2d, 1930 Bugatti. No. 1565, 3d, 1912 Itala. 4d, 1934 Lancia Augusta. 6d, 1927 Fiat Convertable (top up). 10d, 1927 Fiat Convertable (top down).

1985, Oct. 25 ***Perf. 13***

1561-1567 A429 Set of 7 6.50 2.25
Imperf., #1561-1567 17.00 17.00

Souvenir Sheet

With Gum

1568 A429 10d multicolored 5.50 1.25

No. 1568 contains one 40x32mm stamp.

Whales — A430

Designs: No. 1569, 1d, Balaenoptera musculus. No. 1570, 1d, Balaena borealis. No. 1571, 2d, Orcinus orca. No. 1572, 2d, Delphinus. 3d, Megaptera boops. 4d, Balaenoptera physalus. 6d, Eubalaena glacialis.

1985, Nov. 15

1569-1575 A430 Set of 7 8.00 2.50
Imperf., #1569-1575 20.00 20.00

1986 World Cup Soccer Championships, Mexico City — A431

Various soccer plays: No. 1576, 1d, From behind goal. No. 1577, 1d, Goalie from side. No. 1578, 2d, From behind goal. No. 1579, 2d, From in front of goal, vert. 3d, vert. 4d, vert. 6d, vert.

1985, Nov. 30

1576-1582 A431 Set of 7 4.50 1.75
Imperf., #1576-1582 10.00 10.00

Souvenir Sheet

Perf. 13

1583 A431 10d multicolored 4.50 1.25

No. 1583 contains one 40x32mm stamp.

People's Democratic Republic of Laos, 10th Anniv. — A432

a, Woman, dove. b, Woman dancing, natl. arms.

1985, Dec. 2 ***Perf. 11***

1584 A432 1d Pair, #a.-b. 15.00 1.50
#1584a, 1584b singles 2.50

Traditional Musical Instruments A433

#1585, 1d, Stone chimes. #1586, 1d, Large bronze drum. #1587, 2d, Flutes. #1588, 2d, Large red drum. 3d, Monochord. 4d, Moon-shaped lute. 6d, Vietnamese two-string violin.

1985, Dec. 5 ***Perf. 12½x12***

1585-1591 A433 Set of 7 5.25 2.75
Imperf., #1585-1591 12.00 12.00

A434

Socialist Republic of Viet Nam, 40th Anniv.: No. 1592, 10d, Industry. No. 1593, 10d, Agriculture. 20d, Public health. 30d, Education.

1985, Dec. 6 ***Perf. 11***

1592-1595 A434 Set of 4 30.00 15.00

A435

1986, Jan. 6 **Litho.** ***Perf. 11***

1596-1597 A435 50xu, 1d Set of 2 2.00 .80

1st Natl. Elections, 40th anniv.

A436

1986, Jan. 6

1598 A436 1d multicolored 1.00 .45

UN 40th anniv.

A437

Halley's Comet: No. 1599, 2d, Edmond Halley. No. 1600, 2d, Isaac Newton. 3d, Rocket, flags. 5d, Comet.

1986, Feb. 24 ***Perf. 12½***

1599-1602 A437 Set of 4 4.50 1.50
Imperf., #1599-1602 10.00 10.00

A438

Soviet Communist Party, 27th Congress: 50xu, Kremlin, map. 1d, Lenin banner.

1986, Feb. 25 ***Perf. 11***

1603-1604 A438 Set of 2 2.00 .80
Imperf., #1603-1604 36.00

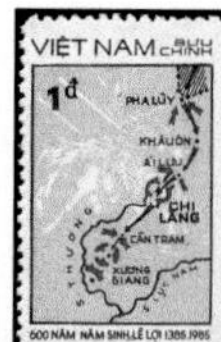

Map of Battle of Xuong Giang — A439

1986, Mar. 1

1605 A439 1d multicolored 1.50 .40

Le Loi, 600th birth anniv.

1986 World Cup Soccer Championships, Mexico City — A440

Various soccer players in action: No. 1606, 1d, Viet Nam at left. No. 1607, 1d, Viet Nam at right. 2d, Viet Nam at left. No. 1609, 3d, Viet Nam at left. No. 1610, 3d, Viet Nam at right. No. 1611, 5d, Viet Nam at left. No. 1612, 5d, Viet Nam at right.

1986, Mar. 3 ***Perf. 12½***

1606-1612 A440 Set of 7 5.00 2.50
Imperf., #1606-1612 9.00 9.00

Souvenir Sheet

Perf. 13

1613 A440 10d multicolored 4.50 1.25

No. 1613 contains one 40x32mm stamp.

1st Manned Space Flight, 25th Anniv. — A441

#1614, 1d, Konstantin Tsiolkovsky. #1615, 1d, Rocket on transporter. 2d, Yuri Gagarin. #1617, 3d, Valentina Tereshkova, vert. #1618, 3d, Alexei Leonov. #1619, 5d, Apollo-Soyuz, crews. #1620, 5d, Soyuz, Salut space station. 10d, Cosmonauts, vert.

1986, Apr. 12 ***Perf. 13***

1614-1620 A441 Set of 7 5.00 2.25
Imperf., #1614-1620 10.00 10.00

Souvenir Sheet

1621 A441 10d multicolored 1.00 1.25

No. 1621 contains one 32x40mm stamp.

Ernst Thalmann (1886-1944), German Politician — A442

1986, Apr. 16 ***Perf. 11***

1622 A442 2d red & black 1.50 .40
Imperf. 20.00

May Day — A443

1986, May 1

1623-1624 A443 1d, 5d, Set of 2 2.00 .40
Imperf., #1623-1624 18.00

Vancouver Expo '86 — A444

Airplanes: No. 1625, 1d, Hawker Hart. No. 1626, 1d, Curtiss Jenny. 2d, PZL-P23. No. 1628, 3d, Yakovlev Yak-11. No. 1629, 3d, Fokker Dr.1. No. 1630, 5d, Boeing P-12 (1920). No. 1631, 5d, Nieuport-Delage NiD.29C1 (1929).

1986, Sept. 30 ***Perf. 13***

1625-1631 A444 Set of 7 5.00 2.00
Imperf., #1625-1631 8.00 8.00

Dam-Strengthening Committee, 40th Anniv. — A445

1986, May 22 ***Perf. 11***

1632 A445 1d carmine 1.00 .45
Imperf. 12.00

Bonsai — A446

Designs: No. 1633, 1d, Ficus glomerata. No. 1634, 1d, Ficus benjamina. 2d, Ulmus tonkinensis. No. 1636, 3d, Persica vulgaris. No. 1637, 3d, Streblus asper. No. 1638, 5d, Pinus khasya. No. 1639, 5d, Podocarpus macrophyllus. 10d, Serissa foetida, horiz.

1986, Dec. 10 ***Perf. 12x12½***

1633-1639 A446 Set of 7 5.50 2.75
Imperf., #1633-1639 15.00 15.00

Souvenir Sheet

Perf. 12½x12

1640 A446 10d multicolored 4.50 4.00

Domestic Cats — A447

Various cats (Background colors): No. 1641, 1d, blue green. No. 1642, 1d, red. 2d, blue. No. 1644, 3d, brown. No. 1645, 3d, blue. No. 1646, 5d, violet. No. 1647, 5d, red, vert.

Perf. 13x12½, 12½x13

1986, June 16

1641-1647 A447 Set of 7 7.50 2.75
Imperf., #1641-1647 16.00 16.00

Traditional Houses — A448

Designs: No. 1648, 1d, Thai den. No. 1649, 1d, Nung. 2d, Thai trang. No. 1651, 3d, Tay. No. 1652, 3d, Hmong. No. 1653, 5d, Dao. No. 1654, 5d, Tay nguyen, vert.

Perf. 12½x12, 12x12½

1986, June 20

1648-1654 A448 Set of 7 5.50 2.75
Imperf., #1648-1654 13.00 13.00

Souvenir Sheet

Perf. 12x12½

1655 A448 10d like #1654 3.50 1.25

Postal Service, 40th Anniv. — A449

Designs: No. 1656, 2d, Telecommunications. No. 1657, 2d, Map, letter carrier. 4d, Soldiers, Nguyen Thi Nghia. 5d, Dish antenna.

1986, Aug. 15 ***Perf. 13***
1656-1659 A449 Set of 4 3.00 1.25
Imperf., #1656-1659 21.00 21.00

A450

Birds: No. 1660, 1d, Merops apiaster. No. 1661, 1d, Cissa chinensis. 2d, Pteruthius erythropterus. No. 1663, 3d, Garrulax leucolophus. No. 1664, 3d, Psarisomus dalhousiae, horiz. No. 1665, 5d, Cyanopica cyanus, horiz. No. 1666, 5d, Motacilla alba. 10d, Copsychus malabaricus.

1986, Aug. 28 ***Perf. 13***
1660-1666 A450 Set of 7 5.00 2.50
Imperf. #1660-1666 12.00 12.00

Souvenir Sheet
Perf. 12½

1667 A450 10d multicolored 5.00 1.25

No. 1667 contains one 32x40mm stamp. Stockholmia '86.

A451

Domestic fowl: No. 1668, 1d, Plymouth Rock. No. 1669, 1d, Maleagris gallopavo. No. 1670, 2d, Ri. No. 1671, 2d, White Plymouth rock. No. 1672, 3d, Leghorn. No. 1673, 3d, Rhode Island red. No. 1674, 3d, Rhode ri. 5d, Gray Plymouth rock hen.

1986, Sept. 15 ***Perf. 12x12½***
1668-1675 A451 Set of 8 5.50 3.00
Imperf., #1668-1675 13.00 13.00

11th Intl. Trade Unions Congress A452

1986, Sept. 16 ***Perf. 12½***
1676 A452 1d blue & red 1.50 .40
Imperf. 16.00

Artifacts, Hung-Voung Period — A453

Designs: No. 1677, 1d, Seated figure, vert. No. 1678, 1d, Knife hilt in form of female figure, vert. 2d, Bronze axe. No. 1680, 3d, Bronze axe, diff. No. 1681, 3d, Bronze bowl. No. 1682, 5d, Bronze pot (round). No. 1683, 5d, Bronze vase (open top).

1986, Oct. 15 ***Perf. 12x12½, 12½x12***
1677-1683 A453 Set of 7 4.50 2.75
Imperf., #1677-1683 11.00 11.00

Souvenir Sheet
Perf. 12x12½

1684 A453 10d like #1677 4.00 4.00

Vietnamese Red Cross, 40th Anniv. — A454

1986, Oct. 20 ***Perf. 12½***
1685 A454 3d rose & greenish blue 1.50 .40
Imperf. 12.00

Sailing Ships — A455

Various sail and oar-powered ships (sail colors): #1686, 1d, bl, grn, yel. #1687, 1d, org. 2d, yel. #1689, 3d, pur & red. #1690, 3d, bl. #1691, 5d, bl, brn, org. #1692, 5d, org.

Perf. 12½x12, 12½x13 (#1688)

1986, Oct. 20
1686-1692 A455 Set of 7 5.50 1.50
Imperf., #1686-1692 15.00

No. 1688 is 38x47mm.

Butterflies A456

Designs: No. 1693, 1d, Catopsilia scylla. No. 1694, 1d, Euploea midamus. 2d, Appias nero. No. 1696, 3d, Danaus chrysippus. No. 1697, 3d, Papilio polytes stichius. No. 1698, 5d, Euploea diocletiana. No. 1699, 5d, Charaxes polyxena.

1987, June 30 ***Perf. 12½***
1693-1699 A456 Set of 7 5.50 2.00
Imperf., #1693-1699 13.00

No. 1696 misspelled "Danais."

Vietnamese Communist Party, 6th Congress A457

1d, Construction projects. 2d, Natl. defense. 4d, Ho Chi Minh. 5d, Intl. cooperation.

1986, Nov. 20 ***Perf. 11***
1700-1703 A457 Set of 4 5.00 1.50
1700a-1703a Perf. 12½ 50.00 50.00
1702b Perf. 11x12½ 27.50 27.50

Souvenir Sheet
Imperf

1704 A457 10d like #1700 4.50 1.25

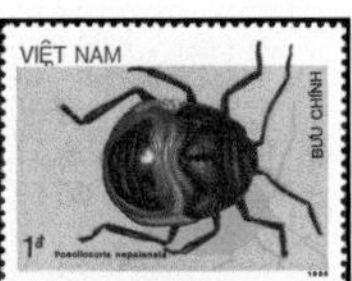

Insects — A458

Designs: No. 1705, 1d, Poecilocoris nepalensis. No. 1706, 1d, Bombus americanorum. 2d, Romalea microptera. No. 1708, 3d, Chalcocoris rutilans. No. 1709, 3d, Chrysocoris sellatus. No. 1710, 5d, Paranthrene palmi. No. 1711, 5d, Crocisa crucifera. 10d, Anabrus simplex.

1987, June 30 ***Perf. 12½***
1705-1711 A458 Set of 7 5.00 2.75
Imperf., #1705-1711 12.00 12.00

Souvenir Sheet

1712 A458 10d multicolored 5.00 1.25

No. 1712 contains one 32x40mm stamp.

Intl. Peace Year — A459

1986, Dec. 7 ***Perf. 11***
1713-1714 A459 1d, 3d, Set of 2 3.00 .80
Imperf., #1713-1714 18.00

Handicrafts A460

Designs: No. 1715, 1d, Round dish. No. 1716, 1d, Rattan handbag. 2d, Rattan foot stool. No. 1718, 3d, Bamboo hand basket. No. 1719, 3d, Muong pannier. No. 1720, 5d, Rattan basket with shoulder straps. No. 1721, 5d, Rattan basket with lid. 10d, Tall rattan basket.

1986, Dec. 10 ***Perf. 11½***
1715-1721 A460 Set of 7 4.50 2.75
Imperf., #1715-1721 9.00 9.00

Souvenir Sheet

1722 A460 10d multicolored 3.50 3.50

A461

1986, Dec. 18 ***Perf. 11***
1723 A461 2d blue green & fawn 1.50 .40

Natl. Resistance, 40th anniv.

A462

Endangered flora: No. 1724, 1d, Fokienia hodginsii. No. 1725, 1d, Amentotaxus yunnanensis. 2d, Pinus kwangtungensis. No. 1727, 3d, Taxus chinensis. No. 1728, 3d, Cupressus torulosa. No. 1729, 5d, Ducampopinus krempfii. No. 1730, 5d, Tsuga yunnanensis. 10d, Abies nukiangensis.

1986, Dec. 26 ***Perf. 12x12½***
1724-1730 A462 Set of 7 4.50 2.75
Imperf., #1724-1730 12.00 12.00

Souvenir Sheet

1731 A462 10d multicolored 4.00 1.25

Elephants A463

Designs: No 1732, 1d, Two elephants. No. 1733, 1d, Female, calf. No. 1734, 3d, Elephant facing right. No. 1735, 3d, Elephant, vert. No. 1736, 5d, Man riding elephant, vert. No. 1737, 5d, Four elephants.

1987, Mar. 10 ***Perf. 12½***
1732-1737 A463 Set of 6 6.50 1.50
Imperf., #1732-1737 15.00 15.00

No. 1737 is 68x27mm.

Vietnamese Legends — A464

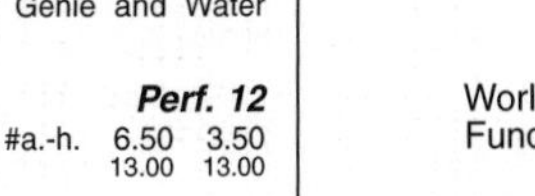

Designs: a, Son Tinh. b, My Nuong. c-e, Battle between Mountain Genie and Water Genie. f-h, Celebration.

1987, Jan. 20 ***Perf. 12***
1738 A464 3d Strip of 8, #a.-h. 6.50 3.50
Imperf. 13.00 13.00

New Year 1987 (Year of the Cat) — A465

1987, Jan. 6 ***Perf. 11***
1739 A465 3d red lilac 1.50 .45
Imperf. 18.00

Natl. Events — A466

Ho Chi Minh and: 10d, August revolution, Aug. 19, 1945. 20d, Proclaiming independence, Sept. 9, 1945. 30d, Victory at Dien Bien Phu, July 7, 1954. 50d, Capture of Saigon, Apr. 30, 1975.

1987, Apr. 12 ***Perf. 11***
1740-1743 A466 Set of 4 5.50 1.50

A467

Champa art: 3d, Temple, Da Nang. 10d, Tower, Na Trang. 15d, Temple, Da Nang (side view). 20d, Dancing girl. 25d, Bust of woman. 30d, Girl playing flute. 40d, Dancing girl, diff.

1987, June 30 ***Perf. 12x12½***
1744-1750 A467 Set of 7 6.50 2.75
Imperf., #1744-1750 12.00 12.00

Souvenir Sheet

1751 A467 50d like #1749 4.50 4.00

A468

Various flowering cacti: 5d, 10d, 15d, 20d, 25d, 30d, 40d.

1987, Dec. 30 ***Perf. 12½***
1752-1758 A468 Set of 7 4.50 2.00
Imperf., #1752-1758 17.50

Souvenir Sheet
Perf. 13

1759 A468 50d multicolored 4.50 1.25

Global Population Reaches 5 Billion — A469

1987, July 11 ***Perf. 13***
1760 A469 5d multicolored 1.50 .45

World Wildlife Fund — A470

Designs: No. 1761, 5d, Concolor gibbon. No. 1762, 5d, Douc monkeys. 15d, Black concolor gibbon. 40d, Douc monkey.

1987, Sept. 23 *Perf. 12½*
1761-1764 A470 Set of 4 9.00 2.00
Imperf., #1761-1764 37.00

A471

Western high plateau costumes: 5d, Male Bana. No. 1766, 20d, Female Bana. No. 1767, 20d, Female Gia Rai. No. 1768, 30d, Male Gia Rai. No. 1769, 30d, Male Ede. 40d, Female Ede.

1987, July 25 *Perf. 12x12½*
1765-1770 A471 Set of 6 5.50 2.50
Imperf., #1765-1770 12.00

A472

1987, July 27 *Perf. 13*
1771 A472 5d multicolored 1.50 .40

Day of the Invalids, 40th anniv.

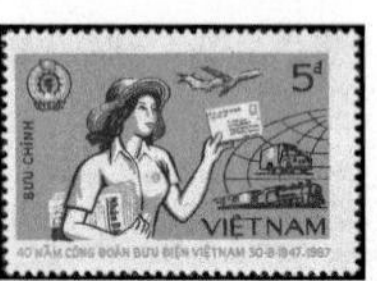
Postal Trade Union, 40th Anniv. — A473

Designs: 5d, Letter carrier, jet, truck, train. 30d, Switchboard operator.

1987, Aug. 30
1772-1773 A473 Set of 2 2.00 1.20

A474

Paintings by Picasso: No. 1774, 3d, *The Three Musicians.* No. 1775, 20d, War. No. 1776, 20d, Peace. No. 1777, 30d, Child with Dove, vert. No. 1778, 30d, Portrait of Gertrude Stein, vert. 40d, Guernica. 50d, Child as Harlequin.

1987, Dec. 30 *Perf. 12½*
1774-1779 A474 Set of 6 5.50 1.75
Imperf., #1774-1779 12.00

Souvenir Sheet

1780 A474 50d multicolored 5.00 1.50

No. 1779 is 44x27mm. No. 1780 contains one 40x32mm stamp.

Coral — A475

Designs: 5d, Epanouis. 10d, Acropora. 15d, Rhizopsammia. 20d, Acropora, diff. 25d, Alcyone, 30d, Corollum. 40d, Cristatella.

1987, Oct. 30 *Perf. 12x12½*
1781-1787 A475 Set of 7 6.50 2.75
Imperf., #1781-1787 12.00

Intl. Year for Housing for the Homeless A476

1987, Sept. 23 *Perf. 13*
1788 A476 5d greenish bl & blk 1.50 .40

Russian Revolution, 70th Anniv. — A477

Designs: 5d, 65d, Industry, agriculture. 20d, Lenin. 30d, Construction. 50d, Ho Chi Minh.

1987, Oct. 6 *Perf. 13*
1789-1792 A477 Set of 4 3.00 1.50

Souvenir Sheet

1793 A477 65d multicolored 4.50 4.00

Hafnia '87 — A478

Seaplanes: 5d, PBY-5. 10d, LeO H-246. 15d, Dornier DO-18. 20d, Short Sunderland. 25d, Rohrbach Rostra. 30d, Chetverikov ARK-3. 40d, CANT Z-509. 50d, Curtiss H-16.

1987, Dec. 30 *Perf. 13*
1794-1800 A478 Set of 7 4.50 2.00
Imperf., #1794-1800 12.50

Souvenir Sheet

1801 A478 50d multicolored 4.00 1.25

No. 1801 contains one 40x32mm stamp.

Czechoslovakia-Viet Nam Friendship Agreement, 10th Anniv. — A479

10d, Handshake. 50d, Flags, buildings.

1987, Oct. 31
1802-1803 A479 Set of 2 3.00 .80
Imperf., 1802-1803 17.00

Viet Nam-Soviet Union Cooperation A480

Designs: 5d, Industry. 50d, Buildings.

1987, Nov. 3
1804-1805 A480 Set of 2 3.00 .80

Mushrooms — A481

Designs: 5d, Polyporellus squamosus. 10d, Clitocybe geotropa. 15d, Tricholoma terreum. 20d, Russula aurata. 25d, Collybia fusipes. 30d, Cortinarius violaceus. 40d, Boletus aereus.

1987, Dec. 30 *Perf. 12½*
1806-1812 A481 Set of 7 4.50 2.00
Imperf., #1806-1812 11.50

Peace — A482

1987, Nov. 10 *Perf. 13*
1813 A482 10d multicolored 1.00 .40

Afro-Asian Solidarity Committee (AAPSO), 30th Anniv. — A483

10d, Hands, dove. 30d, Map, hands, vert.

1987, Nov. 30
1814-1815 A483 Set of 2 2.00 .80
Imperf., #1814-1815 20.00

Victory Over US Bombing Campaign, 15th Anniv. — A484

Designs: 10d, B-52 wreckage. 30d, Children with flowers, wreckage.

1987, Dec. 26
1816-1817 A484 Set of 2 2.50 .80
Imperf., #1816-1817 25.00

Productivity — A485

Designs: 5d, Consumer goods. 20d, Agriculture. 30d, Export products.

1987, Dec. 30
1818-1820 A485 Set of 3 3.00 1.20

Hoang Sa, Truong Sa Islands — A486

Designs: 10d, Ship, sailor. 100d, Maps.

1988, Jan. 19
1821-1822 A486 Set of 2 4.50 .90
Imperf., #1821-1822 17.50

Roses — A487

Various roses: 5d, 10d, 15d, 20d, 25d, 30d, 40d.

1988, Jan. 20 *Perf. 12½*
1823-1829 A487 Set of 7 5.50 2.75
Imperf., #1823-1829 15.00

Souvenir Sheet

Perf. 13

1830 A487 50d multicolored 4.50 1.25

Tropical Fish — A488

Designs: 5d, Red betta splendens. 10d, Labeo bicolor. 15d, Puntis tetrazona. 20d, Brachydania albolineatus. 25d, Puntis conchonius. 30d, Betta splendens, diff. 40d, Botia lecontei.

1988, Jan. 20 *Perf. 13*
1831-1837 A488 Set of 7 5.00 2.00
Imperf., #1831-1837 12.00

Intl. Red Cross, Red Crescent, 125th Anniv. — A489

1988, Feb. 17
1838 A489 10d multicolored 1.00 .40
Imperf. 15.00

Battle of Bach Dang, 700th Anniv. — A490

80d, Fleet of ships. 200d, Battle scene.

1988, Apr. 8
1839-1840 A490 Set of 2 4.50 .80

Tourism — A491

5d, One-pillar pagoda. 10d, Bach Dang River. 15d, Thien Mu Tower, Hue. 20d, Hgu Hanh Mountain, Da Nang. 25d, Nha Trang beach. 30d, Pren Waterfalls. 40d, Market, Ben Thanh. 50d, Cleft Rocks, Quang Ninh.

1988, Apr. 20 *Perf. 12½x12*
1841-1847 A491 Set of 7 5.00 2.00
Imperf., #1841-1847 10.00

Souvenir Sheet

1848 A491 50d multicolored 4.50 1.25

Water Lilies — A492

Designs: 5d, Nymphaea lotus. No. 1850, 10d, Nymphaea pubescens. No. 1851, 10d, Nymphaea nouchali. No. 1852, 20d, Nymphaea rubra. No. 1853, 20d, Nymphaea gigantea. 30d, Nymphaea laydekeri. 50d, Nymphaea capensis.

1988, Apr. 24 *Perf. 12x12½*
1849-1855 A492 Set of 7 5.00 2.00
Imperf., #1849-1855 12.00

Offshore Oil Drilling — A493

1988, Apr. 28 *Perf. 13*
1856 A493 1000d multicolored 8.00 8.50
Imperf. 22.00

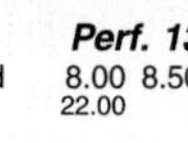

A494

Parrots: No. 1857, 10d, Ara araruna. No. 1858, 10d, Psittacula himalayana. No. 1859, 20d, Aprosmictus erythropterus. No. 1860, 20d, Ara chloroptera. No. 1861, 30d, Ara militaris. No. 1862, 30d, Psittacula alexandri. 50d, Loriculus vernalis. 80d, Ara chloroptera, diff.

1988, May 5 ***Perf. 12x12½***
1857-1863 A494 Set of 7 5.50 2.75
Imperf., #1857-1863 16.00

Souvenir Sheet

1864 A494 80d multicolored 4.00 1.25

A495

Membership in Council of Mutual Economic Assistance, 10th Anniv.: 200d, Map. 300d, Headquarters building.

1988, May 29 ***Perf. 13***
1865-1866 A495 Set of 2 5.50 1.25
Imperf. 20.00

A496

1988, June 1
1867 A496 60d multicolored 1.50 .80
Imperf. 20.00

Vaccinations against disease.

Problems of Peace and Socialism Magazine, 30th Anniv. — A497

1988, July 20
1868 A497 20d multicolored 1.00 .40
Imperf. 12.00

A498

1988, Aug. 20
1869 A498 150d multicolored 1.50 .40
Imperf. 17.00

Pres. Ton Duc Thang, birth cent.

A499

6th Vietnamese Trade Union Congress: 50d, Emblem. 100d, Workers.

1988, Aug. 28
1870-1871 A499 Set of 2 2.00 .80
Imperf., #1870-1871 20.00

Children's Paintings A500

#1872, 10d, My Family. #1873, 10d, My House. #1874, 20d, Fishing. #1875, 20d, Flying Kites. #1876, 30d, Girl playing guitar, animals. #1877, 30d, Children in rain, vert. 50d, Girl holding dove, vert. 80d, Family, diff., vert.

Perf. 12½x12, 12x12½

1988, Sept. 25
1872-1878 A500 Set of 7 5.50 2.50
Imperf., #1872-1878 11.00

Souvenir Sheet

Perf. 12x12½

1879 A500 80d multicolored 4.00 1.25

Hydroelectric Plants — A501

Designs: 2000d, Tri An. 3000d, Hoa Binh.

1988, Sept. 27 ***Perf. 13***
1880-1881 A501 Set of 2 10.00 5.50
Imperf., #1880-1881 35.00

A502

1988, Nov. 3 ***Perf. 13½x13***
1882 A502 50d multicolored 2.00 .45
Imperf. 12.00

Viet Nam-USSR Friendship Agreement, 10th anniv.

A503

Designs: 100d, Fidel Castro. 300d, Flags, Vietnamese, Cuban people.

1988, Dec. 27
1883-1884 A503 Set of 2 2.00 .80
Imperf., #1883-1884 20.00

Cuban revolution, 30th anniv.

Wild Animals — A504

Designs: No. 1885, 10d, Bos banteng. No. 1886, 10d, Bos gaurus. No. 1887, 20d, Axis porcinus. No. 1888, 20d, Tapirus indicus. No. 1889, 30d, Capricornis sumatrensis. No. 1890, 30d, Sus scrofa. 50d, Bubalus bubalus. 80d, Rhinoceros sodaicus.

1988, Dec. 30 ***Perf. 12½***
1885-1891 A504 Set of 7 4.50 2.00
Imperf., #1885-1891 15.00

Souvenir Sheet

1892 A504 80d multicolored 6.50 4.00
Imperf. 20.00

Locomotives A505

Designs: No. 1893, 20d, Kiha 80, Japan. No. 1894, 20d, LRC, Canada. No. 1895, 20d, Hitachi, Japan. No. 1896, 20d, BL-85, USSR. No. 1897, 30d, RC-1, Sweden. No. 1898, 30d, DR-1A, USSR. 50d, T3-136, USSR. 80d, SCNF Z6400.

1988, Dec. 30 ***Perf. 13***
1893-1899 A505 Set of 7 4.50 2.25
Imperf., #1893-1899 12.00

Souvenir Sheet

1900 A505 80d multicolored 4.00 1.25
Imperf. 7.00

No. 1900 contains one 40x32mm stamp.

A506

Fruits, vegetables: No. 1901, 10d, Lagenaria siceraria. No. 1902, 10d, Momordica charantia. No. 1903, 20d, Solanum melongena. No. 1904, 20d, Cucurbita moschata. No. 1905, 30d, Luffa cylindrica. No. 1906, 30d, Benincasa hispida. 50d, Lycopercicon esculentum.

1988, Dec. 30 ***Perf. 12x12½***
1901-1907 A506 Set of 7 5.50 2.75
Imperf., #1901-1907 10.00

A507

Various project spacecraft: No. 1908, 10d, Mars. No. 1909, 10d, Moon. No. 1910, 20d, Saturn. No. 1911, 20d, Inter-planetary. No. 1912, 30d, Venus. No. 1913, 30d, Earth orbital space station. 50d, Cosmos house. 80d, Lander docking with orbiter.

1988, Dec. 30 ***Perf. 13***
1908-1914 A507 Set of 7 4.50 1.50
Imperf., #1908-1914 17.00

Souvenir Sheet

1915 A507 80d multicolored 5.00 1.25

Cosmos Day.
No. 1915 contains one 32x40mm stamp.

Shells — A508

Designs: No. 1916, 10d, Conus miles. No. 1917, 10d, Strombus lentiginosus. No. 1918, 20d, Nautilus. No. 1919, 20d, Bursa rana. No. 1920, 30d, Turbo petholatus. No. 1921, 30d, Oliva erythros. 50d, Mitra eriscopalis. 80d, Tonna tessellata.

1988, Dec. 30 ***Perf. 12½x12***
1916-1922 A508 Set of 7 5.00 2.50
Imperf., #1916-1922 13.00

Souvenir Sheet

1923 A508 80d multicolored 4.50 1.25

India '89 A509

Butterflies: No. 1924, 50d, Anaea echemus. No. 1925, 50d, Ascia monuste. No. 1926, 50d, Juniona evarete. No. 1927, 100d, Phoebis avellaneda. No. 1928, 100d, Eurema proterpia. 200d, Papilio palamedes. 300d, Danaus plexippus. 400d, Parides gundlachiamus.

1989, Jan. 7 ***Perf. 12½***
1924-1930 A509 Set of 7 5.50 2.75
Imperf., #1924-1930 11.00

Souvenir Sheet

1931 A509 400d multicolored 4.50 1.25

No. 1931 contains one 40x32mm stamp. Nos. 1924-1930 printed with se-tenant label.

Natl. Day of Cambodia, 10th Anniv. — A510

Designs: 100d, Soldiers, women working in field. 500d, Viet Nam-Cambodia friendship.

1989, Jan. 7 ***Perf. 13x13½***
1932-1933 A510 Set of 2 2.50 1.20
Imperf., #1932-1933 21.00

India '89 — A511

Designs: No. 1934, 100d, Science, technology. No. 1935, 100d, Agriculture, industry. 300d, Asoka pillar. 600d, Nehru (1889-1964).

1989, Jan. 20 ***Perf. 13***
1934-1937 A511 Set of 4 3.50 1.50

Battle of Dong Da, Bicent. A512

Designs: 100d, Festival. 1000d, Quang Trung defeating Qing invaders.

1989, Feb. 10 ***Perf. 13***
1938-1939 A512 Set of 2 3.00 1.50
Imperf., #1938-1939 21.00

Inter-Parliamentary Union, Cent. — A513

Designs: 100d, Vietnamese membership, 10th anniv. 200d, Centennial emblem.

1989, Mar. 1
1940-1941 A513 Set of 2 2.00 .60

Fishing Boats A513a

Boats from: No. 1942, 10d, Quang Nam. No. 1943, 10d, Quang Tri. No. 1944, 20d, Thua Thien. No. 1945, 20d, Da Nang (sail furled). No. 1946, 30d, Da Nang (under sail). No. 1947, 30d, Quang Tri (under sail). 50d, Hue.

1989, Mar. 20 ***Perf. 12½x12***
1942-1948 A513a Set of 7 5.00 2.25
Imperf., #1942-1948 12.00

Helicopters A514

#1949, 10d, Kamov KA-26. #1950, 10d, Boeing Vertol 234. #1951, 20d, Mil MI-10(V10). #1952, 20d, MBB BO 105. #1953, 30d, Kawasaki Hughes 369HS. #1954, 30d, Bell 206B Jet Ranger, 50d, Mil MI-8. 80d, Puma SA330.

1989, Apr. 12 ***Perf. 12½***

1949-1955 A514 Set of 7 4.50 1.90
Imperf., #1949-1955 14.00

Souvenir Sheet

1956 A514 80d multicolored 4.00 1.25
Imperf. 10.00

No. 1956 contains one 40x32mm stamp.

Bicycles A515

#1957, 10d, Bowden Spacelander. #1958, 10d, Rabasa Derbi. #1959, 20d, Huffy. #1960, 20d, Rabasa Derbi. #1961, 30d, VMX-PL. #1962, 30d, Premier. 50d, Columbia RX5.

1989, May 1 ***Perf. 13***

1957-1963 A515 Set of 7 5.00 1.90
Imperf., #1957-1963 10.00

Turtles — A516

No. 1964, 10d, Cuora trifasciata. No. 1965, 10d, Testudo elegans. No. 1966, 20d, Eretmochelys imbricata. No. 1967, 20d, Platysternon megacephalum. No. 1968, 30d, Dermochelys coriacea. No. 1969, 30d, Chelonia mydas. 50d, Caretta caretta. 80d, Caretta caretta, diff.

1989, May 1 ***Perf. 12½***

1964-1970 A516 Set of 7 7.00 2.25
Imperf., #1964-1970 13.50

Souvenir Sheet

1971 A516 80d multicolored 15.00 1.25
Imperf. 25.00

Finlandia '88 (#1971).

Poisonous Snakes — A517

Designs: No. 1972, 10d, Trimeresurus popeorum. No. 1973, 10d, Trimeresurus mucrosquamatus. No. 1974, 20d, Bungarus fasciatus. No. 1975, 20d, Bungarus candidus. No. 1976, 30d, Calliophis maclellandii. No. 1977, 30d, Ancistrodon acutus. 50d, Ophiophagus hannah, vert.

1989, May 1

1972-1978 A517 Set of 7 5.00 1.90
Imperf., #1972-1978 10.00

Pairs Figure Skating — A518

Various figure skaters: No. 1979, 10d, "Viet Nam" at left. No. 1980, 10d, "Viet Nam" at right. No. 1981, 20d, "Viet Nam" at left. No. 1982, 20d, "Viet Nam" at right, horiz. No. 1983, 30d, "Viet Nam" at left. No. 1984, 30d, "Viet Nam" at right, horiz. 50d, "Viet Nam" at left, horiz.

1989, May 29 ***Perf. 13***

1979-1985 A518 Set of 7 4.50 1.50
Imperf., #1979-1985 11.00

Souvenir Sheet

With Gum

1986 A518 80d multi, horiz. 4.00 1.25
Imperf. 11.00

No. 1986 contains one 40x32mm stamp.

A519

1989, June 5 ***Perf. 13***

1987 A519 100d buff 1.00 .25

Post & Telecommunications.

A520

Ceramics, Li-Tran Period: 50d, Pitcher. No. 1989, 100d, Bowl. No. 1990, 100d, Jug. 200d, Jug, diff. 300d, Vase.

1989, July 1 ***Perf. 12***

1988-1992 A520 Set of 5 3.50 1.50
Imperf., #1988-1992 9.00

Legend of Giong — A521

Designs: 50d, Mother nursing infant. No. 1994, 100d, Giong meets imperial messenger. No. 1995, 100d, Giong riding iron horse, people following. 200d, Giong pulling up bamboo trees. 300d, Giong flying into sky.

1989, July 1 ***Perf. 12½x12***

1993-1997 A521 Set of 5 3.00 1.50
Imperf., #1993-1997 6.50

French Revolution, Bicent. — A522

Designs: 100d, Emblem. 500d, Liberty leading the people, after Delacroix.

1989, July 14 ***Perf. 13½x13***

1998-1999 A522 Set of 2 3.50 .80
Imperf., #1998-1999 9.00

PHILEXFRANCE '89 — A523

Paintings: No. 2000, 50d, Oath of the Tennis Court, by David. No. 2001, 50d, Capture of Louis XVI, horiz. No. 2002, 50d, Liberty, Equality, Fraternity, horiz. No. 2003, 100d, Storming the Bastille. No. 2004, 100d, Death of Marat, by David. 200d, Child and Rabbit, by Prud'hon. 300d, Slave Market, by Gerome, horiz. 400d, Liberty Leading the People, by Delacroix.

1989, July 14 ***Perf. 13***

2000-2006 A523 Set of 7 4.50 2.25
Imperf., #2000-2006 10.00

Souvenir Sheet

2007 A523 400d multicolored 3.50 1.25

No. 2007 contains one 33x44mm stamp.

1989 World Cup Soccer Championships, Italy — A524

Soccer plays: No. 2008, 50d, Dribbling. No. 2009, 50d, Tackling. No. 2010, 50d, Goalie. No. 2011, 100d, Dribbling, diff. No. 2012, 100d, Dribbling, diff., vert. 200d, Preparing to kick, vert. 300d, Heading ball, vert. 400d, Heading ball, diff., vert.

Perf. 13x12½, 12½x13

1989, Aug. 27

2008-2014 A524 Set of 7 4.00 1.75
Imperf., #2008-2014 11.00

Souvenir Sheet

Perf. 13

2015 A524 400d multicolored 4.00 1.25

No. 2015 contains one 32x40mm stamp.

Dogs — A525

#2016, 50d, Dachshund. #2017, 50d, Beagle. #2018, 50d, English setter, vert. #2019, 100d, German short-haired pointer, vert. #2020, 100d, Basset hounds. 200d, German sheperd, vert. 300d, Beagle, diff.

1989, Aug. 20 ***Perf. 12½***

2016-2022 A525 Set of 7 5.50 1.75
Imperf., #2016-2022 10.00

No. 2020 is 68x28mm.

Horses — A526

Designs: No. 2023, 50d, Tennessee Walking. No. 2024, 50d, Appaloosa. No. 2025, 50d, Tersky. No. 2026, 100d, Kladruber. No. 2027, 100d, Welsh cob. 200d, Pinto. 300d, Pony and bridle.

1989, Sept. 23 ***Perf. 13***

2023-2029 A526 Set of 7 5.00 1.75
Imperf., #2023-2029 10.00

No. 2029 is 68x28mm.

Flowers — A527

No. 2030, 50d, Paphiopedilum siamense. No. 2031, 50d, Fuchsia fulgens. No. 2032, 100d, Hemerocallis fulva. No. 2033, 100d, Gloriosa superba. 200d, Strelitzia reginae. 300d, Iris.

1989, Sept. 23 ***Perf. 12½***

2030-2035 A527 Set of 6 5.00 1.50
Imperf., #2030-2035 11.00

German Democratic Republic, 40th Anniv. — A528

1989, Oct. 7 ***Perf. 13***

2036 A528 200d multicolored 1.00 .40

Immunization Campaign A529

#2037, Woman receiving vaccination. #2038, Child receiving oral vaccine. #2039, Clinic.

1989, Oct. 20

2037-2039 A529 100d Set of 3 2.50 .90
Imperf., #2037-2039 25.00

Drawings of Everyday Life, 19th Cent. — A530

Designs: 50d, Assembling plow. No. 2041, 100d, Harrowing. No. 2042, 100d, Irrigating. 200d, Fertilizing. 300d, Harvesting.

1989, Oct. 28 ***Perf. 12x12½***

2040-2044 A530 Set of 5 4.50 1.50
Imperf., #2040-2044 8.50

Horse Paintings, by Xu Beihong (1895-1953) — A531

Various horses: 100d, 200d, 300d, 500d horiz., 800d, 1000d, 1500d.

1989, Dec. 22 ***Perf. 13***

2045-2051 A531 Set of 7 4.25 1.50
Imperf., #2045-2051 9.00

Imperf

Size: 117x72mm

2052 A531 2000d multicolored 7.50 1.25
Imperf. 14.00

Vietnamese Communist Party, 60th Anniv. — A532

Designs: 100d, Ho Chi Minh, tank. 500d, Workers, refinery, field.

1990, Feb. 3 **Litho.** ***Perf. 13***

2053-2054 A532 Set of 2 3.00 1.20
Imperf., #2053-2054 5.50

Ducks A533

a, 100d, Anas platyrhynchos hybrid. b, 300d, Anas penelope. c, 500d, Anas platyrhynchos. d, 1000d, Anas erythrorhyncha. e, 2000d, Anas platyrhynchos, diff. f, 3000d, Anas undulata.

1990, Feb. 15

2055 A533 Block of 6, #a.-f. 3.50 1.50
Imperf. 12.50

Trucks — A534

100d, Mack. 200d, Volvo F89. 300d, Tatra 915 S1. 500d, Hino KZ30000. 1000d, Iveco. 2000d, Leyland DAF Super Comet. 3000d, Kamaz 53212.

1990, Feb. 20

2056-2062 A534 Set of 7 3.50 1.50
Imperf., #2056-2062 5.00

Architectural Sites, Hue A535

#2063, 100d, Tu Duc's Mausoleum. #2064, 100d, Hien Nhon Arch. 200d, Ngo Mon Gate. 300d, Thien Mu Temple. 400d, Palace, gateway.

1990, Feb. 20 ***Perf. 12½x12***

2063-2066 A535 Set of 4 3.00 1.50

Souvenir Sheet

2067 A535 400d multicolored 3.00 1.20

Goldfish — A536

100d, Bulging-eyed, horiz. 300d, Telescopic-eyed, horiz. 500d, Red-headed, horiz. 1000d, Double-tailed. 2000d, Rainbow. 3000d, Comet.

1990, Mar. 20 ***Perf. 13***

2068-2073 A536 Set of 6 3.50 1.50
Imperf., #2068-2073 10.00

Paintings — A537

London '90: 100d, Antonia Zarate, by Goya. 200d, Girl Holding a Paper Fan, by Renoir. 300d, Janet Grizel, by John Russell. 500d, Love Untieing the Belt of Beauty, by Sir Joshua Reynolds. 1000d, Portrait of a Woman, by George Romney. 2000d, Portrait of Madame Ginoux, by Van Gogh. 3000d, Woman in Blue, by Gainsborough. 3500d, Woman in a Straw Hat, by Van Gogh.

1990, Apr. 10

2074-2080 A537 Set of 7 4.50 1.50
Imperf., #2074-2080 7.00

Souvenir Sheet

2081 A537 3500d multicolored 3.00 1.50
Imperf. 5.00

1990 World Cup Soccer Championships, Italy — A538

Various soccer players in action: 100d, 200d, 300d, 500d, 1000d, 2000d, 3000d.

1990, Apr. 19

2082-2088 A538 Set of 7 3.50 1.50
Imperf., #2082-2088 25.00

Souvenir Sheet

2089 A538 3500d multicolored 2.50 1.25

No. 2089 contains one 32x40mm stamp. For overprints see Nos. 2189-2196.

Cats — A539

Various cats: 100d, horiz., 200d, 300d, horiz., 500d, 1000d, horiz., 2000d, 3000d.

1990, May 5

2090-2096 A539 Set of 7 3.50 1.50
Imperf., #2090-2096 6.00

Souvenir Sheet

2097 A539 3500d multicolored 3.00 1.25
Imperf. 5.00

No. 2097 contains one 44x33mm stamp. Belgica '90 (#2097).

Dogs — A540

Various dogs: 100d, 200d, 300d, 500d, 1000d, 2000d, 3000d.

1990, May 15

2098-2104 A540 Set of 7 3.00 1.50
Imperf., #2098-2194 7.00

Souvenir Sheet

2105 A540 3500d Collies 2.50 1.25
Imperf. 7.50

New Zealand '90.

Ho Chi Minh (1890-1969) — A541

Ho Chi Minh and: 100d, Lenin. 300d, Soldiers waving flag. 500d, Hand holding rifle, dove. 1000d, Map. 2000d, Child, dove. 3000d, Stylized globe. 3500d, Flag.

1990, May 17 ***Perf. 13***

2106-2111 A541 Set of 6 3.50 4.00
Imperf., #2106-2111 6.00

Souvenir Sheet

Perf. 12½x13

2112 A541 3500d multicolored 3.00 4.00

No. 2112 contains one 33x44mm stamp.

Dinosaurs A542

100d, Gorgosaurus. 500d, Ceratosaurus. 1000d, Ankylosaurus. 2000d, Ankylosaurus, diff. 3000d, Edaphosaurus.

1990, June 1 ***Perf. 13***

2113-2117 A542 Set of 5 4.50 2.25
Imperf., #2113-2117 10.00

Columbus' Discovery of America, 500th Anniv. — A543

Designs: 50d, Fleet. No. 2119, 100d, Columbus presenting gifts to natives. No. 2120, 100d, Columbus, priest at Rabida. No. 2121, 100d, Columbus at Court of Ferdinand, Isabella. No. 2122, 200d, Map of Caribbean. No. 2123, 200d, Columbus, arms. 300d, Map of Atlantic. 500d, Teotihuacan pot.

1990, June 10 ***Perf. 12½***

2118-2124 A543 Set of 7 4.00 5.50
Imperf., #2118-2124 20.00

Souvenir Sheet

2125 A543 500d multicolored 2.50 3.00

No. 2125 contains one 40x32mm stamp. For overprints see Nos. 2313-2320.

Sailing Ships — A544

Designs: 100d, Viking longship. 500d, Caravel. No. 2128, 1000d, Carrack, 14th-15th cent. No. 2129, 1000d, Flit. No. 2130, 1000d, Carrack, 15th cent., vert. 2000d, Galleon, vert. 3000d, Galleon, diff. 4200d, Egyptian barge.

1990, June 10 ***Perf. 13***

2126-2132 A544 Set of 7 4.00 1.50
Imperf., #2126-2132 14.00

Souvenir Sheet

Perf. 13x12½

2133 A544 4200d multicolored 3.50 1.50
Imperf. 10.00

No. 2133 contains one 44x33mm stamp.

11th Asian Games, Beijing — A545

Designs: 100d, High jump. 200d, Basketball. 300d, Table tennis. 500d, Volleyball. 1000d, Rhythmic gymnastics. 2000d, Tennis. 3000d, Judo. 3500d, Hurdles.

1990, June 20 ***Perf. 13***

2134-2140 A545 Set of 7 4.00 4.00
Imperf., #2134-2140 12.00

Souvenir Sheet

Perf. 12½x13

2141 A545 3500d multicolored 3.00 3.00

No. 2141 contains one 33x44mm stamp.

Nos. 1180-1187 Ovptd. in Red, Green and Black

1990, June 22 ***Perf. 12***

2142-2149 A352 Set of 8 15.00

1990 World Cup Soccer Championships, Italy.

Nos. 1323-1330 Ovptd. in Black and Red

1990, June 22 ***Perf. 12x12½***

2150-2157 A385 Set of 8 15.00

Tourism.

Modern Ships — A546

100d, Freighter. 300d, Container ship. 500d, Cruise ship. 1000d, Liquified natural gas tanker. 2000d, Ro-Ro ship. 3000d, Ferry.

1990, July 20 ***Perf. 13***

2158-2163 A546 Set of 6 4.00 2.25
Imperf., #2158-2163 6.00

Post & Telecommunications Dept., 45th Anniv. — A547

Designs: 100d, Dove, ship, plane. 1000d, Satellite antenna.

1990, Aug. 15 ***Perf. 13x13½***

2164-2165 A547 Set of 2 1.50
Imperf., #2164-2165 3.00

Socialist Republic of Viet Nam, 45th Anniv. — A548

Designs: 100d, Flag, construction projects. 500d, Map, tank, soldiers. 1000d, "VI," ship, communications network. 3000d, Workers, oil rigs. 3500d, Ho Chi Minh.

1990, Sept. 1 ***Perf. 13***

2166-2169 A548 Set of 4 3.50
Imperf., #2166-2169 5.00

Souvenir Sheet

Perf. 12½x13

2170 A548 3500d multicolored 2.00

No. 2170 contains one 33x44mm stamp. Sixth Vietnamese Communist Party Congress (#2168).

Airships A549

Designs: 100d, Henry Gifford, 1871. 200d, Lebandy, 1910. 300d, Graf Zeppelin. 500d, R-101, 1930. 1000d, Soviet, 1936. 2000d, Tissandier, 1883. 3000d, US Navy. 3500d, "Zodiac," 1931.

1990, Sept. 10 ***Perf. 12½***

2171-2177 A549 Set of 7 4.00
Imperf., #2171-2177 11.00

Souvenir Sheet

2178 A549 3500d multicolored 2.00 1.00
Imperf. 7.50

No. 2178 contains one 40x32mm stamp. Helvetia '90, Stamp World London '90.

Fable of Thach Sanh — A550

Designs: a, 100d, Thach Sanh carrying bundles of wood. b, 300d, Ly Thong. c, 500d, Thach Sanh killing python. d, 1000d, Thach Sanh shooting arrow at eagle. e, 2000d, Thach Sanh in prison. f, 3000d, Thach Sanh, princess.

1990, Sept. 20 ***Perf. 13***

2179 A550 Block of 6, #a.-f. 6.00
Imperf. 8.00

Asian-Pacific Postal Training Center, 20th Anniv. — A551

1990, Sept. 25

2180 A551 150d multicolored 1.00
Imperf. 20.00

Nos. 571-578 Ovptd. with Red Cross in Red & "FOR THE FUTURE GENERATION" in various Languages in Black

Language: No. 2181, 12xu, Japanese. No. 2182, 12xu, Italian. No. 2183, 20xu, German.

No. 2184, 20xu, Vietnamese. 30xu, English. 40xu, Russian. 50xu, French. 60xu, Spanish.

1990, Sept. 25 *Perf. 12*
2181-2188 A211 Set of 8 15.00

Position of overprint varies.
Use of these stamps at stated face value is unlikely.

Nos. 2082-2089 Ovptd.

1990, Sept. 25 *Perf. 13*
2189-2195 A538 Set of 7 10.00

Souvenir Sheet

2196 A538 3500d multicolored 8.00

Vietnamese Women's Federation, 60th Anniv. — A552

Designs: 100d, Woman carrying rifle. 500d, Women working in field, laboratory.

1990, Oct. 10
2197-2198 A552 Set of 2 1.50
Imperf., #2197-2198 3.50

Correggio (1494-1534), Painter — A553

Various paintings of the Madonna and Child: No. 2199, 50xu, shown. No. 2200, 50xu, diff. 1d, 2d, 3d, 5d, 6d.

1990, Nov. 13 *Perf. 12½*
2199-2205 A553 Set of 7 4.50
Imperf., #2199-2205 10.00

Souvenir Sheet

2206 A553 10d multicolored 4.00
Imperf. 10.00

No. 2206 contains one 32x40mm stamp.
Dated "1984." Use of these stamps at stated face value is unlikely.

Protection of Forests A554

Designs: 200d, Water conservation, healthy forest. 1000d, SOS, prevent forest fires.

1990, Nov. 15 *Perf. 13*
2207-2208 A554 Set of 2 1.50 .30
Imperf., #2207-2208 5.00

A555

Poisonous mushrooms: 200d, Amanita pantherina. 300d, Amanita phalloides. 1000d, Amanita virosa. 1500d, Amanita muscaria. 2000d, Russula emetica. 3000d, Boletus satanas.

1991, Jan. 21
2209-2214 A555 Set of 6 4.00 2.00
Imperf., #2209-2214 5.50

A555a

1992 Summer Olympics, Barcelona: 200d, Sailing. 300d, Boxing. 400d, Cycling. 1000d, High jump. 2000d, Equestrian. No. 2220, 3000d, Judo. No. 2221, 3000d, Wrestling, horiz. 5000d, Soccer, horiz.

1991, Jan. 31
2215-2221 A555a Set of 7 3.50 2.00
Imperf., #2215-2221 5.50

Souvenir Sheet

2222 A555a 5000d multicolored 2.50 1.25
Imperf., #2222 5.00

No. 2222 contains one 44x33mm stamp.

Nguyen Binh Khiem (1491-1585), Writer — A556

1991, Feb. 15
2223 A556 200d multicolored 1.00 .25
Imperf. 2.50

Discovery of America, 500th Anniv. — A557

Sailing ships: 200d, Marisiliana. No. 2225, 400d, Venetian. No. 2226, 400d, Cromster, vert. No. 2227, 2000d, Nina. No. 2228, 2000d, Pinta. 3000d, Howker, vert. 5000d, Santa Maria.
6500d, Portrait of Columbus.

1991, Feb. 22
2224-2230 A557 Set of 7 4.50 2.00
Imperf., #2224-2230 5.00

Souvenir Sheet

2231 A557 6500d multicolored 3.00 1.25
Imperf. 5.50

Golden Heart Charity — A558

Women wearing traditional costumes: 200d, 500d, 1000d, 5000d.

1991, Feb. 26
2232-2235 A558 Set of 4 3.00 1.25
Imperf., #2232-2235 6.00

Sharks A559

Designs: 200d, Carcharhinus melanopterus. 300d, Carcharhinus amblyrhynchos. 400d, Triakis semifasciata. 1000d, Sphyrna mokarran. 2000d, Triaenodon obesus. No. 2241, 3000d, Carcharias taurus. No. 2242, 3000d, Carcharhinus leucas.

1991, Apr. 6
2236-2242 A559 Set of 7 6.00 2.00
Imperf., #2236-2242 9.00

Endangered Birds — A560

World Wildlife Fund: 200d, Grus vipio. 300d, Grus antigone chick, vert. 400d, Grus japonensis, vert. 1000d, Grus antigone, adults, vert. 2000d, Grus nigricollis, vert. No. 2248, 3000d, Balearica regulorum, vert. No. 2249, 3000d, Bugeranus leucogerranus.

1991, Apr. 20
2243-2249 A560 Set of 7 7.00 2.00
Imperf., #2243-2249 14.00

Shellfish A561

Designs: 200d, 1000d, 2000d, Palinurus, all diff. 300d, Alpheus bellulus. 400d, Periclemenes brevicarpalis. No. 2255, 3000d, Astacus. No. 2256, 3000d, Palinurus, diff.

1991, Apr. 20
2250-2256 A561 Set of 7 4.00 2.00
Imperf., #2250-2256 8.00

Young Pioneers, 50th Anniv. — A562

Designs: 200d, shown. 400d, UN Convention on Children's Rights.

1991, May 15
2257-2258 A562 Set of 2 1.50 .65
Imperf., #2257-2258 3.00

Rally Cars — A563

#2259, 400d, Lada. #2260, 400d, Nissan. 500d, Ford Sierra RS Cosworth. 1000d, Suzuki. 2000d, Mazda 323 4WD. #2264, 3000d, Lancia. #2265, 3000d, Peugeot. 5000d, Peugeot 405.

1991, May 24
2259-2265 A563 Set of 7 4.00 2.25
Imperf., #2259-2265 5.00

Souvenir Sheet

2266 A563 5000d multicolored 3.00 1.25
Imperf. 4.00

No. 2266 contains one 44x33mm stamp.

Locomotives A564

#2267, 400d, Puffing Billy, 1811, vert. #2268, 400d, Fusee, 1829, vert. 500d, Stevens, 1825. 1000d, Crampton #80, 1852. 2000d, Locomotion, 1825. #2272, 3000d, Saint-Lo, 1844. #2273, 3000d, Coutances, 1855. 5000d, Atlantic, 1843.

1991, May 25
2267-2273 A564 Set of 7 4.00
Imperf., #2267-2273 6.00

Souvenir Sheet

2274 A564 5000d multicolored 2.50
Imperf. 4.50

No. 2274 contains one 33x44mm stamp.

Frogs — A565

World Wildlife Fund: 200d, Dendrobates leucomelas. 400d, Rana esculenta. 500d, Mantella aurantiaca. 1000d, Dendrobates tinctorius. 2000d, Hyla halowelli. No. 2280, 3000d, Agalychnis callidryas. No. 2281, 3000d, Hyla aurea.

1991, June 12
2275-2281 A565 Set of 7 7.00 2.50
Imperf., #2275-2281 16.00

7th Vietnamese Communist Party Congress — A566

Designs: 200d, Ho Chi Minh, buildings. 300d, Workers. 400d, Mother, children.

1991, May 15
2282-2284 A566 Set of 3 1.50 .65
Imperf., #2282-2284 3.50

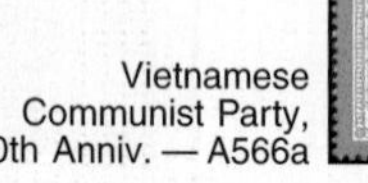

Vietnamese Communist Party, 60th Anniv. — A566a

1991, June 24 **Litho.** *Perf. 13*
2284A A566a 100d red 1.50 1.50
Imperf. 6.50

1992 Winter Olympics, Albertville A567

Designs: 200d, Speed skating, vert. 300d, Free- style skiing, vert. 400d, Bobsled. 1000d, Biathlon. 2000d, Slalom skiing. No. 2290, 3000d, Cross-country skiing, vert. No. 2291, 3000d, Ice dancing, vert. 5000d, Hockey, vert.

1991, July 15
2285-2291 A567 Set of 7 4.00 2.00
Imperf., #2285-2291 4.50

Souvenir Sheet

2292 A567 5000d multicolored 2.50 1.25
Imperf. 3.00

No. 2292 contains one 33x44mm stamp.

Prehistoric Animals — A568

Designs: a, 200d, Arsinoitherium zitteli. b, 500d, Elephas primigenius. c, 1000d, Baluchitherium. d, 2000d, Deinotherium giganteum. e, 3000d, Brontops. f, 3000d, Uinatherium.

1991, July 26
2293 A568 Block of 6, #a.-f. 3.50 3.00
Imperf., #2293 6.00

A569

Golden Heart Charity: 200d, Eye, folded hands. 3000d, Tennis player in wheelchair.

1991, Dec. 19
2294-2295 A569 Set of 2 1.50 .70

A570

Chess pieces: 200d, Pawn. 300d, Knight. 1000d, Rook. 2000d, Queen. No. 2300, 3000d, Bishop. No. 2301, 3000d, King. 5000d, Pawn, Knight, King.

1991, Aug. 20
2296-2301 A570 Set of 6 4.00 2.00
Imperf., #2296-2301 5.00

Souvenir Sheet

2302 A570 5000d multicolored 2.50 1.25
Imperf. 4.00

No. 2302 contains one 33x44mm stamp.

PHILANIPPON '91 — A571

Butterflies: 200d, Attacus atlas. 400d, Morpho cypris. 500d, Troides rotschildi. No. 2306, 1000d, Papilio demetrius. No. 2307, 1000d, Vanessa atalanta. 3000d, Papilio weiskei. 5000d, Apatura ilia substituta. 5500d, Heliconius melpomene.

1991, Aug. 29
2303-2309 A571 Set of 7 3.50 2.25
Imperf., #2303-2309 4.00

Souvenir Sheet

2310 A571 5500d multicolored 3.00 1.25
Imperf. 4.50

No. 2310 contains one 44x33mm stamp.

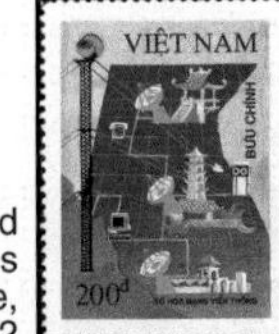
Post and Telecommunications Research Institute, 25th Anniv. — A572

3500d, Communications network, horiz.

1991, Aug.
2311 A572 200d multicolored 1.00 .25
Imperf. 2.00

Souvenir Sheet

2312 A572 3500d multicolored 2.00 1.25
Imperf. 4.00

No. 2312 contains one 44x33mm stamp.

Nos. 2118-2125 Ovptd. in Red

1992, Jan. 15 ***Perf. 12½***
2313-2319 A543 Set of 7 5.50 2.75

Souvenir Sheet

2320 A543 500d multicolored 3.50 1.40

7th Vietnamese Communist Party Congress — A574

200d, Workers, industry, agriculture, atomic energy symbol. 2000d, Map of Asia, hands clasped.

1992, Feb. 3 **Litho.** ***Perf. 13***
2322-2323 A574 Set of 2 1.50 1.75

1992 Winter Olympics, Albertville — A575

Designs: 200d, Biathlon. 2000d, Hockey. 4000d, Slalom skiing. 5000d, Pairs figure skating. 6000d, Downhill skiing.

1992, Feb. 5
2324-2328 A575 Set of 5 3.50 1.75

Miniature Sheet

Columbus' Discovery of America, 500th Anniv. — A576

Designs: a, 4000d, Columbus, flag. b, 6000d, Columbus, natives. c, 8000d, Aboard ship. d, 3000d, Two sailing ships. e, 400d, Columbus' fleet setting sail.

11,000d, Columbus with Ferdinand and Isabella.

1992, Feb. 12
2329 A576 #a.-f. + label 4.00 2.00

Imperf

Size: 102x70mm

2330 A576 11,000d multicolored 3.50 1.25

Airplanes A577

Designs: 400d, Tupolev TU-154M. 500d, Concorde. 1000d, Airbus A-320. 3000d, Airbus A340-300. 4000d, Boeing Dash 8-400. 5000d, Boeing 747-200. 6000d, McDonnell-Douglas MD-11CF.

1992, Mar. 6 ***Perf. 13***
2331-2337 A577 Set of 7 3.50 2.25

A578

Intl. Decade for Natural Disaster Reduction: 400d, Storm system, weather forecasting equipment. 4000d, Man taking water depth readings.

1992, Mar. 23
2338-2339 A578 Set of 2 1.00 .50

A579

1992 Summer Olympics, Barcelona: 400d, Archery. 600d, Volleyball. 1000d, Wrestling. 3000d, Fencing. 4000d, Running. 5000d, Weight lifting. 6000d, Field hockey. 10,000d, Basketball.

1992, Mar. 28
2340-2346 A579 Set of 7 3.50 2.00

Souvenir Sheet

2347 A579 10,000d multicolored 2.50 1.25

No. 2347 contains one 32x43mm stamp.

Motorcycles A580

Designs: 400d, 5000d, Suzuki 500F. 500d, Honda CBR 600F. 1000d, Honda HRC 500F. 3000d, Kawasaki 250F, vert. 4000d, Suzuki RM 250F, vert. 6000d, BMW 1000F. 10,000d, Suzuki RM 250F, diff.

1992, Apr. 8
2348-2354 A580 Set of 7 3.50 2.00

Souvenir Sheet

2355 A580 10,000d multicolored 2.50 1.25

No. 2355 contains one 33x44mm stamp.

Intl. Space Year — A581

400d, Space shuttle launch, vert. 500d, Launch of shuttle Columbia, vert. 3000d, Columbia in space. 4000d, Space station, shuttle Hermes. 5000d, Shuttle Hermes. 6000d, Astronauts, Hubble space telescope, vert.

1992, Apr. 12
2356-2361 A581 Set of 6 3.50 2.00

Saigon Post Office, Cent. — A582

200d, Main entrance. 10,000d, Facade.

1992, Apr. 30 ***Perf. 13***
2362 A582 200d multicolored 1.00 .25
Imperf. 10.00

Souvenir Sheet

Perf. 13½

2363 A582 10,000d multicolored 3.00 1.25

No. 2363 contains one 43x32mm stamp.

European Cup Soccer Championships A583

Various soccer players in action: 200d, 2000d, 4000d, 5000d, 6000d.

1992, May 14 ***Perf. 13***
2364-2368 A583 Set of 5 4.00 2.00

Souvenir Sheet

2369 A583 9000d multicolored 3.00 1.25

No. 2369 contains one 44x33mm stamp.

Spanish Paintings — A584

Designs: 400d, Childhood of the Virgin, by Zurbaran. 500d, Woman with a Jug, by Murillo. 1000d, Portrait of Maria Aptrickaia, by Velazquez. 3000d, Holy Family with St. Katherine, by de Ribera. 4000d, Madonna and Child with Saints Agnes and Thekla, by El Greco. 5000d, Woman with a Jug, by Goya. 6000d, The Naked Maja, by Goya, horiz. 10,000d, Three Women, by Picasso, horiz.

1992, May 30
2370-2376 A584 Set of 7 3.50 2.00

Souvenir Sheet

2377 A584 10,000d multicolored 3.00 1.25

No. 2377 contains one 44x33mm stamp. Expo '92, Seville (#2377).

UN Conference on Environmental Protection, 20th Anniv. — A585

Designs: 200d, Clean, polluted water. 4000d, Graph comparing current development pattern with environmentally safe pattern.

1992, June 1
2378-2379 A585 Set of 2 1.50 .50

A586

Lighthouses: 200d, Cu Lao Xanh. 3000d, Can Gio. 5000d, Vung Tau. 6000d, Long Chau.

1992, June 14 ***Perf. 13½x13***
2380-2383 A586 Set of 4 6.50 1.40

Genoa '92.

Flowers — A587

Designs: 200d, Citrus maxima. 2000d, Nerium indicum. 4000d, Ixora coccinea. 5000d, Cananga oborata. 6000d, Cassia surattensis.

1992, June 28 ***Perf. 13***
2384-2388 A587 Set of 5 3.50 1.40

Birds — A588

Designs: 200d, Ducula spilorrhoa. 2000d, Petrophassa ferruginea. 4000d, Columba livia. 5000d, Lopholaimus antareticus. 6000d, Streptopelia senegalensis, horiz.

1992, July 3
2389-2393 A588 Set of 5 3.50 1.40

Rodents A589

Designs: 200d, 500d, Cavia porcellus, horiz. 3000d, Hystrix indica, horiz. 4000d, Gerbillus gerbillus. 5000d, Petaurista petaurista. 6000d, Oryctolagus cuniculus.

1992, July 26
2394-2399 A589 Set of 6 3.50 2.00

Disabled Soldiers Day, 45th Anniv. — A590

1992, July 27

2400 A590 200d multicolored 1.00 .25
Imperf. 12.50

3rd Phu Dong Games A591

1992, Aug. 1

2401 A591 200d multicolored 1.00 .25

Betta Splendens — A592

Various fish: 200d, 500d, 3000d, 4000d, 5000d, 6000d.

1992, Aug. 15

2402-2407 A592 Set of 6 3.50 2.00

1984 Summer Olympics, Los Angeles — A592a

Designs: No. 2407A, 50xu, Gymnastics. No. 2407B, 50xu, Soccer, vert. 1d, Wrestling. 2d, Volleyball, vert. 3d, Hurdles. 5d, Basketball, vert. 8d, Weight lifting.
10d, Running, vert.

1992, Sept. 1 Litho. *Perf. 12½*

2407A-2407G A592a Set of 7 5.00 5.00

Souvenir Sheet

2407H A592a 10d multi 5.00 5.00

Nos. 2407A-2407G were prepared in 1984 but were not released at that time, because of Viet Nam's boycott of the 1984 Summer Olympics.

Intl. Planned Parenthood Federation, 40th Anniv. — A593

Designs: 200d, Map showing member's locations, vert. 4000d, Anniv. emblem, map.

1992, Oct. 1

2408-2409 A593 Set of 2 1.50 .50

Hanoi Medical School, 90th Anniv. — A594

Designs: 200d, Medical students. 5000d, Alexandre Yersin, school.

1992, Nov. 20

2410-2411 A594 Set of 2 1.50 .50

SOS Children's Villages — A595

Designs: 200d, Adult sheltering child. 5000d, Women, children inside house.

1992, Dec. 22

2412-2413 A595 Set of 2 1.50 .50
Imperf., #2412-2413 10.00

17th Southeast Asian Games, Singapore A596

1993, Jan. 1

2414 A596 200d multicolored 1.00 .25
Imperf. 12.50

Bees — A597

Designs: 200d, Apis dorsata. 800d, Apis koschevnikovi. 1000d, Apis laboriosa. 2000d, Apis cerana japonica. 5000d, Apis cerana cerana. 10,000d, Apis mellifera, vert.

1993, Jan. 15

2415-2420 A597 Set of 6 4.50 2.00
Imperf., #2415-2420 9.00

Fable of Tam Cam — A598

Designs: 200d, Returning from river. 800d, Vision of old man by goldfish pool. 1000d, With unsold rice at market. 3000d, Trying on slipper for prince. 4000d, Rising from lotus flower. 10,000d, Royal couple.

1993, Jan. 18

2421-2426 A598 Set of 6 6.50 2.00
Imperf., #2421-2425 17.00

New Year 1993 (Year of the Rooster) — A599

200d, 5000d, Rooster, hen and chicks.

1993, Jan. 20

2427-2428 A599 Set of 2 2.50 .50
Imperf., #2427-2428 12.50

Medicinal Plants — A600

Designs: 200d, Atractylodes macrocephala. No. 2430, 1000d, Lonicera japonica. No. 2431, 1000d, Quisqualis indica. 3000d, Rehmannia glutinosa. 12,000d, Gardenia jasminoides.

1993, Feb. 27

2429-2433 A600 Set of 5 6.50 1.50

Communications A601

200d, Map, communications equipment. 2500d, Map, Hong Kong-Sri Racha Cable route.

1993, Mar. 1

2434-2435 A601 Set of 2 1.50 .30

Asian Animals — A602

200d, Ailuropoda melanoleuca. 800d, Panthera tigris. 1000d, Elephas maximus. 3000d, Rhinoceros unicornis. 4000d, Hylobates leucogenys. #2441, 10,000d, Neofelis nebulosa. #2442, 10,000d, Bos sauveli.

1993, Mar. 10

2436-2441 A602 Set of 6 5.00 2.00
Imperf., #2436-2441 19.00

Souvenir Sheet

Perf. 13½

2442 A602 10,000d multicolored 3.00 1.25

1994 World Cup Soccer Championships, U.S. — A603

Various soccer players in action.

1993, Mar. 30 *Perf. 13*

2443-2445 A603 200d, 1500d, 7000d, set of 3 3.00 .65

Transportation A604

Designs: 200d, Wheelbarrow. 800d, Buffalo cart. 1000d, Rickshaw, top up. 2000d, Rickshaw with passenger. 5000d, Rickshaw, top down. 10,000d, Horse-drawn carriage.

1993, Apr. 6

2446-2451 A604 Set of 6 5.00 2.00
Imperf., #2446-2451 17.50

500Kv Electricity Lines — A605

1993, May 1

2452-2453 300d, 400d, set of 2 1.75 .30

Polska '93 — A606

Paintings: 200d, Sunflowers, by Van Gogh. No. 2455, 1000d, Young Woman, by Mogidliani. No. 2456, 1000d, Couple in Forest, by Rousseau. 5000d, Harlequin with Family, by Picasso. No. 2458, 10,000d, Female Model, by Matisse, horiz. No. 2459, 10,000d, Portrait of Dr. Gachet, by Van Gogh.

1993, May 7 *Perf. 13*

2454-2458 A606 Set of 5 5.00 1.25
Imperf., #2454-2458 5.50

Souvenir Sheet

Perf. 12½

2459 A606 10,000d multicolored 5.00 1.25

No. 2459 contains one 32x43mm stamp.

Da Lat, Cent. — A607

Orchids: 400d, Paphiopedilum hirsutissimum. No. 2461, 1000d, Paphiopedilum malipoense. No. 2462, 1000d, Paphiopedilum gratrixianum. 12,000d, Paphiopedilum hennisianum.

1993, June 15 *Perf. 13*

2460-2463 A607 Set of 4 5.00 1.50
Imperf., #2460-2463 9.00

Asian Architecture A608

Landmark buildings from: 400d, Thailand, vert. 800d, Indonesia, vert. 1000d, Singapore, vert. No. 2467, 2000d, Malaysia. No. 2468, 2000d, Cambodia. 6000d, Laos. 8000d, Brunei.
10,000d, Thai Binh, Viet Nam, vert.

1993, July 10 Litho.

2464-2470 A608 Set of 7 4.75 1.50
Imperf., #2464-2470 10.00

Souvenir Sheet

Perf. 14x13½

2471 A608 10,000d multicolored 4.00 1.50

7th Trade Union Congress — A608a

Designs: 400d, Industry, communications. 5000d, Hand holding hammer, doves, flowers.

1993, July 28 Litho. *Perf. 13*

2471A-2471B A608a Set of 2 4.50 .40

Crabs — A609

Designs: 400d, Scylla serrata. 800d, Portunus sanguinotentus. 1000d, Charybdis bimaculata. 2000d, Paralithodes brevipes. 5000d, Portunus pelagicus. 10,000d, Lithodes turritus.

1993, July 30

2472-2477 A609 Set of 6 5.50 1.50
Imperf., #2472-2477 9.00

Stamp Day — A610

5000d, Hand holding stamped envelope.

1993, Aug. 15

2478-2479 A610 Set of 2 2.25 .40

Miniature Sheet

Tennis A611

Women tennis players: a, 400d. c, 1000d. Male tennis players: b, 1000d. d, 12,000d.

1993, Sept. 20
2480 A611 #a.-d. + 2 labels 5.50 3.50

A613

Costumes: 400d, Lo Lo. 800d, Thai. 1000d, Dao Do. 2000d, H'mong. 5000d, Kho Mu. No. 2488, 10,000d, Kinh.
No. 2489, 10,000d, Precious gem stones.

1993, Oct. 1 ***Perf. 13***
2483-2488 A613 Set of 6 5.00 1.75

Souvenir Sheet

Perf. 13½

2489 A613 10,000d multicolored 5.25 1.25

Bangkok '93. Issued: Nos. 2483-2488, 10/1/93. No. 2489, 10/10/93.
No. 2489 contains one 43x32mm stamp.

A614

New Year 1994 (Year of the Dog): Various dogs.

1994, Jan. 1
2490-2491 A614 400d, 6000d, set of 2 2.50 .45
Imperf., #2490-2491 4.00

Flowers — A615

#2492, 400d, Prunus persica. #2493, 400d, Chrysanthemum morifolium. #2494, 400d, Rosa chinensis. 15,000d, Delonix regia.

1994
2492-2495 A615 Set of 4 5.50 1.60

Issued: #2492, 1/4; 15,000d, 4/30; #2493, 7/30; #2494, 10/10.

Chess — A616

Designs: 400d, Anatoly Karpov. 1000d, Gary Kasparov. 2000d, Bobby Fischer. 4000d, Emanuel Lasker. No. 2500, 10,000d, Jose Capablanca.
No. 2501, 10,000d, King.

1994, Jan. 20
2496-2500 A616 Set of 5 5.00 1.50
Imperf., #2496-2500 8.00

Souvenir Sheet

2501 A616 10,000d multicolored 3.25 1.25
Imperf. 5.25

Hong Kong '94 — A617

Festivals: 400d, Hoi Lim. 800d, Cham. 1000d, Tay Nguyen. 12,000d, Nam Bo.

1994, Feb. 18
2502-2505 A617 Set of 4 4.50 1.25
Imperf., #2502-2505 6.75

A618

Various opera masks: 400d, 500d, 2000d, 3000d, 4000d, 7000d.

1994, Mar. 15
2506-2511 A618 Set of 6 5.00 1.50
Imperf., #2506-2511 8.50

A619

Various gladiolus hybridus: 400d, 2000d, 5000d, 8000d.

1994, Mar. 30
2512-2515 A619 Set of 4 4.50 1.25
Imperf., #2512-2515 6.75

Japanese Paintings A620

Paintings by: 400d, Utamaro. 500d, Harunobu. 1000d, Hokusai. 2000d, Hiroshige. 3000d, Hokusai, diff. 4000d, Utamaro, diff. 8000d, Choki.

1994, Apr. 9
2516-2522 A620 Set of 7 6.50 1.75
Imperf., #2516-2522 12.00

Insects — A621

Designs: 400d, Cicindela aurulenta. 1000d, Harmonia octomaculata. 6000d, Cicindela tennipes. 7000d, Collyris.

1994, June 15
2523-2526 A621 Set of 4 5.00 1.25
Imperf., #2523-2526 6.75

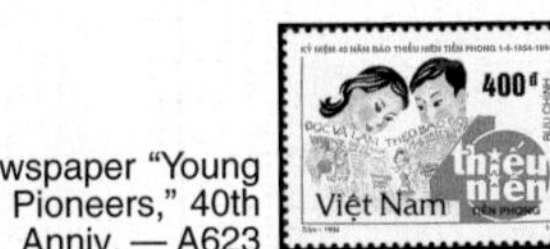

Victory at Dien Bien Phu, 40th Anniv. — A622

Designs: 400d, Soldiers dragging equipment. 3000d, Celebration.

1994, May 7
2527-2528 A622 Set of 2 1.50 .45
Imperf., #2527-2528 1.40

Newspaper "Young Pioneers," 40th Anniv. — A623

1994, May 15 ***Perf. 13x13½***
2529 A623 400d red & black .65 .25

Crocodiles A625

Designs: 400d, Crocodylus porosus. 600d, Alligator mississippiensis. 2000d, Crocodylus niloticus. 3000d, Alligator sinensis. 4000d, Caiman yacare. 9000d, Crocodylus johnsoni. 10,000d, Caiman crocodilus.

1994, June 1 ***Perf. 13x13½***
2532-2537 A625 Set of 6 5.00 1.75
Imperf., #2532-2537 8.00

Souvenir Sheet

Perf. 13½

2538 A625 10,000d multicolored 4.25 1.25
Imperf. 7.00

No. 2538 contains one 43x32mm stamp.

1994 World Cup Soccer Championships, US — A626

Various soccer players in action: 400d, 600d, 1000d, 2000d, 3000d, 11,000d.

1994, Apr. 20 ***Perf. 13***
2539-2544 A626 Set of 6 5.50 1.10
Imperf., #2539-2544 8.00

Souvenir Sheet

Perf. 13½

2545 A626 10,000d multicolored 4.00 1.10
Imperf. 5.00

No. 2545 contains one 32x43mm stamp.

Yersin's Discovery of Plague Bacillus, Cent. — A627

1994, June 15 ***Perf. 13x13½***
2546 A627 400d multicolored .90 .25

UPU, 120th Anniv. — A629

Designs: 400d, UPU emblem, "120." 5000d, World map. 10,000d, UPU emblem, "P," vert.

1994, Aug. 10 ***Perf. 13***
2551-2552 A629 Set of 2 1.75 .45
Imperf., #2551-2552 2.50

Souvenir Sheet

Perf. 14x13½

2553 A629 10,000d multicolored 4.25 1.25
Imperf. 6.00

PHILAKOREA '94 — A630

Birds: 400d, Numenius arquata. 600d, Oceanites oceanicus. 1000d, Fregata minor. 2000d, Morus capensis. 3000d, Lunda cirrhata. 11,000d, Larus belcheri.
10,000d, Collocalia fuciphaga.

1994, Aug. 16 ***Perf. 13x13½***
2554-2559 A630 Set of 6 5.50 1.50
Imperf., #2554-2559 8.00

Souvenir Sheet

Perf. 13½

2560 A630 10,000d multicolored 4.50 1.25
Imperf. 7.50

No. 2560 contains one 43x32mm stamp.

A631

Bamboo: 400d, Bambusa blumeana. 1000d, Phyllostachys aurea. 2000d, Bambusa vulgaris. 4000d, Tetragonocalamus quadrangularis. 10,000d, Bambusa venticosa.

1994, Aug. 17 ***Perf. 13½x13***
2561-2565 A631 Set of 5 5.50 1.50
Imperf., #2561-2565 9.00

Singpex '94.

A632

Various bridges: 400d, 900d, 8000d.

1994, Sept. 20 ***Perf. 13x13½***
2566-2568 A632 Set of 3 3.00 .90

Children's Future — A634

Designs: 400d+100d, Boy helping girl in wheelchair with kite. 2000d, Children dancing, vert.

1994, Oct. 10 **Litho.** ***Perf. 13***
2572-2573 A634 Set of 2 1.00 .40
Imperf., #2572-2573 10.00

A636

People's Army, 50th Anniv.: 400d, People in formation. 1000d, Soldiers, battle map. 2000d, Ho Chi Minh, child. 4000d, Anti-aircraft battery.

1994, Dec. 22
2576-2579 A636 Set of 4 2.25 .75

A637

Intl. Olympic Committee, Cent.: 400d, Flags. 6000d, Pierre de Coubertin.

1994, June 25 ***Perf. 13***
2580-2581 A637 Set of 2 3.00 .90

ICAO, 50th Anniv. — A638

Jets: 400d, In flight. 3000d, On ground.

1994, Dec. 7
2582-2583 A638 Set of 2 1.50 .40

Trams — A639

Designs: 400d, With overhead conductor. 900d, Paris tram. 8000d, Philadelphia mail.

1994, Oct. 10 **Litho.** ***Perf. 13x13½***
2584-2586 A639 Set of 3 3.00 .75

Liberation of Hanoi, 40th Anniv. — A640

Designs: 400d, Greeting soldiers. 2000d, Workers, students, modern technology.

1994, Oct. 10
2587-2588 A640 Set of 2 1.00 .40

New Year 1995 (Year of the Boar) — A641

Stylized boars: 400d, Adult, five young. 8000d, One eating.

1995, Jan. 2 Litho. *Perf. 13*
2589-2590 A641 Set of 2 2.50 .65
Imperf., #2589-2590 12.50

A642

Birds: No. 2591, 400d, Pluvialis apricaria, horiz. No. 2592, 400d, Philetairus socius, horiz. No. 2593, 400d, Oxyruncus cristatus, horiz. No. 2594, 400d, Pandion haliaetus. No. 2595, 5000d, Cariama cristata.

1995, Jan. 20 *Perf. 13x13½, 13½x13*
2591-2595 A642 Set of 5 2.25 .75

A number has been reserved for a souvenir sheet with this set.

A643

Traditional women's attire: 400d, Young women, bicycle. 3000d, Bride. 5000d, Girl in formal dress holding hat.

1995, Feb. 1 *Perf. 13*
2597-2599 A643 Set of 3 2.50 .75
Imperf., #2597-2599 12.50

Vietstampex '95 — A644

1995, Feb. 18
2600 A644 5500d multicolored 2.00 .50

Owls — A645

Designs: 400d, Ketupa zeylonensis. 1000d, Strix aluco. 2000d, Strix nebulosa. 5000d, Strix seloputo. 10,000d, Otus leucotis.
12,500d, Tyto alba.

1995, Mar. 1 *Perf. 13½x13*
2601-2605 A645 Set of 5 5.00 1.50

Souvenir Sheet

Perf. 14x13½

2606 A645 12,500d multicolored 5.00 1.10
Imperf. 6.75

Fish — A646

Designs: 400d, Pomacanthus arcuatus. 1000d, Rhinecanthus rectangulus. 2000d, Pygoplites diacanthus. 4000d, Pomacanthus ciliaris. 5000d, Balistes vetula. 9000d, Balistes conspicillum.

1995, Mar. 20 *Perf. 13*
2607-2612 A646 Set of 6 5.50 1.50

Lenin, 125th Birth Anniv. — A647

1995, Apr. 22 Litho. *Perf. 13*
2613 A647 400d red & black .60 .25

End of World War II, 50th Anniv. — A648

1995, May 2 Litho. *Perf. 13*
2614 A648 400d multicolored *1.00* .25

A649

1996 Summer Olympics, Atlanta: 400d, Hammer throw. 3000d, Cycling. 4000d, Running. 10,000d, Pole vault.
12,500d, Basketball.

1995, Apr. 5 Litho. *Perf. 13*
2615-2618 A649 Set of 4 4.00 1.40

Souvenir Sheet

2619 A649 12,500d multicolored 4.00 1.10

A650

Various balloons: 500d, 1000d, 2000d, 3000d, 4000d, 5000d, 7000d.

1995, May 5
2620-2626 A650 Set of 7 6.50 1.50

Finlandia '95, Intl. Philatelic Exhibition, Helsinki.

Miniature Sheets

Tapirus Indicus A651

No. 2627a, 400d, With young. b, 1000d, Facing left. c, 2000d, Walking right. d, 4000d, Mouth open, left.
No. 2528a, 4000d, Facing right. b, 4000d, Eating leaves. c, 5000d, In water. d, 6000d, Head protruding out of water.

1995, Apr. 25
2627 A651 Sheet of 4, #a.-d. 4.25 3.00
2628 A651 Sheet of 4, #a.-d. 6.00 3.50

World Wildlife Fund (#2627).

Miniature Sheet

Parachutes — A652

No. 2629: a, 400d, One parachutist descending from sky. b, 2000d, Two descending. c, 3000d, One about to touch ground. d, 9000d, Three men on ground with open parachute.

1995, May 24
2629 A652 Sheet of 4, #a.-d. 4.50 2.00

Rhododendrons A653

Designs: 400d, Fleuryi. 1000d, Sulphoreum. 2000d, Sinofalconeri. 3000d, Lyi. 5000d, Ovatum. 9000d, Tanastylum.

1995, June 30
2630-2635 A653 Set of 6 5.50 1.50

Miniature Sheet

Native Folktale A654

a, 400d, Brothers and their parents. b, 1000d, Mother saying farewell to her departing sons. c, 3000d, One brother is transformed into a statue. d, 10,000d, Both brothers transformed into statues.

1995, July 20 Litho. *Perf. 13*
2636 A654 Sheet of 4, #a.-d. 4.25 2.75

A655

400d, Statue of a woman holding child. 3000d, Three women of different races, emblem, horiz.

1995, Aug. 5
2637-2638 A655 Set of 2 1.25 .40

Women's Federation of Viet Nam: 65th anniv. (#2637), 1995 Intl. Women's Conf., Beijing (#2638).

A656

1995, July 26
2639 A656 400d multicolored .60 .25

Admission to Assoc. of Southeast Asian Nations (ASEAN).

Natl. Day — A657

#2640, 400d, Ho Chi Minh, people waving flags, dove of peace. #2641, 400d, Ho Chi Minh holding child. #2642, 1000d, Communist symbol, bridge, electrical wire, Ho Chi Minh Mausoleum. #2643, 1000d, Ho Chi Minh, silhouettes of soldiers, building with flags flying. #2644, 2000d, Soldiers, natl. flag. #2645, 2000d, Antenna, satellite dish, van, olive branch, people on motorcycles.

1995, Aug. 14
2640-2645 A657 Set of 6 3.50 .90

Viet Nam Labor Party, 65th anniv. (No. 2640). Ho Chi Minh, 105th birth anniv. (No. 2641). Evacuation of French troops from North Viet Nam, 40th anniv. (No. 2642). End of war in Viet Nam, 20th anniv. (No 2643). Natl. army, 50th anniv. (No. 2644). Post and Telecommunications Service, 50th anniv. (No. 2645).

Sir Rowland Hill (1795-1879) A658

Design: 4000d, Hill, "penny black."

1995, Aug. 15
2646 A658 4000d multicolored 1.25 .25

Natl. Sports Games — A659

1995, Aug. 30
2647 A659 400d multicolored .65 .25

Singapore '95 — A660

Orchids: 400d, Paphiopedilum druryi. 2000d, Dendrobium orcraceum. 3000d, Vanda. 4000d, Cattelya. 5000d, Paphiopedilum hirsutissimum. 6000d, Christenosia vietnamica haeger.
12,500d, Angraecum sesquipedale.

1995, Sept. 1
2648-2653 A660 Set of 6 6.00 1.40

Souvenir Sheet

2654 A660 12,500d multicolored 4.50 1.25

No. 2654 contains one 32x43mm stamp.

Asian Sites — A661

Designs: 400d, Buildings, monuments, tombs, Hue, Viet Nam. 3000d, Zigzag bridge, West Lake, Hangzhou, China. 4000d, Temple, Macao. 5000d, Peak tram, Hong Kong. 6000d, Pagoda, Peace Memorial Park, Taipei, Taiwan.

1995, Sept. 6
2655-2659 A661 Set of 5 4.75 1.25

UN, 50th Anniv. — A662

1995, Oct. 10
2660 A662 2000d multicolored .75 .25

Total Solar Eclipse, Oct. 10, 1995 — A663

1995, Dec. 23 Litho. *Perf. 13*
2661 A663 400d multicolored .80 .30

Paintings of Women — A664

Designs: 400d, Woman in white dress, flowers, by To Ngoc Van (1906-54) (4-1). 2000d, Washing hair, by Tran Van Can (1906-94) (4-2). 6000d, Standing beside vase of flowers, by To Ngoc Van (4-3). 8000d, Two women, by Tran Van Can (4-4).

1995, Nov. 15 Litho. *Perf. 13*
2662-2665 A664 Set of 4 4.00 3.00

New Year 1996 (Year of the Rat) — A665

Stylized rats: 400d, One carrying fan, one riding horse. 8000d, Four carrying one in palanquin.
13,000d, Marching in parade, carrying banner.

1996, Jan. 2 Litho. *Perf. 13*
2666 A665 400d multicolored .40 .25
2667 A665 8000d multicolored 2.50 1.25

Souvenir Sheet

2668 A665 13,000d multi, vert. 3.50 1.50

No. 2668 contains one 32x43mm stamp.

Dinosaurs A666

Designs: 400d, Tsintaosaurus. 1000d, Archaeopteryx. 2000d, Psittacosaurus. 3000d, Hypsilophodon. 13,000d, Parasaurolophus.

1996, Mar. 6
2669-2673 A666 Set of 5 4.25 3.00

Kingfishers — A667

Designs: 400d, Halcyon smyrnensis. 1000d, Megaceryle alcyon. 2000d, Alcedo Atthis. 4000d, Halcyon coromanda. 12,000d, Ceryle rudis.

1996, Mar. 11
2674-2678 A667 Set of 5 4.50 3.00

Flowers — A668

Various flowers: No. 2679, 400d, brown (5-1). No. 2680, 400d, claret (5-2). No. 2681, 400d, green (5-3). No. 2682, 400d, blue (5-4). No. 2683, 5000d, red (5-5), vert.

Perf. 13x13½, 13½x13

1996, Jan. 10 Litho.
2679-2683 A668 Set of 5 2.00 1.10

8th Vietnamese Communist Party Congress A669

Designs: 400d, Ho Chi Minh (2-1). 3000d, Stylized dove, satellite dish, electrical towers, hammer & sickle, building, olive branch (2-2).

1996, Feb. 3 *Perf. 13*
2684-2685 A669 Set of 2 .85 .60

Asian Sites — A670

Monuments and statues in: 400d, Hanoi. 2000d, Thailand. 3000d, Bhubanesvar, India. 4000d, Kyoto, Japan. 10,000d, Borobudur, Java.

1996, Apr. 10 Litho. *Perf. 13*
2686-2690 A670 Set of 5 4.50 3.00

See Nos. 2773-2777.

Statues — A671

Various statues of men in traditional costumes of early warriors: 400d, 600d, 1000d, 2000d, 3000d, 5000d, 6000d, 8000d.

1996, Feb. 10 Litho. *Perf. 13½x13*
2691-2698 A671 Set of 8 5.50 4.00
Imperf., #2691-2698 15.00

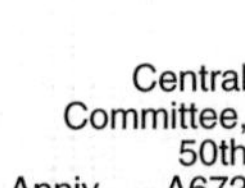

Central Committee, 50th Anniv. — A672

1996, May 22 *Perf. 13*
2699 A672 400d multicolored .50 .25

UNICEF, 50th Anniv. — A673

Designs: 400d, Children of different races, cultures. 7000d, Plant, emblem, water droplets containing representations of education, drinking water, medicine, food.

1996, May 15
2700-2701 A673 Set of 2 2.25 1.50

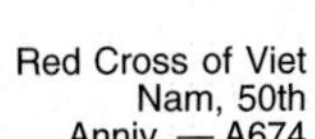

Red Cross of Viet Nam, 50th Anniv. — A674

1996, May 8 *Perf. 13½*
2702 A674 3000d Quotation, Ho Chi Minh 1.00 .50

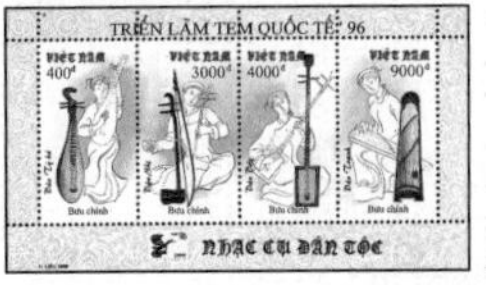

A675

Traditional Musical Instruments: a, 400d, Mandolin. b, 3000d, Bow and string instrument. c, 4000d, Square-shaped guitar-like instrument. d, 9000d, Zither.

1996, Apr. 24 *Perf. 13½x13*
2703 A675 Sheet of 4, #a.-d. 4.50 1.75

China '96 Intl. Philatelic Exhibition.

A676

Insects: 400d, Cincindela japonica. 500d, Calodema wallacei. 1000d, Mylabris oculata. 4000d, Chrysochroa buqueti. 5000d, Ophioniea nigrofasciata. 12,000d, Carabus tauricus.

1996, May 20 *Perf. 13*
2704-2709 A676 Set of 6 5.00 3.50

1996 Summer Olympic Games, Atlanta — A677

Designs: 2000d, Soccer. 4000d, Sailing. 5000d, Field hockey.

1996, July 8
2710-2712 A677 Set of 3 3.00 1.50

Euro '96, European Soccer Championships, Great Britain — A678

Designs: a, 400d, Net, goalie. b, 8000d, Player making shot on goal.

1996, June 1
2713 A678 Pair, #a.-b. 2.00 1.00

No. 2713 is a continuous design.

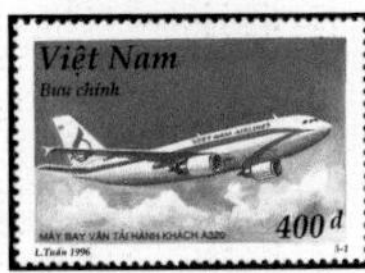

Aircraft A679

400d, Airbus A320. 1000d, AN-72. 2000d, MD-11F. 6000d, RJ-85. 10,000d, B747-400F. 13,000d, Space shuttle carried by Boeing 747.

1996, June 1
2714-2718 A679 Set of 5 4.50 3.00

Souvenir Sheet

Perf. 13½

2719 A679 13,000d multicolored 3.00 2.00

Stamp Day — A680

1996, Aug. 15 *Perf. 13*
2720 A680 400d No. 1L57 (1-1) .50 .25

Paintings by Nguyen Sáng (1923-88) A681

400d, Woman, vase of flowers (2-1). 8000d, Soldiers returning from battle (2-2).

1996, Sept. 10 *Perf. 13*
2721-2722 A681 Set of 2 2.25 1.00

Hue School, Cent. — A682

400d, Women walking beside entrance (2-1). 3000d, View of portals, building (2-2).

1996, Sept. 5
2723-2724 A682 Set of 2 .90 .45

Mushrooms A683

Designs: 400d, Aleuria aurantia. 500d, Morchella conica. 1000d, Anthurus archeri. 4000d, Laetiporus serlphureus. 5000d, Filoboletus manipularis. 12,000d, Tremiscus helvelloides.

1996, Aug. 26 Litho. *Perf. 13*
2725-2730 A683 Set of 6 5.50 4.00

Wild Animals A684

Designs: a, 400d, Pygathrix nemacus. b, 2000d, Panthera tigris. c, 4000d, Rhinoceros sondaicus. d, 10,000d, Balearica regulorum.

1996, Oct. 10 Litho. *Perf. 13*
2731 A684 Sheet of 4, #a.-d. 4.00 4.00

Taipei '96.

Campaign Promoting Iodized Salt — A685

1996, Nov. 2 Litho. *Perf. 13*
2732 A685 400d multicolored .55 .30

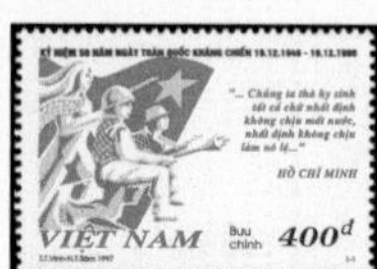

Natl. Liberation Movement, 50th Anniv. — A686

1996, Dec. 19

2733 A686 400d multicolored .55 .30

Fruit — A687

Designs: No. 2734, Hylocereus undatus. No. 2735, Durio zibethinus. No. 2736, Persea americana. No. 2737, Garcinia mangostana. No. 2738, Nephelium lappaceum.

1997, Jan. 2 ***Perf. 13x13½***

2734-2738 A687 400d Set of 5 *2.00* .75

New Year 1997 (Year of the Ox) — A688

Stylized oxen: 400d, Adult, calf. 8000d, Adult.

1997, Jan. 8 **Litho.** ***Perf. 13***

2739-2740 A688 Set of 2 2.50 1.50

Imperf., #2739-2740 12.50

8th Vietnamese Communist Party Congress A689

1997, Feb. 3

2741 A689 400d multicolored .60 .30

Goldfish — A690

Various carassius auratus: 400d, 1000d, 5000d, 7000d, 8000d.

1997, Feb. 5

2742-2746 A690 Set of 5 5.00 3.00

Imperf., #2742-2746 14.50

Souvenir Sheet

Perf. 13½x14

2747 A690 14,000d multicolored 3.50 1.50

No. 2747 contains one 43x32mm stamp. Hong Kong '97 (#2747).

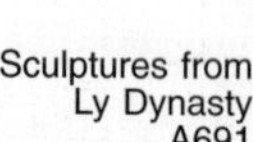

Sculptures from Ly Dynasty A691

Designs: 400d, Serpents in round figure, vert. 1000d, Dragon head, vert. 3000d, People playing instruments. 5000d, Gargoyle. 10,000d, Dragon-head bowl.

1997, Mar. 5

2748-2752 A691 Set of 5 4.50 2.50

Imperf., #2748-2752 14.50

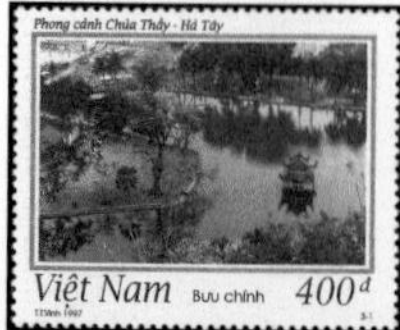

Scenes A692

Designs: 400d, Lake, people in park, Hà Tay. 5000d, Footbridge over river, Lai Chau. 7000d, Houses, fog, trees, Lào Cai.

1997, Mar. 20

2753-2755 A692 Set of 3 3.00 2.00

Huynh Thuc Khang (1876-1947) — A693

1997, Apr. 21 **Litho.** ***Perf. 13½x13***

2756 A693 400d multi .85 .30

Disabled People in Sports — A694

1000d, Tennis. 6000d, Shooting.

1997, Apr. 27 ***Perf. 13***

2757-2758 A694 Set of 2 1.60 1.20

Wild Animals — A695

400d, Chrotogale owstoni. 3000d, Lutra lutra. 4000d, Callosciurus erythraeus. 10,000d, Felis bangalensis.

1997, May 2

2759-2762 A695 Set of 4 4.25 2.75

A696

1997, May 19

2763 A696 400d Women's Union 1.00 .30

A697

Lilium longiflorum (Lilies): 400d, Red. 1000d, White. 5000d, Pink & white. 10,000d, Orange.

1997, Apr. 15 **Litho.** ***Perf. 13***

2764-2767 A697 Set of 4 4.00 2.50

PACIFIC 97 — A698

Suspension bridges: 400d, Golden Gate, San Francisco. 5000d, Raippaluoto. 10,000d, Seto.

1997, May 12

2768-2770 A698 Set of 3 3.50 2.50

Children — A699

400d, UN Convention on the Rights of the Child. 5000d, Breast milk is better.

1997, June 1 **Litho.** ***Perf. 13***

With Gum

2771-2772 A699 Set of 2 1.25 1.00

Asian Sites Type of 1996

Designs: 400d, Pagoda, Hanoi, Viet Nam. 1000d, Ruins of Persepolis, Iran. 3000d, Statue of woman, Iraq. 5000d, Sacred Rock, Kyaikto, Burma. 10,000d, Statue of Buddha lying down, Sr. Lanka.

1997, June 20 **Litho.** ***Perf. 13***

2773-2777 A670 Set of 5 4.50 3.00

Women's Costumes — A700

Various costumes: 400d, Woman holding umbrella, San Chay. 2000d, Woman sewing, wearing jacket tied with sash, Dao quain trang. 5000d, Woman pumping water from well provided by UNICEF, Phù Lá. 10,000d, Woman holding hands in air, Kho Me.

1997, July 8

2778-2781 A700 Set of 4 4.00 2.50

A701

1997, July 11

2782 A701 400d multicolored *4.00* .40

Prevention of AIDS.

ASEAN, 30th Anniv. — A702

1997, Aug. 8 **Litho.** ***Perf. 13***

2783 A702 400d multicolored .60 .25

Monument to War Martyrs & Invalids, 50th Anniv. — A703

1997, July 25

2784 A703 400d multicolored .80 .35

Hibiscus A704

a, 1000d, Hibiscus rosa sinensis. b, 3000d, Hibiscus schizopetalus. c, 5000d, Hibiscus syriacus (pink). d, 9000d, Hibiscus syriacus (yellow).

1997, Aug. 1

2785 A704 Sheet of 4, #a.-d. 4.50 2.50

A705

1997, Aug. 26 **Litho.** ***Perf. 13***

2786 A705 400d multicolored .65 .30

Post and Telecommunications Union, 50th anniv.

A706

Sea horses: 400d, 1000d, Hippocampus (diff.). 3000d, Hippocampus guttulatus. 5000d, Hippocampus kelloggi. 6000d, Hippocampus japonicus. 7000d, Hippocampus hippocampus.

1997, Sept. 4

2787-2792 A706 Set of 6 5.00 4.00

19th Southeast Asian Games — A707

1997, Oct. 11 **Litho.** ***Perf. 13***

2793 A707 5000d multicolored 1.75 .90

Handicrafts A708

Designs: No. 2794, 400d, Lamp. No. 2795, 400d, Two baskets. No. 2796, 400d, Swan-shaped basket. No. 2797, 400d, Deer-shaped basket. 2000d, Basket with handle.

1998, Jan. 1 **Litho.** ***Perf. 13***

2794-2798 A708 Set of 5 1.40 .80

7th Francophone Summit, Hanoi
A709

1997, Sept. 24 Litho. *Perf. 13½x13*
2799 A709 5000d multicolored 2.75 2.00

Birds — A710

400d, Syrmaticus ellioti. 3000d, Lophura diardi. 5000d, Phasianus cholchicus. 6000d, Chrysolophus amherstiae. 8000d, Polyplectron germaini.
14,000d, Lophura imperialis.

1997, Oct. 15 *Perf. 13*
2800-2804 A710 Set of 5 5.50 4.00

Souvenir Sheet
Perf. 13½
2805 A710 14,000d multicolored 3.50 2.50

No. 2805 contains one 43x30mm stamp.

New Year 1998 (Year of the Tiger) — A711

Stylized tigers: 400d, Adult with young. 8000d, Adult.

1998, Jan. 5 *Perf. 13*
2806-2807 A711 Set of 2 2.40 1.50

Sites in Vietnam — A712

Designs: No. 2808, 400d, Rocks, lake, Ninh Thuan. No. 2809, 400d, Lake, cavern, Quang Binh. 10,000d, Village of Quang Nam.

1998, Feb. 2
2808-2810 A712 Set of 3 2.40 1.50

Communist Manifesto, 150th Anniv. — A713

1998, Feb. 3
2811 A713 400d multicolored 1.00 .30

Bonsai — A714

#2812, 400d, Limonia acidissima. #2813, 400d, Deeringia polysperma. #2814, 400d, Pinus merkusii, vert. 4000d, Barringtonia acutangula, vert. 6000d, Ficus elastica, vert. 10,000d, Wrightia religiosa, vert.
No. 2818, Adenium obesum.

1998, Mar. 2
2812-2817 A714 Set of 6 5.25 3.00

Souvenir Sheet
Perf. 13½
2818 A714 14,000d multicolored 3.50 2.00

No. 2818 contains one 43x32mm stamp.

Tet Offensive, 30th Anniv. — A715

1998, Jan. 30 Litho. *Perf. 13*
2819 A715 400d multicolored .80 .30

Opera
A716

Designs: a, 400d, Thi kính bi oan. b, 1000d, Thi mâu lên chúa. c, 2000d, Thi mâu-gia nô. d, 4000d, Thi me dôp-Xa trúong. e, 6000d, Thi kính bi phat va. f, 9000d, Thi kính xin sua.

1998, Apr. 20
2820 A716 Sheet of 6, #a.-f 5.00 3.50

Raptors — A717

Designs: No. 2821, 400d, Pernis apivorus. No. 2822, 400d, Spizaetus ornatus. No. 2823, 400d, Accipter gentilis. 3000d, Buteo buteo. 5000d, Circus melanoleucas. 12,000d, Haliaeetus albicilla.

1998, May 4 Litho. *Perf. 13*
2821-2826 A717 Set of 6 5.00 3.00

Ho Chi Minh City (Saigon), 300th Anniv. — A718

400d, Tank, natl. flag, Ho Chi Minh as young man, building. 5000d, Monument to Ho Chi Minh, symbols of industry, communications, and transportation.
14,000d, Statue of Nguyen Huu Canh (1650-1700), general.

1998, Apr. 30
2827-2828 A718 Set of 2 2.00 .90

Souvenir Sheet
Perf. 14x13½
2828A A718 14,000d multi 4.00 3.00

Orchids — A719

Designs: 400d, Paphiopedilum appletonianum. 6000d, Paphiopedilum helenae.

1998, May 18 Litho. *Perf. 13½*
2829-2830 A719 Set of 2 2.00 1.00

Children's Paintings — A720

UNICEF: 400d, Children, mother in front of home. 5000d, Children on playground.

1998, June 1 *Perf. 13*
2831-2832 A720 Set of 2 1.75 .90

1998 World Cup Soccer Championships, France — A721

Various soccer plays: 400d, 5000d, 7000d.

1998, June 10
2833-2835 A721 Set of 3 3.00 2.00

Sculptures of the Tran Dynasty — A722

Ornate designs: No. 2836, 400d, Serpent. No. 2837, 400d, Two people. 1000d, Shown. 8000d, Person. 9000d, Face.

1998, June 15 Litho. *Perf. 13*
2836-2840 A722 Set of 5 4.50 2.75

Martial Arts — A723

1998, July 13
2841 A723 2000d multicolored 1.00 .50

Intl. Year of the Ocean — A724

1998, Aug. 1 Litho. *Perf. 13*
2842 A724 400d multicolored 1.75 .30

Stamp Day — A725

1998, Aug. 15
2843 A725 400d Bell's telephone 1.00 .30

Ton Duc Thang (1888-1980) — A726

1998, Aug. 20
2844 A726 400d multicolored .85 .30

Moths — A727

Designs: No. 2845, 400d, Antheraea helferi. No. 2846, 400d, Attacus atlas. 4000d, Argema mittrei, vert. 10,000d, Argema maenas, vert.

1998, Aug. 22
2845-2848 A727 Set of 4 4.50 2.50

Paintings by Te Bach Thach (Qi Baishi; 1863-1957) — A728

Various paintings: 400d, Dragonfly & Lotus. 1000d, Chrysanthemum, Cock & Hens. 2000d, Shrimps, 1948. 4000d, Crabs. 6000d, Lotus & Mandarin Ducks. 9000d, Shrimps, 1949.

1998, Sept. 16
2849-2854 A728 Set of 6 5.25 3.25

Legend of the Lake — A729

Designs: No. 2855, Turtle with sword leading boat. No. 2856, Lake.

1998, Oct. 10
2855-2856 A729 400d Set of 2 1.60 .50

Le Thanh Tong (1442-1497)
A730

1998, Oct. 12
2857 A730 400d multicolored .85 .30

Souvenir Sheet

Italia '98, Intl. Philatelic Exhibition — A731

Milan Cathedral.

1998, Oct. 6 *Perf. 13½*
2858 A731 16,000d multicolored 4.50 2.00

8th Trade Union Congress
A732

1998, Oct. 15 Litho. *Perf. 13*
2859 A732 400d multicolored .85 .30

Quy Nhon City, 396th Anniv., Binh Dinh Province, Cent. — A733

1998, Oct. 20
2860 A733 400d multicolored .85 .30

Buoi-Chu Van An Secondary School, 90th Anniv. — A734

Designs: 400d, Students outside school. 5000d, Students listening to speaker.

1998, Nov. 20
2861-2862 A734 Set of 2 1.90 .90

6th ASEAN Congress, Hanoi — A735

1998, Dec. Litho. *Perf. 13*
2863 A735 1000d multicolored .90 .40

Cuban Revolution, 40th Anniv. (in 1999) — A736

1998, Dec. Litho. *Perf. 13*
2864 A736 400d multicolored .90 .30

A737

Paintings: 400d, Birds, tree, flowers (Spring). 1000d, Flowers, ducks (Summer). 3000d, Flowers, rooster (Fall). 12,000d, Tree, flowers, deer & fawn (Winter).

1999, Jan. 4 Litho. *Perf. 13½x13*
2865-2868 A737 Set of 4 4.00 2.00

A738

New Year 1999 (Year of the Cat): 400d, Cat holding tree branch. 8000d, Two cats. 13,000d, Kittens, ball.

1999, Jan. 6 *Perf. 13½*
2869-2870 A738 Set of 2 2.00 1.40

Souvenir Sheet

2871 A738 13,000d multicolored 3.50 2.00

No. 2871 contains one 32x43mm stamp.

Kites — A739

400d, Large bird with long tail. 5000d, Crescent-shaped. 7000d, Bird with long legs.

1999, Feb. 16 Litho. *Perf. 13½x13*
2872-2874 A739 Set of 3 3.50 1.50

Australia '99, World Stamp Expo — A740

Various sailing vessels: #2875, 400d, (4-1). #2876, 400d, (4-2). 7000d, (4-3). 9000d, (4-4).

1999, Mar. 10 Litho. *Perf. 13*
2875-2878 A740 Set of 4 3.75 2.00

Medicinal Plants — A741

Designs: No. 2879, 400d, Kaempferia galanga. No. 2880, 400d, Tacca chantrieri, vert. No. 2881, Alpinia galanga, vert. 6000d, Typhonium trilobatum, vert. 13,000d, Asarum maximum, vert.

1999, Mar. 15
2879-2883 A741 Set of 5 4.50 2.25

Opera Masks — A742

Various masks: 400d (6-1). 1000d (6-2). 2000d (6-3). 5000d (6-4). 6000d (6-5). 10,000d (6-6).

1999, Apr. 16 *Perf. 13½*
2884-2889 A742 Set of 6 5.25 3.50

IBRA'99, World Philatelic Exhibition, Nuremberg — A743

Octopuses: No. 2890, 400d, Octopus gibertianus. No. 2891, 400d, Philonexis catenulata. 4000d, Paroctopus yendol. 12,000d, Octopus vulgaris.

1999, Apr. 20
2890-2893 A743 Set of 4 4.00 2.25

Landscape Paintings of Southern Viet Nam — A744

#2894, 400d, Sun over lake, Cà Mau. #2895, 400d, Rocks protruding out of water, Kien Giang. 12,000d, Traditional huts, Bac Lieu.

1999, May 4 *Perf. 13*
2894-2896 A744 Set of 3 3.50 1.50

Asia-Pacific Telecommunity, 20th Anniv. — A745

1999, May 10 Litho. *Perf. 13x13¼*
2897 A745 400d multi 2.25 1.50

Woodpeckers — A746

Designs: 400d, Chrysocolaptes lucidus. 1000d, Picumnus innominatus. 3000d, Picus rabieri. 13,000d, Blythipicus pyrrhotis.

1999, May 18 Litho. *Perf. 13*
2898-2901 A746 Set of 4 4.50 2.50

UNICEF — A747

Designs: 400d, Girl, hand. 5000d, Boy carrying factory.

1999, June 1 Litho. *Perf. 13*
2902-2903 A747 Set of 2 1.75 .50

Architecture of Late 19th and Early 20th Centuries A748

Designs: No. 2904, 400d, Government Office Building, Hanoi (3-1). No. 2905, 400d, History Museum, Ho Chi Minh City (3-2). 12,000d, Duc Ba Cathedral (3-3).
15,000d, Theater, Hanoi.

1999, June 10 *Perf. 13*
2904-2906 A748 Set of 3 3.00 1.50

Souvenir Sheet
Perf. 13½x14

2907 A748 15,000d multi 4.00 2.00

PhilexFrance '99 (No. 2907). No. 2907 contains one 44x32mm stamp.

Intl. Day to Stop Drug Abuse — A749

1999, June 24 Litho. *Perf. 13*
2908 A749 400d multicolored .85 .25

Da Rang Bridge, Phu Yen — A750

1999, July 1 Litho. *Perf. 13*
2909 A750 400d multi .85 .30

Le Dynasty Sculptures A751

Designs: No. 2910, 1000d, Man Against Tiger (5-1). No. 2911, 1000d, Phoenix (5-2). 3000d, Playing Chess, vert. (5-3). 7000d, Hostler, vert. (5-4). 9000d, Dragon (5-5).

1999, July 1
2910-2914 A751 Set of 5 7.00 5.00

Birth of World's Six Billionth Person — A752

1999, Aug. 2
2915 A752 400d multi .90 .25

Chinese Landscapes A753

Designs: 400d, Park, Beijing (4-1). 2000d, Scenic overlook, Anhwei (4-2). 3000d, Park, Shandong, (4-3). 10,000d, Park, Beijing, diff. (4-4).
14,000d, Great Wall of China.

1999, Aug. 16 *Perf. 13*
2916-2919 A753 Set of 4 4.25 2.50

Souvenir Sheet
Perf. 13½x14

2920 A753 14,000d multi 4.00 2.50

China 1999 World Philatelic Exhibition (No. 2920). No. 2920 contains one 43x32mm stamp.

Boat Races — A754

Races from regions: 400d, North (3-1). 2000d, Central (3-2). 10,000d, South (3-3).

1999, Sept. 10 *Perf. 13*
2921-2923 A754 Set of 3 3.00 2.00

Women's Costumes — A755

Various costumes. #2924, 400d (3-1). #2925, 400d (3-2). #2926, 12,000d (3-3).

1999, Sept. 10
2924-2926 A755 Set of 3 3.50 2.00

Buffalo Fighting Festivals A756

Fighting buffaloes: 400d, (2-1). 5000d, (2-2).

1999, Sept. 15
2927-2928 A756 Set of 2 2.00 .75

Ngo Quyen (898-944), General — A757

1999, Oct. 21
2929 A757 400d multi .90 .30

Nguyen Van Sieu (1799-1872), Teacher, Writer — A758

1999, Nov. 2 Litho. *Perf. 13*
2930 A758 400d multi .90 .30

Tran Xuan Soan (1849-1923), Anti-colonial Leader — A759

1999, Nov. 24
2931 A759 400d multi .90 .30

United Nations Development Program A760

Designs: 400d, Mother and child, farmer, fisherman. 8000d, Villagers, buildings.

1999, Dec. 3
2932-2933 A760 Set of 2 2.75 1.00

Viet Nam in the 20th Century — A761

Designs; No. 2934, 400d, Founding of Viet Nam Communist Party (6-1). No. 2935, 400d, Ho Chi Minh's declaration of country's independence (6-2). No. 2936, 1000d, Conquest of South Viet Nam (6-3). No. 2937, 1000d, People, dam, high tension wire tower, atom (6-4). 8000d, People, satellite, satellite dish, dam, high tension wire tower (6-5). 12,000d, Organizations Viet Nam belongs to (6-6).

2000, Jan. 1 Litho. *Perf. 13*
With Gum
2934-2939 A761 Set of 6 9.00 3.00
2939a Sheet, #2934-2939, without gum 11.00 4.00

New Year 2000 (Year of the Dragon) — A762

Dragon: 400d, Facing right (2-1). 8000d, Facing left (2-2).

2000, Jan. 3 With Gum *Perf. 13½*
2940-2941 A762 Set of 2 4.00 1.50

Intl. Year of Culture and Peace — A763

2000, Jan. 18 With Gum
2942 A763 400d multi .90 .30

Viet Nam Communist Party, 70th Anniv. — A764

#2943, Ho Chi Minh (1890-1969), Pres. (8-1). #2944, Tran Phu (1904-31), 1st Gen. Sec. (8-2). #2945, Le Hong Phong (1902-42), Gen. Sec. (8-3). #2946, Ha Huy Tap (1902-41), Gen. Sec. (8-4). #2947, Nguyen Van Cu (1912-41), Gen. Sec. (8-5). #2948, Truong Chinh (1907-88), Gen. Sec. (8-6). #2949, Le Duan (1907-86), Gen. Sec. (8-7). #2950, Nguyen Van Linh (1915-98), Gen. Sec. (8-8).

2000, Feb. 2 With Gum *Perf. 13*
2943-2950 A764 400d Set of 8 3.50 1.00

Cockfighting A765

Postures: No. 2951, 400d, Song long cuoc (4-1). No. 2952, 400d, Long vu da dao (4-2). 7000d, Song long phuong hoang (4-3). 9000d, Nhan o giap chien (4-4).

2000, Feb. 8 Litho. *Perf. 13*
2951-2954 A765 Set of 4 7.00 2.50
Imperf., #2951-2954 9.00

Bangkok 2000 Stamp Exhibition A766

Palanquins: 400d, Imperial court roofed palanquin (3-1). 7000d, Palanquin without roof (3-2). 8000d, Roofed palanquin (3-3).
15,000d, Palanquin in procession.

2000, Mar. 10 With Gum
2955-2957 A766 Set of 3 5.00 2.50
Souvenir Sheet
2958 A766 15,000d multi 5.00 2.50

Legend of Lac Long Quan and Au Co — A767

Designs: No. 2959, 400d, Lang Long Quan and Au Co marry (6-1). No. 2960, 400d, Au Co, gives birth to 100 sons (6-2). 500d, Au Co takes 50 children to forest (6-3). 3000d, Lac Long Quan takes 50 children to sea (6-4). 4000d, Eldest son, Hung Vuong ascends to throne (6-5). 11,000d, Vietnamese ethnic groups as descendents (6-6).

2000, Apr. 4 *Perf. 13½*
2959-2964 A767 Set of 6 8.00 3.50

Souvenir Sheet

The Stamp Show 2000, London A768

No. 2965 — Fire engines: a, 400d, Iveco Magirus, Germany. b, 1000d, Hino, Japan. c, 5000d, ZIL 103E, Russia. d, 12,000d, FPS.32 Camiva, France.

2000, May 15 *Perf. 13*
2965 A768 Sheet of 4, #a-d 9.00 3.00

Worldwide Fund for Nature — A769

Pseudoryx nghetinhensis: No. 2966, 400d, Head, vine (4-1). No. 2967, 400d, In grass (4-2). 5000d, Near pond (4-3). 10,000d, Head, mountains (4-4).

2000, May 18 With Gum *Perf. 13½*
2966-2969 A769 Set of 4 7.00 2.50
2969a Sheet, 2 each #2966-2969 15.00 5.00

Ho Chi Minh (1890-1969) — A770

2000, May 19 With Gum *Perf. 13*
2970 A770 400d multi .90 .30

World Stamp Expo 2000, Anaheim — A771

Water puppets: No. 2971, 400d, Chu teu (6-1). No. 2972, 400d, Fairy (6-2). No. 2973, 400d, Man plowing field (6-3). 3000d, Female peasant (6-4). 9000d, Drummer (6-5). 11,000d, Fisherman (6-6).

2000, June 28 *Perf. 13½*
2971-2976 A771 Set of 6 8.00 3.50

50th Vietnam Youth Volunteers' Day — A772

2000, July 15 With Gum *Perf. 13*
2977 A772 400d multi .90 .30

Phu Dong Natl. Youth Sports Festival — A773

2000, July 20 With Gum
2978 A773 400d multi .90 .30

Fish — A774

Designs: No. 2979, 400d, Cephalopholis miniatus (6-1). No. 2980, 400d, Pomacanthus imperator (6-2). No. 2981, 400d, Epinephelus merra (6-3). 4000d, Zancius cornutus, vert. (6-4). 6000d, Chaetodon ephippium, vert. (6-5). 12,000d, Heniochus acuminatus, vert. (6-6).
15,000d, Chaetodon lunula.

2000, Aug. 7 *Perf. 13*
2979-2984 A774 Set of 6 8.00 3.00
Souvenir Sheet
Perf. 13½x13¾
2985 A774 15,000d multi 5.00 2.00

Post and Telegraph Dept., 55th Anniv. — A775

2000, Aug. 15 With Gum *Perf. 13*
2986 A775 400d multi .75 .30

People's Police, 50th Anniv. — A776

Designs: 400d, Ho Chi Minh, five policemen. 2000d, Policeman checking documents, vert.

2000, Aug. 19 Litho. *Perf. 13*
With Gum
2987-2988 A776 Set of 2 1.00 .55

Gen. Nguyen Tri Phuong, 200th Anniv. of Birth — A777

2000, Aug. 31 With Gum *Perf. 13½*
2989 A777 400d multi .90 .30

UN Right of the Child Conference, 10th Anniv. — A778

Emblem and: 400d, Boy and girl. 5000d, Five children, vert.

2000, Sept. 8 *Perf. 13*
2990-2991 A778 Set of 2 1.75 1.00

2000 Summer Olympics, Sydney A779

Designs: 400d, Running. 6000d, Shooting. 7000d, Taekwondo, vert.

2000, Sept. 15
2992-2994 A779 Set of 3 3.50 2.25

Gen. Tran Hung Dao, 700th Anniv. of Death. — A780

2000, Sept. 17 With Gum
2995 A780 400d multi .90 .30

Birds — A781

Designs: No. 2996, 400d, Leiothrix argentauris. No. 2997, 400d, Pitta ellioti. No. 2998, 400d, Pomatorinus ferruginosus. 5000d, Dicrurus paradiceus, vert. 7000d, Melanochlora sultanea, vert. 10,000d, Stachyris striolata, vert.

2000, Sept. 28 *Perf. 13½*
2996-3001 A781 Set of 6 8.00 4.00
Souvenir Sheet
Perf. 13½x13¾
3002 A781 15,000d Trena puella 6.00 2.50

No. 3002 contains one 42x31mm stamp. España 2000 Intl. Philatelic Exhibition (No. 3002).

Vietnam Philately Association, 40th Anniv. — A782

2000, Oct. 6 With Gum *Perf. 13*
3003 A782 400d No. 821 .90 .30

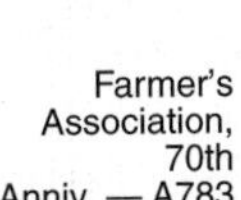

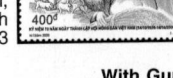

Farmer's Association, 70th Anniv. — A783

2000, Oct. 14 With Gum
3004 A783 400d multi .90 .30

Women's Union, 70th Anniv. — A784

2000, Oct. 14 With Gum
3005 A784 400d multi .90 .30

Hanoi, 990th Anniv. — A785

Designs: 400d, Building, and Ly Thai To, founder of Hanoi. 3000d, Temple, two people, monuments. 10,000d, Peasants with goods, building.
15,000d, People and doves.

2000, Oct. 15 **Perf. 13**
3006-3008 A785 Set of 3 3.50 2.25

Souvenir Sheet
Perf. 13½x13¾

3009 A785 15,000d multi 4.00 2.50

Bats — A786

Designs: No. 3010, 400d, Scotomanes ornatus. No. 3011, 400d, Pteropus lylei. 2000d, Rhinolophus paradoxolophus. 6000d, Eonycteris spelaea. 11,000d, Cynopterus sphinx.

2000, Oct. 14 **Perf. 13**
3010-3014 A786 Set of 5 6.00 3.00

Fatherland Front, 70th Anniv. — A787

2000, Oct. 18 **With Gum**
3015 A787 400d multi .90 .30

6th Natl. Emulation Congress A788

Designs: 400d, People at work. 3000d, Symbols of industry, vert.

2000, Nov. 10 **With Gum**
3016-3017 A788 Set of 2 1.25 .75

Flowers — A789

Designs: 400d, Oxyspora sp. 5000d, Melanstoma villosa, vert.

With Gum

2000, Nov. 15 **Perf. 13½**
3018-3019 A789 Set of 2 3.00 1.00

Hon Khoai Uprising, 60th Anniv. — A790

2000, Dec. 13 **With Gum** **Perf. 13**
3020 A790 400d multi .80 .30

Advent of New Millennium — A791

2001, Jan. 1 **With Gum**
3021 A791 400d multi 1.20 .30

New Year 2001 (Year of the Snake) — A792

Snake and: 400d, Pink flowers. 8000d, Yellow flowers.

2001, Jan. 1 **With Gum** **Perf. 13½**
3022-3023 A792 Set of 2 3.00 1.60

Hong Kong 2001 Stamp Exhibition A793

Fish: 400d, Toxotes microlepis. 800d, Cosmocheilus harmandi. 2000d, Anguilla bicolor pacifica. 3000d, Chitala ornata. 7000d, Megalops cyprinoides. 8000d, Probarbus jullieni.

2001, Jan. 18 **Litho.** **Perf. 13**
3024-3029 A793 Set of 6 6.00 3.00

Nobel Prize, Cent. — A794

2001, Jan. 27 **With Gum** **Perf. 13½**
3030 A794 400d multi .60 .30

Four Seasons A795

No. 3031: a, 400d, Peach blossoms and birds (spring). b, 800d, Cotton rose and pheasant (summer). c, 4000d, Chrysanthemum and phoenix (autumn). d, 10,000d, Pine tree and cranes (winter).

With Gum

2001, Feb. 1 **Perf. 13¼x13**
3031 A795 Sheet of 4, #a-d 6.00 2.50

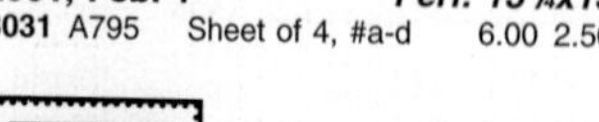

Wild Fruits — A796

Designs: No. 3032, 400d, Rubus cochinchinensis. No. 3033, 400d, Rhizophora mucronata. No. 3034, 400d, Podocarpus neriifolius. No. 3035, 400d, Magnolia pumila. 15,000d, Taxus chinensis.

2001, Feb. 8 **With Gum** **Perf. 13½**
3032-3036 A796 Set of 5 5.50 2.25

Landscapes A797

Designs: No. 3037, 400d, Co Tien Mountain (3-1). No. 3038, 400d, Dong Pagoda, Yen Tu Mountain (3-2). 10,000d, King Dinh Temple (3-3).

2001, Feb. 23 **Perf. 13**
3037-3039 A797 Set of 3 4.50 1.50

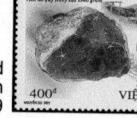

Nhan Dan Newspaper, 50th Anniv. — A798

2001, Mar. 11 **With Gum**
3040 A798 400d multi .80 .30

Rubies Found in Tan Huong — A799

Designs: 400d, 1960-gram ruby. 6000d, 2160-gram "Viet Nam Star."

2001, Mar. 20 **With Gum**
3041-3042 A799 Set of 2 4.00 1.00

Ho Chi Minh Youth Union, 70th Anniv. — A800

2001, Mar. 26 **Litho.** **Perf. 13**
With Gum
3043 A800 400d multi .70 .30

9th Communist Party Congress A801

Designs: 400d, Ho Chi Minh, flag, map (2-1). 3000d, Hammer and sickle, Ngoc Lu bronze drum head, symbols of technology, vert (2-2).

2001, Apr. 18 **With Gum**
3044-3045 A801 Set of 2 1.10 .55

Fauna in Cat Tien Natl. Park — A802

Designs: 400d, Arborophila davidi (4-1). 800d, Stichophthalma uemurai (4-2). 3000d, Rhinoceros sondaicus (4-3). 5000d, Crocodylus siamensis (4-4).

2001, Apr. 3 **Perf. 13½**
3046-3049 A802 Set of 4 5.50 2.00

Mushrooms A803

Designs: No. 3050, 400d, Phallus indusiatus (7-1). No. 3051, 400d, Aseroe arachnoidea (7-2). No. 3052, 400d, Phallus tenuis (7-3). 2000d, Phallus impudicus (7-4). 5000d, Phallus rugulosus (7-5). 6000d, Simblum periphragmoides (7-6). 7000d, Mutinus bambusinus (7-7).

2001, May 2
3050-3056 A803 Set of 7 8.00 3.50

Mushrooms Type of 2001

Design: 13,000d, Pseudocolus schellenbergiae.

2001, May 2 **Litho.** **Perf. 13½x13¾**
3057 A803 13,000d multi 7.00 2.50

No. 3057 contains one 42x31mm stamp.

Ho Chi Minh Young Pioneer's League, 60th Anniv. — A804

2001, May 15 **Litho.** **Perf. 13**
With Gum
3058 A804 400d multi .70 .30

Viet Minh Front, 60th Anniv. — A805

2001, May 19 **With Gum**
3059 A805 400d multi .70 .30

Campaign Against Smoking — A806

2001, May 30 **Perf. 13¼x13½**
With Gum
3060 A806 800d multi .90 .45

Children — A807

Designs: 400d, Two children, UNICEF emblem. 5000d, Five children, UN emblem.

2001, June 1 **Perf. 13½**
3061-3062 A807 Set of 2 2.10 1.00

Children's safety day (#3061); UN Special Session on Children, Washington, DC (#3062).

Diesel Locomotives A808

Designs: No. 3063, 400d, D18E (6-1). No. 3064, 400d, D4H (6-2). 800d, D11H (6-3). 2000d, D5H (6-4). 6000d, D9E (6-5). 7000d, D12E (6-6).

2001, June 5 **Perf. 13**
3063-3068 A808 Set of 6 6.50 3.00

Souvenir Sheet
Perf. 13½x13¾

3069 A808 13,000d D11H, diff. 4.25 2.25

No. 3069 contains one 43x32mm stamp.

Orchids — A809

Designs: No. 3070, 800d, Vanda sp. (6-1). No. 3071, 800d, Dendrobium lowianum (6-2). No. 3072, 800d, Phajus wallichii (6-3). No. 3073, 800d, Habenaria medioflexa (6-4). No. 3074, 800d, Arundina graminifolia, vert. (6-5). 12,000d, Calanthe clavata, vert. (6-6).

Perf. 13½x13¼, 13¼x13½

2001, July 5 With Gum

3070-3075 A809 Set of 6 6.00 2.75

Phila Nippon '01 — A810

Butterflies: No. 3076, 800d, Troides aeacus (6-1). No. 3077, 800d, Inachis io (6-2). No. 3078, 800d, Ancyluris formosissima (6-3). 5000d, Cymothoe sanguris (6-4). 7000d, Taenaris selene (6-5). 10,000d, Trogonoptera brookiana (6-6).

13,000d, Atrophaneura horishanus, vert.

2001, July 16 *Perf. 13½x13¼*

3076-3081 A810 Set of 6 8.00 3.50

Souvenir Sheet

Perf. 13¾x13½

3082 A810 13,000d multi 8.00 2.25

No. 3082 contains one 32x42mm stamp.

2002 World Cup Soccer Championships, Japan and Korea — A811

No. 3083: a, 800d, Player with red shirt. b, 3000d, Player with white shirt.

2001, July 24 With Gum *Perf. 13*

3083 A811 Horiz. pair, #a-b 3.50 1.50

Musical Instruments A812

Designs: No. 3084, 800d, Ho gáo (6-1). No. 3085, 800d, Kenh (6-2). No. 3086, 800d, Dàn tú, vert. (6-3). 2000d, Dàn t'rung, vert. (6-4). 6000d, Trong kinang, vert . (6-5). 9000d, Tính tau, vert. (6-6).

Perf. 13x13¼, 13¼x13

2001, Aug. 4 Litho.

3084-3089 A812 Set of 6 6.00 3.00

Year of Dialogue Among Civilizations — A813

2001, Oct. 9 Litho. *Perf. 13¼x13½*

With Gum

3090 A813 800d multi 1.25 .40

Tran Huy Lieu (1901-69), Writer — A814

2001, Nov. 5 *Perf. 13x12¾*

With Gum

3091 A814 800d multi .90 .40

Nam Cao (1917-51), Writer — A815

2001, Nov. 30 *Perf. 13x13¼*

With Gum

3092 A815 800d multi .90 .45

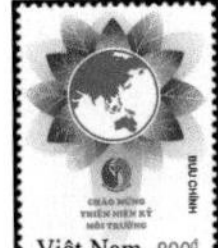

A816

A817

2001 With Gum *Perf. 13½*

3093 A816 800d multi .40 .25

3094 A817 3000d multi 1.25 .45

New Year 2002 (Year of the Horse) — A818

Horse facing: 800d, Right. 8000d, Left. 14,000d, Horse galloping.

2002, Jan. 2 With Gum *Perf. 13½*

3095-3096 A818 Set of 2 3.25 1.10

Souvenir Sheet

Perf. 13½x13¼

3097 A818 14,000d multi 4.25 2.50

No. 3097 contains one 42x31mm stamp.

Opera Costumes — A819

Designs: No. 3098, 1000d, Giáp Tuong Nam (6-1). No. 3099, 1000d, Giáp Tuong Nu (6-2). 2000d, Giáp Tuong Phan Dien (6-3). 3000d, Long Chan (6-4). 5000d, Giáp Tuong Phien (6-5). 9000d, Lung Xiem Quan Giáp (6-6).

2002, Jan. 15 *Perf. 13*

3098-3103 A819 Set of 6 6.50 3.25

Vo Thi Sáu, Heroine, 50th Anniv. of Death — A820

2002, Jan. 23 *Perf. 13x13¼*

3104 A820 1000d multi .90 .40

Program Implementation of 9th Communist Party Congress — A821

Designs: 800d, Map, satellite, buildings, dam, power lines, bridge, computer keyboard (2-1). 3000d, Flag, building, doves, people (2-2).

2002, Feb. 1 *Perf. 13¼x13*

With Gum

3105-3106 A821 Set of 2 1.40 .65

Cacti — A822

Designs: No. 3107, 1000d, Echinocereus albatus (5-1). No. 3108, 1000d, Echinocereus delaetii (5-2). No. 3109, 1000d, Cylindropuntia bigelowii (5-3). 5000d, Echinocereus triglochidatus (5-4). 10,000d, Epiphyllum truncatum (5-5).

2002, Feb. 18 *Perf. 13¼x13½*

3107-3111 A822 Set of 5 6.00 2.50

Victor Hugo (1802-85), French Writer — A823

2002, Feb. 26 *Perf. 13x13¼*

With Gum

3112 A823 1000d multi .90 .45

A824

2002, Feb. 21 Litho. *Perf. 13x13¼*

With Gum

3113 A824 800d multi .90 .45

Birds A825

Designs: 600d, Actinodura sodangorum (6-1). No. 3115, 800d, Garrulax ngoclinhensis (6-2). No. 3116, 800d, Garrulax pectoralis (6-3). No. 3117, 800d, Pomatorhinus hypoleucos (6-4). 5000d, Minla ignotincta (6-5). 8000d, Minla cyanouroptera (6-6).

2002, Mar. 15 Litho. *Perf. 13½*

With Gum

3114-3119 A825 Set of 6 7.00 2.75

Landscapes A826

Designs: No. 3120, 800d, Ganh Son, Binh Thuan (3-1). No. 3121, 800d, Dawn over Tung Estuary, Quang Tri (3-2). 10,000d, Sa Huynh Harbor, Quang Ngai (3-3).

2002, Mar. 15 With Gum

3120-3122 A826 Set of 3 4.50 2.00

Primates — A827

Designs: 600d, Trachypithecus poliocephalus (8-1). 800d, Trachypithecus delacouri (8-2). 1000d, Rhinopithecus avunculus (8-3). 2000d, Pygathrix cinerea (8-4). 4000d, Nomascus concolor (8-5). 5000d, Trachypithecus laotum hatinhensis (8-6). 7000d, Trachypithecus phayrei (8-7). 9000d, Pygathrix nemaeus (8-8).

2002, Apr. 10

3123-3130 A827 Set of 8 8.50 4.50

3130a Souvenir sheet, #3123-3130 + label 8.50 4.50

Bui Thi Xuan, 200th Anniv. of Death — A828

2002, Apr. 13 With Gum *Perf. 13*

3131 A828 1000d multi .90 .45

Souvenir Sheet

2002 World Cup Soccer Championships, Japan and Korea — A829

Color of player or players: a, 1000d, Blue. b, 2000d, Red. c, 5000d, Red violet. d, 7000d, Green.

2002, June 1 With Gum Litho.

3132 A829 Sheet of 4, #a-d 4.00 2.75

Flowers — A830

Designs: 600d, Paphiopedilum concolor (7-1). 800d, Sterculia lanceolata (7-2). 1000d, Schefflera alongensis (7-3). 2000d, Hibiscus tiliaceus (7-4). 3000d, Mussaenda glabra (7-5). 5000d, Boniodendron parviflorum (7-6). 9000d, Bauhinia ornata.

2002, June 5

3133-3139 A830 Set of 7 7.00 3.25

Chau Van Liem, Communist Party Leader, Cent. of Birth — A831

2002, June 28 Litho. *Perf. 13*

With Gum

3140 A831 800d multi .90 .45

Stamp Day A832

2002, July 1 *Perf. 13x12¾*

With Gum

3141 A832 800d multi + label .90 .45

Tay Nguyen Province A833

2002, July 10 Litho. *Perf. 13*

With Gum

3142 A833 800d multi .90 .40

Soft-shell Turtles — A834

Designs: 800d, Pelochelys bibroni (4-1). 2000d, Pelodiscus sinensis. 5000d, Palea steindachneri. 9000d, Trionyx cartilagineus.

2002, July 15 Litho. *Perf. 13½*

3143-3146 A834 Set of 4 6.50 2.60

3146a Souvenir sheet, 2 each #3143-3146 13.00 5.25

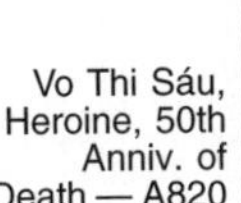

Viet Nam — Laos Diplomatic Relations, 40th Anniv. — A835

2002, July 18 With Gum *Perf. 13*
3147 A835 800d multi .75 .45

Civil Aircraft — A836

Designs: 800d, Super King Air B200 in air (4-1). 2000d, Fokker 70 (4-2). 3000d, ATR-72 (4-3). 8000d, Boeing 767-300 (4-4).
14,000d, Super King Air B200 on ground.

2002, Aug. 1 With Gum *Perf. 13*
3148-3151 A836 Set of 4 6.00 2.25

Souvenir Sheet
Perf. 13½x13¾

3152 A836 14,000d multi 5.00 2.25

Autumn Festival Lanterns — A837

Designs: No. 3153, 800d, Den Ong Sao (4-1). No. 3154, 800d, Den Ong Su (4-2). 2000d, Den Con Tho Om Trang (4-3). 7000d, Den Xep (4-4).

2002, Aug. 16 With Gum *Perf. 13½*
3153-3156 A837 Set of 4 4.00 1.50

Viet Nam Posts and Telecommunications Trade Union, 55th Anniv. — A838

2002, Aug. 23 With Gum *Perf. 13*
3157 A838 800d multi .90 .40

Bridges A839

Designs: No. 3158, 800d, Cau Long Bien (4-1). No. 3159, 800d, Cau Song Han (4-2). 2000d, Cau Truong Tien (4-3). 10,000d, Cau My Thuan (4-4).

2002, Sept. 27 *Perf. 13x13¼*
With Gum
3158-3161 A839 Set of 4 4.50 2.00

Communist Party's Ideology and Culture Commission, 72nd Anniv. — A840

2002, Oct. 10 With Gum *Perf. 13*
3162 A840 800d multi .90 .40

Hanoi Medical University, Cent. — A841

2002, Nov. 15 With Gum
3163 A841 800d multi .90 .40

Teachers' Day — A842

2002, Nov. 20 With Gum
3164 A842 800d multi .90 .40

New Year 2003 (Year of the Ram) — A843

Various goats with background colors of: 800d, Rose pink (2-1). 8000d, Orange (2-2).

2002, Dec. 15 *Perf. 13½*
With Gum
3165-3166 A843 Set of 2 2.50 1.25

Viet Nam — South Korea Diplomatic Relations, 10th Anniv. — A844

Pagoda from: No. 3167, 800d, Viet Nam (2-1). No. 3168, 800d, South Korea (2-2).

2002, Dec. 21 With Gum *Perf. 13*
3167-3168 A844 Set of 2 1.25 .65

Starting with the 2003 issues, stamps are gummed unless otherwise indicated.

Landscapes A845

Designs: 800d, Rung Cao Su, Bình Phuoc (3-1). 3000d, Ao Bà Om, Trà Vinh (3-2). 7000d, Mot nhahn song Rach Gam-Xoài Mút, Tien Giang (3-3).

2003, Feb. 1 Litho. *Perf. 13*
3169-3171 A845 Set of 3 3.00 1.40

Viet Nam Culture Program, 60th Anniv. — A846

2003, Feb. 3
3172 A846 800d multi .90 .30

Viet Nam Cinema Association, 50th Anniv. — A847

2003, Mar. 1
3173 A847 1000d multi .90 .40

Khanh Hoa Province, 350th Anniv. — A848

2003, Mar. 25
3174 A848 800d multi .90 .30

Cycle Rickshaws — A849

Cycle rickshaws from: 800d, Hanoi. 3000d, Ho Chi Minh City. 8000d, Haiphong.

2003, Apr. 1
3175-3177 A849 Set of 3 3.00 1.60

Adventures of the Cricket — A850

2003, May 1 *Perf. 13¼x13½*

3178	Horiz. strip of 6	5.50	2.60
a.	A850 800d Toi là út...	.30	.25
b.	A850 1000d Chang bao...	.35	.25
c.	A850 2000d Toi an han...	.45	.25
d.	A850 3000d Toi và Trui...	.65	.40
e.	A850 5000d Mot ngày...	1.10	.70
f.	A850 8000d Tu nay the...	1.75	1.10

Animals in Ba Vi National Park — A851

Designs: No. 3179, 800d, Manis pentadactyla (4-1). No. 3180, 800d, Petaurista petaurista (4-2). 5000d, Selenarctos thibetanus (4-3). 10,000d, Capricornis sumatraensis (4-4).

2003, June 5 *Perf. 13½*
3179-3182 A851 Set of 4 5.50 2.25

22nd South East Asian Games, Viet Nam — A852

Designs: 800d, Soccer (4-1). 2000d, Hurdles (4-2). 3000d, Kayaking (4-3). 7000d, Wrestling (4-4).
10,000d, Games emblem, mascot, stadium.

2003, July 1 *Perf. 13*
3183-3186 A852 Set of 4 5.00 1.75

Souvenir Sheet
Perf. 13½x13¾

3187 A852 10,000d multi 5.50 1.50

Ninth Congress of Viet Nam Federation of Trade Unions — A853

2003, July 28 *Perf. 13*
3188 A853 800d multi .90 .25

Camellias A854

Designs: 800d, Camellia petelotii (4-1). 1000d, Camellia rubriflora (4-2). 5000d, Camellia vietnamensis (4-3). 6000d, Camellia gilberti (4-4).

2003, Sept. 1 *Perf. 13½*
3189-3192 A854 Set of 4 4.00 1.75

Bangkok 2003 World Philatelic Exhibition.

Orchids — A855

Designs: 800d, Paphiopedilum dianthum (2-1). 8000d, Pleione bulbocodioides (2-2).

2003, Oct. 1 *Perf. 13*
3193-3194 A855 Set of 2 4.25 1.10

Asian Elephants — A856

Designs: 800d, Elephant with trunk extended (4-1). 1000d, Elephants and riders (4-2). 2000d, Elephant with trunk down (4-3). 8000d, Two elephants (4-4)

2003, Oct. 1 *Perf. 13½*
3195-3198 A856 Set of 4 5.00 1.50
3198a Miniature sheet, 2 each #3195-3198 10.00 3.00

My Son World Heritage Site A857

Various ruins: 800d, (3-1). 3000d, (3-2). 8000d (3-3).
10,000d, Temple (43x32mm).

2003, Dec. 1 *Perf. 13x13¼*
3199-3201 A857 Set of 3 6.00 2.00

Souvenir Sheet
Perf. 13½x13¾

3202 A857 10,000d multi 4.50 2.00

New Year 2004 (Year of the Monkey) — A858

Monkeys and: 800d, Apple tree (2-1). 8000d, Palm leaf (2-2).

2003, Dec. 1 *Perf. 13½*
3203-3204 A858 Set of 2 3.00 1.10

Ngo Gia Tu (1908-35), Leader of 1926 Strike — A859

2003, Dec. 30 *Perf. 13¼x13*
3205 A859 800d multi .85 .25

Congratulations — A860

Designs: 800d, Flowers (2-1). 8000d, Bird with envelope (2-2).

2004, Jan. 1 ***Perf. 13 Syncopated***
3206-3207 A860 Set of 2 3.50 1.10

Shells — A861

Designs: 800d, Murex trocheli (3-1). 3000d, Murex haustellum (3-2). 8000d, Chicoreus ramosus (3-3).

2004, Feb. 1 ***Perf. 13***
3208-3210 A861 Set of 3 5.00 1.50

Bamboo Lamps — A862

Various lamps with background colors of: 400d, Yellow (3-1). 1000d, Pale green (3-2). 7000d, Buff (3-3).

Perf. 13 Syncopated
2004, Mar. 1 **Litho.**
3211-3213 A862 Set of 3 3.50 1.10

See Nos. 3352-3363.

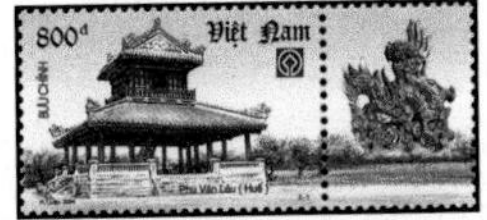
Hué, UNESCO World Heritage Site — A863

Designs: 800d, Pavilion of Edicts (3-1). 4000d, Ngo Mon Gate (3-2). No. 3216, 8000d, Hien Lam Pavilion (3-3).
No. 3217, 8000d, Thai Hoa Palace.

2004, Apr. 1 ***Perf. 13***
Stamp + Label
3214-3216 A863 Set of 3 3.00 1.75
Souvenir Sheet
Perf. 13½x13¾
3217 A863 8000d multi 4.00 1.00

No. 3217 contains one 42x31mm stamp.

Tran Phu (1904-31), Communist Leader — A864

2004, May 1 ***Perf. 13***
3218 A864 800d multi .85 .25

Battle of Dien Bien Phu, 50th Anniv. — A865

Designs: 800d, Soldier, flowers (2-1). 5000d, Dancer, flowers.
8000d, Three dancers, flowers.

2004, May 4 ***Perf. 13***
3219-3220 A865 Set of 2 2.10 .75
Souvenir Sheet
Perf. 13½x13¾
3221 A865 8000d multi 3.50 1.00

FIFA (Fédération Internationale de Football Association), Cent. — A866

2004, May 21 ***Perf. 13***
3222 A866 800d multi 1.50 .25

Thieu Nien Newspaper, 50th Anniv. — A867

2004, June 1
3223 A867 800d multi .85 .25

Bonsai — A868

Designs: 800d, Ficus microcarpa (4-1). 2000d, Premna serratifolia (4-2). 3000d, Ficus pilosa (4-3). 8000d, Ficus religiosa (4-4).

2004, July 1
3224-3227 A868 Set of 4 6.00 1.75

2004 World Stamp Championship, Singapore.

2004 Summer Olympics, Athens — A869

Designs: 800d, Hurdles (4-1). 1000d, Swimming, horiz. (4-2). 6000d, Shooting, horiz. (4-3). 7000d, Taekwondo (4-4).

2004, Aug. 1
3228-3231 A869 Set of 4 5.00 1.90

Naming of Country as Viet Nam, Bicent. — A870

Designs: 800d, Citadel, Hué, lotus flower (2-1). 5000d, Ho Chi Minh, flag (2-2).

2004, Sept. 2
3232-3233 A870 Set of 2 1.90 .75

World Summit on the Information Society, Geneva — A871

2004, Oct. 9
3234 A871 1000d multi .85 .25

Liberation of Hanoi From French, 50th Anniv. — A872

2004, Oct. 10
3235 A872 800d multi .85 .25

Dak Lak Province, Cent. — A873

2004, Nov. 22
3236 A873 800d multi 1.25 .25

Hoi An, UNESCO World Heritage Site — A874

Designs: 800d, Chua Cau. 8000d, Hoi Quán Phúc Kien.

Perf. 13¼x13¾ Syncopated
2004, Dec. 1
3237 A874 800d multi 1.50 .25
Souvenir Sheet
Perf. 13½x13¾
3238 A874 8000d multi 3.50 1.50

No. 3238 contains one 42x31mm stamp.

New Year 2005 (Year of the Rooster) A875

Designs: 800d, Rooster (2-1). 8000d, Hen and chicks.

2004, Dec. 15 ***Perf. 13***
3239-3240 A875 Set of 2 2.75 1.10
3240a Souvenir sheet, #3239-3240 3.00 1.50

Viet Nam Communist Party, 75th Anniv. — A876

2005, Feb. 3
3241 A876 800d multi .85 .25

Gia Lai Province — A877

Perf. 13¼x13¾ Syncopated
2005, Mar. 16 **Litho.**
3242 A877 800d multi .85 .25

Nha Trang Bay A878

Designs: 800d, Boat near shore (2-1). 8000d, Road near shore (2-2).

2005, Apr. 2 ***Perf. 13x12¾***
Stamp + Label
3243-3244 A878 Set of 2 2.25 1.40

Worldwide Fund for Nature (WWF) — A879

Various views of Chrotogale owstoni: 800d, (4-1). 3000d, (4-2). 5000d, (4-3). 8000d, (4-4).

2005, May 2 ***Perf. 13½***
3245-3248 A879 Set of 4 5.00 3.25
Imperf., #3245-3248 12.00
3248a Souvenir sheet, #3245-3248, perf. 13x13½ 5.00 3.50

Liberation of Haiphong, 50th Anniv. — A880

Designs: 800d, Burning airplanes at Cat Bi Airport, Haiphong harbor (2-1). 5000d, Nam Trieu Port (2-2).

2005, May 6 ***Perf. 13x12¾***
Stamp + Label
3249-3250 A880 Set of 2 2.75 .75

People's Police, 60th Anniv. — A881

Medals and: 800d, Marching police, statue of Ho Chi Minh (2-1). 10,000d, Police helping civilians (2-2).

2005, Aug. 10 ***Perf. 13***
3251-3252 A881 Set of 2 2.10 1.40

Posts and Telecommunications Dept., 60th Anniv. — A882

2005, Aug. 15 ***Perf. 13***
Background Color
3253 A882 800d beige .90 .25
Souvenir Sheet
Perf. 13½x13¾
3254 A882 8000d gray 2.00 1.25

August Revolution, 60th Anniv. — A883

Crowd with flags in: 1000d, Hanoi (3-1). 2000d, Hué (3-2). 4000d, Saigon (3-3).

2005, Aug. 19 ***Perf. 13***
3255-3257 A883 Set of 3 2.25 .90
3257a Souvenir sheet, #3255-3257 2.25 .90

Traditional Dress and Houses of Ethnic Groups — A884

No. 3258: a, Ba-na (54-1). b, Bo Y (54-2). c, Brau (54-3). d, Bru-Van Kieu (54-4). e, Cham (54-5). f, Cho-ro (54-6). g, Chu-ru (54-7). h, Chut (54-8). i, Co (54-9). j, Cong (54-10). k, Co-ho (54-11). l, Co Lao (54-12). m, Co-tu (54-13). n, Dao (54-14). o, E-de (54-15). p, Gia-rai (54-16). q, Giay (54-17). r, Gie-Trieng (54-18). s, Ha Nhi (54-19). t, Hoa (54-20). u, Hre (54-21). v, Khang (54-22). w, Khmer (54-23). x, Kho-mu (54-24). y, Kinh (54-25). z, La Chi (54-26). aa, La Ha (54-27). ab, La Hu (54-28). ac, Lao (54-29). ad, Lo Lo (54-30). ae, Lu

(54-31). af, Ma (54-32). ag, Mang (54-33). ah, Mnong (54-34). ai, Mong (54-35). aj, Muong (54-36). ak, Ngai (54-37). al, Nung (54-38). am, O Du (54-39). an, Pa Then (54-40). ao, Phu La (54-41). ap, Pu Peo (54-42). aq, Ra-glai (54-43). ar, Ro-mam (54-44). as, San Chay (54-45). at, San Diu (54-46). au, Si La (54-47). av, Ta-oi (54-48). aw, Tay (54-49). ax, Thai (54-50). ay, Tho (54-51). az, Xinh-mun (54-52). ba, Xo-dang (54-53). bb, Xtieng (54-54).

Perf. 13¾x13¼ Syncopated

2005, Aug. 30

3258 Sheet of 54 + 2 labels 25.00 25.00
a.-bb. A884 800d Any single .25 .25
Complete booklet, #3258a-3258bb 25.00

Thang Long (Hanoi), 1000th Anniv. — A885

People reenacting battles and: 800d, Statue of Gen. Quang Trung, building (3-1). 5000d, Statue of Independence Fighters, building (3-2). No. 3261, 8000d, Statue of Victory Against B-52's, Long Bien Bridge (3-3).

No. 3262, Government officials on dais in Ba Dinh Square.

2005, Oct. 10 Litho. *Perf. 13*
3259-3261 A885 Set of 3 3.00 1.75

Souvenir Sheet

Perf. 13½x13¾

3262 A885 8000d multi 2.50 1.50

New Year 2006 (Year of the Dog) — A886

Designs: 800d, Dog and puppies (2-1). 8000d, Dog (2-2).

2005, Dec. 1 *Perf. 13*
3263-3264 A886 Set of 2 2.50 1.10
3264a Souvenir sheet, #3263-3264 3.00 1.25

National Coat of Arms, 50th Anniv. — A887

2006, Jan. 16 *Perf. 13*
3265 A887 1000d multi .85 .25

10th Vietnamese Communist Party Congress — A888

2006, Feb. 3
3266 A888 800d multi .85 .25

Prime Minister Pham Van Dong (1906-2000) A889

2006, Mar. 1
3267 A889 800d multi .85 .25

Wolfgang Amadeus Mozart (1756-91), Composer A890

2006, Mar. 1
3268 A890 2000d multi 1.50 .35

Léopold Senghor (1906-2001), First President of Senegal — A891

2006, Mar. 20 Litho. *Perf. 13*
3269 A891 800d multi *.85* .25

BirdLife International — A892

Designs: 800d, Lophura edwardsi (5-1). 2000d, Arborophila davidi (5-2). 3000d, Lophura hatinhensis (5-3). 5000d, Polyplectron germaini (5-4, 49x23mm). 8000d, Rheinardia ocellata (5-5, 49x23mm).

Perf. 13¼x14 Syncopated, 13¼x13½ Syncopated (#3273-3274)

2006, Apr. 1
3270-3274 A892 Set of 5 8.00 4.50
3274a Souvenir sheet, #3270-3274 8.00 4.50

2006 World Cup Soccer Championships, Germany — A893

Designs: 800d, One player (1-2). 10,000d, Two players (2-2).

2006, May 1 Litho. *Perf. 13¼x13*
3275-3276 A893 Set of 2 3.50 2.50

Phong Nha - Ke Bang National Park World Heritage Site A894

Designs: 800d, Bi Ky Cave (3-1). 4000d, Xuyen Son Cave (3-2). 8000d, Nuoc Moc Stream (3-3).

12,000d, Tien Cave, vert.

2006, June 1 *Perf. 13x12¾*
3277-3279 A894 Set of 3 7.50 2.50

Souvenir Sheet

Perf. 13¾x13½

3280 A894 12,000d multi 5.00 2.50

No. 3280 contains one 32x43mm stamp.

Animals in Ben En Botanical Gardens — A895

Designs: 800d, Nycticebus bengalensis (4-1). 1000d, Neofelis nebulosa, horiz. (4-2). 7000d, Cuon alpinus, horiz. (4-3). 10,000d, Nomascus leucogenys (4-4).

12,000d, Physignathus cocincinus, horiz.

2006, July 1 *Perf. 13¼x13, 13x13¼*
3281-3284 A895 Set of 4 6.00 3.50

Souvenir Sheet

Perf. 13½x13¾

3285 A895 12,000d multi 5.00 2.50

Flowers — A896

Designs: 800d, Momordica cochinchinensis (4-1). 3000d, Telosma cordata (4-2). 5000d, Momordica charantia (4-3). 8000d, Luffa cylindrica (4-4).

2006, Aug. 1 *Perf. 13*
3286-3289 A896 Set of 4 6.00 3.25

Asia-Pacific Economic Cooperation Summit — A897

2006, Sept. 16
3290 A897 8000d multi 2.25 2.00

Cooperation Between Viet Nam and European Union — A898

2006, Oct. 1 *Perf. 13x13¼*
3291 A898 800d multi *1.00* .25

New Year 2007 (Year of the Pig) — A899

Designs: 800d, Pig and piglets (2-1). 8000d, Pig (2-2).

2006, Dec. 15 *Perf. 13*
3292-3293 A899 Set of 2 3.50 2.00

Tran Te Xuong (1870-1907), Poet — A900

2007, Jan. 20 Litho. *Perf. 13x13¼*
3294 A900 1000d multi .70 .40

Implementation of Resolutions of 10th Communist Party Congress — A901

Perf. 13½x13¼ Syncopated

2007, Feb. 3
3295 A901 800d multi .70 .40

Truong Chinh (1907-88), General Secretary of Communist Party — A902

2007, Feb. 9 *Perf. 13x13¼*
3296 A902 800d multi .70 .40

Le Duan (1907-86), First Secretary of Communist Party — A903

2007, Apr. 7
3297 A903 800d multi .70 .40

Dugong Dugon A904

Various depictions of Dugong dugon: 800d, (4-1). 1000d, (4-2). 7000d, (4-3). 9000d, (4-4).

2007, Aug. 1 Litho. *Perf. 13*
3298-3301 A904 Set of 4 5.50 2.25

Association of South East Asian Nations (ASEAN), 40th Anniv. — A905

Designs: No. 3302, 800d, Secretariat Building, Bandar Seri Begawan, Brunei (10-1). No. 3303, 800d, National Museum of Cambodia (10-2). No. 3304, 800d, Fatahillah Museum, Jakarta, Indonesia (10-3). No. 3305, 800d, Typical house, Laos (10-4). No. 3306, 800d, Malayan Railway Headquarters Building, Kuala Lumpur, Malaysia (10-5). No. 3307, 800d, Yangon Post Office, Myanmar (Burma) (10-6). No. 3308, 800d, Malacañang Palace, Philippines (10-7). No. 3309, 800d, National Museum of Singapore (10-8). No. 3310, 800d, Vimanmek Mansion, Bangkok, Thailand (10-9). No. 3311, 800d, Presidential Palace, Hanoi, Viet Nam (10-10).

2007, Aug. 8 Litho. *Perf. 13x13¼*
3302-3311 A905 Set of 10 5.00 1.25
3311a Miniature sheet of 10, #3302-3311 5.50 1.25

See Brunei No. 607, Burma No. 370, Cambodia No. 2339, Indonesia Nos. 2120-2121, Laos Nos. 1717-1718, Malaysia No. 1170, Philippines Nos. 3103-3105, Singapore No. 1265, and Thailand No. 2315.

Tay Nguyen Tribal Gongs — A906

Various tribal members using gongs: 800d, (3-1). 5000d, (3-2). 8000d, (3-3).

12,000d, Man holding gong.

2007, Nov. 21 Litho. *Perf. 13x13¼*
3312-3314 A906 Set of 3 3.50 1.75

Souvenir Sheet

3314A A906 12,000d multi 3.50 1.50

New Year 2008 (Year of the Rat) — A907

Designs: 800d, Rat at left (2-1). 8000d, Rat at right (2-2).

2007, Dec. 1 *Perf. 13½*
3315-3316 A907 Set of 2 2.50 1.10

Ho Chi Minh (1890-1969) — A908

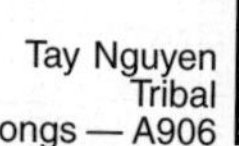

Perf. 13¼x13½

2007, Dec. 31 **Litho.**
3317 A908 1000d dk red & pink .35 .25
3318 A908 3000d dk & lt green .65 .30
3319 A908 4000d dk & lt blue 1.00 .50
Nos. 3317-3319 (3) 2.00 1.05

Vietnamese Cuisine — A909

Designs: 800d, Nem rán (2-1). 9000d, Pho bò (2-2).

2008, Feb. 1 *Perf. 13x13¼*
3320-3321 A909 Set of 2 1.75 1.25

Orchids — A910

Designs: 800d, Calanthe densiflora (4-1). 2000d, Ludisia discolor (4-2). 6000d, Spathoglottis affinis (4-3). 8000d, Calanthe argenteo-striata (4-4).

2008, Mar. 1 **Litho.** *Perf. 13½*
3322-3325 A910 Set of 4 3.50 2.10

2008 Summer Olympics, Beijing — A911

Designs: 800d, Wushu (4-1). 3000d, Swimming (4-2). 5000d, Taekwondo (4-3). 9000d, Canoeing (4-4).

Perf. 14x13½ Syncopated

2008, Mar. 15 **Litho.**
3326-3329 A911 Set of 4 3.50 2.25

Cyprinus Carpio A912

Various depictions of Cyprinus carpio: 800d, (3-1). 6000d, (3-2). 8000d, (3-3).

2008, Apr. 1 *Perf. 13*
3330-3332 A912 Set of 3 3.50 1.90

Vinasat-1 Satellite — A913

2008, Apr. 19 *Perf. 13½*
3333 A913 800d multi .85 .25

Vietnamese Court Music, UNESCO Masterpiece of Intangible Heritage — A914

Inscriptions: 800d, Dai nhac, Bien khanh (3-1). 4000d, Tieu nhac, Dàn Nguyet và Nhi (3-2). 8000d, Luc cúng hoa dang, Kèn Bóp và Sáo (3-3).
9000d, Dai nhac trong le te.

2008, June 3 **Litho.** *Perf. 13x12¾*
3334-3336 A914 Set of 3 3.25 1.60

Souvenir Sheet

Perf. 13x12¾ Syncopated

3337 A914 9000d multi 2.25 1.10

No. 3337 contains one 40x28mm stamp.

Tran Quy Cáp (1870-1908), Progressive Movement Leader — A915

2008, June 8 **Litho.** *Perf. 13*
3338 A915 1000d multi .60 .25

Binh Thuan Province — A916

2008, Sept. 1 *Perf. 13x12¾*
3339 A916 800d multi .60 .25

Seascapes of France and Viet Nam — A917

Designs: 800d, Strait of Bonifacio, France (2-1). 14,000d, Along Bay, Viet Nam (2-2).

2008, Oct. 15
3340-3341 A917 Set of 2 3.50 1.75

See France Nos. 3519-3520.

Lady Trieu's Rebellion, A.D. 248 — A918

Perf. 13¼x13½ Syncopated

2008, Oct. 20
3342 A918 1000d multi .60 .25

Flowers — A919

Designs: 800d, Ceiba chodatii (2-1). 10,000d, Nelumbo nucifera (2-2).

2008, Oct. 25 *Perf. 13*
3343-3344 A919 Set of 2 2.00 1.40

See Argentina Nos. 2508-2509.

Fruit — A920

Designs: 2000d, Durio zibetinus (2-1). 8000d, Hylocereus undatus (2-2).

2008, Nov. 18 **Litho.** *Perf. 13½*
3345-3346 A920 Set of 2 2.00 1.25

See Singapore Nos. 1352-1353.

New Year 2009 (Year of the Ox) — A921

Designs: 2000d, Ox (2-1). 9000d, Ox and calf (2-2).

2008, Dec. 1 **Litho.** *Perf. 13½*
3347-3348 A921 Set of 2 2.00 1.40
3348a Souvenir sheet, #3347-3348 2.50 1.40

Nguyen Khuyen (1835-1909), Poet — A922

2009, Feb. 2 **Litho.** *Perf. 13¼x13*
3349 A922 2000d multi .50 .50

Charles Darwin (1809-82), Naturalist — A923

2009, Feb. 12 *Perf. 13*
3350 A923 2000d multi .85 .50

Border and Coast Guard's Day — A924

2009, Mar. 3 *Perf. 13¼x13*
3351 A924 2000d multi .50 .50

Bamboo Lamps Type of 2004

Perf. 13 Syncopated

2009, May 15 **Litho.**

Background Color

Design of No. 3211

3352 A862 1200d yellow (12-1) .30 .25
3353 A862 2000d lt green (12-2) .35 .25
3354 A862 2500d blue (12-3) .50 .30
3355 A862 4500d gray blue (12-4) .80 .50

Design of No. 3212

3356 A862 5000d gray green (12-5) .85 .55
3357 A862 6500d brn vio (12-6) 1.25 .75
3358 A862 9500d violet (12-7) 1.75 1.10
3359 A862 10,500d red (12-8) 2.00 .75

Design of No. 3213

3360 A862 13,500d fawn (12-9) 2.75 1.00
3361 A862 14,500d brn yel (12-10) 2.90 1.40
3362 A862 17,500d drab (12-11) 3.25 1.75
3363 A862 18,500d olive grn (12-12) 3.50 1.90
Nos. 3352-3363 (12) 20.20 10.50

Opening of the Ho Chi Minh Trail, 50th Anniv. — A925

2009, May 19 *Perf. 13*
3364 A925 2000d multi .60 .30

Praying Mantises — A926

Designs: 1500d, Mantis religiosa (2-1). 12,500d, Tenodera aridifolia (2-2).

2009, July 1 **Litho.** *Perf. 13½*
3365-3366 A926 Set of 2 2.50 1.60

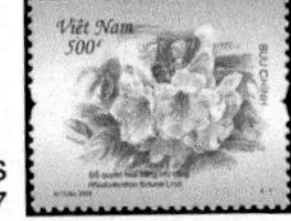

Rhododendrons A927

Designs: 500d, Rhododendron fortunei (4-1). 1200d, Rhododendron simsii (4-2). 4500d, Rhododendron sp. (4-3). 14,500d, Enkianthus quinqueflorus (4-4).

Perf. 13¼x13¾ Syncopated

2009, Aug. 1
3367-3370 A927 Set of 4 4.25 2.40

Fish — A928

Designs: 2000d, Botia macracanthus (4-1). 3000d, Trichopsis pumila (4-2). 6500d, Cynolebias elongatus (4-3). 10,500d, Centropyge flavissima (4-4).
14,500d Scleropages formosus.

2009, Sept. 1 *Perf. 13*
3371-3374 A928 Set of 4 4.50 2.75

Souvenir Sheet

Perf. 13½x13¾

3375 A928 14,500d multi 3.50 1.75

New Year 2010 (Year of the Tiger) — A929

Tiger: 2000d, Walking (2-1). 8500d, Sitting (2-2).

2009, Dec. 1 **Litho.** *Perf. 13x13¼*
3376-3377 A929 Set of 2 2.50 1.25

Viet Nam Communist Party, 80th Anniv. — A930

2010, Feb. 2 **Litho.** *Perf. 13¼x13*
3378 A930 2000d multi .60 .25

Frédéric Chopin (1810-49), Composer A931

2010, Feb. 22 **Litho.** *Perf. 13*
3379 A931 2000d multi .60 .25

Intl. Women's Day — A932

2010, Mar. 3 **Litho.** *Perf. 13x13¼*
3380 A932 3000d multi .70 .40

Pres. Ho Chi Minh (1890-1969) — A933

2010, May 16 Litho. *Perf. 13*
3381 A933 2000d multi .50 .30

BirdLife International A934

Birds: 2000d, Tringa guttifer. 6500d, Calidris pygmeus. 8500d, Larus saundersi.
14,500d, Rynchops albicollis.

2010, May 25 Litho. *Perf. 13x13¼*
3382-3384 A934 Set of 3 2.50 2.00

Souvenir Sheet

Perf. 13½x13¾

3385 A934 14,500d multi 2.50 1.60

Nguyen Huu Tho (1910-96), Acting President A935

2010, July 10 *Perf. 13x13¼*
3386 A935 2000d multi .50 .40

Ta Quang Buu (1910-86), Minister of Higher and Secondary Professional Education A936

2010, July 27
3387 A936 2000d multi .50 .40

Fairy Lilies — A937

Designs: 3500d, Zephyranthes carinata. 10,500d, Zephyranthes ajax.

Perf. 14x13½ Syncopated

2010, July 30
3388-3389 A937 Set of 2 2.50 2.50

Bangkok 2010 Intl. Philatelic Exhibition.

Worldwide Fund for Nature (WWF) — A938

Prionailurus viverrinus: 2000d, At water's edge, facing right. 2500d, In water with fish in mouth. 4500d, Standing on rocks, facing left. 10,500d, Sitting.

2010, Aug. 1 Litho. *Perf. 13*
3390-3393 A938 Set of 4 3.50 3.25
3393a Miniature sheet of 8, 2 each #3390-3393 7.00 7.00

Hanoi, 1000th Anniv. — A939

Dragon and: 2000d, Banner, Hanoi Flag Tower. 2500d, Quan Chuong City Gate, National Conference Center, apartment buildings. 4500d, Long Biên Bridge, Nhât Tân Bridge. 6500d, Hanoi Train Station, Noi Bài Airport.
14,000d, Highways, graduate, computer operators, vert.

2010, Oct. 2 *Perf. 13x13¼*
3394-3397 A939 Set of 4 2.75 2.75

Souvenir Sheet

Perf. 13¾x13½

3398 A939 14,000d multi 2.50 2.50

Viet Nam Stamp Association, 50th Anniv. — A940

2010, Oct. 3 *Perf. 13x13¼*
3399 A940 2000d multi .70 .40

Viet Nam Membership in Association of South East Asian Nations (ASEAN), 15th Anniv. — A941

2010, Oct. 27
3400 A941 8500d multi 1.50 1.50

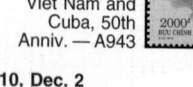

New Year 2011 (Year of the Cat) — A942

Cat: 2000d, Sitting. 10,500d, Lying down.

2010, Dec. 1 *Perf. 13½*
3401-3402 A942 Set of 2 2.25 2.25

Diplomatic Relations Between Viet Nam and Cuba, 50th Anniv. — A943

2010, Dec. 2
3403 A943 2000d multi .50 .40

11th Congress of Vietnamese Communist Party — A944

2011, Jan. 5 *Perf. 13¼x13*
3404 A944 2000d multi .50 .40

UNESCO Intangible Heritage Quan Ho Bac Ninh Folk Songs — A945

Singers: 3000d, Two men with umbrella, two women with hats. 4500d, Two men and two women seated, horiz. 10,500d, Two men with umbrella in boat, two women holding hats.
12,500d, Men and women in boat, horiz.

2011, Jan. 15 *Perf. 13¼x13, 13x13¼*
3405-3407 A945 Set of 3 1.90 1.90

Souvenir Sheet

Perf. 13½x13¾

3408 A945 12,500d multi 1.40 1.40

Ho Chi Minh Communist Youth Union, 80th Anniv. — A946

2011, Mar. 26 Litho. *Perf. 13*
3409 A946 2000d multi .90 .30

Phú Yên, 400th Anniv. A947

2011, Mar. 31 *Perf. 13x12¾*
3410 A947 2000d multi .70 .30

Fauna in Ba Be National Park — A948

Designs: 2000d, Muntiacus muntjac (4-1). 3500d, Gorsachius magnificus (4-2). 6000d, Acanthosaura lepidogaster (4-3). 8500d, Pyxidea mouhoti (4-4).
14,500d, Catopuma temminckii.

2011, May 15 *Perf. 13*
3411-3414 A948 Set of 4 2.50 2.50

Souvenir Sheet

Perf. 13½x13¾

3415 A948 14,500d multi 1.50 1.50

Ho Chi Minh 's Departure From Viet Nam, Cent. — A949

2011, June 5 *Perf. 13*
3416 A949 2000d multi .40 .30

Ernest Hemingway (1899-1961), Writer — A950

2011, July 2 *Perf. 13½*
3417 A950 10,500d multi 1.25 1.25

Dragonflies A951

Designs: 2000d, Lyriothemis mortoni (4-1). 2500d, Trithemis aurora (4-2). 6500d, Rhyothemis obsolescens (4-3). 10,500d, Ictinogomphus decoratus (4-4).

2011, July 11 *Perf. 13½*
3418-3421 A951 Set of 4 2.75 2.75

PhilaNippon '11 Intl. Philatelic Exhibition, Yokohama.

Tran Van Giau (1911-2010), Revolutionary Activist — A952

2011, Sept. 6 *Perf. 13*
3422 A952 2000d multi .40 .30

Decade for Road Safety — A953

Designs: 2000d, Traffic light, police officer teaching students traffic signs (2-1). 6500d, People crossing street in crosswalk (2-2).

2011, Oct. 1 Litho.
3423-3424 A953 Set of 2 1.50 1.25

Mikhail Lomonosov (1711-65), Scientist A954

2011, Nov. 19
3425 A954 8500d multi 1.25 1.25

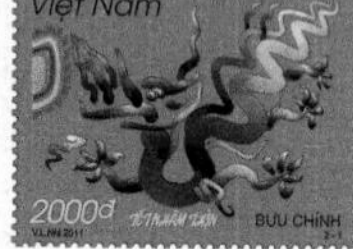

New Year 2012 (Year of the Dragon) A955

Dragon with background color of: 2000d, Bright pink (2-1). 10,500d, Olive green (2-2).

2011, Dec. 1 *Perf. 13x13¼*
3426-3427 A955 Set of 2 2.00 1.75

One-Pillar Pagoda, Hanoi A956

Keo Pagoda, Vu Thu A957

Bridge Pagoda, Hoi An — A958

Perf. 13¾x13½ Syncopated

2012, Jan. 16
3428 A956 2000d rose carmine .30 .25
3429 A956 3000d green .50 .35
3430 A957 3500d brn orange .60 .40
3431 A957 4500d red lilac .70 .60

Perf. 13½x13¾ Syncopated

3432 A958 6500d blue 1.10 .80
3433 A958 10,500d red 1.75 1.25
Nos. 3428-3433 (6) 3.00 3.00

Ao Dais — A959

Designs: 2500d, Woman in brown ao dai with hat (4-1). 3000d, Woman in orange ao dai, woman in red ao dai (4-2). 6000d, Woman in red ao dai holding hat, woman in blue ao dai (4-3). 10,500d, Woman in blue ao dai standing, woman in purple ao dai seated (4-4).

2012, Mar. 8 *Perf. 13*
3434-3437 A959 Set of 4 3.00 3.00

Campaign Against Tuberculosis A960

2012, Mar. 24
3438 A960 2000d multi .40 .30

Asian Pacific Postal Union, 50th Anniv. — A961

2012, Apr. 1
3439 A961 3000d multi .60 .40

Bears — A962

Designs: 2000d, Ursus thibetanus (4-1). 4500d, Ursus malayanus (4-2). 8500d, Ursus malayanus, diff. (4-3). 10,500d, Ursus thibetanus, diff. (4-4).
14,500d, Ursus thibetanus, diff.

2012, Apr. 1 ***Perf. 13x13¼***
3440-3443 A962 Set of 4 3.50 3.00

Souvenir Sheet
Perf. 13½x13¾
3444 A962 14,500d multi 2.00 1.75

Tiled Covered Bridges A963

Bridge in: 2000d, Huong Thuy (3-1). 3000d, Kim Son (3-2). 12,000d, Hai Hậu (3-3).

2012, Apr. 8 ***Perf. 13***
3445-3447 A963 Set of 3 2.75 2.00

Nguyen Huy Tuong (1912-60), Writer — A964

2012, May 6 ***Perf. 13x13¼***
3448 A964 2000d multi .40 .30

Ton That Tung (1912-82), Physician A965

2012, May 10
3449 A965 2000d multi .40 .30

Plumeria Flowers — A966

Designs: 2500d, Plumeria rubra (2-1). 8500d, Plumeria obtusa (2-2).

2012, May 15
3450-3451 A966 Set of 2 1.50 1.50

Pham Hung (1912-88), Politician A967

2012, June 11 ***Perf. 13***
3452 A967 2000d multi .40 .30

Nguyen Van Cu (1912-41), Communist Party General Secretary A968

2012, July 9
3453 A968 2000d multi .40 .30

2012 Summer Olympics, London — A969

Designs: 2000d, Weight lifting (4-1). 3500d, Fencing (4-2). 8500d, Gymnast on pommel horse (4-3). 12,000d, Taekwondo (4-4).

2012, July 12 ***Perf. 13½***
3454-3457 A969 Set of 4 3.00 3.00

Flags, Laotian Prime Minister Kaysone Phomivane and Vietnamese President Ho Chi Minh — A970

Buildings in Laos and Viet Nam — A971

2012, July 18 ***Perf. 13***
3458 A970 2000d multi .25 .25
3459 A971 12,000d multi 1.60 1.60

See Laos Nos. 1860-1861.

Monument to Heroic Mothers, Thach Phu — A972

2012, July 27 ***Perf. 13¼x13***
3460 A972 2000d multi .40 .30

Vo Chi Cong (1912-2011), Politician — A973

2012, Aug. 7 ***Perf. 13***
3461 A973 2000d multi .40 .30

Vu Trong Phung (1912-39), Writer — A974

2012, Oct. 20 ***Perf. 13¼x13***
3462 A974 2000d multi .40 .30

Nguyen Thi Minh Khai (1910-41), Communist Party Leader — A975

2012, Nov. 23 ***Perf. 13x13¼***
3463 A975 2000d multi .40 .30

New Year 2013 (Year of the Snake) — A976

Various snakes and flowers in: 2000d, Orange (2-1). 10,500d, Red violet (2-2).

2012, Dec. 1 ***Perf. 13½***
3464-3465 A976 Set of 2 2.00 1.25

Huynh Tan Phát (1913-89), Politician A977

2013, Feb. 15 **Litho.** ***Perf. 13***
3466 A977 2000d multi .40 .25

Vovinam (Vietnamese Martial Arts) — A978

Various combatants with frame color of: 2000d, Orange yellow (3-1). 6500d, Lilac (3-2). 8500d, Green (3-3).

2013, Mar. 1 **Litho.** ***Perf. 13***
3467-3469 A978 Set of 3 3.00 1.75

Orchids — A979

Designs: 2000d, Dendrobium aphyllum (3-1). 2500d, Dendrobium chrysotoxum (3-2). 17,500d, Dendrobium draconis (3-3).

2013, Apr. 1 **Litho.** ***Perf. 13***
3470-3472 A979 Set of 3 4.00 2.10

Lighthouses — A980

Designs: 2000d, Diêm Diên Lighthouse (4-1). 3000d, Quang Ngai Lighthouse (4-2). 6000d, Dai Lanh Lighthouse (4-3). 14,500d, Kê Gà Lighthouse (4-4).

2013, May 15 **Litho.** ***Perf. 13¼x13***
3473-3476 A980 Set of 4 4.00 2.50

Birds in Xuân Thuy National Park — A981

Designs: 2000d, Platalea minor (4-1). 3500d, Limnodromus semipalmatus (4-2). 6500d, Anas clypeata (4-3). 10,500d, Vanellus cinereus (4-4).
15,000d, Pelecanus philippensis.

2013, June 1 **Litho.** ***Perf. 13***
3477-3480 A981 Set of 4 4.00 2.25

Souvenir Sheet
3481 A981 15,000d multi *2.50* 1.50

Musical Instruments — A982

Designs: 2000d, Ta lu (3-1). 4500d, Kloong put, horiz. (3-2). 12,000d, Goong (3-3).

2013, July 15 **Litho.** ***Perf. 13***
3482-3484 A982 Set of 3 3.50 1.75

Birds — A983

Designs: 2000d, Gallus gallus (2-1). 10,500d, Polyplectron bicalcaratum (2-2).

2013, Sept. 12 **Litho.** ***Perf. 13x13¼***
3485-3486 A983 Set of 2 2.00 1.25

Diplomatic relations between Viet Nam and Singapore, 40th anniv. See Singapore Nos. 1626-1627.

Tran Dai Nghia (1913-97), Military Engineer A984

2013, Sept. 13 **Litho.** ***Perf. 13***
3487 A984 2000d multi .40 .25

Alexandre Yersin (1863-1943), Bacteriologist A985

Yersin as: 2000d, Young man (2-1). 18,500d, Older man (2-2).

2013, Sept. 22 **Litho.** ***Perf. 13***
3488-3489 A985 Set of 2 3.50 2.00

See France Nos. 4480-4481.

Rudolf Diesel (1858-1913), Inventor — A986

2013, Sept. 29 **Litho.** ***Perf. 13¼x13***
3490 A986 2000d multi .40 .25

Tran Huu Tuóc (1913-83), Physician A987

2013, Oct. 13 Litho. *Perf. 13x13¼*
3491 A987 2000d multi .40 .25

New Year 2014 (Year of the Horse) — A988

Horse with background color of: 2000d, Orange (2-1). 10,500d, Red violet (2-2).

2013, Dec. 1 Litho. *Perf. 13½*
3492-3493 A988 Set of 2 2.00 1.25

This stamp depicting Nguyen Chi Thanh, released Dec. 31, 2013, was a gift for standing order customers. It was not made available for sale. Value, $1.25.

Tree Frogs — A989

Designs: 3000d, Rhacophorus puerensis (5-1). 4500d, Rhacophorus annamensis (5-2). 6000d, Rhacophorus robertingeri (5-3). 8000d, Rhacophorus kio (5-4). 10,000d, Rhacophorus rhodopus (5-5).

2014, Apr. 1 Litho. *Perf. 13*
3494-3498 A989 Set of 5 4.50 3.00

Battle of Dien Bien Phu, 60th Anniv. — A990

2014, May 5 Litho. *Perf. 13*
3499 A990 3000d multi .60 .30

Ca Trù Singing, UNESCO Intangible Cultural Heritage — A991

Various musicians and singers: 3000d, (3-1). 8500d, (3-2). 10,500d (3-3).
16,000d, Ca trù musicians and singers, diff.

2014, June 1 Litho. *Perf. 13*
3500-3502 A991 Set of 3 4.00 1.60

Souvenir Sheet

Perf. 13½x13¾

3503 A991 16,000d multi 2.75 1.50

Ngo Mon (Gate of Noon), Hué — A992

Opera House, Ho Chi Minh City — A993

Main Post Office, Ho Chi Minh City — A994

Perf. 13½x13¾ Syncopated

2014, July 1 Litho.

3504	A992	3000d purple	.50	.30
3505	A992	6000d emerald	1.00	.55
3506	A993	6500d blue	1.00	.60
3507	A993	8000d brown	1.25	.75
3508	A994	10,000d red	1.75	.95
3509	A994	12,000d ol brn	2.00	1.10
		Nos. 3504-3509 (6)	7.50	4.25

Endangered Primates — A995

Designs: 3000d, Rhinopithecus avunculus (4-1). 5500d, Trachypithecus poliocephalus (4-2). 8500d, Pygathrix cinerea (4-3). 12,500d, Trachypithecus delacouri (4-4).
18,000d, Nomascus nasutus.

2014, Aug. 11 Litho. *Perf. 13*
3510-3513 A995 Set of 4 5.00 2.75

Souvenir Sheet

Perf. 13¾x13½

3514 A995 18,000d multi 3.00 1.75

25th Intl. Primatological Society Congress, Hanoi.

Truong Dinh (1820-64), Anti-Colonial Military Leader — A996

2014, Aug. 20 Litho. *Perf. 13*
3515 A996 3000d multi .60 .30

Lê Trong Tan (1914-86), General — A997

2014, Oct. 1 Litho. *Perf. 13*
3516 A997 3000d multi .60 .30

New Year 2015 (Year of the Goat) — A998

Goats and flowers with background color of: 3000d, Yellow (2-1). 10,500d, Pink (2-2).

2014, Dec. 1 Litho. *Perf. 13½*
3517-3518 A998 Set of 2 2.25 1.25

Trang An UNESCO World Heritage Site — A999

Designs: 3000d, Den vua Dinh Tiên Hoàng (Co dô Hoa Lu) (3-1). 7000d, Sông Ngô Dong (Tam Coc - Bích Dong) (3-2). 12,000d, Hang Toi (Tràng An) (3-3).
14,000d, Ceremony at temple.

2015, Jan. 23 Litho. *Perf. 13x13¼*
3519-3521 A999 Set of 3 3.00 2.10

Souvenir Sheet

Perf. 13½x13¾

3522 A999 14,000d multi 1.75 1.40

No. 3522 contains one 43x32mm stamp.

A1000

Worship of Hung Kings UNESCO Intangible Cultural Heritage — A1001

Designs: 3000d, Gate, procession (3-1). 7000d, Incense stick holder, worshipers (3-2). 8500d, Rice cakes, worshipers (3-3).
14,000d, Temple.

2015, Apr. 23 Litho. *Perf. 13*
3523-3525 A1000 Set of 3 2.25 1.75

Souvenir Sheet

Perf. 13½x13¾

3526 A1001 14,000d multi 1.60 1.40

General Hoang Van Thai (1915-86) A1002

2015, May 7 Litho. *Perf. 13*
3527 A1002 3000d multi .60 .30

Nguyen Van Linh (1915-98), Communist Party General Secretary A1003

2015, July 1 Litho. *Perf. 13*
3528 A1003 3000d multi .60 .30

Flags and Emblems of Association of South East Asian Nations — A1004

2015, Aug. 7 Litho. *Perf. 13½*
3529 A1004 3000d multi .60 .30
a. Miniature sheet of 10 6.00 6.00

See Brunei No. 656, Burma Nos. 417-418, Cambodia No. 2428, Indonesia No. 2428, Laos No. 1906, Malaysia No. 1562, Philippines No. 3619, Singapore No. 1742, Thailand No. 2875.

Viet Nam Posts and Telecommunications, 70th Anniv. — A1005

2015, Aug. 14 Litho. *Perf. 13*
3530 A1005 3000d multi .60 .30

Climate Change — A1006

Designs: No. 3531, 3000d, Leaf (4-1). No. 3532, 3000d, Wind generator, satellite dish, satellite, helicopter, ship (4-2). 4500d, Wind generator, buildings, foliage (4-3). 12,000d, Globe clock, hands (4-4).

2015, Oct. 14 Litho. *Perf. 13*
3531-3534 A1006 Set of 4 3.25 2.00

Beetles — A1007

Designs: No. 3535, 3000d, Odontolabis cuvera fallaciosa (4-1). No. 3536, 3000d, Cheirotonus battareli (4-2). 4500d, Dorcus titanus westermanni (4-3). 8000d, Jumnos ruckeri tonkinensis (4-4).

2015, Oct. 20 Litho. *Perf. 13½*
3535-3538 A1007 Set of 4 3.00 1.75
3538a Souvenir sheet of 4, #3535-3538 3.00 1.75

New Year 2016 (Year of the Monkey) — A1008

Flowers and: 3000d, Monkey (2-1). 10,500d, Adult and juvenile monkeys (2-2).

2015, Dec. 1 Litho. *Perf. 13½*
3539-3540 A1008 Set of 2 2.25 1.25

A1009

Nguyen Du (1765-1820), Poet — A1010

2015, Dec. 5 Litho. *Perf. 13*
3541 A1009 3000d multi .60 .30

Souvenir Sheet

Perf. 13¾x13½

3542 A1010 15,000d multi 2.50 1.40

Civil Aviation Department, 60th Anniv. A1011

2016, Jan. 10 Litho. *Perf. 13*
3543 A1011 3000d multi .50 .30
Complete booklet, 10 #3543 5.00

12th Congress of Viet Nam Communist Party — A1012

2016, Jan. 18 Litho. *Perf. 13*
3544 A1012 3000d multi .50 .30

Xuan Dieu (1916-85), Poet — A1013

2016, Feb. 2 Litho. *Perf. 13*
3545 A1013 3000d multi .50 .30

Barringtonia Asiatica A1014

Designs: 3000d, Flowers (2-1). 6000d, Plant near coast (2-2).

2016, Apr. 2 Litho. *Perf. 13*
3546-3547 A1014 Set of 2 1.50 .80
3547a Souvenir sheet of 4, 2 each #3546-3547 3.00 1.60

William Shakespeare (1564-1616), Writer — A1015

2016, Apr. 23 Litho. *Perf. 13½*
3548 A1015 3000d multi .50 .30
Complete booklet, 10 #3548 5.00

Relations Between Portugal and Viet Nam, 500th Anniv. — A1016

Flags of Portugal and Viet Nam and: 3000d, Vietnamese ceramic vessel, view of Hoi An (2-1). 12,000d, Portuguese ceramic plate, view of Lisbon (2-2).

2016, July 1 Litho. *Perf. 13*
3549-3550 A1016 Set of 2 2.50 1.40

See Portugal Nos. 3803-3804.

Diplomatic Relations Between Thailand and Viet Nam, 40th Anniv. — A1017

Designs: 3000d, Vietnamese figurines in boat (2-1). 10,500d, Thai figurines in boat (2-2).

2016, Aug. 6 Litho. *Perf. 13*
3551 A1017 3000d multi .50 .30
3552 A1017 10,500d multi 1.50 .95
a. Souvenir sheet of 4, 2 each #3551-3552 5.00 2.50
Complete booklet, 4 #3551, 4 #3552 8.00

See Thailand No. 2927.

Worldwide Fund for Nature (WWF) A1018

Aonyx cinerea: No. 3553, 3000d, Two otters in water (4-1). No. 3554, 3000d, Otter eating fish (4-2). 4500d, Two otters on shore (4-3). 8500d, Two otters on rocks. (4-4).

2016, Sept. 1 Litho. *Perf. 13*
3553-3556 A1018 Set of 4 1.75 1.75
3556a Souvenir sheet of 8, 2 each #3553-3556 3.50 3.50
Complete booklet, 2 each #3553-3556 3.50

Fifth Asian Beach Games, Da Nang — A1019

Designs: 3000d, Beach volleyball (2-1). 8500d, Rowing (2-2).

2016, Sept. 24 Litho. *Perf. 13*
Stamp + Label
3557-3558 A1019 Set of 2 .85 .85
3558a Miniature sheet of 8, 4 each #3557-3558, + 8 labels 3.50 3.50
Complete booklet, #3558a 3.50

Dò'n Ca Tài Tu Musicians (UNESCO Intangible Cultural Heritage List) — A1020

Various musicians: 3000d, On rug by tree (3-1). 4500d, On boats (3-2). 8000d, On rug in front of building (3-3).
12,000d, Two singers.

2016, Oct. 10 Litho. *Perf. 13x12¾*
3559-3561 A1020 Set of 3 1.40 1.40

Souvenir Sheet
Perf. 13½x13¾
3562 A1020 12,000d multi 1.10 1.10

No. 3562 contains one 43x32mm stamp.

Jack London (1876-1916), Writer — A1021

2016, Nov. 22 Litho. *Perf. 13x13¼*
3563 A1021 3000d multi .50 .30
Complete booklet, 10 #3563 5.00

New Year 2017 (Year of the Rooster) — A1022

Designs: 3000d, One rooster (2-1). 10,500d, Two roosters (2-2).

2016, Dec. 20 Litho. *Perf. 13½*
3564-3565 A1022 Set of 2 1.40 1.25
Complete booklet, 4 each #3564-3565 5.50

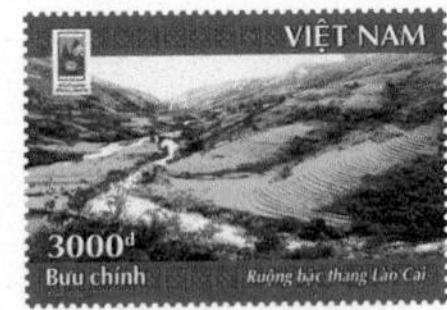
National Tourism Day A1023

Designs: 3000d, Terraced fields, Lào Cai (2-1). 10,500d, Monument on peak of Fanispan (2-2).

2017, Feb. 13 Litho. *Perf. 13¼x13*
3566-3567 A1023 Set of 2 1.25 1.25

Markets A1024

Designs: 3000d, Cho Vùng Cao (3-1). 4500d, Cho Làng (3-2). 6000d, Cho Sông Nuóc (3-3).

2017, Mar. 1 Litho. *Perf. 13x12¾*
3568-3570 A1024 Set of 3 1.25 1.25

General Van Tien Dung (1917-2002) A1025

2017, Apr. 28 Litho. *Perf. 13*
3571 A1025 3000d multi .30 .30

Panax Vietnamensis A1026

Ginseng root and ginseng plant with: 3000d, Red flower. 12,000d, Flower.

2017, June 10 Litho. *Perf. 13*
3572 A1026 3000d multi .30 .30
Complete booklet, 10 #3572 3.00

Souvenir Sheet
Perf. 13½x13¾
3573 A1026 12,000d multi 1.10 1.10

Nelumbo Nucifera A1027

2017, Aug. 8 Litho. *Perf. 13*
3574 A1027 3000d multi .30 .30
Complete booklet, 10 #3574 3.00

Association of Southeast Asian Nations, 50th anniv.

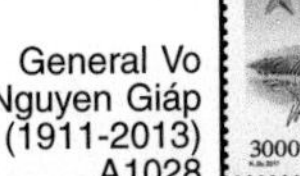

General Vo Nguyen Giáp (1911-2013) A1028

2017, Aug. 25 Litho. *Perf. 13*
3575 A1028 3000d multi .30 .30
Complete booklet, 10 #3575 3.00

Souvenir Sheet
Perf. 13½x13¾
3576 A1028 12,000d multi 1.10 1.10

Artifacts From Hanoi Citadel UNESCO World Heritage Site — A1029

Various artifacts with frame color of: No. 3577, 3000d, Flesh (3-1). No. 3578. 3000d, Light blue (3-2). 8000d, Light yellow green (3-3).
12,000d, Artifact, diff.

2017, Oct. 10 Litho. *Perf. 13*
3577-3579 A1029 Set of 3 1.25 1.25

Souvenir Sheet
Perf. 13¾x13½
3580 A1029 12,000d multi 1.10 1.10

Asia-Pacific Economic Cooperation Economic Leaders Meeting, Da Nang — A1030

2017, Nov. 6 Litho. *Perf. 13*
3581 A1030 3000d multi .30 .30
Complete booklet, 10 #3581 3.00

Russian October Revolution, Cent. — A1031

2017, Nov. 7 Litho. *Perf. 13*
3582 A1031 3000d multi .30 .30
Complete booklet, 10 #3582 3.00

Trung Vuong High School. Hanoi, Cent. — A1032

2017, Nov. 11 Litho. *Perf. 13*
3583 A1032 3000d multi .30 .30
Complete booklet, 10 #3583 3.00

New Year 2018 (Year of the Dog) — A1033

Designs: 3000d, Dog (2-1). 10,500d, Dog and puppy (2-2).

2017, Dec. 1 Litho. *Perf. 13½*
3584-3585 A1033 Set of 2 1.25 1.25
Complete booklet, 4 #3584, 4 #3585 5.00

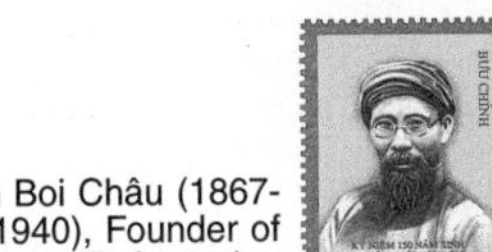
Phan Boi Châu (1867-1940), Founder of Reformation Society — A1034

Perf. 13¼x13½
2017, Dec. 26 Litho.
3586 A1034 3000d multi .30 .30

Sanchi Stupa, India — A1035

Pho Minh Pagoda, Viet Nam — A1036

2018, Jan. 25 Litho. *Perf. 13*
3587 A1035 3000d multi .30 .30
3588 A1036 10,500d multi .95 .95

See India Nos. 2992-2993.

Tet Offensive, 50th Anniv. — A1037

2018, Feb. 8 Litho. *Perf. 13*
3589 A1037 3000d multi .30 .30

Nguyen Binh (1918-66), Poet — A1038

2018, Feb. 13 Litho. *Perf. 13*
3590 A1038 3000d multi .30 .30

Souvenir Sheet

Perf. 13½x13¾

3591 A1038 12,000d multi 1.10 1.10

Bauhinia Variegata A1039

Flowers with denomination at: 3000d, LL (2-1). 8500d, LR (2-2).
14,000d, Flowers, vert.

2018, Mar. 1 Litho. *Perf. 13*

3592-3593 A1039 Set of 2 1.00 1.00
Complete booklet, 4 each #3592, 3593 4.00

Souvenir Sheet

Perf. 13¾x13½

3594 A1039 14,000d multi 1.25 1.25

Dr. Martin Luther King, Jr. (1929-68), Civil Rights Leader — A1040

2018, Apr. 4 Litho. *Perf. 13½*

3595 A1040 3000d multi .30 .30
Complete booklet, 10 #3595 3.00

Karl Marx (1818-83), Political Theorist — A1041

2018, May 5 Litho. *Perf. 13½*

3596 A1041 3000d multi .30 .30
Complete booklet, 10 #3596 3.00

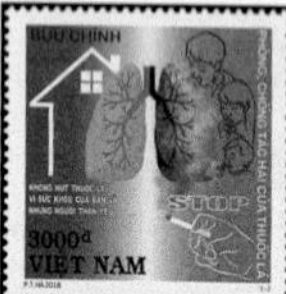

Anti-Smoking Campaign A1042

2018, May 31 Litho. *Perf. 13½*

3597 A1042 3000d multi .30 .30
Complete booklet, 10 #3597 3.00

Marine Life — A1043

Designs: No. 3598, 3000d, Nautilus pompilius (4-1). No. 3599, 3000d, Trochus niloticus (4-2). No. 3600, 3000d, Tridacna maxima (4-3). 10,500d, Mauritia scurra (4-4).
12,000d, Charonia tritonis.

2018, June 23 Litho. *Perf. 13*

3598-3601 A1043 Set of 4 1.75 1.75
3601a Booklet pane of 8, 2 each #3598-3601 3.50 —
Complete booklet, #3601a 3.50

Souvenir Sheet

Perf. 13½x13¾

3602 A1043 12,000d multi 1.10 1.10

Citadel of the Ho Dynasty UNESCO World Heritage Site — A1044

Designs: 3000d, East Gate (3-1). 4500d, West Gate (3-2). 6000d, North Gate (3-3).
12,000d, South Gate.

2018, June 27 Litho. *Perf. 13*

3603-3605 A1044 Set of 3 1.25 1.25

Souvenir Sheet

Perf. 13½x13¾

3606 A1044 12,000d multi 1.10 1.10

Tra Co Communal House, Mong Cai — A1045

2018, July 12 Litho. *Perf. 13*

3607 A1045 3000d multi .30 .30
Complete booklet, 10 #3607 3.00

Fauna of Kon Ka Kinh National Park — A1046

Designs: No. 3608, 3000d, Garrulax konkakinhensis (4-1). No. 3609, 3000d, Acanthosaura nataliae, vert. (4-2). 6500d, Muntiacus truongsonensis (4-3). 10,500d, Pyrops spinolae, vert (4-4).

2018, Aug. 18 Litho. *Perf. 13*

3608-3611 A1046 Set of 4 2.00 2.00
3611a Souvenir sheet of 4, #3608-3611, perf. 13½x13¾, 13¾x13½ 2.00 2.00

Bronze Belt Buckle — A1047

Bronze Jar — A1048

Bronze Sword — A1049

Bronze Lantern — A1050

2018, Oct. 1 Litho. *Perf. 13½*

3612 A1047 3000d multi .25 .25
3613 A1048 4000d multi .35 .35
3614 A1049 6000d multi .55 .55
3615 A1050 8000d multi .70 .70
a. Block or horiz. strip of 4, #3612-3615 1.90 1.90
Complete booklet, 2 each #3612-3615 3.80 3.80
Nos. 3612-3615 (4) 1.85 1.85

National treasures from the Dong Son Bronze Age culure.

Nguyen Trung Truc (1838-68), Anti-Colonial Militia Leader, and Sinking of French Ship L'Espérance A1051

2018, Oct. 6 Litho. *Perf. 13*

3616 A1051 3000d multi .25 .25

Nguyen Hong (1918-82), Writer — A1052

2018, Nov. 5 Litho. *Perf. 13*

3617 A1052 4000d multi .35 .35

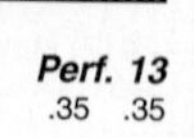

New Year 2019 (Year of the Pig) — A1053

Pig with head at: 4000d, Right (2-1). 15,000d, Left (2-2).

2018, Dec. 1 Litho. *Perf. 13½*

3618-3619 A1053 Set of 2 1.75 1.75
3619a Souvenir sheet of 8, 4 each #3618-3619 7.00 7.00
Complete booklet, 4 each #3618, 3619 7.00

Nelson Mandela (1918-2013), President of South Africa — A1054

2018, Dec. 5 Litho. *Perf. 13*

3620 A1054 4000d multi .35 .35
Complete booklet, 10 #3620 3.50

Diep Minh Chau (1919-2002), Sculptor A1055

2019, Feb. 10 Litho. *Perf. 13*

3621 A1055 4000d multi .35 .35

Hanoi Summit Meeting of U.S. Pres. Donald Trump and North Korean Chairman Kim Jong Un — A1056

2019, Feb. 26 Litho. *Perf. 13*

3622 A1056 4000d multi .35 .35
Complete booklet, 10 #3622 3.50
a. Miniature sheet of 8 3.00 3.00

Ly Thuong Kiet (1019-1105), General A1057

2019, Apr. 1 Litho. *Perf. 13*

3623 A1057 4000d multi .35 .35

Silk Paintings A1058

Designs: No. 3624, 4000d, Bác Hô di công tác, by Nguyen Thu (4-1). No. 3625, 4000d, Ghé tham nhà, by Nguyen Trong Kiêm (4-2). 6000d, Bêp lua Truòng Son, by Vu Giáng Huong (4-3). 15,000d, Hoa trái quê huong, by Lê Thi Kim Bach, vert. (4-4).

Perf. 13½x13, 13x13½

2019, Apr. 1 Litho.

3624-3627 A1058 Set of 4 2.50 2.50

United Nations Day of Vesak — A1059

2019, May 11 Litho. *Perf. 13*

3628 A1059 4000d multi .35 .35

Souvenir Sheet

Perf. 13½x14

3629 A1059 15,000d multi 1.40 1.40

National Liberation Front, 50th Anniv. — A1060

2019, June 6 Litho. *Perf. 13*

3630 A1060 4000d multi .35 .35

Butterflies — A1061

Designs: No. 3631, 4000d, Graphium antiphates (4-1). No. 3632, 4000d, Sasakia charonda (4-2). 6000d, Kallima inachus (4-3). 8000d, Troides aeacus (4-4).
15,000d, Lamproptera meges.

2019, June 11 Litho. *Perf. 13*

3631-3634 A1061 Set of 4 1.90 1.90

Souvenir Sheet

Perf. 14x13½

3635 A1061 15,000d multi 1.40 1.40

China 2019 World Stamp Exhibition, Wuhan, People's Republic of China.

Bridges A1062

Designs: No. 3636, 4000d, Bai Cháy Bridge, Quang Ninh (5-1). No. 3637, 4000d, Nhât Tân Bridge, Hanoi (5-2). 6000d, Trân Thi Ly Bridge, Da Nang (5-3). 8000d, Phú My Bridge, Ho Chi Minh City (5-4). 15,000d, Rach Miêu Bridge, Tiên Giang-Bê Tre (5-5).

2019, July 1 Litho. *Perf. 13*

3636-3640 A1062 Set of 5 3.25 3.25

First Man on the Moon, 50th Anniv. — A1063

2019, July 20 Litho. *Perf. 13½*

3641 A1063 4000d multi .35 .35

Mekong River Fish — A1064

Designs: No. 3642, 4000d, Catlocarpio siamensis (5-1). No. 3643, 4000d, Himantura walga (5-2). 6000d, Pangasianodon gigas (5-3). 8000d, Mystus mysticetus (5-4). 12,000d, Hemibagrus wyckioides (5-5).
15,000d, Pangasius sanitwongsei.

2019, Aug. 1 Litho. *Perf. 13*

3642-3646 A1064 Set of 5 3.00 3.00

Souvenir Sheet

Perf. 13½x14

3647 A1064 15,000d multi 1.40 1.40

Traditional Clothing of Vietnamese Men and Women — A1065

2019, Aug. 8 Litho. *Perf. 13*
3648 A1065 4000d multi .35 .35

Publication of Pres. Ho Chi Minh's Last Testament, 50th Anniv. — A1066

Ho Chi Minh: 4000d, Writing, text and flag of Viet Nam.
15,000d, Standing, tank, symbols of industry and agriculture, flag of Communist Party of Viet Nam, vert.

2019, Aug. 27 Litho. *Perf. 13*
3649 A1066 4000d multi .35 .35

Souvenir Sheet
Perf. 14x13½

3650 A1066 15,000d multi 1.40 1.40

Mohandas K. Gandhi (1869-1948), Indian Nationalist Leader — A1067

2019, Oct. 2 Litho. *Perf. 13*
3651 A1067 4000d multi .35 .35
Complete booklet, 10 #3651 3.50

Ministry of Foreign Affairs, Hanoi — A1068

Viet Nam Fine Arts Museum, Hanoi — A1069

National University, Hanoi — A1070

2019, Nov. 1 Litho. *Perf. 13½x13¼*
3652 A1068 4000d bluish vio .35 .35
3653 A1069 6000d red brown .55 .55
3654 A1070 15,000d blk & dp grn 1.30 1.30
Nos. 3652-3654 (3) 2.20 2.20

Paintings by Leonardo da Vinci (1452-1519) — A1071

Designs: 4000d, Lady with an Ermine. 15,000d, The Last Supper, horiz.

2019, Dec. 5 Litho. *Perf. 13*
3655 A1071 4000d multi .35 .35
Complete booklet, 10 #3655 3.50

Souvenir Sheet

3656 A1071 15,000d multi 1.30 1.30

No. 3656 contains one 47x31mm stamp.

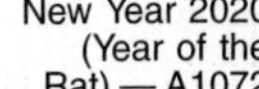

New Year 2020 (Year of the Rat) — A1072

Rat and flowers with background color of: 4000d, Red (2-1). 15,000d, Green (2-2).

2019, Dec. 8 Litho. *Perf. 13½*
3657-3658 A1072 Set of 2 1.75 1.75
3658a Souvenir sheet of 4, 2 each #3657-3658 3.50 3.50
Complete booklet, 4 #3657, 4 #3658 7.00

Communist Party of Viet Nam, 90th Anniv. — A1073

2020, Feb. 3 Litho. *Perf. 13*
3659 A1073 4000d multi .35 .35

Love — A1074

2020, Feb. 14 Litho. *Perf. 13½*
3660 A1074 4000d multi .35 .35
Complete booklet, 10 #3660 3.50

No. 3660 is impregnated with a rose fragrance.

Campaign Against COVID-19 Pandemic — A1075

Designs: 4000d, People wearing protective face masks (2-1). 15,000d, Fist and medical technicians holding test tubes (2-2).

2020, Mar. 31 Litho. *Perf. 13*
3661-3662 A1075 Set of 2 1.75 1.75
Complete booklet, 4 each #3661, 3662 7.00

Lenin (1870-1924), Head of Soviet Union — A1076

2020, Apr. 22 Litho. *Perf. 13½*
3663 A1076 4000d multi .35 .35
Complete booklet, 10 #3663 3.50

Ho Chi Minh (1890-1969), First President of Democratic Republic of Viet Nam — A1077

2020, May 16 Litho. *Perf. 13*
3664 A1077 4000d multi .35 .35
Complete booklet, 10 #3664 3.50

Children's Games A1078

Designs: No. 3665, O an quan (mancala, 4-1). No. 3666, Nhay dây (rope skipping, 4-2). No. 3667, Rong ran lên mây (snake dragon, 4-3). 8000d, Bit mat bat dê (blind man's bluff, 4-4)
19,000d, Kéo co (tug-of-war)..

2020, June 3 Litho. *Perf. 13*
3665 A1078 4000d multi .35 .35
Complete booklet, 10 #3665 3.50
3666 A1078 4000d multi .35 .35
3667 A1078 4000d multi .35 .35
Complete booklet, 10 #3667 3.50
3668 A1078 8000d multi .70 .70
Nos. 3665-3668 (4) 1.75 1.75

Souvenir Sheet
Perf. 13½

3669 A1078 19,000d multi 1.75 1.75

Battle of Bach Dang, 1288 A1079

2020, July 8 Litho. *Perf. 13½*
3670 A1079 4000d multi .35 .35

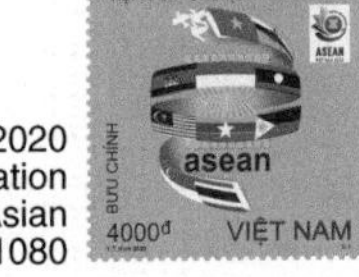

Viet Nam, 2020 Chair of Association of Southeast Asian Nations — A1080

2020, Aug. 7 Litho. *Perf. 13½*
3671 A1080 4000d multi .35 .35
Complete booklet, 10 #3671 3.50

Luong Dinh Cua (1920-75), Agronomist A1081

2020, Aug. 16 Litho. *Perf. 13*
3672 A1081 4000d multi .35 .35

Viet Nam People's Public Security, 75th Anniv. — A1082

2020, Aug. 18 Litho. *Perf. 13*
3673 A1082 4000d multi .35 .35

Souvenir Sheet

National Security Forces, 75th Anniv. A1083

2020, Aug. 18 Litho. *Perf. 13½*
3674 A1083 19,000d multi 1.75 1.75

Artifacts of the Oc Eo Culture — A1084

Designs: 4000d, Statuette of deity Avalokitesvara (3-1). 6000d, Statuette of Buddha (3-2). 8000d, Sculpture of Brahma (3-3). 19,000d, Linga-Yoni, horiz.

Perf. 13¼ Syncopated

2020, Aug. 20 Litho.
3675-3677 A1084 Set of 3 1.60 1.60

Souvenir Sheet
Perf. 13½

3678 A1084 19,000d multi 1.75 1.75

No. 3678 contains one 43x32mm stamp.

Ships of the Vietnamese Coast Guard — A1085

Designs: No. 3679, Ship No. 1013 (4-1). No. 3680, Ship No. 4033 (4-2). 6000d, Ship No. 9004 (4-3). 10,000d, Ship No. 8003 (4-4).
19,000d, Ship No. 8004.

2020, Aug. 27 Litho. *Perf. 13*
3679 A1085 4000d multi .35 .35
3680 A1085 4000d multi .35 .35
Complete booklet, 10 #3680 3.50
3681 A1085 6000d multi .50 .50
3682 A1085 10,000d multi .90 .90
Nos. 3679-3682 (4) 2.10 2.10

Souvenir Sheet
Perf. 13½x13¾

3683 A1085 19,000d multi 1.75 1.75

Paintings of Hanoi's Old Quarter by Bùi Xuân Phái (1920-88) A1086

Bùi Xuân Phái A1087

Designs: 4000d, Hàng Mam Street (2-1). 15,000d, Phat Loc Temple (2-2).

2020, Sept. 1 Litho. *Perf. 13¼x13*
3684 A1086 4000d multi .35 .35
Complete booklet, 10 #3684 3.50
3685 A1086 15,000d multi 1.30 1.30

Souvenir Sheet
Perf. 13x13¼

3686 A1087 19,000d multi 1.75 1.75

Traffic Safety — A1088

Designs: No. 3687, 4000d, "Never drink and drive" (4-1). No. 3688, 4000d, "Buckle up" (4-2). 8000d, "Wear a helmet" (4-3). 12,000d, "Use a child safety seat" (4-4).

2020, Sept. 5 Litho. *Perf. 13½*
3687-3690 A1088 Set of 4 2.40 2.40

To Huu (1920-2002), Poet and Politician A1089

2020, Oct. 8 Litho. *Perf. 13*
3691 A1089 4000d multi .35 .35

Vietnamese Cuisine A1090

Designs: No. 3692, Pho gà (chicken pho, 4-1). No. 3693, 4000d, Nem cuon (spring rolls, 4-2). 6000d, Bún cha (vermicelli and chopped grilled meat, 4-3). 12,000d, Bún thang (vermicelli and chicken noodle soup, 4-4).

2020, Oct. 10 Litho. *Perf. 13*
3692 A1090 4000d multi .35 .35
3693 A1090 4000d multi .35 .35
Complete booklet, 10 #3693 3.50

3694 A1090 6000d multi .50 .50
3695 A1090 12,000d multi 1.10 1.10
Nos. 3692-3695 (4) 2.30 2.30

Kingfishers A1091

Designs: No. 3696, Cayx erithaca (3-1). No. 3697, Alcedo hercules (3-2). 4500d, Pelargopsis capensis (3-3).
15,000d, Halcyon pileata, vert.

2020, Nov. 14 Litho. *Perf. 13½*
3696 A1091 4000d multi .35 .35
3697 A1091 4000d multi .35 .35
Complete booklet, 10 #3697 3.50
3698 A1091 4500d multi .40 .40
Nos. 3696-3698 (3) 1.10 1.10

Souvenir Sheet

3699 A1091 15,000d multi 1.30 1.30

No. 3699 contains one 32x43mm stamp.

Diplomatic Relations Between Viet Nam and Cuba, 60th Anniv. A1092

Designs: 4000d, Castle of Atarés, Havana, Cuba (2-1). 10,000d, Imperial Citadel of Thang Long, Hanoi (2-2).

2020, Dec. 2 Litho. *Perf. 13*
3700-3701 A1092 Set of 2 1.25 1.25
Complete booklet, 4 #3700, 4 #3701 5.00

See Cuba Nos. 6305-6306.

UNESCO Intangible Cultural Heritage of Viet Nam — A1093

UNESCO emblem, Intangible Cultural Heritage emblem, and the scenes from the worshipping of Mother Godesses of the Three Realms: No. 3702, 4000d, Three statues (3-1). No. 3703, 4000d, Woman in costume (3-2). No, 3704, 15,000d, Procession with men in blue costumes (3-3).
No. 3705, 15,000d, Procession with people in yellow and red costumes.

2020, Dec. 6 Litho. *Perf. 13*
3702-3704 A1093 Set of 3 2.00 2.00

Souvenir Sheet

Perf. 13½x13¼

3705 A1093 15,000d multi 1.30 1.30

New Year 2021 (Year of the Ox) — A1094

Designs: 4000d, Ox carrying fruit (2-1). 15,000d, Ox carrying fruit with calf (2-2).

2020, Dec. 12 Litho. *Perf. 13¼*
3706-3707 A1094 Set of 2 1.75 1.75
3707a Souvenir sheet of 4, 2 each #3706-3707 3.50 3.50
Complete booklet, 4 #3706, 4 #3707 7.00

Ludwig van Beethoven (1770-1827), Composer A1095

Designs: 4000d, Musical score, Beethoven and his birthplace in Bonn, Germany. 15,000d, Statue of Beethoven, Vienna, vert.

2020, Dec. 16 Litho. *Perf. 13*
3708 A1095 4000d multi .35 .35
Complete booklet, 10 #3708 3.50

Souvenir Sheet

Perf. 13¾x13½

3709 A1095 15,000d multi 1.30 1.30

13th Congress of the Communist Party of Viet Nam — A1096

2021, Jan. 22 Litho. *Perf. 13*
3710 A1096 4000d multi .35 .35

Campaign Against COVID-19 — A1097

Designs: 4000d+2000d, COVID-19 virus, and methods for protection against spread of virus (2-1). 6000d, Airplane over buildings, hands, hypodermic needle and vials of vaccine (2-2).

2021, Apr. 29 Litho. *Perf. 13*
3711-3712 A1097 Set of 2 1.10 1.10
Complete booklet, 4 #3711, 4 #3712 4.50

Nguyen Co Thach (1921-88), Foreign Minister — A1098

2021, May 14 Litho. *Perf. 13*
3713 A1098 4000d multi .35 .35

A1099

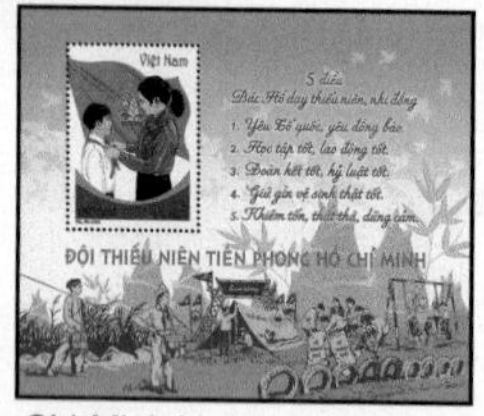

Ho Chi Minh Young Pioneers, 80th Anniv. — A1100

2021, May 15 Litho. *Perf. 13½*
3714 A1099 4000d multi .35 .35

Souvenir Sheet

Perf. 13¾

3715 A1100 15,000d multi 1.30 1.30

A1101

A1102

A1103

Legend of the Watermelon — A1104

2021, June 1 Litho. *Perf. 13*
3716 A1101 4000d multi .35 .35
a. Perf. 13½x13¾ .35 .35
3717 A1102 4000d multi .35 .35
a. Perf. 13¾x13½ .35 .35
3718 A1103 4000d multi .35 .35
a. Perf. 13½x13¾ .35 .35
3719 A1104 6000d multi .55 .55
a. Perf. 13¾x13½ .55 .55
b. Souvenir sheet of 4, #3716a-3719a 1.60 1.60
Nos. 3716-3719 (4) 1.60 1.60

National Treasures — A1105

Designs: No. 3720, 4000d, Gold seal (4-1). No. 3721, 4000d, Gold animal on ball (4-2). 6000d, Gold ciruclar covered container (4-3). 12,000d, Gold box (4-4).

2021, July 31 Litho. *Perf. 13½*
3720-3723 A1105 Set of 4 2.25 2.25

Chickens and Roosters — A1106

Designs: No. 3724, 4000d, Multi-toed chicken and rooster (4-1). No. 3725, 4000d, Dong Tao chicken and rooster (4-2). No. 3726, 4000d, H'mong chicken and rooster (4-3). 12,000d, Lac Thuy chicken and rooster (4-4).

2021, Aug. 25 Litho. *Perf. 13½*
3724-3727 A1106 Set of 4 2.10 2.10

Traffic Safety — A1107

Designs: No. 3728, 4000d, "Turn on lights in the dark" (4-1). No. 3729. 4000d, "Do not drive when drowsy" (4-2). No. 3730, 4000d, "Slow down for safe roads" (4-3). 6000d, "Don't text while driving" (4-4).

2021, Sept. 5 Litho. *Perf. 13½*
3728-3731 A1107 Set of 4 1.60 1.60

Luu Huu Phuoc (1921-89), Composer A1108

2021, Sept. 12 Litho. *Perf. 13*
3732 A1108 4000d multi .35 .35

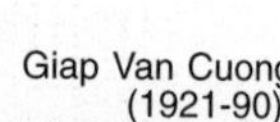
Giap Van Cuong (1921-90), Admiral — A1109

2021, Sept. 13 Litho. *Perf. 13*
3733 A1109 4000d multi .35 .35

Universal Postal Union International Letter Writing Contest, 50th Anniv. — A1110

2021, Oct. 9 Litho. *Perf. 13½*
3734 A1110 4000d multi .35 .35

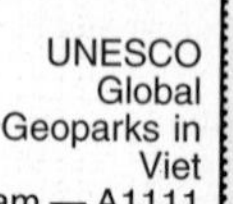
UNESCO Global Geoparks in Viet Nam — A1111

Designs: No. 3735, 4000d, Dong Van Stone Plateau Geopark (3-1). No. 3736, 4000d, Non Cuoc Cao Bang Geopark (3-2). 8000d, Dak Nong Geopark (3-3).
15,000d, Dong Van Stone Plateau Geopark, vert.

2021, Oct. 30 Litho. *Perf. 13*
3735-3737 A1111 Set of 3 1.40 1.40

Souvenir Sheet

Perf. 13¾x13½

3738 A1111 15,000d multi 1.30 1.30

No. 3738 contains one 32x43mm stamp.

New Year 2022 (Year of the Tiger) — A1112

Tiger, kite and flowers with background color of: 4000d, Pink (2-1). 15,000d, Light blue (2-2).

2021, Dec. 1 Litho. *Perf. 13½*
3739-3740 A1112 Set of 2 1.75 1.75
3740a Souvenir sheet of 4, 2 each #3739-3740 3.50 3.50
Complete booklet, 4 #3739, 4 #3740 7.00

SEMI-POSTAL STAMPS

World Communications Year — SP1

No. B1, Hands holding envelope with ITU emblem. No. B2, Satellite dish antenna.

Unwmk.

1983, Nov. 1 Litho. *Perf. 11*
B1-B2 SP1 50xu +10xu Set of 2 3.50 .80

AIR POST STAMP

AP1

Unwmk.

1959, Nov. 20 Litho. *Perf. 11*
C1 AP1 20xu blue & black 9.00 2.00

POSTAGE DUE STAMPS

Democratic Republic of Viet Nam Nos. 1-4 exist with handstamps of "TT" in a diamond. It is unclear to the editors if these stamps were used.

D1

1955 **Typo.** ***Perf. 11½***
J14 D1 50d brown & yellow 11.00 6.00

D2

1958, Dec. 1 **Litho.** ***Perf. 12½***

J15	D2	10d purple & red	.85	.60
J16	D2	20d orange & aqua	2.00	1.00
J17	D2	100d gray blue & red	4.00	2.50
J18	D2	300d olive grn & red	6.00	3.50
		Nos. J15-J18 (4)	12.85	7.60

MILITARY STAMPS

M1

Perf. 12½
1958, May 1 **Litho.** **Unwmk.**
M1 M1 multicolored 14.00 4.50

Invalids in Field Paddy — M2

1959-60 **Litho.** ***Perf. 11***

M2	M2	org brn & brown	7.00	1.00
M3	M2	grey blue & olive	5.00	1.75
		Nos. M2-M3 (2)	12.00	2.75

Issued: No. M2, 3/14/59; No. M3, 7/27/60.

Soldier, Train — M3

1959, July 1
M4 M3 turq blue & black 4.50 1.50

Frontier Guard — M4

1961, Jan. 3
M5 M4 multicolored 13.50 8.00

Naval Patrol — M5

1962, June 15
M6 M5 multicolored 5.00 2.00

Military Medal, Invalid's Badge — M6

1963, Sept. 10
M7 M6 12xu multicolored 4.00 3.75

Rifleman — M7

1964, Aug.
M8 M7 multicolored 4.00 4.00

Rifleman Jumping Wall — M8

1965

M9	M8	red & black	4.00	4.00
M10	M8	yellow green & black	4.00	4.00
		Nos. M9-M10 (2)	8.00	8.00

Issued: No. M9, 7/1; No. M10, 12/25.

Soldier, Guerrilla Woman — M9

1966-67
M11 M9 greenish blue & vio bl 8.00 8.00

Redrawn with two boats at right
M12 M9 olive & brown bl 13.50 12.00

Issued: No. M11, 9/25; No. M12, 6/26/67.

Badge of People's Army — M10

1967, Oct. 10
M13 M10 multicolored 2.50 1.50

M11

1968, Nov. 10
M14 M11 lilac 4.50 1.25

M12

1969, Nov. 15
M15 M12 red & brown red 2.00 1.25

M13

1971, Apr. 27
M16 M13 yellow, brown & red 2.50 1.25

Nguyen Van Be — M14

Design: No. M18, Nguyen Viet Xuan.

1971, Oct. 30 ***Perf. 11***
M17 M14 multicolored 1.75 1.25

Perf. 12½

M18	M14	black, pink & buff	2.50	1.10
M19	M14	black & green	2.50	1.10

M15

M16

1973, Dec. 22 ***Perf. 11***

M20	M15	blue, black & buff	2.00	.50
a.		Perf. 12½	4.50	4.50
M21	M15	red, black & buff ('75)	—	
M22	M16	olive, red & black	2.00	.50
a.		Perf. 12½	4.50	4.50

Issued: No. M21, 5/19/75. On No. M21, the location of "BUU CHINH" and "TEM QUAN DOI" are switched.

Disabled Veteran in Factory — M17

No. M24, Invalid's Badge, open book, vert.

1976, July 27
M23-M24 M17 Set of 2 3.50 1.50

Soldier, Map — M18

1976, Oct. 21
M25 M18 red & black 2.00 1.25

Pilot — M19

No. M27, Tank driver. No. M28, Seaman.

1978
M26-M28 M19 Set of 3 4.50 2.00

Issued: No. M26, 6/3; others, 10/10.

M20

Designs: a, Pilot. b, Badge of People's Army.

1979, Dec. 22
M29 M20 Vertical pair, #a.-b. 3.00 3.50

Types A343a, A359 and

Ho Chi Minh — M21

#M30, Factory militiawoman. #M31, Soldier, woman pointing. #M32, Militiawoman.

1981, Aug. 5

M30	A343a	salmon & multi	1.25	.75
M31	A343a	green & multi	1.25	.75
M32	A359	blue & multi	1.25	.75
M33	M21	blue & tan	1.25	.75
		Nos. M30-M33 (4)	5.00	3.00

Size of No. M32: 13x18mm.

M22

1982, Nov. 9
M34 M22 pink & greenish blue 1.50 1.00

M23

1983, Apr. 30
M35 M23 multicolored 2.00 1.10

Victory at Dien Bien Phu, 30th Anniv. — M24

1984, May 5 **Litho.**
M37 M24 multicolored 1.50 .75

Disabled Soldier Teaching Class — M25

1984, Nov. 10
M38 M25 tan & brown 1.00 .75
Imperf. 15.00

Frontier Forces Type of 1984

1984, Dec. 15
M39 A410 multicolored 1.50 .75

M26

1984, Dec. 22
M40 M26 multicolored 2.00 .50

Policemen and Women — M27

1985, Aug. 30
M41 M27 multicolored 1.50 .60
Imperf. 25.00

M28

1986, Oct. 1
M42 M28 olive brown & black 1.50 .75

M29

1987, Sept. 23
M43 M29 carmine and tan 2.00 1.00

OFFICIAL STAMPS

Harvesting Rice — O1

Denominations in grams or kilograms of rice. Dated 1952.

Perf. 11¼
1953, July Litho. Unwmk.
O1 O1 600g rose 10.00 3.00
O2 O1 1kg ol brown 10.00 4.00
O3 O1 2kg orange 9.00 12.00
O4 O1 5kg gray 15.00 15.00
Nos. O1-O4 (4) 44.00 34.00

Dien Bien Phu Type of 1954

1954-56 *Perf. 11*
O5 A4 600g sepia & ocher 18.00 12.50

No. O5 exists perf 6, Value $60; and also imperf, Value $18.
Issued: #O5, 10/54; perf 6, 12/54; imperf, 1956.

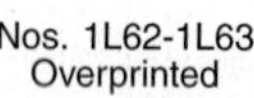

Nos. 1L62-1L63 Overprinted

1955 Typo. *Perf. 7 Rough*
O6-O7 VM2 100g on 2d, 100g on 5d, set of 2 400.00 300.00

Land Reform Type of 1955-56 Inscribed "SU VU" Above Value

1955 Litho. *Perf. 11*
O8-O9 A6 40d, 80d, set of 2 35.00 20.00

Cu Chinh Lan (1930-1952) — O3

Denominations: 20d, 80d, 100d, 500d, 1000d, 2000d, 3000d.

1956, June Litho. *Perf. 11½*
O10-O16 O3 Set of 7 240.00 200.00

4th World Trade Union Congress Type of 1957

Inscribed "SU VU" Above Value

1957, Aug. 1 *Perf. 12½*
O17-O20 A15 20d, 40d, 80d, 100d, set of 4 22.50 15.00

One-Pillar Pagoda — O4

1957-58
O21 O4 150d green and brown
O22 O4 150d orange and slate
Nos. O21-O22 (2) 22.50 10.00

Nos. O21-O22 exist with and without imprint and designer's name. Issued: No. O21, 12/22/57; No. O22, 3/12/58.

Craft Fair, Hanoi — O5

1958, May 30
O23-O24 O5 150d, 200d, set of 2 7.00 5.50

1st World Congress of Young Workers, Prague — O6

1958, June 26
O25 O6 150d lt olive green & red 3.00 1.75

Soldier, Factory, Crops — O7

1958, Aug. 19
O26-O28 O7 50, 150, 200d, set of 3 10.00 7.00

Opening of New Hanoi Stadium — O8

1958, Dec. 31
O29-O32 O8 10d, 20d, 80d, 150d, set of 4 8.50 4.75

Planting Rice — O9

1962, Sept. 1 *Perf. 11*
O33-O35 O9 3, 6, 12xu, set of 3 2.50 2.00

Rural Mail Service — O10

1966, July 1 *Perf. 11*
O36-O37 O10 3xu, 6xu, set of 2 2.50 1.00

VIRGIN ISLANDS

ˈvər-jən ˈī-lənds

LOCATION — West Indies, southeast of Puerto Rico
GOVT. — British colony
AREA — 59 sq. mi.
POP. — 19,107 (1997)
CAPITAL — Road Town

The British Virgin Islands constituted one of the presidencies of the former Leeward Islands colony until it became a colony itself in 1956. For many years stamps of Leeward Islands were used concurrently.

The Virgin Islands group is divided between Great Britain and the United States. See Danish West Indies.

12 Pence = 1 Shilling
20 Shillings = 1 Pound
100 Cents = 1 Dollar (1951)
100 Cents = 1 US Dollar (1962)

Catalogue values for unused stamps in this country are for Never Hinged items, beginning with Scott 88 in the regular postage section and Scott O1 in the officials section.

Values for unused stamps are for examples with original gum as defined in the catalogue introduction. However, Nos. 1-2c are valued without gum as the vast majority of examples are found thus.

Virgin and Lamps A1

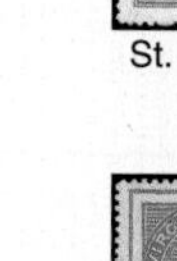

St. Ursula A2

A3

A4

1866 Litho. Unwmk. *Perf. 12*
Toned or White Paper
1 A1 1p green 55.00 65.00
a. Toned paper 57.50 67.50
c. Perf. 15x12, toned paper 6,000. 7,000.
2 A3 6p rose 65.00 100.00
a. Large "V" in "VIRGIN" 325.00 425.00
b. White paper 92.50 125.00
c. As "a," white paper 425.00 500.00

Examples offered as No. 1c frequently have forged perfs.

1867-70 *Perf. 15*
3 A1 1p blue grn ('70) 70.00 75.00
4 A1 1p yel grn ('68) 87.50 87.50
a. Toned paper 95.00 87.50
5 A2 4p lake, *buff* 50.00 65.00
a. 4p lake, *rose* 60.00 82.50
6 A3 6p rose 625.00 625.00
a. Toned paper ('68) 325.00 375.00
7 A4 1sh rose & blk 300.00 300.00
a. Toned paper 400.00 400.00
b. Double lined frame 275.00 350.00
c. As "b," bluish paper 250.00 350.00

Colored Margins
8 A4 1sh rose & blk 82.50 95.00
a. White paper 100.00 115.00
b. Bluish paper 750.00 900.00
c. Central figure omitted 225,000.
Nos. 3-8 (6) 1,215. 1,248.

Examples of No. 8c have perfs. trimmed on one or two sides.

1878 Wmk. 1 *Perf. 14*
9 A1 1p green 95.00 115.00

See #16-17, 19-20. For surcharge see #18.

Queen Victoria — A5

1880 Typo.
10 A5 1p green 82.50 100.00
11 A5 2½p red brown 125.00 140.00

1883-84 Wmk. 2
12 A5 ½p yellow 95.00 95.00
13 A5 ½p green 6.75 17.50
a. Imperf., pair 1,750.
14 A5 1p rose 50.00 55.00
15 A5 2½p ultra ('84) 4.25 16.00
Nos. 12-15 (4) 156.00 183.50

No. 13a probably is a plate proof.

1887 Litho.
16 A2 4p brick red 36.00 67.50
a. 4p brown red 45.00 72.50
17 A3 6p violet 20.00 55.00

No. 8 Handstamp Surcharged in Violet

1888 Unwmk. *Perf. 15*
18 A4 4p on 1sh dp rose & blk, toned paper 145.00 160.00
a. Double surcharge 8,500.
b. Inverted surcharge 55,000.
c. White paper 200.00 225.00

1889 Wmk. 2 *Perf. 14*
19 A1 1p carmine 4.00 10.00
20 A4 1sh brown 42.50 65.00
a. 1sh black brown 75.00 100.00

St. Ursula with Sheaf of Lilies — A7

1899 Engr.
21 A7 ½p yellow grn 4.25 .60
a. "PFNNY" 90.00 125.00
b. "F" without cross bar 90.00 125.00
c. Horiz. pair, imperf. between 13,000.
22 A7 1p red 6.00 2.00
23 A7 2½p ultra 13.00 3.00
24 A7 4p chocolate 6.00 22.50
a. "PENCF" 750.00 1,100.
25 A7 6p dark violet 8.00 3.00
26 A7 7p slate green 14.00 6.50
27 A7 1sh ocher 25.00 37.50
28 A7 5sh dark blue 85.00 95.00
Nos. 21-28 (8) 161.25 170.10

Edward VII — A8

1904 Typo. Wmk. 3
29 A8 ½p violet & bl grn 1.00 .60
30 A8 1p violet & scar 3.25 .55
31 A8 2p violet & bis 7.75 4.00
32 A8 2½p violet & ultra 4.25 2.00
33 A8 3p violet & blk 6.00 2.50
34 A8 6p violet & brn 4.75 2.50
35 A8 1sh green & scar 7.75 7.25
36 A8 2sh6p green & blk 45.00 55.00
37 A8 5sh green & ultra 55.00 75.00
Nos. 29-37 (9) 134.75 149.40

Numerals of 2p, 3p, 1sh and 2sh6p of type A8 are in color on plain tablet.

George V — A9

Die I

For description of dies I and II see "Dies of British Colonial Stamps" in Table of Contents.

1913 Ordinary Paper
38 A9 ½p green 4.25 7.00
39 A9 1p scarlet ('17) 2.25 14.00
40 A9 2p gray 8.50 32.50
41 A9 2½p ultra 10.00 10.00

Chalky Paper
42 A9 3p vio, *yel* 3.00 7.00
43 A9 6p dl vio & red vio 11.00 22.50
44 A9 1sh blk, *green* 3.50 11.00
45 A9 2sh6p blk & red, *bl* 55.00 60.00
46 A9 5sh grn & red, *yel* 50.00 140.00
Nos. 38-46 (9) 147.50 304.00

Numerals of 2p, 3p, 1sh and 2sh6p of type A9 are in color on plain tablet.

1921 Die II Wmk. 4
47 A9 ½p green 17.50 65.00
48 A9 1p carmine 10.00 40.00

For overprints see Nos. MR1-MR2.

Colony Seal — A10

1922 Wmk. 3
49 A10 3p violet, *yel* 1.00 *17.50*
50 A10 1sh black, *emerald* 1.00 *17.50*
51 A10 2sh6p blk & red, *bl* 6.00 *12.50*
52 A10 5sh grn & red, *yel* 52.50 *120.00*
Nos. 49-52 (4) 60.50 *167.50*

1922-28 Wmk. 4
53 A10 ½p green 1.00 *3.00*
54 A10 1p rose red .80 .80
55 A10 1p violet ('27) 2.00 *7.00*
56 A10 1½p rose red ('27) 2.00 *3.00*
57 A10 1½p fawn ('28) 2.75 *1.50*
58 A10 2p gray 1.40 *6.50*
59 A10 2½p ultra 7.00 *25.00*
60 A10 2½p orange ('23) 1.40 2.50
61 A10 3p dl vio, *yel* ('28) 2.50 *12.00*
62 A10 5p dl lil & ol grn 6.00 *50.00*
63 A10 6p dl lil & red vio 2.10 *6.50*
a. 6p dl lil & brt red vio 2.10 *7.00*
64 A10 1sh blk, *emer* ('28) 3.00 *20.00*
65 A10 2sh6p blk & red, *bl* ('28) 20.00 *60.00*
66 A10 5sh grn & red, *yel* ('23) 25.00 *75.00*
Nos. 53-66 (14) 76.95 *272.80*

The ½, 1, 2 and 2½p are on ordinary paper, the others on chalky.

Numerals of 1½p of type A10 are in color on plain tablet.

Common Design Types pictured following the introduction.

Silver Jubilee Issue
Common Design Type

1935, May 6 Engr. *Perf. 11x12*
69 CD301 1p car & dk blue 1.50 7.50
70 CD301 1½p black & ultra 1.50 6.50
71 CD301 2½p ultra & brn 4.00 6.25
72 CD301 1sh brn vio & ind 18.00 35.00
Nos. 69-72 (4) 25.00 55.25
Set, never hinged 32.50

Coronation Issue
Common Design Type

1937, May 12 *Perf. 11x11½*
73 CD302 1p dark carmine .90 2.75
74 CD302 1½p brown .75 2.75
75 CD302 2½p deep ultra .55 1.40
Nos. 73-75 (3) 2.20 6.90
Set, never hinged 2.75

King George VI and Seal of the Colony — A11

1938-47 Photo. *Perf. 14*
76 A11 ½p green .90 .90
77 A11 1p scarlet 1.25 1.00
78 A11 1½p red brown 1.50 1.25
79 A11 2p gray 1.50 1.25
80 A11 2½p ultra 2.00 1.50
81 A11 3p orange 1.25 1.00
82 A11 6p deep violet 3.50 1.00
83 A11 1sh olive bister 2.50 2.00
84 A11 2sh6p sepia 11.00 5.00
85 A11 5sh rose lake 11.00 *6.00*
Nos. 76-87 (12) 49.40 *56.90*
Set, never hinged 75.00

1938 Chalky Paper
76a A11 ½p green .85 3.50
77a A11 1p scarlet 3.15 2.00
78a A11 1½p red brown 3.50 6.50
79a A11 2p gray 3.50 2.50
80a A11 2½p ultramarine 2.50 1.80
81a A11 3p orange 4.25 1.10
82a A11 6p deep violet 6.50 2.75
83a A11 1sh olive bister 12.00 4.50
84a A11 2sh6p sepia 12.00 5.50
85a A11 5sh rose lake 36.00 12.00

Catalogue values for unused stamps in this section, from this point to the end of the section, are for Never Hinged items.

Peace Issue
Common Design Type
Perf. 13½x14

1946, Nov. 1 Engr. Wmk. 4
88 CD303 1½p red brown .25 .25
89 CD303 3p orange .25 .25

Silver Wedding Issue
Common Design Types

1949, Jan. 3 Photo. *Perf. 14x14½*
90 CD304 2½p brt ultra .25 .25

Engr.; Name Typo.
Perf. 11½x11
91 CD305 £1 gray black 16.00 22.00

UPU Issue
Common Design Types
Engr.; Name Typo. on Nos. 93 & 94

1949, Oct. 10 *Perf. 13½, 11x11½*
92 CD306 2½p ultra .40 *2.40*
93 CD307 3p deep orange 1.25 *2.50*
94 CD308 6p red lilac .50 .50
95 CD309 1sh olive .45 .50
Nos. 92-95 (4) 2.60 5.90

University Issue
Common Design Types

1951 Engr. *Perf. 14x14½*
96 CD310 3c red brn & gray blk .40 *2.25*
97 CD311 12c purple & black 1.10 *1.50*

Map of the Islands — A12

1951, Apr. 2 Wmk. 4 *Perf. 14½x14*
98 A12 6c red orange .70 1.75
99 A12 12c purple 1.25 1.00
100 A12 24c olive grn .70 1.25
101 A12 $1.20 carmine 3.50 1.50
Nos. 98-101 (4) 6.15 5.50

Restoration of the Legislative Council, 1950.

Sombrero Lighthouse A13

Map of Jost van Dyke A14

Designs: 3c, Sheep. 4c, Map, Anegada. 5c, Cattle. 8c, Map, Virgin Gorda. 12c, Map, Tortola. 24c, Badge of the Presidency. 60c, Dead Man's Chest. $1.20, Sir Francis Drake Channel. $2.40, Road Town. $4.80, Map, Virgin Islands.

1952, Apr. 15 *Perf. 12½x13, 13x12½*
102 A13 1c gray black .40 2.00
103 A14 2c deep green .85 .25
104 A14 3c choc & gray blk .45 1.25
105 A14 4c red .70 1.60
106 A14 5c gray blk & rose lake 1.40 .70
107 A14 8c ultra .85 *1.25*
108 A14 12c purple 1.25 *1.60*
109 A13 24c dk brown 1.00 .25
110 A14 60c blue & ol grn 4.00 11.00
111 A14 $1.20 ultra & blk 6.00 12.00
112 A14 $2.40 hn brn & dk grn 15.00 *16.00*
113 A14 $4.80 rose car & bl 19.00 19.00
Nos. 102-113 (12) 50.90 66.90

Coronation Issue
Common Design Type

1953, June 2 *Perf. 13½x14*
114 CD312 2c dk green & blk .40 *1.00*

Map of Tortola — A15

Brown Pelican — A16

Designs: 1c, Virgin Islands sloop. 2c, Nelthrop Red Poll bull. 3c, Road Harbor. 4c, Mountain travel. 5c, St. Ursula. 8c, Beach scene. 12c, Boat launching. 24c, White Cedar tree. 60c, Skipjack tuna. $1.20, Treasury Square. $4.80, Magnificent frigatebird.

Perf. 13x12½

1956, Nov. 1 Engr. Wmk. 4
115 A15 ½c claret & blk .45 .25
116 A15 1c dk bl & grnsh bl 1.90 1.10
117 A15 2c black & ver .40 .25
118 A15 3c olive & brt bl .40 .45
119 A15 4c blue grn & brn .45 .45
120 A15 5c gray .50 .25
121 A15 8c dp ultra & org .75 .65
122 A15 12c car & brt ultra 2.50 1.10
123 A15 24c dull red & grn 1.25 1.00
124 A15 60c yel org & dk bl 10.00 12.00
125 A15 $1.20 car & yel grn 2.75 11.00

Perf. 12x11½
126 A16 $2.40 vio brn & dl yel 37.50 16.00
127 A16 $4.80 grnsh bl & dk brn 40.00 16.00
Nos. 115-127 (13) 98.85 60.50

Types of 1956 Surcharged

Perf. 13x12½

1962, Dec. 10 Wmk. 314
128 A15 1c on ½c .25 .25
129 A15 2c on 1c 1.25 .25
130 A15 3c on 2c .25 .25
131 A15 4c on 3c .25 .25
132 A15 5c on 4c .25 .25
133 A15 8c on 8c .35 .35
134 A15 10c on 12c .45 .45
135 A15 12c on 24c .65 .65
136 A15 25c on 60c 3.25 1.25
137 A15 70c on $1.20 .70 3.25

Perf. 12x11½
138 A16 $1.40 on $2.40 10.00 5.00
139 A16 $2.80 on $4.80 10.00 5.00
Nos. 128-139 (12) 27.65 17.20

Freedom from Hunger Issue
Common Design Type

1963, June 4 Photo. *Perf. 14x14½*
140 CD314 25c lilac .50 .50

Red Cross Centenary Issue
Common Design Type
Wmk. 314

1963, Sept. 2 Litho. *Perf. 13*
141 CD315 2c black & red .25 1.00
142 CD315 25c ultra & red .55 .25

Shakespeare Issue
Common Design Type

1964, Apr. 23 Photo. *Perf. 14x14½*
143 CD316 10c ultramarine .45 .45

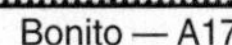

Bonito — A17

Map of Tortola Island — A18

2c, Seaplane at Soper's Hole. 3c, Brown pelican. 4c, Dead Man's Chest (mountain). 5c, Road Harbor. 6c, Fallen Jerusalem Island. 8c, The Baths, Virgin Gorda. 10c, Map of Virgin Islands. 12c, Ferry service, Tortola—St. Thomas. 15c, The Towers. 25c, Plane at Beef Island Airfield. $1, Virgin Gorda Island. $1.40, Yachts, Tortola. $2.80, Badge.

Perf. 13x12½

1964, Nov. 2 Engr. Wmk. 314
144 A17 1c gray ol & dk bl .35 2.40
145 A17 2c rose red & ol .35 .45
146 A17 3c grnsh bl & sep 4.25 2.40
147 A17 4c carmine & blk 1.10 2.40
148 A17 5c green & blk .90 1.60
149 A17 6c orange & blk .35 1.40
150 A17 8c pink & blk .35 1.00
151 A17 10c lt violet & mar 1.60 .45
152 A17 12c vio bl & Prus grn 2.75 3.50
153 A17 15c gray & yel grn .45 3.50
154 A17 25c pur & yel grn 13.00 3.50

Perf. 13x13½
Size: 27x30½mm
155 A18 70c bister brn & blk 5.25 8.00
156 A18 $1 red brn & yel grn 4.25 3.00
157 A18 $1.40 rose & blue 24.00 13.00

Perf. 11½x12
Size: 27x37mm
158 A18 $2.80 rose lilac & blk 26.00 13.00
Nos. 144-158 (15) 84.95 59.60

For surcharges & overprints see Nos. 173-175, 190-191.

ITU Issue
Common Design Type
Perf. 11x11½

1965, May 17 Litho. Wmk. 314
159 CD317 4c yellow & bl grn .25 .25
160 CD317 25c blue & org yel .60 .60

Intl. Cooperation Year Issue
Common Design Type

1965, Oct. 25 Wmk. 314 *Perf. 14½*
161 CD318 1c blue grn & cl .25 .25
162 CD318 25c lt violet & grn .40 .25

Churchill Memorial Issue
Common Design Type

1966, Jan. 24 Photo. *Perf. 14*
Design in Black, Gold and Carmine Rose
163 CD319 1c brt blue .25 .25
164 CD319 2c green .25 .25
165 CD319 10c brown .40 .40
166 CD319 25c violet 1.00 1.00
Nos. 163-166 (4) 1.90 1.90

Royal Visit Issue
Common Design Type

1966, Feb. 22 Litho. *Perf. 11x12*
167 CD320 4c violet blue .25 .25
168 CD320 70c dk car rose 1.50 1.50

Stamps of 1866 — A19

Designs: 5c, R.M.S. Atrato, 1866. 25c, Beechcraft mail plane on Beef Island Airfield and 6p stamp (No. 2). 60c, Landing mail at Road Town, 1866, and 1p stamp (No. 1).

Perf. 12½x13

1966, Apr. 25 Wmk. 314
169 A19 5c grn, yel, red & blk .30 .25
170 A19 10c yel, grn, red, blk & rose .30 .25
171 A19 25c lt grn, bl, red, blk & rose .55 .75
172 A19 60c bl, red, blk, & grn 1.00 1.50
Nos. 169-172 (4) 2.15 2.75

Centenary of Virgin Islands postage stamps.

No. 155 Surcharged

No. 157 Surcharged

No. 158 Surcharged

Perf. 13x12½, 11½x12

1966, Sept. 15 Engr. Wmk. 314
173 A18 50c on 70c 2.00 2.00
174 A18 $1.50 on $1.40 3.75 3.75
175 A18 $3 on $2.80 3.75 3.75
Nos. 173-175 (3) 9.50 9.50

UNESCO Anniversary Issue
Common Design Type

1966, Dec. 1 Litho. *Perf. 14*
176 CD323 2c "Education" .25 .25
177 CD323 12c "Science" .25 .25
178 CD323 60c "Culture" .90 .80
Nos. 176-178 (3) 1.40 1.30

Map and Seal of Virgin Islands — A20

Wmk. 314
1967, Apr. 18 Photo. *Perf. 14½*
179 A20 2c gold, grn & org .25 .25
180 A20 10c gold, rose red, grn & org .25 .25
181 A20 25c gold, red brn, grn & org .25 .25
182 A20 $1 gold, bl, grn & org .45 .45
Nos. 179-182 (4) 1.20 1.20

Introduction of new constitution.

Map of Virgin Islands, Bermuda and C.S. Mercury — A21

10c, Communications center, Chalwell, Virgin Islands. 50c, Cable ship Mercury.

1967, Sept. 14 Wmk. 314 *Perf. 14½*
183 A21 4c green & multi .25 .25
184 A21 10c dp plum & multi .25 .25
185 A21 50c bister & multi .60 .60
Nos. 183-185 (3) 1.10 1.10

Completion of the Bermuda-Tortola, Virgin Islands, telephone link.

Blue Marlin — A22

Designs: 10c, Sergeant fish (cobia). 25c, Peto fish (Wahoo). 40c, Fishing boat, map of Virgin Islands and fishing records.

Perf. 12½x12
1968, Jan. 2 Photo. Wmk. 314
186 A22 2c multicolored .25 *1.00*
187 A22 10c multicolored .25 .25
188 A22 25c multicolored .40 .40
189 A22 40c multicolored .75 .75
Nos. 186-189 (4) 1.65 2.40

Game fishing in Virgin Islands waters.

Nos. 151 and 154 Ovptd. "1968 / INTERNATIONAL / YEAR FOR / HUMAN RIGHTS"

1968, July 1 Engr. *Perf. 13x12½*
190 A17 10c lt violet & maroon .25 .25
191 A17 25c purple & green .40 .40

Martin Luther King, Bible and Sword — A23

1968, Oct. 15 Litho. *Perf. 14*
192 A23 4c dl org, vio & blk .35 .35
193 A23 25c dl org, gray grn & blk .45 .45

Martin Luther King, Jr. (1929-68), American civil rights leader.

DHC-6 Twin Otter — A24

Designs: 10c, Hawker Siddeley 748. 25c, Hawker Siddeley Heron. $1, Badge from cap of Royal Engineers.

1968, Dec. 16 Unwmk. *Perf. 14*
194 A24 2c brn red & multi .25 *1.00*
195 A24 10c grnsh bl, blk & red .40 .25
196 A24 25c ultra, lt bl, org & blk .45 .25
197 A24 $1 green & multi .50 *2.00*
Nos. 194-197 (4) 1.60 3.50

Opening of enlarged Beef Island Airport.

Long John Silver and Jim Hawkins — A25

Scenes from Treasure Island: 10c, Jim's escape from the pirates, horiz. 40c, The fight with Israel Hands. $1, Treasure trove, horiz.

Perf. 13½x13, 13x13½
1969, Mar. 18 Photo. Wmk. 314
198 A25 4c dp car & multi .30 .25
199 A25 10c multicolored .35 .25
200 A25 40c ultra & multi .40 .30
201 A25 $1 black & multi .75 *1.00*
Nos. 198-201 (4) 1.80 1.80

Robert Louis Stevenson (1850-94). The Virgin Islands were used as the setting for "Treasure Island."

Tourist and Rock Grouper — A26

Tourist Publicity: 10c, Yachts in Road Harbor, Tortola, horiz. 20c, Tourists on beach in Virgin Gorda National Park, horiz. $1, Pipe organ cactus and woman tourist.

1969, Oct. 20 Litho. *Perf. 12½*
202 A26 2c multicolored .25 *.55*
203 A26 10c multicolored .25 .25
204 A26 20c multicolored .35 .25
205 A26 $1 multicolored .90 *1.50*
Nos. 202-205 (4) 1.75 2.55

Carib Canoe — A27

Ships: 1c, Santa Maria. 2c, H.M.S. Elizabeth Bonaventure. 3c, Dutch buccaneer, 1660. 4c, Thetis (1827 merchant ship). 5c, Henry Morgan's ship. 6c, Frigate Boreas. 8c, Schooner L'Eclair, 1804. 10c, H.M.S. Formidable. 12c, H.M.S. Nymph burning. 15c, Packet Windsor Castle fighting French privateer. 25c, Frigate Astrea, 1808. 50c, H.M.S. Rhone. $1, Tortola sloop. $2, H.M.S. Frobisher. $3, Booker Line Viking (cargo ship). $5, Hydrofoil Sun Arrow.

Wmk. 314 Sideways
1970, Feb. 16 *Perf. 14½*
206 A27 ½c brn & ocher .25 1.50
207 A27 1c bl, lt grn & vio .25 .50
208 A27 2c red brn, org & gray .45 .75
209 A27 3c ver, bl & brn .35 1.00
210 A27 4c brn, bl & vio bl .35 .40
211 A27 5c grn, pink & blk .35 .25
212 A27 6c lil, grn & blk .45 .25
213 A27 8c lt ol, yel & brn .55 .30
214 A27 10c ocher, bl & brn .60 .40
215 A27 12c sep, yel & dp cl .70 1.25
216 A27 15c org, grnsh bl & brn 3.75 .55
217 A27 25c bl, grnsh gray & pur 3.75 1.50
218 A27 50c rose car, lt grn & brn 3.00 1.60
219 A27 $1 brn, sal pink & dk grn 3.75 3.50
220 A27 $2 gray & yel 7.50 7.00
221 A27 $3 brn, ol bis & dk bl 3.00 5.00
222 A27 $5 lil & gray 3.00 5.00
Nos. 206-222 (17) 32.05 30.75

For overprints see Nos. 235-236.

1973, Oct. 17 Wmk. 314 Upright
206a A27 ½c .85 *5.75*
209a A27 3c 2.00 *2.25*
210a A27 4c 2.00 *4.25*
211a A27 5c 2.00 *2.10*
214a A27 10c 2.40 2.40
215a A27 12c 3.25 3.25
Nos. 206a-215a (6) 12.50 20.00

Wmk. 314 Sideways
1974, Nov. 11 *Perf. 13½*
207a A27 1c 1.25 *2.25*
214b A27 10c 2.50 2.25
215b A27 12c 2.50 3.50
216a A27 15c 3.50 3.25
Nos. 207a-216a (4) 9.75 11.25

"A Tale of Two Cities," by Dickens — A28

Charles Dickens: 10c, "Oliver Twist." 25c, "Great Expectations."

1970, May 4 Litho. *Perf. 14½*
223 A28 5c blk, gray & pink .25 .25
224 A28 10c blk, pale yel grn & blue .35 .35
225 A28 25c blk, yel & lt yel grn .50 *.95*
Nos. 223-225 (3) 1.10 1.55

Hospital Visitor — A29

10c, Girl Scouts receiving 1st aid training at lake side. 25c, Red Cross & Virgin Islands coat of arms.

1970, Aug. 10 Wmk. 314 *Perf. 14*
226 A29 4c multicolored .25 .25
227 A29 10c multicolored .40 .25
228 A29 25c multicolored .75 .75
Nos. 226-228 (3) 1.40 1.25

Centenary of British Red Cross.

Mary Read — A30

Pirates: 10c, George Lowther. 30c, Edward Teach (Blackbeard). 60c, Henry Morgan.

1970, Nov. 16 Wmk. 314 *Perf. 14*
229 A30 ½c dp rose & multi .25 .25
230 A30 10c blue grn & multi .30 .25
231 A30 30c ultra & multi .80 .80
232 A30 60c multicolored 1.25 1.30
Nos. 229-232 (4) 2.60 2.60

Children Spelling out "UNICEF" — A31

1971, Dec. 13
233 A31 15c tan & multi .25 .25
234 A31 30c lt blue & multi .30 .30

25th anniv. of UNICEF.

Nos. 210 and 217 Dated "1972" and Ovptd. "VISIT OF / H.R.H. / THE / PRINCESS MARGARET"

1972, Mar. 7 *Perf. 14½*
235 A27 4c multicolored .40 .40
236 A27 25c multicolored .85 .85

Seaman, 1800 — A32

10c, Boatswain, 1787-1807. 30c, Captain, 1795-1812. 60c, Admiral in full dress uniform, 1787-95.

1972, Mar. 17 *Perf. 14x13½*
237 A32 ½c yellow & multi .25 .25
238 A32 10c brt pink & multi .35 .35
239 A32 30c orange & multi .80 .80
240 A32 60c blue & multi 1.75 1.75
Nos. 237-240 (4) 3.15 3.15

INTERPEX, 14th Intl. Stamp Exhib., NYC, Mar. 17-19.

Silver Wedding Issue, 1972
Common Design Type

Design: Queen Elizabeth II, Prince Philip, sailfish and "Sir Winston Churchill" yacht.

1972, Nov. 24 Photo. *Perf. 14x14½*
241 CD324 15c ultra & multi .25 .25
242 CD324 25c Prus blue & multi .25 .25

Allison Tuna — A33

1972, Dec. 12 Litho. *Perf. 13½x14*
243 A33 ½c Wahoo .25 .25
244 A33 ½c Blue marlin .25 .25
a. Horiz. or vert. pair, #243-244 .25 .25
245 A33 15c shown .45 .45
246 A33 25c White marlin .70 .70
247 A33 50c Sailfish 1.15 1.15
248 A33 $1 Dolphin 2.00 2.00
a. Souvenir sheet of 6, #243-248 11.00 11.00
Nos. 243-248 (6) 4.80 4.80

Game fish.

Lettsom House and Medal — A34

Themes from Quaker History: ½c, Dr. John Coakley Lettsom, vert. 15c, Dr. William Thornton, vert. 30c, US Capitol, Washington, DC, and Dr. Thornton who designed it. $1, Library Hall, Philadelphia, and William Penn.

1973, Mar. 9 Litho. *Perf. 13½*
249 A34 ½c rose & multi .25 .25
250 A34 10c multicolored .25 .25
251 A34 15c multicolored .25 .25
252 A34 30c ultra & multi .35 .35
253 A34 $1 multicolored .75 .75
Nos. 249-253 (5) 1.85 1.85

INTERPEX, 15th Intl. Phil. Exhib., NYC, Mar. 9-11.

Hummingbirds on 1c Coin — A35

Coins and Beach Scenes: 5c, Zenaida doves. 10c, Kingfisher. 25c, Mangrove cuckoos. 50c, Brown pelicans. $1, Magnificent frigate birds.

1973, June 30 Wmk. 314 *Perf. 14½*
254 A35 1c orange & multi .25 *.45*
255 A35 5c lt blue & multi .25 .25
256 A35 10c pale ultra & multi .65 .25
257 A35 25c yellow & multi .75 .25
258 A35 50c lt violet & multi 1.25 1.50
259 A35 $1 ultra & multi 1.75 *2.25*
Nos. 254-259 (6) 4.90 4.95

New Virgin Islands coinage.

Princess Anne's Wedding Issue
Common Design Type

1973, Nov. 16 Wmk. 314 *Perf. 14*
260 CD325 5c citron & multi .25 .25
261 CD325 50c blue grn & multi .25 .25

Virgin and Child, by Bernardino Pintoricchio — A36

Christmas (Paintings of the Virgin and Child by): 3c, Lorenzo Credi. 25c, Carlo Crivelli. 50c, Bernardino Luini.

1973, Dec. 7 *Perf. 14x14½*

262	A36	½c lt green & multi	.25	.25
263	A36	3c rose & multi	.25	.25
264	A36	25c ocher & multi	.25	.25
265	A36	50c lt blue & multi	.30	.30
		Nos. 262-265 (4)	1.05	1.05

Arms of French Minesweeper Canopus — A37

1974, Mar. 22 Wmk. 314 *Perf. 14*

266	A37	5c shown	.25	.25
267	A37	18c USS Saginaw	.30	.30
268	A37	25c HMS Rothesay	.35	.35
269	A37	50c HMCS Ottawa	.50	.50
a.		Souvenir sheet of 4, #266-269	1.75	1.75
		Nos. 266-269 (4)	1.40	1.40

INTERPEX Phil. Exhib., NYC, Mar. 22-24.

Famous Explorers — A38

1974, Aug. 19 *Perf. 14½*

270	A38	5c Columbus	.25	.25
271	A38	10c Sir Walter Raleigh	.25	.25
272	A38	25c Sir Martin Frobisher	.35	.35
273	A38	40c Sir Francis Drake	.65	.65
a.		Souvenir sheet of 4, #270-273	1.60	1.60
		Nos. 270-273 (4)	1.50	1.50

Sea Shells — A39

1974, Sept. 30 *Perf. 13x13½*

274	A39	5c Trumpet triton	.30	.30
275	A39	18c West Indian murex	.70	.70
276	A39	25c Bleeding tooth	1.00	1.00
277	A39	75c Virgin Island latirus	2.50	2.50
a.		Souvenir sheet of 4, #274-277	5.00	5.00
		Nos. 274-277 (4)	4.50	4.50

St. Mary, Aldermanbury, London, — A40

Design: 50c, St. Mary, Fulton, Missouri.

1974, Nov. 30 Wmk. 373 *Perf. 14*

278	A40	10c multicolored	.25	.25
279	A40	50c multicolored	.45	.45
a.		Souvenir sheet of 2, #278-279	.90	.90

Sir Winston Churchill (1874-1965).

Figurehead from "Boreas" — A41

Figureheads: 18c, The Golden Hind. 40c, Crowned lion from the "Superb." 85c, Warrior, from the "Formidable."

Perf. 13½x13

1975, Mar. 14 Wmk. 314

280	A41	5c multicolored	.25	.25
281	A41	18c multicolored	.30	.30
282	A41	40c multicolored	.50	.50
283	A41	85c multicolored	1.15	1.15
a.		Souv. sheet of 4, #280-283, perf. 14	2.75	2.75
		Nos. 280-283 (4)	2.20	2.20

INTERPEX, 17th Phil. Exhib., NYC, Mar. 14-16.

Rock Beauty — A42

Fish: 1c, Squirrelfish. 3c, Queen triggerfish. 5c, Blue angelfish. 8c, Stoplight parrotfish. 10c, Queen angelfish. 12c, Nassau grouper. 13c, Blue tang. 15c, Sergeant major. 18c, Jewfish. 20c, Bluehead wrasse. 25c, Gray angelfish. 60c, Glasseye snapper. $1, Blue chromis. $2.50, French angelfish. $3, Queen parrotfish. $5, Four-eye butterflyfish.

1975 Wmk. 373 *Perf. 14*

Inscribed "1975" Below Design

284	A42	½c shown	.25	.25
285	A42	1c multicolored	.55	.65
286	A42	3c multicolored	1.50	1.75
287	A42	5c multicolored	.35	.45
288	A42	8c multicolored	.35	.45
289	A42	10c multicolored	.35	.45
290	A42	12c multicolored	.55	.65
291	A42	13c multicolored	.55	.65
292	A42	15c multicolored	.55	.65
293	A42	18c multicolored	1.25	1.50
294	A42	20c multicolored	.75	.95
295	A42	25c multicolored	1.60	1.90
296	A42	60c multicolored	1.90	2.40
297	A42	$1 multicolored	2.75	3.25
298	A42	$2.50 multicolored	3.50	5.50
299	A42	$3 multicolored	3.75	5.50
300	A42	$5 multicolored	4.00	6.00
		Nos. 284-300 (17)	24.50	32.95

Issue dates: $5, Aug. 15. Others, June 16.

1977

Inscribed "1977" Below Design

284a	A42	½c multicolored	.55	.55
287a	A42	5c multicolored	1.00	1.00
288a	A42	8c multicolored	1.00	1.00
289a	A42	10c multicolored	1.00	1.00
290a	A42	12c multicolored	1.40	1.40
291a	A42	13c multicolored	1.40	1.40
292a	A42	15c multicolored	1.40	1.40
294a	A42	20c multicolored	2.00	2.00
		Nos. 284a-294a (8)	9.75	9.75

St. Georges Parish School — A43

Designs: 25c, Legislative Council Building. 40c, Mace and gavel of Legislative Council. 75c, Scroll with dates of historical events.

1975, Nov. 27 Litho. Wmk. 373

301	A43	5c ultra & multi	.25	.25
302	A43	25c green & multi	.25	.25
303	A43	40c ocher & multi	.25	.25
304	A43	75c ultra & multi	.25	.25
		Nos. 301-304 (4)	1.00	1.00

Restoration of Legislative Council, 25th anniv.

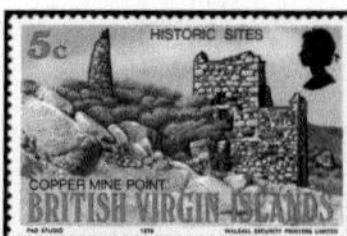

Copper Mine Point — A44

Historic Sites: 18c, Dr. Thornton's Ruin, Pleasant Valley. 50c, Callwood distillery. 75c, The Dungeon.

1976, Mar. 12 Litho. *Perf. 14½*

305	A44	5c red & multi	.25	.25
306	A44	18c red & multi	.25	.25
307	A44	50c red & multi	.40	.40
308	A44	75c red & multi	.60	.60
		Nos. 305-308 (4)	1.50	1.50

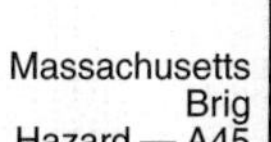

Massachusetts Brig Hazard — A45

Designs: 22c, American Privateer Spy. 40c, Continental Navy Frigate Raleigh. 75c, Frigate Alliance and HMS Trepasy.

1976, May 29 Wmk. 373 *Perf. 14*

309	A45	8c multicolored	.30	.25
310	A45	22c multicolored	.65	.45
311	A45	40c multicolored	1.00	1.00
312	A45	75c multicolored	1.75	1.75
a.		Souvenir sheet of 4, #309-312	6.50	6.50
		Nos. 309-312 (4)	3.70	3.45

American Bicentennial.

Government House, Tortola — A46

Designs: 15c, Government House, St. Croix, vert. 30c, Flags of US and British Virgin Islands, vert. 75c, Arms of British and US Virgin Islands.

1976, Oct. 29 Litho. *Perf. 14*

313	A46	8c green & multi	.25	.25
314	A46	15c green & multi	.25	.25
315	A46	30c green & multi	.25	.25
316	A46	75c green & multi	.55	.55
		Nos. 313-316 (4)	1.30	1.30

US and British Virgin Islands Friendship Day, 5th anniversary.

Holy Bible — A47

8c, Queen visiting Agricultural Station, Tortola, 1966. 60c, Presentation of Holy Bible.

1977, Feb. 7 *Perf. 14x13½*

317	A47	8c silver & multi	.25	.25
318	A47	30c silver & multi	.25	.25
319	A47	60c silver & multi	.25	.25
		Nos. 317-319 (3)	.75	.75

25th anniv. of the reign of Elizabeth II.
For overprints see Nos. 324-326.

Virgin Islands Chart, 1739 — A48

18th Century Maps of Virgin Islands: 22c, 1758. 30c, 1775. 75c, 1779.

1977, June 12 Wmk. 373 *Perf. 13½*

320	A48	8c multicolored	.30	.25
321	A48	22c multicolored	.65	.60
322	A48	30c multicolored	.90	.80
323	A48	75c multicolored	1.90	1.90
		Nos. 320-323 (4)	3.75	3.55

Type of 1977 Inscribed "ROYAL VISIT"

Designs: 5c, Queen visiting Agricultural Station, Tortola, 1966. 25c, Holy Bible. 50c, Presentation of Holy Bible.

1977, Oct. 26 Litho. *Perf. 14x13½*

324	A47	5c yel brn & multi	.25	.25
325	A47	25c dk blue & multi	.25	.25
326	A47	50c purple & multi	.40	.40
		Nos. 324-326 (3)	.90	.90

Caribbean visit of Queen Elizabeth II.

Divers Checking Equipment — A49

Tourist publicity: 5c, Cup coral inside bow of "Rhone." 8c, Sponge growing on superstructure of "Rhone." 22c, Sponge and cup coral. 30c, Scuba diver searching for sponges in cave. 75c, Marine life.

1978, Feb. 10 Wmk. 373 *Perf. 13½*

327	A49	½c multicolored	.25	.25
328	A49	5c multicolored	.25	.25
329	A49	8c multicolored	.25	.25
330	A49	22c multicolored	.55	.25
331	A49	30c multicolored	.75	.75
332	A49	75c multicolored	1.10	1.10
		Nos. 327-332 (6)	3.15	2.85

Corals — A50

1978, Feb. 27 *Perf. 14*

333	A50	8c Fire	.35	.35
334	A50	15c Staghorn	.40	.40
335	A50	40c Brain	.75	.75
336	A50	75c Elkhorn	1.50	1.50
		Nos. 333-336 (4)	3.00	3.00

Elizabeth II Coronation Anniversary Issue

Common Design Types

Souvenir Sheet

1978, June 2 Unwmk. *Perf. 15*

337	Sheet of 6	1.80	1.80
a.	CD326 50c Falcon of the Plantagenets	.30	.30
b.	CD327 50c Elizabeth II	.30	.30
c.	CD328 50c Iguana	.30	.30

No. 337 contains 2 se-tenant strips of Nos. 337a-337c, separated by horizontal gutter.

Lignum Vitae — A51

Flowering Trees: 22c, Ginger thomas. 40c, Dog almond. 75c, White cedar.

1978, Sept. 4 Litho. *Perf. 13x13½*

338	A51	8c multicolored	.25	.25
339	A51	22c multicolored	.40	.40
340	A51	40c multicolored	.50	.50
341	A51	75c multicolored	.60	.60
a.		Souvenir sheet of 4, #338-341	1.25	1.25
		Nos. 338-341 (4)	1.75	1.75

Eurema Lisa — A52

Butterflies: 22c, Dione vanillae. 30c, Heliconius charitonius. 75c, Hemiargus hanno.

1978, Dec. 4 Wmk. 373 *Perf. 14*

342	A52	5c multicolored	.25	.25
343	A52	22c multicolored	.75	.75
a.		Sheet of 9, 6 #342, 3 #343	3.25	3.25
344	A52	30c multicolored	1.00	1.80
345	A52	75c multicolored	2.75	2.25
		Nos. 342-345 (4)	4.75	5.05

Spiny Lobsters — A53

Conservation: 15c, Iguana, vert. 22c, Hawksbill turtle. 75c, Black coral, vert.

1979, Feb. 10 Litho.

346	A53	5c multicolored	.25	.25
347	A53	15c multicolored	.40	.25
348	A53	22c multicolored	.60	.25

349 A53 75c multicolored 1.25 1.25
a. Souvenir sheet of 4, #346-349 3.25 3.25
Nos. 346-349 (4) 2.50 2.00

Strawberry Cactus — A54

Native Cacti: 5c, Snowy cactus. 13c, Barrel cactus. 22c, Tree cactus. 30c, Prickly pear. 75c, Dildo cactus.

1979, May 7 Wmk. 373 *Perf. 14*
350 A54 ½c multicolored .25 .25
351 A54 5c multicolored .25 .25
352 A54 13c multicolored .35 .35
353 A54 22c multicolored .50 .50
354 A54 30c multicolored .55 .55
355 A54 75c multicolored .90 .90
Nos. 350-355 (6) 2.80 2.80

West Indies Girl and Church — A55

Children and IYC Emblem: 10c, African boy and dancers. 13c, Asian girl and children playing. $1, European girl and bicycle.

1979, July 9 *Perf. 14x14½*
356 A55 5c multicolored .25 .25
357 A55 10c multicolored .25 .25
358 A55 13c multicolored .25 .25
359 A55 $1 multicolored .35 .35
a. Souvenir sheet of 4, #356-359 1.25 1.25
Nos. 356-359 (4) 1.10 1.10

International Year of the Child.

No. 118 — A56

Rowland Hill's Signature and: 13c, Virgin Islands No. 11, horiz. 75c, Unissued Great Britain 2d stamp, 1910, horiz. $1, Virgin Islands No. 8c.

1979, Oct. 1 Photo. *Perf. 13½*
360 A56 5c multicolored .25 .25
361 A56 13c multicolored .25 .25
362 A56 75c multicolored .60 .60
Nos. 360-362 (3) 1.10 1.10

Souvenir Sheet

363 A56 $1 multicolored .90 .90

Sir Rowland Hill (1795-1879), originator of penny postage.
For overprints see Nos. 389-390.

Pencil Urchin — A57

½c, Calcified algae. 1c, Purple-tipped sea anemone. 3c, Starfish. 8c, Triton's trumpet. 10c, Christmas tree worms. 13c, Flamingo tongue snails. 15c, Spider crab. 18c, Sea squirts. 20c, True tulip. 25c, Rooster tail conch. 30c, Fighting conch. 60c, Mangrove crab. $1, Coral polyps. $2.50, Peppermint shrimp. $3, West Indian murex. $5, Carpet anemone.

"1979" or "1980" Below Design

1979-80 Litho. *Perf. 14*
364 A57 ½c multicolored .75 *2.50*
365 A57 1c multicolored 1.00 *2.50*
366 A57 3c multicolored 1.50 *2.50*
367 A57 5c shown 1.75 *2.00*
368 A57 8c multicolored 1.75 *1.50*
369 A57 10c multicolored .50 *1.00*
370 A57 13c multicolored 2.00 .75
371 A57 15c multicolored .75 .75
372 A57 18c multicolored 2.25 *4.25*
373 A57 20c multicolored 1.00 *1.90*
374 A57 25c multicolored 1.75 *4.00*
375 A57 30c multicolored 3.00 1.90
376 A57 60c multicolored 2.00 *3.00*
377 A57 $1 multicolored 1.75 *4.00*
378 A57 $2.50 multicolored 1.75 *3.75*
379 A57 $3 multicolored 1.75 *4.00*
380 A57 $5 multicolored 1.75 *4.00*
Nos. 364-380 (17) 27.00 *44.30*

Issued: 5, 8, 10, 15, 20, 25c, $2.50, $3, 12/17/79; others, 4/1/80. Date of year of issue below design.
For overprints see Nos. O1-O15.

"1982" Below Design

1982, Aug. 27 Chalky Paper
367a A57 5c multicolored 1.15 1.15
368a A57 8c multicolored 1.15 1.15
370a A57 13c multicolored 2.25 2.25
371a A57 15c multicolored 2.25 2.25
373a A57 20c multicolored 2.00 2.00
375a A57 30c multicolored 3.00 3.00
Nos. 367a-375a (6) 11.80 11.80

Rotary Athletic Meet, Tortola, Emblem — A58

22c, Paul P. Harris. 60c, Mount Sage National Park. $1, Anniversary emblem.

1980, Mar. 3 Litho. *Perf. 13½x14*
381 A58 8c shown .25 .25
382 A58 22c multicolored .25 .25
383 A58 60c multicolored .40 .40
384 A58 $1 multicolored .70 .70
a. Souvenir sheet of 4, #381-384 1.75 1.75
Nos. 381-384 (4) 1.60 1.60

Rotary International, 75th anniv.

Brown Booby, London 1980 Emblem — A59

25c, Magnificent frigatebird. 50c, White-tailed tropic bird. 75c, Brown pelican.

1980, May 6 Wmk. 373 *Perf. 14*
385 A59 20c shown .25 .25
386 A59 25c multicolored .35 .35
387 A59 50c multicolored .60 .60
388 A59 75c multicolored .80 .80
a. Souvenir sheet of 4, #385-388 2.00 2.00
Nos. 385-388 (4) 2.00 2.00

London 80 Intl. Stamp Exhib., May 6-14.

Nos. 361-362 Overprinted

1980, July 7 Photo. *Perf. 13½*
389 A56 13c multicolored .25 .25
390 A56 75c multicolored .45 .45

Sir Francis Drake — A60

1980, Sept. 26 Litho. *Perf. 14½*
391 A60 8c shown .45 .45
392 A60 15c Queen Elizabeth I .75 .75
393 A60 30c Drake knighted .90 .90
394 A60 75c Golden Hinde 1.90 1.90
a. Souvenir sheet of 4, #391-394 4.00 4.00
Nos. 391-394 (4) 4.00 4.00

400th anniv. of circumnavigation of the world.

Jost Van Dyke — A61

1980, Dec. 1 Wmk. 373 *Perf. 14*
395 A61 2c shown .25 .25
396 A61 5c Peter Island .25 .25
397 A61 13c Virgin Gorda .25 .25
398 A61 22c Anegada .35 .35
399 A61 30c Norman Island .40 .40
400 A61 $1 Tortola .75 .75
a. Souvenir sheet of 1 1.50 1.50
Nos. 395-400 (6) 2.25 2.25

Dancing Lady — A62

1981, Mar. 3 Litho. *Perf. 11*
401 A62 5c shown .25 .25
402 A62 20c Love in the mist .25 .25
403 A62 22c Red pineapple .25 .25
404 A62 75c Dutchman's pipe .85 .85
405 A62 $1 Maiden apple .85 .85
Nos. 401-405 (5) 2.45 2.45

Royal Wedding Issue
Common Design Type

1981, July 22 Litho. *Perf. 14*
406 CD331 10c Bouquet .25 .25
407 CD331 35c Charles, Queen Mother .25 .25
408 CD331 $1.25 Couple .60 .60
Nos. 406-408 (3) 1.10 1.10

#406-408 each se-tenant with decorative label.

Duke of Edinburgh's Awards, 25th Anniv. — A63

1981, Sept. 16 Wmk. 373 *Perf. 14*
409 A63 10c Stamp collecting .25 .25
410 A63 15c Running .25 .25
411 A63 50c Camping .30 .30
412 A63 $1 Duke of Edinburgh .40 .40
Nos. 409-412 (4) 1.20 1.20

Intl. Year of the Disabled — A64

1981, Oct. 19 Litho. *Perf. 14*
413 A64 15c Children .25 .25
414 A64 20c Fort Charlotte Children's Center .30 .30
415 A64 30c Playing music .35 .35
416 A64 $1 Center, diff. .75 .75
Nos. 413-416 (4) 1.65 1.65

A65

Virgin and Child (Christmas): Details from Adoration of the Shepherds, by Rubens. 50c, horiz.

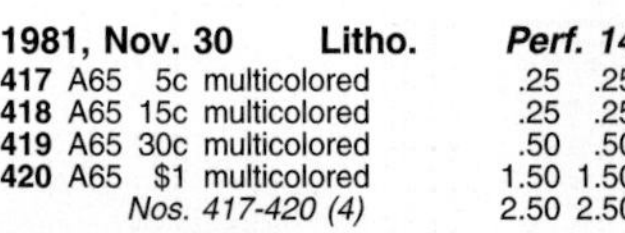

1981, Nov. 30 Litho. *Perf. 14*
417 A65 5c multicolored .25 .25
418 A65 15c multicolored .25 .25
419 A65 30c multicolored .50 .50
420 A65 $1 multicolored 1.50 1.50
Nos. 417-420 (4) 2.50 2.50

Souvenir Sheet

421 A65 50c multicolored 2.50 2.50

A66

Hummingbirds on local flora: 15c, Green-throated carib, erythrina. 30c, Same, bougainvillea. 35c, Antillean crested hummingbird, granadilla passiflora. $1.25, Same, hibiscus.

1982, Apr. 15 Litho. *Perf. 14x14½*
422 A66 15c multicolored .80 .50
423 A66 30c multicolored 1.00 1.00
424 A66 35c multicolored 1.20 1.20
425 A66 $1.25 multicolored 2.50 2.50
Nos. 422-425 (4) 5.50 5.20

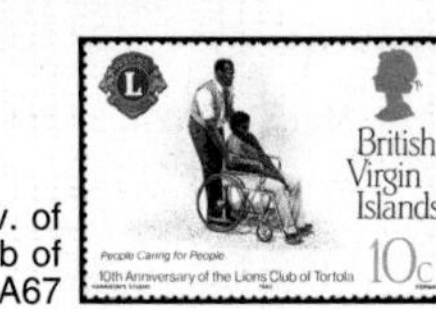
10th Anniv. of Lions Club of Tortola — A67

1982, May 3 *Perf. 13½x14*
426 A67 10c Helping disabled .30 .25
427 A67 20c Headquarters .40 .30
428 A67 30c Map .55 .30
429 A67 $1.50 Emblem 1.75 *2.00*
a. Souvenir sheet of 4, #426-429 3.00 3.00
Nos. 426-429 (4) 3.00 2.85

Princess Diana Issue
Common Design Type

1982, July 1 Litho. *Perf. 14*
430 CD333 10c Arms .25 .25
431 CD333 35c Diana .35 .35
432 CD333 50c Wedding .50 .50
433 CD333 $1.50 Portrait 1.90 1.90
Nos. 430-433 (4) 3.00 3.00

10th Anniv. of Air BVI (Natl. Airline) — A68

1982, Sept. 10 Wmk. 373 *Perf. 14*
434 A68 10c Douglas DC-3 .30 .30
435 A68 15c Britten-Norman Islander .55 .55
436 A68 60c Hawker-Siddeley 2.40 2.40
437 A68 75c Planes 2.75 2.75
Nos. 434-437 (4) 6.00 6.00

Scouting Year — A69

8c, Emblem, Flag raising. 20c, Cub scout, nature study. 50c, Kayak, sea scout. $1, Camp Brownsea Is., Baden-Powell.

1982, Nov. 18
438 A69 8c multicolored .25 .25
439 A69 20c multicolored .35 .35
440 A69 50c multicolored .90 .90
441 A69 $1 multicolored 1.40 1.40
Nos. 438-441 (4) 2.90 2.90

Commonwealth Day — A70

1983, Mar. 14 *Perf. 13½x14*
442 A70 10c Legislature in session .25 .25
443 A70 30c Wind surfing .30 .30
444 A70 35c Globe .35 .35
445 A70 75c Flags 1.25 1.25
Nos. 442-445 (4) 2.15 2.15

Nursing Week — A71

10c, Florence Nightingale (1820-1910), vert. 30c, Nurse, assistant, vert. 60c, Public health. 75c, Peebles Hospital.

1983, May 9 Litho. *Perf. 14½*

446 A71 10c multicolored .60 .25
447 A71 30c multicolored 1.00 .45
448 A71 60c multicolored 1.90 1.25
449 A71 75c multicolored 1.90 1.75
Nos. 446-449 (4) 5.40 3.70

Boat Building — A72

1983, July 25 *Perf. 14*

450 A72 15c First stage .35 .35
451 A72 25c 2nd stage .55 .55
452 A72 50c Launching 1.10 1.10
453 A72 $1 First voyage 2.00 2.00
a. Souvenir sheet of 4, #450-453 4.00 4.00
Nos. 450-453 (4) 4.00 4.00

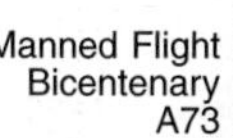

Manned Flight Bicentenary A73

1983, Sept. 15 Wmk. 373 *Perf. 14*

454 A73 10c Grumman Goose .25 .25
455 A73 30c De Havilland Heron .50 .50
456 A73 60c EMB Bandeirante 1.15 1.15
457 A73 $1.25 Hawker-Siddeley 748 2.10 2.10
Nos. 454-457 (4) 4.00 4.00

Christmas — A74

Raphael Paintings: 8c, Madonna & Child with Infant Baptist. 15c, La Belle Jardiniere. 50c, Madonna del Granduca. $1, Terranuova Madonna.

1983, Nov. 7 Litho. *Perf. 14½*

458 A74 8c multicolored .25 .25
459 A74 15c multicolored .25 .25
460 A74 50c multicolored .80 .80
461 A74 $1 multicolored 1.60 1.60
a. Souvenir sheet of 4, #458-461 3.50 3.50
Nos. 458-461 (4) 2.90 2.90

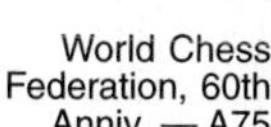

World Chess Federation, 60th Anniv. — A75

10c, Local tournament. 35c, Chess pieces, vert. 75c, 1980 Olympiad, Winning board, vert. $1, Gold medal.

1984, Feb. 20 Litho. *Perf. 14*

462 A75 10c multicolored 1.00 1.00
463 A75 35c multicolored 1.75 1.75
464 A75 75c multicolored 4.25 4.25
465 A75 $1 multicolored 6.75 6.75
Nos. 462-465 (4) 13.75 13.75

Lloyd's List Issue

Common Design Type

15c, Port Purcell, Tortola. 25c, Boeing 747. 50c, Shipwreck of RMS Rhone. $1, Booker Viking.

1984, Apr. 16 Litho. *Perf. 14½x14*

466 CD335 15c multicolored .35 .35
467 CD335 25c multicolored .65 .65
468 CD335 50c multicolored 1.25 1.25
469 CD335 $1 multicolored 2.00 2.00
Nos. 466-469 (4) 4.25 4.25

Souvenir Sheet

UPU Congress — A76

1984, May 16 Wmk. 373 *Perf. 14*

470 A76 $1 Emblem, jet, mailboat 2.75 2.75

1984 Summer Olympics — A77

1984, July 3

471 A77 15c Runners .40 .40
472 A77 15c Runner .40 .40
a. Pair, #471-472 1.25 1.25
473 A77 20c Wind surfers .50 .50
474 A77 20c Wind surfer .50 .50
a. Pair, #473-474 1.50 1.50
475 A77 30c Yachts .60 .60
476 A77 30c Yacht .60 .60
a. Pair, #475-476 2.00 2.00
Nos. 471-476 (6) 3.00 3.00

Souvenir Sheet

477 A77 $1 Torch bearer, vert. 2.50 2.50

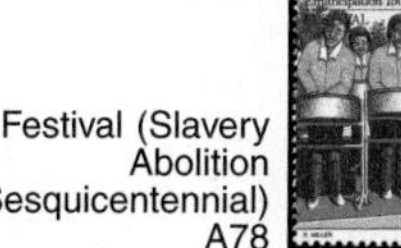

Festival (Slavery Abolition Sesquicentennial) A78

Designs: No. 478: a, Steel band. b, Calypso dancers. c, Dancers (men). d, Woman in traditional dress. e, Parade float.

No. 479 (Sail color of boat(s) in foreground): a, Green & white. b, Red & white, white, purple & white. c, white, yellow & white, blue & white. d, Yellow, red & white. e, Purple & white, white.

Nos. 478 and 479 each in continuous design.

1984, Aug. 14 *Perf. 13½x14*

478 Strip of 5, Parade 1.50 1.50
a.-e. A78 10c, any single .25 .25
479 Strip of 5, Regatta 3.00 3.00
a.-e. A78 30c, any single .45 .45

Local Boats — A79

1984, Nov. 15 Wmk. 373 *Perf. 13*

480 A79 10c Sloop .70 .40
481 A79 35c Fishing boat 1.10 1.10
482 A79 60c Schooner 1.30 1.30
483 A79 75c Cargo boat 1.30 1.60
a. Souvenir sheet of 4, #480-483 4.50 4.50
Nos. 480-483 (4) 4.40 4.40

Four stamps picturing Michael Jackson were printed. The designs were not acceptable to the Virgin Islands so they were not issued. A number of stamps had been distributed in advance for publicity purposes.

New Coinage — A80

1985, Jan. 15 Litho. *Perf. 14½*

484 A80 1c Hawksbill Turtle .25 .25
485 A80 5c Bonito .25 .25
486 A80 10c Great Barricuda .25 .25
487 A80 25c Blue Marlin .55 .55
488 A80 50c Dolphin 1.15 1.25
489 A80 $1 Spotfin Butterfly Fish 2.25 2.25
a. Miniature sheet of 6, #484-489 5.00 5.00
Nos. 484-489 (6) 4.70 4.80

Birds — A81

1985, July 3 Wmk. 373 *Perf. 14*

490 A81 1c Boatswain bird 1.00 2.00
491 A81 2c Night gaulin 1.00 2.00
492 A81 5c Rain bird 1.50 1.50
493 A81 8c Mockingbird 1.50 2.50
494 A81 10c Chinchary 1.75 .50
495 A81 12c Wild pigeon 2.00 1.00
496 A81 15c Bittlin 2.50 1.00
497 A81 18c Blach witch 2.75 3.00
498 A81 20c Pond shakey 2.50 1.25
499 A81 25c Killy-killy 2.50 1.25
500 A81 30c Thrushie 2.50 1.00
501 A81 35c Marmi dove 2.50 1.00
502 A81 40c Little gaulin 3.00 1.25
503 A81 50c Ground dove 3.25 1.25
504 A81 60c Blue gaulin 3.75 4.50
505 A81 $1 Pimleco 4.75 5.50
506 A81 $2 White booby 5.25 8.00
507 A81 $3 Cow bird 7.25 12.50
508 A81 $5 Turtle dove 8.75 15.00
Nos. 490-508 (19) 60.00 66.00

For overprints see Nos. O16-O34.

1987, Oct. 28 Wmk. 384

494a A81 10c .90 .90
496a A81 15c 1.30 1.30
498a A81 20c 1.80 1.80
499a A81 25c 2.25 2.25
501a A81 35c 2.75 2.75
505a A81 $1 8.00 8.00
507a A81 $3 23.00 23.00
Nos. 494a-507a (7) 40.00 40.00

Queen Mother, 85th Birthday — A82

Portraits.

1985, Aug. 26 Litho. *Perf. 12½*

509 A82 10c Facing right .25 .25
510 A82 10c Facing left .25 .25
a. Pair, #509-510 .30 .30
511 A82 25c Facing right .25 .25
512 A82 25c Facing left .25 .25
a. Pair, #511-512 .55 .55
513 A82 50c Facing right .40 .40
514 A82 50c Facing forward .40 .40
a. Pair, #513-514 .85 .85
515 A82 75c Facing right .60 .60
516 A82 75c Facing forward .60 .60
a. Pair, #515-516 1.25 1.25
Nos. 509-516 (8) 3.00 3.00

Souvenir Sheets

1985-86 Litho. *Perf. 13x12½*

517 Sheet of 2 2.25 2.25
a.-b. A82 $1 dull grn & multi 1.10 1.10
518 Sheet of 2 3.00 3.00
a.-b. A82 $1 orange & multi 1.50 1.50
519 Sheet of 2 7.50 7.50
a.-b. A82 $2.50 dl yel & multi 3.75 3.75

Issued: #517, 12/18/85; #518-519, 2/18/86.

For overprints see Nos. 528-531.

Audubon Birth Bicent. — A83

1985, Dec. 17 *Perf. 15*

520 A83 5c Seaside sparrow .25 .25
521 A83 30c Passenger pigeon .50 .50
522 A83 50c Yellow-breasted chat .85 .85
523 A83 $1 American kestrel 1.40 1.40
Nos. 520-523 (4) 3.00 3.00

Exists imperf.

Cruise Ships — A84

1986, Jan. 27

524 A84 35c Flying Cloud .75 .75
525 A84 50c Newport Clipper 1.10 1.10
526 A84 75c Cunard Countess 1.75 1.75
527 A84 $1 Sea Goddess 2.50 2.50
Nos. 524-527 (4) 6.10 6.10

Nos. 511-512, 515-516 Ovptd.

1986, Apr. 17 Litho. *Perf. 12½*

528 A82 25c on No. 511 .50 .50
529 A82 25c on No. 512 .50 .50
530 A82 75c on No. 515 1.75 1.75
531 A82 75c on No. 516 1.75 1.75
Nos. 528-531 (4) 4.50 4.50

Queen Elizabeth II, 60th Birthday A85

12c, Portrait, 1958. 35c, Maundy service. $1.50, Contemporary photograph. $2, Canberra, 1982, vert.

$3, Contemporary photograph, diff.

Perf. 13x12½, 12½x13

1986, Apr. 21 Litho.

532 A85 12c multicolored .25 .25
533 A85 35c multicolored .25 .25
534 A85 $1.50 multicolored .60 .60
535 A85 $2 multicolored .90 .90
Nos. 532-535 (4) 2.00 2.00

Souvenir Sheet

536 A85 $3 multicolored 4.25 4.25

Stamps with blue ribbons and frames omitted were from stock sold when the printer was liquidated.

Wedding of Prince Andrew and Sarah Ferguson A86

1986, July 23 *Perf. 12½*

537 A86 35c Couple, vert. .45 .45
538 A86 35c Sarah, vert. .45 .45
539 A86 $1 Andrew .75 .75
540 A86 $1 Sarah, diff. .75 .75
Nos. 537-540 (4) 2.40 2.40

Stamps of the same denomination exist se-tenant.

Nos. 537-540 overprinted "Congratulations to T.R.H. The Duke & Duchess of York" were not issued.

Traditional Rum Production A87

1986, July 30 *Perf. 14*

541 A87 12c Harvesting sugar cane .50 .50
542 A87 40c Grinding 2.00 2.00
543 A87 60c Distillery 3.25 3.25
544 A87 $1 Transport 5.25 5.25
Nos. 541-544 (4) 11.00 11.00

Souvenir Sheet

545 A87 $2 Up Spirits ceremony, 19th cent. 6.50 6.50

Souvenir Sheet

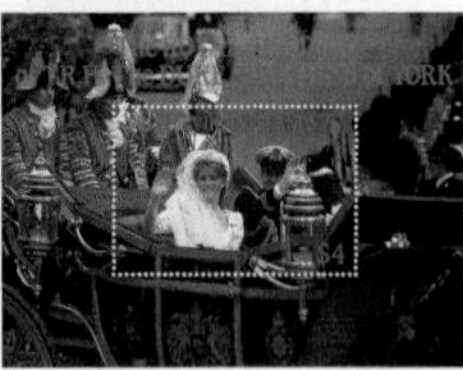

Wedding of Prince Andrew and Sarah Ferguson A88

1986, Oct. 15 Litho. ***Perf. 13x12½***
546 A88 $4 multicolored 3.75 3.75

Cable-Laying Ships — A89

1986, Oct. 15 Wmk. 380 ***Perf. 12½***
547 A89 35c Sentinel .65 .65
548 A89 35c Retriever .65 .65
a. Pair, #547-548 1.30 1.30
549 A89 60c Cable Enterprise 1.10 1.10
550 A89 60c Mercury 1.10 1.10
a. Pair, #549-550 2.25 2.25
551 A89 75c Recorder 1.25 1.25
552 A89 75c Pacific Guardian 1.25 1.25
a. Pair, #551-552 2.50 2.50
553 A89 $1 Great Eastern 1.75 1.75
554 A89 $1 Cable Venture 1.75 1.75
a. Pair, #553-554 3.50 3.50
Nos. 547-554 (8) 9.50 9.50

Souvenir Sheets

555 Sheet of 2 1.30 1.30
a.-b. A89 40c, like #547-548 .65 .65
556 Sheet of 2 1.60 1.60
a.-b. A89 50c, like #549-550 .80 .80
557 Sheet of 2 2.50 2.50
a.-b. A89 80c, like #551-552 1.25 1.25
558 Sheet of 2 4.75 4.75
a.-b. A89 $1.50, like #553-554 2.25 2.25

Cable and wireless in the islands, 20th anniv. Exists Imperf. Value, set of 4 sheets $50.

Souvenir Sheets

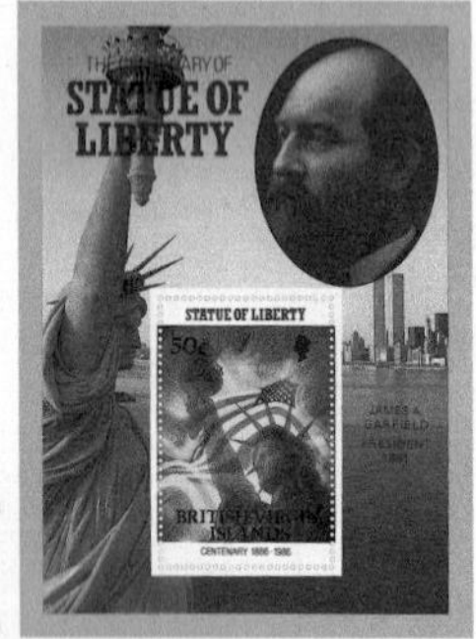

Statue of Liberty, Cent. A90

Various views of the statue.

1986, Dec. 15 Litho. ***Perf. 14***
559 A90 50c multicolored .60 .60
560 A90 75c multicolored 1.00 1.00
561 A90 90c multicolored 1.10 1.10
562 A90 $1 multicolored 1.30 1.30
563 A90 $1.25 multicolored 1.60 1.60
564 A90 $1.50 multicolored 1.90 1.90
565 A90 $1.75 multicolored 2.25 2.25
566 A90 $2 multicolored 2.40 2.40
567 A90 $2.50 multicolored 3.25 3.25
Nos. 559-567 (9) 15.40 15.40

A91

Shipwrecks — A92

12c, Spanish galleon, 18th cent. 35c, HMS Astrea, 1808. 75c, RMS Rhone, 1867. $1.50, SS Rocus, 1929.
$2.50, Brig Volvart, 1918.

1987, Apr. 15 ***Perf. 14***
572 A91 12c multicolored .85 .85
573 A91 35c multicolored 2.40 2.40
574 A91 75c multicolored 4.75 4.75
575 A91 $1.50 multicolored 10.00 10.00
Nos. 572-575 (4) 18.00 18.00

Souvenir Sheet

576 A92 $2.50 multicolored 16.00 16.00

Natl. Flags, Outline Maps — A93

1987, May 28
577 A93 10c Montserrat .25 .25
578 A93 15c Grenada .55 .55
579 A93 20c Dominica .80 .80
580 A93 25c St. Kitts-Nevis 1.00 1.00
581 A93 35c St. Vincent and Grenadines 1.25 1.25
582 A93 50c Virgin Isls. 1.90 1.90
583 A93 75c Antigua & Barbuda 2.75 2.75
584 A93 $1 St. Lucia 4.00 4.00
Nos. 577-584 (8) 12.50 12.50

11th Meeting of the Organization of Eastern Caribbean States.

Botanical Gardens — A94

1987, Aug. 12 Wmk. 384
585 A94 12c Spider lily .75 .75
586 A94 35c Barrel cactus 2.25 2.25
587 A94 $1 Wild plantain 3.25 3.25
588 A94 $1.50 Little butterfly orchid 9.25 9.25
Nos. 585-588 (4) 15.50 15.50

Souvenir Sheet

589 A94 $2.50 White cedar 4.50 4.50

Postal Service Bicent. — A95

Designs: 10c, 18th Cent. packet, #7 canceled "A13." 20c, Map of the islands, #22 canceled "A91." 35c, Tortola Post Office and Customs House, and #5 canceled "Tortola De 20 61." $1.50, Mail plane and #154 canceled "Road town No 2 64 Tortola W.I." $2.50, Late 19th cent. steam packet and #10 canceled "A Tortola Ap 12 70."

1987, Dec. 17 Litho. ***Perf. 14½***
590 A95 10c multicolored .70 .70
591 A95 20c multicolored 1.40 1.40
592 A95 35c multicolored 2.25 2.25
593 A95 $1.50 multicolored 10.00 10.00
Nos. 590-593 (4) 14.35 14.35

Souvenir Sheet

594 A95 $2.50 multicolored 7.00 7.00

Paintings by Titian — A96

10c, Salome, 1512. 12c, Man with the Glove, c. 1520-22. 20c, Fabrizio Salvaresio, 1558. 25c, Daughter of Roberto Strozzi, 1542. 40c, Pope Julius II. 50c, Bishop Ludovico Beccadelli, 1552. 60c, Philip II. $1, Empress Isabella of Portugal, 1548. #603, Emperor Charles V at Muhlberg, 1548. #604, Pope Paul III & His Grandsons, 1546.

Perf. 13½x14

1988, Aug. 11 Unwmk.
595 A96 10c multicolored .65 .65
596 A96 12c multicolored .70 .70
597 A96 20c multicolored .90 .90
598 A96 25c multicolored 1.00 1.00
599 A96 40c multicolored 1.60 1.60
600 A96 50c multicolored 1.75 1.75
601 A96 60c multicolored 1.90 1.90
602 A96 $1 multicolored 2.50 2.50
Nos. 595-602 (8) 11.00 11.00

Souvenir Sheet

603 A96 $2 multicolored 10.00 10.00
604 A96 $2 multicolored 10.00 10.00

1st Annual Open Chess Tournament A97

35c, Pawn & Transporter aircraft over Sir Francis Drake Channel. $1, King & Jose Raul Capablanca (1888-1942), Cuban chess master and world champion from 1921-27. $2, Match scene.

1988, Aug. 25 Unwmk. ***Perf. 14***
605 A97 35c multicolored 4.00 4.00
606 A97 $1 multicolored 11.50 11.50

Souvenir Sheet

607 A97 $2 multicolored 12.50 12.50

1988 Summer Olympics, Seoul — A98

1988, Sept. 8
608 A98 12c Hurdling .65 .65
609 A98 20c Windsurfing 1.10 1.10
610 A98 75c Basketball 3.75 3.75
611 A98 $1 Tennis 4.00 4.00
Nos. 608-611 (4) 9.50 9.50

Souvenir Sheet

612 A98 $2 Running 5.25 5.25

Intl. Red Cross, 125th Anniv. — A99

Safety warnings and steps in administering cardiopulmonary resuscitation (CPR): 12c, "Don't swim alone." 30c, "No swimming during electrical storms." 60c, "Don't eat before swimming." $1, "Proper equipment for boating." No. 617a, Turn victim on back. No. 617b, Position victim's chin so breathing passages are not blocked. No. 617c, Mouth-to-mouth resuscitation. No. 617d, Chest compressions. Nos. 617a-617d vert.

1988, Sept. 26
613 A99 12c multicolored .80 .80
614 A99 30c multicolored 2.00 2.00
615 A99 60c multicolored 3.75 3.75
616 A99 $1 multicolored 6.50 6.50
Nos. 613-616 (4) 13.05 13.05

Souvenir Sheet

617 Sheet of 4 6.25 6.25
a.-d. A99 50c any single 1.10 1.10

#617a-617d has a continuous design.

Visit of Princess Alexandra — A100

Various photographs of the princess.

1988, Nov. 9 Litho. ***Perf. 14***
618 A100 40c shown 2.75 2.75
619 A100 $1.50 multi, diff. 6.00 6.00

Souvenir Sheet

620 A100 $2 multi, diff. 8.00 8.00

World Wildlife Fund — A101

Brown pelicans, Pelecanus Occidentalis: 10c, Pelican in flight. 12c, Perched. 15c, Close-up of head. 35c, Swallowing fish.

1988, Nov. 15
621 A101 10c multicolored 1.50 1.50
622 A101 12c multicolored 1.75 1.75
623 A101 15c multicolored 2.00 2.00
624 A101 35c multicolored 4.00 4.00
Nos. 621-624 (4) 9.25 9.25

Reptiles, Marine Mammals and Birds — A102

20c, Anegada rock iguana. 40c, Virgin gorda dwarf gecko. 60c, Hawksbill turtle. $1, Humpback whale. #629, Northern shoveler, American widgeon & ring-necked ducks. #630, Trunk turtle.

1988, Nov. 15
625 A102 20c multicolored 1.50 1.50
626 A102 40c multicolored 2.00 2.00
627 A102 60c multicolored 3.00 3.00
628 A102 $1 multicolored 7.00 7.00
Nos. 625-628 (4) 13.50 13.50

Souvenir Sheets

629 A102 $2 multicolored 11.50 11.50
630 A102 $2 multicolored 6.50 6.50

Spring Regatta — A103

Various yachts.

1989, Apr. 7 Litho. ***Perf. 14***
631 A103 12c multi, diff., vert. .45 .45
632 A103 40c shown 1.40 1.40
633 A103 75c multi, diff., vert. 2.00 2.00
634 A103 $1 multi, diff. 3.00 3.00
Nos. 631-634 (4) 6.85 6.85

Souvenir Sheet

635 A103 $2 multi, diff., vert. 7.00 7.00

Pre-Columbian Societies and Their Customs A104

1989, May 18
636 A104 10c Hammock .75 .75
637 A104 20c Making a fire .95 .95
638 A104 25c Carvers 1.10 1.10
639 A104 $1.50 Arawak family 5.25 5.25
Nos. 636-639 (4) 8.05 8.05

Souvenir Sheet

640 A104 $2 Ritual 10.00 10.00

Discovery of America 500th anniv. (in 1992).

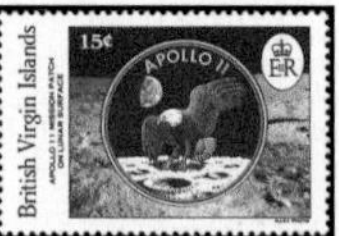

1st Moon Landing, 20th Anniv. — A105

Highlights of the Apollo 11 mission: 15c, Lunar surface, mission emblem. 30c, Buzz Aldrin conducting solar wind experiment. 65c, Raising American flag. $1, Recovery of crew after splashdown. $2, Portrait of crew.

1989, Sept. 28 Litho. *Perf. 14*

641 A105 15c multicolored 1.00 1.00
642 A105 30c multicolored 1.75 1.75
643 A105 65c multicolored 3.50 3.50
644 A105 $1 multicolored 5.00 5.00
Nos. 641-644 (4) 11.25 11.25

Souvenir Sheet

Perf. 13½x14

645 A105 $2 multicolored 11.00 11.00

No. 645 contains one 37x46mm stamp.

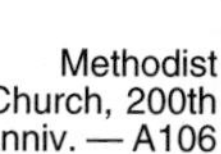

Methodist Church, 200th Anniv. — A106

Designs: 12c, Black Harry, Nathaniel Gilbert preaching. 25c, Book symbolizing role of the church in education. 35c, East End Methodist Church, 1810. $1.25, John Wesley, modern youth choir. $2, Thomas Coke.

1989, Oct. 24 *Perf. 14*

646 A106 12c multicolored .50 .50
647 A106 25c multicolored 1.10 1.10
648 A106 35c multicolored 1.60 1.60
649 A106 $1.25 multicolored 5.75 5.75
Nos. 646-649 (4) 8.95 8.95

Souvenir Sheet

650 A106 $2 multicolored 8.00 8.00

1990 World Cup Soccer Championships, Italy — A107

Various athletes.

1989, Nov. 6

651 A107 5c shown .65 .65
652 A107 10c multi, diff. .65 .65
653 A107 20c multi, diff. 1.25 1.25
654 A107 $1.75 multi, diff. 10.00 10.00
Nos. 651-654 (4) 12.55 12.55

Souvenir Sheet

655 A107 $2 Natl. team 10.00 10.00

Princess Alexandra, Sunset House — A108

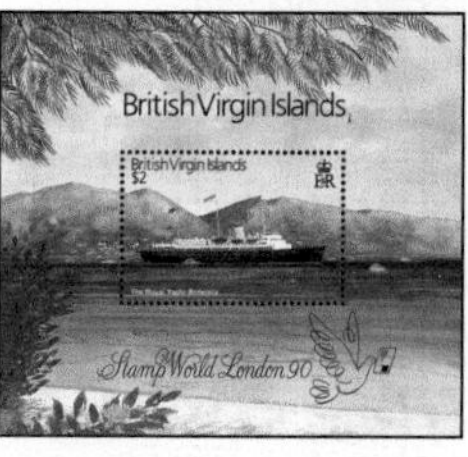

Royal Yacht Britannia A109

b, Princess Margaret, Government House. c, Hon. Angus Ogilvy, Little Dix Bay Hotel. d, Princess Diana & her children, Necker Island Resort.

1990, May 3 Litho. *Perf. 14*

656 Min. sheet of 4 13.00 13.00
a.-d. A108 50c any single 1.25 1.25

Souvenir Sheet

657 A109 $2 multicolored 14.00 14.00

Stamp World London '90.

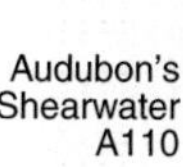

Audubon's Shearwater A110

12c, Red-necked pigeon. 20c, Common gallinule. 25c, Green heron. 40c, Yellow warbler. 60c, Smooth-billed ani. $1, Antillean crested hummingbird. $1.25, Black-faced grassquit.

No. 666, Egg of royal tern. No. 667, Egg of red-billed tropicbird.

1990, May 15

658 A110 5c shown 1.50 1.50
659 A110 12c multicolored 2.25 2.25
660 A110 20c multicolored 2.50 2.50
661 A110 25c multicolored 2.50 2.50
662 A110 40c multicolored 2.75 2.75
663 A110 60c multicolored 3.00 3.00
664 A110 $1 multicolored 3.00 3.00
665 A110 $1.25 multicolored 3.00 3.00
Nos. 658-665 (8) 20.50 20.50

Souvenir Sheets

666 A110 $2 multicolored 6.75 6.75
667 A110 $2 multicolored 6.75 6.75

Blue Tang — A111

1990, June 18

668 A111 10c shown .60 .60
669 A111 35c Glasseye 2.40 2.40
670 A111 50c Slippery Dick 3.50 3.50
671 A111 $1 Porkfish 6.75 6.75
Nos. 668-671 (4) 13.25 13.25

Souvenir Sheet

672 A111 $2 Yellowtail snapper 6.25 6.25

A112

1990, Aug. 30 Litho. *Perf. 14*

673 A112 12c multicolored .40 .40
674 A112 25c multi, diff. .85 .85
675 A112 60c multi, diff. 2.25 2.25
676 A112 $1 multi, diff. 3.00 3.00
Nos. 673-676 (4) 6.50 6.50

Souvenir Sheet

677 A112 $2 multi, diff. 4.75 4.75

Queen Mother, 90th birthday.

A113

Various soccer players.

1990, Dec. 10 Litho. *Perf. 14*

678 A113 12c multicolored .45 .45
679 A113 20c multi, diff. .80 .80
680 A113 50c multi, diff. 1.90 1.90
681 A113 $1.25 multi, diff. 4.00 4.00
Nos. 678-681 (4) 7.15 7.15

Souvenir Sheet

682 A113 $2 multi, diff. 5.75 5.75

World Cup Soccer Championships, Italy.

1992 Summer Olympics, Barcelona A114

1990, Dec. 20 Litho. *Perf. 14*

683 A114 12c Judo .65 .65
684 A114 40c Yachting 2.10 2.10
685 A114 60c Hurdles 3.25 3.25
686 A114 $1 Show jumping 5.50 5.50
Nos. 683-686 (4) 11.50 11.50

Souvenir Sheet

687 A114 $2 Windsurfing 5.50 5.50

Copper Mine Ruins — A115

10c, Cyathea arborea, vert. 35c, Mt. Healthy windmill ruin, vert. $2, Baths, Virgin Gorda.

1991, Mar. 1 Litho. *Perf. 14*

688 A115 10c multicolored .50 .50
689 A115 25c shown 1.25 1.25
690 A115 35c multicolored 2.00 2.00
691 A115 $2 multicolored 9.25 9.25
Nos. 688-691 (4) 13.00 13.00

National Park Trust.

Flowers — A116

1c, Haiti Haiti. 2c, Lobster claw. 5c, Frangipani. 10c, Autograph tree. 12c, Yellow allamanda. 15c, Lantana. 20c, Jerusalem thorn. 25c, Turk's cap. 30c, Swamp immortelle. 35c, White cedar. 40c, Mahoe tree. 45c, Pinguin. 50c, Christmas orchid. 70c, Lignum vitae. $1, African tulip tree. $2, Beach morning glory. $3, Organ pipe cactus. $5, Tall ground orchid. $10, Ground orchid.

1991-92 Litho. *Perf. 14*

No Date Imprint Below Design

692 A116 1c multicolored .25 .25
693 A116 2c multicolored .25 .25
694 A116 5c multicolored .25 .25
695 A116 10c multicolored .25 .25
696 A116 12c multicolored .25 .25
697 A116 15c multicolored .40 .40
698 A116 20c multicolored .55 .55
699 A116 25c multicolored .65 .65
700 A116 30c multicolored .75 .75
701 A116 35c multicolored .85 .85
702 A116 40c multicolored 1.00 1.00
703 A116 45c multicolored 1.10 1.10
704 A116 50c multicolored 1.25 1.25
a. Perf 12 2.00 2.00
705 A116 70c multicolored 1.75 1.75
706 A116 $1 multicolored 2.50 2.50
a. Perf 12 3.25 3.25
707 A116 $2 multicolored 5.00 5.00
a. Perf 12 6.50 6.50
708 A116 $3 multicolored 7.25 7.25
a. Perf 12½x11½ 10.00 10.00
709 A116 $5 multicolored 10.00 10.00
710 A116 $10 multicolored 21.00 21.00
Nos. 692-710 (19) 55.30 55.30

Issued: 1c-$5, 5/1/91; $10, 5/92; Nos. 704a, 706a, 707a, 708a, 8/95.

For overprints see Nos. O37-O51.

1995, June 1 Wmk. 373 Sideways

Inscribed "1995" Below Design

695b A116 10c multicolored .60 *1.60*
697b A116 15c multicolored .80 .50
700b A116 30c multicolored .85 .60
701b A116 35c multicolored 1.00 .65
703b A116 45c multicolored 1.20 1.00
704b A116 50c multicolored 2.75 2.10
707b A116 $2 multicolored 3.75 *6.00*
709b A116 $5 multicolored 10.50 *14.00*
Nos. 695b-709b (8) 21.45 *26.45*

Butterflies — A117

5c, Cloudless sulphur. 10c, Flambeau. 15c, Caribbean buckeye. 20c, Gulf fritillary. 25c, Polydamus swallowtail. 30c, Little sulphur. 35c, Zebra. $1.50, Malachite.

No. 719, Monarch, horiz. No. 720, Red rim, horiz.

Unwmk.

1991, June 28 Litho. *Perf. 14*

711 A117 5c multicolored .50 .50
712 A117 10c multicolored .50 .50
713 A117 15c multicolored .85 .85
714 A117 20c multicolored 1.25 1.25
715 A117 25c multicolored 1.40 1.40
716 A117 30c multicolored 1.75 1.75
717 A117 35c multicolored 2.10 2.10
718 A117 $1.50 multicolored 8.75 8.75
Nos. 711-718 (8) 17.10 17.10

Souvenir Sheets

719 A117 $2 multicolored 8.75 8.75
720 A117 $2 multicolored 8.75 8.75

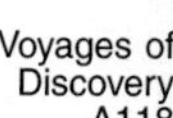

Voyages of Discovery A118

Ships of explorers: 12c, Ferdinand Magellan, 1519-1521. 50c, Rene-Robert de la Salle, 1682. 75c, John Cabot, 1497-1498. $1, Jacques Cartier, 1534. $2, Columbus' ship, 1493 woodcut, vert.

1991, Sept. 20 Litho. *Perf. 14*

721 A118 12c multicolored 2.00 2.00
722 A118 50c multicolored 3.00 3.00
723 A118 75c multicolored 3.75 3.75
724 A118 $1 multicolored 5.00 5.00
Nos. 721-724 (4) 13.75 13.75

Souvenir Sheet

725 A118 $2 multicolored 10.00 10.00

Vincent Van Gogh (1853-1890), Painter A119

Paintings: 15c, Cottage with Decrepit Barn and Stooping Woman. 30c, Paul Gauguin's Armchair, vert. 75c, Breton Women. $1, Vase with Red Gladioli, vert. $2, The Dance Hall in Arles (detail).

1991, Nov. 1 *Perf. 13*

726 A119 15c multicolored 1.25 1.25
727 A119 30c multicolored 1.75 1.75
728 A119 75c multicolored 4.50 4.50
729 A119 $1 multicolored 5.75 5.75
Nos. 726-729 (4) 13.25 13.25

Souvenir Sheet

730 A119 $2 multicolored 12.50 12.50

Christmas — A120

Entire paintings or details by Quinten Massys: 15c, The Virgin and Child Enthroned. 30c, The Virgin and Child Enthroned, diff. 60c, The Adoration of the Magi. $1, Virgin in Adoration. No. 735, The Virgin Standing with Angels. No. 736, The Adoration of the Magi.

1991, Dec. 12 Litho. *Perf. 12*

731 A120 15c multicolored 1.25 1.25
732 A120 30c multicolored 1.75 1.75
733 A120 60c multicolored 3.50 3.50
734 A120 $1 multicolored 4.75 4.75
Nos. 731-734 (4) 11.25 11.25

Souvenir Sheets

Perf. 14½

735 A120 $2 multicolored 7.00 7.00
736 A120 $2 multicolored 7.00 7.00

Mushrooms A121

12c, Agaricus bisporus, vert. 30c, Lentinus edodes. 45c, Hyrocybe acutoconica, vert. $1, Gymnopilus chrysopellus.

$2, Pleurotus ostreatus.

1992, Jan. 15 *Perf. 14*

737 A121 12c multicolored 1.75 1.75
738 A121 30c multicolored 2.10 2.10
739 A121 45c multicolored 3.25 3.25
740 A121 $1 multicolored 5.50 5.50
Nos. 737-740 (4) 12.60 12.60

Souvenir Sheet

741 A121 $2 multicolored 15.00 15.00

Queen Elizabeth II's Accession to the Throne, 40th Anniv.

Common Design Type

1992, Feb. 6 Litho. *Perf. 14*

742 CD348 12c multicolored .40 .40
743 CD348 45c multicolored 1.50 1.50
744 CD348 60c multicolored 2.10 2.10
745 CD348 $1 multicolored 3.50 3.50
Nos. 742-745 (4) 7.50 7.50

Souvenir Sheet

746 CD348 $2 multicolored 8.00 8.00

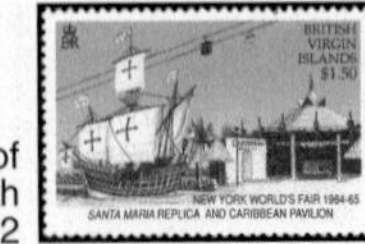

Discovery of America, 500th Anniv. — A122

10c, Queen Isabella. 15c, Columbus' fleet. 20c, Columbus' second coat of arms. 30c, Landing Monument on Watling Island, Columbus' signature. 45c, Columbus. 50c, Flag of Ferdinand & Isabella, Columbus landing on Watling Island. 70c, Convent at La Rabida. $1.50, Replica of Santa Maria at New York World's Fair, 1964-65. #755, Columbus' 2nd fleet. #756, Map.

1992, May 26 Litho. *Perf. 14*

747 A122 10c multi, vert. .90 .90
748 A122 15c multi 1.60 1.60
749 A122 20c multi, vert. 1.60 1.60
750 A122 30c multi 1.60 1.60
751 A122 45c multi, vert. 2.25 2.25
752 A122 50c multi 2.25 2.25
753 A122 70c multi, vert. 2.50 2.50
754 A122 $1.50 multi 3.75 3.75
Nos. 747-754 (8) 16.45 16.45

Souvenir Sheet

755 A122 $2 multicolored 7.50 7.50
756 A122 $2 multicolored 7.50 7.50

1992 Summer Olympics, Barcelona — A123

1992, Aug. Litho. *Perf. 14*

757 A123 15c Basketball 2.50 2.50
758 A123 30c Tennis 2.75 2.75
759 A123 60c Volleyball 3.00 3.00
760 A123 $1 Soccer 3.25 3.25
Nos. 757-760 (4) 11.50 11.50

Souvenir Sheet

761 A123 $2 Olympic flame 14.00 14.00

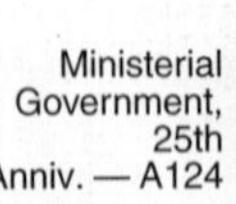

Ministerial Government, 25th Anniv. — A124

Designs: 12c, Social progress and development. 15c, Map of Virgin Islands. 45c, Administration complex. $1.30, International finance.

1993, Apr. Litho. *Perf. 14*

762 A124 12c multicolored .35 .35
763 A124 15c multicolored .40 .40
764 A124 45c multicolored 1.25 1.25
765 A124 $1.30 multicolored 3.75 3.75
Nos. 762-765 (4) 5.75 5.75

Tourism — A125

15c, Swimming from anchored yacht. 30c, Sailboat. 60c, Scuba diver in pink wetsuit. $1, Snorkelers, anchored boat.

#770: a, Trimaran, vert. b, Scuba diver, vert.

1993, Apr. Litho. *Perf. 14*

766 A125 15c multi 1.50 1.50
767 A125 30c multi, vert. 2.00 2.00
768 A125 60c multi 2.50 2.50
769 A125 $1 multi, vert. 3.00 3.00
Nos. 766-769 (4) 9.00 9.00

Souvenir Sheet

770 A125 $1 Sheet of 2, #a.-b. 9.00 9.00

Miniature Sheet

Coronation of Queen Elizabeth II, 40th Anniv. — A126

No. 771: a, 12c, Official coronation photograph. b, 45c, Dove atop Rod of Equity and Mercy. c, 60c, Royal family. d, $1, Recent color photo.

1993, June 2 Litho. *Perf. 13½x14*

771 A126 Sheet, 2 each #a.-d. 12.00 12.00

A souvenir sheet containing a $2 stamp was not an authorized issue. Value $18.

Discovery of Virgin Islands, 500th Anniv. — A127

3c, Ferdinand and Isabella supporting Columbus. 12c, Departure of Columbus. 15c, Departure of second voyage. 25c, Arms, flag of British Virgin Islands. 30c, Columbus, Santa Maria. 45c, Columbus' second fleet at sea. 60c, Rowing ashore. $1, Landing of Columbus. #781, Natives watching ships. #782, Columbus, two ships of his fleet.

1993, Sept. 24 Litho. *Perf. 14*

773 A127 3c multicolored .30 .30
774 A127 12c multicolored .40 .40
775 A127 15c multicolored .55 .55
776 A127 25c multicolored .85 .85
777 A127 30c multicolored 1.10 1.10
778 A127 45c multicolored 1.50 1.50
779 A127 60c multicolored 2.10 2.10
780 A127 $1 multicolored 3.50 3.50
Nos. 773-780 (8) 10.30 10.30

Souvenir Sheets

781 A127 $2 multicolored 7.50 7.50
782 A127 $2 multicolored 7.50 7.50

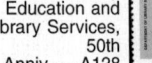

Secondary Education and Library Services, 50th Anniv. — A128

Designs: 5c, Historical documents. 10c, Sporting activities. 15c, Stanley W. Nibbs, educator, vert. 20c, Bookmobile. 30c, Norwell E. Harrigan, educator, vert. 35c, Public library's annual summer program. 70c, Text. $1, High school.

Perf. 14x13½, 13½x14

1993, Dec. Litho.

783 A128 5c multicolored .50 .50
784 A128 10c multicolored 2.50 2.50
785 A128 15c multicolored .70 .70
786 A128 20c multicolored 1.00 1.00
787 A128 30c multicolored 1.60 1.60
788 A128 35c multicolored 1.90 1.90
789 A128 70c multicolored 3.00 3.00
790 A128 $1 multicolored 3.25 3.25
Nos. 783-790 (8) 14.45 14.45

Anegada Ground Iguana — A129

5c, Crawling right. 10c, Head up to right. 15c, View from behind. 45c, Head up to left. $2, Head.

1994, Jan. Litho. *Perf. 14*

791 A129 5c multicolored .90 .90
792 A129 10c multicolored .90 .90
793 A129 15c multicolored 1.25 1.25
794 A129 45c multicolored 2.00 2.00
Nos. 791-794 (4) 5.05 5.05

Souvenir Sheet

795 A129 $2 multicolored 6.25 6.25

World Wildlife Fund.

Rotary Club of Virgin Islands, 25th Anniv. — A130

Designs: 15c, Disaster relief airlift. 45c, Kids, Sea "Kats." 50c, Donated hospital equipment. 90c, Paul P. Harris (1868-1947), founder of Rotary Intl.

1994, June 3 Litho. *Perf. 14*

796 A130 15c multicolored .60 .60
797 A130 45c multicolored 1.35 1.35
798 A130 50c multicolored 1.50 1.50
799 A130 90c multicolored 2.50 2.50
Nos. 796-799 (4) 5.95 5.95

Miniature Sheet of 6

First Manned Moon Landing, 25th Anniv. — A131

Designs: No. 800a, Anniversary emblem. b, Lunar landing training vehicle. c, Apollo 11 lift-off, July 16, 1969. d, Lunar module Eagle in flight. e, Moon landing site approached by Eagle. f, 1st step on Moon, July 20, 1969.

No. 801, Mission patch, crew signatures.

1994, Sept. 30 Litho. *Perf. 14*

800 A131 50c #a.-f. 15.00 15.00

Souvenir Sheet

801 A131 $2 multicolored 14.00 14.00

A132

Previous champions: 15c, Argentina, 1978. 35c, Italy, 1982. 50c, Argentina, 1986. $1.30, W. Germany, 1990.

$2, US flag, World Cup trophy, horiz.

1994, Dec. 16 Litho. *Perf. 14*

802 A132 15c multicolored 1.50 1.50
803 A132 35c multicolored 2.00 2.00
804 A132 50c multicolored 2.25 2.25
805 A132 $1.30 multicolored 5.50 5.50
Nos. 802-805 (4) 11.25 11.25

Souvenir Sheet

806 A132 $2 multicolored 14.00 14.00

1994 World Cup Soccer Championships, US.

UN, 50th Anniv.

Common Design Type

Designs: 15c, Peugeot P4 all-purpose light vehicle. 30c, Foden medium tanker. 45c, Sisu all-terrain vehicle. $2, Westland Lynx AH7 helicopter.

Wmk. 373

1995, Oct. 24 Litho. *Perf. 14*

807 CD353 15c multicolored .45 .45
808 CD353 30c multicolored .90 .90
809 CD353 45c multicolored 1.60 1.60
810 CD353 $2 multicolored 4.50 4.50
Nos. 807-810 (4) 7.45 7.45

A133

Anegada Flamingos.

Wmk. 373

1995, Nov. 15 Litho. *Perf. 13*

811 A133 15c Juveniles .50 .50
812 A133 20c Adults .75 .75
813 A133 60c Adult feeding 2.25 2.25
814 A133 $1.45 Adult feeding chick 4.00 4.00
Nos. 811-814 (4) 7.50 7.50

Souvenir Sheet

815 A133 $2 Chicks 8.50 8.50

Christmas A134

Children's paintings: 12c, House with palm trees. 50c, Santa in boat. 70c, Red house, Christmas tree, presents. $1.30, Dove of peace.

Wmk. 384

1995, Dec. 1 Litho. *Perf. 14*

816 A134 12c multicolored 2.00 2.00
817 A134 50c multicolored 2.75 2.75
818 A134 70c multicolored 3.75 3.75
819 A134 $1.30 multicolored 5.50 5.50
Nos. 816-819 (4) 14.00 14.00

Island Scenes — A135

Designs: 15c, Seine fishing. 35c, Sandy Spit, Jost Van Dyke. 90c, Map of Jost Van Dyke. $1.50, Foxy's wooden boat regatta.

Perf. 13½x13

1996, Feb. 14 Litho. Wmk. 373

820 A135 15c multicolored 1.50 1.50
821 A135 35c multicolored 1.60 1.60
822 A135 90c multicolored 3.50 3.50
823 A135 $1.50 multicolored 5.50 5.50
Nos. 820-823 (4) 12.10 12.10

See Nos. 892-896.

Queen Elizabeth II, 70th Birthday

Common Design Type

Queen in various attire, scenes of Virgin Islands: 10c, Government House, Tortola. 30c, Legislative Council Chambers. 45c, Road Harbor. $1.50, Map of Virgin Islands.

$2, Wearing royal crown.

Perf. 13½x14

1996, Apr. 22 Litho. Wmk. 373

824 CD354 10c multicolored .30 .30
825 CD354 30c multicolored 1.00 1.00
826 CD354 45c multicolored 1.50 1.50
827 CD354 $1.50 multicolored 4.25 4.25
Nos. 824-827 (4) 7.05 7.05

Souvenir Sheet

Perf. 13x13½

828 CD354 $2 multicolored 4.25 4.25

Modern Olympic Games, Cent. — A136

Wmk. 373

1996, May 22 Litho. *Perf. 13*

829 A136 20c Hurdles .65 .65
830 A136 35c Volleyball 1.25 1.25
831 A136 50c Swimming 1.40 1.40
832 A136 $1 Sailing 2.50 2.50
Nos. 829-832 (4) 5.80 5.80

CAPEX '96 — A137

Vintage automobiles: 15c, 1934 Mercedes-Benz 500KA Cabriolet. 40c, 1934 Citroen 12. 60c, 1932 Cadillac V-8 Sport Phaeton. $1.35, 1934 Rolls Royce Phantom II.

$2, 1932 Ford Sport Coupe.

Wmk. 373

1996, June 8 Litho. *Perf. 13½*

833 A137 15c multicolored .35 .35
834 A137 40c multicolored 1.00 1.00
835 A137 60c multicolored 1.75 1.75
836 A137 $1.35 multicolored 3.75 3.75
Nos. 833-836 (4) 6.85 6.85

Souvenir Sheet

837 A137 $2 multicolored 4.25 4.25

UNICEF, 50th Anniv. — A138

Goals of UNICEF for the year 2000: 10c, Educate the child. 15c, Children first. 30c, Children have rights. 45c, No more polio.

Perf. 14x14½

1996, Sept. 16 Litho. Wmk. 373

838 A138 10c multicolored .45 .45
839 A138 15c multicolored .70 .70
840 A138 30c multicolored 1.60 1.60
841 A138 45c multicolored 1.75 1.75
Nos. 838-841 (4) 4.50 4.50

Girl Guiding in Virgin Islands, 25th Anniv. A139

Designs: 10c, Rainbows, arts and crafts. 15c, Brownies, community service. 30c, Guides, campfire. 45c, Rangers, H.M. Queen's birthday parade. $2, Lady Baden-Powell, world chief guide.

Wmk. 373

1996, Dec. 30 Litho. *Perf. 13½*

842 A139 10c multicolored .25 .25
843 A139 15c multicolored .40 .40
844 A139 30c multicolored .70 .70
845 A139 45c multicolored 1.00 1.00
846 A139 $2 multicolored 3.50 3.50
Nos. 842-846 (5) 5.85 5.85

Game Fish — A140

1997, Jan. 6 Wmk. 384 *Perf. 14*

847 A140 1c Mackerel .25 .25
848 A140 10c Wahoo .25 .25
849 A140 15c Barracuda .35 .35
850 A140 20c Tarpon .50 .50
851 A140 25c Tiger shark .60 .60
852 A140 35c Sailfish .85 .85
853 A140 40c Dolphin .95 .95
854 A140 50c Blackfin tuna 1.25 1.25
855 A140 60c Yellowfin tuna 1.50 1.50
856 A140 75c Kingfish 1.75 1.75
857 A140 $1.50 White marlin 3.50 3.50
a. Souvenir sheet of 1, wmk. 373 4.50 4.50
858 A140 $1.85 Amberjack 4.50 4.50
859 A140 $2 Bonito 4.75 4.75
860 A140 $5 Bonefish 12.00 12.00
861 A140 $10 Blue marlin 24.00 24.00
Nos. 847-861 (15) 57.00 57.00

No. 857a, Hong Kong '97.
See Nos. 1020-1023.

Queen Elizabeth II and Prince Philip, 50th Wedding Anniv. A141

#862, Prince with horse. #863, Queen Elizabeth II. #864, Queen riding in open carriage. #865, Prince Philip. #866, Queen holding hat down, Prince. #867, Prince Charles on polo pony.
$2, Queen, Prince riding in open carriage, horiz.

Wmk. 373

1997, July 10 Litho. *Perf. 13*

862 30c multicolored .70 .70
863 30c multicolored .70 .70
a. A141 Pair, #862-863 1.75 1.75
864 45c multicolored 1.00 1.00
865 45c multicolored 1.00 1.00
a. A141 Pair, #864-865 2.50 2.50
866 70c multicolored 1.50 1.50
867 70c multicolored 1.50 1.50
a. A141 Pair, #866-867 4.00 4.00
Nos. 862-867 (6) 6.40 6.40

Souvenir Sheet

868 A141 $2 multicolored 4.50 4.50

Crabs — A142

Wmk. 373

1997, Sept. 11 Litho. *Perf. 13*

869 A142 12c Fiddler .40 .40
870 A142 15c Coral .60 .60
871 A142 35c Blue 1.50 1.50
872 A142 $1 Giant hermit 3.00 3.00
Nos. 869-872 (4) 5.50 5.50

Souvenir Sheet

873 A142 $2 Arrow 5.00 5.00

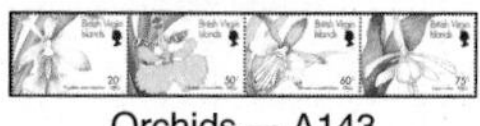

Orchids — A143

Designs: a, 20c, Psychilis macconnelliae. b, 50c, Tolumnia prionochila. c, 60c, Tetramicra canaliculata. d, 75c, Liparis elata.
$2, Dendrobium crumenatum, vert.

Wmk. 373

1997, Nov. 26 Litho. *Perf. 14*

874 A143 Strip of 4, #a.-d. 7.00 7.00

Souvenir Sheet

875 A143 $2 multicolored 4.50 4.50

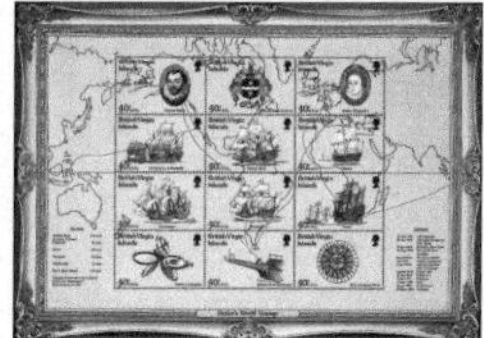

World Voyage of Sir Francis Drake — A144

Portions of map and: No. 876: a, Francis Drake. b, Drake Coat of Arms. c, Queen Elizabeth I. d, Christopher & Marigold. e, Golden Hinde. f, Swan. g, Cacafuego. h, Elizabeth. i, Maria. j, Drake's Astrolabe. k, Golden Hinde beakhead. l, 16th cent. compass rose.
$2, Modern ship named, "Sir Francis Drake."

1997, Dec. 13 *Perf. 14½*

876 A144 40c Sheet of 12, #a.-l. 20.00 20.00

Souvenir Sheet

877 A144 $2 multicolored 5.00 5.00

Diana, Princess of Wales (1961-97)
Common Design Type

Portraits: a, 15c. b, 45c. c, 70c. d, $1.

Perf. 14½x14

1998, Mar. 31 Litho. Wmk. 373

878 CD355 Sheet of 4, #a.-d. 4.50 4.50

No. 878 sold for $2.30 + 20c, with surtax from international sales being donated to the Princess Diana Memorial Fund and surtax from national sales being donated to designated local charity.

Royal Air Force, 80th Anniv.
Common Design Type of 1993 Re-inscribed

Designs: 20c, Fairey IIIF. 35c, Supermarine Scapa. 50c, Westland Sea King HAR3. $1.50, BAe Harrier GR7.
No. 883: a, Curtiss H.12 Large America. b, Curtiss JN-4A. c, Bell Airacobra. d, Boulton-Paul Defiant.

Perf. 13½x14

1998, Apr. 1 Litho. Wmk. 373

879 CD350 20c multicolored .50 .50
880 CD350 35c multicolored 1.00 1.00
881 CD350 50c multicolored 1.50 1.50
882 CD350 $1.50 multicolored 3.50 3.50
Nos. 879-882 (4) 6.50 6.50

Souvenir Sheet

883 CD350 75c Sheet of 4, #a.-d. 8.50 8.50

Marine Life — A145

Designs: 15c, Fingerprint cyphoma. 30c, Long spined sea urchin. 45c, Split crown feather duster worm. $1, Upside down jelly.
$2, Giant anemone.

1998, May 20 Wmk. 384 *Perf. 14½*

884 A145 15c multicolored 1.00 1.00
885 A145 30c multicolored 1.40 1.40
886 A145 45c multicolored 2.10 2.10
887 A145 $1 multicolored 3.75 3.75
Nos. 884-887 (4) 8.25 8.25

Souvenir Sheet

888 A145 $2 multicolored 6.00 6.00

No. 888 is a continuous design.

Childrens' Art Festival — A146

Wmk. 373

1998, Aug. 25 Litho. *Perf. 14*

889 A146 30c Girl in yellow & red, vert. 1.00 1.00
890 A146 45c Dancer, vert. 1.60 1.60
891 A146 $1.30 shown 4.50 4.50
Nos. 889-891 (3) 7.10 7.10

Island Scenes Type of 1996

Designs: 12c, Salt pond. 30c, Shipwreck, HMS Rhone. 70c, Traditional house. $1.45, Salt Island.
$2, Gathering salt.

1998, Oct. 28

892 A135 12c multicolored 1.50 1.50
893 A135 30c multicolored 2.00 2.00
894 A135 70c multicolored 2.50 2.50
895 A135 $1.45 multicolored 4.00 4.00
Nos. 892-895 (4) 10.00 10.00

Souvenir Sheet

896 A135 $2 multicolored 9.00 9.00

Anniversaries and Events — A147

5c, Classes in computer training, woodworking, electronics. 15c, Students playing musical instruments. 30c, Chapel, Mona Campus, Jamaica. 45c, Plaque on wall, university crest. 50c, Dr. John Coakley Lettsom, map of Little Jost Van Dyke island. $1, Crest of the Medical Society of London, building.

Wmk. 384

1998, Dec. 14 Litho. *Perf. 14*

897 A147 5c multicolored .25 .25
898 A147 15c multicolored .40 .40
899 A147 30c multicolored .90 .90
900 A147 45c multicolored 1.25 1.25
901 A147 50c multicolored 1.50 1.50
902 A147 $1 multicolored 1.75 1.75
Nos. 897-902 (6) 6.05 6.05

Comprehensive education in Virgin Islands, 30th anniv. (#897-898). University of West Indies, 50th anniv. (#899-900). Founding of the Medical Society of London by Dr. John Coakley Lettsom, 225th anniv. (#901-902).

Lizards — A148

Designs: 5c, Rock iguana. 35c, Pygmy gecko. 60c, Slippery back skink. $1.50, Wood slave gecko.
No. 907: a, Doctor lizard. b, Yellow-bellied lizard. c, Man lizard. d, Ground lizard.

Perf. 14½x14

1999, Apr. 30 Litho. Wmk. 373

903 A148 5c multicolored .30 .30
904 A148 35c multicolored 1.10 1.10
905 A148 60c multicolored 2.00 2.00
906 A148 $1.50 multicolored 2.75 2.75
Nos. 903-906 (4) 6.15 6.15

Sheet of 4

907 A148 75c #a.-d. 6.50 6.50

Wedding of Prince Edward and Sophie Rhys-Jones
Common Design Type

Perf. 13¾x14

1999, June 15 Litho. Wmk. 384

908 CD356 20c Separate portraits 1.25 1.25
909 CD356 $3 Couple 6.25 6.25

1st Manned Moon Landing, 30th Anniv.
Common Design Type

Designs: 10c, Apollo 11 on launch pad. 40c, Second stage fires. 50c, Artist's rendition of Apollo 11 on moon. $2, Astronauts transfer to lunar module.
$2.50, Looking at earth from moon.

Perf. 14x13¾

1999, July 20 Litho. Wmk. 384

910 CD357 10c multicolored .25 .25
911 CD357 40c multicolored 1.10 1.10
912 CD357 50c multicolored 1.40 1.40
913 CD357 $2 multicolored 4.00 4.00
Nos. 910-913 (4) 6.75 6.75

Souvenir Sheet

Perf. 14

914 CD357 $2.50 multicolored 5.00 5.00

No. 914 contains one 40mm circular stamp.

Shells — A149

Designs: 25c, Measle cowrie. 35c, West Indian top shell. 75c, Zigzag scallop. $1, West Indian fighting conch.
No. 919: a, 5c, Sunrise tellin. b, 10c, King helmet. c, 25c, Like No. 915. d, 35c, Like No. 916. e, 75c, Like No. 917. f, $1, Like No. 918.

Wmk. 373

1999, Nov. 1 Litho. *Perf. 14¼*

915 A149 25c multi .90 .90
916 A149 35c multi 1.50 1.50
917 A149 75c multi 2.50 2.50
918 A149 $1 multi 3.00 3.00
919 A149 Strip of 6, #a.-f. 15.00 15.00
Nos. 915-919 (5) 22.90 22.90

Vignette extends to the top perforations on Nos. 915-918, but does not on stamps from No. 919.

Christmas A150

Churches: 20c, Zion Hill Methodist. 35c, Fat Hogs Bay Seventh Day Adventist. 50c, Ruins of Kingstown St. Philip's Anglican. $1, Road Town St. William's Catholic.

Perf. 13¼x13

1999, Dec. 16 Litho. Wmk. 373

920 A150 20c multi .50 .50
921 A150 35c multi .85 .85
922 A150 50c multi 1.25 1.25
923 A150 $1 multi 2.00 2.00
Nos. 920-923 (4) 4.60 4.60

British Monarchs — A151

a, Henry VII. b, Lady Jane Grey. c, Charles I. d, William III. e, George III. f, Edward VII.

Wmk. 373

2000, Feb. 29 Litho. *Perf. 14*
924 A151 60c Sheet of 6, #a.-f. 8.25 8.25

The Stamp Show 2000, London.

Prince William, 18th Birthday
Common Design Type

William: 20c, As toddler, on chest. 40c, As toddler, standing. 50c, With ski cap & goggles. 60c, Wearing suits & striped shirts. $1, Wearing sweater & bow tie.

Perf. 14¼x13¾, 13¾x14¼
2000, June 21 Litho. Wmk. 373
Stamps With White Border

925 CD359 20c multi .50 .50
926 CD359 40c multi, vert. 1.00 1.00
927 CD359 50c multi, vert. 1.50 1.50
928 CD359 $1 multi 2.50 2.50
Nos. 925-928 (4) 5.50 5.50

Souvenir Sheet
Stamps Without White Border
Perf. 14¼

929 Sheet of 5 9.00 9.00
a. CD359 20c multi .50 .50
b. CD359 40c multi 1.00 1.00
c. CD359 50c multi 1.25 1.25
d. CD359 60c multi 1.60 1.60
e. CD359 $1 multi 2.50 2.50

Queen Mother, 100th Birthday — A152

Various photos. Frame color: 15c, Lilac. 35c, Light green. 70c, Pink. $1.50, Light blue.

Wmk. 373
2000, Aug. 4 Litho. *Perf. 13¾*
930-933 A152 Set of 4 7.50 7.50

Flowering Plants and Trees — A153

10c, Red hibiscus. 15c, Pink oleander. 35c, Yellow bell. 50c, Yellow & white frangipani. 75c, Flamboyant. $2, Bougainvillea.

2000, Sept. 7 *Perf. 13½x13¾*
934-939 A153 Set of 6 10.00 10.00

Millennium A154

Virgin Islands history: 5c, Site of Emancipation Proclamation. 20c Nurse Mary Louise Davies. 30c, Cheyney University, US, founded by Richard Humphries. 45c, Enid Leona Scatliffe, former chief education officer. 50c, H. Lavity Stoutt Community College. $1 Sir J. Olva Georges.
$2, Victoria Cross of Pvt. Samuel Hodge, vert.

Wmk. 373
2000, Nov. 16 Litho. *Perf. 14*
940-945 A154 Set of 6 5.75 5.75
Souvenir Sheet
946 A154 $2 multi 4.75 4.75

Restoration of the Legislative Council, 50th Anniv. — A155

Virgin Islands Councilmen: 10c, Dr. Q. William Osbourne & Arnando Scatliffe. 15c, H. Robinson O'Neal & A. Austin Henley. 20c, Wilfred W. Smith & John C. Brudenell-Bruce. 35c, Howard R. Penn & I. G. Fonseca. 50c, Carlton L. de Castro & Theodolph H. Faulkner. 60c, Willard W. Wheatley. $1, H. Lavity Stoutt.

2000, Nov. 22
947-953 A155 Set of 7 7.00 7.00

Souvenir Sheet

New Year 2001 (Year of the Snake) A156

No. 954: a, 50c, White-crowned dove. b, 50c, Bar-tailed cuckoo dove.

2001, Feb. 1 *Perf. 14½*
954 A156 Sheet of 2, #a-b 6.00 6.00

Hong Kong 2001 Stamp Exhibition.

Visiting Royal Navy Ships — A157

Designs: 35c, HMS Wistaria, 1923-30. 50c, HMS Dundee, 1934-35. 60c, HMS Eurydice, 1787. 75c, HMS Pegasus, 1787. $1, HMS Astrea, 1807. $1.50 HM Yacht Britannia, 1966.

Wmk. 373
2001, Sept. 28 Litho. *Perf. 14*
955-960 A157 Set of 6 17.50 17.50

Nobel Prizes, Cent. — A158

Nobel laureates: 10c, Fridtjof Nansen, Peace, 1922. 20c, Albert Einstein, Physics, 1921. 25c, Sir Arthur Lewis, Economics, 1979. 40c, Saint-John Perse, Literature, 1960. 70c, Mother Teresa, Peace, 1979. $2, Christian Lous Lange, Peace, 1921.

2001, Oct. 5
961-966 A158 Set of 6 15.00 15.00

Reign Of Queen Elizabeth II, 50th Anniv. Issue
Common Design Type

Designs: Nos. 967, 971a, 15c, Princess Elizabeth in uniform. Nos. 968, 971b, 50c, In 1977. Nos. 969, 971c, 60c, Holding flowers. Nos. 970, 971d, 75c, In 1996. No. 971e, $1, 1955 portrait by Annigoni (38x50mm).

Perf. 14¼x14½, 13¾ (#971e)
2002, Feb. 6 Litho. Wmk. 373
With Gold Frames

967 CD360 15c multicolored .60 .60
968 CD360 50c multicolored 1.90 1.90
969 CD360 60c multicolored 2.00 2.00
970 CD360 75c multicolored 2.00 2.00
Nos. 967-971 (4) 6.50 6.50

Souvenir Sheet
Without Gold Frames
971 CD360 Sheet of 5, #a-e 10.00 10.00

Reptiles in Guinness Book Of World Records — A159

Designs: 5c, Estuarine crocodile. 20c, Reticulated python. 30c, Komodo dragon. 40c, Boa constrictor. $1, Dwarf caiman. $2, Sphaerodactylus parthenopion.
$1.50, Head of Sphaerodactylus parthenopion.

Perf. 13¼x13
2002, June 10 Litho. Wmk. 373
972-977 A159 Set of 6 11.50 11.50
977a Sheet of 6, #972-977 11.50 11.50

Souvenir Sheet
978 A159 $1.50 multi 5.00 5.00

Queen Mother Elizabeth (1900-2002)
Common Design Type

Designs: 20c, Wearing tiara (black and white photograph). 60c, Wearing dark blue hat. Nos. 981, 983a, $2, Wearing hat (black and white photograph). Nos. 982, 983b, $3, Wearing pink hat.

Perf. 13¾x14¼
2002, Aug. 5 Litho. Wmk. 373
With Purple Frames

979 CD361 20c multicolored .50 .50
980 CD361 60c multicolored 1.50 1.50
981 CD361 $2 multicolored 4.50 4.50
982 CD361 $3 multicolored 6.00 6.00
Nos. 979-982 (4) 12.50 12.50

Souvenir Sheet
Without Purple Frames
Perf. 14½x14¼
983 CD361 Sheet of 2, #a-b 11.00 11.00

Royal Navy Ships — A160

Designs: 20c, HMS Invincible and HMS Argo. 35c, HMS Boreas and HMS Solebay. 50c, HMS Coventry. $3, HMS Argyll.

Wmk. 373
2002, Aug. 30 Litho. *Perf. 14*
984-987 A160 Set of 4 14.50 14.50

Island Scenes Type of 1996

Designs: 5c, Spring Bay. 40c, Devils Bay. 60c, The Baths. 75c, St. Thomas Bay. $1, Savannah and Pond Bay. $2, Trunk Bay.

2002, Sept. 13
988-993 A135 Set of 6 11.00 11.00

West Indian Whistling Duck — A161

Designs: Nos. 994, 998a, 10c, Duckling and eggs. Nos. 995, 998b, 35c, Duck standing on rock, vert. Nos. 996, 998c, 40c, Duck in water, vert. Nos. 997, 998d, 70c, Two ducks. No. 998e, $2, Duck's head.

Perf. 14¼x13¾, 13¾x14¼
2002, Dec. Litho. Wmk. 373
Stamps With Brown Border
994-997 A161 Set of 4 5.00 5.00

Souvenir Sheet
Stamps Without Brown Border
Perf. 14¼x14½ (Horiz. stamps), 14½ (Vert. stamps)
998 A161 Sheet of 5, #a-e 8.00 8.00

Birdlife International.

Anniversaries and Events — A162

No. 999, 10c: a, Sprinters. b, Cyclists.
No. 1000, 35c: a, Laser class sailboats. b, Women's long jump.
No. 1001, 50c: a, Bareboat class sailboats. b, Racing Cruiser class sailboats.
No. 1002, $1.35: a, Carlos and Esme Downing, founders of Island Sun newspaper. b, Island Sun newspaper and emblem.

Wmk. 373
2003, Mar. 13 Litho. *Perf. 13½*
Horiz. pairs, #a-b
999-1002 A162 Set of 4 11.00 11.00

2002 Commonwealth Games (#999); Admission to Olympic Games, 20th anniv. (#1000); Spring Regatta, 30th anniv. (#1001); Island Sun newspaper, 40th anniv. (#1002).

Head of Queen Elizabeth II
Common Design Type

Wmk. 373
2003, June 2 Litho. *Perf. 13¾*
1003 CD362 $5 multi 10.00 10.00

Coronation of Queen Elizabeth II, 50th Anniv.
Common Design Type

Designs: Nos. 1004, 1006a, 15c, Queen in gown. Nos. 1005, 1006b, $5, Royal Family on Buckingham Palace balcony.

Perf. 14¼x14½
2003, June 2 Litho. Wmk. 373
Vignettes Framed, Red Background

1004 CD363 15c multi .50 .50
1005 CD363 $5 multi 12.00 12.00

Souvenir Sheet
Vignettes Without Frame, Purple Panel
1006 CD363 Sheet of 2, #a-b 12.50 12.50

Prince William, 21st Birthday
Common Design Type

Designs: 50c, William in polo uniform at right. $2, William on polo pony at left.

Wmk. 373
2003, June 21 Litho. *Perf. 14¼*
With Gray Frames

1007 CD364 50c multi 1.00 1.00
1008 CD364 $2 multi 4.00 4.00

Without Gray Frames

1009 Horiz. pair 5.00 5.00
a. CD364 50c multi 1.00 1.00
b. CD364 $2 multi 4.00 4.00
Nos. 1007-1009 (3) 10.00 10.00

Powered Flight, Cent. A163

Designs: 15c, Douglas DC-4. 20c, Boeing Stearman "Kaydet." 35c, B-25 J Mitchell. 40c, F-4B Phantom. 70c, CH-47 Chinook helicopter. $2, AH-64 Apache helicopter.

Perf. 13¼x13¾
2003, Nov. 15 Litho. Wmk. 373
Stamp + Label
1010-1015 A163 Set of 6 12.50 12.50

Christmas — A164

Details from Arrival of the English Ambassadors, by Vittore Carpaccio: 20c, Men standing near railing and pillar. 40c, Men, ships in background. $2.50, Seated man.
No. 1019a (36x36mm), Kneeling man delivering message.

Perf. 13¾x13½
2003, Dec. 15 Litho. Wmk. 373
1016-1018 A164 Set of 3 8.00 8.00

Souvenir Sheet
1019 A164 Sheet, #1016-1018, 1019a 9.50 9.50
a. $1 multi, perf. 13½x13¼ 3.00 3.00

Game Fish Type of 1997
Serpentine Die Cut 12½ on 3 Sides
2004, July 1 Litho. Unwmk.
Self-Adhesive
Booklet Stamps
Size: 21x17mm

1020 A140 15c Barracuda .30 .30
a. Booklet pane of 4 1.20
1021 A140 20c Tarpon .40 .40
a. Booklet pane of 4 1.60
1022 A140 35c Sailfish .70 .70
a. Booklet pane of 4 2.80
Complete booklet, #1020a, 1022a 4.00
1023 A140 40c Dolphin .80 .80
a. Booklet pane of 3 + label 2.40
Complete booklet, #1021a, 1023a 5.25
Nos. 1020-1023 (4) 2.20 2.20

Fruit — A165

2004, July 20 Wmk. 373 *Perf. 13¾*
Inscribed "2004" Below Design

1024 A165 15c Pomegranates .30 .30
1025 A165 20c Cashews .40 .40
1026 A165 35c Tamarinds .70 .70
1027 A165 40c Soursop .80 .80
1028 A165 50c Mangos 1.00 1.00
1029 A165 $2 Guavaberries 4.00 4.00
1030 A165 $5 Mamee apples 10.00 10.00
Nos. 1024-1030 (7) 17.20 17.20

See Nos. 1042-1049.

2007
Inscribed "2007" Below Design

1025a A165 20c multicolored .40 .40
1026a A165 35c multicolored .70 .70
1028a A165 50c multicolored 1.00 1.00
1029a A165 $2 multicolored 4.00 4.00
Nos. 1025a-1029a (4) 6.10 6.10

Virgin Islands Festival, 50th Anniv. — A166

Designs: 10c, Parade. 60c, Horse race. $1, Kayak race. $2.35, Festival Queen.

Wmk. 373
2004, Oct. 26 Litho. *Perf. 13¼*
1031-1034 A166 Set of 4 10.00 10.00

Sports — A167

Designs: 75c, Women soccer players. $1, Runner.

2004, Dec. 30 *Perf. 14*
1035-1036 A167 Set of 2 4.50 4.50

FIFA (Fédération Internationale de Football Association), cent.; 2004 Summer Olympics, Athens.

Caribbean Endemic Bird Festival — A168

Designs: 5c, Black and white warbler. 25c, Worm-eating warbler. 35c, Yellow warbler. 50c, Prothonotary warbler.

No. 1041: a, 10c, Prairie warbler. b, 15c, Yellow-rumped warbler. c, 40c, Black-throated blue warbler. d, 60c, Cape May warbler. e, 75c, Northern parula. f, $2.75, Palm warbler.

Wmk. 373
2005, July 8 Litho. *Perf. 13¾*
1037-1040 A168 Set of 4 3.50 3.50
1041 A168 Miniature sheet, #1037-1040, 1041a-1041f 14.00 14.00

Fruit Type of 2004
2005, Aug. 25 Wmk. 373
Inscribed "2005" Below Design

1042 A165 1c Hog plum .25 .25
a. Inscribed "2007" .25 .25
1043 A165 10c Coco plum .25 .25
1044 A165 25c Sugar apple .50 .50
1045 A165 60c Papaya 1.25 1.25
1046 A165 75c Custard apple 1.50 1.50
1047 A165 $1 Otaheite gooseberry 2.00 2.00
1048 A165 $1.50 Guava 3.00 3.00
1049 A165 $10 Passion fruit 20.00 20.00
Nos. 1042-1049 (8) 28.75 28.75

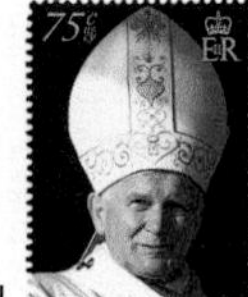

Pope John Paul II (1920-2005) — A169

Wmk. 373
2005, Aug. 18 Litho. *Perf. 14*
1050 A169 75c multi 3.00 3.00

Worldwide Fund for Nature (WWF) — A170

Various depictions of Virgin Islands tree boa: 20c, 30c, 70c, $1.05.

Wmk. 373
2005, Sept. 15 Litho. *Perf. 14*
1051-1054 A170 Set of 4 6.50 6.50
1054a Miniature sheet, 2 each #1051-1054 13.00 13.00

Battle of Trafalgar, Bicent. A171

Designs: 5c, HMS Colossus. 25c, HMS Boreas. 75c, HMS Victory. $3, Admiral Horatio Nelson, vert.

$2.50, HMS Colossus and French ship.

2005, Oct. 18 *Perf. 14x14¾, 14¾x14*
1055-1058 A171 Set of 4 18.00 18.00

Souvenir Sheet
Perf. 13½

1059 A171 $2.50 multi 11.50 11.50

No. 1059 contains one 44x44mm stamp.

Christmas — A172

Flora: 15c, Century plant. 35c, Poinsettia, horiz. 60c, Inkberry. $2.50, Snow on the mountain, horiz.

2005, Nov. 3 *Perf. 14¾x14, 14x14¾*
1060-1063 A172 Set of 4 11.00 11.00

Anniversaries — A173

Designs: 20c, Social Security, 25th anniv. 40c, ZBVI radio station, 40th anniv. 50c, Beef Island Airstrip, 50th anniv. $1, Rotary International, cent.

Wmk. 373
2005, Nov. 16 Litho. *Perf. 13¾*
1064-1067 A173 Set of 4 7.50 7.50

Queen Elizabeth II, 80th Birthday — A174

Queen: 15c, As young woman, in uniform. 75c, Wearing white hat. No. 1070, $1.50, Wearing large earrings. No. 1071, $2, Wearing gray hat with large brim.

No. 1072: a, $1.50, Like 75c. b, $2, Like #1070.

Perf. 14¼x14
2006, July 17 Litho. Wmk. 373
Stamps With White Frames

1068-1071 A174 Set of 4 12.50 12.50

Souvenir Sheet
Stamps Without White Frames

1072 A174 Sheet of 2, #a-b 10.00 10.00

Red Cross Buildings A175

Designs: 20c, New building. $3, Previous building.

Wmk. 373
2007, Aug. 1 Litho. *Perf. 14*
1073-1074 A175 Set of 2 7.00 7.00

Royal Air Force, 90th Anniv. — A176

Designs: 18c, Supermarine Spitfire. 20c, Avro Lancaster. 35c, Douglas C-47 Dakota. 60c, Handley Page Halifax. $1.25 Westland Lysander.

$2.50, Spitfire patrolling D-Day beaches.

Wmk. 373
2008, Apr. 1 Litho. *Perf. 14*
1075-1079 A176 Set of 5 9.00 9.00

Souvenir Sheet

1080 A176 $2.50 multi 6.00 6.00

Princess Diana (1961-97) — A177

Princess Diana in: 60c, Black dress. $3.50, Red dress.

2008, Apr. 7 *Perf. 13¾*
1081 A177 60c multi 1.25 1.25

Souvenir Sheet
Perf. 14¼

1082 A177 $3.50 multi 7.25 7.25

No. 1082 contains one 42x57mm stamp.

Rev. Charles Wesley (1707-88), Hymn Writer — A178

Designs: 20c, Arms. 50c, Wesley. $1.75, Wesley, diff.

2008, May 1 *Perf. 14*
1083-1085 A178 Set of 3 5.00 5.00

2008 Summer Olympics, Beijing — A179

Designs: 15c, Bamboo, runner. 18c, Dragon, yachting. 20c, Lanterns, runner. $1, Fish, yachting.

2008, Aug. 1 *Perf. 13½*
1086-1089 A179 Set of 4 4.00 4.00

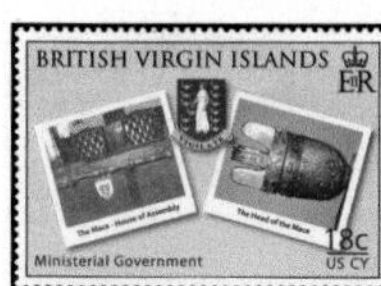

Ministerial Government A180

Arms and: 18c, Mace in House of Assembly, mace head. 35c, House of Assembly, entrance arch. 60c, Henry O. Creque, Ivan Dawson. $2, Paul Wattley, Terrance B. Lettsome.

2008, Aug. 21 *Perf. 14x14¾*
1090-1093 A180 Set of 4 6.50 6.50

End of World War I, 90th Anniv. — A181

Designs: 75c, Sanctuary Wood Cemetery, Ypres, Belgium. 80c, Somme Battlefield, France, horiz. 90c, Lone Pine Cemetery, Gallipoli, Turkey, horiz. $1, War Memorial, Vauquois, France. $1.15, Theipval Memorial, France, horiz. $1.25, Menin Gate, Ypres, Belgium, horiz.

$2, Wreath of Remembrance.

Wmk. 406
2008, Sept. 16 Litho. *Perf. 14*
1094-1099 A181 Set of 6 13.00 13.00

Souvenir Sheet

1100 A181 $2 multi 5.00 5.00

J. R. O'Neal Botanic Gardens — A182

Designs: 20c, Climbing pandanus. 35c, True aloe. 50c, Crown of thorns. $1, Red-eared slider (turtle).

$2.50, Fountain.

Wmk. 373
2009, Mar. 27 Litho. *Perf. 14*
1101-1104 A182 Set of 4 6.00 6.00

Souvenir Sheet

1105 A182 $2.50 multi 6.00 6.00

Ships and Explorers A183

Designs: 15c HMS Ark Royal. 20c, Whydah. 60c, Santa Maria. 70c, RMS Rhone. 90c, Golden Hind. $1.95, HMY Britannia.

$2, Christopher Columbus, vert.

Wmk. 406
2009, May 25 Litho. *Perf. 14*
1106-1111 A183 Set of 6 11.00 11.00

Souvenir Sheet

1112 A183 $2 multi 5.50 5.50

Naval Aviation, Cent. — A184

Victoria Cross recipients: 18c, Lieutenant Robert Hampton Gray. 35c, Lieutenant Commander Eugene Esmonde. 60c, Flight Squadron Lieutenant Rex Warneford. 90c, Squadron Commander Richard Bell Davies.

$2, HMS Illustrious.

2009, June 30
1113-1116 A184 Set of 4 6.00 6.00

Souvenir Sheet

1117 A184 $2 multi 5.50 5.50

Nos. 1113-1116 each were printed in sheets of 8 + central label.

Space Exploration — A185

Designs: 50c, Goddard Rocket Shop, Roswell, New Mexico, 1940. 75c, Vertol VZ-2, 1960. $1, Apollo 11 on launch pad, 1969. $1.25, Space Shuttle flight STS-126 on launch pad, 2008. $2.30, Docking procedure, International Space Station.
$3, Lunar Rover on Moon, painting by Capt. Alan Bean, vert.

2009, July 20 ***Perf. 13¼***
1118-1122 A185 Set of 5 15.00 15.00

Souvenir Sheet

Perf. 13x13¼

1123 A185 $3 multi 7.50 7.50

No. 1123 contains one 40x60mm stamp. Nos. 1118-1122 each were printed in sheets of 6.

Scouting in the Virgin Islands, 75th Anniv. (in 2007) — A185a

2009 Litho. Wmk. 373 ***Perf. 14***
1123A A185a 40c multi — —

Coral Reefs A186

Designs: 20c, Sea turtle. 35c, Fish. 50c, Seahorse, vert. 60c, Shell. $1.50, Coral reef.

Wmk. 406

2010, Mar. 29 Litho. ***Perf. 12½***
1124-1128 A186 Set of 5 7.50 7.50

Construction of New North Sound Post Office Substation — A187

Designs: 20c, John E. George, Sub-postmaster. 50c, New post office substation, horiz. $2, Old post office substation, horiz.

Wmk. 406

2010, May 3 Litho. ***Perf. 12½***
1129-1131 A187 Set of 3 5.50 5.50

East End Methodist Church, 200th Anniv. — A188

Designs: 20c, Church bell. 50c, Church in 2010. 60c, Church in 1977. $2, Church in early 19th cent.

Wmk. 406

2010, Nov. 10 Litho. ***Perf. 13¼***
1132-1135 A188 Set of 4 6.75 6.75

Sailability A189

Various sailors and sailboats with country name and lower panels in: 5c, Dark red. 20c, Violet blue. 25c, Purple. 40c, Green. 50c, Red. $1.50, Orange red.

Wmk. 406

2011, Feb. 24 Litho. ***Perf. 12½***
1136-1141 A189 Set of 6 6.00 6.00

2011 Spring Regatta — A190

Various sailboats with country name and lower panels in: 15c, Green. 35c, Blue, vert. 50c, Olive green, vert. $2, Olive brown.

2011, Mar. 1
1142-1145 A190 Set of 4 6.00 6.00

Souvenir Sheet

Wedding of Prince William and Catherine Middleton — A191

Perf. 14¾x14

2011, Apr. 29 Wmk. 406
1146 A191 $5 multi 10.00 10.00

Coronation of Queen Elizabeth II, 60th Anniv. — A192

Queen Elizabeth II: 20c, And Prince Philip at coronation, 1953. 50c, With Prince Philip on 1966 Virgin Islands visit. $1.50, Walking in Virgin Islands, 1977. $2, With Prince Philip, 2013.

2013, Oct. 1 ***Perf. 13¼x13¾***
1147-1150 A192 Set of 4 8.50 8.50

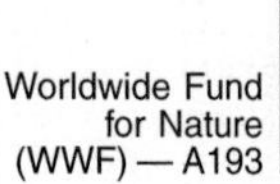
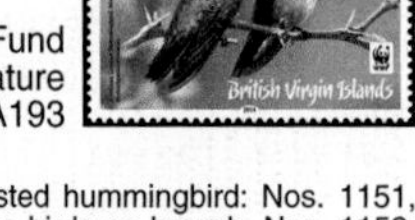

Worldwide Fund for Nature (WWF) — A193

Antillean crested hummingbird: Nos. 1151, 1155a, 35c, Two birds on branch. Nos. 1152, 1155b, 40c, Bird in nest. Nos. 1153, 1155c, 75c, Bird in flight near flowers. Nos. 1154, 1155d, $1.50, Head of bird.
$5, Bird in flight near flowers, diff.

Unwmk.

2014, Jan. 30 Litho. ***Perf. 14***

Stamps With White Frames

1151-1154 A193 Set of 4 6.00 6.00

Stamps Without White Frames

1155 A193 Strip of 4, #a-d 6.00 6.00

Souvenir Sheet

Perf. 14x14¾

1156 A193 $5 multi 10.00 10.00

No. 1156 contains one 48x32mm stamp.

Royal Christenings — A194

Photographs of British royalty with christened infants: 50c, Queen Elizabeth II, 1926. 75c, Prince Charles, 1948. $2, Prince William, 1982. $2.50, Prince George, 2013.

2014, Sept. 25 Litho. ***Perf. 13x13¼***
1157-1160 A194 Set of 4 11.50 11.50

Magna Carta, 800th Anniv. — A195

Designs: 15c, King John approving Magna Carta. 20c, Statue of Justice. 75c, Magna Carta, field of cattails. $2.35, Arms of Virgin Islands, King John.

Perf. 13¼x13½

2015, June 15 Litho.
1161-1164 A195 Set of 4 7.00 7.00

Queen Elizabeth II, 90th Birthday — A196

Photograph of Queen Elizabeth II taken in: 20c, 1940s. 40c, 1977. $1, 1972. $2, 1999.
$4, Queen Elizabeth II in 1954.

2016, Apr. 21 Litho. ***Perf. 14***
1165-1168 A196 Set of 4 7.25 7.25

Souvenir Sheet

1169 A196 $4 multi 8.00 8.00

Queen Elizabeth II, 90th Birthday — A197

Queen Elizabeth II wearing: $10, Pink jacket and hat. $90, Light green jacket and hat.

2016, Dec. 9 Litho. ***Perf. 13½***
1170 A197 $10 multi 20.00 20.00
1171 A197 $90 multi 180.00 180.00

Marine Life — A198

Designs: 10c, Grooved brain coral. 15c, Spiny flower coral. 18c, Elkhorn coral. 40c, Flamingo tongue. 50c, Cushion sea star. 60c, Queen conch. 80c, Caribbean reef squid. $1, Pederson cleaner shrimp. $1.50, Branching vase sponge. $2.50, Common octopus. $5, Spotted eagle ray. $10, Bottlenose dolphins.

2017, July 5 Litho. ***Perf. 13¼x13½***

1172	A198	10c multi	.25	.25
1173	A198	15c multi	.30	.30
1174	A198	18c multi	.40	.40
1175	A198	40c multi	.80	.80
1176	A198	50c multi	1.00	1.00
1177	A198	60c multi	1.25	1.25
1178	A198	80c multi	1.60	1.60
1179	A198	$1 multi	2.00	2.00
1180	A198	$1.50 multi	3.00	3.00
1181	A198	$2.50 multi	5.00	5.00
1182	A198	$5 multi	10.00	10.00
1183	A198	$10 multi	20.00	20.00
		Nos. 1172-1183 (12)	45.60	45.60

Turtles — A199

Designs: 4c, Hawksbill turtle hatchlings. 15c, Head of Green turtle. 20c, Green turtle. 75c, Hawksbill turtle. $2.75, Head of Green turtle, diff.
$5, Head of Hawksbill turtle.

2017, Sept. 6 Litho. ***Perf. 13¼x13½***
1184-1188 A199 Set of 5 8.00 8.00
1188a Vert. strip of 5, #1184-1188 8.00 8.00

Souvenir Sheet

1189 A199 $5 multi 10.00 10.00

No. 1185 was only printed in sheets containing four No. 1188a. Nos. 1184, 1186-1188 were each additionally printed in sheets of 10.

Fish — A200

Designs: 5c, Coney fish. 15c, Balloon fish. 35c, Queen triggerfish. 90c, Red hind. $2, Queen angelfish.
$5, Scrawled filefish.

2017, Nov. 8 Litho. ***Perf. 13¼x13½***
1190-1194 A200 Set of 5 7.00 7.00
1194a Vert. strip of 5, #1190-1194 7.00 7.00

Souvenir Sheet

1195 A200 $5 multi 10.00 10.00

No. 1191 was only printed in sheets containing four No. 1194a. Nos. 1190, 1192-1194 were each additionally printed in sheets of 10.

Wedding of Prince Harry and Meghan Markle — A201

Various photographs of couple: 20c, Prince Harry at left. 50c, Prince Harry at right. $1, On wedding day, standing. $2.50, On wedding day, in coach.
$5, Couple kissing, vert.

Perf. 13¼x13½

2018, Sept. 13 Litho.
1196-1199 A201 Set of 4 8.50 8.50

Souvenir Sheet

Perf. 13½x13¼

1200 A201 $5 multi 10.00 10.00

Flowers — A202

Designs: 20c, Golden trumpet. 40c, Hibiscus. 50c, Oleander. 60c, Frangipani. 75c, White cedar. $2, Bougainvillea. $5, Flamboyant.

2019, Dec. 30 Litho. ***Perf. 13***

1201	A202	20c multi	.40	.40
1202	A202	40c multi	.80	.80
1203	A202	50c multi	1.00	1.00
1204	A202	60c multi	1.25	1.25
1205	A202	75c multi	1.50	1.50
1206	A202	$2 multi	4.00	4.00
1207	A202	$5 multi	10.00	10.00
		Nos. 1201-1207 (7)	18.95	18.95

Dated 2020.

Queen Elizabeth II, 95th Birthday — A203

Photographs of: 15c, Princess Elizabeth wearing Girl Guides uniform, 1942. 20c, Queen Elizabeth II waving at 1953 coronation. 50c, Queen Elizabeth II and Prince Philip, 2003. 75c, Queen Elizabeth II at Badminton Horse Trials, 1968. $1, Queen Elizabeth II in coach, 1971. $3, Queen Elizabeth II at garden party, 2019.
$5, Queen Elizabeth II at knighting ceremony, 2020.

2021, Apr. 21 Litho. ***Perf. 13¼***
1208-1213 A203 Set of 6 11.50 11.50

Souvenir Sheet

1214 A203 $5 multi 10.00 10.00

See Isle of Man No. 2150a.

2020 Summer Olympics, Tokyo — A204

Emblem of Virgin Islands Olympic Committee and Virgin Island athletes: 5c, Elinah Philip, swimmer. 20c, Eldred Henry, shot putter, vert. $1, Kyron McMaster, hurdler, vert. $5, Chantel Malone, long jumper.

2021, July 22 Litho. *Perf. 13½*

1215-1218 A204 Set of 4 12.50 12.50

The 2020 Summer Olympics were postponed until 2021 because of the COVID-19 pandemic.

British Virgin Islands House, London, 20th Anniv. (in 2022) — A205

2023, Jan. 10 Litho. *Perf. 13¾x13¼*

1219 A205 $1 multi 2.00 2.00

WAR TAX STAMPS

Regular Issue of 1913 Overprinted

1916-17 Wmk. 3 *Perf. 14*
Die I

MR1	A9	1p scarlet	.55	*8.00*
a.		1p carmine	2.50	*25.00*
MR2	A9	3p violet, *yellow*	7.00	*26.00*

OFFICIAL STAMPS

Catalogue values for unused stamps in this section are for Never Hinged items.

Nos. 365-368, 370-380 Overprinted "OFFICIAL" in Silver

1985, July Litho. *Perf. 14*

O1	A57	1c multi	.30	1.25
O2	A57	3c multi	.45	1.25
O3	A57	5c multi	.45	.45
O4	A57	8c multi	.55	.60
O5	A57	13c multi	.80	.75
O6	A57	15c multi	.80	.75
O7	A57	18c multi	.90	1.50
O8	A57	20c multi	.90	.80
O9	A57	25c multi	1.25	2.00
O10	A57	30c multi	1.40	1.00
O11	A57	60c multi	2.00	2.50
O12	A57	$1 multi	3.25	3.75
O13	A57	$2.50 multi	5.75	8.00
O14	A57	$3 multi	7.00	10.00
O15	A57	$5 multi	9.50	11.50
		Nos. O1-O15 (15)	35.30	46.10

Nos. 364-380 overprinted in gold and Nos. 364, 369 overprinted in silver exist but were not issued by the Virgin Islands.

Nos. 490-508 Ovptd. "OFFICIAL"

1986 Litho. *Perf. 14*

O16	A81	1c multicolored	.75	2.00
O17	A81	2c multicolored	.50	2.00
O18	A81	5c multicolored	1.50	2.25
O19	A81	8c multicolored	.70	3.00
O20	A81	10c multicolored	1.50	2.25
O21	A81	12c multicolored	1.75	.50
O22	A81	15c multicolored	1.75	.50
O23	A81	18c multicolored	.85	.90
O24	A81	20c multicolored	1.50	1.25
O25	A81	25c multicolored	1.75	1.25
O26	A81	30c multicolored	1.75	1.25
O27	A81	35c multicolored	1.50	1.25
O28	A81	40c multicolored	1.50	1.25
O29	A81	50c multicolored	1.40	2.00
O30	A81	60c multicolored	1.75	2.50
O31	A81	$1 multicolored	2.75	3.50
O32	A81	$2 multicolored	3.00	4.50
O33	A81	$3 multicolored	7.50	9.50
O34	A81	$5 multicolored	12.00	12.00
		Nos. O16-O34 (19)	45.70	53.65

Issue: 1, 5, 10, 15, 20-35c, $5, 7/3; others, 1/28.

Nos. 694-695, 698, 701-706, 708 Ovptd. "OFFICIAL"

1991, Sept. Litho. *Perf. 14*

O37	A116	5c multicolored	.75	*.75*
O38	A116	10c multicolored	.75	*.75*
O41	A116	20c multicolored	.75	*.75*
O44	A116	35c multicolored	1.40	*1.40*
O45	A116	40c multicolored	1.50	*1.50*
O46	A116	45c multicolored	1.75	*1.75*
O47	A116	50c multicolored	1.90	*1.90*
O48	A116	70c multicolored	2.75	*2.75*
O49	A116	$1 multicolored	3.75	*3.75*
O51	A116	$3 multicolored	7.00	*9.50*
		Nos. O37-O51 (10)	22.30	*24.80*

Ovpt. on Nos. O37-O51 is 19mm long. Used values are for c-t-o examples.

Nos. O37-O38, O41, O44-O49, O51 were not available unused until mid-1992.

This set was never used in the Virgin Islands.

Nos. 694-695, 698, 700-706, 708 Ovptd. "OFFICIAL"

1992 Litho. *Perf. 14*

O55	A116	5c multicolored	.25	.25
O56	A116	10c multicolored	.25	.25
O59	A116	20c multicolored	.75	.75
O61	A116	30c multicolored	1.25	1.25
O62	A116	35c multicolored	1.40	1.40
O63	A116	40c multicolored	1.50	1.50
O64	A116	45c multicolored	1.75	1.75
O65	A116	50c multicolored	1.90	1.90
O66	A116	70c multicolored	2.75	2.75
O67	A116	$1 multicolored	3.75	3.75
O69	A116	$3 multicolored	11.50	11.50
		Nos. O55-O69 (11)	27.05	27.05

Ovpt. on Nos. O55-O56, O59, O61-O67, O69 is 15½mm long.

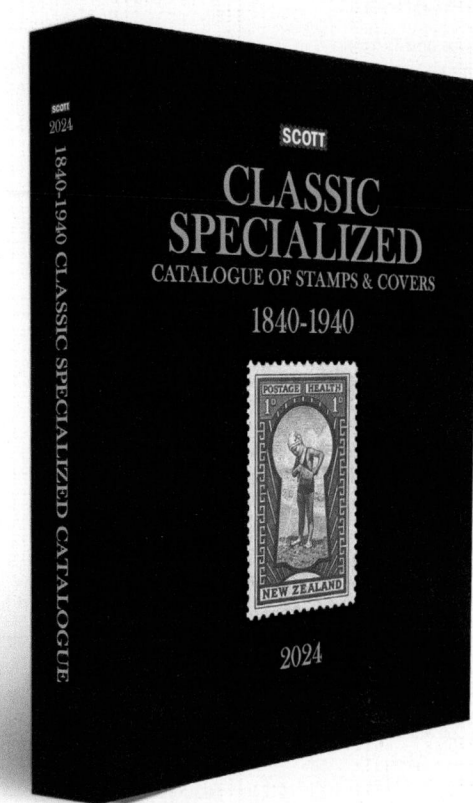

WALLIS & FUTUNA ISLANDS

'wä-ləs and fə-'tü-nə 'ī-ləndz

LOCATION — Group of islands in the South Pacific Ocean, northeast of Fiji
GOVT. — French Overseas Territory
AREA — 106 sq. mi.
POP. — 15,129 (1999 est.)
CAPITAL — Mata-Utu, Wallis Island

100 Centimes = 1 Franc

Catalogue values for unused stamps in this country are for Never Hinged items, beginning with Scott 127 in the regular postage section, Scott B9 in the semi-postal section, Scott C1 in the air-post section, and Scott J37 in the postage due section.

New Caledonia Stamps of 1905-28 Overprinted in Black or Red

1920-28 Unwmk. *Perf. 14x13½*

No.	Type	Description	Unused	Used
1	A16	1c black, *green*	.25	.30
a.		Double overprint	175.00	
2	A16	2c red brown	.25	.30
3	A16	4c blue, *org*	.40	.50
4	A16	5c green	.40	.50
5	A16	5c dull blue ('22)	.40	*.55*
6	A16	10c rose	.40	.65
7	A16	10c green ('22)	.50	.90
8	A16	10c red, *pink* ('25)	2.00	2.25
9	A16	15c violet	.90	1.10
10	A17	20c gray brown	.60	*1.25*
11	A17	25c blue, *grn*	1.25	1.50
12	A17	25c red, *yel* ('22)	.80	1.00
13	A17	30c brown, *org*	1.50	*2.00*
14	A17	30c dp rose ('22)	1.25	*1.75*
15	A17	30c red orange ('25)	.60	.85
16	A17	30c lt green ('27)	1.75	*3.25*
17	A17	35c black, *yel* (R)	.75	1.00
18	A17	40c rose, *grn*	1.10	*1.50*
19	A17	45c violet brn, *pnksh*	1.40	*2.00*
20	A17	50c red, *org*	1.40	*2.10*
21	A17	50c dark blue ('22)	1.50	*2.40*
22	A17	50c dark gray ('25)	2.00	*3.25*
23	A17	65c deep blue ('28)	4.75	*7.50*
24	A17	75c olive green	1.90	*2.60*

Nos. 113, 115-116 Overprinted

No.	Type	Description	Unused	Used
25	A18	1fr blue, *yel grn*	3.50	*5.25*
a.		Triple overprint	240.00	
b.		Double overprint	240.00	
c.		Pair, one stamp without overprint	600.00	
26	A18	1.10fr orange brn ('28)	4.00	*7.25*
27	A18	2fr carmine, *bl*	5.50	*8.50*
28	A18	5fr black, *org* (R)	11.00	*17.00*
		Nos. 1-28 (28)	52.05	*79.00*

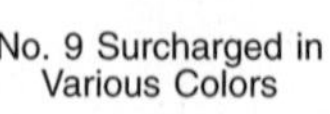

No. 9 Surcharged in Various Colors

1922

No.	Type	Description	Unused	Used
29	A16	0.01c on 15c violet (Bk)	.60	*.95*
30	A16	0.02c on 15c violet (Bl)	.60	*.95*
31	A16	0.04c on 15c violet (G)	.60	*.95*
32	A16	0.05c on 15c violet (R)	.60	*.95*
		Nos. 29-32 (4)	2.40	*3.80*

Stamps and Types of 1920 Surcharged in Black or Red

1924-27

No.	Type	Description	Unused	Used
33	A18	25c on 2fr car, *bl*	.90	1.00
34	A18	25c on 5fr black, *org*	.90	1.00
35	A17	65c on 40c rose red, *grn* ('25)	1.50	*2.00*
36	A17	85c on 75c ol grn ('25)	1.20	*1.60*
37	A17	90c on 75c dp rose ('27)	1.50	*2.75*
38	A18	1.25fr on 1fr dp bl (R; '26)	1.00	*1.40*
39	A18	1.50fr on 1fr dp bl, *bl* ('27)	3.50	*5.50*
a.		Double surcharge	320.00	
b.		Surcharge omitted	290.00	
40	A18	3fr on 5fr red vio ('27)	5.75	*8.00*
a.		Surcharge omitted	250.00	
b.		Double surcharge	325.00	
41	A18	10fr on 5fr ol, *lav* ('27)	27.50	42.50
42	A18	20fr on 5fr vio rose, *yel* ('27)	32.50	50.00
		Nos. 33-42 (10)	76.25	*115.75*

New Caledonia Stamps and Types of 1928-40 Overprinted as in 1920

1930-40 *Perf. 13½, 14x13, 14x13½*

No.	Type	Description	Unused	Used
43	A19	1c brn vio & dp bl	.25	.25
a.		Double overprint	200.00	
b.		Imperf.	50.00	
44	A19	2c dk brn & yel grn	.25	.25
a.		Imperf.	50.00	
45	A19	3c brn vio & ind ('40)	.25	.25
46	A19	4c org & Prus grn	.25	.25
47	A19	5c Prus bl & dp ol	.25	*.40*
48	A19	10c gray lil & dk brn	.25	*.40*
49	A19	15c yel brn & dp bl	.25	*.40*
50	A19	20c brn red & dk brn	.50	*.70*
51	A19	25c dk grn & dk brn	1.00	*1.25*
52	A20	30c gray grn & bl grn	1.00	*1.25*
53	A20	35c Prus grn & dk grn ('38)	1.10	*1.25*
a.		Without overprint	200.00	
54	A20	40c brt red & olive	.95	1.10
55	A20	45c dp bl & red org	1.00	*1.25*
56	A20	45c bl grn & dl grn ('40)	1.00	*1.00*
57	A20	50c violet & brn	1.00	1.10
58	A20	55c bl vio & rose red ('38)	1.75	*2.75*
59	A20	60c vio bl & car ('40)	.25	*.90*
60	A20	65c org brn & bl	1.50	2.00
61	A20	70c dp rose & brn ('38)	1.40	*1.60*
62	A20	75c Prus bl & ol gray	2.40	3.00
63	A20	80c dk cl & grn ('38)	1.40	*1.60*
64	A20	85c green & brown ('38)	3.50	*4.00*
65	A20	90c dp red & brt red	1.90	*2.75*
66	A20	90c ol grn & rose red ('39)	1.10	*1.25*
67	A21	1fr dp ol & sal red	4.00	*4.75*
68	A21	1fr rose red & dk car ('38)	1.60	*2.75*
69	A21	1fr brn red & grn ('40)	.40	.80
70	A21	1.10fr dp grn & brn	26.00	*40.00*
71	A21	1.25fr brn red & grn ('33)	3.00	*3.50*
72	A21	1.25fr rose red & dk car ('39)	1.10	*1.25*
73	A21	1.40fr dk bl & red org ('40)	1.10	*1.40*
74	A21	1.50fr dp bl & bl	1.25	*1.50*
75	A21	1.60fr dp grn & brn ('40)	1.60	*2.00*
76	A21	1.75fr dk bl & red org ('33)	15.00	*16.00*
77	A21	1.75fr vio bl ('38)	1.90	*2.75*
78	A21	2fr red org & brn	1.25	*1.90*
79	A21	2.25fr vio bl ('39)	1.75	*2.40*
80	A21	2.50fr brn & lt brn ('40)	1.50	*2.40*
81	A21	3fr magenta & brn	1.40	*2.00*
82	A21	5fr dk bl & brn	1.75	*2.60*
83	A21	10fr vio & brn, *pnksh*	2.25	*3.50*
84	A21	20fr red & brn, *yel*	3.75	*5.25*
		Nos. 43-84 (42)	95.10	*127.70*

For overprints see Nos. 94-126.

For types A19 and A21 of New Caledonia, with "RF," overprinted as above, see Nos. 126A-126F.

Common Design Types pictured following the introduction.

Colonial Exposition Issue
Common Design Types

1931, Apr. 13 Engr. *Perf. 12½*
Name of Country Typo. in Black

No.	Type	Description	Unused	Used
85	CD70	40c deep green	7.75	8.75
86	CD71	50c violet	7.75	8.75
87	CD72	90c red orange	7.75	8.75
88	CD73	1.50fr dull blue	7.75	8.75
		Nos. 85-88 (4)	31.00	35.00

Colonial Arts Exhibition Issue
Common Design Type
Souvenir Sheet

1937 *Imperf.*

No.	Type	Description	Unused	Used
89	CD78	3fr red violet	19.00	*37.50*
		Never hinged	35.00	
a.		Inscription inverted	3,500.	

New York World's Fair Issue
Common Design Type

1939, May 10 Engr. *Perf. 12½x12*

No.	Type	Description	Unused	Used
90	CD82	1.25fr carmine lake	2.50	3.00
91	CD82	2.25fr ultramarine	2.50	3.00

Petain Issue
New Caledonia Nos. 216A-216B Ovptd. in Lilac or Red

1941 Engr. *Perf. 12½x12*

No.	Type	Description	Unused	Used
92	A21a	1fr bluish green (L)	1.10	
93	A21a	2.50fr dark blue (R)	1.10	

Nos. 92-93 were issued by the Vichy government in France, but were not placed on sale in Wallis & Futuna.

For surcharges, see Nos. B8A-B8B.

Nos. 43-69, 71, 74, 77-78, 80-84 with Additional Overprint in Black

1941-43 *Perf. 14x13½*

No.	Type	Description	Unused	Used
94	A19	1c	2.50	2.50
95	A19	2c	2.50	2.50
96	A19	3c	80.00	80.00
97	A19	4c	3.25	3.25
98	A19	5c	3.25	3.25
99	A19	10c	3.25	3.25
100	A19	15c	3.75	3.75
101	A19	20c	4.50	4.50
102	A19	25c	4.50	4.50
103	A20	30c	4.50	4.50
104	A20	35c	3.25	3.25
105	A20	40c	4.00	4.00
106	A20	45c #55	4.00	4.00
107	A20	45c #56	90.00	90.00
108	A20	50c	3.50	3.50
109	A20	55c	3.50	3.50
110	A20	60c	80.00	80.00
111	A20	65c	3.50	3.50
112	A20	70c	3.50	3.50
113	A20	75c	5.00	5.00
114	A20	80c	3.25	3.25
115	A20	85c	4.00	4.00
116	A20	90c #65	3.50	3.50
117	A21	1fr #68	4.00	4.00
118	A21	1.25fr #71	4.00	4.00
119	A21	1.50fr	3.25	3.25
120	A21	1.75fr #77	3.25	3.25
121	A21	2fr	4.00	4.00
122	A21	2.50fr	160.00	160.00
123	A21	3fr	3.25	3.25
124	A21	5fr	8.00	8.00
125	A21	10fr	60.00	60.00
126	A21	20fr	95.00	95.00
		Nos. 94-126 (33)	667.75	667.75

Types of New Caledonia Without "RF" overprinted as in 1920

1944

No.	Type	Description	Unused	Used
126A	A19	10c gray lil & dk brn	1.25	
126B	A19	15c yel brn & dp bl	1.40	
126C	A21	1fr brn red & grn	2.00	
126D	A21	1.50fr blue	2.50	
126E	A21	10fr vio & brn, *pnksh*	2.50	
126F	A21	20fr red & brn, *yel*	2.75	
		Nos. 126A-126F (6)	12.40	

Nos. 126A-126F were issued by the Vichy government in France, but were not placed on sale in Wallis & Futuna.

Catalogue values for unused stamps in this section, from this point to the end of the section, are for Never Hinged items.

Ivi Poo, Bone Carving in Tiki Design — A1

1944 Unwmk. Photo. *Perf. 11½x12*

No.	Type	Description	Unused	Used
127	A1	5c lt brown	.40	.40
128	A1	10c dp gray blue	.40	.40
129	A1	25c emerald	.40	.40
130	A1	30c dull orange	.40	.40
131	A1	40c dk slate grn	1.40	1.40
132	A1	80c brown red	1.25	1.25
133	A1	1fr red violet	.50	.50
134	A1	1.50fr red	.65	.65
135	A1	2fr gray black	.70	.70
136	A1	2.50fr brt ultra	.90	.90
137	A1	4fr dark purple	1.25	1.25
138	A1	5fr lemon yellow	1.50	1.50
139	A1	10fr chocolate	2.00	2.00
140	A1	20fr deep green	2.00	2.00
		Nos. 127-140 (14)	13.75	13.75

Nos. 127, 129 and 136 Surcharged in Black or Carmine

1946

No.	Type	Description	Unused	Used
141	A1	50c on 5c lt brown	.65	.65
142	A1	60c on 5c lt brown	.65	.65
143	A1	70c on 5c lt brown	.65	.65
144	A1	1.20fr on 5c lt brown	.65	.65
145	A1	2.40fr on 25c emerald	.95	.95
146	A1	3fr on 25c emerald	.95	.95
147	A1	4.50fr on 25c emerald	1.90	1.90
148	A1	15fr on 2.50fr (C)	2.00	2.00
		Nos. 141-148 (8)	8.40	8.40

Military Medal Issue
Common Design Type
Engraved and Typographed

1952, Dec. 1 *Perf. 13*

No.	Type	Description	Unused	Used
149	CD101	2fr multicolored	7.25	7.25

Wallis Islander — A2

Unwmk.

1957, June 11 Engr. *Perf. 13*

No.	Type	Description	Unused	Used
150	A2	3fr dk purple & lil rose	1.00	1.00
151	A2	9fr bl, dl lil & vio brn	1.90	1.90

See Nos. 753a, 753c

Imperforates

Most Wallis and Futuna stamps from 1957 onward exist imperforate in issued and trial colors, and also in small presentation sheets in issued colors.

Flower Issue
Common Design Type

Design: 5fr, Montrouziera, horiz.

1958, Aug. 4 Photo. ***Perf. 12½x12***
152 CD104 5fr multicolored 3.25 3.25

Human Rights Issue
Common Design Type

1958, Dec. 10 Engr. ***Perf. 13***
153 CD105 17fr brt bl & dk bl 4.50 4.50

Women Making Tapa Cloth — A3
Kava Ceremony — A4

17fr, Dancers. 19fr, Dancers with paddles.

1960, Sept. 19 Engr. ***Perf. 13***
154 A3 5fr dk brown, grn & org brn 1.50 1.50
155 A4 7fr dk brown & Prus grn 2.25 2.25
156 A4 17fr ultra, claret & grn 3.00 3.00
157 A3 19fr claret & slate 3.00 3.00
Nos. 154-157 (4) 9.75 9.75

For No. 157 with surcharge, see No. 174.
See No. 753b

Map of South Pacific A4a

1962, July 18 Photo. ***Perf. 13x12***
158 A4a 16fr multicolored 3.75 3.75

5th South Pacific Conf., Pago Pago, 1962.

Sea Shells — A5

1962-63 Engr. ***Perf. 13***
Size: 22x36mm
159 A5 25c Triton 1.00 1.00
160 A5 1fr Mitra episcopalis 1.00 1.00
161 A5 2fr Cypraecassis rufa 1.75 1.75
162 A5 4fr Murex tenuspina 3.00 3.00
163 A5 10fr Oliva erythrostoma 7.00 7.00
164 A5 20fr Cyprae tigris 10.50 10.50
Nos. 159-164,C18 (7) 36.75 31.25

Red Cross Centenary Issue
Common Design Type

1963, Sept. 2 Unwmk. ***Perf. 13***
165 CD113 12fr red lil, gray & car 4.00 4.00

Human Rights Issue
Common Design Type

1963, Dec. 10 Engr.
166 CD117 29fr dk red & ocher 7.00 7.00

Philatec Issue
Common Design Type

1964, Apr. 15 Unwmk. ***Perf. 13***
167 CD118 9fr dk sl grn, grn & red 3.00 3.00

Queen Amelia and Ship "Queen Amelia" — A6

1965, Feb. 15 Photo. ***Perf. 12½x13***
168 A6 11fr multicolored 6.75 6.75

WHO Anniversary Issue
Common Design Type

1968, May 4 Engr. ***Perf. 13***
169 CD126 17fr bl grn, org & lil 5.75 5.75

Human Rights Year Issue
Common Design Type

1968, Aug. 10 Engr. ***Perf. 13***
170 CD127 19fr dk pur, org brn & brt mag 3.25 3.25

Outrigger Canoe — A7

1969, Apr. 30 Photo. ***Perf. 13***
171 A7 1fr multicolored 1.10 1.10
Nos. 171,C31-C35 (6) 32.10 18.85

ILO Issue
Common Design Type

1969, Nov. 24 Engr. ***Perf. 13***
172 CD131 9fr orange, brn & bl 2.75 2.75

UPU Headquarters Issue
Common Design Type

1970, May 20 Engr. ***Perf. 13***
173 CD133 21fr lil rose, ind & ol bis 3.25 3.25

No. 157 Surcharged

1971 Engr. ***Perf. 13***
174 A3 12fr on 19fr 1.30 1.25

Weight Lifting — A8

1971, Oct. 25
175 A8 24fr shown 5.25 5.25
176 A8 36fr Basketball 6.50 6.50
Nos. 175-176,C37-C38 (4) 23.25 19.75

4th South Pacific Games, Papeete, French Polynesia, Sept. 8-19.

De Gaulle Issue
Common Design Type

Designs: 30fr, Gen. de Gaulle, 1940. 70fr, Pres. de Gaulle, 1970.

1971, Nov. 9 Engr. ***Perf. 13***
177 CD134 30fr blue & black 8.00 6.25
178 CD134 70fr blue & black 12.00 10.00

Child's Outrigger Canoe — A9

Designs: 16fr, Children's canoe race. 18fr, Outrigger racing canoe.

1972, Oct. 16 Photo. ***Perf. 13x12½***
Size: 35½x26½mm
179 A9 14fr dk green & multi 8.00 4.25
180 A9 16fr dk plum & multi 8.00 4.25
181 A9 18fr blue & multi 12.00 6.25
Nos. 179-181,C41 (4) 63.00 39.75

Outrigger sailing canoes.

Rhinoceros Beetle — A10

Insects: 25fr, Cosmopolities sordidus (beetle). 35fr, Ophideres fullonica (moth). 45fr, Dragonfly.

1974, July 29 Photo. ***Perf. 13***
182 A10 15fr ol & multi 3.25 2.10
183 A10 25fr ol & multi 4.00 3.00
184 A10 35fr gray bl & multi 7.75 4.00
185 A10 45fr multicolored 7.75 6.00
Nos. 182-185 (4) 22.75 15.10

Georges Pompidou (1911-74), Pres. of France — A11

1975, Dec. 1 Engr. ***Perf. 13***
186 A11 50fr ultra & slate 6.25 5.50

Battle of Yorktown and George Washington A12

American Bicentennial: 47fr, Virginia Cape Battle and Lafayette.

1976, June 28 Engr. ***Perf. 13***
187 A12 19fr blue, red & olive 2.40 1.40
188 A12 47fr blue, red & maroon 4.50 4.00

For overprints see Nos. 205-206.

Conus Ammiralis A13

Sea Shells: 23fr, Cyprae assellus. 43fr, Turbo petholatus. 61fr, Mitra papalis.

1976, Oct. 1 Engr. ***Perf. 13***
189 A13 20fr multicolored 2.50 2.00
190 A13 23fr multicolored 2.50 2.00
191 A13 43fr multicolored 4.75 4.00
192 A13 61fr ultra & multi 7.00 6.50
Nos. 189-192 (4) 16.75 14.50

Father Chanel and Poi Church A14

32fr, Father Chanel and map of islands.

1977, Apr. 28 Litho. ***Perf. 12***
193 A14 22fr multicolored 1.60 1.40
194 A14 32fr multicolored 2.10 1.50

Return of the ashes of Father Chanel, missionary.

Bowl, Mortar and Pestle — A15

Handicrafts: 25fr, Wooden bowls and leather bag. 33fr, Wooden comb, club, and boat model. 45fr, War clubs, Futuna. 69fr, Lances.

1977, Sept. 26 Litho. ***Perf. 12½***
195 A15 12fr multicolored 1.00 .75
196 A15 25fr multicolored 1.90 1.00
197 A15 33fr multicolored 2.10 1.25

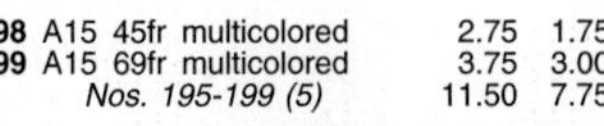

198 A15 45fr multicolored 2.75 1.75
199 A15 69fr multicolored 3.75 3.00
Nos. 195-199 (5) 11.50 7.75

Post Office, Mata Utu — A16

50fr, Sia Hospital, Mata Utu. 57fr, Administration Buildings, Mata Utu. 63fr, St. Joseph's Church, Sigave. 120fr, Royal Palace, Mara Utu.

1977, Dec. 12 Litho. ***Perf. 13***
200 A16 27fr multicolored 1.60 1.40
201 A16 50fr multicolored 2.40 1.80
202 A16 57fr multicolored 2.50 1.80
203 A16 63fr multicolored 3.50 2.75
204 A16 120fr multicolored 8.00 4.50
Nos. 200-204 (5) 18.00 12.25

Nos. 187-188 Overprinted

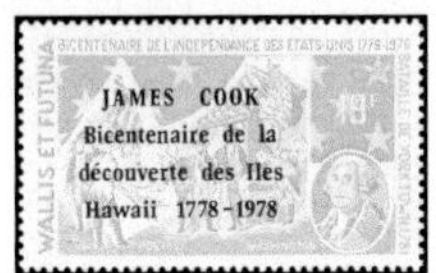

1978, Jan. 20 Engr. ***Perf. 13***
205 A12 19fr multicolored 3.00 2.50
206 A12 47fr multicolored 6.00 4.00

Bicentenary of the arrival of Capt. Cook in the Hawaiian Islands.

Cruiser Triomphant A17

Warships: 200fr, Destroyers Cap des Palmes and Chevreuil. 280fr, Cruiser Savorgnan de Brazza.

1978, June 18 Photo. ***Perf. 13x12½***
207 A17 150fr multicolored 9.00 6.25
208 A17 200fr multicolored 12.50 9.00
209 A17 280fr multicolored 17.00 12.50
Nos. 207-209 (3) 38.50 27.75

Free French warships serving in the Pacific, 1940-1944.

Solanum Seaforthianum A18

Flowers: 24fr, Cassia alata. 29fr, Gloriosa superba. 36fr, Hymenocallis littoralis.

1978, July 11 Photo. ***Perf. 13***
210 A18 16fr multicolored 1.20 .90
211 A18 24fr multicolored 1.45 1.00
212 A18 29fr multicolored 2.00 1.40
213 A18 36fr multicolored 3.50 1.80
Nos. 210-213 (4) 8.15 5.10

Gray Egret — A19

Birds: 18fr, Red-footed booby. 28fr, Brown booby. 35fr, White tern.

1978, Sept. 5 Photo. ***Perf. 13***
214 A19 17fr multicolored 1.50 .90
215 A19 18fr multicolored 2.10 1.00
216 A19 28fr multicolored 2.60 1.40
217 A19 35fr multicolored 3.50 1.60
Nos. 214-217 (4) 9.70 4.90

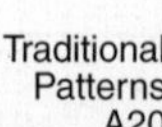

Traditional Patterns A20

Designs: 55fr, Corpus Christi procession. 59fr, Chief's honor guard.

1978, Oct. 3

218 A20 53fr multicolored 2.50 1.80
219 A20 55fr multicolored 3.50 2.10
220 A20 59fr multicolored 4.00 2.50
Nos. 218-220 (3) 10.00 6.40

Human Rights Flame — A21

1978, Dec. 10 Litho. *Perf. 12½*

221 A21 44fr multicolored 1.50 1.30
222 A21 56fr multicolored 2.50 1.80

30th anniversary of Universal Declaration of Human Rights.

Fishing Boat — A22

Designs: 30fr, Weighing young tuna. 34fr, Stocking young tunas. 38fr, Measuring tuna. 40fr, Angler catching tuna. 48fr, Adult tuna.

1979, Mar. 19 Litho. *Perf. 12*

223 A22 10fr multicolored .65 .50
224 A22 30fr multicolored 1.25 .90
225 A22 34fr multicolored 1.35 1.00
226 A22 38fr multicolored 2.25 1.40
227 A22 40fr multicolored 2.75 2.00
228 A22 48fr multicolored 3.75 2.00
a. Souv. sheet of 6, #223-228 + 3 labels 25.00 25.00
Nos. 223-228 (6) 12.00 7.80

Tuna tagging by South Pacific Commission.
For surcharge see No. 261.

Boy with Raft and IYC Emblem A23

Design: 58fr, Girl on horseback.

1979, Apr. 9 Photo. *Perf. 13*

229 A23 52fr multicolored 1.75 1.30
230 A23 58fr multicolored 2.25 1.70

International Year of the Child.

Bombax Ellipticum — A24

64fr, Callophyllum. 76fr, Pandanus odoratissimus.

1979, Apr. 23 Litho. *Perf. 13*

231 A24 50fr multicolored 1.75 1.40
232 A24 64fr multicolored 3.00 1.80
233 A24 76fr multicolored 3.50 2.50
Nos. 231-233 (3) 8.25 5.70

Green and Withered Landscapes A25

1979, May 28 Photo. *Perf. 13*

234 A25 22fr multicolored 1.50 1.10

Anti-alcoholism campaign.

Flowers — A26

20fr, Crinum moorei hook. 42fr, Passiflora. 62fr, Canna indica.

1979, July 16 Photo. *Perf. 12½x13*

235 A26 20fr multicolored .80 .65
236 A26 42fr multicolored 1.75 1.10
237 A26 62fr multicolored 2.40 1.75
Nos. 235-237 (3) 4.95 3.50

See Nos. 279-281.

Swimming A27

1979, Aug. 27 Engr. *Perf. 13*

238 A27 31fr shown 1.90 1.40
239 A27 39fr High jump 2.40 1.80

6th South Pacific Games, Suva, Fiji, Aug. 27-Sept. 8.

Flower Necklaces A28

Design: 140fr, Coral necklaces.

1979, Aug. 27 Litho.

240 A28 110fr multicolored 3.75 2.75
241 A28 140fr multicolored 4.25 3.50

Trees and Birds, by Sutita A29

Paintings by Local Artists: 65fr, Birds and Mountain, by M. A. Pilioko, vert. 78fr, Festival Procession, by Sutita.

1979, Oct. 8 *Perf. 13x12½, 12½x13*

242 A29 27fr multicolored 1.25 1.10
243 A29 65fr multicolored 2.25 1.50
244 A29 78fr multicolored 3.50 2.25
Nos. 242-244 (3) 7.00 4.85

Marine Mantis — A30

Marine Life: 23fr, Hexabranchus sanguineus. 25fr, Spondylus barbatus. 43fr, Gorgon coral. 45fr, Linckia laevigata. 63fr, Tridacna squamosa.

1979, Nov. 5 Photo. *Perf. 13x12½*

245 A30 15fr multicolored 1.00 .75
246 A30 23fr multicolored 1.50 .90
247 A30 25fr multicolored 1.50 1.00
248 A30 43fr multicolored 2.25 1.10
249 A30 45fr multicolored 2.40 1.25
250 A30 63fr multicolored 4.50 2.50
Nos. 245-250 (6) 13.15 7.50

See #294-297. For surcharge see #272.

Transportation Type of 1979

1980, Feb. 29 Litho. *Perf. 13*

251 AP32 1fr like No. C87 .25 .25
252 AP32 3fr like No. C88 .30 .25
253 AP32 5fr like No. C89 .30 .30
Nos. 251-253 (3) .85 .80

Radio Station and Tower — A31

1980, Apr. 21 Litho. *Perf. 13*

254 A31 47fr multicolored 2.25 1.40

Radio station FR3, 1st anniversary.

Jesus Laid in the Tomb, by Maurice Denis A32

1980, Apr. 28 *Perf. 13x12½*

255 A32 25fr multicolored 1.45 .90

Easter 1980.

Gnathodentex Mossambicus A33

27fr, Pristipomoides filamentosus. 32fr, Etelis carbunculus. 51fr, Cephalopholis wallisi. 59fr, Aphareus rutilans.

1980, Aug. 25 Litho. *Perf. 12½x13*

256 A33 23fr multi 1.10 .90
257 A33 27fr multi 1.50 1.00
258 A33 32fr multi 2.25 1.40
259 A33 51fr multi 3.25 2.40
260 A33 59fr multi 3.75 2.75
a. Vert. strip of 5, Nos. 256-260 13.00 13.00

No. 228 Surcharged

1980, Sept. 29 Litho. *Perf. 12*

261 A22 50fr on 48fr multi 3.00 1.80

Sydpex 80 Philatelic Exhibition, Sydney.

13th World Telecommunications Day — A34

1981, May 17 Litho. *Perf. 12½*

262 A34 49fr multicolored 1.60 1.10

Pierre Curie and Laboratory Equipment A35

1981, May 25 Litho. *Perf. 13*

263 A35 56fr multicolored 2.00 1.40

Pierre Curie (1859-1906), discoverer of radioactivity.

Conus Textile — A36

Marine life: 28fr, Favites. 30fr, Cyanophycees. 31fr, Ceratium vultur. 35fr, Amphiprion frenatus. 55fr, Comatule.

1981, June 22 *Perf. 12½x13*

264 A36 28fr multicolored 1.00 .90
265 A36 30fr multicolored 1.10 .90
266 A36 31fr multicolored 1.50 .90
267 A36 35fr multicolored 1.75 1.10
268 A36 40fr shown 2.10 1.40
269 A36 55fr multicolored 2.50 1.60
a. Vert. strip of 6, Nos. 264-269 11.00 11.00

No. 269a is from sheet of 24.

60th Anniv. of Anti-tuberculin Vaccine (Developed by Calmette and Guerin) — A37

1981, July 28 Litho. *Perf. 13*

270 A37 27fr multicolored 1.10 .90

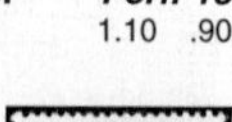

Intl. Year of the Disabled — A38

1981, Aug. 17

271 A38 42fr multicolored 2.00 1.20

No. 245 Surcharged in Red

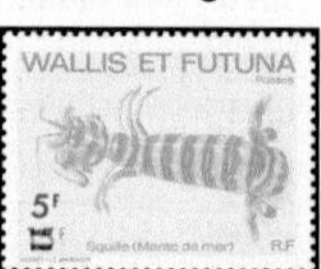

1981, Sept. Photo. *Perf. 13x12½*

272 A30 5fr on 15fr multi .80 .35

Thomas Edison (1847-1931) and his Phonograph, 1878 — A39

1981, Sept. 5 Engr. *Perf. 13*

273 A39 59fr multicolored 1.90 1.40

Battle of Yorktown, 1781 (American Revolution) A40

1981, Oct. 19 Engr. *Perf. 13*

274 A40 66fr Admiral de Grasse 2.00 1.80
275 A40 74fr Sea battle, vert. 3.00 2.75

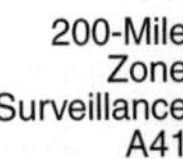

200-Mile Zone Surveillance A41

60fr, Patrol boat Dieppoise. 85fr, Protet.

1981, Dec. 4 Litho. *Perf. 13*
276 A41 60fr multicolored 1.60 1.40
277 A41 85fr multicolored 2.25 2.10

TB Bacillus Centenary — A42

1982, Mar. 24 Litho. *Perf. 13*
278 A42 45fr multicolored 1.75 1.40

Flower Type of 1979 in Changed Colors

1982, May 3 Photo. *Perf. 12½x13*
279 A26 1fr like No. 235 .25 .25
280 A26 2fr like No. 236 .30 .25
281 A26 3fr like No. 237 .30 .30
Nos. 279-281 (3) .85 .80

PHILEXFRANCE '82 Intl. Stamp Exhibition, Paris, June 11-21 — A43

1982, May 12 Engr. *Perf. 13*
282 A43 140fr like No. 25 3.25 2.75

Acanthe Phippium — A44

68fr, Acanthe phippium, diff. 70fr, Spathoglottis pacifica. 83fr, Mussaenda raiateensis, Orchids and rubiaceae.

1982, May 24 Litho. *Perf. 12½x13*
283 A44 34fr shown 1.00 .90
284 A44 68fr multicolored 1.90 1.75
285 A44 70fr multicolored 2.40 1.75
286 A44 83fr multicolored 2.40 2.25
Nos. 283-286 (4) 7.70 6.65

Scouting Year — A45

1982, June 21 *Perf. 12½*
287 A45 80fr Baden-Powell 2.40 1.75

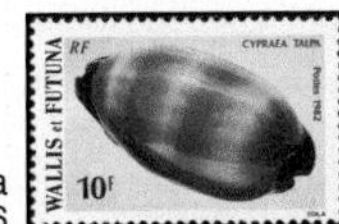

Cypraea Talpa — A46

Porcelaines shells.

1982, June 28 *Perf. 12½x13*
288 A46 10fr shown .30 .30
289 A46 15fr Cypraea vitellus .70 .30
290 A46 25fr Cypraea argus .85 .65
291 A46 27fr Cypraea carneola 1.10 .75
292 A46 40fr Cypraea mappa 1.40 1.10
293 A46 50fr Cypraea tigris 1.75 1.25
Nos. 288-293 (6) 6.10 4.35

Marine Life Type of 1979

1982, Oct. 1 Photo. *Perf. 13x12½*
294 A30 32fr Gorgones milithea 1.25 .75
295 A30 35fr Linckia laevigata 1.75 1.10
296 A30 46fr Hexabranchus sanguineus 2.00 1.50
297 A30 63fr Spondylus barbatus 2.50 2.25
Nos. 294-297 (4) 7.50 5.60

St. Teresa of Jesus of Avila (1515-1582) A48

1982, Nov. 8 Engr. *Perf. 13*
298 A48 31fr multicolored 1.40 .75

See No. 315.

Traditional House — A49

1983, Jan. 20 Litho. *Perf. 13*
299 A49 19fr multicolored .70 .50

Gustave Eiffel (1832-1923), Architect — A50

1983, Feb. 14 Engr. *Perf. 13*
300 A50 97fr multicolored 3.00 2.75

Thai Dancer, 19th Cent. — A51

1983, June 28 Engr. *Perf. 13*
301 A51 92fr multicolored 2.75 1.80

BANGKOK '83 Intl. Stamp Show, Aug. 4-13.

A52

1983, Aug. 25 Litho. *Perf. 13x13½*
302 A52 20fr multicolored .65 .50

World Communications Year.

Cone Shells — A53

10fr, Conus tulipa. 17fr, Conus capitaneus. 21fr, Conus virgo. 22fr, Strombus lentiginosus. 25fr, Lambis chiragra. 35fr, Strombus dentatus. 39fr, Conus vitulinus. 43fr, Lambis scorpius. 49fr, Strombus aurisdianae. 52fr, Conus marmoreus. 65fr, Conus leopardus. 76fr, Lambis crocata.

1983-84 Litho. *Perf. 13½x13*
303 A53 10fr multicolored .25 .25
304 A53 17fr multicolored .65 .50
305 A53 21fr multicolored .65 .50
306 A53 22fr multicolored .55 .50
307 A53 25fr multicolored .65 .60
308 A53 35fr multicolored 1.15 .75
309 A53 39fr multicolored 1.00 .90
310 A53 43fr multicolored 1.40 .90
311 A53 49fr multicolored 1.75 1.40
312 A53 52fr multicolored 1.50 1.40
313 A53 65fr multicolored 1.60 1.60
314 A53 76fr multicolored 2.10 1.60
Nos. 303-314 (12) 13.25 10.90

Issued: 22, 25, 35, 43, 49, 76fr, 3/23/84; others, 10/14/83.

No. 298 Redrawn with Espana '84 Emblem

1984, Apr. 27 Engr. *Perf. 13*
315 A48 70fr multicolored 1.90 1.40

Denis Diderot (1713-1784), Philosopher — A54

100fr, Portrait, encyclopedia title page.

1984, May 11
316 A54 100fr multicolored 2.60 1.75

Nature Protection (Whale) — A55

1984, June 5 Litho. *Perf. 13x12½*
317 A55 90fr Orcina orca 3.25 1.75

4th Pacific Arts Festival A56

1984, Nov. 30 Litho. *Perf. 13*
318 A56 160fr Islanders 3.75 2.50

Lapita Pottery — A57

Ethno-Archaeological Museum: Excavation site, reconstructed ceramic bowl.

1985, Jan. 16 Litho. *Perf. 13*
319 A57 53fr multicolored 1.50 .90

Seashells — A58

1985, Feb. 11
320 A58 2fr Nautilus pompilius .25 .25
321 A58 3fr Murex bruneus .25 .25
322 A58 41fr Casmaria erinaceus 1.30 .90
323 A58 47fr Conus vexillum 1.60 1.00
324 A58 56fr Harpa harpa 2.10 1.10
325 A58 71fr Murex ramosus 2.50 1.60
Nos. 320-325 (6) 8.00 5.10

Victor Hugo, Author (1802-1885) — A59

1985, Mar. 7 Engr.
326 A59 89fr multicolored 2.60 1.60

Bat — A60

1985, Apr. 29 Litho.
327 A60 38fr multicolored 1.60 1.10

Intl. Youth Year — A61

1985, May 20 Litho. *Perf. 12½x13*
328 A61 64fr Children 1.60 1.10

UN, 40th Anniv. A61a

1985, July 12 Engr. *Perf. 13*
328A A61a 49fr Prus grn, dk ultra & red 1.50 .90

Pierre de Ronsard (1524-1585), Poet — A62

1985, Sept. 16 Engr. *Perf. 13*
329 A62 170fr brt bl, sep & brn 5.00 3.50

Dr. Albert Schweitzer A63

1985, Nov. 22 Engr. *Perf. 13*
330 A63 50fr blk, dk red lil & org brn 2.00 1.25

World Food Day — A64

1986, Jan. 23 Litho. *Perf. 12½x13*
331 A64 39fr Breadfruit 1.25 .75

Flamboyants — A65

1986, Feb. 13 ***Perf. 13x12½***
332 A65 38fr multicolored 1.25 1.00

Seashells — A66

1986, Apr. 24 Litho. ***Perf. 13½x13***
333 A66 4fr Lambis truncata .30 .30
334 A66 5fr Charonia tritonis .30 .30
335 A66 10fr Oliva miniacea .45 .35
336 A66 18fr Distorsio anus .65 .65
337 A66 25fr Mitra mitra .95 .75
338 A66 107fr Conus distans 3.00 2.25
Nos. 333-338 (6) 5.65 4.60

Also exists in se-tenant strips of 6 from sheet of 24.

1986 World Cup Soccer Championships, Mexico — A67

1986, May 20 ***Perf. 13x12½***
339 A67 95fr multicolored 2.75 1.80

UNICEF.

Discovery of Horn Islands, 370th Anniv. — A68

No. 340: a, 8fr, William Schouten, ship. b, 9fr, Jacob LeMaire, ship. c, 155fr, Map of Alo & Alofi.

1986, June 19 Engr. ***Perf. 13***
340 A68 Strip of 3, #a.-c. 6.00 4.75

James Watt (1736-1819), Inventor, and Steam Engine — A69

1986, July 11
341 A69 74fr blk & dk red 2.00 1.50

Minesweeper La Lorientaise — A70

7fr, Corvette Commandant Blaison, vert. 120fr, Frigate Balny.

1986, Aug. 7
342 A70 6fr shown .60 .50
343 A70 7fr multicolored .65 .50
344 A70 120fr multicolored 3.25 2.75
Nos. 342-344 (3) 4.50 3.75

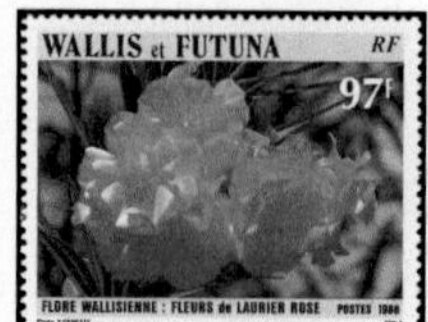

Rose Laurel A71

1986, Oct. 2 Litho. ***Perf. 13x12½***
345 A71 97fr multi 2.60 2.00

Virgin and Child, by Sandro Botticelli — A72

1986, Dec. 12 Litho. ***Perf. 12½x13***
346 A72 250fr multicolored 6.25 4.50

Christmas.

Butterflies — A73

1987, Apr. 2 Litho. ***Perf. 12½***
347 A73 2fr Papilio montrouzieri .40 .35
348 A73 42fr Belenois java .90 .70
349 A73 46fr Delias ellipsis 1.75 .75
350 A73 50fr Danaus pumila 2.25 .95
351 A73 52fr Luthrodes cleotas 2.40 1.00
352 A73 59fr Precis villida 2.80 1.50
Nos. 347-352 (6) 10.50 5.25

World Wrestling Championships A74

1987, May 26 Litho. ***Perf. 12½***
353 A74 97fr multi 3.00 1.90

For overprint see No. 360.

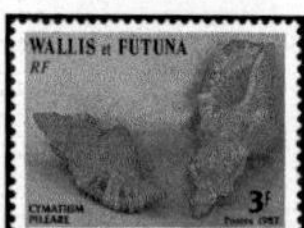

Seashells — A75

1987, June 24 Litho. ***Perf. 13***
354 A75 3fr Cymatium pileare .25 .25
355 A75 4fr Conus textile .25 .25
356 A75 28fr Cypraea mauritiana 1.00 .75
357 A75 44fr Bursa bubo 1.30 1.00
358 A75 48fr Cypraea testudinaria 1.40 1.10
359 A75 78fr Cypraecassis rufa 2.10 1.50
Nos. 354-359 (6) 6.30 4.85

Also exists in se-tenant strips of 6 from sheet of 24.

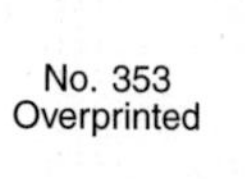

No. 353 Overprinted

1987, Aug. 29 Litho. ***Perf. 12½***
360 A74 97fr multicolored 3.00 2.40

OLYMPHILEX '87, Rome.

Bust of a Girl, by Auguste Rodin (1840-1917) — A76

1987, Sept. 15 Engr. ***Perf. 13***
361 A76 150fr plum 4.50 2.75

See No. 390.

World Post Day — A77

1987, Oct. 9 Litho. ***Perf. 13***
362 A77 116fr multicolored 2.90 1.80

Birds — A78

1987, Oct. 28 ***Perf. 13x12½***
363 A78 6fr Anas superciliosa .35 .35
364 A78 19fr Pluvialis dominica .70 .50
365 A78 47fr Gallicolumba stairi 1.40 .95
366 A78 56fr Arenaria interpres 1.90 1.00
367 A78 64fr Rallus philippensis 2.00 1.10
368 A78 68fr Limosa lapponica 2.25 1.30
Nos. 363-368 (6) 8.60 5.20

Francis Carco (1886-1958), Poet — A79

Design: Carco and views of the Moulin de la Galette and Place du Tertre, Paris.

1988, Jan. 29 Litho. ***Perf. 13***
369 A79 40fr multicolored 2.00 .95

Jean-Francois de Galaup (1741-c.1788), Comte de La Perouse, Explorer — A80

Design: Ships *L'Astrolabe* and *La Boussole,* portrait of La Perouse.

1988, Mar. 21 Engr. ***Perf. 13***
370 A80 70fr org brn, dark blue & olive grn 2.75 2.40

Intl. Red Cross and Red Crescent Organizations, 125th Annivs. — A81

1988, July 4 Engr. ***Perf. 13***
371 A81 30fr blk, dark red & brt blue grn 1.75 1.00

1988 Summer Olympics, Seoul A82

1988, Sept. 1 Engr. ***Perf. 13***
372 A82 11fr Javelin .70 .50
373 A82 20fr Women's volleyball .95 .70
374 A82 60fr Windsurfing 2.00 1.50
375 A82 80fr Yachting 2.90 1.90
a. Souv. sheet of 4, #372-375 + 2 labels, gutter between 8.25 8.25
Nos. 372-375 (4) 6.55 4.60

Intl. Maritime Organization Emblem and Frigate F727 Admiral Charner — A83

1989, Jan. 26 Litho. ***Perf. 13***
376 A83 26fr multi 1.00 .70

Jean Renoir (1894-1979), Film Director, and Scene from *The Grand Illusion* — A84

1989, Feb. 16 Engr. ***Perf. 13***
377 A84 24fr brt lil rose, dark vio brn & brt org 1.35 .75

Antoine Becquerel (1788-1878), Physicist — A85

Perf. 13x12½
1988, Nov. 9 Engr. Unwmk.
378 A85 18fr blk & dark ultra 1.05 .50

Futuna Hydroelectric Plant — A86

Wmk. 385
1989, Apr. 13 Litho. ***Perf. 13½***
379 A86 25fr multi .95 .50

A87

Unwmk.
1988, Oct. 26 Litho. ***Perf. 13***
380 A87 17fr multi .95 .50

World Post Day.

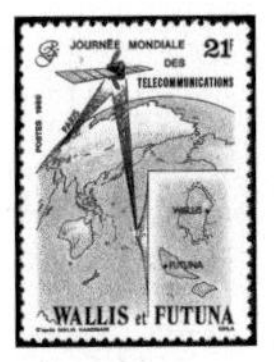
A88

1989, May 17 ***Perf. 12½x13***
381 A88 21fr multi .95 .50

World Telecommunications Day.

Fresco — A89

1989, June 8 ***Perf. 12½***
382 A89 22fr multi 1.00 .50

PHILEXFRANCE '89 — A90

Declaration of Human Rights and Citizenship, Bicent. A91

1989, July 7 **Litho.** ***Perf. 13***
383 A90 29fr multi .90 .70
384 A91 900fr multi 18.50 14.00
a. Souv. sheet of 2, #383-384 + label 25.00 25.00

No. 384 is airmail. No. 384a sold for 1000fr.

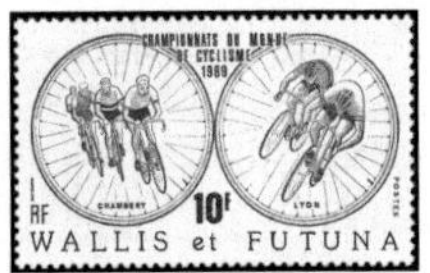
World Cycling Championships — A92

1989, Sept. 14 **Engr.** ***Perf. 13***
385 A92 10fr blk, red brn & emer .65 .45

World Post Day — A93

Unwmk.
1989, Oct. 18 **Litho.** ***Perf. 13***
386 A93 27fr multicolored .95 .50

Landscape A94

1989, Nov. 23 **Litho.** ***Perf. 13***
387 A94 23fr multicolored 1.10 .70

Star of Bethlehem — A95

1990, Jan. 9 **Litho.** ***Perf. 12½***
388 A95 44fr multicolored 1.60 1.00

Fossilized Tortoise — A96

1990, Feb. 15 **Litho.** ***Perf. 12½x13***
389 A96 48fr multicolored 2.75 1.40

Sculpture by Auguste Rodin (1840-1917) — A97

1990, Mar. 15 **Engr.** ***Perf. 13***
390 A97 200fr royal blue 5.50 4.00

1990 World Cup Soccer Championships, Italy — A98

1990, Apr. 16 **Litho.**
391 A98 59fr multicolored 1.75 1.10

Orchids — A99

1990, May 17 **Litho.** ***Perf. 12½***
392 A99 78fr multicolored 2.50 1.50

Mother's Day

Phaeton A100

1990, July 16 ***Perf. 13***
393 A100 300fr multicolored 7.75 4.50
394 A100 600fr Island 16.00 8.50

Moana II — A101

1990, Aug. 16 **Engr.** ***Perf. 13***
395 A101 40fr shown 1.25 .95
396 A101 50fr Moana III 1.75 1.00

Native Huts — A102

1990, Sept. 17 **Litho.** ***Perf. 13x12½***
397 A102 28fr multicolored .95 .50

Stamp Day — A103

1990, Oct. 16 **Litho.** ***Perf. 12½***
398 A103 97fr multicolored 3.25 1.90

Wallis Island Pirogue — A104

1990, Nov. 16 **Litho.** ***Perf. 13x12½***
399 A104 46fr multicolored 1.75 .95

Best Wishes A105

1990, Dec. 17 **Litho.** ***Perf. 13x12½***
400 A105 100fr multicolored 3.00 1.90

Patrol Boats A106

1991 **Engr.** ***Perf. 13***
401 A106 42fr La Moqueuse 1.40 .95
402 A106 52fr La Glorieuse 1.75 1.00

Issue dates: 42fr, Jan. 7; 52fr, Mar. 4.

A107

1991, Feb. 4 **Litho.** ***Perf. 13***
403 A107 7fr Breadfruit picker .30 .30
404 A107 54fr Taro planter 1.75 1.00
405 A107 62fr Spear fisherman 1.90 1.20
406 A107 72fr Native warrior 2.25 1.30
407 A107 90fr Kailao dancer 2.75 1.75
a. Souv. sheet of 5, #403-407 9.50 9.50
Nos. 403-407 (5) 8.95 5.55

Issued: 7fr, 9/2; 54fr, 5/13; 62fr, 4/1; 72fr, 2/4; 90fr, 11/4.

No. 407a sold for 300fr.

Doctors Without Borders, 20th Anniv. — A108

1991, Feb. 18 **Litho.** ***Perf. 13½***
408 A108 55fr multicolored 1.75 1.00

Ultralight Aircraft A108a

1991, June 24
409 A108a 85fr multicolored 2.75 1.80

Portrait of Jean by Auguste Renoir (1841-1919) A109

1991, July 8 **Photo.** ***Perf. 12½x13***
410 A109 400fr multicolored 9.75 8.00

Litho.
Die Cut
Self-Adhesive

411 A109 400fr multicolored 10.00 8.00

Overseas Territorial Status, 30th Anniv. A110

1991, July 29 **Litho.** ***Perf. 13***
412 A110 102fr multicolored 2.75 1.80

Feast of the Assumption A111

1991, Aug. 15 ***Perf. 13x12½***
413 A111 30fr multicolored 1.30 .70

Amnesty Intl., 30th Anniv. — A113

1991, Oct. 7 ***Perf. 13x12½***
414 A113 140fr bl, vio & yel 4.00 2.75

Central Bank for Economic Cooperation, 50th Anniv. — A114

1991, Dec. 2 **Litho.** ***Perf. 13***
415 A114 10fr multicolored .50 .35

Flowers — A115

1fr, Monette allamanda cathartica. 4fr, Hibiscus rosa sinensis. 80fr, Ninuphar.

1991, Dec. 2 ***Perf. 12½x13, 13x12½***
416 A115 1fr multi .25 .25
417 A115 4fr multi, vert. .65 .35
418 A115 80fr multi 2.50 1.50
Nos. 416-418 (3) 3.40 2.10

Christmas A116

1991, Dec. 16 **Litho.** ***Perf. 13***
419 A116 60fr multicolored 1.90 1.20

Maritime Surveillance A117

1992, Jan. 20 Litho. *Perf. 13*
420 A117 48fr multicolored 1.60 1.00

1992 Winter Olympics, Albertville A118

1992, Feb. 17 Litho. *Perf. 13*
421 A118 150fr multicolored 4.00 2.75

Canada '92, Intl. Philatelic Exposition, Montreal — A119

1992, Mar. 25 Engr. *Perf. 13*
422 A119 35fr blk, violet & red 1.25 .70

1992 Summer Olympics, Barcelona A120

1992, Apr. 15 Engr. *Perf. 13*
423 A120 106fr bl grn, grn & bl 3.25 2.25

Granada '92, Intl. Philatelic Exposition — A121

1992, Apr. 17 Engr. *Perf. 12½x12*
424 A121 100fr multicolored 3.00 2.00

Expo '92, Seville A122

1992, Apr. 20 *Perf. 13*
425 A122 200fr bl grn, ol & red brn 5.00 3.75

Chaetodon Ephippium A123

Designs: 22fr, Chaetodon auriga. 23fr, Heniochus monoceros. 24fr, Pygoplites diacanthus. 25fr, Chaetodontoplus conspicillatus. 26fr, Chaetodon unimaculatus. 27fr, Siganus punctatus. 35fr, Zebrasoma veliferum. 45fr, Paracanthurus hepatus. 53fr, Siganus vulpinus.

1992-93 Litho. *Perf. 13*
426 A123 21fr multicolored 1.15 .50
427 A123 22fr multicolored 1.15 .50
428 A123 23fr multicolored 1.15 .50
429 A123 24fr multicolored 1.40 .70
430 A123 25fr multicolored 1.40 .70
431 A123 26fr multicolored 1.40 .70
432 A123 27fr multicolored 1.40 .80
433 A123 35fr multicolored 1.50 .80
434 A123 45fr multicolored 1.60 .95
435 A123 53fr multicolored 1.75 1.25
Nos. 426-435 (10) 13.90 7.40

Issued: 21fr, 26fr, 5/18; 22fr, 7/27; 25fr, 7/27; 23fr, 24fr, 9/14; 35fr, 45fr, 6/21/93; 27fr, 53fr, 9/6/93.

Natives — A125

a, 3 warriors. b, 2 warriors. c, Warrior, 2 boats. d, 2 spear fisherman. e, 3 fisherman.

1992, June 15 Litho. *Perf. 12*
436 A125 70fr Strip of 5, #a.-e. 11.25 9.00
f. Souvenir sheet of 5, #a.-e. 11.25 11.25

#436 has continuous design. #436f sold for 450fr.

Support Ship, "La Garonne" — A126

1992, Oct. 12 Litho. *Perf. 12*
437 A126 20fr multicolored .75 .50

L'Idylle D'Ixelles, by Auguste Rodin (1840-1917) — A127

1992, Nov. 17 Engr. *Perf. 13*
438 A127 300fr lilac & dk blue 8.00 6.00

Miribilis Jalapa — A128

1992, Dec. 7 Litho. *Perf. 12½*
439 A128 200fr multicolored 5.50 3.75

Maritime Forces of the Pacific A129

1993, Jan. 27 Litho. *Perf. 13x12½*
440 A129 130fr multicolored 3.50 2.75

School Art — A130

1993, Feb. 22 Litho. *Perf. 12*
441 A130 56fr multicolored 1.90 1.40

See Nos. 451-452.

Birds — A131

Designs: 50fr, Rallus philippensis swindellsi. 60fr, Porphyrio porphyrio. 110fr, Ptilinopus greyi.

1993, Mar. 20 *Perf. 13½*
442 A131 50fr multicolored 1.50 1.00
443 A131 60fr multicolored 1.75 1.50
444 A131 110fr multicolored 3.25 1.90
Nos. 442-444 (3) 6.50 4.40

Mother's Day — A132

1993, May 30 Litho. *Perf. 12½*
445 A132 95fr Hibiscus 2.00 1.75
446 A132 120fr Siale 2.75 2.75

Admiral Antoine d'Entrecasteaux (1737-1793), French Navigator — A133

1993, July 12 Engr. *Perf. 13*
447 A133 170fr grn bl, red brn & blk 4.00 3.25

Taipei '93 — A134

1993, Aug. 14 Litho. *Perf. 13x12½*
448 A134 435fr multicolored 9.25 9.25

Churches A135

1993, Aug. 15 *Perf. 13*
449 A135 30fr Tepa, Wallis .80 .80
450 A135 30fr Vilamalia, Futuna .80 .80

School Art Type of 1993

1993 Litho. *Perf. 13x13½, 13½x13*
451 A130 28fr Stylized trees .80 .55
452 A130 52fr Family, vert. 1.30 1.00

Issue dates: 28fr, Oct. 18. 52fr, Nov. 8.

Christmas — A136

1993, Dec, 6 *Perf. 13*
453 A136 80fr multicolored 2.00 1.60

Traditional Arts and Crafts Exhibition — A137

1994, Mar. 24 Litho. *Perf. 12½*
454 A137 80fr multicolored 2.40 1.60

Liberation of Paris, 50th Anniv. A138

1994, Apr. 21 Engr. *Perf. 13*
455 A138 110fr black, blue & red 3.00 2.00

Satellite Communications A139

1994, June 23 Litho.
456 A139 10fr multicolored 1.00 1.00

1994 World Cup Soccer Championships, U.S. — A140

1994, June 23
457 A140 105fr multicolored 2.75 2.00

Princesses Ouveennes, 1903 — A141

1994, July 21 Engr. *Perf. 13*
458 A141 90fr blue grn, blk & red 2.25 1.50

Symbols of Playing Cards Suits A142

1994, Aug. 25 Litho. *Perf. 13*
459 A142 40fr multicolored 1.40 .70

Ultra-Light Aircraft A143

1994, Aug. 25
460 A143 5fr multicolored .35 .35

Coconut — A144

1994, Oct. 13 Litho. *Perf. 13*
461 A144 36fr multicolored 1.25 .70

Parrots — A145

1994, Nov. 17 Litho. *Perf. 13x13½*
462 A145 62fr multicolored 2.00 1.25

Grand Lodge of France, Cent. A146

1994, Nov. 24 Engr. *Perf. 13*
463 A146 250fr multicolored 6.50 4.50

Preparing Traditional Meal A147

1995, Jan. 25 Litho. *Perf. 13*
464 A147 80fr multicolored 2.40 1.40

Aerial View of Islands — A148

1995, Feb. 21 *Perf. 13x13½, 13½x13*
465 A148 85fr Nukulaelae 1.75 1.25
466 A148 90fr Nukufetau, vert. 2.00 1.40
467 A148 100fr Nukufotu, Nukuloa 2.10 1.90
Nos. 465-467 (3) 5.85 4.55

Mua College — A149

1995, Apr. 11 *Perf. 12*
468 A149 35fr multicolored 1.20 .70

UN, 50th Anniv. A150

1995, June 26 Litho. *Perf. 13½*
469 A150 55fr multicolored 1.75 1.00

10th South Pacific Games A151

1995, Aug. 1 Litho. *Perf. 13*
470 A151 70fr multicolored 1.90 1.40

Local Plants — A152

1995, Oct. 24 Litho. *Perf. 13½x13*
471 A152 20fr Breadfruit tree .55 .55
472 A152 60fr Tarot 1.30 1.00
473 A152 65fr Kava 1.60 1.40
Nos. 471-473 (3) 3.45 2.95

See Nos. 478-481, 484-485.

Tapa A153

1995, Dec. 12 Litho. *Perf. 13*
474 A153 25fr Native life, vert. .80 .70
475 A153 26fr Fish, sea shells .90 .70

Mothers from the Islands — A154

1996, Jan. 14 Litho. *Perf. 13½x13*
476 A154 80fr multicolored 1.90 1.50

Golf — A155

1996, Jan. 24 *Perf. 13*
477 A155 95fr multicolored 3.25 2.00

Local Plant Type of 1995

1996 Litho. *Perf. 13½x13*
478 A152 27fr Cananga odorata .85 .70
479 A152 28fr Mahoaa 1.10 .70
480 A152 45fr Hibiscus 1.10 .80
481 A152 52fr Ufi 1.30 1.00
Nos. 478-481 (4) 4.35 3.20

Issued: #479, 481, 3/14; #478, 480, 6/20.

Sanglants Swamp A156

1996, June 26 *Perf. 13*
482 A156 53fr multicolored 1.60 1.00

Chess A157

1996, July 17
483 A157 110fr multicolored 2.40 2.00

Local Plant Type of 1995

Designs: 30fr, 48fr, Calladium.

1996, Sept. 17 Litho. *Perf. 13½x13*
Background Color
484 A152 30fr blue green .80 .70
485 A152 48fr lilac 1.15 .90

Francoise Perroton, Missionary A158

1996, Oct. 25 *Perf. 13*
486 A158 50fr multicolored 1.40 1.00

UNICEF, 50th Anniv. — A159

1996, Dec. 4 Litho. *Perf. 13*
487 A159 25fr multicolored .80 .70

CPS, 50th Anniv. — A160

1997, Feb. 6 Litho. *Perf. 13*
488 A160 7fr multicolored .30 .30

Royal Standards A161

1997, Feb. 14 Litho. *Perf. 13x13½*
489 A161 56fr King Lavelua 1.40 1.00
490 A161 60fr King Tuiagaifo 1.40 1.00
491 A161 70fr King Tuisigave 1.75 1.00
Nos. 489-491 (3) 4.55 3.00

Brasseur de Kava — A162

1997, Apr. 17 *Perf. 13½x13*
492 A162 170fr multicolored 4.25 2.75

Island Scenes — A163

Designs: 10fr, Old man telling stories to children seated around campfire. 36fr, Braiding mat, vert. 40fr, Preparing "Kai'umu" (feast).

Perf. 13x13½, 13½x13
1997, May 20 Litho.
493 A163 10fr multicolored .30 .30
494 A163 36fr multicolored 1.00 .80
495 A163 40fr multicolored 1.10 .80
Nos. 493-495 (3) 2.40 1.90

Green Lagoon Turtles — A164

1997, June 18 *Perf. 13x13½*
496 A164 62fr Crawling ashore 1.60 1.00
497 A164 80fr Swimming 2.00 1.40

Festival of Avignon A165

1997, July 31 Litho. *Perf. 13*
498 A165 160fr multicolored 4.00 2.40

Berlin Handicapped Sports Festival — A166

1997, Aug. 12
499 A166 35fr multicolored 1.10 .70

D'Uvéa Karate Club A167

1997, Oct. 15 Litho. *Perf. 13x13½*
500 A167 24fr multicolored .90 .50

Fight Against AIDS — A168

1997, Dec. 1 Litho. *Perf. 13*
501 A168 5fr multicolored 1.00 .35

Christmas A169

1997, Dec, 24
502 A169 85fr Nativity 2.10 1.50

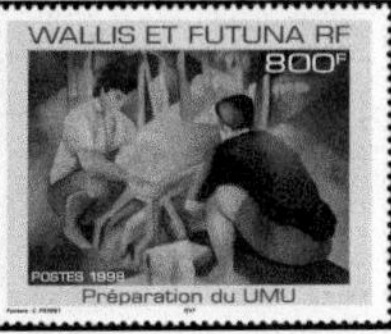
Preparation of UMU A170

1998, Jan. 26
503 A170 800fr multicolored 16.50 11.00

Orchids A171

70fr, Vanda T.M.A. 85fr, Cattleya bow bells. 90fr, Arachnis. 105fr, Cattleya.

1998, Feb. 18 Litho. *Perf. 13*
504 A171 70fr multi, vert. 1.50 1.00
505 A171 85fr multi 1.90 1.25
506 A171 90fr multi, vert. 1.90 1.25
507 A171 105fr multi 2.50 1.50
Nos. 504-507 (4) 7.80 5.00

Telecom 2000 A172

1998, Mar. 24 Litho. *Perf. 13*
508 A172 7fr multicolored .25 .25

Fishing A173

Designs: 50fr, Fisherman casting net into lagoon. 52fr, Fisherman sorting catch.

1998, May 26 Litho. *Perf. 13*
509 A173 50fr multicolored 1.40 .70
510 A173 52fr multicolored 1.40 .70

1998 World Cup Soccer Championships, France — A174

1998, June 10
511 A174 80fr multicolored 2.00 1.40

Insects — A175

1998, July 21 Litho. *Perf. 13x13½*
512 A175 36fr Dragonfly .80 .50
513 A175 40fr Cicada .85 .70

Coral A176

Various corals: a, 4fr. b, 5fr. c, 10fr. d, 15fr.

1998 Litho. *Perf. 13x13½*
514 A176 Strip of 4, #a.-d. 1.25 1.25

52nd Autumn Philatelic Salon A177

1998, Nov. 5 Litho. *Perf. 13½*
515 A177 175fr multicolored 4.00 2.50

World Fight Against AIDS — A178

1998, Dec. 1 *Perf. 13*
516 A178 62fr multicolored 1.60 1.00

Islet of Nuku Taakimoa — A179

1999, Mar. 22 Litho. *Perf. 13*
517 A179 130fr multicolored 3.00 1.80

See No. 594.

Souvenir Sheet

Lagoon Life A180

a, 20fr, Various fish. b, 855fr, Fish, diver.

1999, May 17 Litho. *Perf. 13*
518 A180 Sheet of 2, #a.-b. 18.00 18.00

PhilexFrance '99, World Philatelic Exhibition — A181

1999, July 2 Litho. *Perf. 13*
519 A181 200fr multicolored 4.50 3.25

French Senate, Bicent. A182

1999, Sept. 20 Engr. *Perf. 13*
520 A182 125fr multicolored 3.00 2.00

Territorial Assembly Building A183

1999, Aug. 23 Litho.
521 A183 17fr multicolored .45 .35

Pandanus A184

1999, Oct. 18
522 A184 25fr multicolored .70 .45

Man Making Canoe — A185

1999, Nov. 8
523 A185 55fr multicolored 1.50 .80

French Postage Stamps, 150th Anniv. A186

1999, Dec. 1
524 A186 65fr Wallis & Futuna #86 1.60 1.00

Millennium A187

2000, Jan. 1 Litho. *Perf. 13*
525 A187 350fr multicolored 7.50 4.50

Mata'utu Cathedral — A188

2000, Apr. 28 Photo. *Perf. 13x13¼*
526 A188 300fr multicolored 7.00 3.75

Patrol Boat "La Glorieuse" A189

2000, June 5 Engr. *Perf. 13x12¾*
527 A189 155fr multicolored 4.00 2.40

Sosefo Papilio Makape, First Senator — A190

2000, June 19 *Perf. 12¾x13*
528 A190 115fr multicolored 2.90 1.50

Overseas Broadcasting Institute — A191

2000, July 3 *Perf. 13x12½*
529 A191 200fr multicolored 5.25 2.50

Taro Cultivation A192

2000, July 27 Litho. *Perf. 13*
530 A192 275fr multicolored 6.25 3.50

Souvenir Sheet

2000 Summer Olympics, Sydney — A193

Traditional games, 85fr: a, Spear throwing. b, Sailing. c, Rowing. d, Volleyball.

2000, Sept. 15 Litho. *Perf. 13*
531 A193 #a-d + 2 labels 9.00 9.00

8th Pacific Arts Festival — A194

2000, Oct. 23 *Perf. 13x13¼*
532 A194 330fr multicolored 7.75 4.50

Fish A195

No. 533: a, Coryphaena hippurus. b, Caranx melanpygyus. c, Thunnus albacares.

2000, Nov. 9 Litho. *Perf. 13*
533 Vert. strip of 3 + 2 labels 7.75 7.75
a.-c. A195 115fr Any single 2.40 1.75

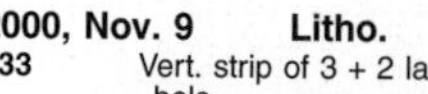

Canonization of St. Marcellin Champagnat, 1st Anniv. — A196

2000, Nov. 13
534 A196 380fr multicolored 9.50 5.00

Talietumu Archaeological Site — A197

2000, Dec. 1 *Perf. 13x13½*
535 A197 205fr multicolored 5.25 2.75

Christmas A198

2000, Dec. 25 *Perf. 13*
536 A198 225fr multicolored 5.75 2.75

Ship "Jacques Cartier" A199

2001, Feb. 26 Engr. *Perf. 13*
537 A199 225fr multicolored 5.50 2.75

Campaign Against Alcoholism — A200

2001, Mar. 14 Litho. *Perf. 13¼x13*
538 A200 75fr multicolored 2.00 1.00

Souvenir Sheet

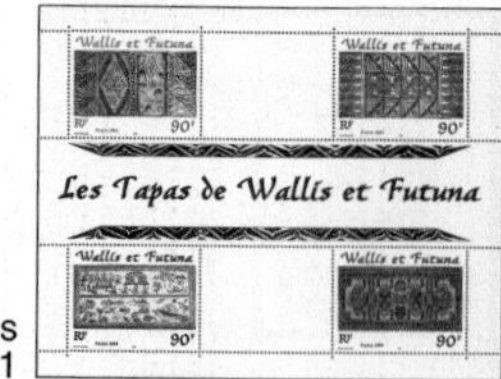

Tapas A201

Tapa with: a, Large diamond, shells, map of islands. b, Triangles and diamonds. c, Scenes of native life, fish, shells, boat. d, Overlapping ovals.

2001, Apr. 14 *Perf. 13*
539 A201 90fr Sheet of 4, #a-d, + 2 labels 9.00 9.00

Children's Drawings of Flowers A202

2001, May 31
540 Horiz. strip of 4 7.00 7.00
a. A202 50fr multi 1.25 1.25
b. A202 55fr multi 1.25 1.25
c. A202 95fr multi 2.10 2.10
d. A202 100fr multi 2.10 2.10

Territorial Status, 40th Anniv. — A203

2001, July 29 Litho. *Perf. 13*
541 A203 165fr multicolored 4.00 2.00

Installation of Mediator, 1st Anniv. — A204

2001, Sept. 26
542 A204 800fr multicolored 16.50 10.00

Year of Dialogue Among Civilizations A205

2001, Oct. 9
543 A205 390fr multicolored 15.00 5.00

5th Autumn Salon — A206

Birds: a, Dacula pacifica. b, Vini australis. c, Tyto alba.

2001, Nov. 8
544 Vert. strip of 3 + 2 labels 10.00 10.00
a.-c. A206 150fr Any single 3.00 3.00

Children's Drawings of Fruit — A207

No. 545, 65fr: a, Custard apple (pomme canelle). b, Breadfruit (fruit de pain).
No. 546, 65fr: a, Pineapple. b, Mango.

2001, Aug. 22 Litho. *Perf. 13*
Vert. Pairs, #a-b
545-546 A207 Set of 2 pairs 6.50 5.00
a. Vert. strip of 4, #545-546 7.00 5.00

Tomb of Futuna King Fakavelikele A208

2001, Dec. 28 Litho. *Perf. 13*
547 A208 325fr multicolored 7.00 3.75

Finemui-Teesi College — A209

2002, Jan. 29 *Perf. 13x13½*
548 A209 115fr multicolored 2.75 1.40

Intl. Women's Day — A210

2002, Mar. 5 Litho. *Perf. 13*
549 A210 800fr Queen Aloisia 16.50 10.00

Arms of Bishop Pompallier — A211

2002, Apr. 19 Engr. *Perf. 13¼*
550 A211 500fr multicolored 11.00 6.50

Uvea Firefighters — A212

Serpentine Die Cut
2002, Apr. 28 Photo.
Self-Adhesive
551 A212 85fr multicolored 2.10 1.40

2002 World Cup Soccer Championships, Japan and Korea — A213

2002, May 31 Litho. *Perf. 13*
552 A213 65fr multicolored 1.75 1.00

World Environment Day — A214

2002, June 5 *Perf. 13x13½*
553 A214 330fr multicolored 6.50 4.00

Traditional Buildings — A215

Designs: No. 554, 50fr, Building with overhanging roof. No. 555, 50fr, Open-air shelter, vert. No. 556, 55fr, Building with two entry ways. No. 557, 55fr, Building with ladder to roof, vert.

2002, Aug. 9 Engr. *Perf. 13¼*
554-557 A215 Set of 4 5.75 2.50

Discovery of the Horn Islands, 1616 — A216

No. 558: a, Jacob Lemaire and compass rose. b, Map of Futuna and Alofi Islands. c, William Schouten and ship.

2002, Aug. 30 Litho. *Perf. 13x13¼*
558 Horiz. strip of 3 9.50 9.50
a.-c. A216 125fr any single 3.00 3.00
d. Souvenir sheet, #558 9.00 9.00

Landscapes A217

No. 559: a, Utua Bay. b, Liku Bay. c, Kingfisher at Vele. d, Aka'Aka Bay.

2002, Sept. 20
559 Horiz. strip of 4 9.50 9.50
a. A217 95fr multi 2.00 1.50
b. A217 100fr multi 2.25 1.50
c. A217 105fr multi 2.25 1.60
d. A217 135fr multi 3.00 1.75

Enygrus Bibroni — A218

2002, Oct. 28 Litho. *Perf. 13¼x13*
560 A218 75fr multicolored 1.90 .75

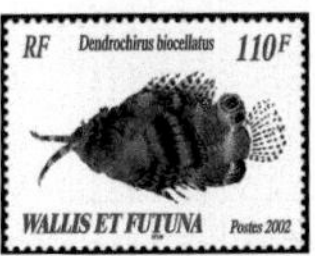
Fish — A219

No. 561: a, Dendrochirus biocellatus. b, Discordipina griessingeri. c, Antennacius nummifer. d, Novaculichthys taeniourus.

2002, Nov. 7 *Perf. 13x13¼*
561 Vert. strip of 4 + 3 labels 9.00 9.00
a.-d. A219 110fr Any single 2.00 1.75

Best Wishes — A220

2002, Dec. 5
562 A220 140fr multicolored 3.00 1.40

Last Avro Lancaster Flight to Wallis, 40th Anniv. — A221

2003, Jan. 26 *Perf. 13*
563 A221 135fr multicolored 3.25 1.75

St. Valentine's Day — A222

2003, Feb. 14 *Perf. 13*
564 A222 85fr multicolored 1.75 1.00

Introduction of the Euro, 1st Anniv. — A223

2003, Feb. 17 *Perf. 12½x12¾*
565 A223 125fr multicolored 3.00 1.80

Values are for examples with surrounding selvage.

Alain Gerbault (1893-1941), Circumnavigator, Aboard Boat "Firecrest" — A224

2003, Mar. 6 Engr. *Perf. 13¼*
566 A224 600fr grn & ol grn 12.00 8.00

Postal Art — A225

Various designs.

2003, Mar. 31 Litho. *Perf. 13*
567 Horiz. strip of 5 2.40 2.40
a. A225 5fr multi .25 .25
b. A225 10fr multi .30 .25
c. A225 15fr multi .35 .35
d. A225 20fr multi .55 .25
e. A225 40fr multi .80 .40

Coral Reefs — A226

Various views.

2003, Apr. 10 *Perf. 13x13¼*
568 Horiz. strip of 4 10.00 10.00
a. A226 95fr multi 1.75 1.75
b. A226 105fr multi 1.90 1.90
c. A226 110fr multi 2.00 2.00
d. A226 115fr multi 2.10 2.10

St. Pierre Chanel (1803-41), Martyred Missionary A227

2003, Apr. 28 Engr. *Perf. 12¼*
569 A227 130fr multicolored 2.60 1.80

2003 Census — A228

2003, June 12 Litho. *Perf. 13*
570 A228 55fr multicolored 1.90 .70

Pacific Legends — A229

Legend of the Coconut Palm: 30fr, Eel. 50fr, Coconut palms, split coconut. 60fr, Split and whole coconuts. 70fr, Coconut palms and clouds.

2003, July 28 Litho. ***Perf. 13x13¼***

571 Horiz. strip of 4 5.00 5.00
a. A229 30fr multi .65 .40
b. A229 50fr multi 1.00 .75
c. A229 60fr multi 1.05 .85
d. A229 70fr multi 1.40 .95
e. Souvenir sheet, #571a-571d 5.25 5.25

Still Life with Maori Statuette, by Paul Gauguin (1848-1903) A230

No. 573a: Study of Heads of Tahitian Women, by Gauguin.

2003 ***Perf. 13***

572 A230 100fr multicolored 2.75 1.60

Souvenir Sheet

573 Sheet, #572, 573a 5.50 5.50
a. A230 100fr multi 2.75 2.25

Issued: No. 572, 7/31; No. 573, 8/20. See New Caledonia No. 929.

Futuna Waterfalls — A231

2003, Aug. 6 ***Perf. 13¼x13***

574 A231 115fr multicolored 2.75 1.75

Frigate Le Nivose — A232

2003, Sept. 15 Engr. ***Perf. 13¼***

575 A232 325fr multicolored 8.00 4.00

Bishop Alexandre Poncet (1884-1973) — A233

2003, Sept. 18 Engr. ***Perf. 13¼***

576 A233 205fr multicolored 4.00 3.00

Arms of Bishop Pierre Bataillon (1810-77) — A234

2003, Oct. 1 Litho. ***Perf. 13¼***

577 A234 500fr multicolored 12.50 7.00

2003 Rugby World Cup, Australia — A235

2003, Oct. 10 ***Perf. 13***

578 A235 65fr multicolored 1.50 .85

Parinari Insularum — A236

2003, Nov. 6 Litho. ***Perf. 13¼x13***

579 A236 250fr multicolored 5.00 3.50

Goddess Havea Hikule'o — A237

2004, Jan. 8

580 A237 85fr multicolored 2.00 1.40

People in Canoe — A238

2004, Jan. 13 ***Perf. 13***

581 A238 75fr multicolored 1.90 1.25

Miniature Sheet

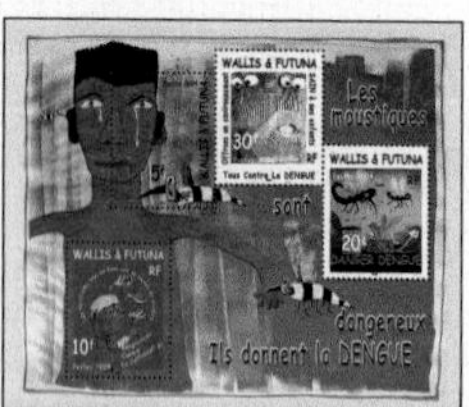

Campaign Against Dengue Fever — A239

No. 582: a, 5fr, Mosquito, crying man. b, 10fr, Mosquitos, man. c, 20fr, Mosquitos, trash. d, 30fr, Mosquitos, sleeping child.

Perf. 13¼x12¾

2004, Feb. 18 Litho.

582 A239 Sheet of 4, #a-d 1.75 1.75

Badminton — A240

2004, Mar. 12 ***Perf. 13¼x13***

583 A240 55fr multicolored 1.40 1.25

Kava Drinkers — A241

2004, Mar. 31 ***Perf. 13x13¼***

584 A241 205fr multicolored 4.00 4.00

Flora — A242

2004, Apr. 22 ***Perf. 13***

585 Horiz. strip of 4 + central label 2.50 2.50
a. A242 15fr Colocasia esculenta .30 .30
b. A242 25fr Carrica papaya .50 .50
c. A242 35fr Artocarpus altilus .70 .70
d. A242 40fr Dioscorea sp. .80 .80

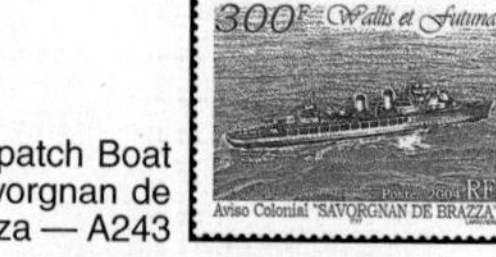

Dispatch Boat Savorgnan de Brazza — A243

Gourdou-Leseurre GL 832 Hy No. 5 and Wallis Island — A244

2004, May 12 Engr. ***Perf. 13¼***

586 A243 300fr multi 6.00 6.00
587 A244 380fr multi 7.50 7.50

Souvenir Sheet

Litho.

588 Sheet of 2 13.00 13.00
a. A243 300fr multi 5.75 5.75
b. A244 380fr multi 7.25 7.25

First flight over Wallis Island, 68th anniv.

Seaweeds — A245

2004, June 26 Litho. ***Perf. 13***

589 Horiz. strip of 3 + 2 alternating labels 10.00 10.00
a. A245 105fr Turbinaria ornata 1.60 1.60
b. A245 155fr Padina melemele 2.40 2.40
c. A245 175fr Tubinaria concoides 2.75 2.75
d. Miniature sheet of 6 + 9 labels 20.00

No. 589 was issued in sheets of 15 with 10 labels.

Miniature Sheet

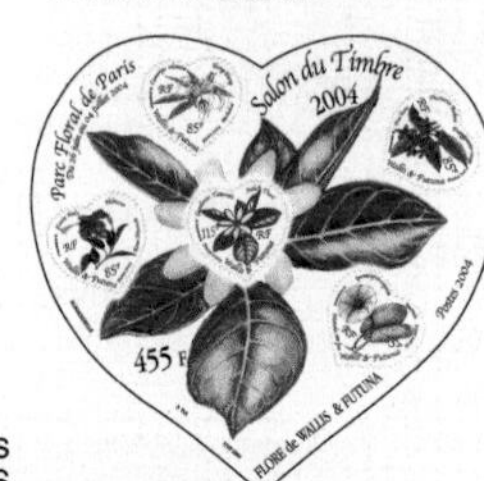

Flowers A246

No. 590: a, Hibiscus rosa-sinensis. b, Cananga odorata. c, Plumeria rubra. d, Ipomeapes caprae. e, Gardenia taitensis.

Serpentine Die Cut 14

2004, June 26 Photo.

Self-Adhesive

590 A246 Sheet of 5 10.00 10.00
a.-d. 85fr Any single 1.90 1.90
e. 115fr multi 2.40 2.40

Salon du Timbre 2004, Paris.

Ninth Pacific Arts Festival, Palau — A247

2004, July 22 Litho. ***Perf. 13x13¼***

591 A247 200fr multicolored 4.00 4.00

Pili'uli Lizard A248

2004, July 26 ***Perf. 13***

592 A248 100fr multicolored 2.50 2.10

Arms of Monsignor Louis Elloy (1829-78) — A249

2004, Sept. 6 Engr. ***Perf. 13¼***

593 A249 500fr multicolored 10.00 10.00

No. 517 Redrawn

2004, Nov. 10 Litho. ***Perf. 13***

594 A179 115fr multi 2.50 2.50

No. 594 shows a 115fr denomination below an obliterated 130fr denomination, the denomination shown on No. 517. This new denomination is not overprinted. No. 594 also has a 2004 year date, rather than an obliterated 1999 year date.

A250

Traditional Houses — A251

2004, Nov. 11 ***Perf. 13¼x13***

595 A250 95fr multicolored 1.90 1.90
596 A251 130fr multicolored 2.75 2.75

Nos. 595-596 were printed in sheets containing four of each stamp plus a large central label.

Miniature Sheet

Cone Shells A252

No. 597: a, Conus eburneus. b, Conus imperialis. c, Conus generalis. d, Gastridium textile.

2005, Jan. 26 ***Perf. 13x13¼***

597 A252 55fr Sheet of 4, #a-d 5.75 5.00

Miniature Sheet

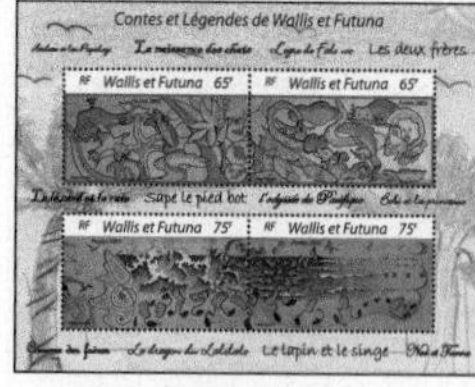

Stories and Legends A253

No. 598: a, 65fr, Whale, bird, crab, eel, turtle. b, 65fr, Fish, octopus, dolphin, butterfly. c, 75fr, Boy, waves, G clef and musical notes. d, 75fr, Musical notes, butterflies.

2005, Jan. 31 ***Perf. 13***

598 A253 Sheet of 4, #a-d 6.75 6.75

Pirogue — A254

2005, Feb. 25 Litho. ***Perf. 13x13¼***
599 A254 330fr multicolored 7.00 7.00

Francophone Week — A255

2005, Mar. 17
600 A255 135fr multicolored 3.00 3.00

Printed in sheets of 10 + 5 labels. See New Caledonia No. 959.

Family Budget Inquiry — A256

2005, Mar. 31 ***Perf. 12¾***
601 A256 205fr multicolored 4.50 4.50

Values are for stamps with surrounding selvage.

Warriors — A257

2005, Apr. 19 ***Perf. 13½x13***
602 Horiz. strip of 5 2.75 2.75
a. A257 5fr blk, red & maroon .25 .25
b. A257 10fr blk, bl & vio blue .25 .25
c. A257 20fr blk, pur & indigo .40 .40
d. A257 30fr blk & red .45 .45
e. A257 50fr blk, lt grn & emerald .80 .80

Traditional Cricket — A258

2005, May 16 ***Perf. 13***
603 A258 190fr multicolored 4.00 4.00

Butterflies — A259

No. 604: a, 40fr, Papilio montrouzieri. b, 60fr, Danaus pumila.

2005, June 30 ***Perf. 13x13¼***
604 A259 Horiz. pair, #a-b 2.25 2.25

Warrior With Spear — A260

Serpentine Die Cut 11
2005, July 14 Self-Adhesive
Booklet Stamp
605 A260 115fr multicolored 2.50 2.40
a. Booklet pane of 10 25.00

Historical Images of Wallis Island A261

2005, July 14 Engr. ***Perf. 13x13¼***
606 Horiz. pair + central label 7.50 7.50
a. A261 155fr Village scene 3.50 3.25
b. A261 175fr Family, house 4.00 3.75

First Noumea to Hihifo Flight, 58th Anniv. A262

2005, Aug. 19
607 A262 380fr multi 8.00 8.00

Souvenir Sheet

Chelomia Mydas — A263

No. 608 — Green turtle: a, Adult entering water. b, Hatchlings entering water. c, Head. d, Swimming underwater.

2005, Aug. 19 Litho. ***Perf. 13x13¼***
608 A263 85fr Sheet of 4, #a-d 8.50 8.50

Arms of Monsignor Jean Armand Lamaze (1833-1906) — A264

2005, Oct. 5 Engr. ***Perf. 13¼***
609 A264 500fr multi 10.50 10.00

Spattoglottis Cinguiculata A265

2005, Oct. 30 Litho. ***Perf. 13***
610 A265 100fr multi 2.00 2.00

Printed in sheets of 10 + 5 labels.

Design of Wallis and Futuna Islands No. 4 — A266

Design of Wallis and Futuna Islands No. 87 — A267

2005, Nov. 10 Litho. ***Perf. 13x13¼***
611 A266 150fr multi 4.00 3.00
612 A267 150fr multi 4.00 3.00

59th Autumn Philatelic Show.

Native Child — A268

2006, Mar. 29 Litho. ***Perf. 13x13¼***
613 A268 75fr multi 1.75 1.60

Monarchical Flags — A269

Designs: 55fr, Kingdom of Uvea. 65fr, Kingdom of Sigave. 85fr, Kingdom of Alo.

Self-Adhesive
Booklet Stamps

2006 Litho. ***Serpentine Die Cut 11***
614 A269 55fr multi 1.20 1.20
a. Booklet pane of 10 12.00
615 A269 65fr multi 1.40 1.40
a. Booklet pane of 10 14.00
616 A269 85fr multi 1.75 1.75
a. Booklet pane of 10 18.00

Issued: 55fr, 6/17; 65fr, 4/18; 85fr, 3/29.

Haka Mai — A270

2006 ***Perf. 13¼x13***
617 A270 190fr multi 4.00 4.00

Removal of Christ from the Cross, by Jean Soane Michon (1926-68) — A271

2006, May 31 Litho. ***Perf. 13¼x13***
618 A271 400fr multi 8.00 8.00

2006 World Cup Soccer Championships, Germany — A272

2006, June 9
619 A272 100fr multi 2.25 2.10

Mata Vai — A273

Mata Tai — A274

2006, June 17 ***Perf. 13x13¼***
620 A273 140fr multi 3.00 3.00
621 A274 200fr multi 4.25 4.25

Historical Images From the 19th Century A275

2006, July 13 Engr. ***Perf. 13x13¼***
622 Horiz. pair + central label 15.00 15.00
a. A275 330fr Girls dancing 7.00 7.00
b. A275 380fr Mua Church 8.00 8.00

Stamp Day — A276

2006, Aug. 5 Litho. ***Perf. 13¼x13***
623 A276 150fr multi 3.50 3.25

Twin Otter Airplane "Ville de Paris", 20th Anniv. A277

2006, Aug. 7 ***Perf. 13***
624 A277 30fr multi 1.00 .65

Territorial Rugby Committee A278

2006, Sept. 9 ***Perf. 12¾x13½***
625 A278 10fr multi 1.00 .25

Uhilamoafa Gravesite — A279

2006, Sept. 12 ***Perf. 13x13¼***
626 A279 290fr multi 6.00 6.00

Arms of Monsignor Joseph Félix Blanc (1872-1962) — A280

2006, Oct. 5 Engr. ***Perf. 13¼***
627 A280 500fr multi 10.50 10.50

Tagaloa, Polynesian Deity — A281

2006, Nov. 8 Litho. ***Perf. 13½x13***
628 A281 150fr multi 3.50 3.50

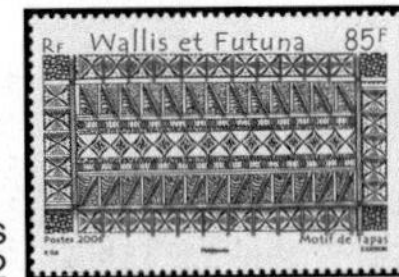
Tapas A282

No. 629: a, Tapas design (shown). b, Mako à Ono. c, Tauasu à Leava. d, Tapas design, diff.

Litho. & Engr.

2006, Nov. 8 ***Perf. 13x13¼***
629 Vert. strip of 4 + central label 8.00 8.00
a.-d. A282 85fr Any single 1.90 1.90

Souvenir Sheet

Christmas — A283

2006, Nov. 8 Litho. *Perf. 13*
630 A283 225fr multi 5.25 5.25

Pio Cardinal Taofinu'u (1923-2006) — A284

2007, Jan. 19 Engr. *Perf. 12½x13*
631 A284 800fr multi 20.00 17.50

Telemedicine — A285

2007, Feb. 28 Litho. *Perf. 13¼x13*
632 A285 5fr multi .75 .25

Audit Office, Bicent. — A286

2007, Mar. 19 Engr. *Perf. 13¼*
633 A286 105fr multi 2.50 2.40

Woman — A287

2007, Mar. 22 Litho. *Perf. 13*
634 A287 75fr multi 1.75 1.75

First Noumea-Hihifo Air Service, 50th Anniv. — A288

2007, Apr. 30 Engr. *Perf. 13x12½*
635 A288 290fr multi 6.75 6.75

Fish A289

2007, May 22 Litho. *Perf. 12¾x13¼*
636 Horiz. pair 2.00 2.00
a. A289 40fr Eviota .90 .90
b. A289 50fr Trimma 1.10 1.10

Secretary General of the Pacific Community, 60th Anniv. — A290

2007, June 28 Litho. *Perf. 13*
637 A290 155fr multi 3.50 3.50

Lolesio Tuita, Javelin Thrower — A291

2007, July 30 Engr. *Perf. 12½x13*
638 A291 330fr purple & red 7.50 7.50

Buildings A292

No. 639: a, House, Tamana. b, Sanctuary of Pierre Chanel, Poi.

2007, July 31 Engr. *Perf. 13x13¼*
639 Horiz. pair with central label 9.00 9.00
a. A292 190fr brown 4.25 4.25
b. A292 200fr brown 4.75 4.75

Discovery of Uvea Island by Samuel Wallis, 240th Anniv. — A293

2007, Aug. 3 Litho.
640 A293 225fr multi 5.25 5.25
a. Souvenir sheet of 1 5.50 5.50

No. 640a sold for 240fr.

Legends of Lomipeau — A294

No. 641 — People and: a, Togitapu Island. b, Uvea Island.

2007, Aug. 3
641 Horiz. pair 1.25 1.25
a. A294 20fr multi .50 .50
b. A294 30fr multi .75 .75

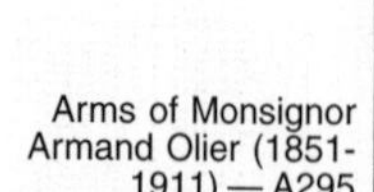

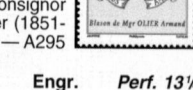

Arms of Monsignor Armand Olier (1851-1911) — A295

2007, Oct. 22 Engr. *Perf. 13¼*
642 A295 500fr multi 12.00 12.00

Emblem of Handisport A296

2007, Oct. 11 Photo. *Perf. 12¾*
643 A296 10fr multi .25 .25

Values are for stamps with surrounding selvage.

2007 Rugby World Cup Championships, France — A297

2007, Oct. 20 Litho. *Perf. 13*
644 A297 205fr multi 5.00 5.00

Printed in sheets of 10 + label.

Dances — A298

Designs: No. 645, 100fr, Mio dance, Futuna. No. 646, 100fr, Kailao Tokotoko dance, Wallis.

2007, Nov. 10 Litho. *Perf. 13¼x13*
645-646 A298 Set of 2 5.00 5.00

Connection to the Internet, 10th Anniv. — A299

2008, Mar. 3 Litho. *Perf. 13x13¼*
647 A299 55fr multi 1.30 1.30

Printed in sheets of 10 + central label.

Coral Reef — A300

2008, Mar. 7
648 A300 95fr multi 2.00 2.00

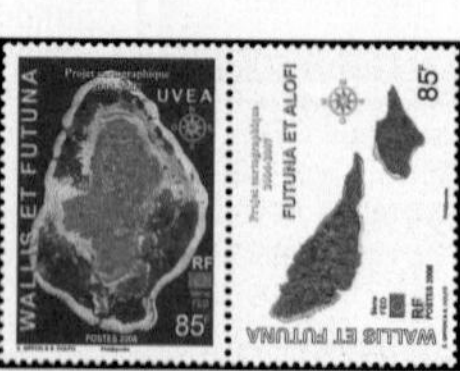

Islands A301

No. 649: a, Uvea. b, Futuna and Alofi, horiz.

Perf. 13¼x13 (#649a), 13x13¼ (#649b)

2008, Mar. 7
649 A301 85fr Pair, #a-b 3.50 3.50

Printed in sheets containing four of each stamp.

Women and Hibiscus Flowers A302

2008, Mar. 7 *Perf. 13*
650 A302 65fr multi 1.75 1.75

Printed in sheets of 10 + 5 labels.

2008 Summer Olympics, Beijing — A303

2008, June 14 *Perf. 13x13¼*
651 A303 75fr multi 2.00 2.00

Intl. Year of Planet Earth A304

2008, June 14 *Perf. 13*
652 A304 190fr multi 5.00 5.00

Souvenir Sheet

653 A304 200fr multi 5.25 5.25

King Tomasi Kulimoetoke II (1918-2007) — A305

2008, July 29 Engr. *Perf. 13¼*
654 A305 380fr orange brown 9.75 9.75

Aglaia Psilopetala A306

2008, July 30 Litho. *Perf. 13*
655 A306 105fr multi 2.75 2.75

Historical Images of Futuna A307

No. 656: a, Women braiding straw. b, Boats returning to island.

2008, July 30 Engr. *Perf. 13x13¼*
656 Horiz. pair with central label 6.75 6.75
a. A307 110fr brown 2.75 2.75
b. A307 155fr brown 4.00 4.00

Stained-glass Windows of Lano Church — A308

Designs: 100fr, St. Theresa. 140fr, St. Peter Chanel.

2008, July 31 Litho. *Perf. 13*
657-658 A308 Set of 2 6.00 6.00

Pirogue Hulls — A309

Various painted pirogue hulls.

2008, Aug. 18 ***Perf. 13x13¼***

659	Horiz. strip of 4	2.75 2.75
a.	A309 5fr multi	.25 .25
b.	A309 20fr multi	.50 .50
c.	A309 40fr multi	.95 .95
d.	A309 50fr multi	1.10 1.10

Lolesio Tuita Stadium — A310

2008, Oct. 28

660 A310 55fr multi 1.25 1.25

Arms of Monsignor Alexandre Poncet (1884-1973) — A311

2008, Oct. 28 Engr. ***Perf. 13¼***

661 A311 500fr multi 11.00 11.00

World Youth Day — A312

2008, Nov. 8 Litho. ***Perf. 13¼x13***

662 A312 10fr multi .25 .25

Pigs A313

No. 663 — Pigs on farm with denomination at: a, UL. b, UR.

2008, Nov. 8 ***Perf. 13x13¼***

663 A313 115fr Horiz. pair, #a-b 5.00 5.00

Fifth French Republic, 50th Anniv. — A314

2008, Nov. 8 Engr. ***Perf. 13¼***

664 A314 225fr multi 5.00 5.00

Louis Braille (1809-52), Educator of the Blind — A315

2009, Mar. 7 Engr. ***Perf. 12¾x13***

665 A315 330fr multi 7.50 7.50

Bougainvillea Spectabilis A316

Flowers with background colors of: No. 666, 55fr, Black. No. 667, 55fr, Green. No. 668, 55fr, Red. No. 669, 55fr, White.

2009, May 4 Litho. ***Perf. 13***

666-669 A316 Set of 4 5.25 5.25

Gobies A317

No. 670: a, Akihito futuna. b, Stiphodon rubromaculatus.

2009, May 7 ***Perf. 12¾x13¼***

670	Horiz. pair	3.00 3.00
a.-b.	A317 65fr Either single	1.50 1.50

St. Theresa of Lisieux (1873-97) — A318

Phil@poste at bottom in: No. 671, White (brown border at bottom). No. 672, Black (brown border at top).

2009, June 27 ***Perf. 13½x13***

671 A318 140fr multi 3.25 3.25
672 A318 140fr multi 3.25 3.25

New Year 2009, (Year of the Ox) — A319

2009, June 30 ***Perf. 13¼x13***

673 A319 95fr multi 2.25 2.25

Pétanque Playing in Wallis & Futuna Islands — A320

2009, July 31

674 A320 105fr multi 2.50 2.50

Arms of Bishop Michel Darmancier (1918-84) — A321

2009, Oct. 30 Engr. ***Perf. 13¼***

675 A321 500fr multi 12.50 12.50

Historical Images A322

No. 676: a, France House. b, Army of Wallisians.

2009, Nov. 5 ***Perf. 13x13¼***

676	Horiz. pair + central label	9.50 9.50
a.-b.	A322 190fr Either single	4.75 4.75

Man Preparing Kava — A323

2009, Nov. 12 Litho. ***Perf. 13¼x13***

677 A323 115fr multi 3.00 3.00

Eiffel Tower on Tapa Cloth — A324

2009, Dec. 8 ***Perf. 13x13¼***

678 A324 85fr brown & black 2.10 2.10

Wallis & Futuna Islands as French Overseas Territory, 50th Anniv. — A325

2009, Dec. 27 Engr. ***Perf. 13¼***

679 A325 205fr multi 5.00 5.00

Arrival of First Doctors on Futuna Island, 50th Anniv. A326

2010, Jan. 3 Litho. ***Perf. 13***

680 A326 800fr multi 18.50 18.50

Gobies A327

2010, Feb. 19 ***Perf. 12¾x13¼***

681	Horiz. pair	2.75 2.75
a.	A327 50fr Sicyopus sasali	1.25 1.25
b.	A327 65fr Stenogobius keletaona	1.50 1.50

A328

A329

A330

Coral Reefs — A331

2010, Mar. 12 Litho. ***Perf. 13x13¼***

682	Horiz. strip of 4	2.40 2.40
a.	A328 10fr multi	.25 .25
b.	A329 20fr multi	.45 .45
c.	A330 30fr multi	.70 .70
d.	A331 40fr multi	.95 .95

Easter — A332

2010, Apr. 2

683 A332 135fr multi 3.25 3.25

Mother's Day — A333

2010, May 28 ***Perf. 13***

684 A333 105fr multi 2.25 2.25

Renewable Energy A334

No. 685: a, Solar panels on ground. b, Solar panels on roof.

2010, June 11

685	Horiz. pair + central label	16.50 16.50
a.-b.	A334 400fr Either single	8.25 8.25

Arms of Bishop Lolesio Fuahea — A335

2010, July 16 Engr. ***Perf. 13¼***

686 A335 500fr multi 11.00 11.00

First Flight to Vele, 40th Anniv. A336

2010, Aug. 24 Litho. ***Perf. 13¼x13***

687 A336 100fr multi 2.25 2.25

Traditional Group Fishing A337

2010, Sept. 24

688 A337 205fr brown 4.75 4.75

Depictions of the Elements — A338

No. 689: a, Water. b, Fire.

2010, Oct. 15 ***Perf. 13***
689 A338 150fr Horiz. pair, #a-b 7.00 7.00

Souvenir Sheet

Cardisoma Carnifex — A338a

No. 689C: d, 95fr, Denomination at LL. e, 130fr, Denomination at UR.

2010, Nov. 6 Litho. ***Perf. 13¼x13***
689C A338a Sheet of 2, #d-e 5.25 5.25

Christmas — A339

2010, Dec. 24 Litho. ***Perf. 13***
690 A339 95fr multi 2.25 2.25

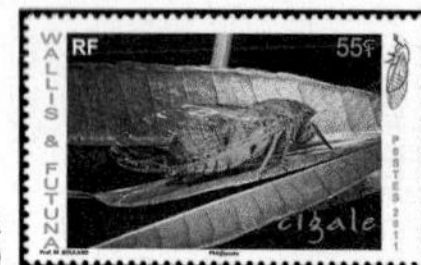

Cicada A340

2011, Jan. 17
691 A340 55fr multi 1.25 1.25

Arms of Bishop Ghislain Marie Raoul Suzanne de Rasilly — A341

2011, Feb. 19 Engr. ***Perf. 13¼***
692 A341 500fr multi 12.00 12.00

French Navy Ship Jacques Cartier, Relief Ship for Victims of Tropical Cyclone Tomas — A342

2011, Mar. 31 Litho. ***Perf. 13***
693 A342 600fr multi 14.50 14.50

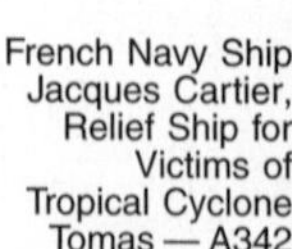

St. Peter Chanel (1803-41) A343

2011, Apr. 28
694 A343 75fr multi 1.75 1.75

Birds A344

No. 695: a, 5fr, Vini australis (30x40mm). b, 20fr, Melipphage foulehaio (30x40mm). c, 115fr, Lalage maculosa futunae (60x40mm).

2011, May 28 ***Perf. 13¼x13***
695 A344 Horiz. strip of 3, #a-c 3.50 3.50

Campaign Against Alcohol — A345

2011, June 28
696 A345 130fr multi 3.25 3.25

Georges Pompidou (1911-74), President of France — A346

2011, July 5 ***Perf. 13x13¼***
697 A346 1000fr multi 24.00 24.00

Territorial Statute, 50th Anniv. — A347

2011, July 16
698 A347 380fr multi 9.25 9.25

Souvenir Sheet

Pacific Games, Noumea, New Caledonia — A348

No. 699: a, 10fr, Track. b, 190fr, Sailing.

2011, Aug. 24
699 A348 Sheet of 2, #a-b 4.75 4.75

Tapa Cloth Designs A349

Designs: 40fr, Flowers and diamonds. 50fr, Shells.

2011, Sept. 24
700-701 A349 Set of 2 2.10 2.10

Wallis Open Air Market, 1st Anniv. — A350

2011, Oct. 2
702 A350 30fr multi .70 .70

Historical Images A351

No. 703: a, Marriage in Mua. b, Marist Sisters, Sofala.

2011, Nov. 4
703 Horiz. pair + central label 6.25 6.25
a. A351 110fr brown 2.50 2.50
b. A351 155fr brown 3.75 3.75

Ninth Pacific Mini-Games, Wallis and Futuna Islands — A352

2012, Jan. 25
704 A352 65fr multi 1.50 1.50

Tekena A353

Fai Koka — A354

2012, Feb. 17
705 A353 75fr multi 1.75 1.75
706 A354 115fr multi 2.60 2.60

First Territorial Assembly A355

2012, Mar. 4
707 A355 200fr multi 4.50 4.50

Corals — A356

Various corals.

2012, Apr. 17 ***Perf. 13x13¼***
708 Horiz. strip of 4 3.25 3.25
a. A356 10fr multi .25 .25
b. A356 30fr multi .70 .70
c. A356 40fr multi .90 .90
d. A356 55fr multi 1.25 1.25

Arrival of Americans, 70th Anniv. A357

2012, May 28 ***Perf. 13***
709 A357 55fr multi 1.25 1.25

Lavelua, King of Uvea, and Chieftains, Circa 1900 A358

2012, June 21 Engr. ***Perf. 13x13¼***
710 A358 380fr bl grn & blk 8.00 8.00

Poetry of the Seas — A359

2012, July 16 Litho. ***Perf. 13***
711 A359 35fr multi .75 .75

Opening of New Payment Office A360

2012, July 27
712 A360 135fr multi 3.00 3.00

Reconstruction of Futuna Upper Administration Delegation Building — A361

2012, Sept. 5
713 A361 95fr multi 2.10 2.10

2013 Oceania Pétanque Tournament, Wallis & Futuna Islands A362

2012, July 7 **Litho.**
714 A362 25fr multi .55 .55

Arms of Bishop Guillaume Douarre (1810-53) — A363

2012, Oct. 18 Engr. ***Perf. 13¼***
715 A363 500fr multi 11.00 11.00

Second Vatican Council, 50th Anniv. A364

2012, Oct. 11 Litho. ***Perf. 13***
716 A364 290fr multi 6.25 6.25

Shells — A365

Various shells.

2012, Nov. 8 ***Perf. 13x13¼***
717 Horiz. strip of 4 3.50 3.50
a. A365 5fr multi .25 .25
b. A365 25fr multi .55 .55
c. A365 35fr multi .75 .75
d. A365 85fr multi 1.90 1.90

Bishop Lolesio Fuahea (1927-2011), First Wallis & Futuna Islands Bishop Born in Oceania — A366

2012, Dec. 2 Engr. *Perf. 13¼x13*
718 A366 1000fr multi 22.00 22.00

A367

Ocean Garden — A368

2013, Jan. 17 Litho. *Perf. 13*
719 A367 85fr multi 2.00 2.00
720 A368 85fr multi 2.00 2.00

Bats A369

2013, Feb. 20 Litho. *Perf. 13*
721 A369 55fr multi 1.25 1.25

Hervé Loste (1926-94), Politician — A370

2013, Mar. 5 Litho. *Perf. 13*
722 A370 800fr multi 17.50 17.50

State High School, 20th Anniv. A371

2013, Mar. 10 Litho. *Perf. 13*
723 A371 65fr multi 1.40 1.40

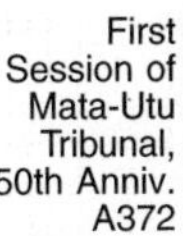

First Session of Mata-Utu Tribunal, 50th Anniv. A372

2013, Apr. 5 Litho. *Perf. 13*
724 A372 190fr multi 4.25 4.25

Discovery of Horn Island (Futuna Island), 400th Anniv. (in 2016) — A373

2013, May 19 Litho. *Perf. 13*
725 A373 330fr multi 7.50 7.50

Story Telling — A374

Traditional Dancers — A375

2013, June 14 Litho. *Perf. 13x13¼*
726 A374 105fr multi 2.40 2.40
727 A375 140fr multi 3.25 3.25

Petelo Sanele Vakalima, Javelin Thrower A376

2013, July 3 Litho. *Perf. 13*
728 A376 75fr multi 1.75 1.75

Sister Marie Françoise Perroton (1796-1873), Missionary — A377

2013, Aug. 10 Engr. *Perf. 13¼x13*
729 A377 400fr beige & blk 9.00 9.00

2013 Pacific Mini-Games, Mata-Utu — A378

No. 730 — Red lizard mascot: a, Serving volleyball, map of Wallis Island. b, Diving for volleyball, map of Futuna Island, horiz. c, Sailing, map of Futuna Island, horiz. d, Weight lifting, map of Futuna Island, horiz. e, Playing rugby, map of Wallis Island. f, Making Taekwondo kick, map of Wallis Island. g, Paddling outrigger canoe, map of Futuna Island, horiz. h, Throwing javelin, map of Wallis Island.

Litho. & Silk-screened
2013, Sept. 2 *Serpentine Die Cut 11*
Self-Adhesive

730 Booklet pane of 8 15.50
a.-h. A378 85fr Any single 1.90 1.90

Bishop Alexandre Poncet (1884-1973) A379

2013, Sept. 18 Engr. *Perf. 13x13¼*
731 A379 150fr black 3.50 3.50

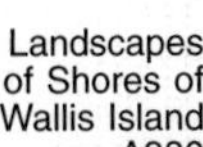

Landscapes of Shores of Wallis Island A380

Designs: 55fr, Fisherman in surf. 65fr, Beach, tree at right.

2013, Oct. 25 Litho. *Perf. 13*
732-733 A380 Set of 2 2.75 2.75

Flowers — A381

Designs: No. 734, 165fr, Hyacinth (jacinth). No. 735, 165fr, Red jasmine (frangipanier).

2013, Nov. 5 Litho. *Perf. 13*
734-735 A381 Set of 2 7.50 7.50

Christmas — A382

2013, Dec. 1 Litho. *Perf. 13*
736 A382 175fr multi 4.00 4.00

New Banknotes A383

Designs: 50fr, 500-franc banknote. 90fr, 1000-franc banknote. 115fr, 5000-franc banknote. 800fr, 10,000-franc banknote.

2014, Jan. 24 Litho. *Perf. 13*
737-740 A383 Set of 4 24.00 24.00

Cyrthandra Futunae — A384

2014, Feb. 18 Litho. *Perf. 13*
741 A384 95fr multi 2.25 2.25

Fai Koka A385

2014, Mar. 5 Litho. *Perf. 13*
742 A385 95fr multi 2.25 2.25

Canonization of Popes — A386

Designs: No. 743, 100fr, Pope John XXIII. No. 744, 100fr, Pope John Paul II.

2014, Apr. 27 Litho. *Perf. 13¼x13*
743-744 A386 Set of 2 4.75 4.75

Chapel and Shrine to St. Peter Chanel, Poi — A387

2014, Apr. 28 Litho. *Perf. 13*
745 A387 130fr multi 3.00 3.00

Mother's Day — A388

2014, May 23 Litho. *Perf. 13¼x13*
746 A388 115fr multi 2.60 2.60

2014 Oceania Weight Lifting Championships, Noumea, New Caledonia — A389

2014, May 27 Litho. *Perf. 13*
747 A389 20fr multi .45 .45

Turtles In Water A390

2014, June 16 Litho. *Perf. 13*
748 A390 65fr multi 1.50 1.50

2014 World Cup Soccer Championships, Brazil — A391

2014, July 12 Litho. *Perf. 13*
749 A391 330fr multi 7.50 7.50

Talietumu Archaeological Site — A392

2014, Aug. 6 Litho. *Perf. 13*
750 A392 75fr multi 1.75 1.75

Miniature Sheet

Tapa Cloths A393

No. 751 — Tapa cloth: a, With geometric design, denomination at UR. b, Depicting people seated around kava bowl. c, With stripes and diamonds, denominations at UL. d,

Depicting canoe, shells, trees and house in octagons.

2014, Sept. 5 Litho. *Perf. 13*
751 A393 85fr Sheet of 4, #a-d 7.25 7.25

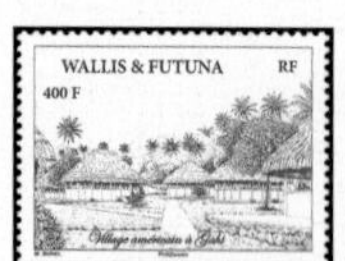

American Village Near Gahi — A394

2014, Oct. 3 Litho. *Perf. 13x13¼*
752 A394 400fr brown 8.50 8.50

Miniature Sheet

Old Stamps A395

No. 753 — Old stamps redrawn in different sizes: a, Stamp like #150. b, Stamp like #155. c, Stamp like #151. d, Stamp like #B9

2014, Nov. 6 Litho. *Perf. 13x13¼*
753 A395 Sheet of 9, #753a-753c, 6 #753d 30.00 30.00
a. 3fr multi .25 .25
b. 7fr multi .25 .25
c. 9fr multi .25 .25
d. 225fr red 4.75 4.75

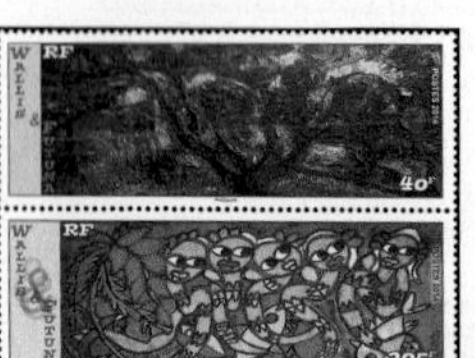

Paintings A396

No. 754 — Painting by: a, 40fr, Nicolai Michoutouchkine. b, 205fr, Aloi Pilioko.

2014, Nov. 8 Litho. *Perf. 13x13¼*
754 A396 Vert. pair, #a-b 5.25 5.25

Benjamin Brial (1923-2004), Politician — A397

2014, Nov. 12 Litho. *Perf. 13*
755 A397 340fr multi 7.00 7.00

Christmas A398

2014, Dec. 23 Litho. *Perf. 13x13¼*
756 A398 85fr multi 1.75 1.75

Women and Children — A399

2015, Jan. 29 Litho. *Perf. 13x13¼*
757 A399 85fr multi 1.60 1.60

Boat Near Beach on Wallis Island A400

2015, Feb. 18 Litho. *Perf. 13*
758 A400 85fr multi 1.60 1.60

Kamilo Gata (1949-2004), Politician — A401

2015, Mar. 27 Litho. *Perf. 13x13¼*
759 A401 600fr multi 11.00 11.00

St. Peter Chanel (1803-41), Missionary A402

2015, Apr. 28 Litho. *Perf. 13*
760 A402 55fr multi 1.10 1.10

Orchids A403

Various orchids: 75fr, 135fr.

2015, May 21 Litho. *Perf. 13*
761-762 A403 Set of 2 4.00 4.00

Emblem of Territorial Committee for Olympics and Sport — A404

2015, June 24 Litho. *Perf. 13*
763 A404 55fr multi 1.00 1.00

Pirogue — A405

2015, July 13 Litho. *Perf. 13x13¼*
764 A405 400fr multi 7.50 7.50

Traditional Women's Clothing — A406

2015, Aug. 31 Litho. *Perf. 13x13¼*
765 A406 330fr multi 6.25 6.25

A407

A408

Lano College, 40th Anniv. — A409

2015, Sept. 3 Litho. *Perf. 13x13¼*
766 Horiz. strip of 3 6.75 6.75
a. A407 55fr multi 1.00 1.00
b. A408 90fr multi 1.75 1.75
c. A409 205fr multi 4.00 4.00

Fugalei, Kaviki and Luaniva Islands A410

2015, Nov. 5 Litho. *Perf. 13*
767 A410 700fr multi 12.50 12.50

Christmas A411

2015, Nov. 23 Litho. *Perf. 13*
768 A411 250fr multi 4.50 4.50

Souvenir Sheet

Cone Shells A412

2016, Jan. 29 Litho. *Perf. 13*
769 A412 Sheet of 2 5.00 5.00
a. 125fr Conus floccatus 2.25 2.25
b. 150fr Conus bullatus 2.75 2.75

Manuia Mobile Phone Service — A413

2016, Feb. 14 Litho. *Perf. 13x13¼*
770 A413 500fr multi 9.25 9.25

Clipper Ship Flying Cloud A414

2016, Mar. 25 Litho. *Perf. 13*
771 A414 300fr multi 5.75 5.75

Eke Dancers — A415

2016, May 4 Litho. *Perf. 13x13¼*
772 A415 105fr multi 2.00 2.00

2016 Festival of Pacific Arts, Guam — A416

2016, May 30 Litho. *Perf. 13*
773 A416 330fr multi 6.25 6.25

Saber Dancer — A417

2016, June 6 Litho. *Perf. 13*
774 A417 135fr multi 2.60 2.60

Campaign Against Diabetes A418

2016, July 13 Litho. *Perf. 13*
775 A418 115fr multi 2.25 2.25

Traditional Fishing, Nukuafo — A419

2016, July 26 Engr. *Perf. 13*
776 A419 800fr dull purple 15.00 15.00

Souvenir Sheet

Butterflies — A420

No. 777: a, Euchrysops cnejus samoa. b, Junonia villida. c, Euploea lewinii eschscholtzii, vert.

2016, Sept. 21 Litho. *Perf. 13*
777 A420 115fr Sheet of 3, #a-c 6.50 6.50

Twin Otter Airplane "Ville de Paris", 30th Anniv. — A421

2016, Nov. 3 Litho. *Perf. 13x13¼*
778 A421 105fr multi 1.90 1.90

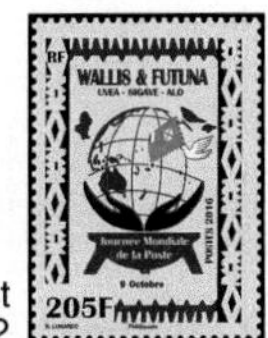

World Post Day — A422

2016, Nov. 3 Litho. ***Perf. 13¼x13***
779 A422 205fr multi 3.75 3.75

Souvenir Sheet

Birds A423

No. 780: a, Fregata ariel. b, Ptilinopus porphyraceus, vert. c, Phaethon rubricauda.

Perf. 13x13¼, 13¼x13 (#780b)
2016, Nov. 30 Litho.
780 A423 95fr Sheet of 3, #a-c 5.25 5.25

Christmas A424

2016, Dec. 20 Litho. ***Perf. 13x13¼***
781 A424 100fr multi 1.75 1.75

Wallis and Futuna Islands Marianne Sculpture — A425

2017, Jan. 31 Litho. ***Perf. 13¼x13***
782 A425 95fr multi 1.75 1.75

Visit of French President François Hollande to Wallis and Futuna Islands A426

2017, Feb. 22 Litho. ***Perf. 13***
783 A426 290fr multi 5.25 5.25

International Women's Day — A427

2017, Mar. 8 Litho. ***Perf. 13***
784 A427 290fr multi 5.25 5.25

St. Peter Chanel (1803-41), Missionary on Futuna Island — A428

2017, Apr. 28 Litho. ***Perf. 13***
785 A428 300fr multi 5.50 5.50

Fire Dancer A429

2017, May 26 Litho. ***Perf. 13***
786 A429 65fr multi 1.25 1.25

Megaptera Novaeangliae and Map of Wallis and Futuna Islands — A430

2017, June 7 Litho. ***Perf. 13***
787 A430 400fr multi 7.75 7.75

World Environment Day.

1957 Wallis & Futuna Islands Soccer Team A431

2017, July 12 Litho. ***Perf. 13***
788 A431 55fr brown 1.10 1.10

Samuel Wallis (1728-95), Discoverer of Wallis & Futuna Islands A432

2017, Aug. 16 Litho. ***Perf. 13***
789 A432 800fr multi 16.00 16.00

Miniature Sheet

Rays A433

No. 790: a, Dasyatis kuhlii (40x30mm). b, Taeniura meyeni (30x40mm). c, Aetobatus narinari (40x30mm). d, Manta alfredi (40x40mm).

2017, Sept. 22 Litho. ***Perf. 13***
790 A433 Sheet of 4 3.25 3.25
a. 5fr multi .25 .25
b. 10fr multi .25 .25
c. 30fr multi .55 .55
d. 115fr multi 2.25 2.25

Hua (Traditional Food) — A434

2017, Oct. 15 Litho. ***Perf. 13***
791 A434 200fr multi 4.00 4.00

Global Warming — A435

No. 792: a, Cyclone Tomas of 2010, map of Futuna Island, rising ocean levels and beach erosion. b, Cyclone Evan of 2012, map of Wallis Island, coral whitening. c, Cyclone Pam of 2015, map of Vanuatu, extreme waves and winds. d, Cyclone Winston of 2016, map of Fiji, acidification of oceans.

2017, Nov. 9 Litho. ***Perf. 13x13¼***
792 Horiz. strip of 4 9.00 9.00
a.-d. A435 115fr Any single 2.25 2.25

The stamp shown above, issued in Nov. 2017, was printed in limited quantities and sold only at a stamp show in Paris, France.

Christmas A436

2017, Dec. 20 Litho. ***Perf. 13***
793 A436 85fr multi 1.75 1.75

Painting by Aloi Pilioko — A437

2018, Jan. 31 Litho. ***Perf. 13***
794 A437 85fr multi 1.75 1.75

New Year 2018 (Year of the Dog) — A438

2018, Feb. 16 Litho. ***Perf. 13***
795 A438 55fr multi 1.10 1.10

Soamako Dance A439

2018, Apr. 28 Litho. ***Perf. 13***
796 A439 500fr multi 10.00 10.00

International Day of Dance

Month of Mary Religious Procession A440

2018, May 2 Litho. ***Perf. 13***
797 A440 380fr multi 7.50 7.50

Inauguration of Tui Samoa Submarine Cable System A441

No. 798 — Ship, cable markers and connection date of: a, Nov. 19, 2017 for Wallis Island. b, Nov. 28, 2017 for Futuna Island.

2018, May 9 Litho. ***Perf. 13***
798 Horiz. pair + 2 labels 3.80 3.80
a.-b. A441 95fr Either single + label 1.90 1.90

2018 World Cup Soccer Championships, Russia — A442

2018, June 18 Litho. ***Perf. 13***
799 A442 150fr multi 3.00 3.00

Bastille Day — A443

2018, July 14 Litho. ***Perf. 13***
800 A443 500fr multi 9.75 9.75

Lavelua Tomasi Kulimoetoke II (1918-2007), 50th King of Wallis Island — A444

2018, July 26 Litho. ***Perf. 13***
801 A444 600fr brown 12.00 12.00

World Youth Day — A445

2018, Aug. 12 Litho. ***Perf. 13***
802 A445 350fr multi 6.75 6.75

Miniature Sheet

Frangipani Flowers — A446

No. 803: a, Red violet flowers, denomination in yellow. b, White flowers, denomination in yellow. c, Pink flowers, denomination in orange. d, Yellow flowers, denomination in orange.

2018, Sept. 5 Litho. *Perf. 13x13¼*
803 A446 55fr Sheet of 4, #a-d 4.25 4.25

Fai Umu Tagata, Futuna Island A447

2018, Sept. 26 Litho. *Perf. 13*
804 A447 40fr multi .80 .80

European Heritage Day.

Mangrove Conservation A448

No. 805: a, Birds and mangrove trees. b, Marine life and mangrove roots. c, Women planting mangrove trees. d, Mature and young mangrove trees and ocean.

2018, Nov. 8 Litho. *Perf. 13x13¼*
805 Horiz. strip of 4 9.00 9.00
a.-d. A448 115fr Any single 2.25 2.25

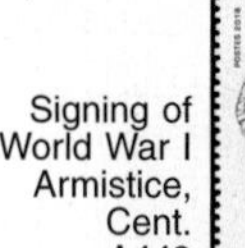

Signing of World War I Armistice, Cent. A449

2018, Nov. 11 Litho. *Perf. 13*
806 A449 390fr multi 7.50 7.50

The stamps shown above, issued in Nov. 2018, were printed in limited quantities and sold only at a stamp show in Paris, France.

Road Safety Campaign A450

2019, Jan. 28 Litho. *Perf. 13*
807 A450 500fr multi 9.75 9.75

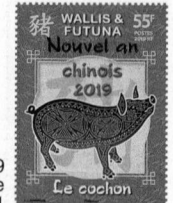

New Year 2019 (Year of the Pig) — A451

2019, Feb. 5 Litho. *Perf. 13*
808 A451 55fr multi 1.10 1.10

Tapaki Dancer — A452

2019, June 20 Litho. *Perf. 13*
809 A452 135fr multi 3.00 3.00

Opening of Wallis & Futuna Islands Language Academy A453

2019, July 12 Litho. *Perf. 13*
810 A453 65fr multi 1.25 1.25

Express Mail Service, 20th Anniv. — A454

2019, Sept. 10 Litho. *Perf. 13*
811 A454 300fr multi 5.50 5.50

2019 Rugby World Cup, Japan — A455

2019, Sept. 20 Litho. *Perf. 13*
812 A455 175fr multi 3.25 3.25

King Vanai and the Battle of Vai — A456

2019, Oct. 17 Litho. *Perf. 13*
813 A456 100fr multi 1.90 1.90

Battle of Vai, 180th anniv.

Cooperation Accord Between Wallis & Futuna Islands and European Union, 20th Anniv. A457

2019, Oct. 17 Litho. *Perf. 13*
814 A457 400fr multi 7.50 7.50

D-Day, 75th Anniv. — A458

2019, Oct. 17 Litho. *Perf. 13*
815 A458 700fr multi 13.00 13.00

World Oceans Day A459

No. 816: a, Uvea Island. b, Futuna and Alofi Islands.

2019, Oct. 17 Litho. *Perf. 13*
816 Horiz. pair + 2 labels 3.50 3.50
a.-b. A459 90fr Either single + label 1.75 1.75

Miniature Sheet

Pacific Games A460

No. 817: a, 5fr, Track and field. b, 10fr, Weight lifting. c, 20fr, Rugby. d, 30fr, Va'a rowing. e, 100fr, Volleyball.

2019, Oct. 30 Litho. *Perf. 13*
817 A460 Sheet of 5, #a-e 3.25 3.25

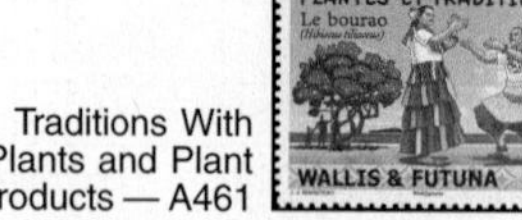

Traditions With Plants and Plant Products — A461

No. 818: a, Dancers wearing Hibiscus tiliaceus flowers. b, Woman with items made with Pandanus odoratissimus fibers. c, Cloth made with Broussonetia papyrifera fibers. d, Man making kava with Piper methysticum.

2019, Nov. 7 Litho. *Perf. 13*
818 Horiz. strip of 4 8.50 8.50
a.-d. A461 115fr Any single 2.10 2.10

The self-adhesive stamp shown above, issued in Nov. 2019, was printed in limited quantities and sold only at a stamp show in Paris, France.

International Black Cat Day — A462

2019, Nov. 20 Litho. *Perf. 13x13¼*
819 A462 65fr multi 1.25 1.25

New Year 2020 (Year of the Rat) — A463

2020, Jan. 25 Litho. *Perf. 13*
820 A463 55fr multi 1.10 1.10

Indigenous Languages of French-Speaking Oceania Areas — A464

2020, Feb. 17 Litho. *Perf. 13*
821 A464 75fr multi 1.40 1.40

International Day of Dance A465

2020, Apr. 29 Litho. *Perf. 13*
822 A465 135fr multi 2.50 2.50

Nature Festival — A466

2020, May 22 Litho. *Perf. 13¼x13*
823 A466 300fr multi 5.75 5.75

Charles de Gaulle's June 18, 1940 Appeal, 80th Anniv. A467

2020, June 18 Litho. *Perf. 13*
824 A467 350fr multi 6.75 6.75

International Night of the Bat — A468

2020, Aug. 31 Litho. *Perf. 13¼x13*
825 A468 65fr multi 1.30 1.30

A469

Campaign Against COVID-19 Pandemic A470

Serpentine Die Cut 6¾x8
2020, Nov. 5 Litho.
Self-Adhesive
826 A469 500fr multi 10.00 10.00
827 A470 500fr multi 10.00 10.00

United Nations, 75th Anniv. A471

2020, Dec. 18 Litho. *Perf. 13*
828 A471 800fr multi 16.50 16.50

Weavers A472

No. 829: a, Purse and female weaver. b, Bowl and male weaver.

2020, Dec. 22 Litho. *Perf. 13*
829 A472 150fr Horiz. pair, #a-b 6.25 6.25

New Year 2021 (Year of the Ox) — A473

2021, Feb. 12 Litho. *Perf. 13*
830 A473 55fr multi 1.10 1.10

A474

A475

A476

Pirogues — A477

2021, Feb. 19 Litho. *Perf. 13x13¼*
831 Horiz. strip of 4 9.75 9.75
a. A474 115fr multi 2.40 2.40
b. A475 115fr multi 2.40 2.40
c. A476 115fr multi 2.40 2.40
d. A477 115fr multi 2.40 2.40

Nos. 831a-831d are each dated 2020.

Coat of Arms of Bishop Susitino Sionepoe — A478

2021, Mar. 24 Litho. *Perf. 13¼x13*
832 A478 500fr multi 10.00 10.00

Miniature Sheet

Birds A479

No. 833; a, 5fr, Gallirallus philippensis (40x30mm). b, 10fr, Porphyrio porphyrio (30x40mm). c, 20fr, Phaethon lepturus (30x40mm). d, 30fr, Egretta sacra (40x40mm).

Perf. 13x13¼ (5fr), 13¼x13 (10fr, 20fr), 13 (30fr)

2021, June 5 Photo.
833 A479 Sheet of 4, #a-d 1.30 1.30

International Day of Forests — A480

2021 Litho. *Perf. 13¼x13*
834 A480 65fr multi 1.30 1.30

Morinda Citrifolia — A481

2021, Aug. 26 Litho. *Perf. 13x13¼*
835 A481 205fr multi 4.25 4.25

Change of Wallis & Futuna Islands Status to Separate French Overseas Territory, 60th Anniv. — A482

2021, Aug. 31 Litho. *Perf. 13*
836 A482 700fr multi + label 14.00 14.00

International Day of Humanitarian Aid — A483

2021, Oct. 15 Litho. *Perf. 13*
837 A483 75fr multi 1.50 1.50

Painting by Aloisio Pilioko (1935-2020) A484

2021, Oct. 15 Litho. *Perf. 13*
838 A484 300fr multi 6.00 6.00

Sharks and Their Teeth — A485

No. 839: a, Nebrius ferrugineus. b, Triaenodon obesus. c, Carcharhinus melanopterus.

2021, Dec. 20 Litho. *Perf. 13x13¼*
839 Horiz. strip of 3 5.25 5.25
a. A485 65fr multi 1.25 1.25
b. A485 95fr multi 1.90 1.90
c. A485 100fr multi 2.00 2.00

Kea Breadfruit A486

2022, Mar. 7 Litho. *Perf. 13*
840 A486 65fr multi 1.25 1.25

World Water Day — A487

2022, Mar. 22 Litho. *Perf. 13*
841 A487 100fr multi 1.90 1.90

Me'e Lakalaka Dancers A488

2022, Apr. 29 Litho. *Perf. 13*
842 A488 380fr multi 6.75 6.75

International Day of Dance.

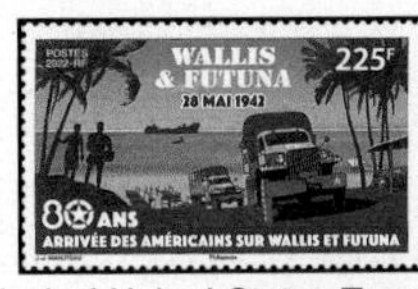
Arrival of United States Troops on Wallis and Futuna Islands, 80th Anniv. A489

2022, May 30 Litho. *Perf. 13*
843 A489 225fr multi 4.00 4.00

Traditional Fishing Customs A490

2022, June 6 Litho. *Perf. 13*
844 A490 400fr multi 7.00 7.00

No. 844 was printed in sheets of 2.

Sygygium Malaccense Leaves Used as Traditional Medicine — A491

2022, June 15 Litho. *Perf. 13x13¼*
845 A491 205fr multi 3.75 3.75

Legend of Mohukele — A492

2022, July 29 Litho. *Perf. 13*
846 A492 330fr multi 5.75 5.75

No. 846 was printed in sheets of 10 + central label.

International Youth Day — A493

2022, Aug. 12 Litho. *Perf. 13*
847 A493 135fr multi 2.25 2.25

Lano Chapel, 175th Anniv. — A494

2022, Oct. 11 Litho. *Perf. 13¼x13*
848 A494 85fr multi 1.40 1.40

Tapa Cloth Depicting Map of Wallis Island and Surrounding Atoll A495

Tapa Cloth Depicting Map of Futuna and Alofi Islands A496

2022, Nov. 3 Litho. *Perf. 13*
849 Horiz. pair 17.50 17.50
a. A495 500fr multi 8.75 8.75
b. A496 500fr multi 8.75 8.75

Syzygium Neurocalyx and Diospyros Major A497

2022, Dec. 23 Litho. *Perf. 13*
850 A497 115fr multi 2.10 2.10

SEMI-POSTAL STAMPS

French Revolution Issue
Common Design Type

Unwmk.

1939, July 5 Photo. *Perf. 13*

Name and Value Typo. in Black

B1	CD83	45c + 25c green	16.00	*22.00*
B2	CD83	70c + 30c brown	16.00	*22.00*
B3	CD83	90c + 35c red org	16.00	*22.00*
B4	CD83	1.25fr + 1fr rose pink	16.00	*22.00*
B5	CD83	2.25fr + 2fr blue	16.00	*22.00*
		Nos. B1-B5 (5)	80.00	110.00
		Set, never hinged	150.00	

New Caledonia Nos. B10 and B12 Ovptd. "WALLIS ET FUTUNA" in Blue or Red, and Common Design Type

1941 Photo. *Perf. 13½*

B6	SP2	1fr + 1fr red	1.75
B7	CD86	1.50fr + 3fr maroon	1.75
B8	SP3	2.50fr + 1fr dark blue	1.75
		Nos. B6-B8 (3)	5.25
		Set, never hinged	9.00

Nos. B6-B8 were issued by the Vichy government in France, but were not placed on sale in Wallis & Futuna.

Nos. 92-93 Srchd. in Black or Red

1944 Engr. *Perf. 12x12½*

B8A	50c + 1.50fr on 2.50fr deep blue (R)	1.90
B8B	+ 2.50fr on 1fr green	1.90

Colonial Development Fund.

Nos. B8A-B8B were issued by the Vichy government in France, but were not placed on sale in Wallis & Futuna.

Catalogue values for unused stamps in this section, from this point to the end of the section, are for Never Hinged items.

Red Cross Issue
Common Design Type

1944 Photo. ***Perf. 14½x14***
B9 CD90 5fr + 20fr red orange 3.00 3.00

The surtax was for the French Red Cross and national relief. See No. 753d.

AIR POST STAMPS

Catalogue values for unused stamps in this section are for Never Hinged items.

Victory Issue
Common Design Type

Perf. 12½

1946, May 8 Unwmk. Engr.
C1 CD92 8fr dark violet 2.25 1.90

Chad to Rhine Issue
Common Design Types

1946

C2	CD93	5fr dark violet	1.40	1.10
C3	CD94	10fr dk slate grn	1.60	1.30
C4	CD95	15fr violet brn	1.60	1.30
C5	CD96	20fr brt ultra	2.40	1.75
C6	CD97	25fr brown orange	2.75	2.10
C7	CD98	50fr carmine	4.00	2.90
		Nos. C2-C7 (6)	13.75	10.45

New Caledonia Nos. C21-C22 Overprinted in Blue

1949, July 4 ***Perf. 13x12½, 12½x13***
C8 AP2 50fr yel & rose red 8.50 7.00
C9 AP3 100fr yel & red brn 15.00 12.00

The overprint on No. C9 is in three lines.

UPU Issue
Common Design Type

1949, July 4 Engr. ***Perf. 13***
C10 CD99 10fr multicolored 11.00 8.25

Liberation Issue
Common Design Type

1954, June 6
C11 CD102 3fr sepia & vio brn 11.00 8.25

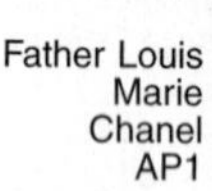

Father Louis Marie Chanel
AP1

1955, Nov. 21 Unwmk. ***Perf. 13***
C12 AP1 14fr dk grn, grnsh bl & ind 2.75 1.40

Issued in honor of Father Chanel, martyred missionary to the Islands.

View of Mata-Utu, Queen Amelia and Msgr. Bataillon
AP2

33fr, Map of islands and sailing ship.

1960, Sept. 19 Engr. ***Perf. 13***
C13 AP2 21fr blue, brn & grn 4.50 4.00
C14 AP2 33fr ultra, choc & bl grn 6.75 6.00

For No. C14 with surcharge, see No. C36.

Shell Diver — AP3

1962, Sept. 20 Unwmk. ***Perf. 13***
C16 AP3 100fr bl, grn & dk red brn 19.00 15.00

Telstar Issue
Common Design Type

1962, Dec. 5
C17 CD111 12fr dk pur, mar & bl 3.75 3.75

Sea Shell Type of Regular Issue

1963, Apr. 1 Engr.
Size: 26x47mm
C18 A5 50fr Harpa ventricosa 12.50 7.00

Javelin Thrower — AP4

1964, Oct. 10 Engr. ***Perf. 13***
C19 AP4 31fr emer, ver & vio brn 19.00 19.00

18th Olympic Games, Tokyo, Oct. 10-25.

ITU Issue
Common Design Type

1965, May 17 Unwmk. ***Perf. 13***
C20 CD120 50fr multicolored 16.00 16.00

Mata-Utu Wharf
AP5

1965, Nov. 26 Engr. ***Perf. 13***
C21 AP5 27fr brt bl, sl grn & red brn 4.50 4.50

French Satellite A-1 Issue
Common Design Type

Designs: 7fr, Diamant rocket and launching installations. 10fr, A-1 satellite.

1966, Jan. 17 Engr. ***Perf. 13***
C22 CD121 7fr crim, red & car lake 3.25 3.25
C23 CD121 10fr car lake, red & crim 3.75 3.75
a. Strip of 2, #C22-C23 + label 8.50 8.50

French Satellite D-1 Issue
Common Design Type

1966, June 2 Engr. ***Perf. 13***
C24 CD122 10fr lake, bl grn & red 3.50 3.50

WHO Headquarters, Geneva, and Emblem — AP6

1966, July 5 Photo. ***Perf. 12½x13***
C25 AP6 30fr org, maroon & bl 3.50 3.50

New WHO Headquarters, Geneva.

Girl and Boy Reading; UNESCO Emblem
AP7

1966, Nov. 4 Engr. ***Perf. 13***
C26 AP7 50fr green, org & choc 5.75 4.25

20th anniv. of UNESCO.

Athlete and Pattern — AP8

Design: 38fr, Woman ballplayer and pattern.

1966, Dec. 8 Engr. ***Perf. 13x12½***
C27 AP8 32fr bl, dp car & blk 4.25 3.00
C28 AP8 38fr emer & brt pink 4.75 4.00

2nd South Pacific Games, Nouméa, 12/8-18.

Samuel Wallis' Ship and Coast of Wallis Island
AP9

1967, Dec. 16 Photo. ***Perf. 13***
C29 AP9 12fr multicolored 6.50 4.75

Bicentenary of the discovery of Wallis Island.

Concorde Issue
Common Design Type

1969, Apr. 17 Engr. ***Perf. 13***
C30 CD129 20fr black & plum 15.00 10.00

Man Climbing Coconut Palm
AP10

32fr, Horseback rider. 38fr, Men making wooden stools. 50fr, Spear fisherman & man holding basket with fish. 100fr, Women sorting coconuts.

1969, Apr. 30 Photo. ***Perf. 13***

C31	AP10	20fr multi	2.50	1.50
C32	AP10	32fr multi	4.25	2.00
C33	AP10	38fr multi	4.50	2.50
C34	AP10	50fr multi	7.25	4.50
C35	AP10	100fr multi	12.50	7.25
		Nos. C31-C35 (5)	31.00	17.75

No. C14 Surcharged with New Value and Three Bars

1971 Engr. ***Perf. 13***
C36 AP2 21fr on 33fr multi 4.00 4.00

Pole Vault
AP11

1971, Oct. 25 Engr. ***Perf. 13***
C37 AP11 48fr shown 4.75 3.00
C38 AP11 54fr Archery 6.75 5.00

4th South Pacific Games, Papeete, French Polynesia, Sept. 8-19.

South Pacific Commission Headquarters, Noumea — AP12

1972, Feb. 5 Photo. ***Perf. 13***
C39 AP12 44fr blue & multi 5.75 4.25

South Pacific Commission, 25th anniv.

Round House and Festival Emblem — AP13

1972, May 15 Engr. ***Perf. 13***
C40 AP13 60fr dp car, grn & pur 7.50 5.00

South Pacific Festival of Arts, Fiji, May 6-20.

Canoe Type of Regular Issue

Design: 200fr, Outrigger sailing canoe race, and island woman.

1972, Oct. 16 Photo. ***Perf. 13x12½***
Size: 47½x28mm
C41 A9 200fr multicolored 35.00 25.00

La Pérouse and "La Boussole"
AP14

Explorers and their Ships: 28fr, Samuel Wallis and "Dolphin." 40fr, Dumont D'Urville and "Astrolabe." 72fr, Bougainville and "La Boudeuse."

1973, July 20 Engr. ***Perf. 13***

C42	AP14	22fr brn, slate & car	11.00	6.00
C43	AP14	28fr sl grn, dl red & bl	12.50	6.00
C44	AP14	40fr brn, ind & ultra	15.00	9.25
C45	AP14	72fr brown, bl & pur	18.00	12.50
		Nos. C42-C45 (4)	56.50	33.75

Charles de Gaulle
AP15

1973, Nov. 9 Engr. ***Perf. 13***
C46 AP15 107fr brn org & dk brn 15.00 11.00

Pres. Charles de Gaulle (1890-1970).

Red Jasmine — AP16

Flowers from Wallis: 17fr, Hibiscus tiliaceus. 19fr, Phaeomeria magnifica. 21fr, Hibiscus rosa sinensis. 23fr, Allamanda cathartica. 27fr, Barringtonia. 39fr, Flowers in vase.

1973, Dec. 6 Photo. ***Perf. 13***

C47	AP16	12fr shown	1.30	1.25
C48	AP16	17fr multicolored	2.00	1.90
C49	AP16	19fr multicolored	2.60	1.90
C50	AP16	21fr multicolored	3.50	2.10
C51	AP16	23fr multicolored	4.50	2.50
C52	AP16	27fr multicolored	5.25	3.00
C53	AP16	39fr multicolored	7.25	6.25
		Nos. C47-C53 (7)	26.40	18.90

UPU Emblem and Symbolic Design — AP17

1974, Oct. 9 **Engr.** ***Perf. 13***
C54 AP17 51fr multicolored 6.50 4.75

Centenary of Universal Postal Union.

Holy Family, Primitive Painting — AP18

1974, Dec. 9 **Photo.** ***Perf. 13***
C55 AP18 150fr multicolored 13.00 10.00

Christmas 1974.

Tapa Cloth AP19

Tapa Cloth: 24fr, Village scene. 36fr, Fish & marine life. 80fr, Marine life, map of islands, village scene.

1975, Feb. 3 **Photo.** ***Perf. 13***
C56 AP19 3fr multicolored 1.00 .65
C57 AP19 24fr multicolored 2.00 1.50
C58 AP19 36fr multicolored 3.25 2.25
C59 AP19 80fr multicolored 6.75 5.25
Nos. C56-C59 (4) 13.00 9.65

DC-7 in Flight — AP20

1975, Aug. 13 **Engr.** ***Perf. 13***
C60 AP20 100fr multicolored 7.25 5.50

First regular air service between Nouméa, New Caledonia, and Wallis.

Volleyball — AP21

1975, Nov. 10 **Photo.** ***Perf. 13***
C61 AP21 26fr shown 1.90 1.20
C62 AP21 44fr Soccer 2.60 1.90
C63 AP21 56fr Javelin 4.25 2.90
C64 AP21 105fr Spear fishing 8.25 6.50
Nos. C61-C64 (4) 17.00 12.50

5th South Pacific Games, Guam, Aug. 1-10.

Lalolalo Lake, Wallis AP22

Landscapes: 29fr, Vasavasa, Futuna. 41fr, Sigave Bay, Futuna. 68fr, Gahi Bay, Wallis.

1975, Dec. 1 **Litho.** ***Perf. 13***
C65 AP22 10fr grn & multi 1.50 .95
C66 AP22 29fr grn & multi 2.50 1.75
C67 AP22 41fr grn & multi 3.50 2.40
C68 AP22 68fr grn & multi 4.75 3.75
Nos. C65-C68 (4) 12.25 8.85

Concorde, Eiffel Tower and Sugar Loaf Mountain AP23

1976, Jan. 21 **Engr.** ***Perf. 13***
C69 AP23 250fr multi 21.00 20.00

1st commercial flight of supersonic jet Concorde from Paris to Rio, Jan. 21.
For overprint see No. C73.

Hammer Throw and Stadium AP24

39fr, Diving, Stadium and maple leaf.

1976, Aug. 2 **Engr.** ***Perf. 13***
C70 AP24 31fr multi 2.75 2.25
C71 AP24 39fr multi 4.00 3.50

21st Olympic Games, Montreal, Canada, July 17-Aug. 1.

De Gaulle Memorial — AP25

Photogravure and Embossed

1977, June 18 ***Perf. 13***
C72 AP25 100fr gold & multi 8.75 7.50

5th anniversary of dedication of De Gaulle Memorial at Colombey-les-Deux-Eglises.

No. C69 Ovptd. in Dark Brown "PARIS NEW-YORK / 22.11.77 / 1er VOL COMMERCIAL"

1977, Nov. 22 **Engr.** ***Perf. 13***
C73 AP23 250fr multicolored 19.00 17.50

Concorde, 1st commercial flight, Paris-NY.

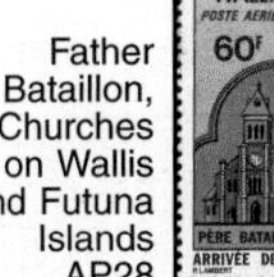

Balistes Niger AP26

Fish: 35fr, Amphiprion akindynos. 49fr, Pomacanthus imperator. 51fr, Zanclus cornutus.

1978, Jan. 31 **Litho.** ***Perf. 13***
C74 AP26 26fr multi 1.75 .75
C75 AP26 35fr multi 2.75 1.00
C76 AP26 49fr multi 3.50 1.25
C77 AP26 51fr multi 4.25 3.25
Nos. C74-C77 (4) 12.25 6.25

Map of Wallis and Uvea Islands AP27

300fr, Map of Futuna and Alofi Islands, horz.

1978, Mar. 7 **Engr.**
C78 AP27 300fr vio bl & grnsh bl 15.00 12.50
C79 AP27 500fr multi 20.00 19.00

Father Bataillon, Churches on Wallis and Futuna Islands AP28

72fr, Monsignor Pompallier, map of Wallis, Futuna and Alofi Islands, outrigger canoe.

1978, Apr. 28 **Litho.** ***Perf. 13x12½***
C80 AP28 60fr multi 2.50 1.75
C81 AP28 72fr multi 2.75 2.00

First French missionaries on Wallis and Futuna Islands.

ITU Emblem AP29

1978, May 17 **Litho.** ***Perf. 13***
C82 AP29 66fr multi 3.00 2.25

10th World Telecommunications Day.

Nativity and Longhouse AP30

1978, Dec. 4 **Photo.** ***Perf. 13***
C83 AP30 160fr multi 7.75 5.50

Christmas 1978.

Popes Paul VI, John Paul I, St. Peter's, Rome AP31

37fr, Pope Paul VI. 41fr, Pope John Paul I.

Perf. 12½x13, 13x12½

1979, Jan. 31 **Litho.**
C84 AP31 37fr multi, vert. 1.75 1.40
C85 AP31 41fr multi, vert. 2.00 1.75
C86 AP31 105fr multi 4.25 3.50
Nos. C84-C86 (3) 8.00 6.65

In memory of Popes Paul VI and John Paul I.

Monoplane of UTA Airlines — AP32

68fr, Freighter Muana. 80fr, Hihifo Airport.

1979, Feb. 28 ***Perf. 13x12½***
C87 AP32 46fr multi 1.50 .95
C88 AP32 68fr multi 1.75 1.50
C89 AP32 80fr multi 2.75 2.00
Nos. C87-C89 (3) 6.00 4.45

Inter-Island transportation.
See Nos. 251-253.

France No. 67 and Eole Weather Satellite AP33

70fr, Hibiscus & stamp similar to #25. 90fr, Rowland Hill & Penny Black. 100fr, Birds, Kano School, Japan 17th cent. & Japan #9.

1979, May 7 **Photo.** ***Perf. 13***
C90 AP33 5fr multi .90 .65
C91 AP33 70fr multi, vert. 3.00 1.90
C92 AP33 90fr multi 3.50 2.50
C93 AP33 100fr multi 4.50 3.75
Nos. C90-C93 (4) 11.90 8.80

Sir Rowland Hill (1795-1879), originator of penny postage.

Cross of Lorraine and People AP34

1979, June 18 **Engr.** ***Perf. 13***
C94 AP34 33fr multi 2.25 1.75

Map of Islands, Arms of France — AP35

1979, July 19 **Photo.** ***Perf. 13***
C95 AP35 47fr multi 2.25 2.00

Visit of Pres. Valery Giscard d'Estaing of France.

Capt. Cook, Ships and Island AP36

1979, July 28
C96 AP36 130fr multi 6.50 4.25

Capt. James Cook (1728-1779).

Telecom Emblem, Satellite, Receiving Station AP37

1979, Sept. 20 **Litho.** ***Perf. 13***
C97 AP37 120fr multi 4.50 3.50

3rd World Telecommunications Exhibition, Geneva, Sept. 20-26.

Virgin of the Crescent Moon, by Albrecht Durer — AP38

1979, Dec. 17 **Engr.** ***Perf. 13***
C98 AP38 180fr red & blk 7.50 6.25

Christmas 1979. See No. C163.

Rotary International, 75th Anniversary — AP39

1980, Feb. 29 **Litho.** ***Perf. 13***
C99 AP39 86fr multi 4.75 3.50

Rochambeau and Troops, US Flag, 1780 — AP40

1980, May 27 Engr. *Perf. 13*
C100 AP40 102fr multi 4.50 3.50

Rochambeau's landing at Newport, RI (American Revolution), bicentenary.

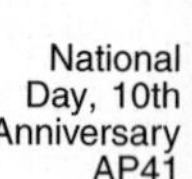

National Day, 10th Anniversary AP41

1980, July 15 Litho. *Perf. 13*
C101 AP41 71fr multi 2.25 1.50

Transatlantic Airmail Flight, 50th Anniversary AP42

1980, Sept. 22 Engr. *Perf. 13*
C102 AP42 122fr multi 4.50 3.50

Fleming, Penicillin Bacilli — AP43

1980, Oct. 20
C103 AP43 101fr multi 4.00 2.50

Alexander Fleming (1881-1955), discoverer of penicillin, 25th death anniversary.

Charles De Gaulle, 10th Anniversary of Death AP44

1980, Nov. 9 Engr. *Perf. 13*
C104 AP44 200fr sep & dk ol grn 8.00 7.25

Virgin and Child with St. Catherine, by Lorenzo Lotto AP45

1980, Dec. 20 Litho. *Perf. 13x12½*
C105 AP45 150fr multi 4.50 3.50

Christmas 1980.

Alan B. Shepard and Spacecraft — AP46

20th Anniv. of Space Flight: 44fr, Yuri Gagarin.

1981, May 11 Litho. *Perf. 13*
C106 AP46 37fr multi 1.20 .95
C107 AP46 44fr multi 1.60 1.40

Vase of Flowers, by Paul Cezanne (1839-1906) AP47

Design: 135fr, Harlequin, by Pablo Picasso.

1981, Oct. 22 Litho. *Perf. 12½x13*
C108 AP47 53fr multi 2.40 1.40
C109 AP47 135fr multi 4.75 3.00

Espana '82 World Cup Soccer AP48

1981-82 Engr. *Perf. 13*
C110 AP48 120fr blk, brn & grn 3.75 2.25
C110A AP48 120fr lil, brn & ol grn 3.75 3.00

Issued: #C110, 11/16/81; #C110A,5/13/82.
For overprint see No. C115.

Christmas 1981 AP49

1981, Dec. 21 Litho. *Perf. 12½*
C111 AP49 180fr multi 5.50 4.25

Tapestry, by Pilioho Aloi — AP50

1982, Feb. 22 Litho. *Perf. 12½x13*
C112 AP50 100fr multi 2.90 2.50

Boats at Collioure, by George Braque (1882-1963) AP51

1982, Apr. 13 Litho. *Perf. 12½x13*
C113 AP51 300fr multi 7.50 5.25

Alberto Santos-Dumont (1873-1932), Aviation Pioneer — AP52

1982, July 24
C114 AP52 95fr multi 3.25 2.40

No. C110 Overprinted with Winner's Name in Blue

1982, Aug. 26 Engr. *Perf. 13*
C115 AP48 120fr multi 4.00 3.00

Italy's victory in 1982 World Cup.

French Overseas Possessions Week, Sept. 18-25 AP53

1982, Sept. 17 Litho.
C116 AP53 105fr Beach 2.50 2.25

Day of the Blind — AP54

1982, Oct. 18 Engr.
C117 AP54 130fr red & blue 3.25 2.00

Christmas 1982 — AP55

Adoration of the Virgin, by Correggio.

1982, Dec. 20 Litho. *Perf. 12½x13*
C118 AP55 170fr multi 4.25 3.00

Wind Surfing (1984 Olympic Event) — AP56

1983, Mar. 4 Litho. *Perf. 13*
C119 AP56 270fr multi 6.50 4.75

World UPU Day AP57

1983, Mar. 30 Litho. *Perf. 13*
C120 AP57 100fr multi 2.75 1.75

Manned Flight Bicentenary — AP58

1983, Apr. 25 Litho. *Perf. 13*
C121 AP58 205fr Montgolfiere 5.50 4.00

Cat, 1926, by Foujita (d. 1968) — AP59

1983, May 20 Litho. *Perf. 12½x13*
C122 AP59 102fr multi 3.75 2.00

Pre-Olympic Year — AP60

1983, July 5 Engr. *Perf. 13*
C123 AP60 250fr Javelin 5.50 4.50

Alfred Nobel (1833-1896) AP61

1983, Aug. 1 Engr. *Perf. 13*
C124 AP61 150fr multi 4.00 2.75

Nicephore Niepce (1765-1833), Photography Pioneer — AP62

1983, Sept. 20 Engr. *Perf. 13*
C125 AP62 75fr dk grn & rose vio 2.50 1.75

Raphael (1483-1520), 500th Birth Anniv. — AP63

1983, Nov. 10 Litho. *Perf. 12½x13*
C126 AP63 167fr The Triumph of Galatea 4.25 3.00

Pandanus AP64

1983, Nov. 30 Litho. *Perf. 13*
C127 AP64 137fr multi 3.50 3.00

Christmas 1983 — AP65

Sistine Madonna, by Raphael.

1983, Dec. 22 Litho. *Perf. 12½x13*
C128 AP65 200fr multi 5.00 4.00

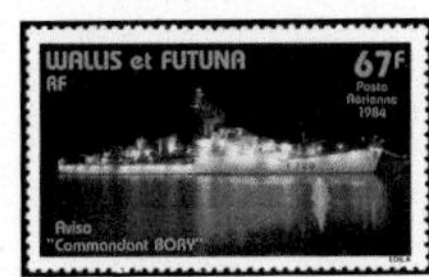

Steamer Commandant Bory — AP66

1984, Jan. 9 ***Perf. 13***
C129 AP66 67fr multi 2.25 1.40

1984 Summer Olympics AP67

1984, Feb. 3 **Litho.** ***Perf. 13***
C130 AP67 85fr Weight lifting 2.40 1.75

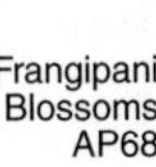

Frangipani Blossoms AP68

1984, Feb. 28 ***Perf. 12½***
C131 AP68 130fr multi 3.25 2.25

Easter 1984 — AP69

1984, Apr. 17 **Litho.** ***Perf. 12½x13***
C132 AP69 190fr Descent from the Cross 4.50 3.25

Homage to Jean Cocteau — AP70

1984, June 30 **Litho.** ***Perf. 13***
C133 AP70 150fr Portrait 4.00 2.90

Soano Hoatau Tiki Sculpture — AP71

1984, July 26
C134 AP71 175fr multi 4.25 3.50

Portrait of Alice, by Modigliani (1884-1920) — AP72

1984, Aug. 20
C135 AP72 140fr multi 3.50 2.50

Ausipex '84 — AP73

1984, Sept. 21 **Litho.** ***Perf. 12½x13***
C136 AP73 180fr Pilioko Tapestry 4.50 3.00

Se-tenant with label showing exhibition emblem.

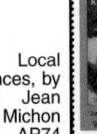

Local Dances, by Jean Michon AP74

1984, Oct. 11 **Photo.** ***Perf. 13***
C137 AP74 110fr multi 3.25 2.00

Altar — AP75

1984, Nov. 5 **Litho.** ***Perf. 13x12½***
C138 AP75 52fr Mount Lulu Chapel 1.50 1.10

Christmas 1984 AP76

1984, Dec. 21 **Litho.** ***Perf. 13x12½***
C139 AP76 260fr Tropical Nativity 6.25 4.00

Pilioko Tapestry AP77

1985, Apr. 3 **Litho.** ***Perf. 13x12½***
C140 AP77 500fr multi 10.00 6.50

The Post in 1926, by Utrillo — AP78

1985, June 17 **Litho.** ***Perf. 12½x13***
C141 AP78 200fr multi 5.00 4.00

Wallis Island Pirogue AP79

1985, Aug. 9 ***Perf. 13***
C142 AP79 350fr multi 7.50 5.00

Ship Jacques Cartier — AP80

1985, Oct. 2 **Engr.** ***Perf. 13x13½***
C143 AP80 51fr Prus bl, brt bl & dk bl 1.40 1.10

Portrait of a Young Woman, by Patrice Nielly — AP81

1985, Oct. 28 **Litho.** ***Perf. 12½x13***
C144 AP81 245fr multi 6.00 4.50

Nativity, by Jean Michon — AP82

1985, Dec. 19 **Litho.** ***Perf. 12½x13***
C145 AP82 330fr multi 7.75 6.50

Halley's Comet AP83

1986, Mar. 6 **Litho.** ***Perf. 13***
C146 AP83 100fr multi 2.60 1.75

Cure of Ars, Birth Bicent. — AP84

1986, Mar. 28 **Litho.** ***Perf. 12½x13***
C147 AP84 200fr multi 5.00 4.25

French Overseas Territory Status, 25th Anniv. AP85

90fr, Queen Amelia. 137fr, July 30 Law, Journal of the Republic.

1986, July 29 **Engr.** ***Perf. 13***
C148 AP85 90fr multicolored 2.25 2.25
C149 AP85 137fr multicolored 3.75 3.75
a. Strip of 2, #C148-C149 + label 6.00 6.00

Queen Amelia's request to France for protection, cent.

World Post Day AP86

1986, Oct. 9 **Litho.** ***Perf. 13***
C150 AP86 270fr multi 6.25 4.00

Statue of Liberty, Cent. — AP87

1986, Oct. 31 **Engr.**
C151 AP87 205fr multi 6.50 5.00

Poi Basilica, 1st Anniv. — AP88

230fr, Fr. Chanel, basilica.

1987, Apr. 30 **Litho.** ***Perf. 13***
C152 AP88 230fr multicolored 5.50 3.75

Telstar Transmitting to Pleumeur-Bodou, France — AP89

1987, May 17 **Engr.** ***Perf. 13***
C153 AP89 200fr gray, brt bl & brn org 5.25 3.75

World Communications Day, 25th anniv. of Telstar.

Piccard, Bathyscaphe Trieste and Stratospheric Balloon — AP90

1987, Aug. 21 **Engr.** ***Perf. 13***
C154 AP90 135fr brt ol grn, dk bl & brt bl 4.00 3.00

Auguste Piccard (1884-1962), physicist.

Arrival of First Missionary, 150th Anniv. AP91

Design: 260fr, Monsignor Bataillon's arrival in 1837, ship and the islands.

1987, Nov. 8 **Engr.** ***Perf. 13***
C155 AP91 260fr brt blue, blk & blue grn 6.25 5.00

Christmas 1987 AP92

1987, Dec. 15 **Litho.** ***Perf. 13x12½***
C156 AP92 300fr multi 6.50 5.00

Garros and Bleriot Aircraft AP93

1988, Feb. 18 Engr. *Perf. 13*
C157 AP93 600fr multi 17.50 10.50

Roland Garros (1888-1918), aviator and tennis player.

Self-portrait with Lace Cravat, by Maurice Quentin de La Tour (1704-88) AP94

1988, Apr. 8 Litho.
C158 AP94 500fr multi 13.00 9.50

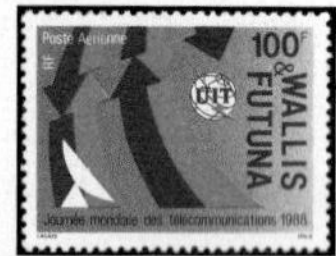
World Telecommunications Day — AP95

1988, May 5 Litho. *Perf. 12½x13*
C159 AP95 100fr multi 2.50 1.90

South Pacific Episcopal Conference AP96

1988, June 1 Litho. *Perf. 13*
C160 AP96 90fr Map, bishop 2.25 1.75

Christmas AP97

Unwmk.

1988, Dec. 15 Litho. *Perf. 13*
C161 AP97 400fr multi 11.00 7.00

Royal Throne — AP98

1989, Mar. 11
C162 AP98 700fr multi 16.00 10.50

Type of 1979

Virgin of the Crescent Moon, by Albrecht Durer

1989, Dec. 21 Engr. *Perf. 13½x13*
C163 AP38 800fr plum 19.00 13.00

Christmas 1989.

Clement Ader (1841-1926), Aviation Pioneer — AP100

1990, June 9 Engr. *Perf. 13*
C164 AP100 56fr multicolored 2.00 1.40

First anniversary of Wallis-Tahiti air link.

Gen. Charles de Gaulle (1890-1979) AP101

1990, Nov. 22 *Perf. 12½x13*
C165 AP101 1000fr multi 24.50 19.00

Father Louis Marie Chanel, 150th Death Anniv. AP102

1991, Apr. 28 Litho. *Perf. 13*
C166 AP102 235fr multicolored 6.50 4.25

French Open Tennis Championships, Cent. — AP103

1991, May 24 Engr. *Perf. 13x12½*
C167 AP103 250fr blk, grn & org 7.50 5.50

Wolfgang Amadeus Mozart, Death Bicent. — AP104

1991, Sept. 23 Engr. *Perf. 13*
C168 AP104 500fr multicolored 13.00 9.50

World Columbian Stamp Expo '92, Chicago AP105

1992, May 22 Litho. *Perf. 13x12½*
C169 AP105 100fr multicolored 3.00 2.25

1992, July 15 *Perf. 13*
C170 AP105 800fr multicolored 19.00 13.00

Genoa '92.

First French Republic, Bicent. AP106

1992, Aug. 17 Engr. *Perf. 13*
C171 AP106 350fr blk, bl & red 9.75 7.50

Louvre Museum, Bicent. AP107

1993, Apr. 12 Engr. *Perf. 13*
C172 AP107 315fr blue, dk blue & red 7.50 5.50

Nicolaus Copernicus, Heliocentric Solar System AP108

1993, May 7 Engr. *Perf. 13*
C173 AP108 600fr multicolored 15.00 9.25

Polska '93.

Second Year of First French Republic, Bicent. AP109

1993, Sept. 22 Engr. *Perf. 13*
C174 AP109 400fr bl, blk & red 9.50 7.50

Wallis Island Landscape AP110

1994, Jan. 26 Litho. *Perf. 13*
C175 AP110 400fr multicolored 11.00 7.50

Hong Kong '94 AP111

1994, Feb. 18 Litho. *Perf. 14x13½*
C176 AP111 700fr multicolored 17.50 12.00

South Pacific Geography Day AP112

1994, May 4 Litho. *Perf. 13*
C177 AP112 85fr multicolored 2.40 1.75

See New Caledonia No. C259.

European Stamp Salon, Paris — AP113

1994, Sept. 22 Litho. *Perf. 13*
C178 AP113 300fr multicolored 8.00 5.00

Antoine de Saint-Exupery (1900-44), Aviator, Author — AP114

1994, Oct. 27 Engr. *Perf. 13*
C179 AP114 800fr multicolored 22.00 15.00

Christmas AP115

1994, Dec. 15 Litho. *Perf. 13*
C180 AP115 150fr multicolored 4.00 3.00

Louis Pasteur (1822-95) AP116

1995, Mar. 25 Litho. *Perf. 13*
C181 AP116 350fr multicolored 8.50 4.75

AP117

1995, Apr. 19 *Perf. 13½x13*
C182 AP117 115fr multicolored 2.75 1.90

University Teacher's Training Institute of the Pacific. See French Polynesia No. 656 and New Caledonia No. 710.

AP118

1995, May 17 *Perf. 13*
C183 AP118 200fr Painting of Cocoa Nuts 4.50 3.00

Intl. Youth Year, 10th Anniv. AP119

1995, July 25 Litho. *Perf. 13*
C184 AP119 450fr multicolored 10.00 6.25

Singapore '95 AP120

1995, Aug. 24 Litho. *Perf. 13*
C185 AP120 500fr multicolored 11.00 6.75

Motion Pictures, Cent. AP121

Lumiere Brothers, film strip.

1995, Sept. 19
C186 AP121 600fr multicolored 13.00 8.50

Charles de Gaulle (1890-1970) AP122

1995, Nov. 14 Engr. *Perf. 13*
C187 AP122 315fr multicolored 8.00 5.50

7th Va'a (Outrigger Canoe) World Championship, Noumea, New Caledonia — AP123

1996, Apr. 24 Litho. *Perf. 13*
C188 AP123 240fr multicolored 6.00 4.25

Sisia College — AP124

1996, May 22 Litho. *Perf. 13½x13*
C189 AP124 235fr multicolored 6.00 4.25

Radio, Cent. AP125

1996, July 25 Engr. *Perf. 13*
C190 AP125 550fr multicolored 13.00 9.25

Modern Olympic Games, Cent. AP126

1996, Aug. 20 Engr. *Perf. 13*
C191 AP126 1000fr blk & dk bl 25.00 17.00

50th Autumn Stamp Salon — AP127

1996, Oct. 24 Litho. *Perf. 13*
C192 AP127 175fr multicolored 4.75 3.00

Campaign to Control Alcoholism AP128

1996, Nov. 19 *Perf. 13x13½*
C193 AP128 260fr multicolored 6.00 4.25

Natl. Center for Scientific Research — AP129

1997, Mar. 14 Litho. *Perf. 13*
C194 AP129 400fr Lapita pottery 8.00 5.50

HIHIFO Air Service AP130

1997, July 8 Litho. *Perf. 13*
C195 AP130 130fr multicolored 3.25 2.10

Sundown Over the Lagoon — AP131

1997, Sept. 22 Litho. *Perf. 13½x13*
C196 AP131 300fr multicolored 7.75 4.25

51st Autumn Stamp Salon AP132

350fr, #C194, 492, 497, 486, C184, C185, 475, C192, C188, 464, 493.
1000fr, Hemispheres, #486, 475, 464, C185, C175, 493, C184, 492, C192, 497, C188, C194, Winged Victory of Samothrace.

1997, Nov. 6 Litho. *Perf. 13*
C197 AP132 350fr multi 7.20 4.75

Imperf

C198 AP132 1000fr multi 21.00 24.00

Marshal Jacques Leclerc (1902-47) AP133

1997, Nov. 28 Litho. *Perf. 13*
C199 AP133 800fr multicolored 18.00 11.50

Alphonse Daudet (1840-97), Writer AP134

1997, Dec. 16 Litho. *Perf. 13*
C200 AP134 710fr multi 18.00 10.00

Alofi Beach AP135

1998, Apr. 21 Litho. *Perf. 13*
C201 AP135 315fr multicolored 7.50 4.25

Cricket — AP136

1998, Sept. 22 Litho. *Perf. 13x13½*
C202 AP136 106fr multicolored 2.75 1.40

Paul Gauguin (1848-1903) AP137

1998, Oct. 27 Litho. *Perf. 13*
C203 AP137 700fr multicolored 16.50 9.25

Garden of Happiness AP138

1998, Nov. 17
C204 AP138 460fr multicolored 11.00 7.25

Polynesian Dancing — AP139

1998, Dec. 15 Litho. *Perf. 13*
C205 AP139 250fr multicolored 6.50 3.50

Kava Porter — AP140

1999, Jan. 18
C206 AP140 600fr multicolored 13.00 8.00

Shells — AP141

95fr, Epitonium scalare. 100fr, Cassis cornuta. 110fr, Charonia tritonis. 115fr, Lambis lambis.

1999, Feb. 15
C207 AP141 95fr multi, vert. 2.25 1.75
C208 AP141 100fr multi, vert. 2.40 1.75
C209 AP141 110fr multi 2.40 1.75
C210 AP141 115fr multi 3.00 1.75
Nos. C207-C210 (4) 10.05 7.00

Finemui AP142

1999, Apr. 19 Engr. *Perf. 12¾*
C211 AP142 900fr multicolored 20.00 11.50

Birds of Nuku Fotu — AP143

a, 10fr, Airgrettes. b, 20fr, Audubon's. c, 26fr, Fregates. d, 54fr, Paille en queue.

1999, June 14 Litho. *Perf. 13x13¾*
C212 AP143 Strip of 4, #a.-d. 3.25 2.50

Wind Song AP144

1999, Nov. 22 Engr. *Perf. 13*
C213 AP144 325fr multi 7.50 4.50

Sunrise Over a Lagoon — AP145

1999, Dec. 20 Litho.
C214 AP145 500fr multi 11.00 7.50

First Transport Flight to Futuna, 30th Anniv. AP146

2000, Aug. 24 Litho. *Perf. 13*
C215 AP146 350fr multi 9.00 4.50

AIR POST SEMI-POSTAL STAMPS

New Caledonia Nos. CB2-CB3 overprinted "ILES WALLIS ET FUTUNA"

1942, June 22 Engr. *Perf. 13*
CB1 SPAP1 1.50fr + 3.50fr green 2.00
CB2 SPAP1 2fr + 6fr yellow brown 2.00

Native children's welfare fund.
Nos. CB1-CB2 were issued by the Vichy government in France, but were not placed on sale in Wallis & Futuna.

Colonial Education Fund

New Caledonia No. CB4 Common Design Type overprinted "ILES WALLIS ET FUTUNA"

1942, June 22
CB3 CD86a 1.20fr + 1.80fr blue & red 2.00

No. CB3 was issued by the Vichy government in France, but was not placed on sale in Wallis & Futuna.

POSTAGE DUE STAMPS

Postage Due Stamps of New Caledonia, 1906, Overprinted in Black or Red

1920 Unwmk. *Perf. 13½x14*

No.	Type	Description	Unused	Used
J1	D2	5c ultra, *azure*	1.00	1.00
J2	D2	10c brn, *buff*	1.10	1.10
J3	D2	15c grn, *grnsh*	1.10	1.10
J4	D2	20c blk, *yel* (R)	1.50	1.50
a.		Double overprint	200.00	
J5	D2	30c carmine rose	1.50	1.50
J6	D2	50c ultra, *straw*	2.40	2.40
J7	D2	60c olive, *azure*	2.90	2.90
a.		Double overprint	200.00	
J8	D2	1fr grn, *cream*	3.75	3.75
		Nos. J1-J8 (8)	15.25	15.25

Type of 1920 Issue Surcharged

1927

No.	Type	Description	Unused	Used
J9	D2	2fr on 1fr brt vio	12.50	12.50
J10	D2	3fr on 1fr org brn	12.50	12.50

Postage Due Stamps of New Caledonia, 1928, Overprinted as in 1920

1930

No.	Type	Description	Unused	Used
J11	D3	2c sl bl & dp brn	.25	.25
a.		Double surcharge	200.00	
b.		Imperf.	200.00	
J12	D3	4c brn red & bl grn	.25	.25
J13	D3	5c red org & bl blk	.25	.25
J14	D3	10c mag & Prus bl	.25	.25
J15	D3	15c dl grn & scar	.35	.35
J16	D3	20c maroon & ol grn	.75	.75
J17	D3	25c bis brn & sl bl	.75	.75
J18	D3	30c bl grn & ol grn	1.40	1.40
J19	D3	50c lt brn & dk red	.85	.85
J20	D3	60c mag & brt rose	1.40	1.40
J21	D3	1fr dl bl & Prus grn	1.40	1.40
J22	D3	2fr dk red & ol grn	1.40	1.40
J23	D3	3fr vio & brn	1.40	1.40
		Nos. J11-J23 (13)	10.70	10.70

Postage Due Stamps of 1930 with Additional Overprint in Black

1943

No.	Type	Description	Unused	Used
J24	D3	2c sl bl & dp brn	35.00	35.00
J25	D3	4c brn red & bl grn	35.00	35.00
J26	D3	5c red org & bl blk	35.00	35.00
J27	D3	10c mag & Prus bl	35.00	35.00
J28	D3	15c dl grn & scar	37.50	37.50
J29	D3	20c mar & ol grn	37.50	37.50
J30	D3	25c bis brn & sl bl	37.50	37.50
J31	D3	30c bl grn & ol grn	37.50	37.50
J32	D3	50c lt brn & dk red	37.50	37.50
J33	D3	60c mag & brt rose	40.00	40.00
J34	D3	1fr dl bl & Prus grn	40.00	40.00
J35	D3	2fr dk red & ol grn	40.00	40.00
J36	D3	3fr violet & brn	40.00	40.00
		Nos. J24-J36 (13)	487.50	487.50

Catalogue values for unused stamps in this section, from this point to the end of the section, are for Never Hinged items.

Thalassoma Lunare — D1

Fish: 1fr, Zanclus cornutus, vert. 5fr, Amphiprion percula.

Perf. 13x13½

1963, Apr. 1 Typo. Unwmk.

No.	Type	Description	Unused	Used
J37	D1	1fr yel org, bl & blk	.60	.60
J38	D1	3fr red, grnsh bl & grn	1.90	2.40
J39	D1	5fr org, bluish grn & blk	3.00	3.50
		Nos. J37-J39 (3)	5.50	6.50

Nos. J37-J39 were reprinted in 1982 on white paper in slightly different shades.

WESTERN UKRAINE

'wes-tərn yü-'krān

LOCATION — In Eastern Central Europe

GOVT. — A former short-lived independent State

A provisional government was established in 1918 in the eastern part of Austria-Hungary but the area later came under Polish administration.

100 Shahiv (Sotykiv) = 1 Hryvnia
100 Heller = 1 Krone

Forgeries of almost all Western Ukraine stamps are plentiful. Particularly dangerous forgeries have been noted for the Kolomyia Issue and for the First and Second Stanyslaviv Issues.

Lviv Issue

Austria Nos. 145-146, 148, 169 Overprinted

Nos. 1-4A are handstamped with an octagonal overprint that reads "ZAKHIDNO UKR. NARODNA REPUBLYKA" ("Western Ukrainian National Republic"), framing the image of a rearing crowned lion.

1918, Nov. 20 *Perf. 12½*

No.	Type	Description	Unused	Used
1	A37	3h bright vio	60.00	425.00
a.		Inverted overprint	200.00	
2	A37	5h light green	55.00	350.00
a.		Inverted overprint	200.00	
3	A37	10h magenta	50.00	350.00
a.		Inverted overprint	190.00	
4	A42	20h dark green	45.00	325.00
a.		Inverted overprint	225.00	
4A	A42	20h light green	250.00	1,000.
		Nos. 1-4A (5)	460.00	2,450.

This issue was in circulation for only two days before Lviv was captured by the Poles on Nov. 22. No examples of Nos. 1-4A used in Lviv are known.

The Western Ukrainian National Republic (ZUNR) government evacuated to the city of Ternopil, which became the provisional capital. ZUNR postal operations were set up in other Western Ukrainian cities, and the Lviv Issue was used in Stanyslaviv (earliest known cancellation date, Dec. 8).). Reports stating that the issue was also used in Khodoriv and Kolomyia must be treated as doubtful since no such examples have ever turned up.

Nos. 1-4 exist in pairs with both normal and inverted overprints. Value $325.

Overprints in alternate colors (violet or red) are proofs. Violet-black overprints are probably transitional color impressions.

Kolomyia Issue

Kolomyia is the main town of the Pokutia region of southwestern Ukraine. Cut off from ZUNR postal officials by wartime conditions and in urgent need of basic value stamps, the Kolomyia postmaster obtained permission from the District Military Command to surcharge remaining Austrian postage stamps to either 5 or 10 sotyks, the equivalent of 5 or 10 heller. These stamps were produced on Dec. 10, under very strict security, by preparing two distinct plates (one for each value) that overprinted 25 stamps at a time (5x5 quarter sections of the Austrian 100-stamp panes). The stamps were placed on sale two days later.

Austria Nos. 168, 145, 147, 149 Surcharged

1918, Dec. 12 Unwmk. *Perf. 12½*

No.	Type	Description	Unused	Used
5	A42	5sot on 15h dl red	95.00	95.00
a.		Inverted overprint	600.00	725.00
b.		Double overprint	1,500.	1,600.
6	A37	10sot on 3h vio	95.00	95.00
7	A37	10sot on 6h dp org	1,750.	1,350.
8	A37	10sot on 12h lt bl	1,650.	1,600.
		Nos. 5-8 (4)	3,590.	3,140.

10 sotyk on 15 heller values are essays; only six were produced.

All inverted surcharges on Nos. 6-8 are forgeries. Double surcharges are forgeries.

First Stanyslaviv Issue

Austrian Stamps of 1916-18 Surcharged in Shahiv (shown) and Hryvnia Currency

At the end of December, 1918, the national government again moved, this time to the city of Stanyslaviv (present-day Ivano-Frankivsk). A shortage of qualified postal personnel resulted in a considerable delay in the creation of new ZUNR postage stamps. In the interim, remaining unoverprinted Austrian stamps were used. Finally, on March 18, 1919, 20 different available Austrian definitive stamps were typograph surcharged at the Dankevych Print Shop in Stanyslaviv.

1919, Mar. 18

No.	Type	Description	Unused	Used
9	A37	3sh on 3h bright vio	20.00	25.00
a.		Double overprint	1,000.	1,500.
10	A37	5sh on 5h light green	20.00	25.00
11	A37	6sh on 6h deep orange	35.00	60.00
12	A37	10sh on 10h mag	30.00	40.00
13	A37	12sh on 12h lt blue	30.00	40.00
a.		Double overprint	325.00	450.00
b.		Double overprint, one on reverse	500.00	210.00
14	A42	15sh on 15h dull red	30.00	40.00
15	A42	20sh on 20h dp grn	30.00	40.00
16	A42	30sh on 30h dull violet	30.00	40.00
17	A39	40sh on 40h ol green	30.00	40.00
18	A39	50sh on 50h dk grn	30.00	40.00
19	A39	60sh on 60h deep blue	30.00	40.00
20	A39	80sh on 80h org brown	30.00	40.00
a.		Inverted overprint	900.00	1,100.
21	A39	1hr on 1k car, *yel*	45.00	50.00
22	A40	2hr on 2k lt blue	45.00	50.00
23	A40	3hr on 3k claret (on #161)	3,500.	3,250.
24	A40	3hr on 3k car rose (on #165)	100.00	125.00
25	A40	3hr on 3k car rose (on #173)	90.00	115.00
26	A40	4hr on 4k dk grn (on #162)	800.00	850.00
27	A40	4hr on 4k yel grn (on #166)	60.00	65.00
28	A40	10hr on 10k deep violet	750.00	800.00
a.		Double overprint	3,000.	3,500.
		Nos. 9-28 (20)	5,735.	5,775.

The 25sh on 25h, type A42, in both light and dull blue shades, never received this overprint. All such stamps are fantasies.

Second Stanyslaviv Issue

The overprinting of a second issue of postage stamps in Stanyslaviv was undertaken in late April. Stamps from several different Austrian stamp series were utilized to create four distinct sets. Most of the stamps available were Austrian postage due, charity or field post stamps. The stamps were typograph surcharged at the Dankevych Print Shop in Stanyslaviv.

Postage Due Stamps of Bosnia, 1904 Surcharged but without Asterisks

1919, April

No.	Type	Description	Unused	Used
29	D1	1sh on 1h blk, red & yel	35.00	45.00
a.		Inverted overprint	70.00	80.00
b.		Double overprint	90.00	100.00
30	D1	2sh on 2h blk, red & yel	15.00	18.00
31	D1	3sh on 3h blk, red & yel	15.00	18.00
a.		Inverted overprint	28.00	45.00
32	D1	4sh on 4h blk, red & yel	135.00	165.00
a.		Inverted overprint	175.00	190.00
b.		Double overprint	300.00	325.00
33	D1	5sh on 5h blk, red & yel	3,250.	—
34	D1	6sh on 6h blk, red & yel	650.00	—
a.		Inverted overprint	750.00	—
b.		Double overprint	850.00	—
35	D1	7sh on 7h blk, red & yel	25.00	30.00
a.		Inverted overprint	40.00	45.00
36	D1	8sh on 8h blk, red & yel	30.00	35.00
a.		Inverted overprint	50.00	60.00
b.		Vertical overprint	2,750.	2,950.
37	D1	10sh on 10h blk, red & yel	1,300.	—
38	D1	15sh on 15h blk, red & yel	675.00	700.00
a.		Inverted overprint	850.00	—
39	D1	20sh on 20h blk, red & yel	6,500.	
a.		Double overprint	8,000.	18,000.
40	D1	50sh on 50h blk, red & yel	375.00	400.00
a.		Inverted overprint	550.00	600.00

Nos. 29-40 were created by overprinting Bosnian 1904 postage due stamps, which had been brought to Stanyslaviv by a Ukrainian military officer returning from the Serbian front. The same printing cliché was used as for the First Stanyslaviv Issue, but the asterisk obliterators were removed.

Most of the overprinting was made using 50-stamp panes (half of a sheet). After one half of the pane (25 positions) was overprinted, it would apparently be turned over and its second half overprinted with the same 25-position block, but as an inverted impression. After overprinting, the pane was torn into two equal 25-stamp halves.

A corrected block was utilized in overprinting, resulting in two types of surcharges on No. 29 (shaha to shahiv) and on Nos. 32, 34 and 38 (shahi to shahiv).

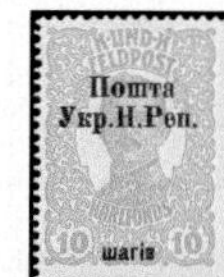

Austrian Military Semipostal Stamps of 1918 Srchd.

No.	Type	Description	Unused	Used
41	MSP7	10sh on 10h gray green	150.00	150.00
a.		Inverted overprint	150.00	160.00
b.		As "a," doubled	280.00	300.00
42	MSP8	20sh on 20h mag	125.00	110.00
a.		Inverted overprint	125.00	120.00
b.		Double overprint	160.00	180.00
43	MSP7	45sh on 45h blue	100.00	110.00
a.		Inverted overprint	100.00	120.00

Nos. 41-43 were printed in the same manner as Nos. 29-40.

Austrian Military Stamps of 1917 Srchd.

No.	Type	Description	Unused	Used
44	M3	1sh on 1h grnsh blue	1,000.	950.00
45	M3	2sh on 2h red orange	150.00	140.00
b.		Double overprint	240.00	230.00
46	M3	3sh olive gray	250.00	225.00
a.		Double overprint	500.00	750.00
47	M3	5sh on 5h olive grn	300.00	275.00
48	M3	6sh on 6h vio	150.00	140.00
49	M3	10sh on 10h org brn	1,000.	950.00
50	M3	12sh on 12h blue	550.00	500.00
a.		Inverted overprint	650.00	600.00
51	M3	15sh on 15h brt rose	500.00	450.00
a.		Inverted overprint	600.00	525.00
52	M3	20sh on 20h red brown	17.00	17.00
b.		Double overprint	1,200.	
53	M3	25sh on 25h ultra	3,500.	4,000.
54	M3	30sh on 30h slate	1,300.	1,200.
55	M3	40sh on 40h ol bister	1,000.	950.00
56	M3	50sh on 50h dp grn	10.00	10.00
a.		Inverted overprint	12.00	12.00
b.		Double overprint	60.00	60.00
57	M3	60sh on 60h car rose	1,000.	950.00
58	M3	80sh on 80h dull blue	50.00	50.00
a.		Inverted overprint	75.00	75.00
59	M3	90sh on 90h dk vio	1,050.	1,000.
60	M4	2hr on 2k rose, *straw*	18.00	18.00
a.		Inverted overprint	35.00	35.00
b.		Perf. 11½	120.00	130.00
c.		"Hryven" instead of "Hryvni"	150.00	250.00
d.		As "c," inverted overprint	300.00	400.00

61 M4 3hr on 3k blue, *grn* 25.00 *25.00*
- *a.* Inverted overprint 40.00 *40.00*
- *b.* Double overprint 70.00 *70.00*

62 M4 4hr on 4k rose, *grn* 25.00 *25.00*
- *a.* Inverted overprint 40.00 *40.00*
- *b.* Double overprint 70.00 *70.00*
- *d.* Perf. 11½ 40.00 *60.00*

63 M4 10hr on 10k dl vio, *gray* *75,000.* *70,000.*

On No. 46a, the second overprint is strongly shifted, causing the overprint to overlap onto adjacent stamps.This causes the stamp to appear to have a triple overprint, but the overprint is double.

Two examples of No. 63 were printed, and neither was ever postally used. The "used" example was cut from a document prepared by the Western Ukrainian economic bureau (Ekonomat) to display the stamps that made up the First and Second Stanyslaviv issues. The specimen stamps on this document were tied with a double-ring bureau cancel that somewhat resembles a regular double-ring postal cancellation.

About half of this issue, where several sheets were available for printing, was overprinted in the manner of Nos. 29-43.

Austrian Stamps of 1916-18 Surcharged

64 A38 15sh on 36h vio (on #J61) 350.00 *450.00*
- *a.* Double overprint 450.00 *550.00*

65 A38 50sh on 42h choc (on #J63) 6,500. *5,000.*

66 A37 3sh on 3h brt violet (on #145) 375.00

67 A37 5sh on 5h lt green (on #146) 375.00
- *a.* Inverted overprint 650.00

68 A37 6sh on 6h deep org (on #147) 1,200. 1,000.

69 A37 10sh on 10h mag (on #148) 375.00
- *a.* Inverted overprint 700.00

70 A37 12sh on 12h lt blue (on #149) 1,050.

71 A38 15sh on 15h rose red (on #150) 850.00 650.00
- *a.* Inverted overprint 1,200. 900.00

72 A42 15sh on 15h dull red (on #168) 450.00 400.00

73 A42 30sh on 30h dull vio (on #171) 450.00
- *a.* Double overprint 700.00

74 A39 40sh on 40h ol grn (on #154) 1,050.

75 M3 50sh on 50h dp grn (on #M61) 1,050.

The two bars in the surcharge were originally created to obliterate the "PORTO" on Nos. 64 and 65 but were subsequently retained for Nos. 66-75.

Third Stanyslaviv Issue

The 12-heller, 20h and 50h, and 2-kronen, 3k, 4k and 10k stamps were delivered in early April 1919; the remaining values (12 in all) were issued May 8, 1919.

Austrian Stamps of 1916-18 Overprinted

1919, May 8

76	A37	3h brt violet	.50	*1.00*
77	A37	5h light green	.50	*1.00*
78	A37	6h deep orange	.50	*1.00*
79	A37	10h magenta	.50	*1.00*
80	A37	12h light blue	.50	*1.00*
81	A42	15h dull red	.50	*1.00*
82	A42	20h deep green	.50	*1.00*
83	A42	25h blue	.50	*1.00*
84	A42	30h dull vio	.50	*1.00*
85	A39	40h olive green	.75	*1.25*
86	A39	50h dark green	.75	*1.25*
87	A39	60h deep blue	.75	*1.25*
88	A39	80h orange brn	1.00	*1.25*
89	A39	90h red violet	1.00	*1.60*
90	A39	1k car, *yel*	1.25	*4.00*
91	A40	2k light blue	2.00	*6.00*
92	A40	3k carmine rose	2.50	*7.50*
93	A40	4k yellow grn	12.00	*17.00*
94	A40	10k deep violet	17.00	*50.00*
		Nos. 76-94 (19)	43.50	*100.10*

Issued: 3h-10h, 15h, 25h-40h, 60h-1k, 5/8; balance of set, 5/13.

A definitive set for Western Ukraine was ordered from the Austrian State Printing Office in March, 1919. Because of the time involved in designing and printing these stamps, Nos. 76-94 were overprinted in Vienna as a provisional issue and were delivered in two shipments. Because travel into and out of Stanyslaviv was becoming more difficult as the month wore on, it was not known whether or not the second shipment, which included the higher values, would arrive. Because of this, the Fourth Stanyslaviv Issue, Nos. 95-103, were overprinted locally.

Fourth Stanislaviv Issue

Austrian Military stamps were typograph surcharged at the Dankevych Print Shop in Stanyslaviv.

Austrian Military Stamps of 1917-18 Surcharged in Black

1919, May 18 ***Perf. 12½***

95 M3 2hr on 2k rose, *straw* 15.00 *17.00*
- *a.* Perf 11½ 150.00 *150.00*

96 M3 3hr on 2k rose, *straw* 15.00 *15.00*
- *a.* Perf 11½ 150.00 *150.00*

97 M3 3hr on 3k grn, *blue* 135.00 *135.00*
- *a.* "5" instead of "3" at left in overprint *1,500.*

98 M3 4hr on 2k rose, *straw* 15.00 *15.00*

99 M3 4hr on 4k rose, *grn* 1,300. *1,300.*

100 M3 5hr on 2k rose, *straw* 15.00 *15.00*
- *a.* Inverted surcharge 800.00

101 M3 10hr on 50h dp grn 35.00 *40.00*
- *a.* Double surcharge 175.00

Austrian Postage Due Stamps of 1916 Srchd., but without Rosettes and Numerals

102 D5 1hr ultra 150.00 *140.00*
103 D5 5hr ultra 1,200. *1,200.*

REGISTRATION STAMPS

Kolomyia Issue

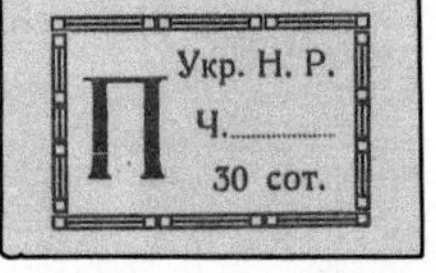

RS1

Without Gum

1918-19 Unwmk. Typeset ***Imperf.***

F1 RS1 30sot black, *rose* 260.00 200.00
F2 RS1 50sot black, *rose* ('19) 160.00 *175.00*

No. F1 was printed on Dec. 10 and issued Dec. 12, 1918, along with the regular Kolomyia Issue (Nos. 5-8). On Dec. 19, the ZUNR government approved an increase in the registered letter rate to 50 sotyks, effective January 1, 1919. New 50-sotyk registration stamps were ordered printed in Kolomyia on 14 January 1919, but were not used until the remaining 30sot stamps were used up at the various post offices. Continued brisk use of these stamps necessitated a second printing of the 50sot stamps two months later. Variations in paper color — from light pink to deep rose — as well as paper thickness occurred in the 30sot and both of the 50sot printings.

Nos. F1-F2a were typographed in vertical panes of five stamps by the Wilhelm Brauner Print Ship in Kolomyia.

Forgeries exist.

OCCUPATION STAMPS

Romanian Occupation of Pokutia

Only the stamps listed below were officially created. Soon after the Romanian occupation ended on Aug. 20, 1919, the C.M.T. handstamps fell into the hands of speculators, and some 37 other Austrian stamps were overprinted. None of these privately-created stamps are known on authentic covers.

Austrian Stamps Surcharged in Dark Violet Blue

1919, June 14 Unwmk. ***Perf. 12½***

On Stamps of 1916-18

N1 A37 40h on 5h lt grn 5.00 *6.00*

N2 A42 60h on 15h dl red 6.00 *7.00*

N3 A42 60h on 20h dp grn 2.50 *3.50*
- *a.* Inverted overprint 3,000.
- *b.* Double overprint 30.00

N4 A42 60h on 25h blue 13.00 *14.00*
- *a.* Inverted overprint 65.00
- *b.* Double overprint 90.00

N5 A42 60h on 30h dl vio 15.00 16.00

N6 A39 1k 20h on 50h dk grn 6.00 *7.00*

N7 A39 1k 20h on 60h dp bl 11.00 *13.00*

N8 A39 1k 20h on 1k car, *yel* 21.00 23.00

On Austrian Postage Due Stamps of 1910-1917

N9 D4 40h on 5h rose red 23.00 *25.00*

N10 D3 1k 20h on 25h car 145.00 *160.00*

N11 D4 1k 20h on 25h rose red 35.00 *40.00*

N12 D4 1k 20h on 30h rose red 20.00 22.00

N13 A38 1k 20h on 50h on 42h choc 32.50 35.00

Arms of Kiev

Arms of Ukraine

Arms of Galicia

First Definitive Issue, May 1919: Letterpress printed at the Austrian State Printing Office on unwatermarked white paper. Inscribed: "Ukrainska Narodnia Republyka Zakhidnia Oblast." ("Ukrainian National Republic Western Province"). Set of 12 values (four of each design), perf 11½ or imperf. Not issued. Value, set of 12: perf $360; imperf $560.

Second Definitive Issue, May 1919: Lithographed and letterpress printed (a two-step process) on unwatermarked white paper. Printer unknown. Inscribed: "Ukrainska Narodnia Respublika Z.O." ("Ukrainian National Republic W(estern) P(rovince)"). Design incorporates the heraldic arms of Ukraine (trident), Kiev (Archangel Michael) and Lviv (lion rampant). 10, 20 and 50 sotyk values imperf; 1 and 10 krone values variably perforated. Not issued. Value, set of 5, $6. Also exists on cream-colored paper.

WEST IRIAN

(Irian Barat)

(West New Guinea)

Stamps formerly listed under West Irian now appear in Volume 1, following United Nations, and Volume 3, following Indonesia.

YEMEN

'ye-mən

LOCATION — Arabian Peninsula, south of Saudi Arabia and bordering on the Red Sea
GOVT. — Republic
AREA — 204,000 sq. mi. (est.)
POP. — 16,942,230 (1999 est.)
CAPITAL — Sana'a (San'a)

40 Bogaches = 1 Imadi
40 Bogaches = 1 Riyal (1962)
100 Fils = 1 Riyal (1975)

The Yemen Arab Republic and the People's Republic of Yemen planned a 30-month unification process scheduled for completion by November 1992. While government ministries merged, both currencies remained valid.

Catalogue values for unused stamps in this country are for Never Hinged items, beginning with Scott 44 in the regular postage section, Scott C1 in the airpost section.

Watermarks

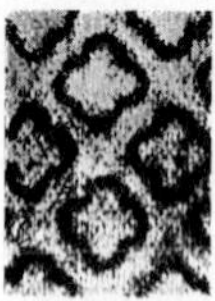

Wmk. 127 — Quatrefoils

Wmk. 258 — Arabic Characters and Y G Multiple

Wmk. 277 — Winged Wheel

For Domestic Postage

A1

Crossed Daggers and Arabic Inscriptions — A2

1926 Unwmk. Typo. *Imperf.*
Laid Paper
Without Gum

1	A1	2½b black	60.00	60.00
2	A1	2½b black, *orange*	60.00	60.00
3	A2	5b black	60.00	60.00
		Nos. 1-3 (3)	180.00	180.00

No. 2 is known crudely perforated 7½ or 9.

Type A1 differs from A2 primarily in the inscription in the left dagger blade.

All come on wove paper. Beware of forgeries, especially those on wove paper.

Replica sheets of Nos. 1-3 exist on both horizontally and vertically laid, watermarked paper. The sheets are marked on the reverse with "CRC / FAC" in san-serif font. Any stamps removed from these replica sheets will contain this marking from 1-4 times on the reverse.

For Foreign and Domestic Postage

A3

Arabic Inscriptions — A4

1930-31 Wmk. 127 *Perf. 14*

7	A3	½b orange ('31)	.35	.30
8	A3	1b green	.70	.50
9	A3	1b yellow grn ('31)	.35	.30
10	A3	2b olive grn	.90	.55
11	A3	2b olive brn ('31)	.55	.50
12	A3	3b dull vio ('31)	.70	.55
13	A3	4b red	.75	1.00
14	A3	4b deep rose ('31)	1.00	.85
15	A3	5b slate gray ('31)	1.25	.90
16	A4	6b dull blue	2.75	1.75
17	A4	6b dp ultra ('31)	1.75	1.25
18	A4	8b lilac rose ('31)	2.00	1.40
19	A4	10b lt brown	5.00	3.50
20	A4	10b brn org ('31)	2.75	1.75
21	A4	20b yel grn ('31)	3.50	2.50
22	A4	1i red brn & lt bl	25.00	14.00
23	A4	1i lil rose & yel grn ('31)	20.00	14.00
		Nos. 7-23 (17)	69.30	45.60

For surcharges and overprints see Nos. 30, 59-62, 166-167, 169-171, 174-176, 246-246Q.

Flags of Saudi Arabia, Yemen and Iraq — A5

1939 Litho. Wmk. 258 *Perf. 12½*

24	A5	4b dl rose & ultra	1.00	.70
25	A5	6b slate bl & ultra	1.25	.90
26	A5	10b fawn & ultra	1.75	1.50
27	A5	14b olive & ultra	3.00	2.75
28	A5	20b yel grn & ultra	4.25	3.50
29	A5	1i claret & ultra	5.00	4.00
		Nos. 24-29 (6)	16.25	13.35

2nd anniv. of the Arab Alliance. Nos. 24-29 exist imperforate. Value set, $20.

For overprints see Nos. C29-C29D.

a

b

c

d

e

Five types of surcharge:
All genuine surcharges are 12-13mm x 15-16mm and were made from steel handstamps.

a. "YEMEN" ½mm from left frameline and ½mm above bottom frameline.
b. "YEMEN" ½mm from left frameline and 1½mm above bottom frameline.
c. "YEMEN" 1½mm from left frameline and ½mm above bottom frameline. Found only on Types A13 and D1.
d. Arabic "4" at the center of the surcharge has been replaced with two vertical strokes. Usually blurred and found only on Type A9.
e. Arabic "4" has been replaced by a pair of crescents. Found only on Type A13.

Values of surcharged stamps are for ordinary examples. Clear, legible surcharges command a premium. Beware of fraudulent rubber-stamped surcharges in violet or grey black ink.

1939 Wmk. 127 *Perf. 14*
No. 7 Handstamped Type "a" in Black

30	A3	4b on ½b orange	*15.00*	*15.00*

See Nos. 44-48, 59-67, 82, 86-87.

A6

A7

1940 Wmk. 258 Litho. *Perf. 12½*

31	A6	½b ocher & ultra	.40	.30
32	A6	1b lt grn & rose red	.40	.30
33	A6	2b bis brn & vio	.50	.30
34	A6	3b dl vio & ultra	.50	.30
35	A6	4b rose & yel grn	.50	.30
36	A6	5b dk gray grn & bis brn	.60	.35
37	A7	6b ultra & yel org	.75	.35
38	A7	8b claret & dp bl	.90	.60
39	A7	10b brn org & yel grn	1.10	.75
40	A7	14b gray grn & vio	1.25	.90
41	A7	18b emerald & blk	1.75	1.50
42	A7	20b yel ol & cerise	2.75	2.00
43	A7	1i vio rose, yel grn & scar	6.50	4.25
		Nos. 31-43 (13)	17.90	12.20
		Set, never hinged	25.00	

No. 36 was used as a 4b stamp in 1957.

For surcharges see Nos. 44-47.

Catalogue values for unused stamps in this section, from this point to the end of the section, are for Never Hinged items.

Nos. 31-34, 36 Handstamped Type "a" in Black

1945-48 *Perf. 12½*

44	A6	4b on ½b	*4.50*	*3.50*
45	A6	4b on 1b ('48)	*4.00*	*4.50*
46	A6	4b on 2b ('48)	*4.50*	*5.00*
47	A6	4b on 3b ('48)	*5.00*	*5.00*
48	A6	4b on 5b ('46)	4.50	3.50

1949-51
Handstamp Type "b" in Black

44a	A6	4b on ½b ('51)	4.00	3.00
45a	A6	4b on 1b ('49)	4.00	3.50
46a	A6	4b on 2b ('49)	4.50	3.50
47a	A6	4b on 3b ('49)	5.00	3.50

Forged surcharges exist.

A8

1946 Frames in Emerald

49	A8	4b black	1.75	.85
50	A8	6b lilac rose	2.50	1.50
51	A8	10b ultra	3.50	1.90
52	A8	14b olive green	6.00	3.25
		Nos. 49-52 (4)	13.75	7.50

Opening of Mutawakkili Hospital. Exist imperforate. Value, set $16.

For overprints see Nos. 168, 172-173.

Mocha Coffee Tree A9

Palace, San'a A10

1947-58 Unwmk. Engr. *Perf. 12½*

53	A9	½b yellow brown	.25	.25
54	A9	1b purple	.70	.40
55	A9	2b ultra	1.40	.90
56	A10	4b red	2.25	1.25
57	A10	5b gray blue	2.50	1.50
58	A9	6b yellow green ('58)	3.50	2.00
		Nos. 53-58 (6)	10.60	6.30

No. 58 was printed in 1947 but not officially issued until June 1958.

Additional values, prepared but not issued, were 10b, 20b and 1i, with views of palaces superimposed on flag, and palace square. These were looted from government storehouses during the 1948 revolution and a number of copies later reached collectors. Values, set: unused $12; used (cto) $9.

For surcharges see Nos. 63-65.

Admission of Yemen to the U.N.

10 postage, 5 airmail and 5 postage due stamps for the Admission of Yemen to the UN were not officially issued for use on domestic mail. Pictured on some of the stamps were Truman, Roosevelt, Churchill and the Statue of Liberty. Value, unused: 10v postage, $35; 5v air post, $22; 5v postage due, $14. The postage and airmail sets exist imperf. Value double that of perforated sets. Covers, scarce and all philatelic, exist to foreign destinations. A few local-use covers are also known.

Nos. 9, 11, 12 and 15 Handstamped Type "a" in Black

1949 Wmk. 127 *Perf. 14*

59	A3	4b on 1b yellow grn	10.00	8.00
60	A3	4b on 2b olive brn	35.00	30.00
61	A3	4b on 3b dull vio	12.00	10.00
62	A3	4b on 5b slate gray	12.00	10.00

Handstamped type "b" were unauthorized.

Nos. 53-55 Handstamped Types "a" and "b" in Black

1949 Unwmk. *Perf. 12½*

63	A9(b)	4b on ½b yel brn	6.00	6.00
64	A9(a)	4b on 1b purple	5.00	5.00
a.		Handstamp type "b"	5.00	5.00
b.		Handstamp type "d"	20.00	15.00
65	A9(a)	4b on 2b ultra	6.00	6.00
a.		Handstamp type "b"	6.00	6.00
b.		Handstamp type "d"	20.00	10.00

Nos. J1-J2 Handstamped Type "b" in Black

1953 Wmk. 258

66	D1	4b on 1b org & yel grn	*20.00*	*25.00*
a.		Handstamp type "c"	*35.00*	*40.00*
67	D1	4b on 2b org & yel grn	*20.00*	*25.00*
a.		Handstamp type "c"	*25.00*	*30.00*

Types "a" and "b" exist inverted, double or horizontal.

Forged surcharges exist.

Parade Ground, San'a — A13

Mosque, San'a — A14

Designs: 5b, Flag of Yemen. 6b, Flag & eagle. 8b, Mocha coffee branch. 14b, Walled city of San'a. 20b, 1i, Ta'iz & its citadel.

1951 Wmk. 277 Photo. *Perf. 14*

68	A13	1b dark brown	.30	.25
69	A13	2b red brown	.60	.25
70	A13	3b lilac rose	.75	.35
71	A14	5b blue & red	1.25	.60
72	A13	6b dk pur & red	1.40	.65
73	A13	8b dk bl & gray grn	1.50	.75
74	A14	10b rose lilac	1.25	.85
75	A14	14b blue green	2.25	1.00

76 A14 20b rose red 3.25 1.75
77 A14 1i violet 7.50 3.00
Nos. 68-77 (10) 20.05 9.45
Nos. 68-77,C3-C9 (17) 44.70 17.70

No. 71 was used as a 4b stamp in 1956. For surcharges see Nos. 82, 86-87.

Palace of the Rock, Wadi Dhahr — A15

Design: 20b, Walls of Ibb.

Engraved and Photogravure

1952 Unwmk. *Perf. 14½, Imperf.*
78 A15 12b choc, bl & dl grn 6.00 6.00
79 A15 20b dp car, bl & brn 9.00 9.00
Nos. 78-79,C10-C11 (4) 31.00 28.00

Flag and View of San'a (Palace in Background) — A16

1952
80 A16 1i red brn, car & gray 12.50 12.50

4th anniv. of the accession of King Ahmed, Feb. 18, 1948. See Nos. 81, C12-C13.

1952 Palace in Foreground
81 A16 30b red brn, car & dk grn 11.00 11.00

Victory of Mar. 13, 1948. See No. C13.

No. 69 Handstamped Type "b" in Black

1951 (?) Wmk. 277 *Perf. 14*
82 A13 4b on 2b red brown 7.50 10.00
a. Handstamp type "c" 11.00 14.00

Surcharge exists without left frameline. Forged surcharges exist. See Nos. 86-87.

Leaning Minaret, Mosque of Ta'iz — A17

1954 Photo. Unwmk.
83 A17 4b deep orange 1.25 .40
84 A17 6b deep blue 2.00 .60
85 A17 8b deep blue green 2.50 1.50
Nos. 83-85,C14-C16 (6) 19.50 6.65

Accession of King Ahmed I, 5th anniv.

Nos. 68 and 70 Handstamped Type "b" in Black

1955 Wmk. 277 *Perf. 14*
86 A13 4b on 1b dk brown 6.50 9.00
a. Handstamp type "c" 20.00 10.00
b. Handstamp type "e" — —
87 A13 4b on 3b lilac rose 9.50 12.50

Yemen Gate, San'a — A18

1956-57 Wmk. 277 *Perf. 14*
87A A18 1b lt brown 1.00 .75
87B A18 5b blue green 1.25 .75
87C A18 10b dark blue ('57) 1.50 .85
Nos. 87A-87C (3) 3.75 2.35

Nos. 87A-87C were prepared for official use, but issued for regular postage. The 1b and 5b were used as 4b stamps. A 20b and 1-imadi of type A18 were not issued. Value unused $25., used (CTO) $15.

Arab Postal Union Issue

Globe — A19

Perf. 13½x13

1957-58 Wmk. 195 Photo.
88 A19 4b yellow brown 1.00 .90
89 A19 6b green ('58) 1.40 1.10
90 A19 16b violet ('58) 2.00 1.50
Nos. 88-90 (3) 4.40 3.50

Arab Postal Union founding, July 1, 1954.

Telecommunications Issue

Globe, Radio and Telegraph — A20

1959, Mar. Wmk. 318 *Perf. 13x13½*
91 A20 4b vermilion 1.50 1.00

Arab Union of Telecommunications. Exists imperf, Value $4.50.

United Arab States Issue

Flags of UAR and Yemen — A21

1959, Mar. 13
92 A21 1b dl red brn & blk .35 .25
93 A21 2b dk blue & blk .45 .35
94 A21 4b sl grn, car & blk .65 .50
Nos. 92-94,C17-C19 (6) 6.95 5.05

First anniversary of United Arab States. No. 94 exists imperf. Value $10.

In 1959 four special sets of stamps were distributed abroad. They honored Human Rights (4v), Yemeni stamps (6v), Automatic Telephone Service (5v) and King Ahmed's Reign (4v). They were overprinted on stamps of either the 1940 issue (type A6) or the 1931 issue (type A4). Although not regularly sold at post offices in Yemen, several values from these sets do appear on covers that passed through normal postal channels. Some values are known with inverted or doubled overprints.

Values for unused sets: Human Rights, $12; Yemeni stamps, $20; Automatic Telephone Service, $20; King Ahmed's Reign, $12.

Arab League Center Issue

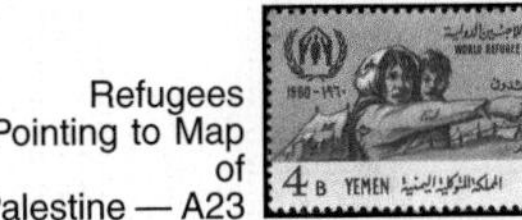

Arab League Center, Cairo — A22

Perf. 13x13½

1960, Mar. 22 Wmk. 328
95 A22 4b dull green & blk .90 .90

Opening of the Arab League Center and the Arab Postal Museum in Cairo. Exists imperf. Value $10.

Refugees Pointing to Map of Palestine — A23

1960, Apr. 7 Photo.
96 A23 4b brown 1.00 .75
97 A23 6b yellow green 1.50 1.25

World Refugee Year, 7/1/59-6/30/60. Exist imperf. Value, set $25.

In 1961 a souvenir sheet was issued containing a 4b gray and 6b sepia in type A18, imperf. Black marginal inscription, "YEMEN 1960," repeated in Arabic. Size: 103x85mm. Value $35.

Torch and Olympic Rings — A24

1960, Dec. Unwmk. *Perf. 14x14½*
98 A24 2b black & lil rose .40 .25
99 A24 4b black & yellow .60 .40
100 A24 6b black & orange 1.00 .60
101 A24 8b brn blk & bl grn 1.50 1.00
102 A24 20b dk bl, org & vio 4.00 2.50
Nos. 98-102 (5) 7.50 4.75

17th Olympic Games, Rome, 8/25-9/11. Exist imperf. Value, set $75. An imperf. souvenir sheet exists, containing one example of No. 99. Size: 100x60mm. Value $40.

UN Emblem Breaking Chains — A25

1961 Unwmk. *Perf. 14x14½*
103 A25 1b violet .25 .25
104 A25 2b green .30 .25
105 A25 3b grnsh blue .40 .25
106 A25 4b brt ultra .50 .35
107 A25 6b brt lilac .60 .50
108 A25 14b rose brown .80 .60
109 A25 20b brown 1.50 1.25
Nos. 103-109 (7) 4.35 3.45

15th anniversary (in 1960) of UN. Exist imperf. Value, set $14. An imperf. souvenir sheet exists, containing one example of No. 106. Blue marginal inscription. Size: 100x60mm. Value $15. For overprints see Nos. 137-143.

Cranes and Ship, Hodeida — A26

1961, June Litho. *Perf. 13x13½*
110 A26 4b multicolored .75 .40
111 A26 6b multicolored 1.25 .75
112 A26 16b multicolored 2.40 1.25
Nos. 110-112 (3) 4.40 2.40

Opening of deepwater port at Hodeida. An imperf. souvenir sheet exists, containing one each of Nos. 110-112. Size: 160x130mm. Value $12.50. For overprints see Nos. 177, 180.

Alabaster Funerary Mask — A27

Designs (ancient sculptures from Marib, Sheba): 2b, Horned animal's head, symbolizing Moon God (limestone). 4b, Bronze head of an Emperor 1st or 2nd century. 8b, Statue of Emperor Dhamar Ali. 10b, Statue of a child, 2nd or 3rd century (alabaster). 12b, Stairs in court of Temple of the Moon God. 20b, Alabaster relief, boy riding monster. 1i, Woman with grapes, relief.

1961, Oct. 14 Photo. *Perf. 11½*
Granite Paper
113 A27 1b salmon, blk & gray .35 .25
114 A27 2b purple & gray .50 .25
115 A27 4b pale brn, gray & blk .70 .25
116 A27 8b brt pink & blk .85 .25
117 A27 10b yellow & blk 1.00 .40
118 A27 12b lt vio bl & blk 1.75 .50
119 A27 20b gray & blk 2.00 .75
120 A27 1i gray ol & blk 4.00 1.25
Nos. 113-120,C20-C21 (10) 14.40 5.15

Exist imperf. Value, set (10), $25. For overprints see Nos. 144-145, 147, 151, 153, 156-158, C24, C25.

Imam's New Palace, San'a — A28

8b, Side view of Imam's palace, San'a, horiz. 10b, Palace of the Rock (Dar al-Hajar).

1961, Nov. 15 Unwmk.
121 A28 4b black & lt bl grn .35 .25
122 A28 8b blk, brt pink & grn .75 .45
123 A28 10b black, sal & grn .85 .50
Nos. 121-123,C22-C23 (5) 5.05 2.05

Exist imperf. Value, set (5) $6. For overprints see #148, 152, 154, C24A, C25A.

Hodeida-San'a Road — A29

1961, Dec. 25 Litho. *Perf. 13½x13*
124 A29 4b multicolored .75 .25
125 A29 6b multicolored .90 .40
126 A29 10b multicolored 1.50 .50
Nos. 124-126 (3) 3.15 1.15

Opening of the Hodeida-San'a highway. A miniature sheet exists containing one each of Nos. 124-126, imperf. Size: 159x129mm. Value $7. For overprints see Nos. 178-179.

Trajan's Kiosk, Philae, Nubia A30

1962, Mar. 1 Photo. *Perf. 11x11½*
127 A30 4b dk red brown 3.00 1.50
128 A30 6b blue green 4.00 2.00

Issued to publicize UNESCO's help in safeguarding the monuments of Nubia. Exist imperf. on toned paper with printer's imprint. Value, set $12.50. A souvenir sheet exists, containing one each of #127-128, imperf. on white paper with printer's imprint at the bottom of the sheet. Size: 100x88½mm. Value $12.50.

Arab League Building, Cairo, and Emblem — A31

1962, Mar. 22 *Perf. 13½x13*
129 A31 4b dark green .70 .25
130 A31 6b deep ultra .85 .40

Arab League Week, Mar. 22-28. A souvenir sheet exists, containing one each of Nos. 129-130, imperf. Size: 94x80mm. Value $3.50. For overprints see Nos. 164-165.

Nurses, Mother and Child — A32

Designs: 4b, Nurse weighing child. 6b, Vaccination. 10b, Weighing infant.

1962, June 20 Unwmk. *Perf. 11½*
131 A32 2b multicolored .60 .25
132 A32 4b multicolored .85 .30
133 A32 6b multicolored 1.00 .40
134 A32 10b multicolored 1.75 .50
Nos. 131-134 (4) 4.20 1.45

Issued for Child Welfare. Exist imperf. Value, set $5. For overprints see Nos. 146, 149-150, 155.

Malaria Eradication Emblem — A33

1962, July 20 ***Perf. 13½x13***

135 A33 4b black & dp org .70 .40
136 A33 6b dk brown & grn 1.00 .60

WHO drive to eradicate malaria. An imperf. souvenir sheet contains one each of Nos. 135-136. Size: 95x79mm. Value $12.50.

No. 136 has laurel leaves added and inscription rearranged.

For overprints see Nos. 189-190.

Nos. 103-109 Overprinted

Perf. 14x14½

1962, Nov. 7 **Photo.** **Unwmk.**

137 A25 1b violet 1.50 1.50
138 A25 2b green 1.50 1.50
139 A25 3b greenish blue 1.50 1.50
140 A25 4b brt ultra 1.50 1.50
141 A25 6b brt lilac 1.50 1.50
142 A25 14b rose brown 1.50 1.50
143 A25 20b brown 1.50 1.50
Nos. 137-143 (7) 10.50 10.50

Exist imperf. and with inverted overprint.

Yemen Arab Republic
Nos. 113-123 and 131-134 Ovptd. in Dark Green or Dark Red

a

b

1963, Jan. 1 ***Perf. 11½***

144 A27 (a) 1b No. 113 (G) .25 .25
145 A27 (a) 2b No. 114 .25 .25
146 A32 (b) 2b No. 131 .35 .35
147 A27 (a) 4b No. 115 (G) .35 .35
148 A28 (a) 4b No. 121 .50 .50
149 A32 (b) 4b No. 132 (G) .50 .50
150 A32 (b) 6b No. 133 .65 .65
151 A27 (a) 8b No. 116 .65 .65
152 A28 (b) 8b No. 122 (G) .90 .90
153 A27 (a) 10b No. 117 .90 .90
154 A28 (a) 10b No. 123 1.60 1.60
155 A32 (b) 10b No. 134 (G) 1.60 1.60
156 A27 (a) 12b No. 118 1.25 1.25
157 A27 (a) 20b No. 119 1.80 1.80
158 A27 (a) 1i No. 120 5.00 5.00
Nos. 144-158,C24-C25A (19) 24.10 24.10

Nos. 144-158, C24-C25A exist imperf. Value, set $45.

The revolution which overthrew the Yemen Monarchy on Sept. 26-27, 1962, three 1962 issues, Nos 127-130 and 135-136 were authorized to be handstamped in black ↔→Yemen Arab Republic↔↓ in Arabic for provisional use. This overprint exists on other values, but their status is questionable.

Nos. 148-150 and 155 exist with double overprints, inverted overprints and with overprints in reversed colors (dark green instead of red and vice versa) on two each of the values. Values for each of these error sets, $20 per set of four.

Proclamation of the Republic — A34

1963, Mar. 15 ***Perf. 11x11½***

159 A34 4b shown .55 .55
160 A34 6b Flag, tank .85 .85

An imperf. souvenir sheet containing Nos. 159-160 exists. Value $10.

See Nos. C26-C28.

UN Freedom From Hunger Campaign — A35

1963, Mar. 21 ***Perf. 11½x11, 11x11½***

162 A35 4b Milk cow, horiz. .90
163 A35 6b shown 1.25

An imperf. souvenir sheet of 2 containing one each Nos. 162-163 exists. Value $12.

For overprints see Nos. 218-218A.

Nos. 129-130 Ovptd. in Dark Red

1963, Sept. 1 ***Perf. 13½x13***

164 A31 4b dark green 6.00 6.00
165 A31 6b deep ultra 6.00 6.00

Nos. 98-100 Overprinted in Black or Red

1963 **Unwmk.** ***Perf. 14x14½***

165A A24 2b black & lil rose 3.00 3.00
165B A24 4b black & yellow (R) 3.00 3.00
165C A24 6b black & orange (R) 3.00 3.00
Nos. 165A-165C (3) 9.00 9.00

Nos. 15-16, 18-23, 50-52 Ovptd. in Black

a

b

1963, Sept. 1

166 A3 (a) 5b No. 15 1.25 1.25
167 A4 (a) 6b No. 16 1.60 1.60
168 A8 (b) 6b No. 50 1.60 1.60
169 A4 (a) 8b No. 18 1.80 1.80
170 A4 (a) 10b No. 19 2.25 2.25
171 A4 (a) 10b No. 20 2.25 2.25
172 A8 (b) 10b No. 51 2.25 2.25
173 A8 (b) 14b No. 52 6.25 6.25
174 A4 (a) 20b No. 21 2.50 2.50
175 A4 (a) 1i No. 22 6.25 6.25
176 A4 (a) 1i No. 23 4.75 4.75
Nos. 166-176 (11) 32.75 32.75

Nos. 168, 172 and 173 exist imperf. Value, set, $18.

Nos. 111-112 and 125-126 Ovptd. in Black

Perf. 13x13½, 13½x13

1963, Sept. 1 **Litho.** **Unwmk.**

177 A26 6b No. 111 1.75 1.75
178 A29 6b No. 125 1.75 1.75
179 A29 10b No. 126 2.50 2.50
180 A26 16b No. 112 2.50 2.50
Nos. 177-180 (4) 8.50 8.50

On Nos. 178-179 the bars eliminate old inscription with text of overprint positioned below and to the right of them, on Nos. 177 and 180, the text is slightly left below the bars.

Nos. 178 and 179 exist with double overprints. Value, set of 2, $25.

Imperf. souvenir sheets of 3 exist containing Nos. 177 and 180 or Nos. 178-179. Value $20 each.

1st Anniv. of the Revolution A36

2b, Flag, torch, candle, vert. 6b, Flag, grain, chain, vert.

Perf. 11½x11, 11x11½

1963, Sept. 26 **Photo.**

186 A36 2b multicolored .35 .30
187 A36 4b shown .55 .45
188 A36 6b multicolored .90 .70
Nos. 186-188 (3) 1.80 1.45

Imperf. souvenir sheet exists containing one each Nos. 186-188. Value $5.

Red Cross, Centennial — A36a

1963, October **Photo.** ***Perf. 13½x13***

188A A36a ¼b bl, blk & red .25 .25
188B A36a ⅓b lil brn, blk & red .25 .25
188C A36a ½b ol grey, blk & red .25 .25
188D A36a 4b vio, black & red .75 .35
188E A36a 8b ocher, blk & red 1.00 .50
188F A36a 20b grn, blk & red 2.00 1.00
Nos. 188A-188F (6) 4.50 2.60

Nos. 188A-188F exist imperf. Value $12. An imperf. souvenir sheet of 2 exists containing one each Nos. 188D-188E. Value $7.50.

Nos. 135-136 Ovptd. in Black

1963, Nov. 25 ***Perf. 13½x13***

189 A33 4b black & dp orange 4.00 4.00
190 A33 6b dk brown & green 4.00 4.00

UN Declaration of Human Rights, 15th Anniv. — A37

1963, Dec. 10 ***Perf. 13½***

191 A37 4b orange & dk brn vio .40 .40
192 A37 6b blue grn & blk .60 .60

Nos. 191-192 exist imperf. Value $6.50. An imperf. souvenir sheet of 2 exists containing one each Nos. 191-192. Value $9.

Olympic Sports — A37a

1964, Mar. 30 **Photo.** ***Perf. 12***

192A A37a ¼b Darts .25 .25
192B A37a ⅓b Table tennis .25 .25
192C A37a ½b Running, vert. .25 .25
192D A37a 1b Volleyball, vert. .45 .40
192E A37a 1½b Soccer, vert. .45 .40
192F A37a 4b Horse racing .65 .50
192G A37a 20b Pole vault 1.35 1.25
i. Souvenir sheet of 1 4.00 4.00
192H A37a 1r Basketball, vert. 2.75 1.50
Nos. 192A-192H (8) 6.40 4.80

Nos. 192F-192H are airmail. Nos. 192A-192H exist imperf. Value $25. An imperf. souvenir sheet containing 1 No. 192F exists. Value $4.

Bagel Spinning and Weaving Factory Inauguration A38

2b, Factory, bobbin, spool, cloth. 4b, Loom machine. 6b, Factory, spool, bolt of cloth.

1964, Apr. 10 ***Perf. 11x11½, 11½x11***

193 A38 2b multicolored .25 .25
193A A38 4b mutlicolored .30 .25
193B A38 6b multicolored .40 .35
193C A38 16b shown 1.10 1.40
Nos. 193-193C (4) 2.05 2.25

Nos. 193-193B vert. An imperf. souvenir sheet of one exists containing No. 193C. Value $3.

No. 193C is air mail.

Hodeida Airport Inauguration A39

1964, Apr. 30 ***Perf. 11½x11***

194 A39 4b Runway .40 .35
194A A39 6b Runway, terminal .55 .50
194B A39 10b Aircraft, terminal, ship at sea .75 .55
Nos. 194-194B (3) 1.70 1.40

An imperf. souvenir sheet of one exists containing No. 194B. Value $3.

1964 New York World's Fair — A39a

Designs: ¼b, 1b, 20b, Manhattan skyline, Sana'a. ⅓b, 4b, Empire State Building, minaret. ½b, 16b, Statue of Liberty, ship loading cranes.

1964, May 10 ***Perf. 12***

195 A39a ¼b brown & multi .25 .25
195A A39a ⅓b grey & multi .25 .25
195B A39a ½b dk bl green & multi .30 .25
195C A39a 1b dk grey & multi .45 .35
195D A39a 4b dk grey & multi .80 .50
195E A39a 16b brown & multi 1.50 1.00
195F A39a 20b red vio & multi 2.00 1.50
Nos. 195-195F (7) 5.55 4.10

Nos. 195E-195F are airmail. An imperf. souvenir sheet containing 1 No. 195F exists. Value $4.

For overprints see Nos. 220-220F.

1964 Summer Olympic Games, Tokyo — A39b

Designs: ¼b, 12b, Globe and flags. ⅓b, 6b, Torch. ½b, 20b, Discus thrower. 1b, Yemen flag. 1½b, 4b, Swimmers, horiz.

1964, June 1 ***Perf. 12***

196 A39b ¼b multicolored .25 .25
196A A39b ⅓b multicolored .25 .25
196B A39b ½b multicolored .30 .25
196C A39b 1b multicolored .40 .30
196D A39b 1½b multicolored .50 .35
196E A39b 4b multicolored .70 .60
196F A39b 6b multicolored .80 .75
196G A39b 12b multicolored 1.50 1.25
196H A39b 20b multicolored 2.25 2.00
i. Souvenir sheet of 1 5.00 5.00
Nos. 196-196H (9) 6.95 6.00

Exist imperf. Value, set $25.

Nos. 196E-196H are airmail.

Boy Scouts A39c

Designs: ¼b, 4b, Raising flag. ⅓b, 1b, 6b, Scouts, tents. ½b, 16b, Bugler. 1½b, 20b, Campfire.

1964, June 20

197 A39c ¼b multicolored .25 .25
197A A39c ⅓b multicolored .25 .25
197B A39c ½b multicolored .25 .25
197C A39c 1b multicolored .35 .25
197D A39c 1½b multicolored .50 .35
197E A39c 4b multicolored .60 .35
197F A39c 6b multicolored .70 .50
197G A39c 16b multicolored 1.50 1.25
i. Souvenir sheet of 1 4.00 4.00
197H A39c 20b multicolored 2.25 1.75
Nos. 197-197H (9) 6.65 5.20

Exist imperf. Value, set $20. An imperf. souvenir sheet containing 1 No. 197H exists. Value, $4.
Nos. 197E-197H are airmail.

Animals — A39d

Designs: ¼b, Baboons. ⅓b, Arabian horses. ½b, 12b, Zebu. 1b, 20b, Lions. 1½b, 4b, Gazelles.

1964, Aug. 15 Photo. ***Perf. 12x11½***

198 A39d ¼b lilac & brown .25 .25
198A A39d ⅓b blue & dk brn .25 .25
198B A39d ½b org & brn .25 .25
198C A39d 1b blue & brn .25 .25
198D A39d 1½b multicolored .40 .25
198E A39d 4b multicolored .65 .40
198F A39d 12b multicolored 1.50 1.00
198G A39d 20b multicolored 3.00 1.25
Nos. 198-198G (8) 6.55 3.90

Exist imperf. Value, set $15.
Nos. 198E-198G are airmail. See Nos. J9-J11.

Flowers — A39e

Designs: ¼b, shown. ⅓b, Crinum. ½b, 12b, Poinsettia. 1b, 4b, Hybrid tea. 1½b, 20b, Peppermint.

1964, Aug. 15 Photo. ***Perf. 11½x12***

199 A39e ¼b multicolored .25 .25
199A A39e ⅓b multicolored .25 .25
199B A39e ½b grn, red & yel .25 .25
199C A39e 1b multicolored .35 .25
199D A39e 1½b red, grn & blk .45 .25
199E A39e 4b multicolored .65 .40
199F A39e 12b dk grn, red & yel 1.50 1.00
199G A39e 20b multicolored 3.00 1.25
Nos. 199-199G (8) 6.70 3.90

Exist imperf. Value, set $12. Nos. 199E-199G are airmail. See Nos. J12-J14.

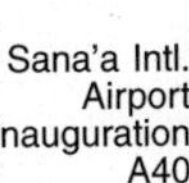

Sana'a Intl. Airport Inauguration A40

1964, Oct. 1

200 A40 1b shown .35 .35
201 A40 2b Terminal, runway, aircraft .35 .35
202 A40 4b like 2b .35 .35
203 A40 8b like 1b .70 .70
Nos. 200-203 (4) 1.75 1.75

An imperf. souvenir sheet of two exists containing one each Nos. 202 and C30. Value $4.
See No. C30.

Arab Postal Union, 10th Anniv. — A41

1964, Oct. 15 ***Perf. 13½***

204 A41 4b multicolored .65 .55

See No. C31.

2nd Arab Summit Conference — A42

1964, Nov. 30

205 A42 4b shown .65 .55
206 A42 6b Conference emblem, map .85 .70

An imperf. souvenir sheet of 2 exists containing one each Nos. 205-206. Value $2.50.
For overprints see Nos. 222-222A.

2nd Anniv. of the Revolution — A43

1964, Dec. 30

207 A43 2b Torch, map .35 .25
208 A43 4b Revolutionary .60 .35
209 A43 6b Flag, 2 candles, map .65 .45
Nos. 207-209 (3) 1.60 1.05

An imperf. souvenir sheet of one exists containing No. 209. Value $2.50.

Birds — A43a

Designs: ¼b, Reef Heron. ½b, Arabian red-legged partridge. ¾b, Eagle owl, vert. 1b, Hammer kop. 1½b, Yemen linnets. 4b, Hoopoes. 6b, Amethyst starlings. 8b, Bald ibis, vert. 12b, Arabian woodpecker, vert. 20b, Bateleur, vert. 1r, Bruce's green pigeon.

Perf. 15x14½, 14½x15

1965, Jan. 30 **Photo.**

Background Color

209A A43a ¼b light violet .50 .25
209B A43a ½b brown olive .75 .25
209C A43a ¾b grey .75 .25
209D A43a 1b olive green 1.00 .40
209E A43a 1½b rose 1.00 .40
209F A43a 4b light blue 2.00 .75
209G A43a 6b blue 2.00 .75
209H A43a 8b bistre 2.00 1.00
209I A43a 12b green 3.00 1.50
209J A43a 20b orange 4.00 2.00
209K A43a 1r blue green 6.00 3.00
Nos. 209A-209K (11) 23.00 10.55

Souvenir Sheet

Imperf

209L A43a 20b rose *15.00 15.00*

Nos. 209A-209K exist imperf. Value, set $35.
Nos. 209G-209K are airmail. For overprints see Nos. 221-221B.

Deir Yassin Massacre — A44

1965, Apr. 30 ***Perf. 11x11½***

210 A44 4b red lil & deep blue .75 .50

See No. C32.

Intl. Telecommunications Union (ITU), Cent. — A45

1965, May 17 ***Perf. 11x11½, 11½x11***

211 A45 4b red & pale blue, vert. .65 .35
212 A45 6b org brn & grn .90 .50

A souvenir sheet of 1 exists containing #212. Value $4.

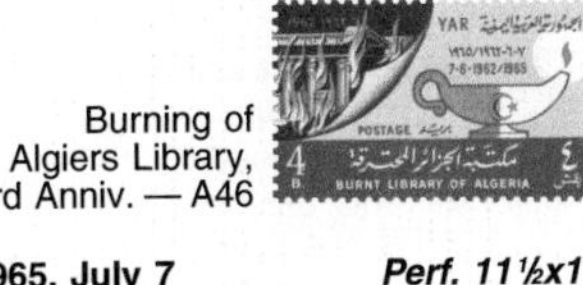

Burning of Algiers Library, 3rd Anniv. — A46

1965, July 7 ***Perf. 11½x11***

213 A46 4b sepia, red & grn .60 .40

See No. C33.

3rd Anniv. of the Revolution A47

1965, Sept. 26

214 A47 4b Tractor, corn, grain .70 .40
214A A47 6b Tractor, tower, buildings .90 .50

An imperf. souvenir sheet of one exists containing No. 214A. Value $3.

Intl. Cooperation Year — A48

1965, Oct. 15 ***Perf. 11x11½***

215 A48 4b shown .70 .55
215A A48 6b UN building, New York 1.00 .60

Nos. 215-215A exist imperf. Value $5. An imperf. souvenir sheet of one exists containing No. 215A. Value $4.

Pres. John F. Kennedy — A48a

Kennedy and: Nos. 216, 216D, Rocket in flight. Nos. 216A, 216G, Launch pads. Nos. 216B-216C, Lift-off. 4b, Capsule in space. 8b, Splash down.

1965, Nov. 29 Photo. ***Perf. 12x11½***

216 A48a ¼b multicolored .25 .25
216A A48a ¼b multicolored .25 .25
216B A48a ¼b multicolored .25 .25
216C A48a ⅓b multicolored .25 .25
216D A48a ½b multicolored .25 .25
216E A48a 4b multicolored .70 .60
216F A48a 8b multicolored 1.60 1.25
216G A48a 12b multicolored 3.00 1.75
Nos. 216-216G (8) 6.55 4.85

Nos. 216F-216G are airmail. Nos. 216-216G exist imperf. Value $12.50. Imperf. souvenir sheets of Nos. 216E-216F exist. Value $5 each.

Astronauts and Cosmonauts — A48b

Spacecraft and: Nos. 217, 8b, Pavel Belyayev. Nos. 217A, 4b, Alexei Leonov. Nos. 217B, 217D, M. Scott Carpenter. Nos. 217C, 16b, Virgil I. "Gus" Grissom. No. 217H, James McDivitt, Edward White.

1965, Dec. 29 Photo. ***Perf. 11½x12***

217 A48b ¼b multicolored .25 .25
217A A48b ¼b multicolored .25 .25
217B A48b ¼b multicolored .25 .25
217C A48b ⅓b multicolored .25 .25
217D A48b ½b multicolored .25 .25
217E A48b 4b multicolored .75 .35
217F A48b 8b multicolored 1.50 1.40
217G A48b 16b multicolored 2.75 2.75
Nos. 217-217G (8) 6.25 5.75

Souvenir Sheet

Imperf

217H A48b 16b multicolored *12.50 12.50*

Exist imperf. Value, set $11.
Nos. 217E-217H are airmail. For overprints see Nos. 225-225H, 229-229D.

Nos. 162-163 Overprinted in Black

a

b

1966, Jan. 15 ***Perf. 11½x11, 11x11½***

218 A35 (a) 4b sal rose & golden brn .90 .90
218A A35 (b) 6b brt pur & yel 1.25 1.25

An imperf. souvenir sheet of two exists containing Nos. 218-218A. Value $8.

Telecommunications — A48c

Designs: No. 219, Light signals. No. 219A, Samuel F.B. Morse, telegraph. No. 219B, Early telephone. No. 219C, Philipp Reis, Thomas Edison, ealry telephone system. No. 219D, Television camera, antenna. No. 219E, Radar dish. No. 219F, Fax machine. No. 219G, Satellite.

1966, Jan. 29 Photo. ***Perf. 12x11½***

219 A48c ¼b red & black .25 .25
219A A48c ¼b grnish bl & blk .25 .25
219B A48c ¼b yel brn & blk .25 .25
219C A48c ⅓b org red & blk .25 .25
219D A48c ½b violet & black .25 .25
219E A48c 4b yel grn & blk .75 .35
219F A48c 6b drab & black 1.25 .65
219G A48c 20b blue & black 2.50 1.25
Nos. 219-219G (8) 5.75 3.50

Nos. 219E-219G are airmail. Nos. 291-219G exist imperf. Value $10. An imperf. souvenir sheet containing 1 No. 219G exists. Value $6.

Nos. 195-195F Overprinted in Black

1966, Feb. 10 Photo. *Perf. 12*

220	A39a	¼b	brown & multi	.50	.50
220A	A39a	⅓b	grey & multi	.50	.50
220B	A39a	½b	dk bl grn & multi	.50	.50
220C	A39a	1b	dk grey & multi	.75	.75
220D	A39a	4b	dk grey & multi	1.25	1.25
220E	A39a	16b	brown & multi	3.00	3.00
220F	A39a	20b	red vio & multi	4.50	4.50
			Nos. 220-220F (7)	11.00	11.00

Nos. 220E-220F are airmail. An imperf. souvenir sheet containing 1 No. 220F exists. Value $10.

Nos. 209A-209C Overprinted in Black or Red

1966, Mar. 5 Photo. *Perf. 12x11½*

Background Color

221	A43a	¼b	light violet	.75	.65
221A	A43a	½b	brown olive	.75	.65
221B	A43a	¾b	grey (R)	1.10	.75
			Nos. 221-221B (3)	2.60	2.05

Nos. 205-206 Ovptd. in Red or Black

1966, Mar. 20 *Perf. 13½*

222	A42	4b	dark green (R)	.60	.40
222A	A42	6b	orange brown	.75	.50

An imperf. souvenir sheet of two exists containing Nos. 222-222A ovptd. in bright pink (4b) or black (6b) with additional inscription at bottom "CASABLANCA / 1965." Value $3.50.

Builders of World Peace — A49

Designs: Nos. 223, 223C, Dag Hammerskjold. Nos. 223A, 4b, John F. Kennedy. Nos. 223B, 223D, Jawaharlal Nehru. 6b, Mohammed Abdel Khaliq Hassuna. 10b, U Thant. 12b, Pope Paul VI.

1966, Mar. 25 Photo. *Perf. 12*

223	A49	¼b	green	.25	.25
223A	A49	¼b	orange brown	.25	.25
223B	A49	¼b	dark grey	.25	.25
223C	A49	⅓b	red brown	.25	.25
223D	A49	½b	violet brown	.25	.25
223E	A49	4b	claret	.75	.35

Size:51x38mm

223F	A49	6b	bl grn & brn	1.00	.50
223G	A49	10b	blue & brown	1.25	.65
223H	A49	12b	red lilac & brn	2.00	1.00
			Nos. 223-223H (9)	6.25	3.75

Exist impref. Value, set $9. Nos. 223F-223H are airmail.

Two imperf. souvenir sheets, 4b and 8b, exist. Values $4 and $6, respectively.

Domesticated Animals — A50

1966, May 5 Photo. *Perf. 12½*

224	A50	¼b	Rooster	.30	.25
224A	A50	¼b	Rabbit	.30	.25
224B	A50	¼b	Donkey	.30	.25
224C	A50	⅓b	Cat	.40	.25
224D	A50	½b	Sheep	.40	.25
224E	A50	4b	Camel	1.00	.50
			Nos. 224-224E (6)	2.70	1.75

Souvenir Sheet

Imperf

224F	A50	22b	Sheep, chickens, geese	4.00	3.00

Nos. 224-224E exist imperf. Value, set $7. No. 224F is airmail.

Nos. 217-217H Overprinted in Black and Red

Luna IX

1966, May 20 Photo. *Perf. 11½x12*

225	A48b	¼b	multicolored	.25	.25
225A	A48b	¼b	multicolored	.25	.25
225B	A48b	¼b	multicolored	.25	.25
225C	A48b	⅓b	multicolored	.25	.25
225D	A48b	½b	multicolored	.25	.25
225E	A48b	4b	multicolored	.45	.30
225F	A48b	8b	multicolored	1.00	.70
225G	A48b	16b	multicolored	1.50	1.20
			Nos. 225-225G (8)	4.20	3.45

Souvenir Sheet

Imperf

225H	A48b	16b	multicolored	*8.00*	*8.00*

Nos. 225-225G exist imperf. Value, set $7.50. Nos. 225E-225H are airmail.

World Cup Soccer Championship, London — A51

1966, May 29 Photo. *Perf. 11*

Background Color

226	A51	¼b	light green	.25	.25
226A	A51	¼b	violet	.25	.25
226B	A51	¼b	dull rose	.25	.25
226C	A51	⅓b	green	.25	.25
226D	A51	½b	orange red	.25	.25
226E	A51	4b	blue	.45	.25
226F	A51	5b	bistre	.60	.30
226G	A51	20b	gold	1.90	1.00
			Nos. 226-226G (8)	4.20	2.80

Nos. 226-226G exist imperf. Value $8. An imperf souvenir sheet containing 1 No. 226G exists. Value $6.

Traffic Day — A52

1966, June 30 *Perf. 11x11½*

227	A52	4b	green & ver	.65	.45
228	A52	6b	green & ver	.75	.50

Nos. 227-228 exist imperf. Value $3. An imperf. souvenir sheet of No. 228 exists. Value $3.50.

Nos. 217-217D Surcharged in Black

Surveyor I.

1966, Aug. 15 Photo. *Perf. 11½x12*

229	A48b	1b on ¼b multi		.65	.50
229A	A48b	¼b	multicolored	.65	.50
229B	A48b	¼b	multicolored	.65	.50
229C	A48b	⅓b	multicolored	.65	.70
229D	A48b	½b	multicolored	1.60	1.25
			Nos. 229-229D (5)	4.20	3.45

A53

Revolution, 6th Anniv. — A53a

1966, Sept. Photo. *Perf. 11½*

230	A53	2b	multicolored	1.50	1.25

Perf. 11x11¼

230A	A53a	4b	multicolored	1.75	1.25
230B	A53a	6b	Factory, tractor, wheat, corn	2.75	1.75
			Nos. 230-230B (3)	6.00	4.25

An imperf. souvenir sheet containing 1 each of Nos. 230A-230B exists. Value $20.

New WHO Headquarters, Geneva — A54

WHO Headquarters, flowers and: Nos. 231, 4b, Galen (129-199). Nos. 231A, 8b, Hippocrates (460-370 BC). Nos. 231B, 16b, Ibn Sina (Avicenna) (980-1037).

1966, Nov. 1 Litho. *Perf. 12½*

231	A54	¼b	multicolored	.25	.25
231A	A54	¼b	multicolored	.25	.25
231B	A54	¼b	multicolored	.25	.25
231C	A54	4b	multicolored	.50	.25
231D	A54	8b	multicolored	1.00	.50
231E	A54	16b	multicolored	2.00	1.00
			Nos. 231-231E (6)	4.25	2.50

Nos. 231C-231E are airmail. Nos. 231-231E exist imperf. Value $10 An imperf. souvenir sheet of 1 No. 231E exists. Value $8.

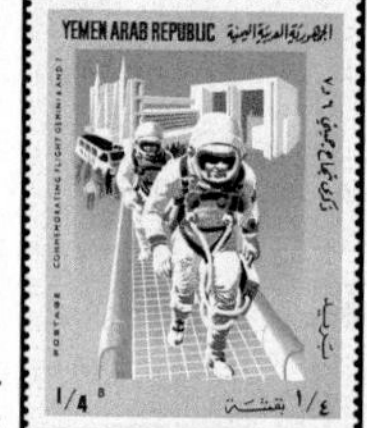

Gemini 6 and 7 Flights — A55

Designs: No. 232, Astronauts. No. 232A, Lift off. No. 232B, Spacecraft, Earth. ⅓b, 2b, Spacecraft in orbit. ½b, 8b, Splash down. 12b, Rendevous.

1966, Dec. 1 Photo. *Perf. 12½*

Background Color

232	A55	¼b	rose	.25	.25
232A	A55	¼b	olive bistre	.25	.25
232B	A55	¼b	blue	.25	.25
232C	A55	⅓b	light blue	.25	.25
232D	A55	½b	blue green	.25	.25
232E	A55	2b	bistre	.50	.25
232F	A55	8b	blue	1.00	.50
232G	A55	12b	violet	1.50	.75
			Nos. 232-232G (8)	4.25	2.75

Nos. 232F-232G are airmail. Nos. 232-232G exist imperf. Value $9. An imperf. souvenir sheet containing 1 No. 232G exists. Value $6.

Nos. 232-232G Overprinted in Red

1966, Dec. 25 Photo. *Perf. 12½*

Background Color

233	A55	¼b	rose	.25	.25
233A	A55	¼b	olive bistre	.25	.25
233B	A55	¼b	blue	.25	.25
233C	A55	⅓b	light blue	.25	.25
233D	A55	½b	blue green	.25	.25
233E	A55	2b	bistre	.45	.30
233F	A55	8b	blue	1.60	1.10
233G	A55	12b	violet	2.00	1.40
			Nos. 233-233G (8)	5.30	4.05

Nos. 233F-233G are airmail. Nos. 233-233G exist imperf. Value $8. An imperf. souvenir sheet containing 1 No. 233G exists. Value $6.

Fruit — A56

1967, Feb. 10 Litho. *Perf. 12½x12*

234	A56	¼b	Figs	.25	.25
234A	A56	¼b	Red apples	.25	.25
234B	A56	¼b	Purple grapes	.25	.25
234C	A56	⅓b	Dates	.25	.25
234D	A56	½b	Apricots	.25	.25
234E	A56	2b	Yellow apples	.55	.30
234F	A56	4b	Oranges	.70	.40
234G	A56	6b	Bananas	.90	.50
234H	A56	8b	Green figs	1.10	.65
234I	A56	10b	Green grapes	1.35	.75
			Nos. 234-234I (10)	5.85	3.85

Exist imperf. Value, set $9. Nos. 234G-234I are airmail. See Nos. J23-J25.

Arab League Day — A57

1967, July Photo. *Perf. 11x11½*

235	A57	4b	violet & brown	.50	.25
235A	A57	6b	dk violet & brown	.75	.40
235B	A57	8b	violet & brown	1.25	.65
235C	A57	20b	dk bl grn & brn	2.00	1.00
235D	A57	40b	dk bl grn & blk	4.00	2.00
			Nos. 235-235D (5)	8.50	4.30

Gamal el-Din el-Afghani (1839-97), advocate of Arab unity.

Intl. Labor Organization (ILO) — A58

1967, Aug. Photo. *Perf. 11½x11*

236	A58	2b	vio & dk blue	.40	.25
236A	A58	4b	car & dk bl grn	.60	.30
236B	A58	6b	grn & dp red lilac	1.00	.50
236C	A58	8b	vio bl & ol bis	1.50	.75
			Nos. 236-236C (4)	3.50	1.80

An imperf. souvenir sheet containing 1 10b No. 236C exists. Value $6.

Agriculture A59

1967, Sept. Photo. *Perf. 11½x11*

237	A59	1b	multicolored	.25	.25
237A	A59	2b	multicolored	.30	.25
237B	A59	4b	multicolored	.35	.25

237C A59 6b multicolored .50 .25
237D A59 8b multicolored .85 .45
237E A59 10b multicolored 1.25 .65
237F A59 12b multicolored 1.50 .75
237G A59 16b multicolored 1.75 .85
237H A59 20b multicolored 2.50 1.25
237I A59 40b multicolored 4.00 2.00
Nos. 237-237I (10) 13.25 6.95

Nos. 237-237E Overprinted in Black

1967, Sept.

238 A59 1b multicolored .40 .25
238A A59 2b multicolored .60 .30
238B A59 4b multicolored 1.00 .50
238C A59 6b multicolored 1.50 .75
238D A59 8b multicolored 2.00 1.00
238E A59 10b multicolored 2.50 1.25
Nos. 238-238E (6) 8.00 4.05

Fifth Anniv. of the Revolution.

Paintings by Flemish Masters — A60

Designs: ¼b, Village Wedding by Bruegel. ⅓b, The Doctor G. Zeile by Van Orley. ½b, H. Fourment and Her Children by Rubens. 3b, The King is Drinking by Jordaens. 6b, Self-Portrait by Van Dyck.

1967, Oct. Photo. *Perf. 13½*

239 A60 ¼b gold & multi .25 .25
239A A60 ⅓b gold & multi .25 .25
239B A60 ½b gold & multi .25 .25
239C A60 3b gold & multi 1.25 .25
239D A60 6b gold & multi 3.00 .55
Nos. 239-239D (5) 5.00 1.55

Nos. 239C-239D are airmail. An imperf. souvenir sheet containing 1 No. 239D exists. Value, $6. Nos. 239-239D exist imperf. with silver frames.

Flemish Painting Type

Paintings by Florentine Masters: ¼b, Portrait of a Young Man by Raphael. ⅓b, E. de Toledo and Her Son by A. Bronzino. ½b, Simoneta Vespucci by P. Di Cosimo. 3b, The Delphic Sibyl by Michelangelo. 6b, Spring by Botticelli.

1967, Nov. 17 Photo. *Perf. 13½*

240 A60 ¼b gold & multi .25 .25
240A A60 ⅓b gold & multi .25 .25
240B A60 ½b gold & multi .25 .25
240C A60 3b gold & multi 1.25 .25
240D A60 6b gold & multi 3.00 .55
Nos. 240-240D (5) 5.00 1.55

Nos. 240C-240D are airmail. An imperf. souvenir sheet containing 1 No. 240D exists. Value, $6. Nos. 240-240D exist imperf. with silver frames.

Flemish Painting Type

Paintings by Spanish Masters: ¼b, The Infanta Margarita by Velazquez. ⅓b, The Knock-Kneed Man by Ribera. ½b, The Beggar by Murillo. 3b, A Knight by El Greco. 6b, The Grape Gathering by Goya.

1967, Nov. 17 Photo. *Perf. 13½*

241 A60 ¼b gold & multi .25 .25
241A A60 ⅓b gold & multi .25 .25
241B A60 ½b gold & multi .25 .25
241C A60 3b gold & multi 1.25 .25
241D A60 6b gold & multi 3.00 .55
Nos. 241-241D (5) 5.00 1.55

Nos. 241C-241D are airmail. An imperf. souvenir sheet containing 1 No. 241D exists. Value, $6. Nos. 241-241D exist imperf. with silver frames.

1968 Winter Olympic Games, Grenoble — A61

Sports: ¼b, Cross-country skiing. ⅓b, Figure skating. ½b, Bobsled. 3b, Ice hockey. 6b, Slalom skiing.

1967, Dec. 9 Photo. *Perf. 11½*

242 A61 ¼b multicolored .25 .25
242A A61 ⅓b multicolored .25 .25
242B A61 ½b multicolored .25 .25
242C A61 3b multicolored 1.20 .25
242D A61 6b multicolored 3.50 .55
Nos. 242-242D (5) 5.45 1.55

An imperf. souvenir sheet containing 1 No. 242D exists. 9.50. Value, $. Nos. 242-242D exist imperf. with different colors.

Paintings by Paul Gauguin — A62

Paintings: No. 243e, Woman in white dress. No. 243f, Woman lying on beach. No. 243Ag, Self-portrait. No. 243Ah, Nevermore. No. 243Bi, Girls from Pouldu. No. 243Bj, Girls from Bretagne. No. 243Ck, La Lune et la Terre. No. 243Cl, Angela. No. 243Dm, Woman. No. 243Dn, Two women.

1968, June Litho. *Perf. 13½*

243 A62 ¼b Pair, #e.-f. .40 .25
243A A62 ⅓b Pair, #g.-h. .40 .25
243B A62 ½b Pair, #i.-j. .40 .25
243C A62 3b Pair, #k.-l. 2.00 .50
243D A62 6b Pair, #m.-n. 3.50 1.00
Nos. 243-243D (5) 6.70 2.25

Nos. 243C-243D are airmail. Nos. 243-243D exist imperf. with gold frames. Value, $9. An imperf. souvenir sheet containing 1 No. 243D exists with either silver or gold frame. Value, each $9.

Paintings by Gaugin Type

Paintings by Van Gogh: No. 244e, Julien Tanguy. No. 244f, Joseph Roulin. No. 244Ag, Sunflowers. No. 244Ah, Church in Auvers. No. 244Bi, Armand Roulin. No. 244Bj, La Berceuse (Madam Roulin). No. 244Ck, Une Arlésienne an Mouemé. No. 244Cl, Marguerite Gachet at piano. No. 244Dm, L'Arlésienne. No. 244Dn, Self-portrait.

1968, June Litho. *Perf. 13½*

244 A62 ¼b Pair, #e.-f. .40 .25
244A A62 ⅓b Pair, #g.-h. .40 .25
244B A62 ½b Pair, #i.-j. .40 .25
244C A62 3b Pair, #k.-l. 2.00 .50
244D A62 6b Pair, #m.-n. 3.50 1.00
Nos. 244-244D (5) 6.70 2.25

Nos. 244C-244D are airmail. Nos. 244-244D exist imperf. with gold frames. Value, $9. An imperf. souvenir sheet containing 1 No. 244D exists with either silver or gold frame. Value, each $9.

Paintings by Gaugin Type

Paintings by Rubens: No. 245e, Head of a little girl. No. 245f, Child's head (Holy Family detail). No. 245Ag, Portrait of a Negro. No. 245Ah, Thomas, Count of Arundel. No. 245Bi, Self-Portrait. No. 245Bj, Isabelle Brandt. No. 245Ck, Woman in a Hat. No. 245Cl, Helene Fourment. No. 245Dm, Rubens' sons. No. 245Dn, The Holy Family.

1968, June Litho. *Perf. 13½*

245 A62 ¼b Pair, #e.-f. .40 .25
245A A62 ⅓b Pair, #g.-h. .40 .25
245B A62 ½b Pair, #i.-j. .40 .25
245C A62 3b Pair, #k.-l. 2.00 .50
245D A62 6b Pair, #m.-n. 3.50 1.00
Nos. 245-245D (5) 6.70 2.25

Nos. 245C-245D are airmail. Nos. 245-245D exist imperf. with gold frames. Value, $9. An imperf. souvenir sheet containing 1 No. 245D exists with either silver or gold frame. Value, each $9.

Nos. 7-23 Overprinted in Black or Red

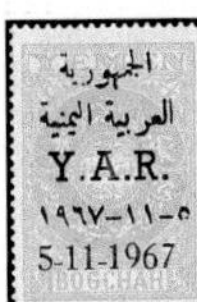

1968 Wmk. 127 *Perf. 14*

246 A3 ½b on No. 7 .75
246A A3 1b On No. 8 (R) .75
246B A3 1b On No. 9 (R) .75
246C A3 2b On No. 10 (R) 1.00
246D A3 2b On No. 11 1.00
246E A3 3b On No. 12 1.25
246F A3 4b On No. 13 1.25
246G A3 4b On No. 14 1.25
246H A3 5b On No. 15 (R) 2.00
246I A4 6b On No. 16 (R) 2.00
246J A4 6b On No. 17 (R) 2.00
246K A4 8b On No. 18 *10.00*
246L A4 10b On No. 19 3.00
246M A4 10b On No. 20 3.00
246N A4 20b On No. 21 4.00
246O A4 1i On No. 22 7.00
246P A4 1i On No. 23 7.00
Nos. 246-246P (17) 48.00

No. 246 exists with a red overprint. No. 246H is known with an inverted overprint.

Flemish Painting Type of 1967

Paintings of Horses: ¼b, Righteous Judge and Warrior of God by Hugo Van Eyck. ⅓b, The Virgin and the Unicorn by Zampieri (Domenichino). ½b, The Prince Baltsar Carlos by Velazquez. 3b, Roman Slave with Horses by Gericault. 6b, The Hunt by Ucello.

1968, July 10 Photo. *Perf. 13½*

247 A60 ¼b gold & multi .25 .25
247A A60 ⅓b gold & multi .25 .25
247B A60 ½b gold & multi .25 .25
247C A60 3b gold & multi 1.75 .35
247D A60 6b gold & multi 3.00 .65
Nos. 247-247D (5) 5.50 1.75

Nos. 247C-247D are airmail. An imperf. souvenir sheet containing 1 No. 247D exists. Value, $11. Nos. 247-247D exist imperf. with silver frames. Value, $7.

Flemish Painting Type of 1967

Paintings by Raphael: ¼b, La Velata. ⅓b, Angelo Doni. ½b, Plato and Aristotle. 3b, A Man. 6b, A Young Woman.

1968, July 10 Photo. *Perf. 13½*

248 A60 ¼b gold & multi .25 .25
248A A60 ⅓b gold & multi .25 .25
248B A60 ½b gold & multi .25 .25
248C A60 3b gold & multi 1.75 .25
248D A60 6b gold & multi 3.00 .55
e. Souvenir sheet of 1 4.00
Nos. 248-248D (5) 5.50 1.55

Nos. 248C-248D are airmail. An imperf. souvenir sheet of No. 248De exists. Nos. 248-248D exist imperf. with silver frames. Value, $7.

Flemish Painting Type of 1967

Paintings by Rembrandt: ¼b, Jan Six. ⅓b, Saskia. ½b, Mars. 3b, H. Stoffels. 6b, Self-portrait.

1968, July 10 Photo. *Perf. 13½*

249 A60 ¼b gold & multi .25 .25
249A A60 ⅓b gold & multi .25 .25
249B A60 ½b gold & multi .25 .25
249C A60 3b gold & multi 1.75 .25
249D A60 6b gold & multi 3.00 .55
e. Souvenir sheet of 1 4.00
Nos. 249-249D (5) 5.50 1.55

Nos. 249C-249D are airmail. An imperf. souvenir sheet of No. 249De exists. Nos. 249-249D exist imperf. with silver frames. Value, $7.

Revolution, 6th Anniversary A63

President and: 2b, Fighters. 4b, Flag. 6b, Roses, vert.

1968, July Litho. *Perf. 12¾*

250 A63 2b multicolored .40 .25
250A A63 4b multicolored .60 .30
250B A63 6b multicolored 1.00 .50
Nos. 250-250B (3) 2.00 1.05

Nos. 250-250B exist imperf. Value $2. An imperf souvenir sheet of No. 250B exists. Value $3.50.

Gold Medalists, 1968 Winter Olympic Games — A64

Various Olympic Gold Medals and: ¼b, Peggy Fleming, USA. ⅓b, Franco Nones, Italy. ½b, Jiri Raska, Czechosovakia. 2b, Hockey Team, USSR. 3b, Jean Claude Killy, France. 4b, Erhard Keller, Germany.

1968, Sept. 10 Litho. *Perf. 13½*

251 A64 ¼b multicolored .25 .25
251A A64 ⅓b multicolored .25 .25
251B A64 ½b multicolored .25 .25
251C A64 2b multicolored 1.00 .25
251D A64 3b multicolored 1.40 .25
251E A64 4b multicolored 2.00 .30
Nos. 251-251E (6) 5.15 1.55

Nos. 251D-251E are airmail. No. 251E exists in perf. and imperf. souvenir sheets of one. Nos. 251-251E exist imperf. with light blue borders. Value, $7.

1968 Summer Olympic Games, Mexico City A65

Ancient Greek art and artifacts of Mexico: ¼b, Greek man, sculpture. ⅓b, Woman on bull, jade mask. ½b, Three people, jaguar. 2b, Two warriors, large carving. 3b, Chariot, mask. 4b, Rider and 2 people, sculpture. No. 252F, Three warriors, Central University City Campus site.

1968, Sept. 30 Litho. *Perf. 13½*

252 A65 ¼b multicolored .25 .25
252A A65 ⅓b multicolored .25 .25
252B A65 ½b multicolored .25 .25
252C A65 2b multicolored 1.20 .25
252D A65 3b multicolored 1.50 .25
252E A65 4b multicolored 1.75 .30
Nos. 251-251E (6) 2.15 1.55

Souvenir Sheet

252F A65 4b multicolored 7.00 1.50

Nos. 252D-252F are airmail. No. 252F contains one 88x35mm stamp. Nos. 252-252F exist imperf. with silver frames. Values: set $7; souvenir sheet, $12.

Olympic Medals Type of 1968

Olympic Gold Medals from: ¼b, 1896, 1908, 1912. ⅓b, 1920, 1924. ½b, 1928, 1932. 2b, 1936, 1948, 1952. 3b, 1956, 1960, 1964. 4b, 1968, 1972.

1968, Oct. 18 Litho. *Perf. 13½*

253 A64 ¼b multicolored .25 .25
253A A64 ⅓b multicolored .25 .25
253B A64 ½b multicolored .25 .25
253C A64 2b multicolored .90 .25
253D A64 3b multicolored 1.20 .25
253E A64 4b multicolored 1.75 .30
Nos. 253-253E (6) 4.60 1.55

Nos. 253D-253E are airmail. No. 253E exists in perf. and imperf. souvenir sheets of one. Nos. 253-253E exist imperf. with light blue borders. Value, $5.

Arms of Winter Olympic Games Host Cities — A66

Designs: ¼b, Ancient ski. ⅓b, Chamonix, 1924; St. Moritz, 1928; Lake Placid, 1932. ½b, Garmisch 1936; St. Moritz, 1948; Oslo, 1952. 2b, Cortina, 1956; Squaw Valley, 1960; Innsbruck, 1964. 3b, Grenoble, 1968. 4b,Sapporo, 1972.

1968, Nov. 23 Litho. *Perf. 13½*
254 A66 ¼b multicolored .25 .25
254A A66 ⅓b multicolored .25 .25
254B A66 ½b multicolored .25 .25
254C A66 2b multicolored .60 .25
254D A66 3b multicolored 1.20 .25
254E A66 4b multicolored 1.75 .30
Nos. 254-254E (6) 4.30 1.55

Nos. 254D-254E are airmail. A perf. and imperf. souvenir sheet containing one each of Nos. 254D-254E exist. Values: perf $7; imperf $14. Nos. 254-254E exist perf. and imperf. with light blue borders. Value, $5.

Arms of Olympic Host Cities Type

Arms of Summer Olympic Games Host Cities: ¼b, Athens, 1896; London, 1908; Stockholm, 1912. ⅓b, Antwerp, 1920; Paris, 1924. ½b, Amsterdam, 1928; Los Angeles, 1932; Berlin, 1936. 2b, London, 1948; Helsinki, 1952. 3b, Melbourne, 1956; Rome, 1960; Tokyo, 1964. 4b, Mexico City, 1968; Munich, 1972.

1968, Dec. 22 Litho. *Perf. 13½*
255 A66 ¼b multicolored .25 .25
255A A66 ⅓b multicolored .25 .25
255B A66 ½b multicolored .25 .25
255C A66 2b multicolored .60 .25
255D A66 3b multicolored 1.20 .25
255E A66 4b multicolored 1.75 .30
Nos. 255-255E (6) 4.30 1.55

Nos. 255D-255E are airmail. A perf. and imperf. souvenir sheet containing one No. 255E exists. Values: perf $7; imperf. $14. Nos. 255-255E exist perf. and imperf. with light blue borders. Value, $5.

Intl. Human Rights Figures — A67

Designs: ¼b, 10b, Dr. Christiaan Barnard with patient, horiz. ⅓b, 2b, Dag Hammarskjold. ¾b, Dr. Barnard. 1b, 4b, Rev. Martin Luther King. 6b, 14b, Robert F. and John F. Kennedy, horiz. 8b, Dr. Barnard with heart, horiz. 12b, 16b, Dr. King and Abraham Lincoln, horiz.

1968 Litho. *Perf. 12½*
256 A67 ¼b multicolored .25 .25
256A A67 ⅓b multicolored .25 .25
256B A67 ¾b multicolored .25 .25
256C A67 1b multicolored .25 .25
256D A67 2b multicolored .90 .25
256E A67 4b multicolored .75 .25
256F A67 6b multicolored 1.50 .35
256G A67 8b multicolored 2.00 .35
256H A67 10b multicolored 2.75 .50
256I A67 12b multicolored 2.75 .55
256J A67 14b multicolored 2.00 .65
256K A67 16b multicolored 2.50 .65
Nos. 256-256K (12) 16.15 4.55

Nos. 256-256K exist imperf. Value: set, $20. Three imperf. souvenir sheets exist; a 10b with Robert and John Kennedy, a 16b with King and Lincoln and a 20b with Dr. Barnard. Value, 3 sheets, $20.

Cultural Olympiad, Mexico City — A68

Paintings in the Louvre, Paris: ¼b, Madeleine by Van Der Weyden. ⅓b, The Gypsy by Frans Hals. ½b, Balthasar Castiglionne by Raphael. 2b, The Lacemaker by Vermeer. 3b, Women and Child by Da Vinci. 4b, Madonna and Child by Botticelli. No. 257F, Mona Lisa by Da Vinci.

1969, Feb. 19 Litho. *Perf. 13½*
257 A68 ¼b silver & multi .25 .25
257A A68 ⅓b silver & multi .25 .25
257B A68 ½b silver & multi .25 .25
257C A68 2b silver & multi .90 .25
257D A68 3b silver & multi 1.20 .25
257E A68 4b silver & multi 1.75 .30
Nos. 257-257E (6) 4.60 1.55

Souvenir Sheet

257F A68 4b gold & multi *7.00 3.50*

Nos. 257D-257F are airmail. Value: set, $6. Nos. 257-257E exist with gold frames. No. 257F has an orange yellow background and exists imperf., as well as both perf and imperf with a blue green background. No. 257C is iinscribed The Embroiderer. No. 257E is inscribed Woman and Child.

Cultural Olympiad Type

Paintings in the Uffizi Gallery, Florence: ¼b, Battista Sforza by Piero Della Francesca. ⅓b, Francesco delle Opere by Perugino. ½b, Francesco Maria della Rovere by Raphael. 2b, Isabel Brandt by Rubens. 3b, Don Garcia de Médicis by Bronzino. 4b, The Birth of Venus (detail) by Botticelli No. 257F, Alegoria della Primavera by Botticelli.

1969, Mar. 29 Litho. *Perf. 13½*
258 A68 ¼b gold & multi .25 .25
258A A68 ⅓b gold & multi .25 .25
258B A68 ½b gold & multi .25 .25
258C A68 2b gold & multi 1.20 .25
258D A68 3b gold & multi 1.50 .25
258E A68 4b gold & multi 1.75 .30
Nos. 258-258E (6) 5.20 1.55

Souvenir Sheet

258F A68 4b gold & multi *7.00 3.50*

Nos. 258D-258F are airmail. Nos. 258-258E exist with gold frames. Value: set, perf or imperf, $6. No. 258F has a red background and exists imperf, as well as perf and imperf with a red orange frame. Value, $14.

Cultural Olympiad Type

Paintings in the Prado, Madrid: ¼b, Charles the First, of England by Van Dyck. ⅓b, The Story of Nastaglio by Botticelli. ½b, Maria Ruthwen by Van Dyck. 2b, Portrait of a Man by Dürer. 3b, Young Girl by Raphael. 4b, Self-portrait by Dürer. No. 257F, A Maja Vestida by Goya.

1969, May 2 Litho. *Perf. 13½*
259 A68 ¼b silver & multi .25 .25
259A A68 ⅓b silver & multi .25 .25
259B A68 ½b silver & multi .25 .25
259C A68 2b silver & multi 1.20 .25
259D A68 3b silver & multi 1.50 .25
259E A68 4b silver & multi 1.75 .30
Nos. 259-259E (6) 5.20 1.55

Souvenir Sheet

259F A68 4b gold & multi *7.00 3.50*

Nos. 259D-259F are airmail. Value: set, $6. Nos. 259-259E exist with bronze frames. No. 258F exists imperf. Value, $14.

Discoveries of the Universe — A69

Spacecraft and Astronomers: No. 260, Vanguard, Ptolemy. No. 260A, Sputknik III, Copernicus. No. 260B, Lunik, Michelangelo. No. 260C, Explorer VI, Tycho Brahe. 3b, Lunik III, Galileo. 6b, Lunik II, Kepler. 10b, Explorer VII, Newton. 14b, Apollo 8.

1969, May 26 Litho. *Perf. 13½*
260 A69 ¼b silver & multi .25 .25
260A A69 ¼b silver & multi .25 .25
260B A69 ⅓b silver & multi .25 .25
260C A69 ⅓b silver & multi .25 .25
260D A69 3b silver & multi .75 .35
260E A69 6b silver & multi 1.25 .65
260F A69 10b silver & multi 2.00 1.00
Nos. 260-260F (7) 5.00 3.00

Souvenir Sheet

260G A69 14b multicolored 6.00 3.00

Nos. 260E-260G are airmail. Nos. 260-260F exist imperf. with lilac-silver frames. A 14b imperf. souvenir sheet with Soyuz 4-5 and Apollo 8 exists.

Discoveries of the Universe Type

Old and New Space Travel: No. 261, Wan Pou, Pioneer IV, Pioneer V. No. 261A, Lucion di Samosa, Sputnik V, Explorer 10, Venus I. No. 261B, Cyrano de Bergerac, Mariner II, Mariner III. No. 261C, Jules Verne, Mariner IV. 2b, Nicolar Kibaltchich, Zond II. 4b, Rocket Lift-off, Venus II, Venus III, Luna X. 22b, Lunar lander, Venus IV. No. 261G, Apollo 9.

1969, July 3 Litho. *Perf. 13½*
261 A69 ¼b silver & multi .25 .25
261A A69 ¼b silver & multi .25 .25
261B A69 ⅓b silver & multi .25 .25
261C A69 ⅓b silver & multi .25 .25
261D A69 2b silver & multi .90 .35
261E A69 4b silver & multi 1.20 .35
261F A69 22b silver & multi 2.75 1.10
Nos. 261-261F (7) 5.85 2.80

Souvenir Sheet

261G A69 6b multicolored *7.00 2.00*

Nos. 261D-261G are airmail. Nos. 261-261F exist imperf. with gold frames. Value: set, $7. A 6b imperf. souvenir sheet with Apollo 9 and a space station exists.

Intl. Labor Organization A70

1969, Aug. 4 Litho. *Perf. 13½*
262 A70 1b Stonemason .25 .25
262A A70 2b Blacksmith .35 .25
262B A70 3b Teacher .50 .25
262C A70 4b Printer .60 .30
262D A70 6b Polisher .75 .35
262E A70 8b Foundry worker 1.00 .50
262F A70 10b Farrier 1.25 .60
Nos. 262-262F (7) 4.70 2.50

Nos. 262D-262F are airmail. Nos. 262-262F exist imperf.

Discoveries of the Universe Type

Spacecraft: No. 263, Mercury Atlas 3, Vostok I, Vostok II, Mercury Atlas 6. No. 263A, Mercury Atlas 8, Vostok III & IV, Mercury Atlas 9, Vostok VI. No. 263B, Voskhod II, Voskhod I, Gemini 3, Gemini 4. No. 263C, Gemini 5-9. 3b, Apollo 8-9. 6b, Soyuz III, Soyuz I, Apollo 7-8. 10b, Gemini 10-12, Apollo 7. No. 263G, Vostok I, Mercury.

1969, Aug. 25 Litho. *Perf. 13½*
263 A69 ¼b multicolored .25 .25
263A A69 ¼b multicolored .25 .25
263B A69 ⅓b multicolored .25 .25
263C A69 ⅓b multicolored .25 .25
263D A69 3b multicolored .90 .35
263E A69 6b multicolored 1.20 .50
263F A69 10b multicolored 2.75 .75
Nos. 263-263F (7) 5.85 2.60

Souvenir Sheet

263G A69 6b multicolored *7.00 3.00*

Nos. 263D-263G are airmail. No. 263G contains one 82x43mm stamp. Nos. 263-263F exist imperf. with light yellow green frames. A 6b imperf. souvenir sheet with Apollo 10 exists.

Napoloen, Birth Bicentennial — A71

Napoleon: ¼b, As artillery lieutenant. ⅓b, As lieutenant colonel, 1792. ½b, As consul. ¾b, On his way to Augsburg. 4b, Crossing over the St. Bernard. 8b, In 1814. 10b, At the height of his career. No. 264G, At his coronation, 1804.

1969, Sept. 16 Litho. *Perf. 13½*
264 A71 ¼b silver & multi .35 .25
264A A71 ⅓b silver & multi .35 .25
264B A71 b silver & multi .40 .25
264C A71 ¾b silver & multi .40 .25
264D A71 4b silver & multi 1.50 .75
264E A71 8b silver & multi 2.00 1.00
264F A71 10b silver & multi 2.50 1.25
Nos. 264-264F (7) 7.50 4.00

Souvenir Sheet

264G A71 4b multicolored *7.00* 2.00

Nos. 264D-264G are airmail. No. 264G contains one 46x69mm stamp. Value, $12. An imperf. 4b souvenir sheet showing a Napoleon bicentennial medal exists. Nos. 264-264F exist imperf. with lilac-silver frames. Value: set, $7.50.

Revolution, 7th Anniv. — A71a

Designs: 2b, Map of Yemen, vert. 4b, Parliament. 6b, Worker, soldier, farmer and student.

1969, Sept. 26 *Perf. 13*
264H A71a 2b multicolored .30 .30
264I A71a 4b multicolored .60 .60
264J A71a 6b multicolored 1.25 1.25
Nos. 264H-264J (3) 2.15 2.15

Nos. 264H-264J exist imperf. Value: set, $4. Nos. 264J also exists in an imperf. souvenir sheet. Value, $7.

Discoveries of the Universe Type

Lunar Research: No. 265, Soyuz IV & V, Apollo 10. No. 265A, Apollo 11. No. 265B, Planned Lunar trips. No. 265C, Lunar surface vehicles. 2b, Lunar vehicles, diff. 4b, Moon base and vehicles. 22b, Soviet lunar project, Apollo 11. No. 265G, Apollo 11.

1969, Oct. 10 Litho. *Perf. 13½*
265 A69 ¼b multicolored .25 .25
265A A69 ¼b multicolored .25 .25
265B A69 ⅓b multicolored .25 .25
265C A69 ⅓b multicolored .25 .25
265D A69 2b multicolored .30 .25
265E A69 4b multicolored .90 .30
265F A69 22b multicolored 2.50 1.00
Nos. 265-265F (7) 4.70 2.55

Souvenir Sheet

265G A69 14b multicolored *9.00* 2.00

Nos. 265D-265G are airmail. No. 263G contains one 63x49mm stamp. Nos. 265-265F exist imperf. with light orange frames. Value: set, $5. A 14b imperf. souvenir sheet with Apollo 11 plaque and astronauts exists. Value, $12.

Cultural Olympiad Type

Paintings in the National Gallery, Washington, DC: ¼b, David by Del Castagno. ⅓b, Elena Grimaldi by Van Dyck. ½b, Girl with her Dueña by Murillo. 2b, Agostina by Corot. 3b, Ginevra Bentivoglio by Ercole Roberti. 4b, Balthasar Coymans by Frans Hals. No. 266F, Ginevra de Benci by Da Vinci.

1969, Nov. Litho. *Perf. 13½*
266 A68 ¼b lilac silver & multi .25 .25
266A A68 ⅓b lilac silver & multi .25 .25
266B A68 ½b lilac silver & multi .25 .25
266C A68 2b lilac silver & multi .90 .25
266D A68 3b lilac silver & multi 1.20 .25
266E A68 4b lilac silver & multi 1.75 .30
Nos. 266-266E (6) 4.60 1.55

Souvenir Sheet

266F A68 4b gold & multi *9.00 2.00*

Nos. 266D-266F are airmail. Nos. 266-266E exist with gold frames. Value, $6. No. 266F contains one 36x69mm stamp. No. 266F exists with a red background instead of blue green and also exists imperf.

Cultural Olympiad Type

Paintings in the National Gallery, London: ¼b, Portrait of a Woman by Van Der Weyden. ⅓b, Portrait of a Young Man by Antonello da Messina. ½b, Portrait of a Young Girl by Mabuse. 2b, The Crab Saleswoman by Hogarth. 3b, Baron Schwiter by Delacroix. 4b, Portrait of an Old Woman by Cézanne. No. 266F, Morning Promenade by Gainsborough.

1969, Dec. Litho. *Perf. 13½*
267 A68 ¼b bluish sil & multi .25 .25
267A A68 ⅓b bluish sil & multi .25 .25
267B A68 ½b bluish sil & multi .25 .25
267C A68 2b bluish sil & multi .90 .25

267D A68 3b bluish sil & multi 1.20 .25
267E A68 4b bluish sil & multi 1.75 .30
Nos. 267-267E (6) 4.60 1.55

Souvenir Sheet

267F A68 4b gold & multi *7.00 2.00*

Nos. 267D-267F are airmail. Nos. 267-267E exist with bronze frames. Value: set, $5. No. 267F contains one 35x74mm stamp. No. 267F exists with an orange yellow background instead of greenish blue and also exists imperf.

Famous French Leaders — A72

Designs: 1¾b, Clovis I. 2b, Charlemagne. 2¼b, Jeanne d'Arc. 2½b, Louis XIV. 3½b, Napoleon I. 5b, Georges Clemenceau. 6b, 10b, Charles de Gaulle.

1969 Litho. *Perf. 13½*
268 A72 1¾b gold & multi .50 .25
268A A72 2b gold & multi .60 .25
268B A72 2¼b gold & multi .65 .25
268C A72 2½b gold & multi .70 .25
268D A74 3½b gold & multi .90 .30
268E A72 5b gold & multi 1.20 .35
268F A72 6b gold & multi 1.50 .45
Nos. 268-268F (7) 6.05 2.10

Souvenir Sheet

268G A72 10b multicolored *11.00 2.00*

Nos. 268-268F exist imperf. with silver frames. Value $7.50. Nos. 268D-268G are airmail. No. 268G contains one 50x83mm stamp. A 10b imperf. souvenir sheet exists depicting DeGaulle, Jeanne d'Arc and Napoleon. Value $12.

Art Treasures of Tutankhamen A73

Tutankhamun: ¼b, Stone bust. ⅓b, Alabaster bust. ½b, Painted bust. 2b, Painted statue. 3b, Gold Mask. 4b, Painted head.

1970, May 20 Litho. *Perf. 13½*
269 A73 ¼b lilac silver & multi .25 .25
269A A73 ⅓b lilac silver & multi .25 .25
269B A73 ½b lilac silver & multi .25 .25
269C A73 2b lilac silver & multi 1.20 .30
269D A73 3b lilac silver & multi 1.75 .35
269E A73 4b lilac silver & multi 2.00 .45
Nos. 269-269E (6) 5.70 1.85

Nos. 269D-269E are airmail. Perf. and imperf. souvenir sheets containing 1 No. 269E exist. Values: perf, $7.50; imperf, $9. These sheets were also overprinted in Red or Green for Roma '70. Values: perf, $7.50; imperf, $9. Nos. 269-269E exist imperf with silver frames. Value, $6.

Art Treasures Type

Treasures of Siam: ¼b, Bronze Buddha head. ⅓b, Stone Buddha head. ½b, Statue from Angkor. 2b, Spirit of Echiffre. 3b, King Pisei. 4b, Buddha on Naga.

1970 Litho. *Perf. 13½*
270 A73 ¼b lilac silver & multi .25 .25
270A A73 ⅓b lilac silver & multi .25 .25
270B A73 ½b lilac silver & multi .25 .25
270C A73 2b lilac silver & multi .90 .30
270D A73 3b lilac silver & multi 1.20 .35
270E A73 4b lilac silver & multi 1.75 .45
Nos. 270-270E (6) 4.60 1.85

Nos. 270D-270E are airmail. Perf. and imperf. souvenir sheets containing 1 No. 270E exist. Values: perf, $7.50; imperf, $9. Nos. 270-270E exist imperf with silver frames. Value, $6.

Art Treasures Type

Treasures of Japan: Various paintings.

1970 Litho. *Perf. 13½*
271 A73 ¼b lilac silver & multi .25 .25
271A A73 ⅓b lilac silver & multi .25 .25
271B A73 ½b lilac silver & multi .25 .25
271C A73 2b lilac silver & multi .90 .30
271D A73 3b lilac silver & multi 1.20 .35
271E A73 4b lilac silver & multi 1.75 .45
f. Souvenir sheet of 1, silver & multi *7.50 2.00*
Nos. 271-271E (6) 4.60 1.85

Nos. 271D-271E, 271Ef are airmail. No. 271Ef has red Expo '70 imprint in the sheet margin. Nos. 271-271E exist imperf with silver frames. No. 271Ef exists imperf. Values: set, $5.50; souvenir sheet, $9.

Expo '70, Osaka, Japan — A74

Various traditional Japanese puppets.

1970, Mar. 15 Litho. *Perf. 13½*
272 A74 ¼b gold & multi .35 .25
272A A74 ⅓b gold & multi .35 .25
272B A74 ½b gold & multi .35 .25
272C A74 2b gold & multi .90 .35
272D A74 3b gold & multi 1.75 .45
272E A74 4b gold & multi 2.25 .55
Nos. 272-272E (6) 5.95 2.10

Nos. 272D-272E are airmail. Nos. 272-272E exist with silver frames (Values: perf, $4; imperf, $7), and imperf. with gold frames (Values: perf, $5.50; imperf, $6). Perf. and imperf. souvenir sheets containing 1 No. 272E exist. Values: perf, $7.50; imperf., $11.

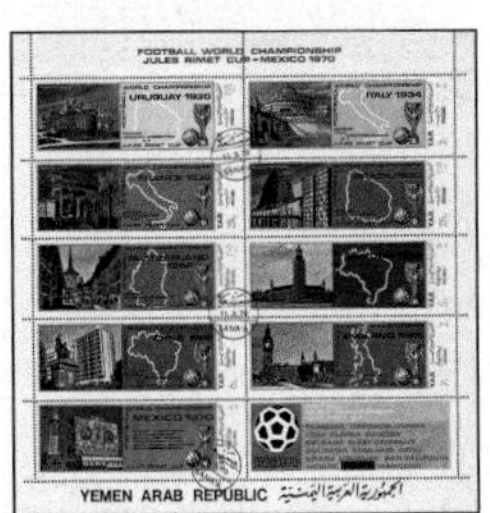

World Cup Soccer Championships, Mexico — A75

1970, Apr. 4 Litho. *Perf. 13½*
273 A75 Sheet of 9 + label 7.00 2.75
c. 1¾b Uruguay 1930 .35 .25
d. 2b Italy 1934 .45 .25
e. 2¼b France 1938 .50 .25
f. 2½b Brazil 1950 .50 .25
g. 3½b Switzerland 1954 .60 .30
h. 5b Sweden 1968 .60 .30
i. 6b Chile 1962 .60 .30
j. 7b England 1966 .70 .35
k. 8b Mexico 1970 .80 .40

Souvenir Sheets

273A A75 4b Pele *9.00*
273B A75 4b Beckenbauer *10.00*

Nos. 273g-273k, 273A-273B are airmail. No. 273B exists imperf.

No. 273k and the adjacent label exist with the name ISRAEL showing and also with the name covered with a black overprint.

Opening of New UPU Headquarters, Bern, Switzerland — A76

Country Views and Europa Stamp Designs: 1⅓b, Austria, Luxembourg, 1956-57 designs. 1¾b, Belgium, Spain, 1958-59 designs. 2¼b, Greece, Portugal, 1960-61 designs. 2½b, Norway, Denmark, 1962-63 designs. 5b, Switzerland, Netherlands, 1964-65 designs. 7b, France, England, 1965-66 Designs. 8b, Germany, Italy, 1968-69 designs. 10b, New UPU Headquarters, 1970 design, UPU emblem.

1970, May 5 Litho. *Perf. 13½*
274 A76 Sheet of 8 5.00 2.25
b. 1⅓b multicolored .40 .25
c. 1¾b multicolored .40 .25
d. 2¼b multicolored .40 .25
e. 2½b multicolored .40 .25
f. 5b multicolored .50 .30
g. 7b multicolored .65 .30
h. 8b multicolored .75 .35
i. 10b multicolored 1.00 .50

Souvenir Sheet

274A A76 10b Liechtenstein 356 *9.00* 2.00

Nos. 274g-274i, 274A are airmail. No. 274 exists imperf with light orange borders. Value, $7. No. 274A contains one 50x50mm stamp. An imperf. 10b souvenir sheet showing Luxembourg 320 exists. Value, $9.

Apollo 12 — A77

Stages of Apollo 12 Mission: 1b, Lift-off. 1¼b, In Lunar orbit. 1⅓b, LM approaches landing site. 1½b, 32 hours on Lunar surface. 4b, Lift-off from the Moon. 4½b, Return to Earth. 7b, Splash down. No. 275A, Astronauts on Lunar surface.

1970, May 11 Litho. *Perf. 13½*
275 A77 Sheet of 7 + label 5.50 2.25
b. 1b multicolored .40 .25
c. 1¼b multicolored .40 .25
d. 1⅓b multicolored .40 .25
e. 1½b multicolored .40 .25
f. 4b multicolored .65 .30
g. 4½b multicolored .75 .30
h. 7b multicolored 1.25 .65

Souvenir Sheet

275A A77 4b multicolored *5.00*

Nos. 274f-275h, 275A are airmail. No. 275 exists imperf with yellow and gold borders. Value, $6. No. 275A contains one 72x56mm stamp. An imperf 4b souvenir sheet exists with the lunar scene reflected in astronaut's helmet.

World Cup Soccer Championships, Mexico — A78

1970, May 20 Litho. *Perf. 13½*
276 A78 Sheet of 6 5.50 2.00
c. ¼b Soviet team .50 .25
d. ⅓b Brazilian team .50 .25
e. ½b English team .50 .25
f. ¾b Italian team .50 .25
g. 4b German team .60 .30
h. 4½b Mexican team .60 .30

Souvenir Sheets

276A A78 6b Stadium *9.00*
276B A78 6b Two players *12.00*

Nos. 276g-276h, 276A-276B are airmail. Nos. 276A-276B each contain a 57x58mm stamp, and exist imperf. No. 276 exists imperf. with silver borders.

World Cup Soccer Championships, Mexico — A79a

No. 277: Various soccer players, pre-Columbian sculptures. Nos. 277A-277B, Players, World Cup trophy, soccer ball.

1970, May 31 Litho. *Perf. 13½*
277 A79a Sheet of 6 4.50 2.00
c. 1b olive grn & multi .50 .25
d. 1¼b blue & multi .50 .25
e. 1⅓b red lil & multi .50 .25
f. 1½b grn & multi .50 .25
g. 3b pink & multi .60 .30
h. 10b org & multi .60 .30

Souvenir Sheets

277A A79a 10b grn & multi *6.00*
277B A79a 10b red & multi *8.50*

Nos. 277g-277h, 277A-277B are airmail. Nos. 277A contains an 85x30mm stamp. No. 277B contains a 49x62mm stamp and exists imperf. No. 277 exists imperf. with light orange background. Value $5. No. 277B also exists imperf. Value $15.

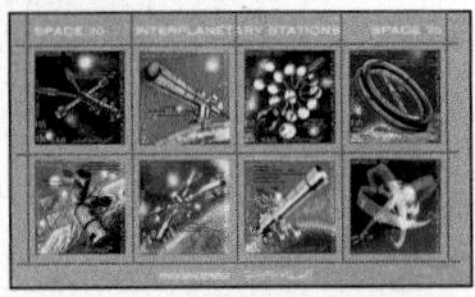

Space '70 Interplanetary Travel A79b

Interplanetary Stations: 1¾b, McDonnel Douglas project 1975-80. 2b, McDonnel Douglas project, diff. 2¼b, Boeing project 1980. 2½b, McDonnel Douglas project 1980-85. 5b, Earth-Moon relay station. 8b, Boeing project 1980-85. 10b, Space telescope. No. 278A, Skylab.

1970, July 21 Litho. *Perf. 13½*
278 A79b Sheet of 7 + label 4.50 2.25
b. 1¾b silver & multi .40 .25
c. 2b silver & multi .40 .25
d. 2¼b silver & multi .40 .25
e. 2½b silver & multi .40 .25
f. 5b silver & multi .60 .30
g. 8b silver & multi .80 .40
h. 10b silver & multi 1.00 .50

Souvenir Sheet

278A A79b 10b multicolored *6.00*

Nos. 278f-278h, 278A are airmail. No. 278 exists imperf with gold borders. Value, $5. No. 278A contains one 67x43mm stamp. An imperf 10b souvenir sheet exists with the a space workshop 1975 design. Value, $7.

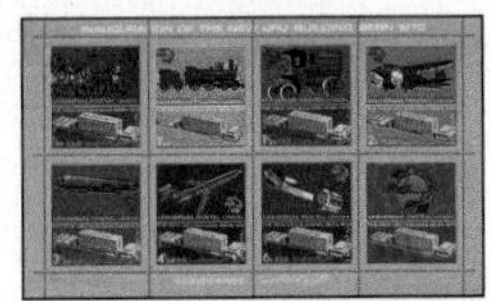

Opening of New UPU Headquarters, Bern, Switzerland — A79c

New UPU Headquarters and: ⅓b, Post coach. 1¼b, Train. 1½b, Early mail truck. 2b, Biplane. 3½b, Zeppelin. 4½b, Jet plane. 6b, Satellite. No. 279A, Zeppelin and post coach.

1970, Aug. 25 Litho. *Perf. 13½*
279 A79c Sheet of 7 + label 4.50 2.25
b. ⅓b silver & multi .40 .25
c. 1¼b silver & multi .40 .25
d. 1½b silver & multi .40 .25
e. 2b silver & multi .40 .25
f. 3½b silver & multi .60 .30
g. 4½b silver & multi .80 .40
h. 6b silver & multi 1.00 .50

Souvenir Sheet

279A A79c 6b multicolored *7.00*

Nos. 279f-279h, 279A are airmail. No. 279 exists imperf with gold borders. Value, $5. No. 279A contains one 44x64mm stamp. An imperf 6b souvenir sheet exists with the a satellite design. Value, $10.

Philympia London 1970 — A79d

Landmarks and stamps: ¼b, Ruins, Greece 163. ½b, Stadium, France 201. ¾b, Statue of Liberty, US719. 1b, Windsor Castle, Great Britain 274. 3b, Statue of She wolf suckling Romulus and Remus, Italy 807. 4b, Tower, Yemen 242C. No. 280A, UPU Headquarters, Germany B89.

1970, Sept. 10 Litho. *Perf. 13½*

280 A79d Sheet of 6 4.25 2.25
- *b.* ¼b greenish silver & multi .30 .25
- *c.* ½b greenish silver & multi .35 .25
- *d.* ¾b greenish silver & multi .40 .25
- *e.* 1b greenish silver & multi .50 .25
- *f.* 3b greenish silver & multi .85 .40
- *g.* 4b greenish silver & multi 1.10 .55

Souvenir Sheet

280A A79d 4b multicolored *7.00*

Nos. 280g, 280A are airmail. No. 280 exists imperf with brownish silver borders. No. 280A contains one 45x51mm stamp, and also exists imperf. An imperf 4b souvenir sheet exists with Mexico C311.

Revolution, 8th Anniv. — A79e

Still Life Paintings by: No. 281b, Courbet. c, No. 281A, Linared. d, Fantin-Latour. e, Renoir, vert. f, Beert, vert.

1970, Sept. 26 Litho. *Perf. 13*

281 Strip of 5 3.00
- *b.-f.* A79e ¼b any single .60

Souvenir Sheet

281A A79e 10b multicolored *4.50*

No. 281 was issued in sheets of 4 strips and also exists imperf.

Arab League, 25th Anniv. — A79f

1970, Oct. 5 Photo. *Perf. 11½x11*

282 A79f 5b org, grn & dark pur .35 —
282A A79f 7b blue, grn & brn .75 —
282B A79f 16b dark olive grn, grn & chalky blue 1.75 —

Nos. 282-282B exist imperf. A perf. souvenir sheet of one exists containing No. 282B. Value, $4.

Munich, 1972 Summer Olympic Games Host City — A79g

City Landmarks: 1b, Glyptothek. 1¾b, Wittelsbach Fountain. 2½b, Maximilianeum. 3b, National Theater. 3½b, Propylaea. 8b, Nymphenburg Castle. 10b, City Hall. No. 283A, Munich Olympic Tower, vert.

1970, Oct. 15 Litho. *Perf. 13½*

283 A79g Sheet of 7 + label 4.50 2.25
- *b.* 1b multicolored .40 .25
- *c.* 1¾b multicolored .45 .25
- *d.* 2½b multicolored .45 .25
- *e.* 3b multicolored .50 .25
- *f.* 3½b multicolored .50 .25
- *g.* 8b multicolored .80 .40
- *h.* 10b multicolored .90 .45

Souvenir Sheet

283A A79g 10b multicolored *3.50*

Nos. 283g-283h, 283A are airmail. No. 283 exists imperf with olive inscriptions at top. Value, $5. No. 283A contains one 30x96mm stamp. An imperf 10b souvenir sheet exists with the Marienplatz.

Sapporo, 1972 Winter Olympic Games Host City — A79h

City Landmarks: 1½b, Sapporor City. 2½b, Olympic Skating Center. 4½b, Makomanai Indoor Ice Arena. 5b, Main Stadium. 7b, Olympic Village. 8b, Bobsled and Luge Courses. 10b, Olympic Jump Hill. No. 283A, Ski Jumper, vert.

1970, Nov. 16 Litho. *Perf. 13½*

284 A79h Sheet of 7 + 2 labels 4.00 2.25
- *b.* 1½b silver & multi .30 .25
- *c.* 2½b silver & multi .30 .25
- *d.* 4½b silver & multi .45 .25
- *e.* 5b silver & multi .45 .25
- *f.* 7b silver & multi .60 .30
- *g.* 8b silver & multi .60 .30
- *h.* 10b multicolored .80 .40

Souvenir Sheet

284A A79h 4b multicolored *5.00*

Nos. 284g-284h, 284A are airmail. No. 284 exists imperf with gold frames and inscriptions. No. 284A contains one 54x74mm stamp. An imperf 4b souvenir sheet exists with a map and speed skater.

German Olympic Medalists — A79i

Medalists: No. 285, 1896-1908 medalists. No. 285A, 1908-1932 medalists. No. 285B, 1936-1956 medalists. No. 285C, 1956-1964 medalists. No. 285D, 1968 medalists, Sapporo & Munich emblems. No. 285E, Summer Olympic medals.

1970, Dec. 15 Litho. *Perf. 13½*

285 A79i ¼b red lilac & multi .25 .25
285A A79i ¼b red lilac & multi .25 .25
285B A79i ⅓b red lilac & multi .25 .25
285C A79i ⅓b red lilac & multi .25 .25
285D A79i 6b red lilac & multi 3.00 1.25
Nos. 285-285D (5) 4.00 2.25

Souvenir Sheet

285E A79i 6b multicolored 7.00 1.75

Nos. 285D-285E are airmail. No. 285E contains 1 54x54mm stamp and exists imperf. Value, $9. Nos. 285-285D exist imperf. Value, $5.

Gamel Abdel Nasser (1918-1970) A79j

Nassar and: No. 286, Sukarno. No. 286A, Nehru. No. 286B, Arif. No. 286C, Hammarskjold. No. 286D, Eisenhower. No. 286E, Abdarrahman al-Iryani. No. 286F, Farmer. No. 286G, Suez Canal. No. 286H, Industrial site. No. 286I, Aswan High Dam. No. 286J, Oil field. No. 286K, Abu Simbel. No. 286L, World map.

No. 286M, Nassar.

1971, Jan. 6 Litho. *Perf. 11*

286 A79j ¼b multicolored .25 .25
286A A79j ¼b multicolored .25 .25
286B A79j ¼b multicolored .25 .25
286C A79j ¼b multicolored .25 .25
286D A79j ½b multicolored .25 .25
286E A79j ½b multicolored 1.00 .50
286F A79j 1b multicolored .35 .25
286G A79j 2b multicolored .40 .25
286H A79j 5b multicolored .50 .25
286I A79j 7b multicolored .65 .30
286J A79j 10b multicolored 1.00 .50
286K A79j 16b multicolored 1.35 .75
Nos. 286-286K (12) 6.50 4.05

Souvenir Sheets

286L A79i 5b multicolored 3.00 1.00
286M A79i 16b multicolored 7.50

No. 286E is 85x81mm. Nos. 286F-286K, 286M are airmail. Nos. 286-286K exist imperf. No. 286M contains one 59x40mm stamp.

Intl. Sports Contribute to World Peace A79k

Sports: ¼b, No. 287, Athens, Pierre de Coubertin. ⅓b, No. 287A, Skier, hurdler. ½b, No. 287B, Figure skater, weightlifter. 2b, Biathlon, Equestrian. 3b, Speed skater, high jump. Nos. 287E-287Ef, Ski jumping, gymnastics.

1971, Jan. 15 Litho. *Perf. 13½*

287 A79k ¼b blk, yel & gold .25 .25
287A A79k ⅓b blk, grn & gold .25 .25
287B A79k ½b blk, pink & gold .25 .25
287C A79k 2b blk, pur & gold .50 .25
287D A79k 3b blk, yel grn & gold .75 .35
287E A79k 4b blk, blue & gold 1.00 .50
- *f.* Souvenir sheet of 1 *5.00 1.50*

Nos. 287-287E (6) 3.00 1.85

Nos. 287D-287E are airmail. No. 287Ef exists imperf. Nos. 287-287E, 287Ef exist imperf with silver borders. Value: set, $4.50; souvenir sheet, $9.

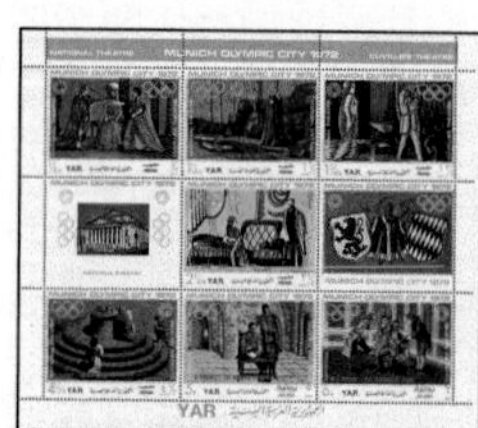

Munich, Olympic Host City — A79l

Composer, opera scenes — No. 288: ½b, Handel, Agrippina. 1¼b, Wagner, Tristan & Isolde. 1¾b, Verdi, Othello. 2¼b, Berg, Lulu. 4½b, Orff, Prometheus. 5b, Wagner, Die Meistersinger. 6b, Mozart, Marriage of Figaro. No. 288A, Richard Wagner (1813-1883), vert.

1971, Feb. 15 Litho. *Perf. 13½*

288 A79l Sheet of 7 + 2 labels 4.50 2.00
- *b.* ½b multicolored .40 .25
- *c.* 1¼b multicolored .40 .25
- *d.* 1¾b multicolored .50 .25
- *e.* 2¼b multicolored .50 .25
- *f.* 4½b multicolored .60 .30
- *g.* 5b multicolored .60 .30
- *h.* 6b multicolored .75 .35

Souvenir Sheet

288A A79l 6b multicolored *7.00 1.50*

Nos. 288g-288h, 288A are airmail. No. 288 exists with light green inscription at top. No. 288A contains one 50x56mm stamp. A 6b imperf. souvenir sheet exists with a portrait of Mozart.

Paintings in Pinakothek Gallery, Munich — A79m

Paintings — No. 289: ¼b, Sebastian by Holbein. ⅓b, Count Philippe by Grein. ¾b, Young Man by Dürer. 1½b, O. Krel by Dürer. 2b, Susanna in the Bath by Altdorfer. 4b, C. Fugger by Amberger. 7b, C. Schuch by Leibl. No. 289A, Count Otto von Wittelsbach, horiz.

1971, Mar. 15 Litho. *Perf. 13½*

289 A79m Sheet of 7 + label 4.50
- *b.* ¼b multicolored .40 .25
- *c.* ⅓b multicolored .40 .25
- *d.* ¾b multicolored .50 .25
- *e.* 1½b multicolored .45 .25
- *f.* 2b multicolored .45 .25
- *g.* 4b multicolored .70 .35
- *h.* 7b multicolored .90 .45

Souvenir Sheet

289A A79m 4b multicolored *7.00 2.00*

Nos. 289g-289h, 289A are airmail. No. 289A contains one 66x46mm stamp. No. 288 exists imperf with inscriptions in light red. A 4b imperf. souvenir sheet exists with Suzanne in the Bath.

Art Type of 1970

Chinese Paintings: ¼b, The Hall of Green Country by Yuan Kiang. ⅓b, Lady at Her Dressing Table by Sou Han. ½b, The Bodhisattva Wen Tchou. 2b, Gatherer of Simples at Tchen Wei by Wou Li. 3b, Buddha by Ting Yun.4b, Li T'ie Kouai by Yen Houei.

1971, Apr. 8 Litho. *Perf. 13½*

290 A73 ¼b lilac silver & multi .25 .25
290A A73 ⅓b lilac silver & multi .25 .25
290B A73 ½b lilac silver & multi .25 .25
290C A73 2b lilac silver & multi .80 .25
290D A73 3b lilac silver & multi 1.25 .35
290E A73 4b lilac silver & multi 1.50 .50
- *f.* Souvenir sheet of 1 *7.00 1.50*

Nos. 290-290E (6) 4.30 1.85

Nos. 290D-290E, 290Ef are airmail. Stamp in No. 290Ef has white borders. No. 290Ef exists imperf. Value, $9.

UN, 25th Anniv. A79n

1971, Apr. 4 Photo. *Perf. 11½x11*

291 A79n 5b dk ol grn, grn & dk vio .55 .45
291A A79n 7b bl, grn & dk bl .90 .75

Exist imperf. Value $6.

Souvenir Sheet

Imperf

291B A79n 16b multicolored 2.00 1.50

Winter Olympic Games, Sapporo A79o

Early Winter Sports: ¼b, Woman on sled. ½b, Skier with bow. 1b, Woman on sled, diff. 1⅓b, Archer on ice skates. 2b, Man on ice skates. 3b, Woman on ice skates. 4b, Man on skis. No. 292A, Sapporo Games emblem, snowflakes, horiz.

1971, Apr. 15 Litho. *Perf. 13¼*

292 A79o Sheet of 7 + label 3.75 2.25
- *b.* ¼b silver & multi .40 .25
- *c.* ½b silver & multi .40 .25
- *d.* 1b silver & multi .40 .25
- *e.* 1⅓b silver & multi .50 .25
- *f.* 2b silver & multi .60 .30
- *g.* 3b silver & multi .80 .40
- *h.* 4b silver & multi .80 .40

Souvenir Sheet

292A A79o 10b multicolored *5.00 1.25*

Nos. 292g-292h, 292A are airmail. No. 292A contains one 66x61mm stamp. No. 292 exists imperf with grayish green borders. A 10b imperf. souvenir sheet exists with Snow Festival.

Summer Olympic Games, Munich A79p

Early Summer Sports: ⅓b, Swimming. 1b, Stone throwing. 1⅓b, Walking, diff. 1¾b, Wrestling. 2¼b, Crossbow. 4½b, Jousting. 7b, Handball. 10b, Gymnastics. No. 293A, Stone throwing, vert.

1971, May 15 Litho. *Perf. 13½*
293 A79p Sheet of 8 4.50 2.25
b. ⅓b gold & multi .30 .25
c. 1b gold & multi .30 .25
d. 1⅓b gold & multi .30 .25
e. 1¾b gold & multi .40 .25
f. 2¼b gold & multi .40 .30
g. 4½b gold & multi .70 .35
h. 7b gold & multi .90 .45
i. 10b gold & multi 1.25 .65

Souvenir Sheet

293A A79p 10b multicolored *5.00 1.50*

Nos. 293g-293i, 293A are airmail. No. 293A contains one 44x78mm stamp. No. 293 exists imperf with silver borders. A 10b imperf. souvenir sheet exists with swimmers.

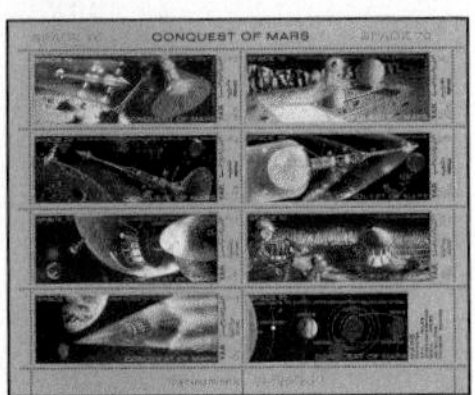

Conquest of Mars — A79q

Stages of Mars exploration: ¼b, Assembly of Photon rocket in Earth orbit. ⅓b, Lunar Base, preparations for Mars mission. ½b, Photon rocket in Lunar orbit. ¾b, Departure for Mars. 3b, In orbit around Phobos. 3½b, Three men on Mars. 6b, Upper stage of Photon rocket returns to Earth. No. 294A, Daedalus, rocket shuttle, Phobos, Mars.

1971, June 15 Litho. *Perf. 13½*
294 A79q Sheet of 7 + label 4.00 2.25
b. ¼b orange & multi .40 .25
c. ⅓b orange & multi .40 .25
d. ½b orange & multi .40 .25
e. ¾b orange & multi .40 .25
f. 3b orange & multi .60 .30
g. 3½b orange & multi .70 .35
h. 6b orange & multi .90 .45

Souvenir Sheet

294A A79q 6b multicolored *5.00 1.50*

Nos. 294f-294h, 294A are airmail. No. 294A contains one 70x51mm stamp. No. 294 exists imperf with light blue borders. A 6b imperf. souvenir sheet exists with Galileo.

Ludwig van Beethoven, Birth Bicent. A79r

Designs: No. 295h, Recital with Beethoven. No. 295i, Chamber music evening. No. 295j, Portrait of Beethoven, Schubert at piano. No. 295k, View of Bonn. No. 295l, View of Vienna. No. 295m, Beethoven's study. 1b, Birth of Beethoven. 2b, Josephine von Brunswick. 5b, Young Beethoven. 7b, 10b, 16b, Beethoven at piano, various.

1971, June 23 Litho. *Perf. 12*
295 A79r Sheet of 3 1.50
h. ¼b bl, blk & grn .50
i. ¼b org, blk & pink .50
j. ½b blue & multi .50
295A A79r Sheet of 3 + 3 labels 1.50
k. ¼b multicolored .50
l. ¼b multicolored .50
m. ½b multicolored .50
295B A79r 1b multicolored .40
295C A79r 2b multicolored .50
295D A79r 5b multicolored .60
295E A79r 7b multicolored .80
295F A79r 10b multicolored .80
295G A79r 16b multicolored 1.00
Nos. 295-296G (8) 7.10

No. 295A contains 2 80x49mm stamps and 1 40x49mm stamp. Imperf. 5b and 16b souvenir sheets exist.

Nos. 295B-295G are airmail.

Art Type of 1970

Indian Paintings: ¼b, Ibrahim Adil Shah II of Bijapur. ⅓b, Head of Apsaras. ½b, Kamodi Ragini. 2b, Virahini. 3b, Krishna and Radha. 4b, Girls Swimming in a Lotus Pond.

1971, Apr. 8 Litho. *Perf. 13½*
296 A73 ¼b lilac silver & multi .25 .25
296A A73 ⅓b lilac silver & multi .25 .25
296B A73 ½b lilac silver & multi .25 .25
296C A73 2b lilac silver & multi .90 .25
296D A73 3b lilac silver & multi 1.20 .35
296E A73 4b lilac silver & multi 1.75 .50
f. Souvenir sheet of 1 *7.00 1.50*
Nos. 296-296E (6) 4.60 1.85

Nos. 296D-296E, 296Ef are airmail. Stamp in No. 296Ef has white borders. No. 296Ef exists imperf.

Olympic Sailing, Kiel, Germany A79s

Olympic sailing yachts: ¼b, 16.5m class, blue spinnaker. ⅓b, 5.5m class. 1¼b, 16.5m class, white spinnaker.2b, Belouga class. 3b, Flying Dutchman class. 4b, Finn class. No. 297A, Finn class, diff.

1971, Sept. 1 Litho. *Perf. 13½*
297 A79s Sheet of 6 4.00 1.65
b. ¼b lilac silver & multi .40 .25
c. ⅓b lilac silver & multi .40 .25
d. 1¼b lilac silver & multi .40 .25
e. 2b lilac silver & multi .60 .30
f. 3b lilac silver & multi .65 .30
g. 4b lilac silver & multi .80 .40

Souvenir Sheet

297A A79s 4b multicolored *7.00 1.50*

Nos. 297g, 297A are airmail. No. 297A contains one 42x64mm stamp and also exists imperf. No. 297exists imperf with gold borders.

1972 Winter Olympic Games, Sapporo A79t

Olympic Sports: ⅓b, Downhill skiing. ¾b, Women's figure skating. 1¼b, 2-man bobsled. 1¾b, Speed skating. 2¼b, Ski jumping. 3½b, Cross-country skiing. 6b, Pairs figure skating. No. 298A, Ski jumping, diff.

1971, Oct. 2 Litho. *Perf. 13½*
298 A79t Sheet of 7 + label 4.50
b. ⅓b silver & multi .45
c. ¾b silver & multi .45
d. 1¼b silver & multi .45
e. 1¾b silver & multi .60
f. 2¼b silver & multi .60
g. 3½b silver & multi .75
h. 6b silver & multi 1.00

Souvenir Sheet

298A A79t 6b multicolored *5.00 1.25*

Nos. 298g-298h, 298A are airmail. No. 298A contains one 73x50mm stamp. No. 298 exists imperf with gray violet borders. Value, $5. A 6b imperf. souvenir sheet exists with Sapporo emblems. Value, $9.

Art Type of 1970

Persian Paintings: ¼b, Murakka Gulshan. ⅓b, Shanname de Baisonghor. ½b, Djami al Tawarikh (drummers). 2b, Murakka Gulshan (fighting bear) . 3b, Djami al Tawarikh (kneeling). 4b, Shanname de Baisonghor (musicians).

1971, Oct. 15 Litho. *Perf. 13½*
299 A73 ¼b lilac silver & multi .25 .25
299A A73 ⅓b lilac silver & multi .25 .25
299B A73 ½b lilac silver & multi .25 .25
299C A73 2b lilac silver & multi .90 .25
299D A73 3b lilac silver & multi 1.20 .35
299E A73 4b lilac silver & multi 2.00 .50
f. Souvenir sheet of 1 *7.00 1.50*
Nos. 299-299E (6) 4.85 1.85

Nos. 299D-299E, 299Ef are airmail. Stamp in No. 299Ef has white borders and exists imperf.

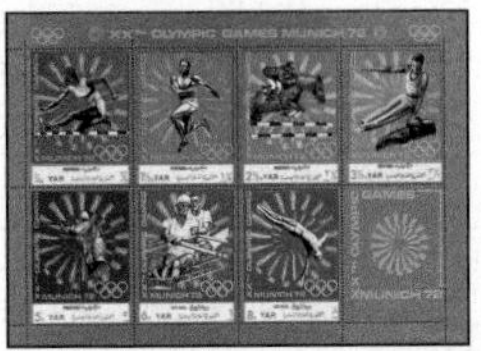

1972 Summer Olympic Games, Munich — A79u

Olympic Sports: ¾b, Women's hurdles. 1½b, Discus. 2½. Equestrian. 3½b, Gymnastics. 5b, Shooting. 6b, Rowing. 8b, Diving. No. 300A, Sprinter at start.

1971, Nov. 4 Litho. *Perf. 13½*
300 A79u Sheet of 7 + label 4.00 2.25
b. ¾b gold & multi .40 .25
c. 1½b gold & multi .40 .25
d. 2½b gold & multi .50 .25
e. 3½b gold & multi .50 .25
f. 5b gold & multi .60 .30
g. 6b gold & multi .60 .30
h. 8b gold & multi .75 .35

Souvenir Sheet

300A A79u 6b multicolored *7.00 1.25*

Nos. 300g-300h, 300A are airmail. No. 300A contains one 44x59mm stamp. No. 300 exists imperf with silver gray borders. A 6b imperf. souvenir sheet exists with equestrian design.

Olympic Medalists Type of 1970 in Diamond Shape

Italian Medalists: No. 301, 1908-1924 medalists. No. 301A, 1928-1936 medalists. No. 301B, 1952-1956 medalists. No. 301C, 1960-1968 medalists. No. 301D, 1968 medalists, Sapporo, Munich emblems. No. 301E, Emblesm of Rome, Tokyo and Munich Games.

1971, Dec. 3 Litho. *Perf. 13½*
301 A79i ¼b silver & multi .25 .25
301A A79i ¼b silver & multi .25 .25
301B A79i ⅓b silver & multi .25 .25
301C A79i ⅓b silver & multi .25 .25
301D A79i 22b silver & multi 3.00 1.25
Nos. 301-301D (5) 4.00 2.25

Souvenir Sheet

301E A79i 14b multicolored 7.00 1.75

Nos. 301D-301E are airmail. No. 301E contains 1 54x54mm stamp. Nos. 301-301D exist imperf. with light green borders. Value, $3.50. A 14b imperf. souvenir sheet with different Olympic emblems exists. Value, $9.

Revolution, 9th Anniv. — A79v

Designs: 7b, View of Sana'a. 18b, Military parade. 24b, Mosque in Sana'a.

1972, Feb. 29 *Perf. 13*
302 A79v 7b multi 1.10
302A A79v 18b multi 2.25
302B A79v 24b multi 3.25
Nos. 302-302B (3) 6.60

An imperf souvenir sheet containing No. 302B exists. Value $3.50.

Arab Postal Union, 25th Anniv. — A79w

1972, Mar. 18 *Perf. 13*
303 A79v 3b multi .40
303A A79w 7b multi .80
303B A79w 10b multi 1.50
Nos. 303-303B (3) 2.70

A 16b souvenir sheet also exists. Value $2.50.

Olympic Medalists Type of 1970 in Diamond Shape

French Medalists: 2b, 1896-1912 medalists. 3b, 1920-1932 medalists. 4b, 1936-1964 medalists. 10b, 1968 medalists, Sapporo, Munich emblems. No. 304D, Olympic Stadia from Tokyo, Mexico City and Munich Games.

1972, Apr. 4 Litho. *Perf. 13½*
304 A79i 2b bl grey & multi .35 .25
304A A79i 3b bl grey & multi .60 .30
304B A79i 4b bl grey & multi .90 .35
304C A79i 10b bl grey & multi 2.25 .75
Nos. 304-304C (4) 4.10 1.65

Souvenir Sheet

304D A79i 4b multicolored 7.00 1.50

Nos. 304B-304D are airmail. No. 304D contains 1 50x33mm stamp. Nos. 304-304C exist imperf. with light blue borders. Value, $5. A 4b imperf. souvenir sheet with different Olympic venues exists. Value, $10.

Art Treasures — A79x

Designs: 1b, Azure stone vase, 1583. 1¼b, Siren of the "Nautilus Cup," 1822. 1⅓b, Neptune vase. 1½b, Emperor Rudolph II's crown, 1602. 3b, Statue of Balthazar, 1724. 4½b, Catherine the Great's carriage, 1779. 7b, Statue of St. George.
6b, The Bath of Diana.

1972, July 31 Litho. *Perf. 13x13½*
305 A79x 1b bluish sil & multi .25 .25
305A A79x 1¼b bluish sil & multi .30 .25
305B A79x 1⅓b bluish sil & multi .35 .25
305C A79x 1½b bluish sil & multi .45 .25
305D A79x 3b bluish sil & multi .85 .30
305E A79x 4½b bluish sil & multi 1.40 .40
305F A79x 7b bluish sil & multi 1.50 .50
Nos. 305-305F (7) 5.10 2.20

Souvenir Sheet

305G A79x 6b multicolored 5.00 2.00

Nos. 305D-305F are airmail. An imperf 6b souvenir sheets with a Jasper Cup, Florence, exists. Value, $9.

10th anniv. of Revolution — A80

1972, Nov. 25 Photo. *Perf. 13*
306 A80 7b lt blue, blk & multi .75 .50
307 A80 10b gray, blk & multi 1.00 .65
Nos. 306-307,C40 (3) 5.75 4.65

For surcharge see No. 318.

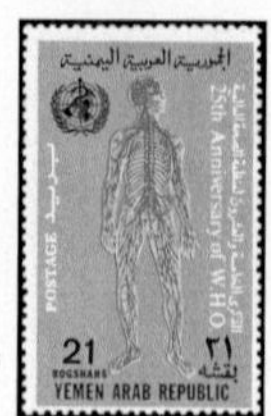

25th Anniv. of WHO — A81

1972, Dec. 1 **Litho.**

308 A81 2b lt yel grn & multi .30 .35
308A A81 21b sky blue & multi 2.00 1.40
308B A81 37b red lilac & multi 4.00 2.25
Nos. 308-308B (3) 6.30 4.00

For surcharge see No. 341A.

Burning of Al-Aqsa Mosque, 2nd Anniv. — A82

1972, Jan. 1 **Photo.** ***Perf. 13½***

309 A82 7b lt bl, blk & multi 1.00 .60
309A A82 18b lt bl, blk & multi 2.00 1.10
Nos. 309-309A,C41 (3) 6.00 4.20

For surcharges see Nos. 319, 341.

25th Anniv. of UNICEF A83

1973, Jan. 15 **Photo.** ***Perf. 13***

310 A83 7b lt bl, blk & multi 1.10 .65
310A A83 10b lt bl, blk & multi 1.60 .80
Nos. 310-310A,C42 (3) 4.60 2.95

For surcharge see No. C46.

UPU Cent. — A84

1974, Nov. 20 **Photo.** ***Perf. 14***

311 A84 10b multicolored .60 .40
311A A84 30b multicolored 1.25 1.50
311B A84 40b multicolored 1.75 1.90
Nos. 311-311B (3) 3.60 3.80

For surcharge see No. 341B.

10th World Hunger Program — A85

1975, Feb. 5 **Litho.** ***Perf. 13½***

313 A85 10b multicolored .50 .25
314 A85 30b multicolored 1.50 1.00
315 A85 63b multicolored 3.00 2.00
Nos. 313-315 (3) 5.00 3.25

12th Anniv. of Revolution — A86

1975, Sept. 25

316 A86 25f Janad Mosque .60 .35
317 A86 75f Althawra Hospital 1.90 .65

Nos. 306, 309 Surcharged in Black with New Values and Bars

1975, Nov. 15 **Photo.** ***Perf. 13½***

318 A80 75f on 7b 2.00 1.00
319 A82 278f on 7b 5.00 4.00

Telephone Cent. — A87

1976, Mar. 10 **Litho.** ***Perf. 14½***

320 A87 25f brt pink & blk .55 .55
321 A87 75f lt grn & blk 1.60 1.60
322 A87 160f lt bl & blk 2.75 2.75
a. Souvenir sheet of 1 3.50 3.00
Nos. 320-322 (3) 4.90 4.90

No. 322a exists both perf. and imperf. Same value.

Coffee Bean Branch — A88

1976, Apr. 25 ***Perf. 14***

323 A88 1f dull lilac .25 .25
324 A88 3f pale gray .25 .25
325 A88 5f lt bl grn .25 .25
326 A88 10f bis brn .25 .25
327 A88 25f golden brn .30 .25
328 A88 50f brt plum .65 .40
329 A88 75f dull pink 1.25 .60

Size: 22x30mm

Perf. 14½

330 A88 1r sky blue 2.00 .70
331 A88 1.50r red lilac 3.00 1.40
332 A88 2r light grn 4.75 1.40
333 A88 5r yel org 12.00 3.00
Nos. 323-333 (11) 24.95 8.75

For surcharges see Nos. 403-407, 592.

2nd Anniv. of Reformation Movement — A89

1976, June 13 **Photo.** ***Perf. 12x12½***

334 A89 75f Industrial Park 1.50 1.50
335 A89 135f Forestry 2.50 2.50

Souvenir Sheet

336 A89 135f Forestry 3.50 3.50

No. 336 contains one stamp (32x47mm).

14th Anniv. of Revolution — A90

Designs: 25f, Natl. Institute of Public Administration. 75f, Housing and population census. 160f, Sanaa University emblem.

1976, Sept. 26 **Photo.** ***Perf. 12x12½***

337 A90 25f buff & multi .65 .65
338 A90 75f yel bis & multi 1.75 1.75
339 A90 160f pale grn & multi 3.25 3.25
Nos. 337-339 (3) 5.65 5.65

Souvenir Sheet

340 A90 160f pale grn & multi 5.00 5.00

No. 340 contains one stamp (33x49mm).

No. 309 Surcharged in Black

1976

341 A82 75f on 7b 2.00 1.50

Nos. 308A, 311B Surcharged in Black or Red

1976 **Photo.** ***Perf. 14***

341A A81 75f on 21b (R) 2.00 1.50
341B A84 160f on 40b 3.50 2.50

Size and location of surcharge varies.

3rd Anniv. of Correction Movement — A91

1977 **Photo.** ***Perf. 14***

342 A91 25f Dish antenna .45 .30
343 A91 75f Computer, technician 1.25 .65
a. Miniature sheet of 1 4.00 4.00

15th Anniv. of September Revolution A92

1977 **Photo.** ***Perf. 13½***

344 A92 25f Sa'ada-San'a Road .45 .35
345 A92 75f Television, Transmitting tower 1.25 .85
346 A92 160f like 25f 2.50 2.00
a. Souvenir sheet of 1 5.00 5.00
Nos. 344-346 (3) 4.20 3.20

25th Anniv. of Arab Postal Union — A93

1978 ***Perf. 14***

347 A93 25f lt yel grn & multi .90 .75
348 A93 60f bis & multi 2.25 1.60
a. Miniature sheet of 1 5.00 4.50

Pres. Hamdi — A94

1978 ***Perf. 11½***

349 A94 25f dk grn & blk .35 .35
350 A94 75f ultra & blk 1.25 1.10
351 A94 160f brn & blk 2.50 1.90
a. Miniature sheet of 1 5.00 5.00
Nos. 349-351 (3) 4.10 3.35

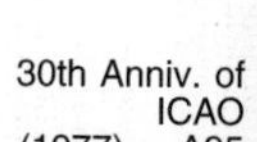

30th Anniv. of ICAO (1977) — A95

1979, Nov. 15 **Photo.** ***Perf. 13½***

352 A95 75f multi 2.10 1.00
353 A95 135f multi 3.25 1.60
a. Miniature sheet of 1 5.00 4.50

Book, World Map, Arab Achievements A96

1979, Dec. 1 ***Perf. 14***

354 A96 25f multi .60 .35
355 A96 75f multi 1.50 1.00
a. Souvenir sheet of 1 3.75 3.25

A97

1980, Jan. 1

356 A97 75f multi 2.00 1.00
357 A97 135f multi, horiz. 3.00 1.60
a. Miniature sheet of 1 5.00 4.50

12th World Telecommunications Day, May 17, 1979.

A98

Dome of the Rock.

1980 **Photo.** ***Perf. 14***

358 A98 5f brt bl & multi .50 .35
359 A98 10f yel & multi 1.00 .65

Palestinian fighters and their families.

Argentina World Cup — A99

World Cup emblem and various players.

1980, Mar. 30

360 A99 25f gold & multi .60 .40
361 A99 30f gold & multi .60 .30
362 A99 35f gold & multi .75 .40
363 A99 50f gold & multi 1.05 .50
Nos. 360-363,C49-C52 (8) 9.80 4.80

Issued in sheets of 8.

Exist imperf. (Value, set $70) and in souvenir sheets (Value, set $60).

International Year of the Child — A100

1980, Apr. 1 ***Perf. 13½***

364 A100 25f Girl, bird 1.75 .50
365 A100 50f Girl, bird, diff. 2.50 .80
366 A100 75f Boy, butterfly, flower 2.60 1.25
Nos. 364-366,C53-C55 (6) 18.85 6.80

Issued in sheets of 6.

Exist imperf. (Value, set $60) and in souvenir sheets (Value, set $60).

World Scouting Jamboree A101

25f, Fishing. 35f, Troup, aircraft. 40f, Mounted bugler, flag. 50f, Telescope, night sky.

1980, May 1 *Perf. 13½x14*

367 A101 25f multicolored .60 .30
368 A101 35f multicolored 1.40 .50
369 A101 40f multicolored 1.40 .50
370 A101 50f multicolored 1.50 .65
Nos. 367-370,C56-C58 (7) 13.05 5.35

Issued in sheets of 6.
Exist imperf. (Value, set $60) and in souvenir sheets (Value, set $60).

Argentina 1978 World Cup Winners A102

World cup emblem and various soccer players.

1980, June 1 *Perf. 14*

371 A102 25f gold & multi .60 .25
372 A102 30f gold & multi .90 .30
373 A102 35f gold & multi .90 .40
374 A102 50f gold & multi 1.35 .40
Nos. 371-374,C59-C62 (8) 12.00 4.35

Exist imperf. (Value, set $60) and in souvenir sheets (Value, set $60).

Hegira, 1400th Anniv. A102a

Designs: 160f, Outside view.

1980, July 1 *Perf. 13½*

375 A102a 25f blk & multi .40 .25
376 A102a 75f car rose & multi 1.40 .60
377 A102a 160f blk & multi 2.40 .75
a. Miniature sheet of 1 5.00 4.00
Nos. 375-377 (3) 4.20 1.60

18th Anniv. of September Revolution — A103

A104

1980, Sept. 26 *Perf. 13½*

378 A103 25f multi .35 .25
379 A104 75f multi 1.10 .65

Souvenir Sheet

380 100f multi 3.00 2.00

No. 380 contains one stamp combining designs A103 and A104 (42x34mm).

Al Aqsa Mosque — A105

Mosques: 25f, Al-Rawda entrance. 100f, Al-Nabwi. 160f, Al-Haram.

1980, Nov. 6 **Photo.** *Perf. 13½*

381 A105 25f multi .40 .25
382 A105 75f multi .90 .50
383 A105 100f multi 2.25 .65
384 A105 160f multi 3.00 1.00
Nos. 381-384 (4) 6.55 2.40

Souvenir Sheet

385 160f multi 6.00 3.25

Islamic Postal Systems Week and Hegira. No. 385 contains one stamp (109x47mm) combining designs of Nos. 382-384.

Intl. Palestinian Solidarity Day — A106

1980, Nov. 29

386 A106 25f lt bl & multi .30 .25
387 A106 75f ver & multi .90 .90

Inscribed 1979.

9th Arab Archaeological Conference — A107

1981, Mar. 1 *Perf. 13½*

388 A107 75f Al Aamiriya Mosque 1.00 .60
389 A107 125f Al Hadi Mosque 1.40 .85
a. Souvenir sheet of 2, #388-389 3.00 3.00

1980 World Tourism Conference, Manila — A108

1981, Apr. 1

390 A108 25f shown .25 .25
391 A108 75f Mosque, houses .55 .30
392 A108 100f Columns, horiz. .70 .45
393 A108 135f Bridge .80 .60
394 A108 160f View of San'a, horiz. 1.20 .60
a. Miniature sheet of 1 5.00 5.00
Nos. 390-394 (5) 3.50 2.20

Sir Rowland Hill (1795-1879), Postage Stamp Inventor A109

25f, Portrait, UPU emblem. 30f, Emblem, stamp of 1963. 50f, Portrait, stamps. 75f, Portrait, globe, jet. 100f, Portrait, stamp collection. 150f, Jets, No. 322.
No. 401, Portrait, vert. No. 402, Portrait, diff.

1981, Sept. 15 **Litho.** *Perf. 14*

395 A109 25f multicolored .90 .50
396 A109 30f multicolored 1.05 .70
397 A109 50f multicolored 1.50 1.00
398 A109 75f multicolored 2.40 1.75
399 A109 100f multicolored 3.25 2.00
400 A109 150f multicolored 6.00 3.00
Nos. 395-400 (6) 15.10 8.95

Souvenir Sheets

401 A109 200f multicolored 10.00

Imperf

402 A109 200f multicolored 20.00

Nos. 398-402 are airmail.
Nos. 395-400 exist imperf and in souvenir sheets (Value, set $45).

Nos. 323-327 Surcharged

1981

403 A88 125f on 1f 1.25 .70
404 A88 150f on 3f 1.50 .85
405 A88 325f on 5f 3.50 2.00
406 A88 350f on 10f 4.00 2.00
407 A88 375f on 25f 4.25 2.50
Nos. 403-407 (5) 14.50 8.05

20th Anniv. of Yemen Airways A110

1983, Apr. 1 **Litho.** *Perf. 14*

408 A110 75f yel & multi 1.00 .50
409 A110 125f red & multi 1.75 .80
410 A110 325f bl & multi 4.00 2.00
Nos. 408-410 (3) 6.75 3.30

Folk Costumes A111

No. 411, Woman carrying waterjar. No. 412, Women, sheep. No. 413, Man, donkeys. No. 414, Man in town square. No. 415, Women, child, well. No. 416, Scholar. No. 417, Woman on beach. No. 418, Camel-drawn plow.
No. 419, Woman. No. 420, Man.

1983, May 1

411 A111 50f multicolored 2.50 1.20
412 A111 50f multicolored 2.50 1.20
413 A111 50f multicolored 2.50 1.20
414 A111 50f multicolored 2.50 1.20
415 A111 75f multicolored 3.75 2.00
416 A111 75f multicolored 3.75 2.00
417 A111 75f multicolored 3.75 2.00
418 A111 75f multicolored 3.75 2.00
Nos. 411-418 (8) 25.00 *12.80*

Souvenir Sheets

419 A111 200f mutlicolored 8.00

Imperf

420 A111 200f mutlicolored 8.00

#411-414 vert. #415-420 are airmail.
Nos. 411-418 exist imperf. (Value, set $60) and in souvenir sheets (Value, set $60).

Sept. 26th Revolution, 20th Anniv. (1982) — A112

1983, Sept. 26 **Litho.** *Perf. 14*

421 A112 100f Communications 1.25 .75
422 A112 150f Literacy 1.75 1.10
423 A112 325f Educational development 4.00 2.40
a. Souvenir sheet of 2, #422, 423 8.00
424 A112 400f Independence 6.00 3.00
Nos. 421-424 (4) 13.00 7.25

World Communications Year — A113

1983, Dec. 15

425 A113 150f lt bl & multi 2.50 1.20
426 A113 325f lt grn & multi 5.00 2.75
a. Souvenir sheet of 1 9.00

Sept. 26 Revolution, 21st Anniv. — A114

1984, Apr. 1 **Litho.** *Perf. 14*

427 A114 100f shown 1.75 .85
428 A114 150f Fist, statue 2.00 1.25
429 A114 325f Gate, tank 4.00 2.00
a. Souvenir sheet of 1 8.00
Nos. 427-429 (3) 7.75 4.10

Israel Aggression Day — A115

1984, Sept. 7

430 A115 150f multi 1.75 .75
431 A115 325f multi 4.50 2.25

Size: 91x120mm

Imperf

432 A115 325f multi *25.00*
Nos. 430-432 (3) 31.25 3.00

Sept. 26 Revolution, 22nd Anniv. — A116

1985, Oct. 1

433 A116 50f Triumphal Arch .75 .35
434 A116 150f San'a Castle walls 2.00 1.25
435 A116 325f Stadium, Govt. Palace, San'a 4.50 2.50
a. Souvenir sheet of 1 8.00
Nos. 433-435 (3) 7.25 4.10

Intl. Anti-Apartheid Year (1978) — A117

1985, Jan. 1

436 A117 150f dp ver & multi 2.00 .90
437 A117 325f grn & multi 4.75 2.40
a. Souvenir sheet of 1 9.00

Intl. Civil Aviation Org., 40th Anniv. — A118

1985, Sept. 20

438 A118 25f multi .40 .25
439 A118 50f multi .60 .25
440 A118 150f multi 1.50 .75
441 A118 325f multi 3.50 1.50
a. Souvenir sheet of 1 6.00 8.00
Nos. 438-441 (4) 6.00 2.75

Arabsat Satellite, 1st Anniv. — A119

1986, Apr. 15 **Litho.** *Perf. 14*

442 A119 150f multi 2.75 1.25
443 A119 325f multi 6.00 2.50
a. Souvenir sheet of 1 9.50

World Telecommunications, 120th Anniv. — A120

1986, May 1

444 A120 150f multi 2.75 1.25
445 A120 325f multi 6.00 2.50
a. Souvenir sheet of 1 9.00

General People's Conference, 2nd Anniv. — A121

1986, May 1

446 A121 150f multi 2.75 1.25
447 A121 325f multi 5.00 2.50
a. Souvenir sheet of 1 6.00 5.00

A122

1986, July 1

448 A122 150f multi 7.25 1.25
449 A122 325f multi 5.00 2.50
a. Souvenir sheet of 1 6.00 5.00

15th Islamic Foreign Ministers' Conference, San'a, Dec. 18-22, 1984.

A123

1986, Oct. 1

450 A123 150f multi 2.50 1.25
451 A123 325f multi 4.50 2.25
a. Souvenir sheet of 1 6.00 5.00

UN 40th anniv.

Arab League, 39th Anniv. — A124

1986, Nov. 15

452 A124 150f multi 2.75 1.50
453 A124 325f multi 5.00 3.00

Natl. Arms — A125

1987, Sept. 26 Litho. *Perf. 14*

454 A125 100f multi 1.00 .30
455 A125 150f multi 1.40 .70
456 A125 425f multi 4.00 2.00
a. Souvenir sheet of 1 4.50 3.50
457 A125 450f multi 4.50 2.25
Nos. 454-457 (4) 10.90 5.25

Sept. 26th Revolution, 25th anniv.
For surcharge see No. 593.

Intl. Youth Year (1985) — A126

1987, Oct. 15 *Perf. 13x13½*

458 A126 150f multi 2.00
459 A126 425f multi 4.00
a. Souvenir sheet of 1 5.00

For surcharge see No. C150.

Drilling of the Republic's First Oil Well, 1984 — A127

1987, Nov. 1 *Perf. 14*

460 A127 150f Oil derrick 2.50
461 A127 425f Derrick, refinery 4.00
a. Souvenir sheet of 1 5.00

For surcharge see No. C151.

General Population and Housing Census, 1986 — A128

1987, Dec. 1

462 A128 150f multi 2.50 1.25
463 A128 425f multi 4.50 2.25
a. Souvenir sheet of 1 5.50 3.00

For surcharge see No. C152.

1986 World Cup Soccer Championships, Mexico — A129

Designs: 100f, 150f, Match scenes, vert. 425f, Match scene and Pique, character trademark.

1988, Jan. 1 Litho. *Perf. 14*

464 A129 100f multi 1.00 .60
465 A129 150f multi, diff. 1.50 1.00
466 A129 425f multi 3.50 1.50
a. Souvenir sheet of 1 6.00 3.00
Nos. 464-466 (3) 6.00 3.10

For surcharge see No. C153.

17th Scouting Conference, San'a — A130

1988, Mar. 1 Litho. *Perf. 14*

467 A130 25f Skin diving .35 .25
468 A130 30f Table tennis .45 .25
469 A130 40f Tennis .55 .30
470 A130 50f Two scouts, flag .65 .30
471 A130 60f Volleyball .75 .35
472 A130 100f Tug-of-war 1.20 .60
473 A130 150f Basketball 1.75 .75
474 A130 425f Archery 5.00 2.00
Nos. 467-474 (8) 10.70 4.80

Souvenir Sheet

475 A130 425f Scout, emblem, hand sign 5.50 4.00

For surcharge see No. C154.

San'a Preservation A131

1988, May 1 Litho. *Perf. 14*

476 A131 25f multicolored .45 .25
477 A131 50f multicolored .85 .45
478 A131 100f multicolored 1.40 .70
479 A131 150f multicolored 1.90 1.00
480 A131 425f multicolored 4.50 2.25
a. Souvenir sheet of 1 6.00 5.00
Nos. 476-480 (5) 9.10 4.65

For surcharge see No. 594.

Battle of Hattin, 800th Anniv. in 1987 — A132

1988 Litho. *Perf. 14*

482 A132 150f multicolored 2.75 1.40
483 A132 425f multicolored 6.75 3.50
a. Souvenir sheet 10.00 10.00

For surcharge see No. C155.

Arab Telecommunication Day, 1987 — A133

1988

484 A133 100f multicolored 1.50 .75
485 A133 150f multicolored 2.25 1.10
486 A133 425f multicolored 5.25 2.50
a. Souvenir sheet 9.00 9.00
Nos. 484-486 (3) 9.00 4.35

For surcharge see No. C156.

A134

Sept. 26 Revolution, 26th Anniv. — A134a

1989, Sept. 30

487 A134 300f multicolored 1.25 .60
488 A134 375f multicolored 1.75 1.00
489 A134a 850f multicolored 3.50 1.75
490 A134a 900f multicolored 3.50 1.75
Nos. 487-490 (4) 10.00 5.10

A souvenir sheet containing one #488 exists. Value, $100.
For surcharges see Nos. 595, 605.

A135

October 14 Revolution, 25th Anniv. — A135a

1989, Oct. 14

491 A135 300f multicolored 1.25 .60
492 A135 375f multicolored 1.75 .85
493 A135a 850f multicolored 3.50 1.75
494 A135a 900f multicolored 3.50 1.75
Nos. 491-494 (4) 10.00 4.95

A souvenir sheet containing one #492 exists. Value, $100.
For surcharges see Nos. 596, 606.

1988 Summer Olympics, Seoul — A136

Game emblem and various events: 300f, Table tennis, basketball, track, boxing. 375f, Soccer game. 850f, Soccer, judo, vert. 900f, Torch bearer.

1989, Nov. 10 Litho. *Perf. 13x13½*

495 A136 300f multicolored 1.50 .75
496 A136 375f multicolored 2.00 1.00
a. Souvenir sheet 10.00 7.50
497 A136 850f multicolored 5.00 2.50
498 A136 900f multicolored 5.00 2.50
Nos. 495-498 (4) 13.50 6.75

For surcharges see Nos. 597, 607.

Palestinian Uprising — A137

375f, Flag raising, vert. 850f, Burning barricades. 900f, Man waving flag, vert.

1989, Dec. 9 *Perf. 13x13½, 13½x13*

499 A137 300f shown 2.00 1.00
500 A137 375f multicolored 3.00 1.50
a. Souvenir sheet of 1 17.50 8.50
501 A137 850f multicolored 5.50 2.75
502 A137 900f multicolored 7.00 3.50
Nos. 499-502 (4) 17.50 8.75

For surcharges see Nos. 598, 608.

Arab Cooperation Council — A138

1990, Feb. 16 Litho. *Perf. 13x13½*

504 A138 300f multicolored 1.25 .65
505 A138 375f multicolored 1.75 .90
a. Souvenir sheet 12.00 9.00
506 A138 850f multicolored 3.50 1.75
507 A138 900f multicolored 3.50 1.75
Nos. 504-507 (4) 10.00 5.05

For surcharges see Nos. 599, 609.

First Exported Oil — A139

1990, Mar. 15 *Perf. 14*

508 A139 300f multicolored 1.25 .60
509 A139 375f multicolored 2.00 1.00
a. Souvenir sheet 10.00 5.00
510 A139 850f multi, diff. 4.00 2.00
511 A139 900f like 850f 4.00 2.00
Nos. 508-511 (4) 11.25 5.60

For surcharges see Nos. 600, 610.

Arab Scout Movement, 75th Anniv. — A140

300f, Scouts holding globe. 850f, Oil rig, scouts, globe.

1990, June 15 Litho. *Perf. 13x13½*

512 A140 300f multicolored 1.25 .60
513 A140 375f like No. 512 1.40 .70
a. Souvenir sheet of 1 7.00 1.00
514 A140 850f multicolored 3.00 1.50
515 A140 900f like No. 514 3.50 1.75
Nos. 512-515 (4) 9.15 4.55

For surcharges see Nos. 601, 611.

Arab Board for Medical Specializations, 10th Anniv. — A141

1990, Apr. 15 Photo. *Perf. 13½x13*

516 A141 300f brt grn & multi 1.25 .60
517 A141 375f lt bl & multi 1.50 .75
a. Sheet of 1, perf. 12½ 5.00 2.50
518 A141 850f lt org & multi 3.25 1.60
519 A141 900f lt vio & multi 3.50 1.75
Nos. 516-519 (4) 9.50 4.70

For surcharges see Nos. 602, 612.

Immunization Campaign A142

300f, 375f, Mother feeding infant, vert.

1990, May 15 ***Perf. 13½x13, 13x13½***

520	A142	300f It bl & multi	1.40	.70
521	A142	375f It org & multi	2.00	1.00
a.		Sheet of 1, perf. 12½	11.00	6.00
522	A142	850f It bl grn & multi	4.00	2.00
523	A142	900f It lake & multi	4.00	2.00
		Nos. 520-523 (4)	11.40	5.70

No. 521a contains one 26x37mm stamp.
For surcharges see Nos. 603, C157.

Republic of Yemen

UN Development Program, 40th Anniv. — A144

1990, Oct. 24 **Litho.** ***Perf. 12***

532	A144	150f multicolored	1.00	.50

For surcharge see No. 622.

Ducks — A145

1990, Sept. 18 **Litho.** ***Perf. 12***

533	A145	10f Pintail swimming	.25	.25
534	A145	20f Wigeon	.25	.25
535	A145	25f Ruddy shelduck	.25	.25
536	A145	40f Gadwall	.30	.25
537	A145	75f Shelduck, male	.50	.30
538	A145	150f Shoveler	1.00	.50
539	A145	600f Teal	4.00	2.00
		Nos. 533-539 (7)	6.55	3.80

Souvenir Sheet

540	A145	460f Pintail in flight	8.00	4.00

For surcharge see No. 623.

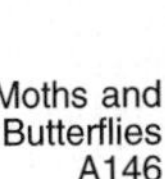

Moths and Butterflies A146

5f, Dirphia multicolor. 20f, Automeris io. 25f, Papilio machaon. 40f, Bhutanitis lidderdalii. 55f, Prepona demophon muson. 75f, Agarista agricola. 700f, Attacus edwardsii.
460f, Daphnis nerii, vert.

1990, Nov. 3 ***Perf. 12½x12***

541	A146	5f multicolored	.25	.25
542	A146	20f multicolored	.25	.25
543	A146	25f multicolored	.25	.25
544	A146	40f multicolored	.35	.25
545	A146	55f multicolored	.45	.30
546	A146	75f multicolored	.55	.30
547	A146	700f multicolored	3.75	2.00
		Nos. 541-547 (7)	5.85	3.60

Souvenir Sheet

Perf. 12x12½

548	A146	460f multicolored	7.50	4.50

Prehistoric Animals — A147

Perf. 12x12½, 12½x12

1990, Nov. 27

549	A147	5f Protembolotherium, vert.	.25	.25
550	A147	10f Diatryma, vert.	.25	.25
551	A147	35f Mammuthus	.25	.25
552	A147	40f Edaphosaurus	.30	.25
553	A147	55f Dimorphodon	.40	.30
554	A147	75f Phororhacos	.50	.30
555	A147	700f Ichthyosaurus, vert.	3.25	1.75
		Nos. 549-555 (7)	5.20	3.35

Size: 61x90mm

Imperf

556	A147	460f Tyrannosaurus, vert.	4.00	2.50

A148

Various domestic cats.

1990, Dec. 26 ***Perf. 12x12½***

557	A148	5f multicolored	.25	.25
558	A148	15f multicolored	.25	.25
559	A148	35f multicolored	.25	.25
560	A148	55f multicolored	.35	.30
561	A148	60f multicolored	.35	.30
562	A148	150f multicolored	.75	.60
563	A148	600f multicolored	2.75	1.50
		Nos. 557-563 (7)	4.95	3.45

Size: 70x90mm

Imperf

564	A148	460f multicolored	5.00	2.50

A149

Mushrooms: 50f, Boletus aestivalis. 60f, Suillus luteus. 80f, Gyromitra esculenta. 100f, Leccinum scabrum. 130f, Amanita muscaria. 200f, Boletus erythropus. 300f, Leccinum testaceoscabrum.
460f, Stropharia aeruginosa.

1991, Mar. 18 **Litho.** ***Perf. 12x12½***

565	A149	50f multicolored	.30	.25
566	A149	60f multicolored	.40	.25
567	A149	80f multicolored	.50	.30
568	A149	100f multicolored	.65	.35
569	A149	130f multicolored	.90	.45
570	A149	200f multicolored	1.50	.55
571	A149	300f multicolored	2.00	.60
		Nos. 565-571 (7)	6.25	2.75

Size: 70x90mm

Imperf

572	A149	460f multicolored	3.00	

Unified Yemen Republic, 1st Anniv. — A150

Designs: 300f, 375f, Eagle crest. 850f, 900f, Hand holding flag, map, sun.

1991, May 22 ***Perf. 13x13½***

573	A150	300f pink & multi	.65	.35
574	A150	375f grn bl multi	.85	.45
a.		Sheet of 1, perf. 12½	2.25	1.50
575	A150	850f It bl & multi	2.00	.65
576	A150	900f bl grn & multi	2.00	.80
		Nos. 573-576 (4)	5.50	2.25

No. 574a contains one 37x27mm stamp.
For surcharges see #604, 613, 624, 627.

Unity Agreement Signed Nov. 30, 1989 — A151

Designs: 300f, 375f, 850f, Fist, flag, map.

1991, May 22 ***Perf. 13½x13***

577	A151	225f multicolored	.45	.25
578	A151	300f org & multi	.70	.35
579	A151	375f yel grn & multi	.90	.50
a.		Sheet of 1, perf. 12½	2.75	1.50
580	A151	650f multicolored	1.40	.70
581	A151	850f red org & multi	1.75	.90
		Nos. 577-581 (5)	5.20	2.70

No. 579a contains one 27x37mm stamp.
For surcharges see #614, 617-619, 625.

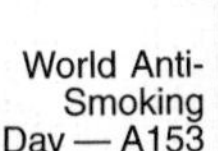

World Anti-Smoking Day — A153

Designs: 300f, 375f, 850f, Man facing skull smoking cigarette.

1991, May 31 ***Perf. 13x13½***

582	A153	225f multicolored	.45	.25
583	A153	300f multicolored	.70	.35
584	A153	375f multicolored	1.00	.50
a.		Sheet of 1, perf. 12½	3.50	1.75
585	A153	650f multicolored	1.50	.75
586	A153	850f multicolored	2.00	1.00
		Nos. 582-586 (5)	5.65	2.85

No. 584a contains one 36x26mm stamp.
For surcharges see Nos. 615, 620, 626.

United Nations, 45th Anniv. — A154

1991, June 26 ***Perf. 13x13½***

587	A154	5r multicolored	1.40	.70
588	A154	8r multicolored	1.75	.90
589	A154	10r multicolored	2.50	1.25
590	A154	12r multicolored	2.75	1.40
		Nos. 587-590 (4)	8.40	4.25

Souvenir Sheet

Perf. 12½

591	A154	6r multicolored	2.50	1.50

No. 591 contains one 37x28mm stamp.

Nos. 329, 456, 480, 489-490, 493-494, 497-498, 501-502, 506-507, 510-511, 514-515, 518-519, 523, 575-576, 581 & 586 Surcharged, "Rials" Spelled Out

1993, Jan. 1 ***Perfs., Etc. as Before***

592	A88	5r on 75f #329	*8.00*	4.00
593	A125	8r on 425f #456	*10.00*	6.00
594	A131	8r on 425f #480	*10.00*	6.00
595	A134a	10r on 900f #490	*10.00*	6.00
596	A135a	10r on 900f #494	*10.00*	6.00
597	A136	10r on 900f #498	*25.00*	15.00
598	A137	10r on 900f #502	*10.00*	6.00
599	A138	10r on 900f #507	*10.00*	6.00
600	A139	10r on 900f #511	*10.00*	6.00
601	A140	10r on 900f #515	*10.00*	6.00
602	A141	10r on 900f #519	*10.00*	6.00
603	A142	10r on 900f #523	*10.00*	6.00
604	A150	10r on 900f #576	*10.00*	6.00
605	A134a	12r on 850f #489	*12.00*	8.00
606	A135a	12r on 850f #493	*12.00*	8.00
607	A136	12r on 850f #497	*25.00*	15.00
608	A137	12r on 850f #501	*12.00*	8.00
609	A138	12r on 850f #506	*12.00*	8.00
610	A139	12r on 850f #510	*12.00*	8.00
611	A140	12r on 850f #514	*12.00*	8.00
612	A141	12r on 850f #518	*12.00*	8.00
613	A150	12r on 850f #575	*12.00*	8.00
614	A151	12r on 850f #581	*12.00*	8.00
615	A153	12r on 850f #586	*12.00*	8.00
		Nos. 592-615 (24)	*288.00*	

Size and location of surcharge varies.

Yemen (PDR) Nos. 441, 443, 447, and Yemen Nos. 577-578, 583 Srchd. Type a or — c

1993 ***Perfs., Etc. as Before***

616	A139(a)	50r on 500f #447	*150.00*	75.00
617	A151(a)	50r on 225f #577	*250.00*	150.00
618	A151(c)	50r on 225f #577		—
a.		Pair, #617-618		
619	A151(a)	100r on 300f #578	*250.00*	150.00
620	A153(a)	100r on 300f #583	*400.00*	200.00
621	A139(a)	200r on 5f #441	*350.00*	200.00
a.		3-Line surcharge		
621B	A139(a)	200r on 20f #443	*350.00*	200.00

Size and location of surcharge varies.

Yemen Republic Nos. 532, 538, 573-574, 579, & 584 Srchd. — a

1993, Sept. 1 ***Perfs., Etc. as Before***

622	A144(a)	50r on 150f #532	*35.00*	*20.00*
623	A145(a)	50r on 150f #538	*35.00*	*20.00*
623A	A153(a)	50r on 225f #582	*400.00*	*200.00*
624	A150(a)	50r on 375f #574	*30.00*	*15.00*
625	A151(a)	50r on 375f #579	*35.00*	*25.00*
626	A153(a)	50r on 375f #584	*35.00*	*25.00*
627	A150(a)	100r on 300f #573	*60.00*	*20.00*

Size and location of surcharge varies.
No. 623 exists with a surcharge similar to surcharge "c."

Yemen People's Democratic Republic Nos. 75, 84B, 204, 208, 216, 232, 235, 244, 267, 335-336, 347, 425, 436-437, 439 & Types Surcharged Type a and

b

1993, Sept. 1 ***Perfs., Etc. as Before***

628	A25(a)	8r on 110f #84B	7.50	4.00
629	A63(a)	8r on 110f #204	7.50	4.00
630	A64(a)	8r on 110f #208	7.50	4.00
631	A66(a)	8r on 110f #216	7.50	4.00
632	A72(a)	8r on 110f #232	7.50	4.00
633	A74(a)	8r on 110r #235	7.50	4.00
634	A76(a)	8r on 110r #244	20.00	10.00
635	A86(a)	8r on 110f #267	7.50	4.00
636	A105(a)	100r on 2d #347	*75.00*	50.00
637	A137(a)	100r on 300f #439	*75.00*	50.00
638	A24(a)	200r on 5f #75	*125.00*	75.00
639	(b)	200r on 15f Soyuz 10 & Salyut 1	*125.00*	75.00
640	A105(b)	200r on 15f #335	*125.00*	75.00
641	(b)	200r on 20f Apollo 8	*125.00*	75.00
642	A105(b)	200r on 20f #336	*125.00*	75.00
643	A131(a)	200r on 20f #425	*200.00*	100.00
644	A134(a)	200r on 75f #436	*125.00*	75.00
645	A135(a)	200r on 250f #437	*125.00*	75.00
		Nos. 628-645 (18)	1,298.	763.00

Size and location of surcharge varies.
No. 582 exists with a 50r type "b" surcharge.
No. 636 exists with a surcharge similar to surcharge "c."

Yemen Unity, 4th Anniv. — A155

Various views of govt. building, San'a.

1994, Sept. 27 Litho. ***Perf. 13½x14***
646 A155 3r multicolored .65 .35
647 A155 5r multicolored 1.20 .50
648 A155 8r multicolored 1.75 .75
649 A155 20r multicolored 4.50 2.00
Nos. 646-649 (4) 8.10 3.60

Souvenir Sheet

650 A155 20r multi, diff. 5.00 3.00

1994 World Cup Soccer Championships, US — A156

2r, Player in yellow shirt dribbling ball, vert. 6r, Player in striped shirt dribbling, vert. 10r, Goal keeper. No. 654, Heading ball, vert.
No. 655, Tackling.

1994, Oct. 1 ***Perf. 14x13½, 13½x14***
651 A156 2r multicolored .55 .25
652 A156 6r multicolored 1.50 .60
653 A156 10r multicolored 2.50 1.00
654 A156 12r multicolored 3.00 1.25
Nos. 651-654 (4) 7.55 3.10

Souvenir Sheet

655 A156 12r multicolored 3.50 2.50

World Day of Environmental Protection — A157

Perf. 14x13½, 13½x14

1995, Oct. 15 Litho.
656 A157 15r Arabian leopard 1.40 .90
657 A157 20r Caracal lynx 1.60 1.00
658 A157 30r Guinea fowl, horiz. 2.40 1.25
Nos. 656-658 (3) 5.40 3.15

Souvenir Sheet

659 A157 50r Partridge, horiz. 5.25 3.50

FAO, 50th Anniv. — A158

Emblem, field, hand holding: 10r, Plant. 25r, Seed. 30r, Fish. 50r, Grain.

1995, Oct. 16 ***Perf. 14x13½***
660 A158 10r violet & multi .90 .50
661 A158 25r claret & multi 1.75 .75
662 A158 30r light blue & multi 2.50 1.00
Nos. 660-662 (3) 5.15 2.25

Souvenir Sheet

663 A158 50r dark blue & multi 2.00

A159

UN, 50th anniv.: Various views of Aden Dam.

1995, Oct. 24 ***Perf. 14x13½, 13½x14***
664 A159 10r multi 1.00 .60
665 A159 20r multi 2.00 .85
666 A159 25r multi, horiz. 2.50 1.25
Nos. 664-666 (3) 5.50 2.70

Souvenir Sheet

667 A159 50r multi, horiz. 5.00 3.00

A160

Naseem Hamed Kashmem, world boxing champion: 10r, With champion belts. 20r, Up close. 25r, Boxing opponent, horiz. 30r, Holding up arm as winner, trainer.
50r, Boxing opponent, diff., horiz.

Perf. 14x13½, 13½x14

1995, Nov. 29
668 A160 10r multicolored 1.00 .40
669 A160 20r multicolored 2.00 .65
670 A160 25r multicolored 2.50 .80
671 A160 30r multicolored 3.00 1.00
Nos. 668-671 (4) 8.50 2.85

Souvenir Sheet

672 A160 50r multicolored 5.00 3.00

Souvenir Sheet

CHINA '96, 9th Asian Intl. Philatelic Exhibition — A161

1996, May 18 Litho. ***Perf. 11½***
673 A161 80r Shanghai 7.50 4.50

1996 Summer Olympic Games, Atlanta — A162

1996, July 19 ***Perf. 14x13½, 13½x14***
674 A162 20r Wrestling, vert. .90 .40
675 A162 50r High jump 1.90 1.20
676 A162 60r Running, vert. 2.10 1.40
677 A162 70r Gymnastics, vert. 2.75 1.75
678 A162 100r Judo, vert. 4.50 2.00
Nos. 674-678 (5) 12.15 6.75

Souvenir Sheet

679 A162 150r Javelin, vert. 10.00 6.50

Landmarks — A163

10r, 70r, 250r, Popular Heritage Museum, Seiyoan. 15r, 40r, 60r, 500r, Rock Palace, Wadi Dhahr, vert. 20r, 100r, 200r, Old Sana'a City. 30r, 50r, 150r, 300r, Al-Mohdhar Minaret, Tarim, vert.

Perf. 13½x14, 14x13½

1996, Sept. 26 Litho.
680 A163 10r org yel & multi .50 .25
681 A163 15r grn yel & multi .75 .25
682 A163 20r lt blue & multi 1.00 .35
683 A163 30r blue & multi 1.25 .40
684 A163 40r salmon & multi 1.75 .55
685 A163 50r green & multi 2.25 .70
686 A163 60r lilac & multi 3.00 .85
687 A163 70r violet & multi 3.50 1.00
688 A163 100r yellow & multi 4.50 1.40
689 A163 150r orange & multi 6.00 1.90
690 A163 200r rose & multi 8.00 2.40
691 A163 250r gray & multi 10.00 2.75
692 A163 300r red & multi 12.50 3.25
693 A163 500r yellow & multi 20.00 4.75
Nos. 680-693 (14) 75.00 20.80

Birds — A164

Designs: 20r, Tyto alba. 50r, Alectoris philbyi. 60r, Gypaetus barbatus. 70r, Alectoris melanocephala. 100r, Chlamydotis undulata.
150r, Ixobrychus minutus, vert.

1996, Oct. 14 Litho. ***Perf. 13½x14***
694 A164 20r multicolored .65 .40
695 A164 50r multicolored 1.60 .80
696 A164 60r multicolored 2.10 1.00
697 A164 70r multicolored 2.25 1.40
698 A164 100r multicolored 3.00 2.00
Nos. 694-698 (5) 9.60 5.60

Souvenir Sheet

Perf. 14x13½

699 A164 150r multicolored 7.50 4.50

Rare Plants in Yemen — A165

Designs: 20r, Parodia masii. 50r, Notocatus cristata. 60r, Adenium obesum socotranum. 70r, Dracaena cinnabari. 100r, Mammillaria erythrosperma.
150r, Parodia maasii, diff.

1996, Nov. 30 ***Perf. 13½x14***
700 A165 20r multicolored .65 .40
701 A165 50r multicolored 1.50 .80
702 A165 60r multicolored 1.80 1.00
703 A165 70r multicolored 2.10 1.40
704 A165 100r multicolored 3.00 2.00
Nos. 700-704 (5) 9.05 5.60

Souvenir Sheet

705 A165 150r multicolored 7.00 4.50

A166

Fish: 20r, Heniochus acuminatus. 50r, 150r, Cheilinus undulatus. 60r, Zebrasoma xanthurum. 70r, Pomacanthus imperator. 100r, Pomacanthus vanthometopon.

1996, Nov. 30
706 A166 20r multicolored .70 .40
707 A166 50r multicolored 1.50 1.00
708 A166 60r multicolored 1.90 1.25
709 A166 70r multicolored 2.75 1.75
710 A166 100r multicolored 3.50 2.50
Nos. 706-710 (5) 10.35 6.90

Souvenir Sheet

711 A166 150r multicolored 8.50 4.50

A167

UNICEF, 50th Anniv.: 20r, Children with books. 50r, Girls clapping hands. 60r, Mother, child. 70r, Mother, three children.
150r, Child making jewelry, horiz.

1996, Dec. 11 ***Perf. 14x13½***
712 A167 20r multicolored .75 .35
713 A167 50r multicolored 1.50 .70
714 A167 60r multicolored 1.80 .85
715 A167 70r multicolored 2.10 1.25
Nos. 712-715 (4) 6.15 3.15

Souvenir Sheet

Perf. 13½x14

716 A167 150r multicolored 6.00 4.00

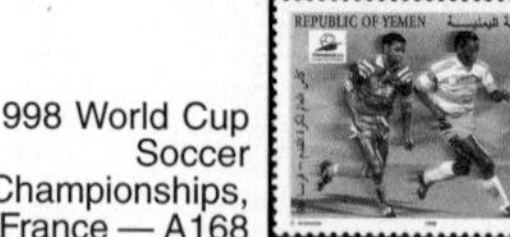

1998 World Cup Soccer Championships, France — A168

Various soccer plays.

1998, June 10 Litho. ***Perf. 13x13½***
717 A168 10r multicolored .40 .25
718 A168 15r multicolored .65 .30
719 A168 35r multicolored 1.40 .65
720 A168 65r multicolored 2.25 1.10
721 A168 75r multicolored 2.50 1.25
a. Souvenir sheet, #717-721 8.00 4.00
Nos. 717-721 (5) 7.20 3.55

Birds — A169

Designs: 10r, Ardeotis arabs. 15r, Neophron percnopterus. 35r, Coracias abyssinicus. 65r, Cinnyricinclus leucogaster. 75r, Melierax metabates.

1998, Sept. 26 Litho. ***Perf. 13***
722-726 A169 Set of 5 8.00 4.00
726a Sheet of 5, #722-726 9.00 5.00

Universal Declaration of Human Rights, 50th Anniv. — A170

15r, Hands in air. 35r, Hands clasped in handshake. 100r, Hands reaching out.

1998, Oct. 12
727-729 A170 Set of 3 6.00 3.00
729a Sheet of 3, #727-729 6.00 4.50

First General Conference of Yemeni Immigrants (in 1999) — A171

Emblem &: 60r, Dhows. 90r, Fort, camel.

2000, May 16 Litho. ***Perf. 14½x14***
730-731 A171 Set of 2 4.50 3.00
731a Souvenir sheet, #730-731 5.50 4.00

Tenth National Day — A172

Background colors: 30r, Light green. 50r, Rose lilac. 70r, Light blue. 150r, Orange.

2000, May 22 ***Perf. 14x14½***
732-734 A172 Set of 3 6.00 4.00

Souvenir Sheet

735 A172 150r multi 6.00 4.00

Plants of Socotra — A173

Designs: 30r, Euphorbia abdalkuri. 70r, Dendrosicyos socotranus. 80r, Caralluma socotrana. 120r, Dracaena cinnabari.
300r, Exacum affine.

2000, July 15
736-739 A173 Set of 4 9.00 5.00

Souvenir Sheet

740 A173 300r multi 10.00 8.00

2000 Summer Olympics, Sydney — A174

Designs: 50r, Judo. 70r, Runner. 80r, Hurdler. 100r, Shooting.
300r, Tennis.

2000, Sept. 15
741-744 A174 Set of 4 8.00 5.00

Souvenir Sheet

745 A174 300r multi 9.50 8.00

Antiquities — A175

Designs: 30r, Stone idols, 3000 B.C. 70r, Statue of Ma'adi Karib, 800 B.C. 100r, Horned griffin, Royal Palace of Shabwa, 300. 120r, Statue of King of Awsan Yasduq Eil, 100 B.C. 320r, Stele with bull's head, 100 B.C., horiz.

2002, June 15 Litho. ***Perf. 13x12¾***
746-749 A175 Set of 4 8.50 8.50

Souvenir Sheet

Imperf

750 A175 320r multi 8.50 8.50

No. 750 contains one 41x26mm stamp.

2002 World Cup Soccer Championships, Japan and Korea — A176

Soccer players with background colors of: 30r, Bister, vert. 70r, Green. 100r, Blue, vert. 120r, Red brown, vert.
No. 755: a, Player's foot and ball. b, World Cup trophy.

2002, May 31 ***Perf. 13x12¾, 12¾x13***
751-754 A176 Set of 4 8.50 8.50

Souvenir Sheet

Perf.

755 A176 160r Sheet of 2, #a-b 8.50 8.50

No. 755 contains two 28mm diameter stamps.

Scouting in Yemen, 75th Anniv. — A177

Designs: 30r, Scout escorting man across street. 60r, Scout digging. 70r, Scouts in rowboat.
160r, Scout saluting, vert.

2002, Apr. 30 ***Perf. 12¾x13***
756-758 A177 Set of 3 4.25 4.25

Souvenir Sheet

Perf. 13x13¼

759 A177 160r multi 5.50 4.25

No. 759 contains one 16x26mm stamp.

Palestinian Intifada — A178

Designs: 30r, Frightened child. 60r, Bleeding child.
90r, Dome of the Rock, horiz.

2002, Apr. 27 ***Perf. 13x12¾***
760-761 A178 Set of 2 2.50 2.50

Imperf

Size: 111x78mm

762 A178 90r multi 2.50 2.50

Poets — A179

Designs: Nos. 763, 30r, 765, 60r, 767a, 70r, Hussain Al-Muhdhar (1931-2000). Nos. 764, 30r, 766, 60r, 767b, 70r, Abdullah Al-Baradony (1929-99).

2002, June 30 Litho. ***Perf. 13x12¾***
763-766 A179 Set of 4 4.50 4.50

Souvenir Sheet

Perf. 13x13¼

767 A179 70r Sheet of 2, #a-b 3.50 3.50

No. 767 contains two 16x28mm stamps.

Revolution, 40th Anniv. — A180

Background colors: 30r, Dull green. 60r, Rose.
90r, Lilac.

2002, Sept. 26 ***Perf. 13x12¾***
768-769 A180 Set of 2 2.25 2.25

Imperf

Size: 110x76mm

770 A180 90r multi 2.50 2.25

World Under-17 Soccer Championships, Finland — A181

Various soccer players with background color of: 30r, Red violet. 50r, Golden brown. 70r, Blue. 100r, Green.
250r, Soccer team and stadium.

2003, Aug. 13 Litho. ***Perf. 12¾x13***
771-774 A181 Set of 4 6.00 6.00

Imperf

Size: 109x74mm

775 A181 250r multi 6.00 6.00

Antiquities — A182

Various sculptures with background colors of: 20r, Pale yellow. 40r, Lilac. 50r, Light green. 150r, Pink.
260r, Black, horiz.

2003, Sept. 26 ***Perf. 13x12¾***
776-779 A182 Set of 4 6.00 6.00

Souvenir Sheet

Perf. 12¾x13

780 A182 260r multi 6.00 6.00

Traditional Women's Clothing — A183

Various women with panel colors of: 30r, Purple. 60r, Yellow green. 70r, Dark green. 100r, Red violet. 150r, Brown.
410r, Purple background, horiz.

2003, Oct. 14 ***Perf. 13x12¾***
781-785 A183 Set of 5 9.00 9.00

Souvenir Sheet

Perf. 12¾x13

786 A183 410r multi 9.00 9.00

Children's Art — A184

Designs: 20r, Girl with flower on globe, vert. 30r, Dove over buildings, vert. 40r, Dove holding swing, vert. 50r, Children in field. 60r, Animals in field. 70r, Street and park.

2003, Oct. 15 ***Perf. 13x12¾, 12¾x13***
787-792 A184 Set of 6 6.00 6.00

Sana'a, 2004 Arabic Cultural Capital — A185

Various buildings with frame colors of: 30r, White. 50r, Purple. 70r, Black. 100r, Dark brown. 150r Red brown.
400r, Buildings, horiz.

2003, Nov. 30 ***Perf. 13x12¾***
793-797 A185 Set of 5 9.00 9.00

Souvenir Sheet

Perf. 12¾x13

798 A185 400r multi 9.00 9.00

FIFA (Fédération Internationale de Football Association), Cent. — A186

2004, May 21 Litho. ***Perf. 13x12¾***
799 A186 100r multi 2.25 2.25

Dated 2005. Stamps did not appear in marketplace until 2005.

2004 Summer Olympics, Athens — A187

Designs: 70r, Running. 80r, Shooting. 100r, Swimming.
250r, Equestrian.

2004, Aug. 13
800-802 A187 Set of 3 5.50 5.50

Souvenir Sheet

803 A187 250r multi 5.50 5.50

Dated 2005. Stamps did not appear in marketplace until 2005.

Telecommunications and Technology — A188

Designs: 60r, Computer chips, "@" symbol, keyboard. 70r, Computer and stylized people, vert. 100r, Yemen Mobile emblem, vert.
400r, Like 70r, vert.

Perf. 12¾x13, 13x12¾

2004, Sept. 26
804-806 A188 Set of 3 5.00 5.00

Souvenir Sheet

807 A188 400r multi 9.00 9.00

Dated 2005. Stamps did not appear in marketplace until 2005.

Spiders — A189

No. 808: a, Tidarren argo. b, Scelidomachus socotranus. c, Habrocestum albopunctatum. d, Rafalus insignipalpis. e, Latrodectus hystrix. f, Atrophothele socotrana.
300r, Like No. 808b.

2004, Oct. 14 ***Perf. 12¾x13***
808 Horiz. strip of 6 6.50 6.50
a.-f. A189 50r Any single 1.00 1.00

Souvenir Sheet

809 A189 300r multi 6.50 6.50

Dated 2005. Stamps did not appear in marketplace until 2005.

Traditional Men's Clothing — A190

Men wearing various outfits with background colors of: 50r, Light yellow. 60r, Green. 70r, Pink. 100r, Blue.
360r, Orange brown.

2004, Oct. 30 ***Perf. 13x12¾***
810-813 A190 Set of 4 6.50 6.50

Souvenir Sheet

814 A190 360r multi 8.00 8.00

Dated 2005. Stamps did not appear in marketplace until 2005.

Handicrafts — A191

No. 815: a, Knife maker holding hammer. b, Textile worker piecing fabric. c, Jeweler. d, Weaver at loom.
3004, Like No. 815a.

2004, Nov. 30
815 Horiz. strip of 4 6.50 6.50
a.-d. A191 70r multi 1.60 1.60

Souvenir Sheet

816 A191 300r multi 6.50 6.50

Dated 2005. Stamps did not appear in marketplace until 2005.

15th National Day — A192

Emblem and: 30r, Industrial plant. 60r, Dam and reservoir. 70r, Man holding flag.
90r, Buildings.

2005, May 22
817-819 A192 Set of 3 3.50 3.50

Souvenir Sheet

820 A192 90r multi 2.00 2.00

United Nations, 60th Anniv. — A193

Symbols of eight goals for a better Yemen: No. 821, 40r, Pregnant woman and doctor. No. 822, 40r, Woman, infant and doctor. No. 823, 40r, Woman reading book. No. 824, 40r, Mosquito, AIDS ribbon, medicine and bottle. No. 825, 40r, Man depositing trash in can, tree, smiling sun. 80r, Goats, hat seller and child. 100r, Woman, man and balance. 120r, Handshake.
130r, UN anniversary emblem.

2005, Oct. 24 Litho. ***Perf. 13x12¾***
821-828 A193 Set of 8 11.00 11.00

Size: 111x83mm

Imperf

829 A193 130r multi 3.00 3.00

No. 829 contains one perforated label lacking a denomination.

Flowers — A194

Various flowers: 50r, 80r, 110r, 130r, 140r, 150r, 300r.

Perf. 13¼x13¾

2007, Sept. 26 **Litho.**
830-835 A194 Set of 6 13.50 13.50

Souvenir Sheet

836 A194 300r multi 6.00 6.00

Insects — A195

Designs: No. 837, 50r, Cheilomenes lunata yemenensis. No. 838, 50r, Pharoscymnus c-luteus. No. 839, 50r, Hippodamia variegata. No. 840, 50r, Cheilomenes propinqua vicina. No. 841, 50r, Brumoides nigrifrons. No. 842, 50r, Serangium buettikeri.
250r, Pharoscymnus c-luteus, diff.

2007, Sept. 26 *Perf. 13¾x13¼*
837-842 A195 Set of 6 6.00 6.00

Souvenir Sheet

843 A195 250r multi 5.00 5.00

Mosques A196

Designs: 50r, Mosque of Prophethood, Hadhramaut. 80r, Al Ameria Mosque, Radaa. 100r, Queen Arwa Mosque, Jebla. 110r, Al Ashrafiah Mosque, Taiz. 120r, Al Aidarous Mosque, Aden. 200r, Al Bukiriah Mosque, Sana'a.
300r, Unidentified mosque.

2007, Oct. 14 *Perf. 13¼x13¾*
844-849 A196 Set of 6 13.50 13.50

Souvenir Sheet

850 A196 300r multi 6.00 6.00

Citadels and Castles — A197

Designs: 50r, Thulaa Citadel, Amran. 80r, Al Tawama Citadels, Hadhramaut. 100r, Serah Castle, Aden. 110r, Sumarah Castle, Ibb. 130r, Al Qahira Castle, Taiz.
300r, Unidentified castle.

2007, Oct. 14
851-855 A197 Set of 5 9.50 9.50

Souvenir Sheet

856 A197 300r multi 6.00 6.00

Marine Life — A198

Designs: 50r, Parupeneus marconema. 80r, Sarda orientalis. 100r, Carcharhinus melanopterus. 110r, Plectorhinchus schotaf. 130r, Panulirus homarus. 160r, Seriola rivoliana.
300r, Panulirus homarus, diff.

2007, Nov. 30
857-862 A198 Set of 6 13.00 13.00

Souvenir Sheet

863 A198 300r multi 6.00 6.00

Yemeni Onyx — A199

Various set and unset onyx stones: 50r, 80r, 100r, 110r, 120r, 130r, 140r, 160r.
250r, Set and unset onyx stones.

2007, Nov. 30 *Perf. 13¾x13¼*
864-871 A199 Set of 8 18.00 18.00

Souvenir Sheet

872 A199 250r multi 5.00 5.00

Natl. Day of Human Rights — A200

Globe, flag, dove, human rights emblem with background color of: 110r, Red violet. 130r, Blue.
250r, Dove and flag, vert.

2007, Dec. 10 *Perf. 13¼x13¾*
873-874 A200 Set of 2 5.00 5.00

Souvenir Sheet

Perf. 13¾x13¼

875 A200 250r multi 5.00 5.00

Yasser Arafat (1929-2004), Palestinian Leader — A201

Palestinian Authority flag and Arafat: 120r, With hand raised. 300fr, With hands not shown, horiz.

2008, Nov. 4 **Litho.** *Perf. 13x12¾*
876 A201 120r multi 2.50 2.50

Size: 110x70mm

Imperf

877 A201 300r multi 6.00 6.00

Opening of Al-Saleh Mosque, Sana'a — A202

Mosque: 80r, Pillars, ceiling and chandeliers. 100r, Interior wall. 120r, Exterior.
300r, Exterior, diff.

2008, Nov. 22 *Perf. 12¾x13*
878-880 A202 Set of 3 6.00 6.00

Size: 109x70mm

Imperf

881 A202 300r multi 6.00 6.00

Gaza — A203

Designs: 60r, Man, boy carrying Palestinian flag. 100r, Barbed wire, children looking through hole in wall, horiz.
120r, Dove and chain.

2009, May 22 *Perf. 13¼x13, 13x13¼*
882-883 A203 Set of 2 3.25 3.25

Souvenir Sheet

884 A203 120r multi 2.50 2.50

Ancient Coins — A204

Various ancient coins: 50r, 60r, 70r, 80r, 100r, 120r. 60r and 80r are vert. 120r is 50x50mm diamond-shaped stamp.

2009, May 22 *Perf. 13x13¼, 13¼x13*
885-889 A204 Set of 5 7.50 7.50

Souvenir Sheet

Perf. 13¼

890 A204 120r multi 2.50 2.50

Ancient Jewelry — A205

Designs: 50r, Bracelet and ring. 60r, Bracelet, horiz. 80r, Necklace and earrings. 100r, Bracelets, horiz. 120r, Necklace. 140r, Bracelets, diff., horiz.
150r, Belt, horiz.

2009, May 22 *Perf. 13¼x13, 13x13¼*
891-896 A205 Set of 6 11.00 11.00

Souvenir Sheet

897 A205 150r multi 3.00 3.00

Horses — A206

Designs: 60r, Head of brown horse with white blaze. 80r, Black horse. 100r, Brown horse with white blaze. 120r, Brown horse with white mane. 140r, White horse.150r, Head of brown horse with white blaze, diff.
200r, Dappled gray horse, vert.

2009, May 22 *Perf. 13x13¼*
898-903 A206 Set of 6 13.00 13.00

Souvenir Sheet

Perf. 13¼x13

904 A206 200r multi 4.25 4.25

Souvenir Sheet

Arab Postal Day A207

No. 905 — Emblem and: a, World map, pigeon. b, Camel caravan.

2009, May 22 *Perf. 12¾*
905 A207 100r Sheet of 2, #a-b 4.25 4.25

Tarim, 2010 Capital of Islamic Culture — A208

Designs: 50r, Palace, yellow and red panel. 60r, Minaret, yellow and green panel. 80r, Al Kaff Palace, orange panel. 100r, Qasr al-Qubba Hotel, black panel.
200r, Palace at night, yellow and brown frame.

2010, Mar. 1 **Litho.** *Perf. 13¼*
906-909 A208 Set of 4 3.50 3.50

Souvenir Sheet

910 A208 200r multi 4.75 4.75

National Day — A209

20th anniversary emblem and background colors of: 60r, Brown and red brown. 80r, Yellow and brown. 200r, Emblem, horiz.

2010, May 22 **Litho.** *Perf. 13*
911-912 A209 Set of 2 3.00 3.00

Souvenir Sheet

913 A209 200r multi 4.25 4.25

2010 World Cup Soccer Championships, South Africa — A210

2010 World Cup emblem, World Cup and various South African stadiums hosting matches: 50r, 60r, 80r, 100r.
No. 918, vert.: a, 50r, 2010 World Cup emblem. b, 100r, World Cup.

2010, June 11
914-917 A210 Set of 4 7.75 7.75

Souvenir Sheet

918 A210 Sheet of 2, #a-b 4.75 4.75

Yemeni Janbiahs (Daggers) A211

Various daggers in sheaths: 50r, 60r, 80r, 100r, 120r. 60r and 100r are vert.
200r, Dagger, diff.

2010, July 21 *Perf. 12¾*
919-923 A211 Set of 5 8.50 8.50

Souvenir Sheet

924 A211 200r multi 4.25 4.25

20th Gulf Cup of Nations Soccer Tournament, Aden — A212

Soccer player at LL and: 60r, Emblem depicting soccer ball, map of Arabian Peninsula. 80r, Soccer players in posed photograph. 100r, Gulf Cup, ring of flags. 120r, Stadium. 150r, Tournament emblem.
250r, Soccer ball with tournament emblem depicting soccer ball and map of Arabian Peninsula.

2010, Nov. 22 *Perf. 13¼*
925-929 A212 Set of 5 7.25 7.25

Souvenir Sheet

930 A212 250r multi 3.50 3.50

AIR POST STAMPS

Catalogue values for unused stamps in this section are for Never Hinged items.

Plane over San'a — AP1

1947 Unwmk. Engr. *Perf. 12½*
C1 AP1 10b bright blue 6.00 2.00
C2 AP1 20b olive green 10.00 2.50

Views Type of Regular Issue

6b, 8b, View of San'a. 10b, Mocha coffee tree. 12b, Palace of the Rock, Wadi Dhahr. 16b, Palace, Ta'iz. 20b, 1i, Parade Ground, San'a.

1951 Wmk. 277 Photo. *Perf. 14*
C3 A14 6b blue 1.40 .50
C4 A14 8b dark brown 1.75 .60
C5 A14 10b dark green 2.25 1.40
C6 A13 12b dark blue 2.50 .80
C7 A14 16b lilac rose 3.00 .80
C8 A13 20b orange brown 3.75 1.25
C9 A13 1i dark red 10.00 3.00
Nos. C3-C9 (7) 24.65 8.35

Nos. C3 and C4 were used provisionally in 1957 for registry and foreign ordinary mail.

Type of Regular Issue

Designs: 12b, Palace of the Rock, Wadi Dhahr. 20b, Walls of Ibb.

Engraved and Photogravure

1952 Unwmk. *Perf. 14½, Imperf.*
C10 A15 12b grnsh blk, bl & brn 8.00 6.50
C11 A15 20b indigo, bl & brn 8.00 6.50

Flag-and-View Type

1952
C12 A16 1i dk brn, car & brt ultra 18.00 18.00

1952 Palace in Foreground
C13 A16 30b yel grn, car & gray 11.00 11.00

Leaning Minaret, Mosque of Ta'iz — AP6

1954 Photo. *Perf. 14*
C14 AP6 10b scarlet 3.25 .90
C15 AP6 12b dull blue 4.00 1.25
C16 AP6 20b olive bister 6.50 2.00
Nos. C14-C16 (3) 13.75 4.15

Accession of King Ahmed I, 5th anniv.

Type of Regular Issue

1959 Wmk. 318 *Perf. 13x13½*
C17 A21 6b orange & blk 1.00 .70
C18 A21 10b red & blk 1.75 1.25
C19 A21 16b brt violet & red 2.75 2.00
Nos. C17-C19 (3) 5.50 3.95

In 1959, four values of the 1931 issue and three values of the 1930 issue overprinted Air Mail 1959 were distributed. Value, set of 7 values, $27.50. Although these stamps were not regularly sold in Yemeni post offices, several values of these sets were used on airmail covers going abroad. Several of these stamps exist with inverted or doubled overprints.

Antiquities of Marib Type

Designs: 6b, Columns, Temple of the Moon God. 16b, Control tower and spillway of 2,700-year-old dam of Marib.

Perf. 11½
1961, Oct. 14 Unwmk. Photo.
C20 A27 6b lt bl grn & blk .85 .25
C21 A27 16b lt blue & blk 2.40 1.00

Exist imperf.
For overprints see Nos. C24, C25.

Yemen Arab Republic Buildings Type

6b, Bab al-Yemen, main gate of San'a, horiz. 16b, Palace of the Rock (Dar al-Hajar).

1961, Nov. 15
C22 A28 6b blk, lt bl & grn .85 .25
C23 A28 16b blk, rose & grn 2.25 .60

For overprints see Nos. C24A, C25A.

Nos. C20-C23 Ovptd. Like Nos. 144-158 in Dark Red or Black

Perf. 11½
1963, Jan. 1 Photo. Unwmk.
C24 A27 (a) 6b No. C20 .90 .90
C24A A28 (b) 6b No. C22 .90 .90
C25 A27 (a) 16b No. C21 2.75 2.75
C25A A28 (a) 16b No. C23 (B) 3.00 3.00

Proclamation of the Republic Type

1963, Mar. 15 *Perf. 11x11½, 11½x11*
C26 A34 8b Bayonette, torch 1.50 1.50
C27 A34 10b Jet, torch, tank 2.00 2.00
C28 A34 16b Flag, chain, torch 2.75 2.75

Nos. C27-C28 horiz.
An imperf. souvenir sheet containing one No. C28 exists. Value $10.

Nos. 25-29 Ovptd. in Black

Wmk. 258
1963, Sept. 1 Litho. *Perf. 12½*
C29 A5 6b slate blue & ultra 1.50 1.50
C29A A5 10b fawn & ultra 1.90 1.90
C29B A5 14b olive & ultra 2.25 2.25
C29C A5 20b yel grn & ultra 3.00 3.00
C29D A5 1i claret & ultra 6.50 6.50
Nos. C29-C29D (5) 15.15 15.15

Exist imperf. Value, set $25.

Spacecraft — AP6a

Various spacecraft.

1963, Dec. 5 Photo. *Perf. 13*
C29E AP6a ¼b multicolored .70 .50
C29F AP6a ⅓b multicolored .70 .50
C29G AP6a ½b multicolored .70 .50
C29H AP6a 4b multicolored 1.50 1.25
C29I AP6a 20b multicolored 5.00 5.00
Nos. C29E-C29I (5) 8.60 7.75

Exist imperf. Value, set $15. An imperf. souvenir sheet containing C29I also exists. Value $10.

Nos. C29E-C29G Overprinted in Black, Red Brown or Brown

1964-1966 Photo. *Perf. 13*
C29J AP6a ¼b On No. C29E 1.25 1.25
C29K AP6a ¼b On No. C29E (RB) 2.50 2.50
C29L AP6a ⅓b On No. C29F 1.25 1.25
C29M AP6a ⅓b On No. C29F (RB) 2.50 2.50
C29N AP6a ½b On No. C29G 1.25 1.25
C29O AP6a ½b On No. C29G (Br) 5.00 5.00
Nos. C29J-C29O (6) 13.75 13.75

Issued: Nos. C29J, C29L, C29N, 12/6/64. Nos. C29K, C29M, 1965. No. C29O, 1966.
Imperf. examples of Nos. C29H-C29I exist with the red brown overprint.

San'a Intl. Airport Type

Perf. 11½x11
1964, Oct. 1 Photo. Unwmk.
C30 A40 6b Sun, buildings, aircraft .70 .70

See note after No. 203.

APU 10th Anniv. Type

1964, Oct. 15 *Perf. 13½*
C31 A41 6b blue grn & blk 1.00 .80

An imperf. souvenir sheet of one exists containing No. C31. Value $3.

Deir Yassin Massacre Type

1965, Apr. 30 *Perf. 11x11½*
C32 A44 6b ver & brt org 1.00 .50

Library Type

1965, July 7 *Perf. 11½x11*
C33 A46 6b sepia, red & int blue .75 .50

An imperf. souvenir sheet of one exists containing No. C33. Value $2.50.

Butterflies — AP6b

Various butterflies.

1966, May 5 Photo. *Perf. 12½*
C33A AP6b 6b multicolored 2.50 2.50
C33B AP6b 8b multicolored 2.50 2.50
C33C AP6b 10b multicolored 5.00 5.00
C33D AP6b 16b multicolored 5.00 5.00
Nos. C33A-C33D (4) 15.00 15.00

Nos. C33A-C33D exist imperf. Value $20.

1968 Winter Olympic Games, Grenoble — AP6c

1967, Nov. 11 Litho. *Perf. 13¼*
C33E AP6c 5b gold & multi 10.00 10.00
C33F AP6c 10b gold & multi 2.10 .70
C33G AP6c 15b gold & multi 3.25 1.00
Nos. C33E-C33G (3) 15.35 11.70

Exist imperf. in silver. Perf. and imperf. souvenir sheets containing one No. C33G exist in both gold and silver. Value, each $30.

Konrad Adenauer (1876-1967) AP6d

1968, June Litho. *Perf. 11*
C33H AP6d 5b gold & black 1.90 .45
C33I AP6d 10b gold, blk & grn 3.75 .75
C33J AP6d 15b gold, blk & blue 5.50 1.00
Nos. C33H-C33J (3) 11.15 2.20

Exist imperf. in silver. Value, $18. Perf. and imperf. souvenir sheets containing one No. C33J exist in both gold and silver. Value, each $18.

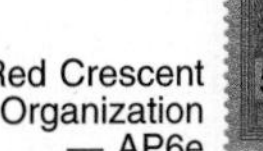

Red Crescent Organization — AP6e

1968 Litho. *Perf. 11*
C33K AP6e 5b gold & multi .90
C33L AP6e 10b gold & multi 1.75
C33M AP6e 15b gold & multi 2.75
Nos. C33K-C33M (3) 5.40

Exist imperf. in silver. Value, $7. An imperf. souvenir sheet containing one No. C33M exists in both silver and gold. Value, each $9.
For surcharge see No. C39A.

Vladimir Komarov (1927-1967), Soviet Cosmonaut — AP6f

1968 Litho. *Perf. 13½*
C33N AP6f 5b gold & multi 1.00
C33O AP6f 10b gold & multi 2.00
C33P AP6f 15b gold & multi 3.00
Nos. C33N-C33P (3) 6.00

Exist imperf. in silver. Value, $7. An imperf. souvenir sheet containing one No. C33P exists in gold. Value, $14.

Nos. C33H-C33J Overprinted in Black for Refugees

1968 Litho. *Perf. 11*
C33Q AP6d 5b gold & black 1.50
C33R AP6d 10b gold, blk & grn 3.00
C33S AP6d 15b gold, blk & blue 4.50
Nos. C33Q-C33S (3) 9.00

Exist imperf. in silver. Perf. and imperf. souvenir sheets containing one No. C33S exist in both gold and silver.

1968 Summer Olympic Games, Mexico City — AP6g

1968, July 2 Litho. *Perf. 13½*
C33T AP6g 5b gold & multi 1.00 .45
C33U AP6g 10b gold & multi 2.00 .75
C33V AP6g 15b gold & multi 3.00 1.25
Nos. C33T-C33V (3) 6.00 2.45

Exist imperf. in silver. Value, $7. Imperf. souvenir sheets containing one No. C33V exists in gold and silver.
For surcharge see No. C39B. Value, each $9.

Universal Declaration of Human Rights, 20th Anniv. — AP6h

1968, Oct. 20 Litho. *Perf. 13½*
C33W AP6g 5b gold & multi 1.00
C33X AP6g 10b gold & multi 2.00
C33Y AP6g 15b gold & multi 3.00
Nos. C33W-C33Y (3) 6.00

Exist imperf. in silver. Value, $7. An imperf. souvenir sheet containing one No. C33Y exists in gold. Value, $10.
For surcharge see No. C39C.

Lenin's Birth Centenary — AP7

1970, Aug. 15 Litho. *Perf. 12x12½*

C34 AP7 6b Public speech 1.40 1.10
C35 AP7 16b Meeting with Arab delegates 3.00 1.90

8th Anniv. of the Revolution AP8

1971, Jan. 24 *Perf. 13*

C36 AP8 5b Country estate .75
C37 AP8 7b Workers 1.10
C38 AP8 16b Handshake, flag, flowers, open book 1.50
Nos. C36-C38 (2) 2.25

A souv. sheet of 1 exists containing. No. C38. Value $5.

No. C38 Overprinted in Black

1971, Jan. 24

C39 AP8 16b multicolored 5.00 3.00

Nos. C33L, C33V and C33X Surcharged in Black

1971, Jan. 24 *Perf. 13*

C39A AP6e 40b On 10b #C33L, "40" is 4.5mm high
d. "40" is 3.5mm high
C39B AP6g 60b On 15b #C33V
f. Missing "B" in surcharge
C39C AP6h 80b On 10b #C33X
e. Missing "B" in surcharge

Revolution Type

1972, Nov. 25 Photo. *Perf. 13*

C40 A80 21b lilac, blk & multi 4.00 3.50

For surcharge see No. C46A.

Al-Aqsa Mosque Type

1973, Jan. 1 Photo. *Perf. 13½*

C41 A82 24b lt bl, blk & multi 3.00 2.50
a. Min. sheet of 1, imperf. 3.00 2.50

UNICEF Type

1973, Jan. 15 Photo. *Perf. 13*

C42 A83 18b lt bl, blk & multi 1.90 1.50
a. Min. sheet of 1, imperf. 3.25 2.50

For surcharge see No. C46.

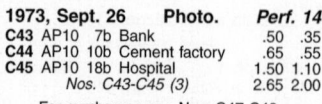

11th Anniv. of Revolution AP10

1973, Sept. 26 Photo. *Perf. 14*

C43 AP10 7b Bank .50 .35
C44 AP10 10b Cement factory .65 .55
C45 AP10 18b Hospital 1.50 1.10
Nos. C43-C45 (3) 2.65 2.00

For surcharges see Nos. C47-C48.

Nos. C40, C42, C43, C45 Surcharged in Black or Red with New Value and Bars

1975, Nov. 15

C46 A83 75f on 18b lt bl, blk & multi 2.50 2.50
C46A A80 75f on 21b #C40 (R) 5.00 5.00
C47 AP10 90f on 7b multi 5.50 2.75
C48 AP10 120f on 18b multi (R) 4.25 4.25
a. Overprinted in black — —
Nos. C46-C48 (4) 17.25 14.50

Argentina 1978 World Cup Type

World cup emblem and various soccer players.

1980, Mar. 30 Photo. *Perf. 14*

C49 A99 60f gold & multi 1.25 .60
C50 A99 75f gold & multi 1.50 .70
C51 A99 80f gold & multi 1.80 .90
C52 A99 100f gold & multi 2.25 1.00
Nos. C49-C52 (4) 4.55 3.20

Two 225f souvenir sheets exist. Value, perf. $12, imperf. $15.

IYC Type

1980, Apr. 1 *Perf. 13½*

C53 A100 80f Girl, bird 3.50 1.25
C54 A100 100f Boy, butterfly, flower 3.50 1.25
C55 A100 150f Boy, butterfly, flower, diff. 5.00 1.75
Nos. C53-C55 (3) 10.50 4.25

Two 200f souvenir sheets exist. Value $12 each.

Scouting Type of 1980

1980, May 1 Photo. *Perf. 13½x14*

C56 A101 60f Bicycling 2.00 .80
C57 A101 75f Fencing 2.40 1.10
C58 A101 120f Butterfly catching 3.75 1.50
Nos. C56-C58 (3) 8.15 3.40

Two 300f souvenir sheets exist. Value $15 each.

Argentina 1978 Winners' Type

World cup emblem and various soccer players.

1980, June 1 Photo. *Perf. 14*

C59 A102 60f gold & multi 1.50 .50
C60 A102 75f gold & multi 2.10 .65
C61 A102 80f gold & multi 2.25 .75
C62 A102 100f gold & multi 2.40 1.10
Nos. C59-C62 (4) 5.50 3.00

Two 225f souvenir sheets exist. Value $12 each.

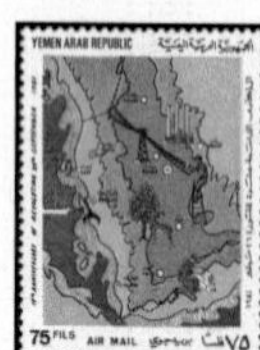

19th Anniv. of Sept. 26th Revolution (1981) — AP11

1982, Jan. 25 Litho. *Perf. 14*

C63 AP11 75f Map .75 .35
C64 AP11 125f Map in sunset 1.00 .50
C65 AP11 325f Dove in natl. colors 3.00 2.00
a. Souvenir sheet of 1 8.00 8.00
C66 AP11 400f Jets 4.00 2.00
Nos. C63-C66 (4) 8.75 4.85

Al-Hasan Ibn Al-Hamadani, Writer AP12

1982, Feb. 1

C67 AP12 125f green & multi 1.25 .60
C68 AP12 325f blue & multi 3.25 1.50

Souvenir Sheet

C69 AP12 375f multi 9.00 9.00

No. C69 contains one stamp (36x46mm).
For surcharge see No. C138.

World Food Day — AP13

Designs: No. C76a, Eggplants. No. C76b, Tomatoes. No. C76c, Beets, peas. No. C76d, Cauliflower, carrots. No. C77a, Dove. No. C77b, Water birds. No. C77c, Fish. No. C77d, Geese.

1982, Mar. 1 Litho. *Perf. 14*

C70 AP13 25f Rabbits 1.25 .45
C71 AP13 50f Rooster, Hens 1.50 .90
C72 AP13 60f Turkeys 1.75 1.00
C73 AP13 75f Sheep 2.50 1.25
C74 AP13 100f Cattle 3.50 1.50
C75 AP13 125f Deer 4.00 1.90
Nos. C70-C75 (6) 14.50 7.00

Souvenir Sheets

C76 Sheet of 4 10.00
a.-d. AP13 100f, any single 2.50
C77 Sheet of 4 10.00
a.-d. AP13 125f, any single 2.50

For surcharges see Nos. C139, C144.
Nos. C70-C75 exist imperf. (Value, set $50) and in souvenir sheets (Value, set $45).

1980 Summer Olympics, Moscow — AP14

1982, Apr. 1

C78 AP14 25f Gymnastics 1.25 .50
C79 AP14 50f Pole vault 1.50 .65
C80 AP14 60f Javelin 1.75 .75
C81 AP14 75f Running 2.50 1.00
C82 AP14 100f Basketball 3.50 1.50
C83 AP14 125f Soccer 4.00 1.75
Nos. C78-C83 (6) 14.50 6.15

Nos. C78-C81 exist imperf. (Value, set $50) and in souvenir sheets (Value, set $45).
Two souvenir sheets of 4 exist: 100f, picturing boxing, wrestling, canoeing, swimming (Value $12.50), and 125f, picturing weight lifting, discus, long jump, fencing (Value $15).
For surcharges see Nos. C140, C145.

Aviation AP15

Various space and aircraft.

1982, May 21

C86 AP15 25f multi 1.25 .50
C87 AP15 50f multi 1.50 .60
C88 AP15 60f multi 1.75 .75
C89 AP15 75f multi 2.50 1.00
C90 AP15 100f multi 3.50 1.40
C91 AP15 125f multi 4.00 1.60
Nos. C86-C91 (6) 14.50 5.85

Nos. C86-C91 exist imperf. (Value set, $50) and in souvenir sheets (Value, set $45).
Two souvenir sheets of 4 exist, 100f and 125f, picturing various aircraft and satellites. Values $12.50 and $15, respectively.
For surcharges see Nos. C141, C146.

Intl. Year of the Disabled AP16

Designs: Nos. C94-C99, Diff. flowers.
No. C100a, Emblem, natl. flag. b, Emblem on globe. c, Natl. colors, UN emblems. d, Disabled man, gifts, nurse.
No. C101a, Flags, globe and nurse. b, UN emblems, natl. flag. c, Emblem, disabled man. d, UN emblem, nurse.

1982, June 1

C94 AP16 25f multi 1.25 .60
C95 AP16 50f multi 1.50 .75
C96 AP16 60f multi 1.75 .90
C97 AP16 75f multi 2.50 1.25
C98 AP16 100f multi 3.50 1.75
C99 AP16 125f multi 4.00 2.00
Nos. C94-C99 (6) 14.50 7.25

Souvenir Sheets

C100 Sheet of 4 12.50
a.-d. AP16 100f, any single 3.00
C101 Sheet of 4 15.00
a.-d. AP16 125f, any single 3.50

Nos. C94-C99 exist imperf. (Value, set $50) and in souvenir sheets (Value, set $45).
For surcharge see No. C147.

Telecommunications Progress — AP17

Designs: 25f, FNRR communication center. 50f, Dish receivers, satellite, globe. 60f, Broadcast towers, dish receivers. 75f, Receivers, birds over plain. 100f, Receivers, satellite, telegraph key. No. C107, Receivers, passenger jet, Earth.
No. C108a, Receivers, Earth. b, Earth, television, flag and camera. c, Computer. d, Skyscraper, Earth, telephone.
No. C109a, Receivers, satellite, ship. b, Communication center, bolts of energy, receivers. c, Receivers, jet, ship, train, car, carriage. d, Radar.

1982, July 1 Litho. *Perf. 14*

C102 AP17 25f multi 1.00 .50
C103 AP17 50f multi 1.25 .60
C104 AP17 60f multi 1.50 .75
C105 AP17 75f multi 2.25 1.00
C106 AP17 100f multi 3.25 1.50
C107 AP17 125f multi 3.75 1.75
Nos. C102-C107 (6) 13.00 6.10

Souvenir Sheets

C108 Sheet of 4 10.00
a.-d. AP17 100f any single 2.50
C109 Sheet of 4 12.00
a.-d. AP17 100f any single 3.00

Nos. C102-C107 exist imperf. (Value, set $50) and in souvenir sheets (Value, set $45).
For surcharges see Nos. C142, C148.

TB Bacillus Centenary AP18

1982, Aug. 1 Litho. *Perf. 14*

C110 AP18 25f multi 1.00 .50
C111 AP18 50f multi 1.25 .60
C112 AP18 60f multi 1.50 .75
C113 AP18 75f multi 2.25 1.00
C114 AP18 100f multi 3.25 1.50
C115 AP18 125f multi 3.75 1.75
Nos. C110-C115 (6) 13.00 6.10

Souvenir Sheets

C116 Sheet of 4, Fruit 14.00
a. AP18 100f, any single 3.50
C117 Sheet of 4, Flowers 14.00
a. AP18 125f, any single 3.50

Nos. C110-C115 exist imperf. (Value, set $20) and in souvenir sheets (Value, set $40).
For surcharges see Nos. C143, C149.

1982 World Cup Soccer Championships, Spain — AP19

Various soccer plays.

1982, Sept. 1 ***Perf. 14***

C118	AP19 25f multi		1.25	.50
C119	AP19 50f multi		1.50	.60
C120	AP19 60f multi		1.75	.75
C121	AP19 75f multi		2.50	1.00
C122	AP19 100f multi		3.50	1.50
C123	AP19 125f multi		4.00	1.75
	Nos. C118-C123 (6)		14.50	6.10

Nos. C118-C123 exist imperf. (Value, set $50) and in souvenir sheets (Value, set $72).

Palestinian Children's Day — AP20

1982, Oct. 20

C126	AP20 75f Boy	1.50	1.00
C127	AP20 125f Girl	2.50	2.00
C128	AP20 325f Boy and girl	6.00	4.00
a.	Souvenir sheet of 1	8.00	8.00
	Nos. C126-C128 (3)	10.00	7.00

Arab Postal Union, 30th Anniv. AP21

1982, Dec. 1

C129	AP21 75f yellow & multi	1.25	1.00
C130	AP21 125f green & multi	2.25	1.75
C131	AP21 325f magenta & multi	4.00	2.00
a.	Souvenir sheet of 1	8.00	8.00
	Nos. C129-C131 (3)	7.50	4.75

1984 Summer Olympics, Los Angeles AP22

1984, Nov. 15

C132	AP22 20f Wrestling	.60	.25
C133	AP22 30f Boxing	.90	.30
C134	AP22 40f Running	1.25	.50
C135	AP22 60f Hurdling	1.50	.70
C136	AP22 150f Pole vault	2.25	1.10
C137	AP22 325f Javelin throw	3.50	1.75
	Nos. C132-C137 (6)	10.00	4.60

Nos. C132-C137 exist imperf. (Value, set $50) and in souvenir sheets (Value, set $50).

Two souvenir sheets of four 75f stamps exist picturing water sports, gymnastics, weightlifting, shot put and discus throwing. Value $12.50 each.

Republic of Yemen

No. C67 Surcharged Nos. 459, 461, 463, 466, 474, 483, 486, 522, C73, C75, C81, C83, C89, C91, C97, C105, C107, C113 & C115 Surcharged with New Value and "AIR MAIL"

1993, Jan. 1 ***Perfs, etc. as Before***

C138	AP12 3r on 125f #C67	7.00	4.00
C139	AP13 3r on 125f #C75	12.00	7.00
C140	AP14 3r on 125f #C83	7.00	4.00
C141	AP15 3r on 125f #C91	7.00	4.00
C142	AP17 3r on 125f #C107	7.00	4.00
C143	AP18 3r on 125f #C115	7.00	4.00
C144	AP13 5r on 75f #C73	12.00	7.00
C145	AP14 5r on 75f #C81	40.00	20.00
C146	AP15 5r on 75f #C89	16.00	7.00
C147	AP16 5r on 75f #C97	8.00	5.00
C148	AP17 5r on 75f #C105	8.00	5.00
C149	AP18 5r on 75f #C113	8.00	5.00
C150	A126 8r on 425f #459	10.00	6.00
C151	A127 8r on 425f #461	10.00	6.00
C152	A128 8r on 425f #463	10.00	6.00
C153	A129 8r on 425f #466	10.00	6.00
C154	A130 8r on 425f #474	10.00	6.00
C155	A132 8r on 425f #483	10.00	6.00
C156	A133 8r on 425f #486	10.00	6.00
C157	A142 12r on 850f #522	15.00	8.00
	Nos. C138-C157 (20)	224.00	126.00

Size and location of surcharge varies.

POSTAGE DUE STAMPS

D1

1942 **Litho.** **Wmk. 258** ***Perf. 12½***

J1	D1 1b org & yel grn	.25	.25
J2	D1 2b org & yel grn	.25	.25
J3	D1 4b org & yel grn	.45	.45
J4	D1 6b org & brt ultra	.55	.55
J5	D1 8b org & brt ultra	.80	.80
J6	D1 10b org & brt ultra	1.00	1.00
J7	D1 12b org & brt ultra	1.50	1.50
J8	D1 20b org & brt ultra	3.00	3.00
	Nos. J1-J8 (8)	7.80	7.80

Yemen had no postage due system. Nos. J1-J8 were used for regular postage.

See Nos. 66-67 for surcharges.

Yemen Arab Republic

Animals Type of Regular Issue Inscribed "Postage Due"

1964, Aug. 15 **Photo.** ***Perf. 12x11½***

J9	A39d 4b Gazelles	1.75	.60
J10	A39d 12b Buffalo	3.50	1.50
J11	A39d 20b Arabian horse	6.50	2.50
	Nos. J9-J11 (3)	11.75	4.60

Flower Type of Regular Issue Inscribed "Postage Due"

1964, Sept. 1 **Photo.** ***Perf. 11½x12***

J12	A39e 4b Like No. 199C	1.40	1.00
J13	A39e 12b Like No. 199B	3.50	2.00
J14	A39e 20b Like No. 199D	5.00	3.50
	Nos. J12-J14 (3)	9.90	6.50

Nos. 209G-209K Overprinted in Black

Perf. 14x14½, 14½x15

1966, Mar. 5 **Photo.**

J15	A43a 6b On No. 209G	4.00	2.50
J16	A43a 8b On No. 209H	4.25	3.00
J17	A43a 12b On No. 209I	6.00	3.50
J18	A43a 20b On No. 209J	10.00	6.50
J19	A43a 1r On No. 209K	20.00	12.50
	Nos. J15-J19 (5)	44.25	28.00

World Cup Soccer Type of Regular Issue Inscribed "Postage Due"

Designs: No. J20, Goalie defending shot on goal. No. J21, Three players. No. J22, Jules Rimet Cup emblem.

1966, May 29 **Litho.** ***Perf. 11***

J20	A51 4b multicolored	1.75	1.25
J21	A51 5b multicolored	3.00	2.00
J22	A51 20b multicolored	6.00	4.00
	Nos. J20-J22 (3)	10.75	7.25

Fruit Type of Regular Issue Inscribed "Postage Due"

1967, Feb. 10 **Litho.** ***Perf. 12½x12***

J23	A56 6b Bananas	1.60	1.25
J24	A56 8b Figs	2.50	1.75
J25	A56 10b Green grapes	3.50	2.25
	Nos. J23-J25 (3)	7.60	5.25

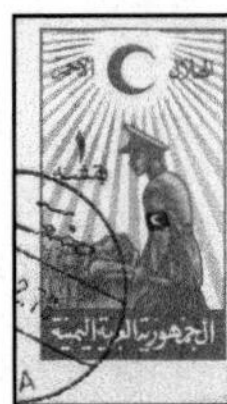

Two stamps of this design were released in 1968 or 1978. While they have been called postal tax stamps, questions about their status and use exist. The editors would like more information about these stamps and would like to examine unused and on cover examples.

YEMEN, PEOPLE'S DEMOCRATIC REPUBLIC OF

'pē-pəls ri-'pə-blik of 'ye-mən

LOCATION — Southern Arabia
GOVT. — Republic
AREA — 111,074 sq. mi.
POP. — 2,030,000 (est. 1981)
CAPITAL — Aden

The People's Republic of Southern Yemen was proclaimed Nov. 30, 1967, when the Federation of South Arabia achieved independence. It consisted of the former British colony of Aden and the protectorates. The name was changed to People's Democratic Republic of Yemen on Nov. 30, 1970. See South Arabia.

The Yemen Arab Republic and the People's Republic of Yemen planned a 30-month unification process scheduled for completion by November 1992. While government ministries merged, both currencies remained valid. A civil war in 1994 delayed the merger.

1,000 Fils = 1 Dinar

Catalogue values for all unused stamps in this country are for Never Hinged items.

People's Republic of Southern Yemen

South Arabia Nos. 3-16 Overprinted in Red or Blue

Nos. 1-10

Nos. 11-14

Perf. 14½x14

1968, Apr. 1 **Photo.** **Unwmk.**

1	A1 5f blue	.25	.25
2	A1 10f lt vio bl	.25	.25
3	A1 15f bl grn	.25	.25
4	A1 20f green	.25	.25
5	A1 25f org brn (B)	.25	.25
6	A1 30f lemon	.25	.25
7	A1 35f red brn (B)	.35	.25
8	A1 50f rose red (B)	.45	.35
9	A1 65f lt yel grn	.60	.40
10	A1 75f rose car (B)	.75	.55
11	A2 100f multi (B)	1.10	.70
12	A2 250f multi	2.25	1.40
13	A2 500f multi (B)	4.50	2.75
14	A2 1d vio & multi	10.00	7.00
	Nos. 1-14 (14)	21.50	14.90

Globe and Flag — A1

Designs: 15f, Revolutionist with broken chain and flames, vert. 50f, Aden Harbor. 100f, Cotton picking.

1968, May 25 **Litho.** ***Perf. 13x12½***

15	A1 10f multi	.25	.25
16	A1 15f multi	.25	.25
17	A1 50f multi	.55	.55
18	A1 100f multi	1.50	1.50
	Nos. 15-18 (4)	2.55	2.55

Independence Day, Nov. 30, 1967.

Girl Scouts at Campfire — A2

Designs: 25f, Three Girl Scouts, vert. 50f, Three Girl Scout leaders.

Perf. 13½

1968, Sept. 21 **Litho.** **Unwmk.**

19	A2 10f ultra & sepia	.50	.50
20	A2 25f org brn & Prus bl	.75	.75
21	A2 50f yel, bl & brn	1.40	1.40
	Nos. 19-21 (3)	2.65	2.65

Girl Scout movement in Southern Yemen, established 1966 (in Aden).

Revolutionary A3

"Freedom-Socialism-Unity" A4

Design: 30f, Radfan Mountains where first revolutionary fell.

1968, Oct. 14 **Unwmk.** ***Perf. 13***

22	A3 20f brn & lt bl	.30	.30
23	A3 30f grn & brn	.45	.45
24	A4 100f ver & yel	1.10	1.10
	Nos. 22-24 (3)	1.85	1.85

Revolution Day (revolution of Oct. 14, 1963).

King of Ausan, Alabaster Statue — A5

Antiquities of Southern Yemen: 35f, African-type sculpture of a man. 50f, Winged bull, Assyrian-type bas-relief, horiz. 65f, Bull's head (Moon God), alabaster plaque, 230 B.C., horiz.

1968, Dec. 28 **Litho.** ***Perf. 13***

25	A5 5f olive & bister	.25	.25
26	A5 35f maroon & lt bl	.50	.50
27	A5 50f bister & blue	1.10	1.10
28	A5 65f lt grnsh bl & lilac	1.40	1.40
	Nos. 25-28 (4)	3.25	3.25

A6

Martyr Monument, Steamer Point, Aden.

1969, Feb. 11 **Litho.** ***Perf. 13***

29	A6 15f yellow & multi	.25	.25
30	A6 35f emerald & multi	.25	.25
31	A6 100f orange & multi	1.50	1.50
	Nos. 29-31 (3)	2.00	2.00

Issued for Martyr Day.

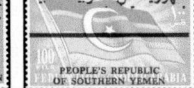

A7

Albert Thomas Monument, Geneva, and ILO emblem.

1969, June 1 Litho. *Perf. 13*

32	A7	10f brt grn, blk & lt brn	.25	.25
33	A7	35f car rose, blk & lt brn	.70	.60

50th anniv. of the ILO, and to honor founder Albert Thomas.

Classroom A8

1969, Sept. 8 Litho. *Perf. 13*

34	A8	35f orange & multi	.50	.35
35	A8	100f yellow & multi	1.40	1.25

International Literacy Day, Sept. 8.

Mahatma Gandhi — A9

1969, Sept. 27 Litho. *Perf. 13*

36	A9	35f lt ultra & vio brn	1.75	.60

Mohandas K. Gandhi (1869-1948), leader in India's fight for independence.

Family — A10

1969, Oct. 1

37	A10	25f lt grn & multi	.50	.40
38	A10	75f car rose & multi	1.40	.90

Issued for Family Day.

UN Headquarters, NYC — A11

1969, Oct. 24 *Perf. 13*

39	A11	20f rose red & multi	.50	.35
40	A11	65f emer & multi	1.40	.70

Issued for United Nations Day.

Map and Flag of Southern Yemen — A12

40f, 50f, Tractors, flag (agricultural progress).

1969, Nov. 30 Litho. Unwmk.

Size: 41x24½mm

41	A12	15f multi	.25	.25
42	A12	35f multi	.45	.25

Size: 37x37mm

43	A12	40f blue & multi	.55	.45
44	A12	50f brown & multi	.90	.60
		Nos. 41-44 (4)	2.15	1.55

Second anniversary of independence.

Map of Arab League Countries, Flag and Emblem — A13

1970, Mar. 22 Unwmk. *Perf. 13*

45	A13	35f lt bl & multi	.85	.35

25th anniversary of the Arab League.

Lenin — A14

1970, Apr. 22 Litho. *Perf. 13*

46	A14	75f multi	1.50	.60

Lenin (1870-1924), Russian communist leader.

Fighter — A15

Designs: 35f, Underground soldier and plane destroyed on ground. 50f, Fighting people hailing Arab liberation flag, horiz.

1970, May 15

47	A15	15f grn, red & blk	.25	.25
48	A15	35f grn, bl, red & blk	.55	.55
49	A15	50f grn, blk & red	.85	.70
		Nos. 47-49 (3)	1.65	1.50

Issued for Palestine Day.

UPU Headquarters, Bern — A16

1970, May 22 Litho. *Perf. 13*

50	A16	15f org & brt grn	.60	.25
51	A16	65f yel & car rose	1.40	.60

New UPU Headquarters in Bern.

Yemeni Costume — A17

Regional Costumes: 15f, 20f, Women's costumes. 50f, Three men of Aden.

1970, July 2 Litho. *Perf. 13*

52	A17	10f yel & multi	.40	.25
53	A17	15f lt lil & multi	.40	.25
54	A17	20f lt bl & multi	.65	.25
55	A17	50f multi	1.25	.45
		Nos. 52-55 (4)	2.70	1.20

Camel and Calf A18

Designs: 25f, Goats. 35f, Arabian oryx. 65f, Socotra dwarf cows.

1970, Aug. 31 Litho. *Perf. 13*

56	A18	15f dk brn & multi	.40	.25
57	A18	25f car rose & multi	.65	.45
58	A18	35f ultra & multi	1.20	.75
59	A18	65f brt grn & multi	2.00	1.25
		Nos. 56-59 (4)	4.25	2.70

A19

35f, Natl. Front Organization Headquarters. 50f, Farm worker, 1970, battle scene, 1963.

1970, Oct. 14 Litho. *Perf. 13*

Size: 41½x29½mm

60	A19	25f multi	.40	.25

Size: 56½x27mm

61	A19	35f multi	.50	.45

Size: 41x24½mm

62	A19	50f multi	1.90	1.25
		Nos. 60-62 (3)	2.80	1.95

7th anniversary of Oct. 14 Revolution.

UN Headquarters, Emblem — A20

1970, Oct. 24 Litho. *Perf. 13*

63	A20	10f org & bl	.45	.25
64	A20	65f brt pink & bl	1.50	.80

25th anniversary of the United Nations.

People's Democratic Republic of Yemen

Temples at Philae A21

1971, Feb. 1 Litho. *Perf. 13½x13*

65	A21	5f violet & multi	.25	.25
66	A21	35f blue & multi	.65	.40
67	A21	65f green & multi	1.60	.90
		Nos. 65-67 (3)	2.50	1.55

UNESCO campaign to save the monuments in Nubia.

Scales, Book and Sword — A22

1971, Mar. 1 *Perf. 13x12½*

68	A22	10f brt pink & multi	.25	.25
69	A22	15f brt grn & multi	.25	.25
70	A22	35f lt ultra & multi	.65	.65
71	A22	50f rose & multi	.85	.85
		Nos. 68-71 (4)	2.00	2.00

First Constitution, 1971.

Men of 3 Races, Human Rights Emblem — A23

1971, Mar. 21

72	A23	20f lt bl & multi	.25	.25
73	A23	35f grn & multi	.75	.75
74	A23	75f lt vio & multi	1.10	1.10
		Nos. 72-74 (3)	2.10	2.10

Intl. year against racial discrimination.

Map and Flag — A24

"Brothers' Blood" Tree, Socotra Island — A25

1971-77 Litho. *Perf. 13½*

75	A24	5f yel & multi	.25	.25
76	A24	10f grn & multi	.25	.25
77	A24	15f yel & multi	.25	.25
78	A24	20f org & multi	.25	.25
79	A24	25f bl & multi	.25	.25
80	A24	35f red org & multi	.35	.25
81	A24	40f vio & multi	.50	.25
82	A24	50f yel grn & multi	.65	.45
82A	A24	60f red & multi	1.40	.60
83	A24	65f pale vio & multi	.90	.65
84	A24	80f org brn & multi	1.00	.80
84A	A24	90f ol & multi	1.40	.75

Perf. 13

84B	A25	110f brn & multi	2.00	.95
85	A25	125f ultra & multi	1.60	1.50
86	A25	250f org & multi	2.90	2.00
87	A25	500f multi	6.00	4.00
88	A25	1d grn & multi	13.50	8.00
		Nos. 75-88 (17)	33.45	21.45

Issued: #82A, 84A-84B, 10/17/77; others, 4/1/71.

See Nos. 332-333. For surcharges see Yemen Nos. 628, 638.

Machine Gun and Map — A26

Designs: 45f, Woman fighter and flame, horiz. 50f, Fighter, factories and rainbow.

1971, June 9 Litho. *Perf. 12½x13*

89	A26	15f multi	.25	.25
90	A26	45f green & multi	.65	.45
91	A26	50f multi	1.10	.75
		Nos. 89-91 (3)	2.00	1.45

Armed revolution in the Arabian Gulf.

Arms with Wrench and Cogwheel — A27

25f, Torch, factories, symbols. 65f, Windmill.

1971, June 22

92	A27	15f blue & multi	*.25*	*.25*
93	A27	25f multi	*.75*	*.55*
94	A27	65f multi	*1.25*	*.75*
		Nos. 92-94 (3)	*2.25*	*1.55*

2nd anniversary of the revolution of June 22, 1969 (Corrective Movement).

A 20f picturing a fighter holding rifle and flag, with flag colors transposed, was withdrawn on day of issue.

Revolutionary Emblem — A28

40f, Map of southern Arabia & flag of republic.

1971, Sept. 26

95	A28	10f yellow & multi	.25	.25
96	A28	40f lt grn & multi	.75	.55

9th anniv. of the revolution of Sept. 26.

Gamal Abdel Nasser — A29

1971, Sept. 28 Litho. *Perf. 12½x13*

97	A29	65f multi	1.25	.75

1st anniv. of the death of Gamal Abdel Nasser (1918-1970), President of Egypt.

UNICEF Emblem, Children of the World — A30

1971, Dec. 11 *Perf. 13x13½*

98 A30 15f org, car & blk .25 .25
99 A30 40f lt ultra, car & blk .40 .35
100 A30 50f yel grn, car & blk .70 .55
Nos. 98-100 (3) 1.35 1.15

25th anniv. of UNICEF.

Pigeons — A31

Birds: 40f, Partridge. 65f, Partridge and guinea fowl. 100f, European kite.

1971, Dec. 22 *Perf. 13½x13*

101 A31 5f bl, blk & car .35 .25
102 A31 40f salmon & multi 1.25 .60
103 A31 65f brt grn, blk & car 3.00 1.10
104 A31 100f yel, blk & car 5.25 2.25
Nos. 101-104 (4) 9.85 4.20

Dhow under Construction A32

Design: 80f, Dhow under sail, vert.

1972, Feb. 15 *Perf. 13½x13, 13x13½*

105 A32 25f bl, brn & yel .75 .45
106 A32 80f lt bl & multi 2.40 1.60

Band — A33

Designs: 25f, 40f, 80f, Various folk dances.

1972, Apr. 8 **Litho.** *Perf. 13*

107 A33 10f lt grn & multi .25 .25
108 A33 25f org & multi .35 .25
109 A33 40f red & multi .80 .45
110 A33 80f blue & multi 1.50 .90
Nos. 107-110 (4) 2.90 1.85

Palestinian Fighter and Barbed Wire — A34

1972, May 15

111 A34 5f emerald & multi .30 .25
112 A34 20f blue & multi .60 .35
113 A34 65f org ver & multi 1.50 .85
Nos. 111-113 (3) 2.40 1.45

Struggle for Palestine liberation.

Militia Women on Parade — A35

Design: 25f, Policemen on parade.

1972, June 20 **Litho.** *Perf. 13½*

114 A35 25f lt bl & multi .60 .25
115 A35 80f bl grn & multi 2.50 1.50
a. Souv. sheet of 2, #114-115 9.00 9.00

Police Day. No. 115a sold for 150f.

Start of Bicycle Race — A36

15f Parade of young women. 40f, Yemeni Guides & Scouts on parade. 80f, Acrobats, vert.

1972, July 20 **Litho.** *Perf. 13½*

116 A36 10f lt bl & multi .40 .25
117 A36 15f multi .55 .25
118 A36 40f buff & multi 1.00 .60
119 A36 80f lt ultra & multi 1.60 .90
Nos. 116-119 (4) 3.55 2.00

Turtle — A37

1972, Sept. 2 **Litho.** *Perf. 13*

120 A37 15f shown .90 .25
121 A37 40f Sailfish 1.10 .70
122 A37 65f Kingfish 1.75 .90
123 A37 125f Spiny lobster 3.25 1.60
Nos. 120-123 (4) 7.00 3.45

Book Year Emblem — A38

1972, Sept. 9

124 A38 40f red, ultra & yel .75 .50
125 A38 65f org, ultra & yel 1.25 .80

International Book Year 1972.

Farm Couple and Fields — A39

1972, Nov. 23 **Litho.** *Perf. 13*

126 A39 10f orange & multi .25 .25
127 A39 25f rose lilac & multi .70 .45
128 A39 40f red & multi 1.25 .80
Nos. 126-128 (3) 2.20 1.50

Lands Day, publicizing land reforms.

Militia — A40

20f, Soldier guarding village. 65f, Industrial, agricultural and educational progress, vert.

1972, Dec. 2 **Litho.** *Perf. 13*

129 A40 5f multi .25 .25
130 A40 20f multi .25 .25
131 A40 65f multi 1.60 1.60
a. Souv. sheet of 3, #129-131, imperf. 4.00 4.00
Nos. 129-131 (3) 2.10 2.10

5th anniversary of independence.

Census Chart — A41

1973, Apr. 3 **Litho.** *Perf. 12½x13½*

132 A41 25f org, emer & ol .25 .25
133 A41 40f rose, bl & vio 1.25 1.25

Population census 1973.

WHO Emblem and "25" — A42

5f, "25" and WHO emblem, vert. 125f, "25" and WHO emblem.

1973, Apr. 7 *Perf. 14x12½, 12½x14*

134 A42 5f multicolored .25 .25
135 A42 20f shown .25 .25
136 A42 125f multicolored 2.10 2.10
Nos. 134-136 (3) 2.60 2.60

25th anniv. of the WHO.

Elephant Bay — A43

Tourist Publicity: 20f, Taweels Tanks Reservoir, vert. 25f, Shibam Town. 100f, Al-Mohdar Mosque, Tarim.

1973, June 9 **Litho.** *Perf. 13*

137 A43 20f multi .25 .25
138 A43 25f multi .25 .25
139 A43 40f multi 1.50 1.50
140 A43 100f multi 1.75 1.75
Nos. 137-140 (4) 3.75 3.75

Office Buildings and Slum, Aden — A44

Design: 80f, Intersection, Aden, vert.

1973, Aug. 4 **Litho.** *Perf. 13*

141 A44 20f multi .25 .25
142 A44 80f multi 1.75 1.75

Nationalization of buildings.

Army Unit — A45

People's Army: 20f, Four marching soldiers. 40f, Sailors on parade. 80f, Tanks.

1973, Sept. 1

143 A45 10f multi .25 .25
144 A45 20f multi .25 .25
145 A45 40f multi 1.00 1.00
146 A45 80f multi 1.40 1.40
Nos. 143-146 (4) 2.90 2.90

FAO Emblem, Loading Food — A46

Design: 80f, Workers and grain sacks.

1973, Dec. 19 **Litho.** *Perf. 13*

147 A46 20f blue & multi .25 .25
148 A46 80f blue & multi 1.50 .90

World Food Program, 10th anniversary.

Letter and UPU Emblem — A47

UPU Emblem and Yemeni Flag — A48

Map of Yemen, UPU Emblem — A49

UPU cent.: 20f, "100" formed by people, and UPU emblem.

1974, Oct. 9 **Litho.** *Perf. 12½x13½*

149 A47 5f multi .25 .25
150 A47 20f multi .45 .25
151 A48 40f multi .70 .70
152 A49 125f multi 1.40 1.25
Nos. 149-152 (4) 2.80 2.45

Irrigation System A50

Progress in Agriculture: 20f, Bulldozer pushing soil. 100f, Tractors plowing field.

1974 **Litho.** *Perf. 13*

153 A50 10f multi .25 .25
154 A50 20f multi .25 .25
155 A50 100f multi 1.50 1.50
Nos. 153-155 (3) 2.00 2.00

Lathe Operator — A51

Industrial progress: 40f, Printers. 80f, Women textile workers, horiz.

1975, May 1 **Litho.** *Perf. 13*

156 A51 10f multi .25 .25
157 A51 40f multi .60 .60
158 A51 80f multi 1.20 1.00
Nos. 156-158 (3) 2.05 1.85

Yemeni Woman — A52

Designs: Various women's costumes.

1975, Nov. 15 **Litho.** *Perf. 11½x12*

159 A52 5f blk & ocher .25 .25
160 A52 10f blk & vio .25 .25
161 A52 15f blk & olive .25 .25
162 A52 25f blk & rose lil .45 .45
163 A52 40f blk & Prus bl .75 .75
164 A52 50f blk & org brn 1.10 1.10
Nos. 159-164 (6) 3.05 3.05

Women Factory Workers, IWY Emblem — A53

1975, Dec. 30 **Litho.** *Perf. 12x11½*

165 A53 40f blk & salmon .60 .60
166 A53 50f blk & yel grn 1.00 1.00

International Women's Year 1975.

Soccer Player and Field — A54

Designs: Different scenes from soccer.

1976, Apr. 1 Litho. *Perf. 11½x12*
167 A54 5f lt bl & brn .25 .25
168 A54 40f yel & green .70 .70
169 A54 80f salmon & vio 1.10 1.10
Nos. 167-169 (3) 2.05 2.05

Rocket Take-off from Moon — A55

15f, Alexander Satalov. 40f, Lunokhod on moon, horiz. 65f, Valentina Tereshkova, rocket.

Perf. 11½x12, 12x11½
1976, Apr. 17 Litho.
170 A55 10f multi .25 .25
171 A55 15f multi .25 .25
172 A55 40f multi 1.00 1.00
173 A55 65f multi 1.25 1.25
Nos. 170-173 (4) 2.75 2.75

Soviet cosmonauts and space program.

Traffic Policemen — A56

1977, Apr. 16 Litho. *Perf. 14*
174 A56 25f red & blk .60 .60
175 A56 60f yel & blk 1.25 1.25
176 A56 75f grn & blk 1.50 1.50
177 A56 110f dp bl & blk 2.00 2.00
Nos. 174-177 (4) 5.35 5.35

Traffic change to right side of road.

APU Emblem — A57

1977, Apr. 12 Litho. *Perf. 13½*
178 A57 20f lt bl & multi .25 .25
179 A57 60f gray & multi .80 .80
180 A57 70f lt grn & multi 1.00 1.00
181 A57 90f bl grn & multi 1.10 1.10
Nos. 178-181 (4) 3.15 3.15

Arab Postal Union, 25th anniversary.

Congress Decree and Red Star — A58

Designs: 25f, Pres. Salim Rubi'a Ali, Council members Ali Nasser Muhamed and Abdul Fattah Ismail. 65f, Women's militia on parade. 95f, Aerial view of textile mill.

1977, May Photo. *Perf. 13*
182 A58 25f grn, gold & dk brn .25 .25
183 A58 35f red, gold & lt bl .50 .50
184 A58 65f bl, gold & lil 1.00 1.00
185 A58 95f org, gold & grn 1.10 1.10
Nos. 182-185 (4) 2.85 2.85

Unification Congress, 1st anniversary.

Afrivoluta Pringlei — A59

Shells: 60f, Festilyria duponti, vert. 110f, Conus splendidulus. 180f, Cypraea 4broderipii.

1977, July 16 Litho. *Perf. 13½*
186 A59 60f multi .95 .70
187 A59 90f multi 1.40 .70
188 A59 110f multi 2.40 1.40
189 A59 180f multi 3.25 2.40
Nos. 186-189 (4) 8.00 5.20

Emblem and Flag — A60

Designs: 20f, Man with broken chain. 90f, Pipeline, agriculture and industry. 110f, Flag, symbolic tree and hands holding tools.

1977, Nov. 30 Litho. *Perf. 13½*
190 A60 5f blk & multi .25 .25
191 A60 20f blk & multi .25 .25
192 A60 90f blk & multi .50 .25
193 A60 110f blk & multi .85 .40
Nos. 190-193 (4) 1.85 1.15

10th anniversary of independence.

Dome of the Rock — A61

1978, May 15 *Perf. 12*
194 A61 5f multi *2.00* .40

Palestinian fighters & families. See #264A.

Festival Emblem and "CUBA" — A62

Designs: 20f, Festival emblem. 90f, Festival emblem as flower. 110f, Festival emblem, dove, young man and woman.

1978, June 22 Litho. *Perf. 14*
195 A62 5f multi .25 .25
196 A62 60f multi .65 .40
197 A62 90f multi .85 .45
198 A62 110f multi 1.10 .70
Nos. 195-198 (4) 2.85 1.80

11th World Youth Festival, Havana.

Silver Ornaments A63

Designs: Various silver ornaments.

1978, July 22 Litho. *Perf. 13½*
199 A63 10f blk & multi .25 .25
200 A63 15f blk & multi .25 .25
201 A63 20f blk & multi .25 .25
202 A63 60f blk & multi .25 .25
203 A63 90f blk & multi 1.00 .65
204 A63 110f blk & multi 1.50 .75
Nos. 199-204 (6) 3.50 2.40

For surcharge see Yemen No. 629.

Yemeni Musical Instruments A64

1978, Aug. 26 *Perf. 14*
205 A64 35f Almarfaai .40 .25
206 A64 60f Almizmar .90 .35
207 A64 90f Alqnboos 1.60 .45
208 A64 110f Simsimiya 2.00 .80
Nos. 205-208 (4) 4.90 1.85

For surcharge see Yemen No. 630.

"V" for Vanguard — A65

1978, Oct. 11 Litho. *Perf. 14*
209 A65 5f multi .25 .25
210 A65 20f multi .25 .25
211 A65 60f multi .40 .25
212 A65 180f multi .85 .50
Nos. 209-212 (4) 1.75 1.25

1st Conf. of Vanguard Party, Oct. 11-13.

Man with Palm, Factories — A66

Designs: 10f, Palm branches, broken chains, horiz. 60f, Candle and "15." 110f, Woman and man with rifle, "15."

1978, Oct. 14
213 A66 10f multi .25 .25
214 A66 35f multi .25 .25
215 A66 60f multi .45 .25
216 A66 110f multi .75 .45
Nos. 213-216 (4) 1.70 1.20

15th Revolution Day.
For surcharge see Yemen No. 631.

Child, Map of Arabia and IYC Emblem — A67

1979, Mar. 20 Litho. *Perf. 13½*
217 A67 15f multi .25 .25
218 A67 20f multi .25 .25
219 A67 60f multi .60 .25
220 A67 90f multi 1.10 .70
Nos. 217-220 (4) 2.20 1.45

International Year of the Child.

Sickle, Star, Tractor, Wheat and Dove — A68

Designs: 35f, Pylon, star, compass, wheat and hammer. 60f, Students, worker and clock. 90f, Woman with raised arms, doves and star.

1979, June 22 Litho. *Perf. 14*
221 A68 20f multi .25 .25
222 A68 35f multi .25 .25
223 A68 60f multi .40 .25
224 A68 90f multi .55 .25
Nos. 221-224 (4) 1.45 1.00

Corrective Movement, 10th anniversary.

Yemen #52, Hill — A69

Hill and: 110f, Yemen #56. 250f, Aden #12.

1979, Aug. 27 Litho. *Perf. 14*
225 A69 90f multi .60 .25
226 A69 110f multi .75 .45

Souvenir Sheet

227 A69 250f multi 2.25 2.25

Sir Rowland Hill (1795-1879), originator of penny postage.

Book, World Map, Arab Achievements A70

1979, Sept. 26 Litho. *Perf. 14*
228 A70 60f multi 1.00 .45

Party Emblem — A71

1979, Oct. 13 *Perf. 14½x14*
229 A71 60f multi .70 .25

Yemeni Socialist Party, 1st anniversary.

Cassia Adenesis — A72

Flowers: 90f, Nerium oleander. 110f, Calligonum comosum. 180f, Adenium obesium.

1979, Nov. 30 Litho. *Perf. 13½*
230 A72 20f multi .25 .25
231 A72 90f multi .90 .50
232 A72 110f multi 1.50 .75
233 A72 180f multi 1.90 .90
Nos. 230-233 (4) 4.55 2.40

For surcharge see Yemen No. 632.

First Anniv. of Iranian Revolution — A73

1980, Feb. 12 Litho. *Perf. 13½*
234 A73 60f multi 1.10 1.10

Dido — A74

1980, Mar. 5 Litho. *Perf. 13½*
235 A74 110f shown 1.00 .50
236 A74 180f Anglia 1.50 .70
237 A74 250f India 2.00 .90
Nos. 235-237 (3) 4.50 2.10

For surcharge see Yemen No. 633.

Basket Maker, London 1980 Emblem — A75

1980, May 6 Litho. *Perf. 14*
238 A75 60f shown .25 .25
239 A75 90f Hubble bubble pipe maker .65 .25
240 A75 110f Weaver .90 .55
241 A75 250f Potter 2.00 1.10
Nos. 238-241 (4) 3.80 2.15

London 1980 Intl. Stamp Exhib., May 6-14.

Hemprich's Skink — A76

1980, May 8 Litho. *Perf. 14*
242 A76 20f shown .25 .25
243 A76 35f Mole viper .60 .25
244 A76 110f Carter's day gecko 1.50 .60
245 A76 180f Cobra 2.50 1.25
Nos. 242-245 (4) 4.85 2.35

For surcharge see Yemen No. 634.

Misha and Olympic Emblem — A77

1980, July 19 Litho. *Perf. 12½x12*
246 A77 110f multi 1.10 .65

For overprint see No. 287.

Farmers Armed — A78

50f, Armed farmers working, horiz. 110f, Sickle (wheat) and fist.

1980, Oct. 17 *Perf. 13½*
247 A78 50f multicolored .50 .25
248 A78 90f shown .75 .50
249 A78 110f multicolored 1.00 .70
Nos. 247-249 (3) 2.25 1.45

10th anniversary of farmers' uprising.

110th Birth Anniversary of Lenin — A79

1980, Nov. 7 Litho. *Perf. 12*
250 A79 35f multi .50 .50

Douglas DC-3 — A80

1981, Mar. 11 Litho. *Perf. 13½*
251 A80 60f shown .75 .50
252 A80 90f Boeing 707 1.50 .75
253 A80 250f DHC Dash 7 3.50 1.60
Nos. 251-253 (3) 5.75 2.85

Democratic Yemen Airlines, 10th anniv.

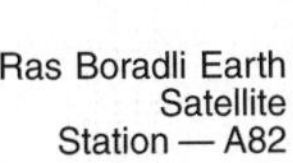

Ras Boradli Earth Satellite Station — A82

1981, June 22 Litho. *Perf. 12*
257 A82 60f multi 1.25 .65

Conocarpus Lancifolius — A83

1981, Aug. 1 Litho. *Perf. 12*
258 A83 90f shown .95 .25
259 A83 180f Ficus vasta 1.75 1.10
260 A83 250f Maerua crassifolia 2.75 1.40
Nos. 258-260 (3) 5.45 2.75

Supreme People's Council, 10th Anniv. — A84

1981, Aug. 18 Litho. *Perf. 15x14½*
261 A84 180f multi 1.50 .90

Desert Fox A85

1981, Sept. 26 Litho. *Perf. 14½*
262 A85 50f shown .70 .25
263 A85 90f South Arabian leopard 1.40 .70
264 A85 250f Ibex 3.25 1.60
Nos. 262-264 (3) 5.35 2.55

No. 194 Redrawn

1981, Oct. 15 Litho. *Perf. 12*
Size: 25x27mm
264A A61 5f multi 1.00 .45

Denomination in upper right.

Tephrosia Apollinea — A86

1981, Nov. 30 Litho. *Perf. 13½*
265 A86 50f shown .75 .25
266 A86 90f Citrullus colocynthis 1.00 .25
267 A86 110f Aloe sqarrosa 1.40 .25
268 A86 250f Lawsonia inermis 3.50 2.00
Nos. 265-268 (4) 6.65 2.75

For surcharge see Yemen No. 635.

Intl. Year of the Disabled — A87

1981, Dec. 12 Litho. *Perf. 14½*
269 A87 50f multi .40 .25
270 A87 100f multi 1.00 .50
271 A87 150f multi 1.50 .85
Nos. 269-271 (3) 2.90 1.60

TB Bacillus Centenary A88

1982, Mar. 24 Litho. *Perf. 14½*
272 A88 50f multi 4.50 .75

30th Anniv. of Arab Postal Union — A89

1982, Apr. 12 Litho. *Perf. 14*
273 A89 100f multi 1.25 .75

1982 World Cup — A90

Designs: Various soccer players.

1982, June 13 Litho. *Perf. 14*
274 A90 50f multi .65 .25
275 A90 100f multi 1.20 .65
276 A90 150f multi 2.00 1.25
277 A90 200f multi 2.60 1.40
a. Souv. sheet of 4, #274-277 6.50 6.50
Nos. 274-277 (4) 6.45 3.55

For overprints see Nos. 281-284.

60th Anniv. of USSR — A93

1982, Dec. 22 Litho. *Perf. 12½x12*
280 A93 50f Flags, arms .65 .45

Nos. 274-277, 277a Ovptd. with Emblem and "WORLD CUP / WINNERS / 1982 / 1st ITALY / 2nd W-GERMANY / 3rd POLAND / 4th FRANCE" in Blue

1982, Dec. 30 Litho. *Perf. 14*
281 A90 50f multi .75 .25
282 A90 100f multi 1.50 1.50
283 A90 150f multi 2.25 2.25
284 A90 200f multi 2.50 2.50
a. Souvenir sheet of 4, #281-284 7.00 7.00
Nos. 281-284 (4) 7.00 6.50

Palestinian Solidarity — A94

1983, Apr. 10 *Perf. 13½x14½*
285 A94 50f Yasser Arafat 1.00 .60
286 A94 100f Arafat, Dome of the Rock 3.00 1.00
a. Souvenir sheet of 1, imperf. 3.00 3.00

No. 246 Ovptd. with TEMBAL '83 Emblem in Yellow

1983, May 21 *Perf. 12½x12*
287 A77 110f multi 10.00 6.00

World Communications Year — A95

Designs: 50f, Correspondent, postrider, ship. 100f, Postman, coach, telegraph. No. 290, Telephones, bus. 200f, Telecommunications. No. 292, Montage.

1983, June 10 *Perf. 13x13½*
288 A95 50f blk & brt bl .75 .25
289 A95 100f multi 1.50 1.50
290 A95 150f multi 2.40 2.40
291 A95 200f multi 2.75 2.75
Nos. 288-291 (4) 7.40 6.90

Souvenir Sheet

292 A95 150f multi 3.00 3.00

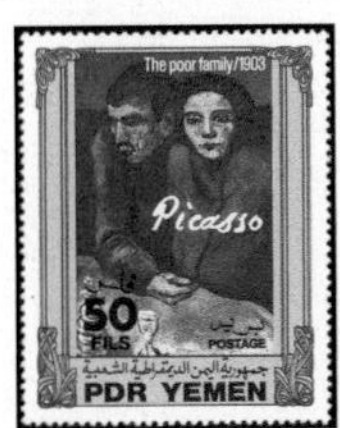
Pablo Picasso (1881-1973), Painter — A96

Paintings: No. 293, The Poor Family, 1903. No. 294, Woman with Crow. No. 295a, The Gourmet. No. 295b, Woman with Child on Beach. No. 295c, Sitting Beggar. No. 296, The Soler Family, horiz.

1983, July 25 *Perf. 14*
293 A96 50f multi 1.00 .30
294 A96 100f multi 2.00 .90

Souvenir Sheets

295 Sheet of 3 17.50 17.50
a. A96 50f multi 1.75 1.75
b. A96 100f multi 4.50 4.50
c. A96 150f multi 6.50 6.50
296 A96 150f multi 12.50 12.50

23rd Pre-Olympics Games, 1984 — A97

1983, July 30
297 A97 25f Show jumping 1.00 .35
298 A97 50f Show jumping, diff. 1.40 .65
299 A97 100f Three-day event 2.50 1.25
Nos. 297-299 (3) 4.90 2.25

Souvenir Sheets

300 Sheet of 4 20.00 20.00
a. A97 20f Bay, vert. 2.50 2.50
b. A97 40f Gray, vert. 2.50 2.50
c. A97 60f Bay, diff., vert. 3.25 3.25
d. A97 80f Arabian 4.50 4.50
301 A97 200f Show jumping, diff., vert. 15.00 15.00

Locomotives A98

1983, Aug. 24 *Perf. 14½x15*
302 A98 25f P8 steam engine, 1905 1.25 .50
303 A98 50f 880 steam, 1915 2.25 .90
304 A98 100f GT 2-4-4, 1923 3.50 1.75
Nos. 302-304 (3) 7.00 3.15

Souvenir Sheets

305 Sheet of 3 20.00 20.00
a. A98 40f D51 steam, 1936 4.75 4.75
b. A98 60f 45 Series, 1937 4.75 4.75
c. A98 100f PT 47, 1948 9.00 9.00
306 A98 200f P36, 1950 20.00 20.00

Ships — A99

1983, Sept. 15 *Perf. 14*
307 A99 50f Europa .60 .50
308 A99 100f World Discoverer 3.00 1.75

Miniature Sheet

309 Sheet of 4 18.00 18.00
a. A99 20f Kruzenstern 1.75 1.75
b. A99 40f Grossherzogin Elisabeth 3.50 3.50
c. A99 60f Sedov 5.50 5.50
d. A99 80f Dar Pomorza 7.50 7.50

Souvenir Sheet

310 A99 200f Gorch Foch 15.00 15.00

Natl. Revolution, 20th Anniv. — A100

1983, Oct. 15 Litho. *Perf. 13½x13*
312 A100 50f shown .90 .45
313 A100 100f Flag, freedom fighter 2.00 1.00

1st Manned Flight, Bicent. — A101

Balloons: 100f, La Montgolfiere prototype. No. 316a, Lunardi's. No. 316b, Charles and Robert's. No. 316c, Wiseman's. No. 316d, Blanchard and Jeffries's. 200f, Five-balloon craft.

1983, Oct. 25 *Perf. 14*

314 A101 50f shown 1.25 .50
315 A101 100f multi 2.50 1.00

Souvenir Sheets

316 Sheet of 4 20.00 20.00
a. A101 20f multi 3.00 3.00
b. A101 40f multi 3.00 3.00
c. A101 60f multi 3.00 3.00
d. A101 80f multi 4.00 4.00
317 A101 200f multi 15.00 15.00

Nos. 314-315 exist imperf. Value, set, $15.

1984 Winter Olympics, Sarajevo — A102

50f, Men's downhill skiing. 100f, Two-man bobsled.

1983, Dec. 28 Litho. *Perf. 14*

318 A102 50f multicolored .90 .40
319 A102 100f multicolored 1.75 .80

Souvenir Sheets

320 Sheet of 3 12.50 12.50
a. A102 40f Ski jumping 3.00 3.00
b. A102 60f Figure skating 3.00 3.00
c. A102 100f Two-man bobsled 3.00 3.00
321 A102 200f Ice hockey 12.50 12.50

1984 Summer Olympics, Los Angeles A103

1984, Jan. 24

322 A103 25f Fencing .45 .25
323 A103 50f Fencing, diff. .90 .45
324 A103 100f Fencing, diff. 1.40 .75
Nos. 322-324 (3) 2.75 1.45

Souvenir Sheets

325 Sheet of 4 15.00 15.00
a. A103 20f Gymnastics 2.75 2.75
b. A103 40f Water polo 2.75 2.75
c. A103 60f Wrestling 2.75 2.75
d. A103 80f Show jumping 2.75 2.75
326 A103 200f Show jumping, diff. 12.50 12.50

Nos. 322-324 exist imperf. Value, set, $15.

Space Flights A104

Designs: 15f, Soyuz 10 and Salyut 1 docking, 1971. 20f, Apollo 8 circling Moon, 1968. 50f, Apollo 11 Moon landing, 1969. 100f, Apollo-Soyuz mission, 1975.
200f, Space Shuttle Columbia.

1984, Apr. 16 Litho. *Perf. 14*

327-330 A104 Set of 4 3.00 2.00

Souvenir Sheet

331 A104 200f multi 7.00 5.50

Nos. 83 and 84B Surcharged with Black Squares

1984, May 26 Litho. *Perf. 13½, 13*

332 A24 50f on 65f multi 10.00 6.00
333 A25 100f on 110f multi 20.00 10.00

Fish — A105

10f, Abalistes stellaris. 15f, Caranx speciocus. 20f, Pomadasys maculatus. 25f, Chaetodon fasciatus. 35f, Pomacanthus imperator. 50f, Rastrelliger kanagurta. 100f, Euthynnus affinis. 150f, Heniochus acuminatus. 200f, Pomacanthus maculosus. 250f, Pterois russelii. 400f, Argyrops spinifer. 500f, Dasyatis uarnak. 1d, Epinephalus chlorostigma. 2d, Drepane longimana.

1984, Nov. 25 Litho. *Perf. 11½*

334 A105 10f multicolored .25 .25
335 A105 15f multicolored .25 .25
336 A105 20f multicolored .30 .25
337 A105 25f multicolored .45 .25
338 A105 35f multicolored .70 .25
339 A105 50f multicolored 1.00 .25
340 A105 100f multicolored 2.00 .45
341 A105 150f multicolored 3.00 .90
342 A105 200f multicolored 4.00 1.00
343 A105 250f multicolored 5.50 1.75
344 A105 400f multicolored 9.00 2.40
345 A105 500f multicolored 11.00 3.25
346 A105 1d multicolored 24.00 7.50
347 A105 2d multicolored 52.50 15.00
Nos. 334-347 (14) 113.95 33.75

For surcharges see Yemen Nos. 636, 640, 642.

Natl. Literacy Campaign A106

1985, Feb. 27 *Perf. 12*

350 A106 50f Girls writing 1.40 .75
351 A106 100f Hand, fountain pen, vert. 2.90 1.20

Victory Parade, Red Square, Moscow, 1945 — A107

1985, May 9 *Perf. 12x12½*

352 A107 100f multi 1.75 .80

Defeat of Nazi Germany, end of World War II, 40th anniv.

12th World Youth and Students Festival — A108

1985, Aug. 3 *Perf. 12*

353 A108 50f Emblem 1.50 .70
354 A108 100f Hand holding emblem 3.00 1.25

UNESCO World Heritage Campaign — A109

1985, Aug. 29

355 A109 50f Shibam city .90 .50
356 A109 50f Close-up of buildings .90 .50
357 A109 100f Windows 1.90 1.90
358 A109 100f Door 1.90 1.90
Nos. 355-358 (4) 5.60 4.80

Nos. 355-357 horiz.

Natl. Socialist Party, 3rd Gen. Cong. — A110

1985, Oct. 10

359 A110 25f Energy .70 .45
360 A110 50f Industry 1.25 .60
361 A110 100f Agriculture 2.40 1.00
Nos. 359-361 (3) 4.35 2.05

UN Child Survival Campaign — A111

1985, Nov. 28

362 A111 50f Mother feeding child 1.75 1.40
363 A111 50f Holding child 1.75 1.40
364 A111 100f Feeding child, diff. 4.00 2.50
365 A111 100f Breastfeeding 4.00 2.50
Nos. 362-365 (4) 11.50 7.80

World Food Day — A112

1986, Jan. 30

366 A112 20f Almihdar Mosque, Aden .90 .25
367 A112 180f Palm trees 4.00 1.75

UN Food and Agriculture Org., 40th anniv.

Lenin, Red Square, Moscow — A113

1986, Feb. 25 *Perf. 12x12½*

368 A113 75f multi 1.75 .70
369 A113 250f multi 4.00 2.00

27th Soviet Communist Party Cong., Moscow.

Costumes Worn at the 1984 Brides Dance Festival — A114

Designs: No. 370, Bride wearing red and green costume, face markings. No. 371, Violet costume. No. 372, Veiled bride. No. 373, Unveiled bride. No. 374, Groom holding dagger. No. 375, Groom holding rifle.

1986, Feb. 27

370 A114 50f multi .80 .50
371 A114 50f multi .80 .50
372 A114 50f multi .80 .50
373 A114 100f multi 1.50 1.25
374 A114 100f multi 1.50 1.25
375 A114 100f multi 1.50 1.25
Nos. 370-375 (6) 6.90 5.25

Revolution Martyrs — A115

1986, Oct. 15 Litho. *Perf. 12*

376 A115 75f Abdul Fattah Ismail 1.10 .70
377 A115 75f Ali Shayaa Hadi 1.10 .70
378 A115 75f Saleh Musleh Kasim 1.10 .70
379 A115 75f Ali Ahmed N. Antar 1.10 .70
Nos. 376-379 (4) 4.40 2.80

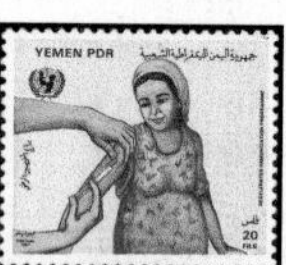

UN Child Survival Campaign — A116

Infant Immunization Program: 20f, Immunizing pregnant woman. 75f, Immunizing infant. 140f, Oral immunization. 150f, Infant, girl, pregnant woman.

1987, Apr. 7 Litho. *Perf. 12*

380 A116 20f multicolored .35 .25
381 A116 75f multicolored 1.10 .70
382 A116 140f multicolored 2.25 1.00
383 A116 150f multicolored 2.25 1.25
Nos. 380-383 (4) 5.95 3.20

1st Socialist Party General Conference A117

1987, July 30 Litho. *Perf. 12*

384 A117 75fr multi 1.10 .45
385 A117 150fr multi 2.25 1.00

October Revolution, Russia, 70th Anniv. — A118

1987, Nov. 7 Litho. *Perf. 12½x12*

386 A118 250f multi 4.50 2.25

Monuments, Ancient City of Shabwa — A119

25f, Royal palace and court. 75f, Palace, diff. 140f, Winged lion bas-relief on stone capital. 150f, The Moon, legend on bronze tablet.

1987, Nov. 18 *Perf. 12*

387 A119 25f multicolored .45 .25
388 A119 75f multicolored 1.10 .55
389 A119 140f multicolored 2.00 1.10
390 A119 150f multicolored 2.25 1.25
Nos. 387-390 (4) 5.80 3.15

Nos. 387-388 horiz.

Natl. Independence, 20th Anniv. — A120

Designs: 5f, Students walking to school. 75f, Family, apartments. 140f, Workers, oil derrick, thermal plant. 150f, Workers, soldier, Workers' Party headquarters.

1987, Nov. 29 *Perf. 12x12½*

391 A120 25f multi .35 .25
392 A120 75f multi 1.00 .45
393 A120 140f multi 2.00 .90
394 A120 150f multi 2.25 1.00
Nos. 391-394 (4) 5.60 2.60

September 26th Revolution, 25th Anniv. — A121

1988, Feb. 27 Litho. *Perf. 13*
395 A121 75f Revolution monument, San'a 1.10 .45

WHO, 40th Anniv. — A122

40f, Sanitary public water supply, vert. 75f, No smoking. 140f, Child immunization. 250f, Health care for all by the year 2000.

1988, Apr. 7 Litho. *Perf. 12*

396	A122	40f multicolored	.45	.30
397	A122	75f multicolored	1.00	.35
398	A122	140f multicolored	1.75	.70
399	A122	250f multicolored	2.75	1.25
		Nos. 396-399 (4)	5.95	2.60

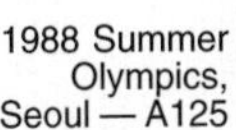

1988 Summer Olympics, Seoul — A125

1988, Sept. 17 Litho. *Perf. 12x12½*

406	A125	40f Weight lifting	.55	.25
407	A125	75f Running	1.00	.45
408	A125	140f Boxing	2.25	1.10
409	A125	150f Soccer	2.40	1.25
		Nos. 406-409 (4)	6.20	3.05

1st Freedom Fighter Killed at the Liberation Front, Radfan Mountains — A126

25f, Freedom fighters, flag, vert. 300f, Anniv. emblem, vert.

Perf. 12½x12, 12x12½
1988, Oct. 12 Litho.

410	A126	25f multicolored	.35	.25
411	A126	75f shown	1.00	.35
412	A126	300f multicolored	4.00	1.75
		Nos. 410-412 (3)	5.35	2.35

October 14th Revolution, 25th anniv.

Indigenous Birds — A127

40f, Treron waalia. 50f, Coracias caudatus lorti, vert. 75f, Upupa epops, vert. 250f, Chlamydotis undulata macqueenii.

1988, Nov. 5 *Perf. 12x12½, 12½x12*

413	A127	40f multicolored	.60	.60
414	A127	50f multicolored	.80	.55
415	A127	75f multicolored	1.40	.80
416	A127	250f multicolored	3.75	2.00
		Nos. 413-416 (4)	6.55	3.95

Handicrafts — A128

Designs: 25f, Incense brazier. 75f, Cage-shaped dress form. 150f, Shell and wicker lidded basket. 250f, Wicker basket.

1988, Nov. 29 Litho. *Perf. 12½x12*

417	A128	25f multi	.25	.25
418	A128	75f multi	1.00	.45
419	A128	150f multi	1.75	1.00
420	A128	250f multi	3.25	1.75
		Nos. 417-420 (4)	6.25	3.45

Aden Harbor and Yemen Port Authority, Cent. — A129

1988, Dec. 5 *Perf. 12x12½*

421	A129	75f Old harbor facility	1.50	.50
422	A129	300f New facility	4.50	2.10

Preservation of San'a City, a Site on the UNESCO World Heritage List — A130

1988, Dec. 15 *Perf. 12x12½, 12½x12*

423	A130	75f shown	1.00	.70
424	A130	250f City view, diff., vert.	4.00	1.75

World Wildlife Fund A131

1989, May 18 Litho. *Perf. 12½x12*

425	A131	20f Sand cat	1.50	.25
426	A131	25f Cat's head	1.50	.30
427	A131	50f Fennec fox	3.00	.50
428	A131	75f Fox's head	4.00	.80
		Nos. 425-428 (4)	10.00	1.85

For surcharge see Yemen No. 643.

Military Forces — A132

Developments of the corrective movement.

1989, Aug. 15 *Perf. 12x12½*

429	A132	25f shown	.35	.25
430	A132	35f Industry	.45	.25
431	A132	40f Agriculture	.55	.25
		Nos. 429-431 (3)	1.35	.75

June 22 Corrective Movement, 20th anniv.

Abdul Fattah Ismail — A133

1989, Aug. 28

432	A133	75f multi	.75	.75
433	A133	150f multi	1.50	1.25

50th Birthday of Abdul Fattah Ismail, 1st secretary-general of the natl. Socialist Party.

Ali Anter Yemeni Pioneer Organization, 15th Anniv. — A134

10f, Drawing by Abeer Anwer. 25f, Girl in pioneer uniform. 75f, Parade, Aden.

Perf. 12x12½, 12½x12
1989, Sept. 29 Litho.

434	A134	10f multicolored	.25	.25
435	A134	25f multicolored	.35	.25
436	A134	75f multicolored	.90	.55
		Nos. 434-436 (3)	1.50	1.05

Nos. 434-435 vert.
For surcharge see Yemen No. 644.

Nehru and the Taj Mahal — A135

1989, Nov. 14 Photo. *Perf. 14*
437 A135 250f blk & golden brn 3.50 1.50

Jawaharlal Nehru, 1st prime minister of independent India.
For surcharge see Yemen No. 645.

Seventy-Day Siege of San'a, 1967-68 — A136

1989, Oct. 25 Litho. *Perf. 12x12½*
438 A136 150f multicolored 4.50 2.50

Coffee Plant — A137

1989, Dec. 20
439 A137 300f multicolored 5.00 2.50

For surcharge see Yemen No. 637.

Seera Rock, Aden, and the Arc de Triomphe, Paris — A138

1989, Dec. 29 Litho. *Perf. 12½x12*
440 A138 250f multicolored 4.25 2.50

French Revolution, bicent.

World Cup Soccer Championships, Italy — A139

Character trademark, soccer plays and flags of participants: 5f, US, Belgium, 1930. 10f, Switzerland, Holland, 1934. 20f, Italy, France, 1938. 35f, Sweden, Spain, 1950. 50f, Federal Republic of Germany, Austria, 1954. Brazil, England, 1958. 500f, Russia, Uruguay, 1962. No. 448, Soccer game.

1990, Apr. 30 Litho. *Perf. 12½x12*

441	A139	5f multicolored	.25	.25
442	A139	10f multicolored	.25	.25
443	A139	20f multicolored	.25	.25
444	A139	35f multicolored	.30	.30
445	A139	50f multicolored	.35	.35
446	A139	60f multicolored	.40	.40
447	A139	500f multicolored	4.00	1.00
		Nos. 441-447 (7)	5.80	2.80

Souvenir Sheet

448 A139 340f multicolored 3.00 3.00

For surcharges see Yemen Nos. 616, 621-621B.

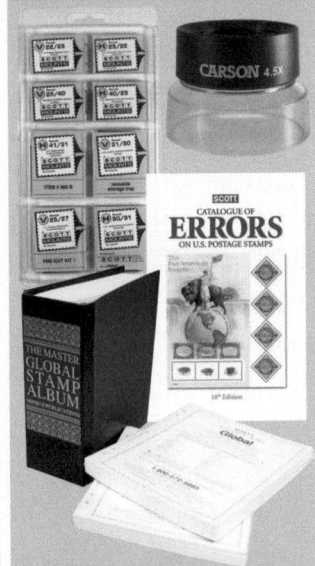

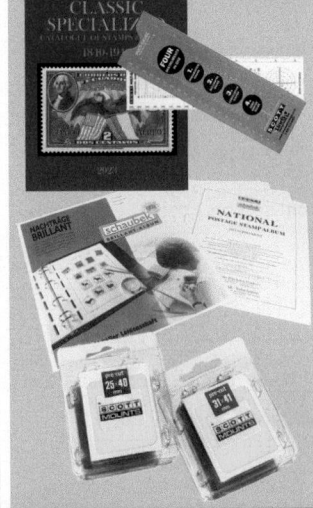

YUGOSLAVIA

yü-gō-'slä-vē-ə

LOCATION — Southern Europe, bordering on the Adriatic Sea
GOVT. — Republic
AREA — 39,500 sq. mi. (est)
POP. — 11,206,847 (1999 est.)
CAPITAL — Belgrade

On December 1, 1918, Bosnia and Herzegovina, Croatia, Dalmatia, Montenegro, Serbia and Slovenia united to form a kingdom which was later called Yugoslavia. A republic was proclaimed November 29, 1945. Other listings may be found under all.

100 Heller = 1 Krone (Bosnia & Herzegovina)
100 Filler = 1 Krone (Croatia-Slavonia)
100 Paras = 1 Dinar (General Issues)

Catalogue values for unused stamps in this country are for Never Hinged items, beginning with Scott 410 in the regular postage section, Scott C50 in the airpost section, Scott F1 in the registered letter section, Scott J67 in the postage due section, Scott RA1 in the postal tax section, and Scott RAJ1 in the postal tax due section.

Counterfeits exist of most of the 1918-19 overprints for Bosnia and Herzegovina, Croatia-Slavonia and Slovenia.

BOSNIA AND HERZEGOVINA

Stamps of Bosnia and Herzegovina, 1910, Overprinted or Surcharged in Black or Red

a

b

c

1918 **Unwmk.** ***Perf. 12½***

1L1	A4(a)	3h olive green	.40	.80
1L2	A4(b)	5h dk grn (R)	.40	.40
1L3	A4(a)	10h carmine	.40	.40
1L4	A4(a)	20h dk brn (R)	.40	.40
1L5	A4(a)	25h deep blue (R)	.40	.40
1L6	A4(b)	30h green	.40	.40
1L7	A4(b)	40h orange	.40	.40
1L8	A4(b)	45h brown red	.40	.40
1L9	A4(b)	50h dull violet	.55	.80
1L10	A4(a)	60h on 50h dl vio	.40	.40
1L11	A4(b)	80h on 6h org brown	.40	.40
1L12	A4(a)	90h on 35h myr green	.40	.40
1L13	A5(c)	2k gray green	.40	.40
1L14	A4(b)	3k on 3h ol grn	2.00	2.75
1L15	A5(c)	4k on 1k mar	4.00	4.75
1L16	A4(b)	10k on 2h vio	6.00	6.75
		Nos. 1L1-1L16 (16)	17.35	20.25

Inverted and double overprints and assorted varieties exist on the stamps for Bosnia and Herzegovina.

Bosnian Girl — A1

1918 **Typo.** ***Perf. 11½***

1L17	A1	2h ultramarine	.40	.40
1L18	A1	6h violet	.80	1.20
1L19	A1	10h rose	.40	.40
1L20	A1	20h green	.40	.40
		Nos. 1L17-1L20 (4)	2.00	2.40

Imperforate stamps of this type (A1) are newspaper stamps of Bosnia.

For surcharges see Nos. 1L21-1L22, 1L43-1L45.

Bosnia and Herzegovina Nos. P1-P2 (Nos. 1L17-1L18, Imperf.) Srchd.

1918 ***Imperf.***

1L21	A1	3h on 2h ultra	.40	.40
a.		Double surcharge	*14.00*	
1L22	A1	5h on 6h violet	.40	.40
a.		Double surcharge	*14.00*	

Stamps of Bosnia and Herzegovina, 1906-17, Ovptd. or Srchd. in Black or Red

d

e

f

1919 ***Perf. 12½***

1L25	A23(d)	3h claret	.40	.80
1L26	A23(e)	5h green	.40	.40
1L27	A23(e)	10h on 6h dark gray	.40	.40
1L28	A24(d)	20h on 35h myr green	.40	.40
1L29	A23(e)	25h ultra	.40	.40
1L30	A23(d)	30h orange red	.40	.40
1L31	A24(d)	45h olive brn	.40	.40
1L32	A27(d)	45h on 80h org brown	.40	.40
a.		Perf. 11½	1.40	1.60
1L33	A24(e)	50h slate blue	100.00	100.00
1L34	A24(e)	50h on 72h dk blue (R)	.40	.40
1L35	A24(d)	60h brown violet	.40	.40
1L36	A27(e)	80h orange brown	.40	.40
a.		Perf. 11½	*35.00*	*30.00*
1L37	A27(d)	90h dark violet	.40	.40
a.		Perf. 11½	3.50	2.75
1L38	A5(f)	2k gray green	.40	.40
a.		Imperf.	35.00	
b.		Perf. 9½	4.50	5.00
1L39	A26(d)	3k car, *green*	.40	.55
1L40	A28(e)	4k car, *green*	1.75	2.50
1L41	A26(d)	5k dk vio, *gray*	1.75	2.75
1L42	A28(e)	10k dk vio, *gray*	3.25	4.00
		Nos. 1L25-1L42 (18)	112.35	115.40

Nos. 1L32, 1L36, 1L37, 1L40 and 1L42 have no bars in the overprint.

Nos. 1L25 to 1L42 exist with inverted overprint or surcharge.

Bosnia and Herzegovina Nos. P2-P4 (Nos. 1L18-1L20, Imperf.) Srchd.

1920 ***Imperf.***

1L43	A1	2h on 6h violet	200.00	180.00
1L44	A1	2h on 10h rose	50.00	50.00
1L45	A1	2h on 20h green	10.00	10.00
		Nos. 1L43-1L45 (3)	260.00	240.00

SEMI-POSTAL STAMPS ISSUES FOR BOSNIA AND HERZEGOVINA

Leading Blind Soldier
SP1

Wounded Soldier
SP2

Semi-Postal Stamps of Bosnia and Herzegovina, 1918 Overprinted

1918 **Unwmk.** ***Perf. 12½, 13***

1LB1	SP1	10h greenish bl	.80	1.00
a.		Overprinted as No. 1LB2	52.50	52.50
1LB2	SP2	15h red brown	2.00	2.00
a.		Overprinted as No. 1LB1	47.50	47.50

Bosnian Semi-Postal Stamps of 1916 Overprinted like No. 1LB2

1LB3	SP1	5h green	125.00	175.00
a.		Overprinted as No. 1LB1	375.00	375.00
1LB4	SP2	10h magenta	100.00	125.00
		Nos. 1LB1-1LB4 (4)	227.80	303.00

Inverted and double overprints exist on Nos. 1LB1-1LB4.

Regular Issue of Bosnia, 1906 Surcharged in Black

Mail Wagon — SP3

Bridge at Mostar
SP4

Scene near Sarajevo
SP5

1919

1LB5	SP3	10h + 10h on 40h org red	1.25	2.00
1LB6	SP4	20h + 10h on 20h dk brown	.60	1.75
1LB7	SP5	45h + 15h on 1k mar	4.75	4.75
		Nos. 1LB5-1LB7 (3)	6.60	8.50

Nos. 1LB5-1LB7 exist with surcharge inverted. Value each $7.50.

SPECIAL DELIVERY STAMPS ISSUES FOR BOSNIA AND HERZEGOVINA

Lightning
SD1 SD2

Bosnian Special Delivery Stamps Overprinted in Black

1918 **Unwmk.** ***Perf. 12½, 13***

1LE1	SD1	2h vermilion	6.00	6.00
a.		Inverted overprint	35.00	
b.		Overprinted as No. 1LE2	47.50	47.50
1LE2	SD2	5h deep green	3.25	3.25
a.		Inverted overprint	18.00	
b.		Overprinted as No. 1LE1	47.50	47.50

POSTAGE DUE STAMPS ISSUES FOR BOSNIA AND HERZEGOVINA

Postage Due Stamps of Bosnia and Herzegovina, 1916, Overprinted in Black or Red

a

b

1918 **Unwmk.** ***Perf. 12½, 13***

1LJ1	D2 (a)	2h red	.25	.25
1LJ2	D2 (b)	4h red	.55	.55
1LJ3	D2 (a)	5h red	.25	.25
1LJ4	D2 (b)	6h red	.90	.90
1LJ5	D2 (a)	10h red	.25	.25
1LJ6	D2 (b)	15h red	6.75	6.75
1LJ7	D2 (a)	20h red	.25	.25
1LJ8	D2 (b)	25h red	.55	.55
1LJ9	D2 (a)	30h red	.55	.55
1LJ10	D2 (b)	40h red	.25	.25
1LJ11	D2 (a)	50h red	1.20	1.20

c

d

1LJ12	D2 (c)	1k dark blue (R)	.55	.55
1LJ13	D2 (d)	3k dark blue (R)	.40	.40
		Nos. 1LJ1-1LJ13 (13)	12.70	12.70

Nos. 1LJ1-1LJ13 exist with overprint double or inverted. Value $3 to $7.

Nos. 1LJ1-1LJ11 exist with type "b" overprint instead of type "a," and vice versa. Value, each $10.

Stamps of Bosnia and Herzegovina, 1900-04, Surcharged

e

f

1919

1LJ14	A2 (e)	2h on 35h blue	.55	.80
1LJ15	A2 (e)	5h on 45h grnsh bl	.95	1.20
1LJ16	A2 (f)	10h on 10 red	.25	.25
1LJ17	A2 (e)	15h on 40h org	.40	.50
1LJ18	A2 (f)	20h on 5h green	.25	.25
1LJ19	A2 (e)	25h on 20h pink	.40	.55
1LJ20	A2 (f)	30h on 30h bis brn	.40	.55
1LJ21	A2 (e)	1k on 50h red lil	.25	.55
1LJ22	A2 (e)	3k on 25h blue	.50	.55

Postage Due Stamps of Bosnia and Herzegovina, 1904 Surcharged

g

h

1LJ23	D1 (g)	40h on 6h blk, red & yel	.25	.25
1LJ24	D1 (h)	50h on 8h blk, red & yel	.25	.25
1LJ25	D1 (h)	200h blk, red & grn	8.00	6.75
1LJ26	D1 (h)	4k on 7h blk, red & yel	.40	.55
		Nos. 1LJ14-1LJ26 (13)	12.85	13.00

Nos. 1LJ14-1LJ26 exist with overprint double or inverted. Value, $3 to $6.

CROATIA-SLAVONIA

Stamps of Hungary Overprinted in Blue

A1

1918 Wmk. 137 *Perf. 15*

On Stamps of 1913

2L1 A1 6f olive green 1.10 2.00
2L2 A1 50f lake, *blue* 1.20 2.00

A2

A3

On Stamps of 1916

2L3 A2 10f violet 100.00 *140.00*
2L4 A3 15f red 100.00 *140.00*

A4

On Hungary Nos. 106-107 White Numerals

2L4A A4 10f rose 1,600. *1,600.*
2L5 A4 15f violet 150.00 150.00
a. Inverted overprint —

On Stamps of 1916-18 Colored Numerals

2L6 A4 2f brown orange .40 .40
2L7 A4 3f red lilac .40 .40
2L8 A4 5f green .40 .40
2L9 A4 6f greenish blue .40 .40
2L10 A4 10f rose red 16.00 12.00
2L11 A4 15f violet .40 .40
2L12 A4 20f gray brown .40 .40
2L13 A4 25f dull blue .40 .40
2L14 A4 35f brown .40 .40
2L15 A4 40f olive green .40 .80

The overprints and surcharges for Croatia-Slavonia exist inverted, double, double inverted, in wrong colors, on wrong stamps, on back, in pairs with one lacking overprint, etc.

A5

A6

2L16 A5 50f red vio & lilac .40 .40
2L17 A5 75f brt bl & pale bl .40 .40
2L18 A5 80f grn & pale grn .40 .40
2L19 A6 1k red brown & cl .40 .40
2L20 A6 2k olive brn & bis .40 .40
2L21 A6 3k dark vio & ind .40 .40
2L22 A6 5k dk brn & lt brn 2.50 3.00
2L23 A6 10k vio brn & vio 16.00 16.00

Stamps of Hungary Overprinted in Blue, Black or Red

No. 2L24

No. 2L27

2L24 A7 10f scarlet (Bl) .40 .40
2L25 A7 20f dark brown (Bk) .40 .40
2L26 A7 25f deep blue (R) .40 .80
2L27 A8 40f olive green (Bl) .40 .40
Nos. 2L6-2L27 (22) 42.10 39.40

Many other stamps of the 1913-18 issues of Hungary, the Semi-Postal Stamps of 1915-16 and Postage Due Stamps were surreptitiously overprinted but were never sold through the post office.

Freedom of Croatia-Slavonia — A9

1918 Unwmk. Litho. *Perf. 11½*

2L28 A9 10f rose 6.50 4.00
2L29 A9 20f violet 6.50 4.00
2L30 A9 25f blue 12.00 8.00
2L31 A9 45f greenish blk 95.00 55.00
Nos. 2L28-2L31 (4) 120.00 71.00

Independence of Croatia, Slavonia and Dalmatia.

#2L28-2L31 exist imperforate, but were not officially issued in this condition.

Excellent counterfeits of #2L28-2L31 exist.

Allegory of Freedom A10

Youth with Standard A11

Falcon, Symbol of Liberty — A12

1919 *Perf. 11½*

2L32 A10 2f brn orange .25 .40
2L33 A10 3f violet .25 .50
2L34 A10 5f green .25 .25
2L35 A11 10f red .25 .25
2L36 A11 20f black brown .25 .25
2L37 A11 25f deep blue .25 .25
2L38 A11 45f dark ol grn .25 .25
2L39 A12 1k carmine rose .25 .25
2L40 A12 3k dark violet .80 .95
2L41 A12 5k deep brown 1.20 .80
Nos. 2L32-2L41 (10) 4.00 4.15

Perf. 12½

2L32a A10 2f 2.90 2.90
2L33a A10 3f 2.90 2.90
2L34a A10 5f 15.00 15.00
2L35a A11 10f 2.90 2.90
2L36a A11 20f 2.90 2.90
Nos. 2L32a-2L36a (5) 26.60 26.60

#2L32-2L41 exist imperf. Value, set $25.

SEMI-POSTAL STAMPS ISSUES FOR CROATIA-SLAVONIA

SP1

SP2

SP3

1918 Wmk. 137 *Perf. 15*

2LB1 SP1 10f + 2f rose red .40 *2.75*
2LB2 SP2 15f + 2f dull violet .40 *.40*
2LB3 SP3 40f + 2f brn carmine .40 *.85*
Nos. 2LB1-2LB3 (3) 1.20 *4.00*

SPECIAL DELIVERY STAMP ISSUE FOR CROATIA-SLAVONIA

SD1

Hungary No. E1 Overprinted in Black

1918 Wmk. 137 *Perf. 15*

2LE1 SD1 2f gray green & red .25 .25

POSTAGE DUE STAMPS ISSUES FOR CROATIA-SLAVONIA

D1

Postage Due Stamps of Hungary Overprinted in Blue

1918 Wmk. Crown (136) *Perf. 15*

2LJ1 D1 50f green & blk 650.00 650.00

Wmk. Double Cross (137)

2LJ2 D1 1f green & red 40.00 40.00
a. Inverted overprint — —
2LJ3 D1 2f green & red 1.20 1.20
2LJ4 D1 10f green & red 1.20 1.20
2LJ5 D1 12f green & red 160.00 160.00
2LJ6 D1 15f green & red .80 .80
2LJ7 D1 20f green & red .80 .80
2LJ8 D1 30f green & red 2.00 2.00
2LJ9 D1 50f green & blk 65.00 65.00
Nos. 2LJ2-2LJ9 (8) 271.00 271.00

NEWSPAPER STAMPS ISSUES FOR CROATIA-SLAVONIA

N1

Hungary No. P8 Overprinted in Black

1918 Wmk. 137 *Imperf.*

2LP1 N1 (2f) orange .40 .40

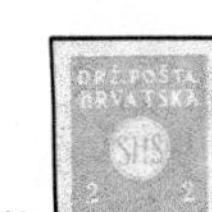
N2

1919 Litho. Unwmk.

2LP2 N2 2f yellow orange .25 1.20

SLOVENIA

Chain Breaker
A1 A2

3, 5, 10, 15f: Chain on right wrist is short, extending only about half way to the frame.

10f: Numerals are 8½mm high.

20, 25, 30, 40f: Distant mountains show faintly between legs of male figure.

40f: Numerals 7mm high. The upright strokes of the "4" extend to the same height; the "0" is 3mm wide.

1919 Unwmk. *Perf. 11½*

Lithographed at Ljubljana Fine Impression

3L1 A1 3f violet .25 .25
3L2 A1 5f green .25 .25
3L3 A1 10f carmine rose .40 .25
3L4 A1 15f blue .25 .25
3L5 A2 20f brown .65 .25
3L6 A2 25f blue .30 .25
3L7 A2 30f lilac rose .30 .25
3L8 A2 40f bister .30 .25
Nos. 3L1-3L8 (8) 2.70 2.00

Various stamps of this series exist imperforate and part perforate. Many shades exist.

See Nos. 3L9-3L17, 3L24-3L28. For surcharges see Nos. 3LJ15-3LJ32.

Allegories of Freedom
A3 A4

King Peter I — A5

3, 5, 15f: The chain on the right wrist touches the bottom tablet.

10f: Numerals are 7½mm high.

15f: Curled end of loin cloth appears above letter "H" in the bottom tablet.

20, 25, 30, 40f: The outlines of the mountains have been redrawn and they are more distinct than on the lithographed stamps.

40f: Numerals 8mm high. The left slanting stroke of the "4" extends much higher than the main vertical stroke. The "0" is 2½mm wide and encloses a much narrower space than on the lithographed stamp.

1919-20 *Perf. 11½*

Typographed at Ljubljana and Vienna Coarse Impression

3L9 A1 3f violet .25 .25
3L10 A1 5f green .30 .25
3L11 A1 10f red .25 .25
3L12 A1 15f blue 1.60 .25
3L13 A2 20f brown .55 .25
3L14 A2 25f blue .50 .25
3L15 A2 30f carmine rose .55 .25
3L16 A2 30f dp red 2.75 .90
3L17 A2 40f orange .55 .25
3L18 A3 50f green .55 .25
a. 50f dark green .55 .25
b. 50f olive green 3.50 1.10
3L19 A3 60f dark blue .85 .25
a. 60f violet blue .85 .25
3L20 A4 1k vermilion .55 .25
a. 1k red orange .55 .25
3L21 A4 2k blue .55 .25
a. 2k dull ultramarine .90 .25
3L22 A5 5k brown lake .80 .25
a. 5k lake 12.00 1.60
b. 5k dull red .60 .25
3L23 A5 10k deep ultra 3.25 .90
Nos. 3L9-3L23 (15) 13.85 5.05

Nos. 3L9-3L23 exist imperf. Value, set $90.

Many of the series exist part perforate.

Many shades exist of lower values.

See Nos. 3L29-3L32, 3L40-3L41.

Serrate Roulette 13½

3L24 A1 5f light grn .25 .25
3L25 A1 10f carmine .25 .25
3L26 A1 15f slate blue .30 .25
3L27 A2 20f dark brown .65 .25
a. Serrate x straight roul. .65 .25
3L28 A2 30f car rose .30 .25
a. Serrate x straight roul. .70 .25
3L29 A3 50f green .30 .25
3L30 A3 60f dark blue .95 .40
a. 60f violet blue 2.25 1.10
3L31 A4 1k vermilion 1.40 .40
a. 1k rose red 1.40 .40
3L32 A4 2k blue 9.00 2.75
Nos. 3L24-3L32 (9) 13.40 5.05

Roulette x Perf. 11½

3L24a A1 5f 150.00 150.00
3L25a A1 10f 55.00 55.00
3L26a A1 15f 175.00 175.00
3L28b A2 30f 55.00 55.00
3L29a A3 50f 5.25 4.00
3L30b A3 60f 55.00 55.00
3L31b A4 1k 55.00 55.00

Thick Wove Paper

1920 Litho. *Perf. 11½*

3L40 A5 15k gray green 7.25 14.50
3L41 A5 20k dull violet 1.40 2.40

On Nos. 3L40-3L41 the horizontal lines have been removed from the value tablets. They are printed over a background of pale brown wavy lines.

Chain Breaker A7

Freedom A8

King Peter I — A9

Pale red wavy lines

Dinar Values:
Type I — Size: 21x30½mm.
Type II — Size: 22x32½mm.

Thin to Thick Wove Paper

1920 *Serrate Roulette 13½*

3L42 A7 5p olive green .25 .25
3L43 A7 10p green .25 .25
3L44 A7 15p brown .25 .25
3L45 A7 20p carmine .40 .40
3L46 A7 25p chocolate .40 .25
3L47 A8 40p dark violet .25 .25
3L48 A8 45p yellow .25 .25
3L49 A8 50p dark blue .25 .25
3L50 A8 60p red brown .25 .25
3L51 A9 1d dark brown (I) .25 .25

Perf. 11½

3L52 A9 2d gray vio (II) .25 .25
3L53 A9 4d grnsh black (I) .30 .30
3L54 A9 6d olive brn (II) .25 .25
3L55 A9 10d brown red (II) .30 .80
Nos. 3L42-3L55 (14) 3.90 4.25

The 2d and 6d have a background of pale red wavy lines, the 10d of gray lines.
Counterfeits exist of No. 3L45.

POSTAGE DUE STAMPS ISSUES FOR SLOVENIA

D1

Ljubljana Print
Numerals 9½mm high

1919 Litho. Unwmk. *Perf. 11½*

3LJ1 D1 5f carmine .25 .25
3LJ2 D1 10f carmine .25 .25
3LJ3 D1 20f carmine .25 .25
3LJ4 D1 50f carmine .25 .25

Nos. 3LJ1-3LJ4 were also printed in scarlet and dark red.

Numerals 8mm high

3LJ5 D1 1k dark blue .45 .30
3LJ6 D1 5k dark blue .65 .50
3LJ7 D1 10k dark blue .90 .75
Nos. 3LJ1-3LJ7 (7) 3.00 2.55

Vienna Print

1920 Numerals 11 to 12 mm high

3LJ8 D1 5f red .25 .25
3LJ9 D1 10f red .25 .25
3LJ10 D1 20f red .25 .25
3LJ11 D1 50f red 1.25 .85

Numerals 7mm high

3LJ12 D1 1k Prussian blue 1.10 .70
a. 1k dark blue 5.00 4.50
3LJ13 D1 5k Prussian blue 1.60 1.25
a. 5k dark blue 8.00 6.75
3LJ14 D1 10k Prussian blue 3.75 3.25
a. 10k dark blue 14.00 15.00
Nos. 3LJ8-3LJ14 (7) 8.45 6.80

Nos. 3LJ8-3LJ14 exist imperf. Value, set $40.

No. 3L4 Surcharged in Red

1920 On Litho. Stamps *Perf. 11½*

3LJ15 A1 5p on 15f blue .25 .25
3LJ16 A1 10p on 15f blue .60 .80
3LJ17 A1 20p on 15f blue .25 .25
3LJ18 A1 50p on 15f blue .25 .25
Nos. 3LJ15-3LJ18 (4) 1.35 1.55

Nos. 3L7, 3L12, 3L26, 3L28, 3L28a Surcharged in Dark Blue

3LJ19 A2 1d on 30f lil rose .25 .25
3LJ20 A2 3d on 30f lil rose .25 .25
3LJ21 A2 8d on 30f lil rose 1.60 .80
Nos. 3LJ19-3LJ21 (3) 2.10 1.30

On Typographed Stamps

3LJ22 A1 5p on 15f pale bl 12.00 2.50
3LJ23 A1 10p on 15f pale bl 35.00 25.00
3LJ24 A1 20p on 15f pale bl 11.00 4.00
3LJ25 A1 50p on 15f pale bl 6.00 7.00
Nos. 3LJ22-3LJ25 (4) 64.00 38.50

3LJ26 A1 5p on 15f slate bl 2.75 .50
3LJ27 A1 10p on 15f slate bl 8.50 3.25
3LJ28 A1 20p on 15f slate bl 2.75 .50
3LJ29 A1 50p on 15f slate bl 2.75 .50
3LJ30 A2 1d on 30f dp rose 2.75 .65
a. Serrate x straight roulette 7.00 4.50
3LJ31 A2 3d on 30f dp rose 5.75 1.75
a. Serrate x straight roulette 8.00 5.50
3LJ32 A2 8d on 30f dp rose 125.00 6.50
a. Serrate x straight roulette 125.00 7.50
Nos. 3LJ26-3LJ32 (7) 150.25 13.65

The para surcharges were printed in sheets of 100, ten horizontal rows of ten. There were: 5p three rows, 10p one row, 20p three rows, 50p three rows. The dinar surcharges were in a setting of 50, arranged in vertical rows of five. There were: 1d five rows, 3d three rows, 8d two rows.

NEWSPAPER STAMPS ISSUES FOR SLOVENIA

Eros — N1

Ljubljana Print

1919 Unwmk. Litho. *Imperf.*

3LP1 N1 2f gray .25 .25
3LP2 N1 4f gray .25 .40
3LP3 N1 6f gray 3.50 4.00
3LP4 N1 10f gray .25 .25
3LP5 N1 30f gray .25 .40
Nos. 3LP1-3LP5 (5) 4.50 5.30

See Nos. 3LP6-3LP13. For surcharges see Nos. 3LP14-3LP23, 4LB1-4LB5.

N2

2 4 6 10

1920 Vienna Print

3LP6 N2 2f gray .25 .25
3LP7 N2 4f gray 6.50 10.00
3LP8 N2 6f gray 1.75 2.75
3LP9 N2 10f gray 14.00 21.00
3LP10 N2 2f blue .25 .30
3LP11 N2 4f blue .25 .25
3LP12 N2 6f blue 125.00 125.00
3LP13 N2 10f blue .25 .25
Nos. 3LP6-3LP13 (8) 148.25 159.80

Nos. 3LP1, 3LP10 Surcharged

a

b

On Ljubljana Print

3LP14 N1 (a) 2p on 2f gray .25 .40
3LP15 N1 (a) 4p on 2f gray .25 .40
3LP16 N1 (a) 6p on 2f gray .40 .65
3LP17 N1 (b) 10p on 2f gray .65 .80
3LP18 N1 (b) 30p on 2f gray .65 .85

On Vienna Print

3LP19 N1 (a) 2p on 2f blue .25 .25
3LP20 N1 (a) 4p on 2f blue .25 .25
3LP21 N1 (a) 6p on 2f blue .25 .25
3LP22 N1 (b) 10p on 2f blue .25 .25
3LP23 N1 (b) 30p on 2f blue .25 .25
Nos. 3LP14-3LP23 (10) 3.45 4.35

The five surcharges were arranged in a setting of 100, in horizontal rows of ten. There were: 2p three rows, 4p three rows, 6p two rows, 10p one row and 30p one row. The sheets were perforated 11½ horizontally between the groups of the different values.

SEMI-POSTAL STAMPS ISSUE FOR CARINTHIA PLEBISCITE

SP1

Nos. 3LP2, 3LP1 Surcharged With Various Designs in Dark Red

1920

4LB1 SP1 5p on 4f gray .25 .25
4LB2 SP1 15p on 4f gray .25 .25
4LB3 SP1 25p on 4f gray .25 .55
4LB4 SP1 45p on 2f gray .25 1.20
4LB5 SP1 50p on 2f gray .25 1.40
4LB6 SP1 2d on 2f gray 2.00 6.00
Nos. 4LB1-4LB6 (6) 3.25 9.65

Nos. 4LB1 to 4LB6 have a different surcharge on each stamp but each includes the letters "K.G.C.A." which signify Carinthian Governmental Commission, Zone A.
Sold at three times face value for the benefit of the Plebiscite Propaganda Fund.

GENERAL ISSUES

For Use throughout the Kingdom

King Alexander A1

King Peter I A2

Unwmk.

1921, Jan. 16 Engr. *Perf. 12*

1 A1 2p olive brown .25 .25
2 A1 5p deep green .25 .25
3 A1 10p carmine .25 .25
4 A1 15p violet .25 .25
5 A1 20p black .25 .25
6 A1 25p dark blue .25 .25
7 A1 50p olive green .25 .25
8 A1 60p vermilion .25 .25
9 A1 75p purple .25 .25
10 A2 1d orange .25 .25
11 A2 2d olive bister .30 .25
12 A2 4d dark green .60 .25
13 A2 5d carmine rose 2.50 .25
14 A2 10d red brown 12.00 .55
Nos. 1-14 (14) 17.90 3.80
Set, never hinged 32.50

Exist imperf. Value, set $125.
For surcharge see No. 27.

Nos. B1-B3 Surcharged in Black, Brown, Green or Blue

a

b

1922-24

15 SP1(a) 1d on 10p .25 .25
16 SP2(b) 1d on 15p ('24) .25 .25
17 SP3(a) 1d on 25p (Br) .25 .25
18 SP2(b) 3d on 15p (G) .80 .25
a. Blue surcharge 1.20 1.20
19 SP2(b) 8d on 15p (G) 1.60 .25
a. Double surcharge 35.00 30.00
b. 9d on 15p (error) 130.00
20 SP2(b) 20d on 15p 10.00 1.00
21 SP2(b) 30d on 15p (Bl) 27.50 2.50
Nos. 15-21 (7) 40.65 4.75
Set, never hinged 60.00

A3

1923, Jan. 23 Engr.

22 A3 1d red brown 2.00 .25
23 A3 5d carmine 3.75 .25
24 A3 8d violet 6.75 .25
25 A3 20d green 27.50 .75
26 A3 30d red orange 72.50 2.75
Nos. 22-26 (5) 112.50 4.25
Set, never hinged 250.00

For surcharge see No. 28.

Nos. 8 and 24 Surcharged in Black or Blue

1924, Feb. 18

27 A1 20p on 60p ver .25 .25
28 A3 5d on 8d violet (Bl) 8.00 .60
Set, never hinged 17.50

The color of the surcharge on No. 28 varies, including blue, blue black, greenish black and black.

A4

A5

1924, July 1 *Perf. 14*

29 A4 20p black .25 .25
30 A4 50p dark brown .25 .25
31 A4 1d carmine .25 .25
32 A4 2d myrtle green .25 .25
33 A4 3d ultramarine .25 .25
34 A4 5d orange brown 1.40 .25
35 A5 10d dark violet 12.50 .25
36 A5 15d olive green 7.50 .25
37 A5 20d vermilion 7.50 .25
38 A5 30d dark green 7.50 1.25
Nos. 29-38 (10) 37.65 3.50
Set, never hinged 80.00

No. 33 Surcharged

1925, June 5
39 A4 25p on 3d ultramarine .35 .25
40 A4 50p on 3d ultramarine .35 .25
Set, never hinged 1.60

King Alexander — A6

1926-27 **Typo.** ***Perf. 13***
41 A6 25p deep green .25 .25
42 A6 50p olive brown .25 .25
43 A6 1d scarlet .25 .25
44 A6 2d slate black .25 .25
45 A6 3d slate blue .30 .25
46 A6 4d red orange .50 .25
47 A6 5d violet .80 .25
48 A6 8d black brown 5.25 .25
49 A6 10d olive brown 4.00 .25
50 A6 15d brown ('27) 15.00 .25
51 A6 20d dark vio ('27) 17.50 .25
52 A6 30d orange ('27) 65.00 .45
Nos. 41-52 (12) 109.35 3.20
Set, never hinged 240.00

For overprints and surcharges see Nos. 53-62, 87-101, B5-B16.

Nos. B7-B16 Overprinted over the Red Surcharge

1928, July
53 A6 1d scarlet .25 .25
a. Surcharge "0.50" inverted
54 A6 2d black .50 .25
55 A6 3d deep blue .80 .50
56 A6 4d red orange 2.00 .60
57 A6 5d bright vio 1.60 .25
58 A6 8d black brown 6.50 .95
59 A6 10d olive brown 12.50 .25
60 A6 15d brown 95.00 3.00
61 A6 20d violet 47.50 3.00
62 A6 30d orange 125.00 9.50
Nos. 53-62 (10) 291.65 18.55
Set, never hinged 725.00

King Alexander — A7

With Imprint at Foot

1931-34 ***Perf. 12½***
63 A7 25p black .25 .25
64 A7 50p green .25 .25
65 A7 75p slate green .40 .25
66 A7 1d red .25 .25
67 A7 1.50d pink .80 .25
68 A7 1.75d dp rose ('34) 1.60 .35
69 A7 3d slate blue 6.00 .25
70 A7 3.50d ultra ('34) 2.40 .35
71 A7 4d deep orange 3.00 .25
72 A7 5d purple 3.00 .25
73 A7 10d dark olive 12.00 .25
74 A7 15d deep brown 12.00 .25
75 A7 20d dark violet 24.00 .25
76 A7 30d rose 12.00 .45
Nos. 63-76 (14) 77.95 3.90
Set, never hinged 175.00

Type of 1931 Issue Without Imprint at Foot

1932-33
77 A7 25p black .25 .25
78 A7 50p green .25 .25
79 A7 1d red .25 .25
80 A7 3d slate bl ('33) 1.00 .25
81 A7 4d deep org ('33) 3.50 .25
82 A7 5d purple ('33) 5.25 .25
83 A7 10d dk olive ('33) 17.00 .25
84 A7 15d deep brn ('33) 27.50 .25
85 A7 20d dark vio ('33) 35.00 .25
86 A7 30d rose ('33) 45.00 .35
Nos. 77-86 (10) 135.00 2.60
Set, never hinged 225.00

See Nos. 102-115.

Nos. 41 to 52 Overprinted

1933, Sept. 5 ***Perf. 13***
87 A6 25p deep green .25 .25
88 A6 50p olive brown .25 .25
89 A6 1d scarlet .75 .25
90 A6 2d slate black 3.25 .70
91 A6 3d slate blue 3.00 .25
92 A6 4d red orange 2.00 .25
93 A6 5d violet 4.00 .25
94 A6 8d black brown 9.25 1.40
95 A6 10d olive brown 16.00 .25
96 A6 15d brown 24.00 1.75
97 A6 20d dark violet 32.50 .80
98 A6 30d orange 32.50 .80
Nos. 87-98 (12) 127.75 7.20
Set, never hinged 240.00

Semi-Postal Stamps of 1926 Overprinted like Nos. 87 to 98 and Four Bars over the Red Surcharge of 1926

1933, Sept. 5
99 A6 25p green .80 .25
100 A6 50p olive brown .80 .25
101 A6 1d scarlet 2.40 .50
Nos. 99-101 (3) 4.00 1.00
Set, never hinged 8.00

Nos. 99-101 exist with double impression of bars. Value, each $5.50 unused, $4.50 used.

King Alexander Memorial Issue
Type of 1931-34 Issues
Borders in Black

1934, Oct. 17
102 A7 25p black .25 .25
103 A7 50p green .25 .25
104 A7 75p slate green .25 .25
105 A7 1d red .25 .25
106 A7 1.50d pink .25 .25
107 A7 1.75d deep rose .25 .25
108 A7 3d slate blue .25 .25
109 A7 3.50d ultramarine .25 .25
110 A7 4d deep orange .40 .25
111 A7 5d purple .60 .25
112 A7 10d dark olive 2.00 .25
113 A7 15d deep brown 4.00 .25
114 A7 20d dark violet 12.00 .25
115 A7 30d rose 10.00 .40
Nos. 102-115 (14) 31.00 3.65
Set, never hinged 50.00

Cyrillic Characters
Latin and Cyrillic inscriptions are transposed within some sets. In some sets some stamps are inscribed in Latin, others in Cyrillic. This will be mentioned only if it is necessary to identify otherwise identical stamps.

King Peter II — A10

1935-36 ***Perf. 13x12½***
116 A10 25p brown black .25 .25
117 A10 50p yel orange .25 .25
118 A10 75p turq green .25 .25
119 A10 1d brown red .25 .25
120 A10 1.50d scarlet .25 .25
121 A10 1.75d cerise .25 .25
122 A10 2d magenta ('36) .25 .25
123 A10 3d brn orange .25 .25
124 A10 3.50d ultramarine .40 .25
125 A10 4d yellow grn 1.20 .25
126 A10 4d slate blue ('36) .25 .25
127 A10 10d bright vio 1.20 .25
128 A10 15d brown 1.20 .25
129 A10 20d bright blue 4.75 .25
130 A10 30d rose pink 2.40 .25
Nos. 116-130 (15) 13.40 3.75
Set, never hinged 25.00

For overprints see Nos. N12, N14, N29.

King Alexander — A11

1935, Oct. 9 ***Perf. 12½x11½, 11½***
131 A11 75p turq green .35 .40
132 A11 1.50d scarlet .35 .40
133 A11 1.75d dark brown .40 .80
134 A11 3.50d ultramarine 2.25 2.50
135 A11 7.50d rose carmine 1.50 2.25
Nos. 131-135 (5) 4.85 6.35

Death of King Alexander, 1st anniv.

Nikola Tesla — A12

1936, May 28 **Litho.** ***Perf. 12½x11½***
136 A12 75p yel grn & dk brn .40 .25
137 A12 1.75d dull blue & indigo .40 .25
Set, never hinged 2.00

80th birthday of Nikola Tesla (1856-1943), electrical inventor.

Memorial Church, Oplenac — A13

1937, July 1
138 A13 3d Prussian grn 1.00 .50
a. Perf. 12½ 15.00 24.00
Never hinged 30.00
139 A13 4d dark blue 1.00 1.20
Set, never hinged 4.00

"Little Entente," 16th anniversary.

Coats of Arms of Yugoslavia, Greece, Romania and Turkey — A14

Perf. 11, 11½, 12½
1937, Oct. 29 **Photo.**
140 A14 3d peacock grn 1.50 .45
141 A14 4d ultramarine 2.00 1.40
Set, never hinged 5.75

Balkan Entente.
Some of the varieties of perfs are scarce.

King Peter II — A16

1939-40 **Typo.** ***Perf. 12½***
142 A16 25p black ('40) .25 .25
143 A16 50p orange ('40) .25 .25
144 A16 1d yellow grn .25 .25
145 A16 1.50d red .25 .25
146 A16 2d dp mag ('40) .25 .25
147 A16 3d dull red brn .25 .25
148 A16 4d ultra .25 .25
148A A16 5d dk blue ('40) .25 .25
148B A16 5.50d dk vio brn ('40) .50 .25
149 A16 6d slate blue 1.00 .25
150 A16 8d sepia 1.20 .25
151 A16 12d bright vio 1.75 .25
152 A16 16d dull violet 2.40 .25
153 A16 20d blue ('40) 2.40 .25
154 A16 30d brt pink ('40) 5.50 .55
Nos. 142-154 (15) 16.75 4.05
Set, never hinged 35.00

For overprints and surcharges see Nos. N1-N11, N13, N15-N28, N30-N35, Croatia 1-25, Serbia 2N1-2N30.

Arms of Yugoslavia, Greece, Romania and Turkey
A17 A18

1940, June 1
155 A17 3d ultramarine .95 .55
156 A18 3d ultramarine .95 .55
a. Pair, #155-156 7.00 13.50
157 A17 4d dark blue .95 .55
158 A18 4d dark blue .95 .55
a. Pair, #157-158 7.00 13.50
Nos. 155-158 (4) 3.80 2.20
Set, never hinged 7.50
Pairs, never hinged 30.00

Balkan Entente.

Bridge at Obod — A19

1940, Sept. 29 **Litho.**
159 A19 5.50d slate grn & pale blue 2.25 3.50
Never hinged 4.00

Zagreb Phil. Exhib.; 500th anniv. of Johann Gutenberg's invention of printing. The first press in the Yugoslav area was located at Obod in 1493.

Issues for Federal Republic

Serbia Nos. 2N37, 2N39 Srchd. in Green or Vermilion

Overprinted with Pale Blue Green Network

1944, Dec. **Unwmk.** ***Perf. 11½***
159A OS4 5d (3d + 2d) rose pink .25 .25
159B OS4 10d (7d + 3d) dk sl grn (V) .25 .25

Similar Srch. on Serbia Nos. 2N37-2N39

1945, Jan. 24 **Without Network**
159C OS4 5d (3d + 2d) rose pink .25 .25
159D OS4 10d (7d + 3d) dk sl grn (V) .25 .25
159E OS4 25d (4d + 21d) ultra (Bk) .25 .25
Nos. 159C-159E (3) .75 .75

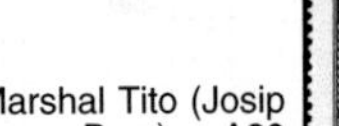

Marshal Tito (Josip Broz) — A20

1945 **Photo.** ***Perf. 12½***
160 A20 25p bright bl grn .25 .25
161 A20 50p deep green .25 .25
162 A20 1d crimson rose 1.20 .25
163 A20 2d dark car rose .25 .25
164 A20 4d deep blue .25 .25
165 A20 5d deep green .25 .40
166 A20 6d dark purple .25 .25
167 A20 9d orange brown .35 .25
168 A20 10d deep rose .25 .40
169 A20 20d orange 1.75 1.60
170 A20 25d dark purple .25 .25
171 A20 30d deep blue .25 .25
Nos. 160-171 (12) 5.55 4.65
Set, never hinged 9.00

Prohor Pcinski Monastery — A21

1945, Aug. 2 **Typo.** ***Perf. 11½***
172 A21 2d red 2.00 2.00
Never hinged 4.00

Formation of the Popular Antifascist Chamber of Deputies of Macedonia, Aug. 2, 1944.

Partisans
A22 A23

Marshal Tito
A24

City of Jajce
A25

Partisan Girl and Flag — A26

1945, Oct. 10 Litho. *Perf. 12½*

173 A22 50p olive gray .25 .25
174 A22 1d blue green .25 .25
175 A23 1.50d orange brown .25 .25
176 A24 2d scarlet .25 .25
177 A25 3d red brown 1.75 .25
178 A24 4d dark blue .30 .25
179 A25 5d dark yel grn 1.00 .25
180 A26 6d black .45 .25
181 A26 9d deep plum .40 .25
182 A23 12d ultramarine .90 .25
183 A22 16d blue .70 .25
184 A23 20d orange ver 1.60 .25
Nos. 173-184 (12) 8.10 3.00
Set, never hinged 17.50

See Nos. 211-214. For surcharges and overprints see Nos. 202-203, 273-282, 286-289, Istria 42, 44, 46, 48, 50, Trieste 5-14.

"Labor" and "Agriculture"
A27 A28

1945, Nov. 29 Photo. *Perf. 12*

185 A27 2d brn carmine 1.75 3.50
186 A28 2d brn carmine 1.75 3.50
187 A27 4d deep blue 1.75 3.50
188 A28 4d deep blue 1.75 3.50
189 A27 6d dk slate grn 1.75 3.50
190 A28 6d dk slate grn 1.75 3.50
191 A27 9d red orange 1.75 3.50
192 A28 9d red orange 1.75 3.50
193 A27 16d bright ultra 1.75 3.50
194 A28 16d bright ultra 1.75 3.50
195 A27 20d dark brown 1.75 3.50
a. Souv. sheet of 2, #191, 195, perf. 11½ 13.50 25.00
196 A28 20d dark brown 1.75 3.50
a. Souv. sheet of 2, #192, 196, perf. 11½ 13.50 25.00
Nos. 185-196 (12) 21.00 42.00
Set, never hinged 42.50
Se-tenant pairs, #185-196 (6) 30.00 30.00
Se-tenant pairs, never hinged 60.00

Constitution for the Democratic Federation of Yugoslavia, Nov. 29, 1945.

Parade of Armed Forces — A31

1946, May 9 Unwmk. *Perf. 12½*

199 A31 1.50d org yel & red .45 .60
200 A31 2.50d cerise & red .95 .85
201 A31 5d blue & red 3.00 1.75
Nos. 199-201 (3) 4.40 3.20
Set, never hinged 8.50

Victory over fascism, 1st anniv.

Type of 1945 Surcharged with New Values in Black

1946, Apr. 1

202 A26 2.50d on 6d bright red .40 .25
203 A26 8d on 9d orange .50 .25
Set, never hinged 1.75

Svetozar Markovic — A32

1946, Sept. 22

204 A32 1.50d blue green .75 .35
205 A32 2.50d dp red lilac .85 .50
Set, never hinged 2.50

Markovic, Serbian socialist, birth cent.

People's Theater, Sofia
A33

Sigismund Monument, Warsaw
A35

Designs: 1d, Prague. 2½d, Victory Monument, Belgrade. 5d, Spassky Tower, Kremlin.

1946, Dec. 8 Litho. *Perf. 11½*

206 A33 ½d dk brn & yel brn 2.00 4.00
207 A33 1d grnsh blk & emer 2.00 4.00
208 A35 1½d dk car rose & rose 2.00 4.00
209 A35 2½d hn brn & brn org 2.00 4.00
210 A35 5d dark bl & blue 2.00 4.00
Nos. 206-210 (5) 10.00 20.00
Set, never hinged 20.00

Pan-Slavic Congress, Belgrade, Dec. 1946.

Types of 1945

1947, Jan. 15 Litho. *Perf. 12½*

211 A26 2.50d red orange .35 .25
212 A25 3d dull red .50 .25
213 A25 5d dark blue 1.40 .25
214 A26 8d orange .90 .25
Nos. 211-214 (4) 3.15 1.00
Set, never hinged 6.00

Gorski Vijenac
A38

Peter P. Nyegosh
A39

1947, June 8 Typo.

215 A38 1.50d Prus grn & blk .50 .80
216 A39 2.50d ol bis & dk car .50 .80
217 A38 5d blue & black .50 .80
Nos. 215-217 (3) 1.50 2.40
Set, never hinged 2.50

Centenary of the Montenegrin national epic "Gorski Vijenac" (Wreath of Mountains) by Nyegosh.

Girls' Physical Training Classes — A40

Girl Runner — A41

Physical Culture Parade — A42

1947, June 15 Litho. *Perf. 11*

218 A40 1.50d brown 1.00 1.00
219 A41 2.50d red 1.00 1.00
220 A42 4d violet blue 1.00 1.00
Nos. 218-220 (3) 3.00 3.00
Set, never hinged 6.00

Natl. sports meet, Belgrade, 6/15-22/47.

Map and Star — A43

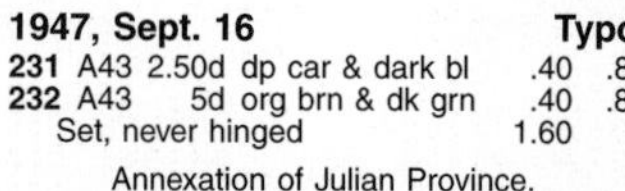

1947, Sept. 16 Typo.

231 A43 2.50d dp car & dark bl .40 .80
232 A43 5d org brn & dk grn .40 .80
Set, never hinged 1.60

Annexation of Julian Province.

Music and One-string Gusle
A44

Vuk Karadzic
A45

1947, Sept. 27 *Perf. 11½x12, 12½*

233 A44 1.50d green .40 .80
234 A45 2.50d orange red .40 .80
235 A44 5d violet blue .40 .80
Nos. 233-235 (3) 1.20 2.40
Set, never hinged 2.40

Centenary of Serbian literature.

Symbols of Industry and Agriculture, Map and Flag — A46

1948, Apr. 8 Litho. *Perf. 12½*

236 A46 1.50d grn, bl & salmon 1.40 2.00
237 A46 2.50d red brn, bl & salmon 1.40 2.00
238 A46 5d dk bl, bl & salmon 1.40 2.00
Nos. 236-238 (3) 4.20 6.00
Set, never hinged 8.00

International Fair, Zagreb, May 8-17.

Danube River Scene — A47

1948, July 30 Unwmk.

239 A47 2d green 2.50 4.25
240 A47 3d carmine 2.50 4.25
241 A47 5d blue 2.50 4.25
242 A47 10d brown orange 2.50 4.25
Nos. 239-242 (4) 10.00 17.00
Set, never hinged 17.50

Danube Conference, Belgrade.

Marchers with Party Flag — A48

1948, July 21 *Perf. 11½, 12½*

243 A48 2d dark green .40 .40
244 A48 3d dark red .60 1.20
245 A48 10d dark blue vio .60 .80
Nos. 243-245 (3) 1.60 2.40
Set, never hinged 3.25

5th Congress of the Communist Party in Yugoslavia, July 21, 1948.

Laurent Kosir — A49

1948, Aug. 21 *Perf. 12½*

246 A49 3d claret .40 .40
247 A49 5d blue .40 .40
248 A49 10d red orange .40 .40
249 A49 12d dull green .40 .40
Nos. 246-249 (4) 1.60 1.60
Set, never hinged 3.25

80th death anniv. of Laurent Kosir, recognized by Yugoslavia as inventor of the postage stamp.

Arms of Bosnia and Herzegovina
A50

Arms of Yugoslavia
A51

1948, Nov. 29 *Perf. 12½, 12x11½*

Arms of Yugoslav Peoples Republics

250 A50 3d green .40 .80
251 A50 3d rose lil (Macedonia) .40 .80
252 A50 3d gray bl (Serbia) .40 .80
253 A50 3d gray (Montenegro) .40 .80
254 A50 3d rose (Croatia) .40 .80
255 A50 3d orange (Slovenia) .40 .80
256 A51 10d deep carmine .60 1.40
Nos. 250-256 (7) 3.00 6.20
Set, never hinged 6.00

The Cyrillic and Latin inscriptions are transposed on Nos. 252, 253 and 255.

Franc Presern — A52

1949, Feb. 8 Photo. *Perf. 11½*

257 A52 3d dark blue .30 .25
258 A52 5d brown orange .30 .25
259 A52 10d olive black 1.00 .80
Nos. 257-259 (3) 1.60 1.30
Set, never hinged 2.75

Death cent. of Franc Presern, poet.

Ski Jump, Planica
A53

Ski Jumper
A54

Perf. 12½x11½

1949, Mar. 20 Litho.

260 A53 10d magenta .40 1.00
261 A54 12d slate gray .80 1.10
Set, never hinged 2.40

Intl. Ski Championships, Planica, Mar. 13-20.

Soldiers
A55

Farmers
A56

Arms and Flags of Macedonia and Yugoslavia — A57

1949, Aug. 2 *Perf. 12½*

262 A55 3d carmine rose .30 .65
263 A56 5d dull blue .40 .80
264 A57 12d red brown 2.00 2.75
Nos. 262-264 (3) 2.70 4.20
Set, never hinged 4.00

Liberation of Macedonia, 5th anniv.
It is reported that No. 264 was not sold to the public at post offices.
For overprints see Nos. C30-C32.

Postal Communications A58

UPU, 75th anniversary: 5d, Plane, locomotive and stagecoach, horiz.

1949, Sept. 8 **Unwmk.**

No.	Type	Description	Unused	Used
265	A58	3d red	1.60	3.25
266	A58	5d blue	.40	.80
267	A58	12d brown	.40	.80
		Nos. 265-267 (3)	2.40	4.85
		Set, never hinged	4.75	

For overprints see Trieste Nos. 15-16.

Locomotives — A60

1949, Dec. 15 **Photo.**

No.	Type	Description	Unused	Used
269	A60	2d Early steam	1.25	2.00
270	A60	3d Modern steam	1.25	2.00
271	A60	5d Diesel	1.25	2.00
272	A60	10d Electric	25.00	24.00
		Nos. 269-272 (4)	28.75	30.00
		Set, never hinged	52.50	

Centenary of Yugoslav railroads.
For overprints see Trieste Nos. 17-20.

Official Stamps Nos. O7 and O8 Surcharged

1949 **Typo.**

No.	Type	Description	Unused	Used
272A	O1	3d on 8d chocolate	.50	.40
272B	O1	3d on 12d violet	.50	.40
		Set, never hinged	2.00	

Stamps of 1945 and 1947 Overprinted or Surcharged in Black

a

b

c

d

1949 **Litho.**

No.	Type	Description	Unused	Used
273	A22 (a)	50p olive gray	.25	.25
274	A22 (a)	1d blue green	.25	.25
275	A24 (b)	2d scarlet	.25	.25
276	A26 (c)	3d on 8d orange	.25	.25
277	A25 (d)	3d dull red	.25	.25
278	A25 (d)	5d dark blue	.25	.25
279	A23 (a)	10d on 20d org ver	.45	.25
280	A23 (a)	12d ultramarine	.40	.25
281	A22 (a)	16d blue	.60	.25
282	A23 (a)	20d orange ver	.60	.25
		Nos. 273-282 (10)	3.55	2.50
		Set, never hinged	6.00	

On No. 279 the surcharge includes a rule below "JUGOSLAVIJA" and "D 10" with two bars over "20D."
See Nos. 286-289.

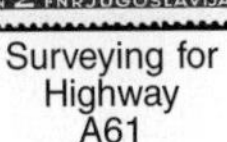

Surveying for Highway A61

Bridge, Map and Automobile A62

Highway Completion Symbolized — A63

1950, Jan. 16 **Photo.** ***Perf. 12½***

No.	Type	Description	Unused	Used
283	A61	2d blue green	.55	.80
284	A62	3d rose brown	.55	.80
285	A63	5d violet blue	.80	1.20
		Nos. 283-285 (3)	1.90	2.80
		Set, never hinged	3.75	

Completion of Belgrade-Zagreb highway, Dec. 1949.

Types of 1945 Overprinted in Black

1950 **Unwmk.** ***Perf. 12½***

No.	Type	Description	Unused	Used
286	A22 (a)	1d brownish org	.40	.25
287	A24 (b)	2d blue green	.40	.25
288	A25 (d)	3d rose pink	.60	.25
289	A25 (d)	5d blue	.60	.25
		Nos. 286-289 (4)	2.00	1.00
		Set, never hinged	4.00	

Marshal Tito — A64

1950, Apr. 30 **Engr.**

No.	Type	Description	Unused	Used
290	A64	3d red	1.00	.80
291	A64	5d dull blue	1.00	.80
292	A64	10d brown	10.00	20.00
293	A64	12d olive black	1.25	2.40
		Nos. 290-293 (4)	13.25	24.00
		Set, never hinged	24.00	

Labor Day, May 1.

Child Eating — A65

1950, June 1 **Photo.**

No.	Type	Description	Unused	Used
294	A65	3d brown red	.80	.45
		Never hinged	1.60	

Issued to publicize Children's Day, June 1.

Boy and Model Plane — A66

Designs: 3d, Glider aloft. 5d, Parachutists. 10d, Aviatrix. 20d, Glider on field.

1950, July 2 **Engr.**

No.	Type	Description	Unused	Used
295	A66	2d dark green	1.60	3.25
296	A66	3d brown red	1.60	3.25
297	A66	5d violet	1.60	3.25
298	A66	10d chocolate	1.60	3.25
299	A66	20d ultramarine	12.00	24.00
		Nos. 295-299 (5)	18.40	37.00
		Set, never hinged	37.50	

Third Aviation Meet, July 2-11.

Map and Chess Symbols — A67

3d, Rook and ribbon. 5d, Globe and chess board. 10d, Allegory of international chess. 20d, View of Dubrovnik, knight and ribbon.

1950, Aug. 20 **Photo.** ***Perf. 11½***

No.	Type	Description	Unused	Used
300	A67	2d red brn & rose brown	.45	.80
301	A67	3d blk brn, gray brn & dl yellow	.45	.80
302	A67	5d dk grn, bl & buff	1.10	.80
303	A67	10d cl, bl & org yel	1.10	2.00
304	A67	20d dk bl, bl & org yellow	22.00	22.50
		Nos. 300-304 (5)	25.10	26.90
		Set, never hinged	50.00	

Intl. Chess Matches, Dubrovnik, Aug. 1950.

Electrification — A68

Designs: 50p, Metallurgy. 2d, Agriculture, 3d, Construction. 5d, Fishing. 7d, Mining. 10d, Fruitgrowing. 12d, Lumbering. 16d, Gathering sunflowers. 20d, Livestock raising. 30d, Book manufacture. 50d, Loading ship.

1950-51 **Unwmk.** **Engr.** ***Perf. 12½***

No.	Type	Description	Unused	Used
305	A68	50p dk brn ('51)	.25	.25
306	A68	1d blue green	.25	.25
307	A68	2d orange	.25	.25
308	A68	3d rose red	.25	.25
309	A68	5d ultramarine	.60	.25
310	A68	7d gray	.60	.25
311	A68	10d chocolate	.60	.25
312	A68	12d vio brn ('51)	2.00	.25
313	A68	16d vio bl ('51)	1.75	.30
314	A68	20d ol grn ('51)	1.75	.25
314A	A68	30d red brn ('51)	4.00	.55
315	A68	50d violet ('51)	21.00	24.00
		Nos. 305-315 (12)	33.30	27.10
		Set, never hinged	55.00	

See Nos. 343-354, 378-384A. For overprints see Trieste Nos. 68-75, 90-92.

Coal and Logs for Export — A69

1950, Sept. 23 **Photo.**

No.	Type	Description	Unused	Used
316	A69	3d red brown	.80	.25
		Never hinged	1.60	

Zagreb International Fair, 1950.

Early Sailing Vessel "Dubrovnik" — A70

Designs: 3d, Partisans in boat. 5d, Loading freighter. 10d, Transatlantic ship "Zagreb." 12d, Sailboats. 20d, Naval gun and ship.

1950, Nov. 29

No.	Type	Description	Unused	Used
317	A70	2d brown violet	.25	.25
318	A70	3d orange brown	.25	.25
319	A70	5d dull green	.25	.25
320	A70	10d chalky blue	.30	.25
321	A70	12d dark blue	.80	.30
322	A70	20d red brown	10.00	2.90
		Nos. 317-322 (6)	11.85	4.20
		Set, never hinged	20.00	

Yugoslav navy.

Partisans with Flag — A71

1951, Mar. 27 **Engr.**

No.	Type	Description	Unused	Used
323	A71	3d red & red brn	3.50	3.50
		Never hinged	7.50	

Yugoslavia's resistance to Nazi Germany, 10th anniv.

Stane Rozman — A72

5d, Post-boy during Slovene insurrection.

1951, Apr. 27 **Photo.**

No.	Type	Description	Unused	Used
324	A72	3d brown red	.25	.25
325	A72	5d dark blue	.60	.40
		Set, never hinged	1.60	

Slovene insurrection, 10th anniv.

Children Painting — A73

1951, June 3

No.	Type	Description	Unused	Used
326	A73	3d red	.80	.25
		Never hinged	1.60	

Issued to publicize Children's Day, June 3.

Zika Jovanovich A74

Serbian Revolutionists A75

1951, July 7

No.	Type	Description	Unused	Used
327	A74	3d brown red	.30	.45
328	A75	5d deep blue	.55	.90
		Set, never hinged	1.60	

Serbian insurrection, 10th anniv.

Sava Kovacevich A76

Kovacevich Leading Revolutionists A77

1951, July 13

No.	Type	Description	Unused	Used
329	A76	3d rose pink	.40	.50
330	A77	5d light blue	1.00	1.10
		Set, never hinged	2.60	

Montenegrin insurrection, 10th anniv.

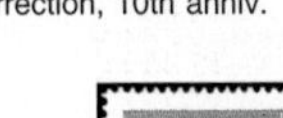

Monument to Marko Oreskovich — A78

1951, July 27

No.	Type	Description	Unused	Used
331	A78	3d shown	.45	.50
332	A78	5d Monument to wounded	.70	.90
		Set, never hinged	2.00	

Croatian insurrection, 10th anniv.

Sium Bolaj A79

Revolutionists A80

1951, July 27

No.	Type	Description	Unused	Used
333	A79	3d rose brown	.40	.50
334	A80	5d blue	.75	.90
		Set, never hinged	2.00	

Revolution in Bosnia and Herzegovina, 10th anniv.

Primoz Trubar — A81

12d, Marko Marulic. 20d, Tsar Stefan Duschan.

1951, Sept. 9 **Engr.**

335	A81	10d slate gray	3.25	6.50
336	A81	12d brown orange	3.25	6.50
337	A81	20d violet	10.00	20.00
		Nos. 335-337 (3)	16.50	33.00
		Set, never hinged	32.50	

Yugoslav cultural anniversaries.
For overprints see Trieste Nos. 40-41.

National Handicrafts — A82

1951, Sept. 15 **Litho.** ***Perf. 11½***

338	A82	3d multicolored	1.75	1.20
		Never hinged	2.50	

Zagreb International Fair, 1951.

Mirce Acev — A83

Monument at Skopje — A84

1951, Oct. 11

339	A83	3d deep plum	.40	.40
340	A84	5d indigo	.80	1.20
		Set, never hinged	2.50	

Macedonian insurrection, 10th anniv.

Soldier and Emblem — A85

1951, Dec. 22 **Photo.** ***Perf. 12½***

341	A85	15d deep carmine	.25	.25
		Never hinged	.50	

Army Day. See No. C54.

Peter P. Nyegosh — A86

1951, Nov. 29 **Engr.**

342	A86	15d deep claret	2.00	.80
		Never hinged	3.25	

Death centenary of Nyegosh. See note after No. 217.

Types of 1950-51

Designs: 15d, Gathering sunflowers. 25d, Agriculture. 35d, Construction. 75d, Lumbering. 100d, Metallurgy.

1951-52 **Engr.**

343	A68	1d gray ('52)	.25	.25
344	A68	2d rose car ('52)	.25	.25
345	A68	5d orange ('52)	.80	.25
346	A68	10d emerald ('52)	4.00	.25
347	A68	15d rose car ('52)	20.00	.25
348	A68	20d purple	2.00	.25
349	A68	25d yel brn ('52)	8.75	.25
350	A68	30d blue	1.00	.25
351	A68	35d red brn ('52)	1.50	.25
352	A68	50d greenish bl	.80	.25
353	A68	75d purple ('52)	2.00	.25
354	A68	100d sepia ('52)	4.00	.25
		Nos. 343-354 (12)	45.35	3.00
		Set, never hinged	90.00	

No. 349 exists with and without printer's inscriptions at bottom, with stamps differing slightly.

Marshal Tito
A87 A88

1952, May 25 **Photo.** ***Perf. 11½***

355	A87	15d shown	.40	.80
356	A88	28d shown	.40	.80
357	A87	50d Tito facing left	19.00	30.00
		Nos. 355-357 (3)	19.80	31.60
		Set, never hinged	40.00	

60th birthday of Marshal Tito.

Child with Ball — A89

1952, June 1 **Litho.** ***Perf. 12½***

358	A89	15d bright rose	3.00	3.00
		Never hinged	6.00	

Issued to publicize Children's Day, June 1.
For overprint see Trieste No. 60.

Girl Gymnast — A90

1952, July 10 ***Perf. 12½***

359	A90	5d shown	.40	.25
360	A90	10d Runner	.60	.25
361	A90	15d Swimmer	.60	.25
362	A90	28d Boxer	1.40	.80
363	A90	50d Basketball	2.00	4.50
364	A90	100d Soccer	24.00	27.50
		Nos. 359-364 (6)	29.00	33.55
		Set, never hinged	55.00	

15th Olympic Games, Helsinki, 1952.
Nos. 359-364 exist imperf. Value $800.
For overprints see Trieste Nos. 51-56.

Split, Dalmatia — A91

1952, Sept. 10 **Litho.**

365	A91	15d shown	.40	.80
366	A91	28d Naval scene	.80	1.75
367	A91	50d St. Stefan	9.00	14.00
		Nos. 365-367 (3)	10.20	16.55
		Set, never hinged	20.00	

Yugoslav navy, 10th anniv.
For overprints see Trieste Nos. 57-59.

Belgrade, 16th Century — A92

1952, Sept. 14 **Engr.** ***Perf. 11½***

368	A92	15d violet brn	6.00	10.00
		Never hinged	10.00	

1st Yugoslav Phil. Exhib., Sept. 14-20. Sold only at the exhibition.

Marching Workers and Congress Flag — A93

1952, Nov. 2 ***Perf. 11½***

369	A93	15d red brown	.60	1.20
370	A93	15d dark vio blue	.60	1.20
371	A93	15d dark brown	.60	1.20
372	A93	15d blue green	.60	1.20
		Nos. 369-372 (4)	2.40	4.80
		Set, never hinged	5.00	

6th Yugoslav Communist Party Congress, Zagreb.
For overprints see Trieste Nos. 61-64.

Nikola Tesla — A94

1953, Jan. 7 **Unwmk.**

373	A94	15d brown carmine	.40	.25
374	A94	30d chalky blue	2.00	.65
		Set, never hinged	4.00	

Death of Nikola Tesla, 10th anniv.
For overprints see Trieste Nos. 66-67.

Woman Pouring Water — A95

Designs: 30d, Hands holding two birds. 50d, Woman holding Urn.

1953, Mar. 24 **Litho.** ***Perf. 11½***

375	A95	15d dark olive green	.40	.65
376	A95	30d chalky blue	.90	.65
377	A95	50d henna brown	8.75	4.50
		Nos. 375-377 (3)	10.05	5.80
		Set, never hinged	20.00	

Issued to honor the United Nations.
See Nos. RA19 and RAJ16. For overprints see Trieste Nos. 76-78.

Types of 1950-52

1953-55 **Litho.** ***Perf. 12½***

8d, Mining. 17d, Livestock raising.

378	A68	1d dull gray	.40	.25
379	A68	2d carmine	1.00	.25
380	A68	5d orange	3.50	.25
381	A68	8d blue	2.50	.25
382	A68	10d yellow green	4.00	.25
383	A68	12d lt vio brown	20.00	.25
384	A68	15d rose red	8.00	.25
384A	A68	17d vio brn ('55)	1.50	.25
		Nos. 378-384A (8)	40.90	2.00
		Set, never hinged	75.00	

For overprints see Trieste Nos. 68-75, 90-92.

Automobile Climbing Mt. Lovcen — A96

30d, Motorcycle & auto at Opatija. 50d, Racers leaving Belgrade. 70d, Auto near Mt. Triglav.

1953, May 10 **Photo.** ***Perf. 12½***

385	A96	15d sal & dp plum	.25	.25
386	A96	30d bl & dark blue	.25	.25
387	A96	50d ocher & choc	.60	.40
388	A96	70d lt bl grn & ol grn	15.00	4.75
		Nos. 385-388 (4)	16.10	5.65
		Set, never hinged	35.00	

Intl. Automobile & Motorcycle Races, 1953.

President Tito — A97

1953, June 28 **Engr.** **Unwmk.**

389	A97	50d deep purple	6.00	8.00
		Never hinged	12.00	

Marshal Tito's election to the presidency, Jan. 14, 1953.
For overprint see Trieste No. 83.

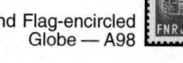

Star and Flag-encircled Globe — A98

1953, July 25 **Engr.; Star Typo.**

390	A98	15d gray & green	1.50	2.40
		Never hinged	3.00	

38th Esperanto Cong., Zagreb, 7/25-8/1.
For overprint see Trieste No. 84.

Macedonian Revolutionary
A99

Nicolas Karev
A100

1953, Aug. 2 **Litho.**

391	A99	15d dark red brown	.30	.65
392	A100	30d dull green	1.75	3.50
		Set, never hinged	4.00	

Macedonian Insurection of 1903, 50th anniv.

Family — A101

1953, Sept. 6 **Photo.**

393	A101	15d deep green	27.50	25.00
		Never hinged	50.00	

Liberation of Istria and the Slovene coast, 10th anniv.
For overprint see Trieste No. 85.

Branko Radicevic — A102

1953, Oct. 1 **Engr.**

394	A102	15d lilac	2.50	2.00
		Never hinged	5.00	

10th death anniv. of Branko Radicevic, poet.
For overprint see Trieste No. 86.

View of Jajce — A103

Designs: 30d, First meeting place. 50d, Marshal Tito addressing Assembly.

1953, Nov. 29 ***Perf. 12½x12***

395	A103	15d dark green	.40	.80
396	A103	30d rose car	.60	1.20
397	A103	50d dark brown	4.00	8.00
		Nos. 395-397 (3)	5.00	10.00
		Set, never hinged	10.00	

2nd Assembly of the Natl. Republic of Yugoslavia, 10th anniv.
For overprints see Trieste Nos. 87-89.

Wildlife
A104

Lammergeier
A105

1954, June 30 Photo. *Perf. 11½*

398	A104	2d	Ground squirrel	.25	.25
399	A104	5d	Lynx	.25	.25
400	A104	10d	Red deer	.40	.25
401	A104	15d	Brown bear	.50	.25
402	A104	17d	Chamois	.80	.25
403	A104	25d	White pelican	1.20	.40
404	A105	30d	shown	1.20	.40
405	A105	35d	Black beetle	1.60	.55
406	A105	50d	Bush cricket	6.00	2.00
407	A105	65d	Adriatic lizard	10.00	10.00
408	A105	70d	Salamander	8.00	10.00
409	A105	100d	Trout	24.00	32.50
			Nos. 398-409 (12)	54.20	57.10
			Set, never hinged	125.00	

See Nos. 497-505. For overprints see Trieste Nos. 93-104.

Catalogue values for unused stamps in this section, from this point to the end of the section, are for Never Hinged items.

Ljubljana, 17th Century — A106

1954, July 29 Engr.

410	A106	15d	multicolored	13.00	13.00

2nd Yugoslav Phil. Exhib., July 29-Aug. 8. Sold for 50d, which included admission to the exhibition.

Revolutionary Flag — A107

30d, Cannon. 50d, Revolutionary seal. 70d, Karageorge.

Engr. & Typo.

1954, Oct. 3 *Perf. 12½*

411	A107	15d	shown	1.60	.45
412	A107	30d	multi	2.25	.80
413	A107	50d	multi	5.00	1.10
414	A107	70d	multi	32.50	15.00
			Nos. 411-414 (4)	41.35	17.35

1st Serbian insurrection, 150th anniv. For overprints see Trieste Nos. 105-108.

Vatroslav Lisinski — A108

30d, Andrea Kacic-Miosic. 50d, Jure Vega. 70d, Jovan Jovanovic-Zmaj. 100d, Philip Visnic.

1954, Dec. 25 Engr.

415	A108	15d	dark green	2.75	1.00
416	A108	30d	chocolate	2.75	1.60
417	A108	50d	dp claret	3.75	3.00
418	A108	70d	indigo	7.50	7.00
419	A108	100d	purple	19.00	19.00
			Nos. 415-419 (5)	35.75	31.60

Scene from "Robinja" A109

"A Midsummer Night's Dream" A110

1955 Photo. *Perf. 12x11½, 12½*

Glazed Paper

420	A109	15d	brown lake	1.50	.90
421	A110	30d	dark blue	5.25	3.00

Festival at Dubrovnik.

Dragon Emblem of Ljubljana — A111

1955 Engr. *Perf. 12½*

422	A111	15d	dk grn & brn	6.25	2.25

1st Intl. Exhib. of Graphic Arts, Ljubljana, July 3-Sept. 3.

Symbol of Sign Language — A112

1955, Aug. 23

423	A112	15d	rose lake	2.50	.60

2nd World Congress of Deaf Mutes, Zagreb, Aug. 23-27.

Hops — A113

Medicinal Plants.

1955, Sept. 24 Photo. *Perf. 11½*

424	A113	5d	shown	.25	.25
425	A113	10d	Tobacco	.25	.25
426	A113	15d	Poppy	.25	.25
427	A113	17d	Linden	.25	.25
428	A113	25d	Chamomile	.25	.25
429	A113	30d	Salvia	.60	.30
430	A113	50d	Dog rose	4.00	2.00
431	A113	70d	Gentian	7.00	2.75
432	A113	100d	Adonis	30.00	19.00
			Nos. 424-432 (9)	42.85	25.30

"Peace" Statue, New York — A114

1955, Oct. 24 Litho. *Perf. 12½*

433	A114	30d	lt bl & blk	1.50	1.10

United Nations, 10th anniversary.

Woman and Dove — A115

1955, Nov. 29 Engr.

434	A115	15d	dull violet	.80	.55

10th anniv. of the "New Yugoslavia."

St. Donat, Zadar A116

Cornice, Cathedral at Sibenik A117

Yugoslav Art: 10d, Relief of a King, Split. 15d, Griffin, Studenica Monastery. 20d, Figures, Trogir Cathedral. 25d, Fresco, Sopocani Monastery. 30d, Tombstone, Radimlje. 40d, Ciborium, Kotor Cathedral. 50d, St. Martin from Tryptich, Dubrovnik. 70d, Figure, Belec Church. 100d, Rihard Jakopic, self-portrait. 200d, "Peace" Statue, New York.

1956, Mar. 24 Photo. *Perf. 11½*

435	A116	5d	blue vio	.45	.25
436	A116	10d	slate grn	.45	.25
437	A116	15d	olive brn	.45	.25
438	A116	20d	brown car	.45	.25
439	A116	25d	black brn	.45	.25
440	A116	30d	dp claret	.45	.25
441	A117	35d	olive grn	1.00	.25
442	A117	40d	red brown	1.75	.50
443	A116	50d	olive brn	2.50	.70
444	A116	70d	dk green	9.25	6.75
445	A116	100d	dark pur	32.50	20.00
446	A116	200d	deep blue	77.50	32.50
			Nos. 435-446 (12)	127.20	62.20

13th Century Tower, Zagreb — A118

1956, Apr. 20 Engr. *Perf. 11½*

Chalky Paper

447	A118	15d	vio brn, bis brn & gray	1.00	.25
a.			Miniature sheet of 4	9.00	—

3rd Yugoslavia Phil. Exhib. (JUFIZ III), Zagreb, May 20-27. No. 447a was sold at the exhibition, tipped into a folder, for 75 dinars.

See No. C56.

Induction Motor — A119

Perf. 11½x12½

1956, July 10 Photo.

448	A119	10d	shown	.50	.25
449	A119	15d	Transformer	.60	.25
450	A119	30d	Electronic controls	1.10	.50
451	A119	50d	Nikola Tesla	4.00	2.00
			Nos. 448-451 (4)	6.20	3.00

Birth cent. of Nikola Tesla, inventor.

Sea Horse A120

Paper Nautilus A121

Designs: 20d, European rock lobster. 25d, "Sea Prince." 30d, Sea perch. 35d, Red mullet. 50d, Scorpion fish. 70d, Wrasse. 100d, Dory.

1956, Sept. 10 *Perf. 11½*

Granite Paper

Animals in Natural Colors

452	A120	10d	bright grn	.50	.30
453	A121	15d	ultra & blk	.50	.30
454	A121	20d	deep blue	.50	.30
455	A121	25d	violet blue	.80	.30
456	A121	30d	brt grnsh bl	.85	.30
457	A121	35d	dk bl green	1.75	.30
458	A121	50d	indigo	6.50	1.90
459	A121	70d	slate grn	8.00	4.00
460	A121	100d	dark blue	32.50	20.00
			Nos. 452-460 (9)	51.90	27.70

Runner — A122

Designs: 15d, Paddling kayak. 20d, Skiing. 30d, Swimming. 35d, Soccer. 50d, Water polo. 70d, Table tennis. 100d, Sharpshooting.

1956, Oct. 24 Litho. *Perf. 12½*

Design and Inscription in Bister

461	A122	10d	dk carmine	.80	.35
462	A122	15d	dark blue	.80	.35
463	A122	20d	ultramarine	1.50	.70
464	A122	30d	olive grn	1.50	.70
465	A122	35d	dark brown	1.50	.70
466	A122	50d	green	1.50	.70
467	A122	70d	brn violet	*50.00*	22.50
468	A122	100d	dark red	*50.00*	22.50
			Nos. 461-468 (8)	107.60	48.50

16th Olympic Games, Melbourne, 11/22-12/8.

Centaury — A123

Medicinal Plants: 15d, Belladonna. 20d, Autumn crocus. 25d, Marsh mallow. 30d, Valerian. 35d, Woolly Foxglove. 50d, Aspidium. 70d, Green Winged Orchid. 100d, Pyrethrum.

Granite Paper

Flowers in Natural Colors

1957, May 25 Photo. *Perf. 11½*

469	A123	10d	dk bl & grn	.25	.25
470	A123	15d	violet	.25	.25
471	A123	20d	lt ol grn & brn	.25	.25
472	A123	25d	dp cl & dk bl	.50	.25
473	A123	30d	lil rose & claret	.90	.25
474	A123	35d	dk gray & dl pur	1.50	.25
475	A123	50d	dp grn & choc	2.50	.75
476	A123	70d	pale brn & grn	4.50	1.60
477	A123	100d	gray & brown	14.00	6.00
			Nos. 469-477 (9)	24.65	9.85

See #538-546, 597-605, 689-694, 772-777.

Hand Holding Factory — A124

1957, June 25 Engr. *Perf. 12½*

478	A124	15d	dark car rose	.40	.25
479	A124	30d	violet blue	1.40	.80

Congress of Workers' Councils, Belgrade, June 25. Exist imperf.

2nd Gymnastic Meet, Zagreb, July 10-14 — A125

Various gymnastic positions.

1957, July 1 Photo.

480	A125	10d	ol grn & blk	.25	.25
481	A125	15d	brn red & blk	.25	.25
482	A125	30d	Prus bl & blk	.80	.25
483	A125	50d	brn & black	3.75	1.25
			Nos. 480-483 (4)	5.05	2.00

Montenegro A126

Natl. Costumes: 15d, Macedonia. 30d, Croatia. 50d, Serbia. 70d, Bosnia and Herzegovina. 100d, Slovenia. 50d, 70d, 100d vert.

1957, Sept. 24 Typo. *Perf. 12½*

Background in Bister Brown

484	A126	10d	dk brn, ultra & red	.40	.25
485	A126	15d	dk brn, blk & red	.40	.25
486	A126	30d	dk brn, grn & red	.40	.25
487	A126	50d	dk brn & green	1.00	.25
488	A126	70d	dk brn & black	1.40	.50
489	A126	100d	dk brn, grn & red	6.50	3.25
			Nos. 484-489 (6)	10.10	4.75

Revolutionists — A127

Lithographed and Engraved

1957, Nov. 7 ***Perf. 11½x12½***
490 A127 15d ocher & red 1.00 .75

Russian Revolution, 40th anniv.

Simon Gregorcic — A128

Famous Yugoslavs: 30d, Anton Linhart, dramatist and historian. 50d, Oton Kucera, physicist. 70d, Stevan Mokranjac, composer. 100d, Jovan Sterija Popovic, writer

1957, Dec. 3 **Engr.** ***Perf. 12½***
491 A128 15d sepia .45 .40
492 A128 30d indigo .60 .40
493 A128 50d reddish brn 1.25 .40
494 A128 70d dl violet 9.00 4.75
495 A128 100d olive grn 15.00 8.00
Nos. 491-495 (5) 26.30 13.95

"Young Man on Fire" — A129

1958, Apr. 22 **Photo.**
496 A129 15d deep plum .80 .25

Union of Yugoslav Communists, 7th congress, Ljubljana, Apr. 22.

Types of 1954

Game birds.

1958, May 25 ***Perf. 11½***
Granite Paper
Birds in Natural Colors

497 A104 10d Mallard .30 .25
498 A104 15d Capercaillie .30 .25
499 A104 20d Ring-necked pheasant .30 .25
500 A105 25d Coot .30 .25
501 A104 30d Water rail .70 .25
502 A105 35d Great bustard 1.25 .25
503 A105 50d Rock partridge 4.50 1.25
504 A104 70d Woodcock 8.25 3.25
505 A105 100d Eurasian crane 17.50 7.50
Nos. 497-505 (9) 33.40 13.50

Stylized Bird — A130

1958, June 14 **Engr.** ***Perf. 12½***
506 A130 15d bluish black .80 .25

Opening of Postal Museum, Belgrade. Exists imperf.

Flag and Laurel — A131

1958, July 1 **Unwmk.**
507 A131 15d brn carmine .50 .30

15th anniv. of victory over Germans at Sutjeska, Bosnia.

Onufrio Well, Dubrovnik — A132

1958, Aug. 10 **Litho.** ***Perf. 12½***
508 A132 15d black & brn 1.50 .30

Marin Drzic, dramatist, 450th birth anniv.

Sisak Steel Works A133

Titograd Hotel and Open-Air Theater A134

Industrial Progress Designs: 2d, Crude oil production. 5d, Shipbuilding. 10d, Sisak steel works. 15d, Jablanica hydroelectric works. 17d, Lumber industry. 25d, Overpass, Zagreb-Ljubljana highway. 30d, Litostroy turbine factory. 35d, Lukavac coke plant. 50d, Bridge at Skopje. 70d, Railroad station, Sarajevo. 100d, Triple bridge, Ljubljana. 200d, Mestrovic station, Zagreb. 500d, Parliament, Belgrade.

1958 **Typo.** ***Perf. 12½ Horiz.***
509 A133 10d green 14.00 6.00
510 A133 15d orange ver 14.00 6.00

Engr. ***Perf. 12½***
511 A133 2d olive .25 .25
512 A133 5d brown red .25 .25
513 A133 10d green .40 .25
514 A133 15d orange ver .40 .25
515 A133 17d deep claret .40 .25
516 A133 25d slate .40 .25
517 A133 30d blue black .40 .25
518 A133 35d rose red .40 .25
519 A134 40d car rose .45 .25
520 A134 50d bright bl .50 .25
521 A134 70d orange ver 1.25 .25
522 A134 100d green 4.75 .25
523 A134 200d red brown 4.50 .25
524 A134 500d intense bl 8.50 .30
Nos. 511-524 (14) 22.85 3.55

Nos. 509-510 are coil stamps.
See #555-562, 627-645, 786-789, 830-840.

Ocean Exploration — A135

1958, Oct. 24 **Unwmk.**
525 A135 15d brown violet .50 .25

Intl. Geophysical Year, 1957-58. Exists imperf. See #C58.

White and Black Hands Holding Scales — A136

1958, Dec. 10 ***Perf. 12½***
526 A136 30d steel blue 1.50 1.00

Universal Declaration of Human Rights, 10th anniv.

Dubrovnik — A137

Tourist attractions: #528, Bled. #529, Postojna grotto. #530, Ohrid. #531, Opatija. #532, Plitvice National Park. #533, Split. #534, Sveti Stefan. #535, Exhibition Hall, Belgrade.

1959, Feb. 16 **Litho.** ***Perf. 12½***
527 A137 10d crim rose & cit .25 .25
528 A137 10d lt grn & lt vio bl .25 .25
529 A137 15d grnsh bl & pur .25 .25
530 A137 15d grn & bright bl .25 .25
531 A137 20d lt grn & grnsh bl .25 .25
532 A137 20d ol bis & brt grn .25 .25
533 A137 30d yel org & purple 1.40 .25
534 A137 30d lt vio bl & gray ol 1.40 .25
535 A137 70d gray & grnsh bl 4.50 2.25
Nos. 527-535 (9) 8.80 4.25

Nos. 527, 530, 532 and 534 are inscribed in Cyrillic characters. See #650-658, 695-700.

Red Flags — A138

1959, Apr. 20 **Unwmk.** ***Perf. 12½***
536 A138 20d multicolored .50 .25

Yugoslav Communist Party, 40th anniv.

Dubrovnik, 15th Century — A139

1959, May 24 **Engr.** ***Perf. 11½***
537 A139 20d yel grn, dk grn & bl *10.00 3.50*

4th Yugoslavia Phil. Exhib. (JUFIZ IV), Dubrovnik.

Flower Type of 1957

Medicinal Plants: 10d, Lavender. 15d, Black Alder. 20d, Scopolia. 25d, Monkshood. 30d, Bilberry. 35d, Juniper. 50d, Primrose. 70d, Pomegranate. 100d, Jimson weed.

1959, May 25 **Photo.**
Granite Paper
Flowers in Natural Colors

538 A123 10d lt bl & dk blue .25 .25
539 A123 15d brt yel & car .25 .25
540 A123 20d dk ol bis & mar .25 .25
541 A123 25d ap grn & dk pur .25 .25
542 A123 30d pink & dk bl .25 .25
543 A123 35d bis brn & vio bl 1.25 .25
544 A123 50d brn & green 3.00 .40
545 A123 70d yel & ocher 4.00 .65
546 A123 100d lt brn & brn 8.50 4.00
Nos. 538-546 (9) 18.00 6.55

Tug of War — A140

Sports: 15d, High jump and runners. 20d, Ring and parallel bar exercises. 35d, Women gymnasts. 40d, Sailors doing gymnastics. 55d, Field ball and basketball. 80d, Swimming. 100d, Festival emblem, vert.

1959, June 26 **Litho.** ***Perf. 12½***
547 A140 10d dk sl grn & ocher .25 .25
548 A140 15d vio bl & sepia .25 .25
549 A140 20d ol bis & dl lil .25 .25
550 A140 35d deep cl & gray .25 .25
551 A140 40d violet & gray .25 .25
552 A140 55d sl grn & ol bis .50 .25
553 A140 80d indigo & olive 3.25 .50
554 A140 100d pur & bister 7.00 3.50
Nos. 547-554 (8) 12.00 5.50

Physical Culture Festival. Exist imperf.

Types of 1958; Designs as before

Designs: 8d, Lumber industry. 15d, Overpass, Zagreb-Ljubljana highway. 20d, Jablanica hydroelectric works. 40d, Titograd Hotel. 55d, Bridge at Skopje. 80d, Railroad Station, Sarajevo.

1959 **Typo.** ***Perf. 12½ Horizontally***
555 A133 15d green 2.50 1.10
556 A133 20d orange ver 3.00 1.10

Engr. ***Perf. 12½***
557 A133 8d deep claret .40 .25
558 A133 15d green .55 .25
559 A133 20d orange ver .95 .25
560 A134 40d bright blue 2.25 .25
561 A134 55d carmine rose 3.50 .25
562 A134 80d orange ver 6.00 .25
Nos. 557-562 (6) 13.65 1.50

Nos. 555-556 are coil stamps.

Fair Emblem — A141

1959, Sept. 5 **Litho.** **Unwmk.**
563 A141 20d lt vio bl & blk 2.00 1.00

50th International Fair at Zagreb.

Athletics — A142

1960, Apr. 25 ***Perf. 12½***
564 A142 15d shown .40 .40
565 A142 20d Swimming .40 .40
566 A142 30d Skiing .40 .40
567 A142 35d Wrestling .40 .40
568 A142 40d Bicycling .40 .40
569 A142 55d Yachting .40 .40
570 A142 80d Horseback riding 5.00 3.50
571 A142 100d Fencing 5.00 3.50
Nos. 564-571 (8) 12.40 9.40

17th Olympic Games.

Hedgehog — A143

1960, May 25 **Photo.** ***Perf. 12x11½***
Animals in Natural Colors

572 A143 15d shown .30 .30
573 A143 20d Red squirrel .30 .30
574 A143 25d Pine marten .30 .30
575 A143 30d Hare .70 .70
576 A143 35d Red fox .70 .70
577 A143 40d Badger .70 .70
578 A143 55d Wolf 1.50 1.50
579 A143 80d Roe deer 1.50 1.50
580 A143 100d Wild boar 4.00 4.00
Nos. 572-580 (9) 10.00 10.00

See Nos. 663-671.

Lenin, 90th Birth Anniv. — A144

1960, June 22 **Engr.** ***Perf. 12½***
581 A144 20d dk grn & slate grn .25 .25

Atomic Accelerator — A145

1960, Aug. 23 **Unwmk.**
582 A145 15d shown *8.00 8.00*
583 A145 20d Generator *8.00 8.00*
584 A145 40d Nuclear reactor *8.00 8.00*
Nos. 582-584 (3) *24.00 24.00*

Nuclear energy exposition, Belgrade. Exist imperf.

Serbian National Theater, Novi Sad — A146

Designs: 20d, Woman from Croatian play. 40d, Edward Rusijan and early plane. 55d, Symbolic hand holding fruit. 80d, Atom and UN emblem.

1960, Oct. 24 ***Perf. 12½***

585 A146 15d gray black .75 .75
586 A146 20d brown .75 .75
587 A146 40d dark gray blue .75 .75
588 A146 55d dull claret 1.00 1.00
589 A146 80d dark green 1.00 1.00
Nos. 585-589 (5) 4.25 4.25

Serbian Natl. Theater, Novi Sad, cent. (#585); Croatian Natl. Theater, Zagreb, cent. (#586); 1st flight in Yugoslavia, 50th anniv. (#587); 15th anniv. of the Yugoslav Republic (#588); UN, 15th anniv. (#589).
Exist imperf.

Ivan Cankar, Writer — A147

Famous Yugoslavs: 20d, Silvije Strahimir Kranjcevic, poet. 40d, Paja Jovanovic, painter. 55d, Dura Jaksic, writer and painter. 80d, Mihajlo Pupin, electro-technician. 100d, Rudjer Boscovich, mathematician.

1960, Dec. 24 **Engr.** ***Perf. 12½***

590 A147 15d dark green .35 .30
591 A147 20d henna brown .35 .30
592 A147 40d olive bister .35 .30
593 A147 55d magenta .35 .30
594 A147 80d dark blue .35 .30
595 A147 100d Prussian bl .35 .30
Nos. 590-595 (6) 2.10 1.80

Exist imperf.

International Atomic Energy Commission Emblem — A148

Engr. & Litho.

1961, May 15 ***Perf. 12½***

596 A148 25d multicolored .50 .25

Intl. Nuclear Electronic Conf., Belgrade.

Flower Type of 1957

Medicinal plants: 10d, Yellow foxglove. 15d, Marjoram. 20d, Hyssop. 25d, Scarlet haw. 40d, Rose mallow. 50d, Soapwort. 60d, Clary. 80d, Blackthorn. 100d, Marigold.

1961, May 25 **Photo.** ***Perf. 11½***

Granite Paper

Flowers in Natural Colors

597 A123 10d lt bl & grnsh bl .30 .30
598 A123 15d gray & chnt .30 .30
599 A123 20d buff & green .30 .30
600 A123 25d lt vio & vio .30 .30
601 A123 40d lt ultra & ultra .30 .30
602 A123 50d lt bl & blue .30 .30
603 A123 60d beige & dk car rose .30 .30
604 A123 80d lt grn & green .30 .30
605 A123 100d redsh brn & choc 12.00 9.00
Nos. 597-605 (9) 14.40 11.40

Victims' Monument, Kragujevac — A149

Monuments: 15d, Stevan Filipovic, Valjevo. 20d, Relief from Insurrection, Bozansko Grahovo. 60d, Victory, Nova Gradiska. 100d, Marshal Tito, Titovo Uzice.

Granite Paper

Gold Frames and Inscriptions

1961, July 3 ***Perf. 12x12½***

606 A149 15d crimson & brn .25 .25
607 A149 20d brn & ol bis .25 .25
608 A149 25d bl grn & gray olive .25 .25
609 A149 60d violet .25 .25
610 A149 100d indigo & black .25 .25
Nos. 606-610 (5) 1.25 1.25

Souvenir Sheet

Imperf

611 A149 500d indigo & black 125.00 125.00

Natl. Insurrection, 20th anniv.

Men of Five Races — A150

National Assembly Building, Belgrade A151

1961, Sept. 1 **Litho.** ***Perf. 11½***

613 A150 25d brown .25 .25

Engr.

614 A151 50d blue green .25 .25
Nos. 613-614,C59-C60 (4) 3.40 2.35

Miniature Sheet

Imperf

615 A150 1000d claret 20.00 17.50

Conference of Non-aligned Nations, Belgrade, Sept. 1961.

St. Clement, 14th Century Wood Sculpture — A152

1961, Sept. 10 **Engr.** ***Perf. 12½***

616 A152 25d sepia & olive 2.00 .65

12th Intl. Congress for Byzantine Studies.

Serbian Women — A153

Regional Costumes: 25d, Montenegro. 30d, Bosnia and Herzegovina. 50d, Macedonia. 65d, Croatia. 100d, Slovenia.

1961, Nov. 28 **Litho.**

617 A153 15d beige, brn & red .25 .25
618 A153 25d beige, red brn & black .25 .25
619 A153 30d beige, brn & dk red .25 .25
620 A153 50d multicolored .25 .25
621 A153 65d brn, red & yel .60 .25
622 A153 100d multicolored 1.60 .75
Nos. 617-622 (6) 3.20 2.00

Luka Vukalovic — A154

1961, Dec. 15 **Engr.**

623 A154 25d slate blue .25 .25

Centenary of Herzegovina insurrection.

Hands with Flower and Rifle — A155

1961, Dec. 22

624 A155 25d red & vio blue .25 .25

20th anniversary of Yugoslav army.

Miladinov Brothers — A156

1961, Dec. 25 **Litho.**

625 A156 25d buff & claret .25 .25

Centenary of Macedonian folksong "Koder"; Dimitri and Konstantin Miladinov, brothers who collected and published folksongs. Monument is at Struga.

Types of 1958; Designs as before

Designs: 5d, Shipbuilding. 8d, Lumber industry. 10d, Sisak steel works. 15d, Overpass. 20d, Jablanica hydroelectric works. 25d, Cable factory, Svetozarevo. 30d, Litostroy turbine factory. 40d, Lukavac coke plant. 50d, Zenica steel works. 65d, Sevojno copper works. 100d, Crude oil production. 150d, Titograd hotel. 200d, Bridge, Skopje. 300d, Railroad station, Sarajevo. 500d, Triple bridge, Ljubljana. 1000d, Mestrovic station, Zagreb. 2000d, Parliament, Belgrade.

1961-62 **Typo.** ***Perf. 12½ Horiz.***

627 A133 10d dark red brn 7.50 .55
628 A133 15d emerald 12.00 .30

Engr. ***Perf. 12½***

629 A133 5d dull orange .25 .25
630 A133 8d gray .25 .25
631 A133 10d dk red brn .25 .25
632 A133 15d emerald .25 .25
633 A133 20d violet blue .50 .25
634 A133 25d vermilion .25 .25
635 A133 30d red brown 6.50 .25
636 A133 40d dp cl ('62) .25 .25
637 A133 50d gray blue 1.60 .25
638 A133 65d green .25 .25
639 A133 100d yel olive 3.25 .25
640 A134 150d carmine ('62) .75 .25
641 A134 200d slate grn ('62) .75 .25
642 A134 300d olive ('62) 1.50 .25
643 A134 500d dull violet 1.25 .25
644 A134 1000d bister brn 4.50 .25
645 A134 2000d claret 10.00 .40
Nos. 629-645 (17) 32.35 4.40

Nos. 627-628 are coil stamps. For surcharges see Nos. 786, 789.

Isis of Kalabsha — A157

Design: 50d, Ramses II, Abu Simbel.

1962, Apr. 7 **Engr.** ***Perf. 12½***

646 A157 25d grnsh blk, *yelsh* .25 .25
647 A157 50d brown, *buff* .25 .25

15th anniv. (in 1961) of UNESCO.

Joy of Motherhood by Frano Krsinic — A158

1962, Apr. 7

648 A158 50d black, *cream* .30 .25

15th anniv. (in 1961) of UNICEF.

Anopheles Mosquito — A159

1962, Apr. 7 **Unwmk.**

649 A159 50d black, *gray* .40 .25

WHO drive to eradicate malaria.

Scenic Type of 1959

Tourist attractions: #650, Portoroz. #651, Jajce. #652, Zadar. #653, Popova Sapka. #654, Hvar. #655, Bay of Kotor. #656, Danube, Iron Gate. #657, Rab. #658, Zagreb.

1962, Apr. 24 **Litho.**

650 A137 15d ol & chlky bl .25 .25
651 A137 15d blue grn & bis .25 .25
652 A137 25d blue & red brn .25 .25
653 A137 25d dk bl & pale bl .25 .25
654 A137 30d blue & brn org .25 .25
655 A137 30d gray & chlky bl .25 .25
656 A137 50d ol & grnsh bl .90 .25
657 A137 50d blue & olive .90 .25
658 A137 100d dk grn & gray bl 7.50 3.00
Nos. 650-658 (9) 10.80 5.00

#651, 653, 655-656 are inscribed in Cyrillic.
Exist imperf.

Marshal Tito, by Augustincic — A160

Design: 50d, 200d, Sideview of bust by Antun Augustincic.

1962, May 25 **Engr.** ***Perf. 12½***

659 A160 25d dark green 1.00 .80
660 A160 50d dark brown 1.00 .80
661 A160 100d dark blue 1.00 .80
662 A160 200d greenish blk 1.00 .80
a. Souv. sheet of 4, #659-662, imperf. 35.00 35.00
Nos. 659-662 (4) 4.00 3.20

70th birthday of Pres. Tito (Josip Broz).

Animal Type of 1960

Designs: 15d, Crested newt. 20d, Fire salamander. 25d, Yellow-bellied toad. 30d, Pond frog. 50d, Pond turtle. 65d, Lizard. 100d, Emerald lizard. 150d, Leopard snake. 200d, European viper (adder).

1962, June 8 **Photo.** ***Perf. 12x11½***

Animals in Natural Colors

663 A143 15d green .50 .50
664 A143 20d purple .50 .50
665 A143 25d chocolate .50 .50
666 A143 30d violet blue .50 .50
667 A143 50d dark red .50 .50
668 A143 65d bright grn .50 .50
669 A143 100d black 1.25 1.25
670 A143 150d brown 1.25 1.25
671 A143 200d car rose 12.50 7.00
Nos. 663-671 (9) 18.00 12.50

Pole Vault — A161

Sports: 25d, Woman discus thrower, horiz. 30d, Long distance runners. 50d, Javelin thrower, horiz. 65d, Shot put. 100d, Women runners, horiz. 150d, Hop, step and jump. 200d, High jump, horiz.

Athletes in Black

1962, July 10 **Litho.** ***Perf. 12½***

672 A161 15d blue .35 .25
673 A161 25d magenta .35 .25
674 A161 30d emerald .35 .25
675 A161 50d red .35 .25
676 A161 65d vio blue .35 .25
677 A161 100d green .70 .25
678 A161 150d orange 3.50 .40
679 A161 200d orange brn 9.50 .80
Nos. 672-679 (8) 15.45 2.70

7th European Athletic Championships, Belgrade, Sept. 12-16. See No. C61.

Child at Play — A162

Litho. & Engr.

1962, Oct. 1 ***Perf. 12½***

680 A162 25d red & black .30 .25

Issued for Children's Week.

Gold Mask, Trebeniste, 5th Century B.C. A163

Bathing the Infant Christ, Fresco, Decani Monastery A164

Yugoslav Art Treasures: 25d, Horseman and bird, bronze vase (5th cent. B.C.). 50d, God Kairos, marble relief. 65d, "The Pigeons of Nerezi," fresco (12th cent.). 150d, Archangel Gabriel, icon (14th cent.).

1962, Nov. 28 **Photo.**

681	A163	25d Prus bl, blk & gold	.25	.25
682	A163	30d gold, saph & blk	.25	.25
683	A164	50d dk grn, brn & gold	.25	.25
684	A164	65d multicolored	.25	.25
685	A164	100d multicolored	.50	.50
686	A163	150d multicolored	1.00	1.00
		Nos. 681-686 (6)	2.50	2.50

Parched Earth and Wheat — A165

1963, Mar. 21 **Engr.** ***Perf. 12½***

687	A165	50d dark brn, *tan*	.40	.40

FAO "Freedom from Hunger" campaign.

Dr. Andrija Mohorovicic and UN Emblem — A166

1963, Mar. 23 **Unwmk.**

688	A166	50d dk blue, *gray*	.40	.40

UN 3rd World Meteorological Day, Mar. 23. Dr. Mohorovicic (1857-1936) was director of the Zagreb meteorological observatory.

Flower Type of 1957

Medicinal Plants: 15d, Lily of the valley. 25d, Iris. 30d, Bistort. 50d, Henbane. 65d, St. John's wort. 100d, Caraway.

1963, May 25 **Photo.** ***Perf. 11½***

Granite Paper

Flowers in Natural Colors

689	A123	15d gray grn & grn	.25	.25
690	A123	25d lt bl, ultra & pur	.25	.25
691	A123	30d gray & black	.25	.25
692	A123	50d redsh brn & red brn	.25	.25
693	A123	65d pale brn & brn	.65	.65
694	A123	100d slate & blk	3.50	2.75
		Nos. 689-694 (6)	5.15	4.40

Scenic Type of 1959

Tourist attractions: 15d, Pula. 25d, Vrnjacka Banja. 30d, Crikvenica. 50d, Korcula. 65d, Durmitor mountain. 100d, Ljubljana.

1963, June 6 **Litho.** ***Perf. 12½***

695	A137	15d multicolored	.25	.25
696	A137	25d multicolored	.25	.25
697	A137	30d multicolored	.25	.25
698	A137	50d multicolored	.25	.25
699	A137	65d multicolored	.25	.25
700	A137	100d multicolored	1.50	.40
		Nos. 695-700 (6)	2.75	1.65

Partisans on the March, by Djordje Andrejevic-Kun A167

Sutjeska (Gorge) A168

Design: No. 702A, As 15d, but inscribed "Vis 1944-1964." 50d, Partisans in battle.

Engr. & Litho.; Litho. (No. 702)

1963-64 ***Perf. 12½, 11½***

701	A167	15d gray & dk sl grn	.25	.25
702	A168	25d dark slate grn	.25	.25
702A	A167	25d gray & dark car rose	.45	.45
703	A167	50d tan & purple	.25	.25
		Nos. 701-703 (4)	1.20	1.20

20th anniv. of the Partisan Battle of Sutjeska (Nos. 701, 702-703); 20th anniv. of the arrival of the Yugoslav General Staff on the island of Vis (No. 702A).

Issued: #702A, 7/27/64; others, 7/3/63.

Gymnast on Vaulting Horse — A169

1963, July 6 **Litho.** ***Perf. 12½***

704	A169	25d shown	.40	.40
705	A169	50d Parallel bars	.80	.40
706	A169	100d Rings	1.20	.40
		Nos. 704-706 (3)	2.40	1.20

5th Gymnastics Europa Prize.

Mother, by Ivan Mestrovic — A170

Sculptures by Mestrovic (1883-1962): 50d, "Reminiscences" (woman). 65d, Head of Kraljevic Marko. 100d, Indian on Horseback.

1963, Sept. 28 **Engr.**

707	A170	25d brown, *cream*	.25	.25
708	A170	50d sl green, *grnsh*	.25	.25
709	A170	65d grnsh blk, *grysh*	.25	.25
710	A170	100d black, *grayish*	1.00	.75
		Nos. 707-710 (4)	1.75	1.50

Children with Toys — A171

1963, Oct. 5 **Litho.**

711	A171	25d multicolored	.40	.25

Issued for Children's Week.

Soldier with Gun and Flag — A172

Litho. & Engr.

1963, Oct. 20 ***Perf. 12½***

712	A172	25d ver, tan & gold	.50	.35

Yugoslavian Democratic Federation, 20th anniv.

Relief from Tombstone, Herzegovina — A173

Art through the centuries: 30d, Horseback trio, Split Cathedral. 50d, King & queen on horseback, Beram Church, Istria. 65d, Archangel Michael, Dominican monastery, Dubrovnik. 100d, Man pouring water, fountain, Ljubljana. 150d, Archbishop Eufrasie, mosaic, Porec Basilica, Istria.

1963, Nov. 29 **Photo.**

713	A173	25d multi	.25	.25
714	A173	30d multi, horiz.	.25	.25
715	A173	50d multi, horiz.	.25	.25
716	A173	65d multi	.25	.25
717	A173	100d multi	.25	.25
718	A173	150d multi	.95	.75
		Nos. 713-718 (6)	2.20	2.00

Issued for the Day of the Republic.

Dositej Obradovic — A174

Famous Yugoslavians: 30d, Vuk Stefanovic Karadzic, reformer of Serbian language. 50d, Franc Miklosic, Slovenian philologist. 65d, Ljudevit Gaj, reformer of Croatian language. 100d, Peter Petrovich Nyegosh, Montenegrin prince, bishop and poet.

Variously Toned Paper

1963, Dec. 10 **Engr.**

719	A174	25d blksh brn	.25	.25
720	A174	30d blksh brn	.25	.25
721	A174	50d blksh brn	.25	.25
722	A174	65d blksh brn	1.00	.25
723	A174	100d blksh brn	1.00	.50
		Nos. 719-723 (5)	2.75	1.50

Vanessa Io — A175

Butterflies & Moths: 30d, Vanessa antiopa. 40d, Daphnis nerii. 50d, Parnassius apollo. 150d, Saturnia pyri. 200d, Papilio machaon.

1964, May 25 **Photo.** ***Perf. 12½***

724	A175	25d multicolored	.40	.40
725	A175	30d multicolored	.40	.40
726	A175	40d multicolored	.40	.40
727	A175	50d multicolored	.40	.40
728	A175	150d multicolored	4.00	4.00
729	A175	200d multicolored	4.00	4.00
		Nos. 724-729 (6)	9.60	9.60

Fireman Rescuing Child — A176

1964, June 14 **Litho.**

730	A176	25d red & black	.25	.25

Centenary of voluntary firemen. Exists imperf.

Runner — A177

1964, July 1 **Unwmk.** ***Perf. 12½***

731	A177	25d shown	.25	.25
732	A177	30d Boxing	.25	.25
733	A177	40d Rowing	.25	.25
734	A177	50d Basketball	.25	.25
735	A177	150d Soccer	5.00	1.00
736	A177	200d Water polo	5.00	1.00
		Nos. 731-736 (6)	11.00	3.00

18th Olympic Games, Tokyo, Oct. 10-25.

UN Flag over Scaffolding — A178

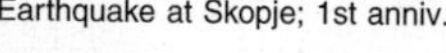
25d, Upheaval of the earth & scaffolding.

1964, July 26 **Engr.**

737	A178	25d red brown	.25	.25
738	A178	50d blue	.25	.25

Earthquake at Skopje; 1st anniv.

Serbian Women — A179

Regional Costumes: 30d, Slovenia. 40d, Bosnia and Herzegovina. 50d, Croatia. 150d, Macedonia. 200d, Montenegro.

Costumes Multicolored

1964, Aug. 5 **Litho.**

740	A179	25d violet & brn	.65	.65
741	A179	30d slate & green	.65	.65
742	A179	40d redsh brn & blk	.65	.65
743	A179	50d blue & black	.65	.65
744	A179	150d dl grn & sepia	2.75	2.75
745	A179	200d tan, red & brn	2.75	2.75
		Nos. 740-745 (6)	8.10	8.10

Exist imperf.

Friedrich Engels — A180

Litho. & Engr.

1964, Sept. 27 ***Perf. 11½***

746	A180	25d shown	.25	.25
747	A180	50d Karl Marx	.25	.25

1st Socialist Intl., London, Sept. 28, 1864. Exist imperf.

Children at Play — A181

1964, Oct. 4 **Litho.** ***Perf. 12½***

748	A181	25d ver, pink & gray grn	.40	.40

Issued for Children's Week. Exists imperf.

The Victor by Ivan Mestrovic — A182

1964, Oct. 20 **Engr.** ***Perf. 11½***

749	A182	25d bister & blk	.25	.25

Liberation of Belgrade, 20th anniv.

Initial from Evangel of Hilandar — A183

Art through the centuries: 30d, Initial from Evangel of Miroslav (musician). 40d, Detail from Cetigne octavo, 1494 (saint with scroll). 50d, Miniature from Evangel of Trogir, 13th cent. (female saint). 150d, Miniature from

Hrvoe Missal, 15th cent. (knight on horseback). 200d, Miniature from 14th cent. manuscript (symbolic fight), horiz.

Perf. 11½x12, 12x11½

1964, Nov. 29 Photo. Unwmk.
750 A183 25d multicolored .25 .25
751 A183 30d multicolored .25 .25
752 A183 40d multicolored .25 .25
753 A183 50d multicolored .25 .25
754 A183 150d multicolored .25 .25
755 A183 200d multicolored .25 .25
Nos. 750-755 (6) 1.50 1.50

Issued for Day of the Republic.

Hand, "Liberty and Equality" — A184

50d, Dove over factory, "Peace and Socialism." 100d, Smokestacks, "Building Socialism."

1964, Dec. 7 ***Perf. 12***
756 A184 25d multicolored .25 .25
757 A184 50d multicolored .25 .25
758 A184 100d multicolored .40 .25
Nos. 756-758 (3) .90 .75

Yugoslav Communist League, 8th congress.

Table Tennis Player — A185

1965, Apr. 15 Litho. ***Perf. 12½***
759 A185 50d shown *4.00 4.00*
760 A185 150d Player at left *4.00 4.00*

28th Table Tennis Championships, Ljubljana, Apr. 15-25. Exist imperf.

Titograd — A186

1965, May 8 Engr.
761 A186 25d shown .25 .25
762 A186 30d Skopje .25 .25
763 A186 40d Sarajevo .25 .25
764 A186 50d Ljubljana .50 .50
765 A186 150d Zagreb .50 .50
766 A186 200d Belgrade .65 .65
Nos. 761-766 (6) 2.40 2.40

Liberation of Yugoslavia from the Nazis, 20th anniv. Exist imperf.

Young Pioneer — A187

1965, May 10 Litho. & Engr.
767 A187 25d blk & tan, *buff* .25 .25

Young Pioneer Games "20 Years of Freedom." Exists imperf.

ITU Emblem and Television Tower — A188

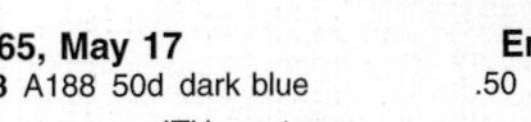

1965, May 17 Engr.
768 A188 50d dark blue .50 .40

ITU, centenary.

Iron Gate, Danube A189

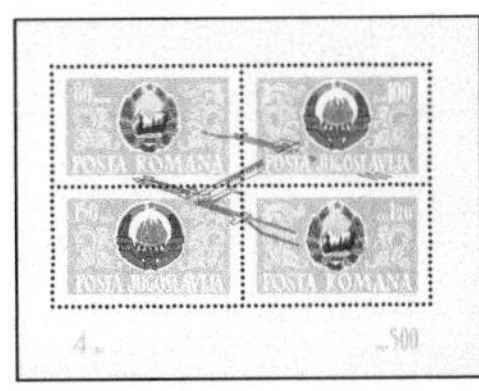

Arms of Yugoslavia and Romania and Djerdap Dam — A190

50d, Iron Gate hydroelectric plant and dam.

1965, May 20 Litho. ***Perf. 12½x12***
769 A189 25d (30b) lt gray bl & dp bl grn .25 .25
770 A189 50d (55b) lt gray bl & car lake .40 .25

Miniature Sheet

Perf. 13½x13

771 A190 Sheet of 4 4.25 4.25
a. 100d multicolored .35 .35
b. 150d multicolored .70 .70

Nos. 769-771 were issued simultaneously by Yugoslavia and Romania to commemorate the start of the construction of the Iron Gate hydroelectric plant. Nos. 769-770 were valid for postage in both countries.

No. 771 contains one each of Nos. 771a, 771b and Romania Nos. 1747a and 1747b. Only Nos. 771a and 771b were valid in Yugoslavia. Sold for 500d.

See Romania Nos. 1745-1747.

Flower Type of 1957

Medicinal Plants: 25d, Milfoil. 30d, Rosemary. 40d, Inula. 50d, Belladonna. 150d, Mint. 200d, Foxglove.

1965, May 25 Photo. ***Perf. 11½***

Granite Paper

Flowers in Natural Colors

772 A123 25d deep carmine .30 .30
773 A123 30d olive bister .30 .30
774 A123 40d red brown .30 .30
775 A123 50d dark blue .30 .30
776 A123 150d violet blue .35 .35
777 A123 200d purple 2.00 2.00
Nos. 772-777 (6) 3.55 3.55

Intl. Cooperation Year Emblem — A191

1965, June 26 Litho. ***Perf. 12½***
778 A191 50d dk bl & dull bl .25 .25

Sibenik — A192

1965, July 6 Unwmk. ***Perf. 12½***
779 A192 25d Rogaska Slatina .40 .40
780 A192 30d shown .40 .40
781 A192 40d Prespa Lake .40 .40
782 A192 50d Prizren .40 .40
783 A192 150d Scutari 1.20 1.20
784 A192 200d Sarajevo 2.00 2.00
Nos. 779-784 (6) 4.80 4.80

Cat — A193

1965, Oct. 3 Litho. ***Perf. 12½***
785 A193 30d maroon & brt yel .45 .25

Issued for Children's Week. Exists imperf.

Nos. 630 and 634 Surcharged in Maroon and Type of 1958

Designs: 20d, Jablanica hydroelectric works. 30d, Litostroy turbine factory.

1965 Engr. ***Perf. 12½***
786 A133 5d on 8d gray 1.00 .50
787 A133 20d emerald .50 .25
788 A133 30d red orange .80 .25
789 A133 50d on 25d vermilion 1.00 .50
Nos. 786-789 (4) 3.30 1.50

Branislav Nusic — A194

Famous Yugoslavs: 50d, Antun Gustav Matos, poet. 60d, Ivan Mazuranic, writer. 85d, Fran Levstik, writer. 200d, Josif Pancic, physician and botanist. 500d, Dimitrije Tucovic, political writer.

1965, Nov. 28 Engr.

Variously Toned Paper

790 A194 30d dull red .25 .25
791 A194 50d indigo .25 .25
792 A194 60d brown .25 .25
793 A194 85d dark blue .25 .25
794 A194 200d dk olive grn .25 .25
795 A194 500d deep claret .60 .45
Nos. 790-795 (6) 1.85 1.70

Marshal Tito — A195

1966, Feb. 4 Litho. ***Perf. 12½***
796 A195 20p bluish grn .40 .25
797 A195 30p rose pink .55 .25

Exists imperf.

Rowing — A196

30p, Long jump. 50p, Ice hockey. 3d, Hockey sticks, puck. 5d, Oars, scull.

1966, Mar. 1 Engr.
798 A196 30p dk car rose .25 .25
799 A196 50p dk purple .25 .25
800 A196 1d gray green .25 .25
801 A196 3d dk red brn 1.75 1.75
802 A196 5d dark blue 1.75 1.75
Nos. 798-802 (5) 4.25 4.25

25th Balkan Games; World ice hockey championship; 2nd rowing championships.

"T" from 15th Century Psalter — A197

Art through the Centuries (Initials from Medieval Manuscripts): 50p, Cyrillic "V," Divosh Evangel, 14th cent. 60p, "R," Gregorius I, Libri moralium, 12th cent. 85p, Cyrillic "P," Miroslav Evangel, 12th cent. 2d, Cyrillic "B," Radomir Evangel, 13th cent. 5d, "F," Passional, 11th cent.

1966, Apr. 25 Photo. ***Perf. 12***
803 A197 30p multicolored .25 .25
804 A197 50p multicolored .25 .25
805 A197 60p multicolored .25 .25
806 A197 85p multicolored .25 .25
807 A197 2d multicolored .25 .25
808 A197 5d multicolored .80 .40
Nos. 803-808 (6) 2.05 1.65

Radio Amateurs' Emblem — A198

1966, May 23 Engr. ***Perf. 12½x12***
809 A198 85p dark blue 2.50 1.20

Union of Yugoslav Radio Amateurs, 20th anniv.; Intl. Congress of Radio Amateurs, Opatija, 5/23-28.

Stag Beetle — A199

Beetles: 50p, Floral beetle. 60p, Oil beetle. 85p, Ladybird. 2d, Rosalia alpina. 5d, Aquatic beetle.

1966, May 25 Photo. ***Perf. 12x12½***
810 A199 30p gray, blk & bis .30 .25
811 A199 50p gray, emer & blk .30 .25
812 A199 60p bluish blk, sl grn & gray .30 .25
813 A199 85p dl org, dp org & black .30 .25
814 A199 2d gray, ultra & blk .30 .25
815 A199 5d tan, brn & blk .55 .25
Nos. 810-815 (6) 2.05 1.50

Serbia No. 2, 1866 — A200

Litho. & Engr.

1966, June 25 ***Perf. 12½***
816 A200 30p shown .25 .25
817 A200 50p No. 3 .25 .25
818 A200 60p No. 4 .25 .25
819 A200 85p No. 5 .25 .25
820 A200 2d No. 6 .45 .35
Nos. 816-820 (5) 1.45 1.35

Souvenir Sheet

Imperf

821 A200 10d No. 1 2.00 2.00

Serbia's first postage stamps, cent.

Leather Shield with Farmer, Soldier and Woman — A201

1966, July 2 ***Perf. 12½***
822 A201 20p pale grn, gold & red brown .25 .25
823 A201 30p buff, gold & dp mag .25 .25
824 A201 85p lt gray, gold & Prus bl .25 .25
825 A201 2d lt bl, gold & vio .25 .25
Nos. 822-825 (4) 1.00 1.00

25th anniversary of National Revolution.

Bishop Strossmayer and Franjo Racki — A202

1966, July 15
826 A202 30p dl ol, blk & buff .25 .25

Centenary of Academy of Arts and Sciences, founded by Bishop Josip Juraj Strossmayer with Racki as first president.

Mostar Bridge, Neretva River — A203

1966, Sept. 24 Engr. *Perf. 12½*

827 A203 30p rose claret 4.00 1.60

400th anniversary of Mostar Bridge.

Medieval View of Sibenik — A204

1966, Sept. 24

828 A204 30p deep plum .25 .25

900th anniversary of Sibenik.

Girl — A205

1966, Oct. 2 Litho.

829 A205 30p ultra, org, red & blk 1.50 1.50

Issued for Children's Week.

Shipbuilding — A206

Designs: 10p, Sisak steel works. 15p, Overpass. 20p, Jablonica hydroelectric works. 30p, Litostroy turbine factory. 40p, Lukavac coke factory. 50p, Zenica steel works. 60p, Cable factory, Svetozarevo. 65p, Sevojno copper works. 85p, Lumber industry. 1d, Crude oil production.

1966 Engr. *Perf. 12½*

830 A206 5p dull orange *1.00 1.00*
831 A206 10p brown *1.00 1.00*
832 A206 15p vio blue *1.00 1.00*
833 A206 20p emerald *.25 .25*
834 A206 30p vermilion *.75 .25*
835 A206 40p dp claret *1.00 1.00*
836 A206 50p gray blue *1.00 1.00*
837 A206 60p red brown *1.00 1.00*
838 A206 65p green *1.00 1.00*
839 A206 85p dl purple *1.00 1.00*
840 A206 1d yel olive *2.00 2.00*
Nos. 830-840 (11) *11.00 10.50*

Issued: 5, 15p, 6/10; 10, 40, 50p, 6/8; 20, 30p, 4/28; 60, 65, 85p, 5/12; 1d, 6/18.
Nos. 830, 832 and 840 exist imperf.
For surcharge see No. 1322.

UNESCO Emblem — A207

1966, Nov. 4 Litho.

841 A207 85p violet blue .25 .25

20th anniversary of UNESCO.

Santa Claus — A208

Designs: 15p, Stylized winter landscape. 30p, Stylized Christmas tree.

1966, Nov. 25 Litho. *Perf. 12½*

842 A208 15p org & dk bl .25 .25
843 A208 20p org & purple .25 .25
844 A208 30p org & sl grn .25 .25

1966, Dec. 23 Photo. *Perf. 12½*

845 A208 15p gold & dk bl .30 .25
846 A208 20p gold & red .30 .25
847 A208 30p gold & green .30 .25
Nos. 842-847 (6) 1.65 1.50

Nos. 842-847 issued for New Year, 1967.

Wolf's Head Coin of Durad I, 1373 — A209

Medieval Coins: 50p, ½d of King Stefan, c. 1461 (arms of Bosnia). 60d, Dinar of Serbia (portrait of Durad Brankovic). 85p, Dinar of Ljubljana, c. 1250 (heraldic eagle). 2d, Dinar of Split, c. 1403-1413 (shield with arms of Duke Hrvoje Vukcic). 5d, Dinar of Emperor Stefan Dusan, c. 1346-1355 (Emperor on horseback).

1966, Nov. 28 Photo.
Coins in Silver, Gray and Black

848 A209 30p ver & blk .25 .25
849 A209 50p ultra & blk .25 .25
850 A209 60p magenta & blk .25 .25
851 A209 85p violet & blk .25 .25
852 A209 2d dk ol bis & blk .25 .25
853 A209 5d brt grn & blk .55 .35
Nos. 848-853 (6) 1.80 1.60

Medicinal Plants — A210

1967, May 25 Photo. *Perf. 11½*
Granite Paper

854 A210 30p Arnica .25 .25
855 A210 50p Flax .25 .25
856 A210 85p Oleander .25 .25
857 A210 1.20d Gentian .25 .25
858 A210 3d Laurel .25 .25
859 A210 5d African rue .80 .80
Nos. 854-859 (6) 2.05 2.05

Youth Day, May 25.

Marshal Tito — A211

Size: 20x27½mm

1967, May 25 Engr. *Perf. 12½*

860 A211 5p orange .25 .25
861 A211 10p dk red brown .25 .25
862 A211 15p dk vio blue .25 .25
863 A211 20p green .25 .25
864 A211 30p vermilion .25 .25
865 A211 40p black .25 .25
866 A211 50p Prussian grn .25 .25
867 A211 60p lilac .25 .25
868 A211 85p deep blue .25 .25
869 A211 1d plum .25 .25
Nos. 860-869 (10) 2.50 2.50

75th birthday of Pres. Tito. Sheets of 15.
Nos. 860-869 were reissued in 1967 with slight differences including thinner paper and slightly darker shades.
See #924-939. For surcharge see #1414.

Coil Stamps

1968-69 Photo. *Perf. 12½ Horiz.*

869A A211 20p green .30 .25
869B A211 30p vermilion .40 .25
869C A211 50p vermilion ('69) .30 .25
Nos. 869A-869C (3) 1.00 .75

EXPO Emblem, Sputnik 1 and Explorer 1 — A212

Spacecraft: 50p, Tiros, Telstar and Molniya. 85p, Luna 9 and lunar satellite. 1.20d, Mariner 4, and Venera 3. 3d, Vostok, Gemini and Agena Rocket. 5d, Astronaut walking in space.

1967, June 26 Photo. *Perf. 11½*

870 A212 30p ultra & multi .25 .25
871 A212 50p yel & multi .25 .25
872 A212 85p slate & multi .25 .25
873 A212 1.20d multicolored .25 .25
874 A212 3d vio & multi .25 .25
875 A212 5d blue & multi 2.75 2.75
Nos. 870-875 (6) 4.00 4.00

EXPO '67, Montreal, Apr. 28-Oct. 27; 18th Congress of the Intl. Astronautical Federation, Belgrade. Exist imperf.

ITY Emblem, St. Tripun's Church, Kotor — A213

Designs (ITY Emblem and): 50p, Municipal Building, Maribor. 85p, Cathedral, Trogir. 1.20d, Fortress gate, Nis. 3d, Drina Bridge, Visegrad. 5d, Daut-pasha's Bath, Skopje.

1967, July 17 Engr.

876 A213 30p slate bl & lt ol .25 .25
877 A213 50p brn & dl vio .25 .25
878 A213 85p dk bl & dp claret .25 .25
879 A213 1.20d dp claret & brn .25 .25
880 A213 3d brn & slate grn .35 .25
881 A213 5d slate grn & brn *3.00* .45
Nos. 876-881 (6) 4.35 1.70

Issued for International Tourist Year, 1967.

Partridge — A214

1967, Sept. 22 Photo. *Perf. 14*

882 A214 30p shown .30 .30
883 A214 50p Pike .30 .30
884 A214 1.20d Red deer .50 .50
885 A214 5d Peregrine falcon 1.25 1.25
Nos. 882-885 (4) 2.35 2.35

Intl. Fishing and Hunting Exposition and Fair, Novi Sad.

Congress Emblem with Sputnik 1 — A215

Litho. & Engr.

1967, Sept. 25 *Perf. 12½*

886 A215 85p dk bl, lt bl & gold .25 .25

18th Congress of the Intl. Astronautical Federation, Belgrade, Sept. 25-30.

Old Theater and Castle, Ljubljana — A216

1967, Sept. 29 Engr. *Perf. 12½*

887 A216 30p sepia & dk grn .25 .25

Centenary of Slovene National Theater.

Child's Drawing: Winter Scene — A217

1967, Oct. 2 Litho.

888 A217 30p multicolored .50 .25

International Children's Week, Oct. 2-8.

Lenin by Mestrovic — A218

1967, Nov. 7 Engr. *Perf. 12½*

889 A218 30p dark purple .25 .25
890 A218 85p olive gray .25 .25

Souvenir Sheet
Imperf

891 A218 10d magenta 8.00 8.00

Russian October Revolution, 50th anniv. Nos. 889-890 exist imperf.

4-Leaf Clover — A219

30p, Chimney sweep. 50p, Horseshoe & flower.

Dated "1968"

1967, Nov. 15 Photo. *Perf. 14*

892 A219 20p shown .25 .25
893 A219 30p Chimney sweep .25 .25
894 A219 50p Horseshoe, flower .25 .25
Nos. 892-894 (3) .75 .75

New Year 1968. See Nos. 957-959.

The Young Sultana, by Vlaho Bucovac A220

Paintings: 85p, The Watchtower, by Dura Jaksic. 2d, Visit to the Family, by Josip Petkovsek. 3d, The Cock Fight, by Paja Jovanovic. 5d, "Spring" (woman and children), by Ivana Kobilca.

Perf. 11½x12, 12x11½

1967, Nov. 28 Engr. & Litho.

895 A220 85p multi, vert. 1.00 .30
896 A220 1d multi 1.00 .30
897 A220 2d multi 1.00 .30
898 A220 3d multi 1.00 .30
899 A220 5d multi, vert. 5.00 2.50
Nos. 895-899 (5) 9.00 3.70

Issued for the Day of the Republic, Nov. 29.
See Nos. 942-946, 995-1000.

Ski Jump — A221

Sport: 1d, Figure skating pair. 2d, Downhill skiing. 5d, Ice hockey.

1968, Feb. 5 Engr. *Perf. 12½*

900 A221 50p dk bl & dk pur .40 .25
901 A221 1d brn & sl green .40 .25
902 A221 2d sl grn & lake .70 .40
903 A221 5d sl grn & dk bl 5.50 3.00
Nos. 900-903 (4) 7.00 3.90

10th Winter Olympic Games, Grenoble, France, Feb. 6-18.

Annunciation — A222

Medieval Icons: 50p, Madonna, St. George's Church, Prizren. 1.50d, St. Sava and St. Simeon. 2d, Christ's descent into hell, Ohrid. 3d, Crucifixion, St. Clement's Church, Ohrid. 5d, Madonna, Church of Our Lady of the Bell Tower, Split.

1968, Apr. 20 Photo. *Perf. 13½*

906 A222 50p gold & multi .25 .25
907 A222 1d gold & multi .25 .25
908 A222 1.50d gold & multi .25 .25
909 A222 2d gold & multi .35 .25
910 A222 3d gold & multi .50 .40
911 A222 5d gold & multi 1.10 1.00
Nos. 906-911 (6) 2.70 2.40

European Bullfinch — A223

Finches: 1d, Goldfinch. 1.50d, Chaffinch. 2d, European greenfinch. 3d, Red crossbill. 5d, Hawfinch.

Birds in Natural Colors

1968, May 25 Photo. *Perf. 11½*

912 A223 50p bister .40 .40
913 A223 1d rose lake .40 .40
914 A223 1.50d gray blue .40 .40
915 A223 2d deep orange .40 .40
916 A223 3d olive green .45 .45
917 A223 5d pale violet 6.50 3.25
Nos. 912-917 (6) 8.55 5.30

Issued for Youth Day. Exist imperf.

800-meter Race for Women — A224

1d, Basketball. 1.50d, Gymnast on vaulting horse. 2d, Rowing. 3d, Water polo. 5d, Wrestling.

Litho. & Engr.

1968, June 28 *Perf. 12½*

918 A224 50p dk brn & dk red brown .40 .40
919 A224 1d Prus bl & blk .40 .40
920 A224 1.50d slate & dk brn .40 .40
921 A224 2d bis & sl grn 1.50 .40
922 A224 3d blk brn & ind 1.50 .40
923 A224 5d dk grn & vio blk 16.00 5.00
Nos. 918-923 (6) 20.20 7.00

19th Olympic Games, Mexico City, 10/12-27.

Tito Type of 1967

1968-72 Engr. *Perf. 12½*

Size: 20x27½mm

924 A211 20p dark blue 1.25 .25
925 A211 25p lake .25 .25
926 A211 30p green .25 .25
927 A211 50p vermilion .75 .25
928 A211 70p black .30 .25
929 A211 75p slate grn .40 .25
930 A211 80p olive 2.00 .25
930A A211 80p red org ('72) .40 .25
931 A211 90p olive .30 .25
932 A211 1.20d dark blue .50 .25
932A A211 1.20d sl grn ('72) .40 .25
933 A211 1.25d deep blue .25 .25
934 A211 1.50d slate grn .40 .25

Size: 20x30½mm

935 A211 2d sepia 2.50 .25
936 A211 2.50d Prussian grn 1.60 .25
937 A211 5d deep plum 1.40 .25
938 A211 10d violet blk 3.00 .35
939 A211 20d bluish black 4.25 .45
Nos. 924-939 (18) 20.20 4.80

The shading of the background of Nos. 924-939 has been changed from the 1967 issue to intensify the contrast around the portrait.

Cannon and Laurel Wreath — A225

1968, Aug. 2 Photo. *Perf. 12½*

940 A225 50p org brn & gold .25 .25

65th anniversary of the Ilinden uprising.

Mother Nursing Twins, Fresco by Jan of Kastav — A226

1968, Sept. 9 Litho.

941 A226 50p black & multi .25 .25

Annexation of Istria and the Slovene Coast to Yugoslavia, 25th anniv. Exists imperf.

Painting Type of 1967

Paintings: 1d, Lake Klansko, by Marko Pernhart. 1.50d, Bavarian Landscape, by Milan Popovic. 2d, Porta Terraferma, Zadar, by Ferdo Quiquerez. 3d, Mt. Triglav seen from Bohinj, by Anton Karinger. 5d, Studenica Monastery, by Djordje Krstic.

Engr. & Litho.

1968, Oct. 3 *Perf. 14x13½*

942 A220 1d gold & multi .25 .25
943 A220 1.50d gold & multi .25 .25
944 A220 2d gold & multi .25 .25
945 A220 3d gold & multi .30 .25
946 A220 5d gold & multi 2.40 .70
Nos. 942-946 (5) 3.45 1.70

Exist imperf.

Aleksa Santic (1868-1924), Poet — A227

1968, Oct. 5 Engr. *Perf. 12½*

947 A227 50p dark blue .25 .25

"Going for a Walk" — A228

1968, Oct. 6 Litho.

948 A228 50p multicolored .25 .25

Issued for Children's Week.

Karl Marx (1818-1883), by N. Mitric — A229

1968, Oct. 11 Engr.

949 A229 50d dk car rose .25 .25

Old Theater and Belgrade Castle — A230

1968, Nov. 22 Engr. *Perf. 12½*

950 A230 50p ol brn & sl grn .25 .25

Serbian National Theater, Belgrade, cent.

Hasan Brkic — A231

Portraits: 75p, Ivan Milutinovic. 1.25d, Rade Koncar. 2d, Kuzman Josifovski. 2.50d, Tone Tomsic. 5d, Mosa Pijade.

1968, Nov. 28 Engr. *Perf. 12½*

951 A231 50p violet black .25 .25
952 A231 75p black .25 .25
953 A231 1.25d red brown .25 .25
a. Souv. sheet, 2 ea #951-953 15.00 15.00
954 A231 2d bluish black .25 .25
955 A231 2.50d slate green .25 .25
956 A231 5d claret 1.25 .50
a. Souv. sheet, 2 ea #954-956 15.00 15.00
Nos. 951-956 (6) 2.50 1.75

2nd Assembly of the National Republic of Yugoslavia, 25th anniv.
No. 954 exists imperf. Value $100.
Nos. 953a and 956a exist imperf.

New Year's Type of 1967

1968, Nov. 25 Photo. *Perf. 14*

Dated "1969"

957 A219 20p Four-leaf clover .25 .25
958 A219 30p Chimney sweep .25 .25
959 A219 50p Horseshoe, flower .25 .25
Nos. 957-959 (3) .75 .75

Issued for New Year 1969.

The Family, by J. Soldatovic — A232

1968, Dec. 10 Engr. *Perf. 12½*

960 A232 1.25d dark blue .25 .25

International Human Rights Year.

ILO Emblem — A233

Litho. & Engr.

1969, Jan. 27 *Perf. 12½*

961 A233 1.25d red & black .25 .25

ILO, 50th anniv.

Dove, Hammer and Sickle Emblem — A234

75p, Graffiti "TITO" & 5-pointed star. 1.25d, 5-pointed crystal. 10d, Marshal Tito in 1943.

Engr. & Photo.

1969, Mar. 11 *Perf. 12½*

962 A234 50p black & red .25 .25
963 A234 75p ol bis & blk .25 .25
964 A234 1.25d red & black .25 .25
Nos. 962-964 (3) .75 .75

Souvenir Sheet

964A Sheet of 9 9.00 9.00
b. A234 10d brown, engr. 5.00 5.00

Communist Federation of Yugoslavia, 50th anniv.; 9th party congress.
No. 964A contains 4 No. 962, 2 each Nos. 963-964, 964b.
Nos. 962-964A exist imperf.

St. Nikita, from Manasija Monastery — A235

Frescoes from Monasteries: 75p, Apostles, Zakopani. 1.25d, Crucifixion, Studenica. 2d, Wedding at Cana, Kalenic. 3d, Angel at the Grave, Milseva. 5d, Pietá, Nerezi.

1969, Apr. 7 Photo. *Perf. 13½*

965 A235 50p gold & multi .25 .25
966 A235 75p gold & multi .25 .25
967 A235 1.25d gold & multi .25 .25
968 A235 2d gold & multi .25 .25
969 A235 3d gold & multi .45 .45
970 A235 5d gold & multi 2.00 .90
Nos. 965-970 (6) 3.45 2.35

Roman Memorial and View of Ptuj — A236

1969, Apr. 23 Engr. *Perf. 11½*

971 A236 50p violet brown .25 .25

1900th anniv. of Ptuj, the Roman Petovio. Issued in sheets of 9 (3x3).

Vasil Glavinov — A237

1969, May 8 *Perf. 12x12½*

972 A237 50p org brn & car lake .25 .25

Vasil Glavinov, Macedonian socialist, birth cent. Issued in sheets of 9 (3x3).

Thin-leafed Peony — A238

Medicinal Plants: 75p, Coltsfoot. 1.25d, Primrose. 2d, Hellebore. 2.50d, Violets. 5d, Anemones.

Flowers in Natural Colors

1969, May 25 Photo. *Perf. 11½*

973 A238 50p yellow brn .25 .25
974 A238 75p dull purple .25 .25
975 A238 1.25d blue .25 .25
976 A238 2d brown .25 .25
977 A238 2.50d plum .25 .25
978 A238 5d green 2.75 2.75
Nos. 973-978 (6) 4.00 4.00

Exist imperf.
See Nos. 1056-1061, 1140-1145.

Eber, by Vasa Ivankovic — A239

Paintings of Sailing Ships: 1.25d, Tare, by Franasovic. 1.50d, Brig Sela, by Vasa Ivankovic. 2.50d, Dubrovnik galleon, 16th century. 3.25d, Madre Mimbelli, by Antoine Roux. 5d, The Virgin Saving Seamen from Disaster, 16th century ikon.

1969, July 10 Photo. *Perf. 11½*

979 A239 50p gold & multi .25 .25
980 A239 1.25d gold & multi .25 .25
981 A239 1.50d gold & multi .25 .25
982 A239 2.50d gold & multi .25 .25
983 A239 3.25d gold & multi .55 .30
984 A239 5d gold & multi 2.75 2.25
Nos. 979-984 (6) 4.30 3.55

Dubrovnik Summer Festival, 20th anniv. Exist imperf.

11th World Games for the Deaf, Belgrade, Aug. 9-16 — A240

1969, Aug. 9 Engr. *Perf. 12½*

985 A240 1.25d dp claret & dl vio .40 .25

Lipice Horse — A241

Horses: 75p, Bosnian mountain horse. 3.25d, Ljutomer trotter. 5d, Half-breed.

1969, Sept. 26 Photo. *Perf. 11½*

986 A241 75p multicolored .25 .25
987 A241 1.25d olive & multi .25 .25
988 A241 3.25d brn & multi .30 .25
989 A241 5d multicolored 3.00 1.50
Nos. 986-989 (4) 3.80 2.25

Zagreb Veterinary College, 50th anniv. Exist imperf.

Children and Birds, by Tanja Vucanik, 13 years — A242

1969, Oct. 5 Litho. *Perf. 12½*

990 A242 50p org, blk & gray .25 .25

Issued for Children's Week.

Arms of Belgrade — A243

Arms: #992, Skopje (bridge & mountain). #993, Titograd (bridge & fortifications).

1969 Litho. *Perf. 12½*

991 A243 50p gold & multi .25 .25
992 A243 50p gold & multi .25 .25
993 A243 50p gold & multi .25 .25
Nos. 991-993 (3) .75 .75

Liberation of capitals of the Federated Republics, 25th anniv. See Nos. 1017-1020.

Josip Smodlaka — A244

1969, Nov. 9 Engr.

994 A244 50p dark blue .25 .25

Smodlaka (1869-1956), leader in Yugoslavia's fight for independence.

Painting Type of 1967

Paintings of Nudes: 50p, The Little Gypsy with the Rose, by Nikola Martinoski. 1.25d, Girl on a Red Chair, by Sava Sumanovic. 1.50d, Woman Combing her Hair, by Marin Tartaglia. 2.50d, Olympia, by Miroslav Kraljevic. 3.25d, The Bather, by Jovan Bijelic. 5d, Woman on a Couch, by Matej Sternen.

Photo. & Engr.

1969, Nov. 29 *Perf. 13½*

995 A220 50p multi, vert. .25 .25
996 A220 1.25d multi, vert. .25 .25
997 A220 1.50d multi, vert. .25 .25
998 A220 2.50d multi .35 .30
999 A220 3.25d multi, vert. .50 .40
1000 A220 5d multi 3.00 2.75
Nos. 995-1000 (6) 4.60 4.20

Exist imperf.

University of Ljubljana, 50th Anniv. — A245

1969, Dec. 9 Engr. *Perf. 11½*

1001 A245 50p slate grn .25 .25

Seal of Zagreb University — A246

Photo. & Engr.

1969, Dec. 17 *Perf. 12½*

1002 A246 50p gold, bl & brn .25 .25

University of Zagreb, 300th anniv.

Common Design Types pictured following the introduction.

Europa Issue, 1969

Common Design Type

1969, Dec. 20 Photo. *Perf. 11½*

1003 CD12 1.25d grnsh gray, buff & brn 1.25 1.25
1004 CD12 3.25d rose lil, gray & dk bl 2.75 2.75

Yugoslavia's admission to CEPT. Exist imperf.

Jovan Cvijic, Geographer — A247

Famous Yugoslavs: 1.25d, Dr. Andrija Stampar, hygienist. 1.50d, Joakim Krcovski, author. 2.50d, Marko Miljanov, Montenegrin patriot-hero. 3.25d, Vaca Pelagic, socialist. 5d, Oton Zupancic, Slovenian poet.

1970, Feb. 16 Engr. *Perf. 12½*

1005 A247 50p reddish brn .25 .25
1006 A247 1.25d brnsh black .25 .25
1007 A247 1.50d lilac .25 .25
1008 A247 2.50d slate grn .25 .25
1009 A247 3.25d reddish brn .25 .25
1010 A247 5d blue vio .25 .25
Nos. 1005-1010 (6) 1.50 1.50

Punishment of Dirce, Pulj — A248

Mosaics from the 1st-4th Centuries: 1.25d, Cerberus, Bitola, horiz. 1.50d, Angel of the Annunciation, Porec. 2.50d, Hunters, Gamzigard. 3.25d, Bull and cherry tree, horiz. 5d, Virgin and Child enthroned, Porec.

1970, Mar. 16 Photo. *Perf. 13½*

1011 A248 50p gold & multi .25 .25
1012 A248 1.25d gold & multi .25 .25
1013 A248 1.50d gold & multi .25 .25
1014 A248 2.50d gold & multi .30 .25
1015 A248 3.25d gold & multi .55 .35
1016 A248 5d gold & multi 1.50 1.50
Nos. 1011-1016 (6) 3.10 2.85

Exist imperf.

Arms Type of 1969

#1017, Sarajevo (arcade). #1018, Zagreb (castle). #1019, Ljubljana (dragon and tower). #1020a, Yugoslavia (embossed coat of arms.)

1970 Litho. *Perf. 12½*

1017 A243 50p gold & multi .25 .25
1018 A243 50p gold & multi .25 .25
1019 A243 50p gold & multi .25 .25
Nos. 1017-1019 (3) .75 .75

Souvenir Sheet

1020 Sheet of 7 15.00 15.00
a. A243 12d gold & black 12.50 12.50

Liberation of Yugoslavia, 25th anniv. No. 1020 contains Nos. 991-993, 1017-1019, 1020a + 2 labels.

Issued: #1017, Apr. 6; #1018, May 8; #1019, May 9; #1020, May 15.

Lenin (1870-1924), by S. Stojanovic — A249

Design: 1.25d, Lenin sculpture facing left.

1970, Apr. 22 Engr.

1021 A249 50p rose lilac .25 .25
1022 A249 1.25d blue gray .25 .25

Basketball — A250

1970, Apr. 25

1023 A250 1.25d plum .25 .25

6th World Basketball Championships, Ljubljana, May 10-23.
Exists imperf.

Europa Issue, 1970

Common Design Type

1970, May 4 Photo. *Perf. 11½*

Size: 32½x23mm

1024 CD13 1.25d lt bl, dk bl & lt grnsh bl .40 .40
1025 CD13 3.25d rose lil, plum & gray .40 .40

Exist imperf.

Istrian Shorthaired Hound — A251

Yugoslav Breeds of Dogs: 1.25d, Yugoslav tricolor hound. 1.50d, Istrian hard-haired hound. 2.50d, Balkan hound. 3.25d, Dalmatian. 5d, Shara mountain dog.

1970, May 25 Photo. *Perf. 11½*

Granite Paper

1026 A251 50p tan & multi .25 .25
1027 A251 1.25d olive & multi .25 .25
1028 A251 1.50d violet & multi .25 .25
1029 A251 2.50d slate & multi .25 .25
1030 A251 3.25d multi .45 .25
1031 A251 5d multi 2.00 2.00
Nos. 1026-1031 (6) 3.45 3.25

Exist imperf.

Telegraph Circuit — A252

1970, June 20 Litho. *Perf. 12½*

1032 A252 50p henna brn, gold & blk .25 .25

Telegraph service in Montenegro, cent.

Bird — A253

1970, Oct. 5

1033 A253 50p multicolored .25 .25

Issued for Children's Week, Oct. 5-11.

Stylized Gymnast — A254

1970, Oct. 22 Engr.

1034 A254 1.25d car & slate .25 .25

17th World Gymnastics Championships, Ljubljana, Oct. 22-27.

UN Emblem and Hand Holding Dove, by Makoto — A255

Litho. & Engr.

1970, Oct. 24 *Perf. 11½*

1035 A255 1.25d dk brn, blk & gold .25 .25

25th anniversary of the United Nations.

Ascension, by Teodor D. Kracum — A256

Baroque Paintings: 75p, Abraham's Sacrifice, by Federiko Benkovic. 1.25d, Holy Family, by Francisek Jelovsek. 2.50d, Jacob's Ladder, by Hristofor Zefarovic. 3.25d, Baptism of Christ, by unknown Serbian painter. 5.75d, The Coronation of Mary, by Tripo Kokolja.

Engr. & Photo.

1970, Nov. 28 *Perf. 13½x14*

1036 A256 50p gold & multi .25 .25
1037 A256 75p gold & multi .25 .25
1038 A256 1.25d gold & multi .25 .25
1039 A256 2.50d gold & multi .25 .25
1040 A256 3.25d gold & multi .45 .25
1041 A256 5.75d gold & multi .75 .70
Nos. 1036-1041 (6) 2.20 1.95

Exist imperf.

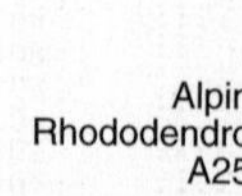

Alpine Rhododendron A257

European Nature Protection Year emblem and: 3.25d, Bearded vulture.

1970, Dec. 14 Photo. *Perf. 11½*

1042 A257 1.25d multi 3.00 3.00
1043 A257 3.25d multi 10.00 10.00

Sheets of 9.

Frano Supilo — A258

Litho. & Engr.

1971, Jan. 25 *Perf. 12½*

1044 A258 50p black & buff .25 .25

Supilo (1870-1917), Croat leader for independence from Austria-Hungary. Sheets of 9.

British, French, Canadian, Italian Satellites — A259

75p, Satellite. 1.25d, Automated moon exploration. 2.50d, Various spacecraft. 3.25d, 1st experimental space station. 5.75d, Astronauts on moon.

1971, Feb. 8 Photo. *Perf. 13½*

1045	A259	50p	multi	.25	.25
1046	A259	75p	multi	.25	.25
1047	A259	1.25d	multi	.25	.25
1048	A259	2.50d	multi, horiz.	.25	.25
1049	A259	3.25d	multi, horiz.	.25	.25
1050	A259	5.75d	multi, horiz.	1.10	1.10
			Nos. 1045-1050 (6)	2.35	2.35

"Space in the service of science." Sheets of 9.

Proclamation of the Commune, Town Hall, Paris — A260

Litho. & Engr.

1971, Mar. 18 *Perf. 11½*

1051 A260 1.25d bis brn & gray brn .25 .25

Centenary of the Paris Commune. Exist imperf.

Europa Issue, 1971

Common Design Type

1971, May 4 Photo. *Perf. 11½*

Size: 33x23mm

1052	CD14	1.50d	Prus bl, pale grn & dk bl	.25	.25
1053	CD14	4d	mag, pink & dk mag	.25	.25

Exist imperf.

Circles — A261

1971, May 5 *Perf. 13½*

1054	A261	50p	shown	.50	.25
1055	A261	1.25d	20 circles	1.40	.70

2nd Congress of Managers of Autonomous States.

Flower Type of 1969

Medicinal Plants: 50p, Common mallow. 1.50d, Common buckthorn. 2d, Water lily. 2.50d, Poppy. 4d, Wild chicory. 6d, Physalis.

1971, May 25 Photo. *Perf. 11½*

Flowers in Natural Colors

1056	A238	50p	lt ultra	.25	.25
1057	A238	1.50d	olive bis	.25	.25
1058	A238	2d	dull blue	.25	.25
1059	A238	2.50d	dark car	.30	.25
1060	A238	4d	dp bister	.65	.65
1061	A238	6d	org brown	4.00	4.00
			Nos. 1056-1061 (6)	5.70	5.65

Exist imperf.

Prince Lazar, Fresco, Lazarica Church — A262

1971, June 28 Photo. *Perf. 13½*

1062 A262 50p gray & multi .25 .25

600th anniversary of founding of Krusevac by Prince Lazar Hrebeljanovic (1329-1389).

View of Krk — A263

Views: 5p, Krusevo. 10p, Castle & mosque, Gradacac. 20p, Church & bridge, Bohinj. 35p, Shore & mountains, Omis. 40p, Peje. 50p, Memorial column, Krusevac. 60p, Logar Valley. 75p, Bridge & church, Bohinj. 80p, Church, Piran. 1d, Street, Bitolj. 1.20d, Minaret, Pocitelj. 1.25d, 1.50d, Gate tower, Hercegnovi. 2d, Cathedral & City Hall Square, Novi Sad. 2.50d, Crna River.

1971-73 Engr. *Perf. 13*

1063	A263	5p	orange ('73)	.25	.25
1064	A263	10p	brown ('72)	.25	.25
1065	A263	20p	vio blk ('73)	.25	.25
1066	A263	30p	ol gray ('72)	.25	.25
a.		30p	green	1.00	.25
1067	A263	35p	brn car ('73)	.25	.25
1068	A263	40p	black ('72)	.25	.25
1069	A263	50p	vermilion	1.50	.25
1070	A263	50p	green ('72)	.25	.25
1071	A263	60p	purple ('72)	.25	.25
1072	A263	75p	slate green	.25	.25
1073	A263	80p	rose red ('72)	1.50	.25
1073A	A263	1d	violet brn	1.50	.45
1073B	A263	1.20d	sl grn ('72)	2.00	.25
1073C	A263	1.25d	deep blue	1.10	.25
1073D	A263	1.50d	bluish blk ('73)	.25	.25
1073E	A263	2d	blue ('72)	1.00	.25
1073F	A263	2.50d	dl pur ('73)	1.00	.25
			Nos. 1063-1073F (17)	12.10	4.45

Issued with and without fluorescent bars.
See type A323. See Nos. 1482-1486, 1599-1600, 1602-1603, 1717. For surcharges see Nos. 1413, 1711-1712, 1765-1766, 1769.

Tourist Issue

Emperor Constantine, 4th Century — A264

Antique Bronzes excavated in Yugoslavia: 1.50d, Boy with fish. 2d, Hercules, replica after Lysippus. 2.50d, Satyr. 4d, Head of Aphrodite. 6d, Citizen of Emona, 1st century tomb.

1971, Sept. 20 Photo. *Perf. 13½*

1074	A264	50p	rose & multi	.25	.25
1075	A264	1.50d	multicolored	.25	.25
1076	A264	2d	multicolored	.25	.25
1077	A264	2.50d	lem & multi	.25	.25
1078	A264	4d	ocher & multi	.25	.25
1079	A264	6d	multicolored	.25	.25
			Nos. 1074-1079 (6)	1.50	1.50

Sheets of 9.

UNICEF Emblem, Children in Balloon — A265

1971, Oct. 4 Litho. *Perf. 13x13½*

1080 A265 50p multicolored .25 .25

Children's Week, Oct. 3-10.

Woman in Serbian Costume, by Katarina Ivanovic — A266

Portraits, 19th Century: 1.50d, The Merchant Ivanisevic, by Anastasije Bocaric. 2d, Ana Kresic, by Vjekoslav Karas. 2.50d, Pavle Jagodic, by Konstantin Danil. 4r, Luiza Pesjakova, by Mihael Stroj. 6d, Old Man and view of Ljubljana, by Matevz Langus.

Engraved and Photogravure

1971, Nov. 29 *Perf. 13½x14*

1081	A266	50p	gold & multi	.25	.25
1082	A266	1.50d	gold & multi	.25	.25
1083	A266	2d	gold & multi	.25	.25
1084	A266	2.50d	gold & multi	.25	.25
1085	A266	4d	gold & multi	.25	.25
1086	A266	6d	gold & multi	.80	.80
			Nos. 1081-1086 (6)	2.05	2.05

See Nos. 1120-1125.

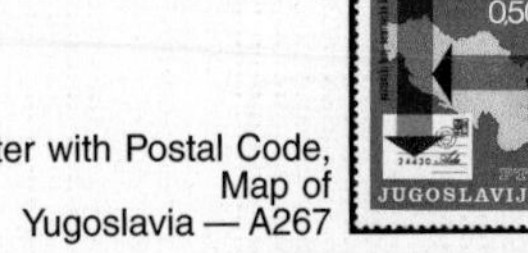

Letter with Postal Code, Map of Yugoslavia — A267

1971, Dec. 15 Photo. *Perf. 13½x14*

1087 A267 50p ultra & multi .25 .25

Introduction of postal code system.

Damjan Gruev (1871-1906), Macedonian Revolutionist — A268

1971, Dec. 22 Engr. *Perf. 12½*

1088 A268 50p dark blue .25 .25

11th Winter Olympic Games, Sapporo, Japan, Feb. 3-13 — A269

Engr. & Typo.

1972, Feb. 3 *Perf. 11½*

1089	A269	1.25d	Speed skating	.25	.25
1090	A269	6d	Slalom	2.50	1.25

Sheets of 9.

First Page of Statute of Dubrovnik — A270

Lithographed and Engraved

1972, Mar. 15 *Perf. 13½*

1091 A270 1.25d gold & multi .25 .25

700th anniversary of the Statute of Dubrovnik, a legal code given by Prince Marko Justiniani.

Ski Jump Track, Planica — A271

1972, Mar. 21 *Perf. 11½*

1092 A271 1.25d blk, lt bl & grn .25 .25

World Ski Jump Championships, Planica, Mar. 22-26.

Water Polo and Olympic Rings — A272

1972, Apr. 17 Litho. *Perf. 12½x12*

1093	A272	50p	shown	.25	.25
1094	A272	1.25d	Basketball	.25	.25
1095	A272	2.50d	Butterfly stroke	.25	.25
1096	A272	3.25d	Boxing	.25	.25
1097	A272	5d	Running	.25	.25
1098	A272	6.50d	Yachting	.40	.40
			Nos. 1093-1098 (6)	1.65	1.65

20th Olympic Games, Munich, Aug. 26-Sept. 10. Sheets of 9.

Europa Issue 1972

Common Design Type

1972, May 4 Photo. *Perf. 11½*

1100	CD15	1.50d	bl, grn & yel	.60	.60
1101	CD15	5d	brt rose, mag & org	.60	.60

Wall Creeper — A275

Birds: 1.25d, Little bustard. 2.50d, Red-billed chough. 3.25d, Spoonbill. 5d, Eagle owl. 6.50d, Rock ptarmigan.

1972, May 8

Birds in Natural Colors

1102	A275	50p	gray violet	.25	.25
1103	A275	1.25d	ocher	.25	.25
1104	A275	2.50d	gray olive	.25	.25
1105	A275	3.25d	light plum	.35	.35
1106	A275	5d	red brown	.65	.65
1107	A275	6.50d	violet	2.50	2.50
			Nos. 1102-1107 (6)	4.25	4.25

Nature protection.

Marshal Tito, by Bozidar Jakac — A276

1972, May 25 Litho. *Perf. 12½*

1108	A276	50p	cream & dk brn	.25	.25
1109	A276	1.25d	gray & indigo	.50	.25

Souvenir Sheet

Imperf

1110 A276 10d gray & blk brn 2.75 2.75

80th birthday of Pres. Tito. Sheets of 9. No. 1110 printed in blocks of 4.

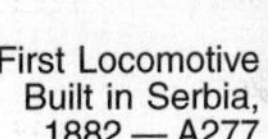

First Locomotive Built in Serbia, 1882 — A277

5d, Modern Yugoslavian electric locomotive.

1972, June 12 Photo. *Perf. 11½*

1111	A277	1.50d	multicolored	.25	.25
1112	A277	5d	multicolored	.80	.30

Intl. Railroad Union, 50th anniv. Exist imperf.

Glider — A278

1972, July 8 Photo. *Perf. 12½*

1113 A278 2d bl gray, gold & blk .25 .25

13th World Gliding Championships, Vrsac Airport, July 9-23. Sheets of 9.
Exists imperf.

Pawn on Chessboard — A279

6d, Chessboard, emblems of King and Queen.

1972, Sept. 18 ***Perf. 11½***

1114 A279 1.50d multi .25 .25
1115 A279 6d multi 1.25 .70

20th Men's and 5th Women's Chess Olympiad, Skopje, Sept.-Oct. Sheets of 9.

Boy on Rocking Horse — A280

1972, Oct. 2 **Litho.** ***Perf. 12½***

1116 A280 80p org & multi .25 .25

Children's Week, Oct. 2-8.

Goce Delchev — A281

1972, Oct. 16 ***Perf. 13***

1117 A281 80p yel grn & blk .25 .25

Delchev (1872-1903), Macedonian freedom fighter.

Grga Martic, by Ivan Mestrovic — A282

1972, Nov. 3 ***Perf. 12½***

1118 A282 80p red, yel grn & blk .25 .25

Brother Grga Martic (1822-1905), Franciscan administrator, educator and poet.

Serbian National Library, Belgrade — A283

1972, Nov. 25 **Engr.** ***Perf. 11½x12***

1119 A283 50p chocolate .25 .25

140th anniversary of the Serbian National Library and opening of new building.

Painting Type of 1971

Still-Life Paintings: 50p, by Milos Tenkovic, horiz. 1.25d, by Jozef Pekovsek. 2.50d, by Katarina Jovanovic, horiz. 3.25d, by Konstantin Danil, horiz. 5d, by Nikola Masic. 6.50d, by Celestin Medovic, horiz.

Perf. 14x13½, 13½x14

1972, Nov. 28 **Engr. & Photo.**

1120 A266 50p gold & multi .25 .25
1121 A266 1.25d gold & multi .25 .25
1122 A266 2.50d gold & multi .25 .25
1123 A266 3.25d gold & multi .25 .25
1124 A266 5d gold & multi .25 .25
1125 A266 6.50d gold & multi .70 .50
Nos. 1120-1125 (6) 1.95 1.75

Exist imperf.

Battle of Stubica, by Krsto Hegedusic A284

6d, Battle of Krsko, by Gojmir Anton Kos.

1973, Jan. 29 **Photo.** ***Perf. 11½***

1126 A284 2d gold & multi .30 .25
1127 A284 6d gold & multi 1.25 .70

Croatian-Slovenian Rebellion, 400th anniv. (2d); Beginning of the peasant rebellions in Slovenia, 500th anniv. (6d). Sheets of 9.

Radoje Domanovic (1873-1908), Serbian Writer — A285

1973, Feb. 3 **Litho.** ***Perf. 12½***

1128 A285 80p tan & brn .40 .25

Sheets of 9.

Skofja Loka — A286

1973, Feb. 15 ***Perf. 11½***

1129 A286 80p brown & buff .30 .25

Millennium of the founding of Skofja Loka. Sheets of 9.

Novi Sad, by Peter Demetrovic A287

Old Engravings: 1.25d, Zagreb, by Josef Szeman. 2.50d, Kotor, by Pierre Mortier. 3.25d, Belgrade, by Mancini. 5d, Split, by Louis-Francois Cassas. 6.50d, Kranj, by Mathaus Merian.

Engraved and Photogravure

1973, Mar. 15 ***Perf. 13½***

1130 A287 50p gold, buff & blk .25 .25
1131 A287 1.25d gold, gray & black .25 .25
1132 A287 2.50d gold & blk .25 .25
1133 A287 3.25d gold & blk .25 .25
1134 A287 5d gold, buff & blk .25 .25
1135 A287 6.50d gold & blk .25 .25
Nos. 1130-1135 (6) 1.50 1.50

Nos. 1130-1131, 1133-1135 exist imperf.

Championship Poster — A288

1973, Apr. 5 **Litho.** ***Perf. 13½x13***

1136 A288 2d multicolored .40 .40

32nd Intl. Table Tennis Championships, Sarajevo, Apr. 5-15. Sheets of 9.

Europa Issue, 1973

Common Design Type

1973, Apr. 30 **Photo.** ***Perf. 11½***

Size: 32½x23mm

1138 CD16 2d dk bl, lil & lt grn .35 .30
1139 CD16 5.50d pur, cit & sal pink .80 .80

Sheets of 9.

Flower Type of 1969

Medicinal Plants: 80p, Birthwort. 2d, Globe thistles. 3d, Olive branch. 4d, Corydalis. 5d, Mistletoe. 6d, Comfrey.

1973, May 25 **Photo.** ***Perf. 11½***

Flowers in Natural Colors

1140 A238 80p orange & grn .25 .25
1141 A238 2d dl bl & blue .25 .25
1142 A238 3d olive & blk .25 .25
1143 A238 4d yel grn & grn .25 .25
1144 A238 5d org & sepia .40 .40
1145 A238 6d lilac & grn 1.75 1.75
Nos. 1140-1145 (6) 3.15 3.15

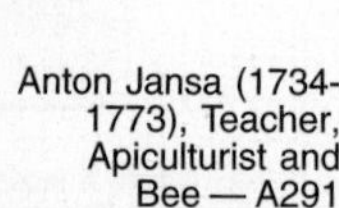

Anton Jansa (1734-1773), Teacher, Apiculturist and Bee — A291

1973, Aug. 25 **Engr.** ***Perf. 12½***

1147 A291 80p black .40 .25

Sheets of 9.

Championship Badge — A292

1973, Sept. 1 **Litho.** ***Perf. 13½x13***

1148 A292 2d multicolored .30 .25

World water sport championships (swimming, water polo, water jumps, figure swimming), Belgrade, Sept. 1-9. Sheets of 9.

"Greeting the Sun," by Ivan Vucovic — A293

1973, Oct. 1 ***Perf. 12½***

1149 A293 80p multicolored 1.20 .80

Children's Week, Oct. 1-7. Sheets of 9.

Post Horn — A294

Coil Stamps

1973-77 **Photo.** ***Perf. 14½x14***

1150 A294 30p brown .25 .25
1151 A294 50p gray blue .25 .25
1152 A294 80p rose red ('74) .40 .25
1153 A294 1d yel grn ('77) .40 .25
1154 A294 1.20d pink ('74) .30 .25
1155 A294 1.50d rose ('77) .40 .25
Nos. 1150-1155 (6) 2.00 1.50

Juraj Dalmatinac, Sculptor, Architect, 500th Anniv. of Death — A295

1973, Oct. 8 **Litho.** ***Perf. 12½***

1158 A295 80p grnsh gray & ol blk .25 .25

Sheets of 9.

Nadezda Petrovic (1873-1915), Self-Portrait A296

Lithographed and Engraved

1973, Oct. 12 ***Perf. 11½***

1159 A296 2d gold & multi .30 .25

Sheets of 9.

Interior, by Marko Celebonovic — A297

Paintings of Interiors by Yugoslav artists: 2d, St. Duja, by Emanuel Vidovic. 3d, Room with Slovak Woman, by Marino Tartaglia. 4d, Painter with Easel, by Miljenko Stancic. 5d, Studio, by Milan Konjovic. 6d, Tavern in Stara Loka, by France Slana.

1973, Oct. 20 **Photo.** ***Perf. 13½***

1160 A297 80p gold & multi .25 .25
1161 A297 2d gold & multi .25 .25
1162 A297 3d gold & multi .25 .25
1163 A297 4d gold & multi .25 .25
1164 A297 5d gold & multi .25 .25
1165 A297 6d gold & multi .45 .40
Nos. 1160-1165 (6) 1.70 1.65

Sheets of 9.

Dragojlo Dudic A298

Lithographed and Engraved

1973, Nov. 29 ***Perf. 12½***

Gray and Indigo

1166 80p shown .25 .25
1167 80p Strahil Pindzur .25 .25
1168 80p Boris Kidric .25 .25
1169 80p Radoje Dakic .25 .25

Gray and Plum

1170 2d Josip Mazar-Sosa .25 .25
1171 2d Zarko Zrenjanin .25 .25
1172 2d Emin Duraku .25 .25
1173 2d Ivan-Lola Ribar .25 .25
a. A298 Sheet of 8, #1166-1173 2.00 2.00

Republic Day, Nov. 29, honoring national heroes who perished during WWII.

Memorial, by O. Boljka, Ljubljana A299

Winged Globe, by D. Dzamonja, at Podgaric A300

Sculptures: 4.50d, Tower by D. Dzamonja, at Kozara. 5d, Memorial, by B. Grabulovski, at Belcista. 10d, Abstract, by M. Zivkovic, at Sutjeska. 50d, Stone "V," by Zivkovic, at Kragujevac.

1974 **Engr.** ***Perf. 12½***

1174 A299 3d slate grn .65 .25
1175 A299 4.50d brn lake 1.00 .25
1176 A299 5d dark vio .90 .25
b. Perf. 13½ 6.00 .40
1177 A300 10d slate grn 1.60 .40
1178 A300 20d dull pur 3.25 .25
1179 A300 50d indigo 4.00 1.00
Nos. 1174-1179 (6) 11.40 2.40

Exist imperf.

1978-82 **Litho.**

1176a A299 5d 2.25 .25
1177a A300 10d ('81) 2.25 .50
1178a A300 20d ('81) 3.25 .50
1179a A300 50d ('82) 4.00 1.00
Nos. 1176a-1179a (4) 11.75 2.25

Metric Measure — A301

1974, Jan. 10 **Litho.** ***Perf. 13***

1180 A301 80p plum & multi .25 .25

Centenary of introduction of metric system.

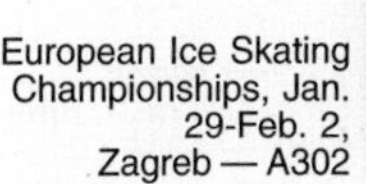

European Ice Skating Championships, Jan. 29-Feb. 2, Zagreb — A302

1974, Jan. 29

1181 A302 2d multicolored .65 .25

Exists imperf.

Diligence, 1874 — A303

Litho. & Engr.

1974, Feb. 25 *Perf. 11½*

1182 A303 80p shown .25 .25
1183 A303 2d New UPU headquarters .25 .25
1184 A303 8d Jet plane .25 .25
Nos. 1182-1184 (3) .75 .75

Centenary of the Universal Postal Union.

Montenegro No. 1 — A304

Litho. & Engr.

1974, Mar. 11 *Perf. 13*

1185 A304 80p shown .25 .25
1186 A304 6d Montenegro No. 7 .30 .25

Centenary of first Montenegrin postage stamps.

Marshal Tito — A305

1974 **Litho.** *Perf. 13*

1193 A305 50p green .25 .25
a. Perf. 13x12½ .40 .25
1196 A305 80p vermilion .25 .25
1198 A305 1.20d slate green .25 .25
1201 A305 2d gray blue .25 .25
a. Perf. 13x12½ .40 .25
b. Perf. 13¼x13½
Nos. 1193-1201 (4) 1.00 1.00

Issued with and without fluorescence.
For surcharge see No. 1415.

Lenin, by Nandor Glid — A306

1974, Apr. 20 **Litho.** *Perf. 13*

1204 A306 2d blk & silver .25 .25

50th death anniv. of Lenin.

Lepenski Vir Statue, c. 4950 B.C. — A307

Europa: 6d, Widow & Child, by Ivan Mestrovic.

1974, Apr. 29 **Photo.** *Perf. 11½*

1205 A307 2d multicolored .40 .40
1206 A307 6d multicolored 1.20 1.20

Exist imperf.

Great Tit — A308

1974, May 25 **Photo.** *Perf. 11½*

1207 A308 80p shown .25 .25
1208 A308 2d Rose .25 .25
1209 A308 6d Cabbage butterfly 1.40 1.10
Nos. 1207-1209 (3) 1.90 1.60

Youth Day. Issued in sheets of 9.

Congress Poster — A309

1974, May 27 **Litho.** *Perf. 11½*

1210 A309 80p gold & multi .25 .25
1211 A309 2d silver & multi .25 .25
1212 A309 6d ocher & multi .40 .40
Nos. 1210-1212 (3) .90 .90

10th Congress of Yugoslav League of Communists, Belgrade, May 27-30.

Radar Ground Station, Ivanjica — A311

1974, June 7 **Engr.** *Perf. 13*

1214 A311 80p shown .25 .25
1215 A311 6d Intelsat IV .50 .25

Opening of first satellite ground station in Yugoslavia at Ivanjica. Sheets of 9.

Games Emblem and Soccer Cup — A312

1974, June 13 **Litho.** *Perf. 13*

1216 A312 4.50d vio bl & multi 1.25 .90

World Cup Soccer Championship, Munich, June 13-July 7. Sheets of 9.

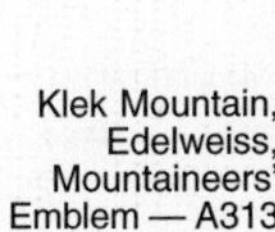

Klek Mountain, Edelweiss, Mountaineers' Emblem — A313

1974, June 15

1217 A313 2d grn & multi .25 .25

Mountaineering in Yugoslavia, cent. Sheets of 9. Exists imperf. Value $40.

Children's Dance, by Jano Knjazovic A314

Paintings: 2d, "Crucified Rooster," by Ivan Generalic, vert. 5d, Laundresses, by Ivan Lackovic, vert. 8d, Dance, by Janko Brasic.

1974, Sept. 9 **Photo.** *Perf. 11½*

1218 A314 80p multi .30 .30
1219 A314 2d multi .30 .30
1220 A314 5d multi .30 .30
1221 A314 8d multi .75 .75
Nos. 1218-1221 (4) 1.65 1.65

Yugoslav primitive art.

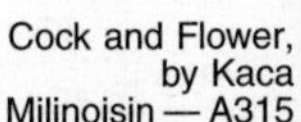

Cock and Flower, by Kaca Milinojsin — A315

Designs (Children's Paintings): 3.20d, Girl and Boy, by Ewa Medrzecka, vert. 5d, Cat and Kitten, by Jelena Anastasijevic.

1974, Oct. 7 **Litho.** *Perf. 13*

1222 A315 1.20d multi .25 .25
1223 A315 3.20d multi .25 .25
1224 A315 5d multi .25 .25
Nos. 1222-1224 (3) .75 .75

Children's Week, Oct. 1-7, and Joy of Europe meeting in Belgrade. Sheets of 9.

Library and Primoz Trubar Statue — A316

1974, Oct. 21 **Engr.** *Perf. 13*

1225 A316 1.20d black .25 .25

Natl. University Library, Ljubljana, 200th anniv. Exists imperf.

White Peonies, by Petar Dobrovic — A317

Paintings of Flowers by Yugoslav artists: 2d, Carnations, by Vilko Gecan. 3d, Flowers, still-life, by Milan Konjovic. 4d, White Vase, by Sava Sumanovic. 5d, Larkspur, by Stane Kregar. 8d, Roses, by Petar Lubarda.

1974, Nov. 28 **Photo.** *Perf. 11½*

1226 A317 80p gold & multi .25 .25
1227 A317 2d gold & multi .25 .25
1228 A317 3d gold & multi .25 .25
1229 A317 4d gold & multi .25 .25
1230 A317 5d gold & multi .25 .25
1231 A317 8d gold & multi .80 .80
Nos. 1226-1231 (6) 2.05 2.05

Sheets of 9.

Title Page and View of Belgrade — A318

1975, Jan. 8 **Litho.** *Perf. 13*

1232 A318 1.20d citron .25 .25
a. Perf. 12½ 30.00 30.00

Sesquicentennial of the first publication of Matica Srpska, literary journal.

Map of Europe and Dove — A319

1975, Jan. 30 *Perf. 12x11½*

1233 A319 3.20d bl & multi .25 .25
1234 A319 8d multi .50 .25

Interparliamentary Union for European Cooperation and Security, 2nd Conference, Belgrade, Jan. 31-Feb. 6. Exist imperf.

Gold-plated Bronze Earring — A320

Antique jewelry in Yugoslav museums: 2.10d, Silver bracelet, 18th cent. 3.20d, Silver gilt belt buckle, 18th cent. 5d, Silver ring with Nike cameo, 14th cent. 6d, Silver necklace, 17th cent. 8d, Bronze gilt bracelet, 14th cent.

1975, Feb. 25 **Photo.** *Perf. 14x13*

1235 A320 1.20d multi .25 .25
1236 A320 2.10d multi .25 .25
1237 A320 3.20d multi .25 .25
1238 A320 5d multi .25 .25
1239 A320 6d multi .25 .25
1240 A320 8d multi .40 .40
Nos. 1235-1240 (6) 1.65 1.65

Svetozar Markovic, by Stevan Bodnarov — A321

1975, Feb. 26 **Engr.** *Perf. 13*

1241 A321 1.20d blue blk .50 .25

Markovic (1846-1875), writer and poet.

Fettered Woman, by Frano Krsinic — A322

1975, Mar. 8 **Photo.** *Perf. 14½x14*

1242 A322 3.20d gold & sepia .25 .25

International Women's Year.

Street, Ohrid — A323

Views: 25p, Budva. 75p, City Hall, Rijeka (Fiume). Nos. 1245, 1246, Street, Ohrid. 1.50d, Church, Bihac. 2.10d, Street and fountain, Hvar. 3.20d, Skofja Loka. 3.40d, Main Square, Vranje. 4.90d, Mosque, Perast.

No Inscription at Bottom

1975-77 **Litho.** *Perf. 13*

1243 A323 25p carmine ('76) 1.20 .25
1244 A323 75p purple ('76) .80 .25
1245 A323 1d dull purple .25 .25
1246 A323 1d dl grn ('76) .40 .25
a. Perf. 13x12½ .40 .25
1247 A323 1.50d rose red ('76) 1.20 .25
a. Perf. 13x12½ 24.00 24.00
1248 A323 2.10d gray green .25 .25
1249 A323 3.20d dull blue .25 .25
1250 A323 3.40d gray grn ('77) .80 .25
a. Perf. 13x12½ 1.60 .25
1251 A323 4.90d dl bl ('76) 2.75 .25
Nos. 1243-1251 (9) 7.90 2.25

See Nos. 1487-1491, 1598, 1601, 1603A, 1713, 1718-1719. For surcharges see Nos. 1382-1383, 1481, 1502, 1545, 1550, 1594-1597A, 1764, 1767-1768, 1770-1771, 1964, 1973.

Nos. 1243, 1246, 1247 exist imperf. Value each, $20.

Europa Issue

Still Life with Eggs, by Mosa Pijade — A325

Painting: 8d, Three Graces, by Ivan Radovic.

1975, Apr. 28

1252 A325 3.20d gold & multi .40 .40
1253 A325 8d gold & multi .40 .40

Exist imperf.

Srem Front Fighters' Monument, by Dusan Dzamonja — A326

1975, May 9 **Litho.** ***Perf. 13½***

1254	A326	3.20d red & multi	.30	.25

Victory over Fascism in WWII; liberation of Yugoslavia, 30th anniv.

Garland Flower — A327

1975, May 24 **Photo.** ***Perf. 14x14½***

1255	A327	1.20d shown	.25	.25
1256	A327	2.10d Garden balsam	.25	.25
1257	A327	3.20d Rose mallow	.25	.25
1258	A327	5d Geranium	.25	.25
1259	A327	6d Crocus	.25	.25
1260	A327	8d Oleander	1.00	1.00
		Nos. 1255-1260 (6)	2.25	2.25

Youth Day.

Kayak — A328

1975, June 20 **Litho.** ***Perf. 13½***

1261	A328	3.20d grnsh bl & multi	.25	.25

9th World Championship of Wild Water Racing, Radika River, June 24-25, and 14th World Championship of Canoe-Slalom, Treska River, June 28-29.

Ambush, Herzegovinian Insurgents, by Ferdo Quiquerez — A329

1975, July 9 **Photo.** ***Perf. 13½x14½***

1262	A329	1.20d gold & multi	.25	.25

Bosnian & Herzegovinian Uprising, cent.

Stjepan Mitrov Ljubisa (1824-1878) — A330

Yugoslav writers: 2.10d, Ivan Prijatelj (1875-1937). 3.20d, Jakov Ignjatovic (1824-89). 5d, Dragojla Jarnevic (1813-75). 6d, Svetozar Corovic (1875-1919). 8d, Ivana Brlic-Mazuranic (1874-1938).

1975, Sept. 16 **Litho.** ***Perf. 13***

1263	A330	1.20d brick red & blk	.25	.25
1264	A330	2.10d dl grn & blk	.25	.25
1265	A330	3.20d ol bis & blk	.25	.25
1266	A330	5d brn org & blk	.25	.25
1267	A330	6d yel grn & blk	.25	.25
1268	A330	8d Prus bl & blk	.30	.30
		Nos. 1263-1268 (6)	1.55	1.55

"Joy of Europe" Children's Meeting, Oct. 2-7, Belgrade — A331

Children's drawings.

1975, Oct. 1 **Litho.** ***Perf. 13½***

1269	A331	3.20d Young Lion	.25	.25
1270	A331	6d Baby Carriage	.70	.65

Peace Dove — A332

1975, Oct. 10

1271	A332	3.20d multi	.25	.25
1272	A332	8d multi	.45	.45

European Security and Cooperation Conference, Helsinki, July 30-Aug. 1. Exist imperf.

Red Cross, "100", Map of Yugoslavia — A333

8d, Red Cross, people seeking help.

1975, Nov. 1 **Litho.** ***Perf. 13½x13***

1273	A333	1.20d red & multi	.25	.25
1274	A333	8d red & multi	.25	.25

Centenary of Red Cross in Yugoslavia.

Soup Kitchen, by Dorde Andrejevic-Kun A334

Social paintings by 20th century Yugoslav artists: 2.10d, People at the Door, by Vinko Grdan. 3.20d, Drunks in Coach, by Marijan Detoni, horiz. 5d, Workers' Lunch, by Tone Kralj, horiz. 6d, Water Wheel, by Lazar Licenoski. 8d, The Hanging, by Krsto Hegedusic.

Perf. 14½x13½, 13½x14½

1975, Nov. 28 **Photo.**

1275	A334	1.20d gold & multi	.25	.25
1276	A334	2.10d gold & multi	.25	.25
1277	A334	3.20d gold & multi	.25	.25
1278	A334	5d gold & multi	.25	.25
1279	A334	6d gold & multi	.25	.25
1280	A334	8d gold & multi	.30	.30
		Nos. 1275-1280 (6)	1.55	1.55

Sheets of 9. No. 1277 exists imperf.

Diocletian's Palace, 304 A.D. — A335

3.20d, House of Ohrid, 19th cent., vert. 8d, Gracanica Monastery, Kosovo, 1321.

1975, Dec. 10 **Engr.** ***Perf. 13½***

1281	A335	1.20d dark brown	.25	.25
1282	A335	3.20d bluish black	.25	.25
1283	A335	8d dk vio brown	.25	.25
		Nos. 1281-1283 (3)	.75	.75

European Architectural Heritage Year 1975. Sheets of 9. Exist imperf.

12th Winter Olympic Games, Feb. 4-15, Innsbruck, Austria — A336

1976, Feb. 4 **Engr.** ***Perf. 13½***

1284	A336	3.20d Ski jump	.25	.25
1285	A336	8d Pair figure skating	.70	.40

Exist imperf.

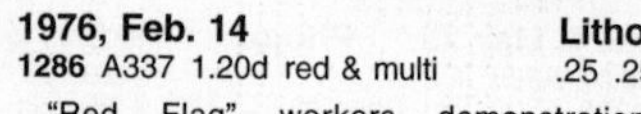
Red Flag — A337

1976, Feb. 14 **Litho.**

1286	A337	1.20d red & multi	.25	.25

"Red Flag" workers demonstration, Kragujevac, Feb. 15, 1876.
Exists imperf. Value $32.50.

Svetozar Miletic (1826-1901), Lawyer, Founder of United Serbian Youth — A338

1976, Feb. 23 ***Perf. 13½x13***

1287	A338	1.20d grnsh gray & dl grn	.25	.25

Borislav "Bora" Stankovic, (1876-1927), Writer — A339

1976, Mar. 31 **Litho.** ***Perf. 13½x13***

1288	A339	1.20d lem, ol & mar	.25	.25

Sheets of 9.

Europa Issue

King Matthias, by Jakob Pogorelec, 1931 — A340

1976, Apr. 26 **Photo.** ***Perf. 11½***

1289	A340	3.20d shown	.25	.25
1290	A340	8d Bowl, 14th cent	.25	.25

Ivan Cankar (1876-1918), Slovenian Writer — A341

1976, May 8 **Litho.** ***Perf. 13½x13***

1291	A341	1.20d orange & plum	.25	.25

Train on Viaduct in Bosnia — A342

Design: 8d, Train on viaduct in Montenegro.

1976, May 15 **Engr.** ***Perf. 13½***

1292	A342	3.20d deep magenta	.25	.25
1293	A342	8d deep blue	.40	.40

Inauguration of the Belgrade-Bar railroad.

Hawker Dragonfly — A343

Fresh-water Fauna: 2.10d, Winkle. 3.20d, Rudd. 5d, Green frog. 6d, Ferruginous duck. 8d, Muskrat.

1976, May 25 **Litho.**

1294	A343	1.20d yel & multi	.40	.40
1295	A343	2.10d bl & multi	.40	.40
1296	A343	3.20d vio & multi	.40	.40
1297	A343	5d multicolored	.80	.80
1298	A343	6d multicolored	.80	.80
1299	A343	8d multicolored	2.75	2.75
		Nos. 1294-1299 (6)	5.55	5.55

Youth Day. Exist imperf.

Vladimir Nazor, Croatian Writer, Birth Cent. — A344

1976, May 29 ***Perf. 13***

1300	A344	1.20d pale lil & dl bl	.25	.25

Battle of Vucji Dol, 1876 — A345

1976, June 16 **Litho.** ***Perf. 13***

1301	A345	1.20d gold, brn & buff	.25	.25

Liberation of Montenegro from Turkey, cent. Exists imperf.

Serbian Pitcher — A346

Water Pitchers: 2.10d, Slovenia. 3.20d, Bosnia-Herzegovina. 5d, Vojvodina 6d, Macedonia. 8d, Kosovo.

1976, June 22 **Photo.** ***Perf. 14x13***

1302	A346	1.20d dk car & multi	.25	.25
1303	A346	2.10d olive & multi	.25	.25
1304	A346	3.20d red & multi	.25	.25
1305	A346	5d brown & multi	.25	.25
1306	A346	6d dk grn & multi	.25	.25
1307	A346	8d dk bl & multi	.35	.35
		Nos. 1302-1307 (6)	1.60	1.60

Exist imperf.

Tesla Monument, Belgrade, and Niagara Falls — A347

1976, July 10 **Engr.** ***Perf. 13***

1308	A347	5d slate grn & indigo	.50	.25

Nikola Tesla (1856-1943), electrical engineer and inventor. Sheets of 9. Exists imperf.

21st Olympic Games, July 17-Aug. 1, Montreal, Canada, — A348

1976, July 17

1309	A348	1.20d Long jump	.25	.25
1310	A348	3.20d Team handball	.25	.25
1311	A348	5d Target shooting	.25	.25
1312	A348	8d Single scull rowing	2.00	1.50
		Nos. 1309-1312 (4)	2.75	2.25

Sheets of 9.

World Map and Peace Dove — A349

1976, Aug. 16 **Litho.** ***Perf. 13***

1313	A349	4.90d multi	.30	.25

5th Summit Conference of Non-Aligned Countries, Colombo, Sri Lanka, Aug. 9-19. Sheets of 9.
Exists imperf. Value $25.

Children's Train — A350

Children's drawings: 4.90d, Navy Day (submarine).

1976, Oct. 2 Litho. *Perf. 13*

1314 A350 4.90d multi .25 .25
1315 A350 8d multi .30 .30

"Joy of Europe" Children's Meeting, Belgrade, Oct. 2-7.
No. 1315 exists imperf.

Herzegovinian Fugitives, by Uros Predic — A351

Historical paintings by 19th-20th century Yugoslav painters: 1.20d, Battle of the Montenegrins, by Djura Jaksic, vert. 2.10d, Nikola S. Zrinjski at Siget, by Oton Ivekovic, vert. 5d, Uprising at Razlovci, by Borko Lazeski. 6d, Enthroning of Slovenian Duke at Gospovetsko Field, by Anton Gojmir Kos. 8d, Break-through at Solun Front, by Veljko Stanojevic.

Perf. 13½x12½, 12½x13½

1976, Nov. 29 Photo.

1316 A351 1.20d gold & multi .25 .25
1317 A351 2.10d gold & multi .25 .25
1318 A351 3.20d gold & multi .25 .25
1319 A351 5d gold & multi .25 .25
1320 A351 6d gold & multi .25 .25
1321 A351 8d gold & multi .80 .80
Nos. 1316-1321 (6) 2.05 2.05

Sheets of 9.

No. 839 Surcharged with New Value and 3 Bars in Rose

1976, Dec. 8 Engr. *Perf. 12½*

1322 A206 1d on 85p dl pur .40 .25

Mateja Nenadovic — A352

1977, Feb. 4 Photo. *Perf. 13½x14*

1323 A352 4.90d multicolored .30 .25

Prota Mateja Nenadovic (1777-1854), Serbian Duke, archbishop and writer.

Rajko Zinzifov — A353

1977, Feb. 10 Litho. *Perf. 13x13½*

1324 A353 1.50d brn & sepia .25 .25

Rajko Zinzifov (1839-1877), writer.

Phlox — A354

Flowers: 3.40d, Lily. 4.90d, Bleeding heart. 6d, Zinnia. 8d, Spreading marigold. 10d, Horseshoe geranium.

1977, Mar. 8 *Perf. 13½x13*

1325 A354 1.50d multi .25 .25
1326 A354 3.40d multi .25 .25
1327 A354 4.90d multi .25 .25
1328 A354 6d multi .30 .25
1329 A354 8d multi .30 .25
1330 A354 10d multi 1.00 .80
Nos. 1325-1330 (6) 2.35 2.05

Exists imperf.

Croatian Music Institute, Zagreb, 150th Anniv. — A355

1977, Apr. 4 Engr. *Perf. 13*

1331 A355 4.90d bl & sepia .40 .40

Alojz Kraigher — A356

1977, Apr. 11 Litho. *Perf. 13½*

1332 A356 1.50d lemon & brn .30 .25

Kraigher (1877-1959), Slovenian writer.

Boka Kotorska, by Milo Milunovic — A357

10d, Zagorje in November, by Ljubo Babie.

1977, May 4 Photo. *Perf. 11½*

1333 A357 4.90d gold & multi .40 .40
1334 A357 10d gold & multi .40 .40

Europa. Issued in sheets of 9.

Marshal Tito, by Omer Mujadzic — A358

1977, May 25 *Perf. 11½x12*

1335 A358 1.50d gold & multi .25 .25
1336 A358 4.90d gold & multi .25 .25
1337 A358 8d gold & multi .30 .30
Nos. 1335-1337 (3) .80 .80

85th birthday of Pres. Tito. Sheets of 9. Exists imperf.

Mountain Range and Gentian — A359

Design: 10d, Plitvice Lakes Falls, trees, robin and environmental protection emblem.

1977, June 6 Litho. *Perf. 13x13½*

1338 A359 4.90d multicolored .25 .25
1339 A359 10d multicolored .70 .50

World Environment Day.

Petar Kocic (1877-1916), Writer — A360

1977, June 15 *Perf. 13½*

1340 A360 1.50d pale grn & brn .30 .25

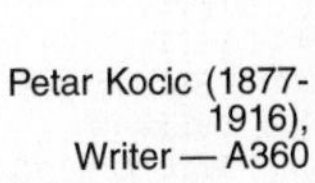

Map of Europe and Peace Dove — A361

1977, June 15 Litho. *Perf. 13½*

1341 A361 4.90d multi .25 .25
1342 A361 10d multi 1.00 1.00

Security and Cooperation Conference, Belgrade, June 15.

Child on Float — A362

Children's drawings: 10d, Fruit picking.

1977, Oct. 3 Litho. *Perf. 13½*

1343 A362 4.90d multi .25 .25
1344 A362 10d multi .50 .40

"Joy of Europe" Children's Meeting.

Sava Congress Center, Belgrade — A363

1977, Oct. 4 Litho. *Perf. 13½*

1345 A363 4.90d bl & multi .25 .25
1346 A363 10d car & multi 1.00 1.00

European Security and Cooperation Conference, Belgrade.
Exist imperf. Value, each $125.

Exhibition Emblem — A364

1977, Oct. 20 Litho. *Perf. 13½*

1347 A364 4.90d gold & multi .30 .25

Balkanfila 1977, 6th Intl. Phil. Exhib. of Balkan Countries, Belgrade, Oct. 24-30.

Double Flute and Shepherd — A365

Landscape and Musician: 3.40d, 4.90d, 6d, Various string instruments. 8d, Bagpipes. 10d, Panpipes.

1977, Oct. 25 Engr. *Perf. 13½*

1348 A365 1.50d och & red brn .25 .25
1349 A365 3.40d green & brn .25 .25
1350 A365 4.90d dk brn & yel .25 .25
1351 A365 6d bl & red brn .25 .25
1352 A365 8d brick red & sep .25 .25
1353 A365 10d sl grn & bis .50 .50
Nos. 1348-1353 (6) 1.75 1.75

Musical instruments from Belgrade Ethnographical Museum.

Ivan Vavpotic, Self-portrait — A366

Self-portraits of Yugoslav artists: 3.40d, Mihailo Vukotic. 4.90d, Kosta Hakman. 6d, Miroslav Kraljevic. 8d, Nikola Martinovski. 10d, Milena Pavlovic-Barili.

Perf. 13½x12½

1977, Nov. 26 Photo.

1354 A366 1.50d gold & multi .25 .25
1355 A366 3.40d gold & multi .25 .25
1356 A366 4.90d gold & multi .25 .25
1357 A366 6d gold & multi .25 .25
1358 A366 8d gold & multi .25 .25
1359 A366 10d gold & multi .65 .65
Nos. 1354-1359 (6) 1.90 1.90

Festival of Testaccio, by Klovic A367

Julija Klovic, by El Greco A368

1978, Jan. 14 Photo. *Perf. 13½*

1360 A367 4.90d multicolored .25 .25
1361 A368 10d multicolored .25 .25

Julija Klovic (1498-1578), Croat miniaturist.

Stampless Cover, Banaviste to Kubin, 1869 — A369

Designs: 3.40d, Mailbox. 4.90d, Ericsson telephone, 1900. 10d, Morse telegraph, 1844.

1978, Jan. 28 *Perf. 13x14*

1362 A369 1.50d multicolored .25 .25
1363 A369 3.40d multicolored .25 .25
1364 A369 4.90d multicolored .25 .25
1365 A369 10d multicolored .25 .25
Nos. 1362-1365 (4) 1.00 1.00

Post Office Museum, Belgrade.

Battle of Pirot — A370

1978, Feb. 20 Litho. *Perf. 13½*

1366 A370 1.50d gold, blk & sl grn 1.75 1.75

Centenary of Serbo-Turkish War.
Exists imperf. Value $40.

Airplanes — A371

1978, Apr. 24 Litho. *Perf. 13½*

1367 A371 1.50d S-49A, 1949 .25 .25
1368 A371 3.40d Galeb, 1961 .25 .25
1369 A371 4.90d Utva-75, 1976 .25 .25
1370 A371 10d Orao, 1974 .80 .80
Nos. 1367-1370 (4) 1.55 1.55

Aeronautical Day.
Exist imperf. Value, each $35.

Europa Issue

View of Golubac — A372

10d, St. Naum Monastery, Ohrid.

1978, May 3 Photo. *Perf. 11½*

1371 A372 4.90d shown .25 .25
1372 A372 10d multicolored .40 .40

Exist imperf.

Boxing Glove — A373

1978, May 5 Litho. *Perf. 13½*

1373 A373 4.90d multicolored .35 .25

Amateur Boxing Championships.
Exists imperf. Value $35.

Honeybee — A374

Bees of Yugoslavia: 3.40d, Halictus scabiosae. 4.90d, Blue carpenter bee. 10d, Large earth bumblebee.

1978, May 25 Photo. *Perf. 11½*

1374 A374 1.50d multi .25 .25
1375 A374 3.40d multi .25 .25
1376 A374 4.90d multi .25 .25
1377 A374 10d multi .95 .95
Nos. 1374-1377 (4) 1.70 1.70

Exist imperf.

Filip Filipovic (1878-1938), Radovan Radovic (1878-1906), Revolutionaries A375

1978, June 19 Litho. *Perf. 13½*

1378 A375 1.50d dk pur & dl ol .25 .25

Marshal Tito A376

Congress Emblem A377

1978, June 20

1379 A376 2d red & multi .25 .25
1380 A377 4.90d red & multi .30 .25

Souvenir Sheet

Imperf

1381 A376 15d red & multi 3.00 3.00

11th Congress of Yugoslav League of Communists, Belgrade, June 20-23.
Nos. 1379-1380 exist imperf. Value, each $35.

Nos. 1246, 1248 Surcharged with New Value and Two Bars in Brown

1978 Litho. *Perf. 13*

1382 A323 2d on 1d *10.00* .25
1383 A323 3.40d on 2.10d .40 .25

Issue dates: #1382, July 17; #1383, Aug. 1.

Conference Emblem over Belgrade — A378

1978, July 25 Photo. *Perf. 13½*

1384 A378 4.90d bl & lt blue .30 .25

Conference of Foreign Ministers of Nonaligned Countries, Belgrade, July 25-29.
Exists imperf. Value $35.

Championship Emblem — A379

1978, Aug. 10 Litho. *Perf. 13½x13*

1385 A379 4.90d multicolored .30 .25

14th Kayak and Canoe Still Water Championships, Lake Sava, Aug. 10-14.

Mt. Triglav, North Rock — A380

1978, Aug. 26 Photo. *Perf. 14*

1386 A380 2d multicolored .25 .25

Bicentenary of first ascent of Mt. Triglav by Slovenian climbers.

Black Lake, Mt. Durmitor — A381

1978, Sept. 20

1387 A381 4.90d shown .25 .25
1388 A381 10d Tara River .55 .30

Protection of the environment.

Night Sky — A382

1978, Sept. 30 Litho. *Perf. 13x12½*

1389 A382 4.90d bl blk, blk & gold .30 .25

29th Congress of International Astronautical Federation, Dubrovnik, Oct. 1-8.

People in Forest — A383

Children's drawings: 10d, Family around pond.

1978, Oct. 2 *Perf. 13½x13*

1390 A383 4.90d multi .35 .25
1391 A383 10d multi .65 .45

"Joy of Europe" Children's Meeting.

Seal on Insurrection Declaration A384

1978, Oct. 5 *Perf. 13½*

1392 A384 2d gold, brn & blk .25 .25

Centenary of Kresna uprising.
Exists imperf. Value $40.

Teachers' Training Institute, Sombor, Bicent. — A385

1978, Oct. 16

1393 A385 2d multicolored .25 .25

Exists imperf.

Croatian Red Cross, Cent. — A386

1978, Oct. 21

1394 A386 2d lt bl, blk & red .25 .25

Metallic Sculpture XXII, by Dusan Dzamonja — A387

Modern Sculptures: 3.40d, Circulation in Space I, by Vojin Bakic, vert. 4.90d, Tectonic Octopode, by Olga Jevric, vert. 10d, Tree of Life, by Drago Trsar.

Perf. 13½x13, 13x13½

1978, Nov. 4 Litho.

1395 A387 2d multicolored .25 .25
1396 A387 3.40d multicolored .25 .25
1397 A387 4.90d multicolored .25 .25
1398 A387 10d multicolored .35 .35
Nos. 1395-1398 (4) 1.10 1.10

Crossing of Neretva Pass, by Ismet Mujezinovic A388

1978, Nov. 10 Litho. *Perf. 13*

1399 A388 2d multicolored .25 .25

35th anniversary of Battle of Neretva. Exists imperf.

Workers Leaving Factory, by Marijan Detoni — A389

Engravings: 3.40d, Workers, by Maksim Sedej. 4.90d, Lumberjacks, by Daniel Ozmo. 6d, Meal Break, by Pivo Karamatijevic. 10d, Hanged Man and Raped Woman, by Djordje Andrejevic Kun.

1978, Nov. 28 Photo. *Perf. 14x13½*

1400 A389 2d gold, blk & buff .25 .25
1401 A389 3.40d gold & black .25 .25
1402 A389 4.90d gold, yel & blk .25 .25
1403 A389 6d gold, buff & blk .25 .25
1404 A389 10d gold, cr & blk .70 .50
Nos. 1400-1404 (5) 1.70 1.50

Republic day.

Larch Cone — A390

1978, Dec. 11 Photo. *Perf. 13x12½*

1405 A390 1.50d shown .25 .25
1406 A390 1.50d Red squirrel .25 .25
1407 A390 2d Sycamore leaves .25 .25
1408 A390 2d Red deer .25 .25
a. Bklt. pane of 8 1.25
1409 A390 3.40d Alder leaves .25 .25
1410 A390 3.40d Partridge .25 .25
1411 A390 4.90d Oak leaves .25 .25
1412 A390 4.90d Grouse .25 .25
a. Bklt. pane of 8 3.25
Nos. 1405-1412 (8) 2.00 2.00

New Year 1979. Nos. 1405-1412 printed se-tenant in sheets of 25.
No. 1408a contains 4 each of Nos. 1407-1408; No. 1412a 2 each of Nos. 1409-1412, with background colors changed. Exist imperf.

Nos. 1064, 868, 1198 Surcharged with New Value and Bars

1978 Engr.; Litho. *Perf. 12½, 13½*

1413 A263 35p on 10p brown 1.60 .30
1414 A211 60p on 85p dp bl 1.60 .30
1415 A305 80p on 1.20d sl grn 1.60 .30
Nos. 1413-1415 (3) 4.80 .90

First Masthead of Politika — A391

1979, Jan. 25 Litho. *Perf. 13½*

1416 A391 2d gold & black .25 .25

Politika daily newspaper, 75th anniv.
Exists imperf. Value $35.

Red Flags and Emblem — A392

1979, Feb. 15

1417 A392 2d red & gold .25 .25

11th Meeting of Self-managers, Kragujevac, Feb. 15-16.
Exists imperf. Value $40.

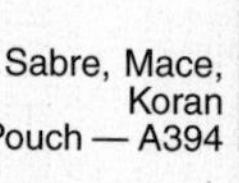

Child and IYC Emblem — A393

1979, Mar. 1 Photo. *Perf. 11½x12*

1418 A393 4.90d gold vio & bl .45 .30

International Year of the Child. Exists imperf.

Sabre, Mace, Koran Pouch — A394

Old Weapons: 3.40d, Pistol and ramrod, Montenegro. 4.90d, Short carbine and powder horn, Slovenia and Croatia. 10d, Oriental rifle and cartridge pouch.

1979, Mar. 26 Photo. *Perf. 14*

1419 A394 2d multicolored .25 .25
1420 A394 3.40d multicolored .25 .25
1421 A394 4.90d multicolored .25 .25
1422 A394 10d multicolored .50 .50
Nos. 1419-1422 (4) 1.25 1.25

5-Pointed Star, Hammer and Sickle — A395

1979, Apr. 20 Photo. *Perf. 13½*

1423 A395 2d multicolored .25 .25
1424 A395 4.90d multicolored .25 .25

Communist and Communist Youth Leagues, 60th anniversary.
Exist imperf. Value, each used, $25.

Cyril and Methodius University and Emblem — A396

1979, Apr. 24 Litho.

1425 A396 2d multicolored .25 .25

Sts. Cyril and Methodius University, Skopje, 30th anniv.

19th Century Belgrade, by C. Goebel — A397

Europa: 10d, Postilion and Ljubljana, 17th century, by Jan van der Heyden.

1979, Apr. 30 Photo. *Perf. 11½*

1426 A397 4.90d multicolored .40 .40
1427 A397 10d multicolored .40 .40

Blue Sow Thistles — A398

Flowers: 3.40d, Anemones. 4.90d, Astragalus. 10d, Alpine trifolium.

1979, May 25 Photo. *Perf. 13½*

1428 A398 2d multicolored .25 .25
1429 A398 3.40d multicolored .25 .25
1430 A398 4.90d multicolored .25 .25
1431 A398 10d multicolored .75 .75
Nos. 1428-1431 (4) 1.50 1.50

Milutin Milankovic, by Paja Jovanovic — A399

1979, May 28

1432 A399 4.90d multi .35 .25

Milutin Milankovic (1879-1958), scientist.

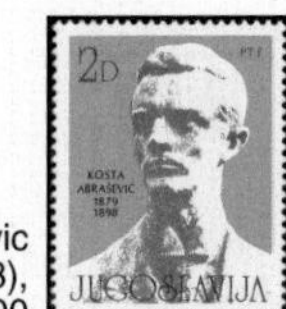

Kosta Abrasevic (1879-1898), Poet — A400

1979, May 29 Litho. *Perf. 13½x13*

1433 A400 2d org, blk & gray .25 .25

Exists imperf. Value, used $40.

Eight-Oared Shell — A401

1979, Aug. 28 Litho. *Perf. 13*

1434 A401 4.90d multicolored .40 .25

9th World Rowing Championship, Lake Bled. Exist imperf. Value $40.

8th Mediterranean Games, Sept. 15-29, Split — A402

1979, Sept. 10

1435 A402 2d Games Emblem .25 .25
1436 A402 4.90d Mascot .25 .25
1437 A402 10d Map, Flags .30 .30
Nos. 1435-1437 (3) .80 .80

Exist imperf. Value, each $30.

Seal, 15th Century — A403

1979, Sept. 14 *Perf. 12½*

1438 A403 2d multicolored .25 .25

Zagreb Postal Service, 450th anniversary. Exists imperf. Value $35.

Lake Palic — A404

Environment Protection: 10d, Lakefront, Prokletije Mountains.

1979, Sept. 20 Photo. *Perf. 14x13½*

1439 A404 4.90d multicolored .25 .25
1440 A404 10d multicolored .65 .40

Bank and Fund Emblems — A405

Engr. & Photo.

1979, Oct. 1 *Perf. 13½*

1441 A405 4.90d multicolored .25 .25
1442 A405 10d multicolored .40 .40

Meeting of the World Bank and International Monetary Fund, Belgrade, Oct. 2-5. Exist imperf. Value, each $25.

"Joy of Europe" — A406

Children's drawings.

1979, Oct. 2 Litho.

1443 A406 4.90d shown .25 .25
1444 A406 10d Child in yard .45 .45

Exist imperf. Value, each $40.

Mihailo Pupin (1854-1935), Physicist, Inventor — A407

1979, Oct. 9 *Perf. 13x13½*

1445 A407 4.90d multicolored .40 .25

Marko Cepenkov — A408

1979, Nov. 15 Litho. *Perf. 13½*

1446 A408 2d multicolored .25 .25

Cepenkov (1829-1920), Macedonian folklorist. Exists imperf.

Pristina University, 10th Anniversary A409

1979, Nov. 17

1447 A409 2d multicolored .25 .25

Exists imperf. Value, used $40.

Radovan Portal, Trogir Cathedral — A410

Romanesque Sculptures: 3.40d, Choir stall, Cathedral of Split. 4.90d, Triforium, Church of the Resurrection, Decani. 6d, Buvina Portal, Cathedral of Split. 10d, Western portal, Church of Our Lady, Studenica.

1979, Nov. 28 Photo.

1448 A410 2d multi .25 .25
1449 A410 3.40d multi .25 .25
1450 A410 4.90d multi .25 .25
1451 A410 6d multi .25 .25
1452 A410 10d multi .35 .35
Nos. 1448-1452 (5) 1.35 1.35

Exist imperf.

Sarajevo University, 30th Anniversary A411

1979, Dec. 1 Litho.

1453 A411 2d multicolored .25 .25

Exists imperf. Value, used $40.

Duro Dakovic and Nikola Hecimovic, Communist Revolutionaries, 50th Death Annivs. — A412

1979, Dec. 10

1454 A412 2d multicolored .25 .25

Exists imperf. Value, used $40.

Sidewheeler Deligrad, 1862-1914 A413

10d, Sidewheeler Serbia, 1917-72.

1979, Dec. 14

1455 A413 4.90d shown .50 .60
1456 A413 10d multicolored 1.00 1.00

Danube Conference. Exist imperf. Value, each $60.

Milton Manaki and Camera — A414

1980, Jan. 21 Litho. *Perf. 13½*

1457 A414 2d pur, yel & brn .25 .25

Manaki (1880-1964), photographer and documentary film maker.

Edward Kardelj, by Zdenko Kalin — A415

1980, Jan. 26

1458 A415 2d multicolored .25 .25

Kardelj (1910-1979), labor movement leader. Exists imperf. Value, used $40.

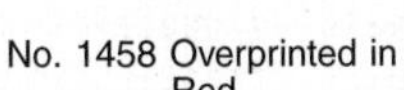

No. 1458 Overprinted in Red

1980, Jan. 26

1459 A415 2d multicolored .25 .25

Ploce renamed Kardeljevo. Exists imperf. Value, used $40.

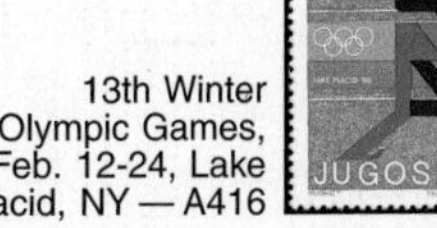

13th Winter Olympic Games, Feb. 12-24, Lake Placid, NY — A416

1980, Feb. 13

1460 A416 4.90d Speed skating .25 .25
1461 A416 10d Cross-country skiing 1.40 1.40

Exist imperf.

University of Belgrade, 75th Anniversary A417

1980, Feb. 27

1462 A417 2d multicolored .25 .25

22nd Summer Olympic Games, July 19-Aug. 3, Moscow — A418

1980, Apr. 21

1463 A418 2d Fencing .25 .25
1464 A418 3.40d Bicycling .25 .25
1465 A418 4.90d Field hockey .25 .35
1466 A418 10d Archery .50 .50
Nos. 1463-1466 (4) 1.25 1.35

Marshal Tito, by Antun Augustincic — A419

Europa: 13d, Tito, by Djordje Prudnikov.

1980, Apr. 28 Photo. *Perf. 11½*
Granite Paper

1467 A419 4.90d multi .25 .25
1468 A419 13d multi 1.00 1.00

Exist imperf. Value, each $15.

Marshal Tito, by Bozidar Jakac — A420

1980, May 4 Litho. *Perf. 13½*

1469 A420 2.50d purplish blk .25 .25
a. Perf. 10½ .30 .25
1470 A420 4.90d gray black .60 .60

Marshal Tito (1892-1980) memorial. Issued in sheets of 8 plus label. Exist imperf. Value, each $25.

Sava Kovacevic (1905-1943), Revolutionary A421

1980, May 11 Litho. *Perf. 13½*

1471 A421 2.50d multicolored .25 .25

Wood Baton and Letter — A422

1980, May 14

1472 A422 2d multicolored .25 .25

1st Tito Youth Relay Race, 35th anniv. Exists imperf. Value $35.

Flying Gunard — A423

1980, May 24 Photo. *Perf. 12*

1473 A423 2d shown .25 .25
1474 A423 3.40d Loggerhead turtle .25 .25
1475 A423 4.90d Sea swallow .30 .30
1476 A423 10d Dolphin 2.25 2.25
Nos. 1473-1476 (4) 3.05 3.05

Emperor Trajan Decius Coin, 3rd Cent. — A424

3rd Century Roman Coins (Illyrian Emperors): 3.40d, Aurelianus. 4.90d, Probus. 10d, Diocletianus.

1980, June 10

1477	A424	2d	multicolored	.25	.25
1478	A424	3.40d	multicolored	.25	.25
1479	A424	4.90d	multicolored	.30	.25
1480	A424	10d	multicolored	.50	.30
			Nos. 1477-1480 (4)	1.30	1.05

No. 1247 Surcharged with New Value and Bars

1980, June 17 Litho. *Perf. 13½*

1481 A323 2.50d on 1.50d .40 .25

Types of 1971-77

Views: 5p, Krusevac. 10p, Gradacac. 20p, Church and bridge, Bohinj. 30p, Krk. 35p, Omis. 40p, Pec. 60p, Logar Valley. 2.50d, Kragujevac. 3.50d, Vrsac. 5.60d, Travnik. 8d, Dubrovnik.

Perf. 13½, 13¼x12½ (#1487), 13¼ (#1486A)

1978-81

1482	A263	5p	deep orange	.40	.25
1483	A263	10p	brown	.40	.40
1483A	A263	20p	purple ('78)	.80	.55
1484	A263	30p	olive gray	.40	.25
1485	A263	35p	brown red	.80	.55
1486	A263	40p	gray	.40	.25
1486A	A263	60p	purple	.40	.25
1487	A323	2.50d	rose red	.80	.25
1488	A323	2.50d	bl gray ('81)	.35	.25
1489	A323	3.50d	red org ('81)	.25	.25
1490	A323	5.60d	gray grn ('81)	.25	.25
1491	A323	8d	gray ('81)	.25	.25
			Nos. 1482-1491 (12)	5.50	3.75

No. 1483A has all three numerals in denomination the same size. On No. 1065 "20" is taller than first "0."

Perf. 13¼x12½

1482a	A263	5p	1.25	.25
1483b	A263	10p	.60	.60
1483Ac	A263	20p	.80	.55
1484a	A263	30p	.80	.40
1485a	A263	35p	1.25	.80
1486b	A263	40p	.55	.25
1486Ac	A263	60p	.55	.40
1487a	A323	2.50d	.50	.25
1488a	A323	2.50d	.25	.25
1489a	A323	3.50d	.25	.25
1490a	A323	5.60d	.25	.25
1491a	A323	8d	.60	.25
		Nos. 1482a-14891a (12)	7.65	4.50

400th Anniversary of Lipica Stud Farm — A425

1980, June 25

1493 A425 2.50d black .25 .25

A426

1980, June 27 *Perf. 13½*

1494 A426 2.50d magenta & red .25 .25

Tito, Basic Law of Self-management, 30th anniv.

A427

1980, June 28 *Perf. 13*

1495 A427 2.50d light green .25 .25

University of Novi Sad, 20th anniv.

Mljet National Park — A428

1980, Sept. 5 Photo. *Perf. 14*

1496	A428	4.90d	shown	.25	.25
1497	A428	13d	Galicica Natl. Park	.25	.25

European Nature Protection Year.

Minerals — A429

1980, Sept. 10 Litho. *Perf. 13½*

1498	A429	2.50d	Pyrrhotine	.35	.35
1499	A429	3.40d	Dolomite	.35	.35
1500	A429	4.90d	Sphalerite	.35	.35
1501	A429	13d	Wulfenite	.80	.80
			Nos. 1498-1501 (4)	1.85	1.85

No. 1244 Surcharged with New Value and Bars

1980, Oct. 15 Litho. *Perf. 13*

1502 A323 5d on 75p purple 2.00 .25

View of Kotor, UNESCO Emblem — A430

1980, Sept. 23 *Perf. 13½*

1503 A430 4.90d multicolored .25 .25

21st UNESCO General Conf., Belgrade,

Children in Garden — A431

Joy of Europe Children's Festival: 13d, 3 faces.

1980, Oct. 2 *Perf. 13½x13*

1504	A431	4.90d	multi	.25	.25
1505	A431	13d	multi	.35	.35

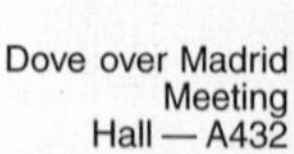

Dove over Madrid Meeting Hall — A432

Lithographed and Engraved

1980, Nov. 11 *Perf. 13½*

1506	A432	4.90d	dk grn & bl grn	.25	.25
1507	A432	13d	dk brn & yel brown	.40	.40

European Security Conference, Madrid.

Federal Flag of Yugoslavia — A433

Republic Day: Socialist Republic flags. Nos. 1508-1515 se-tenant. No. 1511 has Latin letters.

1980, Nov. 28 Litho. *Perf. 12½*

1508	A433	2.50d	Bosnia & Herzegovina	.25	.25
1509	A433	2.50d	Croatia	.25	.25
1510	A433	2.50d	shown	.25	.25
1511	A433	2.50d	Yugoslavia	.25	.25
1512	A433	2.50d	Macedonia	.25	.25
1513	A433	2.50d	Montenegro	.25	.25
1514	A433	2.50d	Serbia	.25	.25
1515	A433	2.50d	Slovenia	.25	.25
			Nos. 1508-1515 (8)	2.00	2.00

Woman with Straw Hat A434

Paintings: 3.40d, Atelier No. 1, by Gabriel Stupica. 4.90d, To the Glory of the Sutjeska Fighters, by Ismet Mujezinovic. 8d, Serenity, by Marino Tartaglia. 13d, Complaint, by Milos Vuskovic.

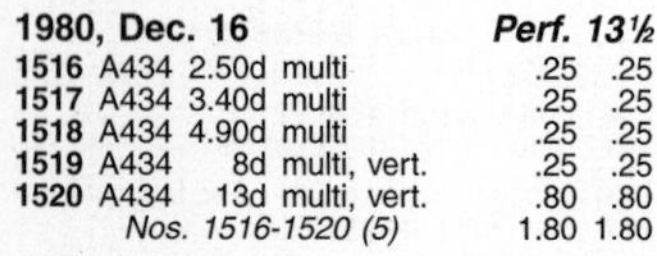

1980, Dec. 16 *Perf. 13½*

1516	A434	2.50d	multi	.25	.25
1517	A434	3.40d	multi	.25	.25
1518	A434	4.90d	multi	.25	.25
1519	A434	8d	multi, vert.	.25	.25
1520	A434	13d	multi, vert.	.80	.80
			Nos. 1516-1520 (5)	1.80	1.80

Ivan Ribar (1881-1968), Politician — A435

1981, Jan. 21 Litho. *Perf. 13½*

1521 A435 2.50d rose red & blk .25 .25

Cementusa Hand Bomb — A436

Partisan Weapons: 5.60d, Rifle. 8d, 52-mm Cannon. 13d, Man-powered tank.

1981, Feb. 16

1522	A436	3.50d	brick red & blk	.25	.25
1523	A436	5.60d	grn & blk	.25	.25
1524	A436	8d	bis brn & blk	.25	.25
1525	A436	13d	rose vio & blk	.50	.50
			Nos. 1522-1525 (4)	1.25	1.25

Monastery of the Virgin, Eleousa, 900th Anniversary A437

1981, Mar. 3

1526 A437 3.50d multicolored 1.10 1.10

Exists imperf. Value $35.

36th World Table Tennis Championship, Novi Sad, Apr. 14-26 — A438

1981, Apr. 14 Litho. *Perf. 13½*

1527 A438 8d multicolored .25 .25

Exists imperf.

Europa Issue

Wedding in Herzegovina, by Nikola Arsenovic — A439

Paintings by Nikola Arsenovic (1823-85): 13d, Witnesses at a Wedding.

1981, May 5 Photo. *Perf. 12*

Granite Paper

1528	A439	8d	multicolored	.30	.25
1529	A439	13d	multicolored	.30	.25

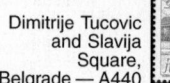

Dimitrije Tucovic and Slavija Square, Belgrade — A440

1981, May 13 Litho. *Perf. 13½*

1530 A440 3.50d bl vio & red .25 .25

Tucovic (1881-1914), Socialist leader. Exists imperf.

Marshal Tito, by Milivoje Unkovic — A441

1981, May 25 Photo. *Perf. 11½x12*

Granite Paper

1531 A441 3.50d gold & dk brn .40 .40

Marshal Tito's 89th birth anniversary. Exists imperf.

Sunflower — A442

1981, May 28 Photo. *Perf. 11½*

Granite Paper

1532	A442	3.50d	shown	.25	.25
1533	A442	5.60d	Hops	.25	.25
1534	A442	8d	Corn	.30	.25
1535	A442	13d	Wheat	.55	.35
			Nos. 1532-1535 (4)	1.35	1.10

Exist imperf.

3rd Autonomous Enterprises Cong. — A443

1981, June 16 Litho. *Perf. 13½*

1536 A443 3.50d multicolored .25 .25

Djordje Petrov (1864-1921), Macedonian Revolutionary — A444

1981, June 22

1537 A444 3.50d bister & black .25 .25

National Insurrection, 40th Anniv. — A445

1981, July 4 *Perf. 12½*

1538	A445	3.50d	red org & tan	.25	.25
1539	A445	8d	red org & tan	.25	.25

Souvenir Sheet

Imperf

1540 A445 30d Tito monument 1.25 1.25

800th Anniv. of Varazdin — A446

1981, Aug. 20 Litho. *Perf. 13½*

1541 A446 3.50d multicolored .25 .25

Parliament Building, Belgrade — A447

1981, Sept. 1

1542 A447 8d red & blue .25 .25

Belgrade Conference of Non-Aligned Countries, 20th anniv.

Serbian Printing Office, 150th Anniv. — A448

1981, Sept. 15

1543 A448 3.50d pale rose & dk bl .25 .25

Fran Levstik (1831-1887), Writer — A449

1981, Sept. 28 ***Perf. 12x11½***

1544 A449 3.50d dl red & gray .25 .25

No. 1251 Surcharged with New Value and Bars

1981, Oct. ***Perf. 13***

1545 A323 5d on 4.90d dl bl .80 .25
a. Perf. 13x12½ 1.60 .40

Joy of Europe Children's Festival — A450

1981, Oct. 2

1546 A450 8d Barnyard .25 .25
1547 A450 13d Skiers .25 .25

125th Anniv. of European Danube Commission A451

8d, Tugboat Karlovac. 13d, Train hauling boat, Sip Canal.

1981, Oct. 28 Litho. ***Perf. 13½***

1548 A451 8d multicolored .25 .25
1549 A451 13d multicolored .70 .70

Nos. 1548-1549 exist imperf. Value, set $75.

No. 1250a Surcharged with New Value and Bars

1981, Oct. 9 Litho. ***Perf. 13x12½***

1550 A323 3.50d on 3.40d gray grn 1.75 .30
a. on #1250 .40 .25

Savings Bank of Yugoslavia, 60th Anniv. — A452

1981, Oct. 31 ***Perf. 11½x12***

1551 A452 3.50d multicolored .25 .25

Intl. Inventions Conference — A453

1981, Nov. 4 ***Perf. 13½***

1552 A453 8d red & gold .25 .25

Nature Protection A454

8d, Plant, Ruguvo Gorge. 13d, Lynx, Prokletjie Mountains.

1981, Nov. 14

1553 A454 8d multicolored .25 .25
1554 A454 13d multicolored .75 .75

August Senoa (1838-1881), Writer — A455

1981, Dec. 12 ***Perf. 11½x12***

1555 A455 3.50d dl gray vio & gldn brn .25 .25

Still Life with a Fish, by Jovan Bijelic (1886-1964) A456

Paintings of Animals: 5.60d, Raven, by Milo Milunovic (1897-1967). 8d, Bird on Blue Background, by Marko Celebonovic (b. 1902). 10d, Horses, by Peter Lubarda (1907-1974). 13d, Sheep, by Nikola Masic (1852-1902).

1981, Dec. 29 Photo. ***Perf. 13½***

1556 A456 3.50d multi .25 .25
1557 A456 5.60d multi .25 .25
1558 A456 8d multi .25 .25
1559 A456 10d multi .25 .25
1560 A456 13d multi .55 .55
Nos. 1556-1560 (5) 1.55 1.55

40th Anniv. of Foca Regulations A457

1982, Jan 14 Litho. ***Perf. 13½***

1561 A457 3.50d Mosa Pijade .25 .25

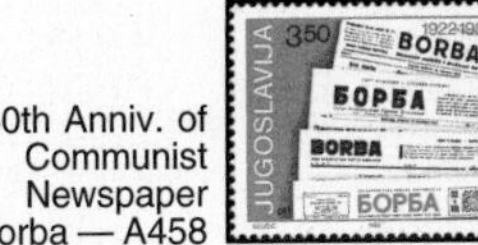

60th Anniv. of Communist Newspaper Borba — A458

1982, Feb. 19 Litho.

1562 A458 3.50d red & blk .25 .25

500th Anniv. of City of Cetinje — A459

1982, Mar. 10

1563 A459 3.50d dull red brn .25 .25

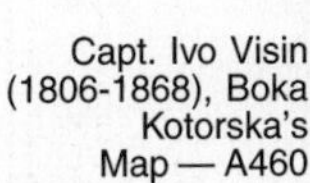

Capt. Ivo Visin (1806-1868), Boka Kotorska's Map — A460

1982, May 5 Photo. ***Perf. 11½***

1564 A460 8d shown .40 .40
1565 A460 15d Ship Splendido .40 .40

Europa, 1st Yugoslavian circumnavigation, 1852-1859.

Male House Sparrow — A461

5.60d, Female house sparrow. 8d, Male field sparrow. 15d, Female field sparrow.

1982, May 24 Litho. ***Perf. 13½***

1566 A461 3.50d shown .25 .25
1567 A461 5.60d multicolored .25 .25
1568 A461 8d multicolored .25 .25
1569 A461 15d multicolored 2.40 2.40
Nos. 1566-1569 (4) 3.15 3.15

See Nos. 1687-1690.

90th Birth Anniv. of Marshal Tito — A462

1982, May 25 Photo. ***Perf. 11½x12***
Granite Paper

1570 A462 3.50d multicolored .25 .25

1982 World Cup — A463

Designs: Soccer ball in various positions.

1982, June 12 ***Perf. 11½***
Granite Paper

1571 Sheet of 4 1.60 1.60
a. A463 3.50d multicolored .25 .25
b. A463 5.60d multicolored .25 .25
c. A463 8d multicolored .25 .25
d. A463 15d multicolored .25 .25

12th Congress of Yugoslavian Communists' League, Belgrade, June 26-29 — A464

1982 June 26 Litho. ***Perf. 13½***

1572 A464 3.50d orange & red .25 .25
1573 A464 8d gray & red .25 .25

Souvenir Sheet
Perf. 12½

1574 Sheet of 2 .80 .80
a. A464 10d like 3.50d .25 .25
b. A464 20d like 8d .55 .55

Exists imperf. Value $250.

Dura Jaksic (1832-1878), Writer, Painter — A465

1982, July 27 Litho. ***Perf. 14***

1575 A465 3.50d Self-portrait .25 .25

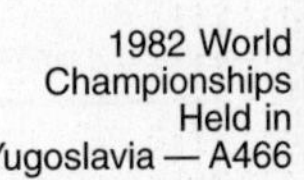

1982 World Championships Held in Yugoslavia — A466

1982, July 30 ***Perf. 13½***

1576 A466 8d Gymnastics .80 .25
1577 A466 8d Kayak .80 .25
1578 A466 8d Weightlifting .80 .25
Nos. 1576-1578 (3) 2.40 .75

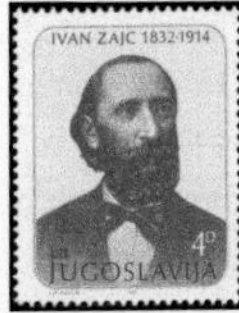

Ivan Zajc (1832-1914), Composer and Conductor — A467

1982, Aug. 3

1579 A467 4d brown .25 .25

Breguet XIX and Potez XXV — A468

6.10d, Super Galeb G-4. 8.80d, Armed boat. 15d, Rocket gun boat.

1982, Sept. 1 Litho. ***Perf. 13½***

1580 A468 4d shown .25 .25
1581 A468 6.10d multicolored .25 .25
1582 A468 8.80d multicolored .25 .25
1583 A468 15d multicolored .50 .50
Nos. 1580-1583 (4) 1.25 1.25

40th anniv. of Air Force/Anti-aircraft Defense and Navy.

Spruce Branch, Tara Natl. Park — A469

15d, Mediterranean monk seal, Kornati.

1982, Sept. 3

1584 A469 8.80d shown .25 .25
1585 A469 15d multicolored .60 .60

14th Joy of Europe Children's Festival A470

1982, Oct. 2

1586 A470 8.80d Traffic .25 .25
1587 A470 15d In the Bath .55 .55

Small Onofrio's Fountain, 15th Cent. — A471

1982, Oct. 23

1588 A471 8.80d multi .25 .25

16th Universal Federation of Travel Agents' Assoc. Cong., Dubrovnik, Oct. 24-30.

600th Anniv. of Hercegnovi A472

1982, Oct. 28

1589 A472 4d multicolored .50 .50

14th Winter Olympic Games, Sarajevo, Feb. 8-19, 1984 — A473

4d, Bridge, Miljacka River. 6.10d, Minaret, Mosque. 8.80d, Evangelical Church. 15d, Street.

1982, Nov. 20 ***Perf. 12½***

1590 A473 4d multicolored .25 .25
1591 A473 6.10d multicolored .25 .25
1592 A473 8.80d multicolored .50 .50
1593 A473 15d multicolored 1.10 1.10
Nos. 1590-1593 (4) 2.10 2.10

Nos. 1488a and 1489a Surcharged In Red, Blue, Black or Red Violet with Two Bars or Shield

1982-83 Litho. ***Perf. 13x12½***

1594 A323 30p on 2.50d (R) .50 .25
1595 A323 50p on 2.50d (Bl) 1.20 .25
1596 A323 60p on 2.50d ('83) .50 .25
1597 A323 1d on 3.50d .25 .25
1597A A323 2d on 2.50d (RV) 1.60 .25
Nos. 1594-1597A (5) 4.05 1.25

Perf. 13

1594a A323 30p on #1488 .40 .25
1595a A323 50p on #1488 .25 .25
1596a A323 60p on #1488 1.00 .25
1597b A323 1d on #1489 .65 .25
Nos. 1594a-1597b (4) 2.30 1.00

Types of 1971-77

Designs: 3d, Skofja Loka. 4d, Pocitelj. 5d, Osijek. 6.10d, like 2.10d. 8.80d, Hercegnovi. 10d, Sarajevo. 16.50d, Ohrid.

1982-83 Litho. *Perf. 13x12½*

1598 A323 3d gray bl .25 .25
1599 A263 4d red org .25 .25
1600 A263 5d grnsh bl ('83) .40 .25
1601 A323 6.10d olive grn .60 .25
1602 A263 8.80d gray .40 .25

Perf. 13½

1603 A263 10d red lil ('83) .25 .25
1603A A323 16.50d dl bl ('83) .25 .25
Nos. 1598-1603A (7) 2.40 1.75

Type styles of Nos. 1600, 1603-1603A differ somewhat from illustrations.

No. 1600 exists imperf. Value $35.

Perf. 13

1598a A323 3d .50 .25
1599a A323 4d .50 .25
1600a A323 5d .40 .25
1601a A323 6.10d .80 .25
1602a A323 8.80d 1.20 .25
1603b A323 10d 1.10 .25
1603c A323 16.50d 1.25 .30
Nos. 1598a-1603c (7) 5.75 1.80

40th Anniv. of Anti-Fascist Council — A474

1982, Nov. 26 *Perf. 13½*

1604 A474 4d Bihac, 1942 .25 .25

The Manuscript, by Janez Bernik (b. 1933) — A475

4d, Prophet on Golden Background, by Joze Ciuha (b. 1924). 6.10d, Journey to the West, by Andrej Jemec (b. 1934). 8.80d, Black Comb with Red Band, by Riko Debenjak (b. 1908). 15d, The Vitrine, by Adriana Maraz (b. 1931).

1982, Nov. 27

1605 A475 4d multi, vert. .25 .25
1606 A475 6.10d multi, vert. .25 .25
1607 A475 8.80d multi, vert. .25 .25
1608 A475 10d multi .25 .25
1609 A475 15d multi .55 .55
Nos. 1605-1609 (5) 1.55 1.55

Uros Predic (1857-1953), Painter — A476

1982, Dec. 7

1610 A476 4d multicolored .25 .25

Union of Pioneers, 40th Anniv. — A477

1982, Dec. 27 *Perf. 12*

1611 A477 4d multicolored .25 .25

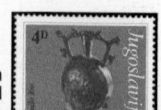

Articles from Museum of Applied Art, Belgrade — A478

Designs: 4d, Lead pitcher, Gnjilane, 16th cent. 6.10d, Silver-plated jug, Macedonia, 18th cent. 8.80d, Goblet, 16th cent., Dalmatia. 15d, Mortar, 15th cent., Kotor.

1983, Feb. 19

1612 A478 4d multicolored .25 .25
1613 A478 6.10d multicolored .25 .25
1614 A478 8.80d multicolored .25 .25
1615 A478 15d multicolored .40 .30
Nos. 1612-1615 (4) 1.15 1.05

Mount Jalovec — A479

1983, Feb. 26

1616 A479 4d blue & lt bl .25 .25

Slovenian Mountaineering Soc., 90th anniv.

Serbian Telephone Service Centenary — A480

1983, Mar. 15

1617 A480 3d Ericsson phone .25 .25

25th Anniv. of Intl. Org. for Maritime Navigation (OMI) — A481

1983, Mar. 17 *Perf. 13½x14*

1618 A481 8.80d multi .25 .25

Edible Mushrooms — A482

4d, Agaricus campestris. 6.10d, Morchella vulgaris. 8.80d, Boletus edulis. 15d, Cantharellus cibarius.

1983, Mar. 21 *Perf. 14*

1619 A482 4d multi .30 .30
1620 A482 6.10d multi .30 .30
1621 A482 8.80d multi .30 .30
1622 A482 15d multi 1.20 1.20
Nos. 1619-1622 (4) 2.10 2.10

Rijeka Railway, 110th Anniv. — A483

No. 1623, Steam engine series 401. No. 1624, Thyristor locomotive 442.

1983, Apr. 5

1623 A483 4d multi .25 .25
1624 A483 23.70d on 8.80d multi .50 .50

No. 1624 not issued without surcharge.

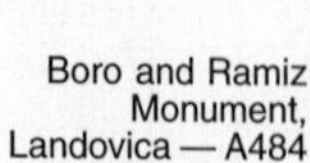

Boro and Ramiz Monument, Landovica — A484

1983, Apr. 10

1625 A484 4d multi .25 .25

Boro Vukmirovic and Ramiz Sadiku, revolutionary martyrs, 40th death anniv.

Ivo Andric (1892-1975), Poet, 1961 Nobel Prize Winner — A485

8.80d, Medal, Travnik Chronicle text. 20d, Portrait, Bridge, Drina River.

1983, May 5 Photo. *Perf. 11½*
Granite Paper

1626 A485 8.80d multicolored .40 .40
1627 A485 20d multicolored .40 .40

Europa.

50th Intl. Agricultural Fair, Novi Sad — A486

1983, May 13 Litho. *Perf. 14*

1628 A486 4d Combine harvester .25 .25

40th Anniv. of Battle of Sutjeska — A487

3d, Assault, by Pivo Karamatijevic.

1983, May 14 *Perf. 12½*

1629 A487 3d multicolored .25 .25

A488

1983, May 25 *Perf. 13½*

1630 A488 4d Tito, Parliament .25 .25
a. Perf. 12½ 1.00 1.00

30th anniv. of election of Pres. Tito.

A489

4d, First mail and passenger car. 16.50d, Mountain road, Kotor.

1983, May 27

1631 A489 4d multi .25 .25
1632 A489 16.50d multi .25 .25

80th anniv. of automobile service in Montenegro.

A490

1983, June 5 *Perf. 14*

1633 A490 23.70d multi .25 .25

UN Conference on Trade and Development, 6th session, Belgrade, June 6-30.

Engraving by Valvasor — A491

1983, June 7 *Perf. 12½*

1634 A491 4d multicolored .25 .25

Town of Pazin millennium.

Triumphal Arch, Titograd — A492

100d, Memorial to S. Filipovic, Valjevo, vert.

1983, June 9 *Perf. 12½*

1635 A492 100d multicolored 2.50 .25
a. Perf. 13x13½ 1.40 .25
1636 A492 200d shown 2.00 .95
a. Perf. 13½x13 3.75 .95

Skopje Earthquake, 20th Anniv. — A493

1983, July 26 Litho. *Perf. 12½*

1637 A493 23.70d deep magenta .25 .25
a. Perf. 13½ .80 .45

For surcharge, see No. 1715.

Sculpture by Ivan Mestrovic — A494

1983, Aug. 15

1638 A494 6d multicolored .25 .25

European Nature Protection A495

16.50d, Gentian, Kopaonik National Park. 23.70d, Chamois, Perucica Gorge.

1983, Sept. 10 Litho. *Perf. 13*

1639 A495 16.50d multi .35 .35
1640 A495 23.70d multi .65 .65

See Nos. 1685-1686.

Joy of Europe — A496

Children's Paintings: 16.50d, Bride and Bridegroom by Verna Paunkonik. 23.70d, Andres and his Mother by Marta Lopez-Ibor.

1983, Oct. 3 Litho. *Perf. 13½*

1641 A496 16.50d multi .25 .25
1642 A496 23.70d multi .65 .65

A497

1983, Oct. 17 Litho. *Perf. 12½*

1643 A497 5d multicolored .25 .25

Kragujevac High School sesquicentenary.

A498

1983, Oct. 17 Litho. *Perf. 13½*

1644 A498 5d multicolored .25 .25

Timok Uprising centenary.

14th Winter Olympic Games, Sarajevo, Feb. 8-19, 1984 — A499

1983, Nov. 25 Engr. *Perf. 13½*

1645 A499 4d Ski jump .25 .25
1646 A499 4d Slalom .25 .25
1647 A499 16.50d Bobsledding .25 .25
1648 A499 16.50d Downhill skiing .25 .25
1649 A499 23.70d Speed skating .50 .50
1650 A499 23.70d Hockey .50 .50
Nos. 1645-1650 (6) 2.00 2.00

Souvenir Sheet

Imperf

1651 A499 50d Emblem 1.75 1.75

Nos. 1645-1651 exist imperf.

Jovan Jovanovic Zmaj (1833-1904), Poet, Neven Masthead — A500

1983, Nov. 24 Litho. *Perf. 12½*

1652 A500 5d multicolored .25 .25

Peasant Wedding, by Pieter Brueghel — A501

Paintings: No. 1654, Susanna with the Old Men, by the "Master of the Prodigal Son." No. 1655, Allegory of Wisdom and Strength, by Paolo Veronese (1528-1588). No. 1656, Virgin Mary from Salamanca, by Robert Campin (1375-1444). No. 1657, St. Ann with Madonna and Jesus, by Albrecht Dürer (1471-1528).

1983, Nov. 26 *Perf. 14*

1653 A501 4d multi .25 .25
1654 A501 16.50d multi .25 .25
1655 A501 16.50d multi .25 .25
1656 A501 23.70d multi .55 .55
1657 A501 23.70d multi .80 .80
Nos. 1653-1657 (5) 2.10 2.10

View of Jajce — A502

1983, Nov. 28 *Perf. 13x12½*

1658 A502 5d multicolored .25 .25

Souvenir Sheet

Imperf

1659 A502 30d Tito .80 .80

40th anniv. of Second Session of the Antifascist Council of the Natl. Liberation of Yugoslavia, Jajce, Nov. 29-30.

World Communications Year — A503

1983, Dec. 10 *Perf. 13½*

1660 A503 23.70d multi .25 .25

Koco Racin (1908-1943), Writer — A504

1983, Dec. 22

1661 A504 5d multicolored .25 .25

Politika Front Page, Oct. 28, 1944 — A505

1984, Jan. 25 Litho. *Perf. 12½*

1662 A505 5d red & black .25 .25

80th anniv. of Politika newspaper and 40th anniv. in Yugoslavia.

Veljko Petrovic (1884-1967), Poet — A506

1984, Feb. 4 Litho. *Perf. 13½*

1663 A506 5d multicolored .25 .25

1984 Winter Olympics — A507

1984, Feb. 8

1664 A507 4d Biathlon .25 .25
1665 A507 4d Giant slalom .25 .25
1666 A507 5d Bobsledding .25 .25
1667 A507 5d Slalom .25 .25
1668 A507 16.50d Speed skating .40 .40
1669 A507 16.50d Hockey .40 .40
1670 A507 23.70d Ski jumping .45 .45
1671 A507 23.70d Downhill skiing .45 .45
Nos. 1664-1671 (8) 2.70 2.70

Souvenir Sheets

Imperf

1672 A507 50d Flame, rings 1.40 1.40
1673 A507 100d Flame, map 2.75 2.75

No. 1664-1671 exist imperf.

Natl. Heroines — A508

Designs: a, Marija Bursac (1902-43). b, Jelena Cetkovic (1916-43). c, Nada Dimic (1923-42). d, Elpida Karamandi (1920-42). e, Toncka Cec Olga (1896-1943). f, Spasenija Babovic Cana (1907-77). g, Jovanka Radivojevic Kica (1922-43). h, Sonja Marinkovic (1916-41).

1984, Mar. 8 Litho. *Perf. 14*

1674 Sheet of 8 + label 3.50 3.50
a.-h. A508 5d any single .25 .25

Slovenia Monetary Institute, 40th Anniv. — A509

1984, Mar. 12 *Perf. 12½*

1675 A509 5d Bond, note .25 .25

Railroad Service in Serbia (Belgrade-Nis) Centenary A510

5d, Train, Central Belgrade Station.

1984, Apr. 9 *Perf. 13*

1676 A510 5d multicolored .25 .25

Jure Franko, Giant Slalom Silver Medalist, 1984 — A511

1984, Apr. 28

1677 A511 23.70d multi .80 .80

Yugoslavia's first Winter Olympic medalist.

Europa (1959-84) — A512

1984, Apr. 30 *Perf. 13½*

1678 A512 23.70d multi .40 .40
1679 A512 50d multi .80 .80

1984 Summer Olympics, Los Angeles — A513

1984, May 14

1680 A513 5d Basketball .55 .55
1681 A513 16.50d Diving .55 .55
1682 A513 23.70d Equestrian .55 .55
1683 A513 50d Running 2.00 2.00
Nos. 1680-1683 (4) 3.65 3.65

Marshal Tito — A514

1984, May 25 *Perf. 13*

1684 A514 5d brown red .25 .25

Nature Type of 1983

Designs: 26d, Centaurea gloriosa (flower), Biokovo Mountain Park. 40d, Anophthalmus (insect), Pekel Cave, Savinja Valley.

1984, June 11 Litho. *Perf. 13½*

1685 A495 26d multicolored .50 .25
1686 A495 40d multicolored .80 .40

Bird Type of 1982

4d, Great black-backed gull. 5d, Black-headed gull. 16.50d, Herring gull. 40d, Common tern.

1984, June 28

1687 A461 4d multicolored .40 .40
1688 A461 5d multicolored .40 .40
1689 A461 16.50d multicolored .40 .40
1690 A461 40d multicolored 3.50 1.50
Nos. 1687-1690 (4) 4.70 2.70

19th Cent. Cradles — A515

1984, Sept. 1 Litho. *Perf. 12½*

1691 A515 4d Bosnia & Herzegovina .25 .25
1692 A515 5d Montenegro .25 .25
1693 A515 26d Macedonia .40 .40
1694 A515 40d Serbia .65 .65
Nos. 1691-1694 (4) 1.55 1.55

Olive Tree, Mirovica — A516

1984, Sept. 1

1695 A516 5d multi .25 .25

Joy of Europe — A517

Children's Drawings: 26d, Traditional costumes. 40d, Girl with doll carriage.

1984, Oct. 2 Litho. *Perf. 14*

1696 A517 26d multicolored .35 .35
1697 A517 40d multicolored .90 .90

City of Virovitica, 750th Anniv. — A518

5d, Engraving, 17th cent.

1984, Oct. 4 *Perf. 13½*

1698 A518 5d multicolored .25 .25

Map, Concentric Waves — A519

1984, Oct. 10

1699 A519 6d Prus bl & brt grn .25 .25

Radio and telegraph service in Montenegro, 80th anniv.

Veterans Conference A520

1984, Oct. 18

1700 A520 26d multicolored .90 .90
1701 A520 40d multicolored 1.20 1.20

Conf. of Veterans on Security, Disarmament & Cooperation in Europe, Belgrade, 10/18-20.

Liberation of Belgrade, 40th Anniv. — A521

1984, Oct. 20

1702 A521 6d "40," arms .25 .25

Miloje Milojevic (1884-1946), Composer — A522

1984, Oct. 27

1703 A522 6d Portrait, score .25 .25

Medals Events, 1984 Summer Olympics — A522a

Designs: a, Wrestling. b, Running. c, Field hockey. d, Shot put. e, Soccer. f, Basketball. g, Netball. h, Rowing.

1984, Nov. 14 Litho. *Perf. 13½*

1704 Sheet of 8 4.00 4.00
a.-h. A522a 26d any single .25 .25

The Tahitians, by Gauguin A523

Paintings by Foreign Artists in Yugoslav Museums: 6d, Portrait of Madame Tatichek, by Ferdinand Waldmuller (1793-1865). No. 1706, The Bathers, by Renoir (1841-1919). No. 1707, At the Window, by Henri Matisse (1869-1954). 40d, Ballerinas, by Edgar Degas (1834-1917).

Perf. 13½x14, 14x13½

1984, Nov. 15

1705 A523 6d multi, vert. .25 .25
1706 A523 26d multi, vert. .25 .25
1707 A523 26d multi, vert. .25 .25
1708 A523 38d multi .50 .50
1709 A523 40d multi .80 .80
Nos. 1705-1709 (5) 2.05 2.05

Nova Macedonia Newspaper, 40th Anniv. — A523a

1984, Nov. 29 *Perf. 13½*
1710 A523a 6d 1st & recent editions .25 .25

Nos. 1602, 1599 and 1637 Surcharged in Red Brown or Black

Types of 1975 and

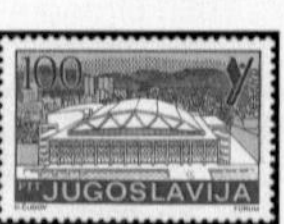

Exhibition Center, Zagreb A524

Bird, Jet, Landscape A525

Designs: 6d, Kikinda. 26d, Korcula. 38d, Maribor. 70d, Trumpeter monument, riverside buildings in Zagreb. 1000d, bird, tail of jet on airfield.

Perf. 13½x12½, 13 (#1713, 1717), 12½ (#1715)

1984-86 **Litho.**
1711 A263 2d on 8.80d 1.75 1.75
a. on #1602a .40 .25
1712 A263 6d on 4d (RBr) .40 .25
a. on #1599a .55 .40
1713 A323 6d lt red brn .40 .25
a. Perf. 13x12½ .80 .25
1715 A493 20d on 23.70d .40 .25
1717 A263 26d dp ultra .40 .25
a. Perf. 13x12½ .50 .25
1718 A323 38d dp lil rose 1.60 .25
a. Perf. 13 .40 .25
1719 A323 70d brt ultra ('85) 1.25 .55
b. Perf. 13 .55 .45

Perf. 14

1719A A524 100d brt org yel & vio .65 .35

Perf. 12½

1720 A525 500d redsh brn & multi ('85) 3.75 1.40
a. Perf. 13¼ 1.75 .65
1721 A525 1000d org brn & multi ('85) 5.50 2.90
a. Perf. 13½ 2.10 1.25
Nos. 1711-1721 (10) 16.10 8.20

Type styles for Nos. 1717-1718 differ somewhat from illustration.

For surcharge, see No. 1973.

Museum Exhibits - Fossils — A526

5d, Aturia aturi. 6d, Pachyophis woodwardi. 33d, Chaetodon hoeferi. 60d, Homo sapiens neanderthalensis.

1985, Feb. 4 **Litho.** *Perf. 12½*
1722 A526 5d multi .25 .25
1723 A526 6d multi .25 .25
1724 A526 33d multi .40 .40
1725 A526 60d multi .90 .90
Nos. 1722-1725 (4) 1.80 1.80

40th Anniv., Monument Protection — A527

1985, Feb. 20 **Litho.** *Perf. 12½*
1726 A527 6d Hopovo church .25 .25

Ski Jumping at Planica, 50th Anniv. — A528

1985, Mar. 15 **Litho.** *Perf. 13½*
1727 A528 6d Three herons in flight 4.75 2.40

European Nature Conservation — A529

1985, Mar. 30 *Perf. 14*
1728 A529 42d Pandion haliaetus 1.25 .80
1729 A529 60d Upupa epops 2.40 1.25

Audubon birth bicentenary, European Information Center for Nature Protection.

A530

Fresco of St. Methodius, St. Naum Monastery, Ohrid.

1985, Apr. 6 **Litho.** *Perf. 11½x12*
1730 A530 10d multicolored 1.75 .80

St. Methodius (d. 885), archbishop of Pannonia and Moravia.

A531

1985, Apr. 16 **Litho.** *Perf. 12½*
1731 A531 6d Clasped hands .25 .25

Osimo Agreements, 10th anniv. Yugoslavia-Italy political and economic cooperation.

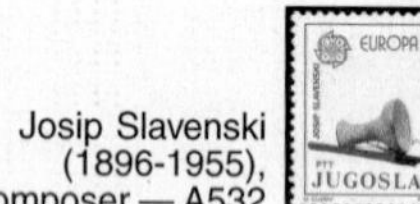

Josip Slavenski (1896-1955), Composer — A532

Europa: 60d, Portrait, block flute, darabukka. 80d, Balkanophonia score, signature.

1985, Apr. 29 *Perf. 14*
1732 A532 60d multi .40 .40
1733 A532 80d multi .80 .80

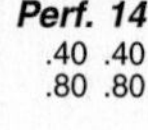

Joachim Vujic, by Dimitrije Avramovic (1815-1855) A533

1985, May 8 *Perf. 12x11½*
1734 A533 10d multi .25 .25

Joachim Vujic Theater, Kragujevac, 150th anniv.

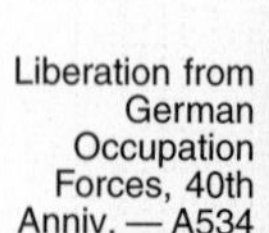

Liberation from German Occupation Forces, 40th Anniv. — A534

1985, May 9 *Perf. 13½*
1735 A534 10d shown .25 .25
1736 A534 10d Order of Natl. Liberation .25 .25

Franjo Kluz (1912-1944), Rudi Cajavec (1911-1942), Breguet-19 Fighter — A535

1985, May 21 *Perf. 13x12½*
1737 A535 10d multi .25 .25

Air Force Day.

Pres. Tito (1892-1980) — A536

1985, May 25 *Perf. 13½*
1738 A536 10d Portrait .50 .25

Cres-Losinj Municipal Tourism Bureau, Cent. — A537

1985, June 12
1739 A537 10d Map, town arms, villa .65 .65

UN 40th Anniv. — A538

1985, June 26 **Litho.** *Perf. 12½*
1740 A538 70d Emblem, rainbow .25 .25

Rowing — A539

1985, June 29 **Litho.** *Perf. 13½*
1741 A539 70d multicolored .40 .40

Souvenir Sheet

1742 A539 100d Course map, arms 1.40 1.40

Intl. European-Danube Rowing Regatta, 30th anniv.

Nautical Tourism — A540

1985, July 1 **Litho.**
1743 A540 8d Sailboat .80 .80
1744 A540 10d Windsurfing .80 .80
1745 A540 50d Sailboat, diff. .80 .80
1746 A540 70d Sailboat, diff. 2.50 2.50
Nos. 1743-1746 (4) 4.90 4.90

F1B Class Motorized Model Plane — A541

1985, Aug. 10 **Litho.** *Perf. 12½x13*
1747 A541 70d multicolored .50 .40

Free Flight World Championships, Livno, Aug. 12-18.

Algae — A542

8d, Corallina officinalis. 10d, Desmarestia viridis. 50d, Fucus vesiculosus. 70d, Padina pavonia.

1985, Sept. 20 *Perf. 14*
1748 A542 8d multicolored .25 .25
1749 A542 10d multicolored .25 .25
1750 A542 50d multicolored .30 .30
1751 A542 70d multicolored 1.50 1.50
Nos. 1748-1751 (4) 2.30 2.30

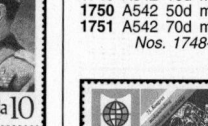

Intl. Federation of Stomatologists, 73rd Congress, Belgrade, Sept. 21-28 — A543

1985, Sept. 21 *Perf. 12x11½*
1752 A543 70d multicolored .40 .40

Children's Drawings — A544

Designs: 50d, Children in a Horse-drawn Cart, by Branka Lukic, age 14, Yugoslavia. 70d, Children in Field, by Suzanne Straathof, age 9, Netherlands.

1985, Oct. 2 *Perf. 14*
1753 A544 50d multicolored .40 .40
1754 A544 70d multicolored 1.25 1.25

Croatian Natl. Theater, Zagreb, 125th Anniv. — A545

1985, Nov. 23 *Perf. 12½*
1755 A545 10d Facade detail .25 .25

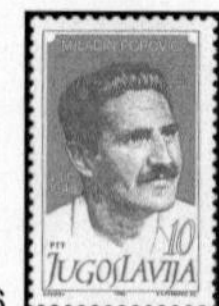

Miladin Popovic — A546

1985, Nov. 26 *Perf. 11½x12*
1756 A546 10d Portrait .25 .25

Popovic (1910-1945), revolutionary.

Natl. Coat of Arms — A547

1985, Nov. 28 *Perf. 13½*
1757 A547 10d multicolored .25 .25

Souvenir Sheet

Imperf

1758 A547 100d multicolored 1.00 1.00

Socialist Federal Republic of Yugoslavia, 40th anniv. No. 1758 contains one stamp 18x27mm.

Royal Procession, by Iromie Wijewardena, Sri Lanka — A548

Paintings from the Art Gallery of Non-aligned Countries, Titograd: 10d, Return from Hunting, by Mama Cangare, Mali. No. 1761, Drum of Coca, by Agnes Ovando Sanz De Franck, Bolivia. No. 1762, The Cock, by Mariano Rodriguez, Cuba, vert. 70d, Three Women, by Quamrul Hassan, Bangladesh, vert.

1985, Dec. 2 *Perf. 14*
1759 A548 8d multicolored .25 .25
1760 A548 10d multicolored .25 .25
1761 A548 50d multicolored .25 .25

1762 A548 50d multicolored .25 .25
1763 A548 70d multicolored 1.40 1.40
Nos. 1759-1763 (5) 2.40 2.40

Nos. 1243, 1482, 1485a, 1490, 1491, 1713a, 1717a, 1603A and 1718 Srchd. in Light Red Brown, Brown or Dark Brown

1985-86 Litho. ***Perf. 13½, 13½x12½***
1764 A323 1d on 25p (B) .80 .25
1765 A263 2d on 5p (DB) .40 .25
a. on #1482a .40 .25
1766 A263 3d on 35p (DB) .25 .25
a. on #1485a .25 .25
1767 A323 4d on 5.60d (B) .25 .25
b. on #1490 .80 .50
1767A A323 5d on 8d (B) .40 .25
c. on #1491a .80 .80
1768 A323 8d on 6d .25 .25
a. on #1713 .25 .25
1769 A263 20d on 26d .25 .25
a. on #1717 7.00 4.00
1770 A323 50d on 16.50d (B) .80 .40
a. on #1603c .80 .40
1771 A323 70d on 38d .80 .50
Nos. 1764-1771 (9) 4.20 2.65

Issued: #1767A, 3/17/86; others, 12/85.

Natl. Automobile Assoc., 40th Anniv. — A549

1986, Feb. 25 ***Perf. 12½***
1772 A549 10d Car .25 .25
1773 A549 70d Helicopter .80 .80

Tara River, Montenegro — A550

1986, Mar. 3 ***Perf. 14***
1774 A550 100d Canyon .40 .40
1775 A550 150d Bridge .80 .80

European nature protection. Sheets of 9.

Studenica Monastery, 800th Anniv. — A551

1986, Mar. 15 ***Perf. 13½***
1776 A551 10d Chapel of Our Lady .55 .40

A552

Various soccer plays.

1986, Apr. 5 Litho. ***Perf. 14***
1777 A552 70d multi .65 .65
1778 A552 150d multi .80 .80

1986 World Cup Soccer Championships, Mexico.

Arrival of St. Clement in Ohrid, 1100th Anniv. — A553

1986, Apr. 12 ***Perf. 12½***
1779 A553 10d Township model *5.00 5.00*

Europa Issue

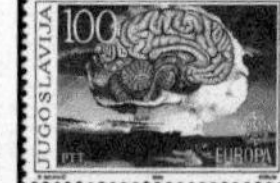
Brain, Mushroom Cloud — A554

1986, Apr. 28 ***Perf. 14***
1780 A554 100d shown .40 .40
1781 A554 200d Injured deer 1.20 .80

European Men's Senior Judo Championships, Belgrade, May 8-11 — A555

1986, May 7 ***Perf. 12½***
1782 A555 70d multi .50 .40

Natl. Costumes — A556

a, Slovenia. b, Vojvodina. c, Croatia. d, Macedonia. e, Serbia. f, Montenegro. g, Kosovo. h, Bosnia & Herzegovina.

1986, May 22 Litho. ***Perf. 12x13***
Booklet Stamps
1783 Bklt. pane of 8 4.50
a.-h. A556 50d any single .55 .55

Yachts, Moscenika Draga Bay — A557

1986, May 23 ***Perf. 14***
1784 A557 50d multi .25 .25
1785 A557 80d multi, diff. .40 .40

Souvenir Sheet
Imperf
1786 A557 100d multi 3.25 3.25

European Sailing Championships, Croatia, May 29-June 7, Flying Dutchman Class. No. 1786 contains one stamp 22x28mm.

Marshal Tito — A557a

1986, May 24 ***Perf. 13x12½***
1787 A557a 10d multicolored .25 .25

Moths and Butterflies — A558

1986, May 26 ***Perf. 14***
1788 A558 10d Eudia pavonia .80 .80
1789 A558 20d Inachis io .80 .80
1790 A558 50d Parnassius apollo .80 .80
1791 A558 100d Apatura iris 1.60 1.60
Nos. 1788-1791 (4) 4.00 4.00

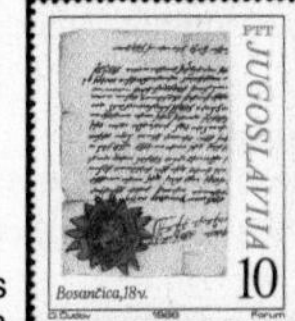
Ancient Manuscripts A558a

Designs: 10d, Evangelical, 18th cent. 20d, Leontijevo Evangelical, 16th cent. 50d, Astrological, Mesopotamia, 15th cent. 100d, Hebrew Haggadah, Spain, 14th cent.

1986, June 12 Litho. ***Perf. 14***
1792 A558a 10d multicolored .25 .25
1793 A558a 20d multicolored .25 .25
1794 A558a 50d multicolored .40 .40
1795 A558a 100d multicolored .80 .65
Nos. 1792-1795 (4) 1.70 1.55

A559

A560

Designs: 20d, Postman on motorcycle. 30d, Postman, resident. 40d, Forklift, mail pallets. 50d, Mail train. 60d, Man posting letters in mailbox. 93d, Open envelope and greetings telegram form. 100d, Postman, mail van. No. 1803, Computer operator facing right. No. 1804, 140d, Computer operator facing left. 120d, Woman sending love letter. 200d, Freighter in high seas. 500d, Postal employee sorting mail. 1000d, Woman at telephone station. 2000d, Aircraft, hemispheres on world map. 30d, 60d, 93d, 106d, 120d, 140d, 500d, 1000d vert.

Perf. 13½, 12½x13½ (20d, 40d, 50d), 14 (100d)

1986-88 Litho.
1796 A559 20d brt pink .40 .25
a. Perf. 13 .40 .25
1797 A559 30d lt brn vio .40 .25
a. Perf. 13x12½ .80 .25
1798 A559 40d brt red .40 .25
a. Perf. 13 .40 .25
1799 A559 50d violet .40 .25
a. Perf. 13 .25 .25
1800 A559 60d lt sage grn .40 .25
1801 A559 93d ultra .40 .25
1802 A559 100d dl magenta .80 .30
1803 A559 106d rose red .40 .25
1804 A559 106d brn org .40 .25
1805 A559 120d dull blue grn .25 .25
1806 A559 140d dull rose .25 .25
1807 A559 200d greenish bl 1.00 .40
a. Perf. 12½ 2.00 1.60
b. Perf. 12½x13½ 6.00 2.00
1808 A559 500d deep blue & beige .40 .40
1809 A559 500d chalky blue & yel .25 .25
1810 A559 1000d vio & blue grn .25 .25
b. Perf. 12½ .55 .50
1810A A560 2000d brt blue, red & brt vio 1.00 .50
Nos. 1796-1810A (16) 7.40 4.60

Size of No. 1802: 19½x18mm.
Issued: 20d, 3/17; 50d, 200d, 6/4; 40d, 7/17; 100d, 6/12; 30d, 7/26; 60d, 6/5/87; #1803, 12/10/87; 93d, 12/16/87; #1804, 1/22/88; #1808, 4/29/88; 1000d, 7/21/88; 20d, 140d, 2000d, #1809, 9/5/88.
See Nos. 1935-1945, 2004-2007, 2013-2015, 2021. For surcharges see Nos. 1877, 1912-1913, 1947-1948, 1972, 1974-1975, 2017, 2019, 2048-2051, 2053.

13th Communist Federations Congress (SKJ) — A561

1986, June 25 ***Perf. 12½***
1811 A561 10d shown .25 .25
1812 A561 20d Star .25 .25

Souvenir Sheet
Imperf
1813 A561 100d Tito .80 .80

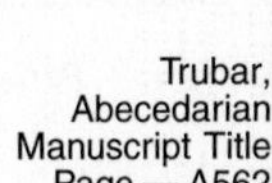
Trubar, Abecedarian Manuscript Title Page — A562

1986, June 28 Litho. ***Perf. 12½x13***
1814 A562 20d multi .55 .40

Primoz Trubar (1508-1568), Slovenian philologist and religious reformer.

Serbian Natl. Theater, Novi Sad, 125th Anniv. — A563

1986, July 28 ***Perf. 14***
1815 A563 40d Thalia .25 .25

Rugovo Dance, Kosovo Province — A564

1986, Sept. 10
1816 A564 40d multi .25 .25

1987 Universiade Games, Zagreb, July 8-19 — A565

1986, Sept. 22 ***Perf. 13½***
1817 A565 30d Volleyball .35 .35
1818 A565 40d Canoeing .35 .35
1819 A565 100d Gymnastics .55 .55
1820 A565 150d Fencing .80 .80
Nos. 1817-1820 (4) 2.05 2.05

18th Joy of Europe Youth Conference — A566

Children's drawings: 100d, Dove, by Tanja Faletic, 14. 150d, Buildings, by Johanna Kraus, 12, DDR.

1986, Oct. 2 ***Perf. 14***
1821 A566 100d multicolored .55 .55
1822 A566 150d multicolored .80 .80

Rotary Switching Apparatus, Village of Bled — A567

1986, Oct. 4 ***Perf. 13½***
1823 A567 40d multicolored .25 .25

Telephone exchanges connected with automatic switching equipment, 50th anniv.

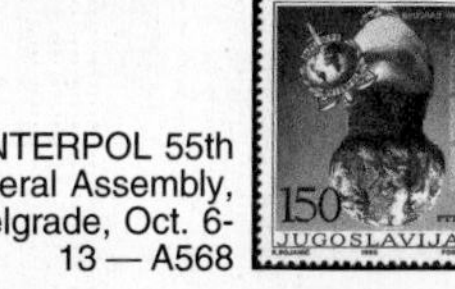
INTERPOL 55th General Assembly, Belgrade, Oct. 6-13 — A568

1986, Oct. 6 ***Perf. 14***
1824 A568 150d multicolored .40 .40

Intl. Brigades, 50th Anniv. — A569

1986, Oct. 21 ***Perf. 13½***
1825 A569 40d multicolored .25 .25

Intl. Peace Year — A570

1986, Nov. 20
1826 A570 150d multicolored .50 .50

Serbian Academy of the Arts and Sciences, Cent. — A571

1986, Nov. 1 **Photo.** ***Perf. 13½***
1827 A571 40d multicolored .25 .25

Paintings by Foreign Artists in the Museum of Contemporary Art, Skopje — A572

No. 1828, Still Life, by Frantisek Muzika, Czechoslovakia. #1829, Disturance, by Rafael Canogar, England. #1830, Iol, by Victor Vasarely, France. #1831, Portrait, by Bernard Buffet, France. #1832, Woman's Head, by Pablo Picasso, Spain.

1986, Dec. 10 **Litho.** ***Perf. 14***
1828 A572 30d multi .25 .25
1829 A572 40d multi .25 .25
1830 A572 100d multi, vert. .40 .40
1831 A572 100d multi, vert. .40 .40
1832 A572 150d multi, vert. .65 .65
Nos. 1828-1832 (5) 1.95 1.95

Wildlife Conservation A573

30d, Lutra lutra. 40d, Ovis musimon. 100d, Cervus elaphus. 150d, Ursus arctos.

1987, Jan. 22 **Litho.** ***Perf. 13½x14***
1833 Strip of 4 + label 8.00 8.00
a. A573 30d multi .65 .65
b. A573 40d multi .65 .65
c. A573 100d multi .65 .65
d. A573 150d multi .65 .65

Label pictures nature reserve.

Rudjer Boscovich (1711-1787), Scientist, and Solar Eclipse over Brera Observatory, Italy — A574

1987, Feb. 13 ***Perf. 14***
1834 A574 150d multicolored .50 .40

European Nature Protection — A575

1987, Mar. 9
1835 A575 150d shown 1.00 1.00
1836 A575 400d Triglav glacial lake 1.50 1.50

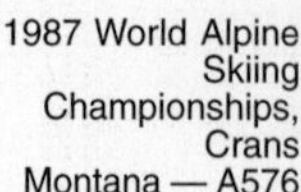

1987 World Alpine Skiing Championships, Crans Montana — A576

1987, Mar. 20 **Litho.** ***Perf. 14***
1837 A576 200d multicolored 2.40 2.40

No. 1837 printed in sheets of 8 plus center label.

Natl. Civil Aviation, 60th Anniv. — A577

1987, Mar. 20 ***Perf. 14***
1838 A577 150d POTEZ-29 .55 .55
1839 A577 400d DC-10 1.20 1.20

Each printed in sheets of 8 plus center label.

Kole Nedelkovski (1912-1941), Poet, Revolutionary A578

1987, Apr. 2 ***Perf. 13½***
1840 A578 40d multicolored .25 .25

Liberation of Montenegro from Turkey, 125th Anniv. — A579

1987, Apr. 16 ***Perf. 13½***
1841 A579 40d Battle flags, folk guitar .25 .25

Slovenian Communist Party, Cebine, 50th Anniv. — A580

1987, Apr. 18 ***Perf. 14***
1842 A580 40d multicolored .25 .25

Europa Issue

Tito Bridge, Krk — A581

1987, Apr. 30 **Litho.** ***Perf. 14***
1843 A581 200d shown .40 .40
1844 A581 400d Bridges over canal .80 .80

Fruit Trees — A582

1987, May 15 **Litho.** ***Perf. 14***
1845 A582 60d Almond .30 .30
1846 A582 150d Pear .90 .90
1847 A582 200d Apple 1.10 1.10
1848 A582 400d Plum 2.25 2.25
Nos. 1845-1848 (4) 4.55 4.55

Tito, 1930, by Mosa Pijade — A583

1987, May 25
1849 A583 60d multi .30 .25

50th anniv. of Tito's assumption of Yugoslavian communist party leadership.

Vuk Stefanovik Karadzic (1787-1864), Linguist and Historian — A584

60d, Bust by Petar Ubavkic, his Trsic residence & Vienna. 200d, Portrait by Uros Knezevic, & alphabet from Karadzic's Serbian Dictionary, 1818.

1987, June 10
1850 A584 60d multi .25 .25
1851 A584 200d multi .40 .40

Zrenjanin Postal Service, 250th Anniv. — A585

1987, June 22 ***Perf. 13½***
1852 A585 60d multi .25 .25

UNIVERSIADE '87, Zagreb, July 8-19 — A586

1987, July 8 **Litho.** ***Perf. 13½***
1853 A586 60d Hurdling .25 .25
1854 A586 150d Basketball .40 .40
1855 A586 200d Balance beam .55 .55
1856 A586 400d Swimming 1.25 1.25
Nos. 1853-1856 (4) 2.45 2.45

Each printed in sheets of eight plus label.

Fire Fighting — A587

1987, July 20 ***Perf. 14***
1857 A587 60d Canadair CL-215 spraying forest .25 .25
1858 A587 200d Fire boat .25 .25

Each printed in sheets of eight plus label.

Monument, Anindol Park, Samobor — A588

1987, Aug. 1 ***Perf. 13½***
1859 A588 60d multi .25 .25

Communist Party of Croatia, 50th anniv.

Sabac High School, 150th Anniv. — A589

1987, Sept. 10 **Litho.** ***Perf. 13½***
1860 A589 80d multi .25 .25

Exhibition Emblem, Balkan Peninsula, Flowers — A590

Clock Tower, Petrovaradin Fortress and Novi Sad — A591

1987, Sept. 19 ***Perf. 14***
1861 A590 250d multi .40 .40

Souvenir Sheet
Imperf

1862 A591 400d multi 1.00 1.00

BALKANFILA XI, Novi Sad, Sept. 19-26.

19th Joy of Europe Conference — A592

Children's drawings: 250d, Girls in forest, by Bedic Aranka, Juguoslavia. 400d, Scarecrow, by Schaffer Ingeborg, Austria.

1987, Oct. 2 **Litho.** ***Perf. 14***
1863 A592 250d multi .75 .75
1864 A592 400d multi .80 .80

Printed in sheets of nine.

Bridges — A593

80d, Arslanagica, Trebinje, 16th cent. 250d, Terzija, Djakovica, 15th cent.

1987, Oct. 15
1865 A593 80d multi .40 .40
1866 A593 250d multi .40 .40

Ship, Dunav-Tisa Channel — A594

1987, Oct. 20 ***Perf. 13½***
1867 A594 80d multi .25 .25

City of Titov Vrbas, 600th anniv.

Astronomical and Meteorological Observatory, Belgrade, Cent. — A595

1987, Nov. 21 ***Perf. 14***
1868 A595 80d multi .25 .25

St. Luke the Evangelist, by Raphael — A596

Paintings by foreign artists in national museums: 200d, Infanta Maria Theresa, by Velazquez. 250d, Nicholas Rubens, Painter's Son, by Rubens. 400d, Louis Laure Sennegon, Painter's Niece, by Jean-Baptiste-Camille Corot (1796-1875).

1987, Nov. 28

1869 A596 80d shown .25 .25
1870 A596 200d multi .40 .40
1871 A596 250d multi .40 .40
1872 A596 400d multi 1.10 1.10
Nos. 1869-1872 (4) 2.15 2.15

Traditional Competitions A597

80d, Bull fighting. 200d, Ljubicevo Horse Games. 250d, Moresca game. 400d, Sinj iron ring.

1987, Dec. 10

1873 A597 80d multi .25 .25
1874 A597 200d multi .40 .40
1875 A597 250d multi .40 .40
1876 A597 400d multi 1.50 1.50
Nos. 1873-1876 (4) 2.55 2.55

No. 1800 Surcharged

1987, Sept. 22 ***Perf. 13½***

1877 A559 80d on 60d sg grn .40 .25

Vinodol Codex, City of Vinodolski, Coat of Arms — A598

1988, Jan. 6 **Litho.** ***Perf. 14***

1878 A598 100d multi .25 .25

Vinodol Codex, 700th anniv.

Intl. Women's Golden Fox Skiing Championships, 25th Anniv. — A599

1988, Jan. 30

1879 A599 350d Slalom, emblem, Mirobor City .25 .25

Printed in sheets of eight plus center label.

World Wildlife Fund — A600

Brown bears (Ursus arctos).

1988, Feb. 1

1880 A600 70d Cub 2.40 1.60
1881 A600 80d Cubs 2.40 1.60
1882 A600 200d Adult, head 2.40 1.60
1883 A600 350d Adult 9.00 4.75
Nos. 1880-1883 (4) 16.20 9.55

1988 Winter Olympics, Calgary — A601

1988, Feb. 13 ***Perf. 14x13½***

1884 A601 350d Slalom .85 .85
1885 A601 1200d Ice hockey 1.25 1.25

Each printed in sheets of 8 plus center label.

Souvenir Sheet

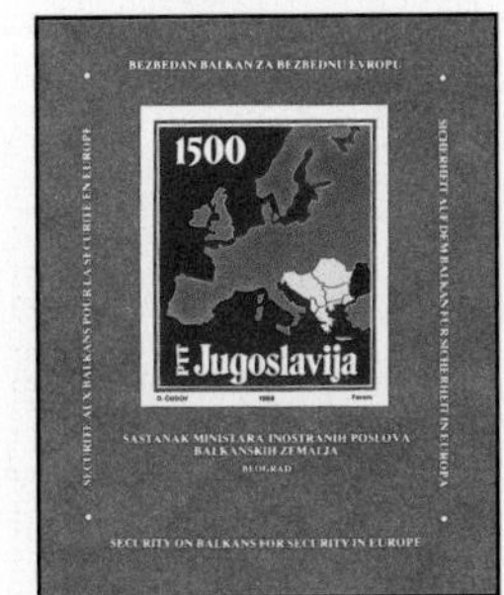

Map of Europe Highlighting Balkan Nations — A602

1988, Feb. 24 **Litho.** ***Imperf.***

1886 A602 1500d multi 1.75 1.75

Congress of Foreign Affairs Ministers from the Balkan Countries, Belgrade, Feb. 24-26.

1988 Summer Olympics, Seoul — A603

South Korean Landscape — A604

1988, Mar. 21 ***Perf. 14x13½***

1887 A603 106d Basketball .55 .55
1888 A603 450d High jump .55 .55
1889 A603 500d Pommel horse .55 .55
1890 A603 1200d Boxing .55 .55
Nos. 1887-1890 (4) 2.20 2.20

Souvenir Sheet

Imperf

1891 A604 1500d multi 2.00 2.00

Nos. 1887-1890 printed in sheets of 8 plus center label.

Europa Issue

Telecommunications A605

1988, Apr. 30 **Litho.** ***Perf. 13½x14***

1892 A605 450d shown .45 .45
1893 A605 1200d Transportation .80 .80

Sea Shells — A606

106d, Gibbula magus. 550d, Pecten jacobaeus. 600d, Tonna galea. 1000d, Argonauta argo.

1988, May 14

1894 A606 106d multicolored .65 .50
1895 A606 550d multicolored .65 .50
1896 A606 600d multicolored 1.00 .80
1897 A606 1000d multicolored 1.50 .80
Nos. 1894-1897 (4) 3.80 2.60

Trial of Tito and Five Comrades, 60th Anniv. — A607

1988, May 25

1898 A607 106d black & brn .25 .25

Palace of Princess Ljubica of Serbia, 1st University Building — A608

1988, June 14 **Litho.** ***Perf. 13½***

1899 A608 106d multi .25 .25

Belgrade University, 150th anniv.

Flowers — A609

600d, Phelypaea boissieri. 1000d, Campanula formanekiana.

1988, July 2 ***Perf. 14***

1900 A609 600d multicolored .80 .80
1901 A609 1000d multicolored 1.25 1.25

European Nature Protection.

Esperanto, Cent. — A610

1988, July 14 ***Perf. 13½***

1902 A610 600d dull vio & ol grn .80 .55

Printed in sheets of 8 plus center label.

Cargo Ships — A611

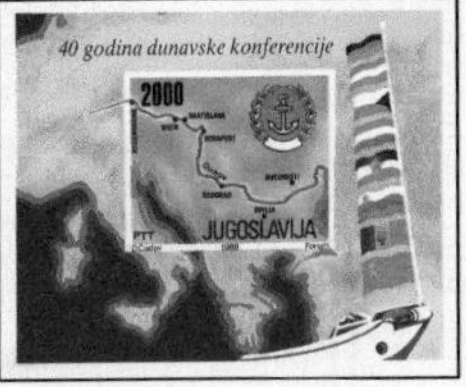

Map of the Danube Basin A612

1988, Aug. 18 **Litho.** ***Perf. 14***

1903 A611 1000d multi .50 .50

Souvenir Sheet

Imperf

1904 A612 2000d multi 3.25 3.25

Danube Conference, 40th anniv.

13th European Junior Basketball Championships, Aug. 21-28 — A613

1988, Aug. 20 ***Perf. 14***

1905 A613 600d multi .40 .40

1st Horse Race in Belgrade, 125th Anniv. — A614

1988, Aug. 27

1906 A614 140d Thoroughbred racing .40 .40
1907 A614 600d Steeplechase .80 .80
1908 A614 1000d Harness racing 1.20 1.20
Nos. 1906-1908 (3) 2.40 2.40

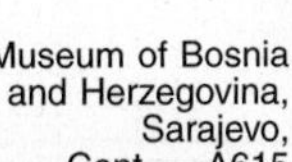

Museum of Bosnia and Herzegovina, Sarajevo, Cent. — A615

140d, Museum, Bosnian bellflower.

1988, Sept. 10 ***Perf. 13½***

1909 A615 140d multicolored .25 .25

Anti-Cancer and AIDS Campaigns — A616

140d, Arm, lobster claw. 1000d, Blood, scream.

1988, Sept. 24 ***Perf. 14***

1910 A616 140d multicolored .25 .25
1911 A616 1000d multicolored .65 .65

Nos. 1801 and 1804 Surcharged

1988, July **Litho.** ***Perf. 13½***

1912 A559 120d on 93d ultra .25 .25
1913 A559 140d on 106d brn org .25 .25

Joy of Europe Youth Conference — A617

Portraits of girls by: 1000d, P. Ranosovic. 1100d, Renoir.

1988, Oct. 1 **Litho.** ***Perf. 14***

1914 A617 1000d multi .65 .65
1915 A617 1100d multi .80 .80

See Nos. 1987-1988.

Slovenski Academy, 50th Anniv. — A618

1988, Oct. 13 **Litho.** ***Perf. 14***

1916 A618 200d multi .25 .25

Museum Exhibits and Places of Origin — A618a

200d, Wood bassinet, traditional wedding (Galicka). #1918, Embroidery, man and woman wearing folk costumes of Vojvodina.

#1919, Scimitar, flintlock, man & woman wearing folk costumes of Kotor (Bokelji). 1100d, Masks (Kurenti).

1988, Oct. 18

1917	A618a	200d multi, vert.	.65	.65
1918	A618a	1000d shown	.65	.65
1919	A618a	1000d multi, vert.	.65	.65
1920	A618a	1100d multi	.65	.65
		Nos. 1917-1920 (4)	2.60	2.60

Woman with Lyre, 4th Cent. B.C. — A618b

Grecian terra cotta figurines: #1922, Eros & Psyche, 2nd cent. BC. #1923, Seated woman, 3rd cent. BC. 1100d, Woman by Stele, 3rd cent. BC.

1988, Oct. 28

1921	A618b	200d multi	.50	.50
1922	A618b	1000d multi	.50	.50
1923	A618b	1000d multi	.50	.50
1924	A618b	1100d multi	.50	.50
		Nos. 1921-1924 (4)	2.00	2.00

Peter II (1813-1851), Prince Bishop and Poet — A618c

Portraits and: 200d, Cetinje Monastery and frontispiece of his principal work. 1000d, Njegos Mausoleum.

1988, Nov. 1

1925	A618c	200d multi	.25	.25
1926	A618c	1000d multi	.55	.55

Postal Service Types of 1986 and

Telephone Receiver and Telephone Card A619

Bird, Posthorn, Simulated Stamp A620

Propeller Plane, Two Arrows and Map — A621

Designs: 170d, 300d, Flower, envelope, mailbox and simulated stamp. 220d, PTT emblem on simulated stamp, mail coach. 800d, Postman on motorcycle. No. 1941, Postman, resident. No. 1942, Mail train. No. 1943, Envelopes, satellite dish. No. 1944, Earth, telecommunications satellite. 100,000d, Bird, open envelope, flower. 170d, 220d, 300d, 2000d, 5000d, No. 1941 vert.

1988-89 Litho. *Perf. 13¼*

1935	A559	170d dl grn	.40	.25
1936	A559	220d brn org	.40	.25
1937	A559	300d ver	.40	.25
1938	A559	800d brt ultra	.25	.25
1939	A619	2000d multi	.25	.25
1940	A620	5000d dk red & ultra	.80	.40
1941	A559	10,000d org & brt lil	.55	.55
1942	A559	20,000d lt ol grn & lt red brn	.55	.55
		Perf. 13½		
1943	A560	10,000d multi	1.25	.55
1944	A560	20,000d multi	.80	.55
1944A	A621	50,000d org & dl bl	1.00	.40
1945	A560	100,000d org & dl grn	.25	.25
		Nos. 1935-1945 (12)	6.90	4.50
		Perf. 12½		
1937a	A559	300d	.40	.25
1938a	A559	800d	.25	.25
1939a	A619	2000d	.25	.25
1940a	A620	5000d	.80	.40
1941a	A559	10,000d	.25	.25
1942a	A559	20,000d	.25	.25
		Nos. 1937a-1941a (5)	1.95	1.40

Issued: 1988 — 170d, 11/17; 220d, 12/6; 1989 — 300d, 5/11; 800d, 2000d, 7/20; 5000d, 1/20; #1941, 11/28; #1942, 12/8; #1943, 3/20; #1944, 7/19; 50,000d, 11/8; 100,000d, 12/4.

See Nos. 2008-2009, 2017, 2052. For surcharges see Nos. 1972, 1974, 2048.

Yugoslavia, 70th Anniv. — A622

1988, Dec. 1 Litho. *Perf. 14*

1946	A622	200d Krsmanovic Hall, Belgrade	.25	.25

Nos. 1805-1806 Surcharged

1988 Litho. *Perf. 13½*

1947	A559	170d on 120d	.80	.25
1948	A559	220d on 140d	.80	.25

Issued: #1947, Dec. 21; #1948, Dec. 15.

Miniature Sheet

Victory of Yugoslavian Athletes at the 1988 Summer Olympics, Seoul — A623

Medals and events: a, Women's air pistol. b, Team handball. c, Table tennis. d, Wrestling. e, Double sculls. f, Basketball. g, Water polo. h, Boxing.

1988, Dec. 31 Litho. *Perf. 14*

1949	A623	Sheet of 8 + label	3.00	3.00
a.-h.		500d any single	.30	.25

Ivan Gundulic (1589-1638), Poet — A624

1989, Jan. 7 *Perf. 13½*

1950	A624	220d multi	.40	.25

World Wildlife Fund — A625

Ducks.

1989, Feb. 23 Litho. *Perf. 14*

1951		Strip of 4 + label	14.00	8.00
a.		A625 300d Anas platyrhynchos	1.25	.50
b.		A625 2100d Anas crecca	3.50	1.75
c.		A625 2200d Anas acuta	3.50	1.75
d.		A625 2200d Anas clypeata	3.50	1.75

Printed in sheets of 20+5 labels. Label pictures WWF emblem.

A626

1989, Mar. 10 *Perf. 13½*

1952	A626	300d Portrait	.25	.25

Publication of The Glory of the Duchy of Kranjska, by Johann Valvasor (1641-1693), 300th anniv.

Flowering Plants — A627

300d, Bulbocodium vernum. 2100d, Nymphaea alba. 2200d, Fritillaria degeniana, vert. 3000d, Orchis simia, vert.

1989, Mar. 20 *Perf. 14*

1953	A627	300d multi	1.00	1.00
1954	A627	2100d multi	1.00	1.00
1955	A627	2200d multi	1.00	1.00
1956	A627	3000d multi	1.00	1.00
		Nos. 1953-1956 (4)	4.00	4.00

6th World Air-Gun Championships, Sarajevo, Apr. 27-30 — A628

1989, Apr. 26

1957	A628	3000d multi	.50	.50

Europa 1989 — A629

1989, Apr. 29

1958	A629	3000d shown	.80	.80
1959	A629	6000d Marbles	.80	.80

15th European Trophy for Natl. Athletic Club Champions, Belgrade, June 3-4 — A630

1989, June 1 Litho. *Perf. 13½*

1960	A630	4000d Pole vault	.80	.80

Printed in sheets of 8+label picturing flags of participating nations.

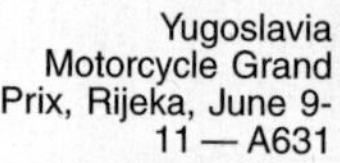

Yugoslavia Motorcycle Grand Prix, Rijeka, June 9-11 — A631

Various race scenes.

1989, June 9 *Perf. 14*

1961	A631	500d multi	.25	.25
1962	A631	4000d multi	.40	.40

Souvenir Sheet

Perf. 14x13½

1963	A631	6000d multi	1.50	1.50

No. 1963 contains one 54x35 stamp.

No. 1246 Surcharged

1989, Apr. 6 Litho. *Perf. 13*

1964	A323	100d on 1d dull grn	.40	.25
a.		Perf. 13x12½	.40	.40

Tito — A632

1989, May 25 *Perf. 13½x14*

1965	A632	300d multi	.25	.25

Early Adriatic Ships — A633

a, Ancient Greek galley. b, Roman galley. c, Crusade galleon, 13th cent. d, Nava of Dubrovnik, 16th cent. e, French ship, 17th cent. f, Vessels, 18th cent. 3000d, View of Dubrovnik seaport, called Ragusa in Italian, from a 17th cent. engraving.

1989, June 10 *Perf. 13½*

1966		Block of 6	2.00	1.50
a.-f.		A633 1000d any single	.30	.25

Souvenir Sheet

1967	A633	3000d multi	.75	.35

No. 1967 contains one 75x32mm stamp. Nos. 1966-1967 printed se-tenant and sold folded in booklet cover.

26th European Basketball Championships A634

Map of Europe, basketball and flags of: No. 1968, France, Yugoslavia, Greece, Bulgaria. No. 1969, Netherlands, Italy, Russia, Spain.

1989, June 20 Litho. *Perf. 13½x14*

1968	A634	2000d multi	.25	.25
1969	A634	2000d multi	.25	.25

Nos. 1968-1969 exist with setenant label.

Defeat of the Serbians at the Battle of Kosovo, 1389 — A635

1989, June 28

1970	A635	500d multi	.25	.25

Danilovgrad Library, Cent. — A636

1989, July 15 Litho. *Perf. 13½*

1971	A636	500d multi	.25	.25

Nos. 1797, 1719, 1935, 1936 Surcharged

1989

1972	A559	400d on 30d lt brn vio	.80	.25
1973	A323	700d on 70d brt ultra	.80	.25
1974	A559	700d on 170d dull green	.80	.25
1975	A559	700d on 220d brn org	.80	.25
		Nos. 1972-1975 (4)	3.20	1.00

Issued: #1975, 7/19; #1974, 8/10; #1972, 8/23; #1973, 12/13.

Kulin Ban Charter, 800th Anniv. — A638

1989, Aug. 29 Litho. *Perf. 14*

1976	A638	500d multi	.25	.25

World Rowing Championships A639

1989, Sept. 2 *Perf. 13½*

1977	A639	10,000d multi	.50	.50

Interparliamentary Union, Cent. — A640

Architecture: No. 1978, Parliament, London (emblem at R). No. 1979, Notre Dame Cathedral (emblem at L).

1989, Sept. 4 *Perf. 13½x14*

1978 A640 10,000d multi .40 .40
1979 A640 10,000d multi .40 .40

A641

View of Belgrade and Maps BEOGRAD '89 — A642

Architecture & antiquities of non-aligned summit host cities: #1980, Belgrade '61, Cairo '64. #1981, Lusaka '70, Algiers '73. #1982, Colombo '76, Havana '79. #1983, New Delhi '83, Harare '76.

1989, Sept. 4

1980 A641 10,000d multi .25 .25
1981 A641 10,000d multi .25 .25
1982 A641 10,000d multi .25 .25
1983 A641 10,000d multi .25 .25
Nos. 1980-1983 (4) 1.00 1.00

Souvenir Sheet

Perf. 14

1984 A642 20,000d multi 1.25 1.25

European Nature Protection — A643

8000d, Paeonia officinalis, Brezovica-Jazinac Lake. 10,000d, Paeonia corallina, Mirusa Canyon.

1989, Sept. 11 *Perf. 14*

1985 A643 8000d multi .40 .40
1986 A643 10,000d multi .40 .40

Joy of Europe Type of 1988

Portraits of children: No. 1987, Child with Lamb, by Jovan Popovic. No. 1988, Girl Feeding Dog, by Albert Cuyp (1620-1691).

1989, Oct. 2 **Litho.** *Perf. 14*

1987 A617 10,000d multi .50 .50
1988 A617 10,000d multi .50 .50

Karpos Uprising, 300th Anniv. — A644

1989, Oct. 20 **Litho.** *Perf. 13½*

1989 A644 1200d ver & dark brn .25 .25

No. 1833c, Cancellation, Quill Pen, Wax Seals and Seal Device on Parchment — A645

1989, Oct. 31 *Perf. 14*

1990 A645 1200d multicolored .25 .25

Stamp Day.

Museum Exhibits — A646

1989, Nov. 2

1991 A646 1200d Pack-saddle maker .25 .25
1992 A646 14,000d Cooper .55 .55
1993 A646 15,000d Winegrower .80 .80
1994 A646 30,000d Weaver 1.40 1.40
Nos. 1991-1994 (4) 3.00 3.00

Religious Paintings A647

2100d, Apostle Matthew, vert. 21,000d, St. Barbara, vert. 30,000d, The Fourth Day of Creation. 50,000d, The Fifth Day of Creation.

1989, Nov. 28 **Litho.** *Perf. 14*

1997 A647 2100d multicolored .25 .25
1998 A647 21,000d multicolored .40 .40
1999 A647 30,000d multicolored .80 .80
2000 A647 50,000d multicolored 1.25 1.25
Nos. 1997-2000 (4) 2.70 2.70

A648

League of Communists 14th Congress — A649

1990, Jan. 20 **Litho.** *Perf. 13½x14*

2001 A648 10,000d Star .30 .25
2002 A648 50,000d Computer .55 .55

Souvenir Sheet

Imperf

2003 A649 100,000d Star, diff. 1.25 1.25

Postal Service Types of 1986-88

10p, Man posting letters in mailbox. 20p, Postal employee sorting mail. 30p, Postman, resident. 40p, Woman at telephone station. 1d, Mail train. 2d, Ship & envelope. 3d, Flower, mailbox, envelope & simulated stamp. 5d, Airplane, letters, map of Europe. 10d, Bird, open envelope, flower. 20d, Woman at telephone station.

Designs for other values as before. 10p, 20p, 30p, 40p, 3d, 5d vert.

1990 *Perf. 12½*

2004 A559 10p br yel grn & vio .50 .25
2005 A559 20p red vio & org .50 .25
2006 A559 30p org & yel grn .25 .25
2007 A559 40p blue grn & red vio .25 .25
2008 A620 50p pur & blue grn .30 .25
2009 A619 60p red org & brt vio .30 .25
2013 A559 1d rose lil & green-ish bl .50 .25
2014 A559 2d red lil & blue .90 .25
2015 A559 3d org & dl blue .90 .30
2017 A619 5d ultra & grnsh blue .90 .45
2019 A559 10d red org & vio bl 1.75 1.40
Nos. 2004-2019 (11) 7.05 4.15

Issued: 10p, 20p, 2/9; 30p, 40p, 1/24; 50p, 1/29; 60p, 2/6; 2d, 2/14; 3d, 2/22; 5d, 1/31; 1d, 5/24; 10d, 6/12.

For surcharges see Nos. 2049-2053, 2168//2176.

1990-92 *Perf. 13¼*

2004a A559 10p br yel grn & vio .50 .25
2005a A559 20p red vio & org 1.40 .70
2006a A559 30p org & yel grn .25 .25
2007a A559 40p blue grn & red vio .25 .25
2008a A620 50p pur & blue grn .30 .25
2009a A619 60p red org & brt vio .30 .30
2013a A559 1d rose lil & green-ish bl 1.75 1.25
2014a A559 2d red lil & blue .65 .45
2015a A559 3d org & dl blue> 2.50 2.25
2017a A619 5d ultra & grnsh blue 1.25 1.00
2019a A559 10d red org & vio bl 7.50 5.50
2021 A559 20d car rose & org .45 .25
Nos. 2004a-2021 (12) 17.10 12.70

Issued: 30p, 40p, 1/24; 50p, 1/29; 5d, 1/31; 60p, 2/6; 10p, 20p, 2/9; 2d, 2/14; 3d, 2/22; 10d, 6/12; 1d, 7/2; 20d, 1/27/92.

For surcharges see Nos. 2049a-2053a, 2168//2176.

Anti-smoking Campaign — A650

1990, Jan. 31 **Litho.** *Perf. 13½x13*

2034 A650 10d gry & yel brn .90 .90

Protected Fish — A651

1990, Feb. 15 *Perf. 13½*

2035 Strip of 4 + label 8.00 8.00
a. A651 1d Esox lucius 1.25 1.25
b. A651 5d Silurus glanis 1.25 1.25
c. A651 10d Lota lota 1.25 1.25
d. A651 15d Perca fluviatilis 1.25 1.25

Zabljak Fortress, Illuminated Manuscript, Coat of Arms — A652

1990, Mar. 9 *Perf. 14x13½*

2036 A652 50p multicolored 1.20 1.20

Enthronement of Djuradj Crnojevic, 500th anniv.

ITU, 125th Anniv. — A653

1990, Mar. 23

2037 A653 6.50d Telegrapher, computer .90 .90

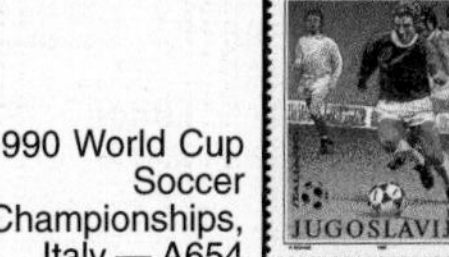

1990 World Cup Soccer Championships, Italy — A654

1990, Apr. 16

2038 A654 6.50d shown 1.40 1.40
2039 A654 10d multi, diff. 1.40 1.40

Europa 1990 — A655

Post offices: 6.50d, PTT Central, Skopje. 10d, Telecommunications Central, Belgrade.

1990, Apr. 23 *Perf. 13½x14*

2040 A655 6.50d multicolored 1.60 1.60
2041 A655 10d multicolored 1.60 1.60

A656

1990, Apr. 30 **Litho.** *Perf. 13½*

2042 A656 6.50d multicolored 1.00 1.00

Labor Day, cent.

A657

Eurovision Song Contest: 10d, Conductor, musical score.

1990, May 5 *Perf. 14x13½*

2043 A657 6.50d multicolored 1.10 1.10
2044 A657 10d multicolored 1.20 1.20

No. 2043 exists with setenant label.

Tennis — A658

1990, May 15 **Litho.** *Perf. 14*

2045 A658 6.50d multicolored 1.40 1.40
2046 A658 10d multicolored 1.40 1.40

Tito — A659

1990, May 25 *Perf. 13½x14*

2047 A659 50p multicolored .30 .30

Nos. 1938, 2004-2009a Surcharged

No. 2048

No. 2049

1990-91 **Litho.** *Perf. 12½*

2048 A559 50p on 800d (#1938a) .45 .25
a. Perf 13¼ (#1938) .45 .25
2049 A559 50p on 20p (#2005) .45 .25
a. Perf 13¼ (#2005a) ('91) 3.50 2.75
2050 A559 1d on 30p (#2006) .45 .25
a. Perf 13¼ (#2006a) 3.50 3.25
2051 A559 2d on 40p (#2007), I .90 .45
a. Type II, perf. 13¼ (#2007a) 1.40 .90
b. Type I, perf. 13¼ (#2007a) 2.25 2.25
2052 A619 5d on 60p (#2009) .45 .25
a. Perf 13¼ (#2009a) 4.50 1.75
2053 A559 10d on 10p (#2004) .45 .25
a. Perf 13¼ (#2004a) 1.00 .55
Nos. 2048-2053 (6) 3.15 1.70

Type II surcharge has 3 instead of 2 bars obliterating old value, new denomination is at bottom of stamp.

Issued: #2048, 2048a, 5/24; #2050, 8/7; #2049, 2049a, 9/18; #2051-2051b, 10/2; #2050a, 1/4/91; #2053, 2053a, 12/12/91; #2052, 2052a, 12/17/91.

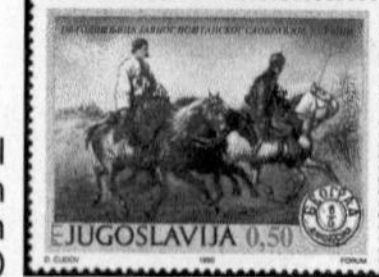

Public Postal Service in Serbia, 150th Anniv. — A660

1990, May 25
2056 A660 50p multicolored 2.25 1.50

Pigeons — A661

1990, June 8 ***Perf. 13½***
2057 A661 50p multicolored .55 .55
2058 A661 5d multicolored 1.10 1.10
2059 A661 6.50d multi, vert. 1.10 1.10
2060 A661 10d multi, vert. 2.75 2.75
Nos. 2057-2060 (4) 5.50 5.50

Mercury Mine at Idrija, 500th Anniv. — A662

Designs: 6.50d, Miners at work, ca. 1490.

1990, June 22 ***Perf. 13½x14***
2061 A662 50p multicolored .25 .25
2062 A662 6.50d multicolored 1.00 1.00

Newspaper "Vjesnik," 50th Anniv. — A663

1990, June 23 ***Perf. 13½***
2063 A663 60p multicolored .70 .70

Serbian Migration, 300th Anniv. — A664

1990, Sept. 20 ***Perf. 14***
2064 A664 1d shown .25 .25
2065 A664 6.50d Caravan .90 .90

European Track & Field Championships, Split — A665

1990, Aug. 27 ***Perf. 13½***
2067 A665 1d Start of race .60 .60
2068 A665 6.50d Runners' feet .90 .90

Souvenir Sheet

2069 A665 10d Runners 2.25 2.25

No. 2069 contains one 54x35mm stamp. A 50p exists but no information on its postal category is available.

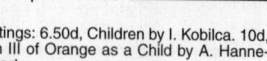

Joy of Europe — A666

Paintings: 6.50d, Children by I. Kobilca. 10d, William III of Orange as a Child by A. Hanneman, vert.

1990, Oct. 2 Litho. ***Perf. 14***
2070 A666 6.50d multicolored 1.10 1.10
2071 A666 10d multicolored 1.50 1.50

Souvenir Sheets

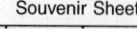

29th Chess Olympics, Novi Sad — A667

1990, Oct. 2 ***Perf. 11½***

Granite Paper

2072 A667 Sheet of 4 8.00 8.00
a. 1d Pawns, knight, bishop, king & queen 1.10 1.10
b. 5d Rook, bishop, knight 1.10 1.10
c. 6.50d King, bishop, knght, pawn 1.10 1.10
d. 10d Chess pieces 1.10 1.10

Imperf

2073 A667 Sheet of 4 8.00 8.00
a. 1d like No. 2072a 1.10 1.10
b. 5d like No. 2072b 1.10 1.10
c. 6.50d like No. 2072c 1.10 1.10
d. 10d like No. 2072d 1.10 1.10

No. 2073 has blue margin inscriptions. Emblems on Nos. 2072a-2072d are in silver, those on Nos. 2073a-2073d are in gold.

Stamp Day — A668

1990, Oct. 2 ***Perf. 14***
2074 A668 2d multicolored .60 .55

150th anniv. of the Penny Black.

European Nature Protection — A669

1990, Nov. 16 Litho. ***Perf. 14***
2075 A669 6.50d Vransko Lake 1.10 1.10
2076 A669 10d Gyps fulvus 1.50 1.50

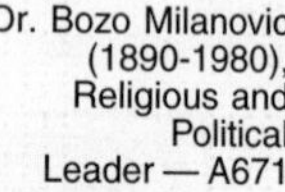

Frescoes A670

Designs: 2d, King Milutin, Monastery of Our Lady, Ljeviska. 5d, Saint Sava, Mileseva Monastery. 6.50d, Saint Elias, Moraca Monastery. 10d, Jesus Christ, Sopocani Monastery.

1990, Nov. 28
2077 A670 2d multicolored .45 .45
2078 A670 5d multicolored .95 .95
2079 A670 6.50d multicolored .95 .95
2080 A670 10d multicolored 1.40 1.40
Nos. 2077-2080 (4) 3.75 3.75

Dr. Bozo Milanovic (1890-1980), Religious and Political Leader — A671

1990, Dec. 20 Litho. ***Perf. 13½***
2081 A671 2d multicolored .30 .30

Religious Carvings A672

Designs: 2d, Christ in the temple. 5d, Nativity scene. 6.50d, Flight from Egypt, horiz. 10d, Entry into Jerusalem, horiz.

1990, Dec. 24 ***Perf. 13½x14, 14x13½***
2082 A672 2d gld, brn, & blk .45 .45
2083 A672 5d gld, brn, & blk .70 .70
2084 A672 6.50d gld, brn, & blk .90 .90
2085 A672 10d gld, brn, & blk 1.10 1.10
Nos. 2082-2085 (4) 3.15 3.15

Protected Birds — A673

1991, Jan. 31 Litho. ***Perf. 14x13½***
2086 Strip of 4 + label 9.00 9.00
a. A673 2d Vanellus vanellus 1.10 1.10
b. A673 5d Lanius senator 1.10 1.10
c. A673 6.50d Grus grus 1.10 1.10
d. A673 10d Mergus merganser 1.10 1.10

Flora — A674

2d, Crocus kosaninii. 6d, Crocus scardicus. 7.50d, Crocus rujanesis. 15d, Crocus adamii.

1991, Feb. 20
2087 A674 2d multicolored .45 .45
2088 A674 6d multicolored .55 .55
2089 A674 7.50d multicolored .60 .60
2090 A674 15d multicolored 2.00 2.00
Nos. 2087-2090 (4) 3.60 3.60

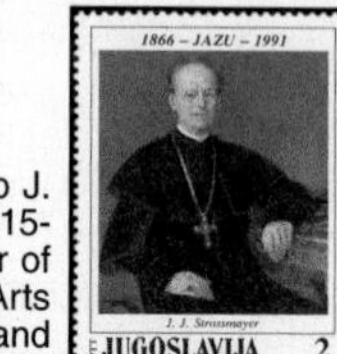

Bishop Josip J. Strossmayer (1815-1905), Founder of Academy of Arts and Sciences — A675

1991, Mar. 4 Litho. ***Perf. 13½x14***
2091 A675 2d multicolored 1.10 .60

Academy of Arts and Sciences, 125th Anniv.

Wolfgang Amadeus Mozart, Composer — A676

1991, Mar. 20 ***Perf. 14***
2092 A676 7.50d multicolored .90 .60

Otto Lilienthal's First Glider Flight, Cent. — A677

Designs: 7.50d, Edvard Rusjan (1886-1911), pilot, aircraft designer. 15d, Otto Lilienthal (1848-1896), aviation pioneer.

1991, Apr. 1
2093 A677 7.50d multicolored 1.10 1.10
2094 A677 15d multicolored 1.40 1.40

Printed in sheets of 8 plus label.

Lhotse I, Himalayas, South Face First Climbed by Tomo Cesen, 1990 — A678

1991, Apr. 24 ***Perf. 14x13½***
2095 A678 7.50d multicolored .90 .55

Europa — A679

Designs: 7.50d, Telecommunications satellite. 15d, Satellite, antenna, telephone.

1991, May 6 ***Perf. 14***
2096 A679 7.50d multicolored .90 .90
2097 A679 15d multicolored 1.75 1.75

Franciscan Monastery, Trsat, 700th Anniv. — A680

1991, May 10 Litho. ***Perf. 13½x14***
2098 A680 3.50d multicolored .80 .25

Governments of Danube River Region Conf., Belgrade — A681

15d, Danube River shipping. 20d, Course of Danube, landmarks, regional animals.

1991, May 15 ***Perf. 13½***
2099 A681 7.50d multicolored 1.00 1.00
2100 A681 15d multicolored 1.50 1.50

Souvenir Sheet

2101 A681 20d multicolored 9.00 9.00

No. 2101 contains one 55x35mm stamp.

Opening of Karavanke Tunnel — A682

Designs: 4.50d, Passage Over Karavanke by J. Valvasor, 17th century. 11d, Entrance to new Karavanke Tunnel.

1991, June 1 ***Perf. 14x13½***
2102 A682 4.50d multicolored .60 .60
2103 A682 11d multicolored .90 .90

Basketball, Cent. — A683

1991, June 15 ***Perf. 13½x14***
2104 A683 11d shown 1.10 1.10
2105 A683 15d Nets, "100" 1.10 1.10

Yugoslavian Insurrection, 50th Anniv. — A684

Designs: 4.50d, Partisan Memorial Medal, 1941. 11d, Medal for Courage.

1991, July 4 Litho. *Perf. 14*

2106	A684	4.50d multicolored	.35	.35
2107	A684	11d multicolored	.70	.70

Yugoslav Natl. Army, 50th Anniv.

Tin Ujevic (1891-1955), Writer — A685

1991, July 5 *Perf. 13½*

2108	A685	4.50d multicolored	.60	.45

Jacobus Gallus (1550-1591), Composer — A686

1991, July 18

2109	A686	11d multicolored	.60	.60

Lighthouses of Adriatic and Danube — A687

Designs: a, Savudrija, 1818. b, Sveti Ivan na pucini, 1853. c, Porer, 1833. d, Stoncica, 1865. e, Olipa, c. 1842. f, Glavat, 1884. g, Veli rat, 1849. h, Vir, 1881. i, Tajerske sestrice, 1876. j, Razanj, 1875. k, Derdap-Danube. l, Tamis-Danube.

1991, July 25 Litho. *Perf. 13½*

2110	A687	10d Bklt. pane of 12, #a.-l.	12.00	12.00

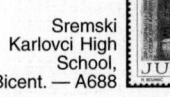

Sremski Karlovci High School, Bicent. — A688

1991, Sept. 12 Litho. *Perf. 14*

2111	A688	4.50d multicolored	.45	.30

European Nature Protection — A689

11d, Palingenia longicauda. 15d, Phalacrocorax pygmaeus.

1991, Sept. 24 *Perf. 13½x14*

2112	A689	11d multicolored	.90	.90
2113	A689	15d multicolored	.90	.90

A690

1991, Sept. 28 *Perf. 14*

2114	A690	4.50d multicolored	.45	.30

Town of Subotica, 600th anniv.

A691

Paintings: 15d, Little Dubravka, by Jovan Bijelic (1886-1964). 30d, Little Girl with a Cat by Mary Cassatt (1845-1926).

1991, Oct. 2

2115	A691	15d multicolored	.70	.70
2116	A691	30d multicolored	1.10	1.10

Joy of Europe.

33rd Intl. Apicultural Congress, APIMONDIA '91 — A692

1991, Sept. 28 Litho. *Perf. 13½x14*

2117	A692	11d multicolored	1.10	.90

Stamp Day, Monument to Prince Michael Obrenovich, Serbia #1 A693

1991, Oct. 31 *Perf. 14*

2118	A693	4.50d multicolored	.60	.25

First Serbia Postage Stamps, 125th Anniv.

Museum Exhibits — A694

Flags and medals: 20d, Vucjido battle flag, medal for courage. 30d, Grahovac battle flag and medal. 40d, Montenegrin state flag, medal for bravery. 50d, Montenegrin court flag, medal of Petrovich Nyegosh Dynasty.

1991, Nov. 28 *Perf. 13½x14*

2119	A694	20d multicolored	.25	.25
2120	A694	30d multicolored	.45	.45
2121	A694	40d multicolored	.60	.60
2122	A694	50d multicolored	.90	.90
		Nos. 2119-2122 (4)	2.20	2.20

Illustrations from Ancient Manuscripts A695

Designs: 20d, Angel carrying Sun around Earth, 17th cent. 30d, Celnica Gospel, menology for April, 14th cent. 40d, Angel from the Annunciation, 13th cent. 50d, Mary Magdalene, 12th cent.

1991, Dec. 12

2123	A695	20d multicolored	.25	.25
2124	A695	30d multicolored	.45	.45
2125	A695	40d multicolored	.60	.60
2126	A695	50d multicolored	.90	.90
		Nos. 2123-2126 (4)	2.20	2.20

Gotse Deltchev (1872-1903), Macedonian Revolutionary — A696

1992, Jan. 29 Litho. *Perf. 13½*

2127	A696	5d multicolored	2.25	2.25

Red Star, European and World Soccer Champions — A697

1992, Jan. 29 Litho. *Perf. 14x13½*

2128	A697	17d multicolored	2.00	2.00

A698

1992, Feb. 8 *Perf. 14x13½*

2129	A698	80d Ski jumping	1.75	1.75
2130	A698	100d Freestyle skiing	1.75	1.75

1992 Winter Olympics, Albertville.

A699

Protected Animals: a, 50d, Lepus europaeus. b, 60d, Pteromys volans. c, 80d, Dryomys nitedula. d, 100d, Cricetus cricetus.

1992, Mar. 10 Litho. *Perf. 14*

2131	A699	Strip of 4, #a.-d. + label	8.00	8.00

Madonna and Child, 14th century, Pec — A700

1992, Mar. 14 *Perf. 13½x14*

2132	A700	80d multicolored	1.00	1.00

Promotion of Breastfeeding.

Ski Association of Montenegro A701

1992, Mar. 25 *Perf. 14x13½*

2133	A701	8d multicolored	5.00	5.00

Skiing in Montenegro, cent.

1860 Fountain, Belgrade — A702

A702a

A702b

A702c

A702d

A702e

A702f

A702g

A702h

A702i

A702j

5d, Griffins, 14th cent. #2136, #2139, Fisherman Fountain, Belgrade. #2138, like #2137. 300d, Kalemegdan Fountain, Belgrade. 500d, Fountain, Sremski Karlovci. #2142, Symbols of Miroslav-Evangelium, 12th cent. 3000d, Fountain, Studenica. 5000d, Fountain, Oplenzu. 10,000d, 500,000d, Health spa, Vrnjacka Banja. 50,000d, Envelopes over map of Europe. #2147, Airplane. #2148, Health spa, Bukovacka Banja.

Inscribed "1992" or "1993"

1992-93 Litho. *Perf. 13¼*

2135	A702a	5d brn & olive	1.00	.25
2136	A702	50d dk bl & lt bl	.45	.25
2137	A702	50d violet	.45	.35
2138	A702	100d lil rose & pink	.45	.25
2139	A702	100d dk grn & lt grn	.25	.25
2140	A702b	300d brn & red brn	.45	.25
2141	A702c	500d dk ol & pale org	.90	.25
a.		Perf. 12½	1.75	1.75
2142	A702d	(A) red, 18x22mm	1.75	.45
a.		Perf. 12½	4.00	.45
b.		Inscribed "1996," Perf. 13¼	2.25	2.25
c.		Inscribed "1996," perf. 12½	.90	.25
d.		Inscribed "1997," perf. 12½	1.50	.25
e.		Inscribed "2002," perf. 12½	5.00	1.50
2143	A702e	3000d red brn	.45	.25
a.		Perf. 12½	2.75	2.25
2144	A702f	5000d vio & yel brn	.45	.25
a.		Perf 12½	3.50	2.75
2145	A702g	10,000d vio bl & grn bl	1.00	.25
2146	A702h	50,000d gray & gray bl	.45	.25
a.		Perf. 12½	1.10	.90
2147	A702i	100,000d red & bl	.90	.45
a.		Perf. 12½	1.10	.90
2148	A702j	100,000d brn red & brn	.90	.25
2149	A702g	500,000d bl & vio	.45	.25
		Nos. 2135-2149 (15)	10.30	4.25

Issued: #2137, 4/1/92; #2139, 5/6/92; 5d, 11/24/92; #2136, 12/15/92; #2138, 12/22/92; 300d, 12/3/92; 500d, 1/14/93; #2142, 4/5/93; #2142a, 1993; #2143, 4/23/93; 5000d, 3/18/93; 10,000d, 11/9/93; 50,000d, 6/10/93; 100,000d, 6/28/93; 100,000d, 12/6/93; 500,000d, 8/10/93.

No. 2142 was valued at 3000d on day of issue.

See No. 2386. For surcharges see Nos. 2220A-2220I, 2253-2254.

Sinking of the Titanic, 80th Anniv. — A703

1992, Apr. 14 *Perf. 14*

2152	A703	150d multicolored	.90	.90

Expo '92, Seville — A704

1992, Apr. 20

2153	A704	150d multicolored	.90	.90

Discovery of America, 500th Anniv. — A705

300d, Columbus, ship. 500d, Columbus' fleet.

1200d, Ships in port.

1992, May 5 Litho. *Perf. 13½x14*

2154	A705	300d multicolored	4.50	4.50
2155	A705	500d multicolored	4.50	4.50

Souvenir Sheet

Perf. 14x13½

2156	A705	1200d multicolored	13.50	13.50

Europa. No. 2156 contains one 54x34mm stamp.

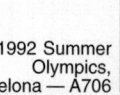

1992 Summer Olympics, Barcelona — A706

1992, May 20 *Perf. 14x13½*

2157 A706 500d Pistol shooting .90 .90
2158 A706 500d Water polo .90 .90
2159 A706 500d Tennis .90 .90
2160 A706 500d Handball .90 .90
Nos. 2157-2160 (4) 3.60 3.60

European Soccer Championships A707

Various soccer plays.

1992, June 1 *Perf. 13½*

2161 A707 1000d shown 1.60 1.60
2162 A707 1000d multicolored 1.60 1.60

Domestic Cats — A708

Designs: No. 2163, Red Persian. No. 2164, White Persian. No. 2165, Yellow tabby. No. 2166, British blue short-hair.

1992, June 25 Litho. *Perf. 13½x14*

Background Color

Cyrillic Letters

2163 A708 1000d blue 1.60 1.60
2164 A708 1000d purple 1.60 1.60

Latin Letters

2165 A708 1000d dark purple 1.60 1.60
2166 A708 1000d brown 1.60 1.60
Nos. 2163-2166 (4) 6.40 6.40

Steam Locomotives A709

Designs: a, JDZ 162. b, JDZ 151. c, JDZ 73. d, JDZ 83. e, JDZ 16. f, Prince Nicholas' coach.

1992, July 3 Litho. *Perf. 14*

2167 A709 1000d Booklet pane of 6, #a.-f. 15.00 15.00

Nos. 2005//2017a Surcharged

1992 *Perfs., Etc. as Before*

2168 A559 2d on 30p #2006 .90 .50
a. Perf 13¼ (#2006a) 1.75 1.00
2169 A559 5d on 20p #2005 1.75 .25
2170 A559 5d on 40p #2007 .90 .50
a. Perf 13¼ (#2007a) 1.75 1.00
2171 A620 10d on 50p #2008 1.75 .25
2172 A621 10d on 5d #2017a .90 .25
2173 A559 20d on 1d #2013 3.00 .90
a. Perf 13¼ (#2013a) 1.75 .90
2174 A621 20d on 5d type of #2017, yel, bl & grn bl 1.00 .50
2175 A559 50d on 2d #2014 10.00 5.00
a. Perf 13¼ (#2014a) 1.75 .25
2176 A559 100d on 3d #2015 6.00 2.00
a. Perf 13¼ (#2015a) 3.50 .25
Nos. 2168-2176 (9) 26.20 10.15

Issued: #2168, 2170, 10/26; #2169, 9/12; #2171, 9/17; #2172, 10/29; #2173, 2175-2176, 8/6; #2174, 11/9.

World Chess Champions — A710

1992, Sept. 14 Litho. *Perf. 14*

2177 A710 500d Bobby Fischer 1.75 1.75
2178 A710 500d Boris Spassky 1.75 1.75

Telephone Service in Vojvodina, Cent. — A711

1892 Telephone, buildings of Novi Sad, Subotica and Zrenjanin.

1992, Oct. 1

2179 A711 10d multicolored 1.40 1.40

Stamp Day — A712

Design: Montenegro #7, musician.

1992, Oct. 2

2180 A712 50d multicolored 1.00 .90

European Art — A713

Europa: No. 2181, Ballet Dancer, by Edgar Degas (1834-1917). No. 2182, Painting of young man, by U. Knezevic.

1992, Oct. 2

2181 A713 500d multicolored 1.40 1.40
2182 A713 500d multicolored 1.40 1.40

European Nature Protection — A714

1992, Nov. 14 *Perf. 13½*

2183 A714 500d Tetrao urogallus 4.00 4.00
2184 A714 500d Pelecanus onocrotalus 4.00 4.00

Publisher Srpska Knjizevna Zadruga, Cent. — A715

1992, Nov. 20 *Perf. 14*

2185 A715 100d multicolored 1.00 1.00

Traditional Architecture A716

Designs: No. 2186, Ancient hut, Zlatibor region. No. 2187, Round house, Morava region. No. 2188, House, on stone cliff, Metohija region. No. 2189, Large estate house, Vojvodina region.

1992, Dec. 12

2186 A716 500d multicolored .80 .80
2187 A716 500d multicolored .80 .80
2188 A716 500d multicolored .80 .80
2189 A716 500d multicolored .80 .80
Nos. 2186-2189 (4) 3.20 3.20

Icons, Mosaics A717

#2190, St. Petka, St. Petka Church, Belgrade. #2191, St. Vasilije-Ostronoski, St. Vasilije-Ostronoski Church, Montenegro. #2192, Mosaic of Simeon Nemanja with model of Blessed Virgin Church, Studenica. #2193, Mosaic of St. Lazar with model of Ravanica Monastery.

1992, Dec. 15

2190 A717 500d multi 1.00 1.00
2191 A717 500d multi 1.00 1.00
2192 A717 500d multi, vert. 1.00 1.00
2193 A717 500d multi, vert. 1.00 1.00
Nos. 2190-2193 (4) 4.00 4.00

Aviation in Yugoslavia, 80th Anniv. — A718

1992, Dec. 24

2194 A718 500d Bleriot XI 1.10 1.10

Diocletian's Reformation of the Roman Empire, 1700th Anniv. — A719

Design: Detail of Roman fresco.

1993, Jan. 28 Litho. *Perf. 13½*

2195 A719 1500d multicolored 1.10 1.10

State Museum, Cetinje, Cent. — A720

1993, Feb. 12 *Perf. 14*

2196 A720 2500d multicolored 1.10 1.10

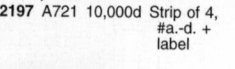

Marine Life — A721

Designs: a, Acipenser sturio. b, Scorpaena scrofa. c, Xiphias gladius. d, Tursiops truncatus.

1993, Mar. 20 *Perf. 13½*

2197 A721 10,000d Strip of 4, #a.-d. + label 8.00 8.00

Serbian Money — A722

#2198, Ancient document, 10 para coins. #2199, 5 dinar banknotes, 5 dinar coins.

1993, Mar. 30

2198 A722 10,000d multicolored 1.40 1.40
2199 A722 10,000d multicolored 1.40 1.40

Restablishment of Serbian monetary system, 125th anniv. (No. 2198). Restoring dinars as Serbian currency, 120th anniv. (No. 2199).

Famous People — A723

Designs: No. 2200, Milos Crnjanski (1893-1977), writer, journalist. No. 2201, Nicola Tesla (1856-1943), physicist. No. 2202, Mihailo Petrovic (1868-1943), mathematician. No. 2203, Aleksa Santic (1868-1924), poet.

1993, Apr. 1

2200 A723 40,000d multicolored 1.40 1.40
2201 A723 40,000d multicolored 1.40 1.40
2202 A723 40,000d multicolored 1.40 1.40
2203 A723 40,000d multicolored 1.40 1.40
Nos. 2200-2203 (4) 5.60 5.60

Joy of Europe — A724

Children's paintings: No. 2204, Girl holding flowers, children, dove, by M. Markovski. No. 2205, Angels, birds, by J. Rugovac.

1993, Apr. 5

2204 A724 50,000d multicolored 1.40 1.40
2205 A724 50,000d multicolored 1.75 1.75

Contemporary Art — A725

Europa: No. 2206, Nude with a Mirror, by M. Milunovic. No. 2207, Composition, by M.P. Barili.

1993, May 5

2206 A725 95,000d multicolored 2.75 2.75
2207 A725 95,000d multicolored 2.75 2.75

A726

A727

A728

A729

A730

Ancient Fortresses: No. 2208, Sutorina, Montenegro. No. 2209, Kalemegdan, Belgrade. No. 2210, Medun, Montenegro. No. 2211, Petrovaradin, near Novi Sad. No. 2212, Bar, Montenegro. No. 2213, Golubac.

1993, July 9 **Booklet Stamps**

2208 A726 900,000d multi 1.00 1.00
2209 A727 900,000d multi 1.00 1.00
2210 A728 900,000d multi 1.00 1.00
2211 A729 900,000d multi 1.00 1.00
2212 A730 900,000d multi 1.00 1.00
2213 A730 900,000d multi 1.00 1.00
a. Booklet pane, #2208-2213 6.00
Complete booklet, #2213a 6.00

Flowers — A731

Colors of various flowers in vases: No. 2214, Yellow, white. No. 2215, Orange, red. No. 2216, Purple, pink, white. No. 2217, Mixed.

1993, July 10 *Perf. 14*

2214 A731 1,000,000d multi 1.40 1.40
2215 A731 1,000,000d multi 1.40 1.40
2216 A731 1,000,000d multi 1.40 1.40
2217 A731 1,000,000d multi 1.40 1.40
Nos. 2214-2217 (4) 5.60 5.60

Electrification of Serbia, Cent. — A732

1993, July 28 *Perf. 13½*

2218 A732 2,500,000d multi .70 .65

European Nature Protection — A733

Designs: No. 2219, Garrulus glandarius. No. 2220, Oriolus oriolus.

1993, Sept. 30

2219 A733 300,000,000d multi *6.25 6.25*
2220 A733 300,000,000d multi *6.25 6.25*

Nos. 2147a, 2135, 2144, 2136 and 2140 Srchd.

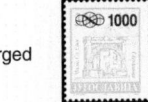

No. 2143 Surcharged

1993 *Perf 13¼*

2220A A702i 10d on 100,000d .90 .90
b. Perf 12½ 1.75 .25
2220B A702a 50d on 5d 1.00 .25
2220C A702f 100d on 5000d 1.00 .25
2220D A702 500d on 50d 1.00 .25
2220E A702e 1000d on 3000d 1.00 .60
b. Perf 12½ 1.00 .25
2220F A702b 10,000d on 300d 1.00 .25
2220G A702a 50,000d on 50d on 5d 2.75 .75
Nos. 2220A-2220G (7) 8.65 3.25

Issued: 50,000d, 11/9/93; others, 10/18/93.
Size and location of surcharge varies.
No 2220G was created by applying three additional "0"s to the "50" surcharge on No. 2220B.

A734

Cooperation on the Danube River — A735

Designs: No. 2221, Ships on river. No. 2222, Ship going down river. 20,000d, Map showing location of Danube River.

1993, Oct. 20 *Perf. 14*

2221 A734 15,000d multicolored 1.40 1.40
2222 A734 15,000d multicolored 1.40 1.40

Souvenir Sheet

2223 A735 20,000d multicolored 2.75 2.75

Post Office in Jagodina, 150th Anniv. — A736

1993, Oct. 30 *Perf. 13½*

2224 A736 12,000d multicolored 1.50 1.00

Stamp Day.

Joy of Europe — A737

Paintings: No. 2225, Boy with Cat, by Sava Sumanovic (1896-1942). No. 2226, Circus Rider, by Georges Rouault (1871-1958).

1993, Nov. 26

2225 A737 2,000,000d multi 1.40 1.40
2226 A737 2,000,000d multi 1.40 1.40

Icons in Monasteries — A738

Designs: No. 2227, The Annunciation, Mileseva. No. 2228, Nativity, Studenica. No. 2229, Madonna and Child, Bogorodica Ljeviska. No. 2230, Flight into Egypt, Oplenac.

1993, Dec. 15

2227 A738 400,000,000d multi 1.00 1.00
2228 A738 400,000,000d multi 1.00 1.00
2229 A738 400,000,000d multi 1.00 1.00
2230 A738 400,000,000d multi 1.00 1.00
Nos. 2227-2230 (4) 4.00 4.00

Traditional Houses — A739

#2231, A-frame huts, Savardak, horiz. #2232, Watchtower. #2233, Stone house on edge of river. #2234, Crmnicka house, Bar, horiz.

1993, Dec. 31

2231 A739 50d multicolored 1.00 1.00
2232 A739 50d multicolored 1.00 1.00
2233 A739 50d multicolored 1.00 1.00
2234 A739 50d multicolored 1.00 1.00
Nos. 2231-2234 (4) 4.00 4.00

Publication of Oktoechos, 500th Anniv. — A740

1994, Jan. 17 Litho. *Perf. 13½*

2235 A740 1000d Text .80 .80
2236 A740 1000d Liturgists .80 .80

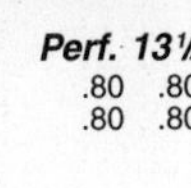

Raptors — A741

Designs: a, Neophron percnopterus. b, Falco cherrug. c, Buteo rufinus. d, Falco naumanni.

1994, Feb. 7

2237 A741 80p Strip of 4, #a.-d. + label 22.50 22.50

Intl. Mimosa Festival, Herceg-Novi — A742

1994, Feb. 28

2238 A742 80p multicolored 1.40 1.40

Natl. Museum, Belgrade, 150th Anniv. — A743

Design: No. 2240, National Theater, Belgrade, 125th anniv., portrait of Prince Milos Obrenovic.

1994, Mar. 19

2239 A743 80p multicolored 1.40 1.40
2240 A743 80p multicolored 1.40 1.40

1994 Winter Olympics, Lillehammer — A744

a, Speed skater. b. Olympic rings, flame. c, Skier.

1994, Apr. 11

2241 A744 60p Strip of 3, #a.-c. 3.25 3.25

Europa — A745

Map of flight route and: 60p, Kodron C61, automobile. 1.80d, Kodron C61 in air over Belgrade.

1994, May 5

2242 A745 60p multicolored 1.75 1.75
2243 A745 1.80d multicolored 2.25 2.25

First night flight Paris-Belgrade-Bucharest-Istanbul, piloted by Louis Guidon, 1923.

Burning of Relics of Holy Sava, 400th Anniv. — A746

1994, May 10 *Perf. 14*

2244 A746 60p multicolored 1.75 1.75

1994 World Cup Soccer Championships, U.S. — A747

60p, Three players with arms raised in victory. 1d, Three players down on ground.

1994, June 10 *Perf. 13½*

2245 A747 60p multicolored 1.40 1.40
2246 A747 1d multicolored 1.40 1.40

A748

1994, July 8

2247 A748 60p Basset hound 1.40 1.40
2248 A748 60p Maltese 1.40 1.40
2249 A748 60p Welsh terrier 1.40 1.40
2250 A748 1d Husky 1.40 1.40
Nos. 2247-2250 (4) 5.60 5.60

A749

1994, July 20

2251 A749 60p multicolored 1.40 1.40

Assembly of Eastern Orthodox Christian nations.

Protecting the Ecology of Montenegro — A750

1994, July 28

2252 A750 50p Tcherna Gora Park 1.40 1.40

Nos. 2148, 2145 Surcharged

1994, July 15 *Perf. 13½*

2253 A702j 10p on 100,000d .50 .50
2254 A702g 50p on 10,000d .90 .65

A751

Monasteries: 1p, Moraca, 13th cent. 5p, Gracanica, 14th cent. 10p, Ostrog. No. 2258-2259, Lazarica, 14th cent. 50p, Studenica, 12th cent. 1d, Sopocani, 13th cent.

Inscribed "1994"

1994 Litho. *Perf. 13¼*

2255 A751 1p bister & purple 1.40 .25
a. Perf 12½, Inscr. "1997" 1.40 .25
2256 A751 5p yel brn & blue 1.40 .25
a. Perf 12½, Inscr. "1998" 1.40 .25
2257 A751 10p magenta & slate .55 .25
a. Perf 12½, Inscr. "1998" .55 .25
2258 A751 20p lil rose & pale vio *.90* .25
2259 A751 20p pale car & gray 35.00 .25
a. Perf 12½, Inscr. "1998" 1.75 .25
2260 A751 50p deep pur & mag .55 .25
a. Inscribed "1997" .55 .25
b. As "a," perf 12½ .55 .25
2261 A751 1d blue & org brown 1.40 .50
a. Perf 12½, Inscr. "1997" 1.40 .50
Nos. 2255-2261 (7) 41.20 2.00

UNESCO (#2260-2261).
Issued: 1p, 5p, #2258, 1d, 8/15; #2259, 9/10; 10p, 50p, 11/10.
Nos. 2262-2271 are unassigned.
For surcharges, see Serbia Nos. 195, 260-261.

A752

1994, Sept. 10

2272 A752 50p multicolored .90 .90

St. Arsenius Seminary, Sremski Karlovci, bicent.

European Nature Protection — A753

Designs: 1d, Fishing pier, Reka Bojana. 1.50d, Lake, Belgrade.

1994, Sept. 20

2273 A753 1d multicolored 2.75 2.75
2274 A753 1.50d multicolored 2.75 2.75

Painting by U. Knezevic — A754

1994, Oct. 5 ***Perf. 14***

2275 A754 1d multicolored 1.75 1.75

Joy of Europe.

Sailing Ships in Bottles A755

a, Revenge, 1585. b, Grand yacht, 1678. c, Santa Maria, 15th cent. d, Nava, 15th cent. e, Mayflower, 1615. f, Carrack, 14th cent.

1994, Oct. 27 ***Perf. 13½***

2276 A755 50p Bklt. pane of 6, #a.-f. 6.00 6.00
Complete booklet, #2276 6.00

Stamp Day — A756

1994, Oct. 31

2277 A756 50p multicolored 4.00 4.00

Drawings on Gravestones — A757

#2278, Man holding umbrella, purse. #2279, 2 men. #2280, Cemetery, stone with man on horse, inscriptions. #2281, Fence, 2 gravestones, cross, man.

1994, Nov. 25

2278 A757 50p multicolored .80 .80
2279 A757 50p multicolored .80 .80
2280 A757 50p multicolored .80 .80
2281 A757 50p multicolored .80 .80
Nos. 2278-2281 (4) 3.20 3.20

Religious Art — A758

#2282, The Annunciation, by D. Bacevic. #2283, Adoration of the Magi, by N. Neskovic. #2284, Madonna and Child, by T.N. Cesljar. #2285, St. John Baptizing Christ, by T. Kracun.

1994, Dec. 15

2282 A758 60p multicolored .80 .80
2283 A758 60p multicolored .80 .80
2284 A758 60p multicolored .80 .80
2285 A758 60p multicolored .80 .80
Nos. 2282-2285 (4) 3.20 3.20

Natl. Symbols — A759

1995, Jan. 26 **Litho.** ***Perf. 13½***

2286 A759 1d Flag 1.50 1.50
2287 A759 1d Arms 1.50 1.50

Sheets of 8

World Chess Champions — A760

#2288: a, Wilhelm Steinitz (1836-1900), Austria. b, Silhouettes of chessman. c, Emmanuel Lasker (1868-1941), Germany. d, Knight. e, Chessman, row of pawns at top. f, José Raúl Capablanca (1888-1942), Cuba. g, Chessman, rook at left. h, Alexander Alekhine (1892-1946), Russia.

#2289: a, Max Euwe, Netherlands. b, Board, pawn in center. c, Mikhail M. Botvinik, Soviet Union. d, Board, queen in middle. e, Board, bishop, knight. f, Vassili Smyslov, Soviet Union. g, Silhouette of knight, rook queen, chessboard. h, Mikhail N. Tal, Soviet Union.

1995

2288 A760 60p #a.-h. + label 10.00 10.00
2289 A760 60p #a.-h. + label 10.00 10.00

Issued: No. 2288, 2/28; No. 2289, 9/1.

Red Star Army Sport Club, 50th Anniv. — A761

1995, Mar. 4

2290 A761 60p bl, red & bister 1.75 1.75

Protection of Nature — A762

a, Salamandra salamandra. b, Triturus alpestris. c, Rana graeca. d, Pelobates syriacus balcanicus.

1995, Mar. 23

2291 A762 60p Strip of 4, #a.-d. + label 10.00 10.00

A763

1995, Apr. 20

2292 A763 60p multicolored 1.50 1.50

Radnicki Soccer Club, Belgrade, 75th anniv.

A764

Europa: 60p, Eagle, mountains. 1.90d, Girl on tricycle, elderly man, woman on park bench, horiz.

1995, May 6

2293 A764 60p multicolored 3.00 2.50
2294 A764 1.90d multicolored 3.00 2.50

A765

1995, May 9

2295 A765 60p multicolored 1.50 1.50

End of World War II, 50th anniv.

A766

1995, May 28

2296 A766 60p multicolored 2.00 2.00

Opening of Vukov-Denkmal Subway Station, Belgrade.

Draba Bertiscea — A767

a, shown. b, Plants, diff. c, Flowers, mountain. d, Plants on rock, stems at right.

1995, June 12

2297 A767 60p Strip of 4, #a.-d. + label 10.00 10.00

European Nature Protection — A768

Designs: 60p, Eremophila alpestris balcanica. 1.90d, Rhinolophus blasii.

1995, July 10

2298 A768 60p multicolored 2.00 2.00
2299 A768 1.90d multicolored 2.50 2.50

Slovakian Folk Festival, by Zuzka Medvedova (1897-1985), Painter A769

1995, Aug. 3

2300 A769 60p multicolored 1.25 1.25

Volleyball, Cent. — A770

1995, Sept. 10

2301 A770 90d multicolored 1.25 1.25

Church of St. Luke, Kotor, 800th Anniv. — A771

1995, Sept. 20

2302 A771 80p multicolored 1.25 1.25

Motion Pictures, Cent. — A772

Designs: 1.10d, Newsreel showing coronation of King Peter II. 2.20d, Auguste and Louis Jean Lumière, film projector.

1995, Oct. 3

2303 A772 1.10d dk brn, lt red brn 1.50 1.50
2304 A772 2.20d dk brn, lt red brn 1.50 1.50

Army Sports Club "Partisan," 50th Anniv. — A773

1995, Oct. 4

2305 A773 80p multi + label 1.25 1.25

UN, 50th Anniv. — A774

1995, Oct. 24

2306 A774 1.10d multicolored 1.25 1.25

Stamp Day — A775

1995, Oct. 31

2307 A775 1.10d multicolored 1.00 1.00

Joy of Europe — A776

Paintings: 1.10d, Young boy by Milos Tenkovic. 2.20d, Young girl by Pierre Bonnard.

1995, Nov. 26

2308 A776 1.10d multicolored 1.50 1.50
2309 A776 2.20d multicolored 1.50 1.50

Children's Day.

Souvenir Sheet

JUFIZ VIII, Natl. Philatelic Exhibition, Budva — A777

Design: Montenegro #37, Serbia #6.

1995, Dec. 13 ***Perf. 14***

2310 A777 2.50d Sheet of 1 + label 2.00 2.00

Christmas — A778

Contemporary religious paintings: No. 2311, Flight into Egypt, by Z. Halupova. No. 2312, Nativity, by D. Milojevic, vert. No. 2313, Outdoor Christmas scene, by M. Rasic, vert. No. 2314, Indoor traditional Christmas scene, by J. Brasic.

1995, Dec. 26 *Perf. 13½*

2311 A778 1.10d multicolored .50 .50
2312 A778 1.10d multicolored .50 .50
2313 A778 2.20d multicolored 1.00 1.00
2314 A778 2.20d multicolored 1.00 1.00
Nos. 2311-2314 (4) 3.00 3.00

Airplanes — A779

1995, Dec. 26

2315 A779 1.10d Saric No. 1 .50 .50
2316 A779 1.10d Douglas DC-3 .50 .50
2317 A779 2.20d Fizir FN 1.00 1.00
2318 A779 2.20d Caravelle 1.00 1.00
Nos. 2315-2318 (4) 3.00 3.00

Battle of Mojkovac, 80th Anniv. — A780

Design: Montenegrins on mountain.

1996, Jan. 6

2319 A780 1.10d multicolored .50 .50

Birth of Sava Sumanovic, Cent. — A781

Design: 1927 Painting, "Drink Boat."

1996, Jan. 22

2320 A781 1.10d multicolored .50 .50

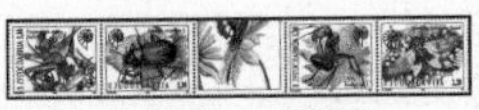
Insects — A782

a, Pyrgomorphela serbica. b, Calosoma sycopanta. c, Formica rufa. d, Ascalaphus macaronius.

1996, Feb. 15

2321 A782 2.20d Strip of 4, #a.-d. + label 7.00 7.00

Protection of nature.

A783

Churches.

1996, Feb. 29 **Litho.** *Perf. 12½*

2322 A783 5d Ljeviska 2.00 1.50
2323 A783 10d Zica 4.00 3.00
2324 A783 20d Decani 8.00 6.00
Nos. 2322-2324 (3) 14.00 10.50

Chess Champions — A784

Designs: a, Tigran Petrosian, Soviet Union. b, Chess pieces, sundial, chess board. c, Boris Spassky, Soviet Union. d, Chess pieces, board, clock showing two time zones. e, Garry Kasparov, Soviet Union. f, Chess pieces, hand holding hour glass. g, Bobby Fischer, US. h, Chess pieces, six clocks. i, Anatoly Karpov, Soviet Union.

1996, Mar. 15 **Litho.** *Perf. 13½*

2325 A784 1.50d Sheet of 9, #a.-i. 6.00 6.00

Olympic Games, Cent. — A786

1.50d, Discus throwers. 2.50d, Runners.

Perf. 13½x13¼

1996, Mar. 30 **Litho.**

2326 A786 1.50d multi .75 .75
2327 A786 2.50d multi 1.25 1.25

1996 Summer Olympics, Atlanta — A787

1996, Apr. 12

2328 A787 1.50d shown 1.50 1.50
2329 A787 1.50d Basketball 1.50 1.50
2330 A787 1.50d Handball 1.50 1.50
2331 A787 1.50d Volleyball 1.50 1.50
2332 A787 1.50d Shooting 1.50 1.50
2333 A787 1.50d Water polo 1.50 1.50
Nos. 2328-2333 (6) 9.00 9.00

1996 Summer Olympic Games, Atlanta A787a

1996, Apr. 12 **Litho.** *Perf. 13*

2334 A787a 5d Sheet of 1 + label 2.00 2.00

Stamp Day — A788

1996, Apr. 30 **Litho.** *Perf. 13½*

2335 A788 1.50d Railway mail car .60 .60

Famous Women Writers — A789

Europa: 2.50d, Isidora Sekulic (1877-1958). 5d, Desanka Maksimovic (1898-1993).

1996, May 7 **Litho.** *Perf. 13½*

2336 A789 2.50d multicolored 2.00 2.00
2337 A789 5d multicolored 2.00 2.00

Serbian Red Cross, 120th Anniv. — A790

1996, May 8

2338 A790 1.50d Dr. Vladan Djordjevic .60 .60

Architectural Education in Yugoslavia, 150th Anniv. — A791

1996, June 1 **Litho.** *Perf. 13½*

2339 A791 1.50d multicolored .60 .60

European Nature Protection — A792

2.50d, Platalea leucorodia. 5d, Plegadis falcinellus.

1996, June 28

2340 A792 2.50d multicolored 1.00 1.00
2341 A792 5d multicolored 2.00 2.00

Prince Peter I Petrovic at Battle of Martinici, 1796 — A793

Design: 2.50d, Prince's Guard at Battle of Kruse (1796), by Valerio, vert.

1996, July 22

2342 A793 1.50d multicolored .50 .50
2343 A793 2.50d multicolored 1.00 1.00

Horse Racing, Ljubicevo — A794

1996, Sept. 2 **Litho.** *Perf. 13½*

2344 A794 1.50d shown .50 .50
2345 A794 2.50d 3 horses racing 1.00 1.00

Fauna — A795

Designs: a, 1.50d, Probosciger aterrimus. b, 2.50d, Goura scheepmakeri. c, 1.50d, Equus burchelli. d, 2.50d, Panthera tigris.

1996, Sept. 25

2346 A795 Strip of 4, #a.-d. + label 8.00 8.00

Belgrade Zoo, 60th anniv.

Children's Day — A796

1996, Oct. 2

2347 A796 1.50d multicolored .70 .70
2348 A796 2.50d Bird 1.25 1.25

Medalists, 1996 Summer Olympic Games — A797

Designs: No. 2349, Shooting, bronze. No. 2350, Shooting, gold. No. 2351, Volleyball, bronze. No. 2352, Basketball, silver.

1996, Oct. 31 **Litho.** *Perf. 13½*

2349 A797 2.50d multicolored 1.40 1.40
2350 A797 2.50d multicolored 1.40 1.40
2351 A797 2.50d multicolored 1.40 1.40
2352 A797 2.50d multicolored 1.40 1.40
Nos. 2349-2352 (4) 5.60 5.60

Savings Accounts, 75th Anniv. — A798

1996, Oct. 31 **Litho.** *Perf. 13½*

2353 A798 1.50d multicolored .70 .70

Soccer in Yugoslavia, Cent. — A799

1996, Nov. 8 **Litho.** *Perf. 13½*

2354 A799 1.50d multicolored .70 .70

Archaeological Finds — A800

Sculptures: No. 2355, God of Autumn. No. 2356, Mother with child. No. 2357, Head of woman. No. 2358, Redheaded goddess.

1996, Nov. 25

2355 A800 1.50d multicolored *.60* .50
2356 A800 1.50d multicolored *.60* .50
2357 A800 2.50d multicolored *1.00* .75
2358 A800 2.50d multicolored *1.00* .75
Nos. 2355-2358 (4) *3.20* 2.50

A801

Christmas (Paintings): No. 2359, Annunciation. No. 2360, Mother of God with Christ. No. 2361, Birth of Christ. No. 2362, Palm Sunday.

1996, Dec. 10

2359 A801 1.50d multicolored *.60* .50
2360 A801 1.50d multicolored *.60* .50
2361 A801 2.50d multicolored *1.00* .75
2362 A801 2.50d multicolored *1.00* .75
Nos. 2359-2362 (4) *3.20* 2.50

A802

1997, Jan. 24 **Litho.** *Perf. 13½*

2363 A802 1.50d multicolored .60 .60

Radomir Putnik Voivode, 150th birth anniv.

25th Intl. Film Festival, Belgrade — A803

1997, Jan. 31

2364 A803 1.50d multicolored .70 .70

Protected Birds — A804

Designs: No. 2365, Dendrocopos major. No. 2366, Nucifraga caryocatactes. No. 2367, Parus cristatus. No. 2368, Erithacus rubecula.

1997, Feb. 21

2365 A804 1.50d multicolored .60 .60
2366 A804 2.50d multicolored .60 .60
2367 A804 1.50d multicolored .90 .90
2368 A804 2.50d multicolored .90 .90
a. Strip of 4, #2365-2368 + label 7.00 7.00

A805

1997, Mar. 17 Litho. *Perf. 13*

2369 A805 1.50d multicolored *1.00 1.00*

St. Achilleus Church, 700th Anniv.

A806

Design: Prince Peter I Petrovic (1747-1830), Bishop of Montenegro.

1997, Apr. 3 *Perf. 13½*

2370 A806 1.50d multicolored *1.00 1.00*

A807

1997, Apr. 19

2371 A807 2.50d multicolored *1.25 1.25*

10th Belgrade Marathon.

A808

1997, Apr. 22 Litho. *Perf. 13½*

2372 A808 2.50d multicolored *1.25 1.25*

Serbian Medical Assoc., 125th anniv.

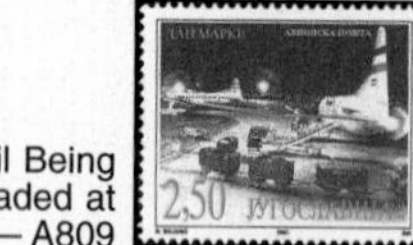
Air Mail Being Loaded at Night — A809

1997, May 3

2373 A809 2.50d multicolored *1.25 1.25*

Stamp Day.

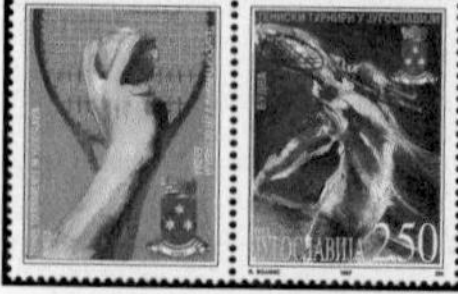
Tennis Tournaments in Yugoslavia — A810

Stylized designs: No. 2374, Player, large racket overhead, Budva. No. 2375, Player with ball flying from racket, Belgrade. No. 2376, Player with racket out in front, Novi Sad.

1997, May 8

2374 A810 2.50d multi + label *1.25 1.25*
2375 A810 2.50d multi + label *1.25 1.25*
2376 A810 2.50d multi + label *1.25 1.25*
Nos. 2374-2376 (3) 3.75 3.75

Stories and Legends — A811

Europa: 2.50d, Shackled Bach Chelik surrounded by creatures. 6d, Bach Chelik in chains, prince fighting with him, princess, castle.

1997, May 30 *Perf. 11½*

2377 A811 2.50d multicolored 2.00 2.00
2378 A811 6d multicolored 2.00 2.00

Each issued in sheets of 8 + label.

European Nature Protection — A812

2.50d, Cerambyx cerdo. 6d, Quercus robur.

1997, June 5

2379 A812 2.50d multicolored 1.00 1.00
2380 A812 6d multicolored 2.00 2.00

Stanislav Binicki (1872-1947) — A813

1997, June 7 *Perf. 13½*

2381 A813 2.50d multicolored 1.00 1.00

Printing of Gorski Vijenac, 150th Anniv. — A814

1997, June 7

2382 A814 2.50d multicolored 1.00 1.00

Flowers — A815

Designs: a, 1.50d, Pelargonium grandiflorum. b, 2.50d, Saintpaulia ionantha. c, 1.50d, Hydrangea macrophylla. d, 2.50d, Oncidium varicosum.

1997, Sept. 10 Litho. *Perf. 13*

2383 A815 Strip of 4, #a.-d. + label 7.00 7.00

Souvenir Sheet

JUFIZ IX, 9th Natl. Philatelic Exhibition — A816

Design: Sculpture, by Dragomir Arambasic, in front of art gallery.

1997, Sept. 10 *Perf. 14*

2384 A816 5d multicolored 2.50 2.50

A817

1997, Sept. 24 *Perf. 13½x14*

2385 A817 2.50d multicolored 1.00 1.00

Serbian Chemical Society, cent.

Type of 1993
Size: 18x18mm

1997, Oct. 2 *Perf. 14*

2386 A702d (A) like #2142 1.00 .25
a. Dated "1999" 1.00 .25

A818

Joy of Europe children's art works: 2.50d, 5d, Busts of people formed from collage of various food products.

1997, Oct. 2

2387 A818 2.50d multicolored 1.00 1.00
2388 A818 5d multicolored 2.00 2.00

"May Assembly in Sremski Karlivoci," by Pavle Simic — A819

1997, Oct. 10 Litho. *Perf. 14*

2389 A819 2.50d multicolored 1.00 1.00

Matica Srpska Gallery, 150th anniv.

A820

Museum exhibits: No. 2390, Two-headed statuette. No. 2391, Parade helmet. No. 2392, Terra cotta statuette. No. 2393, Virgin icon.

1997, Nov. 12

2390 A820 1.50d multicolored .50 .50
2391 A820 1.50d multicolored .50 .50
2392 A820 2.50d multicolored 1.00 1.00
2393 A820 2.50d multicolored 1.00 1.00
Nos. 2390-2393 (4) 3.00 3.00

A821

Icons (Chelandari Serbian Monastery, Mount Athos): No. 2394, Christ. No. 2395, Madonna and Child, 12th cent. No. 2396, Madonna and Child, 13th cent. No. 2397, 3-handed Madonna.

Granite Paper

1997, Dec. 2 *Perf. 11½*

2394 A821 1.50d multicolored .50 .50
2395 A821 1.50d multicolored .50 .50
2396 A821 2.50d multicolored 1.00 1.00
2397 A821 2.50d multicolored 1.00 1.00
Nos. 2394-2397 (4) 3.00 3.00

A822

1998, Jan. 20 Litho. *Perf. 13½*

2398 A822 1.50d Savina *1.00 1.00*
2399 A822 2.50d Donji Brceli *1.00 1.00*

Monasteries of Montenegro.

A823

1998, Feb. 6 *Perf. 14*

2400 A823 2.50d Figure skater 2.00 2.00
2401 A823 6d Skier 2.00 2.00

1998 Winter Olympic Games, Nagano.

Horses — A824

Designs: a, 1.50d, Two running. b, 2.50d, Arabian up close. c, 1.50d, Thoroughbred. d, 2.50d, Thoroughbred running on race track.

1998, Feb. 26 Litho. *Perf. 12x11½*

2402 A824 Strip of 4, #a.-d. + label 10.00 10.00

Intl. Women's Day — A825

1998, Mar. 7 *Perf. 13½*

2403 A825 2.50d multicolored 1.00 1.00

Yugoslav Airlines Assoc., 50th Anniv. — A826

1998, Apr. 24

2404 A826 2.50d multicolored 1.00 1.00

Europa A827

Paintings: 6d, "Dressing the Bride," by Paja Jovanovic (1859-1957). 9d, "Bishop's Congratulations," by Pero Pocek (1878-1963).

1998, May 4 Litho. *Perf. 12*

Granite Paper

2405 A827 6d multicolored 3.00 3.00
2406 A827 9d on 2.50d, multi 3.00 3.00

No. 2406 was not issued without the silver surcharge.

1998 World Cup Soccer Championships, France — A828

1998, May 15 Litho. ***Perf. 13½***

2407 A828 6d shown 1.75 1.75

2408 A828 9d Soccer players, diff. 2.75 2.75

Souvenir Sheet

Danube Commission, 50th Anniv. — A829

1998, May 19 ***Perf. 14***

2409 A829 9d multicolored 4.00 4.00

European Nature Protection — A830

Designs: 6d, Heracium blecicii. 9d, Mola mola, vert.

1998, June 17 Litho. ***Perf. 13¾***

2410 A830 6d multi 1.25 1.25

2411 A830 9d multi 1.75 1.75

Each stamp was printed in sheets of 8 + label.

Famous People of Serbia A831

a, Djura Jaksic (1832-78), poet, painter. b, Nadezda Petrovic (1873-1915), painter. c, Radoje Domanovic (1873-1908), writer. d, Vasilije Mokranjac (1923-1984), composer. e, Streten Stojanovic (1898-1960), sculptor. f, Milan Konjovic (1898-1993), painter. g, Desanka Maksimovic (1898-1993), poet. h, Ivan Tabakovic (1898-1977), painter.

1998, June 30 Litho. ***Perf. 12***

Granite Paper

Sheet of 8 + label

2412 A831 1.50d #a.-h. 3.25 3.25

Souvenir Sheet

Yugoslavia, Winner of World Basketball Championships — A832

1998, Aug. 21 ***Perf. 13½***

2413 A832 10d multicolored 8.00 8.00

Protected Animals — A833

a, 2d, Martes martes. b, 2d, Anthropoides virgo. c, 5d, Lynx lynx. d, 5d, Loxia curvirostra.

1998, Sept. 2

2414 A833 Strip of 4, #a.-d. + label 9.00 9.00

Breaking of the Thessaloniki Front, 80th Anniv. — A834

Designs: No. 2415, 5d, Soldiers and cannons. No. 2416, 5d, Soldiers with machine guns, binoculars.

1998, Sept. 15 Engr. ***Perf. 13½***

2415-2416 A834 Set of 2 3.50 3.50

Stamp Day — A835

1998, Sept. 28

2417 A835 6d Prussian blue 1.40 1.40

Serbian Philatelic Society, 50th anniv.

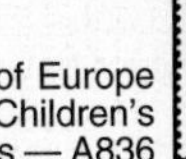

Joy of Europe Children's Drawings — A836

Designs: 6d, Fish. 9d, Fish, diff.

1998, Oct. 2 Litho. ***Perf. 13¾***

2418-2419 A836 Set of 2 3.50 3.50

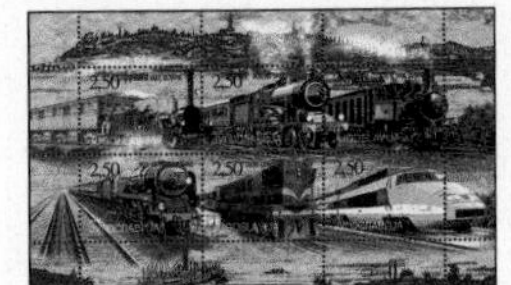

Development of the Railway — A837

Trains: a, 1847. b, 1900. c, 1920. d, 1930. e, Diesel locomotive. f, 1990.

1998, Nov. 3 Litho. ***Perf. 13½***

2420 A837 2.50d Booklet pane of 6, #a.-f. 9.00 9.00

Complete booklet, #2420 9.50

Paintings of Sailing Ships, Maritime Museum, Kotor — A838

#2421, Veracruz, 1873. #2422, Pierino, 1883. #2423, Draghetto, 1865. #2424, Group of ships.

1998, Nov. 11 ***Perf. 12***

Granite Paper

2421 A838 2d multicolored .50 .50

2422 A838 2d multicolored .50 .50

2423 A838 5d multicolored 1.50 1.50

2424 A838 5d multicolored 1.50 1.50

Nos. 2421-2424 (4) 4.00 4.00

Chelandari Monastery, 800th Anniv. — A839

Views of monastery: No. 2425, Looking from center of complex, two trees. No. 2426, Group of taller buildings. No. 2427, Aerial view. No. 2428, Looking across group of buildings, crosses on turrets.

1998, Dec. 9 ***Perf. 14***

2425 A839 2d multicolored .50 .50

2426 A839 2d multicolored .50 .50

2427 A839 5d multicolored 1.25 1.25

2428 A839 5d multicolored 1.25 1.25

Nos. 2425-2428 (4) 3.50 3.50

Third Meeting of Southeast European Postal Ministers — A840

1998, Dec. 17 Litho. ***Perf. 14***

2429 A840 5d multicolored *3.00 3.00*

Souvenir Sheet

Yugoslavia, Silver Medalists at 1998 World Volleyball Championships — A841

1998, Dec. 19 ***Perf. 13½***

2430 A841 10d multicolored *50.00 50.00*

Post and Telecommunications Museum, Belgrade, 75th Anniv. — A842

#2431, Postrider. #No. 2432, Antique telegraph equipment, museum building.

1998, Dec. 21 Engr.

2431 A842 5d olive brown & slate 1.00 1.00

2432 A842 5d red & brown 1.00 1.00

Serbian Monasteries A843

1999, Jan. 14 Litho. ***Perf. 13¾***

2433 A843 2d Visoki Decani .60 .60

2434 A843 5d Grachanica 1.60 1.60

Farm Animals — A844

Designs: a, 2d, Pigs. b, 6d, Goat. c, 2d, Oxen. d, 6d, Long-horn sheep.

1999, Feb. 5 Litho. ***Perf. 13½***

2435 A844 Strip of 4, #a.-d. + label 7.00 7.00

A845

1999, Feb. 24 Litho. ***Perf. 13¼***

2436 A845 6d Scouting 2.00 2.00

A846

1999, Mar. 27

2437 A846 6d brown & buff 1.40 1.40

Yugoslav Bar Association, 70th anniv.

Target

A847 A848

1999 ***Perf. 12¼x12½***

2438 A847 (A) black 5.00 3.00

2439 A848 (A) black & red 20.00 12.00

Issued: No. 2438, 3/27; No. 2439, 4/7. Nos. 2438-2439 sold for 2.04d when issued.

World Table Tennis Championships, Belgrade — A849

1999, Apr. 9 ***Perf. 13¼***

Player colors

2440 A849 6d blue & red 2.00 2.00

2441 A849 6d green & red 2.00 2.00

A850

Europa, National Parks and Reserves: 6d, Falcon, trees, mountains, Kopaonik Natl. Park. 15d, Flowers, mountains, Lovcen Natl. Park.

1999, May 5 Photo. ***Perf. 11¾***

Granite Paper

2442 A850 6d multicolored 6.00 6.00

2443 A850 15d multicolored 6.00 6.00

Each printed in shhets of 8 + 1 central label.

A851

European Nature Protection: 6d, Shovel, spider web. 15d, Thumb squeezing earth.

1999, May 13 ***Perf. 11¾x12***

2444 A851 6d multicolored 2.50 2.50

2445 A851 15d multicolored 2.50 2.50

Mushrooms — A852

Designs: a, Amanita virosa. b, Amanita pantherina. c, Hypholoma fasciculare. d, Ramaria pallida.

1999, June 18 Litho. ***Perf. 11¾x12***

Granite Paper

2446 A852 6d Strip of 4, #a.-d., + central label 10.00 10.00

Central labels differ on sheet.

Famous Montenegrins — A853

Designs: a, Stjepan Mitrov Ljubisa (1824-78). b, Marko Milanov (1833-1901). c, Pero Pocek (1878-1963). d, Risto Stijovic (1894-1974). e, Milo Milunovic (1897-1967). f, Petar Lubarda (1907-74). g, Vuko Radovic (1911-96). h, Mihailo Lalic (1914-92).

1999, June 30 ***Perf. 13¼***
2447 A853 2d Sheet of 8, #a.-h., + central label 3.25 3.25

UPU, 125th Anniv. — A854

1999, Sept. 15 ***Perf. 13¼***
2448 A854 6d shown 1.00 1.00
2449 A854 12d Envelopes circling globe 2.00 2.00

Joy of Europe Children's Drawings — A855

1999, Oct. 1 ***Perf. 13¾***
2450 A855 6d Lion 1.00 1.00
2451 A855 15d Family, vert. 2.50 2.50

Frédéric Chopin (1810-49), Composer — A856

1999, Oct. 15 ***Perf. 13¼***
2452 A856 10d multi 2.25 2.25

No. 2438, Mastheads of "Filatelista" — A857

1999, Oct. 18
2453 A857 10d multi 1.50 1.50

Stamp Day.

A858

Bridges Destroyed by NATO Air Strikes — A859

Bridges: #2454, Varadinski. #2455, Ostruznica. #2456, Murino. #2457, Grdelica. #2458, Bistrica. #2459, Zezeljev.

1999, Oct. 29 ***Perf. 13¾***
2454 A858 2d shown .90 .90
2455 A859 2d shown .90 .90
2456 A859 2d multi .90 .90
2457 A859 6d multi .90 .90
2458 A859 6d multi .90 .90
2459 A859 6d multi .90 .90
Nos. 2454-2459 (6) 5.40 5.40

Millennium — A860

a, 6d, Roman altars, statue of Jupiter. b, 6d, Sculpture of Emperor Trajan and army leaders, mosaic, lamp, lead mirror. c, 6d, Mosaic of Dionysius, arch. d, 6d, Hagia Sophia, mosaic of Madonna and Child, Emperor Constantine. e, 6d, Large cross, candle, fibula, pot. f, 6d, Church, boats, manuscript. g, 15d, Nativity and crucifixion of Christ, boats, farmers.

1999, Nov. 19
2460 A860 Booklet pane of 7, #a.-g., + 2 labels 9.00 9.00
Complete booklet, #2460 9.00

Size of #2460g: 105x55mm.

A861

Bomb Damage — A862

#2461, Bolnice. #2462, Telecommunications complex. #2463, Refinery. #2464, Bolnice, diff. #2465, Telecommunications complex, diff. #2466, Television complex.

1999, Nov. 27 **Litho.** ***Perf. 13¾***
2461 A861 2d shown .50 .50
2462 A862 2d shown .50 .50
2463 A862 2d multi .50 .50
2464 A862 6d multi 1.00 1.00
2465 A862 6d multi 1.00 1.00
2466 A862 6d multi 1.00 1.00
Nos. 2461-2466 (6) 4.50 4.50

A863

Frescoes of Poganovo Monastery, 500th Anniv. — A864

Design A863 has Latin letters, A864 has Cyrillic letters.

1999, Dec. 23
2467 A863 6d shown .80 .80
2468 A864 6d shown .80 .80
2469 A863 6d Fresco, diff. .80 .80
2470 A864 6d Fresco, diff. .80 .80
Nos. 2467-2470 (4) 3.20 3.20

A865

Gold Prospectors in Pec River — A866

Design A865 has Latin letters, A866 has Cyrillic letters.

1999, Dec. 30
2471 A865 6d shown .80 .80
2472 A866 6d shown .80 .80
2473 A865 6d Prospectors, diff. .80 .80
2474 A866 6d Prospectors, diff. .80 .80
Nos. 2471-2474 (4) 3.20 3.20

Krusedol Monastery — A867

2000, Jan. 13 ***Perf. 13¼***
2475 A867 10d shown 1.50 1.50
2476 A867 10d Rakovac Monastery 1.50 1.50

Yugoslavian Archives, 50th Anniv. — A868

2000, Jan. 21
2477 A868 10d multi *25.00 25.00*

Butterflies — A869

No. 2478: a, Nymphalis antiopa. b, Parnalius polyxena. c, Limenitis populi. d, Melanargia galathea.

2000, Feb. 25 **Litho.** ***Perf. 13¾***
2478 Horiz. strip of 4 + central label 18.00 18.00
a.-d. A869 10d Any single 2.50 2.50

Worldwide Fund for Nature — A870

Perdix perdix: a, Pair in snow. b, Pair facing right. c, Bird on nest. d, Pair, one facing left.

2000, Mar. 14 **Litho.** ***Perf. 12x11¾***
2479 A870 10d Strip of 4, #a.-d., + central label 12.00 12.00

Damage from NATO Airstrikes — A871

Various destroyed buildings. Colors: 10d, Blue. 20d, Brown.

2000, Mar. 24 **Engr.** ***Perf. 13¼***
2480-2481 A871 Set of 2 5.00 5.00

Souvenir Sheet

JUFIZ X Philatelic Exhibition, Belgrade — A872

2000, May 2 **Litho.**
2482 A872 15d multi *50.00 50.00*

Nature Protection — A873

Designs: No. 2483, 30d, Feeding chicks by hand. No. 2484, 30d, Map of Europe in tree's leaves, vert.

Perf. 12x11¾, 11¾x12

2000, May 4 **Litho.**
2483-2484 A873 Set of 2 4.00 4.00

Europa — A874

"2000" and: No. 2485, 30d, Astronaut on moon. No. 2486, 30d, Star and mountains.

2000, May 9 ***Perf. 11¾x12***
2485-2486 A874 Set of 2 8.00 8.00

European Soccer Championships A875

Inscriptions in: No. 2487, 30d, Cyrillic letters. No. 2488, 30d, Latin letters.

2000, May 20 **Litho.** ***Perf. 13¾***
2487-2488 A875 Set of 2 6.00 6.00

Postal Services in Serbia, 160th Anniv. — A876

2000, June 7 **Litho.** ***Perf. 13¾***
2489 A876 10d multi *2.00 2.00*

2000 Summer Olympics, Sydney — A877

Map of Australia and: 6d, Kangaroo. 12d, Emu. 24d, Koala and soccer ball. 30d, Parrot.

2000, June 28
2490-2493 A877 Set of 4 7.00 7.00

Stamp Day — A878

2000, Sept. 26 ***Perf. 13¼***
2494 A878 10d multi 4.50 4.50

"Joy of Europe" — A879

Children's art: 30d, Cows. 40d, Cranes, vert.

2000, Oct. 2
2495-2496 A879 Set of 2 3.50 3.50

World Teachers' Day — A880

2000, Oct. 5
2497 A880 10d multi 20.00 20.00

13th Apiarists Congress — A881

2000, Oct. 6
2498 A881 10d multi *5.00 5.00*

Medals Won at 2000 Summer Olympics — A882

Designs: No. 2499, 20d, Water polo (bronze). No. 2500, 20d, Shooting (silver). 30d, Volleyball, vert.

2000, Oct. 23 ***Perf. 13¾***
2499-2500 A882 Set of 2 3.00 3.00

Souvenir Sheet

2501 A882 30d multi 20.00 20.00

No. 2501 contains one 35x46mm stamp.

Millennium — A883

No. 2502: a, Ships. b, Papermaking. c, Galileo and telescopes. d, Steam locomotive and steamship. e, Nikola Tesla, invention of the telephone. f, Astronaut, outer space settlement. g, Ships, airplanes, balloons, horses.

2000, Nov. 2 Litho. ***Perf. 13¾***
2502 A883 Booklet pane of 7 + 2 labels 6.00 —
a.-f. 12d Any single .60 .60
g. 40d multi 2.00 2.00
Booklet, #2502 6.00

Size of No. 2502g: 105x55mm.

Nativity Fresco, Pec — A884

2000, Nov. 7 Litho. ***Perf. 13¾***
2503 A884 A multi *3.50* .50

No. 2503 sold for 3.56d on day of issue.

Serb Clothing From the 1900s — A885

Designs: 6d, Vest, Jagodina. 12d, Dresses, Metochija. 24d, Blouse, Pec. 30d, Vest, Kupres.

2000, Dec. 7
2504-2507 A885 Set of 4 3.00 3.00

Montenegrin Religious Art — A886

Designs: 6d, Madonna and Child, 1573-74. 12d, Nativity, 1666-67. 24d, St. Luke, 1672-73. 30d, Madonna and Child, 1642.

2000, Dec. 19
2508-2511 A886 Set of 4 3.00 3.00

A887 A887a

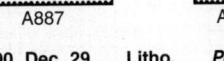

2000, Dec. 29 Litho. ***Perf. 13¾***
2512 A887 6d multi .50 .50
2513 A887a 12d multi .50 .50

Resumption of Yugoslavia's membership in Organization for Security and Cooperation in Europe (#2512), and United Nations (#2513).

Vatoped Monastery, Mount Athos, Greece — A888

Esfigmen Monastery, Mount Athos, Greece — A889

2001, Jan. 26 Litho. ***Perf. 13¼***
2514 A888 10d multi .55 .55
2515 A889 27d multi 1.60 1.60

Matica Srpska, 175th Anniv. — A890

2001, Feb. 16 ***Perf. 13¾***
2516 A890 15d multi 1.10 1.10

Animals — A891

No. 2517: a, Felis leo. b, Ursus maritimus. c, Macaca fuscata. d, Spheniscus humboldti.

2001, Feb. 23
2517 Horiz. strip of 4 + central label 7.25 7.25
a. A891 6d multi .45 .45
b. A891 12d multi .90 .90
c. A891 24d multi 1.10 1.10
d. A891 30d multi 1.40 1.40

Women's World Chess Champions — A892

No. 2518: a, Vera Menchik (1927-44). b, Lyudmila Rudenko (1950-53). c, Yelisavyeta Bykova (1953-56, 1958-62). d, Olga Rubtsova (1956-58). e, Nona Gaprindashvili (1962-78). f, Maia Chiburdanidze (1978-91). g, Zsuzsa Polgar (1996-99). h, Xie Jun (1991-96, 1999-2000).

2001, Mar. 8 ***Perf. 13¼***
2518 A892 10d Sheet of 8, #a-h, + label 4.50 4.50

Famous Men — A893

Designs: 50d, Stevan Mokranjac (1856-1914), composer. 100d, Nikola Tesla (1856-1943), inventor.

2001, Mar. 19 ***Perf. 13¾***
2519-2520 A893 Set of 2 7.25 7.25

Flowers — A894

No. 2521: a, Hibiscus syriacus. b, Nerium oleander. c, Lapageria rosea. d, Sorbus aucuparia.

2001, Apr. 13 ***Perf. 12x11¾***
2521 Horiz. strip of 4 + central label 6.50 6.50
a. A894 6d multi .35 .35
b. A894 12d multi .55 .55
c. A894 24d multi 1.00 1.00
d. A894 30d multi 1.40 1.40

Europa — A895

Designs: 30d, Vratna River. 45d, Jerme Canyon.

2001, May 4 ***Perf. 11¾x12***
2522-2523 A895 Set of 2 6.75 6.75

Serbian Mountaineering Association, Cent. — A896

2001, June 8 ***Perf. 13¼***
2524 A896 15d multi 1.25 1.25

European Nature Protection — A897

Designs: 30d, Bird on branch, Lake Ludasko. 45d, Stork flying above Begej River.

2001, June 22 ***Perf. 12x11¾***
2525-2526 A897 Set of 2 3.75 3.75

14th Cent. Book Illumination — A898

2001, July 2 ***Perf. 13¼***
2527 A898 E multi 1.60 1.60

Sold for 28.70d on day of issue.

Souvenir Sheet

Yugoslavian Victory in European Water Polo Championships — A899

2001, July 5 ***Perf. 13¾***
2528 A899 30d multi 6.50 6.50

Souvenir Sheet

Serbiafila XII Stamp Exhibition — A900

2001, Sept. 8
2529 A900 30d multi 2.50 2.50

Solar Energy — A901

2001, Sept. 19 ***Perf. 13¼***
2530 A901 15d multi 1.60 1.60

Danube Commission — A902

Designs: 30d, Ships, hands raising bridge. 45d, Ship, hand, clock.

2001, Sept. 20 ***Perf. 13¾***
2531-2532 A902 Set of 2 5.50 5.50

Joy of Europe — A903

Paintings: 30d, Child, by Marko Chelebonovic. 45d, Girl Under a Fruit Tree, by Beta Vukanovic.

2001, Oct. 2 ***Perf. 13¼***
2533-2534 A903 Set of 2 5.50 5.50

Yugoslavian Victories in European Sports Championships A904

Designs: No. 2535, 30d, Men's basketball. No. 2536, 30d, Men's volleyball.

2001, Oct. 11
2535-2536 A904 Set of 2 45.00 45.00

Intl. Federation of Philately (FIP), 75th Anniv. — A905

2001, Oct. 24
2537 A905 15d multi 1.60 1.60

Stamp Day.

Minerals — A906

2001, Nov. 2 ***Perf. 13¾***
2538 Horiz. strip of 4 + central label 5.00 5.00
a. A906 7d Antimonite 1.10 1.10
b. A906 14d Calcite 1.10 1.10
c. A906 26.20d Quartz 1.10 1.10
d. A906 28.70d Calcite and galenite 1.10 1.10

Pljevlja Gymnasium, Cent. — A907

2001, Nov. 18 *Perf. 13¼*
2539 A907 15d multi 2.25 2.25

Public Telephone Booths in Serbia, Cent. — A908

2001, Nov. 20
2540 A908 15d multi 1.40 1.40

Christmas — A910

Paintings of the Birth of Jesus Christ: 7d, 14d, 26.20d, 28.70d.

2001, Dec. 1 *Perf. 13¾*
2541-2544 A910 Set of 4 4.50 4.50

Junior World Ice Hockey Championships, Belgrade — A911

2002, Jan. 5 *Perf. 13¼*
2545 A911 14d multi 10.00 10.00

2002 Winter Olympics, Salt Lake City — A912

Designs: 28.70d, Skier. 50d, Four-man bobsled, vert.

2002, Jan. 25 *Perf. 13¼*
2546-2547 A912 Set of 2 25.00 25.00

Jovan Karamata (1902-67), Mathematician — A913

2002, Feb. 1
2548 A913 14d multi 10.00 10.00

Birds — A914

No. 2549: a, Saxicola torquata. b, Saxicola rubetra. c, Parus caeruleus. d, Turdus philomelos.

2002, Feb. 22
2549 Horiz. strip of 4 + central label 10.00 10.00
a. A914 7d multi .65 .65
b. A914 14d multi 1.50 1.50
c. A914 26.20d multi 3.00 3.00
d. A914 28.70d multi 3.50 3.50

Easter — A915

Designs: 7d, Crucifixion, fresco from Studenica Monastery, 1208. 14d, King Milutin's Veil, 1300. 26.20d, Christ's Descent to Hell, silverwork, 1540. 28.70d, Easter egg, Pec Patriarchy, 1980.

2002, Mar. 7 *Perf. 13¾*
2550-2553 A915 Set of 4 9.00 9.00

Bunjevac Women's Clothing — A916

Woman with: 7d, White blouse. 28.70d, Kerchief.

2002, Mar. 29 *Perf. 13¼*
2554-2555 A916 Set of 2 4.50 4.50

Zarko Tomic-Sremac (b. 1900), World War II Hero — A917

2002, Apr. 15
2556 A917 14d multi 12.50 12.50

Danube Fish — A918

No. 2557: a, Rutilus rutilus. b, Acipenser ruthenus. c, Huso huso. d, Stizostedion lucioperca.

2002, Apr. 25 **Litho.** *Perf. 13¼*
2557 Horiz. strip of 4 + central label 18.00 18.00
a. A918 7d multi 1.50 1.50
b. A918 14d multi 2.50 2.50
c. A918 26.20d multi 5.00 5.00
d. A918 28.70d multi 5.00 5.00

Europa — A919

Designs: 28.70d, Trapeze artists. 50d, Tiger trainer.

2002, May 3 *Perf. 13¾*
2558-2559 A919 Set of 2 11.00 11.00

Europa Type
Souvenir Sheet

Design: 45d, Trained horse act.

2002, May 3 **Litho.** *Perf. 13¾*
2560 A919 45d multi 60.00 60.00

No. 2560 contains one 46x35mm stamp.

Civil Aviation in Yugoslavia, 75th Anniv. — A920

Designs: 7d, Potez-29. 28.70d, Boeing 737-300.

Perf. 13¼ Syncopated
2002, June 17 **Litho.**
2561-2562 A920 Set of 2 30.00 30.00

Types of 1993 and 2001
Size: 19x21mm (#2563)

2002, July 25 **Litho.** *Perf. 12½*
2563 A702d A blue *3.00 1.50*

Perf. 13¼
"E" in Green

2564 A898 E multi 7.50 *4.50*

Nos. 2563-2564 were intended for use in Montenegro and were sold there for 13c and 52c in euro currency respectively. The stamps were valid for use in the Serbian section of Yugoslavia.

European Nature Protection — A921

Designs: 28.70d, Tara National Park. 50d, Golija Nature Park.

Perf. 13¼ Syncopated
2002, June 28 **Litho.**
2565-2566 A921 Set of 2 9.00 9.00

Mills — A922

Designs: 7d, Windmill, Melenci. 28.70d, Water mill, Lyuberada.

2002, Sept. 14
2567-2568 A922 Set of 2 9.00 9.00

Liberation of Niskic, 125th Anniv. — A923

2002, Sept. 18 *Perf. 13¾*
2569 A923 14d multi 10.00 9.00

Souvenir Sheet

Victory in 2002 World Basketball Championships — A924

2002, Sept. 20
2570 A924 30d multi 10.00 10.00

Souvenir Sheet

JUFIZ XI Philatelic Exhibition — A925

2002, Sept. 23
2571 A925 30d multi 8.00 8.00

Joy of Europe — A926

Children's art: 28.70d, Boat. 50d, Bird.

2002, Oct. 2
2572-2573 A926 Set of 2 8.50 8.50

Moraca Monastery, 750th Anniv. — A927

2002, Oct. 10
2574 A927 16d multi 20.00 12.00

Nos. 2255-2256 Srchd. in Black or Violet

2002 *Perfs, etc., as Before*
2575 A751 50p on 5p #2256 multi 2.50 1.25
2576 A702g 10d on 10,000d #2145 7.50 6.00
2577 A751 12d on 1p #2255 multi (V) 6.00 4.00
Nos. 2575-2577 (3) 16.00 11.25

Issued: No. 2575, 10/17; No. 2576, 11/28; No. 2577, 12/19.

For stamp like No. 2577, but with black surcharge, see Serbia and Montenegro No. 260.

Intl. Federation of Stamp Dealers Associations, 50th Anniv. — A928

2002, Oct. 24 **Litho.** *Perf. 13¾*
2578 A928 16d multi 7.50 7.50

Serbian Folk Costumes — A929

Paintings of costumes by Olga Benson in Ethnographic Institute of Serbian Academy of Sciences and Arts: a, Man, Kusadak. b, Woman with red headdress, Belgrade. c, Man, Novo Selo. d, Woman in profile, Belgrade.

2002, Nov. 8 *Perf. 13¾*
2579 Horiz. strip of 4, + central label 8.00 8.00
a. A929 16d multi 1.00 1.00
b. A929 24d multi 2.00 2.00
c. A929 26.20d multi 2.00 2.00
d. A929 28.70d multi 2.00 2.00

Christmas — A930

Religious art: 12d, Nativity, Stavronikita Monastery, Mount Athos, Greece, 1546. 16d, Nativity, Chilandari Monastery, Mount Athos, Greece, c. 1618. 26.20d, Nativity, Tretyakov Gallery, Moscow, 15th cent. 28.70d, Adoration of the Magi, by Sandro Botticelli.

2002, Dec. 2
2580-2583 A930 Set of 4 7.00 7.00

Abandoned Dogs — A931

Various dogs.

2003, Jan. 31 *Perf. 13¾*

2584 Horiz. strip of 4, + central label 5.00 5.00
a. A931 16d multi .50 .50
b. A931 24d multi 1.25 1.25
c. A931 26.20d multi 1.25 1.25
d. A931 28.70d multi 1.25 1.25

> Yugoslavia became Serbia & Montenegro on Feb. 4, 2003. See Serbia & Montenegro for subsequent issues.

SEMI-POSTAL STAMPS

Giving Succor to Wounded — SP1

Wounded Soldier — SP2

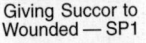

Symbolical of National Unity — SP3

Unwmk.

1921, Jan. 30 **Engr.** *Perf. 12*

B1 SP1 10p carmine .25 .25
B2 SP2 15p violet brown .25 .25
B3 SP3 25p light blue .25 .25
Nos. B1-B3 (3) .75 .75

Nos. B1-B3 were sold at double face value, the excess being for the benefit of invalid soldiers.
Exist imperf. Value $35.
For surcharges see Nos. 15-21.

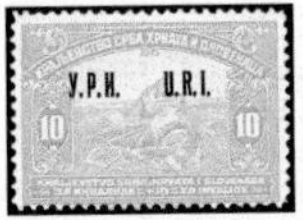

This overprint was applied to 500,000 examples of No. B1 in 1923 and they were given to the Society for Wounded Invalids (Uprava Ratnih Invalida) which sold them for 2d a piece. These overprinted stamps had no franking power, but some were used through ignorance.

Regular Issue of 1926-27 Surcharged in Dark Red

1926, Nov. 1 *Perf. 13*

B5 A6 25p + 25p green .25 .25
B6 A6 50p + 50p olive brn .25 .25
B7 A6 1d + 50p scarlet .25 .25
B8 A6 2d + 50p black .25 .25
B9 A6 3d + 50p slate blue .25 .25
B10 A6 4d + 50p red org .30 .25
B11 A6 5d + 50p brt vio .50 .25
B12 A6 8d + 50p black brn 1.00 .25
B13 A6 10d + 1d olive brn 2.00 .25
B14 A6 15d + 1d brown 8.00 1.00
B15 A6 20d + 1d dark vio 12.00 .55
B16 A6 30d + 1d orange 27.50 3.25
a. Double surcharge
Nos. B5-B16 (12) 52.55 7.05
Set, never hinged 105.00

The surtax on these stamps was intended for a fund for relief of sufferers from floods.
For overprints see Nos. 99-101.

Cathedral at Duvno SP4

King Tomislav SP6

Kings Tomislav and Alexander — SP5

Perf. 12½, 11½x12

1929, Nov. 1 **Typo.**

B17 SP4 50p (+ 50p) olive green .25 .25
B18 SP5 1d (+ 50p) red .60 .40
B19 SP6 3d (+ 1d) blue 1.60 1.10
Nos. B17-B19 (3) 2.45 1.75
Set, never hinged 4.75

Millenary of the Croatian kingdom. The surtax was used to create a War Memorial Cemetery in France and to erect a monument to Serbian soldiers who died there.
No. B18 exists imperf. Value $400.

View of Dobropolje SP7

War Memorial SP8

View of Kajmaktchalan — SP9

1931, Apr. 1 *Perf. 12½, 11½*

B20 SP7 50p + 50p blue grn .25 .25
B21 SP8 1d + 1d scarlet .25 .25
B22 SP9 3d + 3d deep blue .25 .25
Nos. B20-B22 (3) .75 .75

The surtax was added to a fund for a War Memorial to Serbian soldiers who died in France during World War I.

SP10

SP12

SP11

Black Overprint

1931, Nov. 1 *Perf. 12½, 11½x12*

B23 SP10 50p (+ 50p) olive grn .25 *.25*
B24 SP11 1d (+ 50p) red .25 *.25*
B25 SP12 3d (+ 1d) blue .30 .30
Nos. B23-B25 (3) .80 *.80*

Surtax for War Memorial fund.

Rower on Danube at Smederevo SP13

Bled Lake — SP14

Danube near Belgrade — SP15

View of Split Harbor SP16

Zagreb Cathedral SP17

Prince Peter — SP18

1932, Sept. 2 **Litho.** *Perf. 11½*

B26 SP13 75p + 50p dl grn & lt blue .75 1.50
B27 SP14 1d + ½d scar & lt blue .75 1.50
B28 SP15 1½d + ½d rose & green 1.00 2.00
B29 SP16 3d + 1d bl & lt bl 2.00 3.00
B30 SP17 4d + 1d red org & lt blue 9.00 20.00
B31 SP18 5d + 1d dl vio & lilac 9.00 17.00
Nos. B26-B31 (6) 22.50 45.00
Set, never hinged 45.00

European Rowing Championship Races, Belgrade.

King Alexander — SP19

1933, May 25 **Typo.** *Perf. 12½*

B32 SP19 50p + 25p black 6.00 12.00
B33 SP19 75p + 25p yel grn 6.00 12.00
B34 SP19 1.50d + 50p rose 6.00 12.00
B35 SP19 3d + 1d bl vio 6.00 12.00
B36 SP19 4p + 1d dk grn 6.00 12.00
B37 SP19 5d + 1d orange 6.00 12.00
Nos. B32-B37 (6) 36.00 72.00
Set, never hinged 72.50

11th Intl. Congress of P.E.N. (Poets, Editors and Novelists) Clubs, Dubrovnik, May 25-27.
The labels at the foot of the stamps are printed in either Cyrillic or Latin letters and each bears the amount of a premium for the benefit of the local P.E.N. Club at Dubrovnik.

Prince Peter — SP20

1933, June 28

B38 SP20 75p + 25p slate grn .25 .25
B39 SP20 1½d + ½d deep red .25 .25

60th anniv. meeting of the National Sokols (Sports Associations) at Ljubljana, July 1.

Eagle Soaring over City — SP22

1934, June 1 *Perf. 12½*

B40 SP22 75p + 25p green 5.00 9.50
B41 SP22 1.50d + 50p car 7.50 10.00
B42 SP22 1.75d + 25p brown 12.50 10.50
Nos. B40-B42 (3) 25.00 30.00
Set, never hinged 50.00

20th anniversary of Sokols of Sarajevo.

Athlete and Eagle — SP23

1934, June 1

B43 SP23 75p + 25p Prus grn 2.40 4.75
B44 SP23 1.50d + 50p car 2.40 4.75
B45 SP23 1.75d + 25p choc 10.00 14.50
Nos. B43-B45 (3) 14.80 24.00
Set, never hinged 27.50

60th anniversary of Sokols of Zagreb.

Mother and Children SP24 SP25

Perf. 12½x11½

1935, Dec. 25 **Photo.**

B46 SP24 1.50d + 1d dk brn & brown 1.25 1.20
a. Perf. 11½ 12.00 14.50
B47 SP25 3.50d + 1.50d bright ultra & bl 2.00 2.90
Set, never hinged 6.50

The surtax was for "Winter Help."

Queen Mother Marie — SP26

1936, May 3 **Litho.**

B48 SP26 75p + 25p grnsh bl .25 .40
B49 SP26 1.50d + 50p rose pink .25 .45
B50 SP26 1.75d + 75p brown 1.25 1.25
B51 SP26 3.50d + 1d brt bl 1.60 2.75
Nos. B48-B51 (4) 3.35 4.85
Set, never hinged 6.50

Prince Regent Paul — SP27

1936, Sept. 20 **Typo.**

B52 SP27 75p + 50p turq grn & red .40 *.35*
B53 SP27 1.50d + 50p cer & red .40 *.35*
Set, never hinged 1.60

Surtax for the Red Cross.

Princes Tomislav and Andrej SP28 SP29

Perf. 11½x12½, 12½x11½

1937, May 1

B54 SP28 25p + 25p red brn .25 .25
B55 SP28 75p + 75p emerald .25 .40
B56 SP29 1.50d + 1d org red .30 .65
B57 SP29 2d + 1d magenta .60 1.20
Nos. B54-B57 (4) 1.40 2.50
Set, never hinged 2.40

Souvenir Sheet

National Costumes — SP30

1937, Sept. 12 *Perf. 14*

B57A SP30 Sheet of 4 4.75 10.00
Never hinged 9.50
b. 1d blue green 1.00 1.75
c. 1.50d bright violet 1.00 1.75
d. 2d rose red 1.00 1.75
e. 4d dark blue 1.00 1.75

1st Yugoslavian Phil. Exhib., Belgrade. Sold only at the exhibition post office at 15d each.

SP31

SP32

Perf. 11½x12½, 12½x11½

1938, May 1 **Photo.**

B58 SP31 50p + 50p dark brn .25 .30
B59 SP32 1d + 1d dk green .25 .35
B60 SP31 1.50d + 1.50d scar .50 .40
B61 SP32 2d + 2d magenta 1.25 .80
Nos. B58-B61 (4) 2.25 1.85
Set, never hinged 4.00

Surtax for the benefit of Child Welfare. For overprints see Nos. B75-B78.

Bridge and Anti-aircraft Lights — SP33

1938, May 28 *Perf. 11½x12½*

B62 SP33 1d + 50p dk grn .40 .80
B63 SP33 1.50d + 1d scarlet .60 1.20
a. Perf. 11½ 17.50 27.50
B64 SP33 2d + 1d rose vio 1.25 2.40
a. Perf. 11½ 18.00 35.00
B65 SP33 3d + 1.50d dp bl 2.00 4.00
Nos. B62-B65 (4) 4.25 8.40
Set, never hinged 8.00

Intl. Aeronautical Exhib., Belgrade.

Cliff at Demir-Kapiya SP34

Modern Hospital SP35

Runner Carrying Torch — SP36

Alexander I — SP37

Perf. 11½x12½, 12½x11½

1938, Aug. 1

B66 SP34 1d + 1d slate grn & dp grn .45 .40
B67 SP35 1.50d + 1.50d scar .70 .55
B68 SP36 2d + 2d claret & dp rose 1.60 3.25
B69 SP37 3d + 3d dp bl 1.60 3.25
Nos. B66-B69 (4) 4.35 7.45
Set, never hinged 9.00

The surtax was to raise funds to build a hospital for railway employees.

Runner SP38

Shot-Putter SP41

Hurdlers SP39

Pole Vaulter — SP40

1938, Sept. 11

B70 SP38 50p + 50p org brn 1.50 3.00
B71 SP39 1d + 1d sl grn & dp grn 1.50 3.00
B72 SP40 1.50d + 1.50d rose & dk mag 1.50 3.00
B73 SP41 2d + 2d dk blue 3.00 6.00
Nos. B70-B73 (4) 7.50 15.00
Set, never hinged 16.00

Ninth Balkan Games.

Stamps of 1938 Overprinted in Black

a

b

1938, Oct. 1

B75 SP31(a) 50p + 50p dk brn .40 .55
B76 SP32(b) 1d + 1d dk grn .40 .80
B77 SP31(a) 1.50d + 1.50d scar .60 1.20
B78 SP32(b) 2d + 2d mag 1.25 2.40
Nos. B75-B78 (4) 2.65 4.95
Set, never hinged 5.25

Surtax for the benefit of Child Welfare.

Postriders SP43

1d+1d, Rural mail delivery. 1.50d+1.50d, Mail train. 2d+2d, Mail bus. 4d+4d, Mail plane.

1939, Mar. 15 **Photo.** *Perf. 11½*

B79 SP43 50p + 50p buff, bis & brown .35 .75
B80 SP43 1d + 1d sl grn & dp green .35 .75
B81 SP43 1.50d + 1.50d red, cop red & brn car 2.50 2.50
B82 SP43 2d + 2d dp plum & rose lilac 2.50 3.50
B83 SP43 4d + 4d ind & sl bl 3.00 5.00
Nos. B79-B83 (5) 8.70 12.50
Set, never hinged 17.00

Centenary of the present postal system in Yugoslavia. The surtax was used for the Railway Benevolent Association.

The Cyrillic and Latin inscriptions are transposed on Nos. B82 and B83.

Child Eating SP48

Children at Seashore SP49

Boy Planing Board — SP50

Children in Crib — SP51

1939, May 1 *Perf. 12½*

B84 SP48 1d + 1d blk & dp bl green .50 1.00
B85 SP49 1.50d + 1.50d org brn & sal 2.00 3.25
a. Perf. 11½ 80.00 160.00
B86 SP50 2d + 2d mar & vio rose 1.40 2.90
B87 SP51 4d + 4d ind & royal blue 1.40 2.90
Nos. B84-B87 (4) 5.30 10.05
Set, never hinged 10.50

The surtax was for the benefit of Child Welfare.

Czar Lazar of Serbia SP52

Milosh Obilich SP53

1939, June 28 *Perf. 11½*

B88 SP52 1d + 1d sl grn & bl grn 1.60 1.60
B89 SP53 1.50d + 1.50d mar & brt car 1.60 1.60
Set, never hinged 6.50

Battle of Kosovo, 550th anniversary.

Training Ship "Jadran" — SP54

Designs: 1d+50p, Steamship "King Alexander." 1.50d+1d, Freighter "Triglan." 2d+1.50d, Cruiser "Dubrovnik."

1939, Sept. 6 **Engr.**

B90 SP54 50p + 50p brn org .40 .80
B91 SP54 1d + 50p dull grn .80 1.60
B92 SP54 1.50d + 1d dp rose 1.25 2.40
B93 SP54 2d + 1.50d dark bl 2.00 4.00
Nos. B90-B93 (4) 4.45 8.80
Set, never hinged 9.00

Yugoslav Navy and Merchant Marine. The surtax aided a Marine Museum.

Nos. B90-B93 also exist with a small "S" engraver's mark. Set value NH, $160. Location of the mark: On No. B90, above the base of the bowsprit. On No. B91, at the top of the smoke plume just below the "B" in the country name. On No. B92, at the top left of the large numeral "1". On No. B93, in the curve of the numeral "2".

Motorcycle and Sidecar SP58

Racing Car SP59

Motorcycle SP60

Racing Car SP61

1939, Sept. 3 **Photo.**

B94 SP58 50p + 50p multi .50 .80
B95 SP59 1d + 1d multi 1.00 1.60
B96 SP60 1.50d + 1.50d multi 1.40 2.40
B97 SP61 2d + 2d multi 2.50 4.00
Nos. B94-B97 (4) 5.40 8.80
Set, never hinged 10.50

Automobile and Motorcycle Races, Belgrade. The surtax was for the Race Organization and the State Treasury.

Unknown Soldier Memorial — SP62

1939, Oct. 9 *Perf. 12½*

B98 SP62 1d + 50p sl grn & green 1.00 1.60
B99 SP62 1.50d + 1d red & rose red 1.00 1.60
B100 SP62 2d + 1.50d dp cl & vio rose 1.25 2.40
B101 SP62 3d + 2d dp bl & bl 2.50 4.00
Nos. B98-B101 (4) 5.75 9.60
Set, never hinged 11.00

Assassination of King Alexander, 5th anniv. The surtax was used to aid World War I invalids.

Postman Delivering Mail — SP64

Postman Emptying Mail Box — SP65

Parcel Post Delivery Wagon — SP66

Parcel Post SP67

Repairing Telephone Wires SP68

1940, Jan. 1

B102 SP64 50p + 50p brn & deep org .60 1.00
B103 SP65 1d + 1d sl grn & blue grn .60 1.00
B104 SP66 1.50d + 1.50d red brn & scar 1.00 2.40
B105 SP67 2d + 2d dl vio & red lilac 1.25 2.40
B106 SP68 4d + 4d sl bl & bl 4.00 6.50
Nos. B102-B106 (5) 7.45 13.30
Set, never hinged 14.50

The surtax was used for the employees of the Postal System in Belgrade.

Croats' Arrival at Adriatic in 640 SP69

King Tomislav SP70

Death of Matija Gubec
SP71

Anton and Stjepan Radic
SP72

Map of Yugoslavia
SP73

1940, Mar. 1 Typo. *Perf. 11½*

B107	SP69	50p + 50p brn org	.40	.55
B108	SP70	1d + 1d green	.40	.55
B109	SP71	1.50d + 1.50d brt red	1.25	.55
B110	SP72	2d + 2d dk cerise	2.00	2.40
B111	SP73	4d + 2d dark blue	2.00	2.75
		Nos. B107-B111 (5)	6.05	6.80
		Set, never hinged	12.00	

The surtax was used for the benefit of postal employees in Zagreb.

Children Playing in Snow
SP74

Children at Seashore
SP75

1940, May 1 Photo. *Perf. 11½, 12½*

B112	SP74	50p + 50p brn org & org yellow	.25	.40
B113	SP75	1d + 1d sl grn & dk green	.25	.40
B114	SP74	1.50d + 1.50d brn red & scarlet	.60	.80
B115	SP75	2d + 2d mar & vio rose	1.00	1.60
		Nos. B112-B115 (4)	2.10	3.20
		Set, never hinged	4.00	

The surtax was for Child Welfare.

Nos. C11-C14 Surcharged in Carmine

Perf. 11½x12½, 12½x11½

1940, Dec. 23

B116	AP6	50p + 50p on 5d	.25	.25
B117	AP7	1d + 1d on 10d	.25	.40
a.		Perf. 12½	*40.00*	*40.00*
B118	AP8	1.50d + 1.50d on 20d	.80	1.40
B119	AP9	2d + 2d on 30d	.90	1.75
		Nos. B116-B119 (4)	2.20	3.80
		Set, never hinged	4.00	

The surtax was used to fight tuberculosis.
For surcharges see Nos. NB1-NB4.

St. Peter's Cemetery, Ljubljana
SP76

Croatian, Serbian and Slovenian
SP77

Chapel at Kajmaktchalan
SP78

Memorial at Brezje
SP79

1941, Jan. 1 *Perf. 12½*

B120	SP76	50p + 50p gray grn & yel green	.25	.40
B121	SP77	1d + 1d brn car & dl rose	.25	.40
B122	SP78	1.50d + 1.50d myr grn & bl green	.60	1.25
B123	SP79	2d + 2d gray bl & pale lilac	1.00	2.00
		Nos. B120-B123 (4)	2.10	4.05
		Set, never hinged	4.00	

Surtax for the Ljubljana War Veterans Assoc.

Kamenita Gate, Zagreb
SP80

13th Century Cathedral, Zagreb
SP81

1941, Mar. 16 Engr. *Perf. 11½*

B124	SP80	1.50d + 1.50d choc	.60	1.25
B125	SP81	4d + 3d blue blk	.60	1.25
		Set, never hinged	2.75	

2nd Philatelic Exhibition of Croatia, at Zagreb, Mar. 16-27.

Nos. B124-B125 exist perf. 9½ on right side. Value, each $32.50.

No. B124 exists with "S" engraver's mark located next to the lower left window of the building. Value NH $80.

1941, Apr.

B126	SP80	1.50d + 1.50d bl black	12.00	24.00
B127	SP81	4d + 3d choc	12.00	24.00
		Set, never hinged	55.00	

Regional philatelic exhibition at Slavonski Brod. Nos. B126-B127 with gold overprint, "Nezavisna Drzava Hrvatska," are Croatia Nos. B1-B2.

Nos. B126-B127 exist perf. 9½ on right side. Value, each $40 unused, $80 never hinged, $80 used.

No. B126 exists with "S" engraver's mark located next to the lower left window of the building. Value NH $425.

Issues for Federal Republic

Carrying Wounded Soldier
SP82

Child
SP83

1945, Sept. 15 Typo. *Perf. 11½*

B131	SP82	1d + 4d deep ultra	.50	.80
B132	SP83	2d + 6d scarlet	.50	.80
		Set, never hinged	1.90	

The surtax was for the Red Cross.

Russia, Yugoslavia Flags — SP84

1945, Oct. 20 Photo. Unwmk.

B133	SP84	2d + 5d multi	.80	1.60
		Never hinged	1.60	

Liberation of Belgrade, 1st anniv.
Exist imperf. Value $50 unused, $100 never hinged.

Communications Symbols — SP85

1946, May 10 *Perf. 12½*

B134	SP85	1.50d + 1d emer	1.60	3.25
B135	SP85	2.50d + 1.50d car rose	1.60	3.25
B136	SP85	5d + 2d gray bl	1.60	3.25
B137	SP85	8d + 3.50d dl brn	1.60	3.25
		Nos. B134-B137 (4)	6.40	13.00
		Set, never hinged	12.00	

1st PTT Congress since liberation, May 10.

Flag and Young Laborers — SP86

Flag in Red or Carmine and Deep or Dark Blue

1946, Aug. 1 Litho.

B138	SP86	50p + 50p brn & buff	1.00	1.60
B139	SP86	1.50d + 1d dk grn & lt green	1.00	1.60
B140	SP86	2.50d + 2d rose vio & rose lilac	1.00	1.60
B141	SP86	5d + 3d gray bl & blue	1.00	1.60
		Nos. B138-B141 (4)	4.00	6.40
		Set, never hinged	8.00	

The surtax aided railroad reconstruction carried out by Yugoslav youths.

Handstand on Horizontal Bar — SP87

1947, Sept. 5 *Perf. 11½*

B142	SP87	1.50d + 50p dark grn	1.50	1.50
B143	SP87	2.50d + 50p carmine	1.50	1.50
B144	SP87	4d + 50p brt blue	1.50	1.50
		Nos. B142-B144 (3)	4.50	4.50
		Set, never hinged	9.00	

1947 Balkan Games, Sept. 5-7, Ljubljana.

Young Railway Laborers — SP88

1947, Sept. 25 Typo. *Perf. 11½x12*

B145	SP88	1d + 50p orange	.60	.75
B146	SP88	1.50d + 1d yel green	.60	.75
B147	SP88	2.50d + 1.50d car lake	.60	.75
B148	SP88	5d + 2d deep blue	.60	.75
		Nos. B145-B148 (4)	2.40	3.00
		Set, never hinged	4.75	

The surtax was for youth brigades employed in the construction of the Samac-Sarajevo railway.

Symbolizing Protection of "B.C.G." Vaccine
SP89

Dying Serpent
SP91

"Illness" and "Recovery" — SP90

1948, Apr. 1 Litho. *Perf. 12½*

B149	SP89	1.50d + 1d sl blk & red	.40	.80
B150	SP90	2.50d + 2d grnsh gray, ol blk & red	.40	.80
B151	SP91	5d + 3d dk bl & car	.40	.80
		Nos. B149-B151 (3)	1.20	2.40
		Set, never hinged	2.40	

Fight against tuberculosis. The surtax was for the Yugoslav Red Cross.

Juro Danicic — SP92

Portraits: 2.50d+1d, Franjo Racki. 4d+2d, Josip J. Strossmayer.

1948, July 28 *Perf. 11*

B152	SP92	1.50d + 50p blk green	.80	.80
B153	SP92	2.50d + 1d dark red	.80	.80
B154	SP92	4d + 2d dark blue	.80	.80
		Nos. B152-B154 (3)	2.40	2.40
		Set, never hinged	4.75	

Yugoslav Academy of Arts and Sciences, Zagreb, 80th anniv. The surtax was for the Academy.

Shot Put — SP93

1948, Sept. 10 *Perf. 12½*

B155	SP93	2d + 1d shown	.40	.80
B156	SP93	3d + 1d Hurdles	.40	.80
B157	SP93	5d + 2d Pole vault	1.00	1.25
		Nos. B155-B157 (3)	1.80	2.85
		Set, never hinged	3.50	

Balkan and Central Europe Games, 1948. On sale 4 days.

AIR POST STAMPS

Dubrovnik
AP1

Lake Bled
AP2

Falls of Jaice
AP3

Church at Oplenac
AP4

Bridge at Mostar — AP5

Perf. 12½

1934, June 15 Typo. Unwmk.

C1	AP1	50p violet brown	.25	.25
C2	AP2	1d green	.25	.25
C3	AP3	2d rose red	.50	.30
C4	AP4	3d ultramarine	1.40	.45
C5	AP5	10d vermilion	2.75	4.25
		Nos. C1-C5 (5)	5.15	5.50
		Set, never hinged	9.50	

King Alexander Memorial Issue

No. 4 Overprinted in Black

1935, Jan. 1

C6 AP4 3d ultramarine 3.25 4.75
Never hinged 6.50

St. Naum Convent AP6

Port of Rab AP7

Sarajevo — AP8

Ljubljana — AP9

Perf. 11½x12½, 12½x11½

1937, Sept. 12		**Photo.**	
C7 AP6 50p brown		.25	.25
a. Perf. 12½		.25	.25
C8 AP7 1d yellow grn		.25	.25
a. Perf. 12½		.25	.25
C9 AP8 2d blue gray		.25	.25
a. Perf. 12½		.25	.25
C10 AP9 2.50d rose red		.25	.25
a. Perf. 12½		.25	.25
C11 AP6 5d brn violet		.25	.25
a. Perf. 12½		.25	.25
C12 AP7 10d brown lake		.50	.25
a. Perf. 12½		.70	.25
C13 AP8 20d dark green		5.25	8.00
a. Perf. 12½		.70	1.00
C14 AP9 30d ultramarine		18.00	27.50
a. Perf. 12½		1.00	1.75
Nos. C7-C14 (8)		25.00	37.00
Nos. C7-C14, never hinged		47.50	
Nos. C7a-C14a, never hinged		5.50	

For surcharges see Nos. B116-B119, NB1-NB4, NC1-NC8.

Cathedral of Zagreb — AP10

Bridge at Belgrade — AP11

1940, Aug. 15 Litho. *Perf. 12½*

C15 AP10 40d Prus grn & pale green 4.50 *3.50*
C16 AP11 50d bl & pale bl 4.50 *5.00*
Set, never hinged 17.50

For overprints see Nos. NC9-NC10.

Issues for Federal Republic

Plane over Terrace of Kalimegdan, Belgrade AP12

Plane over Dubrovnik AP13

1947, Apr. 21 Typo. *Perf. 11½*

Cyrillic Inscription at Top

C17 AP12 50p ol gray & brn vio .25 .25
C18 AP13 1d mag & ol gray .25 .25
C19 AP12 2d blue & black .25 .25
C20 AP13 5d green & gray .25 .25
C21 AP12 10d olive bis & choc .25 .25
C22 AP13 20d ultra & olive .60 1.25

Roman Inscription at Top

C23 AP12 50p ol gray & brn vio .25 .25
C24 AP13 1d mag & ol gray .25 .25
C25 AP12 2d blue & black .25 .25
C26 AP13 5d green & gray .25 .25
C27 AP12 10d olive bis & choc .25 .25
C28 AP13 20d ultra & olive .60 1.25
Nos. C17-C28 (12) 3.70 5.00
Set, never hinged 4.75

Sheets of each denomination contain alternately stamps with Cyrillic or Roman inscription at top. Value, 6 se-tenant pairs: unused $24; never hinged $47.50.

Laurent Kosir and Birthplace AP14

1948, Aug. 27 Engr.

C29 AP14 15d red violet .60 1.25
Never hinged 1.25

Kosir, recognized by Yugoslavia as inventor of the postage stamp, 80th death anniv. Issued in sheets of 25 stamps and 25 labels.

Nos. 262 to 264 Overprinted in Blue or Carmine

1949, Aug. 25 Unwmk. *Perf. 12½*

C30 A55 3d carmine rose 5.50 8.00
C31 A56 5d dull blue (C) 5.50 8.00
C32 A57 12d red brown 5.50 8.00
Nos. C30-C32 (3) 16.50 24.00
Never hinged 32.50

Liberation of Macedonia, 5th anniv.
It is reported that No. C32 was not sold to the public at the post office.

Souvenir Sheet

Electric Train — AP15

Perf. 11½x12½

1949, Dec. 15 Photo.

C33 AP15 10d lilac rose 90.00 105.00
Never hinged 175.00
a. Imperf. 90.00 105.00
Never hinged 175.00

Centenary of Yugoslav railroads.
For overprint see Trieste No. C17.

Iron Gate, Derdap — AP16

Belgrade AP17

Designs: 2d, Cascades, Plitvice. 3d, Carniola. 6d, Roman bridge, Mostar. 10d, Ohrid. 20d, Gulf of Kotor. 30d, Dubrovnik. 50d, Bled.

Perf. 12½

1951, June 16 Unwmk. Engr.

C34 AP16 1d deep org .25 .25
C35 AP16 2d dk green .25 .25
C36 AP16 3d dark red .25 .25
C37 AP16 6d ultra 2.00 4.00
C38 AP16 10d dark brn .25 .25
C39 AP16 20d grnsh blk .40 .25
C40 AP16 30d dp claret 1.00 .25
C41 AP16 50d dk purple 1.40 .25
C42 AP17 100d dk gray bl 27.50 9.00
Nos. C34-C42 (9) 33.30 14.75
Set, never hinged 65.00

Souvenir Sheet

Imperf

C43 AP17 100d red brn 90.00 175.00
Never hinged 175.00

See Nos. C50-C53. For overprints see Nos. C44, C49, Trieste C22-C32.

Roman Bridge Type of 1951 Overprinted "ZEFIZ 1951" in Carmine

1951, June 16 *Perf. 12½*

C44 AP16 6d dark green 4.00 3.75
Never hinged 8.00

Nos. C43-C44 were issued for Zagreb Philatelic Exhibition, June 16-26.

View on Mt. Kopaonik — AP18

Perf. 12½

1951, July Unwmk. Photo.

C45 AP18 3d shown 1.00 2.00
C46 AP18 5d Mt. Triglav 1.00 2.00
C47 AP18 20d Mt. Kalnik 35.00 *50.00*
Nos. C45-C47 (3) 37.00 54.00
Set, never hinged 70.00

Intl. Union of Mountaineers, 12th Assembly, Bled, July 13-18.

Plane and Parachutists — AP19

1951, Aug. 16 Engr.

C48 AP19 6d carmine 2.00 2.00

Type of 1951 Overprinted in Carmine

C49 AP16 50d blue 32.50 40.00

First World Parachute Championship, Bled, Aug. 16-20.
Nos. C48-C49, never hinged $65.

Catalogue values for unused stamps in this section, from this point to the end of the section, are for Never Hinged items.

Types of 1951

Designs: 5d, Cascades, Plitvice. 100d, Carniola. 200d, Roman bridge, Mostar.

1951-52

C50 AP16 5d yel brn ('52) .40 .25
C51 AP16 100d green 1.75 .25
C52 AP16 200d deep car ('52) 2.50 .30
C53 AP17 500d blue vio ('52) 8.00 .40
Nos. C50-C53 (4) 12.65 1.20

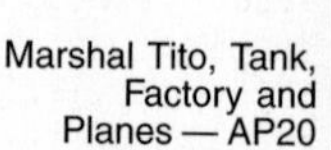

Marshal Tito, Tank, Factory and Planes — AP20

1951, Dec. 22 Unwmk.

C54 AP20 150d deep blue 12.00 10.00

Army Day, Dec. 22; 10th anniv. of the formation of the 1st military unit of "New" Yugoslavia.

Star and Flag-encircled Globe — AP21

1953, July 30 Engr.

C55 AP21 300d bl & grn 190.00 190.00

38th Esperanto Congress, Zagreb, 7/25-8/1.
For overprint see Trieste No. C21.

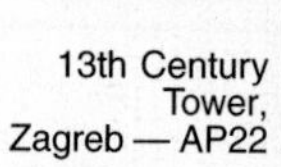

13th Century Tower, Zagreb — AP22

1956, May 20 *Perf. 11½*

Chalky Paper

C56 AP22 30d gray, vio bl & org red 3.25 1.40

Yugoslav Intl. Phil. Exhib., JUFIZ III, Zagreb, May 20-27.

Workers and Cogwheel — AP23

1956, June 15 Photo.

Glossy Paper

C57 AP23 30d car rose & blk 2.50 2.50

10th anniversary of technical education.

Moon and Earth with Satellites — AP24

1958, Oct. 24 Engr. *Perf. 12½*

C58 AP24 300d dark blue 12.00 4.50

Intl. Geophysical Year, 1957-58.

Types of Regular Issue, 1961

1961, Sept. 1 *Perf. 11½*

C59 A150 250d dark purple .90 .60
C60 A151 500d violet blue 2.00 1.25

Type of Athletic Regular Issue, 1962

Souvenir Sheet

Design: Army Stadium, Belgrade.

1962, Sept. 12 Litho. *Imperf.*

C61 A161 600d vio & blk 16.00 16.00

7th European Athletic Championships, Belgrade, Sept. 12-16.

REGISTERED LETTER STAMPS

Catalogue values for unused stamps in this section are for Never Hinged items.

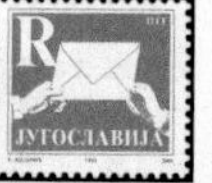

RL1

1993, June 28 Litho. *Perf. 13¼*

F1 RL1 (R) ultra 1.60 .40
a. Perf. 12½ 6.50 .55
b. Dated "1997" 6.50 .40

No. F1 was valued at 11,000d on day of issue. No. F1b issued 2/97.
For surcharge, see Serbia Nos. 194, 274.

Type of 1993

2002, July 25 **Litho.** ***Perf. 12½***

F2 RL1 R red 2.00 1.50

No. F2 was intended for use in Montenegro and was sold there for 39c in euro currency. The stamp was valid for use in the Serbian section of Yugoslavia.

POSTAGE DUE STAMPS

King Alexander — D1

1921 **Typo.** **Unwmk.** ***Perf. 11½***

Red or Black Surcharge

J1 D1 10p on 5p green (R) .25 .25
J2 D1 30p on 5p green (Bk) .25 .25
Set, never hinged .65

D2

D3

1921-22 **Typo.** ***Perf. 11½, Rough***

J3 D2 10p rose .25 .25
J4 D2 30p yellow green .25 .25
J5 D2 50p violet .25 .25
J6 D2 1d brown .30 .25
J7 D2 2d blue .40 .25
J8 D3 5d orange 2.00 .25
J9 D3 10d violet brown 6.00 .45
a. Cliche of 10p in sheet of 10d 190.00 —
J10 D3 25d pink 35.00 1.60
J11 D3 50d green 30.00 1.60
Nos. J3-J11 (9) 74.45 5.15
Set, never hinged 140.00

1924 ***Perf. 9, 10½, 11½, Clean-cut***

J12 D3 10p rose red .25 .25
J13 D3 30p yellow green .35 .40
J14 D3 50p violet .25 .25
J15 D3 1d brown .25 .25
J16 D3 2d deep blue .50 .25
J17 D3 5d orange 1.60 .25
J18 D3 10d violet brown 10.00 .25
J19 D3 25d pink 65.00 1.25
J20 D3 50d green 47.50 1.25
Nos. J12-J20 (9) 125.70 4.40
Set, never hinged 240.00

Nos. J19-J20 do not exist perf 9. Nos. J18-J20 do not exist perf 11½.

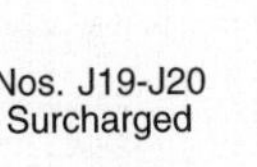

Nos. J19-J20 Surcharged

1928

J21 D3 10d on 25d pink 3.25 .40
J22 D3 10d on 50d green 3.25 .40
a. Inverted surcharge 30.00 18.00
Set, never hinged 13.00

A second type of "1" in surcharge has flag projecting horizontally. Value, each: $24 never hinged; $12 unused; $3.25 used.

Coat of Arms — D4

1931 **Typo.** ***Perf. 12½***

With Imprint at Foot

J23 D4 50p violet 1.40 .25
J24 D4 1d deep magenta 3.00 .25
J25 D4 2d deep blue 9.50 .25
J26 D4 5d orange 2.00 .25
J27 D4 10d chocolate 10.00 1.25
Nos. J23-J27 (5) 25.90 2.25
Set, never hinged 47.50

For overprints see Nos. NJ1-NJ13, Croatia 26-29, J1-J5.

1932 **Without Imprint at Foot**

J28 D4 50p violet .25 .25
J29 D4 1d deep magenta .25 .25
J30 D4 2d deep blue .25 .25
J31 D4 5d orange .25 .25
J32 D4 10d chocolate .25 .25
Nos. J28-J32 (5) 1.25 1.25

Numeral of Value — D5

Overprint in Green, Blue or Maroon

1933 ***Perf. 9, 10½, 11½***

J33 D5 50p vio (G) .25 .25
a. Perf. 10½ .30
J34 D5 1d brown (Bl) .25 .25
a. Perf. 10½ 2.00 1.40
J35 D5 2d blue (M) .25 .25
a. Perf. 10½ 1.00 1.25
J36 D5 5d orange (Bl) .80 .25
J37 D5 10d violet brn (Bl) 4.00 .25
Nos. J33-J37 (5) 5.55 1.25
Set, never hinged 10.50

Issues for Federal Republic

Redrawn Type OD5, German Occupation of Serbia, Overprinted in Black

1945 **Unwmk.** ***Perf. 12½***

J37A OD5 10d red .60 .55
J37B OD5 20d ultramarine .60 .55
Set, never hinged 2.40

In the redrawn design the eagle is replaced by a colorless tablet.

Coat of Arms — D6

1945 **Litho.** ***Perf. 12½***

Numerals in Black

J38 D6 2d brown violet .25 .25
J39 D6 3d violet .25 .25
J40 D6 5d green .25 .25
J41 D6 7d orange brown .25 .25
J42 D6 10d rose lilac .25 .25
J43 D6 20d blue .25 .25
J44 D6 30d light bl grn .40 .35
J45 D6 40d rose red .40 .40

Numerals in Color of Stamp

J46 D6 1d blue green .25 .25
J47 D6 1.50d blue .25 .25
J48 D6 2d vermilion .40 .25
J49 D6 3d violet brown .40 .25
J50 D6 4d rose violet .60 .25
Nos. J38-J50 (13) 4.20 3.50
Set, never hinged 6.50

For overprints see Nos. J64-J66.

Torches and Star — D7

1946-47 **Typo.** **Unwmk.**

J51 D7 50p dp orange ('47) .25 .25
J52 D7 1d orange .25 .25
J53 D7 2d dark blue .25 .25
J54 D7 3d yellow green .25 .25
J55 D7 5d bright purple .25 .25
J56 D7 7d crimson .80 .25
J57 D7 10d brt pink ('47) .80 .25
J58 D7 20d rose lake ('47) 2.00 .55
Nos. J51-J58 (8) 4.85 2.30
Set, never hinged 8.00

See Nos. J67-J79. For overprints see Trieste Nos. J1-J5, J11-J18. For overprints on similar stamps of this type, see Istria and the Slovene Coast Nos. J20-J24.

Nos. J47, J49 and J50 Overprinted in Black

1950 **Litho.**

J64 D6 1.50d blue .25 .25
J65 D6 3d violet brown .25 .25
J66 D6 4d rose violet .25 .30
Nos. J64-J66 (3) .75 .80
Set, never hinged 1.25

Catalogue values for unused stamps in this section, from this point to the end of the section, are for Never Hinged items.

Type of 1946-47

1951-52 **Typo.** ***Perf. 12½***

J67 D7 1d brown ('52) .40 .25
J68 D7 2d emerald .40 .25
J69 D7 5d blue .55 .25
J70 D7 10d scarlet 1.25 .25
J71 D7 20d purple 2.00 .25
J72 D7 30d org yel ('52) 4.00 .25
J73 D7 50d ultramarine 16.00 .40
J74 D7 100d dp plum ('52) 55.00 2.00
Nos. J67-J74 (8) 79.60 3.90

For overprints see Istria Nos. J20-J24, Trieste J11-J18.

1962 **Litho.** ***Perf. 12½***

J75 D7 10d red orange 3.25 .25
J76 D7 20d purple 3.25 .25
J77 D7 30d orange 6.75 .25
J78 D7 50d ultramarine 32.50 .80
J79 D7 100d rose lake 20.00 1.25
Nos. J75-J79 (5) 65.75 2.80

OFFICIAL STAMPS

Issues for Federal Republic

Arms of the Federated People's Republic — O1

Perf. 12½

1946, Nov. 1 **Unwmk.** **Typo.**

O1 O1 50p orange .25 .25
O2 O1 1d blue green .25 .25
O3 O1 1.50d olive green .25 .25
O4 O1 2.50d red .25 .25
O5 O1 4d yellow brown .40 .25
O6 O1 5d deep blue .60 .25
O7 O1 8d chocolate 1.25 .25
O8 O1 12d violet 1.40 .25
Nos. O1-O8 (8) 4.65 2.00
Set, never hinged 8.00

For surcharges see Nos. 272A-272B, Istria 43, 45, 47, 49, 51.

POSTAL TAX STAMPS

Catalogue values for unused stamps in this section are for Never Hinged items.

The tax was for the Red Cross or The Olympic Fund unless otherwise noted.

Red Cross Emblem — PT1

Unwmk.

1933, Sept. 17 **Litho.** ***Perf. 13***

RA1 PT1 50p dark blue & red .65 .25

Obligatory on inland letters during Red Cross Week, Sept. 17-23.
See No. RAJ1.

Dr. Vladen Djordjevic — PT2

1936, Sept. 20 **Typo.** ***Perf. 12***

RA2 PT2 50p brn blk & red .40 .25

Obligatory on inland letters during Red Cross Week, Sept. 20-26.

Aiding the Wounded — PT3

1938, Sept. 18 **Litho.** ***Perf. 12½***

RA3 PT3 50p dk bl, red, yel & grn .40 .25

1940, Sept. 15 **Redrawn**

RA4 PT3 50p slate blue & red .55 .25

The inscription at the upper right of this stamp and the numerals of value are in smaller characters.
Obligatory on all letters during the second week of September.

Issues for Federal Republic

Ruined Dwellings — PT4

1947, Jan. 1 **Litho.** ***Perf. 12½***

RA5 PT4 50p brn & scarlet .25 .25

See No. RAJ2. For overprints see Trieste Nos. RA1, RAJ1.

Red Cross Nurse — PT5

1948, Oct. 1

RA6 PT5 50p dk vio bl & red .25 .25

See No. RAJ3.

Nurse and Child — PT6

1949, Nov. 5

RA7 PT6 50p red & brown .25 .25

See No. RAJ4. For overprints see Trieste Nos. RA2, RAJ2.

Nurse Holding Book — PT7

1950, Oct. 1

RA8 PT7 50p dark green & red .25 .25

Obligatory Oct. 1-8, 1950.
See No. RAJ6.

Hands Raising Red Cross Flag — PT8

1951, Oct. 7

RA9 PT8 50p vio bl & red .25 .25

Obligatory Oct. 7-14.
See No. RAJ6. For overprints see Trieste Nos. RA3, RAJ3.

Nurse — PT9

1952, Oct. 5 **Photo.** ***Perf. 12½***
RA10 PT9 50p gray & carmine .25 .25

For overprint see Trieste No. RA4.

Child Receiving Blood Transfusion — PT10

1953, Oct. 25 **Litho.**
RA11 PT10 2d red vio & red .40 .25

See No. RAJ8. For overprints see Trieste Nos. RA5, RAJ5.

Youths Carrying Flags — PT11

1954, Nov. 1
RA12 PT11 2d gray grn & red .40 .25

See Nos. RAJ9.

Infant — PT11a

1954, Oct. 4
RA12A PT11a 2d brn & salmon 1.25 .65

The tax was for Children's Week.

Girl — PT12

1955, Oct. 2 **Unwmk.** ***Perf. 12½***
RA13 PT12 2d dull red .40 .25

The tax was for child welfare.
See No. RAJ10.

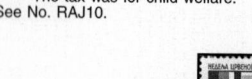

Nurse Opening Window — PT13

1955, Oct. 31
RA14 PT13 2d vio blk & red .25 .25

See No. RAJ11.

Ruins in the Snow — PT14

1956, May 6 ***Perf. 12½***
RA15 PT14 2d sepia & red .30 .25

See No. RAJ12.

Children and Goose — PT15

1956, Sept. 30
RA16 PT15 2d gray green .40 .25

The tax was for child welfare.
See No. RAJ13.

Plane over Temporary Shelter — PT16

1957, May 5 **Litho.**
RA17 PT16 2d lt bl, blk & car .30 .25

See No. RAJ14.

Girl and Boy Pioneers — PT17

1957, Sept. 30 **Unwmk.** ***Perf. 12½***
RA18 PT17 2d rose & gray .30 .25

Children's Week. Obligatory Oct. 2-6.
See No. RAJ15.

Woman Pouring Water — PT17a

1958, May 4 ***Perf. 12½x12***
RA19 PT17a 2d multicolored .40 .25

Issued to honor the United Nations.
On No. RA19 the UN emblem has been left out, Cyrillic inscriptions at left added, country name in Latin letters.
See Nos. 375-377; No. RAJ16.

Playing Children — PT18

1958, Oct. 5 **Litho.** ***Perf. 12½***
RA20 PT18 2d brt yel & black .25 .25

Children's Week, Oct. 5-11.

Helping Hand and Family — PT19

1959, May 3
RA21 PT19 2d blue vio & red .30 .25

Red Cross centenary. Obligatory May 3-9.
See No. RAJ18.

Blackboard, Flower and Fish — PT20

1959, Oct. 5 **Unwmk.**
RA22 PT20 2d ocher & dp gray grn .30 .25

Children's Week. Obligatory on domestic mail, Oct. 5-11.

See No. RAJ19.

"Reconstruction" PT21

1960, May 8 ***Perf. 12½***
RA23 PT21 2d slate & red .30 .25

Obligatory May 8-14. See No. RAJ20.

Girl and Toys — PT22

1960, Oct. 2 **Litho.** ***Perf. 12½***
RA24 PT22 2d red .25 .25

Issued for Children's Week. Obligatory on domestic mail Oct. 2-8.
See No. RAJ21.

Blood Donor Symbolism — PT23

1961, May 7
RA25 PT23 2d multicolored .30 .25

Obligatory May 7-13. Exists imperf. Value $14.
See No. RAJ22.

Bird Holding Flower — PT24

1961, Oct. 1
RA26 PT24 2d orange & violet .25 .25

Children's Week. Exists imperf. Obligatory on domestic mail, Oct. 1-7.
See No. RAJ23.

Bandages and Symbols of Home, Industry, Weather, Transportation, Fire and Flood — PT25

1962, Apr. 30 ***Perf. 12½***
RA27 PT25 5d red brn, gray & red .25 .25

Obligatory on domestic mail May 6-12.
See No. RAJ24.

Centenary Emblem — PT26

1963, May 5 **Unwmk.** ***Perf. 12½***
RA28 PT26 5d dl yel, red & gray .30 .25

Intl. Red Cross, centenary. Exists imperf. Obligatory on all domestic mail during Red Cross Week, May 5-11.
See No. RAJ25.

Parachute Drop of Supplies, Yugoslav Flag — PT27

1964, Apr. 27 **Litho.**
RA29 PT27 5d blue, rose & dk bl .25 .25

Obligatory on domestic mail, May 3-9.

Children in Circle — PT28

1965, May 2 **Litho.** ***Perf. 12½***
RA30 PT28 5d tan & red .25 .25

Obligatory on domestic mail, May 2-8.

Arrows — PT29

1966, Apr. 28 **Litho.** ***Perf. 12½***
RA31 PT29 5p gray & multi .25 .25

Obligatory on domestic mail, May 1-7.

Crosses and Flower — PT30

1967, Apr. 28 **Litho.** ***Perf. 12½***
RA32 PT30 5p vio, red & yel grn .25 .25

Exists imperf.

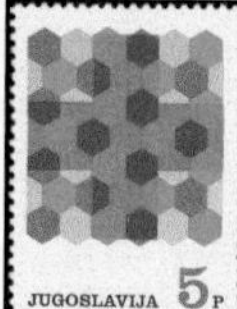
Honeycomb and Red Cross — PT31

1968, Apr. 30 **Litho.** ***Perf. 12***
RA33 PT31 5p multicolored .25 .25

Obligatory on all domestic mail May 5-11.

Aztec Calendar Stone and Olympic Rings — PT32

1968, Oct. 12 ***Perf. 12½***
RA34 PT32 10p black & multi .25 .25

Red Cross, Hands and Globe — PT33

1969, May 18 **Litho.** ***Perf. 12***
RA35 PT33 20p red org, dl red & blk .25 .25

Globe, Olympic Torch and Rings — PT34

1969, Nov. 24 Litho. *Perf. 11¼*
RA36 PT34 10p gold & multi 4.50 .25
a. Perf. 9 12.00 1.90

Yugoslav Olympic Committee, 50th anniv. Exists imperf. Value $125.

Symbolic Flower and People — PT35

1970, Apr. 27 Litho. *Perf. 13*
RA37 PT35 20p vio bl, org & red .25 .25

Olympic Flag — PT36

1970, June 10 Litho. *Perf. 13x13½*
RA38 PT36 10p multicolored .25 .25

Red Cross Encircling Globe — PT37

1971, Apr. 26 Litho. *Perf. 12½*
RA39 PT37 20p blue, yel & red .25 .25

Olympic Rings and Disk — PT38

1971, June 15 Litho. *Perf. 12½*
RA40 PT38 10p blue & black .25 .25

Red Cross and Hemispheres PT39

1972, Apr. 27 *Perf. 13½x13*
RA41 PT39 20p red & multi .25 .25

Olympic Rings, TV Tower, Munich and Sapporo Emblems — PT40

1972, May *Perf. 13x13½*
RA42 PT40 10p ultra & multi .25 .25

Red Cross, Crescent and Lion Emblems — PT41

1973, Apr. 24 Litho. *Perf. 13x13½*
RA43 PT41 20p blue & multi .25 .25

Globe and Olympic Rings — PT42

1973, June 1 Litho. *Perf. 13x13½*
RA44 PT42 10p multicolored .25 .25

Drop of Blood, Red Cross Emblems — PT43

1974, Apr. 25 Litho. *Perf. 13*
RA45 PT43 20p red & multi .25 .25

Olympic Rings — PT44

1974, June 1 Litho. *Perf. 13*
RA46 PT44 10p blue & multi .25 .25

Red Cross, Hands — PT45

1975, Apr. 23 Photo. *Perf. 11½*
RA47 PT45 20p blue, car & blk .25 .25

Olympic Rings — PT46

1975, June 2 Litho. *Perf. 13½*
RA48 PT46 10p multicolored .25 .25

Ruin and Clock — PT47

1975, July 26 Litho. *Perf. 13x13½*
RA49 PT47 30p gray, blk & dk bl .25 .25

Solidarity Week, July 26-Aug. 1. See Nos. RA61-RA62.

Red Crescent, Red Cross, Red Lion — PT48

1976, May 8 Photo. *Perf. 12½x13*
RA50 PT48 20p multicolored .80 .55

1984 Olympics — PT49

1976, July 26 Litho. *Perf. 13½*
RA51 PT49 10p intense blue .25 .25

Fight Tuberculosis, Red Cross — PT50

1977, Sept. 14 Photo.
RA52 PT50 50p multicolored 2.00 .80
RA53 PT50 1d multicolored 2.00 .80

Exist imperf.

1984 Olympics — PT51

1977, Dec. 17 *Perf. 13½x13*
RA54 PT51 10p multicolored .25 .25

Postal Tax Stamps for use in a particular republic or republics fall beyond the scope of this catalogue and are not listed. These stamps, issued since 1977, were not intended for nationwide use. Some of these issues have designs which are similar to stamps used nationwide, most notably those using variations of the Ruin and Clock (PT47) design. Most others show the Red Cross or the Tuberculosis Cross.

Red Crescent, Red Cross, Red Lion — PT52

1978, May 7 Litho. *Perf. 13½*
RA55 PT52 20p on 1d bl & red .50 .25
RA56 PT52 1d blue & red .30 .25

1984 Olympics — PT53

1978, Sept.
RA57 PT53 30p multicolored .35 .25

8th Mediterranean Games, Split, Sept. 15-29 — PT54

1979, Mar. 1 Photo. *Perf. 13½x13*
RA58 PT54 1d violet .25 .25
RA59 PT54 1d greenish blue .25 .25

Red Cross Week — PT55

1979, May 6 *Perf. 13½*
RA60 PT55 1d multicolored .25 .25

Ruin and Clock Type of 1975 Inscribed "1.-7.VI"

1979, June 1
RA61 PT47 30p blk & intense bl .25 .25

Solidarity Week.

Ruin and Clock Type of 1975 Inscribed "1.-7.VI"

1980, June 1 Litho. *Perf. 13x13½*
RA62 PT47 1d black & blue .25 .25

Solidarity Week, June 1-7.

Olympic Week — PT57

1979, Oct. 15 Photo. *Perf. 14*
RA63 PT57 30p blue & red .25 .25

Sculpture, Red Cross — PT58

1980, May 4 Litho. *Perf. 13½*
RA64 PT58 1d multicolored .35 .30

Olympic Week — PT59

1980, Oct. 20 *Perf. 14*
RA65 PT59 50p multicolored .40 .25

SPENS '81, Novi Sad — PT60

1980, Dec. 20 *Perf. 13½*
RA66 PT60 1d multicolored .25 .25

Red Cross — PT61

1981, May 4 Photo.
RA67 PT61 1d multicolored .25 .25

Fight Tuberculosis, Red Cross — PT62

1981, Sept. 14
RA68 PT62 1d multicolored .25 .25

Handshake — PT63

1982, May Litho. *Perf. 13*
RA69 PT63 1d black & red .25 .25

Robert Koch — PT64

1983, Sept. 18 Litho. *Perf. 13*
RA70 PT64 1d multicolored .25 .25

For surcharge see No. RA76.

Fight Tuberculosis, Red Cross — PT65

1983, Sept. 14 Litho. *Perf. 13½*
RA71 PT65 1d bluish grn, blk & red .25 .25
RA72 PT65 2d bluish grn, blk & red .25 .25

1984 Winter Olympics, Sarajevo — PT66

1983, Oct. 20 Litho. *Perf. 12½*
RA73 PT66 2d greenish blue .25 .25

PLANICA 50 — PT67

1985, Apr. 1 Photo. *Perf. 14*
RA74 PT67 2d brt ultra & blue .25 .25

Ruin, Clock and Red Cross — PT68

1987, June 1 Litho. *Perf. 10*
RA75 PT68 30d multicolored .25 .25

Solidarity Week, June 1-7.

No. RA70 Surcharged in Silver

1988, Sept. 14 Litho. *Perf. 13*
RA76 PT64 12d on 1d multi 8.00 8.00

Intl. Red Cross, 125th Anniv. — PT69

1989, May 8 Litho. *Perf. 12x11*
Without Gum
RA77 PT69 20d bl, sil & red .40 .40
RA78 PT69 80d bl, sil & red .40 .40
RA79 PT69 150d bl, sil & red .40 .40
RA80 PT69 160d bl, sil & red .40 .40
Nos. RA77-RA80 (4) 1.60 1.60

Souvenir folders with perf. or imperf. miniature sheets of 4 sold for 3200d.

Ruin, Clock and Red Cross PT70

Building, Clock and Red Cross PT71

1989, June 1 *Perf. 10*
Without Gum
RA81 PT70 250d red & silver .55 .40
Roulette 10
RA82 PT71 400d brt bl gray & red 1.00 .50

Souvenir folders with perf. or imperf. miniature sheets containing one 45x65mm stamp like RA81 sold for 3200d.

Fight TB, Red Cross — PT72

1989, Sept. 14 *Rough Perf. 10½*
Without Gum
RA83 PT72 20d black & red .30 .30
RA84 PT72 200d black & red .30 .30
RA85 PT72 250d black & red .30 .30
RA86 PT72 400d black & red .30 .30
RA87 PT72 650d black & red .30 .30
Nos. RA83-RA87 (5) 1.50 1.50

Red Cross — PT73

1990, May 8 *Perf. 13½*
Without Gum
RA88 PT73 10p green & red .80 .25
Perf. 12½
RA89 PT73 20p green & red .80 .25
a. Perf. 13½ .80 .25
RA90 PT73 30p green & red .80 .25
Nos. RA88-RA90 (3) 2.40 .75

Flowers PT74

Macedonian Red Cross, 45th Anniv. PT75

1990, May 8 *Perf. 10*
Without Gum
RA91 PT74 20p shown .25 .25
RA92 PT74 20p multi, diff. .25 .25
RA93 PT75 20p multicolored .25 .25
a. Block of 3 + label, #RA91-RA93 .80 .80

Souvenir folders with perf. or imperf. miniature sheets of 3 + label sold for 4d.

PT76

1990, Sept. 14 Litho. *Perf. 10*
Without Gum
RA94 PT76 20p blue, org & red .40 .40
RA95 PT76 25p blue, yel & red .40 .40
RA96 PT76 50p blue, yel & red .40 .40
Nos. RA94-RA96 (3) 1.20 1.20

Fight tuberculosis, Red Cross.

PT77

1991, Sept. 14 Litho. *Perf. 12½*
Without Gum
RA97 PT77 1.20d dk bl, yel & red .30 .30
RA98 PT77 2.50d multicolored .30 .30

Required on mail 9/14-21/91.

PT78

1994, May 8 Litho. *Perf. 13½*
RA99 PT78 10p multicolored 1.00 .50

No. RA99 was required on mail 5/8-15/94.

PT79

1994, Sept. 14 Litho. *Perf. 13x13½*
RA100 PT79 10p multicolored 1.00 .50

No. RA100 was required on mail 9/14-21/94.

PT80

1995, May 8 Litho. *Perf. 13½x13*
RA101 PT80 10p multicolored 1.00 .50

No. RA101 was required on mail 5/8-15/95.

PT81

1995, Sept. 9 Litho. *Perf. 13½x13*
RA102 PT81 10p Wilhelm Röntgen 1.00 .50

Fight Tuberculosis. No. RA102 was required on mail 9/9-14/95.

PT82

1996, May 8 Litho. *Perf. 12x12½*
RA103 PT82 15p multicolored .40 .30

No. RA103 was required on mail 5/8-15/96.

PT83

1996, Sept. Litho. *Perf. 12x12½*
RA104 PT83 20p multicolored 2.00 .40

PT84

1997, May 8 Litho. *Perf. 13*
RA105 PT84 20p multicolored 5.00 1.00

No. RA105 was required on mail 5/8-15/97.

Milutin Rankovic (1880-1967), Artist — PT85

1997, Sept. 14 Litho. *Perf. 14*
RA106 PT85 20p multicolored .40 .40

Fight Tuberculosis. No. RA106 was required on mail 9/14-21/97.

PT86

1998, May 8 Litho. *Perf. 13¾*
RA107 PT86 20p multicolored .40 .40

No. RA107 was required on mail 5/8-15/98.

Red Cross — PT87

1999, May 8 Litho. *Perf. 13¾*
RA108 PT87 1d multi 2.00 .50

No. RA108 was required on mail 5/8-5/15/99.

Red Cross — PT88

1999, Sept. 14
RA109 PT88 1d multi 7.00 .70

No. RA109 was required on mail 9/14-9/21/99.

POSTAL TAX DUE STAMPS

Catalogue values for unused stamps in this section are for Never Hinged items.

The tax of Nos. RAJ1-RAJ9, RAJ11-RAJ12, RAJ14 and RAJ18 was for the Red Cross.

Inscribed "PORTO."

Type of Postal Tax Stamp, 1933

1933 Unwmk. Litho. *Perf. 12½*
RAJ1 PT1 50p dull grn & red 1.00 .25
a. Perf. 11½ 20.00 8.00

Type of Postal Tax Stamp, 1947

1947
RAJ2 PT4 50p blue grn & scar .50 .25

For surcharge see Trieste No. RAJ1.

Type of Postal Tax Stamp, 1948

1948
RAJ3 PT5 50p dark grn & red .40 .25

Type of Postal Tax Stamp, 1949

1949
RAJ4 PT6 50p red & violet .55 .25

For overprint see Trieste No. RAJ2.

Cross and Map of Yugoslavia — PTD2

1950 Unwmk. *Perf. 12½*
RAJ5 PTD2 50p red brown & red .40 .25

Exists imperf.

Type of Postal Tax Stamp, 1951

1951
RAJ6 PT8 50p emerald & red .40 .25

For overprint see Trieste No. RAJ3.

Red Cross — PTD3

1952 Unwmk. Photo. *Perf. 12½*
RAJ7 PTD3 50p gray & car .65 .25

For overprint see Trieste No. RAJ4.

Type of Postal Tax Stamp, 1953

1953 Litho.
RAJ8 PT10 2d yel brown & red .80 .40

For overprints see Trieste Nos. RAJ5.

Type of Postal Tax Stamp, 1954

1954 **Litho.**

RAJ9	PT11	2d lilac & red ('54)	.75	.30

Types of Postal Tax Stamps, 1955

1955 **Litho.**

RAJ10	PT12	2d yel grn ('55)	.55	.25
RAJ11	PT13	2d dk vio brn & red ('55)	.80	.25

Types of Postal Tax Stamps, 1956

1956 **Litho.**

RAJ12	PT14	2d blue grn & red ('56)	.55	.25
RAJ13	PT15	2d violet brn ('56)	.55	.25

Types of Postal Tax Stamps, 1957

1957 **Litho.**

RAJ14	PT16	2d gray, blk & car ('57)	.55	.25
RAJ15	PT17	2d lt bl, bis & grn ('57)	.55	.25

Redrawn Type of Regular Issue, 1953

1958 ***Perf. 12½x12***

RAJ16	A95	2d multicolored	.80	.40

See Nos. 375-377; No. RA19.

Child With Toy — PTD4

1958 **Litho.** ***Perf. 12½***

RAJ17	PTD4	2d lt ultra & blk	.55	.25

Issued for Children's Week, Oct. 5-11.

Type of Postal Tax Stamp, 1959

1959

RAJ18	PT19	2d yel org & red	.55	.25

Type of Postal Tax Stamp, 1959

Design: Tree, cock and wheat.

1959

RAJ19	PT20	2d ocher & red brn	.40	.25

Type of Postal Tax Stamp, 1960

1960

RAJ20	PT21	2d vio brn & red	.50	.25

Type of Postal Tax Stamp, 1960

Design: Boy, tools and ball.

1960

RAJ21	PT22	2d Prussian blue	.30	.25

Type of Postal Tax Stamp, 1961

1961, May 7

RAJ22	PT23	2d multicolored	.30	.25

Type of Postal Tax Stamp, 1961

1961, Oct. 1

RAJ23	PT24	2d apple grn & brn	.30	.25

Type of Postal Tax Stamp, 1962

1962, Apr. 30

RAJ24	PT25	5d brn red, bl & red	.30	.25

Type of Postal Tax Stamp, 1963

1963, May 5

RAJ25	PT26	5d red org, red & gray	.50	.25

OFFICES ABROAD

Catalogue values for unused stamps in this section are for Never Hinged items.

King Peter II — A1

1943 **Unwmk.** **Typo.** ***Perf. 12½***

1K1	A1	2d dark blue	.40	*4.00*
1K2	A1	3d slate	.40	*4.00*
1K3	A1	5d carmine	.40	*4.00*
1K4	A1	10d black	.40	*4.00*
		Nos. 1K1-1K4 (4)	1.60	*16.00*

For surcharges see Nos. 1KB1-1KB4.

V. Vodnik A2

Peter Nyegosh A3

3d, Ljudovit Gaj. 4d, Vuk Stefanovic Karadzic. 5d, Bishop Joseph Strossmayer. 10d, Karageorge.

1943, Dec. 1 **Engr.** ***Perf. 12½x13***

1K5	A2	1d red org & black	.40	*8.25*
1K6	A3	2d yel green & blk	.80	*8.50*
1K7	A2	3d dp ultra & blk	.80	*8.75*
1K8	A3	4d dk pur & brn blk	1.60	*9.25*
1K9	A2	5d brn vio & brn blk	1.60	*9.75*
1K10	A3	10d brn & brown blk	5.50	*10.00*
		Nos. 1K5-1K10 (6)	10.70	*54.50*

Souvenir Sheet
Center in Black

1K11	Sheet of 6, #1K5-1K10	65.00

25th anniv. of the Union of Liberated Yugoslavia. Valid on ships of the Yugoslav Navy and Mercantile Marine.

Nos. 1K5-1K10 overprinted diagonally "1945" in London were not issued. In 1950, they were sold by the Yugoslav Government without postal validity. Later they appeared with the additional overprint of the outline of a plane at upper left in carmine or black.

OFFICES ABROAD SEMI-POSTAL STAMPS

Nos. 1K1-1K4 Surcharged in Orange or Black

1943 **Unwmk.** ***Perf. 12½***

1KB1	A1	2d + 12.50d dk bl	2.40	*8.25*
1KB2	A1	3d + 12.50d slate	2.40	*8.25*
1KB3	A1	5d + 12.50d car (Bk)	2.40	*8.25*
1KB4	A1	10d + 12.50d black	2.40	*8.25*
		Nos. 1KB1-1KB4 (4)	9.60	*33.00*

The surtax was for the Red Cross.

LJUBLJANA

(Lubiana, Laibach)

Italian Occupation

Under Italian occupation in 1941, the western half of Slovenia was known as the Province of Ljubljana (Lubiana to the Italians, Laibach to the Germans) and a quisling administration was set up under the profascist General Rupnik.

100 Centesimi = 1 Lira

Yugoslavia Nos. 127, 128, 142-154 Overprinted in Black

1941 **Unwmk.** ***Perf. 12½, 13x12½***

N1	A16	25p black	3.25	4.00
N2	A16	50p orange	3.25	4.00
N3	A16	1d yellow grn	3.25	4.00
N4	A16	1.50d red	3.25	4.00
N5	A16	2d dp magenta	3.25	4.00
N6	A16	3d dl red brn	3.25	4.00
N7	A16	4d ultra	3.25	4.00
N8	A16	5d dark blue	3.25	4.00
N9	A16	5.50d dk vio brn	3.25	4.00
N10	A16	6d slate blue	4.75	9.50
N11	A16	8d sepia	4.75	9.50
N12	A10	10d bright vio	4.75	9.50
N13	A16	12d brt violet	12.00	14.50
N14	A10	15d brown	325.00	525.00
N15	A16	16d dl violet	12.00	14.50
N16	A16	20d blue	24.00	32.50
N17	A16	30d brt pink	52.50	95.00
		Nos. N1-N17 (17)	469.00	746.00
		Set, never hinged	1,100.	

Yugoslavia Nos. 127, 142-154 Overprinted in Black

N18	A16	25p black	3.25	3.25
N19	A16	50p orange	3.25	3.25
N20	A16	1d yellow grn	3.25	3.25
N21	A16	1.50d red	3.25	3.25
N22	A16	2d dp magenta	3.25	3.25
N23	A16	3d dl red brn	3.25	3.25
N24	A16	4d ultra	3.25	3.25
N25	A16	5d dark blue	3.25	3.25
N26	A16	5.50d dk vio brn	3.25	3.25
N27	A16	6d slate blue	3.25	3.25
N28	A16	8d sepia	3.25	3.25
N29	A10	10d brt violet	6.50	4.00
N30	A16	12d bright vio	3.25	3.25
N31	A16	16d dl violet	6.50	4.00
N32	A16	20d blue	20.00	27.50
N33	A16	30d brt pink	110.00	140.00

Yugoslavia Nos. 145, 148 Surcharged in Black

N34	A16	50p on 1.50d red	1.60	2.00
N35	A16	1d on 4d ultra	1.60	2.00
		Nos. N18-N35 (18)	185.20	218.50
		Set, never hinged	400.00	

German Occupation

Stamps of Italy, 1929-42, Overprinted or Surcharged in Blue, Carmine, Black or Green

a

b

c

1944 **Wmk. 140** ***Perf. 14***

N36	A90(a)	5c ol brown	.25	*5.50*
N37	A92(b)	10c dark brn	.25	*5.50*
N38	A93(a)	15c sl grn (C)	.25	*5.50*
N39	A91(b)	20c rose red	.25	*5.50*
N40	A94(a)	25c dp grn (C)	.25	*5.50*
N41	A95(b)	30c ol brown	.25	*5.50*
N42	A93(a)	35c dp bl (C)	.40	*5.50*
N43	A95(b)	50c purple (C)	.25	*7.00*
N44	A94(a)	75c rose red	.25	*10.50*
N45	A91(b)	1 l deep vio	.25	*10.50*
N46	A94(a)	1.25 l dp bl (C)	.25	*4.00*
N47	A92(b)	1.75 l red org	6.00	*24.00*
N48	A93(a)	2 l car lake	.25	*7.00*
N49	A90(c)	2.55 l on 5c ol brn (Bk)	2.40	*12.00*
N50	A94(a)	5 l on 25c dp grn	2.40	*20.00*
N51	A93(b)	10 l purple	10.00	*55.00*
N52	A91(a)	20 l on 20c rose red (G)	12.00	*65.00*
N53	A93(b)	25 l on 2 l car lake (G)	10.00	*125.00*
N54	A92(a)	50 l on 1.75 l red org (C)	40.00	*400.00*
		Nos. N36-N54 (19)	85.95	*778.50*
		Set, never hinged	175.00	

Krizna Jama — A1

Cerknica Lake — A2

Designs: 20c, Railroad Bridge, Borovnica. 25c, Landscape near Ljubljana. 50c, Church, Ribnica. 75c, View, Ljubljana. 1 l, Old Castle, Ljubljana. 1.25 l, Kocevje (Gottschee). 1.50 l, Borovnica Falls. 2 l, Castle, Konstanjevica. 2.50 l, Castle, Turjak. 3 l, Castle, Zuzemperk. 5 l, View of Krk. 10 l, View of Otolac. 20 l, Farm, Carniola. 30 l, Castle and church, Tabor.

Perf. 10½x11½, 11½x10½

1945 **Photo.** **Unwmk.**

N55	A1	5c black	.40	*4.00*
N56	A2	10c red orange	.40	*4.00*
N57	A2	20c brn carmine	.40	*4.00*
N58	A2	25c dk sl green	.40	*4.00*
N59	A1	50c deep violet	.40	*4.00*
N60	A2	75c vermilion	.40	*4.00*
N61	A2	1 l dark ol grn	.40	*4.00*
N62	A1	1.25 l dark blue	.40	*8.00*
N63	A1	1.50 l olive black	.40	*8.00*
N64	A2	2 l ultramarine	.60	*9.50*
N65	A2	2.50 l brown	.60	*9.50*
N66	A1	3 l brt red vio	1.50	*16.00*
N67	A2	5 l dk red brn	1.60	*16.00*
N68	A2	10 l slate green	3.25	*72.50*
N69	A2	20 l sapphire	20.00	*250.00*
N70	A1	30 l rose pink	95.00	*950.00*
		Nos. N55-N70 (16)	126.15	*1,368.*
		Set, never hinged	240.00	

SEMI-POSTAL STAMPS

Italian Occupation

Yugoslavia Nos. B116-B119 with Additional Ovpt. in Black

Perf. 11½x12½, 12½x11½

1941 **Unwmk.**

NB1	AP6	50p + 50p on 5d	9.50	14.50
NB2	AP7	1d + 1d on 10d	9.50	14.50
NB3	AP8	1.50d + 1.50d on 20d	9.50	14.50
NB4	AP9	2d + 2d on 30d	9.50	14.50
		Nos. NB1-NB4 (4)	38.00	58.00
		Set, never hinged	90.00	

German Occupation

Italy Nos. E14 & E15 Srchd. in Red

1944 **Wmk. 140**

NB5	SD4	1.25 l + 50 l green	35.00	*600.00*
NB6	SD4	2.50 l + 50 l dp org	35.00	*600.00*

The surtax aided the Red Cross.

Italy Nos. E4 & E15 Srchd. in Blue or Green

NB7	SD4	1.25 l + 50 l grn (B)	35.00	*600.00*
NB8	SD4	2.50 l + 50 l dp org	35.00	*600.00*
		Nos. NB5-NB8 (4)	140.00	*2,400.*
		Set, never hinged	275.00	

The surtax aided the Homeless Relief Fund.

The German and Slovenian inscriptions in the surcharges are transposed on Nos. NB6 and NB8.

Italy Nos. C12-C14, C16-C18 Srchd. in Blue or Red

Nos. NB9, NB11

Nos. NB10, NB12, NB14

No. NB13

1944 **Wmk. 140**

NB9	AP4	25c + 10 l dk grn	14.00	*400.00*
NB10	AP3	50c + 10 l ol brn	14.00	*400.00*
NB11	AP5	75c + 20 l org brn	14.00	*400.00*

NB12 AP5 1 l + 20 l vio 14.00 *400.00*
NB13 AP6 2 l + 20 l dp bl (R) 14.00 *400.00*
NB14 AP3 5 l + 20 l dk grn 14.00 *400.00*
Nos. NB9-NB14 (6) 84.00 *2,400.*
Set, never hinged 175.00

The surcharge aided orphans.

Italy Nos. C12-C14, C16-C18 Srchd. in Blue or Red

Nos. NB15, NB17

Nos. NB16, NB18, NB20

No. NB19

NB15 AP4 25c + 10 l dk grn 14.00 *400.00*
NB16 AP3 50c + 10 l ol brn 14.00 *400.00*
NB17 AP5 75c + 20 l org brn 14.00 *400.00*
NB18 AP5 1 l + 20 l pur 14.00 *400.00*
NB19 AP6 2 l + 20 l dp bl (R) 14.00 *400.00*
NB20 AP3 5 l + 20 l dk grn 14.00 *400.00*
Nos. NB15-NB20 (6) 84.00 *2,400.*
Set, never hinged 175.00

The surcharge was for winter relief.

AIR POST STAMPS

Italian Occupation

Yugoslavia Nos. C7-C16 Ovptd. like Nos. NB1-NB4

Perf. 12½, 12½x11½, 11½x12½

1941 **Unwmk.**

NC1 AP6 50p brown 11.00 11.00
NC2 AP7 1d yel grn 11.00 11.00
NC3 AP8 2d bl gray 12.50 12.50
NC4 AP9 2.50d rose red 12.50 12.50
NC5 AP6 5d brn vio 20.00 20.00
NC6 AP7 10d brn lake 20.00 20.00
NC7 AP8 20d dark grn 55.00 55.00
NC8 AP9 30d ultra 87.50 95.00
NC9 AP10 40d Prus grn & pale grn 300.00 360.00
NC10 AP11 50d sl bl & gray bl 240.00 240.00
a. Inverted overprint 950.00
Nos. NC1-NC10 (10) 769.50 837.00
Set, never hinged 1,800.

German Occupation

Italy Nos. C12-C14, C16-C19 Overprinted Types "a" and "b" in Carmine, Green or Blue

1944 **Wmk. 140** ***Perf. 14***

NC11 AP4(a) 25c dk grn (C) 10.00 *40.00*
NC12 AP3(b) 50c ol brn (C) 10.00 *125.00*
NC13 AP5(a) 75c org brn (G) 10.00 *40.00*
NC14 AP5(b) 1 l pur (C) 10.00 *125.00*
NC15 AP6(a) 2 l dp bl (Bl) 10.00 *87.50*
NC16 AP3(b) 5 l dk grn (C) 10.00 *125.00*
NC17 AP3(a) 10 l org red (G) 10.00 *87.50*
Nos. NC11-NC17 (7) 70.00 *630.00*

AIR POST SPECIAL DELIVERY STAMP

German Occupation

Italy #CE3 Ovptd. Type "b" in Blue

1944 **Wmk. 140** ***Perf. 14***

NCE1 APSD2 2 l gray blk 10.00 *87.50*

SPECIAL DELIVERY STAMP

German Occupation

Italy #E14 Ovptd. Type "b" in Green

1944 **Wmk. 140** ***Perf. 14***

NE1 SD4 1.25 l green 10.00 *24.00*

POSTAGE DUE STAMPS

Italian Occupation

Yugoslavia Nos. J28-J32 Overprinted in Black Like Nos. N1-N17

1941 **Unwmk.** ***Perf. 12½***

NJ1 D4 50p violet 4.00 4.00
NJ2 D4 1d rose 4.00 4.00
NJ3 D4 2d deep blue 4.00 4.00
NJ4 D4 5d orange 12.00 22.50
NJ5 D4 10d chocolate 12.00 22.50
Nos. NJ1-NJ5 (5) 36.00 57.00
Set, never hinged 80.00

Same Overprinted in Black

NJ6 D4 50p violet 4.00 8.00
NJ7 D4 1d deep magenta 4.00 8.00
NJ8 D4 2d deep blue 8.00 9.50
NJ9 D4 5d orange 55.00 110.00
NJ10 D4 10d chocolate 21.00 40.00
Nos. NJ6-NJ10 (5) 92.00 175.50

Same Overprinted in Black

NJ11 D4 50p violet 4.00 4.00
NJ12 D4 1d deep magenta 6.50 6.50
NJ13 D4 2d deep blue 55.00 110.00
Nos. NJ11-NJ13 (3) 65.50 120.50

German Occupation

Postage Due Stamps of Italy, 1934, Overprinted or Surcharged in Various Colors

d

e

f

g

1944 **Wmk. 140** ***Perf. 14***

NJ14 D6(d) 5c brown (Br) 2.40 *80.00*
NJ15 D6(e) 10c blue (Bl) 2.40 *80.00*
NJ16 D6(d) 20c rose red (R) 1.25 *8.00*
NJ17 D6(e) 25c green (G) 1.25 *8.00*
NJ18 D6(f) 30c on 50c vio (Bk) 1.25 *8.00*
NJ19 D6(g) 40c on 5c brn (Bl) 1.25 *8.00*
NJ20 D6(d) 50c violet (V) 1.25 *8.00*
NJ21 D7(e) 1 l red orange (R) 2.40 *80.00*
NJ22 D7(d) 2 l green (Bl) 2.40 *80.00*
Nos. NJ14-NJ22 (9) 15.85 *360.00*

Fiume-Kupa Zone

Italian Occupation

Four issues of 1941-42 consist of overprints on Yugoslav stamps of 1939-41: (a.) 14 stamps overprinted "ZONA OCCUPATO FIUMANO KUPA" and "ZOFK ZOFK ZOFK." (b.) 3 stamps overprinted as illustrated. (c.) 1 stamp surcharged "MEMENTO AVDERE SEMPER." "L1," etc. (d.) 3 stamps overprinted in arch: "Pro Maternite e Infanzia."

ISSUES FOR ISTRIA AND THE SLOVENE COAST (ZONE B)

Grapes — A1

Olive Branch — A2

Sailboat, Pola — A3

Designs: 50c, Donkey. Nos. 25-26, Ruined home. 2 l, Duino Castle. 5 l, Birthplace of Vladimir Gortan. 10 l, Plowing. Nos. 33-34, Tuna. 30 l, Viaduct at Solkan, Soca River.

Perf. 11½, 12, 10½x11½

1945-46 **Photo.**

23 A1 25c dark green .40 1.00
24 A1 50c red brown .25 .25
25 A1 1 l green .25 .25
26 A1 1 l red .25 .25
27 A2 1.50 l olive brown .25 .25
28 A2 2 l dk Prus grn .25 .25
29 A3 4 l red .25 .25
30 A3 4 l bright blue .25 .40
31 A3 5 l gray black .25 .25
32 A3 10 l brown .25 .25
33 A3 20 l blue 1.60 .85
34 A3 20 l dark violet 3.50 5.25
35 A3 30 l magenta 1.40 .80
Nos. 23-35 (13) 9.15 10.30
Set, never hinged 16.00

The first (Ljubljana) printing is perf. 10½x11½ and consists of Nos. 23-24, 26-28, 30-32, 34-35. The second (Zagreb) printing is perf. 12 and consists of Nos. 23-25, 27-29, 31-33, 35. The third (Belgrade) printing is perf. 11½ and consists of Nos. 25, 28, 40-41.

See Nos. 40-41. For surcharges see Nos. 36-37, J1-J19.

Nos. 33 and 35 Surcharged with New Values and Bars in Black

1946 **Unwmk.** ***Perf. 11½***

36 A3 1 l on 20 l blue .60 1.25
37 A3 2 l on 30 l magenta .60 1.25
Set, never hinged 2.40

Types of 1945

Design: 3 l, Duino Castle

1946, Nov. 30

40 A2 3 l crimson 1.50 1.75
41 A3 6 l ultra 3.25 4.00
Set, never hinged 9.25

Types of Yugoslavia & Official Stamps of 1946 Surcharged in Black

On A26

On O1

1947 **Unwmk.** ***Perf. 12½***

42 A26 1 l on 9d lilac rose .25 .40
43 O1 1.50 l on 50p blue .25 .40
44 A26 2 l on 9d lilac rose .25 .40
45 O1 3 l on 50p blue .25 .40
46 A26 5 l on 9d lilac rose .25 .40
47 O1 6 l on 50p blue .25 .40
48 A26 10 l on 9d lilac rose .25 .40
49 O1 15 l on 50p blue .25 .55
50 A26 35 l on 9d lilac rose .25 .90
51 O1 50 l on 50p blue .25 .90
Nos. 42-51 (10) 5.15
Set, never hinged 2.00

POSTAGE DUE STAMPS

Nos. 23, 24 34 and 35 Surcharged in Black

1945 **Unwmk.** ***Perf. 10½x11***

J1 A3 50c on 20 l dk vio .30 1.
J2 A1 1 l on 25c dk grn 6.00 2.
J3 A3 2 l on 30 l magenta .90 2.
J4 A1 4 l on 50c red brn .70
J5 A1 8 l on 50c red brn .70
J6 A1 10 l on 50c red brn 4.00 1.
J7 A1 20 l on 50c red brn 4.50 3.
Nos. J1-J7 (7) 17.10 11.
Set, never hinged 32.50

Nos. 25 and 35 Surcharged in Black

1945 ***Perf.***

J8 A1 1 l on 1 l green .25
J9 A1 2 l on 1 l green .25
J10 A1 4 l on 1 l green .30
J11 A3 10 l on 30 l magenta 2.50 2.
J12 A3 20 l on 30 l magenta 4.00 4.
J13 A3 30 l on 30 l magenta 4.00 4.
Nos. J8-J13 (6) 11.30 12.

The surcharges are arranged to fit th designs of the stamps.

No. 23 Surcharged in Black

1946

J14 A1 1 l on 25c dark green .40 .
J15 A1 2 l on 25c dark green .70 .
J16 A1 4 l on 25c dark green .40 .

No. 33 Surcharged in Black

J17 A3 10 l on 20 l blue 2.25 1.7
J18 A3 20 l on 20 l blue 5.50 4.5
J19 A3 30 l on 20 l blue 5.25 5.2
Nos. J14-J19 (6) 14.50 13.4
Set, never hinged 25.00

Type of Yugoslavia Postage Due Stamps, 1946, Surcharged in Black

1947

J20 D7 1 l on 1d brt blue grn .25 .5
J21 D7 2 l on 1d brt blue grn .25 .5
J22 D7 6 l on 1d brt blue grn .25 .5
J23 D7 10 l on 1d brt blue grn .25 .5
J24 D7 30 l on 1d brt blue grn .25 .6
Nos. J20-J24 (5) 1.25 2.6
Set, never hinged 1.75

TRIESTE, ZONE A
See listing under Italy, Vol. 3.

TRIESTE

A free territory (1947-1954) on the Adriatic Sea between Italy and Yugoslavia. In 1954 the territory was divided Italy acquiring the northern section and seaport, Yugoslavia the southern section (Zone B).

Catalogue values for all unused stamps in this country are for Never Hinged items.

ZONE B

Issued by the Yugoslav Military Government

100 Centesimi = 1 Lira
100 Paras = 1 Dinar (1949)

See Istria and the Slovene Coast (Zone B) for preceding issues of 1945-47.

Stylized Gymnast and Arms of Trieste — A1

1948 Unwmk. Litho. *Perf. 10½x11*
Inscriptions in:

1 A1 100 l Italian 8.00 4.00
2 A1 100 l Croatian 8.00 4.00
3 A1 100 l Slovene 8.00 4.00
a. Strip of 3, #1-3 95.00 65.00
Nos. 1-3 (3) 24.00 12.00

May Day.

Clasped Hands, Hammer and Sickle — A2

1949 Photo. *Perf. 11½x12½*
4 A2 10 l grnsh blk & ol grn .80 .80

Labor Day, May 1, 1949.
"V.U.J.A. S.T.T." are the initials of "Vojna Uprava Jugoslovenske Armije, Slobodna Teritorija Trsta" (Military Administration Yugoslav Army, Free Territory of Trieste).

Stamps of Yugoslavia, 1945-47 Overprinted in Carmine or Ultramarine

1949, Aug. 15 *Perf. 12½*
5 A22 50p ol gray .40 .30
6 A22 1d bl grn .40 .30
7 A24 2d scar (U) .40 .30
8 A25 3d dl red (U) .40 .30
9 A24 4d dk bl .80 .30
10 A25 5d dk bl .80 .30
11 A26 9d rose vio (U) 5.50 .80
12 A23 12d ultra 5.50 4.00
13 A22 16d blue 8.00 4.75
14 A23 20d org ver (U) 16.00 6.50
Nos. 5-14 (10) 38.20 17.85

The letters of the overprint are set closer and in one line on Nos. 7 and 9.

Yugoslavia Nos. 266 and 267 Overprinted in Carmine

Burelage in Color of Stamp

1949
15 A58 5d blue 10.50 8.00
16 A58 12d brown 10.50 8.00

75th anniv. of the UPU.

Yugoslavia, Nos. 269 to 272, Overprinted in Carmine

1950
17 A60 2d bl grn 4.00 .80
18 A60 3d car rose 4.00 .80
19 A60 5d blue 4.00 2.40
20 A60 10d dp org 16.00 8.00
Nos. 17-20 (4) 28.00 12.00

Workers Carrying Tools and Flag — A3

1950, May 1 Photo.
21 A3 3d violet .55 .55
22 A3 10d carmine 1.00 1.00

Labor Day, May 1, 1950.

Peasant on Ass — A4

Designs: 1d, Cockerel. 2d, Goose. 3d, Bees and honeycomb. 5d, Oxen. 10d, Turkey. 15d, Goats. 20d, Silkworms.

1950 Unwmk. *Perf. 12½*
23 A4 50p dk gray .40 .40
24 A4 1d brn car .40 .40
25 A4 2d dp bl .40 .40
26 A4 3d org brn .40 .40
27 A4 5d aqua 3.25 .40
28 A4 10d brown 3.25 .40
29 A4 15d violet 20.00 8.00
30 A4 20d dk grn 8.00 4.00
Nos. 23-30 (8) 36.10 14.40

1951
31 A4 1d orange brown 1.25 .40
32 A4 3d rose brown 1.60 .40

Worker — A5

1951, May 1
33 A5 3d dark red .80 .40
34 A5 10d brown olive 1.25 .80

Labor Day.

Pietro Paolo Vergerio — A7

1951, Oct. 21 Litho.
37 A7 5d blue 1.00 1.00
38 A7 10d claret 1.00 1.00
39 A7 20d sepia 1.00 1.00
Nos. 37-39 (3) 3.00 3.00

Types of Yugoslavia, 1951, Overprinted "STT VUJA"

1951, Nov.
40 A81 10d brn org (V) 1.00 .70
41 A81 12d grnsh blk (C) 1.00 .70

Bicycle Race — A8

1952 Photo.
42 A8 5d shown .40 .40
43 A8 10d Soccer .40 .40
44 A8 15d Rowing .40 .40
45 A8 28d Sailing 1.60 1.25
46 A8 50d Volleyball 3.25 2.40
47 A8 100d Diving 10.00 4.00
Nos. 42-47 (6) 16.05 8.85

Marshal Tito
A9 A10

1952, May 25 *Perf. 11½*
48 A9 15d dk brn 2.50 1.25
49 A10 28d red brn 2.50 2.00
50 A9 50d dk gray grn 4.75 2.75
Nos. 48-50 (3) 9.75 6.00

60th birthday of Marshal Tito.

Types of Yugoslavia 1952 Overprinted in Carmine

1952, July 26 *Perf. 12½*
51 A90 5d dk brn & sal, *cr* 1.60 .40
52 A90 10d dk grn & grn 1.60 .40
53 A90 15d dk brn & bl, *lil* 1.60 .40
54 A90 28d dk brn & buff, *cr* 1.60 1.60
55 A90 50d dk brn & buff, *yel* 14.00 9.50
56 A90 100d ind & lil, *pink* 32.50 27.50
Nos. 51-56 (6) 52.90 39.80

15th Olympic Games, Helsinki, 1952. Nos. 52, 54, 56 inscribed in Cyrillic characters.
The added "N" in "VUJNA" stands for "Narodna" (Peoples'). See note after No. 4.
Nos. 51-56 exist imperf. Value of set, $950, unused or used.

Yugoslavia Nos. 365 to 367 Overprinted in Carmine

1952, Sept. 13
57 A91 15d deep claret 3.25 2.75
58 A91 28d dark brown 4.00 2.75
59 A91 50d gray 4.75 2.75
Nos. 57-59 (3) 12.00 8.25

Formation of the Yugoslav navy, 10th anniv.

Yugoslavia No. 358 Overprinted in Blue

1952, June 22
60 A89 15d bright rose 1.60 .80

Children's Week.

Yugoslavia Nos. 369-372 Overprinted in Blue or Carmine

1952, Nov. 4
61 A93 15d red brn (Bl) 1.00 .65
62 A93 15d dk vio bl 1.00 .65
63 A93 15d dk brn 1.00 .65
64 A93 15d bl grn 1.00 .65
Nos. 61-64 (4) 4.00 2.60

Issued to publicize the 6th Yugoslavia Communist Party Congress, Zagreb, 1952.

Anchovies and Starfish — A11

1952 Unwmk. Photo. *Perf. 11x11½*
65 A11 15d red brown 4.00 4.00
a. Souvenir sheet, imperf. 55.00 55.00

Capodistria Phil. Exhib., Nov. 29-Dec. 7.
No. 65a contains a 50d dark blue green stamp. Sold for 85d.

Yugoslavia Types of 1952 Overprinted in Various Colors

1953, Feb. 3 *Perf. 12½*
66 A94 15d brn carmine (Bl) .40 .40
67 A94 30d chalky blue (R) 1.60 1.60

10th anniv. of the death of Nikola Tesla.

Stamps or Types of Yugoslavia Overprinted in Various Colors

1953
68 A68 1d gray 9.50 7.25
69 A68 2d car (V) .80 .40
70 A68 3d rose red (R) .80 .40
71 A68 5d orange .40 .40
72 A68 10d emerald (G) .80 .40
73 A68 15d rose red (V) 1.60 .80
74 A68 30d blue (Bl) 4.00 2.40
75 A68 50d grnsh bl (Bl) 8.00 4.00
Nos. 68-75 (8) 25.90 16.05

Nos. 69, 71 and 73 are lithographed.
See Nos. 90-92.

Yugoslavia Nos. 375-377 Overprinted in Various Colors

1953, Apr. 21 *Perf. 11½*
76 A95 15d dk ol grn (O) .25 .25
77 A95 30d chalky blue (O) .40 .40
78 A95 50d henna brown 1.10 1.10
Nos. 76-78 (3) 1.75 1.75

Issued in honor of the United Nations.

Automobile Climbing Mt. Lovcen — A12

Various automobiles and motorcycles.

1953, June 2 *Perf. 12½*
79 A12 15d ocher & choc .40 .40
80 A12 30d lt bl grn & ol grn .40 .40
81 A12 50d salmon & dp plum .40 .40
82 A12 70d bl & dk bl 2.75 2.00
Nos. 79-82 (4) 3.95 3.20

Intl. Automobile and Motorcycle Races, 1953.

Yugoslavia Types of 1953 Overprinted in Carmine

1953, July 8 Engr.
83 A97 50d gray grn (C) 4.00 4.00

Tito's election to the presidency, 1/14/53.

Yugoslavia No. 390 Overprinted in Carmine

1953, July 31
84 A98 15d gray & grn (C) 2.00 2.00

38th Esperanto Cong., Zagreb, July 25-Aug. 1, 1953. See No. C21.

Yugoslavia Types of 1953 Overprinted in Carmine

1953, Sept. 5
85 A101 15d blue (C) 4.00 4.00

Liberation of Istria & the Slovene coast, 10th anniv.

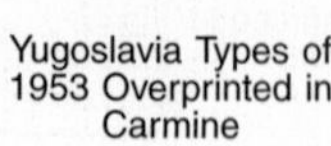
Yugoslavia Types of 1953 Overprinted in Carmine

1953, Oct. 3
86 A102 15d black & gray (C) 1.60 1.25

Cent. of the death of Branko Radicevic, poet.

Stamps or Types of Yugoslavia Overprinted in Various Colors

1953, Nov. 29 ***Perf. 12½x12***
87 A103 15d gray vio (V) 1.10 .80
88 A103 30d claret (Br) 1.10 .80
89 A103 50d dl bl grn (Dk Bl) 1.10 .80
Nos. 87-89 (3) 3.30 2.40

10th anniv. of the 1st republican legislative assembly of Yugoslavia.

Yugoslavia Nos. 380, 382, 384 Overprinted in Various Colors

1954, Mar. 5 ***Perf. 12½***
90 A68 5d org (V) 1.00 .40
91 A68 10d yel grn (C) .80 .40
92 A68 15d rose red (G) 1.00 .40
Nos. 90-92 (3) 2.80 1.20

Overprinted in Carmine

1954 Photo. ***Perf. 11½***
93 A104 2d red brn, sl & cr .80 .40
94 A104 5d gray & dk yel brn .80 .40
95 A104 10d ol grn & dk org brn .80 .40
96 A104 15d dp bl grn & dk org brn .80 .40
97 A104 17d gray brn, dk brn & cr .80 .40
98 A104 25d bis, gray bl & org yel .80 .40
99 A105 30d lil & dk brn .80 .40
100 A105 35d rose vio & bl blk .80 .80
101 A105 50d yel grn & vio brn 1.60 1.25
102 A105 65d org brn & gray blk 4.75 3.25
103 A105 70d bl & org brn 12.00 6.50
104 A105 100d brt bl & blk brn 32.50 25.00
Nos. 93-104 (12) 57.25 39.60

Yugoslavia Types of 1954 Overprinted in Various Colors

1954, Oct. 8 ***Perf. 12½***
105 A107 15d mar, red, ocher & dk bl (Bk) .80 .55
106 A107 30d dk bl, grn, sal buff & choc (G) .80 .55
107 A107 50d brn, bis & red (G) .80 .55
108 A107 70d dk grn, gray grn & choc (R) 1.60 1.25
Nos. 105-108 (4) 4.00 2.90

150th anniv. of the 1st Serbian insurrection.

AIR POST STAMPS

AP1

Perf. 12½x11½

1948, Oct. 17 Photo. Unwmk.
C1 AP1 25 l gray 1.10 .80
C2 AP1 50 l orange 1.10 .80

Economic Exhib. at Capodistria, Oct. 17-24.

Fishermen
AP2

Farmer and Pack Mule
AP3

Mew over Chimneys — AP4

1949, June 1 ***Perf. 11½***
C3 AP2 1 l grnsh bl .40 .40
C4 AP3 2 l red brn .80 .40
C5 AP2 5 l blue .80 .40
C6 AP3 10 l purple 2.40 2.00
C7 AP2 25 l brown 6.50 4.00
C8 AP3 50 l ol grn 8.00 4.00
C9 AP4 100 l deep brown 14.50 6.50
Nos. C3-C9 (7) 33.40 17.70

Italian inscriptions on Nos. C5 and C6, Croatian on No. C7, Slavonic on No. C8.
Nos. C3-C4 exist imperf. Value, each $150.

Nos. C3-C9 Surcharged in Various Colors

No. C14

No. C15

No. C16

1949, Nov. 5
C10 AP2 1d on 1 l (Bk) .40 .40
C11 AP3 2d on 2 l (Br) .80 .40
C12 AP2 5d on 5 l (Bl) .80 .40
C13 AP3 10d on 10 l (V) .80 .40
C14 AP2 15d on 25 l (Br) 16.00 9.50
C15 AP3 20d on 50 l (Gr) 8.00 3.25
C16 AP4 30d on 100 l (Bk) 9.50 4.00
Nos. C10-C16 (7) 36.30 18.35

On Nos. C14 and C15 the original value is obliterated by a framed block, on No. C16 by four parallel lines.

Yugoslavia No. C33 Overprinted in Carmine and Lilac Rose Network
Souvenir Sheet

1950 ***Perf. 11½x12½***
C17 AP15 10d lilac rose 200.00 160.00
a. Imperf. 200.00 160.00

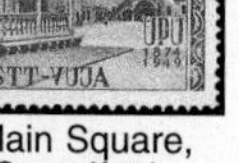
Main Square, Capodistria
AP5

Lighthouse, Pirano
AP6

Design: 25d, Hotel, Portorose.

1952 Unwmk. Photo. ***Perf. 12½***
C18 AP5 5d brown 12.00 12.00
C19 AP6 15d brt bl 8.00 8.00
C20 AP5 25d green 8.00 8.00
Nos. C18-C20 (3) 28.00 28.00

75th anniv. (in 1949) of the UPU.

Type of 1953 Yugoslavia Overprinted in Carmine

1953, July 31
C21 AP21 300d vio & grn 250.00 250.00

38th Esperanto Cong., Zagreb, 7/25-8/1.
Sheets of 12 (12,000 stamps) and sheets of 8 (3,000 stamps in light violet and green).
A private red overprint was applied marginally to 250 sheets of 8: "Esperantski Kongres — 38 — a Universala Kongreso de Esperanto — Congresso del Esperanto."

Air Post Stamps of Yugoslavia in New Colors Overprinted in Various Colors

1954 Engr.
C22 AP16 1d dp pur gray .80 .40
C23 AP16 2d brt grn (G) .80 .40
C24 AP16 3d red brn (Br) .80 .40
C25 AP16 5d chocolate .80 .40
C26 AP16 10d bl grn .80 .40
C27 AP16 20d brn (Br) .80 .40
C28 AP16 30d blue .80 .40
C29 AP16 50d olive blk .80 .60
C30 AP16 100d scar (R) 2.50 2.50
C31 AP16 200d dk bl vio (Bl) 4.75 4.00

Perf. 11x11½
C32 AP17 500d orange (Br) 27.50 20.00
Nos. C22-C32 (11) 41.15 29.90

POSTAGE DUE STAMPS

Yugoslavia Nos. J51 to J55 Overprinted "S T T VUJA" in Two Lines in Ultramarine or Carmine

1949 Unwmk. ***Perf. 12½***
J1 D7 50p dp org .80 .40
J2 D7 1d orange .80 .40
J3 D7 2d dk bl (C) .80 .40
J4 D7 3d yel grn (C) 1.60 .40
J5 D7 5d brt pur (C) 4.00 1.60
Nos. J1-J5 (5) 8.00 3.20

Croakers
D1

Anchovies
D2

1950 Photo.
J6 D1 50p brn org 4.00 .80
J7 D1 1d dp ol grn 4.00 1.60
J8 D2 2d dk grnsh bl 4.00 1.60
J9 D2 3d dk vio bl 4.00 1.60
J10 D2 5d plum 20.00 6.50
Nos. J6-J10 (5) 36.00 12.10

Yugoslavia Nos. J67-J74 Overprinted "STT VUJNA" in Blue or Carmine

1952
J11 D7 1d brown (Bl) .40 .40
J12 D7 2d emerald .40 .40
J13 D7 5d blue .40 .40
J14 D7 10d scar (Bl) .40 .40
J15 D7 20d purple .40 .40
J16 D7 30d org yel (Bl) .40 .40
J17 D7 50d ultra .40 .40
J18 D7 100d dp plum (Bl) 13.50 8.00
Nos. J11-J18 (8) 16.30 10.80

POSTAL TAX STAMPS

Yugoslavia No. RA5 Surcharged in Blue

1948 Unwmk. ***Perf. 12½***
RA1 PT4 2 l on 50p brn & scar 32.50 *32.50*

Obligatory on all mail from May 22-30.

Yugoslavia No. RA7 Overprinted in Black

1950, July 3
RA2 PT6 50p brn & red 2.40 1.25

Yugoslavia No. RA9 Overprinted in Black

1951
RA3 PT8 50p vio bl & red 24.00 16.00

Yugoslavia No. RA10 Overprinted in Carmine

1952
RA4 PT9 50p gray & carmine 1.60 .80

Type of 1953 Yugoslavia Overprinted in Blue

1953
RA5 PT10 2d org brn & red 1.60 .80

The tax of Nos. RA1-RA5 was for the Red Cross.

POSTAL TAX DUE STAMPS

Yugoslavia No. RAJ2 Surcharged Like No. RA1 in Scarlet

1948 Unwmk. *Perf. 12½*
RAJ1 PT4 2 l on 50p bl grn & scar 260.00 240.00

Yugoslavia No. RAJ4 Overprinted in Black

1950, July 3
RAJ2 PT6 50p vio & red 2.40 1.25

Yugoslavia No. RAJ6 Overprinted in Black

1951
RAJ3 PT8 50p emer & red 240.00 225.00

Yugoslavia No. RAJ7 Overprinted in Orange

1952
RAJ4 PTD3 50p gray & car 1.60 1.00

Type of 1953 Yugoslavia Overprinted in Blue

1953
RAJ5 PT10 2d brt car & red 1.60 1.00

ZAIRE

zä-'ir

(Congo Democratic Republic)

LOCATION — Central Africa
GOVT. — Republic
AREA — 905,365 sq. mi.
POP. — 50,481,305 (1999 est.)
CAPITAL — Kinshasa

Congo Democratic Republic changed its name to Republic of the Zaire in November 1971. Issues before that date are listed in Vol. 2 under Congo Democratic Republic.

100 Sengi = 1 Li-Kuta
100 Ma-Kuta = 1 Zaire
100 Centimes = 1 Franc (July 1998)

Catalogue values for all unused stamps in this country are for Never Hinged items.

From 1971 through 1997, imperforates exist of almost all issues. Exceptions are Nos. 756-772, 850-860, 991-999 and 1259-1442.

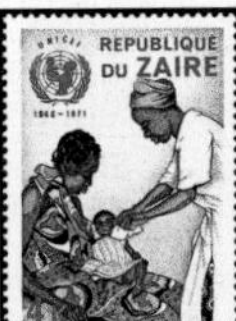

UNICEF Emblem, Child Care — A143

UNICEF Emblem and: 14k, Map of Africa showing Zaire. 17k, Boy in African village.

Perf. 14x13½
1971, Dec. 18 Unwmk.
750 A143 4k gold & multi .50 .25
751 A143 14k lt bl, gold, red & grn 1.25 .75
752 A143 17k gold & multi 2.00 1.10
Nos. 750-752 (3) 3.75 2.10

25th anniv. of UNICEF. For surcharge see No. 1327.

Pres. Mobutu, MPR Emblem — A144

1972 Photo. *Perf. 11½*
753 A144 4k multi 4.00 2.50
754 A144 14k multi 4.00 2.50
755 A144 22k multi 4.00 2.50
Nos. 753-755 (3) 12.00 7.50

5th anniv. of the People's Revolutionary Movement (MPR). For surcharge see #1308.

Zaire Arms A145

Pres. Joseph D. Mobutu A146

1972 Litho. *Perf. 14*
756 A145 10s red org & blk .25 .25
757 A145 40s brt bl & multi .25 .25
758 A145 50s citron & multi .25 .25

Perf. 13
759 A146 1k sky bl & multi .25 .25
760 A146 2k org & multi .25 .25
761 A146 3k multi .25 .25
762 A146 4k emer & multi .25 .25
763 A146 5k multi .25 .25
764 A146 6k multi .25 .25
765 A146 8k cit & multi .40 .25
766 A146 9k multi .50 .25
767 A146 10k lt lil & multi .55 .25
768 A146 14k multi .75 .30
769 A146 17k multi .90 .40
770 A146 20k yel & multi 1.25 .50
771 A146 50k multi 3.00 1.00
772 A146 100k fawn & multi 6.00 2.50
Nos. 756-772 (17) 15.60 7.70

For surcharges and overprints see Nos. 860, 1328, O1-O11.

Same, Denominations in Zaires

1973, Feb. 21
773 A146 0.01z sky bl & multi .25 .25
774 A146 0.02z org & multi .25 .25
775 A146 0.03z multi .25 .25
776 A146 0.04z multi .25 .25
777 A146 0.10z multi .40 .25
778 A146 0.14z multi .60 .55
Nos. 773-778 (6) 2.00 1.80

Inga Dam — A147

1973, Jan. 25 Litho. *Perf. 13½*
790 A147 0.04z multi .35 .25
791 A147 0.14z pink & multi .45 .35
792 A147 0.18z yel & multi .80 .55
Nos. 790-792 (3) 1.60 1.15

Completion of first section of Inga Dam Nov. 24, 1972.

World Map — A148

1973, June 23 Photo. *Perf. 12½x12*
793 A148 0.04z lil & multi .25 .25
794 A148 0.07z multi .35 .25
795 A148 0.18z multi .85 .50
Nos. 793-795 (3) 1.45 1.00

3rd Intl. Fair at Kinshasa, June 23-July 8.

The dark brown ink of the inscription was applied by a thermographic process and varnished, producing a shiny, raised effect.

Hand and INTERPOL Emblem — A149

1973, Sept. 28 Litho. *Perf. 12½*
796 A149 0.06z multi .45 .25
797 A149 0.14z multi .95 .50

50th anniversary of International Criminal Police Organization.

Leopard with Soccer Ball on Globe — A150

1974, July 17 Photo. *Perf. 11½x12*
798 A150 1k multi .25 .25
799 A150 2k multi .25 .25
800 A150 3k multi 1.00 .30
801 A150 4k multi 1.25 .45
802 A150 5k multi 1.50 .60
803 A150 14k multi 4.50 1.10
a. Souvenir sheet, 1 #803 37.50 —
Nos. 798-803 (6) 8.75 2.95

World Cup Soccer Championship, Munich, June 13-July 7.

Foreman-Ali Fight — A151

1974, Nov. 9 Litho. *Perf. 12x12½*
804 A151 1k multi .25 .25
805 A151 4k multi .25 .25
806 A151 6k multi .35 .30
807 A151 14k multi .75 .50
808 A151 20k multi 1.10 .90
Nos. 804-808 (5) 2.70 2.20

World Heavyweight Boxing Championship match between George Foreman and Muhammad Ali, Kinshasa, Oct. 30 (postponed from Sept. 25).

Same, Type of 1974, Denominations in Zaires and Inscribed in Various Colors

1975, Aug. Litho. *Perf. 12x12½*
809 A151 0.01z multi (R) .25 .25
810 A151 0.04z multi (Br) .25 .25
811 A151 0.06z multi (Bk) .30 .30
812 A151 0.14z multi (G) .65 .50
813 A151 0.20z multi (Bk) 1.25 .90
Nos. 809-813 (5) 2.70 2.20

Judge, Lawyers, IWY Emblem — A152

1975, Dec. Photo. *Perf. 11½*
814 A152 1k dull blk & multi .40 .25
815 A152 2k dp rose & multi .50 .25
816 A152 4k dull grn & multi 1.00 .35
817 A152 14k violet & multi 2.25 .50
Nos. 814-817 (4) 4.15 1.35

International Women's Year 1975.

Waterfall — A153

1975 Photo. *Perf. 11½*
818 A153 1k multicolored .30 .25
819 A153 2k lt blue & multi .40 .25
820 A153 3k multicolored .50 .30
821 A153 4k salmon & multi 1.40 .65
822 A153 5k green & multi 1.50 .65
Nos. 818-822 (5) 4.10 2.10

12th General Assembly of the Intl. Union for Nature Preservation (U.I.C.N.), Kinshasa, Sept. 1975.

Okapis — A154

1975
823 A154 1k blue & multi .60 .25
824 A154 2k yellow grn & multi .90 .25
825 A154 3k brown red & multi 1.50 .30
826 A154 4k green & multi 2.40 .50
827 A154 5k yellow & multi 3.25 .60
Nos. 823-827 (5) 8.65 1.90

Virunga National Park, 50th anniversary.

Siderma Maluku Industry — A155

Designs: 1k, Sozacom apartment building, vert. 3k, Matadi flour mill, vert. 4k, Women parachutists. 8k, Pres. Mobutu visiting Chairman Mao, vert. 10k, Soldiers working along the Salongo. 14k, Pres. Mobutu addressing UN Gen. Assembly, Oct. 1974. 15k, Celebrating crowd.

1975
828 A155 1k ocher & multi .50 .25
829 A155 2k yel grn & multi .75 .25
830 A155 3k multi 1.00 .25
831 A155 4k multi 1.50 .25
832 A155 8k dk brn & multi 1.75 .35
833 A155 10k sep & multi 2.00 .50
834 A155 14k bl & multi 5.00 .75
835 A155 15k org & multi 7.00 1.00
Nos. 828-835 (8) 19.50 3.60

10th anniversary of new government.

Tshokwe Mask — A156

Designs: 2k, 4k, Seated woman, Pende. 7k, like 5k. 10k, 14k, Antelope mask, Suku. 15k, 18k, Kneeling woman, Kongo. 20k, 25k, Kuba mask.

1977, Jan. 8 Photo. *Perf. 11½*

836	A156	2k multi	.25	.25
837	A156	4k multi	.25	.25
838	A156	5k gray & multi	.25	.25
839	A156	7k multi	.25	.25
840	A156	10k multi	.30	.25
841	A156	14k multi	.45	.25
842	A156	15k multi	.55	.25
843	A156	18k multi	.65	.35
844	A156	20k multi	1.25	.40
845	A156	25k vio & multi	1.50	.80
		Nos. 836-845 (10)	5.70	3.30

Wood carving and masks of Zaire.

Map of Zaire, UPU Emblem — A157

1977, Apr. Litho. *Perf. 13½*

846	A157	1k org & multi	.35	.25
847	A157	4k dk bl & multi	1.00	.25
848	A157	7k ol grn & multi	1.75	.30
849	A157	50k brn & multi	6.50	4.00
		Nos. 846-849 (4)	9.60	4.80

Cent. of UPU (in 1974).

Congo Stamps of 1968-1971 Srchd. with New Value, Bars and "REPUBLIQUE DU ZAIRE"

1977

850	A126	1k on 10s (#642)	.70	.35
851	A122	2k on 9.6k (#618)	.70	.35
852	A140	10k on 10s (#735)	2.50	.75
853	A134	25k on 10s (#703)	2.75	.50
854	A127	40k on 9.6k (#652)	3.75	2.00
855	A135	48k on 10s (#713)	7.50	3.00
		Nos. 850-855 (6)	17.90	6.95

Congo Nos. 644, 643, 635, 746 Srchd. with New Value, Bars and "REPUBLIQUE DU ZAIRE" in Black or Carmine, Zaire No. 757 Srchd.

1977

856	A126	5k on 30s	1.00	.35
857	A126	10k on 15s (C)	1.00	.35
858	A124	20k on 9.60k	2.25	.75
859	A141	30k on 12k	3.75	.75
860	A145	100k on 40s (C)	9.50	3.00
		Nos. 856-860 (5)	17.50	5.20
		Nos. 850-860 (11)	29.15	17.70

Nos. 850-860 exist with a number of overprint color varieties, as well as with inverted and double overprint errors.

Souvenir Sheet

Adoration of the Kings, by Rubens — A158

1977, Dec. 19 Photo. *Perf. 13½*

861	A158	5z multi	140.00	110.00

Christmas 1977.

Pantodon Buchholzi — A159

Fish: 70s, Aphyosemion striatum. 55, Ctenopoma fasciolatum. 8k, Malapterurus electricus. 10k, Hemichromis bimaculatus. 30k, Marcusenius isidori. 40k, Synodontis nigriventris. 48k, Julidochromis ornatus. 100k, Nothobranchius brieni. 250k, Micralestes interruptus.

1978, Jan. 23 Litho. *Perf. 14*

862	A159	30s multi	.25	.25
863	A159	70s multi	.25	.25
864	A159	5k multi	.25	.25
865	A159	8k multi	.35	.30
866	A159	10k multi	.55	.35
867	A159	30k multi	1.25	.75
868	A159	40k multi	1.75	1.00
869	A159	48k multi	2.00	1.25
870	A159	100k multi	5.50	2.75
		Nos. 862-870 (9)	12.15	7.15

Souvenir Sheet

Perf. 13½

871	A159	250k multi	14.00	14.00

No. 871 contains one 46x35mm stamp. For surcharges see Nos. 1294, 1311.

Soccer Game, Argentina-France A160

Various Soccer Games and Jules Rimet Cup: 3k, Austria-Brazil. 7k, Scotland-Iran. 9k, Netherlands-Peru. 10k, Hungary-Italy. 20k, Fed. Rep. of Germany-Mexico. 50k, Tunisia-Poland. 100k, Spain-Sweden. 500k, Rimet Cup, Games' emblem and cartoon of soccer player, horiz.

1978, Aug. 7 Litho. *Perf. 12½*

872	A160	1k multi	.25	.25
873	A160	3k multi	.25	.25
874	A160	7k multi	.25	.25
875	A160	9k multi	.25	.25
876	A160	10k multi	.25	.25
877	A160	20k multi	.40	.25
878	A160	50k multi	1.10	.60
879	A160	100k multi	2.25	1.25
		Nos. 872-879 (8)	5.00	3.35

Souvenir Sheets

880	A160	500k blue & multi	25.00	25.00
881	A160	500k red & multi	25.00	25.00

11th World Cup Soccer Championship, Argentina, June 1-25. Nos. 880-881 contain one stamp each (47x36mm). Stamp of No. 880 has blue frameline. Stamp of No. 881 has red frame line.

For surcharge see No. 1259.

Mama Mobutu — A161

1978, Oct. 23 Photo. *Perf. 12*

882	A161	8k multi	.30	.30

Mama Mobutu (1941-77), wife of Pres. Mobutu.

Pres. Joseph D. Mobutu — A162

Frame Color

Granite Paper

1978 Photo. *Perf. 12*

883	A162	2k blue	.25	.25
884	A162	5k bister	.25	.25
885	A162	6k Prussian blue	.25	.25
886	A162	8k red brown	.25	.25
887	A162	10k emerald	.25	.25
888	A162	25k red	.25	.25
889	A162	48k purple	.40	.30
890	A162	1z green	.80	.50
		Nos. 883-890 (8)	2.70	2.30

See Nos. 1053, 1055-1056. For surcharges see Nos. 1313, 1333-1336.

Souvenir Sheet

Elizabeth II in Westminster Abbey — A163

1978, Dec. 11 Photo. *Perf. 13½*

891	A163	5z multi	12.00	12.00

Coronation of Queen Elizabeth II, 25th anniv.

Souvenir Sheet

Albrecht Dürer, Self-portrait — A164

1978, Dec. 18 *Perf. 13*

892	A164	5z multi	12.00	12.00

Albrecht Dürer (1471-1528), German painter and engraver.

Leonardo da Vinci and his Drawings A165

History of Aviation: 70s, Planes of Wright Brothers, 1905, and Santos Dumont, 1906. 1k, Bleriot XI, 1909, and Farman F-60, 1909. 5k, Junkers G-38, 1929, and Spirit of St. Louis, 1927. 8k, Sikorsky S-42B, 1934 and Macchi-Castoldi MC-72, 1934. 10k, Boeing 707, 1960, and Fokker F-VII, 1935. 50k, Apollo XI, 1969, and Concorde, 1976. 75k, Helicopter and Douglas DC-10, 1971. 5z, Giffard's balloon, 1852, and Hindenburg LZ 129, 1936.

1978, Dec. 28 Litho. *Perf. 13*

893	A165	30s multi	.25	.25
894	A165	70s multi	.25	.25
895	A165	1k multi	.25	.25
896	A165	5k multi	.35	.25
897	A165	8k multi	.40	.25
898	A165	10k multi	.75	.25
899	A165	50k multi	3.25	1.00
900	A165	75k multi	4.25	1.25
		Nos. 893-900 (8)	9.75	3.75

Souvenir Sheet

Perf. 11½

901	A165	5z multi	16.00	16.00

For overprint and surcharges see Nos. 993, 1173-1181, 1291, 1295, note after 1352.

Pres. Mobutu, Map of Zaire, N'tombe Dancer A166

Pres. Mobutu & Map: 3k, Bird. 4k, Elephant. 10k, Diamond and cotton boll. 14k, Hand holding torch. 17k, Leopard's head and Victoria Regia lily. 25k, Finzia waterfall. 50k, Wagenia fishermen.

1979, Feb. Litho. *Perf. 14x13½*

902	A166	1k multicolored	.25	.25
903	A166	3k multicolored	.25	.25
904	A166	4k multicolored	.25	.25
905	A166	10k multicolored	.25	.25
a.		Souvenir sheet of 4, #902-905	*13.00*	—
906	A166	14k multicolored	.25	.25
907	A166	17k multicolored	.40	.25
908	A166	25k multicolored	.60	.40
909	A166	50k multicolored	1.25	.85
a.		Souvenir sheet of 4, #906-909	*13.00*	—
		Nos. 902-909 (8)	3.50	2.75

Zaire (Congo) River expedition.

A stamp similar to design No. A166, depicting Pres. Mobutu and a flag and printed on gold foil, exists. Value, $50.

Phylloporus Ampliporus — A167

Mushrooms: 5k, Engleromyces goetzei. 8k, Scutellinia virungae. 10k, Pycnoporus sanguineus. 30k, Cantharellus miniatescens. 40k, Lactarius phlebonemus. 48k, Phallus indusiatus. 100k, Ramaria moelleriana.

1979, Mar. Photo. *Perf. 13½x13*

910	A167	30s multicolored	.30	.25
911	A167	5k multicolored	.35	.30
912	A167	8k multicolored	.55	.40
913	A167	10k multicolored	.85	.50
914	A167	30k multicolored	1.75	1.25
915	A167	40k multicolored	2.50	1.50
916	A167	48k multicolored	4.25	2.00
917	A167	100k multicolored	6.25	3.50
		Nos. 910-917 (8)	16.80	9.70

For surcharges see Nos. 1296, 1298, 1312, 1361-1362, 1365-1366, 1368-1369, 1372, 1375.

Souvenir Sheets

Pope John XXIII (1881-1963) — A168

Popes: No. 919, Paul VI (1897-1978). No. 920, John Paul I (1912-78).

1979, June 25 Litho. *Perf. 11½*

918	A168	250k multi	5.00	5.00
919	A168	250k multi	5.00	5.00
920	A168	250k multi	5.00	5.00
		Nos. 918-920 (3)	15.00	15.00

Boy Beating Drum — A169

IYC Emblem on Map of Zaire and: 10k, 20k, Girl, diff. 50k, Boy. 100k, Boys. 300k, Mother and child. 10z, Mother and children, horiz.

1979, July 23 Litho. *Perf. 12½*

921	A169	5k multi	.25	.25
922	A169	10k multi	.25	.25
923	A169	20k multi	.40	.25
924	A169	50k multi	.90	.50

925 A169 100k multi 1.90 1.00
926 A169 300k multi 5.25 2.50
Nos. 921-926 (6) 8.95 4.75

Souvenir Sheet

927 A169 10z multi 14.00 10.50

International Year of the Child.
For surcharges see Nos. 997, 999, 1299, 1306.

Globe and Drummer — A170

1979, July 23
928 A170 1k multi .25 .25
929 A170 9k multi .25 .25
930 A170 90k multi .70 .50
931 A170 100k multi .80 .55
Nos. 928-931 (4) 2.00 1.55

Souvenir Sheet

932 A170 500k multi 5.00 5.00

6th International Fair, Kinshasa. No. 932 contains one 52x31mm stamp.
For overprint & surcharge see #996, 1320.

Globe and School Desk — A171

1979, Dec. 24 Litho. *Perf. 13*
933 A171 10k multi .30 .25

Intl. Bureau of Education, Geneva, 50th anniv.

Adoration of the Kings, by Memling — A172

1979, Dec. 24 *Imperf.*
934 A172 5z multi 6.00 6.00

Christmas 1979.

"Puffing Billy," 1814, Gt. Britain — A173

1.50k, Buddicom No. 33, 1843, France. 5k, "Elephant," 1835, Belgium. 8k, No. 601, 1906, Zaire. 50k, "Slieve Gullion 440," Ireland. 75k, "Black Elephant," Germany. 2z, Type 1-15, Zaire. 5z, "Golden State," US.
10z, Type E.D.75, Zaire.

1980, Jan. 14 Litho. *Perf. 13½x13*
935 A173 50s shown .25 .25
936 A173 1.50k multicolored .25 .25
937 A173 5k multicolored .25 .25
938 A173 8k multicolored .25 .25
939 A173 50k multicolored .75 .25
940 A173 75k multicolored 1.10 .75
941 A173 2z multicolored 2.25 1.90
942 A173 5z multicolored 6.00 6.00
Nos. 935-942 (8) 11.10 9.90

Souvenir Sheet

943 A173 10z multicolored 15.00 15.00

For overprints and surcharges see Nos. 991-992, 994, 1325.

Hill, Belgian Congo No. 257 — A174

1980, Jan. 28 *Perf. 13½x14*
944 A174 2k No. 5 .25 .25
945 A174 4k No. 13 .25 .25
946 A174 10k No. 24 .25 .25
947 A174 20k No. 38 .25 .25
948 A174 40k No. 111 .40 .25
949 A174 150k No. B29 1.25 1.00
950 A174 200k No. 198 1.50 1.25
951 A174 250k shown 1.90 1.50
Nos. 944-951 (8) 6.05 5.00

Souvenir Sheet

952 A174 10z No. 198 11.00 11.00

Sir Rowland Hill (1795-1879), originator of penny postage.
For overprint and surcharge see Nos. 998, 1329.

Albert Einstein (1879-1955), Theoretical Physicist — A175

1980, Feb. 18 *Perf. 13*
953 A175 40s multi .25 .25
954 A175 2k multi .25 .25
955 A175 4k multi .25 .25
956 A175 15k multi .25 .25
957 A175 50k multi .40 .40
958 A175 300k multi 1.60 1.00
Nos. 953-958 (6) 3.00 2.40

Souvenir Sheet

959 A175 5z multi, diff. 4.50 4.50

For surcharges see Nos. 1285, 1290, 1304.

Salvation Army Brass Players A176

50s, Booth Memorial Hospital, NYC. 4.50k, Commissioner George Railton sailing for US mission. 10k, Mobile dispensary, Masina. 20k, Gen. Evangeline Booth, officer holding infant, vert. 75k, Outdoor well-baby clinic. 1.50z, Disaster relief. 2z, Parade, vert. 10z, Gen. & Mrs. Arnold Brown.

1980, Mar. 3 *Perf. 11*
960 A176 50s multi .25 .25
961 A176 4.50k multi .25 .25
962 A176 10k multi .25 .25
963 A176 20k multi .25 .25
964 A176 40k multi .35 .25
965 A176 75k multi .55 .25
966 A176 1.50z multi 1.10 .55
967 A176 2z multi 1.60 .80
Nos. 960-967 (8) 4.60 2.85

Souvenir Sheet

968 A176 10z multi 9.00 9.00

Salvation Army cent. in US. No. 968 contains one 53x38mm stamp and 2 labels.

A set of nine stamps and one souvenir sheet for the 1980 Olympic Games in Moscow was prepared but not issued. Value, set $140.

Souvenir Sheets

Pope John Paul II A177

1980, May 2 Litho. *Perf. 11½*
969 A177 10z multi 17.50 17.50

Visit of Pope John Paul II to Zaire, May.

Baia Castle, by Antonio Pitloo A178

1980, May 5
970 A178 10z multi 6.00 6.00

20th International Philatelic Exhibition, Europa '80, Naples, Apr. 26-May 4.

A179

50k, Woman, line-drawing. 100k, Plutiarch. 500k, Kneeling man, sculpture, vert.

Perf. 12½x13, 13x12½
1980, May 24 Litho.
971 A179 50k multicolored .25 .25
972 A179 100k multicolored .50 .40
973 A179 500k multicolored 2.50 1.75
a. Souvenir sheet of 3 6.00 6.00
Nos. 971-973 (3) 3.25 2.40

Rotary Intl., 75th anniv. No. 973a contains 3 stamps similar to Nos. 971-973, size: 55x35, 35x55mm. Exists imperf.
For surcharge see No. 1313.

Tropical Fish — A180

1k, Chaetodon collaris. 5k, Zebrasoma veliferum. 10k, Euxiphipops xanthometapon. 20k, Pomacanthus annularis. 50k, Centropyge oriculus. 150k, Oxymonacanthus longirostris. 200k, Balistoides niger. 250k, Rhinecanthus aculeatus.
5z, Baliste ondule.

1980, Oct. 20 Litho. *Perf. 14x13½*
974 A180 1k multicolored .25 .25
975 A180 5k multicolored .25 .25
976 A180 10k multicolored .25 .25
977 A180 20k multicolored .25 .25
978 A180 50k multicolored .60 .40
979 A180 150k multicolored 1.40 .55
980 A180 200k multicolored 1.90 .70
981 A180 250k multicolored 2.25 1.00
Nos. 974-981 (8) 7.15 3.65

Souvenir Sheet

981A A180 5z multicolored 4.75 4.75

For surcharge see No. 1307.

Exhibition Emblem, Congo #365 — A181

1980, Dec. 6 Litho. *Perf. 13*
982 Block or strip of 4 2.00 1.75
a. A181 1z denomination at UR, shown .45 .35
b. A181 1z denomination at UL, Belgium #511 .45 .35
c. A181 1z denomination at UR, like #982b .45 .35
d. A181 1z denomination at UL, like #982a .45 .35
983 Block or strip of 4 4.00 3.00
a. A181 2z denomination at UR, Congo #432 .95 .60
b. A181 2z denomination at UL, Belguim # B835 .95 .60
c. A181 2z denomination at UR, like #983b .95 .60
d. A181 2z denomination at UL, like #983a .95 .60
984 Block or strip of 4 6.00 4.50
a. A181 3z denomination at UR, Zaire #755 1.40 .90
b. A181 3z denomination at UL, Belgium # B878 1.40 .90
c. A181 3z denomination at UR, like #984b 1.40 .90
d. A181 3z denomination at UL, like #984a 1.40 .90
985 Block or strip of 4 8.50 6.00
a. A181 4z denomination at UR, Congo #572 1.75 1.10
b. A181 4z denomination at UL, Belgium # B996 1.75 1.10
c. A181 4z denomination at UR, like #985b 1.75 1.10
d. A181 4z denomination at UL, like #985a 1.75 1.10
Nos. 982-985 (4) 20.50 15.25

PHIBELZA, Belgium-Zaire Phil. Exhib.
For surcharge see No. 1342.

Map of Africa, King Leopold I A182

Belgian independence sesquicentennial: 75k, Stanley expedition, Leopold II. 100k, Colonial troops, Albert I. 145k, Protected animals, Leopold III. 270k, Visit of King Baudouin and Queen Fabiola.

1980, Dec. 13 Photo. *Perf. 14*
986 A182 10k multi .45 .25
987 A182 75k multi 1.40 .45
988 A182 100k multi 2.00 .60
989 A182 145k multi 2.50 .80
990 A182 270k multi 4.50 1.25
Nos. 986-990 (5) 10.85 3.35

For surcharges see Nos. 1326, 1331, 1345, 1357, 1408-1412, 1426.

Nos. 935, 936, 898, 939, 900, 931, 925, 951, Overprinted in Red, Silver or Black: 20e Anniversaire-Independence / 1960-1980

1980, Dec. 13 Litho.
991 A173 50s multi .25 .25
992 A173 1.50k multi .25 .25
993 A165 10k multi .25 .25
994 A173 50k multi .40 .25
995 A165 75k multi .60 .25
996 A170 100k multi (S) .90 .50
997 A169 1z on 5z on 100k multi (B) 1.00 .50
998 A174 250k multi 2.00 1.00
999 A169 5z on 100k multi (B) 4.75 2.50
Nos. 991-999 (9) 10.40 5.75

20th anniversary of independence. For surcharges see Nos. 1300, 1316.

Nativity — A183

1980, Dec. 24 *Perf. 13*
1000 A183 10k Shepherds and angels .25 .25
1001 A183 75k Flight into Egypt 1.00 .40
1002 A183 80k Three kings 1.00 .40
1003 A183 145k shown 1.75 .60
Nos. 1000-1003 (4) 4.00 1.65

Souvenir Sheet

1004 A183 10z Church, nativity 5.50 5.50

Christmas 1980. No. 1004 contains one 49x33mm stamp. Exists imperf. For surcharges see Nos. 1301, 1317-1318.

Postal Clerk Sorting Mail, by Norman Rockwell — A184

Designs: Saturday Evening Post covers by Norman Rockwell.

1981, Apr. 27 Litho. *Perf. 14*
1005 A184 10k multi .25 .25
1006 A184 20k multi .25 .25
1007 A184 50k multi .40 .25
1008 A184 80k multi .65 .35
1009 A184 100k multi .70 .40
1010 A184 125k multi 1.10 .45
1011 A184 175k multi 1.25 .65
1012 A184 200k multi 1.40 .75
Nos. 1005-1012 (8) 6.00 3.35

For surcharges see Nos. 1262, 1265, 1269, 1275, 1281, 1354.

First Anniv. of Visit of Pope John Paul II — A185

Scenes of Pope's visit. 50k, 500k, vert.

1981, May 2 *Perf. 13*

1013 A185 5k multi .25 .25
1014 A185 10k multi .25 .25
1015 A185 50k multi .35 .30
1016 A185 100k multi 1.00 .50
1017 A185 500k multi 5.50 2.50
1018 A185 800k multi 7.75 4.25
Nos. 1013-1018 (6) 15.10 8.05

For surcharges see #1190-1194, 1292, 1302, 1343.

Soccer Players — A186

Designs: Soccer scenes.

1981, July 6 **Litho.** *Perf. 12½*

1019 A186 2k multi .25 .25
1020 A186 10k multi .25 .25
1021 A186 25k multi .25 .25
1022 A186 90k multi .50 .25
1023 A186 2z multi 1.00 .55
1024 A186 3z multi 1.60 .85
1025 A186 6z multi 2.75 1.50
1026 A186 8z multi 4.50 3.00
Nos. 1019-1026 (8) 11.10 6.90

Souvenir Sheet

1027 Sheet of 2 6.00 6.00
a. A186 5z like #1019 2.75 2.75
b. A186 5z like #1025 2.75 2.75

ESPANA '82 World Cup Soccer Championship. For surcharges see Nos. 1287, 1303, 1309, 1321.

Intl. Year of the Disabled A187

2k, Archer. 5k, Ear, sound waves. 10k, Amputee. 18k, Cane braille, sunglasses. 50k, Boy with leg braces. 150k, Sign language. 500k, Hands. 800k, Dove.

1981, Nov. 2 **Litho.** *Perf. 14x14½*

1028 A187 2k multicolored .25 .25
1029 A187 5k multicolored .25 .25
1030 A187 10k multicolored .25 .25
1031 A187 18k multicolored .25 .25
1032 A187 50k multicolored .25 .25
1033 A187 150k multicolored .60 .30
1034 A187 500k multicolored 1.50 1.25
1035 A187 800k multicolored 2.75 2.00
Nos. 1028-1035 (8) 6.10 4.80

For surcharges see Nos. 1288, 1293, 1305, 1314.

Souvenir Sheet

Birth Sesqui. of Heinrich von Stephan, UPU Founder A188

Photogravure and Engraved

1981, Dec. 21 *Perf. 11½x12*

1036 A188 15z purple 8.00 8.00

Christmas 1981 — A189

Designs: 25k, 1z, 1.50z, 3z, 5z, Various children. 10z, Holy Family, horiz.

1981, Dec. 21 **Litho.** *Perf. 14*

1037 A189 25k multi .25 .25
1038 A189 1z multi .70 .25
1039 A189 1.50z multi .80 .35
1040 A189 3z multi 1.75 .75
1041 A189 5z multi 2.75 1.25
Nos. 1037-1041 (5) 6.25 2.85

Souvenir Sheet

1042 A189 10z multi 5.50 5.50

13th World Telecommunications Day (1981) — A190

Designs: Symbols of communications and health care delivery.

1982, Feb. 8 **Litho.** *Perf. 13*

1043 A190 1k multi .25 .25
1044 A190 25k multi .25 .25
1045 A190 90k multi .30 .25
1046 A190 1z multi .30 .25
1047 A190 1.70z multi .55 .45
1048 A190 3z multi 1.10 .75
1049 A190 4.50z multi 1.60 1.10
1050 A190 5z multi 1.75 1.25
Nos. 1043-1050 (8) 6.10 4.55

For surcharges see Nos. 1270, 1282.

Pres. Mobutu Type of 1978
Frame Color
Granite Paper

1982 **Photo.** *Perf. 12*

1053 A162 50k purple .25 .25
1055 A162 2z bister .75 .25
1056 A162 5z Prussian blue 2.25 1.25
Nos. 1053-1056 (3) 3.25 1.75

20th Anniv. of African Postal Union (1981) A191

1982, Mar. 8 **Litho.** *Perf. 13*

1057 A191 1z yel grn & gold .50 .40

For surcharges see Nos. 1348, 1352.

1982 World Cup — A192

Designs: Flags and players of finalists.

1982

1058 A192 2k multi .25 .25
1059 A192 8k multi .25 .25
1060 A192 25k multi .25 .25
1061 A192 50k multi .25 .25
1062 A192 90k multi .30 .25
1063 A192 1z multi .45 .30
1064 A192 1.45z multi .55 .45
1065 A192 1.70z multi .85 .70
1066 A192 3z multi 1.40 1.10
1067 A192 3.50z multi 1.90 1.40
1068 A192 5z multi 3.00 2.10
1069 A192 6z multi 3.25 2.50
Nos. 1058-1069 (12) 12.70 9.80

Souvenir Sheet

1070 A192 10z multi 7.50 7.50

Issued: #1058-1069, July 6; #1070, Sept. 21.
For surcharges see #1289, 1315, 1322, 1344, 1435 and footnote after #1336.

9th Conference of Heads of State of Africa and France, Kinshasa, Oct. A193

1982, Oct. 8 **Litho.** *Perf. 13*

1071 A193 75k multi .25 .25
1072 A193 90k multi .25 .25
1073 A193 1z multi .25 .25
1074 A193 1.50z multi .25 .25
1075 A193 3z multi .75 .60
1076 A193 5z multi 1.75 1.25
1077 A193 8z multi 2.00 1.75
Nos. 1071-1077 (7) 5.50 4.60

For surcharges see Nos. 1268, 1271, 1280, 1283, 1347, 1351.

Animals from Virunga Natl. Park A194

1982, Nov. 5

1078 A194 1z Lions .30 .25
1079 A194 1.70z Buffalo 1.00 .75
1080 A194 3.50z Elephants 2.25 1.50
1081 A194 6.50z Antelope 4.00 2.75
1082 A194 8z Hippopotamus 5.75 3.25
1083 A194 10z Monkeys 6.50 4.00
1084 A194 10z Leopard 6.50 4.25
a. Pair, #1083-1084 + label 18.00 18.00
Nos. 1078-1084 (7) 26.30 16.75

#1084a has continuous design.
For surcharge see No. 1430.

Scouting Year — A195

1982, Nov. 29 **Photo.** *Perf. 11½*

Granite Paper

1085 A195 90k Camp .35 .30
1086 A195 1.70z Campfire .90 .55
1087 A195 3z Scout 1.50 1.00
1088 A195 5z First aid 3.25 1.75
1089 A195 8z Flag signals 6.00 3.25
Nos. 1085-1089 (5) 12.00 6.85

Souvenir Sheet

1090 A195 10z Baden-Powell 11.00 11.00

For surcharges see Nos. 1207-1214.

Local Birds — A196

25k, Quelea quelea. 50k, Ceyx picta. 90k, Tauraco persa. 1.50z, Charadrius tricollaris. 1.70k, Cursorius temminckii. 2z, Campethera bennettii. 3z, Podiceps ruficollis. 3.50z, Kaupifalco monogrammicus. 5z, Limnocorax flavirostris. 8z, White-headed vulture.

1982, Dec. 6 **Litho.** *Perf. 13*

1091 A196 25k multicolored .25 .25
1092 A196 50k multicolored .25 .25
1093 A196 90k multicolored .60 .25
1094 A196 1.50z multicolored .65 .40
1095 A196 1.70k multicolored .70 .40
1096 A196 2z multicolored .95 .60
1097 A196 3z multicolored 1.50 .80
1098 A196 3.50z multicolored 1.60 .85
1099 A196 5z multicolored 2.50 1.25
1100 A196 8z multicolored 3.75 2.10
Nos. 1091-1100 (10) 12.75 7.15

All except 3.50z, 8z horiz.
For surcharges see Nos. 1263, 1266, 1272, 1276, 1278, 1284, 1425, 1432, 1438, 1440.

Souvenir Sheet

Christmas — A197

15z, Adoration of the Magi, by van der Goes.

1982, Dec. 20 **Photo.** *Perf. 13½*

1101 A197 15z multicolored 8.00 8.00

Quartz — A198

2k, Malachite, vert. 75k, Gold. 1z, Uraninite. 1.50z, Bournonite, vert. 3z, Cassiterite. 6z, Dioptase, vert. 8z, Cuprite, vert.
10z, Diamonds.

1983, Feb. 13 **Photo.** *Perf. 11½*

Granite Paper

1102 A198 2k multicolored .30 .25
1103 A198 45k shown .40 .25
1104 A198 75k multicolored .75 .25
1105 A198 1z multicolored 1.25 .25
1106 A198 1.50z multicolored 1.75 .80
1107 A198 3z multicolored 3.50 1.50
1108 A198 6z multicolored 6.00 3.00
1109 A198 8z multicolored 8.00 4.00
Nos. 1102-1109 (8) 21.95 10.30

Souvenir Sheet

1110 A198 10z multicolored 10.00 10.00

For surcharges see Nos. 1324, 1330, 1332, 1346.

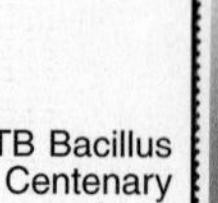

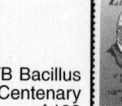

TB Bacillus Centenary A199

1983, Feb. 21 **Litho.** *Perf. 13*

1111 A199 80k multi .25 .25
1112 A199 1.20z multi .40 .35
1113 A199 3.60z multi 1.40 1.00
1114 A199 9.60z multi 4.00 2.25
Nos. 1111-1114 (4) 6.05 3.85

For surcharges see Nos. 1319, 1356, 1358, 1360, 1433, 1436, 1441.

Kinshasa Monuments A200

50k, Zaire Diplomat, vert. 1z, Echo of Zaire. 1.50z, Messengers, vert. 3z, Shield of Revolution, vert. 5z, Weeping Woman. 10z, Militant, vert.

1983, Apr. 25

1115 A200 50k multicolored .25 .25
1116 A200 1z multicolored .25 .25
1117 A200 1.50z multicolored .35 .25
1118 A200 3z multicolored .65 .50
1119 A200 5z multicolored 1.10 .90
1120 A200 10z multicolored 2.40 2.00
Nos. 1115-1120 (6) 5.00 4.15

For surcharges see Nos. 1267, 1279, 1349-1350.

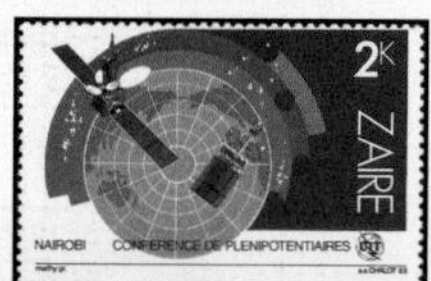

ITU Plenipotentiaries Conference, Nairobi, Sept. 1982 — A201

Various satellites, dish antennae and maps.

1983, June 13 Litho. *Perf. 13*

1121	A201	2k multi	.25	.25
1122	A201	4k multi	.25	.25
1123	A201	25k multi	.25	.25
1124	A201	1.20z multi	.40	.25
1125	A201	2.05z multi	.65	.35
1126	A201	3.60z multi	1.00	.60
1127	A201	6z multi	1.75	1.00
1128	A201	8z multi	2.50	1.40
		Nos. 1121-1128 (8)	7.05	4.35

For surcharges see Nos. 1260-1261, 1264, 1273-1274, 1277, 1355, 1359, 1429, 1434, 1437, 1439, 1442.

Christmas 1983 — A202

Raphael Paintings; No. 1129: a, Virgin and Child. b, Holy Family. c, Esterhazy Madonna. d, Sistine Madonna. No. 1130: a, La Belle Jardiniere. b, Virgin of Alba. c, Holy Family, diff. d, Virgin and Child, diff.

1983, Dec. 26 Photo. *Perf. 13½x13*

1129	A202	Sheet of 4	4.50	4.50
a.-d.		10z, any single	.85	.75
1130	A202	Sheet of 4	5.00	5.00
a.-d.		15z, any single	1.00	.75

Garamba Park A203

10k, Darby's Eland. 15k, Eagles. 3z, Servals. 10z, White rhinoceros. 15z, Lions. 37.50z, Warthogs. No. 1137, Koris bustards. No. 1138, Crowned cranes.

1984, Apr. 2 Litho. *Perf. 13*

1131	A203	10k multi	.25	.25
1132	A203	15k multi	.35	.25
1133	A203	3z multi	.60	.25
1134	A203	10z multi	2.25	1.25
1135	A203	15z multi	2.75	1.75
1136	A203	37.50z multi	6.25	4.25
1137	A203	40z multi	7.00	4.50
1138	A203	40z multi	7.00	4.50
a.		Pair, #1137-1138 + label	16.00	16.00
		Nos. 1131-1138 (8)	26.45	17.00

Nos. 1137-1138 are narrower, 49x34mm, with continuous design.
For surcharge see No. 1428.

World Communications Year — A204

Designs: 10k, Computer operator, Congo River ferry. 15k, Communications satellite. 8.50z, Engineer, Congo River Bridge. 10z, Satellite, ground receiving station. 15z, TV camerawoman filming crowed crane. 37.50z, Satellite, dish antennas. 80z, Switchboard operator, bus.

1984, May 14 Litho. *Perf. 13x12½*

1139	A204	10k multi	.25	.25
1140	A204	15k multi	.25	.25
1141	A204	8.50z multi	.65	.65
1142	A204	10z multi	.70	.70
1143	A204	15z multi	1.10	1.10
1144	A204	37.50z multi	2.75	2.75
1145	A204	80z multi	5.75	5.75
		Nos. 1139-1145 (7)	11.45	11.45

Hypericum Revolutum — A205

Local flowers: 15k, Borreria dibrachiata. 3z, Disa erubescens. 8.50z, Scaevola plumieri. 10z, Clerodendron thompsonii. 15z, Thumbergia erecta. 37.50z, Impatiens niamniamensis. 100z, Canarina eminii.

1984, May 28 Photo. *Perf. 14x13½*

1146	A205	10k multi	.25	.25
1147	A205	15k multi	.25	.25
1148	A205	3z multi	.25	.25
1149	A205	8.50z multi	.80	.80
1150	A205	10z multi	.90	.90
1151	A205	15z multi	1.25	1.25
1152	A205	37.50z multi	3.25	3.25
1153	A205	100z multi	9.00	9.00
		Nos. 1146-1153 (8)	15.95	15.95

1984 Summer Olympics — A206

1984, June 5 Litho. *Perf. 13*

1154	A206	2z Basketball	.25	.25
1155	A206	3z Equestrian	.35	.35
1156	A206	10z Running	1.10	1.10
1157	A206	15z Long jump	1.60	1.60
1158	A206	20z Soccer	2.75	2.75
		Nos. 1154-1158 (5)	6.05	6.05

Souvenir Sheet

Perf. 11½

1159	A206	50z Kayak	5.50	5.50

No. 1159 contains one 31x49mm stamp.
For surcharge see No. 1427.

Manned Flight Bicent. — A207

10k, Montgolfiere, 1783. 15k, Charles & Robert, 1783. 3z, Gustave, 1783. 5z, Santos-Dumont III, 1899. 10z, Stratospheric balloon, 1934. 15z, Zeppelin LZ-129, 1936. 37.50z, Double Eagle II, 1978. 80z, Hot air balloons.

1984, June 28 Litho. *Perf. 14*

1160	A207	10k multi	.25	.25
1161	A207	15k multi	.25	.25
1162	A207	3z multi	.25	.25
1163	A207	5z multi	.50	.40
1164	A207	10z multi	.90	.75
1165	A207	15z multi	1.40	1.00
1166	A207	37.50z multi	3.25	2.75
1167	A207	80z multi	7.25	6.50
		Nos. 1160-1167 (8)	14.05	12.15

For surcharges see Nos. 1413-1420.

Okapi — A208

1984, Oct. 15 Litho. *Perf. 13*

1168	A208	2z Grazing	1.25	.60
1169	A208	3z Resting	2.00	.70
1170	A208	8z Mother and young	3.75	2.25
1171	A208	10z In water	6.00	4.25
		Nos. 1168-1171 (4)	13.00	7.80

Souvenir Sheet

Perf. 11½

1172	A208	50z like 10z	5.25	5.25

World Wildlife Fund. No. 1172 contains one 36x51mm stamp, margin continues the design of the 10z without emblem.
For surcharge see note after No. 1352.

Nos. 893-900 Surcharged in Silver Over Black Bar and With One of Three Different Sabena Airlines Emblems and "1925 1985" in Silver

1985, Feb. 19 *Perf. 13*

1173	A165	2.50z on 30s #893	.35	.25
1174	A165	5z on 5k #896	.90	.50
1175	A165	6z on 70s #894	1.00	.60
1176	A165	7.50z on 1k #895	1.10	.70
1177	A165	8.50z on 10k #898	1.40	.90
1178	A165	10z on 8k #897	1.75	1.25
1179	A165	12.50z on 75k #900	2.00	1.75
1180	A165	30z on 50k #899	3.75	3.25
		Nos. 1173-1180 (8)	12.25	9.20

No. 901 Surcharged in Silver Over Black Bar and With Silver Text "60e ANNIVERSAIRE/1re LIASON AERIENNE/BRUXELLES-KINSHASAL/PAR EDMOND THIEFFRY"

Souvenir Sheet

1985, Feb. 19 *Perf. 11½*

1181	A165	50z on 5z #901	70.00	70.00

OLYMPHILEX '85, Lausanne A209

1985, Apr. 19 *Perf. 13*

1182	A209	1z Swimming	.25	.25
1183	A209	2z Soccer, vert.	.25	.25
1184	A209	3z Boxing	.25	.25
1185	A209	4z Basketball, vert.	.25	.25
1186	A209	5z Equestrian	.40	.40
1187	A209	10z Volleyball, vert.	.85	.85
1188	A209	15z Running	1.25	1.25
1189	A209	30z Cycling, vert.	2.50	2.50
		Nos. 1182-1189 (8)	6.00	6.00

Nos. 1013-1018, 969 Ovptd. and Surcharged with 1 or 2 Gold Bars and "AOUT 1985" in Gold or Black

1985, Aug. 15 *Perf. 13, 11½*

1190	A185	2z on 5k	.25	.25
1191	A185	3z on 10k	.35	.35
1192	A185	5z on 50k	.60	.60
1192A	A185	10z on 100k	1.40	1.40
1192B	A185	15z on 500k	1.90	1.90
1193	A185	40z on 800k	5.50	5.50
		Nos. 1190-1193 (6)	10.00	10.00

Souvenir Sheet

1194	A177	50z on 10z (B)	12.00	12.00

Second visit of Pope John Paul II.

Audubon Birth Bicent. A210

Illustrations of North American bird species by John Audubon: 5z, Great egret. 10z, Yellow-beaked duck. 15z, Small heron. 25z, White-fronted duck.

1985, Oct. 1 *Perf. 13*

1195	A210	5z multicolored	1.25	.60
1196	A210	10z multicolored	1.90	1.10
1197	A210	15z multicolored	4.00	1.50
1198	A210	25z multicolored	6.50	3.00
		Nos. 1195-1198 (4)	13.65	6.20

For surcharges see Nos. 1421-1424.

Natl. Independence, 25th Anniv. — A211

1985, Oct. 23 Photo. *Perf. 12*

Granite Paper

1200	A211	5z multi	.25	.25
1201	A211	10z multi	.45	.45
1202	A211	15z multi	.70	.70
1203	A211	20z multi	1.10	1.10
		Nos. 1200-1203 (4)	2.50	2.50

Souvenir Sheet

Perf. 11½

1204	A211	50z multi	2.50	2.50

UN, 40th Anniv. — A212

1985, Nov. 26

1205	A212	10z Flags, vert.	.50	.50
1206	A212	50z Emblem, UN building	2.75	2.75

Nos. 1087-1088, 1085-1086, 1089-1090 Surcharged

1985, Dec. 2 *Perf. 11½*

Granite Paper

1207	A195	3z on 3z multi	.60	.60
1208	A195	5z on 5z multi	.85	.85
1209	A195	7z on 90k multi	1.10	1.10
1210	A195	10z on 90k multi	1.60	1.60
1211	A195	15z on 1.70z multi	2.50	2.50
1212	A195	20z on 8z multi	3.50	3.50
1213	A195	50z on 90k multi	8.75	8.75
		Nos. 1207-1213 (7)	18.90	18.90

Souvenir Sheet

1214	A195	50z on 10z multi	12.00	12.00

Intl. Youth Year.

Souvenir Sheet

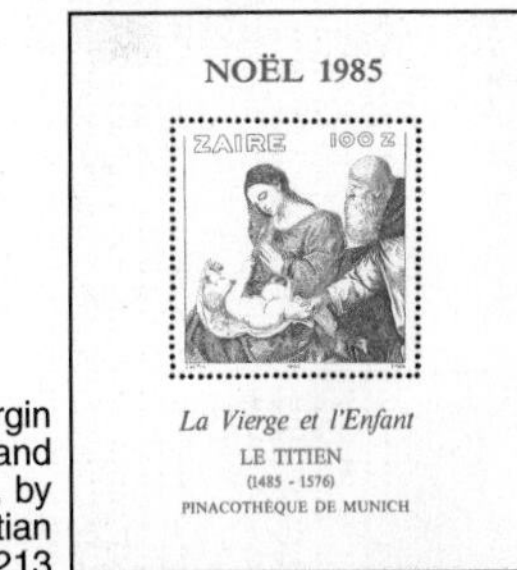

Virgin and Child, by Titian A213

Photogravure and Engraved

1985, Dec. 23 *Perf. 13½*

1215	A213	100z brown	7.00	7.00

Christmas 1985.

Natl. Transit Authority, 50th Anniv. — A214

1985, Dec. 31 *Perf. 13*

1216	A214	7z Kokolo mail ship	.25	.25
1217	A214	10z Steam locomotive	.40	.40
1218	A214	15z Luebo ferry	.60	.60
1219	A214	50z Stanley locomotive	2.00	1.50
		Nos. 1216-1219 (4)	3.25	2.75

Postage Stamp, Cent. — A215

Stamps on stamps: 7z, Belgian Congo No. 30. 15z, Belgian Congo No. B28. 20z, Belgian Congo No. 226. 25z, Zaire No. 1059. 40z, Zaire No. 1152. 50z, Zaire No. 883 and Belgium No. 1094.

1986, Feb. 23 ***Perf. 13***

1220 A215 7z multi .40 .30
1221 A215 15z multi .65 .50
1222 A215 20z multi 1.00 .75
1223 A215 25z multi 1.10 1.00
1224 A215 40z multi 1.75 1.25
Nos. 1220-1224 (5) 4.90 3.80

Souvenir Sheet

Perf. 11½

1225 A215 50z multi 3.25 3.25

No. 1225 contains one 50x35mm stamp.

Beatification of Sister Anuarite Nengapeta, Aug. 15, 1985 — A216

1986, Feb. 21 **Litho.** ***Perf. 13***

1226 A216 10z Pope John Paul II .80 .50
1227 A216 15z Sr. Anuarite 1.10 .70
1228 A216 25z Both portraits 1.60 1.10
Nos. 1226-1228 (3) 3.50 2.30

Souvenir Sheet

Imperf

1229 A216 100z Both portraits, triangular 5.00 5.00

Nos. 1226-1227 vert. No. 1229 contains one quadrilateral stamp, size: 30x36x60mm.
For surcharges see Nos. 1370-1371, 1373, 1376-1377.

Congo Stamp Cent. — A217

1986, Feb. 22 **Litho.** ***Perf. 13***

1230 A217 25z Belgian Congo No. 3 1.25 1.00

Imperfs exist. Value $5.
See Belgium No. 1236.

Indigenous Reptiles — A218

2z, Dasypeltis scaber. 5z, Agama agama. 10z, Python regius. 15z, Chamaeleo dilepis. 25z, Dendroaspis jamesoni. 50z, Naja nigricolis.

1987, Feb. 11 **Litho.** ***Perf. 13***

1231 A218 2z multicolored .25 .25
1232 A218 5z multicolored .25 .25
1233 A218 10z multicolored .50 .50
1234 A218 15z multicolored 1.00 .65
1235 A218 25z multicolored 1.40 1.00
1236 A218 50z multicolored 2.50 2.50
Nos. 1231-1236 (6) 5.90 5.15

Christmas 1987 — A219

Paintings (details) by Fra Angelico: 50z, Virgin and Child, center panel of the Triptych of Cortona, 1435. 100z, The Nativity. 120z, Virgin and Child with Angels and Four Saints, Fiesole Retable. 180z, Virgin and Child with Six Saints, Annalena Retable.

1987, Dec. 24 **Litho.** ***Perf. 13***

1237 A219 50z multi .75 .75
1238 A219 100z multi 1.75 1.75
1239 A219 120z multi 2.25 2.25
1240 A219 180z multi 3.25 3.25
Nos. 1237-1240 (4) 8.00 8.00

French Revolution, Bicent. A220

Designs: 50z, Declaration of the Rights of Man and Citizen. 100z, Abstract art. 120z, Globe showing Africa, South America.

1989 **Litho.** ***Perf. 13½x14½***

1241 A220 40z multicolored .55 .50
1242 A220 50z multicolored .65 .60
1243 A220 100z multicolored 1.40 1.25
1244 A220 120z multicolored 2.00 1.60
Nos. 1241-1244 (4) 4.60 3.95

REGIDESCO, 50th Anniv. — A221

40z, Administration bldg. 50z, Modern factory. 75z, Water works. 120z, Woman drawing water.

1989

1245 A221 40z multicolored .40 .40
1246 A221 50z multicolored .50 .50
1247 A221 75z multicolored .75 .75
1248 A221 120z multicolored 1.40 1.25
Nos. 1245-1248 (4) 3.05 2.90

For surcharge see note after No. 1352.

Fight Against AIDS A222

Designs: 40z, Bowman firing arrow through SIDA. 80z, "SIDA" on Leopard.
150z, World map with AIDS symbols.

1989

1249 A222 30z multicolored 1.00 .90
1250 A222 40z multicolored 1.25 1.25
1251 A222 80z multicolored 2.75 2.50
Nos. 1249-1251 (3) 5.00 4.65

Souvenir Sheet

Perf. 14

1252 A222 150z multicolored 4.75 4.75

For surcharge see note after No. 1352.

Tourist Attractions A223

40z, Waterfalls of Venus. 60z, Rural village. 100z, Kivu Lake. 120z, Niyara Gongo Volcano. 300z, Kisantu Botanical Gardens, vert.

1990 **Litho.** ***Perf. 13½x14½***

1253 A223 40z multicolored .55 .55
1254 A223 60z multicolored .85 .85
1255 A223 100z multicolored 1.40 1.40
1256 A223 120z multicolored 1.75 1.75
Nos. 1253-1256 (4) 4.55 4.55

Souvenir Sheet

Perf. 14½

1257 A223 300z multicolored 4.50 4.50

For surcharge see note after No. 1352.

Souvenir Sheet

Christmas — A224

1990 **Litho.** ***Perf. 14***

1258 A224 500z multicolored 5.00 5.00

Various 1971-1983 Stamps Surcharged in Gold

1990 ***Perfs., Etc. as Before***

1259 A160 20z on 20k #877 .60 .60
1260 A201 40z on 2k #1121 .60 .60
1261 A201 40z on 4k #1122 .60 .60
1262 A184 40z on 10k #1005 .60 .60
1263 A196 40z on 25k #1091 .60 .60
1264 A201 40z on 25k #1123 .60 .60
1265 A184 40z on 50k #1007 .60 .60
1266 A196 40z on 50k #1092 .60 .60
1267 A200 40z on 50k #1115 .60 .60
1268 A193 40z on 75k #1071 .60 .60
1269 A184 40z on 80k #1008 .60 .60
1270 A190 40z on 90k #1045 .60 .60
1271 A193 40z on 90k #1072 .60 .60
1272 A196 40z on 90k #1093 .60 .60
1273 A201 80z on 2k #1121 1.50 1.50
1274 A201 80z on 4k #1122 1.50 1.50
1275 A184 80z on 10k #1005 1.50 1.50
1276 A196 80z on 25k #1091 1.50 1.50
1277 A201 80z on 25k #1123 1.50 1.50
1278 A196 80z on 50k #1092 1.50 1.50
1279 A200 80z on 50k #1115 1.50 1.50
1280 A193 80z on 75k #1071 1.50 1.50
1281 A184 80z on 80k #1008 1.50 1.50
1282 A190 80z on 90k #1045 1.50 1.50
1283 A193 80z on 90k #1072 1.50 1.50
1284 A196 80z on 90k #1093 1.50 1.50
1285 A175 100z on 40s #953 2.10 2.10
1287 A186 100z on 2k #1019 2.10 2.10
1288 A187 100z on 2k #1028 2.10 2.10
1289 A192 100z on 2k #1058 2.10 2.10
1290 A175 100z on 4k #955 2.10 2.10
1291 A165 100z on 5k #896 2.10 2.10
1292 A185 100z on 5k #1013 2.10 2.10
1293 A187 100z on 5k #1029 2.10 2.10
1294 A159 100z on 8k #865 2.10 2.10
1295 A165 100z on 8k #897 2.10 2.10
1296 A167 100z on 8k #912 2.10 2.10
1298 A167 100z on 10k #913 2.10 2.10
1299 A169 100z on 10k #922 2.10 2.10
1300 A165 100z on 10k #993 2.10 2.10
1301 A183 100z on 10k #1000 2.10 2.10
1302 A185 100z on 10k #1014 2.10 2.10
1303 A186 100z on 10k #1020 2.10 2.10
1304 A175 100z on 15k #956 2.10 2.10
1305 A187 100z on 18k #1031 2.10 2.10
1306 A169 100z on 20k #923 2.10 2.10
1307 A180 100z on 20k #977 2.10 2.10
1308 A144 100z on 22k #755 2.10 2.10
1309 A186 100z on 25k #1021 2.10 2.10
1311 A159 100z on 48k #869 2.10 2.10
1312 A167 100z on 48k #916 2.10 2.10
1313 A179 100z on 50k #971 2.10 2.10
1314 A187 100z on 50k #1032 2.10 2.10
1315 A192 100z on 50k #1061 2.10 2.10
1316 A165 100z on 75k #995 2.10 2.10
1317 A183 100z on 75k #1001 2.10 2.10
1318 A183 100z on 80k #1002 2.10 2.10
1319 A199 100z on 80k #1111 2.10 2.10
1320 A170 100z on 90k #930 2.10 2.10
1321 A186 100z on 90k #1022 2.10 2.10
1322 A192 100z on 90k #1062 2.10 2.10
1324 A198 300z on 2k #1102 6.50 6.50
1325 A173 300z on 8k #938 6.50 6.50
1326 A182 300z on 10k #986 6.50 6.50
1327 A143 300z on 14k #751 6.50 6.50
1328 A146 300z on 17k #769 6.50 6.50
1329 A174 300z on 20k #947 6.50 6.50
1330 A198 300z on 45k #1103 6.50 6.50
1331 A182 300z on 75k #987 6.50 6.50
1332 A198 300z on 75k #1104 6.50 6.50
1333 A162 500z on 8k #886 11.50 11.50
1334 A162 500z on 10k #887 11.50 11.50
1335 A162 500z on 25k #888 11.50 11.50
1336 A162 500z on 48k #889 11.50 11.50
Nos. 1259-1336 (74) 204.40 204.40

Size and location of surcharge varies. Some surcharges show "z" before numeral.
100z on #1060 was surcharged in error. Value, $20.

Various 1980-1983 Stamps Surcharged

1991 ***Perfs., Etc., as Before***

1342 A181 1000z on 1z #982a-982d 2.00 2.00
1343 A185 1000z on 100k #1016 .35 .35
1344 A192 1000z on 1z #1063 .35 .35
1345 A182 2000z on 100k #988 .70 .70
1346 A198 2000z on 1z #1105 .70 .70
1347 A193 2500z on 1z #1073 1.40 1.40
1348 A191 3000z on 1z #1057 2.00 2.00
1349 A200 4000z on 1z #1116 2.75 2.75
1350 A200 5000z on 1z #1116 4.00 4.00
1351 A193 10,000z on 1z #1073 5.25 5.25
1352 A191 15,000z on 1z #1057 8.00 8.00
Nos. 1342-1352 (11) 27.50 27.50

Size and location of surcharge varies.

The editors have received from a collector mint stamps bearing the surcharges shown below. There is conflicting data as to the validity of these surcharges, and anyone with information on them is asked to contact the new issues editor.

Du 8 au 15 - 6 - 92
2e Conférence Addis - Abeba
Virus VIH 1 - et VIH 2
EN AFRIQUE
10.000.000 Z

ZAIRE
15.000.000 Z.
Conférence
Nationale
Souveraine
3 mars - 4
décembre
1991 - 1992

Nos. 989, 1010, 1112, 1124 Srchd.

1992, Aug. 18 ***Perfs., Etc. as Before***

1354 A184 50th z on 125k #1010 .60 .60
1355 A201 100th z on 1.20z #1124 .80 .80
1356 A199 150th z on 1.20z #1112 1.40 1.40
1357 A182 200th z on 145k #989 1.75 1.75
1358 A199 250th z on 1.20z #1112 2.25 2.25
1359 A201 300th z on 1.20z #1124 2.75 2.75
1360 A199 500th z on 1.20z #1112 4.50 4.50
Nos. 1354-1360 (7) 14.05 14.05

Size and location of surcharge varies.

#1361-1366

ZAIRE
1 MILLION Z
Cantharellus miniatescens

#1368-1374

1993, Oct. 29 **Photo.** ***Perf. 13½x13***

1361 A167 500th z on 30s #910 .75 .75
1362 A167 500th z on 5k #911 .90 .90
1365 A167 750th z on 8k #912 1.00 1.00
1366 A167 750th z on 10k #913 1.25 1.25
1368 A167 1 mil z on 30k #914 1.50 1.50
1369 A167 1 mil z on 40k #915 1.50 1.50
1370 A167 5 mil z on 48k #916 7.50 7.50
1371 A167 10 mil z on 100k #917 15.00 15.00
Nos. 1361-1371 (8) 29.40 29.40

Nos. 1226-1229 Srchd. in Black or Red

1993, Oct. 29 **Litho.** ***Perf. 13***

1373 A216 3 mil z on 10z #1226 3.00 3.00
1374 A216 3 mil z on 10z #1226 (R)
1375 A216 5 mil z on 15z #1227 4.75 4.75
1376 A216 10 mil z on 25z #1228 9.25 9.25

Souvenir Sheet

Imperf

1377 A216 10 mil z on 100z #1229 13.00 13.00

Size and location of surcharge varies.

ZAIRE 30 NK

Natl. Game Parks, 50th Anniv. — A225

1993 **Litho.** ***Perf. 13***

1403 A225 30k Cape eland .30 .25
1404 A225 50k Elephants .30 .25
1405 A225 1.50z Giant eland 1.25 1.00
1406 A225 3.50z White rhinoceros 3.00 2.00
1407 A225 5z Bongo 4.00 2.50
Nos. 1403-1407 (5) 8.85 6.00

For surcharge see No. 1431.

Nos. 986-900 Surcharged

1994, Apr. 23 **Photo.** ***Perf. 14***

1408 A182 30k on 10k .75 .75
1409 A182 50k on 75k 1.25 1.25
1410 A182 1.50z on 100k 3.75 3.75
1411 A182 3.50z on 145k 7.50 7.50
1412 A182 5z on 270k 11.50 11.50
Nos. 1408-1412 (5) 24.75 24.75

Nos. 1160-1167 Surcharged

1994, Apr. 23 **Litho.** ***Perf. 14***

1413 A207 30k on 10k .75 .75
1414 A207 50k on 15k 1.00 1.00
1415 A207 1.50z on 3z 2.50 2.50
1416 A207 2.50z on 5z 3.75 3.75
1417 A207 3.50z on 10z 5.50 5.50
1418 A207 5z on 15z 8.00 8.00
1419 A207 7.50z on 37.50z 12.50 12.50
1420 A207 10z on 80z 17.50 17.50
Nos. 1413-1420 (8) 51.50 51.50

Nos. 1195-1198 Surcharged

1994, Apr. 23 **Litho.** ***Perf. 13***

1421 A210 50k on 5z 1.75 1.75
1422 A210 1.50z on 10z 5.00 5.00
1423 A210 3.50z on 15z 9.50 9.50
1424 A210 5z on 25z 19.00 19.00
Nos. 1421-1424 (4) 35.25 35.25

Nos. 990, 1079, 1094, 1097, 1113, 1125-1126, 1133, 1155, & 1404 Surcharged in Gold

1994, Aug. 31 ***Perfs., Etc. as Before***

1425 A196 20z on 3z #1097 .40 .40
1426 A182 40z on 270k #990 .40 .40
1427 A203 50z on 3z #1133 .50 .50
1428 A206 75z on 3z #1155 .60 .60
1429 A201 100z on 2.05z #1125 .75 .75
1430 A194 150z on 1.70z #1079 1.25 1.25
1431 A225 200z on 50k #1404 1.50 1.50
1432 A196 250z on 1.50z #1094 1.75 1.75
1433 A199 300z on 3.60z #1113 2.00 2.00
1434 A201 500z on 3.60z #1126 3.25 3.25
Nos. 1425-1434 (10) 12.40 12.40

Size and location of surcharge varies.

Nos. 1067, 1094, 1113, 1125-1126 Surcharged in Gold

No. 1435

No. 1437

1996 ***Perfs., Etc. as Before***

1435 A192 100z on 3.50z #1067 .50 .50
1436 A199 500z on 3.60z #1113 .50 .50
1437 A201 1000z on 2.05z #1125 .50 .50
1438 A196 2500z on 1.50z #1094 1.75 1.75
1439 A201 5000z on 3.60z #1126 3.25 3.25
1440 A196 6000z on 1.50z #1094 3.50 3.50
1441 A199 15,000z on 3.60z #1113 9.00 9.00
1442 A201 25,000z on 3.60z #1126 17.50 17.50
Nos. 1435-1442 (8) 36.50 36.50

1996 Summer Olympic Games, Atlanta — A226

1000z, Equestrian. 12,500z, Boxing. 25,000z, Table tennis. 35,000z, Basketball, vert. 50,000z, Tennis.

1996, July 29 **Litho.** ***Perf. 11½***

1444 A226 1000z multi .25 .25
1445 A226 12,500z multi 1.00 1.00
1446 A226 25,000z multi 3.00 3.00
1447 A226 35,000z multi 4.00 4.00
1448 A226 50,000z multi 4.75 4.75
Nos. 1444-1448 (5) 13.00 13.00

Insects & Spiders — A227

No. 1449: a, Lasius niger. b, Calopterygides. c, Peucetia. d, Sphecides.

1996 **Litho.** ***Perf. 13½***

1449 A227 15,000z Sheet of 4, #a.-d. 15.00 15.00

Minerals — A228

No. 1450: a, Uraninite. b, Malachite. c, Ruby. d, Diamond.
No. 1452, Uranotile, cuprosklodowskite, horiz.

1996

1450 A228 40,000z Sheet of 4, #a.-d. 27.50 27.50

Souvenir Sheet

1452 A228 105,000z multi 20.00 20.00

No. 1452 exists overprinted in silver for Hong Kong Exposition '97.
A number has been reserved for an additional sheet with this set.

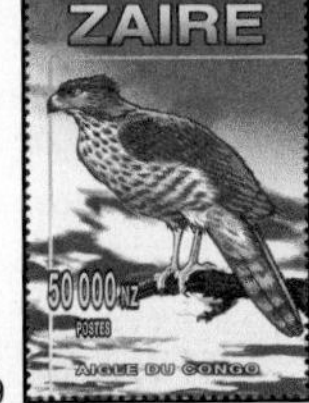

Raptors — A229

No. 1453: a, Congo eagle. b, Crowned eagle. c, Melierax metabates. d, Urotriorchis macrourus.

1996

1453 A229 50,000z Sheet of 4, #a.-d. 30.00 30.00

Butterflies — A230

No. 1454: a, Cymothoe sangaris. b, Colotis zoe. c, Physcaeneura leda. d, Charaxes candiope.

1996

1454 A230 70,000z Sheet of 4, #a.-d. 37.50 37.50

The validity of Nos. 1455-1481 and other stamps from the same time period has been questioned. The editors are attempting to find out more about these stamps.

1998 World Cup Soccer Championships, France — A231

Numbers on players: No. 1455, #12. No. 1456, none. No. 1457, #7. No. 1458, #3.
No. 1459: a, British player. b, Brazilian player.
No. 1460: a-d, Like #1455-1458, but with part of World Cup Trophy behind each player.

1996
1455-1458 A231 35,000z Set of 4 14.00 14.00

Souvenir Sheets

1459 A231 105,000z Sheet of 2, #a.-b. 20.00 20.00
1460 A231 35,000z Sheet of 4, #a.-d. 14.00 14.00

No. 1459 contains 2 42x39mm stamps.
See Nos. 1467-1476.

World Wildlife Fund — A231a

No. 1466 — Pan paniscus: a, With young. b, Two in trees. c, Holding vines. d, Head.

1997
1466 A231a 20,000z Block of 4, #a.-d. 20.00 20.00

1998 World Cup Soccer Championships Type of 1996

African soccer players: No. 1467, 20,000z, Soccer ball at his right. No. 1468, 20,000z, Ball at head. No. 1469, 20,000z, Yellow uniform. No. 1470, 20,000z, Ball on knee.
German soccer players, soccer ball on stamp at: No. 1471, 50,000z, UR. No. 1472, 50,000z, LL. No. 1473, 50,000z, LR. No. 1474, 50,000z, UL.
Nos. 1475a-1475d, 1476a-1476d are like Nos. 1467-1474 but with part of World Cup Trophy behind each player.

1996 **Litho.** ***Perf. 13½***
1467-1470 A231 Set of 4 9.00 9.00
1471-1474 A231 Set of 4 20.00 20.00

Souvenir Sheets

1475 A231 20,000z Sheet of 4, #a.-d. 9.00 9.00
1476 A231 50,000z Sheet of 4, #a.-d. 20.00 20.00

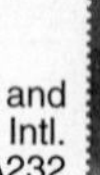

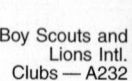

Boy Scouts and Lions Intl. Clubs — A232

No. 1477 — Diceros bicornis: a, Walking forward. b, Walking left, left leg up. c, Facing left. d, Holding head up.
No. 1478 — Panthera leo: a, Cubs. b, Adult male. c, Adult male facing forward, mouth open. d, Adult female on fallen tree.
No. 1479 — Loxodonta africana: a, Walking right, trunk in air. b, Reaching up to tree limb with trunk. c, Walking right, trunk down. d, Mother with calf.
105,000z, Hippopotamus amphibus.

1997 **Litho.** ***Perf. 13x13½***
1477 A232 40,000z Sheet of 4, #a.-d. 13.00 13.00
1478 A232 50,000z Sheet of 4, #a.-d. 17.50 17.50
1479 A232 70,000z Sheet of 4, #a.-d. 24.00 24.00

Souvenir Sheet

1480 A232 105,000z multi 12.00 12.00

Boy Scouts (#1477, 1479-1480). Lions Intl. Clubs (#1478).

Jacqueline Kennedy Onassis (1929-94) — A233

Various portraits.

1997 **Litho.** ***Perf. 13½***
1481 A233 15,000z Sheet of 9, #a.-i. 17.50 17.50

No. 1481 also exists imperf.

Stamps from this country are now being released under the previous name, "Republique Democratique du Congo," or Congo Democratic Republic, despite the resumption of civil war. We will continue to list these stamps under the country's name of Zaire until the situation is resolved.

Diana, Princess of Wales (1961-97) — A234

No. 1482: a, Wearing tiara. b, In white jacket. c, In white hat. d, In polka dotted dress. e, Scarf around neck. f, Low cut evening dress.
No. 1483: a, Wearing tiara. b, Hand under chin. c, Leaning chin on both hands. d, One-shoulder-covered outfit.
No. 1484; a, Red & black dress. b, White jacket, pearls. c, Profile view. d, Wearing tiara.
No. 1485, 400,000z, In black evening dress. No. 1486, 400,000z, Holding flowers.

1998, Aug. 6 **Litho.** ***Perf. 14***
1482 A234 50,000z Sheet of 6, #a.-f. 13.50 7.75
1483 A234 100,000z Sheet of 4, #a.-d. 17.50 10.50
1484 A234 125,000z Sheet of 4, #a.-d. 24.00 14.50

Souvenir Sheets

1485-1486 A234 Set of 2 50.00 25.00

Mother Teresa (1910-97) — A235

1998, Aug. 6
1487 A235 50,000z shown 2.25 1.50

Souvenir Sheet

1488 A235 325,000z Portrait, diff. 11.50 7.50

No. 1487 was issued in sheets of 6.

100 Centimes = 1 Franc (1998)

Native Dwelling A236

Arms A237

Inauguration of Pres. Laurent Kabila — A238

Designs: 1.25fr, Troops and civilians in Kinshasa. 3fr, Flag, crowd, Pres. Kabila breaking chain with sword, horiz.
2.50fr, Gun, arrow, handshake, tractor. 3.50fr, Pres. Kabila.

1999, May 12 **Litho.** ***Perf. 14***
1489 A236 25c multi .25 .25
1490 A237 50c multi .55 .55
1491 A238 75c multi .80 .80
1492 A238 1.25fr multi 1.75 1.75
1493 A238 3fr multi 3.25 3.25
Nos. 1489-1493 (5) 6.60 6.60

Souvenir Sheets

1494 A238 2.50fr multi 2.60 2.60
1495 A238 3.50fr multi 3.75 3.75

Conquest of Kinshasa by troops of Laurent Kabila, 2nd anniv.

Chinese Zodiac Animals A239

No. 1496: a, Rat. b, Ox. c, Tiger. d, Rabbit. e, Dragon. f, Snake. g, Horse. h, Ram. i, Monkey. j, Cock. k, Dog. l, Boar.

1999, Aug. 20 ***Perf. 13¼x13½***
1496 A239 78c Sheet of 12, #a-l 27.50 17.50

A240

A241

A242

A243

Outlaws of the Marsh A244

No. 1497 — Sheet with text starting with "The historical novel. . .": a, 1.45fr, Men fighting. b, 1.50fr, Man uprooting tree. c, 1.60fr, Man with sword in snowstorm. d, 1.70fr, Man with sword, other men at bridge. e, 1.80fr, Three men at table.
No. 1498 — Sheet with text starting with "The main theme. . .": a, 1.45fr, Men and baskets. b, 1.50fr, Man threatening another man with sword. c, 1.60fr, Man attacking tiger. d, 1.70fr, People watching men in martial arts battle. e, 1.80fr, Battling horsemen.
No. 1499 — Sheet with text starting with "The common people. . .": a, 1.45fr, Men fighting in boat. b, 1.50fr, Man with sword fighting man with hatchets. c, 1.60fr, Men near fortified wall. d, 1.70fr, Men fighting on cobblestone street. e, 1.80fr, Archer on horseback at doorway.
No. 1500 — Sheet with text starting with "Today, it is thought. . .": a, 1.45fr, Man seated and other man standing near table. b, 1.50fr, Man setting fire to building. c, 1.60fr, Man in room. d, 1.70fr, Man lifting another man in a battle. e, 1.80fr, Man holding torn scroll.

1999, Aug. 20 ***Perf. 13¼***

Sheets of 5, #a-e

1497-1500 A240 Set of 4 60.00 45.00

Souvenir Sheets

Perf. 13¼x13½

1501 A241 10fr multi 17.50 17.50
1502 A242 10fr multi 17.50 17.50
1503 A243 10fr multi 17.50 17.50
1504 A244 10fr multi 17.50 17.50

A245

A246

African Flora and Fauna A247

Designs: 1fr, Telophorus quadricolor. 1.50fr, Panthera pardus. No. 1507, 2fr, Colotis protomedia. No. 1508, 2fr, Kobus vardoni. No. 1509, 3fr, Canarina abyssinica. No. 1510, 3fr, Smutsia temminckii.
7.80fr, Lion.
No. 1512: a, Okapi. b, Bird, rainbow, waterfalls. c, Giraffe, rainbow, waterfalls. d, Giraffe, waterfall mist. e, Mandrill. f, Chimpanzee. g, Leopard. h, Butterflies. i, Hippopotamus. j, Bird in water. k, Flowers. l, Antelope.
No. 1513: a, Sun. b, Pieris citrina. c, Merops apiaster. d, Lanius collurio. e, Ploceus cucullatus. f, Charaxes pelias. g, Charaxes eupale. h, Giraffa camelopardalis. i, Galago moholi. j, Strelitzia reginae. k, Gazella thomsoni. l, Upupa epops.
No. 1514, 10fr, Taurotragus oryx. No. 1515, 10fr, Hippopotamus amphibus.
No. 1516, 10fr, Warthog.

Perf. 14, 14¼x14¾ (#1511), 14¼x14 (#1516)

2000, Feb. 28
1505-1510 A245 Set of 6 14.50 14.50
1511 A246 7.80fr multi 8.00 8.00
1512 A247 1fr Sheet of 12, #a-l 12.50 12.50
1513 A245 1.50fr Sheet of 12, #a-l 20.00 20.00

Souvenir Sheets

1514-1515 A245 Set of 2 20.00 20.00
1516 A247 10fr multi 10.00 10.00

No. 1516 contains one 42x57mm stamp.

Wild Felines and Canines A248

No. 1517, 1.50fr: a, Felis bengalensis. b, Felis aurata. c, Felis caracal. d, Felis conoclor. e, Felis nigripes. f, Panthera leo. g, Neofelis nebulosa. h, Felis wiedii. i, Acinonyx jubatus. j, Felis pardina. k, Felis yagouaroundi. l, Felis serval.

No. 1518, 2fr: a, Canis mesomelas. b, Otocyon megalotis. c, Speothos venaticus. d, Canis latrans. e, Cuon alpinus. f, Fennecus zerda. g, Urocyon cinereoargenteus. h, Canis lupus. i, Vulpes macrotis. j, Chrysocyon brachyurus. k, Nyctereutes procyonoides. l, Vulpes vulpes.

No. 1519, 10fr, Panthera pardus. No. 1520, 10fr, Alopex lagopus.

2000, Feb. 28 ***Perf. 14***

Sheets of 12, #a-l

1517-1518 A248 Set of 2 40.00 40.00

Souvenir Sheets

1519-1520 A248 Set of 2 17.00 17.00

Millennium A249

2000, June 10

1521 Horiz. strip of 3 12.00 12.00
a. A249 4.50fr multi 1.25 1.25
b. A249 9fr multi 3.25 3.25
c. A249 15fr multi 5.00 5.00

Printed in sheets containing two strips.

A250

A251

Birds — A252

Designs: No. 1522, 3fr, Alopochen aegyptiacus. No. 1523, 3fr, Ardeola ibis. No. 1524, 4.50fr, Oena capensis. No. 1525, 4.50fr, Lybius torquatus. No. 1526, 9fr, Falco tinnunculus. No. 1527, 9fr, Corythaelo cristata.

No. 1528, 4.50fr, Psephotus chrysopterygius chrysopterygius. 8fr, Amazona aestiva. No. 1530, 8.50fr, Are nobilis cumanensis. No. 1531, 9fr, Agapornis roseicollis.

No. 1532, 8.50fr, Lophornis ornata. No. 1533, 9fr, Polytrus guauvunibi.

No. 1534, 9fr: a, Euplectes orix. b, Euplectes ardens. c, Oriolus auratus. d, Plocens cucullatus. e, Amandava subflava. f, Nectarina senegalensis.

No. 1535, 9fr: a, Halcyon malimbicus. b, Tachymarptis melba. c, Haliaeetus vocifer. d, Ardea purpurea. e, Balaeniceps rex. f, Balearica regulorum.

No. 1536: a, Ertoxeres aquila. b, Aglaiolepus kinde. c, Archilochus calobris. d, Trochlus polytaus. e, Chaliostigna herrani. f, Ensifera. g, Chrysolampus mosquitus. h, Phorethornus syrmatophorus. i, Calypre hetervare.

No. 1537, 5fr: a, Eos squamata squamata. b, Aratinga guarouba. c, Aratinga aurea. d, Psuedeos fuscata. e, Agapornis fischeri. f, Aratinga nana nana. g, Aratinga mitrata. h, Trichoglossus haematodus rubitorquis. i, Cacatua galerita galerita.

No. 1538, 5fr: a, Ara macao. b, Neophema elegans. c, Loriculus vernalis. d, Aratinga solstitialis. e, Pionites melancephala. f, Bolborhynchus lineola. g, Ara severa. h, Psephotus chrysopterygius dissimilis. i, Ara militaris.

No. 1539, 15fr, Actophilornis africanus, horiz. No. 1540, 20fr, Ceryle rudis, horiz.

No. 1541, 15fr, Opopsitta diophthalma. No. 1542, 15fr, Ara ararrauna, horiz.

No. 1543, 15fr, Coeligena torgoata. No. 1544, 20fr, Campylopterus hemileicurus.

2000, Aug. 16 ***Perf. 14***

1522-1527 A250 Set of 6 *15.00 15.00*
1528-1531 A251 Set of 4 *13.50 13.50*
1532-1533 A252 Set of 2 *7.75 7.75*

Sheets of 6, #a-f

1534-1535 A250 Set of 2 *47.50 47.50*
1536 A252 4.50fr Sheet of 9, #a-i *18.00 18.00*

Sheets of 9, #a-i

1537-1538 A251 Set of 2 *40.00 40.00*

Souvenir Sheets

1539-1540 A250 Set of 2 *16.00 16.00*
1541-1542 A251 Set of 2 *13.50 13.50*
1543-1544 A252 Set of 2 *16.00 16.00*

Types of 1996 and Unissued Stamps Surcharged

A253

A253a

A253b

A253c

A253d

Designs: 10fr on 70,000z, Colotis zoe. 15fr on 25,000z, Bulbophyllum falcatum. 25fr on 20,000z, Scutellosaurus. 35fr on 15,000z, Sphecides. 45fr on 100,000z, Diamond. 50fr on 35,000z, Termitomyces aurantiacus. 70fr on 50,000z, Melierax metabates. 100fr on 40,000z, Malachite. 150fr on 25,000z, Panda.

No. 1545 surcharged as A253. No. 1548 surcharged as A253d. No. 1551 surcharged as A253a. No. 1552 surcharged as A253b.

2000 **Litho.** ***Perf. 13¼***

1545 A230 10fr on 70,000z multi 7.25 7.25
1546 A253 15fr on 25,000z multi 7.25 7.25
1547 A253a 25fr on 20,000z multi 7.25 7.25
1548 A227 35fr on 15,000z multi 7.25 7.25
1549 A253b 45fr on 100,000z multi 7.25 7.25
1550 A253c 50fr on 35,000z multi 7.25 7.25
1551 A229 70fr on 50,000z multi 7.25 7.25
1552 A228 100fr on 40,000z multi 7.25 7.25
1553 A253d 150fr on 25,000z multi 7.25 7.25

Location of surcharges varies. All surcharged stamps have white margins.

A254

Trains A255

Designs: 1fr, Missouri-Kansas-Texas Line locomotive. 2fr, Spremberg steam locomotive. No. 1556, 3fr, King Class, Great Western Railway. No. 1557, 3fr, Crocodile locomotive. 5fr, Inner-city trains, Great Britain. 6fr, Big Boy, Union Pacific.

No. 1560, 4.50fr: a, Class SU, 2-6-2, Russia. b, Prussian locomotive. c, Zimbabwe locomotive. d, Hunslet 2-8-2, Peru. e, London, Midland & Scottish Railway locomotive. f, London Northeastern Railway locomotive.

No. 1561, 8fr: a, Denver & Rio Grande Western Railroad locomotive. b, Mikado 2-8-2, Louisville & Nashville. c, Mogul, Rio Grande. d, New York Central Railway locomotive. e, Sumpter Valley Railway steam locomotive. f, Three-truck Shay No. 7.

No. 1562, 9.50fr: a, Compagnie du Nord locomotive, France. b, Union Pacific locomotive. c, Great Northern Railway locomotive. d, Liverpool & Manchester Railway locomotive. e, Patentee 2-2-2, London & Birmingham. f, Puffing Billy.

No. 1563, 10fr: a, Chicago, Rock Island & Pacific Railway locomotive. b, Powhattan Arrow, Norfolk & Western. c, Class S-1, New York Central Hudson River Railway. d, Reading Railroad locomotive. e, Great Bear, Great Western Railway. f, Bi-polar, Chicago, Milwaukee, St. Paul & Pacific Railway.

No. 1564, 5fr: a, Beyer-Garratt 50 4-8-2+2-8-4 locomotive. b, Locomotive Express 4-6-2. c, 780CV electric locomotive. d, Electric locomotive on curve. e, Class 2-10-0 Locomotive 56001. f, Electric locomotive on straight track. g, Class 2-8-4 Locomotive 284. h, Class G 6/6 electric locomotive.

No. 1565, 8.50fr: a, Class B-B electric locomotive AE4/4. b, Class EX, Paris-Lyon-Mediterranean. c, Big Boy. d, Tourist car. e, Class 4-8-4 GS-4. f, Class 46 electric locomotive. g, Class-4-6-0 County. h, Class DA Diesel-electric locomotive.

No. 1566, 15fr, New York Central & Hudson River Railway locomotive. No. 1567, 20fr, Mohawk & Hudson Railroad locomotive. No. 1568, 20fr, Broadway Limited, Pennsylvania Railroad. No. 1569, 20fr, Trans-Europe Express.

No. 1570, 20fr, Deltic electric locomotive, Great Britain. No. 1571, 20fr, Diesel-electric locomotive, Canada Pacific.

2001, Jan. 15 **Litho.** ***Perf. 14***

1554-1559 A254 Set of 6 11.50 11.50

Sheets of 6, #a-f

1560-1563 A254 Set of 4 65.00 65.00

Sheets of 8, #a-h

1564-1565 A255 Set of 2 45.00 45.00

Souvenir Sheets

1566-1569 A254 Set of 4 32.50 32.50
1570-1571 A255 Set of 2 14.00 14.00

Ships — A256

Designs: 2.50fr, Clipper. 5fr, Arab bum. 20fr, Flemish galley. 21.70fr, Trabaccolo, vert. 30fr, Dutch galliot. 45.80fr, Japanese coaster.

No. 1578, 10fr: a, Trireme. b, Roman caudicaria. c, 13th cent. warship. d, Byzantine galley. e, Lateneer. f, 14th century cog. g, Arab dhow. h, Hanseatic cog. i, Portuguese galley.

No. 1579, 10fr: a, Egyptian sailing ship. b, Egyptian rowing craft. c, Egyptian seagoing ship. d, Greek galley. e, Etruscan merchantman f, Etruscan fishing skiff. g, Greek merchantman. h, Minoan passenger ship. i, Roman harbor boat.

No. 1580, 10fr: a, Flemish galleon. b, English galleon. c, Carrack. d, Chinese war galley. e, Venetian galley. f, Polacre. g, Hemmena. h, Venetian bragozzo. i, Schooner.

No. 1581, 25fr, Viking drakkar. No. 1582, 25fr, Portuguese caravel, vert. No. 1583, 25fr, HMS Endeavour, vert.

2001, June 22 ***Perf. 14***

1572-1577 A256 Set of 6 14.00 14.00

Sheets of 9, #a-i

1578-1580 A256 Set of 3 30.00 30.00

Souvenir Sheets

Perf. 13¾

1581-1583 A256 Set of 3 16.00 16.00

No. 1581 contains one 50x38mm stamp; Nos. 1582-1583 each contain one 38x50mm stamp.

History of Aviation A257

No. 1584: a, Montgolfier balloon (36x61mm). b, Boxkite and Tiger Moth airplanes (36x61mm). c, Gladiator. d, Eurofighter. e, Mosquito. f, Chipmunk.

No. 1585: a, Blackburn and Spartan Arrow airplanes (36x61mm). b, Tiger Moth. c, Lightning. d, Vulcan B2. e, Tornado.

No. 1586, 25fr, Fox Moth and Avro 540K airplanes. No. 1587, 25fr, Avro 504K and Fox Moth airplanes.

2001, June 22 ***Perf. 14¼***

1584 A257 10fr Sheet of 6, #a-f 10.00 10.00
1585 A257 10fr Sheet of 6, #1584a, 1585a-1585e 10.00 10.00

Souvenir Sheets

Perf. 14¼x14½

1586-1587 A257 Set of 2 12.00 12.00

First Zeppelin Flight, Cent. A258

No. 1588: a, LZ-6. b, LZ-7. c, US Navy airship Akron. c, Lindstrand HS-110 Pittsburgh Tribune-Review airship.

No. 1589, 100fr, LZ-130 Graf Zeppelin II. No. 1590, 100fr, LZ-1.

2001, June 22 ***Perf. 14***

1588 A258 60fr Sheet of 4, #a-d 27.50 27.50

Souvenir Sheets

1589-1590 A258 Set of 2 22.50 22.50

Butterflies — A259

Designs: 5fr, Striped policeman. 21.70fr, Brown-veined white. 45fr, Common dotted border. 45.80fr, Cabbage. 50fr, African migrant. 51.80fr, Mocker swallowtail.

No. 1597, 6fr, horiz.: a, Common grass blue. b, Golden tiger. c, Palla. d, Blue diadem. e, African giant swallowtail. f, African leaf. g, Gold-banded forester. h, Small harvester.

No. 1598, 6fr, horiz.: a, Guinea fowl. b, Forest queen. c, Sweet potato acraea. d, Wanderer. e, Evening brown. f, African ringlet. g, Plain tiger. h, Monarch.

No. 1599, 8fr, horiz.: a, Broad-bordered grass yellow. b, Crimson tip. c, Orange-banded protea. d, Azure hairstreak. e, Marshall's false monarch. f, Blue swallowtail. g, Figtree blue. h, Grass jewel.

No. 1600, 25fr, Long-tailed blue, horiz. No. 1601, 25fr, Chief, horiz. No. 1602, 25fr, Large spotted acraea, horiz.

2001, June 22

1591-1596 A259 Set of 6 25.00 25.00

Sheets of 8, #a-h

1597-1599 A259 Set of 3 37.50 37.50

Souvenir Sheets

1600-1602 A259 Set of 3 17.50 17.50

Flowers and Insects — A260

Designs; 20fr, Aconite, Brazilian frog-hopper. 21.70fr, Larkspur, Mexican cicada. 25fr, Blue orchid, dragonfly. 45.80fr, Spotted blossom orchid, buck moth.

No. 1607, 10fr, horiz.: a, Rein orchids, tiger moth. b, Ivy, Siamese wasp. c, Pink lady's slipper, goat weed emperor. d, Gletscherpetersbart, velvet ant. e, Licorice, viceroy butterfly. f, Grass pink, aphid. g, Ranunculus, spider wasp. h, Clamshell orchid, tropical bee. i, Bog orchids, mayfly.

No. 1608, 10fr, horiz.: a, Common lantana, red-spotted purple butterfly. b, Deep purple lilac, zebra swallowtail. c, Mt. Fujiyama, ruddy copper butterfly. d, Pinafore pink, red admiral butterfly. e, Argemone mexicana, purple hairstreak butterfly. f, Soapwort, sulphur butterfly. g, Lungwort, Buckeye butterfly. h, Wild thyme, pipevine swallowtail. i, Loeselia mexicana, banded purple butterfly.

No. 1609, 10fr, horiz.: a, Cymbidium Stanley Fouraker Highlander, scarlet tiger moth. b, Cymbidium Sparkle "Ruby Lips," Sumatran carpenter bee. c, Dendrobium Sussex, ant lion. d, Cymbidium Vieux Rose Loch Lomond, nachahmend butterfly. e, Cymbidium, cicada-killer wasp. f, Dendrobium Mousmee, spechosoma wasp. g, Arachnis flos-aeris, green lacewing. h, Paphiopedilum, seven-spot ladybug. i, Eulophia quartiniana, damselfly.

No. 1610, 25fr, Jolly Jocker pansy, monarch butterfly, horiz. No. 1611, 25fr, Pink peony, wasp (inscribed erroneously like No. 1610), horiz. No. 1612, 25fr, Plumbago capensis, honey bee, horiz.

2001, June 22 ***Perf. 14***

1603-1606 A260 Set of 4 13.00 13.00

Sheets of 9, #a-i

Perf. 14¼x14½

1607-1609 A260 Set of 3 32.50 32.50

Souvenir Sheets

1610-1612 A260 Set of 3 16.00 16.00

Nos. 1607-1609 each contain nine 37x30mm stamps; Nos. 1610-1612 each contain one 50x37mm stamp.

Tintin in Africa — A261

Designs: 190fr, Tintin with hand above eyes. 461fr, Tintin in car with dog and native.

2001, Dec. 31 **Photo.** ***Perf. 11½***

1613 A261 190fr multi 2.50 2.50

Souvenir Sheet

1614 A261 461fr multi 7.00 7.00

No. 1614 contains one 48x38mm stamp. Examples of No. 1613 with a red overprint for Expo 2010 Shanghai were never put on sale at Congolese post offices.

Imperfs exist. Value: 1613, $15; 1614, $30.

See Belgium Nos. 1875-1876.

Millennium — A261a

Designs: No. 1614A, Patrice Lumumba (1925-61), first Prime Minister of Democratic Republic of the Congo, and Congolese flag. No. 1614B, Neil Armstrong (1930-2012), first man on Moon. No. 1614C, Agricultural worker, farm field and cow. No. 1614D, Congolese drummer and satellite dish. No. 1614E, Dr. Albert Schweitzer (1875-1965), humanitarian and 1952 Nobel Peace laureate. No. 1614F, Dr. Martin Luther King, Jr. (1929-68), civil rights leader and 1964 Nobel Peace laureate. No. 1614G, Nurse examining infant. No. 1614H, Train, ferry and Congolese people in canoe. No. 1614I, Teacher, map and school children. No. 1614J, Aerial view of city.

No. 1614K: l, Charles de Gaulle (1890-1970), president of France. m, Miner and crystals. n, Albert Einstein (1879-1955), physicist. o, Pres. John F. Kennedy (1917-63), p, Mohandas K. Gandhi (1869-1948), Indian nationalist leader. q, Congolese dancer and drummers. r, Congolese art. s, Soccer players. t, Pope John Paul II (1920-2005). u, King Baudouin of Belgium (1930-93).

2001 **Litho.** ***Perf. 11½***

1614A A261a 22fr multi — —
1614B A261a 22fr multi — —
1614C A261a 22fr multi — —
1614D A261a 22fr multi — —
1614E A261a 42fr multi — —
1614F A261a 42fr multi — —
1614G A261a 42fr multi — —
1614H A261a 43fr multi — —
1614I A261a 45fr multi — —
1614J A261a 47fr multi — —

Miniature Sheet

1614K Sheet of 20, #1614A-1614J, 1614l-1614u — —
l.-m. A261a 22fr Either single — —
n. A261a 42fr multi — —
o.-p. A261a 43fr Either single — —
q.-r. A261a 45fr Either single — —
s. A261a 47fr multi — —
t. A261a 48fr multi — —
u. A261a 90fr multi — —

Nos. 1614A-1614J were each issued in sheets of 20.

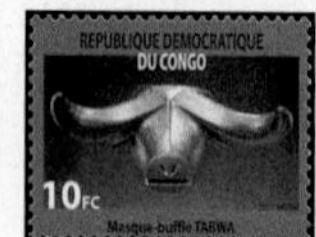

Native Handicrafts — A262

Designs: 10fr, Tabwa buffalo mask. 50fr, Kongo bedpost. 60fr, Loi drum. 150fr, Kuba royal statue, vert. 200fr, Tshokwe mask, vert. 300fr, Luba mask, vert.

2002, Mar. 7 **Litho.** ***Perf. 11½***

1615-1620 A262 Set of 6 13.00 13.00

Lions — A263

Designs: 50fr, Lioness and cub. 75fr, Lion and dead animal. 150fr, Lioness and cubs at water's edge. 250fr, Lion and lioness. 300fr, Lion leaping in water.

2002, Mar. 7 **Litho.** ***Perf. 11½***

1621-1625 A263 Set of 5 13.50 13.50

Flowers — A264

Designs: 25fr, Gloriosa rothschildiana. 50fr, Aworthia cooperi. 125fr, Lithops aucampiae. 250fr, Angraecum sesquipedale.

500fr, Lampranthus coccineus.

2002 **Litho.** ***Perf. 11½***

1626-1629 A264 Set of 4 4.75 4.75

Souvenir Sheet

1630 A264 500fr multi 5.75 5.75

Minerals — A265

Designs: 190fr, Beryl, vert. 340fr, Willemite mimetite. 410fr, Quartz chlorite. 445fr, Allophane copper. 455fr, Rhodochrosite, vert. 480fr, Zircon.

800fr, Anglesite.

Perf. 11½x11¼

2002, Aug. 30 **Litho.**

1631 A265 190fr multi 2.25 2.25
1632 A265 340fr multi 4.00 4.00
1633 A265 410fr multi 5.00 5.00
1634 A265 445fr multi 5.25 5.25
1635 A265 455fr multi 5.25 5.25
1636 A265 480fr multi 5.75 5.75

Souvenir Sheet

1637 A265 800fr multi — —

Worldwide Fund for Nature (WWF) A266

Designs: 20fr, Head of gorilla. 190fr, Adult and juvenile gorillas. 390fr, Gorilla in grass, vert. 455fr, Gorilla eating grass, vert. 1000fr, Head of gorilla, diff.

2002, Aug. 30 **Litho.** ***Perf. 11¾***

1638-1641 A266 Set of 4 15.00 15.00

Souvenir Sheet

1642 A266 1000fr multi — —

Pres. Joseph Kabila — A267

Background color: 195fr, Blue green. 350fr, 800fr, Light blue. 1500fr, Gold.

2002, Dec. 10 **Litho.** ***Perf. 13¼***

1643-1644 A267 Set of 2 5.00 2.00

Souvenir Sheets

1645 A267 800fr multi 7.50 7.50

Litho. & Embossed With Foil Application

1646 A267 1500fr gold & multi 16.00 16.00

Nos. 1645-1646 each contain one 42x50mm stamp.

Numerous stamps on a variety of topics having year dates of 2002-2012 and inscription "Republique Democratique du Congo" apparently were not available in the Congo.

AIDS Prevention A268

AIDS ribbon and text: 320fr, "Une vraie femme ne vend pas son amour propre pour des cadeaux ou de l'argent," head of woman, woman refusing gift from man. 470fr, "Une vraie femme pense à son avenir avant de penser à faire l'amour," head of woman, weomen at school. 490fr, "Je l'aime. Je la protège avec Prudence," man and woman. 530fr, "Un vrai homme ne forcerait jamais une femme à faire l'amour," head of man, men and woman in argument. 550fr, "Un vrai homme ne sera pas forcé à faire l'amour par ses amis," head of man, group of men and woman. 600fr, "Roulez protege," AIDS ribbon on truck. 800fr, "Les apparences sont souvent trompeuses." 1000fr, "Prudence, l'amour de l'avenir."

2016 **Litho.** ***Perf. 13¼x13***

1647-1652 A268 Set of 6 — —

Souvenir Sheets

Size: 120x86mm

1653 A268 800fr multi — —

Size: 86x121mm

1654 A268 1000fr multi — —

Nos. 1649 and 1652 are dated "2005," but Nos. 1647-1652 apparently were not put on sale in the Democratic Republic of Congo until 2016.

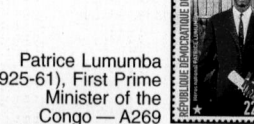

Patrice Lumumba (1925-61), First Prime Minister of the Congo — A269

Designs: 2250fr, No. 1656, Color photograph of Lumumba.

No. 1657 — Various black-and-white photographs of Lumumba with denominations of: a, 2000fr (40x30mm). b, 3000fr, (40x30mm). c, 10,000fr (40x60mm).

2021, June 30 **Litho.** ***Perf. 13¼x13***

1655 A269 2250fr multi — —
1656 A269 10,000fr multi — —

Souvenir Sheet

Perf. 13x13¼

1657 A269 Sheet of 3, #a-c — —

Campaign Against COVID-19 — A270

Denominations: 2000fr, 3000fr, 5000fr, 10,000fr.

2021 **Litho.** ***Perf. 13¼x13***

1658-1661 A270 Set of 4 — —

OFFICIAL STAMPS

Nos. 756-772 Overprinted

1975 **Litho.** ***Perf. 14***

O1 A145 10s red org & blk .25 .25
O2 A145 40s multi .25 .25
O3 A145 50s multi .25 .25

Perf. 13

O4 A146 1k multi .25 .25
O5 A146 2k multi .25 .25
O6 A146 3k multi .25 .25
O7 A146 4k multi .30 .25
O8 A146 5k multi .30 .25
O9 A146 6k multi .45 .25
O10 A146 8k multi .65 .25
O11 A146 9k multi .65 .25
O12 A146 10k multi .80 .25
O13 A146 14k multi 1.25 .40
O14 A146 17k multi 1.50 .45
O15 A146 20k multi 1.50 .60
O16 A146 50k multi 3.75 1.50
O17 A146 100k multi 12.50 4.00
Nos. O1-O17 (17) 25.15 9.95

"SP" are the initials of "Service Public."

ZAMBEZIA

zam-'bē-zē-ə

LOCATION — A former district of the Mozambique Province in Portuguese East Africa
GOVT. — Part of the Portuguese East Africa Colony

The districts of Quelimane and Tete were created from Zambezia. Eventually stamps of Mozambique came into use. See Quelimane and Tete.

1000 Reis = 1 Milreis

King Carlos
A1 A2

Perf. 11½, 12½ (#5, 8, 10-12)

1894 Typo. Unwmk.

1 A1 5r yellow .70 .60
2 A1 10r red violet 1.00 .80
3 A1 15r chocolate 2.00 1.20
a. Perf. 12½ 160.00 115.00
4 A1 20r lavender 2.00 1.20
5 A1 25r blue green 3.25 2.10
6 A1 50r lt blue 3.00 2.10
a. Perf. 12½ 3.00 2.00
7 A1 75r carmine 7.75 6.00
a. Perf. 11½ 120.00 95.00
8 A1 80r yellow grn 7.00 4.50
9 A1 100r brown, *buff* 6.00 3.25
10 A1 150r car, *rose* 8.00 5.25
11 A1 200r dk blue, *bl* 9.00 5.25
a. Perf. 11½ *975.00 1,000.*
b. Perf. 13½ 45.00 35.00
12 A1 300r dk bl, *salmon* 15.00 7.75
a. Perf. 11½ 60.00 40.00
Nos. 1-12 (12) 64.70 40.00

For surcharges and overprints see Nos. 36-47, 73-74, 77-81, 84-88.

1898-1903 ***Perf. 11½***

Name and Value in Black or Red (500r)

13 A2 2½r gray .80 .60
14 A2 5r orange .80 .60
15 A2 10r lt green 1.30 .60
16 A2 15r brown 2.00 1.40
17 A2 15r gray grn ('03) 2.40 2.10
18 A2 20r gray violet 2.00 1.40
19 A2 25r sea green 2.00 1.40
20 A2 25r carmine ('03) 2.00 1.25
21 A2 50r blue 2.00 1.40
22 A2 50r brown ('03) 4.00 3.50
23 A2 65r dull bl ('03) 11.50 9.25
24 A2 75r rose 17.50 8.00
25 A2 75r lilac ('03) 5.00 3.50
26 A2 80r violet 8.50 4.25
27 A2 100r dk bl, *bl* 3.50 2.50
28 A2 115r org brn, *pink* ('03) 16.00 10.00
29 A2 130r brn, *straw* ('03) 16.00 10.00
30 A2 150r brn, *buff* 9.50 5.25
31 A2 200r red vio, *pnksh* 9.50 5.25
32 A2 300r dk bl, *rose* 11.50 5.25
33 A2 400r dull bl, *straw* ('03) 20.00 14.00
34 A2 500r blk, *bl* ('01) 20.00 11.00
35 A2 700r vio, *yelsh* ('01) 25.00 13.00
Nos. 13-35 (23) 192.80 115.50

For surcharges and overprints see Nos. 49-68, 72, 82-83, 93-107.

Stamps of 1894 Surcharged

1902 ***Perf. 11½, 12½ (#41-45, 47)***

36 A1 65r on 10r red vio 13.50 10.00
37 A1 65r on 15r choc 13.50 10.00
38 A1 65r on 20r lav 13.50 10.00
39 A1 65r on 300r bl, *sal* 13.50 10.00
a. Perf. 12½ 13.00 9.75
40 A1 115r on 5r yel 13.50 10.00
41 A1 115r on 25r bl grn 13.50 10.00
42 A1 115r on 80r yel grn 13.50 10.00
43 A1 130r on 75r car 10.00 10.00
a. Perf. 11½ 10.00 10.00
44 A1 130r on 150r car, *rose* 8.00 7.75
45 A1 400r on 50r lt bl 3.25 3.25
a. Perf. 11½ 3.25 3.25
46 A1 400r on 100r brn, *buff* 3.25 3.50
47 A1 400r on 200r bl, *bl* 3.25 3.50

Same Surcharge on No. P1

Perf. 12½

48 N1 130r on 2½r brn 13.50 10.00
a. Double surcharge 27.50 25.00
b. Inverted surcharge 27.50 25.00
Nos. 36-48 (13) 135.75 108.00

Stamps of 1898 Overprinted

1902 ***Perf. 11½***

49 A2 15r brown 4.00 2.00
50 A2 25r sea green 4.00 2.00
51 A2 50r blue 4.00 2.00
52 A2 75r rose 10.00 5.00
Nos. 49-52 (4) 22.00 11.00

No. 23 Surcharged in Black

1905

53 A2 50r on 65r dull blue 9.50 5.75

Stamps of 1898-1903 Overprinted in Carmine or Green

1911

54 A2 2½r gray .50 .30
55 A2 5r orange .50 .30
56 A2 10r light green .60 .35
a. Inverted overprint 21.00 21.00
57 A2 15r gray green .60 .35
58 A2 20r gray violet .85 .50
59 A2 25r carmine (G) 2.50 1.20
60 A2 50r brown .60 *.60*
61 A2 75r lilac 1.90 1.40
62 A2 100r dk bl, *bl* 1.90 1.40
63 A2 115r org brn, *pink* 1.90 1.40
64 A2 130r brown, *straw* 1.90 1.40
65 A2 200r red vio, *pnksh* 1.90 1.40
66 A2 400r dull bl, *straw* 3.00 1.75
67 A2 500r blk & red, *bl* 3.00 1.75
68 A2 700r violet, *yelsh* 3.50 2.50
Nos. 54-68 (15) 25.15 *16.60*

Stamps of 1902-05 Overprinted in Carmine or Green

1914 **Without Gum**

72 A2 50r on 65r dl bl *2,000. 1,800.*
73 A1 115r on 5r yellow 2.50 2.00
74 A1 115r on 25r bl grn 2.50 2.00
75 A1 115r on 80r yel grn 2.50 2.00
76 N1 130r on 2½r brn (G) 2.50 2.00
a. Carmine overprint 24.00 22.50
77 A1 130r on 75r car 2.50 2.00
a. Perf. 12½ 7.50 7.00
78 A1 130r on 150r car, *rose* 2.50 2.00
79 A1 400r on 50r lt bl 3.75 3.50
a. Perf. 12½ 15.50 15.50
80 A1 400r on 100r brn, *buff* 4.00 3.50
a. Inverted surcharge 21.00 21.00
81 A1 400r on 200r bl, *bl* 4.00 3.50

On Nos. 51-52

82 A2 50r blue 2.10 2.00
a. Double surcharge 21.00 21.00
83 A2 75r rose 2.10 2.00
Nos. 73-83 (11) 30.95 26.50

Preceding Issues Overprinted in Carmine

1915

On Surcharged Issue of 1902

84 A1 115r on 5r yellow 1.15 .85
85 A1 115r on 25r bl grn 1.15 .85
86 A1 115r on 80r lt grn 1.15 .85
87 A1 130r on 75r carmine 1.15 .85
a. Perf. 12½ 7.00 4.75
88 A1 130r on 150r car, *rose* 1.15 .85
92 N1 130r on 2½r (down) 1.15 .85

On Nos. 51, 53

93 A2 50r blue 1.15 .85
a. "Republica" inverted 15.00 15.00
94 A2 50r on 65r dull bl 5.00 *3.75*
Nos. 84-94 (8) 13.05 *9.70*

Stamps of 1898-1903 Overprinted Locally in Carmine

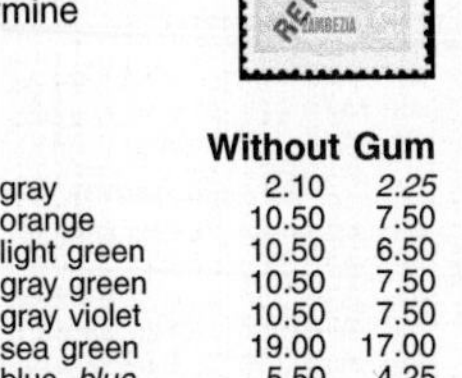

1917 **Without Gum**

95 A2 2½r gray 2.10 *2.25*
96 A2 5r orange 10.50 7.50
97 A2 10r light green 10.50 6.50
98 A2 15r gray green 10.50 7.50
99 A2 20r gray violet 10.50 7.50
100 A2 25r sea green 19.00 17.00
101 A2 100r blue, *blue* 5.50 4.25
102 A2 115r org brn, *pink* 5.50 4.25
103 A2 130r brown, *straw* 5.50 4.25
104 A2 200r red vio, *pnksh* 5.50 4.25
105 A2 400r dull bl, *straw* 5.50 4.75
106 A2 500r blk & red, *bl* 5.50 5.75
107 A2 700r vio, *yelsh* 13.50 8.25
Nos. 95-107 (13) 109.60 84.00

NEWSPAPER STAMP

N1

1894 Unwmk. Typo. ***Perf. 12½***

P1 N1 2½r brown .90 .70

For overprints and surcharges see Nos. 76, 92.

ZAMBIA

'zam-bē-ə

LOCATION — Southern Africa
GOVT. — Republic
AREA — 290,586 sq. mi.
POP. — 9,663,535 (1999 est.)
CAPITAL — Lusaka

The former British protectorate of Northern Rhodesia became an independent republic Oct. 24, 1964, taking the name Zambia. See Northern Rhodesia; see Rhodesia and Nyasaland.

12 Pence = 1 Shilling
20 Shillings = 1 Pound
100 Ngwee = 1 Kwacha (1968)

Catalogue values for all unused stamps in this country are for Never Hinged items.

Pres. Kenneth D. Kaunda, Victoria Falls — A1

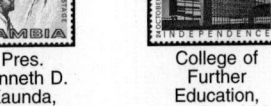

College of Further Education, Lusaka — A2

Perf. 14½x14, 14x14½

1964, Oct. 24 Photo. Unwmk.

1 A1 3p shown .30 .25
2 A2 6p shown .30 .25
3 A1 1sh3p Barotse dancer .30 .30
Nos. 1-3 (3) .90 .80

Zambia's independence, Oct. 24, 1964.

Farmer and Silo
A3

X-Ray Technician
A4

Designs: 2p, Chinyau dancer. 3p, Woman picking cotton. 4p, Angoni bull. 6p, Communications by drum and teletype. 9p, Redwood blossoms and factory. 1sh, Night fishing on Lake Tanganyika. 1sh3p, Woman tobacco worker. 2sh, Tonga basket maker and child. 2sh6p, Elephants in Luangwa Valley Game Reserve. 5sh, Child and school. 10sh, Copper mining. £1, Makishi dancer.

1964, Oct. 24 Photo. ***Perf. 14½***

Size: 23x19mm, 19x23mm

4 A3 ½p emerald, blk & red .30 1.60
5 A4 1p ultra, blk & brn .30 .25
6 A4 2p orange, brn & red .30 .25
7 A4 3p red & black .30 .25
8 A3 4p orange & black .30 .25

Perf. 13½x14½, 14½x13½

Size: 32x23mm, 23x32mm

9 A3 6p Prus grn, brn & org .30 .25
10 A3 9p ultra, brn & dk car rose .30 .25
11 A3 1sh blue, bis & blk .30 .25
12 A4 1sh3p dk bl, ver, blk & yel .30 .25
13 A4 2sh org, blk, brn & ultra .30 .30
14 A3 2sh6p org yel & blk 1.05 .40
15 A3 5sh emerald, blk & yel 1.30 1.05
16 A3 10sh orange & blk 6.25 5.00
17 A4 £1 red, blk, brn & yel 3.15 8.50
Nos. 4-17 (14) 14.75 18.85

ITU Emblem, Old and New Communication Equipment — A5

1965, July 26 Photo. ***Perf. 14***

18 A5 6p brt lilac & gold .30 .25
19 A5 2sh6p gray & gold .90 1.50

Cent. of the ITU.

ICY Emblem — A6

1965, July 26 ***Perf. 14***

20 A6 3p grnsh blue & gold .30 .25
21 A6 1sh3p ultra & gold .50 .50

International Cooperation Year, 1965.

Pres. Kaunda and State House, Lusaka
A7

Clematopsis
A8

Designs: 6p, Fireworks over Independence Stadium. 2sh6p, Tithonia diversifolia.

Perf. 13½x14½

1965, Oct. 18 Unwmk.

22 A7 3p multicolored .30 .25
23 A7 6p ind, yel & brt pink .30 .25

Perf. 14

24 A8 1sh3p pink, yel & brn .30 .25
25 A8 2sh6p brt grn, dp org & brn .30 .25
Nos. 22-25 (4) 1.20 1.00

1st anniv. of independence, Oct. 24.

Inauguration of WHO Headquarters, Geneva — A9

1966, May 18 *Perf. 14*

26 A9 3p rose brn, brt bl & gold .30 .25
27 A9 1sh3p vio bl, brt bl & gold .70 1.00

University of Zambia — A10

1966, July 12 Photo. *Perf. 14*

28 A10 3p brt green & gold .30 .25
29 A10 1sh3p brt purple & gold .30 .25

University of Zambia opening, Mar. 17.

National Assembly Building — A11

1967, May 2 Unwmk. *Perf. 14*

30 A11 3p slate & bronze .30 .25
31 A11 6p yellow grn & bronze .30 .25

Completion of National Assembly Building.

Lusaka Airport — A12

1967, Oct. 2 Photo. *Perf. 13½x14½*

32 A12 6p vio blue & bronze .30 .25
33 A12 2sh6p brown & bronze .65 1.05

Opening of Lusaka International Airport.

Symbols of Agriculture A13

Radio, Telephone and Television A14

Designs: 4p, Emblem of Zambia Youth Service. 1sh, Map showing locations of Zambia coalfields. 1sh6p, Map showing Zambia-Tanzania Road.

Perf. 14½x13½, 13½x14½

1967, Oct. 23

34 A14 4p gray, red & gold .30 .25
35 A13 6p lt vio bl, gold & blk .30 .25
36 A14 9p dull blue, sil & blk .30 .50
37 A14 1sh gold, red, blk & vio bl .50 .25
38 A13 1sh6p bl grn, ultra, gold & blk .75 2.35
Nos. 34-38 (5) 2.15 3.60

Issued to publicize National Development.

Lusaka Cathedral A15

Baobab Tree A16

Designs: 3n, Zambia Airways plane. 5n, National Museum, Livingstone. 8n, Vimbuza dancer. 10n, Woman tobacco picker. 15n, Nudaurelia zambesina butterfly. 20n, Crowned cranes. 25n, Angoni warrior. 50n, Chokwe dancer. 1k, Railroad bridge, Kafue River. 2k, Eland.

Perf. 13½x14½, 14½x13½

1968, Jan. 16 Photo.

Size: 26x22mm, 22x26mm

39 A15 1n bronze & multi .30 .25
a. Booklet pane of 6 1.40
b. Booklet pane of 4 1.40
40 A16 2n bronze & multi .30 .25
41 A15 3n bronze & multi .30 .25
a. Booklet pane of 6 1.40
b. Booklet pane of 4 1.40
42 A16 5n sepia & bronze .30 .25
43 A16 8n bronze & multi .30 .25
44 A16 10n bronze & multi .30 .25

Size: 32x26mm, 26x32mm

45 A15 15n bronze & multi 4.25 .25
46 A16 20n bronze & multi 6.25 .25
47 A16 25n bronze & multi .50 .25
48 A16 50n bronze, org & blk .45 .25
49 A15 1k dk blue & brnz 10.50 .50
50 A15 2k copper & blk 1.30 *1.60*
Nos. 39-50 (12) 25.05 *4.60*

Used values of Nos. 48-50 are for canceled-to-order stamps. Postally used examples sell for more.

Map of Zambia, Arrow Pointing to Ndola — A17

Perf. 14½x14

1968, June 29 Photo. Unwmk.

51 A17 15n brt green & gold .30 .25

Zambia Trade Fair at Ndola.

Children and Human Rights Flame — A18

WHO Emblem — A19

Children — A20

Photogravure; Gold Impressed

1968, Oct. 23 *Perf. 14½x14*

52 A18 3n ultra, dk bl & gold .30 .30
53 A19 10n brt violet & gold .30 .30
54 A20 25n brt blue, blk & gold .30 .75
Nos. 52-54 (3) .90 1.35

Intl. Human Rights Year; 20th anniv. of WHO; 21st anniv. of UNICEF (25n).

Copper Miner — A21

Design: 25n, Worker poling furnace, horiz.

Perf. 14½x13½

1969, June 18 Photo.

55 A21 3n dp violet & copper .30 .25
56 A21 25n yellow, blk & copper 1.05 1.05

50th anniv. of the ILO.

Map of Africa with Zambia — A22

10n, Waterbucks, Kafue National Park, horiz. 15n, Golden perch, Kasaba Bay, horiz. 25n, Carmine bee-eater, Luangwa Valley.

Perf. 13½x14, 14x13½

1969, Oct. 23 Photo.

57 A22 5n ultra, yel & copper .30 .25
58 A22 10n copper & multi .30 .25
59 A22 15n copper & multi .35 .40
60 A22 25n copper & multi 1.05 1.90
Nos. 57-60 (4) 2.00 2.80

International Year of African Tourism.

Nimbus III Weather Satellite — A23

1970, Mar. 23 Litho. *Perf. 13x11*

61 A23 15n multicolored .30 .50

Issued for World Meteorological Day.

"Clean Water" — A24

Designs: 15n, "Nutrition" (infant on scale). 25n, Children's immunization and Edward Jenner, M.D.

1970, July 4 Litho. *Perf. 13x12½*

62 A24 3n multicolored .30 .25
63 A24 15n multicolored .30 .30
64 A24 25n multicolored .65 .75
Nos. 62-64 (3) 1.25 1.30

Issued to publicize preventive medicine and the "Under Five" children's clinics.

Mural by Gabriel Ellison — A25

1970, Sept. 8 Litho. *Perf. 14x14½*

65 A25 15n multicolored .45 .30

Opening of the Conf. of Non-Aligned Nations in Mulungushi Hall (decorated with murals by Mrs. Ellison) in Zambia.

Ceremonial Axe — A26

Traditional Crafts: 5n, Clay pipe bowl with antelope head. 15n, Makishi mask, vert. 25n, The Kuomboka Ceremony (dancers and ceremonial boat).

1970, Nov. 30 Litho. *Perf. 14x14½*

Size: 34x25mm

66 A26 3n dp lil rose & multi .30 .25
67 A26 5n dp org, blk & sepia .30 .25

Perf. 13x13½

Size: 30x45½mm

68 A26 15n dp lil rose & multi .35 .30

Perf. 12½

Size: 71½x23½mm

69 A26 25n violet, blue & multi .60 1.05
a. Souvenir sheet of 4, #66-69 9.00 19.00
Nos. 66-69 (4) 1.55 1.85

Dag Hammarskjold and UN General Assembly A27

Hammarskjold and: 10n, Downed plane. 15n, Dove with olive branch. 25n, Plaque and flowers.

1971, Sept. 18 *Perf. 13½*

70 A27 4n brown & multi .30 .25
71 A27 10n yellow grn & multi .30 .25
72 A27 15n blue & multi .35 .35
73 A27 25n plum & multi .55 .55
Nos. 70-73 (4) 1.50 1.40

10th anniv. of the death of Dag Hammarskjold, (1905-61) Secretary-General of the UN, near Ndola, Zambia.

Red-Breasted Bream — A28

10n, Green-headed bream. 15n, Tiger fish.

1971, Dec. 10

74 A28 4n shown .30 .30
75 A28 10n multicolored .85 .80
76 A28 15n multicolored 2.00 1.10
Nos. 74-76 (3) 3.15 2.20

Christmas.

Cheetah A29

Soil Conservation — A30

1972, Mar. 15 *Perf. 13½x14*

77 A29 4n shown .30 .25
78 A29 10n Lechue .55 .55

Perf. 14x13½

79 A30 15n Cape porcupine .80 .85
80 A30 25n Elephant 2.00 1.40
Nos. 77-80 (4) 3.65 3.05

Conservation Year.

1972, June 30 Litho. *Perf. 14x13½*

10n, Forest conservation. 15n, Water conservation (river view). 25n, Woman in corn field.

Size: 18½x45mm

81 A30 4n shown .30 .25
82 A30 10n multicolored .35 .35

Perf. 13½x14

83 A29 15n multicolored .60 .60
84 A29 25n multicolored 1.10 1.10
Nos. 81-84 (4) 2.35 2.30

Souvenir Sheet

85 Sheet of 4 10.00 *13.50*
a. A30 10n Giraffe and zebra 1.40 *1.90*
b. A30 10n Rhinoceros 1.40 *1.90*
c. A30 10n Hippopotamus and deer 1.40 *1.90*
d. A30 10n Lion 1.40 *1.90*

Conservation Year. Stamp size: 27x50mm.

1972, Sept. 22 *Perf. 13½x14*

4n, Zambian flowers. 10n, Citrus swallowtails and roses. 15n, Bee. 25n, Locusts in corn field.

All horizontal.

Size: 48x35mm

86 A30 4n multicolored .75 .75
87 A30 10n multicolored 2.10 2.10
88 A30 15n multicolored 3.00 3.00
89 A30 25n multicolored 4.50 4.50
Nos. 86-89 (4) 10.35 10.35

Conservation Year.

Mary and Joseph Going to Bethlehem A31

9n, Holy Family. 15n, Adoration of the shepherds. 25n, Kings following the star.

1972, Dec. 1 Litho. *Perf. 14*

No.	Type	Description	Unused	Used
90	A31	4n shown	.30	.25
91	A31	9n multicolored	.30	.25
92	A31	15n multicolored	.30	.25
93	A31	25n multicolored	.35	.35
		Nos. 90-93 (4)	1.25	1.10

Christmas.

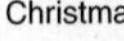

Broken Hill Man — A32

Designs: 4n, Oudenodon and rubidgea (artist's conception; vert.). 10n, Zambiasaurus. 15n, Skull of Luangwa Drysdalli. 25n, Glossoptoris (seed).

Perf. 14x13½, 14

1973, Feb. 1 Litho.

Size: 29x45mm

No.	Type	Description	Unused	Used
94	A32	4n org ver & multi	.65	.35

Size: 37½x21mm

No.	Type	Description	Unused	Used
95	A32	9n org ver & multi	.95	.75
96	A32	10n apple grn & multi	1.10	.95
97	A32	15n lilac & multi	1.50	1.25
98	A32	25n orange brn & multi	2.40	2.40
		Nos. 94-98 (5)	6.60	5.70

Fossils from Luangwa area (except 9n), over 200 million years old.

Meeting of Stanley and Livingstone at Ujiji — A33

4n, Livingstone, the missionary. 9n, Livingstone at Victoria Falls. 10n, Livingstone stopping slave traders. 15n, Livingstone, the physician. 25n, Portrait & tree in Chitumbu, marking burial place of heart.

1973, May 1 *Perf. 13x13½*

No.	Type	Description	Unused	Used
99	A33	3n multicolored	.30	.25
100	A33	4n multicolored	.30	.25
101	A33	9n multicolored	.40	.40
102	A33	10n multicolored	.45	.45
103	A33	15n multicolored	.70	.70
104	A33	25n multicolored	1.10	1.10
		Nos. 99-104 (6)	3.25	3.15

Dr. David Livingstone (1813-73), medical missionary and explorer.

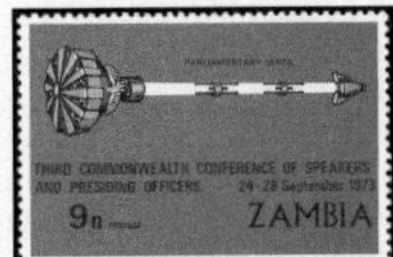

Parliamentary Mace — A34

1973, Sept. 24 Litho. *Perf. 13½x14*

No.	Type	Description	Unused	Used
105	A34	9n tan & multi	.40	.40
106	A34	15n gray & multi	.75	.75
107	A34	25n brt green & multi	1.00	1.00
		Nos. 105-107 (3)	2.15	2.15

Third Commonwealth Conference of Speakers and Presiding Officers, Lusaka.

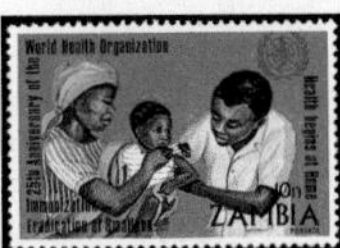

Vaccination A35

WHO Emblem and: 4n, Mother washing infant, vert. 9n, Nurse weighing infant, vert. 15n, Child eating cereal and fruit.

1973, Oct. 16 Litho. *Perf. 14*

No.	Type	Description	Unused	Used
108	A35	4n blue & multi	*52.50*	*35.00*
109	A35	9n orange & multi	.30	.30
110	A35	10n brt grn & multi	.40	.40
111	A35	15n violet & multi	.50	.50
		Nos. 108-111 (4)	*53.70*	*36.20*

WHO, 25th anniv.

A36 A37

Birth of the Second Republic: 4n, UNIP flag. 9n, United National Independence Party Headquarters, Lusaka. 10n, Army band. 15n, Women dancing and singing. 25n, President's parliamentary chair.

1973, Dec. 13 Litho. *Perf. 14x13½*

No.	Type	Description	Unused	Used
112	A36	4n multicolored	*12.00*	*7.50*
113	A36	9n multicolored	.30	.25
114	A36	10n multicolored	.30	.30
115	A36	15n multicolored	.45	.45
116	A37	25n multicolored	.75	.75
		Nos. 112-116 (5)	*13.80*	*9.25*

Pres. Kaunda and his Home During Struggle for Independence A38

4n, Pres. Kaunda at Mulungushi. 15n, Pres. Kaunda holding torch of freedom.

1974, Apr. 28 Litho. *Perf. 14½x14*

No.	Type	Description	Unused	Used
117	A38	4n multi, vert.	.50	.50
118	A38	9n multi	.60	.60
119	A38	15n multi	.90	.90
		Nos. 117-119 (3)	2.00	2.00

50th birthday of Pres. Kenneth Kaunda.

Nakambla Sugar Estate — A39

Designs: 4n, Local market. 9n, Kapiri glass factory. 10n, Kafue hydroelectric plant. 15n, Kafue Bridge. 25n, Conference of Non-aligned Nations, Lusaka, 1970.

1974, Oct. 24 Litho. *Perf. 13½x14*

No.	Type	Description	Unused	Used
120	A39	3n multicolored	.30	.25
121	A39	4n multicolored	.30	.25
122	A39	9n multicolored	.30	.30
123	A39	10n multicolored	.35	.35
124	A39	15n multicolored	.50	.50
125	A39	25n multicolored	.80	.80
		Nos. 120-125 (6)	2.55	2.45

Souvenir Sheet

No.	Type	Description	Unused	Used
126		Sheet of 4	6.00	*10.00*
a.	A39	15n Academic education	1.20	*1.90*
b.	A39	15n Teacher Training College	1.20	*1.90*
c.	A39	15n Technical education	1.20	*1.90*
d.	A39	15n University of Zambia	1.20	*1.90*

10th anniversary of indepencence.

Mobile Post Office — A40

UPU Emblem and: 9n, Rural mail service by Zambia Airways. 10n, Modern Post Office, Chipata. 15n, Ndola Postal Training Center.

1974, Nov. 15

No.	Type	Description	Unused	Used
127	A40	4n multicolored	.30	.25
128	A40	9n multicolored	.30	.25
129	A40	10n multicolored	.30	.25
130	A40	15n multicolored	.30	.30
		Nos. 127-130 (4)	1.20	1.05

Centenary of Universal Postal Union.

Radar by Day — A41

1974, Dec. 16

No.	Type	Description	Unused	Used
131	A41	4n shown	.30	.25
132	A41	9n Radar by night	.30	.30
133	A41	15n Radar at dawn	.50	.50
134	A41	25n Radar station	.85	.90
		Nos. 131-134 (4)	1.95	1.95

Inauguration of Mwembeshi Earth Station, Oct. 21, 1974.

Rhinoceros and Calf — A42

Peanut Harvest A43

2n, Guinea fowl. 3n, Zambian dancers. 4n, Fish eagle. 5n, Bridge, Victoria Falls. 8n, Sitatunga. 9n, Elephant, Kasaba Bay Resort. 10n, Giant pangolin. 15n, Zambezi River source, Monument. 25n, Tobacco field. 50n, Flying doctor service. 1k, Lady Ross's touraco. 2k, Village scene.

1975, Jan. 3 Litho. *Perf. 13½x14*

No.	Type	Description	Unused	Used
135	A42	1n shown	.55	.55
136	A42	2n multicolored	.55	.55
137	A42	3n multicolored	.30	.40
138	A42	4n multicolored	1.00	.25
139	A42	5n multicolored	1.00	1.00
140	A42	8n multicolored	1.00	.90
141	A42	9n multicolored	1.25	.85
142	A42	10n multicolored	.30	.25

Perf. 13

No.	Type	Description	Unused	Used
143	A43	15n multicolored	.35	.25
144	A43	20n shown	1.00	1.40
145	A43	25n multicolored	1.60	.65
146	A43	50n multicolored	4.00	3.00
147	A43	1k multicolored	5.75	2.50
148	A43	2k multicolored	4.00	6.00
		Nos. 135-148 (14)	22.65	18.55

For surcharges see #188-191, 319.

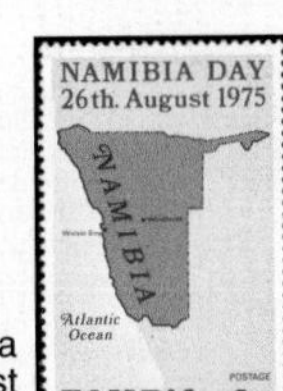

Map of Namibia (South-West Africa) — A44

1975, Aug. 26 Litho. *Perf. 14x13½*

No.	Type	Description	Unused	Used
149	A44	4n green & dk green	.30	.25
150	A44	9n dk blue & gray bl	.30	.25
151	A44	15n yellow & orange	.35	.55
152	A44	25n orange & dp orange	.40	1.10
		Nos. 149-152 (4)	1.35	2.15

Namibia Day.

Sprinkler Irrigation A45

Designs: 9n, Sprinkler irrigation over rows of vegetables. 15n, Furrow irrigation.

1975, Dec. 16 Litho. *Perf. 13*

No.	Type	Description	Unused	Used
153	A45	4n multicolored	.30	.25
154	A45	9p multicolored	.35	.50
155	A45	15n multicolored	.60	1.10
		Nos. 153-155 (3)	1.25	1.85

Intl. Commission on Irrigation and Drainage, 25th anniv.

Julbernardia Paniculata A46

Trees of Zambia: 4n, Sycamore fig. 9n, Baikiaea plurijuga. 10n, Colophospermum. 15n, Uapaca kirkiana. 25n, Pterocarpus angolensis.

1976, Mar. 22 Litho. *Perf. 13*

No.	Type	Description	Unused	Used
156	A46	3n multicolored	.30	.30
157	A46	4n multicolored	.30	.30
158	A46	9n multicolored	.45	.45
159	A46	10n multicolored	.45	.45
160	A46	15n multicolored	.70	.70
161	A46	25n multicolored	.85	.85
		Nos. 156-161 (6)	3.05	3.05

World Forestry Day, Mar. 21.

TAZARA Passenger Train — A47

9n, Train carrying copper. 10n, Clearing the bush. #164, Train carrying heavy machinery. #166b, Track laying. 20n, Reinforcing railroad track. #165, Train carrying various goods. #166d, Completed tracks.

1976, Dec. 10 Litho. *Perf. 13*

No.	Type	Description	Unused	Used
162	A47	4n multicolored	.30	.25
163	A47	9n multicolored	.55	.55
164	A47	15n multicolored	.90	.90
165	A47	25n multicolored	1.50	1.50
		Nos. 162-165 (4)	3.25	3.20

Souvenir Sheet

Perf. 13½x14

No.	Type	Description	Unused	Used
166		Sheet of 4	3.75	3.75
a.	A47	10n multicolored	.35	.35
b.	A47	15n multicolored	.55	.50
c.	A47	20n multicolored	.65	.55
d.	A47	25n multicolored	.90	.70

Completion of Tanzania-Zambia Railroad.

Kayowe Dance — A48

1977, Jan. 18 Litho. *Perf. 13½x14*

No.	Type	Description	Unused	Used
167	A48	4n shown	.30	.25
168	A48	9n Lilombola dance	.30	.25
169	A48	15n Initiation ceremony	.40	.40
170	A48	25n Munkhwele dance	.50	.50
		Nos. 167-170 (4)	1.50	1.40

2nd World Black and African Festival, Lagos, Nigeria, Jan. 15-Feb. 12.

Grimwood's Longclaw — A49

Birds of Zambia: 9n, Shelley's sunbird. 10n, Black-cheeked lovebird. 15n, Locust finch. 20n, White-chested tinkerbird. 25n, Chaplin's barbet.

1977, July 1 Litho. *Perf. 14½*

No.	Type	Description	Unused	Used
171	A49	4n multicolored	.30	.25
172	A49	9n multicolored	.50	.50
173	A49	10n multicolored	.65	.50
174	A49	15n multicolored	1.30	1.50
175	A49	20n multicolored	1.40	1.80
176	A49	25n multicolored	1.60	2.20
		Nos. 171-176 (6)	5.75	6.75

Children Playing with Blocks — A50

Designs: 9n, Women of various races dancing in circle. 15n, Black and white girls with young bird.

1977, Oct. 20 Litho. *Perf. 14x14½*

No.	Type	Description	Unused	Used
177	A50	4n multicolored	.30	.25
178	A50	9n multicolored	.30	.25
179	A50	15n multicolored	.35	.35
		Nos. 177-179 (3)	.95	.85

Combat racism and racial discrimination.

"Glory to God in the Highest" — A51

Christmas: 9n, Nativity. 10n, Three Kings and camel. 15n, Presentation at the Temple.

1977, Dec. 20 Litho. *Perf. 14*

180 A51 4n multicolored .30 .25
181 A51 9n multicolored .30 .25
182 A51 10n multicolored .30 .25
183 A51 15n multicolored .30 .25
Nos. 180-183 (4) 1.20 1.00

Elephant and Road Check — A52

Designs: 18n, Waterbuck and Kafue River boat patrol. 28n, Warthog and helicopter surveillance of National Parks. 32n, Cheetah and armed wildlife guards in Parks and Game Management Areas.

1978, Aug. 1 Litho. *Perf. 14x14½*

184 A52 8n multicolored .30 .30
185 A52 18n multicolored .60 .60
186 A52 28n multicolored .95 .95
187 A52 32n multicolored 1.15 1.15
Nos. 184-187 (4) 3.00 3.00

Anti-poaching Campaign of Zambia Wildlife Conservation Society, Aug. 1978.

Nos. 141, 137, 145 and 143 Srchd. with New Value and 2 Bars

1979, Mar. 15 *Perf. 13½x14, 13*

188 A42 8n on 9n multi .60 .25
189 A42 10n on 3n multi .30 .25
190 A43 18n on 25n multi .30 .25
191 A43 28n on 15n multi .30 .25
Nos. 188-191 (4) 1.50 1.00

Kayowe Dance — A53

Designs: 32n, Kutambala dance. 42n, Chitwansombo drummers. 58n, Lilombola dance.

1979, Aug. 1

192 A53 18n multicolored .30 .30
193 A53 32n multicolored .35 .35
194 A53 42n multicolored .35 .35
195 A53 58n multicolored .50 .50
Nos. 192-195 (4) 1.50 1.50

Commonwealth Summit Conf., Lusaka, Aug. 1-9.

"Why the Zebra is Hornless" — A54

Children's Stories: 18n, Kalulu and the Tug of War. 42n, How the Tortoise got his Shell. 58n, Kalulu and the Lion.

1979, Sept. 21 Litho. *Perf. 14*

196 A54 18n multicolored .30 .25
197 A54 32n multicolored .40 *.55*
198 A54 42n multicolored .45 *.75*
199 A54 58n multicolored .55 *1.00*
a. Souvenir sheet of 4, #196-199 2.50 2.50
Nos. 196-199 (4) 1.70 2.55

International Year of the Child.

Girls of Different Races Holding Emblem — A55

Anti-Apartheid Year (1978): 32n, Boys and toy car. 42n, Infants and butterfly. 58n, Children and microscope.

1979, Nov. 16 Litho. *Perf. 14½x15*

200 A55 18n multicolored .30 .25
201 A55 32n multicolored .35 .35
202 A55 42n multicolored .55 .55
203 A55 58n multicolored .70 .70
Nos. 200-203 (4) 1.90 1.85

Hill, Zambia No. 13 — A56

Hill and: 32n, Mailman & bicycle. 42n, No. Rhodesia #75. 58n, Mailman & oxcart.

1979, Dec. 20 Litho. *Perf. 14½*

204 A56 18n multicolored .30 .25
205 A56 32n multicolored .40 .50
206 A56 42n multicolored .40 .65
207 A56 58n multicolored .45 1.10
a. Souvenir sheet of 4, #204-207 1.75 2.40
Nos. 204-207 (4) 1.55 2.50

Sir Rowland Hill (1795-1879), originator of penny postage.

Nos. 204-207a Overprinted "LONDON 1980"

1980, Mar 6 Litho. *Perf. 15*

208 A56 18n multicolored .30 .40
209 A56 32n multicolored .30 .55
210 A56 42n multicolored .40 .70
211 A56 58n multicolored .60 .85
a. Souvenir sheet of 4 3.00 4.00
Nos. 208-211 (4) 1.60 2.50

London 80 Intl. Stamp Exhib., May 6-14.

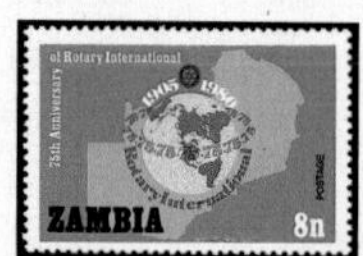

Anniverary Emblem on Map of Zambia — A57

1980, June 18 Litho. *Perf. 14*

212 A57 8n multicolored .30 .25
213 A57 32n multicolored .45 .45
214 A57 42n multicolored .55 .55
215 A57 58n multicolored .70 .70
a. Souvenir sheet of 4, #212-215 2.40 2.40
Nos. 212-215 (4) 2.00 1.95

Rotary International, 75th anniversary.

Running — A58

1980, July 19 Litho. *Perf. 13*

216 A58 18n shown .30 .25
217 A58 32n Boxing .45 .45
218 A58 42n Soccer .55 .55
219 A58 58n Swimming .75 .75
a. Souvenir sheet of 4, #216-219 2.40 2.40
Nos. 216-219 (4) 2.05 2.00

22nd Summer Olympic Games, Moscow, July 19-Aug. 3.

Zaddach's Forester — A59

1980, Sept. 22

220 A59 18n shown .30 .25
221 A59 32n Northern highflier .50 .45
222 A59 42n Zambezi skipper .70 .70
223 A59 58n Modest blue 1.00 1.00
a. Souvenir sheet of 4, #220-223 6.00 6.00
Nos. 220-223 (4) 2.50 2.40

Coat of Arms — A60

1980, Sept. 27 Litho. *Perf. 14½*

224 A60 18n multicolored .30 .25
225 A60 32n multicolored .40 .45
226 A60 42n multicolored .50 .65
227 A60 58n multicolored .60 1.25
Nos. 224-227 (4) 1.80 2.60

26th Commonwealth Parliamentary Association Conference, Lusaka.

A61

Nativity and St. Francis of Assisi (stained glass window), Ndola Church.

1980, Oct. Litho. *Perf. 14*

228 A61 8n multicolored .30 .25
229 A61 28n multicolored .60 .90
230 A61 32n multicolored .60 .90
231 A61 42n multicolored .80 1.25
Nos. 228-231 (4) 2.30 3.30

Christmas and 50th anniv. of Catholic Church in Copperbelt (central Zambia).

Trichilia Emetica Seed Pods, Musikili — A62

Seed Pods: 18n, Afzelia quanzensis, Mupapa. 28n, Erythrina abyssinica, Mulunguti. 32n, Combretum collinum, Mulama.

1981, Mar. 21 Litho. *Perf. 14*

232 A62 8n shown .30 .25
233 A62 18n multicolored .30 .35
234 A62 28n multicolored .35 .70
235 A62 32n multicolored .35 1.15
Nos. 232-235 (4) 1.30 2.45

World Forestry Day.

ITU Emblem — A63

Designs: 18n, 32n, WHO emblem.

1981, May 15 Litho. *Perf. 14½*

236 A63 8n multicolored .35 .35
237 A63 18n multicolored .45 .45
238 A63 28n multicolored .55 .55
239 A63 32n multicolored .60 .60
Nos. 236-239 (4) 1.95 1.95

13th World Telecommunications Day (8n, 28n).

Mask Maker — A64

2n, Blacksmiths. 5n, Potter. 8n, Straw basket fishing. 10n, Roof thatching. 12n, Picking mushrooms ('83). 18n, Millet grinding. 28n, Royal Barge paddler. 30n, Makishi tightrope dancer. 35n, Tonga-ila granary, house. 42n, Cattle herding. 50n, Traditional healer. 75n, Carrying water jugs ('83). 1k, Grinding corn ('83). 2k, Woman smoking pipe.

1981-83

240 A64 1n shown .30 .25
241 A64 2n multicolored .30 .25
242 A64 5n multicolored .30 .25
243 A64 8n multicolored .30 .25
244 A64 10n multicolored .30 .25
244A A64 12n multicolored 3.50 2.75
245 A64 18n multicolored .50 .25
246 A64 28n multicolored .70 .25
247 A64 30n multicolored .70 .25
248 A64 35n multicolored .75 .25
249 A64 42n multicolored .75 1.50

Perf. 14

Size: 37x25mm

250 A64 50n multicolored .75 .25
251 A64 75n multicolored .75 .90
252 A64 1k multicolored .75 .90
253 A64 2k multicolored .75 .90
Nos. 240-253 (15) 11.40 9.45

For surcharges see Nos. 358, 372, 499-506, 596.

Kankobele — A65

Designs: Traditional musical instruments.

1981, Sept. 30 Litho. *Perf. 14½*

254 A65 8n shown .45 .25
255 A65 18n Inshingili .55 .45
256 A65 28n Ilimba .80 1.40
257 A65 32n Bango .80 1.60
Nos. 254-257 (4) 2.60 3.70

Bornite — A66

Designs: Rocks and minerals.

1982, Jan. 5 Litho. *Perf. 14*

258 A66 8n Banded Ironstone 1.10 .25
259 A66 18n Cobaltocalcite 2.15 .90
260 A66 28n Amazonite 2.90 2.50
261 A66 32n Tourmaline 3.10 3.25
262 A66 42n Uranium ore 3.25 4.35
Nos. 258-262 (5) 12.50 11.25

1982, July 1 Litho. *Perf. 14*

263 A66 8n shown 1.05 .35
264 A66 18n Chalcopyrite 2.50 1.40
265 A66 28n Malachite 3.00 3.75
266 A66 32n Azurite 3.00 3.75
267 A66 42n Vanadinite 3.75 4.50
Nos. 263-267 (5) 13.30 13.75

Scouting Year — A67

8n, Scouts, flag. 18n, Baden-Powell. 28n, Horned buffalo, patrol pennat. 1k, Eagle, conservation badge.

1982, Mar. 30 Litho. *Perf. 14*

268 A67 8n multicolored .35 .35
269 A67 18n multicolored .35 .35
270 A67 28n multicolored .35 .35
271 A67 1k multicolored 2.10 2.60
a. Souvenir sheet of 4, #268-271 4.75 5.50
Nos. 268-271 (4) 3.15 3.65

Drilling Rig, 1926 — A68

Steam locomotives.

1983, Jan. 26 *Perf. 14x14½*

272 A68 8n shown .55 .30
273 A68 18n Class B6, 1910 .85 .85
274 A68 28n Borsig engine, 1925 1.35 2.00
275 A68 32n 7th class, 1900 1.75 2.50
Nos. 272-275 (4) 4.50 5.65

Commonwealth Day — A68a

1983, Mar. 10 Litho. *Perf. 14*

276 A68a 12n Cotton picking .30 .25
277 A68a 18n Miners .30 .25
278 A68a 28n Ritual pot, dancers .30 .35
279 A68a 1k Victoria Falls, purple-crested lorie 2.75 3.75
Nos. 276-279 (4) 3.65 4.60

Local Flowers — A69

1983, May 26 Litho. *Perf. 14*

280 A69 12n Eulophia cucullata .30 .25
281 A69 28n Kigelia africana .45 .60
282 A69 35n Protea gaguedi .55 .75
283 A69 50n Leonotis nepotifolia 1.05 *2.25*
a. Souvenir sheet of 4, #280-283, perf. 12x12½ 2.75 *4.00*
Nos. 280-283 (4) 2.35 3.85

Thornicroft's Giraffes — A70

28n, Cookson's wildebeest. 35n, Black lechwe. 1k, Yellow-backed duiker.

1983, July 21 Litho. *Perf. 14*

284 A70 12n shown .65 .65
285 A70 28n multicolored .85 .85
286 A70 35n multicolored 1.20 1.20
287 A70 1k multicolored 2.40 3.25
Nos. 284-287 (4) 5.10 5.95

Tiger Fish — A71

1983, Sept. 29 Litho. *Perf. 14*

288 A71 12n shown .55 .25
289 A71 28n Silver Barbel .85 .70
290 A71 35n Spotted Squeaker .95 2.00
291 A71 38n Red Breasted Bream 1.10 2.00
Nos. 288-291 (4) 3.45 4.95

For surcharge see No. 597.

Christmas — A72

1983, Dec. 12 Litho. *Perf. 14x14½*

292 A72 12n Annunciation .30 .25
293 A72 28n Shepherds .30 .30
294 A72 35n Three Kings .35 .75
295 A72 38n Flight into Egypt .40 1.00
Nos. 292-295 (4) 1.35 2.30

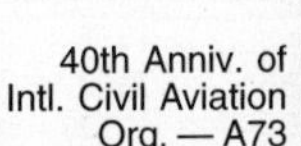

40th Anniv. of Intl. Civil Aviation Org. — A73

1984, Jan. 26 Litho. *Perf. 14*

296 A73 12n Boeing 737, 1983 .30 .25
297 A73 28n Beaver, 1954 .45 .45
298 A73 35n Short Solent Flying Boat, 1948 .55 .55
299 A73 1k DH-66, 1931 1.75 2.50
Nos. 296-299 (4) 3.05 3.75

60th Birthday of Pres. Kaunda — A74

12n, Receiving greetings. 28n, Swearing in, 1983, vert. 60n, Planting cherry tree. 1k, Opening Natl. Assembly, vert.

Perf. 14½x14, 14x14½

1984, Apr. 28 Litho.

300 A74 12n multicolored .30 .30
301 A74 28n multicolored .45 .45
302 A74 60n multicolored .90 2.00
303 A74 1k multicolored 1.10 2.50
Nos. 300-303 (4) 2.75 5.25

1984 Summer Olympics — A75

1984, July 18 Litho. *Perf. 14*

304 A75 12n Soccer .30 .25
305 A75 28n Running .50 .50
306 A75 35n Hurdles .55 .65
307 A75 50n Boxing .75 1.25
Nos. 304-307 (4) 2.10 2.65

Reptiles — A76

1984, Sept. 5 Litho. *Perf. 14*

308 A76 12n Gabon viper .35 .30
309 A76 28n Chameleon .65 .55
310 A76 35n Nile crocodile .75 .65
311 A76 1k Blue-headed agama 1.75 2.25
a. Souvenir sheet of 4, #308-311 4.75 4.75
Nos. 308-311 (4) 3.50 3.75

20th Anniv. of Independence A77

1984, Oct. 22 Litho. *Perf. 14*

312 A77 12n Pres. Kaunda, Mulungushi Rock .30 .30
313 A77 28n Freedom Statue .40 .50
314 A77 1k Produce 1.30 2.00
Nos. 312-314 (3) 2.00 2.80

For surcharge, see No. 599.

Local Mushrooms — A78

12n, Amanita flammeola. 28n, Amanita zambiana. 32n, Termitomyces letestui. 75n, Cantharellus miniatescens.

1984, Dec. 12 Litho. *Perf. 14x14½*

315 A78 12n multicolored 1.25 1.25
316 A78 28n multicolored 1.35 1.35
317 A78 32n multicolored 2.10 2.10
318 A78 75n multicolored 4.00 4.00
Nos. 315-318 (4) 8.70 8.70

For surcharge see No. 600.

No. 146 Surcharged with New Value and Two Bars

1985, Mar. 5 Litho. *Perf. 13½*

319 A43 5k on 50n multi 2.50 3.00

Primates — A79

1985, Apr. 25 Litho. *Perf. 14*

320 A79 12n Chacma baboon .60 .60
321 A79 20n Moloney's monkey .80 .80
322 A79 45n Blue monkey 1.75 1.75
323 A79 1k Vervet monkey 2.60 3.25
Nos. 320-323 (4) 5.75 6.40

For surcharge see No. 604.

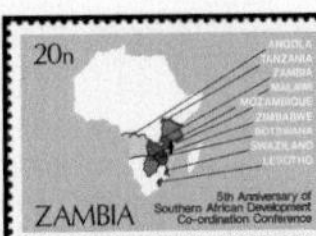

SADCC, 5th Anniv. — A80

1985, July 9 Litho. *Perf. 14*

324 A80 20n Map .80 .80
325 A80 45n Mining 2.10 2.10
326 A80 1k Mulungushi Hall 2.10 2.60
Nos. 324-326 (3) 5.00 5.50

Southern African Development Coordination Conference.

For surcharge see No. 605.

Queen Mother, 85th Birthday — A81 — A81

25n, Portrait in blue, age 80. 45n, Queen Consort at Clarence House, 1963. 55n, With Elizabeth II and Princess Margaret. 5k, With royal family, christening of Prince Harry, 1984.

1985, Aug. 2

327 A81 25n multi, vert. .30 .25
328 A81 45n multi, vert. .30 .25
329 A81 55n multi .30 .25
330 A81 5k multi 1.25 2.00
Nos. 327-330 (4) 2.15 2.75

For surcharges see Nos. 401, 406, 410, 414, 595, 606, 611.

National Anniversaries — A81a

#330A, Pres. Kenneth Kaunda, Mulungushi Rock. #330B, Kaunda, agricultural products. #330C, Freedom statue, flags.

Die Cut Perf. 10

1985, Oct. 23 Embossed

330A-330C A81a 5k gold *15.00 15.00*

United National Independence Party, 26th anniv. (No. 330A); Independence, 20th anniv. (Nos. 330B-330C).

Postal and Telecommunications Corp., 10th Anniv. — A82

20n, Lusaka P.O., 1958. 45n, Livingstone P.O., 1950. 55n, Kalomo P.O., 1902. 5k, Transcontinental Telegraph, 1900.

1985, Dec. 12 *Perf. 13½x13*

331 A82 20n multicolored .60 .60
332 A82 45n multicolored .90 .90
333 A82 55n multicolored 1.00 1.00
334 A82 5k multicolored 3.25 4.25
Nos. 331-334 (4) 5.75 6.75

For surcharges see Nos. 590-593.

UN, 40th Anniv. — A83

1985, Dec. 19 *Perf. 14*

335 A83 20n Boy in cornfield .35 .35
336 A83 45n Emblem .60 .60
337 A83 1k Pres. Kaunda, 1970 1.15 1.50
338 A83 2k Charter signing, 1945 1.75 2.25
Nos. 335-338 (4) 3.85 4.70

For surcharges see #594, 607.

Beetles — A84

35n, Mylabris tricolor. 1k, Phasgonocnema melanianthe. 1.70k, Amaurodes passerinii. 5k, Ranzania petersiana.

1986, Mar. 20

339 A84 35n multicolored .30 .25
340 A84 1k multicolored .40 .45
341 A84 1.70k multicolored .65 .75
342 A84 5k multicolored 2.10 2.25
Nos. 339-342 (4) 3.45 3.70

For surcharges see #609, 612.

Common Design Types pictured following the introduction.

Queen Elizabeth II 60th Birthday

Common Design Type

Designs: 35n, At the Flower Ball, Savoy Hotel, London, 1951. 1.25k, With Prince Andrew at Lusaka Airport, Commonwealth Conf., 1979. 1.70k, With Dr. Kaunda observing natl. anthem. 1.95k, Wearing Queen Mary tiara, state visit to Luxembourg, 1976. 5k, Visiting Crown Agents' offices, 1983.

1986, Apr. 21 Wmk. 384 *Perf. 14*

343 CD337 35n scar, blk & sil .30 .25
344 CD337 1.25k ultra & multi .30 .30
345 CD337 1.70k grn, blk & sil .30 .30
346 CD337 1.95k vio & multi .30 .30
347 CD337 5k rose vio & multi .45 .45
Nos. 343-347 (5) 1.65 1.60

For surcharges see Nos. 402, 405, 407, 411, 415.

Royal Wedding Issue, 1986

Common Design Type

Designs: 1.70k, Sarah Ferguson kissing Prince Andrew. 5k, Andrew in informal dress.

1986, July 23 Litho. *Perf. 14*

348 CD338 1.70k multicolored .30 .30
349 CD338 5k multicolored .80 1.00

1986 World Cup Soccer Championships, Mexico — A85

Various soccer plays.

1986, June 27 Litho. *Perf. 14½*

350 A85 35n multicolored .90 .90
351 A85 1.25k multicolored 2.00 2.00
352 A85 1.70k multicolored 2.40 2.40
353 A85 5k multicolored 3.50 3.50
Nos. 350-353 (4) 8.80 8.80

For surcharges see Nos. 403, 408, 412, 416.

Halley's Comet — A86

Designs: 1.25k, Edmond Halley (1656-1742), by Henry Pegram. 1.70k, Giotto space probe approaching comet. 2k, Youth, astronomer. 5k, Halley's map of the southern constellations.

1986, July 4

354 A86 1.25k multicolored .90 .90
355 A86 1.70k multicolored 1.05 1.05
356 A86 2k multicolored 1.50 1.50
357 A86 5k multicolored 3.00 3.00
Nos. 354-357 (4) 6.45 6.45

For surcharges see Nos. 404, 409, 413, 417.

#244A Surcharged in Light Red Brown

1986, July Litho. *Perf. 14½*

358 A64 20n on 12n multi *15.00* .50

Christmas — A87

Children's drawings.

1986, Dec. 15 Litho. *Perf. 14*

359 A87 35n Nativity .40 .40
360 A87 1.25k Magi 1.40 1.40
361 A87 1.60k Nativity 1.75 1.75
362 A87 5k Angel, house, tree 3.50 3.50
Nos. 359-362 (4) 7.05 7.05

For surcharges see #602, 608.

Tazara Railroad, 10th Anniv. — A88

Locomotive traveling various railway lines.

1986, Dec. 22

363 A88 35n Overpass, Kasama .30 .25
364 A88 1.25k Tunnel 21 vicinity .40 .40
365 A88 1.70k Tunnels 6-7 .55 .55
366 A88 5k Mpika Station grade separation 1.05 1.05
Nos. 363-366 (4) 2.30 2.25

University of Zambia — A89

Designs: 35n, Pres. Kaunda shaking council member's hand. 1.25k, University crest, vert. 1.60k, University statue. 5k, Kaunda laying university building cornerstone, vert.

1987, Jan. 27 Litho. *Perf. 14*

367 A89 35n multicolored .35 .35
368 A89 1.25k multicolored .75 .75
369 A89 1.60k multicolored .85 .85
370 A89 5k multicolored 3.00 4.25
Nos. 367-370 (4) 4.95 6.20

No. 243 Surcharged in Blue

1987 *Perf. 14½*

372 A64 25n on 8n multi .65 .45

Municipal Arms — A90

1987, Mar. 26 *Perf. 14*

373 A90 35n Kitwe .30 .25
374 A90 1.25k Ndola .30 .30
375 A90 1.70k Lusaka .40 .40
376 A90 20k Livingstone 3.00 3.00
Nos. 373-376 (4) 4.00 3.95

For surcharge see No. 603.

Birds — A91

25n, Long-toed fluff tail. 30n, Miombo pied barbet. 35n, Black-and-rufous swallow. 50n, Slaty egret. 1k, Bradfield's hornbill. 1.25k, Margaret's batis. 1.60k, Red-and-blue sunbird. 1.70k, Boehm's bee-eater. 1.95k, Gorgeous bush shrike. 2k, Shoebill. 5k, Taita falcon.

1987-88 *Perf. 11x13*

Size: 20x25½mm

377 A91 25n multicolored 3.50 3.50
378 A91 30n multicolored .30 .30
379 A91 35n multicolored 3.50 3.50

Size: 25x38½mm

Perf. 14

380 A91 50n multicolored .30 .30
381 A91 1k multicolored 3.50 3.50
382 A91 1.25k multicolored 3.50 3.50
383 A91 1.60k multicolored 3.50 3.50
384 A91 1.70k multicolored 3.75 3.75
385 A91 1.95k multicolored 3.75 3.75
386 A91 2k multicolored .50 .50
387 A91 5k multicolored 4.50 4.50
Nos. 377-387 (11) 30.60 30.60

Surcharged

No. 390

No. 392

No. 388, Yellow swamp warbler. No. 389, Olive-flanked robin.

Size: 20x25½mm

388 A91 20n on 1n multi .35 .35
389 A91 75n on 2n multi .35 .35
390 A91 1.65k on 30n #378 .35 .35

Size: 25x38½mm

Perf. 14

391 A91 10k on 50n #380 2.25 2.25
392 A91 20k on 2k #386 3.00 3.00
Nos. 388-392 (5) 6.30 6.30

Issued: #377, 379, 381-385, 387, 9/14/87; #391-392, 3/10/88; others 10/8/87.
Nos. 388-389 not issued without overprint.
See Nos. 433-435, 527-540. For surcharges see Nos. 490, 492-498.

Look-out Tree, Livingstone A92

1.25k, Rafting, Zambezi River. 1.70k, Walking safari, Luangwa Valley. 10k, White pelicans.

1987, June 30 *Perf. 14*

393 A92 35n shown .35 .35
394 A92 1.25k multicolored .40 .40
395 A92 1.70k multicolored 1.75 1.75
396 A92 10k multicolored 6.00 6.00
Nos. 393-396 (4) 8.50 8.50

Zambia Airways, 20th Anniv. — A93

1987, Sept. 21

397 A93 35n De Havilland Beaver .70 .70
398 A93 1.70k DC-10 1.55 1.55
399 A93 5k DC-3 3.50 3.50
400 A93 10k Boeing 707 5.50 5.50
Nos. 397-400 (4) 11.25 11.25

Issues of 1985-86 Surcharged in Gold or Black

1987, Sept. 14 *Perfs. as Before*

401 A81 3k on 25n #327 (G) 1.40 1.40
402 CD337 3k on 35n #343 1.05 1.05
403 A85 3k on 35n #350 1.40 1.40
404 A86 3k on 1.25k #354 (G) 2.40 2.40
405 CD337 4k on 1.25k #344 1.30 1.30
406 A81 6k on 45n #328 2.40 2.40
407 CD337 6k on 1.70k #345 1.90 1.90
408 A85 6k on 1.25k #351 2.40 2.40
409 A86 6k on 1.70k #355 (G) 3.75 3.75
410 A81 10k on 55n #329 (G) 3.50 3.50
411 CD337 10k on 1.95k #346 3.50 3.50
412 A85 10k on 1.70k #352 3.50 3.50
413 A86 10k on 2k #356 (G) 6.50 6.50
414 A81 20k on 5k #330 (G) 6.75 6.75
415 CD337 20k on 5k #347 6.75 6.75
416 A85 20k on 5k #353 6.75 6.75
417 A86 20k on 5k #357 (G) 12.00 12.00
Nos. 401-417 (17) 67.25 67.25

World Food Day — A94

Cattle.

1987, Oct. 1 *Perf. 14½x15*

418 A94 35n Friesian-Holstein .30 .25
419 A94 1.25k Simmental .40 .40
420 A94 1.70k Sussex .40 .40
421 A94 20k Brahma 1.90 1.90
Nos. 418-421 (4) 3.00 2.95

Traditional Heritage — A95

Zambian people.

1987, Oct. 20 *Perf. 13x12½*

422 A95 35n Mpoloto Ne Mikobango .30 .25
423 A95 1.25k Zintaka .30 .30
424 A95 1.70k Mufuluhi .45 .45
425 A95 10k Ntebwe 1.15 1.15
426 A95 20k Kubangwa Aa Mbulunga 2.10 2.10
Nos. 422-426 (5) 4.30 4.25

World Wildlife Fund — A96

Wild Cats A97

50n, Black lechwe drinking water. 2k, Adults and young, horiz. 2.50k, Running, horiz. 10k, Male, diff.
No. 431, Cheetah. No. 432, Caracal.

1987, Dec. 21 Litho. *Perf. 14*

427 A96 50n multicolored *1.50 1.50*
428 A96 2k multicolored *2.75 2.75*
429 A96 2.50k multicolored *2.75 2.75*
430 A96 10k multicolored *6.00 6.00*
Nos. 427-430 (4) *13.00 13.00*

Souvenir Sheets

431 A97 20k multicolored *6.50 6.50*
432 A97 20k multicolored *6.50 6.50*

Bird Type of 1987

1987 Litho. *Perf. 11x13*

433 A91 5n Black-tailed cisticola .35 .35
434 A91 10n White-winged starling .35 .35
435 A91 40n Wattled crane .35 .35
Nos. 433-435 (3) 1.05 1.05

For surcharge see No. 491.

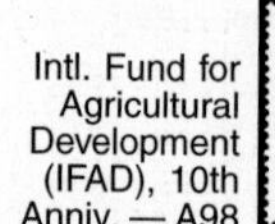

Intl. Fund for Agricultural Development (IFAD), 10th Anniv. — A98

1988, Apr. 2 *Perf. 14*

436 A98 50n Cassava crop .30 .25
437 A98 2.50k Net fishing .55 .55
438 A98 2.85k Cattle breeding .65 .65
439 A98 10k Coffee picking 2.10 2.10
Nos. 436-439 (4) 3.60 3.55

A99

1988, Sept. 12 Litho. *Perf. 12½*

440 A99 50n Breast-feeding .30 .25
441 A99 2k Growth monitoring .55 .55
442 A99 2.85k Immunization .65 .65
443 A99 10k Oral rehydration 2.10 2.10
Nos. 440-443 (4) 3.60 3.55

UN child survival campaign.

A100

1988, Oct. 10 Litho. *Perf. 12½x13*

444 A100 50n Asbestos cement .30 .25
445 A100 2.35k Textiles .50 .50
446 A100 2.50k Tea .55 .55
447 A100 10k Poultry 2.00 2.00
Nos. 444-447 (4) 3.35 3.30

Preferential Trade Area Fair.

Intl. Red Cross and Red Crescent Organizations, 125th Annivs. — A101

1988, Oct. 20 *Perf. 14*

448 A101 50n Famine relief .30 .25
449 A101 2.50k Giving first aid .55 .55
450 A101 2.85k Teaching first aid .70 .70
451 A101 10k Jean-Henri Dunant 2.60 2.60
Nos. 448-451 (4) 4.15 4.10

Endangered Species — A102

1988, Dec. 5 Litho. *Perf. 14*

452 A102 50n Aardvark .30 .30
453 A102 2k Pangolin .60 .60
454 A102 2.85k Wild dog .80 .80
455 A102 20k Black rhinoceros 6.50 6.50
Nos. 452-455 (4) 8.20 8.20

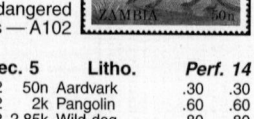

1988 Summer Olympics, Seoul — A103

1988, Dec. 30 Litho. *Perf. 14*

456 A103 50n Boxing .30 .25
457 A103 2k Running .45 .45
458 A103 2.50k Hurdling .55 .55
459 A103 20k Soccer 4.00 4.00
Nos. 456-459 (4) 5.30 5.25

Souvenir Sheets

460 A103 30k Tennis 5.25 5.25
461 A103 30k Martial arts 5.25 5.25

Frogs and Toads — A104

1989, Jan. 25 Litho. *Perf. 12½*

462 A104 50n Red toad .30 .25
463 A104 2.50k Puddle frog .60 .60
464 A104 2.85k Marbled reed frog .75 .75
465 A104 10k Young reed frogs 2.40 2.40
Nos. 462-465 (4) 4.05 4.00

Bats — A105

50n, Common slit-faced. 2.50k, Little free-tailed. 2.85k, Hildebrandt's horseshoe. 10k, Peters' epauletted fruit.

1989, Mar. 22 Litho. *Perf. 12½x13*
466 A105 50n multi .30 .25
467 A105 2.50k multi .70 .70
468 A105 2.85k multi .85 .85
469 A105 10k multi 2.75 2.75
Nos. 466-469 (4) 4.60 4.55

A106

1989, May 2 Litho. *Perf. 12½*
470 A106 50n Map of Zambia .70 .25
471 A106 6.85k Peace dove 2.80 2.80
472 A106 7.85k Papal arms 3.25 3.25
473 A106 10k Victoria Falls 4.75 4.75
Nos. 470-473 (4) 11.50 11.05

State visit of Pope John Paul II, May 2-4.
For surcharges see #614, 616.

Edible Wild Fruits — A107

50n, Parinari curatellifolia. 6.50k, Uapaca kirkiana. 6.85k, Ficus capensis. 10k, Borassus aethiopum.

1989, July 26 Litho. *Perf. 14½x15*
474 A107 50n multicolored .30 .25
475 A107 6.50k multicolored 1.60 2.10
476 A107 6.85k multicolored 1.60 2.10
477 A107 10k multicolored 3.00 3.50
Nos. 474-477 (4) 6.50 7.95

For surcharges see #613, 615.

Grasshoppers A108

1989, Nov. 8 Litho. *Perf. 14x13½*
478 A108 70n Phamphagid .30 .25
479 A108 10.40k Pyrgomorphid 2.10 2.25
480 A108 12.50k Brown katydid 2.50 2.75
481 A108 15k Bush locust 3.00 3.75
Nos. 478-481 (4) 7.90 9.00

No. 480 misspelled "Catydid."

Christmas — A109

Flowers.

1989, Dec. 6 Litho. *Perf. 14½*
482 A109 70n Fireball .30 .25
483 A109 10.40k Flame lily 1.20 1.30
484 A109 12.50k Foxglove lily 1.75 2.00
485 A109 20k Vlei lily 2.75 3.25
Nos. 482-485 (4) 6.00 6.80

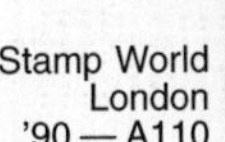

Stamp World London '90 — A110

Designs: 1.20k, Lusaka Main P.O., van, mailman, bicycle. 19.50k, Zambia #220. 20.50k, Rhodesia and Nyasaland #164A, Northern Rhodesia #1. 50k, Great Britain #1, Maltese Cross cancel in red.

Unwmk.
1990, May 2 Litho. *Perf. 14*
486 A110 1.20k multicolored .30 .30
487 A110 19.50k multicolored 2.90 2.90
488 A110 20.50k multicolored 2.90 2.90
489 A110 50k multicolored 5.75 5.75
Nos. 486-489 (4) 11.85 11.85

Nos. 379, 381-387, 433 Surcharged

No. 492

No. 497

1989, July 1 *Perf. 11x13*
490 A91 70n on 35n #379 1.00 .25
491 A91 3k on 5n #433 1.25 .40

Size: 25x38½mm
Perf. 14
492 A91 8k on 1.25k #382 1.50 1.00
493 A91 9.90k on 1.70k #384 1.75 1.75
494 A91 10.40k on 1.60k #383 1.75 1.75
495 A91 12.50k on 1k #381 2.00 2.00
496 A91 15k on 1.95k #385 2.00 2.00
497 A91 20k on 2k #386 3.00 3.00
498 A91 20.35k on 5k #387 3.00 3.00
Nos. 490-498 (9) 17.25 15.15

Nos. 242, 244-245, 247-248 251, 253 Surcharged in Black, Orange Brown, Red Brown, or Violet

a

b

c

1989 *Perf. 14½*
Size: 22x26mm
499 A64(a) 1.20k on 35n #248 (OB) .30 .25
500 A64(b) 3.75k on 5n #242 .40 .40
501 A64(b) 8.11k on 10n #244 1.00 1.00
502 A64(b) 9k on 30n #247 1.00 1.00

Size: 37x25mm
Perf. 14
503 A64(b) 10k on 75n #251 1.00 1.00
504 A64(c) 18.50k on 2k #253 2.00 2.00

Size: 22x26mm
Perf. 14½
505 A64(a) 19.50k on 12n #244A (RB) 4.00 4.00
506 A64(a) 20.50k on 18n #245 (V) 2.00 1.75
Nos. 499-506 (8) 11.70 11.40

Issued: #500-504, 7/1; others, 11/1.

World Cup Soccer Championships, Italy — A111

Soccer players in various positions.

1990, July 7 Litho. *Perf. 14*
507 A111 1.20k multicolored .30 .25
508 A111 18.50k multicolored 2.20 2.20
509 A111 19.50k multicolored 2.20 2.20
510 A111 20.50k multicolored 2.20 2.20
Nos. 507-510 (4) 6.90 6.85

Souvenir Sheet
510A A111 50k multicolored 7.50 7.50

Southern African Development Coordination Conf. (SADCC), 10th Anniv. — A112

Map of SADCC members and: 1.20k, Truck. 19.50k, Telecommunications. 20.50k, Regional cooperation. 50k, Coal transport by cable car.

1990, July 23 *Perf. 12½*
511 A112 1.20k multicolored .30 .25
512 A112 19.50k multicolored 1.60 1.60
513 A112 20.50k multicolored 1.60 1.60
514 A112 50k multicolored 5.50 5.50
Nos. 511-514 (4) 9.00 8.95

Independence, 26th Anniv. — A113

1.20k, Agriculture. 19.50k, Shoe factory. 20.50k, Satellite communications. 50k, Mother and child statue.

1990, Oct. 23 Litho. *Perf. 14*
515 A113 1.20k multicolored .30 .25
516 A113 19.50k multicolored 1.25 1.25
517 A113 20.50k multicolored 1.40 1.40
518 A113 50k multicolored 3.00 3.00
Nos. 515-518 (4) 5.95 5.90

Small Carnivores A114

1990, Nov. 12
519 A114 1.20k Genet .30 .30
520 A114 18.50k Civet 2.40 2.40
521 A114 19.50k Serval 2.60 2.60
522 A114 20.50k African wild cat 2.75 2.75
Nos. 519-522 (4) 8.05 8.05

Intl. Literacy Year — A115

Children's stories — 1.20k, Bird and the Snake. 18.50k, Hare and the Leopard. 19.50k, Mouse and Lion. 20.50k, Hare and the Hippo.

1991, Jan. 11 Litho. *Perf. 14*
523 A115 1.20k multi .30 .30
524 A115 18.50k multi 1.90 1.90
525 A115 19.50k multi 2.75 2.75
526 A115 20.50k multi 3.00 3.00
Nos. 523-526 (4) 7.95 7.95

Bird Type of 1987

10n, Livingstone's flycatcher. 15n, Bar-winged weaver. 30n, Purple-throated cuckoo shrike. No. 530, Red-billed helmet shrike. 1.20k, Western bronze-naped pigeon. 15k, Corn crake. 20k, Dickinson's grey kestrel. 50k, Denham's bustard.

1990-91 Litho. *Perf. 11x13*
527 A91 10n multicolored 1.00 .50
528 A91 15n multicolored 1.00 .50
529 A91 30n multicolored 1.75 .50
530 A91 50n multicolored 1.75 .50
531 A91 50n like #527 1.75 .70
532 A91 1k like #528 2.00 .30
533 A91 1.20k multicolored 2.00 .30
534 A91 2k like #529 2.00 .75
535 A91 3k like #530 2.00 .75
536 A91 5k like #533 2.25 .75

Size: 25x38½mm
Perf. 14
537 A91 15k multicolored 1.75 .70
538 A91 20k multicolored 3.25 2.00
539 A91 20.50k like #538 1.75 1.00
540 A91 50k multicolored 2.75 2.25
Nos. 527-540 (14) 27.00 11.50

Issued: #533, 1k, 2k, 3k, 5k, 20k, 5/7/91; others, 10/30.

Soy Beans — A116

1k, Woman cooking. 2k, Soy bean seed. 5k, Woman feeding child. 20k, Malnourished, healthy children. 50k, Pres. Kaunda, child.

1991, June 28 Litho. *Perf. 13½*
548 A116 1k multicolored .30 .25
549 A116 2k multicolored .30 .25
550 A116 5k multicolored .30 .25
551 A116 20k multicolored 1.75 1.75
552 A116 50k multicolored 3.25 3.25
Nos. 548-552 (5) 5.90 5.75

United Church of Zambia / Rotary Foundation Project.

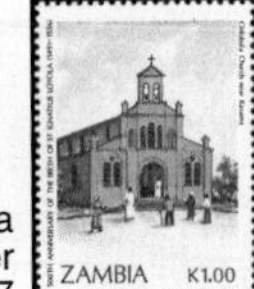
St. Ignatius of Loyola (1491-1556), Founder of Jesuit Order — A117

1k, Chilubula Church near Kasama. 2k, Chikuni Church near Monze. 20k, Bishop Joseph Du Pont. 50k, St. Ignatius of Loyola.

1991, July 18 Litho. *Perf. 13½*
553 A117 1k multicolored .30 .30
554 A117 2k multicolored .30 .30
555 A117 20k multicolored 2.00 2.00
556 A117 50k multicolored 3.75 3.75
Nos. 553-556 (4) 6.35 6.35

Flowering Trees — A118

1k, Baobab. 2k, Dichrostachys cinerea. 10k, Sterospermum kunthianum. 30k, Azanza garckeana.

1991, Nov. 29 Litho. *Perf. 13½*
557 A118 1k multicolored .30 .25
558 A118 2k multicolored .35 .25
559 A118 10k multicolored 2.00 1.50
560 A118 30k multicolored 3.75 3.75
Nos. 557-560 (4) 6.40 5.75

Queen Elizabeth II's Accession to the Throne, 40th Anniv.
Common Design Type

Perf. 14x13½
1992, Feb. 2 Litho. Wmk. 373
561 CD349 4k multicolored .30 .25
562 CD349 32k multicolored 1.00 1.00
563 CD349 35k multicolored 1.15 1.15
564 CD349 38k multicolored 1.15 1.15
565 CD349 50k multicolored 1.60 1.60
Nos. 561-565 (5) 5.20 5.15

For surcharges see Nos. 690-692.

Orchids — A119

1k, Disa hamatopetala. 2k, Eulophia paivaeana. 5k, Eulophia quartiniana. 20k, Aerangis verdickii.

Perf. 13x13½
1992, Feb. 28 Unwmk.
566 A119 1k multi .45 .25
567 A119 2k multi .45 .25
568 A119 5k multi .75 .60
569 A119 20k multi 3.75 3.75
Nos. 566-569 (4) 5.40 4.85

Masks — A120

1992, Mar. 10
570 A120 1k Kasinja .30 .30
571 A120 2k Chizaluke .30 .30
572 A120 10k Mwanapweu 1.25 1.00
573 A120 30k Maliya 3.25 3.75
Nos. 570-573 (4) 5.10 5.35

Antelopes
A121

1992, Sept. 14 Litho. *Perf. 14*
574 A121 4k Bushbuck .30 .25
575 A121 40k Eland 1.00 .75
576 A121 45k Roan antelope 1.00 .75
577 A121 100k Sable antelope 1.90 2.75
Nos. 574-577 (4) 4.20 4.50

Airmail Services, 75th Anniv. — A122

1992, Nov. 24 Litho. *Perf. 14*
578 A122 4k DH66 Hercules .35 .30
579 A122 40k VC10 2.25 .95
580 A122 45k C Class flying boat 2.25 .95
581 A122 100k DC10 3.75 5.00
Nos. 578-581 (4) 8.60 7.20

1992 Summer Olympics, Barcelona — A123

1992, Dec. 28
582 A123 10k 400-meter hurdles .30 .25
583 A123 40k Boxing .60 .40
584 A123 80k Judo 1.25 1.25
585 A123 100k Cycling 3.00 3.00
Nos. 582-585 (4) 5.15 4.90

Christmas
A124

1992, Dec. 23 Litho. *Perf. 14*
586 A124 10k Wise men .30 .25
587 A124 80k Nativity scene 1.35 1.35
588 A124 90k Angels singing 1.60 1.60
589 A124 100k Angel, shepherds 1.60 1.60
a. Souvenir sheet of 4, #586-589 8.00 8.00
Nos. 586-589 (4) 4.85 4.80

For surcharges see Nos. 658-659.

Nos. 331-334 Surcharged

1991, Mar. 4 Litho. *Perf. 13½x13*
590 A82 2k on 20n #331 *35.00* *5.75*
591 A82 2k on 45n #332 *.75* *5.75*
592 A82 2k on 55n #333 — *5.75*
593 A82 2k on 5k #334 *17.50* *5.75*

Stamps of 1981-89 Surcharged in Black or Gold

Perfs. as Before
1991, July 5 Litho.
594 A83 2k on 20n #335 *25.00* *6.00*
595 A81 2k on 25n #327 (G) *47.50* *6.00*
596 A64 2k on 28n #246 —
597 A71 2k on 28n #289 *55.00* —
598 A73 2k on 28n #297 —
599 A77 2k on 28n #313 —
600 A78 2k on 32n #317 *90.00* *8.00*
601 CD337 2k on 35n #343 — *20.00*
602 A87 2k on 35n #359 *75.00* *6.00*
603 A90 2k on 35n #373 *27.50* *6.00*
604 A79 2k on 45n #322 *45.00* *6.00*
605 A80 2k on 45n #325 *40.00* *6.00*
606 A81 2k on 45n #328 *47.50* *6.00*
607 A83 2k on 45n #336 *47.50* *6.00*
608 A87 2k on 1.60k #361 *80.00* *6.00*
609 A84 2k on 1.70k #341 *47.50* *6.00*
611 A81 2k on 5k #330 *17.50* *6.00*
612 A84 2k on 5k #342 *50.00* *6.00*
613 A107 2k on 6.50k #475 *47.50* *6.00*
614 A106 2k on 6.85k #471 *70.00* *6.00*
615 A107 2k on 6.85k #476 *17.50* *6.00*
616 A106 2k on 7.85k #472 *90.00* *6.00*

Numbers have been reserved for additional surcharges in this set.

Waterfalls — A125

1993, Sept. 30 Litho. *Perf. 13½*
617 A125 50k Nkundalila .35 .35
618 A125 200k Chishimba 1.40 1.40
619 A125 250k Chipoma 1.75 1.75
620 A125 300k Lumangwe 2.50 2.50
Nos. 617-620 (4) 6.00 6.00

For surcharges, see Nos. 1011-1014.

Healthy Hearts — A126

1993, Oct. 20 Litho. *Perf. 14½*
621 A126 O Runner 1.10 1.10
622 A126 P Heart 1.10 1.10

No. 621 sold for 50k and No. 622 sold for 80k on date of issue.

Sunbirds — A127

Designs: 20k, Bronze. 50k, Violet-backed. No. 625, Marico. No. 626, Eastern double-collared. 100k, Scarlet-chested. 150k, Bannerman's blue-headed. 200k, Oustalet's. 250k, Red and blue. 300k, Olive. 350k, Green-headed. 400k, Scarlet tufted malachite. 500k, Yellow-bellied. 800k, Copper. 1000k, Orange-tufted. 1500k, Black. 2000k, Green-throated.

1993, May 30 Litho. *Perf. 13*
623 A127 20k multicolored .30 .25
624 A127 50k multicolored .30 .25
625 A127 O multicolored .30 .25
626 A127 P multicolored .30 .30
627 A127 100k multicolored .30 .30
628 A127 150k multicolored .45 .45
629 A127 200k multicolored .55 .55
630 A127 250k multicolored .70 .70
631 A127 300k multicolored .75 .75
632 A127 350k multicolored .95 .95
633 A127 400k multicolored 1.05 1.05
634 A127 500k multicolored 1.30 1.30
635 A127 800k multicolored 2.15 2.15
636 A127 1000k multicolored 2.80 2.80
637 A127 1500k multicolored 4.25 4.25
638 A127 2000k multicolored 5.75 5.75
Nos. 623-638 (16) 22.20 22.05

Nos. 625 sold for 50k and 626 sold for 80k on date of issue.
For surcharge, see Nos. 997, 1090.

Snakes — A128

1994, Sept. 28 Litho. *Perf. 14*
639 A128 50k Tiger snake .25 .25
640 A128 200k Egyptian cobra 1.60 1.60
641 A128 300k African python 2.50 2.50
642 A128 500k Green mamba 4.25 4.25
Nos. 639-642 (4) 8.60 8.60

For surcharges, see Nos. 996, 1007-1010, 1175.

ILO, 75th Anniv. — A129

1995, Apr. 3 Litho. *Perf. 14*
643 A129 100k Road rehabilitation .60 .60
644 A129 450k Block making 2.00 2.00

For surcharge see No. 781A.

Christmas Angels — A130

1995, Aug. 29 *Perf. 14½x14*
645 A130 100k shown .40 .25
646 A130 300k With animals 1.10 .60
647 A130 450k Blowing horn, birds 1.25 1.25
648 A130 500k Playing drum 1.60 1.60
Nos. 645-648 (4) 4.35 3.70

For surcharge, see No. 998.

UN, 50th Anniv. — A131

1995, Dec. 30 Litho. *Perf. 11½*
Granite Paper
649 A131 700k multicolored 1.75 1.75

For surcharges, see Nos. 1038, 1121, 1152.

Natl. Monuments — A132

Designs: 100k, David Livingstone. 300k, Mbereshi Mission. 450k, Von Lettow-Vorbeck. 500k, Niamkolo Church.

1996, Feb. 21 Litho. *Perf. 14*
650 A132 100k multicolored .30 .25
651 A132 300k multicolored .75 .75
652 A132 450k multicolored 1.25 1.25
653 A132 500k multicolored 1.50 1.50
Nos. 650-653 (4) 3.80 3.75

For surcharges, see Nos. 870A, 1015-1018.

World Wildlife Fund — A133

Designs: 200k, Saddle-billed stork. 300k, Black-cheeked lovebird. 500k, Two black-cheeked lovebirds. 900k, Saddle-billed stork with young.

1996, Nov. 27 Litho. *Perf. 14x14½*
654 A133 200k multicolored .50 .50
655 A133 300k multicolored .65 .65
656 A133 500k multicolored 1.00 1.00
657 A133 900k multicolored 1.75 1.75
a. Sheet of 4, #654-657 *100.00* *100.00*
Nos. 654-657 (4) 3.90 3.90

For surcharges, see Nos. 1003-1006.

Nos. 587-588 Surcharged

1996 Litho. *Perf. 14*
658 A124 (0) on 90k #588 1.75 1.75
659 A124 900k on 80k #587 3.00 3.00

No. 658 was valued at 500k on day of issue. Size and location of surcharge varies.

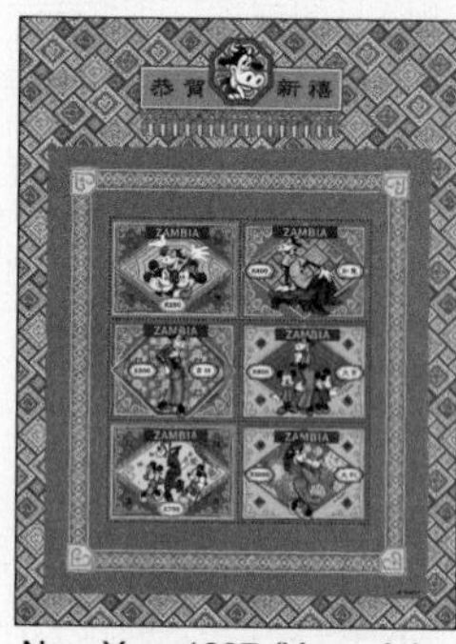
New Year 1997 (Year of the Ox) — A134

Disney characters posing for portrait in Chinese scene, vert.: #660: a, Clarabelle seated. b, Holding scroll. c, Playing musical instrument. d, On bicycle. e, Minnie, Mickey, Clarabelle. f, Holding mirror.

No. 661: a, 250k, Faces of Minnie, Mickey, Clarabelle Cow. b, 400k, Clarabelle seated. c, 500k, Clarabelle standing. d, 600k, Mickey, Clarabelle, Minnie dressed in Chinese outfits. e, 750k, Minnie, Clarabelle, Mickey dancing. f, 1000k, Clarabelle with parasol.

1997, Jan. 28 Litho. *Perf. 14x13½*
660 A134 500k Sheet of 6, #a.-f. 6.50 6.50
661 A134 Sheet of 6, #a.-f. 6.50 6.50

No. 660 contains six 35x61mm stamps.

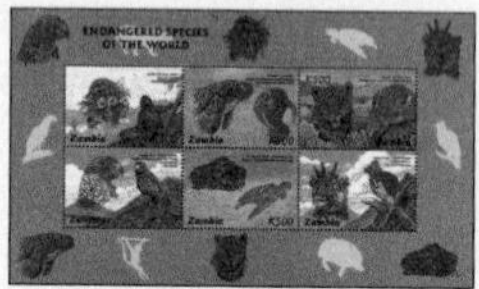
Endangered Species — A135

Species of the world, each 500k: No. 662: a, Spider monkey. b, Manatee. c, Jaguar. d, Puerto Rican parrot. d, Green sea turtle. e, Harpy eagle.

Species of Africa, each 1000k: No. 663a, Black rhinoceros. b, Leopard. c, Chimpanzee. d, Zebra (Grants). e, Mountain gorilla. f, African elephant.

Each, 3000k: No. 664, Lion (African). No. 665, Margay cat.

1997, Feb. 12 *Perf. 14*
662 A135 Sheet of 6, #a.-f. 6.75 6.75
663 A135 Sheet of 6, #a.-f. 13.50 13.50

Souvenir Sheets
664-665 A135 Set of 2 10.00 10.00

Deng Xiaoping (1904-97) — A136

Various portraits of Deng Xiaoping and: 800k, Flags, map of Hong Kong. 1000k, Flag, Hong Kong harbor. 2000k, Hong Kong at night, countdown clock. 2500k, World map with China highlighted.

1997, May 26 Litho. *Perf. 14*
666 A136 800k multicolored 2.50 2.50
667 A136 1000k multicolored 3.50 3.50

Souvenir Sheets
668 A136 2000k multicolored 5.00 5.00
669 A136 2500k multicolored 6.00 6.00

Nos. 666-667 were issued in sheets of 3 each. No. 669 contains one 72x47mm stamp.

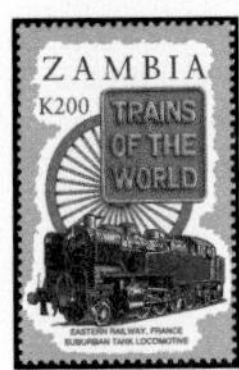
Trains — A137

Locomotives: 200k, Suburban tank, Eastern Railway, France. 300k, Streamlined express, Belgian Natl. Railways. 500k, "Mountain" type express, Union Pacific Railraod. 900k, 2-8-2 "Mikado," Kenya & Uganda Railway. 1000k, 4-6-0 "Royal Scot," LM & S Railway. 1500k, 4-6-0 "Lord Nelson" type, Southern Railway.

No. 676, each 500k: a, Express, German State Railways. b, Express, "Duke of Abercorn," NCC (LMSR), Ireland. c, Heavy freight tank, Netherlands Railways. d, Express, Austrian Federal Railways. e, "Governor" class, Gold Coast Railways. f, 4-8-4 Express, Canadian Natl. Railways.

Each 3000k: No. 677, Diesel-electric passenger, Royal Siamese State Railways. No. 678, "Pacific" type, South African Railways.

1997, June 2

670-675 A137 Set of 6 6.50 6.50
676 A137 Sheet of 6, #a.-f. 6.25 6.25

Souvenir Sheets

677-678 A137 Set of 2 11.00 11.00

Butterflies and Moths — A138

300k, No. 683a, Gaudy commodore. 500k, No. 683b, African moon moth. 700k, No. 683c, Emperor moth. No. 682, 900k, Emperor swallowtail.

1997, Aug. 8 **Litho.** ***Perf. 14***

679-682 A138 Set of 4 9.50 9.50
683 A138 900k Sheet of 4, #a.-c., #682 15.00 15.00

Queen Elizabeth II and Prince Philip, 50th Wedding Anniv. — A139

No. 684, each 500k: a, Queen Elizabeth II. b, Royal arms. c, Queen wearing crown, Prince in uniform. d, Queen, Prince riding in open carriage. e, Buckingham Palace. f, Prince waving.

3200k, Queen, Prince waving from balcony.

1997, Aug. 26 **Litho.** ***Perf. 14***

684 A139 Sheet of 6, #a.-f. 8.00 8.00

Souvenir Sheet

685 A139 3200k multicolored 8.00 8.00

Paul P. Harris (1868-1947), Founder of Rotary, Intl. — A140

1000k, First Rotarians, Silvester Schiele, Harris, Hiram Shorey, Gus Loehr, portrait of Harris.

3200k, Zambian interactors with retirees.

1997, Aug. 27

686 A140 1000k multicolored 4.75 4.75

Souvenir Sheet

687 A140 3200k multicolored 6.25 6.25

Heinrich von Stephan (1831-97), Founder of UPU — A141

Each 1000k, Portrait of Von Stephan and: #688a, World Postal Congress, Berne, 1874. #688b, UPU emblem. #688c, Savannah, paddle steamer, 1819.

3200k, Von Stephan, Prussian postilion, 1715.

1997, Aug. 28

688 A141 Sheet of 3, #a.-c. 6.50 6.50

Souvenir Sheet

689 A141 3200k multicolored 5.00 5.00

Nos. 562-564 Surcharged

1997, Sept. 19 **Litho.** ***Perf. 14x13½***

690 CD349 500k on 35k 1.75 .75
691 CD349 (0) on 32k 1.75 .90
692 CD349 900k on 38k 3.50 3.50
Nos. 690-692 (3) 7.00 5.15

No. 691 was valued at 600k on day of issue.

Owls — A142

300k, #697b, Verreaux's eagle owl. 500k, #697c, Pel's fishing owl. 700k, #697a, Barn owl. #696, Spotted eagle owl.

1997, Dec. 18 **Litho.** ***Perf. 14***

693 A142 300k multicolored .75 .75
694 A142 500k multicolored 1.25 1.25
695 A142 700k multicolored 1.80 1.80
696 A142 900k multicolored 2.20 2.20
Nos. 693-696 (4) 6.00 6.00

Sheet of 4

697 A142 900k #a.-c., #696 9.00 9.00

Christmas — A143

Entire paintings or details, sculpture: No. 698, 50k, Winged Victory of Samothrace. No. 699, 50k, Ognissanti Madonna, by Giotto. No. 700, 100k, Angel, by Antonio Pollaiuolo. No. 701, 100k, Angel of the Annunciation, by Jacopo da Pontormo. No. 702, 500k, No. 703. 1000k, The Virgin and Child Enthroned Among Angels and Saints, by Benozzo Gozzoli.

Each 3200k: No. 704, All of the Rebel Angels, detail, by Rubens. No. 705, The Resurrection of the Dead, by Joseph Christian.

1997, Dec. 18 **Litho.** ***Perf. 14***

698-703 A143 Set of 6 5.25 5.25

Souvenir Sheets

704-705 A143 Set of 2 9.50 9.50

No. 704 incorrectly inscribed "The Virgin and Child Enthroned Among Angels and Saints, by Bonozzo Gozzoli."

Diana, Princess of Wales (1961-97) — A144

Various portraits with color of sheet margin: No. 706, Pale green. No. 707, Pale yellow.

Each 2500k: No. 708, Touching hand of blind man (in sheet margin). No. 709, With Barbara Bush (in sheet margin).

1997

706 A144 500k Sheet of 6, #a.-f. 9.00 9.00
707 A144 700k Sheet of 6, #a.-f. 11.00 11.00

Souvenir Sheets

708-709 A144 Set of 2 10.50 10.50

PAPU (Pan African Postal Union), 18th Anniv. — A145

Designs: 500k, Kobus leche kafuensis. (O), Dove carrying letter over map. 900k, Emblem of dove carrying letter.

1998 ***Perf. 14½***

710 A145 500k multicolored 1.40 1.40
711 A145 (O) multicolored 1.75 1.75
712 A145 900k multicolored 2.25 2.25
Nos. 710-712 (3) 5.40 5.40

No. 711 was valued at 600k on day of issue. For surcharges, see Nos. 1019-1021.

Mahatma Gandhi (1869-1948) A146

Portraits of Gandhi: 250k, As law student in London, 1888. 500k, With Nehru, 1946. No. 715, (O), In front of Red Fort, New Dehli. 900k, At prayer.

2000k, Gandhi at 2nd Round Table Conference, London, 1931.

1998, Jan. 30 **Litho.** ***Perf. 13½***

713-716 A146 Set of 4 16.00 16.00

Souvenir Sheet

717 A146 2000k multicolored 13.00 13.00

No. 715 was valued at 600k on day of issue. Nos. 713, 715-717 are vert.

For surcharges, see Nos. 911-912.

Flowers — A147

Designs: No. 718, Lantana camara. No. 719, Clusia rosea. No. 720, Nymphaea hybrids. No. 721, Portulaca grandiflora.

No. 722: a, Hibiscus rosa-sinensis. b, Plumeria. c, Erythrina variegata. d, Bauhinia blakeana. e, Carissa grandiflora. f, Cordia sebestena. g, Couroupita guianensis. h, Eustoma grandiflorum. i, Passiflora.

3200k, Strelitzia reginae, horiz.

1998, Feb. 27 **Litho.** ***Perf. 14***

718-721 A147 500k Set of 4 4.00 4.00
722 A147 500k Sheet of 9, #a.-i. 9.00 9.00

Souvenir Sheet

723 A147 3200k multicolored 13.00 13.00

New Year 1998 (Year of the Tiger) — A148

Chinese symbols and stylized tigers, each 700k: No. 724: a, Looking right. b, Looking left. c, Facing forward, denomination UL. d, Facing forward, denomination UR.

1500k, Tiger, symbols on both sides.

1998 **Litho.** ***Perf. 14***

724 A148 Sheet of 4, #a.-d. 5.00 5.00

Souenir Sheet

725 A148 1500k multicolored 4.00 4.00

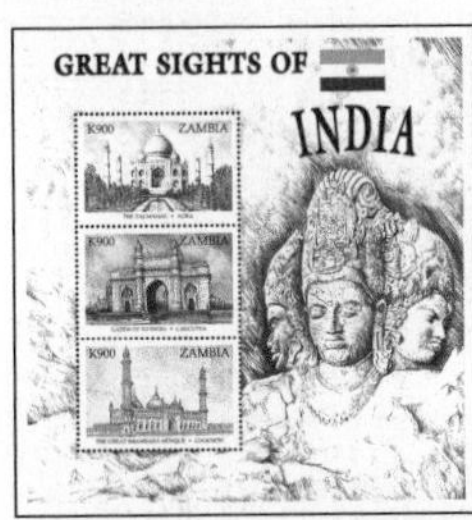
Sites of India — A149

Designs: a, Taj Mahal, Agra. b, Gateway to India, Calcutta. c, Great Imambara Mosque, Lucknow.

1998

726 A149 900k Sheet of 3, #a.-c. 7.25 7.25

Art of India — A150

No. 727, each 700k: a, Ragmala, School of Mewar, 17th cent. b, Babur Nama, Mogul School, 16th cent. c, Hamza Nama, Mogul School, 16th cent. d, Meghamallar, School of Mewar, 16th cent.

2500k, Hindola Raga, School of Deccan, 17th-18th cent.

1998

727 A150 Sheet of 4, #a.-d. 8.25 8.25

Souvenir Sheet

728 A150 2500k multicolored 8.00 8.00

1998 World Cup Soccer Championships, France — A151

No. 729, each 450k: a, Albert, Belgium. b, Bebeto, Brazil. c, Beckenbauer, W. Germany. d, Littbarski, W. Germany. e, Juninho, Brazil. f, Lineker, England. g, Lato, Poland. h, McCoist, Scotland.

No. 730, each 500k: a, Maier, W. Germany, 1974. b, Bellini, Brazil, 1958. c, Kempes, Argentina, 1978. d, Nazassi, Uruguay, 1930. e, Pele, Brazil, 1970. f, Beckenbauer, W. Germany, 1974. g, Combi, Italy, 1934. h, Zoff, Italy, 1982.

No. 731, each 500k: a, Keane, Rep. of Ireland. b, Seaman, England. c, Like #729b. d, Futre, Portugal. e, Ravanelli, Italy. f, Weah, Liberia. g, Bergkamp, Holland. h, Raducioiu, Romania.

Each 3200k: No. 732, Juninho, Brazil. No. 733, Romario, Brazil, horiz. No. 734, McCoist, Scotland, horiz.

1998, Apr. 17 ***Perf. 13½x14, 14x13½***

Sheets of 8, #a-h, + Label

729 A151 multi 5.25 5.25
730-731 A151 Set of 2 13.00 13.00

Souvenir Sheets

732-734 A151 Set of 3 13.50 13.50

Parrots — A152

No. 735, each 500k: a, Rainbow lorikeet. b, Budgerigar, blossom-headed parakeet. c, Blue-yellow macaw. d, Blue-crowned parrot. e, Golden conure. f, Sulphur-crested cockatoo.
No. 736, each 1000k: a, Ara ararauna. b, Ara chloropterd. c, Pale-headed rosellas. d, Northern rosella. e, Gang-gang cockatoo. f, Palm cockatoo.
Each 3200k: No. 737, Mulga parakeet. No. 738, Major Mitchell cockatoo, horiz.

1998, June 1 **Litho.** ***Perf. 14***

735 A152 Sheet of 6, #a.-f. 4.75 4.75
736 A152 Sheet of 6, #a.-f. 9.25 9.25

Souvenir Shets

737-738 A152 Set of 2 14.00 14.00

Mushrooms A153

No. 739, 250k, Red-tufted wood tricholoma. No. 740, 250k, Chlorophyllum molybdites. No. 741, 450k, Stuntz's psilocybe. No. 742, 450k, Lepista sordida. No. 743, 500k, Lepiota. No. 744, 500k, Rosy gomphidius. No. 745, 900k, Cantharellus cybrina. No. 746, 900k, Olive-capped boletus. No. 747, 1000k, Showy volvaria. No. 748, 1000k, Sooty brown waxy cap.
No. 749, each 900k: a, Leller's boletus. b, Short-stemmed russula. c, Anise-scented clitocybe. d, Dung roundhead. e, Oak-loving collybia. f, Wine-red stropharia.
No. 750, each 900k: a, Flat-topped mushroom. b, Alice Eastwood's boletus. c, Pitted milky cap. d, Short-stemmed slippery jask. e, Rose-red russula. f, Zeller's tricholoma.
Each 3200k: No. 751, Honey mushroom. No. 752, Velvet-stemmed flammulina.

1998, July 1

739-748 A153 Set of 10 19.00 19.00

Sheets of 6

749-750 A153 Set of 2 19.00 19.00

Souvenir Sheets

751-752 A153 Set of 2 15.00 15.00

Nos. 749-752 are continuous designs.

Traditional Stories — A154

No. 755, each 2000k: a, like #753. b, like #754.

1998, Dec. 2 **Litho.** ***Perf. 14***

753 A154 300k Luchela nganga .90 .90
754 A154 500k Kasuli 1.40 1.40

Souvenir Sheet

755 A154 Sheet of 2, #a.-b. 6.00 6.00

Christmas.

Orchids — A155

Designs, vert: No. 756, 100k, Paphiopedilum callosum. No. 757, 100k, Phaius tankervilleae. No. 758, 500k, Paphiopedilum fairrieanum. No. 759, 500k, Barkeria lindleyana. No. 760, 1000k, Laelia flava. No. 761, 1000k, Masdervallia unifloria, masdervallia angulifera.
No. 762, each 900k: a, Acacallis cyanea. b, Miltoniopsis phalaenopsis. c, Dendrobium bellatulum. d, Polystachya campyloglossa. e, Pleione bulbocodioides. f, Rhynchostylis gigantea. g, Cattleya lawrenceana. h, Sopbrolaelia. i, Laelia tenebrosa.
No. 763, each 900k: a, Acacallis cyanea, diff. b, Epidendrum gastropodium. c, Laelia rubescens. d, Paphiopedilum dayanum. e, Laelia lobata. f, Dendrobium crepidatum. g, Cattleya nobilior. h, Dendrobium johnsoniae. i, Trichopilia fragrans.
Each 4000k: No. 764, Cattleya maxima, vert. No. 765, Cattleya violacea.

1998, Dec. 23

756-761 A155 Set of 6 5.50 5.50

Sheets of 9

762-763 A155 Set of 2 15.00 15.00

Souvenir Sheets

764-765 A155 Set of 2 13.00 13.00

Classic Cars — A156

Designs: 300k, Ferrari Daytona 365 GTB/4. 500k, Austin Healey Sprite. 900k, Gordon Keeble. 1000k, Alvis TD.
No. 770: a, Mercedes-Benz 300Sl. b, Chevrolet Corvair. c, AC Cobra 427. d, Aston Martin DB5. e, BMW 2002 Turbo. f, Cadillac Eldorado Brougham.
No. 771: a, Mercedes-Benz 280SE 3.5. b, Aston Martin DB2. c, Volkswagen Beetle. d, Lancia Aurelia B20 GT. e, Lamborghini 350 GT. f, Cisitalia 202 Coupe.
No. 771G: h, 1995 Ferrari 750 Pinnafarina. i, 1997 Federrari 312T2/77. j, 1983 Ferrari 208 Turbo. k, 1962 Ferrari Dino 268 SP. l, 1994 Ferrari F355 Berlinetta. m, Ferrari 250 GTE Coupe 2+2 California.
Each 4000k: No. 772, Citroen Light 15. No. 773, Austin Healey MKII 3000.

1998, Dec. 23

766-769 A156 Set of 4 5.00 5.00

Sheets of 6, #a-f

770-771G A156 900k Set of 3 14.00 14.00

Souvenir Sheets

772-773 A156 Set of 2 14.00 14.00

New Year 1999 (Year of the Rabbit) — A157

Various rabbits, denomination at — #774 (each 700k): a, LL. b, LR. c, LL (scratching). d, LR (nose near ground).
2000k, Rabbit, vert.

1999, Jan. 4

774 A157 Sheet of 4, #a.-d. 4.75 4.75

Souvenir Sheet

775 A157 2000k multicolored 4.50 4.50

Trains — A158

Locomotives: No. 776, (0), U20C Diesel electric, 1967. No. 777, 800k, 7th Class No. 70, 1900. No. 778, 800k, 15A Class Beyer-Garrat No. 401, 1950. No. 779, 900k, HP diesel electric, 1966. No. 780, 900k, 20th Class No. 708, 1954.
4000k, 7th Class No. 955, 1892.

1999, Feb. 1 **Litho.** ***Perf. 14½***

776-780 A158 Set of 5 6.25 6.25

Souvenir Sheet

781 A158 4000k multicolored 4.00 4.00

No. 776 was valued at 600k on day of issue.

No. 643 Surcharged

Methods and Perfs as Before

1999, June 1

781A A129 500k on 100k multi

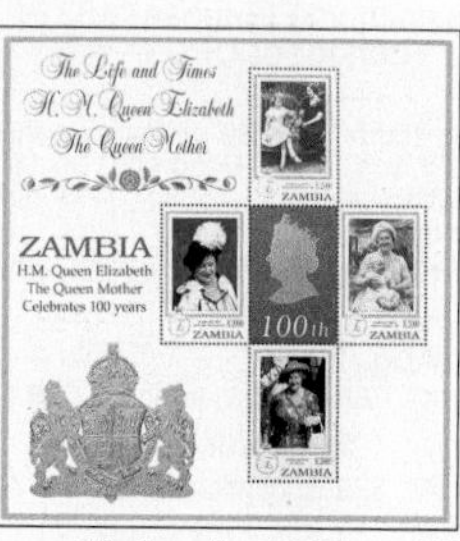

Queen Mother (b. 1900) — A159

No. 782: a, With Princess Elizabeth, 1936. b, Lady of the Garter. c, With Prince Andrew, 1960. d, At Ascot.
5000k, Wedding photograph, 1923.

1999, Sept. 1 ***Perf. 14***

782 A159 2000k Sheet of 4, #a.-d., + label 9.50 9.50

Souvenir Sheet

Perf. 13¾

783 A159 5000k multicolored 6.50 6.50

No. 783 contains one 38x51mm stamp.

Dinosaurs A160

Designs: 50k, Dimetrodon. 100k, Deinonychus. 500k, Protoceratops. 900k, Heterodontosaurus. 1000k, Oviraptor. 1800k, Psittacosaurus.
No. 790, each 900k: a, Stegosaurus. b, Triceratops. c, Brontosaurus. d, Gallimimus. e, Saurolophus. f, Lambeosaurus. g, Centrosaurus. h, Edmontonia. i, Parasaurolophus.
No. 791, each 900k: a, Ceratosaurus. b, Daspletosaurus. c, Baryonyx. d, Ornitholestes. e, Troodon. f, Coelophysis. g, Tyrannosaurus. h, Allosaurus. i, Compsognathus.
Each 4000k: No. 792, Saltasaurus, vert. No. 793, Stygimoloch, vert.

1999, Sept. 27 **Litho.** ***Perf. 14***

784-789 A160 Set of 6 4.50 4.50

Sheets of 9

790-791 A160 Set of 2 14.50 14.50

Souvenir Sheets

792-793 A160 Set of 2 9.00 9.00

Johann Wolfgang von Goethe (1749-1832), German Poet — A161

No. 794, each 2000k: a, A drinking party in Amerbach's cellar. b, Goethe and Friedrich von Schiller. c, Faust falls in love with Margaret.
5000k, Angel.

1999, Oct. 4 **Litho.** ***Perf. 14***

794 A161 Sheet of 3, #a.-c. 5.75 5.75

Souvenir Sheet

795 A161 5000k org brn & brn 5.25 5.25

A162

Cats: 50k, White Devon Rex. 100k, Red Persian. 500k, Chartreux. 900k, Brown tabby Maine Coon.
No. 800, each 1000k, horiz.: a, Tortie point Himalayan. b, Blue mackerel tabby Scottish Fold. c, Chocolate lynx point Balinese. d, Havana Brown. e, Seal point Ragdoll. f, Silver shaded Persian.
No. 801, each 1000k, horiz.: a, Red spotted tabby Exotic Shorthair. b, Blue tortie smoke Persian. c, Brown classic tabby longhaired Scottish Fold. d, Spotted tabby American Bobtail. e, Silver spotted tabby Ocicat. f, Blue British Shorthair.
Each 4000k: No. 802, Silver tabby longhair Persian, horiz. No. 803, Tabby point Siamese.

1999, Oct. 18

796-799 A162 Set of 4 1.60 1.60

Sheets of 6, #a.-f.

800-801 A162 Set of 2 10.00 10.00

Souvenir Sheets

802-803 A162 Set of 2 7.75 7.75

A163

Dogs: 100k, Welsh corgi. 500k, Shetland sheepdog. 900k, Italian greyhound. 1000k, Tibetan spaniel.
No. 808, each 1000k, horiz.: a, Dalmatian. b, Shetland sheepdogs. c, Bearded collie. d, Eskimo. e, Basenji. f, Saluki.
No. 809, each 1000k, horiz.: a, Norwegian elkhound. b, Flat-coated retriever. c, St. Bernard. d, Basset hound, Pembroke Welsh corgi. e, Pembroke Welsh corgi, Pointer. f, Petit Basset Griffon Vendeen.
Each 4000k: No. 810, Whippet. No. 811, Rottweiler.

1999, Oct. 18

804-807 A163 Set of 4 2.50 2.50

Sheets of 6, #a.-f.

808-809 A163 Set of 2 9.50 9.50

Souvenir Sheets

810-811 A163 Set of 2 7.50 7.50

11th Intl. Conference on AIDS in Africa, Lusaka — A164

Designs: 500k, Emblem, waterfalls. 900k, Emblem, close-up view of waterfalls.

1999, Oct. 20

812-813 A164 Set of 2 2.00 2.00

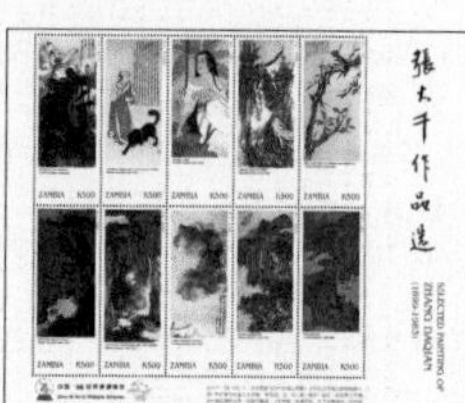
Paintings by Zhang Daqian (1899-1983) — A165

No. 814, each 500k: a, Water Lily in the Rain. b, Chinghai Tribal Girl and a Black Hound. c, Taking a Nap. d, Monkey and Old Tree. e, Bird and Tree of Chin-Chang Mountain. f, Watching Waterfalls. g, On the Way to

Switzerland and Austria. h, A Boat Brings the Wine. i, Brown Landscape. j, Nice Autumn.
No. 815: a, 1000k, White Water Lily, horiz. b, 2000k, Cloudy Waterfalls and Summer Mountain, horiz.

1999, Oct. 21 ***Perf. 13***

814 A165 Sheet of 10, #a.-j. 3.75 3.75
815 A165 Sheet of 2, #a.-b. 2.10 2.10

China 1999 World Philatelic Exhibition, 22nd UPU Congress, Beijing. #815 contains two 52x39mm stamps.

A166

Flora & Fauna — A167

Designs: 50k, Leatherback turtle. 100k, American kestrel. No. 818, 500k, Great blue heron. 900k, Mesene phareus. 1000k, Laelio-cattleya. 1800k, Papilio cresphontes.
Each 500k: No. 822, Cairn's birdwing. No. 823, Pintail. No. 824, Rose. No. 825, Gray tree frog.
No. 826, each 700k: a, White-tailed tropicbird. b, Sooty tern. c, Laughing gull. d, Black skimmer. e, Brown pelican. f, Bottle-nosed dolphin. g, Common dolphin. h, Man in sailboat. i, Blue tang. j, Southern stingray. k, Hammerhead shark. l, Mako shark.
No. 827, each 700k: a, Heliconia. b, Purple-throated Carib. c, St. Vincent parrot. d, Bananaquit. e, prepona meander. f, Unidentified butterfly. g, Hawksbill turtle. h, Black-necked stilt. i, Banded butterflyfish. j, Porkfish. k, Seahorse. l, Chain moray eel.
No. 828: a, Baltimore oriole. b, Chipmunk. c, Blue jay. d, Monarch butterfly. e, Gray heron. f, Mallard. g, Canadian otter. h, American lotus. i, Fowler's toad. j, Bluegill sunfish. k, Rainbow trout. l, Terrapin.
Each 4000k: No. 829, Amazona guildingii. No. 830, Bottle-nosed dolphin, diff. No. 831, Fuchsia. No. 832, Red-banded pereute.

1999, Oct. 27

816-821 A166 Set of 6 5.50 5.50
822-825 A167 Set of 4 2.50 2.50

Sheets of 12, #a.-l.

826-827 A166 Set of 2 14.50 14.50
828 A167 700k multi 7.00 7.00

Souvenir Sheets

829-830 A166 Set of 2 7.50 7.50
831-832 A167 Set of 2 7.50 7.50

IBRA '99 A168

Trains: 1000k, Crampton. 3200k, Post standard 2-8-4 tank locomotive.

1999 ***Perf. 14x14¾***

833-834 A168 Set of 2 3.50 3.50

Souvenir Sheets

PhilexFrance '99 — A169

Each 5000k: #835, Paris-Orleans Railway 4-4-0. #836, paris, Lyon & Mediterranean Railway 2-4-2.

1999 ***Perf. 14¼***

835-836 A169 Set of 2 7.50 7.50

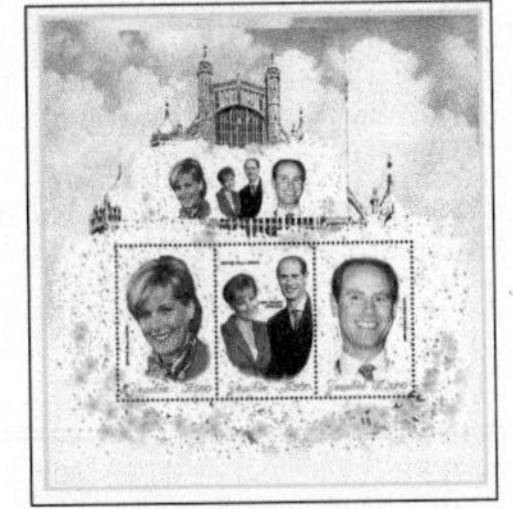

Wedding of Prince Edward and Sophie Rhys-Jones — A170

No. 837: a, 500k, Sophie. b, 900k, Couple. c, 100k, Edward.
3000k, Couple kissing.

1999 ***Perf. 14***

837 A170 Sheet of 3, #a.-c. 3.50 3.50

Souvenir Sheet

838 A170 3000k multi 4.25 4.25

Birds — A171

Designs: 50k, Blacksmith plover. 100k, Sacred ibis. 200k, Purple gallinule. 250k, Purple heron. 300k, Glossy ibis. 400k, Marabou stork. 450k, African spoonbill. 500k, African finfoot. O, No. 847, Knot-billed duck. 600k, Darter. 700k, African skimmer. 800k, Spur-winged goose. 900k, Hammerkop. 1000k, White pelican. 1500k, Black-winged stilt. 2000k, Black-crowned night heron.

1999, Dec. 20 Litho. ***Perf. 14½x15***

839-854 A171 Set of 16 11.50 11.50

No. 847 sold for 500k on day of issue.
Design size of No. 847 is 30½mm wide. See Nos. 927-930.

Flowers — A172

Various flowers making up a photomosaic of Princess Diana, each 1000k.

1999, Dec. 31 ***Perf. 13¾***

855 A172 Sheet of 8, #a.-h. 8.00 8.00

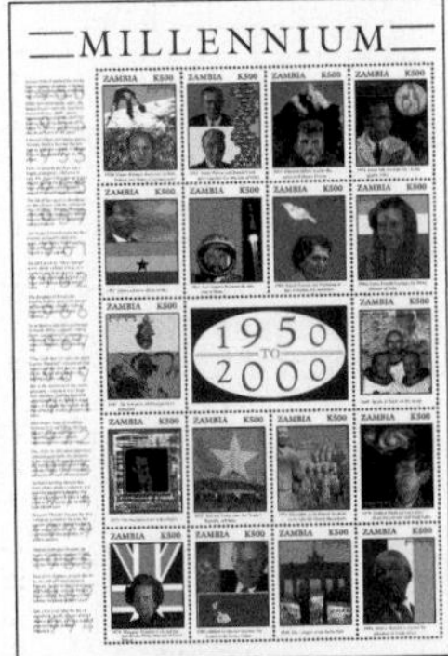

Millennium — A173

Highlights of 1950-2000: a, Venice Biennale shows Jackson Pollock and Abstract Expressionism. b, James Watson and Francis Crick piece together the structure of DNA. c, Edmund Hillary reaches the summit of Mount Everest. d, Jonas Salk's polio vaccine. e, Ghana achieves independence. f, Yuri Gagarin becomes 1st man in space. g, Rachel Carson and the beginning of the environmental movement. h, Indira Gandhi becomes Prime Minister of India. i, 1st successful heart transplant. j, Apollo 11 lands on moon. k, Microprocessor developed. l, Richard Nixon visits People's Republic of China. m, Qin Shi Huang Mausoleum discovered. n, Stephen Hawking proposes new ideas about the universe and black holes. o, Margaret Thatcher elected 1st female Prime Minister of Great Britain. p, Mikhail Gorbachev becomes leader of Soviet Union. q, Fall of the Berlin Wall. r, Nelson Mandela elected Pres. of South Africa.

2000, Feb. 7 ***Perf. 12¾x12½***

856 A173 500k Sheet of 18, #a.-r., + label 12.00 12.00

Butterflies A174

400k, Papilio antimachus. 450k, Amauris niavius. 500k, Charaxes smaragdalis. 800k, Charaxes zelica. 900k, Cymothoe confusa. 1000k, #862, Labobunea ansorgei.
No. 863, each 1000k: a, Palla ussheri. b, Euphaedra aureola. c, Graphium cyrnus nuscyrus. d, Salamis cacta. e, Salamis parhassus. f, Charaxes pelias.
No. 864, each 1000k: a, Large Spotted Acraea. b, Palla (orange wings). c, Palla (blue wings). d, Gold-banded Forester (white wings). e, Figtree blue. f, Gold-banded Forester (pink wings).
No. 865, each 1500k: a, Colotis ione. b, Charaxes acraeoides. c, Euphaedra edwardsi. d, Colotis phisadia. e, Charaxes lydiae. f, Euphaedra eupaulus.
No. 866, each 1500k: a, Papilio zalmoxis. b, Amauris niavius. c, Salamis cytora. d, Salamis temora. e, Charaxes eupale. f, Cymothoe hypatha.
Each 5000k: No. 867, Euphaedra ceres. No. 868, Cymothoe fumana. No. 869, Euphaedra spatiosa. No. 870, Euryphene gambiae.

2000, Feb. 8 ***Perf. 14***

857-862 A174 Set of 6 5.00 5.00

Sheets of 6, #a.-f.

863-864 A174 Set of 2 10.00 10.00
865-866 A174 Set of 2 14.00 14.00

Souvenir Sheets

867-870 A174 Set of 4 16.00 16.00

No. 650 Surcharged

Method and Perf. as Before

2000, Apr. 11

870A A132 700k on 100k multi

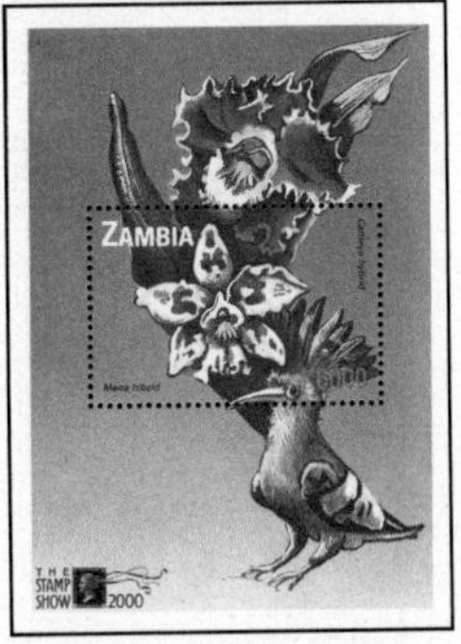

Orchids A175

No. 871, each 1500k: a, Paphiopedilum sioux. b, Phalaenopsis amabilis hybrid. c, Thelymitza ixioides. d, Phalaenopsis schilleriana.
No. 872, each 1500k: a, Miltoniopsis pansy orchid. b, Paphiopedilum venustum. c, Odontoglossum grande. d, Vanda sanderiana alba. e, Phalaenopsis violacea. f, Pleione alishan.
No. 873, each 1500k: a, Cyrtorchis arcuata. b, Cymbioiella rhodochila. c, Unidentified orchid. d, Eulophia quartiana. e, Augraecum montanum. f, Polystacha vulcanica.
No. 874, each 1500k, vert.: a, Catasetum splendens. b, Miltonia spectabilis. c, Stenia pallida. d, Cozacias spatulata. e, Eriopsis sceptzum. f, Paphinia cristata.
Each 6000k: No. 875, Cattleya hybrid. No. 876, Brachycorythis kalbreyeri.

2000, May 16 Litho. ***Perf. 14***

871 A175 Sheet of 4, #a.-d. 5.50 5.50

Sheets of 6, #a.-f.

872-874 A175 Set of 3 20.00 20.00

Souvenir Sheets

875-876 A175 Set of 2 9.00 9.00

The Stamp Show 2000, London.

Popes A176

No. 877: a, Liberius, 352-66. b, Linus, 67-76. c, Lucius I, 253-54. d, Marcellinus, 296-304. e, Mark, 336. f, Pius I, 140-155.
No. 878: a, Simplicius, 468-83. b, Siricius, 384-99. c, Stephen I, 254-57. d, Urban I, 222-30. e, Zephyrinus, 199-217. f, Zosimus, 417-18.
No. 879, Silverius, 536-37. No. 880, Vigilius, 537-55.

2000, July 7 Litho. ***Perf. 13¾***

Sheets of 6, #a-f

877-878 A176 1500k Set of 2 13.00 13.00

Souvenir Sheets

879-880 A176 5000k Set of 2 11.00 11.00

Birds — A177

400k, Great Indian hornbill. 500k, Cockatiel. 600k, Amazonian umbrellabird. 1000k, Unidentified bird. 2000k, Rainbow lorikeet.
No. 886: a, Green aracari. b, Eclectus parrot. c, Crimson topaz. d, King bird of paradise. e, keel-billed toucan. f, Australian king parrot. g, Sailboat. h, Hyacinth macaw.
No. 887: a, Resplendent quetzal. b, Carmine bee-eater. c, Wattled false sunbird. d, Palm trees. e, Sulphur-crested cockatoo. f, Great blue turaco. g, Crimson rosella. h, Malabar pied hornbill.
No. 888: a, Yellow-crowned amazon. b, Green turaco. c, Butterfly and palm trees. d, Plate-billed mountain toucan. e, Scarlet macaw. f, Blue and yellow macaw. g, Guianan cock of the rock. h, Palm cockatoo.
No. 889, Red-crested pochard. No. 890, Toco toucan, horiz. No. 891, Blue and yellow macaw, horiz.

2000, Sept. 8 ***Perf. 14***

881-885 A177 Set of 5 4.50 4.50

Sheets of 8, #a-h

886-888 A177 1500k Set of 3 25.00 25.00

Souvenir Sheets

889-891 A177 5000k Set of 3 12.00 12.00

Birds — A178

Designs: 700k, Red-backed shrike. 800k, Golden pipet. No. 894, 1200k, Orange-breasted sunbird. No. 895, 1400k, Eurasian goldfinch. 1500k, Red-crested turaco. 3000k, Carmine bee-eater.
No. 898, 1000k: a, Gouldian finch. b, Parrot finch. c, Purple grenadier. d, Red bishop. e, Red-crested cardinal. f, Spectacled monarch.

g, Crimson chat. h, Necklaced laughing thrush. i, Chestnut-backed jewel babbler.
No. 899, 1200k: a, Lovely cotinga. b, Andean cock-of-the-rock. c, Orange-bellied leafbird. d, Pin-tailed manakin. e, Pin-tailed broadbill. f, Rufous motmot. g, American goldfinch. h, Double-barred finch. i, Golden-breasted starling.
No. 900, 1400k: a, Campo oriole. b, Hooded warbler. c, Purple honeycreeper. d, Blue-faced honeyeater. e, Scarlet tanager. f, Green-headed tanager. g, Blue-breasted fairy wren. h, Banded pitta. i, Wire-tailed manakin.
No. 901, 5000k, Pin-tailed sandgrouse. No. 902, 5000k, Black bustard.

2000, Sept. 8 Litho. *Perf. 14*
892-897 A178 Set of 6 6.50 6.50

Sheets of 9, #a-i
898-900 A178 Set of 3 22.00 22.00

Souvenir Sheets
901-902 A178 Set of 2 9.50 9.50

African Creation Legends — A179

Designs: Nos, 903, 906a, 600k, Creation in Clay. Nos. 904, 906b, 1000k, The Chameleon and the Lizard. Nos. 905, 906c, 1400k, Why the Stones Do Not Die.

Perf. 14¼x14½
2000, Nov. 10 Litho.
903-905 A179 Set of 3 4.50 4.50

With Brown Frame
906 A179 Horiz. strip of 3, #a-c 6.75 6.75

Souvenir Sheet
No Frame Around Stamp
907 A179 3500k The Rooster in the Sky 5.00 5.00

No. 906 issued in sheets of 9 stamps.
For surcharge, see No. 1106.

Common Market for Eastern and Southern Africa — A180

Designs: 600k, Map of member nations. 700k, Truck crossing border. 1000k, Exchange of money and sale of goods at border.

2000
908-910 A180 Set of 3 4.25 4.25

Nos. 713-714 Surcharged

2000 Method and Perf. as Before
911 A146 1200k on 250k multi
912 A146 1500k on 500k multi

UN High Commissioner for Refugees, 50th Anniv. — A181

Designs: 700k, Children receiving food. 1500k, Woman carrying child.

Perf. 13¾x14¼
2001, Mar. 13 Litho.
915-916 A181 Set of 2 2.50 2.50

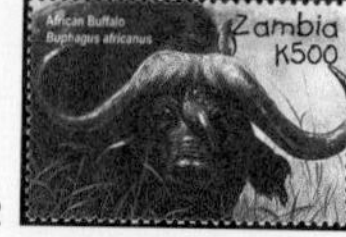
A182

Animals A183

Designs: 500k, African buffalo. 1000k, Cheetah, vert. No. 919, 2000k, Female elephant. 3200k, Ruffed lemur, vert.
No. 921, 2000k: a, Crimson-breasted shrike. b, Common bee-eater. c, Blue monkey. d, Chimpanzee. e, Bush baby. f, Genet.
No. 922, 2000k, horiz.: a, Defassa waterbuck. b, Crowned crane. c, Red hartebeest. d, Pygmy hippopotamus. e, White rhinoceros. f, Giant forest hog.
No. 923, 2000k, horiz.: a, Cheetah. b, Three adult, one young impala. c, Four adult impalas. d, Warthog. e, Two lions. f, Four lions.
No. 924, 6000k, Bull elephant. No. 925, 6000k, Black rhinoceros. No. 926, 6000k, Zebras, vert.

Perf. 13¼x13½, 13½x13¼
2001, Mar. 30
917-920 A182 Set of 4 5.50 5.50

Sheets of 6, #a-f
921-923 A183 Set of 3 22.50 22.50

Souvenir Sheets
924-926 A182 Set of 3 11.00 11.00

Bird Type of 1999

Designs: No. 927, O, Knob-billed duck. No. 928, A, Blacksmith plover. No. 929, B, Sacred ibis. No. 930, C, Purple gallinule.

Perf. 14½x14¾
2001, Mar. 19 Litho.
927-930 A171 Set of 4 3.50 3.50

Nos. 927-930 each sold for 700k, 1200k, 1400k, and 1500k respectively on day of issue. No. 927 is dated "2000" and has a design width of 31½mm. No. 847 has no date and has a design width of 30½mm.
For surcharges, see Nos. 1119, 1120, 1147, 1148, 1178, 1179, 1182.

Total Solar Eclipse, June 21 — A184

Eclipse and: 1000k, Woman. 1500k, Bird. 1700k, Lizard. 1800k, Elephant and man. 2200k, Man.

2001, June 1 Litho. *Perf. 13¾*
931-935 A184 Set of 5 5.00 5.00

Phila Nippon '01, Japan — A185

Designs: No. 936, 500k, Senya Nakamura as Toknatsu, by Kiyomasu Torii I. No. 937, 500k, Kantaro Sanjo II and Monosuke Ichikawa I, by Okumura Masanobu, 1720. No. 938, 1000k, Kantaro Sanjo and Monosuke Ichikawa, by Masanobu, c. 1730. No. 939, 1000k, Standing Figure of a Woman, by Kiyomasu Torii I. 1500k, Ono no Komachi, by Masanobu. 1800k, Dog Bringing a Love Letter, by Shigenaga.

No. 942, 3200k: a, Matsue Nakamura as a Cat Woman, by Shunsho. b, Kantaro Sanjo With Branch of Bamboo, by Kiyomasu Torii I. c, Kinsaku Yamashika I as Peddler, by Kiyomasu Torii I. d, Portrait of an Actor, by Shunsho.
No. 943, 3200k: a, Kumetaro Nakamura I, by Shunsho. b, Actor in Female Role, by Kiyomasu Torii I. c, Kikunojo Segawa Leaning on Sugoroku Board, by Kiyomasu Torii I. d, Gennosuke Ichikawa as a Wakashu, by Kiyomasu Torii I.
No. 944, 6000k, Akashi of the Tamaya, by Ryukoku Hishikawa. No. 945, 6000k, Events of Year in the Floating World, by Moroshige, horiz.

2001, July 4 *Perf. 14*
936-941 A185 Set of 6 4.00 4.00

Sheets of 4, #a-d
942-943 A185 Set of 2 14.00 14.00

Souvenir Sheets
944-945 A185 Set of 2 7.00 7.00

SOS Children's Village — A186

2001, July 30
946 A186 2500k multi 1.90 1.90

Royal Navy Submarines, Cent. — A187

No. 947, horiz.: a, HMS Tabard. b, HMS Opossum. c, HMS Unicorn. d, HMS Churchill. e, HMS Victorious. f, HMS Triumph.
6000k, Lieutenant Commander Malcolm David Wanklyn.

2001, July 30
947 A187 2000k Sheet of 6, #a-f 8.00 8.00

Souvenir Sheet
948 A187 6000k multi 5.75 5.75

Giuseppe Verdi (1813-1901), Opera Composer — A188

No. 949 — Actors in Falstaff : a, Benjamin Luxon (without hat). b, Luxon (with hat). c, Paul Plishka. d, Anne Collin.
8000k, Falstaff.

2001, July 30
949 A188 4000k Sheet of 4, #a-d 9.50 9.50

Souvenir Sheet
950 A188 8000k multi 7.00 7.00

Monet Paintings A189

No. 951, horiz.: a, The Promenade at Argenteuil. b, View of the Argenteuil Plain from the Sannois Hills. c, The Seine at Argenteuil. d, The Basin at Argenteuil.
6000k, Rouen Cathedral Portal, Overcast Weather.

2001, July 30 *Perf. 13¾*
951 A189 1500k Sheet of 4, #a-d 6.50 6.50

Souvenir Sheet
952 A189 6000k multi 6.50 6.50

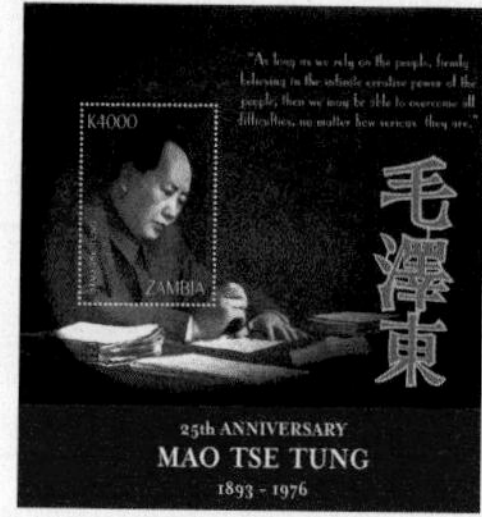
Mao Zedong (1893-1976) — A190

No. 953 — Mao in: a, 1918. b, 1945. c, 1937.
4000k, Portrait.

2001, July 30
953 A190 3200k Sheet of 3, #a-c 7.00 7.00

Souvenir Sheet
954 A190 4000k multi 6.00 6.00

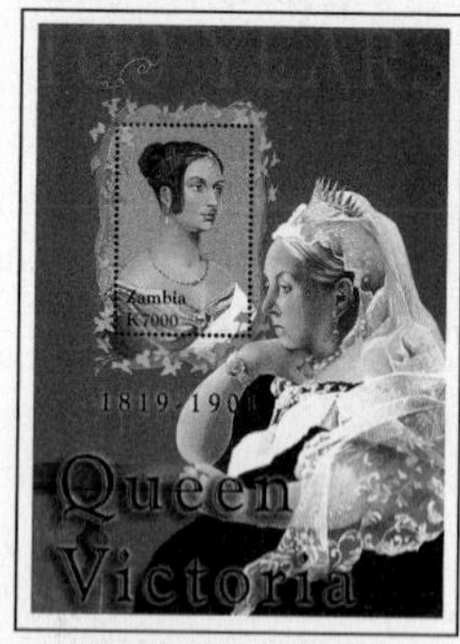
Queen Victoria (1819-1901) — A191

No. 955: a, As child. b, Wearing black dress. c, With child. d, With Prince Albert. e, Wearing crown and red sash. f, Wearing red dress.
7000k, Portrait.

2001, July 30 *Perf. 14*
955 A191 2000k Sheet of 6, #a-f 6.75 6.75

Souvenir Sheet
956 A191 7000k multi 6.00 6.00

Queen Elizabeth II, 75th Birthday A192

No. 957: a, As infant. b, As child. c, As child, in garden. d, Wearing hat.
8000k, Wearing green and black hat.

2001, July 30
957 A192 4000k Sheet of 4, #a-d 6.50 6.50

Souvenir Sheet
958 A192 8000k multi 5.00 5.00

No. 957 contains four 28x42mm stamps.

First Zeppelin Flight, Cent. A193

No. 959: a, LZ-1. b, Parseval PL25. c, LZ-3. d, Baldwin. e, LZ-129. f, Norge Nobile N1.
No. 960, 700k, Graf Zeppelin, vert.

2001, July 30
959 A193 2000k Sheet of 6, #a-f 8.00 8.00

Souvenir Sheet

960 A973 700k multi .40 .40

No. 960 contains one 38x51mm stamp.

Pres. F. J. T. Chiluba — A194

Chiluba: 1000k, Recieving Master's degree. 1500k, Signing forms. 1700k, With arm raised, horiz.
6000k, Receiving Master's degree, diff.

2001 Litho. *Perf. 14*
961-963 A194 Set of 3 3.75 3.75

Souvenir Sheet

964 A194 6000k multi 5.50 5.50

Nobel Prizes, Cent. (in 2001) A195

No. 965, 2000k — Peace laureates: a, Norman E. Borlaug, 1970. b, Lester B. Pearson, 1957. c, Intl. Red Cross, 1944. d, Anwar Sadat, 1978. e, Georges Pire, 1958. f, Linus Pauling, 1962.
No. 966, 2000k — Literature laureates: a, Isaac Bashevis Singer, 1978. b, Gao Xingjian, 2000. c, Claude Simon, 1985. d, Naguib Mahfouz, 1988. e, Camilo Jose Cela, 1989. f, Czeslaw Milosz, 1980.
No. 967, 2000k — Literature laureates: a, Seamus Heaney, 1995. b, Toni Morrison, 1993. c, Günter Grass, 1999. d, Wislawa Szymborska, 1996. e, Dario Fo, 1997. f, José Saramago, 1998.
No. 968, 6000k, George C. Marshall, Peace, 1953. No. 969, 6000k, Gerard Debreu, Economics, 1983. No. 970, 6000k, Robert W. Fogel, Economics, 1993.

2002, Feb. 11 Litho. *Perf. 14*

Sheets of 6, #a-f

965-967 A195 Set of 3 17.50 17.50

Souvenir Sheets

968-970 A195 Set of 3 13.00 13.00

Souvenir Sheet

New Year 2002 (Year of the Horse) A196

2002, Feb. 18 *Perf. 13¼*
971 A196 5000k multi 3.00 3.00

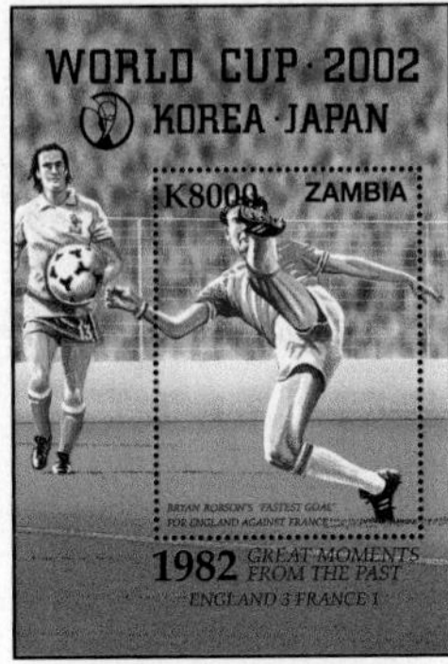

2002 World Cup Soccer Championships, Japan and Korea — A197

No. 972, 2000k: a, Poster from 1954 World Cup, Switzerland. b, Stanly Matthews and English flag. c, Scottish player and flag. d, Belgian player and flag. e, Player and Daejon World Cup Stadium, Korea, horiz.
No. 973, 2000k: a, Ferenc Puskas and Hungarian flag. b, Poster from 1962 World Cup, Chile. c, Spanish player and flag. d, English player and flag. e, Player and Jeonju World Cup Stadium, Korea, horiz.
No. 974, 8000k, Bryan Robson's goal against France, 1982. No. 975, 8000k, Salenko's fifth goal against Cameroon, 1994, horiz.

2002, Feb. 26 *Perf. 14*

Sheets of 5, #a-e

972-973 A197 Set of 2 11.50 11.50

Souvenir Sheets

974-975 A197 Set of 2 10.50 10.50

Size of Nos. 972a-972d, 973a-973d: 28x42mm.

United We Stand — A198

2002, Feb. *Perf. 13½x13¼*
976 A198 3200k multi 2.25 2.25

Issued in sheets of 4.

Reign of Queen Elizabeth, 50th Anniv. — A199

No. 977: a, Wearing blue and white hat. b, Without hat. c, Wearing scarf. d, Wearing tiara.
7500k, With Prince Philip.

2002, July 15 Litho. *Perf. 14¼*
977 A199 3200k Sheet of 4, #a-d 7.00 7.00

Souvenir Sheet

978 A199 7500k multi 4.50 4.50

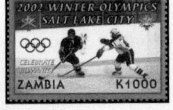

2002 Winter Olympics, Salt Lake City — A200

Designs: 1000k, Ice hockey. 3200k, Cross-country skiing.

2002, July 30 *Perf. 13¼x13¾*
979-980 A200 Set of 2 2.50 2.50

20th World Scout Jamboree, Thailand — A201

No. 981, horiz.: a, Troop hiking. b, Knot tying. c, Archery. d, Fire making.
8000k, Camping.

2002, July 30 *Perf. 14*
981 A201 3200k Sheet of 4, #a-d 6.75 6.75

Souvenir Sheet

982 A201 8000k multi 4.50 4.50

Intl. Year of Mountains — A202

No. 983: a, Mt. Whitney, US. b, Mt. Aconcagua, Argentina and Chile. c, Mt. Mönch, Switzerland. d, Mt. Ararat, Turkey.
9000k, Mt. Everest, Nepal and China.

2002, July 30
983 A202 1500k Sheet of 4, #a-d 4.50 4.50

Souvenir Sheet

984 A202 9000k multi 5.00 5.00

Birds — A203

Designs: 700k, Bee-eater. 1200k, Blue-cheeked bee-eater. 1400k, Boehn's bee-eater. 1500k, Little bee-eater.

2002, Aug. 12
985-988 A203 Set of 4 5.00 5.00

See Nos. 1027-1030. For surcharges, see Nos. 1091, 1231.

Flowers, Butterflies and Mushrooms — A204

No. 989, 2500k — Flowers: a, Camel's foot. b, Christmas bells. c, Impala lily. d, Everlasting. e, Anomatheca grandiflora. f, Soldier lily.
No. 990, 2500k — Butterflies: a, False monarch. b, Golden piper. c, Blue pansy. d, Christmas tree acraea. e, Grass yellow. f, Gold-spotted sylph.
No. 991, 2500k — Mushrooms: a, Copper trumpet. b, King bolete. c, Death cap. d, Fly agaric. e, Chanterelle. f, Deadly fiber cap.
No. 992, 8000k, Arum lily. No. 993, 8000k, African monarch butterfly. No. 994, 8000k, Stump brittle-head mushrooms.

2002, Sept. 9 Litho.

Sheets of 6, #a-f

989-991 A204 Set of 3 20.00 20.00

Souvenir Sheets

992-994 A204 Set of 3 15.00 15.00

Nos. 624, 629, 645 Surcharged

Methods & Perfs as Before

2002, July 1
996 A128 250k on 50k #639 — —
997 A127 300k on 50k #624 — —
998 A130 1000k on 100k #645 — —

Coronation of Queen Elizabeth II, 50th Anniv. — A205

No. 999: a, Wearing crown and pearl necklace. b, Wearing tiara and jeweled necklace. c, Wearing pink and black hat.
10,000k, Wearing flowered dress and hat.

2003, May 19 Litho. *Perf. 14*
999 A205 5000k Sheet of 3, #a-c 8.00 8.00

Souvenir Sheet

1000 A205 10,000k multi 7.50 7.50

Prince William, 21st Birthday A206

No. 1001: a, Wearing bow tie. b, Wearing blue shirt and tie. c, Wearing yellow and black sports shirt.
10,000k, Wearing sweater.

2003, May 19
1001 A206 5000k Sheet of 3, #a-c 7.25 7.25

Souvenir Sheet

1002 A206 10,000k multi 5.00 5.00

Nos. 654-657 Srchd.

Nos. 639-642 Surcharged

Nos. 617-620 Surcharged

Nos. 650-653 Surcharged

Nos. 710-712 Surcharged

Methods & Perfs. as Before

2003, June 26

1003 A133 1000k on 200k #654 25.00 25.00
1004 A133 1000k on 300k #655 25.00 25.00
1005 A133 1000k on 500k #656 25.00 25.00
1006 A133 1000k on 900k #657 25.00 25.00
1007 A128 1700k on 50k #639 1.00 1.00
1008 A128 1700k on 200k #640 1.00 1.00
1009 A128 1700k on 300k #641 1.00 1.00
1010 A128 1700k on 500k #642 1.00 1.00
1011 A125 1800k on 50k #617 1.10 1.10
1012 A125 1800k on 200k #618 1.10 1.10
1013 A125 1800k on 250k #619 1.10 1.10
a. Inverted surcharge 35.00 —
1014 A125 1800k on 300k #620 1.10 1.10
1015 A132 2200k on 100k #650 1.25 1.25
1016 A132 2200k on 300k #651 1.25 1.25
1017 A132 2200k on 450k #652 1.25 1.25
1018 A132 2200k on 500k #653 1.25 1.25
1019 A145 2500k on 500k #710 1.50 1.50
a. Inverted surcharge 35.00
1020 A145 2500k on (O) #711 1.50 1.50
1021 A145 2500k on 900k #712 1.50 1.50
Nos. 1003-1021 (19) 117.90 117.90

Location of surcharges vary on Nos. 1019-1021.

Miniature Sheet

New Year 2003 (Year of the Ram) A207

No. 1022 — Background colors: a, Green. b, Blue violet. c, Maroon. d, Purple.

2003, July 30 Litho. *Perf. 13¼*
1022 A207 3200k Sheet of 4, #a-d 6.50 6.50

Intl. Year of Fresh Water A208

No. 1023: a, Cabora Bassa Dam. b, Lake Kariba. c, Mana Pools National Park. 10,000k, Victoria Falls.

2003, July 30 *Perf. 13½x13¼*
1023 A208 5000k Sheet of 3, #a-c 7.50 7.50

Souvenir Sheet

1024 A208 10,000k multi 5.00 5.00

Powered Flight, Cent. A209

No. 1025: a, Avro 547A. b, Avro 504O with floats. c, Avro 584 Avrocet. d, Avro 504M. 10,000k, Avro 621 Tutor Replica.

2003, July 30 *Perf. 14*
1025 A209 4000k Sheet of 4, #a-d 7.75 7.75

Souvenir Sheet

1026 A209 9000k multi 5.00 5.00

Bird Type of 2002

Designs: 1000k, White-fronted bee-eaters. 1200k, Little bee-eaters. 1500k, Blue-cheeked bee-eater. 1800k, Boehn's bee-eater.

2003, Dec. 26 *Perf. 13¼*
Size: 25x20mm
1027-1030 A203 Set of 4 10.00 10.00

For surcharges, see Nos. 1089, 1109, 1143, 1177.

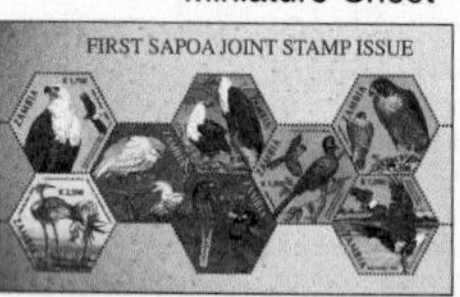

Rotary International in Zambia, 50th Anniv. — A210

Design: 1000k, Rotary emblem and hands. 1200k, Rotary emblem.

2003, Nov. 21 Litho. *Perf. 13*
1031 A210 1000k multi *2.50 2.50*
1032 A210 1200k multi *3.00 3.00*
Nos. 1031-1032 (2) 5.50 5.50

For surcharges, see Nos. 1107, 1123, 1154.

Miniature Sheet

Birds A211

No. 1033: a, 500k, African fish eagles, national bird of Zimbabwe. b, 750k, Cattle egrets, national bird of Botswana. c, 1000k, African fish eagles, national bird of Zambia. d, 1100k, Peregrine falcons, national bird of Angola. e, 1500k, Bar-tailed trogons. f, 1700k, African fish eagles, national bird of Namibia. g, 1800k, Purple-crested louries, national bird of Swaziland. h, 2200k, Blue cranes, national bird of South Africa.

2004, Oct. 11 Litho. *Perf. 14*
1033 A211 Sheet of 8, #a-h 4.50 4.50

See Botswana Nos. 792-793, Namibia No. 1052, South Africa No. 1342, Swaziland Nos. 727-735, and Zimbabwe No. 975.

Independence, 40th Anniv. — A212

Design: 1500k, Vimbuza dancer. 1800k, Kayowe dancer. 2700k, Ngoma dancer. 3300k, Ukishi dancer.

2004, Oct. 23 Litho. *Perf. 13x13¼*
1034 A212 1500k multi 1.25 1.25
1035 A212 1800k multi 1.50 1.50
1036 A212 2700k multi 2.40 2.40
1037 A212 3300k multi 2.80 2.80
Nos. 1034-1037 (4) 7.95 7.95

For surcharges, see Nos. 1112, 1144, 1176.

No. 649 Surcharged

Methods and Perfs As Before

2004, Dec. 28
Granite Paper
1038 A131 1000k on 700k #649 *1.50 1.50*

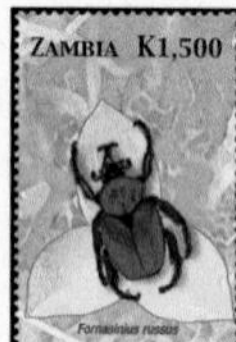

Mammals A213

Designs: No. 1039, 2250k, Acionyx jubatus. No. 1040, 2250k, Phacochoerus aethiopicus. No. 1041, 2250k, Giraffa camelopardalis. 2700k, Syncerus caffer.

No. 1043, vert.: a, Panthera pardus. b, Pan troglodytes. c, Lycaon pictus. d, Equus burchelli.

10,000k, Diceros bicornis, vert.

2005, June 27 Litho. *Perf. 14*
1039-1042 A213 Set of 4 4.25 4.25
1043 A213 3300k Sheet of 4, #a-d 5.75 5.75

Souvenir Sheet

1044 A213 10,000k multi 4.50 4.50

Insects — A214

Designs: 1500k, Fornasinius russus. No. 1046, 2250k, Goliathus giganteus. No. 1047, 2250k, Macrorhina. 2700k, Chelorrhina polyphemus.

No. 1048: a, Sternotomis virescens. b, Cicindela regalis. c, Goliathus meleagris. d, Mecosasms explanta.

10,000k, Meloid.

2005, June 27
1045-1048 A214 Set of 4 3.75 3.75
1049 A214 3300k Sheet of 4, #a-d 5.75 5.75

Souvenir Sheet

1050 A214 10,000k multi 4.50 4.50

Butterflies — A215

Designs: No. 1051, 2250k, Ropalo ceres. No. 1052, 2250k, Morpho portis nymphalidae. No. 1053, 2250k, Phyllocnistis citrella. 2700k, H. misippus.

No. 1055: a, Colotis evippe. b, Papilio lormieri. c, Papilio dardanus. d, Papilio zalmoxis.

10,000k, Epiphora albida druce.

2005, June 27
1051-1054 A215 Set of 4 4.25 4.25
1055 A215 3300k Sheet of 4, #a-d 5.75 5.75

Souvenir Sheet

1056 A215 10,000k multi 4.50 4.50

Orchids — A216

Designs: No. 1057, 1500k, Disa draconis. No. 1058, 1500k, Disa uniflora. No. 1059, 1500k, Disa uniflora orange. 2700k, Phalaenopsis penetrate.

No. 1061: a, Ansellia africana (yellow flower). b, Ansellia africana (spotted flower). c, Cattleya lueddemanniana. d, Laelia tenebrosa.

10,000k, Cymbidium.

2005, June 27
1057-1060 A216 Set of 4 3.25 3.25
1061 A216 3300k Sheet of 4, #a-d 5.75 5.75

Souvenir Sheet

1062 A216 10,000k multi 4.50 4.50

Jesuits in Zambia, Cent. — A217

Designs: 1500k, Bishop Paul Lungu, Map of Zambia. 2550k, Father Torrend, Kasisi Church. 2700k, Father Moreau, Chikuni Church. 3300k, St. Ignatius of Loyola.

2005, June 25 Litho. *Perf. 13¼x13*
1063-1066 A217 Set of 4 4.50 4.50
1066a Souvenir sheet, #1063-1066 4.50 4.50

Dag Hammarskjöld (1905-61), UN Secretary General — A218

Background color: 1500k, Dark blue. 2700k, Blue green.

2005, July 29 Litho. *Perf. 13½*
1067-1068 A218 Set of 2 6.50 6.50
1068a Souvenir sheet of 2, #1067-1068 6.50 6.50

For surcharge, see No. 1145.

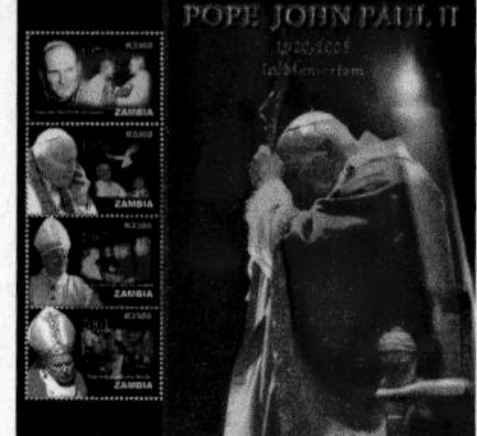

Pope John Paul II (1920-2005) and Pres. Jimmy Carter — A219

Pope John Paul II A220

No. 1070: a, With Sri Chinmoy. b, With boy and dove. c, With Schneider brothers. d, Visiting Ukraine.

2005, Aug. 22 Litho. *Perf. 12¾*
1069 A219 7000k multi 3.00 3.00
1070 A220 3300k Sheet of 4, #a-d 5.75 5.75

No. 1069 was printed in sheets of 4.

A221

Railroads, 200th Anniv. — A222

No. 1071: a, Chinese Class KF 4-8-4. b, Indian Class WP 4-6-2. c, Irish 800 Class 4-6-0. d, French 241A Class 4-8-2.

No. 1072, 1700k: a, British Rail Class 4MT 2-6-4T. b, South African Railways Class 12A. c, Cuban sugar plantation locomotive. d, LNER A4 Pacific facing right. e, LNER A4 Pacific facing left. f, GWR City of Truro 4-4-0. g, British Rail HST Intercity 125. h, Eurostar. i, LNER A3 Flying Scotsman.

No. 1073, 1700k: a, Southern Railway King Arthur Class 4-6-0. b, Berkshire at Kaiiman's Bridge. c, Indian Railways WT Class 2-84 Suburban Tank steam locomotive. d, Ladders on shell of railway car being built. e, Worker on knees inside railway car. f, Yellow staircase next to railway car. g, Workers looking at undercarriage of raised railway car. h, Railway car between blue machinery. i, Model of steam locomotive.

No. 1074, 1700k: a, Great Western Hall Class 4-6-0. b, Argentinian 15B Class 4-8-0. c, Mallet Meter Gauge steam locomotive. d, Worker cutting track. e, Worker and pulley. f, Workers in cherrypicker. g, Workers on tracks and in cherrypickers. h, Workers pouring cement. i, Track workers.

No. 1075, Finnish Class HV2 4-6-0.

No. 1076, 8000k, Orient Express. No. 1077, 8000k, Edinburgh to London train. No. 1078, 800k, Bernina Express.

2005, Aug. 22

1071 A221 4200k Sheet of 4, #a-d 7.50 7.50

Sheets of 9, #a-i

1072-1074 A222 Set of 3 20.00 20.00

Souvenir Sheets

1075 A221 8000k multi 3.50 3.50
1076-1078 A222 Set of 3 10.50 10.50

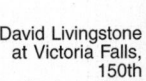

David Livingstone at Victoria Falls, 150th Anniv. — A223

Designs: 1500k, Livingstone, Victoria Falls. 2700k, Statue of Livingstone, railroad bridge.

2006, Jan. 20 Litho. ***Perf. 13x13¼***

1079-1080 A223 Set of 2 2.60 2.60

For surcharges, see Nos. 1113, 1150.

Franciscan Conventuals in Zambia, 75th Anniv. — A224

Design: 2250k, Sister Moon. 2700k, Brother Sun. 3300k, Sister Water.

2006, July 8 Litho. ***Perf. 13¼x13***

1082 A224 2250k multi —
1083 A224 2700k multi —
1084 A224 3300k multi —

An additional stamp was issued in this set. The editors would like to examine any examples.

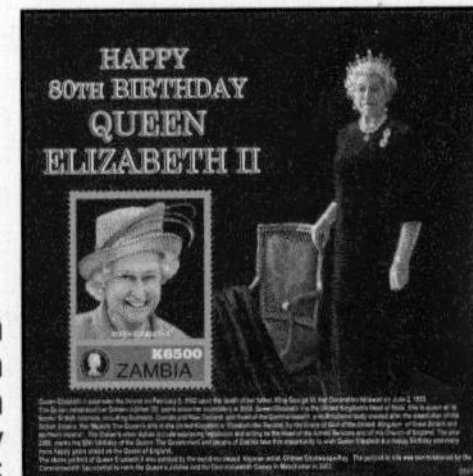

Queen Elizabeth II, 80th Birthday A225

No. 1085 — Queen: a, Wearing crown. b, Wearing necklace. c, Wearing necklace and jacket. d, With Princess Anne.
6500k, Wearing green hat.

2006, Aug. 8 Litho. ***Perf. 13¼***

1085 A225 3200k Sheet of 4, #a-d 6.50 6.50

Souvenir Sheet

1086 A225 6500k multi 3.25 3.25

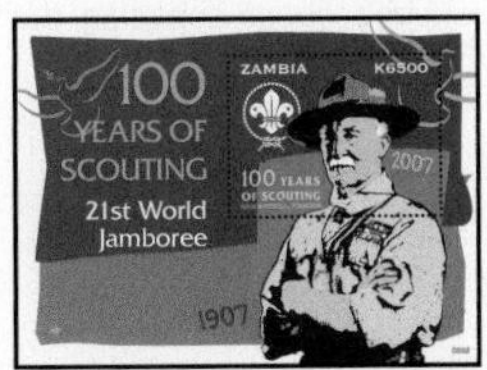

Scouting, Cent. (in 2007) A226

No. 1087, vert. — Scouting emblem, doves, Lord Robert Baden-Powell and background colors of: a, Pink and lilac. b, Yellow and orange. c, Blue and light blue. d, Light green and green.
6500k, Purple and red.

2006, Aug. 8

1087 A226 3200k Sheet of 4, #a-d 9.00 9.00

Souvenir Sheet

1088 A226 6500k multi 6.75 6.75

Nos. 623, 987 and 1028 Surcharged

Methods and Perfs As Before

2007

1089 A203 1500k on 1200k #1028 .70 .70
1090 A127 1850k on 20k #623 .95 .95
1091 A203 3300k on 1400k #987 1.60 1.60
Nos. 1089-1091 (3) 3.25 3.25

Issued: Nos. 1089, 1091, 3/19; No. 1090, 5/30. For surcharge, see No. 1232.

Miniature Sheet

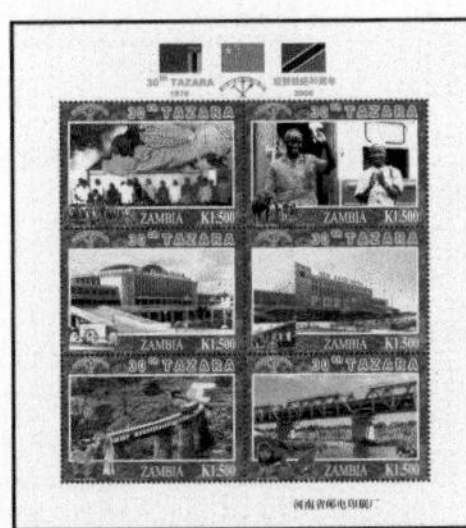
Tazara Railway, 30th Anniv. (in 2006) A227

No. 1092: a, Map of Tanzania and Zambia, waterfall, mountain, people waving, and men signing agreement. b, Men and train, elephant and antelope. c, Dar es Salaam Station, sign and wreaths with Chinese inscriptions. d, New Kapiri Mposhi Station, people near train. e, Train, bridge and tunnel, zebra and giraffe. f, Train on bridge, lion and lioness.

2007, May 28 Litho. ***Perf. 12***

1092 A227 1500k Sheet of 6, #a-f 4.75 4.75

Mammals — A228

Designs: 1500k, Bat-eared fox. 2250k, Spotted hyena. 2700k, Aardwolf. 3300k, Side-striped jackal.

2007, June 29 ***Perf. 13¼x13***

1093-1096 A228 Set of 4 5.25 5.25
1096a Souvenir sheet, #1093-1096 6.00 6.00

For surcharges, see Nos. 1110, 1114, 1122, 1146, 1149, 1151, 1153, 1229.

National Animals — A229

Designs: 1500k, Buffalo (Zambia). 1800k, Nyala (Malawi). 2250k, Nyala (Zimbabwe). 2700k, Burchell's zebra (Botswana). 3300k, Oryx (Namibia).

Litho. With Foil Application

2007, Oct. 9 ***Perf. 13¾***

1097-1101 A229 Set of 5 6.25 6.25

See Botswana No. 838, Malawi No. 752, Namibia Nos. 1141-1142, Zimbabwe Nos. 1064-1068.

Miniature Sheet

2008 Summer Olympics, Beijing — A230

No. 1102: a, Soccer. b, Hurdles. c, Boxing. d, Swimming.

2008, June 8 Litho. ***Perf. 12***

1102 A230 2000k Sheet of 4, #a-d 5.00 5.00

Worldwide Fund for Nature (WWF) — A231

No. 1103 — Greater kudu: a, Two males battling. b, Female and calf. c, Male drinking. d, Female and tree branches.

2008, June 30 ***Perf. 13¼***

1103 Horiz. strip or block of 4 7.25 7.25
a.-d. A231 3000k Any single 1.75 1.75
e. Miniature sheet of 8, 2 each #1103a-1103d 12.50 12.50

Muhammad Ali, Boxer — A232

No. 1104 — Ali: a, In fighting stance without boxing gloves. b, Looking right. c, With gloved fist at chest level. d, With gloved fist near head. e, Pointing. f, Holding Olympic torch.
3200k, Ali wearing crown, with arms raised, and boxing.

2008 ***Perf. 14***

1104 A232 500k Sheet of 6, #a-f 4.50 4.50

Souvenir Sheet

Perf. 13½x13¾

1105 A232 3200k multi 4.50 4.50

No. 1105 contains one 38x50mm stamp. Nos. 1104-1105 were said to have been released in 1998, but did not appear in the marketplace until 2008.

No. 905 Surcharged

Method and Perf. As Before

2008, July 22

1106 A179 1500k on 1400k #905 .90 .90

No. 1032 Surcharged

Method and Perf. As Before

2009, Feb. 17

1107 A210 1500k on 1200k #1032 1.50 1.50

Peonies — A233

2009, Apr. 10 Litho. ***Perf. 13¼***

1108 A233 2000k multi .75 .75

Printed in sheets of 8.

No. 1030 Surcharged

Method and Perf. As Before

2009, May 29

1109 A203 1500k on 1800k #1030 1.50 1.50

No. 1094 Surcharged

No. 1068 Surcharged

No. 1036 Surcharged

No. 1080 Srchd.

No. 1095 Surcharged

2009 Method and Perf. As Before

1110 A228 3300k on 2250k #1094 7.75 7.75
1111 A218 3500k on 2700k #1068 —
1112 A212 3800k on 2700k #1036 — —
1113 A223 4050k on 2700k #1080 —
1114 A228 4950k on 2700k #1095 — —

Issued: Nos. 1110-1111, 1113, 5/29, Nos. 1112, 1114, 12/1.
For surcharges, see Nos. 1150, 1151, 1156, 1228, 1230, 1233.

2010 World Cup Soccer Championships, South Africa — A234

Soccer players, ball, 2010 World Cup mascot and flag of: Nos. 1115, 1118e, 2500k, Zambia. Nos. 1116, 1118h, 4050k, Namibia. Nos. 1117, 1118i, 4950k, South Africa.

No. 1118: a, 900k, Lesotho. b, 1000k, Mauritius. c, 2050k, Botswana. d, 2250k, Zimbabwe. f, 3500k, Malawi. g, 3800k, Swaziland.

2010, Apr. 9 Litho. *Perf. 13½*

On Plain Paper With Olive Brown Background

1115-1117 A234 Set of 3 5.00 5.00

On Gold-faced Paper

1118 A234 Sheet of 9, #a-i 11.00 11.00

See Botswana Nos. 896-905, Lesotho No. , Malawi No. 753, Mauritius No. 1086, Namibia No. 1188, South Africa No. 1403, Swaziland Nos. 794-803, and Zimbabwe Nos.1112-1121.

For surcharges, see Nos. 1155. 1225.

A single sheetlet of 9 omnibus issues exist containing 1118a. See footnote under Namibia 1188.

Nos. 649, 928, 929, 1032 and 1094 Surcharged

Methods and Perfs As Before

2010 ?

1119 A171 2500k on A #928 — —
1120 A171 2500k on B #929 — —
1121 A131 5000k on 700k #649 — —
1122 A228 10,000k on 2250k #1094 — —
1123 A210 10,000k on 1200k #1032 — —

Issued: No. 1120, 11/12/10.

For surcharges, see Nos. 1147, 1148, 1152, 1153, 1154.

Animals — A237

Designs: No. 1137, Boehm's bush squirrel. No. 1140, Sun squirrel.

2012, Oct. Litho. *Perf. 14*

1137 A237 3500k multi —
1140 A237 3500k multi —

Sixteen additional stamps were issued in this set. The editors would like to examine any examples.

Miniature Sheet

Dr. David Livingstone (1813-73), African Missionary and Explorer — A239

No. 1142: a, 25k, Livingstone. b, 30k, Map of northern Zambia, rhinoceros. c, 40k, Map of southwestern Zambia, hippopotamus, antelope. d, 50k, Map of southeastern Zambia, lion.

2013, Mar. 19 Litho. *Perf. 13¼x13*

1142 A239 Sheet of 4, #a-d 54.00 54.00

Nos. 1028, 1036, 1068, 1095-1096, 1113-1114, 1119-1123 Surcharged

No. 1143

Methods and Perfs As Before

2013

1143 A203 1.50k on 1200k #1028 — —
1144 A212 1.50k on 2700k #1036 — —
1145 A218 1.50k on 2700k #1068 — —
1146 A228 1.50k on 2700k #1095 — —
1147 A171 2.50k on 2500k on A #1119 — —
1148 A171 2.50k on 2500k on B #1120 — —
1149 A228 3.80k on 2475k on 3300k #1096 — —
1150 A223 4.05k on 4050k on 2700k #1113 — —
1151 A228 4.95k on 4950k on 2700k #1114 — —
1152 A131 5k on 5000k on 700k #1121 — —
1153 A228 10k on 10,000k on 2250k #1122 — —
1154 A210 10k on 10,000k on 1200k #1123 — —

No. 1116 Surcharged

Methods and Perfs. As Before

2013, July 25

1155 A234 4.05k on 4050k #1116 —

Surcharge on No. 1155 is on the selvage surrounding the stamp.

No. 1112 Surcharged

Method and Perf. As Before

2013, July 25

1156 A212 3.80k on 3800k on 2700k #1112 — —

In 2014, Zambia declared as "illegal" 31 souvenir sheets of one depicting various topics including famous women, actresses, birds, Elvis Presley, mammals, bats, dogs, turtles, and a sheet of 4 and a souvenir sheet depicting the birth of Prince George of Cambridge.

Nos. 639, 928-930, 1030, 1035 Surcharged

Methods and Perfs. As Before

2014, May 2

1175 A128 1.50k on 50k #639 —
1176 A212 1.50k on 1800k #1035 — —
1177 A203 1.50k on 1800k #1030 .95 .95
1178 A171 2.50k on A #928 *1.75* —
1179 A171 2.50k on B #929 *1.75* —
1182 A171 4.95k on C #930 3.25 3.25

Three additional surcharges were issued in this set. The editors would like to examine any examples.

A240

Red Flag Canal, People's Republic of China, 50th Anniv. A241

No. 1184: a, Workers marching to site. b, Waterway under mountain, horiz. c, Building, horiz. d, Workers dangling from cables.

No. 1185: a, Zambian Pres. Kenneth Kaunda. b, Chinese Vice-Premier Li Xiannian.

2014, June 13 Litho. *Perf. 13¼*

1184 A240 7.50k Sheet of 4, #a-d, + label 9.75 9.75

Souvenir Sheet

Perf. 12

1185 A241 15k Sheet of 2, #a-b 9.75 9.75

A242

A243

A244

Animals — A245

Designs: No. 1186, Ratel. No. 1187, Black rhinoceros. No. 1188, Beecroft's flying squirrel. No. 1189, Black lechwe. No. 1190, Chacma baboon. No. 1191, African buffalo. No. 1192, Serval. No. 1193, Common genet. No. 1194, Lion.No. 1195, Red and black squirrel. No. 1196, Blue wildebeest. No. 1197, Hunting dog. No. 1198, African elephant. No. 1199, Boehm' bush squirrel. No. 1200, Klipspringer. No. 1201, Leopard. No. 1202, Sun squirrel. No. 1203, Spotted hyena.

2014, June 26 Litho. *Perf. 14*

1186 A242 1k multi — —
1187 A243 1k multi — —
1188 A244 1k multi — —
1189 A245 1k multi — —
1190 A242 1.50k multi — —
1191 A243 1.50k multi — —
1192 A242 2.50k multi — —
1193 A242 2.50k multi — —
1194 A243 2.50k multi — —
1195 A244 2.50k multi — —
1196 A245 2.50k multi — —
1197 A242 3.50k multi — —
1198 A243 3.50k multi — —
1199 A244 3.50k multi — —
1200 A245 3.50k multi — —
1201 A243 4.95k multi — —
1202 A244 4.95k multi — —
1203 A245 4.95k multi — —

Waterfalls — A246

Designs: 2.50k, Victoria Falls. 3.50k, Lumangwe Falls, vert. 3.80k, Kalambo Falls, vert. 4.05k, Chishimba Falls, vert. 4.95k, Ngonye Falls. 8.35k, Kundalila Falls.

Perf. 13x13¼, 13¼x13

2014, Aug. 28 Litho.

1204-1209 A246 Set of 6 9.00 9.00

Miniature Sheets

Independence, 50th Anniv. — A247

No. 1214 — Dr. Kenneth Kaunda, first President of Zambia: a, With Queen Elizabeth II. b, With British Prime Minister Margaret Thatcher. c, With Archbishop of Canterbury. d, At Independence ceremony. e, With African leaders.

No. 1215: a, Pres. Kaunda. b, Pres. Frederick Chiluba (1943-2011). c, Pres. Levy Mwanawasa (1948-2008). d, Pres. Rupiah Banda. e, Pres. Michael Sata (1937-2014).

No. 1216 — Pres. Sata: a, At inauguration. b, Addressing United Nations.

Litho. With Foil Application

2014, Oct. 23 ***Perf. 13¼***

1214	A247	10k Sheet of 5, #a-e	18.00	18.00
1215	A247	10k Sheet of 5, #a-e	18.00	18.00

Souvenir Sheet

1216	A247	10k Sheet of 2, #a-b	7.25	7.25

Four strips of five stamps were also issued with this set. The editors would like to examine any examples of the strips.

No. 905 Surcharged

Method and Perf. As Before

2017 ?

1217 A179 10k on 1400k #905 —

Friendship Between Zambia and People's Republic of China, 50th Anniv. — A248

Designs: 2.50k, Zambian President Michael Sata and Chinese President Xi Jinping reviewing Chinese troops. 3k, Zambian Pres. Kenneth Kaunda meeting with Chinese Chairman Mao Zedong. 3.50k, Tanzania Zambia Railways train. 3.80k, National Heroes Stadium, Lusaka. 4.05k, Victoria Falls. 4.95k, Great Wall of China.

2015, Feb. 5 **Litho.** ***Perf. 12***

1218-1223 A248 Set of 6 6.25 6.25

No. 1064 Surcharged

Method and Perf. As Before

2018 ?

1224 A217 5k on 2550k #1064 —

No. 1117 Surcharged

Methods and Perfs. As Before

2018

1225 A234 5k on 4950k #1117 — —

Nos. 987, 1090, 1096, 1110, 1111, and 1114 Surcharged

Methods and Perfs. As Before

2022 ?

1228	A228	3.50k on 3300k on 2250k #1110	—	—
1229	A228	3.80k on 3300k #1096	—	—
1230	A228	5k on 4950k on 2700k #1114	—	—
a.		Tripled 5k surcharge	—	—
1231	A203	10k on 1400k #987	—	—
1232	A127	10k on 1850k on 20k #1090	—	—
1233	A218	10k on 3500k on 2700k #1111	—	—

POSTAGE DUE STAMPS

Type of Northern Rhodesia

Perf. 12½

1964, Oct. 24 **Litho.** **Unwmk.**

J1	D2	1p orange	.35	*3.75*
J2	D2	2p dark blue	.35	*3.75*
J3	D2	3p rose claret	.50	*2.75*
J4	D2	4p violet blue	.50	*3.75*
J5	D2	6p purple	.50	*3.75*
J6	D2	1sh emerald	.60	*6.00*
		Nos. J1-J6 (6)	2.80	*23.75*

ZANZIBAR

'zan-zə-ˌbär

LOCATION — Group of islands about twenty miles off the coast of Tanganyika in East Africa

GOVT. — Republic

AREA — 1,044 sq. mi. (approx.)

POP. — 354,360 (est. 1967)

CAPITAL — Zanzibar

Before 1895, unoverprinted stamps of India were used in Zanzibar.

Zanzibar was a British protectorate until Dec. 10, 1963, when it became independent. After a revolt in January, 1964, a republic was established. Zanzibar joined Tanganyika Apr. 26, 1964, to form the United Republic of Tanganyika and Zanzibar (later renamed Tanzania). See Tanzania.

12 Pies = 1 Anna
16 Annas = 1 Rupee
100 Cents = 1 Rupee (1908)
100 Cents = 1 Shilling (1935)

Catalogue values for unused stamps in this country are for Never Hinged items, beginning with Scott 201 in the regular postage section and Scott J18 in the postage due section.

Watermarks

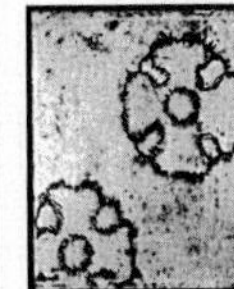

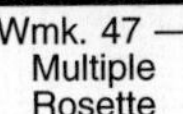

Wmk. 47 — Multiple Rosette

Wmk. 71 — Rosette

Stamps of British India Overprinted

On Stamps of 1882-95

1895 **Wmk. Star (39)** ***Perf. 14***

Blue Overprint

1	A17	½a green	*45,000.*	*6,250.*
2	A19	1a violet brn	3,500.	600.
a.		"Zanzidar"		*28,500.*

1895-96 **Black Overprint**

3	A17	½a green	5.00	5.00
a.		"Zanzidar"	*1,450.*	800.00
b.		"Zanibar"	*1,450.*	*1,900.*
c.		"Zapzibar"		
4	A19	1a violet brn	5.25	4.25
a.		"Zanzidar"	—	*4,000.*
b.		"Zanibar"	1,900.	2,250.
5	A20	1a6p bister brn	5.50	5.00
a.		"Zanzidar"	*4,500.*	1,200.
b.		"Zanizbar"	*2,000.*	
c.		"Zanibar"	*1,800.*	1,750.
d.		"Zapzibar"	*125.00*	*125.00*
6	A21	2a ultra	10.00	9.50
a.		"Zanzidar"	8,500.	3,500.
b.		"Zanibar"	6,750.	2,750.
c.		"Zapzibar"	*150.00*	*160.00*
d.		Double overprint	310.00	
7	A28	2a6p green	10.00	5.50
a.		"Zanzidar"	8,500.	1,800.
b.		"Zanibar"	800.00	*1,400.*
c.		"Zapzibar"		
d.		"Zanzipar"	1,250.	
8	A22	3a orange	13.50	*19.00*
a.		"Zanzidar"	1,150.	*2,150.*
b.		"Zanizbar"	*7,500.*	*8,000.*
9	A23	4a olive grn	22.50	*20.00*
a.		"Zanzidar"	11,500.	4,750.
10	A25	8a red vio	45.00	30.00
a.		"Zanzidar"	11,500.	9,000.

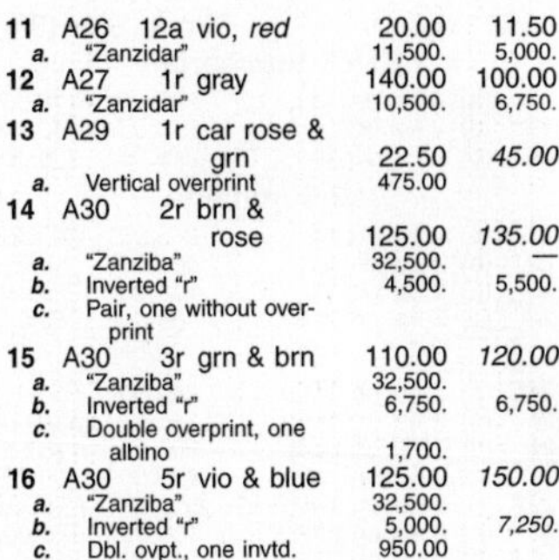

11	A26	12a vio, *red*	20.00	11.50
a.		"Zanzidar"	11,500.	5,000.
12	A27	1r gray	140.00	100.00
a.		"Zanzidar"	10,500.	6,750.
13	A29	1r car rose & grn	22.50	*45.00*
a.		Vertical overprint	475.00	
14	A30	2r brn & rose	125.00	*135.00*
a.		"Zanziba"	32,500.	—
b.		Inverted "r"	4,500.	5,500.
c.		Pair, one without overprint		
15	A30	3r grn & brn	110.00	*120.00*
a.		"Zanziba"	32,500.	
b.		Inverted "r"	6,750.	6,750.
c.		Double overprint, one albino	1,700.	
16	A30	5r vio & blue	125.00	*150.00*
a.		"Zanziba"	32,500.	
b.		Inverted "r"	5,000.	*7,250.*
c.		Dbl. ovpt., one invtd.	950.00	

On Stamp of 1873-76

Wmk. Elephant's Head (38)

17	A14	6a bister	22.50	12.50
a.		"Zanzidar"	11,500.	4,500.
b.		"Zanzibarr"	*8,000.*	*6,500.*
c.		"Zanibar"	900.00	*1,400.*
d.		"Zapzibar"		
e.		Double overprint	325.00	
		Nos. 3-17 (15)	681.75	672.25

Double and triple overprints, with one overprint albino, and color varieties exist for most of the 1-17 overprints. For detailed listings, see *Scott Classic Specialized Catalogue.*

Nos. 4-6 Surcharged

a

b

c d

e

f

1896 **Wmk. Star (39)**

Black Surcharge

18 (a) 2½a on 1a *200.00* *110.00*
19 (b) 2½a on 1a *700.00* *350.00*
20 (c) 2½a on 1a *225.00* *125.00*

Red Surcharge

21 (a) 2½a on 1a *275.00* *725.00*
22 (b) 2½a on 1a *500.00* *1,050.*
23 (c) 2½a on 1a *310.00* *725.00*
24 (a) 2½a on 1a6p *85.00* *60.00*
a. "Zanzidar" *1,700.* *1,450.*
b. "Zanizbar" *5,250.* *2,250.*
24C (b) 2½a on 1a6p *250.00* *550.00*
25 (c) 2½a on 1a6p *145.00* *350.00*
26 (d) 2½a on 1a6p *200.00* *175.00*
27 (e) 2½a on 1a6p *475.00* *400.00*
27A (f) 2½a on 1a6p *27,500.* *18,000.*
28 (a) 2½a on 2a *160.00* *360.00*
28A (b) 2½a on 2a *340.00* *625.00*
29 (c) 2½a on 2a *180.00* *425.00*
30 (d) 2½a on 2a *80.00* *47.50*
31 (e) 2½a on 2a *225.00* *125.00*
31A (f) 2½a on 2a *5,750.* *2,800.*

Certain type varieties are found in the word "Zanzibar" on Nos. 1 to 31A viz: Inverted "q" for "b," broken "p" for "n," "i" without dot, small second "z" and tall second "z." These varieties are found on all values from ½a to 1r inclusive and the tall "z" is also found on the 2r, 3r and 5r.

Double and triple "Zanzibar" with one or two overprints albino exist for most of the 18-31 overprints. For detailed listings, see *Scott Classic Specialized Catalogue.*

Stamps of British East Africa, 1896, Overprinted in Black or Red

1896 **Wmk. Crown and C A (2)**

32 A8 ½a yellow grn 45.00 25.00
33 A8 1a carmine 47.50 20.00
a. Double overprint 825.00 1,000.
34 A8 2½a dk blue (R) 100.00 52.50
35 A8 4½a orange 55.00 65.00
36 A8 5a dark ocher 75.00 45.00
37 A8 7½a lilac 60.00 70.00
Nos. 32-37 (6) 382.50 277.50

A2

Sultan Seyyid Hamed-bin-Thwain
A3

1896, Sept. 20 **Engr.** **Wmk. 71**

38 A2 ½a yel grn & red 4.50 2.50
39 A2 1a indigo & red 4.50 1.90
40 A2 2a red brn & red 5.00 .85
41 A2 2½a ultra & red 19.00 1.60
42 A2 3a slate & red 22.50 12.50
43 A2 4a dk green & red 15.00 6.50
44 A2 4½a orange & red 8.75 8.25
45 A2 5a bister & red 10.00 7.00
a. Half used as 2½a on cover *4,900.*
46 A2 7½a lilac & red 9.00 9.00
47 A2 8a ol gray & red 12.00 9.50
48 A3 1r ultra & red 27.50 12.50
49 A3 2r green & red 35.00 16.00
50 A3 3r violet & red 37.50 20.00
51 A3 4r lake & red 30.00 *20.00*
52 A3 5r blk brn & red 38.00 *27.50*
Nos. 38-52 (15) 278.25 155.60

No. 43 Surcharged in Red

1897

53 A2 (a) 2½a on 4a 110.00 *65.00*
54 A2 (b) 2½a on 4a 350.00 *300.00*
55 A2 (c) 2½a on 4a 140.00 *90.00*
Nos. 53-55 (3) 600.00 *455.00*

1898 **Engr.** **Wmk. 47**

56 A2 ½a yel grn & red 1.75 .45
57 A2 1a indigo & red 6.00 1.40
58 A2 2a red brn & red 12.00 2.25
58A A2 2½a ultra & red 5.50 .45
59 A2 3a slate & red 10.00 1.50
60 A2 4a dk grn & red 4.25 2.25
60A A2 4½a orange & red 17.00 1.50
61 A2 5a bister & red 22.50 2.50
61A A2 7½a lilac & red orange 22.50 3.00
61B A2 8a ol gray & red 22.50 3.50
Nos. 56-61B (10) 124.00 18.80

A4

Sultan Seyyid Hamoud-bin-Mahommed-bin-Said — A5

1899-1901

62 A4 ½a yel grn & red 3.00 .65
63 A4 1a indigo & red 5.00 .25
64 A4 1a car & red ('01) 5.00 .25
65 A4 2a red brn & red 6.00 1.75
66 A4 2½a ultra & red 7.00 1.10
67 A4 3a slate & red 8.00 3.25
68 A4 4a dk green & red 8.50 4.50
69 A4 4½a orange & red 20.00 12.00
70 A4 4½a ind & red ('01) 22.00 19.00
71 A4 5a bister & red 9.50 3.50
72 A4 7½a lilac & red 10.00 *11.00*
73 A4 8a ol gray & red 11.00 *9.00*

Wmk. 71

74 A5 1r ultra & red 27.50 17.50
75 A5 2r green & red 32.50 27.50
76 A5 3r violet & red 55.00 *60.00*
77 A5 4r lilac rose & red 67.50 *77.50*
78 A5 5r gray brown & red 85.00 *110.00*
Nos. 62-78 (17) 382.50 *358.75*

For surcharges see Nos. 94-98.

A6

Monogram of Sultan Ali bin Hamoud — A7

1904, June 8 **Typo.** **Wmk. 47**

79 A6 ½a emerald 3.00 .60
80 A6 1a rose red 3.00 .25
81 A6 2a bister brown 6.00 .50
82 A6 2½a ultra 5.50 .40
83 A6 3a gray 7.00 2.50
84 A6 4a blue green 5.50 1.75
85 A6 4½a black 6.50 2.75
86 A6 5a ocher 8.00 3.50
87 A6 7½a violet 9.50 *9.00*
88 A6 8a olive green 8.00 7.50
89 A7 1r ultra & red 40.00 30.00
90 A7 2r green & red 55.00 *60.00*
91 A7 3r violet & red 70.00 *110.00*
92 A7 4r magenta & red 80.00 *120.00*
93 A7 5r olive & red 85.00 *120.00*
Nos. 79-93 (15) 392.00 *468.75*

Nos. 69-70, 72-73 Surcharged in Black or Lake

g

h

i

1904

94 A4 (g) 1a on 4½a 4.50 *7.50*
95 A4 (g) 1a on 4½a (L) 7.50 *22.50*
96 A4 (h) 2a on 4a (L) 15.00 *22.50*
97 A4 (i) 2½a on 7½a 17.50 *27.50*
a. "Hlaf" 16,000.
b. Thin open "w" in overprint 100.00 120.00
c. Serif on foot of "f" in overprint 190.00 240.00
98 A4 (i) 2½a on 8a 32.50 *47.50*
a. "Hlaf" 15,000. *10,000.*
b. Thin open "w" in overprint 160.00 190.00
c. Serif on foot of "f" in overprint 300.00 350.00
Nos. 94-98 (5) 77.00 *127.50*

Sultan Ali bin Hamoud
A8 A9

A10

Palace of the Sultan — A11

1908-09 **Engr.** **Wmk. 47**

99 A8 1c gray ('09) 2.50 .35
100 A8 3c yellow grn 17.00 .25
101 A8 6c carmine 11.00 .25
102 A8 10c org brn ('09) 7.50 3.00
103 A8 12c violet 20.00 4.25
104 A9 15c ultra & pur 21.00 .45
105 A9 25c brown 8.75 1.25
106 A9 50c dp green 13.00 9.00
107 A9 75c slate ('09) 16.00 *20.00*
108 A10 1r yellow green 50.00 15.00
109 A10 2r violet 30.00 21.00
110 A10 3r yellow brown 45.00 *62.50*
111 A10 4r red 75.00 *120.00*
112 A10 5r blue 85.00 *80.00*
113 A11 10r brn & dk grn 230.00 *375.00*
114 A11 20r yel grn & blk 675.00 *875.00*
115 A11 30r dk brn & blk 775.00 *1,100.*
116 A11 40r org brn & blk 975.00
117 A11 50r lilac & blk 900.00
118 A11 100r blue & blk 1,350.
119 A11 200r black & brn 1,850.
Nos. 99-112 (14) 401.75 *337.30*

It is probable that Nos. 118 and 119 were used only for fiscal purposes.

Sultan Khalifa bin Harub
A12

Dhow
A13

Dhow — A14

1913 ***Perf. 14***

120 A12 1c gray .50 1.00
121 A12 3c yellow grn 1.50 .75
122 A12 6c carmine 1.75 .25
123 A12 10c brown 1.25 *3.75*
124 A12 12c violet 1.50 .75
125 A12 15c ultra 4.25 1.10
126 A12 25c black brn 1.60 *3.00*
127 A12 50c dk green 5.00 *8.25*
128 A12 75c dk gray 3.25 *7.50*
129 A13 1r yellow grn 29.00 *21.00*
130 A13 2r dk violet 22.50 *42.50*
131 A13 3r orange 27.50 *67.50*
132 A13 4r red 45.00 *92.50*
133 A13 5r blue 57.50 *67.50*
134 A14 10r brown & grn 230.00 *440.00*
135 A14 20r yel grn & blk 400.00 *750.00*
136 A14 30r dk brn & blk 425.00 *900.00*
137 A14 40r orange & blk 750.00 *1,200.*
138 A14 50r dull vio & blk 800.00 *1,400.*
139 A14 100r blue & blk 1,000.
140 A14 200r black & brn 1,500.
Nos. 120-134 (15) 432.10 *757.35*

1914-22 **Wmk. 3**

141 A12 1c gray .90 .25
142 A12 3c yellow grn 1.40 .25
143 A12 6c carmine 1.50 .25
144 A12 8c vio, *yel* ('22) 1.75 *7.75*
145 A12 10c dk grn, *yel* ('22) 1.25 *.35*
146 A12 15c ultra 2.00 *8.75*
148 A12 50c dark green 5.25 *8.25*
149 A12 75c deep gray 3.50 *40.00*
150 A13 1r yellow grn 6.00 4.00
151 A13 2r dark violet 20.00 *21.00*
152 A13 3r brown org 27.50 *52.50*
153 A13 4r red 40.00 *95.00*
154 A13 5r blue 19.00 *70.00*
155 A14 10r brown & grn 225.00 *775.00*
Nos. 141-155 (14) 355.05 *1,083.*

1921-29 **Wmk. 4**

156 A12 1c gray .30 *15.00*
157 A12 3c yellow grn 4.50 *10.00*
158 A12 3c orange ('22) .40 .25
159 A12 4c green ('22) .65 *4.00*
160 A12 6c carmine .45 *.55*
161 A12 6c vio, *bl* ('22) .50 .25
162 A12 10c lt brown .85 *18.00*
163 A12 12c violet .65 .35
164 A12 12c carmine ('22) .55 .45
165 A12 15c ultra .70 *15.50*
166 A12 20c dk blue ('22) 1.10 .35
167 A12 25c black brn 1.10 *37.50*
168 A12 50c blue green 5.00 *10.00*
169 A12 75c dark gray 3.00 *70.00*
170 A13 1r yellow grn 7.25 4.00
171 A13 2r dk violet 4.50 *17.50*
172 A13 3r ocher 8.00 *11.00*
173 A13 4r red 17.50 *50.00*
174 A13 5r blue 32.50 *80.00*
175 A14 10r brown & grn 260.00 *525.00*
176 A14 20r green & blk 450.00 *850.00*
Overprinted "SPECIMEN" 160.00
177 A14 30r dk brn & blk ('29) 350.00 *850.00*
Nos. 156-175 (20) 349.50 869.70

Sultan Khalifa bin Harub ("CENTS" with Serifs) — A15

1926-27

184 A15 1c brown 1.10 .25
185 A15 3c yellow org .35 .25
186 A15 4c deep green .35 .50
187 A15 6c dark violet .35 .25
188 A15 8c slate 1.10 5.50
189 A15 10c olive green 1.10 .45
190 A15 12c deep red 3.25 .25
191 A15 20c ultra .65 .40
192 A15 25c violet, *yel* 17.00 3.00
193 A15 50c claret 5.00 .50
194 A15 75c olive brown 40.00 *42.50*
Nos. 184-194 (11) 70.25 53.85
Set, overprinted "SPECIMEN" 240.00

Catalogue values for unused stamps in this section, from this point to the end of the section, are for Never Hinged items.

"CENTS" without Serifs
A16

Dhow
A17

Dhow — A18

1936 ***Perf. 14***

201 A16 5c deep green .25 .25
202 A16 10c black .25 .25
203 A16 15c carmine .30 1.25
204 A16 20c brown org .25 .25
205 A16 25c violet, *yel* .30 .25
206 A16 30c ultra .30 .25
207 A16 40c black brown .30 .25
208 A16 50c claret .40 .25
209 A17 1sh yellow grn 1.50 .25
210 A17 2sh dark violet 5.00 2.00
211 A17 5sh red 30.00 8.00
212 A17 7.50sh blue 40.00 37.50
213 A18 10sh brn org & grn 40.00 32.50
Nos. 201-213 (13) 118.85 83.25

For overprints see Nos. 222-223.

A19

1936, Dec. 9

No.	Type	Description	Unused	Used
214	A19	10c olive grn & blk	4.00	.35
215	A19	20c red violet & blk	6.00	2.75
216	A19	30c deep ultra & blk	16.00	1.00
217	A19	50c red orange & blk	17.50	6.75
		Nos. 214-217 (4)	43.50	10.85

Reign of Sultan Khalifa bin Harub, 25th anniv.

A20

Dhow & Map Showing Zanzibar & Muscat.

Perf. 14

1944, Nov. 20 Engr. Wmk. 4

No.	Type	Description	Unused	Used
218	A20	10c violet blue	1.00	*5.25*
219	A20	20c brown orange	1.50	*3.75*
220	A20	50c Prus green	1.50	.40
221	A20	1sh dull purple	1.50	1.50
		Nos. 218-221 (4)	5.50	10.90

200th anniv. of the Al Busaid Dynasty.

Nos. 202 and 206 Overprinted in Red

1946, Nov. 11

No.	Type	Description	Unused	Used
222	A16	10c black	.25	.50
223	A16	30c ultra	.40	.50

Victory of the Allied Nations in WW II.

Common Design Types pictured following the introduction.

Silver Wedding Issue

Common Design Types

1949, Jan. 10 Photo. *Perf. 14x14½*

No.	Type	Description	Unused	Used
224	CD304	20c orange	.60	1.50

Engraved; Name Typographed

Perf. 11½x11

No.	Type	Description	Unused	Used
225	CD305	10sh light brown	29.00	36.50

UPU Issue

Common Design Types

Engr.; Name Typo. on 30c, 50c

Perf. 13½, 11x11½

1949, Oct. 10 Wmk. 4

No.	Type	Description	Unused	Used
226	CD306	20c red orange	.45	*3.75*
227	CD307	30c indigo	2.50	2.00
228	CD308	50c red lilac	1.00	*3.25*
229	CD309	1sh blue green	1.00	*4.50*
		Nos. 226-229 (4)	4.95	13.50

Sultan Khalifa bin Harub A21

Seyyid Khalifa Schools A22

Perf. 12x12½, 13x12½

1952, Aug. 26 Engr.

No.	Type	Description	Unused	Used
230	A21	5c black	.25	.25
231	A21	10c red orange	.25	.25
232	A21	15c green	2.00	*3.00*
233	A21	20c carmine	.75	.75
234	A21	25c plum	1.10	.25
235	A21	30c blue green	1.10	.25
236	A21	35c ultra	1.00	*5.00*
237	A21	40c chocolate	1.00	*2.00*
238	A21	50c purple	3.25	.25
239	A22	1sh choc & bl grn	.75	.25
240	A22	2sh claret & ultra	3.00	*2.75*
241	A22	5sh carmine & blk	3.00	*6.50*
242	A22	7.50sh emer & gray	27.50	*27.50*
243	A22	10sh gray blk & rose red	12.00	*15.00*
		Nos. 230-243 (14)	56.95	64.00

Sultan Khalifa bin Harub — A23

1954, Aug. 26 *Perf. 12½x12*

No.	Type	Description	Unused	Used
244	A23	15c green	.25	.25
245	A23	20c scarlet	.25	.25
246	A23	30c ultra	.25	.25
247	A23	50c purple	.30	.30
248	A23	1.25sh brown orange	.50	*.75*
		Nos. 244-248 (5)	1.55	1.80

The frames differ on Nos. 245 and 247. Sultan Khalifa bin Harub, 75th birth anniv.

Cloves A24

Dhows A25

Sultan's Barge A26

Malindi Minaret Mosque A27

Kibweni Palace — A28

Sultan Khalifa bin Harub and: 25c, 35c, and 50c Map showing location of Zanzibar. 1sh, 2sh, Dimbani Mosque.

Perf. 11½ (A24), 11x11½ (A25), 14x13½ (A26), 13½x14 (A27), 13x13½ (A28)

1957, Aug. 26 Engr. Wmk. 314

No.	Type	Description	Unused	Used
249	A24	5c dull grn & org	.25	.25
250	A24	10c rose car & brt grn	.25	.25
251	A25	15c dk brn & grn	.25	*3.25*
252	A26	20c ultra	.25	.25
253	A26	25c blk & brn org	.25	*1.50*
254	A25	30c int blk & rose car	.25	*1.50*
255	A26	35c brt grn & ind	.30	.25
256	A27	40c int blk & redsh brn	.25	.25
257	A26	50c dull grn & bl	.35	.30
258	A27	1sh int blk & brt car	.30	.30
259	A25	1.25sh rose car & dk grn	4.00	.45
260	A27	2sh dull grn & org	4.00	2.50
261	A28	5sh ultra	6.00	2.50
262	A28	7.50sh green	15.00	4.50
263	A28	10sh rose carmine	16.00	6.50
		Nos. 249-263 (15)	47.70	24.55

Sultan Seyyid Abdulla bin Khalifa — A29

Designs as before with portrait of Sultan Seyyid Abdulla bin Khalifa.

Perf. 11½ (A29), 11x11½ (A25), 14x13½ (A26), 13½x14 (A27)

1961, Oct. 17 Engr. Wmk. 314

No.	Type	Description	Unused	Used
264	A29	5c dull grn & org	.40	*1.10*
265	A29	10c rose car & brt grn	.40	.25
266	A25	15c dk brn & grn	.90	*3.75*
267	A26	20c ultra	.40	.45
268	A26	25c blk & brn org	1.75	1.75
269	A25	30c int blk & rose car	3.25	3.00
270	A26	35c brt grn & indigo	3.00	*5.00*
271	A27	40c int blk & redsh brn	.40	.25
272	A26	50c dull grn & bl	3.25	.25
273	A27	1sh int blk & brt car	.50	*1.50*
274	A25	1.25sh rose car & dk grn	3.00	*6.50*
275	A27	2sh dull grn & org	1.00	*3.75*

Perf. 13x13½

No.	Type	Description	Unused	Used
276	A28	5sh ultra	4.00	*10.00*
277	A28	7.50sh green	3.75	*19.00*
278	A28	10sh rose carmine	3.75	*11.00*
279	A28	20sh dk brown	19.00	*30.00*
		Nos. 264-279 (16)	48.75	*97.55*

For overprints see Nos. 285-300.

Freedom from Hunger Issue

Common Design Type with Portrait of Sultan Seyyid Abdulla bin Khalifa

1963, June 4 Photo. *Perf. 14x14½*

No.	Type	Description	Unused	Used
280	CD314	1.30sh sepia	1.50	.80

Independent State

Sultan Seyyid Jamshid bin Abdulla and Zanzibar Clove — A30

Designs: 50c, "To Prosperity," arch and sun. 1.30sh, "Religious Tolerance," composite view of churches and mosques, horiz. 2.50sh, "Towards the Light," Mangapwani Cave.

Perf. 12½

1963, Dec. 10 Photo. Unwmk.

No.	Type	Description	Unused	Used
281	A30	30c multicolored	.25	.25
282	A30	50c multicolored	.30	.30
283	A30	1.30sh multicolored	.25	*2.00*
284	A30	2.50sh multicolored	.30	*2.00*
		Nos. 281-284 (4)	1.10	*4.55*

Zanzibar's independence, Dec. 10, 1963. For overprints see Nos. 301-304.

Republic

Nos. 264-279 Overprinted

1964, Feb. 28 As Before

No.	Type	Description	Unused	Used
285	A29	5c dull grn & org	.25	.25
286	A29	10c rose car & brt grn	.25	.25
287	A25	15c dk brn & grn	.25	.25
288	A26	20c ultra	.25	.25
289	A26	25c blk & brn org	.35	.25
290	A25	30c int blk & rose car	.25	.25
291	A26	35c brt grn & ind	.35	.25
292	A27	40c int blk & redsh brn	.25	.25
293	A26	50c dull grn & blue	.35	.25
294	A27	1sh int blk & brt car	.30	.25
295	A25	1.25sh rose car & dk grn	2.25	.90
296	A27	2sh dull grn & org	.85	.45
297	A28	5sh ultra	.85	.50
298	A28	7.50sh green	1.25	7.00
299	A28	10sh rose carmine	2.00	7.00
300	A28	20sh dark brown	3.00	*8.50*
		Nos. 285-300 (16)	13.05	*26.85*

The overprint was applied in England. It is in 2 lines on 40c and 1sh to 20sh. "Jamhuri" means "republic."

Overprint Handstamped

No.	Type	Description	Unused	Used
285a	A29	5c	1.00	.60
286a	A29	10c	1.00	.25
287a	A25	15c	1.50	2.00
288a	A26	20c	1.00	.50
289a	A26	25c	1.75	.25
290a	A25	30c	1.00	.50
291a	A26	35c	1.75	1.00
292a	A27	40c	1.00	1.00
293a	A26	50c	1.75	.25
294a	A27	1sh	1.50	1.25
295a	A25	1.25sh	1.25	1.50
296a	A27	2sh	2.50	1.50
297a	A28	5sh	2.00	1.75
298a	A28	7.50sh	2.50	1.75
299a	A28	10sh	2.50	2.50
300a	A28	20sh	3.00	6.00
		Nos. 285a-300a (16)	27.00	22.60

This overprint was applied locally. It has one line of serifed letters. These are found diagonal, vertical, horizontal, double and inverted. See Nos. 301a-304b. Other stamps with this overprint, including postage dues, were unofficial.

Nos. 281-284 Overprinted

1964, Feb. 28 As Before

No.	Type	Description	Unused	Used
301	A30	30c multi	.25	.25
302	A30	50c multi	.25	.25
303	A30	1.30sh multi	.25	.25
304	A30	2.50sh multi	.25	.25
a.		Green omitted	150.00	
		Nos. 301-304 (4)	1.00	1.00

One-line overprint on 1.30sh.

Overprint Handstamped

No.	Type	Description	Unused	Used
301a	A30	30c	1.00	1.00
302a	A30	50c	.40	.35
303a	A30	1.30sh	1.00	.80
304b	A30	2.50sh	1.50	1.50
c.		Green omitted	425.00	350.00
		Nos. 301a-304b (4)	3.90	3.65

See note after No. 300a.

Moorish Arch, Ax, Sword and Spear — A31

Designs: 10c, 20c, Arch and arrow piercing chain. 25c, 40c, Man with rifle. 30c, 50c, Man breaking chain. 1sh, Man, flag and sun. 1.30sh, Hands breaking chain and cloves, horiz. 2sh, Hands waving flag, horiz. 5sh, Map of Zanzibar and Pemba and flag, horiz. 10sh, Flag and map of Zanzibar and Pemba. 20sh, Flag of Zanzibar, horiz

Perf. 13x13½, 13½x13

1964, June 21 Litho. Unwmk.

No.	Type	Description	Unused	Used
305	A31	5c multicolored	.40	.25
306	A31	10c multicolored	.40	.25
307	A31	15c multicolored	.40	.25
308	A31	20c multicolored	.50	.25
309	A31	25c multicolored	.50	.25
310	A31	30c multicolored	.40	.25
311	A31	40c multicolored	.60	.25
312	A31	50c multicolored	.40	.25
313	A31	1sh multicolored	.50	.25
314	A31	1.30sh multicolored	.30	1.25
315	A31	2sh multicolored	.50	.50
316	A31	5sh multicolored	1.25	*3.00*
317	A31	10sh multicolored	5.25	*4.00*
318	A31	20sh multicolored	5.00	*20.00*
		Nos. 305-318 (14)	16.40	31.00

Soldier and Maps of Zanzibar and Pemba A32

Reconstruction A33

Perf. 13½x13, 13x13½

1965, Jan. 12 Unwmk.

No.	Type	Description	Unused	Used
319	A32	20c green & yel grn	.25	.25
320	A33	30c dk brn & ocher	.25	.25
321	A32	1.30sh vio blue & blue	.25	.25
322	A33	2.50sh purple & rose	.25	1.25
		Nos. 319-322 (4)	1.00	2.00

First anniversary of the revolution.

Zanzibar and Tanzania

Rice Planting — A34

Design: 30c, 1.30sh, Hands holding rice.

Perf. 13x12½

1965, Oct. 17 Litho. Unwmk.

No.	Type	Description	Unused	Used
323	A34	20c blue & blk brn	.25	1.00
324	A34	30c brt pink & blk brn	.25	1.00
325	A34	1.30sh org & blk brn	.25	2.00
326	A34	2.50sh emer & blk brn	.35	5.00
		Nos. 323-326 (4)	1.10	9.00

Issued to publicize agricultural development.

Symbols of Trade, Agriculture, Industry and Education — A35

Designs: 50c, 2.50sh, Soldier and sunburst.

1966, Jan. 12 Litho. *Perf. 12½x13*

No.	Type	Description	Unused	Used
327	A35	20c ultra, red & gray	.25	.25
328	A35	50c black & yel	.25	.25
329	A35	1.30sh multicolored	.30	.35
330	A35	2.50sh black & org	.30	1.00
		Nos. 327-330 (4)	1.10	1.85

2nd anniv. of the revolution of Jan. 12, 1964.

Pres. Abeid Amani Karume and Vice-Pres. Abdulla Kassim Hanga — A36

Design: 50c, 1.30sh, Flag, laurel and hands holding Flame of the Union (inscribed: Jamhuri Tanzania Zanzibar).

1966, Apr. 26 Photo. *Perf. 13½x13*

No.	Type	Description	Unused	Used
331	A36	30c multicolored	.25	.25
332	A36	50c multicolored	.25	.25
333	A36	1.30sh multicolored	.35	.30
334	A36	2.50sh multicolored	.60	1.25
		Nos. 331-334 (4)	1.45	2.05

Union of Tanganyika and Zanzibar, 2nd anniv.

Logging — A37

10c, 1sh, Clove trees & man. 15c, 40c, Cabinetmaker. 20c, 5sh, Lumumba College & book. 25c, 1.30sh, Farmer & tractor. 30c, 2sh, Volunteer farm workers. 50c, 10sh, Street scene, vert.

Perf. 13x12½, 12½x13

1966, June 5 Litho.

No.	Type	Description	Unused	Used
335	A37	5c lemon & vio brn	.70	.80
336	A37	10c brt grn & vio brn	.70	.80
337	A37	15c vio brn & bl	.70	.80
338	A37	20c vio bl & org	.70	.25
339	A37	25c vio brn & yel	.70	.30
340	A37	30c vio brn & dl yel	.80	.25
341	A37	40c vio brn & rose	.90	.25
342	A37	50c green & yel	.90	.25
343	A37	1sh ultra & vio brn	.90	.25
344	A37	1.30sh lt bl grn & vio brn	1.00	3.25
345	A37	2sh brt grn & vio brn	1.00	.60
346	A37	5sh ver & gray	1.50	6.00
347	A37	10sh red brn & yel	2.50	20.00
348	A37	20sh brt pink & vio brn	5.00	35.00
		Nos. 335-348 (14)	18.00	68.80

Symbols of Education A38

1966, Sept. 25 *Perf. 13½x13*

No.	Type	Description	Unused	Used
349	A38	50c blue, blk & org	.25	1.00
350	A38	1.30sh blue, blk & yel grn	.30	1.75
351	A38	2.50sh blue, blk & pink	.80	4.00
		Nos. 349-351 (3)	1.35	6.75

Introduction of free education.

People and Flag — A39

Design: 50c, 1.30sh, Vice-President Abdulla Kassim Hanga, flag and crowd, vert.

Perf. 14x14½, 14½x14

1967, Feb. 5 Litho. Unwmk.

No.	Type	Description	Unused	Used
352	A39	30c multicolored	.25	1.00
353	A39	50c multicolored	.25	1.00
354	A39	1.30sh multicolored	.25	1.25
355	A39	2.50sh multicolored	.40	3.00
		Nos. 352-355 (4)	1.15	6.25

10th anniversary of Afro-Shirazi Party.

Volunteer Workers — A40

Perf. 12½x12

1967, Aug. 20 Photo. Unwmk.

No.	Type	Description	Unused	Used
356	A40	1.30sh multicolored	.30	2.50
357	A40	2.50sh multicolored	.55	6.50

Volunteer (Young) Workers Brigade.

All Zanzibar stamps were withdrawn July 1, 1968, and replaced with current Kenya, Uganda and Tanzania stamps.

In 2013, Tanzania denounced as "illegal" stamps bearing the name "Zanzibar" that had been recently introduced into the philatelic marketplace.

POSTAGE DUE STAMPS

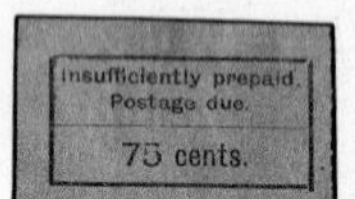

D1

Rouletted 10

1931 Typeset Unwmk.

Thin Paper

Without Gum

No.	Type	Description	Unused	Used
J1	D1	1c blk, *orange*	12.50	150.00
J2	D1	2c blk, *orange*	5.50	75.00
J3	D1	3c blk, *orange*	5.75	75.00
J3A	D1	6c blk, *orange*		8,000.
J4	D1	9c blk, *orange*	3.25	45.00
J4A	D1	12c blk, *orange*	15,000.	12,000.
J4B	D1	12c blk, *green*	1,600.	650.00
J5	D1	15c blk, *orange*	3.25	42.50
J6	D1	18c blk, *orange*	27.50	90.00
a.		18c black, *salmon*	6.00	60.00
J7	D1	20c blk, *orange*	5.00	80.00
J8	D1	21c blk, *orange*	4.00	55.00
J8A	D1	25c blk, *orange*	20,000.	18,000.
J8B	D1	25c blk, *magenta*	2,250.	1,300.
J9	D1	31c blk, *orange*	10.00	130.00
J10	D1	50c blk, *orange*	22.50	275.00
J11	D1	75c blk, *orange*	85.00	750.00

The variety "cent.s" occurs once on each sheet of Nos. J3 to J11 inclusive. For more detailed listings, see the *Scott Classic Specialized* catalog.

D2

1931-33 *Rouletted 5*

Thick Paper

No.	Type	Description	Unused	Used
J12	D2	2c blk, *salmon*	27.50	40.00
J13	D2	3c blk, *rose*	4.00	67.50
J14	D2	6c blk, *yellow*	4.00	40.00
J15	D2	12c blk, *blue*	5.00	32.50
J16	D2	25c blk, *pink*	11.00	145.00
J17	D2	25c blk, *dull violet*	27.50	87.50
		Nos. J12-J17 (6)	79.00	412.50

Catalogue values for unused stamps in this section, from this point to the end of the section, are for Never Hinged items.

D3

1936 Typo. Wmk. 4 *Perf. 14*

No.	Type	Description	Unused	Used
J18	D3	5c violet	8.50	14.00
J19	D3	10c carmine	7.25	3.25
J20	D3	20c green	2.50	6.75
J21	D3	30c brown	18.00	24.00
J22	D3	40c ultra	10.00	30.00
J23	D3	1sh gray	15.50	37.50
		Nos. J18-J23 (6)	61.75	115.50

Chalky paper was introduced in 1956 for the 5c, 30c, 40c, 1sh, and in 1962 for the 10c, 20c. Value for set of 6, unused $3.25, used $110.

See note after No. 300a.

ZIMBABWE

zim-'bä-bwē

LOCATION — Southeastern Africa, bordered by Zambia, Mozambique, South Africa, and Botswana
GOVT. — Republic
AREA — 150,872 sq. mi.
POP. — 11,163,160 (1999 est.)
CAPITAL — Harare

Formerly Rhodesia, the Republic of Zimbabwe was established April 18, 1980.

100 Cents = 1 Dollar

Catalogue values for all unused stamps in this country are for Never Hinged items.

Morganite A69

Black Rhinoceros A70

Odzani Falls — A71

Perf. 14½, 14½x14 (A70)

1980, Apr. 18 Litho.

No.	Type	Description	Unused	Used
414	A69	1c shown	.25	.30
415	A69	3c Amethyst	.25	.30
416	A69	4c Garnet	.25	.25
417	A69	5c Citrine	.25	.25
418	A69	7c Blue topaz	.25	.25
419	A70	9c shown	.25	.25
420	A70	11c Lion	.25	.25
421	A70	13c Warthog	.25	.25
422	A70	15c Giraffe	.25	.25
423	A70	17c Zebra	.25	.25
424	A71	21c shown	.25	.25
425	A71	25c Goba Falls	.30	.30
426	A71	30c Inyangombe Falls	.30	.45
426A	A71	40c Bundi Falls	3.00	4.25
427	A71	$1 Bridal Veil Falls	.40	1.60
428	A71	$2 Victoria Falls	.50	3.00
		Nos. 414-428 (16)	7.25	12.45

No. 426A was issued on a later date.

Rotary International, 75th Anniversary — A72

1980, June 18 *Perf. 14½*

No.	Type	Description	Unused	Used
429	A72	4c multicolored	.25	.25
430	A72	13c multicolored	.25	.25
431	A72	21c multicolored	.30	.25
432	A72	25c multicolored	.35	.35
a.		Souvenir sheet of 4, #429-432	1.40	1.40
		Nos. 429-432 (4)	1.15	1.10

Olympic Rings — A73

1980, July 19

No.	Type	Description	Unused	Used
433	A73	17c multicolored	.45	.45

22nd Summer Olympic Games, Moscow, July 19-Aug. 3.

Gatooma Post Office, 1912 — A74

Post Offices: 7c, Salisbury, 1912. 9c, Umtali, 1901. 17c, Bulawayo, 1895.

1980 Litho. *Perf. 14½*

No.	Type	Description	Unused	Used
434	A74	5c multicolored	.25	.25
435	A74	7c multicolored	.25	.25
436	A74	9c multicolored	.25	.25
437	A74	17c multicolored	.25	.25
a.		Souvenir sheet of 4, #434-437	1.00	1.00
		Nos. 434-437 (4)	1.00	1.00

Post Office Savings Bank, 75th anniv.

Intl. Year of the Disabled — A75

Designs: Various disabilities. Nos. 438-441 form a continuous design.

1981, Sept. 23 Litho. *Perf. 14½*

No.	Type	Description	Unused	Used
438	A75	5c multicolored	.25	.25
439	A75	7c multicolored	.25	.25
440	A75	11c multicolored	.25	.25
441	A75	17c multicolored	.30	.30
		Nos. 438-441 (4)	1.05	1.05

Natl. Tree Day — A76

1981, Dec. 4

No.	Type	Description	Unused	Used
442	A76	5c Msasa	.25	.25
443	A76	7c Mopane	.25	.25
444	A76	21c Flat-crowned acacia	.45	.45
445	A76	30c Pod mahogany	.75	.75
		Nos. 442-445 (4)	1.70	1.70

Rock Paintings — A77

Designs: 9c, Khoisan figures, Gwamgwadza Cave. 11c, Kudus, human figures, Epworth Mission. 17c, Diana's Vow, Rusape. 21c, Giraffes, Gwamgwadza Cave. 25c, Warthog, Mucheka Cave. 30c, Hunters, Shinzwini Shelter.

1982, Mar. 17 Litho. *Perf. 14½*

446 A77 9c multicolored .80 .25
447 A77 11c multicolored 1.00 .25
448 A77 17c multicolored 1.25 .40
449 A77 21c multicolored 1.40 .40
450 A77 25c multicolored 1.60 1.60
451 A77 30c multicolored 1.75 *2.75*
Nos. 446-451 (6) 7.80 5.65

Scouting Year — A78

1982, July 21

452 A78 9c Emblem .30 .25
453 A78 11c Campfire .35 .25
454 A78 21c Map reading .50 .40
455 A78 30c Baden Powell .65 .65
Nos. 452-455 (4) 1.80 1.55

TB Bacillus Centenary — A79

1982, Nov. 17 *Perf. 14½*

456 A79 11c Koch .80 .40
457 A79 30c Scientist examining slide 1.20 *1.75*

Commonwealth Day — A80

Sculptures: 9c, Wing Woman, by Henry Mudzengerere, vert. 11c, Telling Secrets, by Joseph Ndandarika. 30c, Hornbill Man, by John Takawira. $1, The Chief, by Nicholas Mukomberanwa, vert.

1983, Mar. 14 *Perf. 14½*

458 A80 9c multicolored .25 .25
459 A80 11c multicolored .25 .25
460 A80 30c multicolored .25 .25
461 A80 $1 multicolored .40 *1.25*
Nos. 458-461 (4) 1.15 2.00

World Plowing Contest, May A81

No. 463, mechanized plowing.

1983, May 13 Litho. *Perf. 14½*

462 A81 Pair .60 .60
a.-b. 21c, any single .25 .25
463 A81 Pair .80 .80
a.-b. 30c, any single .25 .25

World Communications Year — A82

Means of communication and transportation. Nos. 464-467 vert.

1983, Oct. 12 Litho. *Perf. 14½*

464 A82 9c Mailman .25 .25
465 A82 11c Signaling airplane .25 .25
466 A82 15c Telephone operators .30 .25
467 A82 17c Reading newspapers .40 .25
468 A82 21c Truck on highway .50 .50
469 A82 30c Train .65 *.90*
Nos. 464-469 (6) 2.35 2.40

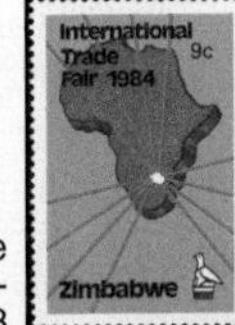

Zimbabwe Intl. Trade Fair, Bulawayo, May 5-13 — A83

1984, Apr. 11 Litho. *Perf. 14½*

470 A83 9c shown .25 .25
471 A83 11c Globe .25 .25
472 A83 30c Emblem .45 .45
Nos. 470-472 (3) .95 .95

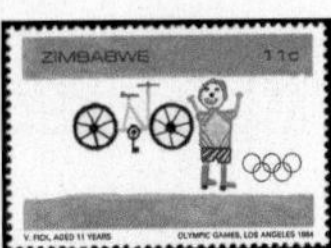

1984 Summer Olympics — A84

Children's Drawings.

1984, July 18 Litho. *Perf. 14½*

473 A84 11c Bicycling .60 .60
474 A84 21c Swimming .50 .50
475 A84 30c Running .60 .60
476 A84 40c Hurdles .70 *1.50*
Nos. 473-476 (4) 2.40 3.20

Heroes' Day — A85

1984, Aug. 8 Litho. *Perf. 14½*

477 A85 9c Heroes .25 .25
478 A85 11c Monument, vert. .25 .25
479 A85 17c Statue, vert. .30 .30
480 A85 30c Bas-relief .50 *.90*
Nos. 477-480 (4) 1.30 1.70

Fish Eagle — A86

1984, Oct. 10 Litho. *Perf. 14½*

481 A86 9c shown .60 .25
482 A86 11c Long crested eagle .65 .25
483 A86 13c Bateleur .70 .70
484 A86 17c Black eagle .90 .90
485 A86 21c Martial eagle 1.25 1.25
486 A86 30c African hawk eagle 1.50 *2.00*
Nos. 481-486 (6) 5.60 5.35

Superheat Engine No. 86, Mashonaland Railways, 1918 — A87

Steam locomotives: 11c, Engine No. 190, North British Locomotive Co., 1926. 17c, Engine No. 424, Beyer Peacock & Co., 1950. Engine No. 726, Beyer Peacock & Co., 1957.

1985, May 15 Litho.

487 A87 9c multicolored .80 .50
488 A87 11c multicolored 1.10 .50
489 A87 17c multicolored 1.60 1.00
490 A87 30c multicolored 3.25 3.25
Nos. 487-490 (4) 6.75 5.25

INTELSAT V — A88

57c, Mazowe Earth Satellite Station.

Perf. 14½x14, 14½

1985, July 8 Litho.

491 A88 26c multicolored 1.60 1.60

Size: 62x23mm

492 A88 57c multicolored 4.00 4.00

Zimbabwe Bird and Tobacco — A89

Agriculture and industry.

Perf. 14¾x14½

1985, Aug. 21 Litho.

493 A89 1c shown .25 .25
a. Perf 14¼x13¾ ('88) *30.00* 2.00
494 A89 3c Corn .25 .25
a. Perf 14¼x13¾ ('88) *10.00* 2.00
495 A89 4c Cotton .25 .25
a. Perf 14¼x13¾ ('88) *40.00* 2.00
496 A89 5c Tea .50 .25
a. Perf 14¼x13¾ ('88) *40.00* 2.00
497 A89 10c Cattle .30 .25
a. Perf 14¼x13¾ ('88) *20.00* 2.00
498 A89 11c Birchenough Bridge .75 .25
499 A89 12c Stamp mill 1.25 .25
500 A89 13c Gold production 3.00 .25
a. Perf 14¼x13¾ ('88) *20.00* *4.00*
501 A89 15c Coal mining 2.75 .25
a. Perf 14¼x13¾ ('88) *40.00* 4.00
502 A89 17c Amethyst mining 3.00 1.25
503 A89 18c Electric train 2.25 2.75
504 A89 20c Kariba Dam 1.50 .25
a. Perf 14¼x13¾ ('88) *20.00* 4.00
505 A89 23c Elephants 4.50 .45
506 A89 25c Zambezi River sunset .65 .30
a. Perf 14¼x13¾ ('88) — *20.00*
507 A89 26c Baobab tree .65 .30
508 A89 30c Great Zimbabwe ruins .75 .70
509 A89 35c Folk dancing .60 .30
510 A89 45c Crushing corn 1.25 .60
511 A89 57c Wood carving .75 .70
512 A89 $1 Mbira drum 1.25 1.00
a. Perf 14¼x13¾ ('88) — *25.00*
513 A89 $2 Mule-drawn scotch cart 2.00 3.00
514 A89 $5 Natl. coat of arms 2.25 4.50
Nos. 493-514 (22) 30.70 18.35

Natl. Archives, 50th Anniv. — A90

Designs: 12c, Gatsi Rusere (c. 1589-1623), ruler of Mashonaland and Zambezi area; mutapa, 17th cent. 18c, Lobengula, ruler of Ndebele State (1870-94), sketch by E. A. Maund, 1889; 1888 Moffat Treaty and elephant seal. 26c, Archives exhibition hall. 35c, Archives building.

1985, Sept. 18 *Perf. 14½*

515 A90 12c multicolored .25 .25
516 A90 18c multicolored .30 .30
517 A90 26c multicolored .45 .45
518 A90 35c multicolored .65 .65
Nos. 515-518 (4) 1.65 1.65

UN Decade for Women — A91

1985, Nov. 13

519 A91 10c Computer operator .70 .70
520 A91 17c Nurse, child 1.00 1.00
521 A91 26c Engineer 1.75 1.75
Nos. 519-521 (3) 3.45 3.45

Harare Conference Center — A92

1986, Jan. 29 Litho. *Perf. 14½*

523 A92 26c Facade 1.00 1.00
524 A92 35c Interior 1.75 1.75

Southern African Development Coordination Conference A93

1986, Apr. 1 *Perf. 14½*

525 A93 12c Grain elevators .50 .50
526 A93 18c Rhinoceros 2.60 2.60
527 A93 26c Map, jet 2.60 2.60
528 A93 35c Map, flags 2.75 2.75
Nos. 525-528 (4) 8.45 8.45

Moths — A94

12c, Jackson's emperor. 18c, Oleander hawk. 26c, Zaddach's emperor. 35c, Southern marbled emperor.

1986, June 18 Litho. *Perf. 14½x14*

529 A94 12c multicolored 1.60 1.60
530 A94 18c multicolored 2.10 2.10
531 A94 26c multicolored 2.75 2.75
532 A94 35c multicolored 3.25 3.25
Nos. 529-532 (4) 9.70 9.70

8th Non-aligned Summit Conference — A95

1986, Aug. 28 Litho. *Perf. 14½x14*

533 A95 26c Victoria Falls 2.75 2.75

Size: 66x26mm

Perf. 14½

534 A95 $1 Great Zimbabwe Enclosure 6.50 6.50

Motoring Cent. — A96

1986, Oct. 8 *Perf. 14½*

535 A96 10c Sopwith, 1921 .75 .75
536 A96 12c Gladiator, 1902 .75 .75
537 A96 17c Douglas, 1920 1.10 1.10
538 A96 26c Ford Model-A, 1930 1.75 1.75
539 A96 35c Schacht, 1909 2.25 2.25
540 A96 40c Benz Velocipede, 1886 2.25 2.25
Nos. 535-540 (6) 8.85 8.85

A97

UN Child Survival Campaign: a, Growth monitoring. b, Breast-feeding. c, Oral rehydration. d, Immunization.

1987, Feb. 11 Litho. *Perf. 14x14½*

541 Block of 4 8.50 8.50
a.-d. A97 12c any single 1.90 1.90

A98

Indigenous owls.

1987, Apr. 15 *Perf. 14½*

542 A98 12c Barred 2.75 2.75
543 A98 18c Pearl-spotted 3.25 3.25
544 A98 26c White-faced 3.75 3.75
545 A98 35c Scops 4.75 4.75
Nos. 542-545 (4) 14.50 14.50

Natl. Girl Guides Movement, 75th Anniv. — A99

1987, June 24

546 A99 15c Commitment .75 .75
547 A99 23c Adventure .90 .90
548 A99 35c Service 1.10 1.10
549 A99 $1 Intl. friendship 2.50 2.50
Nos. 546-549 (4) 5.25 5.25

Duikers and Population Maps — A100

1987, Oct. 7 ***Perf. 14½x14***

550	A100	15c Common gray	.60	.60
551	A100	23c Zebra	.75	.75
552	A100	25c Yellow-backed	.80	.80
553	A100	30c Blue	.90	.90
554	A100	35c Jentink's	1.00	1.00
555	A100	38c Red	1.10	1.10
		Nos. 550-555 (6)	5.15	5.15

Insects — A101

1988, Jan. 12 **Litho.** ***Perf. 14½***

556	A101	15c Praying mantis	.75	.25
557	A101	23c Scarab beetle	1.00	.50
558	A101	35c Short-horned grasshopper	1.50	1.50
559	A101	45c Giant shield bug	1.75	*2.00*
		Nos. 556-559 (4)	5.00	4.25

Natl. Gallery of Art, 30th Anniv. — A102

Sculpture and paintings: 15c, Cockerel, by Arthur Azevedo. 23c, Changeling, by Bernard Matemera. 30c, Spirit Python, by Henry Munyaradzi. 35c, Spirit Bird Carrying People, by Thomas Mukarobgwa, horiz. 38c, The Song of the Shepherd Boy, by George Nene, horiz. 45c, War Victim, by Joseph Muzondo, horiz.

Perf. 14x14½, 14½x14

1988, Apr. 14 **Litho.**

560	A102	15c multicolored	.25	.25
561	A102	23c multicolored	.25	.25
562	A102	30c multicolored	.40	.40
563	A102	35c multicolored	.60	.60
564	A102	38c multicolored	.60	.60
565	A102	45c multicolored	.70	.70
		Nos. 560-565 (6)	2.80	2.80

Aloes and Succulents — A103

15c, Aloe cameronii bondana. 23c, Orbeopsis caudata. 25c, Euphorbia wildii. 30c, Euphorbia fortissima. 35c, Aloe aculeata. 38c, Huernia zebrina.

1988, July 14 ***Perf. 14½***

566	A103	15c multicolored	.35	.35
567	A103	23c multicolored	.55	.55
568	A103	25c multicolored	.55	.55
569	A103	30c multicolored	.60	.60
570	A103	35c multicolored	.60	.70
571	A103	38c multicolored	.75	.85
		Nos. 566-571 (6)	3.40	3.60

Ducks — A104

1988, Oct. 6 **Litho.** ***Perf. 14½x14***

572	A104	15c White-faced duck	.75	.25
573	A104	23c Pygmy goose	.85	.25
574	A104	30c Hottentot teal	.90	.85
575	A104	35c Knob-billed duck	1.00	1.40
576	A104	38c White-backed duck	1.00	1.50
577	A104	45c Maccoa	1.60	*2.75*
		Nos. 572-577 (6)	6.10	7.00

Geckos — A105

1989, Jan. 10 **Litho.** ***Perf. 14½***

578	A105	15c O'Shaughnessy's banded	.80	.25
579	A105	23c Tiger rock	.90	.40
580	A105	35c Tasman's	1.50	1.25
581	A105	45c Bibron's	1.75	2.00
		Nos. 578-581 (4)	4.95	3.90

Wildflowers — A106

1989, Apr. 12 **Litho.** ***Perf. 14½***

582	A106	15c Spotted-leaved arum-lily	.45	.10
583	A106	23c Grassland vlei-lily	.50	.25
584	A106	30c Manica protea	.55	.40
585	A106	35c Flame lily	.65	.40
586	A106	38c Poppy hibiscus	.70	.50
587	A106	45c Blue sesbania	.80	.65
		Nos. 582-587 (6)	3.65	2.30

Fish — A107

15c, Red-breasted bream. 23c, Chessa. 30c, Eastern bottle-nose. 35c, Vundu. 38c, Largemouth black bass. 45c, Tiger fish.

1989, July 12 **Litho.** ***Perf. 14½***

588	A107	15c multicolored	.50	.25
589	A107	23c multicolored	.70	.25
590	A107	30c multicolored	.75	.50
591	A107	35c multicolored	.75	.50
592	A107	38c multicolored	.80	.80
593	A107	45c multicolored	1.00	*1.50*
		Nos. 588-593 (6)	4.50	3.80

See Nos. 696-701.

Endangered Species — A108

1989 **Litho.** ***Perf. 14½x14***

594	A108	15c Black rhinoceros	1.25	.40
595	A108	23c Cheetah	1.25	.45
596	A108	30c Wild dog	1.40	.90
597	A108	35c Pangolin	1.40	1.25
598	A108	38c Brown hyena	1.50	2.00
599	A108	45c Roan antelope	1.60	2.50
		Nos. 594-599 (6)	8.40	7.50

Achievements, 1980-1990 — A109

1990, Apr. 17 **Litho.** ***Perf. 14½x14***

600	A109	15c Unity accord	.45	.25
601	A109	23c Conference center	.50	.25
602	A109	30c Education	.55	.80
603	A109	35c Satellite dish	.65	.90
604	A109	38c Sports stadium	.65	.90
605	A109	45c Agriculture	1.00	*2.50*
		Nos. 600-605 (6)	3.80	5.60

City of Harare, Cent. — A110

15c, Runhare house, 1986. 23c, Market hall, 1894. 30c, Charter house, 1959. 35c, Supreme Court, 1927. 38c, Standard Chartered Bank, 1911. 45c, Town house, 1933.

1990, July 11 **Litho.** ***Perf. 14½***

606	A110	15c multicolored	.40	.25
607	A110	23c multicolored	.60	.25
608	A110	30c multicolored	.65	.45
609	A110	35c multicolored	.75	.90
610	A110	38c multicolored	.75	1.00
611	A110	45c multicolored	.90	1.50
		Nos. 606-611 (6)	4.05	4.35

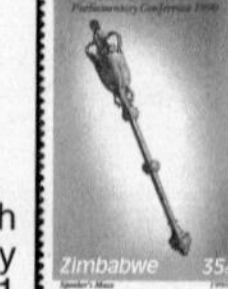

36th Commonwealth Parliamentary Conf. — A111

1990, Sept. 17

612	A111	35c Speaker's mace	.75	.40
613	A111	$1 Speaker's chair	1.75	2.25

Animals A112

Hand Crafts A113

Transportation A114

1c, Tiger fish. 2c, Helmeted guineafowl. 3c, Scrub hare. 4c, Pangolin. 5c, Greater kudu. 9c, Black rhinoceros. 15c, Head rest. 20c, Hand axe. 23c, Gourd, water pot. 25c, Snuff box. 26c, Winnowing basket. 30c, Grinding stone. 33c, Riding bicycles. 35c, Buses. 38c, Train. 45c, Motorcycle, trailer. $1, Jet. $2, Tractor-trailer truck.

Perf. 14, 14½x14 (#620-625), 14¼ (#626-631)

1990, Jan. 2 **Litho.**

614	A112	1c multicolored	.25	.25
a.		Perf 14¾x14½	1.00	.25
615	A112	2c multicolored	1.00	.25
a.		Perf 14¾x14½	1.25	.25
616	A112	3c multicolored	.25	.25
a.		Perf 14¾x14½	1.00	.25
617	A112	4c multicolored	.45	.25
a.		Perf 14x13½	.90	.25
b.		Perf 14¾x14½		
618	A112	5c multicolored	.45	.45
a.		Perf 14¾x14½	1.00	.25
619	A112	9c multicolored	1.50	.40
a.		Perf 14¾x14½	1.50	.40
620	A113	15c multicolored	.30	.25
621	A113	20c multicolored	.25	.25
622	A113	23c multicolored	.25	.25
623	A113	25c multicolored	.25	.25
624	A113	26c multicolored	.60	.40
625	A113	30c multicolored	.40	.40
626	A114	33c multicolored	1.20	.40
627	A114	35c multicolored	1.40	.45
628	A114	38c multicolored	1.75	.45
629	A114	45c multicolored	1.20	.45
630	A114	$1 multicolored	2.10	.90
631	A114	$2 multicolored	1.90	1.60
		Nos. 614-631 (18)	15.50	7.90

Animals — A115

1991, Jan. 15 **Litho.** ***Perf. 14½x14***

632	A115	15c Small-spotted genet	1.00	.25
633	A115	23c Red squirrel	1.10	.30
634	A115	35c Night ape	1.50	1.25
635	A115	45c Bat-eared fox	2.00	1.50
		Nos. 632-635 (4)	5.60	3.30

A116

Traditional musical instruments.

1991, Apr. 16 **Litho.** ***Perf. 14½***

636	A116	15c Hosho	.50	.25
637	A116	23c Mbira	.55	.25
638	A116	30c Ngororombe	.60	.40
639	A116	35c Chipendani	.70	.70
640	A116	38c Marimba	.70	.80
641	A116	45c Ngoma	.80	*1.10*
		Nos. 636-641 (6)	3.85	3.50

Wild Fruits — A117

1991, July 17 **Litho.** ***Perf. 14x14½***

642	A117	20c Snot-apple	.50	.25
643	A117	39c Marula	.55	.30
644	A117	51c Mobola plum	.60	.70
645	A117	60c Water berry	.70	.75
646	A117	65c Northern dwaba berry	.75	.75
647	A117	77c Mahobohobo	.90	1.00
		Nos. 642-647 (6)	4.00	3.75

See Nos. 870-875.

A118

20c, Bridal Veil Falls. 39c, Conference Emblem. 51c, Chinhoyi Caves. 60c, Kariba Dam Wall. 65c, Victoria Falls. 77c, Balancing Rocks.

1991, Oct. 16 **Litho.** ***Perf. 14½***

648	A118	20c multi	.75	.60
649	A118	39c multi	.80	.60
650	A118	51c multi	.90	.80
651	A118	60c multi	1.10	1.10
652	A118	65c multi	1.20	1.20
653	A118	77c multi	1.50	1.30
		Nos. 648-653 (6)	6.25	5.60

Commonwealth Heads of Government meeting, Harare.

Wild Cats — A119

1992, Jan. 8 **Litho.** ***Perf. 14½***

654	A119	20c Lion	1.00	.25
655	A119	39c Leopard	1.50	.50
656	A119	60c Cheetah	2.25	1.75
657	A119	77c Serval	2.50	2.00
		Nos. 654-657 (4)	7.25	4.50

Mushrooms — A120

Designs: 20c, Amanita zambiana. 39c, Boletus edulis. 51c, Termitomyces. 60c, Cantharellus densifolius. 65c, Cantharellus longisporus. 77c, Cantharellus cibarius.

1992, Apr. 8 **Litho.** ***Perf. 14x14½***

658	A120	20c multicolored	.50	.25
659	A120	39c multicolored	.75	.50
660	A120	51c multicolored	.90	.90
661	A120	60c multicolored	1.00	1.00
662	A120	65c multicolored	1.10	1.50
663	A120	77c multicolored	1.25	1.50
		Nos. 658-663 (6)	5.50	5.25

Birds — A121

25c, Blackeyed bulbul. 59c, Fiscal shrike. 77c, Forktailed drongo. 90c, Cardinal woodpecker. 98c, Yellowbilled hornbill. $1.16, Crested francolin.

1992, July 17 **Litho.** ***Perf. 14½***

664	A121	25c multi	.80	.25
665	A121	59c multi	1.10	.45
666	A121	77c multi	1.25	.80
667	A121	90c multi	1.40	.95

668	A121	98c	multi	1.40	.95
669	A121	$1.16	multi	1.50	1.40
			Nos. 664-669 (6)	7.45	4.80

Butterflies — A122

25c, Foxy charaxes. 59c, Orange & lemon. 77c, Emperor swallowtail. 90c, Blue pansy. 98c, African monarch. $1.16, Gaudy commodore.

1992, Oct. 15 Litho. *Perf. 14½x14*

670	A122	25c	multicolored	.90	.25
671	A122	59c	multicolored	1.50	.50
672	A122	77c	multicolored	1.60	1.00
673	A122	90c	multicolored	2.25	1.50
674	A122	98c	multicolored	2.25	1.60
675	A122	$1.16	multicolored	2.50	2.00
			Nos. 670-675 (6)	11.00	6.85

Minerals — A123

1993, Jan. 12 Litho. *Perf. 14½x14*

676	A123	25c	Autunite	1.25	.25
677	A123	59c	Chromite	1.50	.55
678	A123	77c	Azurite	1.75	1.00
679	A123	90c	Coal	2.50	1.50
680	A123	98c	Gold	2.50	1.75
681	A123	$1.16	Emerald	3.00	2.25
			Nos. 676-681 (6)	12.50	7.30

Owls — A124

25c, Wood owl. 59c, Pels fishing owl. 90c, Spotted eagle owl. $1.16, Giant eagle owl.

1993, Apr. 6 Litho. *Perf. 14½*

682	A124	25c	multicolored	2.00	1.00
683	A124	59c	multicolored	2.50	1.50
684	A124	90c	multicolored	4.00	4.50
685	A124	$1.16	multicolored	5.00	6.00
			Nos. 682-685 (4)	13.50	13.00

Household Pottery — A125

1993, July 13 Litho. *Perf. 14½x14*

686	A125	25c	Hadyana	.60	.30
687	A125	59c	Chirongo	.80	.40
688	A125	77c	Mbiya	.90	.80
689	A125	90c	Pfuko	1.00	1.00
690	A125	98c	Tsaya	1.00	1.00
691	A125	$1.16	Gate	1.20	1.20
			Nos. 686-691 (6)	5.50	4.70

Orchids — A126

35c, Polystachya dendrobiflora. $1, Diaphananthe subsimplex. $1.50, Ansellia gigantea. $1.95, Vanilla polyepis.

1993, Oct. 12 Litho. *Perf. 14½*

692	A126	35c	multicolored	.75	.60
693	A126	$1	multicolored	1.75	1.25
694	A126	$1.50	multicolored	2.50	2.50
695	A126	$1.95	multicolored	3.00	3.00
			Nos. 692-695 (4)	8.00	7.35

Fish Type of 1989

1994, Jan. 20 Litho. *Perf. 14½*

696	A107	35c	Hunyani salmon	.45	.25
697	A107	$1	Barbel	.75	.25
698	A107	$1.30	Rainbow trout	.85	.60
699	A107	$1.50	Mottled eel	.90	.65
700	A107	$1.65	Mirror carp	1.00	.80
701	A107	$1.95	Robustus bream	1.05	1.00
			Nos. 696-701 (6)	5.00	3.55

City of Bulawayo, Cent. — A127

1994, Apr. 5 Litho. *Perf. 14½*

702	A127	35c	City Hall	.25	.25
703	A127	80c	Cresta Churchill Hotel	.40	.25
704	A127	$1.15	High Court	.50	.45
705	A127	$1.75	Douslin House	.60	.75
706	A127	$1.95	Goldfields Building	.75	1.00
707	A127	$2.30	Parkade Centre	1.00	1.25
			Nos. 702-707 (6)	3.50	3.95

Export Flowers — A128

1994, July 12 Litho. *Perf. 14½*

708	A128	35c	Strelitzia	.45	.25
709	A128	80c	Protea	.70	.25
710	A128	$1.15	Phlox	.85	.60
711	A128	$1.75	Chrysanthemum	1.00	1.40
712	A128	$1.95	Lillum	1.25	2.25
713	A128	$2.30	Rose	1.50	2.75
			Nos. 708-713 (6)	5.75	7.50

Christmas — A129

Designs: 35c, Archangel Gabriel, Virgin Mary. 80c, Mary, Joseph on way to Bethlehem. $1.15, Nativity scene. $1.75, Angel pointing way to shepherds. $1.95, Magi following star. $2.30, Madonna and child.

1994, Oct. 11 Litho. *Perf. 14½*

714	A129	35c	multicolored	.30	.30
715	A129	80c	multicolored	.40	.30
716	A129	$1.15	multicolored	.60	.50
717	A129	$1.75	multicolored	1.00	.80
718	A129	$1.95	multicolored	1.20	1.00
719	A129	$2.30	multicolored	1.50	1.20
			Nos. 714-719 (6)	5.00	4.10

A130

1c, Corn. 2c, Sugar cane. 3c, Sunflowers. 4c, Sorghum. 5c, Mine workers. 10c, Underground mining. 20c, Coal mining. 30c, Chrome smelting. 40c, Opencast mining. 45c, Underground drilling. 50c, Gold smelting. 70c, Boggie Clock Tower. 80c, Masvingo Watchtower. $1, Hanging tree. $2, Cecil House. $5, The Toposcope. $10, Paper House.

1995-96 Litho. *Perf. 14*

720	A130	1c	multicolored	.25	.50
721	A130	2c	multicolored	.25	.50
722	A130	3c	multicolored	.25	.50
723	A130	4c	multicolored	.25	.50
724	A130	5c	multicolored	.50	.50
725	A130	10c	multicolored	.75	.50
726	A130	20c	multicolored	1.25	.50
727	A130	30c	multicolored	1.50	.50
728	A130	40c	multicolored	1.75	.50
728A	A130	45c	multicolored	1.75	.40
729	A130	50c	multicolored	1.75	.40
730	A130	70c	multicolored	.30	.30
731	A130	80c	multicolored	.30	.30
732	A130	$1	multicolored	.40	.30
733	A130	$2	multicolored	.50	.50
734	A130	$5	multicolored	.50	1.50
735	A130	$10	multicolored	1.75	1.75
			Nos. 720-735 (17)	14.00	9.95

Issued: 45c, 6/3/96; others, 1/17/95.

Insects — A131

35c, Spider-hunting wasp. $1.15, Emperor dragonfly. $1.75, Foxy charaxes. $2.30, Antlion.

1995, Apr. 4 Litho. *Perf. 14½*

736	A131	35c	multicolored	.60	.25
737	A131	$1.15	multicolored	1.15	.55
738	A131	$1.75	multicolored	1.50	2.00
739	A131	$2.30	multicolored	2.00	2.75
			Nos. 736-739 (4)	5.25	5.55

6th All Africa Games, Harare — A132

1995, July 11 Litho. *Perf. 14x14½*

740	A132	35c	Soccer	.40	.25
741	A132	80c	Track	.50	.25
742	A132	$1.15	Boxing	.55	.30
743	A132	$1.75	Swimming	.80	1.00
744	A132	$1.95	Field hockey	2.00	1.75
745	A132	$2.30	Volleyball	1.75	2.00
			Nos. 740-745 (6)	6.00	5.55

UN, 50th Anniv. — A133

1995, Oct. 17 Litho. *Perf. 14½*

746	A133	35c	Health	.25	.25
747	A133	$1.15	Environment	.50	.50
748	A133	$1.75	Food distribution	.60	.60
749	A133	$2.30	Education	.85	.85
			Nos. 746-749 (4)	2.20	2.20

Flowering Trees — A134

1996, Jan. 24 Litho. *Perf. 14½*

750	A134	45c	Fernandoa	.30	.25
751	A134	$1	Round leaf mukwa	.50	.25
752	A134	$1.50	Luckybean tree	.70	.60
753	A134	$2.20	Winter cassia	.85	1.00
754	A134	$2.50	Sausage tree	.90	1.40
755	A134	$3	Sweet thorn	1.00	1.75
			Nos. 750-755 (6)	4.25	5.25

Dams of Zimbabwe A135

1996, Apr. 9 Litho. *Perf. 14½*

756	A135	45c	Mazvikadei	.25	.25
757	A135	$1.50	Mutirikwi	.50	.50
758	A135	$2.20	Ncema	.75	1.00
759	A135	$3	Odzani	1.00	1.50
			Nos. 756-759 (4)	2.50	3.25

Scenic Views — A136

Designs: 45c, Matusadonha Natl. Park. $1.50, Juliasdale Rocky Outcrops. $2.20, Honde Valley. $3, Finger Rocks, Morgenster Mission.

1996, July 18 Litho. *Perf. 14½*

760	A136	45c	multicolored	.25	.25
761	A136	$1.50	multicolored	.50	.50
762	A136	$2.20	multicolored	.75	1.00
763	A136	$3	multicolored	1.00	1.50
			Nos. 760-763 (4)	2.50	3.25

Wood Carvings — A137

1996, Oct. 15 Litho. *Perf. 14½*

764	A137	45c	Frog	.25	.25
765	A137	$1.50	Tortoise	.40	.25
766	A137	$1.70	Kudu	.50	.50
767	A137	$2.20	Chimpanzee	.65	.90
768	A137	$2.50	Porcupine	.70	1.00
769	A137	$3	Rhinoceros	.75	1.25
			Nos. 764-769 (6)	3.25	4.15

Cattle — A138

1997, Jan. 7 Litho. *Perf. 14½*

770	A138	45c	Mashona cow	.30	.25
771	A138	$1.50	Tuli cow	.75	.25
772	A138	$2.20	Nkoni bull	.95	1.00
773	A138	$3	Brahman bull	1.25	1.75
			Nos. 770-773 (4)	3.25	3.25

Convention on Intl. Trade in Endangered Species of Flora and Fauna (CITES) — A139

1997, Apr. 15 Litho. *Perf. 14½*

774	A139	45c	Cycad	.25	.25
775	A139	$1.50	Peregrine falcon	1.00	.75
776	A139	$1.70	Pangolin	.25	.50
777	A139	$2.20	Black rhinoceros	1.00	1.00
778	A139	$2.50	Elephant	1.00	1.00
779	A139	$3	Python	.75	2.00
			Nos. 774-779 (6)	4.25	5.50

Aspects of Rural Life — A140

1997, July 22 Litho. *Perf. 14½*

780	A140	65c	Carving	.25	.25
781	A140	$1	Winnowing	.25	.25
782	A140	$2.40	Dancing	.50	.60
783	A140	$2.50	Plowing	.50	.70
784	A140	$3.10	Stamping	.60	.90
785	A140	$4.20	Fetching water	.90	1.30
			Nos. 780-785 (6)	3.00	4.00

Zimbabwe Railway, Cent. — A141

65c, Passenger coach. $1, 12th Class, No. 257. $2.40, 16A Class, No. 605. $2.50, El 1, No. 4107. $3.10, Jack Tar. $4.20, DE 2, No. 1211.

1997, Oct. 28 Litho. *Perf. 14½*

786	A141	65c	multicolored	.35	.35
787	A141	$1	multicolored	.35	.35
788	A141	$2.40	multicolored	.50	.70
789	A141	$2.50	multicolored	.50	.70
790	A141	$3.10	multicolored	.60	1.00
791	A141	$4.20	multicolored	.80	1.25
			Nos. 786-791 (6)	3.10	4.35

Wildlife — A142

65c, Aardwolf. $2.40, Large gray mongoose. $3.10, Clawless otter. $4.20, Antbear (Aardvark).

1998, Jan. 20 Litho. *Perf. 14½*

792	A142	65c	multicolored	.40	.25
793	A142	$2.40	multicolored	.50	.60
794	A142	$3.10	multicolored	.60	1.00
795	A142	$4.20	multicolored	.75	1.50
			Nos. 792-795 (4)	2.25	3.35

Apiculture — A143

Designs: $1.20, Honeybee on flower. $4.10, Queen, worker, drone. $4.70, Queen, retinue. $5.60, Rural beekeeper. $7.40, Commercial beekeepers. $9.90, Products of the hive.

1998, Apr. 14 **Litho.** ***Perf. 14***

796 A143 $1.20 multicolored .35 .25
797 A143 $4.10 multicolored .50 .50
798 A143 $4.70 multicolored .50 .50
799 A143 $5.60 multicolored .65 .75
800 A143 $7.40 multicolored .90 1.00
801 A143 $9.90 multicolored 1.10 1.25
Nos. 796-801 (6) 4.00 4.25

Fossils — A144

1998, July 21 **Litho.** ***Perf. 14½***

802 A144 $1.20 Fossil fish .80 .25
803 A144 $5.60 Allosaurus footprints 1.10 .70
804 A144 $7.40 Massospondylus 1.50 1.25
805 A144 $9.90 Fossil wood 1.75 1.75
Nos. 802-805 (4) 5.15 3.95

Birds — A145

Designs: $1.20, Yellow-bellied sunbird. $4.10, Lesser blue-eared starling. $4.70, Greyhooded kingfisher. $5.60, Mombo gray tit. $7.40, Chirinda apalis. $9.90, Swynnerton's robin.

1998, Oct. 20 **Litho.** ***Perf. 14***

806 A145 $1.20 multicolored .50 .25
807 A145 $4.10 multicolored .75 .40
808 A145 $4.70 multicolored .75 .50
809 A145 $5.60 multicolored 1.00 1.00
810 A145 $7.40 multicolored 1.00 1.25
811 A145 $9.90 multicolored 1.25 1.50
Nos. 806-811 (6) 5.25 4.90

UPU, 125th Anniv. — A146

$1.20, Counter services at Post Office and Philatelic Bureau. $5.60, Postman delivering mail on bicycle. $7.40, 19th cent. runner, EMS, PTC delivery today. $9.90, Harare Central Sorting Office.

1999, Jan. 19 **Litho.** ***Perf. 14***

812 A146 $1.20 multicolored .25 .25
813 A146 $5.60 multicolored .50 .25
814 A146 $7.40 multicolored 1.25 .70
815 A146 $9.90 multicolored .50 .75
Nos. 812-815 (4) 2.50 1.95

A147

Wild cats of Zimbabwe.

1999, Mar. 16 **Litho.** ***Perf. 14***

816 A147 $1.20 Serval .40 .25
817 A147 $5.60 Cheetah .65 .45
818 A147 $7.40 Caracal .95 1.05
819 A147 $9.90 Leopard 1.25 1.50
Nos. 816-819 (4) 3.25 3.25

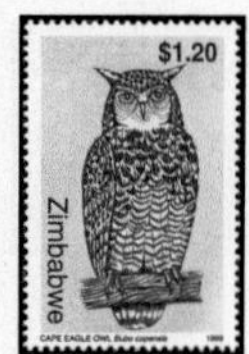

A148

Owls.

1999, June 8 **Litho.** ***Perf. 14¼***

820 A148 $1.20 Cape eagle owl .50 .30
821 A148 $5.60 Grass owl 1.00 .60
822 A148 $7.40 Barn owl 1.00 1.00
823 A148 $9.90 Marsh owl 1.50 1.50
Nos. 820-823 (4) 4.00 3.40

Tourist Activities — A149

1999, Aug. 10 **Litho.** ***Perf. 14¼x14***

824 A149 $2 Canoeing .25 .25
825 A149 $6.70 Rock climbing .60 .50
826 A149 $7.70 Microlighting .65 .60
827 A149 $9.10 White water rafting .80 .80
828 A149 $12 Scenic view 1.00 1.25
829 A149 $16 Viewing game 1.25 2.00
Nos. 824-829 (6) 4.55 5.40

A150

Christmas: $2, Christmas time — Family time. $6.70, Christmas tree in Africa. $7.70, Joy to you this Christmas. $9.10, Christmas time — Flame lily time. $12, Glory to God & Peace on Earth. $16, The House of Christmas.

1999, Oct. 12 **Litho.** ***Perf. 14x14¼***

830 A150 $2 multi .25 .25
831 A150 $6.70 multi .35 .30
832 A150 $7.70 multi .35 .30
833 A150 $9.10 multi .50 .45
834 A150 $12 multi .75 1.00
835 A150 $16 multi 1.00 1.30
Nos. 830-835 (6) 3.20 3.60

A151

Designs: 1c, Nyala. 10c, Construction. 30c, Timber. 50c, Tobacco auction floors. 70c, Harare Central Sorting Office. 80c, New international airport, Harare. $1, Westgate Shopping Complex. $2, Nile crocodile. $3, Pungwe water project. $4, Zebra. $5, Mining. $7, National University of Science and Technology. $10, Ostrich. $15, Cape parrot. $20, Leather products. $30, Lilac-breasted roller. $50, Victoria Falls. $100, Tokwe Mukorsi Dam.

2000, Jan. 25 **Litho.** ***Perf. 14¾***

836 A151 1c multi .25 .25
837 A151 10c multi .25 .25
838 A151 30c multi .25 .25
839 A151 50c multi .25 .25
840 A151 70c multi .25 .40
841 A151 80c multi .70 .50
842 A151 $1 multi .25 .30
843 A151 $2 multi .70 .30
844 A151 $3 multi .25 .25
845 A151 $4 multi 1.00 .25
846 A151 $5 multi 1.10 .30
847 A151 $7 multi .25 .40
848 A151 $10 multi 1.50 .65
849 A151 $15 multi 1.50 1.10
850 A151 $20 multi .60 .80
851 A151 $30 multi 2.50 1.25
852 A151 $50 multi 1.60 1.60
853 A151 $100 multi 2.25 3.00
Nos. 836-853 (18) 15.45 12.10

Sports — A152

2000, Apr. 25 **Litho.** ***Perf. 14***

854 A152 $2 Basketball .25 .25
855 A152 $6.70 Lawn tennis .50 .45
856 A152 $7.70 Netball .50 .50
857 A152 $9.10 Weight lifting .50 .60
858 A152 $12 Taekwondo .75 .80
859 A152 $16 Diving 1.00 1.00
Nos. 854-859 (6) 3.50 3.60

Dr. Joshua Nkomo (1917-99), Vice-President — A153

Designs: $2, $12, Wearing suit. $9.10, $16, Wearing headdress.

2000, June 27 **Litho.** ***Perf. 14x14¼***

Background Color

860 A153 $2 blue .25 .25
861 A153 $9.10 green .80 1.00
862 A153 $12 red 1.10 1.25
863 A153 $16 orange 1.25 1.75
Nos. 860-863 (4) 3.40 4.25

Organizations Combatting Disease — A154

Designs: $2, Ministry of Health. $6.70, Rehabilitation and Prevention of Tuberculosis (RAPT). $7.70, New Start centers. $9.10, Riders for Health. $12, Natl. Aids Coordination Program (NACP). $16, Rotary Intl.

2000, July 18 **Litho.** ***Perf. 14¼x14***

864 A154 $2 multi .30 .30
865 A154 $6.70 multi .50 .50
866 A154 $7.70 multi .50 .50
867 A154 $9.10 multi .60 .60
868 A154 $12 multi .75 .75
869 A154 $16 multi 1.10 1.00
Nos. 864-869 (6) 3.75 3.65

Wild Fruits Type of 1991

$2, Masawu. $6.70, Spiny monkey orange. $7.70, Bird plum. $9.10, Shakama plum. $12, Wild medlar. $16, Wild custard apple.

2000, Oct. 24 **Litho.** ***Perf. 14x14½***

870-875 A117 Set of 6 3.50 3.50

Aviation — A155

Designs: $8, Boeing 737-200. $12, BAe Hawk MK 60. $14, Hawker Hunter FGA-9. $16, Cessna/Reims F-337. $21, Aerospatiale Alouette III helicopter. $28, Boeing 767-200ER.

2001, Jan. 31 **Litho.** ***Perf. 14¼***

876-881 A155 Set of 6 5.50 5.50

Total Solar Eclipse, June 21, 2001 — A156

Designs: $8, Solar prominences. $21, Eclipse path over Africa. $28, Eclipse phases (62x24mm).

Perf. 14¼x14, 14½ ($28)

2001, Apr. 24 **Litho.**

882-884 A156 Set of 3 3.00 3.00

Folklore — A157

Designs: $8, The Hare Who Rode Horseback. $12, The Hippo Who Lost His Hair. $13, The Lion Who Was Saved by a Mouse. $16, The Bush Fowl Who Wakes the Sun. $21, The Chameleon Who Came Too Late. $28, The Tortoise Who Collected Wisdom.

2001, July 24 **Litho.** ***Perf. 14x14¼***

885-890 A157 Set of 6 4.50 4.50
a. Souvenir sheet, #885-890 6.00 6.00

Heroes' Acre — A158

Designs: $8, Main entrance gate. $16, Statue of the Unknown Soldier. $21, General view. $28, Aerial view.

2001, Aug. 7 **Litho.** ***Perf. 14¼x14***

891-894 A158 Set of 4 3.00 3.00

Year of Dialogue Among Civilizations — A159

Winning stamp design entry in: $8, National competition (Three Faces, by Nation Mandla Mguni). $21, International competition.

2001, Oct. 16 **Litho.** ***Perf. 14¼***

895-896 A159 Set of 2 2.50 2.50

Butterflies — A160

Designs: $12, Large blue charaxes. $20, Painted lady. $25, Yellow pansy. $30, Gold-banded forester. $35, Sapphire. $45, Clear-spotted acrea.

2001, Dec. 6 **Litho.** ***Perf. 14¼x14***

897-902 A160 Set of 6 7.50 7.50
902a Souvenir sheet, #897-902 7.50 7.50

Craftsmanship A161

Designs: $12, Knitting and crocheting. $20, Art and design. $25, Basket making. $30, Pottery. $35, Wood carving. $45, Sculpture.

2002, Jan. 22

903-908 A161 Set of 6 7.00 7.00

Gemstones — A162

Designs: $12, Agate. $25, Aquamarine. $35, Diamond. $45, Emerald.

2002, Apr. 23 **Litho.** ***Perf. 14¼x14***

909-912 A162 Set of 4 7.50 7.50

Childline — A163

Children's art: $12, Children embracing. $25, Girl on phone. $35, Teddy bear. $45, Arm with phone receiver.

2002, June 4 Litho. *Perf. 14¼x14*
913-916 A163 Set of 4 6.00 6.00

First Lady Sally Mugabe (1931-92) — A164

Various portraits: $20, $50, $70, $90.

2002, Aug. 6 *Perf. 14x14¼*
917-920 A164 Set of 4 7.00 7.00

Children's Stamp Design Contest Winners — A165

Designs: $20, Mail runner and bicycle at post office, by Agreement Ngwenya. $70, Mail runner and airplane, by Kudzai Chikomo.

2002, Oct. 8 Litho. *Perf. 14¼*
921-922 A165 Set of 2 4.50 4.50

Wild Flowers — A166

Designs: $20, Dissotis princeps. $35, Leonotis nepetifolia. $40, Hibiscus vitifolius. $50, Boophane disticha. $70, Pycnostachys urticifolia. $90, Gloriosa superba.

2002, Oct. 22 *Perf. 14¼x14*
923-928 A166 Set of 6 11.00 11.00
928a Souvenir sheet, #923-928 12.00 12.00

History Society of Zimbabwe, 50th Anniv. — A167

Map of Zimbabwe and: $30, Society emblem. $80, Hourglass, books, diploma. $110, People listening to speaker. $140, Old building.

2003, Jan. 28 Litho. *Perf. 14x14¼*
929-932 A167 Set of 4 5.50 5.50

Harare Intl. Festival of the Arts — A168

Designs: $30, Festival emblem. $80, Emblem and flower. $110, Eye and flowers. $140, Emblem and flowers.

2003, Apr. 22 Litho. *Perf. 14x14¼*
933-936 A168 Set of 4 4.25 4.25

Type of 2000

Designs: ($100), Bateleur eagle. $500, Goliath heron. $1000, White rhinoceros. $5000, Cheetah.

2003, June 24 Litho. *Perf. 14¾*

937	A151	($100) multi	1.00	1.00
938	A151	$500 multi	1.00	1.00
939	A151	$1000 multi	2.00	2.00
940	A151	$5000 multi	5.00	5.00
		Nos. 937-940 (4)	9.00	9.00

No. 937 is inscribed "Standard Postage."

Spiders — A169

Designs: $150, Baboon spider. $200, Rain spider. $600, Black widow spider. $900, Wolf spider. $1250, Violin spider. $1600, Wall spider.

2003, July 30 *Perf. 14¼*
941-946 A169 Set of 6 8.50 8.50
946a Souvenir sheet, #941-946 8.50 8.50

Women Empowerment — A170

Woman in cap and gown with: $300, Globe, hoe and briefcase. $2100, Traditional woman.

2003, Oct. 14 Litho. *Perf. 14¼*
947-948 A170 Set of 2 4.00 4.00

Endangered Medicinal Herbs — A171

Designs: $200, Wild verbena. $500, Pimpernel. $1000, African arrowroot. $3000, Bird pepper. $4200, Wild garlic. $5400, Cleome.

2003, Oct. 28 *Perf. 14x14¼*
949-954 A171 Set of 6 *14.00 14.00*
a. Miniature sheet, #949-954 *17.00 17.00*

Environmental Awareness — A172

Designs: $500, Environment Africa. $3000, Sondela. $4200, Water Africa. $5400, Tree Africa.

2004, Feb. 17 Litho. *Perf. 14x14¼*
955-958 A172 Set of 4 *14.00 14.00*

Medals — A173

Designs: $1500, Zimbabwe Independence Medal. $9000, Bronze Cross of Zimbabwe. $13,000, Silver Cross of Zimbabwe. $16,500, Gold Cross of Zimbabwe.

2004, Apr. 6 Litho. *Perf. 14¼*
959-962 A173 Set of 4 *40.00 40.00*

Aloes — A174

Designs: $1500, Aloe ballii. $3,000, Aloe rhodesiana. $9000, Aloe greatheadii. $10,000, Aloe ortholopha. $13,000, Aloe inyangensis. $16,500, Aloe arborescens.

2004, July 20 Litho. *Perf. 14x14¼*
963-968 A174 Set of 6 *15.00 15.00*
968a Miniature sheet, #963-968 *17.00 17.00*

Co-Vice President Simon Vengai Muzenda (1922-2003) — A175

Background colors: $2300, Red. $12,000, Yellow. $17,000, Green. $22,000, Gray.

2004, Sept. 20 Litho. *Perf. 14x14¼*
969-972 A175 Set of 4 *15.00 15.00*

Conservation A176

Winning art in conservation stamp design contest: $4600, Butterfly, by Kingston Chigidhani. $33,500, Hands and wildlife, by Kudzai Chikomo.

2004, Oct. 26 Litho. *Perf. 14¼x14*
973-974 A176 Set of 2 *7.00 7.00*

Miniature Sheet

Birds A177

No. 975: a, $500, African fish eagles, national bird of Zambia. b, $1000, Purple-crested louries, national bird of Swaziland. c, $2300, African fish eagles, national bird of Zimbabwe. d, $3000, Blue cranes, national bird of South Africa. e, $5000, Cattle egrets, national bird of Botswana. f, $9000, Peregrine falcons, national bird of Angola. g, $12,000, Bar-tailed trogons. h, $17,000, African fish eagles, national bird of Namibia.

2004, Oct. 11 Litho. *Perf. 14*
975 A177 Sheet of 8, #a-h *45.00 45.00*

See Botswana Nos. 792-793, Namibia No. 1052, South Africa No. 1342, Swaziland Nos. 727-735, and Zambia No. 1033.

Birds — A178

Designs: $500, Black-collared barbet. $5000, Gray-headed bush shrike. Z, Red-headed weaver. $10,000, Golden-breasted bunting. $20,000, Cut-throat finch. A, Cabanis's bunting. E, Miombo double-collared sunbird. R, Crested barbet. $50,000, Heuglin's robin. $100,000, Giant kingfisher.

2005, Feb. 8 Litho. *Perf. 14¾x14½*

976	A178	$500 multi	*1.00*	*1.00*
977	A178	$5000 multi	*2.00*	*2.00*
978	A178	Z multi	*2.50*	*2.50*
979	A178	$10,000 multi	*3.00*	*3.00*
980	A178	$20,000 multi	*5.50*	*5.50*
981	A178	A multi	*8.00*	*8.00*
982	A178	E multi	*11.00*	*11.00*
983	A178	R multi	*13.00*	*13.00*
984	A178	$50,000 multi	*13.00*	*13.00*
985	A178	$100,000 multi	*26.00*	*26.00*
		Nos. 976-985 (10)	*85.00*	*85.00*

On day of issue No. 978 sold for $6900, No. 981 sold for $30,000, No. 982 sold for $40,000, and No. 983 sold for $50,000.

Clouds — A179

Designs: $6900, Cirrus. $13,800, Nimbostratus. $30,000, Altocumulus. $40,000, Cumulonimbus.

2005, Apr. 26 *Perf. 14¼*
986-989 A179 Set of 4 *22.50 22.50*

Snakes — A180

Designs: $6900, Banded Egyptian cobra. $13,800, Puff adder. $20,000, Boomslang. $25,000, Mozambique spitting cobra. $30,000, Gaboon viper. $40,000, Black mamba.

2005, July 12 Litho. *Perf. 14¼x14*
990-995 A180 Set of 6 *18.00 18.00*
995a Miniature sheet, #990-995 *25.00 25.00*

Governmental Officials — A181

Designs: $6900, Josiah Tongogara (1940-79), Chief of Defense. $13,800, Herbert Chitepo (1923-75), Director of Public Prosecutions. $30,000, Bernard Chidzero (1927-2002), Minister of Economic Planning. $50,000, Moven Mahachi (1948-2001), Minister of various departments.

2005, Aug. 4 Litho. *Perf. 14x14¼*
996-999 A181 Set of 4 *10.00 10.00*

UNESCO World Heritage Sites — A182

Designs: Z, Soapstone Zimbabwe bird, Great Zimbabwe National Park. $15,500, Wall, Khami Ruins. $52,000, Elephant, Mana Pools National Park. $62,000, Victoria Falls.

2005, Oct. 6 Litho. *Perf. 14¼*
1000-1003 A182 Set of 4 *20.00 20.00*
1003a Souvenir sheet, #1000-1003 *25.00 25.00*

No. 1000 sold for $10,250 on day of issue.

World AIDS Day — A183

Designs: $18,000, Cooking pot, field tender, care for the ill. $80,000, Children teaching AIDS prevention.

2005, Dec. 1 Litho. *Perf. 14¼x14*
1004-1005 A183 Set of 2 *8.75 8.75*

Food — A184

Designs: $25,000, Mushrooms. $35,000, Rapoko, corn and sorghum. $50,000, Pumpkin, watermelon, spiny cucumber. $150,000, Wild fruits. $250,000, Herbs. $300,000, Sweet potato, cassava, peanuts.

2006, Jan. 17 Litho. *Perf. 14x14¼*
1006-1011 A184 Set of 6 *10.00 10.00*
1011a Miniature sheet, #1006-1011 *14.00 14.00*

Pope John Paul II (1920-2005) — A185

Pope: $25,000, Wearing crucifix. $250,000, Holding crucifix.

2006, Feb. 9
1012-1013 A185 Set of 2 10.00 10.00
1013a Souvenir sheet, #1012-1013 12.00 12.00

Water Conservation — A186

Designs: $30,000, Faucet and pail. $225,000, Flood irrigation system. $375,000, Lions at waterhole. $450,000, Kariba Dam.

2006, Apr. 25 Litho. *Perf. 14x14¼*
1014-1017 A186 Set of 4 *18.50 18.50*

National Heroes — A187

Flag and: $60,000, Leopold T. Takawira (1916-70), first vice-president of Zimbabwe African National Union. $350,000, Simon C. Mazorodze (1933-81), health minister. $500,000, Herbert M. Ushewokunze (1933-95), government minister. $650,000, Tichafa S. Parirenyatwa (1927-62), deputy president of Zimbabwe African People's Union.

2006, July 25 Litho. *Perf. 14x14¼*
1018-1021 A187 Set of 4 *15.00 15.00*

Huts — A188

Designs: $100, One hut. $800, Three huts.

2006, Oct. 24 Litho. *Perf. 14¼x14*
1022-1023 A188 Set of 2 12.00 12.00
1023a Souvenir sheet, #1022-1023 *10.00 10.00*

Bridges — A189

Designs: Z, Mpudzi River Bridge. $450, Victoria Falls Bridge. $600, Limpopo River Bridge. $750, Otto Beit Bridge. $800, Kariba Barrage Bridge. $1000, Birchenough Bridge.

2006, Oct. 24
1024-1029 A189 Set of 6 *25.00 25.00*
1029a Souvenir sheet, #1024-1029 *30.00 30.00*

No. 1024 sold for $100 on day of issue.

Trees — A190

Designs: $150, Ziziphuus mauritania. $600, Schlerochra birrea. $750, Jatropha carcus. $1000, Uaparca kirkiana.

2006, Dec. 1 Litho. *Perf. 14x14¼*
1030-1033 A190 Set of 4 *18.00 18.00*
1033a Souvenir sheet, #1030-1033 *18.00 18.00*

Birds — A191

Designs: $50, Hoopoe. $100, Cattle egret. $500, Malachite kingfisher. $1000, Little bee-eater. $2000, Purple-crested lorie. $5000, Purple gallinule. $10,000, African jacana. $20,000, Ground hornbill. $50,000, Gorgeous bush shrike. $100,000, Secretary bird.

Perf. 14¾x14½
2007, Feb. 20 Litho.

1034	A191	$50 multi	*.25*	*.25*
1035	A191	$100 multi	*.25*	*.25*
1036	A191	$500 multi	*.25*	*.25*
1037	A191	$1000 multi	*.35*	*.35*
1038	A191	$2000 multi	*.65*	*.65*
1039	A191	$5000 multi	*1.75*	*1.75*
1040	A191	$10,000 multi	*3.25*	*3.25*
1041	A191	$20,000 multi	*6.50*	*6.50*
1042	A191	$50,000 multi	*12.00*	*12.00*
1043	A191	$100,000 multi	*25.00*	*25.00*
a.		Souvenir sheet, #1034-1043	*65.00*	*65.00*
		Nos. 1034-1043 (10)	*50.25*	*50.25*

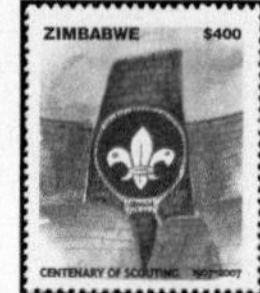

Scouting, Cent. — A192

Scouting emblem and: $400, Great Zimbabwe Ruins. $1500, Map of Zimbabwe. $2000, Centenary emblem. $2500, Map of Africa.

2007, Feb. 20 *Perf. 14x14¼*
1044-1047 A192 Set of 4 *15.00 15.00*

Women — A193

Designs: $7500, Mbuya Nehanda (?-1898), colonial resistance organizer. $29,000, Queen Lozikeyi (c. 1855-1919). $35,000, Mother Patrick (1863-1900), educator. $45,000, Amai Sally Mugabe (1932-92), First Lady.

2007, July 10 *Perf. 14¼*
1048-1051 A193 Set of 4 *9.00 9.00*

Beginning in 2007, Zimbabwean currency began to experience extreme hyperinflation. Starting with Nos. 1052-1055, most stamps are non-denominated, inscribed "Z" for surface-rate letters sent within Zimbabwe, "A" for letters sent to the rest of Africa by air, "E" for letters sent to Europe by air, and "R" for letters sent to the rest of the world by air, with letters being up to 20 grams in weight. Press release information about these stamps probably was printed in advance of their issuance, so it is unknown if the stamps were actually sold to local customers for the rates implied by the release on the stated day of issue at post offices in Zimbabwe. As the Zimbabwean dollar and denominated stamps daily became more and more worthless (with a reissuance of new Zimbabwe dollars eliminating 10 zeroes on Aug. 1, 2008, and yet again eliminating 12 zeroes on Feb. 2, 2009), the editors cannot easily determine selling prices for these stamps.

National Heroes — A194

Designs: Z, Jason Ziyaphapha Moyo (1927-77), second vice-president of Zimbabwe African People's Union. A, Maurice T. Nyagumbo (1924-89), Zimbabwe African National Union senior minister of political affairs. E, Guy Clutton-Brock (1906-95), founder of Cold Comfort Farm Society. R, Chief Rekayi Tangwena (c. 1910-84), senator.

2007, Aug. 9 Litho. *Perf. 14x14¼*
1052-1055 A194 Set of 4 *15.00* —

On day of issue, Nos. 1052-1055 reportedly sold for $3,000, $12,000, $17,000, and $20,000, respectively.

Butterflies — A195

Designs: Z, Mother-of-pearl. A, Citrus swallowtail. E, Orange tip. R, Blue charaxes. $50,000, Crimson tip. $100,000, Painted lady.

2007, Sept. 18
1056-1061 A195 Set of 6 *20.00* —
a. Souvenir sheet, #1056-1061 *25.00* —

On day of issue, Nos. 1056-1059 reportedly sold for $7,500, $29,000, $35,000, and $45,000, respectively.

Life of Children — A196

Winning art in stamp design contest: Z, Boy studying, by John Ndhlovu. $100,000, Mother feeding baby, by Fungai Madzima.

2007, Oct. 9
1062-1063 A196 Set of 2 *15.00* —
a. Souvenir sheet, #1062-1063 *15.00* —

On day of issue, Nos. 1062 reportedly sold for $7,500.

National Animals — A197

Designs: Z, Buffalo (Zambia). A, Nyala (Malawi). E, Burchell's zebra (Botswana). R, Oryx (Namibia). $100,000, Nyala (Zimbabwe).

Litho. With Foil Application
2007, Oct. 9 *Perf. 13¾*
1064-1068 A197 Set of 5 *13.00* —
a. Souvenir sheet, #1064-1068 *20.00* —

On day of issue, Nos. 1064-1067 reportedly sold for $7,500, $29,000, $35,000, and $45,000, respectively. See Botswana No. 838, Malawi No. 752, Namibia Nos. 1141-1142, Zambia Nos. 1097-1101.

St. Valentine's Day — A198

Designs: Z, Heart. A, Cupid. E, Card (5 hearts). R, Rose.

2008, Jan. 24 Litho. *Perf. 14x14¼*
1069-1072 A198 Set of 4 *13.00* —
a. Souvenir sheet, #1069-1072 13.00 —

On day of issue, Nos. 1069-1072 reportedly sold for $25,000, $100,000, $170,000, and $240,000, respectively.

Rodents — A199

Designs: Z, Striped mouse. A, Water rat. E, Angoni vlei rat. R, Woodland dormouse. $5,000,000, Bushveld gerbil. $10,000,000, Namaqua rock mouse.

2008, Apr. 24 *Perf. 14¼*
1073-1078 A199 Set of 6 *15.00* —
a. Souvenir sheet, #1073-1078 *20.00* —

On day of issue, Nos. 1073-1076 reportedly sold for $550,000, $1,900,000, $3,150,000, and $4,600,000, respectively.

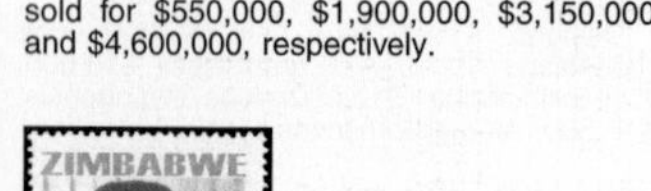

National Heroes — A200

Designs: Z, Johanna Nkomo (1927-2003), wife of Joshua Nkomo. A, Ruth Lottie Nomonde Chinamano (1925-2005), political activist. E, Dr. Swithun Tachiona Mombeshora (1945-2003), National president of Red Cross. R, Willie Dzawanda Musarurwa (1927-90), journalist.

2008, Aug. 5 *Perf. 14x14¼*
1079-1082 A200 Set of 4 *20.00* —

On day of issue, release information states that Nos. 1079-1082 were to be sold for $250,000,000, $50,000,000,000, $90,000,000,000, and $110,000,000,000, respectively, but the stamps were issued after the Aug. 1 revaluation of the currency eliminating 10 zeroes from the denominations.

In December 2008, Zimbabwe's hyperinflation was calculated by *Forbes Asia* at 6.5 times 10 to the 108th power. By the middle of January 2009, virtually all transactions in Zimbabwe were being conducted in foreign currencies, despite law that mandated that the Zimbabwe dollar be used in transactions between parties not having a government license allowing them to conduct transactions in foreign currencies. On January 29, Zimbabwe's finance minister finally made the use of foreign currencies legal for any transactions in Zimbabwe. On February 2, the government revalued the Zimbabwe dollar for the final time, and finally suspended its use on April 12. Selling prices for stamps listed below are stated in US currency, the primary foreign currency used in the country, as well as the currency used in philatelic press releases.

2008 Summer Olympics, Beijing — A201

Emblem of the Zimbabwe Olympic Committee and: Z, Water Cube. A, National Stadium (Bird's Nest). E, Olympic pool. R, Flag of Zimbabwe, medals won by Zimbabwe Olympic athletes.

2009, Jan. 20 Litho. *Perf. 14¼*
1083-1086 A201 Set of 4 *10.00 10.00*

On day of issue, Nos. 1083-1086 reportedly sold in US currency for 50c, $1, $1.50, and $2. respectively.

Paintings — A202

Designs: Zb, Cardoor Scape, bu Cosmos Shiridzinomwa. Zs, Countryside, by James Jali. No. 1089, A, Mountains, by George Churu. No. 1090, A, Barn, by Hilary Kashiri. E, Backyard 1, by Freddy Tauro. R, X in the Land, by Admire Kamudzengere.

2009, Apr. 21
1087-1092 A202 Set of 6 *10.00 10.00*
1092a Souvenir sheet of 6, #1087-1092 *11.00 11.00*

On day of issue, Nos. 1087-1092 sold in US currency for 20c, 25c, 50c, 50c, 75c and $1, respectively.

Wildlife — A203

Designs: Zb, Leopard. Zs, Black rhinonceros. No. 1095, A, African buffalo. No. 1096, A, Lion. E, African elephant. R, All five animals.

2009, June 23
1093-1098 A203 Set of 6 *14.00 14.00*
1098a Souvenir sheet of 6, #1093-1098 *15.00 15.00*

On day of issue, Nos. 1093-1098 sold in US currency for 20c, 25c, 50c, 50c, 75c and $1, respectively.

National Heroes — A204

Flag of Zimbabwe and: Zb, Vitalis Musungwa Gava Zvinavashe (1943-2009), commander of Zimbabwe Defense Forces. Zs, Garikayi Hlomayi Settled Magadzire (1937-96), leader of Zimbabwe National Farmers' Union. A, George Bodzo Nyandoro (1926-94), Minister of Lands, Natural Resources and Rural Development. E, Border "Madzibaba" Gezi (1964-2001), Minister of Youth, Gender and Employment Creation. R, Seugeant Masotsha Ndlovu (1890-1982), union leader.

2009, Aug. 4 ***Perf. 14x14¼***
1099-1103 A204 Set of 5 *12.00 12.00*

On day of issue, Nos. 1099-1103 sold in US currency for 20c, 25c, 50c, 75c and $1, respectively.

Christmas A205

Rural churches: Z, St. Barbara's Catholic Church, Kariba. A, Regina Coeli Catholic Church. E, Elim Evangelical Church, Katerere. R, Free Presbyterian Church, Mbuma.

2009, Dec. 15 ***Perf. 14¼***
1104-1107 A205 Set of 4 8.00 8.00
a. Souvenir sheet, #1104-1107 *8.50 8.50*

On day of issue, Nos. 1104-1107 sold in US currency for 25c, 50c, 75c and $1, respectively.

Zimbabwe, Africa's Paradise — A206

Winning art in stamp design contest by: Z, Fredy Tembo. A, Munashe M. Patsanza. E, Methembe Dhlamini. R, Kudzai Chikomo.

2010, Jan. 19
1108-1111 A206 Set of 4 *10.00 10.00*
1111a Souvenir sheet of 4, #1108-1111 *11.00 11.00*

On day of issue, Nos. 1108-1111 sold in US currency for 25c, 50c, 75c and $1 respectively.

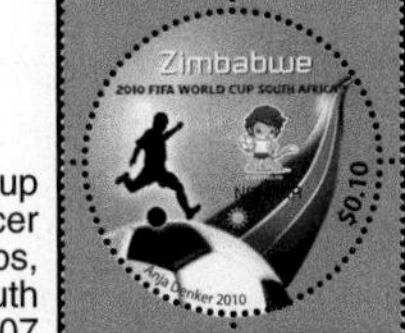

2010 World Cup Soccer Championships, South Africa — A207

Soccer players, ball, 2010 World Cup mascot and flag of: Nos. 1112, 1121a, 10c, Namibia. Nos. 1113, 1121b, 15c, South Africa. Nos. 1114, 1121c, 25c, Zimbabwe. Nos. 1115, 1121d, Z, Botswana. Nos. 1116, 1121e, 50c, Malawi. Nos. 1117, 1121f, A, Mauritius. Nos. 1118, 1121g, 75c, Swaziland. Nos. 1119, 1121h, E, Lesotho. Nos. 1120, 1120i, R, Zambia.

2010, Apr. 9 Litho. ***Perf. 13½***

On Plain Paper With Olive Brown Background

1112-1120 A207 Set of 9 *15.00 15.00*

On Gold-faced Paper

1121 A207 Sheet of 9, #a-i *15.00 15.00*

On day of issue, Nos. 1115 and 1121d sold for 25c, Nos. 1117 and 1121f sold for 50c, Nos. 1119 and 1121h sold for 75c, and Nos. 1120 and 1121i sold for $1.

See Botswana Nos. 896-905, Lesotho No. , Malawi No. 753, Mauritius No. 1086, Namibia No. 1188, South Africa No. 1403, Swaziland Nos. 794-803, and Zambia Nos. 1115-1118.

Single sheetlets of 9 omibus issues exist containing No. 1121a. See footnote under Namibia 1188.

Vice-President Joseph Wilfred Msika (1923-2009) — A208

Zimbabwe flag and various photographs of Msika with panel color of: Z, Yellow. A, Black. E, Dark red. R, Green.

2010, July 27 Litho. ***Perf. 14x14¼***
1122-1125 A208 Set of 4 *8.50 8.50*

On day of issue, Nos. 1122-1125 sold for 25c, 50c, 75c and $1, respectively.

Pan-African Postal Union, 30th Anniv. — A209

2010, Dec. 28 ***Perf. 14¼***
1126 A209 Z multi 1.00 .50

No. 1126 sold for 50c on day of issue.

Railroad Stations — A210

Station in: 25c, Harare. 30c, Kadoma. 85c, Bulawayo. $1, Mutare.

2011, May 26 ***Perf. 14¼x14***
1127-1130 A210 Set of 4 6.50 6.50

National Heroes — A211

Designs: 25c, Tarcissius Malan George Silundika (1929-81), governmental minister. 30c, Julia Zvobgo (1937-2004), politician. 85c, Ariston Maguranyanga Chambati (1934-95), politician. $1, Joseph Luke Culverwell (1918-93), governmental minister.

2011, July 27 ***Perf. 14x14¼***
1131-1134 A211 Set of 4 6.50 6.50

Huts — A212

Designs: 25c, Shona hut. 30c, Ndebele hut. 85c, Manyika hut. $1, Tonga hut.

2011, Nov. 29 ***Perf. 14½x14***
1135-1138 A212 Set of 4 6.50 6.50
1138a Sheet of 4, #1135-1138 6.50 6.50

A213

Sculptures — A214

Designs: 5c, 50c, Tobacco Wither, by Henry Munyaradzi. 25c, Family, by Bernard Matemera. 30c, Mother and Daughters, by Victor Mutongwizo. 75c, $1.50, Bird Carrying Spirit People, by Thomas Mukarobgwa. 85c, Wounded Kudu, by Bakali Manzi. $1, Witch and Her Mate, by Sylvester Mubayi.

2012, Mar. 27 Litho. ***Perf. 14¼***
1139 A213 5c multi .25 .25
1140 A213 25c multi .75 .75
1141 A213 30c multi .75 .75
1142 A213 50c multi 1.25 1.00
a. Souvenir sheet of 4, #1139-1142 3.75 3.75

Perf. 14¼x14

1143 A214 75c multi 1.75 2.00
1144 A214 85c multi 2.00 2.25
1145 A214 $1 multi 2.00 2.25
1146 A214 $1.50 multi 3.50 3.75
a. Souvenir sheet of 4, #1143-1146 10.00 10.00
Nos. 1139-1146 (8) 12.25 13.00

National Heroes — A215

Designs: 30c, Solomon Tapfunmaneyi Ruzambo Mujuru (1945-2011), army officer and politician. 75c, Eddison Jonas Mudadirwa Zvobgo (1935-2004), governmental minister. 85c, Welshman Mabhena (1924-2010), politician. $1, Robson Dayford Manyika (1936-85), governmental minister.

2012, July 24 ***Perf. 14x14¼***
1147-1150 A215 Set of 4 7.00 7.00

Road Safety Campaign — A216

Inscriptions: 30c, Light up 5:30 PM. 75c, Speed/drunk driving. 85c, Obey the code. $1, Visibility.

2012, Aug. 28 ***Perf. 14¼x14***
1151-1154 A216 Set of 4 7.00 7.00

Ants and Termites — A217

Designs: 5c, Honeydew ant. No. 1156, 30c, Philidris ant. No. 1157, 30c, Leaf cutter ant. 75c, Termite and Matabele soldier ant. 85c, Carpenter ant. $1, Termite habitat.

2012, Nov. 20
1155-1160 A217 Set of 6 8.50 8.50
1160a Souvenir sheet of 6, #1155-1160 8.50 8.50

Children's Art — A218

Designs: 30c, Children and rainbow. $1, Corn, mortar, pestle, bowl, head.

2013, Mar. 26
1161-1162 A218 Set of 2 3.00 3.00

Landa John Nkomo (1934-2013), Co-Vice-President A219

Sculpture at Heroes Acre, national flag and: 30c, Nkomo as young man. 75c, Nkomo as older man. 85c, Like 30c. $1, Like 75c.

2013, July 30 ***Perf. 14x14¼***
1163-1166 A219 Set of 4 8.50 8.50

Women's Hairstyles — A220

Designs: 30c, Tonga-Musila. 75c, Shona-Bumhu. 85c, Ndebele-Isicholo. $1, Shangaan-Bhibho.

2013, Dec. 17 Litho. ***Perf. 14¼x14***
1167-1170 A220 Set of 4 7.50 7.50
1170a Souvenir sheet of 4, #1167-1170 7.50 7.50

Export Crops — A221

Designs: 30c, Flowers. 75c, Cotton. 85c, Tea. $1, Tobacco.

2014, Mar. 11 Litho. ***Perf. 14¼x14***
1171-1174 A221 Set of 4 10.00 10.00
1174a Souvenir sheet of 4, #1171-1174 10.00 10.00

Transportation History — A222

Designs: 25c, Donkey-drawn sled, 1890s. No. 1176, 30c, Winston Churchill Train, 1929. No. 1177, 30c, 1928 Model A Ford Phaeton. 75c, De Havilland DH Fox Moth, 1932. 85c, 1946 Bristol Bus. $1, Ox-drawn cart, 1964.

2014, June 3 Litho. ***Perf. 14¼***
1175-1180 A222 Set of 6 9.00 9.00

National Heroes — A223

Designs: 30c, Sabrina Gabriel Mugabe (1929-2010), politician and sister of Pres. Robert Mugabe. 75c, Kumbirai Manyika Kangai (1938-2013), governmental minister. 85c, Stephen Kenneth Sesulelo Vuma (1936-97), politician. $1, Eric Nyakudya Gwanzura (1924-2013), politician.

2014, July 29 Litho. ***Perf. 14x14¼***
1181-1184 A223 Set of 4 7.00 7.00

World Post Day — A224

Designs: 30c, Ancient post runner. 75c, Post rider on horse. 85c, Harare Main Post Office. $1, Post bus.

2014, Oct. 9 Litho. ***Perf. 14¼x14***
1185-1188 A224 Set of 4 7.00 7.00

Frogs — A225

Designs: 30c, Swynnerton's reed frog. 75c, Giant bullfrog. 85c, Bushveld rain frog. $1, Inyanga river frog.

2014, Dec. 9 Litho. ***Perf. 14¼***
1189-1192 A225 Set of 4 7.00 7.00
1192a Souvenir sheet of 4, #1189-1192, imperf. 7.00 7.00

Ruins — A226

Designs: 40c, Chisvingo Ruins. 75c, Dhlo Dhlo Ruins. 85c, Khami Ruins. $1, Nalatale Ruins.

2015, Feb. 24 Litho. ***Perf. 14¼***
1193-1196 A226 Set of 4 7.00 7.00
1196a Souvenir sheet of 4, #1193-1196 7.00 7.00

Victoria Falls — A227

Designs: 10c, Victoria Falls Bridge. 15c, Elephant interaction. 20c, View inside the rain forest. 25c, Makishi dancers. 40c, Zambezi whitewater rafters. 60c, Victoria Falls train station. 75c, Big Tree. 80c, Masks and curios. 85c, Statue of David Livingstone. $1, View of Victoria Falls from Devil's Cataract.

2015, Apr. 30 Litho. ***Perf. 14x14¼***
1197 A227 10c multi .25 .25
1198 A227 15c multi .30 .30
1199 A227 20c multi .40 .40
1200 A227 25c multi .50 .50
1201 A227 40c multi .80 .80
1202 A227 60c multi 1.25 1.25
1203 A227 75c multi 1.50 1.50
1204 A227 80c multi 1.60 1.60
1205 A227 85c multi 1.75 1.75
1206 A227 $1 multi 2.00 2.00
a. Souvenir sheet of 10, #1197-1206 10.50 10.50
Nos. 1197-1206 (10) 10.35 10.35

National Heroes — A228

Designs: 40c, Sunny Ntombiyelanga Takawira (1927-2010), politician. 75c, David Isheunesu Godi Karimanzira (1947-2011), Minister of Education. 85c, Nolan Chipo Makombe (1932-98), Parliament Speaker. $1, Nathan Marwirakuwa Shamuyarira (1929-2014), Minister of Information.

2015, July 30 Litho. ***Perf. 14x14¼***
1207-1210 A228 Set of 4 7.00 7.00

Handicrafts — A229

Designs: 40c, Basketry. 75c, Batik fabrics. 85c, Pottery. $1, Metal sculptures.

2015, Sept. 29 Litho. ***Perf. 14¼x14***
1211-1214 A229 Set of 4 7.00 7.00

Historic Hotels — A230

Designs: 40c, Leopard Rock Hotel. 75c, Bulawayo Club. 85c, Victoria Falls Hotel. $1, Meikles Hotel.

2015, Nov. 28 Litho. ***Perf. 14¼x14***
1215-1218 A230 Set of 4 7.50 7.50

Bank Buildings — A231

Designs: 40c, Standard Bank Ltd. Building, Harare, 1912. 75c, Standard Bank Building, Chegutu, early 1900s. 85c, Barclays Bank Building, Bulawayo, 1912. $1, African Banking Corp. Building, Kadoma, 1913.

2016, Mar. 22 Litho. ***Perf. 14¼x14***
1219-1222 A231 Set of 4 7.50 7.50

National Heroes — A232

Governmental ministers: 40c, Victoria Fikile Chitepo (1927-2016). 75c, Enos Chamunorwa Chikowore (1936-2005). 85c, Josiah Mushore Chinamano (1925-84). $1, Enos Mzombi Nkala (1932-2013).

2016, July 28 Litho. ***Perf. 14x14¼***
1223-1226 A232 Set of 4 8.00 8.00

Campaign Against Pollution — A233

Types of pollution: 10c, Water. 30c, Soil. 40c, Rubbish. 75c, Noise. 85c, Air. $1, Toxic waste.

2016, Aug. 30 Litho. ***Perf. 14½x14***
1227-1232 A233 Set of 6 8.00 8.00

Recreational Fishing — A234

Designs: 40c, Tiger fish. 75c, Largemouth bass. 85c, Fishermen on Lake Mutirikwi. $1, Fishermen on Lake Manyame.

2017, Jan. 30 Litho. ***Perf. 14¼x14***
1233-1236 A234 Set of 4 6.00 6.00
1236a Souvenir sheet of 4, #1233-1236, imperf. 6.00 6.00

Dairy Cows — A235

Breed of cow: 40c, Ayrshire. 75c, Holstein. 85c, Jersey. $1, Red Dane.

2017, Aug. 22 Litho. ***Perf. 14¼***
1237-1240 A235 Set of 4 6.00 6.00
1240a Souvenir sheet of 4, #1237-1240, imperf. 6.00 6.00

National Heroes — A236

Sculpture at Heroes Acre, national flag and: 40c, Cephas George Msipa (1931-2016), politician. 75c, Felix Ngwarati Muchemwa (1945-2016), brigadier general. 85c, Godfrey Guwa Chidyausiku (1947-2017), Chief Justice. $1, Dr. Charles Munhamu Botsio Utete (1938-2016), politician.

2018, Feb. 5 Litho. ***Perf. 14x14¼***
1241-1244 A236 Set of 4 6.00 6.00

Postal officials of Zimbabwe have declared as "illegal" sheets of 4 dated 2009 and 2010 depicting butterflies, sheets of 6 and 9 dated 2011 depicting fire trucks, sheets of 4 and souvenir sheets dated 2015 depicting World Championship ice hockey players, and 76 other souvenir sheets depicting various themes.

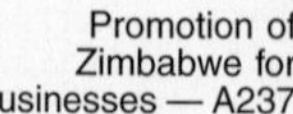

Promotion of Zimbabwe for Businesses — A237

Zimbabwe Pres. Emmerson D. Mnangagwa: 40c, With South African Pres. Cyril Ramaphosa. 75c, Speaking at African Continental Free Trade Area Business Forum. 85c, With International Monetary Fund Managing Director Christine Lagarde. $1, With People's Republic of China Pres. Xi Jinping.

2018, July 18 Litho. ***Perf. 14***
1245-1248 A237 Set of 4 6.00 6.00
1248a Souvenir sheet of 4, #1245-1248, imperf. 6.00 6.00

Ladybugs — A238

Designs: 40c, Seven-spotted ladybug. 75c, Black-and-yellow-spotted ladybug. 85c, Twenty-spotted ladybug. $1, Ladybug in flight.

2018, Oct. 15 Litho. ***Perf. 14***
1249-1252 A238 Set of 4 6.00 6.00
1252a Souvenir sheet of 4, #1249-1252, imperf. 6.00 6.00

Juvenile Animals — A239

Designs: Z, Giraffe. A, Lion. E, Elephant. R, Rhinoceros.

2019, Dec. 17 Litho. ***Perf. 14¼x14***
1253-1256 A239 Set of 4 10.00 10.00
1256a Souvenir sheet of 4, #1253-1256, imperf. 10.00 10.00

On day of issue, No. 1253 sold for 40c; No. 1254, $1; No. 1255, $1.60; No. 1256, $2.

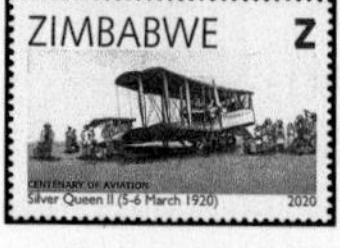

Aviation in Zimbabwe, Cent. — A240

Airplanes: Z, Silver Queen II. A, BOAC Solent. E, Vickers Viscount. R, Boeing 707.

2020, Mar. 5 Litho. ***Perf. 14¼***
1257-1260 A240 Set of 4 10.00 10.00
1260a Souvenir sheet of 4, #1257-1260, imperf. 10.00 10.00

On day of issue, No. 1257 sold for 40c; No. 1258, $1; No. 1259, $1.60; No. 1260, $2.

Musical Instruments — A241

Designs: Z, Hosho. A, Mbira. E, Microphone. R, Guitar.

2021, Feb. 15 Litho. ***Perf. 14¼x14***
1261-1264 A241 Set of 4 10.00 10.00
1264a Souvenir sheet of 4, #1261-1264, imperf. 10.00 10.00

On day of issue, No. 1261 sold for 40c; No. 1262, $1; No. 1263, $1.60; No. 1264, $2.

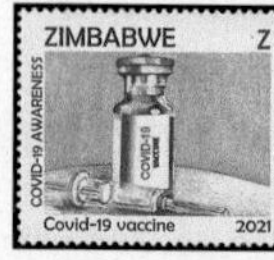

Campaign Against COVID-19 — A242

Designs: Z, COVID-19 vaccine. A, Health care worker checking temperature of patient. E, Hand washing. R, Hand sanitizing.

2021, Mar. 31 Litho. ***Perf. 14¼x14***
1265-1268 A242 Set of 4 10.00 10.00
1268a Souvenir sheet of 4, #1265-1268, imperf. 10.00 10.00

On day of issue, No. 1265 sold for 40c; No. 1266, $1; No. 1267, $1.60; No. 1268, $2.

Independence, 41st Anniv. — A243

Designs: Z, Flag of Zimbabwe. R, Independence torch.

2021, Apr. 16 Litho. ***Perf. 14x14¼***
1269-1270 A243 Set of 2 7.00 7.00

On day of issue, No. 1269 sold for $1 and No. 1270 sold for $2.50.

10th Plenipotentiary Conference of the Pan African Postal Union, Victoria Falls — A244

Designs: Z, Kingdom Hotel. A, Victoria Falls, 40th anniversary emblem.

2021, June 26 Litho. ***Perf. 14¼x14***
1271-1272 A244 Set of 2 5.00 5.00

Pan African Postal Union, 40th anniv. (in 2020). The conference, scheduled for 2020, was postponed until 2021 because of the COVID-19 pandemic. On day of issue, No. 1271 sold for $1 and No. 1272 sold for $1.50.

POSTAGE DUE STAMPS

D1

1981 Litho. ***Perf. 14½***
J20 D1 1c emerald .40 1.10
J21 D1 2c ultramarine .40 1.10
J22 D1 5c lilac .50 1.40
J23 D1 6c yellow .65 2.00
J24 D1 10c red 1.40 4.25
Nos. J20-J24 (5) 3.35 9.85

For surcharge see No. J30.

D2

1985, Aug. 21 Litho. ***Perf. 14½***
J25 D2 1c pale orange .40 .75
J26 D2 2c lilac rose .40 .75
J27 D2 6c light green .40 .75
J28 D2 10c tan .40 .75
J29 D2 13c bright blue .40 .75
Nos. J25-J29 (5) 2.00 3.75

No. J24 Surcharged

1990, Jan. 2 Litho. ***Perf. 14½***
J30 D1 25c on 10c #J24 *11.00 11.00*

D3

1995, Jan. 17 Litho. ***Perf. 14½***
J31 D3 1c yellow .35 .35
J32 D3 2c yellow orange .35 .35
J33 D3 5c rose lilac .35 .35
J34 D3 10c pale blue .35 .35
J35 D3 25c violet .35 .35
J36 D3 40c green .35 .35

J37	D3	60c orange	.35	.35
J38	D3	$1 brown	.55	.55
		Nos. J31-J38 (8)	3.00	3.00

D4

Bird sculpture.

2000, Jan. 25 **Litho.** ***Perf. 14½***

J39	D4	1c blk, lt grn & grn	*.25*	*.25*
J40	D4	10c blk, lt blue & blue	*.25*	*.25*
J41	D4	50c blk, lt brn & brn	*.25*	*.25*
J42	D4	$1 blk, pink & red	*.25*	*.25*
J43	D4	$2 blk, lt yel & yel	*.25*	*.25*
J44	D4	$5 blk, lil & red vio	*.25*	*.25*
J45	D4	$10 blk, lt ver & ver	*.55*	*.55*
		Nos. J39-J45 (7)	2.05	2.05

ZULULAND

'zü-ₑlü-ˌland

LOCATION — Northeastern part of Natal, South Africa
GOVT. — British Colony, 1887-1897
AREA — 10,427 sq. mi.
POP. — 230,000 (estimated 1900)
CAPITAL — Eshowe

12 Pence = 1 Shilling
20 Shillings = 1 Pound

Values for covers are for items posted at Eshowe; all.other postmarks bear premiums.

Stamps of Great Britain Overprinted

1888-93 **Wmk. 30** ***Perf. 14***

1	A54 ½p vermilion	8.75	3.00
2	A40 1p violet	30.00	6.75
3	A56 2p green & red	32.50	55.00
4	A57 2½p vio, *bl* ('91)	45.00	24.00
5	A58 3p violet, *yel*	34.00	25.00
6	A59 4p green & brn	62.50	77.50
7	A61 5p lil & bl ('93)	110.00	*160.00*
8	A62 6p vio, *rose*	25.00	20.00
9	A63 9p blue & lil ('92)	125.00	*135.00*
10	A65 1sh green ('92)	160.00	*175.00*

Wmk. 31

11	A51 5sh rose ('92)	725.00	*800.00*
	Nos. 1-10 (10)	632.75	681.25

Dangerous forgeries exist.
Expertization is recommended for used examples of No. 11.

Natal No. 66 Overprinted

1888-94 **Wmk. 2**

12	A14 ½p green, no period	32.50	*55.00*
a.	Period after "Zululand"	62.50	*97.50*
b.	As "a," double overprint	1,450.	1,600.
d.	As "a," pair, one without ovpt.	*7,500.*	

The varieties formerly listed as Nos. 12c and 12e, No. 12a with inverted overprint and No. 12 with double overprint, are now considered to be forgeries.

Natal No. 71 Ovptd. Like Nos. 1-11

13	A11 6p violet ('94)	70.00	62.50

A1

1891

14	A1 1p lilac	5.00	3.75

By proclamation of the Governor of Zululand, dated June 27th, 1891, No. 14 was declared to be a postage stamp.

A2

1894-96 **Typo.**

15	A2	½p lilac & grn	8.00	7.50
16	A2	1p lilac & rose	7.00	3.25
17	A2	2½p lilac & blue	16.00	12.00
18	A2	3p lilac & brn	11.00	4.00
19	A2	6p lilac & blk	24.00	*25.00*
20	A2	1sh green	52.50	45.00
21	A2	2sh6p grn & blk ('96)	95.00	*115.00*
22	A2	4sh grn & car rose	160.00	*240.00*
23	A2	£1 violet, *red*	675.00	*725.00*
24	A2	£5 vio & blk, *red*	5,750.	*1,900.*
		Overprinted "SPECIMEN"	500.00	
		Nos. 15-23 (9)	1,049.	1,177.
		Nos. 15-23 ovptd. "SPECIMEN"	525.00	

Numerals of Nos. 19-24 are in color on plain tablet. Dangerous forgeries of No. 24 exist.
Expertization is recommended for used examples of No. 24.

Purple or violet cancellations are not necessarily revenue cancels. 14 of the 17 post offices and agencies used violet as well as black postal cancellations.

Zululand was annexed to Natal in Dec. 1897 and separate stamps were discontinued June 30, 1898.

INDEX AND IDENTIFIER

All page numbers shown are those in this Volume 6B.

Postage stamps that do not have English words on them are shown in the Scott *Stamp Illustrated Identifier*. To purchase it visit AmosAdvantage.com or call Amos Media at 800-572-6885.

A & T ovptd. on French Colonies .... Vol. 1A
Aberdeen, Miss. .... Vol. 1A
Abingdon, Va. .... Vol. 1A
Abu Dhabi .... 442, Vol. 1A, Vol. 5A
Abyssinia (Ethiopia) .... Vol. 2B
A.C.C.P., A.D.C.P. .... Vol. 1B
A Certo ovptd. on stamps of Peru .... Vol. 5A
Acores .... Vol. 1B, Vol. 5B
Aden .... Vol. 1A
AEF .... Vol. 2B
Aegean Islands (Greek Occupation) .... Vol. 3A
Aegean Islands (Italian Occupation) .... Vol. 3B
Aeroport International de Kandahar (Afghanistan #679) .... Vol. 1A
Afars and Issas .... Vol. 1A
AFF EXCEP .... Vol. 2B
Afghanistan, Afghan, Afghanes ... Vol. 1A
AFR .... Vol. 5B
Africa, British Offices .... Vol. 3A
Africa, German East .... Vol. 3A
Africa, German South-West .... Vol. 3A
Africa, Italian Offices .... Vol. 3B
Africa Occidental Espanola .... Vol. 6A
Africa Orientale Italiana .... Vol. 3B
Africa, Portuguese .... Vol. 5B
Afrique Equatoriale Francaise .... 375, Vol. 2A, Vol. 2B, Vol. 4B
Afrique Francaise .... Vol. 2B
Afrique Occidentale Francaise ... Vol. 2B
Agion Oros Athoc (Greece) .... Vol. 3A
Aguera, La .... Vol. 1A
Aguinaldo .... Vol. 5A
AHA (Confed. #44X1) .... Vol. 1A
Aimeliik (Palau #686) .... Vol. 5A
Airai (Palau #686) .... Vol. 5A
Aitutaki .... Vol. 1A
Ajman .... 442, Vol. 1A
Aland Islands .... Vol. 2B
Alaouites .... Vol. 1A
Albania .... Vol. 1A
Albania, Greek Occupation .... Vol. 3A
Albania, Italian Offices .... Vol. 3B
Albany, Ga. .... Vol. 1A
Alderney .... Vol. 3A
Aleppo .... Vol. 6A
Alerta ovptd. on stamps of Peru ... Vol. 5A
Alexandretta, Alexandrette .... Vol. 1A
Alexandria, Alexandrie, French Offices .... Vol. 2B
Alexandria, Va. .... Vol. 1A
Alexandroupolis .... Vol. 3A
Algeria, Algerie .... Vol. 1A
Allemagne Duitschland .... Vol. 3A
Allenstein .... Vol. 1A
Allied Military Government (Austria) .... Vol. 1B
Allied Military Gov. (Germany) .... Vol. 3A
Allied Military Government (Italy) ... Vol. 3B
Allied Military Government (Trieste) .... Vol. 3B
Allied Occupation of Azerbaijan .... Vol. 3B
Allied Occupation of Thrace 68
A L'Ocassion de la Journée Internationale de l'Alphabetisation (Afghan. #951) .... Vol. 1A
Alsace .... Vol. 2B
Alsace and Lorraine .... Vol. 2B
Alwar .... Vol. 3B
A.M.G. .... Vol. 1B, Vol. 3A, Vol. 3B
A.M.G./F.T.T. .... Vol. 3B
A.M.G./V.G. .... Vol. 3B
AM Post .... Vol. 3A
Anatolia 299
Ancachs .... Vol. 5A
Andalusian Provinces .... Vol. 6A
Anderson Court House, S.C. ..... Vol. 1A
Andorra, Andorre .... Vol. 1A
Andorre .... Vol. 1A
Angaur (Palau #686) .... Vol. 5A
Angola .... Vol. 1A
Angra .... Vol. 1A
Anguilla .... Vol. 1A, Vol. 5B
Anhwei .... Vol. 2A
Anjouan .... Vol. 1A
Anna surcharged on France .... Vol. 2B
Anna surcharged on Great Britain... Vol. 5A
Anna, Annas .... Vol. 3B
Annam .... Vol. 3B
Annam and Tonkin .... Vol. 1A
Annapolis, Md. .... Vol. 1A
Ano do X Aniversario Comunidade dos Paises de Lingua Portugesa (Angola 1298-1300) .... Vol. 1A
Antigua .... Vol. 1A, Vol. 5B
Antigua & Barbuda .... Vol. 1A
Antioquia .... Vol. 2A
A.O. ovptd. on Congo .... Vol. 3A
AOF on France .... Vol. 2B
A.O.I. ovpt. on Italy .... Vol. 3B
A Payer Te Betalen ....Vol. 1B
A percevoir (see France, French colonies, postage due) .... Vol. 2B, Vol. 3A
Apurimac .... Vol. 5A
A R .... Vol. 4B
A.R. ovptd. on stamps of Colombia .... Vol. 5A
Arabie Saoudite .... Vol. 6A
Arad .... Vol. 3B
A receber (See Portuguese Colonies) .... Vol. 5B
Arequipa .... Vol. 5A
Argentina .... Vol. 1A
Argyrokastron .... Vol. 2B
Arica .... Vol. 5A
Armenia .... 154, Vol. 1A
Armenian stamps ovptd. or surcharged .... 154, Vol. 3A
Army of the North .... Vol. 5B
Army of the Northwest .... Vol. 5B
Aruba .... Vol. 1A
Arwad .... Vol. 5B
Ascension .... Vol. 1A
Assistencia Nacionalaos Tuberculosos .... Vol. 5B
Asturias Province .... Vol. 6A
Athens, Ga. .... Vol. 1A
Atlanta, Ga. .... Vol. 1A
Aunus, ovptd. on Finland .... Vol. 5B
Austin, Miss. .... Vol. 1A
Austin, Tex. .... Vol. 1A
Australia .... Vol. 1A
Australia, Occupation of Japan ... Vol. 1A
Australian Antarctic Territory ...... Vol. 1A
Australian States .... Vol. 1A
Austria .... Vol. 1B
Austria, Allied Military Govt. .... Vol. 1B
Austria, Adm. of Liechtenstein ... Vol. 4A
Austria, Lombardy-Venetia .... Vol. 1B
Austria-Hungary .... Vol. 1B
Austrian Occupation of Italy .... Vol. 3B
Austrian Occupation of Montenegro .... Vol. 4B
Austrian Occupation of Romania ... Vol. 5B
Austrian Occupation of Serbia ... Vol. 6A
Austrian Offices Abroad .... Vol. 1B
Austrian stamps surcharged or overprinted .... 752, Vol. 1B, Vol. 3B, Vol. 5B
Autaugaville, Ala. .... Vol. 1A
Autopaketti, Autorahti .... Vol. 2B
Avisporto .... Vol. 2B
Ayacucho .... Vol. 5A
Aytonomoe .... Vol. 2B
Azerbaijan, Azarbaycan, Azerbaycan, Azerbaidjan .... 154, Vol. 1B, Vol. 3B
Azirbayedjan .... Vol. 3B
Azores .... Vol. 1B, Vol. 5B

B .... Vol. 1B, Vol. 5A, Vol. 6A
B ovptd. on Straits Settlements .... Vol. 1B
Baden .... Vol. 3A
Baghdad .... Vol. 4B
Bahamas .... Vol. 1B
Bahawalpur .... Vol. 5A
Bahrain .... Vol. 1B, Vol. 5A
Baja Cal(ifornia) .... Vol. 4B
Bajar Porto .... Vol. 3B
Baku .... Vol. 1B
Balcony Falls, Va. .... Vol. 1A
Baltimore, Md. .... Vol. 1A
Bamra .... Vol. 3B
Banat, Bacska .... Vol. 3B
Bangkok .... Vol. 1B
Bangladesh .... Vol. 1B
Bani ovptd. on Austria .... Vol. 5B
Bani ovptd. on Hungary .... Vol. 3B
Baranya .... Vol. 3B
Barbados .... Vol. 1B
Barbuda .... Vol. 1B
Barcelona .... Vol. 6A
Barnwell Court House, S.C. .... Vol. 1A
Barranquilla .... Vol. 2A
Barwani .... Vol. 3B
Basel .... Vol. 6A
Bashahr .... Vol. 3B
Basque Provinces .... Vol. 6A
Basutoland .... Vol. 1B
Batavia .... Vol. 5A
Baton Rouge, La. .... Vol. 1A
Batum, Batym (British Occupation) .... Vol. 1B
Bavaria .... Vol. 3A
Bayar Porto .... Vol. 3B
Bayer., Bayern .... Vol. 3A
B.C.A. ovptd. on Rhodesia .... Vol. 1B
B.C.M. .... Vol. 4B
B.C.O.F. .... Vol. 1A
Beaufort, S.C. .... Vol. 1A
Beaumont, Tex. .... Vol. 1A
Bechuanaland .... Vol. 1B
Bechuanaland Protectorate .... Vol. 1B
Beckmann's City Post .... Vol. 1A
Behie 228
Belarus .... Vol. 1B
Belgian (Belgisch) Congo .... Vol. 1B
Belgian East Africa .... Vol. 5B
Belgian Occ. of German East Africa .... Vol. 3A
Belgian Occupation of Germany ... Vol. 3A
Belgien .... Vol. 1B
Belgium, Belgique, Belgie .... Vol. 1B
Belgium (German Occupation) ... Vol. 1B
Belize .... Vol. 1B
Belize, Cayes of .... Vol. 1B
Benadir .... Vol. 6A
Bengasi .... Vol. 3B
Beni .... Vol. 1B
Benin .... Vol. 1B
Benin, People's Republic of ....Vol. 1B
Bequia .... Vol. 5B
Bergedorf .... Vol. 3A
Berlin .... Vol. 3A
Berlin-Brandenburg .... Vol. 3A
Bermuda .... Vol. 1B
Besetztes Gebiet Nordfrankreich ... Vol. 2B
Besieged ovptd. on Cape of Good Hope .... 157, Vol. 2A
Beyrouth, French Offices .... Vol. 2B
Beyrouth, Russian Offices .... Vol. 5B
B. Guiana .... Vol. 1B
B. Hneipoe .... Vol. 2B
Bhopal .... Vol. 3B
Bhor .... Vol. 3B
Bhutan .... Vol. 1B
Biafra .... Vol. 1B
Bijawar .... Vol. 3B
B.I.O.T. ovptd. on Seychelles ..... Vol. 1B
Bishop's City Post .... Vol. 1A
Blagoveshchensk .... Vol. 2B
Bluefields .... Vol. 5A
Bluffton, S.C. .... Vol. 1A
B.M.A. Eritrea .... Vol. 3A
B.M.A. Malaya .... Vol. 6A
B.M.A. Somalia .... Vol. 3A
B.M.A. Tripolitania .... Vol. 3A
Bocas del Toro .... Vol. 5A
Boer Occupation .... Vol. 2A
Bogota .... Vol. 2A
Bohemia and Moravia .... Vol. 2B
Bohmen and Mahren .... Vol. 2B
Boletta, Bollettino .... Vol. 3B, Vol. 6A
Bolivar .... Vol. 2A
Bolivia .... Vol. 1B
Bollo .... Vol. 3B
Bollo Postale .... Vol. 6A
Bophuthatswana .... Vol. 6A
Borneo .... Vol. 5A
Boscawen, N.H. .... Vol. 1A
Bosna i Hercegovina .... 780, Vol. 1B
Bosnia and Herzegovina ..... 780, Vol. 1B
Bosnia, Muslim Gov. in Sarajevo ... Vol. 1B
Bosnia, Croat Administration, Mostar .... Vol. 1B
Bosnia, Serb Administration, Banja Luca .... Vol. 1B
Bosnia stamps overprinted or surcharged .... 780, Vol. 1B, Vol. 3B
Bosnien Herzegowina .... Vol. 1B
Boston, Mass. .... Vol. 1A
Botswana .... Vol. 1B
Boyaca .... Vol. 2A
Brattleboro, Vt. .... Vol. 1A
Braunschweig .... Vol. 3A
Brazil, Brasil .... Vol. 1B
Bremen .... Vol. 3A
Bridgeville, Ala. .... Vol. 1A
British Administration of Bahrain ... Vol. 1B
British Antarctic Territory .... Vol. 1B
British Bechuanaland .... Vol. 1B
British Central Africa .... Vol. 1B
British Colonies - Dies I & II ... See table of contents
British Columbia & Vancouver Is. ... Vol. 2A
British Consular Mail .... Vol. 4B
British Dominion of Samoa .... Vol. 5B
British East Africa .... Vol. 1B
British Forces in Egypt .... Vol. 2B
British Guiana .... Vol. 1B
British Honduras .... Vol. 1B
British Indian Ocean Territory ..... Vol. 1B
British Mandate of Jordan .... Vol. 4A
British Levant .... Vol. 3A
British New Guinea .... Vol. 5A
British North Borneo .... Vol. 5A
British Occupation (of Batum) .... Vol. 1B
British Occupation of Bushire .... Vol. 1B
British Occupation of Cameroun ... Vol. 2A
British Occupation of Crete .... Vol. 2A
British Occupation of Faroe Is. .... Vol. 2B
British Occ. of German East Africa .... Vol. 3A
British Occupation of Iraq .... Vol. 3B, Vol. 4B
British Occupation of Mesopotamia .... Vol. 4B
British Occ. of Orange River Colony .... Vol. 5A
British Occupation overprint ...... Vol. 1B
British Occupation of Palestine ... Vol. 5A
British Occupation of Persia ...... Vol. 1B
British Occupation of Togo 75
British Occ. of Transvaal 155
British Offices in Africa .... Vol. 3A
British Offices in China .... Vol. 3A
British Offices in Morocco .... Vol. 3A
British Offices in Tangier .... Vol. 3A
British Off. in the Turkish Empire ... Vol. 3A
British Protectorate of Egypt ...... Vol. 2B
British Samoa .... Vol. 5B
British Solomon Islands .... Vol. 6A
British Somaliland (Somaliland Protectorate) .... Vol. 6A
British South Africa (Rhodesia) .... Vol. 5B
British stamps surcharged .... Vol. 5A
British Vice-Consulate .... Vol. 4B
British Virgin Islands 712
British Zone (Germany) .... Vol. 3A
Brown & McGill's U.S.P.O. Despatch .... Vol. 1A
Brunei .... Vol. 1B
Brunei (Japanese Occupation) ... Vol. 1B
Brunswick .... Vol. 3A
Buchanan .... Vol. 1A, Vol. 4A
Buenos Aires .... Vol. 1A
Bulgaria, Bulgarie .... Vol. 1B
Bulgarian Occupation of Romania .... Vol. 5B
Bulgarian stamps overprinted or surcharged .... 68, Vol. 3A, Vol. 5B
Bundi .... Vol. 3B
Bundi stamps overprinted .... Vol. 3B
Bureau International .... Vol. 6A
Burgenland .... Vol. 1B
Burgos .... Vol. 6A
Burkina Faso .... Vol. 1B
Burma .... Vol. 1B
Burma (Japanese Occupation) ... Vol. 1B
Burundi .... Vol. 1B
Bushire .... Vol. 1B
Bussahir .... Vol. 3B
Buu-Chinh 653, 654
Buu-Bien 664
Byelorussia .... Vol. 1B

Cabo, Cabo Gracias a Dios ..... Vol. 5A
Cabo Juby, Jubi .... Vol. 2A
Cabo Verde .... Vol. 2A
Cadiz .... Vol. 6A
Caicos 336
Calchi .... Vol. 3B
Cali .... Vol. 2A
Calino, Calimno .... Vol. 3B
Callao .... Vol. 5A
Camb. Aust. Sigillum Nov. .... Vol. 1A
Cambodia, (Int. Com., India) ...... Vol. 3B
Cambodia, Cambodge ... Vol. 2A, Vol. 3B
Camden, S.C. .... Vol. 1A
Cameroons (U.K.T.T.) .... Vol. 2A
Cameroun (Republique Federale) ... Vol. 2A
Campeche .... Vol. 4B
Canada .... Vol. 2A
Canadian Provinces .... Vol. 2A
Canal Zone .... Vol. 1A
Canary Islands, Canarias .... Vol. 6A
Candia .... Vol. 2A
Canouan .... Vol. 5B
Canton, French Offices .... Vol. 2B
Canton, Miss. .... Vol. 1A
Cape Juby .... Vol. 2A

Cape of Good Hope .... Vol. 2A
Cape of Good Hope stamps surchd. (see Griqualand West) ... Vol. 3A
Cape Verde .... Vol. 2A
Carchi .... Vol. 3B
Caribbean Netherlands .... Vol. 2A
Caribisch Nederland .... Vol. 2A
Carinthia .... 782, Vol. 1B
Carlist .... Vol. 6A
Carolina City, N.C. .... Vol. 1A
Caroline Islands .... Vol. 2A
Carpatho-Ukraine .... Vol. 2B
Carriacou & Petite Martinique .... Vol. 3A
Carriers Stamps .... Vol. 1A
Cartagena .... Vol. 2A
Cartersville, Ga. .... Vol. 1A
Carupano 652
Caso .... Vol. 3B
Castellorizo, Castelrosso .... Vol. 2A
Catalonia .... Vol. 6A
Cauca .... Vol. 2A
Cavalla (Greek) .... Vol. 3A
Cavalle, Cavalla (French) .... Vol. 2B
Cayes of Belize .... Vol. 1B
Cayman Islands .... Vol. 2A
CCCP .... Vol. 5B
C.CH. on French Colonies .... Vol. 2A
C.E.F. ovptd. on Cameroun .... Vol. 2A
C.E.F. ovptd. on India .... Vol. 3B
Cefalonia ovptd. on Greece .... Vol. 3B
Celebes .... Vol. 5A
Cent, cents ..... Vol. 1A, Vol. 2B, Vol. 4B, Vol. 5A
Centenaire Algerie RF (France No. 255) .... Vol. 2B
Centenary-1st Postage Stamp (Pakistan #63-64) .... Vol. 5A
Centesimi overprinted on Austria or Bosnia .... Vol. 3B
Centesimi di corona ..... Vol. 1B, Vol. 2B
Centimes .... Vol. 2B
Centimes ovptd. on Austria .... Vol. 1B
Centimes ovptd. on Germany ..... Vol. 3A
Centimos (no country name) ..... Vol. 6A
Centimos ovptd. on France .... Vol. 2B
Central Africa (Centrafricaine) .... Vol. 2A
Central African Republic .... Vol. 2A
Central China .... Vol. 2A
Central Lithuania .... Vol. 2A
Cephalonia .... Vol. 3B
Cerigo .... Vol. 3A, Vol. 3B
Cervantes .... Vol. 6A
Ceska Republica .... Vol. 2B
Ceskoslovenska, Ceskoslovensko .... Vol. 2B
Ceylon .... Vol. 2A
CF .... Vol. 2B
CFA .... Vol. 2B
C.G.H.S. 464
Ch .... Vol. 3B, Vol. 4A
Chachapoyas .... Vol. 5A
Chad .... Vol. 2A
Chahar .... Vol. 2A
Chala .... Vol. 5A
Chamba .... Vol. 3B
Channel Islands .... Vol. 3A
Chapel Hill, N.C. .... Vol. 1A
Charkhari .... Vol. 3B
Charleston, S.C. .... Vol. 1A
Charlotte, N.C. .... Vol. 1A
Charlottesville, Va. .... Vol. 1A
Chateau de Beggen (Luxembourg #1466) .... Vol. 4A
Chateau de Dommeldange (Luxembourg #1467) .... Vol. 4A
Chattanooga, Tenn. .... Vol. 1A
Chekiang .... Vol. 2A
Chemins des Fer .... Vol. 2B
Cherifien Posts .... Vol. 2B
Chiapas .... Vol. 4B
Chiclayo .... Vol. 5A
Chiffre .... See France and French colonies, postage due
Chihuahua .... Vol. 4B
Chile .... Vol. 2A
Chilean Occupation of Peru .... Vol. 5A
Chimarra .... Vol. 2B
China, Chinese .... Vol. 2A
China (Japanese Occupation) .... Vol. 2A
China Expeditionary Force (India) ... Vol. 3B
China, British Offices .... Vol. 3A
China, Formosa .... Vol. 2A, Vol. 4A
China, French Offices .... Vol. 2B
China, German Offices .... Vol. 3A
China, Italian Offices .... Vol. 3B
China, Japanese Offices .... Vol. 4A
China, Northeastern Provinces .... Vol. 2A
China, Offices in Manchuria .... Vol. 2A
China, Offices in Tibet .... Vol. 2A
China, People's Republic .... Vol. 2A
China, People's Republic Regional Issues .... Vol. 2A
China, People's Republic Hong Kong .... Vol. 3B
China, People's Republic Macao ... Vol. 4B
China, Republic of .... Vol. 2A
China, Russian Offices .... Vol. 5B
China, United States Offices ...... Vol. 1A
Chine .... Vol. 2B
Chios .... Vol. 3A
Chita .... Vol. 2B
Chosen .... Vol. 4A
Christiansburg, Va. .... Vol. 1A
Christmas Island .... Vol. 2A
Chungking .... Vol. 2B
C.I.H.S. 464
Cilicia, Cilicie ... Vol. 2A, Vol. 5A, Vol. 6A
Cincinnati, O. .... Vol. 1A
Cinquan Tenaire .... Vol. 5A
Cirenaica .... Vol. 2B
Ciskei .... Vol. 6A
City Despatch Post .... Vol. 1A
City Post .... Vol. 1A
Cleveland, O. .... Vol. 1A
Cluj .... Vol. 3B
c/m .... Vol. 2B
C.M.T. 753
Coamo .... Vol. 1A, Vol. 5B
Cochin .... Vol. 3B
Cochin China .... Vol. 2A
Cochin, Travancore .... Vol. 3B
Co. Ci. ovptd. on Yugoslavia 831
Cocos Islands .... Vol. 2A
Colaparchee, Ga. .... Vol. 1A
Colis Postaux .... Vol. 1B, Vol. 2B, Vol. 3B
Colombia .... Vol. 2A, Vol. 5A
Colombian Dominion of Panama ... Vol. 5A
Colombian States .... Vol. 2A
Colon .... Vol. 5A
Colonie (Coloniali) Italiane .... Vol. 3B
Colonies de l'Empire Francaise ... Vol. 2B
Columbia, S.C. .... Vol. 1A
Columbia, Tenn. .... Vol. 1A
Columbus Archipelago .... Vol. 2B
Columbus, Ga. .... Vol. 1A
Comayagua .... Vol. 3B
Commando Brief .... Vol. 5A
Common Designs .... See table of contents
Commissioning of Maryan Babangida (Nigeria #607) .... Vol. 5A
Communicaciones .... Vol. 6A
Communist China .... Vol. 2A
Comores, Archipel des .... Vol. 2A
Comoro Islands (Comores, Comorien) .... Vol. 2A, Vol. 4B
Compania Colombiana .... Vol. 2A
Confederate States .... Vol. 1A
Congo .... Vol. 1B, Vol. 2A
Congo Democratic Republic .... 835, Vol. 2A
Congo People's Republic (ex-French) .... Vol. 2A
Congo, Belgian (Belge) .... Vol. 1B
Congo Francais .... Vol. 2B
Congo, Indian U.N. Force .... Vol. 3B
Congo, Portuguese .... Vol. 5B
Congreso .... Vol. 6A
Conseil de l'Europe .... Vol. 2B
Constantinople, Georgian Offices .... Vol. 3A
Constantinople, Polish Offices ... Vol. 5B
Constantinople, Italian Offices ... Vol. 3B
Constantinople, Romanian Offices .... Vol. 5B
Constantinople, Russian Offices ... Vol. 5B
Constantinople, Turkey 289
Contribucao Industrial (Macao A14, P. Guinea WT1) .... Vol. 4B, Vol. 5B
Convention States (India) .... Vol. 3B
Coo .... Vol. 3B
Cook Islands .... Vol. 2A
Cook Islands, Niue .... Vol. 5A
Cordoba .... Vol. 1A
Corea, Coree .... Vol. 4A
Corfu .... Vol. 2A, Vol. 3B
Corona .... Vol. 1B, Vol. 2B
Correio, Correios e Telegraphos .... Vol. 5B
Correo Submarino .... Vol. 6A
Correo, Correos (no name) .... Vol. 1A, Vol. 2A, Vol. 5A, Vol. 6A
Corrientes .... Vol. 1A
Cos .... Vol. 3B
Costa Atlantica .... Vol. 5A
Costa Rica .... Vol. 2A
Costantinopoli .... Vol. 3B
Cote d'Ivoire .... Vol. 3B
Cote des Somalis .... Vol. 6A
Council of Europe .... Vol. 2B
Cour Permanente de Justice Internationale .... Vol. 5A
Courtland, Ala. .... Vol. 1A
Cpbnja .... Vol. 6A
Cracow .... Vol. 5B
Crete .... Vol. 2A, Vol. 3B
Crete, Austrian Offices .... Vol. 1B
Crete, French Offices .... Vol. 2B
Crete, Italian Offices .... Vol. 3B
Crimea .... Vol. 5B, Vol. 6A
Croat Administration of Bosnia, Mostar .... Vol. 1B
Croatia .... Vol. 2A
Croatia-Slavonia 780
Croissant Rouge Turc. 294
C.S.A. Postage .... Vol. 1A
CTOT .... Vol. 1B
Cuautla .... Vol. 4B
Cuthbert, GA .... Vol. 1A
Cuba .... Vol. 1A, Vol. 2A
Cuba stamps overprinted .... Vol. 5B
Cuba, U.S. Administration .... Vol. 1A, Vol. 2A
Cucuta .... Vol. 2A
Cuernavaca .... Vol. 4B
Cundinamarca .... Vol. 2A
Curacao .... Vol. 2A, Vol. 5A
Cuzco .... Vol. 5A
C.X.C. on Bosnia and Herzegovina 780
Cyprus .... Vol. 2B
Cyprus, Turkish Republic of Northern 301
Cyrenaica .... Vol. 2B, Vol. 3A, Vol. 4A
Czechoslovakia .... Vol. 2B
Czechoslovak Legion Post .... Vol. 2B
Czech Rep. .... Vol. 2B

D .... Vol. 3B
Dahomey .... Vol. 1B, Vol. 2B
Dakar-Abidjan .... Vol. 2B
Dalmatia .... Vol. 2B
Dalton, Ga. .... Vol. 1A
Danish West Indies .... Vol. 1A, Vol. 2B
Danmark .... Vol. 2B
Dansk-Vestindien .... Vol. 1A, Vol. 2B
Dansk-Vestindiske .... Vol. 1A, Vol. 2B
Danville, Va. .... Vol. 1A
Danzig .... Vol. 2B
Danzig, Polish Offices .... Vol. 5B
Dardanelles .... Vol. 5B
Datia (Duttia) .... Vol. 3B
D.B.L. ovptd. on Siberia and Russia .... Vol. 2B
D.B.P. (Dalni Vostochini Respoublika) .... Vol. 2B
D. de A. .... Vol. 2A
DDR .... Vol. 3A
Debrecen .... Vol. 3B
Deccan (Hyderabad) .... Vol. 3B
Dedeagatch (Greek) .... Vol. 3A
Dedeagh, Dedeagatch (French) ..... Vol. 2B
Deficit .... Vol. 5A
Demopolis, Ala. .... Vol. 1A
Denikin .... Vol. 6A
Denmark .... Vol. 2B
Denmark stamps surcharged ..... Vol. 2B
Denver Issue, Mexico .... Vol. 4B
Den Waisen ovptd. on Italy 832
Despatch (US 1LB, 5LB) .... Vol. 1A
Deutsch-Neu-Guinea .... Vol. 3A
Deutsch-Ostafrika .... Vol. 3A
Deutsch-Sudwest Afrika .... Vol. 3A
Deutsche Bundespost .... Vol. 3A
Deutsche Demokratische Republik .... Vol. 3A
Deutsche Nationalversammlung ... Vol. 3A
Deutsche Post .... Vol. 3A
Deutsche Post Berlin .... Vol. 3A
Deutsche(s) Reich .... Vol. 3A
Deutsche Reich, Nr.21, Nr.16 ..... Vol. 3A
Deutschland .... Vol. 3A
Deutschosterreich .... Vol. 1B
Dhar .... Vol. 3B
Diego-Suarez .... Vol. 2B
Diego-Suarez stamps surcharged .... Vol. 4B
Dienftmarke (Dienstmarke) .... Vol. 3A
Dies I & II, British Colonies ..... See table of contents
Diligencia 465
Dinar 783
Dire-Dawa .... Vol. 2B
Dispatch (US 1LB) .... Vol. 1A
Distrito ovptd. on Arequipa .... Vol. 5A
DJ ovptd. on Obock .... Vol. 6A
Djibouti (Somali Coast) ..... Vol. 2B, Vol. 6A
Dobruja District .... Vol. 5B
Dodecanese Islands ..... Vol. 3A, Vol. 3B
Dollar, ovptd. on Russia .... Vol. 5B
Dominica .... Vol. 2B
Dominican Republic, Dominicana .... Vol. 2B
Don Government .... Vol. 6A
Dorpat .... Vol. 2B
Drzava SHS 780
Dubai .... 442, Vol. 2B, Vol. 5A
Duck Stamps (Hunting Permit) ... Vol. 1A
Duitsch Oost Afrika overprinted on Congo .... Vol. 3A
Duke de la Torre Regency .... Vol. 6A
Dulce et Decorum est Pro Patria Mori (Nepal O1) .... Vol. 5A
Dungarpur .... Vol. 3B
Durazzo .... Vol. 3B
Dutch Guiana (Surinam) .... Vol. 6A
Dutch Indies .... Vol. 5A
Dutch New Guinea .... Vol. 5A
Duttia .... Vol. 3B

EA .... Vol. 1A
E.A.F. overprinted on stamps of Great Britain .... Vol. 3A
East Africa (British) .... Vol. 1B
East Africa (German) .... Vol. 3A
East Africa (Italian) .... Vol. 3B
East Africa and Uganda Protectorates .... Vol. 2B, Vol. 4A
East Africa Forces .... Vol. 3A
East China .... Vol. 2A
Eastern Rumelia .... Vol. 2B
Eastern Rumelia stamps overprinted ... 227
Eastern Silesia .... Vol. 2B
Eastern Szechwan .... Vol. 2A
Eastern Thrace 83
East India .... Vol. 3B
East Saxony .... Vol. 3A
East Timor .... 72, Vol. 1A
Eatonton, Ga. .... Vol. 1A
Ecuador .... Vol. 2B
E.E.F. .... Vol. 5A
Eesti .... Vol. 2B
Egeo .... Vol. 3B
Egiziane (Egypt types A9-A10) ... Vol. 2B
Egypt, Egypte, Egyptiennes ...... Vol. 2B, Vol. 5A
Egypt, French Offices .... Vol. 2B
Eire, Eireann (Ireland) .... Vol. 3B
Ekaterinodar .... Vol. 6A
Elobey, Annobon and Corisco ... Vol. 2B
El Salvador .... Vol. 5B
Elsas, Elfas .... Vol. 2B
Elua Keneta .... Vol. 1A
Emory, Va. .... Vol. 1A
Empire, Franc, Francais .... Vol. 2B
En .... Vol. 4A
England .... Vol. 3A
Epirus .... Vol. 2B
Equateur (Ecuador #19-21) .... Vol. 2B
Equatorial Guinea .... Vol. 2B
Eritrea .... Vol. 2B
Eritrea (British Military Administration) .... Vol. 3A
Escuelas 607
Espana, Espanola .... Vol. 6A
Estado da India .... Vol. 5B
Est Africain Allemand overprinted on Congo .... Vol. 3A
Estensi .... Vol. 3B
Estero .... Vol. 3B
Estland .... Vol. 2B, Vol. 5B
Estonia .... Vol. 2B, Vol. 5B
Etablissments Francais dans l'Inde .... Vol. 2B
Ethiopia, Etiopia, Ethiopie, Ethiopiennes .... Vol. 2B, Vol. 3A
Eupen .... Vol. 3A
Europe .... Vol. 3A
Express Letter .... Vol. 2A

15 August 1947 (Pakistan #23) .... Vol. 5A
500 anos, viaje del descubrimiento de istmo (Panama #897) .... Vol. 5A
F. A. F. L. .... Vol. 6A
Falkland Dependencies .... Vol. 2B
Falkland Islands .... Vol. 2B
Far Eastern Republic .... Vol. 2B
Far Eastern Republic surcharged or ovptd. .... Vol. 6A
Faridkot .... Vol. 3B
Faroe Islands .... Vol. 2B
FCFA ovptd. on France .... Vol. 2B
Federacion 607
Federal Republic (Germany) .... Vol. 3A
Federated Malay States .... Vol. 4B
Fen, Fn. (Manchukuo) .... Vol. 4B
Fernando Po, Fdo. Poo .... Vol. 2B
Feudatory States .... Vol. 3B
Fezzan, Fezzan-Ghadames .... Vol. 4A
Fiera Campionaria Tripoli .... Vol. 4A
Fiji .... Vol. 2B
Fiji overprinted or surcharged ..... Vol. 5A

Filipinas, Filipas. .... Vol. 5A
Fincastle, Va. .... Vol. 1A
Finland .... Vol. 2B
Finnish Occupation of Karelia .... Vol. 4A
Finnish Occupation of Russia ... Vol. 4A, Vol. 5B
Fiume .... Vol. 2B
Fiume-Kupa Zone (Fiumano Kupa) ... 832
Five Cents (Confed. #53X) .... Vol. 1A
Florida 532
F. M. .... Vol. 2B
Foochow, Chinese .... Vol. 2A
Foochow, German .... Vol. 3A
Formosa .... Vol. 2A, Vol. 4A
Foroyar .... Vol. 2B
Forsyth, Ga. .... Vol. 1A
Fort Valley, Ga. .... Vol. 1A
Franc .... Vol. 2B
Franc ovptd. on Austria .... Vol. 1B
Franca ovptd. on stamps of Peru .... Vol. 5A
Francais, Francaise ...... See France and French colonies
France .... Vol. 2B
France (German occupation) ..... Vol. 2B
France D'Outre Mer .... Vol. 2B
Franco Bollo .... Vol. 3B
Franco Marke .... Vol. 3A
Franco Scrisorei .... Vol. 5B
Franklin, N.C. .... Vol. 1A
Franqueo .... Vol. 5A
Franquicia .... Vol. 6A
Fraziersville, S.C. .... Vol. 1A
Fredericksburg, Va. .... Vol. 1A
Free .... Vol. 1A
Frei Durch Ablosung .... Vol. 3A
Freimarke (No Country Name) ... Vol. 3A
French Administration of Andorra .... Vol. 1A
French Administration of Saar ... Vol. 5B
French Colonies .... Vol. 2B
French Colonies surcharged or overprinted .... Vol. 1A, Vol. 2B, Vol. 3A, Vol. 3B, Vol. 4B, Vol. 5A, Vol. 6A
French Commemoratives Index .... Vol. 2B
French Congo .... Vol. 2B
French Equatorial Africa .... 375, Vol. 2A, Vol. 2B, Vol. 4B
French Guiana .... Vol. 2B
French Guinea .... Vol. 2B
French India .... Vol. 2B
French Levant .... Vol. 2B, Vol. 6A
French Mandate of Alaouites ..... Vol. 1A
French Mandate of Lebanon ...... Vol. 4A
French Morocco .... Vol. 2B
French Occupation of Cameroun ... Vol. 2A
French Occupation of Castellorizo .... Vol. 2A
French Occupation of Crete .... Vol. 2A
French Occupation of Germany .... Vol. 3A
French Occupation of Hungary ... Vol. 3B
French Occupation of Libya .... Vol. 4A
French Occupation of Syria .... Vol. 6A
French Occupation of Togo 75
French Oceania .... Vol. 2B
French Offices Abroad .... Vol. 2B
French Offices in China .... Vol. 2B
French Offices in Crete .... Vol. 2B
French Offices in Egypt .... Vol. 2B
French Offices in Madagascar ... Vol. 4B
French Offices in Morocco .... Vol. 2B
French Offices in Tangier .... Vol. 2B
French Offices in Turkish Empire ... Vol. 6A
French Offices in Turkish Empire surcharged .... Vol. 6A
French Offices in Zanzibar .... Vol. 2B
French Polynesia .... Vol. 2B
French Saar .... Vol. 5B
French Southern and Antarctic Territories .... Vol. 2B
French stamps inscribed CFA .... Vol. 2B
French stamps surcharged .... Vol. 2B, Vol. 4B, Vol. 6A
French Sudan .... Vol. 2B
French West Africa .... Vol. 2B
French Zone (Germany) .... Vol. 3A
Frimarke, Frmrk (No Country Name) .... Vol. 2B, Vol. 5A, Vol. 6A
Fujeira .... 442, Vol. 2B
Fukien .... Vol. 2A
Funafuti 371
Funchal .... Vol. 2B

G or GW overprinted on Cape of Good Hope .... Vol. 3A
GAB on French Colonies .... Vol. 3A
Gabon, Gabonaise .... Vol. 3A
Gainesville, Ala. .... Vol. 1A
Galapagos Islands .... Vol. 2B
Galveston, Tex. .... Vol. 1A
Gambia .... Vol. 3A
Gaston, N.C. .... Vol. 1A
Gaza .... Vol. 3B
G & (et) D overprinted on French Colonies .... Vol. 3A
G.E.A. ovptd. .... Vol. 3A, Vol. 6A
General Gouvernement (Poland) ... Vol. 5B
Geneva, Geneve .... Vol. 6A
Georgetown, S.C. .... Vol. 1A
Georgia .... 154, Vol. 3A
Georgia, Offices in Turkey .... Vol. 3A
Georgienne, Republique .... Vol. 3A
German Administration of Albania ... Vol. 1A
German Administration of Danzig .... Vol. 2B
German Administration of Saar ... Vol. 5B
German Democratic Republic .... Vol. 3A
German Dominion of Cameroun ... Vol. 2A
German Dominion of Caroline Islands .... Vol. 2A
German Dominion of Mariana Is. ... Vol. 4B
German Dominion of Marshall Is. ... Vol. 4B
German Dominion of Samoa ...... Vol. 5B
German Dominion of Togo 75
German East Africa .... Vol. 3A
German East Africa (Belgian occ.) .... Vol. 3A
German East Africa (British occ.) .... Vol. 3A
German New Guinea .... Vol. 3A
German New Guinea (New Britain) .... Vol. 5A
German Occupation of Belgium .... Vol. 1B
German Occupation of Estonia ... Vol. 2B
German Occupation of France .... Vol. 2B
German Occupation of Guernsey .... Vol. 3A
German Occupation of Ionian Is. ... Vol. 3B
German Occupation of Jersey ... Vol. 3A
German Occupation of Latvia .... Vol. 4A
German Occupation of Lithuania ... Vol. 5B
German Occupation of Ljubljana 832
German Occupation of Luxembourg .... Vol. 4A
German Occupation of Macedonia .... Vol. 4B
German Occupation of Montenegro .... Vol. 4B
German Occupation of Poland ... Vol. 5B
German Occupation of Romania ... Vol. 5B
German Occupation of Russia ... Vol. 5B
German Occupation of Serbia ... Vol. 6A
German Occupation of Ukraine .... Vol. 5B
German Occupation of Yugoslavia ... 832
German Occupation of Zante .... Vol. 3B
German Offices in China .... Vol. 3A
German Offices in China surcharged .... Vol. 4A
German Offices in Morocco .... Vol. 3A
German Offices in Turkish Empire .... Vol. 3A
German Protectorate of Bohemia and Moravia .... Vol. 2B
German South-West Africa .... Vol. 3A
German stamps surchd. or ovptd. .... Vol. 3A, Vol. 5B, Vol. 6A
German States .... Vol. 3A
Germany .... Vol. 3A
Germany (Allied Military Govt.) ... Vol. 3A
Gerusalemme .... Vol. 3B
Ghadames .... Vol. 4A
Ghana .... Vol. 3A
Gibraltar .... Vol. 3A
Gilbert and Ellice Islands .... Vol. 3A
Gilbert Islands .... Vol. 3A
Giumulzina District 68
Gniezno .... Vol. 5B
Gold Coast .... Vol. 3A
Golfo del Guinea .... Vol. 6A
Goliad, Tex. .... Vol. 1A
Gonzales, Tex. .... Vol. 1A
Gorny Slask 464
Government (U.S. 1LB) .... Vol. 1A
Governo Militare Alleato .... Vol. 3B
G.P.E. ovptd. on French Colonies .... Vol. 3A
Graham Land .... Vol. 2B
Granada .... Vol. 6A
Granadine Confederation, Granadina .... Vol. 2A
Grand Comoro, Grande Comore .... Vol. 3A
Grand Liban, Gd Liban .... Vol. 4A
Great Britain (see also British) .... Vol. 3A
Great Britain, Gaelic ovpt. .... Vol. 3B
Great Britain, Offices in Africa .... Vol. 3A
Great Britain, Offices in China ... Vol. 3A
Great Britain, Offices in Morocco ... Vol. 3A
Great Britain, Offices in Turkish Empire .... Vol. 3A
Greater Rajasthan Union .... Vol. 3B
Greece .... Vol. 3A
Greek Occupation of Albania, North Epirus, Dodecanese Islands ..... Vol. 3A
Greek Occupation of Epirus .... Vol. 3A
Greek Occ. of the Aegean Islands .... Vol. 3A
Greek Occupation of Thrace 83
Greek Occupation of Turkey ... 228, Vol. 3A
Greek stamps overprinted ....77, Vol. 2B
Greenland .... Vol. 3A
Greensboro, Ala. .... Vol. 1A
Greensboro, N.C. .... Vol. 1A
Greenville .... Vol. 4A
Greenville, Ala. .... Vol. 1A
Greenville, Tenn. .... Vol. 1A
Greenville Court House, S.C. ..... Vol. 1A
Greenwood Depot, Va. .... Vol. 1A
Grenada .... Vol. 3A
Grenadines of Grenada .... Vol. 3A
Grenadines of St. Vincent .... Vol. 5B
Grenville .... Vol. 4A
G.R.I. overprinted on German New Guinea .... Vol. 5A
G.R.I. overprinted on German Samoa .... Vol. 5B
G.R.I. overprinted on Marshall Is. ... Vol. 5A
Griffin, Ga. .... Vol. 1A
Griqualand West .... Vol. 3A
Grodno District .... Vol. 4A
Gronland .... Vol. 3A
Grossdeutsches Reich (Germany #529) .... Vol. 3A
Groszy .... Vol. 5B
Grove Hill, Ala. .... Vol. 1A
Gruzija (Georgia) .... Vol. 3A
Guadalajara .... Vol. 4B
Guadeloupe .... Vol. 3A
Guam .... Vol. 1A
Guanacaste .... Vol. 2A
Guatemala .... Vol. 3A
Guayana 652
Guernsey .... Vol. 3A
Guernsey, German Occupation ... Vol. 3A
Guiana, British .... Vol. 1B
Guiana, Dutch .... Vol. 6A
Guiana, French .... Vol. 2B
Guine .... Vol. 3A, Vol. 5B
Guinea .... Vol. 3A, Vol. 6A
Guinea Ecuatorial .... Vol. 2B
Guinea, French .... Vol. 2B
Guinea, Portuguese .... Vol. 5B
Guinea, Spanish .... Vol. 6A
Guinea-Bissau, Guine-Bissau .... Vol. 3A
Guinee .... Vol. 2B, Vol. 3A
Guipuzcoa Province .... Vol. 6A
Gultig 9, Armee .... Vol. 5B
Guyana .... Vol. 3A
Guyane, Guy. Franc. .... Vol. 2B
G.W. ovptd. on Cape of Good Hope .... Vol. 3A
Gwalior .... Vol. 3B

Habilitado-1/2 (Tlacotalpan #1) ... Vol. 4B
Habilitado on Stamps of Cuba ... Vol. 1A, Vol. 2A, Vol. 5A
Habilitado on Telegrafos or revenues .... Vol. 5A, Vol. 6A
Hadhramaut .... Vol. 1A
Hainan Island .... Vol. 2A
Haiti .... Vol. 3B
Hall, A. D. (Confed. #27XU1) ...... Vol. 1A
Hallettsville, Tex. .... Vol. 1A
Hamburg .... Vol. 3A
Hamburgh, S.C. .... Vol. 1A
Hamilton, Bermuda .... Vol. 1B
Hanover, Hannover .... Vol. 3A
Harar .... Vol. 2B
Harper .... Vol. 4A
Harrisburgh, Tex. .... Vol. 1A
Hatay .... Vol. 3B
Hatirasi (Turkey Design PT44) 296
Hatohobei (Palau #686) .... Vol. 5A
Haute Silesie 464
Haute Volta .... Vol. 1B
Haut Senegal-Niger 464
Hawaii, Hawaiian .... Vol. 1A
H B A ovptd. on Russia .... Vol. 6A
Hebrew inscriptions .... Vol. 3B
H.E.H. The Nizam's (Hyderabad) ... Vol. 3B
Heilungkiang .... Vol. 2A
Hejaz .... Vol. 6A
Hejaz-Nejd .... Vol. 6A
Hejaz overprinted .... Vol. 4A, Vol. 6A
Helena, Tex. .... Vol. 1A
Heligoland, Helgoland .... Vol. 3B
Hellas .... Vol. 3A
Helsinki (Helsingfors) .... Vol. 2B
Helvetia, Helvetica (Switzerland) ... Vol. 6A
Heraklion .... Vol. 2A
Herceg Bosna .... Vol. 1B
Herzegovina .... Vol. 1B
Herzogth .... Vol. 3A
H.H. Nawabshah Jahanbegam ... Vol. 3B
H.I. Postage .... Vol. 1A
Hillsboro, N.C. .... Vol. 1A
Hoi Hao, French Offices .... Vol. 2B
Holkar (Indore) .... Vol. 3B
Holland (Netherlands) .... Vol. 5A
Hollandale, Tex. .... Vol. 1A
Holstein .... Vol. 3A
Honan .... Vol. 2A
Honda .... Vol. 2A
Honduras .... Vol. 3B
Honduras, British .... Vol. 1B
Hong Kong .... Vol. 2A, Vol. 3B
Hong Kong (Japanese Occupation) .... Vol. 3B
Hong Kong Special Admin. Region .... Vol. 3B
Hong Kong ovptd. China .... Vol. 3A
Honour's (Hondur's) City .... Vol. 1A
Hopeh .... Vol. 2A
Hopei .... Vol. 2A
Horta .... Vol. 3B
Houston, Tex. .... Vol. 1A
Hrvatska .... 780, Vol. 1B, Vol. 2A
Hrzgl. .... Vol. 3A
Huacho .... Vol. 5A
Hunan .... Vol. 2A
Hungary .... Vol. 1B, Vol. 3B
Hungary (French Occupation) .... Vol. 3B
Hungary (Romanian Occupation) ... Vol. 3B
Hungary (Serbian Occupation) ... Vol. 3B
Huntsville, Tex. .... Vol. 1A
Hupeh .... Vol. 2A
Hyderabad (Deccan) .... Vol. 3B

I.B. (West Irian) .... Vol. 3B
Icaria .... Vol. 3A
ICC ovptd. on India .... Vol. 3B
Iceland .... Vol. 3B
Idar .... Vol. 3B
I.E.F. ovptd. on India .... Vol. 3B
I.E.F. 'D' ovptd. on Turkey .... Vol. 4B
Ierusalem .... Vol. 5B
Ifni .... Vol. 3B
Ile Rouad .... Vol. 5B
Imperio Colonial Portugues .... Vol. 5B
Imposto de Selo .... Vol. 5B
Impuesto (Impto) de Guerra .... Vol. 6A
Inde. Fcaise .... Vol. 2B
Independence, Tex. .... Vol. 1A
Index of U.S. Issues .... Vol. 1A
India .... Vol. 3B, Vol. 5B
India, China Expeditionary Force ... Vol. 3B
India, Convention States .... Vol. 3B
India, Feudatory States .... Vol. 3B
India, French .... Vol. 2B
India, Portuguese .... Vol. 5B
India stamps overprinted .... Vol. 3B, Vol. 4A, Vol. 5A
India, surcharge and crown .... Vol. 6A
Indian Custodial Unit, Korea ...... Vol. 3B
Indian Expeditionary Force .... Vol. 3B
Indian U.N. Force, Congo .... Vol. 3B
Indian U.N. Force, Gaza .... Vol. 3B
Indian Postal Administration of Bahrain .... Vol. 1B
Indo-China, Indo-chine .... Vol. 3B
Indo-China stamps surcharged 662
Indo-China, Int. Commission ..... Vol. 3B
Indonesia .... Vol. 3B, Vol. 5A
Indore .... Vol. 3B
Industrielle Kriegswirschaft .... Vol. 6A
Inhambane .... Vol. 3B
Inini .... Vol. 3B
Inland (Liberia #21) .... Vol. 4A
Inner Mongolia (Meng Chiang) ... Vol. 2A
Insufficiently prepaid 864
Instrucao 88
Instruccion 608
International Bureau of Education .... Vol. 6A
International Commission in Indo-China .... Vol. 3B
International Court of Justice ..... Vol. 5A
International Labor Bureau .... Vol. 6A
International Olympic Committee ... Vol. 6A
International Refugee Organization .... Vol. 6A
International Telecommunication Union .... Vol. 6A
Ionian Islands, IONIKON KPATOE .... Vol. 3B
I.O.V.R. .... Vol. 5B
Iran, Iraniennes .... Vol. 3B
Iran (Bushire) .... Vol. 1B
Iran, Turkish Occupation .... Vol. 3B
Iran with Rs. 10 denomination (Pakistan #1101) .... Vol. 5A
Iraq .... Vol. 3B

Iraq (British Occupation) .... Vol. 3B, Vol. 4B
Ireland .... Vol. 3B
Ireland, Northern .... Vol. 3A
Irian Barat .... Vol. 3B
Isabella, Ga. .... Vol. 1A
Island .... Vol. 3B
Isle of Man .... Vol. 3A
Isole Italiane dell'Egeo .... Vol. 3B
Isole Jonie .... Vol. 3B
Israel .... Vol. 3B
Istria 832
Itaca ovptd. on Greece .... Vol. 3B
Ita-Karjala .... Vol. 4A
Italia, Italiano, Italiane .... Vol. 3B
Italian Colonies .... Vol. 3B
Italian Dominion of Albania .... Vol. 1A
Italian Dominion of Castellorizo ... Vol. 2A
Italian East Africa .... Vol. 3B
Italian Jubaland .... Vol. 5A
Italian Occ. of Aegean Islands ... Vol. 3B
Italian Occupation of Austria .... Vol. 1B
Italian Occupation of Corfu .... Vol. 2A
Italian Occupation of Crete .... Vol. 2A
Italian Occupation of Dalmatia ... Vol. 2B
Italian Occupation of Ethiopia .... Vol. 2B
Italian Occupation of Fiume-Kupa 832
Italian Occupation of Ionian Islands .... Vol. 3B
Italian Occupation of Ljubljana 831
Italian Occupation of Montenegro .... Vol. 4B
Italian Occupation of Yugoslavia 832
Italian Offices Abroad .... Vol. 3B
Italian Offices in Africa .... Vol. 3B
Italian Offices in Albania .... Vol. 3B
Italian Offices in China .... Vol. 3B
Italian Offices in Constantinople Vol. 3B
Italian Offices in Crete .... Vol. 3B
Italian Offices in the Turkish Empire .... Vol. 3B
Italian Social Republic .... Vol. 3B
Italian Somaliland .... Vol. 6A
Italian Somaliland (E.A.F.) .... Vol. 3A
Italian stamps surcharged .... Vol. 1B, Vol. 2B, Vol. 3B
Italian States .... Vol. 3B
Italy (Allied Military Govt.) .... Vol. 3B
Italy (Austrian Occupation) .... Vol. 3B
Italy .... Vol. 3B
Ithaca .... Vol. 3B
Iuka, Miss. .... Vol. 1A
Ivory Coast .... Vol. 3B

J. ovptd. on stamps of Peru .... Vol. 5A
Jackson, Miss. .... Vol. 1A
Jacksonville, Ala. .... Vol. 1A
Jacksonville, Fla. .... Vol. 1A
Jaffa .... Vol. 5B
Jaipur .... Vol. 3B
Jamaica .... Vol. 4A
Jamhuri 863
Jammu .... Vol. 3B
Jammu and Kashmir .... Vol. 3B
Janina .... Vol. 3B
Japan, Japanese .... Vol. 4A
Japan (Australian Occ.) .... Vol. 1A
Japan (Taiwan) .... Vol. 2A, Vol. 4A
Japanese Offices Abroad .... Vol. 4A
Japan Occupation of Brunei .... Vol. 1B
Japan Occupation of Burma .... Vol. 1B
Japan Occupation of China .... Vol. 2A
Japan Occupation of Dutch Indies .... Vol. 5A
Japan Occupation of Hong Kong .... Vol. 3B
Japan Occupation of Johore .... Vol. 4B
Japan Occupation of Kedah .... Vol. 4B
Japan Occupation of Kelantan .... Vol. 4B
Japan Occupation of Malacca .... Vol. 4B
Japan Occupation of Malaya .... Vol. 4B
Japan Occupation of Negri Sembilan .... Vol. 4B
Japan Occupation of Netherlands Indies .... Vol. 5A
Japan Occupation of North Borneo .... Vol. 5A
Japan Occupation of Pahang .... Vol. 4B
Japan Occupation of Penang .... Vol. 4B
Japan Occupation of Perak .... Vol. 4B
Japan Occupation of Philippines .... Vol. 1A, Vol. 5A
Japan Occupation of Sarawak ... Vol. 6A
Japan Occupation of Selangor ... Vol. 4B
Japan Occupation of Sts. Settlements .... Vol. 6A
Japan Occ. of Trengganu .... Vol. 4B
Other Japanese Stamps Overprinted ... Vol. 1B, Vol. 2A, Vol. 4A, Vol. 5A
Jasdan .... Vol. 3B
Java .... Vol. 3B, Vol. 5A
Jedda .... Vol. 6A
Jeend .... Vol. 3B
Jehol .... Vol. 2A
Jersey .... Vol. 3A
Jersey, German Occupation .... Vol. 3A
Jerusalem, Italian Offices .... Vol. 3B
Jerusalem, Russian Offices .... Vol. 5B
Jetersville, Va. .... Vol. 1A
Jhalawar .... Vol. 3B
Jhind, Jind .... Vol. 3B
Johore, Johor .... Vol. 4B
Jonesboro, Tenn. .... Vol. 1A
J. P. Johnson (Confed. #66X1) ... Vol. 1A
Jordan .... Vol. 4A
Jordan (Palestine Occ.) .... Vol. 4A
Journaux .... Vol. 2B
Juan Fernandez Islands (Chile) ... Vol. 2A
Jubile de l'Union Postale Universelle (Switzerland #98) .... Vol. 6A
Jugoslavia, Jugoslavija 783
Junagarh .... Vol. 3B

K .... Vol. 1A
КАЗАКСТАН .... Vol. 4A
Kabul .... Vol. 1A
Kalaallit Nunaat, Kalatdlit Nunat .... Vol. 3A
Kamerun .... Vol. 2A
Kampuchea .... Vol. 2A
Kansu .... Vol. 2A
Karelia, Karjala .... Vol. 4A
Karema ovptd. on Belgian Congo .... Vol. 3A
Karki .... Vol. 3B
Karolinen .... Vol. 2A
Kashmir .... Vol. 3B
Katanga .... Vol. 4A
Kathiri State of Seiyun .... Vol. 1A
Kaunas .... Vol. 4A, Vol. 5B
Kayangel (Palau #686) .... Vol. 5A
Kazakhstan, Kazahstan, Kazakstan .... Vol. 4A
Kedah .... Vol. 4B
Keeling Islands .... Vol. 2A
Kelantan .... Vol. 4B
Kentta Postia .... Vol. 2B
Kenya .... Vol. 4A
Kenya and Uganda .... Vol. 4A
Kenya, Uganda, Tanzania .... Vol. 4A
Kenya, Uganda, Tanganyika .... Vol. 4A
Kenya, Uganda, Tanganyika, Zanzibar .... Vol. 4A
Kerassunde .... Vol. 5B
Kermanshah .... Vol. 3B
K.G.C.A. ovptd. on Yugoslavia 782
K.G.L. .... Vol. 1A, Vol. 2B
Kharkiv 403
Khmer Republic .... Vol. 2A
Khor Fakkan .... Vol. 6A
Kiangsi .... Vol. 2A
Kiangsu .... Vol. 2A
Kiauchau, Kiautschou .... Vol. 4A
Kibris 301
Kibris Cumhuriyeti (Cyprus #198-200) .... Vol. 2B
Kigoma ovptd. on Belgian Congo .... Vol. 3A
Kilis .... Vol. 6A
King Edward VII Land (New Zealand #121a) .... Vol. 5A
Kingman's City Post .... Vol. 1A
Kingston, Ga. .... Vol. 1A
Kionga .... Vol. 4A
Kirghizia .... Vol. 4A
Kiribati .... Vol. 4A
Kirin .... Vol. 2A
Kishangarh, Kishengarh .... Vol. 3B
Kithyra .... Vol. 3A, Vol. 3B
K.K. Post Stempel (or Stampel) .... Vol. 1B
K.K.T.C. (Turk. Rep. N. Cyprus #RA1) 316
Klaipeda .... Vol. 4B
Knoxville, Tenn. .... Vol. 1A
Kolomyia 752
Kolozsvar .... Vol. 3B
Kon .... Vol. 1B, Vol. 2B, Vol. 4A, Vol. 5B, Vol. 6A
Kongeligt .... Vol. 2B
Kop Koh .... Vol. 2B
Korca, Korce (Albania) .... Vol. 1A
Korea .... Vol. 4A
Korea, Democratic People's Republic .... Vol. 4A
Korea (Japanese Offices) .... Vol. 4A
Korea, Indian Custodial Unit .... Vol. 3B
Korea, North .... Vol. 4A
Korea, Soviet occupation .... Vol. 4A
Korea, U.S. Military Govt. .... Vol. 4A
Koritsa .... Vol. 2B
Koror (Palau #686) .... Vol. 5A
Korytsa (Albania #81) .... Vol. 1A
Kos .... Vol. 3B
Kosova .... Vol. 4A
Kosovo .... Vol. 1A, Vol. 4A
Kotah .... Vol. 3B
Kouang Tcheou-Wan .... Vol. 2B
KPHTH (Crete) .... Vol. 2A
Kr., Kreuzer .... Vol. 1B, Vol. 3B
Kraljevstvo, Kraljevina 780
K.S.A. .... Vol. 6A
Kuban Government .... Vol. 6A
K.U.K., K. und K. .... Vol. 1B, Vol. 3B, Vol. 5B
Kunming .... Vol. 2B
Kupa Zone 832
Kurdistan .... Vol. 3B
Kurland, Kurzeme .... Vol. 4A, Vol. 5B
Kurus 294
Kuwait, Koweit .... Vol. 4A, Vol. 5A
Kwangchowan .... Vol. 2B
Kwangsi .... Vol. 2A
Kwangtung .... Vol. 2A
Kweichow .... Vol. 2A
K. Wurtt. Post .... Vol. 3A
Kyiv 403
Kyrgyz Express Post .... Vol. 4A
Kyrgyzstan .... Vol. 4A

La Aguera .... Vol. 1A
Labuan .... Vol. 4A
La Canea .... Vol. 3B
Lady McLeod 157
La Georgie .... Vol. 3A
Lagos .... Vol. 4A
La Grange, Tex. .... Vol. 1A
Laibach 831
Lake City, Fla. .... Vol. 1A
Lanchow .... Vol. 2A
Land Post .... Vol. 3A
Lao, Laos .... Vol. 4A
Laos (Int. Com., India) .... Vol. 3B
L.A.R. .... Vol. 4A
Las Bela .... Vol. 3B
Latakia, Lattaquie .... Vol. 4A
Latvia, Latvija .... Vol. 4A, Vol. 5B
Laurens Court House, S.C. .... Vol. 1A
Lavaca .... Vol. 1A
League of Nations .... Vol. 6A
Lebanon .... Vol. 4A, Vol. 5A, Vol. 6A
Leeward Islands .... Vol. 4A
Lefkas .... Vol. 3A, Vol. 3B
Lei ovptd. on Austria .... Vol. 5B
Lemnos .... Vol. 3A
Lenoir, N.C. .... Vol. 1A
Lero, Leros .... Vol. 3B
Lesbos .... Vol. 3A
Lesotho .... Vol. 4A
Lesser Sundas .... Vol. 5A
Lettland, Lettonia .... Vol. 4A
Letzebuerg .... Vol. 4A
Levant, British .... Vol. 3A
Levant, French .... Vol. 2B, Vol. 6A
Levant, Italian .... Vol. 3B
Levant, Polish .... Vol. 5B
Levant, Romanian .... Vol. 5B
Levant, Russian .... Vol. 5B
Levant, Syrian (on Lebanon) .... Vol. 6A
Lexington, Miss. .... Vol. 1A
Lexington, Va. .... Vol. 1A
Liaoning .... Vol. 2A
Liban, Libanaise .... Vol. 4A
Libau ovptd. on German .... Vol. 4A
Liberia .... Vol. 4A
Liberty, Va. .... Vol. 1A
Libya, Libia, Libye .... Vol. 4A
Libyan Arab Republic .... Vol. 4A
Liechtenstein .... Vol. 4A
Lietuva, Lietuvos .... Vol. 4A
Lifland .... Vol. 5B
Ligne Aeriennes de la France Libre (Syria #MC5) .... Vol. 6A
Lima .... Vol. 5A
Limestone Springs, S.C. .... Vol. 1A
L'Inde .... Vol. 2B
Linja-Autorahti Bussfrakt .... Vol. 2B
Lipso, Lisso .... Vol. 3B
Lithuania .... Vol. 4A, Vol. 5B
Lithuania, Central .... Vol. 2A
Lithuanian Occupation of Memel ... Vol. 4B
Litwa Srodkowa, Litwy Srodkowej .... Vol. 2A
Livingston, Ala. .... Vol. 1A
Livonia .... Vol. 5B
Ljubljana 831
Llanes .... Vol. 6A
L McL 157
Local 289
Local Post .... Vol. 2A
Lockport, N.Y. .... Vol. 1A
Lombardy-Venetia .... Vol. 1B
Lorraine .... Vol. 2B
Losen .... Vol. 6A
Lothringen .... Vol. 2B
Louisville, Ky. .... Vol. 1A
Lourenco Marques, L. Marques .... Vol. 4A
Lower Austria .... Vol. 1B
L P overprinted on Russian stamps .... Vol. 4A
LTSR on Lithuania .... Vol. 4A
Lubeck, Luebeck .... Vol. 3A
Lubiana 831
Lublin .... Vol. 5B
Luminescence .... Vol. 1A
Luxembourg .... Vol. 4A
Lviv 752
Lydenburg 156
Lynchburg, Va. .... Vol. 1A

Macao, Macau .... Vol. 4B
Macedonia .... Vol. 4B
Machin Head definitives .... Vol. 3A
Macon, Ga. .... Vol. 1A
Madagascar, Madagasikara .... Vol. 4B
Madagascar (British) .... Vol. 4B
Madeira .... Vol. 4B, Vol. 5B
Madero Issue (Mexico) .... Vol. 4B
Madison, Ga. .... Vol. 1A
Madison Court House, Fla. .... Vol. 1A
Madrid .... Vol. 6A
Madura .... Vol. 5A
Mafeking .... Vol. 2A
Magdalena .... Vol. 2A
Magyar, Magyarorszag .... Vol. 3B
Magy. Kir. .... Vol. 3B
Majunga .... Vol. 4B
Makedonija .... Vol. 4B
Malacca .... Vol. 4B
Malaga .... Vol. 6A
Malagasy Republic .... Vol. 4B
Malawi .... Vol. 4B
Malaya .... Vol. 4B
Malaya (Japanese Occ.) .... Vol. 4B, Vol. 5A
Malaya (Thai Occ.) .... Vol. 4B
Malaya, Federation of .... Vol. 4B
Malaysia .... Vol. 4B
Malay States .... Vol. 4B
Maldive Islands, Maldives .... Vol. 4B
Malgache Republique .... Vol. 4B
Mali .... Vol. 4B
Malmedy .... Vol. 3A
Malta .... Vol. 4B
Maluku Selatan (So. Moluccas) ... Vol. 6A
Man, Isle of .... Vol. 3A
Manchukuo .... Vol. 4B
Manchukuo stamps overprinted ... Vol. 2A
Manchuria .... Vol. 2A
Manizales .... Vol. 2A
Mapka, Mapok .... Vol. 2B, Vol. 5B
Mariana Islands, Marianen .... Vol. 4B
Marienwerder .... Vol. 4B
Marietta, Ga. .... Vol. 1A
Marion, Va. .... Vol. 1A
Markka, Markkaa .... Vol. 2B
Maroc, Marocco, Marokko .... Vol. 2B, Vol. 3A, Vol. 4B
Marruecos .... Vol. 4B, Vol. 6A
Mars Bluff, S.C. .... Vol. 1A
Marshall Islands, Marschall-Inseln, Marshall-Inseln .... Vol. 4B
Marshall Islands (G.R.I. surch.) .... Vol. 5A
Martinique .... Vol. 4B
Martin's City Post .... Vol. 1A
Mauritania, Mauritanie .... Vol. 4B
Mauritania stamps surcharged ... Vol. 2B
Mauritius .... Vol. 4B
Mayotte .... Vol. 4B
Mayreau .... Vol. 5B
M.B.D. overprinted .... Vol. 3B
McNeel, A.W. .... Vol. 1A
Mecca .... Vol. 6A
Mecklenburg-Schwerin .... Vol. 3A
Mecklenburg-Strelitz .... Vol. 3A
Mecklenburg-Vorpomm .... Vol. 3A
Mecklenburg-Vorpommern .... Vol. 3A
Medellin .... Vol. 2A
Medina .... Vol. 6A
Medio Real .... Vol. 2B
M.E.F. ovptd on Great Britain .... Vol. 3A
Mejico .... Vol. 4B
Melaka .... Vol. 4B
Melekeor (Palau #686) .... Vol. 5A
Memel, Memelgebiet .... Vol. 4B
Memphis, Tenn. .... Vol. 1A
Meng Chiang .... Vol. 2A
Menge .... Vol. 4B
Mengtsz .... Vol. 2B
Merida .... Vol. 4B
Meshed .... Vol. 3B
Mesopotamia (British Occupation) .... Vol. 4B
Metelin .... Vol. 5B

Mexico, Mexicano .... Vol. 4B
Micanopy, Fla. .... Vol. 1A
Micronesia .... Vol. 4B
Middle Congo .... Vol. 4B
Middle East Forces .... Vol. 3A
Mihon .... Vol. 4A
Mil .... Vol. 4A
Militarpost (Milit. Post) .... Vol. 1B
Millbury, Mass. .... Vol. 1A
Milledgeville, Ga. .... Vol. 1A
Miller, Gen. .... Vol. 5B
Milliemes surch. on French Off. in Turkey .... Vol. 2B
Mitau .... Vol. 4A
Milton, N.C. .... Vol. 1A
M. Kir. .... Vol. 3B
Mn. .... Vol. 4A
Mobile, Ala. .... Vol. 1A
Mocambique .... Vol. 4B
Modena, Modones .... Vol. 3B
Moheli .... Vol. 4B
Moldavia .... Vol. 4B, Vol. 5B
Moldova .... Vol. 4B
Moluccas .... Vol. 5A
Monaco .... Vol. 4B
Monastir 228
Mongolia .... Vol. 4B
Mongtseu, Mongtze .... Vol. 2B
Monrovia .... Vol. 4A
Mont Athos .... Vol. 5B
Montenegro .... Vol. 4B
Monterrey .... Vol. 4B
Montevideo 465, 532
Montgomery, Ala. .... Vol. 1A
Montserrat .... Vol. 4B
Moquea, Moquegua .... Vol. 5A
Morelia .... Vol. 4B
Morocco .... Vol. 4B
Morocco (British Offices) .... Vol. 3A
Morocco (German Offices) .... Vol. 3A
Morocco, French .... Vol. 2B
Morocco, Spanish .... Vol. 6A
Morvi .... Vol. 3B
Moschopolis .... Vol. 2B
Mosul .... Vol. 4B
Mount Athos (Greece) .... Vol. 3A
Mount Athos (Turkey) 289
Mount Athos, Russian Offices ... Vol. 5B
Mount Lebanon, La. .... Vol. 1A
Mount Pleasant, NC .... Vol. 1A
Moyen-Congo .... Vol. 4B
Mozambique .... Vol. 4B
Mozambique Co. .... Vol. 4B
MQE ovptd. on French Colonies ... Vol. 4B
Muscat and Oman .... Vol. 5A
Mustique .... Vol. 5B
M.V.iR .... Vol. 5B
Myanmar (Burma) .... Vol. 1B
Mytilene .... Vol. 3A

Nabha .... Vol. 3B
Naciones Unidas .... Vol. 1A
Nagyvarad .... Vol. 3B
Namibia .... Vol. 5A, Vol. 6A
Nandgaon .... Vol. 3B
Nanking .... Vol. 2A
Nanumaga 371
Nanumea 372
Naples, Napoletana .... Vol. 3B
Nashville, Tenn. .... Vol. 1A
Natal .... Vol. 5A
Nations Unies .... Vol. 1A, Vol. 6A
Native Feudatory States, India ... Vol. 3B
Nauru .... Vol. 5A
Navanagar .... Vol. 3B
Navarra .... Vol. 6A
N.C.E. ovptd. on French Colonies .... Vol. 5A
Neapolitan Provinces .... Vol. 3B
Ned. (Nederlandse) Antillen .... Vol. 5A
Ned. (Nederl, Nederlandse) Indie ... Vol. 5A
Nederland .... Vol. 5A
Nederlands Nieuw Guinea .... Vol. 5A
Negeri Sembilan .... Vol. 4B
Negri Sembilan .... Vol. 4B
Nejd .... Vol. 6A
Nejdi Administration of Hejaz ..... Vol. 6A
Nepal .... Vol. 5A
Netherlands .... Vol. 5A
Netherlands Antilles .... Vol. 5A
Netherlands Indies .... Vol. 5A
Netherlands New Guinea .... Vol. 5A
Nevis .... Vol. 5A
New Britain .... Vol. 5A
New Brunswick .... Vol. 2A
New Caledonia .... Vol. 5A
New Caledonia stamps overprinted .... Vol. 5A
Newfoundland .... Vol. 2A
New Granada .... Vol. 2A
New Greece .... Vol. 3A
New Guinea .... Vol. 5A
New Guinea, British .... Vol. 5A
New Guinea, German .... Vol. 3A
New Haven, Conn. .... Vol. 1A
New Hebrides (British) .... Vol. 5A
New Hebrides (French) .... Vol. 5A
New Orleans, La. .... Vol. 1A
New Republic .... Vol. 5A
New Smyrna, Fla. .... Vol. 1A
New South Wales .... Vol. 1A
New York, N.Y. .... Vol. 1A
New Zealand .... Vol. 5A
Nezavisna .... Vol. 2A
N.F. overprinted on Nyasaland Pro. .... Vol. 3A
Ngaraard (Palau #686) .... Vol. 5A
Ngardman (Palau #686) .... Vol. 5A
Ngaremlengui (Palau #686) .... Vol. 5A
Ngchesar (Palau #686) .... Vol. 5A
Ngiwal (Palau #686) .... Vol. 5A
Nicaragua .... Vol. 5A
Nicaria .... Vol. 3A
Nieuwe Republiek .... Vol. 5A
Nieuw Guinea .... Vol. 5A
Niger .... Vol. 5A
Niger and Senegambia .... Vol. 6A
Niger and Upper Senegal 464
Niger Coast Protectorate .... Vol. 5A
Nigeria .... Vol. 5A
Nikolaevsk .... Vol. 6A
Ningsia .... Vol. 2A
Nippon .... Vol. 4A
Nisiro, Nisiros .... Vol. 3B
Niuafo'ou 147
Niue .... Vol. 5A
Niutao 372
Nlle. Caledonie .... Vol. 5A
No Hay Estampillas .... Vol. 2A
N. O. P. O. (Confed. #62XU1) ..... Vol. 1A
Norddeutscher Postbezirk .... Vol. 3A
Noreg (1st stamp #318) .... Vol. 5A
Norfolk, Va. .... Vol. 1A
Norfolk Island .... Vol. 5A
Norge .... Vol. 5A
North Borneo .... Vol. 5A
North China .... Vol. 2A
Northeast China .... Vol. 2A
Northeast Postal Service .... Vol. 2A
Northeastern Provinces (China) ... Vol. 2A
North Epirus (Greek Occupation) ... Vol. 3A
Northern Cook Islands .... Vol. 5A
Northern Cyprus, Turkish Rep. of ... 301
Northern Ireland .... Vol. 3A
Northern Kiangsu .... Vol. 2A
Northern Nigeria .... Vol. 5A
Northern Poland .... Vol. 5B
Northern Rhodesia .... Vol. 5A
Northern Zone, Morocco .... Vol. 4B
North German Confederation ..... Vol. 3A
North Ingermanland .... Vol. 5A
North Viet Nam 662
Northwest China .... Vol. 2A
North West (N. W.) Pacific Islands .... Vol. 5A
Norway .... Vol. 5A
Nossi-Be .... Vol. 5A
Notopher .... Vol. 3A
Nouvelle Caledonie .... Vol. 5A
Nouvelle Hebrides .... Vol. 5A
Nova Scotia .... Vol. 2A
Novocherkassk .... Vol. 6A
Nowa .... Vol. 1B
Nowa Bb ovptd. on Bulgaria ...... Vol. 5B
Nowanuggur .... Vol. 3B
Nowta .... Vol. 6A
Nowte .... Vol. 4B
Noyta ...... 154, Vol. 1B, Vol. 3A, Vol. 4A, Vol. 5B
NP surcharged on Great Britain ... Vol. 5A
Nr. 21, Nr. 16 .... Vol. 3A
N S B ovptd. on French Colonies .... Vol. 5A
N. Sembilan .... Vol. 4B
N.S.W. .... Vol. 1A
Nueva Granada .... Vol. 2A
Nui 373
Nukufetau 373
Nukulaelae 374
Nyasaland (Protectorate) .... Vol. 5A
Nyasaland and Rhodesia .... Vol. 5B
Nyasaland, overprinted .... Vol. 3A
Nyassa .... Vol. 5A
N.Z. .... Vol. 5A

Oakway, S.C. .... Vol. 1A
Oaxaca .... Vol. 4B
Obock .... Vol. 5A
Ob. Ost ovptd. on Germany (Lithuania) .... Vol. 5B
Occupation Francaise .... Vol. 3B
Oceania, Oceanie .... Vol. 2B
Oesterr. Post, Ofterreich .... Vol. 1B
Offentlig Sak, Off. Sak .... Vol. 5A
Oil Rivers .... Vol. 5A
O K C A (Russia) .... Vol. 5B
Oldenburg .... Vol. 3A
Olonets .... Vol. 5B
Oltre Giuba .... Vol. 5A
Oman, Sultanate of .... Vol. 5A
ONU (UN Offices in Geneva #384) .... Vol. 1A
Oradea .... Vol. 3B
Orange River Colony .... Vol. 5A
Oranje Vrij Staat .... Vol. 5A
Orchha, Orcha .... Vol. 3B
Ore surcharged on Denmark ...... Vol. 2B
Orense .... Vol. 6A
Organisation Mondiale de la Sante .... Vol. 6A
Oriental 465
Orts-Post .... Vol. 6A
O.S. .... Vol. 5A
Osten .... Vol. 5B
Osterreich .... Vol. 1B
Ostland .... Vol. 5B
Ottoman, Ottomanes .... 227, Vol. 2B
Oubangi Chari 375
Outer Mongolia .... Vol. 4B
Oviedo .... Vol. 6A
O.V.S. .... Vol. 5A
Oxford, N.C. .... Vol. 1A
O'zbekiston 541

P .... Vol. 2A, Vol. 2B, Vol. 4A, Vol. 6A
P on Straits Settlements .... Vol. 4B
Pacchi Postali .... Vol. 3B, Vol. 6A
Pacific Steam Navigation Co. .... Vol. 5A
Packhoi, Pakhoi .... Vol. 2B
Pahang .... Vol. 4B
Paid (Confed. #35X, etc.) .... Vol. 1A
Paid 5 (US #4X1, 7X1, many Confed.) .... Vol. 1A
Paid 10 (Confed. #76XU, 101XU, 80XU) .... Vol. 1A
Paid 2 Cents (Confed. #2XU) ..... Vol. 1A
Paid 3 Cents (Confed. #2AXU) ... Vol. 1A
Paita .... Vol. 5A
Pakistan .... Vol. 5A
Pakke-porto .... Vol. 3A
Palau .... Vol. 5A
Palestine .... Vol. 2B, Vol. 5A
Palestine (British Administration) ... Vol. 5A
Palestine (Jordan Occ.) .... Vol. 4A
Palestine overprinted .... Vol. 4A
Palestinian Authority .... Vol. 5A
Panama .... Vol. 5A
Panama (Colombian Dom.) .... Vol. 2A, Vol. 5A
Panama Canal Zone .... Vol. 1A
Papua .... Vol. 5A
Papua New Guinea .... Vol. 5A
Para .... 294, Vol. 2B
Para ovptd. on Austria .... Vol. 1B
Para ovptd. on France .... Vol. 2B
Para ovptd. on Germany .... Vol. 3A
Para ovptd. on Italy .... Vol. 3B
Paraguay .... Vol. 5A
Paras .... 227, Vol. 2B
Paras ovpt. on Great Britain .... Vol. 3A
Paras ovpt. on Romania .... Vol. 5B
Paras ovpt. on Russia .... Vol. 5B
Parma, Parm., Parmensi .... Vol. 3B
Pasco .... Vol. 5A
Patiala .... Vol. 3B
Patmo, Patmos .... Vol. 3B
Patterson, N.C. .... Vol. 1A
Patton, N.B. (Confed. #138XU1) ... Vol. 1A
Patzcuaro .... Vol. 4B
Paxos .... Vol. 2A, Vol. 3A, Vol. 3B
PC CP .... Vol. 5B
PD .... Vol. 5B
P.E. (Egypt #4, etc.) .... Vol. 2B
Pechino, Peking .... Vol. 3B
Peleliu (Palau #686) .... Vol. 5A
Pen, Penna .... Vol. 2B
Penang .... Vol. 4B
Penny Post (US 3LB, 8LB) .... Vol. 1A
Penrhyn Island .... Vol. 5A
Pensacola, Fla. .... Vol. 1A
Penybnnka Cpncka .... Vol. 1B
People's Republic of China .... Vol. 2A
Perak .... Vol. 4B
Perlis .... Vol. 4B
Persekutuan Tanah Melayu (Malaya #91) .... Vol. 4B
Persia (British Occupation) .... Vol. 1B
Persia, Persanes .... Vol. 3B
Peru, Peruana .... Vol. 5A
Pesa ovpt. on Germany .... Vol. 3A
Petersburg, Va. .... Vol. 1A
Pfennig, Pfg., Pf. ..... Vol. 2B, Vol. 3A, Vol. 4A
P.G.S. (Perak) .... Vol. 4B
Philadelphia, Pa. .... Vol. 1A
Philippines .... Vol. 2A, Vol. 5A
Philippines (US Admin.) ... Vol. 1A, Vol. 5A
Philippines (Japanese Occ.) ...... Vol. 1A, Vol. 5A
Piast., Piaster ovptd. on Austria .... Vol. 1B
Piaster ovptd. on Germany .... Vol. 3A
Piaster ovptd. on Romania .... Vol. 5B
Piastre, Piastra ovptd. on Italy ... Vol. 3B
Piastre .... 227, Vol. 2B, Vol. 4B
Piastre ovptd. on France .... Vol. 2B
Piastres ovpt. on Great Britain ... Vol. 3A
Piastres ovpt. on Russia .... Vol. 5B
Pies .... Vol. 2A, Vol. 3B
Pietersburg 156
Pilgrim Tercentenary (US #548) ... Vol. 1A
Pilipinas .... Vol. 1A, Vol. 5A
Pisco .... Vol. 5A
Piscopi .... Vol. 3B
Pitcairn Islands .... Vol. 5B
Pittsylvania C.H., Va. .... Vol. 1A
Piura .... Vol. 5A
Plains of Dura, Ga. .... Vol. 1A
Pleasant Shade, Va. .... Vol. 1A
Plum Creek, Tex. .... Vol. 1A
P.O. Paid .... Vol. 1A
Pobres (Spain #RA11) .... Vol. 6A
РОССIЯ, РОССИР .... Vol. 5B
Poczta, Polska .... Vol. 2B, Vol. 5B
Pohjois Inkeri .... Vol. 5A
Pokutia 753
Poland .... Vol. 5B
Poland, exile government in Great Britain .... Vol. 5B
Polish Levant .... Vol. 5B
Polish Offices in Danzig .... Vol. 5B
Polish Offices in Turkish Empire .... Vol. 5B
Polska .... Vol. 5B
Polynesia, French (Polynesie) .... Vol. 2B
Ponce .... Vol. 1A, Vol. 5B
Ponta Delgada .... Vol. 5B
Р.О.П.иТ. .... Vol. 5B
Poonch .... Vol. 3B
Popayan .... Vol. 2A
Port Arthur and Dairen .... Vol. 2A
Porteado .... Vol. 5B
Porte de Conduccion .... Vol. 5A
Porte de Mar .... Vol. 4B
Porte Franco .... Vol. 5A
Port Gibson, Miss. .... Vol. 1A
Port Gdansk .... Vol. 5B
Port Hood, Nova Scotia .... Vol. 2A
Port Lagos .... Vol. 2B
Port Lavaca, Tex. .... Vol. 1A
Porto .... 782, Vol. 1A, Vol. 1B
Porto Gazetei .... Vol. 5B
Porto Pflichtige .... Vol. 3A
Porto Rico .... Vol. 1A, Vol. 2A, Vol. 5B
Port Said, French Offices .... Vol. 2B
Portugal, Portuguesa .... Vol. 5B
Portuguese Africa .... Vol. 5B
Portuguese Congo .... Vol. 5B
Portuguese East Africa (Mozambique) .... Vol. 4B
Portuguese Guinea .... Vol. 5B
Portuguese India .... Vol. 5B
Portuguese India overprinted 88
Posen (Poznan) .... Vol. 5B
Post .... Vol. 3A, Vol. 3B
Post (Postage) & Receipt .... Vol. 3B
Posta .... Vol. 1A, Vol. 6A
Postage(s) .... Vol. 1A, Vol. 3A, Vol. 3B, Vol. 4B, Vol. 5B
Postage Due .... Vol. 1A, Vol. 3A
Postas le hioc .... Vol. 3B
Poste Locale .... Vol. 6A
Postes .... Vol. 1B, Vol. 2B, Vol. 4A
Postes Serbes ovptd. on France ... Vol. 6A
Postgebiet Ob. Ost. .... Vol. 5B
Postmarke .... Vol. 3A
Post Office (US #7X, 9X) .... Vol. 1A
Post Stamp .... Vol. 3B
Postzegel .... Vol. 5A
P.P. ovptd. on French postage dues .... Vol. 2B
P.P.C. ovptd. on Poland .... Vol. 5B
Pre 223
Prefecture issues .... Vol. 4A
Preussen .... Vol. 3A
Priamur .... Vol. 6A
Prince Edward Island .... Vol. 2A
Pristina 228
Province of Canada .... Vol. 2A

Providence (Prov.), R.I. .... Vol. 1A
Prussia .... Vol. 3A
PS .... Vol. 2A, Vol. 3B
P.S.N.C. (Peru) .... Vol. 5A
Puerto Principe .... Vol. 1A, Vol. 2A
Puerto Rico, Pto. Rico .... Vol. 1A, Vol. 2A, Vol. 5B
Puerto Rico (US Admin.) ... Vol. 1A, Vol. 5B
Pul .... Vol. 1A
Pulau Pinang .... Vol. 4B
Puno .... Vol. 5A
Puttialla State .... Vol. 3B

Qatar .... Vol. 5B
Qu'aiti State in Hadhramaut .... Vol. 1A
Qu'aiti State of Shihr and Mukalla .... Vol. 1A
Queensland .... Vol. 1A
Quelimane .... Vol. 5B

R (Armenia) .... Vol. 1A
R (Jind, Iran) .... Vol. 3B
R ovptd. on French Colonies ..... Vol. 2B
Rajasthan .... Vol. 3B
Rajpeepla, Rajpipla .... Vol. 3B
Raleigh, N.C. .... Vol. 1A
Rappen .... Vol. 6A
Rarotonga .... Vol. 2A
Ras al Khaima .... 442, Vol. 5B
R.A.U. .... Vol. 6A
Rayon .... Vol. 6A
Recargo .... Vol. 6A
Redonda (Antigua) .... Vol. 1A
Refugee Relief .... Vol. 3B
Regatul .... Vol. 3B
Reichspost .... Vol. 3A
Reis (Portugal) .... Vol. 5B
Repubblica Sociale Italiana .... Vol. 3B
Republic of China .... Vol. 2A
Republique Arab Unie .... Vol. 6A
Republique Democratique du Congo 835
Reseau d'Etat .... Vol. 2B
Resistance overprinted on Syria ... Vol. 6A
Rethymnon, Retymno .... Vol. 2A
Reunion .... Vol. 2B
R.F. ...... See France or French Colonies
RF - Solidarite Francaise .... Vol. 2B
R H .... Vol. 3B
Rheatown, Tenn. .... Vol. 1A
Rheinland-Pfalz .... Vol. 3A
Rhine Palatinate .... Vol. 3A
Rhodes .... Vol. 3B
Rhodesia .... Vol. 5B
Rhodesia (formerly So. Rhodesia) .... Vol. 5B
Rhodesia and Nyasaland .... Vol. 5B
Rialtar .... Vol. 3B
Riau, Riouw Archipelago .... Vol. 3B
Ricevuta .... Vol. 3B, Vol. 6A
Richmond, Tex. .... Vol. 1A
Rigsbank Skilling .... Vol. 2B
Ringgold, Ga. .... Vol. 1A
Rio de Oro .... Vol. 5B
Rio Muni .... Vol. 5B
RIS on Netherlands Indies .... Vol. 3B
Rizeh .... Vol. 5B
Rn. .... Vol. 4A
RNS .... Vol. 3B
R. O. ovptd. on Turkey .... Vol. 2B
Robertsport .... Vol. 4A
Rodi .... Vol. 3B
Roepiah .... Vol. 5A
Romagna, Romagne .... Vol. 3B
Romana .... Vol. 3B, Vol. 5B
Romania, Roumania .... Vol. 5B
Romania, Occupation, Offices ... Vol. 5B
Romanian Occupation of Hungary .... Vol. 3B
Romanian Occupation of Western Ukraine 753
Romania, Offices in the Turkish Empire .... Vol. 5B
Roman States .... Vol. 3B
Ross Dependency .... Vol. 5A
Rossija .... Vol. 5B
Rostov .... Vol. 6A
Rouad, Ile .... Vol. 5B
Roumelie Orientale .... Vol. 2B
Rpf overprinted on Luxembourg ... Vol. 4A
RSA .... Vol. 6A
R S M (San Marino) .... Vol. 6A
Ruanda ovptd. on Congo .... Vol. 3A
Ruanda-Urundi .... Vol. 5B
Ruffifch-Polen ovptd. on Germany .... Vol. 5B
Rumania, Roumania .... Vol. 5B
Rumanien on Germany .... Vol. 5B
Rupee on Great Britain .... Vol. 5A
Russia .... Vol. 5B
Russia (Finnish Occupation) ..... Vol. 4A, Vol. 5B
Russia (German Occupation) ..... Vol. 5B
Russian Company of Navigation & Trade .... Vol. 5B
Russian Dominion of Poland ...... Vol. 5B
Russian Empire, Finland .... Vol. 2B
Russian Occupation of Crete ..... Vol. 2A
Russian Occupation of Germany ... Vol. 3A
Russian Occupation of Korea .... Vol. 4A
Russian Occupation of Latvia .... Vol. 4A
Russian Occupation of Lithuania ... Vol. 4A
Russian Offices .... Vol. 5B
Russian Offices in China .... Vol. 5B
Russian Offices in Turkish Empire .... Vol. 5B
Russian stamps surch. or ovptd. .... Vol. 1A, Vol. 2B, Vol. 3A, Vol. 4A, Vol. 5B, Vol. 6A
Russian Turkestan .... Vol. 5B
Rustenburg 156
Rutherfordton, N.C. .... Vol. 1A
Rwanda, Rwandaise .... Vol. 5B
Ryukyu Islands .... Vol. 1A

S on Straits Settlements .... Vol. 4B
S A, S.A.K. (Saudi Arabia) .... Vol. 6A
Saar, Saargebiet, Saar Land ...... Vol. 5B
Saba (Caribbean Netherlands #111) .... Vol. 2A
Sabah .... Vol. 4B
Sachsen .... Vol. 3A
Sahara Occidental (Espanol) ...... Vol. 6A
St. Christopher .... Vol. 5B
St. Christopher-Nevis-Anguilla ... Vol. 5B
St. Eustatius (Caribbean Netherlands #112) .... Vol. 2A
Ste. Marie de Madagascar .... Vol. 5B
St. Georges, Bermuda .... Vol. 1B
St. Helena .... Vol. 5B
S. Thome (Tome) E Principe .... Vol. 5B
St. Kitts .... Vol. 5B
St. Kitts-Nevis .... Vol. 5B
St. Louis, Mo. .... Vol. 1A
St. Lucia .... Vol. 5B
St. Martin .... Vol. 5B
St. Pierre and Miquelon .... Vol. 5B
St. Thomas and Prince Islands ... Vol. 5B
St. Vincent .... Vol. 5B
St. Vincent and the Grenadines ..... Vol. 5B
St. Vincent Grenadines .... Vol. 5B
Salamanca Province .... Vol. 6A
Salem, N.C. .... Vol. 1A
Salem, Va. .... Vol. 1A
Salisbury, N.C. .... Vol. 1A
Salonicco, Salonika .... Vol. 3B
Salonika (Turkish) 228
Salonique .... 228, Vol. 5B
Salvador, El .... Vol. 5B
Salzburg .... Vol. 1B
Samoa .... Vol. 5B
Samos .... Vol. 2B, Vol. 3A
San Antonio, Tex. .... Vol. 1A
San Marino .... Vol. 6A
San Sebastian .... Vol. 6A
Santa Cruz de Tenerife .... Vol. 6A
Santa Maura .... Vol. 3A, Vol. 3B
Santander .... Vol. 2A
Sao Paulo .... Vol. 1B
Sao Tome and Principe .... Vol. 5B
Saorstat .... Vol. 3B
Sarawak .... Vol. 4B, Vol. 6A
Sardinia .... Vol. 3B
Sarre overprinted on Germany and Bavaria .... Vol. 5B
Saseno .... Vol. 6A
Saudi Arabia .... Vol. 6A
Saudi Arabia overprinted .... Vol. 4A
Saurashtra .... Vol. 3B
Savannah, Ga. .... Vol. 1A
Saxony .... Vol. 3A
SCADTA .... Vol. 2A
Scarpanto .... Vol. 3B
Schleswig .... Vol. 3A, Vol. 6A
Schleswig-Holstein .... Vol. 3A
Schweizer Reneke 157
Scinde .... Vol. 3B
Scotland .... Vol. 3A
Scutari, Italian Offices .... Vol. 3B
Segel Porto (on Neth. Indies) ..... Vol. 3B
Segnatasse, Segna Tassa .... Vol. 3B
Seiyun .... Vol. 1A
Selangor .... Vol. 4B
Selma, Ala. .... Vol. 1A
Semenov .... Vol. 2B
Sen, Sn. .... Vol. 1A, Vol. 4A, Vol. 5A
Senegal .... Vol. 6A
Senegal stamps surcharged ...... Vol. 2B
Senegambia and Niger .... Vol. 6A
Serb Administration of Bosnia, Banja Luca .... Vol. 1B
Serbia, Serbien .... Vol. 6A
Serbia & Montenego .... Vol. 4B, Vol. 6A
Serbian Occupation of Hungary .... Vol. 3B
Service .... Vol. 3B, Vol. 5A
Sevastopol .... Vol. 6A
Seville, Sevilla .... Vol. 6A
Seychelles .... Vol. 6A
S.H. .... Vol. 3A
Shanghai .... Vol. 2A, Vol. 6A
Shanghai (U.S. Offices) .... Vol. 1A
Shanghai and Nanking .... Vol. 2A
Shansi .... Vol. 2A
Shantung .... Vol. 2A
Sharjah .... Vol. 6A
Shensi .... Vol. 2A
Shihr and Mukalla .... Vol. 1A
Shqipenia, Shqiptare, Shqiperija, Shqiperise (Albania) .... Vol. 1A
S.H.S. on Bosnia and Herzegovina ... 780
S.H.S. on Hungary 780
Siam (Thailand) 1
Siberia .... Vol. 6A
Siberian stamps overprinted or surcharged .... Vol. 2B
Sicily, Sicilia .... Vol. 3B
Siege de la Ligue Arabe (Morocco #44) .... Vol. 4B
Sierra Leone .... Vol. 6A
Sikang .... Vol. 2A
Silesia, Eastern .... Vol. 2B
Silesia, Upper 464
Simi .... Vol. 3B
Sinaloa .... Vol. 4B
Singapore .... Vol. 6A
Sinkiang .... Vol. 2A
Sint Maarten .... Vol. 5B
Sirmoor, Sirmur .... Vol. 3B
Six Cents .... Vol. 1A
Sld. .... Vol. 1B
Slesvig .... Vol. 6A
Slovakia .... Vol. 2B, Vol. 6A
Slovene Coast 832
Slovenia, Slovenija .... Vol. 6A
Slovenia, Italian 831
Slovensko, Slovenska, Slovensky .... Vol. 2B, Vol. 6A
S. Marino .... Vol. 6A
Smirne, Smyrna .... Vol. 3B
Smyrne .... Vol. 5B
S O ovptd. on Czechoslovakia, Poland .... Vol. 2B
Sobreporte .... Vol. 2A
Sociedad Colombo-Alemana ..... Vol. 2a
Sociedade de Geographia de Lisboa .... Vol. 5B
Societe des Nations .... Vol. 6A
Soldi .... Vol. 1B
Solomon Islands .... Vol. 6A
Somali, Somalia, Somaliya .... Vol. 6A
Somalia, B.M.A. .... Vol. 3A
Somalia, E.A.F. .... Vol. 3A
Somali Coast (Djibouti) .... Vol. 6A
Somaliland Protectorate .... Vol. 6A
Sonora .... Vol. 4B
Sonsorol (Palau #686) .... Vol. 5A
Soomaaliya, Sooomaliyeed .... Vol. 6A
Soruth, Sorath .... Vol. 3B
Soudan .... Vol. 2B, Vol. 6A
South Africa .... Vol. 6A
South African Republic (Transvaal) ... 154
South Arabia .... Vol. 6A
South Australia .... Vol. 1A
South Bulgaria .... Vol. 2B
South Borneo .... Vol. 5A
South China .... Vol. 2A
Southern Nigeria .... Vol. 6A
Southern Poland .... Vol. 5B
Southern Rhodesia .... Vol. 6A
Southern Yemen 773
South Georgia .... Vol. 2B, Vol. 6A
South Georgia and South Sandwich Islands .... Vol. 6A
South Kasai .... Vol. 6A
South Korea .... Vol. 4A
South Lithuania .... Vol. 4A
South Moluccas .... Vol. 6A
South Orkneys .... Vol. 2B
South Russia .... Vol. 6A
South Russian stamps surcharged .... Vol. 5B
South Shetlands .... Vol. 2B
South Sudan .... Vol. 6A
South Viet Nam 653
South West Africa .... Vol. 6A
Southwest China .... Vol. 2A
Soviet Union (Russia) .... Vol. 5B
Sowjetische Besatzungs Zone ... Vol. 3A
Spain .... Vol. 6A
Spanish Administration of Andorra .... Vol. 1A
Spanish Dominion of Cuba .... Vol. 2A
Spanish Dominion of Mariana Islands .... Vol. 4B
Spanish Dominion of Philippines ... Vol. 5A
Spanish Dominion of Puerto Rico .... Vol. 5B
Spanish Guinea .... Vol. 6A
Spanish Morocco .... Vol. 6A
Spanish Sahara .... Vol. 6A
Spanish West Africa .... Vol. 6A
Spanish Western Sahara .... Vol. 6A
Sparta, Ga. .... Vol. 1A
Spartanburg, S.C. .... Vol. 1A
SPM ovptd. on French Cols. ...... Vol. 5B
Srbija I Crna Gora .... Vol. 6A
Sri Lanka .... Vol. 6A
Srodkowa Litwa .... Vol. 2A
Stadt Berlin .... Vol. 3A
Stamp (Tibet #O1) 69
Stampalia .... Vol. 3B
Stanyslaviv 753
Statesville, N.C. .... Vol. 1A
Steinmeyer's City Post .... Vol. 1A
Stellaland .... Vol. 6A
Stempel .... Vol. 1B
Straits Settlements .... Vol. 6A
Straits Settlements overprinted ... Vol. 6A
Strombus gigas Linne (Neth. Antilles #1193) .... Vol. 5A
STT Vuja, STT Vujna 832
Styria .... Vol. 1B
S.U. on Straits Settlements .... Vol. 4B
Submarine mail (Correo Submarino) .... Vol. 6A
Sudan .... Vol. 6A
Sudan, French .... Vol. 2B
Suid Afrika .... Vol. 6A
Suidwes-Afrika .... Vol. 6A
Suiyuan .... Vol. 2A
S. Ujong .... Vol. 4B
Sultanate of Oman .... Vol. 5A
Sumatra .... Vol. 3B, Vol. 5A
Sumter, S.C. .... Vol. 1A
Sungei Ujong .... Vol. 4B
Suomi (Finland) .... Vol. 2B
Supeh .... Vol. 2A
Surakarta .... Vol. 3B
Surinam, Suriname, Surinaamse ... Vol. 6A
Suvalki .... Vol. 5B
Sverige .... Vol. 6A
S.W.A. .... Vol. 6A
Swaziland, Swazieland .... Vol. 6A
Sweden .... Vol. 6A
Switzerland .... Vol. 6A
Switzerland, Administration of Liechtenstein .... Vol. 4A
Syria, Syrie, Syrienne .... Vol. 5A, Vol. 6A
Syria (Arabian Government) .... Vol. 6A
Syrie .... Vol. 6A
Syrie-Grand Liban .... Vol. 6A
Szechwan .... Vol. 2A
Szeged .... Vol. 3B

T .... Vol. 1B, Vol. 2B
T ovptd. on stamps of Peru .... Vol. 5A
Tabora ovptd. on Belgian Congo ... Vol. 3A
Tacna .... Vol. 5A
Tadjikistan, Tadzikistan .... Vol. 6A
Tae Han (Korea) .... Vol. 4A
Tahiti .... Vol. 6A
Taiwan (Republic of China) .... Vol. 2A
Taiwan (Formosa) .... Vol. 2A
Taiwan, Japanese .... Vol. 2A, Vol. 4A
Tajikistan .... Vol. 6A
Takca .... Vol. 1B
Takse .... Vol. 1A
Talbotton, Ga. .... Vol. 1A
Talca .... Vol. 2A
Talladega, Ala. .... Vol. 1A
Tallinn .... Vol. 2B
Tanganyika .... Vol. 6A
Tanganyika and Zanzibar .... Vol. 6A
Tanganyika (Tanzania), Kenya, Uganda .... Vol. 4A
Tanger .... Vol. 2B, Vol. 6A
Tangier, British Offices .... Vol. 3A
Tangier, French Offices .... Vol. 2B
Tangier, Spanish Offices .... Vol. 6A
Tannu Tuva .... Vol. 6A
Tanzania .... Vol. 6A
Tanzania-Zanzibar 861
Tartu .... Vol. 2B
Tasmania .... Vol. 1A
Tassa Gazzette .... Vol. 3B
Taxa de Guerra .... Vol. 4B, Vol. 5B
Taxyapom .... Vol. 2B
Tchad .... Vol. 2A
Tchongking .... Vol. 2B
T.C. overprinted on Cochin .... Vol. 3B
T.C., Postalari 227
Te Betalen .... Vol. 1B, Vol. 5A, Vol. 6A
Tegucigalpa .... Vol. 3B

Teheran ... Vol. 3B
Tellico Plains, Tenn. ... Vol. 1A
Temesvar ... Vol. 3B
Ten Cents ... Vol. 1A
T.E.O. ovptd. on Turkey or France ... Vol. 2A, Vol. 6A
Terres Australes et Antarctiques Francaises ... Vol. 2B
Territorio Insular Chileno (Chile #1061) ... Vol. 2A
Teruel Province ... Vol. 6A
Tete ... Vol. 6A
Tetuan ... Vol. 6A
Thailand, Thai ... 1
Thailand (Occupation of Kedah) ... Vol. 4B
Thailand (Occupation of Kelantan) ... Vol. 4B
Thailand (Occupation of Malaya) ... Vol. 4B
Thailand (Occupation of Perlis) ... Vol. 4B
Thailand (Occupation of Trengganu) ... Vol. 4B
Thessaly ... 289
Thomasville, Ga. ... Vol. 1A
Thrace ... 68
Three Cents ... Vol. 1A
Thuringia, Thuringen ... Vol. 3A
Thurn and Taxis ... Vol. 3A
Tibet ... 69
Tibet (Chinese province) ... Vol. 2A
Tibet, Chinese Offices ... Vol. 2A
Tical ... 1
Tientsin (Chinese) ... Vol. 2A
Tientsin (German) ... Vol. 3A
Tientsin (Italian) ... Vol. 3B
Tiflis ... Vol. 3A
Timbre ovptd. on France ... Vol. 2B
Timor ... 70
Timor-Leste ... 72
Timor Lorosae ... 72, Vol. 1A
Tin Can Island ... 147
Tjedan Solidarnosti (Yugoslavia #RA82) ... 830
Tjenestefrimerke ... Vol. 2B, Vol. 5A
Tlacotalpan ... Vol. 4B
Tobago ... 74
Toga ... 118
Togo, Togolaise ... 75
Tokelau Islands ... 112
Tolima ... Vol. 2A
Tonga ... 118
Tongareva ... Vol. 5A
Tonk ... Vol. 3B
To Pay ... Vol. 3A
Toscano ... Vol. 3B
Tou ... Vol. 3B
Touva, Tovva ... Vol. 6A
Transcaucasian Federated Republics ... 154
Trans-Jordan ... Vol. 4A, Vol. 5A
Trans-Jordan (Palestine Occ.) ... Vol. 4A
Transkei ... Vol. 6A
Transvaal ... 154
Transylvania ... Vol. 3B
Trasporto Pacchi ... Vol. 3B
Travancore ... Vol. 3B
Travancore-Cochin, State of ... Vol. 3B
Trebizonde ... Vol. 5B
Trengganu ... Vol. 4B
Trentino ... Vol. 1B
Trieste ... 832, Vol. 1B, Vol. 3B
Trinidad ... 157
Trinidad and Tobago ... 158
Trinidad Society (Trinidad & Tobago #B1) ... 172
Tripoli di Barberia (Tripoli) ... Vol. 3B
Tripoli, Fiera Campionaria ... Vol. 4A
Tripolitania ... 172, Vol. 4A
Tripolitania (B.M.A.) ... Vol. 3A
Tristan da Cunha ... 174
Trucial States ... 188
Tsinghai ... Vol. 2A
Tsingtau ... Vol. 2A, Vol. 4A
T. Ta. C ... 299
Tullahoma, Tenn. ... Vol. 1A
Tumbes (Peru #129-133) ... Vol. 5A
Tunisia, Tunisie, Tunis, Tunisienne ... 188
Turkestan, Russian ... Vol. 5B
Turkey, Turkiye, Turk ... 227
Turkey (Greek Occupation) . 228, Vol. 3A
Turkey in Asia ... 299
Turk Federe Devleti ... 301
Turkish Empire, Austrian Offices ... Vol. 1B
Turkish Empire, British Offices ... Vol. 3A
Turkish Empire, French Offices ... Vol. 2B
Turkish Empire, Georgian Offices ... Vol. 3A
Turkish Empire, German Offices ... Vol. 3A
Turkish Empire, Italian Offices ... Vol. 3B
Turkish Empire, Polish Offices ... Vol. 5B
Turkish Empire, Romanian Offices ... Vol. 5B
Turkish Empire, Russian Offices ... Vol. 5B
Turkish Occupation of Iran ... Vol. 3B
Turkish Republic of Northern Cyprus ... 301
Turkish stamps surcharged or overprinted ... Vol. 2B, Vol. 3A, Vol. 6A
Turkish Suzerainty of Egypt ... Vol. 2B
Turkmenistan, Turkmenpocta ... 316
Turks and Caicos Islands ... 319
Turks Islands ... 338
Tuscaloosa, Ala. ... Vol. 1A
Tuscany ... Vol. 3B
Tuscumbia, Ala. ... Vol. 1A
Tuva Autonomous Region ... Vol. 6A
Tuvalu ... 339
Two Cents (Confed. #53X5) ... Vol. 1A
Two Pence ... Vol. 1A
Two Sicilies ... Vol. 3B
Tyosen (Korea) ... Vol. 4A
Tyrol ... Vol. 1B

UAE ovptd. on Abu Dhabi ... 442
U.A.R. ... 756, Vol. 2B
Ubangi, Ubangi-Shari ... 375
Uganda, U.G. ... 376
Uganda, and Kenya ... Vol. 4A
Uganda, Tanganyika, Kenya ... Vol. 4A
Ukraine, Ukraina ... 402
Ukraine (German Occupation) ... Vol. 5B
Ukraine stamps surcharged ... Vol. 5B
Ukraine, Western ... 752
Ukrainian Soviet Socialist Republic ... 403
Uku Leta ... Vol. 1A
Ultramar ... Vol. 2A
Umm al Qiwain ... 442
UNEF ovptd. on India ... Vol. 3B
UNESCO ... Vol. 2B
U.N. Force in Congo or Gaza (India) ... Vol. 3B
Union Island, St. Vincent ... Vol. 5B
Union Islands ... 112
Union of South Africa ... Vol. 6A
Union of Soviet Socialist Republics ... Vol. 5B
Uniontown, Ala. ... Vol. 1A
Unionville, S.C. ... Vol. 1A
United Arab Emirates ... 442
United Arab Republic (UAR) ... 755, Vol. 2B, Vol. 6A
United Arab Republic, Egypt ... Vol. 2B
United Arab Republic Issues for Syria ... Vol. 6A
United Kingdom ... Vol. 3A
United Nations ... Vol. 1A
United Nations European Office ... Vol. 1A, Vol. 6A
United Nations Offices in Geneva ... Vol. 1A
United Nations Offices in Vienna ... Vol. 1A
United Nations - Kosovo ... Vol. 1A, Vol. 4A
United Nations - West New Guinea ... Vol.1A
United State of Saurashtra ... Vol. 3B
United States Adm. of Canal Zone ... Vol. 1A
United States Adm. of Cuba ... Vol. 1A, Vol. 2A
United States Adm. of Guam ... Vol. 1A
U. S. Adm. of Philippines ... Vol. 1A, Vol. 5A
U. S. Adm. of Puerto Rico ... Vol. 1A, Vol. 5B
U. S. Military Rule of Korea ... Vol. 4A
United States of America ... Vol. 1A
United States of Indonesia ... Vol. 3B
United States of New Granada ... Vol. 2A
United States, Offices in China ... Vol. 1A
Un Real ... Vol. 2B
U.S. Zone (Germany) ... Vol. 3A
Universal Postal Union, Intl. Bureau ... Vol. 6A
UNTEA ovptd. on Netherlands New Guinea ... Vol. 1A, Vol. 3B
UNTEAT ... 72
UPHA ROPA ... Vol. 4B
Upper Austria ... Vol. 1B
Upper Senegal and Niger ... 464
Upper Silesia ... 464
Upper Volta ... Vol. 1B
Urgente ... Vol. 6A
U.R.I. ovptd. on Yugoslavia ... 823
Uruguay ... 465
Urundi ovptd. on Congo ... Vol. 3A
Uskub ... 228
U.S. Mail ... Vol. 1A
U.S.P.O. ... Vol. 1A
U.S.P.O. Despatch ... Vol. 1A
U.S.S.R. ... Vol. 5B
U. S. T.C. overprinted on Cochin ... Vol. 3B
Uzbekistan ... 541

Vaitupu ... 375
Valdosta, Ga. ... Vol. 1A
Valencia ... Vol. 6A
Valladolid Province ... Vol. 6A
Valona ... Vol. 3B
Valparaiso ... Vol. 2A
Vancouver Island ... Vol. 2A
Van Diemen's Land (Tasmania) ... Vol. 1A
Vanuatu ... 562
Varldspost Kongress (Sweden #197) ... Vol. 6A
Vasa ... Vol. 2B
Vathy ... Vol. 2B
Vatican City, Vaticane, Vaticano ... 573
Venda ... Vol. 6A
Venezia Giulia ... Vol. 1B, Vol. 3B
Venezia Tridentina ... Vol. 1B
Venezuela, Veneza., Venezolana ... 607
Venizelist Government ... Vol. 3A
Vereinte Nationen ... Vol. 1A
Vetekeverria ... Vol. 1A
Victoria ... Vol. 1A
Victoria, Tex. ... Vol. 1A
Victoria Land ... Vol. 5A
Vienna ... Vol. 1A, Vol. 1B
Vienna Issues ... Vol. 3B
Viet Minh ... 662
Viet Nam ... 652
Viet Nam Buu Chinh ... 653, 662, 751
Viet Nam Buu Dien ... 664
Viet Nam Cong-Hoa ... 653
Viet Nam Doc-Lap ... 662
Viet Nam Dan-Chu Cong-Hoa ... 662
Viet Nam, Democratic Republic ... 662
Viet Nam, (Int. Com., India) ... Vol. 3B
Viet Nam, North ... 662
Viet Nam, Republic ... 653
Viet Nam, South ... 653
Villa Bella (Brazil #97) ... Vol. 1B
Vilnius ... Vol. 4A, Vol. 5B
Vineta ... Vol. 3A
Virgin Islands ... 712
Vladivostok ... Vol. 2B
Vojna Uprava ... 832
Volksrust ... 157
Vom Empfanger ... Vol. 2B, Vol. 3A
Vorarlberg ... Vol. 1B
V.R. ovptd. on Transvaal ... 155, Vol. 2A
Vryburg ... Vol. 2A
Vuja-STT, Vujna-STT ... 832

Wadhwan ... Vol. 3B
Walachia ... Vol. 5B
Wales & Monmouthshire ... Vol. 3A
Wallis and Futuna Islands ... 726
Walterborough, S.C. ... Vol. 1A
War Board of Trade ... Vol. 6A
Warrenton, Ga. ... Vol. 1A
Warsaw, Warszawa ... Vol. 5B
Washington, Ga. ... Vol. 1A
Watermarks (British Colonies) ... See table of contents
Weatherford, Tex. ... Vol. 1A
Weihnachten Joos van Cleve-Geburt Christi (Austria 2479) ... Vol. 1B
Wenden, Wendensche ... Vol. 5B
Western Army ... Vol. 4A
Western Australia ... Vol. 1A
Western Samoa ... Vol. 5B
Western Szechwan ... Vol. 2A
Western Thrace (Greek Occupation) ... 83
Western Turkey ... Vol. 3A
Western Ukraine ... 752
West Irian ... Vol. 3B
West New Guinea ... Vol. 1A, Vol. 3B
West Saxony ... Vol. 3A
Wet and dry printings ... Vol. 1A
Wharton's U.S. P.O. Despatch ... Vol.1A
White Russia ... Vol. 1B
Wiederaufbauspende ... Vol. 3A
Wilayah Persekutuan ... Vol. 4B
Wilkesboro, N.C. ... Vol. 1A
Williams City Post ... Vol. 1A
Winnsborough, S.C. ... Vol. 1A
Wir sind frei ... Vol. 2B
Wn. ... Vol. 4A
Wohnungsbau ... Vol. 3A
Wolmaransstad ... 157
World Health Organization ... Vol. 6A
World Intellectual Property Organization ... Vol. 6A
World Meteorological Organization ... Vol. 6A
Worldwide ... Vol. 3A
Wrangel issues ... Vol. 5B
Wurttemberg ... Vol. 3A
Wytheville, Va. ... Vol. 1A

Xeimappa ... Vol. 2B

Yambo ... Vol. 6A
Y.A.R. ... 755
Yca ... Vol. 5A
Yemen ... 753
Yemen Arab Republic ... 755
Yemen People's Republic ... 773
Yemen, People's Democratic Rep. ... 773
Yen, Yn. ... Vol. 1A, Vol. 4A
Ykp. H.P., Ykpaiha ... 752
Yksi Markka ... Vol. 2B
Yuan ... Vol. 2A
Yucatan ... Vol. 4B
Yudenich, Gen. ... Vol. 5B
Yugoslavia ... 780
Yugoslavia (German Occupation) ... 832
Yugoslavia (Italian Occupation) ... 831
Yugoslavia (Trieste) ... 832
Yugoslavia (Zone B) ... 833
Yugoslavia Offices Abroad ... 831
Yugoslavia stamps overprinted and surcharged ... Vol. 1B
Yunnan (China) ... Vol. 2A
Yunnan Fou, Yunnansen ... Vol. 2B

Za Crveni Krst (Yugoslavia #RA2) ... 827
Z. Afr. Republiek, Z.A.R. ... 154
Zaire ... 835
Zambezia ... 845
Zambia ... 846
Zante ... Vol. 3B
Zanzibar ... 1026
Zanzibar, French Offices ... Vol. 2B
Zanzibar (Kenya, Uganda, Tanganyika) ... Vol. 4A
Zanzibar-Tanzania ... 861
Z.A.R. ovptd. on Cape of Good Hope ... Vol. 2A
Zelaya ... Vol. 5A
Zentraler Kurierdienst ... Vol. 3A
Zil Eloigne Sesel ... Vol. 6A
Zil Elwagne Sesel ... Vol. 6A
Zil Elwannyen Sesel ... Vol. 6A
Zimbabwe ... 864
Zimska Pomoc ovptd. on Italy ... 832
Zone A (Trieste) ... Vol. 3B
Zone B (Istria) ... 833
Zone B (Trieste) ... 833
Zone Francaise ... Vol. 3A
Zuid Afrika ... Vol. 5A, Vol. 6A
Zuidafrikaansche Republiek ... 154
Zuidwest Afrika ... Vol. 6A
Zululand ... 873
Zurich ... Vol. 6A

INDEX TO ADVERTISERS 2024 VOLUME 6B

ADVERTISER	PAGE
– C –	
Colonial Stamp Co.	Yellow Pages
– G –	
Henry Gitner Philatelists Inc.	573
– K –	
Kelleher & Rogers Ltd.	Inside Front Cover
– M –	
Mystic Stamp Co.	Back Cover
– P –	
Penny Black Stamp Co.	604
Philasearch.com	781, 861
– S –	
Sultan Stamp Center	227

2024
VOLUME 6B
DEALER DIRECTORY
YELLOW PAGE LISTINGS

This section of your Scott Catalogue contains advertisements to help you conveniently find what you need, when you need it...!

Appraisals....................887
Auctions......................887
British Commonwealth..........887
Buying........................887
Canada........................887
Collections...................887
Ducks.........................887
German Colonies...............887
Germany.......................887
New Issues....................887
Stamp Stores.............887, 888
Staits Settlements............888
Supplies......................888
Thailand......................888
Togo..........................888
Tonga.........................888
Topicals......................888
Topicals - Columbus...........888
Transvaal.....................888
Uganda........................888
United States.................888
U.S. - Classics/ Moderns......888
U.S.-Collections Wanted.......888
Want Lists - British Empire 1840-1935 German Cols./Offices.....888
Wanted Worldwide Collections..888
Websites......................888
Worldwide.....................888
Worldwide - Collections.......888

Appraisals

…IAL STAMP COMPANY
…Wilshire Blvd. PH #8
…ngeles, CA 90036
…23-933-9435
…: 323-939-9930
…@colonialstamps.com
…w.colonialstamps.com

…R. ROBERT FRIEDMAN &
…ONS STAMP & COIN
…UYING CENTER
2029 W. 75th St.
Woodridge, IL 60517
PH: 800-588-8100
FAX: 630-985-1588
stampcollections@drbobstamps.com
www.drbobfriedmanstamps.com

Auctions

COLONIAL STAMP COMPANY
5757 Wilshire Blvd. PH #8
Los Angeles, CA 90036
PH: 323-933-9435
FAX: 323-939-9930
info@colonialstamps.com
www.colonialstamps.com

DUTCH COUNTRY AUCTIONS
The Stamp Center
4115 Concord Pike
Wilmington, DE 19803
PH: 302-478-8740
FAX: 302-478-8779
auctions@dutchcountryauctions.com
www.dutchcountryauctions.com

British Commonwealth

ARON R. HALBERSTAM PHILATELISTS, LTD.
PO Box 150168
Van Brunt Station
Brooklyn, NY 11215-0168
PH: 718-788-3978
arh@arhstamps.com
www.arhstamps.com

ROY'S STAMPS
PO Box 28001
600 Ontario Street
St. Catharines, ON
CANADA L2N 7P8
Phone: 905-934-8377
Email: roystamp@cogeco.ca
www.roysstamps.com

THE STAMP ACT
PO Box 1136
Belmont, CA 94002
PH: 650-703-2342
thestampact@sbcglobal.net

Buying

DR. ROBERT FRIEDMAN & SONS STAMP & COIN BUYING CENTER
2029 W. 75th St.
Woodridge, IL 60517
PH: 800-588-8100
FAX: 630-985-1588
stampcollections@drbobstamps.com
www.drbobfriedmanstamps.com

Canada

CANADA STAMP FINDER LLC
2800 N 6th Street, Unit 1-708
St. Augustine, FL 32084
PH: 904-217-2166
Canadian Address:
PO Box 92591
Brampton, ON L6W 4R1
PH: 514-238-5751
Toll Free in North America:
877-412-3106
FAX: 323-315-2635
canadastampfinder@gmail.com
www.canadastampfinder.com

ROY'S STAMPS
PO Box 28001
600 Ontario Street
St. Catharines, ON
CANADA L2N 7P8
Phone: 905-934-8377
Email: roystamp@cogeco.ca
www.roysstamps.com

Collections

DR. ROBERT FRIEDMAN & SONS STAMP & COIN BUYING CENTER
2029 W. 75th St.
Woodridge, IL 60517
PH: 800-588-8100
FAX: 630-985-1588
stampcollections@drbobstamps.com
www.drbobfriedmanstamps.com

Ducks

MICHAEL JAFFE
PO Box 61484
Vancouver, WA 98666
PH: 360-695-6161
PH: 800-782-6770
FAX: 360-695-1616
mjaffe@brookmanstamps.com
www.brookmanstamps.com

German Colonies

COLONIAL STAMP COMPANY
5757 Wilshire Blvd. PH #8
Los Angeles, CA 90036
PH: 323-933-9435
FAX: 323-939-9930
info@colonialstamps.com
www.colonialstamps.com

Germany

HENRY GITNER PHILATELISTS, INC.
PO Box 3077-S
Middletown, NY 10940
PH: 845-343-5151
PH: 800-947-8267
FAX: 845-343-0068
hgitner@hgitner.com
www.hgitner.com

New Issues

DAVIDSON'S STAMP SERVICE
Personalized Service since 1970
PO Box 36355
Indianapolis, IN 46236-0355
PH: 317-826-2620
ed-davidson@earthlink.net
www.newstampissues.com

New Issues

COLONIAL STAMP COMPANY
5757 Wilshire Blvd. PH #8
Los Angeles, CA 90036
PH: 323-933-9435
FAX: 323-939-9930
info@colonialstamps.com
www.colonialstamps.com

Stamp Stores

California

COLONIAL STAMP COMPANY
5757 Wilshire Blvd. PH #8
Los Angeles, CA 90036
PH: 323-933-9435
FAX: 323-939-9930
info@colonialstamps.com
www.colonialstamps.com

Delaware

DUTCH COUNTRY AUCTIONS
The Stamp Center
4115 Concord Pike
Wilmington, DE 19803
PH: 302-478-8740
FAX: 302-478-8779
auctions@dutchcountryauctions.com
www.dutchcountryauctions.com

Florida

DR. ROBERT FRIEDMAN & SONS STAMP & COIN BUYING CENTER
PH: 800-588-8100
FAX: 630-985-1588
stampcollections@drbobstamps.com
www.drbobfriedmanstamps.com

Stamp Stores

Illinois

DR. ROBERT FRIEDMAN & SONS STAMP & COIN BUYING CENTER
2029 W. 75th St.
Woodridge, IL 60517
PH: 800-588-8100
FAX: 630-985-1588
stampcollections@drbobstamps.com
www.drbobfriedmanstamps.com

Indiana

KNIGHT STAMP & COIN CO.
237 Main St.
Hobart, IN 46342
PH: 219-942-4341
PH: 800-634-2646
knight@knightcoin.com
www.knightcoin.com

New Jersey

BERGEN STAMPS & COLLECTIBLES
306 Queen Anne Rd.
Teaneck, NJ 07666
PH: 201-836-8987
bergenstamps@gmail.com

British Commonwealth

British Empire 1840 - 1935

Aden to Zululand Mint & Used
Most complete stock in North America

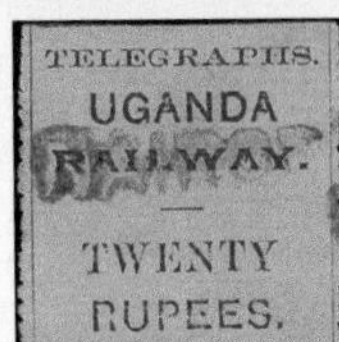

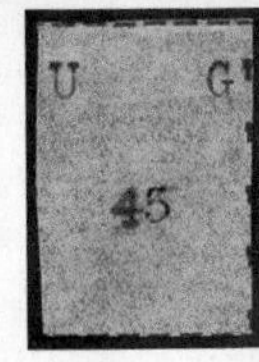

For over 40 years, we have built some of the world's finest collections. Our expert ***Want List Services*** can do the same for you. Over 50 volumes filled with singles, sets and rare stamps, we are sure we have what you need. We welcome your Want Lists in Scott or Stanley Gibbons numbers.

Put our expertise to work for you today! You'll be glad you did!

Colonial Stamp Company

"Rarity and quality are remembered ...long after price is forgotten."

5757 Wilshire Blvd., Penthouse 8
Los Angeles, CA 90036 USA
Tel: +1 (323) 933-9435 Fax: +1 (323) 939-9930

Email: *Info@ColonialStamps.com*
www.ColonialStamps.com

Ask for your free Public Auction Catalogue today!

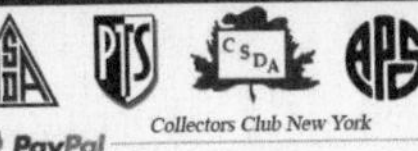

Collectors Club New York

Stamp Stores

New Jersey

TRENTON STAMP & COIN
Thomas DeLuca
Store: Forest Glen Plaza
1800 Highway #33, Suite 103
Hamilton Square, NJ 08690
Mail: PO Box 8574
Trenton, NJ 08650
PH: 609-584-8100
FAX: 609-587-8664
TOMD4TSC@aol.com
www.trentonstampandcoin.com

New York

CHAMPION STAMP CO., INC.
432 West 54th St.
New York, NY 10019
PH: 212-489-8130
FAX: 212-581-8130
championstamp@aol.com
www.championstamp.com

Ohio

HILLTOP STAMP SERVICE
Richard A. Peterson
PO Box 626
Wooster, OH 44691
PH: 330-262-8907 (0)
PH: 330-201-1377 (H)
hilltop@bright.net
hilltopstamps@sssnet.com
www.hilltopstamps.com

Straits Settlements

COLONIAL STAMP COMPANY
5757 Wilshire Blvd. PH #8
Los Angeles, CA 90036
PH: 323-933-9435
FAX: 323-939-9930
info@colonialstamps.com
www.colonialstamps.com

Supplies

BROOKLYN GALLERY COIN & STAMP, INC.
8725 4th Ave.
Brooklyn, NY 11209
PH: 718-745-5701
FAX: 718-745-2775
info@brooklyngallery.com
www.brooklyngallery.com

Thailand

THE STAMP ACT
PO Box 1136
Belmont, CA 94002
PH: 650-703-2342
thestampact@sbcglobal.net

Togo

COLONIAL STAMP COMPANY
5757 Wilshire Blvd. PH #8
Los Angeles, CA 90036
PH: 323-933-9435
FAX: 323-939-9930
info@colonialstamps.com
www.colonialstamps.com

Tonga

COLONIAL STAMP COMPANY
5757 Wilshire Blvd. PH #8
Los Angeles, CA 90036
PH: 323-933-9435
FAX: 323-939-9930
info@colonialstamps.com
www.colonialstamps.com

Topicals

HENRY GITNER PHILATELISTS, INC.
PO Box 3077-S
Middletown, NY 10940
PH: 845-343-5151
PH: 800-947-8267
FAX: 845-343-0068
hgitner@hgitner.com
www.hgitner.com

E. JOSEPH MCCONNELL, INC.
PO Box 683
Monroe, NY 10949
PH: 845-783-9791
ejstamps@gmail.com
www.EJMcConnell.com

Topicals - Columbus

MR. COLUMBUS
PO Box 1492
Fennville, MI 49408
PH: 269-543-4755
David@MrColumbus1492.com
www.MrColumbus1492.com

Transvaal

COLONIAL STAMP COMPANY
5757 Wilshire Blvd. PH #8
Los Angeles, CA 90036
PH: 323-933-9435
FAX: 323-939-9930
info@colonialstamps.com
www.colonialstamps.com

Uganda

COLONIAL STAMP COMPANY
5757 Wilshire Blvd. PH #8
Los Angeles, CA 90036
PH: 323-933-9435
FAX: 323-939-9930
info@colonialstamps.com
www.colonialstamps.com

United States

ACS STAMP COMPANY
2914 W 135th Ave
Broomfield, Colorado 80020
303-841-8666
www.ACSStamp.com

BROOKMAN STAMP CO.
PO Box 90
Vancouver, WA 98666
PH: 360-695-1391
PH: 800-545-4871
FAX: 360-695-1616
info@brookmanstamps.com
www.brookmanstamps.com

U.S. Classics/Moderns

BARDO STAMPS
PO Box 7437
Buffalo Grove, IL 60089
PH: 847-634-2676
jfb7437@aol.com
www.bardostamps.com

U.S.-Collections Wanted

DUTCH COUNTRY AUCTIONS
The Stamp Center
4115 Concord Pike
Wilmington, DE 19803
PH: 302-478-8740
FAX: 302-478-8779
auctions@dutchcountryauctions.com
www.dutchcountryauctions.com

U.S.-Collections Wanted

DR. ROBERT FRIEDMAN & SONS STAMP & COIN BUYING CENTER
2029 W. 75th St.
Woodridge, IL 60517
PH: 800-588-8100
FAX: 630-985-1588
stampcollections@drbobstamps.com
www.drbobfriedmanstamps.com

Want Lists - British Empire 1840-1935 German Cols./Offices

COLONIAL STAMP COMPANY
5757 Wilshire Blvd. PH #8
Los Angeles, CA 90036
PH: 323-933-9435
FAX: 323-939-9930
info@colonialstamps.com
www.colonialstamps.com

Wanted - Worldwide Collections

DUTCH COUNTRY AUCTIONS
The Stamp Center
4115 Concord Pike
Wilmington, DE 19803
PH: 302-478-8740
FAX: 302-478-8779
auctions@dutchcountryauctions.com
www.dutchcountryauctions.com

Websites

ACS STAMP COMPANY
2914 W 135th Ave
Broomfield, Colorado 80020
303-841-8666
www.ACSStamp.com

Worldwide

GUILLERMO JALIL
Maipu 466, local 4
1006 Buenos Aires
Argentina
guillermo@jalilstamps.com
philatino@philatino.com
www.philatino.com (worldwide stamp auctions)
www.jalilstamps.com (direct sale, worldwide stamps)

Worldwide-Collections

DR. ROBERT FRIEDMAN & SONS STAMP & COIN BUYING CENTER
2029 W. 75th St.
Woodridge, IL 60517
PH: 800-588-8100
FAX: 630-985-1588
stampcollections@drbobstamps.com
www.drbobfriedmanstamps.com